THE BREEDON BOOK OF

FOOTBALL RECORDS

THE BREEDON BOOK OF

FOOTBALL RECORDS

1871-2000

For the first time in one book – every FA Premiership, Football League, FA Cup, League Cup, Scottish League, Scottish FA Cup and Scottish League Cup match details and all final tables

compiled by Gordon Smailes

First published in Great Britain by
The Breedon Books Publishing Company Limited
Breedon House, Unit 3, The Parker Centre, Derby, DE21 4SZ.
2000

ISBN 1 85983 214 8

Printed and bound by Butler & Tanner Ltd., Selwood Printing Works, Caxton Road, Frome, Somerset.

Colour separations and jacket printing by GreenShires Group Ltd, Leicester.

Contents

Note: In the results tables for each English League division, 'A' refers to August, 'a' to April; 'M' refers to March, 'm' refers to May; and 'J' refers to January, 'j' refers to June. All the other capital letters are the initial letters of the months concerned (i.e. 'F' refers to February). The notes at the head of each season tell how the make-up of the League was achieved for that campaign. Thus 'Doncaster Rovers failed to gain re-election' at the head of the 1905-06 season means that they were voted out at the 1905 annual meeting.

The Football League

IN 1888, organised football was still an infant, albeit a lusty one, with professionalism having been legalised only three years earlier and the FA Cup only 16 years old. And apart from that competition, then known as the 'English Cup', and the mushrooming local cup competitions, football clubs still had to rely on prestigious friendly games to bring in the crowds. It was a state of affairs which was beginning to pose problems for the leading sides.

Once the thrill of truly competitive cup football had been experienced, friendly matches between even the top teams of the day, had no cutting edge, no real excitement. Further down the scale, the game was often being conducted in a haphazard manner. It was not uncommon for people to arrive and find that the opposition had not turned up, or matches kicked-off so late that spectators had drifted home long before the end.

At the top end of the scale, those clubs which had embraced professionalism now needed money to pay their players. These were the days long before outside commercial activity in football and the clubs could see only one way to finance the signing of better players. The money had to come through the gate, handed over by the paying spectator. It was vital for clubs to find a regular source of income.

One such club was Aston Villa and one of their committee members, William McGregor, a draper with premises near Aston Park, fearing that his club might lose its place as one of the leading sides in the country, suggested a league competition similar to that used in American baseball, although much nearer to home the County Cricket Championship could have provided an example.

His argument was strong: a league would guarantee a definite list of games what McGregor called a 'fixity of fixtures'. And it would provide additional competitive football.

On 2 March 1888, he sent out his now famous letter to Blackburn Rovers, Bolton Wanderers, Preston North End, West Bromwich Albion and to the secretary of his own club, Aston Villa, asking them if they would be interested in forming a football league.

An initial meeting was held on the eve of that year's FA Cup Final, on Friday, 28 March at Anderton's Hotel in Fleet Street, London. Officially in attendance were representatives of Aston Villa, Blackburn Rovers, Burnley, Stoke (who weren't 'City' until 1925), Notts County, West Bromwich Albion and Wolverhampton Wanderers. Preston, who were playing in the Cup Final, did not attend. Nor did Bolton, although as their secretary, John Bentley, had been the only one to respond to McGregor's request for lists of prospective founder-members, presumably McGregor was not too concerned at the Trotters' absence. Derby County's secretary, John Richardson, attended but only to observe.

A further meeting was held on 17 April at Manchester's Royal Hotel. According to the minutes, 11 clubs were represented – all the founder-members except Accrington, although they may have been there – and a name for the competition was settled. McGregor suggested the 'Football Association Union', but this was rejected because of possible confusion with the Rugby Football Union. McGregor's own objection to the name 'Football League' (he thought it might be confused with politically unpopular organisations, the Irish Home Rule League and the Land League) was overruled.

So the Football League began with 12 clubs. They comprised six from Lancashire: Accrington, Blackburn Rovers, Bolton Wanderers, Burnley, Everton and Preston North End; and six from the Midlands: Aston Villa, Derby County, Notts County, Stoke, West Bromwich Albion and Wolverhampton Wanderers. Remarkably, of those dozen founder-members over a century ago, only Accrington (no relation to the later Accrington Stanley) have gone to the wall. Nottingham Forest, The Wednesday (they did not adopt 'Sheffield' until 1929) and a Lancashire side called Halliwell were not accepted by the new organisation.

William McGregor was elected chairman, Harry Lockett of Stoke was the first secretary, and Major William Sudell of Preston North End was the first treasurer. The annual subscription for each club was two guineas (£2.10) and two points were to be awarded for a win and one for a draw. Teams finishing on the same number of points would have to submit to the goal-average, whereby the number scored was divided by the number conceded. It is ironic that this prevailed until 1976 – the dawn of the pocket calculator age – when it was replaced by the much simpler goal-difference used today. Two points for a win continued until 1981, when it was replaced by three points for victory, a move which arguably made the game more entertaining and deterred visiting teams from settling for a draw and only one point.

The first matches in the Football League – five at the onset – were staged on Saturday, 8 September 1888.

Until the League began to keep such records in 1925, football attendance figures were notoriously inaccurate and it apparently relied upon a local journalist casting an eye around a not-always familiar stadium. Indeed, if the exact figure was known, the League ordered that it should not be published. Nevertheless, one has to record that apparently some 26,000 people watched the five opening games, an average of just over 5,000 per match.

The highest 'gate' of the day was the 10,000 who saw Everton beat Accrington 2-1; the lowest, surprisingly, was the local derby game between Wolves and Aston Villa, where 2,500 turned up at Dudley Road.

There were few shocks, although Derby County managed to beat Bolton Wanderers 6-3 at Pikes Lane after trailing 3-0 after only 15 minutes. And the first League game on Merseyside started an hour after the scheduled kick-off when Accrington were late arriving at Anfield where Everton then played.

The identity of the first Football League goalscorer is not known, although it was probably either Preston's Jack Gordon, or his amateur teammate Fred Dewhurst, depending on which account one reads.

A week later Notts County and

Blackburn Rovers made their League debuts. County attracted only 8,000 to Anfield. Blackburn drew 5-5 with Accrington before a 5,000 crowd at Ewood Park.

Until 1891, the referee stood on the touch-line and arbitrated only when the umpires, one from each club, could not agree. Players were not numbered until 1939 and there were no programmes.

The first player to be cautioned in a Football League game was Alec Dick, an Everton full-back who, on 13 October 1888, apparently hit a Notts County player and used foul language. The first offence was not proven and Dick was simply ordered to apologise for using ungentlemanly language.

At the end of the first season, Preston North End were declared League Champions. They were unbeaten in their 22 games and also won the FA Cup without conceding a goal. The four bottom clubs – Stoke, Burnley, Derby and Notts County – were all re-elected. A total of 586 goals were scored at an average of 4.43 per game and only two matches ended scoreless in that first season.

Preston retained the title the following season, at the end of which the Football League lost its first club when Stoke finished bottom and were replaced by Sunderland. It was a particular blow for the League secretary Harry Lockett of Stoke FC. Thus, the position of secretary was now held by a truly impartial individual, a situation that has remained so ever since.

In that second season, the Football League had begun to raise more and more funds by fining clubs for breaches of the regulations, mostly for ineligible players.

That season also saw the League Committee rule that since Aston Villa and Bolton Wanderers, who had both finished on 19 points, were separated by only the tiniest fraction of a goal (0.84314 and 0.84375 respectively) they should be declared as having finished equal eighth, which thus avoided the embarrassment of McGregor's Villa having to apply for re-election.

In 1890-91, a new name appeared on the Football League trophy when Everton took top place. During this season, newcomers Sunderland became the first club to have two points deducted when they fielded goalkeeper Teddy Doig before his qualifying period was ended.

The League also imposed a minimum admission charge of 6d (less than 3p) to games, although they let in ladies free.

In December 1891, concerned at the 'poaching' of players, the Football League and the newly-formed Football Alliance agreed a maximum signing-on fee of £10. It remained so for the next seven decades. A bid to impose a maximum wage in 1891 failed for the time being.

In April 1891 the first inter-League game took place between the Football League and the Football Alliance at Olive Grove, Sheffield. Other fixtures were added and the games were used primarily as fund-raisers for the participating competitions.

At the end of the League's third season Stoke, who had played a season in the Football Alliance, were voted back in with Lancashire club, Darwen. This time there was no team dropping out, the League being extended to 14 clubs.

In their second season of membership, Sunderland took the title and at the 1892 annual meeting it was decided to form a Second Division (although it was initially referred to as the 'Second League') by incorporating many of the clubs from the Football Alliance. West Brom, incidentally, having just won the FA Cup, were exempted from having to apply for re-election even though they had finished in the bottom four.

Nottingham Forest, Newton Heath (later Manchester United) and The Wednesday went straight into what was now effectively the First Division; Darwen, who had just finished bottom, joined the Second Division.

Newcastle East End, Middlesbrough and Middlesbrough Ironopolis (who would amalgamate if accepted) applied for the First Division and, having been rejected, each turned down a Second Division place. Liverpool, a newly-formed club, were also turned down and spent their first season in the Lancashire League, which they won.

The Football League was now expanding into new areas and William McGregor resigned, to be replaced by the Bolton based referee and journalist John Bentley who was to have such an enormous impact on the League's affairs.

Now a two-Division affair, the Football League had to address the problem of promotion and relegation. In April 1892, with Sunderland again the League Champions, six clubs fought out a 19th-century version of today's Play-offs, which were resurrected in 1987. Three from the top of Division Two and three from the bottom of Division One played what were called 'test matches', whilst the bottom four clubs in Division Two had to submit to re-election.

The outcome was that Accrington and Notts County were relegated and Darwen and Sheffield United promoted. Bootle, who had finished outside the re-election zone, resigned anyway and the Second Division was enlarged to 15 clubs with the election of Newcastle United, Rotherham County and Middlesbrough.

The test match idea was eventually dropped in favour of automatic promotion/relegation after the infamous 'game without a shot at goal', when Stoke and Burnley, each needing a point, blatantly contrived a goalless draw at the end of the 1897-98 season.

In 1898-99, the first season of automatic ups and downs, there was a quite remarkable situation when the game between Aston Villa (the eventual Champions) and The Wednesday (who were to finish bottom) on 26 November was abandoned because of bad light with Villa leading 3-1 and just over ten minutes to play. The remaining minutes were played out on 13 March the following year, when Villa added another goal.

New names were now being engraved on the Football League Championship trophy. Aston Villa were the giants up to the turn of the century with five successes, whilst Liverpool and Sheffield United also won the title in that time. Villa were the true football giants of that decade and in 1896-97 they became the second team (and the last for over 60 years) to win the League and FA Cup double. They did it with the names of Athersmith, Devey, Spencer, Reynolds and the Cowans making the headlines, for soccer was now receiving much greater newspaper coverage.

Still there were many changing names in the League's membership and in 1893, Woolwich Arsenal became the first Football League club in London. Meanwhile, the League was being steadily increased in numbers and by 1900 the First and Second Divisions each stood at 18 clubs.

In the early years of this century, Liverpool twice won the title and were relegated in between, and The Wednesday were League Champions in consecutive years.

Liverpool's first title came in 1900-01, despite few changes in playing personnel from the side which had finished in tenth place the previous season. Despite winning their first three games, Liverpool had fallen to eighth by the middle of January and an early exit from the FA Cup meant that the Anfielders had lost three consecutive games. But from 9 February until the end of the season on 29 April, they were unbeaten, conceding only four goals in their last 12 matches. The Merseysiders were thus Champions only eight seasons after joining the Football League.

The Reds were relegated at the end of the 1903-04 season, but in 1905-06 they became the first club to win the First and Second Divisions in consecutive seasons. And they took their second League Championship with the addition of only two players – goalkeeper Sam Hardy and half-back James Bradley – to the side which had stormed to the Second Division title.

Yet a strange twist perhaps helped Liverpool to this second title. On the opening day of the season, centre-forward Jack Parkinson broke his wrist at Woolwich Arsenal's Plumstead ground. Joe Hewitt took over and ended the season as the Reds' leading scorer with 23 goals from only 37 games. Early in the season, Liverpool had languished in the bottom two before an unbeaten run of 16 games swept them to the top.

On 2 September 1899, The Wednesday opened their new ground at Owlerton with a Second Division game against Chesterfield. The ground became known as Hillsborough and Wednesday celebrated the move by winning the Second Division title that season.

After a period of consolidation it was Wednesday's turn to write their name on the Football League trophy. They topped the First Division in 1902-03 and retained the title the following season. Their first success was a close-run affair. When the Owls had completed their programme, Sunderland, the other contenders, still had a game to play. In the event the Wearsiders suffered an unexpected set-back at Newcastle.

On the day their fate was decided, Wednesday were helping to promote professional football in Devon, playing Notts County at Home Park where a 3-0 win earned them the Plymouth Bowl. They retained the League Championship in more comfortable fashion, finishing three points ahead of Manchester City in a season when there was talk of a League and Cup double at Owlerton. They lost to Manchester City in the FA Cup semi-final at Goodison Park. And then City beat Bolton in the Final having, of course, themselves missed out on the double by losing the title to Wednesday.

Manchester United, inspired by the great Billy Meredith, won the First Division title for the first time in 1907-08, the season that United were floated as a public company. Meredith had joined them in May 1906, in the wake of a bribes and illegal payments scandal surrounding his previous club, Manchester City, which had seen him and others receive lengthy suspensions.

Meredith made his United debut after the ban had been lifted on 1 January 1907 and the following season, along with former City colleagues Burgess, Bannister and Sandy Turnbull, all of whom had also been suspended, he helped United to the title.

They were by far the First Division's outstanding team, finishing nine points clear of runners-up Aston Villa, who were themselves only 13 points clear of the bottom club Birmingham. Between them Meredith, Sandy Turnbull and the England winger George Wall scored over 50 of United's goals. Vittorio Pozzo, the man who was to guide Italy to two World Cup triumphs in the 1930s, was then a poor student living in England. He watched United during their Championship season and used some of their techniques in his successful Italian teams.

But the great name in Edwardian soccer was that of Newcastle United, who enjoyed three Championship successes in five seasons as well as appearing in five FA Cup Finals before World War One.

In 1905 they won the title for the first time and almost did the double, losing to Aston Villa in the FA Cup Final. The following season they were again beaten in the Cup Final but lifted another First Division title in 1907. Twelve months later the Magpies lost yet another Cup Final but in 1909 they achieved another Championship triumph, despite an amazing 9-1 defeat by arch-rivals Sunderland at St James' Park. The Cup eventually went to Gallowgate in 1910 when Newcastle beat Barnsley in a replayed Final at Goodison Park. A year later, by now the most consistent team of the decade, they reached the Cup Final once more, this time losing to Barnsley.

There were some great names in the famous black and white stripes – long-serving goalkeeper Jimmy Lawrence, full-backs Carr, McCombie and McCracken, half-backs Veitch, McWilliam and Gardner, and a forward line of Rutherford, Shepherd, Appleyard and Howie. In the history of the game only a handful of clubs can match the dominance which Newcastle United enjoyed in their Edwardian heyday.

Before the Football League closed down during World War One, Manchester United, Aston Villa, Sunderland and Everton had added to their earlier wins and Blackburn Rovers were First Division champions for the first time in 1911-12.

For so long, Blackburn supporters had criticised their club for being too frugal with money. Now the Rovers' board spent on strengthening the team and were rewarded with the League Championship. The major signing was that of Jock Simpson, a right winger who joined Blackburn from Falkirk. This former driver of a horse-drawn omnibus cost Rovers a record £1,800 and he repaid them with some fine performances in the Championship season.

Two seasons later, Blackburn were Champions again. They began the season with five straight wins and that set the pattern for the rest of the campaign. Simpson, Danny Shea (a £2,000 signing from West Ham), Eddie Latheron (a £25 'snip' from non-League football) and Joe Hodkinson (from Second Division Glossop) blended well together. Behind them, one of the League's finest full-back partnerships of long-serving England player Bob Crompton and Arthur Cowell was as reliable as ever.

One outrageous piece of business had been conducted in 1919 when Arsenal, sixth in Division Two in the last pre-war season and heavily in debt after moving to their new stadium at Highbury, were engineered into the First Division by their owner, Sir Henry Norris MP. Each Division was to be extended by two clubs but there was never any justification for Arsenal to be moved up to Division One, where they have remained ever since.

West Brom and Burnley added their names in the first two seasons of post-war football before Liverpool won the title twice in succession. And in 1920-21, the Third Division was formed, by incorporating clubs from the Southern League, although Cardiff City went straight into Division Two and Grimsby Town made up the numbers in the new Third Division with the prospect of some long journeys.

Twelve months later the new section became the Third Division South with the creation of the Third Division North, to which Grimsby where thankfully switched. Now the Football League had four divisions and numbered 88 clubs in all, although the Third Division sides were 'associate members' only.

In 1923-24, Huddersfield Town won the first of three successive Football League Championship titles. The manager who started them on that historic road was a former Northampton Town player called Herbert Chapman. Before Town's third title win, Chapman had moved to Highbury, where he set the Gunners on the road to a similar feat, although he was to die before it was completed.

Huddersfield's first success was not resolved until the very last day of the season, when their 3-0 win over Nottingham Forest, coupled with Cardiff City's 0-0 draw at St Andrew's, was sufficient to give the Yorkshire club the title by 0.024 of a goal. An eight-match run, during which they dropped only four points, clinched the title 12 months later. And the third Championship was achieved after Town again opened the season with ten unbeaten games and finally took the title with a 3-0 win over their 'bogey' team, Bolton Wanderers. There was something of an anticlimax after that when Town lost their last two games.

The Huddersfield team which achieved this treble was skippered by the former Aston Villa forward, Clem Stephenson, who scored 20 goals in 105 appearances in that time. Other stalwarts were Tommy Wilson, Billy Watson, Billy Smith, Sam Wadsworth, George Brown (leading overall scorer with 63 goals), David Steele, Ray Goodall, George Cook, Ted Taylor, Charlie Wilson and Alex Jackson, one of the most gifted forwards of the inter-war period, who joined Huddersfield for a club record fee of £5,000 from Aberdeen.

After Huddersfield's feat, the League trophy ended the 1920s in familiar hands with Newcastle, Everton and Sheffield Wednesday all regaining it. Arsenal began the 1930s with their first Championship and after Everton had interrupted their run in 1931-32, the Gunners were Champions for three seasons on the trot.

Everton's title had been won with the epic contribution of centre-forward Dixie Dean, who scored 45 League goals that season. Of course, that was relatively small beer to Dean, who had netted a record 60 goals in the 1927-28 season and would end his career with 349 League goals in only 399 matches. He also scored a record 37 hat-tricks during his career.

But it was Arsenal who were perhaps the first truly national club, stamping their name indelibly on English football during the 1930s.

Besides the innovative Herbert Chapman – amongst many other things he is credited with evolving the 'stopper' centre-half system to counter the 1925 change in the offside law – there were great players like Alex James and Cliff Bastin, Eddie Hapgood and George Male, Jack Crayston and Wilf Copping, Jack Lambert and then Ted Drake, all of whom became household names. Seven Arsenal players turned out in one England team.

When the Gunners won the title for the first time in 1930-31 they were the first southern club to lift the Championship. The following season, they finished two points behind top club Everton and lost a controversial FA Cup Final to Everton. Then came another Championship, in a season also marked by a sensational FA Cup defeat at the hands of Third Division Walsall, and two more titles quickly followed.

In January 1934, Herbert Chapman died after a short illness. It is impossible to overestimate his contribution to the game and the period 1929-34 will always be known as the 'Chapman Era'. George Allison, one of the club's directors and a well-known journalist, took over as manager of Arsenal and saw the Gunners through to their historic treble.

During the 1920s and '30s, transfer fees had spiralled. In 1928 Arsenal paid a record £10,000 for centre-forward David Jack from Bolton. His fee was 50 per cent higher than the previous record, paid by Aston Villa for Partick Thistle's Jimmy Gibson. And it had all started with the £1,000 which Middlesbrough had paid Sunderland for centre-forward Alf Common in 1905, when 'Boro were criticised for 'buying' their way out of trouble, as though it was not a gentlemanly thing to do. It was an upward trend that would continue in astonishing fashion until by the end of the 20th century transfer fees moved closer to £20 million for the most sought-after world stars.

Although Arsenal remained the country's leading club up to World War Two, they won the title only once more, in 1937-38, with Sunderland, Manchester City (for the first time) and Everton all taking their turn before the competition was again suspended. In the Everton side which won the last post-war League Championship, a 19-year-old centre-forward called Tommy Lawton scored 34 goals. Sadly, like so many of his generation, Lawton was about to lose six years of his career to the war.

Although Liverpool were the first post-war Champions – this was the team of Billy Liddell, Jack Balmer, Albert Stubbins, Phil Taylor, Bob Paisley and company – Arsenal again lifted the title in 1947-48. Their heroes were now Joe Mercer (a member of Everton's pre-war Championship side), George Swindin, Wally Barnes, Laurie Scott, the Compton brothers, Jimmy Logie, Reg Lewis and the veteran centre-forward Ronnie Rooke.

Then a vibrant Portsmouth team, led by Jimmy Dickinson and containing exciting players like Jack Froggatt and Phil Harris, topped the First Division in successive seasons before the 1950s began with Arthur Rowe's newly-promoted Tottenham side, with its delightful 'push and run' style, going straight to the top of the tree.

Rowe's Tottenham side was one of the most purely 'footballing' teams the game has ever seen. They began the 1949-50 season with a long unbeaten run, including two spells of seven consecutive victories. That was enough to give them the Second Division title and they went straight on to head Division One in 1950-51. Despite losing the first game of that season, 4-1 at home to Blackpool, they enjoyed an eight-match winning sequence in October and November and during that time beat Portsmouth (Champions for the previous two 'seasons) 5-l, Newcastle United 7-0 and Stoke City 6-l. There is always a hiccup, however, and bottom club Huddersfield were the only team to take all the points off Spurs that season – and also knocked them out of the FA Cup for good measure.

That great Spurs team included the skilful wing-halves Bill Nicholson and Ronnie Burgess, and delightful forward play from Eddie Baily, Len Duquemin, Les Bennett and Les Medley. Ted Ditchburn kept goal behind full-backs Alf Ramsey and Arthur Wilis.

Spurs' reign was brief, however, as Matt Busby's Manchester United (a club Busby had inherited when they had no ground in the aftermath of the war) and then Arsenal again took the title.

Those early post-war days had been a boom time for soccer attendances. After the, deprivations of war, people wanted entertainment and there were queues everywhere – at cinemas and into speedway, cricket and boxing tournaments. Football, as the true national sport, benefited most and this was a golden age of great stars and huge crowds.

Manager Stan Cullis and England skipper Billy Wright steered Wolves to the Championship in 1953-54 and nobody much begrudged Chelsea, for so long a music-hall joke, their lone success the following season before Manchester United took up the reins again.

This was the United team of Tommy Taylor and Duncan Edwards, Roger Byrne and Eddie Colman. The United team that was to be decimated and then immortalised by the Munich air disaster. In the season that United's dreams came crashing down at the end of an icy German runway, Wolves took the title and retained it the following year.

In 1958 the League format was altered significantly. The top halves of the Third Divisions North and South formed a new Third Division. The rest went into a national Fourth Division. Re-election still had to be avoided until 1987 when the bottom club had no choice but was simply relegated to what is now the GM Vauxhall Conference. It was a shock for Burnley, founder members of the Football League, when, in the first year of Play-offs and relegation from Division Four, they came within one game of going out of the League altogether.

In 1959-60, however, Burnley lifted the Championship before another great Tottenham side blossomed into full fruit. Danny Blanchflower led Bill Nicholson's side to the first modem League and FA Cup double in 1960-61 before Ipswich Town took the title in 1961-62. The names of that Spurs team rolled off the tongue like honey, names like Brown, Baker and Henry, Blanchflower, Norman and Mackay, Jones, Medwin, White, Smith, Greaves, Allen and Dyson.

This was an important era for the Football League. In 1961, led by its chairman, Jimmy Hill, the Professional Footballers' Association successfully campaigned for the abolition of the maximum wage. Now the best players could earn more by moving on and the game was to see the end of such long-serving one-club stars as Tom Finney and Nat Lofthouse. The effect was enormous. The removal of the maximum wage, whilst a move of obvious natural justice, saw the powerful big-city clubs grow more powerful still. Only they could afford the major stars and coupled, eventually, with television saturation of the game, mass car ownership and good motorway links, it began to polarise support for the big clubs. Freedom of contract and the end of the outdated (in labour terms) retain-and-transfer system would also contribute to this development.

That, though, was still some way down the line. Meanwhile, down in the soccer backwater of rural Suffolk, Alf Ramsey, the former Tottenham full-back, was creating a tactical football revolution. Using a withdrawn 'winger' in Jimmy Leadbetter and two fine goalscorers in Ray Crawford and Ted Phillips, he took Ipswich Town from the Second Division to the League Championship. Four years later, Ramsey was weaving, a similar tactical plan to take England to World Cup glory.

Everton, Liverpool (the first of Bill Shankly's major successes) and Manchester United all took the title in the early 1960s, and before the decade was out the Championship had gone back to Anfield and then Old Trafford. After Manchester United won it in 1967 they went on to become the first English club to win the European Cup on a night of high emotion at Wembley.

The first of Busby's successful teams had included several players who were on the books when war broke out – men like Johnny Morris, Stan Pearson, Charlie Mitten, Jack Rowley, Allenby Chilton and Johnny Carey. Now the post-Munich team paraded the skills of Munich survivor Bobby Charlton together with the ultimately wayward genius of George Best and the fiery Denis Law.

Then it was Manchester City's turn for League glory under Joe Mercer and Malcolm Allison, with United finishing runners-up to make it Manchester's season, before Don Revie carried on his Leeds United miracle. Revie had taken a club wallowing in Division Two and eventually turned it into Championship winning material, the first success coming in 1968-69. Leeds United, born out of the disgraced Leeds City, who were kicked out of the League in 1919 for, the cynics may say, being found out when they paid illegal bonuses, were a club who had achieved very little up to then.

Revie changed all that and his side, led by another fiery Scot in Billy Bremner, could practically be pencilled-in every week during that first Championship success as Gary Sprake, Paul Reaney, Terry Cooper, Billy Bremner, Jack Charlton, Norman Hunter, Peter Lorimer, Paul Madeley, Johnny Giles, Eddie Gray, Mick Jones and Mike O'Grady held sway.

After Everton, with their magnificent midfield of Colin Harvey, Howard Kendall and Alan Ball, had another brief taste of success, Arsenal, under manager Bertie Mee, did the double in 1970-71. Many people outside Highbury said they were 'boring' – just as many people outside Elland Road had labelled Leeds 'unscrupulous' – but the feat had been achieved and new Arsenal heroes like Charlie George, John Radford, George Graham, Peter Storey, Ray Kennedy and Frank McLintock were the darlings of Highbury.

Brian Clough took Derby to their first title in 1971-72 – they were to win it again in 1974-75 under former Tottenham star Dave Mackay – but now the Football League was entering the age of Liverpool. Since 1975-76, Liverpool have won the Football League Championship on no less than ten occasions. Occasionally there had been interlopers – Aston Villa, Nottingham Forest, Everton and Arsenal, who won the title in 1988-89 and lifted it again in 1990-91 – but until Manchester United in the last few years of the century threatened to overtake their record, Liverpool had been the most remarkably consistent club in the history of the English top-flight. Successive managers – Bob Paisley, Joe Fagan and Kenny Dalglish – inherited Bill Shankly's legacy and built upon it.

In 1975-76, Paisley steered Liverpool to the League Championship and the UEFA Cup, first won three years earlier. The title was retained the following year and if Liverpool's away form concerned their supporters, their results at the citadel which Anfield had become more than allayed any fears. It has been a familiar story ever since – Liverpool were Champions in 1978-79, 1979-80, 1981-82, 1982-83, 1983-84, 1985-86, 1987-88 and 1989-90.

During that time there have been many Anfield heroes: Keegan, Toshack, Heighway, Callaghan, Hughes, Thompson, Clemence, Neal, Jones, Dalglish, Souness, Smith, the Kennedys, McDermott, Hansen, Johnson, Johnston, Case, Fairclough, Grobbelaar, Lee, Whelan, Lawrenson, Rush, Nicol, Molby, Barnes, Beardsley, Aldridge, McMahon, Gillespie, Houghton. One could go on and on, for there have been so very many headline-making names to come out of Anfield.

And all this, of course, had been achieved by the tremendous consistency of the Liverpool approach, the famous 'boot-room' brigade who had plotted the Reds' seemingly inexorable march over these past two decades.

Indeed, it was hard to imagine a time when Liverpool were not dominating English football. Then the 1991-92 season saw the Reds suffer injury and uncharacteristically fall away in the old First Division. It was a fall from grace which looked like being arrested only as the 21st century began when, under a new manager, Gerard Houllier, Liverpool would have finished in the Champions League places but for a barren last few games of the season.

Back in 1991-92 new challengers in the shape of Leeds United, who lifted the Football League Championship under Howard Wilkinson, appeared to confirm that there was still a chance for a team from outside the ring of Merseyside and London clubs, who had, by and large, made the Football League title their preserve for so many years.

That was the last year of the 'old' First Division. In 1992-93 the FA Premier League began and Manchester United were its first Champions, remarkably the first time that United had finished on top of English football since 1967. But if a whole new generation of fans had arrived since United's last triumph, they did not have long to wait for a repeat. Indeed, when United lifted the Premier League title again in 2000, they had been Champions in six of its eight years. Only Blackburn Rovers, thanks to Jack Walker's millions in 1995, and Arsenal in 1998 had interrupted United's domination.

When the Premier League began, it appeared that far from being a small élite group, the competition did not look much different from the old First Division after all. Then satellite television took an interest, millions of pounds were poured into the game, and the élite – perhaps numbering no more than four or five clubs – emerged in a league of their own with the rest trailing way behind and with no realistic prospect of ever lifting the title.

Perhaps the fairy-tale rise of clubs like Oxford United and Wimbledon, both of whom made it from the Southern League to the old First Division in truly testing times, will never be repeated. Oxford returned whence they came quickly enough but Wimbledon went on to play a part in the Premier League. Wimbledon's story was a remarkable one before their relegation in 2000, and the Premier League has also seen clubs such as Barnsley and Bradford City in its ranks. But they will surely only ever be there to make up the numbers, along with the majority. The real power is with the tiny handful of clubs who, backed by giant media organisations, look not to the domestic game but to Europe and even the world at large.

Truly, the story League football is a remarkable one and a tale that even that great 19th-century visionary, William McGregor, could never have foreseen. Would McGregor approve of the Premier League? Perhaps he would, for he was ever the visionary. After all, was not the original Football League of 1888 just that – a premier competition for the best in the land?

Football League Records
Seasons 1888-89 & 1889-90

Top scorer: J.Goodall (Preston North End) 21 goals.

DIVISION 1

	ACCRINGTON	ASTON VILLA	BLACKBURN R	BOLTON W	BURNLEY	DERBY CO	EVERTON	NOTTS CO	PRESTON N.E.	STOKE	W.B.A.	WOLVERHAMPTON W
1 ACCRINGTON		D15 1-1	J19 0-2	M23 2-3	D01 5-1	O13 6-2	D29 3-1	J26 1-2	O20 0-0	a20 2-0	N24 2-1	O06 4-4
2 ASTON VILLA	O27 4-3		O13 6-1	J12 6-2	D22 4-2	D29 4-2	S22 2-1	S29 9-1	F09 0-2	S15 5-1	J19 2-0	N24 2-1
3 BLACKBURN R	S15 5-5	N17 5-1		D08 4-4	F04 4-2	a15 3-0	N10 3-0	D15 5-2	J12 2-2	O27 5-2	S22 6-2	O20 2-2
4 BOLTON W	D22 4-1	O20 2-3	J26 3-2		S15 3-4	S08 3-6	S29 6-2	M09 7-3	N24 2-5	O13 2-1	N17 1-2	D29 2-1
5 BURNLEY	J12 2-2	J05 4-0	N03 1-7	O06 4-1		J19 1-0	N17 2-2	D29 1-0	D15 2-2	D08 2-1	N10 2-0	O13 0-4
6 DERBY CO	S22 1-1	M09 5-2	N24 0-2	D26 2-3	M02 1-0		O20 2-4	D22 3-2	S29 2-3	J26 2-1	S15 1-2	J12 3-0
7 EVERTON	S08 2-1	O06 2-0	M30 3-1	N03 2-1	N24 3-2	O27 6-2		S15 2-1	J19 0-2	J12 2-1	D01 1-4	F09 1-2
8 NOTTS CO	N10 3-3	D08 2-4	O06 3-3	M05 0-4	O27 6-1	M16 3-5	O13 3-1		N03 0-7	N24 0-3	J12 2-1	J19 3-0
9 PRESTON N.E.	N17 2-0	N10 1-1	D29 1-0	S22 3-1	S08 5-2	D08 5-0	D22 3-0	J05 4-1		O06 7-0	O13 3-0	O27 5-2
10 STOKE	S29 2-4	N03 1-1	D01 2-1	J19 2-2	O20 4-3	a06 1-1	D15 0-0	S22 3-0	N12 0-3		S08 0-2	N17 0-1
11 W.B.A.	N03 2-2	J26 3-3	D22 2-1	N05 1-5	S29 4-3	O06 5-0	F23 1-0	O20 4-2	D26 0-5	D29 2-0		J05 1-3
12 WOLVERHAMPTON W	D08 4-0	S08 1-1	S29 2-2	N10 3-2	S22 4-1	N03 4-1	J26 4-0	F23 2-1	S15 0-4	D22 4-1	D15 2-1	

LEAGUE TABLE
FOOTBALL LEAGUE

	P	W	D	L	F	A	W	D	L	F	A	Pts
Preston N.E.	22	10	1	0	39	7	8	3	0	35	8	40
Aston Villa	22	10	0	1	44	16	2	5	4	17	27	29
Wolverhampton W	22	8	2	1	30	14	4	2	5	20	23	28
Blackburn R	22	7	4	0	44	22	3	2	6	22	23	26
Bolton W	22	6	0	5	35	30	4	2	5	28	29	22
W.B.A.	22	6	2	3	25	24	4	0	7	15	22	22
Accrington S	22	5	3	3	26	17	1	5	5	22	31	20
Everton	22	8	0	3	24	17	1	2	8	11	29	20
Burnley	22	6	3	2	21	19	1	0	10	21	43	17
Derby Co	22	5	1	5	22	20	2	1	8	19	41	16
Notts Co	22	4	2	5	25	32	1	0	10	15	41	12
Stoke	22	3	4	4	15	18	1	0	10	11	33	12

Top scorer: J.Ross (Preston North End) 24 goals.

DIVISION 1

	ACCRINGTON	ASTON VILLA	BLACKBURN R	BOLTON W	BURNLEY	DERBY CO	EVERTON	NOTTS CO	PRESTON N.E.	STOKE	W.B.A.	WOLVERHAMPTON W
1 ACCRINGTON		N30 4-2	S28 2-2	J04 3-1	O19 2-2	N16 6-1	F22 5-3	O12 1-8	M15 2-2	D28 2-1	F08 0-0	J01 6-3
2 ASTON VILLA	D26 1-2		M31 3-0	J25 1-2	S07 2-2	O12 7-1	N23 1-2	S14 1-1	S21 5-3	D07 6-1	O26 1-0	N02 2-1
3 BLACKBURN R	N23 3-2	O19 7-0		D21 7-1	O26 7-1	S21 4-2	D28 2-4	N16 9-1	N02 3-4	J04 8-0	N30 5-0	S14 4-3
4 BOLTON W	S14 2-4	N16 2-0	N09 3-2		M17 2-2	N30 7-1	S21 3-4	O26 0-4	O12 2-6	F08 5-0	D07 7-0	F24 4-1
5 BURNLEY	S21 2-2	O05 2-6	F22 1-2	M01 7-0		M08 2-0	F08 0-1	M15 3-0	S28 0-3	J11 1-3	O12 1-2	N09 1-2
6 DERBY CO	F15 2-3	D28 5-0	F08 4-0	D26 3-2	J04 4-1		O05 2-2	S28 2-0	O19 2-1	O26 2-0	S14 3-1	N23 3-3
7 EVERTON	O26 2-2	J04 7-0	S07 3-2	S28 3-0	S14 2-1	M15 3-0		D07 5-3	N16 1-5	N02 8-0	M08 5-1	S30 1-1
8 NOTTS CO	M13 3-1	N09 1-1	F18 1-1	J11 3-5	N02 1-1	D21 3-1	O19 4-3		M27 0-1	O05 3-1	S21 1-2	D14 0-2
9 PRESTON N.E.	N09 3-1	D25 3-2	D07 1-1	N23 3-1	N30 6-0	J11 5-0	D21 1-2	M01 4-3		S14 10-0	O05 5-0	O26 0-2
10 STOKE	M01 7-1	M17 1-1	D23 0-3	O19 0-1	M10 3-4	S07 1-1	N09 1-2	M24 1-1	N11 1-2		N16 1-3	S28 2-1
11 W.B.A.	D21 4-1	S28 3-0	J11 3-2	N04 6-3	N23 6-1	N09 2-3	M22 4-1	J04 4-2	D26 2-2	M15 2-1		O19 1-4
12 WOLVERHAMPTON W	O05 2-1	D21 1-1	D26 2-4	M15 5-1	D07 9-1	J25 2-1	S16 2-1	S07 2-0	J04 0-1	O12 2-2	D28 1-1	

LEAGUE TABLE
FOOTBALL LEAGUE

	P	W	D	L	F	A	W	D	L	F	A	Pts
Preston N.E.	22	8	1	2	41	12	7	2	2	30	18	33
Everton	22	8	2	1	40	15	6	1	4	25	25	31
Blackburn R	22	9	0	2	59	18	3	3	5	19	23	27
Wolverhampton W	22	6	3	2	28	14	4	2	5	23	24	25
W.B.A.	22	8	1	2	37	20	3	2	6	10	30	25
Accrington S	22	6	4	1	33	25	3	2	6	20	31	24
Derby Co	22	8	2	1	32	13	1	1	9	11	42	21
Aston Villa	22	6	2	3	30	15	1	3	7	13	36	19
Bolton W	22	6	1	4	37	24	3	0	8	17	41	19
Notts Co	22	4	3	4	20	19	2	2	7	23	32	17
Burnley	22	3	1	7	20	21	1	4	6	16	44	13
Stoke	22	2	3	6	18	20	1	1	9	9	49	10

Preston North End, first winners of the Football League and victorious in the FA Cup Final the same season. Back row (left to right, players only): Drummond, Howarth, Russell, Holmes, Graham, Dr Mills-Roberts. Front row: Gordon, J.Ross, Goodall, Dewhurst, Thomson.

Football League Records
Seasons 1890-91 & 1891-92

Top scorer: J.Southworth (Blackburn Rovers) 26 goals. Sunderland were elected in place of Stoke.

DIVISION 1

	ACCRINGTON	ASTON VILLA	BLACKBURN R	BOLTON W	BURNLEY	DERBY CO	EVERTON	NOTTS CO	PRESTON N.E.	SUNDERLAND	W.B.A.	WOLVERHAMPTON W
1 ACCRINGTON		M21 1-3	M04 0-4	J10 2-1	S06 1-1	N08 4-0	S27 1-2	O25 3-2	O11 1-3	N22 4-1	a18 1-0	J01 1-2
2 ASTON VILLA	N15 3-1		D13 2-2	N22 5-0	N08 4-4	O25 4-0	O11 2-2	S13 3-2	M09 0-1	D26 0-0	S27 0-4	M14 6-2
3 BLACKBURN R	S13 0-0	D06 5-1		M07 0-2	N22 5-2	J03 8-0	N08 2-1	M14 1-7	O25 1-0	O11 3-2	D20 2-1	S27 2-3
4 BOLTON W	D13 6-0	O04 4-0	M28 2-0		M21 1-0	S13 3-1	S20 0-5	S06 4-2	N15 1-0	O25 2-5	M14 7-1	D29 6-0
5 BURNLEY	N29 2-0	S20 2-1	O18 1-6	O11 1-2		N15 6-1	M14 3-2	D20 0-1	M07 6-2	S27 3-3	D06 5-4	N01 4-2
6 DERBY CO	D06 1-2	O18 5-4	S06 8-5	D26 1-1	J24 2-4		D13 2-6	D27 3-1	S20 1-3	F07 3-1	N22 3-1	J10 9-0
7 EVERTON	D26 3-2	J01 5-0	N29 3-1	O18 2-0	D27 7-3	O04 7-0		J03 4-2	J10 0-1	N15 1-0	O25 2-3	S13 5-0
8 NOTTS CO	S20 5-0	N29 7-1	N15 1-2	O02 3-1	F10 4-0	S27 2-1	N01 3-1		D06 2-1	D15 2-1	O11 3-2	N22 1-1
9 PRESTON N.E.	N01 1-1	J24 4-1	O04 1-2	S27 1-0	F05 7-0	D20 6-0	N22 2-0	N08 0-0		F21 0-0	S13 3-0	O18 5-1
10 SUNDERLAND	O18 2-2	J10 5-1	N01 3-1	F10 2-0	**S13 2-3**	M21 5-1	D20 1-0	J24 4-0	M14 3-0		N08 1-1	S15 3-4
11 W.B.A.	M07 5-1	N01 0-3	M09 1-0	N03 2-4	O04 3-1	N29 3-4	S06 1-4	O18 1-1	F07 1-3	S20 0-4		D13 0-1
12 WOLVERHAMPTON W	O04 3-0	S06 2-1	D26 2-0	N08 1-0	O25 3-1	O11 5-1	D06 0-1	S22 1-1	N29 2-0	D27 0-3	J03 4-0	

LEAGUE TABLE
FOOTBALL LEAGUE

	P	W	D	L	F	A	W	D	L	F	A	Pts
Everton	22	9	0	2	39	12	5	1	5	24	17	29
Preston N.E.	22	7	3	1	30	5	5	0	6	14	18	27
Notts Co	22	9	1	1	33	11	2	3	6	19	24	26
Wolverhampton W	22	8	1	2	23	8	4	1	6	16	42	26
Bolton W	22	9	0	2	36	14	3	1	7	11	20	25
Blackburn R	22	7	1	3	29	19	4	1	6	23	24	24
Sunderland	22	7	2	2	31	13	3	3	5	20	18	*23
Burnley	22	7	1	3	33	24	2	2	7	19	39	21
Aston Villa	22	5	4	2	29	18	2	0	9	16	40	18
Accrington S	22	5	1	5	19	19	1	3	7	9	31	16
Derby Co	22	6	1	4	38	28	1	0	10	9	53	15
W.B.A.	22	3	1	7	17	26	2	1	8	17	31	12

*Sunderland deducted two points for unapproved registration

Top scorer: J.Campbell (Sunderland) 32 goals. Darwen joined, Stoke rejoined League.

DIVISION 1

	ACCRINGTON	ASTON VILLA	BLACKBURN R	BOLTON W	BURNLEY	DARWEN	DERBY CO	EVERTON	NOTTS CO	PRESTON N.E.	STOKE	SUNDERLAND	W.B.A.	WOLVERHAMPTON W
1 ACCRINGTON		J04 3-2	F27 1-0	N07 0-3	S05 1-0	O10 1-1	a02 1-1	S26 1-1	N21 2-0	J02 1-3	J09 3-0	M05 3-5	J23 4-2	O24 3-2
2 ASTON VILLA	M12 12-2		S05 5-1	O10 1-2	D05 6-1	D26 7-0	J09 6-0	D28 3-4	N07 5-1	a16 3-1	N21 2-1	S28 5-3	S12 5-1	a18 3-6
3 BLACKBURN R	D26 2-2	M05 4-3		N21 4-0	S26 3-3	D25 4-0	J02 0-2	D05 2-2	S12 5-4	O24 2-4	M19 5-3	N07 3-1	M12 3-2	O10 2-0
4 BOLTON W	O03 3-4	a02 1-2	O31 4-2		O24 2-0	S12 1-0	J01 3-1	O17 1-0	M26 2-0	S26 3-0	N14 1-1	S19 4-3	D19 1-1	D05 3-0
5 BURNLEY	N14 2-1	O17 4-1	D12 3-0	M05 1-2		J09 9-0	a16 2-4	F13 1-0	a15 1-0	S07 2-0	S19 4-1	a30 1-2	N28 3-2	M26 1-1
6 DARWEN	S19 5-2	O31 1-5	O17 3-5	S05 1-2	a02 2-6		N28 2-0	N14 3-1	F27 2-3	J01 0-4	O03 9-3	a23 1-7	a16 1-1	M01 1-4
7 DERBY CO	S12 3-1	O03 4-2	M26 1-1	D26 3-2	D19 0-1	N21 7-0		O24 0-3	S19 3-0	D05 1-2	O17 3-3	M19 0-1	F06 1-1	O31 2-1
8 EVERTON	M19 3-0	N28 5-1	S19 3-1	a18 2-5	J02 1-1	S07 5-3	a15 1-2		a16 4-0	O10 1-1	M05 1-0	D25 0-4	N07 4-3	D12 2-1
9 NOTTS CO	N28 9-0	J02 5-2	D19 2-2	O01 2-0	M01 5-1	O24 5-0	F20 2-1	J09 1-3		S05 2-0	S26 1-1	a09 1-0	O10 4-0	N14 2-2
10 PRESTON N.E.	a15 4-1	S19 0-1	N14 3-2	N28 4-0	S21 5-1	a18 4-0	M05 3-0	O31 4-0	D12 6-0		**D25 3-2**	S12 3-1	J09 1-0	**O03 2-0**
11 STOKE	D19 3-1	O24 2-3	N09 0-1	D12 0-1	O10 3-0	D05 5-1	S05 2-1	M12 0-1	F06 1-3	N07 0-1		N28 1-3	a23 1-0	S12 1-3
12 SUNDERLAND	O31 4-1	M26 2-1	a16 6-1	M01 4-1	N21 2-1	D12 7-0	N14 7-1	O03 2-1	D05 4-0	M12 4-1	a02 4-1		O24 4-0	S05 5-2
13 W.B.A.	D05 3-1	N14 0-3	O03 2-2	N02 0-2	D26 1-0	a04 12-0	D12 4-2	S05 4-0	O31 2-2	N21 1-2	a11 2-2	O17 2-5		S19 4-3
14 WOLVERHAMPTON W	S14 5-0	D19 2-0	N28 6-1	a16 1-2	N07 0-0	S28 2-2	S26 1-3	N21 5-1	O17 2-1	a02 3-0	J02 4-1	D26 1-3	D28 2-1	

LEAGUE TABLE
FOOTBALL LEAGUE

	P	W	D	L	F	A	W	D	L	F	A	Pts
Sunderland	26	13	0	0	55	11	8	0	5	38	25	42
Preston N.E.	26	12	0	1	42	8	6	1	6	19	23	37
Bolton W	26	9	2	2	29	14	8	0	5	22	23	36
Aston Villa	26	10	0	3	63	23	5	0	8	26	33	30
Everton	26	8	2	3	32	22	4	2	7	17	27	28
Wolverhampton W	26	8	2	3	34	15	3	2	8	25	31	26
Burnley	26	9	1	3	34	14	2	3	8	15	31	26
Notts Co	26	9	3	1	41	12	2	1	10	14	39	26
Blackburn R	26	8	3	2	39	26	2	3	8	19	39	26
Derby Co	26	6	3	4	28	18	4	1	8	18	34	24
Accrington S	26	7	3	3	24	20	1	1	11	16	58	20
W.B.A.	26	6	3	4	37	24	0	3	10	14	34	18
Stoke	26	5	0	8	19	19	0	4	9	19	42	14
Darwen	26	4	1	8	31	43	0	2	11	7	69	11

Everton's 1890-91 line-up. Back row (left to right, players only): Hannah, Smalley, Doyle. Middle row: Brady, Kirkwood, Holt, Parry, Chadwick. Front row: Latta, Geary, Millward. Goalkeeper Smalley made only one appearance as the Goodison club became the second club to write their name on the Football League Championship trophy. The regular 'keepers were Jardine and Angus.

Football League Records
Season 1892-93

Top scorers: Div 1, J.Campbell (Sunderland) 31 goals; Div 2, G.Wheldon (Small Heath) 24 goals.
Test Matches: 22 Apr Sheffield United 1 Accrington 0 (Nottingham); Darwen 3 Notts County 2 (Ardwick); Small Heath 1 Newton Heath 1 (Stoke); 27 Apr Newton Heath 5 Small Heath 2 (Sheffield). Darwen and Sheffield United promoted, Notts County relegated.
Bootle, Burton Swifts, Crewe Alexandra, Grimsby Town, Lincoln City, Ardwick, Northwich Victoria, Burslem Port Vale, Sheffield United, Small Heath and Walsall Town Swifts were elected to the new Division Two; Newton Heath, Nottingham Forest and Sheffield Wednesday elected straight into Division One.

DIVISION 1

	ACCRINGTON	ASTON VILLA	BLACKBURN R	BOLTON W	BURNLEY	DERBY CO	EVERTON	NEWTON HEATH	NOTTINGHAM F	NOTTS CO	PRESTON N.E.	SHEFFIELD W	STOKE	SUNDERLAND	W.B.A.	WOLVERHAMPTON W
1 ACCRINGTON		a15 1-1	J02 1-1	O08 1-1	J14 0-4	M31 0-3	F25 0-3	N26 2-2	M18 1-1	D10 4-2	N05 1-2	S24 4-2	D26 5-2	S03 0-6	D17 5-4	D31 4-0
2 ASTON VILLA	M25 6-4		D10 4-1	D24 1-1	a04 1-3	O29 6-1	S10 4-1	M06 2-0	O15 1-0	M18 3-1	N26 3-1	J07 5-1	O10 3-2	S17 1-6	N05 5-2	a03 5-0
3 BLACKBURN R	O01 3-3	F11 2-2		N26 3-0	D17 2-0	J07 2-2	S17 2-2	S03 4-3	D31 0-1	D24 1-0	O29 0-0	O15 0-2	F25 3-3	M31 2-2	J28 2-1	N12 3-3
4 BOLTON W	M04 5-2	S24 5-0	M18 2-1		F25 1-0	J02 0-3	O29 4-1	D03 4-1	M31 3-1	M25 4-1	N19 2-4	S17 1-0	O15 4-4	a01 2-1	S10 3-1	O01 3-1
5 BURNLEY	O29 1-3	S05 0-2	D03 0-0	F11 3-0		O08 2-1	a08 3-0	S17 4-1	N26 1-1	O22 3-0	M18 4-2	M31 4-0	S24 3-2	a15 2-3	D31 5-0	a01 2-0
6 DERBY CO	D03 3-3	D17 2-1	O22 3-0	**D26 1-1**	N12 1-0		N05 1-6	F11 5-1	O01 2-3	O19 4-5	S10 1-2	M25 2-2	D24 1-0	a08 1-1	S24 1-1	N26 2-2
7 EVERTON	O22 1-1	O01 1-0	a01 4-0	a03 3-0	D24 0-1	a15 5-0		S24 6-0	S03 2-2	J07 6-0	F11 6-0	N26 3-5	N12 2-2	O08 1-4	J14 1-0	**D10 3-2**
8 NEWTON HEATH	a08 3-3	N19 2-0	N05 4-4	D10 1-0	S10 1-1	D31 7-1	O19 3-4		J14 1-3	N12 1-3	a01 2-1	D24 1-5	M31 1-0	M04 0-5	O08 2-4	O15 10-1
9 NOTTINGHAM F	J07 3-0	N12 4-5	M11 0-1	O20 2-0	D10 2-2	J28 1-0	J12 2-1	O29 1-1		F25 3-1	S24 1-2	D01 2-0	S10 3-4	D03 0-5	M02 3-4	D24 3-1
10 NOTTS CO	F11 2-0	D31 1-4	J14 0-0	O06 2-2	D08 3-1	S17 1-1	D17 1-2	J26 4-0	O08 3-0		O01 3-1	S03 0-1	N05 0-1	N26 3-1	N19 8-1	a08 3-0
11 PRESTON N.E.	a03 0-0	O22 4-1	O08 2-1	S03 2-1	O15 2-0	a17 0-1	D03 5-0	D26 2-1	S17 1-0	M31 4-0		S12 4-1	D31 2-1	J07 1-2	a13 1-1	a10 4-0
12 SHEFFIELD W	S10 5-2	D03 5-3	N19 0-3	N05 4-2	O01 2-0	D10 3-3	F13 0-2	O22 1-0	O03 2-2	a03 3-2	J14 0-5		a01 0-1	O29 3-2	J02 6-0	M11 0-1
13 STOKE	S17 2-2	S12 0-1	a03 2-2	J14 6-0	N19 4-1	S03 1-3	J28 0-1	J07 7-1	O22 3-0	M11 1-0	N14 2-1	D17 2-0		M18 0-1	F11 1-2	O29 2-1
14 SUNDERLAND	O15 4-2	J14 6-0	S24 5-0	F14 3-3	N05 2-0	M11 3-1	J03 4-3	a04 6-0	N19 1-0	S10 2-2	D17 2-0	J28 4-2	O01 3-1		O22 8-1	J02 5-2
15 W.B.A.	N12 4-0	S19 3-2	D26 1-2	N07 1-0	J07 7-1	a01 3-1	O15 3-0	O01 0-0	a03 2-2	O29 4-2	D10 0-1	M18 3-0	N26 1-2	D24 1-3		S17 2-1
16 WOLVERHAMPTON W	N19 5-3	O08 2-1	S10 4-2	O22 1-2	S03 1-0	F25 2-1	M18 2-4	D17 2-0	N05 2-2	S24 3-0	a15 2-1	F11 2-0	D03 1-0	D26 2-0	D27 1-1	

DIVISION 2

	ARDWICK	BOOTLE	BURSLEM P.V.	BURTON S	CREWE A	DARWEN	GRIMSBY T	LINCOLN C	NORTHWICH V	SHEFFIELD U	SMALL HEATH	WALSALL T.S.
1 ARDWICK		S03 7-0	S12 2-0	N26 1-1	F18 3-1	D17 4-2	J30 0-3	a17 3-1	S24 1-1	M04 2-3	O22 2-2	O01 2-0
2 BOOTLE	J21 5-3		S17 1-1	F25 3-2	M25 2-1	D31 5-1	D17 3-1	a15 4-1	D03 2-5	S10 2-0	N05 1-4	M18 7-1
3 BURSLEM P.V.	O10 1-2	N12 0-0		O08 1-0	S24 4-1	O01 2-4	F11 0-1	D03 1-2	M04 4-0	D10 0-10	M25 0-3	D31 3-0
4 BURTON S	J14 2-0	S24 2-1	M18 3-3		S03 7-1	D24 0-2	a08 5-1	D17 4-2	N05 2-0	a01 0-3	O03 2-3	F04 3-2
5 CREWE A	F04 4-1	J07 2-1	N26 5-0	O01 2-4		**F25 2-2**	S10 1-0	J28 4-1	S17 4-2	a12 0-4	D31 1-3	N05 5-6
6 DARWEN	O08 3-1	O22 3-0	N05 4-1	S10 2-3	D03 7-3		M18 6-1	J14 3-1	F14 3-1	N19 3-1	D10 4-3	S24 5-0
7 GRIMSBY T	N05 2-0	O08 3-0	J14 2-0	D03 4-0	D24 4-0	S17 0-1		**F18 2-2**	**S03 2-1**	M31 0-1	**O01 3-2**	a01 3-0
8 LINCOLN C	D24 2-1	a01 5-1	O22 3-4	F11 5-1	D26 1-1	N12 1-1	M04 1-3		F25 5-1	O01 1-0	J07 3-4	M31 3-1
9 NORTHWICH V	S10 0-3	O01 3-2	a08 2-4	M25 2-1	O22 4-1	a15 1-0	J07 5-3	D31 2-1		F18 1-3	D24 0-6	N26 5-2
10 SHEFFIELD U	M25 2-1	N26 8-3	D17 4-0	F06 3-1	M18 4-0	O15 2-0	S26 2-0	S03 4-2	J23 1-1		S17 2-0	J07 3-0
11 SMALL HEATH	a01 3-2	F18 6-2	S03 5-1	N12 3-2	O08 6-0	O29 3-2	F25 8-3	S24 4-1	J14 6-2	D03 1-1		D17 12-0
12 WALSALL T.S.	S17 2-4	D24 4-4	F18 3-0	M04 3-2	J14 3-3	S03 1-2	O22 3-1	O08 2-1	F11 2-3	a15 1-1	S10 1-3	

Edgar Chadwick was one of the great names in football in the 1890s. Born in Blackburn, he had one season with Blackburn Rovers before joining Everton for the inaugural Football League season. He won seven England caps at inside-forward and Championship medals with Everton and Southern League Southampton, whom he joined in 1900 after one season with Burnley.

LEAGUE TABLES

DIVISION 1

	P	W	D	L	F	A	W	D	L	F	A	Pts
Sunderland	30	13	2	0	58	17	9	2	4	42	19	48
Preston N.E.	30	11	2	2	34	10	6	1	8	23	29	37
Everton	30	9	3	3	44	17	7	1	7	30	34	36
Aston Villa	30	12	1	2	50	24	4	2	9	23	38	35
Bolton W	30	12	1	2	43	21	1	5	9	13	34	32
Burnley	30	10	2	3	37	15	3	2	10	14	29	30
Stoke	30	8	2	5	33	16	4	3	8	25	32	29
W.B.A.	30	9	2	4	35	17	3	3	9	23	52	29
Blackburn R	30	5	8	2	29	24	3	5	7	18	32	29
Nottingham F	30	7	2	6	30	27	3	6	6	18	25	28
Wolverhampton W	30	11	2	2	32	17	1	2	12	15	51	28
Sheffield W	30	8	2	5	34	28	4	1	10	21	37	27
Derby Co	30	5	6	4	30	28	4	3	8	22	36	27
Notts Co	30	8	3	4	34	15	2	1	12	19	46	24
Accrington S	30	5	5	5	29	34	1	6	8	28	47	23
Newton Heath	30	6	3	6	39	35	0	3	12	11	50	18

DIVISION 2

	P	W	D	L	F	A	W	D	L	F	A	Pts
Small Heath	22	10	1	0	57	16	7	1	3	33	19	36
Sheffield U	22	10	1	0	35	8	6	2	3	27	11	35
Darwen	22	10	0	1	43	15	4	2	5	17	21	30
Grimsby T	22	8	1	2	25	7	3	0	8	17	34	23
Ardwick	22	6	3	2	27	14	3	0	8	18	26	21
Burton S	22	7	1	3	30	18	2	1	8	17	29	20
Northwich V	22	7	0	4	25	26	2	2	7	17	32	20
Bootle	22	8	1	2	35	20	0	2	9	14	43	19
Lincoln C	22	6	2	3	30	18	1	1	9	15	33	17
Crewe A	22	6	1	4	30	24	0	2	9	12	45	15
Burslem P.V.	22	4	1	6	16	23	2	2	7	14	34	15
Walsall	22	4	3	4	25	24	1	0	10	12	51	13

Small Heath, the first champions of Division Two. Back row (left to right, players only): Bayley, Charsley, Pumfrey, Short, Weston. Middle row: Hallam, Walton, Mobley, Jenkyns, Wheldon, Hands. Front row: Ollis, Devey. Goalkeeper Chris Charsley, an amateur throughout his career, won an England cap and later became chief constable of Coventry and deputy mayor of Weston-super-Mare.

FOOTBALL LEAGUE RECORDS
SEASON 1893-94

Top scorers: Div 1, J.Southworth (Everton) 27 goals; Div 2, F.Mobley (Small Heath) 23 goals.
Test Matches: 28 Apr Small Heath 3 Darwen 1 (Stoke); Liverpool 2 Newton Heath 0 (Blackburn); Preston North End 4 Notts County 0 (Sheffield). Liverpool and Small Heath promoted, Darwen and Newton Heath relegated. Accrington and Bootle resigned. Liverpool, Middlesbrough Ironopolis, Newcastle United, Rotherham Town and Woolwich Arsenal elected to League.

DIVISION 1

	ASTON VILLA	BLACKBURN R	BOLTON W	BURNLEY	DARWEN	DERBY CO	EVERTON	NEWTON HEATH	NOTTINGHAM F	PRESTON N.E.	SHEFFIELD U	SHEFFIELD W	STOKE	SUNDERLAND	W.B.A.	WOLVERHAMPTON W
1 ASTON VILLA		M24 2-1	M03 2-3	O28 4-0	D26 9-0	S30 1-1	S23 3-1	F03 5-1	a14 3-1	N25 2-0	O30 4-0	D09 3-0	S11 5-1	N11 2-1	S02 3-2	M26 1-1
2 BLACKBURN R	N04 2-0		D02 0-1	N18 3-2	D25 4-1	M23 0-2	D16 4-3	M26 4-0	F03 6-1	O07 1-0	J15 4-1	S09 5-1	a14 5-0	O21 4-3	J13 3-0	S23 3-0
3 BOLTON W	N18 0-1	S16 2-1		J06 2-0	O07 1-0	J01 1-1	a16 0-1	D09 2-0	M23 1-1	S30 0-3	O14 0-1	D25 1-1	S02 4-1	a23 2-0	a07 0-3	O21 2-0
4 BURNLEY	a07 3-6	D23 1-0	F03 2-1		S04 5-1	M10 3-1	O07 2-1	O21 4-1	N04 3-1	S09 4-1	D25 4-1	M23 0-1	S30 4-0	D02 1-0	D09 3-0	a14 4-2
5 DARWEN	O14 1-1	S02 2-3	O28 1-3	F06 0-0		a14 2-3	J01 3-3	S30 1-0	D23 0-4	F03 2-1	J06 3-3	D11 2-1	S16 3-1	a07 0-3	N11 2-1	M10 3-1
6 DERBY CO	D02 0-3	M31 5-2	D26 6-1	a02 3-3	N18 2-1		S09 7-3	O07 2-0	D09 3-4	J06 2-1	N04 2-1	O21 3-3	D23 5-2	M07 1-4	S16 2-3	F03 4-1
7 EVERTON	S16 4-2	O14 2-2	M26 3-2	N25 4-3	O21 8-1	N11 1-2		J06 2-0	S04 4-0	O28 2-3	S02 2-3	D23 8-1	a07 6-2	S30 7-1	D30 7-1	M24 3-0
8 NEWTON HEATH	D16 1-3	M12 5-1	M24 2-2	S02 3-2	N04 0-1	M17 2-6	D02 0-3		S23 1-1	a14 1-3	M10 0-2	J13 1-2	M23 6-2	M03 2-4	O14 4-1	N11 1-0
9 NOTTINGHAM F	O07 1-2	N25 0-0	O05 1-0	S16 5-0	M15 4-1	D30 4-2	J18 3-2	a07 2-0		M24 4-2	N18 1-1	O28 1-0	O21 2-0	J13 1-2	S30 2-3	S02 7-1
10 PRESTON N.E.	J18 2-5	N11 0-1	N04 1-0	O14 1-2	S23 4-1	S02 1-0	J13 2-4	D23 2-0	D02 0-2		a07 3-0	M26 1-0	D25 3-3	S16 1-2	M03 3-1	D16 1-3
11 SHEFFIELD U	O02 3-0	M03 3-2	S23 4-2	M26 1-0	S09 2-1	S04 1-2	D09 0-3	N25 3-1	J01 0-2	N20 1-1		O16 1-1	F03 3-3	O07 1-0	O28 0-2	J13 3-2
12 SHEFFIELD W	J06 2-2	S30 4-2	D16 2-1	D26 0-1	J15 5-0	O14 4-0	N04 1-1	S16 0-1	M05 1-0	F06 3-0	N13 1-2		D07 4-1	S02 2-2	S25 2-4	D02 1-4
13 STOKE	O16 3-3	O28 3-1	J13 5-0	N11 4-2	D02 3-1	S23 3-1	M03 3-1	M31 3-1	S09 2-1	N13 2-1	D16 5-0	O07 4-1		M24 2-0	J20 3-1	D30 0-3
14 SUNDERLAND	S09 1-1	D09 2-3	D30 2-1	D16 2-2	M27 4-0	O28 5-0	F06 1-0	D06 4-1	M17 2-0	J01 6-3	J20 4-1	S23 1-1	O14 4-0		N25 2-1	N04 6-0
15 W.B.A.	O21 3-6	J06 2-1	N06 5-2	S23 1-1	D16 2-2	M24 0-1	F03 3-1	S09 3-1	M26 3-0	D04 2-0	D26 3-1	N27 2-2	N04 4-2	D23 2-3		O07 0-0
16 WOLVERHAMPTON W	D23 3-0	D26 5-1	S09 2-1	M03 1-0	S18 2-1	J20 2-4	D04 2-0	O28 2-0	O14 3-1	D09 0-0	S30 3-4	S04 3-1	N25 4-2	J06 2-1	D27 0-8	

DIVISION 2

	ARDWICK	BURSLEM P.V.	BURTON S	CREWE A	GRIMSBY T	LINCOLN C	LIVERPOOL	MIDDLESBROUGH I	NEWCASTLE U	NORTHWICH V	NOTTS CO	ROTHERHAM T	SMALL HEATH	WALSALL T.S.	W ARSENAL
1 ARDWICK		O07 8-1	S11 1-4	a07 1-2	D09 4-1	M31 0-1	S16 0-1	S09 6-1	O21 2-3	J27 4-2	O28 0-0	D26 3-2	S30 0-1	N18 3-0	D30 0-1
2 BURSLEM P.V.	S02 4-2		D16 3-1	S16 4-2	D04 6-1	M10 5-3	a07 2-2	S18 4-0	F03 1-1	S30 3-2	N25 1-0	O21 2-3	S25 5-0	F10 1-2	J06 2-1
3 BURTON S	S20 5-0	J13 5-3		M31 6-1	a07 0-3	F10 1-3	O21 1-1	M17 7-0	S23 3-1	O02 6-2	D30 0-2	S30 4-1	D09 0-2	F24 8-5	N18 6-2
4 CREWE A	F24 1-1	D09 1-1	O07 1-2		J20 3-3	O21 1-1	D28 0-5	S30 5-0	D27 1-1	O28 3-0	S02 0-2	J27 2-0	J13 3-5	D02 1-1	M03 0-0
5 GRIMSBY T	J13 5-0	D02 4-0	S16 2-1	M10 3-2		O28 2-4	M31 0-1	F03 2-1	a14 0-0	S02 7-0.	O21 5-2	F10 7-1	M03 2-1	S30 5-2	D26 3-1
6 LINCOLN C	M24 6-0	F24 2-2	D23 1-1	D25 6-1	S23 1-2		M17 1-1	D26 2-3	O07 2-1	S16 4-1	M23 0-2	S02 1-1	N11 2-5	a07 0-2	F03 3-0
7 LIVERPOOL	D02 3-0	a14 2-1	M03 3-1	M24 2-0	D30 2-0	S09 4-0		O07 6-0	N04 5-1	F03 4-0	N18 2-1	J13 5-1	S23 3-1	D09 3-0	J01 2-0
8 MIDDLESBROUGH I	S23 2-0	J01 3-1	O28 2-1	J06 2-0	N11 2-6	J13 0-0	S02 0-2		D25 1-1	M03 2-1	D16 0-0	D09 6-1	N25 3-0	D30 1-1	F24 3-6
9 NEWCASTLE U	J06 2-1	D30 2-1	M24 4-1	M23 2-1	F24 4-1	J01 5-1	N25 0-0	J02 7-2		J13 3-0	D09 3-0	F17 4-0	O28 0-2	M10 2-0	S30 6-0
10 NORTHWICH V	F10 1-4	S23 1-5	M10 1-1	S09 1-2	F17 0-1	J20 0-3	M28 2-3	a07 2-1	N18 5-3		S11 0-1	M31 1-1	J06 0-7	O07 1-0	D09 2-2
11 NOTTS CO	M15 5-0	O26 6-1	N30 6-2	F17 9-1	O05 3-0	N16 1-2	S30 1-1	N04 3-0	O14 3-1	N23 6-1		J11 4-2	F03 3-1	J20 2-0	S09 3-2
12 ROTHERHAM T	M26 1-3	O28 0-1	N11 2-5	a09 1-4	S09 4-3	D02 2-8	J06 1-4	a14 4-1	J20 2-1	D30 5-4	S16 0-2		M23 2-3	F03 3-2	F06 1-1
13 SMALL HEATH	M17 10-2	M24 6-0	S09 6-1	D06 6-1	O07 5-2	D30 6-0	O14 3-4	D23 2-1	D16 1-4	D02 8-0	a07 3-0	S04 4-3		S16 4-0	O21 4-1
14 WALSALL T.S.	a14 5-2	S09 0-5	J06 3-4	S23 5-1	M24 5-0	M26 5-2	N11 1-1	O21 1-0	D26 1-2	D23 3-0	M12 2-1	S26 3-0	S02 1-3		F12 1-2
15 W ARSENAL	N11 1-0	D25 4-1	a14 0-2	F10 3-2	S25 3-1	F17 4-0	O28 0-5	M10 1-0	S02 2-2	M23 6-0	M24 1-2	N13 3-0	M31 1-4	S11 4-0	

LEAGUE TABLES

DIVISION 1

	P	W	D	L	F	A	W	D	L	F	A	Pts
Aston Villa	30	12	2	1	49	13	7	4	4	35	29	44
Sunderland	30	11	3	1	46	14	6	1	8	26	30	38
Derby Co	30	9	2	4	47	32	7	2	6	26	30	36
Blackburn R	30	13	0	2	48	15	3	2	10	21	38	34
Burnley	30	13	0	2	43	17	2	4	9	18	34	34
Everton	30	11	1	3	63	23	4	2	9	27	34	33
Nottingham F	30	10	2	3	38	16	4	2	9	19	32	32
W.B.A.	30	8	4	3	35	23	6	0	9	31	36	32
Wolverhampton W	30	11	1	3	34	24	3	2	10	18	39	31
Sheffield U	30	8	3	4	26	22	5	2	8	21	39	31
Stoke	30	13	1	1	45	17	0	2	13	20	62	29
Sheffield W	30	7	3	5	32	21	2	5	8	16	36	26
Bolton W	30	7	3	5	18	14	3	1	11	20	38	24
Preston N.E.	30	7	1	7	25	24	3	2	10	19	32	23
Darwen	30	6	4	5	25	28	1	1	13	12	55	19
Newton Heath	30	5	2	8	29	33	1	0	14	7	39	14

DIVISION 2

	P	W	D	L	F	A	W	D	L	F	A	Pts
Liverpool	28	14	0	0	46	6	8	6	0	31	12	50
Small Heath	28	12	0	2	68	19	9	0	5	35	25	42
Notts Co	28	12	1	1	55	14	6	2	6	15	17	39
Newcastle U	28	12	1	1	44	10	3	5	6	22	29	36
Grimsby T	28	11	1	2	47	16	4	1	9	24	42	32
Burton S	28	9	1	4	52	26	5	2	7	27	35	31
Burslem P.V.	28	10	2	2	43	20	3	2	9	23	44	30
Lincoln C	28	5	4	5	31	22	6	2	6	28	36	28
Woolwich A	28	9	1	4	33	19	3	3	8	19	36	28
Walsall	28	8	1	5	36	23	2	2	10	15	38	23
Middlesbrough	28	7	4	3	27	20	1	0	13	10	52	20
Crewe A	28	3	7	4	22	22	3	0	11	20	51	19
Ardwick	28	6	1	7	32	20	2	1	11	15	51	18
Rotherham U	28	5	1	8	28	42	1	2	11	16	49	15
Northwich V	28	3	3	8	17	34	0	0	14	13	64	9

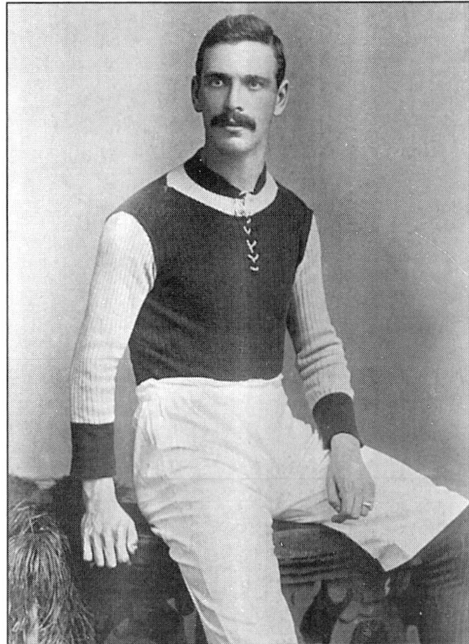

John Devey of Aston Villa, the Football League Champions' leading scorer with 20 goals in 1893-94. In all, Devey won five Championship medals with Villa and appeared in three FA Cup Finals, twice on the winning side. He was restricted to two England caps by the presence by Steve Bloomer and John Goodall. Devey was also a fine cricketer who played for Warwickshire.

Liverpool, Division Two champions in 1893-94. Back row (left to right, players only): McCartney, M.McQueen, Hannah, McOwen, McLean, Dick, Henderson. Front row: Gordon, McVean, McQue, McBride, Bradshaw, Stott, H.McQueen.

Football League Records
Season 1894-95

Top scorers: Div 1, J.Campbell (Sunderland) 22 goals; Div 2, D.Skea (Leicester Fosse) 22 goals.
Test Matches: 27 Apr Bury 1 Liverpool 0 (Blackburn); Derby County 2 Notts County 1 (Leicester); Stoke 3 Newton Heath 0 (Burslem). Bury promoted, Liverpool relegated. Middlesbrough Ironopolis and Northwich Victoria resigned. Burton Wanderers, Bury and Leicester Fosse elected in their place.

DIVISION 1

	ASTON VILLA	BLACKBURN R	BOLTON W	BURNLEY	DERBY CO	EVERTON	LIVERPOOL	NOTTINGHAM F	PRESTON N.E.	SHEFFIELD U	SHEFFIELD W	SMALL HEATH	STOKE	SUNDERLAND	W.B.A.	WOLVERHAMPTON W
1 ASTON VILLA		D08 3-0	J26 2-1	a06 5-0	J05 4-0	a24 2-2	O27 5-0	N24 4-1	N10 4-1	N12 5-0	D03 3-1	S01 2-1	D26 6-0	S15 1-2	O13 3-1	a15 2-2
2 BLACKBURN R	D01 1-3		O13 2-1	N17 1-0	a12 0-0	O20 4-3	S01 1-1	J01 0-0	O27 1-1	D26 3-2	S29 3-1	J05 9-1	S15 6-0	N10 1-1	D22 3-0	M23 5-1
3 BOLTON W	M23 4-3	N03 1-3		O20 1-1	J01 6-0	O06 1-3	D25 1-0	a12 4-1	S15 1-2	J14 6-2	J07 2-2	N24 1-2	S01 2-2	S29 4-1	a13 5-0	D15 6-1
4 BURNLEY	F23 3-3	J12 2-1	J05 1-0		S29 2-0	M16 2-4	S03 3-3	O27 0-1	D08 2-1	D22 2-4	N10 3-0	O13 3-1	a20 1-2	a13 0-3	N24 2-0	S22 2-1
5 DERBY CO	S22 0-2	a06 0-0	D26 2-2	D12 0-2		J12 2-2	J09 0-1	S08 4-2	N24 2-1	D15 4-1	S15 1-2	M30 4-1	J19 1-1	O13 1-2	O27 1-1	J26 1-3
6 EVERTON	J17 4-2	N24 2-1	D08 3-1	M21 3-2	a13 2-3		O13 3-0	S15 6-1	F23 4-2	J26 1-1	S01 3-1	S03 5-0	J07 3-0	O27 2-2	S29 4-1	a08 2-1
7 LIVERPOOL	S08 1-2	S22 2-2	S13 1-2	N03 0-3	M02 5-1	N17 2-2		J12 5-0	a20 2-5	O06 2-2	M30 4-2	D15 3-1	O20 2-0	M25 2-3	J01 4-0	D01 3-3
8 NOTTINGHAM F	O06 2-1	D29 2-3	M16 3-3	S01 2-1	N03 2-1	S22 2-3	a06 3-0		O04 0-2	N17 3-0	J19 2-1	J26 2-0	F23 3-1	D27 2-1	D08 5-3	a13 0-2
9 PRESTON N.E.	J12 0-1	O06 1-1	D01 2-2	J26 4-0	N17 3-2	D15 1-2	a12 2-2	M23 3-1		S08 2-1	a13 3-1	S22 0-1	D25 3-0	D29 1-0	F26 5-0	O20 2-0
10 SHEFFIELD U	O22 2-1	O08 3-0	a15 5-0	S15 2-2	D25 1-4	F26 4-2	D08 2-2	S29 3-2	O13 0-1		J12 1-0	a13 0-2	F09 3-0	M09 4-0	S01 2-1	J19 1-0
11 SHEFFIELD W	N03 1-0	S08 4-1	S22 2-1	O06 4-3	D29 1-1	J01 3-0	J05 5-0	D15 0-0	S03 3-1	O27 2-3		D26 2-0	a17 2-4	M23 1-2	a01 3-2	N17 3-1
12 SMALL HEATH	O20 2-2	M02 1-1	S08 2-0	M23 1-0	M16 3-5	N03 4-4	D29 3-0	D22 1-2	S29 4-4	D01 4-2	M25 0-0		N17 4-2	F09 1-1	F23 1-2	O06 4-3
13 STOKE	S29 4-1	a13 5-1	J12 5-0	M30 5-1	M23 4-1	S08 1-3	N10 3-1	O13 0-3	N12 2-1	S22 1-3	D08 0-2	O27 2-2		J26 2-5	M25 1-1	F04 0-0
14 SUNDERLAND	J02 4-4	D15 3-2	N17 4-0	S08 3-0	S01 8-0	a20 2-1	N24 3-2	J05 2-2	J01 2-0	F23 2-0	F26 3-1	D08 7-1	O06 3-1		S22 3-0	N03 2-0
15 W.B.A.	N17 3-2	J26 2-0	N05 1-1	D29 0-1	O20 2-2	D01 1-4	S15 5-0	a15 1-0	J05 4-5	N03 1-0	a22 6-0	N10 4-1	D15 3-2	D26 0-2		S08 5-1
16 WOLVERHAMPTON W	D22 0-4	F23 3-3	O27 4-2	D26 1-0	D08 2-2	J05 1-0	S29 3-1	N10 1-1	S01 1-3	S03 0-3	O13 2-0	S15 2-1	N24 0-0	J12 1-4	D27 3-1	

DIVISION 2

	BURSLEM P.V.	BURTON S	BURTON W	BURY	CREWE A	DARWEN	GRIMSBY T	LEICESTER F	LINCOLN C	ARDWICK	NEWCASTLE U	NEWTON HEATH	NOTTS CO	ROTHERHAM T	WALSALL T.S.	W ARSENAL
1 BURSLEM P.V.		M04 2-0	O20 1-0	S15 1-2	a20 4-0	N17 0-3	a06 5-0	F23 1-1	M16 7-1	F02 1-2	O06 4-4	D24 2-5	S17 0-3	F16 1-1	S01 1-0	J19 0-1
2 BURTON S	S29 1-0		F16 2-2	a06 0-1	S01 4-0	M16 3-0	S19 2-1	M02 0-5	J26 6-1	N10 2-1	J05 5-3	O20 1-2	D22 2-2	M30 2-0	O01 1-2	S15 3-0
3 BURTON W	M09 4-0	O27 1-2		N17 1-2	J19 4-0	M23 2-2	a13 0-0	F09 1-1	F23 4-1	D26 8-0	a15 9-0	S08 1-0	D08 1-0	O06 4-0	J12 7-0	a20 2-1
4 BURY	N10 4-0	D01 2-0	D22 4-0		S08 4-1	S29 1-0	O06 5-1	D25 4-1	J12 4-1	S01 4-2	N03 4-1	a15 2-1	J01 2-1	S18 2-1	a02 4-1	M02 2-0
5 CREWE A	J05 2-2	O06 1-3	M16 1-2	O20 1-5		F23 2-2	F09 2-1	J12 2-2	O27 1-4	D31 2-3	M09 2-1	D01 0-2	J16 0-3	S22 2-1	S29 2-3	M23 0-0
6 DARWEN	O27 2-0	a20 5-0	S22 2-0	D15 0-1	F16 5-0		J12 4-1	J15 8-2	S08 6-0	a06 4-0	S01 5-0	O06 1-1	J26 2-1	M09 4-3	D01 2-0	J01 3-1
7 GRIMSBY T	J26 4-1	M09 7-1	S29 7-2	J05 3-2	D08 5-0	M30 2-1		S01 4-3	N10 3-0	a20 2-1	S15 3-0	N17 2-1	F05 0-1	O27 4-1	M16 1-0	D26 4-2
8 LEICESTER F	M23 2-1	N17 2-2	S15 1-2	a20 1-0	F18 4-0	N10 2-1	a15 1-0		M04 2-1	M16 3-1	O20 4-4	S22 2-3	D01 5-1	S08 4-2	J05 9-1	J07 3-1
9 LINCOLN C	D08 6-1	S22 3-2	M30 0-2	D26 1-3	a13 5-2	J05 0-2	O20 1-5	a06 1-2		M02 0-2	N17 3-1	D29 3-0	a12 1-3	D25 2-0	F16 1-0	S01 5-2
10 ARDWICK	S08 4-1	a13 4-1	S03 1-1	D08 3-3	a12 4-1	O20 2-4	S22 2-5	M30 1-1	M23 11-3		F09 4-0	N03 2-5	M09 7-1	J01 1-0	O06 6-1	D15 4-1
11 NEWCASTLE U	a12 1-2	S08 6-3	N10 3-1	M16 1-0	D25 6-0	O13 3-2	D01 1-4	S29 2-0	J01 4-2	O27 5-4		a13 3-0	S22 2-2	D15 5-2	D22 7-2	N24 2-4
12 NEWTON HEATH	J01 3-0	D08 5-1	M02 1-1	a12 2-2	S15 6-1	N24 1-1	M23 2-0	O27 2-2	D22 3-0	J05 4-1	a06 5-1		a20 3-3	N10 3-2	a03 9-0	O13 3-3
13 NOTTS CO	F26 10-0	J12 5-1	J05 2-0	N24 2-1	N10 5-1	S15 2-1	O04 3-2	O06 3-0	S29 3-0	O13 1-3	M23 2-1	D15 1-1		M16 4-2	D25 5-0	O27 2-2
14 ROTHERHAM T	M02 2-1	D29 4-1	S01 1-3	N06 2-3	a15 2-0	a13 4-1	J07 3-2	J26 0-1	S15 5-2	O01 3-2	D26 1-0	J12 2-1	N05 1-2		N17 6-1	O20 1-2
15 WALSALL T.S.	S22 2-0	M23 4-1	a16 3-1	O27 0-3	J26 4-0	a15 5-1	S08 4-3	D08 1-3	a20 1-2	S15 1-2	D29 2-3	D26 1-2	M25 2-1	S24 1-2		N10 4-1
16 W ARSENAL	D25 7-0	F23 3-0	J26 1-1	S22 4-2	a06 7-0	D08 4-0	S10 1-3	M09 3-3	O06 5-2	S29 4-2	J12 3-2	M30 3-2	N03 2-1	F09 1-1	a12 6-1	

LEAGUE TABLES

DIVISION 1

	P	W	D	L	F	A	W	D	L	F	A	Pts
Sunderland	30	13	2	0	51	14	8	3	4	29	23	47
Everton	30	12	2	1	47	18	6	4	5	35	32	42
Aston Villa	30	12	2	1	51	12	5	3	7	31	31	39
Preston N.E.	30	9	3	3	32	14	6	2	7	30	32	35
Blackburn R	30	9	5	1	40	15	2	5	8	19	34	32
Sheffield U	30	10	2	3	33	17	4	2	9	24	38	32
Nottingham F	30	10	1	4	33	22	3	4	8	17	34	31
Sheffield W	30	10	2	3	36	19	2	2	11	14	36	28
Burnley	30	8	2	5	28	24	3	2	10	16	32	26
Bolton W	30	8	3	4	45	23	1	4	10	16	39	25
Wolverhampton W	30	7	4	4	24	25	2	3	10	19	38	25
Small Heath	30	6	6	3	35	28	3	1	11	15	46	25
W.B.A.	30	9	2	4	38	21	1	2	12	13	45	24
Stoke	30	7	3	5	35	25	2	3	10	15	42	24
Derby Co	30	4	5	6	23	23	3	4	8	22	45	23
Liverpool	30	6	4	5	38	28	1	4	10	13	42	22

DIVISION 2

	P	W	D	L	F	A	W	D	L	F	A	Pts
Bury	30	15	0	0	48	11	8	2	5	30	22	48
Notts Co	30	12	2	1	50	15	5	3	7	25	30	39
Newton Heath	30	9	6	0	52	18	6	2	7	26	26	38
Leicester C	30	11	2	2	45	20	4	6	5	27	33	38
Grimsby T	30	14	0	1	51	16	4	1	10	28	36	37
Darwen	30	13	1	1	53	10	3	3	9	21	33	36
Burton W	30	10	3	2	49	9	4	4	7	18	30	35
Woolwich A	30	11	3	1	54	20	3	3	9	21	38	34
Manchester C	30	9	3	3	56	28	5	0	10	26	44	31
Newcastle U	30	11	1	3	51	28	1	2	12	21	56	27
Burton S	30	9	2	4	34	20	2	1	12	18	54	25
Rotherham U	30	10	0	5	37	22	1	2	12	18	40	24
Lincoln C	30	8	0	7	32	27	2	0	13	20	65	20
Walsall	30	8	0	7	35	25	2	0	13	12	67	20
Burslem P.V.	30	6	3	6	30	23	1	1	13	9	54	18
Crewe A	30	3	4	8	20	34	0	0	15	6	69	10

Scottish international forward John Bell, who scored 15 goals for runners-up, Everton. He was a 'masterful dribbler' who joined Everton from Dumbarton and later had spells with Spurs, Celtic, New Brighton Tower, Everton (again) and Preston, where he became player-coach.

Sunderland the 1894-95 Football League Champions. Back row (left to right, players only): McNeil, Doig, Wilson, Gow, McCreadie. Middle row: Dunlop, Miller, Hannah, Harvie. Front row: Auld, Gillespy, Campbell, Scott, Johnston.

FOOTBALL LEAGUE RECORDS
SEASON 1895-96

Top scorers: Div 1, J.Campbell (Aston Villa), S.Bloomer (Derby County) 20 goals; Div 2, G.Allan (Liverpool) 26 goals.
Test Matches: 18 Apr Ardwick 1 West Bromwich Albion 1; Liverpool 4 Small Heath 0; 20 Apr West Bromwich Albion 6 Ardwick 1; Small Heath 0 Liverpool 0; 25 Apr Ardwick 3 Small Heath 0; Liverpool 2 West Bromwich Albion 0; 27 Apr Small Heath 8 Ardwick 0; West Bromwich Albion 2 Liverpool 0. Liverpool promoted. Small Heath relegated. Loughborough Town elected in place of Walsall Town Swifts.

DIVISION 1

	ASTON VILLA	BLACKBURN R	BOLTON W	BURNLEY	BURY	DERBY CO	EVERTON	NOTTINGHAM F	PRESTON N.E.	SHEFFIELD U	SHEFFIELD W	SMALL HEATH	STOKE	SUNDERLAND	W.B.A.	WOLVERHAMPTON W
1 ASTON VILLA		O19 3-1	D14 2-0	N02 5-1	D28 2-0	S21 4-1	S30 4-3	J25 3-1	J11 1-0	N16 2-2	M14 2-1	S07 7-3	F22 5-2	O05 2-1	S02 1-0	a06 4-1
2 BLACKBURN R	S28 1-1		D07 3-2	O05 1-0	J04 0-2	F22 0-2	J01 2-3	S14 2-0	O12 3-0	J25 1-0	N23 2-1	M21 2-1	a03 3-1	O26 2-4	F17 1-0	N09 3-1
3 BOLTON W	M07 2-2	N30 1-1		S21 1-0	O05 2-4	J01 2-1	S14 3-1	O19 2-1	M14 1-0	a03 4-1	a25 2-0	F22 4-1	O26 3-1	D21 1-0	a04 2-1	J04 4-0
4 BURNLEY	N23 3-4	a13 6-0	O12 1-2		S14 3-0	a04 2-2	O26 1-1	D21 0-0	S28 1-0	F03 5-0	J04 2-0	a03 1-1	M16 2-0	S09 0-0	J11 3-0	F22 3-1
5 BURY	M21 5-3	a25 2-0	S07 0-3	J01 3-4		N23 1-2	J11 1-1	M24 1-0	D14 1-2	S21 1-0	N09 6-1	O12 4-5	N30 0-1	a03 1-2	N02 3-0	F18 3-0
6 DERBY CO	F08 2-2	a11 0-0	D26 2-1	N09 5-1	O19 2-1		a07 2-1	D07 4-0	M04 1-0	M14 0-2	S28 3-1	N30 8-0	O12 2-1	S14 2-0	D14 4-1	O26 5-2
7 EVERTON	D21 2-0	S21 0-2	a06 1-1	N30 2-1	S09 3-2	a03 2-2		**S07 6-2**	**M07 3-2**	**O05 5-0**	**S02 2-2**	**F03 3-0**	**D14 7-2**	**N16 1-0**	**O19 1-1**	N02 2-0
8 NOTTINGHAM F	a03 0-2	D28 4-2	J11 0-0	M07 2-1	S05 5-0	O05 2-5	O12 2-1		O26 0-1	D14 3-1	a07 1-0	S21 3-0	N28 4-0	J18 3-1	N16 2-0	a04 3-2
9 PRESTON N.E.	D07 4-3	N02 1-1	N09 1-0	O19 1-1	a04 1-1	M28 1-0	J25 1-1	F22 6-0		N30 4-3	a06 0-1	O05 3-2	D25 0-1	J04 4-1	a03 0-0	S07 4-3
10 SHEFFIELD U	S14 2-1	M07 1-1	D30 1-0	M30 1-1	a06 8-0	D21 1-1	N09 1-2	N23 2-1	S30 2-1		D26 1-1	S02 2-0	S28 1-0	O07 1-2	J04 2-0	F08 2-1
11 SHEFFIELD W	J18 1-3	J11 3-0	N02 1-1	D14 1-0	F22 1-3	D28 0-4	F18 3-1	N30 3-0	J01 1-1	S07 1-0		a04 3-0	N16 2-1	O19 3-0	O05 5-3	O12 3-1
12 SMALL HEATH	O26 1-4	F29 2-1	S28 1-2	D26 1-0	M07 1-0	J04 1-3	D07 0-3	N09 1-0	N23 5-2	a07 2-1	F08 1-1		S14 1-2	a11 0-1	D21 2-2	J18 3-2
13 STOKE	J04 1-2	a04 3-0	S02 2-0	D07 2-1	D26 0-2	S07 2-1	a11 1-2	M21 1-0	N11 4-0	N02 4-0	D21 5-0	O19 6-1		M14 5-0	S21 3-1	N23 4-1
14 SUNDERLAND	N09 2-1	S07 2-1	N23 1-0	F18 3-1	S28 0-0	N02 2-2	F22 3-0	F08 1-1	S02 4-1	J11 1-1	M07 2-1	D14 2-1	M28 4-1		J25 7-1	S21 2-2
15 W.B.A.	O12 1-1	a29 3-2	N04 2-3	S07 0-2	M09 1-3	J18 0-0	N23 0-3	S28 3-1	S14 1-2	F22 1-0	O26 2-3	a06 0-0	N09 1-0	D26 1-1		N30 2-1
16 WOLVERHAMPTON W	D26 1-2	D14 1-2	a11 5-0	S02 5-1	a07 1-0	N16 2-0	S28 2-3	M28 6-1	D21 2-1	O19 4-1	S14 4-0	J25 7-2	O05 1-0	D27 1-3	M07 1-2	

DIVISION 2

	BURSLEM P.V.	BURTON S	BURTON W	CREWE A	DARWEN	GRIMSBY T	LEICESTER F	LINCOLN C	LIVERPOOL	LOUGHBOROUGH T	ARDWICK	NEWCASTLE U	NEWTON HEATH	NOTTS CO	ROTHERHAM T	W ARSENAL
1 BURSLEM P.V.		J11 1-0	J18 2-2	O26 2-1	O05 3-3	N16 1-4	M07 1-1	F22 0-1	O21 5-4	a07 1-1	F10 0-1	a20 2-0	M23 3-0	S14 0-4	J25 4-0	F15 0-2
2 BURTON S	M14 2-1		**O26 0-2**	J04 1-1	a11 1-2	N09 2-1	M28 0-2	S30 4-0	F29 0-7	S28 1-2	**N30 1-4**	D07 3-1	F08 4-1	J18 0-0	S14 2-0	D21 3-2
3 BURTON W	S21 2-1	J25 2-1		D28 4-0	S07 3-0	O05 2-1	O19 0-0	a04 4-1	M07 2-1	J20 4-0	N16 4-1	F22 0-3	M18 5-1	a06 1-3	M21 6-1	D14 4-1
4 CREWE A	M25 3-2	N16 1-3	S14 0-1		D07 3-1	M07 0-1	F22 1-1	F08 2-2	M28 0-7	a03 1-2	O19 0-2	J25 3-0	S28 0-2	O05 5-1	N09 3-2	D23 0-1
5 DARWEN	O19 8-2	F15 3-0	J04 3-0	N30 6-1		S14 3-3	S21 4-1	M28 5-0	D14 0-4	F22 1-1	N02 2-3	N09 4-4	D21 3-0	J01 2-0	J13 10-2	M14 1-1
6 GRIMSBY T	J04 6-1	D28 3-0	M28 2-1	F29 2-0	J25 5-0		a11 7-1	S07 4-2	O19 1-0	N30 2-0	S21 5-0	D26 2-1	M14 4-2	M21 3-0	M03 4-0	a04 1-1
7 LEICESTER F	M21 5-0	S07 2-1	S28 1-3	D21 4-1	O26 2-3	a06 1-2		F29 1-3	N30 2-0	O05 5-0	a04 1-2	a07 2-0	J04 3-0	J11 2-1	a03 8-0	J25 1-0
8 LINCOLN C	a18 4-2	O05 1-2	N30 1-2	D26 6-2	M07 1-0	S28 2-5	F15 2-3		D21 0-1	N09 4-1	J11 1-2	D28 4-0	a11 2-0	a03 2-3	F01 5-0	S14 1-1
9 LIVERPOOL	S28 5-1	M21 6-1	S30 4-1	O07 6-1	N23 0-0	F22 3-1	N09 3-1	J25 6-1		D07 1-0	J01 3-1	S14 5-1	O12 7-1	O26 3-0	F18 10-1	J11 3-0
10 LOUGHBOROUGH T	a11 3-0	D26 2-2	N15 1-1	a18 4-1	M21 4-1	D21 0-1	N16 1-4	O26 3-0	S21 2-4		F01 2-4	M07 1-0	S14 3-3	D28 1-3	a06 3-0	F29 2-1
11 ARDWICK	F17 1-0	M07 1-1	N23 1-1	F15 4-0	O12 4-1	O26 2-1	S14 2-0	M14 4-0	a03 1-1	F24 5-1		J04 5-2	D07 2-1	a08 2-0	S09 2-0	S28 1-0
12 NEWCASTLE U	a03 4-2	a04 5-0	F08 4-0	D25 6-0	N16 7-2	J11 1-5	J01 1-0	J02 5-0	O05 1-0	S07 3-0	M21 4-1		O26 2-1	S21 5-1	D21 6-1	J18 3-1
13 NEWTON HEATH	a06 2-1	S21 5-0	F29 1-2	S07 5-0	a03 4-0	J01 3-2	F03 2-0	N16 5-5	N02 5-2	a04 2-0	O05 1-1	O19 2-1		D14 3-0	J11 3-0	N30 5-1
14 NOTTS CO	D07 7-2	F22 5-0	N09 1-4	a04 6-0	S28 4-1	O03 5-3	F08 1-2	O19 2-0	S07 2-3	D25 2-0	F29 3-0	M14 0-1	N23 0-2		N30 0-0	N02 3-4
15 ROTHERHAM T	S07 0-2	S23 1-4	D07 1-6	S21 4-0	D26 3-0	F08 1-0	J18 2-0	M16 2-2	J04 0-5	M14 4-0	N04 2-3	S28 1-1	M07 2-3	N16 1-0		O26 3-0
16 W ARSENAL	D25 2-1	O19 5-0	O12 3-0	M21 7-0	a18 1-3	S02 3-1	D07 1-1	S21 4-0	N16 0-2	J04 5-0	S07 0-1	a06 2-1	N09 2-1	M07 2-0	O05 5-0	

LEAGUE TABLES

DIVISION 1

	P	W	D	L	F	A	W	D	L	F	A	Pts
Aston Villa	30	14	1	0	47	17	6	4	5	31	28	45
Derby Co	30	12	2	1	42	13	5	5	5	26	22	41
Everton	30	10	4	1	40	17	6	3	6	26	26	39
Bolton W	30	12	2	1	34	14	4	3	8	15	23	37
Sunderland	30	10	5	0	36	14	5	2	8	16	27	37
Stoke	30	12	0	3	43	11	3	0	12	13	36	30
Sheffield W	30	10	2	3	31	18	2	3	10	13	35	29
Blackburn R	30	10	1	4	26	18	2	4	9	14	32	29
Preston N.E.	30	8	5	2	31	18	3	1	11	13	30	28
Burnley	30	8	5	2	33	11	2	2	11	15	33	27
Bury	30	7	1	7	32	24	5	2	8	18	30	27
Sheffield U	30	9	4	2	28	12	1	2	12	12	38	26
Nottingham F	30	11	1	3	34	16	0	2	13	8	41	25
Wolverhampton W	30	10	0	5	43	18	0	1	14	18	47	21
Small Heath	30	7	2	6	22	24	1	2	12	17	55	20
W.B.A.	30	5	4	6	18	22	1	3	11	12	37	19

DIVISION 2

	P	W	D	L	F	A	W	D	L	F	A	Pts
Liverpool	30	14	1	0	65	11	8	1	6	41	21	46
Manchester C	30	12	3	0	37	9	9	1	5	26	29	46
Grimsby T	30	14	1	0	51	9	6	1	8	31	29	42
Burton W	30	12	1	2	43	15	7	3	5	26	25	42
Newcastle U	30	14	0	1	57	14	2	2	11	16	36	34
Newton Heath	30	12	2	1	48	15	3	1	11	18	42	33
Woolwich A	30	11	1	3	43	11	3	3	9	16	31	32
Leicester C	30	10	0	5	40	16	4	4	7	17	28	32
Darwen	30	9	4	2	55	22	3	2	10	17	45	30
Notts Co	30	8	1	6	41	22	4	1	10	16	32	26
Burton S	30	7	2	6	24	26	3	2	10	15	43	24
Loughborough T	30	7	3	5	32	25	2	2	11	8	42	23
Lincoln C	30	7	1	7	36	24	2	3	10	17	51	22
Burslem P.V.	30	6	4	5	25	24	1	0	14	18	54	18
Rotherham U	30	7	2	6	27	26	0	1	14	7	71	17
Crewe A	30	5	2	8	22	28	0	1	14	8	67	13

Derby County's side that finished Division One runners-up in 1895-96. Back row (left to right): Methven, A.Staley (trainer), Leiper. Middle row: W.D.Clark (secretary), Cox, A.Goodall, Robinson, Kinsey, J.Staley. Front row: J.Goodall, Paul, Miller, Stevenson, McQueen. On ground: Bloomer, McMillan. Johnny McMillan's son, Stuart, managed the Rams when they won the FA Cup in 1946.

Scottish international Johnny Campbell spent only two seasons with Aston Villa but he scored 39 goals in that time and netted the first-ever goal at Villa Park, in April 1897. He won two Championship medals and an FA Cup winners' medal with them before returning to Celtic.

Football League Records
Season 1896-97

Top scorers: Div 1, S.Bloomer (Derby County) 22 goals; Div 2, T.Boucher and J.Murphy (both Notts County) 22 goals. Test Matches: 17 Apr Notts County 1 Sunderland 0; 19 Apr Sunderland 0 Notts County 0; Burnley 2 Newton Heath 0; 21 Apr Newton Heath 2 Burnley 0; 24 Apr Newton Heath 1 Sunderland 1; 26 Apr Burnley 0 Notts County 1; Sunderland 2 Newton Heath 0. Notts County promoted. Burnley relegated.

Blackpool, Gainsborough Trinity and Walsall replaced Crewe Alexandra, Burslem Port Vale and Rotherham Town. Ardwick became Manchester City.

DIVISION 1

	ASTON VILLA	BLACKBURN R	BOLTON W	BURNLEY	BURY	DERBY CO	EVERTON	LIVERPOOL	NOTTINGHAM F	PRESTON N.E.	SHEFFIELD U	SHEFFIELD W	STOKE	SUNDERLAND	W.B.A.	WOLVERHAMPTON W
1 ASTON VILLA		a17 3-0	M22 6-2	J02 0-3	N07 1-1	O24 2-1	S26 1-2	M13 0-0	D19 3-2	F22 3-1	S12 2-2	N21 4-0	S02 2-1	J16 2-1	O10 2-0	a19 5-0
2 BLACKBURN R	N28 1-5		O17 1-0	O03 3-2	F20 1-2	J16 5-2	M06 4-2	S05 1-0	N14 0-0	O31 0-4	F06 1-3	S19 4-0	M20 2-1	D25 1-2	S01 1-2	J02 2-0
3 BOLTON W	M27 1-2	S12 0-0		M13 2-1	O10 2-0	M06 1-3	D07 2-0	J01 1-4	M20 0-0	O03 3-1	a16 0-2	a10 2-1	O24 4-0	S26 1-0	D19 2-2	a05 1-2
4 BURNLEY	F08 3-4	N07 0-1	F06 0-2		S12 1-0	a05 2-3	O10 2-1	D26 4-1	S19 2-2	O17 2-2	J16 1-1	D19 1-1	J09 1-3	S07 1-1	a10 5-0	M20 0-3
5 BURY	F06 0-2	M27 3-0	O31 2-2	J01 1-1		a10 1-0	M02 3-1	S19 1-2	D25 2-0	S05 0-0	M20 0-1	O17 1-1	N14 4-2	a16 1-1	M13 3-0	N28 3-2
6 DERBY CO	O17 1-3	N21 6-0	D26 1-0	N14 3-2	S26 7-2		a20 0-1	D19 3-2	S05 1-1	M27 2-2	O10 1-3	J09 2-1	N07 5-1	J23 1-0	D25 8-1	S19 4-3
7 EVERTON	S19 2-3	M13 0-3	N14 2-3	N28 6-0	a24 1-2	a16 5-2		O03 2-1	J09 3-1	F06 3-4	O17 1-2	S05 2-1	D19 4-2	D26 5-2	a17 6-3	O31 0-0
8 LIVERPOOL	D25 3-3	O24 4-0	S07 0-2	M27 1-2	D12 3-1	S12 2-0	N21 0-0		O10 3-0	a10 0-0	J02 0-0	a03 2-2	J16 1-0	N07 3-0	S26 0-0	M04 3-0
9 NOTTINGHAM F	M06 2-4	D12 2-1	J16 2-0	O24 4-1	D28 3-0	N18 1-2	M10 3-0	N28 2-0		a08 0-0	S26 2-2	O31 2-2	S12 4-0	N21 2-1	J02 0-1	a10 1-2
10 PRESTON N.E.	a26 0-1	O10 3-1	N21 2-3	S26 5-3	D26 2-2	a19 0-2	a03 4-1	N14 1-1	N07 3-2		O24 1-0	F20 2-2	N28 3-0	S12 5-3	a16 0-0	J16 4-0
11 SHEFFIELD U	O03 0-0	J09 7-0	D29 1-0	S05 1-0	N21 2-2	O31 2-2	J01 1-2	O19 1-1	F20 0-3	M13 0-2		D26 2-0	M27 1-0	S19 3-0	D05 0-1	J23 1-3
12 SHEFFIELD W	N14 1-3	D28 6-0	F27 0-0	M06 1-0	a17 2-0	N28 2-0	O24 4-1	S01 1-2	a05 3-0	J02 1-0	M02 1-1		S26 4-3	O10 0-0	S12 3-1	D12 0-0
13 STOKE	O31 0-2	a10 1-0	S19 2-3	F27 3-2	a12 3-0	D05 2-2	J02 2-3	F06 6-1	O17 3-0	N09 2-1	a15 2-0	J23 0-0		a03 0-1	N21 2-2	S05 2-1
14 SUNDERLAND	J09 4-2	D19 0-1	S05 1-1	M02 1-1	S01 0-1	J02 1-2	D12 1-1	O17 4-3	M13 2-2	J01 1-1	F27 0-1	D05 0-0	F20 4-1		M06 2-1	O03 0-3
15 W.B.A.	S05 3-1	D26 1-0	N02 1-0	a03 3-0	O24 0-0	F06 1-4	J16 1-4	O31 0-1	J23 4-0	S19 1-1	N14 0-1	O03 0-2	D12 1-2	N28 1-0		O17 1-0
16 WOLVERHAMPTON W	D26 1-2	S26 1-1	a20 4-0	N21 2-0	F27 1-1	S01 1-0	S12 0-1	J09 1-2	D05 4-1	D19 1-1	M06 1-1	M13 2-0	O10 1-2	O24 0-1	D28 6-1	

DIVISION 2

	BLACKPOOL	BURTON S	BURTON W	DARWEN	GAINSBOROUGH T	GRIMSBY T	LEICESTER F	LINCOLN C	LOUGHBOROUGH T	MANCHESTER C	NEWCASTLE U	NEWTON HEATH	NOTTS CO	SMALL HEATH	WALSALL	W ARSENAL
1 BLACKPOOL		a19 3-0	S19 5-0	a16 1-0	a24 1-1	J01 1-0	F27 3-0	N14 3-1	M27 4-1	S26 2-2	M13 4-1	O17 4-2	N28 3-2	J23 1-3	F13 3-2	J04 1-1
2 BURTON S	O24 2-2		a16 1-1	N28 2-0	a17 4-0	J16 0-0	S19 2-1	F06 4-0	N07 3-1	D26 5-0	a12 3-0	S05 3-5	J02 1-4	S26 1-1	O05 1-3	M13 1-2
3 BURTON W	M29 3-1	D25 1-0		N14 1-0	J23 3-2	S12 5-1	D19 2-1	a03 2-0	a19 0-1	M06 1-1	D05 0-1	M20 1-2	O03 0-3	F13 2-6	J09 1-0	S14 0-3
4 DARWEN	S12 2-3	O17 5-1	S26 3-0		a10 3-2	M20 3-1	O24 4-1	D19 4-1	F13 5-1	J09 3-1	N07 2-1	M13 0-2	F27 2-1	N21 2-0	D26 12-0	J01 4-1
5 GAINSBOROUGH T	a03 2-0	F13 4-1	N07 2-1	D25 2-4		O03 1-1	F06 0-2	M27 7-0	D05 2-0	S12 1-1	D28 2-0	O21 2-0	M06 3-2	J02 1-3	S26 2-0	D26 4-1
6 GRIMSBY T	F20 2-2	a03 3-0	J02 3-0	M06 4-2	S05 1-1		J23 4-1	S26 3-1	O17 8-1	O24 3-1	D26 3-2	S19 2-0	N21 3-1	D12 2-1	M13 0-1	a08 3-1
7 LEICESTER F	O03 2-1	M06 3-0	J16 2-1	S05 4-1	a19 0-0	D05 4-2		N07 4-1	D25 4-2	a12 3-3	J09 5-0	D28 1-0	S12 2-3	M27 0-1	N28 4-1	F13 6-3
8 LINCOLN C	S05 3-1	M20 1-1	D26 2-3	J16 1-0	F20 0-2	J09 0-3	a10 2-1		O03 0-2	F13 0-1	O24 1-2	a01* 1-3	M31 1-1	M13 1-3	a16 2-1	D05 2-3
9 LOUGHBOROUGH T	J30 4-1	S12 0-2	a17 6-0	J02 4-2	N14 1-0	S02 1-4	S26 0-2	M06 3-0		M17 2-0	F20 3-0	a10 2-0	O24 0-1	D19 2-0	O10 1-2	D12 8-0
10 MANCHESTER C	N07 4-2	N14 3-1	N28 2-1	S19 4-1	F27 4-1	D19 3-1	M13 4-0	S21 3-0	a16 1-1		O17 1-2	O03 0-0	O31 1-4	J01 3-0	J06 5-0	S05 1-1
11 NEWCASTLE U	J16 4-1	M27 2-1	a10 3-0	O03 5-1	M20 1-2	O10 3-0	N14 3-1	J02 2-1	N28 4-1	F06 3-0		J01 2-0	D12 2-2	S12 4-3	M06 2-0	J23 2-0
12 NEWTON HEATH	D26 2-0	J09 1-1	O24 3-0	M02 3-1	S01 2-0	N07 4-2	F20 2-1	S12 3-1	F06 6-0	D25 2-1	S26 4-0		M27 1-1	O10 1-1	S07 2-0	M22 1-1
13 NOTTS CO	M20 3-1	D05 6-1	M13 5-0	F06 4-0	J09 2-0	O01 1-3	O17 6-0	J23 8-0	S05 3-1	O10 3-3	S19 3-1	D19 3-0		a03 1-2	N14 5-2	N07 7-4
14 SMALL HEATH	M06 1-3	O03 1-2	F27 3-2	S14 5-1	O17 2-2	O31 0-1	a16 2-2	S19 1-2	M20 3-0	a19 3-1	S05 3-1	N28 1-0	a10 3-1		D25 3-3	N14 5-2
15 WALSALL	a10 2-0	J23 5-2	S05 2-0	a21 4-0	S19 1-1	F27 0-1	M20 1-1	a17 5-0	O31 5-1	N23 3-2	a03 0-2	S21 2-3	J16 1-3	O24 1-6		O17 5-3
16 W ARSENAL	D19 4-2	F20 3-0	O12 3-0	a19 1-0	O24 6-1	N28 4-2	a17 2-1	D25 6-2	S19 2-0	a28 1-2	a16 5-1	a03 0-2	S26 2-3	M29 2-3	S12 1-1	

LEAGUE TABLES

DIVISION 1

	P	W	D	L	F	A	W	D	L	F	A	Pts
Aston Villa	30	10	3	2	36	16	11	2	2	37	22	47
Sheffield U	30	6	4	5	22	16	7	6	2	20	13	36
Derby Co	30	10	2	3	45	22	6	2	7	25	28	36
Preston N.E.	30	8	4	3	35	21	3	8	4	20	19	34
Liverpool	30	7	6	2	25	10	5	3	7	21	28	33
Sheffield W	30	9	4	2	29	11	1	7	7	13	26	31
Everton	30	8	1	6	42	29	6	2	7	20	28	31
Bolton W	30	7	3	5	22	18	5	3	7	18	25	30
Bury	30	7	5	3	25	15	3	5	7	14	29	30
Wolverhampton W	30	6	4	5	26	14	5	2	8	19	27	28
Nottingham F	30	8	3	4	30	16	1	5	9	14	33	26
W.B.A.	30	7	2	6	18	16	3	4	8	15	40	26
Stoke	30	8	3	4	30	18	3	0	12	18	41	25
Blackburn R	30	8	1	6	27	25	3	2	10	8	37	25
Sunderland	30	4	6	5	21	21	3	3	9	13	26	23
Burnley	30	4	5	6	25	25	2	2	11	18	36	19

DIVISION 2

	P	W	D	L	F	A	W	D	L	F	A	Pts
Notts Co	30	12	1	2	60	18	7	3	5	32	25	42
Newton Heath	30	11	4	0	37	10	6	1	8	19	24	39
Grimsby T	30	12	2	1	44	15	5	2	8	22	30	38
Small Heath	30	8	3	4	36	23	8	2	5	33	24	37
Newcastle U	30	13	1	1	42	13	4	0	11	14	39	35
Manchester C	30	10	3	2	39	15	2	5	8	19	35	32
Gainsborough T	30	10	2	3	35	16	2	5	8	15	31	31
Blackpool	30	11	3	1	39	16	2	2	11	20	40	31
Leicester C	30	11	2	2	44	19	2	2	11	15	37	30
Woolwich A	30	10	1	4	42	20	3	3	9	26	50	30
Darwen	30	13	0	2	54	16	1	0	14	13	45	28
Walsall	30	8	2	5	37	25	3	2	10	16	44	26
Loughborough T	30	10	0	5	37	14	2	1	12	13	50	25
Burton S	30	7	4	4	33	20	2	2	11	13	41	24
Burton W	30	8	1	6	22	22	1	1	13	9	45	20
Lincoln C	30	4	2	9	17	27	1	0	14	10	58	12

England's Charlie Athersmith was one of the game's fastest wingers and altogether scored 85 goals in 307 League and Cup appearances for Aston Villa between 1890-91 and 1900-01. In 1896-97 he won every honour going that season, League Championship, FA Cup winners' medals and international caps.

Notts County, Division Two champions in 1896-97. Back row (left to right, players only): Bramley, Smith, Prescott, Toone, Allsop, Gibson. Front row: Langham, Allen, Murphy, Bull. On ground: Boucher.

Football League Records
Season 1897-98

Top scorers: Div 1, G.Wheldon (Aston Villa) 21 goals; Div 2, H.Boyd (Newton Heath) 23 goals.
Test Matches: 20 Apr Newcastle United 2 Stoke 1; 21 Apr Blackburn Rovers 1 Burnley 3; 23 Apr Stoke 1 Newcastle United 0; Burnley 2 Blackburn Rovers 0; 26 Apr Burnley 0 Stoke 2; 28 Apr Blackburn Rovers 4 Newcastle United 3; 30 Apr Newcastle United 4 Blackburn Rovers 0; Stoke 0 Burnley 0. Burnley and Newcastle United were promoted. Luton Town were elected in place of Burton Wanderers.

DIVISION 1

	ASTON VILLA	BLACKBURN R	BOLTON W	BURY	DERBY CO	EVERTON	LIVERPOOL	NOTTINGHAM F	NOTTS CO	PRESTON N.E.	SHEFFIELD U	SHEFFIELD W	STOKE	SUNDERLAND	W.B.A.	WOLVERHAMPTON W
1 ASTON VILLA		D11 5-1	O02 3-2	S18 3-1	M05 4-1	N13 3-0	O30 3-1	a30 2-0	O16 4-2	F05 4-0	J15 1-2	S01 5-2	a02 1-1	N27 4-3	S04 4-3	a11 1-2
2 BLACKBURN R	S25 4-3		S11 1-3	M19 1-1	N27 1-1	J01 1-1	J08 2-1	J15 1-1	a09 0-1	O09 1-0	N20 1-1	O23 1-1	a08 1-1	D25 2-1	F05 1-3	F26 2-3
3 BOLTON W	N20 2-0	a14 1-2		J03 0-0	J01 3-3	M26 1-0	**D25 0-2**	O23 2-0	S18 1-0	S25 1-0	a08 0-1	O09 0-3	N13 2-1	O30 1-0	a02 2-0	M12 2-1
4 BURY	M12 1-2	a16 1-0	D11 2-1		M29 4-0	O23 0-1	M26 0-2	a04 2-2	N27 0-0	F12 1-0	O09 2-5	S11 3-0	J01 3-3	a08 1-0	O02 3-2	N06 2-1
5 DERBY CO	J22 3-1	S04 3-1	D27 1-0	O16 2-2		S11 5-1	a12 3-1	a11 5-0	D25 1-2	M12 3-1	N13 1-1	F19 1-2	N06 4-1	D11 2-2	S18 3-2	J08 3-2
6 EVERTON	D25 2-1	O02 1-1	S04 2-1	M05 4-2	a08 3-0		O16 3-0	a02 2-0	D11 1-0	M21 1-1	O30 1-4	J08 1-0	J17 1-1	a11 2-0	N27 6-1	S18 3-0
7 LIVERPOOL	a16 4-0	D18 0-1	M19 1-1	M31 2-2	O23 4-2	S25 3-1		N06 1-2	M12 2-0	S11 0-0	F05 0-4	**a11 4-0**	O09 4-0	D27 0-2	J01 1-1	N20 1-0
8 NOTTINGHAM F	M26 3-1	O16 3-1	J08 2-0	a09 3-1	O30 3-4	M12 2-2	N27 2-3		S04 1-1	N13 4-1	S18 1-1	J22 1-0	F19 3-1	O02 1-1	D11 0-1	a08 1-1
9 NOTTS CO	S11 2-3	M05 0-0	N06 1-2	F26 2-1	S25 1-1	J15 3-2	a02 3-2	O09 1-3		O07 1-1	J01 1-3	D04 0-0	O23 4-0	F05 0-1	M19 2-2	D18 2-2
10 PRESTON N.E.	N06 3-1	O30 1-4	O16 0-0	J08 2-1	a09 5-0	N20 1-1	O02 1-1	D25 3-0	a08 3-1		S04 1-3	D18 2-0	M05 0-0	S18 2-0	M31 1-1	N27 1-2
11 SHEFFIELD U	J08 1-0	O04 5-2	F07 4-0	S25 1-1	S01 2-1	F22 0-0	D29 1-2	D04 1-1	F19 0-1	O23 2-1		D27 1-1	S11 4-3	a02 1-0	a11 2-0	J22 2-1
12 SHEFFIELD W	S27 3-0	N13 4-1	N27 3-0	N20 3-0	J15 3-1	F05 2-1	S18 4-2	J01 3-6	O02 3-1	D11 2-1	O16 0-1		D25 4-0	S04 0-1	a09 3-0	M05 2-0
13 STOKE	D18 0-0	S18 2-1	J15 2-0	D27 3-1	O02 2-1	a09 2-0	S04 2-2	N20 1-2	S02 2-0	N08 1-2	D11 2-1	M26 2-1		J08 0-1	O30 0-0	O16 0-2
14 SUNDERLAND	O23 0-0	M12 2-1	F22 2-0	J15 2-1	O09 2-1	D18 0-0	J22 1-0	a23 4-0	J03 2-0	J01 1-0	M05 3-1	S25 1-0	D04 4-0		O16 0-2	S11 3-2
15 W.B.A.	O09 1-1	D27 1-1	N01 2-0	D18 1-0	N20 3-1	N06 2-2	N13 2-1	S11 2-0	a04 0-3	J15 3-1	M26 2-0	M12 0-2	S25 2-0	F19 2-2		O23 2-2
16 WOLVERHAMPTON W	D27 1-1	a02 3-2	a09 2-0	S04 3-0	D04 2-0	O09 2-3	D11 2-1	S25 0-0	O30 3-1	S01 3-0	O02 1-1	a16 5-0	F05 4-2	N13 4-2	D28 1-1	

DIVISION 2

	BLACKPOOL	BURNLEY	BURTON S	DARWEN	GAINSBOROUGH T	GRIMSBY T	LEICESTER F	LINCOLN C	LOUGHBOROUGH T	LUTON T	MANCHESTER C	NEWCASTLE U	NEWTON HEATH	SMALL HEATH	WALSALL	W ARSENAL
1 BLACKPOOL		S11 1-1	O09 2-1	a08 1-0	D18 5-0	a16 1-1	J08 2-1	F19 5-0	a23 4-0	a30 1-0	S18 0-2	D25 2-3	S25 0-1	O16 4-1	a02 1-1	J01 3-3
2 BURNLEY	S04 5-1		O16 2-0	N27 6-1	M12 1-1	D11 6-0	J15 4-0	J01 2-1	M28 9-3	N13 4-0	O30 3-1	O02 3-0	M07 6-3	F05 4-1	S18 4-1	S06 5-0
3 BURTON S	F26 2-1	M05 0-2		F19 2-0	a23 1-1	D01 4-0	N27 2-3	J08 1-1	a08 3-0	D25 2-1	a09 0-0	D18 3-1	S11 0-4	S04 1-3	O02 3-2	J15 1-2
4 DARWEN	N13 3-1	N06 0-1	M26 1-2		J01 2-4	O16 1-0	D18 1-2	S18 3-2	S25 2-1	F26 0-2	S04 2-4	M05 1-3	M19 2-3	O02 1-1	F12 1-2	M12 1-4
5 GAINSBOROUGH T	O02 4-1	a09 0-0	M23 3-2	D24 3-1		S25 2-0	M19 1-0	O16 4-0	M05 4-0	N27 3-3	F26 1-0	D04 1-3	D27 2-1	F19 0-0	J22 1-1	M26 1-0
6 GRIMSBY T	M19 3-0	O23 2-1	F05 7-2	S11 5-0	S04 4-2		S18 0-0	O02 4-2	D04 7-0	J22 1-3	D18 3-4	N06 2-0	a02 1-3	N13 3-1	M05 1-2	F12 1-4
7 LEICESTER F	N06 4-1	O09 0-1	M12 1-1	F05 0-1	a16 3-1	a11 1-0		**F12 3-1**	**D25 4-0**	**S04 1-1**	**a02 0-0**	**a09 1-1**	**N20 1-1**	**M26 2-0**	**O16 3-1**	D04 2-1
8 LINCOLN C	F05 3-2	a08 1-1	J29 3-0	O09 2-2	N13 2-1	D25 1-1	M05 1-4		O23 2-3	D04 4-2	M19 2-1	S25 2-3	N06 1-0	J15 1-2	a09 0-2	D27 2-3
9 LOUGHBOROUGH T	M26 0-2	J22 0-2	D27 3-2	J08 0-1	F05 0-5	a09 2-1	N13 1-1	N27 4-2		O16 2-0	O02 0-3	a11 0-1	**a16 0-0**	S18 0-2	S04 2-1	D18 1-3
10 LUTON T	N29 3-1	M19 2-0	N06 1-1	a11 3-0	S11 4-0	D27 6-0	a08 0-1	D18 9-3	J15 7-0		J01 3-0	F19 3-1	M21 2-2	a02 1-2	F05 6-0	O02 0-2
11 MANCHESTER C	M30 3-3	N20 1-1	a16 9-0	O23 5-0	S01 3-0	O09 3-0	D11 2-1	J24 3-1	S11 3-0	M26 2-1		J08 1-1	D25 0-1	a11 3-3	J03 3-2	S25 4-1
12 NEWCASTLE U	O23 2-0	D27 0-1	S18 3-1	J15 1-0	a02 5-2	M26 4-0	J22 4-2	F26 3-0	J03 3-1	M12 4-1	M16 2-0		O09 2-0	N27 4-0	J01 2-1	S04 4-1
13 NEWTON HEATH	J15 4-0	J12 0-0	J01 4-0	a23 3-2	a08 1-0	N27 2-1	O02 2-0	S04 5-0	M29 5-1	S18 1-2	O16 1-1	N13 0-1		a09 3-1	O30 6-0	F26 5-1
14 SMALL HEATH	J29 2-3	J08 2-2	S25 2-1	D25 5-1	O09 4-3	M12 0-2	S11 2-1	a16 4-0	N06 1-0	F12 4-2	D27 0-1	a12 1-0	O23 2-1		D04 6-0	a23 2-1
15 WALSALL	D27 6-0	**S25 1-2**	O23 4-0	S27 5-0	a11 3-0	N20 1-1	F26 2-1	M12 3-1	O09 3-0	J08 5-0	J15 2-2	S11 2-3	D11 1-1	D18 1-2		N06 3-2
16 W ARSENAL	N27 2-1	a02 1-1	a11 3-0	a09 3-1	S18 4-0	S01 4-1	O23 0-3	S11 2-2	M19 4-0	O09 3-0	F05 2-2	O16 0-0	J08 5-1	M05 4-2	N13 4-0	

LEAGUE TABLES

DIVISION 1

	P	W	D	L	F	A	W	D	L	F	A	Pts
Sheffield U	30	9	4	2	27	14	8	4	3	29	17	42
Sunderland	30	12	2	1	27	8	4	3	8	16	22	37
Wolverhampton W	30	10	4	1	36	14	4	3	8	21	27	35
Everton	30	11	3	1	33	12	2	6	7	15	27	35
Sheffield W	30	12	0	3	39	15	3	3	9	12	27	33
Aston Villa	30	12	1	2	47	21	2	4	9	14	30	33
W.B.A.	30	8	5	2	25	16	3	5	7	19	29	32
Nottingham F	30	7	5	3	30	19	4	4	7	17	30	31
Liverpool	30	7	4	4	27	16	4	2	9	21	29	28
Derby Co	30	10	3	2	40	19	1	3	11	17	42	28
Bolton W	30	9	2	4	18	13	2	2	11	10	28	26
Preston N.E.	30	7	5	3	26	15	1	3	11	9	28	24
Notts Co	30	4	6	5	23	23	4	2	9	13	23	24
Bury	30	8	3	4	25	19	0	5	10	14	32	24
Blackburn R	30	4	7	4	20	22	3	3	9	19	32	24
Stoke	30	8	3	4	21	14	0	5	10	14	41	24

DIVISION 2

	P	W	D	L	F	A	W	D	L	F	A	Pts
Burnley	30	14	1	0	64	13	6	7	2	16	11	48
Newcastle U	30	14	0	1	43	10	7	3	5	21	22	45
Manchester C	30	10	4	1	45	15	5	5	5	21	21	39
Newton Heath	30	11	2	2	42	10	5	4	6	22	25	38
Woolwich A	30	10	4	1	41	14	6	1	8	28	35	37
Small Heath	30	11	1	3	37	18	5	3	7	21	32	36
Leicester C	30	8	5	2	26	11	5	2	8	20	24	33
Luton T	30	10	2	3	50	13	3	2	10	18	37	30
Gainsborough T	30	10	4	1	30	12	2	2	11	20	42	30
Walsall	30	9	3	3	42	15	3	2	10	16	43	29
Blackpool	30	8	4	3	32	15	2	1	12	17	46	25
Grimsby T	30	9	1	5	44	24	1	3	11	8	38	24
Burton S	30	7	3	5	25	21	1	2	12	13	48	21
Lincoln C	30	6	3	6	27	27	0	2	13	16	55	17
Darwen	30	4	1	10	21	32	2	1	12	10	44	14
Loughborough T	30	5	2	8	15	26	1	0	14	9	61	14

Gavin Crawford was one of Woolwich Arsenal's first professional footballers and their skipper for several years. He had already made around 100 senior appearances when the Gunners entered the Football League in 1893. Crawford, a wing-half, later played for Millwall and QPR and was Charlton Athletic's groundsman.

Sheffield United, League Champions in 1897-98. Back row (left to right, players only): Hedley, Johnson, Boyle, Foulke, Almond, Morren. Front row: Bennett, Beers, Needham, Thickett, Priest.

FOOTBALL LEAGUE RECORDS
SEASON 1898-99

Top scorers: Div 1, S.Bloomer (Derby County) 23 goals; Div 2, W.Abbott (Small Heath) 33 goals.
From this season automatic two-up/two-down system of promotion/relegation came into operation. Barnsley, Glossop North End, New Brighton Tower and Burslem Port Vale elected to the League.

LEAGUE TABLES

DIVISION 1

	P	W	D	L	F	A	W	D	L	F	A	Pts
Aston Villa	34	15	2	0	58	13	4	5	8	18	27	45
Liverpool	34	12	3	2	29	10	7	2	8	20	23	43
Burnley	34	11	5	1	32	15	4	4	9	13	32	39
Everton	34	10	2	5	25	13	5	6	6	23	28	38
Notts Co	34	9	6	2	33	20	3	7	7	14	31	37
Blackburn R	34	9	5	3	41	23	5	3	9	19	29	36
Sunderland	34	11	3	3	26	10	4	3	10	15	31	36
Wolverhampton W	34	9	5	3	30	13	5	2	10	24	35	35
Derby Co	34	11	5	1	46	19	1	6	10	16	38	35
Bury	34	9	5	3	31	18	5	2	10	17	31	35
Nottingham F	34	6	6	5	22	18	5	5	7	20	24	33
Stoke	34	10	4	3	29	17	3	3	11	18	35	33
Newcastle U	34	9	3	5	33	18	2	5	10	16	30	30
W.B.A.	34	11	1	5	28	9	1	5	11	14	48	30
Preston N.E.	34	10	4	3	29	14	0	5	12	15	33	29
Sheffield U	34	7	8	2	31	20	2	3	12	14	31	29
Bolton W	34	6	5	6	24	21	3	2	12	13	30	25
Sheffield W	34	8	2	7	26	24	0	6	11	6	37	24

DIVISION 2

	P	W	D	L	F	A	W	D	L	F	A	Pts
Manchester C	34	15	1	1	64	10	8	5	4	28	25	52
Glossop N.E.	34	12	1	4	48	13	8	5	4	28	25	46
Leicester C	34	12	5	0	35	12	6	4	7	29	30	45
Newton Heath	34	12	4	1	51	14	7	1	9	16	29	43
New Brighton	34	13	2	2	48	13	5	5	7	23	39	43
Walsall	34	12	5	0	64	11	3	7	7	15	25	42
Woolwich A	34	14	2	1	55	10	4	3	10	17	31	41
Small Heath	34	14	1	2	66	17	3	6	8	19	33	41
Burslem P.V.	34	12	2	3	35	12	5	3	9	21	22	39
Grimsby T	34	10	3	4	39	17	5	2	10	32	43	35
Barnsley	34	11	4	2	44	18	1	3	13	8	38	31
Lincoln C	34	10	5	2	31	16	2	2	13	20	40	31
Burton S	34	7	5	5	35	25	3	3	11	16	45	28
Gainsborough T	34	8	4	5	40	22	2	1	14	16	50	25
Luton T	34	8	1	8	37	31	2	2	13	14	64	23
Blackpool	34	6	3	8	35	30	2	1	14	14	60	20
Loughborough T	34	5	4	8	31	26	1	2	14	7	66	18
Darwen	34	2	4	11	16	32	0	1	16	6	109	9

DIVISION 1

	ASTON VILLA	BLACKBURN R	BOLTON W	BURNLEY	BURY	DERBY CO	EVERTON	LIVERPOOL	NEWCASTLE U	NOTTINGHAM F	NOTTS CO	PRESTON N.E.	SHEFFIELD U	SHEFFIELD W	STOKE	SUNDERLAND	W.B.A.	WOLVERHAMPTON W
1 ASTON VILLA		N19 3-1	O29 2-1	J14 4-0	J07 3-2	N05 7-1	D17 3-0	a29 5-0	D26 1-0	O22 3-0	a22 6-1	O08 4-2	S24 1-1	M25 3-1	S03 3-1	D03 2-0	a24 7-1	D10 1-1
2 BLACKBURN R	M18 0-0		S10 4-1	D26 0-2	O01 0-0	J14 3-0	O29 1-3	D24 1-3	D10 4-2	D31 3-3	J02 6-0	a15 2-2	a01 2-1	F04 2-0	N12 4-1	O15 3-2	S24 4-1	F18 2-2
3 BOLTON W	a17 0-0	J07 0-2		J03 2-0	D17 0-1	M31 2-1	F25 2-4	a01 2-1	M18 0-0	D10 0-2	O15 0-1	N26 2-2	N12 3-0	S17 0-0	F18 0-2	J21 6-1	S03 3-3	O01 2-1
4 BURNLEY	S17 2-4	N26 2-0	N05 2-0		J21 2-1	M11 2-1	a22 0-0	O22 2-1	O08 2-1	M06 1-1	S03 1-1	S05 3-1	M31 1-0	D03 5-0	a17 1-1	a08 1-0	N19 1-1	D17 4-2
5 BURY	S10 2-1	F14 3-2	a15 3-1	S24 1-1		D31 0-0	M18 3-1	N19 3-0	O22 1-1	D03 2-0	a08 2-0	N05 3-1	O08 1-3	J02 0-0	D24 5-2	M31 1-2	J14 1-1	M14 0-2
6 DERBY CO	M04 1-1	S17 0-0	D26 1-1	N12 2-1	S03 1-2		O15 5-5	D10 1-0	N26 3-1	a20 2-0	F18 4-2	a01 1-0	a22 1-0	J21 9-0	O29 1-1	O01 4-2	J07 4-1	F04 6-2
7 EVERTON	a15 1-1	S01 2-1	O08 1-0	D24 4-0	N26 0-1	a03 1-2		S24 1-2	S10 3-0	J02 1-3	a01 1-2	J14 2-0	D31 1-0	N05 2-0	D10 2-0	M11 0-0	O22 1-0	N19 2-1
8 LIVERPOOL	O15 0-3	a22 2-0	D03 2-0	F18 2-0	a20 1-0	a08 4-0	J21 2-0		a03 3-2	M25 0-1	O01 0-0	N12 3-1	O29 2-1	S03 4-0	F04 1-0	J07 0-0	D17 2-2	S17 1-0
9 NEWCASTLE U	O01 1-1	a08 1-0	N19 4-1	F04 4-1	F18 2-0	M25 2-0	J07 2-2	N05 3-0		M11 0-1	S17 1-2	F25 2-1	O15 1-2	D17 2-2	J21 3-0	a22 0-1	D03 3-0	S03 2-4
10 NOTTINGHAM F	F18 1-0	S03 0-1	a08 1-2	O29 0-1	a01 1-2	D17 3-3	O01 0-0	N26 0-3	N12 2-0		F04 0-0	O06 2-2	M04 2-1	J07 1-1	O15 2-1	S17 1-1	a22 3-0	J21 3-0
11 NOTTS CO	D24 1-0	N05 5-3	a03 2-1	D31 2-2	D10 4-1	O22 2-2	D03 0-1	D27 1-1	J14 3-1	O08 2-2		S24 1-0	S10 2-2	M11 1-0	a15 2-0	N19 5-2	M09 0-0	M25 0-2
12 PRESTON N.E.	F04 2-0	D17 1-1	a29 0-1	O15 1-1	D26 3-1	D03 3-1	S17 0-0	M11 1-2	O29 1-0	N19 1-0	M20 2-0		F18 1-0	a22 1-1	O01 4-2	S03 2-3	a08 4-0	J07 2-1
13 SHEFFIELD U	J21 1-3	D03 1-1	M11 3-1	O01 1-1	F04 4-1	N19 2-1	S03 1-1	J02 0-2	S26 2-2	N05 2-2	J07 2-2	O22 1-1		D26 2-1	S17 1-1	D17 2-0	M25 5-0	S12 1-0
14 SHEFFIELD W	M13 4-1	O08 1-2	J14 1-0	a01 1-0	O15 3-2	S24 3-1	M04 1-2	D31 0-3	a15 1-3	S10 2-1	N12 1-1	S19 2-1	O03 1-1		M27 1-3	F18 0-1	F14 1-2	O29 3-0
15 STOKE	D31 3-0	M11 0-1	O22 2-3	S10 4-1	a22 1-1	S01 0-0	a08 2-1	O08 2-1	S24 0-0	D26 2-1	D17 1-1	N14 2-1	J14 4-1	N19 1-0		M25 1-0	N05 2-1	D03 2-4
16 SUNDERLAND	a01 4-2	a03 0-1	S24 0-0	D10 0-1	O29 3-0	J02 1-0	N12 2-1	S10 1-0	D24 2-3	J14 1-1	M18 1-1	D31 1-0	a29 1-0	O22 2-0	N26 2-0		O08 2-0	M04 3-0
17 W.B.A.	N12 0-1	J21 6-2	D31 1-0	M18 0-1	S17 2-0	S10 1-1	N07 3-0	D26 0-1	a01 2-0	D24 2-0	O29 2-0	D10 2-0	N26 3-0	O01 2-0	M04 0-1	F04 1-0		O15 1-2
18 WOLVERHAMPTON W	a03 4-0	O22 2-1	a04 1-0	a15 4-0	N12 1-2	O08 2-2	a29 1-2	J14 0-0	D31 0-0	S24 0-2	N26 1-0	S10 0-0	D24 4-1	F25 0-0	a01 3-2	N05 2-0	D27 5-1	

Welsh international winger Billy Meredith helped Manchester City into Division One in 1898-99 and later won League Championship and FA Cup winners' medals with Manchester United.

DIVISION 2

	BARNSLEY	BLACKPOOL	BURSLEM P.V.	BURTON S	DARWEN	GAINSBOROUGH T	GLOSSOP N.E.	GRIMSBY T	LEICESTER F	LINCOLN C	LOUGHBOROUGH T	LUTON T	MANCHESTER C	NEW BRIGHTON	NEWTON HEATH	SMALL HEATH	WALSALL	W ARSENAL
1 BARNSLEY		F11 2-1	D31 2-1	a15 2-0	O08 6-0	O22 1-0	D27 1-1	F25 2-2	S24 3-4	a03 1-0	J28 9-0	S10 2-1	N05 1-1	M25 2-1	a04 0-2	J14 7-2	D03 1-1	D24 2-1
2 BLACKPOOL	M15 3-1		S24 0-4	J14 3-0	M31 6-0	a15 4-0	D31 1-2	F18 3-6	a01 2-2	N12 3-0	O08 2-1	N26 2-3	D24 2-4	M04 1-2	a03 0-1	M08 1-1	S10 1-2	M22 1-1
3 BURSLEM P.V.	S03 2-0	J21 6-1		D24 4-1	M18 3-1	N26 2-1	a03 1-2	O01 2-0	N12 0-2	F18 2-1	S17 3-0	M04 4-1	a01 1-1	O15 0-0	F04 1-0	J07 1-0	a15 0-1	S05 3-0
4 BURTON S	D17 5-0	S17 3-1	J28 2-0		N12 4-0	M18 2-1	a01 1-2	J21 1-2	M04 1-1	a12 2-1	J07 1-1	D26 1-1	N26 3-3	F04 1-1	O01 5-1	S03 2-6	M31 0-2	F18 1-2
5 DARWEN	M21 1-1	a08 0-2	J02 1-3	M11 0-2		F11 0-3	F25 0-2	D17 0-2	O01 3-0	J07 1-2	D03 0-1	a11 4-1	O22 0-2	D31 2-4	a22 1-1	M25 1-1	N05 1-1	S17 1-4
6 GAINSBOROUGH T	F18 2-0	D17 7-0	M25 3-2	O26 1-2	O15 2-2		N05 2-4	a22 5-1	F04 4-0	S17 2-2	D26 3-0	O01 2-3	F25 3-1	J07 3-1	S03 0-2	D03 1-1	M11 0-0	J21 0-1
7 GLOSSOP N.E.	M31 1-0	S03 4-1	a08 0-0	D03 5-0	M07 5-0	M04 5-1		J07 4-2	F18 1-3	O01 2-0	a22 4-0	O15 5-0	N12 1-2	J21 5-0	S17 1-2	D17 1-2	M25 2-0	F04 2-0
8 GRIMSBY T	D26 0-1	O22 2-1	F21 3-1	S24 1-3	a15 9-2	D24 0-2	S10 1-1		M31 1-0	M18 1-1	F11 5-0	a01 5-0	a11 1-2	N12 2-2	M04 3-0	O08 2-0	J14 2-1	N26 1-0
9 LEICESTER F	J21 3-1	D03 4-0	M11 1-1	N05 1-0	D26 4-0	O08 1-0	O22 4-2	a03 2-0		S03 3-2	D27 1-0	S17 1-1	F11 1-1	a22 4-1	D17 1-0	a29 0-0	F25 2-2	J07 2-1
10 LINCOLN C	S01 1-0	M11 0-0	O22 1-0	F11 1-1	S10 2-0	J14 1-0	D26 2-2	a08 1-6	D31 3-1		N05 6-0	D24 2-0	S24 3-1	D27 1-2	M25 2-0	M31 2-2	O08 1-1	a15 2-0
11 LOUGHBOROUGH T	M11 2-0	F04 1-3	J14 0-3	S10 1-0	a01 10-0	a03 0-0	D24 1-3	a17 1-3	N26 0-3	M04 2-4		M18 4-1	D10 1-3	a29 6-0	F18 0-1	S24 1-1	D31 1-1	N12 0-0
12 LUTON T	J07 4-1	M25 3-2	N05 0-1	a03 3-0	S24 8-1	J28 4-2	F11 0-2	D03 3-1	J14 1-6	a22 2-0	M31 2-2		O08 0-3	D17 2-3	a08 0-1	M11 2-3	O22 3-2	S03 0-1
13 MANCHESTER C	M04 5-0	a22 4-1	D03 3-1	M25 6-0	F18 10-0	M31 4-0	J02 0-2	S03 7-2	O15 3-1	F22 3-1	D17 5-0	F04 2-0		S17 1-1	D26 4-0	a08 2-0	N19 2-0	O01 3-1
14 NEW BRIGHTON	N26 2-1	N05 4-0	F11 1-0	O08 2-2	D22 7-0	S10 3-2	S24 2-2	M11 2-0	D24 1-0	a01 4-1	F25 3-0	a15 4-0	J14 0-1		N19 0-3	O22 4-0	J28 6-0	D10 3-1
15 NEWTON HEATH	N12 0-0	D10 3-1	O08 2-1	J02 2-2	D24 9-0	D31 6-1	J14 3-0	N05 3-2	a15 2-2	N26 1-0	O22 6-1	a12 5-0	S10 3-0	M18 1-2		F25 2-0	S24 1-0	a01 2-2
16 SMALL HEATH	S17 3-1	D26 5-0	S10 1-2	D31 4-1	N26 8-0	a01 6-1	a15 1-1	F04 2-1	M18 0-3	S05 4-1	J21 6-0	N12 9-0	D27 4-1	F18 3-2	O15 4-1		D24 2-1	M04 4-1
17 WALSALL	a01 1-1	J07 6-0	D17 1-1	a04 7-1	M04 10-0	N12 6-1	N26 2-0	S17 4-1	S26 1-1	F04 3-2	S03 7-0	F18 6-0	M18 1-1	O01 1-1	J21 2-0	a22 2-0		O15 4-1
18 W ARSENAL	a22 3-0	M18 6-0	F25 1-0	O22 2-1	J14 6-0	S24 5-1	F13 3-0	M25 1-1	S10 4-0	D17 4-2	M13 3-1	D31 6-2	a03 0-1	a08 4-0	D03 5-1	N05 2-0	F11 0-0	

FOOTBALL LEAGUE RECORDS
SEASON 1899-1900

Top scorers: Div 1, W.Garraty (Aston Villa) 27 goals; Div 2, J.Wright (Sheffield Wednesday) 24 goals. Chesterfield and Middlesbrough were elected in place of Blackpool and Darwen. Glossop dropped the 'North End' part of their name.

DIVISION 1

	ASTON VILLA	BLACKBURN R	BURNLEY	BURY	DERBY CO	EVERTON	GLOSSOP	LIVERPOOL	MANCHESTER C	NEWCASTLE U	NOTTINGHAM F	NOTTS CO	PRESTON N.E.	SHEFFIELD U	STOKE	SUNDERLAND	W.B.A.	WOLVERHAMPTON W
1 ASTON VILLA		S23 3-1	N25 2-0	O07 2-1	F03 3-2	J13 1-1	S04 9-0	M24 1-0	O21 2-1	N04 2-1	D09 2-2	F17 6-2	a07 3-1	M03 1-1	D23 4-1	D30 4-2	S09 0-2	N11 0-0
2 BLACKBURN R	J20 0-4		J01 2-0	D16 3-2	a14 2-0	N25 3-1	M03 2-2	S30 2-0	S02 4-3	S16 2-3	M05 2-1	a28 2-0	O14 3-0	a13 3-3	M10 3-0	N11 1-2	M24 2-0	a07 2-1
3 BURNLEY	M31 1-2	O07 1-0		O21 1-0	F17 1-2	F03 3-1	D30 3-1	D02 2-1	N04 2-0	N18 1-3	D23 2-2	M03 3-0	a21 0-1	a23 1-0	S09 2-2	J13 3-1	S23 2-0	D09 0-1
4 BURY	J01 2-0	a25 2-0	M14 1-1		D23 1-1	D09 4-1	N11 2-1	O14 2-1	S16 1-4	S30 2-1	D25 2-1	J06 0-1	O28 2-0	J20 2-1	a13 0-1	N25 2-0	a07 1-0	S02 3-0
5 DERBY CO	S30 2-0	D09 0-2	O14 4-1	a28 3-0		a07 2-1	D26 4-1	D25 3-2	J06 0-0	J20 2-1	O28 2-2	S02 0-1	a04 2-0	S16 0-1	N11 2-0	M24 2-0	N25 4-1	D16 0-2
6 EVERTON	S16 1-2	M31 0-0	S30 2-0	a14 2-0	D02 3-0		a16 4-1	J20 3-1	a28 4-0	J06 3-2	O14 2-1	D16 0-2	J01 1-0	S02 1-2	D25 2-0	M10 1-0	N11 1-3	M24 0-1
7 GLOSSOP	D16 1-0	F27 4-2	S02 2-0	M17 0-0	a13 1-3	O21 1-1		a28 1-2	M31 0-2	a14 0-0	S16 3-0	N18 0-0	J06 0-2	D02 2-2	F03 1-2	O07 0-2	a24 1-1	J20 2-3
8 LIVERPOOL	N18 3-3	F03 3-1	a07 0-1	a09 2-0	O07 0-2	S23 1-2	D23 5-2		M03 5-2	M17 2-0	a21 1-0	O21 3-1	D09 1-0	N04 2-2	D30 0-0	S09 0-2	J13 2-0	N25 1-1
9 MANCHESTER C	M19 0-2	D30 1-1	M10 1-0	J13 2-2	S09 4-0	D23 1-2	N25 4-1	O28 0-1		O14 1-0	a09 2-0	S23 5-1	N11 3-1	D25 1-2	a07 1-0	D09 2-1	a21 4-0	S30 1-1
10 NEWCASTLE U	M10 3-2	J13 4-1	M24 2-0	F03 2-1	S23 2-0	S09 2-0	M14 1-0	N11 1-1	a13 0-0		a07 3-1	O07 6-0	N25 0-0	O21 0-0	a21 2-2	D23 2-4	D30 4-2	O28 0-1
11 NOTTINGHAM F	a14 1-1	O21 3-2	a28 4-0	N04 2-2	M03 4-1	F17 4-2	J13 5-0	D16 1-0	D27 2-0	D02 1-0		M17 0-3	S02 3-1	M31 4-0	S23 1-0	a17 1-3	O07 6-1	J06 0-0
12 NOTTS CO	O14 1-4	D23 5-1	O28 6-1	S09 2-2	D30 0-0	a21 2-2	M24 0-0	O05 2-1	J20 1-1	a16 0-0	N11 1-2		M10 3-0	S30 1-2	N25 1-3	a07 3-1	D09 1-2	S16 0-0
13 PRESTON N.E.	D02 0-5	a30 2-0	D16 1-1	M03 1-0	O21 0-0	O07 1-1	S09 1-0	a14 1-3	a16 0-2	M31 4-1	D30 3-0	N04 4-3		N18 0-1	J13 3-0	S23 0-1	F03 5-2	a28 2-0
14 SHEFFIELD U	O28 2-1	S09 3-0	N11 0-0	S23 4-0	J13 1-1	D30 5-0	a07 4-0	M10 1-2	O07 3-0	M26 3-1	N25 3-0	F03 1-1	M24 1-0		D09 1-0	O02 2-2	D23 1-1	O14 5-2
15 STOKE	N13 0-2	N04 2-0	D26 3-0	a16 2-0	M17 1-1	O28 1-1	S30 1-0	S02 3-2	D02 1-0	D16 2-2	J20 0-0	M31 1-0	S16 3-1	a14 1-1		M26 1-2	O21 1-0	S18 1-3
16 SUNDERLAND	S02 0-1	a16 1-0	S16 2-1	M31 1-0	M21 2-0	N04 1-0	F24 0-0	J06 1-0	a14 3-1	a28 1-2	S30 1-0	D02 5-0	J20 1-0	D16 1-1	O14 3-0		M03 3-1	J01 1-2
17 W.B.A.	J06 0-2	a02 1-0	J20 2-0	D02 0-1	M31 0-0	D26 0-0	O14 3-3	S16 2-0	D16 0-0	S02 1-1	a16 8-0	a14 0-0	S30 1-0	N06 1-2	M19 4-0	O28 1-0		M10 3-2
18 WOLVERHAMPTON W	a16 0-1	D02 4-0	a14 3-0	D30 1-0	a21 3-0	M17 2-1	S23 4-0	M31 0-1	F03 1-1	M03 1-1	S09 2-2	J13 2-2	D23 1-3	a17 1-2	O07 0-2	D26 1-0	N04 2-0	

LEAGUE TABLES

DIVISION 1

	P	W	D	L	F	A	W	D	L	F	A	Pts
Aston Villa	34	12	4	1	45	18	10	2	5	32	17	50
Sheffield U	34	11	5	1	40	11	7	7	3	23	22	48
Sunderland	34	12	2	3	27	9	7	1	9	23	26	41
Wolverhampton W	34	8	4	5	28	16	7	5	5	20	21	39
Newcastle U	34	10	5	2	34	15	3	5	9	19	28	36
Derby Co	34	11	2	4	32	15	3	6	8	13	28	36
Manchester C	34	10	3	4	33	15	3	5	9	17	29	34
Nottingham F	34	12	3	2	42	16	1	5	11	14	39	34
Stoke	34	9	5	3	24	15	4	3	10	13	30	34
Liverpool	34	9	4	4	31	19	5	1	11	18	26	33
Everton	34	11	1	5	30	15	2	6	9	17	34	33
Bury	34	12	2	3	29	14	1	4	12	11	30	32
W.B.A.	34	8	6	3	27	11	3	2	12	16	40	30
Blackburn R	34	12	2	3	38	22	1	2	14	11	39	30
Notts Co	34	5	7	5	29	22	4	4	9	17	38	29
Preston N.E.	34	9	3	5	28	20	3	1	13	10	28	28
Burnley	34	10	2	5	28	17	1	3	13	6	37	27
Glossop N.E.	34	4	6	7	19	22	0	4	13	12	52	18

DIVISION 2

	P	W	D	L	F	A	W	D	L	F	A	Pts
Sheffield W	34	17	0	0	61	7	8	4	5	23	15	54
Bolton W	34	14	2	1	47	7	8	6	3	32	18	52
Small Heath	34	15	1	1	58	12	5	5	7	20	26	46
Newton Heath	34	15	1	1	44	11	5	3	9	19	16	44
Leicester C	34	11	5	1	34	8	6	4	7	19	28	43
Grimsby T	34	10	3	4	46	24	7	3	7	21	22	40
Chesterfield	34	10	4	3	35	24	6	2	9	30	36	38
Woolwich A	34	13	1	3	47	12	3	3	11	14	31	36
Lincoln C	34	11	5	1	31	9	3	3	11	15	34	36
New Brighton	34	9	4	4	44	22	4	5	8	22	36	35
Burslem P.V.	34	11	2	4	26	16	3	4	10	13	33	34
Walsall	34	10	5	2	35	18	2	3	12	15	37	32
Gainsborough T	34	8	4	5	37	24	1	3	13	10	51	25
Middlesbrough	34	8	4	5	28	15	0	4	13	11	54	24
Burton S	34	8	5	4	31	24	1	1	15	12	60	24
Barnsley	34	8	5	4	36	23	0	2	15	10	56	23
Luton T	34	5	3	9	25	25	0	5	12	15	50	18
Loughborough T	34	1	6	10	12	26	0	0	17	6	74	8

DIVISION 2

	BARNSLEY	BOLTON W	BURSLEM P.V.	BURTON S	CHESTERFIELD	GAINSBOROUGH T	GRIMSBY T	LEICESTER F	LINCOLN C	LOUGHBOROUGH T	LUTON T	MIDDLESBROUGH	NEW BRIGHTON	NEWTON HEATH	SHEFFIELD W	SMALL HEATH	WALSALL	W ARSENAL
1 BARNSLEY		D26 1-6	J20 3-0	S02 4-1	a17 0-0	F24 5-0	a21 0-1	J06 1-2	N25 0-4	M10 7-0	S16 2-1	F10 5-2	D09 1-1	N11 0-0	M24 1-0	a07 1-1	S30 2-2	a23 3-2
2 BOLTON W	a13 2-0		J02 5-0	a28 5-0	a14 3-0	a21 3-0	F17 1-2	N04 2-2	S23 4-0	D30 7-0	M17 3-0	D02 3-0	J01 2-1	S09 2-1	J13 1-0	F03 1-1	M31 2-0	O21 1-0
3 BURSLEM P.V.	S23 3-1	a23 0-2		O14 2-1	M10 2-0	N11 1-0	S09 2-3	F03 0-2	a21 2-0	N25 3-1	O07 1-0	S04 3-1	D30 1-1	a07 1-0	F12 0-3	D23 3-0	F24 1-0	J13 1-1
4 BURTON S	D30 4-0	D23 2-5	F17 2-2		M31 2-1	a14 1-1	D02 1-2	J13 2-0	O21 0-0	S09 3-1	F03 3-1	M17 5-0	F10 2-2	S23 0-0	O07 0-5	N04 0-3	a13 2-1	a21 2-0
5 CHESTERFIELD	F17 2-1	D06 3-3	N04 0-4	N25 0-4		a07 3-1	F03 3-1	O21 0-0	S09 2-2	a13 1-0	M26 2-0	J27 7-1	J20 5-2	D23 2-1	D30 1-0	J13 0-0	M17 1-3	O07 3-1
6 GAINSBOROUGH T	O21 1-0	D16 1-1	M17 4-0	D26 4-1	D02 3-5		O07 2-3	M03 3-0	J13 3-1	D23 4-2	N04 2-2	M31 5-0	a18 1-1	D30 0-1	S09 0-2	S23 1-4	a30 2-0	F17 1-1
7 GRIMSBY T	D16 8-1	O14 0-0	J06 1-1	a07 6-0	D25 0-3	F10 3-0		a28 6-1	N11 5-2	F24 3-0	S02 3-3	J20 2-0	N25 1-2	D26 0-7	a13 1-2	M24 2-0	S16 4-2	a14 1-0
8 LEICESTER F	S09 1-0	M10 0-0	S30 2-0	S16 1-0	F24 2-2	a16 5-0	D23 3-0		a07 2-0	D25 5-0	J20 2-2	O14 4-1	a21 1-2	M24 2-0	N25 0-0	a17 2-0	D27 2-1	D30 0-0
9 LINCOLN C	M31 1-1	J20 1-0	D16 1-1	F24 3-0	J06 2-0	S16 2-1	a27 1-1	D02 2-0		S30 3-2	M03 2-0	S02 3-0	N04 0-0	F10 1-0	O14 1-2	a13 0-0	D26 3-1	D25 5-0
10 LOUGHBOROUGH T	N04 0-0	S02 2-3	M31 1-2	J06 2-1	a16 0-4	a28 1-2	O21 0-0	N11 0-2	a23 0-1		a17 1-1	a14 1-1	F17 1-2	J13 0-2	S23 0-0	O07 1-2	D02 0-0	M03 2-3
11 LUTON T	J13 3-0	N11 0-2	F10 1-1	S30 5-2	D26 0-3	M10 4-0	D30 0-4	S23 0-0	a16 0-2	M24 4-0		F24 1-1	D23 1-4	N25 0-1	a07 0-1	a21 1-2	O14 4-0	S09 1-2
12 MIDDLESBROUGH	O07 3-0	a07 0-3	M03 1-0	N11 8-1	M24 0-1	N25 0-0	S23 1-0	F17 0-1	D30 1-1	D09 3-0	O21 0-0		J13 5-2	a21 2-0	D23 1-2	S09 1-3	N04 1-1	F03 1-0
13 NEW BRIGHTON	a25 6-2	a16 3-1	S02 2-0	M24 5-0	N06 2-3	O28 5-0	M31 2-1	D16 2-2	M10 3-0	J27 3-0	a28 5-1	S16 1-1		F24 1-4	D25 2-2	N11 2-2	J06 0-1	D02 0-2
14 NEWTON HEATH	M17 3-0	J06 1-2	D02 3-0	J20 4-0	a28 2-1	S02 2-2	M03 1-0	a13 3-2	O07 1-0	S16 4-0	M31 5-0	D16 2-1	O21 2-1		F03 1-0	F17 3-2	a14 5-0	N04 2-0
15 SHEFFIELD W	F27 5-1	S16 2-1	a14 4-0	M12 6-0	S02 5-1	J06 5-1	J01 2-1	M31 2-0	a17 1-0	J20 5-0	D02 6-0	a28 3-0	M03 4-0	S30 2-1		O21 4-0	D16 2-0	M17 3-1
16 SMALL HEATH	D02 5-0	S30 0-0	J27 2-1	M10 2-0	S16 5-3	J20 8-1	F12 0-1	a14 4-1	O02 5-0	F10 6-0	D16 3-0	J06 5-1	M17 2-0	O14 1-0	F24 4-1		S02 3-2	M31 3-1
17 WALSALL	D25 4-2	N25 2-2	O21 0-1	a16 2-0	N11 6-3	M24 1-0	J13 1-1	S25 1-2	D23 3-1	a07 1-0	F17 7-3	M10 1-1	S09 2-1	a17 0-0	a21 1-1	D30 1-0		S23 2-0
18 W ARSENAL	a28 5-1	F24 0-1	S16 1-0	D16 1-1	F10 2-0	O14 2-1	a16 2-0	S02 0-2	M24 2-1	M12 12-0	J06 3-1	S30 3-0	a07 5-0	M10 2-1	N11 1-2	N25 3-0	J20 3-1	

Wing-half Herrod Ruddlesdin was ever-present when Sheffield Wednesday won Division Two in 1899-1900. He later won three England caps and two League Championship medals but died in March 1910, when he was only 33.

Football League Records
Season 1900-01

Top scorers: Div 1, S.Bloomer (Derby County) 23 goals; Div 2, A.Swann (Barnsley) 18 goals.

Blackpool and Stockport County were elected in place of Loughborough Town and Luton Town.

LEAGUE TABLES

DIVISION 1

	P	W	D	L	F	A	W	D	L	F	A	Pts
Liverpool	34	12	2	3	36	13	7	5	5	23	22	45
Sunderland	34	12	3	2	43	11	3	10	4	14	15	43
Notts Co	34	13	2	2	39	18	5	2	10	15	28	40
Nottingham F	34	10	4	3	32	14	6	3	8	21	22	39
Bury	34	11	3	3	31	10	5	4	8	22	27	39
Newcastle U	34	10	5	2	27	13	4	5	8	15	24	38
Everton	34	10	4	3	37	17	6	1	10	18	25	37
Sheffield W	34	13	2	2	38	16	0	8	9	14	26	36
Blackburn R	34	9	4	4	24	18	3	5	9	15	29	33
Bolton W	34	10	5	2	21	12	3	2	12	18	43	33
Manchester C	34	12	3	2	32	16	1	3	13	16	42	32
Derby Co	34	10	4	3	43	18	2	3	12	12	24	31
Wolverhampton W	34	6	10	1	21	15	3	3	11	18	40	31
Sheffield U	34	8	4	5	22	23	4	3	10	13	29	31
Aston Villa	34	8	5	4	32	18	2	5	10	13	33	30
Stoke	34	8	3	6	23	15	3	2	12	23	42	27
Preston N.E.	34	6	4	7	29	30	3	3	11	20	45	25
W.B.A.	34	4	4	9	21	27	3	4	10	14	35	22

DIVISION 2

	P	W	D	L	F	A	W	D	L	F	A	Pts
Grimsby T	34	14	3	0	46	11	6	6	5	14	22	49
Small Heath	34	14	2	1	41	8	5	8	4	16	16	48
Burnley	34	15	2	0	39	6	5	2	10	14	23	44
New Brighton	34	12	5	0	34	8	5	3	9	23	30	42
Glossop N.E.	34	11	2	4	34	9	4	6	7	17	24	38
Middlesbrough	34	11	4	2	38	13	4	3	10	12	27	37
Woolwich A	34	13	3	1	30	11	2	3	12	9	24	36
Lincoln C	34	12	3	2	39	11	1	4	12	4	28	33
Burslem P.V.	34	8	6	3	28	14	3	5	9	17	33	33
Newton Heath	34	11	3	3	31	9	3	1	13	11	29	32
Leicester C	34	9	5	3	30	15	2	5	10	9	22	32
Blackpool	34	7	6	4	20	11	5	1	11	13	47	31
Gainsborough T	34	8	4	5	26	18	2	6	9	19	42	30
Chesterfield	34	6	5	6	25	22	3	5	9	21	36	28
Barnsley	34	9	3	5	34	23	2	2	13	13	37	27
Walsall	34	7	7	3	29	23	0	6	11	11	33	27
Stockport Co	34	9	2	6	25	21	2	1	14	13	47	25
Burton S	34	7	3	7	16	21	1	1	15	18	45	20

DIVISION 1

	ASTON VILLA	BLACKBURN R	BOLTON W	BURY	DERBY CO	EVERTON	LIVERPOOL	MANCHESTER C	NEWCASTLE U	NOTTINGHAM F	NOTTS CO	PRESTON N.E.	SHEFFIELD U	SHEFFIELD W	STOKE	SUNDERLAND	W.B.A.	WOLVERHAMPTON W
1 ASTON VILLA		O29 3-3	D26 3-0	S10 1-0	S29 2-1	S15 1-2	M16 0-2	D01 7-1	N17 2-2	D15 2-1	O13 1-2	S03 4-0	M30 0-0	M09 2-1	S01 2-0	J19 2-2	J05 0-1	O27 0-0
2 BLACKBURN R	D22 2-2		N24 2-0	a13 0-2	M23 1-0	M09 2-1	D29 3-1	S22 1-0	S08 0-0	O06 1-3	a06 0-2	J01 3-1	J12 1-0	O13 2-2	F23 3-2	N10 0-1	O27 1-1	a20 2-0
3 BOLTON W	O06 1-0	M30 1-0		M16 3-2	S01 0-1	D15 1-0	F16 1-0	N03 0-0	O20 3-2	J01 4-2	a05 0-1	S22 1-1	M02 0-0	J05 1-1	D01 1-0	J02 0-0	a13 3-2	a29 1-0
4 BURY	D08 3-1	S29 0-1	N10 3-0		M09 2-1	J01 3-0	a20 0-0	S08 4-0	D22 1-0	M27 0-1	M23 1-0	N24 2-1	D29 1-1	S15 2-0	a05 3-2	O27 0-0	O13 6-1	a06 0-1
5 DERBY CO	a22 3-0	N17 4-0	D29 4-2	N03 5-2		a13 0-1	O06 2-3	M02 2-0	F16 1-1	M16 0-0	S08 2-1	J12 0-0	O20 4-0	a27 3-1	M30 4-1	D26 1-1	D01 4-0	S22 4-5
6 EVERTON	J12 2-1	N03 0-0	a20 2-3	D26 3-3	D08 2-0		S22 1-1	F16 5-2	a08 0-1	M02 4-1	D22 0-1	D29 4-1	O06 3-1	N24 1-1	M16 3-0	a06 1-0	N17 1-0	S08 5-1
7 LIVERPOOL	N10 5-1	S01 3-0	O13 2-1	D15 1-0	D25 0-0	J19 1-2		a13 3-1	M30 3-0	a27 2-0	a08 1-0	O27 3-2	D01 1-2	M23 1-1	J01 3-1	S29 1-2	S15 5-0	M09 1-0
8 MANCHESTER C	a27 4-0	J19 1-3	M09 1-1	J05 1-0	O27 2-0	O13 1-0	D08 3-4		a20 2-1	S15 1-0	N10 2-0	F23 3-1	D22 2-1	S01 2-2	S29 2-0	D25 1-1	a05 1-0	N24 3-2
9 NEWCASTLE U	a17 3-0	J05 1-0	M27 3-0	a27 0-0	O13 2-1	S29 1-0	N24 1-1	D15 2-1		S01 0-0	O27 2-0	M09 3-5	a13 3-0	a06 0-0	S15 2-1	a24 0-2	J19 1-1	N10 3-1
10 NOTTINGHAM F	a20 3-1	a08 0-1	D25 3-0	S22 1-1	N10 1-0	O27 2-1	D22 0-0	J12 4-2	D29 1-2		N24 5-0	O04 4-1	S08 2-0	S29 1-0	O13 1-1	M09 0-0	M13 2-3	D08 2-1
11 NOTTS CO	F16 2-0	D01 2-1	S15 3-1	N17 1-0	J05 2-1	a09 3-2	O20 3-0	M16 0-0	M02 3-1	D26 1-0		M27 6-1	N03 2-4	J19 2-0	a13 2-4	S01 2-2	D15 1-0	O06 4-1
12 PRESTON N.E.	O20 0-2	D08 4-1	M23 1-3	M30 3-1	S15 3-2	S01 1-2	M02 2-2	N17 0-4	N03 0-1	D01 1-1	S29 0-1		M16 3-1	a05 3-2	D25 4-2	J05 1-1	a15 2-3	F16 1-1
13 SHEFFIELD U	N24 2-2	S15 2-1	O27 0-2	S01 0-3	M11 2-1	D25 2-1	a22 0-2	D26 1-1	D08 2-0	J05 0-1	M09 4-2	N10 2-1		D15 1-0	J19 0-4	O13 2-0	S29 1-1	M25 1-1
14 SHEFFIELD W	N03 3-2	F16 1-1	S08 1-0	J12 1-2	D22 2-1	M30 3-1	N17 3-2	D29 4-1	D01 2-2	a09 4-1	S22 4-1	O06 0-1	a29 1-0		M02 4-0	a13 1-0	M16 2-1	J01 2-0
15 STOKE	D29 0-0	O20 2-0	N12 2-1	O06 1-2	N24 0-1	N10 0-2	S08 1-2	J26 2-1	J12 2-0	F16 0-3	S10 1-1	D26 5-0	S22 0-1	O27 2-1		M23 0-0	M09 2-0	D22 3-0
16 SUNDERLAND	S22 0-0	M16 2-0	a08 5-1	M02 4-1	J01 2-1	D01 2-0	F23 0-1	O20 3-0	O06 1-1	N03 0-1	D29 1-1	S08 3-1	F16 3-0	D08 1-0	N17 6-1		M30 3-0	J12 7-2
17 W.B.A.	S08 0-1	M02 1-1	D08 7-2	F16 1-2	S03 1-1	a22 1-2	a29 0-1	O06 3-2	S22 0-1	O20 1-6	N05 1-0	D22 0-1	a30 0-2	N10 1-1	N03 2-2	N24 1-0		D29 1-2
18 WOLVERHAMPTON W	a08 0-0	D15 2-2	S29 1-1	D01 1-1	J19 0-0	J05 1-1	N03 2-1	M30 1-0	M16 1-0	a13 1-0	S03 3-2	O13 2-2	N17 3-0	D26 1-1	a09 0-2	S15 2-2	S01 0-0	

Sam Raybould, Liverpool's leading scorer with 16 goals when they won Division One in 1900-01. In 1902-03 he netted 31, a club record for 30 years.

DIVISION 2

	BARNSLEY	BLACKPOOL	BURNLEY	BURSLEM P.V.	BURTON S	CHESTERFIELD	GAINSBOROUGH T	GLOSSOP	GRIMSBY T	LEICESTER F	LINCOLN C	MIDDLESBROUGH	NEW BRIGHTON	NEWTON HEATH	SMALL HEATH	STOCKPORT CO	WALSALL	W ARSENAL
1 BARNSLEY		S29 0-1	a05 2-1	a06 1-3	S08 3-2	S15 4-1	D22 1-3	a08 2-2	F23 2-3	J01 1-0	O27 0-0	M14 3-1	a20 1-1	a09 6-2	O13 1-2	F09 2-0	D29 2-1	J19 3-0
2 BLACKPOOL	M20 1-1		D08 0-1	a05 2-1	S22 2-0	O13 1-1	S08 1-1	N24 0-0	M09 0-1	D22 1-0	N10 2-0	a06 3-0	D29 1-2	M23 1-2	O27 0-0	F23 3-0	J12 1-0	O06 1-1
3 BURNLEY	M30 4-0	a13 4-0		F16 1-0	S03 2-1	J26 5-1	D25 2-1	J19 5-1	S01 3-0	O20 0-0	J05 1-0	S29 2-0	N03 2-1	S15 1-0	a27 1-0	D15 3-1	M16 0-0	D01 3-0
4 BURSLEM P.V.	D01 3-2	D15 4-0	O13 1-0		M30 4-0	F23 5-1	M16 1-1	S29 0-0	N03 0-0	M02 0-0	S15 2-0	M11 0-2	N17 1-3	J19 2-0	S01 2-2	S03 0-1	D25 2-2	a13 1-0
5 BURTON S	J05 1-1	J19 1-2	M23 1-0	N24 0-2		S01 0-4	a20 1-0	M09 1-3	O13 1-2	O01 0-1	F23 0-0	N10 0-0	D25 1-0	O27 3-1	a15 0-2	S29 3-2	D22 2-1	S15 1-0
6 CHESTERFIELD	J12 1-2	F16 2-0	O06 1-3	O20 1-1	D29 2-0		D01 2-2	S08 0-1	M30 3-3	a05 1-0	a08 2-0	S22 2-3	D26 0-1	D22 2-1	M16 1-1	M02 4-2	a20 1-1	F19 0-1
7 GAINSBOROUGH T	O24 4-2	J05 1-3	M09 3-0	N10 2-1	D15 2-1	a06 2-3		F23 1-1	S29 0-1	M23 0-0	F09 1-1	O27 1-1	N24 4-1	O13 0-1	J19 1-2	S15 2-0	a13 1-0	D29 1-0
8 GLOSSOP	M16 2-1	M30 6-0	S22 0-1	F09 1-2	a05 3-0	D25 1-1	O20 3-1		D15 0-0	O06 3-1	a27 2-0	J12 2-0	F16 0-1	S01 1-0	a13 2-0	D01 6-0	M02 2-0	N17 0-1
9 GRIMSBY T	O20 1-0	J26 2-0	D29 2-1	S08 6-1	F16 5-2	N24 5-2	a05 0-0	a20 1-0		J12 4-1	D01 4-0	D22 2-0	S22 5-2	D08 2-0	N17 1-1	N10 5-1	O06 0-0	M02 1-0
10 LEICESTER F	D25 2-0	a09 3-1	N17 1-1	O27 0-0	D01 5-2	M09 1-3	a08 1-0	F21 1-2	S15 4-0		J19 0-2	O13 1-0	M16 1-1	S29 1-0	J05 1-1	S01 2-2	M30 5-0	D15 1-0
11 LINCOLN C	M02 3-0	M16 3-0	S08 2-0	J12 2-2	O20 2-1	a13 2-0	O06 6-0	D26 1-1	D25 0-1	S22 1-0		D29 1-2	a01 2-0	a05 2-0	M30 3-1	D08 4-0	F16 2-0	J26 3-3
12 MIDDLESBROUGH	D26 3-0	D01 3-1	a09 0-0	O06 4-0	M16 3-1	J19 2-0	M02 9-2	S15 2-2	a27 0-0	F16 2-1	S01 2-0		O20 2-1	J01 1-2	D15 0-1	a13 2-0	M09 2-1	M30 1-1
13 NEW BRIGHTON	D15 2-0	S01 0-0	O27 2-1	M09 1-1	a08 3-1	M23 1-1	M30 3-2	O13 1-0	J19 5-0	N10 0-0	S29 2-0	M25 3-1		F19 2-0	S15 0-0	J01 3-0	D01 5-1	a27 1-0
14 NEWTON HEATH	M13 1-0	D26 4-0	J12 0-1	S22 4-0	M02 1-1	a27 1-0	F16 0-0	D29 3-0	a13 1-0	M20 2-3	D15 4-1	S08 4-0	O06 1-0		D01 0-1	M30 3-1	O20 1-1	M16 1-0
15 SMALL HEATH	F16 3-1	M02 10-1	D22 0-1	D29 2-1	O06 2-0	N10 0-0	S22 6-0	D08 1-0	a01 2-1	S08 0-0	N24 2-0	a20 2-1	J12 4-0	a06 1-0		D26 2-0	a08 2-1	O20 2-1
16 STOCKPORT CO	O06 2-1	O20 0-1	a20 3-2	D22 1-1	a27 2-0	O27 3-1	J12 1-2	a06 1-3	M16 0-1	D29 3-1	M23 1-0	a05 0-1	S08 0-5	N24 1-0	M09 0-0		S22 4-1	F16 3-1
17 WALSALL	S01 3-0	S15 1-2	N10 2-0	M23 2-1	S24 1-5	D15 2-2	D26 3-3	O27 2-1	F09 0-0	N24 2-0	O13 3-0	a22 0-0	a06 3-3	F25 1-1	S29 2-2	J19 1-3		D24 1-0
18 W ARSENAL	S22 1-2	a08 3-1	a06 3-1	D08 3-0	J12 3-1	S29 1-0	S01 2-1	M23 2-0	O27 1-1	N03 2-1	M09 0-0	N24 1-0	D22 2-1	N10 2-1	a22 1-0	O13 2-0	S08 1-1	

Football League Records
Season 1901-02

Top scorers: Div 1, J.Settle (Everton) 18 goals; Div 2, C.Simmons (West Bromwich Albion) 23 goals.
New Brighton Tower resigned and Walsall failed to gain re-election. Bristol City and Doncaster Rovers were elected in their place. Burton Swifts and Wanderers amalgamated to become Burton United.

DIVISION 1

	ASTON VILLA	BLACKBURN R	BOLTON W	BURY	DERBY CO	EVERTON	GRIMSBY T	LIVERPOOL	MANCHESTER C	NEWCASTLE U	NOTTINGHAM F	NOTTS CO	SHEFFIELD U	SHEFFIELD W	SMALL HEATH	STOKE	SUNDERLAND	WOLVERHAMPTON W
1 ASTON VILLA		S14 1-1	N09 1-0	J04 2-0	F15 3-2	S28 1-1	D14 4-1	M29 0-1	M31 2-2	D07 0-0	D28 3-0	S09 2-0	S16 1-2	O26 4-1	D26 1-0	J18 0-0	F01 0-1	N23 2-1
2 BLACKBURN R	J11 4-0		D07 2-0	O05 0-3	a19 3-1	O26 3-1	D25 2-0	a26 1-1	a12 1-4	S07 0-0	J01 1-0	M29 4-2	S21 2-1	N23 2-0	N09 3-1	F15 6-1	M01 0-1	D21 2-0
3 BOLTON W	M08 2-2	a05 4-0		N30 2-2	S14 2-1	a19 1-3	O05 4-0	F22 1-0	J01 3-3	N02 3-1	J02 3-0	S28 1-1	M28 1-0	J18 3-1	J04 4-0	D14 2-1	D28 0-0	O19 2-2
4 BURY	S07 0-0	M28 2-0	M29 2-2		N09 2-0	F15 1-0	J01 1-1	F01 0-0	D07 3-0	a26 4-0	S21 1-1	N23 3-0	J11 1-2	M15 2-0	M01 2-0	O12 4-2	O26 1-0	a12 2-1
5 DERBY CO	O19 1-0	N16 1-1	J11 1-2	M08 1-0		N30 3-1	a01 2-0	O05 1-1	S21 2-0	D26 1-0	N02 1-1	S07 2-0	a28 3-1	a26 2-2	M31 0-0	M22 1-0	a05 1-0	D25 3-1
6 EVERTON	D25 2-3	F22 0-2	D21 1-0	O19 1-1	M29 2-0		M08 0-1	J11 4-0	S02 3-1	S21 0-0	M31 1-0	a12 0-1	O05 2-1	D07 5-0	N23 1-0	N02 1-0	M15 2-0	S07 6-1
7 GRIMSBY T	a12 4-1	O12 2-1	F01 4-1	S28 2-0	S03 1-1	N09 0-2		M15 1-1	F15 3-2	M28 3-0	S14 1-0	J18 1-0	D28 0-1	J04 3-1	D07 1-0	O26 1-2	N23 3-3	M01 3-0
8 LIVERPOOL	N30 1-0	D28 1-0	O26 1-1	a19 1-0	a14 0-2	S14 2-2	a21 2-2		M01 4-0	M22 0-1	D14 0-2	F15 0-1	a05 1-0	O12 1-2	S28 3-1	J04 7-0	D26 0-1	N09 4-1
9 MANCHESTER C	F17 1-0	D14 1-1	O12 1-0	a05 2-0	J18 0-0	M17 2-0	O19 3-0	N02 2-3		M08 2-0	N30 3-1	F01 1-0	M22 4-0	M28 0-3	S14 1-4	a19 2-2	J04 0-3	F22 3-0
10 NEWCASTLE U	a05 2-1	J04 0-3	M01 4-1	D28 1-1	O12 0-1	J18 1-1	N30 5-1	N23 1-0	N09 3-0		a19 3-0	O26 8-0	D14 1-1	F15 2-1	F01 2-0	S14 5-1	S28 0-1	M15 3-1
11 NOTTINGHAM F	a01 1-1	S28 3-0	N23 4-1	J18 2-1	M01 3-1	O12 4-0	J11 0-1	a12 1-1	M29 3-1	M19 0-2		D26 1-0	S07 2-1	N09 1-1	O26 1-1	F01 2-0	F15 2-1	D07 2-0
12 NOTTS CO	N02 0-3	N30 3-0	M31 2-1	M22 2-1	J04 3-2	D14 0-2	S21 3-0	O19 2-2	O05 2-0	O03 0-2	N16 3-0		M08 4-0	S14 6-1	D28 6-1	a05 1-1	a19 2-0	M28 5-3
13 SHEFFIELD U	J01 6-0	J18 4-1	a07 2-0	S14 3-1	O26 3-0	F01 0-0	F11 2-2	D07 2-1	N23 5-0	a12 1-0	J04 2-2	N09 3-0		M01 3-0	F15 1-4	S28 1-1	O12 0-1	M29 0-0
14 SHEFFIELD W	F22 1-0	M22 0-1	S21 5-1	N16 4-1	M17 2-0	a05 1-1	S07 3-1	a01 1-1	D26 2-1	O19 0-0	M08 0-2	J11 4-0	N02 1-0		a19 1-2	N30 3-1	D14 1-1	O05 1-1
15 SMALL HEATH	O12 0-2	M08 2-0	S07 2-0	N02 1-0	a12 5-1	M22 0-1	F22 6-0	S02 0-0	J11 1-0	O05 3-1	a05 1-1	a26 0-0	O19 5-1	D21 1-1		F17 1-1	N30 2-3	S21 1-2
16 STOKE	S21 1-0	O19 2-2	a12 4-0	S02 1-2	N23 1-1	M01 1-2	a14 2-0	S07 1-0	J13 3-0	J11 0-0	O05 1-1	D07 3-0	D26 3-2	M29 1-2	M15 1-0		N09 3-0	N11 3-0
17 SUNDERLAND	O05 1-0	N02 3-2	a26 2-1	a16 3-0	J01 1-0	N16 2-4	M22 3-1	S21 1-1	S07 1-0	M31 0-0	O19 4-0	D21 2-1	S02 3-1	a12 1-2	M29 1-1	M08 2-0		J11 2-0
18 WOLVERHAMPTON W	M22 0-2	M31 3-1	F15 1-2	D14 1-0	S28 0-0	D26 2-1	N02 2-0	M08 3-1	O26 0-0	M10 3-0	S02 2-0	O12 3-1	N30 1-1	F01 1-0	J18 2-1	D28 4-1	S14 4-2	

LEAGUE TABLES

DIVISION 1

	P	W	D	L	F	A	W	D	L	F	A	Pts
Sunderland	34	12	3	2	32	14	7	3	7	18	21	44
Everton	34	11	2	4	31	11	6	5	6	22	24	41
Newcastle U	34	11	3	3	41	14	3	6	8	7	20	37
Blackburn R	34	12	2	3	36	16	3	4	10	16	32	36
Nottingham F	34	11	4	2	32	13	2	5	10	11	30	35
Derby Co	34	11	5	1	26	10	2	4	11	13	31	35
Bury	34	11	5	1	31	9	2	3	12	13	29	34
Aston Villa	34	9	5	3	27	13	4	3	10	15	27	34
Sheffield W	34	9	5	3	30	14	4	3	10	18	38	34
Sheffield U	34	10	5	2	38	13	3	2	12	15	35	33
Liverpool	34	8	3	6	28	16	2	9	6	14	22	32
Bolton W	34	10	6	1	38	17	2	2	13	13	39	32
Notts Co	34	12	2	3	44	19	2	2	13	7	38	32
Wolverhampton W	34	12	3	2	32	13	1	3	13	14	44	32
Grimsby T	34	11	3	3	33	16	2	3	12	11	44	32
Stoke	34	10	4	3	31	12	1	5	11	14	43	31
Small Heath	34	8	5	4	31	14	3	3	11	16	31	30
Manchester C	34	10	3	4	28	17	1	3	13	14	41	28

DIVISION 2

	P	W	D	L	F	A	W	D	L	F	A	Pts
W.B.A.	34	14	2	1	52	13	11	3	3	30	16	55
Middlesbrough	34	15	1	1	58	7	8	4	5	32	17	51
Preston N.E.	34	12	3	2	50	11	6	3	8	21	21	42
Woolwich A	34	13	2	2	35	9	5	4	8	15	17	42
Lincoln C	34	11	6	0	26	4	3	7	7	19	31	41
Bristol C	34	13	1	3	39	12	4	5	8	13	23	40
Doncaster R	34	12	3	2	39	12	1	5	11	10	46	34
Glossop N.E.	34	7	6	4	22	15	3	6	8	14	25	32
Burnley	34	9	6	2	30	8	1	4	12	11	37	30
Burton U	34	8	6	3	32	23	3	2	12	14	31	30
Barnsley	34	9	3	5	36	33	3	3	11	15	30	30
Burslem P.V.	34	7	7	3	26	17	3	2	12	17	42	29
Blackpool	34	9	3	5	27	21	2	4	11	13	35	29
Leicester C	34	11	2	4	26	14	1	3	13	12	42	29
Newton Heath	34	10	2	5	27	12	1	4	12	11	41	28
Chesterfield	34	10	3	4	35	18	1	3	13	12	50	28
Stockport Co	34	8	3	6	25	20	0	4	13	11	52	23
Gainsborough T	34	4	9	4	26	25	0	2	15	4	55	19

DIVISION 2

	BARNSLEY	BLACKPOOL	BRISTOL C	BURNLEY	BURSLEM P.V.	BURTON U	CHESTERFIELD	DONCASTER R	GAINSBOROUGH T	GLOSSOP	LEICESTER F	LINCOLN C	MIDDLESBROUGH	NEWTON HEATH	PRESTON N.E.	STOCKPORT CO	W.B.A.	W ARSENAL
1 BARNSLEY		M08 2-0	D25 2-2	J01 2-2	O05 4-0	S07 3-2	F08 3-2	a05 3-0	O19 2-0	D26 1-4	J11 2-3	a12 2-2	F22 2-7	M22 3-2	S21 0-4	M31 3-1	a19 0-2	D28 2-0
2 BLACKPOOL	N09 2-1		S07 0-2	M29 2-1	J01 1-0	J11 1-0	a12 0-0	O12 3-1	D21 3-0	F01 1-1	M28 4-0	F15 3-0	a26 0-2	S28 2-4	N23 1-4	J18 1-0	O26 2-2	M01 1-3
3 BRISTOL C	M01 3-1	J04 3-0		a12 1-0	M29 4-0	a26 0-2	D07 5-2	F01 3-0	J25 4-0	S28 2-0	N09 2-1	O12 1-1	D21 1-0	J18 4-0	M15 2-0	S14 3-0	F15 1-2	O26 0-3
4 BURNLEY	S28 2-0	N30 2-0	M22 0-1		F22 4-1	O19 0-0	N02 0-0	D28 7-0	M08 6-0	a19 1-1	F01 1-0	J04 1-0	N16 2-2	M28 1-0	O12 0-3	S09 3-0	S14 0-0	J18 0-0
5 BURSLEM P.V.	F01 2-1	a05 0-1	S09 3-0	O26 1-1		M10 2-1	M08 4-2	J04 2-2	M28 1-1	D28 1-0	O12 3-0	S14 1-2	M22 1-1	a19 1-1	F15 0-0	D14 1-1	J18 2-3	S28 1-0
6 BURTON U	J04 2-1	S14 1-1	D28 2-2	F15 5-2	M01 3-0		M15 0-1	N09 1-1	M29 5-0	O26 1-1	J18 2-0	N23 0-6	a12 3-2	O12 0-0	F01 1-1	S28 3-2	D07 1-3	a19 2-0
7 CHESTERFIELD	O12 1-2	M31 3-1	a05 1-0	M01 3-0	N09 4-3	M28 3-1		S14 0-0	M22 2-0	J04 1-0	F15 3-3	J18 0-1	N30 0-0	M17 3-0	O26 2-0	a19 8-1	S28 0-3	F01 1-3
8 DONCASTER R	D07 0-1	F08 4-3	O05 3-0	a26 3-0	S07 3-3	M08 2-0	J11 4-1		S21 3-0	M31 1-2	a12 2-1	M15 1-1	M28 0-0	F22 4-0	a19 4-0	O19 2-0	N23 2-0	M29 1-0
9 GAINSBOROUGH T	F15 0-0	a19 3-0	a02 2-0	N09 1-1	M15 2-3	N30 1-4	N23 0-0	J18 4-1		S14 2-1	O26 3-3	S28 2-2	a05 1-4	J04 1-1	M01 0-1	D28 1-1	F01 1-1	O12 2-2
10 GLOSSOP	M29 1-1	O05 3-1	M04 1-2	D21 0-0	a26 0-1	F22 2-1	S07 3-1	M01 3-1	J11 0-0		D07 1-1	N09 1-1	S21 1-0	O19 0-0	a12 3-1	F08 2-1	M15 1-2	N23 0-1
11 LEICESTER F	S14 2-0	M15 1-0	M08 0-1	O05 2-1	J25 0-1	S21 4-0	O19 3-0	D26 1-0	F22 2-0	a01 1-1		a19 3-1	N02 0-2	N30 3-2	M31 1-0	N23 1-1	D28 0-3	J04 2-1
12 LINCOLN C	M28 1-1	O19 0-0	a21 1-0	S07 1-0	J11 1-1	M22 0-0	S21 4-0	D25 0-0	a16 3-0	M08 1-0	D21 2-0		O05 2-1	D26 2-0	a26 2-1	F22 5-0	M29 1-0	D07 0-0
13 MIDDLESBROUGH	O26 2-1	D28 2-1	a19 2-0	M15 3-0	N23 3-0	J01 5-0	M29 7-1	S28 6-0	D07 3-1	J18 5-0	M01 5-0	F01 0-0		S14 5-0	N09 2-1	J04 6-0	O12 1-2	F15 1-0
14 NEWTON HEATH	N23 1-0	J25 0-1	S21 1-0	F11 2-0	D21 1-0	a21 3-1	a23 2-0	O26 6-0	S07 3-0	F15 1-0	M29 2-0	M01 0-0	a07 1-2		J01 0-2	O05 3-3	N09 1-2	M15 0-1
15 PRESTON N.E.	D14 4-0	M22 1-1	N30 0-0	a07 3-1	O19 2-0	O05 1-0	F22 5-0	D21 3-0	D25 4-1	M28 2-2	S28 5-0	D28 8-0	M08 0-3	D07 5-1		M29 4-0	J04 1-2	S14 2-0
16 STOCKPORT CO	M15 2-3	S21 3-1	J11 1-1	D07 1-2	a12 4-2	a14 2-0	D21 3-0	F15 1-2	a26 2-1	O12 0-0	M24 2-0	O26 2-1	S07 1-3	F01 1-0	a05 0-2		M01 0-2	N09 0-0
17 W.B.A.	D21 3-1	F22 7-2	O19 2-2	J11 3-0	S21 3-1	a05 2-1	S09 4-0	M22 2-2	O05 7-0	S02 0-1	J06 1-0	D09 4-1	D14 2-0	M08 4-0	S07 3-1	D26 3-0		a12 2-1
18 W ARSENAL	S02 2-1	D25 0-0	F22 2-0	S21 4-0	D26 3-1	D21 0-1	O05 3-2	N30 1-0	F08 5-0	M22 4-0	S07 2-0	a05 2-0	O19 0-3	N16 2-0	J11 0-0	M08 3-0	M31 2-1	

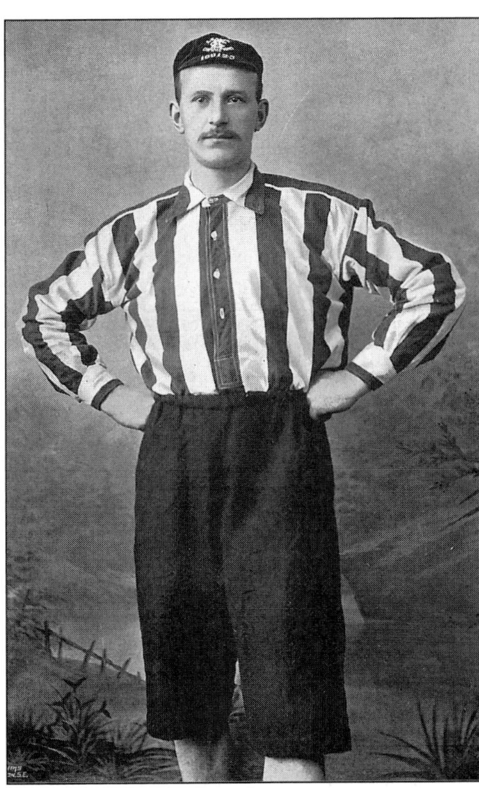

Sunderland's Scottish international goalkeeper Teddy Doig, who spent 14 years with the Roker club from 1890 and later starred for Liverpool.

Football League Records
Season 1902-03

Top scorers: Div 1, S.Raybould (Liverpool) 31 goals; Div 2, W.Gillespie (Manchester City) 30 goals.
Newton Heath became Manchester United.

LEAGUE TABLES

DIVISION 1

	P	W	D	L	F	A	W	D	L	F	A	Pts
Sheffield W	34	12	3	2	31	7	7	1	9	23	29	42
Aston Villa	34	11	3	3	43	18	8	0	9	18	22	41
Sunderland	34	10	5	2	27	11	6	4	7	24	25	41
Sheffield U	34	11	0	6	36	22	6	5	6	22	22	39
Liverpool	34	11	3	3	48	21	6	1	10	20	28	38
Stoke	34	11	2	4	29	11	4	5	8	17	27	37
W.B.A.	34	10	2	5	37	27	6	2	9	17	26	36
Bury	34	14	1	2	41	14	2	2	13	13	29	35
Derby Co	34	13	2	2	34	11	3	1	13	16	36	35
Nottingham F	34	10	3	4	33	22	4	4	9	16	25	35
Wolverhampton W	34	12	2	3	34	17	2	3	12	14	40	33
Everton	34	10	2	5	28	18	3	4	10	17	29	32
Middlesbrough	34	10	3	4	27	16	4	1	12	14	34	32
Newcastle U	34	12	1	4	31	11	2	3	12	10	40	32
Notts Co	34	8	5	4	25	16	4	2	11	16	33	31
Blackburn R	34	9	2	6	27	24	3	3	11	17	39	29
Grimsby T	34	6	5	6	28	22	2	4	11	15	40	25
Bolton W	34	6	2	9	18	20	2	1	14	19	53	19

DIVISION 2

	P	W	D	L	F	A	W	D	L	F	A	Pts
Manchester C	34	15	1	1	64	15	10	3	4	31	14	54
Small Heath	34	17	0	0	57	11	7	3	7	17	25	51
Woolwich A	34	14	2	1	46	9	6	6	5	20	21	48
Bristol C	34	12	3	2	43	18	5	5	7	16	20	42
Manchester U	34	9	4	4	32	15	6	4	7	21	23	38
Chesterfield	34	11	4	2	43	10	3	5	9	24	30	37
Preston N.E.	34	10	5	2	39	12	3	5	9	17	28	36
Barnsley	34	9	4	4	32	13	4	4	9	23	38	34
Burslem P.V.	34	11	5	1	36	16	2	3	12	21	46	34
Lincoln C	34	8	3	6	30	22	4	3	10	16	31	30
Glossop N.E.	34	9	1	7	26	20	2	6	9	17	38	29
Gainsborough T	34	9	4	4	28	14	2	3	12	13	45	29
Burton U	34	9	4	4	26	20	2	3	12	13	39	29
Blackpool	34	7	5	5	32	24	2	5	10	12	35	28
Leicester C	34	5	5	7	20	23	5	3	9	21	42	28
Doncaster R	34	8	5	4	27	17	1	2	14	8	55	25
Stockport Co	34	6	4	7	26	24	1	2	14	13	50	20
Burnley	34	6	7	4	25	25	0	1	16	5	52	20

DIVISION 1

	ASTON VILLA	BLACKBURN R	BOLTON W	BURY	DERBY CO	EVERTON	GRIMSBY T	LIVERPOOL	MIDDLESBROUGH	NEWCASTLE U	NOTTINGHAM F	NOTTS CO	SHEFFIELD U	SHEFFIELD W	STOKE	SUNDERLAND	W.B.A.	WOLVERHAMPTON W
1 ASTON VILLA		J24 5-0	N15 4-2	S20 2-2	S06 0-0	O18 2-1	D27 2-2	D13 1-2	a27 5-0	N29 7-0	J10 3-1	a15 2-1	a18 4-2	D26 1-0	a13 2-0	O04 0-1	N01 0-3	a04 3-1
2 BLACKBURN R	S27 0-2		a04 4-2	O11 0-3	O18 2-4	N08 3-2	J17 2-0	J03 3-1	S01 0-1	a18 3-1	J31 2-2	N29 1-2	S13 2-0	N15 2-1	N01 1-1	D25 0-2	M21 1-0	J01 1-0
3 BOLTON W	M14 0-1	D06 1-2		M28 1-0	J24 2-0	N01 1-3	J02 0-1	O25 1-1	J31 2-1	O11 0-2	N22 1-1	S20 0-1	F28 1-0	S06 0-2	D20 2-3	a11 2-0	J10 0-1	F14 4-1
4 BURY	J17 0-1	a10 1-1	N29 3-0		O04 1-0	J01 4-2	S13 2-1	D27 3-1	a04 3-1	D13 1-0	S27 3-1	M26 3-1	J03 3-1	a06 4-0	D25 2-1	O18 3-1	N15 1-2	a22 4-0
5 DERBY CO	J03 2-0	F14 1-0	S27 5-0	J31 2-0		M28 0-1	a22 2-2	N22 2-1	O11 3-2	O25 0-0	J17 0-1	S13 4-1	D06 1-0	a11 1-0	M14 2-0	N01 5-2	D27 1-0	N08 3-1
6 EVERTON	F14 0-1	a13 0-3	D27 3-1	F28 3-0	N29 2-1		O11 4-2	S27 3-1	J03 3-0	S13 0-1	O25 1-1	a18 2-0	J31 1-0	a04 1-1	N22 0-1	M14 0-3	D13 3-1	J17 2-1
7 GRIMSBY T	a25 0-2	S20 4-1	N08 1-1	J10 2-1	D20 4-1	D25 0-0		a04 3-1	N15 2-2	M21 1-0	S09 0-1	N01 1-1	D13 1-2	O18 0-1	O04 2-2	J24 2-4	a10 4-0	N29 1-2
8 LIVERPOOL	a11 2-1	S06 5-2	D25 5-1	a25 2-0	M23 3-1	a10 0-0	D06 9-2		N01 5-0	M07 3-0	D20 2-1	O18 0-2	M28 2-4	O04 4-2	S20 1-1	M30 1-1	J01 0-2	N15 4-1
9 MIDDLESBROUGH	N22 1-2	a11 4-0	O04 4-3	D06 1-1	a13 3-1	S06 1-0	M14 2-0	F28 0-2		F14 1-0	M28 2-0	J24 2-1	N08 0-2	J10 2-1	a25 1-1	D20 0-1	S20 1-1	O25 2-0
10 NEWCASTLE U	M28 2-0	D20 1-0	a13 2-0	a11 1-0	a10 2-1	a01 3-0	N22 1-0	N08 1-2	O18 0-1		D06 0-2	O04 6-1	M14 0-0	S20 3-0	S06 5-0	a25 1-0	J24 1-0	F28 2-4
11 NOTTINGHAM F	S13 2-0	O04 2-0	M21 1-2	J24 3-0	S20 2-3	O02 2-2	J03 2-1	a18 1-0	N29 1-0	a04 3-2		N15 0-0	D27 2-2	N01 1-4	O18 1-3	a13 5-2	M07 3-1	D13 2-0
12 NOTTS CO	N08 2-1	M28 4-0	J17 1-3	N22 1-0	J10 2-1	D20 2-0	F28 0-1	F14 1-2	S27 2-0	J31 2-2	D26 1-1		O25 1-1	O03 0-3	a11 3-0	D06 0-0	S06 3-1	O11 0-0
13 SHEFFIELD U	D20 2-4	J10 2-1	D26 7-1	S06 1-0	M30 3-2	O04 0-2	a11 3-0	N29 2-0	M07 1-3	N15 2-1	O13 2-0	a10 3-0		S01 2-3	J24 1-3	S20 1-0	O18 1-2	M21 3-0
14 SHEFFIELD W	J01 4-0	M14 0-0	J03 3-0	N08 2-0	D13 0-1	D06 4-1	F14 1-1	J31 3-1	S13 2-0	J17 3-0	F28 1-0	D27 2-0	O11 0-1		M28 1-0	N22 1-0	a18 3-1	S27 1-1
15 STOKE	O11 1-0	D26 0-2	a18 2-0	O25 1-0	N15 2-0	M21 2-0	J31 1-1	J17 1-0	D27 0-2	J03 5-0	F14 3-2	S15 0-2	S27 0-1	N29 4-0		N08 1-1	a04 3-0	S13 3-0
16 SUNDERLAND	J31 1-0	O25 2-2	D13 3-1	F14 3-1	J01 2-0	N15 2-1	S27 5-1	S13 2-1	a18 2-1	D27 0-0	S01 0-1	a04 2-1	J17 0-0	M21 0-1	a10 0-0		N29 0-0	J03 3-0
17 W.B.A.	F28 1-2	N22 5-3	S13 2-1	a20 1-3	a25 3-0	S01 2-1	O25 1-0	O11 1-2	J17 1-0	S27 6-1	N08 2-0	J03 3-2	F14 3-3	D20 2-3	D06 2-1	M28 0-3		J31 2-2
18 WOLVERHAMPTON W	D06 2-1	D27 2-0	O18 3-1	D20 3-2	S01 3-0	S20 1-1	M28 3-0	a27 0-2	D26 2-0	N01 3-0	a11 2-1	a13 2-0	N22 1-3	J24 2-1	J10 1-0	S06 3-3	O04 1-2	

England centre-half Tommy Crawshaw played in two FA Cup winning teams and two League Championship winning sides for Sheffield Wednesday.

DIVISION 2

	BARNSLEY	BLACKPOOL	BRISTOL C	BURNLEY	BURSLEM P.V.	BURTON U	CHESTERFIELD	DONCASTER R	GAINSBOROUGH T	GLOSSOP	LEICESTER F	LINCOLN C	MANCHESTER C	MANCHESTER U	PRESTON N.E.	SMALL HEATH	STOCKPORT CO	W ARSENAL
1 BARNSLEY		J10 6-0	a11 2-0	J01 3-0	a10 1-0	D06 4-0	M21 2-2	J24 2-0	M28 2-3	D20 0-1	O18 1-2	O04 0-0	a14 0-3	a25 0-0	M07 3-0	a13 3-0	S06 2-1	S20 1-1
2 BLACKPOOL	S13 3-3		J01 0-1	F07 2-0	J03 2-5	S27 3-3	a13 2-1	D25 4-0	J17 4-0	O11 2-2	a04 2-0	M21 2-3	D13 0-3	F14 2-0	D27 2-2	N29 0-1	O25 2-0	M07 0-0
3 BRISTOL C	D25 3-3	J31 0-1		M21 3-0	a04 3-0	D27 3-1	S06 2-1	O18 4-2	a18 1-0	J10 1-1	M07 6-1	M30 0-2	N15 3-2	S20 3-1	N29 2-1	N01 1-1	J24 7-1	O04 1-0
4 BURNLEY	F28 1-2	D20 1-1	N22 0-0		O25 3-3	M14 4-1	S08 1-1	S06 1-1	N08 3-2	M28 2-1	J24 1-3	J10 1-0	O04 1-1	D06 0-2	F14 1-1	S20 2-1	a11 3-2	N15 0-3
5 BURSLEM P.V.	a20 2-0	S06 1-1	D06 2-0	M30 3-1		M28 4-2	M07 2-1	S20 3-0	N22 3-1	a11 1-0	F07 2-0	J24 5-1	O18 1-4	D20 1-1	S08 0-0	O04 2-2	N10 3-1	J10 1-1
6 BURTON U	a04 1-1	J24 2-0	a25 0-3	S01 0-0	a13 0-0		D20 1-0	F07 1-0	a11 3-0	S06 2-1	D26 2-3	O18 2-2	M07 0-5	J10 3-1	M21 2-1	F21 0-1	S20 5-1	D25 2-1
7 CHESTERFIELD	N22 3-0	F28 1-1	J03 3-0	O11 2-0	N08 3-0	a18 1-0		M28 1-1	D06 0-1	J17 10-0	S13 5-0	a11 1-0	S27 0-1	J31 2-0	O25 4-2	D27 1-1	F14 4-1	M14 2-2
8 DONCASTER R	S27 2-0	M14 3-0	F14 0-0	a10 2-1	J17 3-2	O11 1-1	N29 3-4		J31 0-0	O25 4-1	a18 0-0	a04 2-1	D27 1-2	F28 2-2	S13 1-2	D13 1-0	N08 2-0	N22 0-1
9 GAINSBOROUGH T	M25 1-2	S20 0-0	D20 2-1	M07 3-0	M21 1-1	a10 3-1	a04 3-2	O04 3-0		a25 1-1	F21 5-1	a15 4-0	O22 0-3	S06 0-1	M14 1-0	O18 1-0	F07 0-0	J24 0-1
10 GLOSSOP	a18 2-2	F17 1-0	S13 0-2	D02 2-0	D09 2-1	J03 3-0	S20 0-3	F24 3-0	D27 4-2		a10 1-2	F28 2-0	M21 0-1	J24 1-3	a04 1-0	M07 0-1	D25 3-1	O18 1-2
11 LEICESTER F	F14 1-2	D06 2-1	N08 2-2	S27 2-1	O11 2-0	F28 0-1	J10 0-2	D20 0-1	D25 4-1	M14 3-2		a14 0-0	J17 1-1	N22 1-1	J31 1-1	S06 1-3	M26 0-2	a11 0-2
12 LINCOLN C	J21 1-3	N22 0-2	O25 1-1	S13 4-1	S27 4-1	F14 4-0	D25 0-0	D06 4-2	O11 1-0	D26 1-0	D27 1-2		J03 1-0	N08 1-3	J17 2-3	a10 0-1	S15 3-1	M28 2-2
13 MANCHESTER C	N24 3-2	a11 2-0	M14 2-2	J31 6-0	F14 7-1	N08 2-0	J24 4-2	J01 4-1	F28 9-0	N22 5-2	S20 3-1	S06 3-1		a10 0-2	O11 1-0	F23 4-0	D06 5-0	D20 4-1
14 MANCHESTER U	D27 2-1	D26 2-2	J17 1-2	a04 4-0	a18 2-1	S13 1-0	O04 2-1	a13 4-0	J03 3-1	S27 1-1	M21 5-1	M07 1-2	D25 1-1		M30 0-1	N15 0-1	M23 0-0	M09 3-0
15 PRESTON N.E.	N08 3-0	a10 3-1	M28 1-0	O18 5-0	F28 5-1	N22 1-1	a20 1-1	J10 5-0	a13 0-0	D06 0-0	O04 2-0	S20 0-1	D26 0-2	a11 3-1		J24 2-1	D20 6-1	S06 2-2
16 SMALL HEATH	O11 2-1	M28 5-1	F28 2-0	J17 3-0	J31 5-1	O25 2-0	D26 2-1	a11 12-0	F14 1-0	N08 3-1	J03 4-3	D20 3-1	S13 4-0	a20 2-1	S27 3-1		N22 2-0	D06 2-0
17 STOCKPORT CO	J03 4-1	F21 4-0	S27 0-1	a13 3-0	D13 0-4	J17 0-2	O18 2-2	M07 1-0	J10 1-1	J31 2-3	N29 2-2	M14 3-1	a04 0-2	O11 2-1	a18 1-1	M21 1-2		J01 0-1
18 W ARSENAL	J17 4-0	N08 2-1	O11 2-1	D27 5-1	S13 3-0	J31 3-0	a10 3-0	M21 3-0	S27 6-1	F14 0-0	a13 0-0	N29 2-1	N01 1-0	O25 0-1	J03 3-1	a04 6-1	F28 3-1	

Football League Records
Season 1903-04

Top scorers: Div 1, S.Bloomer (Derby County) 20 goals; Div 2, P.Smith (Preston North End) 26 goals.
Bradford City were elected in place of Doncaster Rovers.

DIVISION 1

	ASTON VILLA	BLACKBURN R	BURY	DERBY CO	EVERTON	LIVERPOOL	MANCHESTER C	MIDDLESBROUGH	NEWCASTLE U	NOTTINGHAM F	NOTTS CO	SHEFFIELD U	SHEFFIELD W	SMALL HEATH	STOKE	SUNDERLAND	W.B.A.	WOLVERHAMPTON W
1 ASTON VILLA		D12 2-3	a02 0-2	O10 3-0	S26 3-1	N28 2-1	F13 0-1	M19 2-1	N07 3-1	a16 3-1	O24 4-0	F27 6-1	D26 2-1	J16 1-1	J30 3-1	J02 2-0	S12 3-1	N14 2-0
2 BLACKBURN R	a09 0-3		S05 2-2	N07 2-1	O24 0-2	a23 2-3	M12 2-5	D19 1-1	D05 4-0	J01 3-1	N21 3-0	M26 3-0	S26 0-0	F13 1-1	D25 2-0	J30 1-3	O10 2-0	J09 1-1
3 BURY	D05 2-2	J02 3-0		F27 2-2	F13 0-0	D19 2-2	N07 1-3	a09 1-1	M26 0-3	S12 2-2	J01 3-0	N21 0-1	J16 1-0	O10 1-0	O24 2-2	S26 3-1	J30 2-1	a23 0-0
4 DERBY CO	D28 2-2	a11 3-0	O31 2-2		a16 0-1	D25 2-0	J09 2-3	O17 2-2	O03 1-3	N14 2-6	S19 0-1	J23 3-5	a30 0-2	S01 4-1	D26 5-0	N28 7-2	a02 4-2	S05 2-1
5 EVERTON	J23 1-0	S01 3-1	O17 2-1	D19 0-1		a01 5-2	a25 1-0	O03 2-0	S19 4-1	O31 0-2	S05 3-1	J09 2-0	a04 2-0	N28 5-1	a09 0-1	N14 0-1	a18 4-0	a02 2-0
6 LIVERPOOL	M26 1-1	D26 1-2	a16 3-0	O24 3-1	O10 2-2		F27 2-2	F22 1-0	N21 1-0	J02 0-0	N07 2-1	M12 3-0	S12 1-3	J30 0-2	F13 0-0	J16 2-1	S26 1-3	D12 1-2
7 MANCHESTER C	O17 1-0	N14 1-0	a11 3-0	S12 2-1	D26 1-3	O31 3-2		J01 1-1	a01 1-3	a13 0-0	J23 3-0	O03 0-1	N28 1-1	a16 4-0	J02 2-2	a02 2-1	D12 6-3	S19 4-1
8 MIDDLESBROUGH	N21 2-1	a16 0-2	D12 1-0	F13 0-0	J30 3-0	a02 1-0	O24 6-0		M12 1-3	D26 1-1	F27 1-0	N07 4-1	J02 0-1	S26 3-1	O10 2-0	S12 2-3	J16 2-2	N28 1-2
9 NEWCASTLE U	S02 1-1	a02 2-1	N28 3-2	J30 0-0	J16 1-0	M19 1-1	O10 1-0	N14 2-1		D12 3-1	F13 4-1	O24 0-1	a16 4-0	S12 3-1	S26 1-0	D26 1-3	J02 1-0	O31 3-0
10 NOTTINGHAM F	D19 3-7	S19 0-1	J09 2-2	M12 5-1	F27 0-4	S05 2-1	N21 0-3	a23 1-1	a09 1-0		D25 0-1	D05 1-1	J30 0-1	O24 0-1	N25 4-2	O10 3-0	M30 2-0	J23 5-0
11 NOTTS CO	a01 0-0	M19 4-2	N14 0-0	J16 2-2	J02 0-3	O01 4-2	S26 0-3	O31 3-2	O17 3-2	N28 1-3		a04 2-1	a02 1-0	D26 2-0	S12 1-0	D12 2-1	F20 2-3	O03 0-2
12 SHEFFIELD U	O31 1-2	N28 2-2	M19 0-0	S26 3-2	S12 2-1	N14 2-1	D28 5-3	M28 3-0	D25 2-2	a02 2-0	O10 3-1		D12 1-1	J02 1-1	J16 1-1	a16 1-2	D26 4-0	O17 7-2
13 SHEFFIELD W	a23 4-2	J23 3-1	S19 1-1	N21 1-0	N07 1-0	J09 2-1	M26 1-0	S05 4-1	D19 1-1	O03 2-1	F22 2-0	a09 3-0		F27 3-2	M12 1-0	F13 0-0	O24 1-0	J01 4-0
14 SMALL HEATH	S19 2-2	O17 2-1	a04 1-0	a09 1-0	M26 1-1	O03 1-2	D19 0-3	J23 2-2	J09 3-0	S07 3-3	a23 2-0	S05 1-3	O31 0-0		D05 1-0	M05 2-1	N14 0-1	M19 3-0
15 STOKE	O03 2-0	O31 6-2	S01 4-1	a23 1-1	D12 2-3	O17 5-2	S05 1-2	D28 0-0	J23 2-3	M05 2-3	J09 0-2	S19 3-4	N14 3-1	a02 1-0		M19 3-1	N28 5-0	D19 5-1
16 SUNDERLAND	S05 6-1	O03 2-0	J23 6-0	M26 0-3	M12 2-0	S19 2-1	D05 1-1	J09 3-1	J01 1-1	a04 3-1	S01 4-1	D19 2-1	O17 0-1	N07 3-1	N21 3-0		F27 1-1	a01 2-1
17 W.B.A.	J09 1-3	D28 2-1	O03 3-2	D14 0-0	N21 0-0	J23 2-2	a09 2-1	S19 0-0	S05 1-2	O17 1-1	D19 0-0	a23 2-2	[illegible] 0-1	M12 0-1	M26 3-0	O31 1-1		M05 1-2
18 WOLVERHAMPTON W	M12 3-2	S12 1-0	D26 0-0	J02 2-2	D05 2-2	D28 4-2	M21 1-6	M26 2-2	F27 3-2	S26 3-2	J30 1-1	F13 1-0	O10 2-1	N21 1-0	a04 0-0	O24 2-1	N07 1-0	

LEAGUE TABLES

DIVISION 1

	P	W	D	L	F	A	W	D	L	F	A	Pts
Sheffield W	34	14	3	0	34	10	6	4	7	14	18	47
Manchester C	34	10	4	3	35	19	9	2	6	36	26	44
Everton	34	13	0	4	36	12	6	5	6	23	20	43
Newcastle U	34	12	3	2	31	13	6	3	8	27	32	42
Aston Villa	34	13	1	3	41	16	4	6	7	29	32	41
Sunderland	34	12	3	2	41	15	5	2	10	22	34	39
Sheffield U	34	9	6	2	40	21	6	2	9	22	36	38
Wolverhampton W	34	10	6	1	29	23	4	2	11	15	43	36
Nottingham F	34	7	3	7	29	26	4	6	7	28	31	31
Middlesbrough	34	9	3	5	30	17	0	9	8	16	30	30
Small Heath	34	8	5	4	25	19	3	3	11	14	33	30
Bury	34	6	8	3	25	20	1	7	9	15	33	29
Notts Co	34	9	3	5	27	26	3	2	12	10	35	29
Derby Co	34	7	3	7	41	33	2	7	8	17	27	28
Blackburn R	34	7	5	5	29	23	4	1	12	19	37	28
Stoke	34	9	2	6	45	26	1	5	11	9	31	27
Liverpool	34	7	5	5	24	20	2	3	12	25	42	26
W.B.A.	34	4	8	5	19	19	3	2	12	17	41	24

DIVISION 2

	P	W	D	L	F	A	W	D	L	F	A	Pts
Preston N.E.	34	13	4	0	38	10	7	6	4	24	14	50
Woolwich A	34	15	2	0	67	5	6	5	6	24	17	49
Manchester U	34	14	2	1	42	14	6	6	5	23	19	48
Bristol C	34	14	2	1	53	12	4	4	9	20	29	42
Burnley	34	12	2	3	31	20	3	7	7	19	35	39
Grimsby T	34	12	5	0	39	12	2	3	12	11	37	36
Bolton W	34	10	3	4	38	11	2	7	8	21	30	34
Barnsley	34	10	5	2	25	12	1	5	11	13	45	32
Gainsborough T	34	10	2	5	34	17	4	1	12	19	43	31
Bradford C	34	8	5	4	30	25	4	2	11	15	34	31
Chesterfield	34	8	5	4	22	12	3	3	11	15	33	30
Lincoln C	34	9	4	4	25	18	2	4	11	16	40	30
Burslem P.V.	34	10	3	4	44	20	0	6	11	10	32	29
Burton U	34	8	6	3	33	16	3	1	13	12	45	29
Blackpool	34	8	2	7	25	27	3	3	11	15	40	27
Stockport Co	34	7	7	3	28	23	1	4	12	12	49	27
Glossop N.E.	34	7	4	6	42	25	3	2	12	15	39	26
Leicester C	34	5	8	4	26	21	1	2	14	16	61	22

DIVISION 2

	BARNSLEY	BLACKPOOL	BOLTON W	BRADFORD C	BRISTOL C	BURNLEY	BURSLEM P.V.	BURTON U	CHESTERFIELD	GAINSBOROUGH T	GLOSSOP	GRIMSBY T	LEICESTER F	LINCOLN C	MANCHESTER U	PRESTON N.E.	STOCKPORT CO	W ARSENAL
1 BARNSLEY		J09 2-2	a04 1-0	F20 1-2	O03 2-0	a09 1-1	M05 1-0	J23 2-1	M26 0-0	S19 2-0	O17 4-0	a23 3-1	S05 1-1	M12 2-1	a05 0-2	D19 1-0	N21 0-0	O31 2-1
2 BLACKPOOL	S12 0-2		O10 1-4	D26 0-1	a02 0-1	F13 0-5	a01 1-0	F20 4-1	J30 0-0	M19 2-1	D25 3-2	F27 3-0	N07 1-2	J16 2-1	M09 2-1	O24 0-3	S26 4-1	J02 2-2
3 BOLTON W	D25 5-1	J01 3-0		a11 1-0	O31 1-1	J09 1-1	J02 5-0	S01 3-0	D26 4-0	O17 5-0	N14 0-1	J23 4-0	O03 3-1	D12 1-2	a25 0-0	S19 0-2	a16 0-1	N28 2-1
4 BRADFORD C	O24 3-1	a23 0-2	N21 3-3		S19 1-0	M26 3-0	D28 1-1	J09 3-0	M12 2-6	S05 1-3	F06 2-1	a09 1-0	D19 4-0	F27 2-1	J23 3-3	D05 1-1	D12 0-0	a19 0-3
5 BRISTOL C	J30 2-0	D05 5-0	F27 2-0	J16 1-1		N07 6-0	a23 2-1	D19 4-0	O24 3-2	a09 2-1	S12 5-0	N21 4-0	M26 4-0	O10 3-1	J02 1-1	M12 3-1	F13 6-0	S26 0-4
6 BURNLEY	a01 2-2	O17 1-4	S12 0-0	N28 3-2	M05 2-3		S19 1-0	D25 2-1	J02 2-1	F20 2-0	M19 2-4	O03 2-0	F06 2-1	a16 3-1	S07 2-0	J23 2-1	D26 2-0	a02 1-0
7 BURSLEM P.V.	N07 3-0	M12 5-0	S07 2-3	O10 5-2	D26 3-1	J16 2-2		a09 3-1	a16 3-0	M26 3-0	S26 1-1	F13 1-2	F27 6-2	N21 2-2	S12 1-0	J30 0-1	D05 2-0	O24 2-3
8 BURTON U	S26 1-1	M26 1-1	O24 2-1	S12 0-2	a16 2-3	F27 1-2	a04 0-0		F13 4-0	D05 2-1	J02 2-0	M12 1-0	N21 0-0	J30 5-2	D26 2-2	D28 0-0	O10 7-0	J16 3-1
9 CHESTERFIELD	a30 1-0	O03 2-1	a13 1-1	a04 1-1	F20 1-0	S05 0-0	D19 1-1	O17 2-1		F06 6-1	M05 0-0	S19 0-1	J23 2-0	a02 0-1	a01 0-2	J09 0-1	D28 4-1	M19 1-0
10 GAINSBOROUGH T	J16 4-2	N21 3-1	F13 3-1	J02 3-0	a01 3-1	O24 1-2	D29 3-0	a02 1-2	O10 1-0		D26 0-1	a06 4-2	M12 4-0	S26 0-0	a16 0-1	F27 2-0	J30 2-2	S12 0-2
11 GLOSSOP	F13 7-0	D19 0-1	M12 3-3	M01 2-0	J09 1-1	N21 6-2	J23 4-1	S05 0-1	N07 0-2	a23 0-2		D05 1-1	a09 5-0	O24 5-0	S19 0-5	M26 2-2	F27 5-1	O10 1-3
12 GRIMSBY T	D26 5-1	a04 4-0	S26 0-0	S01 2-0	M19 2-0	J30 0-0	O17 3-1	a01 4-0	J16 1-0	M05 3-1	a02 2-0		F20 4-3	J02 1-1	a12 3-1	O10 1-1	S12 2-1	a16 2-2
13 LEICESTER F	J02 2-0	M05 5-1	J30 2-2	a16 1-2	F25 1-0	O10 0-0	D25 1-1	M19 1-3	S26 0-0	a04 2-2	D12 4-2	O24 1-1		S12 2-2	a02 0-1	F13 1-4	J16 3-0	D26 0-0
14 LINCOLN C	D28 0-0	S19 0-0	a09 1-0	a01 1-0	M07 2-6	D19 3-1	M19 3-2	O03 1-0	D05 0-2	J23 0-1	F20 3-1	S05 2-1	J09 6-1		O17 0-0	a23 0-0	D25 3-1	M05 0-2
15 MANCHESTER U	O10 4-0	a09 3-1	N07 0-0	S26 3-1	S05 2-2	M12 3-1	J09 2-0	a23 2-0	D25 3-1	D19 4-2	J16 3-1	M26 2-0	a30 5-2	F13 2-0		N21 0-2	O24 3-1	J30 1-0
16 PRESTON N.E.	a16 1-1	a30 1-0	J16 3-1	a02 4-0	N14 3-0	S26 2-0	O03 3-1	M05 4-0	S12 2-1	D25 2-0	N28 3-0	O31 2-0	O17 4-3	D26 2-1	M19 1-1		J02 1-1	a01 0-0
17 STOCKPORT CO	M19 2-2	J23 2-1	D19 3-2	M05 2-0	O17 1-1	a23 2-2	a02 1-1	F06 1-1	a09 2-0	O03 1-4	a01 3-0	J09 1-1	S19 2-0	N28 4-0	M28 0-3	S05 1-5		J01 0-0
18 W ARSENAL	F27 3-0	S05 3-0	M26 3-0	D25 4-1	M14 2-0	F29 4-0	a25 0-0	S19 8-0	N21 6-0	J09 6-0	a04 2-1	D19 5-1	O26 8-0	N07 4-0	O03 4-0	a09 0-0	M12 5-2	

'Tim' Coleman, the former Northampton Town player who scored 23 goals for Woolwich Arsenal when they were promoted in 1903-04. Coleman later won an England cap and played for Everton, Sunderland, Fulham and Nottingham Forest. He appeared in Arsenal's FA Cup semi-final teams in 1906 and 1907.

FOOTBALL LEAGUE RECORDS
SEASON 1904-05

Top scorers: Div 1, A.Brown (Sheffield United) 22 goals; Div 2, S.Marsh (Bolton Wanderers) 27 goals.
Doncaster Rovers were elected in place of Stockport County.

LEAGUE TABLES

DIVISION 1

	P	W	D	L	F	A	W	D	L	F	A	Pts
Newcastle U	34	14	1	2	41	12	9	1	7	31	21	48
Everton	34	14	2	1	36	11	7	3	7	27	25	47
Manchester C	34	14	3	0	46	17	6	3	8	20	20	46
Aston Villa	34	11	2	4	32	15	8	2	7	31	28	42
Sunderland	34	11	3	3	37	19	5	5	7	23	25	40
Sheffield U	34	13	0	4	39	20	6	2	9	25	36	40
Small Heath	34	11	1	5	32	17	6	4	7	22	21	39
Preston N.E.	34	9	5	3	28	13	4	5	8	14	24	36
Sheffield W	34	10	3	4	39	22	4	2	11	22	35	33
Woolwich A	34	9	5	3	19	12	3	4	10	17	28	33
Derby Co	34	9	4	4	29	19	3	4	10	8	29	32
Stoke	34	10	3	4	26	18	3	1	13	14	40	30
Blackburn R	34	9	3	5	28	18	2	2	13	12	33	27
Wolverhampton W	34	10	2	5	30	23	1	2	14	17	50	26
Middlesbrough	34	7	3	7	21	24	2	5	10	15	32	26
Nottingham F	34	5	3	9	24	28	4	4	9	16	33	25
Bury	34	8	2	7	34	26	2	2	13	13	41	24
Notts Co	34	1	7	9	16	33	4	1	12	20	36	18

DIVISION 2

	P	W	D	L	F	A	W	D	L	F	A	Pts
Liverpool	34	14	3	0	60	12	13	1	3	33	13	58
Bolton W	34	15	0	2	53	16	12	2	3	34	16	56
Manchester U	34	16	0	1	60	10	8	5	4	21	20	53
Bristol C	34	12	3	2	40	12	7	1	9	26	33	42
Chesterfield	34	9	6	2	26	11	5	5	7	18	24	39
Gainsborough T	34	11	4	2	32	15	3	4	10	29	43	36
Barnsley	34	11	4	2	29	13	3	1	13	9	43	33
Bradford C	34	8	5	4	31	20	4	3	10	14	29	32
Lincoln C	34	9	4	4	31	16	3	3	11	11	24	31
W.B.A.	34	8	2	7	28	20	5	2	10	28	28	30
Burnley	34	10	1	6	31	21	2	5	10	12	31	30
Glossop N.E.	34	7	5	5	23	14	3	5	9	14	32	30
Grimsby T	34	9	3	5	22	14	2	5	10	11	32	30
Leicester C	34	8	3	6	30	25	3	4	10	10	30	29
Blackpool	34	8	5	4	26	15	1	5	11	10	33	28
Burslem P.V.	34	7	4	6	28	25	3	3	11	19	47	27
Burton U	34	7	2	8	20	29	1	2	14	10	55	20
Doncaster R	34	3	2	12	12	32	0	0	17	11	49	8

DIVISION 1

	ASTON VILLA	BLACKBURN R	BURY	DERBY CO	EVERTON	MANCHESTER C	MIDDLESBROUGH	NEWCASTLE U	NOTTINGHAM F	NOTTS CO	PRESTON N.E.	SHEFFIELD U	SHEFFIELD W	SMALL HEATH	STOKE	SUNDERLAND	WOLVERHAMPTON W	W ARSENAL
1 ASTON VILLA		J07 3-0	D24 2-0	O15 0-2	S12 1-0	a29 3-2	D10 0-0	N26 0-1	S17 2-0	N12 4-2	S01 1-2	M18 3-0	J21 0-2	O29 2-1	S03 3-0	O01 2-2	a27 3-0	D26 3-1
2 BLACKBURN R	S10 4-0		D31 0-2	J02 3-1	O29 1-0	N12 3-1	a15 0-2	a01 2-0	J21 0-0	M18 1-0	D10 1-1	N26 2-4	O01 0-1	M04 1-4	S17 4-0	D26 2-1	D24 3-0	O15 1-1
3 BURY	a22 2-3	S03 0-2		D26 2-0	O15 1-2	O29 2-4	a01 1-0	M18 2-4	J07 5-1	a21 2-0	N26 0-1	N12 7-1	S17 1-4	J02 1-1	D17 3-1	J21 1-0	D10 3-1	O01 1-1
4 DERBY CO	F11 0-2	O22 1-1	O08 3-2		D27 1-2	M04 0-1	S24 4-2	S10 1-1	F25 3-2	D24 1-1	J14 3-1	D31 2-3	N05 1-0	D10 3-0	N26 3-0	M11 1-0	J28 2-1	N19 0-0
5 EVERTON	O22 3-2	F25 1-0	F11 2-0	D03 0-0		D24 0-0	J28 1-0	J14 2-1	N05 5-1	D31 5-1	S24 1-0	S10 2-0	M11 5-2	a15 2-1	D10 4-1	N19 0-1	O08 2-1	a05 1-0
6 MANCHESTER C	N09 2-1	M11 2-1	F25 3-2	D17 6-0	a21 2-0		F11 3-2	J28 3-2	N19 1-1	J14 2-1	O08 6-1	S24 1-1	a15 1-1	S03 2-1	J07 1-0	D03 5-2	N14 5-1	a08 1-0
7 MIDDLESBROUGH	a08 3-1	D17 2-1	D03 2-2	J21 2-0	O01 1-0	O15 0-1		a29 0-3	M04 0-0	a24 2-5	N12 1-1	O29 0-1	S03 1-3	D26 0-1	M18 2-1	J07 1-3	M25 3-1	S17 1-0
8 NEWCASTLE U	a05 2-0	D03 1-0	N19 3-1	J07 2-0	S17 3-2	O01 2-0	N05 3-0		a08 5-1	J02 1-0	F25 1-0	O15 1-1	D17 6-2	J21 0-1	a21 4-1	a22 1-3	M11 3-0	S03 3-0
9 NOTTINGHAM F	J14 1-1	S24 5-2	S10 5-1	O29 0-1	a24 0-2	M18 2-1	D24 1-1	D10 1-3		N26 2-1	O06 0-1	a01 1-2	D26 2-1	N12 0-2	O01 0-1	O15 2-3	D31 2-2	D27 0-3
10 NOTTS CO	M11 1-2	N19 2-1	N05 0-1	F18 0-0	S03 1-2	S17 1-1	O22 0-0	O08 0-3	M25 1-2		F11 1-3	J28 1-5	D03 2-2	J07 0-0	J21 0-0	a08 2-2	F25 3-4	D17 1-5
11 PRESTON N.E.	D03 2-3	a08 0-0	M25 0-0	S17 2-0	J21 1-1	D26 0-1	M11 2-0	O29 1-0	D17 0-1	O15 3-1		a21 4-0	a22 1-0	O01 2-2	a10 2-1	S03 3-1	N19 2-2	J07 3-0
12 SHEFFIELD U	N19 0-3	M25 3-1	M11 4-0	S03 3-1	J07 1-0	J21 0-3	F25 0-1	F11 1-3	D03 4-0	O01 2-1	O22 1-0		a08 4-2	S17 2-1	D26 5-2	D17 1-0	N05 4-2	D28 4-0
13 SHEFFIELD W	S24 3-2	J28 1-2	J14 4-0	a03 1-1	N12 5-5	N26 2-1	D31 5-0	a26 1-3	O08 2-0	a01 1-0	J02 2-0	D10 1-3		M18 3-1	O15 3-0	D27 1-1	S10 4-0	O29 0-3
14 SMALL HEATH	F25 0-3	N05 2-0	O22 5-0	a08 2-0	D17 1-2	D31 3-1	O08 2-1	S24 2-1	M11 1-2	S10 1-2	J28 2-0	J14 2-0	N19 2-1		a22 0-1	M25 1-1	F11 4-1	D03 2-1
15 STOKE	D31 1-4	J14 4-0	a15 2-0	S01 1-2	a08 2-2	S10 1-0	N19 3-1	O22 1-0	J28 0-0	S24 0-2	N05 1-1	O08 2-1	F11 2-1	a29 1-0		F25 1-3	D03 2-1	M11 2-0
16 SUNDERLAND	J28 2-3	O08 2-1	S24 2-1	N12 3-0	M18 2-3	a01 0-0	S10 1-1	D24 3-1	J02 1-0	S05 5-0	D31 3-2	a24 2-1	O22 3-0	N26 1-4	O29 3-1		J14 3-0	M04 1-1
17 WOLVERHAMPTON W	D17 1-1	a22 2-0	a08 2-0	O01 2-0	D26 0-3	a24 0-3	N26 5-3	N12 1-3	S03 3-2	O29 3-1	M18 0-0	S05 4-2	J07 1-0	O15 0-1	a01 1-3	S17 1-0		J21 4-1
18 W ARSENAL	O08 1-0	F11 2-0	J28 2-1	M18 0-0	a22 2-1	D10 1-0	J14 1-1	D31 0-2	O22 0-3	a15 1-2	S10 0-0	D24 1-0	F25 3-0	a01 1-1	N12 2-1	N05 0-0	S24 2-0	

Newcastle United's Bill Appleyard, one of the great characters of Edwardian football, won two League Championship medals and appeared in two FA Cup Finals for the Magpies.

DIVISION 2

	BARNSLEY	BLACKPOOL	BOLTON W	BRADFORD C	BRISTOL C	BURNLEY	BURSLEM P.V.	BURTON U	CHESTERFIELD	DONCASTER R	GAINSBOROUGH T	GLOSSOP	GRIMSBY T	LEICESTER F	LINCOLN C	LIVERPOOL	MANCHESTER U	W.B.A.
1 BARNSLEY		S10 2-1	a24 2-1	N19 1-0	O22 1-0	D24 1-2	F11 3-0	J28 7-0	M11 1-0	a25 2-1	S24 2-1	N05 0-0	D31 2-2	D03 2-1	M25 2-1	O08 0-2	F25 0-0	a15 1-1
2 BLACKPOOL	J07 6-0		a21 0-2	D17 2-0	N19 2-4	J21 2-0	M11 3-0	F25 1-0	a08 1-1	F11 1-0	O22 2-2	D03 4-1	O01 1-1	S03 0-0	a22 1-0	N05 0-3	M25 0-1	S17 0-0
3 BOLTON W	J02 2-1	O08 3-0		F25 2-0	D31 3-1	S10 4-0	a15 3-1	N19 7-1	F11 4-3	O22 2-0	N05 5-1	J28 4-0	S24 4-1	M25 0-1	N12 4-1	D03 2-0	J03 2-4	D24 2-1
4 BRADFORD C	M18 1-2	a15 3-1	O29 2-1		J28 2-3	a01 4-1	S24 2-1	S10 3-1	O22 0-1	D24 4-1	D31 3-1	F11 1-1	D27 0-0	a24 0-0	M04 0-0	M07 2-4	O08 1-1	N26 3-1
5 BRISTOL C	M29 3-0	M18 2-0	S03 3-4	O01 1-0		M04 0-0	D24 4-2	D10 5-0	J21 2-1	N26 4-1	a01 1-1	S17 2-0	N12 5-0	O15 3-0	a25 2-0	a15 0-1	J07 1-1	O29 2-1
6 BURNLEY	a22 3-0	S24 0-1	J07 0-1	D03 2-1	N05 2-3		F25 5-0	F11 1-1	S05 2-0	J28 4-3	O08 1-3	N19 3-1	D26 1-0	D17 2-0	a08 2-1	O22 0-2	M11 2-0	S03 1-4
7 BURSLEM P.V.	O15 0-2	S05 2-2	D17 1-2	J21 1-1	a22 3-2	O29 3-1		a01 4-2	S17 0-0	M18 2-0	a21 3-2	J07 0-1	M04 2-0	a03 1-3	O01 0-1	N12 1-2	S03 2-2	F18 3-2
8 BURTON U	O01 1-2	D26 0-0	M18 0-1	J07 1-0	a08 2-0	O15 3-1	D03 2-3		S03 0-3	N02 1-0	a24 1-3	a22 2-2	F18 1-0	J21 0-3	S17 2-1	M25 2-1	D17 2-3	a21 0-6
9 CHESTERFIELD	N12 2-0	a29 2-0	O15 1-0	F18 0-0	S24 0-3	N26 1-1	a24 2-1	D31 6-0		a15 4-1	D24 3-2	O08 1-2	a01 0-0	M04 0-0	O29 0-0	S10 1-1	a21 2-0	M18 1-0
10 DONCASTER R	S17 2-0	O15 0-0	D10 0-4	a22 0-1	M25 0-2	O01 0-2	N19 2-2	N05 1-3	D17 0-2		F25 1-5	a08 2-1	a24 0-2	J07 3-0	S03 0-2	M11 1-4	D03 0-1	J21 0-1
11 GAINSBOROUGH T	J21 4-0	F18 1-1	a12 0-4	S03 3-2	D03 4-1	O26 3-1	M25 1-0	M11 2-0	a22 1-1	D26 2-0		D17 0-0	O15 2-1	S17 2-0	J07 2-0	N19 1-2	a08 0-0	O01 4-2
12 GLOSSOP	M04 5-0	a01 0-0	O01 1-2	O15 3-1	D27 0-1	M18 0-0	S10 0-0	D24 1-1	F04 0-1	J14 2-0	a15 3-1		a29 2-0	a21 0-0	F18 3-2	D31 0-2	S24 1-2	M07 2-1
13 GRIMSBY T	S03 0-0	J28 2-0	J21 2-2	a08 0-2	M11 4-0	S17 1-0	N05 0-3	O22 1-0	D03 3-1	O08 2-1	F11 0-0	M25 3-0		a22 2-0	D17 1-0	F25 0-1	N19 0-1	J07 1-3
14 LEICESTER F	a01 2-0	D31 3-1	D27 2-4	M11 1-2	F11 2-1	a15 2-2	O08 3-0	S24 2-0	N05 1-1	S10 3-2	F23 1-1	D26 0-2	D24 5-1		N19 0-1	J28 0-3	O22 0-3	D15 3-1
15 LINCOLN C	N26 2-0	D24 1-0	D26 0-2	N05 1-1	O08 1-3	a21 2-0	J28 3-3	D27 3-1	F25 0-0	D31 3-0	S10 4-1	O22 3-0	a15 0-0	M18 5-1		S24 0-2	F11 3-0	a01 0-2
16 LIVERPOOL	D26 2-1	M04 5-0	a01 1-1	S17 4-1	D17 3-1	a29 3-0	a08 8-1	S01 2-0	J07 6-1	a21 1-0	M18 6-1	S03 2-2	O29 5-0	O01 4-0	J21 1-1		a22 4-0	O15 3-2
17 MANCHESTER U	O29 4-0	a24 3-1	S17 1-2	J02 7-0	S10 4-1	N12 1-0	D31 6-1	a15 5-0	D26 3-0	a01 6-0	D10 3-1	J21 4-1	M18 2-1	F18 4-1	O15 2-0	D24 3-1		M04 2-0
18 W.B.A.	D17 4-1	N07 4-2	a22 0-1	M25 0-2	F25 0-0	D31 1-1	D26 0-1	O08 4-0	N19 0-2	S24 6-1	J28 4-3	M11 1-0	S10 0-2	a08 2-0	D03 2-0	F11 0-2	N05 0-2	

FOOTBALL LEAGUE RECORDS
SEASON 1905-06

Top scorers: Div 1, W.White (Bolton Wanderers) 26 goals; Div 2, W.Maxwell (Bristol City) 27 goals.
Doncaster Rovers failed to gain re-election. Chelsea, Hull City, Leeds City, Clapton Orient and Stockport County were elected to League. Small Heath became Birmingham.

DIVISION 1

	ASTON VILLA	BIRMINGHAM	BLACKBURN R	BOLTON W	BURY	DERBY CO	EVERTON	LIVERPOOL	MANCHESTER C	MIDDLESBROUGH	NEWCASTLE U	NOTTINGHAM F	NOTTS CO	PRESTON N.E.	SHEFFIELD U	SHEFFIELD W	STOKE	SUNDERLAND	WOLVERHAMPTON W	W ARSENAL
1 ASTON VILLA		J20 1-3	D30 0-1	D26 1-1	M03 3-3	a16 6-0	S23 4-0	S11 5-0	O21 2-1	N04 4-1	N18 0-3	F17 3-1	a21 2-1	M17 0-1	D09 4-1	O07 3-0	D23 3-0	S09 2-1	N25 6-0	D27 2-1
2 BIRMINGHAM	S16 2-0		a23 3-0	M26 2-5	a16 0-3	D02 3-1	a09 1-0	J27 1-0	a28 3-2	D26 7-0	J06 0-1	D16 5-0	F10 4-2	S02 1-1	S30 2-0	a14 5-1	O14 2-0	N11 3-0	M24 3-3	O28 2-1
3 BLACKBURN R	S02 1-1	N04 5-1		a02 4-1	D16 3-0	N18 3-0	M17 1-2	J06 0-0	a14 1-1	a28 1-1	J01 1-0	D02 1-1	J27 1-3	a13 1-2	S16 2-1	M31 1-0	S30 3-0	M03 0-3	F24 3-1	O14 2-0
4 BOLTON W	J02 4-1	O21 0-1	O07 1-0		D02 4-0	N04 5-0	M03 3-2	a16 3-2	M31 1-3	a14 2-1	a28 1-1	N18 6-0	F03 2-0	D16 1-2	S02 1-2	M17 1-0	S16 1-2	F17 6-2	J27 3-2	J01 6-1
5 BURY	O28 0-1	J01 1-0	a21 5-0	a07 2-1		D30 0-2	D25 3-2	a02 0-0	S23 2-4	F10 1-1	a13 1-4	J20 2-1	M24 0-0	O14 1-1	N11 2-5	S09 2-2	N25 3-0	D23 3-1	S30 0-1	D09 2-0
6 DERBY CO	S30 1-0	a07 0-0	M24 1-2	M10 0-1	S02 3-1		D09 0-0	F10 0-3	D25 1-2	J06 1-1	J27 2-1	D26 2-2	F24 1-1	S16 3-0	O14 1-0	a28 2-1	O28 1-0	N25 1-0	D16 2-0	N11 5-1
7 EVERTON	J27 4-2	N25 1-2	N11 3-2	O28 3-1	D26 1-2	a14 2-1		S30 4-2	a16 0-3	S02 4-1	S16 1-2	a28 4-1	O14 6-2	J06 1-0	F10 3-2	D16 2-0	a03 -0-3	M24 3-1	a07 2-2	M21 0-1
8 LIVERPOOL	D02 3-0	S23 2-0	S09 1-3	D25 2-2	N04 3-1	O07 4-1	a13 1-1		M03 0-1	M17 6-1	a09 3-0	O21 4-1	D23 2-0	N18 1-1	a21 3-1	F17 2-1	J01 3-1	J20 2-0	D09 4-0	D30 3-0
9 MANCHESTER C	M14 1-4	D23 4-1	D09 1-1	N25 3-1	J27 5-2	a13 1-2	J01 1-0	O28 0-1		S30 4-0	D26 1-4	S09 5-0	N11 5-1	F10 0-0	M10 1-2	D30 2-1	M24 2-0	a21 5-1	S16 4-0	a07 1-2
10 MIDDLESBROUGH	M10 1-2	D25 1-0	D23 1-1	D09 4-4	O07 5-1	S09 0-1	D30 0-0	N11 1-5	a17 6-1		M03 1-0	S23 2-0	N25 4-1	M14 1-2	M24 0-1	J20 2-2	a07 5-0	a13 2-1	O14 3-1	a21 2-0
11 NEWCASTLE U	M24 3-1	S09 2-2	a30 3-0	D23 2-1	O21 3-1	S23 0-1	J20 4-2	N25 2-3	S06 2-2	O28 4-1		O07 3-2	D09 3-1	N04 1-0	a04 2-1	S13 0-3	a24 5-0	D30 1-1	N11 8-0	a16 1-1
12 NOTTINGHAM F	O14 2-2	a21 2-1	a07 1-2	M24 4-0	S16 3-2	a17 0-0	D23 4-3	M14 1-2	J06 0-1	J27 2-1	F10 2-1		D25 1-2	S30 1-0	O28 4-1	a16 3-4	N11 3-1	D09 1-2	S02 3-1	N25 3-1
13 NOTTS CO	D16 2-1	O07 0-0	S23 1-1	S09 3-3	N18 2-2	O21 1-0	F17 0-0	M21 3-0	M17 3-0	M31 1-1	a14 1-0	N04 1-1		D02 2-2	D26 2-3	M03 1-3	D30 1-1	D27 4-1	O05 5-2	J20 1-0
14 PRESTON N.E.	N11 2-0	D30 3-0	F03 2-1	a21 3-0	F17 1-0	J20 3-1	S09 1-1	M24 1-2	O07 2-0	O21 2-1	a26 0-0	S04 3-1	a07 4-1		N25 1-1	S23 0-1	D09 2-0	D25 1-1	O28 3-2	D23 2-2
15 SHEFFIELD U	a14 1-1	D28 3-0	J20 0-2	D30 5-2	M17 1-1	F17 1-0	O07 3-2	D16 1-2	N04 1-3	N18 1-0	D02 2-0	M03 1-4	J01 1-0	M31 0-0		O21 0-2	D25 1-1	S23 4-1	M19 4-1	S09 3-1
16 SHEFFIELD W	F10 2-2	D09 4-2	N25 0-1	N11 1-2	J06 1-1	D23 1-0	a23 3-1	O14 3-2	S02 1-0	S16 3-0	S30 1-1	D27 1-0	O28 3-1	J27 1-1	a18 1-0		a09 2-0	a07 3-3	D26 5-1	M24 4-2
17 STOKE	N13 0-1	F17 2-2	S04 3-0	J20 1-2	M26 4-2	M03 2-2	O21 2-2	D26 2-1	N18 0-0	D02 1-1	D16 1-0	M17 4-0	S02 3-0	a14 3-0	a16 2-1	N04 4-0		O07 1-0	J06 4-0	S23 2-1
18 SUNDERLAND	F28 2-0	M17 3-1	O28 3-0	O14 3-3	a28 0-3	M31 2-0	N18 2-1	S16 1-2	D16 2-0	J01 2-1	S02 3-2	a14 0-1	S30 1-3	a16 2-0	J27 2-0	D02 2-0	F10 1-0		M10 7-2	a25 2-2
19 WOLVERHAMPTON W	M31 4-1	N18 0-0	O21 2-1	S23 2-0	S11 2-2	a21 7-0	D02 2-5	a14 0-2	J20 2-3	F17 0-0	M17 0-2	D30 2-1	a16 6-1	M03 2-3	D23 1-1	S04 0-0	S09 1-2	N04 5-2		O07 0-2
20 W ARSENAL	a13 2-1	M03 5-0	F17 3-2	S30 0-0	a14 4-0	M17 1-0	N04 1-2	S02 3-1	D02 2-0	D16 2-2	D25 4-3	a02 3-1	S16 1-1	S18 2-2	J06 5-1	N18 0-2	J27 1-2	O21 2-0	F10 2-1	

LEAGUE TABLES

DIVISION 1

	P	W	D	L	F	A	W	D	L	F	A	Pts
Liverpool	38	14	3	2	49	15	9	2	8	30	31	51
Preston N.E.	38	12	5	2	36	15	5	8	6	18	24	47
Sheffield W	38	12	5	2	40	20	6	3	10	23	32	44
Newcastle U	38	12	4	3	49	23	6	3	10	25	25	43
Manchester C	38	11	2	6	46	23	8	3	8	27	31	43
Bolton W	38	13	1	5	51	22	4	6	9	30	45	41
Birmingham C	38	14	2	3	49	20	3	5	11	16	39	41
Aston Villa	38	13	2	4	51	19	4	4	11	21	37	40
Blackburn R	38	10	5	4	34	18	6	3	10	20	34	40
Stoke	38	12	5	2	41	15	4	2	13	13	40	39
Everton	38	12	1	6	44	30	3	6	10	26	36	37
Woolwich A	38	12	4	3	43	21	3	3	13	19	43	37
Sheffield U	38	10	4	5	33	23	5	2	12	24	39	36
Sunderland	38	13	2	4	40	21	2	3	14	21	49	35
Derby Co	38	10	5	4	27	16	4	2	13	12	42	35
Notts Co	38	8	9	2	34	21	3	3	13	21	50	34
Bury	38	8	5	6	30	26	3	5	11	27	48	32
Middlesbrough	38	10	4	5	41	23	0	7	12	15	48	31
Nottingham F	38	11	2	6	40	27	2	3	14	18	52	31
Wolverhampton W	38	7	5	7	38	28	1	2	16	20	71	23

DIVISION 2

	P	W	D	L	F	A	W	D	L	F	A	Pts
Bristol C	38	17	1	1	43	8	13	5	1	40	20	66
Manchester U	38	15	3	1	55	13	13	3	3	35	15	62
Chelsea	38	13	4	2	58	16	9	5	5	32	21	53
W.B.A.	38	13	4	2	53	16	9	4	6	26	20	52
Hull C	38	10	5	4	38	21	9	1	9	29	33	44
Leeds U	38	11	5	3	38	19	6	4	9	21	28	43
Leicester C	38	10	3	6	30	21	5	9	5	23	27	42
Grimsby T	38	11	7	1	33	13	4	3	12	13	33	40
Burnley	38	9	4	6	26	23	6	4	9	16	30	38
Stockport Co	38	11	6	2	36	16	2	3	14	8	40	35
Bradford C	38	7	4	8	21	22	6	4	9	25	38	34
Barnsley	38	11	4	4	45	17	1	5	13	15	45	33
Lincoln C	38	10	1	8	46	29	2	5	12	23	43	30
Blackpool	38	8	3	8	22	21	2	6	11	15	41	29
Gainsborough T	38	10	2	7	35	22	2	2	15	9	35	28
Glossop N.E.	38	9	4	6	36	28	1	4	14	13	43	28
Burslem P.V.	38	10	4	5	34	25	2	0	17	15	57	28
Chesterfield	38	8	4	7	26	24	2	4	13	14	48	28
Burton U	38	9	4	6	26	20	1	2	16	8	47	26
Clapton O	38	6	4	9	19	22	1	3	15	16	56	21

DIVISION 2

	BARNSLEY	BLACKPOOL	BRADFORD C	BRISTOL C	BURNLEY	BURSLEM P.V.	BURTON U	CHELSEA	CHESTERFIELD	CLAPTON O	GAINSBOROUGH T	GLOSSOP	GRIMSBY T	HULL C	LEEDS C	LEICESTER F	LINCOLN C	MANCHESTER U	STOCKPORT CO	W.B.A.
1 BARNSLEY		a21 1-1	D23 0-1	M24 2-2	O14 1-2	S23 4-0	O28 3-0	M10 1-2	J20 8-1	F10 4-1	N11 2-1	a07 1-1	S30 2-0	a17 2-0	F24 3-0	a16 0-0	S09 4-2	N25 0-3	J01 4-0	a13 3-0
2 BLACKPOOL	D16 0-0		M03 2-2	J27 1-3	a13 0-1	a14 2-1	S02 2-0	S09 0-1	D02 2-1	a28 3-0	S16 2-2	F10 1-0	M07 2-0	M14 1-2	J01 0-3	M17 0-1	M31 2-0	S30 0-1	O14 2-0	N04 0-3
3 BRADFORD C	a28 0-0	O28 2-1		S30 1-2	F27 0-1	D16 2-0	J06 1-0	S16 1-1	a14 1-0	D26 3-0	J27 1-2	O14 2-0	a07 0-1	M31 0-2	S02 1-0	N18 3-3	D02 2-2	F10 1-5	a17 0-1	M17 0-1
4 BRISTOL C	N18 3-0	S23 2-1	S20 1-0		D02 2-0	M17 4-0	D16 4-0	a28 2-1	N04 3-1	M31 1-0	a13 2-0	S09 2-1	a17 2-0	O21 2-1	a14 2-0	F17 1-2	M03 1-0	D30 1-1	J20 7-0	O07 1-0
5 BURNLEY	F17 2-1	D25 4-1	S04 0-0	a07 2-2		O07 1-3	N11 1-0	M24 2-0	S11 1-1	O21 3-0	N25 1-0	a21 1-0	O28 0-0	J20 1-3	M10 4-3	O02 0-2	S23 2-1	D09 1-3	D23 0-1	D30 0-2
6 BURSLEM P.V.	J27 1-2	S11 1-2	a21 2-1	N11 0-1	F10 2-2		F24 4-1	O30 3-2	S09 4-3	S30 2-1	M10 1-0	N25 3-3	S16 2-2	D25 1-3	O14 2-0	a13 2-0	D30 3-1	M24 1-0	a07 0-0	D23 0-1
7 BURTON U	M03 4-1	D30 1-1	S09 0-1	a21 0-1	M17 1-3	O21 1-0		a07 2-4	F17 4-0	N04 1-0	S06 3-1	O02 1-0	N25 1-0	D26 0-3	N13 1-1	S23 0-0	O07 2-0	D23 0-2	D25 2-0	J20 2-2
8 CHELSEA	N04 6-0	J06 6-0	J20 4-2	D23 0-0	N18 1-0	M03 7-0	D02 3-0		O21 0-1	M17 6-1	a21 1-3	a16 0-0	D09 2-0	S11 5-1	M31 4-0	F05 3-3	F17 4-2	a13 1-1	D30 4-2	S23 1-0
9 CHESTERFIELD	S16 2-0	a07 2-0	D25 1-1	M10 1-2	S30 3-0	J06 2-0	O14 1-0	F24 0-2		J27 1-1	O28 0-0	M24 3-1	S02 1-4	a13 1-2	F10 0-2	D23 3-3	a16 1-2	N11 1-0	N25 3-1	a21 0-3
10 CLAPTON O	O07 0-0	D23 0-0	a13 4-2	N25 0-2	F24 3-0	F03 1-3	M10 0-1	N11 0-3	S23 3-3		M24 1-0	S11 2-0	O14 1-2	S09 0-1	M29 0-0	D30 0-2	J20 3-0	a07 0-1	a21 1-0	a16 0-2
11 GAINSBOROUGH T	M17 1-0	J20 0-1	S23 2-3	D26 1-3	M31 0-1	N04 4-0	a14 5-2	D16 0-2	M03 4-0	D04 2-1		D30 2-0	a28 1-0	F17 3-1	D02 4-1	O07 0-1	O21 2-3	O25 2-2	S09 0-0	a18 2-1
12 GLOSSOP	D02 2-2	O07 4-1	F17 2-3	J06 1-5	D16 1-1	M31 3-2	J01 2-0	D26 2-4	N18 2-0	a14 5-0	S02 1-0		J27 2-0	N04 3-1	a28 1-2	M03 0-0	M17 2-2	S16 1-2	F03 1-0	O21 1-3
13 GRIMSBY T	a05 2-1	O21 1-1	N04 1-0	D27 1-1	M03 2-0	J20 5-0	M31 1-0	a14 1-1	D30 2-0	F17 4-1	D23 2-0	S23 1-1		a21 1-0	M17 1-1	D02 1-1	a13 2-2	S09 0-1	O07 2-0	F03 3-2
14 HULL C	S02 4-1	M24 2-2	N25 5-2	F24 0-3	S16 1-1	a16 3-2	S30 1-1	F10 4-3	O11 3-0	J06 3-1	O14 2-0	M10 1-2	D16 0-1		J27 0-0	a14 0-0	a28 2-1	O28 0-1	N11 3-0	a07 4-0
15 LEEDS C	O21 3-2	a16 3-0	D30 0-2	D09 1-1	F03 1-1	F17 3-1	M24 2-1	N25 0-0	F27 3-0	M03 6-1	a07 1-0	D23 1-0	N11 3-0	S23 3-1		J20 4-1	S11 2-2	a21 1-3	a13 1-1	S09 0-2
16 LEICESTER F	D25 1-0	N11 2-0	M24 2-4	O14 1-2	J06 2-0	D26 2-1	J27 1-1	S30 0-1	D09 1-1	S02 2-1	F10 4-0	O28 2-1	F24 2-0	D07 1-2	S16 0-1		D16 3-1	M29 2-5	M10 2-0	N25 0-0
17 LINCOLN C	J06 4-1	N25 1-1	M10 5-0	O28 0-3	J27 5-0	S02 3-1	F10 5-1	O14 1-4	D26 0-1	S16 2-3	F24 3-0	N11 4-1	D25 3-1	D23 1-4	S30 1-2	a21 3-1		a25 2-3	M24 2-0	D09 1-2
18 MANCHESTER U	M31 5-1	S04 2-1	O07 0-0	S02 5-1	a14 1-0	N18 3-0	a28 6-0	D25 0-0	M17 4-1	D02 4-0	a16 2-0	J20 5-2	J06 5-0	M03 5-0	J15 0-3	O21 3-2	N04 2-1		S23 3-1	F17 0-0
19 STOCKPORT CO	a14 0-0	F17 2-1	O21 1-0	S16 2-3	a28 3-1	D02 3-0	a16 2-0	S02 1-0	M31 0-0	D16 3-3	J06 2-0	S30 5-0	F10 2-2	M17 2-1	D26 2-1	N04 1-1	N18 3-0	J27 0-1		M03 2-2
20 W.B.A.	D26 5-3	M10 5-0	N11 6-1	F10 1-3	S02 1-2	a28 4-1	S16 3-0	J27 1-1	D16 3-0	D25 1-1	S30 4-0	F24 6-0	M24 2-0	D02 1-1	J06 2-1	M31 3-0	a14 1-1	O14 1-0	O28 3-1	

Alex Raisbeck spent 11 seasons with Liverpool, winning two Championship medals, a Division Two winners' medal and eight Scotland caps.

Football League Records
Season 1906-07

Top scorers: Div 1, A.Young (Everton) 28 goals; Div 2, F.Shinton (West Bromwich Albion) 28 goals.

LEAGUE TABLES

DIVISION 1

	P	W	D	L	F	A	W	D	L	F	A	Pts
Newcastle U	38	18	1	0	51	12	4	6	9	23	34	51
Bristol C	38	12	3	4	37	18	8	5	6	29	29	48
Everton	38	16	2	1	50	10	4	3	12	20	36	45
Sheffield U	38	13	4	2	36	17	4	7	8	21	38	45
Aston Villa	38	13	4	2	51	19	6	2	11	27	33	44
Bolton W	38	10	4	5	35	18	8	4	7	24	29	44
Woolwich A	38	15	1	3	38	15	5	3	11	28	44	44
Manchester U	38	10	6	3	33	15	7	2	10	20	41	42
Birmingham C	38	13	5	1	41	17	2	3	14	11	35	38
Sunderland	38	10	4	5	42	31	4	5	10	23	35	37
Middlesbrough	38	11	2	6	33	21	4	4	11	23	42	36
Blackburn R	38	10	3	6	40	25	4	4	11	16	34	35
Sheffield W	38	8	5	6	33	26	4	6	9	16	34	35
Preston N.E.	38	13	4	2	35	19	1	3	15	9	38	35
Liverpool	38	9	2	8	45	32	4	5	10	19	33	33
Bury	38	9	4	6	30	23	4	2	13	28	45	32
Manchester C	38	7	7	5	29	25	3	5	11	24	52	32
Notts Co	38	6	9	4	31	18	2	6	11	15	32	31
Derby Co	38	8	6	5	29	19	1	3	15	12	40	27
Stoke	38	7	6	6	27	22	1	4	14	14	42	26

DIVISION 2

	P	W	D	L	F	A	W	D	L	F	A	Pts
Nottingham F	38	16	2	1	43	13	12	2	5	31	23	60
Chelsea	38	18	0	1	55	10	8	5	6	25	24	57
Leicester C	38	15	3	1	44	12	5	5	9	18	27	48
W.B.A.	38	15	2	2	62	15	6	3	10	21	30	47
Bradford C	38	14	2	3	46	21	7	3	9	24	32	47
Wolverhampton W	38	13	4	2	49	16	4	3	12	17	37	41
Burnley	38	12	4	3	45	13	5	2	12	17	34	40
Barnsley	38	14	2	3	56	21	1	6	12	17	34	38
Hull C	38	11	2	6	41	20	4	5	10	24	37	37
Leeds U	38	10	5	4	38	26	3	5	11	17	37	36
Grimsby T	38	13	2	4	34	16	3	1	15	23	46	35
Stockport Co	38	8	8	3	26	12	4	3	12	16	40	35
Blackpool	38	9	4	6	25	19	2	7	10	8	32	33
Gainsborough T	38	12	3	4	33	20	2	2	15	12	52	33
Glossop N.E.	38	10	4	5	32	21	3	2	14	21	58	32
Burslem P.V.	38	11	5	3	45	26	1	2	16	15	57	31
Clapton O	38	9	7	3	25	13	2	1	16	20	54	30
Chesterfield	38	10	3	6	36	26	1	4	14	14	40	29
Lincoln C	38	10	2	7	29	24	2	2	15	17	49	28
Burton U	38	7	3	9	24	23	1	4	14	10	45	23

Newcastle United's Colin Veitch, another star of Edwardian soccer, played in eight different positions for the Magpies, appeared in five FA Cup Finals and won three Championship medals.

DIVISION 1

	ASTON VILLA	BIRMINGHAM	BLACKBURN R	BOLTON W	BRISTOL C	BURY	DERBY CO	EVERTON	LIVERPOOL	MANCHESTER C	MANCHESTER U	MIDDLESBROUGH	NEWCASTLE U	NOTTS CO	PRESTON N.E.	SHEFFIELD U	SHEFFIELD W	STOKE	SUNDERLAND	W ARSENAL
1 ASTON VILLA		S15 4-1	S01 4-2	a27 0-2	D01 3-2	O13 3-1	M23 2-0	J26 2-1	M30 4-0	F23 4-1	D26 2-0	O27 2-3	N10 0-0	a13 0-0	D24 3-0	D15 5-1	F09 8-1	S10 1-0	J05 2-2	S29 2-2
2 BIRMINGHAM	J19 3-2		M16 2-0	O20 4-2	S03 2-2	D22 3-1	N24 2-1	a06 1-0	S22 2-1	M29 4-0	M02 1-1	D26 0-0	S08 2-4	O06 2-0	D29 3-0	F16 0-0	a25 1-1	N03 2-1	N17 2-0	D08 5-1
3 BLACKBURN R	D29 2-1	N10 1-0		O06 2-3	J19 0-1	D08 4-1	O27 5-1	a08 2-1	S08 1-1	a20 4-0	F16 2-4	D22 4-1	D25 4-0	S22 0-2	J01 1-1	M29 1-1	a06 0-2	O20 3-1	M09 2-1	N24 2-3
4 BOLTON W	D22 1-2	M11 2-3	F09 5-2		M29 1-2	M09 1-0	S15 1-0	O27 1-3	J01 3-0	N24 1-1	J26 0-1	a06 1-0	a20 4-2	D29 0-0	J02 3-0	S08 6-1	N10 0-0	S29 1-1	O13 1-0	M27 3-0
5 BRISTOL C	a06 2-4	S29 0-0	S15 3-0	a02 1-2		O27 2-0	D15 3-0	F09 2-1	D08 3-1	M09 2-0	S01 1-2	N10 3-0	N24 2-1	a27 1-0	M23 1-0	D24 3-3	a24 2-0	J05 4-0	J26 1-1	O13 1-3
6 BURY	F16 0-3	a27 1-0	a13 0-0	N17 2-3	M02 1-1		J05 1-0	D25 1-2	O20 1-3	J19 3-1	M30 1-2	S22 1-1	O06 3-2	N03 3-0	a01 2-0	M16 2-1	S01 0-0	D01 2-0	D15 2-3	S03 4-1
7 DERBY CO	N17 0-1	M30 1-1	M02 2-3	J19 0-1	a20 1-3	S08 2-1		a13 5-2	D01 0-1	S22 2-2	S03 2-2	O06 1-0	N03 0-0	D24 3-0	O20 3-0	D29 3-0	a01 1-0	F16 2-1	M16 1-1	D22 0-0
8 EVERTON	S22 1-2	D01 3-0	N17 2-0	M02 1-0	O06 2-0	J01 1-0	D08 2-0		M29 0-0	S03 9-1	N03 3-0	D29 5-1	J19 3-0	S17 2-2	S08 1-0	O20 4-2	D22 2-0	M16 3-0	M30 4-1	a10 2-1
9 LIVERPOOL	N24 5-2	J26 2-0	J05 0-2	D26 0-2	a13 2-4	S10 2-2	a06 2-0	S29 1-2		O27 5-4	a01 0-1	a17 2-4	M23 4-1	D15 5-1	N10 6-1	a27 2-2	O13 1-2	S01 1-0	S15 1-2	F09 4-0
10 MANCHESTER C	O20 4-2	D25 1-0	D15 0-0	M30 1-1	N03 0-1	S15 2-2	J26 2-2	D26 3-1	M02 1-0		D01 3-0	J02 3-1	F16 1-1	M16 2-1	O06 1-1	N17 0-2	J05 0-1	a13 2-2	a27 2-3	S01 1-4
11 MANCHESTER U	J01 1-0	O27 2-1	O13 1-1	S22 1-2	D29 0-0	N24 2-4	S29 1-1	a22 3-0	D25 0-0	a06 1-1		D08 3-1	D22 1-3	S08 0-0	F23 3-0	J19 2-0	a10 5-0	F09 4-1	M25 2-0	N10 1-0
12 MIDDLESBROUGH	M02 1-0	J01 1-0	a27 0-1	D01 0-0	M16 1-0	J26 3-1	F09 4-1	S01 2-2	N03 0-1	S29 2-3	a13 2-0		O20 0-3	N17 2-0	F16 2-1	M30 0-1	S15 1-3	D15 5-0	D25 2-1	J05 5-3
13 NEWCASTLE U	M16 3-2	J05 2-0	a01 3-1	D15 4-0	M30 3-0	F09 3-2	J01 2-0	S15 1-0	N17 2-0	O13 2-0	F02 5-0	F23 4-0		D01 4-3	O27 2-1	a13 0-0	S29 5-1	M29 1-0	S01 4-2	J26 1-0
14 NOTTS CO	D08 1-1	F09 2-2	J26 1-2	S01 0-0	D22 2-3	M13 1-2	M29 4-0	O13 0-1	a20 2-0	N10 0-0	J05 3-0	a10 2-2	a06 1-0		N24 0-0	a01 4-0	O27 2-2	S15 2-2	S29 0-0	a17 4-1
15 PRESTON N.E.	N03 2-0	S01 2-0	D26 1-0	D08 3-1	N17 3-1	S29 3-2	M09 1-0	J05 1-1	M16 3-1	F09 1-3	D15 2-0	O13 4-2	M02 2-2	M30 0-0		D01 2-1	J26 1-0	a27 2-2	M29 2-0	S15 0-3
16 SHEFFIELD U	a20 0-0	O13 2-0	S29 3-0	J05 2-1	D31 1-1	N10 3-0	S01 2-0	M04 4-1	D22 1-0	M23 1-4	S15 0-2	N24 1-1	D08 0-0	D26 2-1	F02 3-1		a04 2-1	J26 2-0	F09 3-2	O27 4-2
17 SHEFFIELD W	O06 2-1	D15 0-1	D01 3-1	M16 2-0	O20 3-0	D29 1-2	D25 1-1	a27 1-1	F16 2-3	S08 3-1	N17 5-2	J19 0-2	S03 2-2	M02 1-3	S22 2-1	N03 2-2		M30 0-1	a13 2-1	J01 1-1
18 STOKE	S03 0-2	M09 3-0	N12 1-1	D24 3-0	S08 0-3	a06 3-1	O13 2-1	N10 2-0	M11 1-1	D08 3-0	O06 1-2	a20 0-2	D26 1-2	J19 1-1	D22 0-2	S22 1-1	N24 1-1		O27 2-2	a15 2-0
19 SUNDERLAND	S08 2-1	M23 4-1	N03 1-0	F16 1-2	S22 3-3	a20 3-5	N10 0-2	N24 1-0	J19 5-5	D22 1-1	O20 4-1	a01 4-2	M20 2-0	a24 3-1	F13 1-0	O06 1-2	D08 1-1	M02 3-1		a06 2-3
20 W ARSENAL	a01 3-1	a13 2-1	M30 2-0	N03 2-2	F16 1-2	D26 3-1	a27 3-2	D15 3-1	O06 2-1	D29 4-1	M16 4-0	S08 2-0	S22 2-0	O20 1-0	J19 1-0	M02 0-1	M29 1-0	N17 2-1	D01 0-1	

DIVISION 2

	BARNSLEY	BLACKPOOL	BRADFORD C	BURNLEY	BURSLEM P.V.	BURTON U	CHELSEA	CHESTERFIELD	CLAPTON O	GAINSBOROUGH T	GLOSSOP	GRIMSBY T	HULL C	LEEDS C	LEICESTER F	LINCOLN C	NOTTINGHAM F	STOCKPORT CO	W.B.A.	WOLVERHAMPTON W
1 BARNSLEY		S01 3-2	J05 3-1	a18 5-0	O27 3-2	O13 6-1	M30 3-1	M23 2-1	J01 3-2	D15 6-0	D25 3-0	a11 1-1	D26 4-2	N10 3-0	J26 2-2	F09 6-2	S29 0-1	a01 3-1	S15 0-1	D01 0-1
2 BLACKPOOL	D29 2-3		M09 1-0	M29 2-0	D22 0-1	a13 1-1	S08 0-0	O27 0-0	S22 1-3	J01 1-0	O20 4-1	a20 4-3	F16 1-1	D05 1-0	M23 1-0	a06 2-0	N24 1-2	O06 0-1	N10 2-1	J19 1-2
3 BRADFORD C	S08 2-0	N03 3-0		J01 3-1	F12 3-2	a20 2-3	M19 6-3	N10 1-0	M12 5-2	O06 1-1	M02 2-1	D22 1-0	O20 1-0	D29 2-2	N24 3-1	D08 3-0	a06 1-2	F16 1-0	a23 4-0	S22 2-3
4 BURNLEY	N03 2-2	D25 2-1	S03 0-1		O13 6-0	S29 4-0	M16 1-1	F23 0-0	M30 3-0	D01 1-0	a27 1-1	F09 2-0	D15 4-2	M02 1-2	J05 5-0	J26 5-1	S15 2-1	a13 3-0	S01 0-1	N17 3-0
5 BURSLEM P.V.	M02 2-2	a27 3-0	D25 2-3	F16 4-4		J26 0-0	N03 2-0	F09 2-2	N17 3-2	M30 1-0	D15 4-1	S29 3-2	a13 2-1	O20 1-2	S01 1-2	S15 4-2	J05 4-2	D01 5-0	S10 2-1	M16 0-0
6 BURTON U	F16 1-1	O01 0-0	D15 1-0	F02 0-1	S22 2-0		O20 2-1	J05 3-1	N03 2-1	M16 0-0	D01 1-2	J19 2-3	M30 1-2	O06 0-2	M29 0-1	S01 3-4	a01 0-2	N17 0-1	a27 2-0	M02 4-1
7 CHELSEA	N24 2-1	J05 3-0	S15 5-1	N10 2-0	M09 2-1	F23 1-0		a06 7-1	D15 2-1	a27 4-1	S01 9-2	O27 2-0	M29 3-0	M23 2-0	S29 1-0	O13 2-0	F09 0-2	M04 2-0	J26 2-0	a13 4-0
8 CHESTERFIELD	N17 3-2	M02 0-1	M16 3-4	O20 0-1	O06 4-2	S08 2-0	D01 0-0		M29 2-1	D29 7-0	F16 1-3	S22 1-3	J01 3-1	N03 1-0	a13 2-1	a01 1-0	D22 1-1	J19 0-2	M30 2-2	a20 3-2
9 CLAPTON O	a13 1-0	J26 0-0	S29 1-1	N24 2-1	M23 1-1	M09 1-0	a20 0-1	D26 1-2		a01 3-1	S15 3-0	N10 1-0	J05 2-1	a06 1-1	O13 1-0	O27 1-1	F23 0-1	S01 1-1	F09 1-1	D22 4-0
10 GAINSBOROUGH T	a20 1-1	S29 2-0	F09 4-1	a06 0-2	N24 2-0	N10 2-0	D22 1-1	S01 1-0	D25 3-1		J26 2-1	N17 2-1	S15 1-1	D08 1-0	F23 1-2	M09 2-1	O27 2-3	J05 3-1	O13 2-4	O24 1-0
11 GLOSSOP	M29 2-1	F23 0-0	O27 1-2	D22 1-0	a20 4-0	a06 2-2	D29 0-1	O13 3-1	J19 3-0	S22 3-1		F12 1-0	O06 2-4	J01 2-0	N10 2-2	N24 2-1	M23 0-2	F02 2-3	a16 0-0	S08 2-1
12 GRIMSBY T	O20 1-0	D15 0-0	a27 0-2	O06 1-0	M21 2-0	S15 1-1	M02 2-1	J26 3-1	M16 1-2	D26 2-0	a13 2-1		D01 1-3	F16 4-0	a01 0-1	J05 4-0	S01 3-1	M30 3-1	M29 2-1	N03 2-1
13 HULL C	D08 2-0	O13 3-0	M14 0-3	a20 1-1	a01 4-1	N24 3-0	D25 0-1	S29 2-0	S08 2-0	J19 2-4	F09 5-0	a06 4-2		D22 2-1	M09 1-1	M23 1-2	N10 1-2	S22 3-0	O27 0-1	D29 5-1
14 LEEDS C	M16 2-1	F02 1-1	S01 1-1	O27 0-1	F23 2-0	F09 3-1	N17 0-1	M09 1-0	D01 3-2	a13 4-0	a01 1-4	O13 4-3	a27 2-2		S15 1-1	S10 1-1	J26 1-4	D15 6-1	J05 3-2	M30 2-0
15 LEICESTER F	S22 2-1	N17 5-1	M30 1-0	S08 2-0	D29 4-1	D26 3-0	F02 1-1	D08 2-0	F16 2-1	O20 3-1	M16 2-2	S03 2-0	N03 3-0	J19 2-2		D22 3-0	a20 1-2	D25 1-0	D01 3-0	O06 2-0
16 LINCOLN C	O06 1-0	D01 0-1	a13 0-2	S22 1-2	J19 4-0	D29 2-0	F16 0-5	D25 1-0	M02 3-0	N03 4-0	M30 2-1	S08 2-1	N17 0-1	S29 1-1	a27 2-2		M29 1-2	M16 3-1	D15 2-1	O20 0-4
17 NOTTINGHAM F	a02 0-0	M30 3-0	D01 3-0	J19 2-0	S08 2-2	D25 2-0	O06 3-1	O04 3-1	O20 4-0	M02 3-1	N17 2-0	D29 0-3	M16 2-1	S22 3-0	D15 2-1	a24 3-1		N03 2-1	a13 3-1	F16 1-0
18 STOCKPORT CO	D22 0-0	F09 0-0	O13 2-1	D08 2-1	a06 3-0	M23 2-0	J01 1-2	S15 1-1	D29 1-1	S08 1-2	S29 5-0	N24 3-0	J26 1-1	a20 2-2	O27 1-0	N10 1-0	M09 0-0		a08 0-1	M29 0-0
19 W.B.A.	a25 3-1	M16 3-0	N17 3-0	D29 3-2	D26 3-0	D22 5-1	S22 1-2	N24 5-2	O06 5-0	F16 5-0	N03 5-1	D25 6-1	M02 3-0	S08 5-0	a06 0-1	a20 2-1	D08 3-1	O20 1-1		a01 1-1
20 WOLVERHAMPTON W	a06 5-1	S15 1-1	J26 1-1	M23 3-0	N10 6-2	O27 3-0	D08 1-2	D15 2-1	D27 6-1	S03 1-0	J05 4-0	M09 5-0	S01 1-1	N24 3-2	F09 1-0	F23 3-0	O13 2-0	D26 1-1	S29 0-3	

Football League Records
Season 1907-08

Top scorers: Div 1, E.West (Nottingham Forest) 27 goals; Div 2, J.Smith (Hull City) 30 goals.
Burslem Port Vale resigned and Burton United failed to gain re-election, Fulham and Oldham Athletic were elected in their place.

DIVISION 1

	ASTON VILLA	BIRMINGHAM	BLACKBURN R	BOLTON W	BRISTOL C	BURY	CHELSEA	EVERTON	LIVERPOOL	MANCHESTER C	MANCHESTER U	MIDDLESBROUGH	NEWCASTLE U	NOTTINGHAM F	NOTTS CO	PRESTON N.E.	SHEFFIELD U	SHEFFIELD W	SUNDERLAND	W ARSENAL
1 ASTON VILLA		J18 2-3	J04 1-1	S14 2-0	O26 4-4	N23 2-2	D28 0-0	S28 0-2	a04 5-1	N09 2-2	S02 1-4	D14 6-0	N30 3-3	D25 4-0	M02 5-1	M14 3-0	a18 1-0	F15 5-0	S09 1-0	O12 0-1
2 BIRMINGHAM	S21 2-3		M07 1-1	N16 2-1	a25 0-4	S16 0-1	O19 1-1	M28 2-1	J25 1-1	D25 2-1	N02 3-4	O05 1-4	M21 1-1	M30 1-0	D26 0-0	S07 2-0	F08 0-0	D21 2-1	D07 0-2	a11 1-2
3 BLACKBURN R	S07 2-0	N09 1-0		F29 3-2	a11 4-1	S02 1-0	O05 2-0	M14 2-0	a06 1-3	a25 0-0	O19 1-5	S21 2-0	M23 1-1	F08 3-3	D21 1-1	J01 1-1	J25 3-3	D07 2-0	N23 4-2	M28 1-1
4 BOLTON W	a17 3-1	M14 1-0	N02 3-1		D21 1-2	S07 3-6	F08 1-2	N23 3-0	S21 0-4	J01 2-0	a22 2-2	J25 1-1	a01 4-0	O19 1-0	a25 0-1	J02 2-0	O05 1-1	a11 2-1	M28 2-3	D07 3-1
5 BRISTOL C	M11 2-2	D28 0-0	D14 2-2	a18 2-0		O19 1-1	M21 0-0	S02 3-2	N02 2-0	O05 2-1	a04 1-1	M07 0-1	S21 1-1	N30 3-0	J25 2-1	F08 1-3	N16 3-2	S14 0-2	a20 3-0	J04 1-2
6 BURY	M21 2-1	S14 1-0	a17 1-1	J04 2-2	F15 1-1		a18 1-1	J18 3-0	M28 3-1	F29 0-0	J01 0-1	a04 1-4	N16 1-2	D28 0-0	O26 0-0	N09 5-1	D14 3-2	O12 0-2	S28 2-1	S09 3-2
7 CHELSEA	a25 1-3	F15 2-2	D02 1-0	O12 1-3	N23 4-1	D21 3-4		O26 2-1	a20 0-2	D07 2-2	S28 1-4	D26 1-0	S23 2-0	J18 0-4	a29 1-2	a11 0-0	S07 2-4	M14 3-1	F29 2-1	N09 2-1
8 EVERTON	J25 1-0	M18 4-1	N16 4-1	M21 2-1	D26 0-0	S21 6-1	a01 0-3		O05 2-4	S07 3-3	a08 1-3	F08 2-1	a04 2-0	N02 1-0	a20 1-0	S09 2-1	O19 2-1	a25 0-0	a11 0-3	D21 1-1
9 LIVERPOOL	D07 5-0	S28 3-4	S14 2-0	J18 1-0	F29 3-1	a27 2-1	D25 1-4	a17 0-0		M14 0-1	M25 7-4	a18 0-1	D14 1-5	J01 0-0	N09 6-0	N23 1-2	D28 3-0	O26 3-0	O12 1-0	F15 4-1
10 MANCHESTER C	M07 3-2	a17 2-1	D28 2-0	D26 1-0	a21 0-0	N02 2-2	a04 0-3	J04 4-2	N16 1-1		a18 0-0	M21 2-1	O19 1-0	D14 4-2	O12 2-1	a06 5-0	M11 0-2	S28 3-2	S14 0-0	J18 4-0
11 MANCHESTER U	a20 1-2	F29 1-0	F15 1-2	O26 2-1	D07 2-1	D25 2-1	J25 1-0	N09 4-3	S07 4-0	D21 3-1		S09 2-1	F08 1-1	O05 4-0	a11 0-1	a25 2-1	S21 2-1	M28 4-1	M14 3-0	N23 4-2
12 MIDDLESBROUGH	a11 0-1	S04 1-0	J18 3-0	S28 0-1	N09 0-2	D07 0-2	J01 3-1	O12 0-2	D21 3-1	N23 2-0	S14 2-1		a20 2-1	J04 1-1	M14 3-1	M28 1-0	F01 2-0	a08 6-1	F15 3-1	O26 0-0
13 NEWCASTLE U	a08 2-5	N23 8-0	O26 3-0	N09 3-0	J18 2-0	M14 3-0	S14 1-0	D07 2-1	a11 3-1	F15 1-1	O12 1-6	D28 1-1		S28 3-0	S04 1-1	M11 0-0	D26 2-3	J04 2-1	a18 1-3	a17 2-1
14 NOTTINGHAM F	D26 2-2	O26 1-1	O12 3-2	F15 1-0	M28 3-1	a25 1-2	S21 6-0	F29 5-2	S02 3-1	a11 3-1	a17 2-0	S07 0-3	J25 0-0		D07 2-0	D21 2-2	a20 1-1	N23 2-2	N09 4-1	M14 1-0
15 NOTTS CO	N02 0-3	D27 0-0	a18 0-2	D28 0-1	S28 3-1	O03 2-1	N30 2-0	D25 2-1	M07 2-2	F08 1-0	D14 1-1	N16 2-0	O05 0-1	a04 2-0		O19 0-1	M21 0-3	J18 1-2	J04 4-0	S14 2-0
16 PRESTON N.E.	N16 3-0	J04 1-1	D26 1-1	D25 2-0	O12 3-0	M07 3-1	D14 2-4	S14 2-2	M21 3-0	O26 2-4	D28 0-0	N30 1-1	N02 2-0	a18 0-1	F15 1-0		a04 0-0	S02 1-1	J18 3-2	S28 3-0
17 SHEFFIELD U	D21 1-1	O12 1-0	S28 4-2	D30 1-0	M14 2-0	a11 0-2	J04 0-3	F15 2-0	S16 0-0	M28 1-2	J18 2-0	D25 0-0	J01 1-1	S14 2-2	N23 0-1	D07 2-0		N09 1-3	O26 5-3	F29 2-2
18 SHEFFIELD W	O19 2-3	a18 1-4	a04 2-0	D14 5-2	S23 5-3	F08 2-0	N16 3-1	D28 1-2	M09 1-2	J25 5-1	N30 2-0	N02 3-2	S07 3-1	M21 2-1	S21 2-0	O05 1-0	M07 2-0		D26 2-3	D31 6-0
19 SUNDERLAND	O05 3-0	a04 1-0	M21 4-0	N30 1-2	D25 3-3	J25 6-2	N02 3-0	D14 1-2	F08 1-0	S02 2-5	N16 1-2	O19 0-0	D21 2-4	M07 7-2	S07 4-3	S21 4-1	F22 4-1	a17 1-2		J01 5-2
20 W ARSENAL	F08 0-1	D14 1-1	N30 2-0	a04 1-1	S07 0-4	O05 0-0	M07 0-0	a18 2-1	O19 2-1	S21 2-1	M21 1-0	F22 4-1	D25 2-2	N16 3-1	S02 1-1	J25 1-1	N02 5-1	a20 1-1	D28 4-0	

LEAGUE TABLES

DIVISION 1

	P	W	D	L	F	A	W	D	L	F	A	Pts
Manchester U	38	15	1	3	43	19	8	5	6	38	29	52
Aston Villa	38	9	6	4	47	24	8	3	8	30	35	43
Manchester C	38	12	5	2	36	19	4	6	9	26	35	43
Newcastle U	38	11	4	4	41	24	4	8	7	24	30	42
Sheffield W	38	14	0	5	50	25	5	4	10	23	39	42
Middlesbrough	38	12	2	5	32	16	5	5	9	22	29	41
Bury	38	8	7	4	29	22	6	4	9	29	39	39
Liverpool	38	11	2	6	43	24	5	4	10	25	37	38
Nottingham F	38	11	6	2	42	21	2	5	12	17	41	37
Bristol C	38	8	7	4	29	21	4	5	10	29	40	36
Everton	38	11	4	4	34	24	4	2	13	24	40	36
Preston N.E.	38	9	7	3	33	18	3	5	11	14	35	36
Chelsea	38	8	3	8	30	35	6	5	8	23	27	36
Blackburn R	38	10	7	2	35	23	2	5	12	16	40	*36
Woolwich A	38	9	8	2	32	18	3	4	12	19	45	*36
Sunderland	38	11	2	6	53	31	5	1	13	25	44	35
Sheffield U	38	8	6	5	27	22	4	5	10	25	36	35
Notts Co	38	9	3	7	24	19	4	5	10	15	32	34
Bolton W	38	10	3	6	35	26	4	2	13	17	32	33
Birmingham C	38	6	6	7	22	28	3	6	10	18	32	30

*Woolwich Arsenal & Blackburn Rovers finished in equal 14th place

DIVISION 2

	P	W	D	L	F	A	W	D	L	F	A	Pts
Bradford C	38	15	2	2	58	16	9	4	6	32	26	54
Leicester C	38	14	2	3	41	20	7	8	4	31	27	52
Oldham A	38	15	4	0	53	14	7	2	10	23	28	50
Fulham	38	12	2	5	50	14	10	3	6	32	35	49
W.B.A.	38	13	3	3	38	13	6	6	7	23	26	47
Derby Co	38	15	1	3	50	13	6	3	10	27	32	46
Burnley	38	14	3	2	44	14	6	3	10	23	36	46
Hull C	38	15	1	3	50	23	6	3	10	23	39	46
Wolverhampton W	38	11	4	4	34	11	4	3	12	16	34	37
Stoke	38	11	5	3	43	13	5	0	14	14	39	37
Gainsborough T	38	9	4	6	31	28	5	3	11	16	43	35
Leeds U	38	9	6	4	33	18	3	2	14	20	47	32
Stockport Co	38	9	4	6	35	26	3	4	12	13	41	32
Clapton O	38	10	5	4	28	13	1	5	13	12	52	32
Blackpool	38	11	3	5	33	19	0	6	13	18	39	31
Barnsley	38	8	3	8	41	31	4	3	12	13	37	30
Glossop N.E.	38	9	5	5	36	26	2	3	14	18	48	30
Grimsby T	38	8	5	6	27	24	3	3	13	16	47	30
Chesterfield	38	6	6	7	33	38	0	5	14	13	54	23
Lincoln C	38	7	2	10	27	28	2	1	16	19	55	21

DIVISION 2

	BARNSLEY	BLACKPOOL	BRADFORD C	BURNLEY	CHESTERFIELD	CLAPTON O	DERBY CO	FULHAM	GAINSBOROUGH T	GLOSSOP	GRIMSBY T	HULL C	LEEDS C	LEICESTER F	LINCOLN C	OLDHAM A	STOCKPORT CO	STOKE	W.B.A.	WOLVERHAMPTON W
1 BARNSLEY		a18 0-0	J01 1-2	O19 2-3	F08 5-2	S05 2-2	S14 2-4	S28 6-0	M21 1-2	a21 4-1	O05 2-1	J04 4-2	M07 1-3	D14 1-3	J18 2-1	M19 2-1	N30 0-0	D28 0-1	D26 1-3	N16 5-0
2 BLACKPOOL	D21 1-1		M14 2-1	a17 1-0	a25 2-0	S07 5-0	M28 1-0	a11 2-1	J25 0-1	F08 4-0	a01 3-0	N23 1-1	S14 2-3	O19 2-2	D07 4-3	J01 1-0	O05 1-3	F29 1-0	N09 0-1	S21 0-2
3 BRADFORD C	D25 2-0	N16 3-0		a20 2-0	S07 8-1	J25 1-0	D21 3-1	D26 1-3	O19 7-1	N02 2-1	a04 1-1	a11 2-1	O05 5-0	M07 1-5	a25 2-0	S21 1-0	F22 5-0	M21 6-0	N30 0-0	F08 6-2
4 BURNLEY	F15 4-1	D25 2-1	S14 2-1		O26 1-1	N16 3-0	S28 2-2	O12 0-1	a04 2-0	a18 1-0	N02 5-1	J18 5-0	M21 1-0	D28 4-1	S16 1-2	M07 2-1	D14 4-0	S09 3-1	J04 1-1	N30 1-0
5 CHESTERFIELD	O12 1-3	D28 3-2	J04 1-1	F22 2-4		M07 1-1	J18 0-2	J01 1-1	N30 2-2	D14 3-7	O19 0-0	S14 1-2	N16 4-3	a18 2-2	S28 2-1	N02 1-2	M03 4-1	a20 2-4	a17 1-0	M21 2-0
6 CLAPTON O	F29 2-0	J04 1-1	S28 0-3	M14 0-1	N09 5-1		O12 1-0	O26 0-1	a18 2-0	a09 0-0	N30 2-1	S02 1-0	a04 0-0	a20 0-1	M26 2-0	N23 2-0	D28 4-1	S14 3-0	J18 2-2	D14 1-1
7 DERBY CO	D24 3-0	N30 2-1	a18 2-3	J25 1-0	D26 0-0	F08 4-0		S07 0-1	N02 5-2	N16 2-0	D25 4-0	D28 4-1	O19 6-1	F22 1-2	S02 4-0	O05 1-0	M07 3-0	a04 3-0	D14 2-0	a08 3-2
8 FULHAM	J25 2-0	D14 3-0	a17 0-2	F08 2-1	O05 5-0	M18 4-0	J04 0-0		N16 6-0	N30 6-1	S21 0-1	S03 0-1	N02 2-0	a04 5-1	S14 6-1	O19 1-2	M21 0-1	a18 5-1	D28 1-1	a01 2-1
9 GAINSBOROUGH T	N23 0-1	S28 2-1	F15 1-5	D07 2-0	M28 2-1	D21 0-0	F29 1-4	M14 3-3		S14 1-0	D26 3-2	O26 1-2	a22 2-1	J18 1-1	N09 5-1	a11 1-1	J04 3-2	a17 2-0	O12 1-2	O23 0-1
10 GLOSSOP	a17 3-1	O12 2-2	F29 2-2	D21 3-1	a11 3-2	D25 2-1	M14 2-3	a29 1-2	M03 1-0		J25 1-2	N09 5-1	J01 0-2	M24 2-3	F01 3-1	a25 0-0	S21 1-1	F15 2-0	O26 2-1	S07 1-1
11 GRIMSBY T	a09 4-1	O26 2-2	D07 0-1	F29 0-1	a29 4-3	M28 0-0	a20 1-0	J18 0-4	S03 1-4	S28 4-0		a18 1-1	a11 2-0	O12 1-1	J04 0-2	M14 2-0	S14 2-1	N09 1-0	N23 2-2	a17 0-1
12 HULL C	S07 2-0	M21 3-2	D14 0-2	S21 3-1	S26 2-0	O10 5-0	a25 4-0	a20 1-2	F22 0-1	M07 3-2	D21 4-2		F08 4-1	N16 3-2	D25 5-3	J25 3-2	N02 0-0	N30 2-1	a04 4-2	O19 2-0
13 LEEDS C	N09 1-1	a20 1-1	F01 0-1	N23 2-2	M14 0-0	S09 5-2	F15 5-1	F29 0-1	D28 0-0	S02 2-1	D14 4-1	O12 3-2		J04 0-0	O26 2-1	M28 1-2	a17 3-0	J18 0-1	S28 1-0	a18 3-1
14 LEICESTER F	a11 4-0	F15 2-1	N09 2-1	a25 3-1	D21 3-1	D26 0-2	N23 1-3	D07 2-3	S21 3-0	O05 3-1	F08 1-1	M14 3-2	S07 2-2		M28 1-0	D25 4-1	J25 2-1	O26 1-0	F29 3-0	S09 1-0
15 LINCOLN C	S21 0-2	a04 2-0	D28 2-4	O05 1-3	J25 4-0	F15 2-2	a17 1-0	O16 2-4	M07 2-0	M21 0-1	S07 1-0	D26 0-1	F22 5-0	N30 0-3		F08 0-2	N16 1-1	D14 1-2	a18 0-2	N02 3-1
16 OLDHAM A	O26 1-0	D26 3-2	J18 4-0	N09 1-1	F29 4-0	M21 4-1	M30 3-1	F15 3-3	D14 4-1	D28 0-0	N16 2-0	S28 3-0	N30 4-2	a21 1-1	O12 4-0		a18 5-0	J04 3-1	S14 2-1	a04 2-0
17 STOCKPORT CO	M28 2-0	S02 1-1	O26 1-1	a11 1-3	a04 1-0	a25 6-1	N09 2-1	N23 2-0	S07 1-1	J18 3-2	S09 3-0	F29 2-3	D25 2-1	S28 2-1	M14 1-1	D21 2-3		O12 1-2	F15 1-2	J01 1-3
18 STOKE	a25 4-0	N02 3-1	N23 3-0	D26 0-0	S02 1-1	N11 3-0	D07 0-3	D21 6-1	O05 5-0	O19 4-0	M19 5-0	M28 1-1	S21 2-1	a27 0-1	a11 3-0	S07 1-3	F08 1-0		M14 1-1	J25 0-0
19 W.B.A.	a20 1-1	M07 3-0	M28 3-2	S07 5-0	D25 4-0	S21 3-0	a11 1-0	a25 3-1	F08 0-1	F22 1-1	M21 1-2	D07 1-0	J25 1-0	N02 1-1	D21 5-2	N04 1-2	O19 2-0	N16 1-0		O05 1-0
20 WOLVERHAMPTON W	M14 0-1	J18 1-0	O12 0-0	M16 5-1	N23 0-0	a11 2-0	O26 2-2	N09 2-0	D25 1-0	J04 5-0	D28 5-1	F15 1-2	D21 2-0	S14 0-0	F29 3-0	a20 2-1	D26 0-1	S28 2-0	S02 1-2	

'Sandy' Turnbull, one of six Manchester City players banned by the FA in 1906 over illegal payments, was Manchester United's leading scorer when they won their first League Championship in 1907-08.

FOOTBALL LEAGUE RECORDS
SEASON 1908-09

Top scorers: Div 1, B.Freeman (Everton) 38 goals; Div 2, A.Bentley (Derby County) 24 goals.
Stoke resigned and Lincoln City failed to gain re-election. Bradford and Tottenham Hotspur were elected in their place.

LEAGUE TABLES

DIVISION 1

	P	W	D	L	F	A	W	D	L	F	A	Pts
Newcastle U	38	14	1	4	32	20	10	4	5	33	21	53
Everton	38	11	3	5	51	28	7	7	5	31	29	46
Sunderland	38	14	0	5	41	23	7	2	10	37	40	44
Blackburn R	38	6	6	7	29	26	8	7	4	32	24	41
Sheffield W	38	15	0	4	48	24	2	6	11	19	37	40
Woolwich A	38	9	3	7	24	18	5	7	7	28	31	38
Aston Villa	38	8	7	4	31	22	6	3	10	27	34	38
Bristol C	38	7	7	5	24	25	6	5	8	21	33	38
Middlesbrough	38	11	2	6	38	21	3	7	9	21	32	37
Preston N.E.	38	8	7	4	29	17	5	4	10	19	27	37
Chelsea	38	8	7	4	33	22	6	2	11	23	39	37
Sheffield U	38	9	5	5	31	25	5	4	10	20	34	37
Manchester U	38	10	3	6	37	33	5	4	10	21	35	37
Nottingham F	38	9	2	8	39	24	5	6	8	27	33	36
Notts Co	38	9	4	6	31	23	5	4	10	20	25	36
Liverpool	38	9	5	5	36	25	6	1	12	21	40	36
Bury	38	9	6	4	35	27	5	2	12	28	50	36
Bradford C	38	7	6	6	27	20	5	4	10	20	27	34
Manchester C	38	12	3	4	50	23	3	1	15	17	46	34
Leicester C	38	6	6	7	32	41	2	3	14	22	61	25

DIVISION 2

	P	W	D	L	F	A	W	D	L	F	A	Pts
Bolton W	38	14	3	2	37	8	10	1	8	22	20	52
Tottenham H	38	12	5	2	42	12	8	6	5	25	20	51
W.B.A.	38	13	5	1	35	9	6	8	5	21	18	51
Hull C	38	14	2	3	44	15	5	4	10	19	24	44
Derby Co	38	13	5	1	38	11	3	6	10	17	30	43
Oldham A	38	14	4	1	39	9	3	2	14	16	34	40
Wolverhampton W	38	10	6	3	32	12	4	5	10	24	36	39
Glossop N.E.	38	11	5	3	35	17	4	3	12	22	36	38
Gainsborough T	38	12	3	4	30	20	3	5	11	19	50	38
Fulham	38	8	4	7	39	26	5	7	7	19	22	37
Birmingham C	38	10	6	3	35	21	4	3	12	23	40	37
Leeds U	38	12	3	4	35	19	2	4	13	8	34	35
Grimsby T	38	9	5	5	23	14	5	2	12	18	40	35
Burnley	38	8	4	7	33	28	5	3	11	18	30	33
Clapton O	38	7	7	5	25	19	5	2	12	12	30	33
Bradford P.A.	38	9	2	8	30	25	4	4	11	21	34	32
Barnsley	38	11	3	5	36	19	0	7	12	12	38	32
Stockport Co	38	11	2	6	25	19	3	1	15	14	52	31
Chesterfield	38	10	3	6	30	28	1	5	13	7	39	30
Blackpool	38	9	6	4	30	22	0	5	14	16	46	29

DIVISION 1

	ASTON VILLA	BLACKBURN R	BRADFORD C	BRISTOL C	BURY	CHELSEA	EVERTON	LEICESTER F	LIVERPOOL	MANCHESTER C	MANCHESTER U	MIDDLESBROUGH	NEWCASTLE U	NOTTINGHAM F	NOTTS CO	PRESTON N.E.	SHEFFIELD U	SHEFFIELD W	SUNDERLAND	W ARSENAL
1 ASTON VILLA		O03 1-1	F13 1-3	N28 1-1	D26 3-0	J30 0-0	F27 3-1	O31 1-1	D25 1-1	a24 2-1	O17 3-1	D12 0-3	a26 3-0	J09 1-2	N14 1-1	a10 2-4	a09 3-0	S05 1-1	S19 2-0	M13 2-1
2 BLACKBURN R	F15 3-1		M13 1-1	S01 1-1	J23 0-1	O24 2-0	M27 0-0	N28 3-0	S12 1-0	J02 3-2	N14 1-3	D25 0-0	a24 2-4	O10 0-3	D12 0-2	J01 1-1	S26 0-1	O31 2-2	M22 8-1	a10 1-3
3 BRADFORD C	O10 1-1	N07 0-2		D25 0-1	S26 4-1	a20 3-0	N28 1-1	a10 4-1	J23 0-2	S12 0-0	a29 1-0	J02 0-2	M23 1-2	M30 1-1	a24 2-2	a12 2-0	M27 3-1	N14 0-0	O24 0-2	D12 4-1
4 BRISTOL C	a03 0-0	a13 1-4	D26 0-1		M20 4-2	D19 1-0	S05 0-2	J09 1-1	N07 1-0	a28 1-0	a12 0-0	O24 1-1	O03 3-3	D05 2-1	J30 1-0	M17 2-3	N21 1-1	F13 1-1	a17 2-4	S19 2-1
5 BURY	J01 1-2	S19 1-1	J30 2-1	N14 1-2		M31 2-1	F13 2-2	O17 2-2	D12 2-1	a10 1-0	O03 2-2	N28 2-1	M13 1-1	D25 3-2	O31 3-1	M27 0-1	S01 1-2	a24 4-2	S05 4-2	F27 1-1
6 CHELSEA	S26 0-2	F27 1-1	O31 1-1	a26 3-1	S12 4-1		N14 3-3	a29 1-0	J02 3-0	D26 1-2	M13 1-1	a09 3-0	D12 1-2	S21 2-1	a10 3-2	S01 0-0	J23 1-1	O17 2-2	O10 2-0	N28 1-2
7 EVERTON	O24 3-1	N21 4-4	a03 0-1	J02 5-2	O10 4-0	M20 3-2		a24 4-2	a09 5-0	S26 6-3	D05 3-2	J23 1-1	J01 0-1	M24 3-3	D25 0-1	S12 0-1	F20 5-1	D12 1-0	N07 4-0	S07 0-3
8 LEICESTER F	M27 4-2	a03 2-4	D05 1-4	S12 1-1	F20 2-5	N21 5-2	D19 0-2		O10 3-2	M11 3-1	a17 3-2	S26 1-1	J02 0-4	N07 0-3	a12 0-2	J23 0-0	O24 1-1	S01 1-1	M20 4-3	D25 1-1
9 LIVERPOOL	S01 3-2	J09 1-1	S19 4-0	M13 1-2	a17 2-2	S05 2-1	O03 0-1	F13 4-1		N28 1-3	J30 3-1	M27 1-2	O31 2-1	D26 1-1	F27 1-1	N14 2-1	D19 2-1	a10 1-2	a12 3-0	O17 2-2
10 MANCHESTER C	D19 2-0	S05 3-3	J09 4-3	O31 5-1	D05 6-1	D25 1-2	J30 4-0	O03 5-2	a03 4-0		S19 1-2	N14 0-0	F27 0-2	a13 2-1	O17 1-0	M13 4-1	a17 1-3	M27 4-0	S01 1-0	F13 2-2
11 MANCHESTER U	M31 0-2	M20 0-3	N21 2-0	a09 0-1	S07 2-1	N07 0-1	a10 2-2	D12 4-2	S26 3-2	J23 3-1		S12 6-3	D26 1-0	O24 2-2	J01 4-3	J02 0-2	O10 2-1	N28 3-1	M15 2-2	a27 1-4
12 MIDDLESBROUGH	a17 1-0	a12 1-0	S05 1-0	F27 4-0	a03 0-1	J01 1-4	S19 2-3	J30 6-2	N21 1-0	M20 3-0	J09 5-0		O17 0-0	D19 4-0	F13 1-2	O31 4-2	D05 1-2	M13 2-1	S09 0-3	O03 1-1
13 NEWCASTLE U	N21 0-2	D19 2-0	S02 1-0	S09 2-1	N07 3-1	a17 1-3	a12 3-0	S05 2-0	a30 0-1	O24 2-0	D25 2-1	M31 1-0		a03 1-1	S19 1-0	O10 2-0	M20 4-0	J30 1-0	D05 1-9	J09 3-1
14 NOTTINGHAM F	S12 1-2	F13 2-1	O17 2-1	a10 1-1	a12 0-2	O03 2-1	O31 1-2	a21 12-0	O01 5-1	D28 0-2	F27 2-0	a24 4-1	N28 0-4		M27 1-0	D12 1-1	J02 0-2	S19 1-2	J30 4-0	N14 0-1
15 NOTTS CO	M20 1-1	a17 2-3	D19 1-1	S26 0-1	M24 3-2	D05 3-0	D26 0-0	a09 2-3	O24 1-2	F20 5-1	a13 0-1	O10 3-2	J23 0-4	N21 3-0		M10 1-0	N07 3-1	J09 1-0	a03 0-0	S05 2-1
16 PRESTON N.E.	D05 3-2	D26 2-0	a09 0-0	O17 2-1	N21 0-2	S07 6-0	J09 3-3	S19 0-1	M20 2-0	N07 3-0	S05 0-3	M06 1-1	F13 0-1	a17 1-1	O03 0-0		a03 1-1	F27 4-1	D19 1-0	J30 0-0
17 SHEFFIELD U	F06 3-1	J30 0-0	O03 3-0	a05 3-1	M01 2-2	S19 1-3	O17 1-5	F27 2-1	S14 0-2	D12 4-0	F13 0-0	a10 2-0	N14 1-1	S05 1-2	M13 3-2	N28 2-1		D26 2-1	J09 0-2	O31 1-1
18 SHEFFIELD W	J02 4-2	a19 1-2	M20 0-2	O10 2-0	D19 4-3	M22 5-1	a17 2-0	J01 3-1	D05 2-3	N21 3-1	a03 2-0	N07 3-2	S26 2-0	J23 3-0	S12 2-0	O24 1-0	D25 1-0		M29 2-5	D28 6-2
19 SUNDERLAND	J23 4-3	O17 0-1	F27 2-1	D12 0-2	J02 3-1	F13 1-2	M13 2-0	N14 3-1	J01 1-4	a09 2-0	O31 6-1	D26 2-0	a10 3-1	S26 2-1	N28 0-1	a24 2-1	S12 3-1	O03 4-2		M27 1-0
20 W ARSENAL	N07 0-1	D05 0-1	a17 1-0	J23 1-1	O24 4-0	a03 0-0	S02 0-4	D26 2-1	F20 5-0	O10 3-0	D19 0-1	M17 1-1	S12 1-2	M20 1-2	J02 1-0	S26 1-0	a01 1-0	a12 2-0	N21 0-4	

DIVISION 2

	BARNSLEY	BIRMINGHAM	BLACKPOOL	BOLTON W	BRADFORD	BURNLEY	CHESTERFIELD	CLAPTON O	DERBY CO	FULHAM	GAINSBOROUGH T	GLOSSOP	GRIMSBY T	HULL C	LEEDS C	OLDHAM A	STOCKPORT CO	TOTTENHAM H	W.B.A.	WOLVERHAMPTON W
1 BARNSLEY		M13 3-1	O03 4-0	S05 0-1	D12 3-1	a13 1-2	F13 4-0	D26 3-0	J30 1-0	N28 1-2	N14 2-2	O17 1-3	M27 3-1	S19 2-1	J01 2-1	a09 2-0	F27 2-0	J09 1-1	O31 0-2	a24 1-1
2 BIRMINGHAM	N07 2-1		D05 2-2	S02 2-0	S07 3-1	S26 2-0	a17 3-0	O24 1-0	a03 1-1	J23 1-3	J02 2-2	D19 1-2	S12 3-1	N21 1-2	a12 1-0	F20 2-0	D25 4-2	M20 3-3	D28 0-0	O10 1-1
3 BLACKPOOL	S02 1-1	a10 2-0		O31 1-2	M31 2-1	a09 0-0	M13 2-2	J23 1-3	O24 2-2	D26 2-0	D12 3-0	N14 2-1	a24 2-2	F20 2-3	S26 1-0	S12 1-0	M27 2-1	O10 1-1	N28 0-2	J02 3-1
4 BOLTON W	J02 3-0	J01 2-1	M06 3-1		N07 0-1	O24 2-1	F20 4-0	D19 2-0	a30 1-0	O10 0-0	S12 4-0	a03 2-0	S26 2-0	S14 1-0	D25 2-0	D05 3-0	a17 4-1	J23 0-1	S15 1-1	N21 1-1
5 BRADFORD	a17 3-2	O06 1-2	J01 4-3	M13 1-2		O31 2-3	S05 1-0	a03 0-1	a09 2-0	F27 1-1	F06 4-1	D26 1-0	O17 0-2	S01 1-0	a27 2-0	D15 3-4	S19 0-1	D19 0-2	J30 0-0	M20 4-1
6 BURNLEY	D05 3-2	J30 1-1	D25 1-1	F27 1-2	M16 3-3		S01 0-1	N21 0-1	S07 2-0	O17 1-3	O03 5-2	S05 3-2	F13 2-0	D19 1-0	a03 0-0	M20 1-0	J09 5-1	a17 1-2	S19 0-2	N07 3-5
7 CHESTERFIELD	O10 1-0	D12 4-2	N07 3-1	N14 0-2	J02 2-1	a12 1-0		S26 2-0	M17 2-4	J01 2-1	a24 2-1	M27 2-1	F06 1-2	O24 0-4	O03 2-0	J23 1-1	N28 1-2	M08 1-3	a10 2-2	S12 1-1
8 CLAPTON O	D25 1-1	F27 3-2	S19 1-1	a24 0-2	N28 2-0	M27 0-1	J30 1-1		J09 2-0	N14 1-1	O31 2-2	O03 0-2	M13 2-1	J02 1-2	a13 0-0	D12 2-0	F13 5-0	a12 0-0	O17 1-0	a10 1-3
9 DERBY CO	S26 0-0	N28 1-2	F27 1-1	O17 1-0	D28 3-1	D26 1-0	O31 1-1	S12 1-0		a24 2-1	a10 5-0	a21 4-0	D12 2-1	O10 0-0	J23 5-1	J02 1-0	N14 5-0	a28 1-1	a26 2-1	S16 2-1
10 FULHAM	a03 2-2	S19 1-1	a12 3-0	F13 1-2	O24 3-1	M31 3-0	D25 0-0	M20 1-2	D19 1-2		J30 4-0	S02 2-3	O03 5-2	a17 0-3	N21 0-1	N07 3-2	S05 5-1	D05 2-3	J09 2-0	M06 1-1
11 GAINSBOROUGH T	M20 4-1	S05 1-3	a17 1-0	J09 2-1	O10 2-1	a14 1-0	D19 3-0	a28 2-0	O21 0-0	S26 1-1		D28 3-1	J23 0-3	a03 2-0	N07 1-1	O24 1-4	D26 3-2	N21 0-2	a09 2-0	F20 1-0
12 GLOSSOP	M30 3-0	a24 3-1	M20 3-0	N28 0-2	S12 1-1	J02 1-2	N21 2-0	a20 4-0	N07 3-1	a09 0-0	F23 2-2		M16 1-0	M23 2-1	O10 0-0	S26 2-1	a10 3-0	O24 1-1	D12 1-3	J23 3-2
13 GRIMSBY T	N21 0-0	J09 0-3	D19 2-1	J30 1-0	F20 1-1	O10 0-1	D26 1-0	N07 1-0	a17 2-0	M25 2-2	S19 1-2	a12 2-0		D05 0-0	M20 0-1	a20 2-0	S01 3-0	a03 1-2	S05 1-1	O24 3-0
14 HULL C	J23 4-0	M27 4-1	O17 2-0	O03 2-0	D25 2-3	a24 3-2	F27 1-0	S05 3-2	F13 4-0	D12 2-0	N28 5-1	O31 0-0	a10 0-1		J09 4-1	a29 1-0	M13 4-1	S26 1-0	N14 2-2	a12 0-1
15 LEEDS C	S14 2-0	O31 2-0	J30 1-0	D26 1-2	a10 0-3	N28 1-1	a09 3-0	S07 0-0	S19 2-5	M27 2-0	M13 0-2	F13 3-1	N14 4-1	S12 2-0		a24 3-0	O17 2-1	S05 1-0	F27 1-1	D12 5-2
16 OLDHAM A	a12 0-0	O17 2-0	J09 3-1	a10 1-1	M27 2-0	N14 4-1	S19 2-0	a17 2-0	S05 1-1	M13 1-0	F27 2-0	J30 2-1	O31 4-0	a27 2-2	D19 6-0		O03 0-1	D25 1-0	F13 2-0	N28 2-1
17 STOCKPORT CO	O24 2-1	a09 3-2	N21 1-0	D12 1-0	J23 0-1	S12 2-1	a03 2-0	O10 1-1	M20 1-0	J02 1-2	a12 0-1	D05 4-2	J01 0-1	N07 3-1	F20 1-0	M08 1-3		M06 1-3	a24 0-0	S26 1-0
18 TOTTENHAM H	S12 4-0	N14 4-0	F13 4-1	S19 2-1	a24 3-0	D12 4-2	O17 4-0	a09 0-1	O03 0-0	a10 1-0	M27 1-1	F27 3-3	N28 2-0	J30 0-0	J02 3-0	D26 3-0	O31 0-0		M13 1-3	S01 3-0
19 W.B.A.	M24 1-1	D26 1-1	a03 5-1	a12 2-0	S26 1-0	J23 0-0	N02 2-2	F20 1-0	N21 2-0	S12 1-1	D25 2-0	a17 1-0	J02 7-0	M20 1-0	O24 2-1	O10 1-0	D19 2-0	N07 3-0		S07 0-2
20 WOLVERHAMPTON W	D19 2-0	F13 2-0	S05 2-2	M27 1-2	N14 1-1	M13 2-1	J09 3-0	D05 5-1	D25 1-1	O31 0-1	O17 4-0	S19 0-0	F27 0-0	D26 3-0	a17 2-1	a03 1-1	J30 2-0	D28 1-0	O03 0-1	

Scottish international Jimmy Howie of Newcastle United, said to be the best inside-right in the game before World War One. He was a key man in Newcastle's trio of title wins and appeared in four FA Cup Finals.

Football League Records
Season 1909-10

Top scorers: Div 1, J.Parkinson (Liverpool) 30 goals; Div 2, J.Smith (Hull City) 32 goals.
Chesterfield failed to gain re-election, Lincoln City were elected in their place.

DIVISION 1

	ASTON VILLA	BLACKBURN R	BOLTON W	BRADFORD C	BRISTOL C	BURY	CHELSEA	EVERTON	LIVERPOOL	MANCHESTER U	MIDDLESBROUGH	NEWCASTLE U	NOTTINGHAM F	NOTTS CO	PRESTON N.E.	SHEFFIELD U	SHEFFIELD W	SUNDERLAND	TOTTENHAM H	W ARSENAL
1 ASTON VILLA		J29 4-3	J08 3-1	O23 3-1	N06 1-0	M26 4-1	S11 4-1	O09 3-1	D18 3-1	F26 7-1	M25 4-2	a27 4-0	S25 0-0	D04 1-1	a09 3-0	D27 2-1	M12 5-0	F12 3-2	N20 3-2	S01 5-1
2 BLACKBURN R	S18 3-2		M26 4-2	a09 2-0	S13 5-2	D18 5-1	O16 1-0	a11 2-1	J22 1-1	N20 3-2	M05 1-1	S04 2-0	M12 2-2	M25 2-0	D25 2-2	a23 3-1	D04 0-0	N06 0-0	J01 2-0	O02 7-0
3 BOLTON W	S04 1-2	O09 1-2		F19 1-1	a09 4-2	D04 1-3	F12 5-2	M12 0-1	S06 1-2	N06 2-3	F05 1-1	S07 0-4	F26 2-1	J01 3-4	D18 3-1	J22 1-0	J03 0-2	O23 2-1	a23 0-2	S18 3-0
4 BRADFORD C	M05 1-2	N27 2-0	N13 1-0		S04 3-1	J22 0-0	a02 4-1	a30 2-0	O16 1-2	J01 0-2	D27 4-1	M09 3-3	a16 1-1	O02 2-1	M29 2-0	O30 2-0	M25 2-0	D11 3-1	S18 5-1	M19 0-1
5 BRISTOL C	M19 0-0	D11 2-2	N27 1-0	J08 2-0		S08 1-1	a16 1-0	D25 3-1	O30 0-1	M28 2-1	S18 4-1	a25 0-3	a30 4-0	O16 3-1	F19 2-0	N13 0-2	S11 1-1	D28 2-3	O02 0-0	a02 0-1
6 BURY	N13 0-2	a30 2-1	a16 1-2	S11 3-4	S25 1-2		D11 4-2	J01 2-2	M19 1-2	J08 1-1	O02 2-1	O30 1-2	J03 4-1	M05 1-1	O16 3-1	a02 2-0	M09 3-2	D25 0-1	a20 3-1	N27 1-2
7 CHELSEA	J22 0-0	F26 3-1	O02 3-2	N20 0-3	D04 4-1	a23 2-0		N06 0-1	S04 2-1	M26 1-1	F19 2-1	D27 2-1	O23 0-1	S01 2-2	O27 2-0	S18 2-2	a09 4-1	M12 1-4	D18 2-1	M28 0-1
8 EVERTON	M14 0-0	N13 0-2	O30 3-1	D18 1-1	D27 1-0	M28 3-0	M19 2-2		O02 2-3	a23 3-3	a16 1-1	S06 1-4	a02 0-4	S18 2-0	J22 2-1	O16 1-2	S01 1-1	N27 2-1	S04 4-2	M07 1-0
9 LIVERPOOL	a30 2-0	S11 3-1	D25 3-0	F26 1-0	M12 0-1	N06 2-2	J08 5-1	F12 0-1		O09 3-2	D11 0-0	D04 6-5	a20 7-3	a09 2-1	N20 2-0	M25 0-0	O23 3-1	S25 1-4	M26 2-0	J01 5-1
10 MANCHESTER U	O16 2-0	a02 2-0	M19 5-0	S01 1-0	M25 2-1	S04 2-0	N13 2-0	a06 3-2	F19 3-4		a30 4-1	O02 1-1	N27 2-6	S06 2-1	S18 1-1	M05 1-0	D25 0-3	a16 2-0	J22 5-0	O30 1-0
11 MIDDLESBROUGH	M28 3-2	O23 1-3	S25 1-2	D25 3-7	a20 0-0	F12 0-5	O09 0-1	D04 1-1	a23 2-2	D18 1-2		a09 1-1	N06 2-1	M26 2-0	M12 1-0	S01 0-2	J08 4-0	N20 3-2	F26 4-3	S11 5-2
12 NEWCASTLE U	D11 1-0	J08 4-1	S01 1-0	O09 1-0	O23 3-1	M12 2-2	J01 1-0	S25 1-2	a16 1-3	F12 3-4	N27 2-0		S11 1-2	N20 1-3	J03 5-2	a30 0-0	F26 3-1	a13 1-0	N06 1-0	M25 1-1
13 NOTTINGHAM F	J01 1-4	O30 0-4	O16 2-0	D04 1-1	D18 0-0	N03 3-3	M05 0-0	N20 1-0	S18 1-4	a09 2-0	M19 0-1	J22 0-1		S04 2-1	M25 0-0	O02 2-3	a23 0-6	M26 1-3	D27 2-2	M02 1-1
14 NOTTS CO	a16 2-3	D28 2-2	M28 0-0	F12 3-2	F26 0-2	O23 3-1	D25 2-1	a13 2-3	N27 3-1	S25 3-2	N13 2-1	a02 2-2	J08 4-1		N06 3-1	D11 1-2	O09 0-0	S11 1-1	M12 3-0	O07 5-1
15 PRESTON N.E.	N27 1-0	D27 3-2	a30 1-0	S25 2-2	O09 3-0	F26 2-1	J10 2-0	S11 0-1	a02 2-0	F05 1-0	O30 1-0	N13 4-0	S01 0-1	M19 4-0		a16 1-1	F12 1-0	J08 1-0	N22 4-1	D11 3-4
16 SHEFFIELD U	D25 0-1	S25 3-0	S11 2-2	M12 1-2	M26 4-0	N20 2-0	M07 0-0	F26 3-0	D28 4-2	O23 0-1	J01 2-0	D18 4-0	F12 1-4	O18 2-2	D04 5-1		N06 3-3	O09 3-0	a09 1-1	J08 2-0
17 SHEFFIELD W	O30 3-2	a16 2-1	a02 0-0	M28 2-1	J22 2-0	S18 1-4	N27 4-1	S20 1-3	M05 3-0	D27 4-1	S04 1-5	O16 3-1	D11 4-3	F19 0-0	O02 4-1	M19 1-3		a30 1-0	M14 1-1	N13 1-1
18 SUNDERLAND	O02 1-1	M19 0-0	M05 3-0	a23 3-0	J01 4-0	D27 2-3	O30 4-0	a09 0-1	M28 2-1	D04 3-0	a02 2-2	S18 0-2	N13 2-1	J22 0-3	S04 2-1	M16 1-0	D18 2-0		S01 3-1	O16 6-2
19 TOTTENHAM H	a02 1-1	M29 4-0	D11 1-1	J29 0-0	F12 3-2	O09 1-0	a30 2-1	J08 3-0	N13 1-0	S11 2-2	O16 1-3	M19 0-4	D25 2-2	O30 1-3	M05 2-1	N27 2-1	S25 3-0	M25 5-1		a16 1-1
20 W ARSENAL	a11 1-0	F12 0-1	J29 2-0	N06 0-1	N20 2-2	a09 0-0	S25 3-2	O23 1-0	D27 1-1	M12 0-0	J22 3-0	D25 0-3	O09 0-1	D18 1-2	a23 1-3	S04 0-0	M26 0-1	F26 1-2	D04 1-0	

LEAGUE TABLES

DIVISION 1

	P	W	D	L	F	A	W	D	L	F	A	Pts
Aston Villa	38	17	2	0	62	19	6	5	8	22	23	53
Liverpool	38	13	3	3	47	23	8	3	8	31	34	48
Blackburn R	38	13	6	0	47	17	5	3	11	26	38	45
Newcastle U	38	11	3	5	33	22	8	4	7	37	34	45
Manchester U	38	14	2	3	41	20	5	5	9	28	41	45
Sheffield U	38	10	5	4	42	19	6	5	8	20	22	42
Bradford C	38	12	3	4	38	17	5	5	9	26	30	42
Sunderland	38	12	3	4	40	18	6	2	11	26	33	41
Notts Co	38	10	5	4	41	26	5	5	9	26	33	40
Everton	38	8	6	5	30	28	8	2	9	21	28	40
Sheffield W	38	11	4	4	38	28	4	5	10	22	35	39
Preston N.E.	38	14	2	3	36	13	1	3	15	16	45	35
Bury	38	8	3	8	35	30	4	6	9	27	36	33
Nottingham F	38	4	7	8	19	34	7	4	8	35	38	33
Tottenham H	38	10	6	3	35	23	1	4	14	18	46	32
Bristol C	38	9	5	5	28	18	3	3	13	17	42	32
Middlesbrough	38	8	4	7	34	36	3	5	11	22	37	31
Woolwich A	38	6	5	8	17	19	5	4	10	20	48	31
Chelsea	38	10	4	5	32	24	1	3	15	15	46	29
Bolton W	38	7	2	10	31	34	2	4	13	13	37	24

DIVISION 2

	P	W	D	L	F	A	W	D	L	F	A	Pts
Manchester C	38	15	2	2	51	17	8	6	5	30	23	54
Oldham A	38	15	2	2	47	9	8	5	6	32	30	53
Hull C	38	13	4	2	52	19	10	3	6	28	27	53
Derby Co	38	15	2	2	46	15	7	7	5	26	32	53
Leicester C	38	15	2	2	60	20	5	2	12	19	38	44
Glossop N.E.	38	14	1	4	42	18	4	6	9	22	39	43
Fulham	38	9	7	3	28	13	5	6	8	23	30	41
Wolverhampton W	38	14	3	2	51	22	3	3	13	13	41	40
Barnsley	38	15	3	1	48	15	1	4	14	14	44	39
Bradford P.A.	38	12	1	6	47	28	5	3	11	17	31	38
W.B.A.	38	8	5	6	30	23	8	0	11	28	33	37
Blackpool	38	7	7	5	24	18	7	1	11	26	34	36
Stockport Co	38	9	6	4	37	20	4	2	13	13	27	34
Burnley	38	12	2	5	43	21	2	4	13	19	40	34
Lincoln C	38	7	6	6	27	24	3	5	11	15	45	31
Clapton O	38	10	4	5	26	15	2	2	15	11	45	30
Leeds U	38	8	4	7	30	33	2	3	14	16	47	27
Gainsborough T	38	8	3	8	22	21	2	3	14	11	54	26
Grimsby T	38	8	3	8	31	19	1	3	15	19	58	24
Birmingham C	38	7	4	8	28	26	1	3	15	14	52	23

DIVISION 2

	BARNSLEY	BIRMINGHAM	BLACKPOOL	BRADFORD	BURNLEY	CLAPTON O	DERBY CO	FULHAM	GAINSBOROUGH T	GLOSSOP	GRIMSBY T	HULL C	LEEDS C	LEICESTER F	LINCOLN C	MANCHESTER C	OLDHAM A	STOCKPORT CO	W.B.A.	WOLVERHAMPTON W
1 BARNSLEY		S11 5-1	a30 1-0	O02 4-0	O16 0-0	D11 2-1	D28 5-1	F24 2-1	M19 4-1	J08 3-0	N13 2-1	S02 1-2	M17 1-1	N27 3-1	M28 2-1	a02 1-1	S25 2-1	D27 1-0	a14 2-1	O30 7-1
2 BIRMINGHAM	J22 2-1		N27 1-2	D28 0-1	F28 2-1	a02 1-2	D11 1-3	S18 1-1	O16 5-0	S13 2-2	M05 2-4	a16 0-2	O02 1-2	M19 2-1	N13 1-0	O30 1-1	S04 2-2	a30 3-0	J01 0-1	F19 1-0
3 BLACKPOOL	D18 0-0	a09 2-0		M05 0-0	M25 2-3	O16 2-2	N06 1-1	O04 1-1	J22 0-2	N20 1-1	S18 1-0	M12 1-2	J01 3-1	O02 0-1	F19 3-0	S25 0-0	a23 1-3	M26 2-0	D04 2-1	S04 2-0
4 BRADFORD	F12 2-0	M28 5-0	O23 2-1		M12 3-1	O09 3-1	N20 1-2	F26 3-0	a23 2-0	D18 3-3	F08 6-1	N06 0-1	M26 4-2	S11 1-3	S25 4-0	D25 2-0	M08 1-6	D04 2-4	J08 1-0	a09 2-3
5 BURNLEY	F26 2-0	S25 2-0	D25 5-1	O30 1-0		J01 2-0	J08 1-2	O23 2-0	a02 2-1	a18 0-1	N27 3-1	S06 0-1	M19 3-0	D11 5-2	a30 3-0	a16 3-3	O09 1-2	S11 2-2	F12 2-3	N13 4-2
6 CLAPTON O	a07 4-0	N20 3-0	F26 2-1	F19 1-0	D27 2-1		M12 0-2	D18 0-0	S04 2-0	M26 0-0	J22 0-0	O23 0-0	M28 0-2	a25 3-0	O02 1-2	S18 3-2	D04 1-2	N06 2-0	a09 1-3	O25 1-0
7 DERBY CO	D25 2-1	a23 3-1	M19 2-1	a02 1-2	S04 5-2	O30 1-0		J01 3-1	S01 2-2	D04 2-1	O02 6-0	N13 4-0	J22 1-0	O16 0-1	M05 2-0	M16 3-1	M28 1-1	a09 1-0	D18 2-1	S18 5-0
8 FULHAM	O09 3-0	J29 0-0	S13 0-1	O16 3-1	M05 2-1	a30 0-0	M25 0-0		N13 0-1	S11 2-0	a02 3-2	D25 3-1	O30 5-1	a16 2-0	D11 1-1	N27 1-1	F12 1-1	J08 2-0	S25 0-2	M19 0-0
9 GAINSBOROUGH T	N06 0-0	F26 1-0	S11 3-1	D11 3-1	N20 2-0	J08 0-1	S25 2-4	M26 2-0		O09 1-3	a30 1-1	a20 0-1	a09 2-0	M25 0-1	J01 0-0	O27 1-3	M12 0-2	F12 1-0	O23 3-1	D04 0-2
10 GLOSSOP	S04 3-0	D25 4-1	a02 2-3	a30 3-1	S18 2-0	N13 3-1	a28 1-1	J22 0-1	F19 4-0		O16 3-0	N27 2-1	F05 2-1	O30 1-0	M19 0-1	a06 0-3	D27 6-2	D11 1-0	a26 3-2	O02 2-0
11 GRIMSBY T	a26 7-0	O23 0-2	F15 0-1	S01 0-1	a09 5-3	S11 2-0	F12 1-1	N20 0-2	D18 2-1	F26 4-0		S25 2-3	D04 3-1	M28 0-0	J08 1-2	M25 0-1	N06 0-0	O09 0-1	M12 3-0	a23 1-0
12 HULL C	O11 1-0	D04 7-0	O30 1-2	M19 2-1	M28 3-2	M05 3-0	M26 0-0	D27 3-2	S18 5-1	a09 4-2	J01 5-1		S04 3-1	a14 2-1	O16 0-0	O02 1-2	D18 4-0	N20 1-1	a23 5-1	J22 2-2
13 LEEDS C	O23 0-7	F12 2-1	D27 3-2	N13 2-3	N06 1-0	D25 2-1	S11 2-1	M12 2-2	N27 0-0	S25 1-2	a16 3-1	J08 1-1		a30 1-1	S01 5-0	D11 1-3	F26 3-5	M05 0-2	O09 0-1	a02 1-0
14 LEICESTER F	a09 1-1	N06 3-1	F12 3-2	J22 3-0	a23 1-1	S25 4-0	F26 6-0	D04 2-3	D27 9-1	M12 3-1	D25 3-1	O09 3-1	D18 6-2		J29 4-1	S04 1-3	N20 3-0	O23 1-0	M26 2-1	S01 2-1
15 LINCOLN C	a16 2-1	M26 3-2	O09 2-2	M02 1-1	D18 0-0	F12 4-0	O23 2-3	a23 2-2	D25 4-0	N06 1-2	S04 0-0	F26 1-3	D28 0-0	S18 3-1		J22 0-2	a09 0-2	M12 1-0	S29 0-3	M25 1-0
16 MANCHESTER C	M09 0-0	M12 3-0	S02 1-2	J01 3-1	D04 4-0	a13 2-1	O09 2-1	a09 3-1	M28 3-1	O23 3-3	D27 2-0	F12 3-0	a23 3-0	J08 2-0	S11 6-2		M26 0-2	F26 2-1	N06 3-2	D18 6-0
17 OLDHAM A	M14 5-0	J08 1-1	D11 2-0	S18 1-1	F19 1-0	a16 5-0	a26 4-0	O02 0-1	O30 2-0	J01 1-0	M19 4-1	a30 3-0	O16 2-1	a02 2-1	J03 6-1	N13 1-0		D25 3-0	S11 1-2	M05 3-0
18 STOCKPORT CO	J01 5-0	D18 1-1	N13 2-0	a16 2-1	J22 1-1	M19 3-0	N27 1-1	S04 0-2	O02 3-0	a23 5-0	F19 2-1	a02 1-5	S18 0-0	a06 6-2	O30 1-1	O16 1-2	M25 2-0		S01 0-2	M28 1-1
19 W.B.A.	S18 4-3	D27 3-1	a16 0-3	S04 1-0	O02 1-2	N27 3-0	a30 0-0	M29 3-2	M05 5-0	M28 0-0	O30 4-3	D11 0-2	M07 3-1	N13 1-2	a02 1-1	M19 0-0	J22 1-1	S06 0-1		D25 0-1
20 WOLVERHAMPTON W	M12 1-0	O09 4-2	J08 2-1	N27 0-2	M26 3-1	S13 3-1	J29 2-3	N06 1-1	a16 0-0	F12 3-1	D11 8-1	S11 2-2	N20 5-0	D28 4-1	D27 4-2	a30 3-2	O23 1-0	S25 2-1	O16 3-1	

Harry Hampton, a centre-forward who terrorised defenders and made his name by charging goalkeepers. Between 1904-05 and 1919-20 he scored 242 League and Cup goals for Aston Villa.

Football League Records
Season 1910-11

Top scorers: Div 1, A.Shepherd (Newcastle United) 25 goals; Div 2, R.Whittingham (Chelsea) 31 goals.
Grimsby Town failed to gain re-election, Huddersfield Town were elected in their place.

LEAGUE TABLES

DIVISION 1

	P	W	D	L	F	A	W	D	L	F	A	Pts
Manchester U	38	14	4	1	47	18	8	4	7	25	22	52
Aston Villa	38	15	3	1	50	18	7	4	8	19	23	51
Sunderland	38	10	6	3	44	22	5	9	5	23	26	45
Everton	38	12	3	4	34	17	7	4	8	16	19	45
Bradford C	38	13	1	5	33	16	7	4	8	18	26	45
Sheffield W	38	10	5	4	24	15	7	3	9	23	33	42
Oldham A	38	13	4	2	30	12	3	5	11	14	29	41
Newcastle U	38	8	7	4	37	18	7	3	9	24	25	40
Sheffield U	38	8	3	8	27	21	7	5	7	22	22	38
Woolwich A	38	9	6	4	24	14	4	6	9	17	35	38
Notts Co	38	9	6	4	21	16	5	4	10	16	29	38
Blackburn R	38	12	2	5	40	14	1	9	9	22	40	37
Liverpool	38	11	3	5	38	19	4	4	11	15	34	37
Preston N.E.	38	8	5	6	25	19	4	6	9	15	30	35
Tottenham H	38	10	5	4	40	23	3	1	15	12	40	32
Middlesbrough	38	9	5	5	31	21	2	5	12	18	42	32
Manchester C	38	7	5	7	26	26	2	8	9	17	32	31
Bury	38	8	9	2	27	18	1	2	16	16	53	29
Bristol C	38	8	4	7	23	21	3	1	15	20	45	27
Nottingham F	38	5	4	10	28	31	4	3	12	27	44	25

DIVISION 2

	P	W	D	L	F	A	W	D	L	F	A	Pts
W.B.A.	38	14	2	3	40	18	8	7	4	27	23	53
Bolton W	38	17	2	0	53	12	4	7	8	16	28	51
Chelsea	38	17	2	0	48	7	3	7	9	23	28	49
Clapton O	38	14	4	1	28	7	5	3	11	16	28	45
Hull C	38	8	10	1	38	21	6	6	7	17	18	44
Derby Co	38	11	5	3	48	24	6	3	10	25	28	42
Blackpool	38	10	5	4	29	15	6	5	8	20	23	42
Burnley	38	9	9	1	31	18	4	6	9	14	27	41
Wolverhampton W	38	10	5	4	26	16	5	3	11	25	36	38
Fulham	38	12	3	4	35	15	3	4	12	17	33	37
Leeds U	38	11	4	4	35	18	4	3	12	23	38	37
Bradford P.A.	38	12	4	3	44	18	2	5	12	9	37	37
Huddersfield T	38	10	4	5	35	21	3	4	12	22	37	34
Glossop N.E.	38	11	4	4	36	21	2	4	13	12	41	34
Leicester C	38	12	3	4	37	19	2	2	15	15	43	33
Birmingham C	38	10	4	5	23	18	2	4	13	19	46	32
Stockport Co	38	10	4	5	27	26	1	4	14	20	53	30
Gainsborough T	38	9	5	5	26	16	0	6	13	11	39	29
Barnsley	38	5	7	7	36	26	2	7	10	16	36	28
Lincoln C	38	5	7	7	16	23	2	3	14	12	49	24

Enoch 'Knocker' West, who was Manchester United's leading scorer when they won the Division One title in 1910-11 but was later banned for life for allegedly helping to 'fix' a game.

DIVISION 1

	ASTON VILLA	BLACKBURN R	BRADFORD C	BRISTOL C	BURY	EVERTON	LIVERPOOL	MANCHESTER C	MANCHESTER U	MIDDLESBROUGH	NEWCASTLE U	NOTTINGHAM F	NOTTS CO	OLDHAM A	PRESTON N.E.	SHEFFIELD U	SHEFFIELD W	SUNDERLAND	TOTTENHAM H	W ARSENAL
1 ASTON VILLA		O01 2-2	J28 4-1	M11 2-0	D26 4-1	M27 2-1	D24 1-1	O15 2-1	a22 4-2	N26 5-0	N12 3-2	F11 3-1	D10 3-1	S03 1-1	a08 0-2	a14 3-0	O29 2-1	J07 2-1	F25 4-0	S17 3-0
2 BLACKBURN R	a24 0-0		O22 3-0	a08 2-0	J21 6-2	a06 0-1	S10 1-2	N12 2-0	D31 1-0	D24 5-1	D10 3-1	M27 4-1	S01 1-1	O29 1-0	J02 0-1	S24 1-2	N26 6-1	O08 0-1	a22 3-0	F18 1-0
3 BRADFORD C	S24 1-2	F28 1-0		N26 3-1	S10 2-2	N12 3-1	D31 1-3	M14 1-0	D27 1-0	a27 1-0	a08 1-0	O29 2-1	a17 0-1	O15 1-2	D24 1-0	J21 0-1	a04 5-2	a11 3-0	D10 3-0	O08 3-0
4 BRISTOL C	N05 1-2	D03 1-0	a01 0-2		O22 2-0	a29 0-1	F18 1-1	D17 2-1	O08 0-1	J21 3-2	D31 1-0	a15 5-1	F04 1-0	D27 3-2	S24 0-0	M04 0-2	D26 2-2	M18 1-1	S10 0-2	N19 0-1
5 BURY	J02 1-0	S17 2-2	J07 0-1	F25 2-1		F11 0-0	D10 3-0	O01 5-2	a08 0-3	N12 4-2	O29 1-1	J28 1-0	N26 0-0	D17 2-2	M25 1-0	a29 1-1	O15 1-1	a14 0-0	M11 2-1	S03 1-1
6 EVERTON	O22 0-1	N19 6-1	M18 0-0	D24 4-3	O08 2-1		D27 0-1	D03 1-0	S24 0-1	D31 2-0	J02 1-5	a14 2-1	J21 5-0	D10 1-0	S10 2-0	F18 1-0	a22 1-1	M04 2-2	S01 2-0	N05 2-0
7 LIVERPOOL	a29 3-1	J07 2-2	S03 1-2	O15 4-0	a15 2-0	O01 0-2		J28 1-1	N26 3-2	M11 3-0	F27 3-0	S17 2-3	M25 2-1	a08 1-0	N12 3-0	D17 2-0	F11 3-0	D26 1-2	O29 1-2	a17 1-1
8 MANCHESTER C	F18 1-1	M18 0-0	N05 1-3	a22 1-2	S01 5-1	a08 2-1	S24 1-2		J21 1-1	a14 2-1	D24 2-0	N19 1-0	S10 0-1	N26 2-0	D31 0-2	O08 0-4	D10 1-2	O22 3-3	J03 2-1	M04 1-1
9 MANCHESTER U	D17 2-0	S03 3-2	J02 1-0	F11 3-1	D03 3-2	J28 2-2	a01 2-0	S17 2-1		O29 1-2	O15 2-0	J07 4-2	N12 0-0	M25 0-0	M11 5-0	a15 1-1	O01 3-2	a29 5-1	M15 3-2	D26 5-0
10 MIDDLESBROUGH	a01 0-1	a29 2-3	D17 3-2	S17 3-0	M18 2-1	S03 1-0	N05 2-2	D26 0-0	M04 2-2		J28 0-2	J02 2-2	O22 4-1	F11 1-2	F18 2-0	N19 3-1	J07 0-1	D03 1-0	O01 2-0	a15 1-1
11 NEWCASTLE U	M18 1-0	a15 2-2	D03 6-1	S03 0-1	M04 5-1	D26 1-0	O22 6-1	a29 3-3	F18 0-1	S24 0-0		D17 4-1	O08 2-0	J07 3-0	J03 1-1	N05 1-1	a14 0-2	N19 1-1	J21 1-1	a01 0-1
12 NOTTINGHAM F	O08 3-1	N05 5-2	M04 0-2	D10 3-3	S24 1-2	N26 1-1	J21 2-0	M25 0-0	S10 2-1	D27 1-1	a05 0-1		D31 0-2	N12 4-1	O06 1-3	F04 1-2	a08 0-1	F18 1-3	D24 1-2	O22 2-3
13 NOTTS CO	a15 1-2	a14 2-0	D26 1-1	O01 2-0	a01 1-0	S17 0-0	N19 1-0	J07 0-1	M18 1-0	a18 1-0	F11 2-2	S03 1-1		M11 1-0	O29 3-3	D03 0-3	J28 2-0	D17 1-1	O15 1-0	a29 0-2
14 OLDHAM A	D31 1-1	M04 2-0	F18 1-0	a14 1-0	a22 0-0	a15 2-0	D03 3-1	a01 1-1	N19 1-3	O08 1-1	S10 0-2	M18 2-0	N05 2-1		O22 2-1	a17 3-0	D24 1-0	J21 2-1	S24 2-0	M06 3-0
15 PRESTON N.E.	D03 0-1	D26 0-0	a29 2-0	J28 4-0	N19 2-0	J07 0-2	M18 2-1	S03 1-1	N05 0-2	O15 1-1	O01 2-1	S01 0-2	M04 2-0	F25 1-1		a01 1-1	S17 1-3	a15 0-2	F11 2-0	D17 4-1
16 SHEFFIELD U	D28 2-1	J28 1-1	S17 0-1	O29 0-4	D24 3-0	O15 0-1	S19 2-0	F11 2-2	D10 2-0	M27 2-1	a03 0-0	O01 0-1	a08 0-2	D26 1-2	N26 5-0		F25 0-1	S03 1-2	N12 3-0	J07 3-2
17 SHEFFIELD W	M04 1-0	a01 1-0	N19 0-1	J02 2-1	F18 1-0	D17 0-2	O08 1-0	a15 4-1	a17 0-0	S10 1-1	D27 0-2	D03 5-2	S24 1-3	a29 2-0	J21 0-0	O22 2-0		N05 1-1	D31 2-1	M18 0-0
18 SUNDERLAND	S10 3-2	F11 2-2	O01 1-1	N12 3-1	F04 4-1	O29 4-0	J02 4-0	F25 4-0	D24 1-2	a08 3-1	S01 2-1	O15 2-2	a22 1-1	S17 2-1	D10 1-1	D31 0-2	M11 1-2		N26 4-0	J28 2-2
19 TOTTENHAM H	N19 1-2	D17 2-2	a15 2-0	J07 3-2	N05 5-0	a17 0-1	M04 1-0	D27 1-1	O22 2-2	F13 6-2	S17 1-2	D26 1-4	F18 3-0	M27 2-0	O08 1-1	M18 2-1	S03 3-1	a01 1-1		D03 3-1
20 W ARSENAL	M15 1-1	O15 4-1	F11 0-0	M25 3-0	D31 3-2	M11 1-0	a14 0-0	O29 0-1	S01 1-2	D10 0-2	N26 1-2	F25 3-2	D24 2-1	O01 0-0	a22 2-0	S10 0-0	N12 1-0	S24 0-0	a08 2-0	

DIVISION 2

	BARNSLEY	BIRMINGHAM	BLACKPOOL	BOLTON W	BRADFORD	BURNLEY	CHELSEA	CLAPTON O	DERBY CO	FULHAM	GAINSBOROUGH T	GLOSSOP	HUDDERSFIELD T	HULL C	LEEDS C	LEICESTER F	LINCOLN C	STOCKPORT CO	W.B.A.	WOLVERHAMPTON W
1 BARNSLEY		F25 2-3	J28 1-2	a17 0-0	M25 7-0	N26 0-1	J07 3-2	S17 1-2	D24 0-2	N12 4-2	a08 2-2	O01 4-0	N17 1-2	M11 0-1	D10 4-0	a14 1-1	F11 2-2	a22 1-1	O29 1-1	S03 2-2
2 BIRMINGHAM	O22 1-0		a01 2-0	a29 2-1	S10 1-0	J21 1-1	M18 2-1	N19 0-1	F18 2-0	D31 1-1	S24 1-1	D03 1-2	D17 2-1	a14 1-0	F04 2-1	M04 1-0	a15 0-1	O08 1-3	D27 1-1	N05 1-3
3 BLACKPOOL	S24 1-0	N26 3-1		O29 1-1	D24 4-1	a14 1-0	F18 0-2	O22 1-1	J21 0-1	a22 1-2	J02 1-1	M11 1-0	M25 1-1	D10 2-0	D31 1-2	M29 2-0	N12 5-1	S10 2-1	a08 0-0	O08 2-0
4 BOLTON W	J02 4-0	D24 5-1	M04 1-0		O08 1-0	O22 1-1	a26 2-0	F18 2-0	a22 2-1	S24 2-0	N05 3-0	M18 4-0	D03 3-1	S10 2-1	N19 3-0	D31 6-2	a01 3-1	S01 2-2	S05 3-1	J21 4-1
5 BRADFORD	N19 2-3	J07 2-2	a29 1-0	F11 1-1		F18 1-1	a15 2-1	D17 3-0	M18 2-1	O01 1-0	O22 5-0	D26 6-0	S03 0-1	J28 2-0	M04 0-2	a01 3-1	J02 6-0	N05 3-2	S17 3-3	D03 1-0
6 BURNLEY	a01 0-0	S17 2-2	D26 1-1	M20 1-3	O15 1-1		D17 1-1	a29 2-0	N19 2-1	F11 1-0	M04 1-1	S05 0-0	J07 2-1	O01 0-0	N05 4-1	D03 2-1	S03 3-1	M18 5-3	J28 2-0	a15 1-1
7 CHELSEA	S10 3-1	N12 2-2	O15 0-0	O01 3-0	D10 3-0	a22 3-0		F11 1-0	D31 3-2	a08 2-0	D24 3-0	M06 2-0	M20 2-0	N26 2-0	a14 4-1	J21 2-0	O29 7-0	D27 2-0	M29 2-1	S24 2-0
8 CLAPTON O	J21 3-0	M25 2-1	F25 2-1	O15 0-0	a22 1-0	D24 0-2	O08 0-0		S10 1-0	D10 1-0	D26 1-0	O29 4-0	N12 2-0	a08 1-1	a17 1-0	S24 3-1	M11 2-0	D31 1-0	N26 0-0	M20 3-1
9 DERBY CO	a29 5-1	O15 1-0	S17 1-1	D17 2-2	N12 4-2	M25 3-0	S03 1-4	J07 3-1		M15 2-2	N26 4-0	J28 2-1	O08 1-1	O29 2-3	a08 2-2	D26 3-0	O01 5-0	D10 4-1	M01 1-3	D27 2-0
10 FULHAM	M18 0-2	S03 3-0	D17 2-1	J28 2-0	F13 4-0	O08 3-0	D03 1-0	a15 1-1	N05 3-1		F18 1-0	a29 2-2	D26 2-1	S17 0-1	O22 2-1	N19 3-1	a17 0-0	M04 6-2	J07 0-1	a01 0-1
11 GAINSBOROUGH T	O26 1-1	J28 1-0	D27 2-0	M11 1-0	F25 1-2	O29 1-2	a29 3-1	a14 3-1	a01 0-0	O15 0-1		S03 3-0	S17 3-1	F11 1-1	M18 1-2	a15 2-0	J07 1-0	F04 0-0	O01 1-1	D17 1-3
12 GLOSSOP	M28 1-1	a08 2-1	N05 3-1	N12 1-2	a14 0-1	J02 1-1	O22 2-1	M04 1-3	S24 2-2	D24 2-1	D31 3-1		N26 5-2	a22 0-0	S10 2-1	O08 1-0	M25 2-0	J21 3-0	D10 0-2	F18 5-1
13 HUDDERSFIELD T	F18 2-0	a22 7-1	F04 2-2	D10 1-1	D31 0-0	S10 0-1	a18 3-1	M18 2-0	F11 0-3	F28 1-2	J21 2-1	a01 1-0		J02 2-0	S24 3-2	O22 1-2	a08 1-1	J14 4-1	D24 0-2	M04 3-1
14 HULL C	N05 5-1	D26 4-1	a15 1-1	J07 1-1	S24 2-2	D27 3-0	a01 1-1	D03 1-2	M04 2-0	J21 0-0	O08 3-2	D17 1-0	a17 2-2		F18 1-1	M18 2-2	a29 2-1	O22 4-1	S03 1-1	N19 2-2
15 LEEDS C	a15 0-0	O01 1-1	S03 1-2	M25 1-0	O29 2-0	M27 0-0	D26 3-3	D27 1-0	D03 3-2	F25 3-1	N12 4 0	J07 0-2	J28 5-2	O15 1-0		D17 2-3	S17 0-1	a01 4-0	F11 3-1	a29 1-0
16 LEICESTER F	D27 1-1	O29 2-0	O01 2-0	S03 5-0	N26 2-0	a08 1-1	S17 1-0	J28 2-1	a17 1-2	M25 3-2	D10 1-0	F11 1-1	F25 2-1	N12 0-2	a22 2-1		O15 2-0	D24 5-1	M11 2-3	J07 2-3
17 LINCOLN C	O08 1-0	D10 0-1	M18 0-1	N26 1-3	S01 0-0	D31 1-0	M04 0-0	N05 0-0	F08 0-2	a14 1-0	S10 0-0	S14 2-2	D27 2-2	D24 1-4	J21 1-1	F18 2-0		S24 2-0	a22 1-2	O22 1-5
18 STOCKPORT CO	D17 2-2	F13 3-1	J07 1-3	F25 0-1	M11 1-0	N12 4-2	J02 2-2	S03 0-3	a15 3-2	O29 1-1	M25 1-0	S17 2-1	O03 1-0	a24 1-1	N26 0-4	a29 1-0	J28 3-2		O15 0-1	a14 1-0
19 W.B.A.	M04 3-3	a17 1-0	D03 0-1	D26 2-0	J21 3-0	S24 2-1	N19 1-3	a01 3-0	O22 1-1	S10 2-1	a18 2-1	a15 3-1	a29 1-0	D31 0-2	O08 2-0	N05 5-1	D17 3-0	F18 4-2		M18 2-1
20 WOLVERHAMPTON W	D31 1-0	M11 3-1	F11 0-3	S17 3-0	a08 0-0	D10 1-0	J28 0-0	O01 1-0	S05 1-2	N26 5-1	a22 1-1	O15 2-0	O29 0-3	M25 0-0	D24 3-1	S10 1-0	a24 2-1	D26 0-0	N12 2-3	

Football League Records
Season 1911-12

Top scorers: Div 1, H.Hampton (Aston Villa), G.Holley (Sunderland), D.McLean (Sheffield Wednesday) 25 goals; Div 2, B.Freeman (Burnley) 32 goals.

Lincoln City failed to gain re-election, Grimsby Town were elected in their place.

DIVISION 1

	ASTON VILLA	BLACKBURN R	BOLTON W	BRADFORD C	BURY	EVERTON	LIVERPOOL	MANCHESTER C	MANCHESTER U	MIDDLESBROUGH	NEWCASTLE U	NOTTS CO	OLDHAM A	PRESTON N.E.	SHEFFIELD U	SHEFFIELD W	SUNDERLAND	TOTTENHAM H	W.B.A.	W ARSENAL
1 ASTON VILLA		F17 0-3	a05 0-1	D30 0-0	M02 5-2	S23 3-0	D02 5-0	J20 3-1	M30 6-0	N04 2-1	a20 2-0	M16 5-1	D26 6-1	D09 1-0	D23 1-0	O21 2-3	O07 1-3	N18 2-2	S04 0-3	S09 4-1
2 BLACKBURN R	O14 3-1		N11 2-0	M23 3-1	S02 2-0	D09 2-1	F10 1-0	a06 2-0	S30 2-2	J06 2-1	a27 1-1	S16 0-0	a15 1-0	J01 3-0	O28 1-0	D25 0-0	D23 2-2	J27 0-0	a25 4-1	N25 4-0
3 BOLTON W	J01 3-0	M16 2-0		F14 2-0	M30 1-0	O21 1-2	S04 2-1	F17 2-1	a27 1-1	D02 1-0	S02 0-2	a13 3-0	S16 2-1	J27 3-0	J06 0-3	N18 4-2	N04 3-0	D16 1-0	M02 2-0	O07 2-2
4 BRADFORD C	S02 2-1	N18 1-0	S30 1-0		D02 1-0	M02 1-0	a08 0-2	O21 4-1	D26 0-1	a13 2-1	a09 1-1	D16 2-3	J27 0-0	F10 0-1	S16 1-0	M30 5-1	M16 2-1	a27 3-0	N04 4-1	F17 1-1
5 BURY	O28 1-1	D30 1-2	N25 1-3	a06 2-0		D23 1-2	F24 2-2	a20 1-2	O14 0-1	J27 0-2	M09 2-1	S30 0-1	M23 1-1	S16 0-0	F20 3-1	S09 2-2	D25 0-2	F10 2-1	J01 1-0	D09 3-1
6 EVERTON	J27 1-1	a13 1-3	F28 1-0	O28 1-0	a27 1-1		S16 2-1	N11 1-0	J06 4-0	D26 1-0	S30 2-0	a08 1-1	O14 1-1	M23 1-0	F10 3-2	D16 1-0	D02 1-0	S02 2-2	a22 3-0	M27 1-0
7 LIVERPOOL	a06 1-2	O07 1-2	D25 1-0	J01 1-0	O21 1-1	J20 1-3		S09 2-2	N18 3-2	M02 1-1	D09 0-1	N04 3-0	D23 1-0	N25 0-1	a20 2-0	F17 1-1	a05 2-1	M16 1-2	S23 1-3	D30 4-1
8 MANCHESTER C	S16 2-6	D02 3-0	O14 3-1	M28 4-0	D16 2-0	M16 4-0	J06 2-3		S02 0-0	a27 2-0	J27 1-1	D26 4-0	F10 1-3	M09 0-0	S30 0-0	a13 4-0	M30 2-0	a05 2-1	N18 0-2	O28 3-3
9 MANCHESTER U	N25 3-1	a29 3-1	D23 2-0	D25 0-1	F17 0-0	S09 2-1	M23 1-1	D30 0-0		O21 3-4	a06 0-2	M02 2-0	a20 3-1	N11 0-0	D09 1-0	O07 3-1	S23 2-2	N04 1-2	J20 1-2	J01 2-0
10 MIDDLESBROUGH	M09 1-2	S09 2-1	a06 1-0	D09 1-0	S23 1-1	D25 0-0	O28 3-2	D23 3-1	a17 3-0		N11 1-1	F10 4-0	N25 3-0	S30 4-2	M23 1-1	J20 1-1	D30 3-3	O14 2-0	a05 1-0	F24 0-2
11 NEWCASTLE U	D16 6-2	O21 4-2	D30 5-2	S09 0-2	N04 3-2	S06 2-0	a13 1-1	S23 1-0	D02 2-3	M16 0-1		N18 3-2	a05 1-1	F24 1-0	D26 2-2	M02 0-2	F17 3-1	M30 2-0	O07 0-0	J20 1-2
12 NOTTS CO	M13 2-0	J20 1-3	D09 3-2	O05 0-0	F14 2-0	a05 0-1	M09 0-0	D25 0-1	O28 0-1	O07 2-1	M23 1-4		a06 1-1	O14 1-2	N25 2-0	S23 1-0	S09 3-1	F24 2-2	D30 2-0	D23 3-1
13 OLDHAM A	a08 1-2	N04 0-1	J20 3-1	S23 3-0	N18 2-0	F17 3-0	a27 0-1	O07 4-1	D16 2-2	M30 2-0	D25 2-4	D02 1-2		J06 1-0	S02 2-3	M16 1-0	M02 0-0	a13 2-1	O21 3-1	M09 0-0
14 PRESTON N.E.	a13 4-1	D26 2-2	S23 1-2	O07 2-2	J20 1-0	N18 2-1	M30 2-1	N04 2-1	M16 0-0	a22 0-3	D23 2-1	F17 2-1	S09 0-1		a05 3-0	D30 2-3	a20 0-3	M02 0-1	D02 1-1	O21 0-1
15 SHEFFIELD U	O23 0-1	M02 1-1	S09 0-5	M04 7-3	M16 4-0	O07 2-1	D16 3-1	F26 6-2	a13 6-1	N18 1-1	J01 2-1	M30 1-3	D30 4-0	D28 4-2		N04 1-1	O21 1-2	D02 1-2	F17 1-1	S23 2-1
16 SHEFFIELD W	F24 3-0	a08 1-1	M23 0-1	N25 4-2	M18 2-1	a20 1-3	O14 2-2	D09 3-0	F10 3-0	S16 0-2	O28 1-2	J27 3-0	N11 1-0	S02 0-1	M09 1-1		D26 8-0	S30 4-0	D23 4-1	a06 3-0
17 SUNDERLAND	F10 2-2	S06 3-0	M09 0-1	N11 1-1	a08 1-0	a06 4-0	S30 1-2	N25 1-1	J27 5-0	S02 1-0	O14 1-2	J06 5-0	O28 4-2	D16 3-0	F28 0-0	J01 0-0		S16 1-1	D09 3-2	M23 1-0
18 TOTTENHAM H	M23 2-1	S23 0-2	a20 1-0	D23 2-3	O07 2-1	D30 0-1	N11 2-0	a08 0-2	a09 1-1	F17 2-1	N25 1-2	O21 2-2	D09 4-0	O28 6-2	a06 1-1	S04 3-1	J20 0-0		S09 1-0	D25 5-0
19 W.B.A.	S30 2-2	D16 2-0	O28 0-0	a26 0-0	D26 2-0	N25 1-0	J27 1-0	M23 1-1	S16 1-0	a08 3-1	F10 3-1	S02 2-1	a29 0-0	a09 0-2	O14 0-1	a27 1-5	a13 1-0	M13 2-0		N11 1-1
20 W ARSENAL	J06 2-2	a22 5-1	F10 3-0	O14 2-0	a13 1-0	N04 0-1	S02 2-2	M02 2-0	a05 2-1	D16 3-1	S16 2-0	a27 0-3	S30 1-1	a08 4-1	J27 3-1	D02 0-2	N18 3-0	D26 3-1	M16 0-2	

LEAGUE TABLES

DIVISION 1

	P	W	D	L	F	A	W	D	L	F	A	Pts
Blackburn R	38	13	6	0	35	10	7	3	9	25	33	49
Everton	38	13	5	1	29	12	7	1	11	17	30	46
Newcastle U	38	10	4	5	37	25	8	4	7	27	25	44
Bolton W	38	14	2	3	35	15	6	1	12	19	28	43
Sheffield W	38	11	3	5	44	17	5	6	8	25	32	41
Aston Villa	38	12	2	5	48	22	5	5	9	28	41	41
Middlesbrough	38	11	6	2	35	17	5	2	12	21	28	40
Sunderland	38	10	6	3	37	14	4	5	10	21	37	39
W.B.A.	38	10	6	3	23	15	5	3	11	20	32	39
Woolwich A	38	12	3	4	38	19	3	5	11	17	40	38
Bradford C	38	12	3	4	31	15	3	5	11	15	35	38
Tottenham H	38	10	4	5	35	20	4	5	10	18	33	37
Manchester U	38	9	5	5	29	19	4	6	9	16	41	37
Sheffield U	38	10	4	5	47	29	3	6	10	16	27	36
Manchester C	38	10	5	4	39	20	3	4	12	17	38	35
Notts Co	38	9	4	6	26	20	5	3	11	20	43	35
Liverpool	38	8	4	7	27	23	4	6	9	22	32	34
Oldham A	38	10	3	6	32	19	2	7	10	14	35	34
Preston N.E.	38	8	4	7	26	25	5	3	11	14	32	33
Bury	38	6	5	8	23	25	0	4	15	9	34	21

DIVISION 2

	P	W	D	L	F	A	W	D	L	F	A	Pts
Derby Co	38	15	2	2	55	13	8	6	5	19	15	54
Chelsea	38	15	2	2	36	13	9	4	6	28	21	54
Burnley	38	14	5	0	50	14	8	3	8	27	27	52
Clapton O	38	16	0	3	44	14	5	3	11	17	30	45
Wolverhampton W	38	12	3	4	41	10	4	7	8	16	23	42
Barnsley	38	10	5	4	28	19	5	7	7	17	23	42
Hull C	38	12	3	4	36	13	5	5	9	18	38	42
Fulham	38	10	3	6	42	24	6	4	9	24	34	39
Grimsby T	38	9	6	4	24	18	6	3	10	24	37	39
Leicester C	38	11	4	4	34	18	4	3	12	15	48	37
Bradford P.A.	38	10	5	4	30	16	3	4	12	14	29	35
Birmingham C	38	11	3	5	44	29	3	3	13	11	30	34
Bristol C	38	11	4	4	27	17	3	2	14	14	43	34
Blackpool	38	12	4	3	24	12	1	4	14	8	40	34
Nottingham F	38	9	3	7	26	18	4	4	11	20	30	33
Stockport Co	38	8	5	6	31	22	3	6	10	16	32	33
Huddersfield T	38	8	5	6	30	22	5	1	13	20	42	32
Glossop N.E.	38	6	8	5	33	23	2	4	13	9	33	28
Leeds U	38	7	6	6	21	22	3	2	14	29	56	28
Gainsborough T	38	4	6	9	17	22	1	7	11	13	42	23

DIVISION 2

	BARNSLEY	BIRMINGHAM	BLACKPOOL	BRADFORD P.A.	BRISTOL C	BURNLEY	CHELSEA	CLAPTON O	DERBY CO	FULHAM	GAINSBOROUGH T	GLOSSOP	GRIMSBY T	HUDDERSFIELD T	HULL C	LEEDS C	LEICESTER F	NOTTINGHAM F	STOCKPORT CO	WOLVERHAMPTON W
1 BARNSLEY		a08 1-0	S09 1-0	F10 1-0	D25 4-1	S30 1-1	a25 0-2	D23 2-1	a22 0-2	O14 2-2	N25 4-0	a29 1-0	a06 2-2	J01 0-0	S23 1-2	a11 3-4	M23 0-0	D09 1-0	O28 2-1	N11 2-1
2 BIRMINGHAM	S11 1-3		D16 2-1	S02 2-3	N25 0-0	a06 4-0	N11 1-4	M23 4-0	S16 0-4	J06 1-3	F03 2-2	a27 2-0	O28 2-2	a13 1-0	D26 5-1	S30 4-3	O14 4-0	M09 4-2	J27 2-0	F10 3-1
3 BLACKPOOL	J06 0-0	a20 1-0		S16 0-4	D09 1-0	a05 0-0	N25 1-0	a06 1-0	S30 1-0	J27 3-1	M09 0-0	J01 2-0	N11 1-2	D23 3-1	S02 3-2	O14 3-0	O28 1-1	M23 2-0	F10 0-1	a17 1-0
4 BRADFORD	O07 1-0	D30 3-0	F06 0-0		a05 0-1	O14 2-1	D23 1-1	D25 2-1	O28 0-1	M27 0-2	a06 5-0	S23 1-1	D09 4-1	S09 3-1	M20 3-1	N11 1-1	N25 1-1	a20 2-1	M09 1-0	M23 0-2
5 BRISTOL C	D26 0-1	M30 2-1	a13 2-0	a08 1-0		M23 0-3	M09 1-1	N11 1-0	J06 1-1	S02 1-0	O14 2-0	D16 2-0	F24 3-0	D02 3-2	a27 0-0	J27 4-1	F10 0-1	O28 2-2	S16 2-1	S30 0-3
6 BURNLEY	F12 3-0	D02 1-1	D25 1-1	F17 3-1	N18 4-2		O21 2-2	N04 1-0	M16 0-0	M02 5-1	S09 2-0	D30 4-0	S23 1-1	a20 3-0	J20 5-1	S04 4-2	S11 3-0	O07 2-0	M30 4-1	D23 2-1
7 CHELSEA	D16 2-1	M16 0-2	a22 4-1	a27 1-0	N04 2-2	F24 0-2		M02 3-0	S11 1-0	D26 1-0	S30 1-0	D02 1-0	F10 4-1	N18 3-1	a13 1-0	J06 4-2	J27 2-1	O14 2-0	S02 0-0	S16 4-0
8 CLAPTON O	a27 2-0	N18 2-0	D02 2-0	D26 2-0	M16 4-0	M09 1-2	O28 1-4		S02 3-0	a08 4-0	F10 3-0	a13 2-1	O14 1-0	M30 2-1	D16 4-0	S16 2-1	S30 4-1	F24 0-2	J06 4-2	J27 1-0
9 DERBY CO	O21 0-0	F21 0-1	F24 5-1	M02 1-0	S09 3-0	D06 2-0	a08 2-0	D30 5-1		N04 6-1	a20 4-0	O07 5-0	D25 2-1	S23 4-2	F17 2-3	N25 5-2	D09 5-0	a09 1-0	M23 2-0	a06 1-1
10 FULHAM	F17 2-2	S09 2-1	S23 3-0	O21 2-0	D30 2-1	O28 3-4	D25 0-1	a05 0-2	a15 0-0		D09 7-1	a01 0-2	a20 1-3	J20 3-1	O07 0-1	M23 7-2	a06 4-1	D23 2-0	N11 3-1	N25 1-1
11 GAINSBOROUGH T	a10 1-2	O21 0-0	N04 0-0	a24 0-0	F17 2-3	J06 1-0	M20 0-2	O07 0-2	D16 1-1	a13 0-1		M16 1-1	J20 2-3	M02 5-0	O25 0-3	D26 2-1	S02 0-1	S23 1-2	a27 0-0	a05 1-0
12 GLOSSOP	S16 0-2	D23 2-0	D26 1-1	J27 0-0	a20 3-0	S02 1-3	a06 1-2	D09 3-3	F10 3-1	S30 1-1	N11 1-1		M23 5-2	a05 2-3	J06 1-1	F24 2-1	M09 6-0	N25 0-0	O14 1-1	O28 0-1
13 GRIMSBY T	S26 0-0	M02 1-0	M16 1-0	D02 0-0	O21 3-0	J27 1-0	O07 2-1	F17 2-1	D23 0-3	D16 1-0	S16 3-3	a08 0-0		N04 1-2	M30 1-0	J23 1-2	J06 4-0	M21 1-4	D26 2-2	S02 0-0
14 HUDDERSFIELD T	S02 2-1	D09 3-2	a27 4-0	J06 3-1	a06 1-2	D16 1-1	M23 1-3	N25 0-0	J27 0-0	S16 2-0	O28 2-2	D25 3-1	M09 2-0		a09 0-2	F10 1-2	F24 1-2	N11 1-2	S30 2-0	O14 1-1
15 HULL C	J27 0-0	D25 4-0	D30 3-0	S30 5-1	D23 3-0	S16 4-1	D09 1-0	a20 0-2	O14 0-0	F10 2-3	M23 1-1	S09 2-0	N25 1-0	a08 0-1		O28 1-0	N11 4-1	a06 2-1	F24 0-2	M09 3-0
16 LEEDS C	N04 3-2	a05 0-0	F17 1-0	M16 1-2	S23 3-1	D09 1-5	S09 0-0	J20 0-2	M30 0-1	N18 0-2	D25 0-0	O21 2-1	D04 1-2	O07 2-0	M02 0-0		D23 2-1	D30 3-1	a06 1-1	a20 1-1
17 LEICESTER F	N18 0-0	F17 5-2	M02 4-0	M30 3-0	O07 2-0	a08 3-2	S23 2-0	a09 2-0	a13 0-1	D02 2-5	S04 2-0	N04 1-0	S09 0-2	O21 0-2	M16 3-0	a27 2-1		F29 1-1	D16 1-1	D25 1-1
18 NOTTINGHAM F	a13 0-2	N04 0-1	N18 2-1	D16 2-1	M02 2-0	F10 0-1	F17 2-3	O21 3-0	D26 1-3	a27 1-1	J27 2-0	M30 0-1	S30 1-0	M16 3-0	D02 0-0	S02 2-1	S16 4-1		a08 1-2	J06 0-0
19 STOCKPORT CO	M02 1-1	S23 2-0	O07 1-2	N04 1-0	J20 1-0	N25 0-1	D30 0-1	S09 1-1	J01 4-0	M16 2-1	D23 0-3	F17 3-0	a05 3-0	F03 3-1	O21 1-1	a15 3-3	a20 2-3	D25 2-2		D09 1-2
20 WOLVERHAMPTON W	M16 5-0	O07 1-0	O21 3-0	N18 1-1	S04 3-1	a27 2-0	J20 3-1	S23 0-1	D02 0-1	M30 0-0	a08 1-0	M02 1-1	D30 1-2	F17 1-2	N04 8-0	D16 5-0	D26 1-0	S09 1-0	a13 4-0	

Cultured England full-back Bob Crompton, skipper of Blackburn Rovers in 1911-12 when they lifted their first League Championship title.

FOOTBALL LEAGUE RECORDS
SEASON 1912-13

Top scorers: Div 1, D.McLean (Sheffield Wednesday) 30 goals; Div 2, B.Freeman (Burnley) 31 goals.
Gainsborough Trinity failed to gain re-election, Lincoln City were elected in their place.

LEAGUE TABLES

DIVISION 1

	P	W	D	L	F	A	W	D	L	F	A	Pts
Sunderland	38	14	2	3	47	17	11	2	6	39	26	54
Aston Villa	38	13	4	2	57	21	6	8	5	29	31	50
Sheffield W	38	12	4	3	44	23	9	3	7	31	32	49
Manchester U	38	13	3	3	41	14	6	5	8	28	29	46
Blackburn R	38	10	5	4	54	21	6	8	5	25	22	45
Manchester C	38	12	3	4	34	15	6	5	8	19	22	44
Derby Co	38	10	2	7	40	29	7	6	6	29	37	42
Bolton W	38	10	6	3	36	20	6	4	9	26	43	42
Oldham A	38	11	7	1	33	12	3	7	9	17	43	42
W.B.A.	38	8	7	4	30	20	5	5	9	27	30	38
Everton	38	8	2	9	28	31	7	5	7	20	23	37
Liverpool	38	12	2	5	40	24	4	3	12	21	47	37
Bradford C	38	10	5	4	33	22	2	6	11	17	38	35
Newcastle U	38	8	5	6	30	23	5	3	11	17	24	34
Sheffield U	38	10	5	4	36	24	4	1	14	20	46	34
Middlesbrough	38	6	9	4	29	22	5	1	13	26	47	32
Tottenham H	38	9	3	7	28	25	3	3	13	17	47	30
Chelsea	38	7	2	10	29	40	4	4	11	22	33	28
Notts Co	38	6	4	9	19	20	1	5	13	9	36	23
Woolwich A	38	1	8	10	11	31	2	4	13	15	43	18

DIVISION 2

	P	W	D	L	F	A	W	D	L	F	A	Pts
Preston N.E.	38	13	5	1	34	12	6	10	3	22	21	53
Burnley	38	13	4	2	58	23	8	4	7	30	30	50
Birmingham C	38	11	6	2	39	18	7	4	8	20	26	46
Barnsley	38	15	3	1	46	18	4	4	11	11	29	45
Huddersfield T	38	13	5	1	49	12	4	4	11	17	28	43
Leeds U	38	12	3	4	45	22	3	7	9	25	42	40
Grimsby T	38	10	8	1	32	11	5	2	12	19	39	40
Lincoln C	38	10	6	3	31	16	5	4	10	19	36	40
Fulham	38	13	5	1	47	16	4	0	15	18	39	39
Wolverhampton W	38	10	6	3	34	16	4	4	11	22	38	38
Bury	38	10	6	3	29	14	5	2	12	24	43	38
Hull C	38	12	2	5	42	19	3	4	12	18	37	36
Bradford P.A.	38	12	4	3	47	18	2	4	13	13	42	36
Clapton O	38	8	6	5	25	20	2	8	9	9	27	34
Leicester C	38	12	2	5	34	20	1	5	13	16	45	33
Bristol C	38	7	9	3	32	25	2	6	11	14	47	33
Nottingham F	38	9	3	7	35	25	3	5	11	23	34	32
Glossop N.E.	38	11	2	6	34	26	1	6	12	15	42	32
Stockport Co	38	8	4	7	32	23	0	6	13	24	55	26
Blackpool	38	8	4	7	22	22	1	4	14	17	47	26

Charlie Buchan scored 27 goals in 36 games as Sunderland won the title in 1912-13. He just missed being part of a double-winning team when Villa beat Sunderland 1-0 in that year's FA Cup Final.

DIVISION 1

	ASTON VILLA	BLACKBURN R	BOLTON W	BRADFORD C	CHELSEA	DERBY CO	EVERTON	LIVERPOOL	MANCHESTER C	MANCHESTER U	MIDDLESBROUGH	NEWCASTLE U	NOTTS CO	OLDHAM A	SHEFFIELD U	SHEFFIELD W	SUNDERLAND	TOTTENHAM H	W.B.A.	W ARSENAL
1 ASTON VILLA		F15 1-1	D07 1-1	S07 3-1	S02 1-0	O19 5-1	J25 1-1	a05 1-3	J04 2-0	N16 4-2	N02 5-1	D21 3-1	M15 1-0	D26 7-1	a28 4-2	O05 10-0	a23 1-1	M01 1-0	S21 2-4	M24 4-1
2 BLACKBURN R	O12 2-2		O26 6-0	D07 5-0	N23 1-1	D28 0-1	D26 1-2	M10 5-1	a19 2-2	F08 0-0	F10 5-2	N09 2-0	S28 2-1	M22 7-1	a07 3-1	M21 0-1	S09 4-0	S14 6-1	D21 2-4	a05 1-1
3 BOLTON W	a12 2-3	M01 1-1		S21 2-0	S07 1-0	N02 1-1	F15 0-0	D14 1-1	J25 2-2	N30 2-1	N16 3-2	S02 1-2	M29 0-0	M21 3-0	J01 4-2	O19 3-0	a26 1-3	M15 2-0	O05 2-1	J04 5-1
4 BRADFORD C	D28 1-1	a12 0-2	J18 4-1		F22 2-2	D14 2-3	M29 4-1	S14 2-0	M15 2-1	M25 1-0	F04 1-2	F08 2-0	M21 1-0	O12 0-0	S28 3-1	N30 0-0	N02 1-5	a26 3-1	N16 1-1	O26 3-1
5 CHELSEA	M21 1-2	M29 1-6	D28 2-3	O19 0-3		N30 3-1	M15 1-3	S09 1-2	M01 2-1	D25 1-4	D14 2-3	J18 1-0	a26 5-2	S28 1-1	S14 4-2	N16 0-4	O05 2-0	a12 1-0	N02 0-2	F15 1-1
6 DERBY CO	M12 0-1	S07 1-1	M08 3-3	a19 4-0	a05 3-1		S18 1-4	O26 4-2	D21 2-0	O12 2-1	S28 0-2	M22 2-1	F08 1-0	N23 1-2	N09 5-1	M24 1-4	F26 0-3	J18 5-0	D25 1-2	D07 4-1
7 EVERTON	S28 0-1	D25 2-1	O12 2-3	N23 2-1	N09 1-0	M21 2-2		F08 0-2	a05 0-0	J18 4-1	D28 1-0	O26 0-6	S14 4-0	a02 2-3	M12 0-1	a26 3-1	D14 0-4	J01 1-2	D07 1-3	M22 3-0
8 LIVERPOOL	N30 2-0	O19 4-1	a19 5-0	J04 2-1	M24 1-2	M01 2-1	O05 0-2		S21 1-2	M29 0-2	M15 4-2	D26 2-1	N16 0-0	S04 2-0	D21 2-2	F15 2-1	a12 2-5	N02 4-1	J25 2-1	S07 3-0
9 MANCHESTER C	S14 1-0	D14 3-1	S28 2-0	N09 1-3	O26 2-0	a26 1-1	N30 1-0	J18 4-1		D28 0-2	M24 3-0	O12 0-1	J02 4-0	M12 2-0	F08 3-0	a12 2-2	N16 1-0	D25 2-2	M29 2-1	M08 0-1
10 MANCHESTER U	M22 4-0	O05 1-1	a05 2-1	J01 2-0	D26 4-2	F15 4-0	S21 2-0	N23 3-1	S07 0-1		M01 2-3	a19 3-0	N02 2-1	D21 0-0	D07 4-0	J25 2-0	M15 1-3	O19 2-0	J04 1-1	M21 2-0
11 MIDDLESBROUGH	a09 1-1	S21 0-0	M22 4-0	D26 1-1	a19 0-3	J25 4-1	S07 0-0	N09 3-4	M21 0-0	O26 3-2		a05 0-0	a02 1-1	D07 2-2	N23 4-1	J04 0-2	F15 0-2	O05 1-1	J01 3-1	D21 2-0
12 NEWCASTLE U	a26 2-3	M15 0-1	S11 2-1	O05 1-1	S21 3-2	N16 2-4	M01 2-0	J01 0-0	F15 0-1	D14 1-3	N30 3-1		a12 0-0	J04 4-1	D25 1-2	N02 1-0	S07 1-1	M29 3-0	O19 1-1	J25 3-1
13 NOTTS CO	N09 1-1	J25 3-1	N23 1-0	M24 1-1	D21 0-0	O05 0-1	J04 0-1	M22 3-0	S02 0-1	M08 1-2	O19 1-3	D07 0-1		a19 2-1	a05 0-1	S21 1-2	M01 2-1	F15 0-1	S07 1-1	D26 2-1
14 OLDHAM A	S09 2-2	J01 0-0	M25 2-3	F15 0-0	J25 3-2	a15 2-2	N02 2-0	F10 3-1	O19 2-1	a26 0-0	a12 1-0	S14 1-0	D14 4-0		D28 2-0	M15 2-0	S21 3-0	N30 4-1	M01 0-0	O05 0-0
15 SHEFFIELD U	D14 3-2	N02 0-0	D26 0-2	J25 3-2	J04 3-3	M15 4-1	O19 4-1	O14 4-1	O05 1-1	a12 2-1	M31 1-0	D30 1-1	N30 2-0	S07 1-1		M01 0-2	M24 1-3	N16 4-0	F15 1-0	S21 1-3
16 SHEFFIELD W	F08 1-1	S02 2-1	F24 2-2	a05 6-0	M22 3-2	J01 3-3	D21 1-2	O12 1-0	D07 1-0	S28 3-3	S14 3-1	a14 1-2	J18 3-1	N09 5-0	O26 1-0		D25 1-2	D28 2-1	a19 3-2	N23 2-0
17 SUNDERLAND	N23 3-1	S18 2-4	D21 2-1	a30 1-0	F08 4-0	S14 0-2	a09 3-1	D07 7-0	M22 1-0	N09 3-1	O12 4-0	D28 2-0	O26 4-0	J18 1-1	M21 1-0	D26 0-2		S28 2-2	a05 3-1	J01 4-1
18 TOTTENHAM H	O26 3-3	J04 0-1	N09 0-1	D21 2-1	D07 1-0	S21 1-2	S02 0-2	M08 1-0	D26 4-0	M31 1-1	F08 5-3	N23 1-0	N04 0-3	a05 1-0	F22 1-0	S07 2-4	J25 1-2		M21 3-1	a19 1-1
19 W.B.A.	J18 2-2	a26 1-1	F08 2-2	M22 1-1	M08 0-1	D26 0-0	a12 0-0	S28 3-1	N23 0-2	S14 1-2	S04 2-0	a09 1-0	D28 2-0	O26 2-3	O12 3-1	D14 1-1	N30 3-1	M24 4-1		N09 2-1
20 W ARSENAL	S16 0-3	N30 0-1	S14 1-2	M01 1-1	O12 0-1	a12 1-2	N16 0-0	D28 1-1	N02 0-4	S02 0-0	a26 1-1	S28 1-1	D25 0-0	F08 0-0	J18 1-3	M29 2-5	O19 1-3	D14 0-3	M15 1-0	

DIVISION 2

	BARNSLEY	BIRMINGHAM	BLACKPOOL	BRADFORD	BRISTOL C	BURNLEY	BURY	CLAPTON O	FULHAM	GLOSSOP	GRIMSBY T	HUDDERSFIELD T	HULL C	LEEDS C	LEICESTER F	LINCOLN C	NOTTINGHAM F	PRESTON N.E.	STOCKPORT CO	WOLVERHAMPTON W
1 BARNSLEY		M25 1-0	F15 5-3	a03 4-0	M21 7-1	N23 1-4	J25 4-3	a19 0-0	O05 2-1	D07 2-1	S21 3-0	S07 2-0	a05 2-1	J04 2-0	M08 1-0	D21 4-0	J01 1-0	M22 1-1	N09 1-1	O26 3-2
2 BIRMINGHAM	D25 3-1		N30 3-2	D28 1-1	N23 3-0	O12 3-0	D26 1-2	M08 1-1	S09 2-1	O26 0-0	a26 2-1	a12 3-2	F22 3-1	D14 2-2	J18 5-1	N09 4-1	M22 2-0	F08 0-1	S28 1-1	S14 0-0
3 BLACKPOOL	O12 0-1	a05 2-0		N27 0-2	M22 1-1	M21 0-2	S14 2-1	F08 2-0	S28 2-0	J18 1-1	S09 2-1	a19 2-1	D28 1-2	J01 0-3	N23 2-1	F22 1-1	M08 2-1	D21 0-1	D07 1-1	N09 1-2
4 BRADFORD	O19 0-0	S07 0-0	M01 4-2		J01 4-1	a05 2-3	O05 3-1	D21 3-0	F15 2-3	a19 5-0	J25 3-0	J04 2-1	D07 2-0	S21 0-1	N09 2-2	D26 3-0	M24 3-1	N23 0-0	M22 4-2	a16 5-1
5 BRISTOL C	M24 3-0	M29 0-3	N16 0-0	S04 0-0		F08 3-3	a26 1-5	O26 1-0	D25 2-1	F22 3-3	D14 2-2	N30 0-0	O12 1-1	a12 1-1	S14 1-0	M08 2-0	N09 1-2	S28 1-1	J18 7-2	D28 3-1
6 BURNLEY	a23 0-1	F15 3-0	D25 4-0	N30 5-1	O05 2-2		M15 3-1	J04 5-0	N16 5-0	S07 2-1	N02 3-2	O19 4-0	S09 0-0	M01 2-2	D14 5-1	S21 3-1	J25 3-5	S16 2-2	a26 3-2	a12 4-2
7 BURY	S28 2-0	J01 3-0	J04 1-1	F08 2-0	D21 0-1	N09 1-1		a05 0-0	J18 1-0	N23 4-1	S07 4-2	D25 0-2	M22 3-0	M24 1-1	F22 2-2	D07 0-3	a19 2-0	M08 0-0	O26 2-0	O12 1-0
8 CLAPTON O	D14 2-2	N02 0-2	O05 1-0	a26 1-0	M01 0-0	S14 2-0	N30 1-2		a12 2-1	S28 1-0	M29 1-3	M15 1-1	J18 2-1	N16 2-0	D25 1-1	F15 1-2	O19 2-2	D28 1-2	S16 4-1	M21 0-0
9 FULHAM	F08 1-1	M24 3-2	J25 4-2	O12 3-1	a07 0-0	M22 4-2	S21 3-1	D07 1-1		a05 2-0	J04 0-1	S16 2-0	N23 2-0	S07 4-0	O26 1-1	a19 3-1	D21 0-0	N09 3-1	M08 7-0	F22 4-2
10 GLOSSOP	a12 1-0	M01 0-2	S21 2-0	F04 4-3	O19 3-1	D28 1-3	M29 1-1	J25 3-0	J02 2-0		N16 2-0	N02 1-0	S14 0-3	M15 2-1	M21 3-0	O05 0-1	F15 4-3	J01 2-3	F01 2-2	a26 1-3
11 GRIMSBY T	J18 1-1	D21 2-2	S03 1-1	S28 3-0	a19 3-0	M11 2-0	D28 4-0	N23 1-2	S14 2-1	M22 0-0		M24 0-0	N09 2-0	M21 3-2	O12 2-0	a05 0-0	D07 0-0	O26 0-0	F22 4-1	F08 2-1
12 HUDDERSFIELD T	D28 2-0	D07 0-0	D14 3-0	S14 2-0	a05 5-0	F26 1-0	S03 4-0	N09 0-0	M25 5-1	M08 6-0	D26 0-2		O26 5-2	a26 1-0	S28 3-0	M22 5-1	N23 1-1	O12 1-1	F08 3-3	M12 2-1
13 HULL C	D19 0-1	O19 1-2	S07 4-1	a12 5-0	F15 3-1	S26 0-0	N16 2-0	S21 2-1	M29 0-1	a17 2-0	M15 5-0	M01 1-3		N02 6-2	a26 2-1	J25 2-0	O05 2-1	M24 2-2	D25 3-2	D14 0-1
14 LEEDS C	S14 2-0	a19 4-0	D26 0-2	J18 2-0	D07 1-1	O26 4-1	M25 4-2	M22 3-1	D28 2-3	N09 4-0	D25 1-2	D21 0-3	M08 1-0		F08 5-1	N23 2-2	a05 1-0	F22 5-1	O12 2-1	S28 2-2
15 LEICESTER F	N02 1-0	S21 1-2	M29 5-1	M15 3-0	J04 3-1	a19 2-3	O19 3-0	M24 1-0	N30 1-0	D26 1-4	F15 1-0	J25 0-0	D21 3-2	O05 1-1		M25 1-0	S07 3-1	D07 0-3	a05 4-1	N16 0-1
16 LINCOLN C	a26 2-0	M15 0-1	O19 1-0	D25 1-1	N02 2-0	J18 1-3	a12 0-1	O12 1-1	M21 3-0	F08 0-0	F01 3-0	N16 3-1	S28 1-1	M29 3-3	S09 3-0		M01 2-1	S14 0-0	D28 3-2	M24 2-1
17 NOTTINGHAM F	O03 2-0	N16 3-1	N02 1-1	M21 1-2	M15 4-1	S28 2-1	D14 1-1	F22 0-0	a26 2-4	O12 3-2	a12 1-2	M29 0-1	F08 5-0	N30 1-2	D28 4-2	O26 1-2		F05 0-2	S14 2-1	D25 2-0
18 PRESTON N.E.	N16 4-0	O05 1-0	a26 2-1	D14 4-2	J25 5-1	a10 1-1	N02 2-0	S07 0-1	M15 1-0	D25 2-0	M01 2-0	F15 2-1	D26 1-0	O19 3-2	a12 1-0	J04 0-0	S21 1-1		S02 1-1	N30 1-1
19 STOCKPORT CO	M15 0-3	J25 0-1	a12 2-0	N16 1-0	S21 0-1	D21 0-1	M01 1-2	J01 2-0	N02 1-0	M24 1-1	O19 1-1	O05 3-1	M21 3-3	F15 6-0	N04 1-2	S07 2-4	J04 2-1	a19 1-1		M29 5-1
20 WOLVERHAMPTON W	M01 3-0	J04 2-2	M15 4-0	N02 0-0	S07 1-1	D07 0-2	F15 3-1	D26 1-1	O19 2-1	D21 3-1	O05 3-0	S21 2-0	a19 0-1	J25 2-2	M22 1-1	S02 2-0	S16 2-3	a05 2-0	N23 1-0	

Football League Records
Season 1913-14

Top scorers: Div 1, G.Elliott (Middlesbrough) 32 goals; Div 2, S.Stevens (Hull City), J.Peart (Notts County) 28 goals.

DIVISION 1

	ASTON VILLA	BLACKBURN R	BOLTON W	BRADFORD C	BURNLEY	CHELSEA	DERBY CO	EVERTON	LIVERPOOL	MANCHESTER C	MANCHESTER U	MIDDLESBROUGH	NEWCASTLE U	OLDHAM A	PRESTON N.E.	SHEFFIELD U	SHEFFIELD W	SUNDERLAND	TOTTENHAM H	W.B.A.
1 ASTON VILLA		S13 1-3	F25 1-0	D27 0-1	M21 1-0	O25 1-2	a13 3-2	S27 3-1	D06 2-1	S01 1-1	N08 3-1	a25 1-3	a04 1-3	M18 0-0	N22 3-0	D26 3-0	O11 2-0	J17 5-0	D13 3-3	F07 2-0
2 BLACKBURN R	J03 0-0		a04 3-2	O18 0-0	J01 0-0	D06 3-1	O04 3-1	N08 6-0	S06 6-2	F14 2-1	D20 0-1	S20 6-0	S01 3-0	a18 2-1	D25 5-0	J24 3-2	N22 3-2	M23 3-1	F28 1-1	M21 2-0
3 BOLTON W	O18 3-0	N29 1-0		M28 3-0	S20 0-0	F11 1-1	M14 3-1	D13 0-0	F14 2-1	N15 3-0	J03 6-1	F28 1-1	O04 3-1	S06 6-2	J24 0-3	N01 3-1	S01 0-1	a11 2-1	J01 3-0	M07 1-0
4 BRADFORD C	S06 0-0	F25 0-2	N22 5-1		D20 1-1	a04 0-0	J24 0-0	M07 0-1	a13 1-0	O04 3-2	a18 1-1	J03 2-3	D26 2-0	D06 0-1	S17 0-0	S20 2-1	M21 3-1	O25 0-2	F14 2-1	N08 1-0
5 BURNLEY	N15 4-0	S08 1-2	J17 2-2	a27 2-2		S27 6-1	a11 5-1	a10 2-0	M14 5-2	D13 2-0	O11 1-2	a06 1-2	N01 1-0	F07 2-0	F28 3-4	N29 0-0	S13 3-0	D25 0-1	O18 3-1	D27 0-0
6 CHELSEA	F28 0-3	a11 2-0	a13 2-1	N29 2-1	J24 0-0		N15 2-1	a25 2-0	O18 3-0	M28 1-0	S20 0-2	N01 3-2	F14 0-1	J03 2-1	O04 2-0	M14 2-0	D25 2-1	D13 1-1	S06 1-3	S08 1-1
7 DERBY CO	D25 0-2	F07 2-3	N08 3-3	S27 3-1	D06 3-1	M21 0-1		F21 1-0	S01 1-1	J17 2-4	a04 4-2	S10 2-2	D20 2-0	N22 1-2	a18 0-1	S06 3-5	M11 1-1	O11 1-1	J03 4-0	O25 1-2
8 EVERTON	J24 1-4	M14 0-0	a18 1-1	N01 1-1	S01 1-1	D20 0-0	O18 5-0		S20 1-2	F28 1-0	D26 5-0	O04 2-0	J03 2-0	a13 0-2	S06 2-0	F14 5-0	D06 1-1	N15 1-5	M28 1-1	a04 2-0
9 LIVERPOOL	a11 0-1	D27 3-3	O11 2-1	J01 0-1	N08 1-1	M18 3-0	a10 1-0	J17 1-2		D25 4-2	a15 1-2	D13 2-1	N22 0-0	O25 0-3	M21 3-1	a27 2-1	F07 1-2	S13 1-3	N29 2-1	S27 0-0
10 MANCHESTER C	a10 3-1	O11 1-2	M21 0-1	F07 1-0	a18 4-1	N22 2-1	S20 1-2	O25 1-1	D26 1-0		D06 0-2	S06 1-1	a13 0-1	a04 2-1	D20 1-1	J03 2-1	N08 1-2	M18 3-1	J24 2-1	M25 2-3
11 MANCHESTER U	M14 0-6	a25 0-0	S13 0-1	D13 1-1	F14 0-1	J17 0-1	N29 3-3	D25 0-1	N01 3-0	a11 0-1		N15 0-1	F28 2-2	S27 4-1	O18 3-0	a22 2-1	D27 2-1	S08 3-1	O04 3-1	J01 1-0
12 MIDDLESBROUGH	D20 5-2	J17 3-0	O25 2-3	S13 1-1	N22 2-1	M07 2-0	J01 3-2	F07 2-0	a18 4-0	D27 2-0	F21 3-1		D06 3-0	N08 0-0	a04 4-1	a10 2-3	M18 5-2	S27 3-4	a13 6-0	O11 3-0
13 NEWCASTLE U	N29 2-2	a10 0-0	F07 4-3	D25 0-0	M18 3-1	O11 1-0	a25 1-1	S13 0-1	a01 1-2	J01 0-1	O25 0-1	a11 1-0		F21 0-0	N08 2-0	D13 2-1	S27 3-1	D27 2-1	N15 2-0	J17 3-3
14 OLDHAM A	N01 0-1	D13 1-1	D27 2-0	a11 3-1	O04 1-1	S13 3-2	M28 0-0	J01 2-0	F28 2-2	N29 1-3	J24 2-2	M14 3-0	O18 3-0		F14 1-0	N15 1-2	a14 2-0	a25 2-1	S20 3-0	D25 2-0
15 PRESTON N.E.	a01 3-2	D26 1-5	S27 1-1	a10 2-1	O25 2-1	F07 3-3	D13 2-0	D27 1-0	N15 0-1	a25 2-2	M05 4-2	N29 4-1	M14 4-1	O11 0-1		a11 2-4	J17 5-0	S01 2-2	N01 1-2	S13 0-2
16 SHEFFIELD U	J01 3-0	S27 1-1	a06 2-0	J17 1-1	a04 5-0	N08 3-2	D27 2-2	O11 4-1	D20 0-1	S13 1-3	N22 2-0	D25 3-1	a18 2-0	M21 2-1	D06 2-0		O25 0-1	F07 1-0	S01 1-4	M19 1-1
17 SHEFFIELD W	F14 2-3	M28 3-1	D29 1-1	N15 1-3	J03 2-6	D26 3-0	N01 1-3	a11 2-2	O04 4-1	M14 2-2	S06 1-3	O18 2-0	J24 0-0	S22 1-2	S20 2-1	F28 2-1		N29 2-1	a25 2-0	D13 1-4
18 SUNDERLAND	S20 2-0	N01 2-1	D06 3-2	F28 0-1	D26 1-1	a18 2-0	F14 1-0	M21 5-2	J03 1-2	O18 0-0	a10 2-0	J24 4-2	S06 1-2	D20 2-0	J01 3-1	O04 1-2	a04 0-1		M14 2-0	N22 0-0
19 TOTTENHAM H	a18 0-2	O25 3-3	a10 3-0	O11 0-0	F23 2-0	D27 1-2	S13 1-1	N22 4-1	a04 0-0	S27 3-1	F07 2-1	D26 0-1	M21 0-0	J17 3-1	M07 1-0	S08 2-1	D20 1-1	N08 1-4		D06 3-0
20 W.B.A.	O04 1-0	N15 2-0	D20 1-1	M14 2-1	S06 4-1	a14 3-1	F28 2-1	N29 1-1	J24 0-1	N01 0-0	a13 2-1	F14 2-1	S20 1-1	D26 2-2	J03 1-0	O18 2-1	a18 1-1	M28 2-1	a11 1-1	

LEAGUE TABLES

DIVISION 1

	P	W	D	L	F	A	W	D	L	F	A	Pts
Blackburn R	38	14	4	1	51	15	6	7	6	27	27	51
Aston Villa	38	11	3	5	36	21	8	3	8	29	29	44
Middlesbrough	38	14	2	3	55	20	5	3	11	22	40	43
Oldham A	38	11	5	3	34	16	6	4	9	21	29	43
W.B.A.	38	11	7	1	30	16	4	6	9	16	26	43
Bolton W	38	13	4	2	41	14	3	6	10	24	38	42
Sunderland	38	11	3	5	32	17	6	3	10	31	35	40
Chelsea	38	12	3	4	28	18	4	4	11	18	37	39
Bradford C	38	8	6	5	23	17	4	8	7	17	23	38
Sheffield U	38	11	4	4	36	19	5	1	13	27	41	37
Newcastle U	38	9	6	4	27	18	4	5	10	12	30	37
Burnley	38	10	4	5	43	20	2	8	9	18	33	36
Manchester C	38	9	3	7	28	23	5	5	9	23	30	36
Manchester U	38	8	4	7	27	23	7	2	10	25	39	36
Everton	38	8	7	4	32	18	4	4	11	14	37	35
Liverpool	38	8	4	7	27	25	6	3	10	19	37	35
Tottenham H	38	9	6	4	30	19	3	4	12	20	43	34
Sheffield W	38	8	4	7	34	34	5	4	10	19	36	34
Preston N.E.	38	9	4	6	39	31	3	2	14	13	38	30
Derby Co	38	6	5	8	34	32	2	6	11	21	39	27

DIVISION 2

	P	W	D	L	F	A	W	D	L	F	A	Pts
Notts Co	38	16	2	1	55	13	7	5	7	22	23	53
Bradford P.A.	38	15	1	3	44	20	8	2	9	27	27	49
Woolwich A	38	14	3	2	34	10	6	6	7	20	28	49
Leeds U	38	15	2	2	54	16	5	5	9	22	30	47
Barnsley	38	14	1	4	33	15	5	6	8	18	30	45
Clapton O	38	14	5	0	38	11	2	6	11	9	24	43
Hull C	38	9	5	5	29	13	7	4	8	24	24	41
Bristol C	38	12	5	2	32	10	4	4	11	20	40	41
Wolverhampton W	38	14	1	4	33	16	4	4	11	18	36	41
Bury	38	12	6	1	30	14	3	4	12	9	26	40
Fulham	38	10	3	6	31	20	6	3	10	15	23	38
Stockport Co	38	9	6	4	32	18	4	4	11	23	39	36
Huddersfield T	38	8	4	7	28	22	5	4	10	19	31	34
Birmingham C	38	10	4	5	31	18	2	6	11	17	42	34
Grimsby T	38	10	4	5	24	15	3	4	12	18	43	34
Blackpool	38	6	10	3	24	19	3	4	12	9	25	32
Glossop N.E.	38	8	3	8	32	24	3	3	13	19	43	28
Leicester C	38	7	2	10	29	28	4	2	13	16	33	26
Lincoln C	38	8	5	6	23	23	2	1	16	13	43	26
Nottingham F	38	7	7	5	27	23	0	2	17	10	53	23

DIVISION 2

	BARNSLEY	BIRMINGHAM	BLACKPOOL	BRADFORD P.A.	BRISTOL C	BURY	CLAPTON O	FULHAM	GLOSSOP	GRIMSBY T	HUDDERSFIELD T	HULL C	LEEDS C	LEICESTER F	LINCOLN C	NOTTINGHAM F	NOTTS CO	STOCKPORT CO	WOLVERHAMPTON W	W ARSENAL
1 BARNSLEY		O11 1-1	S13 2-1	N22 1-2	F21 3-0	D26 2-0	M07 2-1	a13 1-0	N08 2-0	F07 3-1	J01 2-1	D20 0-2	O25 1-4	D06 3-0	D27 1-0	J17 5-0	a04 0-1	M21 1-0	a18 2-1	S27 1-0
2 BIRMINGHAM	F14 0-0		M14 0-0	S06 1-2	a18 2-2	O18 1-0	a10 2-0	a11 0-1	D25 6-0	N29 1-2	F28 1-4	O04 1-1	D20 0-2	S20 1-0	N01 2-0	N15 2-0	J03 2-1	S03 3-2	J24 4-1	M28 2-0
3 BLACKPOOL	J03 3-1	N08 2-2		D20 2-1	M21 0-1	S20 0-1	a04 0-0	F14 1-1	a11 1-1	M07 1-1	J24 0-1	S06 2-2	N22 2-2	a10 1-0	O04 2-1	F21 2-1	a13 0-0	a18 2-2	J01 2-0	O25 1-1
4 BRADFORD	M28 1-1	D27 5-1	a25 4-1		S13 4-3	N29 3-1	S27 1-0	O18 1-0	F07 2-1	S10 3-0	a11 2-1	N15 2-0	J17 3-1	N01 3-2	D13 3-0	a10 4-0	F28 0-3	O11 0-2	M14 1-0	D25 2-3
5 BRISTOL C	O18 1-1	D13 1-2	N15 1-0	J03 2-0		F28 2-0	D26 3-0	a25 0-1	S03 4-1	a11 1-0	N01 1-0	F14 2-1	a10 1-1	J24 1-0	M14 4-1	M28 1-0	S20 1-1	S06 5-0	O04 0-0	N29 1-1
6 BURY	D25 4-0	F24 3-1	J17 1-0	a04 0-0	O25 3-1		N08 0-0	J01 1-0	M21 1-0	O11 3-1	D27 2-1	a10 2-0	M07 1-1	a18 1-1	S13 1-0	S27 1-0	D06 3-3	N24 1-0	D20 1-4	F07 1-1
7 CLAPTON O	N01 1-0	a13 2-2	N29 2-0	J24 1-0	D25 5-2	M14 1-0		S06 1-0	J03 5-1	a25 0-0	N15 0-0	F28 3-0	M02 3-1	F14 1-0	M28 5-1	a11 3-1	O04 1-0	S20 1-1	O18 2-2	D13 1-0
8 FULHAM	a10 1-2	D06 1-0	O11 0-0	F21 1-6	D20 3-1	S01 1-1	D27 2-0		J17 2-1	N22 2-2	S13 1-0	a18 0-1	D26 0-1	M21 1-2	S27 4-0	O25 2-0	M07 1-2	F07 2-0	a04 1-0	N08 6-1
9 GLOSSOP	M14 5-1	D26 4-1	D06 1-2	O04 2-1	M10 1-1	N15 2-1	S13 0-3	S20 0-1		a10 3-0	M28 2-3	N01 2-1	D27 1-1	O18 0-2	F10 4-0	D16 3-0	F14 0-1	J24 1-1	F28 1-2	a25 0-2
10 GRIMSBY T	O04 1-1	a04 0-2	N01 2-0	F24 0-0	D06 1-0	F14 1-0	D20 2-0	M28 0-3	a13 3-0		O18 2-1	J24 1-3	a18 0-1	J03 3-0	F28 1-3	M14 3-0	S06 0-0	D25 2-0	S20 1-0	N15 1-1
11 HUDDERSFIELD T	a14 3-1	O25 7-0	S27 1-0	D06 0-1	M07 1-2	S06 1-1	M21 1-0	J03 3-1	N22 2-1	F21 1-2		D25 0-3	N08 1-1	D20 1-2	J17 2-1	F07 1-1	a18 2-1	a04 0-2	S09 0-0	O11 1-2
12 HULL C	a25 0-1	F07 0-0	D27 0-0	M21 1-3	O11 0-1	a13 0-1	O25 2-0	D13 1-1	M07 3-0	S27 2-1	D26 4-1		F21 1-0	a04 0-0	O13 1-1	S13 1-0	N22 2-0	N08 3-0	D06 7-1	J17 1-2
13 LEEDS C	F28 3-0	a25 3-2	M28 2-1	S20 5-1	a13 1-0	N01 2-1	a14 0-0	D25 2-1	S06 3-0	D13 4-1	M14 5-1	O18 1-2		O04 2-1	N15 1-0	N29 8-0	J24 2-4	J03 5-1	F14 5-0	a11 0-0
14 LEICESTER F	a11 0-2	J17 0-0	D25 0-1	M07 2-3	S27 3-0	D13 0-0	O11 1-0	N15 3-0	F21 1-3	S13 2-0	a25 0-1	N29 0-4	F07 5-1		a13 2-0	S11 5-1	N08 0-2	O25 2-5	M28 2-3	D27 1-2
15 LINCOLN C	S06 2-2	M07 1-1	F07 1-2	a18 0-3	N08 2-1	J03 1-0	N22 0-0	J24 0-1	a04 1-5	O25 1-3	S20 3-0	M11 0-0	M21 1-0	D26 3-0		O11 1-0	D20 0-0	D06 0-3	a10 1-0	F21 5-2
16 NOTTINGHAM F	S20 0-2	M21 3-1	O18 3-0	a13 1-0	N22 1-1	J24 1-1	D06 1-1	F28 1-1	a18 1-2	N08 4-1	O04 1-1	J03 1-2	a04 2-1	S03 1-3	F14 2-1		D26 1-0	D20 2-2	S06 1-3	M07 0-0
17 NOTTS CO	N29 3-1	S13 5-1	S24 2-0	O25 2-3	J17 4-0	a11 2-0	F07 3-0	N01 4-0	O11 2-2	D27 4-0	D13 3-0	M28 4-1	S27 4-0	M14 4-1	O02 2-1	D25 2-2		F21 2-1	N15 2-0	J01 1-0
18 STOCKPORT CO	N15 1-1	J01 2-0	D13 0-0	F14 3-1	D27 5-1	M28 3-0	J17 0-1	O04 1-3	S27 1-1	D26 2-2	D01 0-0	M14 2-1	S13 2-1	F28 3-0	a11 2-3	a25 2-1	O18 1-2		N01 0-0	a10 2-0
19 WOLVERHAMPTON W	D13 0-1	S27 1-0	D26 1-0	N08 1-0	F07 0-2	a25 3-0	F21 2-1	N29 1-0	O25 1-0	J17 4-1	a13 2-2	a11 1-0	O11 1-3	N22 2-1	S01 1-0	D27 4-1	M21 4-1	M07 3-1		S13 1-2
20 W ARSENAL	J24 1-0	N22 1-0	F28 2-1	D26 2-0	a04 1-1	O04 0-1	a18 2-2	M14 2-0	D20 2-0	a23 2-0	F14 0-1	S20 0-0	D06 1-0	S06 2-1	O18 3-0	N01 3-2	S15 3-0	a13 4-0	J03 3-1	

Danny Shea joined Blackburn from Southern League West Ham United, for £2,000, and was their leading scorer when they won the title again in 1913-14.

Football League Records
Season 1914-15

Top scorers: Div 1, R.Parker (Everton) 35 goals; Div 2, J.Lane (Blackpool) 28 goals.
Woolwich Arsenal dropped 'Woolwich' from their name.

LEAGUE TABLES

DIVISION 1

	P	W	D	L	F	A	W	D	L	F	A	Pts
Everton	38	8	5	6	44	29	11	3	5	32	18	46
Oldham A	38	11	5	3	46	25	6	6	7	24	31	45
Blackburn R	38	11	4	4	51	27	7	3	9	32	34	43
Burnley	38	12	1	6	38	18	6	6	7	23	29	43
Manchester C	38	9	7	3	29	15	6	6	7	20	24	43
Sheffield U	38	11	5	3	28	13	4	8	7	21	28	43
Sheffield W	38	10	7	2	43	23	5	6	8	18	31	43
Sunderland	38	11	3	5	46	30	7	2	10	35	42	41
Bradford P.A.	38	11	4	4	40	20	6	3	10	29	45	41
W.B.A.	38	11	5	3	31	9	4	5	10	18	34	40
Bradford C	38	11	7	1	40	18	2	7	10	15	31	40
Middlesbrough	38	10	6	3	42	24	3	6	10	20	50	38
Liverpool	38	11	5	3	45	34	3	4	12	20	41	37
Aston Villa	38	10	5	4	39	32	3	6	10	23	40	37
Newcastle U	38	8	4	7	29	23	3	6	10	17	25	32
Notts Co	38	8	7	4	28	18	1	6	12	13	39	31
Bolton W	38	8	5	6	35	27	3	3	13	33	57	30
Manchester U	38	8	6	5	27	19	1	6	12	19	43	30
Chelsea	38	8	6	5	32	25	0	7	12	19	40	29
Tottenham H	38	7	7	5	30	29	1	5	13	27	61	28

DIVISION 2

	P	W	D	L	F	A	W	D	L	F	A	Pts
Derby Co	38	14	3	2	40	11	9	4	6	31	22	53
Preston N.E.	38	14	4	1	41	16	6	6	7	20	26	50
Barnsley	38	16	2	1	31	10	6	1	12	20	41	47
Wolverhampton W	38	12	4	3	47	13	7	3	9	30	39	45
Arsenal	38	15	1	3	52	13	4	4	11	17	28	43
Birmingham C	38	13	3	3	44	13	4	6	9	18	26	43
Hull C	38	12	2	5	36	23	7	3	9	29	31	43
Huddersfield T	38	12	4	3	36	13	5	4	10	25	29	42
Clapton O	38	12	5	2	36	17	4	4	11	14	31	41
Blackpool	38	11	3	5	40	22	6	2	11	18	35	39
Bury	38	11	5	3	39	19	4	3	12	22	37	38
Fulham	38	12	0	7	35	20	3	7	9	18	27	37
Bristol C	38	11	2	6	38	19	4	5	10	24	37	37
Stockport Co	38	12	4	3	33	19	3	3	13	21	41	37
Leeds U	38	9	3	7	40	25	5	1	13	25	39	32
Lincoln C	38	9	4	6	29	23	2	5	12	17	42	31
Grimsby T	38	10	4	5	36	24	1	5	13	12	52	31
Nottingham F	38	9	7	3	32	24	1	2	16	11	53	29
Leicester C	38	6	4	9	31	41	4	0	15	16	47	24
Glossop N.E.	38	5	5	9	21	33	1	1	17	10	54	18

DIVISION 1

	ASTON VILLA	BLACKBURN R	BOLTON W	BRADFORD	BRADFORD C	BURNLEY	CHELSEA	EVERTON	LIVERPOOL	MANCHESTER C	MANCHESTER U	MIDDLESBROUGH	NEWCASTLE U	NOTTS CO	OLDHAM A	SHEFFIELD U	SHEFFIELD W	SUNDERLAND	TOTTENHAM H	W.B.A.
1 ASTON VILLA		a02 2-1	D26 1-7	D05 1-2	F13 0-0	O17 3-3	O03 2-1	F10 1-5	a03 6-2	a21 4-1	D19 3-3	M13 5-0	O31 2-1	S02 2-1	a17 0-0	N14 1-0	J16 0-0	S05 1-3	F27 3-1	S19 2-1
2 BLACKBURN R	D25 1-2		S26 2-2	J02 2-2	M29 2-1	N28 6-0	N14 3-2	M13 2-1	S21 4-2	O03 0-1	J23 3-3	a24 4-0	D12 2-3	F13 5-1	S12 4-1	J01 1-2	F27 1-1	O17 3-1	a10 4-1	O31 2-1
3 BOLTON W	J01 2-2	S07 3-2		a02 3-2	N14 3-5	M13 3-1	a14 3-1	O31 0-0	D25 0-1	S19 2-3	S12 3-0	D12 4-0	a10 0-0	O03 1-2	J02 2-0	a26 0-1	O17 0-3	M10 1-1	N28 4-2	F27 1-1
4 BRADFORD	a10 2-2	S05 1-2	O07 1-2		a28 3-0	O31 2-2	O17 3-0	a14 1-2	D12 1-0	a24 3-1	a05 5-0	M27 2-0	N14 1-0	J16 3-1	D25 1-1	N28 2-0	M17 1-1	S19 2-1	M13 5-1	O03 1-4
5 BRADFORD C	O10 3-0	N21 3-0	M20 4-2	O24 3-2		J02 0-0	S09 2-2	D26 0-1	M10 3-2	a06 0-0	N07 4-2	S26 1-1	J23 1-1	a03 3-1	M24 1-0	F06 1-1	a17 1-0	D05 3-1	S12 2-2	D19 5-0
6 BURNLEY	F22 2-1	a03 3-2	N21 5-0	M06 2-0	S05 0-1		a05 2-0	S07 1-0	O24 3-0	J18 1-2	M20 3-0	F06 4-0	S26 2-0	D05 0-0	N07 2-3	O10 1-2	D19 2-3	a17 2-1	J23 3-1	D25 0-2
7 CHELSEA	F06 3-1	M20 1-3	N07 2-1	M01 0-1	a02 2-0	D28 1-4		D19 2-0	O10 3-1	D25 0-0	a19 1-3	J23 2-2	S12 0-3	N21 4-1	O24 2-2	S26 1-1	D05 0-0	a03 3-0	J02 1-1	a17 4-1
8 EVERTON	S26 0-0	N07 1-3	M22 5-3	O10 4-1	D25 1-1	a02 0-2	a26 2-2		F06 1-3	D12 4-1	O24 4-2	S12 2-3	J02 3-0	M20 4-0	M17 3-4	J23 0-0	a03 0-1	N21 7-1	J01 1-1	D05 2-1
9 LIVERPOOL	N28 3-6	a05 3-0	S02 4-3	a17 2-1	O17 2-1	F27 3-0	F13 3-3	O03 0-5		M13 3-2	D26 1-1	N14 1-1	M29 2-2	S05 1-1	D19 1-2	a12 2-1	S19 2-1	J16 2-1	O31 7-2	M24 3-1
10 MANCHESTER C	N25 1-0	F06 1-3	J23 2-1	D19 2-3	S01 4-1	S12 1-0	D26 2-1	a17 0-1	D05 1-1		J02 1-1	O24 1-1	O10 1-1	F22 0-0	a05 0-0	N07 0-0	M20 4-0	M06 2-0	S26 2-1	a03 4-0
11 MANCHESTER U	a26 1-0	S19 2-0	J16 4-1	J01 1-2	M13 1-0	N14 0-2	O31 2-2	F27 1-2	a02 2-0	S05 0-0		a10 2-2	N28 1-0	J30 2-2	S02 1-3	D12 1-2	F13 2-0	O03 3-0	M27 1-1	O17 0-0
12 MIDDLESBROUGH	N07 1-1	D19 1-4	a17 0-0	N21 1-3	F03 3-0	O03 1-1	S19 3-0	J16 5-1	M20 3-0	F27 1-0	D05 1-1		O17 1-1	D25 1-0	a03 4-1	M17 2-2	a05 3-1	J01 2-3	F13 7-5	S05 2-0
13 NEWCASTLE U	a28 3-0	a17 2-1	D05 1-2	M20 1-1	S19 1-0	a14 1-2	M17 2-0	S05 0-1	N07 0-0	F13 2-1	a03 2-0	M10 1-2		D19 1-1	N21 1-2	O24 4-3	S09 0-0	D25 2-5	O03 4-0	S02 1-2
14 NOTTS CO	a05 1-1	O10 1-1	M17 0-0	S12 1-2	N28 0-0	a10 0-0	a28 2-0	N14 0-0	J02 3-1	O17 0-2	S26 4-2	D26 5-1	a24 1-0		J23 2-1	a02 3-1	O31 1-2	F27 2-1	D12 1-2	M13 1-1
15 OLDHAM A	D12 3-3	J16 3-2	S05 5-3	D26 6-2	O31 1-0	a20 1-2	F27 0-0	O17 1-1	a24 0-2	J01 0-0	a06 1-0	N28 5-1	M27 1-0	S19 2-0		a10 3-0	O03 5-2	F01 4-5	N14 4-1	M09 1-1
16 SHEFFIELD U	M20 3-0	D26 1-2	D19 3-1	a03 3-2	O03 1-1	F13 1-0	M08 1-1	S19 1-0	N21 2-1	M29 0-0	a17 3-1	O31 0-1	F27 1-0	D28 1-0	D05 3-0		S05 0-1	a05 1-1	O17 1-1	J16 2-0
17 SHEFFIELD W	S12 5-2	O24 1-1	M01 7-0	S26 6-0	D12 3-3	a24 0-0	a10 3-2	N28 1-4	J23 2-1	N14 2-1	O10 1-0	S01 3-1	J01 2-1	M06 0-0	F06 2-2	J02 1-1		N07 1-2	D25 3-2	M27 0-0
18 SUNDERLAND	J02 4-0	F20 5-1	O10 4-3	J23 3-3	a10 1-1	D12 2-1	N28 2-1	a06 0-3	S12 2-2	O31 0-2	F06 1-0	a02 4-1	D26 2-4	O24 3-1	S26 1-2	S02 3-2	M13 3-1		a24 5-0	N14 1-2
19 TOTTENHAM H	O24 0-2	D05 0-4	a03 4-2	N07 3-0	J16 0-0	S19 1-3	S05 1-1	S02 1-3	M06 1-1	M15 2-2	N21 2-0	O10 3-3	a02 0-0	F20 2-0	M20 1-0	a19 1-1	D26 6-1	D19 0-6		S28 2-0
20 W.B.A.	J23 2-0	M06 0-0	O24 3-0	F06 1-0	a24 3-0	D26 3-0	D12 2-0	a10 1-2	S26 4-0	N28 0-1	F20 0-0	J02 1-0	a05 2-0	N07 4-1	O10 0-0	S12 1-1	N21 0-0	M20 1-2	a06 3-2	

DIVISION 2

	ARSENAL	BARNSLEY	BIRMINGHAM	BLACKPOOL	BRISTOL C	BURY	CLAPTON O	DERBY CO	FULHAM	GLOSSOP	GRIMSBY T	HUDDERSFIELD T	HULL C	LEEDS C	LEICESTER F	LINCOLN C	NOTTINGHAM F	PRESTON N.E.	STOCKPORT CO	WOLVERHAMPTON W
1 ARSENAL		a05 1-0	M13 1-0	O17 2-0	N28 3-0	a10 3-1	O10 2-1	F27 1-2	S12 3-0	S01 3-0	N14 6-0	M27 0-3	S26 2-1	F06 2-0	D26 6-0	O31 1-1	a24 7-0	D12 1-2	J23 3-1	J02 5-1
2 BARNSLEY	J01 1-0		M08 2-1	M13 1-2	O03 2-1	F13 2-0	D26 1-0	a02 1-0	a03 2-2	M20 2-0	S19 0-0	J30 1-0	a17 1-0	D19 2-1	O31 1-0	S05 3-1	F27 3-0	O17 2-1	D05 2-0	N21 2-1
3 BIRMINGHAM	N07 3-0	S12 2-0		N28 3-0	a24 1-1	D25 1-0	M06 1-0	M20 0-2	M01 1-0	J23 11-1	a10 3-0	D12 1-0	M24 2-2	O24 6-3	J02 2-0	N21 2-0	D28 3-0	a05 1-1	O10 0-1	S26 1-2
4 BLACKPOOL	F20 0-2	N07 1-1	a14 3-1		J01 2-0	S12 3-4	F06 5-1	M06 2-1	D19 2-2	N21 3-0	a17 5-0	a02 3-2	J02 1-2	J23 1-0	O24 1-2	M20 0-0	O10 3-0	S26 0-2	a05 4-2	D05 1-0
5 BRISTOL C	a03 1-1	F06 3-1	D19 2-3	S02 2-1		J02 1-0	N21 3-0	D05 2-3	O24 0-0	O10 3-1	D26 7-0	a05 0-1	N07 5-2	M20 1-0	S26 1-0	a17 2-1	J23 1-2	S12 4-0	M06 0-2	F20 0-1
6 BURY	D05 3-1	O10 1-2	D26 1-3	J25 2-2	S05 2-1		a03 3-0	a17 2-0	M06 1-0	F20 5-0	a02 2-2	J01 3-1	M20 0-1	N21 0-0	F06 3-1	D14 1-1	S26 4-2	J23 0-0	N07 2-1	O24 4-1
7 CLAPTON O	F13 1-0	D25 4-2	O31 1-1	O03 2-0	M27 2-0	N28 2-2		O17 0-1	J02 2-1	a05 5-2	M13 2-1	N14 3-1	J23 0-3	S26 2-0	a24 2-0	F27 3-1	D12 0-0	a10 1-1	S12 3-0	S01 1-1
8 DERBY CO	O24 4-0	S02 7-0	N14 1-0	O31 5-0	a10 1-0	D12 2-1	F20 0-3		J23 1-1	J02 1-1	M27 1-1	N28 1-0	F06 4-1	O10 1-2	a05 1-0	M13 3-0	D26 1-0	a24 2-0	S26 1-0	S12 3-1
9 FULHAM	J16 0-1	N28 2-0	O03 2-3	a24 0-1	F27 1-2	O31 6-3	S05 4-0	S19 2-0		a10 2-0	F13 2-1	O17 2-3	a06 4-1	S09 1-0	M27 1-0	M29 3-1	N14 2-1	M13 0-2	D26 1-0	D12 0-1
10 GLOSSOP	S08 0-4	N14 0-1	S19 3-3	M27 1-3	F13 2-1	O17 3-0	a02 3-1	S05 1-1	D05 1-0		J30 0-0	O03 2-2	M16 0-5	D25 0-3	M13 2-3	J16 1-2	O31 1-0	F27 0-1	a17 1-1	a03 0-2
11 GRIMSBY T	M20 1-0	J23 2-3	D05 1-0	D12 2-0	D25 2-3	a05 1-0	N07 2-1	N21 1-2	O10 1-1	S26 1-0		a24 0-0	O24 1-1	M06 2-5	S12 1-0	a03 5-1	J02 4-0	S01 2-2	F20 6-1	F06 1-4
12 HUDDERSFIELD T	N21 3-0	S26 1-0	a17 0-0	D26 5-0	a06 5-3	S08 0-1	M20 1-1	a03 0-0	F20 2-2	F06 0-1	D19 3-1		O31 1-0	N07 1-0	S21 3-1	D05 0-1	S12 4-0	J02 3-1.	O24 2-1	O10 2-0
13 HULL C	a02 1-0	D12 2-1	O17 0-0	S05 1-3	M13 1-1	N14 3-1	S19 0-1	O03 1-0	a05 2-0	a24 2-0	a29 4-1	a15 0-4		J16 2-6	a10 2-1	M11 6-1	N28 3-1	M27 0-1	S03 1-0	D25 5-1
14 LEEDS C	O03 2-2	a24 0-2	F27 2-0	S19 2-0	N14 1-1	M27 2-1	F03 0-1	F13 3-5	S02 0-1	D26 3-0	O31 5-0	M13 1-0	S12 2-3		D12 7-2	O17 3-1	a10 4-0	N28 0-0	J02 1-3	a06 2-3
15 LEICESTER F	D25 1-4	M06 0-1	S05 1-0	F27 2-2	M25 1-3	O03 1-3	J30 1-1	D28 0-6	N21 0-2	N07 3-2	J16 2-0	S19 1-2	D05 1-1	a17 5-1		S02 2-2	O17 3-1	F13 2-3	a03 5-4	M20 0-3
16 LINCOLN C	M06 1-0	J02 3-0	M27 0-1	N14 0-1	D12 3-1	a24 2-3	O24 1-0	N07 0-0	S26 3-1	S12 2-1	N28 2-1	a10 1-1	O10 0-3	F20 0-1	a02 2-3		a05 2-1	D25 3-1	F06 2-2	J23 2-2
17 NOTTINGHAM F	N18 1-1	O24 2-1	S02 1-1	F13 2-1	S19 0-1	F04 1-1	a17 0-1	D25 2-2	M20 2-2	M06 1-0	S05 4-2	J16 3-2	a03 1-0	D05 3-1	F20 1-3	O01 3-2		O03 1-1	N21 1-1	N07 3-1
18 PRESTON N.E.	a17 3-0	F20 5-2	a02 2-0	J30 1-0	F11 4-1	S19 2-0	D05 2-2	D19 1-3	N07 2-1	O24 1-0	S07 3-0	S05 1-1	N21 2-1	a03 2-0	O10 1-0	D26 0-0	F06 2-2		M20 2-0	M06 5-3
19 STOCKPORT CO	S19 1-1	a10 1-2	F13 3-1	D25 0-2	O31 2-2	M13 1-0	J16 2-0	J30 3-2	a02 0-2	D12 2-1	O17 1-1	F27 2-1	J01 3-0	S05 3-1	N28 3-0	O03 1-0	M27 1-0	N14 2-1		a24 2-2
20 WOLVERHAMPTON W	S05 1-0	M27 4-1	a19 0-0	a10 2-0	O17 2-2	F27 1-1	S07 0-0	J16 0-1	a17 2-0	N28 4-0	O03 0-1	F13 4-1	D26 1-2	a05 5-1	N14 7-0	S19 3-1	M13 5-1	O31 2-0	D19 4-1	

In 1914-15, former Glasgow Rangers forward Bobby Parker was Division One's leading scorer, his 35 goals equalling Everton's club record as the Goodison club lifted the title.

FOOTBALL LEAGUE RECORDS
SEASON 1919-20

Top scorers: Div 1, F.Morris (West Bromwich Albion) 37 goals; Div 2, S.Taylor (Huddersfield Town) 35 goals. Glossop resigned after World War One. Coventry City, Gateshead, West Ham United, Stoke and Rotherham County were elected to League. Arsenal were elected to Division One. Leeds City were expelled after eight games and their fixtures taken over by Port Vale. Leicester Fosse became Leicester City.

DIVISION 1

	ARSENAL	ASTON VILLA	BLACKBURN R	BOLTON W	BRADFORD P.A.	BRADFORD C	BURNLEY	CHELSEA	DERBY CO	EVERTON	LIVERPOOL	MANCHESTER C	MANCHESTER U	MIDDLESBROUGH	NEWCASTLE U	NOTTS CO	OLDHAM A	PRESTON N.E.	SHEFFIELD U	SHEFFIELD W	SUNDERLAND	W.B.A.
1 ARSENAL		J24 0-1	O04 0-1	N08 2-2	m01 3-0	O25 1-2	a10 2-0	D06 1-1	D26 1-0	O18 1-1	S08 1-0	J03 2-2	F21 0-3	M27 2-1	A30 0-1	N22 3-1	F07 3-2	a24 0-0	M13 3-0	D20 3-1	S20 3-2	a05 1-0
2 ASTON VILLA	F11 2-1		M20 1-2	a07 3-6	O04 1-0	F28 3-1	J03 2-2	D25 5-2	S01 2-2	F14 2-2	S20 0-1	a26 0-1	D06 2-0	N01 5-3	a05 4-0	a03 3-1	D20 3-0	O18 2-4	N29 4-0	a17 3-1	S06 0-3	N15 2-4
3 BLACKBURN R	S27 2-2	a15 5-1		D20 2-2	J24 3-3	D11 4-1	S13 2-3	M11 3-1	D06 2-0	N01 3-2	F07 0-2	N15 1-4	a24 5-0	S15 0-2	M13 2-0	J01 1-1	a10 0-1	A30 4-0	m01 4-0	O18 1-0	a02 3-0	J03 1-5
4 BOLTON W	N15 2-2	M13 2-1	D27 2-1		A30 1-2	D13 1-1	S01 1-1	F07 1-2	O04 3-0	N29 0-2	J24 0-3	S20 6-2	a10 3-5	m01 2-1	F21 0-3	J03 1-0	M27 1-0	D25 4-1	a24 1-0	J01 2-0	N01 1-0	O18 1-2
5 BRADFORD	a28 0-0	S27 6-1	F23 5-2	S06 2-0		F11 0-0	N29 0-1	O25 1-0	M20 1-1	S03 0-2	N08 1-2	M22 2-1	a06 1-4	D27 1-1	O11 0-1	F14 0-1	S13 2-0	D13 3-3	D26 1-0	F28 3-0	a17 2-2	a03 0-4
6 BRADFORD C	N01 1-1	M17 3-1	N22 3-1	D06 0-1	J03 0-0		m01 2-1	J24 3-1	S20 3-1	N15 3-3	A30 1-3	a05 1-0	M27 2-1	a24 0-1	F07 1-0	D20 3-4	M13 1-1	S10 2-2	a10 1-2	D25 1-1	O18 2-0	O04 3-0
7 BURNLEY	a03 2-1	J17 0-0	S20 3-1	S10 2-1	N22 2-6	S08 1-1		O04 2-3	F28 2-0	a17 5-0	O25 1-2	F14 2-0	N08 2-1	D25 5-3	a02 1-0	S06 2-1	D13 2-1	D27 1-1	O11 2-2	F17 2-0	M20 2-1	M06 2-2
8 CHELSEA	D13 3-1	a02 2-1	F28 2-1	F14 2-3	N01 4-0	F04 1-0	S27 0-1		a17 0-0	S06 0-1	O11 1-0	a03 1-0	J17 1-0	N29 3-1	S13 0-0	M17 2-0	D26 1-0	N15 4-0	D27 1-0	M20 1-1	S01 2-0	a26 2-0
9 DERBY CO	D25 2-1	S08 1-0	D13 0-0	S27 1-2	M27 0-0	S13 3-0	F21 0-2	a24 5-0		a05 2-1	a10 3-0	N29 0-0	A30 1-1	F07 1-2	m01 1-0	O11 3-1	O25 1-1	M13 2-0	J24 5-1	N08 2-1	J03 3-1	D20 0-4
10 EVERTON	O11 2-3	F07 1-1	O25 3-0	N22 3-3	S08 2-0	N08 4-1	a24 2-2	A30 2-3	a02 4-0		D20 0-0	D26 2-0	M13 0-0	a10 5-2	J24 4-0	D06 1-2	F18 0-2	m01 0-1	M27 3-0	J03 1-1	O04 1-3	S20 2-5
11 LIVERPOOL	S01 2-3	S13 2-1	F14 3-0	F04 2-0	N15 3-3	S06 2-1	N01 0-1	O18 0-1	a03 3-0	D27 3-1		M20 1-0	J01 0-0	D13 1-0	S27 1-1	F28 3-0	a05 2-2	N29 1-2	J17 2-0	M10 1-0	D25 3-2	a17 0-0
12 MANCHESTER C	J17 4-1	m01 2-2	N08 8-2	S13 1-4	M13 4-1	J01 1-0	F07 3-1	a10 1-0	N22 3-1	D25 1-1	M27 2-1		O11 3-3	J24 1-0	a24 0-0	S27 4-1	S08 3-1	M17 1-0	A30 3-3	O25 4-2	D27 1-0	D06 2-3
13 MANCHESTER U	F28 0-1	D13 1-2	a17 1-1	a03 1-1	a02 0-1	M20 0-0	N15 0-1	J03 0-2	S06 0-2	M06 1-0	D26 0-0	O18 1-0		O04 1-1	D20 2-1	a26 0-0	F11 1-1	S20 5-1	N01 3-0	S01 0-0	F14 2-0	F25 1-2
14 MIDDLESBROUGH	M20 1-0	O25 1-4	S03 2-2	S17 1-3	D20 1-2	a17 4-0	J01 4-0	N22 0-0	F14 2-0	a03 1-1	D06 3-2	F18 0-2	S27 1-1		N08 0-1	a05 5-2	O11 1-0	J03 4-1	S13 1-0	S06 3-0	M06 0-2	F28 0-0
15 NEWCASTLE U	S06 3-1	J01 2-0	M06 0-0	F28 0-1	O18 4-0	F14 0-1	D26 0-0	S20 3-0	S24 0-0	F11 3-0	O04 3-0	a17 3-0	D27 2-1	D03 0-0		M20 2-1	J03 0-1	N01 1-0	D13 2-1	a03 1-1	N29 2-3	S03 0-2
16 NOTTS CO	N29 2-2	a10 2-1	D25 5-0	J17 2-2	F07 0-2	D27 5-2	A30 2-0	M13 0-1	O18 2-2	D13 1-1	F26 1-0	O04 4-1	m01 0-2	a02 1-1	M27 0-0		a24 2-1	J24 1-2	O02 2-2	S20 3-1	N15 2-2	N01 2-0
17 OLDHAM A	F14 3-0	D27 0-3	a03 0-0	M20 2-0	S20 2-2	M22 0-1	D06 1-0	J01 1-0	N01 3-0	F28 4-1	a02 1-1	S01 1-3	N22 0-3	O18 1-2	J17 1-0	a17 0-0		O04 4-1	N15 4-0	a26 1-0	M08 2-1	S06 2-1
18 PRESTON N.E.	a17 1-1	O11 3-0	S06 0-0	D26 1-1	D06 0-3	S01 1-5	D20 0-1	N08 3-1	M06 1-1	a26 1-1	N22 2-1	F28 1-1	S13 2-3	J17 3-1	O25 2-3	M04 2-0	S27 2-1		a02 2-0	F14 3-0	a03 5-2	M20 0-1
19 SHEFFIELD U	M06 2-0	N22 1-2	O20 2-0	a17 3-2	D25 2-2	a03 0-0	O18 1-3	D20 3-1	F09 0-0	M20 1-1	J03 3-2	S06 3-1	O25 2-2	S20 5-1	D06 2-1	S01 3-0	N08 1-0	J01 2-1		O04 3-0	F28 3-1	F14 1-0
20 SHEFFIELD W	D27 1-2	a29 0-1	O11 0-0	a05 0-2	a19 0-1	D26 1-0	J24 3-1	a06 0-2	N15 2-0	J17 1-0	M13 2-2	N01 0-0	S08 1-3	A30 0-1	M22 0-1	S13 0-0	m01 1-0	F07 0-1	S27 2-1		D13 0-2	N29 0-3
21 SUNDERLAND	S13 1-1	A30 2-1	a05 2-0	O25 2-0	a24 2-0	O11 2-0	M27 3-0	S10 3-2	J17 2-1	S27 2-3	m01 0-1	D20 2-1	F07 3-0	M13 1-1	N22 2-0	N08 3-1	J24 3-0	a10 1-0	M17 3-2	D06 2-1		J01 4-1
22 W.B.A.	a06 1-0	N10 1-2	J17 5-2	O11 4-1	a10 3-1	S27 4-1	M13 4-1	m01 4-0	D27 3-0	S13 4-3	a24 1-1	D13 2-0	J24 2-1	F21 4-1	S08 3-0	O25 8-0	A30 3-1	M27 4-1	F07 0-2	N22 1-3	D26 4-0	

DIVISION 2

	BARNSLEY	BIRMINGHAM	BLACKPOOL	BRISTOL C	BURY	CLAPTON O	COVENTRY C	FULHAM	GRIMSBY T	HUDDERSFIELD T	HULL C	LEEDS C	LEICESTER C	LINCOLN C	NOTTINGHAM F	PORT VALE	ROTHERHAM CO	SOUTH SHIELDS	STOCKPORT CO	STOKE	TOTTENHAM H	WEST HAM U	WOLVERHAMPTON W
1 BARNSLEY		F14 0-5	a17 1-1	a02 0-0	a05 1-3	J03 2-1	M20 1-0	M06 4-1	F09 0-1	a03 3-3	N08 2-3		F28 0-1	O18 5-3	S20 2-2	D26 1-0	O04 4-0	D06 0-1	O25 0-0	S06 1-2	D20 3-0	S01 7-0	N22 4-1
2 BIRMINGHAM	F07 0-0		O11 4-2	J17 1-0	M27 0-2	a24 2-1	S13 4-1	a06 2-0	D27 4-0	S27 4-2	A30 4-1		D26 0-1	M13 7-0	M10 8-0	a10 3-0	N22 2-2	S10 4-0	J24 1-1	D13 2-1	m01 0-1	O25 0-1	N08 2-0
3 BLACKPOOL	a24 0-2	O18 3-0		D27 0-0	a02 1-0	J24 3-0	N29 2-0	N15 1-1	O04 2-0	D13 0-3	M27 2-1	A30 4-2	N01 3-0	S08 6-0	m01 3-2		J01 5-1	F21 0-3	a10 1-0	S20 3-1	F07 0-1	J03 0-0	M13 1-1
4 BRISTOL C	m01 3-1	J03 1-1	D20 0-0		A30 1-0	F07 1-1	N01 1-0	O04 0-3	D06 3-1	N29 2-1	a10 2-2		a05 0-0	S20 6-0	S08 0-0	J24 1-1	O18 2-1	M13 3-1	a24 1-0	N15 1-2	F25 1-2	D26 0-0	M20 1-1
5 BURY	J01 2-0	M20 1-0	D25 1-2	S06 0-1		N22 3-0	a28 2-2	a17 2-2	M06 1-1	S01 2-0	S27 2-0		a03 1-0	D20 3-0	J17 1-1	D06 2-1	F14 4-1	O25 2-1	S13 0-2	F28 1-0	N08 2-1	F11 1-0	O11 2-0
6 CLAPTON O	J17 2-0	a17 2-1	M18 3-0	F14 1-0	N29 2-1		D27 2-2	S04 0-1	a03 3-0	S06 0-1	a02 2-2		a26 3-0	N01 1-0	D13 1-0	N15 2-1	M06 1-2	S27 4-0	D25 2-1	M20 2-1	O18 0-4	F28 1-0	S13 0-0
7 COVENTRY C	M27 1-0	S20 1-3	N22 0-0	O25 0-0	m01 2-1	D20 0-0		O11 0-1	a06 2-0	N08 0-2	F21 0-1	S11 0-4	O04 1-2	a24 2-0	a10 4-2		J03 1-1	J24 1-1	M13 1-1	D25 3-2	A30 0-5	D06 0-0	F07 1-0
8 FULHAM	M13 1-1	a05 1-2	N08 1-2	O13 1-1	a24 1-0	S15 2-1	O18 0-0		D25 2-1	O25 2-2	F07 1-0		S20 5-0	a10 3-0	M27 1-0	m01 4-0	S29 3-0	A30 1-0	F21 4-1	J03 0-0	D06 1-4	N22 1-2	J24 1-1
9 GRIMSBY T	J24 1-1	D20 0-3	S27 1-1	D13 2-2	M13 1-2	a10 2-0	J01 0-1	a02 0-2		S13 1-0	O25 2-1		J03 1-2	F21 2-2	F07 1-0	M27 2-0	N08 0-1	m01 3-1	A30 0-3	N29 2-0	a24 2-0	O11 0-1	S08 0-1
10 HUDDERSFIELD T	a10 4-1	O04 0-0	D06 1-3	N22 1-0	S09 5-0	A30 2-1	N15 5-0	N01 3-0	S20 3-0		M13 2-0		O18 0-0	m01 4-2	a28 2-1	J03 4-1	D25 7-1	F07 2-2	a12 5-0	a06 3-0	J24 1-1	D20 2-0	a14 2-0
11 HULL C	N15 3-1	S06 0-0	M20 0-1	a03 0-0	O04 4-2	O13 3-1	F28 0-1	F14 2-0	N01 4-1	M18 1-4		S20 1-1	F12 5-1	D06 5-2	O18 2-0		a26 1-0	J17 3-0	N22 4-1	S01 3-0	D26 1-3	a17 1-1	D27 10-3
12 LEEDS C			S06 1-0				S03 3-0				S13 1-2												S27 1-1
13 LEICESTER C	M04 0-0	D25 1-0	O25 2-3	a06 2-1	a10 0-5	m01 1-1	S27 1-0	S13 3-2	J17 2-0	O11 0-4	J24 3-2			M27 4-0	M13 0-0	a24 0-1	D06 1-1	N22 0-0	F07 0-2	D20 3-1	S11 2-4	N08 0-0	A30 1-2
14 LINCOLN C	O11 0-4	M06 2-2	S01 0-3	S13 0-0	D27 2-1	O25 2-1	a17 4-1	a03 0-1	F28 2-0	J01 1-3	D13 2-0		M20 0-3		D25 1-4	N22 0-0	J31 0-0	a05 1-1	N08 2-0	F14 2-1	O04 1-1	S06 1-4	J17 4-0
15 NOTTINGHAM F	S13 0-1	F28 1-2	O03 2-0	S01 1-2	J03 1-0	D06 2-1	a03 2-1	M20 0-3	F14 2-0	a17 1-2	O11 0-2		M06 0-0	D26 2-1		F18 0-1	S06 4-1	N08 0-0	S27 1-1	J28 0-2	N22 1-1	a05 2-1	O25 1-0
16 PORT VALE	D25 0-2	a03 1-3		J26 3-1	D13 2-2	N24 4-2		J01 3-4	M20 2-1	M29 0-0			a17 1-2	N29 1-0	J31 4-1		F28 4-2	N10 1-0	a08 2-0	M06 0-3	O27 0-1	F14 1-0	
17 ROTHERHAM CO	S27 1-0	N29 0-3	a05 1-2	O11 2-2	F07 1-2	M13 3-1	J17 4-3	D27 1-1	N15 3-1	D26 1-3	m01 1-2		D13 1-0	J24 3-0	A30 2-0	F21 2-2		a10 1-0	S08 1-0	N01 1-3	M27 1-1	S13 0-1	a24 2-0
18 SOUTH SHIELDS	D13 0-0	S01 1-0	F28 6-0	M10 0-2	N01 0-0	O04 2-0	J31 1-0	S06 2-0	a26 2-0	F14 1-2	J03 7-1		N29 2-0	a02 2-2	N15 5-2	O18 2-0	a03 6-2		D27 3-2	a17 2-2	S20 0-3	M20 3-0	J01 0-0
19 STOCKPORT CO	N01 1-0	M15 2-1	a03 0-0	a17 2-3	S20 1-1	D26 3-1	M06 1-1	F28 2-1	S06 1-2	M20 1-2	N29 3-1		F14 0-2	N15 3-0	O04 0-0	a02 0-4	S01 4-1	D20 1-0		O18 3-1	J03 1-2	a26 1-0	D13 4-1
20 STOKE	A30 2-0	D06 0-1	S13 2-0	N17 2-0	F21 1-1	M27 2-0	D26 6-1	J17 1-0	N22 3-0	a05 0-1	S08 3-1		D27 3-0	F07 1-3	J24 0-2	M13 0-0	O25 3-0	a24 0-0	O11 2-1		a10 1-3	S27 2-1	m01 3-0
21 TOTTENHAM H	D27 4-0	a26 0-0	F14 2-2	F28 2-0	N15 2-1	O11 2-1	S06 4-1	D13 4-0	a17 3-1	F16 2-0	D25 4-0		S01 4-0	S27 6-1	N29 5-2	N01 2-0	M20 2-0	S13 2-0	J17 2-0	a03 2-0		M22 2-0	a02 4-2
22 WEST HAM U	S08 0-2	N01 1-2	J17 1-0	D25 2-0	J24 1-0	M04 0-1	D13 2-0	N29 0-1	O18 1-0	D27 1-1	a24 2-1		N15 1-0	A30 1-1	a02 5-1	F07 3-1	S20 2-1	M27 1-0	m01 3-0	O04 1-1	M13 2-1		a10 4-0
23 WOLVERHAMPTON W	N29 2-4	N15 0-2	M06 0-3	a19 3-1	O18 0-1	S20 1-2	F14 2-0	F23 2-1	S01 6-1	F28 2-3	D20 4-2	O04 2-4	S06 1-1	J03 4-0	N01 4-0		a17 0-1	D26 0-0	D06 2-2	a26 4-0	a05 1-3	a03 1-1	

LEAGUE TABLES

DIVISION 1

	P	W	D	L	F	A	W	D	L	F	A	Pts
W.B.A.	42	17	1	3	65	21	11	3	7	39	26	60
Burnley	42	13	5	3	43	27	8	4	9	22	32	51
Chelsea	42	15	3	3	33	10	7	2	12	23	41	49
Liverpool	42	12	5	4	35	18	7	5	9	24	26	48
Sunderland	42	17	2	2	45	16	5	2	14	27	43	48
Bolton W	42	11	3	7	35	29	8	6	7	37	36	47
Manchester C	42	14	5	2	52	27	4	4	13	19	35	45
Newcastle U	42	11	5	5	31	13	6	4	11	13	26	43
Aston Villa	42	11	3	7	49	36	7	3	11	26	37	42
Arsenal	42	11	5	5	32	21	4	7	10	24	37	42
Bradford P.A.	42	8	6	7	31	26	7	6	8	29	37	42
Manchester U	42	6	8	7	20	17	7	6	8	34	33	40
Middlesbrough	42	10	5	6	35	23	5	5	11	26	42	40
Sheffield U	42	14	5	2	43	20	2	3	16	16	49	40
Bradford C	42	10	6	5	36	25	4	5	12	18	38	39
Everton	42	8	6	7	42	29	4	8	9	27	39	38
Oldham A	42	12	4	5	33	19	3	4	14	16	33	38
Derby Co	42	12	5	4	36	18	1	7	13	11	39	38
Preston N.E.	42	9	6	6	35	27	5	4	12	22	46	38
Blackburn R	42	11	4	6	48	30	2	7	12	16	47	37
Notts Co	42	9	8	4	39	25	3	4	14	17	49	36
Sheffield W	42	6	4	11	14	23	1	5	15	14	41	23

DIVISION 2

	P	W	D	L	F	A	W	D	L	F	A	Pts
Tottenham H	42	19	2	0	60	11	13	4	4	42	21	70
Huddersfield T	42	16	4	1	58	13	12	4	5	39	25	64
Birmingham C	42	14	3	4	54	16	10	5	6	31	18	56
Blackpool	42	13	4	4	40	18	8	6	7	25	29	52
Bury	42	14	4	3	35	15	6	4	11	25	29	48
Fulham	42	11	6	4	36	18	8	3	10	25	32	47
West Ham U	42	14	3	4	34	14	5	6	10	13	26	47
Bristol C	42	9	9	3	30	18	4	8	9	16	25	43
South Shields	42	13	5	3	47	18	2	7	12	11	30	42
Stoke	42	13	3	5	37	15	5	3	13	23	39	42
Hull C	42	13	4	4	53	23	5	2	14	25	49	42
Barnsley	42	9	5	7	41	28	6	5	10	20	27	40
Port Vale	42	11	3	7	35	27	5	5	11	24	35	*40
Leicester C	42	8	6	7	26	29	7	4	10	15	32	40
Clapton O	42	14	3	4	34	17	2	3	16	17	42	38
Stockport Co	42	11	4	6	34	24	3	5	13	18	37	37
Rotherham U	42	10	4	7	32	27	3	4	14	19	56	34
Nottingham F	42	9	4	8	23	22	2	5	14	20	51	31
Wolverhampton W	42	8	4	9	41	32	2	6	13	14	48	30
Coventry C	42	7	7	7	20	26	2	4	15	15	47	29
Lincoln C	42	8	6	7	27	30	1	3	17	17	71	27
Grimsby T	42	8	4	9	23	24	2	1	18	11	51	25

*Port Vale replaced Leeds City

West Brom's Fred Morris scored a record 37 goals when the Throstles won the League Championship in 1919-20. That form earned him two England caps.

Football League Records

Top scorers: Div 1, J.Smith (Bolton Wanderers) 38 goals; Div 2, S.Puddefoot (West Ham United) 29 goals; Div 3, J.Connor (Crystal Palace), E.Simms (Luton Town), G.Whitworth (Northampton Town) 28 goals. Lincoln City failed to gain re-election. Cardiff City and Leeds United were elected to Division Two. Grimsby Town together with the clubs from Division One of the Southern League formed the new Division Three.

Tommy Browell joined Manchester City from Everton for £1,780 and scored 31 goals as City finished Division One runners-up in 1920-21.

DIVISION 1

	ARSENAL	ASTON VILLA	BLACKBURN R	BOLTON W	BRADFORD	BRADFORD C	BURNLEY	CHELSEA	DERBY CO	EVERTON	HUDDERSFIELD T	LIVERPOOL	MANCHESTER C	MANCHESTER U	MIDDLESBROUGH	NEWCASTLE U	OLDHAM A	PRESTON N.E.	SHEFFIELD U	SUNDERLAND	TOTTENHAM H	W.B.A.
1 ARSENAL		S04 0-1	N13 2-0	O09 0-0	a09 2-1	J01 1-2	M19 1-1	D11 1-1	O30 2-0	D27 1-1	N27 2-0	m02 0-0	S11 2-1	A30 2-0	S25 2-2	a23 1-1	F19 2-2	a25 2-1	M26 2-6	J29 1-2	J22 3-2	M28 2-1
2 ASTON VILLA	A28 5-0		a16 3-0	m07 2-0	N20 4-1	F26 1-2	F09 0-0	M28 3-0	a30 1-0	J15 1-3	M12 0-0	J01 0-2	S06 3-1	D25 3-4	a02 0-1	D11 0-0	S25 3-0	O09 1-0	O23 4-0	F12 1-5	S11 4-2	N06 0-0
3 BLACKBURN R	N06 2-2	a09 0-1		N20 2-2	M05 1-0	M25 2-3	J22 1-3	m02 0-0	D04 2-0	S25 0-0	F10 1-2	M26 1-1	O23 0-2	a23 2-0	D18 3-2	M19 3-3	S20 5-1	D25 2-2	F19 1-1	S11 2-0	S04 1-1	O09 5-1
4 BOLTON W	O16 1-1	S15 5-0	N27 2-1		M26 2-0	F05 1-1	M05 1-1	S06 3-1	N13 1-0	M25 4-2	D11 3-1	a23 1-0	S25 3-0	S04 1-1	O30 6-2	a09 3-1	J22 1-1	a04 3-0	M19 2-2	D25 6-2	J01 1-0	S11 3-0
5 BRADFORD	a16 0-1	N27 4-0	F26 1-1	a02 2-1		S25 1-2	O09 1-3	J01 0-2	M12 2-1	A28 3-3	J15 1-1	N13 1-3	a30 1-2	D11 2-4	F12 3-0	O30 0-2	D27 2-1	M28 1-3	S11 2-0	S08 1-1	F05 1-1	m07 0-3
6 BRADFORD C	D18 3-1	M07 3-0	M29 3-4	F16 2-2	O02 2-1		S04 2-0	M26 1-1	D25 2-2	N06 2-2	S18 0-2	F19 0-0	D04 1-2	M19 1-1	O16 0-1	J22 1-1	a23 1-3	m02 6-2	A30 4-0	O23 2-2	a09 1-0	F09 1-1
7 BURNLEY	M12 1-0	F05 7-1	J15 4-1	F26 3-1	O16 1-0	A28 1-4		S25 4-0	F12 2-1	a30 1-1	S06 3-0	D11 1-0	a02 2-1	M25 1-0	S11 2-1	N13 3-1	N27 7-1	D18 2-0	D25 6-0	m07 2-2	O30 2-0	a16 1-1
8 CHELSEA	D04 1-2	M29 5-1	m07 1-2	S01 1-0	D18 4-1	a02 3-1	O02 1-1		S04 1-1	F26 0-1	a16 1-1	D25 1-1	J15 2-1	S18 1-2	a30 1-1	F05 2-0	O23 1-1	N06 1-1	N20 2-1	M12 3-1	O16 0-4	F12 3-0
9 DERBY CO	O23 1-1	a23 2-3	D11 0-1	N06 0-0	M19 1-0	D27 1-1	F23 0-0	A28 0-0		S11 2-4	J01 2-1	a09 0-0	O09 3-0	m02 1-1	N27 0-1	M26 0-1	F05 3-3	J22 1-1	M05 1-1	M28 0-1	A30 2-2	S25 1-1
10 EVERTON	D25 2-4	J22 1-1	O02 2-1	M28 2-3	S04 1-1	N13 2-2	a23 1-1	a06 5-1	S18 3-1		O16 0-0	O30 0-3	F05 3-0	M09 2-0	D11 2-1	S01 3-1	M26 5-2	a09 0-1	S22 3-0	N20 1-1	a27 0-0	J01 2-2
11 HUDDERSFIELD T	N20 0-4	M19 1-0	F05 0-0	D04 0-0	J22 0-0	S11 1-0	A30 1-0	a09 2-0	D18 2-0	O09 0-1		M05 1-2	N06 0-1	M26 5-2	D27 0-1	F23 1-3	m02 3-1	S04 1-0	M29 1-0	S25 0-0	a25 2-0	O23 5-1
12 LIVERPOOL	m07 3-0	D18 4-1	a02 2-0	a30 2-3	N06 0-1	F12 2-1	D04 0-0	D27 2-1	a16 1-1	O23 1-0	F26 4-1		A28 4-2	F09 2-0	M12 0-0	N27 0-1	S11 5-2	S25 6-0	O09 2-2	J15 0-0	M25 1-1	S06 0-0
13 MANCHESTER C	S18 3-1	A30 3-1	O30 0-0	O02 3-1	a23 1-0	D11 1-0	M26 3-0	J22 1-0	O16 0-0	F23 2-0	N13 3-2	S04 3-2		N27 3-0	M25 2-1	m02 3-1	M05 3-1	a20 5-1	a09 2-1	J01 3-1	M09 2-0	D25 4-0
14 MANCHESTER U	S06 1-1	D27 1-3	a30 0-1	A28 2-3	D04 5-1	M12 1-1	M28 0-3	S11 3-1	m07 3-0	F12 1-2	a02 2-0	F05 1-1	N20 1-1		a16 0-1	D18 2-0	O09 4-1	O23 1-0	N06 2-1	F26 3-0	S25 0-1	J15 1-4
15 MIDDLESBROUGH	O02 2-1	M26 1-4	J01 1-1	O23 4-1	F19 2-1	O09 2-1	S18 0-0	a23 0-0	N20 1-0	D04 3-1	D25 2-0	M19 0-1	M28 3-1	a09 2-4		M05 0-0	A28 1-2	A30 0-0	J22 2-2	N06 2-0	m02 1-0	J29 0-1
16 NEWCASTLE U	a30 1-0	D04 2-1	M12 1-2	a16 1-0	O23 2-1	J15 4-0	N06 1-2	F09 1-0	a02 0-1	S08 2-0	F12 1-0	N20 2-0	m07 1-1	J01 6-3	F26 2-0		M25 1-2	S11 4-2	S25 3-0	O09 6-1	D25 1-1	A28 1-1
17 OLDHAM A	F12 1-1	O02 1-1	A30 1-0	J15 0-0	D25 1-0	a30 2-0	N20 2-2	O30 1-2	F14 2-1	a02 0-1	m07 1-2	S18 0-0	F26 2-0	O16 2-2	S04 3-3	M28 0-0		D04 0-2	D18 0-0	a16 2-1	N13 2-5	M12 0-3
18 PRESTON N.E.	F26 0-1	O16 6-1	D27 4-2	F12 1-2	M25 3-3	m07 1-1	J01 0-3	N13 0-1	J15 2-1	a16 1-0	A28 0-1	O02 2-3	M12 0-1	O30 0-0	S06 2-0	S18 3-2	D11 4-0		F07 2-0	a30 1-1	N27 4-1	a02 2-1
19 SHEFFIELD U	a02 1-1	O30 0-0	F12 1-1	M12 2-2	S18 2-0	S06 4-1	D27 1-1	N27 0-1	F26 0-1	O04 2-0	D29 1-1	O16 0-1	a16 1-1	N13 0-0	J15 1-1	O02 0-3	J01 3-0	F05 1-0		A28 1-1	D11 1-1	a30 0-2
20 SUNDERLAND	F05 5-1	F23 0-1	S18 2-0	D27 0-0	S01 5-1	O30 0-0	m02 1-0	M19 1-0	M25 3-0	N27 0-2	O02 2-1	J22 2-1	D18 1-0	M05 2-3	N13 1-2	O16 0-2	a09 1-1	a23 2-2	S04 3-1		M26 0-1	D11 3-0
21 TOTTENHAM H	J15 2-1	S18 1-2	A28 1-2	D18 5-2	F03 2-0	a16 2-0	O23 1-2	O09 5-0	S06 2-0	M12 2-0	a30 1-0	M28 1-0	F12 2-0	O02 4-1	m07 2-2	D27 2-0	N06 5-1	N20 1-2	D04 4-1	a02 0-0		F26 1-0
22 W.B.A.	M29 3-4	N13 2-1	O16 1-1	S18 2-1	m02 0-1	N27 2-0	a09 2-0	M14 1-1	O02 3-0	D18 1-2	O30 3-0	S01 1-1	D27 2-2	J22 0-2	F05 0-1	S04 0-0	M19 0-0	M26 0-3	a23 1-1	D04 4-1	F23 3-1	

DIVISION 2

	BARNSLEY	BIRMINGHAM	BLACKPOOL	BRISTOL C	BURY	CARDIFF C	CLAPTON O	COVENTRY C	FULHAM	HULL C	LEEDS U	LEICESTER C	NOTTINGHAM F	NOTTS CO	PORT VALE	ROTHERHAM CO	SHEFFIELD W	SOUTH SHIELDS	STOCKPORT CO	STOKE	WEST HAM U	WOLVERHAMPTON W
1 BARNSLEY		a02 1-1	D27 0-1	D11 1-1	N27 5-0	F12 0-2	N13 1-0	a30 2-2	F26 3-1	O02 0-0	a16 1-1	J15 2-1	J01 0-0	S06 2-2	M28 3-0	J29 2-1	A28 0-0	S18 1-1	O30 2-0	m07 1-0	M12 1-1	O16 3-2
2 BIRMINGHAM	M26 1-3		O16 3-0	M19 0-0	M05 4-0	S18 1-1	F19 0-0	D04 3-2	M29 1-0	A30 5-1	D18 1-0	O02 5-0	a09 3-0	F05 2-1	m02 4-0	a23 3-2	O30 4-0	S04 1-1	J22 5-0	N27 3-0	D27 2-1	N13 4-1
3 BLACKPOOL	D25 1-0	O09 3-0		A30 1-2	S04 0-1	N20 2-4	S13 2-2	S11 4-0	N06 1-0	M26 1-2	S25 1-0	D04 2-0	J22 1-0	D18 0-2	M05 1-0	F19 0-1	F05 1-1	M19 3-2	a23 1-1	M25 3-1	O23 1-0	a09 3-0
4 BRISTOL C	D04 1-0	M12 0-1	S08 1-1		N13 1-0	J15 0-0	O30 2-0	a16 2-0	F12 2-0	S18 2-1	a02 0-0	J29 1-0	N20 1-0	A28 0-1	D27 3-0	J01 2-4	m07 0-1	M28 4-2	O16 5-1	a30 5-0	F26 1-0	O02 2-0
5 BURY	N20 0-0	F26 0-1	A28 2-2	N06 2-0		J01 3-1	O09 0-1	a02 2-0	J15 1-1	M25 0-0	M12 1-1	S08 4-0	O23 2-2	m07 0-1	J29 1-0	D04 1-0	a30 1-1	D25 1-0	O02 1-1	a16 3-0	F12 1-0	S18 3-1
6 CARDIFF C	M09 3-2	S11 2-1	N27 0-0	J22 1-0	D18 2-1		A30 0-0	D27 0-1	O16 3-0	a23 0-0	M28 1-0	N13 2-0	a04 3-0	O30 1-1	M26 1-2	a11 1-0	D11 1-0	a09 1-0	S04 3-0	F05 0-1	S25 0-0	m02 2-0
7 CLAPTON O	N25 3-2	F12 1-1	m07 0-0	O23 0-0	O16 1-0	S06 2-0		M12 0-0	D04 3-0	D25 1-1	F26 1-0	A28 2-0	O02 2-1	a30 3-0	a25 0-0	N20 2-0	a16 1-0	F05 1-0	S18 5-0	a02 3-2	J15 0-1	M25 0-1
8 COVENTRY C	a23 3-1	D11 0-4	S18 0-2	a09 2-1	M26 1-0	D25 2-4	M19 1-1		F05 0-2	J22 3-2	N27 1-1	M29 1-0	m02 0-0	N13 1-1	A30 0-0	S04 0-1	O02 2-3	O16 1-0	M05 1-1	O30 1-0	O04 0-1	F24 4-0
9 FULHAM	M05 1-0	M25 5-0	N13 1-2	F28 3-0	J22 0-0	O09 0-3	D11 1-0	M14 2-0		m02 3-0	D27 1-0	O30 1-1	M19 2-1	S25 3-1	a09 1-0	M26 1-0	N27 2-0	a23 0-0	A30 3-1	J01 1-3	S11 0-0	A28 2-0
10 HULL C	S25 3-0	S06 1-0	a02 2-1	S11 2-0	M28 1-1	a30 2-0	D27 3-0	J15 1-1	m07 0-0		O23 0-1	a16 1-1	D04 0-3	M12 1-1	N06 1-1	O09 1-1	F26 1-1	N27 0-2	F03 1-1	F12 1-1	S04 2-1	D18 0-1
11 LEEDS U	a09 0-0	J01 1-0	O02 2-0	M26 0-1	M19 1-0	M29 1-2	M05 2-1	D01 4-0	D25 0-0	O30 1-1		S18 3-1	a23 1-1	D11 3-0	S04 3-1	J08 1-0	O16 2-0	S01 1-2	F19 0-2	N13 0-0	J29 1-2	J22 3-0
12 LEICESTER C	J22 2-0	S25 3-0	D11 0-1	F05 0-0	S02 4-0	N06 2-0	S04 2-1	M28 0-1	O23 1-1	a09 0-0	S11 1-1		F19 2-0	N27 0-3	M19 0-0	M05 1-1	J01 2-1	M26 2-0	m02 0-0	D25 3-1	O09 1-0	a28 0-0
13 NOTTINGHAM F	D18 0-0	a16 1-1	J15 3-1	N27 0-1	O30 4-2	F26 1-2	S25 1-1	m07 0-2	M12 5-1	D11 2-0	a30 1-0	F12 1-2		S11 1-0	O09 1-4	D25 6-1	O07 4-2	N13 1-2	M25 1-1	A28 2-2	a02 1-0	F05 1-1
14 NOTTS CO	A30 1-0	F16 0-0	J01 1-2	S04 2-2	m02 2-1	O23 1-2	a23 3-1	N06 1-1	O02 2-1	M19 4-1	D04 1-2	N20 1-1	S18 2-0		F19 0-1	J22 1-0	D27 3-0	M05 2-0	a09 3-0	O16 3-0	M28 1-1	M26 2-1
15 PORT VALE	M25 1-1	m07 0-2	F26 0-1	D25 0-2	F05 3-0	a02 0-0	J01 4-0	S06 0-0	a16 0-0	N13 4-0	A28 2-0	M12 0-0	O16 0-1	F12 1-2		S11 1-1	J15 1-0	O30 0-2	D11 6-1	S25 2-1	a30 1-2	N27 2-3
16 ROTHERHAM CO	F05 1-0	a30 1-1	F12 0-2	S20 0-0	D11 0-5	M12 2-0	N27 0-0	A28 2-3	a02 2-0	O16 1-1	m07 0-2	F26 1-1	D27 0-0	J15 0-0	S18 1-1		N01 2-0	O02 5-4	N13 1-0	S06 1-1	a16 2-0	O30 1-0
17 SHEFFIELD W	S04 0-0	O23 1-2	F07 0-1	m02 2-2	a23 2-0	D04 0-1	a09 1-1	S25 3-0	N20 3-0	M21 3-0	O09 2-0	D18 0-0	A30 0-0	D25 1-1	J22 1-0	M28 2-0		F19 1-1	M26 2-1	S11 1-3	N06 0-1	a11 6-0
18 SOUTH SHIELDS	S11 3-2	A28 3-0	M12 1-0	M25 0-0	D27 2-0	a16 0-1	F02 3-0	O09 4-1	a30 3-0	N20 0-0	S08 3-0	a02 4-3	N06 0-1	F26 1-0	O23 6-1	S25 1-0	F12 2-3		J01 3-1	J15 1-1	m07 0-0	D04 1-2
19 STOCKPORT CO	O23 3-2	J15 0-3	a30 2-2	O09 0-2	S25 1-2	A28 2-5	S11 6-0	F26 3-0	S13 1-1	F05 2-2	F12 3-1	m07 0-0	M28 1-0	a16 1-0	D04 0-0	N06 0-1	a02 0-1	D18 0-0		M12 2-0	N20 2-0	D25 1-2
20 STOKE	m02 3-2	N20 1-2	M28 1-1	a23 0-0	a09 0-1	F14 0-0	M26 0-1	O23 4-1	D18 1-2	a11 1-3	N06 4-0	D27 1-1	S04 4-0	O09 1-0	O02 0-1	A30 2-0	S18 0-1	J22 0-0	M19 1-0		D04 1-0	M10 1-0
21 WEST HAM U	M19 2-1	D25 1-1	O30 1-1	M05 1-0	F19 0-1	O02 1-1	J22 1-0	J01 7-0	S18 2-0	A28 1-1	F05 3-0	O16 0-1	M26 3-0	M25 0-2	a23 1-1	a09 1-0	N13 4-0	m02 2-1	N27 5-0	D11 1-0		S06 1-0
22 WOLVERHAMPTON W	O09 1-1	N06 0-3	a16 3-1	S25 0-0	S11 2-1	m07 1-3	M28 0-2	F12 1-0	S04 1-0	J01 1-3	J15 3-0	a30 3-0	F14 2-1	a02 1-0	N20 2-2	O23 3-0	M12 1-2	D11 3-0	D27 2-0	F26 3-3	A30 1-2	

Joe Lane joined Birmingham from Blackpool, for a club record fee of £3,600, and scored 15 goals as the Blues were promoted to Division One.

SEASON 1920-21

DIVISION 3

	BRENTFORD	BRIGHTON & HA	BRISTOL R	CRYSTAL P	EXETER C	GILLINGHAM	GRIMSBY T	LUTON T	MERTHYR T	MILLWALL	NEWPORT CO	NORTHAMPTON T	NORWICH C	PLYMOUTH A	PORTSMOUTH	Q.P.R.	READING	SOUTHAMPTON	SOUTHEND U	SWANSEA T	SWINDON T	WATFORD
1 BRENTFORD		S11 2-0	N13 0-0	S25 0-4	S04 0-0	J22 3-3	M28 5-0	D11 1-0	a25 0-0	A30 1-0	D18 2-2	M26 1-1	O16 3-1	m02 0-0	M05 1-2	D25 0-2	N27 3-2	O30 1-1	a09 2-2	F05 1-2	F19 0-1	M19 1-0
2 BRIGHTON & H.A.	S18 4-0		O02 2-0	D25 0-2	J22 1-1	M19 1-0	S29 1-3	O30 1-1	S01 0-0	F19 1-0	M05 1-0	m07 3-2	M25 2-0	N13 1-0	a09 3-0	D04 2-1	O16 2-2	F05 1-1	S04 1-0	N27 1-1	M26 0-3	a23 0-3
3 BRISTOL R	N06 2-1	S25 3-1		O09 2-1	m02 5-0	F05 2-0	S11 2-0	M29 5-0	a09 1-1	S04 1-2	S01 3-2	M19 4-2	O23 2-2	a23 2-0	F19 2-2	M25 3-0	D11 3-2	N27 1-2	M26 2-1	D25 1-2	J22 3-1	M05 2-0
4 CRYSTAL P	O02 4-2	D27 3-2	O16 3-0		N27 2-1	M05 4-1	F09 2-0	N13 2-1	S04 3-0	J22 3-2	F19 2-0	a23 5-1	S18 1-0	S01 0-0	M26 3-0	J01 0-0	O30 2-0	M29 1-1	N03 2-3	D11 0-1	M19 1-0	a09 2-2
5 EXETER C	A28 3-0	J15 1-0	m07 1-0	N20 1-1		O09 2-1	F12 1-1	a02 1-0	F05 3-3	S11 4-0	S25 0-1	D04 4-0	S01 1-1	D27 1-1	M28 0-0	F26 0-1	a30 0-1	a16 1-0	O20 0-0	M12 1-2	O23 1-0	N06 1-2
6 GILLINGHAM	J15 1-3	M12 1-0	J29 1-0	F26 0-1	O16 2-1		a02 2-1	m07 0-0	S11 0-0	O30 0-0	N13 1-4	D25 2-5	F12 0-0	O02 0-1	S15 1-1	a16 1-2	S08 1-0	A28 1-1	M25 1-1	a30 2-1	a13 1-1	M16 1-1
7 GRIMSBY T	M25 2-0	J01 2-2	S18 3-1	F05 1-0	F19 2-0	M26 2-0		O16 0-1	O30 1-1	M05 0-2	M19 1-1	A28 2-0	D25 1-1	J22 1-1	a23 0-3	N20 2-1	O02 2-0	D11 3-0	A30 1-0	N13 0-2	a09 3-0	m02 3-0
8 LUTON T	D04 2-0	O23 3-2	J01 1-2	N06 2-2	M26 3-0	D28 5-0	O09 3-1		M05 1-0	a09 0-0	a23 2-2	J22 3-1	N20 4-0	M19 1-1	A30 2-2	O02 2-1	F09 6-0	D25 1-1	m02 4-0	S11 3-0	S04 2-0	M28 1-0
9 MERTHYR T	a30 3-1	S06 4-1	a16 2-2	A28 2-1	J29 7-1	S18 6-1	O23 3-1	F26 4-1		D27 0-1	M28 1-2	N06 1-0	m07 0-0	D18 0-0	F21 2-1	J15 3-1	a02 1-0	M12 1-1	N22 2-0	F12 0-3	O02 2-2	O09 2-0
10 MILLWALL	S06 0-0	F12 0-1	A28 2-0	J15 0-1	S18 2-0	O23 4-0	F26 0-1	a16 0-0	D25 0-0		O16 1-0	J01 1-0	D11 2-0	M28 0-0	O02 1-0	M12 0-0	m07 2-0	a30 0-1	F05 4-2	a02 0-2	N06 5-0	N20 1-0
11 NEWPORT CO	J01 3-1	F26 0-4	S09 0-2	F12 0-1	O02 2-0	N06 1-0	M12 2-1	a30 2-0	M25 0-3	O09 3-1		J29 1-1	J13 2-0	S18 0-0	O23 1-0	a02 1-3	A28 0-1	m07 0-0	D25 1-1	a09 1-1	O21 0-1	D04 0-2
12 NORTHAMPTON T	a02 6-2	m02 1-0	M12 1-2	a30 2-2	D11 3-3	D27 2-0	S04 4-1	J15 1-0	N13 2-2	S13 0-2	F05 0-2		a16 1-0	N27 1-1	O09 1-0	S06 0-3	F26 1-0	F12 2-0	O30 1-0	S25 2-0	M29 1-2	S11 0-1
13 NORWICH C	O09 0-0	M28 3-0	O30 1-1	S11 0-1	S08 0-0	F19 2-1	D27 0-0	N27 3-0	m02 0-0	D04 2-0	J22 3-0	a09 3-3		S04 0-0	M19 2-2	F05 2-0	N13 2-0	S25 0-1	a23 3-1	J01 1-1	M05 3-2	M26 1-1
14 PLYMOUTH A	m07 1-0	N06 5-0	a30 2-1	S08 0-1	D25 0-0	S25 3-1	J15 0-0	M12 1-0	J01 2-1	M25 0-2	S11 5-1	N20 0-2	A28 1-1		a13 2-0	F12 1-0	a16 1-1	a02 0-0	D11 0-0	F26 1-0	O09 0-0	O23 0-2
15 PORTSMOUTH	F26 0-2	a16 3-0	F12 1-0	a02 0-0	M25 2-1	N27 2-2	a30 2-1	S08 3-0	D11 0-0	S25 0-0	O30 0-2	O16 2-0	M12 2-1	F05 1-1		m07 0-0	J15 2-2	S18 0-1	N13 3-0	A28 3-0	D18 1-1	D27 1-0
16 Q.P.R.	D27 1-0	D11 4-0	M28 2-1	D18 3-0	M05 2-1	a09 0-1	N27 2-0	S25 4-1	J22 4-2	M19 0-0	M26 2-0	S02 1-2	F17 2-0	M17 4-0	m02 0-0		S11 2-0	N13 0-0	O09 2-0	O30 1-1	a23 1-0	A28 1-2
17 READING	N20 2-1	O09 0-1	D04 2-1	O23 1-0	a23 0-1	S01 1-2	S25 4-1	F05 0-1	M26 2-0	J29 0-1	S04 4-0	M05 4-0	N06 0-1	a09 1-1	J22 1-0	S18 0-0		D18 0-4	M19 1-1	M28 1-3	D25 2-3	F19 0-0
18 SOUTHAMPTON	O23 3-0	F23 1-0	N20 4-0	M28 1-1	a09 3-0	S04 3-0	D04 0-1	D27 1-1	M19 5-0	a23 1-1	m02 0-0	M09 3-1	O02 1-0	M26 1-0	S11 2-0	N06 2-2	J01 1-2		M05 3-0	O09 3-0	A30 4-0	J22 4-1
19 SOUTHEND U	a16 4-1	A28 2-0	a02 1-0	m07 0-2	J01 0-0	M28 1-0	S06 3-1	F12 1-1	N27 0-1	a06 1-2	D27 2-1	O23 1-2	a30 3-1	D04 2-1	N06 2-1	O16 1-0	M12 1-0	F26 1-0		J15 1-2	S11 1-3	O02 4-1
20 SWANSEA T	a28 1-1	N20 0-0	D27 2-2	D04 0-0	M19 2-1	a23 2-0	N06 3-1	S18 1-1	F19 1-0	M26 0-0	a16 1-2	O02 2-2	S16 5-2	M05 3-0	S04 0-0	O23 1-3	M25 2-1	O16 1-1	J22 2-0		m02 1-1	S02 2-1
21 SWINDON T	F12 1-0	a02 2-0	J15 2-1	M12 1-3	O30 1-1	D11 1-1	a16 0-0	A28 9-1	S25 3-0	N13 4-1	N27 5-0	M28 2-1	F26 4-2	O16 1-1	J01 5-2	a30 0-1	D27 2-0	S06 3-2	**S18 3-0**	m07 0-0		a20 2-0
22 WATFORD	M12 1-0	a30 1-0	F26 2-1	a16 1-1	N13 0-0	J01 3-1	m07 4-2	M25 1-0	O16 1-0	N27 1-0	D11 5-1	S18 7-1	a02 2-0	O30 1-1	D25 3-2	S04 0-2	F12 1-2	J15 0-0	S25 3-0	S08 3-0	F05 0-1	

Crystal Palace, the first champions of Division Three. Back row (left to right, players only): Harry, Nixon, King, Alderson, Irwin, Allen, Dreyer. Second row: Wood, McCracken, Jones, Kennedy, Wells, Wibley, Rhodes, Collier, Little. Front row: Bateman, Smith, Feebury, Cartwright. On ground: Conner, Storey, Menlove, Hann.

LEAGUE TABLES

DIVISION 1

	P	W	D	L	F	A	W	D	L	F	A	Pts
Burnley	42	17	3	1	56	16	6	10	5	23	20	59
Manchester C	42	19	2	0	50	13	5	4	12	20	37	54
Bolton W	42	15	6	0	53	17	4	8	9	24	36	52
Liverpool	42	11	7	3	41	17	7	8	6	22	18	51
Newcastle U	42	14	3	4	43	18	6	7	8	23	27	50
Tottenham H	42	15	2	4	46	16	4	7	10	24	32	47
Everton	42	9	8	4	40	26	8	5	8	26	29	47
Middlesbrough	42	10	6	5	29	21	7	6	8	24	32	46
Arsenal	42	9	8	4	31	25	6	6	9	28	38	44
Aston Villa	42	11	4	6	39	21	7	3	11	24	49	43
Blackburn R	42	7	9	5	36	27	6	6	9	21	32	41
Sunderland	42	11	4	6	34	19	3	9	9	23	41	41
Manchester U	42	9	4	8	34	26	6	6	9	30	42	40
W.B.A.	42	8	7	6	31	23	5	7	9	23	35	40
Bradford C	42	7	9	5	38	28	5	6	10	23	35	39
Preston N.E.	42	10	4	7	38	25	5	5	11	23	40	39
Huddersfield T	42	11	4	6	26	16	4	5	12	16	33	39
Chelsea	42	9	7	5	35	24	4	6	11	13	34	39
Oldham A	42	6	9	6	23	26	3	6	12	26	60	33
Sheffield U	42	5	11	5	22	19	1	7	13	20	49	30
Derby Co	42	3	12	6	21	23	2	4	15	11	35	26
Bradford P.A.	42	6	5	10	29	35	2	3	16	14	41	24

DIVISION 2

	P	W	D	L	F	A	W	D	L	F	A	Pts
Birmingham C	42	16	4	1	55	13	8	6	7	24	25	58
Cardiff C	42	13	5	3	27	9	11	5	5	32	23	58
Bristol C	42	14	3	4	35	12	5	10	6	14	17	51
Blackpool	42	12	3	6	32	19	8	7	6	22	23	50
West Ham U	42	13	5	3	38	11	6	5	10	13	19	48
Notts Co	42	12	5	4	36	17	6	6	9	19	23	47
Clapton O	42	13	6	2	31	9	3	7	11	12	33	45
South Shields	42	13	4	4	41	16	4	6	11	20	30	44
Fulham	42	14	4	3	33	12	2	6	13	10	35	42
Sheffield W	42	9	7	5	31	14	6	4	11	17	34	41
Bury	42	10	8	3	29	13	5	2	14	16	36	40
Leicester C	42	10	8	3	26	11	2	8	11	13	35	40
Hull C	42	7	10	4	24	18	3	10	8	19	35	40
Leeds U	42	11	5	5	30	14	3	5	13	10	31	38
Wolverhampton W	42	11	4	6	34	24	5	2	14	15	42	38
Barnsley	42	9	10	2	31	17	1	6	14	17	33	36
Port Vale	42	7	6	8	28	19	4	8	9	15	30	36
Nottingham F	42	9	6	6	37	26	3	6	12	11	29	36
Rotherham U	42	8	9	4	23	21	4	3	14	14	32	36
Stoke	42	9	5	7	26	16	3	6	12	20	40	35
Coventry C	42	8	6	7	24	25	4	5	12	15	45	35
Stockport Co	42	8	6	7	30	24	1	6	14	12	51	30

DIVISION 3

	P	W	D	L	F	A	W	D	L	F	A	Pts
Crystal Palace	42	15	4	2	45	17	9	7	5	25	17	59
Southampton	42	14	5	2	46	10	5	11	5	18	18	54
Q.P.R.	42	14	4	3	38	11	8	5	8	23	21	53
Swindon T	42	14	5	2	51	17	7	5	9	22	32	52
Swansea T	42	9	10	2	32	19	9	5	7	24	26	51
Watford	42	14	4	3	40	15	6	4	11	19	29	48
Millwall	42	11	5	5	25	8	7	6	8	17	22	47
Merthyr T	42	13	5	3	46	20	2	10	9	14	29	45
Luton T	42	14	6	1	51	15	2	6	13	10	41	44
Bristol R	42	15	3	3	51	22	3	4	14	17	35	43
Plymouth A	42	10	7	4	25	13	1	14	6	10	21	43
Portsmouth	42	10	8	3	28	14	2	7	12	18	34	39
Grimsby T	42	12	5	4	32	16	3	4	14	17	43	39
Northampton T	42	11	4	6	32	23	4	4	13	27	52	38
Newport Co	42	8	5	8	20	23	6	4	11	23	41	37
Norwich C	42	9	10	2	31	14	1	6	14	13	39	36
Southend U	42	13	2	6	32	20	1	6	14	12	41	36
Brighton & H.A.	42	11	6	4	28	20	3	2	16	14	41	36
Exeter C	42	9	7	5	27	15	1	8	12	12	39	35
Reading	42	8	4	9	26	22	4	3	14	16	37	31
Brentford	42	7	9	5	27	23	2	3	16	15	44	30
Gillingham	42	6	9	6	19	24	2	3	16	15	50	28

Arthur Dominy helped Southampton from the Southern League into the Football League and proved a fine captain. He joined Everton in 1926.

FOOTBALL LEAGUE RECORDS

Top scorers: Div 1, A.Wilson (Middlesbrough) 31 goals; Div 2, J.Broad (Stoke) 25 goals; Div 3 N, J.Carmichael (Grimsby Town) 37 goals; Div 3 S, F.Richardson (Plymouth Argyle) 31 goals.

Division Three became the Southern Section and a Northern Section was formed consisting of 16 new clubs plus re-elected Chesterfield, Crewe Alexandra, Lincoln City and Walsall.

Inside-forward Dick Forshaw was an ever-present as Liverpool won the title in successive seasons.

DIVISION 1

	ARSENAL	ASTON VILLA	BIRMINGHAM	BLACKBURN R	BOLTON W	BRADFORD C	BURNLEY	CARDIFF C	CHELSEA	EVERTON	HUDDERSFIELD T	LIVERPOOL	MANCHESTER C	MANCHESTER U	MIDDLESBROUGH	NEWCASTLE U	OLDHAM A	PRESTON N.E.	SHEFFIELD U	SUNDERLAND	TOTTENHAM H	W.B.A.
1 ARSENAL		M25 2-0	N12 5-2	D10 1-1	D12 1-1	m06 1-0	J21 0-0	D26 0-0	J14 1-0	O01 1-0	O29 1-3	M22 1-0	S17 0-1	a05 3-1	a01 2-2	F04 2-1	D24 0-1	S05 1-0	A27 1-2	O15 1-2	a22 1-0	a18 2-2
2 ASTON VILLA	M18 2-0		M11 1-1	S12 1-1	a15 2-1	N12 7-1	J14 2-0	A29 2-1	a17 1-4	F08 2-1	F25 2-0	D03 1-1	S03 4-0	N19 3-1	O29 6-2	D24 1-0	a29 2-0	S17 2-0	D27 5-3	F11 2-0	O01 2-1	O15 0-1
3 BIRMINGHAM	N05 0-1	M15 1-0		N26 1-0	O22 1-1	a22 1-0	A27 2-3	D31 0-1	S05 5-1	S17 1-1	O08 0-2	F04 0-2	a18 3-1	F18 0-1	M25 4-3	J21 0-4	D10 3-0	m06 0-2	D17 2-1	O01 1-0	a01 0-3	D27 0-2
4 BLACKBURN R	D03 0-1	a01 1-2	N19 1-1		D17 1-2	S19 3-1	**F04 3-2**	J02 1-3	A27 1-1	O15 2-2	N12 2-0	M04 0-0	O01 3-1	M25 3-0	a22 2-2	M06 0-2	J14 3-2	D26 3-0	J21 2-3	O29 1-2	m06 1-1	S17 2-3
5 BOLTON W	N19 1-0	a22 1-0	O29 1-2	D24 1-1		S10 3-3	F18 0-1	O15 1-2	J21 0-2	J14 1-0	S24 3-1	M25 1-3	D10 5-0	a08 1-0	m06 4-2	M04 3-2	J02 5-1	A27 2-2	F04 3-1	a17 1-1	S05 1-0	N12 2-0
6 BRADFORD C	a29 0-2	N05 3-2	a15 1-2	A29 1-1	S17 4-3		O01 0-4	M15 1-0	N26 0-1	M11 3-1	a01 4-0	D31 0-0	F25 1-2	D03 2-1	O08 0-2	a17 2-3	S03 3-0	D17 1-0	O22 1-1	M18 0-0	D27 0-4	M08 1-1
7 BURNLEY	F20 1-0	D31 2-1	S03 3-1	F11 1-2	F25 2-0	S24 4-0		M18 1-1	O22 5-0	a29 2-0	D10 1-0	a14 1-1	a15 5-2	D27 4-2	D24 3-1	S10 2-0	M11 0-1	N05 3-3	O08 2-1	S05 2-0	N26 1-0	a08 4-2
8 CARDIFF C	D27 4-3	S05 0-4	J14 3-1	a17 1-3	O08 1-2	J21 6-3	M25 4-2		F08 2-0	N19 2-1	D17 0-0	a22 2-0	N05 0-2	m06 3-1	S24 3-1	a08 1-0	S'0 0-1	F04 3-0	a26 1-1	D03 2-0	A27 0-1	O29 2-0
9 CHELSEA	D31 0-2	a14 1-0	A29 1-2	S03 1-0	J18 0-3	N19 1-0	O29 4-1	F25 1-0		a01 1-0	a10 1-0	S24 0-1	M18 0-0	S10 0-0	D27 1-1	O08 1-1	F11 1-0	D03 0-0	N05 0-2	a15 1-0	D24 1-2	M11 1-1
10 EVERTON	S24 1-1	J21 3-2	S10 2-1	O08 2-0	D31 1-0	M04 2-0	m06 2-0	N26 0-1	a08 2-3		a14 6-2	N05 1-1	D24 2-2	A27 5-0	M01 4-1	S07 2-3	O22 2-2	a10 0-0	a22 1-1	J02 3-0	M15 0-0	D03 1-2
11 HUDDERSFIELD T	O22 2-0	a05 1-0	O15 1-0	N05 3-0	O01 3-0	a08 1-2	D03 1-0	D24 0-1	m06 2-0	a18 1-2		J21 0-1	D26 2-0	F27 1-1	m01 2-1	A27 1-2	N26 1-0	a22 6-0	S06 1-1	S17 1-2	M27 1-1	J14 2-0
12 LIVERPOOL	F25 4-0	D10 2-0	F11 1-0	M11 2-0	M18 0-2	J14 2-1	a17 2-1	a15 5-1	O01 1-1	N12 1-1	D27 2-0		A31 3-2	D17 2-1	N19 4-0	D26 1-0	a01 2-0	O15 4-0	S17 1-1	S03 2-1	O29 1-1	a29 1-2
13 MANCHESTER C	S10 2-0	A27 2-1	a14 1-0	S24 1-1	D03 2-3	F22 3-2	a22 2-0	N12 1-1	M25 0-0	D17 2-1	J02 2-1	S07 1-1		O22 4-1	J21 2-2	m06 1-0	O08 2-1	a05 2-0	a08 2-2	D31 3-0	F04 3-3	N19 6-1
14 MANCHESTER U	M11 1-0	N26 1-0	F25 1-1	M18 0-1	a01 0-1	D10 1-1	D26 0-1	a29 1-1	S17 0-0	S03 2-1	F11 1-1	D24 0-0	O29 3-1		N05 3-5	J14 0-1	a15 0-3	O01 1-1	a17 3-2	J28 3-1	O15 2-1	A29 2-3
15 MIDDLESBROUGH	a08 4-2	O22 5-0	M18 1-1	a15 0-1	a29 4-2	O15 1-2	D17 4-1	O01 0-0	D26 0-1	F11 3-1	M11 5-1	N26 3-1	F01 4-1	N12 2-0		D10 1-1	A29 1-1	a17 1-0	J14 1-1	F25 3-0	S17 0-0	S03 3-2
16 NEWCASTLE U	F11 3-1	D17 1-2	F08 0-1	F25 2-0	M11 2-1	a14 1-2	S17 2-1	a01 0-0	O15 1-0	A31 3-0	S03 1-2	J02 1-1	a29 5-1	D31 3-0	D03 0-0		M18 1-1	O29 3-1	O01 2-1	N19 2-2	N12 0-2	a15 3-0
17 OLDHAM A	D17 2-1	m06 3-1	D03 0-1	D31 1-1	D26 0-0	A27 0-0	M04 0-1	S17 2-1	F04 0-3	O29 0-0	N19 1-1	a08 4-0	O15 0-1	a22 1-1	S05 0-1	M25 0-0		J21 2-0	F18 0-2	N12 3-0	a17 1-0	O01 1-0
18 PRESTON N.E.	A29 3-2	S10 1-0	m01 2-2	D27 2-1	S03 3-1	D24 2-1	N12 2-1	F11 1-1	D10 2-0	M18 1-0	a15 1-1	O08 1-1	M11 1-0	S24 3-2	a14 1-1	O22 2-0	F09 0-0		N26 3-0	a01 1-1	J14 1-2	F25 0-3
19 SHEFFIELD U	S03 4-1	D26 2-3	D24 1-2	F27 0-1	F11 1-0	O29 1-0	O15 0-1	M11 0-2	N12 1-2	a15 1-0	A29 1-1	S10 0-1	a01 1-0	J02 3-0	D31 6-1	S24 1-1	F25 1-0	N19 3-0		a29 4-1	D10 1-0	M18 0-0
20 SUNDERLAND	O08 1-0	F04 1-4	S24 2-1	O22 3-1	a14 6-2	M25 0-0	A31 3-2	D10 4-1	a22 1-2	D26 1-2	S10 2-2	A27 3-0	J14 2-3	J21 2-1	F18 1-1	N26 0-0	N05 5-1	a08 1-0	M04 1-0		a05 2-0	D24 5-0
21 TOTTENHAM H	a15 2-0	S24 3-1	a08 2-1	a29 2-1	A29 1-2	D26 1-0	N19 1-1	S03 4-1	D17 0-0	F25 2-0	M18 1-0	O22 0-1	F11 3-1	O08 2-2	S10 2-4	N05 4-0	a14 3-1	D31 5-0	D03 2-1	M11 1-0		J30 2-0
22 W.B.A.	a17 0-3	O08 0-1	D26 1-0	S10 0-2	N05 0-1	F04 1-1	a01 2-0	O22 2-2	M04 2-2	D10 1-1	D31 3-2	m06 1-4	N26 2-0	S07 0-0	A27 0-0	a22 1-2	S24 0-1	M29 2-0	M25 3-0	D17 2-1	J21 3-0	

Bill Rawlings scored 30 goals for Division Three champions Southampton and was eventually capped by England when playing in Division Two.

DIVISION 2

	BARNSLEY	BLACKPOOL	BRADFORD	BRISTOL C	BURY	CLAPTON O	COVENTRY C	CRYSTAL P	DERBY CO	FULHAM	HULL C	LEEDS U	LEICESTER C	NOTTINGHAM F	NOTTS CO	PORT VALE	ROTHERHAM CO	SHEFFIELD W	SOUTH SHIELDS	STOKE	WEST HAM U	WOLVERHAMPTON W
1 BARNSLEY		F11 3-2	F25 2-0	D26 1-1	S24 3-0	M11 4-0	O08 0-1	A29 3-1	O22 2-1	M06 2-1	a15 4-1	a01 2-2	N12 0-0	a14 2-0	a29 3-0	D24 3-2	D10 0-1	S03 2-0	F27 2-1	M18 2-2	N26 1-1	S10 2-1
2 BLACKPOOL	F04 1-0		D17 1-1	M25 2-0	S05 0-1	J14 2-0	J21 2-1	O29 1-3	A27 4-2	D03 0-2	O01 0-1	S17 1-3	D26 2-0	M04 2-1	O15 1-2	a15 0-1	N12 3-1	N19 0-2	a08 4-0	a14 3-2	m06 3-1	F18 1-3
3 BRADFORD	M22 2-3	D24 0-0		a08 2-1	S10 1-1	D26 3-1	F15 1-2	a18 0-0	J21 5-1	N19 1-2	D10 1-1	N12 0-1	A27 0-1	M25 1-0	F28 2-1	m06 2-0	S24 4-2	O29 2-1	a22 1-0	O15 2-4	S05 2-0	M04 0-0
4 BRISTOL C	D27 3-0	M18 0-1	a11 1-0		D10 2-0	a15 2-1	a17 0-2	F08 1-2	S17 1-2	M11 1-0	O29 1-0	A29 0-0	O01 1-1	D24 0-1	S03 2-2	N05 2-1	F11 1-2	F25 3-1	N26 0-1	a29 2-0	O15 0-1	D31 2-0
5 BURY	O01 1-2	A31 3-0	S17 2-2	D03 5-0		S03 0-0	O22 3-2	M18 1-2	N26 2-0	a29 1-0	F25 4-0	F11 2-1	D17 0-1	D31 1-2	M11 1-0	O08 5-2	a01 0-0	a15 1-2	N05 1-0	F08 0-1	D26 0-1	a14 2-1
6 CLAPTON O	M04 2-1	D31 3-0	D27 1-0	a22 0-1	A27 3-1		F18 4-0	N12 0-0	F04 3-2	D24 4-2	O15 0-2	O01 4-2	J21 0-0	a08 1-2	O29 2-1	S12 2-0	N19 1-2	D10 1-1	m06 0-1	S17 1-0	a17 0-0	M25 1-0
7 COVENTRY C	O15 0-1	J28 0-1	F11 2-2	a18 1-1	O29 1-2	F25 1-2		a29 1-1	N17 1-2	S03 2-0	a01 2-0	M18 1-0	N19 0-0	S10 0-1	a22 4-2	D31 4-1	A29 4-0	D24 2-2	D26 0-1	M11 0-1	O03 2-0	S24 3-1
8 CRYSTAL P	S07 0-1	O22 1-0	a17 1-1	J21 1-1	M25 4-1	N05 1-0	m06 1-1		a22 3-1	O08 2-0	J14 0-2	D24 1-2	a08 1-0	A27 4-1	D26 1-0	F18 0-0	S10 2-0	S24 2-2	F04 1-2	D10 0-2	M04 1-2	D07 1-1
9 DERBY CO	O29 1-0	S03 1-0	F18 1-3	S10 5-1	N19 1-0	F11 3-0	N05 1-0	a15 2-0		D31 1-1	M18 0-0	M11 2-0	D03 0-1	S24 1-2	a01 1-1	D27 3-2	a29 4-0	A29 0-1	a17 0-2	F25 2-4	D24 3-1	O08 2-3
10 FULHAM	J21 0-0	D10 1-0	N26 2-1	M04 0-0	m06 0-1	D17 2-0	A27 5-0	O15 1-1	J14 2-2		S17 6-0	a17 0-1	S05 0-0	F28 2-0	O01 4-0	a08 1-0	O22 4-0	N12 3-1	M25 3-0	D26 2-1	a22 2-0	F04 1-0
11 HULL C	a22 1-3	S24 2-0	D03 3-0	O22 1-0	F18 1-1	O08 2-1	a08 2-0	D31 1-0	M25 1-1	S10 2-1		N19 1-0	M04 5-2	S05 0-1	D17 2-0	J21 2-0	D26 0-1	a14 0-0	A27 1-1	N12 7-1	F04 0-0	m06 2-0
12 LEEDS U	a08 4-0	S10 0-0	N05 3-0	S05 3-0	F04 2-0	S24 2-0	M25 5-2	D17 0-0	M04 2-1	a14 2-0	N26 0-2		F20 3-0	m06 0-0	D10 1-1	A27 2-1	D31 0-2	D26 1-1	O08 0-0	O22 1-2	J21 0-0	a22 0-0
13 LEICESTER C	N05 1-0	D27 1-0	S03 2-1	S24 4-1	D24 0-0	F09 1-0	N26 1-1	a01 2-0	D10 1-1	A29 1-2	M11 0-1	F25 0-0		O08 2-2	M18 3-0	a17 3-0	a15 1-0	a29 1-1	S10 1-0	F11 3-4	J14 2-1	O22 0-1
14 NOTTINGHAM F	a17 1-1	M11 0-0	M18 4-1	D17 1-0	J14 1-2	a01 2-0	S17 1-0	S03 2-1	O01 3-0	F25 0-0	A29 3-2	a29 1-0	O15 0-0		N14 0-0	N19 1-1	F08 1-0	F11 2-0	D10 1-0	a22 3-1	O29 2-0	D26 0-0
15 NOTTS CO	O06 1-4	O08 2-1	D31 3-0	A27 0-2	a05 1-1	O22 0-0	a15 1-1	D27 3-2	a08 1-2	S24 3-0	D24 2-0	D03 4-1	a26 0-0	N05 1-1		F04 1-2	a14 2-0	S10 2-0	J21 2-0	N26 0-0	M29 1-1	S05 4-0
16 PORT VALE	D17 2-3	a22 1-0	a29 1-0	N12 3-1	O15 5-2	A29 3-0	J30 1-2	F25 3-0	D26 1-1	a01 1-1	F13 1-0	S03 0-1	a14 1-1	N26 0-2	F11 0-0		M11 1-0	M18 1-0	O22 1-1	O01 0-1	S17 2-1	D10 0-2
17 ROTHERHAM CO	N07 0-0	N05 0-1	O01 2-0	F20 0-0	a08 1-1	N26 2-0	S05 0-0	S17 1-1	m06 2-0	O29 1-0	D27 2-0	J14 1-0	a22 0-0	J21 0-1	a17 3-0	M04 0-1		O15 0-0	F18 1-1	D17 0-0	M25 0-1	A27 1-0
18 SHEFFIELD W	A27 2-3	N26 5-1	O22 2-1	F18 1-0	a22 4-1	D03 0-0	M13 3-2	O01 1-0	S05 1-1	N05 1-4	a17 0-0	D27 2-1	m06 1-0	F04 0-4	S17 0-0	a03 2-0	O08 1-0		M04 0-3	J14 0-1	a08 2-1	F13 3-1
19 SOUTH SHIELDS	D31 5-2	a01 2-1	a15 1-0	N19 2-0	N12 1-1	a29 1-1	J02 2-1	F11 1-1	a14 3-1	M18 1-0	S03 1-0	O15 0-1	S17 1-0	D03 0-0	M15 0-0	O29 0-1	J28 2-0	M11 0-0		A29 1-1	O01 1-0	D17 0-2
20 STOKE	M25 1-0	a17 1-1	O08 0-1	m06 3-0	J21 1-0	S10 0-0	M04 2-2	D03 5-1	M06 1-1	D27 3-0	N05 0-0	O29 3-0	F04 1-1	a15 1-1	N19 0-0	S24 0-0	D24 1-1	D31 1-1	S05 2-1		A27 2-0	a08 3-0
21 WEST HAM U	N19 4-0	a29 0-2	A29 1-0	O08 3-0	D27 3-2	a14 1-2	D10 3-0	M11 2-0	D17 3-1	a15 1-0	F11 1-1	J28 1-1	D31 1-0	O22 1-0	F25 2-1	S10 3-0	M18 1-2	a01 2-0	S24 1-1	S03 3-0		N05 2-0
22 WOLVERHAMPTON W	S17 2-0	F25 4-0	M11 5-0	J14 2-2	a17 1-1	M18 0-2	O01 1-0	N19 0-1	O15 0-3	F11 0-0	a29 0-2	a15 0-0	O29 1-1	D27 2-0	A29 1-2	D03 2-0	S03 3-1	J28 0-0	D24 3-2	a01 1-1	N12 0-1	

SEASON 1921-22

DIVISION 3 NORTH

	ACCRINGTON S	ASHINGTON	BARROW	CHESTERFIELD	CREWE A	DARLINGTON	DURHAM C	GRIMSBY T	HALIFAX T	HARTLEPOOLS U	LINCOLN C	NELSON	ROCHDALE	SOUTHPORT	STALYBRIDGE C	STOCKPORT CO	TRANMERE R	WALSALL	WIGAN B	WREXHAM
1 ACCRINGTON S		D27 3-0	N26 3-0	S24 3-1	S10 2-0	J14 1-0	N05 5-1	a22 1-0	a17 1-2	M11 4-1	D24 2-0	O08 4-1	S03 4-0	M18 1-2	F11 4-1	a08 1-3	J28 3-0	a29 3-3	F18 4-0	O22 1-0
2 ASHINGTON	J02 2-1		O15 0-2	D24 1-0	O29 0-1	a05 1-0	O01 1-0	A27 1-0	F04 3-1	a22 4-1	N12 4-2	D31 4-0	F18 7-3	a29 2-2	M18 2-3	a14 2-0	M04 1-0	J21 2-3	a08 3-1	S17 2-2
3 BARROW	J07 3-1	O08 2-0		D10 1-0	S24 1-2	N12 0-2	S17 0-1	J21 2-2	F18 1-1	m06 0-1	O22 2-0	D24 0-2	M11 1-0	D27 2-1	a08 2-1	A27 0-2	M25 2-0	F11 3-0	a22 2-0	D31 5-2
4 CHESTERFIELD	O01 0-1	M22 0-1	J02 2-0		O08 1-1	S17 0-3	D17 2-1	D27 4-1	a22 2-0	F04 2-1	J14 3-0	O22 1-2	m06 2-1	F18 2-1	S03 4-0	M04 0-1	a17 3-0	a08 1-0	J21 1-1	N12 3-0
5 CREWE A	S17 2-1	O22 1-2	O01 2-1	O15 1-2		a14 7-3	D31 3-2	a08 1-2	D17 2-1	F18 2-0	J07 0-2	N05 2-1	D26 2-0	a17 1-0	J28 5-1	M25 0-1	S03 1-1	a22 2-0	F04 2-1	m06 3-0
6 DARLINGTON	D31 3-0	J03 5-0	N05 3-0	S10 7-0	D24 0-1		O29 2-2	m06 2-0	A27 2-0	M25 0-0	N19 4-2	S24 0-1	J21 2-1	a08 3-0	F18 3-0	a15 1-0	F04 4-0	J02 5-0	M04 3-0	O15 3-0
7 DURHAM C	N12 3-1	S24 1-0	S10 2-0	N26 3-1	J14 4-2	O22 3-7		F04 1-2	M04 3-1	a18 0-1	J02 2-0	a14 2-0	M25 0-2	S03 2-0	a22 3-1	J21 0-2	a08 3-0	F18 2-0	m06 6-0	D24 3-0
8 GRIMSBY T	a15 2-1	S03 6-1	J28 4-0	D26 2-2	a01 3-0	a29 3-1	F11 5-2		D24 4-1	O08 2-0	a14 3-1	M11 3-1	N26 3-0	O29 0-0	S17 1-1	N12 2-1	J14 5-1	S06 3-1	O01 1-1	F25 2-0
9 HALIFAX T	D10 2-1	F11 2-0	F25 3-2	a15 1-2	a29 5-5	S03 5-1	M11 3-2	J16 2-0		N05 3-0	F16 1-2	a08 3-1	S17 1-1	N26 1-1	O08 2-3	D27 1-0	O01 0-2	D31 1-3	O29 1-2	M25 0-0
10 HARTLEPOOLS U	M04 2-1	a15 2-1	a29 3-1	F11 7-0	F25 1-0	M18 0-0	N19 0-1	O15 0-0	N12 4-0		a01 1-1	J28 6-1	D31 5-3	S17 1-0	J02 0-1	S24 0-0	N26 0-0	O29 1-0	D17 0-0	S03 0-1
11 LINCOLN C	D17 1-1	N05 4-1	O29 1-0	D31 2-1	N26 2-3	D26 0-2	D27 3-0	a17 0-2	J21 3-1	a08 1-1		S10 0-2	F11 1-2	a22 3-1	M04 2-1	m06 0-1	F18 4-1	A27 1-0	M25 3-0	O01 1-0
12 NELSON	O15 0-1	J14 0-2	a17 1-1	O29 2-0	N12 1-2	O01 1-1	D26 3-5	M04 3-0	a01 0-0	J21 0-4	S17 0-0		a22 4-1	F04 3-2	S12 1-0	F18 2-2	m06 0-0	a25 1-0	A27 1-2	J02 4-0
13 ROCHDALE	A27 6-3	F25 2-1	M04 0-1	a29 0-1	D27 2-0	J28 0-2	M18 1-0	N19 0-2	S10 3-3	J14 0-1	F04 0-2	a15 2-2		S24 0-1	N05 2-1	O22 0-1	O08 2-1	D24 7-0	a14 4-2	a01 3-0
14 SOUTHPORT	D26 1-1	M11 0-0	a14 1-0	F25 3-0	J02 2-0	a01 3-1	A27 1-1	O22 7-1	N19 3-0	S10 3-0	a15 0-0	F11 0-1	O01 2-1		D24 5-1	O08 2-1	D10 1-1	N05 3-0	J14 1-1	J28 1-2
15 STALYBRIDGE C	F04 3-1	M25 2-0	a01 3-0	A27 6-0	J21 2-2	F25 1-0	a15 4-3	S10 3-0	O15 2-1	D26 1-3	M11 2-0	D27 2-0	N12 1-0	F28 0-0		D31 0-4	O29 4-0	S24 2-0	N26 0-0	a29 4-1
16 STOCKPORT CO	a01 2-1	a17 3-2	S19 2-0	M11 2-1	M18 1-1	a22 1-0	J28 4-0	N05 0-1	D26 0-0	O01 1-0	a29 2-2	F25 3-0	O29 3-0	O15 2-1	J14 4-0		D24 0-0	N26 3-1	S17 3-0	F11 0-0
17 TRANMERE R	J21 2-4	D26 2-3	M18 2-2	a14 2-0	A27 4-1	F11 0-1	a01 3-3	D31 2-2	S24 2-2	D27 1-2	F25 4-0	a29 4-0	O15 7-0	a18 0-1	O22 4-1	D17 0-2		S10 0-1	N12 2-0	a15 0-0
18 WALSALL	m06 6-1	J28 6-2	F04 3-1	a01 2-1	a15 1-0	a17 0-1	F25 2-0	D10 2-1	J14 4-1	O22 3-1	S03 3-0	M18 2-0	a18 4-0	N12 4-1	O01 2-2	J16 0-2	S17 2-0		O15 4-1	D27 2-2
19 WIGAN B	F25 0-1	a01 1-1	a15 1-2	M13 1-2	F11 2-0	M29 3-3	a29 2-0	S24 1-1	O22 4-3	D24 1-0	M18 3-1	S03 1-4	D10 3-2	D31 3-2	J07 0-2	S10 0-1	N05 0-0	O08 4-2		a17 2-1
20 WREXHAM	O29 2-1	S10 2-0	J14 0-0	N05 6-1	D10 1-0	O08 1-1	J07 3-1	F18 0-1	M18 5-1	A27 0-2	S24 3-1	N26 4-2	a08 1-1	J21 2-0	a14 2-0	M08 0-0	a22 1-3	M04 4-0	D26 3-2	

DIVISION 3 SOUTH

	ABERDARE A	BRENTFORD	BRIGHTON & HA	BRISTOL R	CHARLTON A	EXETER C	GILLINGHAM	LUTON T	MERTHYR T	MILLWALL	NEWPORT CO	NORTHAMPTON T	NORWICH C	PLYMOUTH A	PORTSMOUTH	Q.P.R.	READING	SOUTHAMPTON	SOUTHEND U	SWANSEA T	SWINDON T	WATFORD
1 ABERDARE A		D27 2-0	S10 2-0	D31 2-0	O08 3-3	m06 0-2	a08 6-1	m01 2-0	a10 0-0	a22 0-0	F18 3-0	O29 4-2	M16 1-2	F04 0-0	A27 0-0	N05 4-2	D17 0-1	a18 0-1	N26 1-1	S05 2-1	M25 3-2	S24 3-0
2 BRENTFORD	D26 2-1		a14 4-0	D24 4-2	S24 0-2	a22 5-2	M25 0-1	F18 0-2	A27 0-1	a08 1-0	F04 1-0	O08 1-0	N26 2-1	J21 3-1	N05 2-2	O22 5-1	a18 2-0	J14 1-0	S05 1-0	m06 3-0	M04 3-0	S10 1-1
3 BRIGHTON & H.A.	S17 1-2	a17 2-1		D27 3-1	O29 2-0	S07 3-1	a22 0-1	M18 1-1	F04 1-3	m06 0-1	M04 3-0	N05 7-0	D24 0-2	F18 1-1	J21 3-0	N19 2-1	J14 1-1	O01 0-1	A27 0-0	D10 0-0	a08 2-1	O15 1-1
4 BRISTOL R	J14 5-1	S14 0-0	D26 1-2		S10 4-2	a08 1-3	a10 0-3	F04 2-0	O22 2-0	M25 0-0	J21 3-4	S24 2-0	N12 4-2	A27 1-3	S07 1-1	O08 1-1	N19 2-0	a14 0-0	m06 1-0	a22 0-0	F18 1-1	a18 1-1
5 CHARLTON A	O15 2-1	O01 1-1	O22 1-0	S17 2-0		A27 1-0	S05 0-0	a22 0-1	M04 1-0	J14 2-1	a08 1-1	D10 2-2	D26 2-1	M25 0-0	F18 1-2	D17 1-1	a14 0-1	N28 1-2	F04 4-0	J21 1-0	m06 4-5	N12 1-0
6 EXETER C	a29 0-1	a15 1-0	A31 0-3	a01 2-2	S03 1-0		N19 1-1	D10 0-1	a17 1-0	N12 1-0	D31 2-2	a03 2-0	M11 2-0	D26 0-2	S10 1-4	F25 0-1	M18 1-3	F11 0-0	S24 4-1	O15 1-1	O29 1-4	D24 1-3
7 GILLINGHAM	a01 3-1	M18 0-0	a15 1-0	M11 3-2	A31 2-0	M06 3-0		J14 0-1	S24 5-0	S14 0-1	a14 0-2	D26 3-2	F11 5-2	S10 1-2	O08 1-2	J28 1-2	F25 2-0	S03 2-0	O22 1-0	N12 0-0	D24 2-2	m06 1-1
8 LUTON T	M11 1-2	F25 3-0	M25 2-0	F11 1-2	a15 2-0	S14 4-0	D31 7-0		O08 3-0	D17 1-0	S10 4-0	m06 3-0	S03 2-1	S24 1-0	O22 1-0	a17 3-1	M06 0-1	A29 0-0	N05 3-0	N19 3-0	D27 2-1	a01 1-1
9 MERTHYR T	J28 0-1	S03 2-0	F11 2-1	O29 0-2	M11 1-0	a14 0-0	O01 2-0	O15 2-0		S17 3-1	N12 2-1	M18 2-1	a29 3-0	N26 0-1	D24 2-1	a15 2-0	A29 2-0	m01 0-1	J14 2-2	D26 1-0	D12 4-1	F25 1-2
10 MILLWALL	a15 0-0	a01 1-1	a29 2-0	M18 4-1	D31 0-1	N05 1-0	D10 1-0	D24 1-1	S10 4-0		D26 1-1	A27 0-0	F25 2-2	a14 1-1	S24 1-1	F11 0-0	M11 3-0	D03 0-1	O08 0-0	O29 0-0	N19 0-0	S05 0-0
11 NEWPORT CO	F25 1-0	F11 2-1	M11 0-1	J28 0-1	a27 2-1	J14 1-1	a17 1-1	S17 2-2	N05 0-2	D27 1-0		a15 2-2	O01 1-0	O22 0-0	N26 0-0	A29 0-1	S03 1-0	a29 0-1	S12 2-1	J02 2-3	O15 4-0	M18 0-0
12 NORTHAMPTON T	O22 2-0	O15 2-0	N12 2-0	O01 2-2	J19 1-0	J21 2-3	D27 3-1	a29 2-0	M25 2-0	S03 0-3	a22 2-0		a18 3-0	a08 1-3	M04 0-0	J14 1-0	S17 2-1	a24 0-0	F18 0-2	F04 0-1	S05 2-1	N19 1-0
13 NORWICH C	D10 0-0	N19 0-0	a06 1-1	N05 0-1	D27 2-0	M04 0-0	F04 2-0	A27 0-1	m06 2-0	F23 3-1	S24 2-2	a17 2-0		S08 1-1	a22 2-1	S10 0-0	O29 4-1	O08 2-2	a08 1-1	M25 3-2	J21 1-2	D31 1-1
14 PLYMOUTH A	F11 3-0	J28 4-1	F25 3-1	S03 1-0	M18 3-0	D27 0-0	S17 3-0	O01 2-0	N19 0-0	a17 2-0	O29 1-0	a01 2-0	A29 1-1		D03 0-0	a29 4-0	O15 2-0	a15 1-0	D17 4-0	D31 3-1	N12 1-0	M11 3-0
15 PORTSMOUTH	S03 2-2	N12 1-0	F08 0-0	A31 1-0	F25 1-0	S17 2-0	O15 4-1	O29 1-1	M08 2-1	O01 2-2	N19 4-3	M11 1-1	a15 0-1	D10 3-1		a01 1-0	a29 1-0	M18 0-2	D27 6-0	a14 3-0	J14 1-3	F11 2-0
16 Q.P.R.	N12 1-0	O29 1-1	N26 3-0	O15 1-2	D24 3-1	F18 2-1	J21 1-0	a14 1-0	a22 0-0	F04 6-1	S05 2-1	D31 4-0	S17 2-0	m06 2-0	a08 1-1		O01 1-1	D26 2-2	M25 1-0	M04 1-0	A27 0-0	D10 1-1
17 READING	D24 0-1	D10 0-3	D31 0-0	a05 4-0	a17 1-2	M25 0-0	F18 2-1	J21 2-1	S07 5-0	M15 1-0	A27 1-0	S10 0-0	O22 2-1	O08 0-1	m06 1-1	S24 0-1		N05 0-1	a22 4-0	a08 2-0	F04 1-1	D27 2-1
18 SOUTHAMPTON	a17 1-0	D31 0-0	S24 3-0	D10 1-0	N19 6-0	F04 2-0	A27 2-0	S05 2-1	a08 1-1	J21 4-2	m06 5-0	D24 8-0	O15 2-0	a22 0-0	M25 1-1	D27 1-1	N12 0-0		M04 5-0	F20 1-1	S10 3-1	O29 2-0
19 SOUTHEND U	N19 3-2	A29 1-1	S03 1-2	a29 3-0	F11 1-1	O01 0-1	O29 2-0	N12 0-1	D31 2-1	O15 1-1	D10 0-1	F25 1-1	a01 0-1	D24 1-0	D26 1-2	M18 1-2	a15 2-0	M11 0-0		S17 1-0	a14 1-2	a26 1-4
20 SWANSEA T	A29 1-2	a29 1-0	S12 2-1	a15 8-1	M09 0-0	O08 2-1	N05 2-0	N26 1-1	D27 3-2	O22 3-0	D24 2-2	F11 2-2	M18 1-1	J14 3-0	a17 2-2	M11 1-0	a01 0-0	F25 1-0	S10 1-1		S24 1-3	S03 3-0
21 SWINDON T	M18 2-2	M11 2-1	a01 1-0	F25 0-1	a29 0-0	O22 1-1	M20 0-0	D26 1-1	D10 3-0	N26 1-1	O08 3-2	A29 4-2	m01 6-1	N05 1-2	D31 0-0	S03 2-0	F11 4-0	S17 2-3	a17 6-1	O01 1-0		a15 0-3
22 WATFORD	O01 3-0	S17 0-0	O08 1-0	a17 1-0	N05 2-2	D17 0-0	a29 1-0	a08 4-1	F18 4-1	A31 0-1	M25 1-0	a14 2-2	J14 4-2	M04 0-1	F04 0-3	D03 2-2	D26 2-2	O22 1-1	J21 4-1	A27 0-0	a22 2-2	

LEAGUE TABLES

DIVISION 1

	P	W	D	L	F	A	W	D	L	F	A	Pts
Liverpool	42	15	4	2	43	15	7	9	5	20	21	57
Tottenham H	42	15	3	3	43	17	6	6	9	22	22	51
Burnley	42	16	3	2	49	18	6	2	13	23	36	49
Cardiff C	42	13	2	6	40	26	6	8	7	21	27	48
Aston Villa	42	16	3	2	50	19	6	0	15	24	36	47
Bolton W	42	12	4	5	40	24	8	3	10	28	35	47
Newcastle U	42	11	5	5	36	19	7	5	9	23	26	46
Middlesbrough	42	12	6	3	46	19	4	8	9	33	50	46
Chelsea	42	9	6	6	17	16	8	6	7	23	27	46
Manchester C	42	13	7	1	44	21	5	2	14	21	49	45
Sheffield U	42	11	3	7	32	17	4	7	10	27	37	40
Sunderland	42	13	4	4	46	23	3	4	14	14	39	40
W.B.A.	42	8	6	7	26	23	7	4	10	25	40	40
Huddersfield T	42	12	3	6	33	14	3	6	12	20	40	39
Blackburn R	42	7	6	8	35	31	6	6	9	19	26	38
Preston N.E.	42	12	7	2	33	20	1	5	15	9	45	38
Arsenal	42	10	6	5	27	19	5	1	15	20	37	37
Birmingham C	42	9	2	10	25	29	6	5	10	23	31	37
Oldham A	42	8	7	6	21	15	5	4	12	17	35	37
Everton	42	10	7	4	42	22	2	5	14	15	33	36
Bradford C	42	8	5	8	28	30	3	5	13	20	42	32
Manchester U	42	7	7	7	25	26	1	5	15	16	47	28

DIVISION 2

	P	W	D	L	F	A	W	D	L	F	A	Pts
Nottingham F	42	13	7	1	29	9	9	5	7	22	21	56
Stoke	42	9	11	1	31	11	9	5	7	29	33	52
Barnsley	42	14	5	2	43	18	8	3	10	24	34	52
West Ham U	42	15	3	3	39	13	5	5	11	13	26	48
Hull C	42	13	5	3	36	13	6	5	10	15	28	48
South Shields	42	11	7	3	25	13	6	5	10	18	25	46
Fulham	42	14	5	2	41	8	4	4	13	16	30	45
Leeds U	42	10	8	3	31	12	6	5	10	17	26	45
Leicester C	42	11	6	4	30	16	3	11	7	9	18	45
Sheffield W	42	12	4	5	31	24	3	10	8	16	26	44
Bury	42	11	3	7	35	19	4	7	10	19	36	40
Derby Co	42	11	3	7	34	22	4	6	11	26	42	39
Notts Co	42	10	7	4	34	18	2	8	11	13	33	39
Crystal Palace	42	9	6	6	28	20	4	7	10	17	31	39
Clapton O	42	12	4	5	33	18	3	5	13	10	32	39
Rotherham U	42	8	9	4	17	7	6	2	13	15	36	39
Wolverhampton W	42	8	7	6	28	19	5	4	12	16	30	37
Port Vale	42	10	5	6	28	19	4	3	14	15	38	36
Blackpool	42	11	1	9	33	27	4	4	13	11	30	35
Coventry C	42	8	5	8	31	21	4	5	12	20	39	34
Bradford P.A.	42	10	5	6	32	22	2	4	15	14	40	33
Bristol C	42	10	3	8	25	18	2	6	13	12	40	33

DIVISION 3 NORTH

	P	W	D	L	F	A	W	D	L	F	A	Pts
Stockport Co	38	13	5	1	36	10	11	3	5	24	11	56
Darlington	38	15	2	2	52	7	7	4	8	29	30	50
Grimsby T	38	15	4	0	54	15	6	4	9	18	32	50
Hartlepool U	38	10	6	3	33	11	7	2	10	19	28	42
Accrington S	38	15	1	3	50	15	4	2	13	23	42	41
Crewe A	38	13	1	5	39	21	5	4	10	21	35	41
Stalybridge C	38	14	3	2	42	15	4	2	13	20	48	41
Walsall	38	15	2	2	52	17	3	1	15	14	48	39
Southport	38	11	6	2	39	12	3	4	12	16	32	38
Ashington	38	13	2	4	42	22	4	2	13	17	44	38
Durham C	38	14	0	5	43	20	3	3	13	25	47	37
Wrexham	38	12	4	3	40	17	2	5	12	11	39	37
Chesterfield	38	12	2	5	33	15	4	1	14	15	52	35
Lincoln C	38	11	2	6	32	20	3	4	12	16	39	34
Barrow	38	11	2	6	29	18	3	3	13	13	36	33
Nelson	38	7	6	6	27	23	6	1	12	21	43	33
Wigan B	38	9	4	6	32	28	2	5	12	14	44	31
Tranmere R	38	7	5	7	41	25	2	6	11	10	36	29
Halifax T	38	9	4	6	37	28	1	5	13	19	48	29
Rochdale	38	9	2	8	34	24	2	2	15	18	53	26

DIVISION 3 SOUTH

	P	W	D	L	F	A	W	D	L	F	A	Pts
Southampton	42	14	7	0	50	8	9	8	4	18	13	61
Plymouth A	42	17	4	0	43	4	8	7	6	20	20	61
Portsmouth	42	13	5	3	38	18	5	12	4	24	21	53
Luton T	42	16	2	3	47	9	6	6	9	17	26	52
Q.P.R.	42	13	7	1	36	12	5	6	10	17	32	49
Swindon T	42	10	7	4	40	21	6	6	9	32	39	45
Watford	42	9	9	3	34	21	4	9	8	20	27	44
Aberdare A	42	11	6	4	38	18	6	4	11	19	33	44
Brentford	42	15	2	4	41	17	1	9	11	11	26	43
Swansea T	42	11	8	2	40	19	2	7	12	10	28	41
Merthyr T	42	14	2	5	33	15	3	4	14	12	41	40
Millwall	42	6	13	2	22	10	4	5	12	16	32	38
Reading	42	10	5	6	28	15	4	5	12	12	32	38
Bristol R	42	8	8	5	32	24	6	2	13	20	43	38
Norwich C	42	8	10	3	29	17	4	3	14	21	45	37
Charlton A	42	10	6	5	28	19	3	5	13	15	37	37
Northampton T	42	13	3	5	30	17	0	8	13	17	54	37
Gillingham	42	11	4	6	36	20	3	4	14	11	40	36
Brighton & H.A.	42	9	6	6	33	19	4	3	14	12	32	35
Newport Co	42	8	7	6	22	18	3	5	13	22	43	34
Exeter C	42	7	5	9	22	29	4	7	10	16	30	34
Southend U	42	7	5	9	23	23	1	6	14	11	51	27

Football League Records

Top scorers: Div 1, C.Buchan (Sunderland) 30 goals; Div 2, H.Bedford (Blackpool) 32 goals; Div 3 N, G.Beel (Chesterfield), J.Carmichael (Grimsby Town) 23 goals; Div 3 S, F.Pagnam (Watford) 30 goals.

Goalkeeper Albert Iremonger, dropped after a 6-1 home defeat by Manchester United, he returned for the last game and helped Notts County win promotion.

DIVISION 1

	ARSENAL	ASTON VILLA	BIRMINGHAM	BLACKBURN R	BOLTON W	BURNLEY	CARDIFF C	CHELSEA	EVERTON	HUDDERSFIELD T	LIVERPOOL	MANCHESTER C	MIDDLESBROUGH	NEWCASTLE U	NOTTINGHAM F	OLDHAM A	PRESTON N.E.	SHEFFIELD U	STOKE	SUNDERLAND	TOTTENHAM H	W.B.A.
1 ARSENAL	—	M31 2-0	D09 1-0	a02 1-1	D26 5-0	A28 1-1	S16 2-1	F24 3-1	N11 1-2	D16 1-1	S02 1-0	J20 1-0	M10 3-0	O28 1-2	F10 2-0	M17 2-0	a14 1-1	a28 2-0	D30 3-0	N25 2-3	S30 0-2	O07 3-1
2 ASTON VILLA	a07 1-1	—	M24 3-0	A26 2-0	O21 2-0	D26 3-1	S04 1-3	M30 1-0	a21 3-0	M03 2-1	N25 0-1	F03 2-0	S23 2-2	D16 1-1	J27 4-0	N11 3-0	D30 1-0	D09 0-1	F17 6-0	m05 1-0	O07 2-0	S09 2-0
3 BIRMINGHAM	D02 3-2	M17 1-0	—	O14 1-1	S30 2-0	a28 1-0	N04 0-0	S02 0-1	D16 1-1	D25 0-0	M31 0-1	S16 0-1	O28 2-0	A28 0-2	N18 2-0	F10 2-3	M10 1-0	M12 4-2	S13 2-0	J06 1-2	a14 2-1	J20 0-2
4 BLACKBURN R	J01 0-5	S02 4-2	O07 1-1	—	D16 1-0	O28 2-1	J20 3-1	a28 0-0	S16 5-1	N11 0-0	M12 1-0	D02 0-0	a14 2-0	M10 1-1	M17 2-0	M31 1-0	D25 1-1	S18 1-0	J22 1-5	S23 0-0	F10 1-0	D30 5-1
5 BOLTON W	D25 4-1	O28 3-0	S23 3-0	D23 3-0	—	F10 2-1	D30 0-0	a14 1-1	M30 0-2	O07 1-0	a18 1-1	N25 2-1	M31 1-1	M17 1-0	J02 4-2	S04 3-1	S02 1-1	J20 1-1	N04 1-1	S09 1-1	a11 0-2	D09 3-0
6 BURNLEY	S04 4-1	D25 1-1	m05 0-2	O21 3-1	M12 2-1	—	M30 1-5	N18 1-0	a07 0-1	M24 0-2	S30 2-0	F17 2-0	D09 3-0	O14 0-0	N04 8-2	D16 1-1	J20 2-0	J06 1-4	M03 3-2	a21 2-0	S16 0-1	A26 3-0
7 CARDIFF C	S09 4-1	A28 3-0	N11 1-1	J27 5-0	J06 1-0	a02 2-2	—	M10 6-1	S23 0-2	N25 0-1	O28 3-0	D16 3-1	M17 2-0	F10 5-0	a25 3-1	a28 2-0	M31 1-0	a14 1-0	D02 2-1	O07 2-4	S02 2-3	D26 3-0
8 CHELSEA	F17 0-0	a02 1-1	A26 1-1	m05 1-1	a21 3-0	N25 0-1	M03 1-1	—	F14 3-1	D02 2-2	D30 0-0	a07 1-1	S09 1-1	J20 3-0	D25 2-2	S23 4-0	N11 0-1	O07 0-0	S04 3-2	O21 1-3	D16 0-0	a25 2-2
9 EVERTON	N04 1-0	a14 2-1	D23 2-1	S09 2-0	a02 1-1	M31 1-0	S30 3-1	F10 3-1	—	D30 0-3	O14 0-1	D25 0-0	F28 5-3	S02 3-2	O28 4-2	M10 0-0	a28 1-0	M17 5-1	J20 4-0	D09 1-1	J01 3-1	N25 0-1
10 HUDDERSFIELD T	D23 4-0	M10 3-5	D26 4-0	N04 0-2	O14 0-2	M17 2-0	N18 1-0	D09 3-0	J06 1-0	—	a14 0-0	S30 0-0	S02 0-2	M31 2-0	A28 2-1	O28 3-0	M21 2-0	F10 2-1	S16 1-0	J27 0-1	a28 1-0	a03 4-1
11 LIVERPOOL	A26 5-2	N18 3-0	a07 0-0	F17 3-0	M03 3-0	S23 3-0	O21 3-1	J06 1-0	O07 5-1	a21 1-1	—	M24 2-0	J27 2-0	D02 0-2	D16 2-1	D26 2-1	S16 5-2	M30 2-1	m05 1-0	S06 5-1	N11 0-0	F07 2-0
12 MANCHESTER C	J27 0-0	F10 1-1	S09 0-1	D09 2-1	N18 2-0	F24 1-0	D23 5-1	M31 3-0	D26 2-1	S23 3-1	M17 1-0	—	A28 2-1	a28 0-0	a14 1-1	D30 3-2	O28 2-1	S02 3-3	O14 2-1	a02 1-0	M14 3-0	N11 1-1
13 MIDDLESBROUGH	M03 2-0	S30 2-2	O21 2-1	a21 1-2	a07 1-2	D02 4-1	M24 0-1	S16 2-1	F17 2-4	A26 2-2	J20 0-2	S04 5-0	—	D26 1-1	a02 4-0	O14 2-1	N25 1-1	N04 3-2	D16 3-1	a18 2-0	D30 2-0	m05 0-1
14 NEWCASTLE U	O21 1-1	D23 0-0	S06 0-0	M03 5-1	a16 1-0	O07 0-2	F28 3-1	J27 0-0	A26 2-0	a07 1-0	D09 0-1	m05 3-1	D25 1-1	—	J06 1-0	J01 1-0	S23 3-1	S09 3-0	a21 1-0	N04 2-1	N25 1-1	F14 2-0
15 NOTTINGHAM F	F03 2-1	J20 3-1	N25 1-1	M24 1-0	O05 1-1	N11 1-0	F17 3-2	D26 0-4	O21 2-1	S04 0-1	D23 1-3	a21 2-0	M30 2-1	D30 0-1	—	S16 1-0	O07 3-0	S23 1-0	a07 0-1	A26 1-0	D09 0-1	M03 0-4
16 OLDHAM A	M24 0-0	N04 0-2	F03 2-0	a07 1-0	S11 3-1	D23 1-1	m05 3-1	S30 2-0	M03 1-0	O21 0-3	D25 0-2	J06 0-3	O07 0-0	M30 0-0	S09 2-0	—	D09 2-1	N25 0-2	A26 4-1	F17 0-0	J20 0-3	a21 0-0
17 PRESTON N.E.	a21 1-2	J06 3-2	M03 2-3	D26 1-0	A26 3-1	J27 3-1	a07 3-0	N04 2-0	m05 2-2	F17 1-0	S09 1-3	O21 0-2	N18 1-2	S30 1-0	O14 2-2	D02 5-1	—	D23 2-3	F08 4-2	M24 2-0	a02 2-0	S04 0-0
18 SHEFFIELD U	O02 2-1	D02 1-1	F17 7-1	S04 1-1	J27 2-2	D30 2-1	a21 0-0	O14 0-2	a16 0-1	a09 0-2	a02 4-1	A26 2-0	N11 4-1	S16 2-0	S30 0-0	N18 2-2	D16 2-2	—	O21 2-0	M03 3-1	D26 2-0	a07 3-1
19 STOKE	J06 1-0	F24 1-1	a02 0-0	N18 1-1	N11 2-0	M10 0-1	D09 3-1	A28 1-2	J27 4-1	S09 2-2	a28 0-0	O07 1-1	D23 0-0	a14 1-0	M31 0-1	S02 2-2	F10 4-2	O28 4-0	—	D26 1-2	M17 0-0	S23 0-2
20 SUNDERLAND	N18 3-3	a28 2-0	D30 5-3	S30 4-3	S16 5-1	a14 3-1	O14 2-1	O28 1-1	D02 3-1	J20 1-1	A30 1-0	M30 2-0	F10 2-1	N11 2-0	S02 0-0	F24 2-0	M17 2-2	a11 3-5	J01 2-0	—	M31 2-0	D16 3-2
21 TOTTENHAM H	S23 1-2	O14 1-2	a21 2-0	F14 2-0	F17 0-1	S09 1-3	A26 1-1	D23 3-1	S04 2-0	m05 0-0	N04 2-4	M03 3-1	J06 2-0	N18 0-1	D02 2-1	J27 3-0	M30 1-1	D25 2-1	M24 3-1	a07 0-1	—	O21 3-1
22 W.B.A.	O14 7-0	S16 3-0	J27 1-0	J06 3-0	D02 1-1	S02 2-1	D27 3-0	M17 0-0	N18 0-0	a02 0-2	F10 0-0	N04 2-0	a28 1-0	M14 2-1	M10 0-0	a14 1-0	A28 2-2	M31 4-0	S30 0-1	D23 1-1	O28 5-1	—

Albert Fairclough scored 19 goals to help Bristol City win the Division Three South title. Later he signed for Derby County.

DIVISION 2

	BARNSLEY	BLACKPOOL	BRADFORD C	BURY	CLAPTON O	COVENTRY C	CRYSTAL P	DERBY CO	FULHAM	HULL C	LEEDS U	LEICESTER C	MANCHESTER U	NOTTS CO	PORT VALE	ROTHERHAM CO	SHEFFIELD W	SOUTHAMPTON	SOUTH SHIELDS	STOCKPORT CO	WEST HAM U	WOLVERHAMPTON W
1 BARNSLEY	—	J20 2-2	a02 3-1	A28 2-1	S02 2-1	M31 6-2	N25 1-2	S23 5-0	N11 0-1	D02 1-0	F10 1-0	D30 0-1	a28 2-2	O07 1-0	a14 0-1	D26 2-2	D16 2-4	S09 3-0	M10 5-0	O28 1-1	a16 2-0	M17 1-0
2 BLACKPOOL	J27 0-1	—	S09 3-0	a14 5-1	A28 0-0	M10 0-1	D02 4-0	O07 3-2	N25 3-0	D16 0-0	S02 1-0	D26 1-2	M31 1-0	N11 1-1	M17 0-2	a28 1-0	D30 3-0	S23 1-2	F10 3-0	M30 0-0	O28 4-1	F24 3-1
3 BRADFORD C	a03 2-0	S16 0-2	—	M31 4-0	a28 1-2	F24 4-0	D30 1-1	N25 0-0	D16 2-1	J20 0-2	S30 2-2	O07 1-1	M17 1-2	D09 2-0	M10 0-1	a14 1-1	D26 0-0	N11 1-0	O28 2-0	A28 1-0	S02 2-0	F10 1-1
4 BURY	S06 2-1	a21 3-0	a07 1-0	—	D02 5-1	O14 1-1	O21 2-1	M03 4-1	F14 0-1	A26 1-0	D25 1-1	m05 2-0	N18 2-2	F17 2-2	N11 2-0	D16 1-0	J27 4-0	M24 0-0	S16 1-0	D30 2-0	a02 2-5	S30 3-0
5 CLAPTON O	A26 0-1	S04 0-1	m05 1-0	D09 0-2	—	a02 0-0	F17 3-1	a07 0-0	M03 0-2	F03 2-0	O07 3-0	S09 2-0	N11 1-1	M24 2-1	S23 0-0	D30 5-1	O21 2-2	a21 1-0	D16 0-0	D26 0-2	N25 0-2	J27 4-1
6 COVENTRY C	a07 3-0	M03 1-2	F17 2-1	O07 3-0	a03 2-1	—	S07 2-1	O21 1-0	D11 1-0	m05 0-1	D16 1-2	M24 1-1	S23 2-0	A26 1-2	S09 1-2	N11 2-1	a21 1-1	a30 2-0	J20 0-2	N25 1-0	D30 1-3	D25 7-1
7 CRYSTAL P	N18 2-0	D09 1-1	J06 2-0	O28 1-1	F24 2-0	A30 0-0	—	D26 2-2	S09 0-0	O07 1-1	M17 1-0	S23 0-1	S02 2-3	M30 0-1	D23 2-0	F10 4-0	N11 2-0	J27 1-0	a14 1-1	M10 3-0	M31 1-5	a28 5-0
8 DERBY CO	S30 0-1	O14 1-0	N18 0-2	a11 1-0	M31 0-0	O28 4-0	D25 6-0	—	J20 2-0	M30 0-2	a28 0-1	D16 2-0	M14 1-1	D30 0-0	F10 1-2	M17 1-0	S16 1-1	D02 0-2	N11 1-0	a14 1-2	S04 2-1	S02 1-1
9 FULHAM	N04 0-1	N18 1-1	D23 0-0	F10 3-0	M10 0-0	D09 4-0	S16 2-1	J27 3-1	—	S30 0-0	M31 3-0	M30 2-0	O28 0-0	D26 2-1	S02 1-1	F24 1-2	O14 1-0	J06 1-1	a28 0-1	M17 3-0	a14 0-2	A28 2-0
10 HULL C	D09 2-1	D23 0-0	J27 0-0	S02 2-2	F10 2-1	a28 1-1	O14 1-1	a02 4-2	S23 1-0	—	M10 3-1	N11 1-3	D30 2-1	S16 0-2	A28 3-0	O28 2-3	N18 0-0	D25 1-3	M31 2-0	F24 1-0	M17 1-1	a14 0-0
11 LEEDS U	F24 1-1	A26 1-1	S23 1-0	D26 0-0	O14 0-0	D23 1-0	M24 4-1	m05 1-0	a07 1-1	M03 2-2	—	O21 0-0	J27 0-1	a21 3-0	J06 2-1	M30 2-0	F17 0-0	S04 1-0	N18 0-1	S09 2-0	N04 3-1	D02 1-0
12 LEICESTER C	J06 2-2	D25 1-2	O14 2-0	a28 2-0	S16 2-0	M17 2-1	S30 3-0	D23 0-1	a02 1-1	N04 0-1	O28 2-1	—	a14 0-1	J20 2-1	M31 3-0	A28 3-0	D02 3-1	N18 2-1	F26 3-0	S02 2-0	F15 0-6	M10 7-0
13 MANCHESTER U	J01 1-0	a07 2-1	M21 1-1	N25 0-1	N04 0-0	S30 2-1	A26 2-1	F17 0-0	O21 1-1	J06 3-2	J20 0-0	a21 0-2	—	F21 1-1	O07 1-2	D02 3-0	S04 1-0	M03 1-2	M30 3-0	D16 1-0	D25 1-2	S16 1-0
14 NOTTS CO	O14 1-0	N04 2-0	D02 0-0	M21 1-0	M17 3-1	S02 2-0	a02 0-4	J06 1-2	D25 1-0	S09 0-1	a14 1-0	J27 1-0	F10 1-6	—	O28 1-0	M10 2-0	S30 1-0	D16 1-0	A28 2-0	M31 2-0	a18 2-0	N18 4-1
15 PORT VALE	a21 1-1	F03 2-0	M03 1-2	N04 2-0	S30 3-1	S16 0-1	D16 2-0	F26 2-3	A26 0-1	S04 1-0	D30 1-2	a07 0-0	O14 1-0	O21 0-0	—	N25 0-0	m05 2-2	F17 0-0	D25 3-0	J13 0-2	J20 1-3	M30 1-0
16 ROTHERHAM CO	D25 1-1	m05 1-0	a21 0-2	D23 0-0	J06 0-0	N04 2-0	N06 4-1	M26 3-0	F17 1-3	O21 0-1	a02 3-1	S04 0-0	D09 1-1	M03 1-0	N18 3-1	—	A26 1-2	a07 0-0	S30 2-1	J27 2-1	S16 2-2	O14 3-2
17 SHEFFIELD W	D23 2-3	J06 2-3	D25 2-2	J20 2-0	O28 4-1	a14 3-0	N04 3-1	S09 0-0	O07 1-0	N25 1-0	M19 3-1	D09 2-1	A28 1-0	S23 0-1	a28 2-0	S02 1-0	—	J01 0-0	M17 2-0	F10 4-1	a30 0-2	M31 1-0
18 SOUTHAMPTON	S16 2-2	S30 1-1	N04 2-0	M17 0-3	a14 2-0	F10 3-0	J20 0-2	D09 0-4	D30 2-0	D26 2-1	A28 0-1	N25 0-0	a11 0-0	D23 0-1	M05 3-1	M31 4-2	a02 1-1	—	S02 0-2	a28 1-0	O14 2-0	O28 3-0
19 SOUTH SHIELDS	M03 2-0	M21 1-0	O21 0-0	S09 0-2	D23 3-0	J27 0-0	a21 2-0	N04 3-1	m05 2-0	a07 0-0	N25 0-2	F17 2-1	a02 0-3	S04 1-0	J01 3-1	S23 2-0	M24 1-1	A26 0-0	—	O07 3-0	D09 0-0	J06 1-1
20 STOCKPORT CO	O21 3-1	J01 2-2	S04 1-0	J06 1-0	D25 0-2	N18 5-1	M03 2-2	a21 2-1	M24 0-2	F17 1-1	S16 2-1	A26 4-5	D23 1-0	a07 0-0	D09 0-2	J20 1-0	M15 0-1	m05 3-0	O14 1-1	—	S30 2-1	N04 1-1
21 WEST HAM U	F17 0-0	O21 2-0	A26 1-2	M30 0-0	N18 1-0	J06 1-0	a07 1-1	A28 0-0	a21 1-0	a09 3-0	N11 0-0	F10 2-2	D26 0-2	m05 0-1	J27 0-0	S09 4-0	M03 2-1	O07 1-1	D02 1-0	S23 0-1	—	D23 1-0
22 WOLVERHAMPTON W	M24 3-3	F17 3-4	F19 4-1	S23 1-1	J20 1-3	D26 1-2	m05 1-0	A26 0-1	S04 0-0	a23 3-0	D09 0-1	M03 1-2	S09 0-1	N25 1-0	a02 3-0	O07 3-2	a07 2-0	O21 0-0	D30 1-0	N11 3-1	D16 1-4	—

SEASON 1922-23

DIVISION 3 NORTH

	ACCRINGTON S	ASHINGTON	BARROW	BRADFORD	CHESTERFIELD	CREWE A	DARLINGTON	DURHAM C	GRIMSBY T	HALIFAX T	HARTLEPOOLS U	LINCOLN C	NELSON	ROCHDALE	SOUTHPORT	STALYBRIDGE C	TRANMERE R	WALSALL	WIGAN B	WREXHAM
1 ACCRINGTON S		D26 4-1	F17 3-4	J20 4-3	N04 0-4	J13 0-0	A26 2-1	S30 3-1	J01 4-0	D30 4-1	M10 2-1	m05 1-0	a21 0-1	F03 2-1	M24 3-1	a07 1-0	S16 4-1	D23 2-1	O07 0-0	O21 1-0
2 ASHINGTON	M03 2-5		D23 2-6	a14 2-1	O28 2-0	F10 2-4	S16 3-1	J01 0-0	F17 2-1	M31 3-2	S30 4-2	D09 0-2	O14 0-2	J06 2-0	N25 1-1	N11 0-3	a28 3-1	M17 3-0	S02 2-1	J20 1-1
3 BARROW	F24 5-2	J13 3-0		M31 1-2	S02 3-1	O28 2-0	S30 0-1	a28 2-1	F10 2-0	M24 0-1	O14 0-0	J06 1-3	N04 1-0	J27 4-1	D09 2-0	J02 0-1	a14 2-1	M10 0-0	J01 2-3	S09 1-0
4 BRADFORD	J27 5-1	a21 3-0	a07 3-0		D25 1-0	D23 3-0	F17 2-1	N04 4-1	J06 2-1	S09 2-2	M14 1-1	O21 4-1	A26 6-2	M24 3-0	m05 5-1	N18 1-0	O14 3-0	S23 2-2	a02 1-1	M03 0-1
5 CHESTERFIELD	N11 3-1	O21 2-2	A26 2-1	D09 2-2		S23 2-1	a21 0-0	D30 3-1	O14 3-2	M21 3-0	a07 1-1	a02 3-3	M03 1-2	D26 4-0	F03 3-0	F17 1-0	J01 5-0	S16 6-0	J20 3-1	m05 2-1
6 CREWE A	N25 1-1	F03 3-1	O21 1-0	D16 0-1	S30 2-0		O14 3-0	J20 4-0	N11 3-0	a02 2-1	a21 2-1	a07 3-1	M24 1-0	A26 0-1	F17 1-0	M03 4-1	D30 2-0	M30 0-0	S16 0-1	D25 0-0
7 DARLINGTON	S02 4-0	S09 1-1	S23 3-2	F24 2-0	a14 4-1	a28 5-0		M17 1-0	a02 1-3	F10 0-1	D25 4-0	J13 0-0	D09 2-3	J02 1-1	J27 2-1	J06 1-0	M10 4-0	O21 2-0	M31 2-0	N11 4-1
8 DURHAM C	S23 4-1	a02 1-1	m05 4-1	N11 0-0	J06 1-1	J27 2-0	M24 0-0		S09 0-3	O14 2-2	M03 3-2	F17 7-1	F03 0-1	a21 1-1	A26 1-1	O21 0-0	N25 1-0	D09 0-2	D23 2-2	a07 2-0
9 GRIMSBY T	D25 7-1	F24 7-4	F03 2-0	D30 0-1	O07 3-1	N04 2-3	M30 0-1	S16 1-0		D23 0-1	m05 1-0	a21 1-0	a07 0-2	O21 1-1	M03 2-1	M24 3-0	J20 0-0	N18 1-2	S23 0-0	A26 4-0
10 HALIFAX T	J06 0-0	a07 0-0	M17 3-0	S16 3-0	N25 2-0	D09 1-0	F03 2-1	O07 1-3	J22 1-0		O21 3-0	A26 3-1	D25 2-2	M03 1-0	a21 0-1	m05 2-1	S23 3-1	J20 1-2	N11 0-1	F17 1-1
11 HARTLEPOOLS U	D09 0-0	S23 3-1	O07 2-0	F10 0-1	M31 5-0	a14 1-1	J01 1-0	D26 2-1	a28 2-0	O28 3-2		J02 2-0	J06 5-1	N04 0-2	S09 1-1	J27 4-0	F24 0-1	S02 2-2	M17 0-0	N18 1-1
12 LINCOLN C	a28 0-0	M30 2-0	D30 1-1	O28 0-0	M17 0-0	M31 1-0	N25 1-1	F24 3-1	a14 1-2	S02 0-0	D23 2-1		J20 1-0	S09 0-1	N04 2-0	S23 1-1	F10 2-0	D25 0-2	M10 2-1	O14 2-0
13 NELSON	a14 2-1	O07 1-3	N11 2-1	S02 1-0	M10 4-0	M17 0-0	D23 3-0	F10 4-0	M31 1-1	S12 2-0	D30 4-1	J27 2-1		N25 1-2	S23 2-0	S09 1-0	O28 1-0	a28 3-0	F24 1-0	a24 2-0
14 ROCHDALE	F10 1-1	D30 2-0	J20 3-1	M17 0-3	M30 0-2	S02 1-1	O07 2-2	a14 2-0	O28 0-1	M10 0-1	N11 4-0	S16 1-1	J13 0-3		D23 3-2	a03 2-0	D04 0-0	F24 0-2	a28 3-2	S23 5-0
15 SOUTHPORT	M17 1-2	N18 1-0	M30 2-0	a28 0-0	F10 0-2	J01 2-0	J20 2-1	S02 1-0	M10 3-1	a14 1-3	S16 1-0	N11 3-0	S30 0-1	D25 0-1		O07 0-0	D26 0-0	M31 2-1	O21 1-0	J06 1-0
16 STALYBRIDGE C	M31 1-0	N04 2-1	N25 2-0	D26 1-0	F24 1-2	M10 0-1	D30 4-2	M30 1-0	M17 3-2	a28 4-3	J20 1-1	S30 0-1	S16 2-0	a02 0-0	O14 1-0		S02 4-1	a14 2-0	F20 0-2	D23 3-2
17 TRANMERE R	S09 4-1	D25 1-0	a21 3-0	O07 0-0	D23 2-3	J06 1-2	M03 2-2	J13 5-1	J27 3-2	S30 2-1	F17 1-1	F03 2-0	O21 0-2	a07 2-0	a02 2-0	A26 1-1		N04 2-3	M30 4-2	M24 4-0
18 WALSALL	a02 0-2	M24 2-1	M03 3-1	S30 1-0	S09 0-1	O07 1-1	O28 2-2	a03 2-0	N25 1-0	J27 2-1	A26 2-2	D26 2-0	m05 5-0	O14 0-0	a07 1-0	a21 2-1	N11 2-1		J06 3-1	F10 1-0
19 WIGAN B	O14 2-0	A26 6-1	D26 2-1	N25 3-2	J27 1-0	S09 1-1	a07 3-0	D25 0-2	S30 1-0	N04 0-1	M24 2-0	M03 9-1	F17 3-1	m05 6-0	O28 1-0	a18 3-0	D09 0-0	D30 1-0		a14 1-1
20 WREXHAM	O28 2-0	J27 0-0	S16 0-0	M10 3-0	a28 3-1	D26 2-1	N04 0-0	M31 1-0	S02 1-1	F24 2-1	N25 2-0	O07 0-2	a02 2-1	S30 3-1	D30 1-1	D09 2-1	M17 2-1	F03 1-0	a21 2-1	

DIVISION 3 SOUTH

	ABERDARE A	BRENTFORD	BRIGHTON & HA	BRISTOL C	BRISTOL R	CHARLTON A	EXETER C	GILLINGHAM	LUTON T	MERTHYR T	MILLWALL	NEWPORT CO	NORTHAMPTON T	NORWICH C	PLYMOUTH A	PORTSMOUTH	Q.P.R.	READING	SOUTHEND U	SWANSEA T	SWINDON T	WATFORD
1 ABERDARE A		F17 0-0	m01 0-1	a02 0-1	a21 0-0	M24 3-1	A26 3-1	N25 2-0	O14 2-1	D25 0-0	S30 0-1	J27 6-2	O21 0-2	F03 0-3	a07 2-2	S09 0-2	N04 0-0	m05 0-0	S11 1-1	J06 0-1	M01 3-3	M03 3-1
2 BRENTFORD	F24 0-1		O28 1-2	M31 4-0	D23 0-1	J27 0-3	O14 0-1	S02 2-0	A28 3-2	N04 3-1	a28 1-1	M17 0-0	S30 2-1	S16 1-4	J06 2-0	a14 1-0	S11 1-3	N18 1-1	M30 0-0	M10 0-1	F10 3-0	D26 2-1
3 BRIGHTON & H.A.	D09 3-1	O21 2-1		J20 2-1	M24 2-1	F17 1-0	S06 3-0	O07 3-0	S16 0-1	m05 0-0	a02 2-0	D23 2-1	J06 1-0	A26 0-0	M03 1-0	D25 7-1	S30 2-0	a07 3-1	a21 0-1	N04 1-3	N25 1-1	F21 3-0
4 BRISTOL C	M30 0-0	a07 1-1	J27 3-1		S23 0-1	m05 3-1	F17 1-1	J06 2-1	D09 1-0	F14 3-0	N18 1-1	S09 2-0	M03 1-0	M24 4-0	S04 2-0	N04 2-1	D23 3-2	A26 2-1	O21 5-0	O14 1-0	D26 3-1	a21 3-1
5 BRISTOL R	a14 1-0	a30 1-1	M17 0-0	S30 1-2		N25 1-1	D25 3-3	M10 1-0	F10 1-1	a02 3-0	O28 0-0	A28 3-1	J20 0-0	a23 3-2	N11 0-1	S02 0-1	M26 1-3	S16 1-1	O07 2-0	a28 0-0	M31 2-0	S13 1-2
6 CHARLTON A	M17 1-1	J20 1-1	a16 0-1	a28 1-0	N18 0-0		S16 0-0	F10 3-1	S02 2-1	S30 0-1	N11 0-2	a14 6-0	a02 2-0	D25 3-0	O23 1-0	A28 0-2	O28 1-1	O14 1-0	M12 5-1	M31 3-1	m03 3-1	D30 0-0
7 EXETER C	S02 1-0	O07 0-2	A30 1-0	F24 0-0	D26 0-0	S09 0-0		a28 0-1	**M31 1-2**	D23 2-1	M17 2-1	F10 4-0	J13 1-2	N04 2-0	a02 0-0	M10 2-3	a14 1-2	J06 4-0	D09 2-1	O28 1-0	J20 2-1	S23 1-2
8 GILLINGHAM	N18 4-0	A26 2-0	O14 2-0	D30 1-1	M03 0-1	F14 2-2	m05 2-1		M30 1-0	a21 2-0	D25 3-0	J13 3-0	S06 0-3	a25 5-0	F17 1-0	J20 4-2	S16 0-1	M24 2-1	a07 1-0	S30 2-2	N04 0-0	O21 1-4
9 LUTON T	O07 4-1	S04 4-0	S09 1-1	D02 1-1	F03 1-0	A26 2-2	a07 6-0	a02 2-0		M24 2-1	D30 2-2	N11 1-0	a21 2-1	m05 4-0	O21 2-1	D23 0-2	D26 1-0	F17 1-2	M03 2-0	J20 6-1	S23 3-2	N25 0-1
10 MERTHYR T	D26 0-2	N11 1-0	a28 2-0	F10 0-1	a03 1-1	S23 3-0	a12 3-1	a14 1-0	M17 0-1		M10 1-1	O28 1-0	M05 3-0	N18 0-1	S16 0-1	F24 3-0	M31 0-1	J20 1-1	D30 2-1	S02 2-1	A28 1-1	O07 2-3
11 MILLWALL	S23 1-0	m05 1-1	M30 2-1	N25 1-1	O21 1-0	N04 1-1	M24 3-0	D26 3-1	J06 0-0	M03 1-0		O07 0-0	a07 2-0	a21 3-0	A26 0-0	J01 1-3	J27 0-0	F10 0-0	F17 1-1	D23 0-2	S09 1-1	S04 5-1
12 NEWPORT CO	J20 0-0	M24 0-1	D16 1-0	S16 0-1	S07 4-1	a21 4-0	F03 6-2	D09 2-1	N04 0-3	O21 1-1	O14 0-0		F24 1-1	M10 1-3	m05 1-0	S30 0-0	N18 1-0	a02 3-0	A26 0-2	D27 1-2	J06 2-2	a07 0-1
13 NORTHAMPTON T	O28 3-1	S23 1-1	D30 0-0	M10 2-1	J27 1-0	a03 0-0	N25 3-0	A28 1-0	a14 2-0	D09 1-1	M31 2-1	F17 2-1		O14 1-1	D26 1-0	M17 3-0	a28 4-2	D23 5-0	N11 5-2	F10 1-3	S02 1-2	S09 1-1
14 NORWICH C	F10 1-4	S09 0-2	S02 1-0	M17 2-2	J06 0-0	D26 2-3	N11 6-0	D23 1-1	a28 1-2	N25 1-1	a14 3-2	M03 1-1	O07 1-0		J27 1-0	a07 0-2	A28 1-1	D27 2-0	S23 2-1	F24 1-4	O28 0-0	a02 2-0
15 PLYMOUTH A	M31 2-0	m02 3-0	M10 2-2	A28 5-1	N04 3-0	D09 2-0	M30 5-1	a18 2-0	O28 4-0	S09 2-0	S02 1-0	a28 1-0	D25 1-0	J20 1-1		O14 2-0	F10 2-0	S30 3-0	N25 1-1	a14 2-0	M17 2-0	D23 1-0
16 PORTSMOUTH	S16 1-0	a21 3-0	D26 1-2	N11 1-2	A26 0-0	S06 3-0	M03 3-4	J27 6-1	D16 1-2	F17 1-1	D02 2-0	S23 2-0	M24 0-0	M31 2-1	O07 1-2		J06 1-1	O21 1-0	F03 0-0	N18 0-3	M30 4-1	m05 1-0
17 Q.P.R.	N11 4-1	D09 1-1	S23 0-0	D16 1-2	F17 3-1	O21 1-2	a21 2-0	S09 2-1	D25 4-0	a07 1-1	J20 2-3	N25 1-1	m05 3-2	S04 2-0	M15 2-3	D30 0-1		M03 1-0	M24 1-0	M30 2-1	O07 0-2	A26 1-2
18 READING	a28 1-0	N25 1-0	M31 0-0	S02 0-0	S09 0-1	O07 2-1	D30 1-3	M17 1-1	F24 3-0	J27 1-0	F14 1-2	M30 2-0	D16 0-0	D09 4-1	S23 0-1	O28 0-0	M21 0-0		D26 1-1	A30 4-4	a14 1-0	N11 1-0
19 SOUTHEND U	S25 4-0	a02 1-2	a14 0-0	O28 0-3	O14 0-0	D23 0-0	D16 5-0	M31 1-1	M10 1-3	J06 1-1	F24 4-0	S02 3-1	N04 1-2	S30 3-1	a09 2-1	F10 0-0	M17 2-0	D25 3-1		S16 0-1	a28 2-0	J20 2-1
20 SWANSEA T	D30 5-1	M03 0-0	N11 0-0	O07 4-1	m05 0-1	a07 3-2	O21 5-1	S23 1-0	J27 1-0	A26 1-1	D16 0-1	D26 5-1	F03 4-0	F17 3-1	a21 1-1	N25 2-1	a02 3-0	S04 2-2	S09 1-0		O02 5-0	M24 0-0
21 SWINDON T	D23 5-4	F03 3-0	N18 3-0	D27 0-1	a07 1-0	M03 2-1	J27 2-1	N11 0-1	S30 1-1	S04 4-0	S16 0-0	D30 2-2	A26 2-0	O21 1-2	M24 2-1	a02 3-0	O14 1-0	a21 3-1	m05 3-0	D09 2-1		F17 1-1
22 WATFORD	M10 6-0	D25 2-0	F10 1-2	a14 1-1	D09 0-1	J06 2-2	S30 4-0	O28 5-2	N18 2-1	O14 1-1	A30 0-0	M31 2-1	S16 0-0	M30 2-1	D16 1-0	a28 2-3	S02 0-3	N04 1-0	J27 1-1	M17 2-1	F24 0-3	

LEAGUE TABLES

DIVISION 1

	P	W	D	L	F	A	W	D	L	F	A	Pts
Liverpool	42	17	3	1	50	13	9	5	7	20	18	60
Sunderland	42	15	5	1	50	25	7	5	9	22	29	54
Huddersfield T	42	14	2	5	35	15	7	9	5	25	17	53
Newcastle U	42	13	6	2	31	11	5	6	10	14	26	48
Everton	42	14	4	3	41	20	6	3	12	22	39	47
Aston Villa	42	15	3	3	42	11	3	7	11	22	40	46
W.B.A.	42	12	7	2	38	10	5	4	12	20	39	45
Manchester C	42	14	6	1	38	16	3	5	13	12	33	45
Cardiff C	42	15	2	4	51	18	3	5	13	22	41	43
Sheffield U	42	11	7	3	41	20	5	3	13	27	44	42
Arsenal	42	13	4	4	38	16	3	6	12	23	46	42
Tottenham H	42	11	3	7	34	22	6	4	11	16	28	41
Bolton W	42	11	8	2	36	17	3	4	14	14	41	40
Blackburn R	42	12	7	2	32	19	2	5	14	15	43	40
Burnley	42	12	3	6	39	24	4	3	14	19	35	38
Preston N.E.	42	12	3	6	41	26	1	8	12	19	38	37
Birmingham C	42	10	4	7	25	19	3	7	11	16	38	37
Middlesbrough	42	11	4	6	41	25	2	6	13	16	38	36
Chelsea	42	5	13	3	29	20	4	5	12	16	33	36
Nottingham F	42	12	2	7	25	23	1	6	14	16	47	34
Stoke	42	7	9	5	28	19	3	1	17	19	48	30
Oldham A	42	9	6	6	21	20	1	4	16	14	45	30

DIVISION 2

	P	W	D	L	F	A	W	D	L	F	A	Pts
Notts Co	42	16	1	4	29	15	7	6	8	17	19	53
West Ham U	42	9	8	4	21	11	11	3	7	42	27	51
Leicester C	42	14	2	5	42	19	7	7	7	23	25	51
Manchester U	42	10	6	5	25	17	7	8	6	26	19	48
Blackpool	42	12	4	5	37	14	6	7	8	23	29	47
Bury	42	14	5	2	41	16	4	6	11	14	30	47
Leeds U	42	11	8	2	26	10	7	3	11	17	26	47
Sheffield W	42	14	3	4	36	16	3	9	9	18	31	46
Barnsley	42	12	4	5	42	21	5	7	9	20	30	45
Fulham	42	10	7	4	29	12	6	5	10	14	20	44
Southampton	42	10	5	6	28	21	4	9	8	12	19	42
Hull C	42	9	8	4	29	22	5	6	10	14	23	42
South Shields	42	11	7	3	26	12	4	3	14	9	32	40
Derby Co	42	9	5	7	25	16	5	6	10	21	34	39
Bradford C	42	8	7	6	27	18	4	6	11	14	27	37
Crystal Palace	42	10	7	4	33	16	3	4	14	21	46	37
Port Vale	42	8	6	7	23	18	6	3	12	16	33	37
Coventry C	42	12	2	7	35	21	3	5	13	11	42	37
Clapton O	42	9	6	6	26	17	3	6	12	14	33	36
Stockport Co	42	10	6	5	32	24	4	2	15	11	34	36
Rotherham U	42	10	7	4	30	19	3	2	16	14	44	35
Wolverhampton W	42	9	4	8	32	26	0	5	16	10	51	27

DIVISION 3 NORTH

	P	W	D	L	F	A	W	D	L	F	A	Pts
Nelson	38	15	2	2	37	10	9	1	9	24	31	51
Bradford P.A.	38	14	4	1	51	15	5	5	9	16	23	47
Walsall	38	13	4	2	32	14	6	4	9	19	30	46
Chesterfield	38	13	5	1	49	18	6	2	11	19	34	45
Wigan B	38	14	3	2	45	11	4	5	10	19	28	44
Crewe A	38	13	3	3	32	9	4	6	9	16	29	43
Halifax T	38	11	4	4	29	14	6	3	10	24	32	41
Accrington S	38	14	2	3	40	21	3	5	11	19	44	41
Darlington	38	13	3	3	43	14	2	7	10	16	32	40
Wrexham	38	13	5	1	29	12	1	5	13	9	36	38
Stalybridge C	38	13	2	4	32	18	2	4	13	10	29	36
Rochdale	38	8	5	6	29	22	5	5	9	13	31	36
Lincoln C	38	9	7	3	21	11	4	3	12	18	44	36
Grimsby T	38	10	3	6	35	18	4	2	13	20	34	33
Hartlepool U	38	10	6	3	34	14	0	6	13	14	40	32
Tranmere R	38	11	4	4	41	21	1	4	14	8	38	32
Southport	38	11	3	5	21	12	1	4	14	11	34	31
Barrow	38	11	2	6	31	17	2	2	15	19	43	30
Ashington	38	10	3	6	34	33	1	5	13	17	44	30
Durham C	38	7	9	3	31	19	2	1	16	12	40	28

DIVISION 3 SOUTH

	P	W	D	L	F	A	W	D	L	F	A	Pts
Bristol C	42	16	4	1	43	13	8	7	6	23	27	59
Plymouth A	42	18	3	0	47	6	5	4	12	14	23	53
Swansea T	42	13	6	2	46	14	9	3	9	32	31	53
Brighton & H.A.	42	15	3	3	39	13	5	8	8	13	21	51
Luton T	42	14	4	3	47	18	7	3	11	21	31	49
Millwall	42	9	10	2	27	13	5	8	8	18	27	46
Portsmouth	42	10	5	6	34	20	9	3	9	24	32	46
Northampton T	42	13	6	2	40	17	4	5	12	14	27	45
Swindon T	42	14	4	3	41	17	3	7	11	21	39	45
Watford	42	10	6	5	35	23	7	4	10	22	31	44
Q.P.R.	42	10	4	7	34	24	6	6	9	20	25	42
Charlton A	42	11	6	4	33	14	3	8	10	22	37	42
Bristol R	42	7	9	5	25	19	6	7	8	10	17	42
Brentford	42	9	4	8	27	23	4	8	9	14	28	38
Southend U	42	10	6	5	35	18	2	7	12	14	36	37
Gillingham	42	13	4	4	38	18	2	3	16	13	41	37
Merthyr T	42	10	4	7	27	17	1	10	10	12	31	36
Norwich C	42	8	7	6	29	26	5	3	13	22	45	36
Reading	42	9	8	4	24	15	1	6	14	12	40	34
Exeter C	42	10	4	7	27	18	3	3	15	20	66	33
Aberdare A	42	6	8	7	25	23	3	3	15	17	47	29
Newport Co	42	8	6	7	28	21	0	5	16	12	49	27

FOOTBALL LEAGUE RECORDS

Top scorers: Div 1, W.Chadwick (Everton) 28 goals; Div 2, H.Bedford (Blackpool) 34 goals; Div 3 N, D.Brown (Darlington) 27 goals; Div 3 S, W.P.Haines (Portsmouth) 28 goals.

Stalybridge Celtic resigned. New Brighton, Doncaster Rovers and Bournemouth & Boscombe Athletic were elected to the League.

Outside-left Billy Smith played a major role in Huddersfield Town's hat-trick of League titles and altogether scored 126 goals in 574 appearances during a 21-year playing career at Leeds Road.

DIVISION 1

	ARSENAL	ASTON VILLA	BIRMINGHAM	BLACKBURN R	BOLTON W	BURNLEY	CARDIFF C	CHELSEA	EVERTON	HUDDERSFIELD T	LIVERPOOL	MANCHESTER C	MIDDLESBROUGH	NEWCASTLE U	NOTTINGHAM F	NOTTS CO	PRESTON N.E.	SHEFFIELD U	SUNDERLAND	TOTTENHAM H	W.B.A.	WEST HAM U
1 ARSENAL		F16 0-1	S29 0-0	D01 2-2	O27 0-0	a05 2-0	J19 1-2	D29 1-0	a21 0-1	D15 1-3	M01 3-1	O13 1-2	N03 2-1	A25 1-4	M22 1-0	D27 0-0	m03 1-2	F25 1-3	a12 2-0	N17 1-1	S15 1-0	S10 4-1
2 ASTON VILLA	M12 2-1		S01 0-0	a02 1-0	J26 1-0	O13 1-1	D29 2-1	S15 0-0	S12 1-1	a30 3-1	N17 0-0	A29 2-0	D01 0-0	a21 6-1	a19 2-0	N03 0-0	S29 5-1	D22 2-2	F09 0-1	M15 0-0	O27 4-0	D25 1-1
3 BIRMINGHAM	S22 0-2	A25 3-0		O06 1-1	S10 0-3	F27 2-1	m03 0-0	M22 1-0	D08 0-1	O20 0-1	S05 2-1	D26 3-0	F16 2-1	a05 4-1	J19 0-2	N17 0-0	M01 2-0	a19 0-1	S08 0-2	J05 3-2	D22 0-0	N10 2-0
4 BLACKBURN R	D08 2-0	M01 3-1	O13 4-1		a12 3-1	N03 1-1	M20 2-1	A25 3-0	S15 2-0	D29 1-0	M22 0-0	O20 0-1	F02 2-0	S17 2-1	a05 1-1	J01 4-1	D25 2-0	F16 1-1	N24 3-2	D22 0-1	S29 4-0	J19 0-0
5 BOLTON W	O20 1-2	J19 1-0	J01 1-1	a19 3-0		M01 0-0	S01 2-2	N10 4-0	D29 2-0	N17 3-1	M12 4-1	S15 0-0	M22 2-0	a18 0-1	F16 4-0	D15 7-1	a05 0-0	S03 4-2	O13 1-0	S29 3-1	D25 2-0	D01 1-1
6 BURNLEY	a28 4-1	O06 1-2	F09 1-2	N10 1-2	a01 1-0		a19 1-2	D15 2-0	A27 2-2	a18 1-1	S22 2-0	M17 3-2	D25 0-0	D01 3-2	S08 2-4	S01 1-1	D29 1-0	O27 2-0	M15 0-3	a26 2-2	J26 4-0	N17 5-1
7 CARDIFF C	J26 4-0	J05 0-2	a26 2-0	F09 2-0	A25 3-2	a12 2-0		O13 1-1	M29 0-0	a14 0-0	D22 2-0	N24 1-1	a21 1-0	S29 1-0	D08 4-1	M15 0-2	O20 1-1	D26 3-1	A27 2-1	a07 2-1	N03 3-0	S15 1-0
8 CHELSEA	J05 0-0	S08 0-0	M15 1-1	S01 2-0	N03 0-0	D22 3-2	O06 1-2		F23 1-1	J26 0-1	a18 2-1	a30 3-1	N24 2-0	a19 1-0	D26 1-1	F09 0-6	D08 1-2	S22 1-1	a26 4-1	A27 0-1	M12 0-0	O20 0-0
9 EVERTON	a18 3-1	S19 2-0	D01 2-0	S08 0-0	J05 2-2	S03 3-3	a05 0-0	F16 2-0		S22 1-1	O06 1-0	D22 6-1	J19 1-0	M01 2-2	A25 2-1	O27 3-0	F06 1-1	N10 2-0	D26 2-3	a19 4-2	N17 2-0	M22 2-1
10 HUDDERSFIELD T	D22 6-1	a05 1-0	O27 1-0	J05 1-0	N24 1-0	a22 1-0	M01 2-0	J19 0-1	S29 2-0		N10 3-1	a12 1-1	A25 1-0	F27 1-1	m03 3-0	S15 0-0	S04 4-0	M22 1-0	D08 3-2	D26 2-1	O13 0-0	F16 1-1
11 LIVERPOOL	a02 0-0	N24 0-1	A29 6-2	M15 0-0	F09 3-1	S29 1-0	D15 0-2	J01 3-1	O13 1-2	N03 1-1		J26 0-0	a12 3-1	D25 0-1	O20 4-2	a26 1-0	S15 3-1	D08 2-3	M19 4-2	M29 1-0	S01 0-0	D29 2-0
12 MANCHESTER C	O06 1-0	S05 1-2	a18 1-0	O27 3-1	S08 1-1	F16 2-2	N17 1-1	a05 1-0	D15 2-1	a19 1-1	J19 0-1		M01 3-2	N03 1-1	F13 1-3	D01 1-0	M22 2-2	A25 2-1	S22 4-1	J01 1-0	D29 3-3	m03 2-1
13 MIDDLESBROUGH	N10 0-0	D08 0-2	F23 0-1	M08 2-0	M15 1-2	D26 3-0	J01 0-1	N17 2-0	J26 1-1	S01 2-0	a19 1-1	a02 1-1		O20 1-0	O06 5-2	A29 2-3	D22 1-2	J05 0-1	M29 1-3	S15 0-1	F09 0-1	S29 0-1
14 NEWCASTLE U	S01 1-0	J01 4-1	a09 2-1	A29 2-1	S12 1-0	D08 2-0	S22 1-1	a12 2-1	a02 3-1	F09 0-1	D26 2-1	N10 4-1	O27 3-2		J05 4-0	M19 1-2	N24 3-1	S08 2-2	D22 0-2	J26 2-2	M15 1-1	O13 0-0
15 NOTTINGHAM F	M15 2-1	a12 0-0	J26 1-1	M29 0-0	F23 1-0	S15 0-0	D01 0-1	D25 2-0	S01 1-0	a26 1-1	O27 0-1	F09 1-2	O13 3-1	D29 0-0		S29 1-0	a21 1-1	N17 1-2	M08 1-2	N03 0-0	A27 1-1	D15 2-1
16 NOTTS CO	D26 1-2	N10 0-1	N24 1-1	a18 3-0	D22 1-1	A25 2-1	M22 1-0	M05 0-0	O20 1-1	S08 1-0	m03 1-2	D08 2-0	O04 1-0	F16 1-0	S22 2-1		J19 0-0	a05 0-2	J05 1-2	O06 0-0	a19 1-0	M01 1-1
17 PRESTON N.E.	a26 0-2	S22 2-2	M08 1-0	D26 0-1	M29 0-2	J05 5-0	O27 3-1	D01 1-1	F09 0-1	A27 1-3	S08 0-1	M15 4-1	D15 4-0	N17 1-2	F02 3-1	J26 2-1		O06 1-1	N10 1-2	S01 2-2	M19 1-2	a19 2-1
18 SHEFFIELD U	F09 3-1	D15 2-1	a12 0-2	F23 4-0	A27 0-0	O20 2-1	D25 1-1	S29 1-0	N03 4-0	M15 0-1	D01 1-1	S01 3-0	D29 0-1	S15 2-1	N24 0-0	a07 3-1	O13 4-0		J26 1-1	M08 6-2	a26 2-0	J01 0-2
19 SUNDERLAND	a19 1-1	F13 2-0	S15 1-1	N17 5-1	O06 2-2	M22 0-1	S05 0-3	O17 2-0	J01 3-0	D01 2-1	F16 0-0	S29 5-2	a05 3-2	D15 3-2	M01 1-0	D29 1-1	N03 2-1	J19 2-2		O20 1-0	a18 2-0	A25 0-0
20 TOTTENHAM H	N24 3-0	M22 2-3	D29 1-1	D15 2-1	S22 0-0	m03 1-0	F16 1-1	S03 0-1	a12 2-5	D25 1-0	a05 1-1	a21 4-1	S08 2-1	J19 2-0	N10 3-0	O13 1-3	A25 2-0	M01 1-2	O27 1-1		D01 0-0	a22 0-1
21 W.B.A.	S08 4-0	O20 1-0	D15 0-0	S22 3-3	D26 0-5	J19 0-3	N10 2-4	M01 2-2	N24 5-0	O06 2-4	A25 2-0	J05 2-1	a09 1-1	M22 0-0	S03 3-2	a12 5-0	F16 1-2	m03 3-1	a21 3-1	D08 4-1		a05 0-0
22 WEST HAM U	A27 1-0	D26 1-0	N03 4-1	J26 0-1	D08 0-1	N24 0-0	S08 0-0	O27 2-0	M15 2-1	M27 2-3	J05 1-0	a26 1-2	S22 1-1	O06 1-0	D22 3-2	M08 1-1	a12 3-1	a21 2-2	S01 0-1	F09 0-0	M29 1-0	

Jack Swan was Leeds United's leading scorer in their Division Two championship season. He played for Huddersfield in the 1920 FA Cup Final.

DIVISION 2

	BARNSLEY	BLACKPOOL	BRADFORD C	BRISTOL C	BURY	CLAPTON O	COVENTRY C	CRYSTAL P	DERBY CO	FULHAM	HULL C	LEEDS U	LEICESTER C	MANCHESTER U	NELSON	OLDHAM A	PORT VALE	SHEFFIELD W	SOUTHAMPTON	SOUTH SHIELDS	STOCKPORT CO	STOKE
1 BARNSLEY		F23 3-1	D15 2-1	A27 3-1	a21 2-0	D29 1-0	S01 1-1	a26 5-2	M08 1-3	F09 2-1	M29 0-0	N24 1-3	O27 3-1	D26 1-0	M15 0-0	S29 4-1	F02 3-0	N03 0-0	J26 1-1	S15 1-0	O13 0-0	a19 0-0
2 BLACKPOOL	F16 0-2		M01 2-1	N03 2-0	J19 3-1	m03 3-0	O20 5-0	S29 2-0	D22 4-0	D08 3-0	a18 0-0	a05 1-1	a19 3-1	F06 1-0	D29 1-1	A25 2-2	M22 6-1	O13 1-0	N24 2-0	S03 1-1	D26 0-0	S15 1-1
3 BRADFORD C	D22 3-2	M08 0-2		J26 1-1	D25 2-2	M12 0-0	A27 0-0	O27 0-1	M15 1-2	F23 1-0	a12 2-1	N10 0-0	O13 2-2	D29 0-0	M29 0-2	S15 2-1	N17 2-0	S01 4-1	F09 2-1	a21 0-1	S29 0-1	a26 2-1
4 BRISTOL C	S03 1-1	N10 1-1	J19 0-1		D01 4-1	M22 0-2	S15 2-2	D25 0-0	S29 0-8	O20 0-1	D15 1-0	F16 0-1	M01 0-1	A25 1-2	N17 1-0	a19 0-0	F13 0-0	a18 2-3	O13 1-1	m03 1-0	a05 3-0	D29 1-1
5 BURY	a18 1-1	J26 2-0	J01 3-0	D08 6-0		S22 0-0	a26 5-0	M29 1-1	F09 1-0	A27 2-1	M08 1-0	D22 3-0	J02 2-0	S08 2-0	F23 2-0	O27 2-2	J05 0-0	a12 5-0	A25 1-0	O06 0-1	N03 2-1	M15 1-0
6 CLAPTON O	J05 2-1	a26 1-0	D08 1-1	M15 2-0	S29 1-0		M08 4-0	F09 1-0	S15 2-0	a19 0-0	A27 0-0	O06 0-1	D25 1-0	a18 1-0	S01 5-1	N17 1-2	N03 1-1	F23 0-0	M29 0-0	O20 3-0	D22 1-1	J26 0-2
7 COVENTRY C	A25 2-3	O27 3-1	S03 1-0	S08 1-1	F02 1-0	M01 1-1		D29 0-0	a22 0-1	O06 3-0	D17 0-2	M10 2-1	F16 2-4	N17 1-1	N10 4-0	a05 5-2	J19 1-3	D25 5-1	S22 0-0	a19 1-0	M22 0-0	D15 1-2
8 CRYSTAL P	m03 3-1	S22 3-1	O20 3-0	D26 1-0	a05 1-0	a22 2-1	J05 3-1		D08 0-1	S08 1-1	N03 0-0	S05 1-1	J19 4-3	a19 1-1	O06 1-1	M01 2-3	A25 1-2	D15 3-0	a18 0-0	M22 1-0	F16 1-1	N24 5-1
9 DERBY CO	M01 2-1	D15 2-0	M22 0-0	S22 2-3	F27 0-2	S08 1-0	a21 1-0	D01 5-0		N24 3-3	O13 4-1	a19 2-0	m03 4-0	F16 3-0	D26 6-0	S03 2-1	a05 2-0	D29 1-1	O27 1-0	J19 6-1	A25 4-1	N10 1-1
10 FULHAM	M10 3-0	D01 2-3	F16 1-1	O27 1-1	S03 0-2	a12 0-0	O13 1-1	S15 1-0	N17 3-2		D25 1-1	M22 0-2	a05 1-0	J19 3-1	D15 0-0	D29 0-0	M01 0-0	S29 4-1	N10 3-2	A25 2-3	m03 1-0	a21 3-0
11 HULL C	a05 1-2	a21 2-1	a19 2-0	D22 5-0	M01 0-1	S03 2-2	D08 3-2	N10 2-2	O06 0-1	D26 4-2		S22 1-2	A25 1-1	M22 1-1	S08 2-1	F14 0-0	m03 1-2	N24 1-1	J05 0-0	F16 1-0	J19 1-2	O20 2-0
12 LEEDS U	N17 3-1	M29 0-0	N03 1-0	M19 0-0	D15 1-2	O13 1-0	F09 3-1	A27 3-0	a12 1-1	M15 3-0	S29 5-2		S15 1-2	D01 0-0	a26 1-0	D26 5-0	O27 3-0	J26 1-0	M08 3-0	F27 2-1	a21 4-0	S01 0-0
13 LEICESTER C	O20 2-0	a12 1-2	O06 0-1	M08 5-1	N17 3-0	D26 1-2	F23 2-0	J26 1-0	a26 3-0	M29 2-1	S01 1-1	S08 2-0		N03 2-2	a22 3-1	D15 1-1	S22 2-0	F09 2-1	M15 0-1	D01 4-1	D29 1-1	A27 5-0
14 MANCHESTER U	D25 1-2	F09 0-0	J05 3-0	S01 2-1	S15 0-1	a21 2-2	J02 1-2	a12 5-1	F23 0-0	J26 0-0	M15 1-1	D08 3-1	N10 3-0		M08 0-1	O13 2-0	D22 5-0	a26 2-0	A27 1-0	S29 1-1	O20 3-0	M29 2-2
15 NELSON	M22 4-3	J05 2-3	a05 1-1	N24 2-1	F16 0-5	A25 1-1	N03 3-0	O13 4-2	D25 2-1	D22 1-1	S15 1-1	m03 3-1	a21 1-1	M01 0-2		J19 2-1	a12 1-3	O20 1-1	S11 0-0	F02 0-2	S03 1-1	S29 2-0
16 OLDHAM A	S22 1-1	S01 1-1	S08 0-0	a12 0-0	O20 0-0	D03 1-0	M29 1-1	M08 1-0	A27 2-0	J05 2-1	F09 0-0	D25 2-2	D22 0-0	O06 3-2	J26 1-0		a18 2-0	M15 2-0	a26 1-3	N03 1-0	D08 3-1	F23 0-0
17 PORT VALE	D08 4-1	M15 2-6	N24 2-2	F09 0-2	D29 2-1	N10 1-0	J26 1-1	S01 3-4	M29 2-0	M08 3-1	a26 2-2	O20 0-1	S29 2-1	D15 0-1	a19 0-0	a21 3-0		A27 2-0	M17 1-0	J21 1-1	S15 0-1	O13 2-4
18 SHEFFIELD W	N10 1-0	O06 2-2	A25 0-0	a21 1-0	a19 1-1	F16 1-0	D26 2-0	D22 6-0	J05 1-0	S22 2-1	N17 1-0	J19 0-0	F11 2-1	m03 2-0	O27 5-0	M22 1-2	S03 2-1		S08 1-1	a05 5-0	M01 3-0	D08 3-0
19 SOUTHAMPTON	J19 6-0	N17 3-2	F11 2-0	O06 1-0	S01 3-0	a05 5-0	S29 1-3	a21 1-0	O20 0-0	N03 1-0	D29 2-0	M01 0-1	M22 1-0	S03 0-0	D08 3-0	m03 3-1	F16 1-1	S15 3-0		D15 0-0	a19 0-0	O15 0-1
20 SOUTH SHIELDS	S08 2-0	A27 1-0	a18 0-0	a26 1-1	O13 1-0	O27 1-1	a12 4-2	M15 2-0	J26 3-2	S01 1-0	F23 0-1	J05 2-0	D08 1-2	S22 1-0	F09 3-0	N10 2-0	J01 3-3	M29 1-1	D22 1-2		N24 3-1	M08 1-0
21 STOCKPORT CO	O06 1-1	D25 2-1	S22 1-2	M29 0-0	N10 3-2	M31 2-0	M15 0-0	M10 2-2	S01 0-0	a26 2-1	J26 5-1	a18 1-1	J05 3-1	O27 3-2	A27 1-0	J01 0-1	S08 0-0	M08 1-0	a12 2-3	D10 3-2		F09 0-1
22 STOKE	a12 2-0	S08 2-2	D26 2-0	J05 3-0	M22 0-0	J19 0-1	D22 2-1	N17 1-1	N03 1-1	a22 0-0	O27 1-0	A25 1-1	S03 1-0	a05 3-0	S22 4-0	F16 1-1	O06 1-0	D01 1-1	S24 1-1	M01 0-0	F02 0-0	

Season 1923-24

DIVISION 3 NORTH

	ACCRINGTON S	ASHINGTON	BARROW	BRADFORD	CHESTERFIELD	CREWE A	DARLINGTON	DONCASTER R	DURHAM C	GRIMSBY T	HALIFAX T	HARTLEPOOLS U	LINCOLN C	NEW BRIGHTON	ROCHDALE	ROTHERHAM CO	SOUTHPORT	TRANMERE R	WALSALL	WIGAN B	WOLVERHAMPTON W	WREXHAM
1 ACCRINGTON S		O27 0-1	S25 3-1	F23 2-2	M08 2-0	F11 1-1	S01 2-0	a19 0-0	a30 5-4	J01 2-0	J05 1-2	M17 2-0	J26 3-1	S08 0-0	a26 0-1	M15 3-2	D26 2-0	F09 3-1	O06 0-3	N10 2-2	S22 1-0	M29 1-0
2 ASHINGTON	O20 1-1		M01 2-0	a12 1-0	a26 1-1	O13 3-0	F23 2-1	A27 3-1	S29 2-1	D08 1-0	N03 4-0	a18 0-0	M15 2-1	D22 5-0	J26 1-0	N24 1-2	F09 2-0	M29 3-3	J01 3-1	S15 3-0	J05 1-7	S01 0-2
3 BARROW	S03 0-0	M08 2-2		O13 1-1	O27 2-0	J19 1-2	D25 1-0	D08 0-0	F02 1-2	m03 3-1	a18 1-0	A25 1-2	S15 2-1	a19 2-1	D22 1-2	N10 1-2	J05 1-3	S29 1-1	M22 0-1	F23 2-1	a05 2-2	J12 0-0
4 BRADFORD	F16 1-1	a19 3-1	O06 3-0		F06 2-1	M01 1-1	D08 1-0	D26 4-2	M22 3-0	S03 2-1	J19 1-0	F02 4-0	N03 3-1	A25 1-1	S08 4-2	J05 2-0	S22 2-0	N24 2-0	m03 5-0	a05 4-0	O20 0-1	a22 2-0
5 CHESTERFIELD	M01 3-0	m03 2-0	O20 2-1	D22 2-3		M22 2-1	J05 5-1	S08 2-1	a18 1-1	J19 4-2	M26 1-1	F16 5-1	N24 2-1	S03 1-0	S22 1-1	D25 3-1	O06 4-0	D08 5-0	N10 7-0	a19 1-0	A25 0-0	J01 1-0
6 CREWE A	D08 1-2	O06 1-3	J26 2-0	M08 1-1	M15 0-1		A29 2-1	a26 0-2	N03 0-2	D26 0-0	D22 2-2	a30 2-1	F09 1-2	a18 2-0	J05 0-2	M29 1-0	S01 1-1	F16 1-1	S22 2-0	O27 0-2	S08 0-0	a12 1-1
7 DARLINGTON	A25 2-1	F16 3-2	D26 5-1	N17 3-1	D29 2-1	S05 1-1		O27 1-1	J19 3-2	a19 1-0	m03 0-0	S08 5-0	O13 1-0	a05 3-1	N24 2-2	J01 1-0	D22 3-1	N10 4-1	M01 4-2	F02 3-1	M22 1-1	S22 3-0
8 DONCASTER R	a12 1-2	S03 2-1	D01 2-2	D25 1-1	S15 0-2	m03 4-1	O20 1-0		D15 2-1	M01 2-1	M22 7-0	a05 3-1	D29 3-2	F16 2-0	N03 0-0	S29 0-1	J12 3-0	a21 4-0	J19 3-0	A25 0-0	m01 0-2	O06 1-0
9 DURHAM C	N24 3-0	a05 4-0	F09 1-2	M15 2-0	M29 1-1	N10 3-1	J26 3-2	D22 2-1		J05 0-1	D08 2-2	O20 3-0	F23 1-0	a21 2-1	S01 0-0	a12 3-2	A29 0-1	M01 1-1	S08 1-0	O13 2-2	J01 2-3	a26 4-3
10 GRIMSBY T	a18 2-0	a08 4-0	a26 5-0	A27 2-0	J26 0-0	D25 2-0	a12 3-0	M08 1-1	D29 1-0		S15 1-1	O13 0-1	S29 2-2	O27 0-0	M15 1-0	F09 1-1	M29 1-0	S01 0-0	N17 1-0	M27 1-1	N10 2-0	F23 0-0
11 HALIFAX T	D29 3-0	N10 3-0	a21 1-0	J26 0-0	F09 2-0	J01 2-0	a26 1-4	M15 0-1	M10 2-1	S08 1-3		D25 1-0	S01 1-0	S22 2-1	M29 0-1	F23 0-2	a12 1-0	A27 0-0	O27 3-0	N17 1-2	O06 2-2	M08 0-0
12 HARTLEPOOLS U	D22 3-0	a22 0-1	S01 1-0	F09 0-0	F23 2-3	a21 2-2	S15 0-1	M29 1-1	O27 0-0	O06 1-1	D26 1-3		J01 1-1	N03 0-1	a12 1-2	M08 2-5	a26 1-0	J26 2-1	J05 0-1	S29 0-0	D08 0-1	M15 4-0
13 LINCOLN C	J19 0-2	M22 2-0	S08 4-1	N10 2-3	J12 0-1	F02 0-0	O06 2-0	J05 1-1	F16 3-1	S22 1-3	A25 1-1	S05 1-1		m03 1-0	D25 0-2	D08 2-1	a21 1-1	O27 1-1	a05 2-0	M01 1-1	a12 0-0	D22 4-2
14 NEW BRIGHTON	S15 1-2	D26 1-1	a12 5-0	S01 1-0	A29 0-0	D15 2-1	M29 1-1	F23 2-0	S12 2-0	O20 0-0	S29 2-0	N10 0-0	a26 3-1		M08 1-1	J26 1-2	M15 0-0	O06 0-0	D08 1-0	D29 5-0	D01 0-1	F09 0-0
15 ROCHDALE	m03 4-1	J19 1-0	D15 3-1	S15 3-0	S29 3-0	D29 1-0	a18 0-0	N10 2-0	A25 2-0	M22 4-2	a05 3-0	J12 1-0	D26 1-0	M01 6-2		O13 1-0	J08 2-2	a22 1-0	F02 1-0	S03 1-0	F16 0-0	O27 0-0
16 ROTHERHAM CO	M22 2-0	M17 1-0	N03 2-0	M24 1-0	D26 1-2	N17 1-0	a21 2-0	S22 3-0	a19 5-1	F02 2-1	F16 3-2	M01 5-0	a22 2-0	J19 3-1	O06 0-0		O27 1-1	J12 5-1	A25 0-2	m03 4-0	S03 1-1	S08 2-1
17 SOUTHPORT	D25 1-0	F02 2-0	D29 2-0	S29 1-0	O13 1-0	A25 1-0	a29 1-0	N24 2-2	S04 1-0	a05 3-0	a19 3-0	m03 2-2	a18 3-2	J01 3-0	D08 0-1	O20 0-0		S15 1-1	F16 1-1	J26 1-1	M01 0-0	N03 1-0
18 TRANMERE R	F02 2-0	D25 2-4	S22 3-0	J01 2-1	a05 0-0	F23 1-1	N03 1-4	a18 3-0	M08 1-0	A25 2-1	S06 3-0	J19 2-0	O20 1-3	O13 1-2	a28 2-1	D22 0-1	S08 1-1		a19 3-1	M22 1-0	m03 0-0	J05 1-1
19 WALSALL	O13 2-0	a21 1-1	M15 1-1	a26 2-3	N03 0-1	S29 1-0	M08 2-1	J26 5-2	S15 1-1	N24 2-0	O20 2-0	D29 2-0	M29 0-0	J12 3-0	F09 0-1	S01 1-1	F23 0-1	a12 0-4		D25 3-0	a07 2-1	A27 1-2
20 WIGAN B	N03 2-0	S08 1-1	F16 4-0	M29 0-1	a12 3-1	O20 3-0	F09 2-2	S01 1-0	O06 0-1	D22 4-0	N24 0-1	S22 4-1	M08 0-0	J05 1-0	A27 3-0	a26 3-1	J19 1-1	M15 1-2	D26 2-1		a22 1-1	D08 3-1
21 WOLVERHAMPTON W	S29 5-1	D29 1-0	M29 3-0	O27 2-0	S01 2-1	S15 1-0	M15 2-0	F09 1-0	D26 2-1	N03 4-1	O13 4-0	F11 2-1	a19 3-0	N24 5-1	M26 0-0	A27 3-0	M08 2-1	a26 3-0	D22 0-0	a21 3-3		J26 3-0
22 WREXHAM	a05 1-0	A25 4-0	N24 2-0	a21 2-2	N17 0-0	a19 1-0	S29 0-1	O13 2-2	m03 0-0	F16 1-1	M01 0-1	M22 1-0	M12 2-1	F02 0-0	O20 1-1	S15 1-0	N10 3-0	D26 1-1	S05 0-0	S19 0-0	J19 2-2	

DIVISION 3 SOUTH

	ABERDARE A	BOURNEMOUTH	BRENTFORD	BRIGHTON & HA	BRISTOL R	CHARLTON A	EXETER C	GILLINGHAM	LUTON T	MERTHYR T	MILLWALL	NEWPORT CO	NORTHAMPTON T	NORWICH C	PLYMOUTH A	PORTSMOUTH	Q.P.R.	READING	SOUTHEND U	SWANSEA T	SWINDON T	WATFORD
1 ABERDARE A		S22 1-0	S10 1-2	N10 3-1	M31 2-0	S01 4-1	D29 0-0	M15 1-1	O20 0-1	a22 0-0	S08 1-1	a26 2-0	M08 2-2	A27 0-0	a12 1-2	M17 0-0	M29 1-1	O06 1-0	D26 5-2	F23 4-2	J26 2-2	F09 4-0
2 BOURNEMOUTH	S29 0-1		D25 2-4	D15 1-0	D29 0-1	a26 1-0	S15 1-0	F23 0-0	D08 2-3	a12 3-3	O20 2-0	a05 0-1	F09 2-1	O13 1-2	M15 0-0	a21 0-0	M08 3-1	N24 0-0	N10 0-1	J19 0-0	S01 0-0	S19 1-1
3 BRENTFORD	D08 1-1	D26 2-0		S22 1-2	O13 1-2	F23 0-0	N24 1-0	D22 3-2	S08 2-1	F09 0-0	J05 1-3	J26 0-0	a26 1-0	M08 3-0	A27 1-1	N10 1-1	S01 0-1	a21 4-1	O27 3-1	a12 2-2	M15 2-2	M29 4-1
4 BRIGHTON & H.A.	N03 5-0	D22 5-0	S29 2-0		S15 2-1	M15 3-0	O20 1-0	A29 2-2	D26 4-0	M08 0-0	D08 2-2	M26 4-0	S01 2-0	M29 3-0	F09 4-1	O13 0-4	J26 3-0	J05 4-0	a18 2-0	N24 4-1	a12 1-1	a26 3-0
5 BRISTOL R	N24 2-0	J05 3-4	O06 2-0	S08 2-0		M08 2-0	N03 0-0	S01 2-0	a21 1-1	F23 0-0	D22 4-1	F09 0-0	D08 1-1	M15 3-1	J26 1-1	O27 0-1	A27 2-1	D26 0-0	S22 3-1	a26 2-0	M29 0-1	a12 4-2
6 CHARLTON A	A25 3-1	m03 1-2	F16 3-1	M22 0-2	M01 1-3		a07 1-0	J05 0-0	a05 1-1	S08 1-0	S22 0-1	O06 2-1	D22 0-0	O20 0-0	a21 0-1	M10 1-1	D26 3-0	a19 0-0	S03 4-1	D08 1-3	N03 3-1	N24 1-1
7 EXETER C	J05 1-1	S08 0-2	a02 1-0	O27 0-1	N10 3-1	J26 0-0		a12 2-1	O06 2-1	A29 1-0	a21 2-0	S01 5-0	M29 2-1	F09 1-2	D26 0-4	S12 0-0	a26 3-0	S22 3-2	F23 2-0	M15 1-0	M19 3-1	M08 1-0
8 GILLINGHAM	M22 3-1	F16 1-0	M19 6-0	S05 1-1	A25 1-0	D29 0-1	a19 1-1		J19 0-0	M12 2-1	M01 0-2	O20 2-1	O06 1-1	D25 3-1	N17 1-0	m03 0-2	N03 0-0	F02 1-0	a05 3-2	S29 0-1	a18 1-0	S15 0-0
9 LUTON T	O27 1-0	D01 6-2	S15 2-1	D25 0-0	a18 0-0	M29 0-1	O13 1-0	J26 1-1		M15 1-1	N24 2-0	M08 2-0	A27 1-1	a12 2-1	F23 0-2	S29 4-1	F09 2-0	D15 2-0	D29 4-4	S01 1-2	a26 3-2	N03 0-0
10 MERTHYR T	a21 0-0	a19 4-2	F02 2-0	M01 2-1	F16 1-1	S15 2-1	S06 3-0	D08 0-2	M22 0-0		m03 1-0	D25 3-3	N24 0-0	S29 2-3	J05 1-0	J19 2-2	D22 2-0	a05 1-1	A25 3-2	N03 0-0	O13 2-0	O27 2-1
11 MILLWALL	S15 2-0	O27 4-2	D29 4-1	D01 0-0	D15 1-0	S29 1-0	a18 3-1	M08 5-0	N17 0-1	a26 6-0		a12 2-1	F16 4-3	S01 2-1	M29 1-0	D25 2-0	M15 3-0	N10 0-0	O13 0-0	F09 2-1	A27 1-0	J26 2-0
12 NEWPORT CO	m03 0-0	M29 2-0	a22 3-2	F16 0-0	F02 1-0	O13 0-1	A25 2-0	O27 2-1	M01 1-0	D26 4-4	a19 2-1		S22 1-1	N03 1-0	D15 1-2	S06 2-1	J01 2-1	M22 2-0	S08 5-0	a21 4-1	D01 3-0	D29 1-0
13 NORTHAMPTON T	a07 1-2	F02 3-1	m03 2-3	A25 3-0	S10 0-0	M13 1-0	a05 1-0	O13 2-0	S03 2-0	N17 3-0	F23 2-1	S29 0-0		D29 1-0	N10 1-0	a19 0-4	O20 3-0	J19 3-1	M22 8-0	S15 2-0	D27 1-1	a22 1-2
14 NORWICH C	S03 5-0	O06 1-1	M01 2-3	a05 1-0	M22 3-1	O27 2-2	F14 4-0	D26 1-0	a19 2-0	S22 2-0	A25 1-1	N10 3-1	J05 1-4		S08 0-1	F16 3-1	a21 5-0	m03 2-2	J19 3-1	a28 2-0	N17 2-0	S10 0-0
15 PLYMOUTH A	a19 2-0	M22 4-0	S03 4-1	a30 3-0	J19 2-2	a18 1-1	D25 4-0	N24 3-0	F16 0-0	D29 1-1	a05 1-1	D22 3-2	N03 0-0	S15 2-0		A25 1-2	D08 2-0	M01 2-1	m03 7-1	O20 2-0	S29 1-3	O13 1-0
16 PORTSMOUTH	D22 4-0	a18 3-0	N03 3-0	O06 1-3	O20 1-1	F09 0-0	D08 4-0	a26 3-0	S22 3-0	J26 1-0	D26 0-1	A29 5-0	a12 1-3	F23 4-0	S01 2-1		J05 7-0	S08 1-1	N24 3-0	M29 3-0	a30 4-1	M15 4-0
17 Q.P.R.	a05 3-0	M01 0-1	A25 1-0	J19 1-0	S05 1-2	D25 0-0	m03 2-0	N10 1-1	F02 0-2	D15 3-0	M22 1-1	S12 0-3	O27 3-2	a18 2-1	D01 3-2	D29 0-2		F16 1-4	a19 0-0	O13 2-2	S15 2-2	S29 2-1
18 READING	O13 0-1	N17 1-2	a18 1-0	D29 0-1	D25 3-2	a12 3-1	S29 1-0	F09 4-0	D22 0-1	M29 3-0	N03 2-0	M15 1-1	J26 1-0	a26 3-0	M08 1-2	S15 1-4	F23 4-0		J12 1-0	A29 3-4	O27 1-0	S01 1-1
19 SOUTHEND U	D25 1-1	N03 1-1	O20 3-1	a21 1-0	S29 1-0	A27 2-2	D22 0-0	M29 3-2	J05 1-1	S01 3-1	O06 0-0	S15 2-0	M15 5-1	J26 3-1	a26 0-2	S19 0-1	a12 4-2	D08 2-1		M08 0-0	F09 0-2	M19 3-0
20 SWANSEA T	F16 1-0	J26 1-0	a19 4-0	N17 1-0	m03 3-1	D01 1-0	M22 1-0	S22 3-1	A25 1-0	N10 5-1	M13 1-2	a18 2-1	S08 2-1	D22 1-0	O27 1-0	a05 0-0	O06 2-0	S03 5-1	M01 2-1		D29 1-1	D25 1-0
21 SWINDON T	J19 3-1	A25 3-1	M22 2-1	a19 4-0	a05 0-0	N10 1-1	F16 0-1	a21 4-1	m03 3-2	O06 3-0	S03 1-0	D08 3-0	D26 2-0	N24 4-2	S22 0-1	M01 0-0	S08 0-0	O20 1-0	a02 3-0	J05 1-0		D15 0-0
22 WATFORD	a18 2-0	S05 0-0	a05 0-1	m03 0-0	a19 4-0	N17 1-0	M01 4-1	S08 1-1	N10 0-0	O20 4-0	J19 1-1	J05 8-2	a21 0-2	D08 0-0	O06 0-1	M22 2-3	S22 0-2	A25 2-1	F16 4-1	D26 2-2	D22 0-0	

LEAGUE TABLES

DIVISION 1

	P	W	D	L	F	A	W	D	L	F	A	Pts
Huddersfield T	42	15	5	1	35	9	8	6	7	25	24	57
Cardiff C	42	14	5	2	35	13	8	8	5	26	21	57
Sunderland	42	12	7	2	38	20	10	2	9	33	34	53
Bolton W	42	13	6	2	45	13	5	8	8	23	21	50
Sheffield U	42	12	5	4	39	16	7	7	7	30	33	50
Aston Villa	42	10	10	1	33	11	8	3	10	19	26	49
Everton	42	13	7	1	43	18	5	6	10	19	35	49
Blackburn R	42	14	5	2	40	13	3	6	12	14	37	45
Newcastle U	42	13	5	3	40	21	4	5	12	20	33	44
Notts Co	42	9	7	5	21	15	5	7	9	23	34	42
Manchester C	42	11	7	3	34	24	4	5	12	20	47	42
Liverpool	42	11	5	5	35	20	4	6	11	14	28	41
West Ham U	42	10	6	5	26	17	3	9	9	14	26	41
Birmingham C	42	10	4	7	25	19	3	9	9	16	30	39
Tottenham H	42	9	6	6	30	22	3	8	10	20	34	38
W.B.A.	42	10	6	5	43	30	2	8	11	8	32	38
Burnley	42	10	5	6	39	27	2	7	12	16	33	36
Preston N.E.	42	8	4	9	34	27	4	6	11	18	40	34
Arsenal	42	8	5	8	25	24	4	4	13	15	39	33
Nottingham F	42	7	9	5	19	15	3	3	15	23	49	32
Chelsea	42	7	9	5	23	21	2	5	14	8	32	32
Middlesbrough	42	6	4	11	23	23	1	4	16	14	37	22

DIVISION 2

	P	W	D	L	F	A	W	D	L	F	A	Pts
Leeds U	42	14	5	2	41	10	7	7	7	20	25	54
Bury	42	15	5	1	42	7	6	4	11	21	28	51
Derby Co	42	15	4	2	52	15	6	5	10	23	27	51
Blackpool	42	13	7	1	43	12	5	6	10	29	35	49
Southampton	42	13	5	3	36	9	4	9	8	16	22	48
Stoke	42	9	11	1	27	10	5	7	9	17	32	46
Oldham A	42	10	10	1	24	12	4	7	10	21	40	45
Sheffield W	42	15	5	1	42	9	1	7	13	12	42	44
South Shields	42	13	5	3	34	16	4	5	12	15	34	44
Clapton O	42	11	7	3	27	10	3	8	10	13	26	43
Barnsley	42	12	7	2	34	16	4	4	13	23	45	43
Leicester C	42	13	4	4	43	16	4	4	13	21	38	42
Stockport Co	42	10	7	4	32	21	3	9	9	12	31	42
Manchester U	42	10	7	4	37	15	3	7	11	15	29	40
Crystal Palace	42	11	7	3	37	19	2	6	13	16	46	39
Port Vale	42	9	5	7	33	29	4	7	10	17	37	38
Hull C	42	8	7	6	32	23	2	10	9	14	28	37
Bradford C	42	8	7	6	24	21	3	8	10	11	27	37
Coventry C	42	9	6	6	34	23	2	7	12	18	45	35
Fulham	42	9	8	4	30	20	1	6	14	15	36	34
Nelson	42	8	8	5	32	31	2	5	14	8	43	33
Bristol C	42	5	8	8	19	26	2	7	12	13	39	29

DIVISION 3 NORTH

	P	W	D	L	F	A	W	D	L	F	A	Pts
Wolverhampton W	42	18	3	0	51	10	6	12	3	25	17	63
Rochdale	42	17	4	0	40	8	8	8	5	20	18	62
Chesterfield	42	16	4	1	54	15	6	6	9	16	24	54
Rotherham U	42	16	3	2	46	13	7	3	11	24	30	52
Bradford P.A.	42	17	3	1	50	12	4	7	10	19	31	52
Darlington	42	16	5	0	51	19	4	3	14	19	34	48
Southport	42	13	7	1	30	10	3	7	11	14	32	46
Ashington	42	14	4	3	41	21	4	4	13	18	40	44
Doncaster R	42	13	4	4	41	17	2	8	11	18	36	42
Wigan B	42	12	5	4	39	15	2	9	10	16	38	42
Grimsby T	42	11	9	1	30	7	3	4	14	19	40	41
Tranmere R	42	11	5	5	32	21	2	10	9	19	39	41
Accrington S	42	12	5	4	35	21	4	3	14	13	40	40
Halifax T	42	11	4	6	26	17	4	6	11	16	42	40
Durham C	42	12	5	4	40	23	3	4	14	19	37	39
Wrexham	42	8	11	2	24	12	2	7	12	13	32	38
Walsall	42	10	5	6	31	20	4	3	14	13	39	36
New Brighton	42	9	9	3	28	10	2	4	15	12	43	35
Lincoln C	42	8	8	5	29	22	2	4	15	19	37	32
Crewe A	42	6	7	8	20	24	1	6	14	12	34	27
Hartlepool U	42	5	7	9	22	24	2	4	15	11	46	25
Barrow	42	7	7	7	25	24	1	2	18	10	56	25

DIVISION 3 SOUTH

	P	W	D	L	F	A	W	D	L	F	A	Pts
Portsmouth	42	15	3	3	57	11	9	8	4	30	19	59
Plymouth A	42	13	6	2	46	15	10	3	8	24	19	55
Millwall	42	17	3	1	45	11	5	7	9	19	27	54
Swansea T	42	18	2	1	39	10	4	6	11	21	38	52
Brighton & H.A.	42	16	4	1	56	12	5	5	11	12	25	51
Swindon T	42	14	5	2	38	11	3	8	10	20	33	47
Luton T	42	11	7	3	35	19	5	7	9	15	25	46
Northampton T	42	14	3	4	40	15	3	8	10	24	32	45
Bristol R	42	11	7	3	34	15	4	6	11	18	31	43
Newport Co	42	15	4	2	39	15	2	5	14	17	49	43
Norwich C	42	13	5	3	45	18	3	3	15	15	41	40
Aberdare A	42	9	9	3	35	18	3	5	13	10	40	38
Merthyr T	42	11	8	2	33	19	0	8	13	12	46	38
Charlton A	42	8	7	6	26	20	3	8	10	12	25	37
Gillingham	42	11	6	4	27	15	1	7	13	16	43	37
Exeter C	42	14	3	4	33	17	1	4	16	4	35	37
Brentford	42	9	8	4	33	21	5	0	16	21	50	36
Reading	42	12	2	7	35	20	1	7	13	16	37	35
Southend U	42	11	7	3	35	19	1	3	17	18	65	34
Watford	42	8	8	5	35	18	1	7	13	10	36	33
Bournemouth	42	6	8	7	19	19	5	3	13	21	46	33
Q.P.R.	42	9	6	6	28	26	2	3	16	9	51	31

Top scorers: Div 1, F.Roberts (Manchester City) 31 goals; Div 2, A.Chandler (Leicester City) 33 goals; Div 3 N, D.Brown (Darlington) 39 goals; Div 3 S, J.Fowler (Swansea Town) 28 goals.

Future England full-back Ray Goodall skippered Huddersfield Town to their second successive League Championship win.

DIVISION 1

	ARSENAL	ASTON VILLA	BIRMINGHAM	BLACKBURN R	BOLTON W	BURNLEY	BURY	CARDIFF C	EVERTON	HUDDERSFIELD T	LEEDS U	LIVERPOOL	MANCHESTER C	NEWCASTLE U	NOTTINGHAM F	NOTTS CO	PRESTON N.E.	SHEFFIELD U	SUNDERLAND	TOTTENHAM H	W.B.A.	WEST HAM U
1 ARSENAL		O18 1-1	D26 0-1	O04 1-0	M07 1-0	a18 5-0	O13 0-1	a04 1-1	M21 3-1	F14 0-5	D20 6-1	S06 2-0	S01 1-0	J17 0-2	D27 2-1	N08 0-1	D06 4-0	S20 2-0	N22 0-0	O25 1-0	a14 2-0	M23 1-2
2 ASTON VILLA	a01 4-0		F14 1-0	a29 4-3	N08 2-2	D20 3-0	S01 3-3	D06 1-2	N22 3-1	O04 1-1	D26 2-1	J21 1-4	a10 2-1	S06 0-0	m02 2-0	M21 0-0	a18 1-0	J17 1-1	a04 1-4	M07 0-1	O25 1-0	S20 1-1
3 BIRMINGHAM	D25 2-1	O11 1-0		N01 1-1	S08 1-0	S27 1-0	D13 0-1	S13 2-1	A30 2-2	F28 0-1	F07 0-0	N29 5-2	a25 2-1	M28 1-1	a11 1-1	S15 1-0	J24 3-0	N15 1-1	J03 2-1	S03 0-2	M16 0-0	M14 1-1
4 BLACKBURN R	F07 1-0	S27 1-1	a02 7-1		N22 0-2	J17 0-3	M19 0-1	D20 3-1	D06 3-0	J24 2-3	O25 2-3	S15 3-1	O11 3-1	S01 1-1	a13 0-0	a04 0-2	D25 0-1	D27 2-2	a18 1-1	M21 1-1	N08 1-0	S06 0-1
5 BOLTON W	N01 4-1	M14 4-0	J01 3-0	a22 6-0		F21 5-0	S06 3-3	F07 3-0	J24 1-0	N15 1-0	a10 1-0	a25 2-0	F28 4-2	D13 3-2	D25 1-0	S13 1-0	O11 6-1	a11 3-1	S27 1-2	D27 3-0	S01 1-1	N29 5-0
6 BURNLEY	D13 1-0	a25 1-1	F02 3-2	S13 3-5	O18 0-0		N29 4-0	A30 0-0	S08 0-0	D25 1-5	S20 1-1	N15 2-1	a11 1-0	M14 1-3	M28 0-0	a10 1-1	J03 1-0	N01 1-1	S29 1-2	F14 1-4	O04 0-1	F28 5-4
7 BURY	m02 2-0	S08 4-3	a18 1-4	O18 1-1	J03 1-0	a04 1-0		M21 4-1	M07 1-0	a10 0-1	D06 1-0	S20 0-0	A30 0-2	F11 0-0	J17 3-0	O25 2-1	N22 1-1	O04 1-0	N08 3-0	J01 5-2	D20 0-2	F14 4-2
8 CARDIFF C	N29 1-1	a11 2-1	J17 1-0	a15 3-0	O04 1-2	F11 4-0	N15 4-1		O18 2-1	D13 2-2	S06 3-0	D15 1-3	a01 0-2	F28 3-0	M14 2-0	F14 1-1	m02 0-0	S01 1-1	a13 2-0	M18 0-2	S20 0-1	D26 2-1
9 EVERTON	N15 2-3	M28 2-0	D27 2-1	a11 1-0	S20 2-2	J01 3-2	N01 0-0	F25 1-2		N29 0-2	m02 1-0	O04 0-1	O29 3-1	D25 0-1	F28 3-1	M18 1-0	a13 0-0	a27 1-1	O11 0-3	J17 1-0	S06 1-0	D13 1-0
10 HUDDERSFIELD T	O11 4-0	F07 4-1	O25 0-1	S20 0-0	M21 0-0	D26 2-0	a14 2-0	a18 0-0	a04 2-0		J31 2-0	m02 1-1	F21 1-1	D27 0-0	S02 3-0	N22 0-0	D20 1-0	S06 2-1	D06 4-0	N08 1-2	M11 1-1	J17 1-2
11 LEEDS U	a25 1-0	D25 6-0	O04 0-1	F28 1-1	a14 2-1	J24 0-2	a11 1-0	J03 0-0	S17 1-0	S27 1-1		M28 4-1	D13 0-3	N15 1-1	N29 1-1	S10 1-1	S13 4-0	M14 1-1	A30 1-1	O18 1-0	F14 0-1	N01 2-1
12 LIVERPOOL	J03 2-1	A30 2-4	a04 1-1	O15 0-0	D20 0-0	M21 3-0	J24 4-0	a29 1-2	F07 3-1	N12 2-3	N22 1-0		S13 5-3	F14 1-1	S27 3-0	D26 1-0	N08 3-1	O18 4-1	O25 3-1	a18 1-0	D06 1-1	a10 2-0
13 MANCHESTER C	S17 2-0	a13 1-0	D20 2-2	F14 1-3	O25 2-2	D06 3-3	J31 0-0	N22 2-2	N08 2-2	O18 1-1	a18 4-2	J17 5-0		S20 3-1	S06 4-2	M07 2-1	a04 2-1	F23 2-1	M21 1-3	m02 1-0	D25 1-2	O04 3-1
14 NEWCASTLE U	S13 2-2	J03 4-1	N22 4-0	S10 4-0	a18 0-1	N08 3-0	S27 2-2	O25 1-2	D26 1-1	A30 1-3	M21 4-1	O11 0-0	J24 2-0		F07 4-1	D20 1-0	M07 3-1	J01 0-0	F21 2-0	D06 1-1	a04 0-1	S17 4-1
15 NOTTINGHAM F	A30 0-2	O02 0-2	D06 1-1	a10 0-2	D26 1-1	N22 0-0	S13 2-0	N08 2-1	O25 0-1	S08 0-1	a04 4-0	F04 0-1	J03 0-3	O04 1-1		J24 0-0	M21 0-1	F14 2-3	M07 1-1	D20 1-0	a18 0-1	O18 2-1
16 NOTTS CO	M14 2-1	N15 0-0	m02 0-1	N29 0-0	J17 0-1	a13 2-0	F28 1-1	O11 3-0	S27 3-1	a29 1-1	S01 1-0	D25 1-2	N01 2-0	a25 2-0	S20 0-0		a01 1-0	D13 2-0	F07 4-1	S06 0-0	D27 0-2	a11 4-1
17 PRESTON N.E.	a11 2-0	D13 3-2	S20 1-0	D26 3-2	F14 1-0	S06 0-2	M28 1-1	S15 1-3	a10 1-1	a25 1-4	J17 1-4	M14 4-0	N29 2-3	N01 0-1	N15 3-1	O18 0-1		F28 0-1	N20 1-2	O04 0-3	F12 1-2	D27 3-2
18 SHEFFIELD U	J24 2-1	S13 2-2	M21 4-3	A30 2-3	D06 2-0	a06 4-0	F07 0-1	S08 1-0	D20 1-1	J03 1-1	N08 1-1	M16 0-1	S27 0-5	a13 1-2	O11 1-2	a18 2-0	O25 3-0		D26 2-1	a04 2-0	N22 2-0	S22 1-1
19 SUNDERLAND	M28 2-0	N29 1-1	S06 4-0	D13 1-0	F11 1-0	m02 1-1	M14 1-1	J01 1-0	F14 4-1	a11 1-1	D27 2-1	F28 3-0	N15 3-2	O18 1-1	N01 3-1	O04 0-1	S03 2-0	D25 0-1		S20 4-1	J17 3-0	a25 1-1
20 TOTTENHAM H	F28 2-0	N01 1-3	a10 0-1	N15 5-0	A30 3-0	O11 1-1	D25 1-1	S27 1-1	S13 0-0	M14 1-2	M09 2-1	D13 1-1	N10 1-1	a11 3-0	a25 1-0	J03 1-1	F07 2-0	N29 4-1	J24 1-0		S22 0-1	M28 1-1
21 W.B.A.	a13 2-0	F28 4-1	O18 1-1	M14 1-1	m02 0-0	F07 1-4	a25 1-1	J24 1-0	J03 3-0	N01 1-0	O11 3-1	a11 0-0	D26 3-1	N29 2-0	D13 5-1	A30 1-2	S27 1-1	M30 2-1	S13 2-1	S08 2-0		N15 4-1
22 WEST HAM U	S27 1-0	J24 2-0	N08 0-1	J03 2-0	a04 1-1	O25 2-0	O11 1-1	D25 3-2	a18 4-1	S13 0-0	M07 0-0	a13 0-1	F07 4-0	S08 0-0	a02 0-0	D06 3-0	A30 1-0	a14 6-2	D20 4-1	N22 1-1	M21 2-1	

Former England Schoolboys winger Tommy Glidden helped West Brom into runners-up spot in 1924-25 and later skippered the Throstles in two FA Cup Finals.

DIVISION 2

	BARNSLEY	BLACKPOOL	BRADFORD C	CHELSEA	CLAPTON O	COVENTRY C	CRYSTAL P	DERBY CO	FULHAM	HULL C	LEICESTER C	MANCHESTER U	MIDDLESBROUGH	OLDHAM A	PORTSMOUTH	PORT VALE	SHEFFIELD W	SOUTHAMPTON	SOUTH SHIELDS	STOCKPORT CO	STOKE	WOLVERHAMPTON W
1 BARNSLEY		O04 2-4	J17 3-1	D20 3-3	a04 1-1	N08 3-1	D06 3-0	M09 3-0	a13 1-0	F14 1-2	O25 1-1	m02 0-0	D27 1-0	M21 0-0	O18 1-4	S06 1-3	N22 3-0	a18 1-1	S20 1-0	D26 0-1	M07 1-1	S01 0-0
2 BLACKPOOL	F07 1-2		a10 1-2	N08 1-2	A30 1-0	a18 3-1	O25 0-1	S15 5-1	J24 4-1	J03 0-0	a04 2-1	N22 1-1	O11 1-1	D20 1-2	S13 1-1	a22 4-1	D26 2-2	a01 1-0	S08 5-0	M21 0-1	D06 1-2	S27 2-4
3 BRADFORD C	S13 1-0	a14 1-0		a04 2-0	N08 0-0	F07 1-0	M21 0-0	O18 0-3	A30 1-1	S08 4-1	D20 1-1	a18 0-1	J24 0-1	O25 1-1	O20 2-0	S27 1-1	M07 2-0	N22 1-2	F14 1-0	D06 3-0	D26 1-0	J03 3-1
4 CHELSEA	a25 0-1	M14 3-0	N29 3-0		J24 1-1	A30 1-0	S27 2-2	N15 1-1	O11 0-0	N01 1-0	S08 4-0	a13 0-0	D13 2-0	J03 4-1	F28 2-3	a11 1-0	S13 0-0	F07 1-0	a20 1-1	O18 1-1	a27 2-1	D25 1-0
5 CLAPTON O	N29 0-0	D27 1-0	M14 0-0	S20 0-0		a10 1-2	S06 3-0	F28 0-1	D13 3-0	D25 0-0	F14 0-1	O04 0-1	M28 0-1	S01 5-1	a25 1-1	N15 3-1	O02 1-0	J17 1-0	N01 0-0	F16 1-1	O18 0-2	a11 2-1
6 COVENTRY C	M14 3-2	M09 2-1	O04 0-0	D27 0-3	a14 1-0		S01 1-4	a25 0-0	M28 0-1	a11 0-0	S20 4-2	J17 1-0	N01 2-2	O11 5-1	F12 2-1	F28 0-0	F21 1-1	S15 1-0	D25 0-1	S06 4-2	J31 3-1	N15 2-4
7 CRYSTAL P	a11 0-1	F28 1-2	N15 4-1	a01 1-0	J03 0-1	O01 0-0		N01 2-0	a25 1-2	S13 1-0	O18 0-2	F14 2-1	N29 2-2	m02 0-1	D26 1-2	M28 0-0	A30 0-1	S20 3-1	M14 0-0	O04 3-0	a10 0-1	D13 2-1
8 DERBY CO	S27 1-1	m02 2-2	F25 2-0	M21 1-0	O25 3-0	D20 5-1	M07 3-0		S13 5-1	A30 4-0	D06 0-3	a04 1-0	F07 3-1	D26 1-0	J03 6-1	O11 4-1	S08 2-1	N08 3-0	a13 0-0	N22 2-0	a18 1-2	J24 0-1
9 FULHAM	a14 1-2	S20 1-0	D27 1-1	F14 1-2	a18 0-2	N22 2-0	D20 3-1	J17 0-2		F09 4-0	N08 2-2	M07 1-0	D01 0-0	a04 1-0	O04 0-0	m02 1-1	D06 2-1	a10 1-0	S06 1-1	O25 2-0	M21 1-0	F21 1-0
10 HULL C	O11 5-2	S06 1-1	S01 0-0	M07 1-0	D26 2-1	D06 4-1	J17 5-0	D27 1-1	S27 3-0		N22 2-1	M21 0-1	M19 0-0	a18 1-0	J24 5-0	a13 2-1	D20 4-2	O25 1-1	m02 0-1	N08 3-0	a04 0-0	F07 0-1
11 LEICESTER C	F28 6-0	N29 0-2	a25 1-0	S01 4-0	O11 4-2	J24 5-1	M12 3-1	a11 0-0	M14 4-0	M28 1-0		D27 3-0	S06 0-0	S27 3-0	N15 4-0	D25 7-0	F07 6-1	a14 0-0	D13 1-1	m02 4-0	S13 0-1	N01 2-0
12 MANCHESTER U	S08 1-0	M28 0-0	D13 3-0	J01 1-0	F07 4-2	S13 5-1	O11 1-0	N29 1-1	N01 2-0	N15 2-0	A30 1-0		D26 2-0	J24 0-1	M14 2-0	a25 4-0	S27 2-0	a22 1-1	a11 1-0	a10 2-0	J03 2-0	F28 3-0
13 MIDDLESBROUGH	A30 2-0	F14 4-1	S20 1-0	a18 1-1	N22 1-1	M07 1-1	a04 0-0	O04 1-3	J01 1-3	O18 0-1	J03 1-5	D25 1-1		N08 0-0	a13 1-1	J17 0-1	M21 2-0	D06 0-0	J31 1-1	D20 1-1	O25 1-0	S10 2-0
14 OLDHAM A	N15 2-0	a25 4-1	F28 1-3	S06 0-5	S08 2-1	F14 5-0	O06 0-2	D25 0-1	N29 0-0	D13 1-0	M17 0-1	S20 0-3	M14 0-0		a11 0-2	N01 2-0	a10 1-1	D27 1-1	O18 1-0	J17 0-0	O04 2-0	M28 2-0
15 PORTSMOUTH	F21 0-0	J17 1-1	m02 5-0	O25 0-0	D20 0-2	a04 1-0	D25 0-0	S06 1-1	F07 3-0	S20 2-0	M21 1-1	N08 1-1	a10 3-1	D06 2-2		M30 2-0	a18 1-1	N29 1-1	D27 1-0	M07 1-1	N22 0-0	O11 2-2
16 PORT VALE	J03 2-0	O18 1-2	F02 1-0	D06 1-1	M21 4-2	O25 4-0	N22 3-0	F14 2-1	S08 0-1	a10 1-1	D26 1-2	D20 2-1	S13 2-1	M07 1-0	S15 0-2		N08 1-0	O13 1-1	O04 0-0	a18 4-1	J24 2-0	A30 1-3
17 SHEFFIELD W	M28 1-0	D25 2-6	N01 3-3	J17 2-1	m02 0-0	O18 2-0	D27 0-1	S01 0-1	a11 3-1	a25 5-0	O04 1-4	F23 1-1	N15 2-0	J01 1-0	D13 5-2	M14 0-1		S06 1-0	F28 0-1	S20 3-0	F14 2-1	N29 2-0
18 SOUTHAMPTON	D13 3-1	N01 2-1	a30 2-0	O04 0-0	S13 2-0	m02 3-0	J24 2-0	M14 2-0	D26 1-0	F28 2-2	a13 0-0	O18 0-2	a11 1-1	A30 0-0	S27 0-0	a04 1-0	J03 1-0		N15 1-1	F14 2-1	S08 3-0	a25 1-1
19 SOUTH SHIELDS	J24 5-2	S01 1-3	O11 1-0	N22 1-1	M07 2-0	J01 4-1	N08 1-1	a10 1-0	F25 2-1	a01 2-0	a18 1-1	D06 1-2	S27 0-1	F21 0-0	A30 0-2	F07 3-0	O25 0-1	M21 1-1		a04 0-1	D20 4-0	S13 3-3
20 STOCKPORT CO	D25 1-0	N15 1-0	a11 3-0	F21 4-0	S27 0-1	J03 1-1	F07 1-0	M28 0-0	F28 4-1	M14 0-2	S15 0-2	S01 2-1	a25 1-1	S13 2-0	N01 1-2	F25 0-2	J24 1-0	O11 1-1	N29 0-0		A30 2-0	J01 1-1
21 STOKE	N01 1-1	a11 3-1	J01 0-0	S22 1-0	F21 0-1	S27 4-1	a13 1-1	D13 1-1	N15 1-1	N29 2-0	J17 1-1	S06 0-0	F28 0-1	F07 0-1	M28 2-1	S20 0-1	O11 0-2	S01 2-0	a25 0-0	D27 3-0		M14 0-3
22 WOLVERHAMPTON W	a27 0-1	M23 2-0	S06 2-0	D26 0-1	D06 1-2	M21 3-1	a18 3-1	S20 0-4	O18 2-1	O04 2-1	M30 0-1	O25 0-0	m02 1-0	N22 2-0	F14 0-5	D27 1-0	a04 1-0	D20 3-0	J17 2-1	a13 3-0	N08 1-0	

SEASON 1924-25

DIVISION 3 NORTH

	ACCRINGTON S	ASHINGTON	BARROW	BRADFORD	CHESTERFIELD	CREWE A	DARLINGTON	DONCASTER R	DURHAM C	GRIMSBY T	HALIFAX T	HARTLEPOOLS U	LINCOLN C	NELSON	NEW BRIGHTON	ROCHDALE	ROTHERHAM CO	SOUTHPORT	TRANMERE R	WALSALL	WIGAN B	WREXHAM
1 ACCRINGTON S		F28 2-2	S30 1-2	S08 2-2	J03 2-2	M28 1-0	J01 2-0	M14 3-2	F23 6-0	O04 0-3	S20 2-0	F14 4-1	a25 0-2	S13 2-0	a27 0-1	O18 2-2	A30 2-0	N01 5-1	a22 2-1	a11 1-1	S17 3-1	m02 1-0
2 ASHINGTON	O25 1-2		S13 5-2	a18 1-0	A30 2-1	F21 1-1	D06 4-2	S01 2-0	a10 0-2	M21 0-2	M07 2-0	N22 0-3	J24 2-1	J03 1-1	N08 1-1	J02 4-3	J01 3-1	m02 2-0	S27 1-0	F07 6-1	F14 1-1	D20 2-0
3 BARROW	D26 3-1	J17 3-2		a04 2-1	D20 1-0	S01 2-0	N22 0-4	D27 4-0	S15 2-0	M07 3-2	J31 2-1	N08 1-1	F07 1-2	S20 3-0	O25 1-1	M21 1-0	a18 3-1	S06 1-0	O11 1-1	F21 3-2	a10 0-1	D06 2-2
4 BRADFORD	S01 3-0	D17 7-1	J01 1-1		a13 3-0	F28 6-1	F24 0-0	D25 4-1	O04 4-1	S06 0-1	N15 2-1	J17 3-0	M28 4-0	a11 1-1	D27 5-2	S20 0-0	F21 3-0	a25 1-0	M04 5-1	M14 2-0	N01 2-2	O11 3-0
5 CHESTERFIELD	S06 1-0	D27 1-1	a25 1-1	a10 1-1		J10 1-0	O18 0-1	N01 2-1	M14 6-0	a14 2-0	J17 1-3	O04 4-0	M11 2-0	D26 0-1	S20 3-0	F14 2-0	M30 3-2	F28 1-2	a11 4-1	S08 1-0	N22 3-1	J01 3-0
6 CREWE A	N22 4-2	O18 1-0	S10 3-1	O25 2-1	M21 1-1		J24 0-5	O04 1-1	J31 3-0	a18 3-1	a04 1-1	D20 3-1	S17 1-1	a10 2-1	D06 1-0	D26 2-0	N08 3-1	F14 1-1	A30 0-2	J03 1-1	S13 1-1	M07 1-2
7 DARLINGTON	a10 2-1	a11 2-1	M28 3-0	S27 2-1	F21 3-3	S20 5-1		a25 1-1	D25 0-0	D27 0-0	J02 3-0	S06 2-0	F11 0-1	N15 3-1	S03 3-1	J17 2-0	O11 4-0	D17 2-1	M14 2-1	N01 3-0	F28 5-0	F07 3-1
8 DONCASTER R	N08 4-1	S08 7-3	A30 0-0	D26 1-0	M07 0-1	F07 1-1	D20 0-2		O11 0-0	a04 2-2	M21 0-1	D06 1-0	J03 2-1	a14 1-1	N22 1-0	a18 2-1	O25 4-1	a10 0-1	S13 2-0	J24 2-1	S27 5-0	F21 1-0
9 DURHAM C	M21 2-0	S03 0-0	m02 6-0	F07 1-0	N08 1-1	S27 4-1	a13 2-1	F14 1-0		D06 6-1	N22 1-2	a18 0-1	J01 5-0	a29 3-1	a04 0-0	D20 3-2	M07 1-1	O18 0-0	M18 0-3	S13 0-2	J24 1-1	O25 1-0
10 GRIMSBY T	F07 4-0	J10 1-3	N01 2-1	J03 2-0	S27 0-0	D13 0-0	A30 0-2	J01 1-1	a11 1-1		O11 1-1	S01 2-1	F28 1-2	M14 2-0	F21 2-3	N15 1-1	J24 3-1	M28 3-1	a13 6-1	D25 2-1	a25 4-0	S13 0-1
11 HALIFAX T	J24 2-2	N01 0-0	S27 2-0	m02 1-3	S13 1-0	M12 2-2	a14 1-1	J26 2-0	M28 3-0	F14 1-0		O18 2-0	D25 1-0	F28 2-4	O04 1-2	a13 3-1	J03 4-0	M14 2-0	D20 1-3	D13 1-1	a11 1-2	A30 3-1
12 HARTLEPOOLS U	O11 3-0	M28 0-1	M14 1-0	S13 2-2	F07 1-0	a25 2-0	J03 1-1	a11 2-2	a22 1-0	S10 2-1	F21 1-1		N01 1-1	M25 2-4	a13 0-2	A30 1-1	S27 0-0	O01 1-2	F28 2-1	J01 3-1	D25 1-0	J24 1-1
13 LINCOLN C	D20 3-0	S20 5-0	O04 2-1	N22 0-4	a18 3-1	m02 4-1	M21 0-1	S06 2-0	D27 3-0	O25 0-0	D26 1-1	M07 2-1		M18 2-1	F14 2-0	N08 1-2	D06 3-1	J17 1-1	O18 3-2	a10 0-1	S01 1-0	a04 1-1
14 NELSON	J17 4-1	S06 4-0	J24 2-0	D06 2-2	D25 1-0	a13 7-0	a04 1-1	S09 3-0	S16 7-1	N08 1-0	O25 2-1	M21 2-0	S27 1-0		M07 5-0	N22 1-0	D20 4-1	a21 2-1	F07 4-1	O11 2-1	F21 1-0	a18 2-4
15 NEW BRIGHTON	S27 4-0	M14 4-4	F28 3-0	A30 0-0	J24 2-1	a11 3-0	m02 1-0	M28 0-2	D10 4-0	O18 3-2	F07 3-1	a10 2-0	O11 4-1	N01 5-0		S17 5-0	S13 3-1	J10 1-1	D26 1-0	a25 3-2	D13 3-0	J03 2-1
16 ROCHDALE	F21 0-1	a04 0-0	a28 5-1	J24 2-2	O11 2-1	D25 5-0	S13 2-1	F24 5-2	J10 3-0	m01 2-0	a10 3-1	D27 3-1	M14 3-0	M28 0-1	a14 2-0		F07 4-1	a11 1-0	N01 2-1	F28 3-0	S06 3-2	S27 3-1
17 ROTHERHAM CO	D27 1-1	D25 1-4	M16 0-1	O18 1-1	m02 1-3	M14 1-3	F14 1-1	F28 3-0	N01 1-2	S20 3-0	S06 0-0	J31 1-2	D13 1-1	a25 1-0	J17 2-1	O04 1-3		a14 1-3	S01 2-0	M28 2-0	N15 3-4	a13 0-1
18 SOUTHPORT	M07 3-1	S16 3-0	J03 5-0	D20 3-0	O25 0-2	O11 2-0	a18 1-0	a13 3-0	F21 1-1	N22 3-1	N08 3-1	a04 2-0	S13 4-0	A30 1-0	M21 2-0	D06 0-0	S09 2-0		J24 1-0	S27 1-0	O04 0-1	D25 1-0
19 TRANMERE R	a18 2-1	J31 5-4	F14 4-1	M21 2-0	D06 5-1	D27 2-2	N08 0-1	J17 1-2	S06 1-1	a10 2-3	a25 0-2	O25 4-3	F21 0-0	O04 2-0	J01 1-3	M07 3-1	a04 1-0	S20 1-0		O02 0-1	a14 2-3	N22 2-0
20 WALSALL	D06 1-1	O04 1-0	O18 1-0	N08 0-2	a04 0-0	S06 0-0	M07 2-1	S20 4-0	J17 2-2	D26 2-0	a18 0-2	m02 1-1	a13 2-0	F14 1-2	D20 2-1	O25 0-2	N22 0-1	J31 0-0	J10 2-0		D27 3-1	M21 3-0
21 WIGAN B	a04 1-2	O11 2-0	a13 2-0	M07 1-0	M28 0-0	J17 3-4	O25 1-1	J31 2-2	S20 0-0	D20 3-1	D06 2-0	D26 0-0	S08 4-0	O18 1-1	a18 0-1	J03 2-3	M21 4-1	F07 2-0	m02 4-0	A30 0-0		N08 5-0
22 WREXHAM	S24 1-0	a25 3-1	a11 3-0	F14 1-3	S17 0-0	N01 2-1	O04 0-2	O18 2-1	D13 3-1	J17 1-2	D27 0-0	S20 3-1	O01 0-1	J10 1-1	S06 0-0	J31 1-0	a10 3-1	D26 2-3	M28 4-0	N15 1-1	M14 6-2	

DIVISION 3 SOUTH

	ABERDARE A	BOURNEMOUTH	BRENTFORD	BRIGHTON & HA	BRISTOL C	BRISTOL R	CHARLTON A	EXETER C	GILLINGHAM	LUTON T	MERTHYR T	MILLWALL	NEWPORT CO	NORTHAMPTON T	NORWICH C	PLYMOUTH A	Q.P.R.	READING	SOUTHEND U	SWANSEA T	SWINDON T	WATFORD
1 ABERDARE A		a13 4-2	F16 2-1	O02 1-2	A30 1-2	M14 2-1	M09 2-0	N01 3-1	O18 2-1	F14 1-1	D25 2-0	O04 0-1	J10 1-3	a11 1-1	S20 2-1	O27 3-1	a25 1-1	S13 3-0	M28 3-0	a02 3-1	a23 1-1	N29 2-0
2 BOURNEMOUTH	a10 3-1		O22 2-0	S27 0-0	O11 1-3	a25 0-1	M14 2-1	M25 1-1	J17 3-0	S06 2-1	M28 2-0	F11 0-1	D25 0-0	N01 1-2	S03 0-0	F07 0-1	a22 0-2	J10 0-0	S20 1-0	a11 0-2	F21 0-0	F28 2-1
3 BRENTFORD	S27 2-2	m02 1-2		A30 2-4	S13 1-0	M28 1-1	D26 1-0	N15 2-5	S08 2-1	a10 3-0	F28 2-2	O18 1-0	S15 2-0	a25 1-3	F07 1-1	J03 1-0	O11 0-1	N01 0-1	J10 2-2	M14 3-1	J24 0-0	D13 0-0
4 BRIGHTON & H.A.	M25 4-1	M11 0-1	D27 4-1		F21 1-0	D26 1-0	N15 0-0	a25 2-0	S20 2-0	J17 2-1	O08 3-1	S06 3-3	O04 4-1	M14 0-1	m02 3-1	O11 2-3	M28 5-0	a11 0-1	F28 2-1	D13 0-0	a10 3-1	N01 2-0
5 BRISTOL C	D27 0-1	F14 2-1	J17 3-0	O18 2-1		F28 2-0	S24 1-1	S01 0-1	O04 2-1	M04 2-0	D13 1-0	S20 4-1	N01 2-0	M28 1-0	S06 2-0	a13 2-2	a11 5-0	a25 3-0	M14 5-0	D26 0-0	S17 0-0	N15 1-1
6 BRISTOL R	N08 1-0	D20 1-0	N22 2-0	D25 1-2	O25 0-0		S13 4-0	a10 0-1	a18 0-0	D06 1-1	A30 1-0	a04 1-1	O11 0-1	J24 0-2	M21 3-0	F21 1-1	M18 3-0	a14 1-0	F07 1-3	S08 3-0	M07 0-1	S27 2-0
7 CHARLTON A	a18 5-1	N08 2-2	D25 3-0	M21 1-0	a04 0-1	J17 1-1		S20 1-0	M07 2-0	O25 2-0	F14 3-0	a10 0-2	S06 1-0	S01 0-0	D20 3-2	N22 2-1	O18 2-0	O04 1-2	D27 0-0	F16 0-0	D06 1-0	S18 1-1
8 EXETER C	M07 3-1	a18 2-1	M21 5-1	D20 2-0	S10 0-2	a13 1-1	J24 2-1		D06 3-3	a04 0-1	J03 2-1	N22 0-0	F21 4-3	S27 0-0	N08 1-0	D26 3-0	S13 1-3	A30 1-0	O11 0-1	S24 2-0	O25 1-0	F07 4-0
9 GILLINGHAM	F21 2-0	S13 0-0	S03 1-0	J24 2-0	F07 1-1	F11 0-0	N01 2-0	a11 1-1		D27 4-1	N15 2-1	O22 1-0	a25 1-0	F28 0-1	a10 3-1	S27 0-3	M14 1-0	M28 0-0	D25 3-1	M18 0-0	O11 1-1	S06 0-0
10 LUTON T	O11 0-0	J03 0-2	a13 3-1	S13 3-1	S27 3-0	a11 1-1	F28 1-0	S08 1-1	A30 0-0		M14 6-0	S01 1-1	D13 2-2	S22 2-0	F21 0-0	J24 1-1	N01 3-0	M21 1-0	a25 4-0	M28 0-0	F07 2-2	D26 0-3
11 MERTHYR T	D26 3-1	N22 3-1	O25 4-0	a04 1-2	a18 2-3	M30 1-0	O11 2-1	S06 0-1	M21 0-0	N08 0-0		M07 2-1	S29 1-0	F21 0-2	M23 0-2	D06 1-2	F07 2-3	S20 0-0	S01 1-0	J17 0-2	D20 1-5	a14 0-1
12 MILLWALL	F07 2-1	A30 3-1	F21 3-0	J03 1-1	J24 3-1	S15 0-0	a13 1-0	M28 2-0	m02 2-0	N29 2-2	N01 3-1		a11 3-0	D25 3-1	O11 0-0	S13 0-0	F28 3-0	M14 0-1	D13 2-0	N15 1-2	S27 1-2	a25 0-1
13 NEWPORT CO	M21 1-0	D26 2-0	a04 1-0	F07 0-0	M07 0-2	F14 4-1	a14 2-1	O18 2-1	D20 2-0	a18 1-1	m02 3-0	D06 2-3		S13 1-0	N22 3-0	O25 0-0	A30 0-0	S11 1-1	S27 1-1	a10 3-0	N08 3-1	J24 3-0
14 NORTHAMPTON T	S04 5-0	M07 3-0	D20 0-2	N08 1-0	N22 1-2	S20 5-0	S08 2-1	J31 2-1	O25 1-0	S15 1-0	O18 2-0	D26 0-2	J17 0-2		a18 1-1	M21 5-2	a14 1-0	F14 2-0	S06 0-1	O04 1-3	a04 0-0	D27 1-1
15 NORWICH C	J24 1-1	O09 6-3	O04 3-0	S08 2-2	J03 0-0	N15 1-1	a25 2-1	M14 0-1	a13 0-0	O18 1-1	S27 1-0	F14 2-2	M28 2-1	a23 4-0		A30 1-1	D26 5-0	F28 0-2	a14 0-1	N01 2-0	S13 4-0	D06 2-1
16 PLYMOUTH A	D13 2-0	O04 2-0	S06 7-1	F14 1-0	a10 7-1	O18 3-2	M28 3-2	D25 1-1	J31 2-0	S20 4-0	a11 2-0	J17 1-1	F28 0-2	N15 2-1	D27 5-0		S24 1-0	a20 2-0	a29 6-0	a25 1-1	S08 2-0	M14 1-0
17 Q.P.R.	D20 4-1	M21 0-2	F14 1-0	N22 2-0	D06 3-0	S06 1-2	F21 0-0	J17 1-4	N08 1-1	M07 2-1	O04 1-1	O25 0-0	D27 4-3	a13 2-0	D25 1-2	a04 0-1		J31 1-0	m02 3-1	S20 0-0	a18 1-0	S03 0-0
18 READING	J17 2-0	a04 0-1	M07 3-1	D06 0-0	D20 0-1	m02 4-1	F07 0-0	D27 1-1	N22 0-1	O08 3-0	J24 2-1	N08 1-2	S03 0-1	O11 0-1	O25 2-0	a18 0-0	S27 2-1		a10 2-2	S06 2-0	D26 1-1	F21 3-0
19 SOUTHEND U	N22 2-1	J24 3-0	D06 6-1	O25 2-0	N08 2-0	O04 2-1	A30 0-3	F14 3-0	D26 4-0	D20 2-1	S10 2-1	a18 1-0	J31 0-1	J03 0-1	a04 0-1	M07 0-3	S17 1-0	a13 3-0		O18 1-0	M21 0-0	S13 0-4
20 SWANSEA T	O25 2-2	D06 1-0	N08 7-0	a18 1-0	D25 1-1	S01 2-2	S27 6-1	m02 2-1	a04 2-0	N22 4-1	S13 2-0	M21 2-2	a13 1-0	F07 2-1	M07 2-0	D20 2-0	J24 2-0	a30 1-0	F21 4-0		A30 2-0	O11 3-1
21 SWINDON T	S06 2-0	O18 4-0	S20 2-0	a13 3-0	m02 3-0	N01 3-0	a11 2-2	F28 1-0	F14 2-0	O04 4-1	a25 5-1	J31 1-0	M14 2-2	N29 5-0	J17 1-0	S01 1-0	N15 5-3	D25 2-1	S24 3-0	D27 0-2		M28 0-1
22 WATFORD	a04 0-0	O25 2-1	a18 3-1	M07 0-1	M21 1-0	J31 1-0	m02 0-0	O04 3-0	J03 1-2	D25 1-1	a10 3-1	D20 1-0	S20 0-5	A30 1-0	a11 0-2	N08 1-0	S10 1-0	O18 1-0	J17 0-3	F14 1-3	N22 1-0	

LEAGUE TABLES

DIVISION 1

	P	W	D	L	F	A	W	D	L	F	A	Pts
Huddersfield T	42	10	8	3	31	10	11	8	2	38	18	58
W.B.A.	42	13	6	2	40	17	10	4	7	18	17	56
Bolton W	42	18	2	1	61	13	4	9	8	15	21	55
Liverpool	42	13	5	3	43	20	7	5	9	20	35	50
Bury	42	13	4	4	35	20	4	11	6	19	31	49
Newcastle U	42	11	6	4	43	18	5	10	6	18	24	48
Sunderland	42	13	6	2	39	14	6	4	11	25	37	48
Birmingham C	42	10	8	3	27	17	7	4	10	22	36	46
Notts Co	42	11	6	4	29	12	5	7	9	13	19	45
Manchester C	42	11	7	3	44	29	6	2	13	32	39	43
Cardiff C	42	11	5	5	35	19	5	6	10	21	32	43
Tottenham H	42	9	8	4	32	16	6	4	11	20	27	42
West Ham U	42	12	7	2	37	12	3	5	13	25	48	42
Sheffield U	42	10	5	6	34	25	3	8	10	21	38	39
Aston Villa	42	10	7	4	34	25	3	6	12	24	46	39
Blackburn R	42	7	6	8	31	26	4	7	10	22	40	35
Everton	42	11	4	6	25	20	1	7	13	15	40	35
Leeds U	42	9	8	4	29	17	2	4	15	17	42	34
Burnley	42	7	8	6	28	31	4	4	13	18	44	34
Arsenal	42	12	3	6	33	17	2	2	17	13	41	33
Preston N.E.	42	8	2	11	29	35	2	4	15	8	39	26
Nottingham F	42	5	6	10	17	23	1	6	14	12	42	24

DIVISION 2

	P	W	D	L	F	A	W	D	L	F	A	Pts
Leicester C	42	15	4	2	58	9	9	7	5	32	23	59
Manchester U	42	17	3	1	40	6	6	8	7	17	17	57
Derby Co	42	15	3	3	49	15	7	8	6	22	21	55
Portsmouth	42	7	13	1	28	14	8	5	8	30	36	48
Chelsea	42	11	8	2	31	12	5	7	9	20	25	47
Wolverhampton W	42	14	1	6	29	19	6	5	10	26	32	46
Southampton	42	12	8	1	29	10	1	10	10	11	26	44
Port Vale	42	12	4	5	34	19	5	4	12	14	37	42
South Shields	42	9	6	6	33	21	3	11	7	9	17	41
Hull C	42	12	6	3	40	14	3	5	13	10	35	41
Clapton O	42	8	7	6	22	13	6	5	10	20	29	40
Fulham	42	11	6	4	26	15	4	4	13	15	41	40
Middlesbrough	42	6	10	5	22	21	4	9	8	14	23	39
Sheffield W	42	12	3	6	36	23	3	5	13	14	33	38
Barnsley	42	8	8	5	30	23	5	4	12	16	36	38
Bradford C	42	11	6	4	26	13	2	6	13	11	37	38
Blackpool	42	8	5	8	37	26	6	4	11	28	35	37
Oldham A	42	9	5	7	24	21	4	6	11	11	30	37
Stockport Co	42	10	6	5	26	15	3	5	13	11	42	37
Stoke	42	7	8	6	22	17	5	3	13	12	29	35
Crystal Palace	42	8	4	9	23	19	4	6	11	15	35	34
Coventry C	42	10	6	5	32	26	1	3	17	13	58	31

DIVISION 3 NORTH

	P	W	D	L	F	A	W	D	L	F	A	Pts
Darlington	42	16	4	1	50	14	8	6	7	28	19	58
Nelson	42	18	2	1	58	14	5	5	11	21	36	53
New Brighton	42	17	3	1	56	16	6	4	11	19	34	53
Southport	42	17	2	2	41	7	5	5	11	18	30	51
Bradford P.A.	42	15	5	1	59	13	4	7	10	25	29	50
Rochdale	42	17	2	2	53	16	4	5	12	22	37	49
Chesterfield	42	14	3	4	42	15	3	8	10	18	29	45
Lincoln C	42	13	4	4	39	19	5	4	12	14	39	44
Halifax T	42	11	5	5	36	22	5	6	10	20	30	43
Ashington	42	13	4	4	41	24	3	6	12	27	52	42
Wigan B	42	10	7	4	39	16	5	4	12	23	49	41
Grimsby T	42	10	6	5	38	21	5	3	13	22	39	39
Durham C	42	11	6	4	38	17	2	7	12	12	51	39
Barrow	42	14	4	3	39	22	2	3	16	12	52	39
Crewe A	42	11	7	3	35	24	2	6	13	18	54	39
Wrexham	42	11	5	5	37	21	4	3	14	16	40	38
Accrington S	42	12	5	4	43	23	3	3	15	17	49	38
Doncaster R	42	12	5	4	36	17	2	5	14	18	48	38
Walsall	42	10	6	5	27	16	3	5	13	17	37	37
Hartlepool U	42	9	8	4	28	21	3	3	15	17	42	35
Tranmere R	42	11	3	7	40	29	3	1	17	19	49	32
Rotherham U	42	6	5	10	27	31	1	2	18	15	57	21

DIVISION 3 SOUTH

	P	W	D	L	F	A	W	D	L	F	A	Pts
Swansea T	42	17	4	0	51	12	6	7	8	17	23	57
Plymouth A	42	17	3	1	55	12	6	7	8	22	26	56
Bristol C	42	14	5	2	40	10	8	4	9	20	31	53
Swindon T	42	17	2	2	51	13	3	9	9	15	25	51
Millwall	42	12	5	4	35	14	6	8	7	23	24	49
Newport Co	42	13	6	2	35	12	7	3	11	27	30	49
Exeter C	42	13	4	4	37	19	6	5	10	22	29	47
Brighton & H.A.	42	14	3	4	43	17	5	5	11	16	28	46
Northampton T	42	12	3	6	34	18	8	3	10	17	26	46
Southend U	42	14	1	6	34	18	5	4	12	17	43	43
Watford	42	12	3	6	22	20	5	6	10	16	27	43
Norwich C	42	10	8	3	39	18	4	5	12	14	33	41
Gillingham	42	11	8	2	25	11	2	6	13	10	33	40
Reading	42	9	6	6	28	15	5	4	12	9	23	38
Charlton A	42	12	6	3	31	13	1	6	14	15	35	38
Luton T	42	9	10	2	34	15	1	7	13	15	42	37
Bristol R	42	10	5	6	26	13	2	8	11	16	36	37
Aberdare A	42	13	4	4	40	21	1	5	15	14	46	37
Q.P.R.	42	10	6	5	28	19	4	2	15	14	44	36
Bournemouth	42	8	6	7	20	17	5	2	14	20	41	34
Brentford	42	8	7	6	28	26	1	0	20	10	65	25
Merthyr T	42	8	3	10	24	27	0	2	19	11	50	21

FOOTBALL LEAGUE RECORDS

Top scorers: Div 1, E.Harper (Blackburn Rovers) 43 goals; Div 2, J.Trotter (Sheffield Wednesday) 37 goals; Div 3 N, J.Cookson (Chesterfield) 44 goals; Div 3 S, J.Cock (Plymouth Argyle) 32 goals.

Rotherham County became Rotherham United; Stoke became Stoke City.

When Huddersfield Town won their third successive League Championship in 1925-26, centre-half Tommy Wilson played in all but one game.

DIVISION 1

	ARSENAL	ASTON VILLA	BIRMINGHAM	BLACKBURN R	BOLTON W	BURNLEY	BURY	CARDIFF C	EVERTON	HUDDERSFIELD T	LEEDS U	LEICESTER C	LIVERPOOL	MANCHESTER C	MANCHESTER U	NEWCASTLE U	NOTTS CO	SHEFFIELD U	SUNDERLAND	TOTTENHAM H	W.B.A.	WEST HAM U
1 ARSENAL		a05 2-0	m01 3-0	a03 4-2	O10 2-3	F03 1-2	N14 6-1	O17 5-0	O31 4-1	a17 3-1	S26 4-1	A31 2-2	S12 1-1	M20 1-0	J16 3-2	F13 3-0	D25 3-0	M17 4-0	N28 2-0	A29 0-1	D12 1-0	S21 3-2
2 ASTON VILLA	a02 3-0		O17 3-3	D12 1-2	a26 2-2	A29 10-0	M06 1-1	O31 0-2	a03 3-1	N14 3-0	F03 3-1	M10 2-2	a06 3-0	N28 3-1	S07 2-2	S12 2-2	S26 2-1	M20 2-2	O05 4-2	a17 3-0	F13 2-1	D26 2-0
3 BIRMINGHAM	D19 1-0	F27 2-1		S05 2-0	N07 0-1	a10 1-7	J23 2-3	O10 3-2	S21 3-1	S16 1-3	D05 2-1	O24 1-1	N21 2-0	A31 1-0	a19 2-1	M13 1-1	S19 0-1	F13 2-0	J02 2-1	D25 3-1	S26 3-0	a24 1-0
4 BLACKBURN R	N21 2-3	a24 3-1	J16 4-4		F27 3-0	M13 6-3	A29 1-2	S26 6-3	D25 2-2	F11 2-1	N07 2-2	D19 0-0	D05 1-1	O10 3-3	a10 7-0	O12 1-2	O24 4-1	M01 3-1	S21 3-0	F13 4-2	S12 1-2	M27 1-0
5 BOLTON W	a28 1-1	S19 1-3	J01 5-3	O17 2-2		S16 4-2	J16 3-2	N28 0-1	m01 0-2	D12 6-1	S07 1-0	F06 2-2	a02 0-1	N14 5-1	M17 3-1	A29 2-2	J23 2-1	a17 2-1	a07 3-2	a03 1-1	O31 2-2	O03 1-0
6 BURNLEY	S19 2-2	J02 2-3	D07 3-1	O31 1-3	S09 1-1		a17 2-2	m01 4-1	O17 1-3	F20 1-1	D26 6-3	S05 4-0	O03 2-1	a06 1-2	F06 0-1	a02 1-0	S07 0-0	N14 1-1	M20 5-2	D12 1-2	a03 3-4	J23 2-2
7 BURY	M27 2-2	O24 2-3	S12 2-1	J02 3-1	S05 0-5	D16 8-1		F13 4-1	J01 1-0	a05 0-0	M13 0-2	a24 4-0	a10 0-1	D25 6-5	N21 1-3	N07 1-1	F27 3-1	S26 7-4	O28 2-2	O10 3-0	F24 2-0	D19 4-1
8 CARDIFF C	F27 0-0	M13 2-0	F20 2-0	F06 4-1	a10 0-1	D19 2-3	O03 3-2		S05 2-1	J23 1-2	M27 0-0	N07 5-2	a24 2-2	J02 2-2	O24 0-2	N21 0-0	D05 2-1	a05 0-1	S23 0-1	S21 0-1	D25 3-2	S07 0-1
9 EVERTON	M13 2-3	N21 1-1	S09 2-2	D26 3-0	D19 2-1	F27 1-1	a02 1-1	J16 1-1		O03 2-3	O24 4-2	J30 1-0	F06 3-3	F10 1-1	N07 1-3	a24 3-0	M27 3-0	A29 2-2	M17 2-1	S12 1-1	S16 4-0	D05 2-0
10 HUDDERSFIELD T	D05 2-2	M27 5-1	D28 4-1	a06 3-1	a12 3-0	O10 2-1	S08 2-1	S12 1-1	F13 3-0		F27 3-1	N21 3-0	N25 0-0	S26 2-2	M13 5-0	O24 0-1	D19 2-0	J16 4-1	D26 1-1	M03 2-1	A29 1-1	a10 2-1
11 LEEDS U	F06 4-2	S05 2-2	a17 0-0	M20 2-1	A31 2-1	D25 2-2	O31 2-3	N14 1-0	M06 1-1	O17 0-4		J23 1-0	F20 1-1	D12 3-4	O03 2-0	S16 2-0	J02 2-1	a03 2-0	a06 0-2	m01 4-1	N28 0-1	S19 5-2
12 LEICESTER C	S07 0-1	O10 1-2	M06 1-0	F20 2-1	S26 5-2	J16 3-2	D12 0-2	M20 1-2	N28 1-1	a03 2-0	S12 1-3		A29 3-1	a17 2-3	D28 1-3	F22 3-2	F13 1-0	D26 2-2	N14 4-1	O31 5-3	O17 3-0	a05 1-1
13 LIVERPOOL	J23 3-0	J01 3-1	a03 2-2	a17 2-2	a05 2-2	F13 3-2	N28 0-1	D12 0-2	S26 5-1	M20 1-2	O10 1-1	J02 0-3		O17 2-1	S19 5-0	D25 6-3	S02 2-0	m01 2-2	O31 2-2	M06 0-0	N14 2-0	S05 0-0
14 MANCHESTER C	N07 2-5	a10 4-2	a02 2-4	M17 0-1	M29 1-1	O24 8-3	D26 0-2	A29 3-2	S19 4-4	F06 1-5	a27 2-1	D05 5-1	F27 1-1		S12 1-1	D19 2-2	N21 1-1	N04 2-4	O03 4-1	J16 0-0	J01 3-1	M13 2-0
15 MANCHESTER U	S05 0-1	S02 3-0	N14 3-1	N28 2-0	D25 2-1	S26 6-1	a03 0-1	a28 1-0	M20 0-0	O31 1-1	F13 2-1	S16 3-2	M10 3-3	J23 1-6		O10 2-1	a05 0-1	D12 1-2	a21 5-1	O17 0-0	m01 3-2	J02 2-1
16 NEWCASTLE U	O03 7-0	J23 2-2	O31 1-3	S09 1-7	J02 5-1	J01 1-3	M20 4-0	a03 0-1	D12 3-3	M06 0-2	a05 3-0	S19 3-2	D26 3-0	m01 3-2	a14 4-1		S05 6-3	D09 3-1	O17 0-0	N14 3-1	a17 3-0	F06 4-1
17 NOTTS CO	D26 4-1	F06 1-0	M03 3-0	M06 1-1	S12 3-0	S21 0-1	O17 4-1	a17 2-4	N14 0-3	m01 4-2	A29 1-0	O03 2-2	O01 1-2	a03 1-0	a02 0-3	J16 1-3		O31 2-0	D12 2-0	N28 4-2	M20 0-0	M22 1-1
18 SHEFFIELD U	O24 4-0	N07 4-1	O03 4-1	S19 1-1	D05 2-0	a19 6-1	F06 3-1	J01 11-2	J02 1-1	S05 2-3	N21 2-0	D25 2-4	D19 3-1	O26 8-3	a24 2-0	a10 4-3	M13 3-0		J23 4-1	A31 2-3	F20 3-2	F27 1-1
19 SUNDERLAND	a10 2-1	D19 3-2	A29 3-1	S02 6-2	O24 2-1	N07 2-2	O14 1-0	M31 1-3	O10 7-3	J20 4-1	J01 1-3	M27 3-0	M13 3-2	F13 5-3	D05 2-1	F27 2-2	a24 3-1	S12 6-1		S26 3-0	J16 4-0	N21 4-1
20 TOTTENHAM H	J02 1-1	D05 2-2	D26 2-1	O03 4-2	N21 2-3	a24 0-2	F20 4-2	S14 1-2	J23 1-1	S19 5-5	D19 3-2	M13 1-3	O24 3-1	S05 1-0	F27 0-1	M25 1-0	a10 4-0	S07 3-2	F06 0-2		a02 3-2	N07 4-2
21 W.B.A.	a24 2-1	O03 1-1	F06 5-1	J23 1-1	M13 0-3	N21 5-3	N09 4-0	D26 3-0	S02 1-1	J02 2-2	a10 3-0	F27 3-1	M27 0-3	S23 4-1	D19 5-1	D05 4-0	N07 4-4	O10 2-0	S05 2-5	a05 1-0		O24 7-1
22 WEST HAM U	O05 0-4	D25 5-2	D12 2-2	N14 2-1	F13 6-0	S12 2-0	m01 0-2	A31 3-1	a17 1-0	N28 2-3	J30 4-2	a02 1-1	J16 1-2	O31 3-1	A29 1-0	S26 1-0	O10 1-0	O17 1-3	a03 3-2	M20 3-1	M06 3-0	

Grimsby Town's Jimmy Carmichael was a prolific scorer but perhaps his most spectacular effort was the one he netted against New Brighton in May 1926 to give the Mariners the Division Three North title.

DIVISION 2

	BARNSLEY	BLACKPOOL	BRADFORD C	CHELSEA	CLAPTON O	DARLINGTON	DERBY CO	FULHAM	HULL C	MIDDLESBROUGH	NOTTINGHAM F	OLDHAM A	PORTSMOUTH	PORT VALE	PRESTON N.E.	SHEFFIELD W	SOUTHAMPTON	SOUTH SHIELDS	STOCKPORT CO	STOKE C	SWANSEA T	WOLVERHAMPTON W
1 BARNSLEY		O03 2-0	A31 0-0	J23 2-3	S05 3-1	F06 1-1	a05 0-1	O24 2-2	S19 2-1	M27 0-1	D28 4-1	J02 3-4	N21 2-2	J01 3-0	D19 2-0	M13 1-1	F20 2-0	a24 3-1	F27 1-1	N07 2-1	D05 2-0	M06 1-1
2 BLACKPOOL	F13 4-0		J30 3-0	D25 0-0	O10 3-0	S14 0-1	S12 1-2	D05 2-0	a02 2-2	S07 2-3	J16 3-0	a03 2-1	F27 2-2	S26 2-2	N07 3-1	D19 1-0	A29 2-1	M13 1-0	a10 4-1	M27 0-0	a24 0-0	O24 4-0
3 BRADFORD C	S07 4-1	S19 1-0		J02 4-2	O07 0-3	J23 2-0	F20 0-0	D19 0-0	S05 0-1	a10 2-0	O03 0-1	O24 1-1	D05 0-1	a05 2-0	N21 2-0	D25 1-4	F06 0-5	M27 1-1	a24 2-2	F27 2-1	J20 3-1	M13 1-2
4 CHELSEA	S12 3-2	D26 2-3	A29 2-0		F10 1-3	F20 5-2	a26 2-1	S26 4-0	O03 4-0	a24 0-1	S07 0-0	M13 3-0	D19 0-0	J16 3-1	O24 5-0	a10 0-0	a02 0-0	F27 0-0	N07 3-2	D05 1-1	N21 1-3	M27 3-3
5 CLAPTON O	J16 4-0	M08 2-2	a19 3-1	S19 1-2		O03 1-2	S24 0-1	F27 1-1	F06 0-0	D19 1-0	a02 0-1	N07 1-2	M27 1-1	A29 1-2	a24 1-1	D05 0-0	D25 2-1	O24 1-2	S12 2-1	M13 4-0	a10 2-0	N21 2-1
6 DARLINGTON	S26 2-2	S23 1-3	S12 1-3	O10 1-1	F13 6-0		J16 3-0	M13 1-2	D25 1-2	F27 0-2	A29 0-0	a10 1-0	O24 7-1	J30 4-0	S09 1-1	M27 5-1	S30 3-1	N07 4-1	a17 3-2	N21 1-2	D19 3-3	a24 3-4
7 DERBY CO	a06 4-0	J23 5-2	O10 0-0	D28 4-2	A31 3-1	S05 0-2		M27 3-1	J02 3-1	D05 2-0	F06 2-0	a24 1-0	M13 0-2	D26 2-0	a10 2-0	F27 4-1	S19 2-2	N21 2-0	D19 4-0	O24 7-3	O03 5-0	N07 2-0
8 FULHAM	a19 2-2	a17 1-1	m01 2-0	F06 0-3	O17 0-2	O31 4-0	N14 1-1		M20 1-1	D25 2-0	a03 0-2	J23 2-1	a05 2-3	D12 3-3	O10 2-1	J02 3-0	N28 1-1	F13 2-1	S19 1-0	S05 2-4	A31 0-1	O05 1-2
9 HULL C	J30 2-2	a05 1-2	J16 5-0	F13 0-1	S26 2-0	D26 1-1	A29 0-0	N07 1-0		O24 1-2	O12 4-1	D05 1-2	a24 1-0	S12 3-0	F27 1-1	N21 0-1	S07 4-0	O10 1-3	M13 4-0	a10 1-0	a26 4-2	D19 3-1
10 MIDDLESBROUGH	N14 5-0	S02 3-2	N28 2-5	D12 1-2	m01 1-2	O17 3-2	a17 1-2	D26 4-0	M06 3-3		O31 1-0	O03 2-1	J02 4-1	a03 3-1	S23 5-1	S19 3-0	M20 3-0	J01 1-2	F20 4-0	F06 3-0	J23 0-3	S05 4-1
11 NOTTINGHAM F	D25 4-2	S05 1-1	F13 0-0	A31 1-5	a05 1-0	J02 2-0	S26 1-2	N21 2-2	a21 4-0	M13 1-0		D19 1-1	N07 3-1	O10 2-0	D05 4-0	O24 2-0	J23 1-2	a10 4-1	M27 2-0	a24 1-2	F27 0-2	S19 1-4
12 OLDHAM A	A29 2-1	N21 3-2	M06 3-0	O31 1-1	M20 1-1	F08 0-1	D14 2-0	S12 4-0	a17 2-1	F13 4-1	m01 8-3		O10 1-3	O17 3-2	S26 3-2	S07 1-1	N14 1-0	M16 2-1	J30 3-0	S14 7-2	a02 0-0	D25 1-2
13 PORTSMOUTH	a03 1-2	O17 2-0	a17 3-1	m01 4-0	N14 3-2	M06 2-0	O31 2-2	a02 0-0	D12 2-2	A29 1-5	M20 5-1	F20 0-2		N28 3-2	S30 5-2	F06 1-2	J16 1-2	D07 4-2	D26 4-0	O03 2-0	S19 0-0	J23 3-0
14 PORT VALE	S14 3-0	F06 5-0	a02 2-0	S05 0-6	J02 4-2	S19 6-1	D25 0-1	a24 0-1	J23 3-1	N21 4-0	a12 1-1	F27 3-0	a10 1-1		M27 3-0	N07 4-3	O03 1-1	D19 2-0	O24 2-0	A31 3-0	M13 3-0	D05 3-0
15 PRESTON N.E.	m01 4-2	M20 6-4	a03 3-1	M06 3-1	D12 4-1	a02 0-0	N28 2-1	M25 2-1	O17 4-0	S14 1-0	a17 2-0	F06 2-1	A31 3-2	N14 4-0		J23 0-3	O31 2-2	D26 0-4	O03 5-3	S19 2-0	S05 4-2	J02 1-0
16 SHEFFIELD W	O31 3-0	m01 2-0	D26 5-1	N28 4-1	a17 3-0	N14 4-0	O17 1-4	A29 3-0	a03 2-0	F22 2-0	M22 2-0	D28 5-1	S26 4-2	M20 0-2	S12 5-1		D12 2-1	J16 1-0	S21 6-2	a06 2-0	O10 3-1	F13 2-1
17 SOUTHAMPTON	O10 0-0	J02 2-2	S26 1-2	a05 0-1	D26 2-0	O05 4-1	F10 2-1	a10 2-0	A31 0-2	N07 3-1	S12 2-0	M27 3-1	S05 1-3	F13 2-3	M13 2-0	a24 1-2		D05 0-1	N21 3-0	D19 1-2	O24 4-1	F27 4-2
18 SOUTH SHIELDS	D12 3-0	O31 3-4	N14 1-3	O17 0-0	M24 1-0	M20 2-4	a03 0-0	O03 5-2	M03 1-3	a02 2-2	N28 3-1	S19 0-0	O26 5-1	m01 5-2	a05 1-1	S05 1-1	M06 2-0		F06 4-2	J23 5-1	J02 3-1	S07 3-1
19 STOCKPORT CO	O17 1-1	N28 4-3	D12 1-1	M20 0-0	J23 3-2	D05 1-1	m01 3-0	F09 1-2	O31 0-1	O10 1-2	N14 3-0	S05 1-0	D25 3-3	M06 2-2	F13 1-1	A31 0-2	a03 1-2	S26 4-1		J02 2-1	J01 1-3	a02 1-0
20 STOKE C	M20 1-2	N14 1-3	O17 1-0	a17 1-3	O31 0-0	a03 6-1	M06 0-1	J16 5-0	N28 3-1	S26 4-0	D12 1-1	a26 1-0	F13 2-1	S07 0-3	F22 1-3	a05 0-1	m01 1-1	S12 0-1	A29 3-0		D26 1-1	O10 0-0
21 SWANSEA T	a17 3-0	F25 6-1	M20 1-0	a03 0-0	a12 0-0	m01 1-1	F13 2-0	S21 6-0	N14 2-0	S12 4-0	O17 3-0	a05 3-3	M18 1-0	O31 1-0	J16 4-1	M11 2-2	M29 3-1	A29 1-2	S14 4-0	D25 1-1		S26 2-4
22 WOLVERHAMPTON W	a26 7-1	D12 0-0	O31 1-1	N14 0-0	a03 3-0	M01 1-0	M20 2-0	a12 0-0	m01 3-1	J16 3-1	F08 4-0	D26 2-1	S12 4-1	a17 3-1	A29 3-0	O03 1-2	O17 4-1	S14 2-0	a05 5-1	F20 5-1	F06 2-3	

SEASON 1925-26

DIVISION 3 NORTH

	ACCRINGTON S	ASHINGTON	BARROW	BRADFORD	CHESTERFIELD	COVENTRY C	CREWE A	DONCASTER R	DURHAM C	GRIMSBY T	HALIFAX T	HARTLEPOOLS U	LINCOLN C	NELSON	NEW BRIGHTON	ROCHDALE	ROTHERHAM U	SOUTHPORT	TRANMERE R	WALSALL	WIGAN B	WREXHAM
1 ACCRINGTON S		O31 2-1	M20 2-0	J23 1-4	S05 2-0	O17 3-1	a03 2-0	a14 2-3	S29 3-1	S19 1-0	O03 0-1	S02 1-2	N14 3-1	F20 3-2	J20 0-2	a02 1-3	F06 2-3	m01 4-3	D25 4-3	J02 5-2	a17 4-0	M06 4-2
2 ASHINGTON	M13 3-1		D25 1-4	M27 1-1	D19 0-0	S09 2-0	S12 2-0	F13 6-1	N07 0-1	N21 4-2	D05 0-1	a02 2-0	J30 4-1	A31 5-1	J16 1-1	F27 0-1	a10 4-2	S26 1-1	O24 1-0	a24 2-0	A29 3-3	O10 2-2
3 BARROW	N07 1-2	J01 2-3		N21 0-1	M27 0-3	O10 1-4	J16 0-1	S26 0-2	S14 1-4	a10 0-3	M13 1-2	F27 1-4	S12 3-0	S28 1-0	A29 2-3	O24 1-3	D05 1-2	J30 0-3	a24 3-3	D19 5-2	a02 1-1	F13 4-3
4 BRADFORD	S12 3-0	N14 1-0	a03 3-0		A31 1-0	a17 3-0	M06 3-0	M20 2-0	J30 2-1	D26 0-1	J16 2-2	S26 4-0	O17 4-1	J09 3-0	D16 1-0	F13 3-1	A29 6-1	a06 6-1	O10 3-0	S14 8-0	m01 6-1	O31 1-1
5 CHESTERFIELD	J16 7-2	m01 6-1	N14 3-1	S07 1-1		M17 4-3	O17 4-2	O31 2-2	S12 2-0	a05 2-0	A29 1-0	J30 5-2	J01 2-0	a03 3-1	M06 3-0	S26 1-2	D26 6-1	M20 3-0	F13 4-0	O10 4-0	F24 4-0	a17 3-1
6 COVENTRY C	F27 2-1	a05 2-0	J09 2-0	D05 2-2	a10 2-4		D25 2-1	S12 4-0	O24 3-1	M13 1-1	S26 4-1	a24 5-2	A29 3-2	O03 1-0	a06 0-0	D19 2-2	N07 7-0	J16 0-0	M27 1-2	N21 2-0	S07 0-0	J30 2-0
7 CREWE A	N21 3-0	J23 2-1	S05 4-1	O24 1-2	F27 2-0	D26 2-1		S07 2-2	a10 2-0	a24 1-1	M27 0-1	D05 2-1	O10 3-1	J02 1-4	F06 4-1	M13 3-2	D19 3-1	a21 0-1	N07 1-1	O03 2-1	S19 3-1	a02 2-0
8 DONCASTER R	a24 6-2	O03 2-1	F06 0-1	N07 0-3	M13 3-0	J23 8-1	A31 5-2		D19 4-1	a22 1-4	O24 2-2	M27 2-1	a02 1-0	S19 1-1	S24 2-0	N21 2-2	F27 0-0	D26 6-1	a10 4-0	D05 1-1	F20 1-1	S05 1-1
9 DURHAM C	S09 5-1	M20 0-0	S02 2-1	S19 2-1	J23 5-2	M06 4-1	J09 1-1	m01 3-0		F06 0-0	F20 2-0	a05 0-0	a03 3-2	O17 0-2	a17 0-0	J01 0-2	O03 5-1	N14 3-2	J02 2-1	S05 4-1	O31 2-0	a28 2-1
10 GRIMSBY T	J30 5-2	a03 3-1	F25 4-0	D25 3-0	a02 1-0	O31 2-0	M25 2-0	A29 3-0	S26 3-1		S12 1-0	F13 2-0	M06 4-0	a17 3-0	m01 1-0	O10 3-0	J16 3-0	O17 3-2	S14 8-0	A31 5-1	N14 1-1	M20 1-0
11 HALIFAX T	F13 1-1	J09 0-0	O31 3-2	S05 1-2	J02 2-0	F06 1-0	N14 1-0	M06 0-3	O10 2-1	J23 0-2		S07 2-1	m01 0-2	D12 1-1	a03 1-0	S01 1-1	S19 5-1	M18 3-0	a06 1-1	D26 5-0	a15 2-0	O17 2-1
12 HARTLEPOOLS U	S16 5-1	D26 2-1	O17 2-0	F06 0-3	S19 2-1	D12 3-2	a17 0-0	N14 2-1	D25 1-1	O03 1-1	J01 1-1		J09 4-2	M06 2-0	O31 6-1	J02 4-2	F20 2-1	a03 5-0	S05 3-2	J23 9-3	M20 0-0	m01 5-0
13 LINCOLN C	M27 3-1	S19 2-0	J23 4-3	F27 1-1	S21 2-1	J02 0-3	F20 2-2	a05 3-1	N21 1-0	O24 4-1	D19 0-1	a10 2-1		S05 1-0	O03 3-1	D05 0-2	a24 0-3	S07 3-0	M13 1-3	N07 5-1	F06 2-1	D25 3-2
14 NELSON	O10 1-0	S15 2-2	S08 3-3	a10 2-2	a20 3-3	F13 4-1	A29 2-1	J30 5-3	F27 4-0	D05 1-1	N07 1-1	O24 5-2	J16 5-2		a05 1-1	a24 1-3	M13 3-0	S12 3-3	D19 7-0	M27 2-0	D25 7-0	S26 5-1
15 NEW BRIGHTON	a10 4-1	S05 1-1	J02 2-1	a24 1-1	O24 1-2	a02 5-1	S26 2-3	J01 2-1	D05 1-2	D19 1-4	N21 2-1	M13 3-2	F13 5-0	D26 0-0		N07 3-0	M27 5-1	O10 1-0	S19 3-2	F27 3-2	J23 4-2	S02 2-2
16 ROCHDALE	a05 3-2	O17 1-3	M06 2-1	O03 2-0	F06 2-4	m01 4-1	O31 2-0	a03 4-1	D26 5-0	F20 5-2	S15 2-1	A29 6-0	a17 0-1	M23 2-0	M20 2-1		S08 2-2	J25 3-1	J23 3-2	S19 2-0	J16 2-1	N14 1-2
17 ROTHERHAM U	S26 3-1	F22 5-1	a17 2-1	J02 2-3	D25 0-1	M20 2-1	m01 2-2	O17 1-1	F13 2-0	S05 2-1	J30 1-1	O10 1-0	a19 1-3	O31 1-3	N14 1-0	N02 0-4		M06 5-2	A31 2-0	a06 4-1	a03 1-0	J23 6-2
18 SOUTHPORT	D19 1-3	F06 1-1	S19 2-0	a02 2-1	N07 1-3	S05 1-2	J01 0-0	D25 3-3	M27 6-1	F27 0-1	a24 3-1	N21 1-1	S15 3-2	J23 2-1	F20 3-2	a10 1-7	O24 1-1		D05 2-1	M13 1-1	O03 3-1	J02 0-1
19 TRANMERE R	D26 2-2	M06 1-4	a05 3-0	F20 3-2	O03 0-4	N14 2-1	M20 2-0	J09 1-0	A29 2-1	O01 0-0	a02 3-1	J16 2-0	O31 2-0	m01 4-2	a12 0-1	S12 3-5	J01 3-1	a17 1-0		F06 2-1	O17 5-1	a03 4-1
20 WALSALL	A29 3-3	D12 2-0	m01 1-2	S24 3-1	F20 3-1	a03 4-1	F13 0-3	a17 2-1	J16 0-1	S07 2-2	J25 3-1	S12 1-2	M20 0-0	N14 0-2	O17 3-1	J30 1-5	a05 4-1	O31 2-2	S26 1-3		M06 0-1	J09 5-1
21 WIGAN B	D05 5-0	J02 0-2	D26 4-1	D19 1-3	a24 2-0	A31 5-1	J30 3-1	O10 0-1	M13 4-1	M27 2-2	a10 0-0	N07 1-0	S26 3-3	a06 5-0	S12 3-1	S05 2-2	N21 0-1	F13 3-1	F27 2-2	O24 2-0		J01 6-0
22 WREXHAM	O24 5-6	F20 2-3	O03 0-0	M13 4-2	D05 1-1	S19 3-1	a05 1-1	J16 0-2	a24 3-0	N07 4-1	F27 2-0	D19 2-2	D26 1-1	F06 3-2	S09 1-2	M27 1-0	S12 2-2	A29 3-2	N21 0-2	a10 0-1	S16 1-0	

DIVISION 3 SOUTH

	ABERDARE A	BOURNEMOUTH	BRENTFORD	BRIGHTON & HA	BRISTOL C	BRISTOL R	CHARLTON A	CRYSTAL P	EXETER C	GILLINGHAM	LUTON T	MERTHYR T	MILLWALL	NEWPORT CO	NORTHAMPTON T	NORWICH C	PLYMOUTH A	Q.P.R.	READING	SOUTHEND U	SWINDON T	WATFORD
1 ABERDARE A		D05 3-3	S05 3-0	D26 2-2	S19 3-3	D19 0-1	M13 3-1	a19 2-0	N21 5-0	N07 0-1	O24 2-5	a06 0-0	S07 1-2	F27 2-0	S21 1-0	F20 3-1	F06 6-1	a24 1-0	a10 2-2	O03 2-0	M27 1-1	J02 8-1
2 BOURNEMOUTH	a17 3-0		N14 3-2	F24 0-3	J13 1-1	D25 2-0	F06 4-1	m01 6-1	J16 2-1	O03 1-2	S09 2-2	F20 2-1	M20 0-0	S23 0-2	M13 4-2	a21 2-2	M06 1-2	a05 4-1	S12 1-1	O17 1-2	A29 2-0	a03 3-4
3 BRENTFORD	J16 1-0	M27 0-2		S12 1-6	F20 2-1	F27 4-1	N21 4-0	F13 3-2	a24 2-0	a10 0-0	N07 1-0	D05 1-1	D26 2-0	M13 3-3	A29 3-4	a02 5-1	a26 2-2	S26 1-2	D19 1-0	S07 1-3	O24 3-1	J30 4-3
4 BRIGHTON & H.A.	D25 6-2	a10 3-4	J23 3-2		F06 0-0	a24 2-3	D05 1-0	S19 3-2	M27 1-3	M13 1-2	F27 2-0	N07 3-1	O14 3-1	J02 2-1	a02 2-2	O28 1-1	O03 1-2	O24 2-1	N21 2-2	a21 3-2	D19 3-1	S05 3-1
5 BRISTOL C	J30 1-0	a24 5-0	O10 3-0	S26 1-0		N07 0-0	D19 4-0	O07 1-0	F27 1-0	M27 4-0	D05 5-1	N21 2-1	J16 1-1	a10 1-2	S12 1-1	A29 0-1	a05 2-1	M13 3-1	O24 0-1	D25 1-4	S09 5-1	F13 1-0
6 BRISTOL R	m01 0-3	D26 7-2	O17 1-2	D12 4-0	M20 0-1		a06 4-1	M24 3-1	A31 0-1	S05 2-0	F06 2-2	J23 0-0	a03 0-1	S19 2-2	N14 1-2	J09 2-2	O31 2-3	O03 5-0	a02 4-2	a17 2-0	D28 1-2	M06 2-1
7 CHARLTON A	O31 1-0	S26 5-0	a03 0-2	a17 1-1	m01 3-1	A29 0-1		N14 1-1	S12 1-0	F20 1-0	a05 2-1	N09 0-0	F13 1-4	S03 0-0	M20 3-3	O17 3-0	M25 0-5	D26 1-1	J30 1-2	M06 5-0	J16 2-0	F25 1-1
8 CRYSTAL P	S12 0-1	D19 3-1	O03 2-0	M10 2-1	S23 5-2	O10 0-2	M27 4-1		O24 3-2	N21 0-2	M13 3-0	a10 3-0	A29 1-2	F10 4-2	J16 1-0	D26 2-0	N28 5-5	N07 1-0	a24 3-0	a02 3-0	F27 1-0	S26 4-0
9 EXETER C	a03 4-0	S05 0-1	D28 6-1	N14 2-4	O17 1-1	S09 3-0	J23 5-3	M06 0-1		S19 2-1	F20 2-2	F06 6-2	a17 3-1	O03 2-1	a14 1-0	O31 0-1	D25 4-0	S23 3-0	J02 3-2	M20 0-1	a05 1-2	m01 6-1
10 GILLINGHAM	M20 0-1	F13 1-2	J09 1-3	O31 3-1	N14 0-1	J16 6-3	O10 0-0	a03 1-1	J30 2-0		D25 2-1	S09 3-1	O17 0-0	a02 2-0	S30 1-1	M06 2-0	m01 2-0	A29 3-0	S26 4-1	J20 3-1	S12 0-1	a17 0-1
11 LUTON T	M06 2-1	A31 4-1	M20 4-2	O17 3-3	a17 4-1	S26 1-0	a02 1-0	O31 3-2	O10 1-1	D26 5-3		J02 4-0	m01 2-2	S05 4-2	F22 3-2	N14 3-2	D28 1-1	J30 4-0	S14 0-1	a03 2-0	F13 4-1	J23 5-0
12 MERTHYR T	a05 1-1	O10 0-2	a17 6-0	M20 0-1	a03 3-2	S12 2-3	M15 0-1	J25 4-0	S26 3-1	S03 0-0	A29 2-1		M06 0-2	D25 4-1	O17 5-3	D12 3-1	N14 1-1	J16 1-0	F13 5-2	m01 5-1	F22 2-1	O31 4-1
13 MILLWALL	A31 4-2	N07 0-1	D25 2-1	M22 2-0	S05 3-0	N21 0-0	O03 1-1	J02 1-0	D05 3-0	F27 0-0	D19 7-0	O24 1-1		a24 3-3	O10 4-1	F06 3-1	J23 0-0	M27 3-0	M13 1-0	S19 8-1	a10 3-0	a02 3-0
14 NEWPORT CO	O17 0-0	O01 1-2	O31 2-3	A29 4-3	D28 1-0	J30 3-1	S17 0-0	a17 2-3	F13 3-0	a05 4-0	J16 2-1	D26 3-1	F25 1-0		M06 3-0	m01 1-1	a03 0-3	S12 4-1	O10 1-1	N14 1-0	S26 0-4	M20 3-3
15 NORTHAMPTON T	S14 3-2	O31 1-1	J02 6-1	a06 1-2	J23 1-2	M27 2-0	N07 2-1	S05 4-0	a10 2-1	D28 1-2	a24 0-1	F27 4-1	a26 3-1	O24 2-0		O03 3-2	S19 2-1	D19 3-2	D05 0-1	F06 3-3	N21 2-0	D26 2-2
16 NORWICH C	O10 2-3	S19 3-1	a05 1-0	S14 1-2	J02 1-3	a10 1-0	F27 3-0	D25 4-3	M13 3-1	O24 1-0	M27 2-0	a24 2-2	S26 1-0	D19 0-0	F13 2-1		S05 0-3	N21 1-1	N07 3-1	J23 1-2	D05 2-2	A31 1-1
17 PLYMOUTH A	S26 7-2	O24 7-2	S23 4-0	F13 5-3	a02 3-1	M13 1-2	a24 1-0	S02 6-2	D26 2-2	D19 2-1	a10 4-3	M27 3-0	S12 2-0	N21 3-0	J30 2-4	J16 6-3		D05 3-1	F27 1-3	A29 6-2	N07 1-1	O10 2-1
18 Q.P.R.	F25 1-3	a02 2-2	F06 1-1	M06 0-2	O31 0-2	F13 2-1	D25 2-2	M20 1-3	O08 0-0	J02 0-1	S19 1-0	S05 1-1	D28 3-0	J23 0-2	m01 3-2	a03 0-1	a17 0-4		S03 1-2	M04 2-2	O10 1-1	O17 2-0
19 READING	M24 2-1	J23 5-2	m01 7-1	a03 0-0	M06 1-1	a05 3-0	S19 1-1	D28 2-1	A29 3-2	F06 1-0	S30 3-0	O03 1-1	O31 2-0	F20 2-1	a17 4-2	M20 2-0	O17 1-1	S09 2-1		J16 1-0	D25 2-0	N14 4-1
20 SOUTHEND U	F13 0-1	F27 3-0	S02 3-1	O10 4-0	D26 1-2	D05 3-1	O24 1-2	a05 5-1	N07 3-1	a24 1-1	N21 2-0	D19 5-1	M17 0-2	M27 4-1	S26 6-1	S12 0-1	J02 2-0	a10 2-1	S05 2-2		M13 3-0	S16 0-1
21 SWINDON T	N14 2-1	J02 8-2	M06 2-1	m01 1-0	A31 1-3	S16 4-2	S05 3-0	O17 3-1	a02 2-1	J23 1-0	O03 2-0	S19 0-2	S23 1-1	F06 2-1	a03 1-2	a17 3-1	M20 2-0	F20 2-0	D26 1-1	O31 2-0		a21 5-3
22 WATFORD	A29 2-0	N21 0-0	S19 2-2	J16 3-3	O03 2-2	O24 2-1	a10 1-1	F06 3-0	D19 3-1	D05 3-1	S12 2-0	M13 6-1	a05 0-1	N07 5-1	D25 3-2	S09 3-1	F20 0-1	F27 3-1	M27 0-1	S23 1-4	a24 3-2	

LEAGUE TABLES

DIVISION 1

	P	W	D	L	F	A	W	D	L	F	A	Pts
Huddersfield T	42	14	6	1	50	17	9	5	7	42	43	57
Arsenal	42	16	2	3	57	19	6	6	9	30	44	52
Sunderland	42	17	2	2	67	30	4	4	13	29	50	48
Bury	42	12	4	5	55	34	8	3	10	30	43	47
Sheffield U	42	15	3	3	72	29	4	5	12	30	53	46
Aston Villa	42	12	7	2	56	25	4	5	12	30	51	44
Liverpool	42	9	8	4	43	27	5	8	8	27	36	44
Bolton W	42	11	6	4	46	31	6	4	11	29	45	44
Manchester U	42	12	4	5	40	26	7	2	12	26	47	44
Newcastle U	42	13	3	5	59	33	3	7	11	25	42	42
Everton	42	9	9	3	42	26	3	9	9	30	44	42
Blackburn R	42	11	6	4	59	33	4	5	12	32	47	41
W.B.A.	42	13	5	3	59	29	3	3	15	20	49	40
Birmingham C	42	14	2	5	35	25	2	6	13	31	56	40
Tottenham H	42	11	4	6	45	36	4	5	12	21	43	39
Cardiff C	42	8	5	8	30	25	8	2	11	31	51	39
Leicester C	42	11	3	7	42	32	3	7	11	28	48	38
West Ham U	42	14	2	5	45	27	1	5	15	18	49	37
Leeds U	42	11	5	5	38	28	3	3	15	26	48	36
Burnley	42	7	7	7	43	35	6	3	12	42	73	36
Manchester C	42	8	7	6	48	42	4	4	13	41	58	35
Notts Co	42	11	4	6	37	26	2	3	16	17	48	33

DIVISION 2

	P	W	D	L	F	A	W	D	L	F	A	Pts
Sheffield W	42	19	0	2	61	17	8	6	7	27	31	60
Derby Co	42	17	2	2	57	17	8	5	8	20	25	57
Chelsea	42	10	7	4	42	22	9	7	5	34	27	52
Wolverhampton W	42	15	4	2	55	15	6	3	12	29	45	49
Swansea T	42	13	6	2	50	16	6	5	10	27	41	49
Blackpool	42	12	6	3	41	16	5	5	11	35	53	45
Oldham A	42	14	4	3	52	24	4	4	13	22	38	44
Port Vale	42	15	3	3	53	18	4	3	14	26	51	44
South Shields	42	11	6	4	50	29	7	2	12	24	36	44
Middlesbrough	42	14	1	6	56	28	7	1	13	21	40	44
Portsmouth	42	12	4	5	48	27	5	6	10	31	47	44
Preston N.E.	42	17	2	2	54	28	1	5	15	17	56	43
Hull C	42	11	4	6	40	19	5	5	11	23	42	41
Southampton	42	11	2	8	39	25	4	6	11	24	38	38
Darlington	42	9	5	7	51	31	5	5	11	21	46	38
Bradford C	42	9	5	7	28	26	4	5	12	19	40	36
Nottingham F	42	11	4	6	38	25	3	4	14	13	48	36
Barnsley	42	10	7	4	38	22	2	5	14	20	62	36
Fulham	42	8	6	7	32	29	3	6	12	14	48	34
Clapton O	42	8	6	7	30	21	4	3	14	20	44	33
Stoke C	42	8	5	8	32	23	4	3	14	22	54	32
Stockport Co	42	8	7	6	34	28	0	2	19	17	69	25

DIVISION 3 NORTH

	P	W	D	L	F	A	W	D	L	F	A	Pts
Grimsby T	42	20	1	0	61	8	6	8	7	30	32	61
Bradford P.A.	42	18	2	1	65	10	8	6	7	36	33	60
Rochdale	42	16	1	4	55	25	11	4	6	49	33	59
Chesterfield	42	18	2	1	70	19	7	3	11	30	35	55
Halifax T	42	12	5	4	34	19	5	6	10	19	31	45
Hartlepool U	42	15	5	1	59	23	3	3	15	23	50	44
Tranmere R	42	15	2	4	45	27	4	4	13	28	56	44
Nelson	42	12	8	1	67	29	4	3	14	22	42	43
Ashington	42	11	6	4	44	23	5	5	11	26	39	43
Doncaster R	42	11	7	3	52	25	5	4	12	28	47	43
Crewe A	42	14	3	4	43	23	3	6	12	20	38	43
New Brighton	42	13	4	4	51	29	4	4	13	18	38	42
Durham C	42	14	5	2	45	19	4	1	16	18	51	42
Rotherham U	42	13	3	5	44	28	4	4	13	25	64	41
Lincoln C	42	14	2	5	42	28	3	3	15	24	54	39
Coventry C	42	13	6	2	47	19	3	0	18	26	63	38
Wigan B	42	12	5	4	53	22	1	6	14	15	52	37
Accrington S	42	14	0	7	49	34	3	3	15	32	71	37
Wrexham	42	9	6	6	39	31	2	4	15	24	61	32
Southport	42	9	6	6	37	34	2	4	15	25	58	32
Walsall	42	9	4	8	40	34	1	2	18	18	73	26
Barrow	42	4	2	15	28	49	3	2	16	22	49	18

DIVISION 3 NORTH

	P	W	D	L	F	A	W	D	L	F	A	Pts
Reading	42	16	5	0	49	16	7	6	8	28	36	57
Plymouth A	42	16	2	3	71	33	8	6	7	36	34	56
Millwall	42	14	6	1	52	12	7	5	9	21	27	53
Bristol C	42	14	3	4	42	15	7	6	8	30	36	51
Brighton & H.A.	42	12	4	5	47	33	7	5	9	37	40	47
Swindon T	42	16	2	3	48	22	4	4	13	21	42	46
Luton T	42	16	4	1	60	25	2	3	16	20	50	43
Bournemouth	42	10	5	6	44	30	7	4	10	31	61	43
Aberdare A	42	11	6	4	50	24	6	2	13	24	42	42
Gillingham	42	11	4	6	36	19	6	4	11	17	30	42
Southend U	42	13	2	6	50	20	6	2	13	28	53	42
Northampton T	42	13	3	5	47	26	4	4	13	35	54	41
Crystal Palace	42	16	1	4	50	21	3	2	16	25	58	41
Merthyr T	42	13	3	5	51	25	1	8	12	18	50	39
Watford	42	12	5	4	47	26	3	4	14	26	63	39
Norwich C	42	11	5	5	35	26	4	4	13	23	47	39
Newport Co	42	11	5	5	39	27	3	5	13	25	47	38
Brentford	42	12	4	5	44	32	4	2	15	25	62	38
Bristol R	42	9	4	8	44	28	6	2	13	22	41	36
Exeter C	42	13	2	6	54	25	2	3	16	18	45	35
Charlton A	42	9	7	5	32	23	2	6	13	16	45	35
Q.P.R.	42	5	7	9	23	32	1	2	18	14	52	21

Football League Records

Top scorers: Div 1, J.Trotter (Sheffield Wednesday) 37 goals; Div 2, G.Camsell (Middlesbrough) 59 goals; Div 3 N, A.Whitehurst (Rochdale) 44 goals; Div 3 S, D.Morris (Swindon Town) 47 goals.

Coventry City transferred to Division Three South.

In his second season with Newcastle United, Hughie Gallacher scored 36 goals as the Magpies won the League Championship. He had joined them from Aidrie for £6,500, a record for a Scottish club player.

DIVISION 1

	ARSENAL	ASTON VILLA	BIRMINGHAM	BLACKBURN R	BOLTON W	BURNLEY	BURY	CARDIFF C	DERBY CO	EVERTON	HUDDERSFIELD T	LEEDS U	LEICESTER C	LIVERPOOL	MANCHESTER U	NEWCASTLE U	SHEFFIELD U	SHEFFIELD W	SUNDERLAND	TOTTENHAM H	W.B.A.	WEST HAM U
1 ARSENAL		a15 2-1	a30 3-0	N06 2-2	S01 2-1	F26 6-2	D04 1-0	J01 3-2	A28 2-1	M19 1-2	a02 0-2	F12 1-0	S11 2-2	S18 2-0	D28 1-0	O02 2-2	J22 1-1	O23 6-2	N20 2-3	D18 2-4	a16 4-1	O16 2-2
2 ASTON VILLA	a18 2-3		M19 4-2	J29 4-3	S25 3-4	S04 1-1	S18 1-2	J31 0-0	O09 3-1	D04 5-3	D18 3-0	D28 5-1	a16 2-0	A30 1-1	F19 2-0	J15 1-2	D25 4-0	N20 2-2	M05 3-1	N06 2-3	O23 2-0	a02 1-5
3 BIRMINGHAM	D11 0-0	O30 1-2		A28 3-1	a04 6-1	N13 1-0	S25 2-2	a27 1-2	O16 1-0	S20 1-0	J22 1-3	N27 2-0	J01 2-1	a23 3-0	M12 4-0	a09 2-0	m07 2-3	S13 0-0	S11 2-0	F26 1-0	F05 1-0	D27 0-2
4 BLACKBURN R	a28 1-2	D11 0-2	J15 3-2		a23 0-3	O16 1-5	O04 2-2	m07 1-0	a09 4-4	O02 3-3	D25 4-2	F26 4-1	F12 2-1	O30 2-1	N27 2-1	M12 1-2	N13 3-4	S18 2-2	S20 0-2	S04 1-0	a19 0-0	F14 4-1
5 BOLTON W	S06 2-2	F12 0-2	O02 1-0	D04 5-1		M09 3-1	O23 2-2	S18 2-0	D25 3-1	a16 5-0	a30 4-0	J15 3-0	N20 2-0	J01 2-1	O09 4-0	S04 2-1	a15 4-1	a02 3-2	D18 2-2	M19 2-2	M05 1-1	N06 2-0
6 BURNLEY	O09 2-0	J22 6-3	a02 0-2	M05 3-1	S11 4-3		N06 0-0	A28 4-3	S25 1-0	D18 5-1	O23 2-2	a15 3-2	a30 1-1	D25 4-0	F05 1-0	S06 3-3	M29 2-5	D04 1-0	O12 4-2	N20 5-0	M19 2-1	a16 2-1
7 BURY	m04 3-2	F05 0-1	F12 3-1	S15 0-2	M12 2-0	M26 3-3		O30 2-3	m07 1-2	S01 5-2	A28 2-2	a09 4-2	a15 0-0	N27 0-2	O16 0-3	N13 3-2	D11 4-4	D25 2-0	M30 1-2	O02 0-0	S11 7-3	F26 1-2
8 CARDIFF C	D27 2-0	S11 2-3	N06 1-0	D18 0-1	F05 1-0	J15 0-0	M19 2-1		M16 2-0	a30 1-0	M21 2-0	S06 3-1	D04 0-1	a18 2-0	S25 0-2	S20 1-1	O09 3-0	a16 3-2	O23 3-0	a02 1-2	S04 1-1	N20 1-2
9 DERBY CO	J15 0-2	F26 2-3	M05 4-1	N20 4-5	D27 2-0	F12 4-1	D18 2-0	O02 6-3		a02 0-0	a16 4-4	F19 1-0	N06 4-1	S04 2-1	a18 2-2	S18 1-1	S27 1-0	M19 8-0	D04 4-2	O23 4-1	a30 2-1	D28 3-0
10 EVERTON	O30 3-1	a23 2-2	a18 3-1	F19 1-0	N27 1-1	J01 3-2	S29 2-2	D11 0-1	N13 3-2		O09 0-0	M12 2-1	S18 3-4	S25 1-0	a09 0-0	O16 1-3	M26 2-0	M02 2-1	D25 5-4	J15 1-2	S15 0-0	S04 0-3
11 HUDDERSFIELD T	N13 3-3	m07 0-0	S04 0-2	D27 5-0	D11 1-0	M12 2-0	J15 3-1	O16 0-0	N27 4-2	F26 0-0		O30 4-1	O02 5-3	M26 1-0	a23 0-0	a19 1-0	a09 0-2	F12 4-3	S14 0-0	J29 2-0	A30 4-1	S18 2-1
12 LEEDS U	S25 4-1	S15 3-1	a16 2-1	O09 4-1	A28 2-5	a19 0-2	N20 4-1	A30 0-0	S11 1-0	O23 1-3	M19 1-1		M05 1-1	F23 0-0	J22 2-3	D27 1-2	F05 1-1	D18 4-1	N06 2-2	D04 1-1	a02 3-1	a30 6-3
13 LEICESTER C	F10 2-1	N27 5-1	A30 5-2	S25 4-0	a09 0-1	D11 0-3	a18 1-1	a07 3-1	M26 1-1	F05 6-2	F19 2-4	O16 3-2		M12 3-2	N13 2-3	m07 2-1	O30 2-2	S04 5-3	O09 2-1	S13 2-2	D25 5-0	J15 3-0
14 LIVERPOOL	F05 3-0	S08 2-1	D04 2-1	M19 2-2	D28 3-2	D27 2-2	a16 2-2	a15 5-0	J22 3-2	F12 1-0	N06 2-3	O02 2-4	O23 1-0		A28 4-2	F26 1-2	S11 5-1	M05 3-0	a02 1-2	a30 1-0	N20 2-1	D18 0-0
15 MANCHESTER U	S15 2-2	O02 2-1	O23 0-1	a16 2-0	F26 0-0	S18 2-1	M05 1-2	F12 1-1	a15 2-2	N20 2-1	D04 0-0	S04 2-2	a02 1-0	J15 0-1		F09 3-1	J01 5-0	N06 0-0	a30 0-0	D27 2-1	D18 2-0	M19 0-3
16 NEWCASTLE U	a06 6-1	A28 4-0	N20 5-1	O23 6-1	J22 1-0	S01 1-5	a02 3-1	D25 5-0	F05 3-0	M05 7-3	a15 1-0	J01 1-0	D18 1-1	O09 1-0	S11 4-2		S25 2-0	a30 2-1	M19 1-0	a16 3-2	N06 5-2	D04 2-0
17 SHEFFIELD U	S04 4-0	D27 3-1	D18 4-3	a02 5-3	a18 1-1	O02 2-2	m05 2-0	F26 3-1	S13 1-0	N06 3-3	N20 3-3	S18 1-0	M19 0-3	F07 1-4	A30 2-2	F12 2-1		J15 2-0	a16 2-0	M05 3-3	D04 2-1	O23 0-2
18 SHEFFIELD W	M12 4-2	a09 3-1	a19 4-4	F05 0-3	N13 2-1	a23 2-1	J01 1-3	N29 3-0	O30 2-1	S11 4-0	S25 1-1	m07 1-0	J22 2-2	O16 3-2	M26 2-0	D11 3-2	A28 2-3		F19 4-1	D28 3-1	O09 2-1	S06 1-0
19 SUNDERLAND	a09 5-1	O16 1-1	F16 4-1	J01 2-5	a19 6-2	O06 7-1	S04 3-0	M12 2-2	a23 1-2	D27 3-2	S08 1-1	M26 6-2	J29 3-0	N13 2-1	D11 6-0	O30 2-0	N27 3-0	O02 4-1		S18 3-2	J15 4-1	F12 2-3
20 TOTTENHAM H	m07 0-4	M26 0-1	O09 6-1	J22 1-1	O30 1-0	a09 4-1	F19 1-0	N13 4-1	M12 3-2	A28 2-1	S11 3-3	a23 4-1	S06 2-2	D11 1-2	D25 1-1	N27 1-3	O16 3-1	A30 7-3	F05 0-2		S25 3-0	a15 1-3
21 W.B.A.	N27 1-3	M12 6-2	S18 1-2	a18 2-0	O16 1-1	O30 4-2	J29 3-1	F21 1-2	D11 3-1	S06 3-2	J01 2-2	N13 2-4	D27 0-1	a09 0-1	m07 2-2	M26 4-2	a23 1-0	F26 2-2	A28 3-0	F12 5-0		O02 1-3
22 WEST HAM U	M07 7-0	N13 5-1	D25 1-0	S11 1-5	M26 4-4	N27 2-1	O09 1-2	a09 2-2	J01 1-2	J22 2-1	F05 3-2	D11 3-2	A28 3-3	m07 3-3	O30 4-0	a23 1-1	M12 3-0	O04 1-1	S25 1-2	a18 1-2	F19 1-2	

Goalkeeper Billy Croggins was ever present as Bristol City returned to Division Two. He later won a Division Two medal with Everton.

DIVISION 2

	BARNSLEY	BLACKPOOL	BRADFORD C	CHELSEA	CLAPTON O	DARLINGTON	FULHAM	GRIMSBY T	HULL C	MANCHESTER C	MIDDLESBROUGH	NOTTINGHAM F	NOTTS CO	OLDHAM A	PORTSMOUTH	PORT VALE	PRESTON N.E.	READING	SOUTHAMPTON	SOUTH SHIELDS	SWANSEA T	WOLVERHAMPTON W
1 BARNSLEY		J22 6-1	D11 1-0	a23 3-0	F19 4-2	D27 3-2	D28 5-0	A28 2-1	N13 1-2	F26 1-1	M12 1-1	S25 0-2	O30 4-4	A30 0-1	a18 2-0	O16 2-0	M14 3-0	S11 2-2	m07 5-1	a09 6-1	F05 1-1	M26 4-1
2 BLACKPOOL	S04 6-1		N13 3-0	M26 3-1	D11 6-0	S18 1-1	F26 0-0	D27 6-2	M12 4-0	J29 2-4	a23 2-2	J15 2-2	m07 5-0	O02 2-0	F12 2-0	N27 2-2	O30 2-3	A30 3-1	a09 3-2	a15 6-1	J01 3-1	O16 2-3
3 BRADFORD C	a30 1-1	a02 4-1		S18 0-1	S08 1-3	M05 0-1	M19 1-0	N06 2-2	F26 1-2	D18 4-3	S29 0-1	D04 1-1	a19 1-2	S11 0-1	O23 1-2	A28 1-2	F12 0-1	N20 1-1	J22 2-0	O02 3-1	a16 5-0	D27 1-2
4 CHELSEA	D04 4-2	N06 1-1	F05 5-2		J01 2-1	D18 2-2	S25 2-2	M19 2-0	D25 1-0	a30 0-0	A28 3-0	a16 2-0	S06 2-0	O23 1-0	m04 0-0	M16 2-0	O02 2-1	a02 0-0	S11 2-3	F26 4-1	N20 2-2	a18 1-0
5 CLAPTON O	O02 0-1	a30 1-0	S02 1-1	a28 3-0		N06 0-4	a16 2-3	D04 2-4	F23 1-2	M19 2-4	O09 2-3	O23 2-2	F12 2-1	N20 3-1	a02 4-5	D25 1-2	J15 1-1	D18 5-1	a15 1-0	S04 1-0	M21 1-0	S18 2-0
6 DARLINGTON	D25 3-3	F05 1-3	O16 3-0	m07 2-2	M26 2-1		J22 5-0	S11 2-3	N27 1-3	a15 2-2	O30 1-4	O09 4-2	N13 4-2	A28 0-1	N08 0-4	A30 4-3	D11 0-1	S25 4-2	M12 1-2	a23 8-2	m02 3-1	a09 3-1
7 FULHAM	S13 1-0	O09 1-0	O30 1-1	F12 1-2	N27 2-0	S04 2-1		F19 0-5	m07 3-1	J15 2-5	a09 0-3	A30 2-1	a23 3-0	S18 1-1	M14 0-0	N13 6-2	M12 0-1	D27 1-2	M28 3-0	O16 2-2	a15 4-3	D11 4-1
8 GRIMSBY T	J15 1-3	D25 2-1	M26 4-2	O30 0-0	a23 2-2	M29 2-1	O02 2-0		O16 0-1	S04 2-2	F08 4-7	J01 1-1	J29 1-4	F12 2-5	S18 0-0	a09 4-4	F26 5-2	a15 0-1	N13 0-1	M12 1-1	A30 0-1	m07 6-0
9 HULL C	a02 5-1	O23 3-0	O09 4-0	D27 0-1	S11 4-0	a16 2-1	D18 2-0	M05 2-3		N20 3-2	F05 3-3	N06 1-2	J22 2-0	a30 1-2	D04 2-1	S25 0-0	a18 3-1	S20 1-1	M14 0-0	A30 2-0	M19 2-1	A28 1-0
10 MANCHESTER C	O09 1-1	S11 2-1	m07 8-0	D11 1-0	O30 6-1	a18 7-0	A28 4-2	J22 2-0	a09 2-2		D25 3-5	F19 1-1	M26 4-1	S22 3-0	S01 4-0	M12 4-1	a23 1-0	F05 3-0	O16 3-4	N27 1-2	S25 3-1	N13 2-1
11 MIDDLESBROUGH	O23 5-1	D04 4-4	S22 4-3	J15 0-0	F26 6-0	M19 4-1	N20 6-1	a16 3-0	S18 2-0	D27 2-1		M05 1-0	O02 4-2	a02 3-1	N06 7-3	J01 5-2	S04 0-2	a30 5-0	N27 3-1	M16 5-0	D18 7-1	F12 2-0
12 NOTTINGHAM F	F12 3-1	A28 2-0	a23 3-0	N27 4-1	M12 1-1	F26 5-1	O07 2-0	S06 1-1	M26 3-1	O02 3-3	O16 4-3		F05 2-0	a15 1-1	D27 1-0	m07 0-3	a09 7-0	J22 5-1	D11 3-1	N13 4-2	S11 2-2	O30 1-1
13 NOTTS CO	M19 1-1	D18 2-3	a18 4-0	S13 5-0	S25 3-1	a02 3-1	D04 4-0	a30 3-0	S04 1-0	N06 1-0	F23 2-2	S18 1-2		a16 1-2	N20 2-3	O09 2-1	J01 1-1	M16 2-0	D25 0-1	J15 4-1	O23 1-3	F09 2-2
14 OLDHAM A	J01 0-4	F19 1-3	J29 2-1	M12 1-2	a09 5-2	J15 3-2	F05 2-3	S25 3-1	D11 1-1	S06 1-2	N13 2-1	a18 3-3	N27 5-2		S04 1-0	M26 1-3	O16 5-1	O09 3-1	O30 1-1	m07 3-2	D25 5-2	a23 2-0
15 PORTSMOUTH	a15 1-2	S25 5-0	M12 1-0	O16 2-3	N24 1-1	O25 0-0	S11 2-0	F05 5-2	a23 2-0	J01 2-1	M26 0-1	D25 0-0	a09 9-1	J22 7-2		O30 4-0	m07 5-1	M30 5-0	A28 3-1	D11 1-1	O09 1-0	N27 2-1
16 PORT VALE	M05 3-2	a16 2-4	J15 0-0	S04 0-0	D27 3-0	S20 3-2	a02 7-1	N20 6-1	F12 0-0	O23 0-2	a15 3-1	D18 0-2	F26 6-2	N06 3-0	M19 2-3		M28 2-0	D04 1-1	S27 3-1	S18 4-2	a30 1-1	O02 1-1
17 PRESTON N.E.	a16 2-1	M19 4-1	S25 3-2	M21 0-2	A28 2-2	F19 4-1	O23 2-2	O09 3-2	a15 1-0	D04 2-4	J22 2-2	N20 1-0	A30 4-1	M05 5-2	D18 1-2	S11 4-4		N06 3-1	F05 1-0	D27 4-0	a02 4-0	S27 2-0
18 READING	a06 3-2	S08 0-1	a09 2-3	N13 2-1	m07 0-1	F12 4-2	D25 2-0	a18 1-1	S15 0-1	S18 1-0	a20 2-1	S04 4-0	O16 7-1	F26 6-1	O02 1-2	a23 2-0	a27 3-0		J01 1-0	O30 2-1	J15 3-0	M12 1-2
19 SOUTHAMPTON	D18 3-1	N20 5-3	S04 0-0	a04 1-1	a18 1-2	O23 3-1	N06 4-1	a02 0-0	O02 0-1	a25 1-1	A30 2-1	a30 1-0	D27 2-0	M19 0-1	J15 0-2	S13 2-2	S18 1-1	a16 1-1		F12 6-2	D04 1-1	F26 1-0
20 SOUTH SHIELDS	N20 7-1	a18 2-2	M02 3-3	O09 5-1	J22 2-1	D04 1-0	M05 1-1	O23 3-2	J01 3-1	a16 2-2	S11 0-0	a02 1-1	A28 5-0	D18 4-1	a30 1-0	F05 3-3	D25 1-1	M19 3-0	S25 1-2		N06 0-1	m02 1-2
21 SWANSEA T	S18 5-2	S20 2-0	N27 1-0	a09 2-1	O16 3-2	O02 5-1	a18 4-2	S13 1-1	O30 1-0	F12 1-3	m07 0-1	M10 2-1	M12 0-1	D27 3-0	F26 1-1	D11 2-2	N13 0-0	A28 3-0	a23 2-2	M26 2-0		J22 4-1
22 WOLVERHAMPTON W	N06 9-1	M21 4-1	D25 7-2	A30 0-3	F05 5-0	N20 2-1	a30 2-1	D18 3-4	J15 5-2	a02 4-1	S25 1-2	M19 2-0	S11 0-1	D04 1-1	a16 0-1	a19 1-2	S13 1-2	O23 1-1	O09 2-2	a25 2-0	S04 2-2	

Season 1926-27

Division 3 North

	ACCRINGTON S	ASHINGTON	BARROW	BRADFORD	CHESTERFIELD	CREWE A	DONCASTER R	DURHAM C	HALIFAX T	HARTLEPOOLS U	LINCOLN C	NELSON	NEW BRIGHTON	ROCHDALE	ROTHERHAM U	SOUTHPORT	STOCKPORT CO	STOKE C	TRANMERE R	WALSALL	WIGAN B	WREXHAM
1 ACCRINGTON S		M19 3-0	F19 0-1	D18 2-3	J01 2-1	S25 3-1	a16 2-0	S20 3-0	O09 4-2	F05 7-2	S28 1-1	O23 0-5	N06 2-3	A28 0-1	a30 3-1	J22 2-2	S11 2-4	D04 0-1	D25 2-3	M05 3-5	N20 3-1	a02 1-1
2 ASHINGTON	O30 2-1		a09 3-0	F26 2-2	J03 2-1	a18 4-1	S18 1-1	J01 3-1	N13 3-0	a23 1-0	M26 1-2	M23 1-1	J15 2-3	O16 2-2	O02 4-4	m07 4-1	a11 1-1	F12 0-2	O23 4-3	a04 0-2	J29 1-1	S04 1-1
3 BARROW	O02 1-1	N20 2-2		S11 0-3	a02 1-0	J22 3-1	D18 0-1	F26 2-1	S18 1-1	J15 1-3	F12 0-3	N06 0-1	m02 0-3	S13 2-3	O23 2-2	a18 1-4	D25 1-3	M05 0-0	A30 2-1	M19 1-0	a30 2-2	D04 0-5
4 BRADFORD	m07 6-1	O09 2-0	J29 1-0		F19 5-0	O30 2-0	D25 7-3	D11 3-0	M12 2-1	M26 4-1	O16 3-1	S25 2-2	A30 1-1	J08 5-1	S04 2-2	a09 6-2	N13 3-1	J15 3-0	a23 5-3	F05 5-1	J01 2-1	a18 5-0
5 CHESTERFIELD	A30 1-1	S27 4-1	N13 8-1	O02 3-2		a09 3-0	J29 1-1	M12 7-1	M26 2-0	a19 1-0	O30 4-2	a15 1-1	D25 3-1	m07 2-3	F12 5-2	S13 5-1	a23 3-0	S18 1-1	O16 3-1	F26 2-0	S04 5-2	J15 1-3
6 CREWE A	F12 4-0	a16 2-1	S04 5-0	M19 1-1	N20 0-0		M05 1-3	O02 2-1	J29 1-2	D27 0-1	S18 3-3	a02 2-1	D04 3-2	S06 4-0	J15 2-2	a20 1-0	a15 3-2	O23 0-2	F26 4-1	N06 1-1	D18 2-4	a30 5-1
7 DONCASTER R	a25 2-0	F05 3-1	m07 7-0	D27 4-1	S11 0-3	O16 0-2		a09 5-1	a04 2-0	M12 2-0	a23 1-3	J22 6-0	S25 2-2	M26 3-2	a19 2-2	O30 3-1	S06 1-2	a15 3-1	N13 4-1	A28 2-2	O09 4-1	F19 2-2
8 DURHAM C	D27 2-0	D25 0-2	O09 1-1	a30 2-1	O23 2-1	F19 1-2	N20 2-2		S08 0-1	S25 2-1	a18 4-2	M05 3-3	M19 2-2	J22 1-3	D04 0-1	S11 4-2	F05 1-5	a16 1-2	A28 0-3	D18 3-0	a02 3-1	N06 1-0
9 HALIFAX T	F26 4-3	a02 1-1	F05 5-1	O23 2-0	N06 3-1	S11 3-1	a30 2-1	A30 1-2		J22 2-1	O02 2-1	M19 4-1	N20 2-2	J01 1-0	M05 4-2	D25 1-1	A28 4-1	D18 2-2	a19 2-0	S25 1-1	D04 0-0	a16 0-1
10 HARTLEPOOLS U	S18 3-1	D04 0-1	A28 1-1	N06 2-4	a16 1-2	D25 1-1	O23 3-0	F12 4-0	S04 0-1		J29 1-1	N20 3-2	a30 4-0	F26 3-2	M19 3-1	J01 2-0	J03 1-2	S22 1-3	O02 2-1	a02 2-2	M05 2-1	D18 4-0
11 LINCOLN C	S13 4-0	N06 4-0	S25 3-1	M05 5-1	M19 3-1	F05 3-3	D04 0-0	a15 5-0	F19 3-1	S11 1-2		O09 1-4	a02 4-1	D27 2-3	D18 1-2	A28 1-1	J22 1-3	a30 1-3	S06 1-2	O23 3-3	a16 2-0	N20 2-2
12 NELSON	M12 7-0	S13 4-0	M26 3-0	F12 1-0	a18 0-3	N13 7-1	S04 5-1	O16 1-1	O30 0-0	a09 6-2	F26 2-1		S15 2-0	a05 3-1	S18 5-3	a23 1-2	J08 6-1	J29 1-0	m07 0-2	O02 3-2	J15 4-0	J01 3-0
13 NEW BRIGHTON	M26 0-1	A28 4-0	J08 3-1	S08 3-1	D27 1-0	a23 3-0	F12 0-2	O30 3-1	a09 0-3	D11 2-1	N13 1-1	a27 7-2		M12 1-2	F26 3-0	O16 4-1	m07 1-2	O02 5-0	J22 0-0	a15 3-1	S18 3-1	J29 2-1
14 ROCHDALE	J15 2-1	M05 5-0	a19 5-1	a16 3-0	D18 8-1	A31 3-1	N06 7-2	S04 1-3	a18 2-0	O09 3-0	D25 7-3	a30 2-1	O23 1-1		N20 2-1	S25 1-0	F19 2-0	a02 4-0	J29 3-1	D04 4-4	M19 4-1	S18 3-1
15 ROTHERHAM U	J24 1-1	F19 5-0	M12 2-0	J22 1-1	S25 0-4	A28 2-1	J01 1-3	a23 3-1	O16 2-4	O30 5-3	m07 2-4	F05 2-3	O09 0-0	D11 1-1		N13 1-2	M26 1-2	D27 2-2	J08 2-2	S11 4-1	N01 2-0	A30 2-0
16 SOUTHPORT	S04 2-1	D18 4-1	a15 3-0	N20 2-1	a30 2-1	S28 2-2	M19 2-0	m03 4-5	D27 0-0	A31 1-0	J15 2-3	D04 3-4	M05 7-2	F12 1-1	a02 2-0		O09 2-2	N06 0-3	S18 1-3	a16 6-1	O02 2-2	O23 6-0
17 STOCKPORT CO	F08 3-3	a30 6-2	D27 7-0	a02 1-2	D04 4-0	J01 3-1	A30 1-0	S18 4-0	J15 1-3	a18 3-3	S04 3-3	a16 4-1	D18 1-0	O02 3-0	N06 3-1	F26 2-4		M19 2-2	F12 2-1	N20 0-2	O23 4-1	M05 3-2
18 STOKE C	a23 1-0	S25 7-0	O16 4-0	A28 0-0	F05 3-2	M12 2-1	a18 0-0	J08 4-0	m07 5-1	S13 3-1	J01 2-0	S11 4-1	F19 1-1	N13 3-1	D25 4-1	M26 4-0	O30 0-1		a09 2-0	J22 4-1	A30 2-0	O09 2-0
19 TRANMERE R	a18 2-1	D27 2-1	J01 7-2	D04 1-2	M05 3-2	O09 1-0	a02 1-1	J15 8-3	a15 0-0	F19 2-0	S20 1-1	D18 2-3	S04 4-1	S11 0-1	a16 4-0	F05 3-0	S25 0-0	N20 1-1		a30 6-0	N06 3-1	M19 3-2
20 WALSALL	O16 5-1	S06 0-0	O30 1-0	S18 1-0	O09 0-1	M26 2-3	J15 1-0	m07 1-1	F12 0-1	N13 2-2	M12 1-2	F19 4-1	a18 0-1	a23 4-1	J29 3-2	a25 1-1	a09 1-0	S04 0-1	J24 5-1		D25 3-2	S27 0-1
21 WIGAN B	a09 3-0	S11 1-4	D13 8-0	S20 1-2	M28 1-2	m07 2-2	J08 1-1	N13 3-0	J03 1-1	O16 3-0	F28 3-2	A28 2-1	F05 3-2	O30 0-3	a18 0-0	F19 3-1	M12 2-0	S06 0-3	M26 1-1	D27 5-2		S25 1-1
22 WREXHAM	N13 5-0	J22 1-1	a23 0-2	a15 1-0	A28 3-1	a06 3-1	O02 0-1	M26 3-1	J08 1-2	m07 4-0	a27 1-1	D27 2-2	S11 2-2	F05 2-2	S08 3-0	M12 3-0	O16 2-1	F26 2-6	O30 0-1	S15 1-2	M02 2-0	

Division 3 South

	ABERDARE A	BOURNEMOUTH	BRENTFORD	BRIGHTON & HA	BRISTOL C	BRISTOL R	CHARLTON A	COVENTRY C	CRYSTAL P	EXETER C	GILLINGHAM	LUTON T	MERTHYR T	MILLWALL	NEWPORT CO	NORTHAMPTON T	NORWICH C	PLYMOUTH A	Q.P.R.	SOUTHEND U	SWINDON T	WATFORD
1 ABERDARE A		A28 2-1	a23 3-1	m07 2-2	D25 3-7	a09 2-1	J01 0-0	a18 0-7	F26 2-3	M26 3-1	F12 2-1	M12 0-1	O30 1-2	S06 1-3	S11 0-1	J08 6-1	O16 1-2	J22 5-6	S20 0-2	F05 1-0	D11 1-4	O02 3-2
2 BOURNEMOUTH	J15 3-0		M16 3-1	M02 1-0	a18 2-0	O30 0-1	F26 0-3	F12 1-2	S18 1-1	M12 4-3	S04 4-2	J26 2-0	O16 1-1	M26 0-1	D27 2-1	a09 3-1	a23 0-1	J01 6-2	O02 6-2	m07 3-0	S22 1-2	J29 6-0
3 BRENTFORD	D04 1-4	a02 0-0		A28 4-0	N06 3-0	F12 0-2	M19 2-0	O23 7-3	M05 3-0	F26 6-1	a30 0-0	J01 2-2	a15 1-1	S18 0-0	a16 1-1	J22 1-1	D27 3-0	N20 0-0	S11 4-2	S06 3-1	O02 2-2	D18 3-0
4 BRIGHTON & H.A.	D18 3-1	a16 0-2	J15 1-1		N20 3-0	J29 7-0	a02 3-2	M19 1-1	S01 1-1	F12 5-2	M05 3-2	a15 1-1	O02 4-0	S04 3-1	a30 1-0	D25 2-0	O06 3-2	D04 1-2	N06 4-1	F26 2-1	S18 9-3	O23 4-1
5 BRISTOL C	D27 2-1	a15 2-0	M26 1-0	a09 0-2		F26 3-1	O02 4-1	S18 3-0	J29 5-4	O16 3-2	J15 9-4	a23 6-0	m07 3-0	O30 4-1	S01 4-1	N13 4-3	F09 1-1	S22 4-2	F12 1-0	F23 5-1	M12 2-0	S04 5-0
6 BRISTOL R	N20 4-0	M19 2-1	S25 1-3	S11 0-0	O09 0-5		O23 1-1	D18 1-2	a30 4-1	D28 3-1	a16 2-1	A28 1-2	S06 2-1	a19 1-1	a02 4-0	F05 5-2	J22 1-0	N06 2-2	M05 4-1	D25 5-1	a18 3-1	D04 0-2
7 CHARLTON A	S16 5-1	O09 1-3	O30 1-1	M23 1-0	F19 0-1	M12 3-1		J29 4-2	S04 1-2	m07 1-0	D25 3-0	M03 2-2	J31 3-2	F12 1-1	a28 3-0	M26 5-2	a09 2-0	a18 1-1	S18 2-0	a23 1-0	O16 2-2	J15 2-1
8 COVENTRY C	a19 1-0	S25 6-2	M12 3-1	O30 1-2	F05 2-5	m07 2-2	S11 1-0		D25 3-1	a23 0-0	S06 0-2	N13 4-1	J08 5-1	O16 1-4	O09 3-1	A28 0-3	M26 1-0	F19 3-3	J22 1-0	a09 1-1	D28 1-3	J01 5-1
9 CRYSTAL P	O09 0-0	F05 2-2	O16 4-3	J01 2-0	S11 4-2	M16 7-4	J22 2-1	D27 1-2		F09 1-0	a18 2-2	M26 1-1	a09 1-1	m07 1-6	F19 6-2	M12 3-0	O30 7-1	S25 1-1	A28 2-1	N13 5-3	a23 5-0	S08 0-1
10 EXETER C	N06 2-1	O23 4-0	O09 3-1	S25 0-0	M05 1-1	S15 1-1	D18 1-0	D04 8-1	a16 3-1		a02 5-1	S11 1-2	A28 3-0	a18 1-1	M19 2-1	F19 3-2	F05 1-0	D27 0-2	a30 0-2	J22 2-0	J01 3-1	N20 2-0
11 GILLINGHAM	S25 2-1	J22 1-0	M30 1-2	O16 2-3	A28 1-1	M23 2-0	D27 1-1	S15 2-0	a15 2-1	N13 3-2		F19 0-0	M26 0-1	a23 2-1	J08 0-1	m07 1-2	M12 1-0	S11 4-1	S01 2-2	O30 2-3	a09 4-4	F26 3-0
12 LUTON T	O23 3-3	a30 4-0	A30 2-1	a18 4-0	D04 0-0	J15 1-1	a16 1-0	a02 4-1	N06 1-0	J29 2-2	O02 2-1		S18 2-1	D25 6-0	M05 4-1	S13 2-0	O09 2-2	D18 3-3	N20 2-0	F12 0-0	S04 1-1	M19 2-2
13 MERTHYR T	M19 2-2	M05 4-6	a19 1-0	F19 1-0	D18 1-1	A30 3-2	a30 3-0	a16 1-0	m02 1-2	J15 3-3	N06 2-0	F05 4-1		S13 1-0	S04 1-2	O09 2-0	S25 1-1	O23 5-1	D04 4-0	S11 0-1	D27 1-2	a02 1-1
14 MILLWALL	a16 1-0	N06 1-1	F05 3-0	J22 1-1	M19 0-1	O02 2-3	S25 3-0	M14 1-0	D18 1-0	a15 4-2	D04 2-0	D27 7-0	S20 3-1		N20 4-1	S11 4-2	A28 6-1	a02 1-3	O23 2-1	J01 2-0	F26 4-1	a30 3-1
15 NEWPORT CO	J29 5-2	D25 2-1	a25 0-0	M31 0-1	S09 0-0	N13 1-0	S30 2-1	F26 4-1	O02 2-1	O30 2-0	S18 1-0	O16 3-2	J22 4-3	D11 1-1		J01 1-0	m07 0-0	A28 2-1	a15 0-2	M12 3-0	M26 5-3	F12 2-1
16 NORTHAMPTON T	a30 2-1	N20 2-2	S04 2-3	D27 0-0	a02 2-0	S18 3-0	N06 0-1	J15 2-1	O23 1-1	O02 2-2	D18 2-1	D28 2-1	F26 2-0	a07 1-4	D04 1-2		S06 3-0	a16 2-1	M19 1-0	a19 2-1	F12 1-0	M05 3-2
17 NORWICH C	M05 2-2	D04 4-1	D25 2-1	O28 0-2	a16 1-1	S04 2-0	N20 2-3	N06 3-0	M19 0-1	S18 4-4	O23 0-0	F26 3-2	F12 4-0	J15 0-2	D18 1-0	S20 6-1		a30 0-2	a02 0-1	O02 1-1	J29 2-1	a18 4-0
18 PLYMOUTH A	S04 2-0	S08 1-1	a09 2-1	a23 2-0	m04 4-2	M26 3-2	a15 3-1	O02 3-0	F12 7-1	D25 2-0	J29 0-0	m07 1-0	M12 1-1	N13 1-1	J15 4-1	S01 3-0	a25 2-1		D11 2-0	O16 2-1	O30 3-1	S18 4-0
19 Q.P.R.	S30 3-0	F19 1-1	m05 1-1	M26 2-2	S25 1-2	O16 2-2	F05 2-1	S04 1-1	J15 0-2	F24 1-1	J01 1-1	a09 1-0	a23 5-1	M12 1-1	a18 2-0	O30 4-2	N13 4-0	O09 4-2		J08 3-2	m07 0-1	D25 2-4
20 SOUTHEND U	S18 5-1	D18 0-3	S15 3-1	O09 0-1	a30 0-1	D27 2-1	D04 5-0	N20 3-1	a02 3-1	S04 1-2	M19 1-0	S25 2-1	J29 3-1	A30 1-1	O23 5-0	a18 2-0	F19 3-3	M05 1-2	a16 0-3		J15 2-2	N06 2-0
21 SWINDON T	a02 3-2	S13 2-0	M09 4-2	F05 2-2	O23 2-2	a15 3-5	M05 2-0	a30 2-2	D04 6-1	A30 4-2	N20 1-0	J22 2-0	D25 3-2	O09 3-0	N06 3-1	S25 3-1	S11 3-2	M19 1-2	D18 6-2	A28 5-1		a16 4-2
22 WATFORD	F19 2-2	S11 1-2	m07 0-0	M12 1-0	J22 0-1	a23 3-3	A28 1-0	S01 1-0	S15 1-2	a09 1-0	O09 4-0	O30 2-1	N13 4-1	D28 2-4	S25 0-0	O16 4-0	a15 1-1	F05 1-4	D27 1-2	M26 4-2	J08 2-2	

League Tables

Division 1

	P	W	D	L	F	A	W	D	L	F	A	Pts
Newcastle U	42	19	1	1	64	20	6	5	10	32	38	56
Huddersfield T	42	13	6	2	41	19	4	11	6	35	41	51
Sunderland	42	15	3	3	70	28	6	4	11	28	42	49
Bolton W	42	15	5	1	54	19	4	5	12	30	43	48
Burnley	42	15	4	2	55	30	4	5	12	36	50	47
West Ham U	42	9	6	6	50	36	10	2	9	36	34	46
Leicester C	42	13	4	4	58	33	4	8	9	27	37	46
Sheffield U	42	12	6	3	46	33	5	4	12	28	53	44
Liverpool	42	13	4	4	47	27	5	3	13	22	34	43
Aston Villa	42	11	4	6	51	34	7	3	11	30	49	43
Arsenal	42	12	5	4	47	30	5	4	12	30	56	43
Derby Co	42	14	4	3	60	28	3	3	15	26	45	41
Tottenham H	42	11	4	6	48	33	5	5	11	28	45	41
Cardiff C	42	12	3	6	31	17	4	6	11	24	48	41
Manchester U	42	9	8	4	29	19	4	6	11	23	45	40
Sheffield W	42	15	3	3	49	29	0	6	15	26	63	39
Birmingham C	42	13	3	5	36	17	4	1	16	28	56	38
Blackburn R	42	9	5	7	40	40	6	3	12	37	56	38
Bury	42	8	5	8	43	38	4	7	10	25	39	36
Everton	42	10	6	5	35	30	2	4	15	29	60	34
Leeds U	42	9	7	5	43	31	2	1	18	26	57	30
W.B.A.	42	10	4	7	47	33	1	4	16	18	53	30

Division 2

	P	W	D	L	F	A	W	D	L	F	A	Pts
Middlesbrough	42	18	2	1	78	23	9	6	6	44	37	62
Portsmouth	42	14	4	3	58	17	9	4	8	29	32	54
Manchester C	42	15	3	3	65	23	7	7	7	43	38	54
Chelsea	42	13	7	1	40	17	7	5	9	22	35	52
Nottingham F	42	14	6	1	57	23	4	8	9	23	32	50
Preston N.E.	42	14	4	3	54	29	6	5	10	20	43	49
Hull C	42	13	4	4	43	19	7	3	11	20	33	47
Port Vale	42	11	6	4	50	26	5	7	9	38	52	45
Blackpool	42	13	5	3	65	26	5	3	13	30	54	44
Oldham A	42	12	3	6	50	37	7	3	11	24	47	44
Barnsley	42	13	5	3	56	23	4	4	13	32	64	43
Swansea T	42	13	5	3	44	21	3	6	12	24	51	43
Southampton	42	9	8	4	35	22	6	4	11	25	40	42
Reading	42	14	1	6	47	20	2	7	12	17	52	40
Wolverhampton W	42	10	4	7	54	30	4	3	14	19	45	35
Notts Co	42	11	4	6	45	24	4	1	16	25	72	35
Grimsby T	42	6	7	8	39	39	5	5	11	35	52	34
Fulham	42	11	4	6	39	31	2	4	15	19	61	34
South Shields	42	10	8	3	49	25	1	3	17	22	71	33
Clapton O	42	9	3	9	37	35	3	4	14	23	61	31
Darlington	42	10	3	8	53	42	2	3	16	26	56	30
Bradford C	42	6	4	11	30	28	1	5	15	20	60	23

Division 3 North

	P	W	D	L	F	A	W	D	L	F	A	Pts
Stoke C	42	17	3	1	57	11	10	6	5	35	29	63
Rochdale	42	18	2	1	72	22	8	4	9	33	43	58
Bradford P.A.	42	18	3	0	74	21	6	4	11	27	38	55
Halifax T	42	13	6	2	46	23	8	5	8	24	30	53
Nelson	42	16	2	3	64	20	6	5	10	40	55	51
Stockport Co	42	13	4	4	60	31	9	3	9	33	38	*49
Chesterfield	42	15	4	2	65	24	6	1	14	27	44	47
Doncaster R	42	13	4	4	58	27	5	7	9	23	38	47
Tranmere R	42	13	5	3	54	22	6	3	12	31	45	46
New Brighton	42	14	2	5	49	21	4	8	9	30	46	46
Lincoln C	42	9	5	7	50	33	6	7	8	40	45	42
Southport	42	11	5	5	54	32	4	4	13	26	53	39
Wrexham	42	10	5	6	41	26	4	5	12	24	47	38
Walsall	42	10	4	7	35	22	4	6	11	33	59	38
Crewe A	42	11	5	5	46	28	3	4	14	25	53	37
Ashington	42	9	8	4	42	30	3	4	14	18	60	36
Hartlepool U	42	11	4	6	43	26	3	2	16	23	55	34
Wigan B	42	10	6	5	44	28	1	4	16	22	55	32
Rotherham U	42	8	6	7	41	35	2	6	13	29	57	32
Durham C	42	9	4	8	35	35	3	2	16	23	70	30
Accrington S	42	9	3	9	45	38	1	4	16	17	60	27
Barrow	42	5	6	10	22	40	2	2	17	12	77	22

*Stockport County deducted two points for fielding an ineligible player

Division 3 South

	P	W	D	L	F	A	W	D	L	F	A	Pts
Bristol C	42	19	1	1	71	24	8	7	6	33	30	62
Plymouth A	42	17	4	0	52	14	8	6	7	43	47	60
Millwall	42	16	2	3	55	19	7	8	6	34	32	56
Brighton & H.A.	42	15	4	2	61	24	6	7	8	18	26	53
Swindon T	42	16	3	2	64	31	5	6	10	36	54	51
Crystal Palace	42	12	6	3	57	33	6	3	12	27	48	45
Bournemouth	42	13	2	6	49	24	5	6	10	29	42	44
Luton T	42	12	9	0	48	19	3	5	13	20	47	44
Newport Co	42	15	4	2	40	20	4	2	15	17	51	44
Bristol R	42	12	4	5	46	28	4	5	12	32	52	41
Brentford	42	10	9	2	46	20	3	5	13	24	41	40
Exeter C	42	14	4	3	46	18	1	6	14	30	55	40
Charlton A	42	13	5	3	44	22	3	3	15	16	39	40
Q.P.R.	42	9	8	4	41	27	6	1	14	24	44	39
Coventry C	42	11	4	6	44	33	4	3	14	27	53	37
Norwich C	42	10	5	6	41	25	2	6	13	18	46	35
Merthyr T	42	11	5	5	42	25	2	4	15	21	55	35
Northampton T	42	13	4	4	36	23	2	1	18	23	64	35
Southend U	42	12	3	6	44	25	2	3	16	20	52	34
Gillingham	42	10	5	6	36	26	1	5	15	18	46	32
Watford	42	9	6	6	36	27	3	2	16	21	60	32
Aberdare A	42	8	2	11	38	48	1	5	15	24	53	25

Football League Records

Top scorers: Div 1, W.Dean (Everton) 60 goals; Div 2, J.Cookson (West Bromwich Albion) 38 goals; Div 3 N, J.Smith (Stockport County) 38 goals; Div 3 S, D.Morris (Swindon Town) 38 goals.

Aberdare Athletic failed to gain re-election, Torquay United were elected in their place. Walsall transferred to Division Three South.

Dixie Dean, whose record 60 goals for Everton as they lifted the title will surely never be beaten. Dean scored a hat-trick in the last match, against Arsenal, to clinch the record.

Tom Johnson netted 19 goals as Manchester City won Division Two. The following season he hit 38 goals, still a City record for a Division One season.

DIVISION 1

	ARSENAL	ASTON VILLA	BIRMINGHAM	BLACKBURN R	BOLTON W	BURNLEY	BURY	CARDIFF C	DERBY CO	EVERTON	HUDDERSFIELD T	LEICESTER C	LIVERPOOL	MANCHESTER U	MIDDLESBROUGH	NEWCASTLE U	PORTSMOUTH	SHEFFIELD U	SHEFFIELD W	SUNDERLAND	TOTTENHAM H	WEST HAM U
1 ARSENAL		J21 0-3	M31 2-2	M17 3-2	O29 1-2	A31 4-1	D31 3-1	a06 3-0	F04 3-4	D24 3-2	a14 0-0	O15 2-2	M07 6-3	a28 0-1	N12 3-1	D10 4-1	M28 0-2	S03 6-1	m02 1-1	S17 2-1	J02 1-1	O01 2-2
2 ASTON VILLA	S10 2-2		M17 1-1	N26 2-0	a28 2-2	F08 3-1	S24 1-0	a14 3-1	D27 0-1	D10 2-3	m02 3-0	A27 0-3	J07 3-4	M31 3-1	O08 5-1	O29 3-0	S05 7-2	F11 1-0	D24 5-4	O15 4-2	N12 1-2	a09 1-0
3 BIRMINGHAM	N19 1-1	N05 1-1		F04 2-1	O01 1-1	M24 4-0	O22 2-2	S17 1-3	m05 2-1	J21 2-2	A29 3-1	D03 0-2	a21 2-0	S03 0-0	O15 3-2	a10 0-2	a07 2-0	M10 4-1	M07 1-0	D26 1-1	D31 3-2	D17 1-2
4 BLACKBURN R	N05 4-1	a07 0-1	S24 4-4		J07 1-6	A27 2-1	m05 0-1	S05 0-0	a26 3-2	J02 4-2	O08 1-1	O22 0-0	M10 2-1	S19 3-0	F23 3-0	F11 1-0	a24 6-0	D17 1-0	S10 3-1	D03 0-0	F25 2-1	N19 1-0
5 BOLTON W	M10 1-1	D17 3-1	F11 3-2	S03 3-1		N05 7-1	J21 2-1	D31 2-1	J02 1-3	S05 1-1	F25 0-1	M24 3-3	O22 2-1	a06 3-2	S24 0-0	O08 1-2	N19 3-1	m05 1-1	F29 2-0	a07 1-2	D26 4-1	a21 4-0
6 BURNLEY	S05 1-2	S17 4-2	N12 2-1	D31 3-1	M17 2-2		S03 2-3	D24 2-1	O01 4-2	a28 3-5	D10 0-1	D27 5-1	a06 2-2	N26 4-0	M03 1-1	M31 5-1	O15 2-0	J21 5-3	O29 3-1	F04 3-0	a14 2-2	F18 0-0
7 BURY	A27 5-1	F04 0-0	M03 2-3	D24 2-3	S10 1-0	J07 2-0		a28 3-0	F18 3-0	N26 2-3	M31 2-3	J02 2-1	S19 5-2	a14 4-3	O29 1-4	N12 1-4	D26 4-0	S17 1-0	M17 4-2	O01 5-3	D10 1-2	O15 3-1
8 CARDIFF C	a09 2-2	D03 2-1	F22 2-1	S12 1-1	A27 2-1	m05 3-2	D17 0-1		N19 4-4	D27 2-0	F11 4-0	M10 3-0	N05 1-1	F25 2-0	S10 1-1	S24 3-1	O22 3-1	a07 2-2	J07 1-1	a21 3-1	O08 2-1	M24 1-5
9 DERBY CO	S24 4-0	D26 5-0	D24 4-1	D10 6-0	a14 1-0	F11 3-4	O08 5-2	M31 7-1		N12 0-3	M17 0-0	S10 2-1	F15 2-3	M28 5-0	a28 2-1	S05 1-1	J07 2-2	F25 2-1	N26 4-6	a09 1-0	O29 1-1	A27 2-3
10 EVERTON	m05 3-3	a21 3-2	S10 5-2	a06 4-1	S14 2-2	D17 4-1	a07 1-1	D26 2-1	M24 2-2		S24 2-2	N05 7-1	O15 1-1	O08 5-2	J07 3-1	a18 3-0	M10 0-0	D03 0-0	A27 4-0	N19 0-1	F11 2-5	O22 7-0
11 HUDDERSFIELD T	D03 2-1	O22 1-1	a09 2-0	M14 3-1	O15 1-0	a25 1-2	N19 3-0	O01 8-2	N05 2-1	F04 4-1		D17 3-1	a07 2-4	S17 4-2	a10 2-4	A27 1-3	m05 4-1	a30 0-1	D26 1-0	M10 4-2	J21 4-2	J07 5-2
12 LEICESTER C	F25 3-2	D31 3-0	a14 3-0	a30 6-0	N12 4-2	D26 5-0	a09 2-2	O29 4-1	J21 4-0	M17 1-0	a28 1-2		O08 1-1	O01 1-0	D10 3-3	N26 3-0	F04 6-2	A29 3-1	M31 2-2	S03 3-3	D24 6-1	S17 2-3
13 LIVERPOOL	D27 0-2	S03 0-0	D10 2-3	O29 4-2	M03 4-2	J02 2-2	A31 5-1	M17 1-2	S17 5-2	F25 3-3	N26 4-2	a25 1-1		D24 2-0	M31 1-1	a14 0-0	O01 8-2	D31 2-1	N12 5-2	J21 2-5	a28 2-0	F04 1-3
14 MANCHESTER U	D17 4-1	N19 5-1	J07 1-1	D26 1-1	a09 2-1	a07 4-3	D03 0-1	O15 2-2	O22 5-0	M14 1-0	M07 0-0	F11 5-2	m05 6-1		A27 3-0	S10 1-7	N05 2-0	a21 2-3	S07 1-1	a25 2-1	S24 3-0	M10 1-1
15 MIDDLESBROUGH	a18 2-2	M21 0-0	F25 1-1	S17 2-0	F04 2-5	O22 2-3	M10 6-1	J21 1-2	D17 3-3	S03 4-2	J02 3-1	a21 1-1	N19 1-1	D31 1-2		D26 1-1	D03 5-1	N05 3-0	O01 3-3	m05 0-3	A31 3-1	a07 2-2
16 NEWCASTLE U	a21 1-1	M10 7-5	J02 1-1	O01 0-1	F18 2-2	N19 1-1	M24 2-3	F04 2-0	S14 4-3	S17 2-2	D31 2-3	a07 1-5	D03 1-1	J21 4-1	D27 3-3		D17 1-3	O22 1-0	O15 4-3	N05 3-1	S03 4-1	m05 3-1
17 PORTSMOUTH	O08 2-3	A31 3-1	N26 2-2	N12 2-2	M31 1-0	F25 1-0	D27 1-0	M03 3-0	S03 2-2	O29 1-3	D24 2-1	S24 2-0	F11 1-0	M17 1-0	a14 4-1	a28 0-1		a09 4-1	D10 0-0	F18 3-5	S17 3-0	J21 2-1
18 SHEFFIELD U	J07 6-4	O01 0-3	O29 3-1	a28 2-3	D24 4-3	S10 5-2	M12 3-1	N26 3-4	O15 1-0	a14 1-3	N12 1-7	S05 1-1	A27 1-1	D10 2-1	M17 4-1	a23 1-1	J02 3-1		S24 1-1	a16 5-1	M31 3-1	D26 6-2
19 SHEFFIELD W	O22 1-1	m05 2-0	O08 2-3	J21 4-1	S17 3-0	M10 5-0	N05 4-0	S03 3-3	a07 2-2	D31 1-2	D27 0-5	N19 1-2	M24 4-0	A29 0-2	F11 2-3	F25 0-0	a21 2-0	F04 3-3		D17 0-0	a10 4-2	D03 2-0
20 SUNDERLAND	M14 5-1	F25 2-3	S07 4-2	a14 1-0	N26 1-1	S24 2-3	F11 1-0	D10 0-2	a06 0-1	M31 0-2	O29 3-0	J07 2-2	S10 2-1	N12 4-1	D24 1-0	M17 1-1	A27 3-3	O08 0-1	a28 2-3		M28 0-0	J02 3-2
21 TOTTENHAM H	a07 2-0	M24 2-1	A27 1-0	O15 1-1	F06 1-2	D03 5-0	a21 1-4	M05 1-0	M10 1-2	O01 1-3	S10 2-2	S22 2-1	D17 3-1	F04 4-1	S12 4-2	J07 5-2	M19 0-3	N19 2-2	a06 1-3	O22 3-1		N05 5-3
22 WEST HAM U	F11 2-2	a06 0-0	a28 3-3	M31 4-3	D10 2-0	O08 2-0	F25 1-2	N12 2-0	D31 2-2	M03 0-0	S03 4-2	M12 4-0	S24 3-1	O29 1-2	N26 4-5	D24 5-2	S10 4-2	D27 1-1	a14 1-2	S01 2-4	M17 1-1	

DIVISION 2

	BARNSLEY	BLACKPOOL	BRISTOL C	CHELSEA	CLAPTON O	FULHAM	GRIMSBY T	HULL C	LEEDS U	MANCHESTER C	NOTTINGHAM F	NOTTS CO	OLDHAM A	PORT VALE	PRESTON N.E.	READING	SOUTHAMPTON	SOUTH SHIELDS	STOKE C	SWANSEA T	W.B.A.	WOLVERHAMPTON W
1 BARNSLEY		a28 2-1	O29 2-3	D24 3-1	S24 4-2	J28 8-4	a14 1-4	A27 1-1	S26 2-1	D26 0-3	a10 2-1	M31 0-0	D10 0-1	F20 4-2	J07 2-1	N26 2-0	N12 0-1	O15 0-0	M19 3-1	S10 3-3	M17 2-4	O01 2-2
2 BLACKPOOL	D17 1-3		S24 6-2	J07 2-4	S10 0-1	m05 4-0	J02 4-5	M10 2-1	N19 0-2	O22 2-2	M24 5-3	F25 3-3	A29 1-2	D03 1-6	N05 4-1	D26 3-1	O08 1-0	a21 4-1	F11 3-1	A27 2-2	J28 4-3	a07 3-0
3 BRISTOL C	M10 2-0	F04 2-2		O01 1-1	F18 5-1	O22 3-0	J21 0-0	a21 0-1	D17 1-2	D03 2-0	a07 0-0	D31 1-2	S03 2-1	A31 4-0	N19 1-3	S17 4-1	D26 3-0	m05 1-1	a06 4-0	M24 2-1	O15 0-1	N05 4-1
4 CHELSEA	m05 1-2	S03 3-0	F11 5-2		J28 1-0	J21 2-1	M14 4-0	O22 2-0	a21 2-3	M24 0-1	N19 2-1	S07 5-0	a06 2-1	a07 1-0	M10 2-1	D31 0-0	F25 0-2	D03 6-0	O08 1-0	N05 4-0	S24 1-1	D17 2-0
5 CLAPTON O	F04 2-0	J21 2-5	O08 4-2	S17 2-1		N05 3-2	D31 1-2	M24 0-0	D03 2-1	N19 0-2	a21 2-2	a09 0-1	a16 2-0	D17 0-1	O22 1-1	S03 3-0	A29 2-0	a07 2-2	F25 3-2	M10 1-1	F11 0-0	m05 0-0
6 FULHAM	S17 3-1	D24 2-2	M03 5-0	S10 1-1	M17 2-0		N26 2-2	M26 0-2	O15 1-1	a09 1-1	S15 2-0	D10 2-1	a14 1-1	O01 4-0	A27 2-2	a28 1-0	M31 1-0	F18 2-0	N12 1-5	J07 3-2	O29 3-1	F04 7-0
7 GRIMSBY T	D03 3-1	a06 3-3	S10 1-4	D26 1-1	A27 2-2	a07 1-0		F25 1-1	O22 3-2	N05 4-1	M10 2-1	F11 1-0	O08 1-2	N19 3-0	m05 4-6	A30 3-3	S24 2-2	M24 4-1	M06 1-2	D17 1-2	J07 0-6	a21 0-1
8 HULL C	D31 2-1	O29 2-2	D10 1-1	M03 0-2	N12 2-2	D27 3-2	O15 0-1		F04 3-1	a16 0-0	O01 2-0	a28 1-1	D24 2-2	J21 1-0	S05 0-0	M17 0-1	N26 1-0	S17 1-0	a14 1-0	a06 0-2	M31 1-1	S03 2-0
9 LEEDS U	A29 2-2	M31 4-0	J28 3-2	D10 5-0	a14 4-0	F25 2-1	M03 0-0	S24 2-0		a25 0-1	S10 4-0	M17 6-0	O29 1-0	D27 3-0	F11 2-4	N12 6-2	S03 2-0	D31 3-0	D24 5-1	O08 5-0	N26 1-2	a10 3-0
10 MANCHESTER C	J02 7-3	M03 4-1	a14 4-2	N12 0-1	M31 5-3	a06 2-1	M17 2-0	O08 2-1	S17 2-1		F04 3-3	D24 3-1	O01 3-1	S03 1-0	F25 2-2	O29 4-1	a28 6-1	J21 3-0	N26 4-0	A29 7-4	D10 3-1	D31 3-0
11 NOTTINGHAM F	a09 1-1	N12 4-1	N26 1-1	M31 2-2	D10 4-3	A29 7-0	O29 5-2	F11 1-1	J21 2-2	S24 4-5		S17 2-1	M17 2-1	a26 0-2	O08 3-1	M29 5-3	D24 1-1	S03 7-2	a28 0-2	F25 0-2	a14 0-2	D26 3-2
12 NOTTS CO	N19 9-0	O15 3-1	A27 1-2	O06 0-1	a06 3-0	a21 0-1	O01 3-2	D17 1-1	N05 2-2	m05 2-1	F22 1-2		F04 2-1	O22 2-4	a07 6-2	F18 1-1	S10 0-0	M10 4-1	J07 1-2	D03 2-0	D27 3-0	M24 1-2
13 OLDHAM A	a21 0-1	S05 6-0	J07 4-1	a09 2-1	D27 5-0	D03 4-2	F18 1-0	m05 5-0	M10 0-1	F11 3-2	N05 4-1	S24 0-0		M24 4-1	D17 0-0	O15 3-2	J31 3-1	O22 2-2	S10 3-1	a07 0-1	A27 3-1	N19 3-0
14 PORT VALE	O08 2-1	a14 3-0	S19 5-1	N26 1-1	a28 0-0	F11 4-1	M31 2-2	S10 1-2	D26 1-2	J07 1-2	A27 2-2	M03 3-0	N12 1-0		F06 2-0	D10 3-0	O29 4-0	a06 2-3	M17 0-0	S24 2-0	D24 4-1	F25 2-2
15 PRESTON N.E.	S03 1-2	M17 2-1	M31 5-1	O29 0-3	M03 0-0	D31 1-0	D24 3-0	A29 4-2	O01 5-1	O15 1-0	M05 5-0	N26 4-0	a28 1-1	S17 4-0		a06 4-0	a14 1-2	F04 7-2	D10 2-0	D26 4-2	N12 3-3	J21 5-4
16 READING	a07 1-1	D27 1-0	F15 3-2	A27 1-2	J07 4-0	D17 2-1	S14 2-2	N05 3-0	M24 0-1	M10 1-1	O22 0-2	O08 2-2	F25 1-0	a21 0-0	a09 2-1		F11 0-0	N19 5-1	S24 1-1	m05 0-0	S10 1-4	D03 2-1
17 SOUTHAMPTON	M24 6-1	F18 2-0	D27 3-2	O15 2-4	S05 1-3	N19 5-2	F04 5-0	a07 2-0	J07 1-4	D17 1-1	m05 2-1	J21 5-1	S17 5-2	M10 1-3	D03 0-0	O01 0-0		N05 3-5	A27 3-6	a21 0-2	a09 3-2	O22 4-1
18 SOUTH SHIELDS	F25 0-0	D10 2-2	D24 1-3	a14 2-1	N26 2-2	O08 2-1	N12 1-2	F22 1-0	A27 1-5	S10 0-1	J07 3-4	O29 2-3	M03 0-3	a09 0-1	S24 2-3	M31 0-0	M17 2-1		J02 2-3	F11 3-1	a28 2-3	S12 2-2
19 STOKE C	O22 0-0	O01 2-0	a09 1-0	F20 1-0	O15 2-0	M24 5-1	S17 0-0	D03 3-1	m05 5-1	a07 2-0	D17 1-3	S03 3-0	J21 3-0	N05 0-2	a21 3-2	F04 4-1	D31 2-1	D27 3-1		N19 1-1	S05 1-1	M10 2-2
20 SWANSEA T	J21 3-0	D31 1-0	N12 1-1	M17 0-0	O29 5-0	S03 2-1	a28 3-2	a09 2-0	F18 1-1	S05 5-3	O15 2-0	a14 1-1	N26 0-0	F04 2-0	D27 0-1	D24 0-1	D10 2-0	O01 6-3	M31 1-1		M03 3-2	S17 6-0
21 W.B.A.	N05 1-1	S17 6-3	F25 0-0	F04 3-0	O01 4-1	M10 4-0	S03 3-1	N19 1-1	a07 0-1	a21 1-1	D03 2-3	D26 2-2	D31 0-0	m05 0-0	M24 2-4	J21 5-3	a10 2-1	D17 3-0	A31 2-4	O22 5-2		F18 4-0
22 WOLVERHAMPTON W	F11 2-1	N26 2-4	M17 5-2	a28 1-2	D24 5-3	S24 3-1	D10 0-1	J07 1-1	a09 0-0	A27 2-2	D27 1-0	N12 2-2	M31 3-1	O15 2-1	S10 2-3	a14 2-1	M03 2-1	S05 2-1	O29 1-2	a30 1-1	O08 4-1	

Season 1927-28

DIVISION 3 NORTH

	ACCRINGTON S	ASHINGTON	BARROW	BRADFORD	BRADFORD C	CHESTERFIELD	CREWE A	DARLINGTON	DONCASTER R	DURHAM C	HALIFAX T	HARTLEPOOLS U	LINCOLN C	NELSON	NEW BRIGHTON	ROCHDALE	ROTHERHAM U	SOUTHPORT	STOCKPORT CO	TRANMERE R	WIGAN B	WREXHAM
1 ACCRINGTON S		F04 3-1	D24 5-1	a14 2-1	O15 1-1	D10 0-0	O01 5-0	S17 0-0	J21 1-3	N12 2-0	F18 3-2	S27 2-2	J02 1-0	D31 7-1	D26 2-1	M17 1-0	O29 3-1	M03 4-1	a28 1-0	F15 2-3	S03 2-4	M31 2-0
2 ASHINGTON	S24 1-1		D10 1-0	M03 0-3	A27 2-2	O29 0-0	A29 0-2	F25 2-3	O08 1-2	J02 2-2	S12 3-3	J28 3-1	S10 4-5	a14 5-1	J07 3-2	J14 5-1	a28 6-0	D24 1-3	M31 4-1	N12 3-0	F11 6-3	M17 2-1
3 BARROW	m05 1-0	a21 1-1		O08 0-0	O22 0-0	F11 2-0	N19 1-1	D03 2-0	a07 0-0	J28 1-2	M24 6-2	a06 2-0	N05 3-3	S29 3-1	M10 2-1	A27 1-3	J07 1-1	S10 3-1	D27 2-3	F25 2-1	D17 6-2	S24 2-2
4 BRADFORD	D03 3-3	O22 5-0	F18 1-1		J28 5-0	S10 1-0	M10 2-0	M24 6-3	N19 0-2	A27 4-0	N05 3-2	a07 3-0	D17 3-0	O15 3-2	m05 2-1	D27 4-1	a10 3-1	S05 5-3	O01 2-0	F04 6-2	a21 5-1	J07 2-0
5 BRADFORD C	F25 2-0	D31 5-0	M03 4-1	S17 2-3		D24 3-3	S03 4-1	A31 0-1	a09 1-0	J14 4-0	J21 0-0	O08 2-1	F11 3-1	N12 9-1	S24 3-1	M31 2-2	M14 3-1	a14 2-0	O29 2-2	M17 3-1	D26 3-0	a28 2-0
6 CHESTERFIELD	J14 3-1	M10 3-0	O01 6-0	J21 0-0	m05 2-0		N05 3-2	O22 1-3	M24 1-0	A29 4-2	J07 3-0	D03 1-3	a07 0-1	F18 6-0	D17 2-3	O15 1-3	D27 2-5	a09 5-2	F04 1-1	S17 2-2	N19 0-0	A27 0-1
7 CREWE A	F11 2-3	a06 3-0	M31 4-1	O29 1-3	J07 2-1	M17 4-1		D26 3-3	F25 4-1	D24 5-2	A27 1-1	S24 4-0	M21 0-0	J02 6-1	S10 1-1	a14 1-1	F08 3-2	a28 0-1	N12 3-0	M03 2-3	O08 1-2	S05 1-1
8 DARLINGTON	J28 3-0	O15 5-1	a14 1-1	N12 1-3	J02 1-2	M03 4-2	a09 1-3		F11 3-0	M17 5-0	a06 2-0	S10 5-0	J07 9-2	a16 4-1	A27 3-0	a28 1-0	D24 4-1	O08 3-1	a23 3-1	M31 3-7	S24 1-0	O29 1-3
9 DONCASTER R	S10 0-0	F18 3-2	J14 4-0	M31 2-0	a06 2-1	N12 4-0	O15 3-1	O01 5-0		O29 5-0	D26 1-1	J07 1-1	A27 3-0	a28 4-2	S05 5-1	D24 5-2	S24 2-0	M17 0-1	a14 0-2	m01 5-2	J28 4-1	M03 1-1
10 DURHAM C	M24 2-1	a18 0-0	S17 4-1	D31 0-1	a07 3-2	S07 2-0	m05 5-1	N05 3-3	M10 1-3		D17 1-1	N19 1-0	a21 0-4	F04 3-0	D03 2-1	O01 3-2	F18 1-4	O15 0-0	J21 1-2	S03 1-3	O22 3-0	a09 1-1
11 HALIFAX T	O08 3-1	S05 6-1	A29 5-2	M17 1-1	S10 2-1	S03 1-2	D31 0-0	S19 2-1	D27 0-1	a28 3-1		F11 4-1	S24 3-1	J14 5-1	a23 1-1	a10 1-1	a14 0-0	M26 1-0	M03 1-3	O29 2-2	F25 2-2	D24 4-1
12 HARTLEPOOLS U	a09 0-2	S17 4-1	J02 6-2	J14 1-1	F18 2-3	a14 1-0	F04 4-3	J21 0-1	S03 1-0	D10 2-1	O01 0-1		D26 1-2	M17 4-5	O15 3-3	O29 0-2	M03 1-3	N12 2-1	D24 2-1	a28 2-0	D31 1-1	a21 4-2
13 LINCOLN C	a06 3-1	J21 3-1	M17 5-0	a28 2-0	O01 2-2	a11 0-0	S17 5-2	S03 1-0	D31 2-0	D14 2-1	F04 5-2	D27 1-5		O29 0-0	F18 1-2	M03 3-1	N12 4-1	M31 2-0	O15 2-0	D24 1-1	A29 4-1	a14 5-0
14 NELSON	A27 1-4	D03 1-5	S12 4-0	F25 1-2	M24 0-3	O08 3-3	a21 3-3	a07 4-0	D17 0-1	S24 2-1	N19 3-2	N05 4-2	M10 1-3		O22 0-3	J07 6-3	S10 6-1	M20 1-1	a09 0-4	a24 3-5	m05 3-3	F11 4-0
15 NEW BRIGHTON	D27 3-1	S03 6-0	a18 3-3	D24 1-2	F04 1-1	a28 3-3	J21 5-1	D31 0-0	A31 3-1	a14 4-0	S17 3-1	F25 2-1	O08 2-3	M03 4-0		N12 2-1	M31 1-1	F15 0-1	M17 0-0	O01 0-1	a09 2-1	M07 0-0
16 ROCHDALE	m01 3-2	a07 2-2	D31 3-0	J03 0-4	N19 3-3	F25 5-1	D03 4-0	D17 4-1	m05 1-0	F11 1-0	a21 2-2	M10 0-1	O22 0-3	S03 1-0	M24 0-0		F28 2-1	S24 5-1	A30 2-1	a09 1-2	J21 3-0	O08 3-0
17 ROTHERHAM U	M10 2-1	D17 1-1	S03 3-0	a09 1-0	a21 0-0	D26 1-2	a07 2-0	m05 3-1	F04 2-1	O08 1-1	D03 0-0	O22 5-0	M24 2-4	J21 4-3	N19 0-0	S17 3-1		F11 1-1	D31 0-1	A29 2-1	N05 6-0	F25 0-1
18 SOUTHPORT	O22 5-0	m05 3-3	J21 4-0	A30 2-1	D03 5-1	a06 2-1	D17 3-2	F18 2-0	N05 1-2	F25 3-1	a07 3-1	M24 0-2	N19 3-1	S17 1-2	a21 4-2	F04 3-1	O01 1-1		S03 4-0	D31 0-1	M10 2-1	D26 4-1
19 STOCKPORT CO	D17 3-3	N19 3-0	D26 4-0	F11 2-2	M10 3-0	S24 3-0	M24 1-0	a21 4-0	D03 2-1	S10 2-1	O22 3-0	m05 2-2	J28 2-0	a06 8-0	N05 0-0	J02 5-1	A27 2-0	J07 6-3		O08 1-0	a07 1-1	F27 5-0
20 TRANMERE R	a07 3-2	M24 5-3	O15 5-0	S24 2-2	N05 2-1	J28 6-3	O22 3-3	N19 3-1	a21 0-0	J07 11-1	M10 2-2	D17 1-2	m05 2-2	D27 1-1	F11 4-0	a06 3-0	J02 2-0	A27 1-0	F18 5-2		D03 5-2	S10 2-1
21 WIGAN B	J07 2-0	O01 0-0	a28 1-0	F01 1-3	D27 2-2	M31 3-2	F18 2-1	F04 0-3	S17 1-1	M03 3-0	O15 1-3	A27 0-2	S07 1-3	D10 4-2	a06 2-2	S10 1-2	M17 0-0	O29 1-3	J14 1-3	a14 1-0		N12 3-0
22 WREXHAM	N19 0-1	N05 5-1	F04 5-0	S03 1-1	D17 1-0	D31 1-2	A31 2-0	M10 1-2	O22 1-2	a06 4-0	m05 2-0	S14 3-2	D03 1-0	O01 5-2	a07 0-2	F18 2-1	O15 3-2	D27 3-0	S17 1-0	J21 2-0	M24 5-1	

DIVISION 3 SOUTH

	BOURNEMOUTH	BRENTFORD	BRIGHTON & HA	BRISTOL R	CHARLTON A	COVENTRY C	CRYSTAL P	EXETER C	GILLINGHAM	LUTON T	MERTHYR T	MILLWALL	NEWPORT CO	NORTHAMPTON T	NORWICH C	PLYMOUTH A	Q.P.R.	SOUTHEND U	SWINDON T	TORQUAY U	WALSALL	WATFORD
1 BOURNEMOUTH		J07 1-0	D26 3-1	D03 4-3	a07 3-1	M10 2-3	S24 2-2	F11 2-0	O22 3-0	S10 2-2	N19 2-1	J28 5-0	N05 0-0	a09 1-1	F25 2-1	a21 2-2	S21 1-2	A31 2-3	A27 2-0	O08 1-1	M24 3-1	D17 1-0
2 BRENTFORD	S03 2-1		D31 1-3	a07 5-1	D17 1-1	O22 4-1	F11 2-1	O08 1-1	M24 2-0	J28 4-2	a21 4-0	S24 6-1	M10 3-1	A29 3-0	a06 3-1	D03 0-2	J21 0-3	a23 2-2	N05 1-4	F25 1-2	D05 3-2	m05 1-1
3 BRIGHTON & H.A.	D27 3-2	A27 5-2		a21 5-0	D03 2-2	N05 3-0	J28 4-2	S24 0-2	M10 0-0	J07 3-1	M24 5-0	S10 3-1	S14 1-4	F25 2-1	O08 1-0	N19 4-1	D17 1-3	a06 1-0	m05 4-2	F11 3-0	O22 0-0	a07 1-1
4 BRISTOL R	a14 3-0	S14 1-3	a23 1-0		F25 2-1	S10 1-1	a09 1-1	M17 1-2	J07 2-4	a28 1-2	D27 2-1	D24 1-6	J28 2-1	N12 2-2	M03 3-0	S07 3-1	F11 0-4	M31 1-3	a18 1-0	O29 5-1	A27 5-2	O08 3-1
5 CHARLTON A	a16 1-1	a28 3-2	a14 3-0	O15 2-1		J07 2-1	M17 0-4	O29 0-0	A27 1-0	D24 4-3	S19 0-0	O08 1-1	S10 3-2	M31 2-2	N12 3-2	a06 2-0	S24 1-0	M26 1-2	a30 3-1	M03 1-0	F09 1-3	F11 0-2
6 COVENTRY C	O29 3-2	M03 0-0	M17 2-2	J21 2-3	S03 3-3		F13 2-2	a14 0-0	F18 1-2	N12 4-2	F04 1-2	M31 0-3	a10 0-2	D24 2-4	a28 2-2	S17 1-1	D27 0-0	O15 6-1	S05 4-0	J14 5-1	O01 0-1	D10 2-3
7 CRYSTAL P	F04 6-1	O01 0-2	S17 1-1	a06 3-2	N05 5-0	a21 1-0		A29 2-0	D03 2-2	F18 3-2	D17 2-0	O15 0-4	N19 2-0	S03 1-0	D31 2-1	m05 0-2	O22 1-1	J21 4-1	M24 1-0	M14 3-2	a07 5-1	M10 2-1
8 EXETER C	O01 4-1	F18 0-1	F04 0-3	N05 4-1	M10 2-1	D03 0-1	S07 2-2		a07 2-2	O15 3-2	m05 2-0	a09 2-4	a21 5-1	J21 1-1	S03 2-2	D26 2-0	M24 4-0	S17 3-2	N19 0-0	D31 5-0	D17 3-0	O22 3-3
9 GILLINGHAM	M03 2-1	N12 2-1	O29 0-1	S03 3-1	D31 1-1	O08 1-2	a14 3-1	M28 1-1		M31 0-4	S17 1-1	a25 0-1	F25 4-0	O01 1-3	D24 3-0	J21 3-1	S07 1-2	M17 1-0	a06 0-1	a28 4-1	F04 2-0	D27 0-3
10 LUTON T	J21 3-3	S17 5-2	S03 2-5	D17 2-0	m05 2-1	M24 3-1	O08 6-1	F25 2-1	N19 6-1		D03 5-1	F11 1-1	O22 1-1	M19 2-0	A29 1-3	a07 1-1	N05 0-1	D31 0-0	M10 2-1	a06 5-0	a21 4-1	F04 3-2
11 MERTHYR T	M31 1-1	D10 3-1	N12 4-2	D26 2-3	A29 0-0	S24 3-2	a28 2-2	D24 0-3	M12 3-1	a14 0-0		O03 0-0	F11 0-2	O29 1-3	M17 1-1	J14 1-4	F25 0-4	M03 2-3	O08 8-2	S03 1-3	S10 3-2	a10 3-1
12 MILLWALL	S17 2-0	F04 3-0	J21 6-0	m05 1-0	F18 5-0	N19 9-1	F25 1-1	a06 2-0	a21 6-0	O01 3-2	a07 3-0		M24 5-1	D31 3-0	D27 2-1	D17 2-0	M10 6-1	S03 5-1	O22 3-3	A29 9-1	D03 7-1	N05 4-2
13 NEWPORT CO	M17 4-3	O29 3-0	S01 3-1	S17 3-1	J21 4-3	a09 3-0	a26 0-3	M22 1-0	O15 1-1	M03 7-2	O01 1-1	N12 1-3		a28 4-1	J14 2-2	F04 1-1	a06 1-6	D24 3-2	D26 1-3	a14 2-2	F18 4-1	S03 3-2
14 NORTHAMPTON T	a10 1-1	S05 3-2	O15 1-0	M24 2-0	N19 2-1	m05 2-1	J07 1-1	S10 5-0	F11 1-0	D26 6-5	M10 6-0	A27 5-2	D17 1-2		S24 4-2	O22 2-1	D03 1-0	F18 2-1	a07 3-0	J28 4-4	N05 10-0	a21 5-0
15 NORWICH C	O15 3-3	a09 1-1	F18 0-0	O22 4-2	M24 0-0	D17 0-2	A27 4-1	J07 2-2	m05 0-0	S05 3-0	N05 4-0	a30 2-0	a07 1-1	F04 3-4		M10 2-0	a21 3-1	O01 2-1	D03 1-3	S10 4-0	J28 1-4	N19 1-1
16 PLYMOUTH A	a25 3-1	a14 1-0	M31 2-0	A31 4-1	a09 2-0	J28 4-0	D24 5-1	D27 1-2	S10 2-2	m02 4-0	A27 5-0	D10 3-2	S24 2-0	M03 3-3	O29 4-2		O08 3-0	N12 3-2	F11 3-0	M17 4-1	J07 2-1	F25 0-1
17 Q.P.R.	D24 2-0	S10 2-3	a28 5-0	O01 4-2	F04 3-3	a26 1-5	M03 2-0	N12 0-1	S01 3-3	M17 3-2	O15 0-0	O29 0-1	A27 4-2	a14 0-4	m03 0-0	F18 0-1		J14 3-2	J07 0-1	M31 2-3	a09 1-1	S17 2-1
18 SOUTHEND U	S07 3-0	D26 3-2	a09 0-1	N19 2-1	a21 1-2	F25 3-2	S10 6-1	F15 1-2	N05 1-2	A27 1-0	O22 2-1	J07 0-1	m05 5-1	O08 2-0	F11 1-1	M24 3-0	a07 7-0		M14 1-1	S24 1-0	M10 2-1	D03 3-0
19 SWINDON T	M21 3-2	M17 1-1	D24 4-3	F04 2-1	S17 2-2	A29 6-0	N12 3-3	M31 3-0	a09 6-1	O29 4-2	F18 1-2	M03 3-0	D27 4-1	a25 4-0	a14 1-1	O01 2-2	S03 0-2	a28 0-1		m02 2-2	O15 5-0	J21 4-0
20 TORQUAY U	F18 2-2	O15 2-1	O01 1-1	M10 0-0	O22 1-2	a07 2-3	D27 0-2	A27 1-1	D17 1-1	a09 0-4	J07 2-2	S07 0-1	D03 1-1	S17 1-5	J21 4-2	N05 1-2	N19 1-0	F04 3-3	a21 2-1		m05 1-1	M24 1-1
21 WALSALL	N12 2-3	M31 4-2	M03 3-3	D31 1-2	D27 1-0	F11 7-0	J14 1-1	a28 5-1	S24 7-4	a23 4-1	J21 2-2	a14 2-5	O08 0-3	M17 1-1	S17 1-1	S03 2-1	a10 2-2	O29 0-1	F25 1-2	D10 4-0		A29 2-0
22 WATFORD	a28 2-0	D24 1-1	J14 3-3	F18 2-1	O01 1-2	A27 3-1	O29 2-1	M03 3-2	m02 5-3	S24 1-0	a09 1-1	M17 0-3	J07 2-3	a18 2-0	M31 2-0	O15 1-2	J28 3-3	a14 1-1	S10 2-5	N12 1-2	S07 4-0	

LEAGUE TABLES

DIVISION 1

	P	W	D	L	F	A	W	D	L	F	A	Pts
Everton	42	11	8	2	60	28	9	5	7	42	38	53
Huddersfield T	42	15	1	5	57	31	7	6	8	34	37	51
Leicester C	42	14	5	2	66	25	4	7	10	30	47	48
Derby Co	42	12	4	5	59	30	5	6	10	37	53	44
Bury	42	13	1	7	53	35	7	3	11	27	45	44
Cardiff C	42	12	7	2	44	27	5	3	13	26	53	44
Bolton W	42	12	5	4	47	26	4	6	11	34	40	43
Aston Villa	42	13	3	5	52	30	4	6	11	26	43	43
Newcastle U	42	9	7	5	49	41	6	6	9	30	40	43
Arsenal	42	10	6	5	49	33	3	9	9	33	53	41
Birmingham C	42	10	7	4	36	25	3	8	10	34	50	41
Blackburn R	42	13	5	3	41	22	3	4	14	25	56	41
Sheffield U	42	12	4	5	56	42	3	6	12	23	44	40
Sheffield W	42	9	6	6	45	29	4	7	10	36	49	39
Sunderland	42	9	5	7	37	29	6	4	11	37	47	39
Liverpool	42	10	6	5	54	36	3	7	11	30	51	39
West Ham U	42	9	7	5	48	34	5	4	12	33	54	39
Manchester U	42	12	6	3	51	27	4	1	16	21	53	39
Burnley	42	12	5	4	55	31	4	2	15	27	67	39
Portsmouth	42	13	4	4	40	23	3	3	15	26	67	39
Tottenham H	42	12	3	6	47	34	3	5	13	27	52	38
Middlesbrough	42	7	9	5	46	35	4	6	11	35	53	37

DIVISION 2

	P	W	D	L	F	A	W	D	L	F	A	Pts
Manchester C	42	18	2	1	70	27	7	7	7	30	32	59
Leeds U	42	16	2	3	63	15	9	5	7	35	34	57
Chelsea	42	15	2	4	46	15	8	6	7	29	30	54
Preston N.E.	42	15	3	3	62	24	7	6	8	38	42	53
Stoke C	42	14	5	2	44	17	8	3	10	34	42	52
Swansea T	42	13	6	2	46	17	5	6	10	29	46	48
Oldham A	42	15	3	3	55	18	4	5	12	20	33	46
W.B.A.	42	10	7	4	50	28	7	5	9	40	42	46
Port Vale	42	11	6	4	45	20	7	2	12	23	37	44
Nottingham F	42	10	6	5	54	37	5	4	12	29	47	40
Grimsby T	42	8	6	7	41	41	6	6	9	28	42	40
Bristol C	42	11	5	5	42	18	4	4	13	34	61	39
Barnsley	42	10	5	6	43	36	4	6	11	22	49	39
Hull C	42	9	8	4	25	19	3	7	11	16	35	39
Notts Co	42	10	4	7	47	26	3	8	10	21	48	38
Wolverhampton W	42	11	5	5	43	31	2	5	14	20	60	36
Southampton	42	11	3	7	54	40	3	4	14	14	37	35
Reading	42	9	8	4	32	22	2	5	14	21	53	35
Blackpool	42	11	3	7	55	43	2	5	14	28	58	34
Clapton O	42	9	7	5	32	25	2	5	14	23	60	34
Fulham	42	12	7	2	46	22	1	0	20	22	67	33
South Shields	42	5	5	11	30	41	2	4	15	26	70	23

DIVISION 3 NORTH

	P	W	D	L	F	A	W	D	L	F	A	Pts
Bradford P.A.	42	18	2	1	68	22	9	7	5	33	23	63
Lincoln C	42	15	4	2	53	20	9	3	9	38	44	55
Stockport Co	42	16	5	0	62	14	7	3	11	27	37	54
Doncaster R	42	15	4	2	59	18	8	3	10	21	26	53
Tranmere R	42	14	6	1	68	28	8	3	10	37	44	53
Bradford C	42	15	4	2	59	19	3	8	10	26	41	48
Darlington	42	15	1	5	63	28	6	4	11	26	46	47
Southport	42	15	2	4	55	24	5	3	13	24	46	45
Accrington S	42	14	4	3	49	22	4	4	13	27	45	44
New Brighton	42	10	7	4	45	22	4	7	10	27	40	42
Wrexham	42	15	1	5	48	19	3	5	13	16	48	42
Halifax T	42	11	7	3	47	24	2	8	11	26	47	41
Rochdale	42	13	4	4	45	24	4	3	14	29	53	41
Rotherham U	42	11	6	4	39	19	3	5	13	26	50	39
Hartlepool U	42	10	3	8	41	35	6	3	12	28	46	38
Chesterfield	42	10	4	7	46	29	3	6	12	25	49	36
Crewe A	42	10	6	5	51	28	2	4	15	26	58	34
Ashington	42	10	5	6	54	36	1	6	14	23	67	33
Barrow	42	10	8	3	41	24	0	3	18	13	78	31
Wigan B	42	8	5	8	30	32	2	5	14	26	65	30
Durham C	42	10	5	6	37	30	1	2	18	16	70	29
Nelson	42	8	4	9	50	49	2	2	17	26	87	26

DIVISION 3 SOUTH

	P	W	D	L	F	A	W	D	L	F	A	Pts
Millwall	42	19	2	0	87	15	11	3	7	40	35	65
Northampton T	42	17	3	1	67	23	6	6	9	35	41	55
Plymouth A	42	17	2	2	60	19	6	5	10	25	35	53
Brighton & H.A.	42	14	4	3	51	24	5	6	10	30	45	48
Crystal Palace	42	15	3	3	46	23	3	9	9	33	49	48
Swindon T	42	12	6	3	60	26	7	3	11	30	43	47
Southend U	42	14	2	5	48	19	6	4	11	32	45	46
Exeter C	42	11	6	4	49	27	6	6	9	21	33	46
Newport Co	42	12	5	4	52	38	6	4	11	29	46	45
Q.P.R.	42	8	5	8	37	35	9	4	8	35	36	43
Charlton A	42	12	5	4	34	27	3	8	10	26	43	43
Brentford	42	12	4	5	49	30	4	4	13	27	44	40
Luton T	42	13	5	3	56	27	3	2	16	38	60	39
Bournemouth	42	12	6	3	44	24	1	6	14	28	55	38
Watford	42	10	5	6	42	34	4	5	12	26	44	38
Gillingham	42	10	3	8	33	26	3	8	10	29	55	37
Norwich C	42	9	8	4	41	26	1	8	12	25	44	36
Walsall	42	9	6	6	52	35	3	3	15	23	66	33
Bristol R	42	11	3	7	41	36	3	1	17	26	57	32
Coventry C	42	5	8	8	40	36	6	1	14	27	60	31
Merthyr T	42	7	6	8	38	40	2	7	12	15	51	31
Torquay U	42	4	10	7	27	36	4	4	13	26	67	30

Football League Records

Top scorers: Div 1, D.Halliday (Sunderland) 43 goals; Div 2, J.Hampson (Blackpool) 40 goals; Div 3 N, J.McConnell (Carlisle United) 43 goals; Div 3 S, A.Rennie (Luton Town) 43 goals.

Durham City failed to gain re-election, Carlisle United elected in their place.

Jimmy Seed; the man who inspired Sheffield Wednesday's 'great escape' of 1927-28 then led them to successive League Championship titles.

DIVISION 1

	ARSENAL	ASTON VILLA	BIRMINGHAM	BLACKBURN R	BOLTON W	BURNLEY	BURY	CARDIFF C	DERBY CO	EVERTON	HUDDERSFIELD T	LEEDS U	LEICESTER C	LIVERPOOL	MANCHESTER C	MANCHESTER U	NEWCASTLE U	PORTSMOUTH	SHEFFIELD U	SHEFFIELD W	SUNDERLAND	WEST HAM U
1 ARSENAL		N24 2-5	S15 0-0	M29 1-0	S01 2-0	D22 3-1	M30 7-1	M16 2-1	A29 1-3	a22 2-0	S29 2-0	a27 1-0	a13 1-1	O27 4-4	F02 0-0	D08 3-1	a02 1-2	J19 4-0	N10 2-0	D29 2-2	D26 1-1	O13 2-3
2 ASTON VILLA	a06 4-2		M09 1-2	N17 2-1	O20 3-5	F02 4-2	O13 7-1	S29 1-0	N03 2-3	D01 2-0	a20 4-1	D29 1-0	a02 4-2	S01 3-1	D19 5-1	A27 0-0	S15 1-1	D26 3-2	F20 3-2	m04 4-1	M25 3-1	J19 5-2
3 BIRMINGHAM	M13 1-1	O27 2-4		S22 4-0	D25 0-2	N24 3-6	a27 3-2	a13 0-0	O06 1-4	S08 1-3	J05 1-2	D22 5-1	S10 1-0	M16 0-0	A25 4-1	M02 1-1	M30 0-0	a01 1-0	D08 2-2	F23 4-1	F09 1-0	N10 2-2
4 BLACKBURN R	D25 5-2	M30 2-5	F02 4-1		J19 1-3	m02 1-1	N10 1-1	D22 2-0	D29 3-1	O13 2-1	a01 1-1	D08 0-1	N24 1-1	a27 2-1	S29 2-2	a13 0-3	S24 2-0	S15 4-0	M16 1-1	S01 4-1	S17 2-0	O27 2-0
5 BOLTON W	J05 1-2	a17 3-1	D26 6-2	S08 0-3		D08 0-1	O06 0-1	J01 1-0	S22 3-0	A25 2-3	S03 1-1	N10 4-1	D22 5-0	M30 0-0	a01 1-1	M16 1-1	a13 1-0	O13 4-2	O27 3-1	F09 2-2	F20 2-2	N24 4-1
6 BURNLEY	m04 3-3	S22 4-1	a06 4-0	O20 2-2	a20 3-1		F18 0-0	J05 3-0	M09 2-2	N03 2-0	a16 3-2	F23 5-0	F09 0-1	D25 3-2	N17 2-3	O06 3-4	S10 4-3	D01 4-1	S08 2-1	D15 0-2	A25 3-1	S03 3-3
7 BURY	N17 1-0	F23 2-2	M20 3-1	M23 1-0	m01 3-4	S15 2-1		F02 4-1	m04 3-3	a06 1-2	D01 2-1	J01 2-2	D25 3-1	D29 2-2	a20 1-2	M29 1-3	J19 2-0	M09 0-0	S29 4-0	O20 0-4	N03 1-3	S01 0-3
8 CARDIFF C	N03 1-1	F09 0-2	D01 1-4	m04 1-1	D15 1-1	S01 7-0	S22 4-0		J19 3-0	M23 0-2	N17 0-0	D26 2-1	O06 1-2	a01 1-2	a06 1-3	F23 2-2	D29 2-0	a20 1-1	J26 0-0	M09 3-1	O20 0-1	S10 3-2
9 DERBY CO	S26 0-0	M16 1-0	F16 2-2	A25 5-1	F02 2-1	O27 4-0	D22 3-1	S08 2-0		a02 3-0	D26 1-2	N24 3-4	N10 5-2	a13 2-5	O13 1-1	M30 6-1	a27 1-2	S29 1-0	M02 2-2	S15 6-0	J05 0-0	D08 6-0
10 EVERTON	O06 4-2	a13 0-1	J19 0-2	F23 5-2	D29 3-0	M16 2-0	N24 1-0	N10 1-0	J01 4-0		F02 0-3	O27 0-1	D08 3-1	S29 1-0	S15 2-6	a27 2-4	D22 5-2	S01 4-0	M30 1-3	A29 0-0	D25 0-0	a10 0-4
11 HUDDERSFIELD T	F09 0-1	D08 3-0	S01 0-0	O06 0-2	A27 4-1	N10 7-1	a13 0-2	M30 1-1	D25 0-0	S22 3-1		S15 6-1	a27 1-1	a10 1-3	J19 2-2	O27 1-2	M16 2-1	D29 3-1	N24 6-1	a02 0-0	F23 1-2	D22 4-0
12 LEEDS U	D15 1-1	A25 4-1	m04 0-1	a20 0-1	a29 2-2	O13 2-1	A27 3-1	D25 3-0	a06 1-1	M09 3-1	m01 1-2		J05 4-3	F02 2-2	O20 4-1	S08 3-2	F16 0-0	N03 3-2	a02 2-0	N17 0-2	D01 0-3	S29 4-1
13 LEICESTER C	D01 1-1	a01 4-1	A27 5-3	a06 2-1	m04 6-1	S29 1-1	D26 5-2	F21 2-0	M23 1-0	a20 4-1	D15 4-1	S01 4-4		J19 2-0	M09 3-2	D29 2-1	F02 1-1	O20 10-0	O13 3-1	N03 1-1	N17 1-0	S15 5-0
14 LIVERPOOL	M09 2-4	J05 4-0	N03 1-2	D15 1-1	N17 3-0	D26 8-0	A25 3-0	M29 2-0	D01 3-0	F09 1-2	O20 2-3	S22 1-1	S08 6-3		m04 1-1	F13 2-3	O13 2-1	a17 0-0	S05 1-2	a06 3-2	a20 5-2	M13 2-1
15 MANCHESTER C	S22 4-1	a27 3-0	D29 2-3	F09 1-2	M29 5-1	M30 4-1	J30 6-4	N24 1-1	F23 2-3	J26 5-1	S08 3-2	M02 3-0	O27 2-3	D22 2-3		S01 2-2	N10 2-4	O01 2-1	a13 3-1	D26 2-2	O06 5-3	M16 4-2
16 MANCHESTER U	a20 4-1	J01 2-2	O20 1-0	D01 1-4	N03 1-1	F16 1-0	a01 1-0	O13 1-1	N17 0-1	D15 1-1	M09 1-0	J19 1-2	A25 1-1	S15 2-2	J05 1-2		S29 5-0	m04 0-0	D25 1-1	M23 2-1	a06 3-0	F02 2-3
17 NEWCASTLE U	O20 0-3	M13 2-1	N17 1-0	J01 0-2	D01 4-1	A29 2-7	S08 2-1	A25 1-1	D15 4-1	m04 2-0	N03 4-1	O06 3-2	S22 1-0	F23 2-2	M23 4-0	F09 5-0		a06 0-1	J05 4-2	a20 2-1	M09 4-3	D26 1-0
18 PORTSMOUTH	S08 2-0	D25 3-2	M29 3-1	M13 2-2	F23 4-4	a13 3-1	O27 4-1	D08 0-1	F09 1-5	J05 3-0	A25 1-0	M16 0-2	a10 1-0	N10 0-1	S05 1-0	D22 3-0	N24 0-1		a29 2-3	O06 3-2	S22 4-0	M30 3-0
19 SHEFFIELD U	M23 2-2	O06 1-3	a20 3-2	N03 2-1	M09 1-1	J19 10-0	F09 6-1	S15 3-1	O20 2-1	N17 2-1	a06 1-0	a01 1-1	F23 1-4	S10 1-3	D01 1-3	D26 6-1	S01 3-1	D15 3-0		F02 1-1	m04 4-0	D29 3-3
20 SHEFFIELD W	A25 3-2	D22 4-1	O13 3-0	J05 1-0	S29 0-0	a27 1-1	M02 3-1	O27 1-0	F18 5-0	S03 1-0	J01 1-1	M30 4-2	M16 1-0	N24 3-2	D25 4-0	N10 2-1	D08 3-1	M04 2-1	S22 5-2		S08 2-1	a13 6-0
21 SUNDERLAND	J01 5-1	N10 1-3	S29 3-4	A29 3-1	S15 4-0	D29 2-1	M16 3-1	M02 1-0	S01 4-0	M29 2-2	O13 4-1	a13 2-1	M30 1-2	D08 2-1	F16 3-1	N24 5-1	O27 5-2	F02 5-0	D22 4-4	J19 4-3		a27 4-1
22 WEST HAM U	F23 3-4	S08 4-1	M23 2-1	M09 3-3	a06 3-0	M29 4-0	J05 2-3	S17 1-1	a20 2-2	O20 2-4	m04 1-1	F09 8-2	M04 2-1	O06 1-1	N03 3-0	S22 3-1	D25 1-0	N17 0-1	A25 4-0	D01 3-2	D15 3-3	

Middlesbrough's George Camsell, who scored a record 59 goals when 'Boro stormed to the Division Two title in 1926-27, and hit 30 when they returned to the top flight two seasons later.

DIVISION 2

	BARNSLEY	BLACKPOOL	BRADFORD	BRISTOL C	CHELSEA	CLAPTON O	GRIMSBY T	HULL C	MIDDLESBROUGH	MILLWALL	NOTTINGHAM F	NOTTS CO	OLDHAM A	PORT VALE	PRESTON N.E.	READING	SOUTHAMPTON	STOKE C	SWANSEA T	TOTTENHAM H	W.B.A.	WOLVERHAMPTON W
1 BARNSLEY		S08 3-1	A25 1-2	S29 4-2	J30 0-1	D26 2-0	J01 0-2	N24 2-2	N10 2-2	D22 2-2	F16 1-2	M16 2-0	S22 2-1	M30 6-0	a27 4-1	D08 2-3	M02 4-1	M29 4-2	J05 2-1	a13 4-1	O13 2-0	O27 2-2
2 BLACKPOOL	J19 0-1		M29 3-0	S15 2-1	S01 0-1	F16 0-1	D26 1-1	D08 2-1	M02 3-0	N24 3-0	F02 2-2	M30 3-2	O27 4-0	a13 4-0	D29 3-2	N10 7-0	M16 3-0	O13 2-0	S03 2-2	a27 2-2	S29 0-2	D22 3-0
3 BRADFORD	D29 2-1	a01 5-2		S01 3-2	A27 1-2	F02 2-1	a29 1-0	N10 5-1	M16 3-2	D08 4-0	J19 1-1	a13 2-2	D22 2-0	a27 2-0	O27 7-2	M02 1-0	M30 4-1	S29 2-1	D25 3-1	O13 4-1	S15 4-1	N24 4-1
4 BRISTOL C	F09 3-1	J26 3-2	J05 1-0		S22 0-0	a01 1-0	A25 2-2	M30 0-0	a27 0-1	M16 5-0	O13 2-5	O27 0-4	N10 6-0	D22 2-1	D08 1-0	a13 0-0	O06 1-1	S05 1-1	S08 2-1	N24 2-1	D26 2-3	M02 3-2
5 CHELSEA	S15 1-0	J05 2-3	S05 3-1	F02 3-0		O13 2-2	a01 3-2	a13 0-0	S08 2-0	M30 0-3	S29 3-0	D22 1-1	M02 2-3	N24 3-3	N10 2-1	a27 2-1	O27 1-1	D26 3-1	A25 4-0	D08 1-1	a17 2-5	M16 0-2
6 CLAPTON O	D25 3-1	O06 2-4	S22 1-0	M29 0-1	F23 1-0		M04 3-1	O27 0-2	N24 3-0	S01 1-1	A27 1-4	N10 2-2	a13 2-0	M02 1-0	M30 1-0	D22 1-1	D08 1-1	S08 1-0	F09 1-2	M16 2-3	D29 0-2	a27 2-0
7 GRIMSBY T	A27 2-1	D25 1-4	O06 4-2	D29 3-2	M29 1-0	S15 6-1		S29 0-1	D22 1-4	a27 3-0	S01 2-2	D08 2-2	M30 1-0	N10 3-1	M16 1-0	O27 4-0	N24 2-1	F02 2-1	F23 4-1	M02 2-0	J19 3-1	a13 2-0
8 HULL C	a06 0-0	a20 1-3	M23 1-0	N17 5-1	D01 2-2	M09 0-0	F09 2-3		a01 1-1	a22 4-0	m04 0-1	S08 1-1	A27 1-0	S22 2-0	D25 5-1	O13 3-0	A25 2-2	O20 1-3	D15 1-1	a15 1-1	N03 4-1	J05 1-3
9 MIDDLESBROUGH	M23 1-0	O20 4-1	N03 5-3	D15 3-1	J19 4-5	a06 4-0	m04 3-0	S12 1-1		F23 3-0	a20 1-0	O06 3-1	F20 1-0	D25 5-1	S01 2-3	D29 0-0	S22 1-2	N17 1-0	M09 0-0	J01 3-0	D01 1-1	F09 8-3
10 MILLWALL	m04 0-2	a06 2-1	a20 1-3	N03 3-1	N17 2-1	J05 2-0	D15 4-1	S15 0-0	O13 2-3		M09 1-1	A25 0-1	D25 3-3	J19 2-1	F16 3-1	S29 5-1	M29 2-4	M23 1-3	D01 3-0	F02 5-1	O20 2-2	S03 0-5
11 NOTTINGHAM F	O06 1-3	S22 2-0	S08 3-2	F23 1-1	F09 3-0	S05 0-0	J05 0-1	D22 3-1	D08 1-1	O27 0-4		M02 1-2	a27 3-1	M16 2-2	a13 4-1	N24 1-2	N10 1-1	A25 1-5	F20 2-1	M30 2-2	M29 1-2	D26 2-1
12 NOTTS CO	N03 4-1	N17 3-1	D01 3-3	M09 2-0	M13 4-3	M23 2-0	a20 1-2	J19 6-0	F16 0-3	D29 4-5	O20 1-1		O13 2-0	S01 3-0	S29 0-1	F02 1-1	D25 1-1	D15 1-0	a06 5-1	S15 2-0	A27 3-1	a01 3-0
13 OLDHAM A	F02 1-0	M09 4-2	m04 2-1	M23 1-0	O20 1-0	D01 1-1	N17 0-3	S03 0-1	S15 1-3	D26 4-1	J01 2-0	F23 3-2		a01 1-1	J19 2-1	S01 2-1	F09 3-1	a06 1-0	N03 2-1	D29 3-1	a20 3-0	O06 0-4
14 PORT VALE	N17 3-0	D01 1-0	D15 0-1	m04 5-0	a06 1-0	O20 3-0	M23 0-3	F02 4-1	D26 2-3	S08 5-2	N03 4-2	J05 3-0	M29 2-1		O13 3-2	F25 4-0	S24 1-2	J26 1-2	a20 0-0	S29 2-1	M09 8-1	A25 1-4
15 PRESTON N.E.	D15 2-1	A25 3-1	M09 2-0	a20 2-2	M23 3-0	N17 5-2	N03 5-2	D26 1-0	J05 0-0	O06 3-4	D01 3-2	F09 0-1	S08 3-2	F23 7-1		A27 7-0	J26 0-1	m04 2-2	O20 2-2	M29 2-2	a06 1-1	S22 5-1
16 READING	a20 1-0	M23 4-1	O20 4-0	D01 2-1	D15 3-3	m04 4-2	M09 1-3	F23 3-0	A25 2-3	F09 0-2	a06 0-3	S22 1-2	J05 6-1	O06 2-1	S05 0-0		S08 0-1	N03 1-1	M29 2-0	D26 4-3	N17 5-3	M13 3-0
17 SOUTHAMPTON	O20 1-2	N03 8-2	N17 2-2	F16 2-1	M09 1-2	a20 2-0	a06 3-1	D29 3-2	F02 1-1	a01 3-0	M23 2-1	D26 4-0	S29 2-1	A27 1-2	S15 4-0	J19 2-2		D01 0-0	m04 3-0	S01 1-1	D15 1-1	F23 2-1
18 STOKE C	a01 0-0	F23 1-1	F09 2-0	A27 2-0	D25 0-1	J19 3-1	S22 1-2	M02 1-1	M30 3-2	N10 0-0	D29 1-1	a27 5-0	N24 1-1	S15 2-1	D22 1-1	M16 5-0	a13 3-0		O06 5-0	O27 2-0	S01 4-1	D08 4-3
19 SWANSEA T	S01 2-1	A27 5-5	D26 3-1	J19 0-2	D29 0-1	S29 0-1	O13 2-1	a27 0-1	O27 2-0	a13 2-0	S15 3-5	N24 1-0	M16 3-2	D08 2-0	M02 5-0	a01 0-1	D22 1-1	F16 3-3		N10 4-0	F02 6-1	M30 2-0
20 TOTTENHAM H	D01 2-0	D15 1-2	F23 3-2	a06 1-1	a20 4-1	N03 2-1	O20 2-1	O06 4-1	A27 2-5	S22 2-1	N17 2-1	J26 3-0	A25 4-1	F09 4-2	a01 2-0	D25 2-2	J05 3-2	M09 1-0	M23 1-1		m04 2-0	S08 3-2
21 W.B.A.	F23 6-2	F09 2-2	M11 1-2	D25 1-1	O06 3-0	A25 3-1	S08 1-0	M16 2-0	a13 1-1	a10 3-2	a01 3-0	S03 1-3	D08 1-0	O27 3-1	N24 1-1	M30 5-0	a27 3-1	J05 2-3	S22 5-1	D22 3-2		N10 0-2
22 WOLVERHAMPTON W	M09 3-1	m04 1-5	a06 3-1	O20 2-1	N03 1-1	D15 3-2	D01 2-2	S01 2-4	S29 3-3	A27 0-1	D25 2-3	a02 3-1	F16 0-0	D29 4-0	F02 1-2	S15 2-0	O13 1-1	a20 4-0	N17 0-0	J19 4-2	M23 0-1	

SEASON 1928-29

DIVISION 3 NORTH

	ACCRINGTON S	ASHINGTON	BARROW	BRADFORD C	CARLISLE U	CHESTERFIELD	CREWE A	DARLINGTON	DONCASTER R	HALIFAX T	HARTLEPOOLS U	LINCOLN C	NELSON	NEW BRIGHTON	ROCHDALE	ROTHERHAM U	SOUTHPORT	SOUTH SHIELDS	STOCKPORT CO	TRANMERE R	WIGAN B	WREXHAM
1 ACCRINGTON S		O20 0-1	N03 1-0	D25 0-1	A25 2-3	M23 0-0	J26 2-0	D15 4-0	M09 6-0	O06 1-1	S25 2-2	F23 0-1	m04 4-4	a06 3-1	D01 2-2	J05 1-3	a20 2-0	J01 2-0	F09 2-0	S22 2-0	S08 2-0	N17 4-3
2 ASHINGTON	M02 2-2		S29 1-0	O13 2-8	M16 0-4	F02 0-2	J12 0-5	A27 4-2	F16 4-7	a27 0-3	O27 3-1	D22 1-1	J01 3-2	J19 1-1	S01 2-1	N10 0-1	D29 1-3	D25 1-3	a20 0-1	a13 3-2	M30 1-1	S15 2-2
3 BARROW	M16 2-1	F09 3-0		O27 1-3	N17 1-1	J19 1-2	a29 2-4	J01 3-1	S22 2-2	S15 1-3	N10 2-1	M02 2-3	F23 7-2	D29 0-0	A27 3-3	J12 4-0	a01 1-2	O06 1-1	D22 2-4	a27 1-2	a13 1-0	S01 2-2
4 BRADFORD C	D26 4-1	F23 2-0	M09 8-0		S03 4-2	N03 6-1	S08 4-1	a20 3-0	O20 3-0	F09 2-2	a02 4-1	O06 2-3	D15 0-2	N17 5-2	a06 0-0	A25 11-1	D01 5-0	m04 3-1	S22 2-1	M06 8-0	J05 1-0	M23 5-0
5 CARLISLE U	D29 4-3	N03 5-1	M30 4-1	A30 2-2		a06 1-2	F09 1-0	J19 3-0	M23 1-2	D25 2-1	S01 8-0	J01 3-1	O20 4-0	a20 2-1	D15 4-2	J26 1-1	S13 4-2	M09 5-0	F23 0-5	O06 4-1	S22 2-1	D01 1-1
6 CHESTERFIELD	N10 4-1	S22 4-1	S08 3-0	M16 0-5	M13 1-2		a27 1-0	F23 2-1	J26 0-1	M02 3-2	M30 4-1	O27 1-1	O06 3-2	J01 0-2	M29 2-1	a13 1-2	D26 6-0	F09 3-2	S01 1-2	D22 4-1	a08 0-0	D29 3-1
7 CREWE A	S15 4-0	a06 7-0	a20 3-1	J19 0-0	S29 1-1	D15 6-1		N03 2-0	D01 1-1	D29 3-0	F02 4-2	S01 1-3	M23 1-1	D25 3-0	O20 1-1	a17 3-0	M09 1-1	N17 1-5	S03 2-0	a01 0-1	O13 0-4	m04 3-1
8 DARLINGTON	a27 0-0	S19 4-0	D26 1-2	J02 3-3	S08 0-0	O13 2-2	M16 4-2		a01 1-0	a24 2-0	D22 4-1	a13 2-1	J05 3-2	S29 3-1	F02 5-3	M02 2-1	S15 3-1	A25 2-2	M30 2-3	N10 1-2	O27 3-0	F16 0-0
9 DONCASTER R	O27 4-1	O06 2-1	F02 1-0	M02 1-1	N10 3-0	S15 2-0	D08 0-1	M29 3-1		D22 1-0	M16 4-1	S29 0-0	D26 2-2	S01 1-2	D29 4-2	M30 1-0	A27 4-2	F23 2-1	a27 0-2	a02 2-1	m01 1-2	J19 1-0
10 HALIFAX T	F16 4-2	D15 1-0	J26 2-0	S29 1-1	D26 5-2	O20 1-1	A25 2-2	a06 5-1	m04 2-2		O13 2-0	F02 4-2	D01 1-2	N03 1-1	M23 1-1	a02 3-1	N17 2-1	a20 0-2	S08 1-1	J05 2-0	S17 1-0	M09 1-2
11 HARTLEPOOLS U	a01 1-3	M09 1-3	M23 1-0	J01 1-3	J05 1-0	N17 0-2	S22 2-1	S05 2-0	N03 2-2	F23 3-1		D25 3-2	A25 2-2	D01 5-2	a20 0-2	S08 1-1	D15 4-2	O20 0-5	O06 1-1	F09 4-1	J26 1-3	a06 0-2
12 LINCOLN C	O13 3-1	a01 3-1	O20 5-0	F16 3-4	M29 3-0	M09 1-0	J05 1-0	D01 0-0	F09 2-1	S22 3-0	D26 7-1		a20 5-1	M23 4-0	N17 2-0	S03 1-1	a06 4-1	D15 5-0	J26 1-2	S08 3-1	A25 1-3	N03 1-1
13 NELSON	D22 0-2	D08 5-0	O13 3-4	a27 0-1	M02 1-0	F16 1-0	N10 4-1	S01 2-1	O02 2-4	a13 3-1	D29 1-0	S25 3-4		F02 3-0	S15 3-0	O27 4-2	J19 1-1	S12 1-0	J22 4-1	M30 4-2	M16 2-1	S29 1-3
14 NEW BRIGHTON	F06 2-1	S08 3-2	A25 1-3	M30 0-3	D12 1-0	S10 2-3	D26 2-3	F09 1-0	J05 1-1	M16 1-0	a13 1-3	N10 6-1	S22 0-1		F23 6-1	a27 0-0	O06 3-1	J26 1-0	O27 4-1	M02 1-2	D22 2-2	M29 2-0
15 ROCHDALE	a13 2-1	J05 5-0	S04 4-2	a30 1-3	J12 4-0	a01 2-1	M02 2-1	S22 5-0	A25 1-3	N10 2-2	D08 7-4	M30 0-2	J26 2-1	O13 4-2		D22 2-1	F09 1-1	S08 1-2	M16 1-3	O27 5-1	O06 0-0	D25 4-4
16 ROTHERHAM U	S01 2-1	M23 0-0	a06 2-1	D29 2-2	S15 4-0	D01 2-0	O06 1-2	O20 2-0	N17 1-2	a01 0-0	J19 3-2	A27 3-2	M09 4-0	D15 3-1	m04 5-0		F02 0-2	N03 1-1	D26 3-3	F23 0-1	F09 4-2	a20 2-1
17 SOUTHPORT	a09 3-1	A25 2-1	M29 2-2	a13 0-3	D22 4-3	D25 1-0	O27 6-2	J26 3-1	J01 3-3	M30 1-0	a27 6-2	m04 2-1	S08 5-1	F16 0-0	S29 1-1	S22 2-0		J05 5-0	N10 1-1	M16 1-2	M02 3-0	O13 1-3
18 SOUTH SHIELDS	M29 3-0	D26 0-0	a17 2-2	D22 1-1	O27 5-0	S29 6-3	M30 3-0	D29 1-3	O13 1-0	D08 2-1	M02 1-1	a27 1-0	a01 3-2	S15 0-2	J19 5-2	M16 10-1	S01 4-0		a13 0-1	J12 4-1	N10 2-2	F02 3-2
19 STOCKPORT CO	S29 6-1	S10 4-0	m04 3-2	F02 2-1	O13 2-2	J05 3-1	M29 2-2	N17 7-3	D15 4-1	J19 3-0	F16 3-0	S15 7-3	a06 3-0	M09 2-1	N03 4-0	D25 1-0	M23 2-1	D01 7-1		A25 4-1	J01 2-1	O20 6-2
20 TRANMERE R	F02 1-1	D01 3-2	D15 2-1	S15 1-0	F16 1-2	m04 3-0	J01 1-2	M23 4-0	a20 1-1	S01 2-1	S29 3-0	J19 2-1	N17 6-1	O20 1-3	M09 5-1	O13 3-0	N03 6-1	a06 4-0	D29 2-1		M29 3-2	A27 1-1
21 WIGAN B	J19 5-2	N17 5-1	D01 2-1	S01 2-0	F02 2-2	a20 5-1	F23 4-2	M09 2-0	a06 4-2	A29 1-1	S15 2-0	D29 4-0	N03 1-0	m04 1-1	F16 4-1	S29 1-0	O20 1-0	M23 4-0	a01 4-0	D25 0-1		D15 1-1
22 WREXHAM	M30 4-1	J26 4-0	J05 5-0	N10 2-1	a13 5-1	A25 4-3	D22 1-2	O06 4-3	S08 4-2	O27 2-2	J12 3-1	M16 2-1	F09 3-1	a01 1-1	D26 3-0	D08 2-0	F23 3-1	S22 1-0	M02 2-1	S05 3-1	a27 1-3	

DIVISION 3 SOUTH

	BOURNEMOUTH	BRENTFORD	BRIGHTON & HA	BRISTOL R	CHARLTON A	COVENTRY C	CRYSTAL P	EXETER C	FULHAM	GILLINGHAM	LUTON T	MERTHYR T	NEWPORT CO	NORTHAMPTON T	NORWICH C	PLYMOUTH A	Q.P.R.	SOUTHEND U	SWINDON T	TORQUAY U	WALSALL	WATFORD
1 BOURNEMOUTH		S15 1-1	a01 3-2	O27 6-2	O13 4-2	S29 2-1	a24 2-0	D25 3-1	S08 1-0	a27 4-3	F02 3-3	J05 3-0	M30 0-1	M20 2-0	S05 2-0	D22 4-1	M02 2-3	A25 2-2	a13 2-1	F06 4-3	N10 1-2	M16 3-3
2 BRENTFORD	M13 0-0		D26 5-1	M02 2-0	S03 1-0	F16 1-0	M30 2-4	A25 4-2	D22 1-2	J12 4-1	S29 0-1	S08 2-1	N10 1-3	O13 2-2	M29 4-0	a27 0-2	S22 1-1	J05 1-0	S10 2-0	a13 0-0	M16 1-0	O27 0-1
3 BRIGHTON & H.A.	M29 1-0	D25 3-2		J12 4-0	S15 2-3	S01 0-1	D22 1-5	O06 3-2	N10 2-0	O27 3-1	D29 1-0	S05 2-1	a27 2-1	J19 0-3	F02 3-0	M16 2-1	M30 2-1	F23 2-1	S29 2-2	M02 1-2	m01 2-1	a13 1-1
4 BRISTOL R	M09 1-2	O20 2-0	a06 3-0		a20 3-0	m04 1-1	D25 1-1	N17 1-1	F02 5-3	J19 2-4	F16 1-1	N03 3-0	M29 0-3	D15 1-2	D01 2-0	S15 0-1	S29 1-1	M23 4-1	D29 1-4	S01 2-1	S12 4-1	F23 1-1
5 CHARLTON A	F23 6-2	a22 1-0	J26 3-0	M14 1-2		D26 3-1	M02 1-3	S22 3-1	a17 0-0	N10 1-1	M29 4-1	O06 2-2	S01 2-2	D29 3-1	S08 1-0	M30 2-1	a13 2-2	F09 3-2	O27 4-1	M16 2-0	D22 5-0	a27 2-0
6 COVENTRY C	F09 1-2	O06 1-0	J05 3-0	D22 2-0	D25 0-1		M16 1-3	S08 1-1	J12 1-2	D08 2-0	F23 1-1	S22 6-1	O27 3-1	a01 0-2	A25 3-0	a13 1-4	a27 0-0	J26 1-1	N10 4-1	M30 2-1	M02 1-1	A27 1-1
7 CRYSTAL P	a06 1-3	N17 1-0	m04 1-0	D26 5-2	O20 0-2	N03 0-3		D15 1-0	S05 2-1	m01 3-0	M23 3-0	D01 2-0	S08 1-1	M09 1-0	M06 2-1	O13 1-4	M29 1-4	a20 3-2	F02 6-1	S29 2-0	J05 1-1	A25 3-0
8 EXETER C	D26 6-3	D29 2-3	a17 4-1	M30 2-2	F02 2-5	J19 2-3	a27 1-2		M16 1-4	M02 4-2	S01 1-1	a01 5-0	M20 6-1	S15 2-0	S29 3-1	O27 1-2	N10 1-1	S05 1-2	D22 1-1	O13 1-3	a13 1-1	a10 2-2
9 FULHAM	J19 3-0	m04 1-0	M23 3-1	S22 6-1	a06 2-5	a20 2-2	S10 2-2	N03 0-0		D29 4-2	D15 4-2	O20 4-0	F23 2-3	D01 2-1	N17 2-1	S01 5-2	J26 5-0	M09 2-4	M29 2-0	D25 2-1	O06 5-1	F09 2-3
10 GILLINGHAM	D15 2-2	J26 1-2	M09 1-1	S08 1-0	M23 1-0	a06 1-1	O06 0-1	O20 1-3	A25 2-2		D01 1-0	m04 1-0	F09 0-4	N17 2-1	N03 4-0	D26 2-0	J05 0-0	M29 0-2	F23 0-0	A29 1-1	S22 1-4	a24 0-0
11 LUTON T	S22 2-1	F09 2-1	A25 1-0	O06 4-2	a01 3-0	O13 1-1	N10 5-3	J05 4-0	a27 1-3	a13 8-0		J26 2-0	M16 5-2	S03 4-0	D25 2-1	M11 2-2	D22 3-2	S08 4-2	M30 5-3	a29 1-2	O27 3-1	M02 2-2
12 MERTHYR T	S01 1-0	J19 2-2	A27 1-0	M16 4-0	F16 2-3	F02 2-2	a13 2-2	a02 2-1	M02 4-1	D22 2-3	S15 3-4		J12 2-1	S29 2-2	O13 2-1	D29 2-2	O27 1-2	D25 2-1	a15 0-0	a27 3-0	M30 1-0	N10 2-1
13 NEWPORT CO	N17 0-2	M23 1-1	D15 1-2	a01 2-0	J05 2-0	M09 2-1	J19 1-3	a20 1-1	O13 3-3	S29 5-0	N03 1-2	a06 6-1		O20 0-3	m04 2-2	a18 1-0	S06 0-0	D01 2-2	S15 0-1	F02 4-1	A25 3-1	D25 0-2
14 NORTHAMPTON T	O06 2-0	F23 1-1	S08 1-1	a27 3-1	A25 4-1	a02 3-3	O27 8-1	J26 4-0	a13 3-3	M30 1-0	A30 2-2	F09 4-1	M02 7-0		J05 2-0	S17 3-0	D08 4-2	S22 2-3	M16 1-1	N10 6-1	D26 4-2	D22 3-0
15 NORWICH C	A27 5-1	a01 2-4	S22 3-1	a13 2-1	J19 0-1	D29 3-0	S15 0-1	F09 5-0	M30 2-2	M16 1-2	D26 3-0	F23 3-1	D22 3-1	S01 1-1		N10 0-3	a22 3-1	O06 2-5	M02 1-1	O27 3-0	a27 2-1	m02 5-2
16 PLYMOUTH A	m04 2-0	D15 4-0	N03 1-0	m01 2-0	N17 2-2	D01 3-0	F23 1-1	M09 0-0	J05 4-2	D25 3-0	a20 2-0	A25 4-0	O06 5-2	a06 1-1	M23 4-0		S08 1-2	O20 1-1	A29 3-0	M29 4-0	F09 2-2	S22 2-0
17 Q.P.R.	O20 0-0	F02 2-2	N17 3-2	F09 0-3	D01 2-2	D15 3-1	a01 1-1	M23 1-0	S15 2-1	S01 1-0	m04 1-1	M09 8-0	A30 0-0	a20 4-1	a06 3-0	J19 2-0		N03 3-1	D25 4-2	D29 5-1	F23 2-2	O06 3-2
18 SOUTHEND U	D29 4-4	S01 1-1	O13 1-1	N10 1-0	S29 1-3	S15 0-0	a10 3-0	A27 1-0	O27 0-1	a01 2-0	J19 5-0	D26 5-1	a13 4-2	F02 2-2	F16 5-3	M02 1-1	M16 0-3		a27 1-1	D22 3-0	F20 3-1	M30 1-3
19 SWINDON T	D01 3-3	a06 3-1	F09 2-2	A25 2-1	M09 1-1	M23 1-2	S22 3-2	m04 2-0	a01 1-2	O13 2-1	N17 4-2	a20 2-1	m01 5-2	N03 0-1	O20 1-2	S05 0-0	D26 2-1	D15 3-1		a24 1-1	S08 5-1	J05 5-0
20 TORQUAY U	a20 4-1	D01 4-1	O20 5-1	J05 0-1	N03 3-1	N17 0-2	F09 1-2	F23 1-3	D26 1-1	S05 2-1	a06 2-2	D15 6-2	S22 4-1	M23 0-1	M09 0-3	a01 2-2	A25 3-4	m04 2-1	O06 2-4		J26 3-2	S08 1-0
21 WALSALL	M23 2-1	N03 2-0	a20 1-2	A27 1-3	m04 0-2	O20 0-0	S01 3-1	D01 7-2	F16 2-2	F02 4-0	M09 0-0	N17 1-1	D29 3-1	D25 4-3	D15 3-3	S29 1-1	O13 3-1	a06 4-1	J19 1-1	S15 1-0		a01 4-0
22 WATFORD	N03 0-3	M09 2-0	D01 2-1	O13 1-0	D15 3-1	S05 4-2	D29 3-3	a06 3-0	S29 2-6	S15 1-0	O20 3-2	M23 4-0	D26 3-0	m04 1-1	a20 2-2	F02 6-3	F16 4-1	N17 4-1	S01 3-2	J19 0-2	M29 4-1	

LEAGUE TABLES

DIVISION 1

	P	W	D	L	F	A	W	D	L	F	A	Pts
Sheffield W	42	18	3	0	55	16	3	7	11	31	46	52
Leicester C	42	16	5	0	67	22	5	4	12	29	45	51
Aston Villa	42	16	2	3	62	30	7	2	12	36	51	50
Sunderland	42	16	2	3	67	30	4	5	12	26	45	47
Liverpool	42	11	4	6	53	28	6	8	7	37	36	46
Derby Co	42	12	5	4	56	24	6	5	10	30	47	46
Blackburn R	42	11	6	4	42	26	6	5	10	30	37	45
Manchester C	42	12	3	6	63	40	6	6	9	32	46	45
Arsenal	42	11	6	4	43	25	5	7	9	34	47	45
Newcastle U	42	15	2	4	48	29	4	4	13	22	43	44
Sheffield U	42	12	5	4	57	30	3	6	12	29	55	41
Manchester U	42	8	8	5	32	23	6	5	10	34	53	41
Leeds U	42	11	5	5	42	28	5	4	12	29	56	41
Bolton W	42	10	6	5	44	25	4	6	11	29	55	40
Birmingham C	42	8	7	6	37	32	7	3	11	31	45	40
Huddersfield T	42	9	6	6	45	23	5	5	11	25	38	39
West Ham U	42	11	6	4	55	31	4	3	14	31	65	39
Everton	42	11	2	8	38	31	6	2	13	25	44	38
Burnley	42	12	5	4	55	32	3	3	15	26	71	38
Portsmouth	42	13	2	6	43	26	2	4	15	13	54	36
Bury	42	9	5	7	38	35	3	2	16	24	64	31
Cardiff C	42	7	7	7	34	26	1	6	14	9	33	29

DIVISION 2

	P	W	D	L	F	A	W	D	L	F	A	Pts
Middlesbrough	42	14	4	3	54	22	8	7	6	38	35	55
Grimsby T	42	16	2	3	49	24	8	3	10	33	37	53
Bradford P.A.	42	18	2	1	62	22	4	2	15	26	48	48
Southampton	42	12	6	3	48	22	5	8	8	26	38	48
Notts Co	42	13	4	4	51	24	6	5	10	27	41	47
Stoke C	42	12	7	2	46	16	5	5	11	28	35	46
W.B.A.	42	13	4	4	50	25	6	4	11	30	54	46
Blackpool	42	13	4	4	49	18	6	3	12	43	58	45
Chelsea	42	10	6	5	40	30	7	4	10	24	35	44
Tottenham H	42	16	3	2	50	26	1	6	14	25	55	43
Nottingham F	42	8	6	7	34	33	7	6	8	37	37	42
Hull C	42	8	8	5	38	24	5	6	10	20	39	40
Preston N.E.	42	12	6	3	58	27	3	3	15	20	52	39
Millwall	42	10	4	7	43	35	6	3	12	28	51	39
Reading	42	12	3	6	48	30	3	6	12	15	56	39
Barnsley	42	12	4	5	51	28	4	2	15	18	38	38
Wolverhampton W	42	9	6	6	41	31	6	1	14	36	50	37
Oldham A	42	15	2	4	37	24	1	3	17	17	51	37
Swansea T	42	12	3	6	46	26	1	7	13	16	49	36
Bristol C	42	11	6	4	37	25	2	4	15	21	47	36
Port Vale	42	14	1	6	53	25	1	3	17	18	61	34
Clapton O	42	10	4	7	29	25	2	4	15	16	47	32

DIVISION 3 NORTH

	P	W	D	L	F	A	W	D	L	F	A	Pts
Bradford C	42	17	2	2	82	18	10	7	4	46	25	63
Stockport Co	42	19	2	0	77	23	9	4	8	34	35	62
Wrexham	42	17	2	2	59	25	4	8	9	32	44	52
Wigan B	42	16	4	1	55	16	5	5	11	27	33	51
Doncaster R	42	14	3	4	39	20	6	7	8	37	46	50
Lincoln C	42	15	3	3	58	18	6	3	12	33	49	48
Tranmere R	42	15	3	3	55	21	7	0	14	24	56	47
Carlisle U	42	15	3	3	61	27	4	5	12	25	50	46
Crewe A	42	11	6	4	47	23	7	2	12	33	45	44
South Shields	42	13	5	3	57	24	5	3	13	26	50	44
Chesterfield	42	13	2	6	46	28	5	3	13	25	49	41
Southport	42	13	5	3	52	27	3	3	15	23	58	40
Halifax T	42	11	7	3	42	24	2	6	13	21	38	39
New Brighton	42	11	3	7	40	28	4	6	11	24	43	39
Nelson	42	14	1	6	48	28	3	4	14	29	62	39
Rotherham U	42	12	5	4	44	23	3	4	14	16	54	39
Rochdale	42	12	4	5	55	34	1	6	14	24	62	36
Accrington S	42	11	5	5	42	22	2	3	16	26	60	34
Darlington	42	12	6	3	47	26	1	1	19	17	62	33
Barrow	42	7	6	8	42	37	3	2	16	22	56	28
Hartlepool U	42	9	4	8	35	38	1	2	18	24	74	26
Ashington	42	6	5	10	31	52	2	2	17	14	63	23

DIVISION 3 SOUTH

	P	W	D	L	F	A	W	D	L	F	A	Pts
Charlton A	42	14	5	2	51	22	9	3	9	35	38	54
Crystal Palace	42	14	2	5	40	25	9	6	6	41	42	54
Northampton T	42	14	6	1	68	23	6	6	9	28	34	52
Plymouth A	42	14	6	1	51	13	6	6	9	32	38	52
Fulham	42	14	3	4	60	31	7	7	7	41	40	52
Q.P.R.	42	13	7	1	50	22	6	7	8	32	39	52
Luton T	42	16	3	2	64	28	3	8	10	25	45	49
Watford	42	15	3	3	55	31	4	7	10	24	43	48
Bournemouth	42	14	4	3	54	31	5	5	11	30	46	47
Swindon T	42	12	5	4	48	27	3	8	10	27	45	43
Coventry C	42	9	6	6	35	23	5	8	8	27	34	42
Southend U	42	10	7	4	44	27	5	4	12	36	48	41
Brentford	42	11	4	6	34	21	3	6	12	22	39	38
Walsall	42	11	7	3	47	25	2	5	14	26	54	38
Brighton & H.A.	42	14	2	5	39	28	2	4	15	19	48	38
Newport Co	42	8	6	7	37	28	5	3	13	32	58	35
Norwich C	42	12	3	6	49	29	2	3	16	20	52	34
Torquay U	42	10	3	8	46	36	4	3	14	20	48	34
Bristol R	42	9	6	6	39	28	4	1	16	21	51	33
Merthyr T	42	11	6	4	42	28	0	2	19	13	75	30
Exeter C	42	7	6	8	49	40	2	5	14	18	48	29
Gillingham	42	7	8	6	22	24	3	1	17	21	59	29

Top scorers: Div 1, V.Watson (West Ham United) 41 goals; Div 2, J.Hampson (Blackpool) 45 goals; Div 3 N, F.Newton (Stockport County) 36 goals; Div 3 S, G.Goddard (Queen's Park Rangers) 37 goals.

Ashington failed to gain re-election, York City elected in their place.

Derby County centre-forward Harry Bedford's 30 goals helped the Rams into runners-up spot in 1929-30. His tally equalled the club record set by Alf Bentley in 1909-10.

DIVISION 1

	ARSENAL	ASTON VILLA	BIRMINGHAM	BLACKBURN R	BOLTON W	BURNLEY	DERBY CO	EVERTON	GRIMSBY T	HUDDERSFIELD T	LEEDS U	LEICESTER C	LIVERPOOL	MANCHESTER C	MANCHESTER U	MIDDLESBROUGH	NEWCASTLE U	PORTSMOUTH	SHEFFIELD U	SHEFFIELD W	SUNDERLAND	WEST HAM U
1 ARSENAL		m03 2-4	M15 1-0	M29 4-0	S28 1-2	S14 6-1	O12 1-1	F08 4-0	O19 4-1	D14 2-0	A31 4-0	a18 1-1	a02 0-1	S11 3-2	M12 4-2	N27 1-2	N30 0-1	D26 1-2	a12 8-1	J04 2-3	a28 0-1	N02 0-1
2 ASTON VILLA	S25 5-2		A31 2-1	N30 3-0	F08 2-0	F05 1-2	S09 2-2	O12 5-2	a02 4-1	M15 5-3	J04 3-4	O19 3-0	N16 2-3	D25 0-2	N02 1-0	M29 4-2	a12 2-0	a21 0-1	D14 5-1	S14 1-3	S28 2-1	a26 2-3
3 BIRMINGHAM	N09 2-3	D28 1-1		F01 1-2	M22 3-1	M08 2-0	a05 2-4	N23 0-0	a22 0-2	S07 4-1	F22 1-0	m03 3-0	F15 1-0	D07 3-0	D26 0-1	O05 1-1	S21 5-1	a19 1-0	J18 2-1	O26 1-0	D21 3-1	S04 4-2
4 BLACKBURN R	N23 1-1	a05 2-0	S28 7-5		F22 3-1	N09 8-3	M08 0-3	O26 3-1	S14 4-1	F08 5-2	D07 2-1	J27 3-1	m03 1-0	D21 1-3	J04 5-4	J01 7-0	S16 4-2	M22 1-0	O12 0-1	a19 0-1	D25 5-3	A31 3-3
5 BOLTON W	F01 0-0	O05 3-0	N16 0-0	O19 2-1		D25 1-1	S07 1-2	D28 5-0	N30 2-3	J01 7-1	F15 4-2	M29 1-0	M15 0-2	J18 1-2	M01 4-1	S18 2-2	a09 1-1	S21 2-1	N02 2-1	S25 1-3	a18 3-0	D14 4-1
6 BURNLEY	J18 2-2	S21 1-4	N02 3-1	M15 3-2	D26 2-2		m03 6-2	S02 1-1	N16 3-1	a01 1-3	F01 0-3	F15 1-1	a12 4-1	D28 4-2	M29 4-0	D14 4-1	M11 0-3	S07 4-0	O19 5-0	O05 2-4	S10 2-0	N30 1-1
7 DERBY CO	F19 4-1	S04 4-0	N30 3-1	N02 4-3	J04 2-1	S25 1-3		S14 2-1	D14 5-4	M29 2-2	D26 3-0	a12 2-2	O19 2-2	F01 4-2	M15 1-1	M01 3-1	a26 3-1	O05 3-2	N16 2-1	a21 4-1	A31 3-0	F05 4-3
8 EVERTON	O05 1-1	M05 3-4	M29 2-4	M01 2-2	A31 3-3	a18 3-0	J18 4-0		a12 2-4	N16 0-2	S11 1-1	N30 4-5	J04 3-3	S21 2-3	D14 0-0	O19 3-2	N02 5-2	F01 1-1	a26 3-2	D25 1-4	m03 4-1	M15 1-2
9 GRIMSBY T	F22 1-1	O26 0-2	a18 2-1	J18 5-3	a05 1-1	M22 4-0	a19 2-1	D07 0-3		S24 4-2	M08 1-2	D25 1-4	F01 3-2	N09 2-2	F15 2-2	S21 0-3	S07 4-0	S04 1-1	D28 4-1	F05 0-5	N23 0-1	O05 2-2
10 HUDDERSFIELD T	a19 2-2	N09 1-1	J04 1-1	O05 0-0	D21 0-2	O26 3-0	N23 0-1	a28 1-2	m03 0-1		S14 1-0	A31 3-2	S16 3-0	a05 1-1	a22 2-2	M26 1-0	F01 2-0	D07 2-1	S21 2-2	F22 4-1	M08 0-2	D26 3-0
11 LEEDS U	D28 2-0	S07 4-1	O19 1-0	a12 4-2	O12 2-1	S28 3-0	D25 2-1	S16 2-1	N02 6-0	J18 0-1		M01 1-2	M29 1-1	a22 3-2	a26 3-1	N30 1-2	D14 5-2	S23 1-0	M15 2-2	a09 3-0	F08 5-0	N16 1-3
12 LEICESTER C	a21 6-6	F22 4-3	O17 2-1	S21 1-1	N23 5-2	D21 4-3	D07 0-0	a05 5-4	D26 1-0	D28 1-2	O26 2-2		O05 2-1	a19 3-1	S02 4-1	F01 4-1	J18 6-1	N09 0-5	S07 3-3	M08 2-1	M22 1-2	F20 1-2
13 LIVERPOOL	D21 1-0	M22 2-0	O12 1-1	O09 1-1	N09 3-0	D07 1-3	F22 2-2	S07 0-3	S28 2-0	S04 3-0	N23 1-0	F08 1-1		O26 1-6	J25 1-0	D28 5-2	a21 0-0	M08 2-0	D26 2-0	a05 1-3	a19 0-6	S14 3-1
14 MANCHESTER C	S04 3-1	D26 1-2	a12 1-4	a26 1-1	S14 2-0	A31 2-2	S28 3-0	F05 1-2	M15 3-1	N30 1-1	a21 4-1	D14 3-2	M01 4-3		F08 0-1	N02 3-1	N16 3-0	F26 5-2	M29 2-1	J01 3-3	J04 2-2	O19 4-3
15 MANCHESTER U	O26 1-0	M08 2-3	D25 0-0	S07 1-0	D07 1-1	N23 1-0	N09 3-2	a19 3-3	O12 2-5	a18 1-0	D21 3-1	S11 2-1	S21 1-2	O05 1-3		J18 0-3	D28 5-0	F22 3-0	m03 1-5	a14 2-2	a05 2-1	F01 4-2
16 MIDDLESBROUGH	a09 1-1	N23 2-3	F08 5-1	a21 2-4	m03 3-1	a19 3-1	O26 4-0	F22 1-2	M05 1-5	O12 1-3	a05 1-1	S28 0-2	A31 5-0	M08 1-0	S14 2-3		D26 2-2	D21 2-0	S04 3-1	D07 4-1	N09 3-0	J04 2-0
17 NEWCASTLE U	a05 1-1	D07 2-2	a02 1-1	S04 5-1	O26 2-3	O12 2-1	D21 2-3	M08 1-0	J04 3-1	S28 5-2	a19 2-1	S14 2-1	a18 3-1	M22 2-2	A31 4-1	D25 3-2		N23 4-1	F08 3-5	N09 1-3	F22 3-0	m03 1-0
18 PORTSMOUTH	D25 0-1	a18 1-2	D14 2-1	N16 4-0	F05 3-0	J04 7-1	F08 3-1	S28 1-4	S11 1-1	a12 0-1	m03 0-0	M15 3-0	N02 3-3	O12 2-2	O19 3-0	a26 1-1	M29 2-0		N30 3-1	A31 0-4	S14 1-1	M12 3-1
19 SHEFFIELD U	D16 4-1	a19 3-3	S14 4-2	M03 5-7	M08 2-3	F22 3-1	M22 2-0	D21 2-0	A31 2-3	F17 0-1	N09 3-2	J04 7-1	D25 4-0	N23 1-2	O07 3-1	S09 1-3	O05 1-0	a05 2-3		S28 2-2	O26 4-2	J01 4-2
20 SHEFFIELD W	S07 0-2	J18 3-0	a28 1-1	D14 4-0	S02 1-0	F08 4-1	a22 6-3	D26 4-0	a26 1-0	O19 3-1	S21 1-2	N02 4-0	N30 2-1	m03 5-1	N16 7-2	a12 1-0	M15 4-2	D28 1-1	F01 1-1		O12 1-1	M29 2-1
21 SUNDERLAND	S21 0-1	F01 4-1	a26 2-0	D26 3-1	a21 4-1	J01 3-3	D28 3-1	O02 2-2	M29 2-0	N02 1-0	O05 1-4	N16 2-1	D14 2-3	S07 5-2	N30 2-4	M15 3-2	O19 1-0	J18 1-1	M01 3-2	a30 2-4		a12 4-2
22 WEST HAM U	M08 3-2	D21 5-2	S16 0-1	D28 2-3	a19 5-3	a05 1-0	S21 2-0	N09 3-1	F08 2-0	D25 2-3	M22 3-0	O12 1-2	J18 4-1	F22 3-0	S28 2-1	S07 5-3	S09 5-1	O26 0-1	a18 1-0	N23 1-1	D07 1-1	

Sheffield Wednesday's Jack Allen was the Owls' leading scorer in their Division One title wins of 1928-29 and 1929-30. He was the scorer of Newcastle's controversial goal in the famous 'over the line' Cup Final of 1932.

DIVISION 2

	BARNSLEY	BLACKPOOL	BRADFORD	BRADFORD C	BRISTOL C	BURY	CARDIFF C	CHARLTON A	CHELSEA	HULL C	MILLWALL	NOTTINGHAM F	NOTTS CO	OLDHAM A	PRESTON N.E.	READING	SOUTHAMPTON	STOKE C	SWANSEA T	TOTTENHAM H	W.B.A.	WOLVERHAMPTON W
1 BARNSLEY		O05 2-4	F05 1-1	D21 2-1	M08 3-1	F15 2-1	F22 2-2	N23 2-0	J01 1-1	a05 3-0	a21 1-2	D26 1-1	N09 2-2	m03 2-1	O26 0-0	M22 1-0	A31 3-1	D07 3-1	S28 1-0	J04 2-0	S14 2-2	a19 3-1
2 BLACKPOOL	F08 2-1		S28 1-0	a19 3-0	O26 7-1	S02 2-1	O12 3-0	M22 6-0	D25 1-1	N23 1-2	A31 4-3	S09 5-1	M08 1-2	a18 3-0	F22 5-1	N09 4-2	J04 5-1	a05 0-2	D21 3-0	S14 3-2	M05 1-0	D07 3-2
3 BRADFORD	S21 4-4	F01 5-0		S14 0-2	N09 3-1	O05 2-1	O26 2-0	a05 4-0	M12 1-3	D07 4-2	m03 6-0	S04 5-1	M22 3-3	D26 2-2	M08 5-2	N23 5-2	a22 1-1	a19 3-2	F22 3-0	A31 2-1	J04 5-1	D21 0-0
4 BRADFORD C	a26 0-1	D14 1-1	J18 1-2		O12 3-0	a12 2-1	S28 0-1	S30 4-1	N30 0-1	a21 2-1	M15 1-1	M29 1-1	S02 2-0	N16 2-4	F08 1-1	D25 1-0	N02 2-5	D28 3-0	F19 3-3	M01 0-2	O19 2-2	S07 2-2
5 BRISTOL C	N02 2-1	M01 0-1	M15 0-0	F26 1-3		O19 1-2	D25 2-0	J18 1-1	a21 2-1	S21 4-0	a12 1-0	a26 4-1	D28 0-0	D14 0-4	S18 2-2	S07 5-3	N30 3-1	F01 2-6	S11 2-1	M29 1-0	N16 2-1	O05 1-2
6 BURY	O12 2-1	J01 0-1	F08 5-1	D07 2-4	F22 2-0		D21 4-2	N09 2-2	m03 1-0	a23 2-1	J04 5-1	a18 0-0	O26 2-0	A31 0-2	D25 1-2	M08 2-4	S14 4-2	N23 2-0	a19 1-0	J25 2-1	S28 3-2	a05 3-1
7 CARDIFF C	O19 1-0	F15 4-2	M01 2-0	F01 0-1	D26 1-1	a26 5-1		D28 1-0	D14 1-0	S07 0-1	M29 3-1	a12 1-1	S16 3-1	N30 5-0	S02 2-0	a18 2-1	N16 5-2	J18 1-2	O05 0-0	M15 1-0	N02 3-2	S21 0-0
8 CHARLTON A	M29 2-0	N16 1-4	N30 2-0	m03 1-3	S14 3-1	M15 1-2	A31 4-1		N02 1-1	M17 4-0	F08 1-1	M10 5-0	a07 1-0	O19 1-1	J04 1-1	S28 0-0	a26 4-1	S09 4-4	a18 0-2	D14 1-0	a12 0-1	J01 2-0
9 CHELSEA	S11 2-0	D26 4-0	O12 1-2	a05 3-2	a18 2-1	S23 5-3	a19 1-0	M08 1-1		N09 3-0	S14 3-0	A31 2-0	F22 3-1	J04 1-1	D21 5-0	O26 1-0	J25 2-0	M22 3-2	D07 1-0	S28 3-0	F08 2-0	N23 1-1
10 HULL C	N30 2-0	M29 0-3	a12 0-2	a18 0-0	m01 0-1	N16 1-3	J04 2-2	O12 0-2	M15 1-3		O19 3-2	N02 1-2	S28 0-0	M31 1-0	S14 2-0	F08 4-2	S16 2-0	D25 3-0	A31 1-0	a26 2-0	D14 3-2	m03 2-0
11 MILLWALL	a18 2-1	D28 3-1	S16 1-2	N09 2-2	D07 1-1	S07 2-4	N23 2-0	O05 1-1	J18 0-0	F22 0-0		S21 2-2	a19 2-0	F01 2-1	a05 2-0	D21 3-1	O12 1-1	O26 2-1	M22 0-2	S02 2-5	D25 2-1	M08 4-0
12 NOTTINGHAM F	D25 4-0	m03 0-0	O03 1-1	N23 2-1	D21 5-2	a21 1-2	D07 3-1	O26 0-2	D28 0-0	M08 2-1	F05 1-1		S07 1-1	S14 1-2	a19 2-4	F22 5-0	S28 0-5	N09 2-1	a05 1-0	F08 0-0	O12 0-2	M22 5-2
13 NOTTS CO	M15 3-0	N02 0-2	N16 1-1	S09 2-0	A31 3-1	M01 1-3	S25 2-1	S21 4-0	O19 2-2	F01 4-1	D14 1-1	J04 0-0		a26 1-1	a22 0-3	J18 3-0	a12 1-2	O05 3-3	D26 0-0	N30 0-1	M29 2-1	F15 0-3
14 OLDHAM A	S16 3-2	a21 1-2	D25 5-1	M22 6-1	a19 2-2	D28 2-0	a05 4-1	F22 1-0	S07 4-2	O26 3-1	S28 2-2	J18 0-0	D21 2-2		D07 0-2	S21 0-0	F08 3-2	M08 5-0	N23 4-1	O12 2-0	J01 5-0	N09 6-0
15 PRESTON N.E.	M01 3-1	O19 4-6	N02 4-1	O05 2-2	m03 2-2	D26 1-1	S09 2-3	S07 0-3	a26 1-2	J18 1-2	N30 3-1	D14 1-2	a18 3-1	a12 0-3		D28 2-1	M29 1-1	S21 5-1	F15 0-0	N16 4-0	M15 2-2	F01 1-1
16 READING	N16 1-0	M15 1-1	M29 1-0	D26 1-1	J04 1-6	N02 0-1	a21 2-0	F01 3-1	M01 3-1	O05 1-1	a26 0-1	O19 0-1	S14 2-0	F05 1-1	A31 2-0		D14 1-1	F15 0-0	J25 3-1	a12 3-0	N30 2-2	S04 3-1
17 SOUTHAMPTON	D28 4-0	S07 4-2	a21 2-2	M08 2-1	a05 3-0	J18 0-0	M22 1-1	D21 2-0	S21 4-2	S02 2-2	M03 0-0	F01 2-0	D07 2-2	O05 2-0	N23 1-2	a19 4-3		F22 2-1	N09 2-1	D26 1-0	S09 3-2	O26 3-1
18 STOKE C	a12 3-0	N30 0-1	D14 2-1	A31 2-0	S28 6-2	M29 1-0	S14 1-1	S02 2-1	N16 1-1	D26 3-1	M01 1-0	M15 6-0	F08 1-1	N02 0-2	J25 2-3	O12 2-2	O19 4-0		J04 0-1	m03 1-0	a26 0-3	S30 3-0
19 SWANSEA T	F01 0-2	a26 3-0	O19 2-4	S21 5-0	S02 1-1	D14 2-4	F08 1-0	a21 2-0	a12 3-0	D28 2-0	N16 3-1	N30 1-1	D25 3-2	M29 3-0	O12 4-0	S16 0-1	M15 2-2	S07 2-2		N02 0-1	M01 1-0	J18 2-2
20 TOTTENHAM H	S07 2-1	J18 6-1	D28 1-1	O26 1-1	N23 2-1	S21 2-2	N09 1-2	a19 3-0	F01 3-3	D21 2-2	S23 1-1	O05 1-1	a05 2-0	F15 2-1	M22 1-0	D07 0-0	D25 3-2	O09 3-1	M08 3-0		a18 0-2	F22 4-2
21 W.B.A.	J18 4-2	S21 5-1	S07 5-0	F22 4-2	M22 2-0	F01 5-1	M08 0-2	D07 1-1	O05 2-0	a19 7-1	D26 6-1	M19 1-3	N23 4-2	S02 0-3	N09 2-0	a05 1-0	m03 5-1	D21 2-3	O26 6-2	a21 4-3		D28 7-3
22 WOLVERHAMPTON W	D14 3-0	a12 1-2	a26 4-4	J04 6-0	F08 1-0	N30 2-0	a14 4-0	D26 0-4	M29 0-1	S23 4-2	N02 1-1	N16 2-1	O12 5-1	M15 1-1	S28 4-0	S09 2-1	M01 2-0	a21 2-1	S14 4-1	O19 3-0	A31 2-4	

Season 1929-30

DIVISION 3 NORTH

	ACCRINGTON S	BARROW	CARLISLE U	CHESTERFIELD	CREWE A	DARLINGTON	DONCASTER R	HALIFAX T	HARTLEPOOLS U	LINCOLN C	NELSON	NEW BRIGHTON	PORT VALE	ROCHDALE	ROTHERHAM U	SOUTHPORT	SOUTH SHIELDS	STOCKPORT CO	TRANMERE R	WIGAN B	WREXHAM	YORK C
1 ACCRINGTON S		N02 3-1	J01 7-2	S07 3-0	a12 0-3	D26 3-1	F24 3-3	F01 7-1	S09 3-0	J18 0-3	S24 3-0	N16 5-0	M15 0-2	F15 6-2	O05 2-0	a26 1-1	a21 1-2	M29 0-1	S21 3-3	O19 3-1	M01 1-3	M05 1-1
2 BARROW	M08 3-1		O05 0-2	a05 0-1	a21 1-0	N09 0-1	N23 1-0	D21 0-4	M22 3-0	D07 2-1	F15 0-2	A31 3-0	J04 1-1	F22 2-0	S14 5-1	m03 0-2	O26 1-3	S09 1-4	a19 1-1	F01 4-1	S21 3-3	D25 0-0
3 CARLISLE U	a18 2-1	F08 7-1		N09 6-0	A31 2-0	F22 1-4	M08 1-1	a05 2-0	O26 5-2	M22 2-4	J23 2-2	J25 2-2	S28 1-4	a19 2-0	D07 3-1	S12 4-0	D21 4-1	S14 1-5	N23 4-3	m03 5-0	O12 5-1	J04 2-2
4 CHESTERFIELD	J04 4-2	M12 2-1	M15 3-1		O19 5-1	S14 4-1	S28 2-1	a18 2-0	J25 2-0	F15 2-1	N02 3-0	a07 1-0	a12 1-1	J01 2-0	D26 2-1	M01 2-0	A31 1-2	a26 1-3	S23 1-0	N16 5-0	M29 5-0	F08 3-0
5 CREWE A	D07 2-1	a18 0-0	D28 1-2	F22 2-1		a19 1-2	S21 4-0	N09 4-1	D21 5-2	O26 1-1	S07 4-0	O12 2-3	m03 0-2	N23 6-1	M22 6-1	J18 5-4	a05 2-2	F08 1-1	M08 3-1	S02 2-1	D25 2-0	S28 2-2
6 DARLINGTON	D25 2-4	M15 4-0	O19 3-0	J18 1-4	a28 3-0		S07 6-2	O05 3-2	D28 0-0	S21 1-1	S04 6-1	M29 1-2	N16 0-1	a22 3-0	F15 8-1	D14 2-1	J01 8-3	F19 1-2	F01 7-2	M01 2-0	N02 5-1	a12 5-2
7 DONCASTER R	A31 3-1	M29 4-0	N02 1-4	F01 2-1	a10 2-1	J04 3-1		S23 1-0	S14 0-0	O05 0-0	M01 3-0	a12 1-1	m01 0-2	D26 3-1	a18 2-0	O19 3-1	S02 1-0	M20 1-1	F15 1-1	M15 4-2	N16 4-2	a26 0-3
8 HALIFAX T	S28 1-1	J11 0-1	F20 1-0	a21 3-2	M15 1-3	F08 3-1	S16 1-0		O12 0-0	D25 1-1	M29 1-1	O19 4-0	A31 1-2	S14 2-3	J04 1-1	N16 1-1	J25 0-2	M01 0-3	S09 0-1	a12 2-1	D19 2-0	N02 2-2
9 HARTLEPOOLS U	S02 2-2	N16 2-0	M01 1-0	S21 0-0	a26 5-1	A31 2-5	J18 3-0	F15 3-0		F01 4-0	O19 1-2	J11 1-1	M29 2-0	a21 2-8	J01 5-1	J04 1-1	D25 2-1	a12 0-1	O05 2-0	N02 4-0	M15 5-0	a02 3-1
10 LINCOLN C	S14 3-3	a12 3-0	N16 4-1	O12 2-1	M01 2-2	J25 2-2	F08 3-1	D26 0-1	S28 2-2		M15 4-1	a26 5-3	S16 3-2	A31 0-0	S09 1-1	N02 1-1	J04 2-2	a23 1-0	a21 8-0	M29 2-0	F19 3-0	O19 3-0
11 NELSON	D21 2-1	O12 2-0	D25 2-2	M08 0-2	J04 1-1	S11 0-1	O26 4-1	N23 1-0	F22 3-2	N09 0-0		S28 2-1	F08 2-3	J14 1-0	a05 0-1	A31 2-2	a19 0-1	J25 1-2	M22 0-1	a18 1-3	O01 4-0	S14 3-1
12 NEW BRIGHTON	M22 5-0	D28 5-0	S21 2-1	a19 1-1	F15 3-1	N23 1-3	D07 1-0	F22 4-0	a05 0-0	D21 1-4	F01 2-1		S02 0-1	M08 2-0	O26 2-2	O05 1-3	N09 4-1	a18 3-2	D26 3-0	J18 5-0	S07 2-1	J01 1-1
13 PORT VALE	N09 5-2	S07 5-0	F01 4-0	D07 4-1	S23 2-0	M22 0-2	a05 2-1	D28 3-0	N23 2-1	a19 5-2	O05 3-1	S09 5-1		O26 3-3	F22 7-1	F15 1-0	M08 3-0	D25 1-2	D21 1-0	S21 4-0	J18 3-0	a18 1-1
14 ROCHDALE	O12 4-0	O19 6-1	a29 2-0	S03 2-1	M29 3-1	S17 4-1	D25 2-4	J18 0-3	a18 1-1	a08 3-4	a12 4-1	N02 5-0	M01 0-0		S21 1-2	J11 2-2	F08 2-0	M15 3-1	S07 2-1	D14 2-1	F01 5-4	m03 4-2
15 ROTHERHAM U	F08 2-4	J18 7-0	a12 4-1	D25 1-1	N16 2-1	O12 1-4	a21 1-0	S07 2-0	m03 0-4	S02 1-0	M24 1-2	M01 2-2	O19 2-2	J25 0-4		M29 6-3	S28 0-1	N02 2-2	D28 5-0	F24 4-1	a26 1-3	M15 2-5
16 SOUTHPORT	a19 2-0	J01 0-2	S03 4-3	O26 5-1	S14 0-3	D21 3-0	F22 1-1	M22 4-0	S07 1-1	M08 3-2	D28 0-0	F08 2-1	O12 1-2	a05 2-3	N23 7-1		D07 2-1	S28 1-2	N09 4-4	D25 1-1	a18 5-3	J25 1-0
17 SOUTH SHIELDS	m03 2-2	M01 2-0	a26 5-2	D28 3-1	J11 1-0	a18 3-3	S11 2-1	S21 1-0	D26 3-5	S07 3-1	D14 2-1	M15 1-2	N02 0-0	O05 2-2	F01 5-0	a12 4-0		N16 2-3	S14 1-5	F15 2-2	O19 1-1	M29 4-1
18 STOCKPORT CO	N23 1-0	S02 5-0	J18 7-1	D21 1-0	O05 2-3	a05 4-0	a19 3-0	O26 6-0	M03 5-1	J01 1-1	S21 6-1	m03 2-0	D26 4-2	N09 4-2	M08 6-1	F01 2-2	M22 2-0		F22 3-1	S07 1-1	D28 0-1	F15 2-3
19 TRANMERE R	J25 2-2	F20 5-2	M29 3-0	a22 1-2	N02 1-2	S28 3-0	O12 2-1	S02 3-3	F08 7-1	a18 0-1	N16 2-3	D25 3-1	a26 1-5	J04 2-2	A31 5-4	M15 3-1	J18 3-0	O19 2-0		J11 3-0	a12 2-1	M01 4-4
20 WIGAN B	F22 2-1	S28 2-0	S25 8-0	M22 2-1	J01 2-2	O26 3-2	N09 3-2	D07 2-1	M08 1-3	N23 4-1	a21 2-0	S14 5-0	J25 0-3	D21 3-1	a19 1-1	D26 1-1	O12 1-1	J04 0-1	a05 0-2		F08 2-1	A31 0-2
21 WREXHAM	O26 0-1	M26 3-0	F15 3-3	N23 1-1	D26 1-0	M10 2-2	M22 0-2	a19 2-1	N09 3-5	a05 3-1	m03 5-1	J04 2-1	S14 0-2	S28 8-0	D21 1-0	a21 1-2	F22 1-3	A31 1-1	D07 2-0	O05 2-1		S11 1-1
22 YORK C	a05 2-0	D26 3-1	S07 2-2	O05 1-1	F01 4-2	D07 1-1	D21 2-2	M08 3-0	a19 4-1	F22 1-0	J18 1-0	S18 3-0	a21 0-2	M22 6-0	N09 3-0	S21 0-4	N23 2-2	O12 1-2	O26 0-0	D28 4-0	S04 0-0	

DIVISION 3 SOUTH

	BOURNEMOUTH	BRENTFORD	BRIGHTON & HA	BRISTOL R	CLAPTON O	COVENTRY C	CRYSTAL P	EXETER C	FULHAM	GILLINGHAM	LUTON T	MERTHYR T	NEWPORT CO	NORTHAMPTON T	NORWICH C	PLYMOUTH A	Q.P.R.	SOUTHEND U	SWINDON T	TORQUAY U	WALSALL	WATFORD
1 BOURNEMOUTH		M26 1-2	M12 1-1	a12 3-1	a26 5-1	F01 1-0	S18 2-1	S07 3-0	S11 5-0	D26 1-2	S21 5-1	M15 4-2	M01 1-1	F26 3-1	a21 2-3	N16 1-1	O12 0-0	J18 0-0	M29 1-3	N02 4-1	F08 1-1	O19 3-2
2 BRENTFORD	a19 1-0		D25 5-2	S25 2-1	S04 3-1	O12 3-1	M08 2-0	N23 2-0	F22 5-1	N09 2-1	D07 2-0	S14 6-0	S28 1-0	M22 2-0	O26 3-0	J04 3-0	a21 3-0	a05 2-1	A31 3-2	J25 5-0	D21 6-2	F08 5-0
3 BRIGHTON & H.A.	a05 4-3	D26 2-0		D28 1-0	S25 1-0	a18 1-1	F22 1-2	N09 1-1	D21 5-0	O26 2-0	N23 4-1	S28 4-1	O12 3-2	M08 2-1	S07 6-3	a02 0-1	a19 2-3	M22 1-0	S14 3-0	F08 5-0	D07 4-0	S04 2-1
4 BRISTOL R	a09 2-1	m03 4-1	A31 1-0		a18 0-0	S02 1-3	O26 2-3	M22 1-0	D26 4-1	M08 3-0	a05 2-2	J25 2-2	F08 2-3	N09 2-3	F22 0-1	S14 2-3	D21 4-1	N23 4-2	J04 3-2	S28 2-0	a19 3-1	O12 1-2
5 CLAPTON O	D21 0-0	S16 1-1	m03 4-1	a21 3-0		F08 3-1	N09 2-1	a05 3-0	O26 2-4	M22 2-0	a19 6-1	J04 1-0	M31 3-1	N23 0-0	M08 0-0	A31 0-2	F22 2-4	D07 1-1	D25 2-1	S14 1-1	O12 1-1	S28 1-1
6 COVENTRY C	S28 0-2	F15 2-1	a22 0-2	S09 1-0	O05 5-2		M22 1-0	D07 3-3	M08 3-1	N23 5-0	D21 5-1	A31 2-2	S14 2-0	a05 2-2	N09 3-1	D25 1-0	O26 2-3	a19 5-1	m03 1-2	J04 4-1	F22 4-0	J25 3-1
7 CRYSTAL P	m03 1-1	N02 2-1	O19 2-2	M01 3-0	M15 3-0	N16 4-3		F15 1-1	J04 4-3	F01 5-1	a21 4-1	D14 6-1	S25 1-0	O05 1-3	S14 3-2	a26 3-0	A31 1-1	S11 1-2	N30 1-0	a12 4-2	D26 5-1	M29 1-1
8 EXETER C	J04 1-2	M29 0-0	M15 1-4	N16 5-2	F05 4-0	a12 1-1	O12 6-1		S28 2-1	S04 3-0	A31 2-2	O19 1-1	a26 0-4	a21 6-4	F08 3-0	M01 1-1	J25 0-2	D26 3-1	N02 5-1	S18 0-0	S14 0-2	F19 1-0
9 FULHAM	S02 3-3	O19 2-0	a26 5-1	D25 6-2	M01 2-2	N02 2-0	S07 1-2	F01 2-2		J18 2-1	F15 1-1	F03 5-4	N16 2-1	S21 1-0	D28 3-3	a12 1-3	m03 0-2	O05 2-2	J01 4-1	M29 1-0	a21 3-2	M15 6-1
10 GILLINGHAM	D25 1-5	M15 1-3	M01 2-2	N02 3-3	N16 2-0	M29 0-3	S28 1-1	S11 2-0	S14 0-1		m03 2-0	a26 6-0	a12 5-0	F15 5-2	J25 1-2	F08 0-0	J04 3-1	a18 1-0	O19 0-0	D14 0-2	A31 2-1	J11 1-2
11 LUTON T	J25 1-0	a12 2-1	M29 1-0	M24 3-0	M10 1-2	a26 1-1	a18 2-2	D28 0-4	O12 4-1	S16 2-0		N02 4-0	O19 4-2	D25 1-0	S02 1-1	M15 5-2	F08 2-1	S07 0-3	N16 1-1	M01 3-1	S28 2-3	J18 2-0
12 MERTHYR T	N09 0-1	J18 2-3	F01 2-8	S21 1-1	S07 0-1	a14 2-2	a19 5-2	F22 0-2	a05 3-4	D21 1-1	M08 3-1		m03 5-1	S02 1-0	D07 1-5	F15 0-3	M03 1-4	O26 2-2	F08 3-3	a22 3-0	M22 2-3	D25 2-2
13 NEWPORT CO	O26 1-1	F01 1-3	M03 2-2	O05 2-2	S21 0-0	J18 4-2	a05 0-0	D21 4-1	M22 1-1	D07 5-1	F22 0-0	a10 10-0		a19 2-1	N23 4-4	a21 0-2	N09 4-5	J25 0-0	S05 2-1	D25 2-1	M08 3-2	S07 1-0
14 NORTHAMPTON T	A31 2-0	N16 1-1	N02 1-3	M15 6-1	M29 3-0	a07 2-2	F08 2-0	a22 2-2	M13 3-1	O12 3-1	D26 4-1	S09 2-0	D31 2-0		S28 4-0	O19 1-1	S14 2-1	m03 5-1	M01 3-3	a26 2-2	J04 1-0	a12 2-0
15 NORWICH C	a22 1-0	M01 2-2	J04 2-0	O19 4-2	N02 1-0	M15 10-2	J18 2-2	O05 3-1	A31 0-4	S21 2-0	S09 1-1	a12 5-1	M29 4-1	F01 4-3		a28 1-2	D25 3-0	F15 1-1	a26 1-5	J11 2-0	S16 3-0	N16 3-1
16 PLYMOUTH A	M22 2-1	S07 1-1	S21 1-1	J18 3-0	D28 3-0	D26 3-0	D21 6-1	O26 4-1	D07 3-1	O05 3-0	N09 6-1	O12 2-1	a18 3-1	F22 1-0	a19 4-1		a05 4-0	M08 1-0	M26 5-0	S11 5-0	N23 1-1	m03 2-1
17 Q.P.R.	F15 3-1	a18 2-1	M27 3-1	a26 2-1	O19 1-1	M01 3-1	D28 4-1	S21 2-0	S16 0-0	S07 2-1	O05 1-0	M29 2-0	M15 4-1	J18 0-2	D26 3-2	M13 1-2		F01 2-5	a12 8-3	N16 1-1	S05 2-2	N02 0-0
18 SOUTHEND U	S14 4-1	J11 2-0	N16 0-0	M29 6-0	a12 4-1	a30 1-2	S02 3-2	D25 1-0	F08 1-2	a21 0-0	J04 1-1	M01 6-0	A31 2-1	S16 1-2	O12 1-1	N02 1-1	S28 1-0		M15 3-1	O19 1-1	F19 1-0	a26 1-3
19 SWINDON T	N23 1-1	D28 0-2	J18 0-1	S07 2-2	D26 0-0	S16 1-1	S21 3-1	M08 1-0	a19 1-1	F22 3-0	M22 1-1	O05 6-3	S09 5-1	O26 2-0	D21 2-1	S28 1-2	D07 2-2	N09 5-1		O12 2-1	a05 3-1	a18 1-3
20 TORQUAY U	M08 7-0	S21 2-1	O05 5-2	a02 2-1	J18 0-5	S07 1-3	D07 2-2	m03 2-1	N23 2-4	a19 1-1	O26 2-2	a21 4-0	D26 3-2	D21 0-1	a05 2-2	S04 3-4	M22 1-3	F22 1-1	F15 1-1		N09 5-2	D28 4-0
21 WALSALL	O05 2-2	a26 1-2	a12 2-0	a30 0-0	F15 0-1	O19 3-2	D25 0-0	J18 5-2	a22 2-2	D28 1-2	F01 1-0	N16 6-0	N02 2-1	S07 1-2	m03 1-0	M29 1-3	S09 4-0	S21 1-3	S23 4-0	a09 7-0		M01 1-2
22 WATFORD	F22 0-0	O05 1-2	S18 3-0	F15 4-3	F01 3-0	S21 1-3	N23 1-1	a19 2-1	N09 0-0	a05 4-1	S14 0-4	D26 2-3	J04 2-3	D07 1-2	M22 2-1	S25 0-2	M08 1-1	D21 2-1	a21 4-1	A31 2-0	O26 2-1	

LEAGUE TABLES

DIVISION 1

	P	W	D	L	F	A	W	D	L	F	A	Pts
Sheffield W	42	15	4	2	56	20	11	4	6	49	37	60
Derby Co	42	16	4	1	61	32	5	4	12	29	50	50
Manchester C	42	12	5	4	51	33	7	4	10	40	48	47
Aston Villa	42	13	1	7	54	33	8	4	9	38	50	47
Leeds U	42	15	2	4	52	22	5	4	12	27	41	46
Blackburn R	42	15	2	4	65	36	4	5	12	34	57	45
West Ham U	42	14	2	5	51	26	5	3	13	35	53	43
Leicester C	42	12	5	4	57	42	5	4	12	29	48	43
Sunderland	42	13	3	5	50	35	5	4	12	26	45	43
Huddersfield T	42	9	7	5	32	21	8	2	11	31	48	43
Birmingham C	42	13	3	5	40	21	3	6	12	27	41	41
Liverpool	42	11	5	5	33	29	5	4	12	30	50	41
Portsmouth	42	10	6	5	43	25	5	4	12	23	37	40
Arsenal	42	10	2	9	49	26	4	9	8	29	40	39
Bolton W	42	11	5	5	46	24	4	4	13	28	50	39
Middlesbrough	42	11	3	7	48	31	5	3	13	34	53	38
Manchester U	42	11	4	6	39	34	4	4	13	28	54	38
Grimsby T	42	8	6	7	39	39	7	1	13	34	50	37
Newcastle U	42	13	4	4	52	32	2	3	16	19	60	37
Sheffield U	42	12	2	7	59	39	3	4	14	32	57	36
Burnley	42	11	5	5	53	34	3	3	15	26	63	36
Everton	42	6	7	8	48	46	6	4	11	32	46	35

DIVISION 2

	P	W	D	L	F	A	W	D	L	F	A	Pts
Blackpool	42	17	1	3	63	22	10	3	8	35	45	58
Chelsea	42	17	3	1	49	14	5	8	8	25	32	55
Oldham A	42	14	5	2	60	21	7	6	8	30	30	53
Bradford P.A.	42	14	5	2	65	28	5	7	9	26	42	50
Bury	42	14	2	5	45	27	8	3	10	33	40	49
W.B.A.	42	16	1	4	73	31	5	4	12	32	42	47
Southampton	42	14	6	1	46	22	3	5	13	31	54	45
Cardiff C	42	14	4	3	41	16	4	4	13	20	43	44
Wolverhampton W	42	14	3	4	53	24	2	6	13	24	55	41
Nottingham F	42	9	6	6	36	28	4	9	8	19	41	41
Stoke C	42	12	4	5	41	20	4	4	13	33	52	40
Tottenham H	42	11	8	2	43	24	4	1	16	16	37	39
Charlton A	42	10	6	5	39	23	4	5	12	20	40	39
Millwall	42	10	7	4	36	26	2	8	11	21	47	39
Swansea T	42	11	5	5	42	23	3	4	14	15	38	37
Preston N.E.	42	7	7	7	42	36	6	4	11	23	44	37
Barnsley	42	12	7	2	39	22	2	1	18	17	49	36
Bradford C	42	7	7	7	33	30	5	5	11	27	47	36
Reading	42	10	7	4	31	20	2	4	15	23	47	35
Bristol C	42	11	4	6	36	30	2	5	14	25	53	35
Hull C	42	11	3	7	30	24	3	4	14	21	54	35
Notts Co	42	8	7	6	33	26	1	8	12	21	44	33

DIVISION 3 NORTH

	P	W	D	L	F	A	W	D	L	F	A	Pts
Port Vale	42	17	2	2	64	18	13	5	3	39	19	67
Stockport Co	42	15	3	3	67	20	13	4	4	39	24	63
Darlington	42	14	2	5	71	29	8	4	9	37	44	50
Chesterfield	42	18	1	2	53	15	4	5	12	23	41	50
Lincoln C	42	12	8	1	54	23	5	6	10	29	38	48
York C	42	11	7	3	43	20	4	9	8	34	44	46
South Shields	42	11	6	4	49	32	7	4	10	28	42	46
Hartlepool U	42	13	4	4	50	24	4	7	10	31	50	45
Southport	42	11	5	5	49	31	4	8	9	32	43	43
Rochdale	42	14	3	4	57	30	4	4	13	32	61	43
Crewe A	42	12	5	4	55	28	5	3	13	27	43	42
Tranmere R	42	12	4	5	57	35	4	5	12	26	51	41
New Brighton	42	13	4	4	48	22	3	4	14	21	57	40
Doncaster R	42	13	5	3	39	22	2	4	15	23	47	39
Carlisle U	42	13	4	4	63	34	3	3	15	27	67	39
Accrington S	42	11	4	6	55	30	3	5	13	29	51	37
Wrexham	42	10	5	6	42	28	3	3	15	25	60	34
Wigan B	42	12	4	5	44	26	1	3	17	16	62	33
Nelson	42	9	4	8	31	25	4	3	14	20	55	33
Rotherham U	42	9	4	8	46	40	2	4	15	21	73	30
Halifax T	42	7	7	7	27	26	3	1	17	17	53	28
Barrow	42	9	4	8	31	28	2	1	18	10	70	27

DIVISION 3 SOUTH

	P	W	D	L	F	A	W	D	L	F	A	Pts
Plymouth A	42	18	3	0	63	12	12	5	4	35	26	68
Brentford	42	21	0	0	66	12	7	5	9	28	32	61
Q.P.R.	42	13	5	3	46	26	8	4	9	34	42	51
Northampton T	42	14	6	1	53	20	7	2	12	29	38	50
Brighton & H.A.	42	16	2	3	54	20	5	6	10	33	43	50
Coventry C	42	14	3	4	54	25	5	6	10	34	48	47
Fulham	42	12	6	3	54	33	6	5	10	33	50	47
Norwich C	42	14	4	3	55	28	4	6	11	33	49	46
Crystal Palace	42	14	5	2	56	26	3	7	11	25	48	46
Bournemouth	42	11	6	4	47	24	4	7	10	25	37	43
Southend U	42	11	6	4	41	19	4	7	10	28	40	43
Clapton O	42	10	8	3	38	21	4	5	12	17	41	41
Luton T	42	13	4	4	42	25	1	8	12	22	53	40
Swindon T	42	10	7	4	42	25	3	5	13	31	58	38
Watford	42	10	4	7	37	30	5	4	12	23	43	38
Exeter C	42	10	6	5	45	29	2	5	14	22	44	35
Walsall	42	10	4	7	45	24	3	4	14	26	54	34
Newport Co	42	9	9	3	48	29	3	1	17	26	56	34
Torquay U	42	9	6	6	50	38	1	5	15	14	56	31
Bristol R	42	11	3	7	45	31	0	5	16	22	62	30
Gillingham	42	9	5	7	38	28	2	3	16	13	52	30
Merthyr T	42	5	6	10	39	49	1	3	17	21	86	21

FOOTBALL LEAGUE RECORDS

Top scorers: Div 1, T.Waring (Aston Villa) 49 goals; Div 2, W.Dean (Everton) 39 goals; Div 3 N, J.McConnell (Carlisle United) 37 goals; Div 3 S, P.Simpson (Crystal Palace) 46 goals.

Merthyr Town failed to gain re-election, Thames elected in their place.

Arsenal's David Jack, who scored 31 goals when Arsenal won the League Championship for the first time in 1930-31.

DIVISION 1

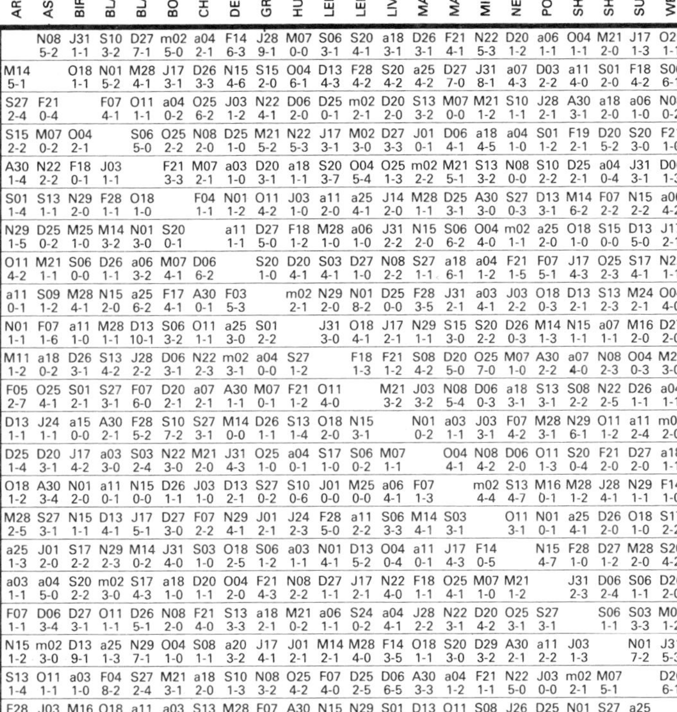

	ARSENAL	ASTON VILLA	BIRMINGHAM	BLACKBURN R	BLACKPOOL	BOLTON W	CHELSEA	DERBY CO	GRIMSBY T	HUDDERSFIELD T	LEEDS U	LEICESTER C	LIVERPOOL	MANCHESTER C	MANCHESTER U	MIDDLESBROUGH	NEWCASTLE U	PORTSMOUTH	SHEFFIELD U	SHEFFIELD W	SUNDERLAND	WEST HAM U
1 ARSENAL		N08 5-2	J31 1-1	S10 3-2	D27 7-1	m02 5-0	a04 2-1	F14 6-3	J28 9-1	M07 0-0	S06 3-1	S20 4-1	a18 3-1	D26 3-1	F21 4-1	N22 5-3	D20 1-2	a06 1-1	O04 1-1	M21 2-0	J17 1-3	O25 1-1
2 ASTON VILLA	M14 5-1		O18 1-1	N01 5-2	M28 4-1	J17 3-1	D26 3-3	N15 4-6	S15 2-0	O04 6-1	D13 4-3	F28 4-2	S20 4-2	a25 4-2	D27 7-0	J31 8-1	a07 4-3	D03 2-2	a11 4-0	S01 2-0	F18 4-2	S06 6-1
3 BIRMINGHAM	S27 2-4	F21 0-4		F07 4-1	O11 1-1	a04 0-2	O25 6-2	J03 1-2	N22 4-1	D06 2-0	D25 0-1	m02 2-1	D20 2-0	S13 3-2	M07 0-0	M21 1-2	S10 1-1	J28 2-1	A30 3-1	a18 2-0	a06 1-0	N08 0-2
4 BLACKBURN R	S15 2-2	M07 0-2	O04 2-1		S06 5-0	O25 2-2	N08 2-0	D25 1-0	M21 5-2	N22 5-3	J17 3-1	M02 3-0	D27 3-3	J01 0-1	D06 4-1	a18 4-5	a04 1-0	S01 1-2	F19 2-1	D20 5-2	S20 3-0	F21 1-0
5 BLACKPOOL	A30 1-4	N22 2-2	F18 0-1	J03 1-1		F21 3-3	M07 2-1	a03 1-0	D20 3-1	a18 1-1	S20 3-7	O04 5-4	O25 1-3	m02 2-2	M21 5-1	S13 3-2	N08 0-0	S10 2-2	D25 2-1	a04 0-4	J31 3-1	D06 1-3
6 BOLTON W	S01 1-4	S13 1-1	N29 2-0	F28 1-1	O18 1-0		F04 1-1	N01 1-2	O11 4-2	J03 1-0	a11 2-0	a25 4-1	J14 2-0	M28 1-1	D25 3-1	A30 3-0	S27 0-3	D13 3-1	M14 6-2	F07 2-2	N15 2-2	a06 4-2
7 CHELSEA	N29 1-5	D25 0-2	M25 1-0	M14 3-2	N01 3-0	S20 0-1		a11 1-1	D27 5-0	F18 1-2	M28 1-0	a06 1-0	J31 2-2	N15 2-0	S06 6-2	O04 4-0	m02 1-1	a25 2-0	O18 1-0	S15 0-0	D13 5-0	J17 2-1
8 DERBY CO	O11 4-2	M21 1-1	S06 0-0	D26 1-1	a06 3-2	M07 4-1	D06 6-2		S20 1-0	D20 4-1	S03 4-1	D27 1-0	N08 2-2	S27 1-1	a18 6-1	a04 1-2	F21 1-5	F07 5-1	J17 4-3	O25 2-3	S17 4-1	N22 1-1
9 GRIMSBY T	a11 0-1	S09 1-2	M28 4-1	N15 2-0	a25 6-2	F17 4-1	A30 0-1	F03 5-3		m02 2-1	N29 2-0	N01 8-2	D25 0-0	F28 3-5	J31 2-1	a03 4-1	J03 2-2	O18 0-3	D13 2-1	S13 2-3	M24 2-1	O04 4-0
10 HUDDERSFIELD T	N01 1-1	F07 1-6	a11 1-0	M28 1-1	D13 10-1	S06 3-2	O11 1-1	a25 3-0	S01 2-2		J31 3-0	O18 4-1	J17 2-1	N29 1-1	S15 3-0	S20 2-2	D26 0-3	M14 1-3	N15 1-1	a07 1-1	M16 2-0	D27 2-0
11 LEEDS U	M11 1-2	a18 0-2	D26 3-1	S13 4-2	J28 2-2	D06 3-1	N22 2-3	m02 3-1	a04 0-0	S27 1-2		F18 1-3	F21 1-2	S08 4-2	D20 5-0	O25 7-0	M07 1-0	A30 2-2	a07 4-0	N08 2-3	O04 0-3	M21 3-0
12 LEICESTER C	F05 2-7	O25 4-1	S01 2-1	S27 3-1	F07 6-0	D20 2-1	a07 2-1	A30 1-1	M07 0-1	F21 1-2	O11 4-0		M21 3-2	J03 3-2	N08 5-4	D06 0-3	a18 3-1	S13 3-1	S08 2-2	N22 2-5	D26 1-1	a04 1-1
13 LIVERPOOL	D13 1-1	J24 1-1	a15 0-0	A30 2-1	F28 5-2	S10 7-2	S27 3-1	M14 0-0	D26 1-1	S13 1-4	O18 2-0	N15 3-1		N01 0-2	a03 1-1	J03 3-1	F07 4-2	M28 3-1	N29 6-1	O11 1-2	a11 2-4	m02 2-0
14 MANCHESTER C	D25 1-4	D20 3-1	J17 4-2	a03 3-0	S03 2-4	N22 3-0	M21 2-0	J31 4-3	O25 1-0	a04 0-1	S17 1-0	S06 0-2	M07 1-1		O04 4-1	N08 4-2	D06 2-0	O11 1-3	S20 0-4	F21 2-0	D27 2-0	a18 1-1
15 MANCHESTER U	O18 1-2	A30 3-4	N01 2-0	a11 0-1	N15 0-0	D26 1-1	J03 1-0	D13 2-1	S27 0-2	S10 0-6	J01 0-0	M25 0-0	a06 4-1	F07 1-3		m02 4-4	S13 4-7	M16 0-1	M28 1-2	J28 4-1	N29 1-1	F14 1-0
16 MIDDLESBROUGH	M28 2-5	S27 3-1	N15 1-1	D13 4-1	J17 5-1	D27 3-0	F07 2-2	N29 4-1	J01 2-1	J24 2-3	F28 5-0	a11 2-2	S06 3-3	M14 4-1	S03 3-1		O11 3-1	N01 0-1	a25 4-1	D26 2-0	O18 1-0	S17 2-2
17 NEWCASTLE U	a25 1-3	J01 2-0	S17 2-2	N29 2-3	M14 0-2	J31 4-0	S03 1-0	O18 2-5	S06 1-2	a03 1-1	N01 4-1	D13 5-2	O04 0-4	a11 0-1	J17 4-3	F14 0-5		N15 4-7	F28 1-0	D27 1-2	M28 2-0	S20 4-2
18 PORTSMOUTH	a03 1-1	a04 5-0	S20 2-2	m02 3-0	S17 4-3	a18 1-0	D20 1-1	O04 2-0	F21 4-3	N08 2-2	D27 1-1	J17 2-1	N22 4-0	F18 1-1	O25 4-1	M07 1-0	M21 1-2		J31 2-3	D06 2-4	S06 1-1	D26 2-0
19 SHEFFIELD U	F07 1-1	D06 3-4	D27 3-1	O11 1-1	D26 5-1	N08 2-0	F21 4-0	S13 3-3	a18 2-1	M21 0-2	a06 1-1	S24 0-2	a04 4-1	J28 2-2	N22 3-1	D20 4-2	O25 3-1	S27 3-1		S06 1-1	S03 3-3	M07 1-2
20 SHEFFIELD W	N15 1-2	m02 3-0	D13 9-1	a25 1-3	N29 7-1	O04 1-0	S08 1-1	a20 3-2	J17 4-1	J01 2-1	M14 2-1	M28 4-0	F14 3-5	O18 1-1	S20 3-0	D29 3-2	A30 2-1	a11 2-2	J03 1-3		N01 7-2	J31 5-3
21 SUNDERLAND	S13 1-4	O11 1-1	a03 1-0	F04 8-2	S27 2-4	M21 3-1	a18 2-0	S10 1-3	N08 3-2	O25 4-2	F07 4-0	D25 2-5	D06 6-5	A30 3-3	a04 1-2	F21 1-1	N22 5-0	J03 0-0	m02 2-1	M07 5-1		D20 6-1
22 WEST HAM U	F28 2-4	J03 5-5	M16 1-2	O18 4-3	a11 3-2	a03 1-4	S13 4-1	M28 0-1	F07 3-4	A30 2-1	N15 1-1	N29 2-0	S01 7-0	D13 2-0	O11 5-1	S08 0-3	J26 3-2	D25 4-3	N01 4-1	S27 3-3	a25 0-3	

Winger Jimmy Stein, a vital member of the Everton side that won the Division Two and Division One titles, and the FA Cup in successive seasons between 1930 and 1933.

DIVISION 2

	BARNSLEY	BRADFORD	BRADFORD C	BRISTOL C	BURNLEY	BURY	CARDIFF C	CHARLTON A	EVERTON	MILLWALL	NOTTINGHAM F	OLDHAM A	PLYMOUTH A	PORT VALE	PRESTON N.E.	READING	SOUTHAMPTON	STOKE C	SWANSEA T	TOTTENHAM H	W.B.A.	WOLVERHAMPTON W
1 BARNSLEY		D06 1-0	S06 2-1	S27 1-0	N08 0-1	a06 2-1	F07 4-0	J17 5-0	O11 1-1	O25 2-3	a18 3-1	S20 1-2	J01 0-4	D27 5-2	M07 1-1	N22 3-2	a04 3-1	F21 4-2	S01 1-0	D20 0-1	D25 0-0	M21 3-0
2 BRADFORD	a11 1-0		F28 1-2	N15 5-2	J31 4-1	M14 5-1	M28 3-0	O18 3-2	N29 4-1	D26 6-0	S06 4-1	D27 4-0	N01 7-1	S08 5-1	S20 2-2	F18 1-3	O04 1-1	m02 2-2	a25 5-1	J17 4-1	D13 3-1	a06 1-1
3 BRADFORD C	J03 1-0	O25 0-4		S13 1-1	N22 2-3	F07 3-1	F04 2-1	A30 3-2	S27 0-3	a18 0-0	M07 1-0	D20 0-0	O11 1-0	S03 2-1	a04 0-0	D06 6-1	M21 4-3	D25 2-2	a07 3-0	N08 2-0	S17 2-3	F21 4-1
4 BRISTOL C	J31 2-1	M21 2-0	J17 0-1		M07 1-1	S17 4-2	O11 1-0	S20 3-0	a03 0-1	F21 1-2	O04 1-4	O25 1-0	S03 2-1	S06 1-1	D20 1-1	a04 1-0	N08 2-1	D06 1-1	D26 2-1	a18 2-1	D27 1-1	N22 0-3
5 BURNLEY	M14 2-2	S27 3-2	M28 1-1	N01 4-2		A30 0-2	a25 1-0	N29 1-1	D13 5-2	O11 2-1	S08 5-2	a03 6-1	F28 2-2	N15 1-2	D25 1-0	S13 8-1	J03 3-2	F07 1-2	O18 2-2	m02 1-0	a11 2-1	F03 4-2
6 BURY	a03 3-1	N08 3-1	O04 3-1	S10 6-0	D27 2-1		S03 3-0	F14 0-1	D25 2-2	N22 5-0	D06 1-0	M21 1-3	S06 2-0	J31 0-3	O25 3-0	D20 2-2	a18 1-0	a04 0-3	J17 2-0	F21 2-0	S20 2-2	M07 1-0
7 CARDIFF C	O04 2-0	N22 0-3	S20 1-1	F14 0-1	D20 4-0	m02 1-3		J31 0-2	S08 1-2	D06 4-4	O25 1-1	F21 0-0	S22 4-1	J17 2-1	a18 0-0	N08 5-0	M07 0-1	M21 3-2	D27 1-0	a06 0-0	S06 3-6	a04 0-3
8 CHARLTON A	S13 1-1	F21 3-1	D27 2-1	J24 0-0	a04 2-1	O11 3-2	S27 4-1		F07 0-7	S06 2-0	D20 1-1	a18 1-1	a06 1-3	D26 3-1	N08 1-3	M21 2-1	N22 3-1	O25 1-2	S15 3-0	M07 1-0	S01 0-4	D06 1-2
9 EVERTON	F18 5-2	a04 4-2	J31 4-2	a06 1-3	a18 3-2	J01 3-2	S17 1-1	O04 7-1		M21 2-0	F21 2-0	D06 6-4	D27 9-1	S20 2-3	S03 2-1	M07 3-2	D20 2-1	N22 5-0	S06 5-1	O25 4-2	J17 2-1	N08 4-0
10 MILLWALL	F28 4-1	D25 1-1	D13 1-1	O18 2-0	F14 2-1	M28 1-0	a11 0-0	J03 6-0	N15 1-3		S20 5-1	J17 1-0	N29 4-1	a25 0-1	O04 5-7	S08 4-0	a03 1-0	A30 1-3	M14 3-1	J31 2-3	N01 2-0	m02 1-1
11 NOTTINGHAM F	D13 3-3	J03 1-0	N01 4-1	F07 6-1	S17 3-3	a11 3-0	F28 3-1	a25 4-3	O18 2-2	J24 2-1		S27 4-1	N15 1-1	M14 1-0	a06 1-4	D25 1-1	m02 3-1	S13 3-0	M28 3-0	F14 2-2	N29 1-6	A30 3-4
12 OLDHAM A	J26 0-0	A30 2-0	a25 3-0	F28 1-3	a06 3-1	N15 3-2	O18 4-2	D13 0-3	a11 3-3	S13 3-1	J31 3-1		M28 2-1	N01 3-3	F14 2-0	J01 1-1	S08 2-1	J03 3-1	N29 2-1	O04 1-2	M23 2-2	D25 2-0
13 PLYMOUTH A	S10 4-0	M07 0-0	F14 0-2	m02 5-3	O25 1-2	J03 3-6	D26 5-1	a03 1-3	A30 2-3	a04 5-0	M21 1-0	N22 1-1		O04 2-1	F21 1-2	a18 3-1	S13 2-3	N08 1-2	S20 0-0	D06 2-0	J31 5-1	D20 3-2
14 PORT VALE	A30 5-2	S22 8-2	m02 1-0	J03 1-0	M21 0-0	S27 0-1	S13 2-0	D25 1-1	J26 1-3	D20 3-2	N08 3-2	M07 2-0	F07 2-1		N22 1-0	F21 2-1	D06 1-0	a18 0-0	O11 2-0	a04 3-0	a03 1-0	O25 0-1
15 PRESTON N.E.	N01 1-1	J29 1-1	N29 4-2	a25 2-2	D26 2-0	F28 3-0	D13 7-0	M14 4-1	m02 2-1	F07 1-3	a03 2-4	O11 1-0	O18 2-1	M28 1-3		J03 3-3	A30 5-0	S27 5-1	a11 0-0	S08 2-1	N15 2-3	S13 5-4
16 READING	M28 6-1	O11 3-0	a11 0-0	N29 4-1	J17 3-1	a25 3-4	M14 3-0	N15 2-0	N01 0-2	S17 2-1	D26 5-2	S03 1-3	D13 1-2	O18 0-3	S06 1-4		S20 1-1	a03 7-3	J31 1-0	D27 1-2	a15 0-3	F07 3-0
17 SOUTHAMPTON	N29 4-0	F07 2-3	N15 4-1	M14 5-1	S06 1-1	D13 5-0	N01 0-1	M28 3-0	a25 2-1	a06 3-1	S01 0-0	S15 1-0	J17 3-3	a11 2-0	D27 2-1	J24 3-2		O11 2-1	F28 1-2	D26 0-3	O18 1-1	S27 2-0
18 STOKE C	O18 0-0	S01 1-1	D26 1-1	a11 3-1	O04 1-1	N29 3-1	N15 1-0	F28 0-0	M28 2-0	D27 2-3	J17 1-0	S06 4-0	M14 0-0	D13 1-0	F02 3-1	a06 2-1	F14 1-3		N01 5-0	S20 2-1	a30 0-1	S15 1-2
19 SWANSEA T	m02 1-0	D20 2-1	a06 1-2	D25 5-2	F21 1-1	S13 5-2	A30 3-2	S08 1-1	J03 2-5	N08 4-1	N22 3-2	a04 0-0	J24 2-0	F14 2-1	D06 2-1	S27 2-1	O25 0-1	M07 1-2		M21 1-2	O04 1-1	a18 1-1
20 TOTTENHAM H	a25 4-2	S13 3-2	M14 3-1	D13 4-1	S01 8-1	O18 3-1	a03 2-2	N01 5-0	M16 1-0	S27 4-1	O11 2-1	F07 4-0	a11 1-1	N29 5-0	S15 0-0	A30 7-1	D25 1-3	J26 3-0	N15 1-1		M28 2-2	J03 1-0
21 W.B.A.	D26 5-0	a18 1-1	S08 1-0	A30 3-0	D06 2-0	J26 2-0	J03 3-2	m02 3-2	S13 1-2	M07 0-0	a04 2-1	N08 2-0	S27 1-2	a06 4-1	M21 2-0	O25 1-0	F21 1-2	D20 4-0	F07 0-0	N22 0-2		O11 2-1
22 WOLVERHAMPTON W	N15 2-0	a07 1-1	O18 0-1	M28 0-1	S20 2-4	N01 7-0	N29 4-1	a11 1-1	M25 3-1	S01 2-0	D27 4-2	D26 3-0	a25 4-3	M11 3-0	J17 2-0	O04 3-1	J31 3-2	S08 5-1	D13 3-1	S06 3-1	F18 1-4	

SEASON 1930-31

DIVISION 3 NORTH

	ACCRINGTON S	BARROW	CARLISLE U	CHESTERFIELD	CREWE A	DARLINGTON	DONCASTER R	GATESHEAD	HALIFAX T	HARTLEPOOLS U	HULL C	LINCOLN C	NELSON	NEW BRIGHTON	ROCHDALE	ROTHERHAM U	SOUTHPORT	STOCKPORT CO	TRANMERE R	WIGAN B	WREXHAM	YORK C
1 ACCRINGTON S		S30 3-1	J24 3-0	O11 1-3	A30 3-1	D15 2-1	M14 2-0	N15 2-1	a11 1-1	O18 0-2	N01 1-3	a25 5-3	F28 3-1	J10 3-0	J01 2-3	F07 3-2	S10 2-0	M28 2-2	S13 5-2	D25 3-0	J03 1-3	S27 4-2
2 BARROW	S01 0-0		J03 7-2	S27 0-3	J29 2-0	J10 3-2	a25 3-1	N01 0-0	M28 3-1	F28 4-0	O18 3-0	F07 3-2	a11 2-1	N15 4-1	S08 0-0	J24 1-0	M05 1-1	M14 1-0	A30 1-3	D13 4-1	a03 2-3	S13 1-2
3 CARLISLE U	S20 7-3	S06 0-1		D27 0-0	O04 4-1	N01 2-1	J01 1-1	F28 2-2	a25 6-2	M28 3-0	a11 1-5	J15 3-6	M14 8-1	O18 2-0	J31 7-1	a03 1-2	J17 4-3	S11 5-1	m02 3-0	N15 6-1	F14 1-1	D26 2-0
4 CHESTERFIELD	F14 7-3	J31 3-1	A30 2-1		S08 2-0	M28 2-1	O18 2-1	a25 8-1	N15 7-0	D13 3-0	J24 0-4	a22 3-2	J10 2-1	M14 1-0	a06 4-1	S13 2-1	O04 2-1	N01 1-1	J01 5-1	a11 3-1	D25 4-0	J03 3-1
5 CREWE A	D27 2-1	D25 6-2	F07 3-5	S17 2-1		J17 2-2	M28 2-1	F04 6-2	M25 0-1	N01 2-1	N15 3-4	M14 2-0	O18 4-2	D17 1-3	S06 3-1	S01 2-3	a06 0-0	a11 1-0	S27 1-2	a25 3-2	J24 2-1	O11 5-1
6 DARLINGTON	a18 1-1	a04 3-2	M07 3-0	N22 5-1	S13 1-2		m02 0-0	F14 2-2	S20 4-1	a06 4-2	S10 2-4	J01 0-1	J03 2-1	J31 3-1	O25 1-1	M21 2-2	D06 2-3	O04 1-2	D20 2-0	A30 2-3	F21 1-1	N08 3-0
7 DONCASTER R	N08 6-1	D20 0-0	a18 2-0	F21 1-0	N22 2-0	S01 1-2		D27 1-1	S18 3-3	S27 1-1	S13 0-2	J24 0-1	O11 2-0	D25 0-0	M21 4-0	S06 3-3	M07 0-0	a03 2-0	D06 6-0	F07 5-1	a04 1-1	O25 0-2
8 GATESHEAD	M21 4-0	M07 4-1	O25 1-0	D20 3-3	a04 2-2	O11 1-1	A30 2-1		m02 3-1	J24 0-0	J03 1-0	S13 0-1	F07 2-0	S08 4-0	N22 0-2	F21 2-0	N08 2-3	a15 2-1	a18 3-0	S27 4-2	D06 4-3	J01 2-1
9 HALIFAX T	D06 1-1	N22 4-0	D20 1-5	M21 1-1	O25 4-0	J24 1-0	S08 0-2	S01 3-0		A30 3-1	D25 1-1	a06 3-2	S13 1-0	O04 1-0	a18 1-0	N08 0-1	a04 0-0	F14 3-0	F21 2-1	J03 0-1	S27 0-0	M07 0-0
10 HARTLEPOOLS U	F21 3-3	O25 3-2	N22 3-5	a18 1-3	M07 2-0	a03 1-1	J31 0-2	S20 2-3	D27 2-1		O04 1-3	F14 0-3	D25 4-0	S06 4-1	D20 4-0	D06 4-2	S01 0-2	J17 1-2	M21 1-2	J01 6-1	N08 2-1	a04 3-0
11 HULL C	M07 1-1	F21 1-1	D06 1-1	S20 3-1	M21 5-1	S15 1-1	J17 8-2	S06 4-0	D26 10-0	a20 5-0		S27 1-3	m02 4-0	a06 3-0	N08 3-1	O25 2-2	D20 5-1	D27 1-1	a04 1-0	O11 0-0	N22 2-3	a18 3-1
12 LINCOLN C	D20 5-2	O04 5-0	a04 5-1	O25 1-1	N08 3-1	D26 1-0	S20 1-0	J17 0-0	a03 4-1	O11 1-0	J31 3-0		S15 2-0	D27 4-0	M07 5-0	a18 1-3	F21 3-3	S06 6-1	N22 1-3	S01 2-0	M21 3-2	D06 4-1
13 NELSON	O25 4-2	D06 0-3	N08 1-2	a04 0-5	F21 1-1	S06 3-1	F14 2-0	O04 2-2	J17 3-2	D26 1-1	S02 0-2	S10 1-2		S20 2-2	D27 0-0	N22 0-0	a18 1-4	J31 1-1	M07 0-4	a03 2-1	D20 2-0	M21 2-5
14 NEW BRIGHTON	a04 0-0	M21 3-1	F21 2-0	N08 3-1	a18 3-0	S27 1-5	D26 2-1	S15 0-0	F07 3-0	J03 1-0	a03 1-1	A30 2-1	J24 2-0		D06 2-1	M07 3-1	N22 1-2	J01 0-2	O11 1-3	S13 0-2	O25 1-1	D20 5-3
15 ROCHDALE	a03 1-6	S15 4-2	S27 1-3	S01 2-3	J03 1-0	a21 1-2	N15 3-5	M28 0-1	F16 2-3	a25 1-2	M14 1-0	N01 4-2	A30 5-4	a11 2-0		O11 6-1	D26 0-4	J10 1-0	J24 1-3	O18 0-4	S13 4-3	F07 2-2
16 ROTHERHAM U	O04 8-1	S20 6-0	a06 1-0	J17 0-1	m02 1-1	N15 0-2	J03 3-0	O18 1-1	M14 2-1	a11 1-1	a27 1-1	D15 2-2	M28 3-0	N01 2-0	F14 1-3		J31 3-3	a25 3-4	D25 4-6	J10 5-2	S08 1-4	A30 2-1
17 SOUTHPORT	S16 3-3	O11 3-2	S13 1-2	F07 3-0	a03 3-1	a11 0-1	N01 2-1	M14 1-0	J13 5-2	m02 2-0	a25 1-0	O18 1-2	J01 8-1	M28 3-0	D25 4-0	S27 4-1		N15 2-0	J03 1-1	a21 3-1	A30 1-1	F17 1-0
18 STOCKPORT CO	N22 4-1	N08 6-0	S15 3-0	M07 2-1	D06 2-0	F07 0-1	a06 2-2	D25 3-1	O11 3-0	S13 3-1	A30 3-2	J03 4-2	S27 1-0	S01 2-0	a04 2-2	D20 5-2	M21 2-0		O25 1-1	J24 4-1	a18 2-2	F21 0-0
19 TRANMERE R	J17 8-0	D27 5-0	S01 2-0	a03 2-0	J31 0-0	a25 1-2	a11 1-2	a06 2-1	O18 2-2	N15 5-4	D13 4-0	M28 3-3	N01 7-1	F14 3-2	S20 7-3	D26 4-2	S06 3-1	F28 3-0		M14 5-1	O04 2-1	S18 4-1
20 WIGAN B	D26 3-2	a18 2-1	M21 1-2	D06 1-5	D20 6-0	D27 2-0	O04 3-0	J31 3-3	S06 3-0	S10 3-2	F14 3-1	m02 0-1	a06 3-1	J17 1-1	F21 3-0	a04 0-0	O25 1-0	S20 2-1	N08 4-3		M07 1-1	N22 3-1
21 WREXHAM	S06 6-1	a06 1-1	O11 2-1	D26 2-1	S20 7-0	O18 2-0	J14 4-1	a11 5-1	J31 3-2	M14 2-0	M28 2-0	N15 2-2	a25 5-1	F28 2-1	J17 1-1	S17 3-2	D27 2-4	D17 3-2	F07 2-2	N01 2-0		S03 3-2
22 YORK C	a06 3-1	J17 4-2	D25 4-0	S06 2-2	F14 4-3	M14 2-1	F28 4-2	a03 4-3	N01 4-1	F04 4-2	M18 3-2	a11 1-1	N15 3-0	a25 4-1	O04 3-0	D27 1-1	S20 3-1	O18 1-2	S10 3-1	M28 2-3	m02 0-1	

DIVISION 3 SOUTH

	BOURNEMOUTH	BRENTFORD	BRIGHTON & HA	BRISTOL R	CLAPTON O	COVENTRY C	CRYSTAL P	EXETER C	FULHAM	GILLINGHAM	LUTON T	NEWPORT CO	NORTHAMPTON T	NORWICH C	NOTTS CO	Q.P.R.	SOUTHEND U	SWINDON T	THAMES	TORQUAY U	WALSALL	WATFORD
1 BOURNEMOUTH		a18 1-0	N22 1-2	O25 4-0	S27 1-1	D26 2-0	D20 0-0	M21 3-1	a06 2-1	N08 2-1	F21 0-0	M07 4-2	D06 1-3	O11 4-1	J28 2-1	S03 2-0	S06 0-0	D27 4-1	F07 3-3	a04 2-2	S17 0-2	S13 1-1
2 BRENTFORD	D18 1-2		O04 3-2	S06 4-0	M28 3-0	O18 1-2	D25 8-2	J31 2-1	S17 4-1	S20 1-1	D27 0-1	J17 3-2	S03 0-4	M14 3-1	S24 2-2	N01 5-3	a03 3-1	a25 5-2	N15 6-1	F14 0-0	F28 6-1	a11 2-1
3 BRIGHTON & H.A.	M28 3-1	F07 1-0		D26 4-0	N01 3-1	a22 2-0	O11 1-1	S06 3-2	a11 1-1	D27 5-0	S17 2-0	a03 5-0	S27 1-1	O18 1-0	M14 1-3	J17 1-1	S03 1-2	O08 1-0	F28 2-4	J28 3-0	a25 3-3	N15 1-0
4 BRISTOL R	F28 2-5	J03 2-5	D25 3-3		a25 4-1	N15 1-0	S13 2-1	S08 1-1	M14 2-1	m02 1-0	S27 5-1	F14 2-0	A30 1-4	a11 3-0	F07 2-2	J14 3-0	J28 2-3	N04 4-1	D17 4-0	a06 3-1	M28 1-2	O18 1-5
5 CLAPTON O	J31 0-0	N22 3-0	M07 1-0	D20 3-1		S06 3-3	a04 3-2	O25 2-3	J17 2-0	F21 0-2	a18 3-2	S03 3-1	M21 2-2	D26 2-0	F14 1-4	a06 2-3	D06 3-1	S20 2-3	S18 2-1	N08 4-0	D27 2-5	O04 4-0
6 COVENTRY C	D25 3-3	F21 0-1	a18 0-0	M21 5-1	J03 4-0		O25 3-5	D06 3-1	m02 2-1	a04 1-2	N08 1-2	N22 6-4	O11 0-1	J24 3-0	A30 1-2	S27 2-0	M07 0-0	S08 4-0	S13 7-1	D20 6-1	F07 2-1	a07 2-2
7 CRYSTAL P	a25 1-0	D26 5-1	F14 0-1	J17 0-2	a20 3-1	F28 1-0		O04 7-2	O18 5-2	J31 5-0	S06 5-1	S20 7-1	S17 0-0	N15 2-1	a11 1-1	M14 4-0	D27 3-1	a03 3-1	M28 2-1	m02 5-0	N01 6-3	D17 6-1
8 EXETER C	N15 4-1	S27 4-0	J03 2-2	S17 0-3	a15 6-1	a11 2-3	F07 4-3		J14 3-2	a06 3-0	S03 1-1	D26 3-0	J28 3-3	A30 1-0	N01 3-3	a25 2-0	O11 1-1	M28 3-1	O18 4-3	S13 2-2	F18 2-5	M14 2-1
9 FULHAM	a03 1-0	S08 1-1	D06 0-1	N08 6-2	S13 2-0	S01 0-0	F21 2-0	a04 4-2		N22 1-1	M07 2-1	M21 0-1	D20 4-2	S27 1-0	J03 3-1	F07 0-2	O25 1-0	D26 6-1	J24 4-2	a18 3-0	O11 5-2	A30 3-2
10 GILLINGHAM	M14 0-0	J28 1-1	A30 0-0	S03 1-1	O18 0-0	J10 2-0	S27 6-2	a03 3-5	M28 3-2		O11 4-0	S10 4-1	S13 0-2	a25 2-1	F28 0-5	D17 2-2	F07 1-0	N15 0-1	D25 3-1	J03 2-3	a11 2-0	N01 4-2
11 LUTON T	O18 2-3	A30 1-1	S08 2-2	J31 4-1	M23 0-1	M14 2-0	J03 1-2	S29 3-1	N01 5-0	F14 4-1		O04 3-1	a06 4-0	J10 1-0	a25 3-0	M28 5-1	S13 2-1	F28 4-0	a11 8-0	D25 3-1	N15 0-0	J28 4-1
12 NEWPORT CO	N01 7-3	S13 0-2	a06 2-0	O11 1-1	m02 1-1	M28 1-1	J26 2-1	D25 4-0	N15 1-3	S15 1-3	F07 3-1		J03 5-2	D18 3-0	O18 2-3	a11 2-3	S27 3-1	M14 3-1	a25 1-1	A30 2-1	J22 1-1	F28 0-2
13 NORTHAMPTON T	a11 2-2	m02 1-2	J31 2-1	D27 1-1	N15 0-0	F14 0-3	S08 0-0	S20 1-0	a25 4-2	J17 0-1	a07 0-0	S06 1-0		N01 3-1	M28 0-0	F28 6-0	D26 4-0	D13 3-0	M14 4-1	O04 0-3	O18 3-0	J15 2-3
14 NORWICH C	F14 2-1	N08 3-0	F21 2-2	D06 1-3	D25 2-0	S20 2-2	M21 2-1	D27 1-2	J31 1-1	D20 4-0	a04 1-0	a18 4-1	M07 1-1		S08 2-2	S06 1-1	N22 0-1	O04 2-0	a06 0-0	O25 3-0	J17 3-1	m02 0-1
15 NOTTS CO	S20 2-0	a04 1-0	N08 2-2	O04 3-0	O11 5-0	D27 4-1	D06 2-2	M07 1-2	S06 6-1	O25 2-1	D20 1-0	F21 5-0	N22 2-2	O02 4-0		D26 2-0	a18 1-1	J17 2-0	S03 4-0	M21 2-0	a03 6-1	J31 1-0
16 Q.P.R.	m02 3-0	M07 3-1	S13 4-1	a04 2-0	a03 4-2	J31 2-0	N08 4-0	D20 7-2	O04 0-2	a18 1-0	N22 3-1	D06 7-1	O25 0-2	J03 3-1	D25 4-1		M21 0-2	F14 1-2	A30 3-0	F21 1-2	S20 3-0	S11 2-3
17 SOUTHEND U	D13 4-0	a06 0-1	m02 0-2	S20 4-0	a11 2-0	N01 2-0	A30 2-4	M18 5-1	F28 2-4	O04 3-2	J17 0-2	J31 6-2	D25 2-1	M28 2-0	D17 2-1	N15 2-0		O18 5-3	J10 1-0	S08 6-3	M14 2-0	a25 1-0
18 SWINDON T	A30 4-1	D20 3-2	a04 1-1	M07 3-1	J24 5-1	S17 4-0	a06 4-4	N22 2-1	D25 4-1	M21 5-2	O25 0-0	N08 4-4	a18 5-1	F07 5-2	S13 1-2	O11 4-1	F21 1-1		S27 3-0	D06 4-0	S03 4-3	J03 2-1
19 THAMES	O04 1-4	M21 2-0	O25 0-0	a18 1-2	S11 3-0	J17 1-2	N22 0-2	F21 1-0	S20 0-0	D26 2-2	D06 1-0	D20 3-1	N08 2-1	a03 2-0	m02 0-0	D27 1-0	a04 3-0	J31 3-2		M07 1-1	S06 4-1	F16 3-2
20 TORQUAY U	J21 4-4	O11 0-3	S20 3-1	S24 3-3	M14 5-2	a25 0-0	S03 3-1	J17 0-0	D17 3-1	S06 3-0	D26 1-1	D27 3-0	F07 3-0	F28 2-0	N15 1-4	O18 6-2	S17 3-1	a11 5-0	N01 5-1		J31 0-1	M28 3-1
21 WALSALL	S08 3-3	O25 1-4	D20 0-0	N22 4-2	A30 4-2	O04 1-2	M07 2-1	a18 2-1	F14 2-0	D06 2-2	M21 0-1	a04 1-0	F21 2-6	S13 7-0	a06 2-1	J24 0-2	N08 1-3	m02 2-2	J03 6-0	S27 0-4		D25 2-2
22 WATFORD	J17 2-0	D06 1-3	M21 5-0	F21 2-2	F07 1-2	a03 4-1	a18 0-2	N08 0-1	D27 2-2	M07 1-0	S20 1-0	O25 6-2	a04 1-2	S03 2-2	S27 0-1	S17 0-4	D20 1-3	S06 3-0	O11 1-0	N22 6-0	D26 2-2	

LEAGUE TABLES

DIVISION 1

	P	W	D	L	F	A	W	D	L	F	A	Pts
Arsenal	42	14	5	2	67	27	14	5	2	60	32	66
Aston Villa	42	17	3	1	86	34	8	6	7	42	44	59
Sheffield W	42	14	3	4	65	32	8	5	8	37	43	52
Portsmouth	42	11	7	3	46	26	7	6	8	38	41	49
Huddersfield T	42	10	8	3	45	27	8	4	9	36	38	48
Derby Co	42	12	6	3	56	31	6	4	11	38	48	46
Middlesbrough	42	13	5	3	57	28	6	3	12	41	62	46
Manchester C	42	13	2	6	41	29	5	8	8	34	41	46
Liverpool	42	11	6	4	48	28	4	6	11	38	57	42
Blackburn R	42	14	3	4	54	28	3	5	13	29	56	42
Sunderland	42	12	4	5	61	38	4	5	12	28	47	41
Chelsea	42	13	4	4	42	19	2	6	13	22	48	40
Grimsby T	42	13	2	6	55	31	4	3	14	27	56	39
Bolton W	42	12	6	3	45	26	3	3	15	23	55	39
Sheffield U	42	10	7	4	49	31	4	3	14	29	53	38
Leicester C	42	12	4	5	50	38	4	2	15	30	57	38
Newcastle U	42	9	2	10	41	45	6	4	11	37	42	36
West Ham U	42	11	3	7	56	44	3	5	13	23	50	36
Birmingham C	42	11	3	7	37	28	2	7	12	18	42	36
Blackpool	42	8	7	6	41	44	3	3	15	30	81	32
Leeds U	42	10	3	8	49	31	2	4	15	19	50	31
Manchester U	42	6	6	9	30	37	1	2	18	23	78	22

DIVISION 2

	P	W	D	L	F	A	W	D	L	F	A	Pts
Everton	42	18	1	2	76	31	10	4	7	45	35	61
W.B.A.	42	14	3	4	40	16	8	7	6	43	33	54
Tottenham H	42	15	5	1	64	20	7	2	12	24	35	51
Wolverhampton W	42	15	2	4	56	25	6	3	12	28	42	47
Port Vale	42	15	3	3	39	16	6	2	13	28	45	47
Bradford P.A.	42	15	4	2	71	24	3	6	12	26	42	46
Preston N.E.	42	12	5	4	55	31	5	6	10	28	33	45
Burnley	42	13	5	3	55	30	4	6	11	26	47	45
Southampton	42	13	4	4	46	22	6	2	13	28	40	44
Bradford C	42	12	5	4	39	26	5	5	11	22	37	44
Stoke C	42	11	6	4	34	17	6	4	11	30	54	44
Oldham A	42	13	5	3	45	28	3	5	13	16	44	42
Bury	42	14	3	4	44	20	5	0	16	31	62	41
Millwall	42	12	4	5	47	25	4	3	14	24	55	39
Charlton A	42	11	4	6	35	33	4	5	12	24	53	39
Bristol C	42	11	5	5	29	23	4	3	14	25	59	38
Nottingham F	42	12	6	3	54	35	2	3	16	26	50	37
Plymouth A	42	10	3	8	47	33	4	5	12	29	51	36
Barnsley	42	13	3	5	42	23	0	6	15	17	56	35
Swansea T	42	11	5	5	40	29	1	5	15	11	45	34
Reading	42	11	2	8	47	33	1	4	16	25	63	30
Cardiff C	42	7	6	8	32	31	1	3	17	15	56	25

DIVISION 3 NORTH

	P	W	D	L	F	A	W	D	L	F	A	Pts
Chesterfield	42	19	1	1	66	22	7	5	9	36	35	58
Lincoln C	42	16	3	2	60	19	9	4	8	42	40	57
Wrexham	42	16	4	1	61	25	5	8	8	33	37	54
Tranmere R	42	16	3	2	73	26	8	3	10	38	48	54
Southport	42	15	3	3	52	19	7	6	8	36	37	53
Hull C	42	12	7	2	64	20	8	3	10	35	35	50
Stockport Co	42	15	5	1	54	19	5	4	12	23	42	49
Carlisle U	42	13	4	4	68	32	7	1	13	30	49	45
Gateshead	42	14	4	3	46	22	2	9	10	25	51	45
Wigan B	42	14	4	3	48	25	5	1	15	28	61	43
Darlington	42	9	6	6	44	30	7	4	10	27	29	42
York C	42	15	3	3	59	30	3	3	15	26	52	42
Accrington S	42	14	2	5	51	31	1	7	13	33	77	39
Rotherham U	42	9	6	6	50	34	4	6	11	31	49	38
Doncaster R	42	9	8	4	40	18	4	3	14	25	47	37
Barrow	42	13	4	4	45	23	2	3	16	23	66	37
Halifax T	42	11	6	4	30	16	2	3	16	25	73	35
Crewe A	42	13	2	6	52	35	1	4	16	14	58	34
New Brighton	42	12	4	5	36	25	1	3	17	13	51	33
Hartlepool U	42	10	2	9	47	37	2	4	15	20	49	30
Rochdale	42	9	1	11	42	50	3	5	13	20	57	30
Nelson	42	6	7	8	28	40	0	0	21	15	73	19

DIVISION 3 SOUTH

	P	W	D	L	F	A	W	D	L	F	A	Pts
Notts Co	42	16	4	1	58	13	8	7	6	39	33	59
Crystal Palace	42	17	2	2	71	20	5	5	11	36	51	51
Brentford	42	14	3	4	62	30	8	3	10	28	34	50
Brighton & H.A.	42	13	5	3	45	20	4	10	7	23	33	49
Southend U	42	16	0	5	53	26	6	5	10	23	34	49
Northampton T	42	10	6	5	37	20	8	6	7	40	39	48
Luton T	42	15	3	3	61	17	4	5	12	15	34	46
Q.P.R.	42	15	0	6	57	23	5	3	13	25	52	43
Fulham	42	15	3	3	49	21	3	4	14	28	54	43
Bournemouth	42	11	7	3	39	22	4	6	11	33	51	43
Torquay U	42	13	5	3	56	26	4	4	13	24	58	43
Swindon T	42	15	5	1	68	29	3	1	17	21	65	42
Exeter C	42	12	6	3	55	35	5	2	14	29	55	42
Coventry C	42	11	4	6	55	28	5	5	11	20	37	41
Bristol R	42	12	3	6	49	36	4	5	12	26	56	40
Gillingham	42	10	6	5	40	29	4	4	13	21	47	38
Walsall	42	9	5	7	44	38	5	4	12	34	57	37
Watford	42	9	4	8	41	29	5	3	13	31	46	35
Clapton O	42	12	3	6	47	33	2	4	15	16	58	35
Thames	42	12	5	4	34	20	1	3	17	20	73	34
Newport Co	42	10	5	6	45	31	1	1	19	24	80	28
Norwich C	42	10	7	4	37	20	0	1	20	10	56	28

FOOTBALL LEAGUE RECORDS

Top scorers: Div 1, W.Dean (Everton) 44 goals; Div 2, C.Pearce (Swansea Town) 35 goals; Div 3 N, B.Hall (Lincoln City) 42 goals; Div 3 N, C.Bourton (Coventry City) 49 goals. Newport County and Nelson failed to gain re-election, Mansfield Town and Chester elected in their place. Walsall transferred to Division Three North. Wigan Borough resigned on 26 October 1931.

Warney Cresswell, the cultured England full-back who missed only two games when Everton became League Champions in 1930-31.

DIVISION 1

	ARSENAL	ASTON VILLA	BIRMINGHAM	BLACKBURN R	BLACKPOOL	BOLTON W	CHELSEA	DERBY CO	EVERTON	GRIMSBY T	HUDDERSFIELD T	LEICESTER C	LIVERPOOL	MANCHESTER C	MIDDLESBROUGH	NEWCASTLE U	PORTSMOUTH	SHEFFIELD U	SHEFFIELD W	SUNDERLAND	W.B.A.	WEST HAM U
1 ARSENAL		O31 1-1	J16 3-0	m07 4-0	F20 2-0	O17 1-1	a02 1-1	M25 2-1	S26 3-2	F17 4-0	D12 1-1	M05 2-1	N28 6-0	J30 4-0	a30 5-0	M19 1-0	S09 3-3	D26 0-2	a16 3-1	S12 2-0	A29 0-1	N14 4-1
2 ASTON VILLA	a25 1-1		N21 3-2	D19 1-5	N07 5-1	O10 2-1	J30 1-3	D05 2-0	O24 2-3	S12 7-0	m07 2-3	A29 3-2	J16 6-1	a09 2-1	D25 7-1	D28 3-0	F27 0-1	a23 5-0	F24 3-1	M28 2-0	M26 2-0	S26 5-2
3 BIRMINGHAM	S05 2-2	a02 1-1		F06 2-1	F03 3-0	O31 2-2	a30 4-0	F20 1-1	J02 4-0	O17 2-1	N28 5-0	N14 2-0	a16 3-1	M29 1-5	M05 3-0	S02 4-1	O03 2-1	S19 1-3	M19 1-2	S23 0-0	D26 1-0	D12 4-1
4 BLACKBURN R	A31 1-1	a30 2-0	S26 1-2		S21 5-1	a02 3-1	M05 2-2	S12 3-2	D25 5-3	O31 3-2	a16 3-0	D12 6-0	M19 1-3	O10 2-2	N14 4-2	O17 0-3	J16 5-3	M28 1-2	A29 1-6	F13 5-2	J30 2-0	N28 2-4
5 BLACKPOOL	O10 1-5	M19 1-3	S12 1-1	S09 2-1		a16 0-3	D25 2-4	A29 2-1	F13 2-0	N28 4-3	a30 2-0	O31 2-3	M05 2-2	S26 2-2	O17 1-2	D12 3-1	M25 1-1	A31 2-0	N14 1-2	J30 3-2	J16 1-2	a02 7-2
6 BOLTON W	M02 1-0	F20 2-1	M12 5-1	N21 3-1	D05 1-2		J01 1-0	a09 1-2	D19 2-1	S09 5-3	F06 1-2	D25 1-0	m07 8-1	a23 1-1	S19 4-2	O03 2-1	S12 4-0	M26 3-1	J16 2-4	N07 3-1	O24 1-0	A29 0-1
7 CHELSEA	N21 2-1	S19 3-6	D19 2-1	O24 1-2	D26 4-1	M25 3-0		N07 2-1	M26 0-0	F20 4-1	S05 0-1	F06 1-0	O03 2-0	D05 3-2	J02 4-0	a14 4-1	M16 0-0	a09 1-1	S09 2-3	M02 2-2	a23 0-2	m07 3-2
8 DERBY CO	M28 1-1	a16 3-1	O10 2-1	J27 1-1	J02 5-0	N28 5-1	M19 1-0		S16 3-0	D12 3-3	a02 3-2	O17 1-1	a30 1-2	S02 2-1	F06 5-2	N14 1-1	S19 2-1	S05 1-3	M05 0-1	D26 3-1	F17 3-1	O31 5-1
9 EVERTON	F06 1-3	M05 4-2	A29 3-2	D26 5-0	O03 3-2	a30 1-0	N14 7-2	S23 2-1		a02 4-2	M19 4-1	N28 9-2	J30 2-1	S12 0-1	D12 5-1	O31 8-1	m07 0-1	F20 5-1	O17 9-3	J16 4-2	M25 2-1	a16 6-1
10 GRIMSBY T	O03 3-1	F02 2-2	F27 1-1	M12 4-3	a09 0-0	S15 2-0	O10 1-2	a23 2-1	N21 1-2		J02 1-4	S19 3-0	F06 5-1	M26 2-1	M25 2-0	S05 1-2	N07 3-1	O24 0-2	m07 3-1	D05 1-3	D19 0-0	D25 2-1
11 HUDDERSFIELD T	a27 1-2	A31 1-1	a09 1-1	D05 1-1	D19 5-0	S26 2-0	J16 2-1	N21 6-0	N07 0-0	A29 1-1		S07 2-1	M29 4-3	a06 1-0	F17 1-1	D26 1-2	M26 1-0	M02 2-2	J30 6-1	O24 4-1	O10 2-2	S12 3-1
12 LEICESTER C	O24 1-2	J02 3-8	M26 3-1	a23 1-0	M12 2-2	D26 1-3	S26 1-0	F27 1-1	a09 0-1	J30 1-2	O15 2-4		S12 2-1	S05 4-0	A31 2-2	M29 4-2	F04 2-1	N07 4-3	O10 3-2	N21 5-0	D05 2-3	F18 2-1
13 LIVERPOOL	a09 2-1	S05 2-0	D05 4-3	N07 4-2	O24 3-2	S02 2-2	a06 2-1	D19 1-1	S19 1-3	S26 4-0	M28 0-3	J27 3-3		N21 4-3	S16 7-2	J02 4-2	a23 1-3	M12 2-1	D25 3-1	M26 1-2	M02 4-1	O10 2-2
14 MANCHESTER C	S19 1-3	N28 3-3	M28 2-1	F20 3-1	F06 7-1	D12 2-1	a16 1-1	S09 3-0	J27 1-0	N14 4-1	O31 3-0	J16 5-1	a02 0-1		M19 1-2	M05 5-1	J01 3-3	O03 1-1	a30 1-2	A29 1-1	S23 2-5	O17 0-1
15 MIDDLESBROUGH	D19 2-5	D26 1-1	O24 2-0	M26 0-2	F27 0-3	J30 3-1	A29 0-2	S26 5-2	a23 1-0	M28 4-0	O03 1-0	m07 1-1	S09 4-1	N07 3-3		F20 2-1	N21 0-1	D05 4-3	S12 4-0	M12 0-1	a09 1-0	J16 3-2
16 NEWCASTLE U	N07 3-2	J01 3-1	m07 0-3	M02 5-3	a27 2-2	F17 3-1	S12 4-1	M26 3-3	m04 0-0	J16 2-0	D25 2-1	M25 3-2	A29 0-1	O24 2-1	O10 3-1		D05 0-0	D19 5-3	S26 4-1	a09 1-2	N21 5-1	J30 2-2
17 PORTSMOUTH	S16 0-3	O17 0-3	F17 2-1	S05 2-0	M28 2-2	M09 3-2	O31 1-0	J30 2-0	S02 0-3	M19 2-0	N14 3-2	a30 0-1	D12 2-0	D26 3-2	a02 2-0	a16 6-0		J02 2-1	N28 2-0	O10 0-0	S26 0-1	M05 3-0
18 SHEFFIELD U	D25 4-1	D12 5-4	J30 1-0	J01 3-2	m07 1-3	N14 4-0	N28 4-2	J16 3-1	O10 1-5	M05 2-1	O17 0-2	M19 2-2	O31 3-0	F15 2-1	a16 2-1	a30 0-3	A29 1-2		a02 1-1	S26 1-1	S12 1-0	S07 6-0
19 SHEFFIELD W	D05 1-3	O03 1-0	N07 5-1	J02 5-1	M26 3-0	S05 7-1	S21 2-2	O24 3-1	F27 1-3	A31 4-1	S19 4-1	F20 3-1	D26 1-1	D19 1-1	J25 1-1	F06 2-0	a09 3-1	N21 2-1		a23 3-2	M12 2-5	M28 6-1
20 SUNDERLAND	a06 2-0	M25 1-1	S16 2-3	O03 2-2	S19 4-0	M19 3-0	O17 2-1	J01 0-0	S05 2-3	a16 2-0	M05 1-3	a02 4-1	N14 1-3	J02 2-5	O31 0-0	N28 1-4	F20 5-1	F06 1-0	D12 3-1		S02 2-1	a30 2-0
21 W.B.A.	J02 1-0	N14 3-0	D25 0-1	S19 4-1	S05 4-0	M05 3-0	D12 4-0	O03 4-0	M28 1-1	a30 5-6	F20 3-2	a16 1-2	O17 1-2	S14 1-1	N28 1-1	a02 2-1	F06 3-0	J25 0-1	O31 1-1	S07 1-0		M19 3-1
22 WEST HAM U	M26 1-1	F06 2-1	a23 2-4	a09 1-3	N21 1-1	J02 3-1	A31 3-1	M12 2-1	D05 4-2	D26 3-1	F01 1-1	O03 1-4	F20 1-0	M02 1-1	S05 0-2	S19 2-1	O24 2-1	S21 1-2	M25 1-2	D19 2-2	N07 1-5	

Another skilful full-back, Tom Parker skippered Arsenal into second place, two points adrift of the Merseysiders.

DIVISION 2

	BARNSLEY	BRADFORD	BRADFORD C	BRISTOL C	BURNLEY	BURY	CHARLTON A	CHESTERFIELD	LEEDS U	MANCHESTER U	MILLWALL	NOTTINGHAM F	NOTTS CO	OLDHAM A	PLYMOUTH A	PORT VALE	PRESTON N.E.	SOUTHAMPTON	STOKE C	SWANSEA T	TOTTENHAM T	WOLVERHAMPTON W
1 BARNSLEY		M05 2-2	A29 1-2	F20 1-1	a16 0-1	S07 0-1	a30 1-4	D12 3-1	J16 0-2	O17 0-0	D26 2-1	M19 3-1	F06 1-1	A31 3-1	O03 0-0	M28 3-0	N28 4-2	a02 3-3	N14 1-0	S12 2-3	J30 3-2	O31 2-2
2 BRADFORD	O24 1-0		N07 1-0	M26 2-0	S26 2-0	a09 2-1	S16 3-0	J30 1-0	D25 3-0	A29 3-1	a23 1-2	S12 4-1	M12 1-1	N21 5-0	D19 2-0	D05 2-2	F17 1-5	O10 2-1	A31 2-1	F27 2-1	J16 2-1	M29 2-1
3 BRADFORD C	J02 9-1	M19 0-0		S19 3-0	N14 1-2	O03 1-3	O17 1-1	a02 3-0	M28 4-1	D12 4-3	m07 0-0	N28 2-2	S05 0-2	F06 2-0	J27 3-3	F20 4-0	a30 0-1	O31 5-2	M05 2-2	D26 5-1	a16 2-0	S07 2-2
4 BRISTOL C	O10 4-0	N14 0-0	J30 0-1		M28 1-6	A29 1-3	N28 1-2	O17 1-1	S26 0-2	a30 2-1	S12 1-4	M05 1-1	S02 3-2	D25 1-1	S23 0-2	J16 0-2	M19 4-2	D12 0-1	a16 0-0	F13 1-1	O31 1-1	a02 0-4
5 BURNLEY	D05 5-3	F06 3-2	M26 1-1	M25 1-2		O24 2-2	J23 0-1	S07 2-2	N21 0-5	O03 2-0	D19 1-1	m07 1-0	a23 1-1	F27 1-4	N07 1-1	M12 2-2	D25 2-2	J02 1-3	S05 3-0	a09 4-1	F20 2-0	S19 1-3
6 BURY	S14 7-1	N28 4-2	F17 0-2	J02 2-1	M05 1-0		D12 6-0	O31 0-1	O10 1-4	a02 0-0	S26 2-0	a30 2-2	M25 2-1	S05 2-1	J01 2-2	J30 2-0	O17 4-1	F03 3-0	M19 0-1	A31 2-1	N14 1-1	a16 1-0
7 CHARLTON A	M07 3-1	S07 2-2	F27 1-0	a09 2-0	S12 0-1	a23 3-0		J16 0-0	O24 0-1	M28 1-0	O10 1-3	A29 3-1	M26 3-1	D05 2-2	N21 2-0	N07 2-1	J30 2-1	S26 2-3	F15 1-1	M12 3-3	D26 2-5	m07 3-2
8 CHESTERFIELD	a23 2-2	S19 3-2	N21 2-2	F27 3-1	J01 5-1	M12 4-1	S05 3-2		a09 1-1	F06 1-3	M26 1-0	F20 1-0	N07 1-4	O24 0-2	A31 1-2	D19 4-0	M28 3-1	D25 1-0	J02 1-3	D05 1-2	O03 4-2	J27 1-2
9 LEEDS U	S05 0-1	D26 3-2	M29 1-1	F06 1-0	a02 3-1	F20 1-0	M05 2-0	N28 3-3		M19 1-4	S07 0-1	a16 1-1	J23 2-2	O03 5-0	S19 0-0	m07 0-2	N14 4-1	a30 1-0	O31 2-0	J02 3-2	D12 1-0	O17 2-1
10 MANCHESTER U	F27 3-0	J02 0-2	a23 1-0	D19 0-1	F17 5-1	N21 1-2	M25 0-2	S26 3-1	N07 2-5		D05 2-0	J30 3-2	O24 3-3	M26 5-1	M12 2-1	a09 2-0	O10 3-2	S02 2-3	S16 1-1	S05 2-1	S12 1-1	D25 3-2
11 MILLWALL	D25 2-0	D12 3-0	A31 6-1	J25 1-0	a30 2-0	F06 2-1	F20 1-0	N14 5-0	S14 2-3	a16 1-1		a02 1-0	J02 4-3	S19 0-0	S05 1-3	O03 2-2	O31 4-1	M05 0-1	O17 1-0	M25 3-1	N28 1-2	M19 1-2
12 NOTTINGHAM F	N07 1-2	J27 6-1	a09 2-1	O24 3-1	O01 1-2	D19 0-2	J02 3-2	O10 4-0	D05 3-3	S19 2-1	N21 1-1		O03 2-1	M12 2-0	F27 3-2	M26 2-1	S16 2-2	M25 2-0	D26 1-1	a23 6-1	F06 1-3	S05 2-0
13 NOTTS CO	S26 2-3	O31 0-2	J16 1-1	m07 3-0	D12 5-0	M28 0-1	N14 2-2	M19 1-1	S12 1-1	M05 1-2	A29 2-0	F13 2-6		S23 1-0	F20 3-0	D25 4-2	a16 1-4	N28 5-0	a02 2-1	J30 1-2	O17 3-1	a30 3-1
14 OLDHAM A	m07 2-2	a02 2-1	S26 1-1	D26 2-1	O17 3-1	J16 1-2	a16 1-0	M05 6-1	F13 2-1	N14 1-5	J30 1-1	O31 2-4	S14 5-2		M25 1-3	S12 3-0	A29 2-2	M19 2-0	D12 1-3	O10 2-0	a30 1-2	N28 0-2
15 PLYMOUTH A	F13 3-0	a30 4-1	S12 3-3	S16 2-1	M19 4-0	D26 5-1	a02 1-1	m07 4-0	J30 3-2	O31 3-1	J16 8-1	O17 5-1	O10 3-4	M28 5-0		A29 1-3	D12 2-1	a16 1-2	N28 1-1	S26 4-2	M05 4-1	N14 3-3
16 PORT VALE	M25 3-0	a16 1-3	O10 2-0	S05 4-2	O31 1-3	S19 1-1	M19 0-1	a30 2-1	A31 1-2	N28 1-2	F13 2-2	N14 2-0	D26 2-0	J25 1-1	J02 2-0		M05 0-1	O17 0-0	F06 3-0	S21 0-4	a02 1-3	D12 1-7
17 PRESTON N.E.	a09 1-2	O03 1-0	D19 5-2	N07 1-1	D26 2-1	F29 0-2	S19 3-2	M25 2-2	M26 0-0	F20 0-0	M12 2-0	S07 1-1	D05 0-0	J02 2-3	a23 5-2	O24 1-4		S05 2-1	F25 2-0	N21 1-0	m07 2-0	F06 4-2
18 SOUTHAMPTON	N21 2-0	F20 0-3	M12 0-1	a23 1-1	A29 3-0	S12 2-1	F06 1-1	D26 1-2	D19 2-1	m07 1-1	O24 3-1	M28 4-0	a09 3-1	N07 1-1	D05 0-6	F27 5-1	J16 3-3		S19 1-2	M26 3-0	S07 2-1	O03 1-3
19 STOKE C	M26 2-0	m07 1-0	O24 3-1	D05 1-1	J16 3-0	N07 3-2	O03 4-0	A29 2-1	M12 3-4	S07 3-0	F27 0-0	D25 2-1	N21 2-2	a23 1-1	a09 3-2	S26 4-0	S12 4-1	J30 2-0		D19 0-0	M28 2-2	F20 2-1
20 SWANSEA T	J23 3-0	O17 1-0	D25 0-1	O03 2-0	N28 5-1	m07 2-0	O31 2-0	a16 1-1	A29 0-2	J16 3-1	M28 4-0	D12 4-1	S19 5-1	F20 1-0	F06 4-1	S07 2-3	a02 0-3	N14 3-4	a30 1-1		M19 1-1	M05 1-1
21 TOTTENHAM H	S19 4-2	S05 3-3	D05 1-5	M12 2-1	O10 1-1	M26 0-0	D25 0-1	F13 3-3	a23 3-1	J23 4-1	a09 1-0	S26 1-3	F27 2-0	D19 3-2	O24 0-1	N21 9-3	A31 4-0	S14 5-2	M25 3-3	N07 6-2		J02 3-3
22 WOLVERHAMPTON W	M12 2-0	M28 6-0	S14 3-1	N21 4-2	J30 3-1	D05 6-0	D28 3-1	S12 6-0	F27 1-1	D26 7-0	N07 5-0	J16 0-0	D19 0-0	a09 7-1	M26 2-0	a23 2-0	S26 3-2	F13 5-1	O10 0-1	O24 2-0	A29 4-0	

Season 1931-32

DIVISION 3 NORTH

	ACCRINGTON S	BARROW	CARLISLE U	CHESTER	CREWE A	DARLINGTON	DONCASTER R	GATESHEAD	HALIFAX T	HARTLEPOOLS U	HULL C	LINCOLN C	NEW BRIGHTON	ROCHDALE	ROTHERHAM U	SOUTHPORT	STOCKPORT CO	TRANMERE R	WALSALL	WIGAN B	WREXHAM	YORK C
1 ACCRINGTON S		a23 2-0	S02 5-3	F27 2-3	S29 2-0	N07 4-0	S05 3-2	a09 1-2	M26 4-0	O24 5-0	D19 1-1	J01 2-2	D05 4-1	J02 3-0	O03 5-2	F10 1-1	F20 2-0	F06 2-2	N21 1-0		D25 5-0	S19 2-1
2 BARROW	F18 3-0		J09 4-1	F20 4-0	a02 2-1	D25 3-4	M19 3-2	J16 3-1	S07 3-1	M28 4-1	F06 0-2	O03 0-2	S12 4-1	N14 4-1	J30 3-0	O31 1-1	a30 4-2	O17 3-1	J02 7-1		a16 1-0	M05 3-1
3 CARLISLE U	m07 3-0	a09 3-1		D19 4-3	S05 2-1	O24 0-2	S19 5-1	M26 0-0	M12 4-0	J02 3-2	D05 0-1	a23 0-3	N21 0-0	J23 4-0	M25 1-2	F06 2-2	D26 1-1	J01 1-1	N07 4-0		S10 2-2	O03 1-1
4 CHESTER	O17 1-0	O10 4-2	a30 4-1		a06 1-0	J16 3-1	J09 1-1	S26 1-1	S12 3-1	S16 2-3	M25 2-0	D25 2-1	F13 2-0	a16 7-2	O31 2-1	a02 4-0	M05 2-1	M19 3-1	J30 5-1	A29 4-0	S30 2-5	N14 3-0
5 CREWE A	S07 3-1	N21 3-2	J16 5-1	a23 1-0		F27 0-1	F06 2-0	N07 3-5	O24 4-3	D19 6-0	a09 4-3	D05 8-1	M26 3-2	S19 1-0	D25 5-0	O03 1-1	D12 2-2	M25 0-0	M12 2-1	S12 4-3	A29 3-0	F20 8-1
6 DARLINGTON	M19 4-1	S02 0-2	M05 0-1	S05 4-1	O17 1-0		a30 2-3	M25 1-2	F13 3-0	J23 6-3	S16 2-1	J02 0-6	J01 3-0	F06 3-1	a02 2-1	F24 0-1	N14 2-0	J20 1-2	O10 2-0	S19 5-0	O31 1-1	a16 4-1
7 DONCASTER R	J16 3-1	N07 0-1	J30 3-3	a09 3-0	S26 2-1	D19 3-2		O21 1-2	O10 3-1	D05 1-3	M26 2-1	N21 0-3	M12 2-1	F13 2-0	S21 2-0	M28 3-0	A29 1-1	m07 2-2	F27 2-1		S12 2-4	D25 1-0
8 GATESHEAD	J09 4-0	S05 4-0	N14 4-0	F06 1-2	M19 3-3	M28 3-2	M05 2-1		D26 1-1	O03 3-1	J23 2-1	S19 2-3	J02 4-0	O31 3-1	D16 4-1	O17 2-0	a16 2-1	F20 3-3	m07 2-0		a02 4-0	S09 6-0
9 HALIFAX T	N14 1-0	S14 1-0	O31 1-1	J23 2-1	M05 4-1	O03 0-3	F20 4-0	D25 1-2		S19 2-0	J02 2-2	S05 3-0	A31 0-0	O17 3-2	J11 1-1	a30 3-0	a02 2-2	a16 0-0	M28 1-2		M19 1-0	a28 4-1
10 HARTLEPOOLS U	M05 1-0	M25 0-2	A29 2-2	S09 2-2	J09 3-1	S12 3-3	a16 5-0	F13 1-2	J30 4-1		D26 2-3	m07 4-3	O10 1-0	D12 3-0	M19 1-4	S23 2-1	O31 2-2	N14 0-5	S26 4-3		O17 0-1	a02 7-2
11 HULL C	a30 3-0	S26 3-0	a16 2-0	M28 0-2	J14 2-4	S07 4-1	N14 4-1	S12 0-1	A29 1-0	D25 3-1		F20 4-1	J30 4-1	a02 4-1	O17 0-1	M19 1-0	F13 4-4	M05 3-0	J16 3-0		m07 5-0	O31 2-3
12 LINCOLN C	M25 5-1	F13 3-1	F24 3-1	D26 4-0	a16 5-1	A29 2-0	a02 1-2	J30 1-0	J16 9-1	A31 6-0	O10 1-0		S26 3-0	J09 3-0	M05 3-1	N14 7-0	O17 1-2	O31 4-2	S12 3-0	S14 3-0	a30 0-0	M19 1-1
13 NEW BRIGHTON	a16 2-1	J23 0-3	a02 4-1	O03 0-1	N14 0-1	D26 0-0	O31 1-0	A29 1-3	m07 2-0	F20 1-1	S19 1-2	F06 2-1		M19 1-1	a30 3-1	M05 3-1	D30 2-1	J16 1-1	S09 0-1		J09 1-1	O17 0-2
14 ROCHDALE	A29 2-2	M26 0-6	S12 4-3	D05 0-3	J30 2-3	S26 1-1	O03 3-1	M12 0-3	F27 1-4	a23 1-3	N21 3-6	a09 3-5	N07 3-2		m07 1-4	F20 0-1	S15 1-0	D26 3-6	O24 0-1		J16 2-4	M28 3-5
15 ROTHERHAM U	F13 2-3	S19 0-2	M28 4-1	M12 3-0	D26 0-2	N21 2-4	S14 6-3	a23 2-1	a09 5-0	N07 1-2	F27 2-0	O24 0-1	D19 2-2	A31 5-0		J02 2-0	S26 1-1	J23 1-0	D05 3-0		O10 0-0	S05 0-1
16 SOUTHPORT	S12 4-2	M12 3-1	S26 2-0	N21 1-1	F13 1-1	a23 3-0	M25 5-0	F27 1-1	D19 2-2	a09 1-2	N07 1-0	M26 1-1	O24 1-0	O10 3-1	A29 3-2		J16 1-0	S08 1-0	D25 5-1		J30 2-0	J01 3-0
17 STOCKPORT CO	O10 3-0	D19 2-0	D25 0-0	O24 0-0	A31 1-2	M26 1-0	J02 1-0	D05 1-1	N21 2-1	M12 3-2	O03 2-0	F27 0-1	a23 3-1	S07 3-1	F06 1-0	S05 0-1		S19 0-1	a09 0-1		M25 5-1	J23 3-2
18 TRANMERE R	S26 8-1	F27 6-1	O10 3-0	N07 2-2	M28 4-1	a09 3-1	A31 0-1	D19 4-3	D05 5-2	M26 5-0	O24 2-2	M12 1-0	S05 5-1	D25 9-1	S12 6-1	S14 2-0	J30 2-2		a23 4-1		F13 3-1	J02 2-2
19 WALSALL	a02 5-5	A29 1-2	M19 3-1	S19 1-1	O31 2-1	F20 1-0	O17 2-0	A31 1-2	M29 4-2	F06 2-3	S05 1-4	J23 0-3	S14 3-0	M05 2-1	a16 3-0	D26 2-1	J09 3-1	F18 2-1		O03 3-0	N14 2-0	D12 2-2
20 WIGAN B			O17 3-2		RESIGNED			O10 2-1	S26 0-1	S05 1-1	S02 3-1	S09 0-3					RESIGNED					
21 WREXHAM	D26 2-1	D05 0-1	S14 1-0	S02 1-1	J02 2-4	M12 3-0	J23 2-1	N21 2-1	N07 2-3	F27 5-3	a23 2-1	D19 1-3	a09 2-1	S05 4-0	F20 1-0	S19 1-1	M28 2-1	O03 2-1	M26 5-1	O24 5-0		F06 2-1
22 YORK C	J30 1-0	O24 1-0	F13 2-4	M26 3-1	O10 3-3	D05 3-0	D26 1-2	S16 3-2	a23 7-2	N21 3-1	M12 0-0	N07 1-1	F27 4-0	M25 5-2	J16 2-0	S02 1-2	S12 1-0	A29 3-2	D19 2-0		S26 3-2	

DIVISION 3 SOUTH

	BOURNEMOUTH	BRENTFORD	BRIGHTON & HA	BRISTOL R	CARDIFF C	CLAPTON O	COVENTRY C	CRYSTAL P	EXETER C	FULHAM	GILLINGHAM	LUTON T	MANSFIELD T	NORTHAMPTON T	NORWICH C	Q.P.R.	READING	SOUTHEND U	SWINDON T	THAMES	TORQUAY U	WATFORD
1 BOURNEMOUTH		D19 1-3	F20 1-2	A29 2-2	N07 3-0	D26 0-1	F27 2-2	S19 4-1	S12 5-2	D05 0-3	O24 0-2	M12 1-1	O03 3-2	M26 1-1	S09 1-0	J16 2-2	N21 2-2	a09 0-0	M28 2-1	a23 4-2	m07 5-0	F06 3-3
2 BRENTFORD	a30 4-2		a02 2-2	O17 4-2	F13 2-3	O31 3-0	S12 4-2	a13 1-1	J16 2-2	D25 0-0	J30 1-1	S26 1-0	J13 1-1	O10 2-0	N14 0-1	A29 1-0	S24 3-0	M25 2-3	M19 2-0	m07 1-0	M05 3-0	a16 1-2
3 BRIGHTON & H.A.	O10 4-1	N21 1-2		S26 2-0	m07 0-0	S12 1-1	D05 4-1	S09 0-3	a09 1-1	N07 2-3	a23 7-0	D19 3-2	D26 4-0	F27 0-0	A29 2-1	F13 1-0	O24 2-0	M12 1-2	J16 1-0	M26 4-1	J30 0-2	M25 2-1
4 BRISTOL R	J02 4-1	F27 2-0	F06 0-4		N21 2-2	S16 2-1	M12 3-1	S05 6-1	O24 2-4	D19 2-2	N07 5-2	M26 3-1	S19 1-1	a09 3-2	O03 0-1	A31 1-1	D05 2-0	a23 0-0	F20 0-2	D26 4-1	M25 1-1	J27 3-2
5 CARDIFF C	M19 0-0	O03 3-2	A31 1-1	a02 3-1		a16 5-0	S14 6-1	O31 1-3	F20 5-2	S19 0-3	M28 1-0	D26 4-1	O17 2-0	J02 5-0	a30 0-2	N14 0-4	S05 5-1	J23 2-3	a13 3-0	F06 9-2	J13 5-2	M05 2-1
6 CLAPTON O	D25 1-2	M12 2-2	J23 2-2	S07 1-0	D05 1-1		M26 5-2	A31 1-3	N07 2-2	F27 0-1	N21 3-1	a09 0-0	S05 4-0	a23 3-2	S19 1-3	M25 3-0	D19 2-2	O03 2-4	F06 4-2	O24 1-1	O10 1-3	J02 2-2
7 COVENTRY C	O17 6-1	J28 0-1	a16 4-3	O31 1-1	S07 2-1	N14 4-2		F06 8-0	S19 4-0	J02 5-5	F13 6-4	O10 3-2	D12 5-1	M28 4-1	J09 3-0	M05 1-0	D25 5-1	A31 0-2	a02 3-2	S05 2-0	M19 3-1	a30 5-0
8 CRYSTAL P	J30 1-1	a23 1-0	S16 2-0	J16 5-0	M12 5-0	m07 0-0	S26 2-2		D19 3-0	a09 2-0	F27 1-0	O24 1-1	J09 2-1	N07 4-0	M25 3-1	S12 1-1	M26 1-1	N21 3-2	D25 0-0	D05 2-1	A29 7-0	O03 2-1
9 EXETER C	J27 1-0	S05 4-1	S30 3-1	M05 1-0	O10 3-1	M19 4-3	J30 3-0	a30 0-1		S02 0-3	S26 4-0	F13 1-1	a16 3-0	S16 0-0	a02 3-0	O17 6-2	M28 4-0	D26 3-0	N14 1-1	J02 4-1	O31 3-1	D16 2-0
10 FULHAM	a16 3-0	D26 2-1	M19 3-0	a30 3-2	J30 4-0	O17 5-1	A29 5-3	J18 4-0	m07 3-1		J16 0-2	S12 3-2	N14 2-1	S26 1-3	O31 4-0	D28 1-3	F13 3-3	O10 1-1	M05 2-2	M28 8-0	S07 10-2	a02 5-0
11 GILLINGHAM	M05 1-4	S19 0-2	a13 0-0	M19 1-0	M25 1-1	a02 0-2	O03 1-3	O17 0-0	F06 0-1	S05 2-1		S09 1-3	a30 2-0	D25 3-2	a16 3-3	O31 1-0	S02 1-1	J02 4-0	J09 2-1	J23 2-0	N14 1-1	F20 0-1
12 LUTON T	O31 1-0	F06 1-1	a30 3-2	N14 3-0	D25 2-1	J11 1-5	F20 3-1	M05 3-0	O03 6-3	J23 1-3	S14 2-0		M25 3-1	A31 1-0	M29 7-1	M19 4-1	J02 6-1	S05 1-3	a16 6-0	S19 2-0	a02 6-1	O17 0-1
13 MANSFIELD T	F13 2-1	a09 2-0	D25 3-3	J30 0-3	F27 1-2	J16 4-3	a23 3-3	O10 1-1	D05 3-1	M26 1-2	D19 3-1	M28 5-2		O24 2-0	m07 5-2	S26 2-2	M12 1-7	N07 4-4	A29 3-2	N21 4-0	S12 2-4	S07 3-2
14 NORTHAMPTON T	N14 1-1	F20 3-0	O17 0-1	D28 6-0	A29 1-0	a21 4-3	M29 3-2	M19 5-0	S07 2-1	F06 0-1	D26 1-0	S28 1-2	M05 3-0		J16 2-2	a02 6-1	J28 2-4	S19 1-2	a30 4-1	O03 0-4	a16 2-0	O31 1-1
15 NORWICH C	S14 1-2	M26 1-0	J02 2-1	F13 6-0	D19 2-0	J30 3-2	a09 6-2	M28 3-2	N21 0-1	M12 2-2	D05 1-1	a23 3-3	A31 1-1	S05 0-0		O10 2-1	F27 0-0	O24 1-1	S12 4-2	N07 7-0	S26 2-0	D26 4-1
16 Q.P.R.	S05 0-3	J02 1-2	O03 1-1	m07 2-1	M26 2-3	M28 3-2	O24 1-1	J28 2-2	F27 1-0	a23 3-1	M10 7-0	N07 3-1	F06 1-1	N21 3-2	F20 2-2		a09 2-0	D05 2-1	S10 1-2	D19 6-0	D26 3-1	S19 4-4
17 READING	a02 3-1	S09 1-2	M05 3-1	a16 3-0	J16 5-1	a30 5-0	D26 2-1	N14 3-0	M25 2-0	O03 4-2	m07 2-0	A29 2-1	O31 4-1	S12 3-2	O17 1-1	J13 3-2		F06 3-1	J30 5-2	J09 5-1	D12 4-1	M19 2-1
18 SOUTHEND U	J13 1-3	M28 1-0	O31 2-0	J09 4-1	S12 1-1	F13 1-3	m07 4-0	a02 1-0	D25 0-1	F20 4-1	A29 2-0	J16 1-1	M19 5-2	J30 0-1	M05 2-0	a16 0-0	S26 1-1		O17 3-0	S07 1-1	a30 4-2	N14 3-0
19 SWINDON T	M25 3-0	N07 1-3	S05 1-2	O10 2-1	a23 1-4	S26 2-3	N21 2-2	D26 3-2	M26 2-1	O24 2-2	a09 4-0	D05 3-2	J02 5-2	D19 3-0	J23 2-0	S16 1-2	S19 0-2	F27 1-2		M12 2-0	F13 3-0	S02 4-1
20 THAMES	D14 4-2	S03 1-1	N14 1-2	D25 0-2	S26 1-2	M05 3-3	J16 5-2	a16 1-3	A29 0-0	M25 0-0	S12 3-0	J30 2-4	a02 6-3	F13 0-2	M19 1-0	a30 3-2	O10 0-0	S17 1-3	O31 1-1		O17 1-1	J18 1-2
21 TORQUAY U	S02 1-1	O24 1-1	S19 1-1	M28 8-1	a09 2-2	F20 3-0	N07 3-3	J02 3-1	M12 2-1	S16 2-3	M26 1-0	N21 1-2	J23 2-2	D05 4-1	F06 2-4	D25 2-3	a23 1-4	D19 2-1	O03 2-1	F27 3-1		S05 3-6
22 WATFORD	S26 4-2	D05 1-4	M28 2-2	S12 5-2	O24 3-0	A29 2-1	D19 2-0	F17 1-2	a23 1-0	N21 3-1	O10 2-0	a13 3-1	S16 4-1	M12 1-2	D25 1-1	J30 2-2	N07 3-2	M26 1-1	m07 4-1	a09 3-2	J16 1-0	

LEAGUE TABLES

DIVISION 1

	P	W	D	L	F	A	W	D	L	F	A	Pts
Everton	42	18	0	3	84	30	8	4	9	32	34	56
Arsenal	42	14	5	2	52	16	8	5	8	38	32	54
Sheffield W	42	14	4	3	60	28	8	2	11	36	54	50
Huddersfield T	42	11	8	2	47	21	8	2	11	33	42	48
Aston Villa	42	15	1	5	64	28	4	7	10	40	44	46
W.B.A.	42	12	4	5	46	21	8	2	11	31	34	46
Sheffield U	42	13	3	5	47	32	7	3	11	33	43	46
Portsmouth	42	14	2	5	37	21	5	5	11	25	41	45
Birmingham C	42	13	5	3	48	22	5	3	13	30	45	44
Liverpool	42	13	4	4	56	38	6	2	13	25	55	44
Newcastle U	42	13	5	3	52	31	5	1	15	28	56	42
Chelsea	42	12	4	5	43	27	4	4	13	26	46	40
Sunderland	42	11	4	6	42	29	4	6	11	25	44	40
Manchester C	42	10	5	6	49	30	3	7	11	34	43	38
Derby Co	42	13	5	3	51	25	1	5	15	20	50	38
Blackburn R	42	12	3	6	57	41	4	3	14	32	54	38
Bolton W	42	15	1	5	51	25	2	3	16	21	55	38
Middlesbrough	42	12	3	6	41	29	3	5	13	23	60	38
Leicester C	42	11	3	7	46	39	4	4	13	28	55	37
Blackpool	42	9	4	8	42	40	3	5	13	23	62	33
Grimsby T	42	11	4	6	39	28	2	2	17	28	70	32
West Ham U	42	9	5	7	35	37	3	2	16	27	70	31

DIVISION 2

	P	W	D	L	F	A	W	D	L	F	A	Pts
Wolverhampton W	42	17	3	1	71	11	7	5	9	44	38	56
Leeds U	42	12	5	4	36	22	10	5	6	42	32	54
Stoke C	42	14	6	1	47	19	5	8	8	22	29	52
Plymouth A	42	14	4	3	69	29	6	5	10	31	37	49
Bury	42	13	4	4	44	21	8	3	10	26	37	49
Bradford P.A.	42	17	2	2	44	18	4	5	12	28	45	49
Bradford C	42	10	7	4	53	26	6	6	9	27	35	45
Tottenham H	42	11	6	4	58	37	5	5	11	29	41	43
Millwall	42	13	3	5	43	21	4	6	11	18	40	43
Charlton A	42	11	5	5	38	28	6	4	11	23	38	43
Nottingham F	42	13	4	4	49	27	3	6	12	28	45	42
Manchester U	42	12	3	6	44	31	5	5	11	27	41	42
Preston N.E.	42	11	6	4	37	25	5	4	12	38	52	42
Southampton	42	10	5	6	39	30	7	2	12	27	47	41
Swansea T	42	12	4	5	45	22	4	3	14	28	53	39
Notts Co	42	10	4	7	43	30	3	8	10	32	45	38
Chesterfield	42	11	3	7	43	33	2	8	11	21	53	37
Oldham A	42	10	4	7	41	34	3	6	12	21	50	36
Burnley	42	7	8	6	36	36	6	1	14	23	51	35
Port Vale	42	8	4	9	30	33	5	3	13	28	56	33
Barnsley	42	8	7	6	35	30	4	2	15	20	61	33
Bristol C	42	4	7	10	22	37	2	4	15	17	41	23

DIVISION 3 NORTH

	P	W	D	L	F	A	W	D	L	F	A	Pts
Lincoln C	40	16	2	2	65	13	10	3	7	41	34	57
Gateshead	40	15	3	2	59	20	10	4	6	35	28	57
Chester C	40	16	2	2	54	22	5	6	9	24	38	50
Tranmere R	40	15	4	1	76	23	4	7	9	31	35	49
Barrow	40	16	1	3	59	23	8	0	12	27	36	49
Crewe A	40	15	3	2	64	24	6	3	11	31	42	48
Southport	40	14	5	1	44	15	4	5	11	14	38	46
Hull C	40	14	1	5	52	21	6	4	10	30	32	45
York C	40	14	3	3	49	24	4	4	12	27	57	43
Wrexham	40	14	2	4	42	25	4	5	11	22	44	43
Darlington	40	12	1	7	41	27	5	3	12	25	42	38
Stockport Co	40	12	3	5	31	15	1	8	11	24	38	37
Hartlepool U	40	10	4	6	47	37	6	1	13	31	63	37
Accrington S	40	14	4	2	56	20	1	2	17	19	60	36
Doncaster R	40	12	3	5	38	27	4	1	15	21	53	36
Walsall	40	12	3	5	42	30	4	0	16	15	55	35
Halifax T	40	11	6	3	36	18	2	2	16	25	69	34
Carlisle U	40	9	7	4	40	23	2	4	14	24	56	33
Rotherham U	40	10	3	7	41	23	4	1	15	22	49	32
New Brighton	40	8	5	7	25	23	0	3	17	13	53	24
Rochdale	40	4	2	14	33	63	0	1	19	15	72	11

Wigan Borough resigned from the League, 26.10.1931

DIVISION 3 SOUTH

	P	W	D	L	F	A	W	D	L	F	A	Pts
Fulham	42	15	3	3	72	27	9	6	6	39	35	57
Reading	42	19	1	1	65	21	4	8	9	32	46	55
Southend U	42	12	5	4	41	18	9	6	6	36	35	53
Crystal Palace	42	14	7	0	48	12	6	4	11	26	51	51
Brentford	42	11	6	4	40	22	8	4	9	28	30	48
Luton T	42	16	1	4	62	25	4	6	11	33	45	47
Exeter C	42	16	3	2	53	16	4	4	13	24	46	47
Brighton & H.A.	42	12	4	5	42	21	5	8	8	31	37	46
Cardiff C	42	14	2	5	62	29	5	6	10	25	44	46
Norwich C	42	12	7	2	51	22	5	5	11	25	45	46
Watford	42	14	4	3	49	27	5	4	12	32	52	46
Coventry C	42	17	2	2	74	28	1	6	14	34	69	44
Q.P.R.	42	11	6	4	50	30	4	6	11	29	43	42
Northampton T	42	12	3	6	48	26	4	4	13	21	43	39
Bournemouth	42	8	8	5	42	32	5	4	12	28	46	38
Clapton O	42	7	8	6	41	35	5	3	13	36	55	35
Swindon T	42	12	2	7	47	31	2	4	15	23	53	34
Bristol R	42	11	6	4	46	30	2	2	17	19	62	34
Torquay U	42	9	6	6	49	39	3	3	15	23	67	33
Mansfield T	42	11	5	5	54	45	0	5	16	21	63	32
Gillingham	42	8	6	7	26	26	2	2	17	14	56	28
Thames	42	6	7	8	35	35	1	2	18	18	74	23

FOOTBALL LEAGUE RECORDS

Top scorers: Div 1, J.Bowers (Derby County) 35 goals; Div 2, E.Harper (Preston North End) 37 goals; Div 3 N, W.McNaughton (Hull City) 41 goals; Div 3 S, C.Bourton (Coventry City) 40 goals.

Thames did not seek re-election. Aldershot and Newport County were elected to League. Mansfield Town transferred to Division Three North.

Cliff Bastin, who scored a record 33 goals for a winger when Arsenal regained the Division One title in 1932-33.

DIVISION 1

	ARSENAL	ASTON VILLA	BIRMINGHAM	BLACKBURN R	BLACKPOOL	BOLTON W	CHELSEA	DERBY CO	EVERTON	HUDDERSFIELD T	LEEDS U	LEICESTER C	LIVERPOOL	MANCHESTER C	MIDDLESBROUGH	NEWCASTLE U	PORTSMOUTH	SHEFFIELD U	SHEFFIELD W	SUNDERLAND	W.B.A.	WOLVERHAMPTON W
1 ARSENAL		a01 5-0	D31 3-0	F25 8-0	F11 1-1	S17 3-2	D10 4-1	O08 3-3	S24 2-1	a29 2-2	D26 1-2	O29 8-2	M04 0-1	J21 2-1	N26 4-2	N12 1-0	a15 2-0	D24 9-2	a14 4-2	S03 6-1	A31 1-2	M18 1-2
2 ASTON VILLA	N19 5-3		O22 1-0	D17 4-0	N05 6-2	S03 6-1	O01 3-1	m06 2-0	M25 2-1	F18 0-3	a22 0-0	S17 4-2	J21 5-2	a08 1-1	D31 3-1	a18 3-0	F04 4-1	O15 3-0	D03 3-6	A29 1-0	M11 3-2	D26 1-3
3 BIRMINGHAM	A27 0-1	M08 3-2		S24 3-1	S10 2-1	a15 2-1	M18 0-0	F01 3-1	J07 4-0	N12 0-2	F11 2-1	a29 0-4	D10 3-0	S07 3-0	O29 1-4	D27 1-2	D24 4-0	a01 4-1	O08 2-1	a17 2-0	a26 1-1	N26 0-0
4 BLACKBURN R	O15 2-3	a29 0-5	F04 2-0		J02 6-5	M18 3-2	D31 1-3	S19 3-3	D26 3-1	M04 4-2	S03 1-1	a01 1-1	N12 2-2	F23 1-0	D24 4-2	D10 2-1	N26 3-2	O29 3-0	J21 1-1	O01 1-3	S17 4-4	a15 1-0
5 BLACKPOOL	O01 1-2	M18 6-2	J21 0-1	a14 3-0		a01 1-3	O29 4-0	D27 4-1	F22 2-1	a15 1-1	A29 2-1	O15 2-1	N26 4-1	F04 1-0	N12 3-1	D24 0-4	M04 0-2	D10 0-3	D31 3-4	S17 3-1	S03 2-4	a29 2-2
6 BOLTON W	F01 0-4	J07 0-1	D03 2-2	N05 4-2	N19 1-0		O15 2-3	M25 1-1	a08 2-4	D26 2-1	m06 5-0	O01 5-0	F04 3-3	O22 2-1	S10 4-3	A27 2-2	F22 4-1	J02 3-3	D17 3-0	M11 0-0	a22 2-2	S05 2-0
7 CHELSEA	a22 1-3	F11 0-1	N05 4-2	A27 2-2	M11 1-0	F25 1-1		O22 1-3	D03 1-0	J07 0-1	a08 6-0	a14 4-1	D27 0-2	D17 3-1	O08 2-1	S24 0-1	S07 4-4	S10 3-0	N19 0-2	m06 1-1	M25 1-2	J28 3-1
8 DERBY CO	F22 2-2	D24 0-0	S17 2-2	A31 2-1	D26 1-1	N12 4-1	M29 0-1		O15 2-0	O29 2-3	D31 5-1	N26 3-2	a01 1-1	O01 4-0	a05 2-2	a29 3-2	a17 2-0	a15 3-0	S03 2-0	F04 3-0	J21 2-2	D10 4-4
9 EVERTON	F04 1-1	N12 3-3	S03 4-1	D27 6-1	O08 2-0	N26 2-2	a15 3-2	F25 4-2		D10 2-0	a17 0-1	M08 6-3	O01 3-1	S17 2-1	a01 0-0	a05 0-0	O29 1-1	m03 1-0	A31 2-1	J21 6-1	D31 1-2	D24 5-1
10 HUDDERSFIELD T	D17 0-1	O08 0-0	M25 0-0	O22 0-3	D03 0-1	D27 2-1	S03 2-0	M11 0-0	a22 0-0		J21 2-2	A29 4-1	a18 3-1	m06 1-0	M15 0-1	F11 4-0	D31 2-2	F01 1-0	a08 4-0	N05 2-1	N19 2-1	S24 3-2
11 LEEDS U	D27 0-0	D10 1-1	O01 1-1	J07 3-1	S05 3-1	D24 4-3	N26 2-0	A27 0-2	a18 1-0	S10 1-1		N12 1-1	M18 5-0	O15 2-1	a29 0-1	a15 6-1	a01 0-1	M04 1-3	S17 3-2	F22 2-3	F04 1-1	O29 2-0
12 LEICESTER C	M11 1-1	F09 3-0	D17 2-2	N19 1-1	M30 3-0	F11 2-0	a18 1-1	a08 4-0	O22 2-2	S05 3-1	M25 3-1		O08 1-2	D03 1-2	S24 1-1	S10 0-3	D27 2-1	A27 1-1	N05 0-0	a22 4-2	m06 6-2	J07 2-2
13 LIVERPOOL	O22 2-3	S10 0-0	a22 1-0	M25 2-2	a08 4-3	S24 0-1	D26 3-0	N19 6-1	F11 7-4	a14 2-2	N05 0-1	F18 1-2		M11 1-1	F01 1-3	J07 3-0	O15 4-3	S07 2-2	m06 4-1	D03 3-3	D17 2-0	A27 5-1
14 MANCHESTER C	S10 2-3	N26 5-2	A31 1-0	O08 2-3	S24 5-1	M08 2-1	m03 1-4	F11 2-1	F01 3-0	D24 3-0	a05 0-0	a15 4-1	O29 1-1		S03 2-3	a01 1-2	D10 3-1	M22 1-0	D26 2-2	D31 2-4	a14 1-0	N12 4-1
15 MIDDLESBROUGH	a08 3-4	A27 0-2	M11 2-2	m06 4-0	M25 2-0	J21 2-1	M01 2-1	N05 0-3	N19 0-2	O15 1-1	D17 0-1	F04 1-1	S17 0-1	J07 2-0		J02 2-3	O01 5-4	D27 2-2	a22 1-1	O22 1-2	D03 3-1	a17 2-1
16 NEWCASTLE U	M25 2-1	a17 3-1	D26 2-1	a22 2-1	m06 1-2	D31 3-1	F04 2-0	D17 0-0	N05 1-2	O01 0-4	D03 3-1	J21 2-1	S03 4-3	N19 2-0	A31 5-1		S17 1-1	F18 2-0	M11 3-1	a08 0-1	O22 3-0	O15 3-2
17 PORTSMOUTH	D03 1-3	S24 2-4	m06 1-1	a08 2-0	O22 2-1	O08 2-1	A31 2-0	a14 2-0	M11 2-2	A27 1-0	N19 3-3	D26 2-1	F25 2-1	a22 1-2	F11 2-0	J28 2-0		J07 1-0	M25 3-0	D17 1-3	N05 3-0	S10 2-0
18 SHEFFIELD U	m06 3-1	a24 1-0	N19 2-1	M11 2-1	a22 1-0	a17 3-2	J21 4-1	D03 4-3	D17 3-2	S17 1-2	O22 0-0	D31 5-2	A29 6-2	N05 2-5	M27 2-0	O08 3-1	S03 2-3		F04 2-3	M25 3-0	a08 1-1	F11 0-0
19 SHEFFIELD W	J02 3-2	a15 0-2	a05 1-1	S10 1-1	A27 4-1	a29 2-0	a01 2-2	J07 0-0	S05 3-1	N26 2-1	F08 2-0	M18 4-1	D24 3-0	D27 2-1	D10 2-1	O29 2-0	N12 2-1	S24 3-3		O15 3-1	O01 3-1	M04 2-0
20 SUNDERLAND	J07 3-2	S07 1-1	a14 1-0	F11 4-2	F01 1-1	O29 7-4	D24 2-1	S24 0-2	S10 3-1	M18 1-2	O08 0-0	D10 2-1	a15 0-0	A27 3-2	M22 0-0	N26 0-2	a29 0-3	N12 2-2	F25 1-2		J02 2-2	a01 0-1
21 W.B.A.	S14 1-1	O29 3-1	O15 1-0	F08 1-3	J07 2-1	D10 4-0	N12 3-2	S10 2-0	A27 3-1	a01 2-1	S24 0-1	D24 4-3	a29 2-1	a17 4-0	a15 0-1	M04 3-2	M18 4-2	N26 0-1	F11 2-0	D26 5-1		O08 4-1
22 WOLVERHAMPTON W	N05 1-7	D27 2-4	a08 1-0	D03 5-3	D17 2-3	A29 4-1	S17 1-2	a22 3-1	m06 4-2	F04 6-4	M11 3-3	S03 1-1	D31 3-1	M25 1-2	a14 2-0	M06 1-1	J21 5-2	O01 5-1	O22 3-5	N19 0-2	F18 3-3	

George Brown led Villa's front line when 'Pongo' Waring was injured in 1932-33 and responded with 33 goals to help Villa into runners-up spot.

DIVISION 2

	BRADFORD	BRADFORD C	BURNLEY	BURY	CHARLTON A	CHESTERFIELD	FULHAM	GRIMSBY T	LINCOLN C	MANCHESTER U	MILLWALL	NOTTINGHAM F	NOTTS CO	OLDHAM A	PLYMOUTH A	PORT VALE	PRESTON N.E.	SOUTHAMPTON	STOKE C	SWANSEA T	TOTTENHAM H	WEST HAM U
1 BRADFORD		J21 2-0	S03 0-4	D03 4-0	F11 3-0	O22 5-1	M11 1-4	a17 1-1	m06 6-0	a05 1-1	N19 3-0	S24 3-1	D17 3-4	A31 1-3	F01 1-0	a22 4-2	D31 2-0	a08 2-1	O08 2-2	M25 1-0	D26 3-3	N05 3-0
2 BRADFORD C	S10 1-0		N12 2-1	D27 3-0	M18 3-0	J07 4-2	A27 2-0	a01 2-2	a18 1-1	a15 1-2	F18 1-5	O29 2-2	F04 1-2	D10 3-0	M04 2-3	O01 7-0	a29 0-0	O15 1-0	D24 1-1	S17 1-1	N26 0-1	S07 5-1
3 BURNLEY	J07 2-0	M25 0-0		m06 1-0	S24 0-1	A27 1-1	O22 3-3	D27 2-0	N05 0-0	O08 2-3	a08 3-0	J31 3-3	a22 2-1	a14 1-1	S10 1-1	N19 1-1	S05 4-0	D03 2-0	F11 1-2	D17 1-2	a24 1-1	M11 4-0
4 BURY	a15 0-0	D26 1-1	D24 5-3		D10 3-1	F25 6-0	O08 1-1	M04 4-1	S24 2-2	N12 2-2	S03 3-0	a01 5-2	A29 3-1	O29 3-3	N26 2-1	D31 0-0	M18 1-2	J21 1-0	a29 3-2	J02 3-0	S17 1-0	F11 6-1
5 CHARLTON A	O01 0-2	N05 0-0	F04 2-2	a22 1-3		m06 2-5	D03 1-2	S03 2-3	N19 4-2	A29 0-1	M25 1-4	O15 3-0	O22 3-3	J21 1-0	F18 4-1	a26 2-1	S17 0-1	D17 2-0	a14 1-0	M11 3-1	D31 0-3	a08 3-1
6 CHESTERFIELD	M04 2-1	S03 1-2	D31 6-0	O15 1-3	D24 2-3		J02 3-2	D10 1-2	D27 3-0	N26 1-1	O01 1-0	M18 0-1	S17 0-0	a29 3-1	O29 1-1	F04 2-2	N12 4-3	F22 1-0	a15 1-2	J21 1-0	a01 1-1	a14 1-0
7 FULHAM	O29 5-2	D31 1-0	M08 2-1	F18 3-3	a15 3-1	S05 2-2		a29 0-1	O15 3-2	a01 3-1	F04 1-1	D24 0-1	J21 3-4	N12 1-0	M18 3-1	S17 1-1	a14 1-0	O01 4-2	N26 1-3	S03 3-1	D10 2-2	D26 4-2
8 GRIMSBY T	a14 5-1	N19 1-1	D26 1-2	O22 1-0	J07 5-5	a22 1-1	D17 1-0		F11 3-3	J31 1-1	N05 1-1	A27 1-1	D03 1-1	F18 5-1	S06 2-3	m06 6-1	O15 5-5	M11 2-2	S10 0-1	a08 2-1	S24 3-2	M25 2-1
9 LINCOLN C	D24 2-2	a14 0-0	M18 1-4	F04 2-1	a01 1-1	D26 5-3	a05 3-0	O01 6-3		a29 3-2	J21 3-0	N26 1-1	D31 1-1	M04 1-3	a15 2-0	S03 0-1	O29 2-1	S17 1-0	D10 2-3	A29 2-0	N12 2-2	O08 6-0
10 MANCHESTER U	O15 2-1	D03 0-1	F22 2-1	M25 1-3	S07 1-1	a08 2-1	N19 4-3	S17 1-1	D17 4-1		O22 7-1	a17 2-1	N05 2-0	F04 2-0	J02 4-0	M11 1-1	O01 0-0	J07 1-2	A27 0-2	m06 1-1	J21 2-1	a22 1-2
11 MILLWALL	a01 1-1	O08 3-3	N26 4-1	J07 5-2	N12 2-1	F11 0-0	S24 2-1	M18 0-1	S10 2-0	M04 2-0		a29 1-1	D27 1-1	D24 6-1	D10 2-0	a17 0-1	a15 1-1	A27 3-0	S05 0-0	F25 3-1	O29 1-4	J30 1-0
12 NOTTINGHAM F	F04 1-1	M11 3-1	S17 1-1	N19 0-2	M16 0-1	N05 2-3	m06 1-0	D31 3-2	a08 2-2	a14 3-2	D17 0-0		F18 3-0	S03 2-3	O01 1-1	M25 1-1	J21 2-1	a22 4-2	D27 1-0	O22 2-2	A29 3-1	D03 2-2
13 NOTTS CO	a29 1-4	S24 2-0	D10 4-2	O06 2-2	M04 3-2	F01 1-1	S10 1-2	a15 1-3	A27 1-1	M18 1-0	D26 1-0	O08 2-4		N26 2-1	N12 4-1	O15 5-0	a01 0-0	a17 1-2	O29 3-4	F11 1-2	D24 3-0	J07 2-0
14 OLDHAM A	S05 1-3	a22 6-1	a17 2-2	M11 2-1	S10 0-0	D17 2-0	M25 1-3	O08 0-1	O22 5-2	S24 1-1	m06 1-0	J07 1-2	a08 5-0		A27 3-1	D03 2-1	D27 0-2	N05 2-0	J31 0-4	N19 0-0	F11 1-5	M13 3-2
15 PLYMOUTH A	S17 3-2	O22 2-1	J21 4-0	a08 1-0	O08 6-1	M11 1-0	N05 2-3	A31 4-0	D03 0-3	D26 2-3	a22 0-0	F11 1-1	M25 0-2	D31 2-1		D17 3-1	S03 5-0	N19 1-1	F25 1-0	F04 1-0	a17 2-2	m06 4-1
16 PORT VALE	D10 3-1	F11 2-0	a01 1-1	A27 1-0	D27 2-1	S24 9-1	J28 1-2	D24 4-2	J07 3-2	O29 3-3	a14 2-0	N12 0-1	M20 4-0	a15 2-4	a29 4-1		N26 0-1	S05 0-2	M04 1-3	O08 2-1	M18 1-1	S10 4-0
17 PRESTON N.E.	A27 2-3	D17 1-4	A30 6-1	N05 1-3	J28 4-2	M25 2-0	a17 1-2	M02 4-2	M11 5-0	F11 3-3	D03 0-1	S10 2-1	N19 3-0	D26 2-2	J07 3-0	a08 3-1		m06 3-1	S24 1-3	a22 1-0	O08 2-6	O22 4-1
18 SOUTHAMPTON	N26 2-0	F25 3-1	a15 3-1	S10 1-0	a29 3-0	O08 2-1	F11 2-2	O29 3-0	J28 4-0	S03 4-2	D31 2-3	D10 0-2	a14 6-2	M18 0-2	a01 2-0	A29 2-2	D24 1-0		N12 1-0	D27 2-0	M04 1-1	S24 4-3
19 STOKE C	F18 4-0	m06 4-1	O01 3-0	D17 2-3	a17 2-0	D03 2-1	a08 0-1	J21 2-0	a22 5-2	D31 0-0	A29 1-2	D26 0-1	M11 0-2	S17 4-0	O15 2-0	O22 1-0	F04 1-1	M25 3-1		N05 2-0	S03 2-0	N19 0-0
20 SWANSEA T	N12 3-1	J28 2-0	a29 2-0	a17 2-1	O29 2-0	S10 3-0	J07 3-0	N26 1-0	S05 3-1	D24 2-1	O15 1-0	M04 0-1	O01 2-0	a01 2-0	S24 0-1	F18 2-0	D10 3-1	D26 2-1	M18 0-2		a15 0-2	A27 1-0
21 TOTTENHAM H	D27 2-0	a08 1-1	O15 4-1	F01 2-1	A27 4-1	N19 4-1	a22 0-0	F04 4-3	M25 3-2	S10 6-1	M11 2-1	S05 0-0	m06 3-1	O01 1-1	a14 0-0	N05 4-0	F18 1-1	O22 5-0	J07 3-2	D03 7-0		D17 2-2
22 WEST HAM U	M20 2-1	A29 2-4	O29 4-4	O01 0-1	N26 7-3	a17 3-1	D27 1-1	N12 5-2	M27 0-0	D10 3-1	S17 3-0	a15 4-3	S03 1-1	O15 5-2	D24 2-2	J21 5-0	M06 1-1	F04 3-1	a01 1-2	D31 3-1	a29 1-0	

SEASON 1932-33

DIVISION 3 NORTH

	ACCRINGTON S	BARNSLEY	BARROW	CARLISLE U	CHESTER	CREWE A	DARLINGTON	DONCASTER R	GATESHEAD	HALIFAX T	HARTLEPOOLS U	HULL C	MANSFIELD T	NEW BRIGHTON	ROCHDALE	ROTHERHAM U	SOUTHPORT	STOCKPORT CO	TRANMERE R	WALSALL	WREXHAM	YORK C
1 ACCRINGTON S		M11 2-0	J28 0-0	S24 3-1	S10 1-4	O08 2-0	N19 2-0	M25 1-1	D03 0-3	A27 4-1	O22 7-1	N05 1-2	J02 6-0	J07 5-4	m03 0-3	A29 5-1	S27 1-1	a08 1-1	m06 3-0	a22 1-3	D17 5-3	F11 5-0
2 BARNSLEY	O29 4-0		a01 3-0	J02 4-1	N12 0-3	D12 7-1	F04 6-2	O01 2-3	J21 2-4	a17 1-1	D26 3-2	F18 1-0	O15 6-2	D10 1-2	a29 3-1	M04 3-1	D24 2-0	S17 2-2	A29 2-1	S03 2-1	D31 5-3	a15 1-1
3 BARROW	S17 5-0	N19 2-3		F25 2-1	O01 2-3	J14 3-0	a22 4-0	D03 3-0	m06 1-2	N05 3-3	M25 3-1	a08 0-2	S03 1-0	F04 2-1	A29 1-1	J21 2-1	D31 2-0	D17 0-3	M11 2-0	F18 1-2	O22 1-1	D27 1-0
4 CARLISLE U	F04 2-2	a08 0-1	O15 0-1		F18 1-1	S01 2-0	a27 3-0	a22 0-2	D26 1-2	M25 5-3	N19 3-1	D03 1-1	J21 3-1	O01 1-3	D31 2-2	S17 0-0	S03 0-0	S29 2-1	N05 0-1	O22 1-1	M11 2-1	a14 5-1
5 CHESTER	J21 4-2	M25 3-1	F11 2-1	O08 4-0		D26 3-1	D03 5-2	a08 2-0	D17 3-1	M11 6-3	N05 3-3	N19 1-1	D31 5-2	S17 3-0	a14 2-0	S03 1-0	A31 1-1	S14 2-2	O22 1-2	S21 1-0	F04 0-3	M29 5-0
6 CREWE A	F18 3-1	a22 2-2	a14 2-0	S05 1-0	D27 0-1		J07 2-4	m06 4-0	M11 2-0	a08 2-1	D03 6-2	D17 1-1	F04 7-0	O15 4-0	J21 3-1	O01 8-0	S17 1-1	O22 2-1	N19 2-0	N05 2-1	M25 2-0	A27 1-0
7 DARLINGTON	a01 2-2	S24 1-1	F15 1-2	a29 5-2	a15 1-1	S03 3-4		S10 2-2	A31 1-3	O08 2-1	F11 1-2	F01 3-2	M18 1-3	J18 2-1	M04 5-1	N12 4-1	O29 1-0	D31 1-1	F25 1-0	a14 1-1	J02 1-2	D24 3-0
8 DONCASTER R	N12 2-2	F11 3-1	a15 1-1	m04 4-2	a27 3-3	D24 5-1	J21 3-1		D31 3-1	M30 5-1	O08 4-1	S24 1-1	O29 2-2	a01 2-0	S17 1-0	M18 1-0	M04 2-1	S03 1-1	D26 2-2	A29 3-2	a14 1-1	a29 3-2
9 GATESHEAD	a15 1-0	S10 1-1	D24 2-3	D27 1-0	a29 3-0	O29 2-1	S07 3-0	A27 4-0		S24 3-0	J28 3-1	J07 2-3	a01 3-2	J02 2-0	M18 3-0	J25 1-1	N12 4-1	a14 0-3	F11 0-2	m03 1-1	O08 4-4	M04 2-2
10 HALIFAX T	D31 0-0	a18 2-1	M18 2-0	N12 0-1	O29 0-2	J18 1-5	F22 4-2	O15 0-0	F04 1-0		A31 4-0	D27 1-3	a29 5-1	M04 3-3	a15 2-0	D24 2-1	D12 1-0	O01 1-3	S03 4-1	S17 4-0	J21 0-0	a01 2-0
11 HARTLEPOOLS U	M04 3-1	D27 6-4	N12 0-1	a01 2-1	M18 3-1	a15 3-2	O01 2-1	F18 4-0	S17 2-2	S07 1-1		O15 0-1	D24 6-3	O29 3-2	J02 3-0	a14 2-0	a29 4-2	F04 1-1	D31 2-3	J21 2-0	S03 3-1	J14 4-2
12 HULL C	M18 4-2	O08 5-1	J19 3-0	a15 6-1	a01 2-0	a29 3-0	S17 3-1	F04 6-1	S03 1-1	D26 3-1	F25 3-0		M04 4-1	N12 5-0	D24 1-1	O29 4-2	O01 4-0	J21 3-0	a17 3-0	D31 0-0	A29 4-1	m01 2-1
13 MANSFIELD T	a17 1-3	a14 0-1	J07 2-1	S10 3-1	A27 1-0	S24 4-0	N05 3-3	M11 2-2	N19 1-2	D17 2-2	m06 7-1	O22 2-1		S05 5-0	D10 4-1	D27 9-2	O08 4-0	M25 1-2	a22 2-0	a08 2-0	D03 0-0	J28 2-0
14 NEW BRIGHTON	S03 2-2	N05 3-5	S24 1-2	F11 2-0	F08 3-1	F25 1-2	a08 7-1	N19 4-4	a22 1-1	O22 0-3	M11 5-2	M25 1-0	A31 1-0		D26 0-3	D31 5-2	a17 2-1	D03 1-1	J21 1-1	D17 2-2	m06 0-2	O08 0-1
15 ROCHDALE	O15 2-0	D17 2-3	S06 0-0	A27 0-1	a17 2-0	S10 1-4	O22 1-1	J28 2-3	N05 1-0	D03 1-0	a22 6-2	m06 3-2	O01 2-1	D27 1-0		F18 2-2	F04 1-3	M11 0-2	a08 0-3	M25 1-1	N19 3-1	J07 1-4
16 ROTHERHAM U	S05 2-3	O22 0-0	S10 1-0	J28 1-0	J07 0-5	F11 5-0	M25 3-1	N05 1-1	a08 1-2	m06 6-1	a17 1-1	M11 3-2	D26 3-0	A27 1-0	O08 2-0		a18 3-1	N19 2-1	D17 2-0	D03 4-1	a22 0-2	S24 1-0
17 SOUTHPORT	D26 2-3	m06 2-0	A27 3-0	J07 4-0	S06 2-1	J28 4-1	M11 5-1	O22 1-0	M25 4-1	J02 1-2	D17 6-3	F11 0-1	F18 5-2	a14 1-1	S24 2-0	O15 2-0		N05 2-1	D03 1-1	N19 2-1	a08 0-0	S10 5-1
18 STOCKPORT CO	J14 2-0	J28 5-4	a29 4-1	D24 0-1	m06 8-5	M04 1-0	A27 5-1	J07 5-1	a17 4-3	F11 6-0	S24 6-2	S10 3-5	N12 2-2	a15 1-1	O29 2-3	a01 1-0	M18 3-1		O08 3-0	D26 5-0	m01 1-0	S05 2-0
19 TRANMERE R	D24 4-0	S05 3-0	O29 1-3	M18 1-2	M04 2-2	a01 5-0	O15 3-1	D27 3-2	O01 4-2	J07 2-3	A27 3-3	a14 2-0	a10 3-0	S10 2-3	J18 3-1	a29 1-0	a15 2-1	F18 2-2		F04 1-3	a24 0-0	N12 2-3
20 WALSALL	D12 1-0	J07 1-1	O08 1-1	M04 5-0	D24 3-1	M18 2-1	a17 4-0	S05 2-0	O15 2-0	F09 4-0	S10 4-1	A27 1-0	J19 8-1	a29 0-0	N12 2-1	a15 1-0	a01 3-1	D27 0-0	S24 3-2		F11 2-3	O29 4-2
21 WREXHAM	a29 1-0	A27 3-0	M04 4-1	O29 2-1	S24 1-2	N12 7-0	D26 3-1	a17 3-0	F18 5-1	S10 5-2	J07 8-1	S07 3-1	a15 1-1	D24 5-0	a01 4-1	M01 5-1	J14 6-0	O15 2-0	S17 1-1	O01 3-0		M18 3-1
22 YORK C	O01 0-0	D03 3-2	a05 3-1	a17 0-1	O15 3-1	D31 4-0	m06 6-1	D17 2-3	O22 2-2	N19 5-3	a08 1-1	a22 1-2	S17 4-3	F18 3-0	S03 2-6	F04 4-3	a26 0-1	A31 2-2	M25 0-1	M11 4-2	N05 2-3	

DIVISION 3 SOUTH

	ALDERSHOT	BOURNEMOUTH	BRENTFORD	BRIGHTON & HA	BRISTOL C	BRISTOL R	CARDIFF C	CLAPTON O	COVENTRY C	CRYSTAL P	EXETER C	GILLINGHAM	LUTON T	NEWPORT CO	NORTHAMPTON T	NORWICH C	Q.P.R.	READING	SOUTHEND U	SWINDON T	TORQUAY U	WATFORD
1 ALDERSHOT		N19 1-1	m06 1-1	M29 1-1	O22 1-0	D26 1-0	S24 1-0	N05 4-0	a14 1-1	J07 3-1	a22 4-1	S10 3-0	D03 2-2	a08 2-1	M11 0-1	O08 1-3	S07 2-0	F11 4-4	A27 1-2	M25 0-1	D17 2-0	F01 2-1
2 BOURNEMOUTH	a01 1-0		F11 1-1	M18 1-1	J28 6-1	N12 2-2	S07 3-2	J07 4-2	S24 3-1	D10 3-2	F25 1-1	a29 1-0	D26 0-2	a17 1-2	S10 1-1	O29 1-1	J18 3-0	M04 0-3	a15 4-0	A27 5-1	O08 1-2	D24 2-2
3 BRENTFORD	D24 2-0	O01 1-1		a26 2-1	a17 2-1	a29 0-0	a01 7-3	O15 4-2	S08 2-1	O29 2-0	J21 0-2	M18 1-2	S17 1-0	F04 6-0	D27 1-0	a15 2-2	D31 2-0	m03 1-1	M04 3-1	F18 1-0	S03 3-1	N12 2-1
4 BRIGHTON & H.A.	O19 0-2	N05 3-0	a22 1-2		m06 7-0	M01 0-3	S10 1-0	O22 0-0	D17 1-0	S07 1-2	a08 2-1	A27 1-0	N19 2-0	M25 1-0	F11 2-1	S24 1-1	D27 4-1	F01 5-3	a14 1-2	M11 5-1	D03 1-1	J07 3-0
5 BRISTOL C	M04 2-2	S17 1-1	a14 1-2	D24 3-4		O15 3-1	a15 3-1	O01 3-0	D26 5-3	N12 3-3	D31 0-1	a01 1-1	S03 5-2	J21 3-2	F18 5-4	a29 1-1	O29 2-3	a26 4-1	M18 5-1	F04 5-1	A31 2-0	J25 2-3
6 BRISTOL R	D27 4-1	M25 1-0	D17 2-4	O08 5-3	M29 1-1		J28 0-0	M11 2-0	m06 1-0	A27 2-3	D03 1-0	J07 1-0	a08 0-0	N19 2-2	O22 4-3	F11 1-1	a17 4-1	S24 1-0	S07 3-1	N05 1-0	a22 0-2	S10 2-0
7 CARDIFF C	F04 2-1	A29 3-0	N19 2-1	J21 1-2	D03 1-1	S17 4-3		D17 6-1	a08 2-2	O15 1-1	N05 1-3	D26 1-0	M11 3-2	O22 1-3	a22 6-0	S03 4-2	O01 2-5	D31 0-1	F18 2-0	m06 3-0	M25 2-1	a14 1-1
8 CLAPTON O	M18 2-3	S03 1-1	F25 1-5	M04 2-0	F11 2-2	O29 0-3	a29 3-0		O08 2-1	J14 4-1	a14 2-2	a15 1-2	A29 0-0	D31 3-1	S24 2-2	S17 0-0	N12 2-2	D24 2-5	a01 0-0	J21 7-1	D26 1-4	D10 2-0
9 COVENTRY C	a18 3-0	F04 3-0	A29 2-3	a29 2-2	D27 6-0	D24 2-0	J14 5-0	F18 5-0		M18 6-2	S03 4-0	N12 4-2	J21 4-0	S17 3-1	O15 3-1	F02 3-5	M04 7-0	a15 3-1	O29 2-3	O01 2-1	D31 5-0	a01 1-3
10 CRYSTAL P	S03 3-0	a22 3-0	M11 2-1	A31 5-0	M25 2-2	D31 2-0	F25 4-1	a08 2-1	N05 1-3		F04 2-2	F11 5-1	m06 3-0	D17 0-0	N19 2-0	a14 4-0	J21 0-1	D26 1-1	S17 4-1	D03 4-3	O22 2-1	O08 0-3
11 EXETER C	a26 0-0	O15 2-3	S10 1-2	J18 4-1	A27 2-0	a15 1-0	M18 1-0	a17 3-0	J07 5-0	S24 1-1		M04 2-1	O01 2-0	F18 4-0	S07 3-1	a01 2-1	a29 2-0	N12 4-1	D24 3-0	D27 5-0	J28 5-0	O29 5-2
12 GILLINGHAM	J21 5-2	D17 4-0	N05 1-3	D31 2-0	N19 4-2	S03 2-0	D27 1-1	D03 3-1	M25 3-0	O01 2-0	O22 1-2		F22 1-1	m06 2-0	a08 5-1	A31 0-2	S17 4-1	a14 4-1	F04 3-2	a22 3-1	M11 1-1	F25 3-3
13 LUTON T	a15 2-1	D27 1-2	F01 5-5	a01 0-0	J07 5-4	M13 1-1	O29 8-1	S05 4-1	S10 4-1	D24 1-1	F11 4-0	O08 2-1		O15 2-2	A27 2-1	N12 1-1	a18 3-1	M18 1-1	a29 3-3	a14 6-2	S24 2-1	a26 3-2
14 NEWPORT CO	J19 2-1	J14 1-1	S24 1-6	N17 5-2	S10 1-1	a01 3-1	M04 4-2	A27 0-2	J28 2-1	a29 1-3	O08 1-1	D24 0-2	a06 3-2		J07 0-3	M18 3-4	a15 5-1	O29 3-3	F09 1-3	S05 1-2	F11 3-1	D26 2-0
15 NORTHAMPTON T	O29 5-2	J21 6-0	D26 1-0	S22 0-0	O08 2-1	M04 1-1	a10 2-0	F04 3-0	F25 5-1	a01 1-0	A29 5-3	J14 1-0	D31 1-0	S03 8-0		D24 2-2	M18 2-1	a29 1-0	N12 0-0	S17 6-0	a18 2-0	a15 0-0
16 NORWICH C	F23 3-2	M11 6-0	D03 3-0	F04 1-0	D17 3-0	O01 1-1	J07 3-1	J28 2-0	a22 2-1	a17 3-0	N19 0-0	S05 2-0	M25 2-1	N05 3-1	m06 2-0		O15 3-2	S10 2-2	D27 1-0	O22 5-2	a08 1-2	A27 1-2
17 Q.P.R.	S01 2-2	a08 3-1	A27 2-3	D26 0-1	M11 1-1	a14 1-1	F11 5-1	M25 2-1	O22 3-3	S10 2-1	D17 1-3	J28 1-1	a22 3-1	D03 6-1	N05 1-1	F25 2-2		O08 0-3	J07 6-1	N19 4-2	m06 1-1	S24 2-1
18 READING	O01 2-2	O22 6-2	a08 1-3	S17 3-0	a22 2-2	F04 3-1	A27 4-2	m06 3-1	D03 3-3	D27 2-3	M25 2-2	a17 4-0	N05 4-1	M11 4-1	D17 4-0	J21 3-2	F18 3-1		O15 1-1	J07 7-1	N19 5-2	S07 2-0
19 SOUTHEND U	D31 5-1	D03 2-1	O22 0-1	a17 2-1	N05 3-1	A29 2-2	O08 2-2	N19 3-3	M11 1-3	F01 1-2	m06 1-2	S24 2-2	D17 2-1	S14 3-0	M25 1-0	D26 2-1	S03 0-1	F25 3-1		a08 0-0	J21 2-1	F11 2-1
20 SWINDON T	N12 3-2	D31 2-0	O08 0-0	N02 5-1	S24 1-4	M18 1-1	D24 6-2	S10 3-3	F11 1-2	a15 1-0	D26 2-2	a26 1-1	a17 1-1	A31 2-0	J28 2-1	M04 2-4	a01 0-0	S03 0-1	M01 2-2		F25 0-0	a29 1-2
21 TORQUAY U	a29 1-0	F18 2-1	J07 1-1	a15 1-0	S07 0-0	a26 1-1	N12 4-1	D27 1-1	A27 3-3	M04 2-1	S17 1-3	O29 1-2	F04 3-1	O01 4-0	a17 5-1	J14 2-2	D24 3-1	a01 1-1	S10 8-1	O15 4-3		M18 3-2
22 WATFORD	S17 2-0	m06 2-1	M25 1-1	S03 0-4	a08 1-0	J21 3-1	a17 2-1	a22 1-1	N19 3-1	F18 1-0	M11 0-0	O15 2-0	O22 4-1	D27 3-2	D03 4-0	D31 1-2	F04 2-2	A31 1-1	O01 2-2	D17 2-2	N05 0-0	

LEAGUE TABLES

DIVISION 1

	P	W	D	L	F	A	W	D	L	F	A	Pts
Arsenal	42	14	3	4	70	27	11	5	5	48	34	58
Aston Villa	42	16	2	3	60	29	7	6	8	32	38	54
Sheffield W	42	15	5	1	46	20	6	4	11	34	48	51
W.B.A.	42	16	1	4	50	23	4	8	9	33	47	49
Newcastle U	42	15	2	4	44	24	7	3	11	27	39	49
Huddersfield T	42	11	6	4	32	17	7	5	9	34	36	47
Derby Co	42	11	8	2	49	25	4	6	11	27	44	44
Leeds U	42	10	6	5	39	24	5	8	8	20	38	44
Portsmouth	42	14	3	4	39	22	4	4	13	35	54	43
Sheffield U	42	14	3	4	50	30	3	6	12	24	50	43
Everton	42	13	6	2	54	24	3	3	15	27	50	41
Sunderland	42	8	7	6	33	31	7	3	11	30	49	40
Birmingham C	42	13	3	5	40	23	1	8	12	17	34	39
Liverpool	42	10	6	5	53	33	4	5	12	26	51	39
Blackburn R	42	11	6	4	48	41	3	4	14	28	61	38
Manchester C	42	12	3	6	47	30	4	2	15	21	41	37
Middlesbrough	42	8	5	8	35	33	6	4	11	28	40	37
Chelsea	42	9	4	8	38	29	5	3	13	25	44	35
Leicester C	42	9	9	3	43	25	2	4	15	32	64	35
Wolverhampton W	42	10	4	7	56	48	3	5	13	24	48	35
Bolton W	42	10	7	4	49	33	2	2	17	29	59	33
Blackpool	42	11	2	8	44	35	3	3	15	25	50	33

DIVISION 2

	P	W	D	L	F	A	W	D	L	F	A	Pts
Stoke C	42	13	3	5	40	15	12	3	6	38	24	56
Tottenham H	42	14	7	0	58	19	6	8	7	38	32	55
Fulham	42	12	5	4	46	31	8	5	8	32	34	50
Bury	42	13	7	1	55	23	7	2	12	29	36	49
Nottingham F	42	9	8	4	37	28	8	7	6	30	31	49
Manchester U	42	11	5	5	40	24	4	8	9	31	44	43
Millwall	42	11	7	3	40	20	5	4	12	19	37	43
Bradford P.A.	42	13	4	4	51	27	4	4	13	26	44	42
Preston N.E.	42	12	2	7	53	36	4	8	9	21	34	42
Swansea T	42	17	0	4	36	12	2	4	15	14	42	42
Bradford C	42	10	6	5	43	24	4	7	10	22	37	41
Southampton	42	15	3	3	48	22	3	2	16	18	44	41
Grimsby T	42	8	10	3	49	34	6	3	12	30	50	41
Plymouth A	42	13	4	4	45	22	3	5	13	18	45	41
Notts Co	42	10	4	7	41	31	5	6	10	26	47	40
Oldham A	42	10	4	7	38	31	5	4	12	29	49	38
Port Vale	42	12	3	6	49	27	2	7	12	17	52	38
Lincoln C	42	11	6	4	46	28	1	7	13	26	59	37
Burnley	42	8	9	4	35	20	3	5	13	32	59	36
West Ham U	42	12	6	3	56	31	1	3	17	19	62	35
Chesterfield	42	10	5	6	36	25	2	5	14	25	59	34
Charlton A	42	9	3	9	35	35	3	4	14	25	56	31

DIVISION 3 NORTH

	P	W	D	L	F	A	W	D	L	F	A	Pts
Hull C	42	18	3	0	69	14	8	4	9	31	31	59
Wrexham	42	18	2	1	75	15	6	7	8	31	36	57
Stockport Co	42	16	2	3	69	30	5	10	6	30	28	54
Chester C	42	15	4	2	57	25	7	4	10	37	41	52
Walsall	42	16	4	1	53	15	3	6	12	22	43	48
Doncaster R	42	13	8	0	52	26	4	6	11	25	53	48
Gateshead	42	12	5	4	45	25	7	4	10	33	42	47
Barnsley	42	14	3	4	60	31	5	5	11	32	49	46
Barrow	42	12	3	6	41	24	6	4	11	19	36	43
Crewe A	42	16	3	2	57	16	4	0	17	23	68	43
Tranmere R	42	11	4	6	49	31	6	4	11	21	35	42
Southport	42	15	3	3	54	20	2	4	15	16	47	41
Accrington S	42	12	4	5	55	29	3	6	12	23	47	40
Hartlepool U	42	15	3	3	56	29	1	4	16	31	87	39
Halifax T	42	12	4	5	39	23	3	4	14	32	67	38
Mansfield T	42	13	4	4	57	22	1	3	17	27	78	35
Rotherham U	42	14	3	4	42	21	0	3	18	18	63	34
Rochdale	42	9	4	8	32	33	4	3	14	26	47	33
Carlisle U	42	8	7	6	34	25	5	0	16	17	50	33
York C	42	10	4	7	51	38	3	2	16	21	54	32
New Brighton	42	8	6	7	42	36	3	4	14	21	52	32
Darlington	42	9	6	6	42	32	1	2	18	24	77	28

DIVISION 3 SOUTH

	P	W	D	L	F	A	W	D	L	F	A	Pts
Brentford	42	15	4	2	45	19	11	6	4	45	30	62
Exeter C	42	17	2	2	57	13	7	8	6	31	35	58
Norwich C	42	16	3	2	49	17	6	10	5	39	38	57
Reading	42	14	5	2	68	30	5	8	8	35	41	51
Crystal Palace	42	14	4	3	51	21	5	4	12	27	43	46
Coventry C	42	16	1	4	75	24	3	5	13	31	53	44
Gillingham	42	14	4	3	54	24	4	4	13	18	37	44
Northampton T	42	16	5	0	54	11	2	3	16	22	55	44
Bristol R	42	13	5	3	38	22	2	9	10	23	34	44
Torquay U	42	12	7	2	51	26	4	5	12	21	41	44
Watford	42	11	8	2	37	22	5	4	12	29	41	44
Brighton & H.A.	42	13	3	5	42	20	4	5	12	24	45	42
Southend U	42	11	5	5	39	27	4	6	11	26	55	41
Luton T	42	12	8	1	60	32	1	5	15	18	46	39
Bristol C	42	11	5	5	59	37	1	8	12	24	53	37
Q.P.R.	42	9	8	4	48	32	4	3	14	24	55	37
Aldershot	42	11	6	4	37	21	2	4	15	24	51	36
Bournemouth	42	10	7	4	44	27	2	5	14	16	54	36
Cardiff C	42	12	4	5	48	30	0	3	18	21	69	31
Clapton O	42	7	8	6	39	35	1	5	15	20	58	29
Newport Co	42	9	4	8	42	42	2	3	16	19	63	29
Swindon T	42	7	9	5	36	29	2	2	17	24	76	29

Football League Records

Top scorers: Div 1, J.Bowers (Derby County) 34 goals; Div 2, E.Glover (Grimsby Town) 42 goals; Div 3 N, A.Lythgoe (Stockport County) 46 goals; Div 3 S, A.Dawes (Northampton Town & Crystal Palace) 27 goals.

The legendary Alex James, who in eight seasons at Highbury helped steer Arsenal to four League titles and two FA Cup triumphs.

DIVISION 1

	ARSENAL	ASTON VILLA	BIRMINGHAM	BLACKBURN R	CHELSEA	DERBY CO	EVERTON	HUDDERSFIELD T	LEEDS U	LEICESTER C	LIVERPOOL	MANCHESTER C	MIDDLESBROUGH	NEWCASTLE U	PORTSMOUTH	SHEFFIELD U	SHEFFIELD W	STOKE C	SUNDERLAND	TOTTENHAM H	W.B.A.	WOLVERHAMPTON W
1 ARSENAL		M10 3-2	A26 1-1	F21 2-1	D16 2-1	M30 1-0	F03 1-2	a07 3-1	D26 2-0	O21 2-0	D02 2-1	S09 1-1	S30 6-0	O14 3-0	N04 1-1	m05 2-0	J06 1-1	N18 3-0	a21 2-1	J31 1-3	S06 3-1	M24 3-2
2 ASTON VILLA	O28 2-3		a14 1-1	M31 1-1	F07 2-0	D09 0-2	D23 2-1	O07 4-3	a30 3-0	A26 2-3	S09 4-2	M07 0-0	N11 3-0	N25 2-3	F10 1-1	a02 3-0	S04 1-0	F24 1-2	S23 2-1	J06 1-5	a28 4-4	D25 6-2
3 BIRMINGHAM	D30 0-0	D02 0-0		S16 2-0	a07 0-3	F21 2-1	S02 2-2	m05 1-3	S30 4-0	M28 3-0	N04 1-2	A30 0-1	J20 0-0	F03 1-2	M24 3-1	D26 4-2	a03 3-0	M10 0-1	N18 1-1	a21 2-0	O14 0-1	O21 0-0
4 BLACKBURN R	O07 2-2	N18 2-1	J29 3-1		O21 4-2	J06 2-1	F24 1-1	D16 2-2	A26 4-2	M24 3-0	M10 3-1	F10 3-0	D25 0-0	S18 3-2	D02 3-2	a07 3-1	S23 3-1	a21 4-1	a02 0-0	J01 1-0	S09 4-0	N04 7-1
5 CHELSEA	a28 2-2	S16 1-0	N25 1-1	M03 3-0		N11 0-2	a14 2-0	S13 2-3	D23 1-1	a23 2-0	F21 2-0	D09 1-2	O14 2-3	O28 2-1	a02 4-0	J20 5-0	M17 0-1	D30 2-0	D26 4-0	S30 0-4	M31 3-2	S02 5-2
6 DERBY CO	a02 2-4	a21 1-1	O07 4-0	S02 1-1	M24 1-0		A30 1-1	O21 1-1	S16 3-1	N04 2-1	N18 3-1	D25 4-1	D30 2-0	J20 1-1	M10 0-1	D16 5-1	F24 1-1	F03 5-1	M17 0-0	a07 4-3	F10 1-1	D02 3-1
7 EVERTON	S23 3-1	m05 2-2	J06 2-0	O14 7-1	D02 2-1	J01 0-3		N04 0-1	a02 2-0	M10 1-1	F10 0-0	F07 2-0	F17 1-1	D26 3-7	a21 1-1	M24 4-0	S09 2-3	a07 2-2	D16 1-0	O21 1-1	A26 1-0	N18 1-2
8 HUDDERSFIELD T	N25 0-1	F21 2-1	D23 0-0	a28 5-3	S04 6-1	M03 2-0	a25 1-0		S09 0-0	O14 5-1	a03 0-2	M31 1-0	D09 2-1	a14 4-1	J06 4-0	S30 6-1	N11 3-2	S16 2-2	A26 2-1	D26 2-0	O28 3-1	F03 3-1
9 LEEDS U	D25 0-1	N04 2-4	F10 1-0	D30 4-0	m05 3-1	J31 0-2	M30 2-2	J20 1-1		a07 8-0	M24 5-1	F24 3-1	A28 5-2	S02 3-0	O21 1-0	a21 1-1	O07 2-1	D02 2-0	M10 3-1	N18 0-0	S23 3-0	D16 3-3
10 LEICESTER C	M08 4-1	D30 1-1	a28 3-7	N11 1-2	S23 1-1	a19 2-0	O28 3-1	F24 1-0	N25 2-2		F01 1-0	S02 0-0	D23 1-2	M31 3-2	O07 2-1	A28 4-0	a14 2-0	D26 3-1	F10 0-0	S09 1-3	D09 0-1	a03 1-1
11 LIVERPOOL	a14 2-3	J20 2-3	M17 4-1	O28 4-0	O07 3-0	M31 4-2	S30 3-2	M30 2-2	N11 4-3	S16 1-3		m02 3-2	M03 6-2	D23 1-2	D25 2-2	S02 3-2	D09 1-3	A30 1-1	P24 1-1	F03 3-1	N25 1-1	D30 1-1
12 MANCHESTER C	J20 2-1	O21 1-0	S06 1-0	S30 3-1	a21 4-2	D26 2-0	S16 2-2	N18 2-2	O14 0-1	J06 1-1	D16 2-1		F03 5-2	M21 1-1	a07 2-1	M10 4-1	A26 2-3	M24 4-2	N04 4-1	D02 2-0	J01 2-7	m05 4-0
13 MIDDLESBROUGH	F10 0-2	M24 1-2	S09 0-3	D26 3-1	F24 2-2	A26 3-1	O07 2-0	a21 3-0	J01 2-1	m05 4-1	O21 4-1	S23 2-1		a02 1-0	D16 2-0	N18 10-3	F07 2-3	N04 6-1	D02 0-4	M10 1-1	J06 3-0	a07 0-0
14 NEWCASTLE U	F24 0-1	a07 1-1	S23 0-0	S06 3-1	M10 2-2	S09 1-1	D25 1-2	D02 3-3	J06 2-0	N18 1-1	J01 9-2	O07 2-2	M30 1-1		A26 2-2	N04 3-1	F10 0-0	D16 2-2	O21 2-1	M24 1-3	J27 1-2	a21 5-1
15 PORTSMOUTH	a18 1-0	S30 3-2	N11 0-2	a14 2-0	M30 0-2	O28 1-0	D09 0-0	S02 3-0	M07 2-1	F21 3-5	D26 1-0	N25 2-0	a30 4-1	D30 2-0		F03 1-1	M31 0-2	J20 3-1	S06 0-0	O14 0-1	D23 2-2	S16 1-1
16 SHEFFIELD U	D23 1-3	J01 3-3	D25 2-1	N25 1-0	S09 4-1	a28 2-0	N11 1-1	F10 1-4	D09 2-1	S04 2-1	J06 2-2	O28 1-1	M31 3-1	M17 4-0	S23 0-1		M03 5-1	O07 1-2	J29 2-0	A26 0-0	a14 0-1	F24 3-1
17 SHEFFIELD W	S02 1-2	A28 1-2	J02 2-1	F03 4-0	N04 2-1	O14 1-1	J20 0-0	M24 1-2	F26 0-2	D02 1-1	a21 1-2	D30 1-1	S16 3-0	S30 3-1	N18 1-2	O21 0-1		m05 2-2	a07 2-0	D16 2-1	D26 3-1	M10 2-1
18 STOKE C	M31 1-1	O14 1-1	O28 1-1	D09 2-0	A26 1-0	S23 0-4	N25 1-2	J29 3-0	a14 1-2	D25 2-1	S04 1-1	N11 0-1	M17 2-0	a28 2-1	S09 2-1	F22 3-0	D23 0-1		J06 3-0	a02 2-0	M08 4-1	S30 1-1
19 SUNDERLAND	D09 3-0	F03 5-1	M31 4-1	M30 3-0	J01 0-0	D23 0-0	a28 3-2	D30 1-1	O28 4-2	S30 2-1	O14 4-1	a11 0-0	a14 2-0	M03 2-0	A30 0-2	S16 5-0	N25 4-0	S02 4-1		F21 6-0	N11 2-2	J20 3-3
20 TOTTENHAM H	S16 1-1	S02 3-2	D09 3-2	D23 4-1	F10 2-1	N25 1-2	M03 3-0	D25 1-3	M31 5-1	J20 0-1	S23 0-3	a14 5-1	O28 2-0	N11 4-0	F24 0-0	D30 4-1	a28 4-3	M30 0-0	O07 3-1		M17 2-1	A28 4-0
21 W.B.A.	S13 1-0	D16 2-1	F24 1-2	J20 0-1	N18 3-1	S30 5-1	D30 3-3	M10 2-3	F03 0-3	a21 2-0	a07 2-2	a02 4-0	S02 3-0	S16 1-1	m05 2-1	D02 3-0	D27 1-1	O21 5-1	M24 6-5	N04 1-2		F17 2-0
22 WOLVERHAMPTON W	N11 0-1	D26 4-3	M03 2-0	M17 5-3	J06 1-1	a14 3-0	M31 2-0	S23 5-2	a28 2-0	a02 1-1	A26 3-2	D23 8-0	N25 0-1	D09 2-1	F07 1-1	O14 3-2	O28 6-2	F10 0-2	S09 1-6	S04 1-0	O07 0-0	

Grimsby Town's Pat Glover, whose 42 goals in 1933-34 saw the Mariners into Division One. It is still a club record.

DIVISION 2

	BLACKPOOL	BOLTON W	BRADFORD	BRADFORD C	BRENTFORD	BURNLEY	BURY	FULHAM	GRIMSBY T	HULL C	LINCOLN C	MANCHESTER U	MILLWALL	NOTTINGHAM F	NOTTS CO	OLDHAM A	PLYMOUTH A	PORT VALE	PRESTON N.E.	SOUTHAMPTON	SWANSEA T	WEST HAM U
1 BLACKPOOL		M24 1-1	m05 1-1	J06 3-2	N04 3-1	M10 1-1	F24 2-0	S04 4-3	D16 3-4	D25 0-0	O07 2-0	N18 3-1	F10 2-2	a21 2-3	F07 2-1	O21 0-0	a07 1-1	S09 1-0	A26 1-2	M30 4-2	S23 2-1	D02 1-1
2 BOLTON W	N11 1-2		J01 0-1	M31 3-0	S23 3-2	F10 4-1	S16 2-0	O28 3-1	S04 0-4	M07 3-3	D23 1-2	J20 3-1	a28 5-0	M30 1-1	a14 1-0	O07 1-0	S02 2-0	N25 3-0	F24 0-2	M17 2-0	D09 2-1	D30 5-1
3 BRADFORD	D23 1-2	D25 1-4		S09 2-1	S06 5-2	a03 5-0	N25 0-1	D09 3-1	S16 2-1	a14 3-1	M31 2-1	O14 6-1	N11 4-0	F03 6-2	O28 3-2	A26 4-2	F17 4-1	M03 2-2	J06 2-1	a28 3-1	M17 5-1	S30 0-0
4 BRADFORD C	S02 1-0	N18 5-1	J20 3-0		M24 2-1	N04 2-1	D26 2-2	a02 1-0	m05 2-1	A30 1-2	F24 3-0	a07 1-1	O07 1-0	D16 3-2	S23 3-1	M10 5-2	D02 3-4	J27 1-2	O21 1-0	D30 2-2	F10 2-1	a21 2-2
5 BRENTFORD	M17 1-0	F03 3-1	A31 2-0	N11 2-1		O07 5-2	D23 2-3	M03 1-2	a02 1-2	S30 2-2	a28 5-0	S16 3-4	D09 3-0	D30 2-1	N25 2-2	F24 2-1	J20 3-0	M31 2-0	D25 3-2	O28 2-0	a14 2-0	S02 4-1
6 BURNLEY	O28 3-2	S30 1-3	M30 1-0	M17 4-2	F17 3-1		a28 1-2	O14 2-1	D30 2-0	D23 3-1	D09 3-1	F03 1-4	a14 2-1	S02 1-0	M31 1-0	D25 0-1	S16 2-2	N11 0-0	S04 1-4	M03 2-1	N25 3-1	J20 4-2
7 BURY	O14 2-5	J02 1-1	a07 2-1	D25 1-0	m05 1-2	D16 1-1		S30 3-3	N18 1-3	F03 3-1	S09 0-2	O21 2-1	J06 5-1	M24 4-2	J01 3-1	a21 1-1	M10 4-0	S11 0-3	D02 2-1	F17 1-0	A26 4-1	N04 2-1
8 FULHAM	A28 1-0	M10 0-2	a21 0-2	M30 0-1	O21 1-1	F24 1-1	F10 2-1		D02 1-0	O07 1-1	S23 1-0	N04 0-2	J29 2-0	a07 3-1	J06 3-0	m05 1-2	M24 3-2	A26 3-0	D16 1-0	D25 1-0	S09 1-0	N18 3-1
9 GRIMSBY T	a28 7-0	A29 2-3	J30 3-2	D23 1-4	M30 2-2	A26 1-0	M31 2-0	a14 3-1		N25 4-1	N11 3-0	D26 7-3	M17 5-2	S30 2-1	M03 2-2	J06 2-1	O14 5-1	S23 1-2	S09 3-0	D09 3-1	O28 3-1	F17 1-1
10 HULL C	D26 3-0	O21 1-0	D02 1-2	S11 2-2	F10 0-1	m05 0-1	S23 3-1	F17 0-0	a07 0-1		F08 2-0	M10 4-1	S09 3-2	N18 2-2	A26 0-1	D16 2-0	N04 5-4	a02 2-1	a21 0-1	O14 1-0	J06 0-0	M24 2-0
11 LINCOLN C	F17 2-2	m05 2-2	N18 2-1	O14 0-1	D16 0-2	a21 4-0	J20 1-2	F03 5-0	M24 3-3	S16 2-1		J06 5-1	A26 0-1	N04 0-0	S04 0-1	D02 1-1	O21 1-1	D25 1-0	a07 0-1	S30 1-1	M30 1-0	M10 0-2
12 MANCHESTER U	M31 2-0	S09 1-5	F24 0-4	N25 2-1	J27 1-3	S23 5-2	M03 2-1	M17 1-0	D25 1-3	O28 4-1	S02 1-1		D23 1-1	A30 0-1	D09 1-2	F10 2-3	D30 0-3	a14 2-0	O07 1-0	N11 1-0	a28 1-1	M30 0-1
13 MILLWALL	S30 0-0	D16 2-1	M24 0-1	F17 1-1	a21 2-0	D02 0-0	S02 0-0	S16 0-1	N04 0-1	J20 2-0	D30 4-1	m05 0-2		M10 0-0	D26 3-2	a07 1-0	M30 0-0	O14 0-3	N18 1-1	a09 1-0	A28 2-1	O21 2-2
14 NOTTINGHAM F	D09 0-0	a02 2-2	S23 3-0	a28 1-2	A26 1-1	J06 0-2	N11 7-2	N25 2-0	F10 4-2	M31 0-1	M17 6-2	S07 1-1	O28 2-0		O07 2-0	S09 1-3	D26 2-1	D23 6-1	F07 2-3	a14 4-1	M03 4-2	O14 0-1
15 NOTTS CO	S16 1-1	D02 1-2	a16 1-0	F03 3-0	a07 1-2	N18 3-1	M30 2-1	S02 4-1	O21 1-2	D30 0-0	S13 2-0	a21 0-0	D25 0-1	F17 1-0		M24 1-1	D16 2-1	S30 3-2	N04 2-2	J20 2-2	F24 1-1	m05 1-2
16 OLDHAM A	M03 2-0	F20 1-3	D30 1-3	O28 4-3	O14 1-4	D26 1-0	D09 2-2	D23 2-2	S02 1-5	a28 7-0	a14 3-0	S30 2-0	N25 1-0	J20 4-1	N11 2-0		F03 1-1	M17 5-1	M30 3-1	A28 1-1	M31 0-0	S16 4-1
17 PLYMOUTH A	N25 0-3	J06 3-0	O07 4-1	a14 3-0	S09 1-1	J27 1-0	O28 3-3	N11 4-0	F24 0-2	M17 1-1	M03 3-0	A26 4-0	a02 1-0	D25 4-3	a28 1-0	S23 1-0		D09 3-0	F10 0-0	M31 0-0	D23 2-2	A30 4-4
18 PORT VALE	J20 1-0	a07 0-0	O21 3-1	S16 3-1	N18 1-0	M24 0-2	A28 4-1	D30 2-2	F05 0-1	M30 3-0	D26 1-0	D02 2-3	F24 5-1	m05 3-1	F10 0-0	N04 2-0	a21 4-0		M10 2-0	S02 2-1	O07 1-0	D16 0-0
19 PRESTON N.E.	D30 3-0	O14 1-1	S02 3-1	M07 0-1	D26 3-2	A28 3-2	a14 0-3	a28 2-0	J20 1-2	D09 5-0	N25 2-1	F21 3-2	M31 4-2	S16 4-0	M17 2-0	a02 1-0	S30 1-1	O28 0-0		D23 3-1	N11 3-0	F03 3-1
20 SOUTHAMPTON	a02 3-2	N04 1-0	D16 5-0	A26 4-1	M10 0-0	O21 2-1	O07 1-0	D26 2-0	a21 4-2	F24 1-1	F10 3-1	M24 1-0	S23 2-3	D02 2-0	S09 3-2	S04 1-0	N18 0-1	J06 1-4	m05 0-1		F05 1-0	a07 3-2
21 SWANSEA T	F03 2-2	a21 0-0	N04 5-1	S30 2-1	D02 2-3	a07 3-0	D30 1-1	J20 1-0	M10 1-1	S02 1-1	a02 1-0	D16 2-1	S04 2-0	O21 1-1	O14 1-1	N18 2-2	m05 2-1	F22 4-0	M24 1-2	S16 1-0		D26 1-1
22 WEST HAM U	a14 1-2	A26 4-2	F10 0-1	D09 1-2	J06 3-2	S09 1-2	M17 3-1	M31 5-1	O07 3-1	N11 2-1	O28 4-1	a02 2-1	M03 1-1	F24 2-1	D23 5-3	F07 1-4	S04 5-1	a28 1-0	S23 6-0	N25 0-0	D25 1-1	

SEASON 1933-34

DIVISION 3 NORTH

	ACCRINGTON S	BARNSLEY	BARROW	CARLISLE U	CHESTER	CHESTERFIELD	CREWE A	DARLINGTON	DONCASTER R	GATESHEAD	HALIFAX T	HARTLEPOOLS U	MANSFIELD T	NEW BRIGHTON	ROCHDALE	ROTHERHAM U	SOUTHPORT	STOCKPORT CO	TRANMERE R	WALSALL	WREXHAM	YORK C
1 ACCRINGTON S		F03 0-9	a28 0-4	D23 2-1	a14 4-1	S02 1-0	O28 0-2	J01 2-0	J03 4-1	S11 5-2	M03 1-1	F17 2-2	S30 1-1	M17 8-0	J20 1-3	N11 2-2	S26 3-2	D30 0-3	S16 2-2	M31 1-0	O14 1-1	J24 4-1
2 BARNSLEY	S23 6-0		M31 3-1	J13 1-0	M17 2-0	F10 3-2	a28 5-2	S09 4-0	N11 2-2	J27 0-0	F19 1-0	D26 5-4	a02 6-1	D23 2-0	O07 4-1	J01 5-1	J06 3-2	a14 2-0	F24 5-1	M03 1-1	A26 3-0	O28 1-0
3 BARROW	D16 2-6	N18 3-4		S04 2-0	F10 9-0	a21 2-0	A26 0-3	F24 5-2	O07 2-1	m05 12-1	D26 5-2	N04 2-2	M24 6-3	J06 3-3	D02 5-3	S09 4-1	O21 3-3	a02 2-0	a07 1-3	J27 5-5	M10 3-1	S23 2-2
4 CARLISLE U	m05 3-0	a07 1-4	A31 0-0		O07 1-0	D16 1-1	J06 6-1	O21 3-3	F24 0-1	M30 6-0	A26 1-0	M24 4-1	N18 3-2	S09 1-2	a21 3-0	J27 0-1	M10 0-0	D26 2-2	D02 2-1	S23 3-2	N04 0-0	F10 3-2
5 CHESTER	D02 7-0	N04 4-2	S30 1-3	F17 3-3		a07 3-2	a02 1-0	D16 8-0	F03 3-1	a21 4-0	S06 1-2	O21 3-3	M10 1-1	D25 0-0	N18 7-1	A26 5-1	m05 1-0	O14 1-1	M24 4-2	J06 0-1	J27 1-2	S09 1-1
6 CHESTERFIELD	J06 1-0	S30 3-0	D13 2-1	a28 4-0	J01 6-1		M03 3-2	D25 0-1	a14 1-1	A26 6-2	S09 4-2	O14 3-1	F17 3-2	O28 4-0	S16 3-0	M17 2-1	M30 2-1	D23 1-0	F03 1-0	N11 1-2	S06 4-0	M31 2-0
7 CREWE A	M10 4-2	D16 4-2	D30 1-3	S02 4-0	M30 3-5	O21 1-2		M24 2-3	D26 4-0	N04 3-2	S16 1-1	D02 1-0	a21 2-1	F10 6-2	F03 4-1	O07 0-2	N18 2-2	J20 2-2	m05 3-1	F24 1-4	a07 1-0	A30 5-3
8 DARLINGTON	a02 3-1	J20 0-4	O14 4-1	M03 1-2	a28 0-4	D26 1-1	N11 1-1		D23 4-0	S06 3-3	M17 4-2	F03 5-3	S16 1-4	M31 1-0	D30 1-1	J24 4-1	F17 4-0	O28 1-2	S02 1-3	J13 2-1	S30 2-1	D09 4-0
9 DONCASTER R	a21 5-1	M24 4-4	F17 3-2	O14 2-1	S23 3-1	D02 1-3	D25 4-0	m05 3-2		D16 5-2	M30 3-0	M10 3-0	N04 1-0	A26 1-0	a07 5-0	J06 2-1	F10 3-0	S04 0-2	N18 2-0	S09 4-0	O21 1-4	J27 3-1
10 GATESHEAD	D26 2-0	S16 1-4	D23 0-0	a02 2-3	a25 1-3	D30 2-1	M17 2-1	A30 2-2	a28 2-4		O28 4-0	S30 6-3	F03 5-3	N11 6-0	S02 2-1	M31 4-1	O14 2-2	M03 0-4	J20 1-2	J17 2-1	F17 0-3	a14 0-2
11 HALIFAX T	O21 2-1	a21 1-1	D25 4-1	D30 3-2	A30 1-0	J20 5-0	J27 3-2	N04 2-0	a02 0-1	M10 2-4		a07 6-2	D02 4-2	S23 1-1	m05 4-2	F10 3-2	M24 6-2	S02 4-2	D16 0-2	O07 2-0	N18 1-3	F24 3-0
12 HARTLEPOOLS U	O07 3-0	D25 0-2	M17 7-0	N11 3-2	M03 1-0	F24 0-3	a14 2-1	S23 6-2	O28 2-2	F10 3-3	J01 5-0		D30 3-1	F14 2-1	A30 2-1	a28 4-0	J27 1-2	M31 3-1	M30 1-1	D23 0-1	S09 4-1	S02 2-0
13 MANSFIELD T	F10 5-0	M30 1-5	N11 0-5	M31 6-0	O28 2-1	O07 0-3	D09 4-1	J27 4-0	M17 1-1	S23 1-1	a14 6-1	A26 1-1		a28 5-2	F24 5-0	D23 3-0	S09 2-2	J13 1-1	A28 0-0	D25 1-2	J06 1-1	M03 0-2
14 NEW BRIGHTON	N04 0-3	m05 0-1	S02 2-2	J20 2-1	D26 0-2	M10 0-0	S30 2-1	N18 3-2	D30 2-2	M24 3-1	F03 3-0	a21 4-1	D16 5-1		O21 0-2	F24 3-1	a07 5-2	S16 2-1	F17 1-0	A30 2-0	D02 0-1	a02 2-1
15 ROCHDALE	S09 0-1	D09 3-1	a14 1-2	F06 0-1	M31 6-0	J27 0-1	S23 2-0	A26 1-0	J13 0-2	J06 2-0	D23 1-2	S05 3-0	O14 2-2	M03 1-1		O28 0-2	D26 3-3	a28 1-1	S30 1-0	M17 3-3	M30 1-2	F20 3-6
16 ROTHERHAM U	M24 3-1	A28 0-2	J20 1-1	S16 0-1	D30 0-3	N04 1-3	F17 3-4	a07 0-0	S02 0-0	N18 3-2	S30 1-2	D16 4-2	m05 1-2	O14 2-2	M10 4-0		D02 0-1	F03 1-1	O21 2-2	a02 1-1	a21 1-3	D26 3-2
17 SOUTHPORT	A29 1-1	S02 2-2	M03 1-3	O28 1-1	D23 3-1	a02 0-0	M31 1-1	O07 3-2	S30 0-0	F24 1-1	N11 1-4	S16 0-2	J20 3-3	J13 4-0	D25 3-0	a14 4-0		M17 1-4	D30 2-2	M20 3-1	F03 1-1	J01 0-0
18 STOCKPORT CO	A26 3-0	D02 1-1	M30 4-1	D25 4-0	F24 4-2	m05 0-0	S09 1-1	M10 6-0	A28 4-3	O21 1-0	J06 13-0	N18 5-2	a07 3-1	J27 5-1	D16 4-1	S23 3-1	N04 9-2		a21 2-1	F10 3-2	M24 7-3	O07 2-1
19 TRANMERE R	F01 2-0	O14 5-2	J18 4-1	a14 3-1	N11 6-1	S23 0-1	D23 5-1	J06 2-2	M31 2-0	S09 2-1	a28 3-2	a02 3-2	S04 3-2	O07 1-0	F10 4-0	M03 1-2	A26 5-0	a23 1-1		O28 1-0	D25 1-2	M17 3-0
20 WALSALL	N18 5-0	O21 5-1	S16 2-4	F03 3-2	S02 5-0	M24 2-2	O14 5-1	D02 3-0	J20 2-0	a07 5-1	F17 2-0	m05 5-0	D26 0-0	S04 2-1	N04 2-0	M30 3-1	a21 4-1	S30 2-0	M10 5-3		D16 3-1	D30 1-0
21 WREXHAM	F24 3-2	D30 4-2	O28 3-2	M17 8-1	S16 0-3	A30 2-3	J13 5-1	F10 6-1	M03 1-1	O07 2-3	M31 0-2	J20 3-1	S02 5-0	a14 5-4	a02 4-1	M07 4-0	S23 2-1	N11 0-1	a11 5-1	a28 4-2		D23 2-3
22 YORK C	a07 3-2	M10 1-1	F03 6-1	S30 4-1	J20 3-2	N18 1-2	S06 4-1	a21 1-1	S16 1-2	D02 1-1	O14 1-0	J06 1-3	O21 1-0	M30 2-1	M24 6-1	D25 0-1	D16 1-0	F17 2-2	N04 1-0	A26 2-2	m05 2-4	

DIVISION 3 SOUTH

	ALDERSHOT	BOURNEMOUTH	BRIGHTON & HA	BRISTOL C	BRISTOL R	CARDIFF C	CHARLTON A	CLAPTON O	COVENTRY C	CRYSTAL P	EXETER C	GILLINGHAM	LUTON T	NEWPORT CO	NORTHAMPTON T	NORWICH C	Q.P.R.	READING	SOUTHEND U	SWINDON T	TORQUAY U	WATFORD
1 ALDERSHOT		D16 0-0	O14 0-1	F03 2-2	M24 0-1	a21 1-3	m05 3-2	S30 0-0	M10 1-1	N18 0-4	D02 0-2	a07 0-2	D25 0-0	J20 3-2	A30 1-1	S16 2-1	S02 3-1	O21 3-0	N04 2-0	F17 1-2	D30 3-0	M30 3-2
2 BOURNEMOUTH	a28 1-2		a18 1-1	M31 5-0	O07 2-0	S09 1-3	D30 1-2	J17 2-0	a02 3-3	F10 1-1	J27 1-3	S23 1-1	D23 4-3	M17 0-0	S02 4-0	N11 2-4	O28 3-2	D25 1-1	F24 1-4	a14 1-1	M03 3-4	A30 3-2
3 BRIGHTON & H.A.	F24 3-1	a21 6-0		S16 5-1	N04 0-2	D02 4-0	D16 1-0	F03 1-1	O21 1-1	M24 4-1	a07 2-1	N18 5-2	M30 1-1	S02 1-1	D26 3-3	J20 1-1	D30 0-1	F17 1-1	M10 1-0	S30 3-0	A30 3-1	m05 2-0
4 BRISTOL C	S23 1-1	N18 3-1	F07 5-0		A26 0-3	M24 3-0	a07 0-1	J06 3-0	D16 0-0	O21 2-2	N04 1-1	M10 1-1	F10 0-0	D26 1-1	O07 2-3	S06 0-1	a02 0-2	a21 1-2	m05 5-1	S09 2-2	F24 2-0	D02 1-0
5 BRISTOL R	N11 4-1	F17 3-0	M17 1-1	D30 5-1		O14 3-1	S30 2-5	M03 2-2	J20 4-1	A30 0-1	M30 1-1	D25 4-2	M31 0-1	a28 2-0	F28 1-1	D23 3-0	a18 4-1	S16 1-0	S02 3-1	O28 3-0	a14 2-1	F03 1-0
6 CARDIFF C	a25 1-2	J20 4-2	a14 1-4	N11 1-5	F24 1-5		S02 1-1	M31 1-2	D26 3-3	O07 4-0	S23 2-1	F10 1-3	a28 0-4	O28 1-1	D23 1-3	M17 0-2	M03 3-1	A28 2-0	M30 1-1	J17 0-1	S16 0-1	D30 4-1
7 CHARLTON A	D23 1-0	A26 4-3	a28 4-3	a23 2-1	F10 2-1	J06 2-0		a14 1-1	F24 2-0	S23 4-2	S09 4-1	J29 2-2	S04 2-0	N11 6-1	M03 1-1	M31 3-3	M17 1-2	M30 0-0	O07 1-3	m02 1-0	O28 6-0	D26 4-3
8 CLAPTON O	F10 9-2	a07 4-1	S23 2-1	S02 4-0	O21 0-0	N18 4-2	D02 1-3		m05 0-0	M10 2-0	M24 4-0	N04 2-1	O07 1-1	A28 3-0	F24 5-1	D30 3-2	D26 2-2	D16 2-3	J20 5-2	J27 1-0	M30 4-1	a21 2-3
9 COVENTRY C	O28 5-1	a03 4-1	M03 2-0	a28 9-0	S09 5-3	D25 4-1	O14 3-2	D23 3-1		J06 5-1	S04 1-3	A26 7-1	M17 2-2	a14 5-2	N11 3-1	D14 0-0	J18 0-1	S30 0-0	J27 2-0	S23 5-1	M31 3-1	F17 2-0
10 CRYSTAL P	M31 4-1	S30 4-1	N11 2-1	M03 0-1	S06 1-2	F17 3-2	F03 1-0	O28 3-2	S02 2-1		O14 0-0	M30 3-2	S13 2-2	D23 1-1	a14 1-2	D25 0-1	a28 4-1	J20 0-0	D30 1-1	M17 0-0	a25 4-1	S16 4-3
11 EXETER C	a14 0-0	S16 4-0	S13 3-0	M17 2-0	a02 0-0	F03 4-0	J20 2-0	N11 0-3	A30 1-0	F24 1-2		O07 2-0	D09 4-2	M03 1-1	a28 0-2	O28 3-4	S30 1-1	D30 4-1	D25 2-0	M31 2-2	D23 4-0	S02 3-1
12 GILLINGHAM	J17 1-2	F03 5-1	M31 3-0	O28 2-1	D26 3-2	S30 6-2	S16 1-1	M17 1-1	D30 3-7	a02 0-5	F17 1-1		a14 1-1	O14 1-0	a11 5-1	M03 1-2	D23 1-4	S02 5-1	A30 0-0	N11 3-3	a28 3-3	J20 3-3
13 LUTON T	D26 1-1	m05 2-0	a02 1-2	S30 3-0	N18 2-2	D16 3-1	A28 2-1	F17 2-0	N04 0-1	a07 2-1	a21 3-2	D02 4-2		S16 1-1	D30 3-1	F03 2-3	J20 4-2	M10 3-1	M24 3-1	O14 2-3	S02 10-2	O21 2-1
14 NEWPORT CO	S09 1-2	N04 1-1	J06 2-2	D25 2-2	D16 1-0	M10 2-2	M24 1-1	S04 1-1	D02 0-0	m05 1-0	O21 1-0	F24 3-1	J27 1-2		S23 2-0	M30 0-0	O07 1-2	a07 1-2	a21 3-0	A26 1-2	F10 0-0	N18 0-3
15 NORTHAMPTON T	S04 0-0	J06 4-1	D25 1-1	F22 2-3	a07 1-2	m05 2-0	O21 1-2	O14 3-0	M24 2-2	D02 4-2	D16 5-3	a21 1-0	A26 2-3	F03 5-3		S30 2-2	S16 2-1	N04 2-4	N18 2-0	a02 2-2	J20 1-1	M10 1-0
16 NORWICH C	J27 2-2	M24 6-1	S09 4-3	A28 7-2	m05 0-0	N04 2-0	N18 3-0	A26 3-0	a21 3-1	D26 2-0	M10 1-1	O21 4-1	S23 4-0	a02 2-1	F10 2-0		F24 1-0	D02 3-2	D16 0-0	J06 3-2	O07 0-2	a07 3-1
17 Q.P.R.	J06 2-4	M10 1-0	A26 2-0	M30 1-0	a21 1-0	O21 4-0	N04 2-1	D25 2-0	a07 0-1	D16 2-1	F10 2-0	m05 5-0	S09 2-1	F17 2-1	J31 2-1	O14 5-2		N18 0-0	D02 4-0	S07 1-0	S23 2-0	M24 0-0
18 READING	M03 3-2	D26 4-0	O07 2-0	a18 1-1	J27 2-2	S06 3-1	a02 1-0	a28 4-0	F10 1-0	S09 0-0	A26 3-1	J06 2-0	O28 4-1	J17 4-0	M17 2-2	a14 1-0	M31 5-0		S23 5-0	D23 2-0	N11 5-2	O14 6-1
19 SOUTHEND U	M17 1-0	O14 1-2	O28 0-0	D23 3-0	J06 2-2	a02 1-1	F17 1-0	S09 2-1	S16 2-1	A26 0-4	D26 3-1	S06 1-2	N11 0-1	M14 3-5	M31 2-0	a28 0-0	a14 0-2	F03 2-2		M03 4-1	J17 3-1	S30 1-1
20 SWINDON T	O07 1-0	D02 3-2	F10 1-1	J20 4-2	M10 1-0	a07 6-3	a21 1-3	S16 3-0	F03 0-1	N04 3-2	N18 1-1	M24 3-1	F24 3-1	D30 1-1	M30 1-1	S02 0-0	A30 3-1	m05 3-1	O21 1-4		D26 2-0	D16 1-0
21 TORQUAY U	A26 0-0	O21 1-0	S06 3-0	O14 2-2	D02 2-1	J27 3-1	M10 1-4	a02 2-1	N18 1-3	a21 2-1	m05 0-2	D16 2-1	J06 0-1	S30 1-2	S09 3-2	F17 1-2	F03 1-1	M24 1-1	a07 3-0	D25 2-0		N04 1-3
22 WATFORD	a02 3-0	S06 1-2	D23 2-0	a14 1-1	S23 0-0	A26 1-2	D25 0-1	D20 6-0	O07 3-3	J31 3-1	J06 2-0	S09 2-1	M03 0-1	M31 3-0	O28 2-0	J13 1-3	N11 0-0	F24 2-0	F10 2-1	a28 4-0	M17 5-0	

LEAGUE TABLES

DIVISION 1

	P	W	D	L	F	A	W	D	L	F	A	Pts
Arsenal	42	15	4	2	45	19	10	5	6	30	28	59
Huddersfield T	42	16	3	2	53	19	7	7	7	37	42	56
Tottenham H	42	14	3	4	51	24	7	4	10	28	32	49
Derby Co	42	11	8	2	45	22	6	3	12	23	32	45
Manchester C	42	14	4	3	50	29	3	7	11	15	43	45
Sunderland	42	14	6	1	57	17	2	6	13	24	39	44
W.B.A.	42	12	4	5	49	28	5	6	10	29	42	44
Blackburn R	42	16	5	0	57	21	2	2	17	17	60	43
Leeds U	42	13	5	3	52	21	4	3	14	23	45	42
Portsmouth	42	11	5	5	31	21	4	7	10	21	34	42
Sheffield W	42	9	5	7	33	24	7	4	10	29	43	41
Stoke C	42	11	5	5	33	19	4	6	11	25	52	41
Aston Villa	42	10	5	6	45	34	4	7	10	33	41	40
Everton	42	9	7	5	38	27	3	9	9	24	36	40
Wolverhampton W	42	13	4	4	50	28	1	8	12	24	58	40
Middlesbrough	42	13	3	5	51	27	3	4	14	17	53	39
Leicester C	42	10	6	5	36	26	4	5	12	23	48	39
Liverpool	42	10	6	5	52	37	4	4	13	27	50	38
Chelsea	42	12	3	6	44	24	2	5	14	23	45	36
Birmingham C	42	8	6	7	29	20	4	6	11	25	36	36
Newcastle U	42	6	11	4	42	29	4	3	14	26	48	34
Sheffield U	42	11	5	5	40	25	1	2	18	18	76	31

DIVISION 2

	P	W	D	L	F	A	W	D	L	F	A	Pts
Grimsby T	42	15	3	3	62	28	12	2	7	41	31	59
Preston N.E.	42	15	3	3	47	20	8	3	10	24	32	52
Bolton W	42	14	2	5	45	22	7	7	7	34	33	51
Brentford	42	15	2	4	52	24	7	5	9	33	36	51
Bradford P.A.	42	16	2	3	63	27	7	1	13	23	40	49
Bradford C	42	14	4	3	46	25	6	2	13	27	42	46
West Ham U	42	13	3	5	51	28	4	8	9	27	42	45
Port Vale	42	14	4	3	39	14	5	3	13	21	41	45
Oldham A	42	12	5	4	48	28	5	5	11	24	32	44
Plymouth A	42	12	7	2	43	20	3	6	12	26	50	43
Blackpool	42	10	8	3	39	27	5	5	11	23	37	43
Bury	42	12	4	5	43	31	5	5	11	27	42	43
Burnley	42	14	2	5	40	29	4	4	13	20	43	42
Southampton	42	15	2	4	40	21	0	6	15	14	37	38
Hull C	42	11	4	6	33	20	2	8	11	19	48	38
Fulham	42	13	3	5	29	17	2	4	15	19	50	37
Nottingham F	42	11	4	6	50	27	2	5	14	23	47	35
Notts Co	42	9	7	5	32	22	3	4	14	21	40	35
Swansea T	42	10	9	2	36	19	0	6	15	15	41	35
Manchester U	42	9	3	9	29	33	5	3	13	30	52	34
Millwall	42	8	8	5	21	17	3	3	15	18	51	33
Lincoln C	42	7	7	7	31	23	2	1	18	13	52	26

DIVISION 3 NORTH

	P	W	D	L	F	A	W	D	L	F	A	Pts
Barnsley	42	18	3	0	64	18	9	5	7	54	43	62
Chesterfield	42	18	1	2	56	17	9	6	6	30	26	61
Stockport Co	42	18	3	0	84	23	6	8	7	31	29	59
Walsall	42	18	2	1	66	18	5	5	11	31	42	53
Doncaster R	42	17	1	3	58	24	5	8	8	25	37	53
Wrexham	42	14	1	6	68	35	9	4	8	34	38	51
Tranmere R	42	16	2	3	57	21	4	5	12	27	42	47
Barrow	42	12	5	4	78	45	7	4	10	38	49	47
Halifax T	42	15	2	4	57	30	5	2	14	23	61	44
Chester C	42	11	6	4	59	26	6	0	15	30	60	40
Hartlepool U	42	14	3	4	54	24	2	4	15	35	69	39
York C	42	11	5	5	44	28	4	3	14	27	46	38
Carlisle U	42	11	6	4	43	23	4	2	15	23	58	38
Crewe A	42	12	3	6	54	38	3	3	15	27	59	36
New Brighton	42	13	3	5	41	25	1	5	15	21	62	36
Darlington	42	11	4	6	47	35	2	5	14	23	66	35
Mansfield T	42	9	7	5	49	29	2	5	14	32	59	34
Southport	42	6	11	4	35	29	2	6	13	28	61	33
Gateshead	42	10	3	8	46	40	2	6	13	30	70	33
Accrington S	42	10	6	5	44	38	3	1	17	21	63	33
Rotherham U	42	5	7	9	31	35	5	1	15	22	56	28
Rochdale	42	7	5	9	34	30	2	1	18	19	73	24

DIVISION 3 SOUTH

	P	W	D	L	F	A	W	D	L	F	A	Pts
Norwich C	42	16	4	1	55	19	9	7	5	33	30	61
Coventry C	42	16	3	2	70	22	5	9	7	30	32	54
Reading	42	17	4	0	60	13	4	8	9	22	37	54
Q.P.R.	42	17	2	2	42	12	7	4	10	28	39	54
Charlton A	42	14	5	2	53	27	8	3	10	30	29	52
Luton T	42	14	3	4	55	28	7	7	7	28	33	52
Bristol R	42	14	4	3	49	21	6	7	8	28	26	51
Swindon T	42	13	5	3	42	25	4	6	11	22	43	45
Exeter C	42	12	5	4	43	19	4	6	11	25	38	43
Brighton & H.A.	42	12	7	2	47	18	3	6	12	21	42	43
Clapton O	42	14	4	3	60	25	2	6	13	15	44	42
Crystal Palace	42	11	6	4	40	25	5	3	13	31	42	41
Northampton T	42	10	6	5	45	32	4	6	11	26	46	40
Aldershot	42	8	6	7	28	27	5	6	10	24	44	38
Watford	42	12	4	5	43	16	3	3	15	28	47	37
Southend U	42	9	6	6	32	27	3	4	14	19	47	34
Gillingham	42	8	8	5	49	41	3	3	15	26	55	33
Newport Co	42	6	9	6	25	23	2	8	11	24	47	33
Bristol C	42	7	8	6	33	22	3	5	13	25	63	33
Torquay U	42	10	4	7	32	28	3	3	15	21	65	33
Bournemouth	42	7	7	7	41	37	2	2	17	19	65	27
Cardiff C	42	6	4	11	32	43	3	2	16	25	62	24

Football League Records

Top scorers: Div 1, E.Drake (Arsenal) 42 goals; Div 2, J.Milsom (Bolton Wanderers) 31 goals; Div 3 N, G.Alsop (Walsall) 39 goals; Div 3 S, R.Allen (Charlton Athletic) 32 goals.

Ted Drake, whose 42 goals in 1934-35 is still an Arsenal record.

DIVISION 1

	ARSENAL	ASTON VILLA	BIRMINGHAM	BLACKBURN R	CHELSEA	DERBY CO	EVERTON	GRIMSBY T	HUDDERSFIELD T	LEEDS U	LEICESTER C	LIVERPOOL	MANCHESTER C	MIDDLESBROUGH	PORTSMOUTH	PRESTON N.E.	SHEFFIELD W	STOKE C	SUNDERLAND	TOTTENHAM H	W.B.A.	WOLVERHAMPTON W
1 ARSENAL		N17 1-2	S29 5-1	S05 4-0	a06 2-2	m04 0-1	N03 2-0	M23 1-1	a20 1-0	J19 3-0	D15 8-0	S01 8-1	O13 3-0	a19 8-0	D29 1-1	D25 5-3	F02 4-1	F20 2-0	M09 0-0	O20 5-1	S15 4-3	D01 7-0
2 ASTON VILLA	M30 1-3		D29 2-2	D22 1-1	D26 0-3	S01 3-2	O13 2-2	F16 3-2	a19 1-1	D08 1-1	J19 5-0	a13 4-2	O27 4-2	a27 0-3	N26 5-4	S29 4-2	N10 4-0	M02 4-1	S15 1-1	F02 1-0	a03 2-3	A27 2-1
3 BIRMINGHAM	F09 3-0	A25 2-1		S22 1-0	O20 0-1	M23 3-2	m04 2-3	N17 3-2	D15 0-4	a22 3-1	N03 2-3	F23 1-3	S08 1-3	F06 4-2	O06 2-1	a06 3-0	D26 0-4	J05 0-0	a20 2-2	D01 2-1	S03 1-2	M09 1-1
4 BLACKBURN R	S17 2-0	m04 5-0	F02 3-1		N17 1-2	D15 2-5	a20 6-2	N03 2-2	D01 4-2	S01 1-1	M09 0-0	D29 0-2	M04 1-0	O13 3-2	D25 0-0	M23 1-0	S15 2-1	S29 0-1	O20 0-0	J01 2-0	J19 3-0	a06 4-2
5 CHELSEA	N24 2-5	D25 2-0	M06 2-2	M30 4-2		D29 1-1	F20 3-0	S29 2-0	O13 2-1	M16 7-1	S01 3-1	D08 4-1	a27 4-2	D22 2-1	a13 1-1	F02 0-0	A29 1-2	O27 0-2	J19 2-2	S15 1-3	N10 2-3	a19 4-2
6 DERBY CO	D22 3-1	J05 1-1	N10 1-1	a27 1-1	A25 3-0		a22 4-1	O13 1-4	S05 4-1	a13 1-2	S15 1-1	N24 1-2	M02 1-2	O27 2-0	M30 0-1	a10 0-3	M20 4-0	S08 0-2	F02 3-1	S29 2-1	D08 9-3	D26 2-0
7 EVERTON	M16 0-2	F23 2-2	D22 2-0	D08 5-2	O06 3-2	J01 2-2		J19 3-1	S22 4-2	M06 4-4	A29 2-1	S15 1-0	N24 1-2	a13 1-1	N10 3-2	S01 4-1	m01 2-2	M30 5-0	D25 6-2	D29 5-2	O27 4-0	F09 5-2
8 GRIMSBY T	N10 2-2	O06 5-1	M30 4-3	M16 1-2	F09 3-1	F23 1-3	S08 0-0		a02 1-1	O27 3-2	a19 3-1	M02 3-2	a13 1-1	D08 2-2	S01 3-0	D29 3-1	D22 3-1	N24 3-1	A28 0-0	D25 3-0	m01 3-0	S22 2-1
9 HUDDERSFIELD T	D08 1-1	a24 1-1	a27 2-2	a13 6-0	F23 3-0	A27 1-0	F02 1-1	S15 1-5		F09 3-1	D26 2-3	N10 8-0	M30 3-0	N24 3-1	M16 2-0	J19 3-4	O27 4-0	D22 1-4	D29 0-3	S01 0-0	M06 3-0	O06 4-1
10 LEEDS U	S08 1-1	a20 1-1	a19 1-1	J05 5-1	N03 5-2	D01 4-2	O20 2-0	M09 3-1	S29 2-0		a06 0-2	S22 0-3	D25 1-2	A25 2-4	M02 3-1	D15 3-3	O13 0-0	S03 4-2	N17 2-4	m04 4-3	F20 4-1	M23 1-1
11 LEICESTER C	a27 3-5	S08 5-0	M16 2-1	O27 0-1	J05 1-0	J31 0-1	S03 5-2	a22 2-2	D25 0-3	N24 1-0		M30 3-1	S22 1-3	M02 3-1	D22 6-3	O13 0-0	D08 0-1	N10' 0-3	S29 0-2	M28 6-0	a13 0-0	A25 1-1
12 LIVERPOOL	J05 0-2	D01 3-1	O13 5-4	A25 2-0	a20 6-0	a06 1-3	M20 2-1	O20 1-1	M23 3-2	F02 4-2	N17 5-1		S05 2-1	D26 2-2	S08 0-1	M09 0-0	F20 1-2	a19 5-0	m04 2-2	D15 4-1	S29 3-2	N03 2-1
13 MANCHESTER C	F23 1-1	M09 4-1	J19 0-0	O06 3-3	D15 2-0	O20 0-1	a06 2-2	D01 1-0	N17 0-0	D26 3-0	F02 6-3	A29 3-1		F09 6-2	a19 2-4	a20 1-2	S01 4-1	S15 3-1	a10 1-0	N03 3-1	D29 3-2	m04 5-0
14 MIDDLESBROUGH	a22 0-1	D15 4-1	S15 0-1	F23 3-3	m04 2-2	M09 1-1	D01 3-2	a20 0-2	a06 2-1	D29 3-3	O20 1-0	J01 2-0	S29 1-2		A29 1-1	N03 3-3	J19 5-3	F02 2-0	F16 0-0	M23 3-1	S01 0-0	N17 2-2
15 PORTSMOUTH	A25 3-3	a06 0-1	a10 2-1	D26 3-1	D01 1-1	N17 5-1	M23 5-1	J05 1-0	N03 5-0	S15 0-0	m04 1-1	J19 1-2	a22 4-2	S05 1-0		O20 4-0	S29 2-1	O13 0-1	D15 2-4	M09 1-1	F02 0-2	a20 0-1
16 PRESTON N.E.	D26 2-1	F09 0-0	N24 0-1	N10 3-1	S22 2-0	O06 0-1	J05 2-2	A25 1-0	S08 2-0	a27 0-2	F23 2-0	O27 2-2	D08 2-4	M16 2-0	M06 1-1		M30 2-1	a13 5-2	a22 1-1	S03 1-0	D22 1-2	J28 2-1
17 SHEFFIELD W	S22 0-0	M23 2-1	D25 2-1	J28 2-2	S03 3-1	N03 1-0	D15 0-0	m04 1-0	M09 1-1	F23 1-0	a20 1-1	O06 4-1	J05 1-0	S08 3-3	F09 3-0	N17 2-1		A25 4-1	D01 2-2	a06 4-0	J01 2-1	O20 3-1
18 STOKE C	O06 2-2	O20 4-1	S01 2-0	F09 3-1	M09 0-1	J19 1-1	N17 3-2	a06 0-0	m04 2-0	A27 8-1	M23 3-0	a22 1-1	J26 2-0	S22 2-0	F23 1-2	D01 3-1	D29 1-1		N03 0-3	a20 4-1	D26 3-0	D15 1-2
19 SUNDERLAND	O27 2-1	F06 3-3	D08 5-1	M02 3-0	S08 4-0	S22 1-4	D26 7-0	S05 3-0	A25 4-1	M30 3-0	F09 2-0	D22 2-3	N10 3-2	O06 1-1	a27 4-1	a19 3-1	a13 2-2	M16 4-1		O13 1-2	N24 0-1	J05 0-0
20 TOTTENHAM H	M06 0-6	S22 0-2	a13 1-1	a19 1-0	J30 1-3	F09 2-2	A25 1-1	D26 2-1	J05 0-0	D22 1-1	O06 2-2	a27 5-1	M16 0-0	N10 3-1	O27 4-1	A27 1-2	N24 3-2	D08 3-2	F23 1-1		M30 0-1	S08 3-1
21 W.B.A.	J30 0-3	N03 2-2	A29 1-2	S08 2-2	M23 2-2	a20 4-3	M09 0-1	D15 4-2	O20 4-1	O06 6-3	D01 4-1	F09 1-1	A25 1-1	J05 6-3	S22 4-2	m04 0-0	a22 1-1	D25 3-0	a06 1-1	N17 4-0		F23 5-2
22 WOLVERHAMPTON W	a13 1-1	S03 5-2	O27 3-1	N24 2-1	a22 6-1	D25 5-1	S29 4-2	F02 0-3	F16 2-3	N10 1-2	D29 3-1	M16 5-3	D22 5-0	M30 5-3	D08 2-3	S15 2-2	M04 2-2	a27 2-1	S01 1-2	J19 6-2	O13 3-2	

Don Welsh, signed from Torquay United, began his Charlton Athletic career as they rose from Division Three South to Division One in consecutive seasons.

DIVISION 2

	BARNSLEY	BLACKPOOL	BOLTON W	BRADFORD	BRADFORD C	BRENTFORD	BURNLEY	BURY	FULHAM	HULL C	MANCHESTER U	NEWCASTLE U	NORWICH C	NOTTINGHAM F	NOTTS CO	OLDHAM A	PLYMOUTH A	PORT VALE	SHEFFIELD U	SOUTHAMPTON	SWANSEA T	WEST HAM U
1 BARNSLEY		M30 2-2	a10 1-1	D29 1-1	a22 2-0	a27 3-3	F02 0-0	N24 3-0	D22 2-0	a13 2-2	J19 0-2	M16 2-1	O27 2-1	D08 1-2	A27 1-1	S29 4-0	M02 1-4	S01 2-0	J01 0-0	O13 1-1	S15 1-0	N10 1-1
2 BLACKPOOL	N17 3-0		m04 1-1	S29 1-0	D01 2-1	S15 2-2	O20 1-0	D29 1-1	F02 1-1	S01 2-1	N03 1-2	A27 4-1	O13 2-1	J19 1-0	a20 3-1	D25 4-0	F16 4-1	M23 3-1	a06 1-0	D15 4-1	M09 2-1	a19 3-2
3 BOLTON W	O06 8-0	D22 4-2		M30 1-2	S22 3-0	m01 2-0	J02 7-0	S01 2-0	N10 4-0	M06 1-2	S03 3-1	D08 1-0	a13 4-0	O27 2-3	J30 5-1	D29 2-0	N24 3-2	F23 2-0	F09 1-1	S08 4-0	a19 1-0	a27 3-1
4 BRADFORD	A25 3-2	F09 0-0	N17 4-0		M09 2-1	a22 2-3	D01 1-1	O06 2-1	D25 0-0	F23 1-2	D15 1-2	J30 1-3	S08 1-1	S03 1-1	N03 0-0	a06 2-0	J05 2-2	m04 1-1	O20 1-3	M23 3-1	a20 3-1	S22 1-3
5 BRADFORD C	a23 1-0	a13 0-2	F02 1-1	O27 3-1		O13 3-0	J19 1-1	D08 0-0	M02 0-0	a27 3-2	D29 2-0	M30 3-3	N10 1-1	D22 4-0	F16 2-0	S15 2-0	M16 0-1	D26 3-0	A27 2-5	S29 1-1	S01 2-0	N24 0-2
6 BRENTFORD	D15 8-1	J26 2-1	N03 1-0	a19 1-0	F23 2-0		N17 6-1	S22 2-1	S05 1-0	F09 2-1	D01 3-1	J05 3-0	A25 2-1	O06 1-1	O20 4-1	M23 2-1	D25 0-0	a20 8-0	m04 3-1	M09 3-2	a06 1-0	S08 4-1
7 BURNLEY	S22 4-1	M05 1-2	D25 2-1	a13 1-2	S08 2-0	M30 0-3		O27 3-3	N24 3-1	M19 1-3	O06 1-2	D22 0-3	a27 1-0	N10 2-1	J05 4-0	a19 4-2	D08 1-2	F09 2-2	J28 0-2	A25 3-0	F23 3-0	S03 5-2
8 BURY	a06 4-1	A25 1-5	J05 2-1	F16 2-4	a20 2-1	F02 4-1	M09 0-0		S29 2-0	J19 0-1	M23 0-1	a19 0-2	S17 1-0	S15 1-0	D15 1-0	O20 2-0	O13 2-1	N17 3-1	D01 3-1	m04 4-1	N03 2-1	D25 2-4
9 FULHAM	m04 1-3	S22 4-1	M23 2-1	D26 2-2	O20 3-1	A27 2-2	a06 2-0	F09 1-2		O06 4-0	a20 3-1	S08 3-2	J05 1-3	F23 2-1	M09 7-0	N17 3-1	A25 3-0	D15 2-0	a19 7-2	N03 3-3	D01 4-1	J26 3-0
10 HULL C	D01 1-1	J05 2-2	O20 0-2	O13 2-0	D15 1-0	S29 2-1	N03 1-3	S08 0-1	F16 1-2		N17 3-2	D26 1-1	a22 1-0	F02 5-0	m04 5-1	M09 1-1	S10 1-1	a06 1-0	a20 0-3	J31 0-0	M23 0-1	S17 4-0
11 MANCHESTER U	S08 4-1	M16 3-2	S12 0-3	a27 2-0	A25 2-0	a13 0-0	M27 3-4	N10 1-0	D08 1-0	M30 3-0		M02 0-1	S22 5-0	N24 3-2	D25 2-1	O13 4-0	D22 3-1	F06 2-1	J05 3-3	J01 3-0	S29 3-1	O27 3-1
12 NEWCASTLE U	N03 4-1	S12 4-1	a20 1-3	S15 0-1	N17 4-2	S01 2-5	m04 2-0	J01 5-1	J19 1-1	D25 6-2	O20 0-1		S29 2-0	D29 2-0	a06 1-1	D15 4-2	F02 3-0	M09 1-2	M23 4-1	D01 1-0	F16 5-1	F23 3-0
13 NORWICH C	M09 0-1	F23 1-1	D01 2-3	J19 3-0	M23 6-1	D29 2-1	D15 2-3	A27 4-1	S01 0-0	a19 3-0	F02 3-2	F09 2-0		D26 3-3	N17 7-2	a20 0-0	S15 3-0	O20 0-0	N03 3-1	a06 4-0	m04 2-2	O06 1-2
14 NOTTINGHAM F	a20 4-1	S08 0-0	M09 0-1	O04 2-2	m04 2-0	F28 0-0	M23 5-0	F06 1-4	O13 1-1	S22 2-1	a06 2-2	A25 5-1	D25 5-2		F09 2-3	N03 4-0	a19 1-3	D01 2-0	D15 2-1	O20 3-1	N17 1-0	J05 2-0
15 NOTTS CO	S03 1-4	D08 3-2	S15 0-2	M16 1-1	O06 2-3	M02 0-1	S01 1-0	a27 1-2	O27 1-1	D22 1-1	D26 1-0	N24 0-1	M30 1-0	S29 3-5		J19 2-1	N10 1-3	a22 3-2	F23 0-1	F02 3-1	D29 4-0	a13 0-2
16 OLDHAM A	F09 1-4	D26 2-3	A25 1-4	N24 1-1	F05 3-1	N10 1-3	a22 1-2	M02 7-2	M30 2-1	O27 5-0	F23 3-1	a27 3-2	D08 4-2	M16 0-5	S08 1-0		a13 1-1	O06 2-0	S22 3-2	J05 0-2	S03 2-2	D22 1-2
17 PLYMOUTH A	O20 3-1	O06 1-2	a06 1-0	S01 2-2	N03 3-1	D26 1-1	a20 2-2	F23 3-0	D29 3-1	A29 6-4	m04 0-2	S22 1-3	F06 0-1	a22 5-2	M23 4-0	D01 2-0		J19 2-1	M09 2-0	N17 4-0	D15 3-2	F09 0-1
18 PORT VALE	J05 4-0	N10 2-2	O13 1-3	D22 1-1	D25 1-0	D08 2-2	S29 3-1	M30 0-1	a27 1-1	N24 1-2	S15 3-2	O27 1-3	M02 1-1	a13 2-0	a19 5-3	F16 2-0	S08 2-2		A25 2-0	S03 4-1	F02 2-1	M16 2-2
19 SHEFFIELD U	D26 2-1	N24 1-1	S29 6-2	M02 3-1	S10 1-2	D22 1-2	S15 0-0	a13 5-3	a22 1-2	D08 3-4	S01 3-2	N10 5-1	M16 1-1	a27 2-1	O13 3-0	F02 2-1	O27 1-2	D29 3-0		F16 6-1	J19 1-1	M30 1-2
20 SOUTHAMPTON	F23 0-1	a27 2-0	J19 1-2	N10 4-1	F09 1-1	O27 1-0	D29 0-0	D22 2-1	M16 1-1	S15 3-0	a22 1-0	a13 2-0	N24 1-4	M02 1-2	S22 1-1	S01 2-2	M30 1-0	A27 0-0	O06 1-1		D26 1-0	D08 2-2
21 SWANSEA T	J31 1-1	O27 2-1	a22 2-1	D08 0-0	J05 3-1	N24 2-4	O13 2-0	M16 1-0	a13 2-0	N10 2-1	F09 1-0	O06 3-4	D22 1-1	M30 3-0	A25 2-1	A27 5-1	a27 3-0	S22 1-1	S08 0-0	D25 0-1		M02 5-4
22 WEST HAM U	M23 4-3	a22 2-1	D15 4-1	F02 2-1	a06 1-0	J19 2-0	A27 1-2	D26 3-0	S15 2-1	D29 1-2	M09 0-0	O13 3-2	F18 1-0	S01 3-1	D01 4-0	m04 2-0	S29 2-1	N03 3-1	N17 2-0	a20 2-1	O20 2-0	

SEASON 1934-35

DIVISION 3 NORTH

	ACCRINGTON S	BARROW	CARLISLE U	CHESTER	CHESTERFIELD	CREWE A	DARLINGTON	DONCASTER R	GATESHEAD	HALIFAX T	HARTLEPOOL U	LINCOLN C	MANSFIELD T	NEW BRIGHTON	ROCHDALE	ROTHERHAM U	SOUTHPORT	STOCKPORT CO	TRANMERE R	WALSALL	WREXHAM	YORK C
1 ACCRINGTON S		D22 5-2	S25 1-0	J05 1-1	D08 1-0	F09 3-0	a22 2-1	J26 1-5	F23 4-2	M30 1-1	S22 0-4	O27 3-0	S19 2-0	A25 1-3	M02 2-5	J12 2-3	S08 1-1	O06 3-1	M16 1-0	a13 3-3	N10 2-2	D26 5-2
2 BARROW	m04 0-2		F23 2-1	a06 4-2	F02 1-1	M09 1-1	D15 4-4	M23 2-1	F16 3-2	S01 2-0	N03 2-0	a22 1-1	S29 3-0	D01 1-2	S03 1-1	J19 2-1	N17 2-1	O20 1-4	D25 1-0	S15 3-1	D29 1-3	a20 0-3
3 CARLISLE U	A30 2-0	O13 0-0		D01 1-3	S29 3-1	N03 1-3	m04 1-2	N17 1-1	O20 5-4	J19 2-4	M23 2-2	J01 2-1	a25 1-1	a20 4-1	a19 0-0	S15 2-1	a06 0-1	M09 1-2	D29 1-1	F02 1-6	S01 0-2	D15 4-0
4 CHESTER	S01 4-0	J16 6-2	a13 3-0		N10 1-1	a19 2-2	J19 3-1	F23 1-3	D29 2-2	M02 5-0	S05 4-1	a27 0-1	M30 3-2	F02 5-4	a03 1-0	O27 4-1	O06 0-2	D25 5-1	D22 0-0	M16 2-1	S29 6-2	S15 5-1
5 CHESTERFIELD	a20 0-0	S22 3-0	F09 3-0	M23 1-2		J19 1-2	D01 2-2	M09 3-2	D15 3-1	J01 4-0	O20 4-0	F23 3-1	J26 0-0	N17 1-0	O06 2-0	D29 2-1	N03 3-3	m04 5-0	A27 0-2	S01 2-0	a19 1-4	a06 3-1
6 CREWE A	S29 4-2	O27 4-3	M16 1-1	a22 1-1	S08 1-0		F16 4-1	A25 1-1	F02 2-1	D08 3-1	J05 1-1	M30 1-0	M02 1-1	S03 2-3	N10 4-1	a27 0-0	D25 2-1	S15 2-3	J12 1-2	D22 1-0	a13 2-0	O13 3-2
7 DARLINGTON	J01 5-0	J12 3-1	D22 5-0	S08 1-0	a13 2-1	O06 6-2		S22 1-1	S05 2-1	N10 0-1	F09 3-0	M02 4-1	m01 1-0	J05 1-0	D26 2-2	M30 4-0	J26 0-0	F23 0-0	O27 2-2	J16 3-2	M16 3-1	A25 2-0
8 DONCASTER R	S15 2-1	N10 2-0	M30 3-0	O13 3-0	O27 0-2	D29 2-0	F02 2-0		J19 5-0	m02 0-1	D26 3-1	a13 1-3	M16 2-1	F16 7-1	J12 1-0	a19 3-5	S03 2-0	S01 3-4	a11 2-0	M02 4-0	a27 2-1	S29 4-1
9 GATESHEAD	O13 1-1	O06 1-0	M02 3-2	A25 2-4	a27 1-4	S22 5-2	A29 3-0	S08 0-0		J12 3-1	J26 2-1	M16 0-2	D22 2-2	D25 2-1	O27 2-0	a13 1-1	J05 1-2	F09 3-2	N10 0-2	F27 1-0	M30 1-0	a19 2-1
10 HALIFAX T	N17 2-1	J05 2-1	S08 4-0	O20 1-0	D25 0-2	a20 1-0	M23 2-1	m04 1-0	a06 4-0		D15 4-1	S22 2-1	A25 2-1	M09 6-2	J26 1-1	S03 2-1	F23 4-3	D01 2-1	F09 1-2	S17 1-1	O06 3-2	N03 5-3
11 HARTLEPOOLS U	F02 4-2	M16 5-2	N10 5-2	A29 0-2	M02 1-1	S01 4-2	S29 0-1	D25 2-1	S15 1-2	a27 0-3		J12 1-5	O27 1-1	O13 2-2	M30 0-0	M06 3-1	a22 4-1	J19 4-0	a13 6-1	D29 2-1	J01 4-3	F16 3-1
12 LINCOLN C	M09 1-0	a19 6-0	D26 4-2	D15 0-0	O13 2-0	N17 1-1	O20 2-4	D01 0-2	N03 5-0	F02 2-3	a06 2-1		S03 4-0	m04 1-0	A25 3-0	S29 4-0	a20 4-1	M23 3-0	J19 2-2	F16 5-1	S15 1-3	J05 3-1
13 MANSFIELD T	D15 2-1	F09 3-2	O06 3-0	N17 1-1	S15 1-0	O20 4-1	a20 2-2	N03 2-0	m04 1-1	D29 4-0	M09 2-1	A29 3-4		a06 2-1	F23 1-0	S01 2-1	M23 2-3	F02 3-2	a19 4-2	J19 4-2	D25 4-0	D01 5-1
14 NEW BRIGHTON	D29 2-1	a13 3-1	F27 5-1	S22 0-2	M30 3-1	A29 1-1	S01 0-1	O06 1-1	D26 3-0	O27 0-0	F23 1-4	D22 0-2	J16 2-1		a27 1-0	M16 3-2	F09 0-0	a19 1-2	S15 0-1	N10 2-2	J12 0-0	J19 4-2
15 ROCHDALE	O20 2-2	A28 0-1	a22 3-1	a20 3-3	F16 0-2	M23 3-0	D25 1-3	a06 0-1	M09 6-1	S15 2-4	N17 3-2	D29 2-0	O13 1-0	D15 3-1		F02 1-3	D01 2-2	N03 0-5	S01 1-1	S29 1-0	J19 3-3	m04 2-0
16 ROTHERHAM U	a06 2-0	S08 0-0	J26 4-1	M09 6-1	A25 2-2	D15 2-2	N17 2-1	a22 1-3	D01 3-0	A27 2-2	m04 0-1	F09 5-0	J05 3-0	N03 1-2	S22 4-0		O20 4-2	a25 2-0	O06 3-1	D26 4-2	F23 2-0	M23 4-1
17 SOUTHPORT	J19 0-0	M30 0-2	J12 0-3	F16 1-1	M16 1-1	D26 2-1	S15 1-4	A28 1-2	S01 1-1	O13 1-2	a19 1-1	a02 3-3	N10 1-2	S29 2-1	a13 2-1	M02 0-3		D29 1-2	a27 4-0	O27 3-2	D22 2-1	F02 0-3
18 STOCKPORT CO	F20 5-1	M02 4-1	O27 2-0	D26 0-1	D22 4-2	F06 4-0	O13 3-0	J05 3-2	S29 5-1	a13 2-1	S08 3-2	N10 1-2	S22 0-2	a22 1-1	M16 3-1	J01 4-0	A25 6-1		M30 1-0	a27 0-3	a29 6-1	S03 0-0
19 TRANMERE R	N03 2-1	D26 2-1	A25 3-1	J01 1-1	S03 2-1	a06 5-1	M09 4-1	a20 0-2	M23 2-2	S29 1-0	D01 3-0	S08 2-1	a22 3-0	J26 0-1	J05 4-1	F16 3-3	D15 4-1	N17 3-1		O13 4-0	F02 1-1	O20 4-0
20 WALSALL	D01 6-0	J26 5-0	S22 1-0	N03 1-1	J05 2-1	m04 4-0	a06 0-0	O20 0-2	a20 5-0	a22 4-1	A25 1-2	O06 0-0	S08 2-2	M23 5-1	F09 0-0	D25 5-2	M09 2-2	D15 3-1	F23 3-0		S03 0-0	N17 2-3
21 WREXHAM	M23 2-2	A25 1-1	J05 4-2	F09 2-2	a22 2-1	D01 2-1	N03 4-0	D15 1-2	N17 3-1	F16 5-0	a20 0-2	J26 2-2	D26 1-3	O20 3-0	S08 2-0	O13 0-1	m04 3-0	a06 2-1	S22 2-2	A29 4-2		M09 2-0
22 YORK C	D25 5-2	a03 1-1	a27 7-0	J26 1-1	M27 1-1	F23 7-3	D29 2-1	F09 1-2	a22 3-0	M16 0-1	O06 3-1	S01 1-2	a13 2-1	S08 1-0	D22 0-1	N10 5-0	S22 3-1	A29 3-1	M02 0-0	M30 4-1	O27 0-0	

DIVISION 3 SOUTH

	ALDERSHOT	BOURNEMOUTH	BRIGHTON & HA	BRISTOL C	BRISTOL R	CARDIFF C	CHARLTON A	CLAPTON O	COVENTRY C	CRYSTAL P	EXETER C	GILLINGHAM	LUTON T	MILLWALL	NEWPORT CO	NORTHAMPTON T	Q.P.R.	READING	SOUTHEND U	SWINDON T	TORQUAY U	WATFORD
1 ALDERSHOT		M02 1-1	F16 1-0	M30 1-0	D25 1-2	S29 2-0	a19 3-2	m01 1-1	a13 3-1	A25 2-2	D22 0-0	M16 4-1	O13 0-1	M06 0-0	a27 3-2	S22 2-0	J05 1-0	N10 2-5	S05 3-2	J30 3-0	S08 2-0	O27 0-0
2 BOURNEMOUTH	O20 4-1		M23 1-0	a22 1-1	D01 3-0	F16 3-1	a06 2-2	J19 1-0	S01 0-2	N17 1-1	D25 3-2	S15 1-1	N03 1-3	D29 3-1	S05 3-1	S29 0-1	m04 0-2	F02 4-1	a20 2-1	M09 1-1	D15 1-2	F23 1-2
3 BRIGHTON & H.A.	O06 3-0	N10 2-0		a27 2-0	A25 3-1	F23 3-1	J05 2-1	J16 3-0	M30 2-0	S08 3-0	O27 6-0	a13 1-1	D26 4-1	D22 0-2	M02 3-1	M16 2-3	J26 5-1	M20 1-0	a19 2-2	F09 2-2	S22 0-0	S05 2-0
4 BRISTOL C	N17 2-0	a19 2-1	D15 1-0		F06 1-1	m04 4-0	M23 1-4	M13 0-0	S29 0-2	N03 0-1	S08 2-0	O13 3-1	M09 0-2	F02 4-2	J05 2-1	D25 1-1	a20 5-1	S05 1-0	O20 2-0	a06 2-0	D01 1-0	A25 3-1
5 BRISTOL R	D26 1-0	a13 4-1	D29 0-0	S15 2-2		a22 3-2	S22 0-0	a27 1-2	O27 2-1	F09 5-3	N10 5-5	D22 4-3	S01 1-1	M02 2-0	M16 5-3	J16 7-1	O06 2-0	M30 3-0	J19 2-1	A29 2-2	F23 1-0	a23 2-0
6 CARDIFF C	F09 1-1	O06 2-1	O13 0-0	D22 3-3	a19 4-1		A25 2-1	a13 3-0	J16 2-4	J05 2-0	a27 5-0	D08 0-2	A27 1-0	M30 3-1	O27 3-4	N10 2-2	S08 2-1	M16 1-1	S10 2-0	S22 1-3	J26 1-1	M02 2-1
7 CHARLTON A	a22 4-0	J12 0-1	S01 3-1	N10 4-1	F02 2-0	D29 3-1		O27 2-1	M02 3-3	O06 2-2	M16 1-0	a27 2-0	J19 4-2	S29 3-1	D08 6-0	M30 0-1	F23 3-1	D22 3-1	S15 3-0	D25 6-0	A27 3-2	a13 5-2
8 CLAPTON O	a20 3-1	S08 0-1	a06 6-0	O06 4-0	D15 5-2	D01 0-1	M09 1-2		A30 0-1	O20 2-0	F09 0-3	a19 2-2	N17 1-1	F23 2-1	S22 4-0	J05 3-2	D26 3-1	A25 2-1	m04 3-0	N03 2-0	M23 3-1	J26 1-1
9 COVENTRY C	D01 0-0	J05 4-1	N17 0-2	F09 1-1	M09 1-0	a06 2-0	O20 4-0	S03 4-0		F23 1-1	S22 1-1	D25 4-0	m04 1-0	O06 5-1	J26 5-0	A25 2-0	M23 4-1	a23 1-2	D15 6-3	a20 3-0	N03 6-0	S08 1-1
10 CRYSTAL P	D29 3-0	M30 1-0	J19 3-0	M16 3-1	S29 2-0	S01 6-1	F16 1-2	M02 1-0	O13 3-1		a20 0-1	O27 2-0	S15 2-1	N10 1-1	a13 6-0	D22 2-0	S05 2-3	a27 3-1	F02 1-0	a19 7-0	D26 2-2	J12 0-0
11 EXETER C	m04 8-1	D26 4-1	M09 3-1	J19 3-0	M23 2-2	D15 2-1	N03 3-1	S29 1-1	F02 2-0	J26 0-6		F16 2-0	O20 1-2	S15 0-1	A25 0-1	S05 3-0	D01 3-0	O13 2-3	J05 4-3	N17 3-3	a06 1-1	a22 1-1
12 GILLINGHAM	N03 1-1	J26 3-1	D01 0-0	F23 1-0	m04 1-1	a20 1-0	D15 3-6	a22 1-0	D26 2-5	M09 2-0	O06 2-1		a06 1-1	A29 1-3	F09 5-0	S08 3-1	O20 0-0	J05 1-1	N17 2-2	M23 2-0	A25 3-0	S22 1-2
13 LUTON T	F23 6-1	M16 4-0	D25 4-0	O27 1-1	J05 6-2	S03 4-0	S08 1-2	M30 3-0	D22 4-0	J30 2-2	M02 4-0	m01 2-2		N24 2-1	a22 4-1	a23 2-2	S22 1-1	a13 2-4	A25 1-1	O06 2-0	F09 3-1	N10 2-2
14 MILLWALL	a06 3-0	S10 2-0	m04 3-1	S22 0-1	O20 0-2	N17 2-2	F09 1-3	O13 1-1	F16 1-3	M23 3-2	J31 1-0	S17 3-2	D15 1-4		S08 2-0	a19 0-1	N03 2-0	D25 2-2	M09 1-0	D01 1-0	a20 4-2	J05 0-0
15 NEWPORT CO	D15 2-0	A27 6-1	O20 1-0	S01 2-0	N03 1-1	M09 4-0	a20 0-2	F02 3-3	S15 2-1	D01 2-3	D29 1-3	S29 2-2	a19 2-4	J19 1-2		O13 1-3	a06 2-1	F28 2-2	M23 0-5	m04 1-2	N17 1-4	D25 0-1
16 NORTHAMPTON T	F02 0-0	F09 0-1	N03 4-1	D26 2-2	a06 1-0	M23 3-0	N17 1-1	S01 3-1	D29 3-4	m04 3-2	A27 2-1	J19 2-1	a20 2-1	a22 1-0	F23 2-0		D15 1-0	S15 1-3	D01 1-1	O20 4-2	M09 3-0	O06 1-0
17 Q.P.R.	S01 2-0	D22 2-1	S15 2-1	J01 4-1	F16 2-0	J19 2-2	O13 0-3	D25 6-3	N10 1-1	A30 3-3	a13 1-1	M02 2-0	F02 3-0	M16 1-0	J12 4-1	a27 3-1		O27 2-0	S29 1-1	D29 1-1	a19 5-1	M30 2-1
18 READING	M23 5-4	S22 4-1	a20 4-4	A29 2-0	N17 5-1	N03 1-1	m04 2-2	D29 0-0	a19 2-0	D15 6-1	F23 2-0	S01 3-0	D01 1-0	D26 2-1	O06 6-1	J30 3-1	M09 0-0		a06 3-2	J19 2-1	O20 3-1	F09 3-2
19 SOUTHEND U	A29 2-1	a10 0-0	a22 3-2	M02 6-0	S08 5-1	D26 2-1	J26 0-3	D22 0-2	a27 1-1	S22 1-4	S01 1-2	M30 0-0	D29 3-3	O27 2-1	N10 0-1	a13 2-1	F09 2-0	m01 6-1		F23 2-0	O06 2-3	M16 0-2
20 SWINDON T	S15 3-2	O27 0-2	S29 4-4	a10 1-0	S05 1-0	F02 2-1	D26 2-2	M16 1-1	m01 0-0	a22 1-1	M30 6-1	N10 3-0	F16 0-1	a13 0-1	D22 0-0	M02 5-3	A25 3-1	S08 1-1	O13 5-0		J05 5-0	a27 2-1
21 TORQUAY U	J19 2-1	a27 1-2	F02 3-0	a13 3-1	O13 1-2	S15 5-2	S05 1-2	N10 4-2	M16 1-0	D25 7-1	J12 3-0	D29 5-0	S29 6-2	M13 1-1	M30 2-1	O27 2-0	a22 7-0	M02 1-1	F16 2-0	S01 2-1		D22 1-3
22 WATFORD	M09 0-1	O13 3-1	A29 0-1	D29 4-0	a20 3-0	O20 1-3	D01 2-0	S15 5-0	J19 2-0	a06 2-0	a19 0-1	F02 3-1	M23 2-2	S01 2-3	D26 7-0	F16 1-1	N17 2-0	S29 1-0	N03 3-1	D15 7-4	m04 3-0	

LEAGUE TABLES

DIVISION 1

	P	W	D	L	F	A	W	D	L	F	A	Pts
Arsenal	42	15	4	2	74	17	8	8	5	41	29	58
Sunderland	42	13	4	4	57	24	6	12	3	33	27	54
Sheffield W	42	14	7	0	42	17	4	6	11	28	47	49
Manchester C	42	13	5	3	53	25	7	3	11	29	42	48
Grimsby T	42	13	6	2	49	25	4	5	12	29	35	45
Derby Co	42	10	4	7	44	28	8	5	8	37	38	45
Liverpool	42	13	4	4	53	29	6	3	12	32	59	45
Everton	42	14	5	2	64	32	2	7	12	25	56	44
W.B.A.	42	10	8	3	55	33	7	2	12	28	50	44
Stoke C	42	12	5	4	46	20	6	1	14	25	50	42
Preston N.E.	42	11	5	5	33	22	4	7	10	29	45	42
Chelsea	42	11	5	5	49	32	5	4	12	24	50	41
Aston Villa	42	11	6	4	50	36	3	7	11	24	52	41
Portsmouth	42	10	5	6	41	24	5	5	11	30	48	40
Blackburn R	42	12	5	4	42	23	2	6	13	24	55	39
Huddersfield T	42	11	5	5	52	27	3	5	13	24	44	38
Wolverhampton W	42	13	3	5	65	38	2	5	14	23	56	38
Leeds U	42	10	6	5	48	35	3	6	12	27	57	38
Birmingham C	42	10	3	8	36	36	3	7	11	27	45	36
Middlesbrough	42	8	9	4	38	29	2	5	14	32	61	34
Leicester C	42	9	4	8	39	30	3	5	13	22	56	33
Tottenham H	42	8	8	5	34	31	2	2	17	20	62	30

DIVISION 2

	P	W	D	L	F	A	W	D	L	F	A	Pts
Brentford	42	19	2	0	59	14	7	7	7	34	34	61
Bolton W	42	17	1	3	63	15	9	3	9	33	33	56
West Ham U	42	18	1	2	46	17	8	3	10	34	46	56
Blackpool	42	16	4	1	46	18	5	7	9	33	39	53
Manchester U	42	16	2	3	50	21	7	2	12	26	34	50
Newcastle U	42	14	2	5	55	25	8	2	11	34	43	48
Fulham	42	15	3	3	62	26	2	9	10	14	30	46
Plymouth A	42	13	3	5	48	26	6	5	10	27	38	46
Nottingham F	42	12	5	4	46	23	5	3	13	30	47	42
Bury	42	14	1	6	38	26	5	3	13	24	47	42
Sheffield U	42	11	4	6	51	30	5	5	11	28	40	41
Burnley	42	11	2	8	43	32	5	7	9	20	41	41
Hull C	42	9	6	6	32	22	7	2	12	31	52	40
Norwich C	42	11	6	4	51	23	3	5	13	20	38	39
Bradford P.A.	42	7	8	6	32	28	4	8	9	23	35	38
Barnsley	42	8	10	3	32	22	5	2	14	28	61	38
Swansea T	42	13	5	3	41	22	1	3	17	15	45	36
Port Vale	42	10	7	4	42	28	1	5	15	13	46	34
Southampton	42	9	8	4	28	19	2	4	15	18	56	34
Bradford C	42	10	7	4	34	20	2	1	18	16	48	32
Oldham A	42	10	3	8	44	40	0	3	18	12	55	26
Notts Co	42	8	3	10	29	33	1	4	16	17	64	25

DIVISION 3 NORTH

	P	W	D	L	F	A	W	D	L	F	A	Pts
Doncaster R	42	16	0	5	53	21	10	5	6	34	23	57
Halifax T	42	17	2	2	50	24	8	3	10	26	43	55
Chester C	42	14	4	3	62	27	6	10	5	29	31	54
Lincoln C	42	14	3	4	55	21	8	4	9	32	37	51
Darlington	42	15	5	1	50	15	6	4	11	30	44	51
Tranmere R	42	15	4	2	53	20	5	7	9	21	35	51
Stockport Co	42	15	2	4	57	22	7	1	13	33	50	47
Mansfield T	42	16	3	2	55	25	3	6	12	20	37	47
Rotherham U	42	14	4	3	56	21	5	3	13	30	52	45
Chesterfield	42	13	4	4	46	21	4	6	11	25	31	44
Wrexham	42	12	5	4	47	25	4	6	11	29	44	43
Hartlepool U	42	12	4	5	52	34	5	3	13	28	44	41
Crewe A	42	12	6	3	41	25	2	5	14	25	61	39
Walsall	42	11	7	3	51	18	2	3	16	30	54	36
York C	42	12	5	4	50	20	3	1	17	26	62	36
New Brighton	42	9	6	6	32	25	5	2	14	27	51	36
Barrow	42	11	5	5	37	31	2	4	15	21	56	35
Accrington S	42	11	5	5	44	36	1	5	15	19	53	34
Gateshead	42	12	4	5	36	28	1	4	16	22	68	34
Rochdale	42	9	5	7	39	35	2	6	13	14	36	33
Southport	42	6	6	9	27	36	4	6	11	28	49	32
Carlisle U	42	7	6	8	34	36	1	1	19	17	66	23

DIVISION 3 SOUTH

	P	W	D	L	F	A	W	D	L	F	A	Pts
Charlton A	42	17	2	2	62	20	10	5	6	41	32	61
Reading	42	16	5	0	59	23	5	6	10	30	42	53
Coventry C	42	14	5	2	56	14	7	4	10	30	36	51
Luton T	42	12	7	2	60	23	7	5	9	32	37	50
Crystal Palace	42	15	3	3	51	14	4	7	10	35	50	48
Watford	42	14	2	5	53	19	5	7	9	23	30	47
Northampton T	42	14	4	3	40	21	5	4	12	25	46	46
Bristol R	42	14	6	1	54	27	3	4	14	19	50	44
Brighton & H.A.	42	15	4	2	51	16	2	5	14	18	46	43
Torquay U	42	15	2	4	60	22	3	4	14	21	53	42
Exeter C	42	11	5	5	48	29	5	4	12	22	46	41
Millwall	42	11	4	6	33	26	6	3	12	24	36	41
Q.P.R.	42	14	6	1	49	22	2	3	16	14	50	41
Clapton O	42	13	3	5	47	21	2	7	12	18	44	40
Bristol C	42	14	3	4	37	18	1	6	14	15	50	39
Swindon T	42	11	7	3	45	22	2	5	14	22	56	38
Bournemouth	42	10	5	6	36	26	5	2	14	18	45	37
Aldershot	42	12	6	3	35	20	1	4	16	15	55	36
Cardiff C	42	11	6	4	42	27	2	3	16	20	55	35
Gillingham	42	10	7	4	36	25	1	6	14	19	50	35
Southend U	42	10	4	7	40	29	1	5	15	25	49	31
Newport Co	42	7	4	10	36	40	3	1	17	18	72	25

Football League Records

Top scorers: Div 1, W.G.Richardson (West Bromwich Albion) 39 goals; Div 2, R.Finan (Blackpool), E.Dodds (Sheffield United) 34 goals; Div 3 N, R.Bell (Tranmere Rovers) 33 goals; Div 3 S, A.Dawes (Crystal Palace) 38 goals.

Raich Carter, Sunderland's dynamic young inside-forward who steered the Wearsiders to the League Championship and the FA Cup in consecutive years.

Jack Bowers, a prolific scorer for Derby in the past, returned after injury to help them to runners-up spot.

DIVISION 1

	ARSENAL	ASTON VILLA	BIRMINGHAM	BLACKBURN R	BOLTON W	BRENTFORD	CHELSEA	DERBY CO	EVERTON	GRIMSBY T	HUDDERSFIELD T	LEEDS U	LIVERPOOL	MANCHESTER C	MIDDLESBROUGH	PORTSMOUTH	PRESTON N.E.	SHEFFIELD W	STOKE C	SUNDERLAND	W.B.A.	WOLVERHAMPTON W
1 ARSENAL		a18 1-0	J04 1-1	O05 5-1	a01 1-1	a04 1-1	a27 1-1	N09 1-1	M25 1-1	S11 6-0	M07 1-1	m02 2-2	D26 1-2	S21 2-3	D09 2-0	F22 2-3	O26 2-1	S14 2-2	F01 1-0	A31 3-1	a10 4-0	N23 4-0
2 ASTON VILLA	D14 1-7		M28 2-1	a25 2-4	O12 1-2	J25 2-2	N16 2-2	S28 0-2	F08 1-1	N02 2-6	D25 4-1	M14 3-3	F29 3-0	a11 2-2	S09 2-7	J04 4-2	S14 5-1	A31 1-2	N30 4-0	S16 2-2	O19 0-7	a10 4-2
3 BIRMINGHAM	S07 1-1	N23 2-2		F01 4-2	M07 0-0	N09 2-1	O05 2-1	M21 2-3	D21 4-2	D26 1-1	D07 4-1	S11 2-0	F15 2-0	J18 0-1	a18 1-0	O26 4-0	a04 0-0	a22 4-1	S21 0-5	a13 2-7	m02 1-3	D28 0-0
4 BLACKBURN R	F08 0-1	D21 5-1	S28 1-2		a04 0-3	J01 1-0	S16 1-0	F22 0-0	O26 1-1	A31 1-0	N09 2-1	J04 0-3	a10 2-2	O12 4-1	M21 2-2	a18 3-1	N23 1-1	D07 3-2	D25 0-1	F15 1-1	S14 3-1	M07 1-0
5 BOLTON W	a29 2-1	F15 4-3	N30 2-0	N02 3-1		A31 0-2	M14 2-3	J04 0-2	S14 2-0	J29 4-0	F01 1-2	M28 3-0	O19 0-0	N16 3-3	O05 3-1	J01 4-0	a10 1-1	S02 1-1	F29 1-2	a11 2-1	D14 3-1	D25 0-3
6 BRENTFORD	N02 2-1	S21 1-2	F29 0-1	S05 3-1	D28 4-0		M28 2-1	m02 6-0	a13 4-1	a11 3-0	S07 1-2	N30 2-2	D14 1-2	M14 0-0	J18 1-0	M25 3-1	D25 5-2	O05 2-2	O19 0-0	N16 1-5	a25 2-2	F01 5-0
7 CHELSEA	O12 1-1	M21 1-0	F08 0-0	m02 5-1	O26 2-1	N23 2-1		a10 1-1	F22 2-2	J04 0-2	a04 1-0	S14 1-0	A31 2-2	D26 2-1	N09 2-1	a22 1-0	a18 5-2	M07 1-2	S04 3-5	S28 3-1	M11 2-2	D21 2-2
8 DERBY CO	M04 0-4	F01 1-3	N16 2-2	O19 1-0	S07 4-0	S18 2-1	a13 1-1		D28 3-3	D14 2-0	J18 2-0	a11 2-1	M28 2-2	N02 3-0	S21 3-2	D26 1-[illegible]	S11 2-0	F19 3-1	M14 0-1	a25 4-0	N30 2-0	O05 3-1
9 EVERTON	N16 0-2	O05 2-2	a25 4-3	M14 4-0	J22 3-3	a10 1-2	O19 5-1	A31 4-0		M28 4-0	S21 1-3	D14 0-0	J04 0-0	F29 2-2	F01 5-2	S11 3-0	m02 5-0	D26 4-3	N02 5-1	N30 0-3	a11 5-3	F15 4-1
10 GRIMSBY T	S03 1-0	a04 4-1	D25 1-0	D28 1-1	S21 3-1	D07 6-1	S07 1-3	a18 4-1	N23 0-4		F22 1-1	S28 0-1	J18 0-0	m02 3-1	O26 1-0	D21 1-2	M07 0-0	M24 4-0	a10 3-0	O12 4-0	F08 4-2	N09 2-1
11 HUDDERSFIELD T	N30 0-0	D26 4-1	a11 1-0	F29 1-1	S28 0-0	J04 2-2	N02 2-0	S14 1-1	J29 2-1	O19 1-0		F08 1-2	M14 1-0	a25 1-1	F19 4-1	a14 1-1	A31 1-0	m02 1-0	N16 2-1	D14 1-0	M28 2-3	S11 3-0
12 LEEDS U	S18 1-1	O26 4-2	S04 0-0	S07 1-4	N23 5-2	M07 1-2	J18 2-0	D07 1-0	a18 3-1	F01 1-2	O05 2-2		S21 1-0	a13 1-1	F22 0-1	M21 1-0	D21 0-1	N09 7-2	D28 4-1	a22 3-0	O12 1-1	a04 2-0
13 LIVERPOOL	D25 0-1	N09 3-2	O12 1-2	a13 4-1	F22 1-1	a18 0-0	D28 2-3	N23 0-0	S07 6-0	S14 7-2	O26 3-0	M18 2-1		S04 0-2	a04 2-2	M07 2-0	D07 2-1	D21 1-0	S18 2-0	F08 0-3	S28 5-0	M21 0-2
14 MANCHESTER C	M11 1-0	D07 5-0	S14 3-1	F19 2-0	M21 7-0	O26 2-1	D25 0-0	a04 1-0	N09 1-0	J01 0-3	J15 1-2	a10 1-3	S11 6-0		M07 6-0	S28 0-0	F22 1-3	N23 3-0	O05 1-2	J04 0-1	A31 1-0	a18 2-1
15 MIDDLESBROUGH	a11 2-2	S04 1-2	D14 0-2	N16 6-1	F08 0-0	S14 0-0	M04 4-1	J29 0-3	S28 6-1	M14 5-1	O12 4-2	O19 1-1	N02 2-2	N30 2-0		A31 3-2	J04 2-0	a13 5-0	a25 0-0	M28 6-0	J01 3-1	S18 4-2
16 PORTSMOUTH	O19 2-1	S07 3-0	M14 0-3	D14 3-1	m02 2-1	O12 1-3	a11 2-0	D25 3-0	S04 2-0	a25 3-2	a10 0-0	N16 2-2	N30 2-1	F01 1-2	D28 1-0		F08 1-1	S21 3-2	M28 2-0	N02 2-2	F29 3-1	J18 1-0
17 PRESTON N.E.	M14 1-0	J18 3-0	N02 3-1	M28 2-0	a13 1-0	D26 2-4	D14 2-0	S02 1-0	S18 2-2	N30 1-0	D28 4-0	a25 5-0	a11 3-1	O19 4-0	S07 0-5	O05 1-1		F01 0-1	F19 1-1	F29 3-2	N16 3-0	S21 2-0
18 SHEFFIELD W	J18 3-2	D28 5-2	O19 3-1	a11 0-0	S09 2-2	F08 3-3	N30 4-1	O12 1-0	F03 3-3	N16 3-0	S16 1-2	F29 3-0	a25 0-0	M28 1-0	a14 0-0	F12 0-1	S28 1-0		D14 0-1	M14 0-0	N02 2-5	S07 0-0
19 STOKE C	S28 0-3	M07 2-3	F06 3-1	D26 2-0	N09 1-2	F22 2-2	S09 3-0	O26 0-0	a04 2-1	a13 1-0	M21 1-0	A31 3-1	m02 2-1	F08 1-0	D21 1-1	N23 2-0	O12 2-1	a18 0-3		S14 0-2	J04 3-2	D07 4-1
20 SUNDERLAND	D28 5-4	J01 1-3	a10 2-1	S21 7-2	D07 7-2	M21 1-3	F01 3-3	D21 3-1	M07 3-3	F19 3-1	a18 4-3	D26 2-1	O05 2-0	S07 2-0	N23 2-1	a04 5-0	N09 4-2	O26 5-1	J18 1-0		S11 6-1	F22 3-1
21 W.B.A.	a13 1-0	a01 0-3	S18 0-0	J18 8-1	a18 2-2	D21 1-0	S21 1-2	M07 0-3	D07 6-1	O05 4-1	N23 1-2	F19 3-2	F01 6-1	D28 5-1	D26 5-2	N09 2-0	M21 2-4	a04 2-2	S07 2-0	S04 1-3		O26 2-1
22 WOLVERHAMPTON W	M28 2-2	a13 2-2	A31 3-1	N30 8-1	D26 3-3	S28 3-2	a25 3-3	F08 0-0	O12 4-0	M04 1-0	S02 2-2	N02 3-0	N16 3-1	D14 4-3	m02 4-0	S14 2-0	a20 4-2	J04 2-1	a11 1-1	O19 3-4	M14 2-0	

DIVISION 2

	BARNSLEY	BLACKPOOL	BRADFORD	BRADFORD C	BURNLEY	BURY	CHARLTON A	DONCASTER R	FULHAM	HULL C	LEICESTER C	MANCHESTER U	NEWCASTLE U	NORWICH C	NOTTINGHAM F	PLYMOUTH A	PORT VALE	SHEFFIELD U	SOUTHAMPTON	SWANSEA T	TOTTENHAM H	WEST HAM U
1 BARNSLEY		N02 1-2	M04 5-1	a13 0-1	S14 3-1	O19 1-1	J27 1-2	a11 2-1	J04 2-0	S28 5-1	D14 3-3	J01 0-3	S09 3-2	N16 2-3	M14 0-2	F19 1-2	A31 4-2	N30 3-2	a25 3-1	M28 0-0	m02 0-0	F08 1-2
2 BLACKPOOL	M21 3-0		F08 4-2	M07 3-3	D26 2-0	J04 2-3	F22 6-2	A31 5-2	N23 1-1	O26 4-1	S28 3-5	D07 4-1	a22 6-0	S04 2-1	S16 1-4	N09 3-1	a18 3-1	O12 3-0	a10 2-1	J29 1-1	a04 2-4	S14 4-1
3 BRADFORD	D07 3-0	O05 3-2		N23 1-1	M07 2-0	a13 1-1	D21 3-0	F26 3-1	N09 1-1	a04 2-1	J01 3-1	O26 1-0	D28 3-2	S21 1-0	F01 1-4	a18 2-2	M21 3-0	S07 3-3	J18 2-1	S16 1-1	F22 2-5	S02 2-0
4 BRADFORD C	a14 1-1	N16 2-1	M28 2-1		S28 0-0	N02 2-0	F08 2-1	M14 3-1	a29 1-0	O12 1-1	m02 2-0	J04 1-0	a01 3-2	N30 0-1	a25 0-0	S09 2-2	S14 1-1	D14 2-1	F29 2-1	O19 2-2	A31 0-1	a11 3-1
5 BURNLEY	J18 3-0	D25 3-2	N16 1-1	F01 3-0		D14 1-1	D28 0-2	M28 1-1	m02 0-2	S07 2-0	a25 2-2	a10 2-2	O05 1-2	a11 1-1	O19 1-0	S21 0-1	S09 5-1	M14 1-1	N02 2-0	N30 5-2	a20 0-0	F29 1-0
6 BURY	F22 3-0	S07 1-1	a10 1-0	M21 1-1	a18 0-4		N23 1-1	J18 5-1	D07 0-0	S21 3-1	O12 3-0	a29 2-3	N09 3-4	D25 0-1	D28 2-6	O26 2-0	a04 5-0	S09 3-2	J01 0-0	F08 2-1	M07 1-1	S28 3-0
7 CHARLTON A	S21 3-0	O19 1-1	a25 3-1	O05 2-1	A31 4-0	M28 5-2		J04 3-0	D26 2-1	J18 4-1	N30 1-0	S09 0-0	F26 4-2	N02 4-1	a11 4-0	F01 1-1	m02 1-1	N16 1-1	M14 2-0	F29 4-1	a13 2-1	D14 2-2
8 DONCASTER R	O26 1-1	D28 0-3	O12 3-2	N09 2-1	N23 1-0	S14 1-0	S07 2-0		a18 0-0	F22 6-1	F08 1-0	a04 0-0	M07 2-2	S16 3-0	D25 0-0	M21 1-2	D07 2-0	a10 0-0	S02 0-1	S28 1-1	D21 2-1	J25 0-2
9 FULHAM	S07 1-1	M28 4-2	M14 4-1	S21 5-1	S18 2-2	M04 7-0	D25 0-0	D14 1-3		D28 3-0	N16 2-0	a01 2-2	F01 3-1	O19 1-1	S02 6-0	J18 2-2	a13 7-0	N02 3-1	a11 0-2	a25 0-1	O05 1-2	N30 4-2
10 HULL C	F01 1-3	a11 0-3	N30 1-1	F20 2-5	J04 1-2	F15 2-3	S14 2-4	O19 2-3	A31 1-1		F29 3-3	m02 1-1	a13 2-3	M14 0-0	N02 2-1	O05 2-1	D26 1-2	a30 2-2	N16 2-2	D14 3-2	S09 1-0	M28 2-3
11 LEICESTER C	a18 2-0	F01 4-1	D25 5-0	S16 2-1	D21 2-0	F20 1-2	a04 4-1	O05 6-0	M07 5-2	D07 2-2		M21 1-1	M19 1-0	J18 1-1	S21 2-1	N23 2-0	N09 2-0	D28 1-3	S07 1-1	S09 4-1	O26 4-1	a13 1-1
12 MANCHESTER U	D26 1-1	F29 3-2	a11 4-0	S07 3-1	a13 4-0	a25 2-1	S04 3-0	N30 0-0	O12 1-0	S18 2-0	N02 0-1		J18 3-1	M28 2-1	D14 5-0	D28 3-2	F08 7-2	O19 3-1	F01 4-0	M14 3-0	S21 0-0	N16 2-3
13 NEWCASTLE U	S04 3-0	a25 1-0	A31 3-3	D26 3-2	F08 1-1	M14 3-0	O12 1-2	N16 2-1	S28 6-2	a10 4-1	O19 3-1	S14 0-2		F29 1-1	N30 5-1	J01 5-0	F05 2-2	M28 3-0	D14 4-1	a11 2-0	J04 1-4	N02 3-3
14 NORWICH C	M07 3-1	S11 0-1	a30 4-1	a04 1-1	O26 2-0	D26 5-3	M21 3-1	m02 2-1	F22 1-0	N09 3-0	S14 1-2	N23 3-5	D07 1-0		a13 4-0	D21 0-0	O12 4-2	S28 0-1	F08 5-1	J04 0-1	a18 1-0	A31 4-3
15 NOTTINGHAM F	N09 6-0	O03 2-2	S28 2-0	D21 1-0	F22 2-0	A31 2-2	O26 0-0	D26 6-2	S11 1-1	M21 0-0	J30 0-1	a18 1-1	a04 1-2	a10 2-2		M07 0-1	N23 9-2	F08 0-1	O12 2-0	S14 2-2	D07 4-1	J04 0-2
16 PLYMOUTH A	O12 7-1	M14 3-2	D14 2-0	S02 0-1	J29 2-0	a11 3-0	S28 4-2	N02 1-3	S14 2-0	F08 0-1	M28 2-1	A31 3-1	m02 1-0	a25 5-1	N16 3-1		J04 4-1	M11 1-1	N30 0-0	a10 1-2	D26 2-1	O19 4-1
17 PORT VALE	D28 0-4	D14 2-2	N02 3-2	J18 2-1	S02 1-1	N30 2-2	S16 2-1	F29 2-0	a10 1-0	M02 4-0	M14 1-1	O05 0-3	S21 3-0	F15 3-1	M28 2-0	S07 2-0		a11 1-1	O19 0-2	N16 0-1	F01 1-5	a25 2-3
18 SHEFFIELD U	a04 2-0	F20 1-0	J04 2-1	a18 3-0	N09 2-0	S02 3-0	M07 2-2	J01 3-0	M26 0-1	D21 7-0	A31 1-2	F22 1-1	N23 5-1	F01 3-2	O05 1-0	D07 0-0	O26 4-0		S21 2-1	D26 4-1	S14 1-1	m02 4-2
19 SOUTHAMPTON	D21 0-1	a13 1-0	S14 3-0	D07 0-0	M21 1-0	S16 0-0	N09 2-5	S09 1-0	O26 1-2	M07 1-0	J04 1-0	S28 2-1	a18 1-3	O05 1-1	F15 7-2	a04 2-0	M30 0-1	F05 0-1		A31 4-3	N23 2-0	D26 2-4
20 SWANSEA T	N23 0-0	S21 1-0	m02 1-2	F22 8-1	a04 1-3	O05 4-1	D07 1-2	F01 2-0	D21 0-2	a18 6-1	S02 2-0	N09 2-1	O26 1-2	S07 4-3	J18 2-1	a13 2-0	M07 3-2	D25 1-3	D28 0-0		M21 1-1	F15 0-1
21 TOTTENHAM H	S16 3-0	N30 3-1	O19 4-0	D28 4-0	O12 5-1	N16 4-3	a10 1-1	a25 3-1	F08 2-2	S02 3-1	a11 1-1	F05 0-0	S07 1-2	D14 2-1	M04 1-1	D25 1-2	S28 5-2	J18 1-1	M28 8-0	N02 7-2		M14 1-3
22 WEST HAM U	O05 2-0	J18 2-1	S09 1-0	O26 1-1	F03 0-0	F01 6-0	a18 1-3	S21 1-2	a04 0-0	N23 4-1	a10 3-2	M07 1-2	M21 4-1	D28 3-2	S07 5-2	F22 4-2	D21 4-0	S16 3-2	D25 0-0	O12 4-0	N09 2-2	

Season 1935-36

DIVISION 3 NORTH

	ACCRINGTON S	BARROW	CARLISLE U	CHESTER	CHESTERFIELD	CREWE A	DARLINGTON	GATESHEAD	HALIFAX T	HARTLEPOOLS U	LINCOLN C	MANSFIELD T	NEW BRIGHTON	OLDHAM A	ROCHDALE	ROTHERHAM U	SOUTHPORT	STOCKPORT CO	TRANMERE R	WALSALL	WREXHAM	YORK C
1 ACCRINGTON S		S21 2-0	M14 0-0	S02 0-3	O05 0-1	D26 2-1	M28 1-0	N16 6-1	J11 2-0	O19 3-2	D28 2-2	a13 1-1	F01 5-2	a11 1-0	S07 2-4	a22 1-1	S24 1-0	F15 1-1	F29 3-1	N02 3-1	D14 0-1	J18 7-2
2 BARROW	J25 0-1		a11 1-1	F08 2-4	A31 1-1	S14 1-1	O19 2-0	m02 3-0	M14 0-0	J23 1-1	O12 0-0	M28 2-2	S02 3-0	N02 3-0	D26 6-2	N16 3-0	S28 0-1	J04 1-0	a25 0-0	a20 1-0	F29 2-1	a13 1-1
3 CARLISLE U	O26 3-1	a30 2-2		N09 1-3	D21 2-1	F22 1-2	A31 3-0	J04 2-0	S12 0-0	O05 0-0	M21 4-1	F15 3-0	a18 3-0	S19 2-1	N23 4-3	J01 1-1	M07 4-0	S28 2-1	S14 0-1	J25 2-1	a10 5-1	a04 0-0
4 CHESTER	S11 4-0	O05 1-2	F29 3-2		D25 1-1	O02 0-1	a11 4-1	J11 4-0	a29 3-1	N02 4-0	a22 4-2	M14 4-0	F15 8-2	S25 1-1	S21 5-2	O19 0-0	A31 5-1	a10 2-0	M28 1-1	N16 2-0	J04 1-1	F01 12-0
5 CHESTERFIELD	F08 0-3	D28 6-1	a25 5-0	D26 1-0		S28 6-0	N02 5-1	M14 2-0	F29 3-1	a27 2-0	a13 0-1	a11 2-1	S07 3-1	N16 3-0	J01 2-2	J11 5-0	O12 5-0	M30 0-0	O19 0-1	J18 3-0	M28 5-0	S02 2-2
6 CREWE A	D25 4-0	J18 3-1	O19 2-0	S18 1-1	F01 5-6		N16 2-0	F29 2-4	M28 3-2	F15 3-2	S02 2-1	a25 1-1	S21 5-1	J29 2-2	D28 3-1	a27 4-1	a10 4-1	O05 0-1	N02 0-0	M14 4-3	a11 3-2	S07 2-1
7 DARLINGTON	N23 2-1	F22 4-1	D28 4-1	D07 1-1	M07 1-2	M21 2-2		J01 5-2	F15 3-2	S07 4-2	a18 1-0	J18 2-1	O26 4-1	O05 5-0	D21 4-0	S21 3-1	a04 3-2	N09 3-1	m02 1-3	S04 1-1	F01 4-2	J02 3-0
8 GATESHEAD	M21 0-0	S18 4-3	S07 1-1	a04 2-0	O26 3-3	N09 2-1	a13 1-1		D25 2-2	F12 1-0	D07 4-0	S21 3-1	F22 3-1	F15 0-0	a18 1-0	F01 1-1	N23 3-1	M07 1-0	S11 1-1	D28 2-2	O05 2-0	D21 0-0
9 HALIFAX T	a04 1-0	O26 3-2	S02 1-0	a18 2-3	N09 2-3	N23 2-4	O12 0-1	D26 1-1		D28 0-1	D21 2-1	S07 1-0	M07 3-0	F01 4-2	O05 2-0	J18 1-0	D07 1-2	M21 0-0	a13 1-0	S16 1-1	S21 4-1	F22 2-0
10 HARTLEPOOLS U	F22 2-1	a04 0-0	F08 1-1	M07 0-2	a18 2-1	O12 1-0	J04 2-1	S14 2-0	A31 1-0		N09 1-1	D25 4-1	D07 4-1	S04 0-1	M21 1-0	a10 5-1	O26 2-1	D21 1-1	J29 2-2	S28 5-0	J01 1-1	N23 4-2
11 LINCOLN C	A31 6-0	F15 2-0	N16 2-0	S14 1-1	a10 0-1	S09 6-2	a20 2-1	a11 5-0	a25 3-1	M18 1-0		N02 1-2	D26 2-0	J25 2-1	F01 5-1	M14 4-0	J04 4-0	S16 3-0	a27 5-0	M28 4-1	O19 3-1	O05 3-2
12 MANSFIELD T	a10 3-1	N23 1-3	O12 1-1	O26 0-0	D07 0-1	D21 1-1	S14 4-2	a14 3-1	J04 3-2	D26 4-0	M07 2-2		a04 2-0	A31 1-0	N09 3-0	m02 8-2	F22 5-1	a18 2-1	S28 2-3	F08 2-2	S11 3-2	M21 5-0
13 NEW BRIGHTON	S28 2-3	S11 2-3	D14 3-0	O12 3-3	J04 1-2	J25 3-1	M14 1-1	O19 1-0	N02 1-4	a11 0-0	J01 0-5	J11 1-0		F29 1-3	a10 2-0	M28 3-0	F08 2-1	S14 2-0	A31 0-0	a25 1-1	N16 0-4	m02 0-2
14 OLDHAM A	D07 3-0	M07 3-1	m02 3-0	F25 1-3	M21 0-0	a04 0-0	F08 2-0	O12 2-2	S28 3-0	S09 2-2	S21 2-3	D28 4-1	N09 6-0		F22 3-3	S07 4-1	a18 4-0	N23 1-3	D25 4-1	a13 2-1	J18 5-2	O26 6-2
15 ROCHDALE	J04 2-2	D25 1-1	M28 0-0	J25 1-1	m02 1-1	A31 2-1	a25 1-1	D14 5-0	F08 2-0	N16 0-1	S28 0-0	F29 3-1	a13 1-0	O19 2-6		N02 1-1	S14 2-1	S10 1-1	a11 0-0	M31 6-4	M14 2-1	F15 2-3
16 ROTHERHAM U	D21 1-3	M21 1-0	D26 4-0	F22 1-2	a04 0-0	a18 3-1	J25 4-0	S28 3-0	S14 2-0	a13 3-0	O26 1-1	S16 2-1	N23 5-0	J04 1-0	M07 6-0		S09 5-0	D07 1-1	F08 1-2	O12 2-0	A31 1-2	N09 5-0
17 SOUTHPORT	m02 2-1	F01 3-1	N02 0-3	D28 2-1	F15 1-0	J01 1-1	J14 4-1	M28 1-1	a11 2-0	M14 1-1	S07 0-3	O19 3-3	O05 2-1	J11 1-1	J18 1-1	S03 2-1		D25 2-3	N16 1-1	F29 1-0	a25 1-1	S21 0-1
18 STOCKPORT CO	O12 1-2	S07 2-1	F01 2-0	a13 2-0	S21 2-2	F08 0-1	F29 2-0	N02 3-1	N16 1-0	a25 2-1	m02 4-0	D14 6-1	J18 1-1	M28 2-0	S02 4-0	a11 1-2	D26 2-0		M14 2-1	O19 0-1	S23 3-2	D28 3-2
19 TRANMERE R	N09 6-0	D21 1-0	J18 4-1	N23 3-1	F22 1-3	M07 4-2	S16 2-0	S02 2-0	a10 0-2	S21 3-1	a04 1-1	F01 4-2	D28 3-1	D26 13-4	D07 5-2	O05 2-2	M21 5-2	O26 4-1		S07 3-1	F15 6-1	a18 3-1
20 WALSALL	M07 2-0	a18 5-1	S21 3-0	M21 1-0	S14 1-1	O26 4-1	S09 4-1	A31 2-0	m02 2-1	F01 6-0	N23 4-1	O05 7-0	D21 1-2	a10 1-2	a04 1-0	F15 0-1	N09 3-1	a14 0-1	J04 0-0		D25 5-0	D07 6-0
21 WREXHAM	a18 3-0	N09 2-0	a13 1-1	S07 1-0	N23 0-1	D07 0-1	S28 3-1	F08 2-4	M11 1-3	S18 1-0	F22 1-1	S04 5-1	M21 3-0	S14 0-1	O26 0-1	D28 2-0	D21 4-2	a04 4-0	O12 4-0	D26 1-1		M07 1-0
22 YORK C	S14 1-1	a10 1-2	J11 2-0	S28 1-2	S11 1-1	J04 4-1	D26 4-1	a25 2-2	O19 2-2	M28 2-2	F08 2-1	N16 7-5	S18 2-0	M14 3-1	O12 2-1	F29 2-1	M18 0-0	A31 0-4	a22 2-0	a11 0-0	N02 1-1	

DIVISION 3 SOUTH

	ALDERSHOT	BOURNEMOUTH	BRIGHTON & HA	BRISTOL C	BRISTOL R	CARDIFF C	CLAPTON O	COVENTRY C	CRYSTAL P	EXETER C	GILLINGHAM	LUTON T	MILLWALL	NEWPORT CO	NORTHAMPTON T	NOTTS CO	Q.P.R.	READING	SOUTHEND U	SWINDON T	TORQUAY U	WATFORD
1 ALDERSHOT		M21 2-0	S07 1-0	F01 0-0	D07 6-1	a18 1-1	M07 1-0	D26 1-2	F22 1-3	D28 3-0	D21 0-2	N23 0-1	O05 1-1	a10 1-1	S02 2-0	a04 3-1	J18 1-3	O26 1-0	N09 1-1	S18 1-3	F15 1-0	S21 1-1
2 BOURNEMOUTH	N16 0-0		F15 1-2	a11 3-0	D26 2-1	F01 4-4	a13 2-0	N02 1-1	J18 2-5	O19 1-1	O05 1-2	S04 2-1	J22 1-2	M14 2-0	S07 4-0	m02 0-1	F29 0-1	S21 4-1	D28 2-1	a25 1-0	M28 1-1	a22 2-2
3 BRIGHTON & H.A.	J04 2-1	O12 0-1		D25 3-0	a18 4-1	M07 1-0	D21 1-3	J25 2-1	a04 2-1	F08 3-1	N09 1-1	F22 1-1	a13 0-0	S28 7-1	N23 5-1	O26 5-1	S04 1-1	D07 4-2	M21 1-3	S14 0-2	A31 3-2	S18 2-1
4 BRISTOL C	S28 1-0	D07 1-0	D26 0-3		S07 0-2	N23 0-2	F22 2-0	O12 0-0	a29 2-0	m02 2-1	a04 2-1	M07 1-2	S14 4-1	S04 1-2	a18 3-2	N09 1-1	a13 0-0	M21 1-1	O26 2-1	F08 5-0	J25 2-0	a01 2-2
5 BRISTOL R	a11 2-2	D25 2-1	N02 5-2	J04 1-1		S11 1-1	J18 1-1	M28 3-2	O05 2-4	a25 6-1	S18 4-3	a10 2-2	F29 2-0	N16 3-0	F01 5-2	A31 0-0	M14 0-1	F15 1-4	S21 3-2	J15 2-1	a14 3-0	O19 0-1
6 CARDIFF C	N02 0-1	S28 1-1	M18 1-0	M28 1-0	S02 0-0		S16 4-1	O19 1-0	D28 1-1	F29 5-2	J25 4-0	F08 2-3	N16 3-1	J18 2-0	a10 0-0	O12 3-2	a11 3-2	S07 2-3	D26 1-1	M14 2-1	a25 1-2	J15 0-2
7 CLAPTON O	a23 0-1	a10 1-1	a25 3-1	O19 2-0	S14 2-0	m02 2-1		J16 0-1	F26 1-0	N16 1-2	D25 3-1	A31 3-0	a02 1-0	M28 4-0	O05 4-0	J04 0-2	N02 1-0	S05 1-0	F01 3-0	a11 1-2	F29 1-1	M14 0-2
8 COVENTRY C	D25 0-2	a18 2-0	S21 5-0	F15 3-1	N23 3-1	F22 5-1	a04 2-0		N09 8-1	J18 3-0	O26 4-0	a27 0-0	S09 5-0	S07 7-1	M07 4-0	M21 5-1	F01 6-1	D28 3-1	D07 3-0	a14 3-1	m02 2-1	O05 2-0
9 CRYSTAL P	O19 2-1	S14 2-0	J15 4-0	a25 6-1	F08 5-3	A31 3-2	O12 2-2	F29 3-1		a11 2-2	J04 1-1	J29 5-1	N02 5-0	D18 6-0	S23 6-1	S28 0-0	M28 0-2	a10 2-0	S11 3-0	D26 5-1	M14 1-0	N16 1-2
10 EXETER C	A31 5-1	F22 1-3	O05 3-3	S18 0-1	D21 3-1	N09 2-0	M21 2-3	S14 1-3	D07 1-0		S28 2-5	O26 1-2	D26 4-3	J25 3-3	a04 3-1	a18 0-0	F15 0-0	M07 4-5	N23 1-0	J04 0-3	a13 1-1	S04 1-3
11 GILLINGHAM	a25 4-2	F08 1-2	F29 1-2	J11 2-1	m02 1-2	S21 3-0	D26 3-0	M14 1-1	S07 0-2	F01 2-2		O12 0-1	M28 1-3	O19 3-0	D28 2-3	S11 0-0	a22 2-2	J18 2-0	a10 2-1	N02 3-1	N16 1-0	a11 0-0
12 LUTON T	M28 2-2	S09 0-0	O19 2-1	D14 1-0	a13 12-0	O05 2-2	D28 5-3	a25 1-1	S21 6-0	M14 3-1	F15 1-2		a11 0-0	N02 7-0	J18 3-3	D26 1-0	S16 2-0	F01 2-1	S07 1-2	N16 2-1	M25 1-0	F29 2-1
13 MILLWALL	F08 1-2	a04 3-0	a10 0-0	J18 1-1	N09 2-1	M21 2-4	S21 1-0	S02 2-2	a18 4-0	D25 2-2	N23 4-1	D07 0-0		S16 2-2	O26 2-1	M07 2-1	D28 2-0	D21 0-1	F22 1-2	O12 1-0	S28 1-1	S07 0-0
14 NEWPORT CO	a13 1-1	O26 0-0	F01 0-2	S09 2-0	M21 1-0	S14 0-0	N23 2-3	J04 2-1	M07 2-5	S21 2-1	M19 4-2	a18 0-2	m02 4-1		D07 5-1	F27 1-2	O05 3-4	N09 1-5	a04 3-1	A31 2-2	D25 1-6	F15 0-5
15 NORTHAMPTON T	S09 3-0	J04 2-1	M28 1-0	N02 0-2	S28 3-3	a13 2-0	F08 2-0	D14 2-4	S16 3-1	J11 1-1	A31 0-0	S14 0-0	M14 2-4	a11 3-0		J25 3-1	N16 1-4	D25 4-2	O12 2-0	F29 0-0	O19 2-1	a25 2-0
16 NOTTS CO	F12 1-2	S18 1-3	M14 1-1	F29 1-1	D28 6-0	F15 2-0	S07 2-0	N16 2-1	F01 3-1	N02 3-1	S04 3-3	D25 0-3	D18 0-0	a25 6-2	S21 3-0		O19 3-0	O05 1-3	J18 1-2	M28 0-0	a11 1-0	a13 0-2
17 Q.P.R.	S14 5-0	N09 2-0	S12 3-2	a10 4-1	O26 4-0	D07 5-1	a18 4-0	S28 0-0	N23 3-0	O12 3-1	M07 5-2	m02 0-0	A31 2-3	F08 1-1	M21 0-1	F22 2-2		a04 0-1	D21 2-1	J25 5-1	J04 2-1	D25 3-1
18 READING	M14 3-1	J25 0-2	a11 3-0	N16 5-2	O12 3-2	J04 4-1	S11 4-1	A31 2-1	a13 0-1	M18 2-0	S14 1-0	S28 2-1	a25 3-1	F29 2-1	D26 5-2	F08 3-1	J15 1-2		m02 2-1	O19 2-0	N02 2-0	M28 3-0
19 SOUTHEND U	F29 2-2	A31 3-3	N16 0-0	M14 0-1	J25 1-1	D25 3-1	S28 2-1	a11 0-0	S04 7-1	M28 4-0	a13 4-2	J04 0-1	O19 6-0	J22 1-2	a22 0-1	S14 0-0	a25 0-1	S18 1-2		a29 1-0	F08 2-1	N02 1-1
20 SWINDON T	m02 3-2	D21 2-3	J18 1-2	O05 1-1	a04 3-0	O26 2-1	D07 2-2	a13 1-2	D25 0-2	S07 1-1	a18 3-0	M21 3-0	F15 3-1	D28 1-1	N09 3-1	N23 2-1	S21 2-2	F22 4-1	M07 1-3		S04 4-1	F01 1-6
21 TORQUAY U	O12 3-1	N23 0-2	D28 1-0	S21 2-0	M07 2-0	J11 2-1	N09 1-0	S18 3-3	O26 3-2	S25 2-1	M21 4-2	a04 2-1	F01 1-3	D26 3-2	F22 3-3	D07 0-1	S07 4-2	a18 0-0	O05 1-1	S11 2-1		J18 2-1
22 WATFORD	J29 0-0	M07 4-1	m02 2-1	A31 0-2	F22 1-2	a04 4-0	O26 1-1	F08 5-0	M21 3-2	S11 1-0	D07 1-2	N09 1-3	J04 2-1	O12 2-5	D21 4-1	a10 1-2	D26 2-1	N23 4-2	a18 5-0	S28 2-1	S14 2-2	

LEAGUE TABLES

DIVISION 1

	P	W	D	L	F	A	W	D	L	F	A	Pts
Sunderland	42	17	2	2	71	33	8	4	9	38	41	56
Derby Co	42	13	5	3	43	23	5	7	9	18	29	48
Huddersfield T	42	12	7	2	32	15	6	5	10	27	41	48
Stoke C	42	13	3	5	35	24	7	4	10	22	33	47
Brentford	42	11	5	5	48	25	6	7	8	33	35	46
Arsenal	42	9	9	3	44	22	6	6	9	34	26	45
Preston N.E.	42	15	3	3	44	18	3	5	13	23	46	44
Chelsea	42	11	7	3	39	27	4	6	11	26	45	43
Manchester C	42	13	2	6	44	17	4	6	11	24	43	42
Portsmouth	42	14	4	3	39	22	3	4	14	15	45	42
Leeds U	42	11	5	5	41	23	4	6	11	25	41	41
Birmingham C	42	10	6	5	38	31	5	5	11	23	32	41
Bolton W	42	11	4	6	41	27	3	9	9	26	49	41
Middlesbrough	42	12	6	3	56	23	3	4	14	28	47	40
Wolverhampton W	42	13	7	1	59	28	2	3	16	18	48	40
Everton	42	12	5	4	61	31	1	8	12	28	58	39
Grimsby T	42	13	4	4	44	20	4	1	16	21	53	39
W.B.A.	42	12	3	6	54	31	4	3	14	35	57	38
Liverpool	42	11	4	6	43	23	2	8	11	17	41	38
Sheffield W	42	9	8	4	35	23	4	4	13	28	54	38
Aston Villa	42	7	6	8	47	56	6	3	12	34	54	35
Blackburn R	42	10	6	5	32	24	2	3	16	23	72	33

DIVISION 2

	P	W	D	L	F	A	W	D	L	F	A	Pts
Manchester U	42	16	3	2	55	16	6	9	6	30	27	56
Charlton A	42	15	6	0	53	17	7	5	9	32	41	55
Sheffield U	42	15	4	2	51	15	5	8	8	28	35	52
West Ham U	42	13	5	3	51	23	9	3	9	39	45	52
Tottenham H	42	12	6	3	60	25	6	7	8	31	30	49
Leicester C	42	14	5	2	53	19	5	5	11	26	38	48
Plymouth A	42	15	2	4	50	20	5	6	10	21	37	48
Newcastle U	42	13	5	3	56	27	7	1	13	32	52	46
Fulham	42	11	6	4	58	24	4	8	9	18	28	44
Blackpool	42	14	3	4	64	34	4	4	13	29	38	43
Norwich C	42	14	2	5	47	24	3	7	11	25	41	43
Bradford C	42	12	7	2	32	18	3	6	12	23	47	43
Swansea T	42	11	3	7	42	26	4	6	11	25	50	39
Bury	42	10	6	5	41	27	3	6	12	25	57	38
Burnley	42	9	8	4	35	21	3	5	13	15	38	37
Bradford P.A.	42	13	6	2	43	26	1	3	17	19	58	37
Southampton	42	11	3	7	32	24	3	6	12	15	41	37
Doncaster R	42	10	7	4	28	17	4	2	15	23	54	37
Nottingham F	42	8	8	5	43	22	4	3	14	26	54	35
Barnsley	42	9	4	8	40	32	3	5	13	14	48	33
Port Vale	42	10	5	6	34	30	2	3	16	22	76	32
Hull C	42	4	7	10	33	45	1	3	17	14	66	20

DIVISION 3 NORTH

	P	W	D	L	F	A	W	D	L	F	A	Pts
Chesterfield	42	15	3	3	60	14	9	9	3	32	25	60
Chester C	42	14	5	2	69	18	8	6	7	31	27	55
Tranmere R	42	17	2	2	75	28	5	9	7	18	30	55
Lincoln C	42	18	1	2	64	14	4	8	9	27	37	53
Stockport Co	42	15	2	4	45	18	5	6	10	20	31	48
Crewe A	42	14	4	3	55	31	5	5	11	25	45	47
Oldham A	42	13	5	3	60	25	5	4	12	26	48	45
Hartlepool U	42	13	6	2	41	18	2	6	13	16	43	42
Accrington S	42	12	5	4	43	24	5	3	13	20	48	42
Walsall	42	15	2	4	58	13	1	7	13	21	46	41
Rotherham U	42	14	3	4	52	13	2	6	13	17	53	41
Darlington	42	16	3	2	60	26	1	3	17	14	53	40
Carlisle U	42	13	5	3	44	19	1	7	13	12	43	40
Gateshead	42	11	10	0	37	18	2	4	15	19	58	40
Barrow	42	9	9	3	33	16	4	3	14	25	49	38
York C	42	10	8	3	41	28	3	4	14	21	67	38
Halifax T	42	12	3	6	34	22	3	4	14	23	39	37
Wrexham	42	12	3	6	39	18	3	4	14	27	57	37
Mansfield T	42	13	5	3	55	25	1	4	16	25	66	37
Rochdale	42	8	10	3	35	26	2	3	16	23	62	33
Southport	42	9	8	4	31	26	2	1	18	17	64	31
New Brighton	42	8	5	8	29	33	1	1	19	14	69	24

DIVISION 3 SOUTH

	P	W	D	L	F	A	W	D	L	F	A	Pts
Coventry C	42	19	1	1	75	12	5	8	8	27	33	57
Luton T	42	13	6	2	56	20	9	6	6	25	25	56
Reading	42	18	0	3	52	20	8	2	11	35	42	54
Q.P.R.	42	14	4	3	55	19	8	5	8	29	34	53
Watford	42	12	3	6	47	29	8	6	7	33	25	49
Crystal Palace	42	15	4	2	64	20	7	1	13	32	54	49
Brighton & H.A.	42	13	4	4	48	25	5	4	12	22	38	44
Bournemouth	42	9	6	6	36	26	7	5	9	24	30	43
Notts Co	42	10	5	6	40	25	5	7	9	20	32	42
Torquay U	42	14	4	3	41	27	2	5	14	21	35	41
Aldershot	42	9	6	6	29	21	5	6	10	24	40	40
Millwall	42	9	8	4	33	21	5	4	12	25	50	40
Bristol C	42	11	5	5	32	21	4	5	12	16	38	40
Clapton O	42	13	2	6	34	15	3	4	14	21	46	38
Northampton T	42	12	5	4	38	24	3	3	15	24	66	38
Gillingham	42	9	5	7	34	25	5	4	12	32	52	37
Bristol R	42	11	6	4	48	31	3	3	15	21	64	37
Southend U	42	8	7	6	38	21	5	3	13	23	41	36
Swindon T	42	10	5	6	43	33	4	3	14	21	40	36
Cardiff C	42	11	5	5	37	23	2	5	14	23	50	36
Newport Co	42	8	4	9	36	44	3	5	13	24	67	31
Exeter C	42	7	5	9	38	41	1	6	14	21	52	27

Football League Records

Top scorers: Div 1, F.Steel (Stoke City) 33 goals; Div 2, J.Bowers (Leicester City) 33 goals; Div 3 N, E.Harston (Mansfield Town) 55 goals; Div 3 S, J.Payne (Luton Town) 55 goals.

Walsall transferred to Division Three South.

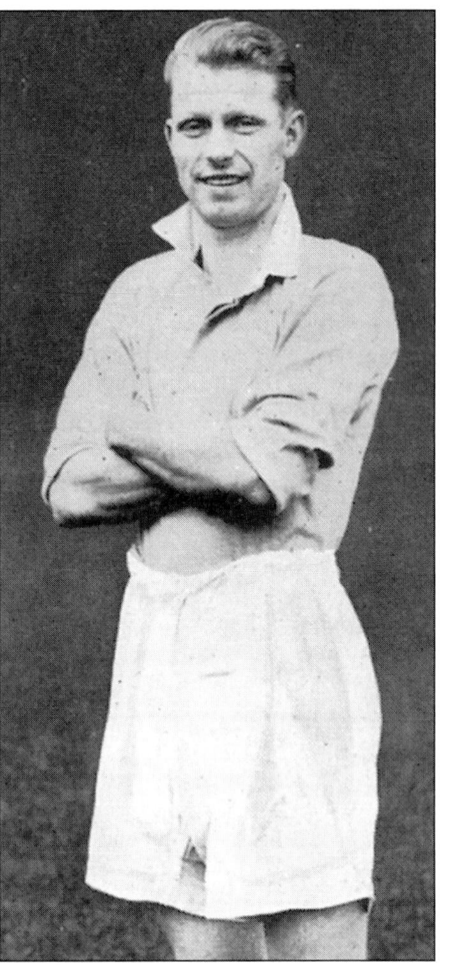

Irish international Peter Doherty, who netted 30 goals when Manchester City won the League Championship. Astonishingly, City were relegated 12 months later.

DIVISION 1

	ARSENAL	BIRMINGHAM	BOLTON W	BRENTFORD	CHARLTON A	CHELSEA	DERBY CO	EVERTON	GRIMSBY T	HUDDERSFIELD T	LEEDS U	LIVERPOOL	MANCHESTER C	MANCHESTER U	MIDDLESBROUGH	PORTSMOUTH	PRESTON N.E.	SHEFFIELD W	STOKE C	SUNDERLAND	W.B.A.	WOLVERHAMPTON W
1 ARSENAL		M20 1-1	m01 0-0	S09 1-1	F24 1-1	D19 4-1	S26 2-2	A29 3-2	O24 0-0	J02 1-1	N07 4-1	M10 1-0	D05 1-3	F06 1-1	N21 5-3	a17 4-0	D25 4-1	O10 1-1	M26 0-0	S12 4-1	a03 2-0	J23 3-0
2 BIRMINGHAM	N14 1-3		O31 1-1	M13 4-0	J23 1-2	J02 0-0	D12 0-1	F27 2-0	S26 2-3	O17 4-2	O10 2-1	F06 5-0	m01 2-2	a10 2-2	M29 0-0	A29 2-1	M27 1-0	N28 1-1	S12 2-4	D25 2-0	S09 1-1	a24 1-0
3 BOLTON W	J01 0-5	M06 0-0		D26 2-2	D19 2-1	D05 2-1	O10 1-3	S12 1-2	S05 1-2	J23 2-2	O24 2-1	F24 0-1	N21 0-2	D28 0-4	N07 1-3	a03 1-0	S07 0-0	M26 1-0	a17 0-0	S26 1-1	M20 4-1	F06 1-2
4 BRENTFORD	S03 2-0	N07 2-1	A29 2-2		S17 4-2	a17 1-0	F06 6-2	J02 2-2	M03 2-3	S12 1-1	M06 4-1	O24 5-2	a03 2-6	O10 4-0	M20 4-1	D05 4-0	M26 1-1	D25 2-1	D19 2-1	J23 3-3	N21 2-1	S26 3-2
5 CHARLTON A	O17 0-2	S19 2-2	a24 1-0	m01 2-1		M29 1-0	N14 2-0	D12 2-0	D26 1-0	a10 1-0	J09 1-0	S05 1-1	F13 1-1	M13 3-0	J30 2-2	D25 0-0	F27 3-1	O31 1-0	S07 2-0	N28 3-1	O03 4-2	M27 4-0
6 CHELSEA	a24 2-0	S05 1-3	a10 0-1	D12 2-1	M26 3-0		O31 1-1	N28 4-0	S02 3-2	M27 0-0	D26 2-1	S16 2-0	F03 4-4	F27 4-2	J09 1-0	O03 1-1	F13 0-0	O17 1-1	D28 1-0	N14 1-3	S19 3-0	M13 0-1
7 DERBY CO	F03 5-4	a17 3-1	F13 3-0	O03 2-3	M20 5-0	M06 1-1		D28 3-1	N21 3-1	M29 3-3	D05 5-3	a03 4-1	F24 0-5	S05 5-4	D19 0-2	O24 1-3	S19 1-2	J09 3-2	N07 2-2	S09 3-0	D26 1-0	S23 5-1
8 EVERTON	D26 1-1	O24 3-3	J09 3-2	S05 3-0	a17 2-2	a03 0-0	D25 7-0		D19 3-0	S26 2-1	M03 7-1	S19 2-0	M20 1-1	M29 2-3	M06 2-3	N21 4-0	J01 2-2	S02 3-1	D05 1-1	F06 3-0	N07 4-2	O10 1-0
9 GRIMSBY T	F27 1-3	F02 1-1	J02 3-1	O17 2-0	A29 0-1	S08 3-0	M27 3-4	a24 1-0		D12 2-2	S19 4-1	J09 2-1	D25 5-3	N14 6-2	O03 5-1	M26 1-0	O31 6-4	M13 5-1	m01 1-3	a12 6-0	F13 2-3	N28 1-1
10 HUDDERSFIELD T	S05 0-0	F20 1-1	S19 2-0	J09 1-1	D05 1-2	N21 4-2	M30 2-0	F03 0-3	a17 0-3		O03 3-0	D19 4-0	N07 1-1	S02 3-1	O24 2-0	M20 1-2	D26 4-2	m01 1-0	a03 2-1	O10 2-1	M10 1-1	D28 4-0
11 LEEDS U	M13 3-4	F13 0-2	F27 2-2	O31 3-1	S12 2-0	A29 2-3	a10 2-0	O17 3-0	J23 2-0	F06 2-1		S26 2-0	S09 1-1	N28 2-1	D25 5-0	m01 3-1	N14 1-0	M27 1-1	J02 2-1	a24 3-0	M30 3-1	a21 0-1
12 LIVERPOOL	O31 2-1	O03 2-0	O17 0-0	F27 2-2	J02 1-2	m01 1-1	N28 3-3	J23 3-2	S12 7-1	a24 1-1	J30 3-0		M26 0-5	M27 2-0	F13 0-2	S09 0-0	M13 1-1	N14 2-2	A29 2-1	D12 4-0	D28 1-2	a10 1-0
13 MANCHESTER C	a10 2-0	S16 1-1	M27 2-2	a07 2-1	O10 1-1	S26 0-0	O17 3-2	N14 4-1	D28 1-1	M13 3-0	S02 4-0	M29 5-1		J09 1-0	D26 2-1	J23 3-1	D12 4-1	a24 4-1	F06 2-1	O31 2-4	S05 6-2	F27 4-1
14 MANCHESTER U	O03 2-0	D05 1-2	D25 1-0	F13 1-3	N07 0-0	O24 0-0	J02 2-2	M26 2-1	M20 1-1	S09 3-1	a03 0-0	N21 2-5	S12 3-2		a17 2-1	F20 0-1	F03 1-1	S19 1-1	M06 2-1	J01 2-1	D19 2-2	A29 1-1
15 MIDDLESBROUGH	M27 1-1	M26 3-1	M13 2-0	N14 3-0	S26 1-1	S12 2-0	a24 1-3	O31 2-0	F06 0-0	F27 5-0	D28 4-2	O10 3-3	A29 2-0	D12 3-2		J02 2-2	N28 2-1	a10 2-0	J23 1-0	O17 5-5	J01 4-1	S09 1-0
16 PORTSMOUTH	D12 1-5	D26 2-1	N28 1-1	a10 1-3	D28 0-1	F06 4-1	F27 1-2	M27 2-2	M29 2-1	N14 1-0	S16 3-0	S02 6-2	S19 2-1	O17 2-1	S05 2-1		a24 0-1	F03 1-0	O10 1-0	M13 3-2	J09 5-3	O31 1-1
17 PRESTON N.E.	D28 1-3	N21 2-2	A31 1-2	M29 1-1	O24 0-0	O10 1-0	J23 5-2	a14 1-0	M10 3-2	A29 1-1	M20 1-0	N07 3-1	a17 2-5	S26 3-1	a03 2-0	D19 1-1		F06 1-1	F24 0-1	J02 2-0	D05 3-2	S12 1-3
18 SHEFFIELD W	F13 0-0	a03 0-3	M29 2-0	D28 0-2	M06 3-1	F20 1-1	S12 2-3	S10 6-4	N07 2-1	S17 2-2	N21 1-2	M20 1-2	D19 5-1	J23 1-0	D05 1-0	S26 0-0	O03 0-1		O24 0-0	A29 2-0	a17 2-3	J02 1-3
19 STOKE C	M29 0-0	J09 2-0	D12 2-2	a24 5-1	A31 1-1	D25 2-0	M13 1-2	a10 2-1	S14 2-0	N28 1-1	S05 2-1	D26 1-1	O03 2-2	O31 3-0	S19 6-2	F13 2-4	O17 0-2	a05 1-0		M27 5-3	F04 10-3	N14 2-1
20 SUNDERLAND	J09 1-1	D28 4-0	F10 3-0	S19 4-1	a03 1-0	M20 2-3	S02 3-2	O03 3-1	D05 5-1	F13 3-2	D19 2-1	a17 4-2	a14 1-3	a21 1-1	F24 4-1	N07 3-2	S05 3-0	D26 2-1	N21 3-0		O24 1-0	M26 6-2
21 W.B.A.	N28 2-4	S02 3-2	N14 0-2	M27 1-0	F06 1-2	J23 2-0	A29 1-3	M13 2-1	O10 4-2	O31 2-1	M29 3-0	D25 3-1	J02 2-2	a24 1-0	m01 3-1	S12 3-1	M22 0-0	a21 2-3	S26 2-2	F27 6-4		O17 2-1
22 WOLVERHAMPTON W	S19 2-0	D19 2-1	O03 2-3	F10 4-0	N21 6-1	N07 1-2	m01 3-1	F13 7-2	a03 5-2	D25 3-1	a17 3-0	D05 2-0	O24 2-1	D26 3-1	A31 0-1	M17 1-1	J09 5-0	S05 4-3	M20 2-1	M29 1-1	a14 5-2	

Left winger Eric Brook, City's second-highest scorer behind Doherty with 20 goals.

DIVISION 2

	ASTON VILLA	BARNSLEY	BLACKBURN R	BLACKPOOL	BRADFORD	BRADFORD C	BURNLEY	BURY	CHESTERFIELD	COVENTRY C	DONCASTER R	FULHAM	LEICESTER C	NEWCASTLE U	NORWICH C	NOTTINGHAM F	PLYMOUTH A	SHEFFIELD U	SOUTHAMPTON	SWANSEA T	TOTTENHAM H	WEST HAM U
1 ASTON VILLA		O24 4-2	N21 2-2	M20 4-0	F20 4-1	S14 5-1	J09 0-0	a03 0-4	D28 6-2	O03 0-0	J30 1-1	S19 0-3	D05 1-3	M30 0-2	D19 3-0	S07 1-1	F13 5-4	M06 2-1	S05 4-0	D26 4-0	N07 1-1	a17 0-2
2 BARNSLEY	F27 0-4		O10 3-2	F06 2-1	S05 2-1	O17 1-1	D12 1-1	A31 2-2	O31 1-1	M27 3-0	N28 4-1	a10 1-0	D28 1-2	D26 1-0	S14 2-1	M13 1-0	N14 1-3	J23 1-1	a24 2-1	J09 0-1	S26 1-0	M29 0-0
3 BLACKBURN R	M27 3-4	F13 1-1		M29 2-0	O03 1-1	N14 3-0	F27 3-1	D26 2-3	N28 5-2	a24 2-5	J01 2-0	O17 0-2	S05 0-0	J30 6-1	S19 1-0	a10 9-1	D12 2-3	S21 3-1	O31 1-0	M13 2-1	D25 0-4	J09 1-2
4 BLACKPOOL	N14 2-3	O03 1-1	M26 2-0		J30 6-0	M13 4-2	O17 2-0	S14 1-2	M27 0-1	D12 3-0	a24 1-1	D28 3-1	D26 6-2	S19 3-0	J09 0-2	N28 7-1	a10 1-1	F13 1-0	F27 2-0	O31 3-2	A31 0-0	S05 1-0
5 BRADFORD	O17 3-3	J02 2-1	F06 1-2	S26 2-1		A29 2-1	a10 2-0	O10 0-1	F27 4-5	N14 1-3	M27 1-0	N28 1-1	S09 1-2	S14 0-3	M30 1-0	O31 3-2	M13 0-0	S12 0-3	D12 3-1	a24 1-1	J23 3-2	D25 2-1
6 BRADFORD C	N11 2-2	F20 3-2	M20 2-2	N07 1-4	D26 2-3		S19 1-3	N21 0-1	M29 2-2	F13 1-0	O03 0-0	J30 1-1	a03 1-2	D19 2-0	a17 2-0	D28 2-1	A31 1-1	O24 3-2	J09 2-2	S05 4-0	M10 2-2	D05 2-1
7 BURNLEY	S12 1-2	a17 3-0	O24 0-0	F24 3-0	D05 2-2	J23 3-0		M06 1-2	J02 3-1	M26 3-3	D25 3-0	S07 0-2	N07 0-0	a03 0-3	N21 3-0	A29 3-0	S14 2-0	D19 1-0	F06 1-3	S26 0-0	O10 3-1	M20 2-1
8 BURY	N28 2-1	S09 2-1	A29 1-1	J01 2-3	F13 3-1	M27 5-0	O31 3-1		a10 4-0	J02 0-4	O17 4-2	F27 1-1	J09 0-1	O03 1-2	F10 3-2	D12 1-1	a24 2-0	D28 2-0	M13 2-1	N14 2-0	M26 5-3	S19 1-1
9 CHESTERFIELD	D25 1-0	M06 2-1	a03 0-4	N21 0-4	O24 4-2	M26 7-1	S05 4-1	D05 1-1		F03 2-3	S19 5-1	J09 4-1	a17 2-5	F20 4-0	A31 3-1	F13 4-2	O03 0-1	N07 2-2	D26 3-0	J01 4-0	M20 1-3	D19 1-1
10 COVENTRY C	F06 1-0	N21 3-0	D19 0-1	a17 1-2	M20 4-0	O10 3-1	M30 0-1	S05 1-3	S26 2-1		D26 1-1	S14 1-1	F25 0-2	N07 2-2	M06 1-1	J23 2-2	S12 2-0	a03 2-0	D25 2-0	A31 2-1	D05 1-0	O24 4-0
11 DONCASTER R	S26 1-0	a03 0-1	m01 0-1	D19 0-4	N21 1-3	F06 1-1	D28 2-0	F20 1-0	J23 0-4	A29 1-1		M26 2-1	O24 0-0	M20 1-2	N07 1-2	S12 0-2	J02 2-1	D05 1-1	A31 2-0	O10 0-0	a17 1-1	M06 1-4
12 FULHAM	J23 3-2	D05 1-0	F20 1-1	D25 0-3	a03 0-0	S26 0-1	S21 2-0	O24 1-1	S12 1-0	m01 0-2	M29 1-0		M06 2-0	N21 3-4	M20 2-3	J02 5-2	A29 2-2	a17 4-0	O10 2-0	F06 5-0	D19 3-3	N07 5-0
13 LEICESTER C	a10 1-0	D25 5-1	J02 1-0	A29 1-2	A31 5-0	N28 4-1	M13 7-3	S12 0-3	D12 3-1	O17 1-0	F27 7-1	O31 2-0		F13 3-2	O03 2-2	a24 2-1	J23 3-2	M29 1-2	N14 2-2	M27 0-0	m01 4-1	F04 2-2
14 NEWCASTLE U	M26 0-2	A29 0-1	S26 2-0	J23 1-2	J01 1-1	a24 2-0	N28 3-0	F06 1-3	O17 1-2	M13 4-2	N14 7-0	M27 1-1	O10 1-0		D25 0-1	M17 3-2	O31 1-1	J02 4-0	a10 3-0	D12 5-1	S12 0-1	S09 5-3
15 NORWICH C	a24 5-1	m01 0-1	J23 0-0	S12 1-2	M29 3-1	D12 0-0	M27 2-2	S26 0-0	S09 2-0	O31 0-3	M13 2-1	N14 3-0	F06 1-2	D28 1-5		O17 4-0	F27 1-2	A29 1-1	N28 4-2	a10 3-0	J02 2-3	O10 3-3
16 NOTTINGHAM F	S02 1-1	N07 4-1	D05 2-0	a03 1-1	M06 3-2	D25 2-1	D26 1-2	a17 1-0	O10 2-2	S19 1-1	J09 2-1	S05 5-3	D19 0-3	O24 0-2	F20 3-4		F03 2-3	M20 1-1	S16 1-1	M29 6-1	a21 3-0	O03 1-0
17 PLYMOUTH A	O10 2-2	M20 1-2	a17 2-0	D05 1-3	N07 2-0	S09 4-4	m01 0-1	D19 3-0	F06 1-1	J09 1-0	S05 7-0	D26 0-3	S19 2-1	M06 1-1	O24 2-0	S26 4-1		N21 2-0	M26 3-1	D25 0-0	a03 2-2	F20 2-0
18 SHEFFIELD U	O31 5-1	S19 2-0	A31 0-1	O10 2-2	J09 3-0	F27 3-1	a24 1-1	D25 1-0	M13 5-0	N28 2-2	a10 3-1	D12 2-0	J01 3-1	S05 2-1	D26 2-0	N14 4-1	M27 2-0		F11 0-0	O17 1-0	F06 3-2	S14 2-0
19 SOUTHAMPTON	J02 2-2	D19 1-3	M06 2-2	O24 5-2	a17 0-0	S12 2-0	O03 1-1	N07 4-1	A29 3-2	D28 1-1	S07 1-0	F13 3-3	M20 1-1	D05 2-0	a03 3-1	m01 0-3	M29 0-0	S26 4-0		J23 2-1	F24 1-0	N21 0-2
20 SWANSEA T	A29 1-2	S12 3-1	N07 1-0	M06 1-1	D19 3-0	J02 3-0	F11 3-0	M20 2-0	m01 4-1	S07 2-0	F13 0-1	O03 3-0	N21 1-3	a17 1-2	D05 2-1	M26 1-0	D28 0-1	F25 2-1	S19 5-1		O24 2-1	a03 0-0
21 TOTTENHAM H	M13 2-2	F03 3-0	D28 5-1	S21 1-2	S19 5-1	O31 5-1	F13 3-0	M29 2-0	N14 5-1	a10 3-1	D12 2-0	a24 1-1	S14 4-2	J09 0-1	S05 2-3	M27 2-1	N28 1-3	O03 2-2	O17 4-0	F27 3-1		D26 2-3
22 WEST HAM U	a26 2-1	M26 0-0	S12 3-1	J02 3-0	D28 1-0	a10 4-1	N14 0-2	J23 5-1	a24 1-1	F27 4-0	O31 1-0	M13 3-3	S26 4-1	A31 0-2	F13 4-1	F06 2-2	O17 1-1	m01 1-0	M27 4-0	N28 2-0	A29 2-1	

Season 1936-37

DIVISION 3 NORTH

	ACCRINGTON S	BARROW	CARLISLE U	CHESTER	CREWE A	DARLINGTON	GATESHEAD	HALIFAX T	HARTLEPOOLS U	HULL C	LINCOLN C	MANSFIELD T	NEW BRIGHTON	OLDHAM A	PORT VALE	ROCHDALE	ROTHERHAM U	SOUTHPORT	STOCKPORT CO	TRANMERE R	WREXHAM	YORK C
1 ACCRINGTON S		D05 5-0	D19 2-1	N21 2-1	M20 4-1	S26 1-0	J23 2-1	M06 3-2	S29 1-2	S12 0-1	A29 1-2	N07 0-3	J02 5-0	M26 1-1	D25 2-3	a03 3-1	J01 3-0	F20 6-3	O10 2-1	O24 4-0	F06 2-2	a17 2-1
2 BARROW	a10 1-0		O10 5-0	J09 1-2	S05 2-2	O31 1-0	M13 3-0	A31 1-2	m01 3-1	N14 2-3	J16 0-4	D26 2-2	M27 2-1	a19 1-2	a24 3-1	S19 3-0	J30 5-1	D25 2-1	O17 0-0	M29 2-0	F27 1-1	F06 2-2
3 CARLISLE U	a24 2-0	F13 2-2		F04 1-1	S19 4-0	N14 2-0	M27 2-1	S05 1-2	M26 2-0	J21 1-1	a15 3-1	J09 1-2	a10 1-1	D25 2-1	O17 5-2	O03 1-0	F27 4-1	S03 1-1	O31 1-0	D26 3-1	M13 2-1	J01 1-1
4 CHESTER	M27 1-1	S12 6-0	S26 4-0		S02 5-0	O17 2-1	a21 6-0	D25 1-1	F06 3-0	O31 3-1	N14 7-3	M29 5-1	M13 4-1	a14 2-1	N28 0-0	J02 2-2	D12 2-1	O10 2-3	a24 1-1	S16 5-2	A29 4-1	J23 3-1
5 CREWE A	N14 2-2	J02 4-1	J23 1-2	S07 1-1		M26 1-1	O17 3-1	S16 0-1	S26 1-1	F27 2-1	M13 2-1	D28 2-1	O31 0-2	M27 1-2	J20 0-1	A29 2-2	a10 0-2	F06 3-2	a19 1-2	O10 2-2	a24 1-1	S12 2-2
6 DARLINGTON	F03 4-1	M06 2-4	M20 1-5	F20 1-3	M29 0-3		D28 0-2	a17 3-3	N21 5-5	J01 2-2	O03 2-2	D19 0-0	F13 1-2	S19 0-3	J09 1-0	O24 4-1	S05 6-3	a03 4-2	D26 1-1	D05 3-2	S09 1-1	N07 1-1
7 GATESHEAD	S19 1-1	N07 1-1	N21 1-0	O24 1-1	F20 2-0	D25 5-0		D19 0-2	a03 2-2	F13 6-3	a07 0-5	J01 3-3	O03 1-1	J09 0-3	S05 0-1	M06 3-1	D26 2-1	D05 5-4	S02 0-0	a17 4-0	M26 0-0	M20 3-2
8 HALIFAX T	O31 3-0	S07 2-1	J02 6-1	D28 1-0	m01 4-1	a19 4-1	a24 2-1		S12 2-0	F06 1-0	F27 2-3	F13 0-0	O17 0-0	a26 0-1	N14 0-1	M29 3-2	M27 4-1	J23 1-1	J16 1-1	S26 2-1	a10 1-2	A29 1-2
9 HARTLEPOOLS U	S02 1-0	J01 3-1	M29 3-0	O03 0-1	J30 4-1	M27 1-3	J16 6-1	J09 5-3		a10 2-2	a24 3-1	S19 3-0	a28 5-0	O17 1-0	F27 2-0	F13 4-1	O31 0-2	D26 2-0	M13 2-4	S05 2-1	N14 2-0	D28 2-0
10 HULL C	J09 0-3	M20 3-2	a03 1-1	M06 1-1	O24 2-0	m01 4-3	O10 3-2	O03 0-0	D05 1-0		S19 1-1	F20 3-0	J30 4-1	S05 2-0	D26 1-1	N07 1-1	A31 2-1	a17 3-2	M29 0-1	D19 5-2	D25 1-0	N21 1-0
11 LINCOLN C	D26 3-3	a03 6-0	a17 3-0	M20 3-0	N07 2-4	F06 4-3	S26 4-0	O24 4-1	D19 3-0	J23 5-0		M06 2-0	S12 1-0	A31 2-0	M29 1-0	N21 5-3	D25 3-0	S05 4-1	S14 0-2	F20 1-0	O10 6-2	D05 3-1
12 MANSFIELD T	M13 2-1	A29 2-1	S12 1-4	M26 5-0	D25 1-4	a24 3-1	m01 3-2	O10 3-0	J23 8-2	O17 5-2	O31 2-2		F27 2-3	N14 1-2	M27 7-1	S09 6-2	J16 4-1	S26 3-0	a10 0-2	F06 2-3	M30 3-0	J02 1-2
13 NEW BRIGHTON	S05 1-1	N21 1-1	D05 1-1	N07 1-0	M06 1-0	O10 2-0	F06 1-1	F20 1-1	a17 4-0	S26 1-1	J09 1-2	O24 0-0		D26 0-2	S02 2-0	M20 5-1	M26 4-0	D19 3-1	D25 1-1	S19 1-2	S16 1-0	a03 4-1
14 OLDHAM A	M29 3-1	a17 4-3	D28 2-1	a03 1-0	N21 1-1	J23 1-1	S12 4-4	N07 1-0	F20 2-0	J02 3-1	S07 1-0	M20 1-1	A29 3-1		S14 5-1	D05 3-0	O10 4-1	O24 3-3	F06 0-2	M06 3-0	S26 2-2	D19 2-2
15 PORT VALE	D28 1-1	D19 3-2	F20 1-0	D05 4-0	a03 0-0	S12 2-2	J02 4-2	M20 3-1	O24 1-0	A29 1-3	M26 1-1	N21 5-1	S07 3-1	m01 1-0		a17 1-1	F06 2-1	M06 0-2	S26 3-0	N07 2-1	J23 0-3	O10 1-1
16 ROCHDALE	a27 4-1	J23 3-1	F06 3-0	S05 0-1	D26 2-0	F27 4-0	O31 0-2	M26 3-5	O10 1-1	M13 4-0	M27 2-3	A31 1-3	N14 4-0	a10 3-0	D12 0-0		a24 1-0	S15 2-1	J09 2-2	D25 2-1	O17 0-6	S26 3-0
17 ROTHERHAM U	m01 2-2	S26 4-1	O24 0-1	a17 2-1	D05 3-2	J02 2-4	A29 3-0	N21 6-0	M06 2-4	S07 0-0	D28 3-1	a03 4-1	M29 3-0	F13 4-4	O03 2-0	D19 1-1		N07 3-0	J23 1-1	M20 3-1	S12 2-2	F20 2-2
18 SOUTHPORT	O17 3-1	M16 3-3	S08 2-1	F13 1-2	O03 1-1	J19 0-0	a10 3-0	S19 2-1	A29 1-1	J16 1-4	J02 2-1	J30 3-2	a24 3-0	F27 2-0	O31 3-3	J01 1-1	M13 4-1		N14 1-1	J09 1-0	M27 1-1	M26 1-4
19 STOCKPORT CO	F13 3-2	F20 4-1	M06 1-2	D19 4-0	a17 1-0	A29 3-3	S07 4-2	a03 0-0	N07 1-1	M26 3-1	m01 2-0	D05 3-1	D28 3-1	O03 4-1	J30 1-0	S12 3-0	S19 4-2	M20 2-1		N21 5-0	J02 2-0	O24 6-0
20 TRANMERE R	a19 1-2	M26 0-0	A29 5-1	J01 5-0	F13 6-1	a10 1-1	a26 6-1	J30 2-1	J02 1-0	D12 2-1	O17 2-2	O03 0-2	J23 3-2	O31 3-3	M13 4-2	J16 4-3	N14 1-2	S12 3-3	M27 2-2		a12 1-1	S07 0-0
21 WREXHAM	O03 1-0	O24 2-1	N07 1-0	D26 1-2	D19 5-0	A31 4-0	M29 6-0	D05 0-2	M20 0-1	a19 2-1	F13 0-3	a17 2-3	J01 4-1	J30 1-1	S19 1-0	F20 0-1	J09 4-2	N21 3-3	S05 0-0	a03 2-0		M06 2-0
22 YORK C	a14 4-2	O03 1-2	m01 5-2	S19 0-2	J09 2-3	M13 3-0	N14 2-0	D26 4-0	D25 4-1	M27 1-1	a10 0-0	S05 1-1	a21 2-1	a24 3-1	F13 1-2	F10 4-1	O17 4-3	M29 4-0	F27 2-1	S02 4-0	O31 3-4	

DIVISION 3 SOUTH

	ALDERSHOT	BOURNEMOUTH	BRIGHTON & HA	BRISTOL C	BRISTOL R	CARDIFF C	CLAPTON O	CRYSTAL P	EXETER C	GILLINGHAM	LUTON T	MILLWALL	NEWPORT CO	NORTHAMPTON T	NOTTS CO	Q.P.R.	READING	SOUTHEND U	SWINDON T	TORQUAY U	WALSALL	WATFORD
1 ALDERSHOT		A29 1-3	J02 0-1	M06 3-0	M26 4-0	a17 0-1	N21 1-1	D19 2-2	O10 1-1	F06 3-0	D05 2-3	D28 1-2	S26 2-0	S09 0-2	M20 0-1	O24 0-0	F20 0-2	J23 1-2	m01 2-1	N07 0-1	a03 4-4	S12 2-2
2 BOURNEMOUTH	D26 2-1		O10 1-0	a17 0-0	S19 3-0	N07 0-2	F20 2-1	M20 3-1	N21 0-0	S02 1-0	M06 2-1	J09 2-1	M29 5-0	a21 3-2	O03 1-0	D05 3-1	a03 2-1	D28 1-0	S05 5-2	D19 3-3	O24 3-2	m01 3-2
3 BRIGHTON & H.A.	S05 1-0	F13 1-0		D05 2-0	J30 5-2	M06 7-2	m01 1-1	N07 1-0	M20 1-0	D26 4-0	O24 2-1	S19 2-2	S02 2-0	O03 1-2	D19 2-2	a03 4-1	N21 1-1	M26 1-0	J09 2-0	a17 5-1	F20 3-0	D25 1-1
4 BRISTOL C	O31 3-0	J27 4-1	a10 1-0		J02 4-1	m01 2-1	J30 4-0	D25 1-0	M26 2-1	M13 2-0	F13 2-3	O17 2-0	N14 3-1	a24 0-1	S19 1-1	A29 3-2	S23 1-2	M27 0-1	a28 1-2	J09 4-1	O03 0-0	J16 2-2
5 BRISTOL R	M29 1-0	J23 4-0	S26 2-0	S05 3-1		N21 5-1	M06 4-0	a03 1-0	D05 4-2	D28 0-3	M20 4-0	D26 2-1	S16 1-1	S12 2-0	O24 2-3	D19 1-1	a17 2-2	O10 1-2	S02 2-1	F20 5-1	N07 3-0	F06 0-1
6 CARDIFF C	a19 4-1	M13 2-1	O31 1-2	S14 3-1	M27 3-1		A31 2-1	J23 1-1	S26 3-1	a24 2-0	S05 3-0	a12 0-1	J09 0-1	N14 2-1	M29 0-2	O10 2-0	F06 1-1	S28 1-1	a10 1-2	D28 0-2	D26 2-2	F27 2-2
7 CLAPTON O	M27 1-1	O17 2-1	S17 2-0	S26 0-0	O31 2-1	S10 0-1		A29 1-1	J02 1-0	J16 2-0	M26 0-2	M13 1-0	a10 1-2	F27 3-1	O10 1-1	J23 0-0	S12 3-2	a29 3-0	N14 1-1	F06 2-0	D28 2-2	a24 1-1
8 CRYSTAL P	a24 3-0	N14 2-2	M13 2-0	D28 1-0	J20 3-0	S19 2-2	D26 2-3		F06 8-0	J30 1-1	J09 0-4	a14 1-0	O17 6-1	M27 2-2	S02 1-2	S23 0-0	O10 3-1	F27 1-1	J16 2-0	M26 0-0	S05 3-1	O31 2-0
9 EXETER C	F13 1-2	M27 1-1	N14 0-4	M29 3-0	a10 3-2	F03 3-1	S05 0-2	O03 3-2		O17 1-1	S19 2-4	M17 1-1	F27 3-1	J20 2-5	D26 1-3	D28 0-3	m01 2-0	O31 2-2	a24 1-1	S02 2-1	J09 3-0	M13 2-1
10 GILLINGHAM	O03 1-2	S09 1-0	A29 1-0	N07 5-3	D25 1-0	D19 0-0	a03 0-2	S26 2-0	F24 2-2		a17 1-0	m01 1-0	J23 4-4	M26 2-0	N21 3-0	M06 0-0	O24 2-1	S12 1-0	F13 4-1	M20 1-0	D05 2-2	J02 2-1
11 LUTON T	a10 5-2	O31 1-0	F27 2-1	O10 4-0	N14 2-0	J02 8-1	M29 2-0	S12 5-2	J23 2-2	a07 5-2		M27 5-0	a24 5-0	M13 3-2	D25 2-1	F06 0-1	S26 4-0	A29 1-0	a21 5-1	m01 2-0	S07 2-0	O17 4-1
12 MILLWALL	D25 4-2	S12 0-2	J23 3-0	F22 3-1	A29 1-2	a03 3-1	N07 2-1	D05 3-0	a17 3-3	S21 3-0	N21 0-2		O10 7-2	J02 1-0	M08 0-0	A31 2-0	D19 0-2	F06 1-2	M26 1-1	O24 1-1	M20 3-1	S26 2-1
13 NEWPORT CO	J30 4-0	M26 4-0	S10 1-4	M20 0-0	m01 2-2	S12 2-3	D05 1-1	F20 1-1	O24 2-0	S19 0-0	D19 2-1	F13 1-2		D28 1-3	a03 2-0	N07 1-2	M06 3-0	J02 6-2	O03 1-1	N21 1-1	a17 1-2	A29 1-3
14 NORTHAMPTON T	A31 5-3	S26 0-0	F06 2-0	D19 5-1	J09 4-1	M20 2-0	O24 1-1	N21 2-0	a03 2-1	M29 5-0	N07 3-1	S05 2-2	D25 3-2		F20 1-1	a17 0-1	D05 2-1	m01 4-3	D26 4-0	S19 3-0	M06 6-3	O10 0-1
15 NOTTS CO	N14 3-0	F06 4-3	a24 0-1	J23 1-0	F27 4-3	M26 4-0	F13 0-0	S07 0-1	A29 3-1	M27 2-0	D28 2-1	O31 1-1	J16 3-1	O17 3-2		S12 1-2	J02 1-0	a10 2-1	M13 3-2	S26 2-0	O01 3-3	D12 2-1
16 Q.P.R.	F27 3-0	a10 1-2	J21 2-3	D26 5-0	a24 2-1	F13 6-0	S19 2-1	m01 1-3	D25 4-0	O31 0-1	O03 2-1	S17 0-1	M13 6-2	F18 3-2	J09 0-2		M26 0-0	N14 7-2	O17 1-1	S05 3-0	F04 2-0	M27 1-2
17 READING	O17 2-0	J20 3-2	M27 2-0	S02 2-1	F24 2-0	O03 3-0	J09 1-1	F13 1-1	S16 1-0	F27 6-2	F10 2-2	a24 3-0	O31 4-4	a10 3-1	S05 4-1	M29 2-0		M13 2-3	D25 2-2	D26 5-1	S19 0-2	N14 3-0
18 SOUTHEND U	S19 2-2	D25 0-0	M29 2-1	N21 3-0	F13 2-3	F20 8-1	a17 0-0	O24 2-1	M06 4-4	J09 0-2	D26 3-0	O03 0-0	S05 9-2	S16 2-0	D05 2-3	M20 3-2	N07 1-1		J30 2-0	a03 0-0	D19 3-0	S02 1-1
19 SWINDON T	S16 5-1	J02 3-1	S12 1-2	O24 0-1	S23 4-1	D05 4-2	M20 1-3	a17 4-0	D19 3-1	O10 3-0	a03 2-2	M29 3-0	F06 1-2	A29 2-0	N07 2-2	F20 1-1	D28 1-2	S26 4-0		M06 4-2	N21 3-0	J23 1-1
20 TORQUAY U	M13 5-1	a24 0-0	D12 0-2	S12 5-2	O17 1-0	D25 1-0	O03 4-1	M29 3-0	S09 0-1	N14 0-2	S16 2-2	F27 0-2	M27 1-2	J23 5-0	J30 2-2	J02 1-1	A29 2-2	J16 1-4	O31 2-0		F13 3-1	a10 4-7
21 WALSALL	J21 0-0	F27 1-1	O17 1-4	F06 1-5	M13 5-2	A29 1-0	D25 3-2	J02 1-0	S12 4-2	a10 2-1	A31 0-1	N14 0-3	a26 1-2	O31 2-2	m01 2-1	S26 2-4	M30 0-1	a24 3-0	M27 5-2	O10 1-0		M26 3-1
22 WATFORD	J09 5-3	S23 4-0	D28 1-0	a03 1-0	O03 3-0	O24 2-0	D19 2-1	M06 3-1	N07 1-1	S05 6-1	F20 1-3	F03 2-2	D26 3-0	F13 4-1	a17 0-2	N21 2-0	M20 6-1	S09 1-3	S19 2-2	D05 4-0	M29 0-0	

LEAGUE TABLES

DIVISION 1

	P	W	D	L	F	A	W	D	L	F	A	Pts
Manchester C	42	15	5	1	56	22	7	8	6	51	39	57
Charlton A	42	15	5	1	37	13	6	7	8	21	36	54
Arsenal	42	10	10	1	43	20	8	6	7	37	29	52
Derby Co	42	13	3	5	58	39	8	4	9	38	51	49
Wolverhampton W	42	16	2	3	63	24	5	3	13	21	43	47
Brentford	42	14	5	2	58	32	4	5	12	24	46	46
Middlesbrough	42	14	6	1	49	22	5	2	14	25	49	46
Sunderland	42	17	2	2	59	24	2	4	15	30	63	44
Portsmouth	42	13	3	5	41	29	4	7	10	21	37	44
Stoke C	42	12	6	3	52	27	3	6	12	20	30	42
Birmingham C	42	9	7	5	36	24	4	8	9	28	36	41
Grimsby T	42	13	3	5	60	32	4	4	13	26	49	41
Chelsea	42	11	6	4	36	21	3	7	11	16	34	41
Preston N.E.	42	10	6	5	35	28	4	7	10	21	39	41
Huddersfield T	42	12	5	4	39	21	0	10	11	23	43	39
W.B.A.	42	13	3	5	45	32	3	3	15	32	66	38
Everton	42	12	7	2	56	23	2	2	17	25	55	37
Liverpool	42	9	8	4	38	26	3	3	15	24	58	35
Leeds U	42	14	3	4	44	20	1	1	19	16	60	34
Bolton W	42	6	6	9	22	33	4	8	9	21	33	34
Manchester U	42	8	9	4	29	26	2	3	16	26	52	32
Sheffield W	42	8	5	8	32	29	1	7	13	21	40	30

DIVISION 2

	P	W	D	L	F	A	W	D	L	F	A	Pts
Leicester C	42	14	4	3	56	26	10	4	7	33	31	56
Blackpool	42	13	4	4	49	19	11	3	7	39	34	55
Bury	42	13	4	4	46	26	9	4	8	28	29	52
Newcastle U	42	11	3	7	45	23	11	2	8	35	33	49
Plymouth A	42	11	6	4	42	22	7	7	7	29	31	49
West Ham U	42	14	5	2	47	18	5	6	10	26	37	49
Sheffield U	42	16	4	1	48	14	2	6	13	18	40	46
Coventry C	42	11	5	5	35	19	6	6	9	31	35	45
Aston Villa	42	10	6	5	47	30	6	6	9	35	40	44
Tottenham H	42	13	3	5	57	26	4	6	11	31	40	43
Fulham	42	11	5	5	43	24	4	8	9	28	37	43
Blackburn R	42	11	3	7	49	32	5	7	9	21	30	42
Burnley	42	11	5	5	37	20	5	5	11	20	41	42
Barnsley	42	11	6	4	30	23	5	3	13	20	41	41
Chesterfield	42	12	3	6	54	34	4	5	12	30	55	40
Swansea T	42	14	2	5	40	16	1	5	15	10	49	37
Norwich C	42	8	6	7	38	29	6	2	13	25	42	36
Nottingham F	42	10	6	5	42	30	2	4	15	26	60	34
Southampton	42	10	8	3	38	25	1	4	16	15	52	34
Bradford P.A.	42	10	4	7	33	33	2	5	14	19	55	33
Bradford C	42	8	8	5	36	31	1	4	16	18	63	30
Doncaster R	42	6	6	9	18	29	1	4	16	12	55	24

DIVISION 3 NORTH

	P	W	D	L	F	A	W	D	L	F	A	Pts
Stockport Co	42	17	3	1	59	18	6	11	4	25	21	60
Lincoln C	42	18	1	2	65	20	7	6	8	38	37	57
Chester C	42	15	5	1	68	21	7	4	10	19	36	53
Oldham A	42	13	7	1	49	25	7	4	10	28	34	51
Hull C	42	13	6	2	39	22	4	6	11	29	47	46
Hartlepool U	42	16	1	4	53	21	3	6	12	22	48	45
Halifax T	42	12	4	5	40	20	6	5	10	28	43	45
Wrexham	42	12	3	6	41	21	4	9	8	30	36	44
Mansfield T	42	13	1	7	64	35	5	7	9	27	41	44
Carlisle U	42	13	6	2	42	19	5	2	14	23	49	44
Port Vale	42	12	6	3	39	23	5	4	12	19	41	44
York C	42	13	3	5	54	27	3	8	10	25	43	43
Accrington S	42	14	2	5	51	26	2	7	12	25	43	41
Southport	42	10	8	3	39	28	2	5	14	34	59	37
New Brighton	42	10	8	3	36	16	3	3	15	19	54	37
Barrow	42	11	5	5	42	25	2	5	14	28	61	36
Rotherham U	42	11	7	3	52	28	3	0	18	26	63	35
Rochdale	42	12	3	6	44	27	1	6	14	25	59	35
Tranmere R	42	10	8	3	52	30	2	1	18	19	58	33
Crewe A	42	6	8	7	31	31	4	4	13	24	52	32
Gateshead	42	9	8	4	40	31	2	2	17	23	67	32
Darlington	42	6	8	7	42	46	2	6	13	24	50	30

DIVISION 3 SOUTH

	P	W	D	L	F	A	W	D	L	F	A	Pts
Luton T	42	19	1	1	69	16	8	3	10	34	37	58
Notts Co	42	15	3	3	44	23	8	7	6	30	29	56
Brighton & H.A.	42	15	5	1	49	16	9	0	12	25	27	53
Watford	42	14	4	3	53	21	5	7	9	32	39	49
Reading	42	14	5	2	53	23	5	6	10	23	37	49
Bournemouth	42	17	3	1	45	20	3	6	12	20	39	49
Northampton T	42	15	4	2	56	22	5	2	14	29	46	46
Millwall	42	12	4	5	43	24	6	6	9	21	30	46
Q.P.R.	42	12	2	7	51	24	6	7	8	22	28	45
Southend U	42	10	8	3	49	23	7	3	11	29	44	45
Gillingham	42	14	5	2	36	18	4	3	14	16	48	44
Clapton O	42	10	8	3	29	17	4	7	10	23	35	43
Swindon T	42	12	4	5	52	24	2	7	12	23	49	39
Crystal Palace	42	11	7	3	45	20	2	5	14	17	41	38
Bristol R	42	14	3	4	49	20	2	1	18	22	60	36
Bristol C	42	13	3	5	42	20	2	3	16	16	50	36
Walsall	42	11	3	7	38	34	2	7	12	25	51	36
Cardiff C	42	10	5	6	35	24	4	2	15	19	63	35
Newport Co	42	7	7	7	37	28	5	3	13	30	70	34
Torquay U	42	9	5	7	42	32	2	5	14	15	48	32
Exeter C	42	9	5	7	36	37	1	7	13	23	51	32
Aldershot	42	5	6	10	29	29	2	3	16	21	60	23

FOOTBALL LEAGUE RECORDS

Top scorers: Div 1, T.Lawton (Everton) 38 goals; Div 2, G.Henson (Bradford) 27 goals; Div 3 N; J.Roberts (Port Vale) 28 goals; Div 3 S, H.Crawshaw (Mansfield Town) 25 goals. Mansfield Town transferred to Division Three South.

England full-back Eddie Hapgood, skippered Arsenal to yet another title.

DIVISION 1

	ARSENAL	BIRMINGHAM	BLACKPOOL	BOLTON W	BRENTFORD	CHARLTON A	CHELSEA	DERBY CO	EVERTON	GRIMSBY T	HUDDERSFIELD T	LEEDS U	LEICESTER C	LIVERPOOL	MANCHESTER C	MIDDLESBROUGH	PORTSMOUTH	PRESTON N.E.	STOKE C	SUNDERLAND	W.B.A.	WOLVERHAMPTON W
1 ARSENAL		a16 0-0	D27 2-1	m07 5-0	a15 0-2	a02 2-2	F19 2-0	F05 3-0	J01 2-1	M19 5-1	S01 3-1	N27 4-1	F02 3-1	a30 1-0	O02 2-1	O30 1-2	O16 1-1	D11 2-0	M05 4-0	S18 4-1	N13 1-1	S04 5-0
2 BIRMINGHAM	D04 1-2		M26 1-1	a09 2-0	D18 0-0	S18 1-1	J22 1-1	O23 1-0	a23 0-3	O02 2-2	N06 2-2	F19 3-2	S15 4-1	D27 2-2	M12 2-2	S01 3-1	S04 2-2	F05 0-2	J01 1-1	F26 2-2	a15 2-1	N20 2-0
3 BLACKPOOL	D25 2-1	N13 0-3		A30 2-2	S20 1-1	a15 1-0	O16 0-2	O02 1-1	S04 1-0	D11 2-2	J01 4-0	M19 5-2	S18 2-4	N27 0-1	F19 2-1	a16 4-2	M05 2-0	a02 1-0	O30 0-1	F05 0-0	a30 3-1	J26 0-2
4 BOLTON W	S15 1-0	N27 1-1	S06 3-0		A28 2-0	M05 1-0	O30 5-5	J22 0-2	S18 1-2	J15 3-1	J26 2-0	a02 0-0	O02 6-1	D11 0-0	a18 2-1	a30 3-1	a16 1-1	O16 1-4	N13 1-0	F19 1-1	M19 3-0	F05 1-2
5 BRENTFORD	a18 3-0	a30 1-2	S16 2-4	J01 1-1		O16 5-2	M09 1-1	F19 2-3	J26 3-0	a02 6-1	S04 2-0	D11 1-1	F05 1-1	M19 1-3	D27 2-1	N13 3-3	O30 2-0	S01 2-1	a16 0-0	O02 4-0	N27 0-2	S18 2-1
6 CHARLTON A	N20 0-3	J29 2-0	a18 4-1	O23 1-1	F26 1-0		D27 3-1	N06 1-2	D04 3-1	S06 0-0	M12 4-0	A28 1-1	D18 2-0	J15 3-0	a23 0-0	S25 1-0	O09 5-1	m07 0-0	M02 3-0	a09 2-1	S11 3-1	M26 4-1
7 CHELSEA	O09 2-2	S11 2-0	F26 1-3	M12 0-0	O23 2-1	a27 1-1		a23 3-0	M26 2-0	S15 1-0	D04 3-1	S08 4-1	a09 4-1	A28 6-1	N20 2-2	J29 0-1	F12 3-1	a15 0-2	S25 2-1	N06 0-0	J15 2-2	D18 0-2
8 DERBY CO	S25 2-0	M05 0-0	F12 3-1	D27 4-2	O09 1-3	M19 3-2	D11 4-0		S15 2-1	a30 1-2	a18 0-4	N13 2-2	J01 0-1	a16 4-1	J29 1-7	O16 1-1	a02 1-0	N27 1-1	F02 4-1	S04 2-2	O30 5-3	S01 1-2
9 EVERTON	A28 1-4	D11 1-1	J15 3-1	J29 4-1	S11 3-0	a16 3-0	N13 4-1	m07 1-1		M05 3-2	S25 1-2	O16 1-1	D27 3-0	F16 1-3	S08 4-1	M19 2-2	a30 5-2	O30 3-5	N27 3-0	a15 3-3	a02 5-3	F19 0-1
10 GRIMSBY T	N06 2-1	F12 4-0	a23 1-0	S04 0-1	N20 0-1	A31 1-1	m07 2-0	D18 0-0	O23 2-1		F26 4-2	S11 1-1	D04 2-1	J29 0-0	a09 3-1	O09 2-1	a15 1-0	J01 1-1	D25 1-5	M29 0-2	S25 1-4	M12 1-0
11 HUDDERSFIELD T	S08 2-1	M19 2-1	A28 3-1	S11 1-0	J15 0-3	O30 1-1	a16 1-2	a19 2-0	F05 1-3	O16 1-2		J29 0-3	F19 0-0	a02 1-2	m07 1-0	N27 3-0	N13 2-0	M16 1-3	m02 3-0	D27 1-1	D11 2-1	O02 1-0
12 LEEDS U	a09 0-1	O09 1-0	N06 1-1	N20 1-1	a23 4-0	J01 2-2	S01 2-0	M26 0-2	F26 4-4	J26 1-1	S18 2-1		M12 0-2	S25 2-0	D18 2-1	D25 5-3	S15 3-1	S04 0-0	a19 2-1	D04 4-3	F12 1-0	O23 1-2
13 LEICESTER C	S11 1-1	m07 1-4	J29 0-1	F12 1-1	S25 0-1	a30 1-0	N27 1-0	A28 0-0	D25 3-1	a16 1-0	O09 2-1	O30 2-4		M05 2-2	J15 1-4	a02 0-1	M19 3-3	N13 1-0	D11 2-0	A30 4-0	O16 4-1	a18 1-1
14 LIVERPOOL	D18 2-0	a06 3-2	a09 4-2	a23 2-1	N06 3-4	S04 1-2	J01 2-2	D04 3-4	O02 1-2	S18 2-1	N20 0-1	F05 1-1	O23 1-1		M26 2-0	a18 1-1	S01 3-2	F02 2-2	S15 3-0	M12 4-0	O09 0-1	F26 0-1
15 MANCHESTER C	F16 1-2	O30 2-0	O09 2-1	a15 1-2	D25 0-2	a06 5-3	a02 1-0	S18 6-1	S01 2-0	N27 3-1	S15 3-2	a30 6-2	S04 3-0	N13 1-3		M09 1-6	F05 2-1	M19 1-2	O16 0-0	F02 0-0	a16 7-1	J01 2-4
16 MIDDLESBROUGH	M12 2-1	S08 1-1	D04 2-2	D18 1-2	M26 0-1	F05 3-1	S18 4-3	F26 4-2	N06 1-2	F19 1-0	a09 0-1	D27 2-0	N20 4-2	a15 1-1	O23 4-0		J26 0-0	O02 2-1	S04 2-1	J01 2-1	m07 4-1	a23 0-3
17 PORTSMOUTH	F26 0-0	J15 1-1	O23 1-2	D04 1-1	M12 4-1	F19 2-1	O02 2-4	N20 4-0	D18 3-1	a18 3-0	M30 3-0	m07 4-0	N06 1-1	S08 1-1	S25 2-2	S11 0-2		D25 3-2	J29 2-0	a23 1-0	A28 2-3	a09 1-0
18 PRESTON N.E.	a23 1-3	S25 2-1	N20 2-0	F26 2-2	S06 1-1	S13 0-1	a18 0-0	a09 4-1	M12 2-1	A28 4-1	O23 1-1	J15 3-1	M09 0-0	S11 4-1	N06 2-2	F16 0-2	D27 1-1		O09 2-1	D18 0-0	J29 1-1	D04 2-0
19 STOKE C	O23 1-1	A28 2-2	M12 1-3	M26 3-2	D04 3-0	O02 2-0	F05 2-1	S11 8-1	a09 1-1	D27 1-1	D18 0-1	a18 0-1	a23 1-2	m07 2-0	F26 3-2	J15 3-0	S18 3-1	F19 1-1		N20 0-0	S06 4-0	N06 1-1
20 SUNDERLAND	J29 1-1	O16 1-0	S25 2-1	O09 3-1	F16 1-0	N27 1-1	M19 1-1	J15 2-0	a18 2-0	N13 2-2	D25 2-1	a16 0-0	S08 1-0	O30 2-3	S11 3-1	A28 3-1	D11 0-2	m04 0-2	a02 1-1		M09 3-0	m07 1-0
21 W.B.A.	M26 0-0	a18 4-3	D18 1-2	N06 2-4	a09 4-3	J26 0-0	S04 4-0	M12 4-2	N20 3-1	F05 2-1	a23 5-1	O02 2-1	F26 1-3	F19 5-1	M16 1-1	S13 3-1	J01 1-2	S18 1-1	A30 0-1	O23 1-6		D27 2-2
22 WOLVERHAMPTON W	J15 3-1	a02 3-2	S11 1-0	S25 1-1	J29 2-1	N13 1-1	a30 1-1	S06 2-2	O09 2-0	O30 1-1	F16 1-4	M05 1-1	a15 10-1	O16 2-0	A28 3-1	M23 0-1	N27 5-0	a16 0-0	M19 2-2	S15 4-0	m02 2-1	

Aston Villa's Frank Broome, one of the most versatile forwards in the game. His 19 goals helped Villa regain their Division One place.

DIVISION 2

	ASTON VILLA	BARNSLEY	BLACKBURN R	BRADFORD	BURNLEY	BURY	CHESTERFIELD	COVENTRY C	FULHAM	LUTON T	MANCHESTER U	NEWCASTLE U	NORWICH C	NOTTINGHAM F	PLYMOUTH A	SHEFFIELD U	SHEFFIELD W	SOUTHAMPTON	STOCKPORT CO	SWANSEA T	TOTTENHAM H	WEST HAM U
1 ASTON VILLA		D28 3-0	S11 2-1	a27 2-0	N13 0-0	M19 2-1	O09 0-2	O30 1-1	S25 2-0	S06 4-1	a02 3-0	O16 2-0	m07 2-0	M09 1-2	F23 3-0	N27 1-0	J29 4-3	J15 3-0	D11 7-1	a19 4-0	a16 2-0	A28 2-0
2 BARNSLEY	D18 0-1		M12 0-0	J01 0-1	O02 2-2	F19 2-2	a09 1-1	a18 1-1	M26 0-0	D27 3-1	F02 2-2	S06 3-0	a23 0-0	m07 2-2	D04 3-2	S18 1-1	N06 4-1	O23 0-2	S04 2-0	N20 2-0	F05 1-1	F26 1-0
3 BLACKBURN R	J27 1-0	O30 5-3		S18 0-0	D11 3-3	a02 2-1	D25 3-3	N27 1-3	S20 2-2	M19 2-2	O16 1-1	N13 2-1	S04 5-3	a16 5-1	A30 2-1	F19 2-3	a18 1-0	O02 4-0	M05 3-0	J01 3-1	a30 2-1	F05 2-1
4 BRADFORD	D27 1-2	A28 4-3	J29 7-1		a16 3-1	N13 1-1	a18 3-2	M19 0-1	F16 1-2	O16 1-1	D11 4-0	M05 2-0	S06 3-0	O30 2-2	O09 2-0	a02 5-1	S25 1-1	S11 2-0	a30 4-1	m07 0-1	N27 3-1	J15 2-1
5 BURNLEY	a05 3-0	F12 1-0	a23 3-1	D04 1-1		A28 2-0	O23 0-2	J15 2-0	D25 1-0	S25 3-2	a15 1-0	J29 2-1	N06 3-0	S11 0-0	F26 0-2	S13 2-0	D18 1-1	N20 4-0	O09 0-0	M12 2-0	S06 2-1	a09 2-0
6 BURY	N06 1-1	O09 0-2	N20 2-1	M26 5-1	J01 4-0		F26 4-0	S11 0-2	F12 4-2	F16 3-4	S13 1-2	S25 1-1	M12 3-1	J29 2-0	S04 2-0	A30 1-0	a23 2-0	a09 2-1	a15 1-3	O23 0-0	D25 1-2	D04 4-3
7 CHESTERFIELD	F19 0-1	N27 0-0	D27 3-0	a15 0-3	M05 0-1	O16 1-2		J29 4-0	J15 0-2	a02 5-2	N13 1-7	a25 2-0	O02 6-2	a30 1-0	S11 2-0	M19 1-0	A28 1-0	S06 5-0	a16 1-0	F05 4-1	O30 2-2	m07 0-1
8 COVENTRY C	M12 0-1	a19 1-0	a09 3-2	N06 0-0	S04 1-0	J27 0-2	S18 2-2		a23 0-1	O09 2-1	A30 1-0	F12 1-0	O23 2-0	S25 1-1	D18 4-0	D27 2-2	N20 0-1	J22 2-0	S13 1-0	F26 5-0	J01 2-1	M26 1-1
9 FULHAM	F05 1-1	N13 0-0	m07 3-1	O02 1-1	D27 2-1	a30 4-0	S04 1-1	D11 3-4		a16 4-1	O30 1-0	N27 1-2	S18 3-4	a02 2-0	J01 2-3	M05 1-1	S06 0-0	a15 1-0	M19 2-0	J22 8-1	O16 3-1	F19 1-1
10 LUTON T	S01 3-2	D25 4-0	N06 4-1	F26 4-2	F05 3-1	O02 0-1	N20 1-1	F19 1-4	D04 4-0		S04 1-0	m07 4-1	D18 1-1	a18 2-2	a09 1-1	F02 2-3	M26 2-2	M12 1-3	J01 6-4	a23 5-1	S18 2-4	O23 2-2
11 MANCHESTER U	N20 3-1	S11 4-1	F26 2-1	a23 3-1	a18 4-0	m07 2-0	M26 4-1	S08 2-2	M12 1-0	J15 4-2		A28 3-0	a09 0-0	D27 4-3	N06 0-0	O02 0-1	O23 1-0	S25 1-2	J29 3-1	D04 5-1	F19 0-1	F23 4-0
12 NEWCASTLE U	F26 2-0	S01 0-1	M26 2-0	O23 3-0	S18 2-2	F05 1-0	a23 3-1	O02 1-2	a09 1-2	S15 1-3	J01 2-2		a15 0-1	F19 3-1	N20 3-1	S04 6-0	D04 1-0	N06 3-0	D25 0-0	D18 1-0	F02 1-0	M12 2-2
13 NORWICH C	S16 1-0	D11 1-0	J15 3-2	S02 1-1	M19 1-0	O30 1-2	F24 2-1	M05 0-2	J29 1-2	a30 0-4	N27 2-3	a18 1-1		O16 2-0	S25 4-0	a16 2-2	S11 3-1	A28 4-3	a02 1-0	O09 1-1	N13 2-1	D27 2-2
14 NOTTINGHAM F	O23 0-2	S15 2-1	D04 3-1	M12 1-0	J26 1-1	S18 1-0	D18 4-2	F05 2-1	N20 0-1	a15 1-0	D28 2-3	O09 0-0	F26 1-2		a23 1-0	J01 2-1	a09 0-1	M26 2-1	S01 1-2	O02 2-1	S04 3-1	N06 0-0
15 PLYMOUTH A	O02 0-3	a16 2-2	S08 2-2	F19 1-0	O16 2-3	J15 2-1	J26 1-1	a30 3-1	A28 4-0	N27 2-4	M19 1-1	a02 2-1	F05 1-1	D11 1-0		O30 2-0	D25 2-4	m07 4-0	N13 2-1	S18 2-2	M09 2-2	a18 2-1
16 SHEFFIELD U	a09 0-0	J29 6-3	O09 1-1	N20 3-1	S20 2-1	S06 2-1	N06 0-2	D25 3-2	O23 2-1	S11 2-0	F17 1-2	J15 4-0	D04 4-1	A28 2-1	M12 0-0		F26 2-1	D18 5-0	S25 2-0	M28 1-1	a18 1-0	a23 3-1
17 SHEFFIELD W	S18 1-2	M19 0-1	a19 1-1	F05 1-0	a30 2-1	D11 2-0	J01 1-0	a02 2-1	S02 2-1	N13 4-0	M05 1-3	a16 3-0	J22 1-0	N27 0-2	D27 1-1	O16 0-1		F19 0-0	O30 3-3	S04 1-1	S16 0-3	O02 1-0
18 SOUTHAMPTON	S04 0-0	M05 2-0	F12 1-0	F02 2-1	a02 0-0	N27 4-1	S01 0-1	a16 0-4	a18 4-0	O30 3-6	F05 3-3	M19 1-0	J01 3-1	N13 2-0	S15 0-0	a30 2-1	O09 5-2		O16 4-1	D25 1-1	D11 2-1	S18 3-3
19 STOCKPORT CO	a23 1-3	J15 1-2	O23 0-1	D18 1-2	F19 3-1	a18 0-1	D04 1-1	m07 1-1	N06 2-0	A28 2-1	S18 1-0	M02 1-3	N20 1-1	S06 1-0	M26 1-3	F05 1-1	M12 2-1	F26 0-0		a09 1-0	O02 3-2	S11 0-0
20 SWANSEA T	a18 2-1	a02 1-0	A28 3-2	S13 0-1	O30 3-1	M05 1-0	S25 1-0	O16 3-3	S11 2-0	D11 1-1	a16 2-2	a30 2-0	F19 1-0	F12 1-0	J29 1-0	N13 3-5	J15 1-1	D27 0-0	N27 0-2		M19 3-2	S06 0-0
21 TOTTENHAM H	D04 2-1	S25 3-0	D18 3-1	a09 2-1	A30 4-0	D27 1-3	M12 2-0	A28 0-0	F26 1-1	J29 3-0	O09 0-1	S11 2-2	M26 4-0	J15 3-0	O23 3-2	a15 1-2	m07 1-2	a23 5-0	F23 2-0	N06 2-0		N20 2-0
22 WEST HAM U	J01 1-1	O16 4-1	S25 2-0	S04 3-1	N27 1-0	a16 3-1	S13 5-0	N13 0-0	O09 0-0	M05 0-0	a30 1-0	O30 1-0	D28 3-3	M19 2-1	a15 0-1	D11 0-2	F12 1-0	J29 3-1	J22 1-0	A30 2-1	a02 1-3	

SEASON 1937-38

DIVISION 3 NORTH

	ACCRINGTON S	BARROW	BRADFORD C	CARLISLE U	CHESTER	CREWE A	DARLINGTON	DONCASTER R	GATESHEAD	HALIFAX T	HARTLEPOOLS U	HULL C	LINCOLN C	NEW BRIGHTON	OLDHAM A	PORT VALE	ROCHDALE	ROTHERHAM U	SOUTHPORT	TRANMERE R	WREXHAM	YORK C
1 ACCRINGTON S		a23 2-0	S25 3-1	A28 1-4	S28 0-0	D04 3-2	N20 2-1	O09 0-1	N06 1-5	J15 3-4	S06 2-1	O23 0-2	F26 0-3	M12 3-1	M26 1-2	a09 2-1	D27 0-1	a15 0-0	F12 3-0	S11 0-1	J03 4-0	J29 1-2
2 BARROW	a25 0-0		M19 0-0	a16 4-2	a30 0-2	O02 1-0	S18 1-1	M05 1-1	S04 1-3	J08 2-1	a18 0-0	A30 1-0	m07 4-1	J01 3-0	J22 2-1	F05 3-0	O16 0-1	F19 1-0	O30 1-2	a02 2-2	D25 0-1	N13 1-2
3 BRADFORD C	F05 2-2	N06 1-0		O02 4-0	S18 2-2	M12 3-1	F26 2-1	J01 2-0	a25 1-1	F19 3-0	N20 4-1	D04 1-2	a09 2-0	a23 3-0	S15 1-1	O23 5-0	S04 3-1	J22 3-2	S01 1-1	D25 1-3	M26 2-2	a19 0-1
4 CARLISLE U	J01 3-1	D04 2-1	F12 2-0		S01 1-3	J08 5-1	M26 3-0	D25 2-2	M12 1-0	S11 5-2	D18 3-1	F26 0-1	S04 0-1	O23 1-1	N06 1-1	N20 3-1	a18 0-1	m07 0-1	O09 1-0	J29 0-0	a23 0-0	S25 2-1
5 CHESTER	m07 3-1	D18 3-1	J29 3-1	S08 1-0		a23 0-3	a09 3-2	F12 4-0	M26 2-1	A28 1-1	F26 6-0	M12 1-3	O23 1-1	N06 1-2	N20 3-3	D04 7-2	O09 4-1	D25 2-3	S25 2-1	J15 1-1	a15 2-1	S11 4-3
6 CREWE A	a16 3-1	F12 4-0	O30 3-1	a09 4-1	a06 1-0		J22 2-2	O16 0-0	J01 1-3	a02 4-0	D27 2-0	S15 0-1	a15 2-0	S01 1-0	S04 0-1	S18 1-2	F05 5-1	a30 3-1	M05 5-0	N13 1-0	O09 1-1	M19 4-2
7 DARLINGTON	a02 3-0	J29 0-1	O16 4-2	N13 3-1	a27 2-1	S11 0-1		a30 1-1	S15 1-2	M19 3-0	F12 2-0	D25 1-3	O09 1-4	a18 1-0	S01 1-0	J15 2-2	D11 2-4	a16 2-1	A28 1-1	O30 0-2	S25 5-3	M16 2-2
8 DONCASTER R	F19 5-1	O23 1-0	A28 4-0	D27 1-3	O02 2-1	F26 0-0	D18 4-0		D04 1-0	a15 2-2	N06 3-3	N20 2-1	M26 3-0	a09 3-0	a23 1-0	S11 3-2	S18 5-0	F05 0-1	J15 3-0	m07 1-1	M12 2-0	m02 2-1
9 GATESHEAD	M19 1-0	J15 6-0	a30 3-0	O30 2-1	N13 3-1	A28 2-0	m07 5-2	a16 2-3		M05 4-1	J29 2-1	F12 3-2	S25 1-1	O09 3-1	a18 0-0	S08 2-1	J08 3-1	a02 0-0	m02 5-0	O16 2-1	S11 2-2	D25 2-2
10 HALIFAX T	S04 1-2	a09 1-1	O09 0-2	J22 0-0	J01 1-1	N20 2-1	N06 1-0	a18 0-1	O23 2-0		a23 0-0	S18 1-0	a25 2-0	F26 2-0	M12 2-1	M26 2-1	S13 2-3	A30 1-3	D27 1-1	S25 1-0	D04 0-0	F14 2-2
11 HARTLEPOOLS U	S01 2-0	a15 1-1	a02 1-1	a30 4-1	O16 0-1	D25 2-2	O02 2-1	M19 0-0	S18 1-3	m04 2-0		S04 2-2	J01 2-0	F02 1-0	F05 2-0	F19 2-1	O30 3-3	M05 4-0	N13 1-2	a16 2-2	m07 2-0	J12 0-0
12 HULL C	M05 0-0	S06 4-0	a16 2-2	O16 2-1	O30 2-2	m07 1-1	D27 4-0	a02 2-1	O02 3-1	J29 0-1	J15 4-0		S11 1-1	F05 1-1	F19 4-1	a18 0-0	N13 4-1	M19 1-1	J13 10-1	a30 0-1	A28 3-2	a25 3-1
13 LINCOLN C	O16 2-0	S13 5-0	J26 4-0	J15 0-1	M05 1-1	a18 3-2	F19 0-0	N13 2-2	F05 3-2	a30 2-0	A28 2-1	J22 2-1		S18 4-1	O02 0-1	D27 1-0	M19 2-0	O30 5-0	a02 1-3	m02 0-1	S06 7-1	a16 2-0
14 NEW BRIGHTON	O30 2-1	A28 2-1	a11 1-1	M05 5-1	M19 4-0	S08 4-0	a15 3-0	J12 1-2	F19 4-1	O16 2-0	S11 4-1	S25 0-0	J29 0-1		m04 1-0	m07 1-1	a02 2-0	N13 2-3	a16 2-2	F12 0-1	J15 1-1	a30 2-1
15 OLDHAM A	N13 1-0	S11 0-0	m07 1-2	M19 3-0	D11 3-2	J15 0-0	S06 3-0	F01 2-1	a15 3-1	O30 2-1	S25 3-1	O09 1-1	F12 2-2	a25 2-1		A28 3-0	a16 4-2	J08 3-1	a30 2-0	M05 2-1	J29 2-0	O16 6-2
16 PORT VALE	J08 4-1	S25 4-0	M05 4-3	a02 2-2	a16 2-2	J29 1-1	S04 1-0	J22 1-1	A30 2-2	N13 0-2	O09 5-1	a15 2-4	D28 1-0	S13 3-2	J01 2-2		a30 4-1	J03 0-0	O16 1-1	M19 1-0	F12 2-0	O30 3-2
17 ROCHDALE	D25 0-1	F26 3-3	J15 2-0	a15 3-1	F19 4-0	S25 1-4	a23 1-1	J29 4-5	a09 2-2	m07 1-1	M12 2-2	M26 0-0	N06 0-1	N20 2-1	D04 1-1	D18 1-1		O02 2-0	S11 3-2	S07 0-0	O23 6-1	A28 0-0
18 ROTHERHAM U	a18 1-1	O09 3-0	S11 2-1	S13 0-1	D27 4-1	D18 1-0	D04 4-2	S25 2-2	N20 1-1	S06 4-1	O23 3-1	N06 2-2	M12 4-0	M26 1-2	a09 2-1	a23 3-2	F12 1-0		J29 1-1	A28 2-1	F26 1-1	J15 3-0
19 SOUTHPORT	O02 2-1	M12 2-0	S06 2-0	F19 1-1	F05 2-2	O23 3-1	J01 1-1	S04 1-3	a23 0-0	D25 2-2	M26 2-0	a09 2-1	N20 1-1	D04 0-0	D18 2-2	F26 1-0	J22 2-0	S18 0-3		a15 1-3	N06 1-2	S14 2-3
20 TRANMERE R	J22 5-0	N20 3-0	D27 2-1	S18 5-0	S04 0-0	M26 2-2	M12 1-1	S13 2-0	F26 4-2	F05 2-0	D04 4-0	D18 3-1	a23 2-0	O02 5-2	O23 1-1	N06 2-1	A30 3-2	J01 0-2	a18 7-2		a09 3-2	O09 1-2
21 WREXHAM	a30 2-0	D27 3-2	N13 2-1	a25 0-0	a18 3-1	F19 1-0	F05 4-0	O30 2-0	J22 0-0	a16 2-0	S13 6-3	J01 0-1	S01 1-0	S04 0-1	S18 1-0	O02 0-0	M05 2-1	O16 2-0	M19 4-1	J12 1-3		a02 1-1
22 YORK C	S18 1-1	M26 1-2	a15 3-1	F05 3-1	J26 4-0	N06 1-2	O23 1-2	S01 2-0	D27 5-1	O02 1-1	a09 1-0	a23 0-1	D04 3-1	D18 3-1	F26 0-0	M12 2-2	J01 0-5	S04 4-1	m07 1-2	F19 2-0	N20 2-1	

DIVISION 3 SOUTH

	ALDERSHOT	BOURNEMOUTH	BRIGHTON & HA	BRISTOL C	BRISTOL R	CARDIFF C	CLAPTON O	CRYSTAL P	EXETER C	GILLINGHAM	MANSFIELD T	MILLWALL	NEWPORT CO	NORTHAMPTON T	NOTTS CO	Q.P.R.	READING	SOUTHEND U	SWINDON T	TORQUAY U	WALSALL	WATFORD
1 ALDERSHOT		a16 2-0	M23 1-2	S18 1-1	M19 0-2	J12 1-1	O16 1-2	J01 1-0	F19 0-1	O02 2-0	O30 1-0	D27 2-1	J22 5-0	N13 0-2	S04 0-1	a30 1-0	S01 0-0	a15 1-0	m07 1-1	M05 1-0	a02 1-0	F05 1-0
2 BOURNEMOUTH	D04 3-0		J22 0-0	M12 0-0	m07 1-3	S25 3-0	S01 2-1	S18 1-0	N20 2-2	M26 2-0	a15 5-4	a23 0-3	O23 1-1	O09 0-0	F26 1-1	S04 1-1	D18 1-1	J01 7-1	a09 1-2	D25 0-0	F12 5-0	N06 0-0
3 BRIGHTON & H.A.	a23 2-1	S11 3-1		N06 1-1	O09 3-0	J29 2-1	D27 2-1	F26 2-1	a09 6-0	N20 1-0	S15 2-0	D18 1-0	M12 1-0	F12 1-2	O23 0-1	J01 3-1	S04 1-1	S01 3-1	D04 3-1	a15 1-1	S25 1-0	M26 1-2
4 BRISTOL C	J29 3-1	O30 2-1	M19 1-1		a30 0-0	M05 0-1	J08 2-0	O09 0-0	J15 4-1	A28 3-1	a27 2-1	S25 0-0	a15 0-0	D27 1-0	m07 3-1	N13 2-0	F12 1-0	a02 4-2	S11 1-1	a16 2-0	O16 3-1	S08 3-1
5 BRISTOL R	N06 0-1	S14 2-1	F19 0-0	D28 1-0		a18 2-1	S18 3-2	a09 1-0	O23 1-1	F26 2-1	S04 0-0	M26 0-2	a23 2-0	A31 0-0	D04 1-1	O02 1-1	N20 2-2	F05 2-1	M12 1-2	J22 2-0	D25 5-2	J01 0-2
6 CARDIFF C	a09 0-1	F05 3-0	S18 4-1	O23 0-0	a15 1-1		J01 2-0	D18 4-2	M26 1-1	N06 4-0	D27 4-1	D04 3-2	F26 3-1	S13 4-1	O02 2-2	J22 2-2	a23 4-1	S04 5-0	N20 2-2	A30 5-2	O09 3-1	M12 1-1
7 CLAPTON O	F26 2-1	S09 3-0	D28 0-3	a09 0-0	J29 1-0	A28 1-1		N06 0-2	D18 2-1	a23 3-0	S25 1-2	O23 2-1	N20 0-2	S11 1-0	M26 2-0	a15 1-1	M12 1-1	m07 1-1	O09 1-0	F12 2-0	J15 2-2	D04 1-1
8 CRYSTAL P	A28 1-1	J29 0-1	O16 3-2	F19 1-1	J19 3-2	a30 1-0	M19 1-0		D28 2-2	a15 3-0	a02 4-0	J15 0-0	O02 3-0	a16 0-1	F05 3-1	M05 4-0	S11 3-1	O30 2-1	S08 0-1	N13 4-1	M16 3-1	S15 4-1
9 EXETER C	O09 0-1	a02 3-1	J12 4-0	S04 3-2	M05 0-0	N13 2-1	a30 2-0	D27 2-2		S18 3-5	O16 4-0	m07 1-5	J01 2-0	O30 4-1	S01 0-3	a16 0-4	a18 0-2	M30 1-1	F12 0-0	F05 2-0	M19 3-2	J22 1-2
10 GILLINGHAM	F12 2-0	N13 0-2	a02 1-1	J01 1-0	O16 0-1	M19 1-0	F23 1-2	a18 2-4	J29 2-1		J22 0-0	O09 2-3	S01 1-0	M05 2-1	M16 2-1	J08 1-5	S15 1-2	a16 2-1	S25 0-0	a30 1-1	O30 3-0	S04 0-0
11 MANSFIELD T	M12 2-0	a18 3-2	m07 1-1	a23 3-5	J15 1-0	D25 3-0	F05 3-1	N20 2-0	F26 2-3	S11 3-1		N06 1-1	D04 1-1	A28 4-1	a09 1-2	F19 3-2	M26 5-1	O02 2-2	O23 2-0	S18 1-1	S08 3-1	D18 0-1
12 MILLWALL	a04 4-0	a25 4-0	a30 2-0	F05 0-3	N13 2-1	a16 1-0	M05 3-0	S04 2-2	S13 2-1	F19 5-0	M19 1-0		S18 4-0	a02 3-0	J24 5-0	A30 1-4	J01 1-1	O16 1-0	a15 0-2	O30 7-0	S20 4-0	O02 1-1
13 NEWPORT CO	S11 4-0	M05 1-1	O30 1-0	a18 0-0	m05 2-2	O16 1-1	a02 3-1	F12 0-0	A28 2-2	S09 2-0	a16 1-0	J29 3-1		a30 0-0	O09 3-0	M19 1-1	S25 2-2	N13 2-0	J15 2-0	J13 0-2	m07 1-2	D27 0-0
14 NORTHAMPTON T	M26 1-0	F19 1-3	O02 3-1	a19 1-0	S06 2-0	m07 0-0	J22 2-0	F03 1-1	M12 1-0	O23 4-1	J01 3-0	N20 0-1	D18 2-0		a23 2-0	F05 0-2	a09 2-2	S18 0-2	N06 1-0	S04 0-3	a18 1-1	F26 3-2
15 NOTTS CO	J15 1-0	O16 1-2	M05 0-3	S22 2-0	a16 1-1	F12 2-0	N13 1-0	S25 0-1	S08 0-0	D27 1-0	O07 2-0	S11 1-1	F19 1-1	D11 5-0		O30 2-2	J29 2-1	M19 0-2	A28 3-0	a02 0-0	a30 3-1	a18 1-2
16 Q.P.R.	D18 3-0	J15 1-2	A28 2-1	M26 0-2	F12 4-0	S11 2-1	a18 3-2	O23 1-0	D04 4-0	a09 2-0	O09 1-1	S09 0-2	N06 0-0	S25 1-1	M12 2-1		F26 3-0	D25 1-0	a23 3-0	m07 6-3	J29 3-1	N20 2-0
17 READING	S08 3-2	a30 4-1	J15 2-1	O02 0-1	a02 4-0	m04 0-0	O30 2-0	J22 3-2	a15 1-0	m07 2-0	N13 3-2	A28 1-0	F05 2-1	J08 4-3	S18 0-2	O16 1-0		M05 3-2	D25 2-1	M19 1-1	a16 2-1	F19 4-1
18 SOUTHEND U	a18 4-1	A28 1-0	S08 2-1	N20 5-0	S25 1-1	J15 3-1	S15 1-2	M12 2-2	a23 1-1	D04 2-0	F12 0-1	F26 1-2	M26 0-2	J29 4-2	N06 2-1	D27 2-1	O23 4-2		D18 0-0	O09 5-1	S11 1-0	a09 2-2
19 SWINDON T	S15 2-0	J26 1-0	a16 0-1	m04 2-3	O30 2-1	a02 2-0	F19 1-0	S01 4-0	O02 3-0	F05 3-0	M05 3-3	a18 1-2	S04 3-2	M19 1-0	J01 1-0	D28. 1-3	D27 0-0	a30 1-1		O16 1-0	N13 1-1	S18 0-2
20 TORQUAY U	O23 1-5	D27 0-0	a18 0-1	D04 1-3	S11 4-1	S08 0-1	O02 3-1	M26 0-0	S25 2-1	D18 1-0	J29 0-1	M12 1-1	a09 0-0	J15 1-2	N20 0-3	S15 0-2	N06 3-2	F19 3-3	F26 1-0		A28 1-0	a23 0-1
21 WALSALL	N20 2-0	O02 2-0	F05 0-3	F26 2-8	D27 5-2	F19 1-0	S04 2-0	a23 1-1	N06 0-2	M12 3-1	m02 2-0	a09 1-1	S13 3-1	a15 1-1	D18 1-0	S18 0-3	D04 2-5	J22 1-5	M26 2-3	J01 0-0		O23 3-1
22 WATFORD	S25 5-1	M19 0-2	N13 1-1	S01 3-1	A28 4-0	O30 4-0	a16 2-0	m07 1-2	S11 0-0	J15 1-1	a30 2-0	F12 1-1	D25 3-0	O16 1-3	a15 2-0	a02 3-1	O09 4-0	J19 3-1	J29 4-0	D28 4-0	M05 2-1	

LEAGUE TABLES

DIVISION 1

	P	W	D	L	F	A	W	D	L	F	A	Pts
Arsenal	42	15	4	2	52	16	6	6	9	25	28	52
Wolverhampton W	42	11	8	2	47	21	9	3	9	25	28	51
Preston N.E.	42	9	9	3	34	21	7	8	6	30	23	49
Charlton A	42	14	5	2	43	14	2	9	10	22	37	46
Middlesbrough	42	12	4	5	40	26	7	4	10	32	39	46
Brentford	42	10	6	5	44	27	8	3	10	25	32	45
Bolton W	42	11	6	4	38	22	4	9	8	26	38	45
Sunderland	42	12	6	3	32	18	2	10	9	23	39	44
Leeds U	42	11	6	4	38	26	3	9	9	26	43	43
Chelsea	42	11	6	4	40	22	3	7	11	25	43	41
Liverpool	42	9	5	7	40	30	6	6	9	25	41	41
Blackpool	42	10	5	6	33	26	6	3	12	28	40	40
Derby Co	42	10	5	6	42	36	5	5	11	24	51	40
Everton	42	11	5	5	54	34	5	2	14	25	41	39
Huddersfield T	42	11	3	7	29	24	6	2	13	26	44	39
Leicester C	42	9	6	6	31	26	5	5	11	23	49	39
Stoke C	42	10	7	4	42	21	3	5	13	16	38	38
Birmingham C	42	7	11	3	34	28	3	7	11	24	34	38
Portsmouth	42	11	6	4	41	22	2	6	13	21	46	38
Grimsby T	42	11	5	5	29	23	2	7	12	22	45	38
Manchester C	42	12	2	7	49	33	2	6	13	31	44	36
W.B.A.	42	10	5	6	46	36	4	3	14	28	55	36

DIVISION 2

	P	W	D	L	F	A	W	D	L	F	A	Pts
Aston Villa	42	17	2	2	50	12	8	5	8	23	23	57
Manchester U	42	15	3	3	50	18	7	6	8	32	32	53
Sheffield U	42	15	4	2	46	19	7	5	9	27	37	53
Coventry C	42	12	5	4	31	15	8	7	6	35	30	52
Tottenham H	42	14	3	4	46	16	5	3	13	30	38	44
Burnley	42	15	4	2	35	11	2	6	13	19	43	44
Bradford P.A.	42	13	4	4	51	22	4	5	12	18	34	43
Fulham	42	10	7	4	44	23	6	4	11	17	34	43
West Ham U	42	13	5	3	34	16	1	9	11	19	36	42
Bury	42	12	3	6	43	26	6	2	13	20	34	41
Chesterfield	42	12	2	7	39	24	4	7	10	24	39	41
Luton T	42	10	6	5	53	36	5	4	12	36	50	40
Plymouth A	42	10	7	4	40	30	4	5	12	17	35	40
Norwich C	42	11	5	5	35	28	3	6	12	21	47	39
Southampton	42	12	6	3	42	26	3	3	15	13	51	39
Blackburn R	42	13	6	2	51	30	1	4	16	20	50	38
Sheffield W	42	10	5	6	27	21	4	5	12	22	35	38
Swansea T	42	12	6	3	31	21	1	6	14	14	52	38
Newcastle U	42	12	4	5	38	18	2	4	15	13	40	36
Nottingham F	42	12	3	6	29	21	2	5	14	18	39	36
Barnsley	42	7	11	3	30	20	4	3	14	20	44	36
Stockport Co	42	8	6	7	24	24	3	3	15	19	46	31

DIVISION 3 NORTH

	P	W	D	L	F	A	W	D	L	F	A	Pts
Tranmere R	42	15	4	2	57	21	8	6	7	24	20	56
Doncaster R	42	15	4	2	48	16	6	8	7	26	33	54
Hull C	42	11	8	2	51	19	9	5	7	29	24	53
Oldham A	42	16	4	1	48	18	3	9	9	19	28	51
Gateshead	42	15	5	1	53	20	5	6	10	31	39	51
Rotherham U	42	13	6	2	45	21	7	4	10	23	35	50
Lincoln C	42	14	3	4	48	17	5	5	11	18	33	46
Crewe A	42	14	3	4	47	17	4	6	11	24	36	45
Chester C	42	13	4	4	54	31	3	8	10	23	41	44
Wrexham	42	14	4	3	37	15	2	7	12	21	48	43
York C	42	11	4	6	40	25	5	6	10	30	43	42
Carlisle U	42	11	5	5	35	19	4	4	13	22	48	39
New Brighton	42	12	5	4	43	18	3	3	15	17	43	38
Bradford C	42	12	6	3	46	21	2	4	15	20	48	38
Port Vale	42	11	8	2	45	27	1	6	14	20	46	38
Southport	42	8	8	5	30	26	4	6	11	23	56	38
Rochdale	42	7	10	4	38	27	6	1	14	29	51	37
Halifax T	42	9	7	5	24	19	3	5	13	20	47	36
Darlington	42	10	4	7	37	31	1	6	14	17	48	32
Hartlepool U	42	10	8	3	36	20	0	4	17	17	60	32
Barrow	42	9	6	6	28	20	2	4	15	13	51	32
Accrington S	42	9	2	10	31	32	2	5	14	14	43	29

DIVISION 3 SOUTH

	P	W	D	L	F	A	W	D	L	F	A	Pts
Millwall	42	15	3	3	53	15	8	7	6	30	22	56
Bristol C	42	14	6	1	37	13	7	7	7	31	27	55
Q.P.R.	42	15	3	3	44	17	7	6	8	36	30	53
Watford	42	14	4	3	50	15	7	7	7	23	28	53
Brighton & H.A.	42	15	3	3	40	16	6	6	9	24	28	51
Reading	42	17	2	2	44	21	3	9	9	27	42	51
Crystal Palace	42	14	4	3	45	17	4	8	9	22	30	48
Swindon T	42	12	4	5	33	19	5	6	10	16	30	44
Northampton T	42	12	4	5	30	19	5	5	11	21	38	43
Cardiff C	42	13	7	1	57	22	2	5	14	10	32	42
Notts Co	42	10	6	5	29	17	6	3	12	21	33	41
Southend U	42	12	5	4	43	23	3	5	13	27	45	40
Bournemouth	42	8	10	3	36	20	6	2	13	20	37	40
Mansfield T	42	12	5	4	46	26	3	4	14	16	41	39
Bristol R	42	10	7	4	28	20	3	6	12	18	41	39
Newport Co	42	9	10	2	31	15	2	6	13	12	37	38
Exeter C	42	10	4	7	37	32	3	8	10	20	38	38
Aldershot	42	11	4	6	23	14	4	1	16	16	45	35
Clapton O	42	10	7	4	27	19	3	0	18	15	42	33
Torquay U	42	7	5	9	22	28	2	7	12	16	45	30
Walsall	42	10	4	7	34	37	1	3	17	18	51	29
Gillingham	42	9	5	7	25	25	1	1	19	11	52	26

FOOTBALL LEAGUE RECORDS

Top scorers: Div 1, T.Lawton (Everton) 35 goals; Div 2, H.Billington (Luton Town) 28 goals; Div 3 N, S.Hunt (Carlisle United) 32 goals; Div 3 S, G.Morton (Swindon Town) 28 goals.

Gillingham failed to gain re-election, Ipswich Town elected in their place. Port Vale transferred to Division Three South.

Wing-half Joe Mercer, a wing-half with a superb tactical brain who played a major part in Everton's League Championship of 1938-39.

DIVISION 1

	ARSENAL	ASTON VILLA	BIRMINGHAM	BLACKPOOL	BOLTON W	BRENTFORD	CHARLTON A	CHELSEA	DERBY CO	EVERTON	GRIMSBY T	HUDDERSFIELD T	LEEDS U	LEICESTER C	LIVERPOOL	MANCHESTER U	MIDDLESBROUGH	PORTSMOUTH	PRESTON N.E.	STOKE C	SUNDERLAND	WOLVERHAMPTON W
1 ARSENAL		S24 0-0	D03 3-1	a10 2-1	M04 3-1	m06 2-0	J21 2-0	F18 1-0	S14 1-2	S10 1-2	O08 2-0	D31 1-0	N05 2-3	N19 0-0	M18 2-0	a15 2-1	a01 1-2	A27 2-0	O22 1-0	D17 4-1	F04 2-0	F01 0-0
2 ASTON VILLA	J28 1-3		M04 5-1	J14 3-1	a15 1-3	S17 5-0	D03 2-0	N19 6-2	S03 0-1	S05 0-3	D24 0-2	F15 4-0	D17 2-1	O22 1-2	F18 2-0	N05 0-2	m06 1-1	O01 2-0	a01 3-0	M18 3-0	D27 1-1	a11 2-2
3 BIRMINGHAM	a08 1-2	O29 3-0		a22 2-1	O08 0-2	D10 5-1	F04 3-4	a26 1-1	O15 3-0	N12 1-0	F25 1-1	M29 1-1	a29 4-0	S07 2-1	a10 0-0	D31 3-3	D26 2-1	N26 2-0	S24 1-3	S10 1-2	A27 1-2	M11 3-2
4 BLACKPOOL	a07 1-0	S10 2-4	D17 2-1		M18 0-0	S19 4-1	N05 0-0	O08 5-1	F04 2-2	A27 0-2	S24 3-1	D26 1-1	N19 1-2	D03 1-1	a01 1-1	F18 3-5	a15 4-0	m06 2-1	M08 2-1	O22 1-1	J25 1-1	D31 1-0
5 BOLTON W	O29 1-1	D10 1-2	F22 3-0	N12 0-1		M11 1-1	A27 2-1	S05 0-2	M25 2-1	O15 4-2	N26 1-1	F25 3-2	J14 2-2	J28 4-0	S17 3-1	a29 0-0	O01 4-1	D31 5-1	a26 0-2	J02 1-3	a08 2-1	a22 0-0
6 BRENTFORD	S08 1-0	F08 2-4	a15 0-1	a29 1-1	N05 2-2		M04 1-0	O22 1-0	O08 1-3	D31 2-0	F04 1-2	A27 2-1	M18 0-1	a01 2-0	N19 2-1	D17 2-5	D03 2-1	F22 2-0	a07 3-1	F18 1-0	S24 2-3	S10 0-1
7 CHARLTON A	D27 1-0	a08 1-0	O01 4-4	M11 3-1	D24 2-1	O29 1-1		a07 2-0	N12 1-0	a22 2-1	M29 3-1	O15 2-1	S03 2-0	S17 1-0	J14 1-3	F11 7-1	J28 3-0	F25 3-3	m06 3-1	A29 4-2	N26 3-0	D10 0-4
8 CHELSEA	O15 4-2	M25 2-1	S17 2-2	M15 1-1	m06 1-1	F25 1-3	a10 1-3		O29 0-2	a08 0-2	M11 5-1	D10 3-0	D27 2-2	S03 3-0	D24 4-1	J28 0-1	J14 4-2	a22 1-0	A31 3-1	O01 1-1	N12 4-0	N26 1-3
9 DERBY CO	a29 1-2	D31 2-1	F18 0-1	O01 2-1	N19 3-0	F11 1-2	M18 3-1	M08 0-1		D27 2-1	F01 4-1	A31 1-0	a01 1-0	a15 1-1	D03 2-2	O22 5-1	D17 1-4	a10 0-1	N05 2-0	S24 5-0	S10 1-0	A27 2-2
10 EVERTON	J14 2-0	a29 3-0	M18 4-2	D24 4-0	F18 2-1	S03 2-1	D17 1-4	D03 4-1	D26 2-2		A31 3-0	J28 3-2	O22 4-0	M08 4-0	O01 2-1	N19 3-0	N05 4-0	S17 5-1	a15 0-0	a01 1-1	a10 6-2	O08 1-0
11 GRIMSBY T	F21 2-1	A27 1-2	O22 1-0	J28 2-0	a01 1-1	O01 0-0	N19 1-1	N05 2-1	S17 1-1	m06 3-0		a07 3-3	D03 3-2	D17 6-1	a15 2-1	S10 1-0	F18 0-2	S06 2-1	M18 1-1	M07 3-1	D31 1-3	D26 2-4
12 HUDDERSFIELD T	S03 1-1	O08 1-1	N19 3-1	D27 3-0	O22 2-1	D24 1-2	F18 4-0	a15 3-1	S07 3-0	S24 3-0	a11 2-0		S17 0-1	N05 2-0	M15 1-1	a01 1-1	M18 0-1	J14 3-0	D17 3-0	D03 1-4	S14 0-1	F04 1-2
13 LEEDS U	M11 4-2	a22 2-0	A31 2-0	M25 1-0	S10 1-2	N12 3-2	D31 2-1	D26 1-1	N26 1-4	F25 1-2	a08 0-1	a19 2-1		O01 8-2	J28 1-1	a10 3-1	F11 0-1	O29 2-2	A27 2-1	m06 0-0	D10 3-3	O15 1-0
14 LEICESTER C	M25 0-2	F25 1-1	S12 2-1	a08 3-4	S24 0-0	N26 1-1	F09 1-5	D31 3-2	D10 2-3	O29 3-0	a22 0-2	M11 0-1	F04 2-0		O08 2-2	D27 1-1	a11 5-3	N12 5-0	S10 2-1	A27 2-2	O15 0-2	m04 0-2
15 LIVERPOOL	N12 2-2	O15 3-0	a07 4-0	N26 1-0	J25 1-2	M25 1-0	S10 1-0	A27 2-1	a08 2-1	F04 0-3	D10 2-2	O29 3-3	S24 3-0	M04 1-1		S07 1-0	S14 3-1	M11 4-4	D31 4-1	D27 1-0	a22 1-1	F25 0-2
16 MANCHESTER U	D10 1-0	M11 1-1	S03 4-1	O15 0-0	A31 2-2	a22 3-0	O08 0-2	S24 5-1	F25 1-1	M29 0-2	J14 3-1	N26 1-1	a07 0-0	D26 3-0	m06 2-0		D24 1-1	a08 1-1	F04 1-1	J21 0-1	O29 0-1	N12 1-3
17 MIDDLESBROUGH	N26 1-1	A31 1-1	D27 2-2	D10 9-2	F04 1-2	a08 3-1	S24 4-0	S10 1-1	a22 2-0	M11 4-4	O15 3-2	N12 4-1	O08 1-2	a10 3-2	J02 3-0	A27 3-1		M29 8-2	J25 2-2	D31 5-1	F25 3-0	O29 1-0
18 PORTSMOUTH	D24 0-0	F04 0-0	a01 2-0	A31 1-0	S03 2-1	D27 2-2	O22 0-2	D17 2-1	a07 1-3	F01 0-1	a19 2-1	S10 4-0	M08 2-0	M18 0-1	N05 1-1	D03 0-0	N19 1-1		F18 0-0	a15 2-0	O08 2-1	S24 1-0
19 PRESTON N.E.	F25 2-1	N26 3-2	J28 5-0	O29 1-1	D27 2-2	a10 2-0	S05 2-0	a29 1-1	M11 4-1	D10 0-1	N12 1-1	a22 3-0	D24 2-0	J14 2-1	S03 1-0	O01 1-1	S17 3-1	O15 2-2		F15 1-1	M25 2-1	a08 4-2
20 STOKE C	a22 1-0	N12 3-1	J14 6-3	F25 1-1	a10 4-1	O15 3-2	a29 1-0	F04 6-1	J28 3-0	N26 0-0	O29 1-2	a08 2-2	S05 1-1	D24 1-0	D26 3-1	S17 1-1	S03 1-3	D10 1-1	O08 3-1		M11 3-1	M29 5-3
21 SUNDERLAND	O01 0-0	D26 1-5	D24 1-0	S17 1-2	D03 2-2	J28 1-1	a01 1-1	M18 3-2	J14 1-0	a07 1-2	S03 1-1	a29 0-0	a15 2-1	F18 2-0	D17 2-3	M04 5-2	O22 1-2	M15 0-2	N19 1-2	N05 3-0		S07 1-1
22 WOLVERHAMPTON W	S17 0-1	a10 2-1	N05 2-1	S03 1-1	D17 1-1	J14 5-2	a15 3-1	a01 2-0	D24 0-0	F22 7-0	D27 5-0	O01 3-0	F18 4-1	A29 0-0	O22 2-2	M18 3-0	M08 6-1	J28 3-0	D03 3-0	N19 3-0	m06 0-0	

Centre-half Bob Pryde dominated Blackburn Rovers' defence as they won the Division Two title in 1938-39.

DIVISION 2

	BLACKBURN R	BRADFORD	BURNLEY	BURY	CHESTERFIELD	COVENTRY C	FULHAM	LUTON T	MANCHESTER C	MILLWALL	NEWCASTLE U	NORWICH C	NOTTINGHAM F	PLYMOUTH A	SHEFFIELD U	SHEFFIELD W	SOUTHAMPTON	SWANSEA T	TOTTENHAM H	TRANMERE R	W.B.A.	WEST HAM U
1 BLACKBURN R		J23 6-4	F18 1-0	D26 1-0	D31 3-0	N05 0-2	a10 2-1	M16 2-0	S24 3-3	F04 3-1	N19 3-0	D03 6-0	M18 3-2	D17 4-0	O08 1-2	J02 2-4	a15 3-0	S10 4-0	O22 3-1	A27 3-2	a01 3-0	S19 3-1
2 BRADFORD	S17 0-4		N05 2-2	F11 3-2	D26 0-0	a01 0-2	J28 1-5	F18 2-1	S03 4-2	J14 1-0	M04 0-1	D24 3-0	D03 1-2	O22 2-2	a15 0-3	O01 3-1	N19 2-1	A29 1-1	M18 0-0	S19 3-0	D17 4-4	a11 1-2
3 BURNLEY	O15 3-2	M11 0-0		O29 0-1	M25 1-2	D24 1-0	S05 2-0	O01 3-2	D10 1-1	F25 2-0	J14 2-0	J28 3-0	S03 2-1	F11 1-0	a07 2-3	a22 1-2	A30 2-1	N12 1-1	D26 1-0	N26 3-1	S17 0-3	a08 1-0
4 BURY	D27 2-4	O08 0-1	M04 1-0		S24 3-1	F18 5-0	A29 0-2	N19 2-5	a07 1-5	J02 1-1	a15 1-1	M18 2-3	O22 2-1	a01 3-0	D03 2-2	D24 2-3	S03 5-2	F04 4-0	D17 3-1	J21 5-0	N05 3-3	S10 1-1
5 CHESTERFIELD	S03 0-2	D27 2-2	N19 3-2	J28 2-1		M04 3-0	a24 0-1	a15 1-2	A29 0-3	D24 3-0	a07 2-0	O22 2-0	D17 7-1	N05 3-1	M18 1-0	S17 3-1	D03 6-1	m06 6-1	a01 3-1	F11 3-0	F18 3-1	O01 1-0
6 COVENTRY C	M11 0-1	N26 3-1	A27 1-1	O15 0-0	O29 2-0		D10 3-1	S05 1-0	M25 0-1	N12 2-1	O01 1-0	a11 2-0	J28 5-1	D26 1-2	a29 0-3	F25 1-0	S10 3-0	a08 3-0	D31 4-0	a22 2-0	F11 1-1	a24 0-0
7 FULHAM	a07 2-3	S24 4-0	S12 0-0	a29 1-2	S10 2-0	a15 1-0		D03 2-1	F04 2-1	O08 2-1	M18 1-1	a01 2-0	N05 2-2	M04 1-2	D17 1-2	a17 2-2	O22 1-1	J23 1-0	F18 1-0	D31 1-0	N19 3-0	A27 3-2
8 LUTON T	O29 1-1	O15 2-2	F04 1-0	M25 2-1	D10 5-0	m06 1-3	a08 2-1		J14 3-0	a22 0-0	A31 2-1	S03 2-1	D27 1-0	J21 3-4	S24 2-0	N26 1-5	a07 6-2	F25 6-3	O08 0-0	M11 3-0	D24 3-1	N12 1-2
9 MANCHESTER C	J28 3-2	D31 5-1	a15 2-0	a10 0-0	a29 3-1	N19 3-0	O01 3-5	S10 1-2		S17 1-6	D03 4-1	D17 4-1	a01 3-0	F18 1-3	O22 3-2	a26 1-1	M18 2-1	A27 5-0	N05 2-0	D27 5-2	M04 3-3	S07 2-4
10 MILLWALL	O01 4-1	S10 3-1	O22 1-1	S05 0-0	A27 3-1	M18 0-0	F11 1-1	D17 2-1	M13 3-1		a01 1-1	M04 6-0	N19 5-0	S24 3-0	F18 4-0	a07 2-0	N05 0-1	D31 1-1	a15 2-0	a29 2-1	D03 1-5	M27 0-2
11 NEWCASTLE U	M25 2-2	O29 1-0	S10 3-2	D10 6-0	J02 0-1	F04 0-4	N12 2-1	a29 2-0	a08 0-2	N26 2-2		D27 4-0	O08 4-0	A27 2-1	D31 0-0	M11 2-1	S24 1-0	a22 1-2	M01 0-1	O15 5-1	S14 5-1	F25 2-0
12 NORWICH C	a08 4-0	A27 1-3	S24 4-0	N12 3-1	F25 2-0	a10 1-1	N26 3-3	D31 2-1	a22 0-0	O29 0-2	M16 1-1		m06 1-0	S10 2-1	F02 1-2	M25 2-2	O08 2-1	O15 3-0	F04 1-2	D10 2-0	S01 2-3	M11 2-6
13 NOTTINGHAM F	N12 1-3	a08 2-0	D31 2-2	F25 1-1	a22 0-1	S24 3-0	M11 1-1	D26 2-4	N26 3-4	M25 3-0	F15 2-0	S07 1-0		a29 2-1	A27 0-2	D10 3-3	F08 0-2	O29 1-2	S10 2-1	F04 2-2	a07 2-0	O15 0-0
14 PLYMOUTH A	a22 1-0	F25 4-1	O08 1-0	N26 0-1	M11 0-0	D27 0-2	O29 0-0	S17 4-1	O15 0-0	J28 2-2	D24 0-1	m03 1-0	A31 3-0		F04 0-1	a08 1-1	m06 2-0	D10 0-0	a10 0-1	N12 3-1	S03 2-1	M25 0-0
15 SHEFFIELD U	a26 0-0	D10 3-1	J02 1-1	a08 1-1	N12 1-1	A29 0-0	a22 2-0	J28 2-2	F25 1-0	O15 2-1	S03 0-0	S17 4-0	D24 0-1	O01 0-1		O29 0-0	D26 5-1	M11 1-2	m06 6-1	M25 2-0	J14 1-1	N26 3-1
16 SHEFFIELD W	S08 3-0	F04 2-0	D17 4-1	A27 2-0	M20 0-0	O22 2-2	D27 5-1	a01 4-1	O08 3-1	a10 3-1	N05 0-2	N19 7-0	a15 1-1	D03 1-2	M04 1-0		F18 2-0	S24 1-1	a29 1-0	S10 2-0	M18 2-1	D31 1-4
17 SOUTHAMPTON	D10 1-3	M25 3-2	a29 2-1	D31 0-0	a08 2-2	J14 0-2	F25 2-1	a10 0-4	N12 1-2	M11 1-1	J28 0-0	F11 3-1	S17 2-2	S14 2-1	D27 2-2	O15 4-3		N26 4-1	A27 1-2	O29 3-1	O01 2-1	a22 0-2
18 SWANSEA T	J14 2-1	a29 2-2	M18 4-0	O01 3-3	S05 1-1	D03 2-4	S17 1-1	O22 2-3	D24 2-0	S03 1-1	D17 0-1	F18 0-1	M04 1-0	a15 2-1	N05 1-2	J28 0-1	a01 1-3		N19 1-1	a10 1-0	D27 3-2	F16 3-2
19 TOTTENHAM H	F25 4-3	N12 2-2	D27 1-0	a22 4-3	N26 2-2	S03 2-1	O15 1-0	F11 0-1	M11 2-3	D10 4-0	S17 1-0	O01 4-1	J14 4-1	a07 1-0	S12 2-2	A29 3-3	D24 1-1	M25 3-0		a08 3-1	J28 2-2	O29 2-1
20 TRANMERE R	D24 1-1	J02 2-1	a01 0-3	S17 3-0	O08 0-1	D17 1-2	S03 0-1	N05 2-3	D26 3-9	A29 2-0	F18 0-3	a15 0-1	O01 1-1	M18 2-0	N19 0-2	J14 1-4	M04 1-1	a07 2-0	D03 0-2		O22 3-1	J28 2-2
21 W.B.A.	N26 2-0	a22 0-2	F01 1-2	M11 6-0	O15 1-0	O08 3-1	M25 3-0	A27 3-0	O29 3-1	a08 0-0	S07 5-2	a29 4-2	a10 0-0	D31 4-2	S10 3-4	N12 5-1	F04 2-0	a19 0-0	S24 4-3	F25 2-0		D10 3-2
22 WEST HAM U	A29 1-2	a07 0-2	D03 1-0	J14 0-0	F04 1-1	S17 4-1	D24 1-0	M18 0-1	m06 2-1	D27 0-0	O22 1-1	N05 2-0	F18 5-0	N19 2-1	a01 0-0	S03 2-3	D17 1-2	O08 5-2	M04 0-2	S24 6-1	a15 2-1	

SEASON 1938-39

DIVISION 3 NORTH

	ACCRINGTON S	BARNSLEY	BARROW	BRADFORD C	CARLISLE U	CHESTER	CREWE A	DARLINGTON	DONCASTER R	GATESHEAD	HALIFAX T	HARTLEPOOLS U	HULL C	LINCOLN C	NEW BRIGHTON	OLDHAM A	ROCHDALE	ROTHERHAM U	SOUTHPORT	STOCKPORT CO	WREXHAM	YORK C
1 ACCRINGTON S		D27 0-2	J14 0-2	J28 2-3	O29 1-1	S17 2-3	F25 2-1	M11 3-0	a10 0-0	M25 1-1	D24 1-2	N12 0-0	O01 1-1	F11 3-4	S03 1-2	S27 1-3	D10 0-5	a22 2-1	O15 1-4	a29 3-2	J07 3-1	a08 3-1
2 BARNSLEY	D26 4-1		S17 4-0	O01 5-2	M11 3-0	J28 3-0	O29 5-2	N12 7-1	O15 1-1	D10 2-0	S03 1-0	M25 2-0	F11 5-1	a29 4-0	J14 1-1	D24 3-0	a22 2-0	S05 2-0	F25 3-1	a10 0-1	a08 2-1	N26 1-0
3 BARROW	S10 2-3	J21 1-2		D26 2-1	a08 5-0	a10 0-1	J07 1-2	F13 2-0	N12 4-4	a29 1-1	F04 0-0	a22 1-1	S05 3-1	A27 2-2	O08 3-0	S24 2-0	O29 3-1	D10 4-1	M25 4-0	D31 0-2	O15 4-0	F25 2-0
4 BRADFORD C	S24 2-1	F04 0-2	D27 3-0		a22 2-0	S05 1-0	M22 4-1	A27 6-2	M15 2-1	F25 1-1	S12 1-0	O15 0-1	D31 6-2	S10 3-0	a10 3-3	O08 1-4	N12 3-0	M25 5-2	a08 2-1	J25 4-0	O29 4-0	D10 6-0
5 CARLISLE U	M04 6-4	N05 3-1	D03 3-0	D17 0-2		a15 1-3	S17 1-0	D31 1-1	O01 2-3	S08 2-2	N19 1-2	A27 2-0	S10 1-2	F18 4-3	a01 1-1	M18 2-0	a29 5-1	F11 3-1	J28 1-1	O22 3-2	D27 1-1	a07 1-3
6 CHESTER	F15 1-0	S24 2-1	a07 1-2	m06 3-2	M01 6-1		a08 4-0	a22 0-0	M25 0-4	O15 2-2	O08 5-1	D27 8-2	A27 1-1	D31 0-0	A31 1-3	F04 4-2	M11 0-0	N12 1-4	a26 2-0	S10 4-3	F25 4-2	O29 5-1
7 CREWE A	O22 2-1	M04 0-0	a01 1-1	a15 0-0	J21 7-1	D03 0-2		S10 2-0	F11 1-2	A27 3-2	M18 2-2	D31 3-2	D17 0-1	S24 6-0	N19 7-1	N05 1-2	a07 4-1	a29 0-0	O01 4-2	F18 2-1	S05 1-0	D27 8-2
8 DARLINGTON	N05 3-0	M18 0-1	a15 3-1	D24 0-4	S03 2-1	D17 3-3	J14 1-0		J28 1-2	D27 5-2	a01 1-0	S07 3-0	F18 0-1	O22 3-1	D03 3-0	N19 3-3	F11 1-2	O01 3-1	S17 0-2	M04 4-3	a07 3-1	a29 1-2
9 DONCASTER R	a07 7-1	F18 1-3	M18 1-1	a20 1-2	F04 1-0	N19 4-1	O08 1-2	S24 4-1		S10 2-3	M04 0-0	J26 3-1	D03 1-0	a15 4-1	N05 4-1	O22 3-2	S12 5-0	D26 1-1	A29 0-0	D17 3-1	D31 0-0	A27 1-0
10 GATESHEAD	N19 4-1	a01 1-1	A31 2-1	O22 0-0	m06 1-1	F18 3-0	D24 0-5	D26 0-2	J14 2-0		a15 2-0	a10 2-0	M04 2-2	N05 4-0	D17 0-3	D03 2-0	J28 2-2	S17 7-1	S03 0-0	M18 4-1	F11 5-1	O01 2-3
11 HALIFAX T	A27 2-0	D31 1-4	O01 1-0	A29 2-2	M25 5-1	F11 1-1	N12 0-0	J09 1-1	O29 0-0	a24 3-3		a08 2-0	a10 1-0	D26 2-0	J28 3-1	S10 0-0	O15 2-1	F25 1-1	M11 1-1	S05 3-3	a22 0-2	J21 2-1
12 HARTLEPOOLS U	M18 2-1	N19 0-1	D17 1-2	F18 1-3	D24 2-1	D26 2-5	S03 0-1	S14 3-0	S17 1-3	a07 3-1	D03 1-0		O22 3-3	M04 2-1	a15 3-2	a01 0-0	O01 4-2	J28 1-1	J14 0-2	N05 4-2	m06 0-0	F11 3-2
13 HULL C	F04 6-1	O08 0-1	S12 4-0	S03 3-2	J14 11-1	D24 3-0	a22 2-1	O15 3-2	a08 0-0	O29 1-0	a07 1-1	F25 4-1		J21 4-2	D26 3-0	A29 0-2	M25 3-3	M09 0-2	a17 2-1	S24 4-4	M11 1-1	N12 2-0
14 LINCOLN C	O08 3-0	A29 2-4	D24 1-1	J14 4-0	O15 2-1	S03 0-3	J28 3-2	F25 3-0	m06 2-5	M11 1-0	D27 0-0	O29 2-2	S17 0-3		S12 0-0	a07 1-0	J11 2-2	a08 0-1	a22 0-1	F04 3-2	N12 8-3	M25 3-3
15 NEW BRIGHTON	D31 4-1	S10 1-2	F11 2-0	a07 2-1	D10 2-3	a29 1-3	M25 1-2	a08 3-0	M11 3-6	a22 0-1	S24 1-0	J18 5-2	D27 6-1	S07 3-2		J21 0-1	F25 3-1	O29 3-0	N12 1-1	A27 0-0	F04 2-3	O15 3-2
16 OLDHAM A	S05 2-0	A27 4-2	J28 1-0	F11 2-1	N12 6-0	O01 1-3	M11 3-0	M25 2-0	F25 0-0	a08 1-3	J14 1-0	J07 4-2	a29 4-1	a10 1-0	S17 1-0		D31 1-2	O15 2-0	O29 2-4	a17 3-1	D10 4-2	a22 6-0
17 ROCHDALE	a15 4-1	D17 2-1	M04 2-2	M18 1-1	A30 2-3	N05 5-2	a10 5-0	O08 6-1	S06 1-1	S24 5-2	F18 4-5	F04 3-4	N19 4-0	a01 4-0	O22 2-0	S03 1-2		D24 0-1	D27 5-0	D03 0-1	J21 0-0	S10 2-2
18 ROTHERHAM U	D17 2-1	S12 0-1	N05 1-2	N19 2-0	O08 4-0	M18 2-0	A29 4-1	F04 3-3	D27 0-0	J21 2-2	O22 0-1	S24 5-1	a01 0-2	D03 1-3	M04 0-0	F18 3-1	A27 7-1		a10 1-0	a15 3-2	S10 3-0	D31 2-0
19 SOUTHPORT	F18 1-0	O22 0-0	N19 4-1	D03 2-2	S24 7-1	a01 2-0	F04 1-2	J21 4-1	a29 0-4	D31 2-0	N05 1-0	S10 2-0	a15 4-0	D17 4-1	M18 1-1	M04 0-0	D26 4-1	a07 1-0		O08 3-0	A27 3-1	S06 1-1
20 STOCKPORT CO	A29 3-0	a07 1-1	S03 3-1	S17 2-0	F25 3-0	J14 0-0	O15 5-1	O29 5-2	a22 1-2	N12 3-2	m06 3-3	M11 5-0	J28 2-2	O01 3-3	D24 1-1	D27 3-1	a08 1-2	J02 5-0	F11 3-1		M25 2-1	a24 3-1
21 WREXHAM	a01 2-0	D03 1-1	F18 3-0	M04 1-1	D26 2-5	O22 3-2	S14 0-4	a10 3-1	S03 3-0	O08 2-0	D17 3-2	A29 3-0	N05 4-2	M18 1-0	O01 1-2	a15 4-1	S17 1-0	J14 2-0	D24 4-3	N19 2-1		J28 1-3
22 YORK C	D03 2-2	a15 2-3	O22 2-3	N05 0-1	a10 4-1	M04 2-2	D26 4-1	A31 1-1	D24 2-2	F04 1-1	S17 3-0	O08 2-0	M18 1-0	N19 1-3	F18 2-0	D17 4-1	J14 0-7	S03 0-1	m06 2-3	a01 1-2	S24 1-0	

DIVISION 3 SOUTH

	ALDERSHOT	BOURNEMOUTH	BRIGHTON & HA	BRISTOL C	BRISTOL R	CARDIFF C	CLAPTON O	CRYSTAL P	EXETER C	IPSWICH T	MANSFIELD T	NEWPORT CO	NORTHAMPTON T	NOTTS CO	PORT VALE	Q.P.R.	READING	SOUTHEND U	SWINDON T	TORQUAY U	WALSALL	WATFORD
1 ALDERSHOT		D17 2-1	F18 1-1	A31 0-1	S07 1-0	D03 1-1	S17 1-0	D27 2-1	a01 2-0	a15 3-1	N05 3-0	J28 1-0	O01 3-0	F11 0-3	a19 1-0	M18 2-0	O22 1-1	N19 1-0	S03 1-0	J14 1-1	M04 3-3	a07 1-1
2 BOURNEMOUTH	a22 4-0		a10 2-0	O15 4-0	M29 5-2	O08 0-0	M25 0-0	A27 1-1	F04 2-0	m06 0-0	S10 1-1	N12 0-1	M11 3-1	O29 3-2	M15 1-1	J21 4-2	A31 0-0	S24 0-4	a08 2-0	J18 2-5	D31 3-1	F25 1-1
3 BRIGHTON & H.A.	O15 0-3	a07 1-1		D27 1-0	a29 6-3	F04 1-2	N12 2-0	F25 0-0	S24 6-1	O08 2-0	D31 3-0	M11 0-0	O29 1-0	a22 2-0	a08 1-0	S10 3-1	S07 2-2	F08 3-0	J07 4-0	M25 2-0	A27 3-1	a26 0-0
4 BRISTOL C	a29 1-0	F18 2-0	D26 2-0		O22 2-1	a01 1-1	J28 3-1	a10 1-1	N19 4-1	D03 3-2	M04 2-0	O01 0-2	F11 0-0	S07 2-1	S03 5-1	N05 2-2	a15 5-1	M18 1-0	J14 1-1	S17 1-3	D17 2-1	D24 2-0
5 BRISTOL R	S12 0-0	D27 1-0	A30 0-1	F25 1-1		S24 1-1	M11 1-0	a17 1-2	J21 4-1	F04 3-3	A27 3-0	O29 0-0	a22 1-0	O15 0-0	J07 0-1	D31 0-0	O08 2-4	S10 4-1	M25 5-0	N12 0-1	a07 2-0	a08 1-1
6 CARDIFF C	a08 2-4	F11 5-0	O01 4-1	J11 2-1	J28 0-2		O15 1-2	M25 0-1	A27 1-2	J14 2-1	a29 0-0	D31 1-2	F25 2-0	a17 4-1	M11 2-4	D26 1-0	S17 0-1	a10 1-0	O29 2-1	a22 3-1	S05 2-1	N12 5-3
7 CLAPTON O	J21 2-0	N19 1-1	M18 2-0	S24 1-1	N05 2-1	F18 1-1		F04 4-0	a07 3-3	D17 1-1	D03 0-0	A27 1-3	D31 3-0	S10 1-1	S08 1-0	a15 2-1	M04 1-2	O22 5-0	a29 5-0	a17 3-0	a01 1-1	O08 0-0
8 CRYSTAL P	D26 3-0	D24 3-0	O22 1-0	a07 3-2	a15 0-0	N19 2-0	O01 4-2		M18 3-2	a01 3-0	D17 6-2	F11 1-1	S07 2-0	a29 5-1	J14 1-0	M04 0-1	D03 0-0	N05 4-3	S17 1-1	J28 1-3	F18 4-0	S03 2-0
9 EXETER C	J07 3-3	O01 0-0	J28 2-2	M25 1-1	S17 2-1	D24 1-1	a10 2-1	N12 4-4		S03 3-0	S07 2-0	F25 3-1	D10 3-2	a08 1-0	O29 1-3	a29 1-1	J14 3-2	D27 3-3	a22 0-0	O15 1-2	F15 3-2	M11 1-3
10 IPSWICH T	a26 7-2	S07 0-2	F11 0-0	a08 4-0	O01 0-0	S10 1-2	a22 3-0	J18 2-1	D31 2-2		D26 5-1	O15 1-4	J21 2-0	F25 0-2	N12 2-0	a10 1-0	m03 2-1	A27 4-2	M11 3-1	O29 1-0	a29 1-0	M25 5-1
11 MANSFIELD T	M11 1-0	J14 2-0	S03 4-2	O29 3-2	D24 1-3	A31 2-2	a08 1-0	a22 0-0	m06 4-2	D27 0-1		J11 0-2	M25 1-1	N12 2-0	J28 2-0	F04 2-2	a07 0-0	O08 3-1	F25 1-1	M08 4-0	S17 0-0	O15 0-0
12 NEWPORT CO	S24 1-0	M18 2-2	N05 2-0	F04 0-2	M04 2-0	S03 3-0	D24 2-1	O08 2-0	O22 0-0	F18 3-2	a01 0-0		S10 1-1	F02 2-1	a29 0-2	D03 2-0	D17 2-0	a15 3-0	D27 6-4	a07 1-0	N19 2-1	S08 1-0
13 NORTHAMPTON T	F04 5-0	N05 2-0	M04 1-4	O08 2-2	D17 2-1	O22 2-1	S03 3-0	m06 0-0	a15 0-0	S17 2-0	N19 3-4	J14 1-0		S24 2-1	D26 2-0	a01 1-0	F18 1-1	D03 2-2	a10 0-2	D24 4-1	M18 4-1	A29 2-0
14 NOTTS CO	O08 1-1	M04 0-1	D17 4-3	m06 0-0	F18 3-1	a15 1-1	J14 1-0	A31 0-1	D03 3-1	O22 2-1	M18 1-1	S17 2-0	J28 1-0		a10 4-0	N19 0-0	O01 2-0	a01 4-1	D24 2-0	S03 5-1	N05 0-0	D27 0-3
15 PORT VALE	A27 1-3	a15 2-0	D03 1-1	D31 4-0	a01 2-1	N05 1-1	m06 1-1	S10 2-0	M04 3-2	M18 0-0	S24 3-0	A29 2-1	D27 0-2	a07 3-1		F18 1-2	N19 0-2	D17 2-2	O01 2-0	F11 0-1	O22 5-1	J21 1-2
16 Q.P.R.	N12 7-0	S17 2-0	J14 1-2	M11 3-1	S03 1-1	D27 5-0	a24 1-1	O29 1-2	S01 5-0	a07 0-0	O01 3-0	a08 0-0	J09 3-0	M25 0-1	O15 2-2		D24 2-2	m06 1-1	F11 2-1	F25 1-1	J28 3-0	a22 1-0
17 READING	F25 5-0	a29 1-0	S14 3-0	D10 2-2	F11 2-0	F01 0-0	O29 2-2	a08 3-1	S10 1-1	S24 2-1	a10 0-0	J21 0-1	O15 5-1	F04 3-1	M25 2-1	A27 2-4		D31 3-0	N12 3-0	M11 3-5	D26 1-1	J11 3-2
18 SOUTHEND U	M25 2-1	J28 2-2	S17 1-1	N12 2-0	J14 3-2	a07 2-0	F25 1-0	M11 3-1	a12 0-1	a19 0-0	F11 2-0	m02 5-0	a08 2-0	a25 1-0	a22 0-0	S07 2-1	S03 2-0		O15 2-3	A31 1-1	O01 2-0	O29 3-0
19 SWINDON T	D31 2-1	D03 4-2	a01 3-2	S10 1-0	N19 2-1	M04 4-1	A31 2-0	J21 2-2	D17 2-1	N05 1-1	O22 1-2	D26 8-0	a07 1-0	A27 4-1	F04 1-1	O08 2-2	M18 4-2	F18 2-1		m06 3-1	a15 1-4	S24 3-0
20 TORQUAY U	S10 1-1	a01 2-0	N19 0-2	J21 3-1	M18 2-2	D17 1-3	D27 2-1	S24 1-2	F18 0-1	M04 1-1	a15 3-0	a10 1-1	A27 1-2	D31 0-2	O08 1-0	O22 2-3	N05 1-1	a29 2-0	S07 1-3		D03 0-1	F04 2-1
21 WALSALL	O29 2-2	S03 1-2	D24 0-2	a22 5-0	a10 2-2	m06 6-3	J12 5-1	O15 1-1	O08 1-2	A29 0-1	F02 0-0	M25 1-1	N12 1-0	M11 3-3	F25 4-0	S24 0-1	D27 3-0	F04 0-2	a24 5-0	a08 5-0		J14 2-0
22 WATFORD	a10 1-1	O22 1-0	a15 1-1	A27 2-2	D03 4-1	M18 1-0	F11 1-0	D31 4-1	N05 4-2	N19 0-0	F18 2-0	S14 1-1	a29 2-0	D26 0-1	S17 2-0	D17 4-1	a01 3-1	M04 3-0	J28 4-1	O01 0-0	S10 4-2	

LEAGUE TABLES

DIVISION 1

	P	W	D	L	F	A	W	D	L	F	A	Pts
Everton	42	17	3	1	60	18	10	2	9	28	34	59
Wolverhampton W	42	14	6	1	55	12	8	5	8	33	27	55
Charlton A	42	16	3	2	49	24	6	3	12	26	35	50
Middlesbrough	42	13	6	2	64	27	7	3	11	29	47	49
Arsenal	42	14	3	4	34	14	5	6	10	21	27	47
Derby Co	42	12	3	6	39	22	7	5	9	27	33	46
Stoke C	42	13	6	2	50	25	4	6	11	21	43	46
Bolton W	42	10	6	5	39	25	5	9	7	28	33	45
Preston N.E.	42	13	7	1	44	19	3	5	13	19	40	44
Grimsby T	42	11	6	4	38	26	5	5	11	23	43	43
Liverpool	42	12	6	3	40	24	2	8	11	22	39	42
Aston Villa	42	11	3	7	44	25	5	6	10	27	35	41
Leeds U	42	11	5	5	40	27	5	4	12	19	40	41
Manchester U	42	7	9	5	30	20	4	7	10	27	45	38
Blackpool	42	9	8	4	37	26	3	6	12	19	42	38
Sunderland	42	7	7	7	30	29	6	5	10	24	38	38
Portsmouth	42	10	7	4	25	15	2	6	13	22	55	37
Brentford	42	11	2	8	30	27	3	6	12	23	47	36
Huddersfield T	42	11	4	6	38	18	1	7	13	20	46	35
Chelsea	42	10	5	6	43	29	2	4	15	21	51	33
Birmingham C	42	10	5	6	40	27	2	3	16	22	57	32
Leicester C	42	7	6	8	35	35	2	5	14	13	47	29

DIVISION 2

	P	W	D	L	F	A	W	D	L	F	A	Pts
Blackburn R	42	17	1	3	59	23	8	4	9	35	37	55
Sheffield U	42	9	9	3	35	15	11	5	5	34	26	54
Sheffield W	42	14	4	3	47	18	7	7	7	41	41	53
Coventry C	42	13	4	4	35	13	8	4	9	27	32	50
Manchester C	42	13	3	5	56	35	8	4	9	40	37	49
Chesterfield	42	16	1	4	54	20	4	8	9	15	32	49
Luton T	42	13	4	4	47	27	9	1	11	35	39	49
Tottenham H	42	13	6	2	48	27	6	3	12	19	35	47
Newcastle U	42	13	3	5	44	21	5	7	9	17	27	46
W.B.A.	42	15	3	3	54	22	3	6	12	35	50	45
West Ham U	42	10	5	6	36	21	7	5	9	34	31	44
Fulham	42	12	5	4	35	20	5	5	11	26	35	44
Millwall	42	12	6	3	44	18	2	8	11	20	35	42
Burnley	42	13	3	5	32	20	2	6	13	18	36	39
Plymouth A	42	9	7	5	24	13	6	1	14	25	42	38
Bury	42	9	5	7	48	36	3	8	10	17	38	37
Bradford P.A.	42	8	6	7	33	35	4	5	12	28	47	35
Southampton	42	9	6	6	35	34	4	3	14	21	48	35
Swansea T	42	8	6	7	33	30	3	6	12	17	53	34
Nottingham F	42	8	6	7	33	29	2	5	14	16	53	31
Norwich C	42	10	5	6	39	29	3	0	18	11	62	31
Tranmere R	42	6	4	11	26	38	0	1	20	13	61	17

DIVISION 3 NORTH

	P	W	D	L	F	A	W	D	L	F	A	Pts
Barnsley	42	18	2	1	60	12	12	5	4	34	22	67
Doncaster R	42	12	5	4	47	21	9	9	3	40	26	56
Bradford C	42	16	2	3	59	21	6	6	9	30	35	52
Southport	42	14	5	2	47	16	6	5	10	28	38	50
Oldham A	42	16	1	4	51	21	6	4	11	25	38	49
Chester C	42	12	5	4	54	31	8	4	9	34	39	49
Hull C	42	13	5	3	57	25	5	5	11	26	49	46
Crewe A	42	12	5	4	54	23	7	1	13	28	47	44
Stockport Co	42	13	6	2	57	24	4	3	14	34	53	43
Gateshead	42	11	6	4	45	24	3	8	10	29	43	42
Rotherham U	42	12	4	5	45	21	5	4	12	19	43	42
Halifax T	42	9	10	2	33	22	4	6	11	19	32	42
Barrow	42	11	5	5	46	22	5	4	12	20	43	41
Wrexham	42	15	2	4	46	28	2	5	14	20	51	41
Rochdale	42	10	5	6	58	29	5	4	12	34	53	39
New Brighton	42	11	2	8	46	32	4	7	10	22	41	39
Lincoln C	42	9	6	6	40	33	3	3	15	26	59	33
Darlington	42	12	2	7	43	30	1	5	15	19	62	33
Carlisle U	42	10	5	6	44	33	3	2	16	22	78	33
York C	42	8	5	8	37	34	4	3	14	27	58	32
Hartlepool U	42	10	4	7	36	33	2	3	16	19	61	31
Accrington S	42	6	5	10	30	39	1	1	19	19	64	20

DIVISION 3 SOUTH

	P	W	D	L	F	A	W	D	L	F	A	Pts
Newport Co	42	15	4	2	37	16	7	7	7	21	29	55
Crystal Palace	42	15	4	2	49	18	5	8	8	22	34	52
Brighton & H.A.	42	14	5	2	43	14	5	6	10	25	35	49
Watford	42	14	6	1	44	15	3	6	12	18	36	46
Reading	42	12	6	3	46	23	4	8	9	23	36	46
Q.P.R.	42	10	8	3	44	15	5	6	10	24	34	44
Ipswich T	42	14	3	4	46	21	2	9	10	16	31	44
Bristol C	42	14	5	2	42	19	2	7	12	19	44	44
Swindon T	42	15	4	2	53	25	3	4	14	19	52	44
Aldershot	42	13	6	2	31	15	3	6	12	22	51	44
Notts Co	42	12	6	3	36	16	5	3	13	23	38	43
Southend U	42	14	5	2	38	13	2	4	15	23	51	41
Cardiff C	42	12	1	8	40	28	3	10	8	21	37	41
Exeter C	42	9	9	3	40	32	4	5	12	25	50	40
Bournemouth	42	10	8	3	38	22	3	5	13	14	36	39
Mansfield T	42	10	8	3	33	19	2	7	12	11	43	39
Northampton T	42	13	5	3	41	20	2	3	16	10	38	38
Port Vale	42	10	5	6	36	23	4	4	13	16	35	37
Torquay U	42	7	5	9	27	28	7	4	10	27	42	37
Clapton O	42	10	9	2	40	16	1	4	16	13	39	35
Walsall	42	9	6	6	47	23	2	5	14	21	46	33
Bristol R	42	8	8	5	30	17	2	5	14	25	44	33

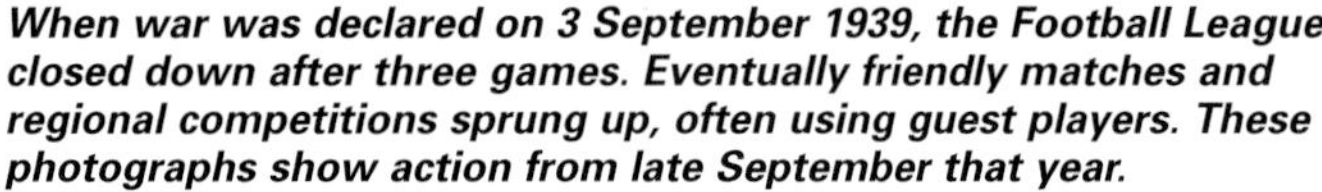

When war was declared on 3 September 1939, the Football League closed down after three games. Eventually friendly matches and regional competitions sprung up, often using guest players. These photographs show action from late September that year.

Top left: Chelsea's England goalkeeper Vic Woodley gathers the ball from an Aldershot attack at the Recreation Ground.
Top right: Charlton goalkeeper Hobbis punches clear from a Millwall attack at The Den.
Bottom left: Oldham defender Shipnan punches the ball away but Manchester United's McKay scored from the resultant penalty.
Bottom right: Brentford centre-forward Holliday is beaten by Chelsea goalkeeper Jackson and defender Salmond at Griffin Park.

SEASON 1939-40

DIVISION 1

Saturday, 26 August 1939

Aston Villa	2	Middlesbrough	0
Chelsea	3	Bolton Wanderers	2
Everton	1	Brentford	1
Huddersfield Town	0	Blackpool	1
Manchester United	4	Grimsby Town	0
Portsmouth	2	Blackburn Rovers	1
Preston North End	0	Leeds United	0
Sheffield United	2	Liverpool	1
Stoke City	4	Charlton Athletic	0
Sunderland	3	Derby County	0
Wolverhampton W	2	Arsenal	2

Monday, 28 August 1939

Aston Villa	1	Everton	2
Blackpool	2	Brentford	1
Stoke City	1	Bolton Wanderers	2

Tuesday, 29 August 1939

Grimsby Town	0	Wolverhampton W	0

Wednesday, 30 August 1939

Arsenal	1	Blackburn Rovers	0
Chelsea	1	Manchester United	1
Derby County	2	Portsmouth	0
Leeds United	0	Charlton Athletic	1
Liverpool	4	Middlesbrough	1
Preston North End	0	Sheffield United	0
Sunderland	1	Huddersfield Town	2

Saturday, 2 September 1939

Arsenal	5	Sunderland	2
Blackburn Rovers	2	Everton	2
Blackpool	2	Wolverhampton W	1
Bolton Wanderers	2	Portsmouth	1
Brentford	1	Huddersfield Town	0
Charlton Athletic	2	Manchester United	0
Derby County	1	Aston Villa	0
Grimsby Town	2	Preston North End	0
Leeds United	0	Sheffield United	1
Liverpool	1	Chelsea	0
Middlesbrough	2	Stoke City	2

DIVISION 2

Saturday, 26 August 1939

Barnsley	4	Nottingham Forest	1
Burnley	1	Coventry City	1
Bury	3	Fulham	1
Chesterfield	2	Bradford	0
Leicester City	4	Manchester City	3
Luton Town	3	Sheffield Wednesday	0
Millwall	3	Newcastle United	0
Newport County	3	Southampton	1
Plymouth Argyle	1	West Ham United	3
Swansea Town	1	West Bromwich Albion	2
Tottenham Hotspur	1	Birmingham	1

Monday, 28 August 1939

Coventry City	3	West Bromwich Albion	3
Millwall	0	Plymouth Argyle	2
Sheffield Wednesday	3	Barnsley	1
West Ham United	2	Fulham	1

Wednesday, 30 August 1939

Birmingham	2	Leicester City	0
Bradford	0	Luton Town	3
Manchester City	1	Bury	1
Southampton	1	Swansea Town	3

Thursday, 31 August 1939

Newport County	1	Tottenham Hotspur	1
Nottingham Forest	2	Newcastle United	0

Saturday, 2 September 1~39

Birmingham	2	Burnley	0
Bradford	2	Millwall	2
Coventry City	4	Barnsley	2
Fulham	1	Luton Town	1
Manchester City	2	Chesterfield	0
Newcastle United	8	Swansea Town	1
Nottingham Forest	2	Newport County	1
Sheffield Wednesday	0	Plymouth Argyle	1
Southampton	3	Bury	0
West Bromwich A	3	Tottenham Hotspur	4
West Ham United	0	Leicester City	2

DIVISION 3 NORTH

Saturday, 26 August 1939

Bradford City	0	Accrington Stanley	2
Darlington	1	Southport	0
Doncaster Rovers	2	Rochdale	0
Gateshead	0	Crewe Alexandra	3
Hartlepools United	1	Barrow	1
Hull City	2	Lincoln City	2
Oldham Athletic	3	Carlisle United	1
Stockport County	0	Halifax Town	3
Tranmere Rovers	3	Rotherham United	1
Wrexham	2	New Brighton	0
York City	2	Chester	2

Monday, 28 August 1939

Barrow	1	Accrington Stanley	2
Halifax Town	2	Oldham Athletic	0
Lincoln City	0	Darlington	2
Rotherham United	2	York City	1

Tuesday, 29 August 1939

Rochdale	1	Wrexham	0
Southport	3	Tranmere Rovers	3

Wednesday, 30 August 1939

Chester	1	Doncaster Rovers	0
Gateshead	3	Hartlepools United	0
New Brighton	2	Bradford City	1

Saturday, 2 September 1939

Accrington Stanley	2	Oldham Athletic	0
Barrow	2	Bradford City	2
Carlisle United	2	Stockport County	0
Chester	2	Tranmere Rovers	0
Crewe Alexandra	0	Hartlepools United	0
Halifax Town	1	Wrexham	1
Lincoln City	4	Gateshead	3
New Brighton	4	Doncaster Rovers	2
Rochdale	1	York City	0
Rotherham United	2	Darlington	2
Southport	1	Hull City	1

DIVISION 3 SOUTH

Saturday, 26 August 1939

Aldershot	0	Bristol City	1
Brighton & Hove A	0	Port Vale	0
Bristol Rovers	2	Reading	2
Clapton Orient	2	Ipswich Town	2
Exeter City	2	Torquay United	2
Mansfield Town	4	Crystal Palace	5
Northampton Town	1	Swindon Town	0
Norwich City	1	Cardiff City	2
Notts County	2	Bournemouth & BA	1
Queen's Park Rangers	2	Watford	2
Southend United	3	Walsall	2

Monday, 28 August 1939

Northampton Town	1	Exeter City	2

Wednesday, 30 August 1939

Bournemouth & BA	2	Queen's Park Rangers	2
Brighton & Hove A	2	Aldershot	1
Bristol City	1	Norwich City	2
Ipswich Town	2	Bristol Rovers	0
Reading	5	Crystal Palace	0
Swindon Town	0	Cardiff City	1
Torquay United	0	Walsall	0
Watford	1	Mansfield Town	2

Thursday, 31 August 1939

Clapton Orient	0	Southend United	0

Saturday, 2 September 1939

Bournemouth & BA	10	Northampton Town	0
Bristol City	3	Brighton & Hove Albion	3
Cardiff City	2	Notts County	4
Crystal Palace	3	Bristol Rovers	0
Ipswich Town	1	Norwich City	1
Port Vale	0	Exeter City	1
Reading	1	Southend United	0
Swindon Town	2	Aldershot	2
Torquay United	2	Mansfield Town	2
Walsall	1	Queen's Park Rangers	0
Watford	1	Clapton Orient	1

LEAGUE TABLES

DIVISION 1

	P	W	D	L	F	A	W	D	L	F	A	Pts
Blackpool	3	2	0	0	4	2	1	0	0	1	0	6
Sheffield U	3	1	0	0	2	1	1	1	0	1	0	5
Arsenal	3	2	0	0	6	2	0	1	0	2	2	5
Liverpool	3	2	0	0	5	1	0	0	1	1	2	4
Everton	3	0	1	0	1	1	1	1	0	4	3	4
Bolton W	3	1	0	0	2	1	1	0	1	4	4	4
Derby Co	3	2	0	0	3	0	0	0	1	0	3	4
Charlton A	3	1	0	0	2	0	1	0	1	1	4	4
Stoke C	3	1	0	1	5	2	0	1	0	2	2	3
Manchester U	3	1	0	0	4	0	0	1	1	1	3	3
Brentford	3	1	0	0	1	0	0	1	1	2	3	3
Chelsea	3	1	1	0	4	3	0	0	1	0	1	3
Grimsby T	3	1	1	0	2	0	0	0	1	0	4	3
Aston Villa	3	1	0	1	3	2	0	0	1	0	1	2
Sunderland	3	1	0	1	4	2	0	0	1	2	5	2
Wolves	3	0	1	0	2	2	0	1	1	1	2	2
Huddersfield T	3	0	0	1	0	1	1	0	1	2	2	2
Portsmouth	3	1	0	0	2	1	0	0	2	1	4	2
Preston NE	3	0	2	0	0	0	0	0	1	0	2	2
Blackburn R	3	0	1	0	2	2	0	0	2	1	3	1
Middlesbrough	3	0	1	0	2	2	0	0	2	1	6	1
Leeds U	3	0	0	2	0	2	0	1	0	0	0	1

DIVISION 2

	P	W	D	L	F	A	W	D	L	F	A	Pts
Luton T	3	1	0	0	3	0	1	1	0	4	1	5
Birmingham	3	2	0	0	4	0	0	1	0	1	1	5
Coventry C	3	1	1	0	7	5	0	1	0	1	1	4
Plymouth A	3	0	0	1	1	3	2	0	0	3	0	4
West Ham U	3	1	0	1	2	3	1	0	0	3	1	4
Leicester C	3	1	0	0	4	3	1	0	1	2	2	4
Tottenham H	3	0	1	0	1	1	1	1	0	5	4	4
Nottingham F	3	2	0	0	4	1	0	0	1	1	4	4
Millwall	3	1	0	1	3	2	0	1	0	2	2	3
Newport Co	3	1	1	0	4	2	0	0	1	1	2	3
Manchester C	3	1	1	0	3	1	0	0	1	3	4	3
WBA	3	0	0	1	3	4	1	1	0	5	4	3
Bury	3	1	0	0	3	1	0	1	1	1	4	3
Newcastle U	3	1	0	0	8	1	0	0	2	0	5	2
Chesterfield	2	1	0	0	2	0	0	0	1	0	2	2
Barnsley	3	1	0	0	4	1	0	0	2	3	7	2
Southampton	3	1	0	1	4	3	0	0	1	1	3	2
Sheffield W	3	1	0	1	3	2	0	0	1	0	3	2
Swansea T	3	0	0	1	1	2	1	0	1	4	9	2
Fulham	3	0	1	0	1	1	0	0	2	2	5	1
Burnley	2	0	1	0	1	1	0	0	1	0	2	1
Bradford	3	0	1	1	2	5	0	0	1	0	2	1

DIVISION 3 NORTH

	P	W	D	L	F	A	W	D	L	F	A	Pts
Accrington S	3	1	0	0	2	0	2	0	0	4	1	6
Halifax T	3	1	1	0	3	1	1	0	0	3	0	5
Chester	3	2	0	0	3	0	0	1	0	2	2	5
Darlington	3	1	0	0	1	0	1	1	0	4	2	5
New Brighton	3	2	0	0	6	3	0	0	1	0	2	4
Rochdale	3	2	0	0	2	0	0	0	1	0	2	4
Crewe A	2	0	1	0	0	0	1	0	0	3	0	3
Wrexham	3	1	0	0	2	0	0	1	1	1	2	3
Tranmere R	3	1	0	0	3	1	0	1	1	3	5	3
Lincoln C	3	1	0	1	4	5	0	1	0	2	2	3
Rotherham U	3	1	1	0	4	3	0	0	1	1	3	3
Carlisle U	2	1	0	0	2	0	0	0	1	1	3	2
Hull C	2	0	1	0	2	2	0	1	0	1	1	2
Gateshead	3	1	0	1	3	3	0	0	1	3	4	2
Barrow	3	0	1	1	3	4	0	1	0	1	1	2
Doncaster R	3	1	0	0	2	0	0	0	2	2	5	2
Southport	3	0	2	0	4	4	0	0	1	0	1	2
Oldham A	3	1	0	0	3	1	0	0	2	0	4	2
Hartlepools U	3	0	1	0	1	1	0	1	1	0	3	2
York C	3	0	1	0	2	2	0	0	2	1	3	1
Bradford C	3	0	0	1	0	2	0	1	1	3	4	1
Stockport Co	2	0	0	1	0	3	0	0	1	0	2	0

DIVISION 3 SOUTH

	P	W	D	L	F	A	W	D	L	F	A	Pts
Reading	3	2	0	0	6	0	0	1	0	2	2	5
Exeter C	3	0	1	0	2	2	2	0	0	3	1	5
Notts Co	2	1	0	0	2	1	1	0	0	4	2	4
Ipswich T	3	1	1	0	3	1	0	1	0	2	2	4
Brighton & HA	3	1	1	0	2	1	0	1	0	3	3	4
Cardiff C	3	0	0	1	2	4	2	0	0	3	1	4
Crystal P	3	1	0	0	3	0	1	0	1	5	9	4
Bournemouth	3	1	1	0	12	2	0	0	1	1	2	3
Bristol C	3	0	1	1	4	5	1	0	0	1	0	3
Mansfield T	3	0	0	0	4	5	1	1	0	4	3	3
Norwich C	3	0	0	1	1	2	1	1	0	3	2	3
Clapton O	3	0	2	0	2	2	0	1	0	1	1	3
Southend U	3	1	0	0	3	2	0	1	1	0	1	3
Torquay U	3	0	2	0	2	2	0	1	0	2	2	3
Walsall	3	1	0	0	1	0	0	1	1	2	3	3
QPR	3	0	1	0	2	2	0	1	1	2	3	2
Watford	3	0	1	1	2	3	0	1	0	2	2	2
Northampton T	3	1	0	1	2	2	0	0	1	0	10	2
Aldershot	3	0	0	1	0	1	0	1	1	3	4	1
Swindon T	3	0	1	1	2	3	0	0	1	0	1	1
Bristol	3	0	1	0	2	2	0	0	2	0	5	1
Port Vale	2	0	0	1	0	1	0	1	0	0	0	1

FOOTBALL LEAGUE RECORDS

Top scorers: Div 1, D.Westcott (Wolverhampton Wanderers) 37 goals; Div 2, C.Wayman (Newcastle United) 30 goals; Div 3 N, C.Jordan (Doncaster Rovers) 41 goals; Div 3 S, D.Clarke (Bristol City) 36 goals.

Birmingham became Birmingham City; Clapton Orient became Leyton Orient.

Billy Liddell began his great Liverpool career as the Reds won the first post-war League Championship.

DIVISION 1

	ARSENAL	ASTON VILLA	BLACKBURN R	BLACKPOOL	BOLTON W	BRENTFORD	CHARLTON A	CHELSEA	DERBY CO	EVERTON	GRIMSBY T	HUDDERSFIELD T	LEEDS U	LIVERPOOL	MANCHESTER U	MIDDLESBROUGH	PORTSMOUTH	PRESTON N.E.	SHEFFIELD U	STOKE C	SUNDERLAND	WOLVERHAMPTON W
1 ARSENAL		J18 0-2	S04 1-3	F08 1-1	N30 2-2	O12 2-2	D14 1-0	M01 1-2	S21 0-1	m31 2-1	a26 5-3	a04 1-2	N16 4-2	m24 1-2	F01 6-2	a12 4-0	D25 2-1	M15 4-1	N02 2-3	O19 1-0	S07 2-2	D28 1-1
2 ASTON VILLA	S14 0-2		m10 2-1	J25 1-1	N16 1-1	S28 5-2	O19 4-0	M29 2-0	J04 2-0	S02 0-1	a12 3-3	D25 2-2	D14 2-1	a26 1-2	N02 0-0	A31 0-1	O12 1-1	m17 4-2	N30 2-3	m26 0-1	a08 4-0	S16 3-0
3 BLACKBURN R	S17 1-2	O05 0-1		D25 1-1	M15 2-1	J01 0-3	m26 1-0	a07 1-2	F15 1-1	S07 4-1	N30 1-1	J18 2-2	M01 1-0	N02 0-0	D14 2-1	N16 1-2	D28 0-1	a12 1-2	O19 2-0	a26 0-2	F01 1-2	S21 1-2
4 BLACKPOOL	O05 2-1	S21 1-0	D26 1-0		M01 0-1	S02 4-2	m17 0-0	N02 1-0	F01 2-1	a07 0-3	N16 2-3	D28 2-1	M29 3-0	N30 3-2	O19 3-1	D14 0-5	S23 4-3	F15 4-0	M15 4-2	a12 0-2	J18 0-5	S07 2-0
5 BOLTON W	a05 1-3	M22 2-1	N09 0-0	O26 1-1		m10 1-0	F19 0-1	D28 1-1	N23 5-1	F22 0-2	S28 1-2	D07 4-0	F03 2-0	S14 1-3	D25 2-2	O12 1-1	S07 1-0	J01 1-2	a04 3-2	S11 3-2	D21 0-1	a19 0-3
6 BRENTFORD	m26 0-1	F01 0-2	m03 0-3	S18 2-1	N02 1-0		N16 1-4	M15 0-2	O05 0-3	D28 1-1	M29 0-1	S07 2-0	N30 1-1	m17 1-1	a12 0-0	a26 0-0	a04 1-3	O19 2-3	D26 2-1	D14 1-4	S21 0-3	J18 4-1
7 CHARLTON A	a19 2-2	F22 1-1	N23 0-2	D21 0-1	O05 2-0	M22 3-0		F01 2-3	D07 2-4	O26 4-1	D26 0-0	M08 0-3	S25 5-0	m10 1-3	S07 1-3	a04 3-3	a05 0-0	J18 0-0	S21 1-2	D28 1-0	S11 5-0	N09 1-4
8 CHELSEA	O26 2-1	N23 1-3	a04 0-2	M08 1-4	A31 4-3	N09 3-2	S28 2-2		a05 3-0	D07 1-1	F08 0-0	a19 1-0	S14 3-0	J04 3-1	S04 0-3	m10 2-0	m26 0-3	D25 1-2	m03 1-4	O12 2-5	M22 2-1	D21 1-2
9 DERBY CO	m10 0-1	S07 1-2	O12 2-1	S28 1-2	M29 1-3	M01 2-1	a12 1-0	N30 3-1		D26 5-1	D14 4-1	m03 1-0	a26 2-1	N16 1-4	M15 4-3	O19 1-1	S04 2-0	N02 2-2	m17 1-2	J18 3-0	D28 5-1	a07 2-1
10 EVERTON	S11 3-2	J01 2-0	J04 1-0	a04 1-1	O19 2-1	A31 0-2	m24 1-1	a12 2-0	D25 4-1		N02 3-3	F01 1-0	m26 4-1	J29 1-0	N16 2-2	N30 2-1	S14 1-0	a26 2-0	D14 2-3	M29 2-2	F15 4-2	O05 0-2
11 GRIMSBY T	D21 0-0	D07 0-3	a05 2-1	M22 2-3	F01 2-2	N23 2-2	D25 3-1	S21 2-1	a19 2-0	M08 2-2		N09 1-0	m17 4-1	O05 1-6	D28 0-0	m03 4-0	O26 3-2	S07· 2-3	J18 2-1	a04 2-5	m10 1-2	S03 0-0
12 HUDDERSFIELD T	a07 0-0	D26 1-0	S14 0-1	A31 1-3	a12 1-0	J04 3-0	N02 5-1	D14 1-4	S11 5-2	S28 1-0	M15 3-2		m10 1-0	O19 1-4	M29 2-2	m17 3-1	J29 1-2	N16 3-0	a26 1-1	N30 1-0	S25 0-0	m26 0-1
13 LEEDS U	M22 1-1	a19 1-1	O26 0-1	N23 4-2	S21 4-0	a05 1-2	S04 0-2	J18 2-1	D21 1-2	N09 2-1	O12 1-0	O05 5-0		F01 1-2	a08 0-2	D25 3-3	m24 0-1	D28 0-3	S07 2-2	m03 1-2	D07 1-1	F22 0-1
14 LIVERPOOL	N23 4-2	D21 4-1	M08 2-1	a05 2-3	J18 0-3	O26 1-0	O12 1-1	S07 7-4	M22 1-1	S21 0-0	F12 5-0	F22 1-0	S28 2-0		m03 1-0	S04 0-1	N09 3-0	a07 3-0	D28 1-2	D26 2-0	a19 1-0	D07 1-5
15 MANCHESTER U	S28 5-2	M08 2-1	a19 4-0	F22 3-0	D26 1-0	D07 4-1	J04 4-1	S18 1-1	N09 4-1	M22 3-0	A31 2-1	N23 5-2	a07 3-1	S11 5-0		S14 1-0	m17 3-0	O05 1-1	m26 6-2	F05 1-1	O26 0-3	a05 3-1
16 MIDDLESBROUGH	D07 2-0	D28 1-2	M22 0-1	a19 1-2	F15 3-1	D21 2-0	a07 1-2	O05 3-2	F22 1-0	a05 4-0	J01 3-0	O26 4-1	D26 3-0	O09 2-2	J18 2-4		N23 3-3	S21 2-0	F01 2-4	S07 5-4	N09 1-3	M08 1-1
17 PORTSMOUTH	D26 0-2	F15 3-2	A31 3-1	S11 0-1	J04 2-0	a07 3-0	N30 3-0	O19 0-2	m31 1-2	J18 2-1	M01 4-1	S21 3-1	N02 4-1	M15 1-2	a26 0-1	M29 3-1		D14 4-4	a12 0-0	N16 1-3	O05 4-1	m03 1-1
18 PRESTON N.E.	N09 2-0	O26 3-1	D07 4-0	O12 2-0	S16 0-4	F22 5-2	S14 5-1	D26 1-1	m26 1-1	D21 2-1	J04 3-0	M22 6-2	A31 3-2	a04 0-0	m10 1-1	J29 0-1	a19 1-1		S04 1-2	S28 1-3	a05 2-2	N23 2-2
19 SHEFFIELD U	j07 2-1	a05 1-2	F22 0-1	N09 4-2	a07 4-2	D25 6-1	m31 1-3	S09 2-2	O26 3-2	a19 2-0	S14 1-1	D21 2-2	J04 6-2	A31 0-1	O12 2-2	S28 2-1	m10 3-1	m24 2-3		j14 2-1	N23 4-2	M22 2-0
20 STOKE C	F22 3-1	N09 0-0	D21 0-0	D07 4-1	S02 1-2	a19 3-1	A31 2-2	F15 6-1	S14 3-2	N23 2-1	a07 3-0	a05 3-0	S16 5-2	D25 2-1	S21 3-2	J04 3-1	M22 1-1	F01 5-0	O05 3-0		m17 0-0	O26 0-3
21 SUNDERLAND	J04 1-4	a04 4-1	S28 1-0	S14 3-2	a26 3-1	m24 2-1	m03 1-1	N16 1-2	A31 3-2	O12 4-1	O19 1-2	S04 3-0	a12 1-0	D14 1-4	M01 1-1	M15 1-0	F08 0-0	N30 0-2	M29 2-1	N02 0-1		D25 0-1
22 WOLVERHAMPTON W	A31 6-1	S11 1-2	m17 3-3	J04 3-1	D14 5-0	S14 1-2	M15 2-0	a26 6-4	a08 7-2	m10 2-3	S23 2-0	O12 6-1	O19 1-0	m31 1-2	N30 3-2	N02 2-4	S28 3-1	M29 4-1	N16 3-1	M01 3-0	D26 2-1	

DIVISION 2

	BARNSLEY	BIRMINGHAM C	BRADFORD	BURNLEY	BURY	CHESTERFIELD	COVENTRY C	FULHAM	LEICESTER C	LUTON T	MANCHESTER C	MILLWALL	NEWCASTLE U	NEWPORT CO	NOTTINGHAM F	PLYMOUTH A	SHEFFIELD W	SOUTHAMPTON	SWANSEA T	TOTTENHAM H	W.B.A.	WEST HAM U
1 BARNSLEY		S14 3-1	D07 3-1	S16 1-0	O26 4-0	N23 1-2	J04 0-2	m03 4-1	M22 1-0	m10 4-0	a19 0-2	a05 4-1	S28 1-1	a04 3-1	A31 3-2	N09 1-3	S09 4-1	D25 4-4	m17 3-1	O12 1-3	m26 2-1	D21 1-2
2 BIRMINGHAM C	J18 1-2		m03 4-0	S07 0-2	D07 3-0	F22 0-0	F15 2-0	a05 2-1	S04 4-0	a19 1-0	N09 3-1	O26 4-0	a07 2-0	S21 1-1	O05 4-0	D21 6-1	N23 3-1	F01 3-1	D25 3-1	D28 1-0	S25 1-0	M22 3-0
3 BRADFORD	a12 1-3	N02 2-0		D14 0-1	S25 2-2	D28 0-0	M15 5-1	O12 1-2	D25 1-2	S04 2-1	m14 1-1	S07 0-0	O19 2-1	N30 2-1	N16 0-1	m26 3-2	M12 1-1	M29 2-3	J18 0-0	a26 2-1	m27 2-4	S28 0-1
4 BURNLEY	S30 2-2	J04 1-0	a19 1-2		m26 1-1	a05 1-1	A31 1-1	O26 2-0	N23 0-0	N09 1-1	D21 0-0	D07 3-0	J28 3-0	S09 3-2	D25 3-0	M22 2-1	F22 2-0	a04 1-0	S28 1-0	F18 0-0	S14 0-2	O12 2-1
5 BURY	M01 4-4	a12 2-0	J01 6-3	N02 2-2		O05 0-2	D14 1-0	A31 7-2	F01 2-3	J18 3-0	S18 2-2	F15 5-2	m17 2-2	O19 0-1	a26 5-0	S21 3-3	D25 4-2	J04 2-1	N16 3-3	m03 1-2	N30 4-0	a04 4-0
6 CHESTERFIELD	M29 2-1	O19 0-1	A31 1-1	N30 0-0	m31 3-1		m26 2-1	S28 1-1	m17 2-0	O12 2-1	J04 0-1	D26 2-3	a26 1-0	N16 2-0	N02 1-1	J01 4-1	j07 4-2	m03 5-0	D14 1-0	a12 0-0	a04 1-1	S14 3-1
7 COVENTRY C	S07 1-1	O12 0-0	N09 0-0	D28 0-3	a19 3-1	O26 1-1		D07 1-0	m10 2-1	D21 0-0	M22 1-1	m24 4-0	S16 1-1	J18 6-0	F01 1-1	m17 1-0	a05 5-1	S21 2-0	a08 3-2	D25 3-1	S02 3-2	N23 2-1
8 FULHAM	O19 6-1	N30 0-1	m31 0-3	m17 1-0	D28 2-0	m10 2-1	a12 2-0		S21 4-2	S07 2-1	M01 2-2	O05 3-2	N16 0-3	D26 4-1	m26 1-1	J18 3-1	a07 1-2	a26 0-0	M15 3-0	N02 1-1	M29 0-1	S09 3-2
9 LEICESTER C	N16 6-0	S12 2-1	D26 2-1	m24 1-4	S28 0-0	S19 0-1	O19 1-0	j07 2-0		m03 2-1	A31 0-3	a08 5-0	D14 2-4	M15 3-0	M01 1-1	O12 4-1	S14 3-5	N02 2-0	a12 0-1	N30 1-1	a26 1-1	J04 4-0
10 LUTON T	N02 3-1	D14 1-3	m24 3-0	M15 1-3	S14 2-0	F15 1-1	a26 1-1	J04 2-0	O05 1-2		a07 0-0	S11 3-0	N30 4-3	m31 6-3	J29 3-2	F01 3-4	A31 4-1	O19 2-2	M29 3-0	N16 3-2	a12 2-0	D26 2-1
11 MANCHESTER C	D14 5-1	M15 1-0	S21 7-2	m10 1-0	S04 3-1	S07 0-0	N16 1-0	J01 4-0	D28 1-0	a04 2-0		J18 1-0	m03 0-2	j14 5-1	M29 2-1	D25 4-3	O12 2-1	N30 1-1	O19 1-1	F01 1-0	N02 5-0	m24 2-0
12 MILLWALL	N30 3-1	m17 0-2	J04 0-1	j07 1-1	O12 1-0	D25 1-1	N02 3-5	j14 1-1	a04 1-0	O07 2-0	S14 1-3		A31 1-4	M29 3-1	M15 4-0	S02 1-1	S28 2-2	N16 3-1	a26 1-1	D14 0-3	O19 1-2	J25 0-0
13 NEWCASTLE U	F01 4-2	a04 2-2	m10 5-0	S21 1-2	N23 1-1	D21 2-1	S11 3-1	M22 1-3	a19 1-1	a05 7-2	O26 3-2	D28 0-2		O05 13-0	J01 3-0	D07 3-2	N09 4-0	F15 1-3	S07 1-1	J18 1-0	D25 2-4	m26 2-3
14 NEWPORT CO	a07 2-1	m26 0-3	m17 1-3	m03 0-3	m24 2-0	M22 3-0	S14 4-2	D25 4-2	N09 2-3	O26 1-3	D07 0-3	N23 3-1	j07 4-2		J04 2-5	m10 1-0	D21 4-3	O24 1-2	O12 2-4	S19 2-4	S28 2-7	a19 1-1
15 NOTTINGHAM F	D28 2-1	m10 1-1	j14 4-0	D26 1-0	D21 2-0	m27 1-0	S28 1-0	a19 2-1	O26 2-0	S21 4-2	N23 0-1	N09 1-2	S05 0-2	S07 6-1		m31 5-1	D07 2-2	J18 6-0	m03 1-1	a07 1-1	O12 1-1	a05 4-3
16 PLYMOUTH A	M15 3-2	a26 0-2	a07 2-4	N16 2-2	J25 3-1	S11 1-0	O05 2-2	S14 2-2	F15 4-0	S28 2-1	D26 2-3	m03 0-2	a12 0-1	N02 4-1	O19 2-0		J04 4-1	M01 2-3	N30 2-1	M29 3-4	D14 2-1	A31 3-1
17 SHEFFIELD W	S02 2-4	M29 1-0	O05 1-2	O19 1-2	D26 2-5	S21 0-1	N30 4-2	S16 1-1	J18 1-3	D28 1-1	m26 1-0	F01 3-0	m24 1-1	a26 2-1	a12 2-0	S07 2-1		D14 3-0	N02 3-0	M01 5-1	N16 2-2	J01 1-1
18 SOUTHAMPTON	D26 1-1	S28 1-0	N23 3-2	a07 0-1	S07 1-1	N09 1-1	F05 5-2	m24 2-0	m26 1-1	F22 1-3	a05 0-1	M22 1-2	O12 1-1	D28 5-1	S14 5-2	O26 5-1	a19 3-1		S04 4-0	m10 1-0	F08 0-1	D07 4-2
19 SWANSEA T	O05 2-2	D26 1-0	S14 1-6	F01 0-2	M22 1-0	a19 1-2	a07 2-3	N09 0-2	D07 3-4	N23 2-0	F22 1-2	m26 0-3	J04 1-2	F15 5-1	S09 3-2	a05 3-1	m10 2-0	O03 4-2		S21 0-2	A31 2-3	O26 2-1
20 TOTTENHAM H	j07 1-1	A31 1-2	D21 3-3	O05 1-1	N09 2-1	D07 3-4	D26 0-0	M08 1-1	a05 2-1	M22 2-1	S28 0-0	a19 2-1	S14 1-1	O07 3-1	a04 2-0	N23 2-1	O26 2-0	S09 2-1	J27 3-1		J04 2-0	m17 0-0
21 W.B.A.	S21 2-5	S18 3-0	O26 1-1	J18 1-1	a05 3-0	a07 3-2	m03 1-1	N23 6-1	D21 4-2	D07 1-2	m31 3-1	m10 2-4	D26 3-2	F01 2-2	m17 5-1	a19 2-5	M22 2-1	O05 2-0	D28 2-1	S07 3-2		N09 2-3
22 WEST HAM U	a26 4-0	N16 0-4	F01 1-1	m31 0-5	a07 3-3	J18 5-0	M29 1-2	S02 3-2	S07 0-2	D25 2-1	O05 1-0	S21 3-1	N02 0-2	F08 3-0	N30 2-2	D28 4-1	m03 2-1	a12 4-0	M01 3-0	O19 2-2	M15 3-2	

Manchester City goalkeeper Frank Swift, a key figure in City's promotion to Division One in 1946-47.

SEASON 1946-47

DIVISION 3 NORTH

	ACCRINGTON S	BARROW	BRADFORD C	CARLISLE U	CHESTER	CREWE A	DARLINGTON	DONCASTER R	GATESHEAD	HALIFAX T	HARTLEPOOLS U	HULL C	LINCOLN C	NEW BRIGHTON	OLDHAM A	ROCHDALE	ROTHERHAM U	SOUTHPORT	STOCKPORT CO	TRANMERE R	WREXHAM	YORK C
1 ACCRINGTON S		D14 1-3	D28 0-0	S24 4-3	N23 1-4	O26 2-3	a19 3-0	F01 0-1	D26 0-3	a04 1-1	F22 2-1	D21 0-0	m31 8-4	m10 3-1	S07 2-3	O05 2-3	M22 2-3	N09 1-0	J18 2-1	D07 2-1	S21 0-1	m14 1-2
2 BARROW	S05 1-3		S07 0-0	D26 3-1	M22 1-0	F22 0-2	D07 2-3	O05 0-1	D21 1-0	S12 3-0	D28 2-0	a19 1-0	O26 1-3	a07 0-1	J18 5-2	m10 2-2	N09 2-3	m03 2-1	S21 1-0	a05 0-1	F01 1-0	N23 0-1
3 BRADFORD C	A31 3-1	J04 5-0		m03 2-2	N09 0-0	S14 1-0	a05 2-0	m24 0-1	a19 2-2	D26 3-1	D21 1-2	D07 1-1	j14 3-0	S09 2-1	S21 1-0	a07 0-1	m31 2-0	O26 5-1	F01 0-2	N23 2-2	O05 2-1	M22 3-2
4 CARLISLE U	J01 4-2	D25 4-1	S19 4-3		a05 3-2	M08 3-3	D21 1-5	S21 2-3	F22 3-1	F15 1-0	O26 5-1	a04 0-2	N09 1-0	O05 3-2	D28 1-2	F01 1-3	N23 1-1	M22 1-1	S07 1-1	a19 4-2	m10 1-1	D07 1-2
5 CHESTER	M29 3-1	N16 3-0	m10 3-0	m31 4-0		F15 2-0	J18 1-1	S04 1-3	F01 0-1	a12 2-0	O05 2-1	S21 5-1	a04 3-0	D14 2-1	N02 2-0	a26 1-0	D25 2-2	S25 2-1	m24 3-0	S07 4-1	S18 2-0	D28 6-0
6 CREWE A	m17 5-0	O19 0-1	J18 2-2	N02 2-0	O12 0-2		D25 3-2	J22 0-3	D28 1-1	M15 2-0	S07 1-1	S09 2-0	J25 0-5	N16 3-0	a26 3-0	M29 2-2	F08 1-2	S28 2-0	m10 3-2	m03 4-3	a12 1-0	a04 2-0
7 DARLINGTON	m03 5-0	a12 0-1	J11 2-0	a26 2-1	S14 3-3	D26 4-0		N02 1-1	a04 2-0	m10 0-1	S11 2-1	F15 0-2	J01 4-3	O19 4-0	M29 1-1	M01 4-1	J04 4-3	A31 4-2	N16 1-2	S28 1-2	j07 1-1	J25 3-1
8 DONCASTER R	S28 5-0	M13 8-0	O12 4-3	J25 9-2	m03 3-0	a05 1-1	M08 5-0		M22 3-0	S14 2-0	N23 5-1	N09 4-1	a12 1-1	J04 0-0	a04 4-2	A31 2-1	D21 1-1	m10 2-0	S16 1-3	O26 2-0	D25 5-0	j07 0-0
9 GATESHEAD	D25 2-1	a26 0-5	J02 1-2	O19 1-3	S28 3-4	A31 2-1	a07 1-0	N16 1-3		m03 6-1	S04 0-1	J01 1-0	J04 3-0	N02 3-0	a12 1-0	m17 2-2	J25 2-0	S14 2-2	J15 1-2	O12 3-1	M29 3-3	m24 1-2
10 HALIFAX T	a07 2-1	S16 3-2	D25 1-2	O12 0-1	D07 1-2	N09 1-2	O05 0-2	J18 4-2	O26 2-1		m24 1-4	m17 2-0	j07 2-3	F01 0-1	S02 1-1	S21 3-0	a05 2-3	N23 1-1	D28 1-2	D21 1-3	S07 0-0	a19 0-3
11 HARTLEPOOLS U	O19 0-2	A31 1-1	a26 0-0	M01 4-1	F08 5-1	J04 5-2	S16 4-1	M29 0-2	m26 1-3	N02 1-4		D25 0-0	S14 2-0	M15 3-0	J11 1-1	N16 0-3	S28 2-1	J25 3-0	a12 1-0	a04 1-0	J01 1-3	O12 1-1
12 HULL C	a26 3-0	m31 1-0	a12 0-2	a07 2-0	M06 1-0	S02 2-2	O12 2-1	M15 0-1	S16 1-2	O19 3-0	D26 1-1		A31 0-0	j07 1-1	m24 0-1	N02 0-1	S14 0-2	J04 4-0	M29 0-3	m10 1-0	N16 1-0	S28 2-2
13 LINCOLN C	N02 1-1	m26 1-0	O19 0-1	M15 3-1	a07 2-2	S21 1-3	S04 2-0	D07 3-5	S07 4-0	N16 3-1	J18 5-2	D28 0-3		M29 5-1	F01 1-3	J22 2-3	O12 4-0	m17 4-2	a26 4-0	D26 2-1	m24 3-1	m03 2-2
14 NEW BRIGHTON	O12 4-0	a04 0-1	S04 0-0	m26 2-2	a19 0-3	M22 4-0	m24 4-1	S07 2-5	M08 2-3	S28 1-1	N09 2-1	O26 1-5	N23 4-2		D26 4-0	J18 1-2	j14 1-0	a05 1-0	J01 1-0	S21 2-1	m31 1-0	m17 0-3
15 OLDHAM A	J04 1-2	S14 0-1	J25 0-1	A31 0-2	m17 1-0	D21 3-1	N23 2-0	a07 0-1	D07 1-1	J01 6-1	a19 0-0	a05 1-2	S28 3-1	D25 2-2		S09 3-2	O26 0-1	F22 2-4	O05 0-0	M22 1-2	F15 1-5	N09 2-2
16 ROCHDALE	m24 5-1	O12 1-1	a04 0-1	S28 6-0	D21 2-1	N23 1-1	O26 3-0	D28 2-3	N09 2-3	J25 1-0	M22 1-0	M08 5-2	a05 2-0	S14 2-2	S17 1-3		a19 1-1	D07 0-0	D25 1-4	m31 3-0	S03 0-1	S07 0-1
17 ROTHERHAM U	N16 4-1	**m24 4-3**	N02 2-1	M29 4-0	D26 3-1	O05 5-1	S07 4-1	a26 3-2	S21 4-0	J13 6-1	F01 4-0	J18 2-0	m10 3-0	a12 3-0	m26 8-0	j07 3-3		a07 2-1	O19 2-1	D28 6-0	m03 3-2	J01 6-1
18 SOUTHPORT	M15 0-1	N02 2-2	M01 0-1	N16 0-2	S10 2-4	F01 2-2	D28 2-2	a19 0-5	J18 2-1	M29 6-1	S21 3-3	S07 3-1	O05 1-3	J11 2-0	O19 2-4	a12 0-2	a04 2-0		F15 4-1	S03 1-2	a26 1-1	D25 0-3
19 STOCKPORT CO	S14 2-0	J25 2-0	S28 4-0	J04 2-0	O26 0-3	a19 3-2	M22 1-0	S09 1-3	a05 2-0	A31 4-1	D07 1-2	N23 2-0	D21 3-2	m03 2-0	F08 4-0	D26 5-2	F22 1-2	O12 2-0		N09 4-0	a04 1-0	m31 4-2
20 TRANMERE R	a12 0-1	J11 1-1	D14 2-0	m24 1-1	J04 3-2	S18 3-2	F01 2-0	M01 3-5	F15 1-0	a26 1-1	a07 4-1	O05 1-3	D25 5-2	J25 3-3	N16 4-2	O19 2-3	A31 1-4	J01 2-0	M15 2-1		N02 0-0	S14 2-1
21 WREXHAM	J25 4-0	S28 1-1	m17 2-0	S14 2-1	m26 0-4	D07 1-0	N09 7-1	D26 0-2	N23 2-0	J04 2-0	a05 4-1	M22 0-1	a19 4-1	A31 3-2	O12 2-1	S25 2-2	S11 1-1	D21 1-1	a07 2-1	j14 0-0		O26 3-1
22 YORK C	J11 0-1	M29 0-2	N16 0-3	a12 2-2	A31 4-4	a07 2-3	S21 3-0	O19 1-4	O05 3-1	m26 2-0	m10 1-4	F01 3-0	S11 2-4	a26 1-2	m21 1-0	J04 2-3	S04 2-3	D26 1-1	N02 3-2	J18 0-1	m27 2-2	

DIVISION 3 SOUTH

	ALDERSHOT	BOURNEMOUTH	BRIGHTON & HA	BRISTOL C	BRISTOL R	CARDIFF C	CRYSTAL P	EXETER C	IPSWICH T	LEYTON O	MANSFIELD T	NORTHAMPTON T	NORWICH C	NOTTS CO	PORT VALE	Q.P.R.	READING	SOUTHEND U	SWINDON T	TORQUAY U	WALSALL	WATFORD
1 ALDERSHOT		S14 2-1	S18 1-3	A31 4-3	J11 0-2	J25 0-1	a26 0-2	m03 2-0	N02 4-1	M15 0-0	a12 1-1	O12 1-1	S28 3-1	F08 1-1	D25 0-0	N16 1-2	a04 1-3	M29 0-0	J04 2-0	M12 0-0	O19 1-2	m17 1-2
2 BOURNEMOUTH	J18 2-2		S21 1-0	F15 0-0	M01 1-3	S18 2-0	N16 4-0	m10 4-1	J01 1-1	a26 2-0	N02 3-1	S07 2-1	D25 0-1	D28 1-2	O05 3-0	S04 1-1	M29 1-0	O19 3-1	a04 5-2	M15 5-0	J15 2-3	a12 0-1
3 BRIGHTON & H.A.	S04 2-1	J25 1-1		J04 1-1	a12 1-2	S28 0-4	m03 1-0	D25 1-6	M15 0-0	N16 2-1	D14 5-0	a04 2-2	F08 3-3	O12 3-2	A31 0-0	M29 0-2	O19 1-4	J15 2-1	S14 1-4	J11 2-0	M01 2-0	N02 1-1
4 BRISTOL C	D28 9-0	O12 1-0	S07 0-0		F01 4-0	a04 2-1	N02 3-0	J18 2-2	J11 1-2	a12 3-0	O19 5-2	D26 2-3	S04 2-1	m03 1-1	S21 3-0	m10 1-1	M15 5-2	a26 2-0	F08 3-1	M01 5-0	N16 1-2	M29 1-2
5 BRISTOL R	a05 0-0	O26 0-2	D07 0-0	S28 0-3		M08 1-0	J04 2-1	a19 1-0	m10 1-1	a07 6-1	J25 1-0	N23 0-3	N09 1-2	M22 4-1	D21 0-0	F15 3-1	A31 2-2	O05 1-3	F22 3-0	S14 3-0	D25 2-2	S09 3-4
6 CARDIFF C	S21 2-1	S09 2-0	F01 4-0	a07 1-1	N02 4-0		M29 0-0	O05 5-0	a26 3-2	j07 1-0	M15 5-0	J18 6-2	D28 6-1	S07 2-1	m10 1-0	O19 2-2	J22 3-0	M01 3-1	S23 5-0	N16 1-0	a12 3-0	m03 1-0
7 CRYSTAL P	D21 0-0	M22 0-1	S11 1-0	m24 0-0	S07 2-1	**N23 1-2**		F22 1-0	O05 1-1	F01 2-0	D28 1-1	a19 2-2	a05 0-1	D07 2-1	O26 1-2	S21 0-0	S18 2-1	J18 0-3	N09 4-1	D25 6-1	a04 1-1	F15 2-0
8 EXETER C	S11 4-1	S28 4-1	D26 2-1	S14 1-3	D14 3-2	m17 0-2	O19 2-1		N16 0-0	M29 3-1	a26 1-0	S18 1-0	O12 3-0	a07 2-2	J04 1-1	M05 3-0	M01 1-3	a12 1-5	J25 1-1	A31 1-1	N02 2-2	M15 1-0
9 IPSWICH T	m26 1-1	a19 2-1	N09 1-2	a05 3-2	S04 0-2	D21 0-1	F08 1-1	M22 2-1		D28 0-0	a07 2-1	O26 1-2	S07 5-0	m17 1-2	N23 2-1	D26 1-1	S28 2-0	m03 1-0	D07 3-1	O12 1-1	J25 2-1	S14 2-0
10 LEYTON O	N09 1-3	m24 2-3	M22 2-1	D07 4-1	a04 3-0	D25 0-1	S28 0-1	J11 3-1	A31 2-2		O12 3-1	M08 2-1	F22 3-0	O26 1-3	a05 5-3	m03 1-1	J25 3-3	S04 1-1	a19 0-0	m10 0-1	S14 1-0	J04 3-1
11 MANSFIELD T	D07 1-3	m03 1-1	a19 0-3	m17 1-3	S21 3-1	N09 1-3	A31 3-1	D21 1-0	a04 4-3	m31 1-3		a05 3-2	M22 4-4	N23 1-0	S14 0-3	O05 0-3	D25 2-2	F01 0-1	O26 1-1	J04 1-0	S18 1-1	O09 2-0
12 NORTHAMPTON T	m29 2-2	J04 2-1	a07 6-1	D25 2-2	M29 1-2	S14 0-2	m17 1-0	S02 1-2	m31 2-2	N02 4-1	J23 3-0		J25 1-0	S28 2-1	m03 1-0	M15 4-4	a26 4-0	N16 2-3	A31 4-1	a12 0-0	a08 0-8	O19 4-1
13 NORWICH C	F01 2-3	D26 1-6	O05 2-3	S18 2-2	M15 3-3	A31 2-1	S26 2-3	F15 1-3	J04 0-1	O19 5-0	N16 3-1	S21 2-3		J18 2-2	a07 3-0	M01 0-1	a12 0-2	N02 1-5	S12 1-5	M29 2-0	m17 0-2	a26 4-2
14 NOTTS CO	O05 2-0	A31 1-0	m10 2-0	S11 0-3	N16 6-0	J04 1-1	a12 0-0	a04 0-0	O19 1-2	m26 1-2	M29 5-1	F01 1-0	S14 3-0		O03 3-2	N02 1-2	m29 1-0	m24 0-2	D25 0-0	J23 0-2	a26 3-1	J25 4-1
15 PORT VALE	D26 4-2	M10 1-0	D28 4-1	F17 2-1	a26 2-1	O12 0-4	m26 4-2	S07 1-2	M29 1-0	J16 2-1	J18 4-1	S09 1-1	a04 1-3	S23 4-1		a12 2-2	N02 5-1	m31 5-1	S28 1-1	O19 2-1	M15 2-2	N16 3-0
16 Q.P.R.	M22 4-1	S25 3-0	N23 2-0	a19 1-0	O12 0-2	m24 2-3	J25 1-2	a05 2-0	D25 1-3	S11 2-0	F08 3-1	N09 1-0	O26 1-1	M08 4-1	D07 2-0		S14 2-0	a04 1-0	D21 7-0	S28 0-0	J04 1-0	A31 2-1
17 READING	a07 1-0	N23 3-2	m17 2-0	N09 2-5	D28 1-1	a05 0-0	S04 10-2	O26 4-0	F01 1-3	S21 2-0	D26 3-0	D21 3-0	D07 4-3	a19 1-1	M08 0-2	J18 1-0		S07 7-2	M22 3-3	S11 2-2	m26 1-1	O05 2-3
18 SOUTHEND U	N23 2-1	m17 2-2	a05 0-0	D21 4-1	F08 2-3	O26 0-2	S14 2-0	D07 2-2	S12 1-1	S19 0-0	S28 1-1	M22 4-0	M08 3-0	N09 3-0	a19 1-1	a07 1-3	J04 0-2		O12 2-0	J25 0-2	A31 3-1	D26 5-0
19 SWINDON T	S07 7-0	a07 1-3	J18 2-2	O05 1-1	O19 1-0	S04 3-2	M15 1-0	S21 2-0	a12 2-1	m17 2-0	M01 6-1	D28 3-1	m03 1-1	D26 4-2	F01 2-1	a26 3-2	N16 2-2	m10 2-1		N02 2-4	M29 4-1	J11 5-0
20 TORQUAY U	a19 0-1	N09 2-2	D21 3-1	O26 2-3	J18 3-0	M22 0-0	D26 2-1	D28 2-1	F15 0-0	O05 3-2	S07 2-2	D07 2-1	N23 2-1	a05 1-2	m24 1-0	m17 0-0	m03 3-0	S21 0-1	M08 1-5		S04 2-0	a07 2-0
21 WALSALL	m10 2-0	a05 3-0	O26 1-1	M22 3-0	D26 2-0	D07 2-3	a07 3-3	m24 2-1	S21 4-2	J18 3-1	S09 0-0	O05 2-0	a19 2-2	D21 2-0	N09 4-1	S07 0-2	O12 2-2	D28 2-2	N23 0-1	m31 2-1		F01 1-3
22 WATFORD	O26 4-1	D07 0-2	m24 1-4	N23 2-3	S18 1-0	a19 2-0	O12 1-0	N09 3-1	J18 2-0	S07 3-1	S04 1-2	m10 1-1	D21 4-1	S21 2-2	M22 2-0	D28 0-2	F08 2-1	D25 4-0	a05 1-1	a04 3-3	S28 0-2	

LEAGUE TABLES

DIVISION 1

	P	W	D	L	F	A	W	D	L	F	A	Pts
Liverpool	42	13	3	5	42	24	12	4	5	42	28	57
Manchester U	42	17	3	1	61	19	5	9	7	34	35	56
Wolverhampton W	42	15	1	5	66	31	10	5	6	32	25	56
Stoke C	42	14	5	2	52	21	10	2	9	38	32	55
Blackpool	42	14	1	6	38	32	8	5	8	33	38	50
Sheffield U	42	12	4	5	51	32	9	3	9	38	43	49
Preston N.E.	42	10	7	4	45	27	8	4	9	31	47	47
Aston Villa	42	9	6	6	39	24	9	3	9	28	29	45
Sunderland	42	11	3	7	33	27	7	5	9	32	39	44
Everton	42	13	5	3	40	24	4	4	13	22	43	43
Middlesbrough	42	11	3	7	46	32	6	5	10	27	36	42
Portsmouth	42	11	3	7	42	27	5	6	10	24	33	41
Arsenal	42	9	5	7	43	33	7	4	10	29	37	41
Derby Co	42	13	2	6	44	28	5	3	13	29	51	41
Chelsea	42	9	3	9	33	39	7	4	10	36	45	39
Grimsby T	42	9	6	6	37	35	4	6	11	24	47	38
Blackburn R	42	6	5	10	23	27	8	3	10	22	26	36
Bolton W	42	8	5	8	30	28	5	3	13	27	41	34
Charlton A	42	6	6	9	34	32	5	6	10	23	39	34
Huddersfield T	42	11	4	6	34	24	2	3	16	19	55	33
Brentford	42	5	5	11	19	35	4	2	15	26	53	25
Leeds U	42	6	5	10	30	30	0	1	20	15	60	18

DIVISION 2

	P	W	D	L	F	A	W	D	L	F	A	Pts
Manchester C	42	17	3	1	49	14	9	7	5	29	21	62
Burnley	42	11	8	2	30	14	11	6	4	35	15	58
Birmingham C	42	17	2	2	51	11	8	3	10	23	22	55
Chesterfield	42	12	6	3	37	17	6	8	7	21	27	50
Newcastle U	42	11	4	6	60	32	8	6	7	35	30	48
Tottenham H	42	11	8	2	35	21	6	6	9	30	32	48
W.B.A.	42	12	4	5	53	37	8	4	9	35	38	48
Coventry C	42	12	8	1	40	17	4	5	12	26	42	45
Leicester C	42	11	4	6	42	25	7	3	11	27	39	43
Barnsley	42	13	2	6	48	29	4	6	11	36	57	42
Nottingham F	42	13	5	3	47	20	2	5	14	22	54	40
West Ham U	42	12	4	5	46	31	4	4	13	24	45	40
Luton T	42	13	4	4	50	29	3	3	15	21	44	39
Southampton	42	11	5	5	45	24	4	4	13	24	52	39
Fulham	42	12	4	5	40	25	3	5	13	23	49	39
Bradford P.A.	42	7	6	8	29	28	7	5	9	36	49	39
Bury	42	11	6	4	62	34	1	6	14	18	44	36
Millwall	42	7	7	7	30	30	7	1	13	26	49	36
Plymouth A	42	11	3	7	45	34	3	2	16	34	62	33
Sheffield W	42	10	5	6	39	28	2	3	16	28	60	32
Swansea T	42	9	1	11	36	40	2	6	13	19	43	29
Newport Co	42	9	1	11	41	52	1	2	18	20	81	23

DIVISION 3 NORTH

	P	W	D	L	F	A	W	D	L	F	A	Pts
Doncaster R	42	15	5	1	67	16	18	1	2	56	24	72
Rotherham U	42	20	1	0	81	19	9	5	7	33	34	64
Chester C	42	17	2	2	53	13	8	4	9	42	38	56
Stockport Co	42	17	0	4	50	19	7	2	12	28	34	50
Bradford C	42	12	5	4	40	20	8	5	8	22	27	50
Rochdale	42	9	5	7	39	25	10	5	6	41	39	48
Wrexham	42	13	5	3	43	21	4	7	10	22	30	46
Crewe A	42	12	4	5	39	26	5	5	11	31	48	43
Barrow	42	10	2	9	28	24	7	5	9	26	38	41
Tranmere R	42	11	5	5	43	33	6	2	13	23	44	41
Hull C	42	9	5	7	25	19	7	3	11	24	34	40
Lincoln C	42	12	3	6	52	32	5	2	14	34	55	39
Hartlepool U	42	10	5	6	36	26	5	4	12	28	47	39
Gateshead	42	10	3	8	39	33	6	3	12	23	39	38
York C	42	6	4	11	35	42	8	5	8	32	39	37
Carlisle U	42	10	5	6	45	38	4	4	13	25	55	37
Darlington	42	12	4	5	48	26	3	2	16	20	54	36
New Brighton	42	11	3	7	37	30	3	5	13	20	47	36
Oldham A	42	6	5	10	29	31	6	3	12	26	49	32
Accrington S	42	8	3	10	37	38	6	1	14	19	54	32
Southport	42	6	5	10	35	41	1	6	14	18	44	25
Halifax T	42	6	3	12	28	36	2	3	16	15	56	22

DIVISION 3 SOUTH

	P	W	D	L	F	A	W	D	L	F	A	Pts
Cardiff C	42	18	3	0	60	11	12	3	6	33	19	66
Q.P.R.	42	15	2	4	42	15	8	9	4	32	25	57
Bristol C	42	13	4	4	56	20	7	7	7	38	36	51
Swindon T	42	15	4	2	56	25	4	7	10	28	48	49
Walsall	42	11	6	4	42	25	6	6	9	32	34	46
Ipswich T	42	11	5	5	33	21	5	9	7	28	32	46
Bournemouth	42	12	4	5	43	20	6	4	11	29	34	44
Southend U	42	9	7	5	38	22	8	3	10	33	38	44
Reading	42	11	6	4	53	30	5	5	11	30	44	43
Port Vale	42	14	4	3	51	28	3	5	13	17	35	43
Torquay U	42	11	5	5	33	23	4	7	10	19	38	42
Notts Co	42	11	4	6	35	19	4	6	11	28	44	40
Northampton T	42	11	5	5	46	33	4	5	12	26	42	40
Bristol R	42	9	6	6	34	26	7	2	12	25	43	40
Exeter C	42	11	6	4	37	27	4	3	14	23	42	39
Watford	42	11	4	6	39	27	6	1	14	22	49	39
Brighton & H.A.	42	8	7	6	31	35	5	5	11	23	37	38
Crystal Palace	42	9	7	5	29	19	4	4	13	20	43	37
Leyton O	42	10	5	6	40	28	2	3	16	14	47	32
Aldershot	42	6	7	8	25	26	4	5	12	23	52	32
Norwich C	42	6	3	12	38	48	4	5	12	26	52	28
Mansfield T	42	8	5	8	31	38	1	5	15	17	58	28

FOOTBALL LEAGUE RECORDS

Top scorers: Div 1, R.Rooke (Arsenal) 33 goals; Div 2, E.Quigley (Sheffield Wednesday) 23 goals; Div 3 N, J.Hutchinson (Lincoln City) 32 goals; Div 3 S, C.Townsend (Bristol City) 29 goals.

Mansfield Town transferred to Division Three North.

Arsenal goalkeeper George Swindin, ever-present in another title-winning season for the Gunners.

DIVISION 1

	ARSENAL	ASTON VILLA	BLACKBURN R	BLACKPOOL	BOLTON W	BURNLEY	CHARLTON A	CHELSEA	DERBY CO	EVERTON	GRIMSBY T	HUDDERSFIELD T	LIVERPOOL	MANCHESTER C	MANCHESTER U	MIDDLESBROUGH	PORTSMOUTH	PRESTON N.E.	SHEFFIELD U	STOKE C	SUNDERLAND	WOLVERHAMPTON W
1 ARSENAL		O11 1-0	a03 2-0	N08 2-1	S10 2-0	F14 3-0	S03 6-0	M20 0-2	a17 1-2	O25 1-1	m01 8-0	N22 2-0	D27 1-2	D06 1-1	S06 2-1	M26 7-0	O04 0-0	J31 3-0	J03 3-2	S20 3-0	A23 3-1	M06 5-2
2 ASTON VILLA	F28 4-2		a14 3-2	S13 0-1	N15 3-1	N29 2-2	M30 2-1	F21 3-0	a07 2-2	S08 3-0	D20 2-2	S27 2-1	a24 2-1	A30 1-1	M22 0-1	D13 1-1	M27 2-1	N01 4-1	O18 2-0	a10 1-0	S01 2-0	D26 1-2
3 BLACKBURN R	N15 0-1	S06 0-0		S15 1-1	N01 4-0	O18 1-2	M27 0-0	J01 1-1	D25 3-4	A23 2-3	S20 4-0	M26 1-2	a10 1-2	F14 1-0	D13 1-1	N29 1-7	M13 1-0	O04 2-3	a24 4-0	F28 2-0	J31 4-3	J03 1-0
4 BLACKPOOL	M27 3-0	J31 1-0	S08 1-0		a05 1-1	a07 0-1	N29 3-1	A23 3-0	M26 2-2	J03 5-0	F14 3-1	S01 4-0	N01 2-0	O04 1-1	a28 1-0	a10 1-0	O18 1-0	D13 0-1	N15 2-1	D25 1-2	S20 0-1	S06 2-2
5 BOLTON W	J01 0-1	a03 1-0	M20 1-0	O25 1-0		J03 1-1	F21 1-0	J31 2-1	a21 0-3	m01 0-0	a17 2-0	O11 1-5	F07 3-0	N22 2-1	M29 0-1	S27 1-3	S06 4-0	S01 1-2	D27 2-3	A23 0-1	N08 3-1	D06 3-2
6 BURNLEY	S27 0-1	a17 1-0	M06 0-0	O11 1-0	A30 2-0		a20 0-2	D06 1-0	A26 0-2	a03 0-1	M20 4-1	m01 2-1	J17 3-0	O25 1-1	S08 0-0	S13 3-0	D20 3-2	D25 1-0	F21 0-0	M26 4-0	N22 4-0	N08 1-1
7 CHARLTON A	A27 2-4	M26 1-1	N08 0-1	a17 2-0	O04 2-1	S20 1-1		O25 3-1	N22 1-5	M06 2-3	D06 2-3	M20 0-0	S17 2-0	a03 0-1	J03 1-2	D25 1-0	F14 2-2	S06 1-2	A23 4-0	J31 0-1	m01 1-0	O11 5-1
8 CHELSEA	N01 0-0	O04 4-2	A27 1-0	D20 2-2	S13 1-1	a24 0-2	M13 3-0		A30 1-0	S20 3-1	D27 2-3	J17 2-4	F28 3-1	M26 2-2	N29 0-4	O18 4-2	D13 1-0	M27 2-0	a10 1-0	N15 4-1	S10 1-1	F14 1-1
9 DERBY CO	N29 1-0	S20 1-3	D27 5-0	M29 1-0	O18 2-1	S03 1-1	a10 0-3	J03 5-1		S06 1-0	O04 4-1	A23 0-0	M31 0-4	S10 0-0	N15 1-1	N01 4-2	a28 2-1	a24 2-1	M27 1-1	D13 1-1	F14 5-1	a14 1-2
10 EVERTON	M13 0-2	S17 3-0	D20 4-1	A30 1-2	D13 2-0	N15 0-3	O18 0-1	a14 2-3	J17 1-3		M29 3-1	S13 1-1	S27 0-3	A27 1-0	a10 2-0	F28 2-1	a24 0-2	N29 2-1	N01 2-0	M27 0-1	D26 3-0	O04 1-1
11 GRIMSBY T	D13 0-4	A23 3-0	F07 2-2	S27 0-1	N29 0-2	N01 1-2	a24 1-3	D25 0-0	F21 2-3	M26 3-0		S17 3-0	M27 0-2	S13 1-0	M17 1-1	N15 0-5	a10 1-0	O18 1-1	S06 0-3	M13 0-0	J03 1-2	S03 0-4
12 HUDDERSFIELD T	a10 1-1	F14 0-1	M29 1-1	A27 2-0	F28 1-2	D13 0-1	N01 0-1	S06 3-1	D20 2-1	a28 1-3	S10 5-1		O18 1-1	D27 1-1	M27 0-2	M13 2-1	A30 0-2	N15 1-0	N29 2-1	a24 0-0	O04 2-2	S20 0-1
13 LIVERPOOL	D25 1-3	D06 3-3	N22 2-1	M20 2-0	S20 0-0	S06 1-1	J01 2-3	O11 3-0	O25 2-2	a21 4-0	N08 3-1	M06 4-0		a17 1-1	S03 2-2	F21 0-1	J31 0-3	A23 3-1	M26 4-0	J03 0-0	a03 0-0	m01 2-1
14 MANCHESTER C	a24 0-0	J03 0-2	S27 1-3	F21 1-0	a10 0-2	M13 4-1	N15 4-0	M29 1-0	S17 3-2	S03 0-1	J31 3-1	D26 1-1	N29 2-0		S20 0-0	M27 2-0	N01 1-0	a21 0-3	D13 4-3	O18 3-0	S06 3-0	A23 4-3
15 MANCHESTER U	J17 1-1	O25 2-0	m01 4-1	D06 1-1	M26 0-2	J01 5-0	A30 6-2	a17 5-0	a03 1-0	N22 2-2	O11 3-4	N08 4-4	A27 2-0	a07 1-1		D20 2-1	D25 3-2	F14 1-1	S13 0-1	O04 1-1	M06 3-1	M20 3-2
16 MIDDLESBROUGH	M29 1-1	m01 1-3	a17 1-1	N22 4-0	F14 4-1	J31 1-2	D27 1-2	M06 0-0	M20 1-1	O11 0-1	a03 4-1	O25 1-0	O04 3-1	N08 2-1	A23 2-2		S20 1-2	J03 1-1	S03 3-0	S06 2-1	D06 2-2	J01 2-4
17 PORTSMOUTH	a21 0-0	N08 2-4	O25 1-1	M06 1-1	J17 2-0	A23 0-1	S27 3-1	m01 2-1	O11 0-0	D06 3-0	N22 4-0	J03 3-2	S13 1-0	M20 1-0	D27 1-3	a14 6-1		M26 1-0	S17 6-0	S03 3-0	a17 2-2	a03 2-0
18 PRESTON N.E.	S13 0-0	M20 3-0	F21 2-1	m01 0-7	A25 1-0	D26 3-2	J17 2-1	N08 2-0	D06 7-4	a17 3-0	M06 2-1	a03 0-2	D20 3-3	O11 2-1	S27 2-1	A30 2-1	M29 1-2		a07 3-3	S17 2-1	O25 2-2	N22 1-3
19 SHEFFIELD U	A30 1-2	M06 3-1	D06 4-1	a03 2-1	D25 2-1	O04 1-1	D20 1-1	N22 3-1	N08 1-2	M20 2-1	J17 4-0	a17 0-1	S08 3-1	m01 2-1	J31 2-1	A25 1-1	J01 1-2	S20 3-1		F14 3-0	O11 3-2	O25 2-2
20 STOKE C	F07 0-0	N22 1-2	O11 2-1	D27 1-1	D20 2-0	M29 3-0	S13 0-1	a03 2-0	m01 1-0	N08 1-1	O25 2-1	D06 1-1	A30 0-2	M06 3-0	F21 0-2	J17 2-4	A25 2-1	S08 0-1	S27 1-1		M20 3-1	a17 2-3
21 SUNDERLAND	D20 1-1	A27 0-0	S13 0-1	a12 1-0	J24 1-2	a10 2-0	D13 0-1	S17 2-3	S27 1-1	D25 2-0	A30 4-2	F21 2-0	N15 5-1	J17 0-1	O18 1-0	a24 3-0	N29 4-1	M13 0-2	F28 1-1	N01 1-0		M26 2-1
22 WOLVERHAMPTON W	O18 1-1	D27 4-1	A30 5-1	J17 1-1	a24 1-0	M27 1-1	F28 2-0	S27 1-0	S13 1-0	F21 2-4	A27 8-1	F07 2-1	D13 1-2	D20 1-0	N01 2-6	S10 1-3	N15 3-1	a10 4-2	M13 1-1	N29 1-2	M29 2-1	

Reg Lewis, his scheming helped Ronnie Rooke score most of Arsenal's goals but Lewis also weighed in with 14 himself.

DIVISION 2

	BARNSLEY	BIRMINGHAM C	BRADFORD	BRENTFORD	BURY	CARDIFF C	CHESTERFIELD	COVENTRY C	DONCASTER R	FULHAM	LEEDS U	LEICESTER C	LUTON T	MILLWALL	NEWCASTLE U	NOTTINGHAM F	PLYMOUTH A	SHEFFIELD W	SOUTHAMPTON	TOTTENHAM H	W.B.A.	WEST HAM U
1 BARNSLEY		D20 0-1	D06 2-2	F14 1-1	N08 2-1	m01 1-2	O25 0-3	D26 0-1	N22 2-0	S10 1-2	A27 3-0	O04 2-0	S20 3-0	M06 1-0	M29 1-1	a17 2-2	J31 2-1	J17 3-1	a03 2-1	O11 2-1	A30 0-1	M20 1-1
2 BIRMINGHAM C	A23 2-3		N22 4-3	J31 0-0	O25 2-0	a17 2-0	O11 0-0	S03 1-1	N08 3-0	O04 3-1	F14 5-1	S20 1-0	S06 2-1	D27 1-0	S10 0-0	a03 2-1	J03 1-1	D06 1-0	M20 0-0	m01 0-0	M29 4-0	M06 0-1
3 BRADFORD	a24 3-2	a10 1-2		F28 1-1	M29 5-3	F14 0-1	J03 1-3	M27 2-2	S10 4-0	N01 3-0	M13 3-1	O18 0-2	O04 2-2	S06 4-0	N15 0-3	S03 3-1	D13 3-0	S20 2-0	D26 1-3	J31 0-2	N29 3-1	A23 4-1
4 BRENTFORD	S27 3-3	S13 1-2	O11 2-1		a17 4-1	O18 0-0	a03 0-3	A30 1-4	m01 2-0	D20 0-2	M26 3-0	D25 2-2	A27 0-3	N08 2-1	J17 1-0	S10 3-1	F21 0-0	O25 1-0	D06 2-2	M20 2-0	F07 1-0	N22 1-1
5 BURY	J24 1-1	M13 1-1	M26 0-4	N29 2-2		J01 1-2	F14 2-0	F28 0-0	A30 4-2	S13 1-0	D13 1-1	a24 0-2	a10 2-2	O04 0-0	O18 3-5	D20 1-0	N15 0-0	S10 1-2	J17 3-0	A27 2-0	N01 1-2	S20 1-2
6 CARDIFF C	D13 1-0	N29 2-0	S27 1-0	M06 1-0	D26 2-2		A23 0-0	N15 1-1	A25 3-0	M27 0-0	N01 0-0	M13 3-0	O11 1-0	J03 6-0	a10 1-1	F21 4-1	S20 3-0	J31 2-1	S08 5-1	S06 0-3	a24 0-5	M26 0-3
7 CHESTERFIELD	M13 1-1	F28 0-3	A30 0-1	N15 4-0	S27 1-2	D20 2-2		D13 4-3	S13 0-3	a24 1-0	N29 3-0	a10 2-3	M27 2-0	J01 2-0	A27 0-1	J17 0-0	N01 1-1	M26 0-2	a14 0-1	D27 3-1	O18 0-2	a07 6-0
8 COVENTRY C	D25 3-2	A25 0-1	N08 5-0	J03 3-0	O11 0-0	a03 1-0	m01 3-0		O25 1-0	S20 5-2	J31 1-2	S06 0-1	A23 4-1	D06 0-1	F21 1-1	M20 1-1	M30 0-0	N22 3-1	M06 0-1	a17 1-1	S15 1-0	F14 0-1
9 DONCASTER R	a10 1-2	M27 0-0	S18 3-0	D13 0-0	J03 1-3	S04 2-2	J31 1-0	M13 0-0		O18 0-1	F28 3-0	M26 1-1	a24 0-2	S20 2-2	N01 0-3	D26 2-0	N29 2-0	O04 0-1	A23 1-1	F14 1-1	N15 2-1	S06 1-0
10 FULHAM	S17 0-1	F21 1-1	M20 0-0	A23 5-0	J31 1-1	N08 4-1	D06 0-0	a28 0-2	M06 0-0		S06 3-2	J03 3-1	M29 1-1	a17 1-0	S27 3-0	O25 0-0	D25 1-1	a03 0-2	O11 0-2	N22 0-2	S03 0-1	m01 1-1
11 LEEDS U	S03 4-1	S27 0-1	O25 2-0	M29 1-1	m01 5-1	M20 4-0	a17 3-0	S13 2-1	O11 0-0	J17 0-1		A23 3-1	D26 0-2	N22 2-1	J24 3-1	M06 2-2	S10 5-0	N08 2-2	J03 0-0	a03 1-3	F21 3-1	D06 2-1
12 LEICESTER C	a05 4-1	a19 0-0	M06 2-0	D27 1-2	D06 2-1	O25 2-1	N22 1-2	J17 2-2	M29 3-2	A30 0-2	D20 2-0		S08 3-2	a03 3-0	S13 2-2	O11 3-1	A25 2-1	M20 2-3	a28 0-0	N08 0-3	S27 1-1	a17 1-3
13 LUTON T	a14 2-1	J17 0-1	F21 3-3	S03 3-0	N22 1-1	F28 1-1	N08 2-1	D20 2-3	D06 2-1	M26 0-3	D27 6-1	S17 2-1		M20 1-2	A30 2-1	m01 2-1	S27 0-0	M06 1-1	a17 0-2	O25 0-0	S13 1-1	a03 0-0
14 MILLWALL	O18 3-3	D25 0-0	J17 0-1	M27 0-1	F21 1-7	A30 0-1	S08 0-2	a24 6-2	F07 1-0	N29 1-2	a10 1-1	N15 0-4	N01 3-1		D13 2-1	S13 2-0	M13 2-0	D20 0-0	S27 3-0	M26 0-0	F28 1-1	S01 1-1
15 NEWCASTLE U	M26 1-0	S17 1-0	a03 2-0	S06 1-0	M06 1-0	N22 4-1	S03 2-3	O04 0-0	M20 2-0	a14 1-0	S20 4-2	J31 2-0	J03 4-1	m01 1-0		N08 0-2	A23 6-1	a17 4-2	O25 5-0	D06 1-0	J01 3-1	O11 1-0
16 NOTTINGHAM F	N29 1-1	N15 0-2	A27 1-2	S17 2-0	A23 2-1	O04 1-2	S06 1-3	N01 4-0	D27 4-2	M13 0-2	O18 1-0	F28 1-0	D13 1-2	J31 5-2	M27 0-0		a24 1-1	F14 0-0	M29 1-1	S20 1-0	a10 3-1	J03 2-1
17 PLYMOUTH A	S13 1-0	A30 0-3	m01 2-2	O04 0-0	a03 0-0	F07 3-0	M20 1-2	M29 1-0	a17 2-2	D27 3-2	S17 1-0	S03 0-0	F14 1-3	O25 1-1	D20 3-0	D06 1-1		O11 0-2	N22 3-1	M06 1-1	J17 2-1	N08 1-1
18 SHEFFIELD W	S06 5-2	a24 0-0	F07 3-1	a12 1-1	S15 2-2	S13 2-1	M29 1-0	a10 1-1	a05 2-0	N15 2-0	M27 3-1	N01 1-1	O18 1-0	A23 3-2	N29 1-0	S27 2-1	F28 1-1		S01 1-2	J03 1-0	D13 1-2	D26 5-3
19 SOUTHAMPTON	N15 4-1	N01 2-0	D27 1-2	a24 2-1	S06 1-0	S17 2-2	S20 3-0	O18 3-1	D20 6-1	a21 1-0	A30 1-2	D13 3-1	N29 3-1	F14 5-1	M13 4-2	M26 2-1	a10 2-3	A27 3-1		O04 1-1	M27 1-1	J31 3-1
20 TOTTENHAM H	M15 0-3	D13 1-2	S13 3-1	N01 4-0	S01 2-2	J17 2-1	D25 3-0	N29 2-1	S27 2-0	a10 0-2	N15 3-1	M27 0-0	a05 0-1	M29 3-2	a24 1-1	a12 0-3	O18 2-0	A30 5-1	F21 0-0		D20 1-1	S15 2-2
21 W.B.A.	J03 0-2	M30 1-1	a17 6-0	S20 3-2	M20 3-3	D06 2-3	M06 1-0	S10 3-1	a03 1-3	A27 2-1	O04 3-2	F14 1-3	J31 1-0	O11 2-1	D26 0-1	N22 3-2	S06 1-1	m01 1-1	N08 1-0	A23 1-0		O25 1-2
22 WEST HAM U	N01 2-1	O18 0-0	D20 0-0	a10 0-1	F07 2-0	M29 4-2	O04 4-0	S27 1-0	J24 2-1	D13 3-0	a24 2-1	N29 1-1	N15 0-0	A25 1-1	F28 0-2	A30 2-1	M27 1-1	D27 1-4	S13 2-0	S08 1-1	M13 0-2	

Season 1947-48

DIVISION 3 NORTH

	ACCRINGTON S	BARROW	BRADFORD C	CARLISLE U	CHESTER	CREWE A	DARLINGTON	GATESHEAD	HALIFAX T	HARTLEPOOLS U	HULL C	LINCOLN C	MANSFIELD T	NEW BRIGHTON	OLDHAM A	ROCHDALE	ROTHERHAM U	SOUTHPORT	STOCKPORT CO	TRANMERE R	WREXHAM	YORK C
1 ACCRINGTON S		S20 0-1	J31 2-0	D06 1-2	N22 1-0	a17 2-1	M06 3-0	O11 1-0	O04 2-0	A23 4-2	J03 2-4	D27 2-1	a03 1-0	S30 5-3	M20 2-3	J01 1-2	m01 0-1	M29 0-0	S06 5-2	O25 1-0	F14 0-2	N08 1-0
2 BARROW	F07 3-0		S11 0-1	M06 2-0	A28 1-0	O11 2-0	a03 0-0	N08 1-2	D26 2-1	M20 1-2	S27 0-2	S13 0-1	m01 1-0	A30 1-1	a17 2-4	a13 0-1	O25 1-3	D20 2-0	F21 0-0	N22 3-0	M26 1-1	D06 1-0
3 BRADFORD C	S13 1-2	S17 1-1		O11 1-1	m01 3-2	F21 1-2	N08 4-0	M20 2-2	M30 2-1	O25 3-1	F07 2-0	J17 2-4	D06 0-1	D20 1-1	N22 0-2	D25 4-0	M06 0-1	A30 4-2	S27 1-0	a03 4-1	A27 1-0	a17 1-3
4 CARLISLE U	D13 2-3	O18 1-2	F28 1-2		F21 2-0	S27 5-2	A23 4-2	J03 1-1	N01 5-2	S06 1-1	J24 0-0	J10 2-5	J01 3-1	N15 2-1	M26 4-1	M27 5-0	J31 0-3	a10 2-3	S20 4-0	D27 4-3	M13 1-2	S04 1-1
5 CHESTER	a10 1-0	S03 0-0	a21 2-1	O04 4-1		S10 4-2	S06 1-1	J31 2-3	O18 0-0	S20 2-0	M17 4-1	N15 1-1	M26 1-2	N01 4-2	A23 2-1	M13 2-1	F14 2-3	M27 0-0	a24 2-2	J03 4-0	F28 4-1	D27 2-3
6 CREWE A	a07 0-0	F28 1-2	O04 3-2	F14 0-2	S17 1-0		J03 4-1	S06 0-1	M13 0-1	J31 2-0	a24 3-1	a10 3-0	A27 0-0	M27 4-0	D25 2-2	N01 2-1	S20 3-3	N15 4-1	a14 4-2	A23 3-2	O18 1-0	M26 1-3
7 DARLINGTON	O18 3-1	N15 2-2	M27 1-1	D20 4-3	J17 1-1	A30 0-1		S01 1-1	J10 4-1	M26 1-0	M13 2-0	F28 1-3	S13 1-2	J24 3-1	S27 0-6	a24 0-0	D25 1-1	J01 1-3	N01 0-0	F21 0-2	a10 3-1	F07 1-1
8 GATESHEAD	F28 4-2	M27 0-2	N01 2-2	A30 1-3	S13 2-1	J17 2-0	A27 1-2		a10 3-0	D25 7-0	O18 0-1	M29 3-2	F07 2-1	a24 3-1	F21 3-5	J10 5-0	D20 1-1	J24 3-2	M13 1-1	J01 3-0	N15 2-2	S27 0-0
9 HALIFAX T	F21 3-3	D25 1-1	M29 0-0	M20 2-1	M06 1-1	O25 4-1	a17 1-1	N22 0-0		a03 0-0	S15 0-2	S27 0-1	O11 1-1	S13 1-2	m01 1-5	J17 2-3	N08 2-1	F07 0-0	S01 4-0	D06 2-2	A23 0-1	J03 0-1
10 HARTLEPOOLS U	a28 4-0	N01 0-3	M13 0-2	J17 1-1	F07 2-1	S13 0-1	M29 3-0	D27 3-2	N15 1-1		F28 3-1	J24 1-2	S27 1-0	J10 1-0	J01 3-1	a10 4-1	A30 2-2	a24 2-0	O18 0-0	A27 1-1	M27 0-2	F21 2-2
11 HULL C	A30 4-2	F14 0-0	S20 2-1	m01 3-1	a17 2-1	a22 2-1	O25 0-3	M06 2-3	S11 1-2	O11 5-0		D20 0-1	N22 1-1	M29 3-0	N08 1-0	A28 0-0	J17 5-3	D26 1-0	J31 1-0	M20 3-0	O04 1-1	a03 1-1
12 LINCOLN C	D25 2-3	J31 2-1	S06 3-0	a17 3-0	a03 4-2	N22 0-0	O11 3-1	M26 3-0	F14 3-1	m01 5-0	A23 2-3		N08 0-0	S10 1-2	O25 0-2	O04 3-0	D06 3-1	S03 3-1	J03 3-0	M06 2-0	S20 2-1	M20 0-0
13 MANSFIELD T	N15 1-0	J24 1-0	a24 1-1	S08 2-3	M29 2-1	S01 3-1	J31 4-0	S20 1-2	F28 3-1	F14 3-2	a10 1-1	M27 0-2		M13 5-0	J03 1-1	O18 1-1	O04 2-1	N01 2-0	a05 1-2	S06 1-3	D27 1-0	A23 1-2
14 NEW BRIGHTON	S03 0-1	J03 1-1	A23 0-2	a03 1-3	M20 0-1	N08 1-2	m01 2-1	D06 1-2	J31 1-0	a17 1-2	M26 1-0	J01 0-1	O25 2-2		O11 2-2	S20 0-0	N22 1-2	F21 2-2	D27 1-0	F14 0-2	S06 1-1	M06 2-1
15 OLDHAM A	N01 1-0	a06 2-1	a10 3-0	M29 2-1	D20 3-1	D26 0-0	F14 3-3	O04 0-1	J24 1-1	S16 0-2	M27 0-0	M13 0-0	A30 1-1	F28 3-0		S13 1-1	A26 1-5	O18 1-1	N15 0-0	S20 0-1	a24 1-4	J17 2-2
16 ROCHDALE	S09 1-3	A23 2-2	D27 2-0	N08 2-1	O25 2-2	M20 1-2	D06 2-1	a17 2-1	S06 2-1	N22 0-2	S02 1-0	a06 1-1	M06 1-2	F07 1-0	J31 2-0		a03 1-0	S27 2-1	M26 1-2	m01 1-1	J03 2-1	O11 3-0
17 ROTHERHAM U	S22 1-0	M13 0-0	O18 4-1	S13 7-2	S27 2-1	F07 5-1	D27 0-0	A23 0-0	M27 3-0	J03 3-2	S06 0-0	a24 0-2	a12 2-1	a10 6-1	S01 4-1	N15 4-1		S15 0-2	F28 4-1	M26 2-0	N01 6-0	J01 3-2
18 SOUTHPORT	M26 1-1	S06 1-2	J03 1-2	N22 0-4	N08 3-0	a03 2-0	S08 2-0	D13 2-1	S20 2-0	a19 2-0	D25 1-2	A26 1-1	M20 1-1	O04 4-0	M06 4-0	F14 2-2	a17 1-2		A23 0-4	O11 1-4	J31 1-0	O25 2-1
19 STOCKPORT CO	J17 1-1	O04 2-3	F14 3-3	F07 2-3	D06 4-1	m01 2-1	M20 1-3	O25 1-1	A25 2-1	M06 2-0	S13 0-0	A30 1-1	a17 5-0	D25 1-2	a03 3-0	M29 4-0	O11 2-2	a26 0-3		N08 2-0	S08 0-1	N22 4-2
20 TRANMERE R	M13 0-1	a10 1-0	N15 2-1	D26 0-3	A30 2-3	D20 2-0	O04 0-1	S09 3-0	a24 0-1	S02 1-0	N01 2-1	O18 1-4	J17 0-1	S27 1-0	F07 1-0	J24 4-1	M29 0-1	F28 2-2	M27 2-3		J10 2-3	S13 4-2
21 WREXHAM	S27 1-1	M29 3-1	S03 4-2	O25 2-1	O11 2-1	M06 1-1	N22 1-2	a03 0-3	D20 6-3	N08 3-1	F21 1-0	F07 3-0	D26 2-1	J17 0-0	D06 1-2	A30 5-1	M20 1-3	S13 2-0	S17 2-0	a17 6-0		m01 3-0
22 YORK C	M27 1-2	a24 0-0	J10 3-3	A25 2-2	D26 2-0	M29 0-1	S20 0-2	F14 3-1	A30 6-0	O04 4-0	N15 2-2	N01 0-1	D20 1-2	O18 3-1	S06 1-0	F28 0-0	S10 2-0	M13 3-3	a10 3-2	J31 1-2	J24 1-1	

DIVISION 3 SOUTH

	ALDERSHOT	BOURNEMOUTH	BRIGHTON & HA	BRISTOL C	BRISTOL R	CRYSTAL P	EXETER C	IPSWICH T	LEYTON O	NEWPORT CO	NORTHAMPTON T	NORWICH C	NOTTS CO	PORT VALE	Q.P.R.	READING	SOUTHEND U	SWANSEA T	SWINDON T	TORQUAY U	WALSALL	WATFORD
1 ALDERSHOT		a10 0-3	S27 1-1	a24 1-1	M26 2-0	S03 2-0	O18 0-0	J10 0-1	F28 0-0	M13 1-2	S17 1-1	a07 2-2	M27 1-0	J17 1-1	S13 1-4	J24 1-2	N01 1-1	N15 0-3	A30 2-2	a21 1-0	D27 3-1	F07 1-1
2 BOURNEMOUTH	N22 1-1		J03 4-1	S13 2-0	D06 3-0	a03 0-0	M29 2-1	J17 4-0	F21 1-1	S17 5-0	a17 2-0	m01 1-3	S03 2-0	O25 3-0	a14 0-1	F07 2-0	D27 0-1	A23 1-0	M20 1-0	N08 6-2	S27 1-1	O11 1-1
3 BRIGHTON & H.A.	F14 1-1	A30 0-2		O18 0-2	J31 3-1	O04 1-1	N15 0-1	J24 4-1	M27 0-0	a10 3-0	S20 2-3	S06 2-0	a24 1-3	D27 2-2	A27 0-5	M13 2-0	a07 1-0	O01 0-1	S17 1-0	M26 2-1	N01 0-4	a28 1-3
4 BRISTOL C	a26 2-4	J31 0-4	M06 1-2		F14 5-2	a17 2-0	D27 1-1	S20 4-0	S17 6-0	S03 1-0	m01 1-1	O11 6-0	J03 1-0	N08 2-1	M20 2-1	F21 0-2	A23 6-0	S06 3-2	a03 2-2	N22 1-2	M26 0-0	O25 1-2
5 BRISTOL R	M29 7-1	a24 1-2	S13 4-1	S27 0-2		S08 1-1	N01 2-2	a28 2-0	M13 0-2	M27 2-3	O04 1-2	F07 2-3	a10 2-0	D20 2-1	A30 0-1	F28 2-3	N15 1-2	S22 2-2	A25 3-1	D26 0-2	O18 2-3	J17 3-0
6 CRYSTAL P	A27 1-0	N15 2-0	a12 0-0	a05 4-0	S17 0-0		F28 1-2	a10 2-1	D20 2-0	O18 2-1	D25 1-0	M29 2-0	N01 1-1	S13 2-0	M15 0-1	a24 2-1	M13 0-0	M27 4-0	J17 1-1	A30 2-1	J24 2-3	S27 1-2
7 EXETER C	M06 4-0	M26 1-1	a03 1-0	D26 3-1	M20 4-0	O11 2-0		S10 1-0	A30 1-1	J31 4-4	O25 1-1	N08 2-0	F14 0-1	a07 0-0	a17 1-2	A27 1-0	S20 0-0	O04 3-1	m01 2-1	J17 0-2	a21 0-6	N22 3-1
8 IPSWICH T	a17 2-0	S06 1-1	O11 4-0	F07 1-0	m01 0-4	N22 3-0	S17 2-0		M29 1-0	D27 3-0	a21 5-2	J31 1-2	A23 2-0	M20 2-1	O25 1-0	S27 1-0	S03 4-0	J03 3-2	N08 0-1	a03 2-1	F21 3-1	M06 1-3
9 LEYTON O	O11 0-3	O04 2-0	N08 2-1	S11 0-2	O25 2-4	A23 1-1	J03 2-4	M26 1-1		S06 2-2	M06 5-0	M20 2-1	S20 2-1	a17 0-0	N22 1-3	D27 2-2	J31 2-0	F14 1-0	D06 0-3	m01 4-1	S04 0-1	a03 0-2
10 NEWPORT CO	O25 2-2	S11 2-2	N22 1-1	A28 1-0	N08 2-2	M06 3-1	S13 3-0	D25 3-1	J17 3-2		M20 1-2	a03 1-1	O04 3-1	m01 0-0	D06 0-0	D20 2-0	F14 1-5	M29 1-1	a08 2-0	O11 0-1	A30 4-2	a17 3-4
11 NORTHAMPTON T	S11 2-1	a29 3-6	F07 4-0	J24 0-4	F21 1-3	D27 3-1	M13 3-1	a24 4-2	O18 1-1	N01 1-1		S27 1-0	N15 1-2	A30 4-1	a08 1-1	M29 1-1	M27 2-0	a10 0-1	M18 0-0	A28 1-0	F28 2-1	S13 0-1
12 NORWICH C	O04 0-1	J24 0-1	J17 2-2	F28 2-3	S20 1-5	M26 3-1	M27 3-0	S13 1-5	N01 3-0	N15 1-2	F14 2-3		a28 0-1	A27 1-2	a21 5-2	O18 2-1	a10 1-0	a24 1-2	D27 2-2	S10 1-1	M13 1-0	A30 1-0
13 NOTTS CO	N08 0-2	A28 1-2	a22 4-0	A30 3-1	N22 4-2	M20 1-0	S27 1-1	a15 0-1	F07 1-4	F21 4-1	a03 3-2	a17 1-2		O11 2-1	S11 1-1	J17 5-1	M26 2-1	D26 5-1	M06 2-1	O25 0-0	S13 1-0	m01 3-3
14 PORT VALE	S06 6-4	M13 2-1	D25 5-0	M27 1-0	A23 1-1	J31 4-1	a24 1-1	N01 4-1	J10 3-0	J24 4-1	J03 1-0	S01 2-0	F28 1-2		M26 0-2	N15 1-0	O04 2-1	O18 1-1	F14 1-0	S20 1-1	a10 0-1	S15 7-0
15 Q.P.R.	J31 0-0	O18 1-0	S04 2-0	N01 2-0	J03 5-2	S20 1-0	S25 3-1	M13 2-0	a10 1-2	a24 1-0	S06 2-0	A23 3-1	S18 4-1	M29 2-1		M27 2-0	O02 3-2	a26 0-0	O04 0-2	F14 3-3	N15 2-1	D27 5-1
16 READING	m01 0-0	S20 3-0	O25 1-0	O04 2-7	O11 0-0	a21 0-0	S03 2-1	F14 1-2	D26 6-2	A23 0-0	M26 1-1	M06 2-4	S06 3-1	a03 2-0	N08 3-2		J03 1-3	J31 4-1	N22 2-3	a17 2-0	S17 0-1	M20 2-0
17 SOUTHEND U	M20 4-0	D26 0-2	a17 2-2	D20 4-0	a03 1-0	O25 2-1	F07 2-0	A27 3-2	S13 2-1	S27 1-0	N08 3-1	N22 0-0	M29 1-2	F21 1-1	m01 0-0	A30 1-1		S10 1-1	O11 1-0	M06 1-0	J17 1-1	J24 1-1
18 SWANSEA T	a03 2-1	D20 3-2	m01 0-0	J17 6-1	a17 0-1	N08 2-0	F21 2-0	A30 1-1	S27 5-0	M26 3-0	N22 5-1	D06 3-2	D27 1-1	M06 2-0	O11 3-1	S13 1-1	S18 3-0		O25 1-0	M20 1-1	F07 1-1	A28 3-0
19 SWINDON T	J03 1-0	N01 0-1	S10 1-1	N15 2-2	S03 1-1	S06 0-0	a14 3-2	M27 0-1	a24 0-1	S20 1-2	A23 0-0	D26 3-2	O18 1-1	S27 1-0	F21 0-0	a10 1-1	F28 0-0	M13 1-0		J31 2-2	a28 0-3	M26 3-0
20 TORQUAY U	A23 2-0	M27 0-1	M29 1-2	a10 2-3	D27 1-2	J03 3-3	S06 1-2	N15 3-0	J24 0-1	F28 4-1	S03 4-2	S17 1-1	M13 2-2	F07 5-0	S27 1-1	a28 1-2	O18 4-1	N01 1-1	S13 1-1		a24 3-2	F21 0-1
21 WALSALL	D25 3-0	F14 0-0	M20 0-0	M29 2-0	M06 2-0	D06 1-1	A23 4-0	O04 1-2	A28 3-1	J03 1-1	O11 2-0	O25 3-2	J31 2-1	N22 1-2	a03 0-1	S11 0-0	S06 6-0	S20 2-1	a17 1-0	a15 1-0		N08 2-0
22 WATFORD	S20 1-2	F28 0-3	A23 2-3	M13 1-1	S06 3-2	F14 0-5	a10 3-1	O18 2-3	N15 2-1	J10 1-2	J31 1-1	J03 2-2	a07 1-3	S10 1-1	D26 0-1	N01 0-1	a24 2-2	S03 4-1	M29 1-0	O04 2-2	M27 2-0	

LEAGUE TABLES

DIVISION 1

	P	W	D	L	F	A	W	D	L	F	A	Pts
Arsenal	42	15	3	3	56	15	8	10	3	25	17	59
Manchester U	42	11	7	3	50	27	8	7	6	31	21	52
Burnley	42	12	5	4	31	12	8	7	6	25	31	52
Derby Co	42	11	6	4	38	24	8	6	7	39	33	50
Wolverhampton W	42	12	4	5	45	29	7	5	9	38	41	47
Aston Villa	42	13	5	3	42	22	6	4	11	23	35	47
Preston N.E.	42	13	4	4	43	35	7	3	11	24	33	47
Portsmouth	42	13	5	3	44	17	6	2	13	24	33	45
Blackpool	42	13	4	4	37	14	4	6	11	20	27	44
Manchester C	42	13	3	5	37	22	2	9	10	15	25	42
Liverpool	42	9	8	4	39	23	7	2	12	26	38	42
Sheffield U	42	13	4	4	44	24	3	6	12	21	46	42
Charlton A	42	8	4	9	33	29	9	2	10	24	37	40
Everton	42	10	2	9	30	26	7	4	10	22	40	40
Stoke C	42	9	5	7	29	23	5	5	11	12	32	38
Middlesbrough	42	8	7	6	37	27	6	2	13	34	46	37
Bolton W	42	11	2	8	29	25	5	3	13	17	33	37
Chelsea	42	11	6	4	38	27	3	3	15	15	44	37
Huddersfield T	42	7	6	8	25	24	5	6	10	26	36	36
Sunderland	42	11	4	6	33	18	2	6	13	23	49	36
Blackburn R	42	8	5	8	35	30	3	5	13	19	42	32
Grimsby T	42	5	5	11	20	35	3	1	17	25	76	22

DIVISION 2

	P	W	D	L	F	A	W	D	L	F	A	Pts
Birmingham C	42	12	7	2	34	13	10	8	3	21	11	59
Newcastle U	42	18	1	2	46	13	6	7	8	26	28	56
Southampton	42	15	3	3	53	23	6	7	8	18	30	52
Sheffield W	42	13	6	2	39	21	7	5	9	27	32	51
Cardiff C	42	12	6	3	36	18	6	5	10	25	40	47
West Ham U	42	10	7	4	29	19	6	7	8	26	34	46
W.B.A.	42	11	4	6	37	29	7	5	9	26	29	45
Tottenham H	42	10	6	5	36	24	5	8	8	20	19	44
Leicester C	42	10	5	6	36	29	6	6	9	24	28	43
Coventry C	42	10	5	6	33	16	4	8	9	26	36	41
Fulham	42	6	9	6	24	19	9	1	11	23	27	40
Barnsley	42	10	5	6	31	22	5	5	11	31	42	40
Luton T	42	8	8	5	31	25	6	4	11	25	34	40
Bradford P.A.	42	11	3	7	45	30	5	5	11	23	42	40
Brentford	42	10	6	5	31	26	3	8	10	13	35	40
Chesterfield	42	8	4	9	32	26	8	3	10	22	29	39
Plymouth A	42	8	9	4	27	22	1	11	9	13	36	38
Leeds U	42	12	5	4	44	20	2	3	16	18	52	36
Nottingham F	42	10	5	6	32	23	2	6	13	22	37	35
Bury	42	6	8	7	27	28	3	8	10	31	40	34
Doncaster R	42	7	8	6	23	20	2	3	16	17	46	29
Millwall	42	7	7	7	27	28	2	4	15	17	46	29

DIVISION 3 NORTH

	P	W	D	L	F	A	W	D	L	F	A	Pts
Lincoln C	42	14	3	4	47	18	12	5	4	34	22	60
Rotherham U	42	15	4	2	56	18	10	5	6	39	31	59
Wrexham	42	14	3	4	49	23	7	5	9	25	31	50
Gateshead	42	11	5	5	48	28	8	6	7	27	29	49
Hull C	42	12	5	4	38	21	6	6	9	21	27	47
Accrington S	42	13	1	7	36	24	7	5	9	26	35	46
Barrow	42	9	4	8	24	19	7	9	5	25	21	45
Mansfield T	42	11	4	6	37	24	6	7	8	20	27	45
Carlisle U	42	10	4	7	50	35	8	3	10	38	42	43
Crewe A	42	12	4	5	41	24	6	3	12	20	39	43
Oldham A	42	6	10	5	25	25	8	3	10	38	39	41
Rochdale	42	12	4	5	32	23	3	7	11	16	49	41
York C	42	8	7	6	38	25	5	7	9	27	35	40
Bradford C	42	10	4	7	38	27	5	6	10	27	39	40
Southport	42	10	4	7	34	27	4	7	10	26	36	39
Darlington	42	7	8	6	30	31	6	5	10	24	39	39
Stockport Co	42	9	6	6	42	28	4	6	11	21	39	38
Tranmere R	42	10	1	10	30	28	6	3	12	24	44	36
Hartlepool U	42	10	6	5	34	23	4	2	15	17	50	36
Chester C	42	11	6	4	44	25	2	3	16	20	42	35
Halifax T	42	4	10	7	25	27	3	3	15	18	49	27
New Brighton	42	5	6	10	20	28	3	3	15	18	53	25

DIVISION 3 SOUTH

	P	W	D	L	F	A	W	D	L	F	A	Pts
Q.P.R.	42	16	3	2	44	17	10	6	5	30	20	61
Bournemouth	42	13	5	3	42	13	11	4	6	34	22	57
Walsall	42	13	5	3	37	12	8	4	9	33	28	51
Ipswich T	42	16	1	4	42	18	7	2	12	25	43	49
Swansea T	42	14	6	1	48	14	4	6	11	22	38	48
Notts Co	42	12	4	5	44	27	7	4	10	24	32	46
Bristol C	42	11	4	6	47	26	7	3	11	30	39	43
Port Vale	42	14	4	3	48	18	2	7	12	15	36	43
Southend U	42	11	8	2	32	16	4	5	12	19	42	43
Reading	42	10	5	6	37	28	5	6	10	19	30	41
Exeter C	42	11	6	4	34	22	4	5	12	21	41	41
Newport Co	42	9	8	4	38	28	5	5	11	23	45	41
Crystal Palace	42	12	5	4	32	14	1	8	12	17	35	39
Northampton T	42	10	5	6	35	28	4	6	11	23	44	39
Watford	42	6	6	9	31	37	8	4	9	26	42	38
Swindon T	42	6	10	5	21	20	4	6	11	20	26	36
Leyton O	42	8	5	8	31	32	5	5	11	20	41	36
Torquay U	42	7	6	8	40	29	4	7	10	23	33	35
Aldershot	42	5	10	6	22	26	5	5	11	23	41	35
Bristol R	42	7	3	11	39	34	6	5	10	32	41	34
Norwich C	42	8	3	10	33	34	5	5	11	28	42	34
Brighton & H.A.	42	8	4	9	26	31	3	8	10	17	42	34

Football League Records

Top scorers: Div 1, W.Moir (Bolton Wanderers) 25 goals; Div 2, C.Wayman (Southampton) 32 goals; Div 3 N, W.Ardron (Rotherham United) 29 goals; Div 3 S, D.McGibbon (Bournemouth & Boscombe Athletic) 30 goals.

Portsmouth outside-left Jack Froggatt received so much fine service from Jimmy Dickinson as Portsmouth took the title in their golden jubilee season.

DIVISION 1

	ARSENAL	ASTON VILLA	BIRMINGHAM C	BLACKPOOL	BOLTON W	BURNLEY	CHARLTON A	CHELSEA	DERBY CO	EVERTON	HUDDERSFIELD T	LIVERPOOL	MANCHESTER C	MANCHESTER U	MIDDLESBROUGH	NEWCASTLE U	PORTSMOUTH	PRESTON N.E.	SHEFFIELD U	STOKE C	SUNDERLAND	WOLVERHAMPTON W
1 ARSENAL		S11 3-1	N06 2-0	a18 2-0	F26 5-0	O09 3-1	m07 2-0	a23 1-2	D25 3-3	O23 5-0	D18 3-0	S08 1-1	D04 1-1	A28 0-1	a09 1-1	N20 0-1	m04 3-2	M12 0-0	J15 5-3	A25 3-0	F05 5-0	S25 3-1
2 ASTON VILLA	J22 1-0		D04 0-3	J01 2-5	A30 2-4	N06 3-1	O23 4-3	M26 1-1	S04 1-1	N20 0-1	S18 3-3	A21 2-1	M12 1-0	F19 2-1	m07 1-1	S13 2-4	O09 1-1	a09 2-0	O02 4-3	a23 2-1	a19 1-1	D27 5-1
3 BIRMINGHAM C	a02 1-1	a30 0-1		a16 1-1	M05 0-0	F05 0-0	F26 1-0	A28 1-0	O30 0-1	F12 0-0	N13 1-0	O16 0-1	S15 4-1	M19 1-0	A25 0-0	D25 2-0	a18 3-0	S11 1-0	N27 1-2	S25 2-1	D11 0-0	D18 0-1
4 BLACKPOOL	a15 1-1	A28 1-0	O23 1-0		F12 1-0	m07 1-1	M26 0-1	M12 2-1	S06 1-1	O09 3-0	D25 0-0	S25 1-0	N20 1-1	A23 0-3	a23 1-1	N06 1-3	a09 1-0	F26 2-2	D18 0-3	D04 2-1	J15 3-3	S11 1-3
5 BOLTON W	O02 1-0	A25 3-0	O09 0-0	S18 2-2		M26 0-1	a09 2-2	m04 1-1	F19 4-0	m07 1-0	S06 1-2	J22 0-3	N06 5-1	a15 0-1	M12 4-1	O23 1-5	a23 1-2	D04 5-3	D27 6-1	N20 2-1	D18 4-1	A28 0-5
6 BURNLEY	M05 1-1	a02 1-1	S18 2-2	D11 2-0	N27 3-0		A31 0-0	F19 3-0	a15 3-1	O02 1-0	O16 1-2	a30 0-2	A21 1-0	a16 0-2	J22 0-0	S04 0-3	J01 2-1	S06 1-0	O30 2-0	D25 1-3	N13 3-1	M19 0-0
7 CHARLTON A	D11 4-3	a16 0-2	O02 1-1	N27 0-0	N13 1-4	A25 3-1		S08 1-1	a30 1-5	a02 3-1	A28 3-1	M19 2-1	S04 3-2	M05 2-3	F19 2-0	S18 0-0	J22 0-1	D25 0-0	O16 2-1	D18 4-1	O30 4-0	a13 2-3
8 CHELSEA	O30 0-1	N27 2-1	J01 2-0	O16 3-3	S04 2-2	S25 1-0	S16 2-2		a16 0-3	S11 6-0	a02 5-0	M05 2-1	a18 1-1	N13 1-1	A21 1-0	S01 2-3	D25 1-2	F05 5-3	M19 1-0	F26 2-2	a30 0-1	D11 4-1
9 DERBY CO	D27 2-1	a27 2-2	a23 1-0	S15 3-1	S25 1-0	a18 2-0	D04 5-1	O23 2-1		M12 3-2	A25 4-1	m04 3-0	M26 2-0	D18 1-3	N06 2-0	a09 2-4	N20 1-0	O09 1-0	A28 2-1	m07 4-1	S11 2-2	F05 3-2
10 EVERTON	a16 0-0	M19 1-3	S04 0-5	M05 5-0	D11 1-0	F26 2-1	a18 1-1	J22 2-1	O16 0-1		O30 2-0	S18 1-1	D25 0-0	a27 2-0	J01 3-1	A21 3-3	S01 0-5	S25 4-1	N13 2-1	S08 2-1	N27 1-0	m04 1-0
11 HUDDERSFIELD T	A21 1-1	F12 0-1	a09 0-0	D27 1-0	S15 0-2	M12 1-0	J01 1-2	N06 3-4	S01 1-1	a23 1-1		a18 0-4	m07 1-0	a06 2-1	N20 0-0	M26 0-2	D04 0-0	O23 0-2	S11 0-0	O09 1-3	S25 2-0	m05 4-0
12 LIVERPOOL	S15 0-1	D18 1-1	M12 1-0	F19 1-1	S11 0-1	D04 1-1	N20 1-1	O09 1-1	O02 0-0	F05 0-0	a15 0-1		a09 0-1	D27 0-2	O23 4-0	a23 1-1	N06 3-1	m07 0-2	A25 3-3	M26 4-0	A28 4-0	a06 0-0
13 MANCHESTER C	a27 0-3	O16 4-1	S08 1-0	M19 1-1	a02 1-0	D18 2-2	J15 0-1	a15 1-0	N27 2-1	D27 0-0	D11 3-1	N13 2-4		S11 0-0	O02 1-0	F19 1-0	S18 1-1	A25 3-2	M05 1-0	A28 0-0	a16 1-1	O30 3-3
14 MANCHESTER U	J01 2-0	S25 3-1	N20 3-0	S01 3-4	a18 3-0	O23 1-1	O09 1-1	a09 1-1	A21 1-2	N06 2-0	S04 4-1	D25 0-0	J22 0-0		m02 1-0	D04 1-1	m07 3-2	a23 2-2	m04 3-2	M12 3-0	a21 1-2	S15 2-0
15 MIDDLESBROUGH	N13 0-1	D11 6-0	S01 1-1	O30 1-0	O16 5-0	S11 4-1	S25 2-4	D18 1-1	a02 1-0	A28 1-0	M19 1-0	a16 0-1	F26 0-1	N27 1-4		a18 3-2	S15 1-1	J15 1-0	a30 3-1	a27 1-1	D27 0-0	M05 4-4
16 NEWCASTLE U	M19 3-2	S08 2-1	D27 1-0	a02 3-1	a16 1-1	J15 1-1	F05 2-0	A25 2-2	N13 3-0	D18 1-0	N27 2-4	O30 1-0	S25 0-0	a30 0-1	a15 1-0		a06 0-5	A28 2-5	D11 3-2	S11 2-2	M05 2-1	O16 3-1
17 PORTSMOUTH	N27 4-1	M05 3-0	a15 3-1	N13 1-1	O30 0-0	A28 1-0	S11 3-1	D27 5-2	M19 1-0	A25 4-0	a30 2-0	a02 3-2	F05 3-1	D11 2-2	S08 1-0	O02 1-0		D18 3-1	S25 3-0	J15 1-0	O16 3-0	a16 5-0
18 PRESTON N.E.	O16 1-1	N13 0-1	J22 0-0	O02 1-3	a30 1-1	S15 0-3	D27 2-3	S18 3-2	M05 0-0	F19 3-1	a16 2-0	D11 3-2	S01 1-3	O30 1-6	S04 6-1	J01 2-1	A21 2-2		a02 4-1	a15 2-1	M19 1-3	N27 1-1
19 SHEFFIELD U	S04 1-1	F26 0-1	M26 4-0	A21 3-2	D25 1-1	a23 0-0	M12 2-0	N20 2-1	J01 3-1	a09 1-1	J22 0-0	A30 1-2	O09 0-2	S18 2-2	D04 1-0	m07 0-0	F19 3-1	N06 3-2		O23 2-2	S06 2-5	a18 1-1
20 STOKE C	A30 1-0	O30 4-2	F19 2-1	a30 3-2	M19 4-0	D27 2-1	A21 2-2	O02 4-3	D11 4-2	S13 1-0	M05 1-3	N27 3-0	J01 2-3	O16 2-1	S18 3-0	J22 1-1	S04 0-1	a18 2-0	a16 0-1		a02 0-0	N13 2-1
21 SUNDERLAND	S18 1-1	a15 0-0	m07 1-1	S04 2-2	A21 2-0	a09 0-0	a23 1-0	D04 3-0	J22 2-1	M26 1-1	F19 0-1	J01 0-2	O23 3-0	O02 2-1	D25 1-0	O09 1-1	M12 1-4	N20 0-0	S15 2-0	N06 1-1		S01 3-3
22 WOLVERHAMPTON W	F19 1-3	D25 4-0	A21 2-2	J22 2-1	J01 2-0	N20 3-0	N06 2-0	m07 1-1	S18 2-2	D04 1-0	O02 7-1	S04 0-0	a23 1-1	S08 3-2	O09 0-3	M12 3-0	O23 3-0	m02 2-1	a19 6-0	a09 3-1	A25 0-1	

Jimmy Dickinson; a magnificent club servant to Portsmouth and the inspiration behind their successive Division One wins. His eventual 764 League appearances were then a record for one club.

DIVISION 2

	BARNSLEY	BLACKBURN R	BRADFORD	BRENTFORD	BURY	CARDIFF C	CHESTERFIELD	COVENTRY C	FULHAM	GRIMSBY T	LEEDS U	LEICESTER C	LINCOLN C	LUTON T	NOTTINGHAM F	PLYMOUTH A	Q.P.R.	SHEFFIELD W	SOUTHAMPTON	TOTTENHAM H	W.B.A.	WEST HAM U
1 BARNSLEY		J01 1-1	F19 0-0	N06 1-2	a23 3-2	S04 1-1	m07 0-1	M12 1-1	S01 1-1	D27 2-1	O23 1-1	a06 3-1	a18 2-0	S18 1-2	S08 4-0	A21 0-0	J22 4-0	O09 4-0	O02 3-0	a09 4-1	D04 2-0	N20 2-3
2 BLACKBURN R	A28 5-3		A23 2-3	m07 2-1	M12 1-2	a15 2-1	M26 0-2	N20 2-0	F05 1-0	J15 3-3	a23 0-0	D04 2-0	N06 7-1	S20 4-1	S11 2-1	S25 2-1	D25 2-0	a09 2-1	D18 1-2	F26 1-1	O23 0-0	O09 0-0
3 BRADFORD	S25 0-2	S01 2-0		O23 3-1	a09 4-1	A21 3-0	a23 1-1	J22 2-1	D25 1-1	F26 0-1	O09 1-1	M12 3-3	m04 0-3	S04 4-1	a18 1-2	S15 2-2	J01 0-0	m07 1-1	a04 2-0	M26 1-1	N20 4-1	N06 2-3
4 BRENTFORD	a02 0-0	D11 0-1	M19 1-0		F19 8-2	D25 1-1	J22 1-1	A21 2-2	a06 0-0	N13 2-0	S01 1-3	S15 1-2	S04 2-1	O16 2-0	a16 2-1	a30 2-2	M05 0-3	J01 2-1	O30 0-0	a18 1-1	S18 0-0	O02 0-0
5 BURY	N27 4-2	O16 3-1	N13 2-1	S25 1-2		M19 0-3	A21 2-2	D25 0-2	S04 2-0	a30 5-1	a18 3-1	m04 1-2	S01 3-1	a02 3-1	D11 1-1	a27 1-1	O30 0-0	S08 2-1	a16 1-0	F05 1-1	J01 4-0	S11 2-0
6 CARDIFF C	J15 0-3	a18 1-0	D18 6-1	D27 2-0	a04 2-1		N06 3-4	a23 3-0	S25 2-1	S11 3-0	D04 2-1	m07 1-1	a09 3-1	A23 3-3	F05 1-0	F26 1-0	S13 3-0	N20 1-1	A28 2-1	O09 0-1	M26 2-2	M12 4-0
7 CHESTERFIELD	D11 3-2	O30 0-0	N27 2-3	S11 0-1	D18 4-0	a02 0-2		F26 0-0	O16 0-1	S08 0-3	S25 3-1	F05 1-1	D27 3-1	a16 1-0	M05 2-1	M19 0-0	N13 2-1	a15 1-1	a30 1-0	J15 1-0	S01 0-0	A28 0-0
8 COVENTRY C	O16 4-0	a16 0-1	S11 2-0	D18 2-1	D27 2-1	N27 0-1	O02 0-2		a02 1-0	M19 4-1	J15 4-1	A28 1-2	F19 1-0	D11 2-0	O30 1-2	N13 1-1	a30 1-1	S18 3-4	M05 2-2	A23 2-0	a19 1-0	S06 1-0
9 FULHAM	A25 1-1	S18 1-1	D27 2-0	a23 2-1	J15 7-2	F19 4-0	M12 2-1	N06 1-0		D18 3-1	a09 1-0	N20 1-0	O23 2-1	a15 4-1	A28 4-0	J22 6-1	O02 5-0	M26 1-1	S08 1-0	D04 1-1	O09 1-2	m07 2-0
10 GRIMSBY T	D25 3-0	S04 1-2	O02 0-3	a09 3-0	D04 2-3	J22 2-2	S14 3-3	O23 4-1	A21 2-3		M26 5-1	N06 1-0	O09 2-2	m03 2-1	A24 1-2	J01 2-2	S18 4-1	M12 2-0	a15 0-1	N20 1-1	m07 1-0	a23 3-0
11 LEEDS U	M19 4-1	J29 1-0	M05 4-2	A25 0-0	F12 0-1	a30 0-0	F19 1-0	S04 4-1	N13 1-1	O30 6-3		D18 3-1	S18 3-1	A28 2-0	a02 1-0	a16 1-0	D11 1-2	J22 1-1	O16 1-1	S08 0-0	O02 1-3	D27 1-3
12 LEICESTER C	O30 1-1	a21 3-1	O16 2-2	S06 0-0	O02 3-2	D11 2-2	S18 2-2	J01 3-1	a16 0-3	a02 1-1	A21 6-2		J22 5-3	M05 1-1	N13 4-2	N27 1-1	A30 2-3	S04 2-2	M19 1-3	D25 1-2	m05 0-3	a18 1-1
13 LINCOLN C	a15 0-1	a02 3-0	D04 3-6	J15 3-1	A25 1-1	N13 0-0	D25 2-2	S25 1-0	M19 0-3	M05 2-3	F05 0-0	S11 2-0		N27 4-4	O16 1-3	O30 1-2	a16 0-0	F26 3-1	D11 1-2	A28 0-0	S15 0-3	D18 4-3
14 LUTON T	F05 1-0	S06 2-0	J15 0-1	M12 2-1	N06 1-0	A30 3-0	N20 1-0	m07 2-0	a18 1-3	S25 1-1	J01 0-0	O09 1-1	a23 6-0		F26 4-3	D25 3-1	A21 0-0	D04 2-1	S11 1-1	O23 1-1	a09 0-1	M26 0-1
15 NOTTINGHAM F	S15 0-1	J22 1-0	a15 2-0	N20 1-2	m07 1-0	S18 0-0	O09 0-1	M26 3-0	J01 0-2	S01 0-0	N06 0-0	a09 2-1	M12 1-1	O02 2-0		S04 1-0	F19 0-0	O23 1-2	D25 2-1	a23 2-2	A21 0-1	D04 3-0
16 PLYMOUTH A	D18 3-1	F19 3-0	S08 3-0	D04 1-0	O09 1-0	O02 0-1	O23 2-2	a09 2-3	S11 3-1	A28 0-2	N20 2-1	a23 1-1	M26 0-0	D27 1-1	J29 1-0		a18 3-1	N06 3-2	A25 1-2	m07 0-5	M12 1-2	F05 2-0
17 Q.P.R.	S11 2-2	D27 4-2	A28 1-0	O09 2-0	M26 3-1	S09 0-0	a09 1-1	D04 0-3	F26 1-0	F05 1-2	m07 2-0	A26 4-1	N20 2-0	D18 0-3	S25 2-1	a15 2-1		a23 1-3	J29 1-3	M12 0-0	N06 0-2	O23 2-1
18 SHEFFIELD W	M05 1-1	N13 3-0	D11 2-1	A28 0-0	S13 1-2	a16 1-1	a19 0-0	F05 2-1	O30 1-2	O16 4-1	S11 3-1	a11 0-1	O02 2-2	a30 0-0	M19 2-1	a02 2-1	N27 2-0		S25 2-0	D18 3-1	D27 2-1	A23 3-0
19 SOUTHAMPTON	F26 3-0	A21 3-0	S18 2-2	M26 2-0	N20 2-0	J01 2-0	D04 1-0	O09 5-2	S15 3-0	a18 0-0	M12 2-1	O23 6-0	F12 4-0	J22 1-1	D27 2-1	S01 2-0	S04 3-0	F19 1-0		N06 3-1	a23 1-1	a09 0-1
20 TOTTENHAM H	N13 4-1	O02 4-0	O30 5-1	a15 2-0	S18 3-1	M05 0-1	S04 4-0	A30 4-0	a30 1-1	a16 5-2	S13 2-2	D27 1-1	J01 1-2	M19 2-1	F12 2-1	D11 3-0	O16 1-0	A21 3-2	a02 0-1		J22 2-0	F19 1-1
21 W.B.A.	a30 2-0	M19 2-1	a16 7-1	F05 2-0	A28 2-3	O30 2-0	A25 0-0	a18 1-0	M05 1-2	D11 5-2	a06 1-0	S25 2-1	S08 5-0	N13 2-1	D18 2-1	O16 3-0	a02 1-1	D25 1-0	N27 2-0	S11 2-2		J15 2-1
22 WEST HAM U	a16 2-0	M05 2-1	a02 4-1	a25 1-1	J22 2-1	O16 3-1	J01 1-2	S13 2-2	D11 1-0	F12 1-0	D25 3-2	a15 4-1	A21 2-2	O30 0-1	a30 0-5	S18 3-0	M19 2-0	A30 2-2	N13 1-1	S25 1-0	S04 1-0	

Season 1948-49

DIVISION 3 NORTH

	ACCRINGTON S	BARROW	BRADFORD C	CARLISLE U	CHESTER	CREWE A	DARLINGTON	DONCASTER R	GATESHEAD	HALIFAX T	HARTLEPOOLS U	HULL C	MANSFIELD T	NEW BRIGHTON	OLDHAM A	ROCHDALE	ROTHERHAM U	SOUTHPORT	STOCKPORT CO	TRANMERE R	WREXHAM	YORK C
1 ACCRINGTON S		F05 1-1	a18 6-0	J29 2-1	M19 3-1	a02 2-0	D18 3-2	D27 2-0	a30 1-2	F26 1-0	D11 1-2	S28 1-2	S11 1-1	O16 5-1	A28 1-1	a27 0-0	A25 2-3	O30 3-1	a16 2-1	J15 0-2	S25 0-1	N13 2-1
2 BARROW	S18 0-0		A21 0-0	O30 0-0	F12 1-1	a05 1-0	a16 1-1	J01 3-1	a02 3-0	A31 0-0	N13 2-0	S04 1-2	a15 1-0	a30 2-1	F19 2-1	J29 0-1	J22 0-2	D27 2-1	M19 2-1	O02 0-0	S07 1-1	O16 5-0
3 BRADFORD C	a19 2-2	J08 0-2		M05 1-2	a16 3-2	a30 1-2	O30 0-2	S18 0-1	O16 1-1	J15 2-1	M19 0-0	F19 4-2	A25 1-0	N13 1-1	D27 2-1	a02 1-0	O02 1-2	J29 4-2	S11 1-1	S08 1-3	A28 1-2	F12 2-2
4 CARLISLE U	a23 4-1	M26 2-0	O09 3-2		A21 2-1	S04 6-2	D27 0-2	F19 3-0	F26 2-1	M12 0-0	a18 0-0	m07 1-1	N06 3-1	S02 2-2	N20 2-0	S16 1-1	D04 1-8	J01 4-2	S18 2-1	a09 2-2	O23 3-2	J22 3-3
5 CHESTER	O23 3-0	m04 4-1	N20 3-0	D18 2-1		D27 1-1	S11 1-2	a09 1-2	A28 1-1	a23 0-1	J15 0-0	N06 0-2	F26 1-1	S25 2-0	M12 2-2	F05 2-1	M26 1-1	a15 2-0	A25 2-0	O09 2-2	D04 2-0	S08 4-1
6 CREWE A	N06 2-0	O09 0-1	a27 2-1	J15 3-0	D25 1-0		S25 3-1	a23 0-0	S11 2-1	m07 0-0	F05 3-0	N20 0-0	M12 3-1	a15 2-1	M26 0-4	F26 1-2	a09 0-3	S06 1-0	A28 3-3	O23 2-0	A25 1-0	J29 2-0
7 DARLINGTON	A21 3-0	N20 2-3	M26 1-5	D25 2-2	J22 3-3	F19 4-1		O23 1-5	S08 1-3	N06 2-1	A25 2-0	M12 0-1	a23 1-2	S04 0-2	m07 2-1	J01 6-1	O09 2-0	S18 0-1	a15 1-1	D04 3-2	a09 3-1	O02 3-1
8 DONCASTER R	D25 0-0	A28 0-0	F05 2-0	S25 2-0	N13 0-0	S23 0-1	M19 1-1		M05 2-1	J22 1-2	O16 0-0	O02 0-0	D18 1-1	a02 2-1	S06 3-0	O30 1-0	a15 0-0	a16 1-2	S30 3-1	A26 2-0	J15 4-2	a30 1-0
9 GATESHEAD	D04 1-1	N06 3-0	M12 6-2	O02 3-0	J01 2-1	J22 4-1	S13 1-3	O09 0-3		O23 1-2	D25 2-1	a18 0-2	a09 0-0	A21 3-0	a23 2-2	A30 2-1	m07 3-2	S04 2-2	F19 0-1	N20 3-3	M26 2-0	S18 1-1
10 HALIFAX T	O02 1-0	A23 1-0	S04 1-1	O16 3-4	J29 1-2	F12 0-0	a02 0-3	S11 1-0	M19 2-2		O30 2-0	S18 2-4	S13 2-2	a16 0-2	a18 3-1	N13 2-1	F19 2-0	a30 0-1	M05 0-1	D25 0-1	D18 2-0	A28 1-2
11 HARTLEPOOLS U	J08 1-0	a09 1-0	O23 1-0	a15 1-0	S04 2-1	S18 4-1	A30 0-1	M12 2-1	D27 1-3	M26 0-0		O09 0-2	N20 1-1	J01 3-1	D04 1-2	A21 6-1	S13 1-4	J22 2-2	O02 0-0	a23 3-0	N06 2-2	F19 2-3
12 HULL C	S09 3-1	J15 3-0	S25 2-0	M23 3-0	a02 3-2	a16 5-0	O16 0-1	m04 0-1	a15 2-0	F05 6-0	M05 2-0		A28 4-0	O30 4-1	A26 6-0	M19 1-1	D25 3-2	N13 5-1	a30 6-1	M30 2-0	S11 3-0	a06 2-3
13 MANSFIELD T	J22 2-0	a18 2-0	A30 1-0	a02 2-0	O02 1-0	O16 5-1	J29 2-2	A21 2-2	N13 1-1	S06 2-1	a16 1-0	J01 1-1		F12 2-0	S18 3-2	a30 2-0	S04 1-2	M05 1-1	O30 4-0	F19 0-0	D27 1-2	M19 3-0
14 NEW BRIGHTON	M12 1-3	a27 3-1	a09 1-0	A25 2-0	F19 1-1	a18 2-1	J15 1-0	N06 0-1	m04 2-2	N20 2-0	A28 1-1	M26 0-0	D04 1-0		O09 0-1	S11 1-2	O23 0-1	O02 0-1	S08 0-2	F05 2-1	a23 2-0	D25 3-1
15 OLDHAM A	J01 4-3	S25 2-1	D25 1-2	a16 1-0	O16 2-1	O30 3-2	F12 7-1	S14 0-2	a12 0-0	a15 2-2	a30 5-1	a26 1-1	F05 4-0	M05 4-2		S04 0-1	A21 1-3	M19 2-1	N13 5-2	S11 0-2	F26 1-1	a02 4-0
16 ROCHDALE	O09 4-1	a23 3-0	N06 1-1	S07 1-0	S18 3-1	O02 3-0	A28 3-4	M26 0-2	A24 3-0	a09 1-0	D18 0-1	O23 1-1	a04 1-0	J22 1-1	J15 1-2		M12 2-0	F19 1-0	D27 2-0	m07 2-1	N20 2-1	a18 2-0
17 ROTHERHAM U	A30 1-0	S11 2-2	F26 2-0	a30 1-1	O30 2-1	N13 6-1	M05 4-3	a18 2-0	D18 1-0	S25 4-0	S06 2-1	D27 0-0	J15 1-0	M19 1-1	a04 2-1	O16 3-1		a02 1-0	F12 2-1	A28 7-0	F05 1-3	a16 2-1
18 SOUTHPORT	M26 3-0	D25 0-0	a23 2-1	A28 2-2	a18 2-1	S14 0-0	F05 1-3	N20 0-2	J15 0-3	a26 2-3	S11 1-2	a09 0-0	O09 1-1	F26 0-1	O23 0-1	S25 3-1	N06 1-3		m02 1-0	M12 2-3	m07 3-0	A23 0-2
19 STOCKPORT CO	N20 2-1	O23 1-2	J22 5-2	F05 2-0	S01 1-1	J01 4-0	a18 2-0	m07 5-1	S25 3-1	O09 3-1	F26 4-0	D04 0-0	M26 2-0	S15 1-0	a09 1-2	D25 2-2	a23 0-1	A21 0-0		N06 4-1	M12 1-0	S04 1-1
20 TRANMERE R	S04 2-2	F26 2-0	S14 1-0	N13 2-1	m02 1-1	M19 2-2	a28 2-1	A31 2-0	a16 1-1	D27 2-2	J29 0-2	A21 1-2	S25 1-0	S18 0-1	J22 1-1	F12 0-0	J01 2-1	O16 1-0	a02 0-0		a15 0-2	O30 0-0
21 WREXHAM	F19 1-0	S15 1-0	J01 5-0	M19 4-0	J08 1-0	S01 2-2	N13 4-3	S04 2-0	O30 1-4	A21 2-1	a02 1-0	J22 0-2	m04 1-1	J29 2-1	O02 1-1	a16 2-0	S18 0-4	F12 2-0	O16 0-0	a18 0-0		M05 3-3
22 YORK C	a09 1-1	M12 2-0	m07 0-2	S11 6-0	S13 2-0	A21 1-3	F26 2-5	J08 2-3	F05 0-1	J01 2-2	S25 4-0	a23 1-3	O23 2-1	D27 2-1	N06 4-0	a15 1-1	N20 6-1	A30 1-3	J15 4-0	M26 1-0	O09 5-1	

DIVISION 3 SOUTH

	ALDERSHOT	BOURNEMOUTH	BRIGHTON & HA	BRISTOL C	BRISTOL R	CRYSTAL P	EXETER C	IPSWICH T	LEYTON O	MILLWALL	NEWPORT CO	NORTHAMPTON T	NORWICH C	NOTTS CO	PORT VALE	READING	SOUTHEND U	SWANSEA T	SWINDON T	TORQUAY U	WALSALL	WATFORD
1 ALDERSHOT		m07 0-0	F05 1-1	D25 0-0	N06 1-5	O09 3-0	S15 1-2	a06 2-0	A21 1-1	S04 5-0	a23 1-2	F26 3-1	a15 4-1	M26 0-1	J01 0-1	M12 0-6	S25 1-0	N20 1-2	S01 1-2	a09 1-3	O23 0-1	J22 0-0
2 BOURNEMOUTH	S29 1-0		S25 0-1	a02 0-0	A25 1-0	S11 2-0	S22 1-0	O02 4-2	M19 3-0	a30 2-0	D18 1-2	O16 5-2	a16 1-2	a15 2-1	O30 2-0	J15 1-3	M05 3-2	A28 1-1	N13 3-0	D25 5-0	S08 2-0	F05 2-1
3 BRIGHTON & H.A.	S18 0-4	F19 1-6		S01 0-0	a09 2-1	M12 1-1	D27 2-0	m07 6-1	J01 3-1	J22 1-2	N06 3-2	a15 0-0	S08 1-0	D04 3-2	S04 1-0	N20 2-0	F26 1-0	a23 0-2	A21 1-1	O23 3-1	M26 1-2	O09 0-0
4 BRISTOL C	D27 1-1	N06 2-1	A25 1-1		F05 1-1	O23 2-0	S11 1-0	a23 2-0	O02 3-0	S08 0-0	m07 1-1	A28 3-0	J15 1-6	N20 3-1	a18 1-1	M26 0-2	D18 2-1	a27 0-0	F19 1-3	O09 0-2	M12 2-2	a09 1-1
5 BRISTOL R	a02 0-2	A30 4-0	N13 0-0	S18 3-1		S13 1-0	F12 3-1	A21 1-6	O16 2-3	S20 2-0	S25 3-1	O30 1-0	a30 2-2	J01 3-2	a16 4-1	a15 4-1	M19 0-0	F26 1-1	M05 1-1	J22 1-0	S04 3-0	D25 3-1
6 CRYSTAL P	M05 2-1	J22 2-1	O16 0-2	M19 4-0	S08 1-0		N13 1-1	S18 1-1	a30 2-1	A28 1-1	D27 0-1	J29 2-2	a02 1-1	F19 1-5	F12 1-1	J08 0-1	a16 2-1	A25 1-1	O30 1-1	a18 0-1	O02 1-3	S04 3-1
7 EXETER C	S08 3-3	a23 2-3	D25 1-1	J22 1-1	m07 2-1	a09 3-1		N20 1-3	F19 3-1	a18 3-0	m04 1-2	A21 5-1	A28 4-1	M12 3-1	O02 2-1	O23 1-2	A25 0-0	M26 1-1	S18 3-1	J15 2-0	O09 2-1	N06 2-1
8 IPSWICH T	a30 4-1	F26 1-0	F12 2-2	J29 2-0	D18 0-1	F05 3-2	a16 2-2		N13 2-2	O30 1-0	A28 5-1	M05 4-2	O16 1-2	S15 3-2	M19 4-1	S11 3-2	a18 1-3	J15 2-0	a02 4-2	A25 5-1	D27 3-2	S25 1-2
9 LEYTON O	D18 1-2	O23 1-2	A28 0-3	F26 3-1	M12 1-1	D04 1-1	S25 5-2	a09 1-1		A26 2-2	O09 5-2	S11 0-3	F05 0-3	N06 3-1	D27 2-0	m07 0-1	J15 2-0	S16 3-1	a15 1-1	N20 3-1	a23 1-1	M26 1-0
10 MILLWALL	J15 1-1	D04 4-0	S11 6-2	S13 4-1	a23 1-1	J01 1-0	a15 2-1	M26 0-0	A30 0-0		N20 3-1	S25 3-2	F26 1-3	O23 3-2	A21 1-1	O09 1-1	F05 1-0	M12 2-0	D25 3-1	N06 1-3	a09 2-1	m07 2-2
11 NEWPORT CO	a28 0-2	A21 1-2	a02 1-1	a07 0-2	F19 2-1	D25 5-0	a30 0-2	J01 3-0	M05 3-2	a16 1-2		M19 2-0	O30 4-3	S04 3-3	O16 2-2	S16 1-1	N13 4-2	a15 2-5	O02 4-1	S18 1-2	J22 1-1	S02 1-1
12 NORTHAMPTON T	O02 2-0	M12 1-0	a18 1-1	J01 3-1	M26 0-1	a23 3-2	D18 4-0	O09 1-1	J22 4-1	F19 4-0	O23 2-1		S02 1-0	D25 1-2	S18 2-2	N06 1-2	S16 2-2	a09 0-1	S04 0-1	D04 0-0	F12 0-1	N20 1-1
13 NORWICH C	a18 0-0	N20 1-1	S15 2-1	S04 4-0	D04 3-0	N06 3-0	J01 3-0	M12 2-0	S18 0-0	O02 1-2	M26 0-0	A25 2-1		O09 3-0	F19 2-0	a09 1-2	D25 3-0	O23 1-0	J22 0-0	m07 0-0	A21 1-2	a23 0-1
14 NOTTS CO	O30 2-0	a18 2-3	a30 1-1	a16 2-1	A28 4-1	S25 5-1	O16 9-0	S09 9-2	a02 2-1	M19 1-3	J15 11-1	D27 2-0	M05 2-1		N13 2-1	F05 1-0	F12 0-0	S11 1-1	S23 1-2	D18 5-0	A26 2-0	F26 4-0
15 PORT VALE	A28 3-0	M26 0-2	J15 3-4	a15 4-2	N20 2-0	m07 0-0	F26 1-1	O23 1-2	D25 3-0	D18 1-0	M12 1-2	F05 1-0	S25 0-0	a09 1-0		A23 3-0	S11 0-2	O09 0-2	S06 2-0	a23 3-1	N06 0-2	J08 3-1
16 READING	O16 2-0	S04 4-2	a16 6-1	O30 2-1	a18 1-0	A21 5-1	M19 2-0	J22 2-1	F12 3-0	M05 2-0	S08 4-1	a02 1-0	N13 2-1	S18 1-4	S01 1-2		a27 2-1	D25 0-2	a30 0-0	O02 4-0	F19 1-0	J01 3-1
17 SOUTHEND U	F19 1-0	O09 0-0	O02 0-0	A21 1-0	O23 0-1	N20 0-1	A31 0-0	a15 1-1	S04 2-2	S18 2-1	a09 0-1	S07 0-1	D27 2-2	m07 3-2	J22 0-0	a23 0-0		N06 0-0	J01 3-4	M26 1-1	a06 2-0	M12 0-1
18 SWANSEA T	a16 2-1	J01 2-0	J29 3-0	a30 2-0	O02 5-0	S02 3-0	O30 6-0	S04 2-0	S09 3-1	O16 2-0	a18 2-1	N13 1-0	M19 2-1	J22 3-1	M05 3-1	D27 2-1	a02 2-2		S30 4-0	F19 6-1	S18 3-1	A21 2-0
19 SWINDON T	A25 3-1	a09 2-2	D18 0-0	S25 2-1	O09 1-1	M26 1-0	F05 1-1	N06 4-0	a18 1-1	D27 2-0	D04 5-2	J15 2-2	S11 3-3	a23 3-0	S15 0-2	a06 1-1	A28 2-1	m07 1-0		M12 1-1	N20 2-1	O23 1-0
20 TORQUAY U	N13 2-2	D27 1-1	M19 1-1	M05 0-2	S11 0-2	a19 2-0	S04 2-1	S01 1-1	a16 7-1	a02 2-1	M23 4-0	a30 3-0	F12 2-1	A21 3-1	M30 0-0	F26 4-2	O30 0-3	S25 0-4	O16 3-1		J01 5-1	S15 3-1
21 WALSALL	M19 0-0	S16 0-0	O30 0-0	O16 0-1	J15 0-1	F26 3-1	M05 4-3	D25 2-1	a28 2-3	N13 5-6	S11 3-1	m07 2-0	D18 4-1	S02 3-2	a02 1-1	S25 2-0	a30 0-3	F05 2-1	a16 0-1	A28 1-1		a18 0-1
22 WATFORD	S11 0-1	S18 0-1	M05 0-0	N13 1-1	D27 0-0	J15 2-0	a02 0-1	F19 1-2	O30 2-1	S29 1-1	A25 2-2	a16 0-1	J29 1-1	O02 1-1	a30 2-1	A28 4-1	O16 0-0	D18 4-2	M19 0-3	S08 1-1	a15 2-0	

LEAGUE TABLES

DIVISION 1

	P	W	D	L	F	A	W	D	L	F	A	Pts
Portsmouth	42	18	3	0	52	12	7	5	9	32	30	58
Manchester U	42	11	7	3	40	20	10	4	7	37	24	53
Derby Co	42	17	2	2	48	22	5	7	9	26	33	53
Newcastle U	42	12	5	4	35	29	8	7	6	35	27	52
Arsenal	42	13	5	3	51	18	5	8	8	23	26	49
Wolverhampton W	42	13	5	3	48	19	4	7	10	31	47	46
Manchester C	42	10	8	3	28	21	5	7	9	19	30	45
Sunderland	42	8	10	3	27	19	5	7	9	22	39	43
Charlton A	42	10	5	6	38	31	5	7	9	25	36	42
Aston Villa	42	10	6	5	40	36	6	4	11	20	40	42
Stoke C	42	14	3	4	43	24	2	6	13	23	44	41
Liverpool	42	5	10	6	25	18	8	4	9	28	25	40
Chelsea	42	10	6	5	43	27	2	8	11	26	41	38
Bolton W	42	10	4	7	43	32	4	6	11	16	36	38
Burnley	42	10	6	5	27	19	2	8	11	16	31	38
Blackpool	42	8	8	5	24	25	3	8	10	30	42	38
Birmingham C	42	9	7	5	19	10	2	8	11	17	28	37
Everton	42	12	5	4	33	25	1	6	14	8	38	37
Middlesbrough	42	10	6	5	37	23	1	6	14	9	34	34
Huddersfield T	42	6	7	8	19	24	6	3	12	21	45	34
Preston N.E.	42	8	6	7	36	36	3	5	13	26	39	33
Sheffield U	42	8	9	4	32	25	3	2	16	25	53	33

DIVISION 2

	P	W	D	L	F	A	W	D	L	F	A	Pts
Fulham	42	16	4	1	52	14	8	5	8	25	23	57
W.B.A.	42	16	3	2	47	16	8	5	8	22	23	56
Southampton	42	16	4	1	48	10	7	5	9	21	26	55
Cardiff C	42	14	4	3	45	21	5	9	7	17	26	51
Tottenham H	42	14	4	3	50	18	3	12	6	22	26	50
Chesterfield	42	9	7	5	24	18	6	10	5	27	27	47
West Ham U	42	13	5	3	38	23	5	5	11	18	35	46
Sheffield W	42	12	6	3	36	17	3	7	11	27	39	43
Barnsley	42	10	7	4	40	18	4	5	12	22	43	40
Luton T	42	11	6	4	32	16	3	6	12	23	41	40
Grimsby T	42	10	5	6	44	28	5	5	11	28	48	40
Bury	42	12	5	4	41	23	5	1	15	26	53	40
Q.P.R.	42	11	4	6	31	26	3	7	11	13	36	39
Blackburn R	42	12	5	4	41	23	3	3	15	12	40	38
Leeds U	42	11	6	4	36	21	1	7	13	19	42	37
Coventry C	42	12	3	6	35	20	3	4	14	20	44	37
Bradford P.A.	42	8	8	5	37	26	5	3	13	28	52	37
Brentford	42	7	10	4	28	21	4	4	13	14	32	36
Leicester C	42	6	10	5	41	38	4	6	11	21	41	36
Plymouth A	42	11	4	6	33	25	1	8	12	16	39	36
Nottingham F	42	9	6	6	22	14	5	1	15	28	40	35
Lincoln C	42	6	7	8	31	35	2	5	14	22	56	28

DIVISION 3 NORTH

	P	W	D	L	F	A	W	D	L	F	A	Pts
Hull C	42	17	1	3	65	14	10	10	1	28	14	65
Rotherham U	42	16	4	1	47	17	12	2	7	43	29	62
Doncaster R	42	10	8	3	26	12	10	2	9	27	28	50
Darlington	42	10	3	8	42	36	10	3	8	41	38	46
Gateshead	42	10	6	5	41	28	6	7	8	28	30	45
Oldham A	42	12	4	5	49	28	6	5	10	26	39	45
Rochdale	42	14	3	4	37	16	4	6	11	18	37	45
Stockport Co	42	13	5	3	44	16	3	6	12	17	40	43
Wrexham	42	12	6	3	35	22	5	3	13	21	40	43
Mansfield T	42	13	6	2	39	15	1	8	12	13	33	42
Tranmere R	42	8	9	4	23	19	5	6	10	23	38	41
Crewe A	42	13	4	4	31	18	3	5	13	21	56	41
Barrow	42	10	8	3	27	13	4	4	13	14	35	40
York C	42	11	3	7	49	28	4	6	11	25	46	39
Carlisle U	42	12	7	2	46	32	2	4	15	14	45	39
Hartlepool U	42	10	5	6	34	25	4	5	12	11	33	38
New Brighton	42	10	4	7	25	19	4	4	13	21	39	36
Chester C	42	10	7	4	36	19	1	6	14	21	37	35
Halifax T	42	8	4	9	26	27	4	7	10	19	35	35
Accrington S	42	11	4	6	39	23	1	6	14	16	41	34
Southport	42	6	5	10	24	29	5	4	12	21	35	31
Bradford C	42	7	6	8	29	31	3	3	15	19	46	29

DIVISION 3 SOUTH

	P	W	D	L	F	A	W	D	L	F	A	Pts
Swansea T	42	20	1	0	60	11	7	7	7	27	23	62
Reading	42	17	1	3	48	18	8	4	9	29	32	55
Bournemouth	42	15	2	4	42	17	7	6	8	27	31	52
Swindon T	42	11	9	1	38	20	7	6	8	26	36	51
Bristol R	42	13	5	3	42	23	6	5	10	19	28	48
Brighton & H.A.	42	11	5	5	32	26	4	13	4	23	29	48
Ipswich T	42	14	3	4	53	30	4	6	11	25	47	45
Millwall	42	12	7	2	42	23	5	4	12	21	41	45
Torquay U	42	12	5	4	45	26	5	6	10	20	44	45
Norwich C	42	11	6	4	32	10	5	6	10	35	39	44
Notts Co	42	15	3	3	68	19	4	2	15	34	49	43
Exeter C	42	12	5	4	45	26	3	5	13	18	50	40
Port Vale	42	11	3	7	32	21	3	8	10	19	33	39
Walsall	42	9	5	7	34	28	6	3	12	22	36	38
Newport Co	42	8	6	7	41	35	6	3	12	27	57	37
Bristol C	42	8	9	4	28	24	3	5	13	16	38	36
Watford	42	6	9	6	24	21	4	6	11	17	33	35
Southend U	42	5	10	6	18	18	4	6	11	23	28	34
Leyton O	42	9	6	6	36	29	2	6	13	22	51	34
Northampton T	42	9	6	6	33	20	3	3	15	18	42	33
Aldershot	42	6	5	10	26	29	5	6	10	22	30	33
Crystal Palace	42	7	8	6	27	27	1	3	17	11	49	27

FOOTBALL LEAGUE RECORDS

Top scorers: Div 1, D.Davis (Sunderland) 25 goals; Div 2, T.Briggs (Grimsby Town) 35 goals; Div 3 N, R.Phillips (Crewe Alexandra), P.Doherty (Doncaster Rovers) 26 goals; Div 3 S, T.Lawton (Notts County) 31 goals.

Peter Harris, Portsmouth's flying outside-right. Along with Jimmy Dickinson he was picked for England's summer tour. Alas, injury ruled him out, but he helped Pompey to another title.

DIVISION 1

	ARSENAL	ASTON VILLA	BIRMINGHAM C	BLACKPOOL	BOLTON W	BURNLEY	CHARLTON A	CHELSEA	DERBY CO	EVERTON	FULHAM	HUDDERSFIELD T	LIVERPOOL	MANCHESTER C	MANCHESTER U	MIDDLESBROUGH	NEWCASTLE U	PORTSMOUTH	STOKE C	SUNDERLAND	W.B.A.	WOLVERHAMPTON W
1 ARSENAL		M29 1-3	S24 4-2	O22 1-0	J21 1-1	A20 0-1	N19 2-3	A31 2-3	F18 1-0	O08 5-2	N05 2-1	J14 1-0	S03 1-2	a01 4-1	D27 0-0	M08 1-1	a15 4-2	m03 2-0	a10 6-0	D24 5-0	S14 4-1	D03 1-1
2 ASTON VILLA	N26 1-1		D10 1-1	S10 0-0	a22 3-0	M25 0-1	a11 1-1	a08 4-0	A23 1-1	S24 2-2	A27 3-1	F18 2-1	M11 2-0	D17 1-0	O15 0-4	J21 4-0	D31 0-1	S05 1-0	O29 1-1	N12 2-0	F25 1-0	D27 1-4
3 BIRMINGHAM C	F04 2-1	a29 2-2		N05 0-2	O01 0-0	S03 0-1	D03 2-0	A20 0-3	D26 2-2	O22 0-0	N19 1-1	M04 2-1	S17 2-3	M18 1-0	a10 0-0	a15 0-0	a01 0-2	O08 0-3	D24 1-0	J14 1-2	A24 2-0	S14 1-1
4 BLACKPOOL	a08 2-1	J14 1-0	M25 1-1		O29 2-0	D27 2-0	S17 2-0	a22 0-0	N12 1-0	a10 0-1	O01 0-0	A20 4-1	O15 0-0	F04 0-0	N26 3-3	A22 1-1	S05 0-0	D24 2-1	D10 4-2	F25 0-1	M11 3-0	S03 1-2
5 BOLTON W	S17 2-2	D03 1-1	F18 1-0	a15 0-0		D24 0-1	M18 3-0	a10 1-0	S05 0-0	M08 1-2	a01 2-1	O08 1-2	J14 3-2	N19 3-0	A31 1-2	O22 1-2	N05 2-2	F04 1-0	A20 4-0	S03 2-1	D26 3-0	a29 2-4
6 BURNLEY	D17 0-0	N05 1-0	D31 1-1	D26 0-0	A27 2-1		a15 1-0	F18 1-2	S10 0-1	D03 5-1	M04 0-0	M18 1-0	a07 0-2	O22 0-0	S24 1-0	a29 3-2	O08 1-2	N19 2-1	S05 2-1	A23 2-2	J21 0-0	a01 0-1
7 CHARLTON A	M11 1-1	a07 1-4	a22 2-0	J21 1-2	N26 0-0	O29 1-1		O15 1-0	D10 1-3	F18 2-0	D31 2-1	S14 2-2	N12 1-3	A27 3-1	F25 1-2	S24 0-3	S10 6-3	D26 1-2	a08 2-0	M25 2-2	D17 1-2	A24 2-3
8 CHELSEA	A24 1-2	O22 1-3	D17 3-0	D03 1-1	a07 1-1	O01 0-1	M08 1-3		A27 1-2	N19 3-2	J21 0-0	a01 3-1	D26 1-1	O08 3-0	S10 1-1	M29 2-1	a29 1-3	N05 1-4	F04 2-2	S07 3-1	D31 2-1	a15 0-0
9 DERBY CO	O01 1-2	A31 3-2	D27 4-1	a01 0-0	m06 4-0	J14 1-1	a29 1-2	D24 2-2		a15 2-0	M18 2-1	O22 4-2	F04 2-2	D03 7-0	A20 0-1	N05 1-0	M29 1-1	M08 2-1	S03 2-3	S17 3-2	a07 3-1	O08 1-2
10 EVERTON	F25 0-1	F04 1-1	a08 0-0	a07 3-0	O15 0-0	a22 1-1	O01 0-1	M11 1-1	O29 1-2		D26 1-1	S03 3-0	A27 0-0	m06 3-1	N12 0-0	D17 3-1	A24 2-1	J14 1-2	N26 2-1	D10 0-2	M29 1-2	S17 1-2
11 FULHAM	M25 2-2	D24 3-0	M11 0-0	F18 1-0	N12 3-0	O15 1-0	S03 1-2	S17 1-1	N26 0-0	D27 0-0		A31 4-1	O29 0-1	J14 1-0	D10 1-0	m06 1-2	S24 2-1	a10 0-1	F25 2-2	a08 0-3	a22 0-1	A20 1-2
12 HUDDERSFIELD T	S10 2-2	O01 1-0	O15 1-0	D17 0-1	F25 2-0	N26 1-2	S07 2-1	N12 1-2	a08 2-0	D31 1-2	A24 2-2		D10 3-2	D26 1-0	M25 3-1	A27 2-2	a11 1-2	S17 0-1	M11 4-0	a22 3-1	O29 1-1	F04 1-0
13 LIVERPOOL	D31 2-0	N19 2-1	J21 2-0	M08 0-1	S10 1-1	a10 0-1	a01 1-0	D27 2-2	S24 3-1	D24 3-1	a15 1-1	m03 2-3		N05 4-0	S07 1-1	O08 2-0	O22 2-2	D03 2-2	A31 1-1	A20 4-2	F18 2-1	M18 0-2
14 MANCHESTER C	N12 0-2	A20 3-3	N26 4-0	S24 0-3	M11 1-1	a08 1-0	D24 2-0	F25 1-1	a22 2-2	S07 0-0	S10 2-0	D27 1-2	M29 1-2		D31 1-2	F18 0-1	J21 1-1	A31 1-0	O15 1-1	O29 2-1	D10 1-1	a10 2-1
15 MANCHESTER U	D26 2-0	M08 7-0	a07 0-2	M18 1-2	A24 3-0	F04 3-2	O08 3-2	J14 1-0	D17 0-1	a01 1-1	a29 3-0	N05 6-0	M15 0-0	S03 2-1		N19 2-0	D03 1-1	a15 0-2	S17 2-2	O01 1-3	A27 1-1	O22 3-0
16 MIDDLESBROUGH	O15 1-1	S17 0-2	O29 1-0	A31 2-0	a08 2-0	D10 4-1	F04 1-0	N26 2-1	M25 3-1	A20 0-1	S07 1-2	D24 3-0	F25 4-1	O01 0-0	M11 2-3		D27 1-0	S03 1-5	a22 2-0	a10 2-0	N12 3-0	J14 2-0
17 NEWCASTLE U	O29 0-3	S03 3-2	N12 3-1	m06 3-0	M25 3-1	F25 0-0	J14 1-0	D10 2-2	M11 2-1	A31 4-0	F04 3-1	a07 0-0	a08 5-1	S17 4-2	a22 2-1	D26 0-1		A20 1-3	O01 4-1	O15 2-2	N26 5-1	D24 2-0
18 PORTSMOUTH	D10 2-1	m06 5-1	F25 2-0	A27 2-3	S24 1-1	M11 2-1	D27 1-0	M25 4-0	O15 3-1	S10 7-0	a07 3-0	J21 4-0	a22 2-1	A24 1-1	O29 0-0	D31 1-1	D17 1-0		N12 0-0	N26 2-2	a08 0-1	O01 1-1
19 STOKE C	m06 2-5	a15 1-0	A27 3-1	a29 1-1	D17 3-2	S12 1-1	O22 0-3	S24 2-3	D31 1-3	M18 1-0	O08 0-2	N19 0-0	A22 0-0	M04 2-0	J21 3-1	D03 1-0	F18 1-0	a01 0-1		D27 2-1	S10 1-3	N05 2-1
20 SUNDERLAND	A27 4-2	a01 2-1	S10 1-1	O08 1-1	D31 2-0	A31 2-1	N05 2-1	m06 4-1	J21 6-1	a29 4-2	O22 2-0	D03 1-1	D17 3-2	a15 1-2	F18 2-2	a07 2-0	M04 2-2	M18 1-1	D26 3-0		S24 2-1	N19 3-1
21 W.B.A.	S07 1-2	O08 1-1	A31 3-0	a26 1-0	D27 2-1	S17 3-0	A20 1-0	S03 1-1	a10 1-0	N05 4-0	D03 4-1	a15 0-0	O01 0-1	a29 0-0	D24 1-2	a01 0-3	M18 1-1	O22 3-0	J14 0-0	F04 0-2		M04 1-1
22 WOLVERHAMPTON W	a22 3-0	D26 2-3	m06 6-1	D31 3-0	D10 1-1	N12 0-0	A29 2-1	O29 2-2	F25 4-1	J21 1-1	D17 1-1	S24 7-1	N26 1-1	a11 3-0	a08 1-1	S10 3-1	A27 2-1	F18 1-0	M25 2-1	M11 1-3	O15 1-1	

Tottenham's Les Medley, the winger who was top scorer when the 'sush and run' team lifted the Division Two title in 1949-50.

DIVISION 2

	BARNSLEY	BLACKBURN R	BRADFORD	BRENTFORD	BURY	CARDIFF C	CHESTERFIELD	COVENTRY C	GRIMSBY T	HULL C	LEEDS U	LEICESTER C	LUTON T	PLYMOUTH A	PRESTON N.E.	Q.P.R.	SHEFFIELD U	SHEFFIELD W	SOUTHAMPTON	SWANSEA T	TOTTENHAM H	WEST HAM U
1 BARNSLEY		a15 1-1	O08 3-2	N19 0-1	O22 1-0	N05 1-0	A20 1-2	S07 4-3	J14 7-2	a01 1-1	D26 1-1	M04 2-2	a10 1-0	a29 4-1	F04 0-1	S17 3-1	S03 2-2	D03 3-4	A24 2-1	O01 5-2	M18 2-0	D24 1-1
2 BLACKBURN R	N12 4-0		S17 0-1	S19 4-1	S03 2-1	A20 1-0	F04 1-1	O29 0-1	a08 3-0	A22 4-2	O15 0-1	J14 3-0	M25 0-0	O01 1-0	a07 2-3	D10 0-0	N26 0-2	D27 0-0	M11 0-0	F25 2-0	D24 1-2	a22 2-0
3 BRADFORD	F25 1-3	J21 2-2		S10 0-2	D26 1-2	S24 3-3	a11 2-0	D10 2-2	O29 4-1	D31 5-1	N26 1-2	A24 2-2	S07 1-0	D17 3-2	N12 1-2	M25 1-0	M11 1-1	A27 1-3	a08 0-0	a22 0-2	F18 1-3	O15 2-1
4 BRENTFORD	a22 3-0	S14 2-0	J14 2-0		D24 2-0	a07 1-0	S17 0-0	M25 2-0	D10 1-0	D26 3-1	M11 0-0	S03 0-1	N12 1-0	F04 0-0	F25 1-0	A31 0-2	a08 1-0	O01 1-1	O29 0-1	O15 0-0	A20 1-4	N26 0-2
5 BURY	M11 2-0	D31 3-0	D27 1-0	A27 1-2		S10 2-2	S07 2-0	F25 0-0	N12 3-1	D17 0-0	D10 2-0	O01 3-0	O15 5-2	S14 5-1	N26 1-1	a22 0-0	M25 1-5	a07 0-0	S24 1-1	a08 1-1	J21 1-2	O29 3-1
6 CARDIFF C	M25 3-0	D17 2-1	F04 1-2	a10 0-0	J14 1-0		O01 2-0	M11 1-0	N26 1-0	S05 2-0	F25 1-0	S17 2-4	O29 0-0	D27 1-0	D10 3-2	a08 4-0	a22 1-2	A22 1-0	a17 1-1	A27 1-0	S03 0-1	N12 0-1
7 CHESTERFIELD	D17 1-0	S24 2-1	a07 1-1	J21 3-1	A24 2-1	F18 0-1		a08 0-1	M11 2-1	S10 0-1	a22 3-1	S12 1-0	D10 0-1	A27 2-0	M25 2-0	O29 2-1	O15 0-1	D31 1-2	N26 0-0	N12 4-1	D27 1-1	F25 1-0
8 COVENTRY C	m06 1-1	M18 1-1	a29 3-1	N05 1-1	O08 1-2	O22 2-1	D03 3-0		D24 1-1	a15 2-0	F04 0-4	D27 1-2	A29 1-0	a01 3-0	J14 0-0	S03 0-0	A20 2-4	F11 3-0	O01 1-2	S17 1-2	M04 0-1	a11 5-1
9 GRIMSBY T	S10 2-2	D03 1-2	M18 4-0	a29 4-1	a15 4-2	a01 0-0	O22 5-2	A27 3-2		F18 1-0	a07 2-0	N05 2-1	D31 6-1	M04 2-2	A31 1-3	D26 1-1	S24 4-0	O08 4-1	D17 1-1	S07 2-1	N19 2-3	J21 2-0
10 HULL C	N26 2-0	S01 3-1	S03 3-3	D27 2-0	A20 3-2	m06 1-1	J14 1-0	N12 2-1	O01 2-2		O29 1-0	D24 4-0	a22 1-1	S17 4-2	O15 4-2	F25 1-1	D10 0-4	F04 1-1	M25 1-2	M11 0-0	a10 1-0	a08 2-2
11 LEEDS U	D27 1-0	a26 2-1	a01 0-0	O22 1-0	a29 4-1	O08 2-0	N19 0-0	S24 3-3	a10 1-0	M18 3-0		D03 1-1	F18 2-1	a15 1-1	D24 3-1	A20 1-1	S14 0-1	N05 1-1	J21 1-0	S03 1-2	J14 3-0	A31 2-2
12 LEICESTER C	O15 2-2	S10 3-3	A29 4-1	D31 1-1	F18 0-2	J21 1-0	S19 0-1	D26 1-0	M25 1-0	A27 1-2	a08 1-1		F25 3-2	F11 0-0	a22 1-0	N12 3-2	O29 1-1	D17 2-2	D10 2-2	N26 0-0	S24 1-2	M11 2-1
13 LUTON T	a07 3-1	N05 5-2	m06 3-1	a15 1-0	M04 2-1	M18 0-0	a29 1-1	A24 2-0	S03 0-0	N19 0-3	O01 1-0	O08 1-0		D03 1-1	S17 1-1	J14 1-2	D24 1-3	a01 0-0	D26 1-1	F04 1-2	O22 1-1	A20 2-2
14 PLYMOUTH A	D10 2-2	F18 0-0	A20 1-1	S24 2-0	m06 2-0	D26 0-0	D24 2-1	N26 1-2	O15 4-2	J21 1-3	N12 1-2	a10 2-1	a08 0-0		O29 1-0	M11 0-2	F25 0-1	S10 0-1	a22 0-0	M25 0-1	A31 0-2	S03 0-3
15 PRESTON N.E.	S24 1-1	a10 3-1	a15 3-0	O08 2-0	a01 3-1	a29 3-0	N05 0-0	S10 1-1	A24 2-0	M04 4-2	A27 1-1	N19 2-1	J21 0-1	M18 0-0		S14 3-2	D26 4-1	O22 0-1	D31 0-3	D17 2-1	D03 1-3	F18 2-1
16 Q.P.R.	J21 0-5	a29 2-3	N05 0-1	A24 3-3	N19 1-0	D03 0-1	M18 3-2	D31 2-0	D27 1-2	O08 1-4	D17 1-1	a15 2-0	S10 3-0	O22 0-2	S07 0-0		F18 1-3	M04 0-0	A27 1-0	a07 0-0	a01 0-2	S24 0-1
17 SHEFFIELD U	D31 1-1	a01 4-0	O22 2-1	D03 1-1	N05 4-4	N19 2-0	M04 1-0	D17 1-1	F04 3-1	a29 5-0	S05 0-1	M18 2-2	A27 2-2	O08 1-1	D27 1-0	O01 1-1		J21 2-0	F11 0-1	A22 1-1	a15 2-1	S10 0-0
18 SHEFFIELD W	a08 2-0	D26 2-0	D24 1-1	F18 3-3	a10 1-0	A29 1-1	S03 4-2	a22 1-1	a26 4-0	S24 6-2	M25 5-2	A20 3-1	N26 1-1	J14 2-4	M11 0-1	O15 1-0	S17 2-1		N12 2-2	O29 3-0	m06 0-0	D10 2-1
19 SOUTHAMPTON	A31 0-0	O22 3-1	D03 3-1	M18 2-3	F04 4-1	M04 3-1	a01 1-0	F18 1-1	A20 1-2	N05 5-0	S17 2-1	a29 5-3	D27 2-1	N19 3-3	S03 1-0	D24 1-2	a10 1-0	a15 1-0		J14 1-2	O08 1-1	m06 3-2
20 SWANSEA T	F18 4-0	O08 2-0	N19 2-0	M04 3-0	D03 1-2	D24 5-1	a15 0-2	J21 1-2	m06 2-1	O22 1-2	D31 1-2	a01 0-0	S24 0-0	N05 2-2	A20 2-1	a10 0-1	S01 1-0	M18 1-2	S10 4-0		a29 1-0	D27 1-0
21 TOTTENHAM H	O29 2-0	A27 2-3	O01 5-0	D17 1-1	S17 3-1	D31 2-0	D26 1-0	O15 3-1	a22 1-2	a07 0-0	S10 2-0	F04 0-2	M11 0-0	A22 4-1	a08 3-2	N26 3-0	N12 7-0	S05 1-0	F25 4-0	D10 3-1		M25 4-1
22 WEST HAM U	A27 2-1	N19 0-2	M04 1-0	a01 2-2	M18 4-0	a15 0-1	O08 1-1	a10 0-1	S17 4-3	D03 2-1	A22 3-1	O22 2-2	D17 0-0	D31 2-2	O01 0-3	F04 1-0	J14 0-0	a29 2-2	S05 1-2	D26 3-0	N05 0-1	

SEASON 1949-50

DIVISION 3 NORTH

	ACCRINGTON S	BARROW	BRADFORD C	CARLISLE U	CHESTER	CREWE A	DARLINGTON	DONCASTER R	GATESHEAD	HALIFAX T	HARTLEPOOLS U	LINCOLN C	MANSFIELD T	NEW BRIGHTON	OLDHAM A	ROCHDALE	ROTHERHAM U	SOUTHPORT	STOCKPORT CO	TRANMERE R	WREXHAM	YORK C
1 ACCRINGTON S		S10 1-0	F11 3-2	D17 1-1	a10 4-0	J21 1-1	N12 3-0	M11 2-2	O29 0-1	J28 1-0	M25 1-2	D31 2-0	A24 2-2	F25 3-0	S27 3-4	a22 1-0	A27 1-4	a08 4-0	O15 4-2	S24 2-0	D26 2-0	F18 0-0
2 BARROW	J14 2-1		M25 1-0	F04 1-3	N12 3-1	a07 0-1	a08 2-1	a22 1-1	F11 1-1	M11 4-0	D26 0-0	S06 0-0	S17 0-1	O15 1-1	D24 3-1	O29 0-1	O01 1-1	F25 1-0	a27 0-1	A30 1-2	S03 2-1	A20 3-2
3 BRADFORD C	a29 5-2	N05 3-2		M04 3-2	D27 1-0	M18 0-2	J14 4-1	A20 1-2	D24 2-1	F04 1-3	S03 1-3	a01 0-1	D03 2-1	S17 2-1	O08 1-1	O01 2-1	N19 1-2	a10 6-0	A31 0-1	O22 2-4	S14 1-0	a15 0-2
4 CARLISLE U	A20 2-1	S24 2-0	J28 3-0		a22 5-1	F18 2-2	O29 0-1	a08 0-0	O15 4-2	N12 0-2	M11 2-1	J21 0-2	D24 1-1	M25 0-0	a07 3-0	F25 2-0	S10 3-1	F11 3-3	S03 2-0	m06 0-0	S01 1-0	D27 4-3
5 CHESTER	a07 1-0	a01 1-0	D26 4-1	D03 2-4		N05 0-1	J21 4-4	D24 3-1	S03 0-3	O01 5-1	J14 3-0	N19 3-1	a29 6-3	F04 2-0	a15 1-1	S14 0-2	M04 4-2	A31 4-1	A20 0-4	M18 0-0	O08 2-1	O22 2-3
6 CREWE A	S17 2-1	a10 1-1	O29 2-2	O01 2-1	M25 1-2		A31 2-0	a19 0-2	a22 3-1	O15 6-3	F11 1-0	D26 3-2	F04 1-1	a08 1-2	S03 1-1	M11 0-1	S05 4-1	N12 1-2	F25 1-0	A20 2-0	J14 1-1	D24 3-3
7 DARLINGTON	a01 0-2	O08 1-1	S10 4-3	M18 1-1	S17 2-1	A24 1-1		S14 2-1	D26 2-3	A27 5-1	a10 1-0	a15 2-0	N05 2-2	D17 3-1	M04 1-1	D31 1-1	O22 2-1	S24 0-2	F18 1-1	a26 0-2	N19 3-1	D03 1-1
8 DONCASTER R	O22 4-1	D03 1-0	D17 1-1	O08 0-0	A27 2-0	M04 0-2	S08 2-1		F04 1-1	a07 4-0	O01 0-0	a29 1-4	a15 0-1	D27 0-0	N05 1-1	A25 0-0	J21 1-0	D31 5-1	J14 3-0	m03 1-1	M18 2-0	a01 1-1
9 GATESHEAD	M18 5-0	a29 3-1	A27 4-2	a15 2-1	D31 4-0	D03 1-1	D27 3-3	S24 1-1		A22 7-1	J02 2-0	F18 2-1	O22 0-1	a10 2-1	a01 2-0	D17 1-3	O08 2-2	S10 3-2	J21 1-0	M04 5-1	N05 0-1	N19 1-1
10 HALIFAX T	M04 1-4	O22 1-0	S24 3-1	a01 1-1	F18 2-1	a15 3-1	D24 1-3	a10 2-2	A29 5-2		A20 1-2	M18 0-1	N19 0-3	S03 3-0	a29 1-1	J21 3-2	N05 4-3	S12 0-0	D27 3-1	O08 0-1	D03 0-0	J14 1-2
11 HARTLEPOOLS U	N05 0-0	D27 2-3	D31 3-0	O22 1-5	S10 5-1	a29 1-6	a07 2-0	F18 1-1	S05 3-5	D17 3-3		O08 2-1	M18 1-3	A22 2-0	N19 0-2	A27 1-2	a15 1-2	J21 1-0	S24 1-0	D03 2-0	a01 3-1	M04 2-0
12 LINCOLN C	S03 1-0	m06 4-0	N12 2-2	S17 2-1	F25 2-0	D27 2-0	O15 2-0	F11 1-0	O01 2-0	O29 1-0	a08 6-0		J14 1-0	M11 1-2	A20 1-2	M25 2-0	F04 0-0	J28 1-1	a22 1-1	a07 0-0	D24 2-0	A24 1-0
13 MANSFIELD T	A29 2-0	J21 1-1	a22 0-2	A27 4-1	F11 0-2	S24 3-0	M25 2-1	O15 1-2	M11 1-0	F25 1-0	O29 7-1	S10 2-1		N12 2-2	D26 3-1	J28 1-1	D31 0-2	D17 1-2	a08 3-0	F18 1-1	a07 1-0	S12 1-0
14 NEW BRIGHTON	N19 3-0	a15 2-0	J21 1-0	N05 3-2	S24 3-3	O08 0-2	A20 1-0	D26 2-2	a07 0-1	D31 1-1	A31 1-0	O22 1-0	a01 1-2		D03 0-0	S10 0-4	M18 0-3	F18 1-0	S07 1-3	D24 0-0	M04 3-1	m06 3-1
15 OLDHAM A	S06 0-1	A27 1-3	a08 2-1	a10 1-1	O15 0-2	D31 2-1	J28 2-0	M25 1-4	N12 1-0	F11 2-1	F25 3-1	D17 0-2	D27 1-0	a22 3-0		S24 0-0	A23 2-2	M11 2-5	O29 3-3	S10 2-1	O01 2-3	J21 2-0
16 ROCHDALE	D03 2-0	M18 2-1	F18 2-2	N19 1-0	S05 0-1	O22 2-1	S03 2-0	A30 0-1	A20 1-3	S17 1-0	D24 4-0	N05 2-0	M04 7-1	J14 4-0	F04 1-0		a01 1-0	D26 2-0	a10 1-1	a15 3-0	a29 1-1	O08 3-1
17 ROTHERHAM U	D24 6-0	F18 1-2	F25 5-2	J14 1-1	S19 3-2	m06 0-0	M11 1-1	S17 0-2	a08 1-2	M25 2-1	O15 5-1	S24 1-3	S03 2-2	O29 3-0	A29 0-1	N12 4-3		a22 4-0	S26 2-1	D26 1-1	A20 2-2	a10 2-1
18 SOUTHPORT	O08 1-0	N19 0-1	a07 1-1	a29 1-2	A22 1-1	a01 2-2	F04 1-1	S03 3-3	J14 0-3	S05 1-1	S17 2-1	M04 1-1	A20 1-1	O01 0-2	O22 3-2	D27 3-2	D03 4-0		D24 1-0	N05 2-1	a15 0-0	M18 1-1
19 STOCKPORT CO	a15 1-0	M04 1-3	A24 1-0	D31 2-0	D17 3-0	N19 4-1	O01 2-1	S10 0-1	S17 2-1	D26 2-0	F04 1-0	D03 1-1	O08 1-0	S14 0-2	M18 1-3	a07 1-1	a29 0-2	A27 3-2		a01 2-1	O22 2-1	NO5 3-1
20 TRANMERE R	F04 0-1	A23 2-1	M11 1-0	S06 0-0	O29 2-1	D17 2-2	F11 3-1	F25 2-4	J28 1-0	a08 2-1	a22 2-1	a10 2-2	O01 2-1	A27 2-1	J14 4-2	O15 1-0	D27 0-2	M25 2-0	N12 2-0		S17 2-1	S03 1-0
21 WREXHAM	D27 1-1	D31 1-0	S07 0-0	A24 1-1	a08 1-1	S10 1-2	F25 2-1	O29 0-1	M25 0-1	a22 2-3	N12 1-0	A27 4-0	a10 0-0	J28 2-2	F18 2-1	F11 3-0	D17 0-1	O15 1-0	M11 0-2	J21 0-0		S24 2-0
22 YORK C	O01 2-1	D17 2-0	O15 1-1	D26 1-1	M11 2-3	A27 1-1	a22 1-1	N12 0-3	F25 1-5	S10 3-1	J28 0-2	A29 1-2	S05 3-3	F11 2-1	S17 0-1	a08 2-2	a07 0-3	O29 0-1	M25 1-1	D31 1-0	F04 5-0	

DIVISION 3 SOUTH

	ALDERSHOT	BOURNEMOUTH	BRIGHTON & HA	BRISTOL C	BRISTOL R	CRYSTAL P	EXETER C	IPSWICH T	LEYTON O	MILLWALL	NEWPORT CO	NORTHAMPTON T	NORWICH C	NOTTINGHAM F	NOTTS CO	PORT VALE	READING	SOUTHEND U	SWINDON T	TORQUAY U	WALSALL	WATFORD
1 ALDERSHOT		N05 0-1	A24 0-1	a10 0-1	a01 3-1	M18 0-0	J21 1-2	a29 5-0	O08 2-0	A27 2-1	D27 4-1	O01 0-0	S14 2-0	F04 1-1	a15 2-0	D03 1-0	M04 2-0	m02 1-1	D31 0-0	S10 3-5	D17 1-0	O22 0-1
2 BOURNEMOUTH	M25 2-1		S24 2-2	S21 3-1	J21 0-2	O01 2-0	A24 2-0	D17 4-0	a10 4-1	O15 1-0	a22 1-1	a08 1-2	m06 2-0	N12 1-2	D31 3-0	A27 2-2	D26 2-1	S10 3-0	M11 1-1	O29 1-2	F25 1-1	S07 0-0
3 BRIGHTON & H.A.	A31 1-1	F04 1-1		S17 2-1	O08 1-2	J07 0-0	a01 0-0	N05 2-1	N19 2-2	m06 1-0	J14 5-0	A27 1-1	S03 1-3	A20 2-2	O22 2-3	M18 2-1	a15 2-1	M04 2-1	D26 0-1	a07 2-1	F18 1-1	D03 2-1
4 BRISTOL C	a07 2-0	a29 3-2	J21 1-2		J14 1-2	D03 2-0	N05 1-0	M18 4-2	a01 0-0	F18 2-1	S03 6-0	A20 3-1	D24 1-2	A30 0-2	M04 4-0	O22 2-0	N19 2-2	O08 1-1	S13 1-0	D26 0-0	S24 2-1	a15 0-1
5 BRISTOL R	N12 2-1	S17 0-0	F25 3-0	S10 2-3		F04 0-0	a10 1-0	A22 2-0	D27 3-0	M11 3-1	a24 3-0	m01 0-0	a22 5-1	a08 0-3	A27 0-3	D17 2-1	S05 2-1	D31 1-1	O29 2-0	M25 2-0	O15 1-1	O01 0-2
6 CRYSTAL P	O29 2-1	F18 1-0	F11 6-0	a22 1-1	S24 1-0		D17 5-3	A27 2-0	A24 1-1	F25 1-0	J28 1-0	N12 0-4	a08 2-0	M25 1-1	S10 1-2	D31 0-1	a07 1-1	J21 2-1	O15 2-2	M11 1-3	S07 2-0	D26 2-0
7 EXETER C	S17 1-0	A31 1-2	N12 2-3	M25 0-0	a07 2-0	A20 2-1		**S24** 1-1	J14 1-1	a26 2-1	O29 3-3	O15 1-3	M11 3-1	F25 0-0	m06 2-2	F18 3-1	S03 3-4	D26 1-1	a22 3-0	F11 1-1	a08 2-1	D24 3-1
8 IPSWICH T	F11 1-0	A20 1-2	M25 2-2	O29 0-0	A31 3-1	D24 4-4	F04 1-0		S17 4-4	a08 0-3	M11 1-0	F25 2-2	O15 3-0	O01 1-2	D27 0-4	m06 2-1	J14 2-0	a10 1-3	J28 3-1	a22 3-1	N12 1-5	S03 1-1
9 LEYTON O	F25 2-7	a07 2-1	a08 0-1	N12 1-0	D26 1-0	S01 2-2	S10 4-1	J21 4-0		a22 1-1	M25 2-1	M11 1-0	O29 1-2	O15 1-1	F18 1-4	S24 1-0	D24 2-1	m06 2-2	F11 1-3	S03 2-1	J28 2-2	A20 0-0
10 MILLWALL	D24 3-0	M04 1-0	S05 5-1	O01 3-1	O22 0-1	O08 2-3	a15 3-1	N19 3-1	D03 3-1		m01 1-2	J14 0-2	S17 1-2	S03 2-1	N05 1-3	a01 3-0	a29 3-1	M18 1-2	A29 1-0	A20 1-3	D27 1-1	a07 1-3
11 NEWPORT CO	D26 6-0	D03 5-0	S10 0-1	D31 6-4	a29 2-3	a15 2-2	M18 1-2	O22 1-0	N05 3-2	S24 4-3		S01 1-4	A20 3-2	a07 4-1	O08 1-1	M04 1-1	a01 1-1	M30 2-1	F18 1-2	S15 1-0	J21 2-1	N19 3-3
12 NORTHAMPTON T	F18 1-1	N19 2-3	D24 2-1	D17 4-2	a15 2-0	a01 2-2	M04 3-3	O08 1-2	O22 3-0	S10 1-0	A25 4-3		a11 3-1	S08 0-0	a29 5-1	D27 1-1	M18 2-0	D03 2-0	J21 0-1	S24 3-0	D31 2-0	N05 0-0
13 NORWICH C	S07 4-0	a15 0-1	D31 1-2	A27 3-0	D03 4-0	N19 2-0	O22 1-2	M04 1-1	M18 4-0	J21 0-2	D17 4-0	a10 2-1		D26 1-1	A24 4-3	O08 0-1	N05 1-1	a29 0-0	S24 4-0	F18 3-3	S10 3-2	a01 2-1
14 NOTTINGHAM F	S24 3-0	a01 3-0	D17 0-1	A24 3-0	N19 2-0	N05 2-0	O08 5-0	F18 2-0	M04 2-1	D31 3-1	a10 3-0	S14 0-1	D27 0-1		D03 1-2	a29 2-0	O22 1-2	a15 1-2	S10 2-1	J21 1-2	A27 1-0	M18 0-1
15 NOTTS CO	J28 3-1	S03 2-0	M11 4-2	O15 4-1	D24 2-0	J14 0-1	S08 3-3	D26 2-0	O01 7-1	M25 2-0	F25 7-0	a27 2-0	S01 5-0	a22 2-0		a07 3-1	F04 4-0	A20 2-0	**N12 3-0**	a08 1-1	O29 1-1	S17 1-0
16 PORT VALE	a22 0-1	D24 1-1	O29 3-0	M11 0-2	A20 1-0	S03 2-0	O01 1-0	S05 2-2	F04 2-0	N12 4-0	O15 1-0	D26 3-1	F25 2-2	F11 1-1	a10 3-1		S17 1-1	A29 0-0	a08 0-1	M27 2-0	M25 2-0	J14 2-0
17 READING	O15 1-3	D27 2-1	S14 3-0	a08 1-0	m06 0-1	a10 1-2	D31 3-2	S10 3-1	A27 5-1	S21 2-0	N12 4-1	O29 3-1	M25 4-1	M11 1-1	S24 0-1	J21 2-1		F18 5-0	D17 4-3	F25 2-0	a22 1-1	A31 1-0
18 SOUTHEND U	a08 3-0	J14 1-0	O15 3-2	F25 2-0	S03 3-1	S17 0-0	D27 1-0	a07 2-2	S06 2-0	O29 3-0	A27 6-0	a22 1-2	F11 1-0	J28 2-3	D17 2-0	A23 1-0	O01 3-2		M25 2-0	N12 2-0	M11 2-2	F04 1-1
19 SWINDON T	S03 2-1	O22 3-1	D27 4-2	m06 1-1	M18 1-0	M04 4-2	D03 7-1	a15 0-3	a29 0-1	A24 1-1	O01 1-1	S17 6-1	F04 1-1	J14 0-5	a01 1-1	N19 0-0	A20 2-0	N05 2-2		D24 1-2	a10 4-3	O08 0-1
20 TORQUAY U	J14 4-0	M18 3-1	a10 0-0	D27 3-3	N05 1-0	O22 1-0	a29 1-4	D03 2-2	D31 4-1	D17 1-0	S07 5-3	F04 1-0	O01 1-1	S17 2-0	N19 0-0	a15 0-0	O08 4-2	a01 2-4	A27 1-0		A24 2-1	M04 2-1
21 WALSALL	A20 0-0	O08 1-1	O01 4-2	F04 1-1	M04 3-1	m06 3-1	N19 3-0	a01 1-3	a15 1-2	D26 0-1	S17 2-0	S03 1-3	J14 1-1	D24 1-3	M18 3-3	N05 1-0	D03 2-0	O22 1-1	a07 0-0	S01 7-1		a29 1-1
22 WATFORD	M11 1-0	S15 4-1	a22 0-0	a20 2-0	F18 0-2	D27 0-0	A27 1-2	D31 6-0	D17 2-1	a10 0-0	a08 0-1	M25 0-0	N12 0-0	O29 1-0	J21 2-1	S10 0-2	A25 1-1	S24 1-0	F25 1-2	O15 1-0	F11 3-0	

LEAGUE TABLES

DIVISION 1

	P	W	D	L	F	A	W	D	L	F	A	Pts
Portsmouth	42	12	7	2	44	15	10	2	9	30	23	53
Wolverhampton W	42	11	8	2	47	21	9	5	7	29	28	53
Sunderland	42	14	6	1	50	23	7	4	10	33	39	52
Manchester U	42	11	5	5	42	20	7	9	5	27	24	50
Newcastle U	42	14	4	3	49	23	5	8	8	28	32	50
Arsenal	42	12	4	5	48	24	7	7	7	31	31	49
Blackpool	42	10	8	3	29	14	7	7	7	17	21	49
Liverpool	42	10	7	4	37	23	7	7	7	27	31	48
Middlesbrough	42	14	2	5	37	18	6	5	10	22	30	47
Burnley	42	9	7	5	23	17	7	6	8	17	23	45
Derby Co	42	11	5	5	46	26	6	5	10	23	35	44
Aston Villa	42	10	7	4	31	19	5	5	11	30	42	42
Chelsea	42	7	7	7	31	30	5	9	7	27	35	40
W.B.A.	42	9	7	5	28	16	5	5	11	19	37	40
Huddersfield T	42	11	4	6	34	22	3	5	13	18	51	37
Bolton W	42	10	5	6	34	22	0	9	12	11	37	34
Fulham	42	8	6	7	24	19	2	8	11	17	35	34
Everton	42	6	8	7	24	20	4	6	11	18	46	34
Stoke C	42	10	4	7	27	28	1	8	12	18	47	34
Charlton A	42	7	5	9	33	35	6	1	14	20	30	32
Manchester C	42	7	8	6	27	24	1	5	15	9	44	29
Birmingham C	42	6	8	7	19	24	1	6	14	12	43	28

DIVISION 2

	P	W	D	L	F	A	W	D	L	F	A	Pts
Tottenham H	42	15	3	3	51	15	12	4	5	30	20	61
Sheffield W	42	12	7	2	46	23	6	9	6	21	25	52
Sheffield U	42	9	10	2	36	19	10	4	7	32	30	52
Southampton	42	13	4	4	44	25	6	10	5	20	23	52
Leeds U	42	11	8	2	33	16	6	5	10	21	29	47
Preston N.E.	42	12	5	4	37	21	6	4	11	23	28	45
Hull C	42	11	8	2	39	25	6	3	12	25	47	45
Swansea T	42	11	3	7	34	18	6	6	9	19	31	43
Brentford	42	11	5	5	21	12	4	8	9	23	37	43
Cardiff C	42	13	3	5	28	14	3	7	11	13	30	42
Grimsby T	42	13	5	3	53	25	3	3	15	21	48	40
Coventry C	42	8	6	7	32	24	5	7	9	23	31	39
Barnsley	42	11	6	4	45	28	2	7	12	19	39	39
Chesterfield	42	12	3	6	28	16	3	6	12	15	31	39
Leicester C	42	8	9	4	30	25	4	6	11	25	40	39
Blackburn R	42	10	5	6	30	15	4	5	12	25	45	38
Luton T	42	8	9	4	28	22	2	9	10	13	29	38
Bury	42	10	8	3	37	19	4	1	16	23	46	37
West Ham U	42	8	7	6	30	25	4	5	12	23	36	36
Q.P.R.	42	6	5	10	21	30	5	7	9	19	27	34
Plymouth A	42	6	6	9	19	24	2	10	9	25	41	32
Bradford P.A.	42	7	6	8	34	34	3	5	13	17	43	31

DIVISION 3 NORTH

	P	W	D	L	F	A	W	D	L	F	A	Pts
Doncaster R	42	9	9	3	30	15	10	8	3	36	23	55
Gateshead	42	13	5	3	51	23	10	2	9	36	31	53
Rochdale	42	15	3	3	42	13	6	6	9	26	28	51
Lincoln C	42	14	5	2	35	9	7	4	10	25	30	51
Tranmere R	42	15	3	3	35	21	4	8	9	16	27	49
Rotherham U	42	10	6	5	46	28	9	4	8	34	31	48
Crewe A	42	10	6	5	38	27	7	8	6	30	28	48
Mansfield T	42	12	4	5	37	20	6	8	7	29	34	48
Carlisle U	42	12	6	3	39	20	4	9	8	29	31	47
Stockport Co	42	14	2	5	33	21	5	5	11	22	31	45
Oldham A	42	10	4	7	32	31	6	7	8	26	32	43
Chester C	42	12	3	6	47	33	5	3	13	23	46	40
Accrington S	42	12	5	4	41	21	4	2	15	16	41	39
New Brighton	42	10	5	6	27	25	4	5	12	18	38	38
Barrow	42	9	6	6	27	20	5	3	13	20	33	37
Southport	42	7	10	4	29	26	5	3	13	22	45	37
Darlington	42	9	8	4	35	27	2	5	14	21	42	35
Hartlepool U	42	10	3	8	37	35	4	2	15	15	44	33
Bradford C	42	11	1	9	38	32	1	7	13	23	44	32
Wrexham	42	8	7	6	24	17	2	5	14	15	37	32
Halifax T	42	9	5	7	35	31	3	3	15	23	54	32
York C	42	6	7	8	29	33	3	6	12	23	37	31

DIVISION 3 SOUTH

	P	W	D	L	F	A	W	D	L	F	A	Pts
Notts Co	42	17	3	1	60	12	8	5	8	35	38	58
Northampton T	42	12	6	3	43	21	8	5	8	29	29	51
Southend U	42	15	4	2	43	15	4	9	8	23	33	51
Nottingham F	42	13	0	8	37	15	7	9	5	30	24	49
Torquay U	42	13	6	2	40	23	6	4	11	26	40	48
Watford	42	10	6	5	26	13	6	7	8	19	22	45
Crystal Palace	42	12	5	4	35	21	3	9	9	20	33	44
Brighton & H.A.	42	9	8	4	32	24	7	4	10	25	45	44
Bristol R	42	12	5	4	34	18	7	0	14	17	33	43
Reading	42	15	2	4	48	21	2	6	13	22	43	42
Norwich C	42	11	5	5	44	21	5	5	11	21	42	42
Bournemouth	42	11	6	4	38	19	5	4	12	19	37	42
Port Vale	42	12	6	3	33	13	3	5	13	14	29	41
Swindon T	42	9	7	5	41	30	6	4	11	18	32	41
Bristol C	42	12	4	5	38	19	3	6	12	22	42	40
Exeter C	42	9	8	4	37	27	5	3	13	26	48	39
Ipswich T	42	9	6	6	36	36	3	5	13	21	50	35
Leyton O	42	10	6	5	33	30	2	5	14	20	55	35
Walsall	42	8	8	5	37	25	1	8	12	24	37	34
Aldershot	42	10	5	6	30	16	3	3	15	18	44	34
Newport Co	42	11	5	5	50	34	2	3	16	17	64	34
Millwall	42	11	1	9	39	29	3	3	15	16	34	32

Football League Records

Top scorers: Div 1, S.Mortensen (Blackpool) 30 goals; Div 2, J.McCormack (Barnsley) 33 goals; Div 3 N, J.Shaw (Rotherham United) 37 goals; Div 3 S, W.Ardron (Nottingham Forest) 36 goals.

Colchester United, Gillingham, Scunthorpe & Lindsey United and Shrewsbury Town elected to League.

Alf Ramsey, a record full-back signing from Southampton who was the final piece in the jigsaw which saw Spurs win the Division One and Two titles in successive seasons.

DIVISION 1

	ARSENAL	ASTON VILLA	BLACKPOOL	BOLTON W	BURNLEY	CHARLTON A	CHELSEA	DERBY CO	EVERTON	FULHAM	HUDDERSFIELD T	LIVERPOOL	MANCHESTER U	MIDDLESBROUGH	NEWCASTLE U	PORTSMOUTH	SHEFFIELD W	STOKE C	SUNDERLAND	TOTTENHAM H	W.B.A.	WOLVERHAMPTON W
1 ARSENAL		M10 2-1	D09 4-4	a21 1-1	D16 0-1	F24 2-5	A23 0-0	O28 3-1	S06 2-1	N25 5-1	S16 6-2	a07 1-2	O14 3-0	J13 3-1	F03 0-0	M23 0-1	S02 3-0	D25 0-3	N11 5-1	A26 2-2	S30 3-0	M24 2-1
2 ASTON VILLA	O21 1-1		F03 0-3	S16 0-1	M17 3-2	D26 0-0	N18 4-2	D23 1-1	D02 3-3	J13 3-0	M03 0-1	S02 1-1	S04 1-3	N04 0-1	O07 3-0	a14 3-3	M31 2-1	m05 6-2	A21 3-1	S30 2-3	A19 2-0	M27 1-0
3 BLACKPOOL	m02 0-1	S23 1-1		M23 2-0	A21 1-2	A26 0-0	O07 3-2	F17 3-1	N04 4-0	S04 4-0	N18 3-1	D25 3-0	m05 1-1	a14 2-1	M17 2-2	M03 3-0	D02 3-2	M31 3-0	J20 2-2	D16 0-1	O21 2-1	S09 1-1
4 BOLTON W	D02 3-0	J20 1-0	M26 1-2		F10 1-1	D16 3-0	S04 1-0	S23 3-0	M03 2-0	D26 0-1	M17 4-0	F17 2-1	A26 1-0	N18 0-2	O21 0-2	O07 4-0	a14 0-1	N04 1-1	S09 1-2	A23 1-4	M31 0-2	a28 2-1
5 BURNLEY	A19 0-1	O28 2-0	A29 0-0	D09 2-0		O14 5-1	M23 2-1	a07 1-0	D26 1-1	a21 0-2	J13 0-1	N25 1-1	M24 1-2	S02 3-1	S16 1-1	S04 1-1	D23 1-0	S30 1-1	M10 1-1	F24 2-0	F03 0-1	N11 2-0
6 CHARLTON A	O07 1-3	D25 2-2	D23 2-3	A19 4-3	M03 0-0		N04 1-2	m05 1-2	O21 2-1	A30 0-0	D02 3-2	J27 1-0	J20 1-2	a28 3-0	a14 1-3	M31 0-1	J13 2-1	M17 2-0	F17 3-0	S02 1-1	N18 2-3	S23 3-2
7 CHELSEA	A30 0-1	a07 1-1	F28 0-2	m05 4-0	M26 0-2	M24 2-3		N25 1-2	S30 2-1	D09 2-0	S02 1-2	a21 1-0	N11 1-0	D23 1-1	J13 3-1	D26 1-4	A19 4-0	F03 1-1	O28 3-0	O14 0-2	S16 1-1	a25 2-1
8 DERBY CO	M17 4-2	A26 4-2	S30 4-1	F03 2-2	N18 1-1	S06 5-0	a14 1-0		a28 0-1	S16 3-2	N04 3-0	J13 1-2	M26 2-4	M31 6-0	M03 1-2	D02 2-3	O21 4-1	D30 1-1	D16 6-5	D25 1-1	O07 1-1	A23 1-2
9 EVERTON	S13 1-1	a21 1-2	M24 0-2	O14 1-1	D25 1-0	M10 0-0	F17 3-0	D09 1-2		F28 1-0	A19 3-2	S16 1-3	O28 1-4	A30 3-2	D23 3-1	S23 1-5	M26 0-0	J13 0-3	N25 3-1	N11 1-2	S02 0-3	a07 1-1
10 FULHAM	a14 3-2	S09 2-1	S13 2-2	D25 0-1	D02 4-1	A23 1-3	a28 1-2	J20 3-5	O07 1-5		O21 1-1	S23 2-1	D16 2-2	M17 2-0	M31 1-1	m02 1-4	N18 4-2	M03 2-0	D30 1-1	M23 0-1	N04 0-1	A26 2-1
11 HUDDERSFIELD T	J20 2-2	O14 4-2	a07 2-1	O28 0-4	S09 3-1	a21 1-1	a18 2-1	M24 2-0	D16 1-2	M10 1-2		N11 2-2	D09 2-3	F17 2-3	S13 0-0	A26 2-1	S23 3-4	A23 3-1	M07 3-4	N25 3-2	M27 1-2	D25 1-2
12 LIVERPOOL	N18 1-3	a25 0-0	D26 1-0	S30 3-3	a14 1-0	M23 1-0	D02 1-0	S09 1-0	J20 0-2	F03 2-0	M31 1-4		A23 2-1	O21 0-0	N04 2-4	F10 2-1	M17 2-1	O07 0-0	A26 4-0	S06 2-1	M03 1-1	D16 1-4
13 MANCHESTER U	M03 3-1	S13 0-0	S02 1-0	D23 2-3	N04 1-1	S16 3-0	M31 4-1	M23 2-0	M17 3-0	A19 1-0	a28 6-0	A30 1-0		F03 1-0	D02 1-2	O21 0-0	O07 3-1	N18 0-0	D26 3-5	J13 2-1	a14 3-0	F17 2-1
14 MIDDLESBROUGH	S09 2-1	M24 2-1	N25 4-3	a07 1-1	D30 3-3	D09 7-3	A26 3-0	N11 1-1	A23 4-0	O28 1-1	S30 8-0	M10 1-1	S23 1-2		D25 2-1	D16 3-1	J20 2-1	M23 1-0	O14 1-1	a21 1-1	S06 2-1	a11 1-2
15 NEWCASTLE U	S23 2-1	a04 0-1	O28 4-2	a18 0-1	J20 2-1	N25 3-2	S09 3-1	O14 3-1	A26 1-1	N11 1-2	S06 6-0	M24 1-1	a21 0-2	m05 1-0		a11 0-0	F17 2-0	D16 3-1	M23 2-2	a07 0-1	A23 1-1	D09 1-1
16 PORTSMOUTH	M26 1-1	N25 3-3	O14 2-0	F24 2-1	m05 2-1	N11 3-3	D25 1-3	a21 2-2	F03 6-3	S30 1-0	D23 1-0	D09 1-3	M10 0-0	A19 1-1	S02 0-0		A30 4-1	S16 5-1	a07 0-0	M24 1-1	J13 2-2	O28 1-4
17 SHEFFIELD W	D30 0-2	N11 3-2	a21 3-1	N25 3-4	A26 0-1	S09 1-2	F24 2-2	a18 4-3	m05 6-0	a07 2-2	F03 3-2	O28 4-1	F26 0-4	S16 0-1	S30 0-0	A21 2-1		S04 1-1	M24 3-0	D09 1-1	D26 3-0	O14 2-2
18 STOKE C	D26 1-0	D09 1-0	N11 1-0	M24 2-1	F17 0-0	O28 2-0	S23 2-1	S02 4-1	S09 2-0	O14 1-1	A28 0-1	F24 2-3	a07 2-0	M26 2-0	A19 1-2	J20 1-2	S11 1-1		a21 2-4	M10 0-0	D23 1-1	N25 0-1
19 SUNDERLAND	M31 0-2	A30 3-3	S16 0-2	J13 1-2	O21 1-1	S30 4-2	M17 1-1	A19 1-0	a14 4-0	S02 0-1	O07 0-0	D23 2-1	D25 2-1	M03 2-1	M26 2-1	N18 0-0	N04 5-1	D02 1-1		F03 0-0	a28 1-1	m05 0-0
20 TOTTENHAM H	D23 1-0	F17 3-2	A19 1-4	A28 4-2	O07 1-0	D30 1-0	M03 2-1	D26 2-1	M31 3-0	M26 2-1	a14 0-2	m05 3-1	S09 1-0	D02 3-3	N18 7-0	N04 5-1	a28 1-0	O21 6-1	S23 1-1		M17 5-0	J20 2-1
21 W.B.A.	F17 2-0	D16 2-0	a04 1-3	N11 0-1	S23 2-1	a07 3-0	J20 1-1	F24 1-2	D30 0-1	M24 0-0	M26 0-2	O14 1-1	N25 0-1	S13 2-3	A30 1-2	S09 5-0	D25 1-3	A26 1-1	D09 3-1	O28 1-2		a21 3-2
22 WOLVERHAMPTON W	N04 0-1	M26 2-3	J13 1-1	S02 7-1	M31 0-1	F03 2-3	O21 2-1	A28 2-3	N18 4-0	D23 1-1	D26 3-1	A19 2-0	S30 0-0	O07 3-4	m02 0-1	M17 2-3	M03 4-0	a14 2-3	S06 2-1	S16 2-1	D02 3-1	

England winger Tom Finney, who helped Preston North End to promotion from Division Two in 1950-51.

DIVISION 2

	BARNSLEY	BIRMINGHAM C	BLACKBURN R	BRENTFORD	BURY	CARDIFF C	CHESTERFIELD	COVENTRY C	DONCASTER R	GRIMSBY T	HULL C	LEEDS U	LEICESTER C	LUTON T	MANCHESTER C	NOTTS CO	PRESTON N.E.	Q.P.R.	SHEFFIELD U	SOUTHAMPTON	SWANSEA T	WEST HAM U
1 BARNSLEY		M03 0-2	M26 3-0	S06 2-3	M31 2-3	N18 0-0	D23 0-0	a14 3-0	D26 0-1	O07 3-1	A30 4-2	J20 1-2	a28 0-0	S09 6-1	D02 1-1	M17 2-0	O21 4-1	N04 7-0	a18 1-1	A19 1-2	F17 1-0	S23 1-2
2 BIRMINGHAM C	O14 2-0		O28 3-2	a25 1-1	J20 3-3	M23 0-0	F17 2-1	S06 1-1	N11 0-2	A26 1-1	M24 2-1	a21 0-1	A23 2-0	N25 3-0	D26 1-0	D30 1-4	S09 1-0	S23 1-1	a07 3-0	F28 2-1	D16 5-0	D09 3-1
3 BLACKBURN R	M23 3-4	M17 2-3		A21 3-2	D25 2-4	O07 2-0	D02 1-1	M03 1-0	F17 4-2	O21 2-0	S23 2-2	F10 2-1	a14 1-0	A26 1-0	N18 4-1	M31 0-0	N04 2-1	a25 2-1	D16 0-2	S11 1-0	J20 3-0	S09 1-3
4 BRENTFORD	S13 0-2	O21 2-1	A30 3-2		F10 4-0	M17 4-0	a14 4-0	O07 0-4	S23 1-1	M31 5-1	J20 2-1	A26 1-2	N18 0-0	D16 1-0	M03 2-0	N04 1-3	F17 2-4	D02 2-1	M23 3-1	D26 4-0	S09 2-1	D30 1-1
5 BURY	N11 0-3	S16 4-1	J01 1-3	D09 2-1		J13 1-2	M23 2-2	S02 1-0	a21 3-1	F03 2-3	N25 0-2	F24 0-1	A19 2-3	O28 4-1	J27 2-0	S30 0-0	A30 3-1	S06 0-1	M10 1-1	M24 1-0	a07 1-1	O14 3-0
6 CARDIFF C	a07 1-1	M26 2-1	F24 1-0	O28 1-1	S09 2-2		S23 1-0	D25 2-1	M10 0-0	D16 5-2	N11 2-1	D09 1-0	F17 2-2	a21 2-1	A28 1-1	A26 2-0	D30 0-2	J20 4-2	N25 2-0	O14 2-2	M24 1-0	S04 2-1
7 CHESTERFIELD	A26 1-2	S30 1-1	a21 4-1	N25 2-2	M26 3-0	F03 0-3		S16 1-1	a07 1-4	A21 2-2	O14 0-0	M10 1-0	S02 1-0	N11 1-1	J13 1-2	D25 0-0	S11 2-0	D16 3-1	M24 0-2	D09 2-3	F24 3-1	O28 1-2
8 COVENTRY C	N25 3-3	S11 3-1	O14 6-1	F24 3-3	D30 5-2	D26 2-1	J20 1-0		O28 3-1	M27 1-0	M10 4-1	A21 1-0	S23 2-1	D09 4-1	F17 0-2	D16 1-2	A26 1-0	S09 3-0	a21 2-3	a07 2-2	N11 3-1	M24 1-0
9 DONCASTER R	D25 3-2	M31 0-1	S30 0-1	F03 0-3	D02 1-1	O21 0-0	N18 1-2	M17 2-1		N04 3-1	J13 2-4	D16 4-4	M03 2-2	M23 5-2	O07 4-3	J20 3-2	a26 2-0	a14 0-2	m05 1-1	A30 0-0	J27 1-0	A26 3-0
10 GRIMSBY T	F24 3-1	D23 1-1	M10 1-1	N11 7-2	S23 2-1	A19 0-0	A30 1-2	M23 1-2	M24 1-0		D30 1-1	N25 2-2	D25 0-2	a07 0-2	S06 4-4	S09 1-4	J20 0-4	F17 2-2	O14 2-2	O28 4-2	D09 4-2	a21 0-1
11 HULL C	A24 3-3	N04 3-2	F03 2-2	S16 3-0	a14 4-0	M31 2-0	M03 2-1	O21 0-2	S09 1-2	S02 2-1		M23 2-0	O07 1-3	m05 5-3	M17 3-3	a28 1-0	D02 0-0	N18 5-1	D26 1-1	S30 4-1	A26 2-1	D16 1-2
12 LEEDS U	S16 2-2	D02 3-0	S02 0-1	D23 1-0	O07 1-1	a28 2-0	O21 2-0	A30 1-0	A19 3-1	a14 1-0	M26 3-0		M31 2-1	S30 2-1	N04 1-1	N18 0-1	M03 0-3	M17 2-2	F03 1-0	J13 5-3	m05 2-0	D26 2-0
13 LEICESTER C	D09 1-2	A28 1-3	N25 2-0	a07 1-2	D16 4-0	S30 1-1	D30 1-0	F03 3-0	O14 2-0	D26 0-0	F24 4-0	N11 1-5		M24 3-1	S16 1-2	S04 1-1	M27 2-3	A26 6-2	S09 2-2	a21 3-1	O28 2-3	M10 1-0
14 LUTON T	J13 1-1	a14 1-1	D23 1-1	A19 2-0	M17 4-2	D02 1-1	M31 3-0	a28 1-1	M26 3-1	N18 4-0	S06 1-2	F17 2-3	N04 0-2		F03 2-2	M03 1-1	O07 1-2	O21 2-0	S16 0-0	S02 0-1	D26 3-1	A30 1-1
15 MANCHESTER C	a21 6-0	D25 3-1	a07 1-0	O14 4-0	A26 5-1	A23 2-1	S09 5-1	S30 1-0	F24 3-3	m05 2-2	O28 0-0	M24 4-1	J20 1-1	S23 1-1		M26 0-0	D16 0-3	a04 5-2	D09 5-3	N25 2-3	M14 1-2	N11 2-0
16 NOTTS CO	O28 2-1	S02 0-1	N11 1-1	M24 2-3	F17 4-2	D23 1-2	D26 1-0	A19 0-2	S16 1-2	J13 3-2	D09 2-2	a07 0-0	m05 2-3	O14 2-2	a30 0-0		S23 1-3	A31 3-3	F24 3-0	M10 2-2	a21 3-2	N25 4-1
17 PRESTON N.E.	M10 7-0	J13 1-0	M24 3-0	S30 4-2	A23 2-0	S02 1-1	S06 4-1	D23 1-1	D09 6-1	S16 2-0	a21 1-0	O14 2-0	M26 3-2	F24 1-0	A19 2-4	F03 3-1		D26 1-0	O28 1-1	N11 3-2	N25 5-1	a07 0-1
18 Q.P.R.	M24 2-1	F03 2-0	D09 3-1	J27 1-1	m05 3-2	S16 3-2	A19 1-1	J13 3-1	N25 1-2	S30 7-1	a07 3-1	O28 3-0	D23 3-0	M10 1-1	S02 1-2	A24 1-0	D25 1-4		N11 2-1	M23 2-0	O14 1-1	F24 3-3
19 SHEFFIELD U	S02 0-2	N18 3-2	A19 0-3	M26 5-1	O21 3-0	a14 1-2	N04 4-1	D02 2-0	S11 0-0	M03 4-2	D25 3-1	S23 2-2	J13 2-1	J20 2-1	a28 0-0	O07 1-2	M17 2-3	M31 2-0		D23 1-2	A28 6-1	F17 1-1
20 SOUTHAMPTON	D16 1-0	O07 0-2	S06 1-1	m05 2-1	N04 1-0	M03 1-1	a28 1-1	N18 5-4	A23 1-1	M17 5-1	F17 2-3	S09 2-0	D02 2-2	D30 1-1	a14 2-1	O21 1-0	M31 3-3	M26 2-2	A26 1-0		S23 2-1	J20 2-2
21 SWANSEA T	S30 1-0	A19 0-1	S16 1-2	J13 2-1	N18 2-0	N04 1-0	O07 2-0	M31 2-1	S02 2-2	a28 1-3	D23 1-0	S07 4-2	M17 2-1	D25 0-2	O21 2-3	D02 2-1	a14 2-1	M03 1-0	A24 1-2	F03 2-1		M26 3-2
22 WEST HAM U	F03 4-2	a28 1-2	J13 2-3	S02 1-2	M03 2-3	m05 0-0	M17 2-0	N04 3-2	D23 0-0	D02 2-1	A19 3-3	D25 3-1	O21 0-0	A24 2-1	M31 2-4	a14 4-2	N18 2-0	O07 4-1	S30 3-5	S16 3-0	M23 1-1	

Season 1950-51

DIVISION 3 NORTH

	ACCRINGTON S	BARROW	BRADFORD	BRADFORD C	CARLISLE U	CHESTER	CREWE A	DARLINGTON	GATESHEAD	HALIFAX T	HARTLEPOOLS U	LINCOLN C	MANSFIELD T	NEW BRIGHTON	OLDHAM A	ROCHDALE	ROTHERHAM U	SCUNTHORPE U	SHREWSBURY T	SOUTHPORT	STOCKPORT CO	TRANMERE R	WREXHAM	YORK C
1 ACCRINGTON S		J27 1-0	S09 3-3	N11 0-2	D26 0-4	O28 1-2	A23 1-0	a07 1-0	m05 2-2	a21 1-0	a25 2-0	O14 3-1	M26 0-2	M24 1-1	J20 1-2	M10 1-2	J01 0-2	F17 0-0	F24 2-0	A26 3-1	D09 2-3	m02 0-2	S23 1-0	S26 2-0
2 BARROW	a16 4-0		D16 2-3	F24 1-3	F10 1-2	a07 2-0	M10 0-1	D09 0-3	N11 1-1	A24 2-0	M24 3-0	a21 3-1	J20 2-3	O28 1-1	A26 2-1	O14 4-3	S23 0-2	S09 1-0	a19 0-0	S07 3-1	S30 1-0	S19 1-2	a12 2-0	M26 2-0
3 BRADFORD	J13 3-0	A19 5-0		S30 3-1	S02 0-2	M24 2-0	a21 1-1	O28 2-1	a18 2-0	O14 2-1	a07 1-1	M10 2-1	S13 1-0	a11 2-1	M26 3-1	A21 0-1	D25 0-4	J27 2-2	N11 2-4	S16 2-0	F24 3-0	F03 4-1	a30 0-1	D23 4-0
4 BRADFORD C	M31 7-0	O07 5-1	F17 4-1		O21 2-4	F10 0-1	J20 1-1	D26 0-3	S09 2-2	A26 2-0	D30 3-1	S06 0-0	N18 2-3	S23 3-0	a28 1-0	M27 2-1	M03 3-4	a14 2-0	a25 1-0	N04 3-0	D16 0-1	A23 2-2	D02 5-3	M17 5-2
5 CARLISLE U	D25 3-1	J01 1-1	D30 1-0	M10 2-1		F24 2-1	M24 2-1	a19 2-1	A24 3-0	a26 1-0	S07 1-0	a07 2-0	F17 2-0	N11 1-0	S09 1-0	O28 4-0	M23 0-0	S23 3-1	O14 2-2	D16 3-1	a21 2-2	A26 3-1	J20 0-2	m03 3-2
6 CHESTER	M17 2-2	N18 1-2	N04 2-0	m05 2-2	O07 1-1		F17 1-1	A26 3-1	S23 2-2	S09 2-1	J20 2-1	a11 2-1	D02 0-1	a25 3-1	A23 3-1	J27 1-3	a14 1-2	a28 4-1	D25 3-1	O21 0-2	a04 3-0	M31 1-3	S06 0-0	M03 3-1
7 CREWE A	A30 3-0	O21 2-0	D02 2-4	S16 1-1	N04 1-1	S30 3-0		J27 5-0	A26 0-1	D25 0-0	D16 3-1	F10 0-4	O07 2-0	J13 2-0	a14 2-1	F03 3-1	M17 1-2	M03 2-0	M23 1-2	a04 1-0	S04 0-2	a28 1-1	N18 1-1	M31 2-4
8 DARLINGTON	N18 3-0	a28 1-1	M17 1-4	a23 2-1	a14 1-0	D23 0-0	a30 2-0		J01 4-2	F17 2-0	M26 0-1	J13 1-1	A30 1-2	S13 5-3	O21 0-0	A19 0-2	J20 2-2	N04 3-2	S02 2-1	M03 1-1	S23 2-1	O07 1-1	M31 1-1	D02 0-3
9 GATESHEAD	A19 7-0	M31 1-0	a14 5-0	J13 2-0	A28 4-3	F03 2-1	D23 4-0	F10 5-2		S04 5-0	D25 0-1	M26 1-2	M17 1-3	S02 4-0	N18 3-2	S16 4-1	O21 0-3	O07 1-0	S30 3-0	a30 1-3	S18 2-0	D02 2-0	M03 0-0	N04 3-0
10 HALIFAX T	D02 2-2	A28 0-0	M03 2-2	D23 1-2	a28 1-0	J13 3-1	D26 1-0	S30 2-2	S11 1-0		J27 1-0	F03 4-1	M31 0-1	A19 0-2	O07 3-0	S02 1-1	N04 1-2	O21 3-3	S16 3-1	a14 4-0	M27 1-0	N18 0-1	M17 1-0	F10 1-3
11 HARTLEPOOLS U	a28 1-0	N04 6-1	N18 3-1	S02 1-1	S11 3-3	S16 1-2	A19 0-2	M23 6-1	D26 3-0	J06 5-2		S30 2-2	O21 1-1	D23 0-1	M03 0-1	J13 0-0	M31 3-1	M17 4-2	F03 1-0	D02 3-2	F10 2-0	a14 2-1	O07 4-1	A28 4-1
12 LINCOLN C	M03 9-1	D02 3-0	O21 1-3	S13 1-4	N18 1-1	A19 2-1	m05 4-1	S09 3-0	M23 2-1	S23 3-1	F17 1-0		D30 3-0	J27 3-0	M31 2-0	D25 4-2	a28 0-2	A23 2-1	D23 5-0	O07 1-2	J20 6-0	M17 2-1	N04 2-1	a14 2-1
13 MANSFIELD T	M23 5-0	S16 4-0	S04 3-2	a07 1-1	S30 2-1	a21 2-1	F24 4-1	A21 2-1	O28 2-1	N11 3-1	M10 1-0	S02 1-1		O14 4-0	D26 3-1	a16 1-0	J13 1-1	A26 1-1	a30 4-0	m05 2-2	M24 2-1	J10 2-1	a23 1-1	F03 3-1
14 NEW BRIGHTON	N04 1-1	M17 1-2	a28 3-3	F03 0-6	M31 0-1	m02 1-0	S09 0-2	S05 2-2	a04 0-1	D16 1-0	A26 1-0	J06 0-1	M03 0-1		D02 2-0	S30 1-5	O07 2-4	N18 1-2	F10 0-0	A22 1-0	D25 1-0	S16 1-1	a14 3-0	O21 0-0
15 OLDHAM A	S16 2-1	D23 0-1	M23 2-3	m01 2-2	J13 1-1	A29 1-0	a17 0-2	M10 2-0	a07 2-3	F24 2-0	O14 5-1	N11 0-0	D25 2-0	a21 3-1		a24 2-0	A19 4-5	S12 3-4	M24 2-1	F03 4-0	O28 1-3	S30 3-4	J27 2-2	S02 2-2
16 ROCHDALE	O21 3-1	M03 1-0	A29 1-2	M26 4-0	M17 4-1	J16 2-3	S23 1-1	m05 0-0	J20 2-0	a10 0-0	S09 3-1	a17 3-0	a14 0-0	F17 1-0	F10 0-1		N18 0-2	D02 2-0	S05 5-0	M31 1-1	A26 1-1	N04 2-3	a28 2-0	O07 0-1
17 ROTHERHAM U	F10 6-2	F03 3-0	D26 2-1	O14 1-0	M26 3-0	a16 0-0	O28 2-3	S16 0-1	M10 1-2	M24 2-0	N11 2-1	a30 3-0	S09 3-0	F24 5-0	m05 3-1	a07 3-0		D30 4-1	a21 2-0	J30 1-1	A21 0-0	S04 1-2	A26 5-0	S30 3-1
18 SCUNTHORPE U	S30 3-0	J13 1-0	J06 1-1	a18 0-0	F03 1-1	D09 2-0	O14 1-1	M24 2-0	F24 2-1	M10 2-2	O28 0-0	A30 1-1	D23 0-0	a07 6-0	S06 1-0	a21 3-0	S02 0-0		A19 0-0	M26 0-0	a30 3-0	F10 1-1	D25 2-0	S16 0-1
19 SHREWSBURY T	O07 0-1	a14 1-0	M31 1-0	J27 2-0	M03 0-3	D26 1-0	M26 0-1	D30 2-2	N25 1-0	J20 2-0	S23 1-0	A26 1-2	a28 1-1	m05 4-2	N04 2-2	S11 0-2	D02 1-2	D16 3-1		M17 1-5	S09 0-3	O21 1-2	A21 2-1	N18 1-0
20 SOUTHPORT	D23 3-0	S12 4-1	J20 2-4	M24 0-1	A19 1-0	M10 0-1	S02 2-0	O14 1-0	J27 1-0	a17 1-1	a21 3-0	F24 0-2	a10 0-1	A29 0-1	S23 1-4	N11 1-1	J09 0-1	M23 2-2	O28 1-2		a07 2-0	S09 0-1	F17 3-1	D26 1-1
21 STOCKPORT CO	a14 0-0	F17 4-1	O07 2-1	A19 3-1	D02 1-2	S02 0-3	S11 3-0	F03 1-0	J31 5-2	M26 2-1	m05 2-0	S16 2-0	N04 3-1	D26 4-0	M17 1-4	D23 2-2	A28 1-3	M31 1-2	J13 2-0	N18 3-2		M03 0-0	O21 2-1	a28 1-0
22 TRANMERE R	S02 1-1	D26 3-0	S23 2-2	A29 3-1	D23 2-2	N11 3-1	a10 3-0	F24 3-2	a21 2-2	a07 3-2	a17 1-0	O28 0-1	M07 2-1	J20 4-3	F17 1-0	M24 2-1	S12 2-1	m05 1-0	M10 0-1	J13 4-0	O14 1-1		M23 1-2	A19 7-2
23 WREXHAM	F03 1-1	S02 1-0	F10 3-1	a21 0-3	S16 2-1	S13 2-0	a07 0-2	N11 3-1	O14 0-0	O28 2-2	F24 1-0	M24 2-3	A19 2-2	a18 0-1	a04 0-2	m02 3-1	D23 0-0	D26 3-1	A30 1-0	S30 3-3	M10 2-0	M26 2-1		J13 4-3
24 YORK C	S04 3-0	M23 0-2	A26 1-3	O28 1-2	J27 1-1	O14 2-2	N11 1-2	a21 1-1	M24 1-1	m05 0-0	A21 3-0	a16 2-2	S23 1-1	M10 2-0	D30 2-2	F24 2-2	F17 3-3	J20 0-0	a07 2-0	D25 2-0	a11 0-0	a25 4-0	S09 3-0	

DIVISION 3 SOUTH

	ALDERSHOT	BOURNEMOUTH	BRIGHTON & HA	BRISTOL C	BRISTOL R	COLCHESTER U	CRYSTAL P	EXETER C	GILLINGHAM	IPSWICH T	LEYTON O	MILLWALL	NEWPORT CO	NORTHAMPTON T	NORWICH C	NOTTINGHAM F	PLYMOUTH A	PORT VALE	READING	SOUTHEND	SWINDON T	TORQUAY U	WALSALL	WATFORD
1 ALDERSHOT		a28 0-1	A26 0-0	a14 0-0	A23 1-1	a11 2-0	m02 3-0	D25 4-2	D02 2-4	O21 0-1	M17 3-1	N18 2-1	D30 3-1	J20 3-0	S09 1-1	F17 1-0	M03 2-2	S23 2-0	O07 1-1	S06 2-2	M23 0-1	m05 1-0	N04 3-0	M31 1-1
2 BOURNEMOUTH	a25 4-0		M10 2-2	A19 1-0	M14 2-0	S13 2-0	O14 5-0	M23 1-1	A23 3-1	F03 2-1	S16 5-0	D23 1-0	O28 2-0	N11 1-0	M24 0-0	F10 3-2	S30 0-2	a07 3-1	m05 1-0	D26 3-1	J27 2-1	a21 0-0	J13 3-1	S02 3-3
3 BRIGHTON & H.A.	D23 1-2	O21 2-1		O07 1-1	S16 2-2	J13 3-1	F03 1-0	M17 4-1	M03 2-2	a14 4-0	D02 3-0	S13 2-3	a18 9-1	M23 5-1	D26 1-1	A30 1-2	N18 0-6	J17 2-2	M31 1-1	N04 2-1	S02 1-0	A19 2-2	a28 1-0	F17 1-1
4 BRISTOL C	a04 1-1	D16 2-0	F24 2-0		S02 1-0	a25 0-2	S06 2-0	A23 3-1	A26 2-0	a18 2-1	S30 4-1	J13 2-1	O14 2-1	O28 1-0	M10 2-2	N11 0-3	D25 1-0	M24 3-1	M26 3-3	J17 0-3	a21 2-0	a07 0-2	F03 3-3	S16 3-0
5 BRISTOL R	A28 3-0	O07 2-0	J20 3-2	D30 2-1		D23 1-1	S09 1-1	M03 3-1	S04 3-0	M31 1-1	N18 2-1	a28 1-0	S23 1-0	m05 1-1	a30 3-3	m03 0-2	N04 3-1	D26 2-0	M17 4-0	O21 4-1	A19 1-0	J31 1-1	a14 1-1	a23 3-0
6 COLCHESTER U	J27 1-0	S07 4-1	S09 4-1	a28 1-1	A26 0-0		D30 1-0	O07 0-1	D16 4-2	N04 2-3	M31 1-0	D02 3-0	J20 1-1	F17 2-1	S23 2-3	D26 0-2	M17 3-0	m05 1-1	O21 1-1	M03 1-3	A31 4-1	M23 3-1	N18 0-1	a14 4-1
7 CRYSTAL P	A19 0-2	M03 0-1	S23 0-2	S13 1-0	J13 1-0	S02 1-3		O21 0-1	O07 4-3	N18 1-3	a14 1-1	J20 1-1	F17 1-1	D25 0-0	a18 0-5	J27 1-6	M31 0-1	M26 0-2	N04 0-3	M17 0-2	D23 2-0	A30 2-1	D02 1-0	a28 1-1
8 EXETER C	D26 3-0	M26 2-1	O28 4-2	A30 1-0	O14 0-2	F24 5-0	M10 1-2		F07 1-2	S16 2-0	J13 0-0	A19 0-1	M24 2-2	a07 1-0	N11 1-2	a21 0-5	F03 3-2	F10 0-3	S30 1-3	a18 1-0	S13 1-0	a04 0-0	S02 1-0	D23 3-3
9 GILLINGHAM	a21 3-0	A30 2-2	O14 1-1	D23 1-2	S13 1-0	A19 0-0	F24 0-0	J17 9-4		S30 0-1	F03 1-0	S02 4-3	M10 0-1	M24 3-1	O28 2-2	a07 1-4	m05 1-2	N11 1-1	D25 0-3	M23 0-0	m02 2-1	F10 2-0	S16 4-1	J13 3-1
10 IPSWICH T	M10 5-2	S23 1-0	F10 3-0	m05 2-0	N11 2-3	M24 3-0	a07 1-1	J20 1-0	F17 5-1		A23 2-2	D25 2-1	a21 2-1	A19 1-1	a11 0-1	F24 1-3	A26 2-0	S13 2-2	D30 0-2	S09 1-0	O28 4-1	O14 3-1	J06 3-1	M26 2-1
11 LEYTON O	O28 1-0	J20 2-0	a21 2-1	m03 0-2	a07 1-0	D09 1-1	F10 2-0	S09 1-3	S23 4-0	A31 2-0		a19 0-2	a12 0-3	S07 1-0	J11 3-1	O14 0-4	a26 1-2	F24 2-3	A26 2-0	D30 1-1	M24 2-1	M10 5-1	M23 2-1	D26 1-2
12 MILLWALL	a07 1-0	A26 3-0	S04 1-1	S09 5-3	a11 1-0	a21 2-0	S16 1-0	a25 5-0	D30 4-3	D26 4-0	S18 3-1		F24 2-4	M10 2-1	O14 1-1	M24 1-1	M23 1-1	O28 2-2	J10 1-3	A21 1-1	F10 1-0	N11 4-1	S30 2-0	F03 4-0
13 NEWPORT CO	S02 7-0	a30 1-0	m05 3-0	M03 0-1	F03 2-1	S16 2-0	S30 2-4	N04 0-3	O21 1-0	D02 1-2	a28 0-0	O07 2-3		S21 2-2	a25 1-1	A19 0-2	a14 2-0	A31 2-1	N18 5-0	M31 6-1	J13 2-1	D23 2-1	D26 3-0	S14 2-2
14 NORTHAMPTON T	S16 1-0	M31 0-1	M27 0-0	M17 2-2	a19 1-1	S30 2-1	D26 2-0	N18 4-1	N04 4-1	D16 2-1	S14 3-3	O21 1-2	a05 1-4		A31 1-2	S02 2-2	a28 1-3	D23 1-1	D02 1-1	a14 1-1	F03 1-2	J13 1-0	O07 1-1	M03 6-0
15 NORWICH C	J13 2-2	N04 3-0	D27 1-1	O21 0-0	S30 2-0	F03 1-1	m05 3-1	M31 3-0	M17 2-0	a28 1-3	F01 3-1	M03 2-1	M26 2-1	A23 0-0		D23 2-0	D02 1-0	A19 2-0	a14 2-1	N18 3-0	S16 2-0	S02 1-1	S13 1-0	O07 3-1
16 NOTTINGHAM F	S30 7-0	a14 1-0	A23 4-0	M31 0-0	M26 2-1	D25 0-0	J06 1-0	D02 2-2	N18 9-2	O07 0-0	M03 0-1	N04 2-0	m02 2-1	a25 2-2	A26 4-2		S06 4-1	S09 2-1	J20 1-1	a28 3-0	a18 2-1	F03 3-1	O21 4-0	M17 2-1
17 PLYMOUTH A	O14 5-1	F17 3-1	a07 3-3	D26 2-0	M24 0-0	O28 7-1	N11 4-0	S23 0-1	a18 2-0	D23 2-1	A19 2-1	M26 2-2	F10 1-1	a09 4-1	a21 2-1	S13 0-2		S02 1-0	S09 2-0	J20 2-0	M10 5-1	F24 1-0	A30 1-1	J10 3-1
18 PORT VALE	F03 3-1	N18 3-1	a23 0-1	N04 1-3	D25 0-0	a16 1-1	a26 2-2	a30 2-0	M31 4-3	S04 1-0	O07 3-1	m03 0-1	A24 1-0	A26 0-3	a02 2-1	J13 1-1	M05 2-1		a28 0-0	D02 3-1	S30 2-1	S16 1-0	M03 1-1	O21 2-1
19 READING	F24 7-1	a18 0-0	N11 7-0	M23 4-2	O28 0-0	M10 3-2	M24 1-1	F17 4-2	D26 1-1	S02 2-0	D23 4-0	m02 1-1	a07 5-0	a21 2-0	F14 3-1	S16 0-2	J13 4-0	J27 3-0		S23 0-2	O14 3-1	S13 0-0	A19 2-1	A30 1-0
20 SOUTHEND U	S12 4-2	D25 6-1	M24 3-1	J31 1-1	M10 1-1	O14 4-2	O28 5-2	m05 5-1	M26 4-0	J13 1-0	S02 0-1	A29 0-3	N11 3-0	F10 3-0	a07 0-2	a10 3-2	S16 1-0	a21 1-1	F03 3-3		F24 8-2	S30 3-0	D23 0-1	A19 5-1
21 SWINDON T	M26 4-0	J06 2-1	D30 0-0	D02 1-0	D16 1-2	A23 1-1	A26 2-0	S06 1-0	a28 2-0	M17 2-0	N04 2-0	a14 0-1	S09 2-0	S23 1-0	J20 1-0	m05 2-3	O21 1-2	F17 2-1	M03 1-1	O07 4-1		D25 2-1	M31 1-1	N18 3-2
22 TORQUAY U	S27 1-2	D02 0-2	D16 3-1	N18 4-1	J17 1-2	M26 4-1	A23 4-1	a28 2-0	a14 1-2	M03 0-1	O21 2-1	M31 2-1	A26 3-4	S09 1-1	D30 1-5	S23 3-2	O07 1-3	J20 3-2	S06 2-1	F17 2-2	D26 1-0		M17 3-2	N04 3-2
23 WALSALL	F10 3-1	S09 0-1	m03 1-0	S23 3-1	F15 1-2	a07 4-2	a21 0-0	D30 0-2	J20 2-1	J27 2-0	M26 1-1	F17 4-0	D25 0-0	F24 1-0	S07 0-1	M10 0-2	A24 1-1	O14 2-0	D16 1-2	A26 1-2	N11 1-0	O28 3-1		a19 1-0
24 WATFORD	N11 1-2	D30 2-1	S30 1-1	J20 1-2	a21 1-0	F10 2-0	D09 1-0	A26 1-2	S09 5-0	M23 0-2	D25 2-0	S23 0-0	S07 0-2	O14 0-1	F24 0-2	O28 1-1	J27 1-1	M10 2-0	A24 3-1	D16 1-3	a07 1-2	M24 2-2	m05 1-3	

LEAGUE TABLES

DIVISION 1

	P	W	D	L	F	A	W	D	L	F	A	Pts
Tottenham H	42	17	2	2	54	21	8	8	5	28	23	60
Manchester U	42	14	4	3	42	16	10	4	7	32	24	56
Blackpool	42	12	6	3	43	19	8	4	9	36	34	50
Newcastle U	42	10	6	5	36	22	8	7	6	26	31	49
Arsenal	42	11	5	5	47	28	8	4	9	26	28	47
Middlesbrough	42	12	7	2	51	25	6	4	11	25	40	47
Portsmouth	42	8	10	3	39	30	8	5	8	32	38	47
Bolton W	42	11	2	8	31	20	8	5	8	33	41	45
Liverpool	42	11	5	5	28	25	5	6	10	25	34	43
Burnley	42	9	7	5	27	16	5	7	9	21	27	42
Derby Co	42	10	5	6	53	33	6	3	12	28	42	40
Sunderland	42	8	9	4	30	21	4	7	10	33	52	40
Stoke C	42	10	5	6	28	19	3	9	9	22	40	40
Wolverh'pton W	42	9	3	9	44	30	6	5	10	30	31	38
Aston Villa	42	9	6	6	39	29	3	7	11	27	39	37
W.B.A.	42	7	4	10	30	27	6	7	8	23	34	37
Charlton A	42	9	4	8	35	31	5	5	11	28	49	37
Fulham	42	8	5	8	35	37	5	6	10	17	31	37
Huddersfield T	42	8	4	9	40	40	7	2	12	24	52	36
Chelsea	42	9	4	8	31	25	3	4	14	22	40	32
Sheffield W	42	9	6	6	43	32	3	2	16	21	51	32
Everton	42	7	5	9	26	35	5	3	13	22	51	32

DIVISION 2

	P	W	D	L	F	A	W	D	L	F	A	Pts
Preston N.E.	42	16	3	2	53	18	10	2	9	38	31	57
Manchester C	42	12	6	3	53	25	7	8	6	36	36	52
Cardiff C	42	13	7	1	36	20	4	9	8	17	25	50
Birmingham C	42	12	6	3	37	20	8	3	10	27	33	49
Leeds U	42	14	4	3	36	17	6	4	11	27	38	48
Blackburn R	42	13	3	5	39	27	6	5	10	26	39	46
Coventry C	42	15	3	3	51	25	4	4	13	24	34	45
Sheffield U	42	11	4	6	44	27	5	8	8	28	35	44
Brentford	42	13	3	5	44	25	5	5	11	31	49	44
Hull C	42	12	5	4	47	28	4	6	11	27	42	43
Doncaster R	42	9	6	6	37	32	6	7	8	27	36	43
Southampton	42	10	9	2	38	27	5	4	12	28	46	43
West Ham U	42	10	5	6	44	33	6	5	10	24	36	42
Leicester C	42	10	4	7	42	28	5	7	9	26	30	41
Barnsley	42	9	5	7	42	22	6	5	10	32	46	40
Q.P.R.	42	13	5	3	47	25	2	5	14	24	57	40
Notts Co	42	7	7	7	37	34	6	6	9	24	26	39
Swansea T	42	14	1	6	34	25	2	3	16	20	52	36
Luton T	42	7	9	5	34	23	2	5	14	23	47	32
Bury	42	9	4	8	33	27	3	4	14	27	59	32
Chesterfield	42	7	7	7	30	28	2	5	14	14	41	30
Grimsby T	42	6	8	7	37	38	2	4	15	24	57	28

DIVISION 3 NORTH

	P	W	D	L	F	A	W	D	L	F	A	Pts
Rotherham U	46	16	3	4	55	16	15	6	2	48	25	71
Mansfield T	46	17	6	0	54	19	9	6	8	24	29	64
Carlisle U	46	18	4	1	44	17	7	8	8	35	33	62
Tranmere R	46	15	5	3	51	26	9	6	8	32	36	59
Lincoln C	46	18	1	4	62	23	7	7	9	27	35	58
Bradford P.A.	46	15	3	5	46	23	8	5	10	44	49	54
Bradford C	46	13	4	6	55	30	8	6	9	35	33	52
Gateshead	46	17	1	5	60	21	4	7	12	24	41	50
Crewe A	46	11	5	7	38	26	8	5	10	23	34	48
Stockport Co	46	15	3	5	45	26	5	5	13	18	37	48
Rochdale	46	11	6	6	38	18	6	5	12	31	44	45
Scunthorpe U	46	10	12	1	32	9	3	6	14	26	48	44
Chester C	46	11	6	6	42	30	6	3	14	20	34	43
Wrexham	46	12	6	5	37	28	3	6	14	18	43	42
Oldham A	46	10	5	8	47	36	6	3	14	26	37	40
Hartlepool U	46	14	5	4	55	26	2	2	19	9	40	39
York C	46	7	12	4	37	24	5	3	15	29	53	39
Darlington	46	10	8	5	35	29	3	5	15	24	48	39
Barrow	46	12	3	8	38	27	4	3	16	13	49	38
Shrewsbury T	46	11	3	9	28	30	4	4	15	15	44	37
Southport	46	9	4	10	29	25	4	6	13	27	47	36
Halifax T	46	11	6	6	36	24	0	6	17	14	45	34
Accrington S	46	10	4	9	28	29	1	6	16	14	72	32
New Brighton	46	7	6	10	22	32	4	2	17	18	58	30

DIVISION 3 SOUTH

	P	W	D	L	F	A	W	D	L	F	A	Pts
Nottingham F	46	16	6	1	57	17	14	4	5	53	23	70
Norwich C	46	16	6	1	42	14	9	8	6	40	31	64
Reading	46	15	6	2	57	17	6	9	8	31	36	57
Plymouth A	46	16	5	2	54	19	8	4	11	31	36	57
Millwall	46	15	6	2	52	23	8	4	11	28	34	56
Bristol R	46	15	7	1	46	18	5	8	10	18	24	55
Southend U	46	15	4	4	64	27	6	6	11	28	42	52
Ipswich T	46	15	4	4	48	24	8	2	13	21	34	52
Bournemouth	46	17	5	1	49	16	5	2	16	16	41	51
Bristol C	46	15	4	4	41	25	5	7	11	23	34	51
Newport Co	46	13	4	6	48	25	6	5	12	29	45	47
Port Vale	46	13	6	4	35	24	3	7	13	25	41	45
Brighton & H.A.	46	11	8	4	51	31	2	9	12	20	48	43
Exeter C	46	11	4	8	33	30	7	2	14	29	55	42
Walsall	46	12	4	7	32	20	3	6	14	20	42	40
Colchester U	46	12	5	6	43	25	2	7	14	20	51	40
Swindon T	46	15	4	4	38	17	3	0	20	17	50	40
Aldershot	46	11	8	4	37	20	4	2	17	19	68	40
Leyton O	46	13	2	8	36	28	2	6	15	17	47	38
Torquay U	46	13	2	8	47	39	1	7	15	17	42	37
Northampton T	46	8	9	6	39	30	2	7	14	16	37	36
Gillingham	46	10	7	6	41	30	3	2	18	28	71	35
Watford	46	8	5	10	29	28	1	6	16	25	60	29
Crystal Palace	46	6	5	12	18	39	2	6	15	15	45	27

Football League Records

Top scorers: Div 1, G.Robledo (Newcastle United) 33 goals; Div 2, D.Dooley (Sheffield Wednesday) 46 goals; Div 3 N, A.Graver (Lincoln City) 36 goals; Div 3 S, R.Blackman (Reading) 39 goals.

New Brighton failed to gain re-election, Workington elected in their place. Shrewsbury Town transferred to Division Three South.

When Manchester United won the title in 1951-52, Jack Rowley's 30 goals included hat-tricks in the first two games and stood as a club record until beaten by Dennis Viollet eight years later.

Derek Dooley burst upon the scene in 1951-52 when his 46 goals in only 30 appearances helped Sheffield Wednesday to the Division Two title. Sadly, in February 1953, he broke a leg against Preston and had to have the limb amputated.

DIVISION 1

	ARSENAL	ASTON VILLA	BLACKPOOL	BOLTON W	BURNLEY	CHARLTON A	CHELSEA	DERBY CO	FULHAM	HUDDERSFIELD T	LIVERPOOL	MANCHESTER C	MANCHESTER U	MIDDLESBROUGH	NEWCASTLE U	PORTSMOUTH	PRESTON N.E.	STOKE C	SUNDERLAND	TOTTENHAM H	W.B.A.	WOLVERHAMPTON W
1 ARSENAL		J05 2-1	a14 4-1	N24 4-2	O13 1-0	M13 2-1	A29 2-1	S15 3-1	O27 4-3	A18 2-2	S05 0-0	J26 2-2	D08 1-3	M22 3-1	a16 1-1	D25 4-1	F16 3-3	a19 4-1	S01 3-0	S29 1-1	N10 6-3	D22 2-2
2 ASTON VILLA	S08 1-0		J19 4-0	D15 1-1	M22 4-1	N10 0-2	a15 7-1	A25 4-1	a05 4-1	S10 1-0	S22 2-0	D29 1-2	O13 2-5	N24 2-0	D08 2-2	F09 2-0	O27 3-2	F16 2-3	A27 2-1	M08 0-3	a19 2-0	D25 3-3
3 BLACKPOOL	a11 0-0	S15 0-3		a05 1-0	F16 1-0	O13 1-2	A18 1-2	J26 2-1	M08 4-2	D22 3-1	D26 2-0	S29 2-2	a19 2-2	O27 2-2	N10 6-3	A27 0-0	S10 0-3	N24 4-2	J05 3-0	D08 1-0	M22 2-0	S01 3-2
4 BOLTON W	a12 2-1	A18 5-2	N17 1-0		J26 1-4	S29 2-1	M15 3-0	F02 1-2	a14 2-1	O20 2-1	M29 1-1	D01 2-1	S01 1-0	S03 3-1	A22 0-0	N03 0-3	S15 1-1	D22 1-1	O06 1-1	J05 1-1	D25 3-2	M01 2-2
5 BURNLEY	M01 0-1	N03 2-1	O06 2-0	S22 1-3		D15 1-0	D01 1-1	M15 0-1	A25 1-0	a12 0-2	A21 0-0	O20 0-0	a11 1-1	D29 7-1	J19 2-1	a26 1-0	D25 0-2	F09 4-0	M29 0-1	S03 1-1	S08 6-1	N17 2-2
6 CHARLTON A	O20 1-3	a24 0-1	M01 2-0	F09 1-0	A18 1-0		a26 1-1	N03 3-3	D29 3-0	D01 4-0	O06 2-0	M15 0-0	S12 2-2	S08 4-3	S22 3-0	D22 0-2	A29 4-2	a14 4-0	N17 2-1	D25 0-3	J19 3-3	a12 1-0
7 CHELSEA	A22 1-3	a14 2-2	D15 2-1	O27 1-3	a19 4-1	D08 1-0		S05 0-1	S08 2-1	S15 2-1	A25 1-3	D25 0-3	N10 4-2	F16 5-0	M12 1-0	D29 1-1	N24 0-0	M22 1-0	S29 2-1	a30 0-2	O13 1-3	J26 0-1
8 DERBY CO	J19 1-2	D22 1-1	S22 1-1	D08 5-2	O27 1-0	M22 1-3	m03 1-1		N10 5-0	D26 2-1	F09 1-1	S08 1-3	F16 0-3	a05 3-1	a19 1-3	a14 1-0	M08 4-3	S01 4-2	A18 3-4	O13 4-2	N24 2-1	A29 1-3
9 FULHAM	M15 0-0	N17 2-2	O20 1-2	a11 1-2	D22 1-2	S01 3-3	J05 1-2	m01 3-0		a26 1-0	M01 1-1	N03 1-2	D26 3-3	J19 6-0	F09 1-1	O06 2-3	A18 2-3	S12 5-0	a12 0-1	A29 1-2	S22 1-0	D01 2-2
10 HUDDERSFIELD T	D15 2-3	S19 3-1	A25 1-3	M08 0-2	N24 1-3	a19 1-0	J19 1-0	D25 1-1	D08 1-0		D29 1-2	A22 5-1	M22 3-2	S22 1-0	O13 2-4	S08 0-1	a05 2-0	O27 0-2	a15 2-2	N10 1-1	F16 3-0	S29 1-7
11 LIVERPOOL	S12 0-0	J26 1-2	D25 1-1	N10 1-1	A29 3-1	F16 1-1	D22 1-1	S29 2-0	O13 4-0	S01 2-1		a14 1-2	N24 0-0	M08 1-1	M22 3-0	A18 0-2	D08 2-2	a05 2-1	S15 2-2	a19 1-1	O27 2-5	J05 1-1
12 MANCHESTER C	S22 0-2	S01 2-2	F09 0-0	a19 0-3	M12 0-1	O27 4-2	D26 3-1	J05 4-2	M22 1-1	A29 3-0	a11 1-2		S15 1-2	N10 2-1	N24 2-3	J01 0-1	O13 1-0	D08 0-1	D22 3-1	F16 1-1	a05 1-2	A18 0-0
13 MANCHESTER U	a26 6-1	M01 1-1	D01 3-1	D29 1-0	a14 6-1	S05 3-2	a21 3-0	O06 2-1	D25 3-2	N03 1-1	a12 4-0	J19 1-1		A22 4-2	A25 2-1	N17 1-3	S29 1-2	S08 4-0	O20 0-1	J26 2-0	D15 5-1	M15 2-0
14 MIDDLESBROUGH	N03 0-3	a12 2-0	M15 1-0	a23 2-0	S01 5-0	J05 2-1	O06 0-0	N17 0-0	S15 2-0	J26 2-1	O20 3-3	M29 2-2	A29 1-4		a14 2-1	M01 2-1	D22 2-5	D26 3-0	D01 0-2	A18 2-1	F09 0-1	a26 4-0
15 NEWCASTLE U	N17 2-0	a26 6-1	a07 1-3	A29 0-1	S15 7-1	J26 6-0	O20 3-1	D01 2-1	S29 0-1	M01 6-2	N03 1-1	a12 1-0	D22 2-2	a11 0-2		M15 3-3	J05 3-0	A18 6-0	D26 2-2	S01 7-2	a23 1-4	O06 3-1
16 PORTSMOUTH	D26 1-1	S29 2-0	A22 1-3	M22 3-0	D08 2-2	A25 1-0	S01 1-0	a11 3-1	F16 4-0	J05 3-1	D15 1-3	S05 1-0	a05 1-0	O13 5-4	O27 3-1		a19 1-2	N10 4-1	J26 0-2	N24 2-0	M12 1-1	S15 2-3
17 PRESTON N.E.	O06 2-0	M15 2-2	S05 3-1	J19 2-2	J01 1-2	A22 3-0	a12 1-0	O20 0-1	D15 0-1	N17 5-2	a26 4-0	M01 1-1	F09 1-2	A25 0-1	S08 1-2	D01 2-2		S22 2-0	N03 4-2	a14 1-1	D29 1-0	M29 3-0
18 STOKE C	D01 2-1	O06 4-1	a12 2-3	A25 1-2	S29 2-1	S17 1-2	N03 1-2	D29 3-1	S03 1-1	M15 0-0	N17 1-2	a26 3-1	J05 0-0	m03 3-2	D15 4-5	M29 2-0	J26 0-0		M01 1-1	S15 1-6	A20 1-1	O20 1-0
19 SUNDERLAND	D29 4-1	S05 1-3	S08 1-3	F16 0-2	N10 0-0	a05 1-1	F09 4-1	D15 3-0	N24 2-2	a11 7-1	J19 3-0	A25 3-0	M08 1-2	a19 3-1	D25 1-4	S22 3-1	M22 0-0	O13 0-1		O27 0-1	D08 3-3	J01 1-1
20 TOTTENHAM H	F09 1-2	O20 2-0	a26 2-0	S08 2-1	S10 1-1	D26 2-3	N17 3-2	M01 5-0	A20 1-0	a02 1-0	D01 2-3	O06 1-2	S22 2-0	D15 3-1	D29 2-1	a12 3-1	F23 1-0	J19 2-0	M15 2-0		A25 3-1	N03 4-2
21 W.B.A.	a21 3-1	D01 1-2	N03 1-1	D26 3-2	J05 1-1	S15 1-1	M01 0-1	a12 1-0	J26 0-2	O06 0-0	M15 3-3	N17 3-2	A18 3-3	S29 2-3	S05 3-3	O20 5-0	S01 1-1	A29 1-0	a26 1-1	D22 3-1		a14 2-1
22 WOLVERHAMPTON W	A25 2-1	D26 1-2	D29 3-0	O13 5-1	a05 1-2	N24 2-2	S22 5-3	A22 1-2	a19 2-2	F09 0-0	S08 2-1	D15 2-2	O27 0-2	D08 4-0	F16 3-0	J19 1-1	N10 1-4	M08 3-0	F23 0-3	M22 1-1	a15 1-4	

DIVISION 2

	BARNSLEY	BIRMINGHAM C	BLACKBURN R	BRENTFORD	BURY	CARDIFF C	COVENTRY C	DONCASTER R	EVERTON	HULL C	LEEDS U	LEICESTER C	LUTON T	NOTTINGHAM F	NOTTS CO	Q.P.R.	ROTHERHAM U	SHEFFIELD U	SHEFFIELD W	SOUTHAMPTON	SWANSEA T	WEST HAM U
1 BARNSLEY		M22 1-2	a14 1-2	N24 0-0	S29 3-3	O27 2-0	S15 1-0	a19 1-1	D08 1-0	D15 2-2	O13 3-1	N10 3-3	S05 1-2	a05 1-1	S12 2-1	D25 3-1	M08 0-1	S01 3-4	F16 5-4	A25 3-1	J26 2-3	J05 1-1
2 BIRMINGHAM C	N03 2-1		N17 0-1	J05 1-2	A18 2-1	a11 3-2	M01 3-1	S15 2-2	J26 1-2	M29 2-2	A22 1-1	D22 2-0	a26 3-1	S01 0-2	D01 2-0	a12 1-0	D25 4-0	M15 3-0	S12 0-0	S29 1-1	O06 1-1	O20 2-1
3 BLACKBURN R	a11 2-1	a05 1-4		D08 3-0	S15 1-2	N10 0-1	S01 0-1	A27 3-3	F16 1-0	D25 1-0	O27 2-3	N24 2-1	J26 2-1	a19 3-2	S29 2-0	J01 4-2	M22 1-1	A18 1-5	M12 0-0	O13 0-1	J05 3-1	D22 3-1
4 BRENTFORD	a12 1-1	S08 1-0	a26 1-1		O20 4-0	D29 1-1	N03 1-0	a30 1-0	A27 1-0	D01 2-1	D15 2-1	J19 1-3	M01 3-3	S22 1-1	O06 1-0	F09 0-0	A25 2-0	N17 4-1	a11 2-3	D25 1-2	M15 3-1	a21 1-1
5 BURY	F09 3-0	D15 3-0	J19 0-2	M08 1-0		D08 1-1	D25 0-2	O27 1-1	M22 1-0	S22 3-1	N24 1-2	F16 1-4	A25 0-1	O13 2-0	D29 2-1	S08 3-1	a19 3-1	J01 1-0	a05 1-2	N10 8-2	a11 4-1	A29 4-0
6 CARDIFF C	M15 3-0	a14 3-1	a21 3-1	S01 2-0	a26 3-0		O06 4-1	J05 2-1	S15 3-1	N03 1-0	m03 3-1	A18 4-0	D01 3-0	D22 4-1	a12 1-0	N17 3-1	A20 2-4	S17 1-1	S29 2-1	J26 1-0	D26 3-0	M01 1-1
7 COVENTRY C	J19 0-0	O13 1-1	D29 1-2	M22 2-1	D26 3-0	F16 2-1		N10 1-2	a05 2-1	S08 1-4	D08 4-2	M08 1-3	a15 5-2	O27 3-3	D15 0-2	A25 0-0	S03 2-1	S22 1-1	a19 0-2	N24 3-1	A20 3-2	F09 1-2
8 DONCASTER R	D01 1-2	J19 0-5	A22 1-0	S05 1-2	M15 1-1	S08 1-0	M29 1-0		D25 3-1	a26 0-1	A25 2-0	S22 2-2	O20 1-1	F09 0-1	M01 1-5	O06 4-0	D29 0-3	a12 2-1	D15 1-1	a14 0-1	N03 3-0	N17 4-1
9 EVERTON	a26 1-1	S22 1-3	O06 0-2	A22 1-0	N03 2-2	J19 3-0	N17 4-1	D26 1-1		a11 5-0	D29 2-0	F09 2-0	M15 1-3	S05 1-0	O20 1-5	M01 3-0	S08 3-3	D01 1-0	A25 3-3	D15 3-0	M29 2-1	a12 2-0
10 HULL C	A18 0-0	N10 0-1	D26 3-0	a19 4-1	J26 5-0	M22 0-0	J05 5-0	D08 2-0	a14 1-0		M08 3-2	a05 3-1	S29 1-2	N24 1-4	S20 1-3	A30 4-1	O27 3-3	D22 2-1	O13 0-1	F16 0-0	S15 5-2	S01 1-1
11 LEEDS U	M01 1-0	A29 1-1	M15 1-0	A18 1-1	a12 2-1	S12 2-1	a26 3-1	D22 0-0	S01 1-2	O20 2-0		D26 2-1	N17 1-1	a14 0-0	M29 1-0	N03 3-0	F09 3-0	O06 3-1	S15 3-2	J05 1-1	D01 1-1	J26 3-1
12 LEICESTER C	M29 1-2	A25 4-0	a12 2-1	S15 1-1	O06 1-1	D15 3-0	O20 3-1	J26 2-1	S29 1-2	N17 1-0	D25 1-2		S01 3-3	J05 3-1	a26 1-1	D01 4-0	a15 2-0	N03 5-5	A20 3-1	S03 3-0	M01 1-1	M15 3-1
13 LUTON T	m03 4-2	D08 2-4	S22 1-1	O13 0-2	D22 2-1	a19 2-2	a14 2-1	M12 1-4	O27 1-1	F09 1-1	a05 2-1	D29 1-2		F16 3-3	S08 6-0	J19 0-1	N24 1-1	A29 2-1	N10 5-3	M22 2-1	A18 2-2	D26 6-1
14 NOTTINGHAM F	N17 3-3	D29 0-1	D01 1-0	J26 2-0	M01 1-0	A25 2-3	M15 3-1	S29 1-1	S12 2-0	a12 4-0	a11 1-1	S08 2-2	O06 2-0		J19 3-2	a26 3-1	D15 4-2	M29 0-2	D26 2-1	A22 3-0	O20 2-2	N03 0-0
15 NOTTS CO	A30 4-0	a19 5-0	F09 0-1	F16 5-2	S01 2-1	N24 1-1	A18 2-1	O13 1-0	M08 0-0	S06 4-0	N10 1-2	D08 2-3	J05 5-4	S15 2-2		S22 0-0	a05 0-3	D25 3-1	M22 2-2	O27 3-4	D22 2-0	a14 1-0
16 Q.P.R.	D26 1-1	N24 0-2	S03 2-1	S29 3-1	J05 3-2	a05 1-1	D22 1-4	F16 0-2	O13 4-4	A20 1-1	M22 0-0	a19 1-0	S15 0-0	D08 4-3	J26 1-4		N10 2-3	a14 4-2	O27 2-2	M08 2-1	S01 1-1	A18 2-0
17 ROTHERHAM U	O20 4-0	D26 1-2	N03 3-0	D22 1-1	D01 4-3	A27 2-0	F23 0-1	S01 2-0	J05 1-1	M15 1-1	S29 4-2	a14 0-2	a12 0-1	A18 1-2	N17 2-0	M29 1-0		M01 3-1	J26 3-3	S15 4-1	a26 1-3	O06 2-1
18 SHEFFIELD U	D29 1-2	O27 4-2	D15 1-1	a05 1-4	S10 1-0	M12 6-1	J26 1-2	N24 2-1	a19 1-2	A25 4-1	F16 3-0	M22 5-0	A20 3-0	N10 1-4	D26 1-0	m03 1-2	O13 1-0		S08 7-3	D08 2-2	S29 5-0	S15 6-1
19 SHEFFIELD W	O06 2-1	S03 1-1	O20 2-0	a14 2-0	N17 2-1	F09 4-2	D01 3-1	A18 3-1	D22 4-0	M01 6-0	J19 1-2	A27 1-0	a02 4-0	D25 1-1	N03 6-0	M15 2-1	S22 3-5	J05 1-3		S01 3-1	a12 1-1	a26 2-2
20 SOUTHAMPTON	D22 1-1	F09 2-0	M01 2-1	D26 2-1	M29 4-2	S22 1-1	a12 2-2	S12 2-0	A18 1-0	O06 1-1	S08 0-0	F23 2-0	N03 2-3	A29 5-2	M15 4-0	O20 1-1	J19 3-1	a26 0-1	D29 1-4		N17 3-2	D01 1-2
21 SWANSEA T	S22 2-1	F16 4-0	S08 5-1	O27 1-1	a14 0-2	D25 1-1	A30 7-1	M22 1-2	N10 0-2	J19 3-0	a19 4-1	O13 1-0	D15 0-3	M08 1-2	A25 1-1	D29 2-3	D08 5-0	F09 3-1	N24 1-2	a05 1-1		S13 2-1
22 WEST HAM U	S08 2-1	M08 0-1	A25 3-1	N10 1-0	A23 1-1	O13 1-1	S29 3-1	a05 3-3	N24 3-3	D29 2-0	S22 2-0	O27 2-3	D25 3-0	M22 3-1	a11 2-1	D15 4-2	F16 2-1	J19 5-1	D08 0-6	a19 4-0	S06 2-2	

Season 1951-52

DIVISION 3 NORTH

	ACCRINGTON S	BARROW	BRADFORD	BRADFORD C	CARLISLE U	CHESTER	CHESTERFIELD	CREWE A	DARLINGTON	GATESHEAD	GRIMSBY T	HALIFAX T	HARTLEPOOLS U	LINCOLN C	MANSFIELD T	OLDHAM A	ROCHDALE	SCUNTHORPE U	SOUTHPORT	STOCKPORT CO	TRANMERE R	WORKINGTON	WREXHAM	YORK C
1 ACCRINGTON S		S15 1-1	a30 5-1	O20 0-1	D22 0-2	N03 4-2	a11 2-0	a26 2-3	D26 1-3	A18 1-2	J26 0-3	S25 2-2	M01 0-0	M29 1-3	A22 1-0	O06 1-2	a02 0-0	N17 2-2	D01 0-0	S01 0-3	a12 1-1	J05 0-0	S29 4-2	M15 2-1
2 BARROW	J19 3-1		M27 0-2	N17 1-0	S22 0-1	D01 1-0	J12 2-0	M01 2-1	M15 2-2	O20 2-1	S13 3-1	A25 0-0	M29 2-1	a26 1-2	D29 1-1	N03 0-1	S08 4-0	F23 2-1	O06 0-0	F09 1-3	D26 2-0	a11 1-0	A23 3-1	a12 0-0
3 BRADFORD	F23 1-1	A18 3-1		J19 2-1	S17 0-1	O06 3-0	J05 3-3	M29 3-2	a12 2-0	N17 2-0	D22 3-2	S22 6-1	a26 1-2	M01 1-1	F09 0-1	D01 1-0	a15 1-1	O20 2-2	N03 2-2	A27 4-2	M15 2-3	F13 2-1	S01 5-0	D26 2-1
4 BRADFORD C	M08 1-3	a05 2-2	S15 2-2		O27 1-2	D29 1-0	D08 1-0	S12 0-2	a14 3-1	m03 1-1	a23 0-2	D25 3-2	J26 0-2	A25 1-1	F16 2-1	S29 5-2	O13 3-0	M26 1-0	A22 2-1	M22 2-3	J23 2-0	N10 1-0	a19 3-2	S08 3-3
5 CARLISLE U	A25 4-1	J26 0-1	S06 1-0	M15 1-0		M29 0-0	J01 2-3	D29 2-0	O06 1-1	D26 0-0	S29 1-2	A23 2-2	O20 2-1	N17 1-4	F02 0-0	M01 3-3	M06 1-1	a12 3-0	a26 0-2	J05 2-1	D01 1-0	S15 0-1	a11 2-0	N03 2-1
6 CHESTER	M22 3-1	a19 0-0	F16 4-2	S01 1-0	N10 4-2		D26 3-0	a14 2-0	a02 2-0	S29 0-3	D08 0-3	O13 5-1	J05 3-3	F02 0-1	M08 1-5	S15 1-2	O27 4-0	A22 3-1	F23 2-1	a05 0-0	S05 4-1	a23 2-2	A18 2-1	D22 0-1
7 CHESTERFIELD	a14 2-0	F02 2-0	S08 0-0	a26 2-2	F23 3-0	D25 2-0		N03 0-0	N17 4-2	M29 1-0	A18 3-1	J19 3-1	D01 2-2	O06 2-2	S22 1-1	a12 1-0	F09 5-1	M01 3-0	M15 2-0	S10 0-1	O20 1-1	A27 3-1	D22 3-0	D29 2-1
8 CREWE A	D08 3-3	O13 1-1	N10 3-4	S03 0-1	S01 1-1	a11 1-2	M22 2-1		A18 3-0	D22 4-2	M08 1-2	a05 4-1	A29 4-2	F09 0-2	a23 1-0	J12 3-1	a19 1-0	S22 2-2	S08 1-0	D26 1-0	J19 2-1	F16 2-0	O27 2-2	F23 0-0
9 DARLINGTON	D25 4-5	O27 1-2	m03 3-0	a11 3-1	F16 1-2	S22 1-1	a05 3-0	D15 0-1		F13 3-2	M22 0-2	a19 0-2	S19 2-1	J19 1-1	D08 2-1	S05 2-2	A22 2-1	S08 2-3	A25 1-1	O13 1-2	D29 2-2	M08 2-1	N10 2-1	F09 1-0
10 GATESHEAD	M26 1-0	M08 2-0	a05 0-1	F23 2-2	D25 1-1	F09 1-0	N10 1-1	A25 1-0	J23 2-2		O27 1-1	A27 3-0	S10 2-0	S22 3-1	a19 4-1	a02 1-0	D08 1-0	J19 2-1	D29 3-0	F16 0-2	S08 4-1	O13 4-1	M22 1-1	a14 1-1
11 GRIMSBY T	S22 2-1	S05 1-0	A25 3-0	a12 2-1	F09 4-1	a26 2-1	a30 2-0	O20 0-1	N03 3-0	M15 2-0		D29 8-1	N17 2-0	A22 2-3	S08 1-1	M29 3-1	J19 4-0	D25 3-2	M01 4-1	a11 4-0	O06 1-0	m03 5-0	F02 1-0	D01 0-0
12 HALIFAX T	S03 0-4	D22 0-1	M10 0-0	D26 1-1	S10 1-2	M01 4-1	S15 0-0	N17 2-3	D01 4-1	a12 0-1	S01 3-0		F09 2-0	O20 1-3	a14 1-0	a26 1-0	a28 1-0	M15 2-1	M29 0-1	M24 1-2	N03 1-0	A18 3-1	J05 2-0	O06 1-1
13 HARTLEPOOLS U	O13 4-2	N10 3-1	D08 2-1	S22 2-1	M08 1-0	S08 2-1	a19 4-1	A20 3-0	F23 2-0	S03 1-0	a05 2-1	S29 6-1		D29 1-1	D25 2-0	a14 1-1	F16 1-1	A25 3-1	J16 3-1	O27 0-1	a30 0-1	M22 0-1	J01 1-0	J19 3-2
14 LINCOLN C	N10 2-2	D08 3-0	O13 2-0	D22 2-1	a05 2-2	J23 4-1	F16 5-1	S29 11-1	S15 7-2	J26 1-0	A29 0-2	M08 4-1	S01 4-3		O27 1-2	J05 4-0	M22 2-0	S12 4-1	a14 4-0	a23 2-1	F23 3-0	a19 7-0	D26 3-2	A18 3-1
15 MANSFIELD T	A27 3-0	S01 2-1	S29 1-0	O06 2-1	J12 1-2	O20 3-1	J26 2-1	a12 2-1	a26 3-2	D01 2-3	J05 2-2	a15 4-2	D26 0-1	M15 1-0		F23 2-1	S17 1-1	N03 4-1	N17 4-0	A18 1-0	M29 3-0	D22 3-2	S15 3-0	M01 1-1
16 OLDHAM A	F16 3-1	M22 3-1	a19 1-2	F09 2-1	O13 2-0	J19 11-2	a22 3-0	F02 5-2	S11 3-2	A21 2-0	N10 1-1	D08 2-0	a11 5-2	S08 4-1	m03 5-3		D25 1-1	D29 2-0	a29 2-1	M08 1-0	A25 3-0	O27 0-1	a05 2-1	S22 2-0
17 ROCHDALE	J15 3-1	J05 4-1	a14 1-1	M01 1-1	A18 0-4	M15 0-5	S29 2-0	D01 1-0	A28 6-2	a26 0-3	S15 0-0	F23 0-2	O06 3-0	N03 0-1	S04 1-0	D26 2-2		M29 1-2	a12 1-0	D22 0-0	N17 3-2	S01 2-0	J26 1-5	O20 0-2
18 SCUNTHORPE U	a05 3-1	m01 0-0	M08 0-0	A18 1-0	a24 1-1	A30 2-2	O13 1-1	J26 2-0	J05 5-2	S15 1-1	D26 1-3	O27 2-1	D22 2-0	S06 1-3	M22 4-1	S01 2-2	N10 3-1		S29 1-1	a19 1-1	a14 2-0	D08 3-1	F16 0-0	J17 1-1
19 SOUTHPORT	a19 0-0	F16 2-2	M22 0-0	A28 1-1	D08 2-1	m03 1-0	O27 4-1	J05 1-1	D22 3-0	S01 0-2	O13 2-0	N10 3-2	F02 2-0	a11 0-3	a05 0-1	A18 0-0	a22 1-2	F09 5-1		S15 0-1	S22 1-0	D25 4-2	M08 2-1	S11 2-1
20 STOCKPORT CO	D29 6-0	S29 2-2	A20 1-0	N03 1-2	S08 1-1	N17 0-0	S03 2-1	D25 4-2	M01 5-0	O06 0-0	a14 1-1	J12 6-2	M15 0-1	a12 1-1	D15 2-1	O20 0-0	A25 1-0	D01 1-1	J19 3-1		a26 2-0	J26 5-0	F23 0-0	M29 3-1
21 TRANMERE R	a22 3-1	D25 3-1	O27 1-2	F06 3-1	a19 3-2	S11 3-1	M08 2-0	S15 1-0	S01 3-0	J05 5-1	F16 2-3	M22 1-2	A18 4-1	J01 2-2	N10 1-1	D22 0-4	a05 4-3	a11 3-1	J26 5-1	D08 2-0		S29 3-1	O13 3-1	A28 2-0
22 WORKINGTON	S08 0-2	a14 3-1	J24 2-3	M29 0-1	J19 1-2	a12 2-2	A22 3-1	O06 3-1	O20 2-1	M01 1-2	F23 2-4	J01 2-1	N03 1-1	D01 0-3	A25 0-1	M15 0-1	D29 1-1	a26 0-0	D26 6-1	S22 0-3	F09 1-2		S05 2-0	N17 1-0
23 WREXHAM	F09 1-0	A29 2-4	D29 3-2	D01 3-0	a14 3-1	S26 3-2	A25 0-3	M15 4-0	M29 1-1	N03 2-1	J12 2-0	S08 2-1	a12 0-0	D25 4-2	J19 3-1	N17 1-0	S22 2-0	O06 1-2	O20 3-0	a30 0-0	M01 0-1	S12 0-0		a26 1-1
24 YORK C	O27 6-1	a21 2-1	D25 1-0	J05 3-1	M22 0-0	A25 4-2	S01 1-0	m03 3-0	S29 2-1	a11 1-0	a19 1-1	F16 6-2	S15 3-1	M31 1-0	O13 3-0	J26 5-0	M08 1-1	a28 0-1	S03 0-2	N10 0-1	A20 1-1	a05 5-1	D08 4-2	

DIVISION 3 SOUTH

	ALDERSHOT	BOURNEMOUTH	BRIGHTON & HA	BRISTOL C	BRISTOL R	COLCHESTER U	CRYSTAL P	EXETER C	GILLINGHAM	IPSWICH T	LEYTON O	MILLWALL	NEWPORT CO	NORTHAMPTON T	NORWICH C	PLYMOUTH A	PORT VALE	READING	SHREWSBURY T	SOUTHEND U	SWINDON T	TORQUAY U	WALSALL	WATFORD
1 ALDERSHOT		O20 1-3	N03 0-2	D01 1-0	D29 1-3	S29 1-1	a30 3-0	J26 4-1	a16 2-1	a12 1-1	S05 0-1	M15 2-1	O06 4-0	A18 0-1	S15 2-0	J05 1-2	a26 4-1	D26 0-2	F23 1-1	M01 2-2	a11 4-0	N17 1-3	A29 3-1	D22 2-0
2 BOURNEMOUTH	M08 0-2		D29 3-1	A22 0-0	M22 1-0	a19 5-0	D08 1-2	a23 0-4	A25 3-3	F23 2-2	D25 3-2	S08 0-2	S29 5-1	a14 3-0	a05 1-2	N10 1-2	S05 0-1	J16 1-2	O13 2-0	J26 2-1	S15 4-1	J12 3-1	F16 2-1	O27 0-0
3 BRIGHTON & H.A.	M22 4-2	S01 0-1		a14 1-1	a05 1-1	A18 5-1	D26 4-3	D08 2-1	F23 0-0	S12 5-1	O13 3-1	D22 0-0	S15 1-2	S29 2-0	a19 2-0	a23 2-3	D15 2-1	J26 1-0	O27 1-0	J05 5-0	F16 4-0	A29 3-4	M08 5-1	N10 4-1
4 BRISTOL C	a19 1-1	A28 1-0	a11 4-1		S15 1-1	M08 2-0	O27 2-0	O13 1-1	J12 3-2	S22 0-2	N10 1-1	S11 2-1	A18 3-1	D29 2-0	F16 2-5	D26 1-1	J05 1-0	D22 1-3	a22 3-0	F06 6-0	M22 2-1	F09 2-2	a05 2-0	D08 1-3
5 BRISTOL R	S01 5-1	N03 1-2	N17 5-0	J19 2-0		a14 6-0	S03 4-0	m01 2-2	a12 5-0	a26 1-0	F27 1-0	M29 2-1	O20 1-1	O06 2-2	S29 1-1	J26 1-2	D25 4-1	M01 1-2	A25 3-3	M15 2-0	A20 1-0	D01 5-0	a28 5-1	S08 0-1
6 COLCHESTER U	F09 0-2	D01 1-1	m01 0-0	O20 4-1	a11 2-1		A25 1-2	F02 1-0	D26 1-0	M01 1-0	S08 0-1	a26 2-2	N17 2-1	N03 2-5	A23 1-1	S13 1-0	M15 0-0	a03 4-1	S22 2-2	a12 1-0	D29 2-0	O06 0-0	J19 3-2	m03 1-0
7 CRYSTAL P	J12 0-2	a26 2-2	D25 1-2	M15 2-1	S12 0-1	D22 2-2		A18 2-1	O06 0-2	O20 3-1	J19 2-1	D29 1-1	a12 1-1	m03 3-3	F23 2-0	A29 0-1	N03 3-1	N17 1-2	F09 1-1	D01 1-0	S08 0-1	M01 1-1	S22 2-1	a14 2-0
8 EXETER C	S22 0-4	a12 2-2	a26 2-0	M01 0-0	J16 0-1	F23 0-0	M26 0-1		A22 4-2	O06 2-1	D29 6-1	D01 0-3	M29 3-4	M15 0-3	S05 2-4	a14 1-0	O20 2-0	N03 1-4	J19 4-2	N17 2-2	A25 1-2	D25 4-0	S08 1-0	F09 3-0
9 GILLINGHAM	N10 3-3	D22 0-2	F02 2-3	m03 5-0	a23 2-1	D25 1-2	F16 4-4	A29 2-1		a11 1-1	M08 1-1	A18 1-1	J05 2-3	J26 2-1	D08 1-2	a19 1-2	S29 4-2	S15 1-1	M22 0-0	S01 2-0	O13 4-0	S12 3-0	O27 4-1	a05 1-0
10 IPSWICH T	a23 2-3	F02 3-1	S05 5-0	J26 1-1	D08 1-2	O13 0-2	M08 1-1	F16 2-4	a14 1-1		M22 1-0	A29 3-0	D22 3-1	J05 3-2	D25 0-2	S29 2-2	S15 2-0	S01 4-2	a05 1-0	A18 4-1	O27 1-5	J30 2-0	N10 0-1	a19 3-0
11 LEYTON O	S12 0-1	D26 1-0	M01 2-3	m01 2-0	F07 3-3	J05 7-0	S15 0-4	S01 3-0	O20 1-0	N03 2-0		O06 0-0	a26 1-1	a12 2-1	D22 3-3	A18 1-0	N17 2-0	D01 0-4	a14 4-1	F09 1-4	J26 1-0	M15 0-1	S19 3-0	A29 0-0
12 MILLWALL	O27 3-2	J05 3-1	A25 0-3	S19 3-2	N10 1-1	D08 1-1	S01 3-1	a19 4-0	M31 3-1	A22 4-0	F16 2-0		J26 2-0	a30 2-1	a23 2-1	a05 0-2	a11 1-1	S29 3-2	M08 0-0	S15 2-0	D26 0-0	F23 4-1	O13 2-1	M22 1-0
13 NEWPORT CO	F16 4-2	F09 2-0	J19 1-1	a28 1-0	M08 2-2	a05 0-1	a24 1-0	N10 4-0	S08 1-1	A25 2-1	a03 1-0	S22 2-1		A20 2-0	M22 2-2	O27 3-3	F23 1-1	S17 3-1	D25 3-1	J17 3-0	a19 0-0	D29 1-2	a11 4-2	O13 2-5
14 NORTHAMPTON T	J24 6-2	a15 5-3	F09 3-0	S01 1-2	F16 2-0	M22 2-0	N10 5-2	O27 3-1	S22 2-1	S08 1-0	a24 4-0	J12 1-1	S06 5-0		M08 1-2	O13 3-1	S27 3-1	F23 0-3	D08 6-0	S20 4-3	a05 1-0	J19 2-4	a19 4-1	D26 1-4
15 NORWICH C	J19 1-2	N17 2-0	D01 0-1	O06 1-0	F09 1-0	A29 5-2	F02 1-0	S12 1-1	a26 5-0	D26 2-0	A25 1-0	a12 1-0	N03 1-2	O20 2-1		a30 3-0	M01 2-3	M15 2-1	S08 3-2	a02 1-0	m03 2-0	a14 7-0	D29 8-0	S22 3-0
16 PLYMOUTH A	S08 2-1	M29 4-1	a12 2-2	D25 2-2	S22 1-2	S05 3-1	A22 5-0	J12 2-1	D01 4-2	F09 2-0	M19 3-0	N17 5-0	M15 5-0	M01 2-0	J16 3-1		O06 3-0	O20 3-2	D29 6-1	N03 2-0	F13 3-0	a26 2-2	A25 3-0	J19 3-1
17 PORT VALE	D08 4-1	S10 2-2	J12 1-1	S08 1-0	D26 1-1	O27 1-1	M22 2-0	M08 3-0	F09 1-0	J19 0-0	a05 3-0	m01 2-1	M24 4-2	D22 0-0	O13 0-0	F16 1-0		A18 0-2	a19 1-0	A27 0-0	N10 2-2	S22 2-2	a21 1-0	S01 1-1
18 READING	D25 5-1	m03 5-0	S22 1-4	A25 3-0	O13 4-2	N10 4-2	a05 3-1	M22 2-1	J19 2-1	D29 4-0	a19 1-1	F09 2-0	S12 1-2	F02 2-0	O27 1-1	M08 2-0	F20 5-1		A22 6-2	a14 5-2	a23 2-0	S08 6-1	D08 3-0	F16 4-1
19 SHREWSBURY T	F02 5-1	M01 2-0	M15 1-1	a12 2-0	D22 2-1	J26 1-0	S29 2-1	S15 2-1	N03 2-2	N17 0-2	S24 3-0	O20 0-1	D26 1-4	a26 3-1	J05 0-2	S01 1-3	D01 2-0	A27 2-1		O06 0-1	J24 0-1	M29 1-1	S03 1-2	A18 2-3
20 SOUTHEND U	O13 7-1	S22 1-0	S08 2-0	F27 5-1	O27 2-1	a22 3-2	a19 4-0	a05 0-0	D29 3-1	a29 5-0	S29 1-0	J19 0-1	m03 2-1	S11 2-0	N10 2-1	M22 1-1	A21 0-0	a11 2-0	F16 2-2		D08 2-2	A25 2-2	D26 3-0	M08 5-1
21 SWINDON T	a14 1-1	J19 2-0	O06 0-2	N03 0-0	A29 0-0	S01 2-1	J05 0-2	D22 3-1	M01 2-1	M15 1-2	S22 2-0	D25 2-2	D01 1-1	N17 1-1	A18 1-1	F27 2-2	a28 2-0	a12 2-0	a30 1-2	a26 1-0		O20 2-1	F09 1-1	S12 0-1
22 TORQUAY U	a05 6-1	A18 2-2	A22 0-1	S29 1-2	a19 4-2	F16 3-1	O13 1-5	D26 5-1	S05 2-1	m03 2-0	O27 1-1	F02 2-5	S01 1-2	S15 1-2	S19 1-2	D08 3-2	J26 2-3	J05 0-3	N10 3-2	D22 1-3	M08 9-0		M22 1-1	a23 2-0
23 WALSALL	A23 1-0	O06 2-2	O20 1-1	N17 2-0	A18 1-0	S15 1-3	J26 3-0	J05 1-2	M15 1-0	M29 1-3	J24 2-4	M01 1-2	a14 0-1	D01 3-0	S01 4-0	D22 2-5	a12 3-0	a26 2-0	S13 0-4	D25 2-0	S29 0-0	N03 2-3		F02 3-1
24 WATFORD	A25 2-2	M15 1-2	a03 3-1	a26 3-1	J05 0-3	J16 0-1	a11 2-0	S29 1-1	N17 2-2	D01 1-1	A23 0-1	N03 1-2	M01 1-1	D25 2-4	J26 1-1	S15 1-3	D29 2-0	O06 3-1	J12 4-1	O20 0-0	S06 1-7	a12 1-2	F23 2-0	

LEAGUE TABLES

DIVISION 1

	P	W	D	L	F	A	W	D	L	F	A	Pts
Manchester U	42	15	3	3	55	21	8	8	5	40	31	57
Tottenham H	42	16	1	4	45	20	6	8	7	31	31	53
Arsenal	42	13	7	1	54	30	8	4	9	26	31	53
Portsmouth	42	13	3	5	42	25	7	5	9	26	33	48
Bolton W	42	11	7	3	35	26	8	3	10	30	35	48
Aston Villa	42	13	3	5	49	28	6	6	9	30	42	47
Preston N.E.	42	10	5	6	39	22	7	7	7	35	32	46
Newcastle U	42	12	4	5	62	28	6	5	10	36	45	45
Blackpool	42	12	5	4	40	27	6	4	11	24	37	45
Charlton A	42	12	5	4	41	24	5	5	11	27	39	44
Liverpool	42	6	11	4	31	25	6	8	7	26	36	43
Sunderland	42	8	6	7	41	28	7	6	8	29	33	42
W.B.A.	42	8	9	4	38	29	6	4	11	36	48	41
Burnley	42	9	6	6	32	19	6	4	11	24	44	40
Manchester C	42	7	5	9	29	28	6	8	7	29	33	39
Wolverh'pton W	42	8	6	7	40	33	4	8	9	33	40	38
Derby Co	42	10	4	7	43	37	5	3	13	20	43	37
Middlesbrough	42	12	4	5	37	25	3	2	16	27	63	36
Chelsea	42	10	3	8	31	29	4	5	12	21	43	36
Stoke C	42	8	6	7	34	32	4	1	16	15	56	31
Huddersfield T	42	9	3	9	32	35	1	5	15	17	47	28
Fulham	42	5	7	9	38	31	3	4	14	20	46	27

DIVISION 2

	P	W	D	L	F	A	W	D	L	F	A	Pts
Sheffield W	42	14	4	3	54	23	7	7	7	46	43	53
Cardiff C	42	18	2	1	52	15	2	9	10	20	39	51
Birmingham C	42	11	6	4	36	21	10	3	8	31	35	51
Nottingham F	42	12	6	3	41	22	6	7	8	36	40	49
Leicester C	42	12	6	3	48	24	7	3	11	30	40	47
Leeds U	42	13	7	1	35	15	5	4	12	24	42	47
Everton	42	12	5	4	42	25	5	5	11	22	33	44
Luton T	42	9	7	5	46	35	7	5	9	31	43	44
Rotherham U	42	11	4	6	40	25	6	4	11	33	46	42
Brentford	42	11	7	3	34	20	4	5	12	20	35	42
Sheffield U	42	13	2	6	57	28	5	3	13	33	48	41
West Ham U	42	13	5	3	48	29	2	6	13	19	48	41
Southampton	42	11	6	4	40	25	4	5	12	21	48	41
Blackburn R	42	11	3	7	35	30	6	3	12	19	33	40
Notts Co	42	11	5	5	45	27	5	2	14	26	41	39
Doncaster R	42	9	4	8	29	28	4	8	9	26	32	38
Bury	42	13	2	6	43	22	2	5	14	24	47	37
Hull C	42	11	5	5	44	23	2	6	13	16	47	37
Swansea T	42	10	4	7	45	26	2	8	11	27	50	36
Barnsley	42	8	7	6	39	33	3	7	11	20	39	36
Coventry C	42	9	5	7	36	33	5	1	15	23	49	34
Q.P.R.	42	8	8	5	35	35	3	4	14	17	46	34

DIVISION 3 NORTH

	P	W	D	L	F	A	W	D	L	F	A	Pts
Lincoln C	46	19	2	2	80	23	11	7	5	41	29	69
Grimsby T	46	19	2	2	59	14	10	6	7	37	31	66
Stockport Co	46	12	9	2	47	17	11	4	8	27	23	59
Oldham A	46	19	2	2	65	22	5	7	11	25	39	57
Gateshead	46	14	7	2	41	17	7	4	12	25	32	53
Mansfield T	46	17	3	3	50	23	5	5	13	23	37	52
Carlisle U	46	10	7	6	31	24	9	6	8	31	33	51
Bradford P.A.	46	13	6	4	51	28	6	6	11	23	36	50
Hartlepool U	46	17	3	3	47	19	4	5	14	24	46	50
York C	46	16	4	3	53	19	2	9	12	20	33	49
Tranmere R	46	17	2	4	59	29	4	4	15	17	42	48
Barrow	46	13	5	5	33	19	4	7	12	24	42	46
Chesterfield	46	15	7	1	47	16	2	4	17	18	50	45
Scunthorpe U	46	10	11	2	39	23	4	5	14	26	51	44
Bradford C	46	12	5	6	40	32	4	5	14	21	36	42
Crewe A	46	12	6	5	42	28	5	2	16	21	54	42
Southport	46	12	6	5	36	22	3	5	15	17	49	41
Wrexham	46	14	5	4	41	22	1	4	18	22	51	39
Chester C	46	13	4	6	46	30	2	5	16	26	55	39
Halifax T	46	11	4	8	31	23	3	3	17	30	74	35
Rochdale	46	10	5	8	32	34	1	8	14	15	45	35
Accrington S	46	6	8	9	30	34	4	4	15	31	58	32
Darlington	46	10	5	8	39	34	1	4	18	25	69	31
Workington	46	8	4	11	33	34	3	3	17	17	57	29

DIVISION 3 SOUTH

	P	W	D	L	F	A	W	D	L	F	A	Pts
Plymouth A	46	19	3	1	70	19	10	5	8	37	34	66
Reading	46	19	2	2	73	23	10	1	12	39	37	61
Norwich C	46	18	1	4	55	15	8	8	7	34	35	61
Millwall	46	16	5	2	46	21	7	7	9	28	32	58
Brighton & H.A.	46	15	4	4	57	24	9	6	8	30	39	58
Newport Co	46	13	7	3	45	26	8	5	10	32	50	54
Bristol R	46	14	5	4	60	20	6	7	10	29	33	52
Northampton T	46	17	1	5	65	31	5	4	14	28	43	49
Southend U	46	16	6	1	56	17	3	4	16	19	49	48
Colchester U	46	12	7	4	32	22	5	5	13	24	55	46
Torquay U	46	10	3	10	53	42	7	7	9	33	56	44
Aldershot	46	11	4	8	40	27	7	4	12	38	62	44
Port Vale	46	11	11	1	33	16	3	4	16	17	50	43
Bournemouth	46	11	4	8	42	30	5	6	12	27	45	42
Bristol C	46	13	6	4	44	26	2	6	15	14	43	42
Swindon T	46	9	9	5	29	22	5	5	13	22	46	42
Ipswich T	46	12	4	7	45	31	4	5	14	18	43	41
Leyton O	46	12	5	6	39	26	4	4	15	16	42	41
Crystal Palace	46	9	7	7	32	28	6	2	15	29	52	39
Shrewsbury T	46	11	3	9	35	29	2	7	14	27	57	36
Watford	46	7	7	9	34	37	6	3	14	23	44	36
Gillingham	46	10	7	6	47	31	1	6	16	24	50	35
Exeter C	46	10	4	9	40	36	3	5	15	25	50	35
Walsall	46	11	3	9	38	31	2	2	19	17	63	31

Football League Records

Top scorers: Div 1, C.Wayman (Preston North End) 24 goals; Div 2, A.Rowley (Leicester City) 39 goals; Div 3, N.J.Whitehouse (Carlisle United) 29 goals; Div 3 S, G.Bradford (Bristol Rovers) 33 goals.

Port Vale transferred to Division Three North.

Peter Goring, who won an FA Cup winners' medal in 1950, was an important member of the Arsenal side which won the title in 1952-53, scoring ten goals.

DIVISION 1

	ARSENAL	ASTON VILLA	BLACKPOOL	BOLTON W	BURNLEY	CARDIFF C	CHARLTON A	CHELSEA	DERBY CO	LIVERPOOL	MANCHESTER C	MANCHESTER U	MIDDLESBROUGH	NEWCASTLE U	PORTSMOUTH	PRESTON N.E.	SHEFFIELD W	STOKE C	SUNDERLAND	TOTTENHAM H	W.B.A.	WOLVERHAMPTON W
1 ARSENAL		D20 3-1	O04 3-1	a15 4-1	m01 3-2	M07 0-1	S13 3-4	a06 2-0	F18 6-2	a04 5-3	N22 3-1	A27 2-1	N08 2-1	O25 3-0	S10 3-1	M19 1-1	O11 2-2	a18 3-1	A30 1-2	F07 4-0	M21 2-2	J17 5-3
2 ASTON VILLA	A23 1-2		S06 1-5	O04 1-1	a04 2-0	a29 2-0	D26 1-1	J24 1-1	J03 3-0	M07 4-0	O25 0-0	S20 3-3	O11 1-0	m01 0-1	F18 6-0	N08 1-0	a18 4-3	M25 1-1	S01 3-0	N22 0-3	a07 1-1	S15 0-1
3 BLACKPOOL	F21 3-2	J17 1-1		A30 3-0	O11 4-2	M25 0-1	S27 8-4	S15 3-1	a03 2-1	a18 3-1	D06 4-1	D25 0-0	N22 1-1	N08 0-2	D20 3-2	A25 1-1	O25 0-1	a15 1-1	S13 2-0	M07 2-0	a04 2-0	F07 2-0
4 BOLTON W	D25 4-6	F21 0-0	J03 4-0		N08 1-2	a18 0-1	J01 1-2	S06 1-1	A23 2-0	O11 2-2	M07 1-0	J24 2-1	F18 5-3	D06 4-2	S20 0-5	M25 0-3	N22 1-1	O25 2-1	a03 5-0	a04 2-3	a22 0-1	S01 2-1
5 BURNLEY	D13 1-1	N15 1-0	M03 0-1	M28 0-1		J24 0-0	a25 2-0	O18 1-1	O04 1-2	D25 2-0	S08 2-1	M14 2-1	A23 0-1	S06 2-1	N01 3-2	a03 2-2	S20 1-1	A26 3-2	a11 5-1	F17 3-2	J03 5-0	N29 0-0
6 CARDIFF C	a22 0-0	a25 1-2	N01 2-2	M11 1-0	S13 0-0		F28 0-1	M28 3-3	M14 2-0	a06 4-0	F21 6-0	N15 1-2	S03 1-1	D27 0-0	a11 0-1	F07 0-2	A30 4-0	S27 2-0	D13 4-1	J17 0-0	S17 1-2	D20 0-0
7 CHARLTON A	J24 2-2	M18 5-1	F23 2-0	S10 2-0	a22 0-0	O11 3-1		O04 2-2	S20 3-1	N08 3-2	a04 1-2	a03 2-2	M21 2-0	M07 0-0	A27 2-2	a18 2-1	J17 3-0	N22 5-1	D20 3-1	a30 3-2	O25 0-0	A30 2-2
8 CHELSEA	a03 1-1	S13 4-0	S10 4-0	J17 1-0	M07 0-2	N08 0-2	F21 0-1		A27 1-1	M23 3-0	a29 3-1	D20 2-3	a18 1-1	a04 1-2	A30 2-0	O11 5-3	M21 1-0	D27 0-0	F07 3-2	O25 2-1	N22 0-2	S27 1-2
9 DERBY CO	S27 2-0	A30 0-1	a06 1-1	D20 4-3	F21 1-3	O25 1-1	F07 1-1	S03 3-2		N22 3-2	a18 5-0	S10 2-3	a04 3-3	M21 0-2	D26 3-0	a29 0-1	M07 2-1	D06 4-0	J17 3-1	O11 0-0	N08 1-1	S13 2-3
10 LIVERPOOL	N15 1-5	O18 0-2	N29 2-2	M04 0-0	D26 1-1	a03 2-1	M28 1-2	a25 2-0	a11 1-1		J17 0-1	D13 1-2	S20 4-1	O04 5-3	S13 1-1	D20 2-2	A27 1-0	A30 3-2	M14 2-0	S10 2-1	F14 3-0	N01 2-1
11 MANCHESTER C	a11 2-4	M14 4-1	a25 5-0	O18 1-2	S17 0-0	O04 2-2	N15 5-1	D13 4-0	N29 1-0	S06 0-2		A30 2-1	J24 5-1	F14 2-1	F28 2-1	a22 0-2	a03 3-1	D20 2-1	N01 2-5	A27 0-1	S20 0-1	M28 3-1
12 MANCHESTER U	S03 0-0	F07 3-1	D26 2-1	S13 1-0	O25 1-3	a04 1-4	a06 3-2	A23 2-0	J01 1-0	a20 3-1	J03 1-1		D06 3-2	N22 2-2	J17 1-0	M07 5-2	N08 1-1	O11 0-2	S27 0-1	M25 3-2	a18 2-2	F21 0-3
13 MIDDLESBROUGH	M28 2-0	M04 1-0	a11 5-1	S27 1-2	D20 2-2	A27 3-0	N01 1-0	N29 4-0	N15 1-0	F07 2-3	S13 5-4	a25 5-0		a06 2-1	D13 3-2	A30 1-1	J01 2-2	J17 0-0	O18 1-2	D27 0-4	O04 4-2	M14 1-1
14 NEWCASTLE U	M14 2-2	D13 2-1	M28 0-1	a25 2-3	J17 0-0	D25 3-0	O18 3-2	N15 2-1	N01 1-0	F21 1-2	S27 2-0	a11 1-2	a03 1-0		N29 1-0	S13 4-3	D20 1-5	F07 1-2	S10 2-2	A30 1-1	J01 3-5	F28 1-1
15 PORTSMOUTH	S17 2-2	S27 1-1	A23 0-2	F07 3-1	M21 2-1	N22 0-2	S03 1-1	J03 2-0	D27 2-2	J24 3-1	O11 2-1	S06 2-0	m02 1-4	a18 5-1		O25 2-5	a04 5-2	M07 1-1	F21 5-2	N08 2-1	D06 1-2	a03 2-2
16 PRESTON N.E.	a25 2-0	M28 1-3	J01 4-2	N01 2-2	a06 2-1	S20 2-3	N29 2-1	F28 2-1	D13 3-0	A23 1-1	D26 6-2	O18 0-5	J03 3-0	J24 2-1	M14 4-0		F14 1-0	S10 3-0	N15 3-2	O04 1-0	S06 1-0	a11 1-1
17 SHEFFIELD W	M02 1-4	N29 2-2	M14 2-0	a11 1-1	F07 2-4	J03 2-0	S06 0-3	N01 1-0	O18 2-0	S03 0-2	a06 1-1	M28 0-0	S17 2-0	A23 2-2	N15 3-4	S27 1-1		F21 1-0	a25 4-0	S13 2-0	D26 4-5	D13 2-3
18 STOKE C	N29 1-1	N01 1-4	D13 4-0	M14 1-2	S01 1-3	F14 0-0	a11 1-0	D26 1-1	a25 1-2	J03 3-1	A23 2-1	F28 3-1	S06 1-0	S20 1-0	O18 2-4	S15 0-0	O04 1-3		M28 3-0	a06 2-0	J24 5-1	N15 1-2
19 SUNDERLAND	J03 3-1	J01 2-2	J24 1-1	a06 2-0	N22 2-1	a27 4-2	A23 2-1	S20 2-1	S06 2-1	O25 3-1	M21 3-3	F18 2-2	M07 1-1	S17 0-2	O04 1-1	a04 2-2	D06 2-1	N08 1-1		a18 1-1	O11 1-0	D27 5-2
20 TOTTENHAM H	S20 1-3	a11 1-1	O18 4-0	N15 1-1	S27 2-1	S06 2-1	D13 2-0	M14 2-3	M12 5-2	S15 3-1	S01 3-3	N01 1-2	D25 7-1	J03 3-2	M28 3-3	F21 4-4	J24 2-1	a03 1-0	N29 2-2		A23 3-4	a25 3-2
21 W.B.A.	N01 2-0	a06 3-2	N15 0-1	D13 0-1	A30 1-2	S10 1-0	M14 3-1	a11 0-1	M28 2-2	S27 3-0	F07 2-1	N29 3-1	F21 3-0	A27 1-0	a25 2-0	J17 2-1	D27 0-1	S13 3-2	F28 1-1	D20 2-1		O18 1-1
22 WOLVERHAMPTON W	S06 1-1	S08 2-1	S20 2-5	A25 3-1	a18 5-1	A23 1-0	J03 1-2	F18 2-2	J24 3-1	M21 3-0	N08 7-3	O04 6-2	O25 3-3	O11 2-0	a06 4-1	N22 0-2	J31 3-1	a04 3-0	D26 1-1	D06 0-0	M07 2-0	

Geoff Bradford, whose 33 goals in 1952-53 helped Bristol Rovers win promotion from Division Three South.

DIVISION 2

	BARNSLEY	BIRMINGHAM C	BLACKBURN R	BRENTFORD	BURY	DONCASTER R	EVERTON	FULHAM	HUDDERSFIELD T	HULL C	LEEDS U	LEICESTER C	LINCOLN C	LUTON T	NOTTINGHAM F	NOTTS CO	PLYMOUTH A	ROTHERHAM U	SHEFFIELD U	SOUTHAMPTON	SWANSEA T	WEST HAM U
1 BARNSLEY		M21 1-3	a06 1-4	D26 0-2	N08 3-2	D20 2-2	S10 2-3	a29 1-1	J17 2-4	O04 5-1	M07 2-2	a18 0-3	F14 1-1	O25 2-3	A27 0-2	N22 1-2	O11 0-3	F07 2-3	S13 1-3	a04 0-1	A30 3-1	D06 2-0
2 BIRMINGHAM C	N01 3-1		a11 1-2	D13 3-1	F21 0-2	a06 2-1	a25 4-2	A30 1-4	O18 0-2	N15 4-3	S17 2-2	S13 3-1	M28 2-2	S03 2-2	N29 0-5	F07 3-2	D25 4-0	D20 4-0	M14 1-2	S27 2-0	M11 1-4	J17 2-0
3 BLACKBURN R	a03 2-0	N22 1-2		J17 3-0	a18 4-0	S13 2-1	A30 3-1	M07 2-2	S27 1-1	S08 2-0	N08 1-1	D25 2-0	S01 0-2	a04 1-1	D20 2-1	J01 3-2	M21 1-3	O25 0-1	F21 1-2	D06 3-0	F07 3-0	O11 3-0
4 BRENTFORD	D25 4-0	m01 1-2	S06 3-2		F14 2-2	F21 1-0	S20 2-4	N08 2-2	S03 1-3	J03 1-0	a18 3-3	O25 4-2	A23 1-0	a22 1-1	J24 1-1	M07 5-0	N22 1-2	a04 1-1	S17 0-0	O11 3-0	a03 0-0	M21 1-4
5 BURY	M28 5-2	O04 3-0	N29 1-0	S27 3-0		F28 2-1	D13 0-5	D20 1-1	M14 1-1	a11 2-1	A27 2-2	J17 1-4	N15 2-2	a03 1-0	a25 2-0	S13 0-1	J01 3-2	D27 2-0	N01 0-4	F07 0-0	O18 1-3	A30 1-1
6 DONCASTER R	A23 1-1	a03 1-0	J24 3-3	O04 0-2	O11 1-1		F18 3-0	J31 0-0	S09 1-1	S06 3-1	D06 0-0	M21 0-0	J03 2-0	a30 1-0	S20 1-0	a22 2-0	a18 1-1	N22 2-1	D26 0-2	M07 1-0	A27 2-3	N08 1-1
7 EVERTON	J01 2-1	D06 1-1	J03 0-3	F07 5-0	a15 3-0	S27 7-1		M25 3-3	a06 2-1	A23 0-2	N22 2-2	M07 2-2	a22 0-3	a18 1-1	S06 3-0	O11 1-0	a04 2-0	N08 0-1	S03 0-0	J24 2-2	F21 0-0	O25 2-0
8 FULHAM	D13 3-1	J03 3-1	O18 2-1	M28 5-0	A23 2-0	N15 1-3	N01 3-0		N29 0-2	F28 2-1	J24 2-1	S03 4-6	O04 4-2	S06 2-0	M14 0-1	S17 6-0	S20 2-1	F18 4-1	a25 1-2	D26 1-1	a11 3-1	a06 2-3
9 HUDDERSFIELD T	S06 6-0	M07 1-1	F14 0-3	A27 0-0	O25 2-0	S17 3-1	a07 8-2	a18 4-2		S20 1-1	A23 1-0	a04 1-0	J24 5-0	O11 3-0	O04 1-2	N08 1-0	m01 4-0	D06 1-0	J03 1-1	M21 5-0	D25 3-0	N22 0-1
10 HULL C	F21 2-2	a04 2-0	S15 3-0	A30 2-2	N22 0-2	J17 1-1	D20 1-0	O11 3-1	F07 0-2		M21 1-0	a16 1-1	a06 1-1	N08 0-2	D27 3-1	D06 6-0	O25 0-1	M07 3-2	S27 4-0	a18 1-0	S13 1-1	A25 1-0
11 LEEDS U	O18 4-1	S10 0-1	M28 0-3	N29 3-2	S03 2-0	a25 1-1	a11 2-0	S13 2-0	D20 2-1	N01 3-1		S27 0-1	M14 2-1	D27 2-2	a22 2-1	F21 3-1	A30 1-1	J17 4-0	F28 0-3	S24 1-1	D13 5-1	F07 3-2
12 LEICESTER C	N29 2-2	J24 3-4	D27 2-1	M14 2-3	S06 3-2	N01 4-2	O18 4-2	A25 6-1	N15 2-1	D13 5-0	F14 3-3		a25 3-2	S20 1-1	F28 1-1	A23 3-0	O04 2-0	a07 3-2	a11 0-0	J03 4-1	M28 2-1	S08 0-0
13 LINCOLN C	S27 1-1	N08 1-1	A27 4-1	D20 0-0	a04 4-0	A30 2-0	D26 1-1	F21 2-2	S13 2-2	a03 2-1	O25 1-1	D06 3-2		M21 1-2	S10 2-3	a18 3-0	M07 0-0	O11 1-3	F07 3-2	N22 2-2	J17 3-1	m01 3-1
14 LUTON T	M14 6-0	A27 0-1	N15 6-0	a25 0-1	a06 4-1	D13 1-2	N29 4-2	J17 2-0	F28 0-2	M28 3-2	D26 2-0	F07 2-0	N01 4-0		a11 3-0	S27 5-1	D20 1-0	A30 2-1	O18 4-1	F21 1-2	S10 3-1	S13 0-0
15 NOTTINGHAM F	S03 3-0	a18 0-2	A23 1-2	S13 3-0	D06 4-1	F07 2-2	J17 3-3	O25 0-1	F21 1-0	D26 4-1	a04 2-1	O11 1-3	S17 1-1	N22 4-3		J03 1-0	N08 3-1	M21 4-3	a06 1-1	a29 2-3	S27 6-4	M07 0-0
16 NOTTS CO	a11 1-0	S20 2-0	D13 5-0	O18 4-0	J24 2-1	M14 4-3	M05 2-2	S11 1-1	M28 1-0	a25 2-0	O04 3-2	D20 2-2	N29 1-1	F19 1-2	A30 3-2		a03 0-4	A28 2-1	N15 0-3	S06 1-2	N01 3-4	D27 1-1
17 PLYMOUTH A	F28 4-0	D27 2-1	N01 3-1	a11 1-0	S17 0-0	N29 0-0	N15 1-0	F07 3-1	D13 0-2	M14 1-2	J03 0-1	F21 2-1	O18 0-0	A23 2-1	M28 0-3	a06 2-2		S13 4-3	S06 5-2	S03 3-1	a25 3-2	S27 1-1
18 ROTHERHAM U	S20 3-1	A23 1-1	M14 0-0	N15 4-1	D26 6-1	a11 4-2	M28 2-2	S27 1-0	a25 0-0	O18 2-1	S06 3-1	a06 0-0	F28 3-2	J03 1-3	N01 2-3	S01 2-3	J24 2-3		D13 0-2	S15 2-2	N29 2-1	F21 1-1
19 SHEFFIELD U	J24 3-0	O25 2-2	O04 3-0	S08 3-2	M21 3-1	D25 2-2	A25 1-0	D06 2-1	A30 0-2	a29 0-2	O11 2-1	N22 7-2	S20 6-1	M07 1-1	S22 2-0	a04 2-1	J17 5-0	J01 1-4		N08 5-3	D20 7-1	a18 3-1
20 SOUTHAMPTON	N15 1-2	a15 1-1	a25 6-1	F28 0-2	S20 1-2	O18 3-3	S13 1-1	D27 5-3	N01 0-2	N29 5-1	a06 2-2	A30 5-2	a11 1-0	O04 1-3	D13 2-2	J17 1-1	A27 2-3	S10 2-3	M28 4-4		M14 1-4	D20 1-2
21 SWANSEA T	J03 3-0	O11 1-1	S20 1-1	a06 3-2	M07 2-0	S04 2-1	O04 2-2	N22 1-1	D27 3-3	J24 3-0	a16 3-2	N08 1-1	S06 1-1	S18 4-2	F14 2-1	M21 5-1	D06 2-2	a18 0-0	A23 1-2	O25 1-2		a04 4-1
22 WEST HAM U	a25 3-1	S06 1-2	F28 0-0	N01 3-1	J03 3-2	M28 1-3	M14 3-1	a03 1-2	a11 0-1	S01 0-0	S20 2-2	S15 4-1	D13 5-1	J24 0-1	O18 3-2	D25 2-2	F18 0-1	O04 2-4	N29 1-1	A23 1-0	N15 3-0	

SEASON 1952-53

DIVISION 3 NORTH

	ACCRINGTON S	BARROW	BRADFORD	BRADFORD C	CARLISLE U	CHESTER	CHESTERFIELD	CREWE A	DARLINGTON	GATESHEAD	GRIMSBY T	HALIFAX T	HARTLEPOOLS U	MANSFIELD T	OLDHAM A	PORT VALE	ROCHDALE	SCUNTHORPE U	SOUTHPORT	STOCKPORT CO	TRANMERE R	WORKINGTON	WREXHAM	YORK C
1 ACCRINGTON S		F21 1-0	J01 3-2	a11 1-1	A27 1-0	N01 1-1	J17 1-1	O18 1-1	a25 1-0	D13 1-1	S27 1-2	S10 1-1	D20 1-1	J31 2-2	a06 0-2	M14 1-1	N29 2-1	M28 2-1	F28 1-2	N15 1-4	S13 0-2	A30 0-1	D27 1-2	F07 1-0
2 BARROW	O04 2-0		S06 2-0	F28 5-1	N15 0-0	D13 3-0	J01 2-1	N29 1-2	M14 2-2	N01 2-2	S08 1-1	F19 5-1	M28 2-1	S20 3-0	J24 4-3	a25 1-2	O18 2-1	A23 2-1	a11 1-1	A25 1-0	a06 2-0	D26 3-0	J03 1-1	J31 1-0
3 BRADFORD	a22 4-0	J17 1-0		S20 2-2	N01 2-2	N29 1-0	J31 0-1	N15 1-0	F28 3-0	O18 3-0	A30 0-3	D26 1-2	M14 1-1	O04 1-1	M11 0-0	a11 2-2	A25 2-1	a25 1-1	M28 1-0	D13 1-1	S10 1-0	a06 6-1	S13 1-2	D20 2-3
4 BRADFORD C	S24 3-2	O11 2-2	F07 2-1		a07 7-2	J03 2-2	N08 2-1	S17 1-3	F21 4-3	D25 3-1	M07 1-0	a18 5-0	O01 1-1	a20 2-1	a29 0-0	A23 1-0	S27 0-3	S06 0-0	J10 2-2	J24 3-0	M21 5-3	a04 4-0	S03 3-1	O25 1-1
5 CARLISLE U	S04 4-4	a04 0-0	M21 1-3	a03 4-4		O04 1-1	a30 3-0	S20 1-2	S11 4-2	D20 2-2	S25 3-0	O11 1-2	A30 4-1	M07 1-0	O25 0-0	F14 2-0	J10 5-0	D25 8-0	J24 2-0	J01 2-1	M12 4-0	D06 3-1	N08 1-0	a18 1-1
6 CHESTER	M21 2-0	a29 2-1	a18 0-3	A30 2-0	F21 1-2		M07 2-0	a22 2-2	S13 6-3	F07 2-0	J31 0-2	N08 2-1	S27 0-1	a04 2-2	S24 0-1	a06 2-2	D06 3-0	S17 1-1	M25 0-0	D20 4-0	O11 3-2	O25 1-1	a15 1-2	A27 1-1
7 CHESTERFIELD	S06 3-0	O01 1-1	J10 1-1	M28 1-1	D13 4-2	O18 2-1		A27 1-0	a11 3-0	N29 1-1	D27 3-2	J03 2-1	a25 2-0	A23 4-1	S15 1-2	F28 1-0	N15 1-0	M14 1-1	S20 1-2	N01 2-1	S27 1-2	J24 1-1	a06 2-1	F21 1-2
8 CREWE A	M07 3-2	a18 1-1	a04 2-3	S10 1-1	F07 2-2	S29 4-1	S01 2-1		A30 0-1	J17 4-3	a29 1-2	O25 1-1	S13 2-0	M21 1-0	N08 0-1	D26 1-4	D20 4-2	a03 2-0	S27 2-0	J14 2-0	F21 1-0	O11 4-0	S24 3-3	D06 3-0
9 DARLINGTON	M25 1-0	O25 1-0	O11 1-3	O04 4-1	S17 0-0	J24 3-2	S24 3-1	J03 1-1		a03 1-0	M21 1-1	a29 0-2	J31 3-0	J01 2-1	S03 0-5	S06 0-2	D26 3-2	S20 1-0	A23 3-1	a20 1-0	a04 1-2	a18 1-0	M07 2-2	N08 0-1
10 GATESHEAD	a29 5-0	M21 3-1	M07 3-2	D27 2-2	A23 2-0	S20 4-1	a18 2-4	S06 6-1	a06 5-1		N08 2-0	F04 3-1	S08 1-1	S01 1-2	O11 1-0	J24 1-1	J01 3-1	F18 1-1	J03 1-2	O04 2-0	S22 0-1	a15 1-1	O25 1-0	a04 1-1
11 GRIMSBY T	F14 3-0	S17 2-1	J03 2-3	O18 0-0	a11 2-3	J13 5-4	D25 0-0	a25 1-0	N01 2-0	M28 0-0		S20 2-0	N15 7-0	J24 5-1	S06 1-1	D13 1-1	M14 3-2	S03 1-0	N29 1-0	F28 0-1	O01 3-1	O04 2-0	A23 2-0	a03 2-1
12 HALIFAX T	S15 3-0	S27 1-0	D27 2-4	N29 1-1	F28 2-1	M28 3-1	A30 3-1	M14 1-3	D13 3-2	J12 1-3	F07 3-2		A25 3-2	a06 1-2	S29 2-2	N01 1-2	a25 3-1	N15 2-1	O18 4-1	a11 3-0	J17 0-0	D20 5-2	F21 0-0	S13 0-0
13 HARTLEPOOLS U	A23 4-1	N08 2-0	O25 0-1	J01 0-0	J03 1-0	F14 2-2	a20 2-0	J24 2-1	J10 1-0	S15 0-0	a04 2-0	S01 0-0		O11 2-0	M07 4-1	S20 2-0	a03 2-1	O04 1-1	S06 3-0	D27 0-2	a18 4-1	a29 2-2	M21 1-2	S22 2-1
14 MANSFIELD T	a13 0-0	F07 2-2	F21 1-1	a25 3-1	O18 2-1	N15 2-2	D20 1-4	N01 3-0	S29 3-2	A25 2-0	S13 1-1	a07 2-1	F28 2-0		D27 0-2	M28 1-0	D13 2-1	a11 1-0	M14 2-2	N29 2-2	A30 1-0	S08 0-0	S27 0-2	J17 1-1
15 OLDHAM A	a03 3-0	S13 3-0	S27 2-1	D13 2-0	M14 2-4	a11 2-1	S09 1-1	M28 0-1	A26 5-0	M03 1-1	J17 1-1	a21 1-0	O18 4-2	D26 1-0		N15 0-1	O04 1-0	N29 0-1	N01 3-0	a25 1-1	D20 5-2	J13 4-1	F07 4-2	A30 2-1
16 PORT VALE	O25 0-1	a13 3-0	S22 1-0	D20 0-0	S27 0-0	a03 1-1	O11 3-0	D27 3-1	J17 2-1	S13 1-1	a30 4-0	M21 1-1	F07 3-0	N08 1-1	a04 1-1		A30 5-2	M16 4-0	F21 0-0	S08 2-0	A25 2-0	M07 2-0	a18 0-0	a20 2-0
17 ROCHDALE	a18 1-0	M07 6-2	S02 1-0	M24 2-1	J31 1-2	S06 3-1	a04 0-2	A23 0-1	D27 3-1	S30 2-3	O25 0-2	a14 1-1	a06 3-1	a29 1-0	F21 3-1	J03 1-1		J24 2-2	S16 0-0	S20 2-2	N08 3-0	S23 2-0	O11 4-1	M21 0-3
18 SCUNTHORPE U	N08 5-2	D20 1-2	M26 1-2	J17 4-0	D27 1-2	S11 1-1	O25 1-0	a06 2-0	F07 2-0	S27 0-0	A28 0-1	a04 1-1	F21 0-0	S25 0-1	a18 1-1	J31 1-2	S13 5-1		O02 3-0	A30 2-2	M07 2-0	M21 2-1	a27 1-2	O11 2-0
19 SOUTHPORT	O11 1-0	S23 3-2	N08 2-2	J31 3-0	S13 2-0	D26 2-0	F07 1-0	F14 3-0	D20 3-0	A30 3-2	a18 4-3	M07 1-1	J17 0-0	O25 1-3	M21 1-0	O04 0-0	S09 1-0	J01 2-3		a03 3-0	a21 1-2	A25 2-0	a04 1-0	a14 2-0
20 STOCKPORT CO	a04 3-1	S01 6-1	a29 2-0	S13 6-1	S29 3-0	A23 4-1	M21 4-1	J31 2-4	S27 2-2	F21 3-1	O11 2-2	S22 1-1	D25 1-1	a18 2-2	a13 1-1	S15 0-2	F07 2-0	J03 1-1	a06 3-0		O25 3-2	N08 6-0	J17 3-1	M07 1-1
21 TRANMERE R	J24 2-0	a03 2-0	S16 4-0	N01 3-1	a25 4-1	F28 4-0	F14 3-1	O04 1-0	N15 5-2	a11 2-0	J01 2-1	S06 0-0	N29 0-2	J03 1-0	A23 0-0	S02 1-1	M28 1-0	O18 0-1	D13 1-1	M14 1-0		S20 3-0	J31 4-2	a28 1-3
22 WORKINGTON	J03 3-0	D27 3-1	a03 2-2	N15 3-2	S06 1-1	M14 1-2	S13 2-3	F28 4-0	N29 3-1	a25 0-2	F21 3-1	A23 2-0	D13 1-1	S17 0-1	J31 1-1	O18 1-1	a11 1-2	N01 0-3	S03 2-4	M28 0-2	F07 2-0		a22 4-0	S27 1-3
23 WREXHAM	D26 3-1	A30 4-0	J24 0-3	A25 2-1	M28 3-0	a25 7-0	a03 2-2	a11 1-0	O18 4-2	M14 1-0	D20 3-1	O04 2-1	N01 3-2	F14 1-0	S20 2-2	N29 3-1	F28 3-0	D13 2-3	N15 3-2	S06 5-2	J21 1-0	O01 3-0		S10 1-1
24 YORK C	S20 2-0	J10 1-1	A23 3-1	M14 0-0	N29 1-0	S01 0-0	O04 0-0	D13 2-1	M28 3-0	N15 1-2	a06 2-0	J24 2-2	a11 1-0	S06 2-0	J03 1-2	S29 1-0	N01 2-0	F28 0-2	a25 3-1	O18 3-0	D26 2-0	F14 1-3	S15 2-1	

DIVISION 3 SOUTH

	ALDERSHOT	BOURNEMOUTH	BRIGHTON & HA	BRISTOL C	BRISTOL R	COLCHESTER U	COVENTRY C	CRYSTAL P	EXETER C	GILLINGHAM	IPSWICH T	LEYTON O	MILLWALL	NEWPORT CO	NORTHAMPTON T	NORWICH C	Q.P.R.	READING	SHREWSBURY T	SOUTHEND U	SWINDON T	TORQUAY U	WALSALL	WATFORD
1 ALDERSHOT		A27 1-0	M14 1-2	N15 1-2	a29 0-0	A30 0-0	D26 4-1	M28 0-1	a03 1-1	a22 3-2	D13 1-1	a25 2-0	S10 1-2	N01 2-2	N29 2-1	D20 1-2	S20 4-1	S06 2-2	F14 4-2	F28 1-1	J24 2-2	a11 0-2	O04 2-0	O18 1-2
2 BOURNEMOUTH	S03 0-3		O01 2-1	a06 4-1	N08 1-2	O11 1-0	O25 3-0	J31 4-2	M21 2-1	S24 4-2	S06 2-1	J03 4-1	a04 1-1	S17 1-2	A23 0-1	M07 0-0	m02 1-0	J24 2-0	a15 2-0	S27 5-1	F07 1-1	D27 0-1	a18 5-1	F21 4-1
3 BRIGHTON & H.A.	O25 4-2	a22 2-0		J03 0-1	a18 2-1	M21 0-0	a04 1-1	A23 4-1	S24 4-2	m02 5-0	F14 1-4	S20 3-1	a15 1-0	D27 2-2	J24 1-1	N08 2-3	O11 2-0	O04 1-1	S03 3-1	S17 2-2	M07 1-2	S06 2-1	a03 4-2	J31 1-2
4 BRISTOL C	a04 0-0	a03 1-1	A30 2-2		F07 0-0	S23 3-2	a28 1-0	S13 5-0	D06 4-1	O11 4-0	S09 4-2	a21 2-1	A26 0-0	J17 2-0	O04 2-3	a18 0-1	M21 4-4	J10 1-1	O25 3-2	D26 5-0	N08 4-2	F14 4-4	M07 6-1	D20 5-1
5 BRISTOL R	J31 4-1	M28 2-1	N29 7-0	S20 0-0		S15 3-1	F21 5-2	D13 2-0	S27 0-0	S06 3-1	M14 3-0	O18 2-1	J24 1-1	a25 3-1	F28 1-1	S29 3-1	D27 2-1	N01 4-0	A23 2-1	N15 2-1	a06 1-2	S01 3-0	J03 2-0	a11 0-3
6 COLCHESTER U	J03 1-2	F28 1-1	N01 0-0	a11 3-1	S11 0-3		a03 0-1	M19 3-0	J31 3-1	O04 1-1	A23 0-0	D13 3-1	a23 0-0	M28 3-3	a25 1-2	m02 0-4	J24 1-1	A28 2-1	S20 1-0	O18 3-3	S06 3-1	N29 4-1	F14 6-1	M14 1-1
7 COVENTRY C	D27 3-0	M14 2-3	N15 3-1	a25 2-2	O04 1-1	a06 2-2		N29 4-2	S29 1-0	S20 2-1	F28 2-0	S01 3-0	F14 4-1	a11 0-1	S15 1-1	J15 2-1	J03 2-0	O18 4-0	S06 0-0	N01 2-1	A23 1-2	D13 7-2	J24 3-1	M28 1-0
8 CRYSTAL P	N08 3-0	J10 1-0	D20 2-1	J24 1-3	m01 1-0	a04 3-1	a18 2-2		a15 2-0	A27 0-0	a22 1-1	O04 2-2	J17 0-1	A30 2-1	F14 4-3	S24 1-1	O25 4-2	S10 0-3	M07 1-2	a06 0-0	M21 3-0	S20 2-2	O11 4-1	a29 1-0
9 EXETER C	a06 2-2	N01 5-1	a11 1-5	D13 1-1	F14 0-0	J21 2-0	a22 1-0	a25 2-0		J24 0-0	O18 1-1	F28 0-1	S20 1-0	N29 3-2	A27 2-0	S10 1-0	A23 2-2	M14 2-0	J03 2-2	M28 0-2	D26 1-2	O04 4-1	S06 6-1	N15 1-1
10 GILLINGHAM	O01 2-0	a11 1-2	D13 1-2	F28 0-1	J17 0-4	F21 1-1	F07 0-0	S03 1-0	S13 1-0		M28 1-1	N01 3-2	A30 0-1	D20 1-1	M14 1-1	S27 0-3	J10 3-0	N15 2-1	a03 4-2	N29 1-1	S17 0-0	O18 2-1	D26 3-1	a25 2-1
11 IPSWICH T	m01 2-1	J17 2-1	S27 1-0	S17 1-0	O25 1-5	D20 2-2	O11 3-0	O01 2-0	M07 0-1	N08 1-1		M25 0-1	M21 1-6	F21 3-0	a06 1-1	A27 2-1	a18 0-1	A30 1-2	S24 2-1	S13 0-0	a15 1-1	J14 2-2	a04 5-0	F07 1-1
12 LEYTON O	a16 4-1	A30 2-2	F07 3-0	O02 1-3	M07 3-3	a30 5-3	A28 1-2	F21 0-0	O11 2-0	M21 1-1	D26 3-1		O25 1-4	S27 2-1	J10 0-1	a03 3-1	S25 5-0	D20 1-1	a04 0-0	J17 3-0	a18 2-2	S08 4-1	N08 4-1	S13 2-0
13 MILLWALL	S17 0-0	N15 3-1	a25 1-1	S03 1-1	S13 3-0	a27 3-1	S27 2-0	S06 0-0	F07 0-0	J03 3-1	N01 3-2	M14 0-0		D13 3-0	O18 1-2	F21 2-3	a03 2-1	M28 1-0	D26 4-1	a11 4-1	J31 3-0	F28 3-0	A23 3-0	N29 1-1
14 NEWPORT CO	M21 2-1	S11 2-1	D25 0-3	S06 4-3	a13 2-2	N08 0-1	S25 4-4	J03 3-2	a18 1-0	A23 1-2	O04 1-3	F14 0-1	a30 1-3		S20 4-1	a04 1-1	M07 2-0	a23 1-0	O11 4-2	J15 0-1	O25 3-0	J24 3-0	S04 3-2	a03 1-1
15 NORTHAMPTON T	a18 4-0	D20 5-1	S13 5-3	F21 0-2	O11 2-2	a16 2-0	S11 3-1	S27 5-1	S04 3-1	O25 3-1	a07 2-0	J31 3-1	M07 1-1	F07 5-0		a30 3-3	a04 4-2	D26 6-1	N08 3-1	A30 4-3	S25 3-1	a23 3-3	M21 2-1	J17 4-1
16 NORWICH C	A23 5-0	O18 1-1	M28 3-2	N29 0-0	a22 0-0	D26 3-0	J31 1-1	a11 5-1	S17 2-0	F14 3-2	S03 1-0	a06 5-1	O04 2-2	N15 2-0	D13 1-2		S06 2-0	F28 3-0	J24 2-1	M14 3-1	J03 1-1	a25 3-0	S20 3-0	N01 5-2
17 Q.P.R.	F07 2-2	D13 2-1	F28 3-3	N01 2-1	D26 0-1	S13 1-0	A30 0-4	M14 1-1	D20 1-1	J31 1-1	N29 2-2	a11 0-1	a06 1-3	O18 4-2	N15 2-2	J17 3-1		a25 1-0	a20 1-0	O04 3-2	S27 1-1	M28 0-1	S08 4-2	A25 2-2
18 READING	J17 2-3	S13 1-3	F21 0-0	J31 4-0	M21 2-0	S03 2-0	M07 1-0	S17 4-1	O25 3-1	a04 3-2	J03 1-1	A23 2-0	N08 5-0	O01 2-1	a13 2-0	O11 0-1	a29 2-0		a18 5-3	F07 1-0	m01 4-1	a03 4-1	a11 0-0	S27 3-0
19 SHREWSBURY T	S27 2-1	a25 1-0	A28 0-0	M14 0-1	D20 0-1	F07 3-0	J17 1-0	O18 1-1	A30 1-3	a06 3-1	a11 2-2	N15 2-0	D27 2-4	F28 1-1	M28 2-4	S13 1-8	O02 0-3	N29 1-1		D13 7-1	F21 2-1	N01 2-1	F05 1-0	S11 3-1
20 SOUTHEND U	O11 1-1	F14 0-0	S09 1-2	a29 0-4	a04 2-1	M07 4-0	M21 1-0	a03 2-2	N08 1-1	a18 3-1	J24 2-0	S06 1-0	S23 2-1	J31 1-0	J03 3-1	O25 1-2	F21 2-0	S20 3-1	m01 2-2		S02 3-0	A23 3-1	D06 2-1	S30 1-0
21 SWINDON T	S13 3-2	S20 1-2	O18 3-0	M28 0-0	a03 1-3	J17 0-1	D20 2-3	N01 3-6	D27 5-2	S10 0-0	a25 2-0	M18 1-1	J14 1-2	M14 2-0	a11 3-0	A30 2-1	F14 1-3	D13 2-0	O04 2-2	A27 1-3		N15 2-0	O01 1-2	F28 0-0
22 TORQUAY U	S24 1-2	D26 5-1	J17 1-2	S27 1-2	A27 1-0	a18 5-1	m02 2-1	F07 1-1	F21 5-2	M07 3-2	J31 4-1	S17 5-0	O11 1-0	S13 3-3	O01 3-0	a15 4-1	N08 1-1	a06 2-0	M21 4-0	D20 4-2	a04 3-1		O25 0-3	A30 2-2
23 WALSALL	F21 0-0	a30 2-2	a06 3-0	O18 3-3	A30 3-5	S27 0-3	S13 1-1	F28 2-4	J17 2-2	D27 1-3	N15 1-3	M28 1-0	D20 0-2	A28 1-3	N01 1-5	F07 3-2	S18 1-1	S25 2-0	J15 4-4	a25 1-1	a23 1-2	M14 2-0		D13 0-0
24 WATFORD	M07 1-1	O04 3-0	J14 2-3	A23 4-1	S25 2-3	O25 2-0	N08 1-1	D26 2-0	a04 3-1	a16 0-0	S20 1-0	J24 1-0	a18 1-1	a06 0-1	S06 2-1	M21 3-2	S04 1-1	F14 2-1	S18 1-1	a23 1-1	O11 2-1	J03 1-1	J10 3-0	

LEAGUE TABLES

DIVISION 1

	P	W	D	L	F	A	W	D	L	F	A	Pts
Arsenal	42	15	3	3	60	30	6	9	6	37	34	54
Preston N.E.	42	15	3	3	46	25	6	9	6	39	35	54
Wolverh'pton W	42	13	5	3	54	27	6	8	7	32	36	51
W.B.A.	42	13	3	5	35	19	8	5	8	31	41	50
Charlton A	42	12	8	1	47	22	7	3	11	30	41	49
Burnley	42	11	6	4	36	20	7	6	8	31	32	48
Blackpool	42	13	5	3	45	22	6	4	11	26	48	47
Manchester U	42	11	5	5	35	30	7	5	9	34	42	46
Sunderland	42	11	9	1	42	27	4	4	13	26	55	43
Tottenham H	42	11	6	4	55	37	4	5	12	23	32	41
Aston Villa	42	9	7	5	36	23	5	6	10	27	38	41
Cardiff C	42	7	8	6	32	17	7	4	10	22	29	40
Middlesbrough	42	12	5	4	46	27	2	6	13	24	50	39
Bolton W	42	9	4	8	39	35	6	5	10	22	34	39
Portsmouth	42	10	6	5	44	34	4	4	13	30	49	38
Newcastle U	42	9	5	7	34	33	5	4	12	25	37	37
Liverpool	42	10	6	5	36	28	4	2	15	25	54	36
Sheffield W	42	8	6	7	35	32	4	5	12	27	40	35
Chelsea	42	10	4	7	35	24	2	7	12	21	42	35
Manchester C	42	12	2	7	45	28	2	5	14	27	59	35
Stoke C	42	10	4	7	35	26	2	6	13	18	40	34
Derby Co	42	9	6	6	41	29	2	4	15	18	45	32

DIVISION 2

	P	W	D	L	F	A	W	D	L	F	A	Pts
Sheffield U	42	15	3	3	60	27	10	7	4	37	28	60
Huddersfield T	42	14	4	3	51	14	10	6	5	33	19	58
Luton T	42	15	1	5	53	17	7	7	7	31	32	52
Plymouth A	42	12	5	4	37	24	8	4	9	28	36	49
Leicester C	42	13	6	2	55	29	5	6	10	34	45	48
Birmingham C	42	11	3	7	44	38	8	7	6	27	28	48
Nottingham F	42	11	5	5	46	32	7	3	11	31	35	44
Fulham	42	14	1	6	52	28	3	9	9	29	43	44
Blackburn R	42	12	4	5	40	20	6	4	11	28	45	44
Leeds U	42	13	4	4	42	24	1	11	9	29	39	43
Swansea T	42	10	9	2	45	26	5	3	13	33	55	42
Rotherham U	42	9	7	5	41	30	7	2	12	34	44	41
Doncaster R	42	9	9	3	26	17	3	7	11	32	47	40
West Ham U	42	9	5	7	38	28	4	8	9	20	32	39
Lincoln C	42	9	9	3	41	26	2	8	11	23	45	39
Everton	42	9	8	4	38	23	3	6	12	33	52	38
Brentford	42	8	8	5	38	29	5	3	13	21	47	37
Hull C	42	11	6	4	36	19	3	2	16	21	50	36
Notts Co	42	11	5	5	41	31	3	3	15	19	57	36
Bury	42	10	6	5	33	30	3	3	15	20	51	35
Southampton	42	5	7	9	45	44	5	6	10	23	41	33
Barnsley	42	4	4	13	31	46	1	4	16	16	62	18

DIVISION 3 NORTH

	P	W	D	L	F	A	W	D	L	F	A	Pts
Oldham A	46	15	4	4	48	21	7	11	5	29	24	59
Port Vale	46	13	9	1	41	10	7	9	7	26	25	58
Wrexham	46	18	3	2	59	24	6	5	12	27	42	56
York C	46	14	5	4	35	16	6	8	9	25	29	53
Grimsby T	46	15	5	3	47	19	6	5	12	28	40	52
Southport	46	16	4	3	42	18	4	7	12	21	42	51
Bradford P.A.	46	10	8	5	37	23	9	4	10	38	38	50
Gateshead	46	13	6	4	51	24	4	9	10	25	36	49
Carlisle U	46	13	7	3	57	24	5	6	12	25	44	49
Crewe A	46	13	5	5	46	28	7	3	13	24	40	48
Stockport Co	46	13	8	2	61	26	4	5	14	21	43	47
Chesterfield	46	13	6	4	40	23	5	5	13	25	40	47
Tranmere R	46	16	4	3	45	16	5	1	17	20	47	47
Halifax T	46	13	5	5	47	31	3	10	10	21	37	47
Scunthorpe U	46	10	6	7	38	21	6	8	9	24	35	46
Bradford C	46	14	7	2	54	29	0	11	12	21	51	46
Hartlepool U	46	14	6	3	39	16	2	8	13	18	45	46
Mansfield T	46	11	9	3	34	25	5	5	13	21	37	46
Barrow	46	15	6	2	48	20	1	6	16	18	51	44
Chester C	46	10	7	6	39	27	1	8	14	25	58	37
Darlington	46	13	4	6	33	27	1	2	20	25	69	34
Rochdale	46	12	5	6	41	27	2	0	21	21	56	33
Workington	46	9	5	9	40	33	2	5	16	15	58	32
Accrington S	46	7	9	7	25	29	1	2	20	14	60	27

DIVISION 3 SOUTH

	P	W	D	L	F	A	W	D	L	F	A	Pts
Bristol R	46	17	4	2	55	19	9	8	6	37	27	64
Millwall	46	14	7	2	46	16	10	7	6	36	28	62
Northampton T	46	18	4	1	75	30	8	6	9	34	40	62
Norwich C	46	16	6	1	56	17	9	4	10	43	38	60
Bristol C	46	13	8	2	62	28	9	7	7	33	33	59
Coventry C	46	15	5	3	52	22	4	7	12	25	40	50
Brighton & H.A.	46	12	6	5	48	30	7	6	10	33	45	50
Southend U	46	15	5	3	41	21	3	8	12	28	53	49
Bournemouth	46	15	3	5	49	23	4	6	13	25	46	47
Watford	46	12	8	3	39	21	3	9	11	23	42	47
Reading	46	17	3	3	53	18	2	5	16	16	46	46
Torquay U	46	15	4	4	61	28	3	5	15	26	60	45
Crystal Palace	46	12	7	4	40	26	3	6	14	26	56	43
Leyton O	46	12	7	4	52	28	4	3	16	16	45	42
Newport Co	46	12	4	7	43	34	4	6	13	27	48	42
Ipswich T	46	10	7	6	34	28	3	8	12	26	41	41
Exeter C	46	11	8	4	40	24	2	6	15	21	47	40
Swindon T	46	9	5	9	38	33	5	7	11	26	46	40
Aldershot	46	8	8	7	36	29	4	7	12	25	48	39
Q.P.R.	46	9	9	5	37	34	3	6	14	24	48	39
Gillingham	46	10	7	6	30	26	2	8	13	25	48	39
Colchester U	46	9	9	5	40	29	3	5	15	19	47	38
Shrewsbury T	46	11	5	7	38	35	1	7	15	30	56	36
Walsall	46	5	9	9	35	46	2	1	20	21	72	24

FOOTBALL LEAGUE RECORDS

Top scorers Div 1, J.Glazzard (Huddersfield Town) 29 goals; Div 2, J.Charles (Leeds United) 42 goals; Div 3 N, G.Ashman (Carlisle United) 30 goals; Div 3 S, J.English (Northampton Town) 28 goals.

England half-back Billy Wright, skipper of the Wolves side which lifted the Division One title in 1953-54.

Veteran centre-forward Tommy Lawton, a star with Everton before the war, he later played for Chelsea, Brentford and Notts County before joining Arsenal in 1953-54. His strike rate was then only moderate but he played a few games as the Gunners finished 12th.

DIVISION 1

	ARSENAL	ASTON VILLA	BLACKPOOL	BOLTON W	BURNLEY	CARDIFF C	CHARLTON A	CHELSEA	HUDDERSFIELD T	LIVERPOOL	MANCHESTER C	MANCHESTER U	MIDDLESBROUGH	NEWCASTLE U	PORTSMOUTH	PRESTON N.E.	SHEFFIELD U	SHEFFIELD W	SUNDERLAND	TOTTENHAM H	W.B.A.	WOLVERHAMPTON W
1 ARSENAL		a06 1-1	D28 1-1	N14 4-3	O17 2-5	F13 1-1	M13 3-3	S08 1-2	A22 0-0	a10 3-0	S19 2-2	M27 3-1	a24 3-1	N28 2-1	a16 3-0	O03 3-2	S01 1-1	O31 4-1	J23 1-4	F27 0-3	D12 2-2	S05 2-3
2 ASTON VILLA	A29 2-1		S12 2-1	O31 2-2	a10 5-1	D19 1-2	N28 2-1	F06 2-2	F20 2-2	F27 2-1	A24 3-0	M13 2-2	N14 5-3	O17 1-2	J16 1-1	a24 1-0	S26 4-0	M31 2-1	S14 3-1	D12 1-2	a20 6-1	D26 1-2
3 BLACKPOOL	D26 2-2	J23 3-2		N28 0-0	A31 2-0	a16 4-1	F27 3-1	A22 2-1	S05 3-1	a24 3-0	O03 2-0	a10 2-0	M13 0-0	D12 1-3	S07 1-1	M31 4-2	J02 2-2	O17 1-2	F13 3-0	N14 1-0	O31 4-1	S19 0-0
4 BOLTON W	a03 3-1	M20 3-0	a17 3-2		a16 0-0	F06 3-0	D26 3-1	N21 2-2	D05 0-0	A29 2-0	O10 3-2	S12 0-0	A26 3-2	J16 2-2	N07 6-1	F13 0-2	J01 2-1	S09 2-1	M06 3-1	O03 2-0	D19 2-1	O24 1-1
5 BURNLEY	M06 2-1	N21 3-2	A25 2-1	a19 1-1		O24 3-0	D19 2-0	a03 1-2	a17 2-1	F06 1-1	M20 3-1	F20 2-0	J16 5-0	S26 1-2	O10 1-0	D25 2-1	N07 2-1	A29 4-1	D05 5-1	S07 4-2	S12 1-4	A19 4-1
6 CARDIFF C	S26 0-3	A22 2-1	a19 0-1	S19 1-1	M13 1-0		O31 5-0	D28 0-0	S02 2-1	N28 3-1	J23 0-3	N14 1-6	D12 1-0	M27 2-1	M03 3-2	F27 2-1	S16 2-0	a24 2-2	S05 1-1	O17 1-0	a10 2-0	J02 1-3
7 CHARLTON A	O24 1-5	a17 1-1	O10 4-2	D25 1-0	A22 3-1	M20 3-2		J02 1-1	N07 2-1	S26 6-0	D05 2-1	a19 1-0	S12 8-1	F25 0-0	M06 3-1	S17 2-1	a03 3-0	J16 4-2	A19 5-3	S03 0-1	F06 1-1	N21 0-2
8 CHELSEA	S15 0-2	S19 1-2	D19 5-1	a10 2-0	N14 2-1	D26 2-0	A29 3-1		J23 2-2	O31 5-2	a16 0-1	D12 3-1	O17 1-1	a24 1-2	A25 4-3	N28 1-0	S05 1-2	F27 0-1	O03 2-2	M27 1-0	M17 5-0	F13 4-2
9 HUDDERSFIELD T	D19 2-2	O03 4-0	J16 0-0	a24 2-1	N28 3-1	A26 2-0	M27 4-1	S12 3-1		O17 2-0	S09 1-1	O31 0-0	S26 2-1	M13 3-2	A29 5-1	D12 2-2	F06 2-2	N14 2-0	D26 2-1	a10 2-5	F27 0-2	a20 2-1
10 LIVERPOOL	N21 1-2	O10 6-1	D05 5-2	J02 1-2	S19 4-0	a17 0-1	F13 2-3	M20 1-1	M06 1-3		N07 2-2	A22 4-4	a19 4-1	A26 2-2	A19 3-1	S05 1-5	O24 3-0	O03 2-2	a03 4-3	J23 2-2	D26 0-0	S16 1-1
11 MANCHESTER C	F06 0-0	S02 0-1	F24 1-4	F27 3-0	O31 3-2	S12 1-1	a24 3-0	a19 1-1	S16 0-1	a07 0-2		S05 2-0	a10 5-2	N14 0-0	S26 2-1	O17 1-4	D26 2-1	D12 3-2	J02 2-1	M17 4-1	N28 2-3	A22 0-4
12 MANCHESTER U	N07 2-2	O24 1-0	N21 4-1	J23 1-5	O03 1-2	a03 2-3	a16 2-0	A19 1-1	M20 3-1	D19 5-1	J16 1-1		S09 2-2	A29 1-1	a17 2-0	S19 1-0	D05 2-2	D25 5-2	O10 1-0	F13 2-0	A26 1-3	M06 1-0
13 MIDDLESBROUGH	D05 2-0	a03 2-1	O24 0-1	S02 3-2	S05 1-3	A19 0-0	J23 0-2	M06 3-3	F13 0-3	a16 0-1	N21 0-1	S16 1-4		D25 2-3	M20 2-2	A22 0-4	O10 2-0	S19 4-1	a17 0-0	J02 3-0	F24 1-1	N07 3-3
14 NEWCASTLE U	a17 5-2	M06 0-1	J01 2-1	S05 2-3	F13 3-1	N07 4-0	O03 0-2	D05 1-1	O24 0-2	S02 4-0	a03 4-3	J02 1-2	D26 2-3		N21 1-1	J23 0-4	M20 4-1	a16 3-0	A22 2-1	S19 1-3	S16 3-7	O10 1-2
15 PORTSMOUTH	a19 1-1	S05 2-1	S16 4-4	M27 3-2	F27 3-2	O03 1-1	O17 3-1	S02 3-2	J02 5-2	D12 5-1	F13 4-1	N28 1-1	O31 0-2	a10 2-0		N14 1-3	A22 3-4	a07 2-1	S19 4-1	D26 1-1	a24 3-0	J23 2-0
16 PRESTON N.E.	F24 0-1	D05 1-1	N07 2-3	S26 3-1	D26 2-1	O10 1-2	S09 2-0	a17 1-0	A19 1-2	J16 2-1	M06 4-0	F06 1-3	D19 1-0	S12 2-2	a03 4-0		N21 2-1	A26 6-0	O24 6-2	a16 2-1	A29 0-2	M20 0-1
17 SHEFFIELD U	A24 1-0	a26 2-1	A29 3-4	D12 3-0	M27 2-1	S07 0-1	N14 1-1	J16 1-3	S19 3-6	M13 3-1	D25 2-2	a24 1-3	F27 2-2	O31 3-1	D19 3-1	a10 1-1		S12 2-0	a19 1-3	N28 5-2	O17 1-2	O03 3-3
18 SHEFFIELD W	M20 2-1	N07 3-1	M06 1-2	S16 2-1	J02 2-0	D05 2-1	S05 1-2	O10 2-0	a03 1-4	F24 1-1	A19 2-0	D26 0-1	F06 4-2	S23 3-0	O24 4-4	S02 4-2	J23 3-2		N21 2-2	A22 2-1	S26 2-3	a17 0-0
19 SUNDERLAND	S12 7-1	J01 2-0	S26 3-2	O17 1-2	a24 2-1	J16 5-0	D12 2-1	F20 1-2	D25 1-1	N14 3-2	A29 4-5	F27 0-2	N28 0-2	D19 1-1	F06 3-1	a07 2-2	a16 2-2	a10 2-4		O31 4-3	M31 2-1	A26 3-2
20 TOTTENHAM H	O10 1-4	A19 1-0	a03 2-2	M03 3-2	S16 2-3	M06 0-1	A26 3-1	N07 2-1	N21 1-0	S12 2-1	O24 3-0	S26 1-1	A29 4-1	F06 3-0	D25 1-1	a19 2-6	a17 2-1	D19 3-1	M20 0-3		J16 0-1	D05 2-3
21 W.B.A.	A19 2-0	a19 1-1	M20 2-1	A22 1-1	J23 0-0	N21 6-1	S19 2-3	O24 5-2	O10 4-0	D25 5-2	a17 1-0	S02 2-0	O03 2-1	S09 2-2	D05 2-3	J02 3-2	M06 2-2	F13 4-2	N07 2-0	S05 3-0		a03 0-1
22 WOLVERHAMPTON W	J16 0-2	D24 1-2	F06 4-1	M24 1-1	D12 1-2	A29 3-1	a10 5-0	S26 8-1	a19 4-0	S07 2-1	D19 3-1	O17 3-1	M27 2-4	F27 3-2	S12 4-3	O31 1-0	F20 6-1	N28 4-1	A31 3-1	a24 2-0	N14 1-0	

DIVISION 2

	BIRMINGHAM C	BLACKBURN R	BRENTFORD	BRISTOL R	BURY	DERBY CO	DONCASTER R	EVERTON	FULHAM	HULL C	LEEDS U	LEICESTER C	LINCOLN C	LUTON T	NOTTINGHAM F	NOTTS CO	OLDHAM A	PLYMOUTH A	ROTHERHAM U	STOKE C	SWANSEA T	WEST HAM U
1 BIRMINGHAM C		N07 0-0	O24 5-1	M06 1-1	N21 0-0	M20 3-0	a17 0-1	D05 5-1	S19 2-2	A19 2-0	O03 3-3	S05 1-2	O10 1-0	S09 5-1	a19 2-2	D25 3-0	a03 2-1	S02 3-0	J02 2-3	J23 1-0	A22 6-0	F13 2-0
2 BLACKBURN R	a10 3-0		A31 2-2	A22 1-1	O03 4-2	J01 0-3	D25 2-0	S19 0-0	O17 5-1	J23 3-1	O31 2-2	a16 3-0	J02 6-0	M27 2-0	N14 2-0	S05 2-0	F13 4-0	N28 2-3	D12 3-0	F27 3-0	a24 1-0	M13 4-1
3 BRENTFORD	M13 2-0	A27 1-4		S05 0-3	a16 2-1	D19 0-0	S10 1-4	O03 1-0	A29 2-1	F13 2-2	O17 2-1	a24 1-3	J23 0-1	a10 0-1	O31 1-1	S19 0-0	D25 3-1	N14 1-0	N28 0-1	D12 0-0	M27 3-1	F27 3-1
4 BRISTOL R	O17 1-1	D19 1-2	J16 0-0		S07 2-0	A29 3-0	A24 0-1	D28 0-0	D12 2-1	O03 4-2	F27 1-1	N28 3-0	S19 0-1	O31 3-3	M13 1-0	F13 1-1	a16 1-0	a10 3-1	M27 1-0	a24 3-2	N14 0-1	S12 2-2
5 BURY	M27 1-1	F20 0-0	J30 1-1	S16 3-1		D25 4-0	S26 2-1	S05 2-2	O31 1-3	a07 3-0	N14 4-4	O17 2-5	S02 1-1	a24 0-1	N28 2-1	A22 3-3	J23 1-0	D12 3-0	F27 3-0	M13 0-6	S19 1-2	a10 2-0
6 DERBY CO	O31 2-4	S09 2-2	A22 4-1	J02 0-1	D26 3-1		a19 2-0	F13 2-6	F27 3-3	S19 2-0	M13 0-2	D12 2-1	S05 2-0	N14 1-2	a10 1-2	J23 0-0	O03 3-1	M27 1-4	a24 1-1	S02 1-1	N28 4-2	O17 2-1
7 DONCASTER R	N14 3-1	D26 0-2	S16 3-0	S02 1-0	F13 0-1	a16 1-3		J23 2-2	M13 2-2	S05 4-1	a10 0-0	F27 0-2	A22 1-1	N28 1-3	M27 1-3	J02 4-2	S19 1-0	a24 3-3	O03 1-2	O17 1-0	D12 1-0	O31 2-0
8 EVERTON	a24 1-0	F06 1-1	F24 6-1	D25 4-0	J16 0-0	S26 3-2	S12 4-1		N14 2-2	S02 2-0	N28 2-1	O31 1-2	a16 3-1	D19 2-1	D12 3-3	S23 3-2	A29 3-1	F27 8-4	M13 3-0	a10 1-1	O17 2-2	M27 1-2
9 FULHAM	F06 5-2	M06 2-3	J02 4-1	A20 4-4	M20 3-0	O10 5-2	O24 1-2	a17 0-0		N21 5-1	S12 1-3	S02 1-1	D05 4-1	F20 5-1	S26 3-1	a03 4-3	N07 3-1	D25 3-1	S16 2-4	A22 0-1	a19 4-3	J16 3-4
10 HULL C	D12 3-0	S12 0-2	S26 2-0	a12 4-1	A29 3-0	F06 3-0	J16 3-1	A24 1-3	M27 2-1		a24 1-1	a10 0-3	D26 3-0	F27 1-2	S07 3-0	a16 0-2	D19 8-0	O17 2-0	O31 1-0	N14 1-2	M13 4-3	N28 2-1
11 LEEDS U	F20 1-1	M20 3-2	M06 4-0	O10 3-3	a17 3-4	O24 3-1	N07 3-1	a03 3-1	J23 1-2	D05 0-0		J02 7-1	F13 5-2	a19 2-1	D26 0-2	A19 6-0	N21 2-1	S16 1-1	A22 4-2	S05 1-1	S02 3-2	S19 1-2
12 LEICESTER C	J16 3-4	a19 4-0	D05 6-0	a03 1-0	M06 2-0	A19 2-2	O10 2-0	M20 2-2	A24 2-2	N07 1-3	A29 5-0		N21 9-2	F06 2-1	S12 1-0	a17 2-2	O24 1-0	S26 4-2	D25 4-1	S07 4-0	F23 4-1	D19 2-1
13 LINCOLN C	F27 0-1	A29 8-0	S12 2-1	F06 1-2	A26 0-0	J16 2-2	D19 0-2	a19 1-1	a24 4-2	D28 3-0	S26 2-0	M27 3-1		M13 1-1	O17 2-2	O03 3-0	S09 3-1	O31 2-0	N14 4-3	N28 1-1	a10 3-1	D12 1-2
14 LUTON T	S16 2-0	N21 2-1	N07 1-1	M20 1-1	D05 3-2	a17 2-1	a03 2-0	A22 1-1	O03 1-2	O10 3-1	a16 1-1	S19 2-2	O24 1-0		A26 0-1	M06 2-1	A19 4-4	J02 2-1	J23 1-1	F13 0-1	S05 2-0	D26 3-1
15 NOTTINGHAM F	a16 1-1	a17 0-1	M20 2-1	O24 3-1	a03 2-2	N07 4-2	N21 2-2	A19 3-3	F13 4-1	S16 2-0	D25 5-2	J23 3-1	M06 4-2	S02 2-1		O10 5-0	D05 1-1	A22 3-0	S05 4-1	S19 5-4	J02 2-1	O03 4-0
16 NOTTS CO	D26 2-1	J16 0-5	F06 2-0	S26 1-5	D19 0-0	S12 0-1	A29 1-5	S10 0-2	N28 0-0	a19 1-1	D12 2-0	N14 1-1	F20 1-1	O17 1-2	F27 1-1		A27 2-0	M13 2-0	a10 1-2	M27 2-1	O31 3-0	a24 3-1
17 OLDHAM A	N28 2-3	S26 1-0	D26 2-0	a19 0-0	S12 0-0	F20 0-0	F06 2-2	a29 0-4	a10 2-3	A22 0-0	M27 4-2	a06 0-2	S14 1-0	D12 1-2	a24 1-3	S01 1-3		S05 1-1	O17 2-3	O31 1-0	F27 2-2	N14 3-1
18 PLYMOUTH A	A24 2-2	a03 1-1	a17 3-2	N07 3-3	A19 1-1	N21 3-2	D05 0-0	O10 4-0	D26 2-2	M06 2-2	S07 1-1	F13 0-3	M20 1-2	A29 2-2	D19 1-0	O24 3-3	J16 5-0		S19 0-2	O03 1-1	J23 1-1	a19 2-1
19 ROTHERHAM U	A29 1-0	A20 1-4	a03 1-1	N21 1-1	O10 1-0	D05 5-2	a29 4-0	O24 1-2	S07 3-2	M20 3-2	D19 2-4	D26 1-1	a17 4-1	S12 2-1	J16 3-0	N07 0-1	M06 7-0	F06 2-1		S21 2-2	S26 2-1	A24 5-0
20 STOKE C	S12 3-2	O10 3-0	A19 1-1	D05 3-2	O24 4-0	A24 2-2	M06 2-2	N07 2-4	D19 1-3	a17 0-1	J16 4-0	S14 2-2	a03 4-1	S26 1-1	F06 1-1	N21 0-1	M20 0-1	a26 3-2	a19 1-1		D28 5-0	A29 1-1
21 SWANSEA T	D19 1-3	D05 2-1	N21 1-0	a17 3-1	F06 2-1	a03 2-1	A19 0-1	M06 0-2	a16 2-0	O24 1-0	A27 4-3	O03 0-0	N07 4-2	J16 1-1	A29 2-1	M20 2-2	O10 4-0	S12 0-1	F13 0-2	D26 2-2		S10 1-1
22 WEST HAM U	S26 1-2	O24 2-1	O10 0-1	J23 1-1	N07 5-0	M06 0-0	M20 2-1	N21 1-1	S05 3-1	a03 1-0	F06 5-2	A22 4-1	A19 5-0	D25 1-0	F20 1-1	D05 1-2	a17 0-1	a16 2-2	A31 3-0	a12 2-2	S14 4-1	

Season 1953-54

DIVISION 3 NORTH

	ACCRINGTON S	BARNSLEY	BARROW	BRADFORD	BRADFORD C	CARLISLE U	CHESTER	CHESTERFIELD	CREWE A	DARLINGTON	GATESHEAD	GRIMSBY T	HALIFAX T	HARTLEPOOLS U	MANSFIELD T	PORT VALE	ROCHDALE	SCUNTHORPE U	SOUTHPORT	STOCKPORT CO	TRANMERE R	WORKINGTON	WREXHAM	YORK C
1 ACCRINGTON S		O24 3-0	S19 3-2	M20 0-0	F13 0-1	S28 2-2	a28 1-0	O03 2-2	a03 2-1	M06 0-0	J30 2-2	S16 3-1	D26 3-0	O10 2-0	J23 5-1	N07 2-2	a07 1-0	J01 0-1	a17 1-1	A22 2-1	a19 0-1	A26 4-2	S05 1-2	D05 2-0
2 BARNSLEY	M13 5-0		a24 3-2	A29 2-1	J09 4-2	O17 1-1	S02 3-0	S05 4-1	S16 1-1	J23 5-1	M31 0-2	O31 0-0	F27 1-2	S19 3-2	N28 2-1	D19 0-1	N14 2-1	a19 0-1	S23 2-1	M27 4-1	a21 3-0	O03 4-2	a10 3-0	D26 2-1
3 BARROW	a20 4-3	D05 0-1		J01 4-1	S14 3-0	S12 1-1	O10 2-1	D19 2-2	D28 3-1	a17 2-2	a03 0-0	S26 4-0	J16 1-1	a26 1-1	S21 4-2	A24 0-0	a19 4-2	M20 1-2	M06 2-3	F20 1-0	A29 2-1	N07 0-1	D25 1-0	O24 4-1
4 BRADFORD	O31 6-4	J02 0-2	M17 2-1		A22 4-0	M13 2-4	S30 5-0	M10 1-1	A31 1-1	S05 2-2	S19 3-1	M27 4-1	O17 4-2	J23 5-0	a24 1-0	S16 1-2	a10 2-2	O03 2-2	D28 1-1	N14 3-2	F27 1-2	F24 3-1	N28 2-0	a19 2-0
5 BRADFORD C	S26 1-0	A19 1-0	S09 1-0	D19 3-0		F06 1-0	M06 1-0	A29 2-0	O10 3-0	D05 2-0	a28 2-2	F20 3-0	S12 2-0	a17 1-1	A26 2-2	a07 1-1	D26 4-0	N07 1-3	O24 4-1	a20 1-1	J16 1-0	a03 1-1	S23 1-2	M20 1-0
6 CARLISLE U	S22 2-1	M06 2-4	J23 2-2	O24 0-1	S19 2-0		a03 1-1	F13 2-3	N07 5-0	O10 1-1	D26 1-0	S01 3-3	a16 5-0	J30 2-3	S05 5-0	M20 0-0	A22 7-0	D05 5-1	a27 3-2	S15 2-0	O03 0-2	J01 2-2	J02 0-0	a17 1-1
7 CHESTER	a10 3-0	A26 1-1	F27 1-1	S23 2-3	O17 3-0	N14 0-1		M13 2-2	a19 2-0	S16 2-2	J02 5-0	N28 1-1	M27 3-1	A22 1-1	M24 0-2	D26 0-1	D12 2-0	J23 0-0	F13 1-0	a24 1-2	O31 1-2	S05 3-0	O03 2-1	S19 3-1
8 CHESTERFIELD	F20 0-0	J16 1-1	A22 1-1	M24 5-1	J02 2-3	S26 5-0	O24 4-0		M06 0-2	A19 1-1	a17 1-1	a19 1-0	F06 1-2	D05 2-1	J01 0-0	O10 1-2	S28 2-1	a03 1-0	M20 2-0	D26 4-0	S12 2-1	a26 1-0	A31 1-0	N07 3-2
9 CREWE A	N14 0-3	S07 3-2	J30 2-0	A26 1-1	F27 1-2	M27 0-0	a16 1-0	O17 2-0		A22 1-0	S05 3-1	a10 1-1	O31 3-1	J02 3-0	D26 0-0	S28 0-0	a24 2-1	S19 1-1	O03 0-0	N28 1-5	M13 1-2	J23 2-3	a12 1-2	F13 1-1
10 DARLINGTON	O17 4-1	S12 1-1	N28 1-3	J16 2-1	a24 1-0	F27 3-2	S09 1-0	M31 3-2	D19 0-1		O03 0-2	M13 3-0	J30 1-1	M24 0-1	a10 1-2	A29 0-3	M27 0-0	D26 3-0	A26 0-1	O31 1-0	S19 2-1	a19 3-0	N14 0-2	J01 1-3
11 GATESHEAD	J09 4-0	S26 0-0	N14 1-0	a07 0-1	a10 1-0	D25 2-2	A29 2-1	N28 3-3	J16 2-0	F20 1-2		F27 7-1	D12 4-0	a19 1-3	M27 1-3	S12 1-0	M13 2-1	A24 0-0	D19 1-0	O17 4-2	a24 2-1	S21 4-1	O31 3-1	S07 3-0
12 GRIMSBY T	S09 2-0	M20 0-1	F13 1-0	N07 0-0	O03 1-0	A26 3-2	a17 0-0	a16 1-1	a28 3-1	O24 1-0	O10 2-0		S23 2-1	M06 3-0	S19 0-2	a03 2-2	S05 3-2	A22 0-1	D05 1-2	J02 1-0	D25 1-0	J30 1-0	J23 0-0	A19 3-0
13 HALIFAX T	D25 2-0	O10 1-2	S05 2-0	M06 2-2	J23 0-1	a19 2-0	N07 1-1	S19 2-1	M20 1-0	J09 0-0	A19 0-0	S28 2-0		F20 1-0	J02 2-0	O24 0-1	S14 1-1	a17 0-3	a03 1-2	A31 0-1	a29 1-1	D05 3-0	A22 0-2	a27 2-3
14 HARTLEPOOLS U	F27 0-1	F06 0-1	a10 2-2	S12 0-2	N28 1-1	a12 1-1	D19 2-0	a24 0-1	A29 0-0	S26 1-0	a16 1-0	O17 3-0	O03 2-0		N14 3-1	J16 2-1	O31 6-0	S21 3-2	S07 1-1	M13 6-0	a05 1-2	D26 2-2	M27 1-1	A24 2-2
15 MANSFIELD T	S12 1-1	a17 2-0	S28 2-3	D05 1-1	A31 0-0	J16 2-1	J09 2-1	S14 2-2	D25 6-0	D12 6-0	N07 1-1	F06 5-1	A29 3-1	a03 1-0		A19 1-2	F20 2-0	O24 2-1	O10 4-2	S26 3-1	D19 2-0	M20 0-2	a19 4-0	M06 7-2
16 PORT VALE	M30 1-0	A22 0-0	A31 4-0	S07 2-0	a01 3-0	O31 1-0	D25 1-0	F27 2-2	S21 1-0	a29 1-1	J23 0-0	N14 2-0	M15 2-0	S05 3-1	a05 1-1		N28 6-0	F13 0-0	a16 0-0	a10 7-0	O17 2-0	S19 2-0	a24 2-0	O03 5-0
17 ROCHDALE	A29 1-0	a03 1-1	a16 1-0	a27 0-1	D25 3-2	D19 2-1	D28 4-0	S22 0-1	D05 4-1	N07 3-0	O24 0-1	J16 4-1	S08 0-1	M20 2-2	O03 1-0	a17 0-0		O10 1-1	F06 2-0	S12 0-0	A25 0-1	M06 4-2	F13 6-2	J09 1-2
18 SCUNTHORPE U	M18 1-2	a16 6-0	O31 3-2	F20 4-1	M27 2-1	a24 2-1	S12 1-0	N14 2-1	F06 2-2	D25 1-1	S03 1-1	D19 2-1	N28 3-2	O01 0-0	M13 2-2	S26 0-2	F27 1-1		J16 1-1	a01 2-0	a10 3-1	S17 4-1	O17 3-1	A29 3-0
19 SOUTHPORT	N28 5-3	J01 5-2	O17 0-1	D25 1-0	M13 0-1	a10 3-0	S26 0-1	O31 2-1	F20 1-2	S01 3-0	A22 2-4	a24 2-1	N14 1-0	S15 2-1	F27 2-1	a19 0-0	S19 1-1	S05 4-3		a28 1-2	M27 0-0	J02 1-1	J30 4-0	J23 1-1
20 STOCKPORT CO	D19 1-1	N07 3-0	O03 5-1	a03 4-1	a16 5-0	S07 3-2	D05 5-0	D25 6-1	a17 1-0	M20 2-0	M06 0-1	A29 3-2	A24 1-1	O24 1-0	F13 3-2	a26 1-1	J23 1-2	M10 1-1	A19 1-1		S21 6-0	O10 2-0	S19 2-2	J16 0-1
21 TRANMERE R	a16 1-0	M03 0-1	J02 1-0	O10 1-1	S05 0-1	F20 1-2	M20 2-1	J23 1-2	O24 1-0	M10 1-0	D05 1-4	D26 2-4	S26 1-0	J01 3-2	A22 2-5	M06 1-3	S01 5-1	a27 1-1	N07 2-0	S29 2-2		a17 4-2	S15 6-1	a03 1-1
22 WORKINGTON	A31 3-1	F20 2-0	M27 1-1	S26 1-1	N14 2-2	J09 2-2	J16 2-0	a10 2-1	S12 1-2	a16 1-1	S28 2-0	M17 2-0	a24 3-1	D25 0-0	O31 1-1	F06 2-0	O17 0-1	S07 1-3	A29 0-1	F27 0-0	N28 2-1		M13 1-1	D19 5-2
23 WREXHAM	J16 4-2	a28 1-1	D26 1-2	a17 2-0	S30 0-1	A29 4-2	F20 2-1	A26 1-2	A19 1-1	a03 4-2	M20 5-1	S12 4-0	D19 5-0	N07 2-0	a16 2-0	D05 1-1	S26 2-0	M06 3-1	a07 2-1	F06 1-0	S09 3-0	O24 8-0		O10 1-1
24 YORK C	a24 1-2	D25 0-2	M13 5-2	a16 0-0	O31 3-2	N28 1-3	F06 2-1	M27 1-3	S26 0-3	S21 3-3	S14 1-1	a12 1-2	a10 1-1	A31 5-0	O17 5-1	F24 0-1	J30 1-2	J02 2-0	S12 2-1	S05 0-0	N14 0-0	A22 0-0	F27 5-2	

DIVISION 3 SOUTH

	ALDERSHOT	BOURNEMOUTH	BRIGHTON & HA	BRISTOL C	COLCHESTER U	COVENTRY C	CRYSTAL P	EXETER C	GILLINGHAM	IPSWICH T	LEYTON O	MILLWALL	NEWPORT CO	NORTHAMPTON T	NORWICH C	Q.P.R.	READING	SHREWSBURY T	SOUTHAMPTON	SOUTHEND U	SWINDON T	TORQUAY U	WALSALL	WATFORD
1 ALDERSHOT		O24 1-2	D05 2-3	F13 2-5	J23 3-0	A19 4-2	S19 1-2	D25 1-2	N07 1-2	M06 3-0	a16 1-1	O10 1-1	S30 2-0	a03 3-1	A22 0-0	J02 1-4	F20 2-2	S16 1-0	S05 1-1	a17 4-0	S02 1-0	a28 4-1	a07 3-1	M20 3-1
2 BOURNEMOUTH	a24 1-1		S19 1-1	O17 5-2	a19 4-2	S09 1-0	F27 2-0	M13 4-1	J09 4-1	S30 2-3	J02 1-2	A22 4-1	N28 1-1	A26 2-1	a10 2-0	a07 0-1	S05 1-1	N14 2-1	D25 3-1	J23 0-1	O31 4-0	O03 1-2	M27 1-1	F13 1-3
3 BRIGHTON & H.A.	a10 3-2	F06 3-0		N28 2-1	N14 1-0	S12 3-1	M13 3-0	F27 2-1	J16 3-1	S26 1-2	A26 2-1	F20 4-0	O17 4-2	A29 3-2	a24 0-0	a30 3-1	J09 3-2	a16 2-3	M27 2-1	S09 3-2	a07 1-1	D19 1-2	D26 5-3	S23 3-3
4 BRISTOL C	S26 4-0	M06 1-1	M20 1-1		S05 3-0	O24 1-0	J23 4-0	S15 5-1	A19 1-1	O10 2-3	F06 1-0	a19 2-1	D26 3-0	N07 2-1	S30 3-1	A22 1-2	a17 3-1	a29 3-1	J02 1-0	D05 4-1	F20 5-1	a03 3-0	S01 4-1	a27 2-1
5 COLCHESTER U	S12 3-0	a16 1-1	a03 1-1	J16 0-2		O10 0-3	A29 4-1	S03 0-1	M06 0-1	D19 1-2	D05 1-0	a17 3-0	J09 2-2	O24 1-1	S17 0-1	D25 5-0	M20 2-4	F20 3-1	O01 0-1	a29 0-1	F06 2-2	A20 3-1	S26 1-1	N07 2-2
6 COVENTRY C	O31 2-1	S14 2-0	J23 1-2	a24 3-0	F27 2-1		O17 0-0	N28 2-0	A31 2-1	D25 1-3	A22 4-0	S28 0-0	a10 1-2	O03 0-0	a26 1-0	a12 3-1	J02 1-1	M13 2-1	a20 2-1	S05 1-0	M27 0-0	F13 4-0	N14 2-0	S19 0-1
7 CRYSTAL P	F06 0-0	O10 3-1	a28 1-1	S12 1-2	J02 0-1	M06 3-1		J30 0-0	O24 1-2	a19 1-1	a17 2-2	J16 2-3	S16 3-0	A20 2-2	D25 1-0	S30 0-3	D05 1-0	S02 3-2	A22 4-3	M20 4-2	S26 3-2	N07 4-1	F20 1-0	a03 1-1
8 EXETER C	D26 1-3	a28 1-0	O10 0-1	S09 0-1	A26 1-2	M20 4-0	J09 7-0		D05 1-2	a03 1-2	A19 2-1	N07 4-1	J23 1-0	a17 1-0	S19 0-2	F13 0-0	O24 2-0	A29 0-1	O03 4-0	M06 1-1	S23 3-1	J16 1-2	D19 2-1	a19 2-1
9 GILLINGHAM	M27 1-3	J30 1-0	S05 0-0	O31 2-2	O17 2-0	A26 2-0	a24 3-2	a10 0-1		S16 1-1	S30 1-2	D25 2-0	D12 0-1	F13 2-1	O03 3-1	a16 1-0	A22 3-0	N28 2-0	F27 2-0	J02 3-1	N14 1-0	S19 0-4	M13 3-0	J23 2-3
10 IPSWICH T	O17 4-0	S23 2-1	F13 2-3	F27 2-1	A22 3-0	D26 4-1	a16 2-0	N14 1-1	S09 6-1		S05 3-1	J02 1-1	M13 1-2	m01 2-1	N28 1-1	a10 2-1	J23 0-1	M27 0-0	a07 2-1	S19 1-1	a24 2-0	A26 2-1	O31 3-0	O03 1-0
11 LEYTON O	a19 1-2	A29 5-0	S03 0-2	S19 4-1	a10 3-1	D19 1-0	a08 2-0	O31 3-1	S24 3-1	J16 1-2		S12 2-2	M27 3-0	D26 2-0	N14 3-1	M18 2-2	F13 2-1	a24 2-0	N28 1-4	O03 1-1	F27 1-1	S10 3-2	O17 2-1	a22 1-1
12 MILLWALL	F27 2-0	D19 2-1	O03 0-2	a16 1-0	a26 0-0	S21 1-2	S05 2-2	M27 2-1	D26 3-1	A29 1-2	J23 0-3		N14 3-1	S07 1-0	M13 1-3	N28 4-0	S19 2-0	O31 3-1	a10 2-1	F13 2-1	O17 6-1	J09 2-2	a24 3-0	A24 1-0
13 NEWPORT CO	S21 2-2	M20 4-0	M06 1-0	D25 3-2	a22 1-1	D05 2-1	S07 1-3	S12 0-3	a17 1-0	a26 1-2	N07 1-1	a03 0-0		F06 2-0	F13 4-1	O03 2-1	A20 4-1	J16 2-1	A24 0-4	O24 3-2	D19 2-0	a16 2-0	A29 4-2	O10 0-1
14 NORTHAMPTON T	N14 6-2	S03 2-1	J02 4-2	M27 3-0	a24 3-0	F20 0-1	O31 6-0	a08 2-2	S26 1-1	M25 1-0	D25 2-2	S17 4-2	S19 1-0		a20 2-0	F27 2-1	S21 1-1	a10 1-0	O17 3-0	D19 5-0	M13 2-0	J23 3-1	N28 5-1	S05 4-1
15 NORWICH C	D19 3-3	D05 1-3	O24 1-0	S23 1-1	S09 2-1	a17 2-1	D26 2-1	F06 1-2	F24 0-0	M20 1-2	a03 3-1	a28 4-3	S26 2-0	a19 4-1		A26 2-2	N07 2-3	S12 1-0	m01 1-0	A19 1-0	A29 2-2	O10 0-1	J16 3-0	M06 4-1
16 Q.P.R.	A29 0-2	a17 2-1	A19 1-2	D19 0-1	D26 0-0	J30 0-3	S21 1-1	S26 0-0	a19 3-1	D05 3-1	a26 2-1	M20 4-0	F20 5-1	O10 1-1	A31 0-2		a03 2-0	F06 0-0	S07 0-1	N07 1-0	J16 0-2	M06 5-1	S12 2-0	O24 0-4
17 READING	O03 6-1	J16 0-1	M24 2-1	a07 0-2	N28 2-0	A29 4-3	a10 4-1	a24 4-1	D19 0-1	S12 3-1	S26 1-1	M31 2-4	O31 4-1	S30 2-0	M27 4-4	N14 3-1		O17 1-1	M13 4-1	A26 2-0	a19 3-1	D25 2-4	F27 0-2	S09 4-1
18 SHREWSBURY T	S07 0-2	a03 1-1	a19 3-1	J30 4-3	O03 3-1	J09 1-1	A24 1-1	J02 1-1	M20 0-0	N07 1-1	O24 3-3	m01 3-1	S05 2-1	D05 2-4	J23 4-0	S19 1-1	M06 0-3		F13 3-2	O10 2-1	D26 1-0	a17 2-1	S21 4-1	A22 6-4
19 SOUTHAMPTON	J16 2-0	D26 2-1	N07 1-0	A29 4-2	S23 2-1	a19 2-1	D19 3-1	F20 2-0	O10 1-0	a17 1-1	M20 4-1	D05 4-2	S02 4-0	M06 1-0	M24 0-0	S16 3-1	a28 1-1	S26 4-2		a03 3-5	S12 3-1	O24 2-2	M17 0-0	A19 2-0
20 SOUTHEND U	a13 2-1	S12 2-1	S15 2-0	a10 0-1	M13 3-0	J16 2-2	N28 1-2	O17 0-1	A29 1-1	F06 3-1	F24 2-1	S26 1-2	a24 0-1	A22 2-0	O31 5-2	M27 4-1	S01 1-2	F27 3-0	N14 2-1		J30 3-1	S30 1-0	a16 3-1	D26 3-0
21 SWINDON T	A26 3-1	A19 2-1	a17 0-1	O03 5-0	S19 3-0	N07 1-1	F13 1-1	S30 2-4	a03 2-1	O24 1-2	O10 2-1	M06 2-1	A22 7-1	a28 0-0	J02 0-0	S05 0-1	a16 1-0	D25 2-1	J23 0-1	J09 3-0		M20 6-1	S16 3-0	D05 2-2
22 TORQUAY U	M13 3-0	F20 2-0	A22 2-3	N14 4-0	O31 3-1	S26 1-1	M27 1-0	S05 3-2	F06 3-3	S02 1-1	S16 2-3	J30 2-2	a19 3-2	S12 1-1	F27 2-4	O17 2-2	D26 2-2	D12 2-0	a24 1-1	S23 1-1	N28 2-1		a10 3-1	J02 2-2
23 WALSALL	J30 0-2	N07 1-0	D25 3-1	A27 0-0	F13 2-3	a03 1-0	O03 1-0	A22 1-1	a29 1-1	A19 0-2	M06 4-2	O24 0-2	J02 0-1	M20 0-1	S05 1-4	J23 2-0	O10 1-3	O01 0-0	S19 1-0	a19 2-0	S10 0-1	D05 1-3		a17 0-0
24 WATFORD	N28 6-1	S26 2-3	S29 1-1	M13 2-0	M27 3-0	F06 1-0	N14 4-1	a16 0-2	S12 6-1	M03 1-0	a30 3-1	S01 2-1	F27 1-0	J16 1-1	O17 1-3	a24 0-2	S15 3-0	D19 3-1	O31 2-0	D25 2-2	a10 2-1	A29 3-1	F24 3-1	

LEAGUE TABLES

DIVISION 1

	P	W	D	L	F	A	W	D	L	F	A	Pts
Wolverh'pton W	42	16	1	4	61	25	9	6	6	35	31	57
W.B.A.	42	13	5	3	51	24	9	4	8	35	39	53
Huddersfield T	42	13	6	2	45	24	7	5	9	33	37	51
Manchester U	42	11	6	4	41	27	7	6	8	32	31	48
Bolton W	42	14	6	1	45	20	4	6	11	30	40	48
Blackpool	42	13	6	2	43	19	6	4	11	37	50	48
Burnley	42	16	2	3	51	23	5	2	14	27	44	46
Chelsea	42	12	3	6	45	26	4	9	8	29	42	44
Charlton A	42	14	4	3	51	26	5	2	14	24	51	44
Cardiff C	42	12	4	5	32	27	6	4	11	19	44	44
Preston N.E.	42	12	2	7	43	24	7	3	11	44	34	43
Arsenal	42	8	8	5	42	37	7	5	9	33	36	43
Aston Villa	42	12	5	4	50	28	4	4	13	20	40	41
Portsmouth	42	13	5	3	53	31	1	6	14	28	58	39
Newcastle U	42	9	2	10	43	40	5	8	8	29	37	38
Tottenham H	42	11	3	7	38	33	5	2	14	27	43	37
Manchester C	42	10	4	7	35	31	4	5	12	27	46	37
Sunderland	42	11	4	6	50	37	3	4	14	31	52	36
Sheffield W	42	12	4	5	43	30	3	2	16	27	61	36
Sheffield U	42	9	5	7	43	38	2	6	13	26	52	33
Middlesbrough	42	6	6	9	29	35	4	4	13	31	56	30
Liverpool	42	7	8	6	49	38	2	2	17	19	59	28

DIVISION 2

	P	W	D	L	F	A	W	D	L	F	A	Pts
Leicester C	42	15	4	2	63	23	8	6	7	34	37	56
Everton	42	13	6	2	55	27	7	10	4	37	31	56
Blackburn R	42	15	4	2	54	16	8	5	8	32	34	55
Nottingham F	42	15	5	1	61	27	5	7	9	25	32	52
Rotherham U	42	13	4	4	51	26	8	3	10	29	41	49
Luton T	42	11	7	3	36	23	7	5	9	28	36	48
Birmingham C	42	12	6	3	49	18	6	5	10	29	40	47
Fulham	42	12	3	6	62	39	5	7	9	36	46	44
Bristol R	42	10	7	4	32	19	4	9	8	32	39	44
Leeds U	42	12	5	4	56	30	3	8	10	33	51	43
Stoke C	42	8	8	5	43	28	4	9	8	28	32	41
Doncaster R	42	9	5	7	32	28	7	4	10	27	35	41
West Ham U	42	11	6	4	44	20	4	3	14	23	49	39
Notts Co	42	8	6	7	26	29	5	7	9	28	45	39
Hull C	42	14	1	6	47	22	2	5	14	17	44	38
Lincoln C	42	11	6	4	46	23	3	3	15	19	60	37
Bury	42	9	7	5	39	32	2	7	12	15	40	36
Derby Co	42	9	5	7	38	35	3	6	12	26	47	35
Plymouth A	42	6	12	3	38	31	3	4	14	27	51	34
Swansea T	42	11	5	5	34	25	2	3	16	24	57	34
Brentford	42	9	5	7	25	26	1	6	14	15	52	31
Oldham A	42	6	7	8	26	31	2	2	17	14	58	25

DIVISION 3 NORTH

	P	W	D	L	F	A	W	D	L	F	A	Pts
Port Vale	46	16	7	0	48	5	10	10	3	26	16	69
Barnsley	46	16	3	4	54	24	8	7	8	23	33	58
Scunthorpe U	46	14	7	2	49	24	7	8	8	28	32	57
Gateshead	46	15	4	4	49	22	6	9	8	25	33	55
Bradford C	46	15	6	2	40	14	7	3	13	20	41	53
Chesterfield	46	13	6	4	41	19	6	8	9	35	45	52
Mansfield T	46	15	5	3	59	22	5	6	12	29	45	51
Wrexham	46	16	4	3	59	19	5	5	13	22	49	51
Bradford P.A.	46	13	6	4	57	31	5	8	10	20	37	50
Stockport Co	46	14	6	3	57	20	4	5	14	20	47	47
Southport	46	12	5	6	41	26	5	7	11	22	34	46
Barrow	46	12	7	4	46	26	4	5	14	26	45	44
Carlisle U	46	10	8	5	53	27	4	7	12	30	44	43
Tranmere R	46	11	4	8	40	34	7	3	13	19	36	43
Accrington S	46	12	7	4	41	22	4	3	16	25	52	42
Crewe A	46	9	8	6	30	26	5	5	13	19	41	41
Grimsby T	46	14	5	4	31	15	2	4	17	20	62	41
Hartlepool U	46	10	8	5	40	21	3	6	14	19	44	40
Rochdale	46	12	5	6	40	20	3	5	15	19	57	40
Workington	46	10	9	4	36	22	3	5	15	23	58	40
Darlington	46	11	3	9	31	27	1	11	11	19	44	38
York C	46	8	7	8	39	32	4	6	13	25	54	37
Halifax T	46	9	6	8	26	21	3	4	16	18	52	34
Chester C	46	10	7	6	39	22	1	3	19	9	45	32

DIVISION 3 SOUTH

	P	W	D	L	F	A	W	D	L	F	A	Pts
Ipswich T	46	15	5	3	47	19	12	5	6	35	32	64
Brighton & H.A.	46	17	3	3	57	31	9	6	8	29	30	61
Bristol C	46	18	3	2	59	18	7	3	13	29	48	56
Watford	46	16	3	4	52	23	5	7	11	33	46	52
Northampton T	46	18	4	1	63	18	2	7	14	19	37	51
Southampton	46	17	5	1	51	22	5	2	16	25	41	51
Norwich C	46	13	5	5	43	28	7	6	10	30	38	51
Reading	46	14	3	6	57	33	6	6	11	29	40	49
Exeter C	46	12	2	9	39	22	8	6	9	29	36	48
Gillingham	46	14	3	6	37	22	5	7	11	24	44	48
Leyton O	46	14	5	4	48	26	4	6	13	31	47	47
Millwall	46	15	3	5	44	24	4	6	13	30	53	47
Torquay U	46	10	10	3	48	33	7	2	14	33	55	46
Coventry C	46	14	5	4	36	15	4	4	15	25	41	45
Newport Co	46	14	4	5	42	28	5	2	16	19	53	44
Southend U	46	15	2	6	46	22	3	5	15	23	49	43
Aldershot	46	11	5	7	45	31	6	4	13	29	55	43
Q.P.R.	46	10	5	8	32	25	6	5	12	28	43	42
Bournemouth	46	12	5	6	47	27	4	3	16	20	43	40
Swindon T	46	13	5	5	48	21	2	5	16	19	49	40
Shrewsbury T	46	12	8	3	48	34	2	4	17	17	42	40
Crystal Palace	46	11	7	5	41	30	3	5	15	19	56	40
Colchester U	46	7	7	9	35	29	3	3	17	15	49	30
Walsall	46	8	5	10	22	27	1	3	19	18	60	26

Football League Records

Top scorers Div 1, R.Allen (West Bromwich Albion) 27 goals; Div 2, T.Briggs (Blackburn Rovers) 33 goals; Div 3 N, D.Travis (Oldham Athletic), J.Connor (Stockport County), A.Bottom (York City) 30 goals; Div 3 S, E.Morgan (Gillingham) 31 goals.

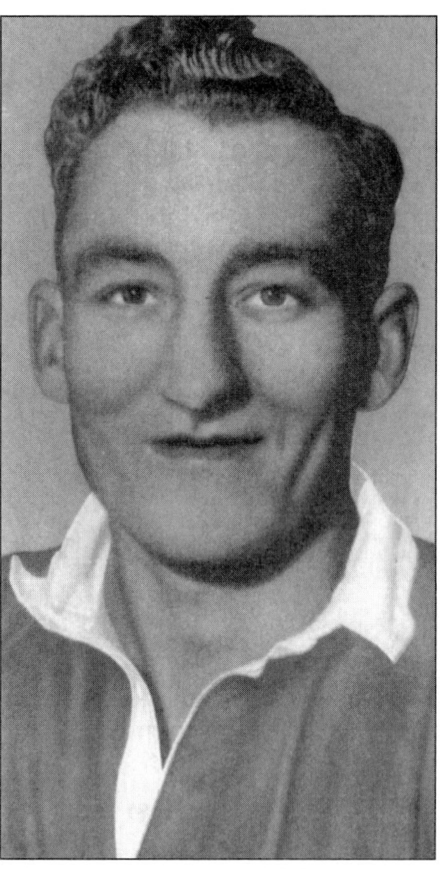

Forward Roy Bentley, one of the stars of the Chelsea side which lifted the Division One title for the first time in 1954-55.

DIVISION 1

	ARSENAL	ASTON VILLA	BLACKPOOL	BOLTON W	BURNLEY	CARDIFF C	CHARLTON A	CHELSEA	EVERTON	HUDDERSFIELD T	LEICESTER C	MANCHESTER C	MANCHESTER U	NEWCASTLE U	PORTSMOUTH	PRESTON N.E.	SHEFFIELD U	SHEFFIELD W	SUNDERLAND	TOTTENHAM H	W.B.A.	WOLVERHAMPTON W
1 ARSENAL		M12 2-0	a09 3-0	M26 3-0	S25 4-0	a08 2-0	D11 3-1	D25 1-0	A31 2-0	N13 3-5	F19 1-1	S14 2-3	a23 2-3	A21 1-3	O16 0-1	F05 2-0	S11 4-0	F26 3-2	O30 1-3	S04 2-0	J01 2-2	N27 1-1
2 ASTON VILLA	O23 2-1		J22 3-1	F12 3-0	a02 3-1	D04 0-2	S18 1-2	M05 3-2	O09 0-2	O02 0-0	N06 2-5	a30 2-0	D28 2-1	S13 1-2	S04 1-0	N20 1-3	a16 3-1	J01 0-0	A23 2-2	A21 2-4	M19 3-0	a12 4-2
3 BLACKPOOL	D04 2-2	S11 0-1		A23 2-3	a11 1-0	a16 0-0	S20 1-1	O23 1-0	a02 4-0	D18 1-1	M19 2-0	N20 1-3	A28 2-4	N06 2-0	D25 2-2	O09 1-2	a30 1-2	F19 2-1	F05 0-0	S25 5-1	M05 3-1	J15 0-2
4 BOLTON W	N06 2-2	S25 3-3	S01 3-0		a30 0-1	M19 0-0	A21 3-2	J01 2-5	a16 2-0	a27 1-0	O09 4-1	O23 2-2	S11 1-1	N20 2-1	S06 3-1	M09 2-1	M05 1-0	a08 2-2	M02 3-0	D25 1-2	a02 2-4	F05 6-1
5 BURNLEY	F12 3-0	N13 2-0	a08 0-1	O16 2-0		A21 1-0	F26 3-0	A31 1-1	S04 0-2	a09 1-1	S06 3-1	J01 2-0	D11 2-4	J22 0-1	O30 1-0	D25 2-2	O02 2-1	M12 2-0	a23 0-1	N27 1-2	S18 0-2	M26 1-0
6 CARDIFF C	a11 1-2	a09 0-1	N27 1-2	O30 2-2	D18 0-3		M12 4-3	M23 0-1	F12 4-3	S11 1-1	A28 2-1	S18 3-0	F26 3-0	O02 4-2	a23 1-1	A25 2-5	S08 1-1	N13 5-3	D11 0-1	M26 1-2	D25 3-2	a30 3-2
7 CHARLTON A	M05 1-1	F05 6-1	S16 3-3	D18 2-0	O09 3-1	O23 4-1		M19 0-2	N20 5-0	A28 2-1	A26 2-3	a16 1-1	a26 1-1	a02 1-1	a11 2-2	a30 0-4	D04 3-1	D25 3-0	S25 1-3	m05 1-2	N06 1-3	S11 1-3
8 CHELSEA	D27 1-1	D11 4-0	M12 0-0	A28 3-2	A23 1-0	S04 1-1	O30 1-2		S18 0-2	F26 4-1	D18 3-1	J22 0-2	O16 5-6	F12 4-3	N27 4-1	S06 0-1	a08 1-1	a23 3-0	M29 2-1	N13 2-1	O02 3-3	a09 1-0
9 EVERTON	A25 1-0	m04 0-1	N13 0-1	N27 0-0	J15 1-1	S25 1-1	a23 2-2	F05 1-1		M23 4-0	S11 2-2	F23 1-0	O30 4-2	a08 1-2	M26 2-3	A28 1-0	D18 2-3	D11 3-1	O16 1-0	a09 1-0	S08 1-2	D27 3-2
10 HUDDERSFIELD T	a02 0-1	F23 1-2	A21 1-3	S04 2-0	D04 0-1	m02 2-0	J01 0-0	O09 1-0	O23 2-1		a30 3-1	M19 0-0	F05 1-3	a16 2-0	A30 2-1	M05 0-4	N06 1-2	S13 3-0	D27 1-1	a12 1-0	N20 3-3	S25 2-0
11 LEICESTER C	O02 3-3	M26 4-2	O30 2-2	m04 4-0	S13 2-2	J01 2-1	A30 0-1	A21 1-1	a20 2-2	O16 1-3		S04 0-2	a09 1-0	S18 3-2	M12 4-0	a11 0-1	D27 0-1	N27 4-3	N13 1-1	a23 2-0	F12 6-3	D11 1-2
12 MANCHESTER C	S08 2-1	O16 2-4	a23 1-6	M16 4-2	A28 0-0	F05 4-1	N27 1-5	S11 1-1	O02 1-0	O30 2-4	J15 2-2		S25 3-2	D25 3-1	N13 1-2	D18 3-1	A25 5-2	M30 2-2	a09 1-0	D11 0-0	a08 4-0	a20 3-0
13 MANCHESTER U	N20 2-1	D27 0-1	J01 4-1	J22 1-1	M05 1-0	O09 5-2	S04 3-1	a30 2-1	M19 1-2	S18 1-1	D04 3-1	F12 0-5		O23 2-2	A21 1-3	N06 2-1	a02 5-0	S01 2-0	a11 2-2	S15 2-1	a16 3-0	F23 2-4
14 NEWCASTLE U	D18 5-1	S08 5-3	a25 1-1	a23 0-0	S11 2-1	a27 3-0	N13 3-1	S25 1-3	a11 4-0	N27 2-2	F05 2-0	D27 2-0	a18 2-0		D11 2-1	a20 3-3	A28 1-2	a09 5-0	F26 1-2	O16 4-4	A25 3-0	O30 2-3
15 PORTSMOUTH	a30 2-1	a27 2-2	D27 3-0	S15 1-0	M19 0-2	N20 1-3	a08 2-0	a16 0-0	N06 5-0	A25 4-2	O23 2-1	a02 1-0	D18 0-0	M05 3-1		F19 2-0	O09 6-2	S25 2-1	S11 2-2	F05 0-3	D04 6-1	A28 0-0
16 PRESTON N.E.	S18 3-1	a23 0-3	F26 3-1	a09 2-2	D27 0-1	S01 7-1	O16 1-2	S15 1-2	J01 0-0	D11 2-3	a08 2-4	A21 5-0	M26 0-2	S04 3-3	O02 1-1		F12 1-2	O30 6-0	N27 3-1	M12 1-0	J22 3-1	N13 3-3
17 SHEFFIELD U	a18 1-1	N27 1-3	O16 2-1	D11 2-0	F19 1-0	S13 1-3	a09 5-0	S20 1-2	A21 2-5	M26 2-2	D25 1-1	A30 0-2	N13 3-0	J01 6-2	m02 5-2	S25 0-5		S18 1-0	M14 1-0	O30 4-1	S04 1-2	a23 1-2
18 SHEFFIELD W	O09 1-2	A28 6-3	O02 2-1	a11 3-2	O23 1-1	a02 1-1	D27 2-2	N20 1-1	M05 2-2	S06 4-1	a16 1-0	N06 2-4	A23 2-4	D04 0-3	F12 1-3	M19 2-0	F05 1-2		J15 1-2	S11 2-2	a30 5-0	D18 2-2
19 SUNDERLAND	M19 0-1	S01 0-0	S18 2-0	O02 1-1	N20 2-2	M05 1-1	F12 1-2	N06 3-3	a30 3-0	D25 1-1	a02 1-1	D04 3-2	a08 4-3	O09 4-2	J22 2-2	a16 2-1	O23 2-2	S04 2-0		J01 1-1	A21 4-2	S15 0-0
20 TOTTENHAM H	J15 0-1	D18 1-1	F12 3-2	D27 2-0	a16 0-3	N06 0-2	O02 1-4	a02 2-4	D04 1-3	a11 1-1	N20 5-1	M05 2-2	S08 0-2	a30 2-1	S18 1-1	O23 3-1	M19 5-0	J22 7-2	A28 0-1		O09 3-1	A25 3-2
21 W.B.A.	A28 3-1	O30 2-3	D11 0-1	N13 0-0	F05 2-2	D27 1-0	M26 2-1	M09 2-4	S15 3-3	a23 2-1	S25 6-4	a11 2-1	N27 2-0	S01 4-2	a09 3-1	S11 2-0	M12 3-3	O16 1-2	D18 2-2	a27 1-2		M16 1-0
22 WOLVERHAMPTON W	a16 3-1	a11 1-0	S04 1-0	S18 1-2	N06 5-0	O16 1-1	J22 2-1	D04 3-4	D25 1-3	F12 6-4	M05 5-0	O09 2-2	O02 4-2	M19 2-2	J01 2-2	a02 1-1	N20 4-1	A21 4-2	S08 2-0	A30 4-2	O23 4-0	

Birmingham City's Peter Murphy, whose goals helped the St Andrew's club back to Division One.

DIVISION 2

	BIRMINGHAM C	BLACKBURN R	BRISTOL R	BURY	DERBY CO	DONCASTER R	FULHAM	HULL C	IPSWICH T	LEEDS U	LINCOLN C	LIVERPOOL	LUTON T	MIDDLESBROUGH	NOTTINGHAM F	NOTTS CO	PLYMOUTH A	PORT VALE	ROTHERHAM U	STOKE C	SWANSEA T	WEST HAM U
1 BIRMINGHAM C		N13 3-1	A25 2-1	S25 1-3	O30 1-1	M16 4-1	M30 3-2	S11 0-0	S08 4-0	M02 2-0	F05 3-3	D11 9-1	a20 2-1	a11 3-0	D25 0-1	a23 1-1	a09 3-1	N27 7-2	A28 3-1	D18 2-0	O16 2-0	M26 1-2
2 BLACKBURN R	a02 3-3		F05 8-3	a30 1-1	S13 5-2	D27 7-2	D18 3-1	N20 4-0	O09 4-1	D04 1-2	a08 1-0	S11 4-3	a16 0-0	N06 9-0	M05 0-1	J15 4-5	S25 2-2	F19 2-1	O23 4-1	M19 2-0	A28 4-1	A23 5-2
3 BRISTOL R	A30 1-1	S18 2-1		M19 2-1	S04 4-1	J01 1-0	F12 4-1	a02 1-0	N20 4-0	O23 5-1	N06 2-2	S06 3-0	O09 3-2	a30 2-2	a16 2-1	D27 1-4	a08 3-1	A21 1-0	M05 1-0	D04 1-1	O02 7-0	J22 2-4
4 BURY	F12 0-1	D11 2-1	O30 3-1		O16 2-2	F26 1-4	A28 1-3	a08 4-1	S18 2-1	S04 5-3	D18 3-1	M12 3-4	A24 2-1	O02 0-1	a20 1-1	N27 1-2	M26 3-1	N13 2-2	S20 2-2	D27 1-1	a09 2-1	a23 4-1
5 DERBY CO	M19 0-0	S08 0-3	F19 1-1	M05 2-3		S25 5-0	A25 3-4	a30 3-0	N06 2-0	O09 2-4	D04 3-0	A28 3-2	M02 0-0	O23 1-2	a02 1-2	D18 1-1	S11 2-2	F05 6-1	N20 2-3	a16 1-2	a08 1-4	D27 0-0
6 DONCASTER R	m04 1-5	D25 1-3	A28 2-2	O09 1-0	F12 2-0		S15 4-0	D04 2-2	M19 1-1	a02 0-1	M05 1-1	D18 4-1	a30 0-3	a16 3-1	N06 0-3	a08 4-2	J15 3-2	S27 1-0	F05 0-4	a20 1-1	A25 2-1	O02 2-1
7 FULHAM	O09 2-1	A21 5-1	S25 2-3	J01 0-0	S01 2-0	S08 5-2		a16 0-1	M05 4-1	a30 1-3	N20 3-2	F05 1-2	O23 3-1	a02 1-2	D04 1-1	S11 3-1	F19 2-3	D25 3-1	M19 1-1	N06 2-2	a20 5-1	a11 0-0
8 HULL C	a25 0-3	a09 1-4	N13 0-1	a11 1-0	D11 1-1	a23 1-1	N27 0-0		S04 4-2	A21 0-2	A30 4-0	M26 2-2	D27 0-4	S18 1-0	J01 2-3	O30 5-2	F26 0-2	O16 2-1	O02 1-2	F12 1-1	M12 4-3	S13 0-1
9 IPSWICH T	S15 1-2	F26 1-1	a09 1-0	F05 2-3	M26 2-1	O30 5-1	O16 2-4	a18 2-0		S25 1-2	S11 1-2	D27 2-0	A28 3-1	S01 6-1	M09 2-1	D11 0-1	N27 2-1	M12 1-0	D18 2-2	S22 0-1	a23 1-1	N13 0-3
10 LEEDS U	O02 1-0	a23 2-0	M12 2-0	J15 1-0	F26 1-0	N13 1-0	D11 1-1	D18 3-0	F12 4-1		A28 2-3	N27 2-2	a11 4-0	D25 1-1	S18 1-1	a09 2-0	O30 3-2	M26 3-0	A25 2-4	S08 0-1	S11 5-2	O16 2-1
11 LINCOLN C	S18 1-1	a11 2-1	M26 0-2	A21 3-2	a23 3-0	O16 5-1	a09 2-2	A25 0-1	a27 1-1	J01 2-0		O30 3-3	S08 1-2	F12 3-3	S04 2-1	M16 1-2	N13 3-2	m04 0-1	D27 2-3	O02 1-4	N27 2-2	D11 2-1
12 LIVERPOOL	a30 2-2	J22 4-1	S15 5-3	O23 1-1	J01 2-0	A21 3-2	S18 4-1	N06 2-1	D25 6-2	a16 2-2	M19 2-4		a02 4-4	D04 3-1	N20 1-0	O02 3-1	S01 3-3	a11 1-1	O09 3-1	M05 2-4	F12 1-1	S04 1-2
13 LUTON T	S04 1-0	N27 7-3	a27 2-0	S01 3-2	O02 2-0	D11 3-0	M12 3-0	D25 1-1	J01 3-2	a08 0-0	S15 2-1	N13 3-2		J22 2-0	A21 3-0	M26 3-1	O16 3-1	a23 4-2	F12 4-0	S18 3-1	O30 1-2	a09 2-0
14 MIDDLESBROUGH	a08 2-5	M26 4-3	D11 1-0	a27 1-1	M12 3-1	N27 3-1	N13 4-2	F05 1-2	A25 0-1	D27 1-0	S25 2-1	a23 1-2	S11 0-2		S08 1-4	O16 2-0	D18 4-1	a09 2-0	J15 5-1	A28 1-2	F26 4-2	O30 6-0
15 NOTTINGHAM F	D27 0-2	O16 1-2	N27 1-0	S11 2-3	N13 3-0	M26 3-1	a23 2-0	A28 0-1	O02 2-0	F05 1-1	J15 1-1	a09 3-1	D18 1-5	S15 4-2		S25 0-1	M12 2-0	O30 2-3	a08 0-2	A25 0-3	D11 0-0	m02 1-1
16 NOTTS CO	D04 3-2	S04 3-1	D25 2-0	a16 2-1	A21 2-3	a11 4-0	a27 0-0	M19 3-1	a30 2-1	N20 1-2	O23 2-1	M03 0-3	N06 3-3	M05 1-3	F12 4-1		S09 2-0	S02 1-1	a02 3-2	O09 1-0	S18 2-1	J01 5-1
17 PLYMOUTH A	N20 1-0	F12 0-2	a11 0-1	N06 2-4	J22 1-0	S04 1-2	O02 3-2	O09 1-2	a16 2-0	M19 3-1	a02 1-0	A23 1-0	M05 2-1	A21 2-2	O23 1-2	S15 1-3		J01 0-0	D04 2-1	a30 2-0	D25 2-2	S18 1-1
18 PORT VALE	a16 2-0	O02 0-3	D18 1-0	a02 1-0	S18 3-0	J22 1-1	D27 4-0	M05 3-0	O23 3-3	N06 0-1	O09 1-3	a08 4-3	D04 1-1	N20 1-1	M19 1-2	A23 1-1	A28 1-0		a30 1-0	a25 0-1	S06 1-0	F12 1-1
19 ROTHERHAM U	J01 0-2	M12 5-1	O16 6-2	S06 4-2	a09 2-1	S18 2-3	O30 2-3	F19 2-0	A21 3-2	A30 3-0	D25 3-0	m02 6-1	S25 2-0	S04 3-0	a11 3-2	N13 2-0	a23 2-0	D11 3-0		a18 2-1	a25 2-0	N27 2-2
20 STOKE C	A21 2-1	O30 1-1	a23 2-0	D25 3-2	N27 3-1	a09 3-0	M26 1-1	S25 0-0	a11 3-0	S13 0-1	F19 4-2	O16 2-0	F05 0-0	J01 1-2	A30 2-0	M28 3-0	D11 3-1	S04 0-0	S11 1-2		N13 4-1	M12 0-2
21 SWANSEA T	M05 0-3	J01 2-3	M31 1-1	N20 1-1	a11 3-0	S02 3-0	S04 2-2	O23 1-0	D04 6-1	J22 2-0	a16 3-1	S25 3-2	M19 2-1	O09 2-0	a30 3-2	F05 3-0	D27 4-2	S16 7-1	N06 2-1	a02 3-5		A21 5-2
22 WEST HAM U	N06 2-2	A30 2-5	S11 5-2	D04 3-3	D25 1-0	F24 0-1	a08 2-1	S06 1-1	a02 4-0	M05 2-1	a30 0-1	a26 0-3	N20 2-1	M19 2-1	O09 2-0	A28 3-0	F05 6-1	S25 2-0	a16 1-2	O23 3-0	D18 3-3	

Season 1954-55

Division 3 North

	ACCRINGTON S	BARNSLEY	BARROW	BRADFORD	BRADFORD C	CARLISLE U	CHESTER	CHESTERFIELD	CREWE A	DARLINGTON	GATESHEAD	GRIMSBY T	HALIFAX T	HARTLEPOOLS U	MANSFIELD T	OLDHAM A	ROCHDALE	SCUNTHORPE U	SOUTHPORT	STOCKPORT CO	TRANMERE R	WORKINGTON	WREXHAM	YORK C
1 ACCRINGTON S		S27 2-3	J01 6-3	M12 4-3	J29 1-0	S01 3-2	F26 3-0	J03 4-1	S18 1-0	a23 3-0	N27 6-2	O16 3-0	D27 3-1	a09 2-5	J22 3-2	S08 4-0	O30 5-4	F19 2-1	A21 1-1	N13 0-1	M26 3-1	S04 2-0	S25 2-0	a11 2-2
2 BARNSLEY	S22 1-2		S18 3-0	S01 2-1	a11 1-0	a23 3-1	m04 4-2	a09 3-0	N27 3-1	N13 4-1	M26 3-0	D27 1-3	J01 3-0	O30 0-0	O02 1-0	A21 2-2	m03 2-0	S15 1-0	a27 0-0	M12 2-0	O16 4-1	F12 3-1	J08 4-2	S04 1-0
3 BARROW	A28 1-2	F05 3-1		N13 3-1	S25 3-2	M12 2-1	O30 2-0	a21 2-0	O16 0-3	A23 1-1	D27 0-1	M26 2-0	S20 1-3	a18 0-2	D18 2-2	F19 3-1	a09 4-2	S11 1-3	S13 2-1	a23 2-0	N27 1-0	a08 2-2	J15 1-1	m05 1-5
4 BRADFORD	O23 3-2	A23 1-0	a02 3-0		D18 2-0	S06 0-2	D27 3-0	S20 1-3	J29 2-1	F19 1-1	S25 2-2	a11 2-1	D04 0-1	F05 1-0	M19 0-0	a30 0-2	A28 1-1	O09 0-0	a25 1-0	S11 2-1	M30 0-0	N06 3-1	M05 0-0	a16 1-3
5 BRADFORD C	m04 0-3	a12 0-2	F12 2-1	A21 1-1		N27 2-0	a23 0-0	N13 1-1	a09 2-0	M26 3-0	O30 1-1	a20 4-0	S04 2-0	M12 0-1	S22 1-0	J01 0-1	S01 1-0	D25 2-4	S18 0-1	O16 2-3	m02 2-1	O02 0-1	S15 2-2	a04 2-3
6 CARLISLE U	A24 1-0	D04 2-4	O23 4-0	S14 3-2	a16 1-0		S21 1-2	F05 1-2	S25 4-0	S11 0-1	m03 1-2	J29 3-1	a02 4-0	A28 3-2	O09 1-2	a26 5-2	D25 7-2	a30 1-2	M19 2-1	D18 3-3	a08 1-2	M05 0-4	F19 1-0	N06 4-5
7 CHESTER	O09 1-1	a30 0-2	M19 3-1	D25 2-0	D04 1-0	S29 1-2		S25 1-0	F19 3-1	F05 0-2	S11 1-2	S15 1-0	D11 1-3	J15 1-0	M05 1-0	a16 0-0	a08 1-2	J08 2-4	a20 0-0	A28 1-0	D18 0-1	O23 0-2	A25 1-0	a02 1-2
8 CHESTERFIELD	a30 6-1	a25 3-1	O09 4-1	S27 1-3	a02 2-1	S18 2-1	F12 5-3		a13 0-0	A28 2-0	D18 1-3	O02 1-0	M19 2-1	a08 3-0	M30 4-1	N06 1-3	m02 3-1	a16 2-0	M05 2-1	D27 3-7	S06 2-1	A30 2-0	D04 3-1	O23 0-3
9 CREWE A	F05 0-3	a16 1-2	M05 5-1	J08 2-1	a27 1-0	F12 4-1	O02 1-3	S11 2-2		M30 2-2	A28 1-1	S27 2-0	N06 0-0	D18 1-1	A25 2-1	a02 4-1	S15 2-2	D04 1-1	O23 2-3	a08 4-4	D27 3-0	O09 1-1	a30 2-2	M19 2-3
10 DARLINGTON	D04 3-3	a02 0-1	S01 3-2	O02 3-0	N06 4-0	a20 1-1	S18 4-1	J01 0-2	S04 2-1		a11 5-1	F12 1-3	O23 1-0	D27 0-1	a30 3-1	M19 0-2	S29 2-2	a27 1-1	O09 2-0	S15 0-0	J29 2-2	A21 1-2	a16 2-2	M05 1-0
11 GATESHEAD	a16 1-1	N06 0-4	D25 3-1	M09 3-2	M19 2-1	S04 0-0	M30 0-0	A21 1-3	J01 1-0	a08 1-1		S18 1-0	M05 4-0	S06 3-0	D04 4-0	O23 2-2	O02 0-1	a02 0-1	A30 1-0	M23 4-4	S27 3-1	a30 3-2	a25 0-1	O09 1-1
12 GRIMSBY T	M05 2-1	D25 1-3	N06 1-0	a08 1-0	a30 1-4	M08 2-0	S08 3-1	F19 1-2	S22 2-1	S25 0-2	F05 1-1		a16 0-1	S11 1-0	O23 3-2	D04 1-1	D18 1-1	A24 1-4	a02 0-1	J15 1-0	A28 2-2	M19 0-1	O09 1-3	a27 2-1
13 HALIFAX T	D25 1-1	A28 1-1	S29 1-2	a23 0-0	a18 0-0	N13 5-3	a09 3-1	O30 2-0	M26 3-3	M12 4-1	O16 4-0	N27 3-2		M28 1-0	S08 1-2	S11 0-0	M16 1-2	D18 3-1	O02 0-1	A25 1-2	S18 0-0	J29 2-2	a11 2-0	F12 3-3
14 HARTLEPOOLS U	a25 1-3	M19 0-3	a30 0-0	S18 0-1	O23 0-0	J01 1-0	S04 3-1	a11 2-0	A21 2-1	D25 1-0	S13 0-0	M23 3-2	O09 1-0		a16 1-2	M05 2-0	F12 3-1	N06 4-2	M30 2-1	S27 2-1	O02 4-0	D04 3-2	a02 3-0	A30 1-0
15 MANSFIELD T	S11 2-2	F19 1-1	A21 0-5	O30 2-1	S27 1-0	F26 1-1	O16 2-1	S04 2-0	A30 4-2	a18 3-1	a23 0-1	M12 3-0	S13 2-1	N27 0-2		J29 1-3	M26 3-2	S25 2-1	a11 3-0	a09 0-0	N13 3-1	J01 2-0	F05 2-1	D27 1-2
16 OLDHAM A	S13 0-1	D18 4-1	O02 3-2	a18 5-0	A28 1-1	a09 2-1	N27 2-1	M26 4-1	N13 4-0	O30 3-1	M12 1-2	a23 4-0	m02 1-2	O16 0-1	J08 1-1		S04 0-0	a08 1-1	F12 1-0	F26 1-1	A24 2-1	S21 2-1	D25 2-1	S18 3-2
17 ROCHDALE	M19 0-0	O09 3-0	a27 4-1	J01 3-2	A25 1-2	D27 1-2	a11 2-0	J29 0-0	S08 1-1	S22 2-2	F19 4-0	A21 0-3	a30 2-2	S25 2-1	N06 2-0	a20 2-1		M05 2-0	a16 0-0	F05 1-0	S11 2-0	a02 2-1	O23 2-1	D04 1-1
18 SCUNTHORPE U	O02 4-0	S09 1-0	J22 3-0	m05 1-1	D27 1-0	a18 1-1	J29 1-1	N27 2-1	a23 3-1	a09 1-0	N13 0-2	S02 1-0	A21 2-2	M26 5-1	F12 2-0	a11 6-1	O16 2-2		S04 2-0	O30 3-0	M12 1-2	S18 1-1	S30 1-0	J01 1-2
19 SOUTHPORT	D18 1-1	S11 0-2	S07 2-1	a09 1-0	F05 1-0	O30 4-1	M26 1-1	O16 0-0	M12 1-0	F26 0-0	A24 1-2	N13 2-2	F19 4-0	m02 1-0	a08 1-0	S25 1-0	N27 1-0	m07 1-1		D11 1-1	a23 0-0	D27 1-2	A28 1-2	S28 2-2
20 STOCKPORT CO	a02 0-0	O23 1-0	D04 1-2	J22 6-0	M05 1-1	A21 5-2	J01 3-0	D25 3-2	a11 6-1	S06 3-0	J29 2-1	S04 0-0	A30 2-1	S20 0-2	a25 2-2	O09 3-2	S18 1-4	M19 4-2	a30 0-2		F12 2-0	a16 0-1	N06 4-0	F21 1-2
21 TRANMERE R	N06 3-1	M05 0-1	a16 0-4	S04 3-3	O09 2-0	a11 6-1	A21 1-1	S14 0-0	D25 1-2	M09 0-1	S21 1-2	J01 2-0	F05 1-2	F19 3-1	a02 2-1	A31 2-1	J22 3-1	O23 1-2	D04 2-2	S25 1-1		a26 1-1	M19 1-2	a30 1-0
22 WORKINGTON	J15 0-1	S25 1-0	a11 0-0	M26 1-3	F19 1-1	O16 1-0	M12 1-1	A25 2-3	F26 3-3	D18 6-1	a20 4-0	O30 2-2	m04 1-0	a23 0-1	A28 2-2	S29 3-0	N13 1-0	F05 1-1	D25 0-1	N27 4-1	a09 1-0		S11 2-1	S15 2-1
23 WREXHAM	F12 3-1	J29 3-0	S04 3-0	O16 1-0	S08 1-3	O02 1-1	S01 2-1	a23 0-2	a20 5-0	N27 2-2	a09 2-0	m04 5-0	a08 1-1	N13 1-4	S18 1-3	D27 2-1	M12 0-0	S22 0-1	J01 2-2	M26 1-4	O30 1-2	M30 1-1		A21 2-6
24 YORK C	a08 1-1	J15 1-3	m02 1-4	N27 1-2	S11 0-1	a13 2-1	N13 5-0	M16 3-2	O30 3-1	O16 3-1	F26 2-1	a09 0-0	S25 2-1	A23 1-0	D25 3-1	F05 2-1	a23 2-0	A28 2-3	S20 1-1	O02 4-0	a18 1-0	S06 0-0	D18 3-3	

Division 3 South

	ALDERSHOT	BOURNEMOUTH	BRENTFORD	BRIGHTON & HA	BRISTOL C	COLCHESTER U	COVENTRY C	CRYSTAL P	EXETER C	GILLINGHAM	LEYTON O	MILLWALL	NEWPORT CO	NORTHAMPTON T	NORWICH C	Q.P.R.	READING	SHREWSBURY T	SOUTHAMPTON	SOUTHEND U	SWINDON T	TORQUAY U	WALSALL	WATFORD
1 ALDERSHOT		S01 1-1	N06 2-3	a30 2-2	M05 0-2	D25 2-2	a02 1-1	S18 3-0	a08 4-2	M19 0-2	D04 0-1	a16 3-0	S22 0-0	F12 3-4	D18 4-1	S15 2-0	S04 3-1	J08 2-0	a27 2-0	A28 1-0	J22 0-0	O23 2-1	O09 4-0	O02 3-0
2 BOURNEMOUTH	A25 4-0		M19 1-2	D04 1-1	a27 0-1	F05 2-0	D18 2-1	S22 4-1	S11 2-0	O23 1-2	M05 0-3	O09 0-1	J15 3-3	a11 0-1	S25 1-3	A28 2-2	a30 0-0	N06 3-1	a20 1-1	F19 2-1	S08 1-1	a16 0-2	a02 1-1	D25 1-1
3 BRENTFORD	M26 1-1	O30 1-3		J22 2-3	F12 2-2	O16 3-2	A28 2-3	a09 3-0	F26 1-0	S23 3-0	a08 2-0	D25 3-1	m02 1-0	N27 1-3	M12 1-0	S04 1-1	S16 2-2	A26 2-2	D18 0-3	m05 2-2	N13 4-2	S18 4-2	O02 0-2	a23 3-2
4 BRIGHTON & H.A.	m04 5-3	a23 1-1	S11 3-4		O02 0-1	F26 1-1	m07 2-0	N13 1-0	M23 5-3	a11 1-0	a20 1-0	D18 1-2	S18 4-1	a09 2-1	O16 0-1	O30 4-1	S22 3-2	S08 0-0	A28 1-2	M12 2-1	M26 3-1	F12 1-1	A25 3-0	N27 3-1
5 BRISTOL C	O16 6-1	a09 2-2	S25 2-1	F19 3-2		S14 4-0	F05 2-0	a19 3-0	O30 2-0	D18 1-4	A28 5-0	M09 5-1	a23 0-0	M26 5-1	J08 0-1	N27 1-1	D25 2-1	a11 4-1	S11 2-0	F26 3-2	M12 3-0	A31 1-1	S21 5-3	N13 1-0
6 COLCHESTER U	D27 1-1	S18 3-3	M05 3-2	O09 2-4	S09 0-2		O23 0-1	J01 2-0	S02 1-2	a28 2-2	a02 2-2	N06 0-2	O02 1-0	S04 4-1	S23 1-0	F12 1-0	a16 0-2	D04 2-4	a30 3-5	a08 2-0	A21 0-0	M31 0-2	M19 2-2	J22 1-3
7 COVENTRY C	N13 2-1	A21 1-0	J01 1-0	S04 2-1	S18 1-3	M12 0-0		N27 4-1	O16 1-1	S06 4-1	S20 2-2	a12 4-1	a04 3-2	a23 0-0	a18 4-0	m02 5-1	A23 2-1	O02 3-0	D25 1-1	m04 1-4	a09 1-0	J22 0-1	F12 5-3	O30 3-2
8 CRYSTAL P	F05 3-2	S29 2-1	a27 1-1	a02 1-0	a30 1-2	A28 0-0	a16 1-0		D18 1-1	J08 0-2	F19 1-1	M19 1-1	D25 2-1	S01 3-1	m04 2-0	a08 2-1	O09 1-1	M05 2-2	D04 1-2	S11 2-2	S25 0-0	N06 1-1	O23 3-1	S15 1-1
9 EXETER C	a11 0-1	J22 1-1	O09 3-2	J29 3-1	M19 0-1	A25 2-2	M05 0-0	A21 2-0		a02 1-1	N06 1-7	a30 1-4	F12 1-1	J01 3-1	S08 0-1	S18 2-1	a27 3-1	a16 1-0	O23 0-1	S29 2-1	D25 2-1	F19 1-2	D04 1-1	S04 0-0
10 GILLINGHAM	O30 0-2	M12 0-2	S29 2-1	a08 1-1	A21 1-1	a09 2-1	S15 2-1	J29 2-1	N13 1-1		S25 0-0	F19 1-1	M26 4-2	F26 2-2	N27 2-1	a20 3-1	J22 5-1	S04 3-3	A25 1-0	a23 1-1	S18 2-1	D27 3-1	J01 3-2	O16 0-1
11 LEYTON O	a23 1-5	O16 3-1	a11 0-1	D27 0-0	J01 4-1	N13 2-0	S30 1-0	O02 2-1	M26 5-0	F12 2-2		A26 1-0	M17 1-2	J29 2-1	a09 1-2	M12 3-0	S18 2-0	J22 5-0	S09 4-1	N27 5-1	O30 1-0	A21 2-1	S04 1-0	F26 0-1
12 MILLWALL	N27 3-1	F26 1-1	D27 2-2	A21 2-0	S04 1-3	M26 5-2	a08 3-1	O30 5-2	m02 2-2	O02 3-2	A30 1-0		M12 1-1	S13 1-0	N13 0-0	O16 0-1	F12 2-2	S18 2-0	S20 2-0	a09 1-4	a23 1-0	J01 4-1	J22 1-0	J29 1-0
13 NEWPORT CO	S30 2-1	S04 1-1	a21 3-1	F05 1-3	D04 2-2	F19 0-0	O09 1-1	D27 0-1	S25 2-1	N06 1-3	a30 1-2	O23 2-1		A21 0-1	A26 1-1	J22 4-0	a02 3-1	a28 1-1	M05 0-1	S16 3-2	a08 2-2	M19 1-1	a16 1-0	J01 0-2
14 NORTHAMPTON T	S25 2-1	a12 5-0	a16 1-2	a27 1-0	N06 2-0	a18 6-1	D04 1-0	A26 1-1	A28 2-0	O09 4-1	J08 2-2	S09 0-1	D18 2-2		S11 1-1	D27 1-3	M05 2-6	O23 3-1	M19 2-1	F05 6-2	D11 1-0	a02 1-0	a30 1-1	S30 0-1
15 NORWICH C	A21 4-3	F12 0-1	O23 1-0	M05 0-0	J29 0-1	S29 0-2	a30 1-1	S04 2-0	S15 3-0	a16 1-2	a27 1-1	a02 2-1	S01 2-0	J22 3-2		O02 1-1	D04 0-1	M19 2-0	N06 2-0	D27 3-3	J01 2-1	O09 5-1	a11 2-1	S18 3-1
16 Q.P.R.	S07 5-0	J01 1-1	J15 1-1	M19 3-2	a16 1-1	S25 4-1	J29 3-2	a11 1-0	F05 1-2	a30 1-1	O23 2-0	M05 1-2	S11 2-0	D25 1-0	F19 2-1		N06 2-3	a02 2-0	O09 2-2	A30 1-1	S27 3-1	D04 4-2	a25 1-1	A21 2-1
17 READING	a20 2-2	M30 1-0	S08 0-0	S29 0-2	D27 0-2	N27 4-0	S01 2-2	F26 5-0	a09 0-0	S11 2-2	F05 0-2	S25 0-0	N13 2-1	O16 0-1	a23 1-1	M26 3-1		J01 1-2	F19 0-1	O30 1-1	J29 2-1	a11 3-2	A21 2-2	M12 1-1
18 SHREWSBURY T	J29 1-0	a25 3-0	A30 2-2	S13 3-0	D11 0-2	a23 2-0	F19 1-0	O16 1-1	N27 1-1	m02 1-1	S11 0-2	F05 3-2	a09 3-0	M12 4-0	O30 2-1	N13 1-0	A28 2-3		S25 3-1	D18 2-3	m06 7-0	S27 3-2	D27 2-2	a18 2-1
19 SOUTHAMPTON	a09 1-1	J29 0-0	A21 6-4	J01 3-2	J22 2-1	J08 0-1	D27 1-0	a23 2-2	M12 3-0	S01 3-1	S15 1-0	S29 3-0	O16 2-0	O30 4-0	M26 3-1	F26 2-2	O02 3-1	F12 2-1		N13 3-0	N27 1-1	S04 0-0	S18 2-1	a11 2-0
20 SOUTHEND U	J01 0-1	O02 2-2	a30 3-2	O23 4-0	O09 3-2	a11 4-2	N06 1-0	J22 3-2	S21 0-0	D04 3-1	a16 1-2	a26 1-0	S07 1-1	S18 4-1	D25 4-1	A24 2-2	M19 0-0	A21 4-1	a02 0-1		S04 4-1	M05 1-2	J29 2-1	F12 1-3
21 SWINDON T	S11 1-0	S15 0-2	a02 1-1	N06 0-2	O23 2-2	D18 1-1	a27 3-0	F12 0-0	D27 2-0	F05 2-1	M19 0-0	D04 1-1	a11 1-3	O02 0-1	A28 1-0	S22 2-0	m04 2-0	O09 2-1	a16 1-0	a20 0-1		a30 0-0	M05 2-2	S01 6-1
22 TORQUAY U	M12 2-2	N27 0-1	F05 4-2	S25 2-1	A25 2-2	m04 2-1	S11 1-2	M26 2-2	O02 1-0	D25 1-3	D18 2-7	A28 4-2	O30 2-3	N13 5-2	F26 2-0	a23 3-2	a25 3-1	S22 2-0	J15 2-2	O16 4-1	a06 1-1		S08 2-0	a09 2-2
23 WALSALL	M31 2-2	N13 6-1	F19 2-2	S02 0-2	S30 1-3	O30 3-1	S25 1-1	M12 1-4	a23 1-0	A28 0-1	m05 1-4	S11 1-1	N27 3-3	a04 6-1	a12 2-1	a09 4-1	D18 4-0	D25 4-0	F05 0-0	m02 4-1	O16 1-2	S16 2-4		M26 0-1
24 WATFORD	F19 0-0	D27 1-0	D04 2-2	a16 0-0	a02 0-2	S11 2-0	M19 1-0	S07 7-1	m06 1-1	M05 1-1	O09 1-3	M30 5-3	A28 3-2	S21 1-1	F05 2-2	D18 1-1	O23 1-3	a30 2-1	a08 2-1	S25 1-1	A24 3-0	a26 4-1	N06 4-0	

League Tables

Division 1

	P	W	D	L	F	A	W	D	L	F	A	Pts
Chelsea	42	11	5	5	43	29	9	7	5	38	28	52
Wolverh'pton W	42	13	5	3	58	30	6	5	10	31	40	48
Portsmouth	42	13	5	3	44	21	5	7	9	30	41	48
Sunderland	42	8	11	2	39	27	7	7	7	25	27	48
Manchester U	42	12	4	5	44	30	8	3	10	40	44	47
Aston Villa	42	11	3	7	38	31	9	4	8	34	42	47
Manchester C	42	11	5	5	45	36	7	5	9	31	33	46
Newcastle U	42	12	5	4	53	27	5	4	12	36	50	43
Arsenal	42	12	3	6	44	25	5	6	10	25	38	43
Burnley	42	11	3	7	29	19	6	6	9	22	29	43
Everton	42	9	6	6	32	24	7	4	10	30	44	42
Huddersfield T	42	10	4	7	28	23	4	9	8	35	45	41
Sheffield U	42	10	3	8	41	34	7	4	10	29	52	41
Preston N.E.	42	8	5	8	47	33	8	3	10	36	31	40
Charlton A	42	8	6	7	43	34	7	4	10	33	41	40
Tottenham H	42	9	4	8	42	35	7	4	10	30	38	40
W.B.A.	42	11	5	5	44	33	5	3	13	32	63	40
Bolton W	42	11	6	4	45	29	2	7	12	17	40	39
Blackpool	42	8	6	7	33	26	6	4	11	27	38	38
Cardiff C	42	9	4	8	41	38	4	7	10	21	38	37
Leicester C	42	9	6	6	43	32	3	5	13	31	54	35
Sheffield W	42	7	7	7	42	38	1	3	17	21	62	26

Division 2

	P	W	D	L	F	A	W	D	L	F	A	Pts
Birmingham C	42	14	4	3	56	22	8	6	7	36	25	54
Luton T	42	18	2	1	55	18	5	6	10	33	35	54
Rotherham U	42	17	1	3	59	22	8	3	10	35	42	54
Leeds U	42	14	4	3	43	19	9	3	9	27	34	53
Stoke C	42	12	5	4	38	17	9	5	7	31	29	52
Blackburn R	42	14	4	3	73	31	8	2	11	41	48	50
Notts Co	42	14	3	4	46	27	7	3	11	28	44	48
West Ham U	42	12	4	5	46	28	6	6	9	28	42	46
Bristol R	42	15	4	2	52	23	4	3	14	23	47	45
Swansea T	42	15	3	3	58	28	2	6	13	28	55	43
Liverpool	42	11	7	3	55	37	5	3	13	37	59	42
Middlesbrough	42	13	1	7	48	31	5	5	11	25	51	42
Bury	42	10	5	6	44	35	5	6	10	33	37	41
Fulham	42	10	5	6	46	29	4	6	11	30	50	39
Nottingham F	42	8	4	9	29	29	8	3	10	29	33	39
Lincoln C	42	8	6	7	39	35	5	4	12	29	44	36
Port Vale	42	10	6	5	31	21	2	5	14	17	50	35
Doncaster R	42	10	5	6	35	34	4	2	15	23	61	35
Hull C	42	7	5	9	30	35	5	5	11	14	34	34
Plymouth A	42	10	4	7	29	26	2	3	16	28	56	31
Ipswich T	42	10	3	8	37	28	1	3	17	20	64	28
Derby Co	42	6	6	9	39	34	1	3	17	14	48	23

Division 3 North

	P	W	D	L	F	A	W	D	L	F	A	Pts
Barnsley	46	18	3	2	51	17	12	2	9	35	29	65
Accrington S	46	18	2	3	65	32	7	9	7	31	35	61
Scunthorpe U	46	14	6	3	45	18	9	6	8	36	35	58
York C	46	13	5	5	43	27	11	5	7	49	36	58
Hartlepool U	46	16	3	4	39	20	9	2	12	25	29	55
Chesterfield	46	17	1	5	54	33	7	5	11	27	37	54
Gateshead	46	11	7	5	38	26	9	5	9	27	43	52
Workington	46	11	7	5	39	23	7	7	9	29	32	50
Stockport Co	46	13	4	6	50	27	5	8	10	34	43	48
Oldham A	46	14	5	4	47	22	5	5	13	27	46	48
Southport	46	10	9	4	28	18	6	7	10	19	26	48
Rochdale	46	13	7	3	39	20	4	7	12	30	46	48
Mansfield T	46	14	4	5	40	28	4	5	14	25	43	45
Halifax T	46	9	9	5	41	27	6	4	13	22	40	43
Darlington	46	10	7	6	41	28	4	7	12	21	45	42
Bradford P.A.	46	11	7	5	29	21	4	4	15	27	49	41
Barrow	46	12	4	7	39	34	5	2	16	31	55	40
Wrexham	46	9	6	8	40	35	4	6	13	25	42	38
Tranmere R	46	9	6	8	37	30	4	5	14	18	40	37
Carlisle U	46	12	1	10	53	39	3	5	15	25	50	36
Bradford C	46	9	5	9	30	26	4	5	14	17	29	36
Crewe A	46	8	10	5	45	35	2	4	17	23	56	34
Grimsby T	46	10	4	9	28	32	3	4	16	19	46	34
Chester C	46	10	3	10	23	25	2	6	15	21	52	33

Division 3 South

	P	W	D	L	F	A	W	D	L	F	A	Pts
Bristol C	46	17	4	2	62	22	13	6	4	39	25	70
Leyton O	46	16	2	5	48	20	10	7	6	41	27	61
Southampton	46	16	6	1	49	19	8	5	10	26	32	59
Gillingham	46	12	8	3	41	28	8	7	8	36	38	55
Millwall	46	14	6	3	44	25	6	5	12	28	43	51
Brighton & H.A.	46	14	4	5	47	27	6	6	11	29	36	50
Watford	46	11	9	3	45	26	7	5	11	26	36	50
Torquay U	46	12	6	5	51	39	6	6	11	31	43	48
Coventry C	46	15	5	3	50	26	3	6	14	17	33	47
Southend U	46	13	5	5	48	28	4	7	12	35	52	46
Brentford	46	11	6	6	44	36	5	8	10	38	46	46
Norwich C	46	13	5	5	40	23	5	5	13	20	37	46
Northampton T	46	13	5	5	47	27	6	3	14	26	54	46
Aldershot	46	12	6	5	44	23	4	7	12	31	48	45
Q.P.R.	46	13	7	3	46	25	2	7	14	23	50	44
Shrewsbury T	46	14	5	4	49	24	2	5	16	21	54	42
Bournemouth	46	7	8	8	32	29	5	10	8	25	36	42
Reading	46	7	10	6	32	26	6	5	12	33	47	41
Newport Co	46	8	8	7	32	29	3	8	12	28	44	38
Crystal Palace	46	9	11	3	32	24	2	5	16	20	56	38
Swindon T	46	10	8	5	30	19	1	7	15	16	45	37
Exeter C	46	9	7	7	30	31	2	8	13	17	42	37
Walsall	46	9	6	8	49	36	1	8	14	26	50	34
Colchester U	46	7	6	10	33	40	2	7	14	20	51	31

FOOTBALL LEAGUE RECORDS

Top scorers: Div 1, N.Lofthouse (Bolton Wanderers) 33 goals; Div 2, W.Gardiner (Leicester City) 34 goals; Div 3 N, R.Crosbie (Grimsby Town) 36 goals; Div 3 S, R.Collins (Torquay United) 40 goals.

Centre-forward Tommy Taylor, who was killed in the Munich air disaster. In 1955-56, his 25 goals were a big contribution to Manchester United winning the League Championship.

DIVISION 1

	ARSENAL	ASTON VILLA	BIRMINGHAM C	BLACKPOOL	BOLTON W	BURNLEY	CARDIFF C	CHARLTON A	CHELSEA	EVERTON	HUDDERSFIELD T	LUTON T	MANCHESTER C	MANCHESTER U	NEWCASTLE U	PORTSMOUTH	PRESTON N.E.	SHEFFIELD U	SUNDERLAND	TOTTENHAM H	W.B.A.	WOLVERHAMPTON W
1 ARSENAL		O01 1-0	a14 1-0	D17 4-1	D31 3-1	N26 0-1	A23 3-1	O29 2-4	A27 1-1	F21 3-2	a02 2-0	M31 3-0	S06 0-0	M17 1-1	O15 1-0	S17 1-3	M06 3-2	N12 2-1	F04 3-1	J14 0-1	D10 2-0	D27 2-2
2 ASTON VILLA	F11 1-1		S05 0-0	S10 1-1	S24 0-2	M19 2-0	A27 2-0	M03 1-1	J21 1-4	M31 2-0	D31 3-0	N12 1-0	D17 0-3	O15 4-4	O29 3-0	D26 1-3	D10 3-2	a14 3-2	A29 1-4	N26 0-2	a28 3-0	a03 0-0
3 BIRMINGHAM C	D03 4-0	S21 2-2		M24 1-2	a21 5-2	J14 1-2	a07 2-1	F04 4-0	N05 3-0	D26 6-2	N19 5-0	S17 0-0	O22 4-3	A20 2-2	A31 3-1	F25 3-2	S03 0-3	D24 0-2	O08 1-2	O01 3-0	a02 2-0	M10 0-0
4 BLACKPOOL	A20 3-1	J14 6-0	N12 2-0		M30 0-0	A29 1-1	O01 2-1	O15 5-0	S05 2-1	D10 4-0	D26 4-2	F18 3-2	F04 0-1	N26 0-0	M17 5-1	D24 2-3	O29 2-6	M31 1-1	S03 7-3	a14 0-2	M03 5-1	S17 2-1
5 BOLTON W	S03 4-1	F18 1-0	D10 6-0	a02 1-3		M31 0-1	S07 4-0	A27 1-3	D17 4-0	O15 1-1	J02 2-2	O29 4-0	D26 1-3	N12 3-1	a14 3-2	J14 4-0	N26 0-0	M03 2-1	S17 0-3	M21 3-2	M17 4-0	O01 2-1
6 BURNLEY	a07 0-1	N05 2-0	S10 3-2	A22 0-2	O22 2-0		F25 0-2	a02 2-1	M10 5-0	A27 0-1	O08 2-0	S05 3-1	D03 2-2	S24 0-0	D31 3-1	N19 3-0	D26 1-2	F11 1-1	M24 4-0	D17 2-0	J21 1-2	a21 1-2
7 CARDIFF C	a28 1-2	D24 1-0	N26 2-1	F11 1-0	A31 1-0	O15 2-2		D10 3-1	D26 1-1	N12 3-1	S24 1-2	a14 2-0	J14 4-1	O29 0-1	M07 1-1	a02 2-3	F18 3-1	S17 3-2	A20 3-1	a23 0-0	M31 1-3	S03 1-9
8 CHARLTON A	M10 2-0	N19 3-1	S24 2-0	F25 1-2	D24 3-1	M30 2-1	a21 0-0		O08 1-2	S10 0-2	D03 4-1	A20 2-2	N05 5-2	D27 3-0	J21 0-2	O22 6-1	S15 2-1	S01 3-2	a07 2-1	D31 1-2	F11 5-1	M24 0-2
9 CHELSEA	D24 2-0	S17 0-0	M21 1-2	a28 2-1	A20 0-2	O29 0-0	D27 2-1	F22 3-1		a14 6-1	A29 0-0	a02 0-0	O01 2-1	M03 2-4	D10 2-1	S03 1-5	M31 0-1	N26 1-0	J14 2-3	O15 2-0	N12 2-0	F04 2-3
10 EVERTON	O08 1-1	O22 2-1	D27 5-1	a21 1-0	F25 1-0	D24 1-1	M24 2-0	J14 3-2	D03 3-3		N05 5-2	S03 0-1	N19 1-1	S14 4-2	F11 0-0	F04 0-2	A20 0-4	M30 1-4	M10 1-2	S17 2-1	A31 2-0	a07 2-1
11 HUDDERSFIELD T	a03 0-1	S03 1-1	M07 1-1	D27 3-1	a28 3-1	F18 1-0	F04 1-2	a14 4-0	A24 1-3	M17 1-0		O15 0-2	S17 3-3	M31 0-2	N12 2-6	A20 1-0	O01 2-2	O29 1-2	D24 4-0	D10 1-0	N26 1-0	J14 1-3
12 LUTON T	O22 0-0	M24 2-1	J21 0-1	O08 3-1	M10 0-0	a28 2-3	D03 3-0	D17 2-1	M30 2-2	D31 2-2	F25 1-2		a21 3-2	F11 0-2	S10 4-2	a07 1-0	A31 2-1	D27 2-1	N19 8-2	A27 2-1	S24 0-2	N05 5-1
13 MANCHESTER C	A31 2-2	A20 2-2	M31 1-1	S24 2-0	D27 2-0	a14 1-3	S10 3-1	M21 0-2	F11 2-2	M07 3-0	J21 1-0	D10 3-2		S03 1-0	N26 1-2	J02 4-1	O15 0-2	a11 3-1	a02 4-2	N12 1-2	O29 2-0	D24 2-2
14 MANCHESTER U	N05 1-1	F25 1-0	D17 2-1	a07 2-1	M24 1-0	F04 2-0	M10 1-1	D26 5-1	N19 3-0	S07 2-1	O22 3-0	O01 3-1	D31 2-1		M30 5-2	a21 1-0	S17 3-2	J14 3-1	D03 2-1	A24 2-2	A27 3-1	O08 4-3
15 NEWCASTLE U	F25 2-0	M10 2-3	A24 2-2	N05 1-2	D03 3-0	S03 3-1	N19 4-0	S17 4-1	a21 1-1	O01 1-2	M24 1-1	J14 4-0	a07 3-1	a02 0-0		O08 2-1	D24 5-0	A20 4-2	D27 3-1	F04 1-2	J02 0-3	O22 3-1
16 PORTSMOUTH	J21 5-2	D27 2-2	O15 0-5	A27 3-3	S10 3-3	M03 3-1	M30 1-1	M31 4-0	D31 4-4	S24 1-0	D17 5-2	N26 0-0	a28 2-4	D10 3-2	F22 0-2		N12 0-2	M17 1-1	O01 2-1	O29 4-1	a14 1-1	A24 2-1
17 PRESTON N.E.	N19 0-1	a21 0-1	D31 1-1	M10 3-3	a07 0-1	D27 4-2	O08 1-2	S07 2-2	O22 2-3	D17 0-1	F11 1-2	A24 2-1	F25 0-3	J21 3-1	A27 4-3	M24 2-1		S24 0-2	N05 2-2	a02 3-3	S10 0-1	D03 2-0
18 SHEFFIELD U	M24 0-2	D03 2-2	A27 0-3	O22 2-1	N19 1-3	O01 1-2	J21 2-1	A22 0-0	a07 2-1	a02 1-1	M10 3-1	D26 0-4	O08 1-1	S10 1-0	D17 2-1	N05 1-3	F04 3-1		a21 2-3	S05 2-0	D31 2-2	m02 3-3
19 SUNDERLAND	S24 3-1	A24 5-1	a18 1-0	D31 0-0	J21 0-0	N12 4-4	D17 1-1	N26 3-2	S10 4-3	O29 0-0	A27 4-1	M07 1-2	M30 0-3	a14 2-2	D26 1-6	F11 4-2	M21 2-2	D10 3-2		M31 3-2	O15 2-1	J02 1-1
20 TOTTENHAM H	S10 3-1	a07 4-3	F11 0-1	D03 1-1	O08 0-3	A20 0-1	N05 1-1	S03 2-3	F25 4-0	J21 1-1	a21 1-2	D24 2-1	M24 2-1	A31 1-2	S24 3-1	M10 1-1	M30 0-4	a28 3-1	O22 2-3		D26 4-1	N19 2-1
21 W.B.A.	a21 2-1	O08 1-0	a03 0-2	N19 1-2	N05 2-0	S17 1-0	O22 2-1	O01 3-3	M24 3-0	A24 2-0	a07 1-2	F04 3-1	M10 0-4	D24 1-4	S07 1-1	D03 4-0	J14 3-2	S03 2-1	F25 3-0	D27 1-0		A20 1-1
22 WOLVERHAMPTON W	D26 3-3	a02 0-0	O29 1-0	J21 2-3	F11 4-2	D10 3-1	D31 0-2	N12 2-0	S24 2-1	N26 1-0	S10 4-0	M17 1-2	A27 7-2	F18 0-2	M31 2-1	A31 3-1	a14 2-1	O15 3-2	a28 3-1	a18 5-1	D17 3-2	

Roy Shiner, a colourful goalscorer who helped Sheffield Wednesday back into Division One.

DIVISION 2

	BARNSLEY	BLACKBURN R	BRISTOL C	BRISTOL R	BURY	DONCASTER R	FULHAM	HULL C	LEEDS U	LEICESTER C	LINCOLN C	LIVERPOOL	MIDDLESBROUGH	NOTTINGHAM F	NOTTS CO	PLYMOUTH A	PORT VALE	ROTHERHAM U	SHEFFIELD W	STOKE C	SWANSEA T	WEST HAM U
1 BARNSLEY		F25 2-1	S24 0-0	N19 4-3	S03 3-3	M24 2-2	D24 3-0	D03 2-1	A20 2-1	J14 0-1	O08 1-0	M10 0-5	J21 0-4	a21 1-1	A31 3-1	O22 1-2	D27 1-2	S14 3-2	N05 0-3	a07 1-0	a02 3-2	F11 1-1
2 BLACKBURN R	O15 5-1		O29 4-6	F04 2-0	M31 3-1	O01 1-1	A29 1-0	M30 2-0	D10 2-3	D24 2-3	A20 0-2	S03 3-3	a14 2-1	J02 2-2	M03 2-0	J14 2-1	N12 7-1	a30 3-1	D26 2-2	S17 3-0	N26 3-0	M17 4-1
3 BRISTOL C	F04 2-0	a21 2-0		O22 1-1	S17 3-1	a07 4-1	J14 2-1	N05 5-2	S03 0-1	F25 1-1	D03 5-1	O08 2-1	O01 2-0	M24 0-0	D24 1-3	D27 6-0	a02 0-0	A30 5-2	N19 3-2	M10 0-1	A20 2-1	S06 3-1
4 BRISTOL R	F18 1-1	S24 1-0	M03 0-3		N12 4-2	A27 4-2	M17 2-2	J21 4-2	O29 4-1	D26 2-1	F11 3-0	a28 1-2	N26 7-2	S10 4-1	a14 2-0	M30 2-1	D17 1-2	M31 1-4	D31 4-2	A22 4-2	O15 1-2	D10 1-1
5 BURY	D31 3-0	O08 0-4	J21 1-1	M24 0-1		N05 5-1	A20 1-5	F25 3-2	A30 1-0	M10 3-1	D24 3-3	O22 1-4	S10 1-1	D03 1-2	M30 4-0	a07 7-1	F11 2-2	D27 2-1	a21 2-5	N19 1-0	S19 2-4	S24 1-1
6 DONCASTER R	N12 1-1	F11 2-2	N26 3-2	D24 2-1	M17 2-3		O29 4-2	S24 3-0	a14 1-2	S05 6-2	D27 2-0	M30 1-0	m03 0-1	J21 1-3	O15 1-1	S01 3-1	D10 3-0	S03 1-1	S10 2-2	A20 2-4	M31 3-1	M26 2-1
7 FULHAM	A27 5-1	A24 3-0	S10 3-0	N05 3-5	D17 3-1	a21 4-0		O08 5-0	M30 1-2	O22 3-2	M10 3-0	a07 3-1	D31 4-1	m02 4-3	S07 1-1	N19 2-1	S24 1-4	F11 1-1	D03 1-2	M24 2-0	D26 4-1	J21 3-1
8 HULL C	a14 4-1	a02 0-3	M17 1-3	S17 1-2	O15 2-3	a10 1-1	M31 2-2		a28 1-4	A20 2-4	A29 2-1	D24 1-2	O29 2-2	D27 0-3	D10 2-0	S03 0-1	F18 2-1	N26 0-3	O01 2-2	m01 3-2	M03 1-4	**N12 3-1**
9 LEEDS U	D17 3-1	M10 1-2	D31 2-1	a21 2-1	A22 1-0	D03 3-0	a02 6-1	S05 1-0		a07 4-0	O22 1-0	N19 4-2	A27 2-0	O08 3-0	D26 1-0	M24 4-2	J21 1-1	S24 4-1	F25 2-1	N05 1-0	F11 2-2	S10 3-3
10 LEICESTER C	S10 0-0	A27 0-2	O15 2-2	D27 4-2	D10 5-0	a28 3-0	M03 2-1	D17 1-2	N26 5-2		D31 4-0	S17 3-1	M31 1-1	A22 5-2	F18 4-0	F04 5-1	O29 4-1	M17 3-1	a02 1-2	O01 3-1	N12 6-1	a14 2-1
11 LINCOLN C	M31 4-0	D17 3-0	a14 2-0	O01 2-0	A27 4-2	D26 1-1	D10 6-1	A24 2-0	M03 1-1	S03 7-1		m02 2-0	O15 1-2	a02 1-3	N26 2-0	S17 1-0	M17 1-0	N12 1-1	S07 2-2	a25 2-1	F18 3-1	O29 1-1
12 LIVERPOOL	D10 1-1	D31 1-2	M31 2-1	S07 0-2	M03 4-2	a02 1-2	N26 7-0	A27 3-0	F29 1-0	J21 3-1	S10 2-1		S24 1-1	D17 5-2	N12 2-1	O01 4-1	a14 4-1	O29 2-0	A24 0-3	D26 2-2	M17 4-1	O15 3-1
13 MIDDLESBROUGH	S17 1-1	D03 1-0	F11 2-1	a07 0-1	J14 1-3	N19 4-1	S03 1-1	a21 5-1	D24 5-3	O08 4-3	a18 4-2	F04 1-2		N05 3-2	A20 3-0	M10 1-2	J02 1-1	a02 0-1	M24 2-2	O22 1-3	A31 4-1	D26 2-0
14 NOTTINGHAM F	O29 1-0	a28 1-1	N12 0-2	J14 1-1	a14 0-2	S17 5-0	O15 1-0	D26 2-1	M31 2-0	A31 2-0	a03 2-2	A20 1-3	M17 2-4		O01 0-2	D24 3-1	N26 2-2	M03 1-0	F04 0-1	S03 2-3	D10 2-1	a18 0-0
15 NOTTS CO	A25 2-2	O22 1-2	A27 3-2	D03 5-2	a02 2-1	F25 3-2	S15 3-4	M10 0-2	D27 2-1	N19 1-1	a07 2-2	M24 2-1	D17 5-0	F11 1-3		N05 3-0	S10 0-0	J21 1-2	O08 1-1	a21 1-3	S24 1-5	D31 0-1
16 PLYMOUTH A	M03 3-0	S10 1-0	D26 5-0	a02 0-1	N26 1-4	A22 2-2	F18 0-0	D31 1-1	N12 4-3	S24 0-1	J21 1-4	F11 4-0	D10 4-0	A27 1-2	M17 1-1		O15 1-1	a14 3-1	D17 1-1	S05 0-1	O29 0-1	M31 0-1
17 PORT VALE	D26 1-2	M24 4-1	M30 2-0	A20 1-1	O01 1-1	M10 2-0	F04 2-1	N19 0-1	S17 2-0	a21 2-3	N05 1-1	D03 1-1	a28 3-2	a07 0-2	J14 3-1	F25 3-1		D24 4-1	O22 0-1	O08 1-0	S03 3-0	A22 2-1
18 ROTHERHAM U	S05 0-0	N19 3-2	A22 1-3	O08 1-0	D26 1-3	D31 3-3	O01 2-3	a07 0-2	a23 0-2	N05 3-1	M24 2-2	a21 0-1	a03 2-1	O22 2-1	S17 1-1	D03 0-0	A27 1-0		M10 2-3	a28 0-1	m03 2-3	D17 3-2
19 SHEFFIELD W	M21 3-0	D27 5-1	F18 2-1	S03 4-2	O29 3-3	J14 5-2	a14 2-3	F11 4-1	O15 4-0	S12 1-1	a28 5-3	A31 1-1	N12 3-1	S24 1-2	M31 1-0	A20 5-2	M03 4-0	D10 0-2		D24 4-0	S17 2-2	N26 1-1
20 STOKE C	N26 2-1	J21 1-2	D10 4-2	A29 1-2	a16 0-2	D17 5-2	N12 1-2	S10 4-1	M17 2-1	F11 2-0	S24 3-0	D27 3-2	M03 2-5	D31 1-1	O29 0-2	S12 4-1	M31 1-1	O15 1-0	A27 2-0		a14 5-0	a02 3-0
21 SWANSEA T	a28 3-1	a07 2-1	D17 2-1	F25 1-2	S08 5-3	O08 2-0	D27 2-0	O22 4-1	O01 1-1	M24 6-1	N19 0-2	N05 2-1	A25 2-1	M10 0-1	F04 5-1	a21 2-2	D31 0-0	S10 4-1	J21 2-1	D03 0-0		A27 4-2
22 WEST HAM U	O01 4-0	N05 2-3	a28 3-0	M10 2-1	M19 3-2	O22 6-1	S17 2-1	M24 1-1	J14 1-1	D03 1-3	a21 2-4	F25 2-0	D27 1-0	N19 1-2	S03 6-1	O08 4-0	A29 0-2	A20 1-1	a07 3-3	M30 2-0	D24 5-1	

SEASON 1955-56

DIVISION 3 NORTH

	ACCRINGTON S	BARROW	BRADFORD	BRADFORD C	CARLISLE U	CHESTER	CHESTERFIELD	CREWE A	DARLINGTON	DERBY CO	GATESHEAD	GRIMSBY T	HALIFAX T	HARTLEPOOLS U	MANSFIELD T	OLDHAM A	ROCHDALE	SCUNTHORPE U	SOUTHPORT	STOCKPORT CO	TRANMERE R	WORKINGTON	WREXHAM	YORK C
1 ACCRINGTON S		S10 2-0	S26 7-0	M03 2-0	S24 1-0	J21 4-0	S14 5-1	a14 5-1	D24 2-1	N26 2-0	A20 2-2	F11 0-1	J28 2-2	O15 1-0	a02 3-1	M31 2-2	A24 3-0	O29 2-0	a30 4-2	S03 3-1	a28 0-0	N12 5-1	F18 3-1	M17 1-3
2 BARROW	J14 3-1		A25 2-2	J28 3-1	F11 0-0	S24 1-2	a28 3-1	N26 5-0	S03 0-1	M17 1-2	D24 4-0	J02 0-0	F18 2-2	a14 3-2	S17 4-1	O29 4-1	S15 2-0	M03 2-2	A20 0-2	O15 2-0	D27 1-1	M31 2-0	M30 0-3	N12 0-1
3 BRADFORD	a23 1-0	A29 3-2		O15 1-1	a28 2-1	S12 1-1	S03 0-5	O29 2-0	O01 3-0	M03 2-4	F04 3-1	D27 2-1	a14 1-1	M31 1-3	M17 0-3	a03 4-1	D24 3-3	A20 2-0	S17 0-3	N12 2-0	a18 4-5	F18 4-0	N26 4-2	M14 2-1
4 BRADFORD C	O22 2-1	a21 1-1	a16 5-0		a02 0-0	O08 1-1	a07 3-5	J21 3-1	M10 3-0	S10 2-1	N05 3-1	S21 0-2	S07 2-0	S24 2-0	a25 4-2	D17 0-0	D03 2-2	D26 4-3	M24 2-0	F11 4-1	J07 5-0	A27 2-0	A24 4-3	D31 3-1
5 CARLISLE U	F04 0-4	O01 2-0	J02 4-1	M30 0-0		a24 4-1	A20 1-1	N12 4-1	S17 2-0	M31 0-3	J14 2-1	S13 1-2	A30 2-2	M17 0-3	a12 5-2	J28 3-1	D27 1-2	F18 1-2	S03 4-0	N26 4-1	D24 0-3	M03 2-4	O15 0-1	O29 3-1
6 CHESTER	S17 1-1	F04 1-0	S07 0-0	F18 1-1	S28 3-3		D27 2-1	M17 0-0	J14 2-1	N12 2-5	S03 3-0	A31 2-0	M30 1-0	N26 0-1	O15 4-3	M03 3-2	a28 0-0	m02 3-5	D24 1-3	a14 1-4	A20 0-0	O29 1-0	O01 2-1	M31 2-2
7 CHESTERFIELD	S07 0-1	S21 2-0	D31 5-1	N26 1-1	D17 2-1	D26 2-1		J28 8-0	A24 2-1	F18 2-0	J02 3-0	A27 1-0	M17 3-0	M03 2-3	M31 2-1	O15 1-0	S10 7-2	a14 2-0	O01 5-1	O29 2-3	F04 2-0	S17 2-4	N12 2-0	a02 3-1
8 CREWE A	D03 0-3	a07 0-1	M10 4-2	S17 1-4	M24 3-1	a11 0-0	a21 0-3		F25 1-1	S05 2-1	S21 1-0	N05 0-0	J14 1-4	D27 1-3	D24 2-1	O01 1-2	O22 2-0	F04 1-2	M30 1-1	A20 3-1	O08 4-0	a25 2-1	S03 1-2	A24 1-2
9 DARLINGTON	A27 2-0	D31 4-2	F11 4-1	O29 1-1	J21 3-5	S10 0-1	A31 2-1	O15 4-1		a14 1-0	D27 0-0	S24 0-1	M03 1-2	D17 0-0	F18 3-1	N12 2-1	S28 2-0	M31 1-0	a28 0-1	a02 0-0	S14 6-2	M17 2-2	J28 2-2	N26 1-4
10 DERBY CO	a07 6-2	M07 2-1	O22 4-0	J14 4-1	N05 3-0	M24 3-1	O08 3-0	S14 3-3	D03 6-2		F25 4-1	M10 1-3	S03 4-1	a28 3-2	A20 4-0	M19 2-0	a21 2-0	S17 2-2	A31 2-0	D27 2-0	a02 0-0	O01 2-2	D24 2-0	S28 3-2
11 GATESHEAD	D17 4-0	A27 3-2	S24 3-0	M31 4-1	S10 2-3	D31 1-1	S26 3-3	a28 4-1	D26 0-1	O15 2-4		J21 2-0	O29 1-1	M30 2-1	J28 3-0	M17 1-3	F11 4-1	N12 1-0	S12 2-0	F18 2-1	A22 3-3	N26 4-3	M03 2-1	a14 3-2
12 GRIMSBY T	O01 3-0	S27 3-0	D26 2-0	a28 2-0	S06 1-0	A23 6-1	D24 3-0	M31 5-1	a17 1-0	O29 2-1	S17 3-1		O15 4-0	N12 1-0	N26 2-0	F18 5-1	A20 1-1	M30 0-1	a25 2-0	M17 3-0	S03 1-0	J28 1-2	a14 1-0	M03 2-1
13 HALIFAX T	a21 2-0	O08 1-0	D03 6-0	S12 3-2	A22 2-2	a02 0-1	J07 3-0	S10 2-0	O22 3-0	D31 2-2	M10 3-3	a30 0-1		J21 0-2	F11 1-1	D26 5-1	a07 1-1	a28 0-3	N05 0-1	S24 1-0	M24 0-2	D17 2-0	S26 1-1	A27 2-4
14 HARTLEPOOLS U	m03 0-0	D03 1-0	N05 3-1	F04 1-0	a30 3-0	a07 3-1	O22 3-0	D26 6-1	A20 3-0	S19 2-0	a02 3-1	M24 1-2	S17 3-2		S03 4-2	J02 1-0	M10 1-0	O01 0-2	O08 1-0	D24 0-0	a21 4-0	A29 1-0	J14 3-2	S05 0-1
15 MANSFIELD T	M30 3-2	J21 4-0	a09 5-0	S26 0-0	D03 0-1	F25 3-0	N05 0-1	A27 1-1	O08 3-3	D17 1-1	a21 3-1	a07 0-2	O01 3-1	D31 5-1		S05 2-0	M24 6-0	A22 3-2	O22 0-1	S10 2-2	M10 6-0	S19 0-0	F04 6-1	D26 3-1
16 OLDHAM A	N05 1-3	M10 6-1	a02 5-1	A20 1-1	a21 2-2	O22 4-1	F25 2-2	F11 1-1	M24 3-3	S24 1-1	J07 1-2	O08 1-1	D27 1-3	S27 3-2	S12 1-1		D31 2-2	D24 2-1	a07 1-1	A30 3-2	D03 4-1	S10 0-1	a28 1-1	J21 2-2
17 ROCHDALE	A29 1-1	S05 5-1	A27 4-2	a14 3-1	D26 5-2	S21 4-2	a18 1-5	M03 1-0	a24 1-0	J28 0-5	O01 1-1	D17 2-0	N26 2-1	O29 1-4	N12 1-1	S03 4-4		O15 3-2	F04 1-3	M31 0-0	S17 1-3	M30 1-0	M17 1-0	F18 3-1
18 SCUNTHORPE U	M10 2-3	O22 2-0	D17 4-2	D27 2-0	O08 4-0	a21 2-1	D03 2-0	S24 1-1	N05 0-1	J21 0-2	M24 1-1	a02 0-1	S21 1-0	F11 5-1	A31 3-0	A27 2-1	M22 1-2		a18 0-1	a26 1-5	a07 2-1	D31 3-1	S07 1-1	S10 1-1
19 SOUTHPORT	D26 1-1	D17 2-1	J21 3-0	N12 3-1	D31 3-0	A27 1-0	F11 1-0	a02 5-0	S20 0-1	A23 2-5	S06 2-0	S10 2-0	M31 2-0	F18 0-0	M03 1-1	N26 1-1	S24 2-0	M17 2-2		J28 1-1	S27 1-0	a14 0-0	O29 1-1	O15 3-3
20 STOCKPORT CO	D31 1-2	F25 4-1	M24 0-0	O01 1-0	a07 8-1	D03 2-1	M10 2-1	D17 2-1	M30 2-1	D26 2-1	O08 1-2	F15 0-0	F04 3-1	A27 4-0	J14 7-2	A22 0-0	N05 0-0	S26 3-2	a21 4-0		O22 7-0	S05 4-5	S17 4-0	a28 4-1
21 TRANMERE R	S20 4-1	D26 1-1	S10 4-1	M17 1-1	A27 0-1	D17 4-0	S24 0-1	F18 2-1	S06 0-1	M30 0-1	A30 1-1	D31 0-1	N12 2-1	J28 2-2	O29 1-0	a14 0-3	J21 2-1	N26 2-1	J02 1-2	M03 2-1		O15 2-0	M31 0-2	O01 2-1
22 WORKINGTON	M24 0-0	N05 6-1	O08 4-0	D24 2-1	O22 4-0	M10 0-0	J21 0-1	S28 1-0	J07 2-0	F11 0-3	a07 6-1	a21 0-0	A20 2-0	A24 5-1	a28 2-1	J14 4-3	a02 0-1	S03 1-2	D03 2-3	S14 0-1	F25 3-0		D27 3-1	S24 0-0
23 WREXHAM	O08 1-4	a02 0-0	a07 1-0	A31 2-1	F25 5-2	F11 0-0	M24 3-0	D31 4-2	a21 2-1	A27 3-1	O22 1-1	D03 1-0	a25 1-2	S10 1-3	S24 2-0	S21 1-1	J07 0-0	S14 0-1	M10 2-1	J21 0-1	N05 3-1	D26 0-1		D17 4-5
24 YORK C	a16 0-1	M24 3-2	a21 5-0	S03 0-2	M10 3-1	N05 3-0	M30 3-1	A29 1-1	a07 4-0	a23 1-0	D03 1-0	O22 3-4	D24 5-0	S12 3-0	D27 1-1	S17 2-0	O08 1-2	a09 0-0	F25 0-1	S19 1-0	F11 2-4	F04 1-1	A20 1-3	

DIVISION 3 SOUTH

	ALDERSHOT	BOURNEMOUTH	BRENTFORD	BRIGHTON & HA	COLCHESTER U	COVENTRY C	CRYSTAL P	EXETER C	GILLINGHAM	IPSWICH T	LEYTON O	MILLWALL	NEWPORT CO	NORTHAMPTON T	NORWICH C	Q.P.R.	READING	SHREWSBURY T	SOUTHAMPTON	SOUTHEND U	SWINDON T	TORQUAY U	WALSALL	WATFORD
1 ALDERSHOT		a07 1-3	O08 4-1	D31 0-3	M24 1-0	F25 2-2	A27 1-1	M10 1-0	D03 2-2	S24 0-3	N05 1-1	a21 2-1	A24 1-0	S14 2-0	a18 0-0	D26 1-2	D17 4-4	J21 2-0	S10 3-2	O22 3-3	a28 1-1	S28 1-2	F11 2-1	a02 1-1
2 BOURNEMOUTH	N26 2-2		A27 0-0	J28 2-0	A24 3-1	D17 0-1	a14 1-0	D26 0-0	S24 1-2	F18 1-1	a28 3-1	J21 4-0	O29 0-0	M31 0-0	S28 0-1	N12 1-0	S10 2-1	M30 2-0	O01 1-3	S07 4-1	M17 4-0	M03 2-0	O15 2-0	D31 4-0
3 BRENTFORD	F18 2-0	D24 2-1		M03 4-2	J14 2-2	a23 1-1	O15 3-0	F04 2-0	A20 1-4	N12 3-2	S17 1-0	S12 2-2	a14 1-1	a02 2-1	S03 1-2	A30 2-0	D26 2-2	M17 1-1	O29 2-1	O01 2-1	M12 1-2	N26 1-3	M31 2-2	S19 0-0
4 BRIGHTON & H.A.	S03 5-2	a21 4-1	O22 3-0		a07 2-0	M10 2-1	J14 5-0	M24 1-0	J21 5-0	S28 3-0	a18 1-1	a02 2-1	D26 4-1	D24 4-0	D03 6-0	A20 1-1	O08 3-1	F11 3-2	S24 5-0	N05 4-0	S14 2-0	a28 3-2	A24 3-0	F25 2-3
5 COLCHESTER U	N12 4-0	S01 1-0	S10 0-3	N26 3-3		D31 2-0	M31 2-4	D17 5-1	S29 1-1	D26 3-3	S15 2-1	F11 1-2	O15 2-1	M17 2-0	a28 3-2	O29 4-1	S24 0-3	J28 2-0	a14 3-2	A27 3-6	M03 5-0	F18 3-2	M30 1-1	J21 4-1
6 COVENTRY C	O15 1-1	A20 3-1	S26 2-1	O29 3-2	S03 2-0		M03 1-3	S17 2-2	S12 2-0	M31 3-1	J14 3-0	D27 5-1	D10 3-0	F18 0-1	D24 5-3	a03 4-1	a28 0-0	N12 2-1	M17 2-0	M19 0-0	O01 6-0	a14 1-2	N26 1-0	A29 3-0
7 CRYSTAL P	D24 1-0	D03 1-3	F25 0-2	S10 1-2	J07 1-1	O22 3-0		N05 0-1	a21 1-3	F11 1-0	M24 1-2	D31 2-2	a28 1-0	A20 2-3	a07 2-0	S14 1-1	M30 2-3	S24 0-1	J21 0-2	M10 1-2	D27 0-2	A31 3-0	S28 2-0	O08 1-2
8 EXETER C	O29 2-1	D27 2-0	S24 2-3	N12 0-5	A20 0-0	J21 2-3	M17 6-1		a28 2-1	a14 2-2	D24 1-1	A31 3-1	a02 2-0	M03 3-1	S14 1-1	O15 2-0	S28 0-2	N26 3-0	a11 3-2	S10 0-1	F18 1-2	S03 0-0	J28 1-1	F11 1-2
9 GILLINGHAM	a14 2-0	m02 2-1	D17 1-2	S17 1-0	a25 2-1	S07 1-1	J28 1-1	S21 2-1		O15 0-0	A24 0-1	S10 4-3	M17 3-2	N26 0-2	O01 3-1	M31 0-2	D31 2-0	F18 3-1	M30 1-2	D27 2-3	N12 4-0	O29 1-3	M03 0-1	A27 3-0
10 IPSWICH T	F04 2-1	O08 1-0	M24 1-1	a25 2-1	D27 3-1	J07 1-0	O01 3-3	D03 2-2	F25 1-1		a21 2-0	O22 6-2	D24 3-2	S17 1-0	M30 4-1	J14 4-1	M10 3-3	S21 2-1	A24 4-2	a07 3-0	S03 6-2	A20 0-2	S07 5-2	N05 0-0
11 LEYTON O	M17 8-3	S22 3-0	J21 2-1	M31 0-1	S08 6-0	S10 3-1	N12 8-0	A27 1-1	S01 2-0	m03 1-2		a26 2-1	F18 3-1	O29 1-1	D26 2-2	M03 7-1	F11 1-0	a14 5-2	N26 4-0	D31 3-0	O15 4-0	M30 3-2	D17 4-0	S24 3-1
12 MILLWALL	J28 3-3	S17 4-0	S05 4-0	M30 2-4	O01 0-1	D26 0-2	S03 1-1	A22 2-0	J14 5-0	M03 0-5	a30 5-0		N12 2-4	a14 4-1	m04 1-0	N26 2-0	A27 4-0	O15 1-2	F18 3-2	a28 5-0	M31 1-1	M17 3-2	O29 3-2	D17 1-1
13 NEWPORT CO	S01 0-1	M10 1-0	D03 1-2	D27 1-0	F25 0-0	a21 4-2	S22 0-1	M30 1-2	N05 3-2	A27 2-1	O08 3-0	M24 1-4		S29 0-1	O22 2-2	O01 2-1	J07 2-3	D17 1-2	S08 1-0	a19 2-0	a12 1-0	S10 2-1	D31 2-0	a07 0-1
14 NORTHAMPTON T	S08 3-2	a12 2-1	a03 1-0	A27 3-0	N05 0-2	O08 2-1	D17 1-1	O22 3-0	a07 0-2	J21 0-5	M10 0-1	D03 4-0	a26 5-0		M24 1-1	S19 5-2	a21 1-2	S10 1-0	D31 3-1	F25 1-1	S01 2-1	F11 2-0	S24 3-1	D27 1-3
15 NORWICH C	M31 0-1	a25 0-2	D31 1-0	a14 3-3	S21 1-1	A27 1-0	N26 3-1	S07 2-1	F11 5-1	a02 3-2	D27 2-2	S24 4-1	M03 2-3	N12 4-1		M17 1-0	J21 2-1	A24 3-1	J28 1-4	D17 7-2	O29 4-1	O15 0-0	a12 3-2	S10 4-1
16 Q.P.R.	D27 2-2	M24 0-1	A22 1-1	D17 2-1	M10 6-2	M30 1-2	S05 0-3	F25 1-0	J07 2-2	S10 1-1	O22 0-1	a07 4-0	F11 0-0	a28 3-2	N05 2-3		D03 3-3	D31 1-1	A27 4-0	O08 1-2	S26 1-0	S24 3-1	J21 3-2	a21 3-2
17 READING	A20 0-5	J14 0-2	D27 5-2	F18 0-2	F27 1-3	S21 1-0	a02 1-0	a25 1-2	S03 1-2	O29 1-5	O01 0-1	D24 4-1	M31 3-0	J28 4-1	S17 2-2	a14 3-1		M03 0-1	O15 1-1	A31 4-1	N26 0-1	N12 0-3	M17 2-0	S14 6-1
18 SHREWSBURY T	S17 3-3	a02 1-1	N05 1-1	O01 2-1	a21 2-1	M24 3-0	a30 2-0	a07 2-0	O08 3-1	a28 1-1	D03 1-4	F25 3-1	A20 5-0	J14 1-1	A29 6-0	S03 1-1	O22 3-0		S26 2-0	a23 1-1	D24 1-1	S12 1-2	D26 2-1	M10 0-0
19 SOUTHAMPTON	J14 3-1	F11 3-2	M10 1-1	F04 1-2	D03 3-0	N05 3-0	S17 3-1	M31 5-0	a02 1-1	A31 2-2	a07 1-2	O08 3-0	S14 3-3	S03 2-3	a21 2-5	D24 4-0	F25 5-2	J07 1-1		M24 0-0	A20 2-1	D27 6-2	S21 4-1	O22 2-0
20 SOUTHEND U	M03 3-2	S14 4-1	F11 2-2	M17 1-2	D24 4-0	S24 3-0	O29 4-3	J14 6-0	D26 2-2	N26 2-3	S03 0-0	S21 3-1	S17 4-1	O15 2-0	A20 3-1	F18 5-1	A24 1-0	M31 1-0	N12 2-1		M30 0-0	m02 2-3	a14 3-2	a25 1-0
21 SWINDON T	S21 1-1	N05 2-2	a21 0-1	S07 0-0	O22 3-1	F11 1-1	D26 0-0	O08 0-1	M24 0-1	D31 0-1	F25 1-2	F29 1-0	S24 1-2	A24 0-1	M10 1-1	a25 0-1	a07 0-0	A27 2-1	D17 1-1	a02 1-1		J21 2-1	S10 1-2	D03 0-0
22 TORQUAY U	a25 5-0	O22 0-0	a07 3-1	S21 0-0	O08 1-2	D03 0-0	A24 1-1	D31 3-1	M10 1-1	D17 2-2	a02 1-3	N05 3-0	J14 1-1	O01 3-1	F25 1-1	F04 2-0	M24 0-0	S07 5-0	D26 3-2	a21 2-2	S17 4-0		A27 3-2	F29 4-1
23 WALSALL	O01 4-2	F25 0-0	m03 1-2	S01 2-2	a02 0-0	a07 2-0	a26 4-0	a21 3-1	O22 2-1	S15 1-3	A20 0-2	M10 2-1	S03 3-3	a16 2-0	O08 2-0	S17 2-2	N05 1-0	D27 1-0	a28 1-3	D03 3-1	J14 4-0	D24 1-4		M24 2-1
24 WATFORD	M30 1-1	S03 0-2	a28 0-2	O15 1-3	S17 1-1	A23 2-1	F18 0-2	O01 2-3	D24 0-1	M17 0-2	F04 0-4	A20 4-2	N26 1-1	D26 2-2	J14 1-1	J28 0-1	S06 1-0	O29 3-4	M03 1-0	S27 3-2	a14 2-1	M31 2-1	N12 4-2	

LEAGUE TABLES

DIVISION 1

	P	W	D	L	F	A	W	D	L	F	A	Pts
Manchester U	42	18	3	0	51	20	7	7	7	32	31	60
Blackpool	42	13	4	4	56	27	7	5	9	30	35	49
Wolverh'pton W	42	15	2	4	51	27	5	7	9	38	38	49
Manchester C	42	11	5	5	40	27	7	5	9	42	42	46
Arsenal	42	13	4	4	38	22	5	6	10	22	39	46
Birmingham C	42	12	4	5	51	26	6	5	10	24	31	45
Burnley	42	11	3	7	37	20	7	5	9	27	34	44
Bolton W	42	13	3	5	50	24	5	4	12	21	34	43
Sunderland	42	10	8	3	44	36	7	1	13	36	59	43
Luton T	42	12	4	5	44	27	5	4	12	22	37	42
Newcastle U	42	12	4	5	49	24	5	3	13	36	46	41
Portsmouth	42	9	8	4	46	38	7	1	13	32	47	41
W.B.A.	42	13	3	5	37	25	5	2	14	21	45	41
Charlton A	42	13	2	6	47	26	4	4	13	28	55	40
Everton	42	11	5	5	37	29	4	5	12	18	40	40
Chelsea	42	10	4	7	32	26	4	7	10	32	51	39
Cardiff C	42	11	4	6	36	32	4	5	12	19	37	39
Tottenham H	42	9	4	8	37	33	6	3	12	24	38	37
Preston N.E.	42	6	5	10	32	36	8	3	10	41	36	36
Aston Villa	42	9	6	6	32	29	2	7	12	20	40	35
Huddersfield T	42	9	4	8	32	30	5	3	13	22	53	35
Sheffield U	42	8	6	7	31	35	4	3	14	32	42	33

DIVISION 2

	P	W	D	L	F	A	W	D	L	F	A	Pts
Sheffield W	42	13	5	3	60	28	8	8	5	41	34	55
Leeds U	42	17	3	1	51	18	6	3	12	29	42	52
Liverpool	42	14	3	4	52	25	7	3	11	33	38	48
Blackburn R	42	13	4	4	55	29	8	2	11	29	36	48
Leicester C	42	15	3	3	63	23	6	3	12	31	55	48
Bristol R	42	13	3	5	53	33	8	3	10	31	37	48
Nottingham F	42	9	5	7	30	26	10	4	7	38	37	47
Lincoln C	42	14	5	2	49	17	4	5	12	30	48	46
Fulham	42	15	2	4	59	27	5	4	12	30	52	46
Swansea T	42	14	4	3	49	23	6	2	13	34	58	46
Bristol C	42	14	4	3	49	20	5	3	13	31	44	45
Port Vale	42	12	4	5	38	21	4	9	8	22	37	45
Stoke C	42	13	2	6	47	27	7	2	12	24	35	44
Middlesbrough	42	11	4	6	46	31	5	4	12	30	47	40
Bury	42	9	5	7	44	39	7	3	11	42	51	40
West Ham U	42	12	4	5	52	27	2	7	12	22	42	39
Doncaster R	42	11	5	5	45	30	1	6	14	24	66	35
Barnsley	42	10	5	6	33	35	1	7	13	14	49	34
Rotherham U	42	7	5	9	29	34	5	4	12	27	41	33
Notts Co	42	8	5	8	39	37	3	4	14	16	45	31
Plymouth A	42	7	6	8	33	25	3	2	16	21	62	28
Hull C	42	6	4	11	32	45	4	2	15	21	52	26

DIVISION 3 NORTH

	P	W	D	L	F	A	W	D	L	F	A	Pts
Grimsby T	46	20	1	2	54	10	11	5	7	22	19	68
Derby Co	46	18	4	1	67	23	10	3	10	43	32	63
Accrington S	46	17	4	2	61	19	8	5	10	31	38	59
Hartlepool U	46	18	2	3	47	15	8	3	12	34	45	57
Southport	46	12	9	2	39	18	11	2	10	27	35	57
Chesterfield	46	18	1	4	61	21	7	3	13	33	45	54
Stockport Co	46	16	4	3	65	22	5	5	13	25	39	51
Bradford C	46	16	5	2	57	25	2	8	13	21	39	49
Scunthorpe U	46	12	4	7	40	26	8	4	11	35	37	48
Workington	46	13	4	6	47	20	6	5	12	28	43	47
York C	46	12	4	7	44	24	7	5	11	41	48	47
Rochdale	46	13	5	5	46	39	4	8	11	20	45	47
Gateshead	46	15	4	4	56	32	2	7	14	21	52	45
Wrexham	46	11	5	7	37	28	5	5	13	29	45	42
Darlington	46	11	6	6	41	28	5	3	15	19	45	41
Tranmere R	46	11	4	8	33	25	5	5	13	26	59	41
Chester C	46	10	8	5	35	33	3	6	14	17	49	40
Mansfield T	46	13	6	4	59	21	1	5	17	25	60	39
Halifax T	46	10	6	7	40	27	4	5	14	26	49	39
Oldham A	46	7	12	4	48	36	3	6	14	28	50	38
Carlisle U	46	11	3	9	45	36	4	5	14	26	59	38
Barrow	46	11	6	6	44	25	1	3	19	17	58	33
Bradford P.A.	46	13	4	6	47	38	0	3	20	14	84	33
Crewe A	46	9	4	10	32	35	0	6	17	18	70	28

DIVISION 3 SOUTH

	P	W	D	L	F	A	W	D	L	F	A	Pts
Leyton O	46	18	3	2	76	20	11	5	7	30	29	66
Brighton & H.A.	46	20	2	1	73	16	9	5	9	39	34	65
Ipswich T	46	16	6	1	59	28	9	8	6	47	32	64
Southend U	46	16	4	3	58	25	5	7	11	30	55	53
Torquay U	46	11	10	2	48	21	9	2	12	38	42	52
Brentford	46	11	8	4	40	30	8	6	9	29	36	52
Norwich C	46	15	4	4	56	31	4	9	10	30	51	51
Coventry C	46	16	4	3	54	20	4	5	14	19	40	49
Bournemouth	46	13	6	4	39	14	6	4	13	24	37	48
Gillingham	46	12	3	8	38	28	7	7	9	31	43	48
Northampton T	46	14	3	6	44	27	6	4	13	23	44	47
Colchester U	46	14	4	5	56	37	4	7	12	20	44	47
Shrewsbury T	46	12	9	2	47	21	5	3	15	22	45	46
Southampton	46	13	6	4	60	30	5	2	16	31	51	44
Aldershot	46	9	9	5	36	33	3	7	13	34	57	40
Exeter C	46	10	6	7	39	30	5	4	14	19	47	40
Reading	46	10	2	11	40	37	5	7	11	30	42	39
Q.P.R.	46	10	7	6	44	32	4	4	15	20	54	39
Newport Co	46	12	2	9	32	26	3	7	13	26	53	39
Walsall	46	13	5	5	43	28	2	3	18	25	56	38
Watford	46	8	5	10	31	39	5	6	12	21	46	37
Millwall	46	13	4	6	56	31	2	2	19	27	69	36
Crystal Palace	46	7	3	13	27	32	5	7	11	27	51	34
Swindon T	46	4	10	9	18	22	4	4	15	16	56	30

FOOTBALL LEAGUE RECORDS

Top scorers: Div 1, J.Charles (Leeds United) 38 goals; Div 2, A.Rowley (Leicester City) 44 goals; Div 3 N, R.Straw (Derby County) 37 goals; Div 3 S, E.Phillips (Ipswich Town) 42 goals.

Elegant England left-back Roger Byrne skippered Manchester United to a second successive Championship. He, too, was a Munich victim.

DIVISION 1

	ARSENAL	ASTON VILLA	BIRMINGHAM C	BLACKPOOL	BOLTON W	BURNLEY	CARDIFF C	CHARLTON A	CHELSEA	EVERTON	LEEDS U	LUTON T	MANCHESTER C	MANCHESTER U	NEWCASTLE U	PORTSMOUTH	PRESTON N.E.	SHEFFIELD W	SUNDERLAND	TOTTENHAM H	W.B.A.	WOLVERHAMPTON W
1 ARSENAL		N03 2-1	D22 4-0	a19 1-1	N17 3-0	A21 2-0	A18 0-0	a20 3-1	D26 2-0	F23 2-0	a06 1-0	M09 1-3	O06 7-3	S29 1-2	S15 0-1	J12 1-1	S04 1-2	F02 6-3	D01 1-1	O20 3-1	S01 4-1	M23 0-0
2 ASTON VILLA	M16 0-0		O27 3-1	S01 3-2	S29 0-0	N10 1-0	M13 4-1	A18 3-1	N24 1-1	J12 5-1	F02 1-1	a27 1-3	F04 2-2	D08 1-3	O13 3-1	F18 2-2	M30 2-0	a13 5-0	a08 2-2	S15 2-4	A27 0-0	a22 4-0
3 BIRMINGHAM C	A25 4-2	a10 1-2		N03 2-2	O06 0-0	D29 2-0	S22 2-1	N17 4-2	J19 0-1	M09 1-3	a20 6-2	O20 3-0	a27 3-3	D15 3-1	S05 6-1	A22 3-1	S08 3-0	D25 4-0	a06 1-2	D01 0-0	a23 2-0	F09 2-2
4 BLACKPOOL	a22 2-4	D29 0-0	M16 3-1		D15 4-2	m01 1-0	D08 3-1	S22 3-2	a13 1-0	A27 5-2	D25 1-1	S08 4-0	F09 4-1	O27 2-2	N24 2-3	M30 5-0	O13 4-0	M02 3-1	J19 1-2	S03 4-1	N10 0-1	A25 3-2
5 BOLTON W	M30 2-1	F09 0-0	F20 3-1	A18 4-1		N24 3-0	S15 2-0	S12 2-0	O27 2-2	a27 1-1	J12 5-3	a19 2-2	D26 1-0	N10 2-0	D08 3-1	a13 1-1	M02 2-3	M16 3-2	S05 2-1	S01 1-0	O13 1-1	S22 0-3
6 BURNLEY	A28 3-1	a15 2-1	S01 2-0	O06 2-2	a06 1-0		D22 6-2	D01 2-1	A18 2-0	S03 2-1	O20 0-0	N03 1-1	a20 0-3	a19 1-3	F02 3-2	S15 1-1	D25 2-2	S29 4-1	M09 2-0	a29 1-0	J12 1-0	N17 3-0
7 CARDIFF C	D15 2-3	a03 1-0	F02 1-2	M09 3-4	J19 2-0	A25 3-3		M23 2-3	S08 1-1	D01 1-0	O06 4-1	a06 0-0	N03 1-1	a27 2-3	A22 5-2	a22 0-2	D29 2-3	S05 2-1	N17 1-0	a20 0-3	S29 0-0	F23 2-2
8 CHARLTON A	O13 1-3	D15 0-2	M30 1-0	F02 0-4	S20 2-1	a13 1-2	N10 0-2		M16 3-1	S29 1-2	A23 1-2	A25 1-2	S15 1-0	F18 1-5	O27 1-1	M02 1-3	D08 3-4	S08 4-4	D29 3-2	a19 1-1	N24 3-2	D25 2-1
9 CHELSEA	D25 1-1	a06 1-1	S15 1-0	D01 2-2	F23 2-2	D15 2-0	J12 1-2	N03 1-3		a20 5-1	D29 1-1	N17 4-1	M09 4-2	S05 1-2	a22 6-2	S29 3-3	A25 1-0	S19 0-0	M23 0-2	O06 2-4	F02 2-4	O20 3-3
10 EVERTON	O27 4-0	S08 0-4	D08 2-0	A22 2-3	A25 2-2	S12 1-0	a13 0-0	F09 5-0	O13 0-3		D15 2-1	J19 2-1	a22 1-1	M06 1-2	M30 2-1	N10 2-2	F27 1-4	N24 1-0	S22 2-1	D26 1-1	M16 0-1	D29 3-1
11 LEEDS U	N24 3-3	S22 1-0	O13 1-1	D26 5-0	S08 3-2	M11 1-1	F16 3-0	A29 4-0	S01 0-0	A18 5-1		F09 1-2	S12 2-0	M30 1-2	M16 0-0	D08 4-1	O27 1-2	N10 3-1	a22 3-1	M02 1-1	a13 0-0	J19 0-0
12 LUTON T	D08 1-2	S05 0-0	a03 0-0	J12 0-2	a22 1-0	M16 0-2	N24 3-0	D22 4-2	M30 0-4	S15 2-0	S29 2-2		S01 3-2	a13 0-2	F16 4-1	M20 1-0	N10 1-1	O13 2-0	A18 6-2	F02 1-3	O27 0-1	A22 1-0
13 MANCHESTER C	M20 2-3	A25 1-1	N10 3-1	S29 0-3	D25 1-3	O13 0-1	M16 4-1	J19 5-1	D08 5-4	a19 2-4	S05 1-0	D29 3-2		F02 2-4	M02 1-2	N24 5-1	a13 0-2	O27 4-2	S08 3-1	A22 2-2	M30 2-1	D15 2-3
14 MANCHESTER U	F09 6-2	M09 1-1	A18 2-2	F23 0-2	M25 0-2	a22 2-0	D26 3-1	O06 4-2	J01 3-0	O20 2-5	N17 3-2	D01 3-1	S22 2-0		J12 6-1	S01 3-0	A29 3-2	S15 4-1	a20 4-0	a06 0-0	a29 1-1	N03 3-0
15 NEWCASTLE U	J19 3-1	a20 1-2	J01 3-2	a06 2-1	M09 4-0	S22 1-1	A29 1-0	F23 3-1	a19 1-2	N17 0-0	N03 2-3	O06 2-2	O20 0-3	S08 1-1		A18 2-1	F09 1-2	D29 1-2	D22 6-2	M23 2-2	D26 5-2	D01 2-1
16 PORTSMOUTH	S08 2-3	O06 5-1	A29 3-4	N17 0-0	D01 1-1	J19 1-0	a19 1-0	O20 1-0	F09 2-2	M23 3-2	M09 2-5	M13 2-2	a06 0-1	D29 1-3	D15 2-2		S22 2-2	A25 3-1	m01 3-2	N03 2-3	a27 0-1	a20 1-0
17 PRESTON N.E.	S10 3-0	N17 3-3	J12 1-0	a20 0-0	O20 2-2	D26 1-0	S01 6-0	M09 4-3	a27 1-0	O06 0-0	F23 3-0	M23 2-0	D01 3-1	A20 1-3	S29 1-0	F02 7-1		a19 1-0	N03 6-0	A18 1-4	S15 3-2	a06 1-0
18 SHEFFIELD W	S22 2-4	D01 2-1	a29 3-0	O20 1-2	N03 1-2	F09 0-0	S12 5-3	J12 3-1	A22 4-0	a06 2-2	M26 2-3	a20 3-0	F23 2-2	J19 2-1	S01 4-0	a09 3-1	a22 3-1		O06 3-2	N17 4-1	A18 4-2	M09 2-1
19 SUNDERLAND	a13 1-0	D25 1-0	N24 0-1	S15 5-2	A22 3-0	D08 2-1	M30 1-1	S01 8-1	N10 1-3	F02 1-1	a19 2-0	D15 1-0	J12 1-1	O13 1-3	A25 1-2	O27 3-3	M16 0-0	F16 5-2		S29 0-2	M13 1-4	J01 2-3
20 TOTTENHAM H	M13 1-3	J19 3-0	a13 5-1	a27 2-1	D29 4-0	O27 2-0	O13 5-0	a22 6-2	F20 3-4	D25 6-0	A25 5-1	S22 5-0	A29 3-2	N24 2-2	N10 3-1	M16 2-0	D15 1-1	M30 1-1	F09 5-2		D08 2-2	S08 4-1
21 W.B.A.	D29 0-2	A22 2-0	a22 0-0	a03 1-3	a20 3-2	S08 2-2	F09 1-2	a06 2-2	S22 2-1	N03 3-0	D01 0-0	F23 4-0	N17 1-1	A25 2-3	D25 1-0	S05 2-1	J19 0-0	D15 1-4	O20 2-0	M09 1-1		O06 1-1
22 WOLVERHAMPTON W	N10 5-2	a23 3-0	S29 3-0	D22 4-1	F02 3-2	M30 1-2	O27 3-1	F16 7-3	M02 3-1	S01 2-1	S15 1-2	A29 5-4	A18 5-1	M16 1-1	a13 2-0	O13 6-0	N24 4-3	D08 2-1	S12 2-2	J12 3-0	a15 5-2	

Derby County centre-forward Ray Straw, whose 37 goals took the Rams out of Division Three North. Straw later signed for Coventry and was the first player to appear in all six divisions of the Football League.

DIVISION 2

	BARNSLEY	BLACKBURN R	BRISTOL C	BRISTOL R	BURY	DONCASTER R	FULHAM	GRIMSBY T	HUDDERSFIELD T	LEICESTER C	LEYTON O	LINCOLN C	LIVERPOOL	MIDDLESBROUGH	NOTTINGHAM F	NOTTS CO	PORT VALE	ROTHERHAM U	SHEFFIELD U	STOKE C	SWANSEA T	WEST HAM U
1 BARNSLEY		S15 3-3	J12 3-0	O13 0-2	M30 1-1	M02 3-1	a22 1-1	N24 2-0	N10 0-5	F27 2-0	M16 3-0	S05 5-2	O27 4-1	A25 1-3	S29 1-1	a13 1-1	D15 2-0	D26 1-1	S01 1-6	D08 2-2	A22 2-3	F02 1-2
2 BLACKBURN R	J19 2-0		F09 3-1	D08 2-0	O27 6-2	N10 2-2	D25 2-0	M16 2-0	a13 3-2	M02 1-1	O13 3-3	A25 3-4	F16 2-2	N24 1-0	J01 2-2	a19 1-1	S08 2-4	D29 3-2	S22 3-1	M30 1-0	D15 5-3	A27 0-2
3 BRISTOL C	S08 1-2	S29 3-0		S22 5-3	M16 2-0	M30 4-0	S04 0-3	N10 0-2	O27 2-1	D08 0-2	a13 4-2	D15 5-1	O13 2-1	M02 2-1	A21 1-5	F20 3-0	D29 3-3	A25 2-1	J19 5-1	N24 1-2	a27 3-1	a19 1-1
4 BRISTOL R	F23 1-1	a20 0-1	F02 0-0		D26 6-1	D22 6-1	N17 4-0	A18 1-0	S10 4-0	S15 1-2	A27 3-2	N03 0-1	a22 0-0	J12 0-2	a06 3-2	F09 3-0	D01 2-1	M09 4-2	O06 3-1	S01 4-0	M23 1-1	O20 1-1
5 BURY	N17 1-2	M09 2-2	N03 2-3	D25 7-2		S29 4-4	O06 0-1	F02 2-3	S08 1-3	S17 4-5	D29 1-3	a20 1-0	A25 0-2	A21 3-2	F23 1-2	D15 2-1	a06 1-0	O20 1-4	M23 0-1	J01 0-1	J19 1-3	D01 3-3
6 DONCASTER R	O20 5-2	M23 1-1	N17 4-1	A25 2-4	F09 1-1		D01 4-0	a22 0-1	S22 4-0	D15 0-2	J19 6-1	O06 3-1	S08 1-1	D26 2-1	M09 1-1	D29 4-2	a20 4-0	A22 1-1	a06 1-0	S10 4-0	F23 0-1	N03 3-0
7 FULHAM	a19 2-0	D26 7-2	S12 2-1	M30 3-2	F16 1-3	a13 3-0		O13 3-1	S01 1-0	N10 2-2	D08 3-1	J19 0-1	M02 1-2	M16 1-2	D22 0-1	N24 5-1	F09 6-3	S22 3-1	A29 1-2	O27 1-0	S08 7-3	A18 1-4
8 GRIMSBY T	a06 4-1	N03 1-3	M23 0-3	D15 3-2	S22 0-1	a19 4-2	F23 3-1		J19 1-2	D25 2-2	S08 0-0	F09 2-0	D29 0-0	S04 3-2	D01 0-0	A25 2-1	O20 1-0	a20 3-2	N17 1-2	A28 4-1	O06 5-0	M09 2-1
9 HUDDERSFIELD T	M23 2-0	D01 0-2	M09 2-1	S03 2-1	J12 1-2	F02 0-1	D29 1-1	S15 2-1		A20 1-2	A25 3-0	O20 0-1	D15 0-3	a23 0-1	O06 1-0	D26 3-0	N17 3-1	a06 1-0	N03 1-4	S29 2-2	a20 2-2	F23 6-2
10 LEICESTER C	O06 5-2	O20 6-0	a20 1-1	J19 7-2	S12 3-0	A18 3-1	M23 1-3	J26 4-3	A29 2-2		a22 1-4	M09 4-3	F09 3-2	S01 1-1	N17 0-0	S22 6-3	F23 2-1	D01 5-2	J12 5-0	D22 3-2	N03 1-1	a06 5-3
11 LEYTON O	N03 2-0	F23 1-1	D01 2-2	A23 1-1	S01 4-3	S15 1-1	a20 0-2	J12 1-1	D22 3-1	a19 1-5		a06 2-1	D26 0-4	S29 1-1	A18 1-4	a27 2-2	M23 3-2	N17 2-1	M09 1-2	F02 2-2	O20 3-0	O06 1-2
12 LINCOLN C	a27 4-1	D22 1-2	A18 1-1	M16 1-0	D08 2-0	F16 4-1	S15 1-0	S29 1-0	M02 1-2	O27 2-3	N24 0-2		M30 3-3	a13 1-1	J12 0-2	N10 1-0	A22 4-0	a19 3-3	D26 4-1	O13 0-1	F02 0-2	S01 0-2
13 LIVERPOOL	M09 2-1	O06 2-3	m01 2-1	a19 4-1	D22 2-0	J12 2-1	O20 4-3	S01 3-2	A18 2-3	S29 2-0	D25 1-0	N17 4-0		F02 1-2	a20 3-1	A29 3-3	N03 4-1	M23 4-1	D01 5-1	S15 0-2	a06 2-0	a27 1-0
14 MIDDLESBROUGH	D22 1-2	a06 2-1	O20 4-1	S08 3-2	A29 2-2	D25 3-2	N03 3-1	S12 2-1	a22 7-2	D29 1-3	F09 1-2	D01 3-0	S22 1-1		M23 2-2	J19 0-0	O06 3-1	F23 0-1	a20 3-1	A18 1-1	M09 6-2	N17 3-1
15 NOTTINGHAM F	F09 7-1	S06 2-1	A30 2-2	N24 1-1	O13 5-1	O27 2-1	A25 3-1	a13 2-1	F21 0-0	M30 1-2	D15 1-2	S08 1-1	D08 1-0	N10 0-4		m01 2-4	S22 4-2	J19 3-1	a22 2-1	M16 4-0	D29 4-3	a15 3-0
16 NOTTS CO	D01 3-2	a23 2-0	O06 1-1	S29 0-2	A18 2-2	S01 1-2	a06 0-0	D22 0-1	D24 1-2	F02 0-0	S13 1-3	M23 3-0	A23 1-1	S15 2-1	O20 1-2		M09 3-1	N03 1-5	F23 2-2	J12 5-0	N17 1-4	a20 4-1
17 PORT VALE	A18 0-0	J12 0-3	S01 3-1	a13 2-3	N24 3-2	D08 4-1	S29 2-1	M02 3-0	M30 1-2	O13 2-3	N10 1-2	A27 1-1	M16 1-2	F16 2-1	F02 1-7	O27 1-2		a27 2-1	M25 0-6	a29 2-2	a19 0-2	S15 0-0
18 ROTHERHAM U	D25 0-0	S01 0-2	D22 6-1	O27 0-0	M02 1-1	A27 0-1	F02 4-3	D08 2-1	N24 3-3	a13 1-1	M30 2-0	a22 3-0	N10 2-2	O13 2-3	S15 3-2	M16 0-0	J01 1-0		A18 0-4	F16 1-0	S29 6-1	J12 0-1
19 SHEFFIELD U	D29 5-0	F02 0-2	S15 1-1	F16 0-0	N10 1-1	N24 4-0	A20 5-2	M30 2-0	M16 2-0	S08 1-1	O27 2-3	D25 2-0	a13 3-0	D08 2-1	a27 0-4	O13 5-1	A25 4-2	D15 2-7		M02 1-1	J01 2-2	S29 1-0
20 STOKE C	a20 3-0	N17 4-1	a06 0-2	D29 2-1	a22 2-0	S03 1-1	M09 0-2	A20 1-0	F09 5-1	A25 3-1	S22 7-1	F23 8-0	J19 1-0	D15 3-1	N03 2-1	S08 6-0	O10 3-1	O06 6-0	O20 3-3		D01 4-1	M23 0-1
21 SWANSEA T	A30 2-3	A18 5-1	D26 5-0	N10 2-3	S15 3-0	O13 4-2	J12 4-5	F16 3-1	D08 4-2	M16 2-3	M02 1-0	S22 1-2	N24 1-1	O27 2-2	S01 1-4	M30 2-1	a22 2-2	F09 1-0	S13 4-1	a13 1-0		D22 3-1
22 WEST HAM U	S22 2-0	A20 1-3	a22 3-1	M02 1-2	a13 1-0	M16 1-1	D15 2-1	O27 0-1	O13 0-2	N24 2-1	F16 2-1	D29 2-1	S03 1-1	M30 1-1	D25 2-1	D08 2-1	J19 2-1	S08 1-1	F09 3-2	N10 1-0	A25 1-2	

Season 1956-57

DIVISION 3 NORTH

	ACCRINGTON S	BARROW	BRADFORD	BRADFORD C	CARLISLE U	CHESTER	CHESTERFIELD	CREWE A	DARLINGTON	DERBY CO	GATESHEAD	HALIFAX T	HARTLEPOOLS U	HULL C	MANSFIELD T	OLDHAM A	ROCHDALE	SCUNTHORPE U	SOUTHPORT	STOCKPORT CO	TRANMERE R	WORKINGTON	WREXHAM	YORK C
1 ACCRINGTON S		A29 4-1	M25 5-0	S24 0-2	J26 1-2	F02 4-0	S15 1-1	M23 5-0	O06 4-2	N03 0-0	D01 2-0	O20 4-0	S29 2-1	a22 0-3	S01 3-3	D22 2-2	a06 2-1	J01 0-1	J12 4-2	a08 4-0	S12 1-0	a20 2-1	M09 1-0	A18 3-0
2 BARROW	A20 3-1		F09 1-0	M02 4-0	D26 3-0	M30 3-0	N10 2-1	D29 3-0	S24 3-1	S08 2-2	S22 1-2	S03 1-0	N24 3-1	J26 1-2	O27 2-0	a13 2-1	D15 2-0	A25 1-2	M16 1-1	J01 0-3	F16 5-0	a22 5-2	J19 2-1	O13 1-2
3 BRADFORD	O13 2-0	S29 4-1		J19 2-0	F16 1-3	M02 3-1	N24 2-0	D15 4-3	F02 3-1	A25 3-2	S08 0-1	J05 2-1	a27 0-2	S17 4-1	N10 1-4	M16 2-2	a23 0-0	S03 1-2	M30 2-3	A20 3-2	a13 1-2	D26 1-3	D29 0-4	O27 0-2
4 BRADFORD C	S19 1-2	O20 0-2	S15 2-0		F09 3-2	S01 1-0	D22 3-2	D01 5-1	a20 1-2	a03 0-2	A29 3-1	M23 1-0	J12 1-1	a06 2-1	S12 4-3	a22 4-1	N03 1-1	M09 3-1	A18 3-1	S22 1-1	D25 4-1	m01 2-3	O06 2-1	J26 0-2
5 CARLISLE U	M19 2-2	D25 1-1	O06 2-1	S29 1-4		S15 3-0	J12 4-2	N03 2-1	O09 1-2	M09 1-3	F23 3-2	a06 0-0	F02 2-1	a09 1-3	D22 6-1	A18 2-2	a30 2-1	M23 0-0	S01 1-2	S25 3-3	a19 2-2	O20 1-1	D01 2-2	J01 2-0
6 CHESTER	S22 0-2	a29 2-0	O20 2-0	D29 1-2	J19 1-2		S12 3-4	O06 4-1	a06 0-3	A22 2-2	a20 4-1	M09 1-1	A25 0-1	M23 1-1	J26 6-2	a10 1-0	D01 2-2	F23 2-2	a22 2-0	S08 1-4	F09 1-1	N03 1-0	D15 0-0	S26 3-4
7 CHESTERFIELD	J19 1-0	M23 3-2	a06 4-1	A25 1-1	S08 2-2	S05 3-0		A22 2-0	m01 4-1	a19 2-2	O20 6-0	D01 2-1	D15 5-1	N03 3-1	D25 1-0	J01 1-0	F23 2-2	O06 1-0	J26 6-0	D29 1-0	S22 3-1	M09 2-2	a20 2-1	F09 3-4
8 CREWE A	N10 3-4	S01 1-1	A18 2-0	a13 1-0	M16 2-2	F16 0-0	A29 0-4		D22 1-3	J05 2-5	S03 0-3	F02 1-3	O13 1-2	J12 2-3	a27 6-4	M02 2-2	S29 1-6	S19 2-1	D25 0-0	O27 0-1	M30 0-0	S15 0-1	a22 3-0	N24 1-1
9 DARLINGTON	F16 0-0	S19 1-1	S22 0-5	a27 3-2	A22 0-1	N24 5-1	M30 4-1	A25 3-0		D29 1-1	J19 7-0	a19 0-1	M02 3-1	D25 1-1	M16 1-3	O27 1-0	J01 4-3	D15 1-2	N10 1-0	S29 3-1	O13 1-1	J26 4-2	S08 1-5	a13 2-4
10 DERBY CO	M16 2-2	J12 3-3	D22 6-1	O13 0-2	O27 3-0	A29 3-0	a22 7-1	J26 4-0	S01 1-1		A18 5-3	S29 6-0	F16 2-0	S15 1-0	M02 4-0	N24 3-2	S19 3-0	D25 4-0	a27 2-0	a13 2-0	N10 4-0	F02 2-3	S12 1-0	M30 1-0
11 GATESHEAD	a13 1-1	F02 2-2	J12 1-3	A20 1-2	O13 4-2	a27 4-1	M02 1-3	S10 1-1	S15 1-2	D15 1-1		D25 2-1	S01 4-3	S29 2-0	M30 1-1	N10 2-3	J05 2-1	a22 0-0	N24 3-1	F16 1-5	O27 3-1	S17 1-2	A25 4-2	M16 0-2
12 HALIFAX T	M02 0-1	S10 3-2	J26 3-1	N10 0-2	N24 1-3	O27 2-1	a13 2-1	S22 1-0	a22 3-2	F09 1-0	a15 0-1		M16 2-0	A18 1-0	F16 2-1	A27 1-1	S08 2-1	J19 1-0	O13 3-1	M30 3-2	a27 4-0	D22 4-2	S24 1-2	S01 0-0
13 HARTLEPOOLS U	F09 2-1	a06 2-0	a20 2-1	S08 2-0	S22 2-1	D22 2-2	A18 5-1	F23 2-0	O20 2-1	O06 2-1	D29 4-1	N03 0-1		J01 3-3	a19 2-1	J26 4-1	M09 0-0	D01 0-0	S10 5-2	J19 4-1	S24 5-1	M23 2-1	A27 2-1	D26 2-0
14 HULL C	a19 2-1	M18 3-0	S24 2-0	N24 1-0	a27 0-0	N10 2-0	M16 3-2	S08 2-0	D26 1-1	J19 3-3	F09 1-1	D15 3-1	M30 2-0		a13 1-2	O13 2-1	A25 2-0	D29 2-2	O27 2-1	M02 5-3	A20 4-1	S03 0-2	S22 1-2	F16 1-1
15 MANSFIELD T	D29 1-3	M09 1-3	M23 2-1	S03 3-1	A25 5-1	J05 1-1	a08 3-0	a20 2-1	N03 7-3	O20 1-2	D08 2-4	O06 2-0	a23 4-1	D01 2-1		S22 2-4	A20 2-3	F09 1-1	a29 1-2	D15 4-2	S08 3-0	a15 2-2	a06 3-1	J19 4-1
16 OLDHAM A	A25 2-4	D01 0-1	N03 3-1	a19 1-1	D15 2-2	D25 0-0	S18 3-3	O20 2-0	M09 3-2	a06 1-2	M23 1-2	A21 4-3	a16 0-0	F23 1-3	F02 1-1		J19 0-1	a20 1-1	S29 2-1	S10 2-0	D29 1-0	O06 1-0	a30 1-2	S08 3-1
17 ROCHDALE	N24 0-2	A18 1-0	a22 2-1	M16 4-1	M30 2-1	a13 2-1	O13 1-0	F09 1-1	S12 3-0	S26 3-1	J26 0-0	J12 1-1	O27 1-0	M05 4-3	A29 0-0	S15 0-2		S22 3-0	F16 6-1	N10 2-2	M02 1-0	S01 0-0	D26 0-2	a27 1-0
18 SCUNTHORPE U	M30 2-3	D22 1-1	S13 2-2	O27 1-1	N10 1-2	O13 3-0	F16 5-1	S27 5-1	A18 1-2	D26 1-4	a19 1-2	S15 6-1	a13 1-2	S01 1-1	S29 0-1	a27 0-0	F02 1-0		A30 1-0	M16 2-3	N24 1-4	J12 2-1	a04 4-3	M02 2-1
19 SOUTHPORT	S08 3-5	N03 0-0	J01 5-1	D15 1-5	D29 4-1	a19 1-1	M26 0-0	a24 0-1	M23 1-0	a20 3-2	a06 2-3	F23 1-1	S04 1-6	M09 1-0	S18 1-1	F09 2-0	O06 0-1	A21 2-2		A25 0-1	J19 1-0	D01 0-1	O20 1-1	S22 1-1
20 STOCKPORT CO	D25 2-1	a20 2-1	A27 4-0	F02 1-1	S17 2-0	J12 2-1	S01 2-1	M09 2-0	F09 5-2	D01 3-2	O06 1-1	a29 2-2	S15 2-4	O20 1-2	A18 2-1	S03 2-1	M23 3-1	N03 1-3	D22 2-0		J05 3-1	a06 0-1	F23 4-0	a22 3-0
21 TRANMERE R	S04 1-2	O06 0-2	D01 0-3	a15 0-0	a22 0-1	S29 3-1	F02 2-2	J01 3-0	a08 2-2	M23 0-1	M09 0-0	a20 0-2	S18 0-1	A28 2-4	J12 3-1	S01 2-1	O20 2-2	a06 4-2	S15 1-1	J26 2-2		M13 1-1	N03 2-4	D22 3-3
22 WORKINGTON	a27 4-1	a19 0-1	D25 0-1	M30 5-1	M02 2-0	M16 0-1	O27 2-1	J19 4-0	J05 6-2	S22 2-1	S26 2-1	A25 3-1	N10 1-1	S12 4-3	O13 3-3	F16 0-0	D29 5-0	S08 2-2	a13 2-0	N24 4-1	D15 3-2		F09 3-0	A29 3-2
23 WREXHAM	O27 5-2	S15 5-0	S01 2-0	F16 1-2	a13 6-4	A18 2-2	a27 1-3	a19 5-0	J12 5-0	S05 0-2	D22 4-1	S19 3-2	A22 2-2	F02 5-2	N24 0-0	M30 4-4	D25 4-1	a10 1-1	M02 1-1	O13 2-3	M16 1-0	S29 3-0		N10 1-1
24 YORK C	D15 3-1	F23 1-0	M09 1-2	J05 3-1	S03 2-0	S17 0-1	S29 1-2	a06 2-1	D01 1-0	a29 1-1	N03 1-0	D29 1-2	D25 3-3	O06 2-1	S15 2-0	J12 2-1	a20 4-0	O20 0-2	F02 9-1	a19 0-0	A25 1-0	A20 2-2	M23 1-0	

DIVISION 3 SOUTH

	ALDERSHOT	BOURNEMOUTH	BRENTFORD	BRIGHTON & HA	COLCHESTER U	COVENTRY C	CRYSTAL P	EXETER C	GILLINGHAM	IPSWICH T	MILLWALL	NEWPORT CO	NORTHAMPTON T	NORWICH C	PLYMOUTH A	Q.P.R.	READING	SHREWSBURY T	SOUTHAMPTON	SOUTHEND U	SWINDON T	TORQUAY U	WALSALL	WATFORD
1 ALDERSHOT		D26 3-2	A25 0-2	S19 1-4	D01 2-1	a27 0-1	a20 2-1	N03 1-4	A22 0-0	S29 3-1	S05 3-0	M09 3-1	a10 4-0	a06 0-0	a19 0-2	O06 4-2	D29 1-4	S15 1-1	M23 1-1	O20 5-3	D15 2-2	J26 0-1	F02 4-1	J12 3-1
2 BOURNEMOUTH	D24 3-2		F09 3-0	S08 1-1	F23 1-1	a19 1-2	D01 2-2	M09 3-1	J19 3-1	A22 1-0	D29 6-1	O20 2-1	a27 4-1	O06 1-1	N03 2-1	M23 1-0	a20 2-1	S05 6-1	D15 1-0	a06 1-1	S22 7-0	A25 0-0	S19 2-2	m03 4-0
3 BRENTFORD	D22 2-2	S29 2-2		S04 2-5	a06 1-1	M23 1-1	O20 1-1	a20 3-0	S18 3-2	F02 1-1	M04 5-0	D01 0-0	O06 2-1	a27 1-1	A18 4-1	a19 2-0	M09 4-0	J12 3-1	N03 4-0	M12 3-2	A21 4-1	D25 0-0	S15 6-2	S01 1-5
4 BRIGHTON & H.A.	S26 2-2	J12 2-2	S12 1-2		N03 0-0	O20 2-1	a22 1-1	O06 3-0	D26 3-1	S01 3-2	F02 3-2	M23 2-0	M09 5-0	a20 3-0	a06 3-1	D01 1-0	a27 8-3	A18 4-3	F23 1-0	F09 1-1	J05 2-0	S15 6-0	D22 1-3	A29 2-2
5 COLCHESTER U	a13 1-1	O13 3-0	N24 1-0	M16 0-0		J05 3-2	A27 3-3	S24 4-0	N10 0-0	F16 0-0	O27 2-1	F02 1-0	D22 5-1	D25 1-1	J12 2-1	S01 1-1	S15 3-2	S29 6-0	S10 3-1	A18 3-2	M30 1-1	M02 2-1	a19 2-1	a29 2-0
6 COVENTRY C	M30 5-1	a23 4-2	N10 1-1	M02 1-2	J26 2-4		a01 3-3	A18 1-0	O27 4-1	S24 1-1	O13 1-2	a08 2-0	J12 3-1	S10 3-2	F02 1-4	S15 5-1	S29 0-1	a13 3-3	A20 2-1	S01 2-0	M16 3-0	F16 3-2	D08 2-2	N24 0-2
7 CRYSTAL P	O27 2-1	a13 1-1	M02 0-2	a19 2-2	A22 2-4	A25 1-1		S08 0-0	F16 1-2	N24 1-3	S15 2-2	S19 2-1	S29 1-1	D15 4-1	J26 2-1	D25 2-1	S05 1-1	N10 0-1	D29 1-2	F02 2-0	O13 0-0	m01 1-1	M30 3-0	M16 0-0
8 EXETER C	M16 1-1	m01 1-2	O27 1-1	F16 1-3	S19 0-2	D15 4-2	J12 2-1		O13 4-0	a13 1-2	a22 1-1	S05 2-0	F02 0-0	A22 0-0	D26 2-1	S29 0-0	J26 1-1	M30 5-1	A25 0-4	S15 6-1	M02 3-2	S01 1-1	N24 0-1	N10 1-2
9 GILLINGHAM	A29 6-2	S15 1-0	S26 2-1	D25 0-0	M23 1-2	a20 1-2	O06 4-1	F23 2-1		J12 1-1	S29 1-3	a27 1-1	J26 1-2	N03 1-1	D01 0-3	M09 0-1	a06 0-0	D22 1-1	O20 0-0	a19 0-2	S05 3-0	F02 1-1	S01 2-1	A18 0-3
10 IPSWICH T	F09 4-1	A29 1-0	S22 4-0	D29 4-0	O06 3-1	S19 4-0	a06 4-2	D01 3-0	S08 1-1		A25 0-2	F23 5-0	M23 0-1	a22 3-1	a20 2-1	N03 4-0	O20 4-2	J26 5-1	M09 2-0	a27 3-3	J19 4-1	D15 6-0	S12 2-2	D26 4-1
11 MILLWALL	S10 1-5	S01 3-4	M18 1-1	S22 4-3	a20 3-1	F23 3-2	J19 3-0	a19 1-3	F09 2-1	D22 2-2		N03 1-0	D01 1-0	O20 5-1	a27 2-2	a06 2-0	M23 1-0	A27 0-0	O06 0-0	M09 0-0	D26 2-1	J12 7-2	A18 1-0	S24 1-1
12 NEWPORT CO	m02 3-0	M07 5-3	a13 3-0	N10 0-0	S22 1-0	M21 3-0	S27 2-2	S13 1-1	M30 4-0	O13 1-0	M16 0-0		A18 3-0	F09 3-1	S01 4-1	D22 1-1	J12 1-2	a19 2-0	a04 2-3	A30 2-1	N24 2-1	O27 3-0	F16 2-2	S15 3-0
13 NORTHAMPTON T	O13 4-2	M30 2-2	F16 5-1	a30 1-0	A25 1-0	S08 4-0	F09 1-0	S22 1-1	J05 4-1	N10 2-1	a13 2-1	D15 0-3		D29 1-1	S17 2-0	S06 3-0	A23 3-0	O27 1-1	J19 2-1	D25 2-2	a23 2-0	N24 3-0	M16 2-3	M02 1-2
14 NORWICH C	N24 1-1	F20 1-3	M30 1-1	O27 1-1	D26 1-2	S05 3-0	A18 1-0	A29 1-0	M16 1-3	a19 1-2	M02 2-0	S29 1-1	S01 2-1		S15 3-0	J12 1-2	F02 2-5	m01 3-0	N28 0-3	D22 1-2	N10 2-4	O13 1-2	J05 2-2	a13 1-2
15 PLYMOUTH A	a22 2-2	M16 2-0	D15 2-0	N24 2-0	S08 2-2	S22 0-0	M11 0-1	J05 5-0	a13 2-0	O27 1-2	M30 0-0	a10 3-2	S24 4-3	J19 3-2		A20 1-2	A25 0-6	O13 1-1	F09 2-1	S10 0-0	a29 1-0	N10 0-0	M02 2-4	F16 3-3
16 Q.P.R.	F16 0-1	N10 2-1	a22 2-2	a13 0-0	D29 1-1	J19 1-1	D26 4-2	F09 5-3	a29 5-0	M16 0-2	N24 0-0	A25 1-1	S10 1-0	S08 3-1	A27 3-0		D15 1-1	M02 2-1	S22 1-2	M25 3-0	S24 3-0	M30 0-1	O27 1-0	O13 3-1
17 READING	S01 2-1	O27 0-4	m01 2-0	M30 2-2	J19 0-3	F09 3-0	S12 1-2	M13 4-0	N24 4-0	M02 1-3	N10 3-0	S08 0-0	A29 1-1	S22 2-1	D22 3-2	A18 1-0		F16 2-2	M25 2-4	S26 3-2	a13 1-0	M16 3-1	O13 3-0	a22 1-2
18 SHREWSBURY T	J19 2-2	S10 0-0	S08 3-2	D15 4-0	F09 1-3	D01 5-0	M23 1-1	a27 1-2	A25 1-0	M28 1-1	A20 2-0	a22 2-0	a20 2-0	M09 4-5	F23 3-1	O20 0-0	O06 1-1		a06 0-0	N03 0-0	D29 7-3	S17 1-1	a29 3-2	S22 1-0
19 SOUTHAMPTON	N10 1-0	A18 3-0	M16 3-3	O13 1-0	S05 2-1	A29 1-1	S01 3-0	D22 2-2	M02 0-1	m01 0-2	F25 4-0	m04 3-0	S15 2-0	O03 2-0	S29 2-2	F02 1-2	D26 4-1	N24 4-0		J12 1-2	O27 2-1	a22 1-0	a13 3-1	M30 3-1
20 SOUTHEND U	M02 2-4	N24 2-1	O13 1-0	S29 3-1	D15 3-2	D29 1-2	S22 1-1	J19 2-0	a22 5-0	M30 2-0	m01 1-0	A22 3-3	D26 0-1	A25 0-0	S05 0-1	a15 3-0	S19 4-0	M16 1-2	S08 1-2		F16 1-0	a13 2-0	N10 2-0	O27 2-0
21 SWINDON T	A18 1-2	F02 2-1	A29 1-3	J26 3-0	a27 4-1	N03 2-2	F23 3-1	O20 3-5	S12 2-3	S15 3-1	a10 1-0	a06 1-0	a22 4-0	M23 1-1	M09 0-3	S19 1-0	D01 3-2	S01 1-2	a20 0-0	O06 3-2		S29 1-2	J12 1-2	D22 2-0
22 TORQUAY U	M13 4-2	D22 1-0	D26 2-0	J19 1-0	O20 4-2	O06 3-1	M09 3-0	D29 1-0	S22 3-3	A18 4-1	S08 7-2	a20 4-0	a06 2-0	F23 7-1	M23 1-1	a27 3-0	N03 3-1	S26 1-1	a19 2-0	D01 3-3	F09 7-0		A29 2-0	S12 3-0
23 WALSALL	S22 5-1	S27 0-0	J19 7-0	A25 3-2	a22 2-1	M09 1-1	a27 1-2	a06 2-0	D29 2-2	S06 2-0	D15 7-1	O06 0-0	N03 2-2	J26 6-3	O20 1-0	a20 0-2	F23 3-2	D25 1-1	D01 1-1	M23 0-1	S08 1-2	A23 0-1		F09 2-0
24 WATFORD	S08 3-0	M26 1-1	D29 1-1	A21 2-1	M09 0-0	a06 1-0	N03 1-4	M23 1-1	D15 2-3	D25 2-1	S18 2-0	J19 5-0	O20 2-1	D01 3-3	O06 0-1	F23 2-4	a19 1-0	F02 2-3	a27 4-2	a20 1-1	A25 3-4	S04 4-1	S29 1-0	

LEAGUE TABLES

DIVISION 1

	P	W	D	L	F	A	W	D	L	F	A	Pts
Manchester U	42	14	4	3	55	25	14	4	3	48	29	64
Tottenham H	42	15	4	2	70	24	7	8	6	34	32	56
Preston N.E.	42	15	4	2	50	19	8	6	7	34	37	56
Blackpool	42	14	3	4	55	26	8	6	7	38	39	53
Arsenal	42	12	5	4	45	21	9	3	9	40	48	50
Wolverh'pton W	42	17	2	2	70	29	3	6	12	24	41	48
Burnley	42	14	5	2	41	21	4	5	12	15	29	46
Leeds U	42	10	8	3	42	18	5	6	10	30	45	44
Bolton W	42	13	6	2	42	23	3	6	12	23	42	44
Aston Villa	42	10	8	3	45	25	4	7	10	20	30	43
W.B.A.	42	8	8	5	31	25	6	6	9	28	36	42
Birmingham C	42	12	5	4	52	25	3	4	14	17	44	*39
Chelsea	42	7	8	6	43	36	6	5	10	30	37	*39
Sheffield W	42	14	3	4	55	29	2	3	16	27	59	38
Everton	42	10	5	6	34	28	4	5	12	27	51	38
Luton T	42	10	4	7	32	26	4	5	12	26	50	37
Newcastle U	42	10	5	6	43	31	4	3	14	24	56	36
Manchester C	42	10	2	9	48	42	3	7	11	30	46	35
Portsmouth	42	8	6	7	37	35	2	7	12	25	57	33
Sunderland	42	9	5	7	40	30	3	3	15	27	58	32
Cardiff C	42	7	6	8	35	34	3	3	15	18	54	29
Charlton A	42	7	3	11	31	44	2	1	18	31	76	22

*Birmingham City & Chelsea finished in equal 12th position

DIVISION 2

	P	W	D	L	F	A	W	D	L	F	A	Pts
Leicester C	42	14	5	2	68	36	11	6	4	41	31	61
Nottingham F	42	13	4	4	50	29	9	6	6	44	26	54
Liverpool	42	16	1	4	53	26	5	10	6	29	28	53
Blackburn R	42	12	6	3	49	32	9	4	8	34	43	52
Stoke C	42	16	2	3	64	18	4	6	11	19	40	48
Middlesbrough	42	12	5	4	51	29	7	5	9	33	31	48
Sheffield U	42	11	6	4	45	28	8	2	11	42	48	46
West Ham U	42	12	4	5	31	24	7	4	10	28	39	46
Bristol R	42	12	5	4	47	19	6	4	11	34	48	45
Swansea T	42	12	3	6	53	34	7	4	10	37	56	45
Fulham	42	13	1	7	53	32	6	3	12	31	44	42
Huddersfield T	42	10	3	8	33	27	8	3	10	35	47	42
Bristol C	42	13	2	6	49	32	3	7	11	25	47	41
Doncaster R	42	12	5	4	51	21	3	5	13	26	56	40
Leyton O	42	7	8	6	34	38	8	2	11	32	46	40
Grimsby T	42	12	4	5	41	26	5	1	15	20	36	39
Rotherham U	42	9	7	5	37	26	4	4	13	37	49	37
Lincoln C	42	9	4	8	34	27	5	2	14	20	53	34
Barnsley	42	8	7	6	39	35	4	3	14	20	54	34
Notts Co	42	7	6	8	34	32	2	6	13	24	54	30
Bury	42	5	3	13	37	47	3	6	12	23	49	25
Port Vale	42	7	4	10	31	42	1	2	18	26	59	22

DIVISION 3 NORTH

	P	W	D	L	F	A	W	D	L	F	A	Pts
Derby Co	46	18	3	2	69	18	8	8	7	42	35	63
Hartlepool U	46	18	4	1	56	21	7	5	11	34	42	59
Accrington S	46	15	4	4	54	22	10	4	9	41	42	58
Workington	46	16	4	3	60	25	8	6	9	33	38	58
Stockport Co	46	16	3	4	51	26	7	5	11	40	49	54
Chesterfield	46	17	5	1	60	22	5	4	14	36	57	53
York C	46	14	4	5	43	21	7	6	10	32	40	52
Hull C	46	14	6	3	45	24	7	4	12	39	45	52
Bradford C	46	14	3	6	47	31	8	5	10	31	37	52
Barrow	46	16	2	5	51	22	5	7	11	25	40	51
Halifax T	46	16	2	5	40	24	5	5	13	25	46	49
Wrexham	46	12	7	4	63	33	7	3	13	34	41	48
Rochdale	46	14	6	3	38	19	4	6	13	27	46	48
Scunthorpe U	46	9	5	9	44	36	6	10	7	27	33	45
Carlisle U	46	9	9	5	44	36	7	4	12	32	49	45
Mansfield T	46	13	3	7	58	38	4	7	12	33	52	44
Gateshead	46	9	6	8	42	40	8	4	11	30	50	44
Darlington	46	11	5	7	47	36	6	3	14	35	59	42
Oldham A	46	9	7	7	35	31	3	8	12	31	43	39
Bradford P.A.	46	11	2	10	41	40	5	1	17	25	53	35
Chester C	46	8	7	8	40	35	2	6	15	15	49	33
Southport	46	7	8	8	31	34	3	4	16	21	60	32
Tranmere R	46	5	9	9	33	38	2	4	17	18	53	27
Crewe A	46	5	7	11	31	46	1	2	20	12	64	21

DIVISION 3 SOUTH

	P	W	D	L	F	A	W	D	L	F	A	Pts
Ipswich T	46	18	3	2	72	20	7	6	10	29	34	59
Torquay U	46	19	4	0	71	18	5	7	11	18	46	59
Colchester U	46	15	8	0	49	19	7	6	10	35	37	58
Southampton	46	15	4	4	48	20	7	6	10	28	32	54
Bournemouth	46	15	7	1	57	20	4	7	12	31	42	52
Brighton & H.A.	46	15	6	2	59	26	4	8	11	27	39	52
Southend U	46	14	3	6	42	20	4	9	10	31	45	48
Brentford	46	12	9	2	55	29	4	7	12	23	47	48
Shrewsbury T	46	11	9	3	45	24	4	9	10	27	55	48
Q.P.R.	46	12	7	4	42	21	6	4	13	19	39	47
Watford	46	11	6	6	44	32	7	4	12	28	43	46
Newport Co	46	15	6	2	51	18	1	7	15	14	44	45
Reading	46	13	4	6	44	30	5	5	13	36	51	45
Northampton T	46	15	5	3	49	22	3	4	16	17	51	45
Walsall	46	11	7	5	49	25	5	5	13	31	49	44
Coventry C	46	12	5	6	52	36	4	7	12	22	48	44
Millwall	46	13	7	3	46	29	3	5	15	18	55	44
Plymouth A	46	10	8	5	38	31	6	3	14	30	42	43
Aldershot	46	11	5	7	43	35	4	7	12	36	57	42
Crystal Palace	46	7	10	6	31	28	4	8	11	31	47	40
Exeter C	46	8	8	7	37	29	4	5	14	24	50	37
Gillingham	46	7	8	8	29	29	5	5	13	25	56	37
Swindon T	46	12	3	8	43	33	3	3	17	23	63	36
Norwich C	46	7	5	11	33	37	1	10	12	28	57	31

Football League Records

Top scorers: Div 1, R.Smith (Tottenham Hotspur) 36 goals; Div 2, B.Clough (Middlesbrough)40 goals; Div 3 N, A.Ackerman (Carlisle United) 35 goals; Div 3 S, D.Reeves (Southampton), S.McGrory. (Southend United) 31 goals.

Norman Deeley, the winger who was a star of Wolves' League Championship triumph in 1957-58.

DIVISION 1

	ARSENAL	ASTON VILLA	BIRMINGHAM C	BLACKPOOL	BOLTON W	BURNLEY	CHELSEA	EVERTON	LEEDS U	LEICESTER C	LUTON T	MANCHESTER C	MANCHESTER U	NEWCASTLE U	NOTTINGHAM F	PORTSMOUTH	PRESTON N.E.	SHEFFIELD W	SUNDERLAND	TOTTENHAM H	W.B.A.	WOLVERHAMPTON W
1 ARSENAL		O02 4-0	O19 1-3	J11 2-3	F18 1-2	a19 0-0	M08 5-4	S10 2-3	S28 2-1	S14 3-1	A31 2-0	N02 2-1	F01 4-5	N30 2-3	a21 1-1	N16 3-2	D14 4-2	M22 1-0	D21 3-0	F22 4-4	A27 2-2	a07 0-2
2 ASTON VILLA	D26 3-0		D21 0-2	F01 1-1	a08 4-0	M08 3-0	F22 1-3	A31 0-1	A26 2-0	S28 5-1	S14 2-0	D14 1-2	M31 3-2	O19 4-3	a30 1-1	N02 2-1	N30 2-2	a19 2-0	J11 5-2	N16 1-1	a05 2-1	S23 2-3
3 BIRMINGHAM C	M01 4-1	A24 3-1		N23 0-0	O26 5-1	J18 2-3	D28 3-3	M29 2-1	a12 1-1	a26 0-1	M15 1-1	O05 4-0	D07 3-3	S07 1-4	S04 0-2	a07 4-1	S21 3-1	M12 1-0	N09 2-3	S11 0-0	D26 3-5	O12 1-5
4 BLACKPOOL	S07 1-0	S21 1-1	M22 4-2		D28 2-3	N16 2-4	N02 2-1	a23 0-1	A24 3-0	D25 5-1	A26 1-2	O19 2-5	S09 1-4	a05 3-2	M08 3-0	N30 2-1	a04 1-2	F22 2-2	O05 7-0	D14 0-2	a19 2-0	J18 3-2
5 BOLTON W	O05 0-1	a04 4-0	M08 1-0	A31 3-0		D14 2-1	N30 3-3	D26 1-5	F01 0-2	J11 2-3	D21 1-2	a05 0-2	S14 4-0	a19 1-1	N16 2-0	S28 1-0	a21 0-4	N02 5-4	S11 2-2	O19 3-2	F22 2-2	S04 1-1
6 BURNLEY	D07 2-1	O26 3-0	S14 3-1	M29 2-1	a26 3-1		F01 2-1	M01 0-2	N23 3-1	N09 7-3	F15 1-2	D25 2-1	M15 3-0	S28 0-2	S09 3-1	D21 3-1	A27 2-0	a04 2-0	O12 6-0	J11 2-0	A31 2-2	a12 1-1
7 CHELSEA	O26 0-0	O12 4-2	A31 5-1	M15 1-4	a12 2-2	S21 6-1		J11 3-1	D07 2-1	N23 4-0	N09 1-3	A28 2-3	a26 2-1	J18 2-1	a04 0-0	D25 7-4	F08 0-2	O05 1-0	M29 0-0	D21 2-4	S11 2-2	M11 1-2
8 EVERTON	O16 2-2	D28 1-2	N16 0-2	N20 0-0	D25 1-1	O19 1-1	S07 3-0		a04 0-1	F15 2-2	F01 0-2	a19 2-5	S04 3-3	F22 1-2	D14 1-1	M22 4-2	M08 4-2	N30 1-1	S14 3-1	a05 3-4	N02 1-1	A24 1-0
9 LEEDS U	M19 2-0	S04 4-0	N30 1-1	D21 2-1	S21 2-1	M22 1-0	a19 0-0	a07 1-0		A31 2-1	S11 0-2	N16 2-4	J11 1-1	D14 3-0	S14 1-2	F22 2-0	N02 2-3	a05 2-2	S25 2-1	M08 1-2	O19 1-1	O05 1-1
10 LEICESTER C	J18 0-1	F08 6-1	D14 2-2	D26 2-1	S07 2-3	a05 5-3	M22 3-2	O05 2-2	D28 3-0		a08 4-1	F22 8-4	A24 0-3	N02 2-1	O19 3-1	M08 2-2	N16 1-3	S18 4-1	A28 4-1	a19 1-3	N30 3-3	S21 2-3
11 LUTON T	D28 4-0	J18 3-0	N02 3-0	S04 2-0	A24 1-0	O05 3-2	a05 0-2	S21 0-1	S18 1-1	a07 2-1		M08 1-2	D26 2-2	N16 0-3	N30 3-1	a19 2-1	F22 1-3	O19 2-0	F08 7-1	M22 0-0	D14 5-1	S07 3-1
12 MANCHESTER C	M15 2-4	a26 1-2	M05 1-1	M01 4-3	N09 2-1	D26 4-1	S04 5-2	D07 6-2	M29 1-0	O12 4-3	O26 2-2		D28 2-2	a07 2-1	J11 1-1	S14 2-1	S11 2-0	O09 2-0	a12 3-1	S28 5-1	F01 4-1	N23 3-4
13 MANCHESTER U	S21 4-2	O05 4-1	a19 0-2	S18 1-2	J18 7-2	N02 1-0	D14 0-1	A28 3-0	S07 5-0	D21 4-0	D25 3-0	A31 4-1		a23 1-1	F22 1-1	O19 0-3	a05 0-0	N16 2-1	a04 2-2	N30 3-4	M08 0-4	a21 0-4
14 NEWCASTLE U	a12 3-3	M01 2-4	J11 1-2	N09 1-2	D07 1-2	a28 1-3	S14 1-3	O12 2-3	a26 1-2	M15 5-3	M29 3-2	a14 4-1	N23 1-2		D25 1-4	S11 2-0	O05 0-2	S25 0-0	F01 2-2	A31 3-1	D21 3-0	O26 1-1
15 NOTTINGHAM F	N09 4-0	N23 4-1	A28 1-1	O26 1-2	M29 0-0	S18 7-0	a07 1-1	a26 0-3	J18 1-1	M01 3-1	a12 1-0	S07 2-1	O12 1-2	D26 2-3		F01 2-0	A24 2-1	D28 5-2	D07 2-0	F15 1-2	S28 0-2	M15 1-4
16 PORTSMOUTH	M29 5-4	M15 1-0	a04 3-2	a12 1-2	F08 2-2	A24 0-0	D26 3-0	N23 3-2	O12 1-2	O26 2-0	D07 5-0	J18 2-1	a16 3-3	S18 2-2	S21 1-4		D28 0-2	S07 3-2	a26 0-2	A28 5-1	M19 2-2	N09 1-1
17 PRESTON N.E.	a26 3-0	a12 1-1	F01 8-0	a07 2-1	N23 3-0	S04 2-1	S28 5-2	O26 3-1	M15 3-0	M29 4-1	O12 1-0	S18 6-1	N09 1-1	M19 2-1	D21 2-0	A31 4-0		D26 3-0	M01 3-0	S14 3-1	J11 3-1	D07 1-2
18 SHEFFIELD W	N23 2-0	D07 2-5	S28 5-3	O12 0-3	M15 1-0	a07 1-2	F15 2-3	a12 2-1	N09 3-2	S11 2-1	M01 2-1	D21 4-5	M29 1-0	S04 1-0	A31 1-2	J11 4-2	D25 4-4		O26 3-3	F01 2-0	S14 1-2	a26 2-1
19 SUNDERLAND	A24 0-1	S07 1-1	a05 1-6	F15 1-4	S18 1-2	F22 2-3	N16 2-2	J18 1-1	D26 2-1	S04 3-2	S28 3-0	N30 2-1	a07 1-2	S21 2-0	a19 3-0	D14 1-1	O19 0-0	M08 3-3		N02 1-1	M22 2-0	D28 0-2
20 TOTTENHAM H	O12 3-1	M29 6-2	S18 7-1	a26 2-1	M12 4-1	S07 3-1	A24 1-1	N09 3-1	O26 2-0	D07 1-4	N23 3-1	F08 5-1	a12 1-0	D28 3-3	O05 3-4	S04 3-5	J18 3-3	S21 4-2	M15 0-1		a04 0-0	D26 1-0
21 W.B.A.	S04 1-2	N09 3-2	O01 0-0	D07 1-1	O12 2-2	D28 5-1	S18 1-1	M15 4-0	M12 1-0	a12 6-2	a26 4-2	S21 9-2	O26 4-3	A24 2-1	F08 3-2	O05 3-1	S07 4-1	J18 3-1	N23 3-0	a07 0-2		M29 0-3
22 WOLVERHAMPTON W	a08 1-2	S16 2-1	F22 5-1	S14 3-1	A28 6-1	N30 2-1	O19 2-1	D21 2-0	F19 3-2	F01 5-1	J11 1-1	M22 3-3	S28 3-1	M08 3-1	N02 2-0	a05 1-0	a19 2-0	D14 4-3	A31 5-0	O02 4-0	N16 1-1	

John Dick netted 21 goals as West Ham returned to Division One. Only three players have scored more than his 166 goals for the Hammers overall.

DIVISION 2

	BARNSLEY	BLACKBURN R	BRISTOL C	BRISTOL R	CARDIFF C	CHARLTON A	DERBY CO	DONCASTER R	FULHAM	GRIMSBY T	HUDDERSFIELD T	IPSWICH T	LEYTON O	LINCOLN C	LIVERPOOL	MIDDLESBROUGH	NOTTS CO	ROTHERHAM U	SHEFFIELD U	STOKE C	SWANSEA T	WEST HAM U
1 BARNSLEY		S18 0-2	N30 4-1	A24 2-2	a19 1-1	O19 4-1	D28 3-0	M08 1-1	J18 1-0	N16 3-3	M22 2-3	S04 5-1	a05 3-0	a08 1-3	D14 2-1	S21 1-1	D26 1-1	N02 3-0	a23 0-2	F22 1-2	S07 1-0	S28 1-0
2 BLACKBURN R	S09 3-1		M24 5-0	J18 2-0	N16 4-0	D14 1-1	S21 3-1	a07 3-2	O05 1-1	M08 3-0	O19 1-1	A24 0-0	a19 4-1	S07 0-1	F22 3-3	N30 3-3	D28 3-0	a05 5-0	D25 1-0	N02 1-0	F08 2-2	A26 2-1
3 BRISTOL C	a12 5-0	N09 0-0		O12 3-2	a07 2-0	J18 1-2	D25 2-1	S21 2-2	D07 0-5	S10 3-2	O05 1-3	M15 1-0	S07 2-2	M01 4-0	A24 1-2	D28 0-0	O26 3-1	F08 0-1	M29 1-4	S03 2-1	a26 1-2	N23 1-1
4 BRISTOL R	D21 1-1	S14 4-0	a05 3-3		O19 0-2	N16 1-0	A26 5-2	F22 2-1	a04 2-2	D14 0-7	a19 1-1	F01 3-1	M22 4-0	F19 3-0	M08 3-1	N02 5-0	S28 5-2	N30 1-3	J11 2-2	S16 2-0	D26 3-0	A31 2-3
5 CARDIFF C	D07 7-0	M29 4-3	a04 2-3	M26 0-2		S21 0-3	O12 3-2	F08 3-1	a26 3-0	S04 1-3	S11 1-0	N09 1-1	J18 1-1	O26 3-2	D28 6-1	S07 0-2	M15 2-0	O05 2-2	N23 0-0	D26 5-2	A24 0-0	a12 0-3
6 CHARLTON A	M01 4-2	a26 3-4	S14 1-0	M29 2-3	F01 3-1		N09 2-2	D25 2-0	O26 2-2	A31 2-0	D21 7-6	D07 4-1	S12 3-2	N23 4-1	S28 5-1	F15 6-2	a12 4-1	a04 4-0	A29 3-1	J11 3-0	M15 1-1	O12 0-3
7 DERBY CO	A31 1-4	F01 0-3	D26 5-2	S04 2-1	a05 0-2	M22 1-3		N16 1-0	D21 3-3	a19 1-0	N30 2-4	S28 2-2	N02 2-0	S18 3-2	O19 2-1	M08 2-1	F15 2-1	F22 3-4	S14 2-0	D14 0-0	a07 1-0	J11 2-3
8 DONCASTER R	O28 1-1	a04 1-5	F01 2-1	N23 3-2	S28 0-1	D26 1-2	M29 1-2		M15 1-6	J11 3-3	A31 0-3	a26 1-1	A28 2-0	a12 1-3	F19 1-1	S18 3-2	D07 4-0	D21 3-2	O12 2-2	S14 0-1	N09 3-0	M01 1-2
9 FULHAM	S14 1-1	a23 1-1	a19 3-4	a07 3-0	D14 2-0	M08 3-1	A24 2-0	N02 4-1		F22 6-0	N16 2-1	S18 0-0	O19 3-1	D26 4-1	S07 2-2	a21 0-1	S04 1-0	m01 3-1	S28 6-3	N30 3-4	D28 2-0	F01 2-2
10 GRIMSBY T	M29 2-1	O26 3-4	S17 1-1	a26 3-2	A27 1-1	D28 4-2	D07 3-2	S07 3-1	N23 3-1		S21 4-1	M01 0-2	A24 7-2	F08 4-0	D25 3-1	a04 4-1	O12 2-0	J18 3-1	M15 1-3	a22 0-0	a12 2-2	N09 1-2
11 HUDDERSFIELD T	N09 0-5	M05 2-1	F19 0-0	D07 0-0	S18 1-1	A24 3-3	a12 0-0	D28 2-2	M29 0-3	F01 1-0		O12 3-0	a08 2-0	a26 0-1	S04 2-1	D25 1-0	J18 3-0	S07 1-3	O26 1-1	S28 1-0	N23 2-2	M15 3-1
12 IPSWICH T	A28 3-0	D21 2-1	N02 4-2	S21 3-2	M22 3-1	a19 1-4	F08 2-2	D14 2-0	S11 1-1	O19 3-2	a05 4-0		N30 5-3	J18 1-1	N16 3-1	F22 1-1	S07 2-1	A31 1-2	a07 1-0	M08 1-3	O05 0-1	D26 2-1
13 LEYTON O	O12 2-1	D07 5-1	J11 4-0	N09 1-3	S14 4-2	S19 3-2	M15 1-1	S05 2-0	M13 1-3	D21 5-1	a04 3-1	a12 2-0		M29 1-0	F01 1-0	S28 4-0	N23 2-2	D25 6-2	a26 0-1	A31 0-2	O26 5-1	F20 1-4
14 LINCOLN C	a07 1-3	J11 1-1	a23 4-0	O05 0-1	a30 3-1	F22 2-3	S11 1-1	N30 1-1	D25 0-1	S28 1-4	D14 1-1	S14 2-1	N16 2-0		N02 0-1	M22 2-3	F01 2-2	a19 2-0	A31 2-2	a05 1-3	S04 4-0	D21 1-6
15 LIVERPOOL	a26 1-1	N23 2-0	D21 4-3	O26 2-0	A31 3-0	F08 3-1	M05 2-0	O05 5-0	J11 2-1	D26 3-2	A28 1-1	M29 3-1	S21 3-0	M15 1-0		J18 0-2	N09 4-0	N27 2-0	a12 1-0	a07 3-0	O12 4-0	D07 1-1
16 MIDDLESBROUGH	F01 3-1	a12 2-3	A31 0-0	M15 4-3	J11 4-1	O05 2-0	O26 3-2	S11 5-0	O12 2-0	a07 5-1	D26 0-1	N23 5-2	M19 2-0	N09 3-1	S14 2-2		M29 3-1	A28 2-2	D07 1-2	D21 1-3	M01 2-1	a26 1-3
17 NOTTS CO	D25 2-3	A31 1-1	M08 0-1	a23 0-0	N02 5-2	N30 2-1	O05 1-0	a19 0-5	A29 1-5	a05 2-0	S14 1-1	J11 0-3	F22 0-1	S21 1-0	M22 0-2	N16 2-0		D14 1-0	D21 1-0	O19 1-2	S12 2-4	a08 1-0
18 ROTHERHAM U	M15 4-1	O12 1-2	S28 4-1	a12 2-0	a21 3-1	a07 1-5	N23 0-2	A24 2-1	N09 3-1	F15 2-0	J11 1-1	D28 1-4	D26 2-2	D07 1-2	S19 2-2	S05 1-4	a26 1-3		M01 1-6	F01 0-2	M29 5-2	O26 1-2
19 SHEFFIELD U	O05 0-0	D26 4-2	N16 0-3	S07 2-0	F22 3-0	S02 0-3	J18 0-1	a05 3-0	a28 1-1	N02 3-1	M08 3-2	a08 1-1	D14 0-2	D28 4-0	N30 1-1	a19 3-2	A24 1-0	O19 2-0		M22 3-0	S21 2-2	S16 2-1
20 STOKE C	N23 3-1	M15 2-4	A26 3-0	S09 3-5	N04 3-0	S07 2-2	a26 2-1	J18 0-0	a12 1-2	O05 4-1	F08 1-1	O26 5-1	D28 1-3	O12 1-1	S23 1-2	A24 4-1	M01 0-1	S21 4-1	N09 2-3		D09 6-2	M29 1-4
21 SWANSEA T	J11 4-2	S28 0-4	D14 5-1	D25 6-4	D21 0-1	N02 1-3	a08 7-0	M22 4-3	A31 4-4	N30 0-2	F22 1-1	F15 0-0	M08 1-2	A29 5-1	a05 0-2	O19 1-4	S19 1-3	N16 1-3	F01 0-2	a19 4-1		S14 3-2
22 WEST HAM U	F08 1-1	S02 1-1	F22 3-2	D28 6-1	N30 1-1	a05 0-0	S07 2-1	O19 1-1	S21 3-2	M22 2-0	N02 5-2	D25 1-1	O05 3-2	A24 2-2	a19 1-1	D14 2-1	a04 3-1	M08 8-0	S09 0-3	N16 5-0	J18 6-2	

SEASON 1957-58

DIVISION 3 NORTH

	ACCRINGTON S	BARROW	BRADFORD	BRADFORD C	BURY	CARLISLE U	CHESTER	CHESTERFIELD	CREWE A	DARLINGTON	GATESHEAD	HALIFAX T	HARTLEPOOLS U	HULL C	MANSFIELD T	OLDHAM A	ROCHDALE	SCUNTHORPE U	SOUTHPORT	STOCKPORT CO	TRANMERE R	WORKINGTON	WREXHAM	YORK C
1 ACCRINGTON S		a24 3-2	D28 5-2	M15 2-2	M05 3-0	S07 3-2	S30 1-2	S16 0-4	D26 2-0	a12 0-0	N23 3-0	a14 2-1	A24 1-2	O26 3-0	M29 4-1	O05 1-1	S02 3-2	O12 2-1	J18 2-2	M01 3-2	a04 2-1	N09 3-0	D14 2-1	S21 3-0
2 BARROW	S28 3-1		S16 0-0	a21 1-2	F01 4-2	a07 2-3	F15 4-1	J01 4-1	a12 0-1	N09 2-1	D07 1-2	a26 0-3	S30 3-3	S02 0-0	O26 2-1	S14 2-2	O12 2-1	M29 0-1	A24 1-0	J11 1-1	D25 1-4	M01 0-0	N23 2-2	D28 1-0
3 BRADFORD	A31 1-3	S09 1-1		O12 0-0	D21 1-4	J04 4-1	J11 3-0	S14 2-0	M15 3-1	a14 4-1	A26 2-2	D07 0-2	S28 2-3	a12 4-4	F15 0-2	a07 1-3	N09 2-2	M01 1-2	D25 3-5	N23 1-0	F01 1-0	a26 3-3	O26 2-0	S25 0-2
4 BRADFORD C	N02 1-1	a05 4-1	M22 2-1		M08 3-3	D14 1-1	a19 5-0	a29 0-0	J18 2-1	O05 3-1	M11 0-1	D28 3-0	N30 0-1	a08 1-0	D26 1-1	O19 0-0	S07 1-0	a24 2-3	S18 2-0	A24 2-1	F22 3-0	O01 0-0	S21 3-1	S04 3-2
5 BURY	J01 1-1	S21 4-1	A24 1-0	O26 1-0		D28 3-0	D25 1-2	S23 1-0	a26 2-0	N23 5-0	M29 4-1	S02 1-0	a07 3-3	M01 1-1	N09 0-2	F08 4-0	F15 4-1	a12 2-1	S07 4-1	F12 1-1	S16 8-2	M15 3-0	O12 3-0	J18 4-1
6 CARLISLE U	J11 6-1	a14 2-1	J01 2-3	a26 0-3	A31 0-2		S14 3-2	F01 2-2	N09 2-0	M01 5-2	F18 5-1	N23 2-1	F15 1-2	O12 0-1	A27 3-4	D21 1-1	M29 1-0	O26 3-4	O01 4-0	a12 3-1	S28 3-1	D25 2-2	M15 4-0	S10 2-1
7 CHESTER	a30 5-1	O05 2-2	S07 1-2	N09 0-0	D26 0-0	J18 0-0		a07 0-0	A28 3-2	O12 0-1	a12 1-1	M01 1-1	D28 2-1	M15 1-1	N23 1-2	J04 0-0	a16 2-0	D14 1-2	S21 1-1	O26 3-0	A24 1-3	M29 4-3	S18 0-1	F08 9-2
8 CHESTERFIELD	S11 1-0	J04 4-3	J18 1-1	M29 0-1	a23 1-1	S21 1-3	a04 2-1		D07 1-1	a26 2-0	O12 5-3	O26 1-1	S07 2-1	N09 0-0	a12 1-4	D26 2-1	M01 2-2	A24 1-1	a16 0-0	M15 2-1	D28 2-1	N23 3-0	S04 3-2	O05 2-0
9 CREWE A	D25 4-1	N30 1-4	N02 3-0	S14 2-2	D14 0-1	a19 0-0	S02 0-3	a05 1-2		a04 2-2	D21 2-2	F15 1-2	M08 2-1	F01 1-2	A31 1-0	M22 0-2	a21 0-0	S18 0-2	a23 3-2	S28 1-2	O19 0-4	J11 0-3	O02 2-0	F22 3-4
10 DARLINGTON	N30 0-2	a19 3-0	a05 4-0	F19 4-0	F22 3-2	O19 1-2	M22 2-3	D14 2-0	a07 3-0		S14 2-2	O02 5-0	S04 1-3	a23 2-2	F01 2-0	a28 3-1	S18 4-2	D28 1-1	M19 1-2	D26 1-0	S07 2-1	S28 3-1	A24 2-1	N02 2-0
11 GATESHEAD	F22 1-3	N02 0-2	S02 2-4	J01 0-0	J04 1-2	a05 3-2	N30 3-2	M22 3-0	A24 3-1	J18 4-0		S16 0-0	S21 0-0	D26 3-1	a14 2-1	a19 1-0	a07 3-2	S07 1-2	O19 2-1	O14 3-0	D14 2-3	F15 3-0	D28 1-1	M24 0-0
12 HALIFAX T	a05 0-2	D14 3-1	M29 2-0	A31 3-2	A26 1-2	F22 5-0	O19 2-1	M08 3-2	O05 2-0	S23 1-0	S09 4-1		a19 3-0	J11 2-2	a08 4-0	S21 4-0	a29 4-1	D26 0-1	N30 4-1	S14 0-0	N02 1-1	D21 2-2	a21 0-0	M22 2-1
13 HARTLEPOOLS U	D21 1-1	S23 4-1	F08 0-0	a12 2-0	a04 2-1	O05 0-1	A31 2-1	J11 0-2	O26 1-1	A26 5-1	F01 2-2	N09 5-0		N23 5-1	a26 2-0	S09 4-1	M15 1-3	a28 1-2	J01 2-1	M29 1-2	S14 1-1	O12 1-0	M01 1-2	D25 2-2
14 HULL C	M25 1-0	A26 1-1	N30 3-3	a07 1-3	O19 2-1	M22 4-0	N02 3-0	a19 1-0	S21 1-0	M10 2-1	D25 1-1	S07 5-2	F22 1-1		S30 1-1	a05 9-0	J18 2-1	O05 2-0	D14 3-2	D28 1-0	M17 0-0	S09 3-2	F08 2-0	A24 0-1
15 MANSFIELD T	J25 0-2	M08 4-2	O05 2-1	D25 5-2	a19 6-4	S02 2-0	F22 3-1	N30 1-1	D28 2-1	S21 4-2	a28 3-0	a07 2-1	D14 5-1	S23 1-3		N02 4-4	A24 2-4	J18 3-5	a05 3-0	S09 2-2	M22 4-1	M10 6-3	S07 2-1	O19 2-1
16 OLDHAM A	F15 0-3	J18 1-1	a04 4-2	M01 1-1	S28 1-3	A24 1-0	a22 5-1	D25 2-1	O12 1-0	M29 2-2	N09 0-0	F01 2-4	S17 4-0	a15 1-1	M15 1-1		a26 0-0	N23 2-1	D28 3-2	S03 2-4	O01 1-0	O26 4-1	a12 4-1	S07 2-3
17 ROCHDALE	A28 3-0	M22 1-1	a19 1-2	J11 0-2	O05 1-1	M11 1-0	a05 1-1	O19 3-4	J04 3-0	S11 5-4	a04 0-0	S28 5-1	N02 7-0	S14 2-1	D21 3-0	D14 1-3		S25 1-4	F22 2-0	F01 3-0	M08 2-0	A31 1-0	D25 2-0	N30 2-1
18 SCUNTHORPE U	M22 1-0	a17 1-0	O19 6-2	S28 0-2	N30 1-0	m01 3-1	a26 2-1	D21 1-1	S12 3-2	A31 5-0	J11 2-1	O31 1-1	a05 2-0	F20 2-0	S14 3-3	F22 1-1	O03 2-0		N02 1-0	M13 4-0	S05 1-0	F01 2-2	a07 1-0	a19 1-2
19 SOUTHPORT	S14 3-3	D21 0-4	D26 2-1	S10 0-2	J11 2-2	S24 2-0	F01 2-4	S28 5-2	M29 2-0	O26 0-3	M01 1-0	a12 0-3	J04 0-0	a26 1-2	M31 4-1	A31 2-1	N23 0-2	M15 1-2		O12 1-0	F15 0-3	A27 0-1	N09 1-3	a04 0-1
20 STOCKPORT CO	O19 0-0	S07 2-0	F22 3-0	D21 0-4	a05 4-0	N30 4-1	M08 2-2	N02 4-1	F08 5-1	D25 4-1	S23 5-1	J18 4-2	a14 2-1	A31 1-0	S16 3-3	A26 3-0	S21 0-3	a21 2-1	M22 1-2		a19 2-1	a04 0-2	O05 1-1	D14 2-1
21 TRANMERE R	a07 0-1	D26 1-1	S21 5-0	N23 4-1	S09 1-1	F08 0-1	D21 2-2	A31 1-2	M01 5-2	J11 2-1	a26 2-1	M15 2-0	J18 3-2	M29 4-4	O12 1-2	S23 1-1	O26 3-1	A26 1-4	O05 2-1	N09 2-2		a12 1-0	a30 2-1	J01 6-1
22 WORKINGTON	a19 0-1	O19 0-1	D14 1-2	S25 1-1	N02 3-0	D26 2-1	J25 5-3	F22 0-2	S07 3-2	F08 2-2	O05 1-1	A24 4-4	M22 1-0	S18 3-2	a23 4-0	M08 4-2	D28 1-2	S21 3-2	S04 2-0	a07 1-1	N30 1-2		J18 4-2	a05 0-0
23 WREXHAM	a26 1-0	F22 0-0	M08 1-1	F01 1-1	M22 2-0	N02 1-0	S11 1-0	A28 2-2	S25 0-1	D21 2-0	A31 1-2	J04 2-1	O19 3-1	S28 6-0	J11 4-2	N30 2-2	D26 2-0	a04 1-0	a19 1-0	F15 1-0	a05 2-2	S14 1-1		a16 2-2
24 YORK C	F01 0-3	A31 0-0	S30 3-0	A26 2-0	S14 2-1	S16 0-5	S28 1-2	F15 3-3	N23 3-1	m01 3-0	O26 2-2	O12 1-1	D26 2-2	D21 3-1	M01 3-1	J11 2-2	a12 1-0	N09 0-0	a07 1-0	a26 0-0	a23 4-0	a28 3-0	M29 1-2	

DIVISION 3 SOUTH

	ALDERSHOT	BOURNEMOUTH	BRENTFORD	BRIGHTON & HA	COLCHESTER U	COVENTRY C	CRYSTAL P	EXETER C	GILLINGHAM	MILLWALL	NEWPORT CO	NORTHAMPTON T	NORWICH C	PLYMOUTH A	PORT VALE	Q.P.R.	READING	SHREWSBURY T	SOUTHAMPTON	SOUTHEND U	SWINDON T	TORQUAY U	WALSALL	WATFORD
1 ALDERSHOT		M22 0-0	N02 0-2	O02 2-3	a16 2-1	a19 1-1	O19 4-1	F15 2-2	S28 2-0	F01 2-2	a04 2-1	S04 0-0	J25 2-1	D28 3-3	A24 0-1	a23 1-1	J11 1-0	D14 0-1	D25 1-5	S18 0-2	S14 2-1	M08 1-1	N30 1-3	F22 2-2
2 BOURNEMOUTH	N23 5-1		J18 1-0	S04 1-3	S21 1-1	S18 0-0	D28 3-1	O26 2-1	M15 2-1	N09 4-0	M29 4-3	a04 1-1	F08 3-1	a12 0-0	a30 3-1	M01 4-1	D25 4-1	O02 3-1	F15 5-2	O12 2-1	a26 1-1	S07 2-0	J04 1-2	A24 2-1
3 BRENTFORD	M15 4-2	S14 4-2		a28 1-0	A31 3-3	S28 1-3	D25 0-3	A27 1-0	O12 1-0	M01 4-1	N23 2-1	S10 7-1	J11 7-1	N09 2-0	a26 4-1	D21 1-1	M11 2-1	F15 2-0	a12 0-0	M29 4-2	O26 0-0	a07 0-1	F01 2-1	O01 0-0
4 BRIGHTON & H.A.	S25 0-1	A28 2-1	a19 1-1		D14 5-2	O19 3-0	M22 3-2	A31 2-2	D21 5-2	a07 4-2	O05 5-3	a05 1-4	S21 0-1	S11 3-2	J04 0-0	J11 1-1	N02 1-2	M08 2-1	F08 1-1	S14 3-1	D26 1-0	N30 1-1	F22 2-0	a30 6-0
5 COLCHESTER U	N09 1-1	F01 3-2	D28 1-1	M29 1-2		F15 4-1	a07 1-1	O12 3-0	M01 3-2	O26 2-1	a12 1-1	S30 1-0	S14 1-2	a26 1-2	N23 2-1	S02 2-1	S09 1-3	a21 3-0	m01 4-2	J11 1-0	M15 1-3	A24 3-0	S28 1-1	D26 4-0
6 COVENTRY C	M17 6-0	S09 0-3	F08 0-0	M01 2-2	O05 1-0		J18 2-2	N09 6-1	a26 1-1	N23 1-4	S02 1-2	D28 1-1	a21 2-1	M29 1-1	D25 1-0	M15 1-1	A24 1-0	a08 5-0	O12 0-0	O26 1-0	a12 0-1	S21 2-1	M24 4-1	S07 2-2
7 CRYSTAL P	M01 1-1	A31 3-0	D26 2-1	N23 2-4	a04 1-1	S14 2-0		M29 2-0	S11 3-0	A28 0-1	N09 2-2	F15 1-3	D21 0-3	O26 3-0	M15 1-0	a16 2-3	S28 2-2	F01 3-0	a26 1-4	a12 2-0	O12 4-1	O02 1-1	J11 4-1	a23 4-2
8 EXETER C	O05 3-0	M08 1-2	S04 3-5	D28 2-0	F22 4-3	a05 1-0	D14 0-1		S25 1-3	S11 2-0	J18 0-2	N30 0-1	O19 2-2	F08 4-2	S21 1-0	a07 0-0	M22 1-1	a16 2-1	S07 2-2	A24 0-5	a23 0-1	D26 5-1	N02 2-1	a19 1-2
9 GILLINGHAM	F08 1-1	a16 1-1	F22 3-2	A24 0-1	O19 2-3	a30 3-2	S18 3-0	O02 1-1		a23 1-0	S07 0-1	a19 1-2	M08 1-0	S21 1-0	J18 0-2	D25 1-1	N30 2-1	M22 1-3	D28 2-1	a04 2-0	O05 2-1	S04 1-0	a05 3-0	D14 1-1
10 MILLWALL	S21 3-3	a05 0-2	O19 0-1	a04 2-2	M08 1-4	J04 4-1	S02 3-0	S16 3-0	M17 3-1		D28 1-2	D14 0-0	N02 2-2	J18 0-1	S07 2-1	S30 5-0	a19 0-0	N30 1-3	A24 1-2	D26 1-2	F08 1-1	F22 1-2	J25 1-3	O05 2-3
11 NEWPORT CO	a07 3-2	D14 3-1	M22 1-2	F15 1-2	N30 2-2	A29 2-2	a05 0-0	S14 0-0	J11 5-0	A31 1-2		M08 0-1	a19 1-0	D25 0-2	N11 2-1	F01 4-2	O28 0-0	F22 2-0	J04 1-1	S28 1-0	D21 4-1	M06 3-2	S12 2-0	N02 2-1
12 NORTHAMPTON T	A29 0-0	a08 4-0	S16 3-1	N09 2-4	S26 4-1	A31 4-0	O05 1-2	a12 9-0	M27 3-1	M29 7-2	O26 0-3		D26 0-1	O12 5-0	M01 3-2	N23 1-5	S14 1-2	J11 2-0	M15 1-3	a26 1-3	F01 3-0	a24 1-0	D21 3-0	F08 2-3
13 NORWICH C	a26 1-3	S28 2-2	S07 3-2	F01 0-0	J18 1-1	M05 1-1	A24 3-2	M01 3-2	O26 2-0	M15 1-1	a16 5-2	O09 2-2		N23 1-0	a12 3-0	O12 2-0	O23 2-2	S18 2-0	M29 0-2	S04 0-2	N09 1-1	D28 3-1	F15 2-1	a07 1-1
14 PLYMOUTH A	A31 4-2	N30 3-1	a05 0-0	S16 2-1	O09 1-1	D14 4-0	M08 1-0	S28 1-0	F01 2-1	S14 1-0	D26 1-0	F22 3-0	M22 0-1		a04 1-0	F15 3-1	A26 1-0	D21 2-2	S30 4-0	a21 2-3	J11 2-2	N02 1-0	a19 2-1	O19 2-1
15 PORT VALE	D21 6-1	a19 2-3	M24 0-1	a23 2-2	M22 2-0	D26 0-1	N02 4-0	F01 3-2	S14 2-0	J11 1-1	S30 2-2	O19 3-0	N30 2-2	a07 0-0		S28 2-1	F22 1-2	S02 0-0	S16 4-0	F15 1-3	A31 3-1	a05 2-1	D14 2-1	M08 5-0
16 Q.P.R.	M03 0-1	O19 3-0	A24 1-0	S07 0-1	A26 1-0	N02 3-0	a19 4-2	a04 1-1	D26 1-1	S23 3-0	S21 1-1	M22 1-0	F22 1-1	O05 1-0	F08 2-1		M17 3-0	a28 3-0	J18 3-2	D28 1-1	S16 2-1	D14 1-1	M08 1-0	N30 3-0
17 READING	S07 3-0	D26 2-0	a23 1-2	M15 1-1	S18 7-0	D21 3-1	F08 2-2	N23 2-0	a12 4-0	F19 4-1	M01 1-0	J18 5-2	O02 1-2	S04 1-3	O12 3-0	J25 3-0		A31 2-2	O26 1-0	N09 1-1	M29 0-4	O05 1-0	a04 3-1	S21 1-1
18 SHREWSBURY T	M29 5-1	S23 0-4	O05 0-2	O26 2-0	J04 0-0	a07 1-3	S21 0-0	a26 1-0	N23 2-1	a12 0-1	O12 1-1	S07 3-1	S09 0-0	A24 2-0	A26 1-0	N09 2-1	D28 0-2		M01 1-3	M15 1-1	D07 1-3	F08 3-0	D26 2-0	J18 1-1
19 SOUTHAMPTON	D26 2-2	O05 7-0	N30 4-2	S28 5-0	a19 3-2	F22 7-1	J25 2-1	J11 6-0	A31 5-1	D21 3-2	a23 2-1	N02 2-1	D14 7-3	S25 0-1	S11 0-3	S14 5-0	M08 0-1	O19 2-2		F01 2-2	O09 1-3	M22 4-2	A28 4-1	a05 5-0
20 SOUTHEND U	S11 1-2	F22 2-0	D14 0-0	J18 0-2	S07 2-3	M08 5-1	N30 1-1	D21 2-0	a07 2-0	D25 2-0	F08 1-1	m02 6-3	A28 5-2	a16 2-1	O05 1-1	A31 6-0	a05 2-1	N02 5-1	S21 3-2		S25 2-3	a19 0-0	O19 4-1	M22 2-1
21 SWINDON T	J18 3-0	J25 1-0	M08 4-1	D25 2-2	N02 4-0	N30 2-1	F22 0-0	J04 5-1	F15 1-1	S28 3-0	A24 4-0	S21 5-1	a05 1-2	S07 1-0	D28 0-0	S11 1-1	D14 1-1	a19 1-0	a07 1-0	O02 2-1		O19 3-1	M22 2-3	S04 0-0
22 TORQUAY U	O26 2-1	J11 3-1	a04 0-1	a12 2-0	D21 1-3	F01 1-0	S25 1-1	D25 1-3	A28 3-2	O12 2-3	a26 2-2	a16 1-0	A31 1-1	M15 0-2	N09 1-1	M29 3-1	F15 1-4	S28 0-2	N23 1-1	a29 2-2	M01 2-2		S14 2-1	S11 1-0
23 WALSALL	a12 0-0	a24 3-1	S21 0-2	O12 2-3	F08 3-0	M10 4-1	S07 2-1	M15 3-0	N09 1-1	a26 4-2	S19 3-0	A24 2-1	O05 2-1	M03 0-2	M29 3-0	O26 1-2	a07 0-0	D25 0-1	S05 1-1	M01 1-1	N23 1-1	J18 0-0		D28 1-3
24 WATFORD	O12 1-3	D21 1-1	S24 4-1	a26 0-1	O15 1-1	J11 1-0	M25 2-1	D07 5-4	M29 3-0	F15 3-0	M15 2-2	S28 0-2	a04 1-4	M01 0-2	O26 0-2	a12 0-0	F01 1-1	S14 3-0	N09 3-0	N23 1-1	A27 0-0	S17 1-0	A31 1-1	

LEAGUE TABLES

DIVISION 1

	P	W	D	L	F	A	W	D	L	F	A	Pts
Wolverh'pton W	42	17	3	1	60	21	11	5	5	43	26	64
Preston N.E.	42	18	2	1	63	14	8	5	8	37	37	59
Tottenham H	42	13	4	4	58	33	8	5	8	35	44	51
W.B.A.	42	14	4	3	59	29	4	10	7	33	41	50
Manchester C	42	14	4	3	58	33	8	1	12	46	67	49
Burnley	42	16	2	3	52	21	5	3	13	28	53	47
Blackpool	42	11	2	8	47	35	8	4	9	33	32	44
Luton T	42	13	3	5	45	22	6	3	12	24	41	44
Manchester U	42	10	4	7	45	31	6	7	8	40	44	43
Nottingham F	42	10	4	7	41	27	6	6	9	28	36	42
Chelsea	42	10	5	6	47	34	5	7	9	36	45	42
Arsenal	42	10	4	7	48	39	6	3	12	25	46	39
Birmingham C	42	8	6	7	43	37	6	5	10	33	52	39
Aston Villa	42	12	4	5	46	26	4	3	14	27	60	39
Bolton W	42	9	5	7	38	35	5	5	11	27	52	38
Everton	42	5	9	7	34	35	8	2	11	31	40	37
Leeds U	42	10	6	5	33	23	4	3	14	18	40	37
Leicester C	42	11	4	6	59	41	3	1	17	32	71	33
Newcastle U	42	6	4	11	38	42	6	4	11	35	39	32
Portsmouth	42	10	6	5	45	34	2	2	17	28	54	32
Sunderland	42	7	7	7	32	33	3	5	13	22	64	32
Sheffield W	42	12	2	7	45	40	0	5	16	24	52	31

DIVISION 2

	P	W	D	L	F	A	W	D	L	F	A	Pts
West Ham U	42	12	8	1	56	25	11	3	7	45	29	57
Blackburn R	42	13	7	1	50	18	9	5	7	43	39	56
Charlton A	42	15	3	3	65	33	9	4	8	42	36	55
Liverpool	42	17	3	1	50	13	5	7	9	29	41	54
Fulham	42	13	5	3	53	24	7	7	7	44	35	52
Sheffield U	42	12	5	4	38	22	9	5	7	37	28	52
Middlesbrough	42	13	3	5	52	29	6	4	11	31	45	45
Ipswich T	42	13	4	4	45	29	3	8	10	23	40	44
Huddersfield T	42	9	8	4	28	24	5	8	8	35	42	44
Bristol R	42	12	5	4	52	31	5	3	13	33	49	42
Stoke C	42	9	4	8	49	36	9	2	10	26	37	42
Leyton O	42	14	2	5	53	27	4	3	14	24	52	41
Grimsby T	42	13	4	4	54	30	4	2	15	32	53	40
Barnsley	42	10	6	5	40	25	4	6	11	30	49	40
Cardiff C	42	10	5	6	44	31	4	4	13	19	46	37
Derby Co	42	11	3	7	37	36	3	5	13	23	45	36
Bristol C	42	9	5	7	35	31	4	4	13	28	57	35
Rotherham U	42	8	3	10	38	44	6	2	13	27	57	33
Swansea T	42	8	3	10	48	45	3	6	12	24	54	31
Lincoln C	42	6	6	9	33	35	5	3	13	22	47	31
Notts Co	42	9	3	9	24	31	3	3	15	20	49	30
Doncaster R	42	7	5	9	34	40	1	6	14	22	48	27

DIVISION 3 NORTH

	P	W	D	L	F	A	W	D	L	F	A	Pts
Scunthorpe U	46	16	5	2	46	19	13	3	7	42	31	66
Accrington S	46	16	4	3	53	28	9	5	9	30	33	59
Bradford C	46	13	7	3	42	19	8	8	7	31	30	57
Bury	46	17	4	2	61	18	6	6	11	33	44	56
Hull C	46	15	6	2	49	20	4	9	10	29	47	53
Mansfield T	46	16	3	4	68	42	6	5	12	32	50	52
Halifax T	46	15	5	3	52	20	5	6	12	31	49	51
Chesterfield	46	12	8	3	39	28	6	7	10	32	41	51
Stockport Co	46	15	4	4	54	28	3	7	13	20	39	47
Rochdale	46	14	4	5	50	25	5	4	14	29	42	46
Tranmere R	46	12	6	5	51	32	6	4	13	31	44	46
Wrexham	46	13	8	2	39	18	4	4	15	22	45	46
York C	46	11	8	4	40	26	6	4	13	28	50	46
Gateshead	46	12	5	6	41	27	3	10	10	27	49	45
Oldham A	46	11	7	5	44	32	3	10	10	28	52	45
Carlisle U	46	13	3	7	56	35	6	3	14	24	43	44
Hartlepool U	46	11	6	6	45	26	5	6	12	28	50	44
Barrow	46	9	7	7	36	32	4	8	11	30	42	41
Workington	46	11	6	6	46	33	3	7	13	26	48	41
Darlington	46	15	3	5	53	25	2	4	17	25	64	41
Chester C	46	7	10	6	38	26	6	3	14	35	55	39
Bradford P.A.	46	8	6	9	41	41	5	5	13	27	54	37
Southport	46	8	3	12	29	40	3	3	17	23	48	28
Crewe A	46	6	5	12	29	41	2	2	19	18	52	23

DIVISION 3 SOUTH

	P	W	D	L	F	A	W	D	L	F	A	Pts
Brighton & H.A.	46	13	6	4	52	30	11	6	6	36	34	60
Brentford	46	15	5	3	52	24	9	5	9	30	32	58
Plymouth A	46	17	4	2	43	17	8	4	11	24	31	58
Swindon T	46	14	7	2	47	16	7	8	8	32	34	57
Reading	46	14	5	4	52	23	7	8	8	27	28	55
Southampton	46	16	3	4	78	31	6	7	10	34	41	54
Southend U	46	14	5	4	56	26	7	7	9	34	32	54
Norwich C	46	11	9	3	41	28	8	6	9	34	42	53
Bournemouth	46	16	5	2	54	24	5	4	14	27	50	51
Q.P.R.	46	15	6	2	40	14	3	8	12	24	51	50
Newport Co	46	12	6	5	40	24	5	8	10	33	43	48
Colchester U	46	13	5	5	45	27	4	8	11	32	52	47
Northampton T	46	13	1	9	60	33	6	5	12	27	46	44
Crystal Palace	46	12	5	6	46	30	3	8	12	24	42	43
Port Vale	46	12	6	5	49	24	4	4	15	18	34	42
Watford	46	9	8	6	34	27	4	8	11	25	50	42
Shrewsbury T	46	10	6	7	29	25	5	4	14	20	46	40
Aldershot	46	7	9	7	31	34	5	7	11	28	55	40
Coventry C	46	10	9	4	41	24	3	4	16	20	57	39
Walsall	46	10	7	6	37	24	4	2	17	24	51	37
Torquay U	46	9	7	7	33	34	2	6	15	16	40	35
Gillingham	46	12	5	6	33	24	1	4	18	19	57	35
Millwall	46	6	6	11	37	36	5	3	15	26	55	31
Exeter C	46	10	4	9	37	35	1	5	17	20	64	31

FOOTBALL LEAGUE RECORDS

Top scorers: Div 1, J.Greaves (Chelsea) 33 goals; Div 2, B. Clough (Middlesbrough) 42 goals; Div 3, E.Towers (Brentford) 32 goals; Div 4, A.Rowley (Shrewsbury Town) 37 goals.

The two sections of Division Three formed the new Third and Fourth Divisions. Scunthorpe & Lindsey United dropped '& Lindsey' from their name.

Ron Flower, another England half-back who skippered Wolverhampton Wanderers to the Division One title.

DIVISION 1

	ARSENAL	ASTON VILLA	BIRMINGHAM C	BLACKBURN R	BLACKPOOL	BOLTON W	BURNLEY	CHELSEA	EVERTON	LEEDS U	LEICESTER C	LUTON T	MANCHESTER C	MANCHESTER U	NEWCASTLE U	NOTTINGHAM F	PORTSMOUTH	PRESTON N.E.	TOTTENHAM H	W.B.A.	WEST HAM U	WOLVERHAMPTON W
1 ARSENAL		D13 1-2	m04 2-1	M14 1-1	N29 1-4	S09 6-1	A26 3-0	a11 1-1	J17 3-1	F24 1-0	A30 5-1	D27 1-0	S20 4-1	F28 3-2	N01 3-2	N15 3-1	a25 5-2	D20 1-2	S13 3-1	O04 4-3	M28 1-2	O18 1-1
2 ASTON VILLA	O22 1-2		A23 1-1	F18 1-0	S20 1-1	O25 2-1	a18 0-0	J31 3-1	N08 2-4	M07 2-1	a04 1-2	M21 3-1	D06 1-1	D27 0-2	O04 2-1	S06 2-3	A25 3-2	N22 2-0	M30 1-1	O11 1-4	J03 1-2	S08 1-3
3 BIRMINGHAM C	a14 4-1	D20 4-1		a22 3-0	D13 4-2	a08 1-3	S13 2-1	a25 4-1	F21 2-1	S17 4-1	S27 4-2	A30 0-1	D26 6-1	N29 0-4	N15 1-0	O18 0-3	N01 2-2	F07 5-1	a11 5-1	S03 0-6	F28 3-0	M14 0-3
4 BLACKBURN R	O25 4-2	S27 2-3	N08 3-2		S15 0-0	D06 1-1	M07 4-1	D25 0-3	M21 2-1	N22 2-4	A25 5-0	a20 3-1	a18 2-1	M02 1-3	D20 3-0	M27 3-0	F07 2-1	O11 4-1	A30 5-0	a04 0-0	F21 1-2	S13 1-2
5 BLACKPOOL	a18 1-2	F07 2-1	a20 2-0	S08 1-1		M07 4-0	O11 1-1	M27 5-0	O25 1-1	a04 3-0	M21 2-1	D06 3-0	N22 0-0	A30 2-1	A25 3-0	F21 1-0	S13 1-1	D25 4-2	D20 0-0	N08 1-1	S27 2-0	a13 0-1
6 BOLTON W	S17 2-1	M18 1-3	S06 2-0	a25 3-1	O18 4-0		S27 1-2	M04 6-0	D27 0-3	A23 4-0	M27 3-3	J31 4-2	S03 4-1	N15 6-3	D13 1-1	S20 3-2	N29 2-1	F21 2-1	M28 4-1	J03 2-1	N01 0-2	a11 2-2
7 BURNLEY	S02 3-1	N29 3-1	J31 0-1	O18 0-0	M17 3-1	a14 0-1		O04 4-0	S09 3-1	J03 3-1	D27 3-3	S20 2-2	A23 3-4	M28 4-2	a25 2-2	N01 0-2	a11 2-1	M27 1-0	D13 3-1	S06 1-3	M14 1-0	N15 0-2
8 CHELSEA	N22 0-3	S13 2-1	D06 1-0	D27 0-2	M30 3-1	O11 0-1	F21 1-3		a18 3-1	N08 2-0	O25 5-2	M07 3-3	a04 2-0	D20 2-3	S10 6-5	S27 4-1	J17 2-2	M21 3-1	A27 4-2	a22 0-2	F07 3-2	A30 6-2
9 EVERTON	S06 1-6	M28 2-1	O04 3-1	N01 2-2	M14 3-1	D26 1-0	S17 1-2	N29 3-1		S20 3-2	D20 0-1	M30 3-1	J31 3-1	O18 3-2	A30 0-2	a11 1-3	D13 2-1	A27 1-4	F28 2-1	F18 3-3	N15 2-2	a25 0-1
10 LEEDS U	S27 2-1	O18 0-0	S10 0-0	a11 2-1	N15 1-1	D20 3-4	A30 1-1	M28 4-0	F07 1-0		S13 1-1	A26 1-1	F21 0-4	N01 1-2	N29 3-2	D13 1-0	F28 1-1	J17 1-3	M14 3-1	D27 0-1	a25 1-0	M31 1-3
11 LEICESTER C	J03 2-3	N15 6-3	M18 2-4	S03 1-1	N01 0-3	M30 0-0	D26 1-1	M14 0-3	A23 2-0	J31 0-1		O04 3-1	S06 3-1	a25 2-1	F28 0-1	N29 0-3	M28 3-1	S17 2-2	O18 3-4	S20 2-2	a11 1-1	D13 1-0
12 LUTON T	D26 6-3	N01 2-1	J03 0-1	D13 1-1	a25 1-1	S13 0-0	F07 6-2	O18 2-1	M27 0-1	S03 1-1	F21 4-3		S17 5-1	a11 0-0	M28 4-2	a09 5-1	a22 3-1	S27 4-1	N15 1-2	A23 1-1	S06 4-1	N29 0-1
13 MANCHESTER C	F07 0-0	a25 0-0	D27 4-1	N29 0-1	a11 0-2	A27 3-3	D20 1-4	N15 5-1	S13 1-3	O04 2-1	a29 3-1	S10 1-1		S27 1-1	M14 5-1	M28 1-1	O18 3-2	A30 1-1	N01 5-1	M30 0-2	D13 3-1	F28 1-4
14 MANCHESTER U	O11 1-1	D26 2-1	a18 1-0	S06 6-1	J03 3-1	a04 3-0	N08 1-3	A23 5-2	M07 2-1	M21 4-0	D06 4-1	N22 2-1	F14 4-1		J31 4-4	S03 1-1	M27 6-1	O08 0-2	S20 2-2	O25 1-2	S17 4-1	F21 2-1
15 NEWCASTLE U	M21 1-0	F21 1-0	a29 1-1	A23 1-5	S03 1-0	a22 2-0	D06 5-2	S17 1-2	J03 4-0	a18 2-2	O11 3-1	N08 1-0	O25 4-1	S13 1-1		D26 1-3	S27 2-0	M07 1-2	J17 1-2	N22 1-2	M30 3-1	F07 3-4
16 NOTTINGHAM F	a04 1-1	a20 2-0	M07 1-7	M31 1-1	O04 2-0	F07 3-0	M21 1-2	a15 1-3	N22 2-1	a22 0-3	a18 1-4	O11 3-1	N08 4-0	A27 0-3	D27 3-0		A30 5-0	O25 0-1	S10 1-1	D06 1-1	S13 4-0	D20 1-3
17 PORTSMOUTH	D06 0-1	S03 5-2	M21 1-1	S20 2-1	J31 1-2	a18 0-1	N22 4-2	S06 2-2	a15 2-3	O11 2-0	N08 4-1	O25 2-2	M07 3-4	M30 1-3	M11 1-5	J03 0-1		a04 1-2	O04 1-1	S17 2-6	A23 1-2	D26 3-5
18 PRESTON N.E.	A23 2-1	a11 4-2	S20 3-0	F28 1-2	D26 0-3	O04 0-0	M30 0-4	N01 2-0	S01 3-1	S06 1-2	S22 3-1	a06 0-0	J03 2-0	D13 3-4	O18 3-4	M16 3-5	N15 3-1		a25 2-2	J31 2-4	N29 2-1	M28 1-2
19 TOTTENHAM H	J31 1-4	M27 3-2	N22 0-4	J03 3-1	A23 2-3	N08 1-1	a08 2-2	S03 4-0	O11 10-4	O25 2-3	M07 6-0	a04 3-0	M21 3-1	F07 1-3	S06 1-3	S17 1-0	F21 4-4	D06 1-2		a18 5-0	D26 1-4	S27 2-1
20 W.B.A.	F21 1-1	a29 1-1	A27 2-2	N15 2-3	M28 3-1	A30 1-1	M11 2-4	D13 4-0	S27 2-3	D26 1-2	F07 2-2	a15 2-0	M31 3-0	M14 1-3	a11 2-2	a25 2-0	S10 1-2	S13 1-1	N29 4-3		O18 2-1	N01 2-1
21 WEST HAM U	N08 0-0	A30 7-2	O11 1-2	O04 6-3	F16 1-0	M21 4-3	O25 1-0	S20 4-2	a04 3-2	D06 2-3	N22 0-3	a13 0-0	a20 5-1	S08 3-2	M27 3-0	J31 5-3	D20 6-0	a18 1-1	D25 2-1	M07 3-1		A25 2-0
22 WOLVERHAMPTON W	M07 6-1	S17 4-0	O25 3-1	J31 5-0	S06 2-0	N22 1-2	a04 3-3	J03 1-2	D06 1-0	F14 6-2	a22 3-0	a18 5-0	O11 2-0	O04 4-0	S20 1-3	A23 5-1	D27 7-0	N08 2-0	M02 1-1	M21 5-2	S03 1-1	

DIVISION 2

	BARNSLEY	BRIGHTON & HA	BRISTOL C	BRISTOL R	CARDIFF C	CHARLTON A	DERBY CO	FULHAM	GRIMSBY T	HUDDERSFIELD T	IPSWICH T	LEYTON O	LINCOLN C	LIVERPOOL	MIDDLESBROUGH	ROTHERHAM U	SCUNTHORPE U	SHEFFIELD U	SHEFFIELD W	STOKE C	SUNDERLAND	SWANSEA T
1 BARNSLEY		F14 0-2	A27 4-7	M07 0-0	D20 3-2	S10 7-1	O11 0-0	a18 2-4	O04 3-1	A30 1-0	O25 3-0	a29 1-3	N22 2-2	M30 0-2	D27 1-0	J31 1-1	M21 0-1	S20 1-3	D06 0-1	N08 2-1	a04 0-2	a20 3-1
2 BRIGHTON & H.A.	S27 1-1		J17 2-2	N08 1-1	S13 2-2	A30 2-2	a22 3-1	D27 3-0	S10 2-0	F07 2-0	a04 4-1	O25 2-2	M21 2-1	S24 2-2	D20 4-6	F21 3-0	M07 2-1	M30 2-0	O11 1-3	a18 2-2	D06 2-0	N22 2-2
3 BRISTOL C	S02 3-1	S06 3-0		M21 1-1	D26 2-3	O04 2-4	D06 1-3	N08 1-1	F24 1-0	S16 2-1	M27 3-0	a18 0-1	a21 1-0	S20 1-3	F14 2-2	A23 6-1	N22 0-1	J03 3-1	a04 1-2	M07 2-1	O25 4-1	O11 4-0
4 BRISTOL R	O18 0-2	F28 2-0	N01 1-2		S08 2-0	a25 2-1	S22 2-1	S13 0-0	N15 7-3	M28 1-1	D27 1-1	D20 1-3	F07 3-0	a11 3-0	N29 3-1	M14 4-1	A30 4-0	D13 1-1	a30 2-1	F21 1-0	S27 2-1	M30 4-4
5 CARDIFF C	A23 0-1	J31 3-1	D27 1-0	S17 2-4		M31 1-2	M21 0-0	a04 1-2	S20 4-1	S03 3-2	O11 1-2	D06 2-1	N08 3-0	F14 3-0	O04 3-2	J03 1-0	a18 0-2	S06 3-1	N22 2-2	O25 2-1	a22 2-1	M07 0-1
6 CHARLTON A	S18 4-0	J03 2-3	F21 4-1	D06 4-3	M30 0-0		a18 1-2	a23 2-1	S06 2-1	D27 2-1	M21 5-1	N22 4-1	O25 3-2	J31 2-3	S20 1-0	S04 5-2	a04 2-3	A23 1-1	N08 3-3	O11 1-2	M07 3-2	F14 2-1
7 DERBY CO	M28 3-0	D13 1-3	a25 4-1	S03 3-2	N01 1-3	N29 3-2		F07 2-0	F28 3-0	D20 3-1	S17 3-2	A30 1-2	S27 1-0	N15 3-2	a11 0-3	O18 1-1	J17 3-1	M14 2-1	S13 1-4	M30 3-0	F21 2-0	D26 3-1
8 FULHAM	N29 5-2	D26 3-1	F28 1-0	J31 1-0	N15 2-1	D13 2-1	S20 4-2		M28 3-0	a11 1-0	S06 3-2	F14 5-2	S17 4-2	O18 0-1	M14 3-2	a25 4-0	O04 1-1	N01 4-2	M27 6-2	A23 6-1	S03 6-2	J03 1-2
9 GRIMSBY T	F21 3-3	S16 1-1	S13 2-0	a04 1-2	F07 5-1	a14 1-5	N08 3-0	O11 2-2		S27 2-1	N22 2-3	a21 4-1	A26 4-2	D20 2-3	A30 3-2	M27 1-1	O25 1-1	D25 1-2	M07 0-2	D06 2-2	M21 1-1	a18 0-1
10 HUDDERSFIELD T	J03 2-1	S20 3-2	S09 0-1	O11 1-2	A27 3-0	D25 1-0	A23 1-1	N22 2-1	F14 2-0		M07 3-0	M21 0-0	a04 2-1	O04 5-0	M30 5-1	S06 3-0	D06 0-1	J31 0-2	a18 1-2	a22 1-2	N08 1-1	O25 3-2
11 IPSWICH T	M14 3-1	N15 5-3	M30 1-1	D26 0-2	M28 3-3	N01 3-1	S10 1-1	J17 1-2	a11 2-1	O18 0-0		A27 2-1	S13 4-1	N29 2-0	a25 2-1	D13 1-0	D20 3-1	a30 1-0	A30 0-2	S27 0-2	F07 0-2	F21 3-2
12 LEYTON O	S06 5-1	M14 2-2	N29 4-2	A23 1-3	a25 3-0	a11 6-1	J03 1-3	S27 0-2	D13 0-1	N01 2-5	S04 2-0		F21 0-0	F28 1-3	N15 5-2	M28 2-0	S13 2-1	O18 1-1	F07 0-2	D26 0-1	M30 6-0	S18 0-0
13 LINCOLN C	a11 2-1	N01 4-2	D13 0-2	S20 4-1	F28 4-2	M14 3-3	F14 1-4	S10 2-4	S03 4-4	N15 1-1	J31 3-1	O04 2-0		M28 2-1	O18 1-1	N29 1-0	M27 3-3	a25 1-2	D27 0-1	J03 3-1	A23 3-1	S06 1-2
14 LIVERPOOL	M27 3-2	S03 5-0	F07 3-2	N22 2-1	S27 1-2	S13 3-0	a04 3-0	M07 0-0	A23 3-3	F21 2-2	a18 3-1	N08 3-0	O11 3-2		a08 1-2	D27 4-0	a22 3-0	S10 2-1	O25 3-2	M20 3-4	J03 3-1	D06 4-0
15 MIDDLESBROUGH	D26 3-1	A23 9-0	S27 0-0	a18 2-2	F21 1-1	F07 1-3	N22 5-0	O25 2-3	M11 1-0	J01 3-1	D06 2-3	a04 4-2	M07 1-2	S06 2-1		S17 1-2	N08 6-1	S03 0-0	a22 2-2	J31 0-0	O11 0-0	M21 6-2
16 ROTHERHAM U	S13 3-0	O04 0-1	D20 1-2	O25 3-3	A30 1-0	A28 4-3	M07 3-0	D06 4-0	M30 2-1	a30 0-1	a23 1-2	O11 1-1	a18 1-0	D26 0-1	S11 1-4		F07 1-0	a15 2-2	M21 1-0	a04 0-0	N22 0-4	N08 3-3
17 SCUNTHORPE U	N01 1-0	O18 2-3	a11 3-3	J03 0-0	D18 1-0	N15 3-3	S06 2-2	F21 1-2	M14 1-3	a25 0-3	A23 1-1	J31 2-0	M30 3-1	D13 1-2	F28 0-3	S20 2-0		M28 1-3	S27 1-4	S18 1-1	D26 3-2	S04 3-1
18 SHEFFIELD U	F07 5-0	M31 3-1	A30 4-0	a20 5-2	a27 1-1	D20 5-0	O25 1-2	M21 2-0	D27 2-1	S13 0-0	N08 2-0	M07 2-3	D06 6-1	S15 2-0	A25 0-1	S27 2-0	O11 4-1		F21 1-0	N22 2-1	a18 3-1	a04 2-0
19 SHEFFIELD W	a25 5-0	M28 2-0	N15 2-3	S06 3-1	a11 3-1	F27 4-1	J31 1-1	M30 2-2	O18 6-0	N29 4-1	J03 3-1	S20 2-0	D26 7-0	a14 1-0	D13 2-0	N01 5-0	F14 2-0	O04 2-0		S03 4-1	S17 6-0	A23 2-1
20 STOKE C	F28 2-1	N29 3-0	O18 2-1	O04 2-2	M14 0-1	M28 2-1	O22 2-1	D20 4-1	a25 4-0	D13 5-1	F16 1-0	D27 3-2	A30 1-0	N01 0-2	S13 3-1	N15 3-0	S10 4-3	a11 1-2	A27 3-0		a06 0-0	S20 3-0
21 SUNDERLAND	N15 2-2	a25 4-1	M14 3-1	F14 3-1	D13 0-2	O18 0-3	O04 3-0	A27 1-2	N01 1-0	F28 1-0	S20 0-2	J01 4-0	D20 2-0	A30 2-1	M28 0-0	a11 1-1	D27 3-1	N29 4-1	S10 3-3	S06 3-1		J31 2-1
22 SWANSEA T	D13 2-1	a11 4-2	M28 1-0	M27 2-1	a15 1-3	S27 2-2	D27 4-4	A30 1-2	N29 1-1	M14 0-1	O04 4-2	S11 3-3	J17 3-1	a25 3-3	N01 5-2	F28 3-0	A28 3-0	N15 0-2	D20 4-0	F07 1-0	S13 5-0	

Sheffield Wednesday's Alan Finney helped the Owls win Division Two in 1958-59. Altogether, Finney made 503 League and Cup appearances for Wednesday, scoring 90 goals.

Season 1958-59

DIVISION 3

	ACCRINGTON S	BOURNEMOUTH	BRADFORD C	BRENTFORD	BURY	CHESTERFIELD	COLCHESTER U	DONCASTER R	HALIFAX T	HULL C	MANSFIELD T	NEWPORT CO	NORWICH C	NOTTS CO	PLYMOUTH A	Q.P.R.	READING	ROCHDALE	SOUTHAMPTON	SOUTHEND U	STOCKPORT CO	SWINDON T	TRANMERE R	WREXHAM
1 ACCRINGTON S		M26 3-2	S27 1-3	S12 1-1	M14 0-2	S29 3-1	S17 1-1	M11 2-0	D26 4-2	F07 0-1	A30 2-0	A27 2-2	M23 0-2	D20 3-0	a25 1-1	N01 2-4	D13 4-3	M28 4-2	O08 0-0	O17 3-0	a11 2-2	F18 0-0	N29 3-1	F21 1-1
2 BOURNEMOUTH	M30 5-2		O25 4-0	N08 0-0	J03 2-0	N22 2-1	D27 1-1	S20 1-0	A27 3-0	D06 1-0	J24 3-3	a29 1-1	S24 2-0	a18 0-0	F14 1-1	S06 2-0	S10 0-1	J31 0-0	O11 2-1	A23 1-4	a22 2-0	a04 3-3	O04 4-0	M07 0-0
3 BRADFORD C	F14 0-0	M14 0-1		D20 3-0	M10 1-0	S10 1-0	O18 1-3	a11 3-0	O04 1-3	A30 2-1	A27 1-1	a22 1-0	N01 2-2	D27 4-1	D13 0-0	a25 1-0	F28 1-2	N29 7-1	S20 2-3	M28 6-1	M31 4-2	O01 1-2	S06 2-0	J31 3-2
4 BRENTFORD	J31 2-1	M28 1-1	A23 4-0		N29 0-0	O04 1-1	N01 2-1	S02 0-1	S20 2-0	S30 1-1	S09 2-0	F14 3-0	a30 0-4	a21 4-0	M27 3-0	a11 1-0	M14 3-1	D13 2-1	S06 2-0	a25 6-1	O18 1-4	D25 2-2	F28 5-2	J03 2-1
5 BURY	O25 3-1	A30 5-1	a04 2-2	a18 1-1		M30 1-0	D20 0-0	J01 5-0	M07 3-1	J24 2-1	a28 2-2	O11 0-0	a14 3-2	F07 0-1	S08 1-1	F14 3-1	S22 1-1	O04 6-1	M21 1-0	S13 2-3	A26 3-3	N22 0-0	D26 4-2	N08 3-0
6 CHESTERFIELD	S22 0-1	a11 1-0	S15 2-0	F21 1-2	M27 3-0		N29 2-2	O25 2-0	A23 2-3	J01 2-1	F07 3-1	J03 3-1	D13 1-1	S13 1-0	N01 1-2	F28 2-3	a25 1-0	O18 0-0	A25 3-3	S06 4-0	a13 1-0	S27 1-3	M28 3-2	D26 1-1
7 COLCHESTER U	S08 1-0	D26 3-1	M07 3-2	M21 0-4	A23 1-3	a18 1-0		J31 1-0	a27 3-1	O25 1-3	a04 1-3	N22 3-2	A25 2-1	F23 4-1	S20 2-0	J03 3-0	a20 3-1	S06 2-1	M27 1-3	S29 0-1	O04 8-2	N08 1-0	F14 1-1	O11 1-1
8 DONCASTER R	a04 3-0	F07 5-1	N22 0-3	A28 1-0	O09 0-1	M14 2-1	O16 2-1		N08 1-2	a23 0-2	O11 0-2	M21 1-0	S27 0-1	M07 2-1	O02 4-6	S09 2-0	F24 2-5	D27 1-1	J24 3-2	F21 2-1	A30 4-1	M27 2-0	D20 2-0	a18 1-1
9 HALIFAX T	D27 0-2	S01 0-1	F21 3-3	F07 0-0	O18 4-2	D20 3-2	a30 4-1	M28 5-1		S27 1-2	J17 0-0	S22 3-1	M31 1-1	A30 1-1	a20 0-1	M14 2-1	a11 4-1	N01 2-1	S08 2-0	F28 1-0	N29 4-3	S13 1-0	a25 3-0	a15 4-1
10 HULL C	S20 4-2	N01 5-3	J03 4-0	S22 3-1	a25 2-0	O06 3-1	M14 3-0	D13 5-1	F14 4-0		D26 5-2	O04 2-3	M28 3-3	S15 5-0	A23 1-1	N29 1-0	O18 2-0	a11 2-1	J31 3-0	J10 3-2	F28 3-1	S01 0-0	M30 1-0	S06 1-0
11 MANSFIELD T	J03 3-2	a25 1-4	S01 2-1	S15 1-1	D13 0-2	S20 2-1	F02 3-2	F28 3-1	S06 4-3	D27 1-1		J31 2-1	a06 1-1	F14 3-0	O18 1-4	O04 3-4	M28 1-0	M30 0-0	A23 1-6	a11 1-4	N01 2-1	a13 0-0	M14 0-2	S22 3-1
12 NEWPORT CO	S04 2-1	D13 4-1	O09 3-2	S27 0-1	F28 1-1	A30 0-1	m04 0-1	N01 3-1	O02 0-2	F21 1-3	S13 1-0		D20 2-2	M16 3-1	M28 0-1	O20 3-1	N29 2-1	M14 1-0	D25 4-2	a13 3-1	a25 2-0	F07 3-0	M09 3-0	S18 2-1
13 NORWICH C	O11 2-4	O01 2-2	M21 4-2	a04 4-1	S06 3-2	a29 2-1	S03 1-2	F04 3-0	M30 3-1	N08 0-1	a18 1-0	A23 3-0		N22 3-3	O04 1-1	J31 5-1	D26 1-0	S20 2-1	M07 3-1	J03 4-0	S17 1-3	a08 1-1	a22 0-0	O25 2-2
14 NOTTS CO	A23 1-1	N29 4-3	D26 1-3	O09 0-0	S20 1-1	J31 3-1	a25 0-1	O18 2-2	J03 4-4	S11 1-1	S27 3-4	S06 1-1	a11 1-3		M14 1-2	M30 0-1	J10 3-1	F28 1-1	S25 1-2	D13 1-4	M28 0-2	F21 1-0	N01 1-1	S04 2-0
15 PLYMOUTH A	M04 2-4	S27 3-1	a29 1-1	M30 1-1	S18 3-0	M21 2-0	F07 1-1	S22 4-0	a04 1-1	D20 1-1	M07 8-3	N08 3-2	F21 0-1	O25 3-0		D26 3-2	S13 2-2	S04 2-1	a18 1-0	O08 3-1	J17 2-1	O11 3-2	A30 4-0	N22 2-2
16 Q.P.R.	M21 3-1	J17 0-4	M16 3-0	N22 1-2	S27 2-1	O11 2-2	A30 4-2	S15 3-1	O25 3-1	a18 1-1	F21 1-1	M07 4-2	S13 2-1	M27 2-1	D27 2-1		D20 2-0	a20 3-0	N08 2-2	F07 1-3	S29 0-0	a27 2-1	A25 1-1	a04 5-0
17 READING	a29 5-0	S17 2-0	O11 3-2	O25 3-1	S29 1-0	J24 1-2	O08 0-0	S06 2-0	N22 3-0	a15 2-0	N08 3-3	a18 1-3	D27 3-1	a04 3-1	J31 0-2	A23 2-2		J03 3-0	F21 4-1	S03 3-0	F14 2-1	M21 3-1	S20 0-0	M30 2-1
18 ROCHDALE	N08 1-0	S13 2-1	a18 0-3	a27 0-0	F21 1-0	M07 0-0	M16 0-1	D26 1-0	M21 1-0	N22 0-1	M27 2-2	O25 1-1	F07 1-2	O11 1-2	A25 0-2	O07 2-2	A30 1-0		a04 1-0	S27 1-1	D20 0-2	S10 1-1	S23 1-4	J24 3-1
19 SOUTHAMPTON	a22 3-1	F28 0-0	F07 1-2	M09 0-6	N01 4-2	S01 0-0	M30 3-0	a25 1-1	S17 5-0	S13 6-1	D20 3-2	D27 3-3	O18 1-1	O01 3-0	N29 5-1	M28 1-0	O04 3-3	F02 6-1		M14 3-2	D13 2-1	A30 1-1	a11 2-3	S27 1-2
20 SOUTHEND U	M07 4-2	D20 2-0	N08 1-1	a08 2-0	J31 1-0	J17 2-5	S24 1-1	O04 5-0	O11 3-2	a04 1-1	N22 5-1	M30 1-0	A30 1-0	a29 5-2	J24 0-0	S20 4-0	A27 2-2	F14 3-1	O25 1-1		D27 3-1	a18 0-2	S10 1-3	M21 4-1
21 STOCKPORT CO	N22 0-0	O06 3-1	M27 1-1	M07 1-1	S01 0-1	a04 1-1	F21 0-1	J03 2-0	a18 0-1	O11 2-1	M21 4-1	M02 2-1	S08 2-3	N08 1-1	S06 2-2	S22 2-3	S27 0-1	A23 1-0	a27 4-0	O20 0-1		O25 2-0	J31 1-0	F07 2-2
22 SWINDON T	S06 1-2	J10 0-1	S24 2-2	D26 1-1	a11 0-0	F14 1-2	M28 2-0	M30 0-0	J31 0-2	A27 2-0	a22 2-1	S20 2-1	a25 4-3	O04 3-1	F28 3-4	D13 2-0	N01 2-0	S17 2-1	J03 3-1	N29 2-1	M14 3-0		O18 1-2	A23 1-0
23 TRANMERE R	a18 9-0	F21 4-0	F23 3-1	O11 1-2	D27 4-0	N08 2-0	S27 3-3	A23 3-0	J24 1-2	M27 1-0	O25 2-2	a04 2-1	O06 0-1	M21 0-3	M16 2-0	S01 2-0	F07 2-1	S29 2-1	N22 2-0	S15 1-1	S13 3-1	M07 3-1		J01 1-2
24 WREXHAM	O04 2-2	O18 1-0	S13 3-3	A30 2-1	M28 0-0	D27 3-4	F28 2-0	N29 2-1	a22 1-1	a29 5-1	O01 2-1	S10 0-0	a13 1-2	A27 3-2	a11 1-1	a08 1-0	M27 0-1	a25 1-0	F14 1-3	N01 3-1	S20 3-1	D20 1-0	D13 2-5	

DIVISION 4

	ALDERSHOT	BARROW	BRADFORD	CARLISLE U	CHESTER	COVENTRY C	CREWE A	CRYSTAL P	DARLINGTON	EXETER C	GATESHEAD	GILLINGHAM	HARTLEPOOLS U	MILLWALL	NORTHAMPTON T	OLDHAM A	PORT VALE	SHREWSBURY T	SOUTHPORT	TORQUAY U	WALSALL	WATFORD	WORKINGTON	YORK C
1 ALDERSHOT		A30 0-1	D13 3-3	D20 4-0	F28 1-0	O01 0-4	J10 0-0	D26 1-2	S04 1-4	a22 1-0	S13 8-1	M30 4-2	M14 2-4	F14 4-2	a11 1-3	J17 1-3	S20 0-4	S17 0-0	N01 3-2	M28 1-4	O04 0-5	O18 0-0	N29 2-0	a25 0-1
2 BARROW	J03 3-4		F28 2-3	S29 1-3	N01 1-2	O04 0-3	a25 0-2	M14 1-0	S20 2-1	S01 1-0	A23 0-3	S15 2-2	a21 1-1	S06 3-1	D13 2-2	M30 2-1	O18 1-2	F14 3-4	a11 3-0	N29 2-2	J31 0-0	M28 0-4	J01 2-2	D27 2-3
3 BRADFORD	a27 5-1	O11 0-2		M07 0-3	S27 3-0	N08 2-0	J01 0-2	F07 5-0	N22 1-2	M21 0-3	J17 4-1	O25 2-0	S01 4-1	J24 4-1	M27 1-2	D26 2-1	S13 0-2	a04 3-1	S15 3-0	S29 3-1	a18 3-2	F21 1-1	A23 3-2	J03 2-1
4 CARLISLE U	A23 1-0	S23 1-0	O18 1-1		M28 4-3	F14 1-6	D13 2-0	N01 3-3	M11 1-1	O04 1-2	M30 4-2	A26 1-2	a11 1-0	J03 0-2	S09 2-1	M03 3-0	M14 0-3	S20 0-0	N29 5-0	a25 0-1	S06 1-1	M16 2-0	D26 3-2	F28 0-0
5 CHESTER	O11 2-2	M21 2-0	F14 2-0	N08 2-1		a18 1-1	a22 0-1	S03 3-2	a29 1-0	N22 4-2	M07 0-1	a04 1-2	O08 1-1	D27 0-0	S06 2-3	O25 5-2	O04 1-2	J24 3-5	M30 2-1	A23 0-2	S17 2-0	O01 2-1	J31 1-2	S20 2-2
6 COVENTRY C	S22 7-1	F21 2-0	M28 0-0	S27 1-2	N29 5-1		F28 3-2	a11 2-0	A23 0-0	S13 2-0	S15 4-1	F07 1-1	D13 4-1	O06 1-0	O18 2-0	S01 1-0	M16 1-0	J03 3-2	S06 1-0	D26 3-0	M31 0-0	a25 1-0	M14 4-0	N01 2-0
7 CREWE A	a04 5-0	J24 5-0	O08 4-1	F17 3-1	A30 2-4	O11 1-1		D20 4-1	O25 2-1	M05 0-0	N22 0-0	F21 0-2	S13 0-2	N08 4-1	S01 1-2	a18 5-0	M27 2-0	M07 2-4	F07 1-1	S27 1-1	M21 5-3	J17 1-3	S18 2-0	O01 2-4
8 CRYSTAL P	D27 4-1	O25 2-2	S20 2-0	M21 0-2	A27 3-3	N22 1-1	A23 6-2		J24 4-1	a04 1-1	O11 3-1	N08 4-1	O01 1-2	F21 4-0	J03 1-1	M07 4-0	F14 1-1	a18 4-3	O08 1-0	M27 3-1	a29 1-3	S17 3-0	S06 1-1	J31 0-0
9 DARLINGTON	A25 2-3	F07 5-2	a11 1-1	S13 0-1	D13 0-0	D20 1-4	M14 1-1	a25 1-4		A30 1-1	F21 3-2	a16 1-2	D27 3-1	S18 0-2	N01 2-2	S27 1-1	N29 2-0	J01 2-1	F28 4-0	O18 3-2	O01 2-3	O08 1-1	M28 1-1	M18 0-1
10 EXETER C	O08 2-0	A28 4-0	N01 4-0	F21 2-1	a11 1-1	J31 2-1	D27 3-0	a15 3-1	J03 2-2		a06 1-1	S27 3-0	a25 3-0	M30 3-1	F28 3-4	S10 3-2	M28 3-4	S06 1-0	D13 3-2	S20 2-2	A23 3-0	N29 3-0	O18 1-0	M14 0-2
11 GATESHEAD	J31 1-0	D20 4-0	S06 1-4	M27 4-1	O18 0-1	S08 1-1	a11 0-0	F28 1-3	O04 1-3	O27 1-2		a20 2-0	N01 3-0	S20 1-2	N29 4-1	A30 2-1	J01 0-4	A25 1-2	M28 1-1	a13 1-0	F14 2-1	M14 1-0	a25 0-3	D13 1-0
12 GILLINGHAM	M27 3-0	S10 4-2	M14 1-1	S01 1-1	J17 3-3	S20 2-0	O04 3-0	M28 1-1	S06 0-0	F14 0-2	O08 3-0		N29 4-1	A23 1-2	D26 4-1	O01 3-2	N01 0-2	J31 2-1	a25 2-0	a08 3-2	J03 4-2	a11 2-1	F28 5-1	O18 2-2
13 HARTLEPOOLS U	O25 0-3	a04 10-1	A25 3-0	N22 1-2	J01 1-3	a27 2-1	J31 2-1	S22 4-1	D26 1-0	J24 3-3	M21 0-0	a18 3-1		M07 3-1	S20 3-0	N08 4-0	S08 1-5	A23 0-2	J03 1-1	S06 2-4	O11 1-1	M27 4-3	F14 0-3	O04 1-5
14 MILLWALL	S27 4-0	J17 3-0	a25 1-1	A30 1-0	D25 0-1	a20 1-1	M28 2-0	O04 2-1	S08 1-2	M27 1-1	F07 0-2	D20 2-0	O18 3-2		J10 3-0	S13 4-2	D13 4-2	S22 0-0	M14 1-1	N01 2-0	S01 1-3	F28 4-1	a11 1-1	N29 5-2
15 NORTHAMPTON T	N22 1-0	a30 2-0	M31 4-1	a06 0-0	a13 4-0	M07 4-0	A28 3-0	A30 3-0	M21 1-3	O11 1-1	a18 1-0	D27 4-2	F07 2-1	a04 0-1		J24 2-1	D20 2-4	O25 3-3	S27 3-1	F21 1-1	N08 3-2	S13 2-1	S25 1-1	O09 1-2
16 OLDHAM A	S06 0-1	M27 2-0	D27 1-0	a28 2-0	M14 3-5	A26 2-0	N29 2-1	O18 3-0	F14 1-3	S15 2-1	J03 3-0	S22 3-1	M28 1-0	J31 1-3	a25 2-1		F28 0-2	O04 3-1	a20 2-0	a11 1-0	S20 1-4	N01 3-5	D13 1-0	A23 0-1
17 PORT VALE	F07 3-2	M07 4-1	J31 4-2	O25 1-1	F21 4-0	a04 3-0	M30 1-1	S27 2-3	a18 1-1	N08 5-3	D26 8-0	M21 3-1	S15 1-1	a27 5-2	A23 1-4	O11 0-0		N22 2-0	S29 4-1	O06 3-1	J23 2-1	S01 1-3	M02 2-0	S06 2-2
18 SHREWSBURY T	S08 3-1	S27 1-2	J10 0-1	F07 4-1	a25 3-0	A30 4-1	O18 2-2	N29 2-1	M30 1-0	a30 3-0	S01 1-1	S13 3-2	D20 3-0	S29 1-2	M14 4-0	F21 0-0	a11 4-3		D26 6-2	F28 5-0	a20 2-0	D13 4-2	N01 1-1	M28 2-2
19 SOUTHPORT	M21 0-1	N22 0-0	S09 1-0	a18 0-1	M27 1-1	a14 1-2	S20 3-0	J01 0-2	O11 2-0	a28 0-1	N08 2-2	J24 2-1	A30 1-1	O25 2-1	F14 1-2	a04 1-1	S23 2-2	D25 0-1		J31 2-2	M07 1-1	D20 0-3	O04 3-0	S02 1-0
20 TORQUAY U	N08 1-1	a18 1-0	S22 2-1	F25 0-0	D20 4-0	D27 1-1	F14 6-2	M30 0-2	M07 4-1	F07 3-4	a04 0-1	a29 3-1	J17 1-3	M21 2-0	O04 4-2	N22 2-1	a22 1-1	O11 1-4	S13 1-0		O25 1-2	A30 2-3	S04 4-1	S17 1-1
21 WALSALL	F21 2-4	S13 3-1	N29 3-2	a14 5-0	S11 2-2	M30 3-0	O31 6-0	D13 0-2	S25 0-0	M17 3-0	S27 0-1	A30 1-2	F28 0-0	A28 2-1	M28 2-1	F07 3-0	a25 1-1	O09 2-3	O18 5-1	M14 2-2		D26 3-2	a09 3-0	a11 5-0
22 WATFORD	M07 2-1	N08 1-1	O04 2-1	a04 2-2	O14 4-2	J24 1-4	S06 0-1	S09 2-2	a21 0-0	a18 2-1	O25 5-1	N22 2-2	M30 4-1	O11 1-1	J31 3-1	M21 2-1	A26 0-2	m07 1-4	A23 5-1	J03 1-2	D27 1-2		S20 3-0	F14 2-3
23 WORKINGTON	a18 1-0	O08 2-2	D20 2-1	D27 0-1	S13 1-0	O25 2-2	S10 1-0	M16 0-4	N08 3-3	M07 2-2	D05 4-2	O11 0-1	S27 3-0	N22 1-1	O01 3-3	a22 2-0	A30 2-2	M21 1-1	F21 2-0	A25 3-3	a04 0-1	F07 3-1		M30 2-2
24 YORK C	J24 0-0	D26 1-0	A30 4-0	O11 1-1	F07 1-1	M21 0-0	S22 4-0	S13 1-1	a04 2-1	O25 0-2	a27 1-0	M07 3-1	F21 1-1	a18 3-3	a20 2-1	D20 3-1	a15 0-0	N08 2-0	A25 2-0	S08 1-0	N22 3-2	S27 0-0	M27 2-2	

LEAGUE TABLES

DIVISION 1

	P	W	D	L	F	A	W	D	L	F	A	Pts
Wolverh'pton W	42	15	3	3	68	19	13	2	6	42	30	61
Manchester U	42	14	4	3	58	27	10	3	8	45	39	55
Arsenal	42	14	3	4	53	29	7	5	9	35	39	50
Bolton W	42	14	3	4	56	30	6	7	8	23	36	50
W.B.A.	42	8	7	6	41	33	10	6	5	47	35	49
West Ham U	42	15	3	3	59	29	6	3	12	26	41	48
Burnley	42	11	4	6	41	29	8	6	7	40	41	48
Blackpool	42	12	7	2	39	13	6	4	11	27	36	47
Birmingham C	42	14	1	6	54	35	6	5	10	30	33	46
Blackburn R	42	12	3	6	48	28	5	7	9	28	42	44
Newcastle U	42	11	3	7	40	29	6	4	11	40	51	41
Preston N.E.	42	9	3	9	40	39	8	4	9	30	38	41
Nottingham F	42	9	4	8	37	32	8	2	11	34	42	40
Chelsea	42	13	2	6	52	37	5	2	14	25	61	40
Leeds U	42	8	7	6	28	27	7	2	12	29	47	39
Everton	42	11	3	7	39	38	6	1	14	32	49	38
Luton T	42	11	6	4	50	26	1	7	13	18	45	37
Tottenham H	42	10	3	8	56	42	3	7	11	29	53	36
Leicester C	42	7	6	8	34	36	4	4	13	33	62	32
Manchester C	42	8	7	6	40	32	3	2	16	24	63	31
Aston Villa	42	8	5	8	31	33	3	3	15	27	54	30
Portsmouth	42	5	4	12	38	47	1	5	15	26	65	21

DIVISION 2

	P	W	D	L	F	A	W	D	L	F	A	Pts
Sheffield W	42	18	2	1	68	13	10	4	7	38	35	62
Fulham	42	18	1	2	65	26	9	5	7	31	35	60
Sheffield U	42	16	2	3	54	15	7	5	9	28	33	53
Liverpool	42	15	3	3	57	25	9	2	10	30	37	53
Stoke C	42	16	2	3	48	19	5	5	11	24	39	49
Bristol R	42	13	5	3	46	23	5	7	9	34	41	48
Derby Co	42	15	1	5	46	29	5	7	9	28	42	48
Charlton A	42	13	3	5	53	33	5	4	12	39	57	43
Cardiff C	42	12	2	7	37	26	6	5	10	28	39	43
Bristol C	42	11	3	7	43	27	6	4	11	31	43	41
Swansea T	42	12	5	4	52	30	4	4	13	27	51	41
Brighton & H.A.	42	10	9	2	46	29	5	2	14	28	61	41
Middlesbrough	42	9	7	5	51	26	6	3	12	36	45	40
Huddersfield T	42	12	3	6	39	20	4	5	12	23	35	40
Sunderland	42	13	4	4	42	23	3	4	14	22	52	40
Ipswich T	42	12	4	5	37	27	5	2	14	25	50	40
Leyton O	42	9	4	8	43	30	5	4	12	28	48	36
Scunthorpe U	42	7	6	8	32	37	5	3	13	23	47	33
Lincoln C	42	10	5	6	45	37	1	2	18	18	56	29
Rotherham U	42	9	5	7	32	28	1	4	16	10	54	29
Grimsby T	42	7	7	7	41	36	2	3	16	21	54	28
Barnsley	42	8	4	9	34	34	2	3	16	21	57	27

DIVISION 3

	P	W	D	L	F	A	W	D	L	F	A	Pts
Plymouth A	46	14	7	2	55	27	9	9	5	34	32	62
Hull C	46	19	3	1	65	21	7	6	10	25	34	61
Brentford	46	15	5	3	49	22	6	10	7	27	27	57
Norwich C	46	13	6	4	51	29	9	7	7	38	33	57
Colchester U	46	15	2	6	46	31	6	8	9	25	36	52
Reading	46	16	4	3	51	21	5	4	14	27	42	50
Tranmere R	46	15	3	5	53	22	6	5	12	29	45	50
Southend U	46	14	6	3	52	26	7	2	14	33	54	50
Halifax T	46	14	5	4	48	25	7	3	13	32	52	50
Bury	46	12	9	2	51	24	5	5	13	18	34	48
Bradford C	46	13	4	6	47	25	5	7	11	37	51	47
Bournemouth	46	12	9	2	40	18	5	3	15	29	51	46
Q.P.R.	46	14	6	3	49	28	5	2	16	25	49	46
Southampton	46	12	7	4	57	33	5	4	14	31	47	45
Swindon T	46	13	4	6	39	25	3	9	11	20	32	45
Chesterfield	46	12	5	6	40	26	5	5	13	27	38	44
Newport Co	46	15	2	6	43	24	2	7	14	26	44	43
Wrexham	46	12	6	5	40	30	2	8	13	23	47	42
Accrington S	46	10	8	5	42	31	5	4	14	29	56	42
Mansfield T	46	11	5	7	38	42	3	8	12	35	56	41
Stockport Co	46	9	7	7	33	23	4	3	16	32	55	36
Doncaster R	46	13	2	8	40	32	1	3	19	10	58	33
Notts Co	46	5	9	9	33	39	3	4	16	22	57	29
Rochdale	46	8	7	8	21	26	0	5	18	16	53	28

DIVISION 4

	P	W	D	L	F	A	W	D	L	F	A	Pts
Port Vale	46	14	6	3	62	30	12	6	5	48	28	64
Coventry C	46	18	4	1	50	11	6	8	9	34	36	60
York C	46	12	10	1	37	17	9	8	6	36	35	60
Shrewsbury T	46	15	5	3	59	24	9	5	9	42	39	58
Exeter C	46	16	4	3	55	24	7	7	9	32	37	57
Walsall	46	13	5	5	56	25	8	5	10	39	39	52
Crystal Palace	46	12	8	3	54	27	8	4	11	36	44	52
Northampton T	46	14	5	4	48	25	7	4	12	37	53	51
Millwall	46	13	6	4	46	23	7	4	12	30	46	50
Carlisle U	46	11	6	6	37	30	8	6	9	25	35	50
Gillingham	46	14	6	3	53	27	6	3	14	29	50	49
Torquay U	46	11	5	7	45	32	5	7	11	33	45	44
Chester C	46	10	5	8	39	33	6	7	10	33	51	44
Bradford P.A.	46	15	1	7	51	29	3	6	14	24	48	43
Watford	46	10	6	7	46	36	6	4	13	35	43	42
Darlington	46	7	8	8	37	36	6	8	9	29	32	42
Workington	46	9	10	4	40	32	3	7	13	23	46	41
Crewe A	46	11	5	7	52	32	4	5	14	18	50	40
Hartlepool U	46	11	4	8	50	41	4	6	13	24	47	40
Gateshead	46	11	3	9	33	30	5	5	13	23	55	40
Oldham A	46	15	0	8	39	29	1	4	18	20	55	36
Aldershot	46	8	4	11	37	45	6	3	14	26	52	35
Barrow	46	6	6	11	34	45	3	4	16	17	59	28
Southport	46	7	8	8	26	25	0	4	19	15	61	26

Football League Records

Top scorers: Div 1, D.Viollet (Manchester United) 32 goals; Div 2, B.Clough (Middlesbrough) 39 goals; Div 3, D.Reeves (Southampton) 39 goals; Div 4, C.Holton (Watford) 42 goals.

Irish international inside-forward Jimmy McIlroy guided Burnley to the title in 1959-60.

DIVISION 1

	ARSENAL	BIRMINGHAM C	BLACKBURN R	BLACKPOOL	BOLTON W	BURNLEY	CHELSEA	EVERTON	FULHAM	LEEDS U	LEICESTER C	LUTON T	MANCHESTER C	MANCHESTER U	NEWCASTLE U	NOTTINGHAM F	PRESTON N.E.	SHEFFIELD W	TOTTENHAM H	W.B.A.	WEST HAM U	WOLVERHAMPTON W
1 ARSENAL		O31 3-0	F06 5-2	S26 2-1	S15 2-1	D12 2-4	a09 1-4	F20 2-1	a15 2-0	M26 1-1	M15 1-1	D26 0-3	S12 3-1	a23 5-2	F27 1-0	S01 1-1	O17 0-3	A22 0-1	S05 1-1	N28 2-4	N14 1-3	J02 4-4
2 BIRMINGHAM C	a16 3-0		a30 1-0	N21 2-1	M19 2-5	a27 0-1	S09 1-1	a02 2-2	O24 2-4	O03 2-0	S19 3-4	N07 1-1	D05 4-2	S05 1-1	A26 4-3	M05 4-1	J23 2-1	O10 0-0	J02 0-1	a18 1-7	D26 2-0	A22 0-1
3 BLACKBURN R	S19 1-1	N28 2-1		D25 1-0	A31 1-0	O17 3-2	M30 1-0	S21 3-1	A22 4-0	a27 3-2	a23 0-1	a15 0-2	F13 2-1	O31 1-1	a09 1-1	J02 1-2	O03 1-4	S05 3-1	F27 1-4	N14 3-2	D12 6-2	J23 0-1
4 BLACKPOOL	F13 2-1	a09 0-1	D26 1-0		A22 3-2	a23 1-1	D12 3-1	a18 0-0	J02 3-1	O17 3-3	S14 3-3	A31 0-0	O03 1-3	F27 0-6	N14 2-0	S05 0-1	O31 0-2	J23 0-2	N28 2-2	M26 2-0	M12 3-2	S19 3-1
5 BOLTON W	S09 0-1	D12 4-1	A26 0-3	D19 0-3		F27 2-1	a23 2-0	A29 2-1	S19 3-2	O31 1-1	N28 3-1	M09 2-2	a18 3-1	N14 1-1	M12 1-4	F13 1-1	a09 2-1	O03 1-0	M26 2-1	O17 0-0	S12 5-1	D26 2-1
6 BURNLEY	M19 3-2	S26 3-1	M05 1-0	O10 1-4	D05 4-0		J16 2-1	A25 5-2	a30 0-0	D19 0-1	a15 1-0	a16 3-0	O24 4-3	D28 1-4	F06 2-1	N21 8-0	S08 2-1	a02 3-3	M01 2-0	S12 2-1	A29 1-3	N07 4-1
7 CHELSEA	N21 1-3	S16 4-2	N07 3-1	M19 2-3	O10 0-2	S05 4-1		O24 1-0	F13 4-2	J23 1-3	J02 2-2	M05 3-0	a02 3-0	S02 3-6	D26 2-2	a16 1-1	A22 4-4	D05 0-4	a15 1-3	F24 2-2	S19 2-4	a30 1-5
8 EVERTON	O03 3-1	N14 4-0	S16 2-0	a15 4-0	J02 0-1	S02 1-2	M12 6-1		S05 0-0	a23 1-0	O31 6-1	A22 2-2	D26 2-1	N28 2-1	M25 1-2	J23 6-1	F27 4-0	S19 2-1	a09 2-1	D12 2-2	O17 0-1	F13 0-2
9 FULHAM	a18 3-0	M12 2-2	D19 0-1	A29 1-0	F06 1-1	N28 1-0	S26 1-3	J16 2-0		F27 5-0	a09 1-1	S12 4-2	A26 5-2	M26 0-5	O17 4-3	O03 3-1	N14 1-2	D28 1-2	D12 1-1	a23 2-1	O31 1-0	S09 3-1
10 LEEDS U	N07 3-2	M09 3-3	O24 0-1	M05 2-4	a16 1-0	A22 2-3	S12 2-1	O10 3-3	D05 1-4		S02 1-1	J02 1-1	M19 4-3	S16 2-2	S26 2-3	a30 1-0	a19 2-1	N21 1-3	D26 2-4	F06 1-4	J16 3-0	a02 0-3
11 LEICESTER C	O24 2-2	F06 1-3	O10 2-3	S09 1-1	a30 1-2	a18 2-1	A29 3-1	a16 3-3	N21 0-1	A26 3-2		D05 3-3	M05 5-0	F24 3-1	S12 0-2	a02 0-1	D26 2-2	N07 2-0	S26. 1-1	J16 0-1	D19 2-1	M19 2-1
12 LUTON T	D28 0-1	M26 1-1	a18 1-1	A26 0-1	S05 0-0	O31 1-1	O17 1-2	D19 2-1	J23 4-1	A29 0-1	F27 2-0		S09 1-2	a09 2-3	D12 3-4	S19 1-0	N28 1-3	F13 0-1	N14 1-0	M12 0-0	a23 3-1	O03 1-5
13 MANCHESTER C	J23 1-2	F27 3-0	S26 2-1	M09 2-3	a15 1-0	m02 1-2	N14 1-1	D28 4-0	S02 3-1	D12 3-3	O17 3-2	S16 1-2		S19 3-0	N28 3-4	A22 2-1	a23 2-1	J02 4-1	O31 1-2	a09 0-1	M30 3-1	S05 4-6
14 MANCHESTER U	O10 4-2	J16 2-1	a16 1-0	D05 3-1	a02 2-0	D26 1-2	A26 0-1	a30 5-0	N07 3-3	S09 6-0	O03 4-1	N21 4-1	F06 0-0		A29 3-2	M19 3-1	F13 1-1	O24 3-1	S12 1-5	D19 2-3	a18 5-3	M05 0-2
15 NEWCASTLE U	D05 4-1	S02 1-0	N21 3-1	a02 1-1	O24 0-2	S19 1-3	D28 1-1	N07 8-2	M05 3-1	F13 2-1	J23 0-2	M19 3-2	a30 0-1	J02 7-3		O10 2-1	S05 1-2	a15 3-3	A22 1-5	S16 0-0	O03 0-0	a16 1-0
16 NOTTINGHAM F	A26 0-3	O17 0-2	A29 2-2	J16 0-0	S26 2-0	a09 0-1	O31 3-1	S12 1-1	F20 2-2	N28 4-1	N14 1-0	F06 2-0	D19 1-2	D12 1-5	a23 3-0		M26 1-1	S09 2-1	M12 1-3	D28 1-2	F27 3-1	a19 0-0
17 PRESTON N.E.	M05 0-3	S12 3-2	M01 5-3	a16 4-1	N21 1-0	S15 1-0	D19 4-5	D05 0-0	a02 4-1	a18 1-1	D28 1-1	a30 2-0	O10 1-5	S26 4-0	J16 1-2	N07 1-0		M19 3-4	F06 1-1	A29 1-1	A25 1-1	O24 4-3
18 SHEFFIELD W	D19 5-1	a23 2-4	J16 3-0	S12 5-0	F24 1-0	N14 1-1	F27 1-1	F06 2-2	D26 1-1	a09 1-0	a06 2-2	S26 2-0	A29 1-0	M30 4-2	a18 2-0	S16 0-1	D12 2-2		O17 2-1	O31 2-0	N28 7-0	S02 2-2
19 TOTTENHAM H	J16 3-0	A29 0-0	D05 2-1	a30 4-1	N07 0-2	O03 1-1	a18 0-1	N21 3-0	M19 1-1	D28 1-4	F13 1-2	a02 1-1	a16 0-1	J23 2-1	D19 4-0	O24 2-1	S19 5-1	M05 4-1		A26 2-2	S09 2-2	O10 5-1
20 W.B.A.	a30 1-0	a19 1-1	a02 2-0	N07 2-1	M05 1-1	J23 0-0	O03 1-3	M19 6-2	O10 2-4	S19 3-0	S05 5-0	O24 4-0	N21 2-0	A22 3-2	S09 2-2	D26 2-3	J02 4-0	a16 3-1	S02 1-2		M09 3-2	D05 0-1
21 WEST HAM U	a02 0-0	D28 3-1	M19 2-1	O24 1-0	J23 1-2	J02 2-5	F06 4-2	M05 2-2	a16 1-2	S05 1-2	A22 3-0	O10 3-1	N07 4-1	a15 2-1	F20 3-5	D05 4-1	A31 2-1	a30 1-1	S14 1-2	S26 4-1		N21 3-2
22 WOLVERHAMPTON W	A29 3-3	D19 2-0	S12 3-1	F06 1-1	D28 0-1	M30 6-1	N28 3-1	S26 2-0	S16 9-0	N14 4-2	D12 0-3	F23 3-2	J16 4-2	O17 3-2	O31 2-0	a18 3-1	M16 3-3	A26 3-1	a23 1-3	F27 3-1	a11 5-0	

Peter McParland, another Irish international star. His performances at outside-left helped Aston Villa back to Division One.

DIVISION 2

	ASTON VILLA	BRIGHTON & HA	BRISTOL C	BRISTOL R	CARDIFF C	CHARLTON A	DERBY CO	HUDDERSFIELD T	HULL C	IPSWICH T	LEYTON O	LINCOLN C	LIVERPOOL	MIDDLESBROUGH	PLYMOUTH A	PORTSMOUTH	ROTHERHAM U	SCUNTHORPE U	SHEFFIELD U	STOKE C	SUNDERLAND	SWANSEA T
1 ASTON VILLA		D19 3-1	a09 2-1	J16 4-1	D12 2-0	N14 11-1	M15 3-2	F06 4-0	D28 1-1	S12 3-1	S26 1-0	M01 1-1	M30 4-4	O17 1-0	O31 2-0	S14 5-2	a23 3-0	N28 5-0	F27 1-3	a18 2-1	A31 3-0	A29 1-0
2 BRIGHTON & H.A.	A22 1-2		M12 5-1	M02 2-2	N14 2-2	O17 1-1	D12 2-0	S02 3-2	a09 1-1	D28 1-4	S16 1-1	a18 3-3	F27 1-2	a23 3-2	S19 2-2	S05 3-1	M26 0-0	O31 0-1	N28 0-2	J23 1-0	J02 2-1	S26 1-2
3 BRISTOL C	N21 0-5	O24 0-1		O10 2-1	J16 0-3	S15 1-2	F20 0-1	a16 2-3	S12 0-1	a18 5-1	D05 1-1	M19 1-0	S01 1-0	S26 2-0	D28 2-1	N07 2-0	A29 2-3	D19 0-2	F06 2-2	a30 1-2	a02 1-0	M05 2-2
4 BRISTOL R	S05 1-1	O03 4-5	F27 2-1		O31 1-1	S21 2-2	N28 2-1	a15 2-0	M26 1-0	S07 2-1	A22 2-2	J02 3-3	D12 0-2	a09 0-2	a23 2-0	S19 2-0	M12 3-1	O17 1-1	N14 3-2	F13 3-1	J23 3-1	D26 3-1
5 CARDIFF C	a16 1-0	a02 1-4	S05 4-2	a30 2-2		J02 5-1	S16 2-0	M05 2-1	F20 3-2	O24 3-2	O10 5-1	F13 6-2	A22 3-2	A26 2-0	a19 0-1	M19 1-4	S19 1-4	J23 4-2	D26 2-0	N21 4-4	D05 2-1	N07 2-1
6 CHARLTON A	a02 2-0	M05 3-1	S09 4-2	A26 2-2	A29 2-1		S26 6-1	D05 1-1	J16 3-2	a16 1-3	M19 0-0	N21 2-2	D26 3-0	F06 1-0	F20 5-2	a30 6-1	D19 2-2	a18 5-2	S12 1-1	O24 1-2	N07 3-1	O10 2-2
7 DERBY CO	O24 2-2	a16 0-1	O03 3-0	M19 1-0	S09 1-2	F24 1-2		a02 3-2	a18 1-3	N21 3-0	N07 1-1	a30 3-1	S19 1-2	A29 1-7	J23 1-0	O10 1-0	A26 1-1	D28 3-0	D19 1-1	J16 2-0	M05 0-1	D05 1-2
8 HUDDERSFIELD T	S19 0-1	A26 2-0	D12 6-1	a18 0-1	O17 0-1	a23 4-0	N14 2-2		M12 1-0	D19 3-1	S05 1-1	J23 3-0	N28 1-0	M26 2-0	a09 2-0	O03 6-3	F27 2-1	A29 2-0	O31 0-1	D28 2-3	F13 1-1	S09 4-3
9 HULL C	D26 0-1	N21 3-1	J23 1-1	N07 3-1	O03 0-0	S05 0-4	a15 1-1	O24 1-1		a30 2-0	M05 1-2	O10 0-5	J02 0-1	S14 3-3	A22 3-1	D05 1-3	F13 1-0	S19 0-2	A31 0-2	M17 4-0	a16 0-0	a02 3-1
10 IPSWICH T	J23 2-1	D26 3-0	a15 1-3	S16 3-0	M12 1-1	D12 1-1	a09 1-1	A22 1-4	O31 2-0		J02 6-3	S05 3-0	a23 0-1	N14 1-0	N28 3-3	F13 1-1	O17 2-3	F27 1-0	M26 2-0	O03 4-0	S19 6-1	A26 4-1
11 LEYTON O	F13 0-0	S10 3-2	a23 3-1	D19 1-2	F27 3-4	N28 2-0	M26 3-0	J16 2-1	O17 3-1	A29 4-1		S19 4-0	a09 2-0	O31 5-0	N14 2-3	D26 1-2	S12 2-3	D12 1-1	M17 1-1	A27 2-1	O03 1-1	a15 2-1
12 LINCOLN C	O03 0-0	a15 2-1	N28 3-1	A29 0-1	S26 2-3	a09 5-3	O31 6-2	S12 0-2	F27 3-0	J16 0-1	F06 2-2		N14 4-2	M12 5-2	M26 0-1	A26 0-2	D12 0-1	a23 2-1	O17 2-0	S09 3-0	D28 0-0	D19 2-0
13 LIVERPOOL	N07 2-1	O10 2-2	A26 4-2	a16 4-0	D19 0-4	D28 2-0	a06 4-1	M19 2-2	A29 5-3	D05 3-1	N21 4-3	a02 1-3		S12 1-2	S26 4-1	O24 1-1	a18 3-0	S09 2-0	J16 3-0	M05 5-1	a30 3-0	F20 4-1
14 MIDDLESBROUGH	M05 0-1	D05 4-1	F13 6-3	N21 5-1	S02 1-1	S19 3-0	J02 3-0	N07 1-0	S09 4-0	a02 4-1	a30 2-2	O24 3-2	J23 3-3		S05 6-2	A22 0-0	D28 3-0	O03 3-1	a18 1-2	a16 1-0	O10 1-1	M19 2-0
15 PLYMOUTH A	a30 3-0	F06 3-2	D26 1-4	D05 5-3	J30 1-1	O03 6-4	S12 0-5	N21 1-3	D19 3-2	M19 3-1	a02 1-0	N07 0-2	F13 1-1	J16 2-2		M05 1-1	S07 1-0	A24 4-0	A29 1-1	O10 2-3	O24 0-0	a16 3-1
16 PORTSMOUTH	S09 1-2	J16 2-2	M26 2-0	F06 4-5	N28 1-1	O31 2-2	F27 2-3	F20 0-2	a23 1-1	S26 0-2	D28 1-1	S02 1-2	M12 2-1	D19 6-3	O17 1-0		a09 2-0	N14 4-0	D12 0-2	A29 2-2	a18 1-2	S12 1-3
17 ROTHERHAM U	D05 2-1	N07 1-0	J02 3-1	O24 3-0	F06 2-2	A22 3-3	A31 1-2	O10 1-1	S26 1-0	M05 1-4	J23 1-1	a16 1-0	a19 2-2	D26 0-2	S16 1-1	N21 2-1		S05 1-1	M02 0-0	a02 3-0	M19 1-0	a30 1-1
18 SCUNTHORPE U	M19 1-2	a30 1-2	A22 1-1	M05 3-4	S12 1-2	a15 1-1	D26 3-2	J02 0-2	F06 3-0	O10 2-2	a16 2-1	D05 5-0	S17 1-1	F20 1-1	S03 2-0	a02 1-0	J16 2-1		S26 1-1	N07 1-1	N21 3-1	O24 3-1
19 SHEFFIELD U	O10 1-1	M19 4-1	S19 5-2	a02 1-1	D28 2-1	J23 2-0	A22 2-1	a30 2-0	A24 6-0	N07 1-0	O24 0-2	M05 3-2	S05 2-1	a19 0-0	J02 4-0	a16 0-0	O03 2-3	F13 2-1		D05 0-1	S07 1-2	N21 3-3
20 STOKE C	S30 3-3	S12 1-3	O31 1-3	S26 0-1	a09 0-1	M12 1-3	S05 2-1	D26 1-1	N28 3-1	M30 1-2	S02 2-1	S16 6-1	O17 1-1	D12 2-5	F27 1-0	J02 4-0	N14 2-3	M26 1-3	a23 1-2		A22 3-1	F06 4-2
21 SUNDERLAND	A26 1-0	A29 0-0	N14 3-2	S12 2-2	a23 1-1	M26 1-3	O17 3-1	S26 0-0	D12 1-3	F06 0-1	F20 1-4	D26 2-4	O31 1-1	F27 2-2	M12 4-0	a15 2-0	N28 1-2	a09 1-0	S16 5-1	D19 0-2		J16 4-0
22 SWANSEA T	J02 1-3	F13 2-2	a26 6-1	D28 3-0	M26 3-3	F27 5-2	a23 1-3	S17 3-1	N14 0-0	S03 2-1	a18 1-0	A22 2-1	O03 5-4	N28 3-1	D12 6-1	J23 1-1	O31 2-2	M12 3-1	a09 2-1	S19 2-2	S05 1-2	

Season 1959-60

DIVISION 3

	ACCRINGTON S	BARNSLEY	BOURNEMOUTH	BRADFORD C	BRENTFORD	BURY	CHESTERFIELD	COLCHESTER U	COVENTRY C	GRIMSBY T	HALIFAX T	MANSFIELD T	NEWPORT CO	NORWICH C	PORT VALE	Q.P.R.	READING	SHREWSBURY T	SOUTHAMPTON	SOUTHEND U	SWINDON T	TRANMERE R	WREXHAM	YORK C
1 ACCRINGTON S		J09 2-1	S07 2-1	F06 0-4	M11 3-4	N28 1-3	D05 1-3	D12 1-2	S26 0-2	J16 2-4	a09 0-5	M21 0-1	a18 0-0	O17 3-4	F27 1-3	S12 1-2	S28 0-0	A24 2-2	O31 2-2	M26 0-4	O12 3-1	D19 1-3	A29 2-2	M30 4-0
2 BARNSLEY	a23 5-0		M19 1-0	O24 2-0	A22 1-2	F13 2-2	F20 3-1	J02 2-1	M05 1-0	N07 3-3	S19 1-2	J23 2-2	a16 0-2	S16 2-0	S30 1-0	D12 2-1	D26 3-3	a19 0-0	O07 1-0	S05 4-1	S02 0-3	N21 2-0	a02 6-1	O10 1-1
3 BOURNEMOUTH	S16 3-1	N28 1-1		S26 3-2	O17 1-2	a09 2-1	a18 1-1	M12 3-2	F20 2-2	S12 4-2	m04 1-0	M26 6-0	S23 4-1	F27 0-0	S02 3-0	F06 1-1	O31 1-1	D19 2-2	a23 1-3	D12 0-0	D26 3-1	A29 2-1	J16 1-3	O07 2-0
4 BRADFORD C	S19 4-5	M12 0-0	F13 0-0		a23 0-2	O17 0-0	S05 1-0	O31 0-0	S15 1-3	D28 2-2	F27 1-2	S01 4-1	J23 6-2	N28 1-1	a09 3-1	a18 3-1	M26 0-2	M15 2-3	D12 2-0	S29 3-1	J02 1-0	O03 1-0	O13 2-2	A22 2-0
5 BRENTFORD	O24 3-0	D19 3-0	M05 1-0	m03 4-0		S08 1-1	M08 3-0	O06 2-0	M19 3-1	F20 0-2	S22 1-1	a15 1-1	a30 1-2	S26 3-4	F06 2-0	a16 1-1	J16 2-2	S12 2-1	A29 2-2	D28 3-1	a02 2-1	O10 2-1	A25 3-1	N21 1-2
6 BURY	M19 0-1	S26 0-2	N21 0-2	M05 0-0	S15 1-0		a16 1-1	A22 3-1	O10 2-1	a30 1-1	J23 2-2	S05 4-1	J30 0-1	S29 1-0	a15 3-1	O24 2-0	O06 1-0	D28 2-1	F20 1-2	J02 3-0	F06 0-3	a02 4-1	N07 3-2	S01 2-0
7 CHESTERFIELD	D26 0-3	O03 4-1	a15 4-0	J16 1-2	M26 1-0	O31 0-2		J09 1-1	S12 0-3	D19 2-2	a23 2-1	N28 0-1	J01 2-0	D12 2-1	M12 4-1	A29 0-4	F27 2-1	O17 2-2	A24 3-2	a09 1-0	S26 1-3	S21 2-0	S07 5-1	F06 2-0
8 COLCHESTER U	a30 5-1	A29 2-2	O24 1-2	a16 2-1	O12 2-1	D19 3-0	a02 1-0		J30 0-0	A24 2-2	S07 1-0	S21 3-0	N07 2-1	F20 3-0	S26 3-1	D28 2-0	S12 4-2	F06 3-2	M21 1-1	a15 2-3	N21 0-0	M05 4-0	O10 3-1	M19 2-2
9 COVENTRY C	F13 2-1	O17 2-1	O03 4-0	S07 2-2	N28 2-1	F27 0-1	J23 1-0	a23 3-1		a19 0-2	A24 0-1	A22 2-0	S19 1-1	a09 2-1	M07 1-1	S21 0-0	a30 1-1	M26 1-1	M12 4-1	O31 2-0	S05 3-1	O05 1-0	D25 5-3	J02 5-2
10 GRIMSBY T	S05 4-0	M26 2-0	J23 1-1	D26 1-3	O03 1-3	D12 2-2	A22 5-1	S01 4-1	a15 3-0		M12 3-2	O17 2-1	J02 0-1	O31 1-1	a23 1-1	O13 3-1	a09 0-1	N28 2-1	a26 3-2	F27 1-1	S15 3-0	S19 1-1	F13 3-1	S29 2-2
11 HALIFAX T	N21 0-2	F06 5-0	a02 1-0	O10 4-0	S28 1-0	S12 1-0	a28 0-1	S14 3-2	A31 2-2	O24 1-2		J02 4-2	M19 2-1	J09 0-1	D26 1-1	M05 3-1	a11 2-2	O05 1-2	S26 3-1	A22 2-1	a16 3-1	N07 0-3	a30 2-0	J16 1-2
12 MANSFIELD T	a02 4-1	S12 1-4	N07 3-4	A24 0-0	a18 0-1	J16 1-5	M19 4-1	S28 1-3	a04 2-4	M05 3-2	A29 1-1		N21 3-1	D26 3-2	a25 6-3	O10 4-3	S26 4-4	F20 1-0	F06 4-2	S14 1-1	M28 1-2	a30 0-2	O24 6-2	a16 2-0
13 NEWPORT CO	a15 1-3	O31 4-0	S28 5-2	S12 2-0	D12 4-2	a23 3-1	O12 3-1	M26 3-2	F15 2-0	A29 0-2	N28 5-1	a09 0-1		M12 1-1	O19 4-3	J16 2-3	A24 3-2	F27 1-3	M07 5-1	M21 1-1	F20 1-3	S07 2-1	F29 4-1	S26 3-2
14 NORWICH C	M05 4-0	S09 0-0	O10 2-3	M19 0-0	F13 2-1	S23 2-0	a30 3-0	O03 3-2	N21 1-4	a16 1-1	a18 3-0	D28 5-1	O24 1-0		S12 5-1	J30 1-0	A29 4-2	M30 1-1	D19 1-2	a27 4-3	N07 3-2	A26 3-0	F06 3-1	a02 1-0
15 PORT VALE	O10 2-0	S21 1-0	A24 1-0	N21 0-2	S19 3-1	a18 3-0	O24 3-1	F13 1-1	a02 0-1	F10 2-1	D28 7-0	O12 4-1	M05 2-1	J23 2-1		M19 0-0	D19 4-1	A29 0-3	S07 1-1	O03 3-1	a30 6-1	J16 1-1	a16 3-1	N07 2-0
16 Q.P.R.	J23 5-1	a30 1-0	S19 3-0	a15 5-0	O31 2-4	M12 2-0	M28 3-3	D26 3-1	S28 2-1	O05 0-0	O17 3-0	F27 2-0	S05 3-0	a23 0-0	N28 2-2		M07 2-0	a09 1-1	M26 0-1	A31 0-0	A22 2-0	F13 2-1	O03 2-1	S14 0-0
17 READING	S23 2-0	D30 3-2	a16 2-2	a27 1-0	S05 3-3	O14 0-1	O10 6-3	J23 2-1	D12 4-2	N21 1-2	O03 1-1	F13 3-2	S02 0-1	J02 0-2	A22 2-3	a02 2-0		S09 2-3	a15 2-0	S19 4-1	M05 3-0	J30 5-4	M19 0-1	O24 1-0
18 SHREWSBURY T	A31 5-0	a18 2-2	A22 0-0	a02 3-0	J23 1-1	D26 0-2	M05 2-4	S19 4-1	N07 3-2	M19 5-2	a25 2-2	O03 6-3	O10 6-2	S05 1-3	J02 2-1	N21 1-1	S14 3-2		S28 1-1	F13 1-3	O24 3-0	a16 0-0	J30 3-2	D12 4-0
19 SOUTHAMPTON	a16 5-1	O14 2-1	F24 4-3	a30 2-0	J02 2-0	O03 0-2	S02 4-3	S05 4-2	O24 5-1	a02 1-1	F13 3-2	S19 5-2	D26 2-0	A22 2-2	S16 3-2	N07 2-1	a18 1-0	S23 6-3		J23 3-1	O10 5-1	M19 1-1	N21 3-0	M05 3-1
20 SOUTHEND U	N07 6-1	F29 2-2	a30 3-0	S21 2-1	D26 2-0	A29 0-4	N21 1-2	a18 1-0	a16 1-0	O10 3-0	D19 3-0	S07 0-2	a02 3-2	O05 1-0	F22 2-1	A24 3-2	F06 2-0	S26 2-1	S12 2-4		M19 1-3	O24 7-1	M05 1-1	J30 1-1
21 SWINDON T	O07 0-1	A26 1-1	D28 2-0	A29 5-3	J09 0-0	S19 1-0	F13 1-1	a09 4-3	m04 2-0	S09 3-2	O31 1-1	a23 2-1	O03 1-0	M26 0-1	D12 2-3	D19 2-1	O17 0-4	M12 4-2	F27 0-3	N28 2-0		a18 1-1	S23 4-1	S12 1-1
22 TRANMERE R	A22 5-1	a09 2-0	J02 1-1	F29 2-3	F27 2-1	a25 2-0	S28 3-0	O17 1-1	O12 3-1	F22 2-0	M28 1-1	D12 4-2	S14 2-2	A31 0-0	S05 6-0	S26 0-3	a23 0-1	O31 3-3	N28 2-4	M12 1-0	a15 2-2		S12 4-1	D26 2-2
23 WREXHAM	J02 2-3	M09 1-0	S05 1-2	O07 4-3	S02 3-2	M26 1-1	O28 2-3	F27 1-1	D26 1-3	S26 2-1	D12 2-1	M12 3-0	A22 0-0	S19 1-2	O31 1-0	m04 1-1	N28 2-1	a23 1-1	a09 2-1	O17 3-1	S30 1-2	J23 1-0		a18 3-1
24 YORK C	O03 3-0	F27 0-0	O12 3-2	D19 1-1	a09 0-1	A24 1-0	S19 1-0	N28 2-3	A29 1-1	S21 3-3	S05 1-2	O31 2-1	F12 2-0	M16 1-2	M26 2-0	S07 2-1	M12 2-3	a30 0-1	O17 2-2	a23 2-3	J23 1-0	D28 3-0	a15 3-0	

DIVISION 4

	ALDERSHOT	BARROW	BRADFORD	CARLISLE U	CHESTER	CREWE A	CRYSTAL P	DARLINGTON	DONCASTER R	EXETER C	GATESHEAD	GILLINGHAM	HARTLEPOOLS U	MILLWALL	NORTHAMPTON T	NOTTS CO	OLDHAM A	ROCHDALE	SOUTHPORT	STOCKPORT CO	TORQUAY U	WALSALL	WATFORD	WORKINGTON
1 ALDERSHOT		A29 6-1	M12 6-1	N28 0-2	F27 3-2	D28 6-1	O17 1-0	S02 3-0	O07 1-1	M26 1-0	S21 3-2	J16 3-1	D19 3-0	F06 1-2	F20 3-0	a23 1-1	a09 2-0	J09 0-0	S12 0-0	O31 1-0	S26 1-3	a30 0-2	M16 2-2	S16 3-1
2 BARROW	J02 3-0		O17 3-3	a09 5-1	D26 3-0	S05 0-0	F27 0-1	A22 4-1	S14 1-1	O31 3-3	A31 2-2	S12 0-1	D12 2-2	S26 2-2	a25 0-1	N28 4-3	J09 2-0	S28 3-0	F06 3-1	M12 5-1	m02 1-1	a23 2-3	M26 2-1	a18 2-1
3 BRADFORD	O24 3-2	M05 2-0		A29 1-1	F20 1-1	S26 2-2	O07 3-1	M19 1-0	a16 3-3	S21 1-0	N07 4-2	O10 3-0	F06 6-2	S07 1-1	a07 3-0	J16 1-1	D19 2-0	a02 0-0	D26 3-0	a19 1-1	a30 2-2	S12 1-3	A24 1-1	N21 3-2
4 CARLISLE U	a19 0-0	N21 0-1	J02 1-3		S01 2-1	S29 4-2	A22 2-2	J30 1-0	O10 2-0	J23 0-4	a30 4-0	a02 0-1	a15 1-1	M19 3-3	M05 0-2	O06 2-0	F13 0-1	M29 1-1	N07 1-0	S05 0-4	O24 2-0	S15 1-1	S19 1-0	D26 0-1
5 CHESTER	O10 5-1	D28 3-2	O03 1-1	A26 0-1		S12 0-0	F13 0-1	M05 1-1	a02 2-0	S07 1-0	O24 4-2	F06 4-2	J16 1-1	J30 2-1	N21 1-1	D19 2-1	S23 0-0	M19 2-1	a30 2-2	O14 1-2	a16 1-1	A29 1-3	a18 0-1	N07 3-1
6 CREWE A	D26 3-2	J16 3-2	F13 4-1	S23 3-0	J23 2-1		S19 1-1	O10 5-0	N07 2-0	O14 1-1	M05 4-1	a30 1-2	A29 1-0	a16 2-0	a02 0-1	A26 2-1	a18 2-2	O24 1-3	M16 5-1	O03 4-2	N21 1-2	D19 1-5	S09 1-3	M19 2-0
7 CRYSTAL P	M05 1-1	O10 9-0	a27 1-0	D19 2-1	S26 3-4	F06 4-0		O24 2-0	N21 4-0	a15 1-0	M19 2-2	D28 3-3	S12 5-2	O28 1-2	a16 0-1	A29 1-1	S02 3-2	N07 4-0	F20 2-2	S16 3-1	J30 1-1	J16 1-2	S23 8-1	a02 0-1
8 DARLINGTON	A24 4-0	D19 3-1	O31 4-3	a23 2-1	O17 0-0	F27 1-1	M12 1-1		m04 2-2	a25 0-1	a15 2-1	A29 2-1	D28 2-0	S12 1-1	S26 3-2	D12 5-2	N28 1-3	S16 0-0	J16 5-0	M26 1-2	F06 1-0	S30 0-2	a09 0-3	O07 0-3
9 DONCASTER R	O15 1-2	S08 1-4	N28 2-0	F27 4-1	M08 2-0	M26 4-0	a09 1-2	O03 0-1		D12 0-1	F13 1-0	a15 3-0	O31 5-1	A27 0-0	A29 3-2	O17 0-4	D28 0-0	S19 2-1	S24 5-0	a23 1-0	D19 1-3	M12 1-1	S05 1-0	J23 2-0
10 EXETER C	N07 3-1	M19 2-2	S30 3-1	S12 1-3	S17 2-0	O07 2-4	a18 2-2	a02 0-0	a30 4-2		N21 2-1	O24 2-0	F20 5-0	O10 2-2	A22 1-1	F06 3-3	J16 4-3	a16 4-1	M05 1-1	S02 2-1	D28 1-0	S26 1-2	A29 2-0	J30 1-0
11 GATESHEAD	S28 4-1	A24 3-1	M26 1-2	D12 1-0	M12 0-1	O17 4-2	O31 0-2	a18 1-3	S26 5-0	a09 1-0		D19 2-2	F27 1-1	J16 1-0	F06 1-3	S07 0-0	a23 2-0	O05 1-2	A29 1-0	J09 2-1	S12 0-2	a25 3-0	N28 1-3	M28 2-1
12 GILLINGHAM	S05 3-1	J23 1-0	F27 2-0	m06 3-1	S19 3-1	D12 1-1	m04 0-0	J02 2-0	a18 2-1	M12 2-1	A22 5-4		a23 3-1	F20 3-1	S16 2-1	a09 0-1	M26 2-2	S03 2-0	S26 4-1	O17 0-2	O07 1-0	N28 2-0	O31 2-0	S30 2-2
13 HARTLEPOOLS U	A22 3-0	a30 0-1	S19 3-0	a18 1-2	S05 2-3	J02 2-0	J23 0-1	D26 1-2	M19 2-6	O03 4-3	O10 3-0	J30 3-1		N21 0-2	N07 1-4	S21 2-4	S07 2-2	M05 0-1	a16 3-2	F13 2-1	a02 4-0	A31 1-2	M23 0-0	O24 1-4
14 MILLWALL	S19 2-0	F13 3-3	S14 2-0	O31 1-1	a23 7-1	N28 1-4	D12 1-0	J23 5-2	A31 1-1	F27 2-3	S05 4-0	O03 3-3	a09 4-0		S28 2-1	M26 1-1	M12 0-1	J02 2-0	O05 2-2	M07 3-2	a15 2-0	J09 1-1	O17 2-2	A22 3-0
15 NORTHAMPTON T	O03 2-0	a11 6-0	a23 3-1	O17 2-2	a09 1-0	a28 0-0	N28 0-2	F13 3-1	J02 3-1	D19 1-1	S19 2-0	S10 2-1	M26 3-0	S21 0-3		M12 4-2	F27 8-1	J23 3-1	a19 2-2	D12 1-1	A27 3-0	O31 0-1	D28 1-2	S05 0-0
16 NOTTS CO	J30 5-3	a16 1-2	S05 0-1	O15 2-1	A22 2-1	S03 4-1	J02 7-1	a30 5-4	M05 3-4	S19 3-0	S17 4-0	N21 3-1	O01 4-0	N07 2-1	O24 2-1		O03 3-1	D26 2-1	a02 4-1	J23 3-0	M19 1-1	a18 2-1	F13 2-1	O10 2-0
17 OLDHAM A	N21 0-1	a02 1-0	A22 2-0	S26 0-1	S29 0-0	a15 2-4	A24 1-0	a16 1-3	D26 1-1	S05 1-2	J30 1-1	N07 3-1	S15 1-2	O24 1-1	O10 0-1	m03 0-3		a30 1-0	M19 0-1	J02 0-0	M05 0-2	a12 2-4	J23 0-0	F06 2-2
18 ROCHDALE	a18 2-0	S22 4-1	M15 0-1	O03 3-0	O31 0-0	M12 4-2	M26 4-0	S08 2-0	F06 2-0	N28 3-0	O13 2-0	A27 1-0	O17 2-0	A29 0-1	S12 2-2	D28 1-4	D12 2-0		D19 1-0	a09 3-0	J16 4-2	F27 0-2	a23 3-3	S26 1-1
19 SOUTHPORT	J23 0-4	S19 1-0	D28 1-1	M26 1-1	D12 3-1	a23 0-1	O03 3-1	S05 0-1	m02 1-1	O17 3-2	J02 1-0	F13 1-1	N28 2-1	a25 1-0	a15 0-4	J09 1-2	O31 1-0	A22 2-2		F27 3-0	S15 1-2	a09 1-4	M12 1-1	S01 2-2
20 STOCKPORT CO	M19 1-1	O24 1-0	a15 0-0	J16 0-0	O05 3-0	F29 1-0	S07 0-1	N07 1-0	J30 2-0	A24 1-0	a02 0-0	M05 1-1	S26 2-1	D28 2-2	a30 3-0	S12 3-1	A29 3-1	N21 2-1	O10 1-0		S21 0-1	F06 2-0	D19 4-0	a16 2-0
21 TORQUAY U	F13 2-1	O03 3-2	D12 1-1	M12 2-1	N28 1-2	a09 5-2	a23 2-1	S19 1-2	A22 2-1	D26 2-3	J23 1-0	a27 2-0	J09 3-0	a18 2-2	S02 5-3	O31 3-1	O17 4-1	S05 1-1	S09 4-0	S30 4-0		M26 2-1	F27 2-1	J02 2-1
22 WALSALL	D12 1-0	J29 2-1	J23 2-1	S10 0-1	J02 2-1	A22 3-1	S05 3-0	S22 1-0	O24 5-2	M22 2-2	D26 2-2	a16 2-3	A25 2-2	a02 2-1	M19 1-2	a19 2-2	O13 2-1	O10 4-2	N21 8-0	S19 3-1	N07 3-2		O03 3-4	M05 2-2
23 WATFORD	a02 1-3	N07 2-0	S01 1-0	F06 3-1	a15 4-2	S15 2-0	S29 4-2	N21 2-1	J16 1-2	J02 5-2	a16 5-0	M19 3-1	O13 7-2	M05 0-2	M01 3-1	S26 4-2	S12 6-0	a26 2-1	O24 2-1	A22 0-0	O10 0-1	m03 2-2		D12 3-2
24 WORKINGTON	S10 3-3	a15 1-1	a09 0-1	D29 1-0	M26 5-0	O31 5-0	F25 1-1	O15 1-1	S12 2-0	a23 2-1	O03 1-1	S24 1-1	M12 3-0	D19 4-0	J16 5-1	F27 0-1	S19 2-0	F13 2-0	A27 1-1	N28 1-1	A29 0-2	O17 0-3	a30 0-1	

LEAGUE TABLES

DIVISION 1

	P	W	D	L	F	A	W	D	L	F	A	Pts
Burnley	42	15	2	4	52	28	9	5	7	33	33	55
Wolverh'pton W	42	15	3	3	63	28	9	3	9	43	39	54
Tottenham H	42	10	6	5	43	24	11	5	5	43	26	53
W.B.A.	42	12	4	5	48	25	7	7	7	35	32	49
Sheffield W	42	12	7	2	48	20	7	4	10	32	39	49
Bolton W	42	12	5	4	37	27	8	3	10	22	24	48
Manchester U	42	13	3	5	53	30	6	4	11	49	50	45
Newcastle U	42	10	5	6	42	32	8	3	10	40	46	44
Preston N.E.	42	10	6	5	43	34	6	6	9	36	42	44
Fulham	42	12	4	5	42	28	5	6	10	31	52	44
Blackpool	42	9	6	6	32	32	6	4	11	27	39	40
Leicester C	42	8	6	7	38	32	5	7	9	28	43	39
Arsenal	42	9	5	7	39	38	6	4	11	29	42	39
West Ham U	42	12	3	6	47	33	4	3	14	28	58	38
Everton	42	13	3	5	50	20	0	8	13	23	58	37
Manchester C	42	11	2	8	47	34	6	1	14	31	50	37
Blackburn R	42	12	3	6	38	29	4	2	15	22	41	37
Chelsea	42	7	5	9	44	50	7	4	10	32	41	37
Birmingham C	42	9	5	7	37	36	4	5	12	26	44	36
Nottingham F	42	8	6	7	30	28	5	3	13	20	46	35
Leeds U	42	7	5	9	37	46	5	5	11	28	46	34
Luton T	42	6	5	10	25	29	3	7	11	25	44	30

DIVISION 2

	P	W	D	L	F	A	W	D	L	F	A	Pts
Aston Villa	42	17	3	1	62	19	8	6	7	27	24	59
Cardiff C	42	15	2	4	55	36	8	10	3	35	26	58
Liverpool	42	15	3	3	59	28	5	7	9	31	38	50
Sheffield U	42	12	5	4	43	22	7	7	7	25	29	50
Middlesbrough	42	14	5	2	56	21	5	5	11	34	43	48
Huddersfield T	42	13	3	5	44	20	6	6	9	29	32	47
Charlton A	42	12	7	2	55	28	5	6	10	35	59	47
Rotherham U	42	9	9	3	31	23	8	4	9	30	37	47
Bristol R	42	12	6	3	42	28	6	5	10	30	50	47
Leyton O	42	12	4	5	47	25	3	10	8	29	36	44
Ipswich T	42	12	5	4	48	24	7	1	13	30	44	44
Swansea T	42	12	6	3	54	32	3	4	14	28	52	40
Lincoln C	42	11	3	7	41	25	5	4	12	34	53	39
Brighton & H.A.	42	7	8	6	35	32	6	4	11	32	44	38
Scunthorpe U	42	9	7	5	38	26	4	3	14	19	45	36
Sunderland	42	8	6	7	35	29	4	6	11	17	36	36
Stoke C	42	8	3	10	40	38	6	4	11	26	45	35
Derby Co	42	9	4	8	31	28	5	3	13	30	49	35
Plymouth A	42	10	6	5	42	36	3	3	15	19	53	35
Portsmouth	42	6	6	9	36	36	4	6	11	23	41	32
Hull C	42	7	6	8	27	30	3	4	14	21	46	30
Bristol C	42	8	3	10	27	31	3	2	16	33	66	27

DIVISION 3

	P	W	D	L	F	A	W	D	L	F	A	Pts
Southampton	46	19	3	1	68	30	7	6	10	38	45	61
Norwich C	46	16	4	3	53	24	8	7	8	29	30	59
Shrewsbury T	46	12	7	4	58	34	6	9	8	39	41	52
Grimsby T	46	12	7	4	48	27	6	9	8	39	43	52
Coventry C	46	14	6	3	44	22	7	4	12	34	41	52
Brentford	46	13	6	4	46	24	8	3	12	32	37	51
Bury	46	13	4	6	36	23	8	5	10	28	28	51
Q.P.R.	46	14	7	2	45	16	4	6	13	28	38	49
Colchester U	46	15	6	2	51	22	3	5	15	32	52	47
Bournemouth	46	12	8	3	47	27	5	5	13	25	45	47
Reading	46	13	3	7	49	34	5	7	11	35	43	46
Southend U	46	15	3	5	49	28	4	5	14	27	46	46
Newport Co	46	15	2	6	59	36	5	4	14	21	43	46
Port Vale	46	16	4	3	51	19	3	4	16	29	60	46
Halifax T	46	13	3	7	42	27	5	7	11	28	45	46
Swindon T	46	12	6	5	39	30	7	2	14	30	48	46
Barnsley	46	13	6	4	45	25	2	8	13	20	41	44
Chesterfield	46	13	3	7	41	31	5	4	14	30	53	43
Bradford C	46	10	7	6	39	28	5	5	13	27	46	42
Tranmere R	46	11	8	4	50	29	3	5	15	22	46	41
York C	46	11	5	7	38	26	2	7	14	19	47	38
Mansfield T	46	11	4	8	55	48	4	2	17	26	64	36
Wrexham	46	12	5	6	39	30	2	3	18	29	71	36
Accrington S	46	4	5	14	31	53	7	0	16	26	70	27

DIVISION 4

	P	W	D	L	F	A	W	D	L	F	A	Pts
Walsall	46	14	5	4	57	33	14	4	5	45	27	65
Notts Co	46	19	1	3	66	27	7	7	9	41	42	60
Torquay U	46	17	3	3	56	27	9	5	9	28	31	60
Watford	46	17	2	4	62	28	7	7	9	30	39	57
Millwall	46	12	8	3	54	28	6	9	8	30	33	53
Northampton T	46	13	6	4	50	22	9	3	11	35	41	53
Gillingham	46	17	4	2	47	21	4	6	13	27	48	52
Crystal Palace	46	12	6	5	61	27	7	6	10	23	37	50
Exeter C	46	13	7	3	50	30	6	4	13	30	40	49
Stockport Co	46	15	6	2	35	10	4	5	14	23	44	49
Bradford P.A.	46	12	10	1	48	25	5	5	13	22	43	49
Rochdale	46	15	4	4	46	19	3	6	14	19	41	46
Aldershot	46	14	5	4	50	22	4	4	15	27	52	45
Crewe A	46	14	3	6	51	31	4	6	13	28	57	45
Darlington	46	11	6	6	40	30	6	3	14	23	43	43
Workington	46	10	8	5	41	20	4	6	13	27	40	42
Doncaster R	46	13	3	7	40	23	3	7	13	29	53	42
Barrow	46	11	8	4	52	29	4	3	16	25	58	41
Carlisle U	46	9	6	8	28	28	6	5	12	23	38	41
Chester C	46	10	8	5	37	26	4	4	15	22	51	40
Southport	46	9	7	7	30	32	1	7	15	18	60	34
Gateshead	46	12	3	8	37	27	0	6	17	21	59	33
Oldham A	46	5	7	11	20	30	3	5	15	21	53	28
Hartlepool U	46	9	2	12	40	41	1	5	17	19	68	27

Football League Records

Top scorers: Div 1, J.Greaves (Chelsea) 41 goals; Div 2, R.Crawford (Ipswich Town) 39 goals; Div 3, A.Richards (Walsall) 36 goals; Div 4, T.Bly (Peterborough United) 52 goals.

Gateshead failed to gain re-election, Peterborough United were elected in their place.

Danny Blanchflower, creative right-half for Spurs and Northern Ireland. Blanchflower skippered Tottenham to their historic League and Cup double in 1960-61.

DIVISION 1

	ARSENAL	ASTON VILLA	BIRMINGHAM C	BLACKBURN R	BLACKPOOL	BOLTON W	BURNLEY	CARDIFF C	CHELSEA	EVERTON	FULHAM	LEICESTER C	MANCHESTER C	MANCHESTER U	NEWCASTLE U	NOTTINGHAM F	PRESTON N.E.	SHEFFIELD W	TOTTENHAM H	W.B.A.	WEST HAM U	WOLVERHAMPTON W
1 ARSENAL		O15 2-1	S06 2-0	M11 0-0	a08 1-0	D10 5-1	D17 2-5	F11 2-3	N12 1-4	N26 3-2	a03 4-2	F25 1-3	J14 5-4	O29 2-1	S17 5-0	A27 3-0	A23 1-0	D26 1-1	S10 2-3	O01 1-0	M25 0-0	a22 1-5
2 ASTON VILLA	M04 2-2		O22 6-2	J21 2-2	D31 2-2	a04 4-0	N05 2-0	S12 2-1	A20 3-2	S03 3-2	N19 2-1	O01 1-3	D03 5-1	S17 3-1	O08 2-0	a01 1-2	a15 1-0	a29 4-1	F11 1-2	M28 0-1	A29 2-1	D24 0-2
3 BIRMINGHAM C	S14 2-0	M11 1-1		M25 1-1	a22 0-2	D17 2-2	a27 0-1	a03 2-1	O15 1-0	D10 2-4	J14 1-0	N26 0-2	M22 3-2	N12 3-1	D26 2-1	S24 3-1	S10 1-3	A27 1-1	a08 2-3	A31 3-1	F25 4-2	O29 1-2
4 BLACKBURN R	O22 2-4	S10 4-1	N05 2-0		D27 2-0	S24 3-1	O08 1-4	N19 2-2	S19 3-1	M31 1-3	D03 5-1	J14 1-1	M18 4-1	D17 1-2	a29 2-4	A24 4-1	M04 1-0	a01 1-1	A27 1-4	a15 2-1	M20 4-1	F04 2-1
5 BLACKPOOL	N19 1-1	A27 5-3	D03 1-2	D24 2-0		S10 0-1	M21 0-0	N05 6-1	S24 1-4	S05 1-4	O08 2-5	D17 5-1	a29 3-3	M31 2-0	a15 2-1	O22 4-0	F18 0-1	M15 0-1	A22 1-3	a01 0-1	F04 3-0	M04 5-2
6 BOLTON W	a01 1-1	a03 3-0	A20 2-2	F11 0-0	J21 3-1		N19 3-5	M04 3-0	S03 4-1	S17 3-4	O22 0-3	D24 2-0	N05 3-1	O01 1-1	D03 2-1	a15 3-1	a29 1-1	M18 0-1	S07 1-2	O08 0-1	D31 3-1	A24 0-2
7 BURNLEY	A20 3-2	M25 1-1	S17 2-1	F25 1-1	O29 1-2	a08 2-0		S03 1-2	M11 4-4	D26 1-3	O01 5-0	D10 3-2	A30 1-3	O15 5-3	D31 5-3	M31 4-1	S06 5-0	F11 3-4	a22 4-2	J21 0-1	a18 2-2	N12 5-3
8 CARDIFF C	S24 1-0	S07 1-1	M31 0-2	a08 1-1	M24 0-2	O15 0-1	J14 2-1		D10 2-1	N12 1-1	D17 2-0	O28 2-1	F04 3-3	N26 3-0	F22 3-2	S10 1-3	A27 2-0	A24 0-1	M11 3-2	D26 3-1	a22 1-1	F25 3-2
9 CHELSEA	a15 3-1	D17 2-4	M04 3-2	S07 5-2	F11 2-2	J14 1-1	O22 2-6	a01 6-1		O01 3-3	F04 2-1	A24 1-3	N19 6-3	D24 1-2	N05 4-2	a29 4-3	M18 1-1	a26 0-2	a03 2-3	D03 7-1	S10 3-2	A27 3-3
10 EVERTON	a29 4-1	M22 1-2	a01 1-0	a03 2-2	S14 1-0	F04 1-2	D27 0-3	a15 5-1	F18 1-1		M04 1-0	A27 3-1	O24 4-2	A24 4-0	N19 5-0	M18 1-0	O08 0-0	D03 4-2	D17 1-3	N05 1-1	S24 4-1	S10 3-1
11 FULHAM	M31 2-2	a08 1-1	S03 2-1	a22 1-1	F25 4-3	M11 2-2	F22 0-1	A20 2-2	S17 3-2	O15 2-3		N12 4-2	D26 1-0	D10 4-4	A31 4-3	S13 1-0	S24 2-0	J21 1-6	M25 0-0	D31 1-2	O29 1-1	N26 1-3
12 LEICESTER C	O08 2-1	a19 3-1	a29 3-2	S03 2-4	A20 1-1	D26 2-0	a01 2-2	a10 3-0	A31 1-3	D31 4-1	a15 1-2		a26 1-2	J21 6-0	F11 5-3	D03 1-1	N04 5-2	N19 2-1	S17 1-2	O22 2-2	a03 5-1	S14 2-0
13 MANCHESTER C	S03 0-0	a22 4-1	O01 2-1	O29 4-0	a19 1-1	M25 0-0	A24 2-1	S17 4-2	a08 2-1	M11 2-1	D24 3-2	O15 3-1		M04 1-3	J21 3-3	D17 1-2	M31 2-3	S07 1-1	F25 0-1	F11 3-0	N12 1-2	D10 2-4
14 MANCHESTER U	M18 1-1	F04 1-1	a15 4-1	A20 1-3	a03 2-0	F18 3-1	a12 6-0	a29 3-3	D26 6-0	A31 4-0	a01 3-1	S10 1-1	D31 5-1		O22 3-2	O24 2-1	D03 1-0	N05 0-0	J16 2-0	N19 3-0	S14 6-1	S24 1-3
15 NEWCASTLE U	F04 3-3	F25 2-1	D24 2-2	N26 3-1	N12 4-3	a22 4-1	A27 0-1	O01 5-0	M25 1-6	a08 0-4	A24 7-2	S24 1-3	S10 1-3	M11 1-1		J14 2-2	D17 0-0	M31 0-1	O29 3-4	S14 3-2	D10 5-5	O15 4-4
16 NOTTINGHAM F	D31 3-5	D10 2-0	F11 1-0	A31 1-1	M11 0-0	N12 2-2	a03 3-1	J21 2-1	N26 2-1	O29 1-2	S21 4-2	a22 2-2	A20 2-2	F25 3-2	S03 0-2		D24 2-0	O01 1-2	O15 0-4	S17 1-2	a08 1-1	M25 1-1
17 PRESTON N.E.	A30 2-0	N12 1-1	J21 2-3	O15 2-0	O01 1-0	a18 0-0	S13 2-3	D31 1-1	O29 0-2	F25 1-0	F11 2-0	M25 0-0	a03 1-1	a22 2-4	A20 2-3	D26 0-1		S17 2-2	D10 0-1	S03 2-1	M11 4-0	a08 1-2
18 SHEFFIELD W	D23 1-1	N26 1-2	D31 2-0	D10 5-4	O15 4-0	O29 2-0	S24 3-1	A31 2-0	F25 1-0	a22 1-2	S10 2-0	a08 2-2	S14 3-1	M25 5-1	a03 1-1	F21 1-0	F04 5-1		N12 2-1	A20 1-0	S03 1-0	M11 0-0
19 TOTTENHAM H	J21 4-2	S24 6-2	N19 6-0	D31 5-2	A31 3-1	S14 3-1	D03 4-4	N02 3-2	M31 4-2	A20 2-0	N05 5-1	F04 2-3	O10 1-1	S03 4-1	M22 1-2	a26 1-0	a01 5-0	a17 2-1		a29 1-2	D24 2-0	F22 1-1
20 W.B.A.	F18 2-3	O29 0-2	A24 1-2	N12 1-2	D10 3-1	F25 3-2	S10 0-2	D27 1-1	a22 3-0	M25 3-0	A27 2-4	M11 1-0	S24 6-3	a08 1-1	S05 6-0	F04 1-2	J14 3-1	D17 2-2	N26 1-3		O15 1-0	a03 2-1
21 WEST HAM U	N05 6-0	A22 5-2	O08 4-3	O01 3-2	S17 3-3	A27 2-1	a29 1-2	D03 2-0	J21 3-1	F11 4-0	M18 1-2	M31 1-0	a15 1-1	S05 2-1	a01 1-1	N19 2-4	O22 5-2	J14 1-1	D26 0-3	M04 1-2		D17 5-0
22 WOLVERHAMPTON W	D03 5-3	D26 3-2	M18 5-1	S17 0-0	S03 1-0	A31 3-1	a15 2-1	O08 2-2	D31 6-1	J21 4-1	a29 2-4	S07 3-2	a01 1-0	F11 2-1	M08 2-1	N05 5-3	N19 3-0	O22 4-1	O01 0-4	J28 4-2	A20 4-2	

Terry Bly, the prolific scorer who helped former Midland League club Peterborough United make such a great impression as members of the Football League.

DIVISION 2

	BRIGHTON & HA	BRISTOL R	CHARLTON A	DERBY CO	HUDDERSFIELD T	IPSWICH T	LEEDS U	LEYTON O	LINCOLN C	LIVERPOOL	LUTON T	MIDDLESBROUGH	NORWICH C	PLYMOUTH A	PORTSMOUTH	ROTHERHAM U	SCUNTHORPE U	SHEFFIELD U	SOUTHAMPTON	STOKE C	SUNDERLAND	SWANSEA T
1 BRIGHTON & H.A.		A27 6-1	O15 3-5	D17 3-2	a22 2-1	S07 2-4	S24 2-1	A24 1-1	a08 1-0	J14 3-1	N12 1-0	F18 0-1	F25 2-2	M31 2-0	N26 2-2	S10 1-0	D27 1-1	M11 0-0	F04 0-1	O29 0-1	D10 1-2	M25 0-0
2 BRISTOL R	D31 0-1		N26 3-1	F11 1-1	O29 1-2	S03 1-1	A29 4-4	S17 4-2	O15 3-1	a04 4-3	F25 4-1	A20 2-3	a08 3-1	N12 2-5	M11 2-0	S12 2-1	J21 3-3	a22 3-1	M20 4-2	D10 1-0	M25 1-0	O01 4-2
3 CHARLTON A	M04 3-1	a01 2-1		D03 3-1	M31 2-3	O08 0-2	a29 2-0	M18 2-0	F11 3-0	N19 1-3	S17 4-1	O22 6-6	A31 0-1	D26 6-4	O01 7-4	a15 4-3	A20 1-1	D31 2-3	N05 1-3	S03 3-1	S07 2-2	J21 6-2
4 DERBY CO	A20 4-1	S24 1-1	a22 2-3		M25 1-1	a24 1-4	D24 2-3	J21 3-1	M11 3-1	F18 1-4	O15 4-1	A31 1-0	N26 0-0	a08 4-1	O29 6-2	a03 3-0	S03 2-5	D10 2-0	S14 2-2	S17 1-1	N12 1-1	F25 2-3
5 HUDDERSFIELD T	D03 0-1	a29 4-0	a03 2-2	N05 1-3		a01 1-3	J21 0-1	a15 1-0	D31 4-1	O22 2-4	A20 1-1	M18 1-0	F21 1-1	S24 1-5	S03 3-3	M04 0-1	N19 1-2	S14 0-1	O08 3-1	D26 0-0	F04 4-2	A31 3-1
6 IPSWICH T	S13 4-0	J14 3-2	F25 2-1	A27 4-1	N26 4-2		F18 4-0	D17 6-2	N12 3-1	S10 1-0	M25 0-1	M31 3-1	D27 4-1	D10 3-1	a08 2-2	F04 1-1	A30 2-0	O15 0-1	S24 3-3	M11 2-1	a22 4-0	O29 0-3
7 LEEDS U	F10 3-2	A24 1-1	O29 1-0	D27 3-3	S10 1-4	O01 2-5		S07 1-3	a22 7-0	D17 2-2	M08 1-2	S17 4-4	M11 1-0	O15 2-1	D10 0-0	A27 2-0	a25 2-2	M25 1-2	J14 3-0	N12 0-1	F25 2-4	a08 2-2
8 LEYTON O	A31 2-1	F04 3-2	D10 1-1	S10 2-1	M21 2-0	A20 1-3	S14 0-1		O29 1-2	S24 1-3	M11 2-1	M14 1-1	a22 1-0	M07 1-1	M25 2-1	F20 2-1	D31 2-1	S03 1-4	M29 1-1	a10 3-1	a08 0-1	O15 2-2
9 LINCOLN C	N19 2-1	M04 1-2	S24 2-2	O22 3-4	A27 0-0	a15 1-4	D03 2-3	a29 2-0		O08 1-2	D27 1-1	a01 5-2	F04 1-4	S10 3-1	D17 2-3	A24 0-1	N05 0-2	F22 0-5	M18 0-3	M31 1-1	J14 1-2	S14 2-0
10 LIVERPOOL	S03 2-0	M31 3-0	a08 2-1	O01 1-0	M11 3-1	J21 1-1	A20 2-0	F11 5-0	F25 2-0		S07 2-2	D31 3-4	N12 2-1	M24 1-1	O15 3-3	D26 2-1	S17 3-2	N26 4-2	A31 0-1	a22 3-0	O29 1-1	D10 4-0
11 LUTON T	a15 3-1	O08 4-2	a26 4-1	M04 1-1	D17 1-0	N05 3-2	a01 1-1	O22 0-1	D26 3-0	S14 2-1		N19 6-1	S10 0-2	J14 3-2	A24 1-0	M18 2-1	a29 0-0	S24 1-4	D03 4-1	F23 4-1	A27 3-3	M31 2-2
12 MIDDLESBROUGH	O01 2-2	D17 1-1	M11 2-2	A24 1-2	D10 2-1	a03 3-1	F04 3-0	D26 2-0	N26 1-1	A27 1-1	a08 2-1		O15 2-0	F25 3-1	a22 3-0	J14 2-2	S21 1-3	O29 3-1	S10 5-0	M25 1-0	S24 1-0	N12 3-1
13 NORWICH C	O08 2-2	N19 2-1	A24 4-0	a01 0-2	O01 2-0	D26 0-3	O22 3-2	D03 3-2	S17 5-1	a15 2-1	J21 2-1	M04 4-1		S07 1-0	F11 3-1	N05 3-1	M18 0-1	A20 1-1	a29 5-0	D31 1-0	a03 3-0	S03 0-0
14 PLYMOUTH A	a03 1-2	a15 5-0	D27 6-4	N19 4-2	F11 2-1	M18 1-2	M04 3-1	a01 3-2	J21 1-1	N05 0-4	S03 1-1	O08 3-3	S14 3-0		S17 5-1	a29 3-3	D03 3-1	A31 2-0	O22 1-3	A20 3-1	O01 1-0	D31 1-0
15 PORTSMOUTH	a01 4-0	a19 3-0	F18 1-1	a29 3-2	J14 1-3	N19 1-0	M18 3-1	N05 1-2	A20 3-0	M04 2-2	A31 3-2	J28 0-3	S24 3-0	F04 0-2		O08 2-2	a15 2-2	a03 1-2	D31 1-1	S07 1-0	S10 2-1	D27 1-1
16 ROTHERHAM U	a18 5-2	S07 4-0	N12 2-3	a04 1-1	O15 2-2	S17 1-1	D31 1-3	O01 2-1	A29 2-0	D27 1-0	D10 5-2	S03 1-2	M25 0-2	O29 0-0	F25 1-0		F11 4-0	a08 1-2	A20 1-0	N26 0-0	M11 0-0	a22 3-3
17 SCUNTHORPE U	D23 2-2	S10 2-1	a11 0-0	J14 1-2	a08 0-1	A25 4-0	a03 3-2	A27 2-2	M25 3-1	F04 2-3	O29 1-0	S15 1-1	D10 2-1	a22 2-0	N12 5-1	S24 1-1		F25 1-1	F18 2-0	O15 1-1	N26 3-3	M11 1-2
18 SHEFFIELD U	O22 2-1	D03 2-3	A27 1-0	a19 3-1	S06 3-1	M07 1-3	N05 3-2	J14 4-1	O01 2-1	a01 1-1	F11 2-1	a29 4-1	D17 1-1	A23 3-0	S20 3-1	N19 3-1	O08 2-0		a15 2-1	J21 4-1	D27 0-1	S17 3-0
19 SOUTHAMPTON	S17 4-2	D26 4-2	M25 1-2	S07 5-1	F25 4-2	F11 1-1	S03 2-4	a03 1-1	D10 2-3	A24 4-1	a22 3-2	J21 3-2	O29 2-2	M11 1-1	A27 5-1	D17 3-2	O01 4-2	N12 0-1		a08 0-1	O15 3-2	N26 5-0
20 STOKE C	a29 0-2	M18 2-0	J16 5-3	M20 2-1	D24 2-2	O22 2-4	a15 0-0	O08 1-2	a03 0-0	m03 3-1	O01 3-0	N05 1-1	A27 1-1	D17 9-0	S12 1-0	a01 1-4	M04 2-0	S10 2-0	N19 1-2		A22 0-0	F11 1-3
21 SUNDERLAND	M18 2-1	N05 2-0	S14 2-2	a15 1-2	S17 1-2	D03 2-0	O08 2-3	N19 4-1	S03 2-2	a29 1-1	D31 7-1	F11 2-0	M31 0-3	F22 2-1	J21 4-1	O22 1-1	a01 2-0	D26 1-1	a17 3-1	A31 4-0		A20 2-1
22 SWANSEA T	N05 2-3	F28 2-1	S10 3-3	O08 2-1	A23 2-0	a29 2-1	N19 3-2	M04 1-0	S06 1-2	M18 2-0	a03 3-1	a15 3-2	J14 4-1	A27 1-2	D26 4-0	M14 2-1	O24 2-2	F04 3-0	a01 4-1	S24 0-0	D17 3-3	

Season 1960-61

DIVISION 3

	BARNSLEY	BOURNEMOUTH	BRADFORD C	BRENTFORD	BRISTOL C	BURY	CHESTERFIELD	COLCHESTER U	COVENTRY C	GRIMSBY T	HALIFAX T	HULL C	NEWPORT CO	NOTTS CO	PORT VALE	Q.P.R.	READING	SHREWSBURY T	SOUTHEND U	SWINDON T	TORQUAY U	TRANMERE R	WALSALL	WATFORD
1 BARNSLEY		S17 2-3	F11 5-2	O22 1-1	D31 2-0	D03 3-1	a15 3-1	S14 3-0	A20 4-1	D26 3-2	a03 1-1	S28 1-0	a24 1-3	J21 5-2	a01 5-1	S03 3-3	A31 1-1	m03 4-2	N19 2-1	M18 2-1	a12 1-0	O08 2-1	a29 2-2	M22 0-1
2 BOURNEMOUTH	F04 1-2		S10 2-2	O08 0-1	A31 2-2	N19 0-3	a01 1-0	F18 4-4	S28 2-1	O05 2-1	a29 1-2	S12 2-2	S24 2-2	D31 1-3	M18 1-1	A20 1-0	D27 2-0	D03 2-2	J28 3-2	M04 2-1	O22 1-3	J14 2-1	a15 0-3	M31 0-1
3 BRADFORD C	S24 1-4	F14 3-1		M04 3-1	A20 2-0	a15 0-1	N19 3-2	M07 0-1	A30 4-1	S13 1-3	F04 2-2	D26 0-0	F18 1-2	S03 2-2	F28 3-3	D31 1-1	M23 2-1	a29 1-1	a01 2-1	O22 2-1	M18 0-3	a03 1-1	M14 1-2	O08 2-2
4 BRENTFORD	M11 0-0	a22 2-2	O15 2-2		D10 2-0	S17 1-5	F11 2-2	M25 0-0	F25 1-1	N12 0-1	D31 2-0	a08 2-2	O29 2-4	a03 3-0	a25 0-0	S27 2-0	m02 2-1	S03 4-0	O01 1-1	D23 2-1	S06 2-3	A20 4-1	J21 3-1	A23 2-1
5 BRISTOL C	A27 4-0	A23 1-0	D17 1-2	a29 3-0		M18 1-2	O22 3-0	S10 5-0	O04 2-0	F04 2-1	N19 3-2	S24 1-2	J14 3-0	S20 2-1	O08 3-4	D26 1-1	F18 2-0	a01 0-0	M04 2-0	S06 1-1	M31 2-2	a15 2-0	F21 2-0	M14 4-1
6 BURY	F25 2-1	a08 1-1	J07 2-2	F04 1-0	O29 1-0		A30 3-3	S20 4-0	M11 1-0	a04 2-0	O04 4-1	a22 3-0	D10 4-1	N12 7-0	A27 3-1	M25 1-0	O15 3-0	J02 3-1	M21 2-0	S10 3-0	F14 6-0	F18 3-0	D26 3-4	S24 0-2
7 CHESTERFIELD	M27 5-1	N12 0-1	a08 4-1	S24 1-1	M11 3-0	A22 2-2		D10 2-3	O15 4-1	D17 2-3	S05 3-0	M31 1-2	F25 1-0	M25 3-1	J14 0-0	O29 0-1	a22 2-2	D26 2-3	A27 0-3	F04 1-1	S10 2-0	J02 1-1	S26 1-2	F18 2-0
8 COLCHESTER U	S05 4-2	O01 0-1	a24 2-4	J28 2-4	J21 0-1	S26 0-2	a29 4-3		S03 4-3	A22 1-1	M04 3-1	A20 4-0	D26 1-1	F11 1-2	a15 2-0	S17 0-1	D31 2-2	O08 1-1	D03 2-0	a01 3-1	N19 3-3	O22 0-3	M31 0-4	M18 1-4
9 COVENTRY C	D17 5-2	S19 1-0	A22 2-2	D02 2-0	a24 2-1	O22 1-2	M03 3-1	J14 2-0		S10 0-0	a01 2-0	F04 4-0	A27 4-1	D26 2-2	a04 1-1	S05 4-4	S24 2-1	J30 3-2	O08 3-0	a28 1-1	F20 5-1	N19 4-1	M18 1-2	a14 0-1
10 GRIMSBY T	D20 3-2	a25 0-1	S06 1-0	a01 0-0	S17 5-2	M31 2-2	A20 0-0	A30 2-1	a18 2-3		O22 6-1	D31 2-0	S20 2-1	O01 1-1	D03 0-5	F11 3-1	S03 3-1	M04 0-2	a29 1-0	N28 3-2	a15 4-2	M18 4-1	O08 3-1	J28 1-3
11 HALIFAX T	a10 1-0	D10 2-1	S17 3-2	A27 1-0	a08 2-1	a24 0-2	S12 2-1	O15 2-1	N12 2-2	M11 0-0		O29 3-0	a22 2-1	F25 0-1	S26 3-3	a17 1-1	M25 1-0	F11 1-1	D24 6-2	D17 1-1	A22 3-2	S10 5-0	O01 1-0	J14 0-0
12 HULL C	S19 2-0	S05 2-0	D27 3-0	N19 3-0	F13 3-3	O08 0-1	a03 2-2	D17 1-1	S17 1-1	A27 2-3	M18 4-2		A22 5-1	O03 3-1	a29 2-2	O01 3-1	a20 1-0	O22 3-1	J14 0-1	a15 0-0	D03 2-3	J28 4-2	M04 2-1	a01 3-2
13 NEWPORT CO	M13 2-3	F11 2-0	O01 1-0	M18 0-1	S03 4-1	a29 0-0	D05 5-1	D22 3-2	M20 3-3	S26 1-1	O08 1-1	A29 3-1		S17 2-2	F13 2-1	J23 1-3	A20 5-2	a03 1-1	a15 1-2	J28 2-0	a01 2-2	M04 1-0	S15 4-2	M06 5-1
14 NOTTS CO	S10 5-1	A27 3-2	J14 2-1	a04 0-0	S29 3-0	a01 0-3	J28 1-0	S24 4-2	D27 3-0	F18 0-1	M23 1-1	a27 2-1	F04 6-0		O22 2-2	A25 2-1	S08 4-2	a15 2-1	M18 1-2	O08 1-0	M04 0-1	a29 4-1	N19 3-1	D17 3-1
15 PORT VALE	N12 2-0	O29 3-0	M25 2-4	O03 3-2	a22 1-1	D31 4-3	S03 7-1	F06 3-0	M31 3-1	F25 3-2	S19 2-3	D10 4-1	a08 3-1	M11 1-3		O15 0-1	S17 1-1	A29 4-1	J21 4-0	F18 4-1	S24 0-3	D26 5-0	A20 1-1	S05 3-0
16 Q.P.R.	J14 4-2	D17 3-1	A27 1-0	S19 0-0	D27 1-1	J28 3-1	M18 1-2	F04 3-2	S12 2-1	S24 2-0	a15 5-1	F18 2-1	S10 2-0	A29 2-0	M04 1-0		O03 5-2	N19 1-1	O22 2-1	M31 3-1	O08 3-3	D03 9-2	a01 1-0	a29 2-1
17 READING	A24 0-1	D26 4-3	S21 3-1	a14 4-0	O01 1-1	M04 1-3	O08 2-0	A27 2-1	F11 0-0	J14 3-1	J28 1-1	S10 2-4	D17 2-3	S14 2-0	F04 2-1	a26 3-1		M18 2-1	a03 3-0	D03 1-1	a29 5-1	a01 1-2	O22 3-2	N19 1-1
18 SHREWSBURY T	O01 1-2	F25 2-1	a12 2-0	J14 3-0	N12 4-2	S07 2-1	D27 4-2	a22 2-2	M25 2-1	O15 2-1	S24 1-1	M11 0-0	a17 5-0	M08 4-0	A24 1-1	a08 4-1	O29 6-1		S21 2-2	A27 1-1	D17 2-1	F04 1-2	a26 1-2	S10 2-2
19 SOUTHEND U	a08 2-0	M25 0-0	N12 0-0	F18 1-1	O15 1-0	A20 0-3	D31 1-1	F25 2-1	a22 4-1	D10 1-1	D26 2-2	S03 3-1	J07 4-2	O29 3-1	S10 2-1	M11 0-0	a04 0-1	S26 1-1		S24 0-2	F04 3-2	S12 1-2	A29 1-2	O03 6-1
20 SWINDON T	a19 1-0	O15 0-1	M11 4-0	J07 1-1	O19 3-1	J21 4-0	S17 2-0	N12 0-2	D10 1-2	a08 3-0	A20 1-1	a12 1-1	M25 2-0	a22 1-0	O01 6-0	a03 1-0	F25 1-1	D31 2-2	F11 1-1		a26 3-1	A31 1-0	S03 1-0	S28 1-2
21 TORQUAY U	M25 1-1	M11 0-1	O29 2-1	S14 1-1	a03 0-0	S03 1-1	J21 3-0	a08 1-1	O01 3-0	F06 0-0	S01 1-1	F25 1-2	N12 0-0	O15 2-2	F11 1-1	a22 1-6	D10 4-2	A20 2-0	S17 2-1	O05 1-1		S22 5-2	D31 3-0	D23 2-2
22 TRANMERE R	a22 2-1	S03 4-3	M31 1-0	D19 2-0	F27 3-2	O01 1-7	a24 1-1	M11 7-2	a08 2-0	O29 3-6	J21 6-2	M24 1-0	O15 2-4	D10 2-3	D27 3-3	F25 1-2	N12 1-1	S17 4-2	S05 2-1	A22 2-2	S26 2-2		F11 1-4	A27 0-2
23 WALSALL	D10 1-0	J09 2-0	F25 4-0	S10 4-0	M25 4-0	D23 1-0	S20 2-1	a03 3-0	O28 1-1	a22 2-1	F18 0-0	O15 1-0	S06 2-2	a08 2-1	D17 6-2	N12 4-3	M11 2-2	O03 3-2	A23 5-1	M21 2-1	A27 3-0	S24 3-1		F04 5-2
24 WATFORD	O15 1-2	a03 0-1	a22 2-2	A30 6-1	F25 0-1	F11 1-1	O01 3-1	O29 2-2	a11 7-2	M25 2-0	S03 4-3	N12 2-2	M11 4-1	A20 2-2	S13 0-0	D10 0-3	a08 2-0	J21 3-1	a25 3-0	S20 1-0	D27 3-0	D31 2-2	S17 2-0	

DIVISION 4

	ACCRINGTON S	ALDERSHOT	BARROW	BRADFORD	CARLISLE U	CHESTER	CREWE A	CRYSTAL P	DARLINGTON	DONCASTER R	EXETER C	GILLINGHAM	HARTLEPOOLS U	MANSFIELD T	MILLWALL	NORTHAMPTON T	OLDHAM A	PETERBOROUGH U	ROCHDALE	SOUTHPORT	STOCKPORT CO	WORKINGTON	WREXHAM	YORK C
1 ACCRINGTON S		F18 1-0	S26 0-0	D24 1-2	M11 1-0	S10 2-0	J14 1-3	D17 2-3	D10 2-2	a03 2-2	a08 0-1	S12 3-0	F25 3-0	M25 1-4	A29 3-3	O03 3-2	S24 5-1	a11 3-2	O29 2-0	a22 2-1	N12 4-1	F04 1-2	O14 0-3	a19 2-0
2 ALDERSHOT	O01 3-1		S17 2-1	S03 3-0	a22 2-1	S07 3-2	D27 5-0	M25 2-1	O29 1-3	N12 5-0	F25 3-1	J21 0-1	a08 4-0	A20 2-0	F11 0-2	D31 2-2	A31 4-0	O15 1-1	D10 3-0	M11 1-0	a03 3-2	S28 0-0	M27 0-0	a26 6-1
3 BARROW	S19 1-1	F04 2-0		N26 5-0	M25 0-2	A27 3-0	D17 3-4	F25 0-3	a03 1-1	O15 2-1	a22 1-1	a17 0-1	M11 2-1	J07 1-1	S05 2-1	S24 1-0	S10 1-2	D10 2-1	N12 1-0	D27 0-1	m01 3-1	J14 0-4	O29 1-1	A22 1-1
4 BRADFORD	m01 2-2	J14 1-0	O01 4-0		a08 0-0	A22 1-0	S19 2-0	M11 3-1	O15 1-0	O29 1-1	S17 5-2	F11 0-0	M25 1-3	a22 2-1	a24 2-1	S10 1-3	A27 5-1	a20 1-0	J07 2-1	F25 1-0	D10 4-2	D17 4-0	N12 3-1	S05 3-3
5 CARLISLE U	O22 3-1	D03 2-2	J28 1-0	N19 2-2		M31 3-1	O08 0-1	F04 2-0	S10 4-4	S24 2-1	D17 2-2	J02 1-3	F18 2-2	S27 3-1	M18 1-2	a15 2-1	a29 3-0	A27 3-3	S06 1-2	J14 1-0	A23 1-4	D27 2-4	a11 1-0	M04 1-1
6 CHESTER	J21 2-3	S14 2-0	D31 0-0	A31 3-1	a03 3-2		F11 0-0	J07 3-0	a08 0-3	a22 1-2	O29 4-4	A20 2-2	D10 1-2	O15 3-3	S03 1-4	M08 0-2	D26 3-1	M25 1-2	F25 3-1	N12 1-0	M11 0-0	N26 2-2	O01 1-0	S17 2-1
7 CREWE A	S03 0-1	D26 2-1	A20 0-1	S28 1-1	F25 3-0	S24 5-2		a22 1-2	a19 1-1	D10 1-1	M25 2-0	A31 2-1	S17 3-0	M11 1-2	D31 2-2	S07 0-2	O05 2-1	N12 3-1	O15 3-0	a08 0-1	O29 4-1	F18 1-2	M31 2-1	J21 1-5
8 CRYSTAL P	A20 9-2	a19 2-1	O08 4-2	O22 4-1	S17 1-1	J28 5-1	D03 0-0		A24 3-2	D31 5-1	D27 0-0	M04 2-0	S03 2-2	O01 4-1	M31 0-2	M18 2-3	a01 2-1	S07 0-2	F11 4-1	S28 5-0	a26 2-1	N19 4-2	J21 3-2	a29 1-0
9 DARLINGTON	a29 3-2	M18 2-2	M31 2-3	M04 0-0	J21 0-0	N19 5-1	a15 0-1	A31 0-1		A20 1-0	a24 3-0	O08 2-2	D31 4-0	F11 3-2	S19 5-2	O22 1-1	J28 0-1	D26 2-2	S17 1-0	S14 1-0	O01 2-0	a01 1-1	S03 1-2	D03 2-1
10 DONCASTER R	M31 1-0	a01 3-1	M04 3-0	M18 2-0	F11 1-0	D03 2-1	a29 6-0	A27 1-5	D17 4-0		S06 2-1	O22 2-3	J21 5-3	a25 2-3	O08 3-0	J28 0-2	N19 2-1	S20 1-2	O01 3-2	A23 0-1	D26 3-1	a15 3-4	S17 3-1	J14 0-2
11 EXETER C	N19 2-4	O08 1-0	D03 2-2	F04 4-2	A20 0-0	M18 4-1	M16 0-1	D26 2-3	O05 1-3	S14 2-0		a29 2-0	S26 2-1	S03 0-2	a15 2-3	a03 1-3	M04 3-0	S24 3-4	D31 1-0	F18 2-1	J21 2-1	O22 0-0	A31 1-0	a01 2-1
12 GILLINGHAM	S07 2-1	S10 5-2	a27 2-2	S24 3-4	N12 1-1	D17 3-0	A24 0-0	O15 1-2	F25 0-1	M11 2-0	D10 4-2		O29 5-1	m03 0-0	D27 1-2	a12 0-1	J14 2-3	O01 4-4	a08 0-0	a03 2-0	a22 1-1	A27 4-2	M25 0-3	S21 3-2
13 HARTLEPOOLS U	O08 4-1	N19 3-1	O22 0-2	J28 2-4	O01 0-1	a29 4-4	F04 1-2	J14 2-4	A27 5-0	S10 2-1	S19 0-0	M18 1-0		D27 3-2	M04 2-2	a01 4-2	a15 5-1	A22 0-2	a24 2-0	D17 1-5	S05 0-2	D03 4-1	F11 0-0	J02 1-3
14 MANSFIELD T	M22 0-0	D17 2-0	N19 5-1	a12 1-2	S19 1-3	M04 3-1	O22 1-1	F18 1-2	S24 2-1	a17 1-2	J14 2-3	a15 1-0	D26 2-1		a01 5-1	a29 4-2	a03 1-2	S10 1-0	A22 0-2	F04 1-2	A27 2-2	O08 2-0	S12 0-3	M18 1-3
15 MILLWALL	A22 2-2	S24 2-2	S12 3-0	O03 5-1	O29 4-2	J14 5-1	A27 2-3	a03 0-2	S26 0-1	F25 0-1	J07 2-2	D26 1-2	O15 5-2	N12 3-0		F18 3-1	F04 0-1	a22 4-3	M25 4-1	D10 3-1	a08 3-0	S10 0-3	M11 2-0	D17 3-2
16 NORTHAMPTON T	a25 2-1	A27 2-1	F11 3-0	J21 0-1	M21 0-0	S19 3-2	S13 4-1	O29 1-2	M11 1-1	M25 3-0	a04 3-1	S17 3-1	N12 3-3	D10 1-0	O01 2-2		D17 1-0	F25 0-3	a22 5-1	O15 3-1	S03 4-2	A29 3-2	a08 3-0	D27 3-0
17 OLDHAM A	F11 5-2	A23 0-2	J21 3-1	D31 4-0	D10 5-2	D27 4-1	a25 1-0	N12 4-3	M25 3-3	a08 1-1	O15 5-2	S03 1-1	J07 2-1	M31 3-1	S17 2-3	A20 1-2		M11 1-1	S27 0-2	O29 3-2	F25 3-0	S12 3-5	a22 0-2	O01 3-1
18 PETERBOROUGH U	a15 3-0	M04 7-1	a29 6-2	a03 3-1	D31 5-0	M13 6-0	a01 4-1	S12 4-1	D24 5-1	S26 6-2	F11 7-1	F18 2-0	A29 3-2	J21 2-1	D03 4-2	O08 3-3	O22 2-2		S03 4-3	O03 3-4	S17 0-1	M18 2-1	A20 3-0	N19 1-1
19 ROCHDALE	M18 3-2	a29 1-1	a01 0-0	a15 2-3	S13 2-1	O08 2-0	M04 3-0	S24 2-2	F04 1-0	F18 2-1	A27 3-1	N19 2-0	O03 4-0	A30 1-2	J28 4-0	D03 1-1	S20 3-0	a18 2-2		S10 0-1	a10 1-1	a03 2-0	D26 2-1	O22 0-0
20 SOUTHPORT	D03 3-0	O22 1-1	D26 4-1	O08 2-3	S03 3-0	a01 1-2	N19 2-0	S20 3-3	S06 1-4	A30 1-1	O01 2-0	M31 1-2	A20 2-0	S17 2-1	a29 4-1	M04 2-0	M18 2-0	a25 3-3	J21 0-1		F11 1-0	J28 3-0	D31 2-2	a15 2-2
21 STOCKPORT CO	a01 0-3	M31 2-0	a15 1-0	a29 2-3	A29 2-0	O22 1-1	M18 0-1	O03 5-2	F18 2-1	D27 1-0	S10 0-0	M06 2-0	S12 1-1	D31 1-0	N19 3-1	a17 1-1	O08 0-1	F04 0-6	A20 1-0	S24 2-0		M04 1-0	S26 1-0	M13 2-0
22 WORKINGTON	S17 2-1	S21 0-4	S03 3-1	A20 1-3	D26 2-1	O05 1-0	O01 0-0	a08 1-0	N12 1-3	J07 1-3	M11 3-1	D31 2-0	a22 2-0	F24 1-3	J21 2-2	A24 3-0	S07 1-1	O29 0-3	M31 3-0	M25 3-1	O15 1-0		D10 3-1	F10 2-0
23 WREXHAM	M04 3-0	a15 3-1	M18 1-0	a01 0-1	O05 2-1	F18 1-2	a03 0-1	S10 1-2	M15 3-1	F04 2-2	A25 3-1	M08 0-0	S24 1-0	S07 2-0	O22 0-1	N19 2-2	D03 2-2	D17 0-1	D27 2-0	A27 3-0	S21 1-3	a29 2-1		O08 4-0
24 YORK C	D31 1-0	O03 4-1	A29 2-0	S12 2-0	O15 4-0	F04 2-0	S10 3-1	D10 0-2	a22 4-1	S03 1-1	N12 6-1	S26 0-0	M31 4-0	O29 3-2	A20 3-2	D26 0-1	F18 1-0	a08 0-1	M11 2-0	M20 2-0	M25 0-0	S24 4-0	F25 2-1	

LEAGUE TABLES

DIVISION 1

	P	W	D	L	F	A	W	D	L	F	A	Pts
Tottenham H	42	15	3	3	65	28	16	1	4	50	27	66
Sheffield W	42	15	4	2	45	17	8	8	5	33	30	58
Wolverh'pton W	42	17	2	2	61	32	8	5	8	42	43	57
Burnley	42	11	4	6	58	40	11	3	7	44	37	51
Everton	42	13	4	4	47	23	9	2	10	40	46	50
Leicester C	42	12	4	5	54	31	6	5	10	33	39	45
Manchester U	42	14	5	2	58	20	4	4	13	30	56	45
Blackburn R	42	12	3	6	48	34	3	10	8	29	42	43
Aston Villa	42	13	3	5	48	28	4	6	11	30	49	43
W.B.A.	42	10	3	8	43	32	8	2	11	24	39	41
Arsenal	42	12	3	6	44	35	3	8	10	33	50	41
Chelsea	42	10	5	6	61	48	5	2	14	37	52	37
Manchester C	42	10	5	6	41	30	3	6	12	38	60	37
Nottingham F	42	8	7	6	34	33	6	2	13	28	45	37
Cardiff C	42	11	5	5	34	26	2	6	13	26	59	37
West Ham U	42	12	4	5	53	31	1	6	14	24	57	36
Fulham	42	8	8	5	39	39	6	0	15	33	56	36
Bolton W	42	9	5	7	38	29	3	6	12	20	44	35
Birmingham C	42	10	4	7	35	31	4	2	15	27	53	34
Blackpool	42	9	3	9	44	34	3	6	12	24	39	33
Newcastle U	42	7	7	7	51	49	4	3	14	35	60	32
Preston N.E.	42	7	6	8	28	25	3	4	14	15	46	30

DIVISION 2

	P	W	D	L	F	A	W	D	L	F	A	Pts
Ipswich T	42	15	3	3	55	24	11	4	6	45	31	59
Sheffield U	42	16	2	3	49	22	10	4	7	32	29	58
Liverpool	42	14	5	2	49	21	7	5	9	38	37	52
Norwich C	42	15	3	3	46	20	5	6	10	24	33	49
Middlesbrough	42	13	6	2	44	20	5	6	10	39	54	48
Sunderland	42	12	5	4	47	24	5	8	8	28	36	47
Swansea T	42	14	4	3	49	26	4	7	10	28	47	47
Southampton	42	12	4	5	57	35	6	4	11	27	46	44
Scunthorpe U	42	9	8	4	39	25	5	7	9	30	39	43
Charlton A	42	12	3	6	60	42	4	8	9	37	49	43
Plymouth A	42	13	4	4	52	32	4	4	13	29	50	42
Derby Co	42	9	6	6	46	35	6	4	11	34	45	40
Luton T	42	13	5	3	48	27	2	4	15	23	52	39
Leeds U	42	7	7	7	41	38	7	3	11	34	45	38
Rotherham U	42	9	7	5	37	24	3	6	12	28	40	37
Brighton & H.A.	42	9	6	6	33	26	5	3	13	28	49	37
Bristol R	42	13	4	4	52	35	2	3	16	21	57	37
Stoke C	42	9	6	6	39	26	3	6	12	12	33	36
Leyton O	42	10	5	6	31	29	4	3	14	24	49	36
Huddersfield T	42	7	5	9	33	33	6	4	11	29	38	35
Portsmouth	42	10	6	5	38	27	1	5	15	26	64	33
Lincoln C	42	5	4	12	30	43	3	4	14	18	52	24

DIVISION 3

	P	W	D	L	F	A	W	D	L	F	A	Pts
Bury	46	18	3	2	62	17	12	5	6	46	28	68
Walsall	46	19	4	0	62	20	9	2	12	36	40	62
Q.P.R.	46	18	4	1	58	23	7	6	10	35	37	60
Watford	46	12	7	4	52	27	8	5	10	33	45	52
Notts Co	46	16	3	4	52	24	5	6	12	30	53	51
Grimsby T	46	14	4	5	48	32	6	6	11	29	37	50
Port Vale	46	15	3	5	63	30	2	12	9	33	49	49
Barnsley	46	15	5	3	56	30	6	2	15	27	50	49
Halifax T	46	14	7	2	42	22	2	10	11	29	56	49
Shrewsbury T	46	13	7	3	54	26	2	9	12	29	49	46
Hull C	46	13	6	4	51	28	4	6	13	22	45	46
Torquay U	46	8	12	3	37	26	6	5	12	38	57	45
Newport Co	46	12	7	4	51	30	5	4	14	30	60	45
Bristol C	46	15	4	4	50	19	2	6	15	20	49	44
Coventry C	46	14	6	3	54	25	2	6	15	26	58	44
Swindon T	46	13	6	4	41	16	1	9	13	21	39	43
Brentford	46	10	9	4	41	28	3	8	12	15	42	43
Reading	46	13	5	5	48	29	1	7	15	24	54	40
Bournemouth	46	8	7	8	34	39	7	3	13	24	37	40
Southend U	46	10	8	5	38	26	4	3	16	22	50	39
Tranmere R	46	11	5	7	53	50	4	3	16	26	65	38
Bradford C	46	8	8	7	37	36	3	6	14	28	51	36
Colchester U	46	8	5	10	40	44	3	6	14	28	57	33
Chesterfield	46	9	6	8	42	29	1	6	16	25	58	32

DIVISION 4

	P	W	D	L	F	A	W	D	L	F	A	Pts
Peterborough U	46	18	3	2	85	30	10	7	6	49	35	66
Crystal Palace	46	16	4	3	64	28	13	2	8	46	41	64
Northampton T	46	16	4	3	53	25	9	6	8	37	37	60
Bradford P.A.	46	16	5	2	49	22	10	3	10	35	52	60
York C	46	17	3	3	50	14	4	6	13	30	46	51
Millwall	46	13	3	7	56	33	8	5	10	41	53	50
Darlington	46	11	7	5	41	24	7	6	10	37	46	49
Workington	46	14	3	6	38	28	7	4	12	36	48	49
Crewe A	46	11	4	8	40	29	9	5	9	21	38	49
Aldershot	46	16	4	3	55	19	2	5	16	24	50	45
Doncaster R	46	15	0	8	52	33	4	7	12	24	45	45
Oldham A	46	13	4	6	57	38	6	3	14	22	50	45
Stockport Co	46	14	4	5	31	21	4	5	14	26	45	45
Southport	46	12	6	5	47	27	7	0	16	22	40	44
Gillingham	46	9	7	7	45	34	6	6	11	19	32	43
Wrexham	46	12	4	7	38	22	5	4	14	24	34	42
Rochdale	46	13	7	3	43	19	4	1	18	17	47	42
Accrington S	46	12	4	7	44	32	4	4	15	30	56	40
Carlisle U	46	10	7	6	43	37	3	6	14	18	42	39
Mansfield T	46	10	3	10	39	34	6	3	14	32	44	38
Exeter C	46	12	3	8	39	32	2	7	14	27	62	38
Barrow	46	10	6	7	33	28	3	5	15	19	51	37
Hartlepool U	46	10	4	9	46	40	2	4	17	25	63	32
Chester C	46	9	7	7	38	35	2	2	19	23	69	31

FOOTBALL LEAGUE RECORDS

Top scorers: Div 1, R.Crawford (Ipswich Town), D.Kevan (West Bromwich Albion) 33 goals; Div 2, R.Hunt (Liverpool) 41 goals; Div 3, C.Holton (Watford & Northampton Town) 37 goals; Div 4, R.R.Hunt (Colchester) 37 goals.

Ray Crawford, one of the architects of Ipswich Town's remarkable climb from Division Two to League Championship winners.

DIVISION 1

	ARSENAL	ASTON VILLA	BIRMINGHAM C	BLACKBURN R	BLACKPOOL	BOLTON W	BURNLEY	CARDIFF C	CHELSEA	EVERTON	FULHAM	IPSWICH T	LEICESTER C	MANCHESTER C	MANCHESTER U	NOTTINGHAM F	SHEFFIELD U	SHEFFIELD W	TOTTENHAM H	W.B.A.	WEST HAM U	WOLVERHAMPTON W
1 ARSENAL		M31 4-5	S23 1-1	M03 0-0	O07 3-0	J13 1-2	A19 2-2	M17 1-1	N04 0-3	m01 2-3	D26 1-0	a23 0-3	A29 4-4	S09 3-0	O21 5-1	N18 2-1	a28 2-0	N14 1-0	D23 2-1	F03 0-1	D02 2-2	a14 3-1
2 ASTON VILLA	N11 3-1		O28 1-3	F03 1-0	S23 5-0	a07 3-0	M24 0-2	m01 2-2	A26 3-1	D16 1-1	F24 2-0	D09 3-0	a21 8-3	N25 2-1	S18 1-1	a23 5-1	J13 0-0	O16 1-0	F21 0-0	M14 1-0	S09 2-4	O02 1-0
3 BIRMINGHAM C	F10 1-0	M17 0-2		M30 2-1	N04 1-1	S30 2-1	S16 2-6	D02 3-0	O21 3-2	a24 0-0	A19 2-1	J20 3-1	S02 1-5	D26 1-1	M03 1-1	A30 1-1	a14 3-0	D23 1-1	a28 2-3	S20 1-2	N18 4-0	O07 3-6
4 BLACKBURN R	O14 0-0	S16 4-2	N11 2-0		A28 1-1	a21 2-3	F24 2-1	A19 0-0	F10 3-0	a07 1-1	N25 0-2	S18 2-2	O28 2-1	D09 4-1	a10 3-0	J20 2-1	S30 1-2	a26 0-2	a23 0-1	M24 1-1	M28 1-0	S02 2-1
5 BLACKPOOL	F24 0-1	F10 1-2	M24 1-0	A21 2-1		O14 2-1	a23 1-1	D23 3-0	S30 4-0	N11 1-1	a07 2-1	O28 1-1	M10 2-1	a21 3-1	S02 2-3	S16 1-3	a03 2-4	N25 1-3	A19 1-2	D09 2-2	S04 2-0	J20 7-2
6 BOLTON W	S02 2-1	N18 1-1	F17 3-2	D02 1-1	M03 0-0		a11 0-0	J20 1-1	M31 4-2	a04 1-1	S20 2-3	A19 0-0	a23 1-0	F03 0-2	M17 1-0	a14 6-1	N04 2-0	A30 4-3	O09 1-2	S23 3-2	a28 1-0	O21 1-0
7 BURNLEY	D16 0-2	N04 3-0	F03 7-1	a17 0-1	a20 2-0	A26 3-1		O21 2-1	a28 1-1	S23 2-1	F20 2-1	A22 4-3	S05 2-0	J13 6-3	a14 1-3	a03 0-0	D02 4-2	D26 4-0	M17 2-2	S09 3-1	M03 6-0	N18 3-3
8 CARDIFF C	O28 1-1	D26 1-0	a21 3-2	D16 1-1	A26 3-2	S09 1-2	M14 1-1		S06 5-2	D09 0-0	M23 0-3	N25 0-3	a07 0-4	F24 0-0	S16 1-2	S30 2-2	A23 1-1	N11 2-1	J13 1-1	O18 2-2	a23 3-0	F09 2-3
9 CHELSEA	M24 2-3	D23 1-0	M09 1-1	S23 1-1	F16 1-0	N11 1-0	D09 1-2	S20 2-3		O28 1-1	S02 0-0	a21 2-2	O14 1-3	a07 1-1	A30 2-0	A19 2-2	S09 6-1	F24 1-0	D26 0-2	N25 4-1	F03 0-1	a20 4-5
10 EVERTON	S30 4-1	A19 2-0	a20 4-1	N18 1-0	M30 2-2	D26 1-0	F10 2-2	a28 8-3	M17 4-0		D23 3-0	S16 5-2	J20 3-2	S06 0-2	D02 5-1	O07 6-0	O21 1-0	S02 0-4	N04 3-0	A30 3-1	a14 3-0	M03 4-0
11 FULHAM	a11 5-2	O07 3-1	D16 0-1	a14 2-0	N18 0-1	S06 2-2	S30 3-5	N04 0-1	J13 3-4	A26 2-1		F10 1-2	S16 2-1	A23 3-4	a28 2-0	M03 1-1	M17 5-2	J20 0-2	a17 1-1	a23 1-2	O21 2-0	D02 0-1
12 IPSWICH T	a20 2-2	a28 2-0	S09 4-1	S05 2-1	M17 1-1	D16 2-1	A29 6-2	a14 1-0	D02 5-2	F03 4-2	S23 2-4		D26 1-0	A26 2-4	N18 4-1	N04 1-0	M03 4-0	M09 2-1	O21 3-2	J13 3-0	O07 4-2	M31 3-2
13 LEICESTER C	A23 0-1	D02 0-2	J13 1-2	M17 2-0	O21 0-2	a24 1-1	S20 2-6	N18 3-0	a11 2-0	S09 2-0	F03 4-1	M28 0-2		D16 2-0	a04 4-3	a28 2-1	O07 4-1	S23 1-0	a30 2-3	A26 1-0	F17 2-2	N04 3-0
14 MANCHESTER C	J20 3-2	a14 1-0	a11 1-4	a28 3-1	D02 2-4	S16 2-1	S02 1-3	O07 1-2	N18 2-2	S20 1-3	A30 2-1	D23 3-0	A19 3-1		F10 0-2	O21 3-0	M31 1-1	a20 3-1	M03 6-2	F21 3-1	N04 3-5	M17 2-2
15 MANCHESTER U	a16 2-3	J15 2-0	O14 0-2	A26 6-1	J13 0-1	O28 0-3	N25 1-4	F03 3-0	A23 3-2	a21 1-1	D09 3-0	a07 5-0	N11 2-2	S23 3-2		D26 6-3	a23 0-1	M24 1-1	S09 1-0	F24 4-1	D16 1-2	S30 0-2
16 NOTTINGHAM F	a07 0-1	a24 2-0	A22 2-1	S09 1-2	F03 3-4	N25 0-1	N11 3-2	F17 2-1	D16 3-0	F24 2-1	O14 1-1	M24 1-1	D09 0-0	M10 1-2	M20 1-0		A26 2-0	a21 3-1	S23 2-0	O28 4-4	J13 3-0	S19 3-1
17 SHEFFIELD U	D09 2-1	S02 0-2	N25 3-1	F20 0-0	D26 2-1	M24 3-1	a21 2-0	A28 1-0	J20 3-1	M14 1-1	O28 2-2	O14 2-1	F24 3-1	N11 3-1	a24 2-3	D22 2-0		S16 1-0	S04 1-1	a07 1-1	S23 1-4	A19 2-1
18 SHEFFIELD W	S20 1-1	M03 3-0	A26 5-1	O21 1-0	a14 3-2	A23 4-2	a30 4-0	a03 2-0	O07 5-3	J13 3-1	S09 1-1	S30 1-4	F10 1-2	a23 1-0	N04 3-1	D02 3-0	F03 1-2		N18 0-0	D16 2-1	M17 0-0	a28 3-2
19 TOTTENHAM H	A26 4-3	S30 1-0	D09 3-1	a20 4-1	D16 5-2	F24 2-2	O28 4-2	S02 3-2	D30 5-2	M24 3-1	N11 4-2	M14 1-3	N25 1-2	O14 2-0	J20 2-2	F10 4-2	a09 3-3	a07 4-0		a21 1-2	A23 2-2	S16 1-0
20 W.B.A.	S16 4-0	O21 1-1	S06 0-0	N04 4-0	a28 7-1	F10 6-2	J20 1-1	M03 5-1	a14 4-0	A23 2-0	a24 2-0	S02 1-3	D23 2-0	S30 2-2	O07 1-1	M17 2-2	N18 3-1	A19 0-2	D02 2-4		M31 0-1	D26 1-1
21 WEST HAM U	a21 3-3	J20 2-0	a06 2-2	D26 2-3	S18 2-2	D09 1-0	O14 2-1	a20 4-1	S16 2-1	N25 3-1	a30 4-2	F24 2-2	S30 4-1	M24 0-4	A19 1-1	S02 3-2	F10 1-2	O28 2-3	A28 2-1	N11 3-3		D18 4-2
22 WOLVERHAMPTON W	N25 2-3	A28 2-2	F24 2-1	J13 0-2	S09 2-2	M10 5-1	a07 1-1	S23 1-1	a23 1-1	O14 0-3	a21 1-3	N11 2-0	M24 1-1	O28 4-1	F28 2-2	S27 2-1	D16 0-1	D09 3-0	F03 3-1	M28 1-5	A26 3-2	

Roger Hunt, whose 41 goals in Liverpool's Division Two promotion season of 1961-62 is still a club record.

DIVISION 2

	BRIGHTON & HA	BRISTOL R	BURY	CHARLTON A	DERBY CO	HUDDERSFIELD T	LEEDS U	LEYTON O	LIVERPOOL	LUTON T	MIDDLESBROUGH	NEWCASTLE U	NORWICH C	PLYMOUTH A	PRESTON N.E.	ROTHERHAM U	SCUNTHORPE U	SOUTHAMPTON	STOKE C	SUNDERLAND	SWANSEA T	WALSALL
1 BRIGHTON & H.A.		D30 1-0	S02 0-2	a10 2-2	D09 1-2	N11 2-2	A22 1-3	a07 0-1	S16 0-0	O14 2-1	O28 2-0	M10 0-4	a20 2-1	a21 3-2	N25 0-0	F10 0-3	D16 0-3	F24 0-0	S05 2-1	S30 1-1	A26 2-2	M24 3-2
2 BRISTOL R	D26 0-1		A28 0-1	a20 2-2	N11 1-4	M10 1-1	S23 4-0	S16 2-1	A19 0-2	D09 1-0	N25 0-2	a07 2-1	F27 2-1	O14 4-3	F24 2-1	D22 4-2	S18 2-1	M24 1-0	J20 0-2	S02 2-3	O28 4-1	a21 2-2
3 BURY	J13 2-1	A22 2-0		S15 1-2	M24 2-2	a21 1-2	a20 1-1	M13 0-1	F10 0-3	F24 2-1	M10 2-1	O14 2-7	D16 2-3	N25 1-1	a07 2-1	S30 2-1	A26 4-1	S09 0-2	D26 0-2	S19 3-2	N11 1-1	O24 2-1
4 CHARLTON A	S09 2-3	a23 2-1	F03 1-0		O28 4-0	N25 0-2	D16 3-1	M24 1-2	S30 0-4	S23 0-1	O14 1-0	F24 1-1	A26 2-2	a07 3-1	D09 4-0	S20 0-2	J13 3-3	M06 1-0	A22 2-2	D26 2-0	a21 3-2	M10 3-3
5 DERBY CO	a28 2-0	M31 4-1	N04 3-0	M17 0-1		S30 1-0	D02 3-3	J20 1-2	O21 2-0	A23 2-0	D16 3-2	a23 1-2	a14 1-1	F10 2-2	S16 3-2	M03 1-1	N18 2-2	D26 1-1	J13 2-0	O07 1-1	S06 6-3	A26 1-3
6 HUDDERSFIELD T	M31 2-0	O21 4-1	D02 2-0	a14 0-2	a09 4-0		M03 2-1	S27 1-1	N18 1-2	J13 1-2	F03 0-0	S09 2-1	O07 1-1	A23 5-1	a02 2-2	a28 0-3	a23 1-2	A26 1-0	M17 3-0	N04 0-0	M26 3-1	S23 4-2
7 LEEDS U	A30 1-1	F10 0-0	a24 0-0	A19 1-0	a21 0-0	O14 1-0		N11 0-0	D23 1-0	M24 2-1	a07 2-0	J27 0-1	S20 0-1	F24 2-3	S30 1-2	S02 1-3	D26 1-4	O28 1-1	S16 3-1	J20 1-0	M10 2-0	N25 4-1
8 LEYTON O	N18 4-1	F03 2-3	a28 2-0	N04 2-1	S09 2-0	S20 3-0	M31 0-0		M17 2-2	a20 0-0	A26 2-0	D16 2-0	D02 2-0	S29 1-2	F09 0-2	O21 1-1	a14 0-1	A21 1-3	O07 3-0	M03 1-1	D26 1-0	J13 3-0
9 LIVERPOOL	F03 3-1	D16 2-0	S23 5-0	a30 2-1	M10 4-1	a07 1-1	A26 5-0	O28 3-3		N11 1-1	F24 5-1	O04 2-0	J13 5-4	D09 2-1	M24 4-1	M28 4-1	S09 2-1	a21 2-0	a23 2-1	A23 3-0	N25 5-0	O14 6-1
10 LUTON T	M03 2-1	a28 2-0	O07 4-0	F10 1-6	A30 4-2	S02 3-4	N04 3-2	a23 1-3	M31 1-0		S27 3-2	F17 1-0	M17 1-2	D23 0-2	A19 4-1	D02 4-3	O21 1-2	S16 1-4	N18 0-0	a14 1-2	J20 5-1	a11 2-0
11 MIDDLESBROUGH	M16 4-0	a14 5-0	O21 2-1	M03 3-2	A19 3-4	S16 1-0	N18 1-3	D23 2-3	O07 2-0	S20 2-4		M07 3-0	a28 2-1	J20 1-1	S02 1-0	A30 5-1	N04 1-2	S30 1-1	D02 2-2	M31 0-1	F10 1-3	a24 3-0
12 NEWCASTLE U	O21 5-0	N18 5-2	M03 1-2	O07 4-1	a20 3-0	J20 1-1	a28 0-3	A19 0-0	S20 1-2	S30 4-1	D26 3-4		N04 0-0	S02 0-2	D23 0-2	M31 1-0	M17 2-1	F10 3-2	a14 2-0	D02 2-2	S16 2-2	A23 1-0
13 NORWICH C	a23 3-0	S30 2-2	A19 3-1	D23 2-2	N25 3-2	F24 1-2	S06 2-0	a21 0-0	S02 1-2	O28 0-4	D09 5-4	M24 0-0		D26 0-2	N11 2-0	J20 0-1	A23 2-2	M10 1-1	F10 1-0	S16 3-1	O14 2-1	a07 3-1
14 PLYMOUTH A	D02 5-0	M03 3-1	a14 1-2	N18 2-1	S23 2-3	A30 4-2	O07 1-1	F17 2-1	a28 2-3	A26 0-3	S09 1-1	J13 1-1	D30 3-1		S20 1-0	N04 2-5	M31 3-1	D16 4-0	O21 3-1	M17 3-2	a23 0-0	F03 2-1
15 PRESTON N.E.	a14 3-1	O07 1-0	N18 1-2	a28 2-0	F03 1-0	D26 1-0	a09 1-1	S23 3-2	N04 1-3	D16 2-0	J13 4-3	A26 0-1	M30 2-0	S26 1-1		M17 2-0	D02 4-1	a23 1-1	M03 1-2	O21 0-1	A22 1-1	S09 2-3
16 ROTHERHAM U	S23 2-1	A26 4-0	F17 2-0	S26 3-2	O14 2-2	D08 3-3	J12 2-1	M09 2-1	D26 1-0	a21 1-1	a03 0-1	N11 0-0	S09 3-1	M24 1-3	O28 2-2		F02 0-1	N25 4-2	D16 1-2	a24 0-3	a07 1-2	F24 2-2
17 SCUNTHORPE U	A19 3-3	S05 2-1	D22 1-2	S01 6-1	a06 2-0	a24 1-3	F20 2-1	N24 0-2	J20 1-1	M10 2-0	M23 1-1	O27 3-2	A29 2-0	N11 5-1	a20 2-1	S15 5-2		O13 5-1	S29 2-2	F10 3-1	F23 2-0	M06 2-1
18 SOUTHAMPTON	O07 6-1	N04 0-2	J20 5-3	M31 1-2	D30 2-1	D23 3-1	M17 4-1	A30 1-2	D02 2-0	F03 3-0	F21 1-3	S23 1-0	O21 2-2	A19 1-2	O18 0-0	a14 2-1	M03 6-4		a28 5-1	N18 2-0	S02 5-1	S06 1-1
19 STOKE C	S18 0-1	S09 2-1	a11 1-3	A28 4-0	S02 1-1	O28 3-0	F03 2-1	F24 0-1	a24 0-0	a07 2-1	a21 2-0	N25 3-1	S23 3-1	M10 2-0	O14 1-1	A19 1-2	F17 1-0	D09 3-2		D23 1-0	M24 0-0	N11 2-1
20 SUNDERLAND	F17 0-0	J13 6-1	S27 3-0	M14 4-1	F24 2-1	M24 3-1	S09 2-1	O14 2-1	A30 1-4	N25 2-2	N11 2-1	a21 3-0	F03 2-0	O28 5-0	M21 0-0	a23 4-0	S23 4-0	a07 3-0	A26 2-1		D09 7-2	D16 3-0
21 SWANSEA T	D23 3-0	M17 1-1	M31 0-1	D02 1-0	S19 3-1	A19 1-1	O21 2-1	D30 1-3	m04 4-2	S09 3-2	S23 3-3	F02 3-2	M03 0-3	a24 5-0	A29 1-2	N18 2-2	O07 2-1	J13 0-1	N04 1-0	a28 1-1		F17 1-3
22 WALSALL	N04 2-2	D02 0-0	M17 3-0	O21 2-2	D23 2-0	F10 2-2	a14 1-1	S02 1-5	M03 1-1	D26 2-0	a23 1-2	A29 1-0	N18 5-0	S16 1-0	J20 2-1	O07 5-0	a28 4-1	S19 0-2	M30 3-1	A19 4-3	S30 0-0	

SEASON 1961-62

DIVISION 3

	BARNSLEY	BOURNEMOUTH	BRADFORD	BRENTFORD	BRISTOL C	COVENTRY C	CRYSTAL P	GRIMSBY T	HALIFAX T	HULL C	LINCOLN C	NEWPORT CO	NORTHAMPTON T	NOTTS CO	PETERBOROUGH U	PORTSMOUTH	PORT VALE	Q.P.R.	READING	SHREWSBURY T	SOUTHEND U	SWINDON T	TORQUAY U	WATFORD
1 BARNSLEY		F09 2-2	a07 1-2	O28 2-2	N11 7-3	M09 2-1	S16 0-3	J27 0-3	M27 1-2	a23 1-0	D26 0-1	A30 1-1	O11 3-2	O14 2-0	D09 0-3	J20 2-2	M24 2-1	A26 2-4	S02 2-3	a21 1-1	F24 1-1	S27 6-2	m02 4-2	S30 3-0
2 BOURNEMOUTH	S23 5-0		D09 2-2	a07 1-1	a21 2-1	N11 1-1	a20 1-0	M24 2-3	S09 2-1	S06 1-1	D16 0-0	M10 2-1	S27 3-2	O04 2-1	F24 1-1	F17 2-0	O14 1-0	F03 3-1	J27 1-0	A23 0-0	O28 3-0	J13 0-0	A26 3-1	D30 4-1
3 BRADFORD	N18 3-2	a28 1-2		a04 1-2	S23 2-0	O16 0-0	M07 2-0	a24 0-1	O21 2-0	M03 1-0	A23 2-0	O25 4-1	O07 1-2	A26 3-2	S09 6-2	M31 2-1	F03 2-1	a14 3-3	S06 1-3	J13 1-1	M14 4-0	M17 2-2	F17 3-1	D02 1-1
4 BRENTFORD	M17 1-1	N18 2-2	D26 2-0		O10 0-2	S19 2-1	a13 4-2	m01 0-2	A22 0-2	m03 0-2	D02 1-0	J13 3-1	a27 3-0	F02 0-1	F17 2-0	O21 3-2	a20 1-2	D16 1-4	A26 1-2	S23 4-0	S09 0-0	O07 1-0	M03 0-2	M30 3-1
5 BRISTOL C	M31 0-0	D02 2-1	F10 6-1	O03 3-0		a24 3-2	a28 2-2	S29 3-0	a14 4-3	O07 1-1	F03 2-0	S05 1-2	A22 1-0	D16 6-0	J13 1-2	M06 0-4	S09 0-1	N18 2-0	F06 5-0	A26 0-1	S26 3-2	O21 5-3	M17 4-1	M03 2-1
6 COVENTRY C	O20 1-1	M30 0-1	O09 3-0	S25 2-0	a23 1-1		N17 0-2	D26 2-0	S04 3-1	a28 0-2	M02 2-2	A25 3-0	D02 1-0	S09 2-2	S23 1-3	a14 2-0	a16 0-1	M16 2-3	D16 1-0	F03 4-1	J13 3-3	A21 2-1	O06 2-2	M12 1-0
7 CRYSTAL P	F03 1-3	a23 0-0	M24 0-0	J27 2-2	D09 2-3	a07 2-2		N11 4-1	J13 4-3	M21 1-2	S20 1-3	O28 2-0	S06 1-4	A23 4-1	O14 5-2	S23 1-2	a21 0-0	S09 2-2	M10 3-4	F24 2-1	S30 2-2	A26 3-1	D16 7-2	O11 1-1
8 GRIMSBY T	a14 4-0	J06 3-0	a23 3-2	S05 1-0	F17 1-0	a10 2-0	M30 0-0		M17 3-0	D02 1-0	O07 4-1	D16 1-0	M03 3-2	J13 2-1	F03 2-1	N18 1-0	S23 1-1	O21 1-1	S26 4-0	S09 2-1	A26 3-1	O10 0-1	A22 2-3	a28 5-3
9 HALIFAX T	A19 3-1	J20 3-1	a18 2-3	A28 1-0	J27 3-4	a30 0-2	S02 1-1	O28 3-3		F10 2-1	a24 0-3	O14 0-0	S30 1-3	a09 1-2	N11 2-1	D23 0-1	a07 3-3	m03 1-1	F23 2-1	M24 1-2	a21 0-2	M19 2-0	F19 1-0	S16 2-0
10 HULL C	a20 4-0	a12 2-1	O14 0-1	M24 3-0	F24 3-2	D09 3-1	D26 2-4	a21 2-1	S23 1-2		J13 1-0	a07 4-0	A26 1-0	M10 2-1	D16 1-1	J06 0-1	A31 3-1	F16 3-1	N11 0-1	O28 3-1	J27 0-0	F03 0-1	S09 4-0	S21 1-0
11 LINCOLN C	J31 2-2	A19 0-2	A30 3-2	a21 3-3	S16 1-1	O14 1-2	S27 3-2	F23 1-1	a23 0-1	S02 0-3		M23 3-2	J20 0-0	a06 2-2	M10 1-2	m02 2-2	O28 1-1	a30 0-5	D09 2-3	F07 1-2	N11 2-0	F16 2-2	S23 1-3	D23 0-0
12 NEWPORT CO	A21 0-2	O21 0-1	S18 1-2	S02 6-1	O16 3-1	D23 1-2	M17 2-1	A19 0-2	M05 0-1	N18 0-2	M26 4-0		M31 0-0	F17 2-0	O02 2-3	F05 0-5	M12 1-1	O07 2-4	M19 0-0	a16 3-2	S23 0-3	D02 2-2	a28 0-3	a14 0-0
13 NORTHAMPTON T	O03 3-1	S18 0-3	F24 2-0	D09 5-0	A29 0-1	a21 4-1	O17 1-1	O14 7-0	F17 3-1	D23 2-0	S09 2-2	N11 5-0		J27 1-2	O28 2-2	M20 2-2	S02 1-1	a24 1-1	M24 1-0	M10 3-1	a07 3-1	S23 1-2	F03 1-2	D16 2-0
14 NOTTS CO	M03 0-2	O12 3-2	D23 4-2	S16 3-1	A19 1-0	J20 2-0	A31 0-0	S02 2-0	a28 0-0	a03 3-0	N18 1-0	S30 8-1	a14 1-4		S07 2-2	O07 2-1	S21 2-3	D02 0-0	F10 2-2	D26 3-2	a23 2-0	a12 0-1	M31 2-0	M17 1-0
15 PETERBOROUGH U	a28 4-2	O07 1-2	M19 1-0	S30 6-0	S02 3-4	F10 2-3	M03 4-1	S16 2-1	M31 5-1	A19 3-2	O21 5-4	O09 2-1	M17 0-2	a30 2-0		D02 0-1	D23 1-3	F19 5-1	a23 1-0	S25 0-3	D26 4-1	N18 3-2	a14 2-1	A28 4-3
16 PORTSMOUTH	S09 3-2	S30 1-1	N11 4-2	M10 4-0	M24 5-0	J27 3-2	F10 2-1	a07 0-2	A26 1-1	O11 2-1	S06 0-0	S16 2-2	D26 4-1	F24 0-0	a21 0-3		D09 1-0	J13 4-1	O28 2-0	O14 3-1	A23 1-0	D16 2-2	S27 2-0	a23 2-1
17 PORT VALE	M05 2-0	M19 1-0	S16 3-2	a23 3-0	J20 0-2	S30 2-0	D02 0-1	F10 0-2	N18 1-1	A21 4-0	M17 4-0	D26 3-0	J13 1-1	S25 1-0	A26 0-1	a28 2-3		M31 2-3	O09 2-1	D16 4-1	S04 0-0	a14 1-1	O21 4-1	O07 1-3
18 Q.P.R.	M19 3-0	S16 1-1	a11 1-2	A19 3-0	a07 4-1	O28 4-1	J20 1-0	M10 3-2	S25 6-2	S30 1-1	O09 1-3	F24 4-0	a23 2-0	a21 2-0	M24 3-3	S02 0-1	N11 2-1		A21 3-6	D09 3-1	O14 5-3	S04 6-1	D30 6-0	F10 1-2
19 READING	J12 0-0	a14 0-1	m02 3-1	D23 4-0	D26 2-2	A19 4-0	O20 2-1	S20 1-2	O06 3-2	M30 1-1	a27 4-0	S08 2-1	a11 2-0	S23 4-2	a20 3-2	M16 0-3	O04 0-0	A30 0-2		F17 3-0	F02 3-1	M02 1-1	D02 1-0	N17 3-2
20 SHREWSBURY T	D02 4-1	A30 2-2	S02 4-1	F10 1-3	D23 2-2	S16 1-1	O07 1-5	J20 1-2	M14 0-0	M17 2-0	a14 0-0	a23 4-1	O21 1-3	M28 3-0	S20 3-4	M03 0-1	A19 4-2	a28 1-2	S30 4-1		O25 1-1	M30 1-3	N18 1-1	O18 5-1
21 SOUTHEND U	O07 1-2	M17 0-0	A19 2-1	J20 0-0	S18 1-0	S02 2-0	F17 2-2	D23 2-0	D02 2-1	a14 2-1	M31 0-0	F10 1-0	N18 1-3	a20 3-2	D30 1-1	A28 2-2	O16 4-1	M03 2-3	S16 0-2	O02 1-1		a28 0-2	J06 2-1	O21 0-1
22 SWINDON T	S19 1-1	S02 1-1	O28 3-2	F23 5-2	M10 0-4	A29 3-3	D23 5-0	O03 0-0	a16 6-0	S16 1-1	S30 4-0	a21 3-0	F10 2-2	M23 1-0	a07 3-2	A19 1-3	a30 1-0	O17 0-0	O13 4-1	N11 1-2	D09 0-0		a20 0-1	J20 3-1
23 TORQUAY U	S07 6-2	D22 2-1	S30 1-3	O14 3-1	O28 1-3	F24 1-0	A19 1-2	A30 1-2	O11 2-3	J20 4-2	F10 3-4	D09 3-2	S16 1-2	N11 3-3	a02 1-3	S20 0-2	M10 2-0	D26 2-2	a21 0-0	a07 3-1	M24 2-2	a23 3-0		S02 3-4
24 WATFORD	F17 3-1	D26 0-0	a21 0-2	N11 2-1	O14 1-1	M23 0-1	O03 3-2	D09 2-1	F03 0-0	S26 1-1	A26 3-3	J27 3-1	A19 0-0	O28 3-1	A22 2-3	a20 0-0	F24 2-0	S23 3-2	a06 1-1	S05 1-1	M09 1-3	S09 2-0	J13 4-1	

DIVISION 4

	ACCRINGTON S	ALDERSHOT	BARROW	BRADFORD C	CARLISLE U	CHESTER	CHESTERFIELD	COLCHESTER U	CREWE A	DARLINGTON	DONCASTER R	EXETER C	GILLINGHAM	HARTLEPOOLS U	MANSFIELD T	MILLWALL	OLDHAM A	ROCHDALE	SOUTHPORT	STOCKPORT CO	TRANMERE R	WORKINGTON	WREXHAM	YORK C
1 ACCRINGTON S		S23 0-2	S25 2-2	F03 0-2	S09 1-0	A26 0-1	J27 0-0	J13 0-4	O14 1-0	A21 3-1					S04 0-0	D09 0-2	O02 1-0	F24 0-2		F16 1-2	D16 1-1	N11 0-4	O28 0-2	
2 ALDERSHOT	F09 2-2		M09 3-1	A26 2-2	D16 0-1	a04 6-2	S02 1-1	a23 1-0	M24 1-0	S30 6-1	J26 3-1	N11 1-1	S27 4-0	O09 1-1	O14 4-2	F24 0-2	S16 3-1	O28 3-0	S06 2-0	J20 4-1	A23 3-1	a21 3-1	a07 3-1	D09 2-0
3 BARROW	S18 3-1	O21 2-2		M17 1-1	M26 0-3	N18 3-2	S30 1-0	M31 4-0	A19 3-0	a09 3-0	J01 4-1	D23 3-0	O09 7-0	a28 5-1	A28 1-1	a30 2-2	O07 3-1	a20 0-1	D02 1-1	M03 3-1	a14 2-0	S16 1-1	S02 0-2	F10 0-0
4 BRADFORD C	S16 0-1	M14 2-1	O28 1-1		a23 3-2	A30 2-0	O18 0-2	D26 4-1	N11 3-3	F10 3-2	a25 2-0	a07 5-1	F24 5-2	S30 5-1	M10 6-1	O14 2-4	M20 1-1	M23 1-0	O11 1-0	S02 1-3	a11 3-1	D09 1-1	m02 5-3	A19 2-2
5 CARLISLE U	J20 2-0	A19 2-1	M24 0-0	a20 2-4		m01 2-0	F24 3-1	A29 1-1	a06 3-0	S16 1-0	D09 1-0	J27 2-1	O14 1-2	F10 1-0	O28 1-0	M10 3-2	S02 2-0	N11 2-2	S30 2-1	D23 1-0	O10 0-3	D26 1-2	M13 1-0	S27 3-2
6 CHESTER	D23 0-0	D26 2-3	a07 2-3	A23 1-2	S06 1-1		M10 4-1	O11 2-2	a21 1-0	S02 2-2	S27 2-3	D09 1-1	O28 1-1	J20 4-4	N11 0-1	M24 2-4	A19 1-0	J27 2-3	S16 2-0	a23 2-0	F09 1-1	F24 1-3	S30 1-1	O14 1-1
7 CHESTERFIELD		J13 2-3	F17 2-2	S18 2-1	O07 1-3	O21 4-1		M03 4-1	a30 3-1	N18 1-1	a20 3-0	A28 2-0	S09 3-2	M31 2-0	S23 0-4	F03 2-3	D02 2-3	a16 1-0	a09 3-2	a28 3-2	M17 1-2	A19 0-1	D26 1-5	D23 1-1
8 COLCHESTER U	S02 3-2	a20 3-0	N11 1-1	D30 9-1	A21 2-0	O02 5-2	O14 3-3		J27 5-3	J20 2-0	a30 5-3	a21 2-0	M10 6-0	S16 6-1	M23 2-0	O28 2-2	D23 5-1	a07 1-1	F10 2-0	A19 3-0	S30 3-0	S25 6-1	D09 2-4	F24 3-1
9 CREWE A	M02 4-0	M07 2-0	D16 1-1	M31 1-2	N18 3-0	D02 1-1	S06 2-1	a14 4-0		O07 5-1	F10 2-0	J20 3-1	A23 5-2	S20 3-0	a20 3-2	F14 2-1	O21 3-5	A26 2-1	J13 3-1	M17 3-2	a28 3-0	S30 2-0	S16 0-3	O11 0-0
10 DARLINGTON	A28 1-1	F17 2-0	D26 1-0	S23 3-3	F03 2-1	J13 2-0	a07 4-4	S09 0-2	F24 2-1		O28 1-0	O14 1-0	J27 1-1	a23 1-2	M19 3-1	a21 1-5	S04 3-0	S18 2-0	D16 1-2	O02 3-0	A26 2-1	M24 1-1	M10 1-0	N11 0-0
11 DONCASTER R	F27 1-1	a13 2-1	J20 3-2	D02 2-0	a28 1-2	S19 2-0	a23 0-0	S05 1-4	S23 3-0	M17 1-2		F16 3-1	D16 2-1	M10 2-2	J12 0-1	A26 1-2	M30 0-0	F03 1-2	M03 1-2	N18 1-1	O07 6-1	A22 1-1	O10 0-2	D26 1-2
12 EXETER C	O21 3-0	M31 2-1	A26 3-0	N18 1-2	a14 4-0	a28 5-0	A23 4-1	D02 0-2	S09 2-1	M03 0-1	S30 1-5		D26 1-3	O07 1-1	D16 2-1	a23 1-1	M17 3-3	J13 1-3	S19 1-1	J06 4-3	F03 1-0	O11 3-1	F10 1-1	a11 2-1
13 GILLINGHAM	D02 5-1	S20 0-1	O04 3-2	O07 3-1	M03 4-1	M17 0-0	J20 5-1	O21 2-1	A30 0-1	a14 2-2	A19 2-2	D30 2-2		N18 4-0	F17 2-2	S23 3-1	a28 0-2	m03 4-2	M31 4-0	F03 1-1	J06 0-1	D23 4-2	a23 2-3	S02 1-2
14 HARTLEPOOLS U		O02 0-2	D09 2-3	F17 1-3	S23 0-3	S09 1-3	N11 1-2	F03 1-1	S25 2-1	a20 2-0	O21 3-0	F24 0-0	a07 1-3		a21 0-1	J27 2-0	A21 1-1	D16 3-1	A26 4-2	S04 2-2	J13 0-0	O28 0-1	O14 1-4	M24 0-2
15 MANSFIELD T		M02 4-1	A21 0-1	O21 0-1	M17 5-2	M30 3-0	F10 2-2	J15 4-0	a23 1-1	a28 3-0	S02 4-0	A19 3-1	S30 3-1	D02 3-1		O16 0-0	M26 2-0	D26 0-1	a14 3-1	O07 2-0	N18 1-2	J20 4-1	D23 1-2	S16 3-1
16 MILLWALL		O07 2-1	S04 1-0	M03 1-2	O21 3-0	J06 2-0	S16 2-1	M17 2-0	D30 4-3	D02 4-2	M05 2-0	a20 2-0	F10 0-0	a14 3-2	O02 4-0		F17 2-0	A28 1-1	N18 1-1	S18 1-3	M31 3-0	S02 5-0	A19 0-1	J20 2-1
17 OLDHAM A	O11 5-0	F03 2-1	F24 3-2	S09 2-2	J13 5-0	D16 4-1	a21 3-1	A26 2-2	M10 2-0	m02 0-1	N11 3-1	O28 1-1	D09 1-1	A30 5-2	N15 2-3	S30 4-2		O14 2-2	D26 2-1	S23 0-0	a23 2-0	a07 0-2	M24 1-1	M13 1-0
18 ROCHDALE	O07 1-0	M17 1-0	a23 0-2	J31 4-1	M31 1-1	a14 3-2	O11 1-1	N18 0-1	M13 3-0	O18 1-3	S16 2-3	S02 3-0	S06 3-1	A19 3-1	a11 3-2	A23 4-1	M03 3-1		a28 2-0	O21 3-3	D02 1-0	F10 1-3	J20 2-1	S30 3-1
19 SOUTHPORT		m01 2-1	a21 0-0	O03 2-1	F16 0-0	F03 1-0	M24 0-2	S23 3-0	S02 2-0	A19 1-4	O14 3-1	S25 1-1	N11 1-1	D23 0-1	M05 2-1	a07 3-1	D30 0-5	D09 3-0		A22 2-1	S09 2-1	M10 1-1	F24 4-2	O28 3-1
20 STOCKPORT CO	S29 2-0	S08 3-1	O14 3-0	J13 3-1	A26 1-2	a20 0-1	M12 2-1	D16 1-4	O28 0-1	O09 3-0	a06 2-1	M23 1-0	S16 3-1	a09 1-1	F23 2-1	S25 1-1	F10 1-1	M09 5-2	A28 1-4		D26 3-0	M19 3-1	N11 1-2	a21 2-1
21 TRANMERE R	A19 2-0	A28 1-2	N24 2-1	S04 3-2	O02 0-3	S23 4-1	O28 1-0	F17 5-2	D09 1-6	M12 0-0	F23 3-2	S16 3-4	M24 4-2	S01 3-2	a07 2-0	N11 5-1	a20 3-1	a21 2-0	J19 3-1	M26 1-3		O14 3-2	S25 2-0	M09 2-2
22 WORKINGTON		D02 2-1	F03 1-2	a28 5-3	M07 2-1	O07 4-1	D16 2-0	S21 1-2	F17 0-1	a04 2-1	A30 0-0	O04 3-1	A26 5-1	M17 1-1	S09 1-1	J13 2-2	N18 0-2	S23 2-1	O21 3-0	a14 1-1	M03 2-1		a11 1-0	a23 0-0
23 WREXHAM		N18 2-1	J13 1-1	a14 2-1	D02 2-2	F17 0-0	M28 4-2	a28 0-0	F03 1-1	O21 5-0	O18 3-1	S23 1-2	a20 3-0	M03 10-1	A26 5-0	D16 2-2	a04 2-1	S09 3-0	O07 2-3	M30 0-1	S20 4-0	S04 2-3		A30 2-1
24 YORK C	N18 1-0	a28 0-1	S23 5-0	D16 4-0	S18 1-1	M03 5-1	A26 4-0	O07 5-0	O02 4-2	M31 2-1	a02 5-2	S04 2-1	J13 4-0	M19 2-0	F03 2-1	S09 0-1	a14 4-1	F17 2-1	M16 2-2	D02 1-0	O21 1-2	a20 4-0	A21 3-2	

LEAGUE TABLES

DIVISION 1

	P	W	D	L	F	A	W	D	L	F	A	Pts
Ipswich T	42	17	2	2	58	28	7	6	8	35	39	56
Burnley	42	14	4	3	57	26	7	7	7	44	41	53
Tottenham H	42	14	4	3	59	34	7	6	8	29	35	52
Everton	42	17	2	2	64	21	3	9	9	24	33	51
Sheffield U	42	13	5	3	37	23	6	4	11	24	46	47
Sheffield W	42	14	4	3	47	23	6	2	13	25	35	46
Aston Villa	42	13	5	3	45	20	5	3	13	20	36	44
West Ham U	42	11	6	4	49	37	6	4	11	27	45	44
W.B.A.	42	10	7	4	50	23	5	6	10	33	44	43
Arsenal	42	9	6	6	39	31	7	5	9	32	41	43
Bolton W	42	11	7	3	35	22	5	3	13	27	44	42
Manchester C	42	11	3	7	46	38	6	4	11	32	43	41
Blackpool	42	10	4	7	41	30	5	7	9	29	45	41
Leicester C	42	12	2	7	38	27	5	4	12	34	44	40
Manchester U	42	10	3	8	44	31	5	6	10	28	44	39
Blackburn R	42	10	6	5	33	22	4	5	12	17	36	39
Birmingham C	42	9	6	6	37	35	5	4	12	28	46	38
Wolverh'pton W	42	8	7	6	38	34	5	3	13	35	52	36
Nottingham F	42	12	4	5	39	23	1	6	14	24	56	36
Fulham	42	8	3	10	38	34	5	4	12	28	40	33
Cardiff C	42	6	9	6	30	33	3	5	13	20	48	32
Chelsea	42	7	7	7	34	29	2	3	16	29	65	28

DIVISION 2

	P	W	D	L	F	A	W	D	L	F	A	Pts
Liverpool	42	18	3	0	68	19	9	5	7	31	24	62
Leyton O	42	11	5	5	34	17	11	5	5	35	23	54
Sunderland	42	17	3	1	60	16	5	6	10	25	34	53
Scunthorpe U	42	14	4	3	52	26	7	3	11	34	45	49
Plymouth A	42	12	4	5	45	30	7	4	10	30	45	46
Southampton	42	13	3	5	53	28	5	6	10	24	34	45
Huddersfield T	42	11	5	5	39	22	5	7	9	28	37	44
Stoke C	42	13	4	4	34	17	4	4	13	21	40	42
Rotherham U	42	9	6	6	36	30	7	3	11	34	46	41
Preston N.E.	42	11	4	6	34	23	4	6	11	21	34	40
Newcastle U	42	10	5	6	40	27	5	4	12	24	31	39
Middlesbrough	42	11	3	7	45	29	5	4	12	31	43	39
Luton T	42	12	1	8	44	37	5	4	12	25	34	39
Walsall	42	11	7	3	42	23	3	4	14	28	52	39
Charlton A	42	10	5	6	38	30	5	4	12	31	45	39
Derby Co	42	10	7	4	42	27	4	4	13	26	48	39
Norwich C	42	10	6	5	36	28	4	5	12	25	42	39
Bury	42	9	4	8	32	36	8	1	12	20	40	39
Leeds U	42	9	6	6	24	19	3	6	12	26	42	36
Swansea T	42	10	5	6	38	30	2	7	12	23	53	36
Bristol R	42	11	3	7	36	31	2	4	15	17	50	33
Brighton & H.A.	42	7	7	7	24	32	3	4	14	18	54	31

DIVISION 3

	P	W	D	L	F	A	W	D	L	F	A	Pts
Portsmouth	46	15	6	2	48	23	12	5	6	39	24	65
Grimsby T	46	18	3	2	49	18	10	3	10	31	38	62
Bournemouth	46	14	8	1	42	18	7	9	7	27	27	59
Q.P.R.	46	15	3	5	65	31	9	8	6	46	42	59
Peterborough U	46	16	0	7	60	38	10	6	7	47	44	58
Bristol C	46	15	3	5	56	27	8	5	10	38	45	54
Reading	46	14	5	4	46	24	8	4	11	31	42	53
Northampton T	46	12	6	5	52	24	8	5	10	33	33	51
Swindon T	46	11	8	4	48	26	6	7	10	30	45	49
Hull C	46	15	2	6	43	20	5	6	12	24	34	48
Bradford P.A.	46	13	5	5	47	27	7	2	14	33	51	47
Port Vale	46	12	4	7	41	23	5	7	11	24	35	45
Notts Co	46	14	5	4	44	23	3	4	16	23	51	43
Coventry C	46	11	6	6	38	26	5	5	13	26	45	43
Crystal Palace	46	8	8	7	50	41	6	6	11	33	39	42
Southend U	46	10	7	6	31	26	3	9	11	26	43	42
Watford	46	10	9	4	37	26	4	4	15	26	48	41
Halifax T	46	9	5	9	34	35	6	5	12	28	49	40
Shrewsbury T	46	8	7	8	46	37	5	5	13	27	47	38
Barnsley	46	9	6	8	45	41	4	6	13	26	54	38
Torquay U	46	9	4	10	48	44	6	2	15	28	56	36
Lincoln C	46	4	10	9	31	43	5	7	11	26	44	35
Brentford	46	11	3	9	34	29	2	5	16	19	64	34
Newport Co	46	6	5	12	29	38	1	3	19	17	64	22

DIVISION 4

	P	W	D	L	F	A	W	D	L	F	A	Pts
Millwall	44	16	3	3	47	18	7	7	8	40	44	56
Colchester U	44	17	4	1	78	24	6	5	11	26	47	55
Wrexham	44	12	6	4	56	23	10	3	9	40	33	53
Carlisle U	44	15	3	4	35	22	7	5	10	29	41	52
Bradford C	44	14	5	3	58	32	7	4	11	36	54	51
York C	44	17	2	3	62	19	3	8	11	22	34	50
Aldershot	44	16	4	2	56	20	6	1	15	25	40	49
Workington	44	12	6	4	40	23	7	5	10	29	47	49
Barrow	44	12	7	3	49	20	5	7	10	25	38	48
Crewe A	44	16	3	3	53	24	4	3	15	26	46	46
Oldham A	44	12	7	3	47	26	5	5	12	30	44	46
Rochdale	44	14	3	5	47	28	5	4	13	24	43	45
Darlington	44	13	5	4	37	24	5	4	13	24	49	45
Mansfield T	44	14	3	5	51	19	5	3	14	26	47	44
Tranmere R	44	15	2	5	53	37	5	2	15	17	44	44
Stockport Co	44	13	3	6	42	27	4	6	12	28	42	43
Southport	44	13	5	4	36	25	4	4	14	25	46	43
Exeter C	44	11	5	6	43	32	2	6	14	19	45	37
Chesterfield	44	11	3	8	43	38	3	6	13	27	49	37
Gillingham	44	10	6	6	48	30	3	5	14	25	64	37
Doncaster R	44	8	5	9	34	29	3	2	17	26	56	29
Hartlepool U	44	6	5	11	27	35	2	6	14	25	66	27
Chester C	44	5	9	8	36	37	2	3	17	18	59	26

Accrington Stanley resigned from the League 6.3.1962.

Top scorers: Div 1, J.Greaves (Tottenham Hotspur) 37 goals; Div 2, R.Tambling (Chelsea) 35 goals; Div 3, G.Hudson (Coventry City) 30 goals; Div 4, K.Wagstaff (Mansfield Town) 34 goals.

Accrington Stanley resigned, Oxford United were elected in their place.

Everton's Alex Young, the Scottish international inside-forward who became such a hero at Goodison. His vision steered the Merseysiders to the Division One title in 1962-63.

DIVISION 1

	ARSENAL	ASTON VILLA	BIRMINGHAM C	BLACKBURN R	BLACKPOOL	BOLTON W	BURNLEY	EVERTON	FULHAM	IPSWICH T	LEICESTER C	LEYTON O	LIVERPOOL	MANCHESTER C	MANCHESTER U	NOTTINGHAM F	SHEFFIELD U	SHEFFIELD W	TOTTENHAM H	W.B.A.	WEST HAM U	WOLVERHAMPTON W
1 ARSENAL		S04 1-2	A21 2-0	M23 3-1	D08 2-0	F16 3-2	m11 2-3	M26 4-3	m14 3-0	N24 3-1	S22 1-1	D15 2-0	M09 2-2	a20 2-3	A25 1-3	a06 0-0	N10 1-0	S08 1-2	F23 2-3	a12 3-2	O13 1-1	O27 5-4
2 ASTON VILLA	S10 3-1		M16 4-0	J19 0-0	S01 1-1	D01 5-0	N17 2-1	a01 0-2	N03 1-2	S29 4-2	m15 3-1	O20 1-0	m18 2-0	m08 3-1	a09 1-2	m04 0-2	S15 1-2	a13 0-2	A20 2-1	O06 2-0	A18 3-1	a16 0-2
3 BIRMINGHAM C	A29 2-2	O27 3-2		D08 3-3	a20 3-6	a03 2-2	S08 5-1	a16 0-1	S22 4-1	a06 0-1	m18 3-2	A25 2-2	N24 0-2	O13 2-2	m10 2-1	N10 2-2	M23 0-1	M30 1-1	D15 0-2	S19 0-0	m01 3-2	M09 3-4
4 BLACKBURN R	N03 5-5	S08 4-1	a27 6-1		M25 3-3	M29 5-0	O06 2-3	N17 3-2	M16 0-1	D15 0-1	O20 2-0	D01 1-1	A25 1-0	m01 4-1	M02 2-2	A20 2-5	S17 1-2	a12 3-0	m20 3-0	a13 3-1	S22 0-4	m13 5-1
5 BLACKPOOL	a27 3-2	M29 4-0	D01 1-1	a23 4-1		N17 3-1	M20 0-0	a13 1-2	O20 0-0	A20 1-0	a08 1-1	M02 3-2	D15 1-2	S22 2-2	O06 2-2	S03 2-1	a15 3-1	M16 2-3	S08 1-2	N03 0-2	m13 0-0	A25 0-2
6 BOLTON W	S29 3-0	a20 4-1	a24 0-0	N24 0-0	a06 3-0		A22 2-2	S15 0-2	A25 1-0	S08 1-3	m11 2-0	a15 0-1	m13 1-0	N10 3-1	S05 3-0	O27 1-0	M09 3-2	m06 0-4	D08 1-0	M25 1-2	M23 3-0	O13 3-0
7 BURNLEY	S01 2-1	a06 3-1	m14 3-1	a02 1-0	S29 2-0	A28 2-1		A18 1-3	a12 4-0	D08 3-1	S04 1-1	S15 2-0	M23 1-3	O27 0-0	m04 0-1	a20 0-0	O13 5-1	D29 4-0	N24 2-1	a30 2-1	M09 1-1	N10 2-0
8 EVERTON	a24 1-1	O13 1-1	a15 2-2	a06 0-0	N10 5-0	m04 1-0	D15 3-1		m11 4-1	O27 3-1	S08 3-2	S05 3-0	S22 2-2	M23 2-1	A22 3-1	M09 2-0	N24 3-0	A25 4-1	a20 1-0	S29 4-2	D08 1-1	F23 0-0
9 FULHAM	S15 1-3	M23 1-0	m04 3-3	O27 0-0	M09 2-0	m01 2-1	a15 1-1	S01 1-0		O13 1-1	A18 2-1	S29 0-2	a20 0-0	N24 2-4	D26 0-1	F23 3-1	A29 2-2	S19 4-1	N10 0-2	m18 1-2	a06 2-0	D08 0-5
10 IPSWICH T	M30 1-1	m21 1-1	N17 1-5	A18 3-3	A28 5-2	m17 4-1	a27 2-1	M19 0-3	M02 0-1		O06 0-1	a13 1-1	M05 2-2	S11 0-0	N03 3-5	S01 1-1	D21 1-0	D01 2-0	M16 2-4	O20 1-1	a15 2-3	S22 2-3
11 LEICESTER C	F09 2-0	D08 3-3	S29 3-0	M09 2-0	N24 0-0	S01 4-1	S19 3-3	F12 3-1	D15 2-3	F23 3-0		D26 5-1	O13 3-0	a06 2-0	a16 4-3	A25 2-1	O27* 3-1	A22 3-3	M23 2-2	S15 1-0	N10 2-0	a20 1-1
12 LEYTON O	A18 1-2	M09 0-2	D22 2-2	a20 1-1	O13 0-2	a12 0-1	m07 0-1	S12 3-0	F16 1-1	N10 1-2	a03 0-2		m02 2-1	F23 1-1	S08 1-0	M23 0-1	D08 2-2	S22 2-4	O27 1-5	A29 2-3	S01 2-0	N24 0-4
13 LIVERPOOL	N14 2-1	F13 4-0	m08 5-1	D22 3-1	A18 1-2	O06 1-0	N03 1-2	a08 0-0	D01 2-1	S15 1-1	M02 0-2	N17 5-0		A29 4-1	a13 1-0	a18 0-2	S01 2-0	a29 0-2	a12 5-2	M20 2-2	S12 2-1	F16 4-1
14 MANCHESTER C	D01 2-4	A25 0-2	M02 2-1	S29 0-1	m04 0-3	a13 2-1	M26 2-5	N03 1-1	M29 2-3	S05 2-1	N17 1-1	O06 2-0	A22 2-2		m15 1-1	a12 1-0	a24 1-3	O20 3-2	m11 1-0	a27 1-5	S08 1-6	D15 3-3
15 MANCHESTER U	m06 2-3	N24 2-2	S01 2-0	O13 0-3	F23 1-1	S12 3-0	S22 2-5	A29 0-1	a01 0-2	M23 0-1	a15 2-2	m18 3-1	N10 3-3	S15 2-3		D08 5-1	a20 1-1	m01 1-3	M09 0-2	A18 2-2	O27 3-1	a22 2-1
16 NOTTINGHAM F	N17 3-0	S22 3-1	a13 0-2	A28 2-0	S11 2-0	M16 1-0	D01 2-1	N13 3-4	O06 3-1	m10 2-1	F19 0-2	N03 1-1	S08 3-1	a15 1-1	m20 3-2		A18 2-1	M02 0-3	m18 1-1	m14 2-2	D29 3-4	a30 2-0
17 SHEFFIELD U	a13 3-3	m01 2-1	N03 0-2	S05 1-1	a16 0-0	O20 4-1	M02 1-0	M30 2-1	A22 2-0	A25 2-1	M26 0-0	a26 2-0	m11 0-0	a03 3-1	D01 1-1	D15 3-1		O06 2-2	S22 3-1	N17 1-0	F16 0-2	S08 1-2
18 SHEFFIELD W	m18 2-3	N10 0-0	S15 5-0	a15 4-0	O27 0-0	A18 1-1	a23 0-1	D22 2-2	S12 1-0	a20 0-3	A29 0-3	m04 3-1	D08 0-2	M09 4-1	S29 1-0	O13 2-2	m15 3-1		a08 3-1	S01 3-1	N24 1-3	M23 3-1
19 TOTTENHAM H	O06 4-4	A29 4-2	A18 3-0	S15 4-1	J19 2-0	a27 4-1	M30 1-1	D01 0-0	a13 1-1	D26 5-0	N03 4-0	M27 2-0	a15 7-2	S01 4-2	O24 6-2	S29 9-2	m04 4-2	N17 1-1		M02 2-1	D22 4-4	S12 1-2
20 W.B.A.	a15 1-2	m11 1-0	S12 1-0	N10 2-5	M23 1-2	S22 5-4	A25 1-2	m07 0-4	S08 6-1	M09 6-1	m04 2-1	A22 2-1	O27 1-0	D08 2-1	D15 3-0	N24 1-4	a06 1-2	J12 0-3	O13 1-2		a20 1-0	a03 2-2
21 WEST HAM U	M02 0-4	D15 1-1	O06 5-0	m04 0-1	S14 2-2	N03 1-2	O22 1-1	a27 1-2	N17 2-2	a12 1-3	a13 2-0	m11 2-0	S03 1-0	m18 6-1	M18 3-1	a22 4-1	S29 1-1	a02 2-0	A25 1-6	D01 2-2		A20 1-4
22 WOLVERHAMPTON W	a08 1-0	a15 3-1	O24 0-2	S01 4-2	m09 2-0	M20 4-0	a13 7-2	O06 0-2	a27 2-1	m04 0-0	D01 1-3	M30 2-1	S29 3-2	A18 8-1	N17 2-3	S15 1-1	J19 0-0	N03 2-2	S19 2-2	M16 7-0	A29 0-0	

Dennis Viollet, the former Manchester United star who helped lift Stoke City back to Division One.

DIVISION 2

	BURY	CARDIFF C	CHARLTON A	CHELSEA	DERBY CO	GRIMSBY T	HUDDERSFIELD T	LEEDS U	LUTON T	MIDDLESBROUGH	NEWCASTLE U	NORWICH C	PLYMOUTH A	PORTSMOUTH	PRESTON N.E.	ROTHERHAM U	SCUNTHORPE U	SOUTHAMPTON	STOKE C	SUNDERLAND	SWANSEA T	WALSALL
1 BURY		N03 1-0	S22 3-1	a16 2-0	a13 3-3	O06 2-0	M30 1-1	S18 3-1	A18 1-0	N17 1-0	D01 0-0	J19 0-3	M02 1-2	a02 2-0	O20 0-0	M19 0-5	S01 0-2	m07 1-1	m14 2-1	D29 3-0	A30 2-0	a27 0-0
2 CARDIFF C	M23 3-1		a06 1-2	F23 1-0	D22 1-0	S12 5-3	m18 3-0	D08 0-0	O13 1-0	S01 1-2	A18 4-4	A29 2-4	m01 2-1	S22 1-2	m06 1-1	N10 4-1	O27 4-0	M09 3-1	N24 1-1	a20 5-2	S15 5-2	a15 2-2
3 CHARLTON A	F09 0-0	N17 2-4		D22 1-4	a27 0-0	O20 0-3	a13 1-0	a15 1-2	S01 2-0	D01 3-4	a23 1-2	M02 0-2	M16 6-3	M30 2-0	N03 2-1	S29 2-3	S15 1-0	m18 2-1	S18 0-3	A28 2-2	A18 2-2	O06 3-2
4 CHELSEA	a12 2-0	O06 6-0	A25 5-0		M27 3-1	a13 2-1	M02 1-2	a30 2-2	a01 3-1	O20 3-2	N03 4-2	N17 2-0	D01 1-1	m21 7-0	a27 2-0	D15 3-0	A22 3-0	S10 2-0	m11 0-1	S08 1-0	S22 2-2	M30 0-1
5 DERBY CO	N24 0-0	A25 1-2	D08 2-3	O27 1-3		S22 2-4	D15 2-1	O13 0-0	M23 1-0	a15 3-3	S19 0-1	m06 3-0	M20 3-2	m10 4-0	S08 1-0	a20 3-2	a06 6-2	N10 3-1	A22 1-1	F23 2-2	M09 0-2	a24 2-0
6 GRIMSBY T	m18 5-1	S18 1-2	M09 2-1	N24 0-3	m04 0-0		D29 1-1	N10 1-1	a20 3-1	S29 3-4	S15 0-1	S01 0-2	D15 1-1	A21 1-1	a12 2-0	O13 1-2	A25 3-0	D08 4-1	O27 1-1	M23 1-2	a06 1-0	a30 3-1
7 HUDDERSFIELD T	N10 0-1	S08 1-0	N24 2-0	O13 1-0	A18 3-3	a24 0-0		S01 1-1	M09 2-0	a29 0-0	a16 2-1	S12 0-0	a01 4-2	m13 1-3	S22 1-0	a06 1-0	M23 2-0	O27 2-3	a20 3-3	D08 0-3	m06 4-1	A29 4-0
8 LEEDS U	S05 1-2	a27 3-0	a16 4-1	S15 2-0	M02 3-1	M30 3-0	m11 0-1		m04 3-0	O06 2-3	O20 1-0	N03 3-0	N17 6-1	D01 3-3	a13 4-1	A22 3-4	a03 1-0	S29 1-1	D15 3-1	A25 1-0	m18 5-0	M13 3-0
9 LUTON T	D15 2-1	a24 2-3	m11 4-1	D26 0-2	N03 1-2	D01 2-2	M16 3-2	S22 2-2		M25 4-3	M30 2-3	a13 4-2	a27 3-0	O06 3-3	S05 0-2	A25 2-3	a15 1-0	A29 3-2	S08 0-0	m13 0-3	m01 3-1	N17 4-3
10 MIDDLESBROUGH	a06 0-0	m11 3-2	a20 2-1	M09 1-0	a12 5-1	F16 0-1	A25 0-5	m06 2-1	O27 0-2		A22 4-2	m21 6-2	S22 3-0	S07 4-2	m15 2-0	N24 2-1	N10 4-3	M23 1-2	D08 2-2	D15 3-3	O13 2-2	S12 2-3
11 NEWCASTLE U	a20 1-3	D15 2-1	a03 3-2	M23 2-0	S12 0-0	M27 0-0	a12 1-1	M09 1-1	N10 3-1	A29 6-1		S22 2-1	S08 3-1	A25 1-1	m11 2-2	D08 4-1	N24 1-1	a06 4-1	m01 5-2	O13 1-1	O27 6-0	m08 0-2
12 NORWICH C	S08 1-1	A22 0-0	O13 1-4	a06 4-1	S29 2-0	m11 0-0	S05 2-3	M23 3-2	N24 3-3	D29 3-4	m04 1-2		A25 2-1	a16 5-3	D15 1-1	F23 4-2	D08 3-3	a20 1-0	M09 6-0	O27 4-2	N10 5-0	S15 2-1
13 PLYMOUTH A	O13 0-0	D26 4-2	O27 6-1	a20 2-1	S15 2-1	A18 2-0	S29 1-1	a06 3-1	D08 3-1	F09 4-5	J19 0-2	D22 1-0		S19 2-0	A22 7-1	M09 2-2	F23 2-3	a12 2-1	M23 0-1	N10 1-1	N24 1-0	S01 3-0
14 PORTSMOUTH	O27 2-1	m04 2-0	N10 3-3	S29 0-2	S01 1-0	A29 2-1	S15 1-1	a20 3-0	F23 3-1	m18 1-1	D22 3-1	a15 0-2	S12 1-2		m01 1-2	M23 1-2	M09 1-2	O13 1-1	a06 0-3	N24 3-1	D08 0-0	A18 4-1
15 PRESTON N.E.	M09 0-2	S29 2-6	M23 4-1	D08 1-3	m18 1-0	a15 0-0	m04 2-0	N24 4-1	S11 3-1	S15 0-1	S01 2-1	A18 2-2	A28 0-0	D26 4-2		O27 2-2	O13 3-1	F23 1-0	N10 1-1	a06 1-1	a20 6-3	M19 4-2
16 ROTHERHAM U	S15 1-5	M29 2-1	a30 1-2	A18 0-1	N30 2-2	m07 0-0	N17 0-2	A28 2-1	D21 2-1	a13 4-1	a27 3-1	O05 0-3	O20 3-2	N03 0-0	M16 3-1		m17 1-0	S01 2-0	D26 1-2	S11 4-2	a15 2-1	m04 1-2
17 SCUNTHORPE U	m10 1-0	M15 2-2	m07 2-0	A28 3-0	N16 2-1	D21 1-1	N02 2-2	a23 0-2	a12 2-0	M29 1-1	S04 2-1	a26 3-1	O06 2-2	O19 1-2	M26 4-1	S08 1-0		A18 2-1	S22 0-0	a30 1-1	S11 1-0	N30 2-0
18 SOUTHAMPTON	A25 0-3	O31 3-5	S08 1-0	S19 2-1	m01 5-0	m13 4-1	M20 3-1	m15 3-1	A22 2-2	N03 6-0	N17 3-0	D01 3-1	a15 1-1	M02 4-2	O06 1-0	m11 1-0	D15 1-1		m22 2-0	S22 2-4	a22 3-0	a13 2-0
19 STOKE C	S29 2-0	a13 1-0	S12 6-3	S01 0-0	A29 3-3	M16 4-1	D01 2-1	A18 0-1	m18 2-0	a27 0-1	O06 3-1	O20 3-0	N03 2-2	N17 3-1	M30 3-0	a01 3-1	m04 2-3	S15 3-1		a15 2-1	M27 2-0	M02 3-0
20 SUNDERLAND	D26 0-1	D01 2-1	A22 1-0	m18 0-1	O06 3-0	N03 6-2	a27 1-1	D22 2-1	S15 3-1	A18 3-1	M02 0-0	M20 7-1	M30 1-1	a13 1-0	N17 2-1	S05 2-0	S29 0-0	m04 4-0	a12 0-0		S01 3-1	O20 5-0
21 SWANSEA T	A23 3-0	S04 2-1	D15 2-1	F09 2-0	O19 2-0	N17 1-0	O06 1-2	S08 0-2	S29 1-0	M02 1-1	M16 1-0	a09 2-0	a13 2-1	a27 0-0	D01 1-1	a16 2-2	S18 1-0	D26 1-1	A25 2-1	m11 3-4		N03 3-0
22 WALSALL	D08 3-1	a16 2-1	m24 1-2	N10 1-5	M16 1-3	S08 4-1	A21 1-1	O27 1-1	a06 1-1	S04 1-0	S29 0-6	m14 3-1	M26 2-2	D15 3-5	A25 4-1	S22 1-0	a20 1-1	N24 1-1	O13 0-0	M09 2-3	M23 0-1	

Season 1962-63

DIVISION 3

	BARNSLEY	BOURNEMOUTH	BRADFORD	BRIGHTON & HA	BRISTOL C	BRISTOL R	CARLISLE U	COLCHESTER U	COVENTRY C	CRYSTAL P	HALIFAX T	HULL C	MILLWALL	NORTHAMPTON T	NOTTS CO	PETERBOROUGH U	PORT VALE	Q.P.R.	READING	SHREWSBURY T	SOUTHEND U	SWINDON T	WATFORD	WREXHAM
1 BARNSLEY		a02 2-2	a30 1-4	A28 2-0	M16 1-1	N27 4-0	a16 2-0	a27 2-3	O05 2-1	m22 0-4	S04 1-0	S22 1-2	a13 4-1	S08 1-1	J12 3-1	D21 0-2	M29 2-1	m10 0-0	m13 1-0	N17 1-0	D01 2-2	A18 1-1	O20 4-1	O02 2-1
2 BOURNEMOUTH	M20 1-1		A22 2-2	m08 1-0	S05 1-1	a06 1-1	a20 5-1	S01 1-1	a12 1-1	O27 3-0	N10 1-1	M09 3-0	S15 1-1	F23 3-0	D22 3-1	A18 3-3	S29 2-0	O13 2-1	N24 1-0	m04 0-0	m18 0-0	D08 0-0	S19 1-0	M23 3-1
3 BRADFORD	O13 1-1	A29 1-1		D08 1-5	S29 2-5	a20 2-2	S12 3-1	A18 1-1	S24 0-0	N10 2-1	J04 1-1	M23 3-1	S01 2-2	M09 2-3	a16 5-0	M06 2-2	S15 2-1	O27 0-3	m04 3-2	M26 2-1	M19 2-2	D26 2-0	O10 1-0	a06 3-1
4 BRIGHTON & H.A.	A21 2-0	a13 0-1	a27 3-1		M19 1-0	S22 1-1	O09 1-0	M30 3-0	D01 2-2	J12 1-2	F02 0-1	A25 2-1	M16 0-2	a12 0-5	N17 1-3	S18 0-3	M02 3-1	D15 2-2	O06 2-4	O20 1-1	J26 0-0	S04 1-1	m04 1-4	S08 1-3
5 BRISTOL C	O27 5-2	S11 1-0	F16 4-2	D26 1-2		a23 4-1	F23 2-2	A28 1-2	O02 1-1	m07 1-1	D08 2-2	a06 3-1	A18 2-2	M23 3-1	a30 1-1	M09 1-1	S01 2-0	N10 2-4	m18 4-2	D22 3-1	a16 6-3	O13 2-2	S22 3-3	m03 0-2
6 BRISTOL R	S18 3-2	N17 1-2	D01 3-3	F09 4-1	S15 1-2		S29 1-1	m14 2-0	a13 2-2	A25 2-0	S08 5-2	D15 2-5	O20 2-0	A21 2-2	M30 1-1	S04 3-1	O06 1-1	a15 0-0	F26 1-0	M02 2-0	M16 1-2	O09 2-0	a27 3-1	m11 1-1
7 CARLISLE U	a12 2-1	N30 0-3	a23 3-0	O02 1-0	O05 2-5	a02 4-0		N17 3-1	a27 0-1	S08 2-2	S22 1-0	m11 2-1	m14 4-3	D15 1-2	M12 4-2	A21 1-4	O20 1-1	A24 2-5	m06 1-1	M16 2-1	M30 1-2	S18 0-0	D26 2-1	m23 2-1
8 COLCHESTER U	D08 1-1	m11 3-1	D15 1-4	N10 4-1	A20 1-0	M22 1-0	a06 2-1		A25 0-0	O13 1-2	O27 1-1	M04 2-3	S29 2-5	S15 2-2	S08 2-2	a20 2-0	S10 0-1	a22 2-1	S24 4-2	O08 3-2	m04 3-1	m06 0-2	a16 3-2	M08 1-1
9 COVENTRY C	F23 2-0	a16 1-2	S18 3-1	a20 1-1	O23 4-2	a29 5-0	D08 3-2	F26 2-2		M23 1-0	a06 5-4	O27 2-2	a08 2-0	O13 1-1	A18 2-0	D29 3-3	m04 0-1	M09 4-1	S29 2-1	S15 0-0	S01 3-4	A28 2-0	S04 3-1	N10 3-0
10 CRYSTAL P	S29 1-2	M16 1-0	M30 6-0	S01 2-2	a13 3-2	M20 2-1	m18 3-0	M27 0-1	m15 0-0		A18 0-0	m01 1-1	D26 3-0	O10 1-2	O20 1-1	a24 0-2	a27 2-1	S12 1-0	D01 2-1	A29 2-2	O06 2-3	S15 0-0	N17 0-1	a15 5-0
11 HALIFAX T	S11 2-0	M30 3-1	a13 4-4	S15 2-1	a27 2-5	m18 2-3	M26 2-4	M15 1-2	N17 2-4	D15 2-2		a15 0-2	m21 3-0	S24 1-3	m07 2-1	O08 2-0	a03 0-4	A27 1-4	m11 1-2	O06 2-2	O19 0-1	S29 4-3	D01 1-3	A25 2-0
12 HULL C	m04 0-2	O20 1-1	M13 1-0	D22 2-1	N17 4-0	A18 3-0	A31 3-1	O06 2-2	m07 2-0	S20 0-0	a12 2-0		S13 4-1	S29 2-0	m20 1-1	S15 3-2	D01 0-1	a25 4-1	a13 0-1	a27 2-2	D29 1-2	m18 1-1	M30 1-0	A23 1-3
13 MILLWALL	m18 4-1	M11 1-0	m11 3-1	O27 2-2	D15 4-2	M09 2-1	M23 2-0	F16 2-1	S08 3-3	a01 1-1	O13 1-1	S03 5-1		a20 1-3	S22 0-2	a06 0-1	A27 0-0	D08 0-0	a12 4-1	S17 1-2	O01 3-1	N10 3-4	A25 6-0	F23 2-4
14 NORTHAMPTON T	a23 4-2	O06 2-2	O20 3-1	a16 3-0	a08 5-1	A28 2-0	m09 2-0	M12 3-1	M02 0-0	O02 3-1	S17 7-1	m24 3-0	D01 1-1		a02 2-2	S01 2-3	N17 0-0	S22 1-0	M30 5-0	a13 1-0	a27 5-3	M26 1-1	M16 1-0	S11 8-0
15 NOTTS CO	S01 2-0	A25 2-0	a12 3-2	a06 0-1	S20 3-2	N10 1-3	M21 1-0	m17 6-0	D15 1-1	M09 0-2	M23 5-0	O13 1-1	m04 3-3	D26 2-1		D08 2-0	O11 1-0	F23 3-2	S06 1-0	S29 1-5	S15 2-1	a20 2-0	A23 1-3	O27 3-2
16 PETERBOROUGH U	A25 4-2	D15 3-0	O06 2-0	O15 3-1	O20 3-1	S10 1-0	A27 2-2	D01 6-2	D26 0-3	S22 0-0	O01 1-1	M25 1-3	N17 6-0	m11 0-4	a27 0-0		M18 3-1	S08 1-2	M16 1-1	a02 2-3	a13 1-3	a15 3-1	M02 4-0	F16 1-3
17 PORT VALE	N09 1-0	m13 0-3	m06 2-1	O13 1-2	m11 3-1	m20 2-0	M09 2-0	S03 4-2	S22 2-1	D08 4-1	a22 2-0	a20 1-0	A20 1-1	a06 3-1	O01 1-1	M23 3-2		a29 3-2	A25 2-0	a12 0-0	S24 5-1	O27 2-1	S08 1-3	D15 2-2
18 Q.P.R.	S15 2-1	M02 1-0	M16 1-2	A18 2-2	M30 3-1	a12 3-5	D22 2-2	a01 1-2	m22 1-3	S03 4-1	A20 5-0	O22 4-1	a27 2-3	F09 1-3	O06 0-1	m18 0-0	a13 3-1		N17 3-2	D01 0-0	a08 1-0	S01 2-2	m13 2-2	S17 1-2
19 READING	M22 4-1	O03 2-1	S21 4-1	F23 4-5	S08 0-3	m08 1-0	O12 2-0	S19 4-1	m01 4-1	a19 0-1	A31 4-2	M20 2-2	a15 2-0	N10 2-1	S12 1-1	O26 0-1	D22 4-3	a05 1-1		A18 5-0	A29 1-3	M08 1-2	a03 0-0	M11 3-0
20 SHREWSBURY T	a06 1-3	S22 2-1	S07 1-2	M09 2-1	A25 3-3	O13 7-2	O27 1-1	O03 1-2	m20 2-1	A22 3-1	F23 4-2	D08 1-4	S26 3-3	m01 1-0	a24 2-2	N10 5-4	a15 2-1	a20 0-3	D15 2-1		S12 6-0	M23 1-2	m11 3-0	D26 4-2
21 SOUTHEND U	a20 0-0	S08 0-1	A25 3-1	M23 1-1	a15 2-2	O27 3-2	N10 2-0	S22 2-3	m11 1-1	m20 1-0	M09 1-1	D26 0-1	a22 2-1	D08 5-1	m13 1-2	m06 2-1	S17 2-0	S29 1-3	A20 2-0	S03 3-1		a06 1-1	D15 1-1	O13 2-0
22 SWINDON T	D15 2-1	a27 2-1	a02 2-1	S11 5-1	M02 3-2	O02 3-0	a30 2-0	a13 6-1	A21 4-1	F02 1-0	m04 1-1	S08 2-0	M30 1-0	A25 2-3	D01 3-1	a12 2-3	M16 2-3	J12 5-0	O20 1-1	m14 1-0	N17 4-1		O06 3-1	S22 3-0
23 WATFORD	M12 0-0	S25 0-1	O02 3-2	S29 2-0	M26 1-4	D08 0-1	D29 5-1	a15 1-1	S11 6-1	a06 1-4	a20 2-1	N10 4-2	a30 0-2	O27 4-2	A28 4-0	O13 2-3	m18 1-2	M23 2-5	S15 4-0	S01 4-3	A18 3-1	F23 3-3		a09 3-1
24 WREXHAM	m08 2-1	m15 1-0	N17 3-1	m18 0-0	D01 2-1	S01 5-2	S15 2-1	O20 4-1	a01 5-1	a12 3-4	m01 3-1	A29 2-0	O06 5-1	O24 1-4	M16 5-1	S29 4-4	A18 0-1	O10 3-1	a27 1-1	M20 2-0	M02 1-1	F27 0-0	a13 0-0	

DIVISION 4

	ALDERSHOT	BARROW	BRADFORD C	BRENTFORD	CHESTER	CHESTERFIELD	CREWE A	DARLINGTON	DONCASTER R	EXETER C	GILLINGHAM	HARTLEPOOLS U	LINCOLN C	MANSFIELD T	NEWPORT CO	OLDHAM A	OXFORD U	ROCHDALE	SOUTHPORT	STOCKPORT CO	TORQUAY U	TRANMERE R	WORKINGTON	YORK C
1 ALDERSHOT		A22 2-1	M20 3-1	O20 0-0	O06 2-2	M06 1-0	O10 2-2	D15 2-3	D01 3-1	a13 1-1	m11 0-1	S19 3-2	a03 1-2	M30 2-3	m18 2-1	O24 1-1	S15 0-0	M16 2-0	A25 4-2	a27 2-2	a12 1-1	S29 2-3	N17 2-2	a08 4-1
2 BARROW	A27 1-1		D22 1-1	F16 1-1	D01 4-3	O06 2-0	M30 2-3	D26 4-1	m06 4-0	M02 0-2	N17 1-1	a15 2-0	S15 2-1	M16 3-2	m13 3-0	a29 3-2	A18 3-2	a22 1-1	S10 6-2	a13 1-0	m04 0-0	S01 1-1	O20 5-1	a27 2-1
3 BRADFORD C	S22 0-2	A25 3-0		a13 2-1	M16 2-0	M30 1-1	O20 1-0	S08 3-0	O03 2-3	D01 2-3	m08 1-1	m11 1-1	M13 2-2	a03 1-3	m01 3-4	D15 1-3	a15 1-4	N17 1-2	M27 0-2	O06 3-2	A22 2-1	O24 2-1	a27 2-2	m15 1-2
4 BRENTFORD	M09 4-2	S29 2-1	N10 5-2		D26 2-1	m04 2-1	a30 3-1	F23 1-3	D15 1-0	S08 3-1	A21 1-2	O02 4-0	a20 3-2	A25 1-3	O27 3-1	D08 2-1	M23 4-0	S22 1-0	O13 3-3	S18 2-1	M12 2-2	a06 4-0	m23 4-3	a15 2-1
5 CHESTER	F23 0-2	a19 1-0	O27 2-0	a03 1-2		m22 0-2	S19 1-2	A29 1-2	m11 1-1	S22 3-1	D15 1-0	D07 1-0	a06 3-2	S08 0-2	O13 2-2	M13 1-0	M09 2-1	a15 1-0	O03 6-1	A25 0-1	N10 3-1	M23 0-0	m08 1-1	S12 0-0
6 CHESTERFIELD	M23 3-1	m20 1-1	m06 0-1	S15 1-1	S29 1-1		a12 1-2	M09 6-1	A20 3-1	A25 1-1	a29 0-2	O13 2-2	S01 2-2	S17 4-4	N10 1-2	a22 0-0	a06 1-0	m17 1-3	O27 6-0	S03 1-2	D08 2-0	a20 4-0	D15 1-1	a01 1-1
7 CREWE A	O03 2-1	a03 2-1	M09 5-0	S12 3-0	a22 3-0	a17 2-0		D08 2-1	S08 3-0	m22 1-0	A25 2-2	a20 4-1	N10 1-1	m08 3-0	M13 4-1	a06 2-3	O13 3-2	M27 1-2	D15 2-2	m11 1-2	M23 1-1	O27 2-0	S22 0-1	A29 1-0
8 DARLINGTON	A18 1-1	M18 2-1	m17 2-1	O06 1-3	A20 2-1	O20 2-1	a27 1-4		N17 5-1	M16 0-1	D01 2-0	S10 0-2	S29 0-0	a13 2-1	D22 4-2	a15 1-1	S01 2-1	a08 3-0	N24 1-3	M29 5-1	m06 1-3	S15 2-3	m13 3-1	M11 2-1
9 DONCASTER R	a20 2-1	M23 2-2	O09 1-1	A18 0-2	S01 1-2	A28 0-0	m18 1-1	a06 2-0		a02 1-1	S15 1-0	N10 2-3	M09 3-0	a15 1-1	D08 2-2	O27 1-1	S29 4-2	O30 2-2	m04 0-0	F09 1-2	O13 2-0	a25 2-1	D26 2-0	D22 3-2
10 EXETER C	N10 4-2	O13 0-2	a20 0-2	m17 2-2	m04 2-1	D22 2-2	S29 1-1	O27 1-3	S12 0-1		a15 0-0	M09 3-1	O03 1-1	A22 0-3	a06 1-0	F23 2-1	m08 1-1	S01 0-2	M23 2-1	D26 0-1	A18 0-3	D08 2-1	S20 1-0	S15 2-1
11 GILLINGHAM	S01 1-0	a06 2-3	O13 2-1	A29 1-4	A18 2-1	D26 2-1	D22 4-0	a20 1-0	m01 1-0	a12 4-0		M30 5-1	M23 3-0	S22 0-1	a24 3-1	N10 4-3	m20 2-1	S12 2-1	D08 3-1	S08 1-0	O27 4-2	M09 0-0	F16 2-2	S26 0-0
12 HARTLEPOOLS U	S24 1-2	a12 1-1	S01 2-2	a22 2-1	a27 0-3	a08 1-1	D01 1-5	S03 0-2	a13 1-1	O20 0-2	a01 1-1		m04 3-0	m13 3-4	A18 2-3	S29 0-1	D22 1-2	O06 4-0	A27 4-0	N17 3-0	S15 0-3	m18 0-2	M16 2-2	a29 1-1
13 LINCOLN C	D26 2-4	m18 1-2	S26 3-2	D01 1-3	N17 1-3	m11 1-3	a13 1-2	m01 2-1	O19 1-2	O10 4-1	m15 2-1	S22 4-1		M27 2-6	S12 6-3	S08 1-2	A29 1-0	a27 3-0	a15 0-2	M16 0-0	D21 3-0	A18 4-2	O06 3-2	M29 2-4
14 MANSFIELD T	M18 2-2	O27 5-0	a29 3-1	D22 1-2	m18 4-0	O22 3-0	S15 2-2	N10 6-0	a16 4-2	A27 1-0	m04 0-0	M23 3-1	O13 2-0		a20 2-1	M09 4-2	D08 3-2	A18 1-0	a06 6-1	S29 0-1	a08 1-2	O01 6-1	S10 0-0	S01 2-0
15 NEWPORT CO	S08 2-2	S17 6-0	S29 2-0	M16 1-4	M04 0-1	O01 2-3	O06 5-1	A25 2-2	a27 2-4	N17 4-0	a13 2-0	D15 2-1	S03 2-1	D01 1-1		A20 0-0	m23 1-0	m20 1-1	M11 1-0	m04 3-1	M18 1-0	D10 1-2	a01 2-2	O18 1-3
16 OLDHAM A	S12 2-0	S22 2-1	A18 2-1	a27 2-1	M30 2-0	a13 2-1	N17 2-2	a12 1-0	M16 4-0	O06 1-2	O10 2-1	m08 6-1	J19 4-1	O20 3-2	A29 3-2		S26 2-0	F02 5-1	D26 11-0	J26 2-1	S01 1-1	F27 1-1	M02 2-2	D01 3-2
17 OXFORD U	m01 1-1	D15 4-1	a12 2-1	m11 2-1	O20 3-0	N17 0-0	m15 0-0	m04 4-2	M20 3-3	M30 0-3	O06 2-3	A25 6-2	A22 2-1	a27 3-0	S22 5-1	S19 1-1		a13 0-0	S08 0-0	O03 1-1	S05 1-1	a04 2-2	D01 2-1	M16 0-2
18 ROCHDALE	O27 1-1	O02 6-0	a06 2-1	M20 3-5	a16 0-0	S08 3-2	D29 2-0	O13 1-1	O23 3-1	m11 3-0	M05 1-1	M12 2-1	m07 1-0	D15 3-1	M23 3-3	S15 1-1	N10 2-1		M09 1-0	O16 1-0	a20 3-0	m23 2-0	A25 3-2	S29 1-0
19 SOUTHPORT	a22 1-1	S03 3-3	S15 3-3	M02 1-0	O08 4-1	M16 0-2	A18 1-3	M04 4-2	M30 2-1	a29 1-3	a27 0-0	A20 1-1	a12 0-0	N17 3-2	S01 2-1	a02 2-1	m18 4-2	O20 1-1		D01 2-0	S28 4-4	m07 0-0	a13 6-3	O06 2-1
20 STOCKPORT CO	D08 3-0	N10 1-3	a22 3-1	N24 2-1	M18 1-0	S10 0-1	S01 1-1	a01 0-1	S22 2-1	D29 4-3	m18 0-0	a06 4-1	O27 1-2	m20 1-1	S15 1-1	M23 2-1	O08 1-1	A27 1-0	a20 0-2		M09 1-2	O13 2-2	a12 2-3	A18 1-1
21 TORQUAY U	a15 3-1	S08 2-1	A29 4-1	M29 1-1	a13 1-0	a27 2-1	M06 1-2	S22 1-1	M02 2-2	D15 3-0	M16 0-0	F02 2-0	A25 0-0	O06 3-3	F27 3-1	F20 2-0	S12 2-2	D01 2-1	F16 5-1	O20 2-2		m01 1-0	O04 2-0	N17 1-0
22 TRANMERE R	m04 1-3	m11 2-0	S10 1-1	M04 1-2	m13 3-0	D01 4-1	M16 2-1	M25 3-1	O06 2-3	a27 2-1	O20 2-1	S08 6-1	D15 3-0	a22 5-1	a12 0-0	A25 1-2	M11 3-0	M30 3-2	S21 7-1	M02 3-1	S17 1-1		A20 0-1	a13 2-1
23 WORKINGTON	a06 0-1	M09 3-5	D08 2-3	S01 3-1	S15 3-0	A18 0-0	m04 0-1	M23 2-0	M28 1-0	S24 3-1	S29 5-2	O27 0-0	F23 1-1	M14 3-2	m11 4-0	O13 0-1	a19 0-0	D22 1-0	N10 2-0	a15 4-0	a22 1-2	A28 1-0		m18 3-0
24 YORK C	O13 0-0	D08 1-1	M22 3-0	a12 1-1	N12 0-0	S22 3-4	A20 2-0	O01 5-1	A25 1-0	M18 3-3	S17 0-3	M25 2-0	a22 3-1	m11 2-1	M08 2-0	a20 5-2	O26 1-2	m04 1-0	m20 1-1	D15 3-1	a05 1-0	N10 1-2	S08 1-2	

LEAGUE TABLES

DIVISION 1

	P	W	D	L	F	A	W	D	L	F	A	Pts
Everton	42	14	7	0	48	17	11	4	6	36	25	61
Tottenham H	42	14	6	1	72	28	9	3	9	39	34	55
Burnley	42	14	4	3	41	17	8	6	7	37	40	54
Leicester C	42	14	6	1	53	23	6	6	9	26	30	52
Wolverh'pton W	42	11	6	4	51	25	9	4	8	42	40	50
Sheffield W	42	10	5	6	38	26	9	5	7	39	37	48
Arsenal	42	11	4	6	44	33	7	6	8	42	44	46
Liverpool	42	13	3	5	45	22	4	7	10	26	37	44
Nottingham F	42	12	4	5	39	28	5	6	10	28	41	44
Sheffield U	42	11	7	3	33	20	5	5	11	25	40	44
Blackburn R	42	11	4	6	55	34	4	8	9	24	37	42
West Ham U	42	8	6	7	39	34	6	6	9	34	35	40
Blackpool	42	8	7	6	34	27	5	7	9	24	37	40
W.B.A.	42	11	1	9	40	37	5	6	10	31	42	39
Aston Villa	42	12	2	7	38	23	3	6	12	24	45	38
Fulham	42	8	6	7	28	30	6	4	11	22	41	38
Ipswich T	42	5	8	8	34	39	7	3	11	25	39	35
Bolton W	42	13	3	5	35	18	2	2	17	20	57	35
Manchester U	42	6	6	9	36	38	6	4	11	31	43	34
Birmingham C	42	6	8	7	40	40	4	5	12	23	50	33
Manchester C	42	7	5	9	30	45	3	6	12	28	57	31
Leyton O	42	4	5	12	22	37	2	4	15	15	44	21

DIVISION 2

	P	W	D	L	F	A	W	D	L	F	A	Pts
Stoke C	42	15	3	3	49	20	5	10	6	24	30	53
Chelsea	42	15	3	3	54	16	9	1	11	27	26	52
Sunderland	42	14	5	2	46	13	6	7	8	38	42	52
Middlesbrough	42	12	4	5	48	35	8	5	8	38	50	49
Leeds U	42	15	2	4	55	19	4	8	9	24	34	48
Huddersfield T	42	11	6	4	34	21	6	8	7	29	29	48
Newcastle U	42	11	8	2	48	23	7	3	11	31	36	47
Bury	42	11	6	4	28	20	7	5	9	23	27	47
Scunthorpe U	42	12	7	2	35	18	4	5	12	22	41	44
Cardiff C	42	12	5	4	50	29	6	2	13	33	44	43
Southampton	42	15	3	3	52	23	2	5	14	20	44	42
Plymouth A	42	13	4	4	48	24	2	8	11	28	49	42
Norwich C	42	11	6	4	53	33	6	2	13	27	46	42
Rotherham U	42	11	3	7	34	30	6	3	12	33	44	40
Swansea T	42	13	5	3	33	17	2	4	15	18	55	39
Portsmouth	42	9	5	7	33	27	4	6	11	30	52	37
Preston N.E.	42	11	6	4	43	30	2	5	14	16	44	37
Derby Co	42	10	5	6	40	29	2	7	12	21	43	36
Grimsby T	42	8	6	7	34	26	3	7	11	21	40	35
Charlton A	42	8	4	9	33	38	5	1	15	29	56	31
Walsall	42	7	7	7	33	37	4	2	15	20	52	31
Luton T	42	10	4	7	45	40	1	3	17	16	44	29

DIVISION 3

	P	W	D	L	F	A	W	D	L	F	A	Pts
Northampton T	46	16	6	1	64	19	10	4	9	45	41	62
Swindon T	46	18	2	3	60	22	4	12	7	27	34	58
Port Vale	46	16	4	3	47	25	7	4	12	25	33	54
Coventry C	46	14	6	3	54	28	4	11	8	29	41	53
Bournemouth	46	11	12	0	39	16	7	4	12	24	30	52
Peterborough U	46	11	5	7	48	33	9	6	8	45	42	51
Notts Co	46	15	3	5	46	29	4	10	9	27	45	51
Southend U	46	11	7	5	38	24	8	5	10	37	53	50
Wrexham	46	14	6	3	54	27	6	3	14	30	56	49
Hull C	46	12	6	5	40	22	7	4	12	34	47	48
Crystal Palace	46	10	7	6	38	22	7	6	10	30	36	47
Colchester U	46	11	6	6	41	35	7	5	11	32	58	47
Q.P.R.	46	9	6	8	44	36	8	5	10	41	40	45
Bristol C	46	10	9	4	54	38	6	4	13	46	54	45
Shrewsbury T	46	13	4	6	57	41	3	8	12	26	40	44
Millwall	46	11	6	6	50	32	4	7	12	32	55	43
Watford	46	12	3	8	55	40	5	5	13	27	45	42
Barnsley	46	12	6	5	39	28	3	5	15	24	46	41
Bristol R	46	11	8	4	45	29	4	3	16	25	59	41
Reading	46	13	4	6	51	30	3	4	16	23	48	40
Bradford P.A.	46	10	9	4	43	36	4	3	16	36	61	40
Brighton & H.A.	46	7	6	10	28	38	5	6	12	30	46	36
Carlisle U	46	12	4	7	41	37	1	5	17	20	52	35
Halifax T	46	8	3	12	41	51	1	9	13	23	55	30

DIVISION 4

	P	W	D	L	F	A	W	D	L	F	A	Pts
Brentford	46	18	2	3	59	31	9	6	8	39	33	62
Oldham A	46	18	4	1	65	23	6	7	10	30	37	59
Crewe A	46	15	4	4	50	21	9	7	7	36	37	59
Mansfield T	46	16	4	3	61	20	8	5	10	47	49	57
Gillingham	46	17	3	3	49	23	5	10	8	22	26	57
Torquay U	46	14	8	1	45	20	6	8	9	30	36	56
Rochdale	46	16	6	1	48	21	4	5	14	19	38	51
Tranmere R	46	15	3	5	57	25	5	7	11	24	42	50
Barrow	46	14	7	2	52	26	5	5	13	30	54	50
Workington	46	13	4	6	42	20	4	9	10	34	48	47
Aldershot	46	9	9	5	42	32	6	8	9	31	37	47
Darlington	46	13	3	7	44	33	6	3	14	28	54	44
Southport	46	11	9	3	47	35	4	5	14	25	71	44
York C	46	12	6	5	42	25	4	5	14	25	37	43
Chesterfield	46	7	10	6	43	29	6	6	11	27	35	42
Doncaster R	46	9	10	4	36	26	5	4	14	28	51	42
Exeter C	46	9	6	8	27	32	7	4	12	30	45	42
Oxford U	46	10	10	3	44	27	3	5	15	26	44	41
Stockport Co	46	9	7	7	34	29	6	4	13	22	41	41
Newport Co	46	11	6	6	44	29	3	5	15	32	61	39
Chester C	46	11	5	7	31	23	4	4	15	20	43	39
Lincoln C	46	11	1	11	48	46	2	8	13	20	43	35
Bradford C	46	8	5	10	37	40	3	5	15	27	53	32
Hartlepool U	46	5	7	11	33	39	2	4	17	23	65	25

Top scorers: Div 1, J.Greaves (Tottenham Hotspur) 35 goals; Div 2, R.Saunders (Portsmouth) 33 goals; Div 3, A.Biggs (Bristol Rovers) 30 goals; Div 4, H.McIlmoyle (Carlisle United) 39 goals.

Scottish international forward Ian St John scored 21 goals when Liverpool won the League Championship in 1963-64. The following year his glorious headed goal won the FA Cup for the Merseysiders.

DIVISION 1

	ARSENAL	ASTON VILLA	BIRMINGHAM C	BLACKBURN R	BLACKPOOL	BOLTON W	BURNLEY	CHELSEA	EVERTON	FULHAM	IPSWICH T	LEICESTER C	LIVERPOOL	MANCHESTER U	NOTTINGHAM F	SHEFFIELD U	SHEFFIELD W	STOKE C	TOTTENHAM H	W.B.A.	WEST HAM U	WOLVERHAMPTON W
1 ARSENAL		S10 3-0	N05 4-1	a11 0-0	N23 5-3	S07 4-3	F08 3-2	M14 2-4	D10 6-0	J18 2-2	O05 6-0	D21 0-1	D07 1-1	S21 2-1	O26 4-2	M28 1-3	M24 1-1	F29 1-1	O15 4-4	A27 3-2	N09 3-3	A24 1-3
2 ASTON VILLA	O19 2-1		M30 0-3	A31 1-2	J11 3-1	N02 3-0	a04 2-0	S14 2-0	O07 0-1	M21 2-2	N30 0-0	a18 1-3	F19 2-2	N16 4-0	D14 3-0	S28 0-1	M07 2-2	A26 1-3	S16 2-4	F22 1-0	F01 2-2	D28 2-2
3 BIRMINGHAM C	D28 1-4	M31 3-3		M13 2-2	N09 3-2	A24 2-1	J18 0-0	M28 3-4	O05 0-2	D21 0-0	S21 1-0	S04 2-0	a22 3-1	S07 1-1	N23 3-3	a25 3-0	F08 1-2	a11 0-1	F29 1-2	S11 0-1	D07 2-1	O26 2-2
4 BLACKBURN R	N30 4-1	D21 2-0	N16 3-0		M27 1-2	O09 3-0	O19 1-2	S16 2-2	M21 1-2	O05 2-0	a18 3-1	M07 5-2	A24 1-2	F22 1-3	F08 2-0	S04 2-2	N02 1-1	S21 1-0	S07 7-2	a04 0-2	D28 1-3	J18 1-1
5 BLACKPOOL	a04 0-1	S07 0-4	M20 3-0	M30 3-2		M07 2-0	F22 1-1	D26 1-5	N02 1-1	S30 1-0	O19 2-2	N30 3-3	D21 0-1	S16 1-0	O05 1-0	A24 2-2	a18 2-2	F08 1-0	J18 0-2	N16 1-0	S02 0-1	S21 1-2
6 BOLTON W	J11 1-1	M28 1-1	D14 0-2	F29 0-5	O26 1-1		M30 2-1	a11 1-0	S04 1-3	F08 2-1	S18 6-0	S14 0-0	N09 1-2	O05 0-1	F01 2-3	a08 3-0	D28 3-0	O12 3-4	D07 1-3	A31 1-2	N23 1-1	a24 0-4
7 BURNLEY	S28 0-3	N23 2-0	S14 2-1	O01 3-0	O12 1-0	M31 1-1		A27 0-0	J11 2-3	S10 4-1	D14 3-1	M10 2-0	a14 0-3	D26 6-1	D07 1-1	O26 1-2	A31 3-1	M28 1-0	a21 7-2	F01 3-2	M03 3-1	N09 1-0
8 CHELSEA	N16 3-1	J18 1-0	N02 2-3	S11 1-0	D28 1-0	N30 4-0	S04 2-0		a18 1-0	M07 1-2	F22 4-0	a06 1-0	S07 1-3	O02 1-1	M30 1-0	D21 3-2	O19 1-2	O05 3-3	S21 0-3	M21 3-1	A24 0-0	F08 2-3
9 EVERTON	O02 2-1	F28 4-2	F18 3-0	N09 2-4	M28 3-1	S11 2-0	S07 3-4	D07 1-1		A24 3-0	J18 1-1	D28 0-3	F08 3-1	D21 4-0	M14 6-1	O15 4-1	S21 3-2	N23 2-0	O26 1-0	M27 1-1	a25 2-0	a11 3-3
10 FULHAM	S14 1-4	N09 2-0	A31 2-1	F19 1-1	F29 1-1	S28 3-1	S18 2-1	O26 0-1	D14 2-2		D26 10-1	F01 2-1	M14 1-0	M27 2-2	O12 0-0	N23 3-1	A28 2-0	a25 3-3	M28 1-1	J11 1-1	a11 2-0	D07 4-1
11 IPSWICH T	F18 1-2	a11 4-3	F01 3-2	D07 0-0	a25 4-3	O01 1-3	A24 3-1	O12 1-3	S14 0-0	D28 4-2		M30 1-1	O26 1-2	S03 2-7	M28 4-3	F29 1-0	J11 1-4	N09 0-2	N23 2-3	S28 1-2	D20 3-2	a14 1-0
12 LEICESTER C	A31 7-2	D07 0-0	A28 3-0	O26 4-3	a11 2-3	J18 1-0	O05 0-0	N23 2-4	D26 2-0	S21 0-1	M31 2-1		M28 0-2	F08 3-2	F29 1-1	N09 0-1	S11 2-0	J11 2-1	a25 0-1	D14 0-2	M18 2-2	O14 0-1
13 LIVERPOOL	a18 5-0	O05 5-2	F22 2-1	D14 1-2	A31 1-2	M20 2-0	N30 2-0	J11 2-1	S28 2-1	N16 2-0	M07 6-0	N02 0-1		a04 3-0	A28 1-2	F01 6-1	O09 3-1	D26 6-1	M30 3-1	O19 1-0	S14 1-2	S16 6-0
14 MANCHESTER U	F01 3-1	a06 1-0	J11 1-2	O28 2-2	S11 3-0	F19 5-0	D28 5-1	M23 1-1	A31 5-1	M30 3-0	A28 2-0	S28 3-1	N23 0-1		a25 3-1	a13 2-1	D14 3-1	D07 5-2	N09 4-1	S14 1-0	O26 0-1	M28 2-2
15 NOTTINGHAM F	M07 2-0	A24 0-1	a04 4-0	S28 1-1	F15 0-1	S21 3-1	a18 1-3	M31 0-1	N16 2-2	F22 2-0	N02 3-1	O08 2-0	S03 0-0	O19 1-2		D26 3-3	M21 3-2	J18 0-0	D21 1-2	N30 0-3	S17 3-1	S07 3-0
16 SHEFFIELD U	N02 2-2	F08 1-1	O19 3-0	A28 0-1	D14 1-0	N16 0-1	M07 2-0	A31 1-1	F22 0-0	a04 1-0	O09 3-1	M21 0-1	S21 3-0	N30 1-2	D28 1-2		S14 1-1	S11 4-1	O05 3-3	a18 2-1	J11 2-1	M31 4-3
17 SHEFFIELD W	M30 0-4	O26 1-0	S28 2-1	M28 5-2	D07 1-0	D26 3-0	D21 3-1	F29 3-2	F01 0-3	S04 3-0	S07 3-1	O02 1-2	M04 2-2	A24 3-3	N09 3-1	J18 3-0		a08 2-0	a13 2-0	F15 2-2	O12 3-0	N23 5-0
18 STOKE C	O09 1-2	S04 2-2	N30 4-1	F01 3-1	S28 1-2	F22 0-1	N02 4-4	M04 2-0	a04 3-2	O19 1-1	M21 9-1	S07 3-3	a29 3-1	a18 3-1	S14 0-1	S18 0-2	N16 4-4		A24 2-1	M07 1-1	M31 3-0	D21 0-2
19 TOTTENHAM H	F22 3-1	J25 3-1	O02 6-1	J11 4-1	S14 6-1	a18 1-0	N16 3-2	F01 1-2	M07 2-4	N02 1-0	a04 6-3	O19 1-1	M27 1-3	M21 2-3	A31 4-1	F15 0-0	N30 1-1	D14 2-1		D28 0-2	S28 3-0	S04 4-3
20 W.B.A.	S04 4-0	O12 4-3	S18 3-1	N23 1-3	M13 2-1	D21 1-1	S21 0-0	N09 1-1	M31 4-2	S07 3-0	F08 2-1	A24 1-1	a25 2-2	J18 1-4	a11 2-3	D07 2-0	O05 1-3	O26 2-3	D26 4-4		M28 0-1	F29 3-1
21 WEST HAM U	M21 1-1	S21 0-1	a17 5-0	D26 2-8	A26 3-1	a04 2-3	O07 1-1	D14 2-2	O19 4-2	N30 1-1	A30 2-2	N16 2-2	J18 1-0	M07 0-2	S09 0-2	S07 2-3	F22 4-3	M27 4-1	F08 4-0	N02 4-2		O05 1-1
22 WOLVERHAMPTON W	D14 2-2	D26 3-3	M07 5-1	S14 1-5	F01 1-1	O19 2-2	M21 1-1	S28 4-1	N30 0-0	a18 4-0	N16 2-1	F22 1-2	S09 1-3	N02 2-0	J11 2-3	M30 1-1	a04 1-1	A31 2-1	A28 1-4	O02 0-0	F17 0-2	

Bobby Collins, the great Scottish midfield general on whose talent Don Revie launched his great sides. Collins missed only one game as Leeds were promoted from Division Two in 1963-64.

DIVISION 2

	BURY	CARDIFF C	CHARLTON A	DERBY CO	GRIMSBY T	HUDDERSFIELD T	LEEDS U	LEYTON O	MANCHESTER C	MIDDLESBROUGH	NEWCASTLE U	NORTHAMPTON T	NORWICH C	PLYMOUTH A	PORTSMOUTH	PRESTON N.E.	ROTHERHAM U	SCUNTHORPE U	SOUTHAMPTON	SUNDERLAND	SWANSEA T	SWINDON T
1 BURY		S17 4-1	F22 0-2	O08 1-2	O19 1-1	M07 0-2	D21 1-2	N02 1-2	S28 1-1	a04 1-1	N30 1-2	J18 1-1	S03 4-2	S21 2-2	a13 3-2	a18 2-1	A24 4-2	M31 3-2	a21 1-5	S07 0-1	M21 3-2	F18 1-0
2 CARDIFF C	S11 2-1		M07 1-1	a04 2-1	O02 0-0	N16 2-1	S21 0-0	F22 2-1	A28 2-2	N02 1-1	M20 2-2	O05 1-0	A24 3-1	N30 3-1	S07 1-2	D26 0-4	J17 2-1	a08 3-1	a18 2-4	F08 0-2	O19 1-1	M30 1-0
3 CHARLTON A	O12 3-0	O26 5-2		F01 2-0	S17 2-1	S14 5-2	a25 0-2	M30 1-2	F15 4-3	A31 2-4	J11 1-2	M28 1-1	a11 3-1	S28 1-0	F29 0-1	S03 3-0	N09 4-3	N23 0-1	D14 2-2	D07 0-0	D28 3-1	M14 2-2
4 DERBY CO	M14 2-1	N23 2-1	S21 1-1		F08 0-0	A31 2-0	M28 1-1	S11 1-0	O26 1-3	D28 2-2	D14 1-2	J11 0-0	F29 2-1	J18 3-1	a25 3-1	O05 1-2	D07 1-4	J25 2-2	M30 3-2	O16 0-3	A28 3-0	a11 3-0
5 GRIMSBY T	M28 1-0	a15 0-2	S10 0-2	S28 1-3		F01 2-2	N09 0-2	D26 1-1	O12 1-1	J11 3-1	S14 2-1	D07 4-1	O26 3-1	F15 1-1	N23 0-3	M27 0-3	F29 1-3	a11 2-0	A31 2-2	a25 2-2	D13 1-1	A28 1-2
6 HUDDERSFIELD T	O26 2-1	F29 2-1	a07 2-1	D21 0-0	S21 1-2		O12 0-2	O05 2-1	a11 0-2	M31 1-0	D28 3-0	a13 0-1	N09 1-1	S07 4-3	D07 1-1	F08 2-2	M28 0-3	a25 3-2	S03 4-0	A24 0-2	S10 1-0	N23 2-0
7 LEEDS U	A31 3-0	F01 1-1	N02 1-1	O19 2-2	M21 3-1	F22 1-1		a04 2-1	J11 1-0	O09 2-0	M30 2-1	D14 0-0	S28 4-2	a18 1-1	S11 3-1	N16 1-1	A28 1-0	F15 1-0	M07 3-1	D26 1-1	N30 2-1	S14 0-0
8 LEYTON O	a25 1-1	a13 4-0	M26 0-3	S18 3-0	D28 0-0	F24 2-3	N23 0-2		D07 0-2	F01 3-2	S28 1-0	N09 0-0	D21 1-1	S03 1-0	O26 3-6	A24 2-2	a11 0-2	M14 2-2	S14 1-0	a06 2-5	J11 4-0	M28 2-1
9 MANCHESTER C	F08 1-1	S04 4-0	O05 1-3	M07 3-2	F22 0-4	N30 5-2	S07 3-2	a18 2-0		M17 1-0	a04 3-1	S21 3-0	M27 5-0	O09 1-1	A24 0-2	O19 2-3	D21 6-1	D26 8-1	M21 1-1	J18 0-3	N02 1-0	S18 0-0
10 MIDDLESBROUGH	N23 2-0	a24 3-1	D21 2-3	D26 3-0	S07 6-0	M30 1-1	M14 1-3	S21 2-0	F29 2-2		A26 3-0	a10 1-0	D07 0-1	A24 5-0	O12 3-1	J18 3-0	S09 2-2	M28 2-0	O05 1-0	O26 2-0	F08 2-1	N09 1-1
11 NEWCASTLE U	a11 0-4	N09 0-4	S07 5-0	A24 3-1	J18 4-0	D26 2-0	M27 0-1	F08 3-0	N23 3-1	S04 2-0		O26 2-3	a25 2-0	D21 1-1	O02 1-0	S21 2-4	a08 5-2	D07 3-1	S11 2-2	M14 1-0	O05 4-1	F29 4-1
12 NORTHAMPTON T	S13 1-2	F15 2-1	O19 1-2	S07 0-1	a18 1-2	O08 1-0	O01 0-3	M21 1-2	F01 2-1	N30 3-2	M07 2-2		S16 3-2	F18 0-0	M31 2-1	N02 0-3	D26 1-3	S03 2-0	a04 2-0	D21 5-1	N16 2-3	S28 4-0
13 NORWICH C	A28 0-1	D14 5-1	N30 1-3	N16 3-0	M07 2-0	M21 2-2	F08 2-2	A31 1-2	M30 1-2	a18 1-1	N02 3-1	S11 3-3		a04 1-1	J18 3-1	O02 2-1	S21 2-2	S07 2-1	O19 1-1	O05 2-3	F22 3-0	D26 3-2
14 PLYMOUTH A	F01 1-0	a11 1-1	F08 1-1	S14 0-0	O05 3-2	J11 0-0	D07 0-1	A28 2-2	M14 2-1	D14 2-0	A31 3-4	O12 0-3	N23 1-2		N09 0-4	S18 0-2	a25 0-0	F29 3-1	D28 1-1	O02 1-1	M30 3-2	O26 2-4
15 PORTSMOUTH	D28 3-3	J11 5-0	N16 4-1	N02 1-1	a04 2-2	a18 2-1	S18 1-1	M07 4-3	D14 2-2	F22 1-0	O19 5-2	M30 3-0	S14 1-1	M21 1-2		N30 1-2	O05 2-1	F01 3-4	S28 2-0	S04 2-4	O09 0-0	A31 1-4
16 PRESTON N.E.	D07 3-0	D28 4-0	A27 3-1	F17 0-2	M30 1-0	S28 2-1	M03 2-0	D14 0-0	M28 2-0	S14 2-2	F01 3-0	a25 2-1	M17 3-0	S09 0-0	a11 0-0		N23 2-2	O26 1-0	J11 2-1	N09 1-1	A31 3-3	O12 1-0
17 ROTHERHAM U	D14 6-2	S13 1-0	M20 5-0	a18 2-0	N16 1-0	O19 3-1	S03 2-2	N30 2-4	A31 1-2	S17 2-1	F22 2-3	D28 1-0	F01 4-0	N02 3-1	F15 4-2	a04 4-2		S28 2-1	O01 2-3	M30 2-2	M07 3-0	J11 0-0
18 SCUNTHORPE U	M26 0-0	A30 1-2	a04 1-1	M20 3-2	N30 2-2	N02 1-0	O05 0-1	O01 0-0	D28 2-4	O19 1-0	a18 2-0	A27 1-2	J11 2-2	N16 1-0	S21 1-1	M07 1-0	F08 4-3		F22 1-2	S09 1-1	S12 2-2	D14 3-0
19 SOUTHAMPTON	F29 0-1	D07 3-2	A24 6-1	a01 6-4	D21 6-0	A28 1-1	O26 1-4	J18 3-0	N09 4-2	F15 2-2	S18 2-0	N23 3-1	M28 3-0	D26 1-2	F08 2-3	S07 4-5	a27 6-1	J29 7-2		a11 0-0	S21 4-0	a25 5-1
20 SUNDERLAND	J11 4-1	S28 3-3	a18 2-1	F22 3-0	N02 3-0	D14 3-2	D28 2-0	N16 4-1	S14 2-0	M07 0-0	O09 2-1	A31 0-2	F19 0-0	O19 1-0	A28 3-0	M21 4-0	M27 2-0	S18 1-0	N30 1-2		a04 1-0	F01 6-0
21 SWANSEA T	N09 0-2	M28 3-0	D26 1-2	S03 2-1	A24 1-1	S17 1-2	a11 0-3	S07 1-0	a25 3-3	S28 2-1	M17 0-1	a07 1-1	O15 3-1	M31 2-1	a21 1-1	D20 5-1	O26 4-2	J16 4-1	M03 6-0	N23 1-2		D07 3-0
22 SWINDON T	O05 2-1	M27 1-2	O01 2-2	N30 0-0	S03 2-1	a04 1-2	J18 2-2	O19 5-0	S10 3-0	M21 2-0	N16 0-0	F08 2-3	D28 2-2	M07 2-1	D21 2-0	F22 1-4	S07 3-1	A24 3-0	N02 1-2	S21 1-0	a18 2-1	

Season 1963-64

DIVISION 3

	BARNSLEY	BOURNEMOUTH	BRENTFORD	BRISTOL C	BRISTOL R	COLCHESTER U	COVENTRY C	CREWE A	CRYSTAL P	HULL C	LUTON T	MANSFIELD T	MILLWALL	NOTTS CO	OLDHAM A	PETERBOROUGH U	PORT VALE	Q.P.R.	READING	SHREWSBURY T	SOUTHEND U	WALSALL	WATFORD	WREXHAM
1 BARNSLEY		S21 2-1	O19 1-1	N02 2-4	O29 1-2	D14 1-1	D26 1-1	a04 1-0	N30 2-0	J17 2-2	S06 3-1	a18 1-1	A31 1-1	M03 2-1	O08 2-2	M31 3-2	a20 0-0	O04 3-1	M20 0-3	M07 2-1	A27 0-1	F22 1-3	S17 0-0	F08 3-0
2 BOURNEMOUTH	F01 4-1		D28 2-0	O19 0-1	M27 1-0	J11 2-2	M21 2-1	a22 3-0	J04 4-3	S28 1-0	F22 3-1	O05 0-0	S14 4-0	N02 1-1	A28 1-0	S18 3-0	M07 3-0	O16 4-2	N30 1-2	a18 2-0	D14 1-0	a04 1-1	A31 2-0	O30 2-0
3 BRENTFORD	a25 1-1	a13 2-0		A27 1-2	O12 2-5	M14 3-1	O05 2-3	D21 2-2	S07 2-1	a28 1-3	F08 2-6	O29 4-0	O26 3-1	A24 4-1	a11 2-0	N23 2-0	O01 1-2	F29 2-2	S21 4-2	M30 0-1	M28 3-0	J18 1-1	N09 1-2	O15 9-0
4 BRISTOL C	M14 5-2	a25 3-1	S10 3-3		A24 3-0	M28 3-1	O15 0-1	J18 1-1	S21 1-1	O26 1-0	O29 5-1	M27 2-3	N09 0-0	S07 2-0	F29 3-1	O11 3-1	D21 0-0	M10 2-1	O05 0-2	O01 2-2	a11 2-2	F08 5-1	N23 2-0	F11 4-0
5 BRISTOL R	O22 1-1	M31 2-3	F22 3-1	D14 4-0		S28 3-1	a04 0-1	O19 1-2	M07 1-3	O08 4-0	a13 1-2	N30 3-2	F15 2-2	a18 4-0	A31 0-1	J11 2-2	D28 4-4	S17 0-0	a21 2-5	M21 7-0	S14 3-1	N02 3-0	F01 1-2	A27 1-1
6 COLCHESTER U	A24 4-1	S07 1-2	N02 1-2	F24 1-1	F08 2-3		O19 2-1	F22 4-0	a15 1-1	D21 1-1	a18 1-1	M07 1-1	S30 2-0	N30 4-0	O05 2-3	O28 4-1	a04 1-2	S21 2-0	D26 2-1	a20 1-0	O14 3-3	S09 0-0	M31 1-1	J18 4-1
7 COVENTRY C	D28 3-1	F29 2-2	F15 2-2	O08 2-1	N23 4-2	a25 1-0		S17 5-1	A24 5-1	F01 2-2	J18 3-3	S28 0-3	J03 3-0	S10 2-0	M28 4-1	N09 3-2	M31 1-1	a11 4-2	S07 0-0	O22 8-1	M13 2-5	D21 1-0	O26 2-2	O12 3-0
8 CREWE A	N23 1-2	N09 1-0	A31 1-1	S14 2-0	a25 4-1	O12 1-1	O02 2-2		O23 0-2	M28 1-4	A28 1-0	D14 3-2	a11 1-0	S28 0-1	J25 1-0	D26 0-0	J31 1-0	O26 2-0	M27 2-2	J11 3-2	F14 1-2	O08 0-1	F29 0-1	M14 1-2
9 CRYSTAL P	a11 1-2	M28 2-1	J11 1-0	F01 1-0	O26 1-0	F29 0-0	D14 1-1	O30 1-0		N23 2-2	O02 1-1	A31 3-1	O12 2-1	F15 2-0	a25 1-3	J25 1-0	S28 2-0	M14 1-0	S11 4-1	S14 3-0	D28 3-0	M18 1-0	O09 2-0	N09 2-1
10 HULL C	S14 2-2	F08 3-4	a18 0-0	M07 4-4	F26 0-2	A31 0-0	S21 2-1	M11 2-1	a04 1-1		M21 2-0	D26 3-1	J11 0-0	a22 4-1	M27 0-1	A28 0-0	N02 4-1	O30 3-0	F22 1-1	O19 4-2	O02 1-0	N30 3-1	D14 2-2	O05 4-2
11 LUTON T	J11 2-3	O12 1-0	S28 0-2	O23 1-4	M28 4-2	J25 3-1	S14 1-3	S11 3-3	S18 0-4	F29 2-1		F01 0-2	D28 1-3	M30 2-0	N09 1-2	M14 2-3	O09 1-0	N23 4-4	D21 2-1	F15 2-0	O26 4-1	A24 1-0	a25 2-1	a11 3-1
12 MANSFIELD T	M09 2-1	F15 1-1	O21 2-2	M30 4-0	a11 2-0	O26 1-1	F08 3-2	A24 2-1	D21 1-1	D28 2-0	S21 1-1		a25 4-1	S16 4-0	N23 1-1	M28 4-1	S09 1-1	O12 1-0	J18 2-1	O07 3-1	N09 4-1	S07 2-1	a06 1-1	F29 3-1
13 MILLWALL	a13 4-2	J18 3-0	M07 1-3	a20 0-1	O05 0-1	S16 0-1	a18 0-0	N30 1-0	F22 0-1	S07 0-1	D26 3-0	O19 0-1		a04 6-1	O28 2-1	O14 0-2	M16 3-1	F08 2-2	A24 2-0	N02 2-2	M27 1-1	M21 2-1	A26 0-3	S21 1-4
14 NOTTS CO	M28 1-1	M14 1-3	D14 2-0	J11 1-1	a09 3-4	a11 3-1	A29 0-3	F08 0-0	O05 1-1	J25 0-1	M26 1-1	O03 1-0	N23 2-0		D28 4-2	F01 0-0	S14 2-0	a25 2-2	O17 0-1	A31 0-1	F29 1-1	O24 0-1	O12 1-2	O26 3-0
15 OLDHAM A	O16 2-0	S11 2-4	N30 4-1	M21 1-2	D21 2-2	F15 2-2	J22 2-0	a18 3-2	O19 3-1	M30 1-1	a22 0-1	a04 1-0	O23 1-2	D26 2-0		S14 4-2	S07 1-0	A24 2-1	N02 3-1	F22 2-4	F01 0-3	M07 2-4	S28 1-0	O02 3-2
16 PETERBOROUGH U	M30 3-2	S30 2-1	a04 3-0	F22 4-2	S07 2-2	O21 4-0	a20 2-0	D28 3-2	a18 1-1	S09 5-1	N02 0-0	J04 1-3	O07 2-3	S21 5-1	J18 0-0		M23 1-1	D21 2-1	M07 1-0	N30 2-2	S28 3-0	O19 1-2	F15 0-1	A24 5-2
17 PORT VALE	N09 1-0	O26 0-0	S16 3-0	A31 4-1	D26 1-0	N23 0-2	M30 1-1	S21 4-0	F08 1-2	a13 1-0	O14 1-0	A26 1-0	M28 1-0	J18 0-1	J11 1-0	F29 1-2		a06 2-0	O28 0-0	D14 1-1	O12 4-1	O05 2-2	a11 0-0	a25 5-0
18 Q.P.R.	a27 2-2	O07 1-0	M20 2-2	D28 0-2	S30 1-0	F01 0-0	N30 3-6	M07 2-0	N02 3-4	O21 0-2	a29 1-1	F22 2-0	S28 2-0	O19 3-2	D14 3-2	A31 3-0	a18 3-0		a14 4-2	S09 3-4	J11 4-5	m01 3-0	S14 1-0	M27 1-0
19 READING	F29 6-1	a11 2-0	F01 4-3	F15 1-1	N09 3-1	D28 5-3	J11 2-2	M30 2-2	A28 0-0	O12 2-0	A31 1-1	S14 4-3	D14 1-0	O09 3-2	M14 0-1	O26 1-0	O23 1-0	M28 1-2		S28 2-0	a25 4-2	S18 0-1	J25 2-0	N23 2-1
20 SHREWSBURY T	O26 3-1	J25 5-2	M31 1-1	S18 2-0	F29 0-1	N09 1-1	O30 0-0	S07 3-0	J18 1-1	a25 5-1	O05 1-0	O16 2-0	M14 0-1	D21 5-2	O12 2-0	a11 0-0	A24 1-0	A26 1-2	F08 2-1		N23 2-2	S21 2-1	M28 3-0	D28 1-2
21 SOUTHEND U	S09 4-1	A24 1-1	M16 2-1	N30 1-1	J18 3-4	O07 0-0	N02 1-2	O05 1-1	D26 2-1	S16 1-1	M07 0-1	a20 2-1	M30 1-1	M20 3-1	S21 2-2	F08 2-0	F22 1-1	S07 1-3	O19 2-0	a04 7-1		a18 1-1	O21 3-0	D21 1-1
22 WALSALL	O11 4-4	N23 0-2	S14 2-2	S28 1-1	M14 2-3	A27 1-1	A31 0-3	O14 2-1	M30 2-2	a11 1-1	D14 4-0	J11 3-1	F28 0-2	O29 2-1	O26 1-1	a25 2-0	F15 2-1	N09 0-2	O01 1-1	F01 1-1	D07 2-0		D28 1-3	M28 0-2
23 WATFORD	O01 2-1	D21 3-0	a21 2-2	a04 2-2	S21 3-2	M27 3-1	M07 1-1	M21 4-1	O15 3-1	A24 3-3	O19 2-0	N02 3-0	S10 2-2	F22 2-0	F08 2-1	O05 1-2	N30 1-1	J18 3-1	a18 1-0	J04 2-1	O29 3-1	D26 5-3		S07 4-2
24 WREXHAM	S27 7-2	O23 3-4	O09 2-4	a18 1-1	S11 1-2	S14 5-4	F22 1-1	N02 1-1	a22 2-2	F15 3-1	N30 2-0	M20 2-0	F01 3-0	M07 4-0	S18 0-4	D14 2-3	O19 1-2	M30 0-1	a03 0-3	D26 2-3	A31 1-3	J04 4-0	J11 3-1	

DIVISION 4

	ALDERSHOT	BARROW	BRADFORD	BRADFORD C	BRIGHTON & HA	CARLISLE U	CHESTER	CHESTERFIELD	DARLINGTON	DONCASTER R	EXETER C	GILLINGHAM	HALIFAX T	HARTLEPOOLS U	LINCOLN C	NEWPORT CO	OXFORD U	ROCHDALE	SOUTHPORT	STOCKPORT CO	TORQUAY U	TRANMERE R	WORKINGTON	YORK C
1 ALDERSHOT		N30 8-2	O19 0-3	O23 2-3	M21 1-0	F08 3-2	M09 2-1	M07 0-2	D21 1-2	N02 4-2	S18 0-1	M30 1-1	J18 0-0	A24 4-1	O09 2-0	D26 2-0	a22 2-0	a18 1-1	S11 3-1	F22 7-0	S21 1-0	S07 5-4	O05 4-0	a04 5-2
2 BARROW	a11 0-2		O05 2-2	J25 2-3	M30 1-1	M16 2-2	S09 2-2	J01 5-2	O12 3-1	O14 0-2	O26 1-1	N09 0-3	A24 0-0	F28 1-2	a25 2-0	S21 1-1	S07 1-1	D20 1-2	M14 1-3	F07 1-2	a13 1-0	D28 1-1	J18 1-1	S30 1-2
3 BRADFORD	F29 2-1	F15 1-0		O12 1-3	S14 2-1	O26 1-1	F01 4-0	A31 0-1	N23 4-1	J11 3-1	J25 3-2	D14 1-0	N09 4-4	a11 3-1	D28 0-1	A26 2-5	O08 5-2	O23 2-2	M28 3-0	S17 2-2	a27 1-1	a25 4-2	M30 1-0	S28 1-3
4 BRADFORD C	O30 3-0	a04 7-1	F22 1-0		N02 3-1	O05 2-2	M21 1-1	O19 4-2	S07 1-2	M07 2-1	A24 1-2	S11 0-2	S21 0-0	D21 2-0	M31 4-0	O16 2-1	a18 2-1	N30 2-0	O02 2-0	J29 1-0	F08 2-1	J18 0-3	a22 0-2	J04 3-2
5 BRIGHTON & H.A.	N09 3-1	M27 2-0	J18 0-1	M14 1-2		a25 1-3	O29 0-0	S21 1-1	D07 2-0	F08 4-0	D26 1-2	F29 2-1	a11 3-0	F15 4-1	O26 5-1	D21 1-2	O01 2-1	S10 3-1	O12 1-0	S07 1-2	N23 3-0	J25 1-1	A24 1-2	O17 3-0
6 CARLISLE U	S27 4-0	a17 4-1	M07 4-0	F04 1-2	F24 0-1		a04 3-1	N02 1-0	A24 3-3	M21 6-0	A26 3-0	O15 3-1	S07 3-0	O01 7-1	O22 5-0	F22 3-3	S20 2-1	a21 1-0	M27 5-2	O18 0-0	J18 0-1	D21 5-2	D28 3-1	N30 4-0
7 CHESTER	a25 2-0	A28 2-0	S21 1-0	N09 3-0	O23 0-0	N23 4-2		F08 4-2	O16 0-1	O05 1-1	O12 2-0	O26 1-0	J25 5-2	D28 2-1	M13 3-1	S07 3-0	A24 0-2	O02 2-0	F29 5-0	J18 2-1	a11 2-1	M28 0-2	D21 2-1	M30 1-1
8 CHESTERFIELD	O26 4-0	M28 1-1	D21 1-2	F29 3-2	F01 1-0	M14 2-0	S28 1-0		a11 2-1	S14 3-3	a13 0-1	D26 0-3	a25 2-2	J25 0-2	O12 1-3	S16 0-1	M27 0-0	a06 1-1	J11 1-0	A24 1-1	N09 1-1	N23 1-1	S09 2-2	F15 1-0
9 DARLINGTON	A31 0-1	F22 3-3	a04 2-2	J11 1-2	a20 1-2	D14 1-6	O07 1-0	N30 3-2		a18 2-0	F15 1-1	F01 1-1	S09 0-0	O21 0-0	S14 1-1	M23 3-1	M07 3-0	O19 3-2	S28 2-2	J04 2-3	S16 2-0	M30 3-5	N02 1-1	D28 4-2
10 DONCASTER R	M14 1-1	O08 3-1	S07 3-2	O25 2-1	S28 1-1	N09 1-1	F15 3-2	J18 1-1	J25 10-0		F01 1-0	O12 1-2	N23 3-1	M28 2-2	F29 0-0	A24 1-1	S10 0-1	M24 2-0	D28 3-0	D21 4-1	a25 1-0	a11 1-2	S17 2-3	O22 0-0
11 EXETER C	O02 0-0	M07 0-0	a18 2-3	D14 4-1	D28 0-0	S11 1-0	F22 3-0	a21 6-1	O05 1-1	S21 3-1		J11 0-0	O09 0-0	F08 2-1	A31 0-0	a04 3-1	M21 3-2	N02 0-1	S14 1-1	N29 2-0	M27 0-0	O23 5-0	J04 2-1	O19 1-0
12 GILLINGHAM	M27 2-0	a08 3-1	A24 2-0	A28 0-0	O19 1-0	O09 2-0	M07 2-1	D28 1-0	S21 2-1	F22 1-1	S07 0-0		O05 2-1	J18 2-0	S18 1-0	a18 1-1	a15 2-0	J04 0-0	D21 5-1	a22 0-0	O23 2-0	F08 2-2	N30 3-1	N02 1-0
13 HALIFAX T	S14 3-3	D14 1-0	M21 2-1	F01 0-1	N30 2-2	J11 1-2	a18 1-0	**M04 3-2**	A26 2-2	a04 0-2	O14 2-0	F15 0-0		M30 4-1	S28 0-2	M07 2-0	F22 3-1	M11 3-2	O28 4-1	N02 4-2	A31 5-1	S16 2-0	O19 1-3	a20 2-0
14 HARTLEPOOLS U	D14 1-4	O19 0-0	N30 4-2	A31 1-0	O05 2-2	S16 0-6	D26 2-0	a17 1-0	J01 0-2	a20 2-1	S28 1-1	S14 0-0	M27 1-1		J11 1-2	a06 1-1	N02 2-1	M07 1-1	F01 2-3	a04 3-0	A26 1-4	M23 3-2	M21 1-2	F22 0-1
15 LINCOLN C	O16 3-3	a29 3-0	D26 3-0	M30 1-2	M07 0-2	O30 0-2	N02 3-2	F22 5-2	J18 3-1	O19 3-1	D21 1-1	O02 0-3	F08 4-0	S07 4-2		a22 2-1	N30 3-2	a04 2-0	A24 2-0	S11 1-0	O05 3-2	S21 0-1	a18 0-2	M20 3-2
16 NEWPORT CO	D28 2-1	F03 3-0	S09 4-0	O07 3-1	A31 2-0	O12 1-4	J11 0-1	S30 0-1	N09 1-2	D14 1-0	N23 0-1	a30 0-1	O26 4-2	a25 2-1	M28 4-2		M02 1-0	S28 1-1	a11 3-0	M30 3-1	F29 0-3	M14 0-2	O21 0-0	S14 0-0
17 OXFORD U	M28 1-1	J11 0-0	O16 2-1	M11 1-1	S18 1-3	F01 1-2	D14 2-1	M30 1-2	O26 5-0	A28 0-1	N09 0-2	N23 3-1	O12 2-2	M14 5-1	a11 2-0	O05 2-1		S14 1-1	a25 0-0	O30 1-0	D26 1-0	a29 0-2	F08 2-1	A31 4-4
18 ROCHDALE	F25 2-2	A31 1-3	O30 0-0	a11 1-2	A28 1-1	M28 1-1	M04 1-0	O16 0-1	F29 2-1	M31 2-2	M14 1-3	a25 2-1	D28 4-1	O26 2-0	N23 2-2	F08 0-1	J18 0-0		N09 4-0	O05 1-0	J11 1-2	O12 1-1	S21 5-0	D14 2-0
19 SOUTHPORT	A27 4-1	N02 3-3	a21 0-1	S17 3-3	F22 3-3	M30 3-0	O19 0-2	S07 0-1	F08 3-1	D26 3-0	J18 1-1	A31 1-1	O22 3-1	S21 2-1	D14 1-0	N30 4-2	a13 1-1	M20 2-1		a18 2-0	O07 1-0	O05 2-0	a04 0-3	M07 0-3
20 STOCKPORT CO	O12 2-2	S28 5-0	S30 2-1	D28 2-1	J11 1-1	F29 0-3	S14 1-0	D14 2-1	a25 2-0	A31 1-3	a11 0-0	M28 2-0	M14 1-2	N23 1-0	A26 4-0	M27 1-0	O21 0-0	F15 1-0	J25 1-4		O26 0-0	N09 1-1	O14 0-0	F01 2-0
21 TORQUAY U	F01 3-0	a22 1-1	N02 6-2	S28 4-0	a03 3-0	S14 3-1	N30 5-0	M20 1-1	O03 3-1	a08 1-0	M30 1-1	O30 1-0	D21 3-2	S11 4-2	F15 2-2	O19 8-3	D28 0-0	S07 1-0	O14 3-1	M06 4-0		A24 1-1	F21 2-1	a17 0-1
22 TRANMERE R	J10 3-0	D26 1-1	J03 3-1	S13 0-1	a17 1-2	A30 6-1	J01 3-3	a03 2-1	M27 0-2	N29 3-0	O28 2-1	S27 0-0	S30 2-2	O07 2-3	J31 3-0	N02 2-3	O18 1-3	F21 2-1	F14 2-0	M20 4-2	D14 3-1		M06 0-2	A26 1-0
23 WORKINGTON	F14 4-0	S13 4-1	M27 1-1	M28 1-0	D14 1-0	D26 2-2	A31 1-1	A27 1-2	M14 3-0	O01 4-1	a25 0-0	a11 1-0	F28 2-4	N09 2-0	J25 1-1	F24 2-0	S27 3-1	F01 3-0	N23 2-1	O08 1-1	O11 2-1	O25 4-2		J10 1-0
24 YORK C	N23 1-2	S16 1-2	F08 2-0	a25 1-0	O07 2-3	a11 0-0	M27 1-0	O05 2-0	a06 3-1	O28 3-1	F28 1-2	a27 0-1	M28 1-3	O12 0-1	N09 0-0	J18 3-0	D21 0-2	A24 0-3	O25 4-1	S20 2-0	J25 1-1	S09 1-2	S07 0-1	

LEAGUE TABLES

DIVISION 1

	P	W	D	L	F	A	W	D	L	F	A	Pts
Liverpool	42	16	0	5	60	18	10	5	6	32	27	57
Manchester U	42	15	3	3	54	19	8	4	9	36	43	53
Everton	42	14	4	3	53	26	7	6	8	31	38	52
Tottenham H	42	13	3	5	54	31	9	4	8	43	50	51
Chelsea	42	12	3	6	36	24	8	7	6	36	32	50
Sheffield W	42	15	3	3	50	24	4	8	9	34	43	49
Blackburn R	42	10	4	7	44	28	8	6	7	45	37	46
Arsenal	42	10	7	4	56	37	7	4	10	34	45	45
Burnley	42	14	3	4	46	23	3	7	11	25	41	44
W.B.A.	42	9	6	6	43	35	7	5	9	27	26	43
Leicester C	42	9	4	8	33	27	7	7	7	28	31	43
Sheffield U	42	10	6	5	35	22	6	5	10	26	42	43
Nottingham F	42	9	5	7	34	24	7	4	10	30	44	41
West Ham U	42	8	7	6	45	38	6	5	10	24	36	40
Fulham	42	11	8	2	45	23	2	5	14	13	42	39
Wolverh'pton W	42	6	9	6	36	34	6	6	9	34	46	39
Stoke C	42	9	6	6	49	33	5	4	12	28	45	38
Blackpool	42	8	6	7	26	29	5	3	13	26	44	35
Aston Villa	42	8	6	7	35	29	3	6	12	27	42	34
Birmingham C	42	7	7	7	33	32	4	0	17	21	60	29
Bolton W	42	6	5	10	30	35	4	3	14	18	45	28
Ipswich T	42	9	3	9	38	45	0	4	17	18	76	25

DIVISION 2

	P	W	D	L	F	A	W	D	L	F	A	Pts
Leeds U	42	12	9	0	35	16	12	6	3	36	18	63
Sunderland	42	16	3	2	47	13	9	8	4	34	24	61
Preston N.E.	42	13	7	1	37	14	10	3	8	42	40	56
Charlton A	42	11	4	6	44	30	8	6	7	32	40	48
Southampton	42	13	3	5	69	32	6	6	9	31	41	47
Manchester C	42	12	4	5	50	27	6	6	9	34	39	46
Rotherham U	42	14	3	4	52	26	5	4	12	38	52	45
Newcastle U	42	14	2	5	49	26	6	3	12	25	43	45
Portsmouth	42	9	7	5	46	34	7	4	10	33	36	43
Middlesbrough	42	14	4	3	47	16	1	7	13	20	36	41
Northampton T	42	10	2	9	35	31	6	7	8	23	29	41
Huddersfield T	42	11	4	6	31	25	4	6	11	26	39	40
Derby Co	42	10	6	5	34	27	4	5	12	22	40	39
Swindon T	42	11	5	5	39	24	3	5	13	18	45	38
Cardiff C	42	10	7	4	31	27	4	3	14	25	54	38
Leyton O	42	8	6	7	32	32	5	4	12	22	40	36
Norwich C	42	9	7	5	43	30	2	6	13	21	50	35
Bury	42	8	5	8	35	36	5	4	12	22	37	35
Swansea T	42	11	4	6	44	26	1	5	15	19	48	33
Plymouth A	42	6	8	7	26	32	2	8	11	19	35	32
Grimsby T	42	6	7	8	28	34	3	7	11	19	41	32
Scunthorpe U	42	8	8	5	30	25	2	2	17	22	57	30

DIVISION 3

	P	W	D	L	F	A	W	D	L	F	A	Pts
Coventry C	46	14	7	2	62	32	8	9	6	36	29	60
Crystal Palace	46	17	4	2	38	14	6	10	7	35	37	60
Watford	46	16	6	1	57	28	7	6	10	22	31	58
Bournemouth	46	17	4	2	47	15	7	4	12	32	43	56
Bristol C	46	13	7	3	52	24	7	8	8	32	40	55
Reading	46	15	5	3	49	26	6	5	12	30	36	52
Mansfield T	46	15	8	0	51	20	5	3	15	25	42	51
Hull C	46	11	9	3	45	27	5	8	10	28	41	49
Oldham A	46	13	3	7	44	35	7	5	11	29	35	48
Peterborough U	46	13	6	4	52	27	5	5	13	23	43	47
Shrewsbury T	46	13	6	4	43	19	5	5	13	30	61	47
Bristol R	46	9	6	8	52	34	10	2	11	39	45	46
Port Vale	46	13	6	4	35	13	3	8	12	18	36	46
Southend U	46	9	10	4	42	26	6	5	12	35	52	45
Q.P.R.	46	13	4	6	47	34	5	5	13	29	44	45
Brentford	46	11	4	8	54	36	4	10	9	33	44	44
Colchester U	46	10	8	5	45	26	2	11	10	25	42	43
Luton T	46	12	2	9	42	41	4	8	11	22	39	42
Walsall	46	7	9	7	34	35	6	5	12	25	41	40
Barnsley	46	9	9	5	34	29	3	6	14	34	65	39
Millwall	46	9	4	10	33	29	5	6	12	20	38	38
Crewe A	46	10	5	8	29	26	1	7	15	21	51	34
Wrexham	46	9	4	10	50	42	4	2	17	25	65	32
Notts Co	46	7	8	8	29	26	2	1	20	16	66	27

DIVISION 4

	P	W	D	L	F	A	W	D	L	F	A	Pts
Gillingham	46	16	7	0	37	10	7	7	9	22	20	60
Carlisle U	46	17	3	3	70	20	8	7	8	43	38	60
Workington	46	15	6	2	46	19	9	5	9	30	33	59
Exeter C	46	12	9	2	39	14	8	9	6	23	23	58
Bradford C	46	15	3	5	45	24	10	3	10	31	38	56
Torquay U	46	16	6	1	60	20	4	5	14	20	34	51
Tranmere R	46	12	4	7	46	30	8	7	8	39	43	51
Brighton & H.A.	46	13	3	7	45	22	6	9	8	26	30	50
Aldershot	46	15	3	5	58	28	4	7	12	25	50	48
Halifax T	46	14	4	5	47	28	3	10	10	30	49	48
Lincoln C	46	15	2	6	49	31	4	7	12	18	44	47
Chester C	46	17	3	3	47	18	2	5	16	18	42	46
Bradford P.A.	46	13	5	5	50	34	5	4	14	25	47	45
Doncaster R	46	11	8	4	46	23	4	4	15	24	52	42
Newport Co	46	12	3	8	35	24	5	5	13	29	49	42
Chesterfield	46	8	9	6	29	27	7	3	13	28	44	42
Stockport Co	46	12	7	4	32	19	3	5	15	18	49	42
Oxford U	46	10	7	6	37	27	4	6	13	22	36	41
Darlington	46	8	9	6	40	37	6	3	14	26	56	40
Rochdale	46	9	8	6	36	24	3	7	13	20	35	39
Southport	46	12	6	5	42	29	3	3	17	21	59	39
York C	46	9	3	11	29	26	5	4	14	23	40	35
Hartlepool U	46	8	7	8	30	36	4	2	17	24	57	33
Barrow	46	4	10	9	30	36	2	8	13	21	57	30

Football League Records

Top scorers: Div 1, A.McEvoy (Blackburn Rovers), J.Greaves (Tottenham Hotspur) 29 goals; Div 2, G.O'Brien (Southampton) 34 goals; Div 3, K.Wagstaff (Mansfield Town & Hull City) 34 goals; Div 4, A.Jeffrey (Doncaster Rovers) 36 goals.

George Best, the wayward genius whose skills lit up Manchester United's title-winning season of 1964-65.

DIVISION 1

	ARSENAL	ASTON VILLA	BIRMINGHAM C	BLACKBURN R	BLACKPOOL	BURNLEY	CHELSEA	EVERTON	FULHAM	LEEDS U	LEICESTER C	LIVERPOOL	MANCHESTER U	NOTTINGHAM F	SHEFFIELD U	SHEFFIELD W	STOKE C	SUNDERLAND	TOTTENHAM H	W.B.A.	WEST HAM U	WOLVERHAMPTON W
1 ARSENAL		A29 3-1	a06 3-0	S08 1-1	a19 3-1	O17 3-2	S26 1-3	O31 3-1	F20 2-0	F13 1-2	J23 4-3	D12 0-0	N28 2-3	O06 0-3	M06 1-1	A25 1-1	D26 3-2	S12 3-1	F23 3-1	a03 1-1	N14 0-3	J02 4-1
2 ASTON VILLA	D19 3-1		a12 3-0	S05 0-4	J16 3-2	N28 1-0	A31 2-2	O05 1-2	O31 2-0	A22 1-2	a20 1-0	F06 0-1	a28 2-1	M20 2-1	a17 2-1	S19 2-0	N14 3-0	S14 2-1	a03 1-0	O17 0-1	M31 2-3	M22 3-2
3 BIRMINGHAM C	N07 2-3	F13 0-1		a24 5-5	O24 3-0	S12 2-1	N21 1-6	S26 3-5	A26 2-2	a26 3-3	a10 2-0	O10 0-0	a19 2-4	D12 1-1	J23 1-1	F27 0-0	A29 1-2	D05 4-3	J02 1-0	S09 1-1	D26 2-1	M13 0-1
4 BLACKBURN R	S16 1-2	J02 5-1	O31 3-1		S02 4-1	F24 1-4	F13 0-3	M06 0-2	N28 2-0	D28 0-2	S26 3-1	A29 3-2	a03 0-5	a27 1-1	O17 4-0	J29 0-1	O07 1-1	M23 3-2	a19 3-1	N14 4-2	M20 4-0	S12 4-1
5 BLACKPOOL	a16 1-1	S12 3-1	M06 3-1	A24 4-2		D12 2-4	a26 3-2	O17 1-1	a03 3-0	S07 4-0	F13 1-1	J02 2-3	N14 1-2	N28 0-2	F20 2-2	A29 1-0	a17 1-1	S26 3-1	S28 1-1	M20 3-0	O31 1-2	J23 1-1
6 BURNLEY	F27 2-1	a10 2-2	J16 2-0	O10 1-1	A22 2-2		a24 6-2	S05 1-1	D26 4-0	O24 0-1	N07 2-1	D05 1-5	O06 0-0	S08 2-2	D19 3-1	M13 4-1	a20 1-0	M27 0-0	A25 2-2	F06 0-1	S19 3-2	N21 1-1
7 CHELSEA	F06 2-1	A26 2-1	a03 3-1	O03 5-1	D26 2-0	O31 0-1		N14 5-1	S12 1-0	S19 2-0	J02 4-1	a16 4-0	S30 0-2	F22 0-1	M22 3-0	S09 1-1	O17 4-0	A29 3-1	M10 3-1	a17 2-2	N28 0-3	D12 2-1
8 EVERTON	a24 1-0	M13 3-1	F06 1-1	O24 2-3	F27 0-0	J02 2-1	M31 1-1		a16 2-0	N07 0-1	N21 2-2	a12 2-1	S08 3-3	A25 1-0	S12 1-1	O10 1-1	D12 1-1	a10 1-1	A29 4-1	D26 3-2	O03 1-1	D05 5-0
9 FULHAM	D05 3-4	a24 1-1	S02 3-1	a09 3-2	N21 3-3	D28 0-1	J16 1-2	a19 1-1		M13 2-2	O10 5-2	N07 1-1	S05 2-1	J23 4-1	S16 1-2	M27 2-0	S26 1-4	F27 1-0	F13 4-1	D19 3-1	A22 1-2	O24 2-0
10 LEEDS U	N11 3-1	D12 1-0	N14 4-1	D26 1-1	S16 3-0	M15 5-1	J23 2-2	M20 4-1	S30 2-2		S12 3-2	A26 4-2	a17 0-1	S26 1-2	O31 4-1	a20 2-0	a05 3-1	J02 2-1	O17 3-1	N28 1-0	a03 2-1	A29 3-2
11 LEICESTER C	S19 2-3	a19 1-1	N28 4-4	F06 2-3	O05 3-2	M20 0-2	S05 1-1	a03 2-1	F24 5-1	J16 2-2		S09 2-0	A29 2-2	O17 3-2	N14 0-2	D26 2-2	a26 0-1	D12 0-1	O31 4-2	S30 4-2	a17 1-0	A26 3-2
12 LIVERPOOL	A22 3-2	S26 5-1	F24 4-3	D19 3-2	S05 2-2	a17 1-1	a19 2-0	S19 0-4	M20 3-2	S02 2-1	O13 0-1		O31 0-2	N14 2-0	O07 3-1	J16 4-2	a03 3-2	D28 0-0	N28 1-1	a06 0-3	O17 2-2	F13 2-1
13 MANCHESTER U	a26 3-1	O24 7-0	D16 1-1	N21 3-0	M22 2-0	F13 3-2	M13 4-0	S16 2-1	M15 4-1	D05 0-1	a12 1-0	a24 3-0		S12 3-0	D28 1-1	N07 1-0	J23 1-1	O10 1-0	S26 4-1	A22 2-2	S02 3-1	F27 3-0
14 NOTTINGHAM F	M13 3-0	N07 4-2	A22 4-3	D05 2-5	a10 2-0	S15 3-1	O10 2-2	S01 3-1	S19 2-3	F06 0-0	F27 2-1	a01 2-2	J16 2-2		a19 0-0	N21 2-2	F13 3-1	O24 5-2	D26 1-2	S05 0-0	D19 3-2	a24 0-2
15 SHEFFIELD U	O24 4-0	D05 4-2	S19 3-1	F27 1-1	O10 1-3	A29 2-0	N07 0-2	J16 0-0	S09 1-1	a24 0-3	M26 0-2	M13 3-0	D26 0-1	a20 0-2		J02 2-3	A26 0-1	N21 3-0	D12 3-3	O03 1-1	F06 2-1	a10 0-2
16 SHEFFIELD W	S02 2-1	M15 3-1	O17 5-2	A22 1-0	D19 4-1	S23 5-1	S16 2-3	F20 0-1	N14 1-1	a19 3-0	D28 0-0	S12 1-0	M20 1-0	a03 0-0	S05 0-2		N28 1-1	F13 2-0	a17 1-0	O31 1-1	M06 2-0	S26 2-0
17 STOKE C	D28 4-1	M27 2-1	M17 2-1	M13 1-1	D05 4-2	a19 2-0	F27 0-2	A22 0-2	F06 3-1	O10 2-3	O24 3-3	N21 1-1	S19 1-2	O03 1-1	S02 0-1	a10 4-1		a24 3-1	S09 2-0	J16 2-0	S05 3-1	N07 0-2
18 SUNDERLAND	J16 0-2	S09 2-2	a17 2-1	S19 1-0	F06 1-0	N14 3-2	D19 3-0	N28 4-0	O17 0-0	S05 3-3	A22 3-3	D26 2-3	F24 1-0	M06 4-0	a03 3-1	a28 3-0	O31 2-2		M20 2-1	S02 2-2	F20 3-2	a16 1-2
19 TOTTENHAM H	O10 3-1	N21 4-0	S05 4-1	a16 5-2	M13 4-1	S02 4-1	O24 1-1	D19 2-2	O05 3-0	F27 0-0	a24 6-2	a09 3-0	F06 1-0	D28 4-0	A22 2-0	D05 3-2	S16 2-1	N07 3-0		S19 1-0	J16 3-2	M27 7-4
20 W.B.A.	N21 0-0	F27 3-1	S16 0-2	M26 0-0	N07 1-3	S26 1-2	D05 0-2	M23 4-0	A29 2-2	a12 1-2	M13 6-0	O24 3-0	D12 1-1	J02 2-2	F13 0-1	a24 1-0	S12 5-3	A26 4-1	J23 2-0		a19 4-2	O10 5-1
21 WEST HAM U	M27 2-1	O10 3-0	D28 2-1	N07 1-1	a23 2-1	J23 3-2	a12 3-2	F13 0-1	D12 2-0	N21 3-1	D05 0-0	F27 2-1	A24 3-1	A28 2-3	S26 3-1	O24 1-2	J02 0-1	M13 2-3	S12 3-2	a16 6-1		S07 5-0
22 WOLVERHAMPTON W	S05 0-1	D26 0-1	S30 0-2	J16 4-2	S19 1-2	a03 1-2	A22 0-3	a17 2-4	M30 0-0	D19 0-1	S02 1-1	a26 1-3	O17 2-4	O31 1-2	N28 1-0	F06 3-1	M20 3-1	a20 3-0	N14 3-1	M15 3-2	S14 4-3	

Midfielder Dave Hilley was outstanding in Newcastle's promotion season. Hugely creative, he also scored 12 goals as the Magpies topped Division Two.

DIVISION 2

	BOLTON W	BURY	CARDIFF C	CHARLTON A	COVENTRY C	CRYSTAL P	DERBY CO	HUDDERSFIELD T	IPSWICH T	LEYTON O	MANCHESTER C	MIDDLESBROUGH	NEWCASTLE U	NORTHAMPTON T	NORWICH C	PLYMOUTH A	PORTSMOUTH	PRESTON N.E.	ROTHERHAM U	SOUTHAMPTON	SWANSEA T	SWINDON T
1 BOLTON W		F13 0-1	a28 1-0	M29 1-1	A29 1-3	O10 3-0	N07 3-1	D15 1-0	J23 0-0	a24 0-0	a10 4-0	S16 4-2	a19 1-1	D26 0-0	F27 5-2	S26 6-1	N21 3-2	S12 5-1	O24 2-0	S02 3-0	M13 2-1	M26 1-1
2 BURY	O02 2-1		a03 1-2	a20 2-0	N13 5-0	F06 3-1	D19 2-1	M19 0-2	M05 0-1	S08 2-1	D28 0-2	F23 3-2	O17 1-2	a17 1-4	S19 1-0	O06 0-2	S01 1-1	N27 1-1	a27 0-1	O30 3-3	S04 2-2	A22 6-1
3 CARDIFF C	S05 1-3	N21 4-0		N07 2-1	a19 3-1	a10 0-0	O10 2-1	S16 1-1	A22 0-0	M27 0-2	M12 2-2	J15 6-1	S19 1-1	F06 0-2	D05 1-3	D19 4-0	O24 1-0	A26 3-3	a24 3-2	M24 2-2	a06 5-0	F27 2-0
4 CHARLTON A	M06 1-3	a19 1-2	M22 2-2		O31 3-0	S15 1-2	J16 1-3	a17 0-0	a03 4-0	D28 2-0	A22 2-1	O06 0-2	S01 0-1	F20 1-1	O03 2-1	N28 3-2	D19 3-3	N14 2-3	F06 1-1	O17 2-5	S19 1-0	S05 3-2
5 COVENTRY C	D19 0-0	M27 2-1	a20 0-2	M13 2-0		N21 0-0	S15 0-2	O03 2-3	S01 5-3	N07 1-1	O24 2-2	S05 3-0	J16 5-4	S19 0-1	a10 3-0	A22 2-0	F27 1-2	D28 3-0	D05 3-5	F06 1-1	a24 3-0	O10 3-2
6 CRYSTAL P	a07 2-0	S26 0-2	N28 0-0	S30 3-1	a03 2-2		A22 2-3	N14 3-0	O07 1-1	F13 1-0	a19 1-1	O17 3-1	a17 1-1	O31 1-2	J16 2-0	S19 2-1	D26 4-2	M17 1-0	S05 2-1	M20 0-2	D19 3-3	S02 3-1
7 DERBY CO	M20 2-3	A29 3-1	F20 1-0	S12 4-4	S09 2-1	D12 3-3		O07 2-0	a17 2-3	J02 1-0	J30 2-0	N14 3-3	a03 0-3	N28 2-2	A26 0-1	O31 3-2	S26 4-0	O17 3-1	M24 2-2	M06 2-1	a19 3-4	F13 4-1
8 HUDDERSFIELD T	A22 1-1	N07 0-2	S29 3-1	O24 0-1	F13 2-1	M27 2-0	a24 3-1		D28 0-0	M13 0-0	F27 1-0	M30 1-0	S05 0-1	J16 2-0	N21 0-0	S02 1-2	O10 2-1	a19 3-0	a10 1-0	S19 0-3	D05 4-0	F06 2-1
9 IPSWICH T	S19 1-4	D05 1-0	D12 1-1	N21 1-1	A25 1-3	a24 3-2	O24 2-1	D26 3-2		a10 1-1	M27 4-1	F06 5-2	O03 3-1	S15 0-0	J02 3-0	J16 2-2	N07 7-0	A29 1-5	O10 4-4	a19 2-0	F27 3-0	M13 0-0
10 LEYTON O	S28 3-1	S14 1-0	N14 1-3	D26 4-2	a28 1-3	O03 0-1	S05 1-4	O31 1-0	N28 0-0		A31 4-3	a16 1-1	F20 2-1	O17 2-2	F06 2-3	M31 2-0	A22 5-2	a03 2-1	S19 2-1	a17 0-0	J16 2-3	D19 0-3
11 MANCHESTER C	N28 2-4	D26 0-0	O31 2-0	a28 2-1	a17 1-1	a16 0-2	S19 2-0	O17 2-3	N14 4-0	A26 6-0		M06 1-1	O14 3-0	A29 0-2	S09 0-2	a03 2-1	S05 2-0	M20 4-3	O03 2-1	F20 3-1	F06 1-0	J16 1-2
12 MIDDLESBROUGH	S07 5-2	O10 3-3	S12 0-0	a24 1-2	J02 2-3	F27 0-0	M27 1-2	A29 0-0	S26 2-4	a19 2-0	D05 0-1		D26 0-2	A24 1-0	O24 2-0	F13 1-3	a09 4-1	J23 1-1	M13 3-5	D12 4-1	N07 4-0	N21 4-1
13 NEWCASTLE U	a16 2-0	F27 2-3	J23 2-0	A24 1-1	S12 2-0	O24 2-0	N21 2-2	J02 2-1	F13 2-2	O10 5-0	a24 0-0	D28 2-1		D12 5-0	M13 2-0	S16 2-1	D05 3-0	S26 5-2	N07 3-1	A29 2-1	M27 3-1	a10 1-0
14 NORTHAMPTON T	M02 4-0	O24 2-0	S26 1-0	O10 1-0	J23 1-1	M13 1-1	a10 2-2	S11 3-2	S29 3-2	F27 2-0	D19 2-0	S01 1-1	S08 1-0		N07 0-0	a20 3-1	a24 1-1	F13 2-1	M27 1-0	J02 2-2	N21 2-1	D05 2-1
15 NORWICH C	O17 3-2	J23 1-1	M06 2-1	F13 2-0	N28 1-0	S12 1-2	S02 5-2	a03 0-2	S05 2-1	S26 2-0	S16 4-1	a17 2-0	O31 1-1	M20 1-1		F20 3-0	a20 3-1	O07 4-2	D19 3-0	N14 2-2	A22 2-1	J30 3-1
16 PLYMOUTH A	F06 1-3	a24 2-2	A29 3-1	a10 1-5	D12 2-3	J23 1-1	M13 1-1	A26 0-0	S12 1-1	D05 1-1	N21 3-2	O03 1-0	S30 2-1	a19 5-2	O10 1-0		M27 2-1	J02 0-1	F27 1-1	F17 4-0	O24 2-1	N07 2-1
17 PORTSMOUTH	a03 3-0	A26 2-1	a17 1-0	A29 2-3	O17 0-2	D28 1-1	F06 3-1	F20 3-0	M20 0-2	D12 1-1	J02 1-1	N28 2-1	M06 1-2	O07 3-3	a19 4-0	N14 0-1		O31 1-0	S30 2-0	S12 0-3	O03 1-0	S19 5-0
18 PRESTON N.E.	J16 2-2	a10 2-2	A31 1-1	M26 2-1	D26 3-2	D05 1-0	F27 2-2	a20 2-0	D19 4-1	N21 3-0	N07 2-5	S19 4-3	F06 2-0	O03 2-2	a24 3-1	S05 1-3	M13 6-1		A22 0-0	N02 0-0	O10 2-2	O24 2-1
19 ROTHERHAM U	a17 0-0	S12 3-0	O06 3-1	S26 3-2	M06 0-2	J02 1-0	D28 1-1	N28 2-3	F20 2-2	a06 3-0	F13 0-0	O31 2-3	M20 1-1	N14 1-1	A29 4-0	O17 4-2	S15 1-0	D12 2-2		a03 1-3	A25 4-2	a19 1-0
20 SOUTHAMPTON	A26 3-2	M13 3-1	F13 1-1	F27 4-0	S26 4-1	N07 0-1	D05 3-3	J23 3-3	a21 1-1	O24 2-2	O10 1-0	A22 0-3	D19 0-1	S05 2-0	M27 1-0	D26 5-0	J16 2-2	S16 3-1	N21 6-1		a10 3-1	a24 2-1
21 SWANSEA T	O31 2-0	J02 2-2	D26 3-2	J23 1-3	S29 1-1	A29 2-1	a20 2-1	M06 2-2	O17 1-1	S12 2-5	S26 3-0	M20 1-2	N14 3-1	a03 1-2	D12 0-0	a17 3-0	F13 0-0	M23 4-0	S01 0-3	N28 3-3		S15 4-0
22 SWINDON T	N14 1-3	D12 2-0	O17 3-3	J02 2-0	F20 4-1	A25 2-0	O03 4-2	S26 4-1	O31 3-1	A29 1-0	S12 0-1	a03 0-1	N28 1-6	M23 4-2	D26 0-1	M20 2-3	J23 0-0	a17 2-2	a16 3-2	O13 2-1	S08 3-0	

SEASON 1964-65

DIVISION 3

	BARNSLEY	BOURNEMOUTH	BRENTFORD	BRISTOL C	BRISTOL R	CARLISLE U	COLCHESTER U	EXETER C	GILLINGHAM	GRIMSBY T	HULL C	LUTON T	MANSFIELD T	OLDHAM A	PETERBOROUGH U	PORT VALE	Q.P.R.	READING	SCUNTHORPE U	SHREWSBURY T	SOUTHEND U	WALSALL	WATFORD	WORKINGTON
1 BARNSLEY		O10 2-2	N07 3-1	N03 1-2	M13 0-2	a10 1-2	M26 1-2	F27 0-0	S15 1-0	M30 1-0	S30 1-1	J30 3-0	a24 2-3	O24 0-1	D28 3-2	N21 0-2	A22 0-0	S04 1-1	S25 2-0	D18 6-2	J16 1-4	F13 0-1	O20 4-0	a20 0-3
2 BOURNEMOUTH	F20 1-0		a19 0-1	N28 1-2	S30 1-1	F06 0-4	O14 3-1	A26 2-2	a03 1-2	S05 1-2	J09 2-3	S19 4-0	J16 2-0	S09 0-0	D19 0-1	O03 3-0	M06 2-0	A22 3-2	O17 2-1	O28 2-1	D26 2-1	a17 4-0	O31 0-0	M20 4-0
3 BRENTFORD	M20 1-0	a16 2-1		D26 2-1	S26 1-1	D19 6-1	J16 1-0	O20 2-1	S19 2-0	S15 2-0	O27 1-3	A22 2-2	A31 1-0	F13 2-2	O06 3-1	S05 4-0	F20 5-2	a17 2-1	a27 4-0	O17 2-0	O31 2-1	a03 0-0	N28 5-1	a07 3-0
4 BRISTOL C	A25 5-1	a09 0-0	M02 3-2		F13 2-1	O23 1-2	O10 1-1	J30 1-1	S26 1-2	M26 4-0	J23 1-2	M13 1-0	N07 1-1	a24 2-0	N21 3-1	F27 3-0	O13 2-0	S29 2-0	D12 2-2	a20 3-0	S08 4-0	A29 5-1	J02 1-1	S12 5-0
5 BRISTOL R	O31 1-0	O06 4-2	F06 1-2	O03 1-1		S05 5-2	S19 2-2	a16 1-1	O27 3-0	S01 5-3	M06 1-1	D19 3-2	A22 4-1	O20 0-0	S15 4-0	J16 4-0	D26 3-1	O17 1-0	M20 2-0	F23 0-0	a17 2-2	M16 0-1	a03 1-0	N28 4-0
6 CARLISLE U	N28 4-0	S26 3-4	A28 0-1	a16 1-1	J02 1-2		D12 4-1	M09 2-1	O17 3-1	J09 3-1	F20 0-0	O07 1-1	a20 3-0	S12 2-0	F13 2-1	A24 1-1	O30 2-0	M16 1-2	M06 3-1	M19 2-1	a02 4-3	O27 2-1	S08 1-1	D26 1-0
7 COLCHESTER U	J09 4-1	O19 4-3	S12 0-3	F20 2-3	J23 1-1	A22 0-1		F13 1-1	D28 2-1	O05 0-1	S05 1-2	A31 0-1	S14 0-1	S26 2-2	a16 0-1	D19 2-0	O17 1-2	O31 2-2	a03 2-1	a17 0-4	M20 3-1	N28 2-1	M06 0-0	O26 1-1
8 EXETER C	O17 3-0	a28 1-3	O14 0-0	M06 0-1	a19 0-1	S19 0-0	O03 2-0		N28 1-1	D19 4-1	a03 0-2	J16 5-1	S05 2-3	O08 2-1	A22 4-2	F06 2-1	M31 2-2	D26 2-2	J08 1-3	S16 0-1	F20 1-1	O31 0-1	M20 1-0	M22 0-0
9 GILLINGHAM	S09 1-0	N21 1-1	J23 1-0	F06 2-0	a24 1-3	F27 1-0	D26 2-1	a10 0-1		N07 0-0	S12 1-0	O24 5-0	M13 0-0	J30 2-1	M26 2-0	O10 2-0	O03 2-2	a16 2-1	A26 0-0	O21 5-0	S30 1-0	D12 4-0	A29 5-2	J02 5-1
10 GRIMSBY T	S19 3-2	J02 2-2	S09 2-1	M09 0-2	A25 1-1	O21 1-1	S30 2-0	A29 2-1	M20 1-1		O31 3-0	O03 2-2	F06 1-1	D12 3-1	S12 2-0	a16 2-0	a03 0-0	M06 1-1	a06 3-0	N28 2-2	O28 1-0	F20 2-2	O17 1-0	a17 0-1
11 HULL C	O07 7-0	M27 2-1	a24 2-1	S19 3-2	J30 3-2	O09 1-0	J02 5-1	N21 3-1	J16 1-1	M13 3-3		F27 3-1	O24 1-1	a10 2-1	N07 0-2	D28 4-0	F06 3-1	O12 1-0	S09 1-2	O03 1-2	a19 0-0	A26 2-0	D12 1-1	A29 2-2
12 LUTON T	a07 5-1	F17 0-1	D12 4-2	O31 0-0	A29 0-2	O01 1-1	A26 3-1	S12 1-2	a17 0-2	F13 1-1	O17 1-3		O21 1-1	J02 2-0	S26 1-1	S09 1-1	M20 2-0	a03 3-1	O28 1-1	M10 2-7	N28 0-1	a16 1-3	D26 2-4	a29 0-0
13 MANSFIELD T	O26 4-3	S12 0-0	A24 4-1	M20 3-0	D12 3-0	a19 2-0	S07 0-1	J02 2-1	O31 3-1	S26 2-2	a17 2-1	O12 2-0		A29 4-1	M29 0-0	S28 2-2	M15 8-1	N28 2-1	O03 3-2	a03 1-0	a05 6-1	D28 2-0	F20 3-0	O17 3-5
14 OLDHAM A	a17 1-1	S15 1-1	O03 1-1	O28 7-3	O14 1-2	J16 2-3	F06 3-1	S28 2-0	M06 2-0	A22 1-5	N28 2-1	S05 0-2	D19 2-1		S01 3-1	S19 0-1	a16 5-3	F20 1-2	O31 2-1	D28 1-3	O17 0-2	M20 1-3	J27 2-0	a03 0-2
15 PETERBOROUGH U	D26 4-1	A29 4-3	S28 3-1	a03 0-1	S07 3-1	O03 1-2	a19 4-1	D12 0-0	a28 1-0	J16 3-1	M20 2-1	F06 2-0	S19 4-5	A24 5-0		O12 2-2	N28 6-1	O26 2-1	M08 2-2	M15 4-1	S05 4-2	O17 3-2	a17 2-1	O31 0-4
16 PORT VALE	a03 2-0	F13 1-2	J02 2-1	O17 1-2	S12 1-1	A31 1-3	A29 1-2	S26 0-1	F20 0-4	a20 2-3	D26 0-3	S14 1-0	O05 2-2	M15 2-1	O19 0-1		a17 0-0	M20 2-0	N28 0-1	O31 1-1	J08 2-2	a26 2-1	O26 2-2	M29 2-0
17 Q.P.R.	D11 3-2	J29 1-1	O09 1-3	O19 1-0	D28 3-1	M12 1-2	F26 5-0	a23 0-0	F13 3-1	N21 1-1	S25 2-1	N06 7-1	M26 2-0	a19 1-1	a10 3-2	O23 3-1		S07 0-1	A28 2-1	O05 2-1	A24 2-0	J01 1-0	S11 2-2	a05 2-1
18 READING	J02 1-1	D12 1-0	O24 1-1	O07 1-1	F27 1-1	M27 1-2	M13 1-1	a07 2-2	a19 3-0	M24 2-0	O21 3-3	N21 1-2	a10 2-1	O10 1-0	a24 4-2	N07 1-1	S16 5-3		S12 2-0	A26 3-1	A29 2-0	J23 0-2	S26 6-2	F13 1-0
19 SCUNTHORPE U	F05 2-3	F26 3-1	M26 2-0	A22 5-2	N07 1-1	J29 0-1	N20 0-0	O24 0-0	N03 2-3	D26 2-1	S15 1-1	a24 8-1	F12 0-1	M12 1-1	O10 2-3	a09 0-0	D18 2-1	J15 1-1		S04 3-2	S18 2-1	O13 4-0	a20 0-2	S29 1-1
20 SHREWSBURY T	A29 3-3	a24 1-2	F27 1-0	a19 1-5	O10 2-1	N07 2-2	O24 3-0	S08 1-0	O13 2-0	a10 1-3	F13 0-4	M26 0-2	N03 1-1	D26 1-3	a07 1-1	M13 0-0	a12 3-2	S01 4-0	J02 3-2		D12 1-3	S11 3-1	J23 2-2	S26 6-1
21 SOUTHEND U	S12 2-0	D28 2-1	M13 0-1	S14 0-4	O24 6-3	N21 1-0	N07 6-3	O10 0-0	O05 3-1	a24 4-0	a16 2-1	a10 5-0	J30 1-4	F27 6-1	J02 2-0	M26 2-1	A31 0-0	D19 2-2	J23 0-1	A22 1-0		S26 0-0	F13 0-1	O12 3-0
22 WALSALL	O03 1-1	O24 0-1	N21 4-3	D19 2-4	M27 2-0	D05 1-0	a10 2-1	M13 2-1	A22 0-1	O10 1-0	a06 3-3	a19 0-1	D26 2-1	N07 1-2	F27 0-1	J30 0-0	S05 4-1	S19 4-1	O20 1-2	J16 1-1	F06 2-3		O06 0-4	S15 1-4
23 WATFORD	M16 1-1	M13 2-0	a10 1-1	S05 2-2	N21 1-1	S17 0-0	J30 3-0	N07 1-0	D19 1-2	F27 1-1	A22 2-1	D28 2-0	O10 3-1	M27 3-2	O24 1-1	a24 1-0	J16 0-2	F06 5-1	a16 5-0	S19 2-2	O03 2-1	S29 3-0		M08 3-2
24 WORKINGTON	a16 0-0	N07 2-0	M17 1-1	J15 1-0	a09 2-1	D28 0-1	a23 1-0	M26 0-1	S05 1-1	O24 2-2	D19 1-3	O09 1-0	F26 1-5	N21 0-0	M12 1-0	A22 4-1	S18 0-0	O02 0-2	O06 2-0	F05 2-2	O19 3-1	O28 3-1	A25 2-0	

DIVISION 4

	ALDERSHOT	BARROW	BRADFORD	BRADFORD C	BRIGHTON & HA	CHESTER	CHESTERFIELD	CREWE A	DARLINGTON	DONCASTER R	HALIFAX T	HARTLEPOOLS U	LINCOLN C	MILLWALL	NEWPORT CO	NOTTS CO	OXFORD U	ROCHDALE	SOUTHPORT	STOCKPORT CO	TORQUAY U	TRANMERE R	WREXHAM	YORK C
1 ALDERSHOT		J30 2-1	A26 1-1	O28 1-1	O31 0-2	A22 3-1	S05 2-0	O03 5-2	a19 0-1	D19 3-0	S19 2-0	a03 3-0	M30 3-2	a17 0-0	F06 2-1	J16 1-2	M20 4-1	N28 1-2	S09 0-3	F20 2-0	M17 2-5	S30 3-0	O19 5-0	O17 1-0
2 BARROW	M27 2-0		N21 2-1	O03 1-0	D12 1-4	a16 2-1	M13 1-2	D28 1-2	J02 3-1	N07 1-2	F27 1-0	J16 4-2	A24 2-2	F06 0-5	O10 1-4	O24 2-0	A29 1-1	S19 2-2	a10 1-1	O19 0-1	S28 2-1	a24 0-2	J11 0-2	S07 0-2
3 BRADFORD	A31 3-1	a03 3-2		S15 3-3	M20 2-0	D28 3-1	D22 1-0	F06 2-3	O03 3-1	A22 5-2	D05 5-1	N28 4-0	O31 3-1	O27 4-0	S19 2-2	S05 2-2	J30 1-0	a17 0-0	O13 0-0	O17 1-0	F20 4-2	a21 1-1	S29 0-0	M06 0-0
4 BRADFORD C	a24 2-0	F13 1-3	S09 0-2		a06 4-1	A25 1-3	a10 0-0	M13 5-2	O24 2-3	F03 0-3	M27 3-1	a19 4-0	S12 0-1	O21 1-2	N07 1-0	N21 0-2	S26 2-1	O07 0-2	D26 2-1	A29 1-1	D12 2-3	F27 1-2	O10 4-1	J02 1-2
5 BRIGHTON & H.A.	M13 2-0	A22 3-1	N07 2-2	S19 3-3		F06 4-4	F27 5-0	J09 3-1	a26 3-1	O24 1-1	D26 2-1	D19 5-0	O20 4-0	J16 2-0	S15 1-0	O10 6-0	A25 0-0	S05 3-0	M26 3-1	a19 3-1	O03 3-1	a10 2-1	N21 5-1	O06 3-1
6 CHESTER	D12 6-2	a19 4-1	D26 3-0	F10 3-1	S26 3-1		F24 4-0	N07 2-2	M13 4-5	a24 3-0	N21 1-0	O07 4-0	J23 5-1	S16 3-1	M26 4-3	a10 4-1	F13 2-1	M10 0-1	O10 3-1	J02 4-0	A29 0-1	O24 3-2	F27 6-1	S12 4-1
7 CHESTERFIELD	J02 0-1	O31 2-0	A29 2-4	N28 3-1	O17 1-1	a17 1-3		S28 2-1	M29 3-0	S12 1-0	O03 3-0	M20 3-1	F20 1-0	a03 2-3	a16 2-1	F06 0-0	M06 2-1	J30 1-1	D12 1-2	S19 2-0	a05 2-1	S07 1-0	A24 0-0	D28 1-1
8 CREWE A	F13 4-1	D26 6-2	S26 1-1	O31 2-1	O28 3-2	M20 5-1	O07 0-2		A29 1-2	a16 4-4	S08 2-2	F20 2-3	a17 5-0	M06 1-1	A26 1-1	M10 2-1	D12 2-2	O17 1-1	J23 4-1	a03 3-2	J29 2-0	J02 1-1	S12 1-0	N28 2-3
9 DARLINGTON	J01 4-1	S05 1-2	F13 1-2	M22 3-1	a17 2-0	O31 2-0	O19 2-2	D19 0-2		O05 2-2	A31 5-1	F22 2-3	N28 3-1	O17 1-3	A22 0-1	S14 5-1	O26 2-0	F20 2-0	S26 3-2	M15 3-2	M20 1-2	S12 2-1	a05 5-1	a03 1-0
10 DONCASTER R	A29 1-0	M20 4-2	D12 1-1	a17 0-0	M06 2-1	a06 1-4	J16 2-0	a19 3-1	S29 6-3		F06 4-0	J30 0-1	O17 1-2	N28 4-0	O03 1-0	S18 0-0	O31 2-2	a03 2-2	A25 1-2	D26 3-0	S05 2-0	a27 1-0	S08 1-1	F20 4-3
11 HALIFAX T	J23 3-3	O17 3-2	S12 2-3	J30 0-3	D28 1-1	a03 3-4	F13 2-1	S15 2-0	A25 4-0	S26 2-4		M16 2-1	O06 2-1	M20 1-2	O19 2-0	a19 1-1	F20 1-3	O31 1-2	J02 2-1	a17 0-1	N28 0-1	D12 0-1	A29 2-1	O27 1-1
12 HARTLEPOOLS U	N21 1-1	S12 3-0	a10 2-0	a16 2-2	A29 1-1	S28 1-1	N07 1-1	O10 2-4	D26 4-3	M29 1-1	O24 4-0		D12 3-0	O03 1-0	F27 2-4	M13 2-2	J02 1-1	F06 1-1	a05 2-1	S07 4-3	S21 1-0	J23 2-0	a24 1-0	A24 2-2
13 LINCOLN C	O24 3-1	S23 1-0	M12 2-2	J16 0-2	O14 0-1	S19 2-2	O10 0-2	F17 1-2	a10 2-0	F27 0-2	S30 2-3	A22 4-2		S05 2-2	a24 4-3	D26 1-0	S09 0-2	D18 1-1	N07 3-0	O03 6-0	F06 0-1	N20 1-2	M26 0-2	a16 0-1
14 MILLWALL	a05 5-0	S26 3-1	a24 1-0	O12 3-0	S12 2-0	S07 1-0	N21 4-2	O24 0-0	F27 1-1	a10 1-1	N07 5-1	F13 0-0	J02 2-1		M13 4-0	M27 4-1	J23 2-2	a16 0-0	S29 0-0	D12 1-0	A24 2-2	O10 1-0	D26 2-2	A29 1-1
15 NEWPORT CO	S26 2-1	F20 2-2	J23 4-3	M19 4-2	S07 1-1	J30 0-1	a19 4-1	A31 2-2	D12 2-1	F13 1-0	O12 0-2	O17 2-0	O26 7-0	O31 2-2		S28 3-1	D26 0-3	M29 2-3	S12 5-0	N28 2-0	a03 4-0	A29 1-1	J02 2-0	a17 2-0
16 NOTTS CO	S12 0-0	M06 4-1	J02 3-3	a03 1-0	F20 1-2	N28 1-1	S26 5-1	O22 2-0	S10 4-2	J23 5-2	a20 4-0	O31 1-0	D28 2-1	a29 1-2	O08 1-0		O17 0-0	M20 0-0	A29 0-0	O29 2-0	a17 0-0	A27 2-4	D12 1-3	O03 3-1
17 OXFORD U	N07 0-0	D19 7-0	M27 3-0	F06 3-1	M31 2-2	O03 3-2	O24 1-0	A22 4-2	a24 1-0	M13 1-0	O10 1-0	S05 3-0	S16 2-0	S19 0-2	F17 4-1	F27 4-0		J16 2-2	N21 1-1	O07 2-0	a19 3-0	J09 1-0	a09 4-0	O21 2-0
18 ROCHDALE	a10 3-1	J23 3-0	J09 4-3	S30 3-1	M22 2-2	O14 2-1	M26 1-2	F27 1-0	O10 1-1	N21 2-1	M13 3-0	S26 3-0	A29 2-0	a21 0-2	O24 2-0	N07 1-1	S12 3-3		a24 2-0	A26 4-0	S07 1-0	D28 0-1	F13 2-1	D12 1-2
19 SOUTHPORT	S21 3-1	N28 0-4	O19 1-1	D28 0-4	J30 1-2	F20 2-2	A22 1-0	S18 2-3	F06 3-3	A31 3-5	S05 5-2	a17 1-1	M20 4-4	O05 0-0	J16 5-3	D19 0-0	a03 0-3	O26 1-0		M06 1-1	O17 0-1	O03 2-2	a19 0-2	O31 0-1
20 STOCKPORT CO	O10 2-1	O12 1-0	F27 0-2	M08 2-0	a16 1-4	S04 4-5	J23 0-1	N20 1-1	M26 0-0	D28 2-0	M22 2-0	S14 0-1	F13 3-1	A22 1-4	a10 2-0	a23 0-1	S28 0-0	F15 1-2	O23 2-2		J16 0-2	N06 2-3	M12 3-2	S25 1-2
21 TORQUAY U	D26 5-2	O07 6-2	O10 1-1	A22 2-2	F13 0-1	D19 3-2	a24 0-2	M27 0-1	N07 2-0	J02 2-4	a10 2-0	O19 2-1	S26 0-2	M31 0-0	N21 2-2	F24 2-1	a21 1-1	S16 2-1	F27 2-0	S12 1-0		M13 2-1	O24 3-4	J23 1-3
22 TRANMERE R	O05 3-1	O26 3-0	a16 0-0	O16 5-1	N27 4-2	M29 4-1	S14 4-0	S04 1-0	J15 2-1	O19 3-0	A22 5-2	S18 5-1	a02 4-0	F19 1-0	D18 3-2	A31 4-0	a17 2-4	D26 4-1	F12 3-1	M19 1-1	O30 3-1		S25 6-0	J29 2-1
23 WREXHAM	O12 4-0	a17 3-3	O07 4-1	F20 3-2	a03 1-2	O17 4-2	M17 1-2	J16 3-3	S19 4-2	S16 0-2	D19 1-1	O28 3-0	J30 5-3	a27 0-1	S05 4-2	A22 4-0	N28 1-1	O03 2-3	a16 1-1	O31 4-1	a28 2-3	F06 3-2		M20 2-0
24 YORK C	F27 1-0	S14 2-0	O24 0-1	S05 5-2	S28 2-1	J16 3-2	D26 7-1	a09 3-1	N21 2-1	O09 4-2	a24 4-0	A31 0-0	a19 3-0	D19 3-1	M01 5-1	F13 2-1	O12 2-1	A22 2-1	M12 3-2	F06 3-0	S18 1-2	M26 4-0	N07 2-1	

LEAGUE TABLES

DIVISION 1

	P	W	D	L	F	A	W	D	L	F	A	Pts
Manchester U	42	16	4	1	52	13	10	5	6	37	26	61
Leeds U	42	16	3	2	53	23	10	6	5	30	29	61
Chelsea	42	15	2	4	48	19	9	6	6	41	35	56
Everton	42	9	10	2	37	22	8	5	8	32	38	49
Nottingham F	42	10	7	4	45	33	7	6	8	26	34	47
Tottenham H	42	18	3	0	65	20	1	4	16	22	51	45
Liverpool	42	12	5	4	42	33	5	5	11	25	40	44
Sheffield W	42	13	5	3	37	15	3	6	12	20	40	43
West Ham U	42	14	2	5	48	25	5	2	14	34	46	42
Blackburn R	42	12	2	7	46	33	4	8	9	37	46	42
Stoke C	42	11	4	6	40	27	5	6	10	27	39	42
Burnley	42	9	9	3	39	26	7	1	13	31	44	42
Arsenal	42	11	5	5	42	31	6	2	13	27	44	41
W.B.A.	42	10	5	6	45	25	3	8	10	25	40	39
Sunderland	42	12	6	3	45	26	2	3	16	19	48	37
Aston Villa	42	14	1	6	36	24	2	4	15	21	58	37
Blackpool	42	9	7	5	41	28	3	4	14	26	50	35
Leicester C	42	9	6	6	43	36	2	7	12	26	49	35
Sheffield U	42	7	5	9	30	29	5	6	10	20	35	35
Fulham	42	10	5	6	44	32	1	7	13	16	46	34
Wolverh'pton W	42	8	2	11	33	36	5	2	14	26	53	30
Birmingham C	42	6	8	7	36	40	2	3	16	28	56	27

DIVISION 2

	P	W	D	L	F	A	W	D	L	F	A	Pts
Newcastle U	42	16	4	1	50	16	8	5	8	31	29	57
Northampton T	42	14	7	0	37	16	6	9	6	29	34	56
Bolton W	42	13	6	2	46	17	7	4	10	34	41	50
Southampton	42	12	6	3	49	25	5	8	8	34	38	48
Ipswich T	42	11	7	3	48	30	4	10	7	26	37	47
Norwich C	42	15	4	2	47	21	5	3	13	14	36	47
Crystal Palace	42	11	6	4	37	24	5	7	9	18	27	45
Huddersfield T	42	12	4	5	28	15	5	6	10	25	36	44
Derby Co	42	11	5	5	48	35	5	6	10	36	44	43
Coventry C	42	10	5	6	41	29	7	4	10	31	41	43
Manchester C	42	12	3	6	40	24	4	6	11	23	38	41
Preston N.E.	42	11	8	2	46	29	3	5	13	30	52	41
Cardiff C	42	10	7	4	43	25	3	7	11	21	32	40
Rotherham U	42	10	7	4	39	25	4	5	12	31	44	40
Plymouth A	42	10	7	4	36	28	6	1	14	27	51	40
Bury	42	9	4	8	36	30	5	6	10	24	36	38
Middlesbrough	42	8	5	8	40	31	5	4	12	30	45	35
Charlton A	42	8	5	8	35	34	5	4	12	29	41	35
Leyton O	42	10	4	7	36	34	2	7	12	14	38	35
Portsmouth	42	11	4	6	36	22	1	6	14	20	55	34
Swindon T	42	12	3	6	43	30	2	2	17	20	51	33
Swansea T	42	9	7	5	40	29	2	3	16	22	55	32

DIVISION 3

	P	W	D	L	F	A	W	D	L	F	A	Pts
Carlisle U	46	14	5	4	46	24	11	5	7	30	29	60
Bristol C	46	14	6	3	53	18	10	5	8	39	37	59
Mansfield T	46	17	4	2	61	23	7	7	9	34	38	59
Hull C	46	14	6	3	51	25	9	6	8	40	32	58
Brentford	46	18	4	1	55	18	6	5	12	28	37	57
Bristol R	46	14	7	2	52	21	6	8	9	30	37	55
Gillingham	46	16	5	2	45	13	7	4	12	25	37	55
Peterborough U	46	16	3	4	61	33	6	4	13	24	41	51
Watford	46	13	8	2	45	21	4	8	11	26	43	50
Grimsby T	46	11	10	2	37	21	5	7	11	31	46	49
Bournemouth	46	12	4	7	40	24	6	7	10	32	39	47
Southend U	46	14	4	5	48	24	5	4	14	30	47	46
Reading	46	12	8	3	45	26	4	6	13	25	44	46
Q.P.R.	46	15	5	3	48	23	2	7	14	24	57	46
Workington	46	11	7	5	30	22	6	5	12	28	47	46
Shrewsbury T	46	10	6	7	42	38	5	6	12	34	46	42
Exeter C	46	8	7	8	33	27	4	10	9	18	25	41
Scunthorpe U	46	9	8	6	42	27	5	4	14	23	45	40
Walsall	46	9	4	10	34	36	6	3	14	21	44	37
Oldham A	46	10	3	10	40	39	3	7	13	21	44	36
Luton T	46	6	8	9	32	36	5	3	15	19	58	33
Port Vale	46	7	6	10	27	33	2	8	13	14	43	32
Colchester U	46	7	6	10	30	34	3	4	16	20	55	30
Barnsley	46	8	5	10	33	31	1	6	16	21	59	29

DIVISION 4

	P	W	D	L	F	A	W	D	L	F	A	Pts
Brighton & H.A.	46	18	5	0	68	20	8	6	9	34	37	63
Millwall	46	13	10	0	45	15	10	6	7	33	30	62
York C	46	20	1	2	63	21	8	5	10	28	35	62
Oxford U	46	18	4	1	54	13	5	11	7	33	31	61
Tranmere R	46	20	2	1	72	20	7	4	12	27	36	60
Rochdale	46	15	4	4	46	22	7	10	6	28	31	58
Bradford P.A.	46	14	8	1	52	22	6	9	8	34	40	57
Chester C	46	19	1	3	75	26	6	5	12	44	55	56
Doncaster R	46	13	6	4	46	25	7	5	11	38	47	51
Crewe A	46	11	8	4	55	34	7	5	11	35	47	49
Torquay U	46	11	5	7	41	33	10	2	11	29	37	49
Chesterfield	46	13	5	5	36	22	7	3	13	22	48	48
Notts Co	46	12	7	4	43	23	3	7	13	18	50	44
Wrexham	46	12	5	6	59	37	5	4	14	25	55	43
Hartlepool U	46	11	10	2	44	28	4	3	16	17	57	43
Newport Co	46	14	5	4	54	26	3	3	17	31	55	42
Darlington	46	14	2	7	52	30	4	4	15	32	57	42
Aldershot	46	14	3	6	46	25	1	4	18	18	59	37
Bradford C	46	9	2	12	37	36	3	6	14	33	52	32
Southport	46	5	9	9	35	45	3	7	13	23	44	32
Barrow	46	9	4	10	30	38	3	2	18	29	67	30
Lincoln C	46	8	4	11	35	33	3	2	18	23	66	28
Halifax T	46	9	4	10	37	37	2	2	19	17	66	28
Stockport Co	46	8	4	11	30	34	2	3	18	14	53	27

Football League Records

Top scorers: W.Irvine (Burnley) 29 goals; Div 2, M.Chivers (Southampton) 30 goals; Div 3, L.Allen (Queen's Park Rangers) 30 goals; Div 4, K.Hector (Bradford) 44 goals.

Ron Yeats, Liverpool's giant centre-half and one of the dominant figures in yet another Championship success.

DIVISION 1

	ARSENAL	ASTON VILLA	BLACKBURN R	BLACKPOOL	BURNLEY	CHELSEA	EVERTON	FULHAM	LEEDS U	LEICESTER C	LIVERPOOL	MANCHESTER U	NEWCASTLE U	NORTHAMPTON T	NOTTINGHAM F	SHEFFIELD U	SHEFFIELD W	STOKE C	SUNDERLAND	TOTTENHAM H	W.B.A.	WEST HAM U
1 ARSENAL		D04 3-3	O23 2-2	M05 0-0	F05 1-1	S04 1-3	M12 0-1	O09 2-1	m05 0-3	m07 1-0	J08 0-1	S25 4-2	M26 1-3	S28 1-1	S14 1-0	N06 6-2	D28 5-2	A21 2-1	a23 1-1	M08 1-1	a05 1-1	N20 3-2
2 ASTON VILLA	a30 3-0		F19 3-1	S11 3-0	a16 2-1	N27 2-4	D11 3-2	M12 2-5	A23 0-2	A28 2-2	M26 0-3	a06 1-1	J01 4-2	a02 1-2	J15 3-0	J29 0-2	O30 2-0	N13 0-1	S06 3-1	S25 3-2	O16 1-1	F07 1-2
3 BLACKBURN R	J15 2-1	S04 0-2		m02 1-3	J01 0-2	O16 0-1	O30 1-2	S01 3-2	M19 2-3	a08 0-2	F05 1-4	m07 1-4	N13 4-2	D11 6-1	N27 5-0	O02 0-0	a30 1-2	S15 0-1	F26 2-0	m09 0-1	a16 0-1	S18 1-2
4 BLACKPOOL	O16 5-3	F26 0-1	D25 4-2		A30 1-3	J01 1-2	J15 2-0	A21 2-2	M28 1-0	S06 4-0	S04 2-3	O30 1-2	a20 1-1	a30 3-0	a16 0-3	a08 2-1	N27 2-1	D11 1-1	S18 1-2	F05 0-0	N13 1-1	M19 2-1
5 BURNLEY	A28 2-2	N20 3-1	O09 1-4	A24 3-1		J29 1-2	F19 1-1	J08 1-0	m07 0-1	D18 4-2	a23 2-0	S11 3-0	M12 1-0	S07 4-1	M26 4-1	O23 2-0	a11 2-1	D28 4-1	a09 1-0	D04 1-1	S25 2-0	N06 3-1
6 CHELSEA	F19 0-0	m16 0-2	m04 1-0	O09 0-1	A21 1-1		S11 3-1	F05 2-1	N06 1-0	O23 0-2	D04 0-1	M12 2-0	S25 1-1	D28 1-0	a11 1-0	m07 2-0	S15 1-1	S01 1-2	F22 3-2	J08 2-1	a25 2-3	a09 6-2
7 EVERTON	S18 3-1	J08 2-0	O05 2-2	O23 0-0	S04 1-0	F26 2-1		D18 2-0	N20 0-0	N06 1-2	M19 0-0	a25 0-0	a11 1-0	A21 5-2	M15 3-0	a09 1-3	A31 5-1	F05 2-1	D04 2-0	O09 3-1	S07 2-3	J11 2-2
8 FULHAM	J01 1-0	S18 3-6	A25 5-2	J29 0-0	D11 2-5	A28 0-3	O16 3-2		a08 1-3	a18 0-4	F26 2-0	J15 0-1	O30 2-0	N27 1-4	N13 1-1	S08 0-0	a16 4-2	a30 1-1	M19 3-0	S04 0-2	a02 2-1	O02 3-0
9 LEEDS U	N13 2-0	S01 2-0	S25 3-0	M26 1-2	O30 1-1	a04 2-0	a16 4-1	a12 0-1		M12 3-2	D28 0-1	J12 1-1	a30 3-0	O16 6-1	S04 2-1	S11 2-2	J01 3-0	J15 2-2	A21 1-0	S15 2-0	D11 4-0	F05 5-0
10 LEICESTER C	O30 3-1	F05 2-1	a12 2-0	S14 0-3	O16 0-1	M21 1-1	m04 3-0	D28 5-0	S18 3-3		A21 1-3	N13 0-5	a16 1-2	O02 1-1	a30 2-1	M19 1-0	D11 4-1	J01 1-0	S04 4-1	S01 2-2	N27 2-1	m09 2-1
11 LIVERPOOL	D11 4-2	O02 3-1	N17 5-2	F19 4-1	N27 2-1	a30 2-1	S25 5-0	S11 2-1	D27 0-1	J29 1-0		J01 2-1	O16 2-0	N13 5-0	O30 4-0	A25 0-1	a06 1-0	a16 2-0	F12 4-0	M12 1-0	J15 2-2	S15 1-1
12 MANCHESTER U	M19 2-1	m09 6-1	N06 2-2	a27 2-1	F26 4-2	S18 4-1	D15 3-0	O23 4-1	m19 1-1	a09 1-2	O09 2-0		S15 1-1	F05 6-2	S01 0-0	N20 3-1	A21 1-0	S04 1-1	J08 1-1	D18 5-1	D27 1-1	D04 0-0
13 NEWCASTLE U	O02 0-1	O09 1-0	a09 2-1	N06 2-0	S18 3-2	M19 0-1	a08 0-0	m07 1-1	m16 2-0	N20 1-5	D18 0-0	S08 1-2		S04 2-0	A21 2-2	a23 0-2	F05 2-0	F26 3-1	M05 2-0	O23 0-0	A25 0-1	J08 2-1
14 NORTHAMPTON T	A25 1-1	N06 2-1	J08 2-1	D04 2-1	S15 1-2	D27 2-3	J29 0-2	a23 2-4	M05 2-1	M26 2-2	a09 0-0	A28 1-1	F19 3-1		M12 3-3	O09 0-1	S25 0-0	a12 1-0	a25 2-1	N20 0-2	S10 3-4	O23 2-1
15 NOTTINGHAM F	S07 0-1	O23 1-2	a23 0-3	N20 2-1	M08 1-0	a12 1-2	D27 1-0	a26 1-2	F19 0-4	D04 2-0	m10 1-1	A24 4-2	J29 1-2	S18 1-1		J08 1-0	m07 1-0	M19 4-3	D18 0-0	N06 1-0	A28 3-2	O09 5-0
16 SHEFFIELD U	a25 3-0	A21 1-0	M29 2-0	a11 0-1	J15 2-1	O30 1-2	N13 2-0	S15 2-0	F26 1-1	S25 2-2	S01 0-0	a16 3-1	N27 3-2	J01 2-2	D11 1-1		S18 1-0	O16 3-2	F05 2-2	D28 1-3	a30 0-2	S04 5-3
17 SHEFFIELD W	D27 4-0	a27 2-0	D04 2-1	a04 3-0	m09 0-2	m02 1-1	A25 3-1	N20 1-0	O09 0-0	J08 1-2	N06 0-2	J29 0-0	A28 1-0	M19 3-1	S11 3-1	M12 2-2		M30 4-1	O23 3-1	a09 1-1	F19 1-2	D18 0-0
18 STOKE C	J29 1-3	a09 2-0	S08 3-2	J08 4-1	D27 3-1	A25 2-2	A28 1-1	D04 3-2	O23 1-2	O09 1-0	N20 0-0	F19 2-2	S11 4-0	F12 6-2	S25 1-0	M25 2-0	m04 3-1		N06 1-1	a23 0-1	M12 1-1	m07 1-0
19 SUNDERLAND	a20 0-2	S15 2-0	S11 1-0	M12 2-1	N13 0-4	a16 2-0	a30 2-0	S25 2-2	J29 2-0	F19 0-3	a11 2-2	D11 2-3	J03 2-0	O30 3-0	O16 3-2	A28 4-1	J26 0-2	a02 2-0		M26 2-0	J01 1-5	S01 2-1
20 TOTTENHAM H	S11 2-2	M19 5-5	J29 4-0	A27 4-0	a30 0-1	D11 4-2	J01 2-2	F19 4-3	S08 3-2	A25 4-2	S18 2-1	O16 5-1	J15 2-2	a16 1-1	a02 2-3	D27 1-0	N13 2-3	N27 2-2	O06 3-0		O30 2-1	a08 1-4
21 W.B.A.	a11 4-4	F11 2-2	N20 2-1	a09 2-1	M19 1-2	O02 1-2	S15 1-1	N06 6-2	J08 1-2	a22 5-1	O23 3-0	m04 3-3	S01 1-2	F26 1-1	F05 5-3	D04 1-1	S04 4-2	S18 6-2	O09 4-1	m07 2-1		A21 3-0
22 WEST HAM U	a16 2-1	M05 4-2	M12 4-1	S25 1-1	a02 1-1	N13 2-1	N27 3-0	M26 1-3	A28 2-1	S11 2-5	S06 1-5	a30 3-2	D11 4-3	J15 1-1	J01 0-3	F19 4-0	O16 4-2	O30 0-0	A23 1-1	a25 2-0	J29 4-0	

Mike Summerbee was Joe Mercer's first signing when he took over at Maine Road in 1965. Summerbee helped City back to Division One and then shared in all City's domestic and European triumphs.

DIVISION 2

	BIRMINGHAM C	BOLTON W	BRISTOL C	BURY	CARDIFF C	CARLISLE U	CHARLTON A	COVENTRY C	CRYSTAL P	DERBY CO	HUDDERSFIELD T	IPSWICH T	LEYTON O	MANCHESTER C	MIDDLESBROUGH	NORWICH C	PLYMOUTH A	PORTSMOUTH	PRESTON N.E.	ROTHERHAM U	SOUTHAMPTON	WOLVERHAMPTON W
1 BIRMINGHAM C		M19 0-1	a22 1-3	D18 4-0	N06 4-2	J08 2-1	S04 2-2	N20 0-1	A21 2-1	a09 5-5	D28 2-1	m03 4-1	S08 2-2	D04 3-1	A25 1-1	O09 1-0	F26 1-0	S18 1-3	F05 1-1	m07 3-0	O23 0-1	a11 2-2
2 BOLTON W	S25 1-2		J08 1-2	F26 2-1	O23 2-1	m04 4-0	A21 4-2	N06 4-2	S01 3-0	D18 0-1	S15 1-1	M12 3-1	M26 2-0	N20 1-0	a11 6-0	m07 1-1	F05 0-1	S04 2-0	M16 1-3	a25 1-3	O09 2-3	D04 2-1
3 BRISTOL C	N27 2-0	N13 2-2		F11 2-1	S25 1-1	M12 2-0	m03 0-0	S11 1-1	J01 1-1	M25 1-1	S04 2-1	m10 4-1	a30 2-0	F05 1-1	D11 2-2	A31 0-0	O30 0-0	a02 1-0	O16 1-0	A21 2-1	a08 0-1	D28 0-1
4 BURY	O16 5-1	N16 1-1	S07 1-2		J29 1-1	m10 2-1	M05 3-0	A24 1-1	N13 2-2	A28 4-1	a19 0-4	J01 1-1	J15 3-0	a12 2-1	O30 2-0	S18 2-5	a30 1-0	D11 1-0	a16 5-0	O02 6-1	F19 1-3	M19 1-0
5 CARDIFF C	a02 1-3	M05 1-1	M18 2-1	A21 1-0		a08 1-1	N10 3-1	O06 1-2	a30 1-0	A25 2-1	N27 0-1	O30 1-0	N13 3-1	S18 4-3	m03 5-3	m10 0-2	J01 5-1	O16 1-2	D11 1-3	F26 0-0	D27 3-5	S04 1-4
6 CARLISLE U	N13 1-0	O30 1-1	S17 5-0	D27 4-1	a12 2-0		J01 3-1	M18 2-2	D11 3-1	S07 2-1	a30 2-0	a02 3-1	a15 1-0	F26 1-2	M08 2-1	A21 4-1	O16 1-3	J15 2-1	O02 0-2	S03 1-0	A31 1-0	F05 2-1
7 CHARLTON A	F19 2-1	J29 0-1	O23 1-4	a23 0-1	S14 5-2	O09 3-2		a26 2-0	M26 1-0	m07 2-2	S25 0-2	A28 2-0	S11 3-0	m13 2-3	M12 1-0	m18 2-1	A31 1-1	D27 2-2	a08 5-2	N06 2-2	D04 2-2	J08 1-1
8 COVENTRY C	a16 4-3	a02 2-2	F26 2-2	A31 1-0	M26 3-1	S25 3-2	O16 3-1		S18 0-1	a12 3-2	D11 0-3	N13 3-1	N27 1-1	S04 3-3	a30 2-1	D28 2-0	J15 5-1	O30 3-2	J01 5-1	F05 2-2	S14 5-1	A21 2-1
9 CRYSTAL P	J29 1-0	A25 1-1	O09 2-1	J08 1-0	D04 0-0	m07 2-0	O02 2-0	M12 0-1		a23 1-1	S11 2-1	D27 3-1	A28 2-1	D18 0-2	F19 1-1	N06 0-0	a08 3-1	S08 4-1	M19 1-1	O23 2-2	N20 1-0	a09 0-1
10 DERBY CO	O30 5-3	O16 2-0	O02 2-1	F05 4-1	S01 1-5	S15 3-1	D11 2-0	a11 1-0	N27 4-0		a16 4-1	J15 2-2	a02 1-3	M19 1-2	N13 5-0	S04 3-1	M05 1-2	J01 3-1	a30 1-0	S18 1-3	A21 0-3	F26 2-2
11 HUDDERSFIELD T	M15 2-0	S07 1-0	F19 3-0	N06 2-0	a23 1-1	D04 2-0	M19 1-1	m07 0-2	F26 1-1	N20 1-3		A24 1-0	J29 1-1	O09 0-0	A28 6-0	a09 0-0	O02 2-1	a11 2-0	S18 2-1	D18 4-0	J08 2-0	O23 1-1
12 IPSWICH T	M26 0-1	S18 2-0	N20 0-0	O09 3-4	a09 2-1	N06 1-0	F05 1-4	J08 1-0	F11 2-2	O23 2-2	A31 2-2		a11 3-2	a23 1-1	S07 2-1	M19 2-0	S04 4-1	F26 1-0	A21 1-0	D04 0-0	D18 3-0	m07 5-2
13 LEYTON O	S13 2-1	O02 1-0	D04 0-4	O23 2-2	J08 1-1	N20 2-1	F26 1-2	a23 1-1	F05 0-2	N06 0-0	A21 0-2	a08 1-4		m07 2-2	a18 2-3	M28 0-0	S18 0-1	M19 0-0	S04 2-2	A30 1-4	m09 1-1	O09 0-3
14 MANCHESTER C	a30 3-1	a16 4-1	A28 2-2	a08 1-0	M12 2-2	S11 2-1	O30 0-0	F19 1-0	O16 3-1	S25 1-0	J01 2-0	N27 2-1	D11 5-0		J29 3-1	O27 0-0	a02 1-1	N13 3-1	J15 0-0	J12 3-1	m18 0-0	A25 2-1
15 MIDDLESBROUGH	A31 1-1	a12 1-1	M05 4-2	a09 1-0	N20 3-4	a23 0-2	S18 2-2	D04 1-1	S04 2-2	J08 0-0	F05 1-3	S14 3-2	D27 2-1	A21 1-1		O22 0-1	M19 0-1	O26 5-2	F26 2-1	O09 4-0	N06 0-0	D18 3-1
16 NORWICH C	J01 2-2	D11 3-0	A25 0-0	M12 4-0	A28 3-2	J29 2-0	a16 2-0	D27 1-1	a02 2-1	F19 0-1	O30 1-1	S25 1-0	O16 2-1	S15 3-3	a27 1-2		N27 0-0	a30 1-3	N13 1-1	a11 1-2	S11 3-4	O02 0-3
17 PLYMOUTH A	S11 6-1	A28 1-3	a09 0-2	D04 2-2	O09 2-2	M14 0-0	A25 3-0	O23 1-2	a11 1-2	D27 0-0	M25 0-0	F19 3-0	M12 1-1	N06 1-0	S25 2-2	a23 2-0		J29 3-1	S08 0-1	J08 5-2	m07 2-3	N20 2-2
18 PORTSMOUTH	M12 0-1	F19 1-0	N06 2-4	m07 4-0	D18 3-1	O23 4-1	D28 3-1	a09 2-0	S15 1-1	O09 1-1	a06 2-1	S11 1-0	S25 4-1	J08 2-2	M25 4-1	D04 0-3	A21 4-1		S01 4-1	N20 1-1	F05 2-5	a23 2-0
19 PRESTON N.E.	A28 3-3	a19 0-1	D18 1-1	N20 2-1	m07 9-0	a25 2-1	a11 3-3	O09 0-0	S25 2-0	D04 2-0	M12 1-1	J29 0-1	F19 1-2	O23 0-3	S11 1-1	J08 0-0	S13 2-0	A23 4-1		a09 1-1	a23 1-1	N06 2-2
20 ROTHERHAM U	D11 3-4	N27 2-1	J29 1-2	M25 2-1	S11 6-4	m12 3-3	m09 0-0	A28 1-1	J15 3-0	M12 3-0	O16 0-0	a30 0-0	A24 2-1	m04 0-1	J01 4-1	a12 2-1	N13 2-0	a16 3-3	O30 6-3		S25 1-0	S07 4-3
21 SOUTHAMPTON	M05 0-1	J01 5-1	a11 2-2	S04 6-2	a20 3-2	A25 1-0	a30 1-0	S08 1-0	a16 1-0	J29 3-1	N13 0-1	O16 1-2	O30 1-0	O02 0-1	a02 3-1	F26 2-2	D11 4-1	A28 2-2	N27 5-2	M19 1-1		S18 9-3
22 WOLVERHAMPTON W	a12 2-0	a30 3-1	D27 1-1	S25 3-0	F19 2-1	A28 3-0	N13 2-2	J29 0-1	O30 1-0	S11 4-0	J15 2-1	D11 4-1	J01 2-1	A30 2-4	O16 3-0	M26 2-1	a16 0-0	N27 8-2	a02 3-0	S13 4-1	M12 1-1	

Season 1965-66

DIVISION 3

	BOURNEMOUTH	BRENTFORD	BRIGHTON & HA	BRISTOL R	EXETER C	GILLINGHAM	GRIMSBY T	HULL C	MANSFIELD T	MILLWALL	OLDHAM A	OXFORD U	PETERBOROUGH U	Q.P.R.	READING	SCUNTHORPE U	SHREWSBURY T	SOUTHEND U	SWANSEA T	SWINDON T	WALSALL	WATFORD	WORKINGTON	YORK C
1 BOURNEMOUTH		a26 0-1	N20 0-1	D28 1-0	D17 0-1	F19 1-1	M26 1-0	m10 1-1	N06 2-2	a08 0-0	m07 1-0	S14 1-1	O09 2-3	J08 1-1	O23 3-2	a23 1-2	S25 2-0	S11 0-0	A24 2-1	M12 1-0	A21 0-1	a09 2-0	F05 1-1	M05 1-0
2 BRENTFORD	m17 1-0		a11 2-0	F05 0-5	N20 1-2	m28 0-2	N23 3-2	a09 2-4	m07 0-3	N06 1-2	O23 0-0	F26 5-1	J08 1-0	A21 6-1	a23 1-1	O09 0-1	S14 4-0	M01 2-0	S18 2-0	M05 0-1	M19 2-2	m10 1-1	O02 0-1	S04 0-1
3 BRIGHTON & H.A.	a16 1-2	a08 2-0		J01 4-3	S11 2-1	M26 0-1	O05 1-2	A28 1-2	J29 6-4	S25 2-2	m13 3-1	M08 2-0	M12 1-0	N23 0-2	F19 1-1	F12 0-1	D11 1-1	N27 9-1	O30 1-1	a30 1-0	a02 2-1	D27 2-0	m20 3-1	O15 3-1
4 BRISTOL R	D27 0-0	A28 1-1	O09 0-0		a23 2-0	N06 0-0	J29 2-1	m06 1-2	F19 6-0	J08 1-1	O19 4-0	S18 3-1	N20 1-1	a12 1-0	a09 0-0	M29 2-0	A24 3-2	M05 3-1	M19 2-1	S07 0-1	O02 3-0	O23 1-1	N09 2-2	F26 0-0
5 EXETER C	O16 1-0	a16 5-0	m03 2-0	N27 1-0		D04 3-1	m21 2-0	O02 1-4	M19 2-2	O06 1-2	A21 4-0	D11 1-2	M05 2-5	S18 0-0	a27 1-2	S04 4-0	a02 0-0	J15 1-1	D27 1-1	O30 1-1	a13 0-2	F05 1-2	J01 2-1	a30 0-2
6 GILLINGHAM	S04 2-0	O30 1-0	O02 3-1	a02 2-0	A25 1-1		M05 3-2	F23 0-3	m03 2-0	A28 1-0	a27 3-0	a16 1-2	J29 1-1	m18 3-1	M23 2-4	M19 0-1	O16 0-1	a11 1-0	N27 2-0	J01 1-0	a30 1-0	S18 2-2	D11 1-0	m21 0-0
7 GRIMSBY T	O02 2-0	A24 3-2	S15 3-1	A21 1-1	J08 1-1	O23 3-1		a23 1-0	a09 0-1	m28 2-0	D18 3-1	S04 1-1	N06 3-0	m07 4-2	N20 3-3	a08 1-3	m04 2-1	m17 1-0	F26 2-2	D27 2-2	S18 3-1	O09 2-1	M19 1-0	F05 3-1
8 HULL C	O30 3-0	a30 4-1	F05 1-0	D11 6-1	a20 6-1	M09 1-0	N27 1-1		F26 4-0	D27 1-0	O06 5-1	a11 2-1	m17 2-1	S04 1-3	S25 3-3	A21 3-2	a16 2-1	m20 1-0	J01 4-1	S01 1-0	O16 3-2	N24 3-1	J15 6-0	S18 1-4
9 MANSFIELD T	m23 1-0	D11 2-0	A21 3-1	S04 2-0	S25 0-0	M14 0-0	a30 2-1	S11 1-2		a25 1-1	F21 1-0	J01 1-4	M26 1-7	F05 2-1	M12 0-2	M07 2-2	M21 0-3	m09 2-0	O16 3-0	a16 1-5	J15 0-3	O04 2-2	O30 0-1	a11 4-1
10 MILLWALL	a12 1-0	a02 1-0	M19 3-2	O25 3-3	S13 3-0	F05 2-0	O30 2-1	D28 3-0	m16 2-0		S04 1-0	N27 2-0	N22 4-1	O02 2-1	M05 3-0	S18 2-2	J15 4-2	J01 2-0	a30 1-0	O16 1-0	D11 1-1	F26 0-0	A21 2-0	a16 2-0
11 OLDHAM A	D11 2-2	J15 1-1	m18 1-0	O30 2-0	J29 3-1	S11 5-3	O16 1-4	O13 2-2	M05 1-1	M01 0-2		m21 3-0	A28 2-4	m25 0-2	A25 2-2	O02 1-3	J01 0-1	S17 1-0	a16 1-0	a12 1-1	M15 1-2	M18 0-1	a30 1-1	m10 3-0
12 OXFORD U	N03 2-1	S11 2-0	O23 0-0	M12 1-0	m07 0-1	N20 0-4	F19 2-0	a08 0-2	O09 4-1	a23 3-1	J08 3-3		a09 1-0	D18 1-3	M26 2-0	m28 0-3	A28 0-1	A25 3-2	a27 2-2	J29 0-3	D27 7-1	N06 1-2	M05 0-2	S25 4-1
13 PETERBOROUGH U	J01 1-0	m21 3-0	S18 2-2	a16 5-2	m09 2-0	A21 1-0	a02 1-1	a25 4-1	O02 3-2	A23 0-2	F05 0-1	a30 2-3		M19 1-1	M28 0-0	F26 3-1	O30 4-1	O16 4-0	D11 5-2	J15 2-3	O04 3-1	S04 2-2	a11 1-1	N27 1-0
14 Q.P.R.	m21 5-0	J29 1-0	A23 4-1	a08 4-1	M12 1-0	a25 1-3	D11 3-0	F19 3-3	A28 1-2	M26 6-1	m02 1-1	O16 2-3	S25 2-1		S11 0-2	O04 1-0	a30 2-1	a16 2-1	J15 6-2	N27 3-2	O30 2-1	F15 1-1	a02 4-1	J01 7-2
15 READING	M07 1-0	N27 2-0	S03 0-0	a29 0-1	m18 4-1	S15 2-2	m23 0-0	M18 0-1	S17 2-1	F12 1-1	M30 3-2	O01 0-1	D27 2-1	m13 2-1		F05 2-0	m20 4-1	O29 1-0	a13 2-1	a01 0-2	J01 3-0	A21 1-2	O15 1-1	D11 3-0
16 SCUNTHORPE U	N27 3-0	J01 3-2	M05 2-2	O16 3-0	F19 2-1	S25 0-1	a12 2-2	J29 2-4	A25 0-1	M12 4-4	M26 1-1	O30 1-2	S11 1-1	S14 1-2	A28 2-0		D28 1-4	a30 0-0	a02 1-1	D11 2-1	m21 4-2	m17 1-1	a16 4-1	J15 4-1
17 SHREWSBURY T	M19 0-2	O06 0-0	m06 3-1	N01 1-0	N06 4-0	M30 2-1	m02 3-1	N20 2-2	a22 2-1	O22 2-0	O09 3-1	F05 4-0	m12 3-1	a09 0-0	J08 3-3	D27 1-4		O01 3-0	S03 5-0	m18 1-1	M24 1-2	a11 0-0	S17 1-1	A21 4-1
18 SOUTHEND U	F26 1-2	M07 1-0	a22 0-0	F12 2-0	O23 4-2	a08 5-2	a25 3-1	N06 0-2	J08 1-0	O08 0-2	M11 0-2	N22 2-1	D18 2-0	N20 1-3	m27 2-1	m13 0-1	M14 2-0		A21 2-0	S24 4-2	F05 5-3	m06 1-0	O25 3-1	S13 2-3
19 SWANSEA T	N23 5-0	M12 1-1	m28 2-2	S25 3-0	J22 1-0	a23 0-3	S11 1-0	O09 4-2	M01 1-2	a09 0-2	N20 4-1	m17 3-2	m07 1-1	O23 4-2	a11 5-4	N06 3-4	F19 4-0	J29 5-0		A28 1-1	m24 1-0	J08 4-2	S14 1-6	M25 7-2
20 SWINDON T	S18 0-0	F12 2-1	a09 3-2	O05 4-3	m28 2-2	O09 0-1	m10 0-0	J08 3-1	N20 6-2	M15 1-0	a11 0-1	A21 0-0	O23 3-0	a23 2-1	N06 5-0	m07 0-0	a26 0-0	M19 4-0	F05 2-2		S04 0-0	M26 0-1	m03 0-1	O19 6-0
21 WALSALL	J29 2-1	S25 1-1	N06 2-1	M26 1-1	a11 1-1	a09 6-1	M12 1-0	D17 2-4	O23 2-1	m07 1-4	a23 2-2	m04 1-1	S14 2-0	m28 0-1	O09 3-0	J08 3-0	S11 3-0	A28 3-0	M05 1-1	F19 5-0		N20 3-0	A24 1-1	m17 2-0
22 WATFORD	a30 1-0	O16 1-1	M22 0-1	J15 2-0	A28 3-0	M12 1-0	J01 1-1	A24 1-1	S14 2-1	S11 0-1	S25 4-0	a02 1-1	F19 1-0	M05 1-2	J29 1-2	a26 2-1	a08 1-0	D11 4-1	m13 0-1	O02 2-0	a16 0-1		N27 1-2	O30 3-2
23 WORKINGTON	A28 2-2	M26 1-1	J07 1-0	a26 0-0	O09 6-1	m07 1-0	S25 1-0	O22 3-0	m27 2-0	J28 0-0	a09 0-1	F11 2-1	a21 1-1	N05 1-1	m09 1-0	N19 1-2	M11 1-3	F19 3-1	O04 7-0	S11 0-3	M30 1-0	a23 1-0		M15 2-1
24 YORK C	F12 0-2	M28 1-1	D17 0-1	S10 1-5	a09 2-0	J08 1-2	A27 1-1	M12 1-2	a08 2-1	N19 2-1	N05 2-2	M18 1-4	a23 1-1	O09 2-2	m06 1-2	D04 1-3	J29 2-2	O04 0-3	O01 5-1	A23 0-2	a25 0-3	J21 1-0	D27 3-3	

DIVISION 4

	ALDERSHOT	BARNSLEY	BARROW	BRADFORD	BRADFORD C	CHESTER	CHESTERFIELD	COLCHESTER U	CREWE A	DARLINGTON	DONCASTER R	HALIFAX T	HARTLEPOOLS U	LINCOLN C	LUTON T	NEWPORT CO	NOTTS CO	PORT VALE	ROCHDALE	SOUTHPORT	STOCKPORT CO	TORQUAY U	TRANMERE R	WREXHAM
1 ALDERSHOT		a23 1-1	F19 3-1	a27 5-1	a09 5-2	O09 2-2	S15 1-3	N20 1-3	m07 1-0	M23 0-1	M12 1-1	a08 0-0	S11 5-0	O23 2-0	A28 3-1	O06 2-1	M09 0-0	F12 3-0	J29 2-3	S25 3-0	N06 1-0	F16 3-2	J08 1-3	M26 2-2
2 BARNSLEY	M15 2-1		O15 3-0	a15 1-1	A28 4-2	N23 0-2	S03 0-0	F26 1-1	J29 0-1	O01 3-1	O29 1-5	D27 1-2	J15 2-2	a26 0-1	J01 3-0	a29 2-2	F12 1-1	A24 1-0	M08 5-0	m13 4-0	M18 1-2	D11 1-0	S17 4-0	m10 3-0
3 BARROW	S04 2-2	D18 1-5		F05 5-2	O23 2-0	N20 4-1	M19 3-2	O09 3-0	a18 1-1	m07 1-1	D27 2-1	J08 3-0	O04 2-0	m12 2-2	a25 0-1	F26 2-2	a23 2-1	N06 2-2	O02 0-2	S13 3-3	M05 1-0	S18 2-0	a11 1-1	A21 4-2
4 BRADFORD	N01 5-1	N20 7-2	A28 2-3		a23 5-1	a12 0-1	J04 3-1	J08 1-0	a09 2-1	O23 0-2	S11 0-1	M26 2-1	a19 4-1	D18 4-2	J29 1-3	F12 6-1	O09 4-0	m07 1-2	A24 1-2	M12 2-1	m24 3-1	O04 1-1	N06 1-1	S25 4-2
5 BRADFORD C	a30 1-1	F05 1-0	J15 0-0	F16 3-0		M05 1-2	a11 1-1	S04 1-2	A25 0-1	M19 2-0	m16 1-1	M16 0-1	O30 1-3	O02 2-0	O16 2-2	D11 3-2	a27 0-4	J12 2-0	J01 2-1	a20 3-0	S18 1-7	A21 4-1	F26 2-4	m12 4-1
6 CHESTER	J01 3-2	O06 3-3	a16 0-0	a08 2-4	F12 4-0		O30 3-0	D28 2-1	O27 3-0	F05 3-2	a30 1-4	S25 1-0	N27 2-0	S04 4-2	m28 1-1	O16 6-1	F26 1-1	M26 2-0	a02 1-2	D11 1-0	A21 1-0	J15 1-1	S15 3-1	S18 4-2
7 CHESTERFIELD	A23 1-1	F19 3-1	S25 2-2	D27 0-3	a08 1-1	M28 2-2		m07 2-4	O09 3-1	N20 1-2	a25 1-1	O23 3-2	M25 1-3	J08 1-0	M12 1-3	A21 1-2	N06 0-0	D18 3-1	S11 4-1	m02 3-2	a23 2-1	F05 1-1	a09 0-0	S06 1-1
8 COLCHESTER U	a16 0-0	S11 4-0	J01 2-2	F28 6-3	F19 0-1	D27 1-1	D11 3-0		A28 1-1	a25 0-1	J15 2-1	A23 1-0	O16 2-0	M05 3-0	a08 2-2	N27 3-2	N22 4-1	J29 3-0	S18 2-0	O30 0-0	O02 3-2	a30 0-2	M19 2-1	a02 1-1
9 CREWE A	D11 2-0	A21 0-1	O29 2-1	a30 2-5	S15 7-1	m18 1-1	J01 1-0	F05 0-2		S17 0-1	m11 0-1	F23 3-0	a01 3-1	M18 7-0	J15 2-0	M02 2-2	O01 1-0	M09 0-0	O16 3-1	a15 2-1	m04 1-1	a08 2-1	S04 1-2	N27 0-1
10 DARLINGTON	O30 4-3	M26 2-1	D11 1-0	M14 4-1	S25 3-0	A28 0-1	a16 4-1	m16 2-0	M12 1-1		a11 3-2	M28 2-0	D28 1-1	A23 0-2	a30 1-0	m09 0-1	J29 1-0	S11 2-1	F28 3-1	J01 2-0	O04 3-0	m21 0-0	M07 0-1	O16 2-0
11 DONCASTER R	S17 3-2	m03 2-1	D28 1-1	F25 6-2	N06 1-1	a09 1-1	F15 1-0	D04 2-0	J08 4-1	a12 6-3		a22 2-2	A24 4-0	A21 4-0	N23 1-1	M19 1-0	m06 0-3	N19 1-0	M04 2-0	F05 1-1	O09 1-0	O02 0-1	D18 3-1	S04 2-0
12 HALIFAX T	a12 3-4	D28 2-2	J22 2-1	O01 1-0	O05 3-2	M18 2-0	F12 4-1	S14 1-1	M05 1-0	S03 2-2	M08 2-3		a15 1-0	F26 2-2	m16 3-0	D31 4-4	S18 0-1	m10 2-0	O29 4-1	a29 1-2	F05 0-1	O16 0-2	A21 2-2	D10 4-0
13 HARTLEPOOLS U	F26 3-0	O23 1-2	m09 3-0	S04 2-3	m21 1-1	a23 2-0	O02 1-2	D18 0-1	N06 4-1	D27 1-1	S13 2-0	N20 1-2		m07 3-1	M05 2-0	S18 5-2	a09 2-0	J08 2-0	m16 0-0	A21 3-1	a08 2-1	M19 0-2	O09 0-0	F05 4-2
14 LINCOLN C	J15 2-1	M22 4-1	a30 4-0	O15 1-1	M25 1-0	F19 2-2	M09 0-2	F12 0-2	S24 1-1	S15 4-1	J28 0-3	S11 3-3	D11 2-1		N27 2-2	O30 1-1	A28 1-2	M12 0-1	a16 2-0	a08 4-0	M15 1-2	a02 1-1	O06 1-0	J01 0-2
15 LUTON T	F05 3-1	O09 5-4	m19 3-2	A21 3-1	D18 2-3	J08 5-2	S18 1-2	a11 1-1	O23 4-0	a09 2-0	O07 4-3	N06 4-1	F12 2-1	a23 0-0		S04 2-1	N20 5-1	m14 5-0	M19 4-1	D28 2-0	m07 2-0	F26 3-2	M26 2-1	S16 1-0
16 NEWPORT CO	N22 3-1	a09 1-0	S11 3-2	M07 3-1	m07 2-2	m23 3-2	J31 3-4	m28 2-1	M21 1-0	N08 3-0	S25 4-0	O09 3-1	M12 3-0	m02 0-0	m25 3-1		O25 1-2	a11 0-1	A28 1-1	M25 1-1	J08 1-0	S13 3-2	N19 0-0	m16 2-2
17 NOTTS CO	O16 2-0	M05 0-1	N27 0-2	J01 2-0	m18 2-1	S11 3-3	a02 2-0	O07 1-0	M26 0-1	A21 0-0	D11 1-2	M12 1-1	a30 1-0	F05 2-1	a16 1-1	J15 1-1		S25 3-1	m21 3-3	S04 1-2	S16 1-1	O30 1-1	m13 1-2	a11 3-1
18 PORT VALE	M05 2-1	S13 1-1	m02 0-0	D11 3-3	a04 0-0	O02 5-2	O16 1-1	A21 1-0	O04 2-0	F26 3-1	a16 0-1	a27 2-0	M21 0-0	S18 3-0	O30 1-2	a12 3-0	M19 0-1		J15 2-1	N27 4-1	S04 2-0	J01 0-0	F05 2-3	a30 1-0
19 ROCHDALE	A21 1-0	a11 2-1	M25 4-0	S14 2-3	O08 5-1	N05 3-0	F26 1-1	M11 0-1	D18 2-1	a22 1-2	F12 0-1	a19 0-1	a26 3-1	N20 0-1	S24 1-2	F05 2-1	J08 0-2	O22 1-0		O05 3-0	a09 4-0	S04 2-3	m06 3-5	D27 6-0
20 SOUTHPORT	M18 0-2	a04 3-1	A23 1-1	S17 2-1	J08 4-0	m07 2-0	M21 1-0	m10 0-1	N20 1-1	O08 1-1	A28 2-1	a09 1-0	J29 4-1	a11 5-1	D27 3-2	O02 2-0	F19 1-0	a23 2-1	N22 4-0		D17 2-0	a25 3-3	O23 1-1	F26 2-2
21 STOCKPORT CO	m16 1-2	S24 1-0	F11 5-2	O29 2-3	M21 1-1	J28 0-1	N26 2-1	M25 1-0	S10 2-0	N22 1-1	J01 1-1	A27 3-0	a11 1-2	F21 2-1	D10 4-1	m20 2-1	A23 1-3	F18 3-0	a29 3-1	O15 2-2		a15 1-0	S06 1-2	J14 2-4
22 TORQUAY U	D27 5-1	O20 3-0	M12 0-1	N23 2-1	J29 4-3	O23 1-0	A28 2-0	a09 0-1	a11 2-1	J08 0-4	M26 0-0	m02 1-0	S25 2-0	N06 4-1	S11 2-0	A25 1-0	m09 2-0	O09 1-0	F19 4-0	S22 1-1	N20 1-4		a23 2-1	F12 3-1
23 TRANMERE R	O18 5-2	M11 1-0	a08 1-2	a01 1-2	S10 2-2	A23 1-0	a29 3-2	S24 2-0	F18 3-1	M04 1-2	O15 1-0	J28 5-2	J01 6-1	N22 3-2	N03 2-0	a15 0-1	D27 0-3	A27 1-0	D10 6-2	J14 0-2	a25 6-2	N26 0-1		O29 6-3
24 WREXHAM	O02 4-0	J08 6-3	J29 3-1	M19 3-2	N20 1-1	M12 2-1	O25 2-1	N06 2-3	a23 1-4	D18 1-2	F19 4-3	m07 2-2	A28 1-1	O09 0-1	A23 2-0	a25 0-1	a08 1-3	m04 1-0	M30 2-2	S11 3-1	O23 1-4	M05 0-2	S29 1-5	

LEAGUE TABLES

DIVISION 1

	P	W	D	L	F	A	W	D	L	F	A	Pts
Liverpool	42	17	2	2	52	15	9	7	5	27	19	61
Leeds U	42	14	4	3	49	15	9	5	7	30	23	55
Burnley	42	15	3	3	45	20	9	4	8	34	27	55
Manchester U	42	12	8	1	50	20	6	7	8	34	39	51
Chelsea	42	11	4	6	30	21	11	3	7	35	32	51
W.B.A.	42	11	6	4	58	34	8	6	7	33	35	50
Leicester C	42	12	4	5	40	28	9	3	9	40	37	49
Tottenham H	42	11	6	4	55	37	5	6	10	20	29	44
Sheffield U	42	11	6	4	37	25	5	5	11	19	34	43
Stoke C	42	12	6	3	42	22	3	6	12	23	42	42
Everton	42	12	6	3	39	19	3	5	13	17	43	41
West Ham U	42	12	5	4	46	33	3	4	14	24	50	39
Blackpool	42	9	5	7	36	29	5	4	12	19	36	37
Arsenal	42	8	8	5	36	31	4	5	12	26	44	37
Newcastle U	42	10	5	6	26	20	4	4	13	24	43	37
Aston Villa	42	10	3	8	39	34	5	3	13	30	46	36
Sheffield W	42	11	6	4	35	18	3	2	16	21	48	36
Nottingham F	42	11	3	7	31	26	3	5	13	25	46	36
Sunderland	42	13	2	6	36	28	1	6	14	15	44	36
Fulham	42	9	4	8	34	37	5	3	13	33	48	35
Northampton T	42	8	6	7	31	32	2	7	12	24	60	33
Blackburn R	42	6	1	14	30	36	2	3	16	27	52	20

DIVISION 2

	P	W	D	L	F	A	W	D	L	F	A	Pts
Manchester C	42	14	7	0	40	14	8	8	5	36	30	59
Southampton	42	13	4	4	51	25	9	6	6	34	31	54
Coventry C	42	14	5	2	54	31	6	8	7	19	22	53
Huddersfield T	42	12	7	2	35	12	7	6	8	27	24	51
Bristol C	42	9	10	2	27	15	8	7	6	36	33	51
Wolverh'pton W	42	15	4	2	52	18	5	6	10	35	43	50
Rotherham U	42	12	6	3	48	29	4	8	9	27	45	46
Derby Co	42	13	2	6	48	31	3	9	9	23	37	43
Bolton W	42	12	2	7	43	25	4	7	10	19	34	41
Birmingham C	42	10	6	5	41	29	6	3	12	29	46	41
Crystal Palace	42	11	7	3	29	16	3	6	12	18	36	41
Portsmouth	42	13	4	4	47	26	3	4	14	27	52	40
Norwich C	42	8	7	6	33	27	4	8	9	19	25	39
Carlisle U	42	16	2	3	43	19	1	3	17	17	44	39
Ipswich T	42	12	6	3	38	23	3	3	15	20	43	39
Charlton A	42	10	6	5	39	29	2	8	11	22	41	38
Preston N.E.	42	7	10	4	37	23	4	5	12	25	47	37
Plymouth A	42	7	8	6	37	26	5	5	11	17	37	37
Bury	42	12	5	4	45	25	2	2	17	17	51	35
Cardiff C	42	10	3	8	37	35	2	7	12	34	56	34
Middlesbrough	42	8	8	5	36	28	2	5	14	22	58	33
Leyton O	42	3	9	9	19	36	2	4	15	19	44	23

DIVISION 3

	P	W	D	L	F	A	W	D	L	F	A	Pts
Hull C	46	19	2	2	64	24	12	5	6	45	38	69
Millwall	46	19	4	0	47	13	8	7	8	29	30	65
Q.P.R.	46	16	3	4	62	29	8	6	9	33	36	57
Scunthorpe U	46	9	8	6	44	34	12	3	8	36	33	53
Workington	46	13	6	4	38	18	6	8	9	29	39	52
Gillingham	46	14	4	5	33	19	8	4	11	29	35	52
Swindon T	46	11	8	4	43	18	8	5	10	31	30	51
Reading	46	13	5	5	36	19	6	8	9	34	44	51
Walsall	46	13	7	3	48	21	7	3	13	29	43	50
Shrewsbury T	46	13	7	3	48	22	6	4	13	25	42	49
Grimsby T	46	15	6	2	47	25	2	7	14	21	37	47
Watford	46	12	4	7	33	19	5	9	9	22	32	47
Peterborough U	46	13	6	4	50	26	4	6	13	30	40	46
Oxford U	46	11	3	9	38	33	8	5	10	32	41	46
Brighton & H.A.	46	13	4	6	48	28	3	7	13	19	37	43
Bristol R	46	11	10	2	38	15	3	4	16	26	49	42
Swansea T	46	14	4	5	61	37	1	7	15	20	59	41
Bournemouth	46	9	8	6	24	19	4	4	15	14	37	38
Mansfield T	46	10	5	8	31	36	5	3	15	28	53	38
Oldham A	46	8	7	8	34	33	4	6	13	21	48	37
Southend U	46	15	1	7	43	28	1	3	19	11	55	36
Exeter C	46	9	6	8	36	28	3	5	15	17	51	35
Brentford	46	9	4	10	34	30	1	8	14	14	39	32
York C	46	5	7	11	30	44	4	2	17	23	62	27

DIVISION 4

	P	W	D	L	F	A	W	D	L	F	A	Pts
Doncaster R	46	15	6	2	49	21	9	5	9	36	33	59
Darlington	46	16	3	4	41	17	9	6	8	31	36	59
Torquay U	46	17	2	4	43	20	7	8	8	29	29	58
Colchester U	46	13	7	3	45	21	10	3	10	25	26	56
Tranmere R	46	15	1	7	56	32	9	7	7	37	34	56
Luton T	46	19	2	2	65	27	5	6	12	25	43	56
Chester C	46	15	5	3	52	27	5	7	11	27	43	52
Notts Co	46	9	8	6	32	25	10	4	9	29	28	50
Newport Co	46	14	6	3	46	24	4	6	13	29	51	48
Southport	46	15	6	2	47	20	3	6	14	21	49	48
Bradford P.A.	46	14	2	7	59	31	7	3	13	43	61	47
Barrow	46	12	8	3	48	31	4	7	12	24	45	47
Stockport Co	46	12	4	7	42	29	6	2	15	29	41	42
Crewe A	46	12	4	7	42	23	4	5	14	19	40	41
Halifax T	46	11	6	6	46	31	4	5	14	21	44	41
Barnsley	46	11	6	6	43	24	4	4	15	31	54	40
Aldershot	46	12	6	5	47	27	3	4	16	28	57	40
Hartlepool U	46	13	4	6	44	22	3	4	16	19	53	40
Port Vale	46	12	7	4	38	18	3	2	18	10	41	39
Chesterfield	46	8	9	6	37	35	5	4	14	25	43	39
Rochdale	46	12	1	10	46	27	4	4	15	25	60	37
Lincoln C	46	9	7	7	37	29	4	4	15	20	53	37
Bradford C	46	10	5	8	37	34	2	8	13	26	60	37
Wrexham	46	10	4	9	43	43	3	5	15	29	61	35

Football League Records

Top scorers: Div 1, R.Davies (Southampton) 37 goals; Div 2, R.Gould (Coventry City) 24 goals; Div 3, R.Marsh (Queen's Park Rangers) 30 goals; Div 4, E.Phythian (Hartlepools United) 23 goals.

The legendary Bobby Charlton, a key figure in another Manchester United success he went on to help United to European Cup glory.

DIVISION 1

	ARSENAL	ASTON VILLA	BLACKPOOL	BURNLEY	CHELSEA	EVERTON	FULHAM	LEEDS U	LEICESTER C	LIVERPOOL	MANCHESTER C	MANCHESTER U	NEWCASTLE U	NOTTINGHAM F	SHEFFIELD U	SHEFFIELD W	SOUTHAMPTON	STOKE C	SUNDERLAND	TOTTENHAM H	W.B.A.	WEST HAM U
1 ARSENAL		A27 1-0	S17 1-1	D03 0-0	F04 2-1	a25 3-1	N19 1-0	N05 0-1	O01 2-4	M28 1-1	J14 1-0	M03 1-1	O08 2-0	a22 1-1	M25 2-0	S06 1-1	D26 4-1	m06 3-1	D17 2-0	J07 0-2	O22 2-3	A23 2-1
2 ASTON VILLA	D31 0-1		J14 3-2	a22 0-1	S17 2-6	m06 2-4	a08 1-1	O08 3-0	F04 0-1	O01 2-3	S03 3-0	D03 2-1	A20 1-1	N19 1-1	O22 0-0	A22 0-1	S05 0-1	M25 2-1	D27 2-1	M04 3-3	N05 3-2	M28 0-2
3 BLACKPOOL	J21 0-3	S10 0-2		F11 0-2	M27 0-2	a22 0-1	D03 0-1	M25 0-2	A22 1-1	S05 1-2	S24 0-1	O08 1-2	O22 6-0	M04 1-1	a08 0-1	D17 1-1	A27 2-3	N19 0-1	J07 1-1	N05 2-2	m06 1-3	D26 1-4
4 BURNLEY	a29 1-4	N26 4-2	O01 1-0		F25 1-2	m13 1-1	A23 3-0	S03 1-1	O15 5-2	M18 1-0	O29 2-3	F04 1-1	J14 0-2	M28 0-2	A20 4-0	a01 2-0	N12 4-1	D26 0-2	a15 1-0	S17 2-2	D31 5-1	D10 4-2
5 CHELSEA	S24 3-1	J21 3-1	M24 0-2	O08 1-3		D03 1-1	M04 0-0	m06 2-2	S07 2-2	D24 1-2	F11 0-0	N05 1-3	M25 2-1	A24 2-1	N19 1-1	A27 0-0	J07 4-1	a22 1-0	S10 1-1	O26 3-0	a10 0-2	D17 5-5
6 EVERTON	N12 0-0	a01 3-1	N26 0-1	S06 1-1	a19 3-1		D17 3-2	F04 2-0	O29 2-0	A27 3-1	a29 1-1	A23 1-2	O01 1-1	D23 0-1	J14 4-1	O15 2-1	M18 0-1	S03 0-1	m16 4-1	M22 0-1	S17 5-4	F25 4-0
7 FULHAM	a19 0-0	N12 5-1	a29 2-2	A29 0-0	O29 1-3	A20 0-1		S17 2-2	D27 4-2	F25 2-2	N26 4-1	M27 2-2	F04 5-1	m13 2-3	S03 0-1	M18 1-2	D10 3-1	D31 4-1	a01 3-1	O01 3-4	J14 2-2	O15 4-2
8 LEEDS U	O15 3-1	F25 0-2	D10 1-1	J07 3-1	a01 1-0	S24 1-1	J21 3-1		N12 3-1	m03 2-1	M18 0-0	A27 3-1	D26 5-0	S10 1-1	M28 2-0	m15 1-0	O29 0-1	F11 3-0	S07 2-1	D17 3-2	A24 2-1	N26 2-1
9 LEICESTER C	F11 2-1	S24 5-0	A31 3-0	N05 5-1	m09 3-2	M04 2-2	D26 0-2	a10 0-0		J18 2-1	M28 2-1	N30 1-2	m06 4-2	O08 3-0	a22 2-2	J07 0-1	S10 1-1	D03 4-2	J21 1-2	M25 0-1	N19 2-1	A27 5-4
10 LIVERPOOL	M27 0-0	F11 1-0	m13 1-3	N09 2-0	D26 2-1	D31 0-0	O08 2-2	N19 5-0	A20 3-2		A30 3-2	M25 0-0	a07 3-1	N05 4-0	D03 1-0	S10 1-1	J21 2-1	M04 2-1	S24 2-2	m06 0-0	a22 0-1	J07 2-0
11 MANCHESTER C	S10 1-1	a19 1-1	F04 1-0	M04 1-0	O01 1-4	N19 1-0	a22 3-0	m08 2-1	M24 1-3	A24 2-1		J21 1-1	N05 1-1	D03 1-1	m06 1-1	J02 0-0	D17 1-1	a12 3-1	A27 1-0	O08 1-2	M25 2-2	S07 1-4
12 MANCHESTER U	O29 1-0	a29 3-1	F25 4-0	S24 4-1	O15 1-1	A31 3-0	M28 2-1	D31 0-0	M18 5-2	D10 2-2	S17 1-0		S03 3-2	F11 1-0	D27 2-0	N12 2-0	a18 3-0	m13 0-0	N26 5-0	J14 1-0	A20 5-3	a01 3-0
13 NEWCASTLE U	F25 2-1	D17 0-3	M18 2-1	S10 1-1	D10 2-2	F11 0-3	S24 1-1	D24 1-2	a01 1-0	N12 0-2	O15 2-0	M11 0-0		J21 0-0	A31 1-0	N26 3-1	a29 3-1	M24 3-1	O29 0-3	A27 0-2	S07 1-3	a26 1-0
14 NOTTINGHAM F	N26 2-1	a15 3-0	O29 2-0	M27 4-1	A30 0-0	D26 1-0	S06 2-1	J14 1-0	F25 1-0	O15 1-1	m02 2-0	O01 4-1	S17 3-0		D31 3-1	D10 1-1	a01 3-1	A20 1-2	N12 3-1	F04 1-1	S03 2-1	M18 1-0
15 SHEFFIELD U	D10 1-1	M18 3-3	N12 1-1	D17 1-1	a17 3-0	S10 0-0	J07 4-0	M27 1-4	N26 0-1	a28 0-1	a01 1-0	D26 2-1	A23 0-1	A27 1-2		F04 1-0	F25 2-0	J21 2-1	O15 2-0	S06 2-1	O01 4-3	O29 3-1
16 SHEFFIELD W	m13 1-1	A31 2-0	A20 3-0	m06 7-0	D31 6-1	N05 1-2	O22 1-1	D03 0-0	S03 1-1	J14 0-1	D27 1-0	a10 2-2	a22 0-0	M25 0-2	S24 2-2		F11 4-1	O08 1-3	M28 5-0	N19 1-0	a19 1-0	S17 0-2
17 SOUTHAMPTON	D27 2-1	m13 6-2	D31 1-5	a08 4-0	S03 0-3	O25 1-3	M25 4-2	M04 0-2	J14 4-4	S17 1-2	A20 1-1	N19 1-2	D03 2-0	m06 2-1	O08 2-3	O01 4-2		N05 3-2	A31 3-1	a22 0-1	M29 2-2	F04 6-2
18 STOKE C	a01 2-2	D10 6-1	a15 2-0	D27 4-3	N26 1-1	J07 2-1	A27 1-2	O01 0-0	a29 3-1	O29 2-0	N12 0-1	S07 3-0	M27 0-1	D17 1-2	S17 3-0	F25 0-2	O15 3-2		M18 3-0	A24 2-0	F04 1-1	S10 1-1
19 SUNDERLAND	A20 1-3	D26 2-1	S03 4-0	N19 4-3	J14 2-0	M25 0-2	m06 3-1	m13 0-2	S17 2-3	F04 2-2	D31 1-0	a22 0-0	M04 3-0	a19 1-0	N05 4-1	M24 2-0	A24 2-0	O25 2-1		D03 0-1	O08 2-2	O01 2-4
20 TOTTENHAM H	S03 3-1	O29 0-1	O15 1-3	J21 2-0	M18 1-1	M27 2-0	F11 4-2	A20 3-1	D10 2-0	a01 2-1	F25 1-1	S10 2-1	D31 4-0	S24 2-1	m13 2-0	a15 2-1	N26 5-3	A31 2-0	m03 1-0		D27 0-0	N12 3-4
21 W.B.A.	M18 0-1	O15 2-1	a01 3-1	A27 1-2	N12 0-1	J21 1-0	S10 5-1	A31 2-0	a15 1-0	N26 2-1	D10 0-3	D17 3-4	m13 6-1	J07 1-2	F11 1-2	O29 1-2	M27 3-2	S24 0-1	F25 2-2	D26 3-0		a28 3-1
22 WEST HAM U	A29 2-2	M24 2-1	D27 4-0	M25 3-2	A20 1-2	O08 2-3	N05 6-1	a22 0-1	D31 0-1	S03 1-1	m13 1-1	m06 1-6	N19 3-0	O26 3-1	a04 0-2	J21 3-0	S24 2-2	J14 1-1	F11 2-2	m09 0-2	D03 3-0	

Coventry City goalkeeper Bill Glazier, part of manager Jimmy Hill's Sky Blue revolution at Highfield Road.

DIVISION 2

	BIRMINGHAM C	BLACKBURN R	BOLTON W	BRISTOL C	BURY	CARDIFF C	CARLISLE U	CHARLTON A	COVENTRY C	CRYSTAL P	DERBY CO	HUDDERSFIELD T	HULL C	IPSWICH T	MILLWALL	NORTHAMPTON T	NORWICH C	PLYMOUTH A	PORTSMOUTH	PRESTON N.E.	ROTHERHAM U	WOLVERHAMPTON W
1 BIRMINGHAM C		O29 1-1	a01 2-2	O15 4-0	S10 1-3	D10 1-2	M18 1-2	N12 4-0	J07 1-1	N26 3-1	a15 2-0	a28 0-1	M27 2-1	F25 2-2	F11 2-0	D26 3-0	A27 2-1	S27 0-0	A30 3-0	J21 3-1	S24 2-3	D17 3-2
2 BLACKBURN R	M04 1-0		a25 0-0	F11 1-0	O08 2-1	S10 4-1	D27 2-0	A24 2-1	M25 0-1	A27 2-1	D17 0-0	F18 2-0	a08 4-1	S24 1-2	D03 1-0	a22 3-0	O22 0-0	N19 3-0	N05 2-2	S07 2-0	m06 1-1	J21 0-0
3 BOLTON W	N05 3-1	M27 0-1		a19 0-0	M25 3-1	J21 3-1	S07 3-0	D17 2-1	O22 1-1	M11 0-0	A27 3-1	S10 1-0	N19 2-1	F11 1-1	m06 5-0	D03 1-2	M04 1-1	a22 1-2	a08 0-1	O08 4-2	A24 2-2	S24 0-0
4 BRISTOL C	M25 3-1	O01 2-2	D26 1-1		m06 3-3	A27 1-2	F04 3-0	S06 4-0	J21 2-2	A23 0-1	M28 4-1	D17 1-1	M04 2-1	S10 1-1	N19 1-1	a07 1-0	O08 1-0	N05 1-0	O21 3-3	D03 2-0	a22 1-2	J07 1-0
5 BURY	J14 0-2	F25 1-2	O14 2-1	D10 2-1		a15 2-0	O01 0-2	M18 2-1	F04 0-1	a01 1-1	O29 2-2	N12 0-0	D31 3-2	a28 1-2	M28 0-1	S20 1-2	S17 2-0	A20 1-0	S03 1-3	D27 3-4	S06 5-2	N26 2-1
6 CARDIFF C	m06 3-0	J14 1-1	S17 2-5	D31 5-1	N19 3-0		S03 4-2	F03 4-1	a22 1-1	D26 1-2	O01 1-1	S07 1-1	O08 2-4	A20 0-2	M04 1-1	D14 4-2	D03 2-0	M25 4-1	M22 0-0	a08 4-0	N04 0-0	A31 0-3
7 CARLISLE U	O22 2-0	D26 1-2	m13 6-1	S24 2-1	F11 2-0	J07 3-0		M28 1-0	O08 2-1	D17 3-0	A23 0-0	A27 2-1	N05 2-0	J21 2-1	a22 2-1	N19 2-0	S27 1-0	a08 0-0	M04 5-1	m06 1-1	D03 2-3	S10 1-3
8 CHARLTON A	m12 1-0	A30 0-0	A20 0-1	S27 5-0	O22 4-0	S24 5-0	M24 1-0		F18 1-2	S10 1-1	J07 3-1	J21 1-2	a22 1-3	D20 2-1	D31 0-0	m06 3-0	N05 0-0	D03 1-0	N19 0-2	M11 2-0	O08 2-0	F11 1-3
9 COVENTRY C	S03 1-1	O15 2-0	M18 1-1	S17 1-0	S24 3-0	N26 3-2	F25 2-1	O29 1-0		N12 1-2	a01 2-2	a15 1-0	A20 1-0	D09 5-0	m13 3-1	M28 2-0	J14 2-1	A30 1-0	D31 5-1	F11 2-1	D26 4-2	a29 3-1
10 CRYSTAL P	a22 2-1	D31 2-1	S03 3-2	A31 2-1	N05 3-1	D27 3-1	A20 4-2	J14 1-0	a08 1-1		S17 2-1	F11 1-1	m06 4-1	M27 0-2	M25 1-2	O08 5-1	N19 0-0	F04 2-1	D03 0-2	M07 1-0	O22 1-1	m13 4-1
11 DERBY CO	N19 1-2	A20 2-3	D31 2-2	M27 2-0	M04 3-1	F11 1-1	A31 0-1	S03 0-2	N05 1-2	J21 2-0		S24 4-3	D03 2-3	S28 2-2	O08 5-1	J14 4-3	a08 1-1	m06 1-1	a22 0-0	O22 5-1	M25 2-0	D26 0-3
12 HUDDERSFIELD T	D03 3-1	S03 3-1	J14 2-1	A20 2-0	a08 4-2	m13 3-1	D31 1-1	S17 4-1	N19 3-1	O01 0-2	F04 1-0		D27 1-0	A30 1-0	O22 2-0	M25 0-2	a22 0-1	O08 1-1	m06 1-1	N05 1-0	M04 3-0	M27 0-1
13 HULL C	M28 0-2	N12 2-3	a15 1-1	O29 0-2	A27 2-0	F25 1-0	a01 1-2	N26 2-2	D17 2-2	D10 6-1	a27 1-3	D26 2-0		M18 1-1	J21 2-0	S23 6-1	S20 5-0	F11 4-2	S28 2-0	J07 2-2	S10 1-0	O15 3-1
14 IPSWICH T	O08 3-2	F04 1-1	O01 2-2	J14 0-0	D03 2-0	D17 0-0	S17 1-2	D26 0-0	m06 1-1	M28 2-0	S06 4-3	A23 3-0	O22 5-4		a08 4-1	N05 6-1	a18 0-2	M04 1-1	M25 4-2	a22 0-0	N19 3-2	A27 3-1
15 MILLWALL	O01 3-1	a29 1-1	D10 2-0	a15 3-2	M24 2-0	O29 1-0	N26 2-1	A27 0-0	S05 1-0	O15 1-1	F25 3-2	M18 1-3	S17 2-1	N12 1-0		S03 1-0	D26 2-1	J14 1-2	F04 1-1	S19 2-0	D17 2-0	a01 1-1
16 NORTHAMPTON T	D27 2-1	N26 2-1	a29 2-1	N12 2-1	A30 0-0	M18 2-0	a15 3-3	J17 1-1	M11 0-0	F25 1-0	S10 0-2	O15 0-1	F04 2-2	a01 1-1	J07 1-2		S06 1-2	S17 2-1	O01 2-4	D17 1-5	A27 3-1	O29 0-4
17 NORWICH C	D31 3-3	M18 0-1	O29 1-0	F25 1-0	J21 2-0	a29 3-2	O15 2-0	a01 1-1	S10 1-1	a15 4-3	N12 4-1	N26 0-0	A31 0-2	S03 1-2	D27 1-1	m13 1-0		M27 3-1	A20 0-0	S24 1-1	F11 1-0	D10 1-2
18 PLYMOUTH A	S07 1-1	a15 4-0	N26 2-0	a01 1-2	D17 4-1	O15 7-1	N12 1-2	a29 2-1	A24 4-2	S24 1-0	D10 1-2	F25 2-3	O01 3-1	O29 1-1	S10 3-1	J21 1-0	M24 2-2		D27 0-0	A27 1-0	J07 1-0	M18 0-1
19 PORTSMOUTH	A24 4-5	a01 1-1	N12 2-1	M18 1-1	J07 1-2	M27 1-2	O29 2-1	a15 1-2	A27 0-2	a29 1-1	N26 0-3	D10 1-1	S07 0-1	O15 4-2	S24 0-1	F11 3-2	D17 3-3	D26 2-1		S10 2-0	J21 3-2	F25 2-3
20 PRESTON N.E.	S17 3-0	S26 3-0	F25 1-3	a29 2-2	D24 2-2	N12 4-0	D10 2-3	O15 2-1	O01 3-2	O29 1-0	M18 2-0	a01 1-2	S03 4-2	N26 2-0	O24 2-1	A20 2-1	F04 3-1	D31 2-0	J14 1-0		M28 1-1	a15 1-2
21 ROTHERHAM U	F04 3-2	D10 2-1	A30 0-1	N26 3-3	m13 3-0	a01 4-1	a29 2-3	F25 2-0	D27 1-1	M18 0-1	O15 0-0	O29 4-2	J14 1-1	a15 0-2	A20 3-1	D31 1-2	O01 2-1	S03 4-2	S17 0-1	M27 2-1		N12 2-2
22 WOLVERHAMPTON W	A20 1-2	S17 4-0	F04 5-2	S03 1-1	a22 4-1	S21 7-1	J14 1-1	O01 1-0	D03 1-3	S07 1-1	D24 5-3	M28 1-0	M25 4-0	D31 0-0	N05 2-0	M04 1-0	m06 4-1	O22 2-1	O08 3-1	N19 3-2	a08 2-0	

SEASON 1966-67

DIVISION 3

	BOURNEMOUTH	BRIGHTON & HA	BRISTOL R	COLCHESTER U	DARLINGTON	DONCASTER R	GILLINGHAM	GRIMSBY T	LEYTON O	MANSFIELD T	MIDDLESBROUGH	OLDHAM A	OXFORD U	PETERBOROUGH U	Q.P.R.	READING	SCUNTHORPE U	SHREWSBURY T	SWANSEA T	SWINDON T	TORQUAY U	WALSALL	WATFORD	WORKINGTON
1 BOURNEMOUTH		S28 2-1	M27 0-0	D26 1-1	F25 1-1	N12 4-1	J21 1-0	m13 0-0	S24 1-0	a15 1-3	F18 1-1	A27 2-1	D17 0-0	D10 1-1	O15 1-3	a01 2-2	J28 0-0	N16 0-3	a26 1-0	O29 1-4	O01 1-0	a29 3-0	M18 0-0	S10 0-2
2 BRIGHTON & H.A.	S07 0-3		N19 3-2	a22 1-1	O19 5-0	S03 0-0	M04 2-2	S17 0-2	O08 1-0	J14 1-0	m06 1-1	N05 2-0	a08 2-0	O01 5-2	D27 2-2	D31 0-1	M25 2-2	D03 2-1	M08 3-2	A20 2-2	a12 0-1	F04 2-3	M27 1-0	O22 0-0
3 BRISTOL R	M24 1-1	a15 2-2		J14 4-1	O04 3-0	F25 4-2	O18 4-1	M18 0-0	D27 1-0	O15 4-4	D31 2-2	F11 2-1	S24 2-1	a01 1-1	a29 2-1	S27 2-1	O24 1-1	S03 1-0	A20 3-3	S17 3-0	N12 1-0	O29 4-2	D10 0-3	M11 0-1
4 COLCHESTER U	D27 2-0	m13 3-2	S10 3-1		a29 2-3	O15 5-0	M11 0-0	O29 4-0	O17 2-2	M18 3-0	A20 2-3	S24 3-2	J21 1-2	N12 1-4	D10 1-3	F25 2-0	F11 0-1	D31 3-1	M24 3-1	S26 2-1	a15 1-0	a01 5-1	S03 2-1	a10 2-2
5 DARLINGTON	O08 1-2	N14 3-1	a22 0-3	D03 0-4		J14 3-2	O22 1-1	F04 1-0	M04 0-0	S17 1-1	D26 0-3	a08 2-3	N19 1-2	a10 5-0	M27 0-0	S03 0-1	N05 2-1	m06 1-1	S05 1-0	D31 2-1	F18 0-0	O01 0-1	A20 1-0	M25 1-1
6 DONCASTER R	a08 1-1	m16 1-1	O07 3-2	M03 1-4	S09 0-4		a21 2-3	D23 3-2	N18 2-2	N15 4-6	M25 0-4	M10 1-1	S06 2-1	D17 3-1	J21 1-1	a25 0-2	m05 3-0	O21 2-1	N05 4-1	F11 1-0	A27 2-1	M28 2-1	S23 0-0	D03 2-1
7 GILLINGHAM	S17 0-0	O15 2-0	N16 1-0	F18 2-1	M18 1-2	m13 3-1		D10 2-0	J14 0-0	a29 5-2	O01 5-1	M27 1-0	D27 3-1	O05 2-2	O29 2-2	a15 0-2	D17 0-1	a26 1-1	F04 0-0	N12 1-0	F25 0-0	S03 0-0	a01 4-1	A27 1-1
8 GRIMSBY T	a22 1-0	J21 2-3	O22 0-0	M25 0-0	S24 4-1	D26 4-1	m06 4-0		D03 1-2	M24 1-2	a08 2-1	O08 1-0	M04 1-0	m02 1-1	F11 1-1	O19 2-0	S07 7-1	N05 1-1	N19 2-1	a05 3-4	S10 1-0	A27 3-1	a12 0-2	D17 4-1
9 LEYTON O	F04 1-0	F25 3-2	D26 0-2	N14 3-3	O15 1-2	a15 4-1	S09 0-1	a29 1-1		m12 4-2	a10 2-0	D17 2-2	M27 2-1	S17 1-1	M18 0-0	N11 3-2	A27 3-1	F18 2-2	O01 1-0	a01 0-0	S05 0-0	m19 0-2	O29 1-1	m27 2-1
10 MANSFIELD T	N19 1-0	S10 2-1	M04 2-0	O22 2-0	J21 2-2	O17 3-1	D03 4-1	M28 4-0	a22 1-1		N05 4-5	S05 2-4	O08 1-1	A27 0-0	S24 1-7	F22 4-2	D27 3-1	M25 0-1	a08 1-2	a24 1-3	O31 4-2	D17 4-1	F11 2-1	m06 0-1
11 MIDDLESBROUGH	M11 3-1	D10 1-0	A27 1-2	D17 4-0	D27 4-0	O29 2-0	F11 1-1	N12 0-1	a24 3-1	a01 1-0		S10 0-2	m16 4-1	m13 2-1	S26 2-2	M18 2-2	J21 2-1	M27 1-0	O17 4-1	O15 4-0	a29 4-0	a15 0-2	F25 3-0	S24 3-2
12 OLDHAM A	D31 1-1	a01 4-1	O01 3-0	F04 4-0	N12 4-0	F18 1-0	M29 2-1	F24 0-1	A20 3-1	S27 0-0	J14 0-1		a25 1-1	M18 1-0	a15 0-1	D10 1-3	O18 2-0	S17 4-1	S03 4-1	a28 1-0	O29 5-0	O15 6-2	m13 1-1	D27 3-0
13 OXFORD U	A20 1-1	N12 1-2	F04 4-1	S17 1-1	a15 3-2	S28 6-1	D26 1-1	O15 3-1	M24 0-0	F25 2-1	S03 1-1	a12 3-1		O29 0-3	m13 2-1	O01 1-3	F18 2-1	J14 2-1	D31 2-3	D10 0-0	a01 2-2	M18 1-2	a29 0-0	O19 3-0
14 PETERBOROUGH U	m06 2-0	F11 2-1	N05 1-1	a08 2-1	a24 2-0	A20 3-3	S05 2-0	S03 2-1	J21 0-2	D31 3-1	a22 1-2	O22 3-1	M25 2-3		F20 0-2	M28 2-1	M04 1-0	N19 0-2	D03 4-4	D23 1-2	S24 0-1	J14 2-1	O17 2-2	O08 3-0
15 Q.P.R.	M07 4-0	D26 3-0	D03 3-0	m06 2-1	M24 4-0	S17 6-0	M25 2-0	O01 5-1	O22 4-1	F04 0-0	S06 4-0	N19 0-1	a22 3-1	M11 0-0		J14 2-1	a08 5-1	A20 2-2	O08 4-2	S03 3-1	N15 2-1	a25 0-0	D31 4-1	N05 4-1
16 READING	N05 0-0	A27 1-1	S07 1-2	O08 2-3	S21 1-0	a12 4-0	N19 2-1	N16 6-0	a08 1-0	M11 2-2	O22 0-0	m06 2-1	F11 1-2	M27 2-2	S10 2-2		D03 4-0	M03 2-0	M25 2-0	S24 2-1	D17 2-1	D27 3-1	J21 1-1	a22 2-0
17 SCUNTHORPE U	S03 0-1	O28 0-1	a24 3-1	S30 3-1	M31 2-0	D09 2-1	A20 1-2	S27 0-0	D30 2-2	D23 2-1	S17 3-2	N15 1-1	M10 2-2	O14 1-0	N12 0-2	a28 0-2		F04 2-0	J14 4-3	m12 1-2	M17 3-1	F24 2-0	a14 1-0	M27 4-1
18 SHREWSBURY T	O19 4-1	a29 0-0	N02 3-4	A27 2-1	D10 3-0	M18 2-1	a12 3-1	a01 0-1	M11 6-1	O29 1-0	M29 1-0	J21 3-1	S10 1-0	a15 1-1	D17 0-0	O15 1-0	S24 4-3		D27 2-2	F25 3-1	S21 3-2	N12 1-2	S26 1-1	F11 3-1
19 SWANSEA T	a04 0-1	M11 1-1	D17 2-2	M27 1-0	S27 1-1	a01 6-0	S24 1-1	a15 2-0	F11 2-0	N12 0-1	N15 4-4	A29 3-0	A27 0-1	a29 3-3	F25 1-3	O29 5-2	S10 0-1	D26 5-2		M18 2-2	D10 0-0	m13 4-1	O15 2-2	J21 5-2
20 SWINDON T	M25 1-0	D17 1-1	J21 0-1	S06 1-1	A27 4-0	O01 0-1	a08 2-0	F28 3-1	N05 5-1	a11 3-1	M04 4-1	D03 6-3	m06 3-0	D26 4-1	m02 1-1	F04 0-1	a22 2-1	O08 2-2	O22 4-0		M28 0-0	a18 3-2	S10 1-2	N19 3-0
21 TORQUAY U	F11 3-2	a26 5-0	a08 2-1	N19 5-0	M11 2-0	D31 4-0	O08 4-1	J14 3-1	S28 1-1	S03 1-2	D03 2-1	M25 4-0	N05 1-0	F04 1-0	O19 1-1	A20 3-0	O22 1-1	a22 0-2	m06 2-4	M27 1-0		S17 5-2	D14 1-0	M04 5-1
22 WALSALL	D03 3-0	S24 2-1	M25 1-1	N04 1-0	F11 1-1	M27 4-0	O11 3-0	D31 1-0	m06 1-1	A20 1-2	N19 2-1	M03 1-1	O22 2-0	S10 1-1	a11 2-0	D26 3-1	O08 2-0	a08 2-2	a22 1-1	O18 1-1	J21 0-1		M11 0-1	S06 2-0
23 WATFORD	O22 3-0	M24 1-1	m06 3-1	m09 0-0	D17 2-0	F04 4-1	N05 1-1	a25 3-1	M25 1-3	O01 0-1	O08 2-0	a22 2-2	D03 2-0	N15 3-1	A27 1-0	S17 1-0	N19 0-1	S06 1-0	M03 1-1	J14 2-0	D26 2-1	F18 2-1		a08 2-1
24 WORKINGTON	J14 0-0	M17 2-1	F18 0-2	J28 1-0	O28 1-2	a29 3-1	D31 1-3	A20 2-1	S02 3-1	D10 2-4	F04 1-2	D26 1-1	N16 0-0	F25 1-0	a01 0-2	m13 1-2	M28 1-0	m17 2-3	S16 6-3	a15 1-3	O14 1-2	S28 4-0	N12 1-2	

DIVISION 4

	ALDERSHOT	BARNSLEY	BARROW	BRADFORD	BRADFORD C	BRENTFORD	CHESTER	CHESTERFIELD	CREWE A	EXETER C	HALIFAX T	HARTLEPOOLS U	LINCOLN C	LUTON T	NEWPORT CO	NOTTS CO	PORT VALE	ROCHDALE	SOUTHEND U	SOUTHPORT	STOCKPORT CO	TRANMERE R	WREXHAM	YORK C
1 ALDERSHOT		S17 3-2	N11 0-1	M18 1-2	F18 0-3	S03 3-1	O15 3-0	a29 4-0	a01 1-0	M24 1-0	D31 0-1	A20 1-1	O26 1-0	F04 4-1	J14 5-0	F25 4-1	O29 0-1	O01 4-0	D26 5-2	S28 4-1	D10 1-1	N14 1-1	a26 2-0	a15 0-0
2 BARNSLEY	J21 1-1		A30 2-3	a01 2-0	D26 1-1	A20 0-1	O29 1-2	S02 0-3	a15 1-0	O24 2-1	M27 4-1	M11 1-2	D10 2-1	S10 2-1	D31 1-1	M18 0-0	N12 1-0	F25 3-1	F11 1-2	O15 0-0	S27 1-2	a11 2-2	S23 2-2	a28 0-1
3 BARROW	a08 1-1	M25 2-0		F04 1-0	M04 0-1	m06 1-0	S16 1-1	M24 2-1	a24 3-2	O08 5-0	J02 1-0	S26 2-3	F18 2-1	N19 3-0	M06 1-0	J14 0-1	O01 2-2	D31 2-0	a22 1-0	S03 2-2	A20 1-1	O22 0-0	N05 1-1	O17 1-1
4 BRADFORD	O22 1-1	F15 1-3	S24 0-1		N05 2-0	N19 2-2	D31 2-3	F08 2-0	J21 1-4	m06 2-2	M25 1-0	D03 1-2	a11 2-1	a22 0-0	a08 3-1	A20 4-1	S10 1-1	F18 0-3	O08 1-2	M28 0-0	O18 0-1	S06 2-3	M04 1-3	F11 1-0
5 BRADFORD C	M11 4-1	D27 1-1	O15 5-2	S03 2-3		O01 2-0	D10 2-3	a01 3-1	F25 0-3	J14 1-1	F04 1-2	S17 3-0	O29 2-1	N16 2-1	a26 1-2	a29 3-1	S28 2-0	a15 4-1	D17 2-1	M08 3-3	N12 0-1	A27 1-0	M27 3-3	M18 1-0
6 BRENTFORD	O11 1-0	D17 3-1	D10 0-3	a15 1-1	F11 2-0		N12 4-0	F25 1-0	a29 0-2	a11 3-1	O18 1-0	D27 1-2	S27 2-2	A27 1-0	M27 1-1	a01 1-0	m13 2-0	M18 4-0	J21 1-1	O29 2-1	O15 2-1	S24 1-1	S10 1-1	F18 1-1
7 CHESTER	M04 0-0	a22 1-0	J21 1-1	A27 0-3	m06 1-0	a08 1-2		a12 2-1	S10 0-3	D03 0-2	N19 0-2	M25 1-0	F11 0-1	O22 0-0	N05 4-2	M24 1-2	J28 1-3	O19 3-2	S07 1-1	F18 2-1	D26 1-1	D17 0-1	O08 1-3	S24 3-1
8 CHESTERFIELD	D03 1-1	N05 1-0	M27 1-2	D27 4-1	J28 0-1	O08 3-0	a24 0-2		F18 0-0	a22 1-0	M04 1-1	O22 1-0	A27 3-1	m06 0-0	S05 0-1	O01 1-1	m08 2-1	S17 0-0	N19 2-1	F04 2-1	J14 2-1	a08 3-1	M25 4-0	D17 1-0
9 CREWE A	N05 2-1	N19 2-2	a12 3-2	S16 1-3	O08 1-0	m10 1-0	J14 3-1	M11 2-1		S05 2-2	m06 1-1	F11 1-2	a05 3-0	a08 3-1	M25 3-2	S03 4-1	F03 1-0	A20 2-1	O22 1-0	D31 1-1	M24 1-1	M04 1-2	a22 1-2	D26 2-0
10 EXETER C	M27 1-1	N16 0-3	F25 1-2	D10 4-1	S10 2-2	a25 1-0	a29 2-0	O29 1-1	S27 2-0		O01 3-2	F04 1-0	M18 1-0	F18 2-1	D26 0-0	m13 1-0	S17 0-1	N12 0-0	A27 0-1	a15 0-0	a01 0-3	J28 1-4	D17 4-1	O15 3-1
11 HALIFAX T	A27 2-2	M28 1-1	D26 1-4	m13 0-0	S23 2-2	N15 3-2	a15 2-1	O15 1-0	D10 1-0	F11 0-0		a11 2-1	F25 0-0	D17 1-1	M11 2-2	N12 5-2	a29 2-2	O29 1-1	S09 2-2	a01 2-0	M18 0-1	J21 2-1	m16 3-1	S27 2-1
12 HARTLEPOOLS U	D17 3-2	F18 1-1	S05 2-1	a29 2-0	J21 1-0	D26 2-2	J30 3-2	M18 3-2	O01 1-2	S24 3-1	a24 1-3		O15 5-0	M24 2-1	S19 0-1	a15 2-1	D10 2-1	a01 2-1	J06 1-2	N12 1-1	O29 1-0	S10 0-2	A27 2-1	F25 4-2
13 LINCOLN C	M25 0-4	m06 0-1	M11 2-1	a26 2-2	a22 1-4	S07 3-1	O01 2-3	D31 2-1	N16 1-1	O22 1-1	O07 3-3	M04 3-0		D03 8-1	A20 2-2	F04 2-1	D27 0-1	J14 0-2	a08 2-2	S17 0-4	S02 0-1	N05 2-0	N19 1-1	M24 2-2
14 LUTON T	S24 4-0	J14 1-1	a15 3-1	O29 2-2	O20 0-0	D31 3-0	M18 1-0	D10 3-2	N12 2-1	M11 4-0	A20 2-0	M27 0-2	a29 2-1		S03 3-1	O15 2-5	a01 1-1	S29 3-1	a12 1-0	F25 0-0	S17 0-3	D27 2-0	F11 3-1	m13 5-1
15 NEWPORT CO	S10 1-2	A27 2-0	a29 0-1	N12 0-0	a10 1-1	M28 1-1	a03 2-3	S26 4-1	m13 2-1	D27 3-2	m01 3-0	O17 0-2	M13 0-0	O24 2-0		O29 1-0	a17 1-1	O15 2-2	S24 3-0	M18 0-0	F25 1-1	F13 1-2	J21 1-1	D10 4-2
16 NOTTS CO	O08 3-0	O22 0-3	S10 2-2	D17 2-1	D03 1-3	N05 3-2	M28 3-0	F11 0-2	N01 1-1	M25 0-1	a08 2-1	N19 0-0	S24 2-1	M04 1-2	a22 2-1		A27 0-0	D27 2-0	M10 1-0	O19 0-1	a26 2-2	m06 0-0	S07 2-2	J21 2-0
17 PORT VALE	a22 0-2	a08 3-1	F11 2-1	J14 0-0	S05 3-2	M25 1-3	S03 1-1	O17 2-3	S24 1-1	J21 2-0	D03 0-1	m06 0-0	m03 2-2	N05 1-0	N19 2-0	D31 0-0		M28 5-0	M04 1-3	A20 2-1	M11 0-2	O08 1-1	O22 0-2	a24 4-1
18 ROCHDALE	F11 2-1	O08 1-1	A27 1-3	M11 1-0	N19 0-1	O22 1-3	M01 0-1	J21 2-1	D17 0-1	a08 1-0	a22 3-0	N05 3-2	S10 1-0	S06 3-0	M04 2-0	J27 1-1	M27 1-2		D03 1-2	a10 1-1	S24 1-0	M25 1-2	m06 1-3	m02 2-2
19 SOUTHEND U	D27 4-0	S30 3-0	O28 1-3	F25 4-0	A20 2-1	S17 3-0	S26 5-1	a15 4-1	M17 1-1	D31 0-0	J14 1-0	S02 2-0	N12 3-0	a24 2-0	F04 1-0	F18 1-0	O14 4-1	a29 0-0		D10 0-1	m13 0-1	M27 0-0	N14 1-1	M31 2-1
20 SOUTHPORT	S05 1-0	M04 3-0	O10 4-1	M27 1-0	M25 2-1	a22 2-0	M11 4-3	S24 1-2	A26 4-1	N19 1-1	N05 2-0	a08 3-1	J21 2-1	O08 4-1	O22 1-0	S19 2-1	D17 0-0	a24 1-2	m06 1-0		F11 4-0	D03 1-0	D26 1-0	S10 2-0
21 STOCKPORT CO	m05 1-0	S05 2-1	D16 2-1	N14 4-0	a07 1-0	M03 1-2	D23 1-1	S09 3-1	M27 1-1	N04 1-0	O21 2-1	a21 2-0	m26 4-5	J20 1-0	O07 0-0	a10 2-0	F17 1-1	F03 2-2	M25 4-1	S30 1-0		N18 1-0	D02 1-0	A26 3-1
22 TRANMERE R	O17 2-2	a24 3-3	M17 1-2	S26 2-2	D30 3-1	F03 0-0	A20 0-0	N11 1-0	O14 5-0	S03 1-1	S16 1-0	J13 2-0	M31 1-0	D26 1-0	S30 2-1	m17 3-0	F24 2-1	m12 3-1	M24 1-2	a28 1-2	a14 3-0		F17 2-1	O28 2-1
23 WREXHAM	a10 2-0	F04 2-2	a01 1-1	O15 6-0	M24 1-1	J14 0-0	F25 3-1	m13 3-2	O29 1-1	A20 0-0	S03 4-0	D31 4-1	a15 0-0	O01 2-0	S17 2-2	S26 3-2	M18 2-1	D10 4-2	O17 2-0	a03 1-1	a29 2-2	M11 0-0		N12 1-1
24 YORK C	N19 1-2	D03 0-3	N14 1-2	S30 3-1	O22 4-1	M11 0-0	F04 1-1	A20 1-1	D27 0-2	M03 2-4	S05 4-3	O07 1-1	M27 3-1	M25 5-1	m05 2-1	S16 4-1	a10 3-1	S02 1-1	N04 2-1	J14 2-0	D31 1-2	a21 0-1	a07 4-0	

LEAGUE TABLES

DIVISION 1

	P	W	D	L	F	A	W	D	L	F	A	Pts
Manchester U	42	17	4	0	51	13	7	8	6	33	32	60
Nottingham F	42	16	4	1	41	13	7	6	8	23	28	56
Tottenham H	42	15	3	3	44	21	9	5	7	27	27	56
Leeds U	42	15	4	2	41	17	7	7	7	21	25	55
Liverpool	42	12	7	2	36	17	7	6	8	28	30	51
Everton	42	11	4	6	39	22	8	6	7	26	24	48
Arsenal	42	11	6	4	32	20	5	8	8	26	27	46
Leicester C	42	12	4	5	47	28	6	4	11	31	43	44
Chelsea	42	7	9	5	33	29	8	5	8	34	33	44
Sheffield U	42	11	5	5	34	22	5	5	11	18	37	42
Sheffield W	42	9	7	5	39	19	5	6	10	17	28	41
Stoke C	42	11	5	5	40	21	6	2	13	23	37	41
W.B.A.	42	11	1	9	40	28	5	6	10	37	45	39
Burnley	42	11	4	6	43	28	4	5	12	23	48	39
Manchester C	42	8	9	4	27	25	4	6	11	16	27	39
West Ham U	42	8	6	7	40	31	6	2	13	40	53	36
Sunderland	42	12	3	6	39	26	2	5	14	19	46	36
Fulham	42	8	7	6	49	34	3	5	13	22	49	34
Southampton	42	10	3	8	49	41	4	3	14	25	51	34
Newcastle U	42	9	5	7	24	27	3	4	14	15	54	33
Aston Villa	42	7	5	9	30	33	4	2	15	24	52	29
Blackpool	42	1	5	15	18	36	5	4	12	23	40	21

DIVISION 2

	P	W	D	L	F	A	W	D	L	F	A	Pts
Coventry C	42	17	3	1	46	16	6	10	5	28	27	59
Wolverh'pton W	42	15	4	2	53	20	10	4	7	35	28	58
Carlisle U	42	15	3	3	42	16	8	3	10	29	38	52
Blackburn R	42	13	6	2	33	11	6	7	8	23	35	51
Ipswich T	42	11	8	2	45	25	6	8	7	25	29	50
Huddersfield T	42	14	3	4	36	17	6	6	9	22	29	49
Crystal Palace	42	14	4	3	42	23	5	6	10	19	32	48
Millwall	42	14	5	2	33	17	4	4	13	16	41	45
Bolton W	42	10	7	4	36	19	4	7	10	28	39	42
Birmingham C	42	11	5	5	42	23	5	3	13	28	43	40
Norwich C	42	10	7	4	31	21	3	7	11	18	34	40
Hull C	42	11	5	5	46	25	5	2	14	31	47	39
Preston N.E.	42	14	3	4	44	23	2	4	15	21	44	39
Portsmouth	42	7	5	9	34	37	6	8	7	25	33	39
Bristol C	42	10	8	3	38	22	2	6	13	18	40	38
Plymouth A	42	12	4	5	42	21	2	5	14	17	37	37
Derby Co	42	8	6	7	40	32	4	6	11	28	40	36
Rotherham U	42	10	5	6	39	28	3	5	13	22	42	36
Charlton A	42	11	4	6	34	16	2	5	14	15	37	35
Cardiff C	42	9	7	5	43	28	3	2	16	18	59	33
Northampton T	42	8	6	7	28	33	4	0	17	19	51	30
Bury	42	9	3	9	31	30	2	3	16	18	53	28

DIVISION 3

	P	W	D	L	F	A	W	D	L	F	A	Pts
Q.P.R.	46	18	4	1	66	15	8	11	4	37	23	67
Middlesbrough	46	16	3	4	51	20	7	6	10	36	44	55
Watford	46	15	5	3	39	17	5	9	9	22	29	54
Reading	46	13	7	3	45	20	9	2	12	31	37	53
Bristol R	46	13	8	2	47	28	7	5	11	29	39	53
Shrewsbury T	46	15	5	3	48	24	5	7	11	29	38	52
Torquay U	46	17	3	3	57	20	4	6	13	16	34	51
Swindon T	46	14	5	4	53	21	6	5	12	28	38	50
Mansfield T	46	12	4	7	48	37	8	5	10	36	42	49
Oldham A	46	15	4	4	51	16	4	6	13	29	47	48
Gillingham	46	11	9	3	36	18	4	7	12	22	44	46
Walsall	46	12	8	3	37	16	6	2	15	28	56	46
Colchester U	46	14	3	6	52	30	3	7	13	24	43	44
Leyton O	46	10	9	4	36	27	3	9	11	22	41	44
Peterborough U	46	12	4	7	40	31	2	11	10	26	40	43
Oxford U	46	10	8	5	41	29	5	5	13	20	37	43
Grimsby T	46	13	5	5	46	23	4	4	15	15	45	43
Scunthorpe U	46	13	4	6	39	26	4	4	15	19	47	42
Brighton & H.A.	46	10	8	5	37	27	3	7	13	24	44	41
Bournemouth	46	8	10	5	24	24	4	7	12	15	33	41
Swansea T	46	9	9	5	50	30	3	6	14	35	59	39
Darlington	46	8	7	8	26	28	5	4	14	21	53	37
Doncaster R	46	11	6	6	40	40	1	2	20	18	77	32
Workington	46	9	3	11	35	35	3	4	16	20	54	31

DIVISION 4

	P	W	D	L	F	A	W	D	L	F	A	Pts
Stockport Co	46	16	5	2	41	18	10	7	6	28	24	64
Southport	46	19	2	2	47	15	4	11	8	22	27	59
Barrow	46	12	8	3	35	18	12	3	8	41	36	59
Tranmere R	46	14	6	3	42	20	8	8	7	24	23	58
Crewe A	46	14	5	4	42	26	7	7	9	28	29	54
Southend U	46	15	5	3	44	12	7	4	12	26	37	53
Wrexham	46	11	12	0	46	20	5	8	10	30	42	52
Hartlepool U	46	15	3	5	44	29	7	4	12	22	35	51
Brentford	46	13	7	3	36	19	5	6	12	22	37	49
Aldershot	46	14	4	5	48	19	4	8	11	24	38	48
Bradford C	46	13	4	6	48	31	6	6	11	26	31	48
Halifax T	46	10	11	2	37	27	5	3	15	22	41	44
Port Vale	46	9	7	7	33	27	5	8	10	22	31	43
Exeter C	46	11	6	6	30	24	3	9	11	20	36	43
Chesterfield	46	13	6	4	33	16	4	2	17	27	47	42
Barnsley	46	8	7	8	30	28	5	8	10	30	36	41
Luton T	46	15	5	3	47	23	1	4	18	12	50	41
Newport Co	46	9	9	5	35	23	3	7	13	21	40	40
Chester C	46	8	5	10	24	32	7	5	11	30	46	40
Notts Co	46	10	7	6	31	25	3	4	16	22	47	37
Rochdale	46	10	4	9	30	27	3	7	13	23	48	37
York C	46	11	5	7	45	31	1	6	16	20	48	35
Bradford P.A.	46	7	6	10	30	34	4	7	12	22	45	35
Lincoln C	46	7	8	8	39	39	2	5	16	19	43	31

FOOTBALL LEAGUE RECORDS

Top scorers: Div 1, G.Best (Manchester United) R.Davies (Southampton) 28 goals; Div 2, J.Hickton (Middlesbrough) 24 goals; Div 3, D.Rogers (Swindon Town) 25 goals; Div 4, L.Massie (Halifax Town), R.Chapman (Port Vale) 25 goals.
Leyton Orient dropped 'Leyton' from their name.

Francis Lee joined Manchester City from Bolton for £60,000 in October 1967 and at the end of the season had won a League Championship medal.

DIVISION 1

	ARSENAL	BURNLEY	CHELSEA	COVENTRY C	EVERTON	FULHAM	LEEDS U	LEICESTER C	LIVERPOOL	MANCHESTER C	MANCHESTER U	NEWCASTLE U	NOTTINGHAM F	SHEFFIELD U	SHEFFIELD W	SOUTHAMPTON	STOKE C	SUNDERLAND	TOTTENHAM H	W.B.A.	WEST HAM U	WOLVERHAMPTON W
1 ARSENAL		a27 2-0	D30 1-1	S02 1-1	N11 2-2	O28 5-3	m07 4-3	a13 2-1	A28 2-0	S23 1-0	F24 0-2	F10 0-0	D23 3-0	J13 1-1	a30 3-2	a15 0-3	A19 2-0	O14 2-1	S16 4-0	m11 2-1	N25 0-0	M16 0-2
2 BURNLEY	D02 1-0		N04 1-1	A19 2-1	D30 2-1	S30 2-0	m11 3-0	a15 1-1	O24 1-1	M02 0-1	F17 2-1	N18 2-0	O07 1-1	m04 0-2	D23 2-1	M23 2-0	a20 4-0	S16 3-0	S02 5-1	a06 0-0	A29 3-3	F03 1-1
3 CHELSEA	D26 2-1	a22 2-1		S30 1-1	O14 1-1	A26 1-1	M20 0-0	M16 4-1	F12 3-1	a16 1-0	N25 1-1	A23 1-1	F03 1-0	S06 4-2	N11 3-0	S02 2-6	S16 2-2	a27 1-0	a13 2-0	D16 0-3	O28 1-3	a29 1-0
4 COVENTRY C	J06 1-1	D16 5-1	F10 2-1		N25 0-2	N11 0-3	a13 0-1	a27 0-1	D26 1-1	S09 0-3	M16 2-0	J20 1-4	A29 1-3	A26 2-2	F24 3-0	S05 2-1	a15 2-0	O28 2-2	O14 2-3	S23 4-2	D08 1-1	M30 1-0
5 EVERTON	a06 2-0	D26 2-0	a20 2-1	M02 3-1		m21 5-1	S16 0-1	a09 2-1	F03 1-0	N04 1-1	A19 3-1	M23 1-0	D02 1-0	N18 1-0	a15 1-0	O07 4-2	m04 3-0	D23 3-0	A29 0-1	O24 2-1	S05 2-0	S02 4-2
6 FULHAM	M23 1-3	F10 4-3	D23 2-2	a06 1-1	S09 2-1		J06 0-5	J20 0-1	D02 1-1	O21 2-4	a12 0-4	a20 2-0	N18 2-0	M13 0-1	F28 2-0	m04 2-2	m01 0-2	A28 3-2	D30 1-2	O07 1-2	S23 0-3	A19 1-2
7 LEEDS U	N04 3-1	S20 2-1	O07 7-0	N18 1-1	J20 2-0	S02 2-0		S23 3-2	m04 1-2	M23 2-0	N08 1-0	O25 2-0	M13 1-1	a06 3-0	D30 3-2	J13 5-0	D02 2-0	A19 1-1	a17 1-0	a20 3-1	F10 2-1	D23 2-1
8 LEICESTER C	N18 2-2	a16 0-2	O25 2-2	D02 0-0	S30 0-2	S16 1-2	F03 2-2		O07 2-1	a06 1-0	D23 2-2	N04 2-2	m04 4-2	M02 3-1	A30 3-0	a20 4-1	m11 0-0	S02 0-2	A19 2-3	M23 2-3	D30 2-4	J13 3-1
9 LIVERPOOL	A22 2-0	M16 3-2	S09 3-1	D30 1-0	S23 1-0	a27 4-1	D09 2-0	F24 3-1		D16 1-1	N11 1-2	A26 6-0	m11 6-1	a12 1-2	O28 1-0	J20 2-0	S30 2-1	a13 2-1	a29 1-1	J06 4-1	O14 3-1	N25 2-1
10 MANCHESTER C	F03 1-1	N25 4-2	a12 1-0	M09 3-1	a29 2-0	M16 5-1	O28 1-0	N11 6-0	A19 0-0		S30 1-2	S06 2-0	S02 2-0	S16 5-2	a25 1-0	A30 4-2	D23 4-2	F24 1-0	D09 4-1	D30 0-2	a13 3-0	O14 2-0
11 MANCHESTER U	O07 1-0	S09 2-2	M02 1-3	O25 4-0	D16 3-1	a15 3-0	A23 1-0	A26 1-1	a06 1-2	M27 1-3		m04 6-0	M23 3-0	a20 1-0	J20 4-2	N18 3-2	N04 1-0	m11 1-2	S23 3-1	D02 2-1	J06 3-1	D26 4-0
12 NEWCASTLE U	S30 2-1	a13 1-0	A30 5-1	S16 3-2	O28 1-0	O14 2-1	M16 1-1	a03 0-0	D23 1-1	m11 3-4	D09 2-2		J13 0-0	F03 1-0	N25 4-0	A19 3-0	S02 1-1	D26 2-1	a27 1-3	a12 2-2	N11 1-0	F24 2-0
13 NOTTINGHAM F	A26 2-0	F24 1-0	S23 3-0	A22 3-3	a22 1-0	a13 2-2	N25 0-2	M19 2-1	S05 0-1	J06 0-3	O28 3-1	S09 4-0		D16 1-0	O14 0-0	F10 2-2	D26 3-0	M30 0-3	M16 0-0	J20 3-2	a16 1-1	N11 3-1
14 SHEFFIELD U	S09 2-4	D09 1-0	m11 1-2	D23 2-0	a13 0-1	a23 2-3	N11 1-0	N25 0-0	a15 1-1	J20 0-3	O14 0-3	S23 2-1	A19 1-3		S02 0-1	D30 4-1	A29 1-0	M16 1-2	F26 3-2	F10 1-1	a27 1-2	O28 1-1
15 SHEFFIELD W	m04 1-2	A26 2-1	a06 2-2	O07 4-0	a16 0-0	S06 4-2	D26 0-1	A23 2-1	M23 1-2	D02 1-1	S16 1-1	M02 1-1	a20 0-0	J06 1-1		N04 2-0	O23 1-1	F03 0-1	J17 1-2	N18 2-2	D16 4-1	S30 2-2
16 SOUTHAMPTON	a10 2-0	O28 2-2	J06 3-5	m11 0-0	F26 3-2	M08 2-1	S09 1-1	O14 1-5	S16 1-0	A23 3-2	a13 2-2	D16 0-0	S30 2-1	D26 3-3	M30 2-0		F03 1-2	N25 3-2	N11 1-2	A26 4-0	M16 0-0	a27 1-1
17 STOKE C	D16 0-1	O14 0-2	J20 0-1	a16 3-3	D09 1-0	N25 0-1	a23 3-2	S06 3-2	m15 2-1	A26 3-0	M30 2-4	J06 2-1	D30 1-3	A23 1-1	M16 0-1	S23 3-2		N11 2-1	O28 2-1	S09 0-0	F26 2-0	a13 0-2
18 SUNDERLAND	a20 2-0	J20 2-2	D02 2-3	M23 1-1	A26 1-0	A23 3-0	D16 2-2	J06 0-2	N18 1-1	O07 1-0	S06 1-1	D30 3-3	N04 1-0	O25 2-1	S23 0-2	M02 0-3	a06 3-1		F10 0-1	m04 0-0	S09 1-5	a15 2-0
19 TOTTENHAM H	J20 1-0	M30 5-0	N18 2-0	a20 4-2	A23 1-1	D26 2-2	a12 2-1	D16 0-1	N04 1-1	m04 1-3	F03 1-2	D02 1-1	O25 1-1	O07 1-1	S09 2-1	a06 6-1	M23 3-0	S30 3-0		M01 0-0	A26 5-1	S06 2-1
20 W.B.A.	S06 1-3	N11 8-1	A19 0-1	F03 0-1	M16 2-6	F24 2-1	O14 2-0	O28 0-0	S02 0-2	D26 3-2	a29 6-3	a15 2-0	S16 2-1	S30 4-1	a13 1-1	D23 0-0	M13 3-0	a02 0-0	N25 2-0		m01 3-1	A30 4-1
21 WEST HAM U	M29 1-1	A21 4-2	M23 0-1	m04 0-0	m11 1-1	F03 7-2	S30 0-0	D26 4-2	a20 1-0	N18 2-3	S02 1-3	a06 5-0	a12 3-0	D02 3-0	A19 2-3	O23 0-1	O07 3-4	a24 1-1	D23 2-1	D11 2-3		S16 1-2
22 WOLVERHAMPTON W	O23 3-2	S23 3-2	m04 3-0	N04 2-0	J06 1-3	D16 3-2	A26 2-0	S09 1-3	M02 1-1	a20 0-0	D30 2-3	O07 2-2	a06 6-1	M23 1-3	M19 2-3	D02 2-0	N18 3-4	M09 2-1	m11 2-1	A23 3-3	J20 1-2	

Brian Kidd made his senior Manchester United debut in 1967-68 and ended the campaign with a European Cup winners' medal as well as helping United to runners-up spot in Division One.

DIVISION 2

	ASTON VILLA	BIRMINGHAM C	BLACKBURN R	BLACKPOOL	BOLTON W	BRISTOL C	CARDIFF C	CARLISLE U	CHARLTON A	CRYSTAL P	DERBY CO	HUDDERSFIELD T	HULL C	IPSWICH T	MIDDLESBROUGH	MILLWALL	NORWICH C	PLYMOUTH A	PORTSMOUTH	PRESTON N.E.	Q.P.R.	ROTHERHAM U
1 ASTON VILLA		O07 2-4	M23 1-2	O21 3-2	a20 1-1	m04 2-4	D30 2-1	N04 1-0	J20 4-1	S23 0-1	J06 2-1	D02 0-0	N18 2-3	a06 2-2	F10 0-1	M02 3-1	D16 4-2	A28 0-1	a16 1-0	S09 1-0	m11 1-2	A26 3-1
2 BIRMINGHAM C	F24 2-1		S16 1-1	F03 1-2	A19 4-0	D26 4-1	a13 0-0	J13 1-3	m07 4-0	N25 1-0	a02 3-1	D23 6-1	S04 6-2	S02 0-0	S26 6-1	S30 2-3	M16 0-0	a16 2-2	O14 2-2	N11 3-0	D09 2-0	O28 4-1
3 BLACKBURN R	M13 2-1	J20 1-2		a03 2-1	S23 2-1	S09 2-0	a27 1-1	A23 1-0	M09 3-2	M16 2-1	D26 3-0	F14 0-0	A26 2-0	S06 2-1	J06 3-0	D16 2-0	F24 0-0	a24 1-1	N25 2-2	a13 0-1	M30 0-1	D09 3-1
4 BLACKPOOL	M16 1-0	S23 1-0	a15 2-1		F10 1-1	J20 1-1	N11 3-1	D26 1-1	a13 2-0	O14 2-0	D09 1-1	S04 2-0	J06 3-1	A21 0-0	S09 3-0	A26 1-4	N25 0-2	M30 2-0	a27 2-0	D16 4-1	O28 0-1	F24 1-1
5 BOLTON W	N25 2-3	D16 1-1	F03 2-1	S30 1-2		a17 1-0	A26 1-1	S16 2-3	N22 2-0	a27 2-2	O28 5-3	S02 3-1	A23 6-1	M09 1-2	D26 2-0	S06 1-1	O14 2-0	D09 1-2	a13 1-2	M30 0-0	F24 1-1	M16 0-2
6 BRISTOL C	F27 0-0	D30 3-1	J13 0-0	S16 2-4	a02 1-1		O14 1-1	S02 1-0	N25 0-2	F24 2-1	N10 1-0	A19 2-3	S30 3-3	D22 1-1	S05 0-0	F03 0-2	D05 0-2	a13 2-0	M16 3-0	a27 4-1	A22 0-2	M29 0-1
7 CARDIFF C	D26 3-0	N18 1-3	D02 3-2	a06 1-3	D23 1-3	M02 0-1		a20 1-0	m11 0-0	A30 4-2	S23 1-5	m04 0-0	M22 2-3	O07 1-1	O24 3-0	D05 2-2	S09 3-1	A19 1-1	J06 3-0	F10 2-0	a16 1-0	J20 2-2
8 CARLISLE U	M30 1-2	S09 1-1	A29 1-0	D30 1-3	J20 3-0	J06 0-0	N25 1-3		M16 0-0	O28 3-0	a13 1-1	S23 2-1	D16 1-1	F10 4-1	A26 2-2	a16 1-1	D09 2-2	a27 2-0	F23 1-1	O14 4-1	N11 3-1	S05 4-1
9 CHARLTON A	S16 3-0	D02 3-1	M01 3-0	N18 0-2	a06 2-0	a20 1-2	S05 1-1	O21 2-2		M05 0-1	D16 1-2	F17 4-2	m04 5-1	M23 0-1	O07 2-2	J06 1-0	D26 3-3	S30 1-0	O03 4-1	A26 0-0	F03 3-3	a12 4-1
10 CRYSTAL P	F03 0-1	a20 0-0	O23 1-0	M02 3-1	D02 0-3	O07 2-0	S27 2-1	M23 1-1	S09 3-0		A26 1-0	a06 0-1	J20 0-1	m01 1-3	m04 1-3	N18 2-2	a16 6-0	S06 5-0	D26 2-2	m15 2-0	S30 1-0	D16 1-0
11 DERBY CO	S02 3-1	N04 2-2	D30 2-2	m04 1-3	M23 2-1	a06 3-1	F03 3-4	N18 0-1	A19 3-2	D23 1-1		O21 1-0	a20 1-2	M02 2-3	D02 2-4	O07 3-3	M09 1-1	S16 1-0	S30 0-1	a15 1-2	F17 4-0	S27 4-1
12 HUDDERSFIELD T	a27 0-0	A26 2-3	S30 2-1	m11 1-3	J06 1-1	D16 0-3	D09 1-0	F03 1-1	M30 4-1	N11 1-1	M16 3-1		D26 2-0	S16 1-4	a16 1-0	A22 1-0	a13 2-0	F24 0-1	S09 2-2	O28 1-1	N25 1-0	O14 2-0
13 HULL C	a13 3-0	m11 0-1	D22 1-1	S02 0-1	A30 1-2	F10 4-2	O27 1-2	A19 1-0	D09 1-1	S16 1-1	N25 3-0	D30 1-1		a15 1-1	S23 0-2	J13 1-1	N11 0-2	M16 0-2	M30 1-1	F24 1-1	O14 2-0	a25 2-1
14 IPSWICH T	N11 2-1	J06 2-1	m11 1-1	A29 1-1	S09 1-1	A26 5-0	F24 4-2	S30 3-1	O28 3-2	M30 2-2	O14 4-0	J20 2-0	a16 2-0		D16 1-2	D26 2-1	S23 0-0	N25 1-1	D09 1-2	M16 4-0	a27 2-2	a13 2-0
15 MIDDLESBROUGH	S30 1-1	A29 1-1	S02 0-0	J13 0-0	D30 1-2	m11 2-1	M09 2-3	D23 4-0	F24 1-1	D09 3-0	a27 2-2	a15 3-2	F03 2-1	A19 0-2		S16 0-1	M30 2-0	O14 5-0	O28 1-0	N25 5-0	a13 3-1	N11 1-1
16 MILLWALL	O14 1-2	F10 1-1	A19 1-2	O24 1-1	F16 3-0	S23 1-1	M30 3-1	a15 1-0	S02 0-0	a13 5-1	F24 1-1	A29 1-1	S09 1-1	D30 1-1	J20 4-0		a27 1-0	O28 3-0	N11 3-2	D09 2-0	M16 1-1	N25 0-0
17 NORWICH C	A19 1-0	O21 4-2	O07 1-0	a20 1-2	M02 3-1	M23 3-2	m08 1-0	m04 2-1	D30 1-1	a15 2-1	S06 3-2	N18 0-1	a06 2-2	F03 3-4	N04 2-1	D02 5-2		S02 2-0	S16 1-3	A23 1-3	D23 0-0	F10 2-2
18 PLYMOUTH A	A23 2-1	a15 1-2	F17 2-1	M09 2-2	m04 1-2	N18 0-1	D16 0-0	D02 3-1	F10 1-4	m11 2-1	J20 3-4	O07 1-1	O21 2-5	a20 0-1	M02 0-1	M23 2-1	J10 2-2		A26 1-2	S23 1-2	D26 0-1	S09 0-1
19 PORTSMOUTH	a15 2-2	M02 1-2	a20 2-1	D02 3-1	N18 3-0	O21 2-0	S02 3-1	O07 2-1	S27 4-0	D30 2-2	F10 3-2	J13 3-1	N04 3-0	m04 1-2	M23 2-0	a06 0-0	J20 3-0	D23 0-0		S06 2-1	A19 1-1	S23 1-1
20 PRESTON N.E.	M18 2-1	a06 0-0	N18 3-5	A19 0-2	N04 1-1	D02 0-1	S30 3-0	M02 0-2	D23 4-1	S02 0-0	a16 1-1	M23 3-1	O07 3-2	O21 1-1	a20 0-0	m04 0-1	A28 1-0	F03 2-0	m11 3-1		S16 0-2	D26 2-2
21 Q.P.R.	S05 3-0	m04 2-0	D12 3-1	M23 2-0	O07 1-0	A29 3-1	a12 1-0	a06 1-0	S23 2-1	F10 2-1	S09 0-1	a20 3-0	M09 1-1	D02 1-0	N18 1-1	O21 3-1	A26 2-0	D30 4-1	D16 2-0	J20 2-0		J06 6-0
22 ROTHERHAM U	D23 0-2	M23 1-1	m04 1-0	O07 1-2	O21 2-2	N04 1-0	S16 3-2	m11 1-2	a16 1-1	A19 0-3	A28 1-3	M02 1-0	D02 1-3	N18 1-3	a06 0-1	a20 2-0	S30 1-3	M19 1-0	F03 1-1	D30 1-0	S02 1-3	

Season 1967-68

Division 3

	BARROW	BOURNEMOUTH	BRIGHTON & HA	BRISTOL R	BURY	COLCHESTER U	GILLINGHAM	GRIMSBY T	ORIENT	MANSFIELD T	NORTHAMPTON T	OLDHAM A	OXFORD U	PETERBOROUGH U	READING	SCUNTHORPE U	SHREWSBURY T	SOUTHPORT	STOCKPORT CO	SWINDON T	TORQUAY U	TRANMERE R	WALSALL	WATFORD
1 BARROW		A26 1-1	D02 1-1	O02 1-0	D16 1-1	N13 5-0	O21 0-1	M02 2-0	a06 1-0	J20 0-1	N04 4-0	D30 4-1	M09 3-0	S09 1-2	a15 1-0	m11 2-1	m04 3-0	F10 3-1	a20 3-0	S04 1-1	O07 3-0	N18 2-1	M23 1-1	S23 0-0
2 BOURNEMOUTH	D23 3-0		a12 2-2	A19 3-1	J13 1-0	S23 1-2	a06 4-0	N04 1-0	D02 0-0	m11 3-0	a20 0-2	M09 0-0	S02 2-1	F10 3-3	O21 2-0	S04 1-0	O07 1-1	O04 4-1	J20 1-0	M02 2-1	M23 1-1	m04 3-0	N18 1-1	D26 0-1
3 BRIGHTON & H.A.	a27 1-1	a15 2-3		N25 1-1	S02 1-0	F24 0-0	D26 3-0	O23 3-1	F03 1-1	M16 3-0	S30 0-2	a13 0-1	J27 0-0	O14 1-1	M20 1-1	N11 3-1	A26 3-0	M30 1-0	m01 3-0	D16 0-0	S25 0-1	S16 2-0	F28 1-0	O28 1-0
4 BRISTOL R	O24 1-0	D16 2-0	a20 3-1		M09 3-1	A26 1-1	M02 1-1	O07 3-0	a30 0-2	S09 2-0	M23 2-0	F17 4-3	S26 1-1	N14 2-1	D26 1-0	F10 4-0	D02 4-1	S23 1-3	N18 0-2	m04 1-2	a12 1-0	a06 3-1	O21 2-3	J20 0-2
5 BURY	A19 1-2	S09 4-0	J17 4-0	F27 4-2		J20 2-0	N04 3-2	M23 2-0	a19 1-0	F10 3-1	N18 3-1	S05 3-1	D23 1-1	S23 4-0	M02 2-0	O03 4-3	a12 2-0	D30 3-2	m04 5-3	O07 1-1	O21 5-1	D02 3-3	a06 2-1	m11 2-0
6 COLCHESTER U	S02 3-2	F03 0-1	O07 0-0	D23 2-0	S16 0-0		N18 2-2	a06 1-3	m04 1-1	D30 1-2	D02 2-1	A19 0-0	M25 1-2	m11 1-5	M23 2-5	F26 1-0	M02 0-3	S25 1-1	a12 1-1	O21 2-1	N04 3-5	F10 1-2	a20 2-2	O02 2-1
7 GILLINGHAM	M16 3-0	N11 0-0	D30 1-1	O14 0-0	M30 2-0	a13 1-0		S09 1-0	M09 2-3	a27 2-1	A19 2-0	F24 1-0	O28 2-1	N25 3-2	S23 3-0	a15 3-1	m11 0-1	S02 1-4	O04 3-1	F10 3-1	J20 1-1	S27 1-1	D23 0-1	a24 0-0
8 GRIMSBY T	O14 0-1	M30 2-1	O04 4-2	F24 3-2	O28 3-1	N11 1-2	M13 1-1		A19 0-0	N25 0-0	D23 0-0	a12 0-1	M16 0-1	a13 1-1	F10 1-1	S16 2-1	D30 0-1	a24 2-0	S06 3-1	m11 3-2	S23 1-1	M20 3-0	S02 3-0	a27 0-1
9 ORIENT	N11 4-2	a27 1-0	S23 1-2	M30 2-2	N25 1-0	a22 1-1	m07 0-4	D16 1-0		a15 0-0	O24 1-3	O28 0-2	a13 1-0	D30 3-0	N13 1-0	M16 2-1	J20 1-1	O14 3-0	F10 2-2	S09 0-0	A26 0-2	m11 0-1	S25 2-0	F24 0-1
10 MANSFIELD T	S16 1-2	F17 1-1	O21 1-3	M11 3-0	S30 1-1	D26 2-1	D02 0-1	a20 1-1	a16 0-0		S25 3-2	S02 1-1	F03 1-0	O23 2-3	a06 2-2	D23 3-0	M23 0-1	A19 4-2	M02 1-0	N04 2-2	N18 2-0	O07 0-3	m04 0-3	M09 1-2
11 NORTHAMPTON T	M30 3-0	N25 1-0	F10 2-2	O28 4-5	a13 0-1	a27 2-2	D16 1-1	A26 3-0	O03 2-1	S05 1-1		M16 1-2	N11 1-1	a23 3-1	S09 1-2	O14 1-0	S23 2-2	F24 1-1	M19 4-1	J20 2-0	N14 1-0	D26 0-1	M09 3-0	a16 1-1
12 OLDHAM A	D26 3-1	M12 1-1	N18 3-0	m11 3-5	S26 1-2	D16 2-1	O07 0-1	a16 2-1	M23 2-2	N14 1-0	O21 2-0		O24 3-1	A26 0-2	m04 1-3	S23 3-4	a20 0-0	J20 2-0	a06 4-1	D02 0-2	F10 0-1	N04 2-1	M02 0-3	S09 2-0
13 OXFORD U	a03 3-1	N15 3-2	m04 2-0	S06 0-2	A26 5-4	S09 3-1	M23 3-0	O21 2-1	N18 2-0	S23 2-0	a06 1-0	O04 3-1		J20 3-1	O07 2-0	D30 2-3	D16 2-2	m11 1-0	D02 2-2	a12 0-0	M02 2-0	a20 1-0	N04 4-0	F10 1-0
14 PETERBOROUGH U	J13 0-1	S30 2-0	M02 2-3	S02 4-1	F03 0-2	F17 3-1	a20 3-0	N18 3-2	D26 3-2	O02 2-0	m04 4-0	D23 2-1	S16 1-1		N04 2-3	A19 1-1	O21 0-1	M09 1-0	O07 2-0	M23 1-1	a06 2-0	a15 1-1	D02 2-1	S04 5-1
15 READING	a12 3-0	M16 1-0	M09 1-0	D30 2-1	O14 3-4	O28 1-0	F03 3-1	S30 3-0	S02 4-2	N11 2-1	F14 0-0	a24 0-1	F24 1-1	M30 0-1		a27 2-1	S27 0-0	N25 1-1	A19 3-0	O04 2-1	m11 4-0	D23 3-0	S16 2-2	a13 2-0
16 SCUNTHORPE U	F17 2-4	S26 1-1	a06 1-3	S30 1-1	O24 3-1	M09 5-1	J26 2-1	J20 0-3	O21 1-1	A25 3-3	M02 1-1	F03 2-0	D26 1-1	D15 2-1	D01 1-2		N17 0-0	S09 1-0	N03 0-2	a19 3-1	m03 2-0	M22 1-1	O07 2-5	N14 1-1
17 SHREWSBURY T	a24 1-0	F24 1-0	D23 0-0	a27 0-0	a15 1-0	O14 4-0	F17 1-2	D26 3-2	S16 2-2	O28 2-1	F03 2-0	N25 4-2	A19 2-0	M16 1-1	S06 2-1	a13 4-0		N11 3-2	S02 0-0	M09 0-1	O25 5-0	M05 1-1	S30 0-1	M30 3-1
18 SOUTHPORT	S29 1-0	O23 1-1	N04 1-0	F03 2-1	D26 2-2	S04 2-3	N13 4-1	m03 0-1	M01 0-0	D16 3-1	O07 1-3	S15 1-0	F16 1-0	a01 2-1	a19 2-1	m06 1-1	a05 0-0		M22 4-3	N18 1-1	D02 0-2	O20 2-0	a15 2-0	A26 2-0
19 STOCKPORT CO	N24 1-0	S15 3-1	S08 2-0	a13 3-1	a22 4-2	a15 1-0	O23 1-1	S25 1-1	S29 2-0	O13 1-0	F17 4-0	N10 0-2	a26 0-4	F23 2-2	D15 3-0	M29 4-1	N13 4-2	O30 4-3		A25 2-0	J26 0-0	F02 5-2	D29 0-0	M15 2-0
20 SWINDON T	S26 0-1	O14 4-0	A19 2-1	a23 4-1	F24 2-3	M16 1-1	S30 2-2	F27 5-0	M12 4-0	M30 1-1	S16 4-0	a27 0-0	a16 1-1	O28 0-0	O24 5-1	N25 2-0	M19 0-0	a13 3-3	D19 2-0		D30 1-0	S02 3-1	F03 3-0	N11 2-0
21 TORQUAY U	F24 0-2	O28 2-1	S06 1-1	a15 2-0	M16 3-0	M30 3-0	S16 2-1	F03 1-0	a01 1-1	a13 0-2	S02 0-0	S30 2-1	O14 1-1	N11 3-1	F17 2-1	a25 2-1	O04 3-0	a27 2-2	M09 3-0	D26 1-1		A19 1-0	J13 4-1	N25 1-0
22 TRANMERE R	a13 0-0	a22 0-0	J19 2-2	N10 3-3	a26 2-0	S29 4-2	S04 2-1	a29 1-2	M25 3-0	F23 1-1	D30 2-2	M29 1-0	N24 1-1	a12 0-1	A25 1-2	O27 2-0	S08 4-1	M15 0-2	S22 2-1	N13 3-2	D15 2-3		O23 2-0	O13 1-2
23 WALSALL	O28 4-0	a13 1-1	m11 1-2	M16 2-1	N11 2-1	N25 1-1	A26 3-0	N14 2-0	S05 5-0	a23 2-1	a02 4-0	O14 3-1	M29 0-1	a27 3-2	J20 2-2	F24 0-0	F10 1-2	a16 1-1	D26 0-1	S23 3-2	S09 1-1	O03 5-1		D16 1-1
24 WATFORD	F03 3-2	D30 0-2	M23 4-0	S16 4-0	F17 1-1	O24 1-1	m04 3-0	D02 7-1	O07 1-1	M19 1-2	a12 5-1	J16 1-2	S30 2-0	S26 4-1	N18 3-0	S02 4-0	N04 2-0	D23 0-1	O21 5-0	a06 2-0	a20 2-1	M01 3-2	A19 1-2	

Division 4

	ALDERSHOT	BARNSLEY	BRADFORD	BRADFORD C	BRENTFORD	CHESTER	CHESTERFIELD	CREWE A	DARLINGTON	DONCASTER R	EXETER C	HALIFAX T	HARTLEPOOLS U	LINCOLN C	LUTON T	NEWPORT CO	NOTTS CO	PORT VALE	ROCHDALE	SOUTHEND U	SWANSEA T	WORKINGTON	WREXHAM	YORK C
1 ALDERSHOT		M02 1-1	N18 1-1	N15 3-3	a20 0-0	F10 2-1	M13 3-0	S09 2-0	O04 0-0	a06 2-1	D26 0-0	A26 1-1	J27 2-0	D16 3-2	M20 0-1	a12 0-0	J20 0-0	S23 2-0	D02 2-1	M23 1-3	O07 1-1	S06 5-0	O21 3-1	m04 2-2
2 BARNSLEY	O14 1-0		S26 2-0	N11 1-0	a15 3-0	a23 2-1	S15 0-0	F24 3-1	a13 1-0	A19 1-0	J27 2-1	M30 0-0	F10 4-0	O28 2-1	D23 2-2	m11 4-2	N25 3-1	a26 2-0	O03 1-1	S02 1-1	S23 3-0	M16 2-1	M05 2-2	D30 1-0
3 BRADFORD	F24 1-1	S04 1-1		S30 1-2	S23 1-0	M16 0-2	O28 2-1	J27 1-2	N11 1-2	F17 1-1	M30 0-1	a22 0-1	A26 0-1	a27 1-5	D30 2-1	N13 0-2	a13 1-4	O14 2-2	J20 0-0	O23 0-1	D16 1-2	N25 1-1	a16 0-1	S09 1-1
4 BRADFORD C	S02 1-3	a06 1-0	F10 1-2		M09 2-3	a15 2-2	S27 3-1	O18 2-1	D23 1-0	m04 1-1	A19 2-1	F03 0-1	M23 1-1	S16 2-1	D02 2-0	O21 3-0	D26 5-1	O04 2-1	O07 0-0	a20 2-1	N04 4-1	J24 1-0	N18 3-1	M02 0-0
5 BRENTFORD	N25 1-1	J06 0-1	F03 2-1	J27 0-1		O28 3-1	M30 1-1	a13 2-1	F24 2-0	S30 4-2	N11 5-1	S16 0-0	D16 0-1	a23 1-3	F17 0-2	A26 3-1	O14 2-1	M16 3-1	S09 4-0	D26 1-2	S26 2-1	a27 2-1	O24 0-0	N14 3-1
6 CHESTER	S30 2-5	m04 1-1	O21 0-0	a16 2-3	M23 3-0		a03 3-0	S06 0-4	F03 0-1	M02 2-3	S16 3-1	O25 3-2	a20 0-2	D30 6-0	O07 1-3	N18 2-1	D16 1-3	A26 1-1	N04 0-1	J27 0-0	D02 2-3	F17 1-2	N15 1-1	a06 1-1
7 CHESTERFIELD	F17 1-2	J20 2-3	M23 2-0	S04 2-1	N04 2-1	S09 3-1		D16 4-1	S30 3-1	O21 2-0	F03 1-1	a16 0-0	D02 3-1	O23 2-0	M02 0-0	a20 1-2	A26 4-0	N13 3-0	a06 0-2	O07 3-1	m04 3-1	D26 0-0	M09 3-1	N18 3-1
8 CREWE A	M27 1-1	N18 3-3	M09 4-0	F17 1-1	O07 2-0	S27 2-0	A19 1-1		S02 1-1	D30 2-2	D23 2-0	S30 5-1	N04 2-1	F03 2-1	m04 2-1	M23 1-1	O25 4-0	a12 1-1	M02 2-1	D02 1-0	a06 2-0	S16 3-2	a20 0-0	O21 0-0
9 DARLINGTON	O23 6-2	O07 0-2	a06 0-0	A26 2-2	N18 2-3	S23 0-2	F10 1-1	a01 0-0		N04 1-1	F17 0-1	D16 0-0	D30 2-3	S25 1-1	M23 1-2	m04 1-0	S09 2-2	J20 2-2	a20 2-0	O21 1-1	M04 2-0	a12 1-0	M02 1-1	D02 3-1
10 DONCASTER R	N11 3-0	D15 1-2	m10 2-0	a23 2-2	F10 2-0	O14 0-0	M15 1-0	D26 2-2	M29 2-1		O28 3-1	a26 0-0	N14 0-1	N25 0-0	O03 2-0	S09 1-1	M08 3-1	a13 0-0	S23 2-0	a16 2-1	A26 1-2	F24 3-0	S05 2-2	J19 2-0
11 EXETER C	D30 3-0	M09 2-0	m01 0-0	D16 4-1	a06 0-3	J20 1-0	S23 1-1	A26 1-4	m11 0-0	M23 0-1		S27 0-0	m04 0-0	a12 0-1	O21 0-5	D02 2-1	N15 3-3	S09 3-1	N18 3-1	M02 0-2	F10 1-3	O25 1-0	O07 2-2	a20 3-1
12 HALIFAX T	D23 2-2	N04 1-1	m04 1-0	S23 1-0	J20 3-0	O31 2-2	a15 0-2	M05 0-1	A19 2-0	D02 2-3	S04 1-1		O21 3-0	J13 1-0	a20 0-1	M02 4-1	m10 0-1	D30 0-1	M09 2-0	N18 1-2	a02 2-2	S02 2-1	a06 2-2	O07 2-1
13 HARTLEPOOLS U	M09 1-0	S29 2-1	D22 2-0	O27 1-0	A19 2-0	N24 0-0	a26 2-1	M30 1-1	D26 1-0	S01 0-0	a01 3-1	M15 0-0		O13 1-1	J13 2-1	O23 2-0	N10 3-1	F24 2-2	S04 1-1	S16 0-1	m11 2-0	a13 2-1	F03 3-0	a12 1-0
14 LINCOLN C	A19 1-1	M23 0-1	D02 5-1	J20 2-0	m04 1-0	D26 3-0	O04 2-2	S23 2-4	S06 1-2	a20 2-0	a15 1-1	S09 1-0	M02 1-2		N18 2-3	O07 2-1	F10 1-3	m11 0-1	J06 3-2	a06 4-2	O21 3-0	D23 3-0	N04 0-2	J27 1-3
15 LUTON T	M30 3-1	A26 2-0	D26 2-0	a27 1-3	m11 2-1	a13 0-0	O14 1-0	a24 4-0	F26 3-1	O25 5-3	M16 0-0	N25 2-0	S09 1-0	F24 4-2		J20 1-1	a12 2-0	M09 2-0	F10 4-1	S27 3-1	N15 4-0	N11 4-0	D16 2-1	S23 3-1
16 NEWPORT CO	a15 0-2	F17 3-0	S02 4-0	M16 0-3	D23 2-2	F24 1-1	N25 0-3	O31 0-0	a23 1-0	F27 2-1	a27 1-1	O14 0-1	O03 2-0	a13 0-1	S16 1-1		M30 1-0	N21 1-1	A19 1-1	F06 2-0	D30 3-0	a29 2-1	S30 3-2	S05 2-1
17 NOTTS CO	S16 0-1	a20 1-4	O07 0-0	D30 1-0	M02 2-1	A19 1-2	D23 1-0	O04 1-0	J13 0-0	m01 0-2	S02 1-0	F17 1-3	a06 0-3	S30 0-0	a15 2-2	N04 3-1		S06 0-0	O21 2-0	m04 4-3	N18 3-2	F03 2-1	D02 1-1	M23 1-1
18 PORT VALE	F03 0-3	D02 2-0	M02 4-0	O23 1-2	O21 4-1	D23 4-4	S02 0-1	a15 0-2	S16 0-1	O07 4-2	M25 1-0	D26 2-1	N18 2-3	F16 1-1	J26 0-0	a06 0-1	S25 4-1		M23 1-1	A19 1-2	a20 4-2	S30 4-2	m04 1-1	N04 1-0
19 ROCHDALE	a27 0-2	O23 1-0	S16 1-1	a13 3-2	M18 1-1	M30 1-1	N11 1-4	O14 1-1	N25 1-0	F03 2-0	F24 2-2	a29 2-1	S25 1-1	S02 1-2	S30 2-2	D16 4-3	M16 0-0	O28 3-1		F17 0-1	a15 1-2	J27 1-3	D30 3-0	A26 3-2
20 SOUTHEND U	O27 1-1	N13 4-1	O02 2-1	N25 1-1	D30 1-0	M08 5-1	a13 1-1	a26 0-0	M15 2-2	a08 1-2	O14 1-0	F24 2-2	J20 2-1	N11 2-1	S04 3-0	S22 2-2	a22 0-1	D15 1-1	m10 3-1		S08 1-0	M29 7-0	A25 3-1	F10 0-1
21 SWANSEA T	a13 1-0	F03 1-1	A19 1-1	M30 0-0	S05 2-1	a27 1-0	a23 0-1	N11 1-2	M09 0-1	D23 3-1	S30 1-1	O28 2-1	m06 0-2	M16 2-2	S02 2-2	D26 4-2	F24 2-0	N25 4-2	a16 1-0	M19 2-2		O14 5-2	S16 2-0	O03 1-1
22 WORKINGTON	S28 3-2	O21 0-1	a20 2-2	S09 0-1	D02 2-0	m11 1-0	D30 3-1	J20 2-2	a15 0-1	N17 2-2	O04 1-0	N15 1-1	O07 2-1	A26 2-4	a06 0-1	M09 1-1	S23 5-1	F10 1-1	m04 0-1	N04 2-2	M02 3-1		M23 1-2	D16 1-1
23 WREXHAM	M16 2-1	S09 2-0	a12 3-0	F24 0-2	O02 1-2	S02 2-0	M18 3-0	N25 1-0	O14 3-1	S25 0-0	a13 0-0	N11 2-0	S23 6-0	M30 2-1	A19 1-1	F10 0-1	a27 2-0	a22 1-0	D26 2-0	O16 4-1	J20 2-1	O28 5-0		m11 3-1
24 YORK C	a22 2-3	D26 1-1	M25 6-2	O14 0-1	S02 0-1	N11 4-1	F24 0-2	M16 1-1	a27 1-1	S16 1-2	N25 4-0	a13 1-2	a15 0-2	M09 1-0	F03 1-1	S25 0-1	O28 4-2	M30 5-1	D23 4-1	S30 2-2	O23 2-1	A19 1-1	F17 3-1	

LEAGUE TABLES

DIVISION 1

	P	W	D	L	F	A	W	D	L	F	A	Pts
Manchester C	42	17	2	2	52	16	9	4	8	34	27	58
Manchester U	42	15	2	4	49	21	9	6	6	40	34	56
Liverpool	42	17	2	2	51	17	5	9	7	20	23	55
Leeds U	42	17	3	1	49	14	5	6	10	22	27	53
Everton	42	18	1	2	43	13	5	5	11	24	27	52
Chelsea	42	11	7	3	34	25	7	5	9	28	43	48
Tottenham H	42	11	7	3	44	20	8	2	11	26	39	47
W.B.A.	42	12	4	5	45	25	5	8	8	30	37	46
Arsenal	42	12	6	3	37	23	5	4	12	23	33	44
Newcastle U	42	12	7	2	38	20	1	8	12	16	47	41
Nottingham F	42	11	6	4	34	22	3	5	13	18	42	39
West Ham U	42	8	5	8	43	30	6	5	10	30	39	38
Leicester C	42	7	7	7	37	34	6	5	10	27	35	38
Burnley	42	12	7	2	38	16	2	3	16	26	55	38
Sunderland	42	8	7	6	28	28	5	4	12	23	33	37
Southampton	42	9	8	4	37	31	4	3	14	29	52	37
Wolverh'pton W	42	10	4	7	45	36	4	4	13	21	39	36
Stoke C	42	10	3	8	30	29	4	4	13	20	44	35
Sheffield W	42	6	10	5	32	24	5	2	14	19	39	34
Coventry C	42	8	5	8	32	32	1	10	10	19	39	33
Sheffield U	42	7	4	10	25	31	4	6	11	24	39	32
Fulham	42	6	4	11	27	41	4	3	14	29	57	27

DIVISION 2

	P	W	D	L	F	A	W	D	L	F	A	Pts
Ipswich T	42	12	7	2	45	20	10	8	3	34	24	59
Q.P.R.	42	18	2	1	45	9	7	6	8	22	27	58
Blackpool	42	12	6	3	33	16	12	4	5	38	27	58
Birmingham C	42	12	6	3	54	21	7	8	6	29	30	52
Portsmouth	42	13	6	2	43	18	5	7	9	25	37	49
Middlesbrough	42	10	7	4	39	19	7	5	9	21	35	46
Millwall	42	9	10	2	35	16	5	7	9	27	34	45
Blackburn R	42	13	5	3	34	16	3	6	12	22	33	43
Norwich C	42	12	4	5	40	30	4	7	10	20	35	43
Carlisle U	42	9	9	3	38	22	5	4	12	20	30	41
Crystal Palace	42	11	4	6	34	19	3	7	11	22	37	39
Bolton W	42	8	6	7	37	28	5	7	9	23	35	39
Cardiff C	42	9	6	6	35	29	4	6	11	25	37	38
Huddersfield T	42	10	6	5	29	23	3	6	12	17	38	38
Charlton A	42	10	6	5	43	25	2	7	12	20	43	37
Aston Villa	42	10	3	8	35	30	5	4	12	19	34	37
Hull C	42	6	8	7	25	23	6	5	10	33	50	37
Derby Co	42	8	5	8	40	35	5	5	11	31	43	36
Bristol C	42	7	7	7	26	25	6	3	12	22	37	36
Preston N.E.	42	8	7	6	29	24	4	4	13	14	41	35
Rotherham U	42	7	4	10	22	32	3	7	11	20	44	31
Plymouth A	42	5	4	12	26	36	4	5	12	12	36	27

DIVISION 3

	P	W	D	L	F	A	W	D	L	F	A	Pts
Oxford U	46	18	3	2	49	20	4	10	9	20	27	57
Bury	46	19	3	1	64	24	5	5	13	27	42	56
Shrewsbury T	46	14	6	3	42	17	6	9	8	19	32	55
Torquay U	46	15	6	2	40	17	6	5	12	20	39	53
Reading	46	15	5	3	43	17	6	4	13	27	43	51
Watford	46	15	3	5	59	20	6	5	12	15	30	50
Walsall	46	12	7	4	47	22	7	5	11	27	39	50
Barrow	46	14	6	3	43	13	7	2	14	22	41	50
Peterborough U	46	14	4	5	46	23	6	6	11	33	44	*50
Swindon T	46	13	8	2	51	16	3	9	11	23	35	49
Brighton & H.A.	46	11	8	4	31	14	5	8	10	26	41	48
Gillingham	46	13	6	4	35	19	5	6	12	24	44	48
Bournemouth	46	13	7	3	39	17	3	8	12	17	34	47
Stockport Co	46	16	5	2	49	22	3	4	16	21	53	47
Southport	46	13	6	4	35	22	4	6	13	30	43	46
Bristol R	46	14	3	6	42	25	3	6	14	30	53	43
Oldham A	46	11	3	9	37	32	7	4	12	23	33	43
Northampton T	46	10	8	5	40	25	4	5	14	18	47	41
Leyton O	46	10	6	7	27	24	2	11	10	19	38	41
Tranmere R	46	10	7	6	39	28	4	5	14	23	46	40
Mansfield T	46	8	7	8	32	31	4	6	13	19	36	37
Grimsby T	46	10	7	6	33	21	4	2	17	19	48	37
Colchester U	46	6	8	9	29	40	3	7	13	21	47	33
Scunthorpe U	46	8	9	6	36	34	2	3	18	20	53	32

*Peterborough United deducted 19 points for irregular bonuses – automatically demoted to Division Four.

DIVISION 4

	P	W	D	L	F	A	W	D	L	F	A	Pts
Luton T	46	19	3	1	55	16	8	9	6	32	28	66
Barnsley	46	17	6	0	43	14	7	7	9	25	32	61
Hartlepool U	46	15	7	1	34	12	10	3	10	26	34	60
Crewe A	46	13	10	0	44	18	7	8	8	30	31	58
Bradford C	46	14	5	4	41	22	9	6	8	31	29	57
Southend U	46	12	8	3	45	21	8	6	9	32	37	54
Chesterfield	46	15	4	4	47	20	6	7	10	24	30	53
Wrexham	46	17	3	3	47	12	3	10	10	25	41	53
Aldershot	46	10	11	2	36	19	8	6	9	34	36	53
Doncaster R	46	12	8	3	36	16	6	7	10	30	40	51
Halifax T	46	10	6	7	34	24	5	10	8	18	25	46
Newport Co	46	11	7	5	32	22	5	6	12	26	41	45
Lincoln C	46	11	3	9	41	31	6	6	11	30	37	43
Brentford	46	13	4	6	41	24	5	3	15	20	40	43
Swansea T	46	11	8	4	38	25	5	2	16	25	52	42
Darlington	46	6	11	6	31	27	6	6	11	16	26	41
Notts Co	46	10	7	6	27	27	5	4	14	26	52	41
Port Vale	46	10	5	8	41	31	2	10	11	20	41	39
Rochdale	46	9	8	6	35	32	3	6	14	16	40	38
Exeter C	46	9	7	7	30	30	2	9	12	15	35	38
York C	46	9	6	8	44	30	2	8	13	21	38	36
Chester C	46	6	6	11	35	38	3	8	12	22	40	32
Workington	46	8	8	7	35	29	2	3	18	19	58	31
Bradford P.A.	46	3	7	13	18	35	1	8	14	12	47	23

Top scorers: Div 1, J.Greaves (Tottenham Hotspur) 27 goals; Div 2, J.Toshack (Cardiff City) 22 goals; Div 3, D.Rogers (Swindon Town) 22 goals; Div 4, G.Talbot (Chester) 22 goals.

Hartlepools United became Hartlepool.

Mick Jones, Leeds' first £100,000 signing, was their leading scorer when they won Division One in 1968-69.

DIVISION 1

	ARSENAL	BURNLEY	CHELSEA	COVENTRY C	EVERTON	IPSWICH T	LEEDS U	LEICESTER C	LIVERPOOL	MANCHESTER C	MANCHESTER U	NEWCASTLE U	NOTTINGHAM F	Q.P.R.	SHEFFIELD W	SOUTHAMPTON	STOKE C	SUNDERLAND	TOTTENHAM H	W.B.A.	WEST HAM U	WOLVERHAMPTON W
1 ARSENAL		F15 2-0	N23 0-1	O12 2-1	D07 3-1	F18 0-2	a12 1-2	A13 3-0	A17 1-1	A27 4-1	D26 3-0	N09 0-0	F01 1-1	A31 2-1	J11 2-0	M29 0-0	S14 1-0	S28 0-0	M24 1-0	D21 2-0	O26 0-0	a07 3-1
2 BURNLEY	N30 0-1		S28 2-1	A31 1-1	a08 1-2	N02 1-0	O19 5-1	D28 2-1	O05 0-4	M04 2-1	S14 1-0	A17 1-0	M01 3-1	J18 2-2	a12 2-0	A20 3-1	D14 1-1	a23 1-2	M29 2-2	M15 2-2	O08 3-1	N16 1-1
3 CHELSEA	a14 2-1	a05 2-3		M10 2-1	S07 1-1	O05 3-1	N30 1-1	O19 3-0	J18 1-2	N02 2-0	M15 3-2	a04 1-1	A14 1-1	a19 2-1	A28 1-0	N16 2-3	M05 1-0	F22 5-1	A31 2-2	A17 3-1	S21 1-1	D14 1-1
4 COVENTRY C	D14 0-1	M22 4-1	S10 0-1		S21 2-2	N30 0-2	N16 0-1	a01 1-0	a22 0-0	O19 1-1	a08 2-1	S07 2-1	a19 1-1	F25 5-0	M08 3-0	N02 1-1	M18 1-1	M04 3-1	S17 1-2	A27 4-2	A24 1-2	O05 0-1
5 EVERTON	a29 1-0	A13 3-0	M29 1-2	a12 3-0		J18 2-2	a22 0-0	N30 7-1	A27 0-0	O05 2-0	M10 0-0	a14 1-1	A31 2-1	N16 4-0	S14 3-0	D14 1-0	O19 2-1	N02 2-0	A17 0-2	S28 4-0	a01 1-0	J28 4-0
6 IPSWICH T	A24 1-2	J11 2-0	D26 1-3	M25 0-0	N09 2-2		A20 2-3	m03 2-1	S14 0-2	M11 2-1	F01 1-0	O12 1-4	D21 2-3	A27 3-0	a25 2-0	a12 0-0	S28 3-1	a04 1-0	O26 0-1	D07 4-1	N23 2-2	A10 1-0
7 LEEDS U	S21 2-0	D21 6-1	F15 1-0	F01 3-0	N23 2-1	F12 2-0		a19 2-0	A31 1-0	a05 1-0	J11 2-1	D26 2-1	a30 1-0	A14 4-1	D07 2-0	M01 3-2	A17 2-0	A28 1-1	N09 0-0	O26 0-0	O12 2-0	S07 2-1
8 LEICESTER C	a08 0-0	O26 0-2	D21 1-4	S28 1-1	m14 1-1	A17 1-3	S14 1-1		a12 1-2	A21 3-0	D07 2-1	J11 2-1	N09 2-2	M12 2-0	N23 1-1	A31 3-1	M15 0-0	m05 2-1	a29 1-0	O12 0-2	F01 1-1	O09 2-0
9 LIVERPOOL	M31 1-1	D26 1-1	N09 2-1	N23 2-0	O08 1-1	a19 4-0	a28 0-0	S21 4-0		A10 2-1	O12 2-0	O26 2-1	F15 0-2	S07 2-0	F01 1-0	D03 1-0	A20 2-1	A24 4-1	D21 1-0	J11 1-0	D07 2-0	a05 1-0
10 MANCHESTER C	O09 1-1	D07 7-0	J11 4-1	D21 4-2	D26 1-3	A31 1-1	S28 3-1	a04 2-0	m12 1-0		A17 0-0	m05 1-0	O26 3-3	M15 3-1	N09 0-1	S14 1-1	M29 3-1	a12 1-0	O12 4-0	N23 5-1	a30 1-1	A14 3-2
11 MANCHESTER U	O05 0-0	a19 2-0	A24 0-4	A21 1-0	A10 2-1	N16 0-0	N02 0-0	m17 3-2	D14 1-0	M08 0-1		S21 3-1	a05 3-1	M19 8-1	M22 1-0	O19 1-2	M24 1-1	J18 4-1	A28 3-1	a02 2-1	S07 1-1	N30 2-0
12 NEWCASTLE U	J18 2-1	M08 1-0	A21 3-2	M29 2-0	A24 0-0	D14 2-1	O05 0-1	N02 0-0	m17 1-1	N16 1-0	a12 2-0		A28 1-1	O19 3-2	a09 3-2	N30 4-1	a30 5-0	M22 1-1	S28 2-2	S14 2-3	A10 1-1	a21 4-1
13 NOTTINGHAM F	N16 0-2	A10 2-2	a08 1-2	S14 0-0	a25 1-0	O19 1-2	F25 0-2	J18 0-0	N30 0-1	M24 1-0	M31 0-1	O08 2-4		M04 1-0	A20 0-0	M11 1-0	O05 3-3	D14 1-0	a12 0-2	M22 3-0	M08 0-1	N02 0-0
14 Q.P.R.	M22 0-1	N09 0-2	S14 0-4	D07 0-1	F01 0-1	O08 2-1	J24 0-1	A10 1-1	M29 1-2	A24 1-1	O26 2-3	D21 1-1	N23 2-1		O12 3-2	S28 1-1	a12 2-1	A20 2-2	F15 1-1	D26 0-4	J11 1-1	M08 0-1
15 SHEFFIELD W	M01 0-5	S21 1-0	O09 1-1	A17 3-0	a19 2-2	S07 2-1	a01 0-0	a14 1-3	N16 1-2	J18 1-1	A31 5-4	A14 1-1	a07 0-1	D14 4-0		D28 0-0	N30 2-1	O05 1-1	m12 0-0	M05 1-0	a05 1-1	O19 0-2
16 SOUTHAMPTON	S07 1-2	a07 5-1	F01 5-0	J11 1-0	O12 2-5	S21 2-2	A10 1-3	M22 1-0	A14 2-0	a19 3-0	D21 2-0	F15 0-0	D07 1-1	a05 3-2	O26 1-1		A28 2-0	M08 1-0	N23 2-1	N09 2-0	D26 2-2	A24 2-1
17 STOKE C	a19 1-3	O12 1-3	O26 2-0	N09 0-3	D21 0-0	a05 2-1	M08 1-5	A24 1-0	a07 0-0	S07 1-0	N23 0-0	D07 1-0	D26 3-1	S21 1-1	a22 1-1	O09 1-0		A10 2-1	J11 1-1	F01 1-1	A14 0-2	M22 4-1
18 SUNDERLAND	a05 0-0	N23 2-0	D07 3-2	O26 3-0	J11 1-3	A14 3-0	O09 0-1	S07 2-0	M15 0-2	S21 0-4	N09 1-1	A31 1-1	O12 3-1	a07 0-0	D26 0-0	A17 1-0	M01 4-1		F01 0-0	M10 0-1	D21 2-1	a19 2-0
19 TOTTENHAM H	A10 1-2	S07 7-0	M22 1-0	a04 2-0	M08 1-1	M18 2-2	J18 0-0	O05 3-2	O19 2-1	D14 1-1	O09 2-2	a02 0-1	S21 2-1	J29 3-2	A24 1-2	a22 2-1	N02 1-1	N16 5-1		A21 1-1	a19 1-0	F22 1-1
20 W.B.A.	O19 1-0	A24 3-2	M08 0-3	O09 6-1	a05 1-1	a23 2-2	a09 1-1	D14 1-1	N02 0-0	a16 2-0	A14 3-1	a19 5-1	S07 2-5	O05 3-1	A10 0-0	J18 1-2	N16 2-1	N30 3-0	a07 4-3		a14 3-1	S21 0-0
21 WEST HAM U	a21 1-2	A26 5-0	a12 0-0	M14 5-2	A19 1-4	M21 1-3	D14 1-1	N16 4-0	F22 1-1	N30 2-1	M29 0-0	M01 3-1	A17 1-0	N02 4-3	S28 1-1	O05 0-0	a08 0-0	O19 8-0	S14 2-2	A31 4-0		M24 3-1
22 WOLVERHAMPTON W	A21 0-0	F01 1-1	O12 1-1	a15 1-1	O26 1-2	M01 1-1	M29 0-0	A28 1-0	S28 0-6	a08 3-1	F15 2-2	N23 5-0	J11 1-0	A17 3-1	D21 0-3	M15 0-0	A31 1-1	S14 1-1	D07 2-0	a12 0-1	N09 2-0	

Kevin Hector, the king of the Baseball Ground as his goals helped Brian Clough's Derby County back to Division One.

DIVISION 2

	ASTON VILLA	BIRMINGHAM C	BLACKBURN R	BLACKPOOL	BOLTON W	BRISTOL C	BURY	CARDIFF C	CARLISLE U	CHARLTON A	CRYSTAL P	DERBY CO	FULHAM	HUDDERSFIELD T	HULL C	MIDDLESBROUGH	MILLWALL	NORWICH C	OXFORD U	PORTSMOUTH	PRESTON N.E.	SHEFFIELD U
1 ASTON VILLA		a12 1-0	M15 1-1	A31 0-1	a08 1-1	A26 1-0	F15 1-0	D26 2-0	O26 0-0	D07 0-0	O12 1-1	M29 0-1	A17 1-1	J11 1-0	S14 1-1	N23 1-0	A19 1-1	D21 2-1	S28 2-0	F01 2-0	N09 0-1	M01 3-1
2 BIRMINGHAM C	S21 4-0		J18 3-1	N16 1-0	M25 5-0	D14 2-0	S17 1-3	O08 2-0	a05 3-0	a07 0-0	M08 0-1	J14 1-1	O05 5-4	S07 5-1	N30 5-2	a19 3-1	O19 1-2	A10 1-2	N02 0-1	A24 5-2	M21 3-1	M04 2-2
3 BLACKBURN R	A24 2-0	N09 3-2		A28 1-1	a19 2-3	M22 1-3	D21 3-0	J11 1-0	O12 0-2	N23 0-1	a28 1-2	A10 1-1	a05 2-2	D07 0-0	M08 1-1	M25 1-1	S07 2-4	O26 3-0	S18 1-0	a07 3-1	D26 1-0	S21 1-0
4 BLACKPOOL	M22 1-1	F01 2-1	O07 0-1		S07 1-0	A24 2-2	N23 6-0	N09 1-2	D21 1-0	J11 2-3	O26 3-0	M08 2-3	S21 2-2	D26 0-0	A10 2-0	D07 1-1	a19 1-0	M19 2-1	a07 1-0	O12 1-1	S16 1-1	a05 1-1
5 BOLTON W	S18 4-1	N23 0-0	S14 1-1	M29 1-4		a07 1-0	A17 2-0	D21 1-2	D26 0-1	O12 3-0	J11 2-2	S28 1-2	M15 3-2	O26 2-3	a12 1-0	F01 0-0	O09 0-4	D04 1-1	M01 1-1	D07 1-0	a16 0-0	A31 4-2
6 BRISTOL C	O08 1-0	O12 0-0	A31 1-0	M15 1-1	A20 2-2		D07 2-1	S28 0-3	F15 3-0	D26 2-0	F25 1-1	S14 0-0	M01 6-0	N09 0-1	M29 1-1	J11 3-0	a08 0-0	N23 0-1	a12 2-0	O26 2-2	F01 2-1	A17 1-1
7 BURY	N30 3-2	a08 1-2	O19 1-3	M26 2-0	M07 2-1	a15 1-2		A21 3-3	A10 3-2	A27 2-3	A24 2-1	J25 0-1	D28 5-1	a05 1-1	J18 0-0	S21 2-3	O05 0-0	M22 1-2	D14 3-1	a18 3-2	S07 0-1	N16 0-2
8 CARDIFF C	O05 1-1	A28 4-0	N02 2-1	F12 1-0	O19 0-2	J25 3-0	a07 2-0		S21 2-1	A14 0-1	A10 0-4	N16 1-1	M24 0-2	a19 0-2	D28 3-0	S07 2-0	D14 2-0	M07 3-1	F08 5-0	M21 2-2	A24 1-0	N30 4-1
9 CARLISLE U	D28 0-1	S28 2-3	D14 4-1	O19 1-0	O05 1-1	N30 3-0	M01 2-0	a12 1-0		A17 1-1	M29 1-2	M11 1-1	N16 2-0	A31 0-0	N04 1-0	M15 3-0	F22 1-0	S14 0-4	A27 0-2	A13 0-0	a07 1-0	J18 0-1
10 CHARLTON A	F22 1-1	A20 3-1	a15 4-0	N02 0-0	D14 2-2	O05 0-0	O08 2-2	a04 4-1	M08 1-1		M22 1-1	J18 2-0	N30 5-3	S21 1-0	N16 1-1	a05 2-0	A10 3-4	A24 2-1	O19 1-0	S07 2-1	a19 0-1	M25 2-1
11 CRYSTAL P	D14 4-2	A17 3-2	N16 1-0	J25 1-2	N02 2-1	O19 2-1	M15 1-0	M01 3-1	S07 5-0	A31 3-3		N30 1-2	a19 3-2	A14 2-1	F22 2-0	a04 0-0	M19 4-2	A28 2-0	M26 1-1	a05 3-1	S21 1-2	O05 1-1
12 DERBY CO	S07 3-1	O26 1-0	M01 4-2	A17 1-1	a05 5-1	a19 5-0	J11 2-0	F01 2-0	N23 3-3	N09 2-1	M05 0-1		S18 1-0	M15 1-0	A28 2-2	D26 3-2	S21 1-0	D07 1-1	A31 2-0	D21 2-1	O12 1-0	a07 1-0
13 FULHAM	M08 1-1	D26 2-0	S28 1-1	a12 0-0	A24 0-2	A10 1-0	O26 0-0	D07 1-5	F01 0-2	F15 0-1	S13 1-0	a02 0-1		N23 4-3	A21 0-0	D21 0-3	M22 2-0	O12 1-3	M29 0-1	N09 2-2	F26 2-1	O09 2-2
14 HUDDERSFIELD T	N02 3-1	M29 0-0	a30 2-1	O05 2-1	M04 3-0	J18 4-1	S28 4-1	S14 3-0	M22 2-0	a12 0-0	a08 0-0	A24 2-0	a15 3-0		D14 0-3	O08 3-0	N16 0-2	A20 2-2	N30 2-1	A10 0-0	M08 1-1	O19 1-0
15 HULL C	a19 1-0	a15 1-2	A17 1-3	M01 2-2	S21 1-0	S07 1-1	N08 3-0	O26 3-3	J11 1-2	F01 5-2	D07 2-0	O09 1-0	a07 4-0	O12 3-0		A31 3-0	a05 2-0	D26 0-1	M14 0-0	N23 2-2	D20 1-1	S18 1-1
16 MIDDLESBROUGH	M04 0-0	S14 3-1	N30 2-0	F22 2-1	N16 0-0	D03 4-1	a12 2-3	M29 0-0	A24 1-0	S28 1-0	A20 4-0	O05 0-0	O19 2-0	A27 1-1	M22 5-3		J18 1-1	a08 0-0	J24 2-0	M08 1-0	A10 2-1	J28 3-1
17 MILLWALL	a04 0-1	D21 1-3	M28 2-2	S14 1-2	A26 3-1	S16 2-2	D26 1-0	O12 2-0	D07 1-1	M01 3-2	N23 0-2	a12 0-1	A31 2-0	F01 5-1	S28 2-3	N09 2-0		J11 3-1	A17 2-1	F15 0-0	O26 0-0	M14 1-0
18 NORWICH C	O19 1-1	M01 1-1	a23 3-1	N30 0-1	J18 2-0	M26 1-1	A31 2-2	A17 3-1	a19 2-1	M15 0-1	O09 0-1	a16 1-4	D14 2-0	a07 1-0	O05 1-2	A14 0-2	N02 0-3		N16 1-1	S21 0-1	a05 1-1	S07 2-0
19 OXFORD U	a05 1-0	J11 1-2	a04 2-1	A21 0-0	A10 1-1	S21 0-0	O12 2-2	N23 0-2	O09 0-1	D21 0-1	N09 0-2	M22 0-2	S07 1-0	F15 3-0	A24 1-1	O26 2-4	M08 1-0	F01 0-2		M05 3-1	D07 2-1	a19 1-0
20 PORTSMOUTH	N16 2-0	M15 0-0	A21 0-1	D14 1-0	F22 2-2	D28 1-1	S13 1-2	A31 1-3	a09 2-1	M29 4-1	S28 3-3	O19 0-1	J18 3-1	M01 1-2	F08 1-0	A17 3-0	N30 3-0	a12 5-2	O05 3-0		O09 1-1	N02 2-1
21 PRESTON N.E.	J18 1-0	A31 4-1	O05 1-1	a08 1-0	N30 1-4	N16 1-0	M29 3-0	M15 0-1	S30 2-2	S14 1-1	a12 0-0	D14 0-0	N25 0-0	A17 1-0	O19 1-0	M01 1-2	M03 0-1	S28 1-3	F22 2-1	A26 0-0		M17 2-2
22 SHEFFIELD U	A10 3-1	D07 2-0	a12 3-0	S28 2-1	M22 5-2	M08 2-1	F01 5-0	M11 2-2	N09 0-1	O26 2-0	D26 1-1	A20 2-0	A27 1-0	D21 0-0	a08 1-1	O12 1-3	A24 1-0	M29 1-0	S14 1-2	J11 2-0	N23 4-0	

Season 1968-69

DIVISION 3

	BARNSLEY	BARROW	BOURNEMOUTH	BRIGHTON & HA	BRISTOL R	CREWE A	GILLINGHAM	HARTLEPOOL	ORIENT	LUTON T	MANSFIELD T	NORTHAMPTON T	OLDHAM A	PLYMOUTH A	READING	ROTHERHAM U	SHREWSBURY T	SOUTHPORT	STOCKPORT CO	SWINDON T	TORQUAY U	TRANMERE R	WALSALL	WATFORD
1 BARNSLEY		A10 2-3	J11 1-0	S28 4-0	M04 4-2	N09 2-2	A24 0-1	D21 2-1	S14 2-2	O08 3-1	a08 2-0	a25 2-1	M08 0-1	N23 0-0	O26 1-0	M21 0-1	D26 1-0	S17 2-1	a29 2-0	F01 1-1	a12 1-0	M29 2-2	O12 0-0	a22 3-2
2 BARROW	M01 0-1		F01 0-2	A31 1-1	a21 3-0	O26 2-0	S16 2-1	J11 1-2	S28 3-1	A17 0-0	S14 3-0	M03 0-2	O07 2-1	N09 1-0	M17 0-0	a04 2-0	O12 2-1	M29 0-0	D26 3-3	F15 0-3	M15 2-0	a12 1-0	N23 1-1	D21 1-4
3 BOURNEMOUTH	N02 3-0	a28 1-0		O05 2-0	M15 0-0	A28 4-0	N30 2-0	M01 4-0	a25 0-1	F08 0-2	D14 2-1	M29 3-2	J18 3-1	A17 0-1	a04 1-1	D28 1-0	A31 2-0	O19 2-1	S14 1-0	S18 2-0	N06 3-0	J04 3-4	S28 1-0	a12 1-3
4 BRIGHTON & H.A.	a05 4-1	M22 4-1	D26 4-1		N09 3-1	J25 3-1	a19 0-2	M19 1-1	a04 2-0	S21 1-0	A10 1-2	N23 1-1	A24 6-0	M05 0-0	D20 2-0	S07 2-2	F01 3-0	M08 4-0	J11 1-1	O12 1-3	A28 1-1	a16 2-2	F15 3-0	O26 0-1
5 BRISTOL R	F18 4-2	N04 4-2	A24 3-2	J18 1-1		M21 1-0	O19 5-1	S06 2-1	F24 0-1	M31 0-0	M25 6-2	a04 2-1	O05 1-0	a19 1-1	a05 1-3	D13 1-1	A27 1-2	N30 2-1	a15 2-0	S21 2-1	M11 1-1	N02 0-2	M08 0-1	A10 1-1
6 CREWE A	J18 1-4	D28 1-1	O07 0-2	N06 1-0	A31 6-1		a30 4-2	A17 1-0	J04 2-0	J29 2-0	O18 2-1	S14 2-2	M12 3-0	M01 2-1	S18 1-2	N30 1-0	M14 0-1	a21 3-3	M29 1-1	a04 1-2	D14 2-1	O05 2-3	a11 0-1	S28 2-3
7 GILLINGHAM	M14 1-1	a07 2-0	a22 0-0	S14 5-0	D21 0-2	M26 1-0		F01 2-2	A17 2-2	A31 1-3	S28 1-1	J25 2-0	a16 2-0	O26 1-0	D26 2-2	O09 2-0	N23 4-1	a12 0-0	O12 0-0	M05 2-0	M29 0-0	M01 1-1	N09 4-0	J11 0-5
8 HARTLEPOOL	O18 2-1	N01 1-4	A10 1-1	F22 2-5	M28 1-0	m05 0-0	M10 1-1		a21 0-0	D14 1-0	O04 1-1	a11 3-0	F24 0-2	O14 1-1	M22 2-0	J18 0-3	S13 0-0	N06 2-2	S28 0-0	A24 0-0	J04 2-2	N29 2-4	a04 1-1	S16 2-1
9 ORIENT	a19 1-1	a05 1-2	M17 1-0	O21 3-2	N23 2-1	M03 2-0	M08 1-1	O26 0-1		S07 0-0	A24 1-0	D09 0-0	S21 3-0	F15 1-2	J25 4-2	A10 3-3	a28 4-0	M22 0-2	M26 2-0	D26 1-0	a09 0-1	S09 0-0	F01 0-0	N09 1-1
10 LUTON T	A28 5-1	M26 5-1	N23 1-1	a12 3-0	M19 3-0	F26 2-0	M22 1-1	O12 3-0	M29 2-1		S18 4-2	O26 2-1	A10 4-0	D21 2-0	F01 2-1	A24 3-1	M05 2-1	a08 0-0	a25 4-1	N09 2-0	S28 1-0	S14 3-1	J25 1-0	a30 2-1
11 MANSFIELD T	a14 0-0	a19 4-2	O12 3-1	M01 3-2	O26 0-0	D21 2-1	a05 2-0	D26 2-0	M15 0-2	a07 1-0		N09 0-2	S07 4-0	a28 1-0	J11 1-1	S21 0-1	m09 1-2	A26 3-1	F01 0-0	N23 2-0	A17 2-1	A31 1-1	a25 2-1	m05 3-0
12 NORTHAMPTON T	N30 3-1	J28 4-0	S07 1-3	F25 1-1	S17 2-2	a19 0-1	N05 0-1	S21 0-0	D14 4-1	D28 0-2	J18 0-0		F22 1-1	a05 1-1	M08 4-2	O05 1-0	a08 3-4	M11 1-0	A27 1-1	N26 2-6	N02 1-1	O19 2-1	M22 3-1	S10 2-0
13 OLDHAM A	A17 1-1	A27 0-1	M25 2-0	M15 2-0	D26 2-1	F01 3-0	a04 1-0	N23 1-2	a12 3-1	M01 0-1	M28 2-2	a29 1-1		J11 0-2	F18 1-1	S17 0-0	J25 2-2	S14 0-1	M04 5-2	O26 2-3	A31 3-1	S28 1-2	D20 1-0	O12 0-3
14 PLYMOUTH A	S23 0-0	J18 4-1	M08 1-1	J04 1-1	S14 3-1	A10 2-2	D28 1-1	O09 3-0	N30 2-1	O19 2-0	N06 1-0	S28 0-1	N02 1-1		A24 3-1	M12 1-2	M29 1-1	D14 0-4	a12 2-2	M22 2-1	O05 1-2	F22 1-0	S18 1-0	a08 1-2
15 READING	J29 3-2	a23 0-1	a16 0-1	O18 1-0	S27 2-1	a07 3-1	O04 3-2	A30 7-0	N06 0-1	M12 1-1	N02 2-1	A16 1-0	N30 4-1	M14 1-2		M24 1-0	a11 2-4	J18 1-0	F28 4-2	O09 0-1	M31 1-1	D14 2-0	M28 2-2	S13 0-1
16 ROTHERHAM U	A31 0-0	a15 3-1	O26 1-1	M29 1-1	O12 3-2	a25 3-0	A27 1-0	N09 1-1	M01 3-1	M15 2-2	a12 3-0	J21 0-1	a08 1-2	F01 0-1	M04 4-1		D21 1-0	S28 3-1	J25 4-1	m02 1-1	S14 1-0	A17 4-1	J11 0-1	N23 0-2
17 SHREWSBURY T	O05 0-0	D14 1-0	M22 1-0	M12 1-2	O09 1-0	A24 1-1	m05 1-1	a19 1-1	N02 1-0	J08 3-1	N30 1-1	a16 1-0	N05 0-1	S07 1-0	S21 3-3	O19 1-0		m02 5-1	a07 2-1	a05 1-1	a23 1-0	J18 0-1	A10 0-1	M08 1-1
18 SOUTHPORT	a07 1-0	S06 1-0	D20 2-1	A17 2-3	a23 3-0	N22 4-0	S20 4-2	J24 3-0	A30 2-2	a14 1-1	O07 3-2	M26 2-0	a18 3-1	O11 2-0	N08 1-1	a05 0-0	M17 5-0		O25 5-0	J11 1-1	m06 2-2	M14 2-2	D26 2-1	M03 1-1
19 STOCKPORT CO	M31 1-1	O04 4-1	a18 0-1	N01 3-1	a08 0-1	S06 2-1	D13 5-0	a05 1-0	O18 5-2	N29 2-0	M10 1-1	O07 1-0	J06 0-0	S20 2-3	A10 2-2	N04 3-1	S16 4-3	D28 3-0		M08 2-1	J17 1-2	a21 1-0	A23 2-2	M21 4-2
20 SWINDON T	M25 2-0	m05 2-0	a08 3-0	D14 1-0	a12 2-2	a15 1-0	F25 1-0	F04 1-1	O05 1-0	J18 0-0	a22 1-0	M01 1-0	J28 5-1	A31 3-0	A27 0-0	F22 1-0	S28 3-0	N02 5-1	A17 1-0		O19 2-1	F18 1-0	S14 1-0	M29 0-1
21 TORQUAY U	S21 3-1	A24 3-1	J25 0-0	O09 1-1	F01 0-1	O12 2-0	S07 2-0	M03 3-0	a16 0-0	a04 1-1	a30 0-1	J11 2-0	M22 3-1	F05 0-1	N23 1-0	a19 1-0	O26 2-0	A10 3-0	N09 0-1	D21 0-1		a07 2-5	S30 4-2	F15 2-1
22 TRANMERE R	S06 3-1	S20 0-3	M03 2-1	O14 0-2	J10 1-2	D26 0-1	A10 2-0	a24 1-0	O07 3-0	a18 0-2	M21 2-1	D20 2-1	a05 6-2	M17 2-2	O11 2-1	M07 0-0	N08 3-1	A23 1-0	N22 1-1	J24 3-5	S16 0-1		O25 2-1	J31 0-3
23 WALSALL	D14 3-0	F25 1-1	a05 0-0	N30 4-0	A17 2-2	S20 1-1	J28 2-1	a15 1-2	M11 2-1	N05 2-0	a01 3-1	A31 0-1	O19 2-1	a07 1-1	S07 2-2	N02 0-0	M01 2-0	O05 3-0	M15 2-0	a19 0-2	F22 0-1	M25 1-1		O08 0-0
24 WATFORD	N04 1-2	O19 4-0	S21 1-0	D28 1-0	M01 1-0	a05 4-0	N02 2-1	a07 0-0	J18 0-0	O05 1-0	F22 2-1	M14 3-0	D14 2-0	a15 1-0	a19 1-0	F08 5-1	A17 2-0	a01 1-0	A31 0-1	S07 0-0	N30 0-0	M11 3-1	A27 0-0	

DIVISION 4

	ALDERSHO	BRADFORD	BRADFORD C	BRENTFORD	CHESTER	CHESTERFIELD	COLCHESTER U	DARLINGTON	DONCASTER R	EXETER C	GRIMSBY T	HALIFAX T	LINCOLN C	NEWPORT CO	NOTTS CO	PETERBOROUGH U	PORT VALE	ROCHDALE	SCUNTHORPE U	SOUTHEND U	SWANSEA T	WORKINGTON	WREXHAM	YORK C
1 ALDERSHOT		O09 4-1	O12 2-1	J11 1-2	D21 4-0	F15 2-0	F01 1-2	S20 0-0	N23 1-2	D26 2-0	a19 3-1	A24 0-2	a04 0-1	J04 4-0	M22 0-0	M19 1-4	M05 3-0	N09 0-0	O26 3-2	S18 2-1	M08 5-2	S07 0-1	A10 2-1	J25 2-0
2 BRADFORD	A26 0-1		J25 0-0	N23 0-2	O12 1-1	O26 0-1	N09 2-1	a05 1-3	D21 2-1	S09 2-1	S07 1-1	m12 0-0	S16 1-1	S21 1-5	A24 1-1	a02 0-2	m05 0-1	J11 1-4	F01 2-2	a08 0-3	A10 1-1	a19 1-0	M08 1-2	M26 1-0
3 BRADFORD C	D14 1-1	N06 1-0		S28 3-0	A17 2-0	A31 2-1	S14 1-1	a25 0-0	M01 1-1	a07 1-0	M12 1-1	J18 1-1	O19 2-0	N30 1-1	D07 1-1	a29 2-1	a16 2-2	a12 1-1	M29 3-0	m02 3-2	F12 1-0	D28 0-1	O05 1-3	O09 5-0
4 BRENTFORD	N02 2-4	a21 3-0	m05 2-1		a30 2-1	S07 1-0	A10 4-0	N04 0-1	a14 1-0	M22 0-1	F22 4-2	N30 1-1	J18 2-2	O05 1-1	M26 0-0	a19 2-0	A24 3-1	A26 1-1	M08 2-1	M10 1-1	D14 2-1	J04 0-3	O19 1-1	S21 5-1
5 CHESTER	O19 3-1	D14 4-1	M08 0-0	S18 2-2		S21 2-0	A24 5-1	J04 1-2	S03 2-1	a19 0-1	M26 0-1	M12 2-2	a23 2-0	F22 4-0	J18 3-1	a05 2-3	S06 2-0	a08 2-1	M22 0-2	N02 1-2	O05 3-0	N30 0-2	N06 1-1	A10 2-0
6 CHESTERFIELD	N30 1-2	D28 1-1	M22 0-1	M29 1-2	a12 2-0		S16 0-2	N02 2-2	S28 0-1	M08 2-0	D14 0-0	N04 2-0	M17 1-1	a21 2-1	O05 0-2	A28 2-0	A10 3-1	S14 1-1	a08 1-2	a25 0-0	J18 2-0	O19 0-1	M10 0-1	A24 1-1
7 COLCHESTER U	M10 2-0	J18 3-0	a18 1-1	F28 2-1	M14 1-1	a04 1-0		O19 0-0	A31 1-2	a05 1-0	O04 2-1	a21 0-0	M24 1-1	D14 2-1	F22 1-1	a14 2-2	S20 1-0	A17 0-0	A26 0-4	N29 4-0	a25 0-1	N04 3-0	N02 2-1	S07 1-0
8 DARLINGTON	a12 1-0	S28 2-0	m09 1-3	J25 3-1	M03 2-2	J11 1-3	a28 1-1		D26 0-0	O26 1-2	A17 0-0	M29 0-1	A31 5-0	O07 1-0	S14 3-2	N09 3-3	F01 1-0	O12 0-0	N23 0-1	m05 2-3	a08 3-0	M01 6-2	S16 1-0	a21 3-2
9 DONCASTER R	F25 7-0	O18 4-1	A10 1-1	a08 5-0	O08 4-3	a05 0-0	M22 1-0	O04 0-1		S07 3-1	N29 2-1	J14 0-0	N02 0-2	F04 2-2	M11 0-0	S20 1-0	a19 2-0	S17 2-0	A23 4-3	J18 2-0	N06 0-0	a22 0-0	D14 0-0	M07 2-1
10 EXETER C	O05 0-0	F24 4-2	S18 2-3	A31 2-2	S14 2-2	A17 3-0	S28 1-1	M24 2-0	M29 0-0		N02 2-2	a24 2-1	N06 3-0	M12 2-0	O19 0-0	M01 0-1	O08 3-1	M15 2-2	a12 3-1	D14 1-2	N30 0-1	M31 1-0	M18 5-3	a09 5-0
11 GRIMSBY T	S14 0-2	M29 2-0	F01 1-5	m03 0-2	O26 0-0	O12 1-2	D26 2-4	M08 1-1	m05 1-3	J11 1-2		a04 0-1	a12 1-1	A10 3-0	S17 2-0	D21 2-2	N23 1-1	D07 2-0	J25 0-1	S28 0-0	A24 1-2	A27 0-1	M22 1-1	N09 3-0
12 HALIFAX T	m03 1-0	A31 3-0	N09 1-1	a28 2-0	F01 0-0	M25 0-0	M04 2-1	S07 0-4	O26 4-1	N23 2-1	a15 0-0		A17 0-1	a19 3-0	O08 3-1	O12 2-1	D21 2-1	m08 1-0	D26 2-0	M01 1-1	a05 2-1	a07 3-0	S21 2-0	J11 0-4
13 LINCOLN C	a16 2-1	a07 3-2	D21 2-0	N09 1-0	N23 2-0	O16 2-2	O26 0-3	M22 2-1	J11 1-1	J25 3-2	S21 3-0	M08 0-0		A24 1-0	A10 5-0	M05 1-1	D26 0-1	F01 0-0	F15 1-2	A28 2-1	S07 0-1	a05 4-1	a19 0-0	O12 3-0
14 NEWPORT CO	S28 3-4	a12 1-0	F15 1-3	D26 1-1	M17 2-5	N23 1-2	O12 1-0	A26 0-0	M03 0-0	F01 2-1	F28 2-0	S14 2-0	M15 2-1		M29 0-0	J11 4-2	N08 0-0	F10 1-1	F24 1-1	A31 4-1	S16 2-1	A17 0-0	a08 0-2	O26 1-1
15 NOTTS CO	A31 0-2	M15 5-0	J11 0-2	O26 0-2	N09 3-2	D26 2-1	m02 2-0	a19 0-0	F01 1-1	D21 3-1	a07 2-1	A28 1-2	M01 0-0	S07 3-1		J25 2-1	O12 0-0	a28 1-1	M05 1-0	A17 2-2	S21 0-3	a16 0-0	a05 5-0	N23 0-0
16 PETERBOROUGH U	a21 2-0	N30 6-1	A24 2-2	S14 2-1	S28 1-2	O07 3-0	a08 0-1	J29 1-1	a12 0-1	A10 1-1	O19 1-1	F05 0-0	J13 0-0	N02 1-1	N04 1-0		M08 0-1	M29 0-1	S16 3-2	O05 1-0	M10 2-2	F24 1-1	J04 2-3	M22 2-1
17 PORT VALE	M24 0-0	a25 1-1	a08 1-1	M15 4-1	M29 2-1	M01 0-1	a12 0-0	M10 1-0	S14 0-2	S30 1-0	a21 1-0	O19 1-1	O05 1-1	J18 5-0	D14 0-2	A17 1-0		A31 1-1	S28 4-1	N04 1-1	D28 1-0	N02 3-1	N30 1-0	S16 3-0
18 ROCHDALE	J18 3-0	N02 6-0	S21 6-0	O07 0-0	a14 4-1	a19 0-0	M08 4-0	F24 2-0	a07 0-0	A24 1-1	J04 6-1	a30 1-0	M10 2-1	N04 0-1	N30 0-0	S07 1-1	M22 1-0		A10 3-2	m10 3-0	O19 0-1	O05 0-0	a23 2-1	a05 2-1
19 SCUNTHORPE U	a29 4-1	D06 1-0	S06 1-0	A17 1-1	A30 2-2	a15 0-1	O08 2-3	m02 0-0	M14 0-2	S21 2-1	N06 1-2	O04 0-1	N30 0-0	O18 1-0	J04 2-1	a07 1-2	a05 0-1	M01 0-0		m12 4-1	N01 3-1	J28 0-1	M25 1-0	a18 2-1
20 SOUTHEND U	a07 4-2	a14 5-0	N22 2-0	J31 4-0	J10 1-2	M03 2-2	F14 3-1	A23 1-1	N09 2-0	O11 6-1	a05 0-1	A10 2-1	O07 3-0	a28 1-0	M07 4-0	D26 2-1	F24 1-1	O26 1-3	M17 0-3		a18 4-0	S20 1-0	S06 1-0	D20 1-2
21 SWANSEA T	A17 2-2	M01 3-0	M04 0-2	O12 2-3	D26 0-5	N09 0-0	N23 2-0	a15 1-1	J25 0-1	m05 2-0	M15 1-1	S28 1-0	M29 5-0	a07 3-2	a12 3-0	F01 0-0	O26 1-0	D21 3-0	J11 2-0	S14 2-2		A31 0-0	A27 0-0	M18 2-1
22 WORKINGTON	M28 1-0	S14 3-1	O26 0-0	M05 1-0	F15 0-0	D21 1-1	J24 0-1	A10 1-2	M19 1-1	N09 3-0	O09 2-0	S18 1-1	S28 1-1	m08 3-2	a08 1-1	N23 1-0	J11 0-0	D26 1-2	O12 1-1	a12 0-0	M22 0-3		A24 0-0	a30 2-0
23 WREXHAM	M01 2-0	A17 3-0	M31 1-1	D21 2-0	J25 1-1	F01 1-1	J11 0-3	a04 2-1	O12 3-1	a21 2-2	A31 2-0	a12 2-2	S14 0-1	a14 4-0	S28 3-2	O26 0-0	a28 2-0	N23 3-2	N09 0-1	M28 3-3	O07 2-0	m05 1-0		a16 2-1
24 YORK C	N04 2-1	O05 4-2	A26 1-1	a12 2-1	a28 4-2	M15 3-1	M29 2-0	N30 1-1	A17 1-1	O28 0-2	J18 2-5	m05 0-0	D14 1-1	D28 0-0	a23 2-0	A31 2-1	a04 3-1	S28 0-0	S14 2-1	O19 1-1	m02 0-2	M10 2-1	F24 1-0	

LEAGUE TABLES

DIVISION 1

	P	W	D	L	F	A	W	D	L	F	A	Pts
Leeds U	42	18	3	0	41	9	9	10	2	25	17	67
Liverpool	42	16	4	1	36	10	9	7	5	27	14	61
Everton	42	14	5	2	43	10	7	10	4	34	26	57
Arsenal	42	12	6	3	31	12	10	6	5	25	15	56
Chelsea	42	11	7	3	40	24	9	3	9	33	29	50
Tottenham H	42	10	8	3	39	22	4	9	8	22	29	45
Southampton	42	13	5	3	41	21	3	8	10	16	27	45
West Ham U	42	10	8	3	47	22	3	10	8	19	28	44
Newcastle U	42	12	7	2	40	20	3	7	11	21	35	44
W.B.A.	42	11	7	3	43	26	5	4	12	21	41	43
Manchester U	42	13	5	3	38	18	2	7	12	19	35	42
Ipswich T	42	10	4	7	32	26	5	7	9	27	34	41
Manchester C	42	13	6	2	49	20	2	4	15	15	35	40
Burnley	42	11	6	4	36	25	4	3	14	19	57	39
Sheffield W	42	7	9	5	27	26	3	7	11	14	28	36
Wolverh'pton W	42	7	10	4	26	22	3	5	13	15	36	35
Sunderland	42	10	6	5	28	18	1	6	14	15	49	34
Nottingham F	42	6	6	9	17	22	4	7	10	28	35	33
Stoke C	42	9	7	5	24	24	0	8	13	16	39	33
Coventry C	42	8	6	7	32	22	2	5	14	14	42	31
Leicester C	42	8	8	5	27	24	1	4	16	12	44	30
Q.P.R.	42	4	7	10	20	33	0	3	18	19	62	18

DIVISION 2

	P	W	D	L	F	A	W	D	L	F	A	Pts
Derby Co	42	16	4	1	43	16	10	7	4	22	16	63
Crystal Palace	42	14	4	3	45	24	8	8	5	25	23	56
Charlton A	42	11	8	2	39	21	7	6	8	22	31	50
Middlesbrough	42	13	7	1	36	13	6	4	11	22	36	49
Cardiff C	42	13	3	5	38	19	7	4	10	29	35	47
Huddersfield T	42	13	6	2	37	14	4	6	11	16	32	46
Birmingham C	42	13	3	5	52	24	5	5	11	21	35	44
Blackpool	42	9	8	4	33	20	5	7	9	18	21	43
Sheffield U	42	14	4	3	41	15	2	7	12	20	35	43
Millwall	42	10	5	6	33	23	7	4	10	24	26	43
Hull C	42	10	7	4	38	20	3	9	9	21	32	42
Carlisle U	42	10	5	6	25	17	6	5	10	21	32	42
Norwich C	42	7	6	8	24	25	8	4	9	29	31	40
Preston N.E.	42	8	8	5	23	19	4	7	10	15	25	39
Portsmouth	42	11	5	5	39	22	1	9	11	19	36	38
Bristol C	42	9	9	3	30	15	2	7	12	16	38	38
Bolton W	42	8	7	6	29	26	4	7	10	26	41	38
Aston Villa	42	10	8	3	22	11	2	6	13	15	37	38
Blackburn R	42	9	6	6	30	24	4	5	12	22	39	37
Oxford U	42	8	5	8	21	23	4	4	13	13	32	33
Bury	42	8	4	9	35	33	3	4	14	16	47	30
Fulham	42	6	7	8	20	28	1	4	16	20	53	25

DIVISION 3

	P	W	D	L	F	A	W	D	L	F	A	Pts
Watford	46	16	5	2	35	7	11	5	7	39	27	64
Swindon T	46	18	4	1	38	7	9	6	8	33	28	64
Luton T	46	20	3	0	57	14	5	8	10	17	24	61
Bournemouth	46	16	2	5	41	17	5	7	11	19	28	51
Plymouth A	46	10	8	5	34	25	7	7	9	19	24	49
Torquay U	46	13	4	6	35	18	5	8	10	19	28	48
Tranmere R	46	12	3	8	36	31	7	7	9	34	37	48
Southport	46	14	8	1	52	20	3	5	15	19	44	47
Stockport Co	46	14	5	4	49	25	2	9	12	18	43	46
Barnsley	46	13	6	4	37	21	3	8	12	21	42	46
Rotherham U	46	12	6	5	40	21	4	7	12	16	29	45
Brighton & H.A.	46	12	7	4	49	21	4	6	13	23	44	45
Walsall	46	10	9	4	34	18	4	7	12	16	31	44
Reading	46	13	3	7	41	25	2	10	11	26	41	43
Mansfield T	46	14	5	4	37	18	2	6	15	21	44	43
Bristol R	46	12	6	5	41	27	4	5	14	22	44	43
Shrewsbury T	46	11	8	4	28	17	5	3	15	23	50	43
Leyton O	46	10	8	5	31	19	4	6	13	20	39	42
Barrow	46	11	6	6	30	23	6	2	15	26	52	42
Gillingham	46	10	10	3	35	20	3	5	15	19	43	41
Northampton T	46	9	8	6	37	30	5	4	14	17	31	40
Hartlepool U	46	6	12	5	25	29	4	7	12	15	41	39
Crewe A	46	11	4	8	40	31	2	5	16	12	45	35
Oldham A	46	9	6	8	33	27	4	3	16	17	56	35

DIVISION 4

	P	W	D	L	F	A	W	D	L	F	A	Pts
Doncaster R	46	13	8	2	42	16	8	9	6	23	22	59
Halifax T	46	15	5	3	36	18	5	12	6	17	19	57
Rochdale	46	14	7	2	47	11	4	13	6	21	24	56
Bradford C	46	11	10	2	36	18	7	10	6	29	28	56
Darlington	46	11	6	6	40	26	6	12	5	22	19	52
Colchester U	46	12	8	3	31	17	8	4	11	26	36	52
Southend U	46	15	3	5	51	21	4	10	9	27	40	51
Lincoln C	46	13	6	4	38	19	4	11	8	16	33	51
Wrexham	46	13	7	3	41	22	5	7	11	20	30	50
Swansea T	46	11	8	4	35	20	8	3	12	23	34	49
Brentford	46	12	7	4	40	24	6	5	12	24	41	48
Workington	46	8	11	4	24	17	7	6	10	16	26	47
Port Vale	46	12	8	3	33	15	4	6	13	13	31	46
Chester C	46	12	4	7	43	24	4	9	10	33	42	45
Aldershot	46	13	3	7	42	23	6	4	13	24	43	45
Scunthorpe U	46	10	5	8	28	22	8	3	12	33	38	44
Exeter C	46	11	8	4	45	24	5	3	15	21	41	43
Peterborough U	46	8	9	6	32	23	5	7	11	28	34	42
Notts Co	46	10	8	5	33	22	2	10	11	15	35	42
Chesterfield	46	7	7	9	24	22	6	8	9	19	28	41
York C	46	12	8	3	36	25	2	3	18	17	50	39
Newport Co	46	9	9	5	31	26	2	5	16	18	48	36
Grimsby T	46	5	7	11	25	31	4	8	11	22	38	33
Bradford P.A.	46	5	8	10	19	34	0	2	21	13	72	20

FOOTBALL LEAGUE RECORDS

Top scorers: Div 1, J.Astle (West Bromwich Albion) 25 goals; Div 2, J.Hickton (Middlesbrough) 24 goals; Div 3, G.Jones (Bury) 26 goals; Div 4, A.Kinsey (Wrexham) 27 goals.

Joe Royle, whose 23 goals were a vital factor in Everton's League Championship win of 1969-70.

DIVISION 1

	ARSENAL	BURNLEY	CHELSEA	COVENTRY C	CRYSTAL P	DERBY CO	EVERTON	IPSWICH T	LEEDS U	LIVERPOOL	MANCHESTER C	MANCHESTER U	NEWCASTLE U	NOTTINGHAM F	SHEFFIELD W	SOUTHAMPTON	STOKE C	SUNDERLAND	TOTTENHAM H	W.B.A.	WEST HAM U	WOLVERHAMPTON W
1 ARSENAL		D13 3-2	J17 0-3	O04 0-1	M30 2-0	N08 4-0	A09 0-1	O25 0-0	A19 1-1	M14 2-1	N22 1-1	S20 2-2	D27 0-0	A23 2-1	S06 0-0	D06 2-2	F07 0-0	F28 3-1	S16 2-3	O07 1-1	a04 2-1	M28 2-2
2 BURNLEY	S13 0-1		a15 3-1	N15 0-0	O11 4-2	F14 1-1	M07 1-2	S27 0-1	A26 1-1	D26 1-5	A30 1-1	N29 1-1	N01 0-1	F21 5-0	O18 4-2	M24 1-1	M27 1-1	A16 3-0	A19 0-2	M21 2-1	J31 3-2	J10 1-3
3 CHELSEA	S27 3-0	S17 2-0		N01 1-0	A30 1-1	O11 2-2	N15 1-1	A16 1-0	J10 2-5	a18 2-1	D20 3-1	M21 2-1	F25 0-0	M07 1-1	M25 3-1	D26 3-1	M17 1-0	J31 3-1	a04 1-0	O18 2-0	A20 0-0	S13 2-2
4 COVENTRY C	J31 2-0	M28 1-1	F28 0-3		S13 2-2	A16 1-1	O25 0-1	D26 3-1	S27 1-2	M03 2-3	J10 3-0	N08 1-2	N22 1-0	S16 3-2	M14 1-1	M31 4-0	a04 0-3	M24 1-1	D06 3-2	A12 3-1	O11 2-2	A30 1-0
5 CRYSTAL P	N01 1-5	F11 1-2	D27 1-5	D13 0-3		D06 0-1	O08 0-0	M28 1-1	O18 1-1	A27 1-3	a06 1-0	A09 2-2	O04 0-3	J17 1-1	F21 0-2	M14 2-0	S06 3-1	A13 2-0	A23 0-2	S20 1-3	M24 0-0	N22 2-1
6 DERBY CO	F21 3-2	A09 0-0	F11 2-2	O08 1-3	M21 3-1		S06 2-1	A20 3-1	M30 4-1	N01 4-0	O18 0-1	O04 2-0	D13 2-0	N29 0-2	J17 1-0	S10 3-0	A23 0-0	N15 3-0	S20 5-0	D27 2-0	M07 3-0	a04 2-0
7 EVERTON	F14 2-2	N22 2-1	M28 5-2	F21 0-0	A16 2-1	D20 1-0		J10 3-0	A30 3-2	D06 0-3	D23 1-0	A19 3-0	J24 0-0	N01 1-0	A26 2-1	S27 4-2	O18 6-2	O11 3-1	M14 3-2	a01 2-0	S13 2-0	J31 1-0
8 IPSWICH T	M31 2-1	J17 0-1	N18 1-4	A23 0-1	N15 2-0	A12 0-1	S20 0-3		a21 3-2	O18 2-2	N01 1-1	F10 0-1	S06 2-0	A09 0-0	O04 1-0	a04 2-0	M07 1-1	M21 2-0	D27 2-0	D13 0-1	N29 1-0	S16 1-1
9 LEEDS U	A13 0-0	a04 2-1	S20 2-0	J17 3-1	F28 2-0	O25 2-0	D27 2-1	N08 4-0		N22 1-1	a18 1-3	S06 2-2	A23 1-1	O29 6-1	D13 2-0	M28 1-3	O04 2-1	N19 2-0	A09 3-1	F10 5-1	D17 4-1	D06 3-1
10 LIVERPOOL	N29 0-1	A23 3-3	A09 4-1	S06 2-1	a03 3-0	F28 0-2	M21 0-2	M24 2-0	M07 0-0		A12 3-2	D13 1-4	F16 0-0	O04 1-1	M16 3-0	O25 4-1	S20 3-1	S09 2-0	O07 0-0	J17 1-1	N15 2-0	N08 0-0
11 MANCHESTER C	F18 1-1	J06 1-1	S06 0-0	S20 3-1	M11 0-1	M27 0-1	A23 1-1	F28 1-0	N29 1-2	A20 0-2		N15 4-0	O08 2-1	F07 1-1	A09 4-1	N08 1-0	J17 0-1	a04 0-1	D13 1-1	O04 2-1	M21 1-5	O25 1-0
12 MANCHESTER U	J10 2-1	M17 3-3	D06 0-2	M30 1-1	F14 1-1	J31 1-0	A13 0-2	O11 2-1	J26 2-2	S13 1-0	M28 1-2		A27 0-0	O18 1-1	a15 2-2	A16 1-4	N01 1-1	A30 3-1	N22 3-1	a08 7-0	S27 5-2	D26 0-0
13 NEWCASTLE U	A30 3-1	M30 0-1	O25 0-1	a14 4-0	J31 0-0	S13 0-1	S17 1-2	D20 4-0	D26 2-1	O11 1-0	A16 1-0	a04 5-1		N15 3-1	A13 3-1	F11 2-1	M21 3-1	N08 3-0	F28 1-2	F06 1-0	M02 4-1	S27 1-1
14 NOTTINGHAM F	D26 1-1	O25 1-1	N22 1-1	a07 1-4	S27 0-0	M14 1-3	F28 1-1	a10 1-0	A16 1-4	J31 1-0	O11 2-2	M31 1-2	M28 2-2		D06 2-1	S13 2-1	A12 0-0	J24 2-1	N08 2-2	A26 1-0	A30 1-0	D20 4-2
15 SHEFFIELD W	D20 1-1	F28 2-0	N08 1-3	J28 0-1	O25 0-0	S27 1-0	a04 0-1	J31 2-2	S13 1-2	A30 1-1	a22 1-2	S17 1-3	A20 1-0	M21 2-1		O11 1-1	N15 0-2	D26 2-0	M30 0-1	M10 2-0	J10 2-3	A16 2-3
16 SOUTHAMPTON	M21 0-2	S06 1-1	A23 2-2	O18 0-0	N29 1-1	a15 1-1	J17 2-1	A27 4-2	N15 1-1	M11 0-1	a08 0-0	O08 0-3	S20 1-1	D13 1-2	F07 4-0		D27 0-0	M07 1-1	O04 2-2	A09 0-2	N01 1-1	A20 2-3
17 STOKE C	O11 0-0	N08 2-1	a13 1-2	A27 2-0	D20 1-0	D26 1-0	M30 0-1	N22 3-3	J31 1-1	J10 0-2	S27 2-0	F28 2-2	D06 0-1	A20 1-1	M28 2-1	A30 2-1		S13 4-2	O25 1-1	a15 3-2	A16 2-1	F14 1-1
18 SUNDERLAND	O18 1-1	O08 0-1	O04 0-0	A09 0-0	A20 0-0	M28 1-1	a08 0-0	D06 2-1	N01 0-0	a15 0-1	A27 0-4	D27 1-1	M27 1-1	S20 2-1	A23 1-2	N22 2-2	D13 0-3		J17 2-1	S06 2-2	F21 0-1	M14 2-1
19 TOTTENHAM H	m02 1-0	A13 4-0	A27 1-1	M21 1-2	D26 2-0	J10 2-1	M11 0-1	A30 3-2	F14 1-1	A16 0-2	S13 0-3	a13 2-1	O18 2-1	M27 4-1	N01 1-0	J31 0-1	F21 1-0	S27 0-1		N15 2-0	D20 0-2	O11 0-1
20 W.B.A.	A16 0-1	D06 0-1	M30 3-1	A20 0-1	J10 3-2	A30 0-2	N08 2-0	S13 2-2	O11 1-1	S27 2-2	J31 3-0	O25 2-1	M14 2-2	a04 4-0	N22 3-0	F20 1-0	S17 1-3	J27 3-1	M28 1-1		D26 3-1	F28 3-3
21 WEST HAM U	A25 1-1	O04 3-1	A11 2-0	F11 1-2	N08 2-1	N22 3-0	D13 0-1	M14 0-0	a02 2-2	M28 1-0	D06 0-4	J17 0-0	A09 1-0	D27 1-1	S20 3-0	F28 0-0	O06 3-3	O25 1-1	S06 0-1	A23 1-3		M31 3-0
22 WOLVERHAMPTON W	N15 2-0	S20 1-1	D13 3-0	a10 0-1	M18 1-1	A27 1-1	O04 2-3	J24 2-0	M21 1-2	M30 0-1	F21 1-3	A23 0-0	J17 1-1	S06 3-3	O08 2-2	A13 2-1	A09 3-1	N29 1-0	F07 2-2	N01 1-0	O18 1-0	

The much-travelled Frank Worthington had a particularly happy time at Huddersfield Town, where he scored 18 goals when Town won the Division Two title in 1969-70.

DIVISION 2

	ASTON VILLA	BIRMINGHAM C	BLACKBURN R	BLACKPOOL	BOLTON W	BRISTOL C	CARDIFF C	CARLISLE U	CHARLTON A	HUDDERSFIELD T	HULL C	LEICESTER C	MIDDLESBROUGH	MILLWALL	NORWICH C	OXFORD U	PORTSMOUTH	PRESTON N.E.	Q.P.R.	SHEFFIELD U	SWINDON T	WATFORD
1 ASTON VILLA		O18 0-0	M21 1-1	N15 0-0	N19 3-0	F21 0-2	F07 1-1	N12 1-0	F25 1-0	O08 4-1	S20 3-2	A27 0-1	a08 2-0	S06 2-2	A09 0-1	M31 0-0	J17 3-5	O04 0-0	N01 1-1	a13 1-0	A23 0-2	D13 0-2
2 BIRMINGHAM C	M30 0-2		O11 3-0	D26 2-3	F24 2-0	J31 2-2	O25 1-1	S27 1-1	J10 3-0	D06 2-2	a04 2-4	F14 0-1	M14 0-0	N22 2-0	S16 3-1	A16 1-3	A19 1-1	M28 1-0	A30 3-0	S13 2-1	N08 2-0	F28 0-0
3 BLACKBURN R	D06 2-0	M04 1-1		N12 2-1	N08 3-1	N22 3-3	O08 1-0	M28 1-0	a08 3-0	a04 0-2	A23 2-1	O25 3-1	S06 4-0	S20 4-0	O04 3-1	M14 2-0	D27 0-3	D13 4-2	S17 0-1	F28 1-2	A09 2-0	J17 1-0
4 BLACKPOOL	M28 2-1	A23 2-0	A18 0-0		O25 1-1	M14 1-0	O04 3-2	D06 1-1	F28 2-0	D13 2-0	M18 0-1	N08 1-1	J17 1-1	F07 1-1	O06 0-0	N22 1-0	A09 2-1	S15 0-0	a04 1-1	M30 1-0	S06 3-2	S20 0-3
5 BOLTON W	S17 2-1	S06 2-0	M30 1-0	F21 0-2		N01 3-1	M18 0-1	a04 0-0	M21 1-1	J17 1-1	D13 2-1	N12 2-3	F11 2-1	A09 4-1	a09 0-0	O18 1-1	S20 0-1	A23 2-0	N29 6-4	N15 0-0	O04 0-1	O08 2-3
6 BRISTOL C	N08 1-0	O04 2-0	M07 4-0	N29 2-1	M27 2-2		A23 0-2	O25 0-0	S23 6-0	D27 1-2	O07 3-1	F28 0-0	D13 0-0	J17 1-1	S20 4-0	N11 2-0	F07 3-0	S06 0-0	N15 2-0	a04 0-1	M21 3-3	A09 1-0
7 CARDIFF C	O11 4-0	F21 3-1	A16 0-0	J31 2-2	A30 2-1	D29 1-0		F14 1-1	D20 1-0	M14 0-1	N01 6-0	S13 1-1	A27 1-0	a15 0-0	O18 0-1	M28 0-0	M25 2-0	N22 2-1	S27 4-2	J10 3-0	A13 2-2	D06 3-1
8 CARLISLE U	A19 1-1	J17 4-3	N15 0-1	M21 1-2	A26 2-1	M31 2-1	A09 2-3		M07 1-1	O04 0-2	S06 2-1	a14 2-2	A23 1-0	D13 4-0	D27 2-1	F21 1-1	N01 3-3	S20 1-0	O18 3-2	N29 0-1	O07 2-2	F10 5-0
9 CHARLTON A	M14 1-0	S20 0-1	O18 0-0	N01 0-2	D06 1-1	a14 2-1	S06 0-0	N22 2-1		F07 1-2	J17 1-4	M28 0-5	M03 0-2	O07 2-2	D13 3-0	A26 1-0	O04 2-2	A09 2-1	M31 1-1	A19 3-2	D27 1-1	A23 0-0
10 HUDDERSFIELD T	A16 2-0	M21 2-0	A26 0-1	S13 2-0	S27 1-0	A30 3-0	J24 1-0	J31 1-0	O11 4-0		M30 2-2	M10 1-1	O18 0-0	N01 0-0	F21 1-1	F24 1-0	N15 4-0	A19 3-2	J20 2-0	D26 2-1	M24 1-1	a14 3-1
11 HULL C	M10 3-1	A27 0-0	D26 3-0	A29 1-0	S13 4-2	A16 2-0	M31 1-1	D20 2-4	S27 1-1	O25 2-3		M14 4-1	M28 3-2	J24 2-1	A13 1-0	O11 3-1	a15 3-3	N08 3-1	F14 1-2	J31 2-3	F28 1-1	N22 1-1
12 LEICESTER C	a04 1-0	A09 3-1	M17 2-1	M31 0-0	A20 2-2	O18 2-0	D13 1-2	S17 1-2	N15 2-2	S20 1-1	D17 2-2		O08 2-1	D27 1-1	A23 3-0	N01 2-1	S06 2-1	F25 3-0	a18 2-1	M21 2-1	J17 0-2	O04 3-1
13 MIDDLESBROUGH	A30 1-0	D16 4-2	J13 4-1	S27 0-2	O11 4-0	S13 2-0	a04 2-1	D26 0-2	N08 2-0	M31 1-1	N15 1-0	A16 2-1		A12 3-1	M21 0-0	J10 2-0	M07 2-1	F28 1-1	J31 1-0	M17 1-0	S16 0-0	O25 3-1
14 MILLWALL	M16 2-0	M11 6-2	J20 3-1	O11 1-3	F14 2-0	S27 1-1	D15 1-2	S13 4-2	A16 1-1	F28 1-0	M21 2-1	A30 0-1	A18 1-1		N15 1-0	J31 0-0	D08 3-1	M30 2-1	D26 2-0	O25 1-0	a04 3-1	N08 1-0
15 NORWICH C	F14 3-1	a15 6-0	J31 0-1	A16 3-1	N22 1-0	J10 4-1	F28 1-1	A30 1-0	S13 1-1	N08 1-2	A20 2-1	D26 3-0	M11 2-0	M28 2-1		S27 2-0	A27 0-0	O25 1-2	O11 1-0	D20 1-1	M30 1-0	a18 1-1
16 OXFORD U	O25 2-2	O08 2-0	N29 1-0	a18 2-0	F28 3-1	M18 2-0	N15 1-1	N08 1-0	a04 1-1	A09 1-2	F07 0-0	M27 0-1	S20 1-1	O04 0-0	J17 1-0		A23 0-2	F18 3-1	M21 0-0	S17 0-0	D13 0-0	S06 2-1
17 PORTSMOUTH	S27 0-0	N12 1-1	A30 2-0	F14 2-3	J10 1-1	O11 0-0	N08 3-0	F28 4-0	J31 5-1	M28 1-3	S17 1-4	D20 2-3	N22 2-3	M14 0-1	a04 1-4	J24 2-1		D06 4-0	S13 1-3	A16 1-5	O25 3-1	a01 3-1
18 PRESTON N.E.	J31 1-1	N15 4-1	S13 0-0	a13 0-3	D26 1-3	J24 0-1	a20 1-2	J10 3-1	M16 4-1	N10 1-3	F21 3-3	O11 2-1	N01 0-1	O18 1-1	M31 1-1	A30 0-1	M21 1-2		A16 0-0	S27 2-1	N29 3-1	A25 3-0
19 Q.P.R.	F28 4-2	D27 2-1	a14 2-3	A26 6-1	M14 0-4	M28 2-2	J17 2-1	M27 0-0	O25 1-1	S06 4-2	A09 3-0	N22 1-1	O04 4-0	A23 3-2	F17 4-0	D06 1-2	D13 2-0	O07 0-0		N08 2-1	S20 2-0	N11 2-1
20 SHEFFIELD U	N22 5-0	D13 6-0	N01 4-0	O18 2-3	M28 0-1	A26 2-1	S20 1-0	M13 1-0	A12 2-0	A23 0-0	O04 3-0	D06 1-0	A09 3-0	M31 3-1	S06 1-0	a15 5-1	O07 5-0	J17 2-0	F24 2-0		F09 1-2	D27 1-1
21 SWINDON T	D26 1-1	M31 4-1	a20 1-0	a07 1-1	J31 3-2	D06 1-1	A19 2-1	A16 2-2	A30 5-0	N22 2-1	O18 1-0	S27 1-1	a14 0-3	S30 2-1	N01 2-0	S13 0-0	M03 3-1	M14 1-0	J10 0-0	O11 2-1		M28 1-0
22 WATFORD	S13 3-0	N01 2-3	S27 0-2	J10 0-1	A16 0-0	F14 2-0	M21 2-1	O11 1-2	D26 1-1	S17 1-1	M06 1-1	J31 2-1	M27 2-3	F24 1-1	a07 1-1	D20 2-0	O18 4-0	a04 0-0	A20 0-1	A30 1-2	N15 0-0	

Season 1969-70

DIVISION 3

	BARNSLEY	BARROW	BOURNEMOUTH	BRADFORD C	BRIGHTON & HA	BRISTOL R	BURY	DONCASTER R	FULHAM	GILLINGHAM	HALIFAX T	LUTON T	MANSFIELD T	ORIENT	PLYMOUTH A	READING	ROCHDALE	ROTHERHAM U	SHREWSBURY T	SOUTHPORT	STOCKPORT CO	TORQUAY U	TRANMERE R	WALSALL
1 BARNSLEY		O04 2-1	A09 1-0	F07 3-2	N22 1-2	O07 2-0	D13 3-3	D27 2-1	F21 3-3	J17 5-1	N01 2-0	M31 2-1	M28 1-1	S20 1-2	F09 0-1	A26 4-3	M03 1-0	M13 1-0	M17 1-1	O18 1-1	A23 1-0	a07 3-0	a14 1-1	S06 2-0
2 BARROW	J31 1-1		M21 1-1	D01 0-1	F16 1-1	N29 1-1	F21 3-1	M09 1-1	A30 3-1	O18 1-1	S29 0-1	F14 2-1	S13 0-1	A25 1-1	N01 1-1	J24 2-2	D20 2-0	S27 1-2	M27 2-0	D26 1-0	M07 4-1	O11 0-4	A16 0-3	F23 0-1
3 BOURNEMOUTH	F14 3-1	M04 0-0		M28 0-0	D26 0-0	O25 2-2	a04 2-0	N26 3-1	O11 2-2	N22 2-1	S27 0-0	A16 0-1	a18 1-0	F28 0-2	M14 1-3	J10 1-2	S29 0-3	A30 1-0	S17 3-3	J31 1-0	N08 1-0	S13 1-2	D20 2-2	M27 2-2
4 BRADFORD C	O11 1-1	a08 3-3	J24 8-1		S27 1-0	M07 2-4	M30 0-1	M21 3-0	F14 0-0	N01 1-0	D26 2-1	S13 1-1	a22 0-1	a15 0-1	O18 1-0	O01 4-0	F04 0-3	J31 0-1	F21 2-2	A30 1-0	N29 1-0	A16 2-1	F25 1-1	A27 3-0
5 BRIGHTON & H.A.	M07 2-0	S20 2-0	A23 1-1	J17 2-1		O04 0-3	D27 2-0	J03 1-0	N01 2-1	S06 3-1	M11 4-0	O18 1-2	a15 1-2	D13 0-0	O07 2-0	M27 2-1	A27 2-0	a08 2-1	F07 1-0	M21 1-0	M18 1-0	N29 2-2	F21 2-0	A09 1-1
6 BRISTOL R	A16 3-3	M14 2-1	F21 5-2	N22 1-1	J31 0-2		O18 2-1	M31 1-1	S13 3-2	a14 1-2	A30 2-0	F10 3-0	J10 4-1	M28 1-0	A26 3-1	D26 1-1	S27 3-3	O11 3-0	N01 1-3	F14 2-0	a07 1-0	J24 3-1	S30 3-0	M03 3-1
7 BURY	S13 1-2	O25 4-0	A26 1-0	N08 0-2	A30 1-2	F28 2-2		a14 1-1	A16 1-0	M03 1-3	J31 1-1	J24 1-3	S30 1-0	M14 0-1	M28 3-1	S27 2-1	D06 2-1	F14 2-1	a07 2-2	O11 4-3	J03 4-1	F16 1-0	J10 8-0	N22 4-2
8 DONCASTER R	A30 1-0	M28 3-2	a07 2-1	M03 1-1	S30 2-0	N08 3-1	S16 1-1		J31 0-1	M14 1-0	J10 0-1	O11 2-0	A16 2-0	M30 0-1	N21 1-1	J20 2-3	J23 3-1	D26 1-2	a04 2-1	S27 1-0	O24 0-1	a09 1-0	S13 2-1	F28 0-0
9 FULHAM	O25 0-0	D27 2-1	F06 1-1	A09 0-0	M30 4-1	D13 3-1	O08 2-4	O04 1-1		A23 2-1	a15 2-1	a08 0-1	N22 1-1	J02 1-1	S20 4-3	a20 2-1	M14 2-0	F28 3-2	S06 3-1	A27 3-2	J17 1-1	N08 1-1	M28 1-1	M18 4-0
0 GILLINGHAM	S27 1-3	F28 0-1	a25 0-0	M27 1-1	D20 0-1	S17 1-0	M21 1-0	F18 2-1	D26 2-0		a22 2-0	A30 0-2	a10 3-3	O25 0-1	N26 4-0	A16 1-3	S13 2-2	J10 1-1	M11 2-1	O01 2-4	a04 0-2	J31 2-4	O11 0-0	N08 1-3
1 HALIFAX T	F28 0-2	J27 3-0	J17 4-1	A23 0-0	M28 1-0	D27 1-1	O04 2-0	S20 1-1	S16 0-8	M17 1-1		a04 0-0	O25 1-2	O07 1-1	D13 2-0	M14 1-1	N08 3-1	M03 4-2	A09 1-0	D06 1-0	S06 1-0	M31 1-1	N22 2-2	a24 0-1
2 LUTON T	N08 1-1	A09 3-0	O07 0-0	D13 5-0	F28 1-1	S06 4-0	M17 0-0	F07 4-0	N25 1-0	D27 1-2	A26 1-1		M14 2-2	A23 3-2	J17 0-2	M28 5-0	N22 2-0	M27 2-1	S20 2-2	a14 1-0	O04 2-0	O25 1-1	M03 2-0	a11 3-0
3 MANSFIELD T	M09 2-0	D13 4-2	M16 2-0	S06 2-1	S15 1-0	S20 1-1	F23 3-1	O06 1-2	a06 2-3	A09 1-0	F21 3-3	a20 0-0		D27 4-1	O04 1-2	O18 2-1	N03 1-2	a04 2-0	J17 2-0	a01 5-0	M23 4-1	M21 2-0	N01 1-2	A23 0-0
4 ORIENT	F16 4-2	a04 2-0	N01 3-0	S15 2-1	S13 1-1	M09 0-0	J26 3-0	O18 2-0	S29 3-1	a27 1-2	A16 1-0	D26 1-0	A30 1-0		M27 4-1	O11 0-1	a11 2-2	D20 1-1	a25 1-0	a20 3-2	M21 3-0	S27 1-1	J31 2-0	N24 2-0
5 PLYMOUTH A	S29 0-0	M31 1-0	N29 0-1	F28 0-1	A16 0-1	a04 2-2	M11 2-2	M07 0-0	J10 2-0	F25 2-2	S13 1-0	S27 1-3	J31 1-0	N08 1-0		F14 1-1	O11 2-3	J24 0-3	M21 4-2	D20 1-1	S17 2-0	D26 6-0	A30 2-1	O25 1-0
6 READING	a04 6-2	M18 6-3	S20 2-0	J14 1-0	N08 1-0	A23 1-5	J17 3-2	S06 1-0	M21 0-4	O08 1-0	F11 4-1	M11 0-1	M30 1-0	F07 3-2	A09 2-1		F28 1-0	O25 1-1	D27 3-1	a22 8-0	D13 3-1	S17 1-1	a08 1-1	O04 2-3
7 ROCHDALE	M21 1-1	S06 1-0	J26 0-1	S20 1-2	a04 2-1	J17 0-0	A23 3-3	M16 2-0	a18 0-1	D13 0-0	M30 5-0	a25 1-2	N24 2-1	A09 0-3	F07 2-1	N01 3-2		S15 4-2	O04 3-0	F21 1-1	O06 2-0	M09 1-1	O18 4-0	a09 1-2
8 ROTHERHAM U	D02 2-0	J17 5-0	D27 3-0	O04 2-3	N25 2-0	F07 0-0	A09 4-3	A23 0-1	O18 0-0	S20 0-1	M21 1-1	N01 1-1	A26 2-2	S06 0-0	M17 1-0	F21 1-1	a14 3-1		O07 1-2	M10 2-0	J13 0-0	M23 2-1	M31 0-1	D13 4-1
9 SHREWSBURY T	J24 1-1	N08 1-1	a15 2-0	O25 1-0	O11 2-2	M30 0-0	N26 3-3	A27 0-0	D20 1-1	M28 2-2	F14 3-1	J10 5-1	S27 0-0	N22 1-1	a18 3-0	A30 0-0	J31 1-0	A16 1-0		S13 1-2	F28 3-1	O01 1-0	D26 2-0	M14 1-1
0 SOUTHPORT	M27 0-1	A23 1-0	O04 3-0	a24 1-0	M03 2-0	A09 0-0	F06 4-0	J17 2-2	a03 0-2	a17 1-1	a07 1-0	S16 0-3	N08 0-1	M17 1-0	S06 0-0	N22 6-2	O25 0-3	M28 2-1	D13 0-2		S20 1-1	F28 4-2	M14 2-0	O08 0-1
1 STOCKPORT CO	D26 1-0	N22 2-2	M30 0-2	M14 0-2	J23 0-1	N24 0-1	N01 1-0	F21 3-1	S27 1-4	A25 1-0	F02 0-1	J31 1-1	O11 1-3	M02 0-2	a13 0-1	S13 2-2	A16 0-1	O13 1-1	O18 1-1	J10 0-0		A30 0-1	a24 0-1	M28 2-2
2 TORQUAY U	N26 1-1	F07 1-1	D13 2-2	O08 2-1	M14 2-1	M18 1-2	S06 3-0	A09 2-1	M27 1-1	O04 3-2	O18 0-1	F21 2-2	M04 0-2	J17 0-1	A23 1-2	D05 1-1	M28 3-0	N22 0-0	a22 3-0	N01 0-0	S10 3-0		A27 5-1	S20 0-0
3 TRANMERE R	S15 0-1	O06 5-0	S06 1-5	M16 1-0	O25 2-0	a17 5-2	S20 3-2	D13 1-3	a27 1-0	a20 0-0	M06 1-1	M21 3-2	F28 1-1	O04 1-1	a06 3-1	N24 1-5	M27 0-0	N08 2-2	A23 3-1	N29 0-1	A09 3-0	a03 1-1		J17 0-0
4 WALSALL	D20 3-2	S16 1-0	O18 2-1	a04 2-0	F25 0-3	M21 2-1	M24 1-1	O31 1-3	J27 1-3	M31 0-1	O11 2-1	S30 1-3	D26 1-0	a07 2-0	a17 2-2	a14 4-1	A30 1-4	S13 0-2	N29 3-2	A16 4-0	a22 0-0	J10 0-1	S27 0-0	

DIVISION 4

	ALDERSHOT	BRADFORD	BRENTFORD	CHESTER	CHESTERFIELD	COLCHESTER U	CREWE A	DARLINGTON	EXETER C	GRIMSBY T	HARTLEPOOL	LINCOLN C	NEWPORT CO	NORTHAMPTON T	NOTTS CO	OLDHAM A	PETERBOROUGH U	PORT VALE	SCUNTHORPE U	SOUTHEND U	SWANSEA T	WORKINGTON	WREXHAM	YORK C
1 ALDERSHOT		a20 4-2	a24 1-2	N22 3-1	A27 1-0	N01 1-1	A16 4-1	F25 4-0	a15 1-0	M28 2-2	O01 4-1	O11 1-1	A30 1-1	O18 5-2	S27 2-0	M30 1-0	F21 1-0	J31 2-0	J10 3-1	M14 2-1	D26 2-2	D20 3-1	S13 0-2	N26 4-1
2 BRADFORD	A09 2-0		S20 0-1	J19 1-2	S06 1-1	F07 0-1	M02 0-0	F28 0-1	D27 2-1	A23 1-1	M31 3-0	M28 0-3	M13 1-1	O04 1-2	O25 1-3	M16 0-0	O06 2-3	N08 1-2	a04 0-5	J17 1-0	N22 0-2	S15 2-0	N24 2-3	D13 2-0
3 BRENTFORD	M21 0-0	J10 1-1		a04 2-0	F21 0-1	a18 2-0	D26 1-1	A30 1-1	M27 2-0	N24 3-0	F23 3-0	S29 2-1	D20 1-0	M07 1-0	A16 1-0	O18 1-1	N01 5-2	J24 1-0	O11 3-0	S15 3-1	S13 2-2	J31 1-0	S27 0-0	M09 0-0
4 CHESTER	a30 2-1	O01 1-0	A27 1-2		O18 1-2	a01 1-0	S27 2-1	J31 1-3	N01 2-0	a15 3-1	O11 2-1	J10 1-2	F25 2-0	F21 2-1	S13 0-1	M11 2-1	M21 2-3	D20 1-1	F14 1-1	N26 2-0	A16 2-2	A30 3-0	D26 2-0	N29 3-0
5 CHESTERFIELD	a04 4-2	a17 4-0	O25 1-0	F28 0-1		M21 2-0	S29 1-0	D26 2-0	N24 2-1	N08 1-2	A30 3-0	J24 4-0	S13 4-0	M09 2-1	O11 5-0	N29 3-1	a27 3-1	A16 0-1	J31 2-1	M31 3-0	a21 0-0	S27 4-0	F25 2-0	S15 3-1
6 COLCHESTER U	M27 3-1	O11 2-1	M14 1-1	O25 0-1	M02 4-1		S13 1-0	D20 2-1	M28 2-1	N22 3-2	J10 1-1	a22 2-0	J31 1-1	a06 0-3	D26 2-1	a13 3-1	A25 2-1	A30 0-0	S29 0-2	N08 0-2	S27 1-1	J24 3-0	A16 2-0	F28 3-0
7 CREWE A	O08 1-0	M21 0-0	A23 1-2	J17 3-0	a24 2-1	D13 0-1		N29 2-0	F07 1-1	O04 3-0	a10 3-0	N26 3-1	F21 1-1	A09 2-0	A27 1-1	S20 1-1	S06 2-0	a15 0-0	N01 0-2	J27 5-3	M27 0-1	O18 1-0	M11 2-3	M18 3-0
8 DARLINGTON	M16 0-2	N01 1-1	D27 1-2	O04 1-2	A23 0-1	S06 3-2	M14 2-0		O06 4-0	F07 0-0	a22 4-0	N22 0-3	A25 0-0	D13 2-2	M28 1-2	J17 1-1	S20 1-2	M02 2-2	M30 2-0	A09 0-2	a13 2-1	F23 1-1	O18 2-1	a27 1-0
9 EXETER C	S17 2-1	A30 3-0	N08 2-2	M30 1-0	a07 1-1	M11 2-1	O11 3-0	A16 1-2		O25 0-1	J24 6-0	J31 1-2	D26 1-1	M21 1-0	J10 1-1	M07 0-2	N29 1-1	S27 1-2	D20 4-1	F28 3-0	O01 6-0	S13 5-1	F14 1-0	a04 2-1
0 GRIMSBY T	M10 2-2	D26 2-2	a07 2-1	S16 4-1	M27 1-0	a28 5-3	J31 0-2	O11 0-1	F21 2-0		A16 2-0	S27 0-2	S30 1-1	a18 0-1	J03 2-1	N01 4-1	O18 0-0	J10 2-0	S13 1-1	a04 2-2	J24 0-2	F14 1-1	A30 0-0	M21 0-0
1 HARTLEPOOL	F02 1-3	O18 5-2	A09 0-0	F07 1-2	D27 0-0	S20 0-0	N22 1-1	N24 1-3	M16 2-0	O06 0-1		M14 0-3	a13 0-1	S06 1-1	M02 4-0	O04 1-1	J17 4-2	M28 0-2	F20 1-2	D13 2-1	A25 3-0	M27 1-0	N01 1-3	A23 2-2
2 LINCOLN C	F07 1-1	M23 5-2	J03 1-0	S20 2-0	M18 0-2	A09 3-3	a08 2-1	a25 1-0	O04 1-0	J17 2-0	a18 3-0		M27 3-0	D27 0-0	a15 2-4	S06 0-1	D13 3-0	A27 0-0	O18 1-2	A23 3-3	F21 0-0	N01 1-1	M21 0-0	O08 4-0
3 NEWPORT CO	D27 3-4	N29 5-1	S06 1-0	M16 3-1	D13 0-2	O04 4-1	O25 0-0	a04 2-1	A23 2-0	a25 1-0	S15 1-1	N08 3-1		J17 0-2	F28 1-0	O06 2-1	F07 0-1	M30 1-1	M09 3-0	S20 4-0	a06 1-2	M21 0-1	M07 1-2	A09 1-2
4 NORTHAMPTON T	F28 4-0	J31 3-0	N22 1-1	N08 0-1	M28 0-1	N25 1-1	F23 1-2	S13 1-1	M02 2-0	M14 3-1	D20 0-1	A30 1-1	S27 4-1		S30 3-1	A26 0-0	a14 2-2	D26 2-0	F18 2-1	O25 2-0	a10 4-1	O28 3-0	O11 0-1	M31 2-2
5 NOTTS CO	J17 3-0	M30 5-2	O08 1-0	D13 3-0	F07 1-1	A23 1-1	a04 0-1	M11 4-1	S20 4-0	S06 2-1	M21 1-0	S17 2-0	O18 4-1	a24 2-0		A09 0-0	D27 2-2	a08 1-2	N29 3-1	M18 2-0	N01 0-1	a21 0-3	F21 3-2	O04 0-2
6 OLDHAM A	O25 4-2	J24 0-0	M31 4-1	M28 5-0	M14 1-0	S16 1-2	a21 2-1	S27 1-1	N22 1-1	F28 0-2	J31 1-0	F10 1-1	A16 3-0	a04 0-2	F14 5-0		a07 4-2	S13 2-3	A30 1-3	M03 3-0	O11 0-1	D26 1-2	O01 2-3	N08 3-1
7 PETERBOROUGH U	N08 4-1	A16 2-1	F28 0-0	a18 0-0	N22 1-2	a04 1-1	F25 3-0	J10 3-2	M14 1-1	M30 1-0	S27 4-0	S13 2-1	O11 4-0	S17 1-0	A30 1-0	N26 8-1		a22 0-0	D26 2-2	M28 3-4	J31 1-1	S30 1-1	a10 5-2	O25 3-1
8 PORT VALE	O04 0-0	F21 4-1	M16 0-0	S06 3-0	O06 1-1	a25 1-1	S15 2-0	M21 4-0	J17 2-0	S20 1-0	M09 3-0	a04 0-0	N01 3-1	A23 4-1	a18 1-1	D13 1-0	A09 0-0		M23 1-2	F23 3-0	O18 0-0	N29 3-1	a01 1-0	F07 1-1
9 SCUNTHORPE U	S20 0-0	A26 2-0	F10 1-1	A09 2-3	O04 1-2	J27 1-1	M31 0-1	N08 2-0	S06 0-0	D13 1-1	O25 3-1	F28 2-1	M28 4-0	M17 1-0	M14 2-3	D27 2-1	A23 2-1	N22 2-1		O07 2-0	M03 1-2	N25 1-0	a14 1-3	J17 1-1
0 SOUTHEND U	N29 2-2	S27 1-1	a13 2-2	a06 4-2	N01 0-0	F21 2-1	A30 2-0	a10 2-0	O18 1-1	A25 1-3	S13 0-2	D26 2-2	J10 3-2	M27 2-2	J24 2-5	M21 1-0	M09 2-0	S29 1-1	A15 3-0		D20 2-1	O11 3-1	J31 1-0	m01 1-0
1 SWANSEA T	A23 1-1	M07 5-0	D13 1-0	O07 2-1	A09 0-0	J17 1-0	N08 3-0	S16 3-1	F24 0-0	M17 2-0	a04 3-0	O25 2-2	N25 1-1	S20 3-2	M31 1-1	F07 4-0	O04 4-1	F28 0-0	M21 2-1	S06 2-0		M23 0-0	F17 1-2	D27 2-1
2 WORKINGTON	S06 1-2	a15 1-0	O04 1-2	F18 1-1	J17 1-1	M18 1-1	F28 1-0	O25 1-0	D13 1-2	A09 0-0	N08 1-3	M30 1-1	M04 3-0	O08 2-0	N22 0-2	A23 1-0	J15 1-1	M14 3-2	a08 2-2	F06 5-0	M28 0-0		A27 2-0	S20 1-1
3 WREXHAM	D13 1-1	a06 4-0	J17 1-0	A23 2-0	S20 2-1	O06 4-2	M28 2-2	M27 6-2	A09 3-0	a20 3-2	F28 1-0	M02 0-0	N22 3-0	a27 3-0	N08 2-0	a18 1-1	M16 2-1	O25 1-1	S15 2-1	O04 4-0	M14 1-1	a04 4-1		S06 4-0
4 YORK C	a07 2-0	S13 4-1	M28 4-2	M13 0-0	a13 1-1	O18 4-2	a17 0-0	S29 2-1	A25 1-0	M02 1-1	D26 0-0	A16 2-0	a21 2-1	N01 1-1	J31 1-2	F21 0-0	M27 3-0	O11 0-1	S27 3-2	N22 1-0	A30 3-0	F09 1-0	a24 2-1	

LEAGUE TABLES

DIVISION 1

	P	W	D	L	F	A	W	D	L	F	A	Pts
Everton	42	17	3	1	46	19	12	5	4	26	15	66
Leeds U	42	15	4	2	50	19	6	11	4	34	30	57
Chelsea	42	13	7	1	36	18	8	6	7	34	32	55
Derby Co	42	15	3	3	45	14	7	6	8	19	23	53
Liverpool	42	10	7	4	34	20	10	4	7	31	22	51
Coventry C	42	9	6	6	35	28	10	5	6	23	20	49
Newcastle U	42	14	2	5	42	16	3	11	7	15	19	47
Manchester U	42	8	9	4	37	27	6	8	7	29	34	45
Stoke C	42	10	7	4	31	23	5	8	8	25	29	45
Manchester C	42	8	6	7	25	22	8	5	8	30	26	43
Tottenham H	42	11	2	8	27	21	6	7	8	27	34	43
Arsenal	42	7	10	4	29	23	5	8	8	22	26	42
Wolverh'pton W	42	8	8	5	30	23	4	8	9	25	34	40
Burnley	42	7	7	7	33	29	5	8	8	23	32	39
Nottingham F	42	8	9	4	28	28	2	9	10	22	43	38
W.B.A.	42	10	6	5	39	25	4	3	14	19	41	37
West Ham U	42	8	8	5	28	21	4	4	13	23	39	36
Ipswich T	42	9	5	7	23	20	1	6	14	17	43	31
Southampton	42	3	12	6	24	27	3	5	13	22	40	29
Crystal Palace	42	5	6	10	20	36	1	9	11	14	32	27
Sunderland	42	4	11	6	17	24	2	3	16	13	44	26
Sheffield W	42	6	5	10	23	27	2	4	15	17	44	25

DIVISION 2

	P	W	D	L	F	A	W	D	L	F	A	Pts
Huddersfield T	42	14	6	1	36	10	10	6	5	32	27	60
Blackpool	42	10	9	2	25	16	10	4	7	31	29	53
Leicester C	42	12	6	3	37	22	7	7	7	27	28	51
Middlesbrough	42	15	4	2	36	14	5	6	10	19	31	50
Swindon T	42	13	7	1	35	17	4	9	8	22	30	50
Sheffield U	42	16	2	3	50	10	6	3	12	23	28	49
Cardiff C	42	12	7	2	38	14	6	6	9	23	27	49
Blackburn R	42	15	2	4	42	19	5	5	11	12	31	47
Q.P.R.	42	13	5	3	47	24	4	6	11	19	33	45
Millwall	42	14	4	3	38	18	1	10	10	18	38	44
Norwich C	42	13	5	3	37	14	3	6	12	12	32	43
Carlisle U	42	10	6	5	39	28	4	7	10	19	28	41
Hull C	42	11	6	4	43	28	4	5	12	29	42	41
Bristol C	42	11	7	3	37	13	2	6	13	17	37	39
Oxford U	42	9	9	3	23	13	3	6	12	12	29	39
Bolton W	42	9	6	6	31	23	3	6	12	23	38	36
Portsmouth	42	8	4	9	39	35	5	5	11	27	45	35
Birmingham C	42	9	7	5	33	22	2	4	15	18	56	33
Watford	42	6	8	7	26	21	3	5	13	18	36	31
Charlton A	42	7	8	6	23	28	0	9	12	12	48	31
Aston Villa	42	7	8	6	23	21	1	5	15	13	41	29
Preston N.E.	42	7	6	8	31	28	1	6	14	12	35	28

DIVISION 3

	P	W	D	L	F	A	W	D	L	F	A	Pts
Orient	46	16	5	2	43	15	9	7	7	24	21	62
Luton T	46	13	8	2	46	15	10	6	7	31	28	60
Bristol R	46	15	5	3	51	26	5	11	7	29	33	56
Fulham	46	12	9	2	43	26	8	6	9	38	29	55
Brighton & H.A.	46	16	4	3	37	16	7	5	11	20	27	55
Mansfield T	46	14	4	5	46	22	7	7	9	24	27	53
Barnsley	46	14	6	3	43	24	5	9	9	25	35	53
Reading	46	16	3	4	52	29	5	8	10	35	48	53
Rochdale	46	11	6	6	39	24	7	4	12	30	36	46
Bradford C	46	11	6	6	37	22	6	6	11	20	28	46
Doncaster R	46	13	4	6	31	19	4	8	11	21	35	46
Walsall	46	11	4	8	33	31	6	8	9	21	36	46
Torquay U	46	9	9	5	36	22	5	8	10	26	37	45
Rotherham U	46	10	8	5	36	19	5	6	12	26	35	44
Shrewsbury T	46	10	12	1	35	17	3	6	14	27	46	44
Tranmere R	46	10	8	5	38	29	4	8	11	18	43	44
Plymouth A	46	10	7	6	32	23	6	4	13	24	41	43
Halifax T	46	10	9	4	31	25	4	6	13	16	38	43
Bury	46	13	4	6	47	29	2	7	14	28	51	41
Gillingham	46	7	6	10	28	33	6	7	10	24	31	39
Bournemouth	46	8	9	6	28	27	4	6	13	20	44	39
Southport	46	11	5	7	31	22	3	5	15	17	44	38
Barrow	46	7	9	7	28	27	1	5	17	18	54	30
Stockport Co	46	4	7	12	17	30	2	4	17	10	41	23

DIVISION 4

	P	W	D	L	F	A	W	D	L	F	A	Pts
Chesterfield	46	19	1	3	55	12	8	9	6	22	20	64
Wrexham	46	17	6	0	56	16	9	3	11	28	33	61
Swansea T	46	14	8	1	43	14	7	10	6	23	31	60
Port Vale	46	13	9	1	39	10	7	10	6	22	23	59
Brentford	46	14	8	1	36	11	6	8	9	22	28	56
Aldershot	46	16	5	2	52	22	4	8	11	26	43	53
Notts Co	46	14	4	5	44	21	8	4	11	29	41	52
Lincoln C	46	11	8	4	38	20	6	8	9	28	32	50
Peterborough U	46	13	8	2	51	21	4	6	13	26	48	48
Colchester U	46	14	5	4	38	22	3	9	11	26	41	48
Chester C	46	14	3	6	39	23	7	3	13	19	43	48
Scunthorpe U	46	11	6	6	34	23	7	4	12	33	42	46
York C	46	14	7	2	38	16	2	7	14	17	46	46
Northampton T	46	11	7	5	41	19	5	5	13	23	36	44
Crewe A	46	12	6	5	37	18	4	6	13	14	33	44
Grimsby T	46	9	9	5	33	24	5	6	12	21	34	43
Southend U	46	12	8	3	40	28	3	2	18	19	57	40
Exeter C	46	13	5	5	48	20	1	6	16	9	39	39
Oldham A	46	11	4	8	45	28	2	9	12	15	37	39
Workington	46	9	9	5	31	21	3	5	15	15	43	38
Newport Co	46	12	3	8	39	24	1	8	14	14	50	37
Darlington	46	8	7	8	31	27	5	3	15	22	46	36
Hartlepool U	46	7	7	9	31	30	3	3	17	11	52	30
Bradford P.A.	46	6	5	12	23	32	0	6	17	18	64	23

Football League Records

Top scorers: Div 1, A.Brown (West Bromwich Albion) 28 goals; Div 2, J.Hickton (Middlesbrough) 25 goals; Div 3, G.Ingram (Preston North End), D.Roberts (Mansfield Town) 22 goals; Div 4, E.MacDougall (Bournemouth & Boscombe Athletic) 42 goals.

Bradford failed to gain re-election, Cambridge United were elected in their place. Swansea Town became Swansea City.

John Radford, who netted 15 League goals in Arsenal's double-winning season of 1970-71.

DIVISION 1

	ARSENAL	BLACKPOOL	BURNLEY	CHELSEA	COVENTRY C	CRYSTAL P	DERBY CO	EVERTON	HUDDERSFIELD T	IPSWICH T	LEEDS U	LIVERPOOL	MANCHESTER C	MANCHESTER U	NEWCASTLE U	NOTTINGHAM F	SOUTHAMPTON	STOKE C	TOTTENHAM H	W.B.A.	WEST HAM U	WOLVERHAMPTON W
1 ARSENAL		M20 1-0	a20 1-0	a03 2-0	a06 1-0	N14 1-1	O31 2-0	O17 4-0	A25 1-0	F20 3-2	S01 0-0	N28 2-0	F06 1-0	A22 4-0	a17 1-0	O03 4-0	D26 0-0	m01 1-0	S05 2-0	S19 6-2	J09 2-0	D12 2-1
2 BLACKPOOL	N07 0-1		D26 1-1	O24 3-4	D12 1-0	a26 3-1	F20 0-1	S19 0-2	O17 2-2	N28 0-2	M13 1-1	A17 0-0	J16 3-3	m01 1-1	a03 0-1	a17 2-3	S05 0-3	O03 1-1	a12 0-0	A22 3-1	F27 1-1	F06 0-2
3 BURNLEY	S12 1-2	a10 1-0		S01 0-0	O10 0-0	O31 2-1	a24 1-2	J09 2-2	N14 2-3	M27 2-2	A29 0-3	A15 1-2	D19 0-4	A25 0-2	J30 1-1	N21 2-1	M06 0-1	F23 1-1	M20 0-0	D05 1-1	a13 1-0	S26 2-3
4 CHELSEA	A29 2-1	M06 2-0	a26 0-1		a24 2-1	a10 1-1	A15 2-1	A26 2-2	M20 0-0	S26 2-1	M27 3-1	a12 1-0	O10 1-1	J09 1-2	D05 1-0	F17 2-0	O31 2-2	N21 2-1	N14 0-2	J30 4-1	D19 2-1	S12 2-2
5 COVENTRY C	O24 1-3	F13 2-0	a17 3-0	S19 0-1		N21 2-1	a27 0-0	O03 3-1	S05 0-0	J09 1-0	F26 0-1	M13 1-0	N07 2-1	a13 2-1	m01 2-0	O17 2-0	A22 1-0	D05 1-0	a03 0-0	D26 1-1	F08 0-1	A25 0-1
6 CRYSTAL P	M13 0-2	S02 1-0	F27 0-2	J13 0-0	F20 1-2		D12 0-0	m01 2-0	M24 0-3	F06 1-0	N07 1-1	J16 1-0	A19 0-1	a17 3-5	A22 1-0	S05 2-0	O03 3-1	a03 3-2	S19 0-3	O17 3-0	O24 1-1	N28 1-1
7 DERBY CO	F27 2-0	N21 2-0	S19 1-0	O17 1-2	S02 3-4	F17 1-0		a17 3-1	a03 3-2	A26 2-0	O24 0-2	N07 0-0	M13 0-0	D26 4-4	S05 1-2	M31 1-2	a12 0-0	A22 2-0	O03 1-1	m01 2-0	D05 2-4	J09 1-2
8 EVERTON	A15 2-2	a24 0-0	A18 1-1	J16 3-0	a12 3-0	S26 3-1	O10 1-1		F06 2-1	S12 2-0	D19 0-1	F20 0-0	A29 0-1	F23 1-0	O24 3-1	N07 1-0	D12 4-1	M13 2-0	N28 0-0	F27 3-3	M30 0-1	a10 1-2
9 HUDDERSFIELD T	J16 2-1	A15 3-0	M13 0-1	N07 0-1	M27 1-0	S12 0-2	A29 0-0	D05 1-1		O10 1-0	a12 0-0	D19 0-0	a10 1-0	J30 1-2	F13 1-1	O24 0-0	A18 3-1	F27 0-1	S01 1-1	N21 2-1	S26 1-1	a24 1-2
10 IPSWICH T	N21 0-1	J30 2-1	S05 3-0	m01 0-0	A18 0-2	D05 1-2	J16 0-1	a06 0-0	a17 2-0		F23 2-4	O24 1-0	F26 2-0	S19 4-0	M13 1-0	A22 0-0	a03 1-3	O17 2-0	M23 1-2	O03 2-2	N07 2-1	S01 2-3
11 LEEDS U	a26 1-0	N14 3-1	a03 4-0	S05 1-0	O31 2-0	M20 2-1	M06 1-0	A22 3-2	O03 2-0	D12 0-0		F06 0-1	N28 1-0	O17 2-2	D26 3-0	m01 2-0	S19 1-0	N18 4-1	J09 1-2	a17 1-2	A26 3-0	F20 3-0
12 LIVERPOOL	J30 2-0	J09 2-2	O17 2-0	O03 1-0	N14 0-0	A25 1-1	M20 2-0	N21 3-2	A22 4-0	M29 2-1	D05 1-1		J12 0-0	S05 1-1	a06 1-1	S19 3-0	m01 1-0	D26 0-0	a17 0-0	a02 1-1	F16 1-0	O31 2-0
13 MANCHESTER C	D05 0-2	A26 2-0	A22 0-0	a17 1-1	M20 1-1	J09 1-0	N14 1-1	a03 3-0	D26 1-1	O31 2-0	J30 0-2	a26 2-2		m05 3-4	O03 1-1	a09 1-3	O17 1-1	S19 4-1	m01 0-1	S05 4-1	N21 2-0	M06 0-0
14 MANCHESTER U	D19 1-3	S26 1-1	J16 1-1	A19 0-0	S12 2-0	O10 0-1	a10 1-2	S02 2-0	N28 1-1	a24 3-2	A15 0-1	a19 0-2	D12 1-4		F27 1-0	M13 2-0	F20 5-1	N07 2-2	F06 2-1	O24 2-1	A29 1-1	a12 1-0
15 NEWCASTLE U	O10 1-1	A29 1-2	N28 3-1	F06 0-1	S26 0-0	D19 2-0	M27 3-1	M18 2-1	D12 2-0	N14 0-0	a10 1-1	S12 0-0	a12 0-0	O31 1-0		A26 1-1	M20 2-2	J09 0-2	F20 1-0	a28 3-0	a24 1-1	A15 3-2
16 NOTTINGHAM F	a13 0-3	O10 3-1	F20 1-0	D12 1-1	A15 2-0	M27 3-1	N28 2-4	M20 3-2	M06 1-3	D19 0-1	S26 0-0	a24 0-1	S12 0-1	N14 1-2	J16 2-1		F06 2-0	a27 0-0	O31 0-1	A18 3-3	a10 1-0	A29 4-1
17 SOUTHAMPTON	a10 1-2	M27 1-1	O24 2-0	F27 0-0	D19 3-0	m04 6-0	S12 4-0	F16 2-2	J09 1-0	A29 1-0	a24 0-3	S26 1-0	A15 1-1	N21 1-0	N07 2-0	D05 4-1		J30 2-1	A25 0-0	M13 1-0	a27 1-2	O10 1-2
18 STOKE C	S26 5-0	a13 1-1	D12 0-0	F20 1-2	F06 2-1	A29 0-0	D19 1-0	N14 1-1	O31 3-1	A15 0-0	S12 3-0	a10 0-1	a24 2-0	M20 1-2	A19 3-0	S02 0-0	N28 0-0		m05 0-1	J16 2-0	O10 2-1	a07 1-0
19 TOTTENHAM H	m03 0-1	S12 3-0	N07 4-0	M13 2-1	A29 1-0	a24 2-0	a07 2-1	J30 2-1	a28 1-1	a10 2-0	A19 0-2	O10 1-0	S26 2-0	D05 2-2	N21 1-2	M10 0-1	J16 1-3	O24 3-0		F17 2-2	A15 2-2	D19 0-0
20 W.B.A.	a24 2-2	D19 1-1	F06 1-0	N28 2-2	a10 0-0	A15 0-0	S26 2-1	O31 3-0	F20 2-1	a12 0-1	O10 2-2	A29 1-1	M27 0-0	M06 4-3	S02 1-2	J09 0-1	N14 1-0	A26 5-2	D12 3-1		S12 2-1	M20 2-4
21 WEST HAM U	A17 0-0	O31 2-1	O03 3-1	A22 2-2	N28 1-2	M06 0-0	F06 1-4	S05 1-2	m01 0-1	M20 2-2	J16 2-3	D12 1-2	F20 0-0	a03 2-1	S19 0-2	F24 2-0	A31 1-1	a17 1-0	O17 2-2	a09 2-1		N14 3-3
22 WOLVERHAMPTON W	M02 0-3	D05 1-0	m01 1-0	F13 1-0	J16 0-0	J30 2-1	A19 2-4	D26 2-0	S19 3-1	a28 0-0	N21 2-3	F27 1-0	O24 3-0	O03 3-2	O17 3-2	a03 4-0	a17 0-1	S05 1-1	A22 0-3	N07 2-1	M13 2-0	

Tony Hateley, another much-travelled goalscorer, who played in Notts County's Fourth Division championship side of 1970-71.

DIVISION 2

	BIRMINGHAM C	BLACKBURN R	BOLTON W	BRISTOL C	CARDIFF C	CARLISLE U	CHARLTON A	HULL C	LEICESTER C	LUTON T	MIDDLESBROUGH	MILLWALL	NORWICH C	ORIENT	OXFORD U	PORTSMOUTH	Q.P.R.	SHEFFIELD U	SHEFFIELD W	SUNDERLAND	SWINDON T	WATFORD
1 BIRMINGHAM C		a10 1-0	F20 4-0	J09 2-0	M27 2-0	D19 1-0	S26 1-1	a13 0-0	O20 0-0	A29 1-1	S01 0-1	F06 3-1	N28 2-2	N14 1-0	S12 1-1	a24 1-1	A15 2-1	O10 0-1	D12 1-0	M20 3-1	O31 2-1	M06 2-0
2 BLACKBURN R	D26 2-2		S19 0-2	m01 2-2	M13 1-1	F20 0-2	F06 1-0	D12 0-1	O03 2-2	J16 1-0	a09 1-1	a17 0-2	O24 2-1	A22 0-0	S21 0-0	F27 1-1	S02 0-2	N07 1-3	a03 3-2	N28 0-1	S05 1-0	O17 2-3
3 BOLTON W	N21 3-0	a24 1-1		O24 1-0	S12 0-2	a10 0-3	O10 4-0	M27 0-0	F27 0-3	A15 4-2	F13 0-3	M13 1-1	N07 0-1	S30 0-1	S26 0-2	D19 1-1	A29 2-2	J16 2-1	A19 2-1	a12 1-3	D05 0-3	J30 0-1
4 BRISTOL C	S29 2-1	S26 1-1	M06 1-1		A29 1-0	N28 2-1	D19 2-2	S12 3-3	a27 0-1	a09 3-2	J16 0-2	F20 3-2	D12 0-1	F06 0-0	O10 0-4	a10 2-0	a24 0-0	M27 0-1	O31 1-2	A15 4-3	M20 2-1	N14 3-0
5 CARDIFF C	S05 2-0	N14 4-1	a07 1-0	a03 1-0		M06 4-0	F20 1-1	O31 5-1	O17 2-2	N28 0-0	O03 3-4	A22 2-2	S19 1-1	m01 1-0	F06 1-0	O28 1-0	M20 1-0	S02 1-1	J09 4-0	D12 3-1	D26 1-1	a17 0-1
6 CARLISLE U	A22 0-3	N21 1-0	D26 1-0	J30 2-1	O24 1-1		J09 1-1	S01 2-0	a03 0-1	M13 1-0	O17 1-0	O02 3-0	a17 4-2	S05 2-0	N07 3-2	D05 6-0	F13 3-0	F27 1-0	m01 3-0	O20 0-0	S19 2-1	a13 2-1
7 CHARLTON A	m01 1-1	D05 2-4	a17 4-1	A22 1-1	N21 2-1	S29 1-1		J16 0-1	S19 0-1	O24 1-1	M13 1-0	S05 1-3	a09 2-1	a03 2-0	F26 2-0	N07 2-2	a20 0-3	F13 0-2	O17 2-3	a27 1-1	O03 2-1	M02 1-2
8 HULL C	O03 0-1	F23 0-0	S05 1-0	a12 1-0	F27 1-1	a28 1-2	O21 2-0		D05 3-0	N07 0-2	A22 1-0	S19 2-0	m01 1-0	a17 5-2	M13 0-1	J30 0-1	N21 1-1	O24 1-1	D26 4-4	J09 4-0	O16 2-0	a03 1-0
9 LEICESTER C	J16 1-4	a13 1-1	O31 1-0	S02 4-0	A15 0-1	A29 2-2	a24 1-0	F06 0-0		S12 1-0	S30 3-2	D12 2-1	F20 2-1	N28 4-0	M27 0-0	S26 2-0	D19 0-0	a10 0-0	M10 1-0	O10 1-0	N14 3-1	M20 1-1
10 LUTON T	a03 3-2	O20 2-0	O17 2-0	O03 3-0	m04 3-0	N14 3-3	M06 1-1	M20 3-1	a12 1-3		S05 1-0	M30 1-1	A22 0-0	S19 4-0	S01 4-0	N21 2-1	J09 0-0	D05 2-1	a17 2-2	O31 1-2	m01 1-1	F13 1-0
11 MIDDLESBROUGH	a27 0-0	S12 1-1	D12 1-0	O20 1-0	a13 1-1	A15 2-1	N14 3-0	D19 1-0	J09 1-0	M27 2-1		N28 1-0	F06 5-0	M20 0-1	A29 0-2	O10 3-2	S26 6-2	a24 1-1	F20 1-0	a10 2-2	M06 3-0	O31 2-2
12 MILLWALL	D05 2-1	O10 2-0	N14 2-0	N21 2-0	D19 2-1	a05 2-1	M27 2-0	a24 4-0	M01 0-0	a10 4-0	J30 1-0		J23 2-2	M06 0-1	A15 1-2	A29 0-0	O31 3-0	S14 1-2	M20 1-0	S26 0-0	J09 2-2	O19 3-0
13 NORWICH C	J30 2-2	M06 2-1	M20 2-1	F13 3-2	a24 1-2	O10 1-1	S12 2-0	S26 0-2	N21 2-2	D19 1-1	D05 1-1	S02 1-0		O31 4-2	a12 1-1	A15 1-1	a10 3-0	A29 1-0	N14 0-0	M27 3-0	O21 1-0	J09 2-1
14 ORIENT	M13 0-2	D19 1-1	J09 3-1	D05 1-1	S26 0-0	M27 1-1	A29 0-0	O10 0-1	M29 0-1	a24 1-2	N07 0-0	O24 0-0	F26 1-0		a10 0-0	a26 1-1	a12 0-1	A15 3-1	O19 1-1	S12 1-0	F13 1-0	N21 1-1
15 OXFORD U	a09 1-0	J09 2-1	m01 1-1	a17 1-0	D05 1-0	M20 1-1	O31 2-1	N14 0-3	S05 1-0	a28 2-1	a03 2-2	O17 2-3	O03 1-1	M10 0-1		M24 1-1	O21 1-3	J30 1-2	A22 1-1	M06 0-0	N21 0-0	S19 2-1
16 PORTSMOUTH	S19 1-0	O31 4-1	A22 4-0	M10 1-1	J16 1-3	F06 1-4	M20 2-0	N28 2-2	m01 1-2	F20 0-1	a17 1-1	a03 0-2	O17 0-2	S02 1-1	D12 1-0		M06 2-0	S30 1-5	S05 2-0	N14 2-1	a12 0-2	O03 5-0
17 Q.P.R.	O17 5-2	a27 2-0	a03 4-0	S19 2-1	N07 0-1	D12 1-1	N28 1-4	F20 1-1	A22 1-3	S29 0-1	m01 1-1	F27 2-0	M23 0-1	O03 5-1	J16 2-0	O24 2-0		M13 2-2	a06 1-0	F06 2-0	a17 4-2	S05 1-1
18 SHEFFIELD U	a17 3-0	M20 5-0	O20 2-2	S05 3-3	a27 5-1	O31 2-2	D12 3-0	M09 1-2	D26 2-1	F06 2-1	S19 1-1	a13 2-0	a03 0-0	O17 3-1	N28 3-0	J09 2-0	N14 1-1		O03 3-2	F20 1-0	A22 2-1	m01 3-0
19 SHEFFIELD W	F13 3-3	A29 1-1	S02 1-1	F27 2-0	A26 1-2	S26 3-0	A15 1-0	a10 1-1	O24 0-3	O10 1-5	N21 3-2	N07 1-0	M13 2-1	J16 2-1	D19 1-1	M30 3-1	S12 1-0	a12 0-0		a24 1-2	J30 2-2	D05 2-1
20 SUNDERLAND	N07 2-1	J30 3-2	O03 4-1	O17 1-0	F13 0-4	J16 2-0	S02 3-0	O07 0-1	a17 0-0	F27 0-0	D26 2-2	m01 0-1	S05 2-1	a09 1-0	O24 0-1	M13 0-0	D05 3-1	N21 0-0	S19 3-1		a03 5-2	A22 3-3
21 SWINDON T	F27 1-2	M27 3-0	F06 3-1	N07 2-1	a10 2-2	a24 0-0	a13 1-1	A15 1-1	M13 0-1	S26 0-0	O24 3-0	S29 3-0	J16 3-2	D12 1-1	F20 3-0	S12 2-1	O10 1-0	D19 3-0	N28 3-0	A29 2-0		S01 1-1
22 WATFORD	O24 2-1	A15 2-1	N28 1-1	M13 0-3	O10 0-1	S12 0-0	a10 1-1	A29 1-2	N07 0-1	D12 0-1	F26 1-0	J16 0-4	S30 2-0	F20 0-0	a24 2-1	a09 0-0	M27 1-2	S26 0-0	F06 3-0	D19 1-1	a28 1-2	

Season 1970-71

Division 3

	ASTON VILLA	BARNSLEY	BRADFORD C	BRIGHTON & HA	BRISTOL R	BURY	CHESTERFIELD	DONCASTER R	FULHAM	GILLINGHAM	HALIFAX T	MANSFIELD T	PLYMOUTH A	PORT VALE	PRESTON N.E.	READING	ROCHDALE	ROTHERHAM U	SHREWSBURY T	SWANSEA C	TORQUAY U	TRANMERE R	WALSALL	WREXHAM
1 ASTON VILLA		a12 0-0	D05 1-0	O03 0-0	S30 1-1	N11 1-0	O17 0-0	S05 3-2	J30 1-0	S23 2-1	M13 1-1	A31 0-1	A22 1-1	J16 1-0	S19 2-0	m04 2-1	a17 1-0	F13 1-0	D26 2-0	a03 3-0	N07 0-1	O24 1-0	M17 0-0	m01 3-4
2 BARNSLEY	S12 1-1		D19 2-0	F06 1-0	J02 0-4	A28 1-1	J16 1-0	O31 0-1	A15 0-1	S29 3-1	S26 2-2	a10 1-0	N28 2-0	a13 1-0	F20 0-1	a24 3-0	M06 2-2	O10 2-1	M20 2-1	N14 0-0	M09 2-0	M26 0-0	a27 1-2	J23 3-1
3 BRADFORD C	F06 1-0	A22 1-0		a12 2-3	F20 1-1	M13 1-3	m01 1-0	D26 3-0	a28 2-3	M17 0-1	F27 0-1	N20 1-1	S19 0-1	J23 1-1	O02 0-2	S30 0-1	a03 3-0	N07 1-1	S05 1-0	a17 0-2	O24 2-0	J16 1-1	O17 0-0	S23 1-3
4 BRIGHTON & H.A.	a09 1-0	D05 1-2	S12 1-2		S26 0-0	M27 1-0	N07 1-2	J09 3-0	M10 3-2	M13 3-1	a24 0-2	D19 2-0	a28 1-1	O10 0-0	F27 0-0	a10 2-0	O21 1-1	A29 1-1	F13 1-2	N25 2-2	A15 0-0	M31 0-0	J30 2-2	O24 2-0
5 BRISTOL R	J09 1-2	M16 3-0	N10 4-2	m01 1-3		O24 0-1	O03 3-2	S22 2-0	F13 0-1	a17 2-0	D05 1-0	O20 2-0	a13 1-3	S01 3-0	a03 0-0	N07 4-0	O17 2-2	F27 0-2	A22 2-2	D26 0-0	M23 1-1	M13 0-1	S19 3-0	S05 3-2
6 BURY	F20 3-1	a03 0-0	N14 1-1	S05 0-2	M06 3-0		a06 1-1	O03 2-3	M20 2-0	A22 2-1	O20 1-1	J23 0-0	a17 3-0	O31 2-3	S22 0-1	F06 5-1	M16 0-2	a27 0-1	S19 1-1	m01 1-1	J09 1-0	N28 0-0	D26 1-1	O17 1-2
7 CHESTERFIELD	A15 2-3	O21 4-2	S26 0-1	M20 2-1	a12 2-0	S12 0-0		F20 4-0	M26 0-0	S02 2-0	O10 5-0	J02 2-2	N14 2-0	M10 3-0	N28 0-0	A29 4-0	F10 1-1	a10 1-1	M06 2-0	O31 0-0	a24 5-0	D19 2-0	J09 1-1	F06 1-0
8 DONCASTER R	M26 2-1	F26 1-0	a10 3-1	S29 2-0	M09 0-1	a13 2-0	N10 2-1		a24 0-1	F13 2-2	S11 1-2	A15 1-2	J16 0-0	J02 1-2	N06 1-1	O10 2-0	a27 1-2	D19 0-2	J30 1-1	D05 1-2	S26 0-1	A29 2-2	O23 1-2	M13 2-1
9 FULHAM	N28 0-2	O17 1-1	S02 5-0	S23 1-0	M02 2-1	N07 2-1	S05 2-0	S19 1-1		D28 1-0	O24 3-1	F06 0-0	O03 1-1	F20 4-1	m01 0-1	J16 1-1	a07 2-0	M13 1-0	a17 0-0	A22 4-1	F26 4-0	S28 2-0	a03 1-0	M17 1-0
10 GILLINGHAM	M10 0-0	J09 2-1	J12 2-1	N14 1-1	O10 1-4	D19 1-2	a28 1-1	J23 0-1	a10 1-3		A29 2-1	S26 2-2	M20 0-2	a24 1-1	F06 2-1	A15 0-0	F20 0-0	M27 2-1	O31 0-2	M06 0-0	S12 1-2	a12 0-0	O21 2-1	N28 1-2
11 HALIFAX T	N14 2-1	m01 4-1	O31 1-2	S19 0-1	F06 0-0	J16 3-0	a17 1-0	D12 4-0	M06 2-1	a03 2-1		M20 0-1	S22 4-1	N28 2-0	O17 1-0	J23 4-0	D26 1-4	S29 1-3	O03 2-0	M15 2-2	J11 2-0	F20 4-3	S05 2-1	A22 2-0
12 MANSFIELD T	a26 2-0	D26 1-2	J30 3-5	A22 1-0	J16 4-1	F13 1-0	M15 2-2	O17 2-1	D05 1-0	m01 2-0	N07 3-2		S04 1-5	S28 2-0	a17 3-1	O24 0-0	O03 3-2	N09 1-1	a03 1-1	a13 2-0	M13 0-0	F27 6-2	O14 2-2	S19 1-1
13 PLYMOUTH A	D19 1-1	F01 2-1	a24 1-3	S02 1-1	S12 0-0	O10 3-4	M13 1-1	O21 1-1	a12 1-1	N07 2-1	J02 1-1	M27 0-0		A29 2-1	O24 1-1	M24 4-0	J09 2-2	S26 4-1	N11 4-4	F13 2-3	a10 1-2	A15 0-1	D05 3-1	F27 2-2
14 PORT VALE	O19 2-0	O03 1-1	F12 0-0	a17 2-1	a26 2-0	F27 0-0	S21 0-2	M15 1-0	N09 0-1	S19 1-1	J30 0-1	J09 2-0	a03 2-1		S05 1-0	M13 3-1	A22 4-1	O24 1-0	a12 0-1	O17 4-0	D05 0-1	N07 2-2	m01 1-1	D26 0-3
15 PRESTON N.E.	a24 0-0	N09 3-1	a13 1-1	O31 1-1	A29 3-2	M08 2-0	J30 1-0	M20 4-0	S26 1-1	D05 1-0	A15 1-1	O10 2-1	M06 1-0	M27 1-0		S12 4-1	N14 3-1	m04 3-0	J09 2-0	O19 1-1	D19 2-2	a10 1-1	F13 1-0	A31 3-2
16 READING	O31 3-5	S19 2-0	J09 1-1	a21 0-3	M20 0-2	D05 1-5	a03 1-1	a17 1-0	O21 1-1	O17 3-2	F13 1-1	M06 1-0	M17 0-2	N14 2-1	a12 1-0		m01 1-1	J30 4-2	S23 2-1	S05 3-1	N11 2-1	S02 1-1	A22 1-2	O03 0-0
17 ROCHDALE	O10 1-1	O24 1-0	A29 0-0	J16 3-3	A15 1-1	F22 2-0	F13 2-0	A31 1-0	S12 1-2	N10 0-1	a10 0-3	a12 1-1	N02 1-1	D19 0-3	M13 1-2	S26 1-2		a24 4-3	D05 1-2	J30 0-0	M27 2-0	M08 0-0	F27 2-0	N07 4-1
18 ROTHERHAM U	J23 1-1	a17 1-0	M20 1-1	a03 2-0	O31 1-1	S01 3-2	D26 1-2	A22 2-0	N14 1-1	S05 0-0	J09 2-2	F20 2-1	m01 1-1	M06 2-1	M16 1-1	N28 2-1	S19 5-1		O17 1-1	S22 2-0	O20 3-1	F06 2-0	O03 1-0	a12 1-1
19 SHREWSBURY T	a10 2-1	N06 1-0	M27 1-1	M24 0-1	D18 1-4	a23 2-0	O24 1-1	N27 0-3	O10 0-1	F26 0-0	a14 2-2	A28 5-2	F20 1-1	S12 7-3	S30 0-1	M10 3-1	F06 0-2	A15 4-2		a28 1-0	a20 1-0	S25 3-1	M13 1-1	J16 1-0
20 SWANSEA C	A29 1-2	M12 0-2	O10 2-0	F20 1-0	a10 1-3	S26 3-0	F27 1-0	F05 1-1	D19 4-1	O24 1-0	m04 3-1	S12 2-4	M30 0-2	A15 0-2	J15 2-2	M27 5-0	N28 4-2	M09 1-1	S01 5-0		a12 0-1	a24 0-0	N07 1-1	S29 3-0
21 TORQUAY U	M20 1-1	S21 0-1	M06 1-1	O16 1-0	N28 1-1	S30 2-1	S18 1-1	m01 2-1	O31 3-1	a13 2-3	a28 2-0	N14 0-0	D26 2-1	F05 1-1	A22 3-1	F19 0-4	S04 3-0	J15 3-1	m06 1-0	O03 2-1		F01 4-2	a16 1-2	a02 1-2
22 TRANMERE R	M05 1-1	S04 2-2	O19 3-1	M15 3-0	N13 0-2	J29 0-0	A21 0-0	a02 1-0	J08 0-3	O02 1-0	N09 0-1	O30 4-1	O16 1-0	M22 1-1	D26 3-3	a26 0-0	a19 0-2	D04 5-0	a30 1-0	S18 0-0	F12 0-0		a09 0-0	D12 1-1
23 WALSALL	J02 3-0	S01 1-2	A15 1-2	N28 1-0	a24 1-2	a10 3-0	S29 2-1	M06 1-2	A29 3-2	J16 3-0	M27 0-0	M09 0-1	F06 1-0	S26 3-1	J27 0-1	D19 1-2	O31 0-3	a13 0-1	N14 0-1	M19 0-1	O10 1-4	S12 2-0		F20 3-1
24 WREXHAM	S26 2-3	F13 1-0	F22 2-0	m07 1-1	M27 1-0	A15 3-2	D05 0-3	N14 0-0	J02 2-2	M01 3-4	D19 2-2	a24 4-0	O31 4-0	a10 1-1	a26 1-1	a09 2-0	M20 3-1	S12 1-1	O19 2-1	J09 1-1	A29 1-0	O10 4-1	N09 2-1	

Division 4

	ALDERSHOT	BARROW	BOURNEMOUTH	BRENTFORD	CAMBRIDGE U	CHESTER	COLCHESTER U	CREWE A	DARLINGTON	EXETER C	GRIMSBY T	HARTLEPOOL	LINCOLN C	NEWPORT CO	NORTHAMPTON T	NOTTS CO	OLDHAM A	PETERBOROUGH U	SCUNTHORPE U	SOUTHEND U	SOUTHPORT	STOCKPORT CO	WORKINGTON	YORK C
1 ALDERSHOT		O24 3-0	A15 2-0	J16 1-0	S30 2-2	a09 1-0	F26 0-1	M27 0-0	O10 2-2	F20 2-2	N28 3-2	a24 1-0	S26 0-2	F06 1-1	a10 1-1	A29 0-1	M10 1-1	D19 2-2	S11 0-1	M29 2-2	F22 2-1	a28 5-0	N07 1-1	M13 0-1
2 BARROW	M06 1-1		J02 1-2	F06 0-1	N28 2-1	O10 1-4	A31 0-2	A29 0-1	A15 1-1	N14 1-1	F20 0-1	M27 3-0	S12 1-4	J23 3-1	a24 2-1	D19 1-2	a10 1-1	S26 2-3	M08 1-2	M20 2-0	a12 0-2	O31 2-2	O19 0-3	J09 0-2
3 BOURNEMOUTH	O17 1-1	M17 0-0		a17 1-0	O03 3-0	M06 3-1	S18 4-1	N28 2-2	M20 1-0	J27 4-1	A22 2-1	N14 3-0	O31 3-0	a03 2-2	J23 4-2	F06 1-1	J16 5-0	A31 1-0	S30 0-2	a09 4-0	F20 0-1	S05 2-0	S23 1-0	m01 4-0
4 BRENTFORD	O19 2-3	D05 2-1	O10 1-2		a26 1-2	A15 1-2	M29 1-0	M08 3-1	S26 1-0	O31 5-0	N14 2-0	F24 1-0	D19 2-1	M20 0-3	a09 3-0	a24 2-2	M27 1-1	S12 1-1	a10 0-1	M06 4-2	A29 0-1	J09 3-0	m07 3-0	N09 6-4
5 CAMBRIDGE U	J09 1-1	J30 3-3	a13 0-2	A31 1-0		M08 1-1	D05 2-1	a24 1-0	J02 2-0	M06 2-0	M20 2-3	S26 2-0	A15 1-1	N14 3-2	D19 0-2	a10 2-1	A29 3-1	O10 1-1	M27 1-1	O31 0-3	S12 0-0	O19 1-1	N09 1-2	F13 1-1
6 CHESTER	O03 1-2	a17 2-1	O24 4-2	O17 1-2	S23 2-1		A22 2-1	F20 1-0	F06 2-1	S19 3-1	O07 5-0	N28 0-1	S02 1-0	m01 2-1	J16 2-2	J23 2-1	N07 0-1	F27 2-0	M13 2-0	M17 2-0	S30 1-0	D26 3-0	a03 1-0	a12 1-1
7 COLCHESTER U	O30 5-2	a26 4-1	a23 1-1	N28 4-0	F05 2-1	D18 0-1		S25 3-0	M08 2-0	M20 1-1	F22 1-0	A15 1-0	a10 1-1	F20 4-2	A29 1-1	S12 2-3	O09 1-2	a09 3-0	M22 2-0	N13 1-1	M27 1-0	m07 1-1	J08 2-1	O19 1-0
8 CREWE A	S05 0-3	a03 1-0	J30 3-3	S23 5-3	S19 1-2	N11 6-3	m01 0-3		J09 3-0	a09 4-1	M17 4-0	O21 1-0	F13 3-1	D26 2-0	M13 3-0	a28 1-2	F27 0-1	D05 1-3	O24 3-1	a17 1-2	N07 1-0	O03 2-3	O17 1-0	A22 3-4
9 DARLINGTON	a17 1-2	O17 3-1	N07 1-0	m01 2-1	M15 2-0	D05 5-1	S21 0-0	S28 0-1		S05 3-2	D26 5-1	a26 2-0	J30 3-2	S19 2-1	O24 0-0	J16 2-3	F13 3-1	M13 1-0	N09 3-0	a03 0-4	F27 1-1	A22 1-0	a12 0-1	O03 2-0
10 EXETER C	N11 4-1	M13 4-2	a10 0-0	F27 1-0	O24 1-0	a24 3-1	N07 2-2	S12 6-2	M27 2-1		O21 4-0	O10 1-1	a12 0-0	J09 1-1	F09 1-1	S26 0-1	D19 0-2	A29 3-2	A15 1-1	S02 2-0	D12 2-1	F13 2-1	F16 0-1	D05 0-2
11 GRIMSBY T	J30 0-2	N10 3-1	D19 1-0	M13 1-5	N07 2-0	M27 2-2	a20 3-1	m04 2-0	a10 1-1	J16 1-2		A29 1-1	M09 1-1	a27 2-0	S12 0-2	O10 2-1	A15 4-1	a24 2-1	a09 1-0	S29 2-0	S26 1-2	D05 1-2	F27 1-0	O24 3-1
12 HARTLEPOOL	S19 1-1	S05 2-1	M13 2-1	M15 0-0	m01 0-0	J30 0-2	O17 1-2	J16 0-2	A31 2-2	a17 3-0	a03 2-2		D05 0-0	O03 2-2	F27 2-2	S30 2-1	N09 0-1	N07 1-2	F13 1-1	S21 0-1	O24 1-2	a09 3-0	A22 1-1	D26 2-1
13 LINCOLN C	m01 4-4	a09 0-3	F27 1-2	A22 2-0	O17 0-1	a28 2-0	D26 1-2	J23 2-2	N28 2-1	O03 4-1	S23 3-0	F06 2-0		M17 1-1	N18 1-3	F20 0-1	M13 2-1	O24 2-1	N07 4-1	S19 1-2	J16 3-0	a17 1-1	S05 3-1	a03 4-5
14 NEWPORT CO	D05 1-2	F12 3-2	A29 0-2	N07 0-1	M12 2-0	S26 0-1	N10 1-3	a10 1-3	a24 3-1	S29 0-1	S01 0-1	a13 2-0	a20 2-2		A15 0-1	M09 2-1	S12 1-4	M27 2-0	O10 2-3	J15 3-0	D19 2-2	M02 3-1	O24 2-2	F26 0-3
15 NORTHAMPTON T	D26 2-0	S19 1-0	F13 2-3	O03 1-0	A22 2-1	O20 3-1	a03 2-1	N14 1-1	M05 2-0	M16 2-2	a13 0-4	O31 2-0	J09 2-1	O17 1-0		M20 1-1	D05 1-3	N10 2-0	J30 1-0	m01 0-2	S01 2-1	S22 1-1	a17 5-0	S05 3-2
16 NOTTS CO	a03 3-0	A22 3-1	D05 2-1	S19 0-0	D26 4-1	F13 2-1	a12 4-0	S02 5-1	O21 3-0	m01 1-1	a17 1-0	J09 3-0	N11 0-0	S23 2-0	N07 1-0		O24 2-0	J30 6-0	F27 3-0	S05 2-1	M13 3-1	M17 5-1	O03 2-2	O17 2-1
17 OLDHAM A	S22 5-2	D26 2-1	O20 2-2	S05 5-1	a03 4-1	M20 1-1	a17 4-0	O31 5-3	J23 3-1	A22 2-1	O17 1-0	M30 2-0	N14 4-2	D12 4-0	F06 1-1	M06 1-3		J09 3-0	O06 1-1	O03 2-0	N28 2-4	m01 1-1	S19 1-3	M15 1-1
18 PETERBOROUGH U	A22 1-0	m01 4-0	a28 3-1	a12 1-2	a17 2-3	O31 1-0	O03 1-2	F06 3-1	N14 0-1	a03 1-3	S19 1-1	M20 5-0	M06 1-1	S05 2-1	F20 1-0	N28 1-1	S30 2-1		J16 1-2	D26 4-0	J23 1-0	O17 5-1	M17 3-1	S23 2-1
19 SCUNTHORPE U	a13 2-1	S22 1-1	J09 1-1	D26 1-1	S05 0-0	N14 0-2	M16 2-0	M06 1-1	F20 0-0	O17 3-0	O03 1-2	J23 2-1	M20 3-1	a17 0-1	N28 2-2	O03 0-1	S01 2-3	O20 5-2		A22 3-0	F06 2-0	a03 1-2	m01 4-0	S19 0-1
20 SOUTHEND U	F12 2-2	N06 2-3	S11 1-2	O24 4-3	F26 1-1	F22 1-1	M12 1-1	O09 0-2	A28 0-0	a28 0-0	J08 1-1	M10 2-0	m03 1-1	O21 3-0	S25 1-0	M26 1-0	a12 3-0	a05 1-2	D18 2-2		A15 1-1	N09 2-1	D04 1-1	J29 1-0
21 SOUTHPORT	M17 3-3	O02 1-0	N10 0-1	a03 2-0	a09 0-1	J09 2-0	S04 2-1	M19 1-0	O30 0-3	S21 0-2	S08 1-0	M05 5-0	O20 1-0	A21 6-1	a26 2-1	N14 0-2	J29 1-4	F12 3-2	D04 5-1	O16 3-0		S18 1-0	D26 1-0	a16 2-2
22 STOCKPORT CO	A31 1-0	F26 2-0	M26 1-1	S28 1-0	J15 0-1	a10 0-1	O23 0-0	a12 2-2	D18 1-1	J22 0-3	F05 1-0	S11 2-1	O09 4-3	N27 3-2	D12 1-1	F22 1-0	S25 1-1	A15 0-0	A28 2-0	F19 0-0	a23 3-0		M12 1-0	N06 1-0
23 WORKINGTON	M20 4-0	J16 2-1	M10 1-0	M24 1-1	F20 3-1	A29 1-0	S30 1-1	A15 1-1	S12 0-0	N28 1-0	O31 1-0	D19 0-1	M27 2-1	M06 2-1	O10 2-0	a08 0-1	a24 0-0	M31 2-1	S26 0-0	F06 1-1	a10 2-1	N13 0-1		a27 1-0
24 YORK C	N13 3-1	O12 4-3	S26 1-1	F20 0-0	M01 3-0	S12 1-1	J16 1-1	D19 1-0	a09 2-0	F06 2-2	M05 4-1	a10 4-0	A29 2-0	O30 1-0	M27 4-1	A15 0-0	a19 0-1	M08 2-1	a24 2-0	N27 3-0	O09 2-0	M19 2-1	A31 1-0	

LEAGUE TABLES

DIVISION 1

	P	W	D	L	F	A	W	D	L	F	A	Pts
Arsenal	42	18	3	0	41	6	11	4	6	30	23	65
Leeds U	42	16	2	3	40	12	11	8	2	32	18	64
Tottenham H	42	11	5	5	33	19	8	9	4	21	14	52
Wolverh'pton W	42	13	3	5	33	22	9	5	7	31	32	52
Liverpool	42	11	10	0	30	10	6	7	8	12	14	51
Chelsea	42	12	6	3	34	21	6	9	6	18	21	51
Southampton	42	12	5	4	35	15	5	7	9	21	29	46
Manchester U	42	9	6	6	29	24	7	5	9	36	42	43
Derby Co	42	9	5	7	32	26	7	5	9	24	28	42
Coventry C	42	12	4	5	24	12	4	6	11	13	26	42
Manchester C	42	7	9	5	30	22	5	8	8	17	20	41
Newcastle U	42	9	9	3	27	16	5	4	12	17	30	41
Stoke C	42	10	7	4	28	11	2	6	13	16	37	37
Everton	42	10	7	4	32	16	2	6	13	22	44	37
Huddersfield T	42	7	8	6	19	16	4	6	11	21	33	36
Nottingham F	42	9	4	8	29	26	5	4	12	13	35	36
W.B.A.	42	9	8	4	34	25	1	7	13	24	50	35
Crystal Palace	42	9	5	7	24	24	3	6	12	15	33	35
Ipswich T	42	9	4	8	28	22	3	6	12	14	26	34
West Ham U	42	6	8	7	28	30	4	6	11	19	30	34
Burnley	42	4	8	9	20	31	3	5	13	9	32	27
Blackpool	42	3	9	9	22	31	1	6	14	12	35	23

DIVISION 2

	P	W	D	L	F	A	W	D	L	F	A	Pts
Leicester C	42	12	7	2	30	14	11	6	4	27	16	59
Sheffield U	42	14	6	1	49	18	7	8	6	24	21	56
Cardiff C	42	12	7	2	39	16	8	6	7	25	25	53
Carlisle U	42	16	3	2	39	13	4	10	7	26	30	53
Hull C	42	11	5	5	31	16	8	8	5	23	25	51
Luton T	42	12	7	2	40	18	6	6	9	22	25	49
Middlesbrough	42	13	6	2	37	16	4	8	9	23	27	48
Millwall	42	13	5	3	36	12	6	4	11	23	30	47
Birmingham C	42	12	7	2	30	12	5	5	11	28	36	46
Norwich C	42	11	8	2	34	20	4	6	11	20	32	44
Q.P.R.	42	11	5	5	39	22	5	6	10	19	31	43
Swindon T	42	12	7	2	38	14	3	5	13	23	37	42
Sunderland	42	11	6	4	34	21	4	6	11	18	33	42
Oxford U	42	8	8	5	23	23	6	6	9	18	25	42
Sheffield W	42	10	7	4	32	27	2	5	14	19	42	36
Portsmouth	42	9	4	8	32	28	1	10	10	14	33	34
Orient	42	5	11	5	16	15	4	5	12	13	36	34
Watford	42	6	7	8	18	22	4	6	11	20	38	33
Bristol C	42	9	6	6	30	28	1	5	15	16	36	31
Charlton A	42	7	6	8	28	30	1	8	12	13	35	30
Blackburn R	42	5	8	8	20	28	1	7	13	17	41	27
Bolton W	42	6	5	10	22	31	1	5	15	13	43	24

DIVISION 3

	P	W	D	L	F	A	W	D	L	F	A	Pts
Preston N.E.	46	15	8	0	42	16	7	9	7	21	23	61
Fulham	46	15	6	2	39	12	9	6	8	29	29	60
Halifax T	46	16	2	5	46	22	6	10	7	28	33	56
Aston Villa	46	13	7	3	27	13	6	8	9	27	33	53
Chesterfield	46	13	8	2	45	12	4	9	10	21	26	51
Bristol R	46	11	5	7	38	24	8	8	7	31	26	51
Mansfield T	46	13	7	3	44	28	5	8	10	20	34	51
Rotherham U	46	12	10	1	38	19	5	6	12	26	41	50
Wrexham	46	12	8	3	43	25	6	5	12	29	40	49
Torquay U	46	12	6	5	37	26	7	5	11	17	31	49
Swansea C	46	11	5	7	41	25	4	11	8	18	31	46
Barnsley	46	12	6	5	30	19	5	5	13	19	33	45
Shrewsbury T	46	11	6	6	37	28	5	7	11	21	34	45
Brighton & H.A.	46	8	10	5	28	20	6	6	11	22	27	44
Plymouth A	46	6	12	5	39	33	6	7	10	24	30	43
Rochdale	46	8	8	7	29	26	6	7	10	32	42	43
Port Vale	46	11	6	6	29	18	4	6	13	23	41	42
Tranmere R	46	8	11	4	27	18	2	11	10	18	37	42
Bradford C	46	7	6	10	23	25	6	8	9	26	37	40
Walsall	46	10	1	12	30	27	4	10	9	21	30	39
Reading	46	10	7	6	32	33	4	4	15	16	52	39
Bury	46	7	9	7	30	23	5	4	14	22	37	37
Doncaster R	46	8	5	10	28	27	5	4	14	17	39	35
Gillingham	46	6	9	8	22	29	4	4	15	20	38	33

DIVISION 4

	P	W	D	L	F	A	W	D	L	F	A	Pts
Notts Co	46	19	4	0	59	12	11	5	7	30	24	69
Bournemouth	46	16	5	2	51	15	8	7	8	30	31	60
Oldham A	46	14	6	3	57	29	10	5	8	31	34	59
York C	46	16	6	1	45	14	7	4	12	33	40	56
Chester C	46	17	2	4	42	18	7	5	11	27	37	55
Colchester U	46	14	6	3	44	19	7	6	10	26	35	54
Northampton T	46	15	4	4	39	24	4	9	10	24	35	51
Southport	46	15	2	6	42	24	6	4	13	21	33	48
Exeter C	46	12	7	4	40	23	5	7	11	27	45	48
Workington	46	13	7	3	28	13	5	5	13	20	36	48
Stockport Co	46	12	8	3	28	17	4	6	13	21	48	46
Darlington	46	15	3	5	42	22	2	8	13	16	35	45
Aldershot	46	8	10	5	32	23	6	7	10	34	48	45
Brentford	46	13	3	7	45	27	5	5	13	21	35	44
Crewe A	46	13	1	9	49	35	5	7	11	26	41	44
Peterborough U	46	14	3	6	46	23	4	4	15	24	48	43
Scunthorpe U	46	9	7	7	36	23	6	6	11	20	38	43
Southend U	46	8	11	4	32	24	6	4	13	21	42	43
Grimsby T	46	13	4	6	37	26	5	3	15	20	45	43
Cambridge U	46	9	9	5	31	27	6	4	13	20	39	43
Lincoln C	46	11	4	8	45	33	2	9	12	25	38	39
Newport Co	46	8	3	12	32	36	2	5	16	23	49	28
Hartlepool U	46	6	10	7	28	27	2	2	19	6	47	28
Barrow	46	5	5	13	25	38	2	3	18	26	52	22

Football League Records

Top scorers: Div 1, F.Lee (Manchester City) 33 goals; Div 2, R.Latchford (Birmingham City) 23 goals; Div 3, E.MacDougall (AFC Bournemouth) 35 goals; Div 4, P.Price (Peterborough United) 28 goals.

Bournemouth & Boscombe Athletic became AFC Bournemouth.

Derby County skipper Roy McFarland missed only four games as the Rams won the League Championship for the first time in their history.

DIVISION 1

	ARSENAL	CHELSEA	COVENTRY C	CRYSTAL P	DERBY CO	EVERTON	HUDDERSFIELD T	IPSWICH T	LEEDS U	LEICESTER C	LIVERPOOL	MANCHESTER C	MANCHESTER U	NEWCASTLE U	NOTTINGHAM F	SHEFFIELD U	SOUTHAMPTON	STOKE C	TOTTENHAM H	W.B.A.	WEST HAM U	WOLVERHAMPTON W
1 ARSENAL		A14 3-0	D11 2-0	N27 2-1	F12 2-0	J01 1-1	J22 1-0	O30 2-1	S11 2-0	S25 3-0	m08 0-0	N13 1-2	a25 3-0	O09 4-2	a01 3-0	A24 0-1	M28 1-0	A28 0-1	m11 0-2	D18 2-0	a22 2-1	a08 2-1
2 CHELSEA	O16 1-2		S04 3-3	a08 2-1	S18 1-1	J29 4-0	J08 2-2	D27 2-0	D11 0-0	F19 2-1	M11 0-0	A21 2-2	A18 2-3	a22 3-3	N06 2-0	M29 2-0	O23 3-0	a24 2-0	N27 1-0	S01 1-0	M25 3-1	O02 3-1
3 COVENTRY C	m01 0-1	D17 1-1		O22 1-1	A24 2-2	a04 4-1	N06 2-1	J22 1-1	O09 3-1	D04 1-1	N20 0-2	a15 1-1	a01 2-3	A28 1-0	S11 1-1	a18 3-2	J01 1-0	A14 1-1	S25 1-0	M17 0-2	M21 1-1	F19 0-0
4 CRYSTAL P	a11 2-2	N20 2-3	F12 2-2		M28 0-1	S25 2-1	a29 0-0	N13 1-1	D18 1-1	a03 1-1	A24 0-1	J22 1-2	S11 1-3	A14 2-0	A28 1-1	D04 5-1	a01 2-3	a26 2-0	J01 1-1	O09 0-2	O30 0-3	M18 0-2
5 DERBY CO	O23 2-1	J01 1-0	J29 1-0	N06 3-0		D18 2-0	a15 3-0	M22 1-0	a01 2-0	M18 3-0	m01 1-0	D04 3-1	A14 2-2	a03 0-1	F19 4-0	N20 3-0	A28 2-2	S11 4-0	O09 2-2	S25 0-0	A18 2-0	M04 2-1
6 EVERTON	S18 2-1	A24 2-0	O02 1-2	M21 0-0	S04 0-2		D27 2-2	O16 1-1	F12 0-0	a15 0-0	N13 1-0	M11 1-2	A31 1-0	O30 1-0	m02 1-1	A21 0-1	N20 8-0	D04 0-0	M01 1-1	J22 2-1	J08 2-1	M25 2-2
7 HUDDERSFIELD T	A17 0-1	A28 1-2	a11 0-1	D11 0-1	N27 2-1	a01 0-0		a08 1-3	S25 2-1	A14 2-2	F12 0-1	O30 1-1	O09 0-3	J29 0-0	O26 0-1	M21 0-0	D18 0-2	J01 0-0	M28 1-1	S11 1-0	N13 1-0	a22 0-1
8 IPSWICH T	F19 0-1	a01 1-2	A17 3-1	M04 0-2	A31 0-0	A14 0-0	N20 1-0		A28 0-2	S11 1-2	D04 0-0	a18 2-1	D18 0-0	S25 0-0	O09 1-1	a15 0-0	M18 1-1	O23 2-1	a03 2-1	J01 2-3	J29 1-0	N06 2-1
9 LEEDS U	M25 3-0	m01 2-0	M11 1-0	S04 2-0	D27 3-0	O23 3-2	a05 3-1	J08 2-2		N06 2-1	S18 1-0	O16 3-0	F19 5-1	S01 5-1	M27 6-1	J22 1-0	M04 7-0	N20 1-0	A25 1-1	D04 3-0	O02 0-0	A21 0-0
10 LEICESTER C	a04 0-0	O30 1-1	a22 1-0	O02 0-0	A21 0-2	N27 0-0	O16 2-0	M25 1-0	M22 0-0		J08 1-0	S04 0-0	a08 2-0	N13 3-0	A18 2-1	S18 0-1	S01 0-1	J29 2-1	D11 0-1	F12 0-1	M11 2-0	D27 1-2
11 LIVERPOOL	N06 3-2	O09 0-0	a08 3-1	J29 4-1	D11 3-2	M04 4-0	O23 2-0	a22 2-0	J01 0-2	A28 3-2		F26 3-0	S25 2-2	M18 5-0	A14 3-1	F19 2-0	S11 1-0	M28 2-1	D18 0-0	a01 2-0	N27 1-0	A17 3-2
12 MANCHESTER C	M04 2-0	M18 1-0	N27 4-0	A18 4-0	a22 2-0	O09 1-0	F19 1-0	D11 4-0	A14 0-1	D18 1-1	S01 1-0		N06 3-3	S11 2-1	J01 2-2	O23 2-1	S25 3-0	a01 1-2	A28 4-0	M01 2-1	a08 3-1	J29 5-2
13 MANCHESTER U	A20 3-1	J22 0-1	D27 2-2	M25 4-0	O16 1-0	M08 0-0	M11 2-0	S04 1-0	O30 0-1	N20 3-2	a03 0-3	a12 1-3		F12 0-2	D04 3-2	O02 2-0	a15 3-2	a29 3-0	N13 3-1	A23 3-1	S18 4-2	J08 1-3
14 NEWCASTLE U	M11 2-0	D04 0-0	J08 4-2	O16 1-2	O02 0-1	F19 0-0	A25 0-0	a05 0-1	a19 1-0	M04 2-0	A21 3-2	M25 0-0	O23 0-1		N20 2-1	D27 1-2	N06 3-1	m08 0-0	J22 3-1	m03 4-2	S04 2-2	S18 2-0
15 NOTTINGHAM F	D27 1-1	M14 2-1	M25 4-0	J08 0-1	O30 0-2	D11 1-0	O02 1-2	M11 0-2	N27 0-2	J22 1-2	O16 2-3	S18 2-2	a22 0-0	a08 1-0		S04 2-3	A24 2-3	A31 0-0	F12 0-1	N13 4-1	A21 1-0	a25 1-3
16 SHEFFIELD U	J29 0-5	S25 1-0	N13 2-0	a22 1-0	a08 0-4	M18 1-1	A31 3-1	N27 7-0	A17 3-0	J01 1-1	O30 1-1	F12 3-3	a04 1-1	a01 1-0	D18 2-1		A14 3-1	O09 2-3	S11 2-2	A28 0-0	F29 3-0	D11 2-2
17 SOUTHAMPTON	O02 0-1	a18 2-2	S18 3-1	D27 1-0	J08 1-2	a08 0-1	S04 1-2	A21 0-0	N13 2-1	a11 1-0	M25 0-1	a04 2-0	N27 2-5	F26 1-2	J29 4-1	O16 3-2		A17 3-1	a22 0-0	O30 1-1	D11 3-3	M11 1-2
18 STOKE C	J08 0-0	N13 0-1	O16 1-0	A21 3-1	M25 1-1	a22 1-1	S18 1-0	F12 3-3	a08 0-3	A25 3-1	O02 0-0	D27 1-3	D11 1-1	N27 3-3	a10 0-2	M11 2-2	J22 3-1		O30 2-0	m05 1-1	a04 0-0	S04 0-1
19 TOTTENHAM H	N24 1-1	a15 3-0	M31 1-0	S18 3-0	M11 0-1	N06 3-0	A21 4-1	O02 2-1	J29 1-0	a29 4-3	S04 2-0	J08 1-1	M04 2-0	A18 0-0	O23 6-1	M25 2-0	D04 1-0	F19 2-0		N20 3-2	D27 0-1	O16 4-1
20 W.B.A.	S04 0-1	a27 4-0	A21 1-1	M11 1-1	a05 0-0	A18 2-0	M25 1-1	S18 1-2	a22 0-1	O23 0-1	D27 1-0	O02 0-2	J29 2-1	D11 0-3	M04 1-0	J08 2-2	F19 3-2	N06 0-1	a08 1-1		O16 0-0	N27 2-3
21 WEST HAM U	D04 0-0	S11 2-1	A30 4-0	F19 1-1	J22 3-3	A28 1-0	M04 3-0	A23 0-0	M31 2-2	O09 1-1	a15 0-2	N20 0-2	J01 3-0	D18 0-1	M18 4-2	N06 1-2	m01 1-0	S25 2-1	a01 2-0	A14 0-1		O23 1-0
22 WOLVERHAMPTON W	N20 5-1	a12 0-2	O30 1-1	A31 1-0	N13 2-1	S11 1-1	D04 2-2	F26 2-2	m08 2-1	a01 0-1	J22 0-0	A24 2-1	A28 1-1	J01 2-0	S25 4-2	a28 1-2	O09 4-2	D18 2-0	A14 2-2	a15 0-1	F12 1-0	

Charlie Aitken, one of Aston Villa's all-time greats. Altogether he made 656 full League and Cup appearances for them and was a great inspiration when they returned from Division Three in 1971-72.

DIVISION 2

	BIRMINGHAM C	BLACKPOOL	BRISTOL C	BURNLEY	CARDIFF C	CARLISLE U	CHARLTON A	FULHAM	HULL C	LUTON T	MIDDLESBROUGH	MILLWALL	NORWICH C	ORIENT	OXFORD U	PORTSMOUTH	PRESTON N.E.	Q.P.R.	SHEFFIELD W	SUNDERLAND	SWINDON T	WATFORD
1 BIRMINGHAM C		a04 2-1	S18 1-0	F19 2-0	D27 3-0	A21 3-2	S04 4-1	N27 3-1	a25 2-0	M25 1-0	a22 1-1	a08 1-0	M04 4-0	N06 2-0	O02 0-0	J08 6-3	O23 2-2	M11 0-0	D11 0-0	O16 1-1	J29 4-1	S28 4-1
2 BLACKPOOL	S25 1-1		J22 1-0	a01 4-2	A16 3-0	N06 2-0	a29 5-0	F19 2-1	D18 1-1	N20 0-1	a03 3-1	M18 0-0	S11 1-2	O09 4-1	a15 2-0	a24 1-2	D04 1-1	O23 1-1	A28 1-0	M04 1-1	A14 4-1	J01 5-0
3 BRISTOL C	J01 1-0	S28 4-0		D18 0-2	A31 2-0	N19 1-4	F19 2-0	N06 1-2	S11 4-0	D04 0-0	A28 2-1	A14 3-3	S25 0-1	O23 5-3	a29 4-2	J29 1-1	a01 4-1	M04 2-0	M18 1-0	a15 3-1	M31 1-0	O09 2-1
4 BURNLEY	O30 1-1	D27 2-1	S04 1-1		O16 3-0	M11 3-1	a04 3-1	M25 1-1	F12 0-2	A21 2-1	N13 5-2	a22 2-0	J29 1-0	S28 6-1	J08 1-1	D11 1-3	a25 1-0	S18 1-0	F26 5-3	O02 0-1	N27 1-2	a08 3-0
5 CARDIFF C	a01 0-0	J29 3-4	a26 2-3	A14 2-2		a15 3-1	O23 6-1	M04 1-0	A28 1-1	a29 1-1	J01 1-0	O09 1-2	F19 0-0	a12 1-0	M21 1-1	D01 3-2	M29 5-2	N06 0-0	S11 3-2	N20 1-2	S25 0-1	D18 2-0
6 CARLISLE U	M21 2-2	F26 2-0	a08 2-0	O09 0-3	N27 2-1		S28 5-2	a22 3-1	S25 2-1	F12 0-0	M14 3-0	a04 3-3	D18 3-0	J01 2-0	O30 2-1	N13 1-0	A14 0-0	D11 1-4	J29 2-2	a25 1-2	A28 0-0	S11 2-0
7 CHARLTON A	D18 1-1	D11 2-3	O30 2-0	S25 2-0	F12 2-2	J22 1-1		a08 2-2	A14 1-0	F26 2-0	S11 0-2	a25 0-2	a01 0-2	M31 1-2	N13 3-0	a22 1-1	J01 2-1	N27 2-1	O09 2-2	O19 2-2	M18 3-1	A28 2-0
8 FULHAM	a18 0-0	O30 2-1	F26 2-0	S11 0-2	N13 4-3	D04 0-1	N20 1-0		O09 1-0	J22 3-1	D18 2-2	a01 1-0	A28 0-0	S25 2-1	O12 1-1	F12 1-1	M18 0-0	A31 0-3	M28 4-0	a29 0-0	J01 2-4	A14 3-0
9 HULL C	S01 1-0	S04 1-0	M25 1-1	O23 1-2	J08 0-0	a03 2-0	O16 2-3	M11 4-0		O02 0-0	D11 4-3	N27 0-0	N06 1-2	M04 1-1	A21 1-0	S18 1-3	F19 3-2	a08 1-1	a22 1-0	D27 2-3	S29 2-0	J29 4-0
10 LUTON T	S11 0-0	a08 1-4	a22 0-0	M18 1-0	D11 2-2	O23 0-2	N06 1-2	S28 2-0	a04 0-1		S25 3-2	J01 2-1	A14 1-1	D18 2-0	F05 1-2	N27 3-2	A28 1-1	J29 1-1	a01 3-1	F19 1-2	O09 0-0	M04 0-0
11 MIDDLESBROUGH	D04 0-0	O02 1-0	J08 1-0	M04 1-0	S18 1-0	D27 2-2	M25 2-2	S04 2-0	a29 3-0	M31 0-0		O19 1-0	a15 1-0	N20 1-0	M11 2-1	O16 2-1	N06 0-1	A21 3-2	A31 2-1	J22 2-0	F19 2-0	O23 2-1
12 MILLWALL	N20 3-0	A21 1-0	O16 3-1	D04 1-1	M11 1-1	O02 2-1	A30 2-1	D27 4-1	a15 2-1	S18 2-2	J29 1-0		O23 2-1	F19 2-1	M25 2-0	M31 1-0	a29 2-0	J08 0-0	S27 1-1	S04 1-1	M04 2-2	N06 3-2
13 NORWICH C	N13 2-2	M25 5-1	a04 2-2	O13 3-0	O30 2-1	S04 1-0	D27 3-0	J08 2-1	M15 2-0	O16 3-1	N27 2-0	F12 2-2		S01 0-0	S18 3-2	A21 3-1	J22 1-1	O02 0-0	a08 1-0	M11 1-1	a22 1-0	D11 1-1
14 ORIENT	m02 0-1	M11 0-1	F12 2-0	J22 1-0	A21 4-1	S18 2-1	O02 3-2	a03 1-0	N13 1-0	S04 0-0	a08 1-1	O30 2-2	a24 1-2		O16 1-1	M24 2-1	O18 3-2	D27 2-0	N27 0-3	J08 5-0	D11 0-1	a22 1-0
15 OXFORD U	M31 0-1	N27 3-1	D11 0-0	A28 2-1	a22 1-0	F19 3-1	M04 2-1	J29 1-0	M18 2-2	S01 1-1	O09 0-0	S11 1-2	J01 0-2	A14 1-1		a08 2-2	D18 2-0	S29 3-1	S25 1-0	O23 2-0	N06 1-1	a01 0-0
16 PORTSMOUTH	A28 1-0	S01 1-3	O20 1-1	a29 1-2	J22 2-0	M04 1-0	D04 0-0	O23 6-3	J01 0-0	a15 0-3	A14 2-1	S25 1-1	M18 2-1	S11 3-2	N20 2-0		O09 1-1	F19 1-0	D18 1-2	N06 2-2	a01 1-2	a03 2-2
17 PRESTON N.E.	F12 0-0	a22 1-4	D27 1-0	A30 1-3	O02 1-2	O16 3-0	S18 2-1	A21 2-0	O30 3-1	J08 0-1	a17 1-0	D11 4-0	S28 0-2	J29 1-1	S04 1-0	M11 4-0		M25 1-1	N13 1-0	a04 1-3	m01 2-2	N27 2-0
18 Q.P.R.	O09 1-0	F12 0-1	N13 3-0	J01 3-1	m02 3-0	a29 3-0	a15 2-0	a25 0-0	N20 2-1	O19 1-0	M18 1-0	A28 1-1	a03 0-0	a01 1-0	J22 4-2	O30 1-1	S11 2-1		A14 3-0	D04 2-1	D18 3-0	S25 3-0
19 SHEFFIELD W	a29 1-2	J08 1-2	A21 1-5	N06 2-1	M25 2-2	O20 2-1	a10 2-1	O02 4-0	D04 2-1	D27 2-2	a26 1-0	J22 1-1	N20 1-1	a17 3-1	a03 0-0	S04 1-1	M04 1-0	O16 0-0		S18 3-0	O23 1-0	F19 2-1
20 SUNDERLAND	A14 1-1	N13 0-0	N27 1-1	a03 4-3	a08 1-1	S01 0-3	J29 3-0	D11 2-1	a01 0-1	O30 2-2	S29 4-1	D18 3-3	O09 1-1	A28 2-0	F12 3-0	M01 3-2	S25 4-3	a22 0-1	J01 2-0		S11 1-0	a17 5-0
21 SWINDON T	O19 1-1	O16 1-0	O02 0-1	a15 0-1	a04 3-1	J08 0-0	A21 2-1	S18 4-0	J22 2-1	a18 2-1	O30 0-1	N13 0-2	D04 0-1	a29 2-2	F26 4-0	D27 3-1	N20 1-1	S04 0-0	F12 1-0	M25 1-1		a25 2-0
22 WATFORD	J22 0-1	S18 1-0	M11 0-2	N20 2-1	S04 2-2	M25 1-2	J08 0-3	O16 1-2	O20 1-2	N13 2-1	F12 0-1	F26 0-1	a29 1-1	D04 0-1	D27 0-1	O02 1-0	a15 1-0	M31 0-2	O30 1-1	A21 1-1	S01 0-0	

SEASON 1971-72

DIVISION 3

	ASTON VILLA	BARNSLEY	BLACKBURN R	BOLTON W	BOURNEMOUTH	BRADFORD C	BRIGHTON & HA	BRISTOL R	CHESTERFIELD	HALIFAX T	MANSFIELD T	NOTTS CO	OLDHAM A	PLYMOUTH A	PORT VALE	ROCHDALE	ROTHERHAM U	SHREWSBURY T	SWANSEA C	TORQUAY U	TRANMERE R	WALSALL	WREXHAM	YORK C
1 ASTON VILLA		J22 2-0	O30 4-1	D18 3-2	F12 2-1	D04 3-0	S11 2-0	a03 2-1	m05 1-0	J01 1-0	S22 0-1	N13 1-0	a10 1-0	A14 3-1	F26 2-0	A28 2-0	O09 1-2	J19 3-0	a01 2-0	a29 5-1	O20 2-0	M18 0-0	S25 2-0	F05 1-0
2 BARNSLEY	S28 0-4		a08 0-0	a01 1-0	N27 0-0	O23 0-2	a04 0-1	J01 0-0	O09 1-4	S11 1-2	J29 1-1	a22 2-1	N06 2-1	J15 2-2	M21 0-0	S25 3-3	M18 1-1	A28 1-3	D18 0-1	F19 0-0	A31 0-0	A14 4-2	M08 2-1	M04 2-1
3 BLACKBURN R	F19 1-1	F05 4-0		S11 0-3	a26 2-1	N06 1-0	a12 2-2	M27 1-2	D18 1-0	m08 2-0	O23 1-1	O20 0-2	D04 0-1	M18 3-2	J22 3-1	O09 3-0	A14 2-1	M31 1-0	S25 1-2	M04 1-0	a15 4-1	J01 1-1	A28 2-1	J15 3-0
4 BOLTON W	S04 2-0	D27 0-0	M25 1-0		A21 0-0	M15 0-0	D04 1-1	F19 0-0	M04 1-0	S29 1-1	O02 2-0	J08 1-2	O16 2-1	J29 2-1	M11 3-0	a12 2-1	a29 2-2	a15 2-0	O23 0-0	a19 2-0	a03 1-0	M22 0-1	N06 0-2	S18 0-1
5 BOURNEMOUTH	O23 3-0	a15 0-0	A31 1-0	M18 1-2		M04 3-0	a01 1-1	M08 2-0	S25 1-0	D18 3-1	F19 1-1	J22 2-0	a29 2-0	F05 1-0	O19 3-2	S11 4-1	A28 3-1	A14 3-1	O09 2-1	N06 1-0	m03 0-0	F23 0-0	J01 4-0	D04 2-2
6 BRADFORD C	a22 0-1	F12 0-2	F26 1-2	m10 0-3	N13 2-2		M18 2-1	D18 1-1	S11 2-2	A28 2-1	J15 2-2	N27 2-3	J29 2-2	M20 0-1	a08 0-0	a01 1-1	J01 1-0	S25 2-1	A14 0-2	a26 0-1	O30 1-1	O09 3-0	a03 0-2	S29 3-1
7 BRIGHTON & H.A.	M25 2-1	O02 0-0	a19 3-0	a22 1-1	D27 2-0	A21 3-1		S29 3-1	N27 2-1	N13 2-1	J08 1-0	S18 1-1	M15 0-1	F26 3-0	O16 1-1	m03 1-1	a26 2-1	O30 2-0	J29 1-0	M31 3-1	M11 2-0	F12 1-2	a08 3-2	S04 0-2
8 BRISTOL R	O02 0-1	S18 3-0	M14 3-0	O30 2-0	a18 1-2	S04 7-1	J22 2-2		m02 3-1	a08 1-0	M11 2-1	a04 0-2	M25 1-0	N27 2-2	D27 2-1	F12 5-2	N09 1-2	N13 3-1	a25 2-1	J08 2-0	A21 2-1	F26 2-1	a22 3-1	O16 5-4
9 CHESTERFIELD	a19 0-4	M11 0-0	S04 2-0	N13 2-1	a05 0-0	M25 0-1	a15 0-1	a29 1-3		F12 2-1	S18 2-0	A21 1-2	O02 0-1	O30 2-1	J08 2-1	F26 2-0	a12 0-1	O20 0-0	D04 1-2	O16 2-0	M15 2-2	J22 1-1	O06 1-0	D27 2-1
10 HALIFAX T	S18 0-1	M25 2-0	D27 0-1	J22 0-1	S04 1-0	J08 2-1	M04 0-5	F05 2-1	O23 2-0		O16 1-1	a18 3-1	M11 0-0	N15 0-1	a04 2-0	O19 2-2	N06 1-1	a29 0-0	a15 0-1	M14 0-0	O02 3-2	D04 3-1	F19 4-1	A21 3-1
11 MANSFIELD T	a24 1-1	O18 0-0	F12 1-0	M27 1-0	O29 0-5	a29 1-1	A28 0-3	O09 0-0	J01 2-1	A14 0-0		F26 1-1	F05 2-1	D18 2-3	N13 0-1	M18 3-1	S25 0-1	M20 2-2	S11 0-2	D04 0-0	J22 1-1	a01 1-1	m01 1-1	a15 0-0
12 NOTTS CO	M04 0-3	D04 3-0	J29 1-0	A28 1-2	S29 1-1	a15 2-0	J01 1-0	S25 2-3	M18 1-4	a12 3-1	N06 2-0		O23 2-0	O09 1-0	a26 2-1	A14 4-0	M22 1-1	S11 1-0	a03 5-0	m03 2-1	a29 1-0	D18 3-0	a01 1-0	F19 2-2
13 OLDHAM A	N27 0-6	F26 6-0	D11 1-1	A14 2-2	M21 3-1	O19 0-2	J15 2-4	S11 3-2	M31 1-1	O09 0-0	a08 2-1	F12 0-1		S25 0-1	O30 1-0	J01 3-2	m05 5-1	D18 1-4	M28 1-0	J22 1-0	N13 3-1	A28 1-3	M18 0-2	A31 1-0
14 PLYMOUTH A	O16 3-2	M14 2-1	A21 1-0	O12 2-0	O02 1-1	a18 1-4	N06 1-2	a15 2-1	F19 1-0	a25 1-1	S04 3-1	M11 1-1	a03 0-0		M25 0-0	J22 4-1	M04 2-1	D04 1-2	m02 4-1	D27 3-1	S18 2-2	S13 3-2	O23 1-2	J08 4-0
15 PORT VALE	N06 4-4	a29 1-0	S27 0-0	O09 1-1	J29 1-1	F05 1-0	A14 1-1	a01 0-0	A28 0-2	S25 1-0	M04 1-0	A30 0-3	F19 1-0	S11 0-0		m12 1-1	m08 1-2	J01 2-1	M18 3-0	a15 0-0	D04 2-1	a03 1-1	D18 1-0	O23 4-3
16 ROCHDALE	J08 1-0	a03 0-2	M11 2-1	a24 2-2	M25 1-1	D27 0-1	a29 1-2	O23 3-1	N06 0-2	J29 3-2	A21 2-1	O16 1-1	S18 1-1	S27 3-2	M13 3-2		D04 2-1	F05 0-0	F19 1-1	O02 5-0	S03 2-1	a15 0-0	M04 1-0	a17 1-2
17 ROTHERHAM U	M11 0-2	A21 3-0	O16 2-1	m02 2-0	J08 0-0	S18 2-0	A31 2-4	J29 0-0	a08 0-1	F26 3-2	a03 3-1	M14 2-2	D27 3-1	N13 4-3	a18 3-0	a22 5-1		F12 2-1	S28 4-0	S04 2-2	M25 0-0	O30 1-1	N27 2-2	O02 1-1
18 SHREWSBURY T	M15 1-1	J07 1-0	O02 7-1	N26 1-0	O15 3-2	a04 3-0	F19 3-5	M04 2-2	J28 3-4	m03 3-0	a19 4-2	M25 1-1	S04 2-4	a22 1-2	S18 0-0	a08 2-1	O23 0-1		N05 3-0	A21 2-0	D27 0-0	S01 4-1	S29 2-1	M10 2-1
19 SWANSEA C	D27 1-2	S04 2-0	a04 0-1	F12 3-2	M11 1-2	O16 2-0	O19 2-1	A31 2-0	a22 1-3	N27 3-0	M24 1-1	O02 1-1	a18 0-0	a08 1-1	A21 0-1	O30 1-0	J22 0-2	F26 1-0		S18 0-0	J08 1-1	N13 2-0	a11 0-2	M14 2-1
20 TORQUAY U	a12 2-1	O30 1-2	N13 3-1	m05 1-1	F26 0-2	S01 2-1	S25 2-2	A28 1-1	A14 3-2	M22 2-0	a22 0-1	a08 1-1	S29 0-2	a01 2-1	N27 3-0	S13 1-1	D18 0-1	M18 2-0	J01 1-4		F12 0-1	S11 2-2	O09 2-3	J29 0-1
21 TRANMERE R	J28 0-1	a24 0-0	N26 1-3	S24 0-0	a07 1-2	F19 4-1	O08 2-0	M17 0-1	m15 1-2	M31 2-3	S27 2-2	m08 2-1	M04 2-2	J01 3-2	a21 3-2	D17 2-0	S10 0-0	m10 0-4	A27 0-0	O22 2-0		M27 3-3	A14 2-1	N05 2-0
22 WALSALL	A21 1-1	O16 1-1	S18 0-0	a08 1-1	M14 1-1	M11 3-0	O23 0-1	N06 2-0	S28 1-1	a21 0-0	D27 2-1	S04 1-2	J08 2-3	a11 1-0	O02 2-0	N26 3-0	F19 0-0	a25 4-1	M04 4-0	M25 1-0	a18 4-1		J29 2-1	a04 2-1
23 WREXHAM	M31 0-2	a17 2-0	J08 1-1	F26 1-2	S18 1-3	O02 2-1	F05 1-2	D04 1-1	M20 2-0	O30 2-0	M13 1-1	D27 1-1	A21 3-1	F12 0-2	S04 1-2	N13 1-3	a15 0-0	J22 2-1	a29 2-0	M11 1-2	O16 3-0	O18 3-1		M25 2-0
24 YORK C	a08 0-1	N13 1-1	a29 0-1	J01 0-0	a22 0-2	J21 3-1	D18 1-2	A14 0-0	a01 4-1	M18 1-1	N27 1-2	O30 0-2	a24 0-0	A28 2-3	F12 2-1	M20 2-0	M31 2-0	O09 1-1	J24 1-1	O18 3-1	F26 5-0	S25 2-0	S11 1-1	

DIVISION 4

	ALDERSHOT	BARROW	BRENTFORD	BURY	CAMBRIDGE U	CHESTER	COLCHESTER U	CREWE A	DARLINGTON	DONCASTER R	EXETER C	GILLINGHAM	GRIMSBY T	HARTLEPOOL	LINCOLN C	NEWPORT CO	NORTHAMPTON T	PETERBOROUGH U	READING	SCUNTHORPE U	SOUTHEND U	SOUTHPORT	STOCKPORT CO	WORKINGTON
1 ALDERSHOT		J15 1-1	M18 1-2	M04 2-2	M31 1-1	S01 0-0	O09 0-2	a12 0-0	O23 3-0	a08 3-0	a01 0-0	D18 0-2	N27 1-1	F19 2-0	a22 0-0	J01 3-0	J29 0-2	N06 1-1	A28 1-2	S25 1-1	S11 0-0	S29 1-1	m03 4-0	A14 2-2
2 BARROW	M13 1-1		a24 0-3	D27 1-1	N27 1-1	M25 2-0	N06 2-2	A21 2-1	a17 0-4	J08 1-2	M20 0-0	a08 1-0	S04 0-0	a03 2-0	O02 2-2	M04 1-0	A14 0-1	M11 0-2	S27 0-0	O23 0-1	F19 2-1	S18 0-2	J28 3-2	a22 2-0
3 BRENTFORD	A21 1-1	A30 4-0		O16 2-0	a08 2-1	M31 1-1	M04 0-2	D27 1-0	J08 6-2	a17 2-1	a22 1-0	N27 1-3	M25 2-0	S04 6-0	M13 2-0	N06 3-1	O02 6-1	S18 5-1	J29 1-2	F19 0-3	O23 1-2	D11 1-0	S27 2-0	M27 2-0
4 BURY	N13 3-1	a01 4-0	A14 0-2		S11 0-1	F26 3-1	A28 3-0	F12 2-0	J22 3-2	a11 3-3	S25 4-3	M21 5-0	a22 1-1	O19 1-1	O30 0-1	M31 3-0	N27 4-2	a25 1-1	J01 2-1	O09 3-1	D18 2-0	a08 2-1	M18 4-0	M09 2-0
5 CAMBRIDGE U	O02 1-1	a15 1-0	F05 1-1	M25 0-2		O16 2-0	O23 4-2	S04 3-2	S18 6-0	M11 1-1	S29 0-1	a26 2-1	D27 3-1	M15 2-1	a03 0-0	F19 0-1	A21 1-1	a19 2-5	N06 4-1	a29 2-0	D04 1-1	J08 0-0	M04 2-0	M20 0-0
6 CHESTER	a26 0-0	S11 0-0	S25 0-0	N06 2-0	A14 1-1		a03 2-1	a22 0-0	F19 2-1	N27 1-1	J01 1-2	A28 5-1	a08 1-2	O23 4-0	M21 2-1	a01 3-0	S29 3-2	M04 1-1	M18 2-0	a19 0-0	O09 1-1	J29 1-1	J15 0-0	D18 2-1
7 COLCHESTER U	M11 1-0	F26 0-1	N13 1-1	J08 0-0	F12 1-1	O01 1-0		S17 4-2	M24 4-3	M13 1-2	N26 3-0	O29 2-2	a17 0-1	A20 1-0	O15 5-2	a24 2-3	M31 2-0	D27 1-1	a10 2-1	J21 1-1	O18 1-0	S03 1-0	a21 3-2	a07 1-0
8 CREWE A	a29 2-1	M18 1-0	a01 2-1	O23 0-0	D18 1-1	D04 3-1	J01 2-4		F05 1-1	S29 0-1	M31 0-1	S11 0-1	J29 0-1	a15 1-2	S01 3-1	m03 1-2	M04 0-1	F19 2-0	S25 2-0	A28 0-2	J15 1-2	N06 2-1	A14 3-1	O09 0-0
9 DARLINGTON	F12 4-2	M27 0-1	A28 0-0	S27 0-0	J01 2-1	O30 1-1	S11 2-0	a08 1-1		F26 4-1	J15 2-1	m01 0-0	N13 3-2	a24 1-2	N27 3-3	S25 0-0	M20 5-2	J29 1-1	D18 1-0	M31 0-1	M18 2-3	a22 0-0	O09 1-2	a01 4-0
10 DONCASTER R	F05 2-1	A28 0-1	M21 0-3	a29 4-1	O09 1-1	a15 0-0	J15 2-0	J21 0-0	N06 4-0		S11 2-1	a04 1-1	a25 2-1	M04 2-1	O19 2-0	A14 4-2	O22 1-1	D04 3-2	a01 1-1	D18 0-2	S25 0-2	F19 2-1	J01 2-2	M18 0-0
11 EXETER C	D27 1-0	a29 7-1	D04 0-1	a03 3-2	J22 3-4	S18 1-1	a15 3-3	O02 3-1	M15 3-0	M25 1-0		O20 1-1	A21 3-4	a19 1-0	M11 1-2	F05 1-0	J08 1-3	S04 3-2	F19 0-0	N06 1-0	M04 0-0	O16 1-3	O23 2-0	a26 0-2
12 GILLINGHAM	S04 0-1	F05 1-1	a15 0-1	M15 2-0	S01 2-0	J08 1-0	F19 0-2	M25 2-1	O16 4-2	O02 2-0	J29 0-2		M11 0-1	S18 1-0	a19 3-3	O23 1-2	D27 4-1	a03 1-1	M04 4-2	D04 0-1	a29 0-0	A21 2-1	N06 3-2	S29 0-0
13 GRIMSBY T	a15 3-3	D18 2-0	S11 3-1	D04 4-1	a01 2-1	F05 1-0	M21 3-0	O19 2-3	M04 2-0	A31 3-1	m02 3-0	O09 2-1		N06 3-2	J22 2-2	J15 4-2	F19 4-2	a29 3-2	M31 2-0	A14 4-1	J01 4-1	O23 0-1	S25 4-1	A28 1-1
14 HARTLEPOOL	O30 0-1	S25 4-3	D18 1-2	J29 3-1	J15 1-2	F12 2-1	M18 3-2	N27 1-0	A30 2-3	N13 0-0	M27 1-0	J01 3-1	F26 0-1		a08 2-1	O09 0-1	a22 2-0	S27 1-0	A14 3-1	a01 1-0	A28 2-2	a10 1-0	M31 5-0	S11 1-3
15 LINCOLN C	D04 2-2	a12 3-2	J15 4-1	F19 2-0	S25 3-1	a29 4-0	A14 2-0	a26 0-0	a15 0-1	J29 2-0	O09 4-1	M09 1-1	S29 3-0	F05 2-1		A28 3-1	N06 2-0	O23 3-2	S11 0-0	M18 1-0	a01 0-0	M04 2-1	D18 2-1	J01 1-0
16 NEWPORT CO	S18 2-3	N13 2-1	F26 0-0	O02 2-1	O30 3-0	D27 1-0	A31 2-1	a18 2-0	a04 4-0	O16 1-3	a08 0-0	F12 1-2	M13 2-1	M10 0-2	D11 2-0		S04 1-1	A21 1-1	a22 2-1	m01 1-0	J22 2-0	M24 2-2	a11 1-0	N27 0-1
17 NORTHAMPTON T	O19 2-3	O15 2-0	a03 0-0	a15 2-2	M18 1-2	J22 4-2	S25 1-1	N12 4-1	a29 1-2	F12 1-1	A28 1-1	a01 6-1	O30 3-0	D04 2-1	F26 2-3	D18 1-1		F05 1-1	O09 5-0	J01 0-2	a11 1-1	a25 0-0	S10 2-0	J15 1-2
18 PETERBOROUGH U	F26 0-0	O09 7-0	J01 2-2	A30 2-0	M09 2-0	N13 2-0	a01 4-0	O30 2-0	O18 1-3	a22 2-0	D18 3-3	S25 2-1	M27 0-2	J22 2-2	F12 4-4	M18 3-1	a08 1-0		m01 3-2	S11 0-1	A14 2-0	N27 2-0	A28 4-2	a04 1-1
19 READING	J08 2-0	J22 1-0	O20 2-1	S18 0-2	F26 1-0	A21 1-0	a29 2-4	a03 1-0	S04 2-0	D27 3-1	O30 3-1	N13 1-2	O02 1-3	O16 3-0	M25 0-1	D04 4-2	M11 2-1	M15 2-1		a15 2-0	M22 1-4	a19 1-1	a26 2-2	F12 0-0
20 SCUNTHORPE U	a04 1-0	F12 2-1	O30 0-0	M11 3-0	a11 2-1	D11 2-0	S28 2-0	J08 2-0	O02 3-1	S04 0-0	F26 3-0	a22 3-3	O16 1-2	D27 2-2	A21 2-1	J29 1-0	S17 0-0	M25 0-0	N27 1-1		a25 1-1	M14 1-0	a08 0-2	N13 2-0
21 SOUTHEND U	M24 1-0	O29 1-0	F12 3-1	S04 0-0	a21 1-2	M10 4-2	J28 1-4	M13 4-1	A20 3-0	M31 2-1	N12 3-0	m03 2-2	S17 3-1	J07 3-1	D27 2-1	S27 3-1	a17 4-1	O15 2-1	a07 4-1	A30 2-3		O01 2-1	N26 4-2	F26 2-0
22 SOUTHPORT	J22 0-0	J01 1-0	O08 0-0	F05 0-1	A27 4-1	O18 4-3	D18 3-0	F26 4-2	D04 2-1	O30 3-0	A14 4-0	M18 1-0	F12 1-0	a28 1-0	N12 1-1	S10 4-2	A30 4-0	a15 2-4	m04 5-2	J15 1-1	a03 0-1		a01 1-0	S24 2-2
23 STOCKPORT CO	a17 0-0	O18 1-3	J21 0-1	A20 2-2	N12 3-0	M13 0-0	D03 2-2	O15 3-1	M10 2-1	S17 1-2	F12 0-4	F26 2-1	a03 0-2	O01 2-1	S03 4-2	a28 4-4	M24 3-1	J07 0-0	A30 0-1	F05 0-0	a14 2-2	D27 1-1		O29 1-1
24 WORKINGTON	O16 5-0	D04 0-1	a29 3-0	a19 1-0	O20 0-1	S04 0-0	F05 1-0	M11 1-0	D27 0-0	A21 2-0	S01 0-0	J22 1-1	J08 0-0	M25 0-0	S18 0-0	a15 3-0	M15 2-0	O02 4-1	O23 5-0	M04 2-1	N06 3-1	M31 0-0	F19 1-1	

LEAGUE TABLES

DIVISION 1

	P	W	D	L	F	A	W	D	L	F	A	Pts
Derby Co	42	16	4	1	43	10	8	6	7	26	23	58
Leeds U	42	17	4	0	54	10	7	5	9	19	21	57
Liverpool	42	17	3	1	48	16	7	6	8	16	14	57
Manchester C	42	16	3	2	48	15	7	8	6	29	30	57
Arsenal	42	15	2	4	36	13	7	6	8	22	27	52
Tottenham H	42	16	3	2	45	13	3	10	8	18	29	51
Chelsea	42	12	7	2	41	20	6	5	10	17	29	48
Manchester U	42	13	2	6	39	26	6	8	7	30	35	48
Wolverh'pton W	42	10	7	4	35	23	8	4	9	30	34	47
Sheffield U	42	10	8	3	39	26	7	4	10	22	34	46
Newcastle U	42	10	6	5	30	18	5	5	11	19	34	41
Leicester C	42	9	6	6	18	11	4	7	10	23	35	39
Ipswich T	42	7	8	6	19	19	4	8	9	20	34	38
West Ham U	42	10	6	5	31	19	2	6	13	16	32	36
Everton	42	8	9	4	28	17	1	9	11	9	31	36
W.B.A.	42	6	7	8	22	23	6	4	11	20	31	35
Stoke C	42	6	10	5	26	25	4	5	12	13	31	35
Coventry C	42	7	10	4	27	23	2	5	14	17	44	33
Southampton	42	8	5	8	31	28	4	2	15	21	52	31
Crystal Palace	42	4	8	9	26	31	4	5	12	13	34	29
Nottingham F	42	6	4	11	25	29	2	5	14	22	52	25
Huddersfield T	42	4	7	10	12	22	2	6	13	15	37	25

DIVISION 2

	P	W	D	L	F	A	W	D	L	F	A	Pts
Norwich C	42	13	8	0	40	16	8	7	6	20	20	57
Birmingham C	42	15	6	0	46	14	4	12	5	14	17	56
Millwall	42	14	7	0	38	17	5	10	6	26	29	55
Q.P.R.	42	16	4	1	39	9	4	10	7	18	19	54
Sunderland	42	11	7	3	42	24	6	9	6	25	33	50
Blackpool	42	12	6	3	43	16	8	1	12	27	34	47
Burnley	42	13	4	4	43	22	7	2	12	27	33	46
Bristol C	42	14	3	4	43	22	4	7	10	18	27	46
Middlesbrough	42	16	4	1	31	11	3	4	14	19	37	46
Carlisle U	42	12	6	3	38	22	5	3	13	23	35	43
Swindon T	42	10	6	5	29	16	5	6	10	18	31	42
Hull C	42	10	6	5	33	21	4	4	13	16	32	38
Luton T	42	7	8	6	25	24	3	10	8	18	24	38
Sheffield W	42	11	7	3	33	22	2	5	14	18	36	38
Oxford U	42	10	8	3	28	17	2	6	13	15	38	38
Portsmouth	42	9	7	5	31	26	3	6	12	28	42	37
Orient	42	12	4	5	32	19	2	5	14	18	42	37
Preston N.E.	42	11	4	6	32	21	1	8	12	20	37	36
Cardiff C	42	9	7	5	37	25	1	7	13	19	44	34
Fulham	42	10	7	4	29	20	2	3	16	16	48	34
Charlton A	42	9	7	5	33	25	3	2	16	22	52	33
Watford	42	5	5	11	15	25	0	4	17	9	50	19

DIVISION 3

	P	W	D	L	F	A	W	D	L	F	A	Pts
Aston Villa	46	20	1	2	45	10	12	5	6	40	22	70
Brighton & H.A.	46	15	5	3	39	18	12	6	5	43	29	65
Bournemouth	46	16	6	1	43	13	7	10	6	30	24	62
Notts Co	46	16	3	4	42	19	9	9	5	32	25	62
Rotherham U	46	12	8	3	46	25	8	7	8	23	27	55
Bristol R	46	17	2	4	54	26	4	10	9	21	30	54
Bolton W	46	11	8	4	25	13	6	8	9	26	28	50
Plymouth A	46	13	6	4	43	26	7	4	12	31	38	50
Walsall	46	12	8	3	38	16	3	10	10	24	41	48
Blackburn R	46	14	4	5	39	22	5	5	13	15	35	47
Oldham A	46	11	4	8	37	35	6	7	10	22	28	45
Shrewsbury T	46	13	5	5	50	29	4	5	14	23	36	44
Chesterfield	46	10	5	8	25	23	8	3	12	32	34	44
Swansea C	46	10	6	7	27	21	7	4	12	19	38	44
Port Vale	46	10	10	3	27	21	3	5	15	16	38	41
Wrexham	46	10	5	8	33	26	6	3	14	26	37	40
Halifax T	46	11	6	6	31	22	2	6	15	17	39	38
Rochdale	46	11	7	5	35	26	1	6	16	22	57	37
York C	46	8	8	7	32	22	4	4	15	25	44	36
Tranmere R	46	9	7	7	34	30	1	9	13	16	41	36
Mansfield T	46	5	12	6	19	26	3	8	12	22	37	36
Barnsley	46	6	10	7	23	30	3	8	12	9	34	36
Torquay U	46	8	6	9	31	31	2	6	15	10	38	32
Bradford C	46	6	8	9	27	32	5	2	16	18	45	32

DIVISION 4

	P	W	D	L	F	A	W	D	L	F	A	Pts
Grimsby T	46	18	3	2	61	26	10	4	9	27	30	63
Southend U	46	18	2	3	56	26	6	10	7	25	29	60
Brentford	46	16	2	5	52	21	8	9	6	24	23	59
Scunthorpe U	46	13	8	2	34	15	9	5	9	22	22	57
Lincoln C	46	17	5	1	46	15	4	9	10	31	44	56
Workington	46	12	9	2	34	7	4	10	9	16	27	51
Southport	46	15	5	3	48	21	3	9	11	18	25	50
Peterborough U	46	14	6	3	51	24	3	10	10	31	40	50
Bury	46	16	4	3	55	22	3	8	12	18	37	50
Cambridge U	46	11	8	4	38	22	6	6	11	24	38	48
Colchester U	46	13	6	4	38	23	6	4	13	32	46	48
Doncaster R	46	11	8	4	35	24	5	6	12	21	39	46
Gillingham	46	11	5	7	33	24	5	8	10	28	43	45
Newport Co	46	13	5	5	34	20	5	3	15	26	52	44
Exeter C	46	11	5	7	40	30	5	6	12	21	38	43
Reading	46	14	3	6	37	26	3	5	15	19	50	42
Aldershot	46	5	13	5	27	20	4	9	10	21	34	40
Hartlepool U	46	14	2	7	39	25	3	4	16	19	44	40
Darlington	46	9	9	5	37	24	5	2	16	27	58	39
Chester C	46	10	11	2	34	16	0	7	16	13	40	38
Northampton T	46	8	9	6	43	27	4	4	15	23	52	37
Barrow	46	8	8	7	23	26	5	3	15	17	45	37
Stockport Co	46	7	10	6	33	32	2	4	17	22	55	32
Crewe A	46	9	4	10	27	25	1	5	17	16	44	29

FOOTBALL LEAGUE RECORDS

Top scorers: Div 1, B.Robson (West Ham United) 28 goals; Div 2, D.Givens (Queen's Park Rangers) 23 goals; Div 3, A.Horsfield (Charlton Athletic) 26 goals; Div 4, F.Binney (Exeter City) 27 goals.

Barrow failed to gain re-election, Hereford United were elected in their place.

Burnley's Martin Dobson, a long-serving midfielder who played a major part in getting the Clarets back into Division One.

DIVISION 1

	ARSENAL	BIRMINGHAM C	CHELSEA	COVENTRY C	CRYSTAL P	DERBY CO	EVERTON	IPSWICH T	LEEDS U	LEICESTER C	LIVERPOOL	MANCHESTER C	MANCHESTER U	NEWCASTLE U	NORWICH C	SHEFFIELD U	SOUTHAMPTON	STOKE C	TOTTENHAM H	W.B.A.	WEST HAM U	WOLVERHAMPTON W
1 ARSENAL		S26 2-0	S02 1-1	N04 0-2	M26 1-0	M31 0-1	N18 1-0	O14 1-0	D02 2-1	F17 1-0	S16 0-0	O28 0-0	J06 3-1	J27 2-2	D26 2-0	M03 3-2	S30 1-0	A19 2-0	a14 1-1	D16 2-1	A29 1-0	A15 5-2
2 BIRMINGHAM C	D23 1-1		O07 2-2	M24 3-0	A26 1-1	F10 2-0	S23 2-1	D30 1-2	a30 2-1	D09 1-1	a07 2-1	S09 4-1	M10 3-1	A15 3-2	N25 4-1	A12 1-2	O21 1-1	a21 3-1	N04 0-0	a28 3-2	a23 0-0	F27 0-1
3 CHELSEA	J20 0-1	M03 0-0		a23 2-0	N25 0-0	D30 1-1	D23 1-1	S23 2-0	A12 4-0	N11 1-1	A23 1-2	A26 2-1	a28 1-0	O28 1-1	D09 3-1	F10 4-2	a21 2-1	a07 1-3	a03 0-1	O14 3-1	S09 1-3	M06 0-2
4 COVENTRY C	A22 1-1	O28 0-0	S30 1-3		M02 2-0	a14 0-2	D02 1-0	M31 2-1	a02 0-1	J06 3-2	a17 1-2	O14 3-2	J27 1-1	S16 0-3	D16 3-1	N18 3-0	A19 1-1	S02 2-1	F17 0-1	D26 0-0	N11 3-1	A29 0-1
5 CRYSTAL P	O21 2-3	M06 0-0	M31 2-0	O07 0-1		A15 0-0	N04 1-0	a14 1-1	N18 2-2	a20 0-1	A19 1-1	A29 1-0	D16 5-0	S02 2-1	S30 0-2	M13 0-1	D26 3-0	F17 3-2	J27 0-0	S16 0-2	M24 1-3	M10 1-1
6 DERBY CO	N25 5-0	S16 1-0	A19 1-2	D09 2-0	N11 2-2		a28 3-1	a30 3-0	M03 2-3	O14 2-1	S02 2-1	A23 1-0	D26 3-1	D16 1-1	J06 1-0	O28 2-1	F17 4-0	F14 0-3	S30 2-1	J27 2-0	a21 1-1	m04 3-0
7 EVERTON	a21 0-0	D26 1-1	a17 1-0	a07 2-0	A22 1-1	A29 1-0		O28 2-2	O14 1-2	J27 0-1	M03 0-2	N11 2-3	A19 2-0	S30 3-1	a03 2-2	M17 2-1	S16 0-1	J06 2-0	D16 3-1	S02 1-0	N25 1-2	D09 0-1
8 IPSWICH T	M10 1-2	A19 2-0	D26 3-0	D05 2-0	D09 2-1	O21 3-1	M24 0-1		N04 2-2	S30 0-2	D16 1-1	a07 1-1	F17 4-1	J06 1-0	A15 1-2	a28 1-1	J27 2-2	S16 2-0	S02 1-1	M17 2-0	O07 1-1	a21 2-1
9 LEEDS U	m09 6-1	D16 4-0	F17 1-1	O21 1-1	a21 4-0	O07 5-0	M10 2-1	A23 3-3		S16 3-1	S30 1-2	N25 3-0	a18 0-1	D26 1-0	S02 2-0	N11 2-1	A30 1-0	J27 1-0	J06 2-1	A19 2-0	D09 1-0	M24 0-0
10 LEICESTER C	A12 0-1	a14 0-1	A16 1-1	A26 0-0	D23 2-1	M10 0-0	S09 1-2	a24 1-1	F10 2-0		A30 3-2	J20 1-1	N04 2-2	M31 0-0	O21 1-2	F24 0-0	O07 1-0	M24 2-0	N18 0-1	D02 3-1	D30 2-1	S23 1-1
11 LIVERPOOL	F10 0-2	D02 4-3	N04 3-1	D23 2-0	D30 1-0	J20 1-1	O07 1-0	F24 2-1	a23 2-0	a28 0-0		A12 2-0	A15 2-0	N18 3-2	M24 3-1	S23 5-0	M10 3-2	O21 2-1	M31 1-1	a14 1-0	A26 3-2	S09 4-2
12 MANCHESTER C	M24 1-2	J27 1-0	M27 0-1	M10 1-2	a28 2-3	N04 4-0	A16 0-1	D02 1-1	M31 1-0	S02 1-0	F17 1-1		N18 3-0	a18 2-0	A19 3-0	a14 3-1	D16 2-1	D26 1-1	S16 2-1	S30 2-1	O21 4-3	O07 1-1
13 MANCHESTER U	A26 0-0	O14 1-0	A30 0-0	S09 0-1	a11 2-0	S23 3-0	J24 0-0	A12 1-2	D23 1-1	A23 1-1	N11 2-0	a21 0-0		M17 2-1	a07 1-0	a23 1-2	N25 2-1	D09 0-2	O28 1-4	M03 2-1	J20 2-2	F10 2-1
14 NEWCASTLE U	S09 2-1	N11 3-0	M24 1-1	F10 1-1	J20 2-0	F28 2-0	a25 0-0	A26 1-2	S23 3-2	J01 2-2	a21 2-1	D23 2-1	O21 2-1		O07 3-1	D30 4-1	D09 0-0	M10 1-0	A30 0-1	A23 1-1	a07 1-2	A12 2-1
15 NORWICH C	S23 3-2	M31 1-2	a14 1-0	M07 1-1	a24 2-1	A26 1-0	A12 1-1	N11 0-0	J20 1-2	M17 1-1	O28 1-1	D30 1-1	D02 0-2	F24 0-1		S09 1-1	A23 0-0	A30 2-0	O14 2-1	N18 2-0	F10 0-1	D23 1-1
16 SHEFFIELD U	O07 1-0	F17 0-1	S16 2-1	a21 3-1	a07 2-0	M24 3-1	O21 0-1	A29 0-0	A15 0-2	D16 2-0	D26 0-3	D09 1-1	S30 1-0	A19 1-2	J27 2-0		S02 3-1	N04 0-0	m02 3-2	J06 3-0	M10 0-0	N25 1-2
17 SOUTHAMPTON	a23 2-2	M17 2-0	N18 3-1	D30 2-1	S23 2-0	A12 1-1	F10 0-0	S09 1-2	a28 3-1	M03 0-0	O14 1-1	M06 1-1	M31 0-2	a14 1-1	N04 1-0	J20 1-1		A15 1-0	D02 1-1	O28 2-1	D23 0-0	A26 1-1
18 STOKE C	D30 0-0	N18 1-2	D02 1-1	M26 2-1	A12 2-0	D23 4-0	A26 1-1	a04 1-0	S09 2-2	O28 1-0	M17 0-1	S23 5-1	a14 2-2	O14 2-0	a28 2-0	A23 2-2	N11 3-3		M14 1-1	M31 2-0	F24 2-0	a24 2-0
19 TOTTENHAM H	D09 1-2	A23 2-0	O21 0-1	A12 2-1	S09 2-1	a18 1-0	F24 3-0	J20 0-1	A26 0-0	a21 1-1	N25 1-2	F10 2-3	M24 1-1	a28 3-2	M10 3-0	D23 2-0	a07 1-2	O07 4-3		N11 1-1	S23 1-0	a30 2-2
20 W.B.A.	F28 1-0	A30 2-2	M10 1-1	S23 1-0	F10 0-4	S09 2-1	a11 4-1	D23 2-0	M28 1-1	a07 1-0	D09 1-1	a25 1-2	O07 2-2	N04 2-3	a21 0-1	A26 0-2	M24 1-1	N25 2-1	A16 0-1		A12 0-0	O21 1-0
21 WEST HAM U	a28 1-2	S30 2-0	J27 3-1	A14 1-0	O28 4-0	N18 1-2	M31 2-0	M02 0-1	a14 1-1	A19 5-2	J06 0-1	M17 2-1	S02 2-2	D02 1-1	S16 4-0	O14 3-1	a20 4-3	D16 3-2	D26 2-2	F17 2-1		N04 2-2
22 WOLVERHAMPTON W	N11 1-3	S02 3-2	D16 1-0	a28 3-0	O14 1-1	D02 1-2	a14 4-2	N18 0-1	O28 0-2	D26 2-0	J27 2-1	M03 5-1	S16 2-0	F17 1-1	a23 3-0	M31 1-1	J06 0-1	S30 5-3	A19 3-2	M20 2-0	A22 3-0	

Despite missing several games through injury, John Toshack still managed 13 goals for Liverpool in their 1972-73 Championship season.

DIVISION 2

	ASTON VILLA	BLACKPOOL	BRIGHTON & HA	BRISTOL C	BURNLEY	CARDIFF C	CARLISLE U	FULHAM	HUDDERSFIELD T	HULL C	LUTON T	MIDDLESBROUGH	MILLWALL	NOTTINGHAM F	ORIENT	OXFORD U	PORTSMOUTH	PRESTON N.E.	Q.P.R.	SHEFFIELD W	SUNDERLAND	SWINDON T
1 ASTON VILLA		N11 0-0	S02 1-1	a14 1-0	J06 0-3	J27 2-0	A29 1-0	M03 2-3	A19 2-0	D02 2-0	N18 0-2	O28 1-1	S30 1-0	D26 2-2	D16 1-0	M31 2-1	M17 2-0	F17 1-1	O14 0-1	a24 2-1	S27 2-0	S16 2-1
2 BLACKPOOL	O17 1-1		A19 6-2	N18 3-0	D26 1-2	M07 1-0	N04 0-0	M17 2-0	F17 1-1	M31 4-3	M03 1-1	S30 0-1	S02 2-1	a23 2-0	S16 1-1	O14 2-1	D02 3-1	a14 2-0	O28 2-0	D16 1-2	A28 0-0	J27 2-0
3 BRIGHTON & H.A.	J20 1-3	D30 1-2		A12 1-1	N18 0-1	N04 2-2	M21 1-0	S09 2-1	M10 2-1	O07 1-1	F10 2-0	D02 0-2	S20 1-3	a28 2-2	a14 2-1	S23 2-2	a23 1-1	M31 2-0	D23 1-2	O21 3-3	A26 2-2	M24 3-1
4 BRISTOL C	M27 3-0	a21 3-0	F17 3-1		D16 0-1	D26 1-0	a07 4-1	S26 1-1	S30 0-0	a28 2-1	O28 0-1	S16 1-1	A19 2-2	O14 1-1	J27 2-2	M17 0-0	M03 3-1	a23 2-1	N11 1-2	S02 1-2	N25 1-0	J06 3-0
5 BURNLEY	A26 4-1	S23 4-3	a21 3-0	F24 1-1		O21 3-0	A12 2-2	D30 2-2	F03 2-1	F10 4-1	a24 3-0	S26 0-0	M24 2-1	N25 1-0	N11 1-2	D23 1-1	M20 4-0	A29 2-0	S09 1-1	M10 0-1	a16 2-0	O07 2-1
6 CARDIFF C	S09 0-2	A26 1-2	S27 1-1	S23 1-3	M17 0-1		F10 1-0	N25 3-1	a21 4-1	m09 0-2	A12 2-1	O14 2-0	A30 1-0	N11 2-1	M03 3-1	J19 2-0	D29 0-2	O28 3-0	a18 0-0	D09 4-1	m07 1-1	a07 1-1
7 CARLISLE U	a28 2-2	S26 2-3	D16 5-1	D02 1-2	F17 1-1	S16 4-0		O14 2-1	J06 0-0	a14 0-1	M31 2-0	J27 1-1	a24 0-1	S02 1-2	M17 1-0	N18 2-1	O28 1-0	D26 6-1	M03 1-3	S30 1-1	N11 4-3	A19 3-0
8 FULHAM	O07 2-0	O21 2-0	J27 5-1	N04 5-1	A19 1-1	M31 1-1	M10 1-0		S16 1-1	S20 2-0	M27 0-1	J06 2-1	D26 1-0	D16 3-1	S30 1-1	a14 2-0	N18 0-0	S02 1-3	O17 0-2	F17 1-0	M24 1-2	a20 0-0
9 HUDDERSFIELD T	D30 1-1	A12 1-0	O14 0-2	N14 0-1	a14 0-2	N18 2-1	A26 1-1	F10 1-0		D23 1-3	J20 1-2	M17 1-1	M31 1-0	M03 1-1	O28 1-1	S09 2-0	a28 2-0	D02 0-0	M06 2-2	N04 1-0	S23 1-1	S19 1-1
10 HULL C	a07 1-2	N25 1-2	M02 2-0	A29 2-0	S16 1-1	D16 1-1	D09 1-1	N11 2-2	a23 0-0		a10 4-0	D26 3-1	F17 0-2	A19 0-0	S02 2-0	O27 0-1	O14 5-1	J27 6-2	S26 4-1	J06 1-1	a21 0-2	S30 3-2
11 LUTON T	a21 0-0	O07 2-2	S16 2-1	M24 1-3	S30 2-2	F17 1-1	N25 0-1	a07 1-0	S02 4-1	O21 1-2		a23 0-1	D16 2-2	J27 1-0	J06 1-1	A30 0-1	O18 2-2	A19 1-0	D09 2-2	D26 0-0	M10 1-0	N04 0-1
12 MIDDLESBROUGH	M24 1-1	F02 2-0	a07 1-1	F10 2-1	N04 3-3	M10 2-0	S09 1-0	A26 1-2	O21 2-1	S23 1-0	D23 0-1		O07 1-0	D09 0-0	a28 3-2	D30 1-0	F24 3-0	S19 0-0	J20 0-0	a21 3-0	A12 2-1	N25 0-2
13 MILLWALL	a23 1-1	J20 1-1	N11 3-0	D30 3-0	O28 1-1	a28 1-1	D23 1-0	S23 1-3	N25 1-0	A12 2-0	F26 3-2	M02 1-0		S25 2-1	O14 2-0	F10 3-1	A26 0-2	M17 4-1	a21 0-1	a07 2-1	S09 0-1	D09 1-1
14 NOTTINGHAM F	S23 1-1	D23 4-0	A29 1-0	M10 1-0	M31 3-0	S19 2-1	J20 2-1	F24 2-1	O07 1-1	M13 1-2	S09 0-1	a14 1-3	N04 3-2		D02 2-1	A26 2-1	A12 0-0	N18 0-1	F10 0-0	M24 3-0	a24 1-0	O21 2-2
15 ORIENT	F24 4-0	F10 2-0	D09 1-0	S09 0-2	S18 1-1	O07 0-0	O21 2-1	a23 3-2	M24 3-1	J20 0-0	A26 0-1	A28 2-0	M10 3-1	a07 3-0		A12 1-1	D23 0-1	N03 1-2	S23 2-2	N25 3-2	a30 1-1	a21 1-0
16 OXFORD U	N25 2-0	M10 0-1	D26 3-0	O21 0-2	a20 0-2	S02 2-1	a21 1-1	D09 0-0	J27 2-0	M23 5-2	a28 2-1	A19 4-0	S16 2-1	J06 1-0	F17 2-1		N04 1-3	S30 0-2	a07 2-0	S20 1-0	O07 5-1	D16 1-0
17 PORTSMOUTH	O21 0-1	a07 1-0	S30 2-0	O07 0-3	S02 0-2	A19 3-1	M24 0-0	a21 1-2	A30 1-2	M10 2-2	N11 2-2	D16 0-0	J06 1-1	F17 2-0	a20 1-0	S27 1-0		S16 0-1	N25 0-1	J27 1-0	D09 2-3	D26 1-1
18 PRESTON N.E.	A12 0-1	D09 0-3	N25 4-0	D23 3-3	a28 1-1	M24 0-0	S23 1-0	J20 0-3	a07 0-0	S09 1-0	D30 2-0	N11 0-1	O21 1-0	a21 2-1	S25 0-0	a24 0-1	F10 0-5		A26 1-1	O07 1-1	M19 1-3	M10 1-1
19 Q.P.R.	M10 1-0	M24 4-0	a24 2-0	S19 1-1	J27 2-0	S30 3-0	O07 4-0	a28 2-0	F06 3-1	N04 1-1	a14 2-0	S02 2-2	N18 1-3	S16 3-0	D26 3-1	D02 0-0	M31 5-0	J06 3-0		A19 4-2	O21 3-2	F17 5-0
20 SHEFFIELD W	D23 2-2	F28 2-0	M17 1-1	M14 3-2	O14 0-1	a14 1-0	a23 0-0	A12 3-0	S27 3-2	A26 4-2	S23 4-0	N18 2-1	D02 2-2	O28 1-2	M31 2-0	N11 0-1	S09 2-1	M03 2-1	D30 3-1		F10 1-0	A16 2-1
21 SUNDERLAND	N04 2-2	a28 1-0	J06 4-0	M31 2-2	D02 0-1	a23 2-1	M27 2-1	O28 0-0	a10 3-0	N18 1-1	O14 0-2	F17 4-0	J27 2-0	S30 4-1	A19 1-0	M03 1-0	a14 2-0	D16 0-0	m09 0-3	S16 1-1		S02 3-2
22 SWINDON T	F10 1-3	S09 0-0	O28 2-2	A26 2-1	M02 0-1	F27 3-0	M12 2-0	D23 2-2	N11 1-1	a24 2-1	S26 0-2	M31 1-0	a14 0-0	M17 0-0	N18 3-1	F24 1-3	S23 1-1	O14 3-2	A12 2-2	A29 1-0	J20 1-1	

SEASON 1972-73

DIVISION 3

	BLACKBURN R	BOLTON W	BOURNEMOUTH	BRENTFORD	BRISTOL R	CHARLTON A	CHESTERFIELD	GRIMSBY T	HALIFAX T	NOTTS CO	OLDHAM A	PLYMOUTH A	PORT VALE	ROCHDALE	ROTHERHAM U	SCUNTHORPE U	SHREWSBURY T	SOUTHEND U	SWANSEA C	TRANMERE R	WALSALL	WATFORD	WREXHAM	YORK C
1 BLACKBURN R		S02 0-3	a14 2-1	J06 2-1	F17 0-0	O28 3-1	M14 0-1	N04 0-0	D02 3-0	M07 2-0	a28 1-1	S20 3-1	O14 0-1	A19 1-1	a20 2-1	S30 3-0	J27 0-0	D16 2-1	M17 3-0	M31 2-2	O25 2-0	S16 0-0	M03 1-1	F03 2-0
2 BOLTON W	M28 0-1		A12 3-0	a28 2-0	N11 2-0	F20 3-0	S27 1-0	F10 2-0	a16 3-0	D30 2-2	A26 2-1	S09 2-0	D23 2-0	M17 2-1	N25 2-1	O14 0-0	M21 2-0	O28 1-1	O11 3-0	S23 2-0	M03 3-1	a07 1-1	J30 1-0	a21 3-0
3 BOURNEMOUTH	M20 3-0	F17 2-0		D26 3-2	D16 0-0	N25 3-1	A19 2-2	M24 1-1	A29 1-0	M10 1-1	a07 2-0	O21 0-1	S26 4-0	O24 4-2	F03 4-0	S02 1-1	S30 2-0	S16 2-0	a21 2-0	O07 1-1	a20 0-1	J06 3-0	N11 1-0	J27 2-3
4 BRENTFORD	A26 4-0	A28 2-1	S23 1-1		S25 2-1	F26 1-0	N11 3-1	F24 0-1	A12 0-1	a20 1-1	D30 1-1	J20 0-2	F10 5-0	O28 1-0	J13 1-1	M03 1-0	a07 1-2	M17 1-2	S09 0-2	O09 2-0	O14 2-0	M19 1-1	D23 1-0	N25 2-0
5 BRISTOL R	A12 3-0	S19 1-1	F24 2-0	N04 3-1		D23 2-1	A29 2-2	A26 2-1	D30 4-1	N07 1-0	F10 3-3	S23 2-0	J30 4-1	M06 0-0	M10 3-0	D02 5-1	O21 5-1	M31 1-2	a20 3-1	J13 2-0	a14 2-1	M24 2-1	S09 2-0	O07 1-2
6 CHARLTON A	M24 1-2	D16 2-3	M31 1-1	N28 2-1	a24 3-3		F03 2-2	M10 1-1	M06 1-0	S19 6-1	O21 4-2	O07 3-0	D02 2-0	J06 1-0	J27 1-2	S16 2-0	A19 1-2	D26 0-0	A29 6-0	N04 1-1	F16 1-1	S30 2-1	a14 2-1	S02 1-0
7 CHESTERFIELD	S23 3-1	N04 0-1	D30 1-1	S20 3-0	a28 0-1	O18 1-0		D23 2-1	F07 2-0	F24 0-2	A12 4-1	A26 2-2	S09 1-2	M31 2-1	O07 3-2	a14 2-1	M24 2-0	M07 2-4	J13 1-0	a24 2-0	D02 3-0	O21 0-0	F10 1-2	M10 0-0
8 GRIMSBY T	S26 2-0	S16 2-0	O28 0-1	D16 4-0	J06 2-0	O14 0-2	a20 2-1		M17 0-0	D02 3-1	N11 6-2	a28 1-1	M06 0-1	S30 1-0	A19 2-1	D26 1-0	F13 3-2	O24 3-1	M03 2-0	a14 2-0	J27 6-2	S02 2-0	M31 0-1	F17 1-2
9 HALIFAX T	a07 2-2	S30 1-1	a28 2-0	a04 3-2	A19 3-0	a21 3-0	S02 0-1	O21 1-1		O07 0-1	J13 0-3	M24 2-1	N11 2-2	F03 0-0	D26 0-1	J27 1-0	F27 0-1	a24 2-1	N25 1-1	M10 2-1	S16 0-1	O24 1-1	A22 2-2	M13 1-0
10 NOTTS CO	a21 0-0	A19 1-0	O14 0-2	S30 1-0	F03 2-0	N11 3-1	D16 2-0	a07 4-0	M03 3-0		N25 2-4	M21 2-0	O28 1-1	S16 2-2	O25 2-0	a23 2-0	F17 1-0	J27 2-0	S27 2-0	a28 4-1	S02 1-1	D26 1-0	M17 1-0	J06 1-0
11 OLDHAM A	A29 1-2	J06 2-0	D02 1-1	A19 1-1	S16 3-0	M17 0-1	M27 3-0	S19 1-2	a14 1-1	M31 1-1		N04 7-1	M03 1-0	a20 0-0	S30 1-0	O24 3-0	S02 2-1	F03 0-1	O28 2-0	M07 3-1	D16 2-1	J27 2-1	O14 2-2	D26 1-1
12 PLYMOUTH A	N11 1-2	J27 1-0	M17 1-0	S02 0-1	D26 3-2	M03 5-0	F20 2-2	A29 3-1	O28 2-1	a14 1-4	S26 1-3		M31 2-1	m01 3-2	F17 4-1	F06 3-0	S16 3-0	A19 2-0	O14 3-1	D02 0-1	S30 0-2	a23 1-1	M06 1-0	O24 1-1
13 PORT VALE	M10 2-1	a23 2-2	N04 2-1	S16 1-0	S02 2-1	a07 3-1	J27 2-1	a21 3-0	S18 2-1	M24 1-1	O07 0-2	N25 1-1		a09 0-0	F26 4-1	D16 2-0	O23 1-1	S30 3-1	M19 3-1	O21 0-0	D26 1-2	F03 1-0	A28 3-2	A19 2-1
14 ROCHDALE	D30 0-1	O21 2-2	J29 1-0	M24 0-1	D09 0-0	A26 0-2	N25 1-2	a23 3-2	O09 0-0	F10 4-1	D23 0-0	F24 0-6	A12 0-0		a07 0-1	N11 0-2	M10 1-1	a28 3-2	M12 1-1	S09 1-1	S25 2-1	O07 1-0	S23 1-0	M19 1-0
15 ROTHERHAM U	D23 1-1	M31 1-0	O10 2-7	M06 2-1	O14 1-1	S09 2-1	M03 1-0	D30 2-0	S23 0-1	J30 1-4	a23 2-3	A12 1-0	A26 7-0	D02 0-0		O28 2-1	S19 2-0	a14 1-0	F10 0-2	F24 1-2	M17 2-0	N04 1-0	J20 1-1	a28 1-2
16 SCUNTHORPE U	a24 1-1	M10 1-1	J20 1-1	O07 1-0	a07 0-2	F10 0-2	M20 0-1	S23 1-2	S08 0-3	D23 1-0	M13 0-0	O10 1-1	F24 0-1	S19 1-2	M24 2-1		N25 1-0	N04 0-0	A12 1-0	D30 1-5	A29 2-1	a21 1-0	A26 1-1	O21 1-0
17 SHREWSBURY T	S09 2-0	a13 0-2	a24 0-0	D02 2-0	M16 4-2	D30 0-2	O27 2-0	O10 3-2	A25 0-0	A12 0-0	J19 2-2	F09 1-1	M27 2-3	O14 3-2	N11 1-1	M30 4-2		M02 1-0	S23 2-1	D22 0-0	M06 1-1	A29 0-0	F23 0-0	S26 1-0
18 SOUTHEND U	F24 0-1	M24 1-1	F09 2-2	O21 4-0	N24 0-0	S22 1-1	a21 5-1	M12 2-0	D22 1-1	S09 2-1	O09 0-1	D29 3-1	a20 5-0	A28 1-2	M19 1-0	S25 1-0	O06 2-0		A25 3-1	J20 1-0	N10 2-0	M09 0-0	A12 0-1	a06 3-0
19 SWANSEA C	O21 2-2	a04 2-3	M06 1-0	J26 2-1	S30 0-2	a28 2-1	O24 2-1	O07 6-2	M31 2-0	N04 3-0	M24 0-0	M09 1-1	a14 0-1	S02 2-3	S16 0-1	F03 2-1	D26 0-2	J06 1-1		S19 1-1	A19 2-1	F27 2-1	D01 3-1	J29 1-3
20 TRANMERE R	N24 1-1	D26 1-1	M02 0-0	F02 6-2	O23 1-1	S25 4-0	S29 1-0	M19 1-1	O13 1-1	A28 0-2	a21 0-1	a06 2-2	M16 2-0	F06 0-1	D15 2-0	A18 2-1	a20 1-0	S01 3-1	N10 1-1		J05 3-1	F16 1-0	O27 4-0	S15 1-0
21 WALSALL	J13 0-2	O07 3-2	D23 1-0	M10 3-0	M19 4-3	A12 3-2	a07 3-2	S09 1-0	m01 0-1	J23 1-3	F24 3-0	a25 1-3	S23 2-0	N04 0-2	O21 1-0	a28 1-1	a21 1-0	S19 3-1	F19 1-1	A26 2-0		N25 1-3	O10 2-0	M24 0-0
22 WATFORD	F10 1-3	D02 2-1	A26 3-2	a14 2-2	O28 2-1	a20 1-1	M17 0-0	J20 1-2	M28 2-1	S23 1-0	S09 2-1	D23 3-2	O10 1-1	M02 0-0	S27 1-1	M06 5-1	a28 0-1	O14 1-0	F24 0-1	A12 1-0	M31 1-0		M14 0-0	N11 2-2
23 WREXHAM	O07 0-0	O30 1-3	O02 1-1	a23 4-1	J27 2-2	M19 2-2	S16 1-0	N25 3-2	N04 0-0	O21 2-0	M10 1-1	a21 1-2	a27 5-0	D26 3-3	S02 1-0	J06 1-2	D16 0-0	F17 4-2	a07 1-0	M23 0-0	F03 2-1	A19 1-0		S30 3-1
24 YORK C	O09 1-0	M05 0-1	S09 0-0	M31 0-1	M03 0-0	J20 1-1	O14 2-0	A12 0-0	F24 2-1	A26 1-1	S23 0-0	M26 1-2	D30 0-0	a14 1-2	A28 0-1	M17 3-1	N04 2-1	D02 2-0	D23 3-0	F10 4-1	O28 0-0	S18 0-0	a20 1-1	

DIVISION 4

	ALDERSHOT	BARNSLEY	BRADFORD C	BURY	CAMBRIDGE U	CHESTER	COLCHESTER U	CREWE A	DARLINGTON	DONCASTER R	EXETER C	GILLINGHAM	HARTLEPOOL	HEREFORD U	LINCOLN C	MANSFIELD T	NEWPORT CO	NORTHAMPTON T	PETERBOROUGH U	READING	SOUTHPORT	STOCKPORT CO	TORQUAY U	WORKINGTON
1 ALDERSHOT		O28 0-2	D16 2-1	O14 2-0	a24 1-1	J27 1-1	F03 2-0	M07 3-0	J13 3-1	M17 1-0	N11 0-0	D26 0-0	S27 2-1	M31 2-0	J06 0-0	S16 0-1	M02 0-2	J17 3-0	a14 2-1	S30 1-0	S02 2-2	O25 2-0	F17 2-1	A19 2-0
2 BARNSLEY	M24 0-2		F17 1-2	a21 0-1	A19 3-1	S30 0-0	S16 4-0	S26 2-2	O21 0-2	A29 4-2	a06 1-1	S02 1-1	D08 2-1	N11 0-0	a24 4-1	D26 1-1	N25 2-1	M10 2-0	O07 3-2	D16 0-0	J27 0-1	J06 1-3	O24 0-0	F06 1-0
3 BRADFORD C	F24 1-0	A12 3-1		M28 0-0	M02 0-1	O04 0-1	N04 3-0	F10 2-2	D23 7-0	a23 4-3	D30 4-0	M31 3-1	S23 0-2	A26 1-1	D02 3-1	O14 1-1	O11 2-1	S09 2-1	J20 1-4	O28 1-1	a28 0-2	M07 1-0	M17 1-0	a14 2-2
4 BURY	M10 1-2	M06 2-1	O24 0-0		D16 1-1	F17 1-1	a23 4-0	D02 0-1	O07 1-0	M31 5-0	O21 2-1	A19 2-1	M24 1-1	a14 3-0	S16 0-4	J27 1-0	A29 0-0	S19 2-2	N04 3-1	a10 4-0	F03 0-1	D26 1-2	S02 0-0	S30 3-0
5 CAMBRIDGE U	D23 2-2	D30 1-1	O07 2-1	F24 2-2		M24 1-0	O20 3-0	J31 1-0	A12 0-3	A26 3-1	J20 1-3	N04 3-1	S09 1-1	O11 1-0	M07 2-1	a28 3-2	F10 3-1	D09 3-1	S23 3-1	a14 1-0	M10 2-2	S20 1-0	D02 0-0	M31 1-0
6 CHESTER	S09 0-0	a20 0-0	N11 1-1	A12 2-0	O28 1-1		A30 4-0	S23 2-1	F10 5-0	F20 1-2	D23 0-1	a14 1-0	O11 2-0	F24 0-1	O14 2-1	M17 2-2	D30 0-2	M28 3-0	A26 8-2	M07 2-0	S26 0-0	D01 2-0	M31 1-2	M03 1-3
7 COLCHESTER U	O09 2-3	F10 1-2	S25 0-0	D23 2-1	M16 0-1	a27 2-3		S08 5-1	J19 1-0	F24 1-1	a16 1-2	a30 4-0	D29 1-1	A12 1-0	M03 0-2	O28 1-1	A26 1-3	S22 2-2	a09 1-0	M30 2-2	N10 3-1	a13 3-0	M05 1-1	O13 1-1
8 CREWE A	a21 0-2	N04 1-0	S16 1-2	a07 2-1	O25 1-1	D26 1-1	J27 1-2		N25 0-0	S20 0-1	O07 1-0	S30 1-1	M10 2-0	A30 2-1	S02 1-1	D16 0-4	M21 0-0	M24 1-0	O21 0-2	m02 0-0	a18 0-2	F03 0-1	A19 1-1	J06 2-0
9 DARLINGTON	A28 1-4	M17 0-0	a20 1-0	M03 1-1	F17 3-3	S16 1-1	S02 2-1	M31 3-1		O28 0-1	S25 0-0	F03 2-3	N11 1-2	M05 2-2	A19 1-1	S30 2-3	O14 2-3	a14 0-0	D02 2-2	O23 0-2	J06 0-7	J27 2-0	D16 0-3	a09 2-1
10 DONCASTER R	O21 1-0	a27 0-0	S29 1-0	N25 4-1	J06 0-0	O24 0-0	D16 1-0	N11 0-2	M23 2-0		M20 5-1	J26 0-1	a07 2-1	S26 0-0	D26 1-1	A19 0-1	a21 1-5	O06 3-0	M09 1-1	a24 0-2	S15 2-0	S01 2-2	F03 1-0	F16 1-1
11 EXETER C	S20 1-0	D02 2-1	A19 5-1	M17 1-1	S02 3-1	a23 0-0	S30 1-0	M03 0-0	N04 1-1	a14 0-1		D16 3-2	A28 1-1	O14 1-0	N06 2-0	J06 4-2	O28 0-0	M31 4-1	F12 1-1	a03 0-0	F17 0-1	S16 3-0	D26 3-2	J27 4-2
12 GILLINGHAM	S23 1-2	J20 5-1	N25 4-2	D30 2-2	S26 1-2	D09 1-0	a06 2-1	a23 3-2	O10 4-0	S08 3-0	F24 1-0		J13 2-0	F10 2-0	M17 1-1	N11 2-1	A12 0-0	A25 1-3	D23 2-0	O14 1-0	a21 2-0	a28 3-0	M02 1-1	O28 0-2
13 HARTLEPOOL	N04 1-1	a14 1-4	D26 1-0	O28 1-1	J27 0-0	F03 0-0	A19 2-1	O14 1-1	S18 0-0	D02 0-0	a28 0-0	O23 2-0		M03 0-1	F17 1-0	a20 1-1	M16 1-0	M05 2-0	M31 0-1	S02 1-2	S30 0-2	D16 0-0	J06 1-0	S16 1-0
14 HEREFORD U	N25 1-0	S19 1-2	J06 1-0	D09 1-0	F03 2-1	J17 3-1	F17 4-1	a28 1-0	M12 1-0	N04 3-2	M10 1-0	S16 0-0	O07 0-0		J27 2-1	O25 3-1	a07 2-0	O21 2-0	M24 3-0	A19 3-0	D26 2-2	a18 1-0	S30 2-1	S02 0-0
15 LINCOLN C	A26 0-2	D23 1-2	a07 2-1	F10 2-2	a21 2-1	M10 1-0	O07 3-2	J20 1-1	F28 1-0	S23 2-1	J13 2-2	O21 1-0	A12 1-2	S09 4-1		N25 1-1	F24 0-2	O11 1-1	a20 1-0	N11 0-0	M21 3-1	M24 5-3	S27 3-1	a28 1-1
16 MANSFIELD T	F10 2-0	S23 3-1	M10 4-1	S09 1-1	A30 3-1	O21 4-1	M24 1-1	F24 5-1	a24 5-0	D30 0-0	A26 3-0	S18 2-0	D23 2-0	J13 1-1	M31 0-2		M26 0-0	A12 1-0	O09 4-2	D02 1-1	O07 3-3	N04 1-0	a14 2-1	M05 4-0
17 NEWPORT CO	O07 2-1	M31 1-1	F06 0-0	a28 4-3	S16 0-2	A19 3-2	J06 1-0	a14 0-0	M09 0-0	M06 1-0	M24 2-0	F17 5-1	O21 5-1	N28 0-1	D16 2-2	S02 0-1		N04 1-0	S19 1-1	D26 1-0	O24 3-1	S30 1-0	J23 2-1	a24 2-0
18 NORTHAMPTON T	a07 0-2	O14 2-2	J27 1-2	N11 0-1	S30 2-2	S01 1-0	D26 4-0	O28 1-0	M20 2-2	M02 0-2	N25 1-2	J06 2-1	a21 3-1	M17 0-4	F03 0-0	F16 1-0	S26 0-1		a28 1-3	S16 1-1	D15 0-1	F13 1-1	a23 0-2	O24 1-0
19 PETERBOROUGH U	M19 1-0	M02 6-3	S02 3-0	S25 1-1	D26 1-1	J06 2-2	O23 2-2	M17 4-3	a07 1-1	O14 3-1	a21 1-1	a24 0-1	N25 3-0	O28 1-1	S30 2-2	F03 1-0	N11 1-0	A28 1-2		J27 4-2	A19 0-1	F17 2-3	S16 0-1	D16 2-1
20 READING	a23 0-0	F24 0-0	M24 2-0	A26 0-0	M21 1-0	a21 2-1	N25 0-1	A12 1-1	F21 1-0	D23 1-0	O11 2-0	M10 3-1	J20 1-0	D30 0-1	S20 1-1	a07 2-0	S23 5-0	F10 3-0	S09 2-0		O21 1-1	O07 0-0	F28 3-0	N04 2-0
21 SOUTHPORT	J20 3-1	S09 1-0	S11 3-1	O11 2-1	O13 1-1	N03 3-2	S20 1-0	D22 2-0	A26 2-1	F09 2-2	A12 1-0	M06 0-0	a23 1-1	S22 2-0	a14 1-0	M02 3-1	J30 0-2	F23 1-2	D30 2-1	M16 4-1		M30 1-0	O27 2-1	D01 2-1
22 STOCKPORT CO	m04 1-1	A25 2-0	a21 3-1	S22 0-0	N10 2-2	a06 2-1	M19 2-0	O09 0-0	S08 3-1	J19 2-1	F09 1-0	S11 2-3	F23 0-1	D22 1-1	O28 2-1	S25 2-1	a23 1-0	D29 0-0	A12 3-2	M02 2-2	N24 2-0		O13 2-0	M16 3-0
23 TORQUAY U	A12 1-1	J13 0-0	O21 1-2	J20 0-1	a07 1-2	N25 1-2	a20 0-0	D30 0-0	F24 2-1	O11 1-0	S23 0-2	O07 0-0	A26 1-0	a24 0-0	N04 2-0	M21 1-1	S09 2-2	D23 2-1	F10 1-0	a28 2-2	M24 2-0	M10 0-0		S20 3-0
24 WORKINGTON	D30 2-1	O11 3-2	M21 1-1	a20 2-0	N25 5-1	O07 3-1	M10 1-0	A26 1-1	S23 2-1	A12 2-0	S09 3-1	M24 1-1	F10 0-0	J20 2-1	A30 0-3	D09 2-0	D23 3-2	J13 3-0	F23 2-2	S27 0-0	a07 2-0	O21 2-0	N11 2-2	

LEAGUE TABLES

DIVISION 1

	P	W	D	L	F	A	W	D	L	F	A	Pts
Liverpool	42	17	3	1	45	19	8	7	6	27	23	60
Arsenal	42	14	5	2	31	14	9	6	6	26	29	57
Leeds U	42	15	4	2	45	13	6	7	8	26	32	53
Ipswich T	42	10	7	4	34	20	7	7	7	21	25	48
Wolverh'pton W	42	13	3	5	43	23	5	8	8	23	31	47
West Ham U	42	12	5	4	45	25	5	7	9	22	28	46
Derby Co	42	15	3	3	43	18	4	5	12	13	36	46
Tottenham H	42	10	5	6	33	23	6	8	7	25	25	45
Newcastle U	42	12	6	3	35	19	4	7	10	25	32	45
Birmingham C	42	11	7	3	39	22	4	5	12	14	32	42
Manchester C	42	12	4	5	36	20	3	7	11	21	40	41
Chelsea	42	9	6	6	30	22	4	8	9	19	29	40
Southampton	42	8	11	2	26	17	3	7	11	21	35	40
Sheffield U	42	11	4	6	28	18	4	6	11	23	41	40
Stoke C	42	11	8	2	38	17	3	2	16	23	39	38
Leicester C	42	7	9	5	23	18	3	8	10	17	28	37
Everton	42	9	5	7	27	21	4	6	11	14	28	37
Manchester U	42	9	7	5	24	19	3	6	12	20	41	37
Coventry C	42	9	5	7	27	24	4	4	13	13	31	35
Norwich C	42	7	9	5	22	19	4	1	16	14	44	32
Crystal Palace	42	7	7	7	25	21	2	5	14	16	37	30
W.B.A.	42	8	7	6	25	24	1	3	17	13	38	28

DIVISION 2

	P	W	D	L	F	A	W	D	L	F	A	Pts
Burnley	42	13	6	2	44	18	11	8	2	28	17	62
Q.P.R.	42	16	4	1	54	13	8	9	4	27	24	61
Aston Villa	42	12	5	4	27	17	6	9	6	24	30	50
Middlesbrough	42	12	6	3	29	15	5	7	9	17	28	47
Bristol C	42	10	7	4	34	18	7	5	9	29	33	46
Sunderland	42	12	6	3	35	17	5	6	10	24	32	46
Blackpool	42	12	6	3	37	17	6	4	11	19	34	46
Oxford U	42	14	2	5	36	18	5	5	11	16	25	45
Fulham	42	11	6	4	32	16	5	6	10	26	33	44
Sheffield W	42	14	4	3	40	20	3	6	12	19	35	44
Millwall	42	12	5	4	33	18	4	5	12	22	29	42
Luton T	42	6	9	6	24	23	9	2	10	20	30	41
Hull C	42	9	7	5	39	22	5	5	11	25	37	40
Nottingham F	42	12	5	4	32	18	2	7	12	15	34	40
Orient	42	11	6	4	33	18	1	6	14	16	35	36
Swindon T	42	8	9	4	28	23	2	7	12	18	37	36
Portsmouth	42	7	6	8	21	22	5	5	11	21	37	35
Carlisle U	42	10	5	6	40	24	1	7	13	10	28	34
Preston N.E.	42	6	8	7	19	25	5	4	12	18	39	34
Cardiff C	42	11	4	6	32	21	0	7	14	11	37	33
Huddersfield T	42	7	9	5	21	20	1	8	12	15	36	33
Brighton & H.A.	42	7	8	6	32	31	1	5	15	14	52	29

DIVISION 3

	P	W	D	L	F	A	W	D	L	F	A	Pts
Bolton W	46	18	4	1	44	9	7	7	9	29	30	61
Notts Co	46	17	4	2	40	12	6	7	10	27	35	57
Blackburn R	46	12	8	3	34	16	8	7	8	23	31	55
Oldham A	46	12	7	4	40	18	7	9	7	32	36	54
Bristol R	46	17	4	2	55	20	3	9	11	22	36	53
Port Vale	46	15	6	2	41	21	6	5	12	15	48	53
Bournemouth	46	14	6	3	44	16	3	10	10	22	28	50
Plymouth A	46	14	3	6	43	26	6	7	10	31	40	50
Grimsby T	46	16	2	5	45	18	4	6	13	22	43	48
Tranmere R	46	12	8	3	38	17	3	8	12	18	35	46
Charlton A	46	12	7	4	46	24	5	4	14	23	43	45
Wrexham	46	11	9	3	39	23	3	8	12	16	31	45
Rochdale	46	8	8	7	22	26	6	9	8	26	28	45
Southend U	46	13	6	4	40	14	4	4	15	21	40	44
Shrewsbury T	46	10	10	3	31	21	5	4	14	15	33	44
Chesterfield	46	13	4	6	37	22	4	5	14	20	39	43
Walsall	46	14	3	6	37	26	4	4	15	19	40	43
York C	46	8	10	5	24	14	5	5	13	18	32	41
Watford	46	11	8	4	32	23	1	9	13	11	25	41
Halifax T	46	9	8	6	29	23	4	7	12	14	30	41
Rotherham U	46	12	4	7	34	27	5	3	15	17	38	41
Brentford	46	12	5	6	33	18	3	2	18	18	51	37
Swansea C	46	11	5	7	37	29	3	4	16	14	44	37
Scunthorpe U	46	8	7	8	18	25	2	3	18	15	47	30

DIVISION 4

	P	W	D	L	F	A	W	D	L	F	A	Pts
Southport	46	17	4	2	40	19	9	6	8	31	29	62
Hereford U	46	18	4	1	39	12	5	8	10	17	26	58
Cambridge U	46	15	6	2	40	23	5	11	7	27	34	57
Aldershot	46	14	6	3	33	14	8	6	9	27	24	56
Newport Co	46	14	6	3	37	18	8	6	9	27	26	56
Mansfield T	46	15	7	1	52	17	5	7	11	26	34	54
Reading	46	14	7	2	33	7	3	11	9	18	31	52
Exeter C	46	13	8	2	40	18	5	6	12	17	33	50
Gillingham	46	15	4	4	44	20	4	7	12	19	38	49
Lincoln C	46	12	7	4	38	27	4	9	10	26	30	48
Stockport Co	46	14	7	2	38	18	4	5	14	15	35	48
Bury	46	11	7	5	37	19	3	11	9	21	32	46
Workington	46	15	7	1	44	20	2	5	16	15	41	46
Barnsley	46	9	8	6	32	24	5	8	10	26	36	44
Chester C	46	11	6	6	40	19	3	9	11	21	33	43
Bradford C	46	12	6	5	42	25	4	5	14	19	40	43
Doncaster R	46	10	8	5	28	19	5	4	14	21	39	42
Torquay U	46	8	10	5	23	17	4	7	12	21	30	41
Peterborough U	46	10	8	5	42	29	4	5	14	29	47	41
Hartlepool U	46	8	10	5	17	15	4	7	12	17	34	41
Crewe A	46	7	8	8	18	23	2	10	11	20	38	36
Colchester U	46	8	8	7	36	28	2	3	18	12	48	31
Northampton T	46	7	6	10	24	30	3	5	15	16	43	31
Darlington	46	5	9	9	28	41	2	6	15	14	44	29

FOOTBALL LEAGUE RECORDS

Top scorers: Div 1, M.Channon (Southampton) 21 goals; Div 2, D.McKenzie (Nottingham Forest) 26 goals; Div 3, W.Jennings (Watford) 26 goals; Div 4, B.Yeo (Gillingham) 31 goals.

Billy Bremner, the tenacious Scottish midfielder and skipper of Leeds' 1973-74 Championship team.

DIVISION 1

	ARSENAL	BIRMINGHAM C	BURNLEY	CHELSEA	COVENTRY C	DERBY CO	EVERTON	IPSWICH T	LEEDS U	LEICESTER C	LIVERPOOL	MANCHESTER C	MANCHESTER U	NEWCASTLE U	NORWICH C	Q.P.R.	SHEFFIELD U	SOUTHAMPTON	STOKE C	TOTTENHAM H	WEST HAM U	WOLVERHAMPTON W
1 ARSENAL		O06 1-0	F02 1-1	N17 0-0	D01 2-2	a20 2-0	D22 1-0	O20 1-1	A28 1-2	S08 0-2	N03 0-2	M23 2-0	A25 3-0	J01 0-1	J12 2-0	a30 1-1	S11 1-0	M02 1-0	S22 2-1	F16 0-1	a06 0-0	D04 2-2
2 BIRMINGHAM C	F23 3-1		a16 2-2	S11 2-4	D26 1-0	S01 0-0	O27 0-2	S29 0-3	D29 1-1	N24 3-0	S15 1-1	J19 1-1	M16 1-0	D08 1-0	a27 2-1	a23 4-0	M30 1-0	N10 1-1	a13 0-0	A28 1-2	D15 3-1	O13 2-1
3 BURNLEY	D15 2-1	a12 2-1		A28 1-0	S01 2-2	S15 1-1	M16 3-1	F09 0-1	N10 0-0	a13 0-0	D26 2-1	S29 3-0	O27 0-0	a27 1-1	D08 1-0	O13 2-1	J19 1-2	a22 3-0	N24 1-0	S11 2-2	F23 1-1	D29 1-1
4 CHELSEA	a13 1-3	S05 3-1	M13 3-0		S15 1-0	J19 1-1	N10 3-1	O13 2-3	D15 1-2	D08 3-2	D29 0-1	F09 1-0	M30 1-3	M16 1-0	O26 3-0	F23 3-3	S01 1-2	N24 4-0	a27 0-1	a15 0-0	D26 2-4	S29 2-2
5 COVENTRY C	a27 3-3	M02 0-1	J01 1-1	J12 2-2		S18 1-0	O06 1-2	N03 0-1	a13 0-0	D22 1-2	A28 1-0	S11 2-1	F02 1-0	S22 2-2	F26 1-0	M23 0-1	N24 3-1	S08 2-0	M09 2-0	A25 1-0	O20 0-1	D08 1-0
6 DERBY CO	D08 1-1	J01 1-1	J12 5-1	A25 1-0	a15 1-0		S08 2-1	M23 2-0	N24 0-0	O20 2-1	S12 3-1	A29 1-0	F16 2-2	F02 1-0	O06 1-1	N03 1-2	a13 4-1	S22 6-2	M02 1-1	D22 2-0	M09 1-1	a27 2-0
7 EVERTON	S29 1-0	M09 4-1	O20 1-0	M23 1-1	F23 1-0	D29 2-1		S01 3-0	J19 0-0	A28 1-1	D08 0-1	D26 2-0	a23 1-0	N24 1-1	a13 4-1	S15 1-0	D15 1-1	a27 0-3	S11 1-1	N03 1-1	O13 1-0	F09 2-1
8 IPSWICH T	M16 2-2	D22 3-0	S22 3-2	F26 1-1	M30 3-0	N10 3-0	J01 3-0		D08 0-3	A25 1-1	a13 1-1	N24 2-1	S08 2-1	S04 1-3	M02 1-1	a15 1-0	a27 0-1	F02 7-0	J12 1-1	O06 0-0	F05 1-3	O27 2-0
9 LEEDS U	F05 3-1	S08 3-0	M23 1-4	F02 1-1	N17 3-0	a06 2-0	A25 3-1	a20 3-2		F26 1-1	O20 1-0	M09 1-0	S22 0-0	M02 1-1	D22 1-0	D01 2-2	a15 0-0	J12 2-1	O06 1-1	J01 1-1	N03 4-1	S05 4-1
10 LEICESTER C	D29 2-0	a06 3-3	N17 2-0	a20 3-0	S29 0-2	M16 0-1	M02 2-1	J19 5-0	O13 2-2		S01 1-1	S15 1-1	S05 1-0	N10 1-0	a29 3-0	D15 2-0	F23 1-1	O27 0-1	a16 1-1	D01 3-0	F09 0-1	D26 2-2
11 LIVERPOOL	a24 0-1	J12 3-2	M02 1-0	S08 1-0	F05 2-1	S04 2-0	a20 0-0	N17 4-2	M16 1-0	J01 1-1		a16 4-0	D22 2-0	O06 2-1	F02 1-0	a06 2-1	O27 1-0	F26 1-0	A25 1-0	S22 3-2	D01 1-0	N10 1-0
12 MANCHESTER C	N10 1-2	A25 3-1	D22 2-0	S22 3-2	S05 1-0	F06 1-0	a02 1-1	a06 1-3	O27 0-1	J12 2-0	a12 1-1		M13 0-0	M27 2-1	S08 2-1	N17 1-0	M16 0-1	O06 1-1	J01 0-0	F02 0-0	a20 2-1	M30 1-1
13 MANCHESTER U	J19 1-1	O20 1-0	a03 3-3	N03 2-2	D15 2-3	O13 0-1	a15 3-0	D29 2-0	F09 0-2	S12 1-2	S29 0-0	a27 0-1		a13 1-0	N24 0-0	S01 2-1	D26 1-2	D08 0-0	A29 1-0	M23 0-1	S15 3-1	F23 0-0
14 NEWCASTLE U	S01 1-1	a20 1-1	a10 1-2	O20 2-0	F09 5-1	D15 0-2	a06 2-1	S12 3-1	D26 0-1	M23 1-1	F23 0-0	O13 1-0	N17 3-2		a15 0-0	S29 2-3	D29 1-0	A29 0-1	N03 2-1	m11 0-2	J19 1-1	S15 2-0
15 NORWICH C	S15 0-4	M20 2-1	a20 1-0	M09 2-2	O13 0-0	F23 2-4	N17 1-3	D26 1-2	S29 0-1	N03 1-0	D15 1-1	D29 1-1	a06 0-2	a17 1-1		A29 0-0	F09 2-1	S12 2-0	M23 4-0	O20 1-1	S01 2-2	J19 1-1
16 Q.P.R.	O27 2-0	S22 2-2	F27 2-1	O06 1-1	N10 3-0	M30 0-0	J12 1-0	a12 0-1	a27 0-1	F02 0-0	N24 2-2	a09 3-0	J01 3-0	D22 3-2	F05 1-2		D08 0-0	A25 1-1	S08 3-3	M02 3-1	S04 0-0	M16 0-0
17 SHEFFIELD U	S04 5-0	N03 1-1	A25 0-2	J01 1-2	a06 0-1	N17 3-0	F02 1-1	M12 0-3	a16 0-2	O06 1-1	a08 1-0	O20 1-2	M02 0-1	S08 1-1	S22 1-0	a20 1-1		D22 4-2	F16 0-0	J12 2-2	M23 1-0	F05 1-0
18 SOUTHAMPTON	D26 1-1	M23 0-2	N03 2-2	a06 0-0	D29 1-1	M05 1-1	D01 2-0	D15 2-0	S15 1-2	M18 1-0	O13 1-0	F23 0-2	a20 1-1	F05 3-1	S04 2-2	J19 2-2	S29 3-0		O20 3-0	N17 1-1	a15 1-1	S01 2-1
19 STOKE C	M30 0-0	N17 5-2	a06 4-0	J27 1-0	O27 3-0	D26 0-0	S05 0-0	S15 1-1	F23 3-2	a15 1-0	J19 1-1	S01 1-1	a29 1-0	a03 2-1	N10 2-0	D29 4-1	O13 1-2	M16 4-1		a20 1-0	S29 2-0	D15 2-3
20 TOTTENHAM H	O13 2-0	F06 4-2	S05 2-3	a03 1-2	J19 2-1	S29 1-0	M30 0-2	F23 1-1	S01 0-3	a27 1-0	m08 1-1	D15 0-2	N10 2-1	O27 0-2	M16 0-0	D26 0-0	S15 1-2	a13 3-1	D08 2-1		D29 2-0	N24 1-3
21 WEST HAM U	N24 1-3	F02 0-0	O06 0-1	M02 3-0	M16 2-3	O27 0-0	F16 4-3	A27 3-3	M30 3-1	S22 1-1	a27 2-2	D08 2-1	J12 2-1	A25 1-2	J01 4-2	S10 2-3	N10 2-2	a12 4-1	D22 0-2	S08 0-1		a13 0-0
22 WOLVERHAMPTON W	a15 3-1	F16 1-0	S08 0-2	D22 2-0	a20 1-1	a09 4-0	S22 1-1	M09 3-1	S11 0-2	a23 1-0	M23 0-1	N03 0-0	O06 2-1	J12 1-0	A25 3-1	O20 2-4	A28 2-0	J01 2-1	F02 1-1	a06 1-1	N17 0-0	

New Middlesbrough manager Jack Charlton appointed Stuart Boam captain and Boam led 'Boro to the Division Two championship in 1973-74.

DIVISION 2

	ASTON VILLA	BLACKPOOL	BOLTON W	BRISTOL C	CARDIFF C	CARLISLE U	CRYSTAL P	FULHAM	HULL C	LUTON T	MIDDLESBROUGH	MILLWALL	NOTTINGHAM F	NOTTS CO	ORIENT	OXFORD U	PORTSMOUTH	PRESTON N.E.	SHEFFIELD W	SUNDERLAND	SWINDON T	W.B.A.
1 ASTON VILLA		a15 0-1	F27 1-1	O20 2-2	O06 5-0	M13 2-1	O23 2-1	S19 1-1	N17 1-1	F02 0-1	J12 1-1	J01 0-0	a24 3-1	D22 1-1	S22 2-2	S08 2-0	M23 4-1	A25 2-0	N03 1-0	a20 1-2	a06 1-1	M02 1-3
2 BLACKPOOL	a16 2-1		M02 0-2	M19 2-2	F16 2-1	a20 4-0	S17 1-0	O22 2-0	a06 1-2	D22 3-0	S22 0-0	S08 1-0	O20 2-2	O06 0-1	J12 1-1	F02 2-0	N03 5-0	M23 3-0	J01 0-0	D01 0-2	N17 2-0	A25 2-3
3 BOLTON W	O13 1-2	D26 1-1		J20 2-1	a06 1-1	F23 2-0	S15 2-0	a02 0-0	S01 1-0	M23 1-0	a15 2-1	O20 0-1	S29 1-0	N17 1-3	S11 1-1	N03 2-1	D29 4-0	a20 0-2	F16 4-2	D05 1-0	D15 2-0	M09 1-1
4 BRISTOL C	M16 0-1	O27 0-1	A25 1-0		F02 3-2	a06 2-0	N10 0-1	M30 0-1	S18 3-1	S08 1-3	D22 1-1	F26 5-2	a12 1-0	D01 2-2	J01 0-2	M02 0-0	a20 0-2	J12 0-0	S22 2-0	N17 2-0	O23 1-0	O06 1-1
5 CARDIFF C	F23 0-1	O13 1-0	N24 1-0	D15 0-1		J19 2-2	a30 1-1	S15 0-0	S29 1-3	N14 0-0	a13 3-2	M23 1-3	D08 1-1	J26 1-0	a27 1-1	S12 5-0	S01 1-1	M09 2-0	O20 0-1	D29 4-1	D26 2-1	N03 0-1
6 CARLISLE U	a27 2-0	D08 2-3	O06 1-0	N24 2-1	A25 1-1		M16 1-0	O27 3-0	N10 4-0	J01 2-0	O23 1-1	D22 1-1	a13 2-1	S08 3-0	F02 3-0	S22 2-1	S18 0-2	M02 2-2	J12 2-2	a16 1-0	M30 5-1	F25 0-1
7 CRYSTAL P	S11 0-0	O02 1-2	J12 0-0	M23 3-1	S22 3-3	O20 0-1		a16 0-2	a20 0-2	O06 1-2	S08 2-3	N17 1-1	N03 0-1	A25 1-4	M03 0-0	F17 2-0	a06 0-0	F03 2-0	D22 0-0	M09 3-0	D01 4-2	J01 1-0
8 FULHAM	O02 1-0	S12 0-0	S22 1-0	N03 2-1	J12 0-1	M09 0-2	a12 1-3		D01 0-0	M05 2-1	M19 0-4	A25 2-0	M23 2-0	F16 2-0	S08 0-3	D22 3-1	N17 2-0	O06 0-0	F02 4-1	O20 0-2	a20 4-1	a06 0-0
9 HULL C	a13 1-1	N24 1-0	J01 0-0	O02 2-1	D22 1-1	M23 1-1	D08 3-0	a27 2-0		M09 1-3	F16 1-3	J12 1-1	S11 0-0	F02 1-0	O06 1-1	A25 0-0	O20 4-1	S08 1-0	M02 2-1	N03 2-0	a15 0-1	S22 0-0
10 LUTON T	D15 1-0	S29 3-0	N10 2-1	D29 1-0	D12 1-0	S01 6-1	F23 2-1	D26 1-1	O27 2-2		M30 0-1	a20 3-0	J19 2-2	F05 1-1	M16 3-1	a16 0-1	S15 3-3	a06 4-2	N17 2-1	m01 3-4	O13 2-1	D01 0-2
11 MIDDLESBROUGH	S15 0-0	F09 0-0	a09 0-0	S29 2-0	N17 3-0	S11 1-0	D29 2-0	S01 0-2	O13 1-0	N03 2-1		M09 2-1	D15 1-0	a06 4-0	O02 3-2	M23 1-0	J19 3-0	D11 3-0	a20 8-0	D26 2-1	F23 2-1	O20 0-0
12 MILLWALL	S01 1-1	D29 2-2	M16 2-1	O13 0-2	N10 2-0	S29 1-2	a13 3-2	J20 1-0	S15 3-0	D08 0-1	O27 0-1		F23 0-0	M30 0-0	N24 0-1	a27 0-0	D26 1-1	O22 5-1	S17 1-0	D15 2-1	F16 3-0	a12 1-0
13 NOTTINGHAM F	O27 1-2	M16 2-0	D22 3-2	a16 1-1	a20 2-1	N17 2-0	M30 1-2	N10 3-0	O23 0-0	A25 4-0	F02 5-1	O06 3-0		M03 0-0	F26 2-1	J01 1-1	M26 2-0	S22 1-1	S08 2-1	a06 2-2	S18 2-0	J12 1-4
14 NOTTS CO	S29 2-0	F23 0-3	a13 0-0	a27 2-1	a15 1-1	D29 0-3	J20 1-3	O13 2-1	D15 3-2	S11 1-1	N24 2-2	N03 3-3	D26 0-1		D08 2-4	O02 0-0	F09 4-0	O20 2-1	M09 1-5	S01 1-4	S15 2-0	M23 1-0
15 ORIENT	m03 1-1	S15 3-2	O22 3-0	S01 0-1	D01 1-2	D15 0-1	D26 3-0	D29 1-0	F23 1-1	O20 2-0	S17 0-0	a06 1-1	O13 2-1	a20 1-1		M10 1-1	a15 2-1	N03 2-2	M23 0-1	J19 2-1	S29 0-0	N17 2-0
16 OXFORD U	D29 2-1	D15 2-2	M30 0-2	D26 5-0	O24 4-2	a23 0-1	O13 1-1	S26 0-0	J19 1-1	a12 1-1	N10 0-2	J26 0-3	S01 1-0	S19 2-1	O27 1-1		F23 3-0	N17 1-1	a06 1-0	S15 0-1	M17 1-1	a20 1-0
17 PORTSMOUTH	N10 2-0	M30 0-0	S08 0-2	D08 1-0	J01 1-0	O02 2-1	N24 2-2	a13 3-0	M16 3-1	J12 0-0	A25 0-1	M02 0-0	a27 0-2	S22 1-2	a12 0-0	O06 2-1		D22 3-0	F20 1-1	S11 1-1	O27 3-1	F03 1-1
18 PRESTON N.E.	J19 0-0	N10 1-3	D08 2-1	S15 1-1	O27 2-2	D26 0-1	D15 1-1	F23 0-1	D29 2-0	N24 2-2	a27 2-4	S11 2-0	F10 2-1	M16 0-2	M30 0-1	a13 0-0	S29 2-1		a12 0-0	O13 1-0	S01 1-1	O01 3-1
19 SHEFFIELD W	a01 2-4	S01 0-0	a27 1-0	F10 3-1	M16 5-0	S15 1-0	S29 4-0	D15 0-3	D26 1-1	a13 2-2	D08 2-2	O03 3-2	D29 1-1	O27 0-0	N10 1-2	N24 0-1	O13 1-2	a15 1-0		F23 0-1	J19 2-1	S12 3-1
20 SUNDERLAND	D08 2-0	a27 2-1	N13 3-0	a13 1-2	S08 1-1	a12 2-1	O27 0-0	M16 1-0	M30 1-0	S22 0-1	M02 0-2	F02 4-0	N24 0-0	J01 1-2	A25 1-1	J12 0-0	M05 3-0	F16 2-1	O06 3-1		N10 4-1	D22 1-1
21 SWINDON T	N24 1-0	a13 1-0	F03 2-2	S11 0-1	M02 1-1	N03 2-2	a27 0-1	D08 1-1	J26 1-1	F26 0-2	O06 0-1	S22 1-3	O02 0-0	F19 1-4	D22 2-2	O20 1-0	M09 1-2	J01 3-1	A25 3-1	M23 0-2		S08 1-0
22 W.B.A.	D26 2-0	J19 1-1	O27 0-0	F23 2-2	M30 2-2	O13 1-1	S01 1-0	N24 2-0	M19 2-3	a27 1-1	M16 0-4	a17 1-1	S15 3-3	N10 2-1	a13 1-0	D08 1-0	D15 1-2	S18 0-2	O24 2-0	S29 1-1	D29 2-0	

Season 1973-74

DIVISION 3

	ALDERSHOT	BLACKBURN R	BOURNEMOUTH	BRIGHTON & HA	BRISTOL R	CAMBRIDGE U	CHARLTON A	CHESTERFIELD	GRIMSBY T	HALIFAX T	HEREFORD U	HUDDERSFIELD T	OLDHAM A	PLYMOUTH A	PORT VALE	ROCHDALE	SHREWSBURY T	SOUTHEND U	SOUTHPORT	TRANMERE R	WALSALL	WATFORD	WREXHAM	YORK C
1 ALDERSHOT		a27 4-0	O24 1-3	M03 0-1	J27 2-3	a13 6-0	O27 2-1	M27 2-2	M16 1-0	D08 2-1	F03 1-0	J12 1-0	O06 0-1	S19 3-2	N10 0-0	M13 4-0	S22 2-2	F17 3-3	J01 4-0	A25 0-0	S08 1-0	M30 1-0	N14 5-1	D22 2-2
2 BLACKBURN R	a24 1-2		M23 4-3	O06 3-1	S22 0-2	O20 2-0	O24 1-1	J12 2-1	S19 1-0	a15 1-1	J01 1-2	M27 1-0	M02 0-1	N03 2-0	a06 1-1	a20 3-1	J27 2-0	A25 1-0	F03 2-1	F17 0-0	D22 0-2	N17 5-0	m01 1-2	S08 4-0
3 BOURNEMOUTH	S12 3-0	N10 1-2		J01 0-0	A25 0-3	D08 1-0	N14 1-0	S08 0-1	a13 1-1	a24 1-1	M02 3-2	D22 1-0	F02 0-3	a12 0-0	M16 2-2	O03 2-0	F16 1-0	J25 1-3	O06 2-0	S22 2-1	J12 1-0	O27 1-0	a27 0-1	M27 1-3
4 BRIGHTON & H.A.	D26 0-1	F23 3-0	S01 0-2		D01 2-8	a03 4-1	S15 1-2	N17 0-0	F09 1-1	O13 0-1	M10 2-1	M23 1-2	S19 1-2	D29 1-0	M20 2-1	J20 2-1	O20 2-0	a15 0-2	O24 4-0	a20 1-3	a06 2-1	S29 0-1	F27 2-1	N03 0-0
5 BRISTOL R	a02 2-1	M12 3-0	J19 3-0	a27 1-1		S29 1-0	S01 2-1	N03 1-0	D29 1-1	S15 2-0	S11 1-1	M08 2-1	a13 1-2	D26 4-2	O13 1-1	M05 1-1	O02 1-0	D08 4-0	N13 3-1	a16 1-0	M23 0-2	F23 1-0	M19 1-0	O20 0-0
6 CAMBRIDGE U	N17 1-2	M16 0-2	a20 2-1	J27 1-1	D22 2-2		N10 1-0	F02 1-2	M30 0-1	O27 0-1	F17 2-0	J01 2-2	S22 1-1	m01 3-1	O24 4-2	a06 3-3	S08 2-1	J12 3-2	A25 2-0	M27 1-0	M03 0-0	S19 3-2	a16 2-1	O06 0-0
7 CHARLTON A	m03 2-0	S11 4-3	a06 0-0	J12 0-4	J01 1-1	M23 2-0		S22 3-3	a15 2-1	O02 5-2	S08 2-0	J26 2-1	M26 4-1	N17 2-0	D01 2-0	O20 3-0	F03 3-3	M03 2-1	D22 0-1	O06 1-0	F17 0-1	a20 1-3	N03 0-0	A25 2-4
8 CHESTERFIELD	J05 0-0	S15 3-0	D29 2-1	a13 1-0	M30 0-0	M13 3-0	F09 3-1		S01 1-0	F23 1-1	D08 1-1	O24 0-2	M16 1-0	J19 1-0	S29 2-1	D26 1-0	a27 0-2	N14 0-0	O27 4-2	N10 1-0	a17 1-0	O13 3-1	a03 2-2	S19 0-2
9 GRIMSBY T	O20 1-0	O02 4-2	N17 1-1	S22 0-0	S08 1-1	N03 1-0	a12 5-0	J01 1-1		S11 4-1	A25 1-3	F02 2-1	a24 2-1	a06 3-0	a20 2-0	J26 5-1	D22 1-2	M26 2-1	F16 2-1	J12 5-0	N06 1-0	a29 2-2	M23 1-1	M02 1-2
10 HALIFAX T	a20 0-0	a16 1-1	N03 1-1	F16 2-2	J12 0-0	M10 0-1	S18 2-1	O06 2-0	a09 1-2		S22 1-1	M02 0-0	A25 0-0	M23 1-0	N17 1-0	a22 1-0	M26 1-0	S08 0-0	J27 1-1	D22 2-1	F03 3-1	a06 0-0	O20 1-2	a30 2-1
11 HEREFORD U	M20 0-2	S01 1-0	D26 0-2	O27 3-0	O24 0-0	O13 0-0	D29 2-3	a20 2-1	J19 2-1	M13 3-1		N17 0-1	N10 3-4	F20 0-1	F23 2-1	a03 2-1	a15 1-1	M16 1-2	M30 3-0	S19 0-2	D01 3-1	S15 1-1	S29 2-0	a06 0-0
12 HUDDERSFIELD T	S15 1-0	J29 1-0	S29 1-1	N10 2-2	O27 1-2	S01 2-1	a02 2-0	S11 1-0	M20 1-0	D26 4-0	a13 0-0		D08 2-1	O13 2-1	D29 3-0	F23 5-0	N13 1-0	M30 0-1	a27 3-1	M16 0-0	O09 2-2	J19 1-2	a24 2-1	a16 0-1
13 OLDHAM A	F23 2-0	D26 2-3	M19 4-2	O02 0-1	N17 1-1	M05 6-1	a30 0-2	O20 0-0	a02 3-1	J19 3-2	M23 1-1	a20 6-0		S29 1-0	S01 1-1	O13 3-1	N03 3-0	S11 2-0	a12 6-0	a06 2-2	M09 2-1	D29 0-3	S15 0-0	M12 2-1
14 PLYMOUTH A	O02 2-1	M30 2-1	a15 2-0	S08 0-1	M02 1-0	a27 4-1	a16 1-0	A25 1-1	N13 1-0	N10 1-1	M26 0-1	F16 1-1	m03 0-0		O27 2-0	S11 5-0	O06 2-2	F02 1-1	J12 4-1	J01 2-0	S22 2-1	M16 2-0	D08 1-2	m06 0-2
15 PORT VALE	M23 0-1	N12 1-2	O20 0-0	F02 2-1	F17 3-1	S10 2-1	a27 3-1	D22 0-1	D08 1-1	a13 1-1	O06 1-3	S08 4-2	J01 3-0	M10 2-1		N03 3-1	A25 3-0	S22 0-0	M02 2-1	J26 1-0	M25 1-1	a16 1-2	O01 1-0	J12 2-2
16 ROCHDALE	a15 2-2	D08 1-2	S17 3-3	A25 1-1	M25 0-1	F05 0-2	M16 1-1	M02 1-2	O27 1-1	a27 1-1	F26 1-1	O06 1-1	F16 1-3	O22 1-3	M30 1-1		J12 3-2	D22 1-1	S22 2-2	S08 0-1	J01 0-1	N10 1-3	a13 0-0	F03 1-3
17 SHREWSBURY T	F10 0-0	a02 3-0	O13 1-1	M16 1-0	S18 0-2	D29 2-0	M19 3-3	D01 0-1	S29 1-1	J05 0-2	a16 1-1	a06 3-0	M30 0-2	F23 0-0	J19 0-1	S15 2-0		O27 1-2	N10 2-0	O23 1-3	a20 0-0	D26 3-2	S01 0-1	N17 0-2
18 SOUTHEND U	O13 2-1	J19 1-1	a01 2-2	a12 0-2	a19 0-0	S14 3-1	D26 2-0	a05 1-3	a22 4-1	D29 1-2	O19 2-1	N03 5-2	O22 2-2	M18 2-0	F09 1-0	S29 1-2	M10 2-0		S17 0-1	D01 1-1	N17 2-1	A31 2-3	F24 1-1	M24 3-3
19 SOUTHPORT	S01 3-0	a08 2-2	F24 1-0	S10 1-1	a05 1-0	J19 0-0	S29 1-2	M09 1-1	O12 0-1	a01 1-1	N02 1-1	D01 0-0	a15 0-2	S15 1-1	D26 0-1	M10 0-0	M23 1-0	O01 0-0		N17 2-2	O19 1-1	J05 1-1	D29 0-2	a19 1-1
20 TRANMERE R	J20 0-1	O12 1-1	F10 1-1	D08 4-1	a12 0-0	a22 5-2	F24 2-0	M23 1-2	S14 0-0	S28 0-1	O08 0-0	O19 1-1	F04 0-2	S01 2-0	a01 3-0	D29 1-1	S10 1-0	a26 2-0	a13 3-1		N02 3-0	a08 1-0	D26 0-1	M09 0-0
21 WALSALL	D29 3-2	S29 2-0	S15 1-2	N13 0-1	N10 0-0	D26 3-0	O13 4-0	a15 2-0	F23 3-1	M19 2-2	a27 3-1	S17 3-0	O27 1-1	F10 0-4	a30 0-0	S01 0-0	D08 2-0	a13 1-2	M17 2-0	M30 0-1		a02 2-2	J20 3-0	O16 0-0
22 WATFORD	N03 2-1	a13 0-0	M09 1-1	D22 1-0	O06 0-0	O03 3-0	D08 1-3	F16 2-1	a27 1-2	N12 0-0	J12 2-1	A25 1-1	S08 0-1	O20 0-3	a24 2-1	M23 4-0	M02 1-0	J01 1-0	M27 4-0	F02 4-2	J26 1-3		S12 2-0	S22 1-1
23 WREXHAM	a06 0-0	O27 2-2	D01 0-1	M25 1-0	F02 1-0	a12 2-1	M30 4-0	M04 2-1	N10 1-1	M16 2-1	D22 5-0	S22 0-0	J12 1-2	a20 5-2	S17 0-0	N17 3-0	J01 3-1	O06 5-1	S08 3-2	M02 0-0	A25 2-0	O22 1-0		F20 1-0
24 YORK C	S29 3-1	D29 1-0	M06 4-1	M30 3-0	M16 2-1	F24 2-0	J19 0-1	O01 0-0	D26 1-1	S01 1-1	N12 0-0	a12 2-1	a27 1-1	a03 1-1	S15 3-1	J05 2-1	a13 0-1	N10 1-0	D08 4-0	O27 2-0	S10 1-1	F10 2-2	O12 1-0	

DIVISION 4

	BARNSLEY	BRADFORD C	BRENTFORD	BURY	CHESTER	COLCHESTER U	CREWE A	DARLINGTON	DONCASTER R	EXETER C	GILLINGHAM	HARTLEPOOL	LINCOLN C	MANSFIELD T	NEWPORT CO	NORTHAMPTON T	PETERBOROUGH U	READING	ROTHERHAM U	SCUNTHORPE U	STOCKPORT CO	SWANSEA C	TORQUAY U	WORKINGTON
1 BARNSLEY		O06 2-2	D22 2-1	N03 3-2	J27 1-1	A25 0-1	N17 2-1	F24 1-0	O23 2-0	M23 3-0	M26 3-1	a20 2-0	S18 0-1	S08 1-1	O20 1-1	a06 0-2	a16 0-0	F03 3-2	M03 1-0	J01 5-0	S22 4-0	M10 1-0	J12 1-0	F17 4-0
2 BRADFORD C	F23 3-0		D08 1-1	D29 4-2	O27 1-1	a27 1-1	S29 0-1	D26 3-0	S01 1-1	J20 1-0	O31 0-0	M06 2-0	F10 4-0	N14 3-1	a03 3-0	O13 1-1	S15 1-1	N10 4-3	S12 2-1	O03 2-1	M17 0-1	M20 3-1	M30 2-1	a13 3-2
3 BRENTFORD	S29 5-1	a20 2-0		F09 1-2	N17 3-0	a16 0-0	a01 3-0	D15 0-0	S15 2-0	S01 0-1	D01 0-3	J19 1-2	F23 2-1	N03 4-1	D26 1-1	M18 3-1	O13 0-1	S17 0-1	O20 1-1	M09 2-1	a06 0-0	J05 0-2	S10 0-0	M23 1-1
4 BURY	M30 2-0	S08 3-0	S22 3-0		O06 3-1	F03 2-0	M17 2-0	O02 5-1	a13 3-1	a12 0-0	F17 3-2	S11 1-0	N13 2-1	J27 2-0	a27 5-0	O27 3-1	N10 0-2	J12 1-0	D22 3-1	M26 0-0	M03 1-1	D08 0-2	A25 4-0	J01 3-1
5 CHESTER	a03 3-1	M10 1-0	a13 0-0	F24 1-1		N14 0-4	D26 1-0	F10 1-0	O13 3-0	S15 0-1	O20 2-4	A31 3-1	S29 2-3	O03 1-1	D29 3-0	m01 0-0	M20 2-1	a27 0-0	N03 1-0	M23 2-0	a16 2-1	J19 1-0	D08 1-1	S12 1-0
6 COLCHESTER U	J19 2-0	D01 4-0	a12 2-1	M19 1-1	a05 1-1		S01 3-2	O12 3-0	a02 3-0	S28 1-0	a20 0-2	F22 3-0	J05 4-1	M22 1-0	S15 4-1	D29 1-0	D26 1-1	S11 0-0	M08 0-1	O19 2-0	N17 3-1	F08 2-0	O02 2-2	N02 3-0
7 CREWE A	a13 0-1	D22 1-0	J26 0-0	O20 1-0	M03 1-0	J01 1-2		N03 1-1	D08 4-0	M10 2-5	A25 1-0	M23 1-3	a27 2-1	S22 1-1	O03 4-1	a16 0-2	N14 2-1	M27 2-1	S08 1-8	J12 1-0	O06 1-3	S12 0-0	F17 0-0	F03 1-0
8 DARLINGTON	a27 4-2	M03 2-1	S08 1-2	S17 0-0	S22 1-2	F16 1-0	M30 3-0		O27 1-0	O22 1-0	J12 1-3	a16 1-1	M17 0-3	D22 1-0	a13 0-1	N10 2-3	D08 2-2	J01 2-1	O06 1-1	F03 3-0	J26 1-1	N12 1-1	J27 0-0	A25 0-0
9 DONCASTER R	S11 1-0	J01 2-2	J12 1-2	N17 1-1	F17 1-2	J27 2-0	a20 0-2	M10 0-0		a06 1-0	D22 1-2	O20 2-2	a16 2-0	M26 0-0	M22 2-0	a23 2-1	O02 3-1	O06 0-0	F03 1-2	M02 1-0	A25 1-1	N03 3-1	S07 0-1	S22 5-2
10 EXETER C	N10 6-1	A25 0-0	J01 2-1	a15 0-3	J12 2-1	D22 1-0	O27 2-0	S12 3-0	N14 1-2		O06 2-1	O03 2-0	a13 0-1	M09 1-1	D08 0-1	M16 1-1	M30 1-2	S22 0-1	a30 0-0	a22 4-0	M27 2-1	a27 2-0	M02 4-2	S08 1-1
11 GILLINGHAM	J05 1-1	a15 2-0	a27 1-0	O13 3-0	M17 1-0	D08 4-1	J20 3-0	S15 0-1	S29 5-1	F23 2-1		F10 3-0	a24 2-0	a13 2-2	S01 1-1	D26 3-1	a03 1-0	M30 0-1	O03 1-1	S12 7-2	O27 2-1	D29 1-1	N10 2-1	N14 4-0
12 HARTLEPOOL	D08 1-2	M27 1-0	A25 1-0	O22 1-1	J01 0-0	O06 0-0	N10 1-0	a12 1-2	M17 3-0	S17 1-3	S22 2-1		O27 0-2	F17 4-0	N12 0-1	J05 1-0	a27 0-1	S08 1-2	J12 2-0	D22 3-0	F03 3-0	a13 0-1	J26 0-0	M03 3-0
13 LINCOLN C	O03 1-1	S22 0-1	O06 3-2	a06 4-3	D22 2-2	M27 0-1	D01 4-2	O20 2-1	a15 3-3	N17 2-1	F03 2-3	M09 0-1		M03 1-1	N03 3-0	a20 1-1	S12 1-1	F17 0-2	J27 2-1	A25 1-0	S08 1-1	M23 2-2	J01 3-0	J12 2-0
14 MANSFIELD T	D29 2-2	a06 0-0	M30 1-1	a01 1-2	S17 3-0	N10 2-2	F10 1-2	S29 1-0	a29 2-0	M18 3-3	N17 2-2	O13 2-0	D26 4-3		F24 2-1	S01 2-0	J20 2-1	M16 1-1	D01 3-0	a20 2-2	O22 5-0	S15 2-1	O27 2-1	a17 2-0
15 NEWPORT CO	M17 1-0	a22 2-2	M02 1-1	D01 1-0	S08 0-2	J12 1-3	S18 4-2	N17 2-0	N09 3-1	J27 2-1	J01 3-3	a06 0-0	M30 0-1	O09 2-0		O23 3-1	O27 0-1	A25 0-0	S22 1-0	F17 2-1	D22 3-1	a16 2-1	F03 2-2	M25 4-0
16 NORTHAMPTON T	N13 2-1	F17 3-0	F02 0-0	M09 3-1	M26 3-3	S07 0-0	a15 1-1	M24 5-0	a27 3-1	O20 1-2	M03 0-0	N03 1-0	D08 1-0	J01 2-0	S11 1-0		a13 0-1	J27 3-3	A25 3-1	S21 2-0	J12 2-0	O02 2-0	O05 0-0	D22 1-0
17 PETERBOROUGH U	a15 3-0	J12 1-1	F16 1-0	M23 2-2	F02 0-0	M02 2-0	a06 4-0	a20 1-0	S17 5-1	N03 2-0	m01 4-2	D01 2-0	O22 1-0	A25 2-1	M09 2-0	N17 3-0		D22 2-0	M25 2-0	S08 1-0	J01 3-2	O20 3-0	S22 1-1	O06 2-0
18 READING	M20 1-0	M24 0-0	O03 1-0	S15 2-2	a22 3-0	O24 1-1	J05 2-0	S01 2-0	F24 5-0	F10 4-1	N03 0-1	D29 1-1	O13 0-0	O20 3-0	J19 1-1	a03 1-2	S29 1-1		N17 1-0	a06 0-0	a20 1-1	D26 1-2	a12 4-0	M10 2-0
19 ROTHERHAM U	D26 2-1	O23 2-1	M16 1-1	S29 1-0	M30 3-2	O27 0-0	D29 1-1	F23 0-1	M19 1-2	O13 4-0	S18 1-1	S15 2-2	a02 2-0	a27 2-1	F10 1-1	J20 1-2	m11 3-1	a13 1-1		a15 1-1	N10 1-2	S01 1-0	N13 1-0	D08 1-1
20 SCUNTHORPE U	S01 3-0	S18 2-1	O27 4-1	a30 1-2	N10 2-1	M16 1-0	S14 0-0	M19 1-0	D26 2-1		O23 1-1	S29 1-1	J19 1-1	D08 5-3	O13 0-0	F10 1-2	D29 2-1	N13 1-0	a16 3-0		M30 2-1	F23 0-0	a13 0-0	a27 0-1
21 STOCKPORT CO	F10 1-1	O20 0-1	N12 1-1	D26 3-2	a15 0-1	D15 0-3	F24 0-0	a01 1-2	J20 0-0	J05 0-1	M10 2-0	a22 1-1	D29 2-2	S10 1-1	S28 1-1	S14 2-2	S01 1-1	D08 0-0	M23 0-1	N02 3-1		O13 0-1	a26 2-1	O01 1-1
22 SWANSEA C	O27 2-0	F03 0-1	M26 0-0	a20 0-1	A25 2-0	S22 2-0	O23 2-0	a06 0-0	M30 0-0	D01 2-0	S08 0-3	N17 0-0	N10 3-0	J12 2-0	a15 1-1	S18 1-1	M16 0-2	M03 2-1	J01 4-2	O06 1-2	F17 3-0		D22 0-1	J27 1-0
23 TORQUAY U	S15 1-1	N03 1-0	O24 3-0	J19 1-2	a20 2-2	S19 0-4	O13 2-1	J05 0-0	D29 3-0	D26 0-0	M23 0-1	a03 0-2	S01 2-1	M10 4-0	D15 3-2	F24 1-0	m07 1-2	a15 1-1	a06 3-0	N17 1-1	D01 2-2	S29 3-1		O20 3-0
24 WORKINGTON	O13 1-0	N17 1-0	N10 0-2	S01 0-0	O24 1-1	M30 1-4	a24 0-0	J20 5-2	F10 3-1	D15 3-1	a06 3-3	D26 0-2	S15 1-1	a15 0-0	J05 3-2	S29 1-0	F24 4-1	O27 0-0	a20 0-2	a10 1-2	S19 1-1	a03 1-0	M17 3-1	

LEAGUE TABLES

DIVISION 1

	P	W	D	L	F	A	W	D	L	F	A	Pts
Leeds U	42	12	8	1	38	18	12	6	3	28	13	62
Liverpool	42	18	2	1	34	11	4	11	6	18	20	57
Derby Co	42	13	7	1	40	16	4	7	10	12	26	48
Ipswich T	42	10	7	4	38	21	8	4	9	29	37	47
Stoke C	42	13	6	2	39	15	2	10	9	15	27	46
Burnley	42	10	9	2	29	16	6	5	10	27	37	46
Everton	42	12	7	2	29	14	4	5	12	21	34	44
Q.P.R.	42	8	10	3	30	17	5	7	9	26	35	43
Leicester C	42	10	7	4	35	17	3	9	9	16	24	42
Arsenal	42	9	7	5	23	16	5	7	9	26	35	42
Tottenham H	42	9	4	8	26	27	5	10	6	19	23	42
Wolverh'pton W	42	11	6	4	30	18	2	9	10	19	31	41
Sheffield U	42	7	7	7	25	22	7	5	9	19	27	40
Manchester C	42	10	7	4	25	17	4	5	12	14	29	40
Newcastle U	42	9	6	6	28	21	4	6	11	21	27	38
Coventry C	42	10	5	6	25	18	4	5	12	18	36	38
Chelsea	42	9	4	8	36	29	3	9	9	20	31	37
West Ham U	42	7	7	7	36	32	4	8	9	19	28	37
Birmingham C	42	10	7	4	30	21	2	6	13	22	43	37
Southampton	42	8	10	3	30	20	3	4	14	17	48	36
Manchester U	42	7	7	7	23	20	3	5	13	15	28	32
Norwich C	42	6	9	6	25	27	1	6	14	12	35	29

DIVISION 2

	P	W	D	L	F	A	W	D	L	F	A	Pts
Middlesbrough	42	16	4	1	40	8	11	7	3	37	22	65
Luton T	42	12	5	4	42	25	7	7	7	22	26	50
Carlisle U	42	13	5	3	40	17	7	4	10	21	31	49
Orient	42	9	8	4	28	17	6	10	5	27	25	48
Blackpool	42	11	5	5	35	17	6	8	7	22	23	47
Sunderland	42	11	6	4	32	15	8	3	10	26	29	47
Nottingham F	42	12	6	3	40	19	3	9	9	17	24	45
W.B.A.	42	8	9	4	28	24	6	7	8	20	21	44
Hull C	42	9	9	3	25	15	4	8	9	21	32	43
Notts Co	42	8	6	7	30	35	7	7	7	25	25	43
Bolton W	42	12	5	4	30	17	3	7	11	14	23	42
Millwall	42	10	6	5	28	16	4	8	9	23	35	42
Fulham	42	11	4	6	26	20	5	6	10	13	23	42
Aston Villa	42	8	9	4	33	21	5	6	10	15	24	41
Portsmouth	42	9	8	4	26	16	5	4	12	19	46	40
Bristol C	42	9	5	7	25	20	5	5	11	22	34	38
Cardiff C	42	8	7	6	27	20	2	9	10	22	42	36
Oxford U	42	8	8	5	27	21	2	8	11	8	25	36
Sheffield W	42	9	6	6	33	24	3	5	13	18	39	35
Crystal Palace	42	6	7	8	24	24	5	5	11	19	32	34
Preston N.E.	42	7	8	6	24	23	2	6	13	16	39	*31
Swindon T	42	6	7	8	22	27	1	4	16	14	45	25

*Preston North End had one point deducted for fielding an ineligible player

DIVISION 3

	P	W	D	L	F	A	W	D	L	F	A	Pts
Oldham A	46	13	6	4	50	23	12	6	5	33	24	62
Bristol R	46	15	6	2	37	15	7	11	5	28	18	61
York C	46	13	8	2	37	15	8	11	4	30	23	61
Wrexham	46	15	6	2	44	15	7	6	10	19	28	56
Chesterfield	46	14	6	3	31	16	7	8	8	24	26	56
Grimsby T	46	14	6	3	48	21	4	9	10	19	29	51
Watford	46	12	6	5	34	21	7	6	10	30	35	50
Aldershot	46	13	6	4	47	22	6	5	12	18	30	49
Halifax T	46	9	11	3	23	15	5	10	8	25	36	49
Huddersfield T	46	14	5	4	37	16	3	8	12	19	39	47
Bournemouth	46	11	5	7	25	23	5	10	8	29	35	47
Southend U	46	10	7	6	40	30	6	7	10	22	32	46
Blackburn R	46	13	4	6	38	21	5	6	12	24	43	46
Charlton A	46	13	5	5	43	29	6	3	14	23	44	46
Walsall	46	11	7	5	37	19	5	6	12	20	29	45
Tranmere R	46	10	8	5	31	15	5	7	11	19	29	45
Plymouth A	46	13	6	4	37	17	4	4	15	22	37	44
Hereford U	46	10	5	8	31	25	4	10	9	22	32	43
Brighton & H.A.	46	10	3	10	31	31	6	8	9	21	27	43
Port Vale	46	12	6	5	37	23	2	8	13	15	35	42
Cambridge U	46	11	7	5	36	27	2	2	19	12	54	35
Shrewsbury T	46	7	7	9	24	24	3	4	16	17	38	31
Southport	46	4	14	5	19	20	2	2	19	16	62	28
Rochdale	46	1	12	10	24	38	1	5	17	14	56	21

DIVISION 4

	P	W	D	L	F	A	W	D	L	F	A	Pts
Peterborough U	46	19	4	0	49	10	8	7	8	26	28	65
Gillingham	46	16	5	2	51	16	9	7	7	39	33	62
Colchester U	46	16	5	2	46	14	8	7	8	27	22	60
Bury	46	18	3	2	51	14	6	8	9	30	35	59
Northampton T	46	14	7	2	39	14	6	6	11	24	34	53
Reading	46	11	9	3	37	13	5	10	8	21	24	51
Chester C	46	13	6	4	31	19	4	9	10	23	36	49
Bradford C	46	14	7	2	45	20	3	7	13	13	32	48
Newport Co	46	13	6	4	39	23	3	8	12	17	42	*45
Exeter C	46	12	5	6	37	20	6	3	13	21	35	†44
Hartlepool U	46	11	4	8	29	16	5	8	10	19	31	44
Lincoln C	46	10	8	5	40	30	6	4	13	23	37	44
Barnsley	46	15	5	3	42	16	2	5	16	16	48	44
Swansea C	46	11	6	6	28	15	5	5	13	17	31	43
Rotherham U	46	10	9	4	33	22	5	4	14	23	36	43
Torquay U	46	11	7	5	37	23	2	10	11	15	34	43
Mansfield T	46	13	8	2	47	24	0	9	14	15	45	43
Scunthorpe U	46	12	7	3	33	17	2	5	16	14	47	†42
Brentford	46	9	7	7	31	20	3	9	11	17	30	40
Darlington	46	9	8	6	29	24	4	5	14	11	38	39
Crewe A	46	11	5	7	28	30	3	5	15	15	41	38
Doncaster R	46	10	7	6	32	22	2	4	17	15	58	35
Workington	46	10	8	5	33	26	1	5	17	10	48	35
Stockport Co	46	4	12	7	22	25	3	8	12	22	44	34

*Newport County had one point deducted for fielding an ineligible player. †Scunthorpe United awarded points after Exeter City failed to turn up

FOOTBALL LEAGUE RECORDS

Top scorers: Div 1, M.Macdonald (Newcastle United) 21 goals; Div 2, B.Little (Aston Villa) 20 goals; Div 3, R.McNeil (Hereford United) 31 goals; Div 4, R.Clarke (Mansfield Town) 28 goals.

Manchester United's Stuart Pearson, signed by Tommy Docherty from Hull for £200,000. His 17 goals in 1974-75 helped United straight back to Division One.

DIVISION 1

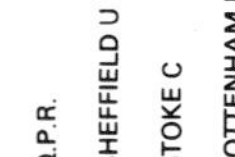

	ARSENAL	BIRMINGHAM C	BURNLEY	CARLISLE U	CHELSEA	COVENTRY C	DERBY CO	EVERTON	IPSWICH T	LEEDS U	LEICESTER C	LIVERPOOL	LUTON T	MANCHESTER C	MIDDLESBROUGH	NEWCASTLE U	Q.P.R.	SHEFFIELD U	STOKE C	TOTTENHAM H	WEST HAM U	WOLVERHAMPTON W
1 ARSENAL		M15 1-1	S07 0-1	J11 2-1	D26 1-2	a08 2-0	N16 3-1	M01 0-2	A20 0-1	a12 1-2	D14 0-0	F01 2-0	S21 2-2	A24 4-0	N30 2-0	M18 3-0	O12 2-2	M31 1-0	M29 1-1	a26 1-0	O26 3-0	N02 0-0
2 BIRMINGHAM C	S28 3-1		F01 1-1	M25 2-0	N02 2-0	O05 1-2	S14 3-2	J18 0-3	D28 0-1	O15 1-0	A20 3-4	D21 3-1	a19 1-4	N16 4-0	A17 0-3	O19 3-0	M22 4-1	a29 0-0	D07 0-3	F18 1-0	M18 1-1	A31 1-1
3 BURNLEY	M22 3-3	N09 2-2		D28 2-1	A27 1-2	A31 3-0	M31 2-5	O26 1-1	O15 1-0	S14 2-1	F08 2-0	M08 1-1	J18 1-0	O12 2-1	D21 1-1	N23 4-1	D07 3-0	F22 2-1	a26 0-0	a12 3-2	S28 3-5	A17 1-2
4 CARLISLE U	D07 2-1	S21 1-0	a01 4-2		D14 1-2	a05 0-0	O19 3-0	M29 3-0	J18 2-1	N23 1-2	M01 0-1	O05 0-1	M15 1-2	S24 0-0	A27 0-1	D26 1-2	F22 1-2	F08 0-1	S07 0-2	A24 1-0	N09 0-1	a19 1-0
5 CHELSEA	S14 0-0	F08 2-1	A21 3-3	A17 0-2		N13 3-3	M08 1-2	a26 1-1	M31 0-0	J18 0-2	N09 0-0	A31 0-3	D07 2-0	a12 0-1	M22 1-2	F22 3-2	D28 0-3	a23 1-1	O26 3-3	O12 1-0	D21 1-1	S28 0-1
6 COVENTRY C	N23 3-0	a12 1-0	M01 0-3	O26 2-1	A24 1-3		A27 1-1	S21 1-1	F22 3-1	N09 1-3	M15 2-2	N30 1-1	S24 2-1	S07 2-2	a26 0-2	D14 2-0	F08 1-1	M28 2-2	D26 2-0	F15 1-1	O12 1-1	J11 2-1
7 DERBY CO	F22 2-1	D26 2-1	S21 3-2	a26 0-0	S25 4-1	A21 1-1		D14 0-1	N23 2-0	F08 0-0	O12 1-0	J11 2-0	M29 5-0	a01 2-1	O26 2-3	S07 2-2	N09 5-2	A24 2-0	M15 1-2	M01 3-1	a12 1-0	a09 1-0
8 EVERTON	A31 2-1	N30 4-1	a04 1-1	D21 2-3	O19 1-1	M31 1-0	A17 0-0		M22 1-1	S28 3-2	J11 3-0	N16 0-0	F25 3-1	N02 2-0	D28 1-1	O05 1-1	M08 2-1	a19 2-3	A20 2-1	F01 1-0	O15 1-1	S14 0-0
9 IPSWICH T	A27 3-0	a01 3-2	A24 2-0	N30 3-1	S21 2-0	N16 4-0	F25 3-0	S07 1-0		O12 0-0	M29 2-1	N02 1-0	D26 0-1	O26 1-1	J11 2-0	M15 5-4	a12 2-1	M01 0-1	S24 3-1	D14 4-0	a26 4-1	F01 2-0
10 LEEDS U	O05 2-0	A24 1-0	D26 2-2	F25 3-1	N30 2-0	F01 0-0	N02 0-1	M15 0-0	a19 2-1		M31 2-2	a05 0-2	S07 1-1	M01 2-2	N16 2-2	M29 1-1	A21 0-1	S21 5-1	D14 3-1	D04 2-1	J11 2-1	O19 2-0
11 LEICESTER C	A17 0-1	A28 1-1	N02 1-0	A31 1-1	F01 1-1	S28 0-1	a19 0-0	D07 0-2	D20 0-1	D28 0-2		M19 1-1	O05 0-0	M08 1-0	a09 1-0	a05 4-0	S14 3-1	O19 3-0	J18 1-1	N16 1-2	a01 3-0	M22 3-2
12 LIVERPOOL	N09 1-3	M29 1-0	S24 0-1	a12 2-0	M01 2-2	J18 2-1	D07 2-2	F22 0-0	F08 5-2	O26 1-0	A24 2-1		D14 2-0	D26 4-1	O12 2-0	M25 4-0	a26 3-1	M15 0-0	S21 3-0	S07 5-2	N23 1-1	A27 2-0
13 LUTON T	M25 2-0	O12 1-3	N30 2-3	S28 3-1	J11 1-1	M08 1-3	D21 1-0	a09 2-1	S14 1-4	M22 2-1	a12 3-0	A17 1-2		a26 1-1	O16 0-1	F08 1-0	A31 1-1	N09 0-1	F22 0-0	O26 1-1	A28 0-0	D28 3-2
14 MANCHESTER C	O16 2-1	F22 3-1	a19 2-0	M19 1-2	O05 1-1	M22 1-0	D28 1-2	F08 2-1	a23 1-1	A31 2-1	N23 4-1	S14 2-0	O19 1-0		M28 2-1	J18 5-1	S28 1-0	D07 3-2	N09 1-0	A21 1-0	A17 4-0	D21 0-0
15 MIDDLESBROUGH	J18 0-0	D14 3-0	M29 2-0	A20 0-2	S07 1-1	O19 4-4	a05 1-1	M18 2-0	D07 3-0	F22 0-1	D10 3-0	a19 1-0	A24 1-1	S21 3-0		N09 0-0	N23 1-3	D26 1-0	M01 2-0	M15 3-0	F08 0-0	O05 2-1
16 NEWCASTLE U	a23 3-1	a26 1-2	F15 3-0	S14 1-0	N16 5-0	A17 3-2	M22 0-2	a12 0-1	S28 1-0	D21 3-0	O26 0-1	F12 4-1	N02 1-0	N30 2-1	F01 2-1		M31 2-2	A21 2-2	O12 2-2	J11 2-5	A31 2-0	O16 0-0
17 Q.P.R.	a19 0-0	S07 0-1	J11 0-1	N16 2-1	M18 1-0	N02 2-0	F01 4-1	S24 2-2	O05 1-0	A27 1-1	D26 4-2	O19 0-1	M01 2-1	M15 2-0	F25 0-0	S21 1-2		D14 1-0	A24 0-1	M29 0-1	N30 0-2	a05 2-0
18 SHEFFIELD U	D28 1-1	O26 3-2	N16 2-2	N02 2-1	F15 2-1	D20 1-0	O15 1-2	O12 2-2	A31 3-1	a01 1-1	a26 4-0	S28 1-0	F01 1-1	J11 1-1	S14 1-0	A27 2-1	A17 1-1		a12 2-0	N30 0-1	M22 3-2	M08 1-0
19 STOKE C	D21 0-2	J11 0-0	O19 2-0	M22 5-2	a05 3-0	S14 2-0	S28 1-1	A28 1-1	M18 1-2	A17 3-0	N30 1-0	M31 2-0	N16 4-2	F01 4-0	A31 1-1	a19 0-0	N27 1-0	O05 3-2		N02 2-2	D28 2-1	F15 2-2
20 TOTTENHAM H	O19 2-0	N23 0-0	O05 2-3	O16 1-1	a19 2-0	D28 1-1	A31 2-0	N09 1-1	A17 0-1	a28 4-2	F22 0-3	M22 0-2	a05 2-1	A28 1-2	S28 1-2	D07 3-0	D21 1-2	J18 1-3	F08 0-2		S14 2-1	M28 3-0
21 WEST HAM U	a28 1-0	S25 3-0	M15 2-1	F01 2-0	M29 0-1	a19 1-2	O05 2-2	A24 2-3	O19 1-0	D07 2-1	S21 6-2	F19 0-0	A19 2-0	D14 0-0	N02 3-0	F28 0-1	J18 2-2	S07 1-2	M28 2-2	D26 1-1		N16 5-2
22 WOLVERHAMPTON W	F08 1-0	M01 0-1	D14 4-2	O12 2-0	M15 7-1	D07 2-0	J18 0-1	D26 2-0	N09 2-1	a26 1-1	S07 1-1	A20 0-0	M31 5-2	M29 1-0	a12 2-0	A24 4-2	O26 1-2	S24 1-1	N23 2-2	S21 2-3	F22 3-1	

Archie Gemmill, Derby's Scottish midfield dynamo, who in the absence of the injured Roy McFarland, proved an inspirational captain as the Rams lifted the League Championship for the second time.

DIVISION 2

	ASTON VILLA	BLACKPOOL	BOLTON W	BRISTOL C	BRISTOL R	CARDIFF C	FULHAM	HULL C	MANCHESTER U	MILLWALL	NORWICH C	NOTTINGHAM F	NOTTS CO	OLDHAM A	ORIENT	OXFORD U	PORTSMOUTH	SHEFFIELD W	SOUTHAMPTON	SUNDERLAND	W.B.A.	YORK C
1 ASTON VILLA		O12 1-0	M05 0-0	J11 2-0	D26 1-0	a09 2-0	F08 1-1	A28 6-0	F22 2-0	S21 3-0	A24 1-1	O02 3-0	N09 0-1	a12 5-0	S07 3-1	N29 0-0	N23 2-0	O26 3-1	M15 3-0	a26 2-0	M29 3-1	D14 4-0
2 BLACKPOOL	a19 0-3		A24 2-1	F15 2-0	M15 0-0	S24 4-0	J18 1-0	O05 1-2	O19 0-3	S07 1-0	D14 2-1	M29 0-0	D07 3-1	D26 1-0	A20 0-0	N16 0-0	a05 2-2	N02 3-1	M01 3-0	F01 3-2	M31 2-0	S21 1-1
3 BOLTON W	A31 1-0	O22 0-0		M22 0-2	J18 5-1	O19 2-1	D28 0-0	a19 1-1	M08 0-1	F01 2-0	F15 0-0	N02 2-0	S28 1-1	N12 1-1	O05 2-0	D21 3-1	A17 3-0	S14 0-1	N16 3-2	M31 0-2	D07 0-1	a05 1-1
4 BRISTOL C	D07 1-0	N23 0-1	S07 2-1		a01 1-1	D26 0-0	a26 3-1	J18 2-0	N09 1-0	M15 2-1	M29 0-1	D14 1-0	O26 3-0	M01 3-1	A24 0-0	N05 3-0	F08 3-1	a12 1-0	S21 2-0	O12 1-1	F22 2-1	S24 0-0
5 BRISTOL R	S14 2-0	S28 1-3	N30 1-0	D28 1-4		O05 1-0	M11 1-2	A31 2-0	M28 1-1	O19 2-0	F01 0-2	a05 4-2	A17 0-0	J11 2-1	N16 0-0	F15 1-0	D21 0-1	S17 1-1	N02 0-1	M22 2-1	O22 2-1	a19 1-3
6 CARDIFF C	D28 3-1	M08 1-1	a26 1-2	S14 0-1	a12 2-2		D11 0-0	S28 1-2	A31 0-1	F14 0-1	J11 2-1	N16 2-1	D21 0-0	O26 3-1	F01 0-0	A17 1-1	a02 1-0	M22 0-0	N29 2-2	N02 2-0	O12 0-2	O16 3-2
7 FULHAM	N02 3-1	N30 1-0	M28 2-1	O19 1-1	S25 0-0	A24 4-0		F01 1-1	O05 1-2	M04 0-0	S21 4-0	J11 0-1	A28 3-0	M15 0-0	D26 0-0	a22 0-0	a19 2-2	F25 2-1	M24 3-2	N16 1-3	D14 1-0	S07 0-2
8 HULL C	A20 1-1	a12 1-0	O12 2-0	N30 1-0	M01 2-0	M15 1-1	N09 2-1		N23 2-0	S24 1-1	S07 0-0	D26 1-3	F08 1-0	S21 1-1	M29 0-0	J11 1-0	F22 0-0	a26 1-0	D14 1-1	O26 3-1	A24 1-0	M31 2-0
9 MANCHESTER U	N16 2-1	a26 4-0	S25 3-0	F01 0-1	S21 2-0	M01 4-0	a12 1-0	F15 2-0		A24 4-0	M15 1-1	S07 2-2	O12 1-0	M31 3-2	D14 0-0	N02 4-0	A28 2-1	J11 2-0	O26 1-0	N30 3-2	D26 2-1	M29 2-1
10 MILLWALL	a01 1-3	M22 0-0	N09 1-1	S28 1-0	a26 1-1	J25 5-1	A31 2-0	M08 2-0	S16 0-1		a12 1-1	A19 3-0	J18 3-0	F08 0-0	D07 1-1	S14 0-0	D28 0-0	D21 2-1	O12 4-0	A17 1-4	O26 2-2	F22 1-3
11 NORWICH C	a30 1-4	A17 2-1	N23 2-0	D21 3-2	N09 0-1	D07 1-1	M31 1-2	M22 1-0	S28 2-0	O05 2-0		a19 3-0	S14 3-0	F22 1-0	a05 2-0	D28 1-0	O19 2-0	A31 1-1	A21 1-0	M08 0-0	F08 3-2	J18 2-3
12 NOTTINGHAM F	M08 2-3	D21 0-0	F08 2-3	A17 0-0	O26 1-0	F22 0-0	D07 1-1	S14 4-0	M22 0-1	A27 2-1	O12 1-3		D28 0-2	N09 1-0	J18 2-2	A31 1-2	S17 1-2	a01 1-0	a12 0-0	S28 1-1	a26 2-1	N23 2-1
13 NOTTS CO	F01 1-3	J11 0-0	M15 1-1	a05 1-2	D14 3-2	M29 0-2	A20 1-1	N02 5-0	a19 2-2	N30 2-1	D26 1-1	M25 2-2		A24 1-0	S24 1-1	O19 4-1	O05 1-1	N16 3-3	S07 3-2	F15 0-0	S21 0-0	M01 2-1
14 OLDHAM A	O05 1-2	S14 1-0	F04 1-0	A31 2-0	D07 3-4	a05 4-0	S28 1-0	M28 0-1	D28 1-0	N02 1-1	N16 2-2	F01 2-0	O15 1-0		a19 0-0	M22 1-1	M08 2-0	A17 2-1	F15 1-1	D21 0-0	J18 0-0	O19 2-3
15 ORIENT	M22 1-0	A27 0-0	a12 0-0	a15 1-0	F22 1-0	N09 1-1	S14 0-0	D21 0-0	A17 0-2	J11 2-1	O26 0-3	N30 1-1	M08 0-1	O12 3-1		M31 1-1	A31 1-1	S28 1-0	a26 2-1	D28 1-1	N23 0-2	F08 1-0
16 OXFORD U	J18 1-2	F22 0-0	M29 2-1	O23 2-0	N23 2-1	D14 1-0	O26 2-1	D07 3-1	F08 1-0	D26 3-1	J25 2-1	F28 1-1	a26 1-2	S07 1-0	S21 1-2		N09 1-0	O12 1-0	S25 0-4	a12 1-0	M15 1-1	A24 3-1
17 PORTSMOUTH	F18 2-3	O26 0-0	D14 2-0	N02 0-1	M29 3-0	S21 2-2	O12 0-0	N16 1-1	O15 0-0	M31 1-0	a26 0-3	A24 2-0	a12 1-1	S24 1-1	F28 3-0	F01 2-1		N30 1-0	D26 1-2	J11 4-2	S07 1-3	M15 1-0
18 SHEFFIELD W	a23 0-4	F08 0-0	D26 0-2	O05 1-1	A24 1-1	S07 1-2	N23 1-0	O19 2-1	D07 4-4	M29 0-1	a08 0-1	S21 2-3	F22 0-1	D14 1-1	M15 0-1	a19 1-1	J18 0-2		M31 0-1	O02 0-2	S25 0-0	N09 3-0
19 SOUTHAMPTON	S28 0-0	A31 1-1	F22 0-1	M28 0-1	F08 3-0	a22 2-0	D21 0-0	A17 3-3	a05 0-1	a18 3-2	A27 1-1	O05 0-1	M22 3-2	J25 1-0	O19 4-2	M18 2-1	S14 2-1	D28 0-1		J14 1-1	N09 1-0	D07 2-1
20 SUNDERLAND	O19 0-0	N09 1-0	S21 0-0	a19 3-0	S07 5-1	F08 3-1	F22 1-2	a05 1-0	J18 0-0	D14 2-0	S24 0-0	M15 0-0	N23 3-0	M25 2-2	M28 3-0	O05 2-0	D07 4-1	O15 3-0	A24 3-1		M01 3-0	D26 2-0
21 W.B.A.	D21 2-0	D28 2-0	a08 0-1	N16 1-0	N06 2-2	a19 2-0	A17 0-1	S18 2-2	S14 1-1	a05 2-1	N02 1-1	O19 0-1	a02 4-1	N30 1-0	F15 1-0	S28 3-0	M22 2-1	M08 4-0	F01 0-3	A31 1-0		O05 2-0
22 YORK C	A17 1-1	a01 0-0	O26 1-3	M08 1-0	O12 3-0	A27 1-0	M22 3-2	D28 3-0	D21 0-1	N16 2-1	N30 1-0	F14 1-1	A31 2-2	a26 0-0	N01 0-1	S17 1-1	S28 3-0	J31 3-0	J10 1-1	S14 0-1	a12 1-3	

Season 1974-75

DIVISION 3

	ALDERSHOT	BLACKBURN R	BOURNEMOUTH	BRIGHTON & HA	BURY	CHARLTON A	CHESTERFIELD	COLCHESTER U	CRYSTAL P	GILLINGHAM	GRIMSBY T	HALIFAX T	HEREFORD U	HUDDERSFIELD T	PETERBOROUGH U	PLYMOUTH A	PORT VALE	PRESTON N.E.	SOUTHEND U	SWINDON T	TRANMERE R	WALSALL	WATFORD	WREXHAM
1 ALDERSHOT		F22 1-1	J18 1-2	M31 2-1	O19 1-1	N09 3-0	D07 1-0	S21 0-1	J25 2-1	D26 2-1	M15 0-0	O02 3-1	M19 2-2	A24 1-0	a05 5-0	S04 4-3	O05 2-1	S07 1-2	M29 3-0	F12 0-1	F28 2-0	a19 0-0	F08 3-1	S25 1-2
2 BLACKBURN R	N16 2-0		O05 1-0	S07 1-0	N02 1-0	J11 3-1	a19 2-0	A24 3-2	N06 1-1	O02 4-1	M19 1-1	S21 1-0	M29 1-0	M28 1-1	F01 0-1	F15 5-2	O19 2-2	D26 3-0	S25 1-0	M01 2-0	M15 2-1	a05 3-3	N30 0-0	a28 0-0
3 BOURNEMOUTH	N30 1-0	a12 0-0		S21 2-0	N16 2-1	O26 1-2	F25 0-0	M01 0-2	O12 4-0	A24 2-0	O23 0-1	M29 0-1	D26 2-1	J04 1-1	m05 2-1	J11 3-7	N02 1-2	M15 1-0	S07 0-0	M31 1-1	M18 0-0	F01 0-1	a26 4-2	O02 0-2
4 BRIGHTON & H.A.	D28 2-0	M22 0-1	M26 2-1		S28 0-0	M08 1-1	A31 2-1	J25 2-0	A17 1-0	a05 4-3	O16 3-1	a16 0-0	F22 2-1	a19 2-0	a23 2-0	D21 2-2	S18 1-1	O19 0-4	D07 2-0	N09 1-1	F08 3-1	a09 1-0	S14 2-0	O05 3-3
5 BURY	a26 2-1	F08 1-2	F22 1-0	M15 2-1		O12 2-1	F04 1-1	S24 0-0	N09 2-2	F11 0-1	S07 1-1	D26 4-1	M28 3-0	S21 3-0	N05 3-0	O26 0-1	J11 3-1	O01 2-0	A24 0-1	M18 0-0	M29 3-1	N30 2-0	a12 1-0	M01 2-2
6 CHARLTON A	F01 3-1	D07 2-1	a05 2-3	S24 2-1	a19 0-1		O19 3-2	J01 4-1	J17 1-0	F28 2-1	M29 1-1	M18 3-1	A24 2-0	S07 1-0	O05 3-0	N02 0-2	F15 2-2	a29 3-1	M15 2-1	S21 3-3	O01 3-3	N16 4-2	O22 4-1	J04 1-1
7 CHESTERFIELD	J11 0-2	O12 1-2	O16 0-0	M01 2-4	F15 2-0	a26 2-0		S07 1-1	a12 2-1	M29 2-1	S21 2-0	F19 1-1	M15 4-1	D26 3-0	N16 2-0	N30 1-2	F01 1-0	M31 0-0	M19 1-1	O02 0-2	S25 1-0	N02 2-2	O26 4-4	A24 3-1
8 COLCHESTER U	J04 0-0	a22 2-0	A31 1-0	F15 2-2	m02 3-2	S14 3-0	M22 1-2		D20 1-1	O05 4-2	N15 5-0	a04 2-0	N06 1-2	F01 3-2	D28 4-1	S17 1-0	O15 2-0	a19 2-2	O29 1-1	M04 2-0	D06 2-1	S28 1-2	A17 1-1	N02 1-1
9 CRYSTAL P	F15 3-0	O22 1-0	a19 4-1	M18 3-0	F01 2-2	N30 2-1	O05 1-4	M25 2-1		a29 4-0	O01 3-0	F28 1-1	J04 2-2	M15 1-1	N02 1-1	N16 3-3	a05 1-1	S24 1-0	D26 1-1	S07 6-2	A24 2-1	O19 1-0	J11 1-0	S21 2-0
10 GILLINGHAM	S14 0-0	a09 1-1	a23 1-0	O26 2-1	S18 1-0	A31 0-1	D21 4-0	a12 2-1	D28 3-1		a26 2-0	N09 4-0	O12 2-3	J11 3-2	S28 1-1	M31 2-2	M22 0-0	N06 2-1	F08 2-1	F22 3-1	J25 2-3	A17 2-2	M08 2-1	N30 2-1
11 GRIMSBY T	S28 2-0	A17 1-2	M08 0-0	O08 3-2	M22 2-0	D21 1-1	M28 2-0	F22 1-1	a08 2-1	O19 2-1		D07 2-1	M04 0-0	O05 1-2	S14 1-2	a22 1-1	A31 3-0	a05 2-1	J18 0-0	F08 2-0	N09 3-2	D28 0-0	S17 2-2	a19 2-0
12 HALIFAX T	a08 1-0	a01 1-1	D21 3-2	N30 1-0	S14 0-1	A17 2-2	S17 1-3	O26 1-1	A31 3-1	F01 1-1	J11 1-1		a26 2-2	N16 2-1	M08 2-1	D28 1-1	S28 1-1	N02 3-0	O15 3-1	O12 0-0	a12 0-0	a22 1-0	M22 2-0	F15 1-0
13 HEREFORD U	A17 2-0	D21 6-3	S14 0-1	N16 2-0	D28 1-1	a23 2-2	S28 5-0	O23 3-1	S18 2-0	a19 1-1	F15 3-2	O19 0-0		N02 1-1	A31 2-0	M08 1-5	M31 1-0	O05 2-2	a05 1-0	D07 2-1	J18 2-0	M22 2-0	S04 0-1	F01 1-0
14 HUDDERSFIELD T	a22 2-2	D28 1-2	D03 2-2	O12 1-0	a01 0-0	M22 1-3	S14 2-0	N09 3-2	S28 0-1	D07 0-2	a12 1-0	F22 1-2	F08 2-1		A17 1-2	a08 0-2	M08 3-1	J18 0-1	M04 4-1	O26 2-2	a26 0-0	D21 3-2	A31 3-1	O22 0-0
15 PETERBOROUGH U	O26 1-1	N09 1-0	a16 3-0	A24 2-0	O16 3-1	a12 1-1	F22 0-2	M28 1-0	F08 1-1	M15 0-0	D26 1-3	S25 1-1	M01 1-1	M19 2-1		a26 1-0	N30 0-2	S21 0-0	O02 1-0	M29 0-0	a30 1-2	J11 0-0	O12 1-0	S07 2-1
16 PLYMOUTH A	O15 1-0	F04 2-1	D07 1-0	M29 2-2	a05 2-1	F08 1-1	J18 3-0	a15 1-0	F22 0-1	S21 1-1	A24 2-1	M28 2-0	S24 1-0	O01 2-0	O19 2-0		a19 1-1	M18 2-1	F28 1-0	D26 4-3	S07 4-1	O05 2-1	N09 1-1	M15 0-3
17 PORT VALE	a12 3-1	a26 1-4	F08 0-0	a28 1-0	D07 1-0	M03 1-0	N09 3-2	S30 2-2	O26 2-1	S07 2-1	M01 1-0	M15 2-1	S21 3-0	D14 4-0	J18 1-3	O12 2-0		M29 2-1	a01 0-0	A24 2-2	D26 1-0	N04 1-1	F22 0-0	M17 2-0
18 PRESTON N.E.	M22 3-1	S14 0-0	S28 5-2	a26 1-0	S03 3-0	S17 2-0	D28 2-1	O12 0-2	M08 1-1	O22 1-0	O26 2-0	F08 1-0	a12 2-2	N30 4-0	a01 1-1	A17 1-0	D21 1-0		N09 1-4	F18 2-0	F22 1-0	A31 3-2	a22 2-2	J11 3-1
19 SOUTHEND U	D23 1-1	M08 2-2	M21 0-0	J11 1-0	a21 1-0	S27 2-1	A17 2-1	a25 1-1	S13 0-1	N01 2-2	N29 3-0	S02 4-0	O25 0-0	F15 1-0	O07 1-2	A30 2-1	D28 1-3	F01 1-1		a11 2-0	O11 1-0	S16 3-0	M28 0-0	N16 1-1
20 SWINDON T	S17 3-2	A31 2-0	D28 2-1	F04 1-0	A17 0-2	a01 2-0	N05 1-0	N30 4-1	M22 1-1	N16 1-0	N02 3-2	a19 3-1	J11 1-0	a05 4-1	D21 0-1	S14 2-0	a22 3-2	F15 1-0	O05 2-0		S03 0-0	M08 3-0	S28 2-2	O19 2-1
21 TRANMERE R	A31 2-0	S27 1-1	A17 0-1	N02 1-2	D21 0-0	a07 0-1	M07 1-2	J10 2-0	m07 2-0	F14 1-1	J31 3-1	O04 3-1	N29 6-1	O19 1-2	a09 1-0	M21 1-3	S13 1-0	N15 3-1	a18 2-1	O21 3-0		M28 3-0	D28 2-2	a03 0-1
22 WALSALL	O11 3-0	O26 1-3	N09 2-0	O01 6-0	J18 3-0	F22 0-1	F08 2-2	M15 5-2	a25 3-0	M18 1-1	J14 2-0	A24 1-1	S07 3-1	M29 2-0	D07 0-1	a12 0-0	O08 0-0	F28 2-0	F04 3-0	S24 2-0	S21 1-0		F19 2-0	D26 2-1
23 WATFORD	N02 1-1	J18 0-0	O19 1-0	D26 1-1	O05 2-1	N06 0-2	a05 2-2	M19 1-2	D07 1-2	S25 0-0	J04 3-2	S07 2-2	O02 1-1	F28 1-0	a19 0-3	F01 1-3	N16 3-2	A24 3-2	S21 2-0	M15 1-0	a14 1-0	a29 2-3		M29 1-2
24 WREXHAM	M08 4-0	N25 1-1	a07 1-1	a12 2-1	A31 3-1	D28 0-3	a21 0-0	F08 2-1	M31 0-0	J18 0-1	O12 2-3	F04 4-0	N09 2-1	N04 3-0	M22 1-2	S28 5-1	A17 2-2	D07 1-1	F22 1-1	a26 1-2	O26 1-0	S14 0-0	D21 5-1	

DIVISION 4

	BARNSLEY	BRADFORD C	BRENTFORD	CAMBRIDGE U	CHESTER	CREWE A	DARLINGTON	DONCASTER R	EXETER C	HARTLEPOOL	LINCOLN C	MANSFIELD T	NEWPORT CO	NORTHAMPTON T	READING	ROCHDALE	ROTHERHAM U	SCUNTHORPE U	SHREWSBURY T	SOUTHPORT	STOCKPORT CO	SWANSEA C	TORQUAY U	WORKINGTON
1 BARNSLEY		F01 2-2	N02 1-1	S17 1-1	A31 0-1	M08 1-1	a19 1-1	F15 0-1	A17 1-0	O19 2-1	N16 0-2	O15 1-3	S28 2-1	D21 5-1	a05 2-0	M22 5-3	F25 1-1	S03 2-2	J18 1-0	J04 3-0	S13 2-0	a22 1-0	D07 0-1	O05 0-1
2 BRADFORD C	N09 2-0		O23 1-0	M22 1-1	S14 2-0	A17 1-2	J18 1-1	O12 2-0	S04 0-1	J29 3-0	a12 1-2	F08 1-1	S18 0-1	a23 2-1	F22 1-3	D28 1-0	a16 1-1	A31 3-0	O26 1-2	D21 1-2	S28 2-0	M31 1-2	D14 3-0	D07 1-1
3 BRENTFORD	F08 3-0	N04 0-0		S14 1-0	M22 1-1	S28 1-0	D07 3-0	a12 1-1	D28 2-0	F22 1-0	O12 1-1	N09 2-3	a01 0-0	A17 1-0	J25 1-0	M08 3-0	S16 3-4	D21 2-0	a26 2-1	a21 1-0	a07 3-0	A31 1-0	O26 3-1	J18 2-2
4 CAMBRIDGE U	J14 2-0	S06 0-1	D26 2-0		S03 3-0	a04 2-0	M14 1-0	M28 4-1	O18 1-1	O01 3-2	S21 5-0	S24 2-2	N16 1-1	N01 3-4	M18 1-0	F01 1-1	N30 0-0	a19 2-0	O15 0-2	O04 1-0	J11 1-0	F15 2-0	F28 3-1	A23 3-0
5 CHESTER	M01 2-1	D26 1-0	S07 2-0	O23 1-1		O19 2-0	a16 1-0	O02 3-0	a05 1-1	A24 3-0	M19 4-1	M15 0-0	F15 4-1	F01 4-1	S25 2-0	N02 4-0	J11 0-1	O05 1-0	J04 1-1	a19 3-0	N30 3-1	N16 3-0	S21 3-0	M29 0-0
6 CREWE A	S25 1-1	M19 0-0	M15 1-1	O26 0-0	a26 0-1		M29 2-1	S21 2-1	O23 2-1	S07 2-0	A24 1-0	D26 0-2	O12 1-2	J18 3-1	J04 1-0	D07 0-1	M05 1-0	F08 1-1	F28 0-0	N09 0-0	F22 2-0	a12 2-2	O02 0-1	D14 0-0
7 DARLINGTON	O12 0-0	N30 0-3	J11 2-1	S28 6-0	D28 1-1	D21 1-0		a26 4-1	M08 2-0	N09 1-2	O26 1-4	a12 2-1	a21 3-0	M22 2-0	F08 0-1	S16 1-2	a01 0-1	S14 3-1	J25 1-2	S02 1-1	A31 0-2	A17 3-2	O14 2-2	O21 2-0
8 DONCASTER R	J24 1-1	a19 4-1	O05 2-1	D21 0-1	N05 1-1	a01 2-1	O19 1-3		a22 3-3	D07 3-0	O15 2-2	F22 4-3	A31 0-2	M08 2-0	J18 1-1	S13 4-1	S28 0-0	S17 1-1	N08 1-3	D28 1-1	A17 2-1	M21 3-2	F08 3-0	a05 0-0
9 EXETER C	D14 4-2	O02 1-0	M31 1-0	a26 1-4	O26 1-0	N06 2-0	S25 4-1	A24 2-1		J04 1-0	M01 1-2	S07 0-1	a12 3-1	D07 2-2	S21 0-2	J18 2-1	F22 0-4	N09 0-0	M29 1-0	F08 1-0	J24 4-1	O12 1-2	D26 0-0	M15 1-0
10 HARTLEPOOL	a26 4-3	F15 1-2	N16 3-2	a07 1-1	a21 1-0	M22 1-1	F01 2-0	J11 2-1	M10 0-3		F12 2-0	O26 2-1	A17 2-0	J01 2-0	N06 2-3	D21 5-0	S14 3-2	M28 1-0	a12 1-1	A31 1-1	M08 1-1	S28 0-2	O12 0-0	N02 3-0
11 LINCOLN C	F22 3-0	O05 2-1	a19 1-1	M31 0-0	A17 2-1	a23 0-0	a05 1-1	N13 4-0	A31 5-0	J17 2-0		F25 0-0	a09 5-2	S14 2-2	D06 1-1	S28 3-0	M22 2-0	D28 1-0	F08 3-0	S18 1-1	J20 2-0	M08 1-3	N08 3-1	O19 3-0
12 MANSFIELD T	O21 2-1	N02 3-0	F01 1-1	M07 2-1	S27 0-0	S14 0-0	O05 4-2	N16 5-2	M21 3-2	a05 2-0	a14 3-1		D28 3-0	O28 3-0	O19 1-1	A30 2-0	D21 1-1	a21 7-0	D07 3-1	A17 2-1	a01 1-1	O07 3-0	J18 3-0	a19 1-0
13 NEWPORT CO	M15 3-4	J04 2-1	S21 1-0	F22 1-2	J25 3-0	a19 1-1	A24 2-1	F28 0-2	O05 1-2	M17 2-0	M03 1-1	M31 2-1		O18 2-1	a15 2-2	a05 3-2	F08 1-1	D07 2-0	S07 2-4	J17 1-0	N09 3-3	S03 3-0	M29 2-1	S24 3-1
14 NORTHAMPTON T	M28 2-1	A24 1-2	J04 0-0	F08 1-2	N09 2-0	N29 3-0	S06 3-0	S24 2-0	J11 1-1	a01 3-0	D26 1-0	M25 0-2	a25 3-2		F28 0-3	N05 0-1	a12 1-1	F11 3-0	S21 3-3	F22 1-1	O11 4-1	O26 5-1	a15 1-1	O01 3-0
15 READING	O26 0-3	N16 1-1	F15 1-0	A17 2-0	M08 2-1	S18 1-1	N02 3-0	N30 2-0	a02 3-0	F24 0-0	J11 1-0	a26 1-1	S14 3-0	A31 3-2		a09 2-1	a23 1-1	M22 1-1	O12 1-2	S28 4-1	D28 1-3	D21 1-2	a12 1-0	F01 3-0
16 ROCHDALE	S07 3-1	F17 1-1	S23 0-0	N09 0-0	F08 0-1	J11 3-0	J04 2-0	D26 2-0	N30 1-1	M29 3-0	M15 1-1	M01 0-1	O26 2-4	O21 2-2	S30 0-2		O12 1-2	F22 4-2	M17 0-0	M11 3-3	a12 3-0	a26 1-0	A24 1-1	S21 2-0
17 ROTHERHAM U	M31 2-0	S24 4-0	F04 3-0	J18 0-0	D07 1-2	F15 1-1	S21 1-1	M15 1-0	N16 1-1	D26 1-2	S07 2-2	M29 2-1	N02 1-1	O05 1-3	A24 2-1	a19 3-1		a05 3-2	O01 0-0	O19 3-0	N05 3-0	F01 1-0	M18 3-1	M01 1-0
18 SCUNTHORPE U	O01 1-0	M01 1-2	a15 1-2	O12 2-0	a12 1-3	N02 1-1	D26 1-1	J04 0-0	F01 2-1	S21 1-1	a01 1-1	A24 0-1	J11 4-1	F15 2-1	S07 0-1	N16 2-2	O26 0-3		M15 1-0	O15 3-3	a26 0-0	N30 1-2	S24 0-2	M18 2-1
19 SHREWSBURY T	N30 3-1	a05 3-2	O19 1-0	D28 1-0	S17 2-0	A31 0-1	F15 2-0	F01 7-4	D21 2-2	O05 0-1	N02 0-4	J11 0-1	M22 1-0	M31 6-0	a19 2-0	A17 1-1	a08 3-1	S28 5-0		M08 1-0	a22 0-0	S14 2-0	N05 2-0	N16 2-0
20 SOUTHPORT	S20 1-0	M28 1-2	A24 3-0	a11 2-2	O11 2-1	J31 1-1	O01 1-0	M31 2-1	N02 3-0	F28 0-0	a28 3-2	M18 1-1	N30 1-3	N15 0-0	D13 2-0	F14 1-0	a26 2-0	a08 1-0	S25 1-2		O25 2-1	J10 3-0	S06 1-1	D26 2-2
21 STOCKPORT CO	D26 0-3	M14 1-1	S30 1-1	D06 1-0	J17 1-1	N15 1-0	F28 2-1	M17 0-2	F15 3-2	O28 1-1	J20 0-0	S20 3-2	J31 1-1	a18 1-0	M31 1-0	O04 2-3	O21 1-0	O19 3-2	A24 0-3	a04 0-0		N01 2-1	J03 0-0	S06 1-3
22 SWANSEA C	A24 0-3	S21 1-1	F28 0-1	M04 2-1	F22 0-1	O05 2-1	A27 1-0	S07 3-3	a19 0-2	M15 1-0	S24 2-1	O01 1-2	O15 2-0	a05 1-0	M29 1-2	O18 3-3	N08 0-2	J18 1-0	D26 1-4	D06 2-2	F08 1-0		M28 0-1	J04 0-1
23 TORQUAY U	J11 1-1	O19 0-1	a05 3-2	A31 1-0	M31 3-0	S04 1-0	N16 0-0	N02 2-0	S14 2-2	a19 2-1	F01 1-3	N30 0-2	D21 0-1	S28 0-1	O05 2-1	a23 3-0	A17 0-3	M08 1-1	O23 1-1	M22 3-2	S18 2-2	D28 0-0		F15 2-1
24 WORKINGTON	a12 1-2	J11 0-0	N30 0-1	a23 1-2	D21 0-0	D28 3-0	N06 1-2	O26 0-3	S28 0-1	a15 1-1	a26 0-2	O12 1-3	M08 3-1	a09 2-2	N08 2-1	M31 2-1	A31 0-2	A17 1-1	F22 0-2	S14 0-1	M22 1-0	S18 2-0	J25 2-1	

LEAGUE TABLES

DIVISION 1

	P	W	D	L	F	A	W	D	L	F	A	Pts
Derby Co	42	14	4	3	41	18	7	7	7	26	31	53
Liverpool	42	14	5	2	44	17	6	6	9	16	22	51
Ipswich T	42	17	2	2	47	14	6	3	12	19	30	51
Everton	42	10	9	2	33	19	6	9	6	23	23	50
Stoke C	42	12	7	2	40	18	5	8	8	24	30	49
Sheffield U	42	12	7	2	35	20	6	6	9	23	31	49
Middlesbrough	42	11	7	3	33	14	7	5	9	21	26	48
Manchester C	42	16	3	2	40	15	2	7	12	14	39	46
Leeds U	42	10	8	3	34	20	6	5	10	23	29	45
Burnley	42	11	6	4	40	29	6	5	10	28	38	45
Q.P.R.	42	10	4	7	25	17	6	6	9	29	37	42
Wolverh'pton W	42	12	5	4	43	21	2	6	13	14	33	39
West Ham U	42	10	6	5	38	22	3	7	11	20	37	39
Coventry C	42	8	9	4	31	27	4	6	11	20	35	39
Newcastle U	42	12	4	5	39	23	3	5	13	20	49	39
Arsenal	42	10	6	5	31	16	3	5	13	16	33	37
Birmingham C	42	10	4	7	34	28	4	5	12	19	33	37
Leicester C	42	8	7	6	25	17	4	5	12	21	43	36
Tottenham H	42	8	4	9	29	27	5	4	12	23	36	34
Luton T	42	8	6	7	27	26	3	5	13	20	39	33
Chelsea	42	4	9	8	22	31	5	6	10	20	41	33
Carlisle U	42	8	2	11	22	21	4	3	14	21	38	29

DIVISION 2

	P	W	D	L	F	A	W	D	L	F	A	Pts
Manchester U	42	17	3	1	45	12	9	6	6	21	18	61
Aston Villa	42	16	4	1	47	6	9	4	8	32	26	58
Norwich C	42	14	3	4	34	17	6	10	5	24	20	53
Sunderland	42	14	6	1	41	8	5	7	9	24	27	51
Bristol C	42	14	5	2	31	10	7	3	11	16	23	50
W.B.A.	42	13	4	4	33	15	5	5	11	21	27	45
Blackpool	42	12	6	3	31	17	2	11	8	7	16	45
Hull C	42	12	8	1	25	10	3	6	12	15	43	44
Fulham	42	9	8	4	29	17	4	8	9	15	22	42
Bolton W	42	9	7	5	27	16	6	5	10	18	25	42
Oxford U	42	14	3	4	30	19	1	9	11	11	32	42
Orient	42	8	9	4	17	16	3	11	7	11	23	42
Southampton	42	10	6	5	29	20	5	5	11	24	34	41
Notts Co	42	7	11	3	34	26	5	5	11	15	33	40
York C	42	9	7	5	28	18	5	3	13	23	37	38
Nottingham F	42	7	7	7	24	23	5	7	9	19	32	38
Portsmouth	42	9	7	5	28	20	3	6	12	16	34	37
Oldham A	42	10	7	4	28	16	0	8	13	12	32	35
Bristol R	42	10	4	7	25	23	2	7	12	17	41	35
Millwall	42	8	9	4	31	19	2	3	16	13	37	32
Cardiff C	42	7	8	6	24	21	2	6	13	12	41	32
Sheffield W	42	3	7	11	17	29	2	4	15	12	35	21

DIVISION 3

	P	W	D	L	F	A	W	D	L	F	A	Pts
Blackburn R	46	15	7	1	40	16	7	9	7	28	29	60
Plymouth A	46	16	5	2	38	19	8	6	9	41	39	59
Charlton A	46	15	5	3	51	29	7	6	10	25	32	55
Swindon T	46	18	3	2	43	17	3	8	12	21	41	53
Crystal Palace	46	14	8	1	48	22	4	7	12	18	35	51
Port Vale	46	15	6	2	37	19	3	9	11	24	35	51
Peterborough U	46	10	9	4	24	17	9	3	11	23	36	50
Walsall	46	15	5	3	46	13	3	8	12	21	39	49
Preston N.E.	46	16	5	2	42	19	3	6	14	21	37	49
Gillingham	46	14	6	3	43	23	3	8	12	22	37	48
Colchester U	46	13	7	3	45	22	4	6	13	25	41	47
Hereford U	46	14	6	3	42	21	2	8	13	22	45	46
Wrexham	46	10	8	5	41	23	5	7	11	24	32	45
Bury	46	13	6	4	38	17	3	6	14	15	33	44
Chesterfield	46	11	7	5	37	25	5	5	13	25	41	44
Grimsby T	46	12	8	3	35	19	3	5	15	20	45	43
Halifax T	46	11	10	2	33	20	2	7	14	16	45	43
Southend U	46	11	9	3	32	17	2	7	14	14	34	42
Brighton & H.A.	46	14	7	2	38	21	2	3	18	18	43	42
Aldershot	46	13	5	5	40	21	1	6	16	13	42	*38
Bournemouth	46	9	6	8	27	25	4	6	13	17	33	38
Tranmere R	46	12	4	7	39	21	2	5	16	16	36	37
Watford	46	9	7	7	30	31	1	10	12	22	44	37
Huddersfield T	46	9	6	8	32	29	2	4	17	15	47	32

*Aldershot had one point deducted for fielding an unregistered player.

DIVISION 4

	P	W	D	L	F	A	W	D	L	F	A	Pts
Mansfield T	46	17	6	0	55	15	11	6	6	35	25	68
Shrewsbury T	46	16	3	4	46	18	10	7	6	34	25	62
Rotherham U	46	13	7	3	40	19	9	8	6	31	22	59
Chester C	46	17	5	1	48	9	6	6	11	16	29	57
Lincoln C	46	14	8	1	47	14	7	7	9	32	34	57
Cambridge U	46	15	5	3	43	16	5	9	9	19	28	54
Reading	46	13	6	4	38	20	8	4	11	25	27	52
Brentford	46	15	6	2	38	14	3	7	13	15	31	49
Exeter C	46	14	3	6	33	24	5	8	10	27	39	49
Bradford C	46	10	5	8	32	21	7	8	8	24	30	47
Southport	46	13	7	3	36	19	2	10	11	20	37	47
Newport Co	46	13	5	5	43	30	6	4	13	25	45	47
Hartlepool U	46	13	6	4	40	24	3	5	15	12	38	43
Torquay U	46	10	7	6	30	25	4	7	12	16	36	42
Barnsley	46	10	7	6	34	24	5	4	14	28	41	41
Northampton T	46	12	6	5	43	22	3	5	15	24	51	41
Doncaster R	46	10	9	4	41	29	4	3	16	24	50	40
Crewe A	46	9	9	5	22	16	2	9	12	12	31	40
Rochdale	46	9	9	5	35	22	4	4	15	24	53	39
Stockport Co	46	10	8	5	26	27	2	6	15	17	43	38
Darlington	46	11	4	8	38	27	2	6	15	16	40	36
Swansea C	46	9	4	10	25	31	6	2	15	21	42	36
Workington	46	7	5	11	23	29	3	6	14	13	37	31
Scunthorpe U	46	7	8	8	27	29	0	7	16	14	49	29

FOOTBALL LEAGUE RECORDS

Top scorers: Div 1, E.MacDougall (Norwich City) 23 goals; Div 2, D.Hales (Charlton Athletic) 28 goals; Div 3, R.McNeil (Hereford United) 35 goals; Div 4, R.Moore (Tranmere Rovers) 34 goals.

Liverpool and England goalkeeper Ray Clemence was in the middle of a remarkably consistent run as the Reds gained another Championship trophy. Clemence did not miss a League game for four seasons.

DIVISION 1

	ARSENAL	ASTON VILLA	BIRMINGHAM C	BURNLEY	COVENTRY C	DERBY CO	EVERTON	IPSWICH T	LEEDS U	LEICESTER C	LIVERPOOL	MANCHESTER C	MANCHESTER U	MIDDLESBROUGH	NEWCASTLE U	NORWICH C	Q.P.R.	SHEFFIELD U	STOKE C	TOTTENHAM H	WEST HAM U	WOLVERHAMPTON W
1 ARSENAL		J10 0-0	F21 1-0	D20 1-0	O11 5-0	N08 0-1	S20 2-2	a17 1-2	D06 1-2	S06 1-1	F24 1-0	O04 2-3	N22 3-1	O25 2-1	M16 0-0	A26 2-1	D27 2-0	J31 1-0	A23 0-1	a03 0-2	M20 6-1	a13 2-1
2 ASTON VILLA	S13 2-0		S27 2-1	O25 1-1	A30 1-0	a19 1-0	N22 3-1	M06 0-0	A16 1-2	N29 1-1	a10 0-0	A27 1-0	F21 2-1	a24 2-1	J17 1-1	D13 3-2	J31 0-2	N08 5-1	M27 0-0	O11 1-1	D26 4-1	F24 1-1
3 BIRMINGHAM C	N15 3-1	a03 3-2		S20 4-0	M20 1-1	D06 2-1	A23 0-1	a13 3-0	O18 2-2	D20 2-1	M13 0-1	F14 2-1	A19 0-2	F07 2-1	S23 3-2	F28 1-1	S06 1-1	O04 2-0	D27 1-1	a17 3-1	N01 1-5	J10 0-1
4 BURNLEY	A16 0-0	F28 2-2	a10 1-0		a24 1-3	J17 1-2	A19 1-1	F07 0-1	S27 0-1	F17 1-0	D06 0-0	M13 0-0	a19 0-1	A30 4-1	D26 0-1	S13 4-4	O18 1-0	F24 3-1	N01 0-1	M20 1-2	D13 2-0	N15 1-5
5 COVENTRY C	M13 1-1	a13 1-1	N29 3-2	O04 1-2		A19 1-1	D19 1-2	S06 0-0	F28 0-1	a03 0-2	O18 0-0	A23 2-0	F07 1-1	S23 0-1	M27 1-1	N15 1-0	N01 1-1	J10 1-0	S20 0-3	D27 2-2	F14 2-0	a17 3-1
6 DERBY CO	F18 2-0	D27 2-0	M27 4-2	S06 3-0	J31 2-0		a21 1-3	O04 1-0	N01 3-2	a17 2-2	F28 1-1	S20 1-0	S24 2-1	N29 3-2	A27 3-2	M13 3-1	A23 1-5	D20 3-2	M24 1-1	J10 2-3	N15 2-1	O18 3-2
7 EVERTON	a10 0-0	O18 2-1	D13 5-2	J31 2-3	A16 1-4	A30 2-0		D06 3-3	M20 1-3	N01 1-1	S27 0-0	N15 1-1	D23 1-1	a19 3-1	S13 3-0	J17 1-1	M13 0-2	A26 3-0	a07 2-1	F24 1-0	a24 2-0	F28 3-0
8 IPSWICH T	D26 2-0	N01 3-0	A30 4-2	A26 0-0	J17 1-1	a24 2-6	M27 1-0		D13 2-1	O18 1-1	S13 2-0	a07 2-1	a10 3-0	S27 0-3	A16 0-3	S23 2-0	N15 1-1	N29 1-1	M13 1-1	J31 1-2	a19 4-0	F17 3-0
9 LEEDS U	M27 3-0	D20 1-0	N22 3-0	a03 2-1	O25 2-0	M02 1-1	N29 5-2	A23 1-0		D27 4-0	A26 0-3	a17 2-1	O11 1-2	F21 0-2	N08 3-0	J31 0-3	O04 2-1	a14 0-1	J10 2-0	S20 1-1	M09 1-1	S06 3-0
10 LEICESTER C	J17 2-1	M20 2-2	A16 3-3	N08 3-2	S27 0-3	D26 2-1	M06 1-0	N22 0-0	a20 2-1		A30 1-1	J31 1-0	a24 2-1	O11 0-0	D13 1-0	a10 0-0	F25 0-1	F21 1-1	A27 1-1	O25 2-3	S13 3-3	D06 2-0
11 LIVERPOOL	D02 2-2	S20 3-0	O11 3-1	M27 2-0	N22 1-1	O25 1-1	a03 1-0	J10 3-3	F07 2-0	a06 1-0		D27 1-0	N08 3-1	M06 0-2	F21 2-0	N29 1-3	D20 2-0	S06 1-0	a17 5-3	A23 3-2	A19 2-2	O04 2-0
12 MANCHESTER C	a24 3-1	F07 2-1	N08 2-0	O11 0-0	D13 4-2	a10 4-3	F21 3-0	O25 1-1	D26 0-1	A20 1-1	a19 0-3		S27 2-2	S13 4-0	A30 4-0	A16 3-0	D06 0-0	M06 4-0	S24 1-0	N22 2-1	J17 3-0	M20 3-2
13 MANCHESTER U	O18 3-1	N15 2-0	J31 3-1	D27 2-1	A27 1-1	F25 1-1	a17 2-1	S20 1-0	M13 3-2	O04 0-0	F18 0-0	m04 2-0		M27 3-0	N29 1-0	N01 1-0	J10 2-1	A23 5-1	a21 0-1	S06 3-2	F28 4-0	D20 1-0
14 MIDDLESBROUGH	F28 0-1	O04 0-0	A26 2-0	F14 1-1	F24 2-0	M20 0-2	D27 1-1	a03 2-0	N15 0-0	M13 0-1	N01 0-1	J10 1-0	D06 0-0		J31 3-3	a06 0-1	S20 0-0	a17 3-0	S06 3-0	D20 1-0	O18 3-0	A23 1-0
15 NEWCASTLE U	N01 2-0	S06 3-0	a07 4-0	a17 0-1	D06 4-0	F07 4-3	J10 5-0	D20 1-1	M31 2-3	A23 3-0	N15 1-2	a14 2-1	M20 3-4	A20 1-1		O18 5-2	a03 1-2	D27 1-1	M03 0-1	O04 2-2	M13 2-1	S20 5-1
16 NORWICH C	F07 3-1	A23 5-3	O25 1-0	J10 3-1	F21 0-3	O11 0-0	S06 4-2	M31 1-0	A20 1-1	S20 2-0	M20 0-1	D20 2-2	M17 1-1	N08 0-1	N22 1-2		a17 3-2	a03 1-3	O04 0-1	M06 3-1	D06 1-0	D27 1-1
17 Q.P.R.	a19 2-1	A19 1-1	J17 2-1	N22 1-0	M06 4-1	D13 1-1	O11 5-0	F21 3-1	a24 2-0	S23 1-0	A16 2-0	M27 1-0	S13 1-0	a10 4-2	S27 1-0	D26 2-0		O25 1-0	N29 3-2	N08 0-0	A30 1-1	F07 4-2
18 SHEFFIELD U	A19 1-3	F14 2-1	m04 1-1	S23 2-1	S13 0-1	A16 1-1	F07 0-0	M20 1-2	A30 0-2	N15 1-2	J17 0-0	N01 2-2	D13 1-4	D26 1-1	a19 1-0	S27 0-1	F28 0-0		O18 0-2	D06 1-2	a10 3-2	M13 1-4
19 STOKE C	D13 2-1	D06 1-1	a19 1-0	M06 4-1	a10 0-1	S27 1-0	N08 3-2	O11 0-1	S13 3-2	F07 1-2	D26 1-1	a02 0-0	A30 0-1	J17 1-0	O25 1-1	a24 0-2	M20 0-1	N22 2-1		F21 1-2	A16 1-2	A20 2-2
20 TOTTENHAM H	S27 0-0	M13 5-2	D26 1-3	N29 2-1	a19 4-1	S13 2-3	D10 2-2	A20 1-1	a10 0-0	F28 1-1	D13 0-4	O18 2-2	J17 1-1	A16 1-0	a24 0-3	A30 2-2	F14 0-3	M27 5-0	N15 1-1		F07 1-1	N01 2-1
21 WEST HAM U	N29 1-0	a17 2-2	M06 1-2	A23 3-2	N08 1-1	F21 1-2	O04 0-1	D27 1-2	F23 1-1	J10 1-1	J31 0-4	S06 1-0	O25 2-1	N22 2-1	O11 2-1	M27 0-1	J24 1-0	S20 2-0	D20 3-1	A25 1-0		a03 0-0
22 WOLVERHAMPTON W	A30 0-0	S23 0-0	S13 2-0	F21 3-2	D26 0-1	N22 0-0	O25 1-2	N08 1-0	J17 1-1	M27 2-2	m04 1-3	N29 0-4	A16 0-2	D13 1-2	a10 5-0	a19 1-0	A26 2-2	O11 5-1	J31 2-1	M16 0-1	S27 0-1	

Sunderland's Bryan 'Pop' Robson, who played a major role in the Wearsiders' winning the Division Two title in 1975-76, when he scored 13 goals.

DIVISION 2

	BLACKBURN R	BLACKPOOL	BOLTON W	BRISTOL C	BRISTOL R	CARLISLE U	CHARLTON A	CHELSEA	FULHAM	HULL C	LUTON T	NOTTINGHAM F	NOTTS CO	OLDHAM A	ORIENT	OXFORD U	PLYMOUTH A	PORTSMOUTH	SOUTHAMPTON	SUNDERLAND	W.B.A.	YORK C
1 BLACKBURN R		S24 0-2	N08 1-1	S06 1-2	M06 1-2	a16 1-0	N29 2-0	O25 1-1	O04 0-1	N04 1-0	a03 3-0	D27 1-4	M27 2-1	A23 4-1	D20 1-1	N22 0-0	J31 3-1	F21 0-3	J28 1-1	S20 0-1	O11 0-0	a17 4-0
2 BLACKPOOL	F24 1-1		M06 1-1	a03 2-1	O25 1-4	a17 2-1	J10 2-1	N22 0-2	D20 1-1	J31 2-2	O04 3-2	N04 1-1	N29 1-0	S06 1-1	A23 1-0	F21 2-0	M27 0-0	O11 0-0	S20 4-3	a20 1-0	N08 0-1	D27 0-0
3 BOLTON W	M23 0-1	N01 1-0		D20 1-0	a28 3-1	N15 0-0	O04 5-0	M27 2-1	A23 2-2	F28 1-0	J27 3-0	a03 0-0	O18 2-1	a17 4-0	S20 1-1	M02 0-1	M13 0-0	N04 4-1	S06 3-0	D27 2-1	N29 1-2	a13 1-2
4 BRISTOL C	J17 1-0	S27 2-0	A16 1-0		A30 1-1	D06 0-0	O11 4-0	a10 2-2	M20 0-0	D13 3-0	M06 3-0	F21 0-2	a24 1-2	F24 1-0	N07 0-0	S12 4-1	D26 2-2	a20 1-0	F07 1-1	A19 3-0	O25 0-2	N22 4-1
5 BRISTOL R	N01 1-1	F28 1-1	S23 2-2	a16 0-0		S20 0-1	S06 0-0	N29 1-2	J10 1-0	M13 0-1	D27 0-1	O04 4-2	F14 0-0	D20 1-0	a03 1-1	M27 0-1	N15 0-0	J31 2-0	a17 2-0	O18 1-0	N04 1-1	A23 2-1
6 CARLISLE U	A30 0-1	D26 1-0	F21 3-2	M27 0-1	a10 4-2		O25 1-1	D13 2-1	J31 2-2	a20 0-0	O11 1-1	M06 1-1	J17 1-2	N04 2-1	N22 1-2	A16 1-1	a24 2-0	S13 2-1	N29 1-0	F24 2-2	S27 1-1	N08 1-0
7 CHARLTON A	M20 2-1	S13 1-1	a24 0-4	M12 2-2	J17 3-0	F27 4-2		a19 1-1	F17 3-2	S26 1-0	D03 1-5	F24 2-2	A16 1-2	O18 3-1	M23 1-1	A29 2-1	D12 2-0	D26 1-3	O31 4-1	N15 1-2	a09 2-1	J31 3-2
8 CHELSEA	F28 3-1	O18 2-0	D06 0-1	S20 1-1	M20 0-0	A23 3-1	D27 2-3		a06 0-0	F18 0-0	a16 2-2	S06 0-0	N15 2-0	J10 0-3	a17 0-2	A27 3-1	N01 2-2	F25 2-0	M13 1-1	D20 1-0	J31 1-2	O04 0-0
9 FULHAM	a24 1-1	A16 0-0	D13 1-2	N29 1-2	S13 0-2	A20 3-0	N08 1-1	S27 2-0		a10 1-1	N22 2-0	O11 0-0	D26 3-2	M27 1-0	O25 1-1	J17 1-1	a19 0-0	M06 0-1	M09 1-0	F07 2-0	A30 4-0	F21 2-0
10 HULL C	F06 0-1	A19 1-0	O25 2-2	A23 3-1	O11 0-0	D27 2-3	a03 2-2	N08 1-2	S20 1-2		D20 1-2	J10 1-0	S23 0-2	a16 3-0	S06 1-0	M06 2-0	N29 4-0	N22 1-0	O04 0-0	a17 1-4	F21 2-1	M27 1-1
11 LUTON T	S27 1-1	a24 3-0	S13 0-2	N01 0-0	a19 3-1	M13 3-0	M27 1-1	A30 3-0	O18 1-0	A16 2-0		J31 1-1	a10 1-1	N15 2-3	N29 1-0	D26 3-2	S24 1-1	J17 3-1	M02 1-0	F28 2-0	D13 2-1	N04 4-0
12 NOTTINGHAM F	a20 1-0	F07 3-0	S27 1-2	N15 1-0	a24 3-0	N01 4-0	S24 1-2	J17 1-3	M13 1-0	S13 1-2	O21 0-0		A30 0-1	F28 4-3	M27 1-0	a10 4-0	A16 2-0	D13 0-1	O18 3-1	M17 2-1	D26 0-2	N29 1-0
13 NOTTS CO	D06 3-0	M20 1-2	N22 1-1	O04 1-1	N08 1-1	S06 1-0	D20 2-0	F21 3-2	a17 4-0	F24 1-2	S20 1-0	a13 0-0		D27 5-1	a27 2-0	O11 0-1	N04 1-0	O25 2-0	A23 0-0	a03 0-0	M06 0-2	J10 4-0
14 OLDHAM A	D13 2-1	J17 1-0	D26 2-1	O07 2-4	A16 2-0	F07 2-2	N22 2-0	S13 2-1	D06 2-2	A30 1-0	F21 1-1	O25 0-0	a19 2-2		M06 1-1	N08 1-1	S27 3-2	a10 5-2	O21 3-2	M20 1-1	a24 0-1	O11 2-0
15 ORIENT	A16 1-1	D12 0-1	a10 0-0	F14 0-1	S26 0-0	O18 1-0	M02 0-1	D26 3-1	F28 2-0	J17 1-0	M20 3-0	D06 1-1	A19 1-1	N01 2-0		a24 2-1	S13 1-0	A29 0-1	N15 2-1	M13 0-2	a20 0-0	S23 1-0
16 OXFORD U	O18 0-0	N15 1-3	A20 2-0	J10 1-1	D06 2-1	D20 0-0	a16 1-0	F07 1-1	S06 1-3	N01 2-3	a17 1-3	S20 0-1	M13 2-1	F14 1-1	O04 2-1		F28 2-2	M20 1-0	D27 1-2	A23 1-1	N12 0-1	a03 1-0
17 PLYMOUTH A	O21 2-2	D06 1-2	O11 2-3	J24 0-0	F21 3-0	O04 2-1	A23 1-0	M06 0-3	D27 4-0	M20 1-1	F24 3-0	D20 1-0	F07 1-3	a03 2-1	J10 3-0	O25 2-1		N08 3-1	a16 1-0	S06 1-0	N22 2-1	S20 1-1
18 PORTSMOUTH	N15 0-1	M13 2-0	F07 0-1	D27 0-1	O21 1-2	J10 1-0	a17 2-2	S23 1-1	N01 0-1	O18 1-1	S06 0-2	A23 1-1	F28 1-3	S20 1-1	a13 2-1	N29 0-2	F14 2-0		a06 0-1	O04 0-0	M27 0-1	D20 0-1
19 SOUTHAMPTON	S13 2-1	a10 3-1	J17 0-0	A26 3-1	D26 3-0	M20 1-1	a12 3-2	O11 4-1	F24 2-1	a24 1-0	N08 3-1	N22 0-3	D13 2-1	J31 3-2	F21 3-0	a19 2-1	A29 1-0	S27 4-0		D06 4-0	A16 3-0	O25 2-0
20 SUNDERLAND	a10 3-0	A30 2-0	a19 2-1	M23 1-1	N22 1-1	S23 3-2	F21 4-1	A16 2-1	A26 2-0	D26 3-1	O25 2-0	N08 3-0	S27 4-0	N29 2-0	O11 3-1	D13 1-0	J17 2-1	a24 2-0	M27 3-0		S13 2-0	M30 1-0
21 W.B.A.	M13 2-2	M31 0-0	M20 2-0	M17 0-1	F07 3-0	a03 3-0	S20 1-1	A20 0-0	a14 3-1	N15 2-0	A23 1-0	a17 2-0	N01 0-0	O04 1-1	D27 1-1	F25 2-0	O18 1-0	D06 3-1	D19 0-2	J10 0-0		S06 2-2
22 YORK C	D26 2-1	a19 1-1	A30 1-2	O18 1-4	D13 0-0	F14 1-2	O21 1-3	a24 2-2	N15 1-0	D06 1-2	F07 2-3	M20 3-2	S13 1-2	M13 1-0	F24 0-2	S27 2-0	a10 3-1	A16 2-1	F28 2-1	N01 1-4	J17 0-1	

Season 1975-76

DIVISION 3

	ALDERSHOT	BRIGHTON & HA	BURY	CARDIFF C	CHESTER	CHESTERFIELD	COLCHESTER U	CRYSTAL P	GILLINGHAM	GRIMSBY T	HALIFAX T	HEREFORD U	MANSFIELD T	MILLWALL	PETERBOROUGH U	PORT VALE	PRESTON N.E.	ROTHERHAM U	SHEFFIELD W	SHREWSBURY T	SOUTHEND U	SWINDON T	WALSALL	WREXHAM
1 ALDERSHOT		a17 1-1	J10 1-1	O22 2-1	M13 1-1	F14 3-1	O18 2-2	D27 1-0	N01 3-0	a07 0-3	A23 1-2	D20 0-2	S06 2-1	S24 1-1	M24 1-0	F07 2-0	S20 1-1	F28 3-0	N15 1-1	M27 1-1	O04 2-1	a14 0-1	N29 3-2	a03 2-3
2 BRIGHTON & H.A.	D30 4-1		N04 2-1	A30 0-1	S13 6-0	S27 3-0	J17 6-0	F24 2-0	a19 1-1	M17 4-2	F21 1-0	D06 4-2	J31 1-0	F03 1-0	M06 5-0	a10 3-0	O11 1-0	A16 3-0	a24 1-1	M10 2-2	N08 2-0	M20 2-0	S10 1-2	O25 3-2
3 BURY	A30 1-1	F07 1-1		m04 0-1	a27 1-0	S13 3-1	a12 0-0	D06 0-1	A16 2-0	M06 1-1	O25 0-0	M20 2-3	S23 2-1	S27 2-0	M16 2-1	a19 1-2	F21 2-0	a10 4-0	D26 0-0	M30 2-1	O11 1-0	O21 5-0	J17 1-1	N08 0-1
4 CARDIFF C	J31 1-0	J10 0-1	A23 1-1		F28 2-0	O31 4-3	N15 2-0	S06 0-1	F14 4-1	a03 2-1	S20 0-0	a14 2-0	J20 1-0	M27 0-0	D27 5-2	F25 1-1	a07 1-0	M13 1-1	O18 2-0	N29 3-0	D22 3-1	a17 0-0	N04 0-0	O04 3-0
5 CHESTER	O11 1-0	J24 3-0	a16 0-0	O25 1-1		M20 2-1	S24 1-0	m04 2-1	D06 2-2	S06 1-2	a07 2-1	O04 0-1	J10 1-1	N08 3-1	S20 1-1	F21 1-0	D27 3-0	F07 3-1	O21 1-0	M06 1-0	A23 1-1	D20 2-1	M16 1-1	a17 1-3
6 CHESTERFIELD	N08 5-2	a07 2-1	F11 3-2	M06 1-1	N29 1-1		N05 6-1	A23 1-2	J31 0-1	a16 4-3	D20 1-2	S20 2-3	a17 1-2	O25 2-2	S06 1-1	J24 0-1	O04 3-0	M27 1-0	S24 1-0	O11 2-1	D27 1-2	a03 4-0	F21 2-1	J10 1-1
7 COLCHESTER U	M16 2-0	S20 2-0	O04 0-0	F21 3-2	F24 1-0	F07 2-3		J10 0-3	M20 2-2	D27 1-0	S06 0-1	J24 1-4	A23 0-2	M23 0-1	a16 1-1	O25 1-0	a03 1-1	O21 0-0	D06 2-1	N08 1-1	a17 2-1	a06 1-2	O11 2-0	D20 0-2
8 CRYSTAL P	a20 0-0	S23 0-1	M27 1-0	a10 0-1	A16 2-0	a28 0-0	A30 3-2		D30 0-1	O11 3-0	a13 1-1	O21 2-2	N29 4-1	M30 0-0	N08 1-1	M09 2-2	M16 2-0	S13 2-0	S27 1-1	J17 1-1	O25 1-1	F07 3-3	J06 0-1	F21 1-1
9 GILLINGHAM	M06 1-1	D27 1-0	a03 2-0	N08 2-2	M27 2-0	O21 2-2	N29 0-1	a17 1-2		A23 3-0	O04 1-1	a06 3-4	S20 3-1	F21 3-1	D20 2-2	O11 2-1	S06 1-0	S23 0-0	F07 0-0	M16 2-1	a13 1-2	J10 3-2	O25 2-3	J24 1-1
10 GRIMSBY T	S27 1-0	O18 2-1	N01 0-0	A16 2-0	a10 2-0	J03 3-0	a19 0-1	M13 1-2	a24 2-1		S23 2-2	F14 1-0	N15 4-1	S13 2-1	F07 1-1	M30 1-1	N29 0-0	D26 4-1	J17 1-1	A30 3-2	M27 2-2	F28 1-0	M09 1-2	N11 3-2
11 HALIFAX T	a24 1-3	N15 1-3	F28 0-2	J17 1-1	S27 5-2	M30 1-0	a26 1-1	N01 1-3	M09 1-1	F24 2-1		O18 0-1	F14 1-2	A16 1-2	D06 0-1	D26 1-3	N04 2-1	a19 0-1	M02 0-0	S13 0-0	M23 1-0	M13 0-2	A30 2-1	M20 0-1
12 HEREFORD U	M31 2-1	M27 1-1	N29 2-0	F04 4-1	M10 5-0	J17 4-2	S13 0-0	J31 1-1	S27 1-1	N08 3-2	M17 1-2		F11 1-0	a10 0-0	O25 2-4	A16 0-0	a28 3-1	a24 3-2	A30 3-1	a19 3-1	F21 2-1	S24 1-0	D26 1-3	O11 2-0
13 MANSFIELD T	a10 1-0	M01 1-0	F23 1-1	S13 1-4	A30 1-1	D26 0-1	a24 0-0	M20 1-1	J17 1-1	F21 1-0	N08 1-1	F07 2-2		M08 1-1	O11 1-1	J03 3-1	O25 0-1	M29 1-1	a19 3-0	A16 1-2	M15 3-1	D06 3-1	S27 4-1	M06 0-0
14 MILLWALL	F25 4-1	a16 3-1	a07 0-0	D06 1-3	F14 1-0	F28 2-0	N01 1-1	D20 2-1	N15 2-2	J24 1-1	a03 1-0	S06 1-0	O04 1-0		a17 2-0	M20 1-0	J10 2-0	O18 3-1	M13 1-0	N04 0-0	S20 2-1	D27 0-0	J31 2-1	A23 2-1
15 PETERBOROUGH U	S13 1-1	N01 1-0	O18 4-0	a19 0-0	J17 3-0	a10 0-1	J14 3-1	F18 2-0	M31 1-1	N04 4-2	M27 1-0	F27 0-3	M13 0-3	D26 1-1		A30 0-0	J31 2-0	S27 1-3	M10 2-2	a24 3-2	N29 3-2	N15 3-1	A16 0-0	S24 2-0
16 PORT VALE	N03 0-1	S06 1-1	D27 2-1	S22 2-1	N15 0-1	O18 1-1	F28 3-2	O04 0-0	M13 1-1	D20 4-3	a17 1-1	a03 1-1	a20 2-2	N29 2-0	J10 2-0		A23 1-1	N01 1-0	F16 1-0	J31 0-0	F09 1-1	S20 3-0	M27 1-2	a05 3-1
17 PRESTON N.E.	J17 1-0	M13 1-0	N15 0-0	S27 3-1	a19 0-0	M09 3-1	A16 2-1	O18 0-0	a10 4-0	M20 0-0	F07 2-1	N01 3-4	F28 0-2	A30 2-1	O21 2-1	a24 3-0		J13 3-2	M30 4-2	F03 0-2	F24 5-1	F14 4-2	S13 3-1	D06 0-1
18 ROTHERHAM U	O25 2-2	a03 1-1	S06 3-3	O11 1-0	N04 0-1	D06 2-0	J31 2-0	F03 4-1	F24 2-0	a17 3-0	D27 0-1	A23 1-1	D20 2-1	M16 1-2	a06 1-1	M06 1-2	a20 1-1		M20 1-0	F21 0-1	J10 2-0	O04 0-2	N08 3-1	S20 2-1
19 SHEFFIELD W	F21 3-1	A23 3-3	a17 1-0	M17 1-3	J31 2-0	M24 1-3	M27 1-0	a07 1-0	N05 1-0	S20 4-0	a20 1-0	J10 1-2	D27 0-0	O11 4-1	O04 2-2	N08 0-3	D20 2-2	N29 0-0		O25 1-1	a29 2-1	J24 0-2	M06 2-1	S06 1-0
20 SHREWSBURY T	D06 5-3	O04 1-2	D20 1-3	M20 3-1	N01 2-0	M13 0-2	F14 1-0	S20 2-4	O18 1-0	J10 1-0	J24 2-0	D27 2-1	a02 1-2	F07 1-0	A23 3-1	O21 1-0	a17 1-0	N15 0-2	a13 0-0		a06 3-1	S06 3-0	F24 1-1	a21 1-2
21 SOUTHEND U	M08 0-2	F17 4-0	M13 2-0	M29 0-2	a23 2-0	a19 1-1	D26 2-0	F27 1-2	M01 2-2	D05 5-2	O20 4-1	J26 1-3	O17 2-2	J16 0-0	M19 0-0	S13 3-3	S22 0-2	A30 1-2	A16 2-1	S27 1-3		O31 3-0	a09 2-2	F06 2-1
22 SWINDON T	F10 6-3	N29 3-2	J31 2-1	D26 4-0	M30 2-1	A16 0-1	S27 0-1	N04 1-2	A30 2-2	O25 3-0	O11 3-1	F24 0-1	M27 0-2	a20 0-2	F21 0-3	J17 2-1	N08 1-3	M09 1-1	S13 2-1	a10 3-0	M06 0-0		a24 5-1	a29 2-2
23 WALSALL	M20 4-1	D20 2-0	S20 0-1	F07 2-3	O18 1-0	N15 1-0	M13 1-1	S16 1-1	F27 4-0	O04 2-0	J10 2-0	a17 0-0	a06 0-1	O21 1-1	a03 2-2	D06 3-1	J24 3-1	F13 5-1	D02 2-2	S22 2-0	S06 2-3	A23 1-1		D27 2-2
24 WREXHAM	A16 3-1	F28 3-0	F14 2-1	M08 1-1	D26 1-1	A30 1-0	D13 1-1	N15 1-3	S13 2-0	J31 1-0	N29 1-1	M13 2-1	N01 1-0	J03 1-1	F23 3-0	S27 1-0	M27 1-2	J17 3-0	a10 3-0	F09 2-3	a27 2-2	O18 2-0	a19 0-3	

DIVISION 4

	BARNSLEY	BOURNEMOUTH	BRADFORD C	BRENTFORD	CAMBRIDGE U	CREWE A	DARLINGTON	DONCASTER R	EXETER C	HARTLEPOOL	HUDDERSFIELD T	LINCOLN C	NEWPORT CO	NORTHAMPTON T	READING	ROCHDALE	SCUNTHORPE U	SOUTHPORT	STOCKPORT CO	SWANSEA C	TORQUAY U	TRANMERE R	WATFORD	WORKINGTON
1 BARNSLEY		M09 2-0	M27 1-1	a10 1-1	M30 4-0	S12 1-1	F14 1-0	S24 0-1	O21 0-0	F28 3-1	N29 2-3	a19 0-1	M13 3-1	A30 3-1	O18 4-2	D26 2-1	J03 1-0	a24 2-0	N15 2-2	N01 0-0	F07 0-0	J17 1-0	A16 1-0	S27 0-0
2 BOURNEMOUTH	O04 1-1		J10 2-1	S24 3-0	N01 3-0	F07 1-0	A23 1-2	S06 0-1	a16 1-0	a03 4-2	D20 1-0	a26 1-1	S20 2-0	N29 0-0	a07 0-1	O22 2-1	N15 1-0	M13 3-3	J24 2-0	D27 2-0	a17 0-0	O18 4-2	F14 4-1	M27 1-0
3 BRADFORD C	D06 2-1	A30 0-1		A16 1-1	a24 1-2	a19 4-1	N01 2-0	O22 3-4	F07 0-0	N15 1-2	S24 2-2	M31 1-5	m03 3-0	a10 1-2	M13 1-1	J17 3-0	D26 0-0	M10 1-1	O18 1-2	F28 0-0	M20 3-1	S13 3-0	S27 1-0	J14 1-0
4 BRENTFORD	S06 1-0	F23 1-2	a03 2-2		F28 0-0	M20 0-0	D20 3-0	J24 0-1	a17 5-1	A23 1-1	a05 0-0	M13 1-0	O04 1-3	J31 2-1	D27 2-2	D06 3-0	N01 5-2	O18 1-0	S20 2-1	a16 1-0	J10 1-1	F14 0-1	N15 1-0	N03 4-0
5 CAMBRIDGE U	D20 1-1	M06 0-1	A23 0-0	O25 2-1		O11 1-1	O04 1-0	a03 3-3	J24 0-1	a16 4-0	S20 0-0	O21 2-4	a06 0-1	N08 0-1	a21 2-2	F21 0-0	F07 2-2	M20 2-2	S06 0-1	J10 3-1	D27 2-1	D06 3-3	S23 4-1	M16 4-1
6 CREWE A	J23 1-1	N05 1-0	D27 1-3	N29 1-0	M13 1-2		S20 2-0	J10 1-2	a07 0-0	O04 0-0	a14 0-2	N01 2-3	a17 4-0	M27 0-1	A23 3-3	S24 0-0	O18 1-0	F13 4-0	a03 3-1	D20 2-1	S06 6-0	N15 1-0	M03 2-2	J31 0-0
7 DARLINGTON	N08 2-0	a24 2-0	M22 2-2	M29 2-0	D13 1-1	J17 0-0		O25 2-2	O11 0-0	N03 1-2	F21 0-3	S27 0-0	M27 4-0	S13 0-1	N29 0-1	a20 4-0	A16 2-0	J03 2-0	F23 0-1	a28 1-1	M15 1-0	a10 2-0	A30 1-0	D26 1-0
8 DONCASTER R	F24 2-2	a10 1-1	J30 1-1	S15 1-1	A16 0-2	A30 3-1	F27 3-2		M20 0-0	F14 3-0	N04 4-1	D26 2-4	N15 5-1	M09 0-4	N01 1-1	J20 1-2	a19 0-1	S27 5-2	M13 3-1	O18 2-1	D06 0-1	D13 3-0	J17 1-2	M30 1-0
9 EXETER C	J31 2-0	J02 1-0	N04 0-0	D26 0-0	S13 1-2	S27 2-2	M13 1-1	N28 1-0		O18 3-1	M27 4-1	J17 0-0	F28 3-0	D13 0-0	F13 4-1	M09 1-0	a23 5-4	A16 2-0	O31 2-0	N14 3-0	F25 0-0	A29 0-2	a19 1-3	a10 1-0
10 HARTLEPOOL	O25 1-0	A16 1-1	F21 2-2	a24 1-0	F18 2-2	M10 1-3	F07 2-3	N08 2-1	O13 2-1		M06 1-1	A30 2-2	N29 4-1	D26 3-0	S22 2-4	M31 3-0	S13 1-2	J17 0-0	O22 3-0	M27 1-0	O11 0-1	S27 1-2	a10 2-1	a20 0-2
11 HUDDERSFIELD T	M20 1-2	M30 0-0	a29 0-0	S27 2-1	J17 2-0	J27 1-0	N15 1-0	F07 1-2	D06 0-1	N01 2-0		S13 0-1	O18 2-1	A16 1-1	F28 3-0	A30 0-0	a10 1-1	a19 1-2	F14 2-2	M13 2-0	O21 2-3	D26 1-0	a24 1-0	M09 2-0
12 LINCOLN C	D27 2-1	O25 1-0	D20 4-2	O11 3-1	J31 3-0	M06 2-0	a07 2-1	a17 5-0	S20 4-1	J10 3-0	M23 0-0		a03 4-1	M17 3-1	S06 3-1	N08 2-0	N28 3-0	F25 6-0	a16 2-0	O04 4-0	A23 4-2	N04 2-2	M26 5-1	F21 4-1
13 NEWPORT CO	O11 1-0	J17 3-1	N08 3-1	M08 1-0	S27 2-0	D26 2-2	D06 4-1	F21 2-3	O25 3-3	M20 0-1	M17 1-2	A16 3-1		a20 1-1	O20 0-0	a10 1-1	A30 0-0	S13 2-0	F07 2-2	F23 1-2	M05 0-2	J03 1-5	M31 0-2	a24 2-3
14 NORTHAMPTON T	J10 5-0	M20 6-0	S05 4-2	O21 3-1	F14 4-2	D06 2-1	J24 3-2	O03 2-1	D20 3-1	a17 5-2	a03 1-1	O18 1-0	D27 3-0		a15 4-1	F07 1-1	F27 2-1	N15 1-0	a23 4-0	S19 0-0	a06 2-2	M12 1-1	N01 3-0	S23 2-1
15 READING	M17 0-0	S27 2-1	O11 2-1	a19 1-0	D26 1-0	a24 3-1	M20 4-1	M06 0-1	N08 4-3	F25 1-0	O25 2-0	a10 1-1	M02 1-0	J03 1-0		A16 2-0	D13 1-0	A30 1-0	D06 5-0	N05 1-0	F21 0-0	M31 5-0	S13 3-0	J17 1-0
16 ROCHDALE	a17 0-0	F10 2-2	S20 0-0	M27 1-2	N14 1-1	M22 0-1	D27 1-0	a16 1-0	O04 0-1	D20 1-1	M01 0-0	F14 0-0	S06 4-3	N03 0-2	a03 0-0		M12 1-1	F28 2-0	a05 2-3	A23 2-1	J24 2-2	N01 4-1	O18 2-1	N29 1-1
17 SCUNTHORPE U	a20 1-0	F21 2-0	a17 2-0	M06 2-1	N04 0-1	M16 1-0	a03 2-1	D27 2-1	A23 0-1	M02 5-1	S06 0-1	M20 0-2	J10 1-2	O25 0-2	O04 2-1	O11 1-3		D06 1-2	D20 0-0	a06 1-1	S20 3-1	F24 2-2	F10 0-1	N08 3-0
18 SOUTHPORT	A23 0-0	O10 0-2	O03 1-2	M16 2-0	N29 2-4	N07 2-2	a16 2-0	a06 1-1	a02 1-0	S19 2-4	D27 1-2	S24 1-2	J24 3-0	F21 0-1	J10 1-2	O25 0-1	M26 1-1		a17 2-0	S05 1-1	D19 1-3	J31 0-0	N04 1-2	M05 2-1
19 STOCKPORT CO	F20 1-1	S12 0-0	M15 2-1	J16 2-0	J01 0-1	A16 0-0	S22 0-0	O10 1-2	M05 2-1	J30 2-0	N08 0-1	a12 0-3	N03 0-1	A22 1-3	M26 1-1	S26 0-1	M29 0-0	D26 1-0		N28 3-2	O24 1-0	a19 0-2	D12 2-2	A30 4-1
20 SWANSEA C	M05 3-1	a20 1-1	O25 3-1	a26 2-2	A30 1-0	J03 4-0	O21 2-0	M16 2-1	F20 0-3	D06 3-1	O11 1-1	M09 2-2	S23 2-2	J16 1-1	F06 5-1	a23 1-1	S27 2-0	a10 2-0	M19 5-0		N08 3-0	A16 1-1	D26 4-2	S13 1-0
21 TORQUAY U	N05 2-0	D30 2-1	N29 1-0	A30 2-3	a19 0-0	a10 2-1	O18 2-4	M27 2-2	S24 1-0	M13 1-1	F17 1-3	a24 2-2	N01 1-1	S27 0-1	N15 0-0	S13 1-0	J17 1-0	M31 2-1	F28 4-1	F14 0-2		M10 2-1	J03 1-0	A16 1-0
22 TRANMERE R	S19 1-0	M15 2-0	a26 3-3	N07 5-1	M26 3-2	F20 2-1	S05 2-0	A22 2-2	J09 1-1	a06 1-2	a17 3-0	F06 2-0	a14 3-1	O10 2-0	D19 2-0	M06 0-1	S22 2-1	O20 1-0	D27 5-0	a02 3-0	O03 7-1		N28 3-0	O24 6-0
23 WATFORD	a03 1-0	N08 1-1	a06 3-0	F21 3-2	F24 1-0	O25 2-1	J10 2-0	S20 2-1	D27 2-0	S06 2-1	A23 0-2	D06 1-3	D20 3-1	M06 0-1	J24 2-1	M16 3-0	O21 1-0	F07 2-0	O04 1-1	a17 2-1	a16 0-0	M20 2-2		O11 2-0
24 WORKINGTON	a07 1-7	D06 1-3	a16 0-3	F07 1-1	O18 1-0	O22 0-3	a17 0-0	D20 3-1	S06 1-0	D27 1-2	O04 0-2	N15 0-3	A23 1-2	F25 1-0	S20 0-2	M20 0-0	F14 2-3	J09 2-1	J10 1-2	J24 1-1	a03 1-3	F28 0-1	M13 1-3	

LEAGUE TABLES

DIVISION 1

	P	W	D	L	F	A	W	D	L	F	A	Pts
Liverpool	42	14	5	2	41	21	9	9	3	25	10	60
Q.P.R.	42	17	4	0	42	13	7	7	7	25	20	59
Manchester U	42	16	4	1	40	13	7	6	8	28	29	56
Derby Co	42	15	3	3	45	30	6	8	7	30	28	53
Leeds U	42	13	3	5	37	19	8	6	7	28	27	51
Ipswich T	42	11	6	4	36	23	5	8	8	18	25	46
Leicester C	42	9	9	3	29	24	4	10	7	19	27	45
Manchester C	42	14	5	2	46	18	2	6	13	18	28	43
Tottenham H	42	6	10	5	33	32	8	5	8	30	31	43
Norwich C	42	10	5	6	33	26	6	5	10	25	32	42
Everton	42	10	7	4	37	24	5	5	11	23	42	42
Stoke C	42	8	5	8	25	24	7	6	8	23	26	41
Middlesbrough	42	9	7	5	23	11	6	3	12	23	34	40
Coventry C	42	6	9	6	22	22	7	5	9	25	35	40
Newcastle U	42	11	4	6	51	26	4	5	12	20	36	39
Aston Villa	42	11	8	2	32	17	0	9	12	19	42	39
Arsenal	42	11	4	6	33	19	2	6	13	14	34	36
West Ham U	42	10	5	6	26	23	3	5	13	22	48	36
Birmingham C	42	11	5	5	36	26	2	2	17	21	49	33
Wolverh'pton W	42	7	6	8	27	25	3	4	14	24	43	30
Burnley	42	6	6	9	23	26	3	4	14	20	40	28
Sheffield U	42	4	7	10	19	32	2	3	16	14	50	22

DIVISION 2

	P	W	D	L	F	A	W	D	L	F	A	Pts
Sunderland	42	19	2	0	48	10	5	6	10	19	26	56
Bristol C	42	11	7	3	34	14	8	8	5	25	21	53
W.B.A.	42	10	9	2	29	12	10	4	7	21	21	53
Bolton W	42	12	5	4	36	14	8	7	6	28	24	52
Notts Co	42	11	6	4	33	13	8	5	8	27	28	49
Southampton	42	18	2	1	49	16	3	5	13	17	34	49
Luton T	42	13	6	2	38	15	6	4	11	23	36	48
Nottingham F	42	13	1	7	34	18	4	11	6	21	22	46
Charlton A	42	11	5	5	40	34	4	7	10	21	38	42
Blackpool	42	9	9	3	26	22	5	5	11	14	27	42
Chelsea	42	7	9	5	25	20	5	7	9	28	34	40
Fulham	42	9	8	4	27	14	4	6	11	18	33	40
Orient	42	10	6	5	21	12	3	8	10	16	27	40
Hull C	42	9	5	7	29	23	5	6	10	16	26	39
Blackburn R	42	8	6	7	27	22	4	8	9	18	28	38
Plymouth A	42	13	4	4	36	20	0	8	13	12	34	38
Oldham A	42	11	8	2	37	24	2	4	15	20	44	38
Bristol R	42	7	9	5	20	15	4	7	10	18	35	38
Carlisle U	42	9	8	4	29	22	3	5	13	16	37	37
Oxford U	42	7	7	7	23	25	4	4	13	16	34	33
York C	42	8	3	10	28	34	2	5	14	11	37	28
Portsmouth	42	4	6	11	15	23	5	1	15	17	38	25

DIVISION 3

	P	W	D	L	F	A	W	D	L	F	A	Pts
Hereford U	46	14	6	3	45	24	12	5	6	41	31	63
Cardiff C	46	14	7	2	38	13	8	6	9	31	35	57
Millwall	46	16	6	1	35	14	4	10	9	19	29	56
Brighton & H.A.	46	18	3	2	58	15	4	6	13	20	38	53
Crystal Palace	46	7	12	4	30	20	11	5	7	31	26	53
Wrexham	46	13	6	4	38	21	7	6	10	28	34	52
Walsall	46	11	8	4	43	22	7	6	10	31	39	50
Preston N.E.	46	15	4	4	45	23	4	6	13	17	34	48
Shrewsbury T	46	14	2	7	36	25	5	8	10	25	34	48
Peterborough U	46	12	7	4	37	23	3	11	9	26	40	48
Mansfield T	46	8	11	4	31	22	8	4	11	27	30	47
Port Vale	46	10	10	3	33	21	5	6	12	22	33	46
Bury	46	11	7	5	33	16	3	9	11	18	30	44
Chesterfield	46	11	5	7	45	30	6	4	13	24	39	43
Gillingham	46	10	8	5	38	27	2	11	10	20	41	43
Rotherham U	46	11	6	6	35	22	4	6	13	19	43	42
Chester C	46	13	7	3	34	19	2	5	16	9	43	42
Grimsby T	46	13	7	3	39	21	2	3	18	23	53	40
Swindon T	46	11	4	8	42	31	5	4	14	20	44	40
Sheffield W	46	12	6	5	34	25	0	10	13	14	34	40
Aldershot	46	10	8	5	34	26	3	5	15	25	49	39
Colchester U	46	9	6	8	25	27	3	8	12	16	38	38
Southend U	46	9	7	7	40	31	3	6	14	25	44	37
Halifax T	46	6	5	12	22	32	5	8	10	19	29	35

DIVISION 4

	P	W	D	L	F	A	W	D	L	F	A	Pts
Lincoln C	46	21	2	0	71	15	11	8	4	40	24	74
Northampton T	46	18	5	0	62	20	11	5	7	25	20	68
Reading	46	19	3	1	42	9	5	9	9	28	42	60
Tranmere R	46	18	3	2	61	16	6	7	10	28	39	58
Huddersfield T	46	11	6	6	28	17	10	8	5	28	24	56
Bournemouth	46	15	5	3	39	16	5	7	11	18	32	52
Exeter C	46	13	7	3	37	17	5	7	11	19	30	50
Watford	46	16	4	3	38	18	6	2	15	24	44	50
Torquay U	46	12	6	5	31	24	6	8	9	24	39	50
Doncaster R	46	10	6	7	42	31	9	5	9	33	38	49
Swansea C	46	14	8	1	51	21	2	7	14	15	36	47
Barnsley	46	12	8	3	34	16	2	8	13	18	32	44
Cambridge U	46	7	10	6	36	28	7	5	11	22	34	43
Hartlepool U	46	10	6	7	37	29	6	4	13	25	49	42
Rochdale	46	7	11	5	27	23	5	7	11	13	31	42
Crewe A	46	10	7	6	36	21	3	8	12	22	36	41
Bradford C	46	9	7	7	35	26	3	10	10	28	39	41
Brentford	46	12	7	4	37	18	2	6	15	19	42	41
Scunthorpe U	46	11	3	9	31	24	3	7	13	19	35	38
Darlington	46	11	7	5	30	14	3	3	17	18	43	38
Stockport Co	46	8	7	8	23	23	5	5	13	20	53	38
Newport Co	46	8	7	8	35	33	5	2	16	22	57	35
Southport	46	6	6	11	27	31	2	4	17	14	46	26
Workington	46	5	4	14	19	43	2	3	18	11	44	21

FOOTBALL LEAGUE RECORDS

Top scorers: Div 1, M.Macdonald (Arsenal), A.Gray (Aston Villa) 25 goals; Div 2, M.Walsh (Blackpool) 26 goals; Div 3, P.Ward (Brighton & Hove Albion) 32 goals; Div 4, B.Joicey (Barnsley) 25 goals.

Emlyn Hughes, the powerful, adaptable footballer who captained Liverpool to another Championship and also led them to their first European Cup Final victory in 1977.

DIVISION 1

	ARSENAL	ASTON VILLA	BIRMINGHAM C	BRISTOL C	COVENTRY C	DERBY CO	EVERTON	IPSWICH T	LEEDS U	LEICESTER C	LIVERPOOL	MANCHESTER C	MANCHESTER U	MIDDLESBROUGH	NEWCASTLE U	NORWICH C	Q.P.R.	STOKE C	SUNDERLAND	TOTTENHAM H	W.B.A.	WEST HAM U
1 ARSENAL		a25 3-0	N06 4-0	A21 0-1	a23 2-0	m03 0-0	S18 3-1	M05 1-4	J03 1-1	a02 3-0	N20 1-1	S04 0-0	D18 3-1	m07 1-1	D04 5-3	J15 1-0	O02 3-2	O16 2-0	F05 0-0	a11 1-0	M08 1-2	F19 2-3
2 ASTON VILLA	O20 5-1		S18 1-2	O23 3-1	N20 2-2	M02 4-0	F05 2-0	S04 5-2	m07 2-1	S25 2-0	D15 5-1	m04 1-1	N06 3-2	a05 1-0	D18 2-1	a23 1-0	m20 1-1	m16 1-0	M23 4-1	a20 2-1	m23 4-0	A21 4-0
3 BIRMINGHAM C	J18 3-3	m10 2-1		a09 3-0	M05 3-1	O02 5-1	m14 1-1	D07 2-4	A24 0-0	a30 1-1	A28 2-1	N27 0-0	J22 2-3	O16 3-1	a02 1-2	F12 3-2	O30 2-1	a16 2-0	D11 2-0	M19 1-2	S11 0-1	D27 0-0
4 BRISTOL C	J22 2-0	a02 0-0	O26 0-1		N06 0-0	M15 2-2	M05 1-2	O02 1-2	m10 1-0	O16 0-1	m16 2-1	F19 1-0	m07 1-1	D18 1-2	F05 1-1	N20 3-1	M19 1-0	A24 1-1	S04 4-1	a12 1-0	a05 1-2	S18 1-1
5 COVENTRY C	N27 1-2	a16 2-3	S25 2-1	m19 2-2		a25 2-0	D11 4-2	D27 1-1	A28 4-2	O02 1-1	m10 0-0	m14 0-1	A24 0-2	J22 1-1	O16 1-1	S11 2-0	N09 2-0	a30 5-2	O30 1-2	a02 1-1	a19 1-1	a09 1-1
6 DERBY CO	D15 0-0	a09 2-1	M12 0-0	O30 2-0	M09 1-1		a16 2-3	m14 0-0	F12 0-1	D27 1-0	S11 2-3	a30 4-0	A28 0-0	A25 0-0	J22 4-2	a06 2-2	m11 2-0	a02 2-0	N27 1-0	O16 8-2	S25 2-2	a20 1-1
7 EVERTON	M01 2-1	A28 0-2	D18 2-2	S25 2-0	m07 1-1	N20 2-0		A24 1-1	N06 0-2	F12 1-2	M22 0-0	O05 2-2	a05 1-2	D29 2-2	m24 2-0	a19 3-1	J22 1-3	S11 3-0	m19 2-0	M26 4-0	m16 1-1	O23 3-2
8 IPSWICH T	S25 3-1	F12 1-0	a11 1-0	M12 1-0	a05 2-1	D18 0-0	J15 2-0		N20 1-1	S11 0-0	D04 1-0	O23 1-0	J03 2-1	a23 0-1	m07 2-0	F15 5-0	A28 2-2	F26 0-1	N23 3-1	A21 3-1	N06 7-0	M22 4-1
9 LEEDS U	O30 2-1	D11 1-3	F02 1-0	a30 2-0	F05 1-2	S04 2-0	m04 0-0	a16 2-1		N27 2-2	O23 1-1	D27 0-2	O02 0-2	M05 2-1	S18 2-2	M23 3-2	m14 0-1	N10 1-1	a09 1-1	F19 2-1	A21 2-2	a26 1-1
10 LEICESTER C	O23 4-1	M05 1-1	D04 2-6	M26 0-0	M12 3-1	a12 1-1	S04 1-1	F19 1-0	m16 0-1		O27 0-1	A21 2-2	N20 1-1	M15 3-3	m04 1-0	N06 1-1	S18 2-2	S29 1-0	J15 2-0	D18 2-1	m07 0-5	F05 2-0
11 LIVERPOOL	a16 2-0	O30 3-0	F05 4-1	N27 2-1	S04 3-1	F19 3-1	O16 3-1	a30 2-1	a02 3-1	N09 5-1		a09 2-1	m03 1-0	O02 0-0	M05 1-0	A21 1-0	D11 3-1	D27 4-0	J01 2-0	S18 2-0	J15 1-1	m14 0-0
12 MANCHESTER C	F12 1-0	A25 2-0	a19 2-1	S11 2-1	D18 2-0	D04 3-2	m10 1-1	a02 2-1	a08 2-1	J22 5-0	D29 1-1		S25 1-3	a11 1-0	N06 0-0	M01 2-0	O16 0-0	A28 0-0	M09 1-0	m07 5-0	N20 1-0	O02 4-2
13 MANCHESTER U	m14 3-2	J01 2-0	A21 2-2	J19 2-1	J15 2-0	F05 3-1	D27 4-0	O30 0-1	M12 1-0	a16 1-1	F16 0-0	M05 3-1		S18 2-0	F19 3-1	O23 2-2	a30 1-0	a09 3-0	N10 3-3	S04 2-3	M23 2-2	N27 0-2
14 MIDDLESBROUGH	F15 3-0	D27 3-2	M22 2-2	m14 0-0	A21 1-0	J15 2-0	a09 2-2	N27 0-2	S25 1-0	O30 0-1	M12 0-1	D07 0-0	a26 3-0		S04 1-0	O09 1-0	a16 0-2	J01 0-0	S11 2-1	F05 2-0	O23 1-0	a29 1-1
15 NEWCASTLE U	a30 0-2	m14 3-2	O23 3-2	A28 0-0	M23 1-0	A21 2-2	N24 4-1	M09 1-1	M02 3-0	a09 0-0	S25 1-0	F16 2-2	S11 2-2	M26 1-0		M12 5-1	N27 2-0	O30 1-0	D27 2-0	F26 2-0	O06 2-0	a16 3-0
16 NORWICH C	A25 1-3	N27 1-1	S04 1-0	a16 2-1	F19 3-0	S18 0-0	a30 2-1	a09 0-1	O16 1-2	J01 3-2	J22 2-1	O30 0-2	a02 2-1	M09 1-0	O02 3-2		D27 2-0	J29 1-1	m14 2-2	M05 1-3	F05 1-0	N10 1-0
17 Q.P.R.	M12 2-1	S11 2-1	m23 2-2	a26 0-1	a11 1-1	N06 1-1	A21 0-4	m16 1-0	M08 0-0	F26 3-2	m07 1-1	M22 0-0	a19 4-0	N20 3-0	a23 1-2	O05 2-3		S25 2-0	O23 2-0	J11 2-1	S04 1-0	a04 1-1
18 STOKE C	M23 1-1	O02 1-0	N20 1-0	a20 2-2	F16 2-0	O23 1-0	F19 0-1	S18 2-1	a12 2-1	M19 0-1	a11 0-0	F05 0-2	m11 3-3	N06 3-1	M15 0-0	m07 0-0	M05 1-0		A21 0-0	a23 0-0	D18 0-2	S04 2-1
19 SUNDERLAND	A28 2-2	O16 0-1	m07 1-0	F11 1-0	J03 0-1	a23 1-1	O02 0-1	M19 1-0	D29 0-1	A24 0-0	N06 0-1	S18 0-2	a11 2-1	F19 4-0	a08 2-2	D18 0-1	a02 1-0	J22 0-0		N20 2-1	F22 6-1	M05 6-0
20 TOTTENHAM H	D27 2-2	a30 3-1	O20 1-0	N13 0-1	O23 0-1	M23 0-0	O30 3-3	J22 1-0	S11 1-0	m14 2-0	M09 1-0	D11 2-2	F12 1-3	A28 0-0	A25 0-2	S25 1-1	a09 3-0	N27 2-0	a16 1-1		M12 0-2	J01 2-1
21 W.B.A.	a09 0-2	N10 1-1	F28 2-1	D27 1-1	S17 1-1	M05 1-0	N27 3-0	M16 4-0	J22 1-2	D11 2-2	A25 0-1	a16 0-2	O16 4-0	a02 2-1	M19 1-1	A28 2-0	F12 1-1	m14 3-1	a30 2-3	O02 4-2		O30 3-0
22 WEST HAM U	S11 0-2	J22 0-1	a08 2-2	F26 2-0	m04 2-0	m07 2-2	a02 2-2	O16 0-2	O06 1-3	A28 0-0	D18 2-0	M12 1-0	m16 4-2	D04 0-1	N20 1-2	a11 1-0	A23 1-0	F12 1-0	S25 1-1	N06 5-3	J03 0-0	

Wolves centre-forward John Richards scored 15 times as the Molineux club topped Division Two.

DIVISION 2

	BLACKBURN R	BLACKPOOL	BOLTON W	BRISTOL R	BURNLEY	CARDIFF C	CARLISLE U	CHARLTON A	CHELSEA	FULHAM	HEREFORD U	HULL C	LUTON T	MILLWALL	NOTTINGHAM F	NOTTS CO	OLDHAM A	ORIENT	PLYMOUTH A	SHEFFIELD U	SOUTHAMPTON	WOLVERHAMPTON W
1 BLACKBURN R		S04 0-1	A21 3-1	S18 0-0	D27 2-2	F05 2-1	a06 1-3	a30 0-0	O23 0-2	m14 1-0	N27 1-0	N13 1-0	O30 1-0	M26 2-0	J01 1-3	O09 6-1	F19 2-0	M12 2-2	M02 2-0	M05 1-0	a20 3-0	a16 0-2
2 BLACKPOOL	F12 1-1		M12 1-0	J22 4-0	a09 1-1	a02 1-0	D27 0-0	a16 2-2	S25 0-1	N27 3-2	F14 2-1	J01 0-0	a30 1-0	S11 4-2	O16 1-0	F26 1-1	A24 0-2	A28 3-0	O09 0-2	N13 1-0	m14 1-0	O30 2-2
3 BOLTON W	J22 3-1	O02 0-3		O16 1-0	N09 2-1	m10 2-1	M22 3-4	N27 1-0	F26 2-2	O30 2-1	a30 3-1	S11 5-1	D21 2-1	A28 3-1	D27 1-1	F12 4-0	a02 3-0	A24 2-0	M05 3-0	a09 1-2	a16 3-0	m14 0-1
4 BRISTOL R	M08 0-0	A21 1-4	m17 2-2		a16 1-1	J15 1-1	D11 2-1	O30 1-1	O05 2-1	F12 2-1	N13 2-3	N27 3-0	J01 1-0	M12 0-0	a30 1-1	S25 5-1	A28 0-0	S11 1-0	O23 1-1	m14 3-1	a09 2-3	D27 1-5
5 BURNLEY	a08 3-1	D28 0-0	a12 0-0	N20 1-1		D04 0-0	F26 2-0	O16 4-4	a23 1-0	A24 3-1	F12 1-1	S25 0-0	A28 1-2	D18 1-3	a02 0-1	m07 3-1	N06 1-0	O09 3-3	J03 0-2	M12 1-0	S11 2-0	J22 0-0
6 CARDIFF C	A28 2-1	O23 2-2	O09 3-2	A25 1-2	a30 0-1		m14 1-1	J22 1-1	M12 1-3	J01 3-0	D27 3-1	D11 1-1	a16 4-2	S24 0-0	N27 0-3	S11 2-3	F12 3-1	M02 0-1	M26 0-1	O30 0-2	N10 1-0	a09 2-2
7 CARLISLE U	D29 1-1	O12 1-1	N06 0-1	m07 2-3	S18 2-1	D18 4-3		O02 4-2	F05 0-1	M19 1-2	S14 2-2	S04 1-1	O16 1-1	N20 0-1	M05 1-1	J03 0-2	a12 1-1	D04 1-0	a23 3-1	F19 4-1	J22 0-6	a19 2-1
8 CHARLTON A	D04 4-0	N20 1-2	a22 1-1	J03 4-3	a26 5-2	A21 0-2	M11 1-0		a11 4-0	A28 1-1	F25 1-1	O09 3-1	S10 4-3	a08 3-2	J14 2-1	J29 1-1	m07 2-1	F15 2-0	N05 3-1	O23 3-2	S24 6-2	F12 1-1
9 CHELSEA	a02 3-1	M05 2-2	S18 2-1	M19 2-0	N27 2-1	O02 2-1	A28 2-1	N10 2-1		D27 2-0	J01 5-1	m14 4-0	a09 2-0	F12 1-1	a16 2-1	A25 1-1	O16 4-3	J22 1-1	F19 2-2	a30 4-0	O30 3-1	D11 3-3
10 FULHAM	D14 2-0	a23 0-0	J03 0-2	S04 1-0	J15 2-2	N06 1-2	N16 2-0	F05 1-1	a08 3-1		S25 4-1	O23 0-0	F26 1-2	D28 2-3	A21 2-2	N20 1-5	D04 5-0	m07 6-1	a11 2-0	M26 3-2	M11 1-1	S11 0-0
11 HEREFORD U	a23 1-0	m07 1-1	D15 3-3	a11 1-1	S04 3-0	a06 2-2	m04 0-0	S18 1-2	N06 2-2	M05 1-0		A21 1-0	M19 0-1	a20 3-1	M02 0-1	O23 1-4	N20 0-0	D18 2-3	F09 1-1	M23 2-2	m11 2-0	O02 1-6
12 HULL C	a12 1-0	N06 2-2	F19 2-2	a23 0-1	M05 4-1	m07 1-2	F12 3-1	M19 0-0	D18 1-1	a02 1-0	J22 1-1		A24 3-1	F15 0-0	O02 1-0	a08 0-1	D28 0-1	a19 1-1	N20 3-1	S17 1-1	A28 4-0	O16 2-0
13 LUTON T	F15 2-0	D04 0-0	m07 1-1	N06 4-2	F05 2-0	N20 2-1	M26 5-0	F19 2-0	D29 4-0	S18 0-2	O09 2-0	J24 2-1		a12 1-2	S04 1-1	a23 4-2	M08 1-0	a11 0-0	M12 1-1	A21 2-0	O23 1-4	M05 2-0
14 MILLWALL	O16 0-1	F19 1-1	F05 3-0	O02 2-0	m14 2-0	M05 0-2	a16 1-1	D27 1-1	S04 3-0	a09 0-0	O30 4-2	a30 2-1	N13 4-2		D11 0-2	J22 2-5	M19 2-1	a02 0-1	S18 3-0	N27 0-1	A25 0-0	J01 1-1
15 NOTTINGHAM F	N06 3-0	M26 3-0	a06 3-1	D04 4-2	O23 5-2	a23 0-1	S25 5-1	A25 1-1	N20 1-1	J22 3-0	S11 4-3	M12 2-0	F12 1-2	m07 1-0		M08 1-2	a27 3-0	M29 3-0	D18 1-1	O09 6-1	M22 2-1	A28 1-3
16 NOTTS CO	M19 0-0	S18 2-0	S04 0-1	M05 2-1	M02 5-1	F19 1-0	O30 2-1	m14 0-1	F15 2-1	a16 0-0	a01 3-2	D27 1-1	N27 0-4	A21 1-2	a09 1-1		O02 1-0	O16 0-1	F05 2-0	M28 2-1	a30 3-1	N13 1-1
17 OLDHAM A	S11 2-0	J15 1-0	O23 2-2	F05 4-0	F15 3-1	S04 3-2	N13 4-1	M22 1-1	a19 0-0	a30 1-0	a16 3-5	a09 3-0	m14 1-2	O09 2-1	O30 1-0	M12 1-1		S25 0-0	A21 2-2	D27 1-2	N27 2-1	M15 0-2
18 ORIENT	O02 0-1	m10 0-1	M15 2-2	F19 2-0	M19 0-1	S18 3-0	a30 0-0	a09 0-0	A21 0-1	D11 0-0	m14 1-1	m17 1-1	D27 1-0	M08 1-1	N13 0-1	M26 1-0	M05 0-2		S04 2-2	a16 0-2	a26 2-3	N27 2-4
19 PLYMOUTH A	A24 4-0	M19 2-0	S25 1-1	a02 1-1	O30 0-1	O16 2-2	N27 0-1	J01 1-0	S11 2-3	N13 2-2	a09 2-1	a16 1-2	O02 1-0	F26 2-2	m02 1-2	A28 1-2	J22 2-2	F12 1-2		D11 0-0	D27 1-1	a30 0-0
20 SHEFFIELD U	S25 1-1	a12 1-5	D28 2-3	D18 2-3	O02 1-0	M08 3-0	S11 3-0	a02 3-0	D03 1-0	O16 1-1	A28 1-1	F26 1-1	J22 0-3	m03 1-1	M19 2-0	N06 1-0	a05 2-1	N20 1-1	m07 1-0		F12 2-2	A24 2-2
21 SOUTHAMPTON	m07 2-0	D18 3-3	N20 1-3	D29 2-1	F19 2-0	a11 3-2	A21 1-2	M05 2-1	D07 1-1	O02 4-1	O16 1-0	F05 2-2	a02 1-0	J15 0-2	S18 1-1	D04 2-1	a23 4-0	N06 2-2	a08 4-1	S04 1-1		m03 1-0
22 WOLVERHAMPTON W	N20 1-2	M01 2-1	D18 1-0	a05 1-0	A21 0-0	a26 4-1	O23 4-0	S04 3-0	m07 1-1	F19 5-1	M12 2-1	M26 2-1	S25 1-2	N06 3-1	F05 2-1	a11 2-2	S18 5-0	a23 1-0	D04 4-0	F09 2-1	O05 2-6	

SEASON 1976-77

DIVISION 3

	BRIGHTON & HA	BURY	CHESTER	CHESTERFIELD	CRYSTAL P	GILLINGHAM	GRIMSBY T	LINCOLN C	MANSFIELD T	NORTHAMPTON T	OXFORD U	PETERBOROUGH U	PORTSMOUTH	PORT VALE	PRESTON N.E.	READING	ROTHERHAM U	SHEFFIELD W	SHREWSBURY T	SWINDON T	TRANMERE R	WALSALL	WREXHAM	YORK C
1 BRIGHTON & H.A.		M19 1-1	J15 3-0	D18 2-1	O02 1-1	D29 2-0	F19 3-0	J29 4-0	a02 3-1	J03 2-0	A21 3-2	O16 1-0	a06 4-0	a23 1-0	F05 2-0	a12 2-0	S04 3-1	m03 3-2	M15 4-0	N06 4-0	M05 1-1	O05 7-0	N27 0-2	S18 7-2
2 BURY	O09 3-0		S18 2-0	m07 3-1	F19 0-1	N26 3-1	A21 2-0	a11 3-0	M12 2-0	F15 1-1	M26 2-1	S25 4-1	a23 1-0	a08 3-0	O23 3-2	J29 1-0	J15 1-1	N06 1-3	m03 0-1	O26 0-1	S04 2-1	D18 0-2	M01 0-2	F05 4-2
3 CHESTER	A24 0-1	M08 1-0		a23 1-2	F12 2-1	F22 1-0	M19 2-0	m03 1-0	O16 1-0	N27 2-1	A28 1-3	O02 2-1	a11 1-1	m07 1-1	S11 0-0	F01 3-1	M05 1-3	F15 1-0	D28 1-2	D18 2-1	J22 1-0	N06 1-0	a08 1-2	a02 1-0
4 CHESTERFIELD	m14 1-1	D04 7-0	N10 1-0		a30 0-2	M12 1-0	F16 0-1	S25 1-4	D27 0-1	A21 0-0	m04 2-0	a16 0-0	F05 1-2	M30 4-0	J29 1-1	O09 4-0	a09 1-0	F26 2-0	M26 1-1	S04 0-1	N03 0-0	O23 1-0	S11 0-6	O30 2-0
5 CRYSTAL P	M12 3-1	S11 2-1	S04 1-2	N27 0-0		a05 3-1	J15 2-1	m07 4-1	S25 2-0	D18 1-1	O09 2-2	F26 0-0	F22 2-1	F01 2-0	M22 1-0	N06 1-1	O23 2-1	a23 4-0	O26 2-1	a12 5-0	F05 1-0	J03 3-0	m03 2-1	A21 1-0
6 GILLINGHAM	a09 0-1	a30 1-0	a16 1-0	O02 2-1	D27 0-3		N02 1-1	O16 0-1	N13 3-1	S04 1-1	J29 1-1	M22 1-1	S18 2-1	F19 1-1	O30 1-1	A21 2-2	D04 1-2	M19 1-0	F15 2-1	M05 2-2	m14 3-0	F05 1-0	a02 2-0	m03 2-0
7 GRIMSBY T	S11 2-0	J22 2-0	O09 0-0	N06 1-2	A24 0-1	a11 1-1		a08 1-2	F12 0-1	J29 0-1	F26 1-2	A28 2-2	N27 1-0	J03 2-4	S25 1-0	D18 2-1	M12 1-1	D28 1-1	a23 2-1	m07 2-0	a02 1-0	m03 2-2	N30 3-0	O16 1-0
8 LINCOLN C	a20 2-2	N03 2-3	M29 3-3	M05 3-2	M02 3-2	M26 4-0	D27 2-0		F15 3-2	F05 5-4	a16 0-1	m11 1-1	M15 2-1	S04 2-0	a30 2-0	O23 3-1	O29 2-2	O02 1-1	A21 1-1	S18 0-0	N13 2-2	J18 4-1	M18 1-1	a09 2-0
9 MANSFIELD T	O23 1-1	O02 5-0	M26 1-1	a11 2-1	M05 1-0	a23 2-2	S04 3-0	N06 3-1		m07 3-0	F07 3-0	M19 1-1	m02 2-0	D28 2-1	A21 3-1	N08 4-0	F05 3-1	J11 1-0	a12 1-0	N27 1-1	S18 1-1	F28 3-0	D18 2-0	F19 4-1
10 NORTHAMPTON T	O30 0-2	a09 3-0	a29 0-0	J22 2-1	M15 3-0	F12 1-2	a19 0-0	A28 1-0	M08 0-1		N13 1-0	N02 2-2	O15 3-1	M19 3-0	J01 0-1	S11 1-2	D27 1-4	J15 0-2	F26 5-3	a01 1-1	J07 3-4	S25 0-1	O01 0-2	a16 3-0
11 OXFORD U	J22 1-0	O16 2-2	F05 2-0	J08 3-2	M19 0-1	D11 3-1	S18 5-2	O26 1-2	S07 0-3	a23 1-0		a02 2-3	N06 2-1	N27 0-0	S04 2-2	D29 1-0	F19 1-2	D18 1-1	M01 4-2	a08 0-0	O02 1-1	a12 0-0	m07 2-2	M05 0-2
12 PETERBOROUGH U	M26 2-0	M05 0-1	M11 3-2	O06 0-3	S18 0-0	N06 0-1	F05 3-1	a26 1-2	O09 2-1	a12 3-1	O23 2-0		J03 4-2	m04 1-1	J15 0-0	S14 2-1	A21 0-2	N27 1-2	J29 2-1	S29 1-0	F19 0-0	m07 3-5	a23 0-2	S04 3-0
13 PORTSMOUTH	D27 1-0	N13 1-1	N02 2-1	A28 0-1	a09 0-0	F26 3-2	a30 1-2	S11 1-1	J18 2-2	M26 2-1	J01 1-1	O30 0-0		O23 1-1	D04 0-0	S25 0-2	a16 5-1	F12 0-3	M12 2-0	A24 2-1	a19 0-3	O09 1-1	J22 0-1	m14 3-1
14 PORT VALE	N13 2-2	D27 0-1	M14 1-0	A23 1-1	a26 4-1	S11 1-2	O30 2-0	M21 1-0	a09 1-4	O08 2-1	a30 2-1	M07 1-1	a02 1-0		N01 0-0	F28 1-0	m14 1-4	A28 2-0	S25 1-2	J22 2-2	a16 1-1	M11 0-0	O16 2-3	F07 0-2
15 PRESTON N.E.	A28 1-1	a02 0-1	F19 3-4	a19 2-2	O16 2-1	a26 1-0	M05 2-1	N27 3-0	J22 1-2	N06 3-0	F12 2-1	O12 6-2	m07 0-0	S14 4-0		a23 3-0	S18 0-0	M29 4-1	D17 2-1	F08 2-0	M19 1-0	a11 0-1	M15 2-1	O02 4-2
16 READING	N03 2-3	F26 1-3	O30 2-0	M19 2-0	J01 0-0	J22 1-2	m14 2-0	a02 1-2	a16 1-0	F19 2-4	a09 2-0	D27 1-0	M05 2-0	S18 1-1	N13 0-2		m11 0-3	O16 0-1	F05 0-0	O02 4-1	a30 0-0	S04 2-1	S08 2-0	F16 1-1
17 ROTHERHAM U	F12 0-0	A24 3-0	S25 1-1	D28 1-0	a02 1-1	m07 1-0	O02 3-2	M08 1-0	A28 3-0	a11 2-0	S11 1-1	J22 0-0	O26 2-2	D18 1-1	F26 2-0	m03 1-2		a12 0-1	N06 1-0	a23 1-1	O16 1-2	N27 1-0	F15 2-0	M19 1-1
18 SHEFFIELD W	J08 0-0	J25 1-0	O05 3-0	S18 4-1	N09 1-0	O09 2-0	a09 1-0	M12 1-1	O30 0-2	A25 2-1	m14 2-0	a30 4-0	S04 1-1	F05 1-2	a16 1-0	M26 2-1	N02 1-3		O23 0-1	F19 3-1	D04 3-1	A21 0-0	M05 3-1	D27 3-2
19 SHREWSBURY T	D04 1-0	J11 0-1	a09 2-0	O16 3-0	a16 1-1	A24 4-2	N13 2-1	J22 2-1	N02 0-0	S18 3-0	O30 1-0	a19 2-1	O02 4-1	M05 1-1	m14 1-2	A28 2-0	F01 0-0	a02 1-1		M19 2-2	D27 2-2	F19 1-2	F12 3-2	a30 2-1
20 SWINDON T	m10 2-1	a16 0-1	m14 2-1	F12 3-0	N02 1-1	S25 2-2	M08 4-1	F26 2-2	a30 0-1	O23 5-1	D27 1-0	a09 0-4	m17 4-3	A21 1-0	m03 0-1	M11 2-2	N13 2-4	S11 5-2	O09 1-0		O30 1-1	M26 2-2	A28 3-2	M29 5-1
21 TRANMERE R	S25 1-3	M28 1-2	A21 0-1	a12 2-1	A27 1-0	D17 2-0	O22 2-0	a23 2-2	M21 4-0	m02 2-1	M11 1-1	S11 2-0	J28 1-3	O25 1-1	O08 0-0	N26 2-1	M25 0-1	m06 1-0	a08 2-1	F21 0-1		D28 0-0	N05 0-0	J31 4-4
22 WALSALL	a16 1-0	m14 3-3	M22 1-0	a02 2-2	O30 0-0	A28 1-2	F01 1-0	S14 1-3	a19 1-2	M05 0-3	N02 2-2	D03 1-1	M19 1-1	O02 3-1	D27 0-1	F12 6-1	a30 0-1	J22 5-1	S11 3-3	O16 2-0	a09 2-0		F26 2-3	N13 1-2
23 WREXHAM	a30 0-0	O30 0-0	D27 4-2	F19 3-1	m11 2-4	O23 2-1	a16 3-2	O09 3-0	m14 0-1	M12 3-1	D04 1-1	N10 2-0	A21 2-0	M24 6-2	a09 2-0	J15 3-1	a18 2-1	S25 2-2	S04 1-0	F05 2-2	M07 2-0	S18 1-0		N01 1-1
24 YORK C	F26 0-1	A28 2-2	O23 0-2	J25 2-1	J22 2-1	J08 2-2	M26 1-1	F22 2-2	S11 0-1	O26 1-4	S25 2-1	F12 2-1	D18 1-4	N06 1-0	M12 0-2	m07 1-1	O09 1-1	a11 0-2	N27 0-3	a19 4-2	S07 1-0	a23 0-0	a12 0-0	

DIVISION 4

	ALDERSHOT	BARNSLEY	BOURNEMOUTH	BRADFORD C	BRENTFORD	CAMBRIDGE U	COLCHESTER U	CREWE A	DARLINGTON	DONCASTER R	EXETER C	HALIFAX T	HARTLEPOOL	HUDDERSFIELD T	NEWPORT CO	ROCHDALE	SCUNTHORPE U	SOUTHEND U	SOUTHPORT	STOCKPORT CO	SWANSEA C	TORQUAY U	WATFORD	WORKINGTON
1 ALDERSHOT		M26 0-1	J03 1-0	A21 2-1	S10 1-1	m18 1-3	a05 1-1	J29 1-1	M12 1-2	J15 1-0	M02 2-2	m04 0-0	N27 3-0	O23 1-0	F26 4-0	O27 0-2	a23 1-1	N06 0-0	A28 1-0	O09 2-0	S25 2-2	F12 0-1	a12 2-1	m07 2-0
2 BARNSLEY	O16 1-0		J29 3-1	S25 2-2	J22 2-0	a22 2-1	N27 0-1	O19 2-2	S11 1-1	M19 1-1	m03 3-4	D29 1-0	D18 3-0	O02 2-1	A28 2-0	m07 2-0	N06 5-1	O26 3-1	a02 1-0	F26 1-0	F12 1-0	N09 2-1	M09 1-1	a11 4-0
3 BOURNEMOUTH	O30 4-1	a19 1-0		D04 1-1	J01 3-1	F26 0-1	S25 0-0	O23 0-0	a16 0-1	m14 3-1	O09 2-0	J22 3-0	F12 2-0	J08 1-0	N02 1-0	M12 1-1	S11 2-2	A28 2-0	N13 5-0	a30 3-0	D27 1-1	a09 1-1	M26 2-1	A24 1-1
4 BRADFORD C	F09 3-1	M05 0-0	m07 1-1		O02 3-2	N06 0-0	D18 1-0	a11 1-0	A28 3-1	a02 3-1	J29 1-1	O27 3-0	D22 2-2	M19 3-1	O16 3-1	a06 3-0	m04 4-0	a23 2-0	F12 1-0	S11 3-3	A25 4-1	F26 3-2	N27 0-0	J03 4-1
5 BRENTFORD	F19 0-1	A21 0-1	N06 3-2	M12 4-0		N27 0-2	J03 1-4	m02 0-0	O23 0-3	S04 2-2	a12 1-0	J29 2-1	a23 3-1	F05 1-3	O09 1-1	F22 3-2	m07 4-2	a08 1-0	S18 3-0	J15 4-0	M26 4-0	M05 3-2	M23 3-0	O25 5-0
6 CAMBRIDGE U	a09 4-1	N13 0-0	S18 2-0	J01 2-1	a30 3-2		A21 2-0	F19 2-0	J29 4-0	m03 3-0	F05 1-1	a01 4-0	M19 2-0	N02 1-1	D27 3-1	J15 0-0	O15 1-0	O02 2-3	a16 5-1	D04 2-2	m14 2-3	O29 4-1	S04 4-0	M05 4-1
7 COLCHESTER U	D27 1-0	a29 1-0	M04 1-0	m14 2-1	O30 2-1	J21 0-1		S18 3-2	D04 4-0	a15 1-0	S04 3-1	A24 3-0	O16 6-2	a19 3-1	J01 5-0	F05 1-0	a02 1-1	M19 0-1	J18 4-1	N12 1-0	a08 1-1	N01 4-0	F19 1-0	O01 3-1
8 CREWE A	a20 1-0	D27 1-0	a02 2-1	N03 1-0	J08 3-2	S11 1-0	F26 1-0		M16 1-1	a30 1-2	M11 2-0	O16 3-1	A28 3-1	m14 0-0	M23 2-0	S25 1-1	F12 2-1	A25 1-1	a09 0-0	a06 2-1	O30 3-1	a16 2-1	O09 2-0	J22 1-1
9 DARLINGTON	O02 2-1	F19 2-1	O25 4-0	F05 0-0	a02 2-2	a18 0-2	m07 2-0	a23 4-0		M05 1-3	N27 2-1	N06 0-0	a08 3-1	S18 2-0	A23 1-0	a12 0-2	M07 5-2	F21 0-0	M19 2-1	S03 0-2	J22 0-4	O16 2-1	D18 0-0	D28 3-2
10 DONCASTER R	S14 1-2	O09 2-1	D18 0-0	O22 2-3	F12 5-0	J08 1-1	O25 3-2	N27 3-0	S25 4-0		m07 0-3	a12 3-0	N05 2-1	M25 2-0	S10 1-0	J11 2-0	a11 3-0	D28 0-3	J22 3-1	M11 1-0	F26 2-1	A28 0-4	a23 1-0	a19 6-3
11 EXETER C	m14 3-0	J08 1-0	M19 1-1	a20 0-0	N03 3-2	A28 1-1	F12 1-0	O02 3-0	a30 1-0	D04 0-2		F26 1-0	J22 3-1	N12 2-0	a09 1-0	S11 2-1	S29 2-0	a02 3-1	O30 3-1	a16 2-1	J01 2-0	D27 3-0	M05 2-2	O16 0-0
12 HALIFAX T	M22 2-0	a09 0-1	A21 2-3	a16 2-1	a19 0-0	O23 0-2	M08 1-2	M26 3-0	F14 2-1	N02 6-0	S18 1-2		S24 1-0	D27 0-0	a30 0-0	S04 0-0	O09 0-1	F19 3-1	m14 1-1	O30 2-1	N09 1-0	F08 2-0	M12 1-1	F05 6-1
13 HARTLEPOOL	a30 0-2	m14 0-2	S04 0-1	a09 0-1	N13 2-0	O09 2-2	M26 2-2	F05 3-0	D27 1-1	J01 0-0	A21 2-2	M05 1-0		O30 0-1	a16 0-1	O23 2-0	M12 3-0	S18 1-1	M28 1-1	N01 1-1	a18 2-2	J08 4-0	J15 1-0	F19 2-0
14 HUDDERSFIELD T	a02 2-0	M12 1-0	m03 0-0	O09 3-0	A28 1-0	a12 1-2	M21 0-0	D18 0-1	F26 3-1	O16 2-1	a23 0-1	a05 1-0	F15 4-1		F12 3-0	N26 2-1	D28 1-0	m07 1-1	S14 1-0	S25 2-0	S11 2-2	J22 2-1	O26 2-2	N06 2-1
15 NEWPORT CO	S18 2-1	M28 1-1	a12 1-0	M26 2-0	M18 3-1	a05 4-2	F22 1-2	m07 2-1	J14 0-1	M01 1-2	a26 0-3	N27 1-1	O26 1-1	S04 1-1		a23 3-0	J28 0-0	m10 3-0	M04 3-1	A21 0-1	O22 0-2	O02 0-0	m03 3-0	m17 1-0
16 ROCHDALE	a16 2-1	J25 2-3	O02 0-0	D27 0-1	m14 2-3	A23 2-2	A28 1-0	M05 0-1	N01 2-2	O30 1-0	F19 1-2	F12 4-1	a02 0-1	a30 2-2	N13 0-0		J22 5-0	O16 0-0	M01 3-0	a09 1-1	J08 1-0	a26 0-1	S18 3-1	M19 0-3
17 SCUNTHORPE U	N13 1-3	F08 1-2	F19 0-0	J08 2-1	J25 2-1	M26 0-2	O23 2-0	S03 4-0	O30 3-0	D27 1-1	M15 4-1	M19 2-1	O02 2-0	a09 0-4	a19 1-0	A21 0-1		M05 1-0	N02 1-1	m14 2-2	a16 0-3	a30 0-0	F05 0-0	S18 3-1
18 SOUTHEND U	J01 5-0	a15 1-1	F04 2-2	N12 4-1	D27 2-1	M11 0-1	O08 0-0	J15 1-0	m02 0-0	a09 2-1	O23 2-0	S10 1-1	F25 1-0	D04 1-1	O29 1-1	M25 3-0	S24 1-1		a29 3-2	J28 0-0	M15 1-2	m13 0-3	A21 2-1	S03 2-0
19 SOUTHPORT	F05 0-1	O22 1-0	a22 0-0	S03 0-4	M08 1-2	O26 0-0	m03 1-3	D29 0-0	O08 0-0	A21 2-2	J03 1-1	D18 0-0	m07 1-2	J15 2-2	S25 0-1	N06 1-1	a12 2-1	N27 0-0		M26 1-0	M11 1-3	S11 1-1	J29 1-3	a08 1-1
20 STOCKPORT CO	M19 0-0	S17 2-1	N26 1-0	M28 1-1	A23 2-0	m06 0-0	a22 1-1	N05 1-2	F11 2-2	O01 2-1	O25 0-0	J31 1-1	M07 1-0	M04 2-3	J21 2-1	D29 0-1	D17 1-0	a18 0-0	O15 2-2		A27 3-0	a01 2-1	a11 2-2	J07 1-0
21 SWANSEA C	M05 4-2	S04 2-1	a11 3-0	M01 2-3	O15 5-3	D18 3-1	D29 2-1	J04 3-0	A21 2-1	S18 1-1	N06 0-0	a23 2-1	J29 4-2	a26 2-1	a02 3-1	m03 3-2	D11 2-0	a12 2-0	O02 2-1	M22 4-4		M18 4-1	m07 1-4	N27 4-0
22 TORQUAY U	S04 0-1	J15 1-0	F16 2-1	S18 0-3	S25 1-1	J03 2-2	a11 2-2	O27 5-0	M26 2-0	F05 0-1	a08 0-1	m07 3-2	m04 1-0	A21 1-0	M12 1-0	J29 2-0	N27 1-3	D18 0-0	M23 0-0	O23 1-2	O09 2-1		N06 3-1	a23 3-1
23 WATFORD	N02 1-1	O30 1-0	O16 1-1	a30 1-1	a09 0-1	F12 2-0	S11 2-1	M19 3-1	m14 1-1	M29 5-1	S25 4-1	O02 0-0	A24 4-0	a16 2-0	J11 2-0	F26 3-1	A28 2-1	J22 1-1	a19 2-0	D27 1-1	D04 2-0	J01 4-0		a02 2-0
24 WORKINGTON	F16 1-1	N03 0-1	M09 1-1	O29 0-1	a16 1-3	S25 0-2	M12 2-4	A21 1-0	a09 2-3	J29 1-1	M26 1-3	A28 1-1	S11 1-1	J01 3-2	m14 0-1	O09 0-2	F26 1-0	F12 0-3	D27 2-2	m04 2-2	a30 1-3	N13 2-4	O23 0-1	

LEAGUE TABLES

DIVISION 1

	P	W	D	L	F	A	W	D	L	F	A	Pts
Liverpool	42	18	3	0	47	11	5	8	8	15	22	57
Manchester C	42	15	5	1	38	13	6	9	6	22	21	56
Ipswich T	42	15	4	2	41	11	7	4	10	25	28	52
Aston Villa	42	17	3	1	55	17	5	4	12	21	33	51
Newcastle U	42	14	6	1	40	15	4	7	10	24	34	49
Manchester U	42	12	6	3	41	22	6	5	10	30	40	47
W.B.A.	42	10	6	5	38	22	6	7	8	24	34	45
Arsenal	42	11	6	4	37	20	5	5	11	27	39	43
Everton	42	9	7	5	35	24	5	7	9	27	40	42
Leeds U	42	8	8	5	28	26	7	4	10	20	25	42
Leicester C	42	8	9	4	30	28	4	9	8	17	32	42
Middlesbrough	42	11	6	4	25	14	3	7	11	15	31	41
Birmingham C	42	10	6	5	38	25	3	6	12	25	36	38
Q.P.R.	42	10	7	4	31	21	3	5	13	16	31	38
Derby Co	42	9	9	3	36	18	0	10	11	14	37	37
Norwich C	42	12	4	5	30	23	2	5	14	17	41	37
West Ham U	42	9	6	6	28	23	2	8	11	18	42	36
Bristol C	42	8	7	6	25	19	3	6	12	13	29	35
Coventry C	42	7	9	5	34	26	3	6	12	14	33	35
Sunderland	42	9	5	7	29	16	2	7	12	17	38	34
Stoke C	42	9	8	4	21	16	1	6	14	7	35	34
Tottenham H	42	9	7	5	26	20	3	2	16	22	52	33

DIVISION 2

	P	W	D	L	F	A	W	D	L	F	A	Pts
Wolverh'pton W	42	15	3	3	48	21	7	10	4	36	24	57
Chelsea	42	15	6	0	51	22	6	7	8	22	31	55
Nottingham F	42	14	3	4	53	22	7	7	7	24	21	52
Bolton W	42	15	2	4	46	21	5	9	7	29	33	51
Blackpool	42	11	7	3	29	17	6	10	5	29	25	51
Luton T	42	13	5	3	39	17	8	1	12	28	31	48
Charlton A	42	14	5	2	52	27	2	11	8	19	31	48
Notts Co	42	11	5	5	29	20	8	5	8	36	40	48
Southampton	42	12	6	3	40	24	5	4	12	32	43	44
Millwall	42	9	6	6	31	22	6	7	8	26	31	43
Sheffield U	42	9	8	4	32	25	5	4	12	22	38	40
Blackburn R	42	12	4	5	31	18	3	5	13	11	36	39
Oldham A	42	11	6	4	37	23	3	4	14	15	41	38
Hull C	42	9	8	4	31	17	1	9	11	14	36	37
Bristol R	42	8	9	4	32	27	4	4	13	21	41	37
Burnley	42	8	9	4	27	20	3	5	13	19	44	36
Fulham	42	9	7	5	39	25	2	6	13	15	36	35
Cardiff C	42	7	6	8	30	30	5	4	12	26	37	34
Orient	42	4	8	9	18	23	5	8	8	19	32	34
Carlisle U	42	7	7	7	31	33	4	5	12	18	42	34
Plymouth A	42	5	9	7	27	25	3	7	11	19	40	32
Hereford U	42	6	9	6	28	30	2	6	13	29	48	31

DIVISION 3

	P	W	D	L	F	A	W	D	L	F	A	Pts
Mansfield T	46	17	6	0	52	13	11	2	10	26	29	64
Brighton & H.A.	46	19	3	1	63	14	6	8	9	20	26	61
Crystal Palace	46	17	5	1	46	15	6	8	9	22	25	59
Rotherham U	46	11	9	3	30	15	11	6	6	39	29	59
Wrexham	46	15	6	2	47	22	9	4	10	33	32	58
Preston N.E.	46	15	4	4	48	21	6	8	9	16	22	54
Bury	46	15	2	6	41	21	8	6	9	23	38	54
Sheffield W	46	15	4	4	39	18	7	5	11	26	37	53
Lincoln C	46	12	9	2	50	30	7	5	11	27	40	52
Shrewsbury T	46	13	7	3	40	21	5	4	14	25	38	47
Swindon T	46	12	6	5	48	33	3	9	11	20	42	45
Gillingham	46	11	8	4	31	21	5	4	14	24	43	44
Chester C	46	14	3	6	28	20	4	5	14	20	38	44
Tranmere R	46	10	7	6	31	23	3	10	10	20	30	43
Walsall	46	8	7	8	39	32	5	8	10	18	33	41
Peterborough U	46	11	4	8	33	28	2	11	10	22	37	41
Oxford U	46	9	8	6	34	29	3	7	13	21	36	39
Chesterfield	46	10	6	7	30	20	4	4	15	26	44	38
Port Vale	46	9	7	7	29	28	2	9	12	18	43	38
Portsmouth	46	8	9	6	28	26	3	5	15	25	44	36
Reading	46	10	5	8	29	24	3	4	16	20	49	35
Northampton T	46	9	4	10	33	29	4	4	15	27	46	34
Grimsby T	46	10	6	7	29	22	2	3	18	16	47	33
York C	46	7	8	8	25	34	3	4	16	25	55	32

DIVISION 4

	P	W	D	L	F	A	W	D	L	F	A	Pts
Cambridge U	46	16	5	2	57	18	10	8	5	30	22	65
Exeter C	46	17	5	1	40	13	8	7	8	30	33	62
Colchester U	46	19	2	2	51	14	6	7	10	26	29	59
Bradford C	46	16	7	0	51	18	7	6	10	27	33	59
Swansea C	46	18	3	2	60	30	7	5	11	32	38	58
Barnsley	46	16	5	2	45	18	7	4	12	17	21	55
Watford	46	15	7	1	46	13	3	8	12	21	37	51
Doncaster R	46	16	2	5	47	25	5	7	11	24	40	51
Huddersfield T	46	15	5	3	36	15	4	7	12	24	34	50
Southend U	46	11	9	3	35	19	4	10	9	17	26	49
Darlington	46	13	5	5	37	25	5	8	10	22	39	49
Crewe A	46	16	6	1	36	15	3	5	15	11	45	49
Bournemouth	46	13	8	2	39	13	2	10	11	15	31	48
Stockport Co	46	10	10	3	29	19	3	9	11	24	38	45
Brentford	46	14	3	6	48	27	4	4	15	29	49	43
Torquay U	46	12	5	6	33	22	5	4	14	26	45	43
Aldershot	46	10	8	5	29	19	6	3	14	20	40	43
Rochdale	46	8	7	8	32	25	5	5	13	18	34	38
Newport Co	46	11	6	6	33	21	3	4	16	9	37	38
Scunthorpe U	46	11	6	6	32	24	2	5	16	17	49	37
Halifax T	46	11	6	6	36	18	0	8	15	11	40	36
Hartlepool U	46	8	9	6	30	20	2	3	18	17	53	32
Southport	46	3	12	8	17	28	0	7	16	16	49	25
Workington	46	3	7	13	23	42	1	4	18	18	60	19

Top scorers: Div 1, R.Latchford (Everton) 30 goals; Div 2, R.Hatton (Blackpool) 22 goals; Div 3, A.Bruce (Preston North End) 27 goals; Div 4, S.Phillips (Brentford), A.Curtis (Swansea City) 32 goals.

Workington failed to gain re-election, Wimbledon were elected in their place. Hartlepool became Hartlepool United.

Bolton's Neil Whatmore netted 19 goals when the Trotters won the Division Two title in 1977-78. Altogether he scored 121 goals in 338 games for them.

DIVISION 1

	ARSENAL	ASTON VILLA	BIRMINGHAM C	BRISTOL C	CHELSEA	COVENTRY C	DERBY CO	EVERTON	IPSWICH T	LEEDS U	LEICESTER C	LIVERPOOL	MANCHESTER C	MANCHESTER U	MIDDLESBROUGH	NEWCASTLE U	NORWICH C	NOTTINGHAM F	Q.P.R.	W.B.A.	WEST HAM U	WOLVERHAMPTON W
1 ARSENAL		F04 0-1	O29 1-1	M18 4-1	D26 3-0	N12 1-1	N26 1-3	A23 1-0	J02 1-0	D10 1-1	S17 2-1	O04 0-0	M04 3-0	a01 3-1	a29 1-0	a15 2-1	F28 0-0	S03 3-0	O15 1-0	M25 4-0	O01 3-0	J14 3-1
2 ASTON VILLA	S10 1-0		O01 0-1	J28 1-0	a15 2-0	D26 1-1	M25 0-0	A27 1-2	a29 6-1	a26 3-1	M04 0-0	a01 0-3	A24 1-4	O29 2-1	N12 0-1	a17 2-0	O15 3-0	a05 0-1	J02 1-1	D10 3-0	M18 4-1	S23 2-0
3 BIRMINGHAM C	M21 1-1	F25 1-0		D27 3-0	D31 4-5	O08 1-1	O22 3-1	D17 0-0	a11 0-0	J14 2-3	N19 1-1	S03 0-1	a22 1-4	A20 1-4	F04 1-2	S17 3-0	a08 2-1	D03 0-2	O04 2-1	F28 1-2	M28 3-0	N05 2-1
4 BRISTOL C	O22 0-2	S03 1-1	M25 0-1		M21 3-0	a29 1-1	N12 3-1	M11 0-1	D10 2-0	O08 3-2	J14 0-0	a15 1-1	F17 2-2	a25 0-1	N26 4-1	a01 3-1	F04 3-0	D31 1-3	O01 2-2	D26 3-1	S17 3-2	A20 2-3
5 CHELSEA	M27 0-0	N19 0-0	A24 2-0	O29 1-0		A27 1-2	S10 1-1	D03 0-1	J21 5-3	O01 1-2	O05 0-0	M04 3-1	m05 0-0	F11 2-2	O15 0-0	M18 2-2	D17 1-1	N05 1-0	m02 3-1	J02 2-2	D27 2-1	a22 1-1
6 COVENTRY C	D17 1-2	M21 2-3	M04 4-0	D03 1-1	J14 5-1		A20 3-1	a08 3-2	O22 1-1	S03 2-2	M11 1-0	F04 1-0	O04 4-2	D31 3-0	S17 2-1	a04 0-0	D27 5-4	a22 0-0	N19 4-1	O01 1-2	N05 1-0	M28 4-0
7 DERBY CO	m09 3-0	D27 0-3	M18 1-3	D17 1-0	M11 1-1	J02 4-2		N05 0-1	A24 0-0	S17 2-2	a22 4-1	M08 4-2	D03 2-1	S03 0-1	O01 4-1	M04 1-1	O29 2-2	J14 0-0	M27 2-0	O15 1-1	N19 2-1	a08 3-1
8 EVERTON	D31 2-0	J14 1-0	N12 2-1	O15 1-0	a29 6-0	N26 6-0	a01 2-1		a15 1-0	M25 2-0	F04 2-0	a05 0-1	O01 1-1	D26 2-6	D10 3-0	O29 4-4	S17 3-0	A20 1-3	M04 3-3	O04 3-1	F18 2-1	S03 0-0
9 IPSWICH T	A20 1-0	D03 2-0	O15 5-2	a22 1-0	S03 1-0	M18 1-1	D31 1-2	N19 3-3		F04 0-1	D17 1-0	S17 1-1	N05 1-0	J14 1-2	M21 1-1	O01 2-1	M27 4-0	a25 0-2	D27 3-2	M04 2-2	O29 0-2	m09 1-2
10 LEEDS U	a22 1-3	O05 1-1	A27 1-0	M04 0-2	F25 2-0	J21 2-0	a12 2-0	D27 3-1	S10 2-1		M28 5-1	O15 1-2	D17 2-0	S24 1-1	M18 5-0	J02 0-2	N05 2-2	N19 1-0	D03 3-0	A24 2-2	a08 1-2	M27 2-1
11 LEICESTER C	F11 1-1	O08 0-2	a15 1-4	A27 0-0	a26 0-2	O15 1-2	D10 1-1	S10 1-5	N12 2-1	O29 0-0		N26 0-4	J02 0-1	M25 2-3	D26 0-0	a29 3-0	M18 2-2	S24 0-3	J21 0-0	a01 0-1	A24 1-0	F25 1-0
12 LIVERPOOL	a25 1-0	N05 1-2	J21 2-3	N19 1-1	O08 2-0	S10 2-0	S24 1-0	O22 0-0	a18 2-2	M11 1-0	a08 3-2		m01 4-0	F25 3-1	J02 2-0	A23 2-0	a22 3-0	m04 0-0	D17 1-0	A27 3-0	D03 2-0	D27 1-0
13 MANCHESTER C	O08 2-1	D31 2-0	D10 3-0	S24 2-0	N26 6-2	a25 3-1	a29 1-1	F25 1-0	a01 2-1	N12 2-3	A20 0-0	O29 3-1		S10 3-1	M25 2-2	D26 4-0	S03 4-0	a11 0-0	F11 2-1	a15 1-3	J14 3-2	O22 0-2
14 MANCHESTER U	N05 1-2	M29 1-1	J02 1-2	F08 1-1	S17 0-1	A24 2-1	J21 4-0	M27 1-2	A27 0-0	M01 0-1	D27 3-1	O01 2-0	M15 2-2		M04 0-0	O15 3-2	N19 1-0	D17 0-4	a08 3-1	M18 1-1	a22 3-0	D03 3-1
15 MIDDLESBROUGH	D03 0-1	D17 1-0	S10 1-2	a08 2-0	a04 2-0	a11 1-1	F25 3-1	a22 0-0	S24 1-1	O22 2-1	M27 0-1	A20 1-1	D27 0-2	O08 2-1		A27 2-0	D31 2-2	M29 2-2	N05 1-1	J21 1-0	a25 1-2	N19 0-0
16 NEWCASTLE U	N19 1-2	a08 1-1	M15 1-1	N05 1-1	O22 1-0	S24 1-2	O08 1-2	M24 0-2	F25 0-1	A20 3-2	D03 2-0	D31 0-2	M29 2-2	M11 2-2	J14 2-4		a26 2-2	D28 0-2	a22 0-3	S10 0-3	S03 2-3	D17 4-0
17 NORWICH C	S24 1-0	M11 2-1	N26 1-0	S10 1-0	N12 0-0	M25 1-2	M29 0-0	M15 0-0	D26 1-0	a01 3-0	O22 2-0	D10 2-1	J21 1-3	a15 1-3	A24 1-1	O05 2-1		F25 3-3	A27 1-1	a29 1-1	J02 2-2	O08 2-1
18 NOTTINGHAM F	J21 2-0	S17 2-0	a29 0-0	A23 1-0	a01 3-1	D10 2-1	A27 3-0	J02 1-1	O04 4-0	a15 1-1	M14 1-0	D26 1-1	O15 2-1	N12 2-1	O29 4-0	M25 2-0	O01 1-1		a18 1-0	N26 0-0	M04 2-0	F04 2-0
19 Q.P.R.	a11 2-1	A20 1-2	a25 0-0	F25 2-2	S24 1-1	a15 2-1	D26 0-0	O08 1-5	M25 3-3	a29 0-0	S03 3-0	N12 2-0	S17 1-1	N26 2-2	a01 1-0	D10 0-1	J14 2-1	O22 0-2		O29 2-1	M14 1-0	D31 1-3
20 W.B.A.	D27 1-3	a22 0-3	S24 3-1	M27 2-1	A20 3-0	F25 3-3	a18 1-0	a25 3-1	O08 1-0	D31 1-0	N05 2-0	J14 0-1	N19 0-0	O22 4-0	S03 2-1	a12 2-0	D03 0-0	m02 2-2	M22 2-0		D17 1-0	S17 2-2
21 WEST HAM U	F25 2-2	O22 2-2	D26 1-0	F11 1-2	M25 3-1	a01 2-1	a15 3-0	S24 1-1	M24 3-0	N26 0-1	D31 3-2	a29 0-2	A27 0-1	D10 2-1	O03 0-2	J21 1-0	A20 1-3	O08 0-0	S10 2-2	N12 3-3		M11 1-2
22 WOLVERHAMPTON W	A27 1-1	m02 3-1	a01 0-1	J02 0-0	D10 1-3	O29 1-3	O04 1-2	J21 3-1	N26 0-0	D26 3-1	O01 3-0	M25 1-3	M18 1-1	a29 2-1	a15 0-0	N12 1-0	M04 3-3	S10 2-3	A23 1-0	M14 1-1	O15 2-2	

Peter Withe, a key member of the Nottingham Forest side that won the League Championship for the first time. Three years later, Withe helped Villa to the title.

DIVISION 2

	BLACKBURN R	BLACKPOOL	BOLTON W	BRIGHTON & HA	BRISTOL R	BURNLEY	CARDIFF C	CHARLTON A	CRYSTAL P	FULHAM	HULL C	LUTON T	MANSFIELD T	MILLWALL	NOTTS CO	OLDHAM A	ORIENT	SHEFFIELD U	SOUTHAMPTON	STOKE C	SUNDERLAND	TOTTENHAM H
1 BLACKBURN R		S10 1-2	a26 0-1	a08 0-1	M11 0-1	M27 0-1	A27 3-0	O08 2-1	D03 3-0	M15 4-0	M24 1-1	F11 2-0	N19 3-1	D17 2-1	J02 1-0	F25 4-2	S24 1-0	a22 1-1	N05 2-1	O22 2-1	D27 1-1	A24 0-0
2 BLACKPOOL	F04 5-2		D27 0-2	D03 0-1	S03 3-1	M28 1-1	O01 3-0	J14 5-1	O04 3-1	a18 1-2	M11 3-0	O22 2-1	a22 1-2	N19 2-2	M07 2-2	A20 1-1	D31 0-0	N05 1-1	D17 0-1	a08 1-1	M27 1-1	S17. 0-2
3 BOLTON W	O03 4-2	M25 2-1		M04 1-1	a15 3-0	J02 1-2	D10 6-3	N12 2-1	a18 2-0	a29 0-0	J21 1-0	O29 2-1	O15 2-0	A23 2-1	D26 2-0	S10 1-0	a01 2-0	A27 2-1	M18 0-0	O01 1-1	M07 2-0	N26 1-0
4 BRIGHTON & H.A.	N26 2-2	a29 2-1	O08 1-2		D26 1-1	F11 2-1	O29 4-0	a25 1-0	O22 1-1	M25 2-0	S10 2-1	S27 3-2	J21 5-1	A27 3-2	a01 2-1	D10 1-1	N12 1-0	S24 2-1	J02 1-1	M11 2-1	F25 2-1	a15 3-1
5 BRISTOL R	O15 4-1	J21 2-0	N19 0-1	a18 0-4		M04 2-2	J02 3-2	F25 2-2	D27 3-0	A27 0-0	D03 1-1	S10 1-2	O04 3-1	N05 2-0	A23 2-2	S24 0-0	F11 2-1	a08 4-1	O29 0-0	a22 4-1	D17 3-2	M18 2-3
6 BURNLEY	D26 2-3	O29 0-1	A20 0-1	S17 0-0	O08 3-1		a15 4-2	D10 1-0	S03 1-1	a25 2-0	O22 1-1	a29 2-1	M14 2-0	O01 0-2	N12 3-1	M25 4-1	N26 0-0	M11 4-1	F04 3-3	J14 1-0	D31 0-0	a01 2-1
7 CARDIFF C	J14 1-1	F25 2-1	a22 1-0	M24 1-0	A20 1-1	N19 2-1		D31 1-0	a08 2-2	S24 3-1	D17 0-0	O08 1-4	S17 1-1	D28 4-1	m03 2-1	O22 1-0	m09 0-1	D03 1-6	M29 1-0	N05 2-0	J28 5-2	S03 0-0
8 CHARLTON A	M04 2-2	A27 3-1	D17 2-1	O04 4-3	S30 3-1	a22 3-2	a04 0-0		M24 1-0	J02 0-1	a08 0-1	J21 0-0	N05 2-2	F28 0-2	M17 0-0	F10 2-2	S10 2-1	N19 3-0	D27 1-3	M28 3-2	D03 3-2	O15 4-1
9 CRYSTAL P	a29 5-0	a25 2-2	S24 2-1	M18 0-0	M25 1-0	J21 1-1	N26 2-0	O29 1-1		O01 2-3	A27 0-1	D26 3-3	A23 3-1	J02 1-0	D10 2-0	a01 0-0	a15 1-0	F11 1-0	O15 1-2	M04 0-1	S10 2-2	N12 1-2
10 FULHAM	S03 0-0	O08 1-1	D03 2-0	D28 2-1	J14 1-1	O04 4-1	M07 1-0	A20 1-1	F25 1-1		N19 2-0	M10 1-0	M27 0-2	a22 0-1	S17 5-1	D30 0-2	O22 1-2	M24 2-0	a07 1-1	D17 3-0	N05 3-3	F04 1-1
11 HULL C	O29 0-1	O15 2-0	S03 0-0	F04 1-1	a29 0-1	M18 1-3	N12 4-1	N26 0-2	J14 1-0	a15 0-1		a01 1-1	O01 0-2	M04 3-2	M25 1-1	D26 0-1	D10 2-2	D31 2-3	a11 0-3	S17 0-0	A20 3-0	O04 2-0
12 LUTON T	S17 0-0	M18 4-0	M21 2-1	D31 1-0	F08 1-1	D03 1-2	M04 3-1	S03 7-1	M27 1-0	O15 1-0	N05 1-1		D17 1-1	O04 1-0	O01 2-0	J14 0-1	A20 1-0	D27 4-0	a22 1-2	N19 1-2	a08 1-3	F22 1-4
13 MANSFIELD T	a15 2-2	D10 1-3	M11 0-1	S03 1-2	a24 3-0	S24 4-1	F11 2-2	a01 0-3	D31 1-3	D26 2-1	F25 1-0	N12 3-1		S10 0-0	O29 1-3	N26 0-2	a29 1-1	O08 1-1	J14 1-2	A20 2-1	O22 1-2	M25 3-3
14 MILLWALL	N12 1-1	a15 2-0	D31 1-0	J14 0-1	a01 1-3	F25 1-1	M25 1-1	S24 1-1	A20 0-3	D10 0-3	O08 1-1	a25 1-0	m02 1-0		N26 0-0	a29 2-0	M21 2-0	O22 1-1	S17 3-0	S03 0-0	a18 3-1	D26 1-3
15 NOTTS CO	A20 1-1	S24 1-1	M27 1-1	N05 1-0	D31 3-2	D17 3-0	S10 1-1	O22 2-0	a22 2-0	a04 1-1	D27 2-1	F25 2-0	M21 1-0	a08 1-1		M11 3-2	O08 1-1	a25 1-2	S03 2-3	D03 2-0	N19 2-2	J14 3-3
16 OLDHAM A	O01 0-2	J02 2-1	F18 2-2	a22 1-1	a04 4-1	D27 2-0	M18 1-1	S17 1-1	N05 1-1	A23 2-0	M27 2-1	A27 1-0	a08 0-1	D03 2-2	O15 2-1		J21 2-1	D17 3-0	N19 1-1	O04 1-1	M24 1-1	M04 1-1
17 ORIENT	a04 0-0	A23 1-4	N05 1-1	D17 0-1	S17 2-1	a18 3-0	O15 2-1	m03 0-0	N19 0-0	M17 1-1	a22 2-1	J02 0-0	D03 4-2	O29 0-0	M04 0-0	S03 5-3		M27 3-1	a25 1-1	D27 2-0	J14 2-2	O01 1-1
18 SHEFFIELD U	D10 2-0	a01 0-0	J14 1-5	a04 2-0	N26 1-1	O15 2-1	a29 0-1	a15 1-0	S17 0-2	O29 2-1	A23 2-0	M25 4-1	M04 2-0	M18 5-2	O04 4-1	N12 1-0	D26 2-0		O01 3-2	M14 1-2	S03 1-1	J02 2-2
19 SOUTHAMPTON	a01 5-0	N12 2-0	O22 2-2	A20 1-1	M27 3-1	S10 3-0	D26 3-1	M25 4-1	M11 2-0	N26 2-0	S24 1-0	D10 0-1	A27 1-0	F11 2-3	J21 3-1	a15 2-2	O04 1-0	F25 2-1		D31 1-0	O08 4-2	a29 0-0
20 STOKE C	M18 4-2	N26 1-2	F25 0-0	O15 1-0	D10 3-2	A27 2-1	a01 2-0	D26 4-0	O08 0-2	N12 2-0	M08 1-0	a15 0-0	J02 1-1	a12 2-1	a29 1-1	a26 3-0	M25 5-1	S10 4-0	A24 1-0		S24 0-0	O29 1-3
21 SUNDERLAND	M25 0-1	D26 2-1	S17 0-2	O01 0-2	N12 5-1	A23 3-0	O04 1-1	a29 3-0	M14 0-0	a01 2-2	J02 2-0	N26 1-1	M18 1-0	O15 2-0	a15 3-1	O29 3-1	A27 1-1	J21 5-1	M04 0-0	a04 1-0		D10 1-2
22 TOTTENHAM H	D31 4-0	F11 2-2	a08 1-0	N19 0-0	O22 9-0	N05 3-0	J21 2-1	M11 2-1	D17 2-2	S10 1-0	a26 1-0	S24 2-0	D27 1-1	M27 3-3	A27 2-1	O08 5-1	F25 1-1	A20 4-2	D03 0-0	M22 3-1	a22 2-3	

SEASON 1977-78

DIVISION 3

	BRADFORD C	BURY	CAMBRIDGE U	CARLISLE U	CHESTER	CHESTERFIELD	COLCHESTER U	EXETER C	GILLINGHAM	HEREFORD U	LINCOLN C	OXFORD U	PETERBOROUGH U	PLYMOUTH A	PORTSMOUTH	PORT VALE	PRESTON N.E.	ROTHERHAM U	SHEFFIELD W	SHREWSBURY T	SWINDON T	TRANMERE R	WALSALL	WREXHAM
1 BRADFORD C		N12 2-1	A20 4-0	M11 2-2	S10 2-2	D31 1-3	J07 1-2	a15 1-2	M01 2-1	O22 0-0	D03 2-2	A27 2-3	S28 2-1	S24 0-1	a01 1-0	M08 1-1	O08 1-1	F25 3-0	O29 3-2	S27 2-0	a26 2-1	M14 2-0	a29 2-3	D26 2-1
2 BURY	a08 2-2		J07 5-2	D31 1-1	N19 1-1	O22 0-0	D27 1-1	J21 5-0	S13 2-2	a25 1-1	A20 1-0	D10 3-2	O08 0-0	a22 1-1	M11 0-0	F25 3-0	M27 1-1	N05 1-1	S03 3-0	S24 0-3	J28 0-0	S27 1-0	M14 0-1	M24 2-3
3 CAMBRIDGE U	J14 4-1	N08 3-0		O08 2-0	J28 0-0	a15 2-0	O22 2-0	a29 2-1	A27 2-3	M11 2-0	N12 5-0	O29 2-1	J02 1-0	F11 3-0	M25 1-0	D26 2-0	F25 1-1	S24 1-1	D03 3-0	M07 2-0	S27 5-2	S10 1-0	a01 2-1	a25 1-0
4 CARLISLE U	O15 1-1	a01 0-3	M04 1-1		S20 0-0	O29 2-1	O01 1-3	a03 2-0	M18 1-0	a11 2-0	O04 2-3	S17 2-2	M07 0-0	A27 0-0	N12 3-1	D03 1-1	S10 3-1	F07 2-1	J02 1-0	a15 1-0	a29 2-2	J14 2-2	D26 2-0	M27 1-4
5 CHESTER	F04 3-2	a15 1-0	S02 0-0	M01 2-2		D03 2-1	J21 2-1	a01 2-1	S17 2-2	A20 4-1	D31 2-2	a12 3-1	a29 4-3	O08 1-1	a26 2-0	N12 2-1	M24 1-2	M11 2-1	S14 2-1	D26 1-0	O22 1-0	F25 0-0	M27 1-1	S28 1-1
6 CHESTERFIELD	N05 2-0	M18 2-1	N19 2-1	M28 2-1	a22 1-2		O05 0-0	O01 0-0	a26 5-2	S14 2-1	M01 0-0	J02 3-0	A27 2-0	a08 4-1	J28 3-0	J14 2-0	D27 0-1	M27 0-0	M04 2-2	S07 3-1	m03 3-1	D10 1-1	O15 0-1	S17 1-0
7 COLCHESTER U	A23 3-0	M25 1-0	M17 2-1	F25 2-2	A27 2-0	a04 2-0		D09 3-1	J13 1-1	O08 0-0	D26 1-1	O14 1-1	O28 3-0	S09 3-1	M07 4-0	S27 2-3	S24 0-0	m03 0-0	a29 1-1	a01 1-2	N11 2-0	J27 0-0	J02 1-1	a15 1-1
8 EXETER C	N19 1-0	A27 2-2	D03 2-4	S26 0-1	J02 1-1	a18 0-0	a22 0-0		a08 2-1	D27 1-0	M11 3-0	N05 2-1	F11 1-0	M28 0-0	S24 0-1	S10 4-1	O22 2-0	M08 1-0	O12 2-1	J28 1-1	M22 0-0	a26 4-2	J14 1-1	O08 0-1
9 GILLINGHAM	S03 4-1	M07 1-4	J21 3-1	O22 1-1	F21 1-0	S27 3-0	A20 1-3	N12 1-0		J07 4-0	a29 0-0	S10 2-1	M25 0-0	F25 1-1	D26 0-0	a04 1-1	M11 2-1	O08 2-1	a15 2-1	O29 1-1	D31 2-2	S24 1-1	D03 3-1	a01 0-0
10 HEREFORD U	M18 2-1	O05 1-0	O15 0-0	S24 1-0	J14 2-2	M08 2-1	M04 1-0	M25 4-0	S07 2-0		a05 1-1	O01 2-1	D26 0-0	J28 1-3	a15 0-2	O29 1-1	F11 0-0	S10 2-3	a01 0-1	J02 1-1	D03 1-1	A27 0-1	N12 3-2	a29 1-1
11 LINCOLN C	a22 3-2	J14 0-0	a08 4-1	a26 2-1	N05 2-1	S23 1-0	M27 0-0	O15 1-2	D10 0-2	S28 0-0		M08 1-0	S10 0-1	J02 2-2	F11 1-0	M28 3-0	N19 2-2	M24 3-3	M18 3-1	A26 1-3	O08 3-1	D27 1-1	A24 2-2	F24 0-1
12 OXFORD U	J21 3-1	a29 0-0	J11 2-3	F11 0-0	S24 4-1	a01 1-1	M11 3-0	D31 0-0	F04 1-1	F25 3-0	S14 1-0		a26 3-3	O22 2-1	S28 0-0	M25 1-1	S03 1-0	A20 2-3	N12 1-0	D03 1-1	D26 3-3	O08 1-0	a15 3-1	M01 2-1
13 PETERBOROUGH U	a04 5-0	M04 2-1	N05 2-0	S13 2-1	D10 0-0	a11 2-0	M14 1-0	S17 1-1	D27 1-1	M28 2-1	F04 0-1	O04 1-0		N19 1-0	A20 0-0	M17 1-1	D31 1-0	a08 1-0	F22 2-1	O15 2-1	a18 2-0	a22 1-0	O01 0-0	S03 2-2
14 PLYMOUTH A	m01 6-0	D03 0-1	S17 0-1	J21 0-1	M04 2-2	N12 2-0	F04 1-1	D26 2-2	O01 1-3	S03 2-0	M13 1-2	M18 2-1	a15 1-0		O29 3-1	a29 3-2	A20 0-0	a11 1-1	a04 1-1	O04 2-2	M25 0-2	O15 0-1	O13 3-3	D31 0-1
15 PORTSMOUTH	J02 3-1	O15 1-1	D27 2-2	a08 3-3	O04 0-0	S03 3-0	S13 0-0	F28 1-1	M27 1-1	N19 2-0	S17 0-2	a04 0-2	J14 2-2	M21 1-5		N15 1-1	a22 0-2	D10 3-3	O01 2-2	M18 2-0	J20 1-2	N05 2-5	M04 1-2	F04 0-1
16 PORT VALE	S12 1-0	O01 1-2	M28 1-1	a22 0-1	a08 0-0	A20 1-3	a24 0-3	F08 4-0	O10 2-2	M22 1-0	S03 2-1	D27 1-1	O22 0-0	D09 3-3	J07 2-0		N05 0-0	D31 3-0	S17 0-0	M04 1-2	M11 1-0	N19 1-1	F28 2-2	a11 1-1
17 PRESTON N.E.	M04 3-1	D26 4-0	O01 2-0	F04 2-1	O29 2-1	M25 0-0	F28 4-0	M18 0-0	O15 2-0	S17 0-0	a15 4-0	F21 3-2	a01 0-1	J14 5-2	D03 3-1	J02 2-0		A27 3-2	O04 2-1	a29 2-2	S13 1-1	O25 2-1	a04 1-0	N12 1-3
18 ROTHERHAM U	O01 2-1	J02 0-3	M14 1-0	S03 0-0	O15 1-1	D26 1-2	S17 1-0	S13 1-0	M04 2-0	a18 1-0	O29 0-0	J14 2-0	N12 0-1	O11 1-2	a29 0-1	a01 2-0	a25 2-1		M25 1-2	a04 0-0	a15 1-3	M18 2-0	O04 3-0	D03 2-2
19 SHEFFIELD W	M21 2-0	J28 3-2	a22 0-0	N05 3-1	M07 1-1	O08 1-0	D03 1-2	J17 2-1	N19 0-0	D31 1-0	O22 2-0	a08 2-1	S24 0-1	S27 1-1	F25 0-0	F11 3-1	a18 1-0	D27 1-0		S10 0-1	A20 1-1	M27 1-0	A27 0-0	m03 2-1
20 SHREWSBURY T	D27 4-0	a18 5-3	S13 3-3	N19 0-3	M25 0-0	J31 1-1	D31 1-0	S03 0-2	D06 1-2	N05 3-0	J21 0-1	a22 1-0	M11 0-0	a25 3-1	O22 6-1	O08 3-0	D10 0-0	S27 4-1	F28 0-0		J25 2-3	a08 3-1	S17 0-0	A20 2-1
21 SWINDON T	O04 0-1	S16 1-1	a04 0-0	D10 2-2	M17 1-1	S10 2-1	a08 0-0	O29 4-0	N05 3-2	a22 1-0	M04 1-0	M27 3-2	A23 2-0	D27 3-1	A27 3-1	O15 1-1	M07 0-2	N19 2-0	J14 2-2	S30 5-0		J02 1-0	a11 2-3	M14 1-2
22 TRANMERE R	S16 0-0	a03 0-0	F03 0-1	A20 3-2	S30 5-0	a28 1-1	S02 1-0	O03 2-1	a11 1-1	J20 2-1	M25 3-1	D16 4-1	D02 0-2	M10 1-1	D30 2-0	a14 2-1	J06 1-0	O21 2-2	D26 3-1	N12 2-0	M31 1-1		O28 0-1	S12 3-1
23 WALSALL	D10 1-1	S10 1-2	D31 0-0	M25 0-0	D27 3-0	M11 2-2	N05 4-2	A20 1-3	a22 2-1	a08 2-0	F07 3-1	N19 2-1	F25 1-0	M07 1-0	O08 1-1	S24 2-0	S27 0-0	m01 3-1	a25 1-1	F11 3-0	S03 2-0	J17 0-0		O22 0-1
24 WREXHAM	M25 2-0	O29 3-1	O03 4-1	D27 3-1	a03 1-2	F11 1-1	N19 2-1	M04 2-1	J02 3-3	D10 2-1	O01 1-0	A22 2-2	m01 0-0	N05 2-0	S10 2-0	A27 1-1	a08 0-0	a22 7-1	O15 1-1	J14 0-0	S24 2-1	M06 6-1	M18 1-0	

DIVISION 4

	ALDERSHOT	BARNSLEY	BOURNEMOUTH	BRENTFORD	CREWE A	DARLINGTON	DONCASTER R	GRIMSBY T	HALIFAX T	HARTLEPOOL U	HUDDERSFIELD T	NEWPORT CO	NORTHAMPTON T	READING	ROCHDALE	SCUNTHORPE U	SOUTHEND U	SOUTHPORT	STOCKPORT CO	SWANSEA C	TORQUAY U	WATFORD	WIMBLEDON	YORK C
1 ALDERSHOT		S10 0-0	O29 2-0	D26 1-0	S28 2-0	F28 3-2	A27 1-0	M17 4-2	a15 0-0	a29 3-0	J28 3-3	O08 2-2	a01 2-1	a04 1-1	S24 2-0	D03 4-0	M25 3-0	J02 0-0	A24 2-1	F25 2-2	N12 3-0	O15 1-0	M08 3-1	J14 1-1
2 BARNSLEY	F07 2-0		M31 3-0	N12 0-0	D26 4-0	J07 2-1	M04 0-0	O14 1-2	a04 3-2	O29 3-2	M18 1-1	S03 1-0	a15 2-3	D03 4-1	A20 4-0	S13 3-0	D31 1-1	M25 2-1	F18 0-1	a11 0-2	O04 2-0	S17 1-0	a29 3-2	O01 2-1
3 BOURNEMOUTH	M24 0-0	J02 2-2		F04 3-2	J14 1-0	N19 2-0	O05 0-1	a22 1-0	S17 0-0	M04 1-0	D10 1-0	M28 4-2	M17 1-1	O25 1-0	a08 1-0	J21 1-1	S03 0-3	O01 3-1	N05 1-0	D27 0-1	M14 1-1	a04 1-2	O15 1-2	S13 2-1
4 BRENTFORD	M27 2-0	a08 2-0	S10 1-1		J28 5-1	a22 2-0	a18 2-2	D10 3-1	O01 4-1	M18 2-0	J02 1-1	D27 3-3	A20 3-0	A27 1-1	M06 4-0	S24 2-0	O29 1-0	O15 0-0	a03 4-0	N19 0-2	M04 3-0	O03 0-3	A22 4-1	N05 1-0
5 CREWE A	a25 0-2	M27 2-1	A20 3-1	S03 4-6		D31 2-2	a22 2-0	N19 0-2	F22 0-0	O01 1-0	D27 1-1	S14 2-0	O14 3-2	M17 1-1	N05 2-1	J07 1-1	F01 0-1	a11 2-0	D09 1-1	a08 2-1	S17 2-0	M24 2-2	M04 0-0	O05 1-0
6 DARLINGTON	S17 1-1	S06 0-2	a15 1-0	D02 1-3	a01 2-0		M18 1-1	J14 1-2	S13 2-1	M25 1-2	O15 2-2	F04 2-1	O04 2-0	J02 2-0	J24 1-0	a29 1-1	N12 2-0	D26 3-0	O01 2-2	S03 1-1	a03 0-0	a18 0-0	O29 3-1	M04 0-2
7 DONCASTER R	a11 4-3	O08 2-1	a25 0-0	S17 3-1	D03 2-0	O21 1-2		F28 0-1	D31 1-1	a15 2-0	F25 4-3	A20 2-2	N12 4-2	a29 2-2	M10 1-1	D26 1-1	S27 2-0	S20 2-1	F04 1-0	J10 1-1	a01 1-0	S03 0-1	M25 0-2	M28 1-1
8 GRIMSBY T	O22 1-0	M11 1-0	D03 0-2	a29 2-1	a15 2-2	A20 2-0	S24 0-0		D26 0-0	S13 2-1	M24 1-0	F25 1-0	M25 0-1	N12 0-1	S03 2-1	O08 0-0	a01 2-0	a25 2-0	J21 0-0	a18 2-1	D31 3-1	a11 1-1	O04 3-1	F04 3-2
9 HALIFAX T	N19 2-1	S27 1-1	F28 0-0	F25 1-1	S10 1-1	M07 0-2	N05 0-1	M27 0-0		A23 3-0	O08 0-0	a08 3-1	A27 0-1	a18 2-4	D17 3-1	M28 2-2	S24 0-1	M18 2-1	D27 1-1	D10 3-1	O15 0-0	a22 1-1	J14 1-2	J02 2-0
10 HARTLEPOOL U	D10 2-2	M24 1-2	O08 0-1	O22 3-1	F25 1-1	D27 2-1	N19 0-2	M07 3-1	F07 1-1		a25 3-2	a22 1-1	a11 0-2	S24 2-1	S27 1-0	S03 1-0	M11 1-0	F28 2-1	a08 2-0	D31 0-4	A20 1-2	N05 1-2	S10 2-0	M14 4-2
11 HUDDERSFIELD T	S03 1-1	O22 2-0	a29 2-0	a01 1-3	M25 3-0	M11 2-1	O01 4-1	O29 1-3	M04 2-2	O04 3-1		J21 2-0	a04 0-1	a15 0-2	J07 3-1	D31 4-1	D26 2-0	D02 3-1	S17 0-0	A20 0-0	S13 1-1	M14 1-0	D17 3-0	a11 1-2
12 NEWPORT CO	M04 2-1	F28 3-1	D26 3-2	M25 1-2	M07 1-0	S10 1-1	J14 1-0	O01 3-0	N12 2-0	D03 4-2	A27 2-0		J02 5-3	a01 0-0	F11 3-0	O04 3-1	a29 1-2	a15 1-1	O15 2-2	S24 1-0	O29 0-0	M17 2-2	a25 0-1	S06 2-1
13 NORTHAMPTON T	D31 1-1	N19 1-1	O22 1-0	J14 2-2	M11 0-0	a25 2-2	a08 0-0	D27 2-1	M14 1-2	S17 5-3	S27 3-1	N05 2-4		O08 0-2	O11 3-1	F25 1-2	M21 0-0	F04 1-0	S13 2-1	a22 3-1	S03 1-0	M28 0-2	F28 0-3	D10 1-1
14 READING	O05 1-0	a22 0-0	J07 0-0	a12 0-0	O22 2-0	N05 2-1	D10 3-0	a08 0-0	S03 2-1	F18 2-3	N19 1-0	D31 2-0	M04 0-0		D28 4-3	M11 1-0	A20 0-1	S17 3-1	M27 2-1	M24 1-4	F08 3-3	S14 1-3	O01 2-2	a26 1-0
15 ROCHDALE	m01 0-0	J14 1-1	N12 1-1	S13 1-2	J02 0-2	A27 2-0	O15 3-1	M20 1-3	O04 3-1	a04 0-1	O17 0-0	S17 0-1	O29 1-1	a24 1-0		a15 1-1	D03 1-2	a01 2-1	M04 2-1	F27 2-1	a29 1-3	O01 2-3	D26 3-0	M18 1-2
16 SCUNTHORPE U	a22 1-1	M07 1-0	A26 0-0	M14 1-1	A23 3-0	D10 3-0	M27 0-0	M03 2-1	O29 2-0	a18 2-0	N05 1-1	a04 2-0	O01 2-2	O15 0-1	N19 1-0		S10 1-2	J14 0-2	J02 3-0	S27 1-0	M18 0-1	a08 0-1	S17 3-0	D27 2-1
17 SOUTHEND U	D27 3-1	N04 0-0	J27 5-1	M24 2-1	A26 1-0	a07 2-0	a03 4-0	J02 1-1	F17 5-0	O14 1-1	M27 1-3	D09 4-2	A22 0-0	J13 0-2	a21 3-1	F03 2-0		M04 4-2	O03 0-2	S12 2-1	S30 4-0	N19 1-0	M17 1-0	S16 0-0
18 SOUTHPORT	N05 1-1	D27 1-1	F25 0-0	M11 1-3	S23 1-2	M27 1-0	M07 1-1	S27 2-2	O21 1-2	A27 1-1	a22 1-1	N19 3-3	S09 3-1	M14 1-1	D31 3-1	A20 1-1	O07 0-0		M24 2-0	a04 0-3	J07 0-0	D10 2-2	a17 0-5	a07 4-1
19 STOCKPORT CO	J06 2-1	S23 3-0	D30 2-1	S26 1-1	a28 1-2	F24 1-0	S09 1-1	A26 2-0	M25 1-3	N11 6-0	F27 0-1	M10 2-0	M06 1-2	D26 2-0	O07 2-0	M31 1-1	a24 1-0	O28 2-1		O22 2-0	a14 3-0	A20 1-3	D02 2-2	J27 2-0
20 SWANSEA C	O01 1-0	A27 2-1	M25 1-0	a15 2-1	N12 5-0	J28 1-2	A23 3-0	S16 2-0	a29 2-0	a01 8-0	J14 1-0	F17 4-0	D03 2-4	O29 2-1	S10 3-0	a25 3-1	M07 0-0	O04 1-1	M17 3-1		D26 1-1	M03 3-3	J02 3-0	O15 1-1
21 TORQUAY U	a08 1-2	a26 3-1	S24 1-1	O08 2-1	M01 1-2	S26 0-0	J02 2-0	N05 3-1	M11 2-2	J14 0-0	M08 2-1	M22 2-0	J28 2-1	S10 3-0	D10 3-0	O22 4-2	a18 0-1	O12 2-2	N19 2-0	M27 2-4		D27 2-3	A27 1-1	a22 3-0
22 WATFORD	M11 1-0	F11 0-0	S27 2-1	a25 1-1	O29 5-2	S24 2-1	J28 6-0	S06 1-0	D03 1-1	J02 1-0	S10 2-0	O22 2-0	D26 3-0	M07 1-0	F25 1-0	N12 4-1	a15 1-1	a29 3-2	J13 1-0	O08 2-1	M25 1-0		a01 2-0	A27 1-3
23 WIMBLEDON	S13 1-2	D10 0-0	M11 3-1	J07 1-1	O08 0-0	N07 1-1	D28 3-3	a04 2-2	A20 3-3	F20 3-0	a08 2-0	S27 3-0	S24 2-0	F24 1-1	M27 5-1	F11 0-0	O22 1-3	S03 2-2	a22 2-0	N05 1-1	J21 0-1	D31 1-3		N19 2-1
24 YORK C	A20 1-2	F24 1-2	M07 0-0	D31 3-2	a04 1-1	O07 1-2	O28 2-1	S10 1-2	M31 1-1	D26 1-0	S24 1-1	J07 2-0	a29 0-3	S27 2-0	O21 2-2	M24 0-2	F28 1-2	N12 2-1	S02 2-1	M11 2-1	D03 0-0	J21 0-4	a15 1-1	

LEAGUE TABLES

DIVISION 1

	P	W	D	L	F	A	W	D	L	F	A	Pts
Nottingham F	42	15	6	0	37	8	10	8	3	32	16	64
Liverpool	42	15	4	2	37	11	9	5	7	28	23	57
Everton	42	14	4	3	47	22	8	7	6	29	23	55
Arsenal	42	14	5	2	38	12	7	5	9	22	25	52
Manchester C	42	14	4	3	46	21	6	8	7	28	30	52
W.B.A.	42	13	5	3	35	18	5	9	7	27	35	50
Coventry C	42	13	5	3	48	23	5	7	9	27	39	48
Aston Villa	42	11	4	6	33	18	7	6	8	24	24	46
Leeds U	42	12	4	5	39	21	6	6	9	24	32	46
Manchester U	42	9	6	6	32	23	7	4	10	35	40	42
Birmingham C	42	8	5	8	32	30	8	4	9	23	30	41
Derby Co	42	10	7	4	37	24	4	6	11	17	35	41
Norwich C	42	10	8	3	28	20	1	10	10	24	46	40
Middlesbrough	42	8	8	5	25	19	4	7	10	17	35	39
Wolverh'pton W	42	7	8	6	30	27	5	4	12	21	37	36
Chelsea	42	7	11	3	28	20	4	3	14	18	49	36
Bristol C	42	9	6	6	37	26	2	7	12	12	27	35
Ipswich T	42	10	5	6	32	24	1	8	12	15	37	35
Q.P.R.	42	8	8	5	27	26	1	7	13	20	38	33
West Ham U	42	8	6	7	31	28	4	2	15	21	41	32
Newcastle U	42	4	6	11	26	37	2	4	15	16	41	22
Leicester C	42	4	7	10	16	32	1	5	15	10	38	22

DIVISION 2

	P	W	D	L	F	A	W	D	L	F	A	Pts
Bolton W	42	16	4	1	39	14	8	6	7	24	19	58
Southampton	42	15	4	2	44	16	7	9	5	26	23	57
Tottenham H	42	13	7	1	50	19	7	9	5	33	30	56
Brighton & H.A.	42	15	5	1	43	21	7	7	7	20	17	56
Blackburn R	42	12	4	5	33	16	4	9	8	23	44	45
Sunderland	42	11	6	4	36	17	3	10	8	31	42	44
Stoke C	42	13	5	3	38	16	3	5	13	15	33	42
Oldham A	42	9	10	2	32	20	4	6	11	22	38	42
Crystal Palace	42	9	7	5	31	20	4	8	9	19	27	41
Fulham	42	9	8	4	32	19	5	5	11	17	30	41
Burnley	42	11	6	4	35	20	4	4	13	21	44	40
Sheffield U	42	13	4	4	38	22	3	4	14	24	51	40
Luton T	42	11	4	6	35	20	3	6	12	19	32	38
Orient	42	8	11	2	30	20	2	7	12	13	29	38
Notts Co	42	10	9	2	36	22	1	7	13	18	40	38
Millwall	42	8	8	5	23	20	4	6	11	26	37	38
Charlton A	42	11	6	4	38	27	2	6	13	17	41	38
Bristol R	42	10	7	4	40	26	3	5	13	21	51	38
Cardiff C	42	12	6	3	32	23	1	6	14	19	48	38
Blackpool	42	7	8	6	35	25	5	5	11	24	35	37
Mansfield T	42	6	6	9	30	34	4	5	12	19	35	31
Hull C	42	6	6	9	23	25	2	6	13	11	27	28

DIVISION 3

	P	W	D	L	F	A	W	D	L	F	A	Pts
Wrexham	46	14	8	1	48	19	9	7	7	30	26	61
Cambridge U	46	19	3	1	49	11	4	9	10	23	40	58
Preston N.E.	46	16	5	2	48	19	4	11	8	15	19	56
Peterborough U	46	15	7	1	32	11	5	9	9	15	22	56
Chester C	46	14	8	1	41	24	2	14	7	18	32	54
Walsall	46	12	8	3	35	17	6	9	8	26	33	53
Gillingham	46	11	10	2	36	21	4	10	9	31	39	50
Colchester U	46	10	11	2	36	16	5	7	11	19	28	48
Chesterfield	46	14	6	3	40	16	3	8	12	18	33	48
Swindon T	46	12	7	4	40	22	4	9	10	27	38	48
Shrewsbury T	46	11	7	5	42	23	5	8	10	21	34	47
Tranmere R	46	13	7	3	39	19	3	8	12	18	33	47
Carlisle U	46	10	9	4	32	26	4	10	9	27	33	47
Sheffield W	46	13	7	3	28	14	2	9	12	22	38	46
Bury	46	7	13	3	34	22	6	6	11	28	34	45
Lincoln C	46	10	8	5	35	26	5	7	11	18	35	45
Exeter C	46	11	8	4	30	18	4	6	13	19	41	44
Oxford U	46	11	10	2	38	21	2	4	17	26	46	40
Plymouth A	46	7	8	8	33	28	4	9	10	28	40	39
Rotherham U	46	11	5	7	26	19	2	8	13	25	49	39
Port Vale	46	7	11	5	28	23	1	9	13	18	44	36
Bradford C	46	11	6	6	40	29	1	4	18	16	57	34
Hereford U	46	9	9	5	28	22	0	5	18	6	38	32
Portsmouth	46	4	11	8	31	38	3	6	14	10	37	31

DIVISION 4

	P	W	D	L	F	A	W	D	L	F	A	Pts
Watford	46	18	4	1	44	14	12	7	4	41	24	71
Southend U	46	15	5	3	46	18	10	5	8	20	21	60
Swansea C	46	16	5	2	54	17	7	5	11	33	30	56
Brentford	46	15	6	2	50	17	6	8	9	36	37	56
Aldershot	46	15	8	0	45	16	4	8	11	22	31	54
Grimsby T	46	14	6	3	30	15	7	5	11	27	36	53
Barnsley	46	15	4	4	44	20	3	10	10	17	29	50
Reading	46	12	7	4	33	23	6	7	10	22	29	50
Torquay U	46	12	6	5	43	25	4	9	10	14	31	47
Northampton T	46	9	8	6	32	30	8	5	10	31	38	47
Huddersfield T	46	13	5	5	41	21	2	10	11	22	34	45
Doncaster R	46	11	8	4	37	26	3	9	11	15	39	45
Wimbledon	46	8	11	4	39	26	6	5	12	27	41	44
Scunthorpe U	46	12	6	5	31	14	2	10	11	19	41	44
Crewe A	46	11	8	4	34	25	4	6	13	16	44	44
Newport Co	46	14	6	3	43	22	2	5	16	22	51	43
Bournemouth	46	12	6	5	28	20	2	9	12	13	31	43
Stockport Co	46	14	4	5	41	19	2	6	15	15	37	42
Darlington	46	10	8	5	31	22	4	5	14	21	37	41
Halifax T	46	7	10	6	28	23	3	11	9	24	39	41
Hartlepool U	46	12	4	7	34	29	3	3	17	17	55	37
York C	46	8	7	8	27	31	4	5	14	23	38	36
Southport	46	5	13	5	30	32	1	6	16	22	44	31
Rochdale	46	8	6	9	29	28	0	2	21	14	57	24

Football League Records

Top scorers: Div 1, F.Worthington (Bolton Wanderers) 24 goals; Div 2, B.Robson (West Ham United) 24 goals; Div 3, R.Jenkins (Watford) 29 goals; Div 4, J.Dungworth (Aldershot) 26 goals.

Southport failed to gain re-election, Wigan Athletic were elected in their place.

Kenny Dalglish, a £440,000 signing from Celtic, he was top scorer for Liverpool in 1978-79 and went on to share in many Anfield triumphs as a player and manager.

DIVISION 1

	ARSENAL	ASTON VILLA	BIRMINGHAM C	BOLTON W	BRISTOL C	CHELSEA	COVENTRY C	DERBY CO	EVERTON	IPSWICH T	LEEDS U	LIVERPOOL	MANCHESTER C	MANCHESTER U	MIDDLESBROUGH	NORWICH C	NOTTINGHAM F	Q.P.R.	SOUTHAMPTON	TOTTENHAM H	W.B.A.	WOLVERHAMPTON W
1 ARSENAL		O07 1-1	D30 3-1	S16 1-0	M10 2-0	a16 5-2	a03 1-1	D16 2-0	N18 2-2	N04 4-1	A19 2-2	D02 1-0	M24 1-1	S23 1-1	F10 0-0	a28 1-1	J13 2-1	S02 5-1	O21 1-0	a10 1-0	D26 1-2	F24 0-1
2 ASTON VILLA	a25 5-1		M03 1-0	M07 3-0	N18 2-0	a28 2-1	M28 1-1	a11 3-3	S16 1-1	m02 2-2	D26 2-2	a16 3-1	N04 1-1	O14 2-2	O27 0-2	D16 1-1	S30 1-2	M20 3-1	S02 1-1	M24 2-3	m11 0-1	A19 1-0
3 BIRMINGHAM C	m05 0-0	O21 0-1		N21 3-0	N25 1-1	S23 1-1	M10 0-0	A26 1-1	D09 1-3	a03 1-1	F10 0-1	S09 0-3	O07 1-2	N11 5-1	A22 1-3	M27 1-0	a21 0-2	M06 3-1	a07 2-2	F24 1-0	a24 1-1	a14 1-1
4 BOLTON W	M26 4-2	m05 0-0	S02 2-2		A19 1-2	F24 2-1	N04 0-0	S09 2-1	a03 3-1	a21 2-3	O07 3-1	m01 1-4	O21 2-2	D22 3-0	a14 0-0	S23 3-2	N25 0-1	a07 2-1	M24 2-0	m08 1-3	N18 0-1	D09 3-1
5 BRISTOL C	O28 1-3	A26 1-0	M31 2-1	N11 4-1		a10 3-1	D26 5-0	D02 1-0	S30 2-2	F03 3-1	a28 0-0	D16 1-0	D30 1-1	M03 1-2	M17 1-1	A22 1-1	O14 1-3	a03 2-0	S16 3-1	J13 0-0	a17 1-0	N21 0-1
6 CHELSEA	m14 1-1	D09 0-1	F03 2-1	O14 4-3	D23 0-0		F21 1-3	a04 1-1	A19 0-1	m05 2-3	S02 0-3	M03 0-0	S16 1-4	N25 0-1	a21 2-1	O28 3-3	a07 1-3	M17 1-3	a14 1-2	N18 1-3	S30 1-3	M24 1-2
7 COVENTRY C	N25 1-1	a07 1-1	O28 2-1	M17 2-2	a14 3-2	S09 3-2		N21 4-2	D23 3-2	O07 2-2	S23 0-0	M06 0-0	F24 0-3	M20 4-3	N11 2-1	A26 4-1	A22 0-0	D09 1-0	a21 4-0	F10 1-3	M03 1-3	m05 3-0
8 DERBY CO	a21 2-0	D23 0-0	N18 2-1	M21 3-0	a07 0-1	O07 1-0	S02 0-2		M24 0-0	F28 0-1	M10 0-1	F24 0-2	A19 1-1	D09 1-3	m05 0-3	F10 1-1	a14 1-2	N25 2-1	S23 2-1	O21 2-2	S16 3-2	N04 4-1
9 EVERTON	A26 1-0	J31 1-1	a28 1-0	a16 1-0	F10 4-1	N11 3-2	a10 3-3	A22 2-1		F24 0-1	D16 1-1	O28 1-0	D26 1-0	N21 3-0	S09 2-0	M30 2-2	M10 1-1	M03 2-1	O07 0-0	D30 1-1	m01 0-2	S23 2-0
10 IPSWICH T	M17 2-0	S09 0-2	a17 3-0	D16 3-0	S23 0-1	D30 5-1	M13 1-1	a16 2-1	O14 0-1		D02 2-3	A22 0-3	M31 2-1	A26 3-0	N21 2-1	D26 1-1	M03 1-1	O28 2-1	F10 0-0	a28 2-1	N11 0-1	J20 3-1
11 LEEDS U	N11 0-1	a14 1-0	S30 3-0	a25 5-1	D09 1-1	N22 2-1	F03 1-0	O28 4-0	a21 1-0	a07 1-1		m17 0-3	J13 1-1	A23 2-3	D23 3-1	M03 2-2	m15 1-2	m04 4-3	N25 4-0	S16 1-2	O14 1-3	A26 3-0
12 LIVERPOOL	a07 3-0	m08 3-0	F13 1-0	S30 3-0	a21 1-0	O21 2-0	S16 1-0	O14 5-0	M13 1-1	M24 2-0	N04 1-1		N18 1-0	a14 2-0	N25 2-0	F21 6-0	D09 2-0	A19 2-1	m05 2-0	S02 7-0	F03 2-1	M20 2-0
13 MANCHESTER C	A22 1-1	m15 2-3	m01 3-1	M03 2-1	m05 2-0	J20 2-3	O14 2-0	N11 1-2	a14 0-0	N25 1-2	S09 3-0	A26 1-4		F10 0-3	a24 1-0	F27 2-2	D23 0-0	a21 3-1	D09 1-2	S23 2-0	O28 2-2	a07 3-1
14 MANCHESTER U	F03 0-2	F24 1-1	A19 1-0	a11 1-2	O21 1-3	m16 1-1	a16 0-0	a28 0-0	S02 1-1	N18 2-0	M24 4-1	D26 0-3	S30 1-0		O07 3-2	a25 1-0	S16 1-1	F28 2-0	N04 1-1	D16 2-0	D30 3-5	m07 3-2
15 MIDDLESBROUGH	S30 2-3	M10 2-0	M24 2-1	D26 1-1	N04 0-0	D16 7-2	A19 1-2	M13 3-1	M06 1-2	S02 0-0	a10 1-0	m11 0-1	a17 2-0	M27 2-2		O14 2-0	F03 1-3	S16 0-2	N18 2-0	M31 1-0	a28 1-1	O21 2-0
16 NORWICH C	D09 0-0	a21 1-2	S16 4-0	F03 0-0	M24 3-0	M10 2-0	N18 1-0	S30 3-0	N25 0-1	a14 0-1	O21 2-2	O07 1-4	S02 1-1	a07 2-2	F24 1-0		m05 1-1	J31 1-1	A19 3-1	N04 2-2	J13 1-1	M07 0-0
17 NOTTINGHAM F	S09 2-1	a04 4-0	D16 1-0	M31 1-1	F24 2-0	M28 6-0	M24 3-0	D26 1-1	N04 0-0	O21 1-0	a16 0-0	a28 0-0	m09 3-1	a18 1-1	S23 2-2	M14 2-1		N18 0-0	m02 1-0	A19 1-1	S02 0-0	O07 3-1
18 Q.P.R.	F13 1-2	S23 1-0	m07 1-3	D02 1-3	O07 1-0	N04 0-0	a28 5-1	M31 2-2	O21 1-1	m11 0-4	D30 1-4	N11 1-3	D16 2-1	S09 1-1	J20 1-1	a13 0-0	A26 0-0		F24 0-1	D26 2-2	A22 0-1	F10 3-3
19 SOUTHAMPTON	M03 2-0	N21 2-0	D02 1-0	A22 2-2	F20 2-0	D26 0-0	D16 4-0	F03 1-2	F17 3-0	S30 1-2	M31 2-2	a24 1-1	a28 1-0	a30 1-1	A26 2-1	N11 2-2	O28 0-0	O14 1-1		a16 3-3	a13 1-1	S09 3-2
20 TOTTENHAM H	D23 0-5	A23 1-4	O14 1-0	O28 2-0	S09 1-0	A26 2-2	S30 1-1	M03 2-0	m05 1-1	D09 1-0	J20 1-2	N22 0-0	F03 0-3	a21 1-1	a07 1-2	M17 0-0	N11 1-3	a14 1-1	M28 0-0		m14 1-0	N25 1-0
21 W.B.A.	a14 1-1	N25 1-1	N04 1-0	A26 4-0	J01 3-1	M14 1-0	O21 7-1	M26 2-1	a07 1-0	A19 2-1	F24 1-2	S23 1-1	a04 4-0	m05 1-0	D09 2-0	S09 2-2	m18 0-1	M24 2-1	m08 1-0	O07 0-1		a21 1-1
22 WOLVERHAMPTON W	O14 1-0	N11 0-4	D26 2-1	a28 1-1	S02 2-0	A22 0-1	D30 1-1	a24 4-0	F03 1-0	S16 1-3	N18 1-1	a10 0-1	M27 1-1	O28 2-4	M03 1-3	a16 1-0	a30 1-0	S30 1-0	J17 2-0	a03 3-2	D16 0-3	

Dave Swindlehurst of Crystal Palace, top scorer with 14 goals when the Selhurst Park club inched their way to the Division Two championship.

DIVISION 2

	BLACKBURN R	BRIGHTON & HA	BRISTOL R	BURNLEY	CAMBRIDGE U	CARDIFF C	CHARLTON A	CRYSTAL P	FULHAM	LEICESTER C	LUTON T	MILLWALL	NEWCASTLE U	NOTTS CO	OLDHAM A	ORIENT	PRESTON N.E.	SHEFFIELD U	STOKE C	SUNDERLAND	WEST HAM U	WREXHAM
1 BLACKBURN R		D09 1-1	a04 0-2	a14 1-2	M28 1-0	F28 1-4	S30 1-2	A19 1-1	m09 2-1	S16 1-1	O14 0-0	a21 1-1	a25 1-3	N18 3-4	M14 0-2	S02 3-0	M24 0-1	a07 2-0	N25 2-2	J17 1-1	m05 1-0	O28 1-1
2 BRIGHTON & H.A.	a28 2-1		a16 3-0	M03 2-1	A22 0-2	D26 5-0	a13 2-0	F17 0-0	O14 3-0	F03 3-1	D16 3-1	N21 3-0	D30 2-0	M31 0-0	S09 1-0	D02 2-0	S30 5-1	M17 2-0	J20 1-1	A26 2-0	O28 1-2	N11 2-1
3 BRISTOL R	O07 4-1	M20 1-2		a21 2-0	F10 2-0	S02 4-2	N18 5-5	a14 0-1	A19 3-1	M10 1-1	S09 2-0	D09 0-3	N04 2-0	F24 2-2	M24 0-0	O21 2-1	m05 0-1	N25 2-1	D23 0-0	a07 0-0	J20 0-1	S23 2-1
4 BURNLEY	D26 2-1	O21 3-0	D16 2-0		M31 1-1	D30 0-0	M24 2-1	N04 2-1	N18 5-3	A19 2-2	M13 2-1	m08 0-1	a10 1-0	S02 2-1	O07 1-0	a28 0-1	M10 1-1	M06 1-1	F24 0-3	S23 1-2	S09 3-2	a16 0-0
5 CAMBRIDGE U	O21 0-1	M24 0-0	S30 1-1	N25 2-2		J13 5-0	S16 1-1	D23 0-0	a14 1-0	N18 1-1	F03 0-0	M20 2-1	S02 0-0	M10 0-1	D09 3-3	N04 3-1	O07 1-0	m05 1-0	A19 0-1	a21 0-2	a07 0-0	F24 1-0
6 CARDIFF C	S23 2-0	a14 3-1	m07 2-0	m05 1-1	S09 1-0		N04 1-4	N25 2-2	D23 2-0	O21 1-0	a25 2-1	a07 2-1	M10 2-1	O07 2-3	A26 1-3	F24 1-0	A19 2-2	a21 4-0	M24 1-3	D09 1-1	m11 0-0	m14 1-0
7 CHARLTON A	F10 2-0	D23 0-3	A26 3-0	A22 1-1	M06 2-3	M17 1-1		M27 1-1	N25 0-0	F24 1-0	N21 1-2	M10 2-4	O21 4-1	S22 1-1	m05 2-0	O06 0-2	a07 1-1	D09 3-1	a14 1-4	N11 1-2	a21 0-0	S09 1-1
8 CRYSTAL P	N11 3-0	O07 3-1	D26 0-1	m11 2-0	a10 1-1	M31 2-0	a17 1-0		O28 0-1	D16 3-1	A22 3-1	J20 0-0	D02 1-0	a28 2-0	S23 1-0	D30 1-1	F24 0-0	N21 3-1	F10 1-1	S09 1-1	A26 1-1	M03 1-0
9 FULHAM	N03 1-2	F24 0-1	N10 3-0	A26 0-0	D26 5-1	a11 2-2	M31 3-1	M10 0-0		a28 3-0	D30 1-0	S23 1-0	D16 1-3	D02 1-1	F10 1-0	a16 2-2	O21 5-3	S09 2-0	O07 2-0	J20 2-2	N21 0-0	A22 0-1
10 LEICESTER C	J20 1-1	S23 4-1	O28 0-0	N11 2-1	A26 1-1	M03 1-2	O14 0-3	a20 1-1	M21 1-0		M28 3-0	m05 0-0	M17 2-1	S09 0-1	J01 2-0	F10 5-3	D23 1-1	A23 0-1	a07 1-1	a14 1-2	N25 1-2	N22 1-1
11 LUTON T	F24 2-1	a21 1-1	J16 3-2	a07 4-1	S23 1-1	S16 7-1	S02 3-0	M24 0-1	m05 2-0	N04 0-1		a14 2-2	N18 2-0	O21 6-0	A19 6-1	M10 2-1	D09 1-2	F10 1-1	F06 0-0	N25 0-3	F26 1-4	O07 2-1
12 MILLWALL	D16 1-1	S02 1-4	a28 0-3	S30 0-2	a17 2-0	D02 2-0	O28 0-2	S16 0-3	a24 0-0	a04 2-0	D26 0-2		A19 2-1	M24 0-1	N04 2-3	a10 2-0	m22 0-2	O14 1-1	N18 3-0	M03 0-1	m14 2-1	m17 2-2
13 NEWCASTLE U	S09 3-1	m05 1-3	m02 3-0	D23 3-1	N22 1-0	O28 3-0	M03 5-3	a07 1-0	a21 0-0	O07 1-0	A26 1-0	N11 1-0		a18 1-2	N25 1-1	S23 0-0	a04 4-3	a14 1-3	D09 2-0	F24 1-4	A23 0-3	m08 2-0
14 NOTTS CO	A26 2-1	N25 1-0	O14 2-1	N21 1-1	O28 1-1	M27 1-0	F03 1-1	D09 0-0	a07 1-1	a24 0-1	M03 3-1	A22 1-1	S30 1-2		a14 0-0	S16 1-0	a21 0-0	M13 4-1	m05 0-1	D23 1-1	N11 1-0	m01 1-1
15 OLDHAM A	a13 5-0	M06 1-3	A22 3-1	m14 2-0	a28 4-1	N18 2-1	D30 0-3	a03 0-0	S30 0-2	a16 2-1	N11 2-0	m11 4-1	M31 1-3	D26 3-3		D16 0-0	S16 2-0	M03 1-1	S02 1-1	O28 0-0	O14 2-2	a24 1-0
16 ORIENT	N21 2-0	a07 3-3	M03 1-1	D09 2-1	M17 3-0	O14 2-2	M20 2-1	m05 0-1	M27 1-0	S30 0-1	O28 3-2	D23 2-1	F03 2-0	J20 3-0	a21 0-0		N25 2-0	N11 1-1	S09 0-1	A22 3-0	a14 0-2	A26 0-1
17 PRESTON N.E.	A22 4-1	F10 1-0	D30 1-1	O28 2-2	a24 0-2	N11 2-1	D12 6-1	O14 2-3	M03 2-2	a17 4-0	a28 2-2	S09 0-0	a16 0-0	D16 1-1	M20 1-1	M31 1-1		A26 2-2	S23 0-1	N21 3-1	M17 0-0	D26 2-1
18 SHEFFIELD U	m02 0-1	N04 0-1	M31 1-0	S16 4-0	D30 3-3	D16 2-1	a28 2-1	S02 0-2	F06 1-1	m08 2-2	S30 1-1	F24 0-2	D26 1-0	a10 5-1	O21 4-2	A19 1-2	N18 0-1		M10 0-0	O07 3-2	a02 3-0	a17 1-1
19 STOKE C	M31 1-2	S27 2-2	a17 2-0	O14 3-1	N11 1-3	A23 2-0	D26 2-2	S30 1-1	a04 2-0	D02 0-0	a16 0-0	A26 2-0	a28 0-0	D30 2-0	N22 4-0	M14 3-1	F28 1-1	O28 2-1		M27 0-1	M03 2-0	D16 3-0
20 SUNDERLAND	a16 0-1	N18 2-1	D02 5-0	F03 3-1	D16 0-2	a28 1-2	A19 1-0	M14 1-2	S16 1-1	D26 1-1	M31 1-0	O21 3-2	O14 1-1	a13 3-0	M10 3-0	M24 1-0	S02 3-1	a25 6-2	N04 0-1		S30 2-1	M07 1-0
21 WEST HAM U	D30 4-0	M10 0-0	S16 2-0	a24 3-1	D02 5-0	a16 1-1	D16 2-0	N18 1-1	S02 0-1	M31 1-1	a09 1-0	O07 3-0	M24 5-0	A19 5-2	F24 3-0	D26 0-2	N04 3-1	S23 2-0	O21 1-1	F10 3-3		a28 1-1
22 WREXHAM	M10 2-1	A19 0-0	m10 0-1	M21 0-1	O14 2-0	S30 1-2	a02 1-1	O21 0-0	M24 1-1	S02 0-0	m07 2-0	N25 3-0	S16 0-0	N04 3-1	a07 2-0	N18 3-1	a14 2-1	F28 4-0	a21 0-1	m05 1-2	D09 4-3	

Season 1978-79

DIVISION 3

	BLACKPOOL	BRENTFORD	BURY	CARLISLE U	CHESTER	CHESTERFIELD	COLCHESTER U	EXETER C	GILLINGHAM	HULL C	LINCOLN C	MANSFIELD T	OXFORD U	PETERBOROUGH U	PLYMOUTH A	ROTHERHAM U	SHEFFIELD W	SHREWSBURY T	SOUTHEND U	SWANSEA C	SWINDON T	TRANMERE R	WALSALL	WATFORD
1 BLACKPOOL		m05 0-1	a07 1-2	S02 3-1	D23 3-0	S12 0-0	F10 2-1	a24 1-1	S26 2-0	F20 3-1	O07 2-0	O21 2-0	A19 1-0	D09 0-0	M10 0-0	N18 1-2	N04 0-1	M20 5-0	F24 1-2	a21 1-3	m15 5-2	a14 2-0	S16 2-1	M24 1-1
2 BRENTFORD	M31 3-2		O07 0-1	D30 0-0	M10 6-0	A26 0-3	A21 1-0	N11 0-0	S23 0-2	S09 1-0	S25 2-1	a28 1-0	N04 3-0	J20 0-0	D26 2-1	a23 1-0	a17 2-1	M26 2-3	a13 3-0	F10 1-0	m08 1-2	O21 2-0	D02 1-0	F24 3-3
3 BURY	M06 1-3	m15 2-3		a13 2-2	S30 1-1	O14 3-1	a28 2-2	M03 4-2	A26 2-2	O28 1-1	a16 2-2	D30 0-0	M20 1-1	m19 1-0	S12 1-2	D26 3-2	m01 0-0	M31 3-0	A22 3-3	N11 0-1	M27 0-1	F27 1-0	O17 1-1	S16 1-2
4 CARLISLE U	N11 1-1	a21 1-0	F13 1-2		a14 1-1	A22 1-1	S08 4-0	D09 1-1	a07 1-0	M27 2-2	J20 2-0	F10 1-0	m05 0-1	M20 4-1	O07 1-1	O21 1-1	F24 0-0	M17 1-1	S23 0-0	S25 2-0	O28 2-0	M06 2-0	A26 1-0	a24 1-0
5 CHESTER	a13 4-2	O28 3-1	F10 1-1	D26 1-2		M28 3-0	J17 2-2	A26 3-0	F21 1-1	N11 2-1	M07 5-1	M31 1-1	M03 4-1	S08 1-1	O18 0-0	M14 0-1	a28 2-2	a16 0-0	M21 0-1	S23 2-0	S27 2-0	F24 1-1	A23 2-1	O07 2-1
6 CHESTERFIELD	M14 1-3	N18 0-0	F24 2-1	M24 2-3	N04 3-1		O18 2-1	S09 0-1	m19 0-2	a04 1-2	a17 1-3	a16 1-0	S02 1-1	S23 3-1	A19 1-3	a28 1-0	D26 3-3	M07 2-1	S27 3-2	O07 2-1	F28 1-1	M10 5-2	M31 0-0	O21 0-2
7 COLCHESTER U	S30 3-1	M24 1-1	D09 0-0	a02 2-1	S12 2-1	a24 0-0		F02 2-2	m07 2-2	a21 2-1	J23 2-0	M09 1-0	a14 1-1	m04 4-2	N03 2-1	S02 0-0	N18 1-0	S15 1-0	O20 1-1	A19 2-2	O06 3-2	a06 1-0	F27 2-0	D23 0-1
8 EXETER C	O18 3-0	S02 2-2	O21 2-1	a28 3-2	N18 0-1	J13 3-1	S27 2-1		O07 0-0	S23 3-1	D30 3-2	A19 0-0	J20 2-0	F10 1-0	a17 1-0	M31 2-0	M24 2-2	S13 0-1	D02 0-0	F24 2-1	a11 1-2	N04 3-0	D26 3-1	M10 0-0
9 GILLINGHAM	F03 2-0	J27 0-0	N18 3-3	D02 0-0	S16 1-0	S30 2-1	a16 3-0	m14 2-0		O14 2-0	O17 4-2	M24 0-0	M10 2-1	M03 1-0	D30 2-0	A19 0-0	S12 0-0	a28 2-0	D26 1-0	N04 2-0	M31 2-2	J13 3-2	a10 3-1	S02 2-3
10 HULL C	a16 0-0	M06 1-0	M10 4-1	A19 1-1	S02 3-0	S16 1-1	M13 1-0	m07 1-0	F24 0-1		M31 0-0	D26 3-0	S30 0-1	O07 1-1	m01 2-1	M24 1-0	a13 1-1	F03 1-1	a24 2-0	O21 2-2	a28 1-1	N18 2-1	S12 4-1	N04 4-0
11 LINCOLN C	m07 1-2	M21 1-0	m09 1-4	S16 1-1	a07 0-0	D23 0-1	O13 0-0	a21 0-1	a25 2-4	m05 4-2		N04 0-1	D09 2-2	a14 0-1	N18 3-3	a04 3-0	S02 1-2	m02 1-2	M10 1-1	M24 2-1	O21 0-3	A19 2-1	S29 1-1	S13 0-5
12 MANSFIELD T	M03 1-1	D09 2-1	a21 3-0	S30 1-0	m05 2-0	m21 2-1	O28 1-1	M26 1-1	A21 1-1	a14 0-2	m11 2-0		m14 1-1	D23 1-1	M12 5-0	m19 0-1	S16 1-1	m07 2-2	A26 1-1	a23 2-2	N11 0-1	N13 0-0	O14 1-3	a07 0-3
13 OXFORD U	M28 1-0	a04 0-1	S09 0-0	M31 5-1	O21 0-0	N11 1-1	D26 2-0	S16 3-2	O28 1-1	F10 1-0	a28 2-1	S27 3-2		F24 0-2	a11 3-2	D02 1-0	a25 1-1	A23 0-1	M07 0-0	A26 0-2	a16 0-1	O07 0-0	D30 2-1	J27 1-1
14 PETERBOROUGH U	a28 1-2	S16 3-1	N04 2-2	S12 0-0	J13 2-1	m08 0-0	M31 1-2	S30 1-1	O21 1-1	m11 3-0	D26 0-1	a17 1-2	O14 1-1		M24 2-1	a16 1-1	A19 2-0	D06 0-2	D30 0-1	M10 2-0	a24 2-1	S02 1-0	F03 0-3	N18 0-1
15 PLYMOUTH A	O28 0-0	a14 2-1	a03 3-0	F17 2-0	a24 2-2	D16 1-1	M17 1-1	F27 4-2	a21 2-1	a07 3-4	A26 2-1	S09 1-4	F20 0-1	N14 3-2		S30 2-0	J27 2-0	O14 1-1	N11 1-1	m05 2-2	S16 2-0	F03 2-2	M03 1-0	D09 1-1
16 ROTHERHAM U	A26 2-1	O17 1-0	a14 2-1	M03 1-3	a21 0-1	D09 1-0	N11 1-0	m05 2-1	M27 1-1	S05 0-2	S09 2-0	S23 2-0	a07 0-0	m01 1-1	F10 1-0		O07 0-1	O28 1-2	F06 2-1	M06 0-1	F24 1-3	D23 3-2	m14 4-1	S26 2-1
17 SHEFFIELD W	m17 2-0	M13 1-0	S26 0-0	O14 0-0	D09 0-0	a14 4-0	A26 0-0	O24 2-1	M06 2-1	m19 2-3	N11 0-0	a03 1-2	O17 1-1	M27 3-0	S23 2-3	m07 2-1		M03 0-0	S09 3-2	a07 0-0	m11 2-1	a21 1-2	O28 0-2	m05 2-3
18 SHREWSBURY T	S09 2-0	A19 1-0	m05 1-0	N04 0-0	J30 1-0	a21 1-1	J19 2-0	m17 4-1	D09 1-1	S26 1-0	S23 2-0	O07 2-2	M24 0-0	a07 2-0	F24 2-0	m10 3-1	O21 2-2		F09 2-0	D23 3-0	A26 0-0	a24 2-1	N10 1-1	a14 1-1
19 SOUTHEND U	O14 4-0	D23 1-1	M24 0-0	M12 1-1	A19 0-1	F02 2-0	M02 1-1	a06 0-1	a14 0-1	O23 3-0	O27 2-0	N17 1-1	S11 2-0	a21 0-0	S01 2-1	S15 2-1	F13 2-1	S29 0-1		D08 0-2	M16 5-3	m04 0-1	a30 1-0	a02 1-0
20 SWANSEA C	D30 1-0	S30 2-1	S02 2-0	F02 0-0	F27 2-2	m11 2-1	M27 4-1	O14 1-0	M16 3-1	M02 5-3	A22 3-0	O17 3-2	N18 1-1	O28 4-1	M31 2-1	S12 4-4	D02 4-2	a10 1-1	a28 3-2		D26 1-2	S16 4-3	a17 2-2	M20 3-2
21 SWINDON T	S23 0-1	S12 2-0	A19 2-1	M10 0-0	F03 2-0	a07 1-0	M20 1-2	a03 1-1	m05 3-1	D09 2-0	M03 6-0	S02 1-0	m02 2-0	O17 3-1	J20 1-3	O14 1-0	S30 3-0	N18 2-1	N04 1-0	a14 0-1		M24 4-1	J16 4-1	a21 2-0
22 TRANMERE R	D26 0-2	M03 0-1	S22 0-0	a16 1-1	O13 6-2	O27 1-1	m09 1-5	M16 2-2	D09 1-1	A26 1-3	M26 0-0	a30 1-2	F16 1-0	N10 1-0	S25 2-1	a18 1-1	F19 1-1	O16 2-2	M30 1-2	a03 1-2	A21 1-1		a27 0-0	F10 1-1
23 WALSALL	F06 2-1	a07 2-3	a24 0-1	N18 1-2	M24 2-1	m05 0-1	S23 2-2	a14 2-2	M20 0-1	J06 1-2	M13 4-1	F24 1-1	a21 0-1	S26 4-1	O21 2-1	N04 0-1	M10 0-2	S02 1-1	O07 1-1	F20 1-1	S09 4-1	D09 2-0		A19 2-4
24 WATFORD	A22 5-1	O14 2-0	J20 3-3	O17 2-1	m02 1-0	M03 2-0	a13 0-3	O28 1-0	N11 1-0	m14 4-0	J06 2-0	D02 1-1	S23 4-2	A26 1-2	a28 2-2	F03 2-2	M31 1-0	D26 2-2	a17 2-0	S09 0-2	D30 2-0	S30 4-0	M27 3-1	

DIVISION 4

	ALDERSHOT	BARNSLEY	BOURNEMOUTH	BRADFORD C	CREWE A	DARLINGTON	DONCASTER R	GRIMSBY T	HALIFAX T	HARTLEPOOL U	HEREFORD U	HUDDERSFIELD T	NEWPORT CO	NORTHAMPTON T	PORTSMOUTH	PORT VALE	READING	ROCHDALE	SCUNTHORPE U	STOCKPORT CO	TORQUAY U	WIGAN A	WIMBLEDON	YORK C
1 ALDERSHOT		O17 1-0	M20 1-0	S12 6-0	M10 3-0	S30 1-1	D09 2-1	N04 2-0	S02 1-0	O14 1-1	M03 2-0	a07 1-0	M24 2-3	a14 2-0	S23 0-2	J13 1-1	F06 2-2	N18 1-0	F03 2-0	D23 3-2	J20 1-0	a21 1-0	A19 1-1	m05 1-0
2 BARNSLEY	a24 2-0		M06 1-0	N18 0-1	M24 3-1	a30 1-1	a03 3-0	m08 2-1	A19 4-2	a12 1-0	a16 2-1	S16 1-0	M10 1-0	O07 1-1	M30 1-1	D26 6-2	S30 3-1	a28 0-3	M13 4-1	F24 4-4	S12 1-2	O21 0-0	N04 3-1	S02 3-0
3 BOURNEMOUTH	O07 0-1	a07 0-2		a21 1-0	J13 0-1	N18 2-2	F03 7-1	O21 0-0	M10 1-0	S02 0-1	F24 1-1	S12 2-0	A19 3-1	F21 0-0	S29 3-1	F06 3-1	a14 0-0	S16 3-1	M24 0-0	a23 3-1	N04 1-0	m05 2-1	D23 1-2	D09 1-2
4 BRADFORD C	M07 0-2	A26 1-2	D30 2-1		a28 6-0	M31 0-0	a30 1-0	a16 1-3	S27 3-0	m02 1-2	A23 2-1	O28 1-1	S23 1-3	N11 3-0	M28 2-0	O18 2-3	M13 2-3	D26 1-0	M03 1-1	S09 1-1	a11 3-1	m07 1-1	a04 1-0	O14 2-1
5 CREWE A	O27 1-1	A23 0-2	S09 1-0	D09 1-2		F23 1-1	F13 2-4	S23 0-3	F10 1-0	O21 0-1	F06 0-0	M28 3-3	M13 0-1	a10 2-4	N11 0-0	A25 1-5	a07 0-2	m18 1-2	m05 0-2	S27 2-2	O07 6-2	a14 1-1	a25 1-2	a21 0-1
6 DARLINGTON	a03 2-1	S26 0-0	A26 0-0	m05 1-1	O13 1-1		a14 3-2	S09 0-1	F27 2-1	m07 0-1	N11 2-1	A22 1-0	a07 1-0	m14 0-0	m11 2-0	O28 4-0	O17 1-2	M03 0-2	D23 2-2	M27 0-1	S23 1-2	D09 1-1	a21 1-1	M06 0-1
7 DONCASTER R	a28 1-1	S23 2-2	S26 1-1	N04 2-0	a16 2-0	D26 2-3		M31 0-1	a17 1-1	M23 0-0	J30 1-0	F27 0-2	O21 0-0	F10 2-0	O17 2-3	S12 1-3	M20 2-2	D02 1-0	S01 0-0	O07 2-0	O10 1-0	F24 0-1	M09 1-0	N18 1-2
8 GRIMSBY T	M17 0-0	a21 2-0	M03 1-0	J09 5-1	F27 2-2	J16 7-2	m05 3-4		N18 2-1	S16 0-1	O28 1-1	F03 2-1	D09 1-0	O17 4-3	O14 1-0	a03 1-0	A19 1-2	S30 4-0	a14 1-1	a07 2-1	S02 3-0	M24 3-1	S12 2-2	D23 3-0
9 HALIFAX T	N11 1-1	M27 0-2	O28 0-2	a26 2-0	S30 0-0	S16 0-2	M06 0-0	A26 1-2		m14 2-4	m09 1-0	a14 2-3	m05 1-2	a21 2-2	M03 2-0	O14 0-3	D09 0-0	m07 2-1	m18 2-3	A22 2-1	a03 1-0	D16 1-2	a07 2-1	S12 0-1
10 HARTLEPOOL U	F24 2-2	D23 1-1	N11 0-0	a07 2-2	M03 2-2	O07 0-2	A19 3-4	J20 1-0	S23 3-1		S09 2-1	m05 2-0	S25 0-0	m17 2-0	A25 1-1	m10 1-2	a21 0-0	O28 5-1	O17 1-1	M13 1-3	F10 3-2	a03 1-1	D09 1-1	a14 1-1
11 HEREFORD U	O21 1-1	F28 1-1	O14 0-0	M24 3-1	S16 6-1	S02 1-0	a21 2-0	M10 0-1	N04 2-2	M07 1-0		a25 3-0	D22 0-3	D09 4-3	m07 0-1	S30 1-0	S13 0-0	M21 2-2	a07 3-1	a14 1-0	N18 3-1	A19 0-0	m05 0-0	F03 1-0
12 HUDDERSFIELD T	D02 0-0	m02 1-0	M13 2-1	M10 0-0	A19 0-0	M24 2-2	S09 2-1	S26 2-0	D26 2-0	M31 2-0	O17 2-3		F24 0-1	S23 1-0	a28 2-0	a16 3-2	S02 1-1	a17 1-0	N18 3-2	a04 0-0	a30 1-1	O07 1-1	O21 3-0	N04 1-0
13 NEWPORT CO	A22 1-2	O28 1-1	m01 2-0	F27 2-4	S12 1-2	D02 2-1	M03 3-0	a28 1-1	M31 2-0	F02 3-2	a11 4-1	O14 2-1		M16 2-1	a16 1-2	D30 1-0	J13 3-2	O17 0-0	a18 2-0	A26 1-2	D26 1-1	N10 2-1	S16 1-3	S30 1-1
14 NORTHAMPTON T	D26 2-3	a26 0-1	a16 4-2	S02 1-0	a17 3-1	S12 4-1	S30 3-0	a24 1-2	D30 2-1	A23 1-1	a28 2-1	M06 2-3	N04 3-1		D02 0-2	M13 1-0	O14 2-2	M31 1-0	S15 1-0	O21 2-2	M24 1-2	M10 2-4	N18 1-1	a03 1-0
15 PORTSMOUTH	m15 1-1	m05 0-1	F10 1-1	A19 0-1	S02 3-0	N04 3-0	a24 4-0	F24 1-3	O21 3-1	N18 3-0	O07 1-0	D09 1-0	F20 2-1	a07 1-0		S16 2-0	D23 4-0	J13 1-1	S12 0-0	a21 1-1	M10 1-0	S26 1-0	a14 0-0	M24 1-1
16 PORT VALE	S09 1-1	a14 3-2	S23 1-2	a24 2-1	N18 2-2	M10 2-1	J16 1-3	O07 1-1	F24 0-1	N04 2-0	m01 1-1	J01 1-0	a21 1-1	S26 2-2	M21 0-0		m05 0-3	S02 1-1	A19 2-2	D09 2-1	O21 1-2	J09 2-1	M24 1-0	a07 0-0
17 READING	a16 4-0	F10 1-0	D26 1-0	O07 3-0	D06 3-0	a25 1-0	S16 3-0	M28 4-0	a28 1-0	F26 3-1	F21 3-0	N11 1-1	S09 2-1	F24 5-1	a13 2-0	M31 0-0		A23 2-0	M16 0-1	O28 3-3	S27 1-0	A26 2-0	m02 1-0	O21 3-0
18 ROCHDALE	A26 1-1	D09 0-3	a03 2-1	a14 1-0	N04 2-1	O21 2-1	a07 2-0	M13 2-5	O07 1-1	M10 1-1	S23 0-2	a11 0-2	a23 1-0	m05 4-1	S09 0-2	N11 0-1	M24 1-0		a21 1-0	m01 2-0	m09 1-0	M19 0-2	S25 0-0	A19 1-2
19 SCUNTHORPE U	S26 2-0	S09 0-1	A22 1-0	O21 3-2	M31 0-1	a10 1-0	N11 0-0	D26 2-1	a16 1-0	a24 3-1	D16 4-2	A25 3-1	O07 2-3	M20 0-3	a03 2-2	M27 2-0	N04 0-3	D30 0-4		S23 1-0	a28 2-2	m01 0-1	m08 2-0	M10 2-3
20 STOCKPORT CO	a09 2-2	O13 0-0	O16 1-0	J12 1-0	M05 4-3	A19 3-0	F21 0-1	D04 2-1	M23 1-2	S11 4-0	D26 0-2	S29 3-1	N17 1-1	M02 2-1	D29 4-2	a27 0-0	M09 0-0	a16 3-0	F26 0-2		M30 0-1	N03 0-1	S01 0-1	S15 2-0
21 TORQUAY U	S16 2-1	J31 3-2	M17 0-1	F14 1-2	F20 3-0	J27 1-0	M28 2-1	N11 3-1	S09 2-0	S30 4-1	A26 1-0	a21 2-1	a14 2-0	A19 0-1	O28 2-1	M03 2-2	F03 1-1	O14 1-1	D09 0-1	m05 1-0		a07 1-1	F28 1-6	a25 3-0
22 WIGAN A	D30 3-2	M03 1-1	M31 1-0	S16 1-3	D26 1-0	a28 2-2	O14 1-0	A23 0-3	O18 1-0	a16 2-2	M28 0-0	F17 2-1	S02 2-3	O28 2-0	F03 2-0	a13 5-3	N18 3-0	S13 3-0	S30 1-0	M17 2-0	M14 3-1		F14 1-2	F28 1-1
23 WIMBLEDON	M27 3-1	m14 1-1	a10 4-0	S30 2-1	O17 1-1	m17 2-0	O28 3-2	M20 0-1	D02 2-1	a28 3-1	M31 2-0	M03 2-1	M06 0-0	A26 4-1	D26 2-4	A22 1-0	S23 1-0	F03 3-2	O14 3-1	N11 2-0	a16 5-0	S09 2-1		m11 2-1
24 YORK C	M31 1-1	N11 0-1	a28 2-1	F24 2-2	m01 1-0	a16 5-2	A26 1-1	a13 0-0	M13 2-0	D26 1-1	S26 1-0	m19 1-3	M20 1-2	S09 1-0	A22 5-3	m07 4-0	M03 0-1	M27 2-1	O28 1-0	m14 1-0	O17 0-0	S23 0-1	O07 1-4	

LEAGUE TABLES

DIVISION 1

	P	W	D	L	F	A	W	D	L	F	A	Pts
Liverpool	42	19	2	0	51	4	11	6	4	34	12	68
Nottingham F	42	11	10	0	34	10	10	8	3	27	16	60
W.B.A.	42	13	5	3	38	15	11	6	4	34	20	59
Everton	42	12	7	2	32	17	5	10	6	20	23	51
Leeds U	42	11	4	6	41	25	7	10	4	29	27	50
Ipswich T	42	11	4	6	34	21	9	5	7	29	28	49
Arsenal	42	11	8	2	37	18	6	6	9	24	30	48
Aston Villa	42	8	9	4	37	26	7	7	7	22	23	46
Manchester U	42	9	7	5	29	25	6	8	7	31	38	45
Coventry C	42	11	7	3	41	29	3	9	9	17	39	44
Tottenham H	42	7	8	6	19	25	6	7	8	29	36	41
Middlesbrough	42	10	5	6	33	21	5	5	11	24	29	40
Bristol C	42	11	6	4	34	19	4	4	13	13	32	40
Southampton	42	9	10	2	35	20	3	6	12	12	33	40
Manchester C	42	9	5	7	34	28	4	8	9	24	28	39
Norwich C	42	7	10	4	29	19	0	13	8	22	38	37
Bolton W	42	10	5	6	36	28	2	6	13	18	47	35
Wolverh'pton W	42	10	4	7	26	26	3	4	14	18	42	34
Derby Co	42	8	5	8	25	25	2	6	13	19	46	31
Q.P.R.	42	4	9	8	24	33	2	4	15	21	40	25
Birmingham C	42	5	9	7	24	25	1	1	19	13	39	22
Chelsea	42	3	5	13	23	42	2	5	14	21	50	20

DIVISION 2

	P	W	D	L	F	A	W	D	L	F	A	Pts
Crystal Palace	42	12	7	2	30	11	7	12	2	21	13	57
Brighton & H.A.	42	16	3	2	44	11	7	7	7	28	28	56
Stoke C	42	11	7	3	35	15	9	9	3	23	16	56
Sunderland	42	13	3	5	39	19	9	8	4	31	25	55
West Ham U	42	12	7	2	46	15	6	7	8	24	24	50
Notts Co	42	8	10	3	23	15	6	6	9	25	45	44
Preston N.E.	42	7	11	3	36	23	5	7	9	23	34	42
Newcastle U	42	13	3	5	35	24	4	5	12	16	31	42
Cardiff C	42	12	5	4	34	23	4	5	12	22	47	42
Fulham	42	10	7	4	35	19	3	8	10	15	28	41
Orient	42	11	5	5	32	18	4	5	12	19	33	40
Cambridge U	42	7	10	4	22	15	5	6	10	22	37	40
Burnley	42	11	6	4	31	22	3	6	12	20	40	40
Oldham A	42	10	7	4	36	23	3	6	12	16	38	39
Wrexham	42	10	6	5	31	16	2	8	11	14	26	38
Bristol R	42	10	6	5	34	23	4	4	13	14	37	38
Leicester C	42	7	8	6	28	23	3	9	9	15	29	37
Luton T	42	11	5	5	46	24	2	5	14	14	33	36
Charlton A	42	6	8	7	28	28	5	5	11	32	41	35
Sheffield U	42	9	6	6	34	24	2	6	13	18	45	34
Millwall	42	7	4	10	22	29	4	6	11	20	32	32
Blackburn R	42	5	8	8	24	29	5	2	14	17	43	30

DIVISION 3

	P	W	D	L	F	A	W	D	L	F	A	Pts
Shrewsbury T	46	14	9	0	36	11	7	10	6	25	30	61
Watford	46	15	5	3	47	22	9	7	7	36	30	60
Swansea C	46	16	6	1	57	32	8	6	9	26	29	60
Gillingham	46	15	7	1	39	15	6	10	7	26	27	59
Swindon T	46	17	2	4	44	14	8	5	10	30	38	57
Carlisle U	46	11	10	2	31	13	4	12	7	22	29	52
Colchester U	46	13	9	1	35	19	4	8	11	25	36	51
Exeter C	46	14	6	3	38	18	3	9	11	23	38	49
Hull C	46	12	9	2	36	14	7	2	14	30	47	49
Brentford	46	14	4	5	35	19	5	5	13	18	30	47
Oxford U	46	10	8	5	27	20	4	10	9	17	30	46
Southend U	46	11	6	6	30	17	4	9	10	21	32	45
Blackpool	46	12	5	6	38	19	6	4	13	23	40	45
Sheffield W	46	9	8	6	30	22	4	11	8	23	31	45
Plymouth A	46	11	9	3	40	27	4	5	14	27	41	44
Chester C	46	11	9	3	42	21	3	7	13	15	40	44
Rotherham U	46	13	3	7	30	23	4	7	12	19	32	44
Mansfield T	46	7	11	5	30	24	5	8	10	21	28	43
Bury	46	6	11	6	35	32	5	9	9	24	33	42
Chesterfield	46	10	5	8	35	34	3	9	11	16	31	40
Peterborough U	46	8	7	8	26	24	3	7	13	18	39	36
Walsall	46	7	6	10	34	32	3	6	14	22	39	32
Tranmere R	46	4	12	7	26	31	2	4	17	19	47	28
Lincoln C	46	5	7	11	26	38	2	4	17	15	50	25

DIVISION 4

	P	W	D	L	F	A	W	D	L	F	A	Pts
Reading	46	19	3	1	49	8	7	10	6	27	27	65
Grimsby T	46	15	5	3	51	23	11	4	8	31	26	61
Wimbledon	46	18	3	2	50	20	7	8	8	28	26	61
Barnsley	46	15	5	3	47	23	9	8	6	26	19	61
Aldershot	46	16	5	2	38	14	4	12	7	25	33	57
Wigan A	46	14	5	4	40	24	7	8	8	23	24	55
Portsmouth	46	13	7	3	35	12	7	5	11	27	36	52
Newport Co	46	12	5	6	39	28	9	5	9	27	27	52
Huddersfield T	46	13	8	2	32	15	5	3	15	25	38	47
York C	46	11	6	6	33	24	7	5	11	18	31	47
Torquay U	46	14	4	5	38	24	5	4	14	20	41	46
Scunthorpe U	46	12	3	8	33	30	5	8	10	21	30	45
Hartlepool U	46	7	12	4	35	28	6	6	11	22	38	44
Hereford U	46	12	8	3	35	18	3	5	15	18	35	43
Bradford C	46	11	5	7	38	26	6	4	13	24	42	43
Port Vale	46	8	10	5	29	28	6	4	13	28	42	42
Stockport Co	46	11	5	7	33	21	3	7	13	25	39	40
Bournemouth	46	11	6	6	34	19	3	5	15	13	29	39
Northampton T	46	12	4	7	40	30	3	5	15	24	46	39
Rochdale	46	11	4	8	25	26	4	5	14	22	38	39
Darlington	46	8	8	7	25	21	3	7	13	24	45	37
Doncaster R	46	8	8	7	25	22	5	3	15	25	51	37
Halifax T	46	7	5	11	24	32	2	3	18	15	40	26
Crewe A	46	3	7	13	24	41	3	7	13	19	49	26

Football League Records

Top scorers: Div 1, P.Boyer (Southampton) 23 goals; Div 2, C.Allen (Queen's Park Rangers) 28 goals; Div 3, T.Curran (Sheffield Wednesday) 22 goals; Div 4, C.Garwood (Aldershot & Portsmouth) 27 goals.

Alan Hansen, the tall, elegant defender who made 38 appearances in yet another Liverpool Championship-winning season.

DIVISION 1

	ARSENAL	ASTON VILLA	BOLTON W	BRIGHTON & HA	BRISTOL C	COVENTRY C	CRYSTAL P	DERBY CO	EVERTON	IPSWICH T	LEEDS U	LIVERPOOL	MANCHESTER C	MANCHESTER U	MIDDLESBROUGH	NORWICH C	NOTTINGHAM F	SOUTHAMPTON	STOKE C	TOTTENHAM H	W.B.A.	WOLVERHAMPTON W
1 ARSENAL		F09 3-1	F23 2-0	N03 3-0	M11 0-0	D08 3-1	M22 1-1	J19 2-0	N17 2-0	A21 0-2	J12 0-1	N24 0-0	O06 0-0	A25 0-0	S15 2-0	D21 1-1	m05 0-0	a05 1-1	O20 0-0	D26 1-0	a26 1-1	S29 2-3
2 ASTON VILLA	S22 0-0		N03 3-1	A22 2-1	A25 0-2	D19 3-0	F02 2-0	M01 1-0	J12 2-1	M22 1-1	N24 0-0	D08 1-3	F27 2-2	S08 0-3	M19 0-2	M26 2-0	a05 3-2	O06 3-0	N17 2-1	a26 1-0	O13 0-0	M10 1-3
3 BOLTON W	O13 0-0	A18 1-1		J12 0-2	D01 1-1	a15 1-1	O27 1-1	M15 1-2	D26 1-1	D15 0-1	S22 1-1	O09 1-1	N17 0-1	a07 1-3	a08 2-2	M11 1-0	M01 1-0	A25 2-1	a19 2-1	M22 2-1	S08 0-0	m03 0-0
4 BRIGHTON & H.A.	A18 0-4	M03 1-1	S01 3-1		a07 0-1	M01 1-1	D26 3-0	D01 2-0	m03 0-0	S15 2-0	O13 0-0	N10 1-4	D29 4-1	M15 0-0	a19 2-1	O27 2-4	M29 1-0	S22 0-0	D15 0-0	J19 0-2	F16 0-0	a08 3-0
5 BRISTOL C	O27 0-1	D29 1-3	a12 2-1	J01 2-2		O09 1-0	M01 0-2	N10 0-2	F19 2-1	J19 0-3	A18 2-2	M15 1-3	N24 1-0	O13 1-1	a22 3-1	a26 2-3	S22 1-1	D21 0-1	S15 0-0	D08 1-3	a05 0-0	S01 2-0
6 COVENTRY C	m03 0-1	a29 1-2	S15 3-1	O20 2-1	A21 3-1		a19 2-1	a07 2-1	O06 2-1	D01 4-1	N10 3-0	J19 1-0	F09 0-0	D15 1-2	J01 2-0	S01 2-0	D29 0-3	F23 3-0	N03 1-3	S29 1-1	M08 0-2	M29 1-3
7 CRYSTAL P	N10 1-0	S15 2-0	M08 3-1	a05 1-1	O20 1-1	N24 0-0		S01 4-0	F23 1-1	S29 4-1	a12 1-0	a26 0-0	N03 2-0	M29 0-2	D29 1-2	J01 0-0	D08 1-0	A21 0-0	F09 0-1	O06 1-1	J26 2-2	J19 1-0
8 DERBY CO	S08 3-2	O20 1-3	O06 4-0	a12 3-0	M22 3-3	D26 1-2	J12 1-2		A25 0-1	N17 0-1	a05 2-0	D22 1-3	a26 3-1	F02 1-3	S22 1-0	D08 0-0	N24 4-1	F16 2-2	M08 2-2	F23 2-1	N03 2-1	A22 0-1
9 EVERTON	M28 0-1	S01 1-1	a05 3-1	D08 2-0	S29 0-0	M15 1-1	O13 3-1	D29 1-1		F09 0-4	N13 5-1	M01 1-2	D22 1-2	O27 0-0	N10 0-2	A18 2-4	J01 1-0	a26 2-0	M18 2-0	N24 1-1	a28 0-0	S15 2-3
10 IPSWICH T	O09 1-2	N10 0-0	a26 1-0	F02 1-1	S08 1-0	a12 3-0	F19 3-0	M29 1-1	S22 1-1		M14 1-0	O13 1-2	D08 4-0	M01 6-0	O27 1-0	a05 4-2	A18 0-1	N24 3-1	S01 3-1	D21 3-1	J01 4-0	D29 1-0
11 LEEDS U	S01 1-1	a19 0-0	F09 2-2	F23 1-1	N03 1-3	M22 0-0	D01 1-0	J01 1-0	A22 2-0	O06 2-1		S15 1-1	S29 1-2	m03 2-0	a02 2-0	D29 2-2	J19 1-2	M08 2-0	a08 3-0	O20 1-2	N17 1-0	D15 3-0
12 LIVERPOOL	a19 1-1	m03 4-1	A21 0-0	M22 1-0	O06 4-0	S08 4-0	D15 3-0	a08 3-0	O20 2-2	F23 1-1	M19 3-0		M11 2-0	D26 2-0	D01 4-0	S22 0-0	F19 2-0	J12 1-1	a01 1-0	N17 2-1	A25 3-1	N03 3-0
13 MANCHESTER C	M15 0-3	a07 1-1	M29 2-2	A25 3-2	a19 3-1	S22 3-0	A18 0-0	D15 3-0	a02 1-1	m03 2-1	F16 1-1	O27 0-4		N10 2-0	O10 1-0	M01 0-0	O13 1-0	S08 0-1	D26 1-1	J12 1-1	F02 1-3	D01 2-3
14 MANCHESTER U	D29 3-0	a23 2-1	F27 2-0	O06 2-0	F23 4-0	a26 2-1	N17 1-1	S15 1-0	M12 0-0	O20 1-0	D08 1-1	a05 2-1	M22 1-0		S01 2-1	N24 5-0	D22 3-0	N03 1-0	S29 4-0	a12 4-1	A22 2-0	F09 0-1
15 MIDDLESBROUGH	m19 5-0	S29 0-0	D21 3-1	N24 1-1	N17 1-0	a05 1-2	A25 1-1	F09 3-0	M22 2-1	M11 1-1	D26 3-1	m06 1-0	A21 3-0	J12 1-1		S08 1-0	a26 0-0	D08 0-1	F23 1-3	N03 0-0	O06 2-1	O20 1-0
16 NORWICH C	a02 2-1	D01 1-1	S29 2-1	M08 2-2	D15 2-0	J12 1-0	a07 2-1	m03 4-2	N03 0-0	D26 3-3	A25 2-1	F09 3-5	O20 2-2	a19 0-2	F27 0-0		S15 3-1	N17 2-1	O06 2-2	A22 4-0	M22 1-1	F23 0-4
17 NOTTINGHAM F	D01 1-1	D26 2-1	O20 5-2	N17 0-1	F09 0-0	A25 4-1	m03 4-0	a19 1-0	m09 1-0	N03 2-0	S08 0-0	S29 1-0	F23 4-0	a02 2-0	F16 2-2	a30 2-0		M22 2-0	A22 1-0	M11 4-0	J12 3-1	O06 3-2
18 SOUTHAMPTON	J01 0-1	M15 2-0	D29 2-0	F09 5-1	a29 5-2	O13 2-3	O09 4-1	S29 4-0	D15 1-0	a19 0-1	O27 1-2	S01 3-2	J19 4-1	A18 1-1	m03 4-1	M29 2-0	N10 4-1		D01 3-1	S15 5-2	M01 1-1	a07 0-3
19 STOKE C	M01 2-3	M29 2-0	N24 1-0	a26 1-0	F02 1-0	A18 3-2	S22 1-2	O27 3-2	S08 2-3	J12 0-1	D21 0-2	a23 0-2	a05 0-0	F16 1-1	O13 0-0	M15 2-1	O10 1-1	a12 1-2		A25 3-1	D08 3-2	N10 0-1
20 TOTTENHAM H	a07 1-2	D15 1-2	N10 2-0	S08 2-1	m03 0-0	F27 4-3	M15 0-0	O13 1-0	a19 3-0	a02 0-2	M01 2-1	M29 2-0	S01 2-1	D01 1-2	A18 1-3	O10 3-2	O27 1-0	F02 0-0	D29 1-0		S22 1-1	a23 2-2
21 W.B.A.	D15 2-2	F23 1-2	M18 4-4	S29 2-2	D26 3-0	O27 4-1	a01 3-0	A18 0-0	D01 1-1	a07 0-0	M29 2-1	D29 0-2	S15 4-0	O10 2-0	M14 0-0	N10 2-1	S01 1-5	O20 4-0	m03 0-1	F09 2-1		a19 0-0
22 WOLVERHAMPTON W	m16 1-2	O27 1-1	D08 3-1	D21 1-3	J12 3-0	N17 0-3	S08 1-1	O09 0-0	F02 0-0	A25 3-0	a26 3-1	F26 1-0	a12 1-2	S22 3-1	M01 0-2	O13 1-0	m12 3-1	D26 0-0	M22 3-0	a05 1-2	N24 0-0	

Kevin Drinkell, the local boy made good who scored 16 goals when Grimsby Town won the Division Three title in 1979-80.

DIVISION 2

	BIRMINGHAM C	BRISTOL R	BURNLEY	CAMBRIDGE U	CARDIFF C	CHARLTON A	CHELSEA	FULHAM	LEICESTER C	LUTON T	NEWCASTLE U	NOTTS CO	OLDHAM A	ORIENT	PRESTON N.E.	Q.P.R.	SHREWSBURY T	SUNDERLAND	SWANSEA C	WATFORD	WEST HAM U	WREXHAM
1 BIRMINGHAM C		S01 1-1	D15 2-0	N10 1-0	D29 2-1	S15 1-0	M11 5-1	A18 3-4	D01 1-2	a19 1-0	S29 0-0	m03 3-3	a01 2-0	F09 3-1	M15 2-2	J01 2-1	O27 1-0	O09 1-0	O20 2-0	M29 2-0	a07 0-0	F23 2-0
2 BRISTOL R	J12 1-0		D01 0-0	F02 0-0	S29 1-1	O20 3-0	F23 3-0	a04 1-0	a23 1-1	A21 3-2	N17 1-1	O06 2-3	D15 2-0	M08 1-2	M11 3-3	N03 1-3	A25 2-1	a19 2-2	D26 4-1	S08 1-1	m03 0-2	M22 1-0
3 BURNLEY	a26 0-0	a12 1-1		N24 5-3	O13 0-2	A21 1-1	O06 0-1	F02 2-1	M22 1-2	N17 0-0	D26 3-2	A25 0-1	S08 1-1	N03 1-2	M01 1-1	M08 0-3	a05 0-0	S22 1-1	J12 0-0	D08 1-0	F19 0-1	D21 1-0
4 CAMBRIDGE U	M22 2-1	S15 4-1	a19 3-1		F09 2-0	F23 1-0	S29 0-1	D15 4-0	A21 1-1	N03 1-2	M08 0-0	a08 2-3	D26 3-3	O22 1-1	m03 3-2	D01 2-1	J12 2-0	J19 3-3	O06 0-1	A25 2-2	a01 2-0	N17 2-0
5 CARDIFF C	A25 1-2	F16 0-1	F23 2-1	S22 0-0		M08 3-1	O20 1-2	D26 1-0	a08 0-1	O06 2-1	M22 1-1	N03 3-2	D01 1-0	N17 0-0	D15 0-2	A22 1-0	S08 1-0	m03 1-1	a07 1-0	F02 1-0	a19 0-1	J12 1-0
6 CHARLTON A	F02 0-1	M01 4-0	O09 3-3	O13 1-1	O27 3-2		M29 1-2	a08 0-1	D15 2-0	a04 1-4	A25 1-1	D26 0-0	N09 2-1	J12 0-1	A18 0-3	a19 2-2	S22 2-1	M15 0-4	m03 1-2	F26 0-0	D01 1-0	S08 1-2
7 CHELSEA	S08 1-2	O13 1-0	M15 2-1	F16 1-1	M01 1-0	N17 3-1		O27 0-2	D26 1-0	a07 1-1	J12 4-0	a19 1-0	m03 3-0	M22 1-0	D01 2-0	a02 0-2	F02 2-4	A18 0-0	D15 3-0	S22 2-0	N14 2-1	A25 3-1
8 FULHAM	N03 2-4	F26 1-1	S15 3-1	a26 1-2	a15 2-1	a22 1-0	M08 1-2		F09 0-0	S29 1-3	a12 1-0	O20 1-3	M28 0-1	A22 0-0	S01 1-0	J19 0-2	D08 2-1	D29 0-1	F23 1-2	N24 0-0	N10 1-2	O06 0-2
9 LEICESTER C	a12 2-1	J01 3-0	N10 1-1	O10 2-1	D21 0-0	a26 2-1	a05 1-0	S22 3-3		S01 1-3	F02 1-0	S08 1-0	M01 0-1	D08 2-2	M29 1-2	D29 2-0	M15 2-0	O27 2-1	F20 1-1	A18 2-0	O13 1-2	N24 2-0
10 LUTON T	N24 2-3	O09 3-1	M29 1-1	A18 1-1	M14 1-2	D21 3-0	J01 3-3	F16 4-0	J12 0-0		D08 1-1	F02 2-1	S22 0-0	A25 2-1	O27 1-1	N10 1-1	a12 0-0	O13 2-0	S08 5-0	a05 1-0	M01 1-1	a26 2-0
11 NEWCASTLE U	F20 0-0	M29 3-1	a07 1-1	O27 2-0	N10 1-0	D29 2-0	S01 2-1	D01 2-0	S15 3-2	m03 2-2		a02 2-2	A18 3-2	N19 2-0	O10 0-0	D15 4-2	O13 1-0	J01 3-1	a19 1-3	M01 0-2	M15 0-0	S22 1-0
12 NOTTS CO	D08 1-1	M15 0-0	D29 2-3	J01 0-0	A18 4-1	a05 0-0	N24 2-3	M01 1-1	J19 0-1	S15 0-0	D22 2-2		O13 1-1	a26 1-1	N10 2-1	S01 1-0	O09 5-2	M29 0-1	S22 0-0	a12 1-2	O27 0-1	F26 1-1
13 OLDHAM A	D21 1-0	a26 2-1	M04 2-1	a05 1-1	a12 0-3	M22 4-3	D08 1-0	N17 0-1	O20 1-1	F09 2-1	N03 1-0	F23 1-0		O06 1-0	S15 3-2	S29 0-0	N24 0-2	S01 3-0	M08 4-1	F19 1-1	a29 0-0	A21 2-3
14 ORIENT	S22 2-2	O27 2-1	A18 2-2	M01 2-0	M29 1-1	S01 1-1	N10 3-7	O09 1-0	m03 0-1	D29 2-2	S08 1-4	D15 1-0	M14 1-1		a19 2-2	a08 1-1	F16 0-1	D01 2-1	a30 0-0	O13 1-0	J01 0-4	F02 4-0
15 PRESTON N.E.	O06 0-0	S22 3-2	O20 3-2	D08 2-2	a26 2-0	N03 1-1	a12 1-1	J12 3-2	N17 1-1	M08 1-1	A21 1-0	M22 2-0	F02 0-1	N24 2-2		F23 0-3	D26 3-0	F16 2-1	A25 1-1	D21 1-2	S08 1-1	a05 0-0
16 Q.P.R.	a05 1-1	A18 2-0	O27 7-0	a12 2-2	O09 3-0	N24 4-0	D18 2-2	S08 3-0	A25 1-4	M22 2-2	a26 2-1	J12 1-3	F16 4-3	F12 0-0	O13 1-1		N17 2-1	M01 0-0	F02 3-2	M14 1-1	S22 3-0	D08 2-2
17 SHREWSBURY T	M08 1-0	D29 3-1	J01 2-0	S01 1-2	J19 1-2	F09 3-1	S15 3-0	m03 5-2	O06 2-2	D01 1-2	F23 3-1	A21 1-1	a19 0-1	S29 1-0	a01 1-3	M29 3-0		a08 1-2	N03 2-2	N10 1-0	D15 3-0	O20 3-1
18 SUNDERLAND	A22 2-0	N24 3-2	F09 5-0	S08 2-0	D08 2-1	O06 4-0	N03 2-1	A25 2-1	M08 0-0	F23 1-0	a05 1-0	N17 3-1	J12 4-2	a12 1-1	S29 1-1	O20 3-0	D21 2-1		M22 1-1	a26 5-0	m12 2-0	D26 1-1
19 SWANSEA C	F29 0-1	a05 2-0	S01 2-1	M14 2-4	J01 2-1	D08 1-0	a26 1-1	O13 4-1	S29 0-2	M04 2-0	N24 2-3	F09 0-1	O27 2-0	D21 0-1	D29 1-0	S15 1-2	A18 2-0	N10 3-1		O09 1-0	M29 2-1	a12 1-0
20 WATFORD	N17 1-0	J19 0-0	m03 4-0	D29 0-0	S15 1-1	S29 2-1	F09 2-3	a19 4-0	N03 1-3	D26 0-1	O20 2-0	D01 2-1	a07 1-0	F23 0-3	a09 0-0	O06 1-2	M22 0-1	D15 1-1	A21 0-0		S01 2-0	M18 3-1
21 WEST HAM U	a22 1-2	D08 2-1	S29 2-1	D21 3-1	N24 3-0	m05 4-1	A20 0-1	M22 2-3	F23 3-1	O20 1-2	O06 1-1	M11 1-2	A25 1-0	a05 2-0	J19 2-0	F09 2-1	a26 1-3	S15 2-0	N17 2-0	J12 1-1		N03 1-0
22 WREXHAM	O13 1-0	N10 1-2	a04 1-0	M29 1-0	S01 0-1	J19 3-2	D29 2-0	M15 1-1	a19 0-1	D15 3-1	F09 1-0	S29 1-0	O08 1-1	S15 2-1	J01 2-0	m03 1-3	M01 0-1	a07 0-1	D01 1-0	O27 3-0	A18 1-0	

SEASON 1979-80

DIVISION 3

	BARNSLEY	BLACKBURN R	BLACKPOOL	BRENTFORD	BURY	CARLISLE U	CHESTER	CHESTERFIELD	COLCHESTER U	EXETER C	GILLINGHAM	GRIMSBY T	HULL C	MANSFIELD T	MILLWALL	OXFORD U	PLYMOUTH A	READING	ROTHERHAM U	SHEFFIELD U	SHEFFIELD W	SOUTHEND U	SWINDON T	WIMBLEDON
1 BARNSLEY		O02 1-1	D21 2-1	M15 1-0	N06 2-1	M01 1-1	O27 1-1	O09 0-1	F16 1-2	N10 2-2	O13 2-0	a05 0-1	a22 3-1	S08 1-0	S22 2-1	J26 2-0	a26 0-0	A25 2-0	M04 0-0	M25 0-0	A18 0-3	D01 1-2	J12 1-2	a11 4-0
2 BLACKBURN R	S19 0-1		F09 2-0	M01 3-0	m03 1-2	O10 1-2	N07 2-0	N14 1-0	O27 3-0	F27 1-1	M14 3-1	S01 0-0	a04 1-0	D26 0-0	A18 1-1	D08 2-1	O13 1-0	a19 4-2	S29 0-3	a07 1-0	a22 1-2	S15 1-1	M29 2-0	J19 3-0
3 BLACKPOOL	a04 1-1	S22 2-1		O13 5-4	O10 1-2	a07 2-1	m03 0-0	N07 2-2	F29 1-0	M15 1-0	A18 2-1	J26 0-3	D26 2-2	a19 1-1	M29 2-2	J05 1-2	F16 1-3	D08 5-2	S15 3-2	O02 2-3	N10 1-1	J18 1-0	O27 0-1	S01 3-0
4 BRENTFORD	O06 3-1	O20 2-0	F23 2-1		a08 0-0	a19 0-3	D26 2-2	S01 3-1	N10 1-0	S17 0-2	J05 0-2	S15 1-0	D08 7-2	a07 2-0	m03 1-0	D15 1-1	M08 0-0	N03 2-2	M29 0-1	O22 1-2	J19 2-2	S29 2-0	D29 1-3	F09 0-1
5 BURY	O23 2-2	a29 1-2	A21 3-0	D21 4-2		M04 0-2	S01 2-0	D01 2-0	J29 0-1	J19 3-0	M29 0-2	S18 1-1	S15 0-1	F23 0-2	N10 3-0	F09 1-2	N03 2-1	M08 1-0	a05 1-0	O20 1-2	a12 1-0	O06 1-1	a26 0-0	S29 1-2
6 CARLISLE U	O20 3-1	A21 1-1	M18 2-0	D01 3-1	A25 1-0		S29 2-2	a05 0-2	a26 2-0	F09 4-1	S08 1-2	D21 0-2	F23 3-2	O23 1-1	J12 4-0	M08 2-2	M22 2-1	a15 3-3	S18 3-1	N17 1-0	F26 0-2	N03 4-0	a12 2-1	O06 1-1
7 CHESTER	M08 0-0	O24 0-0	D29 1-0	a05 1-1	J12 1-0	F20 1-0		a23 1-0	a12 2-1	M26 1-3	a30 0-2	A22 3-1	O20 2-1	N17 1-0	S08 1-1	M22 1-0	O06 1-0	S22 0-2	D21 3-1	A25 1-1	D01 2-2	a26 2-1	M19 1-0	N03 3-1
8 CHESTERFIELD	A21 2-0	M22 0-1	O23 0-0	J12 1-0	a19 2-0	D26 3-2	a07 2-0		S08 3-0	m03 3-0	a01 0-0	F23 2-3	S18 1-1	N03 2-0	D08 3-2	O06 2-2	A25 3-1	N17 7-1	F09 3-0	J05 2-1	S29 2-1	M08 1-0	M25 2-1	O20 0-0
9 COLCHESTER U	S29 0-0	M08 0-1	O19 3-1	M22 6-1	a07 2-1	D07 1-1	J08 1-1	J18 0-1		a02 0-0	D26 2-2	F08 2-1	N02 1-1	S18 2-1	a19 0-0	m02 3-0	N16 5-2	O05 1-1	D29 1-1	A21 1-0	S15 0-0	F22 2-1	A31 2-3	O23 4-0
10 EXETER C	M22 2-1	a12 2-0	O06 1-0	O03 0-0	S08 1-0	S22 1-2	O13 1-0	J26 1-2	D21 3-1		F16 3-1	N03 1-2	M08 2-2	A25 2-1	F02 2-1	N17 0-0	J01 2-2	M01 1-0	D01 1-1	J12 3-1	a26 1-0	O24 4-2	a05 4-1	A22 0-2
11 GILLINGHAM	F23 1-1	O06 1-2	N03 1-1	a12 0-1	N17 2-1	J19 1-1	S15 2-2	F26 0-1	a05 2-2	S29 1-0		O20 0-1	M04 1-0	M08 2-0	A25 1-1	O23 4-0	m03 0-1	J12 1-1	a26 0-1	M22 3-0	M18 1-1	N13 1-0	D01 0-0	S18 1-0
12 GRIMSBY T	D26 3-0	J12 1-2	A25 4-3	F02 5-1	O02 1-0	a04 2-0	O09 0-2	O13 1-1	S22 1-2	A18 4-1	M01 1-0		a07 1-1	D08 2-1	M15 2-0	a19 2-0	S08 1-0	J15 2-1	O27 2-0	m03 4-0	N06 3-1	M22 1-0	F16 2-0	N17 1-0
13 HULL C	N17 0-2	D21 0-1	a05 3-1	a26 2-1	m05 0-1	O13 2-0	M01 1-0	O02 2-1	A18 0-2	O27 2-2	S22 0-0	M25 2-2		J12 3-1	F16 1-0	A25 2-2	a12 1-0	M22 0-1	N06 1-1	S08 3-1	O09 1-1	m03 1-0	M14 1-0	D01 1-1
14 MANSFIELD T	a14 1-4	a05 0-1	D01 1-1	M10 0-0	O13 1-0	N06 2-1	M29 2-1	A18 3-2	O01 0-1	D29 0-1	O27 2-0	a26 0-0	S01 1-1		M01 1-0	S15 1-0	D21 0-0	F16 2-2	O08 5-1	S22 3-4	M15 1-1	a12 3-1	N10 1-1	J26 1-1
15 MILLWALL	F09 2-2	N03 1-0	N17 2-0	M18 3-1	M22 0-1	S01 1-0	J19 3-1	a26 2-0	D01 1-2	S15 5-1	D29 2-0	O06 2-0	S29 3-2	O20 2-2		F23 3-0	A21 2-1	O23 2-0	a12 0-0	M08 1-1	S18 3-3	F12 1-2	M04 6-2	a05 2-2
16 OXFORD U	S01 1-0	a26 0-1	a12 0-2	O10 0-2	S22 3-1	O27 1-0	N10 0-1	M14 1-2	J12 0-2	M29 2-0	N07 1-1	D01 0-1	D29 3-0	F02 3-1	O13 1-2		O31 1-1	S08 4-0	A18 5-1	F16 1-1	M01 0-2	a05 1-0	F06 2-2	M19 4-1
17 PLYMOUTH A	D08 2-1	F23 0-1	S29 2-2	O27 0-1	A18 2-0	N10 4-2	M15 1-0	D29 1-0	M29 2-0	a07 2-0	J26 2-2	J19 1-1	J05 5-1	a01 0-0	O09 1-1	S18 1-1		D26 2-0	O20 1-0	a19 4-1	S01 1-3	a22 0-0	N06 2-0	S15 3-0
18 READING	D29 7-0	D01 1-1	a26 0-1	A18 2-2	O27 3-1	S15 2-0	F09 2-1	M29 2-2	M14 2-0	O20 2-1	S01 1-3	a12 1-1	N10 3-0	S29 1-0	N07 2-0	M26 2-0	a05 1-0		F20 1-1	F23 2-1	D21 0-2	S19 1-1	O10 2-1	M05 3-0
19 ROTHERHAM U	a07 1-1	F05 1-3	m06 0-2	N17 4-2	D26 0-2	O02 4-1	a01 2-0	S22 2-0	A25 3-0	a19 2-0	D08 2-1	M08 0-0	O23 2-1	A21 2-1	M25 2-1	N03 0-2	M01 3-1	m03 1-1		O06 1-2	O13 1-2	J12 2-1	S08 3-0	M22 0-0
20 SHEFFIELD U	S15 2-0	J01 2-1	S18 3-1	N06 0-2	M01 0-0	M29 0-2	F26 1-1	a29 0-2	O09 1-2	S01 3-1	N10 4-0	D29 1-1	J19 1-1	F09 1-0	O27 0-1	S29 3-1	D01 3-2	O13 2-0	M15 1-0		a05 1-1	D21 2-0	A18 2-1	a26 2-1
21 SHEFFIELD W	N03 0-2	A25 0-3	M22 4-1	S08 0-2	F05 5-1	m03 0-0	a19 3-0	F16 3-3	F02 3-0	D08 0-1	a07 1-0	O23 2-0	A21 0-0	O06 0-0	O02 2-0	O20 2-2	J12 0-1	a01 1-1	F23 5-0	D26 4-0		N17 2-0	S22 4-2	M08 3-1
22 SOUTHEND U	a19 2-1	F02 0-1	S07 1-2	F16 3-2	M14 0-0	A18 1-0	D07 4-1	O26 0-0	O12 0-1	N05 4-0	O29 0-3	N09 1-0	J25 3-0	M17 1-1	a07 1-0	D26 1-1	S21 4-1	F25 2-2	S01 0-2	a04 2-1	M29 1-1		F29 1-0	D29 1-3
23 SWINDON T	m03 0-1	N17 2-0	M08 2-1	A25 4-0	D08 8-0	M11 0-0	S18 3-1	S15 2-1	a22 2-3	D26 2-3	a19 3-0	S29 3-0	O06 0-0	M22 2-1	a29 1-0	a07 1-1	O23 2-1	A21 0-0	a15 6-2	N03 3-2	F09 1-2	O20 1-0		F23 2-1
24 WIMBLEDON	M11 1-2	S08 1-0	J12 1-2	S22 0-0	F26 0-1	M14 0-0	A18 2-3	M01 1-1	N06 3-3	O09 2-2	F12 1-0	M29 3-6	a19 3-2	m03 3-2	a22 2-2	a15 1-3	F19 3-1	a07 1-1	N10 0-1	D08 1-1	O27 3-4	A25 0-1	O13 2-0	

DIVISION 4

	ALDERSHOT	BOURNEMOUTH	BRADFORD C	CREWE A	DARLINGTON	DONCASTER R	HALIFAX T	HARTLEPOOL U	HEREFORD U	HUDDERSFIELD T	LINCOLN C	NEWPORT CO	NORTHAMPTON T	PETERBOROUGH U	PORTSMOUTH	PORT VALE	ROCHDALE	SCUNTHORPE U	STOCKPORT CO	TORQUAY U	TRANMERE R	WALSALL	WIGAN A	YORK C
1 ALDERSHOT		D26 0-1	O06 3-1	S22 3-0	F02 1-1	a19 1-1	N17 3-1	J12 0-2	M08 3-3	N03 0-2	O23 2-0	A21 0-1	O13 2-0	O30 2-0	a07 1-2	A25 3-1	M22 3-0	S08 2-0	J26 2-0	M01 1-1	m06 0-0	F16 1-1	m03 0-3	D08 2-2
2 BOURNEMOUTH	a05 3-1		M08 1-1	a26 0-1	D29 1-0	N17 0-0	S22 0-1	O06 2-1	O23 2-2	O20 1-3	M22 0-0	A25 3-2	D21 2-2	D01 0-0	O02 0-1	a12 3-1	N03 4-0	M25 3-3	F02 2-0	J01 1-2	F16 2-1	A21 1-1	S08 1-2	F23 0-0
3 BRADFORD C	M15 2-0	O27 2-2		A18 4-0	a05 3-0	J26 3-1	N07 2-0	D21 2-0	a26 1-0	N10 0-0	S08 1-1	a22 3-0	O10 3-1	J12 1-1	M01 0-0	O02 2-0	J01 1-2	S22 2-0	O13 6-1	a12 1-1	A25 2-0	D01 0-1	F16 2-1	M29 1-2
4 CREWE A	F09 1-0	D07 0-0	N03 2-0		N17 0-0	O06 1-2	J12 2-1	M08 2-1	F23 1-0	S19 1-3	A22 0-2	M22 0-3	S29 2-1	F01 1-4	F12 1-1	S07 0-2	O20 2-1	a07 1-1	a19 1-0	A24 2-2	D26 0-0	O24 1-2	a04 2-1	m03 2-0
5 DARLINGTON	S15 0-0	m03 0-1	F26 3-4	M29 0-0		a04 2-1	O13 1-1	J19 0-1	J26 1-1	a08 2-3	M04 1-1	a19 1-1	N10 0-0	O27 1-1	M15 1-1	M01 1-1	A31 3-1	N06 3-1	O02 3-0	F16 2-0	D08 3-1	S22 1-3	A18 2-2	O09 2-1
6 DONCASTER R	D01 1-1	M29 1-0	S01 0-3	a22 1-1	D21 0-1		O09 2-1	M11 0-2	a11 1-0	D29 1-2	F02 1-1	S22 1-3	A18 2-1	N09 2-1	O26 2-0	J12 2-3	a26 2-0	F16 5-0	M01 1-1	S11 5-3	O02 1-1	a05 1-1	O13 3-1	N06 2-0
7 HALIFAX T	M29 1-0	F09 2-0	O23 0-1	S01 3-1	F23 1-1	A21 1-1		S29 2-1	S15 1-0	D26 2-1	D08 1-0	O06 2-1	M04 2-1	D29 0-0	a19 1-2	N10 0-0	S18 1-0	a08 2-2	a22 1-3	a29 3-3	N03 0-0	O20 2-1	M19 0-0	a07 1-1
8 HARTLEPOOL U	S01 1-0	M15 3-1	a04 0-1	O27 3-1	S08 3-1	a08 1-2	F16 1-2		N10 3-0	J26 1-1	a19 0-0	D08 0-0	M29 2-1	M01 1-2	A18 0-3	O13 2-1	D29 1-1	O09 3-2	N06 1-2	S22 2-2	J05 2-1	F02 2-2	a15 1-1	D26 3-1
9 HEREFORD U	O27 0-1	N07 2-1	D08 0-2	O13 2-0	A25 1-0	J05 2-2	F02 2-0	M22 2-1		a19 1-3	a02 0-0	a07 0-2	M01 0-1	F16 0-1	D26 0-0	O10 0-0	N17 1-1	m03 1-1	M15 2-0	O03 0-0	S08 1-2	J12 0-1	S22 2-1	A18 3-1
10 HUDDERSFIELD T	A18 2-0	M01 2-0	M22 0-0	O02 3-0	J01 2-1	A25 3-0	a05 5-0	m03 2-1	D01 0-1		J12 3-2	S08 2-1	N06 5-0	M15 0-0	O13 1-3	S22 7-1	D21 5-1	a15 2-1	F16 5-0	a26 4-2	N17 1-1	a12 1-1	O09 4-0	O27 2-2
11 LINCOLN C	M19 1-1	N10 1-1	J30 1-0	O10 3-0	a12 2-1	S15 1-1	a25 4-0	N30 3-3	F06 2-0	S01 2-0		F16 2-1	F13 0-0	A18 0-1	M29 1-0	M15 3-0	a05 0-0	O13 4-0	O27 1-0	J26 2-0	S22 3-0	O03 2-2	F29 4-0	D29 1-1
12 NEWPORT CO	O09 4-2	J26 0-0	S15 1-2	N10 1-1	D01 4-0	F26 2-1	M14 5-2	a26 1-0	J01 1-0	J18 2-2	S29 1-1		S18 2-1	D21 1-1	N06 4-3	A18 2-1	a12 1-0	D15 2-1	M29 3-1	a05 3-0	O13 2-0	D29 0-1	O27 3-2	S01 2-0
13 NORTHAMPTON T	F23 2-1	a08 0-1	A22 1-2	F16 1-0	M22 2-0	N03 1-0	S07 0-0	N17 2-1	O20 2-0	O23 4-2	a07 0-0	O02 3-2		S22 1-0	m03 0-2	F02 3-1	M08 0-0	D08 0-0	D26 2-0	M18 3-0	O06 2-1	A25 1-2	a19 1-1	J05 2-0
14 PETERBOROUGH U	S19 1-3	a19 2-0	m03 1-0	S15 3-0	M08 3-0	M22 3-2	A25 2-1	O20 2-0	S29 2-0	O06 1-3	N03 3-1	a08 0-1	F09 0-0		D08 0-0	J26 3-0	F23 2-0	J05 3-1	a07 1-1	O24 2-1	A22 1-2	N17 1-3	D26 1-2	M05 2-1
15 PORTSMOUTH	J01 1-3	S18 4-0	O20 4-1	a12 1-1	O06 4-3	M08 2-0	D01 3-1	N03 2-1	a05 0-0	F23 4-1	N17 4-0	O23 0-2	D29 6-1	a26 4-0		D21 2-2	F09 3-0	A25 6-1	S08 1-0	A21 3-0	F02 1-1	M22 1-2	J12 1-1	S29 5-2
16 PORT VALE	D29 0-2	J05 1-1	S17 1-2	F20 2-0	O20 2-0	m03 3-0	M22 1-0	F23 1-1	A20 0-1	F09 1-1	O06 1-2	N03 2-0	S15 5-0	S01 0-1	a01 2-3		S29 5-1	D26 1-0	D07 1-2	N17 1-1	O22 0-1	M08 2-2	a07 1-1	a19 1-2
17 ROCHDALE	D04 2-1	A18 0-2	a07 0-1	M01 0-0	J11 2-2	F12 3-2	O02 2-2	A24 1-0	m06 0-2	a01 0-2	M11 1-1	a29 2-0	O26 3-2	O12 0-0	S22 1-2	F15 0-2		a18 0-1	O09 0-1	a15 0-0	m02 2-0	S08 1-1	N06 0-2	M14 0-2
18 SCUNTHORPE U	a22 1-1	S01 2-1	F09 3-3	M04 1-1	O23 3-0	S28 0-0	D21 1-0	A21 1-3	D29 1-0	S14 1-1	F23 1-0	O20 1-3	a25 3-0	a12 1-0	J26 1-0	a05 1-0	N30 2-0		N10 1-1	N03 1-1	M08 2-2	O06 2-2	M29 1-3	S18 6-1
19 STOCKPORT CO	a11 0-4	S14 1-1	F22 2-2	N30 2-1	S17 1-1	O19 0-3	m02 4-1	O22 0-0	O05 2-1	S28 1-2	M08 2-1	N17 0-5	a04 2-0	J21 1-0	M10 1-1	a25 0-1	A20 1-1	M21 1-2		D21 4-0	J11 2-2	N02 1-0	A25 1-2	F08 1-0
20 TORQUAY U	O20 2-1	a07 0-0	M05 2-3	D29 1-0	S29 4-0	J19 2-2	O27 3-0	a23 3-1	S19 1-1	D08 3-1	m03 2-5	D26 2-0	S01 2-2	N07 2-0	O10 2-1	M29 1-1	S15 3-0	A18 3-0	a02 0-0		a19 3-1	F23 0-1	M14 2-2	N10 4-3
21 TRANMERE R	D21 1-2	S28 0-5	D28 4-0	a05 2-0	a26 1-2	S17 1-0	A18 2-0	a11 1-0	M25 0-0	M29 0-0	F09 1-0	F22 0-2	M14 1-1	O08 3-0	S14 4-1	N12 1-1	J25 5-1	O26 1-2	A31 0-1	N30 2-0		M04 0-1	M10 1-3	O19 1-2
22 WALSALL	S29 1-1	O09 0-0	a19 1-1	N06 1-0	F09 1-1	D26 3-1	M01 2-0	S15 3-1	S01 3-2	J05 1-1	S18 3-0	m03 2-4	J26 5-1	M29 2-3	N10 1-1	O27 2-1	F19 2-0	M15 1-1	A18 2-1	O13 1-1	a07 2-0		D08 1-1	a01 3-1
23 WIGAN A	M05 2-1	F06 2-1	S29 4-1	D21 2-0	N03 4-1	a30 0-0	a12 3-1	S19 2-1	F09 1-1	A22 1-2	O20 2-1	M08 0-1	D01 0-0	a05 2-1	S01 1-2	M26 3-1	O24 1-1	N17 4-1	D29 3-1	O06 0-3	M22 0-0	a26 3-0		S15 2-5
24 YORK C	a26 1-1	O12 1-1	N17 2-2	J26 2-2	A21 3-1	O23 1-3	F12 2-2	a05 2-1	N03 3-1	M08 0-4	A25 0-2	J12 2-1	a12 1-2	S08 0-2	F16 1-0	D01 5-1	O06 3-2	O02 2-0	S22 2-2	M22 1-0	M01 0-1	D21 0-1	F02 1-2	

LEAGUE TABLES

DIVISION 1

	P	W	D	L	F	A	W	D	L	F	A	Pts
Liverpool	42	15	6	0	46	8	10	4	7	35	22	60
Manchester U	42	17	3	1	43	8	7	7	7	22	27	58
Ipswich T	42	14	4	3	43	13	8	5	8	25	26	53
Arsenal	42	8	10	3	24	12	10	6	5	28	24	52
Nottingham F	42	16	4	1	44	11	4	4	13	19	32	48
Wolverh'pton W	42	9	6	6	29	20	10	3	8	29	27	47
Aston Villa	42	11	5	5	29	22	5	9	7	22	28	46
Southampton	42	14	2	5	53	24	4	7	10	12	29	45
Middlesbrough	42	11	7	3	31	14	5	5	11	19	30	44
W.B.A.	42	9	8	4	37	23	2	11	8	17	27	41
Leeds U	42	10	7	4	30	17	3	7	11	16	33	40
Norwich C	42	10	8	3	38	30	3	6	12	20	36	40
Crystal Palace	42	9	9	3	26	13	3	7	11	15	37	40
Tottenham H	42	11	5	5	30	22	4	5	12	22	40	40
Coventry C	42	12	2	7	34	24	4	5	12	22	42	39
Brighton & H.A.	42	8	8	5	25	20	3	7	11	22	37	37
Manchester C	42	8	8	5	28	25	4	5	12	15	41	37
Stoke C	42	9	4	8	27	26	4	6	11	17	32	36
Everton	42	7	7	7	28	25	2	10	9	15	26	35
Bristol C	42	6	6	9	22	30	3	7	11	15	36	31
Derby Co	42	9	4	8	36	29	2	4	15	11	38	30
Bolton W	42	5	11	5	19	21	0	4	17	19	52	25

DIVISION 2

	P	W	D	L	F	A	W	D	L	F	A	Pts
Leicester C	42	12	5	4	32	19	9	8	4	26	19	55
Sunderland	42	16	5	0	47	13	5	7	9	22	29	54
Birmingham C	42	14	5	2	37	16	7	6	8	21	22	53
Chelsea	42	14	3	4	34	16	9	4	8	32	36	53
Q.P.R.	42	10	9	2	46	25	8	4	9	29	28	49
Luton T	42	9	10	2	36	17	7	7	7	30	28	49
West Ham U	42	13	2	6	37	21	7	5	9	17	22	47
Cambridge U	42	11	6	4	40	23	3	10	8	21	30	44
Newcastle U	42	13	6	2	35	19	2	8	11	18	30	44
Preston N.E.	42	8	10	3	30	23	4	9	8	26	29	43
Oldham A	42	12	5	4	30	21	4	6	11	19	32	43
Swansea C	42	13	1	7	31	20	4	8	9	17	33	43
Shrewsbury T	42	12	3	6	41	23	6	2	13	19	30	41
Orient	42	7	9	5	29	31	5	8	8	19	23	41
Cardiff C	42	11	4	6	21	16	5	4	12	20	32	40
Wrexham	42	13	2	6	26	15	3	4	14	14	34	38
Notts Co	42	4	11	6	24	22	7	4	10	27	30	37
Watford	42	9	6	6	27	18	3	7	11	12	28	37
Bristol R	42	9	8	4	33	23	2	5	14	17	41	35
Fulham	42	6	4	11	19	28	5	3	13	23	46	29
Burnley	42	5	9	7	19	23	1	6	14	20	50	27
Charlton A	42	6	6	9	25	31	0	4	17	14	47	22

DIVISION 3

	P	W	D	L	F	A	W	D	L	F	A	Pts
Grimsby T	46	18	2	3	46	16	8	8	7	27	26	62
Blackburn R	46	13	5	5	34	17	12	4	7	24	19	59
Sheffield W	46	12	6	5	44	20	9	10	4	37	27	58
Chesterfield	46	16	5	2	46	16	7	6	10	25	30	57
Colchester U	46	10	10	3	39	20	10	2	11	25	36	52
Carlisle U	46	13	6	4	45	26	5	6	12	21	30	48
Reading	46	14	6	3	43	19	2	10	11	23	46	48
Exeter C	46	14	5	4	38	22	5	5	13	22	46	48
Chester C	46	14	6	3	29	18	3	7	13	20	39	47
Swindon T	46	15	4	4	50	20	4	4	15	21	43	46
Barnsley	46	10	7	6	29	20	6	7	10	24	36	46
Sheffield U	46	13	5	5	35	21	5	5	13	25	45	46
Rotherham U	46	13	4	6	38	24	5	6	12	20	42	46
Millwall	46	14	6	3	49	23	2	7	14	16	36	45
Plymouth A	46	13	7	3	39	17	3	5	15	20	38	44
Gillingham	46	8	9	6	26	18	6	5	12	23	33	42
Oxford U	46	10	4	9	34	24	4	9	10	23	38	41
Blackpool	46	10	7	6	39	34	5	4	14	23	40	41
Brentford	46	10	6	7	33	26	5	5	13	26	47	41
Hull C	46	11	7	5	29	21	1	9	13	22	48	40
Bury	46	10	4	9	30	23	6	3	14	15	36	39
Southend U	46	11	6	6	33	23	3	4	16	14	35	38
Mansfield T	46	9	9	5	31	24	1	7	15	16	34	36
Wimbledon	46	6	8	9	34	38	4	6	13	18	43	34

DIVISION 4

	P	W	D	L	F	A	W	D	L	F	A	Pts
Huddersfield T	46	16	5	2	61	18	11	7	5	40	30	66
Walsall	46	12	9	2	43	23	11	9	3	32	24	64
Newport Co	46	16	5	2	47	22	11	2	10	36	28	61
Portsmouth	46	15	5	3	62	23	9	7	7	29	26	60
Bradford C	46	14	6	3	44	14	10	6	7	33	36	60
Wigan A	46	13	5	5	42	26	8	8	7	34	35	55
Lincoln C	46	14	8	1	43	12	4	9	10	21	30	53
Peterborough U	46	14	3	6	39	22	7	7	9	19	25	52
Torquay U	46	13	7	3	47	25	2	10	11	23	44	47
Aldershot	46	10	7	6	35	23	6	6	11	27	30	45
Bournemouth	46	8	9	6	32	25	5	9	9	20	26	44
Doncaster R	46	11	6	6	37	27	4	8	11	25	36	44
Northampton T	46	14	5	4	33	16	2	7	14	18	50	44
Scunthorpe U	46	11	9	3	37	23	3	6	14	21	52	43
Tranmere R	46	10	4	9	32	24	4	9	10	18	32	41
Stockport Co	46	9	7	7	30	31	5	5	13	18	41	40
York C	46	9	6	8	35	34	5	5	13	30	48	39
Halifax T	46	11	9	3	29	20	2	4	17	17	52	39
Hartlepool U	46	10	7	6	36	28	4	3	16	23	36	38
Port Vale	46	8	6	9	34	24	4	6	13	22	46	36
Hereford U	46	8	7	8	22	21	3	7	13	16	31	36
Darlington	46	7	11	5	33	26	2	6	15	17	48	35
Crewe A	46	10	6	7	25	27	1	7	15	10	41	35
Rochdale	46	6	7	10	20	28	1	6	16	13	51	27

Football League Records

Top scorers: Div 1, P.Withe (Aston Villa), S.Archibald (Tottenham Hotspur) 20 goals; Div 2, D.Cross (West Ham United) 22 goals; Div 3, A.Kellow (Exeter City) 25 goals; Div 4, A.Cork (Wimbledon) 23 goals.

West Ham United and England midfielder Trevor Brooking, who was probably at the peak of his career when the Hammers won the Division Two title in 1980-81.

Gary Shaw, the only Birmingham-born player in Aston Villa's 1980-81 Championship side. He scored 18 goals that season.

DIVISION 1

	ARSENAL	ASTON VILLA	BIRMINGHAM C	BRIGHTON & HA	COVENTRY C	CRYSTAL P	EVERTON	IPSWICH T	LEEDS U	LEICESTER C	LIVERPOOL	MANCHESTER C	MANCHESTER U	MIDDLESBROUGH	NORWICH C	NOTTINGHAM F	SOUTHAMPTON	STOKE C	SUNDERLAND	TOTTENHAM H	W.B.A.	WOLVERHAMPTON W
1 ARSENAL		m02 2-0	M31 2-1	N01 2-0	J31 2-2	a20 3-2	N22 2-1	D27 1-1	a11 0-0	O04 1-0	M28 1-0	F24 2-0	D20 2-1	F28 2-2	O21 3-1	S27 1-0	A19 1-1	S13 2-0	O18 2-2	A30 2-0	N15 2-2	D06 1-1
2 ASTON VILLA	N29 1-1		D13 3-0	O22 4-1	A30 1-0	F21 2-1	S13 0-2	a14 1-2	N15 1-1	N01 2-0	J10 2-0	J31 1-0	M14 3-3	a25 3-0	A20 1-0	a18 2-0	M28 2-1	D26 1-0	O04 4-0	O18 3-0	a08 1-0	S20 2-1
3 BIRMINGHAM C	O07 3-1	O11 1-2		F07 2-1	A16 3-1	N08 1-0	m02 1-1	D20 1-3	a21 0-2	D06 1-2	S06 1-1	M21 2-0	A23 0-0	a04 2-1	F20 4-0	N11 2-0	J17 0-3	O25 1-1	D27 3-2	N22 2-1	S20 1-1	M17 1-0
4 BRIGHTON & H.A.	a04 0-1	D20 1-0	S13 2-2		M07 4-1	D27 3-2	O07 1-3	N11 1-0	m02 2-0	a20 2-1	F21 2-2	O25 1-2	N22 1-4	N08 0-1	S20 2-0	O11 0-1	F24 2-0	M21 1-1	D06 2-1	J31 0-2	A30 1-2	A16 2-0
5 COVENTRY C	A23 3-1	J17 1-2	N15 2-1	O04 3-3		S06 3-1	S27 0-5	F28 0-4	N01 2-1	M14 4-1	A19 0-0	J10 1-1	a11 0-2	D26 1-0	O18 0-1	N29 1-1	a25 1-0	a18 2-2	O21 2-1	M28 0-1	D13 3-0	F07 2-2
6 CRYSTAL P	D26 2-2	S27 0-1	a11 3-1	a18 0-3	F17 0-3		F28 2-3	S13 1-2	M28 0-1	O18 2-1	N15 2-2	N29 2-3	N01 1-0	A23 5-2	D13 4-1	a25 1-3	O21 3-2	J10 1-1	M14 0-1	A19 3-4	O04 0-1	J17 0-0
7 EVERTON	J10 1-2	F07 1-3	N29 1-1	D13 4-3	F21 3-0	S20 5-0		J17 0-0	M14 1-2	A19 1-0	O18 2-2	D26 0-2	M28 0-1	a18 4-1	a11 0-2	A23 0-0	O04 2-1	a25 0-1	N15 2-1	N01 2-2	O21 1-1	S06 2-0
8 IPSWICH T	a18 0-2	S06 1-0	J13 5-1	A19 2-0	S20 2-0	F07 3-2	A30 4-0		O04 1-1	N15 3-1	D13 1-1	a25 1-0	O18 1-1	F17 1-0	D26 2-0	J10 2-0	m13 2-3	J31 4-0	M28 4-1	M14 3-0	N01 0-0	F21 3-1
9 LEEDS U	N08 0-5	A16 1-2	D26 0-0	N29 1-0	a04 3-0	O25 1-0	O11 1-0	M31 3-0		A30 1-2	a18 0-0	O08 1-0	S20 0-0	N12 2-1	J31 1-0	D13 1-0	J10 0-3	F14 1-3	F21 1-0	S13 0-0	m06 0-0	M21 1-3
10 LEICESTER C	M07 1-0	a04 2-4	a25 1-0	D26 0-1	O11 1-3	M21 1-1	N12 0-1	A16 0-1	J17 0-1		A23 2-0	N08 1-1	F07 1-0	D13 1-0	N29 1-2	F28 1-1	a18 2-2	O08 1-1	S06 0-1	S27 2-1	J10 0-2	O25 2-0
11 LIVERPOOL	O25 1-1	N22 2-1	F14 2-2	S27 4-1	N11 2-1	A16 3-0	M21 1-0	O11 1-1	D27 0-0	J31 1-2		m19 1-0	a14 0-1	O07 4-2	A30 4-1	N08 0-0	F28 2-0	a03 3-0	m02 0-1	D06 2-1	S13 4-0	D20 1-0
12 MANCHESTER C	S06 1-1	A23 2-2	O18 0-1	M28 1-1	N22 3-0	m02 1-1	a20 3-1	D06 1-1	D20 1-0	M31 3-3	O04 0-3		F21 1-0	J17 3-2	N01 1-0	F07 1-1	N15 3-0	S20 1-2	A20 0-4	O22 3-1	M14 2-1	D27 4-0
13 MANCHESTER U	O11 0-0	O08 3-3	J31 2-0	J10 2-1	N08 0-0	a04 1-0	O25 2-0	M21 2-1	F28 0-1	S13 5-0	D26 0-0	S27 2-2		A16 3-0	a25 1-0	M18 1-1	N29 1-1	D13 2-2	A30 1-1	F17 0-0	a18 2-1	N12 0-0
14 MIDDLESBROUGH	S20 2-1	D06 2-1	N01 1-2	a11 1-0	a21 0-1	J31 2-0	D27 1-0	m02 2-1	A19 3-0	O21 1-0	m05 1-2	A30 2-2	N15 1-1		O04 6-1	S06 0-0	O18 1-1	F21 3-1	F07 1-0	D20 4-1	M28 2-1	N22 2-0
15 NORWICH C	M21 1-1	N12 1-3	S27 2-2	F28 3-1	D20 2-0	O29 1-1	N08 2-1	a20 1-0	A23 2-3	m02 2-3	J17 0-1	a04 2-0	D06 2-2	M17 2-0		O25 1-1	S13 1-0	A16 5-1	N22 1-0	D27 2-2	F14 0-2	O11 1-1
16 NOTTINGHAM F	F21 3-1	D27 2-2	A20 2-1	M14 4-1	m02 1-1	D06 3-0	J31 1-0	N22 1-2	O22 2-1	S20 5-0	a11 0-0	S13 3-2	O04 1-2	M03 1-0	M28 2-1		N01 2-1	A30 5-0	D20 3-1	N15 0-3	O18 2-1	a20 1-0
17 SOUTHAMPTON	N11 3-1	O25 1-2	A30 3-1	S06 3-1	D06 1-0	D20 4-2	M17 3-0	N08 3-3	N22 2-1	D27 4-0	S20 2-2	A16 2-0	M07 1-0	M21 1-0	F07 2-1	a04 2-0		O11 1-2	J31 2-1	a20 1-1	F21 2-2	O07 4-2
18 STOKE C	F07 1-1	a20 1-1	M28 0-0	O18 0-0	D27 2-2	N22 1-0	D06 2-2	A23 2-2	S06 3-0	D20 1-0	N01 2-2	M18 2-1	O22 1-2	S27 1-0	N15 3-1	F18 1-2	M14 1-2		a11 2-0	O04 2-3	A20 0-0	m02 3-2
19 SUNDERLAND	D13 2-0	M07 1-2	a18 3-0	a25 1-2	M21 3-0	O11 1-0	A16 3-1	O25 0-2	S27 4-1	F14 1-0	N29 2-4	N12 2-0	J28 2-0	S13 0-1	J10 3-0	O08 2-2	A23 1-2	N08 0-0		F28 1-1	D26 0-0	a04 0-1
20 TOTTENHAM H	J17 2-0	M21 2-0	J10 1-0	A23 2-2	O25 4-1	N12 4-2	a04 2-2	D17 5-3	F07 1-1	F21 1-2	a25 1-1	D13 2-1	S06 0-0	O11 3-2	a18 2-3	A16 2-0	D26 4-4	M11 2-2	S20 0-0		N29 2-3	N08 2-2
21 W.B.A.	A16 0-1	N08 0-0	F28 2-2	J17 2-0	O08 1-0	M07 1-0	M31 2-0	a04 3-1	D06 1-2	N22 3-1	F07 2-0	O11 3-1	D27 3-1	O25 3-0	S06 3-0	M21 2-1	S27 2-1	N25 0-0	a20 2-1	m02 4-2		A23 1-1
22 WOLVERHAMPTON W	a25 1-2	F28 0-1	O04 1-0	N15 0-2	S13 0-1	A30 2-0	m04 0-0	S27 0-2	O18 2-1	M28 0-1	N25 4-1	a18 1-3	A19 1-0	J10 3-0	M14 3-0	D26 1-4	D13 1-1	N29 1-0	N01 2-1	a30 1-0	J31 2-0	

DIVISION 2

	BLACKBURN R	BOLTON W	BRISTOL C	BRISTOL R	CAMBRIDGE U	CARDIFF C	CHELSEA	DERBY CO	GRIMSBY T	LUTON T	NEWCASTLE U	NOTTS CO	OLDHAM A	ORIENT	PRESTON N.E.	Q.P.R.	SHEFFIELD W	SHREWSBURY T	SWANSEA C	WATFORD	WEST HAM U	WREXHAM
1 BLACKBURN R		a18 0-0	a11 1-0	N29 2-0	O22 2-0	N15 2-3	O18 1-1	F14 1-0	S20 2-0	S13 3-0	a25 3-0	M28 0-0	A20 1-0	J31 2-0	D26 0-0	O04 2-1	M14 3-1	A30 2-0	N01 0-0	J10 0-0	D13 0-0	F21 1-1
2 BOLTON W	D27 1-2		O18 1-1	S06 2-0	N01 6-1	F07 4-2	O04 2-3	J24 3-1	N22 1-1	m02 0-3	A23 4-0	N25 3-0	F24 2-0	D06 3-1	O21 2-1	D19 1-2	A19 0-0	M14 0-2	S20 1-4	a11 2-1	M28 1-1	a20 1-1
3 BRISTOL C	N08 2-0	D13 3-1		A23 0-0	J10 0-1	D26 0-0	a18 0-0	O25 2-2	M10 1-1	O07 2-1	O11 2-0	S20 0-1	N29 1-1	a04 3-1	N15 0-0	F21 0-1	F07 1-0	a25 1-1	S06 0-1	J17 0-0	A19 1-1	M21 0-2
4 BRISTOL R	m02 0-1	F14 2-1	J31 0-0		O04 0-1	F28 0-1	M14 1-0	N22 1-1	A30 2-2	D27 2-4	S27 0-0	D19 1-1	S13 0-0	A16 1-1	M28 2-0	N11 1-2	O18 3-3	a11 1-1	a21 1-2	N04 3-1	N01 0-1	D06 0-1
5 CAMBRIDGE U	D20 0-0	a04 2-3	N22 2-1	M07 1-3		M21 2-0	S13 0-1	A16 3-0	m02 5-1	O25 1-3	N08 2-1	a20 1-2	O11 3-1	N11 1-0	F14 1-0	D06 1-0	J24 0-2	F28 3-1	J17 3-1	A23 3-1	S27 1-2	O07 1-0
6 CARDIFF C	A16 1-2	S13 1-1	a20 2-3	S20 2-1	O17 1-2		O31 0-1	m02 0-0	D06 1-1	N22 1-0	F25 1-0	F20 0-1	J31 0-2	A30 4-2	a11 1-3	O22 1-0	M04 0-0	M28 2-2	D27 3-3	O04 1-0	m06 0-0	N12 1-0
7 CHELSEA	M21 0-0	M07 2-0	D27 0-0	O08 2-0	F07 3-0	a04 0-1		N12 1-3	O11 3-0	a20 0-2	O25 6-0	m02 0-2	N08 1-0	D20 0-1	S20 1-1	A30 1-1	N22 2-0	J31 3-0	D06 0-0	F21 0-1	S06 0-1	A16 2-2
8 DERBY CO	S06 2-2	A30 1-0	M28 1-0	J10 2-1	N15 0-3	N29 1-1	A20 3-2		F07 2-1	D31 2-2	a18 2-0	a11 2-2	D26 4-1	F21 1-1	m06 1-2	O18 3-3	O04 3-1	N01 1-1	M31 0-1	D13 1-1	N26 2-0	S20 0-1
9 GRIMSBY T	F28 0-0	J10 4-0	O04 1-0	J17 2-0	N29 3-1	a25 0-1	D13 2-0	S13 0-1		S27 0-0	D26 0-0	M14 2-1	a18 0-0	F14 2-0	A19 0-0	N01 0-0	O21 0-0	N15 1-0	M28 1-0	O18 1-1	a11 1-5	A23 1-0
10 LUTON T	F07 3-1	N29 2-2	M14 3-1	a18 1-0	M28 0-0	J10 2-2	D26 2-0	A23 1-2	F21 0-2		J17 0-1	O04 0-1	a25 1-2	S20 2-1	D13 4-2	a11 3-0	N01 3-0	O18 1-1	O21 2-2	A19 1-0	N15 3-2	S06 1-1
11 NEWCASTLE U	a15 0-0	J31 2-1	D20 0-0	F21 0-0	a11 2-1	S06 2-1	M28 1-0	D27 0-2	a20 1-1	A30 2-1		A20 1-1	S20 0-0	m02 3-1	M14 2-0	F07 1-0	N15 1-0	O22 1-0	O18 1-2	N01 2-1	O04 0-0	N22 0-1
12 NOTTS CO	O25 2-0	A16 2-1	F28 2-1	O11 3-1	m05 2-0	S27 4-2	N29 1-1	N08 0-0	O07 0-0	M07 0-1	N11 0-0		D13 0-2	M21 1-0	a18 0-0	S06 2-1	A23 2-0	J10 0-0	F07 2-1	a25 1-2	J17 1-1	a05 1-1
13 OLDHAM A	N11 1-0	S27 1-1	m02 2-0	F07 1-0	M15 2-2	A23 2-0	a11 0-0	a20 0-2	D27 1-2	D06 0-0	F28 0-0	O21 0-1		N22 0-1	N01 1-1	A16 1-0	S06 2-0	O04 0-0	D20 2-2	M28 2-1	O18 0-0	F17 1-3
14 ORIENT	A23 1-1	a26 2-2	N01 3-1	N15 2-2	A19 3-0	J17 2-2	O21 0-1	S27 1-0	S06 2-0	M01 0-0	N29 1-1	O18 0-2	J10 2-3		O04 4-0	M31 4-0	M28 2-0	D13 1-0	a11 1-1	D26 1-1	a18 0-2	F07 2-1
15 PRESTON N.E.	a21 0-0	M24 1-2	A16 1-1	O25 0-0	S06 2-0	N08 3-1	F28 1-0	D06 0-3	D02 2-4	O11 1-0	O07 2-3	D27 2-2	a04 1-2	M07 3-0		N22 3-2	a14 2-1	S27 0-0	m02 1-3	F07 2-1	A23 0-0	D20 1-1
16 Q.P.R.	M07 1-1	O11 3-1	S27 4-0	A19 4-0	a25 5-0	F03 2-0	J17 1-0	M21 3-1	a04 1-0	N08 3-2	S13 1-2	F14 1-1	N15 2-0	O07 0-0	J10 1-1		F28 1-2	N29 0-0	A23 0-0	a18 0-0	D26 3-0	O25 0-1
17 SHEFFIELD W	O07 2-1	N11 2-0	S13 2-1	D13 4-1	a18 4-1	O11 2-0	J10 0-0	M07 0-0	a28 1-2	a04 3-1	A16 2-0	J31 1-2	F14 3-0	O25 2-2	A30 3-0	S20 1-0		D26 1-1	F21 2-0	N29 1-0	m08 0-1	N08 2-1
18 SHREWSBURY T	J17 1-1	O07 1-2	D06 4-0	N08 3-1	S20 2-1	O25 2-0	A23 2-2	a04 1-0	A16 1-1	D19 0-1	M21 1-0	N22 1-1	M07 2-2	O11 1-2	F21 3-0	m02 3-3	a21 2-0		N11 0-0	S06 2-1	F07 0-2	D27 1-2
19 SWANSEA C	a04 2-0	F28 3-0	M17 0-0	D26 2-1	A30 1-1	a18 1-1	a25 3-0	O11 3-1	O24 1-0	a27 2-2	D13 4-0	S13 1-1	O07 3-0	N08 0-2	N28 3-0	J31 1-2	S27 2-3	A19 2-1		D16 1-0	J10 1-3	M06 3-1
20 WATFORD	N22 1-1	N08 3-1	A30 1-0	M21 3-1	J31 0-0	M07 4-2	S27 2-3	O07 1-1	D20 3-1	N11 0-1	a04 0-0	D06 2-0	O25 2-1	a17 2-0	S13 2-1	D27 1-1	m02 2-1	F14 1-0	A16 2-1		F28 1-2	O11 1-0
21 WEST HAM U	O11 2-0	O25 2-1	N11 5-0	a04 2-0	F21 4-2	O07 1-0	F14 4-0	D20 3-1	N08 2-1	A16 1-2	M07 1-0	A30 4-0	M21 1-1	D27 2-1	J31 5-0	a21 3-0	D06 2-1	S13 3-0	N22 2-0	S20 3-2		m02 1-0
22 WREXHAM	S27 0-1	D26 0-1	O21 1-0	a25 3-1	D13 0-0	A19 0-1	N15 0-4	F28 2-2	J31 0-2	M31 0-0	J10 0-0	N01 1-1	A30 3-2	S13 3-1	O18 0-1	M28 1-1	a11 4-0	a18 1-2	O04 1-1	m04 0-1	N29 2-2	

Season 1980-81

DIVISION 3

	BARNSLEY	BLACKPOOL	BRENTFORD	BURNLEY	CARLISLE U	CHARLTON A	CHESTER	CHESTERFIELD	COLCHESTER U	EXETER C	FULHAM	GILLINGHAM	HUDDERSFIELD T	HULL C	MILLWALL	NEWPORT CO	OXFORD U	PLYMOUTH A	PORTSMOUTH	READING	ROTHERHAM U	SHEFFIELD U	SWINDON T	WALSALL
1 BARNSLEY		D20 2-0	S30 0-1	M28 3-2	N04 3-1	O04 0-0	N01 2-0	a20 1-1	a07 3-0	a10 1-0	N29 2-2	J31 3-3	S13 1-0	N11 5-0	O18 2-0	m02 4-1	O21 1-1	J10 2-1	A16 1-2	F21 2-3	a28 1-0	A30 2-1	S20 2-0	D27 3-0
2 BLACKPOOL	a25 1-0		S20 0-3	a18 0-0	M28 0-1	M25 0-2	D26 2-3	O22 0-3	O18 1-1	D06 0-0	F14 0-2	O04 4-0	J31 1-2	S13 2-2	M04 0-0	N01 2-4	a12 1-1	M14 1-0	A30 0-2	J17 0-0	A20 0-0	O01 2-1	N15 1-1	F21 1-0
3 BRENTFORD	S15 1-1	F28 2-0		J03 0-0	M14 1-1	N15 0-1	O18 0-1	a11 3-2	D26 2-1	N03 0-1	S13 1-3	O20 3-3	J17 0-0	S27 2-2	A18 1-0	O04 0-1	N01 3-0	M28 0-1	F14 2-2	A23 1-2	a25 2-1	a18 1-1	D06 1-1	J24 4-0
4 BURNLEY	D02 0-1	D27 4-1	O25 2-0		a21 0-3	F17 0-1	F28 1-0	A23 1-0	S06 1-0	F07 1-0	M07 3-0	N29 3-2	a14 4-2	S16 2-0	S27 5-0	A16 1-1	m02 1-1	D20 2-1	J27 1-3	N08 1-2	O11 1-1	O07 3-2	a04 0-0	N11 0-0
5 CARLISLE U	O07 2-2	O28 2-0	O11 1-2	D26 3-2		a25 1-2	J31 3-0	S27 2-6	D06 4-0	M31 1-1	N08 2-2	S13 0-0	N11 1-1	M21 2-0	S16 2-1	A30 1-4	F28 0-0	F14 2-0	a04 0-0	F10 0-0	a18 0-1	A16 0-3	M17 2-1	M07 1-1
6 CHARLTON A	M07 1-1	O25 2-1	A16 3-1	A30 2-0	D20 2-1		S13 1-0	N29 1-0	S20 1-2	F21 1-0	D27 1-1	m02 2-1	a04 1-2	J10 3-2	M17 0-0	N11 3-0	a21 0-0	J31 1-1	a14 1-2	O28 4-2	N08 2-0	O11 2-0	M21 0-0	O07 2-0
7 CHESTER	a04 2-2	a17 2-1	J10 0-0	S20 0-0	A23 1-0	F07 4-0		D27 2-1	F21 0-0	S06 1-0	O25 0-1	D20 1-2	O29 0-2	O08 4-1	J24 0-1	D03 1-1	A16 0-1	N12 1-0	m02 0-1	O11 1-0	M21 0-1	N08 3-2	M07 1-0	D06 1-0
8 CHESTERFIELD	D26 0-0	M21 3-2	N08 2-1	J31 3-0	F21 1-0	J17 0-1	a18 2-0		S30 3-0	m08 1-0	a04 0-0	A30 2-0	A16 2-1	O11 1-0	D06 3-0	S20 3-2	F14 2-1	S13 2-2	M07 3-0	m05 3-2	O07 2-0	N11 1-0	a07 2-2	O25 1-2
9 COLCHESTER U	O11 2-2	J10 3-2	a20 0-2	F14 2-1	m02 1-0	F28 2-0	S27 1-1	S16 1-1		F03 1-2	N11 3-2	D27 2-1	M07 1-2	O28 2-0	S13 3-0	D20 1-0	N29 3-0	A16 2-2	O07 1-0	M22 1-2	O25 0-0	a04 1-1	N08 1-0	A23 1-1
10 EXETER C	N08 0-1	m02 0-0	O08 0-0	S13 0-0	N29 2-0	S27 4-3	a29 2-2	D20 2-2	A30 4-0		S17 1-0	A16 2-1	O11 1-4	J31 1-3	F28 2-0	D27 2-2	N12 1-1	a21 1-1	J14 2-0	a04 3-1	M18 2-1	M21 1-1	O25 3-4	J10 0-3
11 FULHAM	J16 2-3	S05 1-2	F07 1-1	O04 0-2	a11 2-3	a18 1-0	M17 0-1	N01 1-1	A20 1-0	O01 0-1		M14 3-2	D06 2-2	A29 0-0	O22 1-1	M28 2-1	O18 0-4	N04 0-0	F21 3-0	a25 1-2	N15 1-1	D26 2-1	J31 2-0	S20 2-1
12 GILLINGHAM	A23 1-1	M07 3-1	M21 2-0	a07 0-0	F07 0-1	D06 0-1	a25 2-1	J24 1-0	a18 0-0	N15 1-5	O11 1-0		S16 0-0	O25 2-0	D26 1-2	S06 3-2	S27 1-1	F28 0-1	N08 0-1	A19 2-0	J03 0-0	O28 2-2	O07 0-0	a03 1-0
13 HUDDERSFIELD T	F07 1-0	A23 1-1	N29 3-0	O21 0-0	A19 1-1	N01 0-1	M28 0-0	N15 2-0	O04 2-0	a07 5-0	m02 4-2	S30 1-0		D27 5-0	a11 0-1	J10 4-1	N04 2-0	O18 2-0	D20 0-0	S06 4-1	J24 1-0	S20 1-0	F21 0-2	a21 1-1
14 HULL C	A19 1-2	F07 2-1	F21 0-0	S30 0-0	O21 0-1	O18 0-2	N04 0-0	M14 0-0	M17 0-1	A23 3-3	a07 0-1	M28 2-2	a18 2-1		N15 3-1	m07 3-1	O04 0-1	N01 1-0	S20 2-1	D06 2-0	D26 1-2	a25 1-1	a14 0-0	S06 0-1
15 MILLWALL	M21 1-1	O07 0-0	N11 2-2	F21 2-2	S30 3-0	S06 2-0	A30 1-0	m02 0-2	F07 3-1	S20 1-0	J10 3-1	a20 0-0	N08 2-1	A16 1-1		J31 0-0	D20 2-1	N29 1-1	D27 0-0	M08 2-1	a04 0-1	O25 1-4	O11 3-1	O28 0-1
16 NEWPORT CO	D06 0-0	a04 3-1	M07 1-1	N15 1-2	m05 4-0	A19 1-2	D13 1-1	F28 5-1	a25 1-0	a18 2-1	O28 2-1	F14 1-1	O25 3-2	N08 4-0	A23 2-1		S13 0-1	S27 0-2	O11 2-1	O07 0-0	J16 0-1	J03 4-0	D26 0-2	a07 1-1
17 OXFORD U	M24 1-1	N08 0-2	a04 1-1	D06 0-2	S20 1-2	D26 1-0	N15 1-0	S06 0-3	J17 2-1	A20 1-2	M21 2-0	F21 1-1	O08 0-2	M07 1-1	a29 1-0	F07 0-1		A30 0-0	O25 1-2	a18 2-1	O29 1-1	J31 2-0	O01 0-0	O11 1-1
18 PLYMOUTH A	O25 1-3	O11 0-2	O28 0-1	a25 2-1	S06 4-1	A23 1-1	A19 2-0	F07 1-0	N15 1-1	D26 0-2	O07 2-1	S20 4-1	M17 0-0	a04 0-0	J17 2-0	F21 3-2	J24 3-0		M21 1-0	S30 2-1	D06 3-1	a14 1-0	a18 0-0	N08 2-0
19 PORTSMOUTH	N15 0-1	J24 3-3	S06 0-2	O18 4-2	N01 2-1	S16 1-0	N29 2-0	O04 1-0	N04 2-1	F10 5-0	S27 1-0	a11 0-0	a25 1-2	F28 2-1	a18 2-1	M14 0-0	M29 1-1	O21 1-3		D26 0-0	A23 3-1	J10 1-0	A19 1-0	F07 2-0
20 READING	S27 3-2	N29 3-0	J31 0-0	a11 1-3	J10 3-1	M28 1-3	J02 3-0	O18 2-3	O22 1-0	N01 2-1	D20 0-0	N12 0-1	F14 2-1	m02 2-0	O04 4-1	F18 1-1	D27 0-1	S17 1-1	a20 2-1		F28 1-1	S13 1-0	A30 4-1	A16 2-0
21 ROTHERHAM U	S06 2-0	N11 4-0	D20 4-1	M31 1-0	D27 3-0	a11 3-0	O21 0-0	N04 0-0	M28 2-0	O04 3-1	A16 2-2	O18 2-0	A30 0-0	a20 1-1	N01 3-0	N29 1-0	J10 0-0	m02 2-1	J31 3-0	S20 2-0		F21 2-1	F07 1-0	S30 2-1
22 SHEFFIELD U	M31 1-1	S16 4-2	D27 0-0	N04 0-0	N15 2-2	M14 3-2	a07 2-0	A19 2-0	N01 3-0	O18 3-1	a21 1-2	J17 0-1	F28 2-2	D20 3-1	M28 2-3	O14 2-0	A23 1-0	O04 0-0	D06 1-0	F07 2-0	S27 1-2		S06 3-0	m02 0-1
23 SWINDON T	F28 2-0	A16 1-2	m02 0-0	N01 0-3	O18 1-1	O21 0-3	O04 1-2	J10 0-1	a11 3-0	M28 2-2	A23 3-4	N04 0-0	S27 1-0	N29 3-1	M14 0-0	a20 1-1	S16 1-0	D27 3-0	N11 0-2	J24 3-1	S13 2-1	F14 5-2		D19 3-1
24 WALSALL	a18 1-1	S27 2-2	A30 2-3	A20 3-1	O04 4-3	N04 2-2	J17 2-1	M28 4-3	J31 3-1	O21 1-3	M01 1-2	N01 3-3	D26 2-2	F14 1-1	J03 0-0	O18 1-0	M14 0-3	a11 1-3	S13 2-0	N15 2-2	S16 0-2	N29 4-4	a25 2-1	

DIVISION 4

	ALDERSHOT	BOURNEMOUTH	BRADFORD C	BURY	CREWE A	DARLINGTON	DONCASTER R	HALIFAX T	HARTLEPOOL U	HEREFORD U	LINCOLN C	MANSFIELD T	NORTHAMPTON T	PETERBOROUGH U	PORT VALE	ROCHDALE	SCUNTHORPE U	SOUTHEND U	STOCKPORT CO	TORQUAY U	TRANMERE R	WIGAN A	WIMBLEDON	YORK C
1 ALDERSHOT		O07 0-0	a04 1-1	S05 1-0	A23 2-0	F21 2-1	O25 1-0	D06 2-1	M07 2-1	D26 4-0	S30 0-0	S20 1-0	J03 0-0	N08 0-0	F07 0-0	O11 0-0	N15 0-0	a18 1-2	J17 3-0	O28 2-1	M22 3-2	J24 0-1	A19 2-0	a25 1-1
2 BOURNEMOUTH	N04 0-2		F14 4-0	a11 2-2	O21 0-0	M14 3-3	D06 1-2	J17 2-1	S16 1-0	A19 1-0	a25 0-1	O18 0-1	A23 0-0	F28 4-1	M28 0-0	S27 2-1	O04 2-2	D26 2-1	J03 0-1	J24 1-1	S13 1-0	N01 3-0	a18 0-1	N15 1-1
3 BRADFORD C	N01 1-0	S06 1-1		M28 0-2	O04 2-2	N04 3-0	D26 1-1	F11 0-0	a19 2-0	m15 0-1	O22 1-2	M14 0-2	S17 3-1	J28 1-1	O18 2-1	M08 2-1	A23 0-0	M04 2-1	A20 1-1	F07 2-0	S27 0-3	a11 3-3	N15 2-0	D06 1-1
4 BURY	F14 0-0	N08 3-0	O25 2-2		S16 1-3	A30 1-2	M31 2-0	J31 0-0	N11 0-0	O28 2-1	m04 1-1	S13 4-1	O07 1-2	M07 1-1	S27 2-1	M21 3-1	a18 6-1	A16 1-2	a25 0-1	O11 3-0	a04 2-2	F28 0-0	N29 1-0	D26 2-0
5 CREWE A	J31 0-0	J10 0-2	M07 1-0	O01 2-2		D20 1-1	O11 0-0	S20 2-1	a03 2-0	O07 5-0	A30 0-3	N29 1-2	M21 3-1	D27 1-0	m01 0-0	O25 1-0	F14 1-0	O29 1-1	F21 2-0	A16 0-1	N12 3-0	D13 1-2	S13 0-3	N08 1-1
6 DARLINGTON	S27 1-2	O11 1-2	O07 2-1	J24 2-1	a25 2-1		N11 5-0	a18 3-1	D26 3-0	M08 2-1	M10 0-0	F15 2-2	A16 1-0	M21 2-0	m05 1-1	O28 4-4	S16 0-1	O25 0-2	A23 2-2	a05 1-0	N08 2-0	S13 3-1	M17 4-1	J03 0-0
7 DONCASTER R	J10 3-1	m02 2-1	a21 2-0	O21 1-0	M13 1-1	A19 2-0		O18 0-0	J24 1-2	S06 5-1	O04 0-1	D19 2-1	F06 1-1	A23 0-4	N15 2-0	N29 1-2	M27 1-0	S19 1-0	a10 2-1	S30 2-0	D27 1-0	N04 1-1	N01 2-1	F20 3-2
8 HALIFAX T	m02 1-0	N29 1-2	O28 2-0	A23 4-2	M24 1-0	D27 1-2	M21 0-3		N08 1-2	O25 0-0	F14 1-3	A16 0-2	a04 0-1	N11 2-3	D20 2-2	a20 2-0	S13 1-0	O11 1-5	J24 2-0	M07 2-1	J10 1-1	S16 0-1	S27 0-1	O07 3-1
9 HARTLEPOOL U	O04 1-0	S30 1-0	D27 2-2	A19 1-2	N01 6-2	a17 2-0	A30 1-0	a11 3-0		S20 2-0	O18 2-0	O21 0-1	S06 2-3	D20 1-1	J10 3-0	J31 2-2	N04 2-0	F21 1-3	M28 1-0	N29 0-2	m02 3-0	N15 3-1	M14 2-3	F07 1-0
10 HEREFORD U	a20 0-0	N12 1-0	D20 4-0	J10 0-1	N05 0-0	O04 0-1	F14 1-3	M28 0-1	F28 3-0		N01 0-2	J31 2-1	S27 4-1	m02 1-1	O22 2-3	S17 3-0	a11 2-1	S13 0-0	m06 2-0	D27 0-1	A16 1-1	N29 1-1	O18 1-1	A30 1-1
11 LINCOLN C	S17 0-1	D20 2-0	J10 1-1	D06 2-1	J24 2-1	m02 1-0	M07 1-1	S06 3-0	M21 2-0	a04 1-0		D27 1-1	O25 8-0	A16 1-1	a20 1-0	O08 3-0	S27 2-2	N08 2-1	F07 1-0	N12 5-0	O29 2-0	A23 2-0	F28 0-0	O11 1-1
12 MANSFIELD T	a06 1-2	M21 1-1	O11 1-0	F07 2-0	J17 4-1	S06 1-0	m06 1-1	N15 0-1	M16 0-1	A23 4-0	a18 2-0		O27 2-0	O25 2-1	J24 5-0	a04 2-2	D26 1-0	M07 0-1	D06 1-0	N08 1-1	O06 1-1	S27 3-1	S15 1-0	A18 0-1
13 NORTHAMPTON T	O21 2-0	J31 0-1	S30 0-1	N04 5-3	O17 4-1	N15 2-2	S13 0-2	O31 2-1	F14 3-1	a14 0-0	M28 1-1	J10 0-1		a21 2-2	D27 5-1	D20 3-2	M13 3-3	S23 2-0	O03 0-1	m01 1-0	N29 3-1	F03 1-1	a11 1-1	S19 2-0
14 PETERBOROUGH U	a11 0-0	S20 1-0	A30 2-2	O04 2-0	a18 2-1	O18 1-0	J31 0-1	A20 2-2	a25 1-1	D06 3-0	N15 1-0	M28 1-0	D26 3-0		N01 1-1	S13 2-2	O22 0-2	O01 5-2	N04 1-2	F21 1-3	M18 4-1	M13 0-0	M04 1-1	J17 3-0
15 PORT VALE	S13 0-1	O27 0-2	a14 2-1	F21 1-3	D05 2-2	S20 4-2	A16 3-0	a26 0-0	O25 1-1	M16 4-0	D20 0-1	A30 0-0	a18 1-1	a04 1-1		N08 1-1	M03 2-2	N10 1-0	S29 2-0	O06 3-1	O11 5-1	F14 3-0	J31 2-3	M07 2-0
16 ROCHDALE	M14 0-2	F21 0-0	S20 0-2	O18 2-1	J03 2-0	M28 0-0	J17 2-2	D26 1-1	A23 1-1	S30 0-0	N04 1-0	N01 1-4	m03 0-1	F07 2-3	a12 2-1		A19 4-0	D06 0-2	D12 2-1	S06 2-1	J24 3-1	O04 3-0	O21 2-0	a18 3-2
17 SCUNTHORPE U	A16 2-2	M06 1-1	J31 1-0	D27 2-2	S06 1-1	S30 3-0	O28 1-1	F07 2-2	O07 3-3	N08 3-1	F21 2-2	a20 2-0	O11 0-2	J10 1-1	F24 1-1	N11 1-1		M22 2-1	S19 2-0	O25 0-2	D20 2-0	m02 4-4	A30 1-2	a04 3-2
18 SOUTHEND U	D27 3-0	a17 2-1	D12 3-1	N15 1-0	M27 3-0	J09 1-0	F27 0-0	M13 5-1	S26 4-0	F06 2-0	a11 0-0	O03 2-0	J23 0-0	S15 1-0	A18 5-1	m01 1-1	O17 2-0		O31 2-0	D19 3-1	A20 2-0	O20 1-0	N03 1-0	S05 3-0
19 STOCKPORT CO	N29 1-0	O24 2-1	N10 1-2	D19 1-2	S26 1-3	J30 0-1	N07 2-1	A29 1-1	O27 0-2	O10 0-0	S13 0-0	m01 2-1	M06 1-2	O06 3-4	S15 2-1	A16 2-2	F27 2-0	a03 1-0		F16 4-1	a20 1-0	D27 0-1	F13 0-0	M20 2-0
20 TORQUAY U	M29 2-0	A30 2-0	S13 2-0	M14 3-1	N15 1-0	N01 0-2	S16 2-3	O04 1-0	J17 2-1	a18 0-1	A20 1-2	a12 1-1	D06 3-3	S27 2-0	N05 4-0	F14 2-0	F04 2-1	a25 0-3	O22 1-2		M01 2-1	O18 2-0	D26 2-3	a08 1-2
21 TRANMERE R	O17 3-1	F06 0-1	M10 1-1	O31 3-1	A18 0-1	a10 3-1	a17 1-1	O20 2-0	D05 2-2	a29 2-1	M03 0-0	N03 1-0	J16 3-2	S05 1-2	M24 1-2	A29 3-1	a24 1-2	J30 2-2	D26 1-0	S19 1-0		M29 2-3	O03 3-0	S29 5-0
22 WIGAN A	A30 1-0	a04 0-1	N08 0-1	S20 2-1	D26 0-0	F07 3-1	O08 3-0	O01 4-1	A16 0-3	F11 1-0	J31 0-2	F21 2-0	N12 3-0	O11 1-1	S06 1-0	M07 0-1	D06 1-1	J03 0-1	a18 2-1	M21 2-0	O25 1-1		a25 1-0	O29 1-0
23 WIMBLEDON	N11 4-0	D27 2-0	A16 2-2	m02 2-4	F07 2-0	D06 1-1	a04 1-0	F21 3-0	O11 5-0	M22 0-0	S20 0-1	S30 2-1	N08 1-0	O28 2-1	A23 1-0	a28 4-1	J19 2-2	O07 0-1	S06 1-2	a20 1-0	M07 2-1	M31 1-0		O25 3-0
24 YORK C	D20 4-1	A16 4-0	m02 0-3	a14 0-1	a11 2-0	O21 1-2	S27 0-1	N04 1-1	S13 0-1	J24 1-2	M14 1-0	N11 2-0	m05 1-2	M24 1-2	O04 4-1	D27 1-2	N01 1-0	F14 0-1	O18 1-0	A23 0-0	S23 4-1	J10 2-1	M28 0-1	

LEAGUE TABLES

DIVISION 1

	P	W	D	L	F	A	W	D	L	F	A	Pts
Aston Villa	42	16	3	2	40	13	10	5	6	32	27	60
Ipswich T	42	15	4	2	45	14	8	6	7	32	29	56
Arsenal	42	13	8	0	36	17	6	7	8	25	28	53
W.B.A.	42	15	4	2	40	15	5	8	8	20	27	52
Liverpool	42	13	5	3	38	15	4	12	5	24	27	51
Southampton	42	15	4	2	47	22	5	6	10	29	34	50
Nottingham F	42	15	3	3	44	20	4	9	8	18	24	50
Manchester U	42	9	11	1	30	14	6	7	8	21	22	48
Leeds U	42	10	5	6	19	19	7	5	9	20	28	44
Tottenham H	42	9	9	3	44	31	5	6	10	26	37	43
Stoke C	42	8	9	4	31	23	4	9	8	20	37	42
Manchester C	42	10	7	4	35	25	4	4	13	21	34	39
Birmingham C	42	11	5	5	32	23	2	7	12	18	38	38
Middlesbrough	42	14	4	3	38	16	2	1	18	15	45	37
Everton	42	8	6	7	32	25	5	4	12	23	33	36
Coventry C	42	9	6	6	31	30	4	4	13	17	38	36
Sunderland	42	10	4	7	32	19	4	3	14	20	34	35
Wolverh'pton W	42	11	2	8	26	20	2	7	12	17	35	35
Brighton & H.A.	42	10	3	8	30	26	4	4	13	24	41	35
Norwich C	42	9	7	5	34	25	4	0	17	15	48	33
Leicester C	42	7	5	9	20	23	6	1	14	20	44	32
Crystal Palace	42	6	4	11	32	37	0	3	18	15	46	19

DIVISION 2

	P	W	D	L	F	A	W	D	L	F	A	Pts
West Ham U	42	19	1	1	53	12	9	9	3	26	17	66
Notts Co	42	10	8	3	26	15	8	9	4	23	23	53
Swansea C	42	12	5	4	39	19	6	9	6	25	25	50
Blackburn R	42	12	8	1	28	7	4	10	7	14	22	50
Luton T	42	10	6	5	35	23	8	6	7	26	23	48
Derby Co	42	9	8	4	34	26	6	7	8	23	26	45
Grimsby T	42	10	8	3	21	10	5	7	9	23	32	45
Q.P.R.	42	11	7	3	36	12	4	6	11	20	34	43
Watford	42	13	5	3	34	18	3	6	12	16	27	43
Sheffield W	42	14	4	3	38	14	3	4	14	15	37	42
Newcastle U	42	11	7	3	22	13	3	7	11	8	32	42
Chelsea	42	8	6	7	27	15	6	6	9	19	26	40
Cambridge U	42	13	1	7	36	23	4	5	12	17	42	40
Shrewsbury T	42	9	7	5	33	22	2	10	9	13	25	39
Oldham A	42	7	9	5	19	16	5	6	10	20	32	39
Wrexham	42	5	8	8	22	24	7	6	8	21	21	38
Orient	42	9	8	4	34	20	4	4	13	18	36	38
Bolton W	42	10	5	6	40	27	4	5	12	21	39	38
Cardiff C	42	7	7	7	23	24	5	5	11	21	36	36
Preston N.E.	42	8	7	6	28	26	3	7	11	13	36	36
Bristol C	42	6	10	5	19	15	1	6	14	10	36	30
Bristol R	42	4	9	8	21	24	1	4	16	13	41	23

DIVISION 3

	P	W	D	L	F	A	W	D	L	F	A	Pts
Rotherham U	46	17	6	0	43	8	7	7	9	19	24	61
Barnsley	46	15	5	3	46	19	6	12	5	26	26	59
Charlton A	46	14	6	3	36	17	11	3	9	27	27	59
Huddersfield T	46	14	6	3	40	11	7	8	8	31	29	56
Chesterfield	46	17	4	2	42	16	6	6	11	30	32	56
Portsmouth	46	14	5	4	35	19	8	4	11	20	28	53
Plymouth A	46	14	5	4	35	18	5	9	9	21	26	52
Burnley	46	13	5	5	37	21	5	9	9	23	27	50
Brentford	46	7	9	7	30	25	7	10	6	22	24	47
Reading	46	13	5	5	39	22	5	5	13	23	40	46
Exeter C	46	9	9	5	36	30	7	4	12	26	36	45
Newport Co	46	11	6	6	38	22	4	7	12	26	39	43
Fulham	46	8	7	8	28	29	7	6	10	29	35	43
Oxford U	46	7	8	8	20	24	6	9	8	19	23	43
Gillingham	46	9	8	6	23	19	3	10	10	25	39	42
Millwall	46	10	9	4	30	21	4	5	14	13	39	42
Swindon T	46	10	6	7	35	27	3	9	11	16	29	41
Chester C	46	11	5	7	25	17	4	6	13	13	31	41
Carlisle U	46	8	9	6	32	29	6	4	13	24	41	41
Walsall	46	8	9	6	43	43	5	6	12	16	31	41
Sheffield U	46	12	6	5	38	20	2	6	15	27	43	40
Colchester U	46	12	7	4	35	22	2	4	17	10	43	39
Blackpool	46	5	9	9	19	28	4	5	14	26	47	32
Hull C	46	7	8	8	23	22	1	8	14	17	49	32

DIVISION 4

	P	W	D	L	F	A	W	D	L	F	A	Pts
Southend U	46	19	4	0	47	6	11	3	9	32	25	67
Lincoln C	46	15	7	1	44	11	10	8	5	22	14	65
Doncaster R	46	15	4	4	36	20	7	8	8	23	29	56
Wimbledon	46	15	4	4	42	17	8	5	10	22	29	55
Peterborough U	46	11	8	4	37	21	6	10	7	31	33	52
Aldershot	46	12	9	2	28	11	6	5	12	15	30	50
Mansfield T	46	13	5	5	36	15	7	4	12	22	29	49
Darlington	46	13	6	4	43	23	6	5	12	22	36	49
Hartlepool U	46	14	3	6	42	22	6	6	11	22	39	49
Northampton T	46	11	7	5	42	26	7	6	10	23	41	49
Wigan A	46	13	4	6	29	16	5	7	11	22	39	47
Bury	46	10	8	5	38	21	7	3	13	32	41	45
Bournemouth	46	9	8	6	30	21	7	5	11	17	27	45
Bradford C	46	9	9	5	30	24	5	7	11	23	36	44
Rochdale	46	11	6	6	33	25	3	9	11	27	45	43
Scunthorpe U	46	8	12	3	40	31	3	8	12	20	38	42
Torquay U	46	13	2	8	38	26	5	3	15	17	37	41
Crewe A	46	10	7	6	28	20	3	7	13	20	41	40
Port Vale	46	10	8	5	40	23	2	7	14	17	47	39
Stockport Co	46	10	5	8	29	25	6	2	15	15	32	39
Tranmere R	46	12	5	6	41	24	1	5	17	18	49	36
Hereford U	46	8	8	7	29	20	3	5	15	9	42	35
Halifax T	46	9	3	11	28	32	2	9	12	16	39	34
York C	46	10	2	11	31	23	2	7	14	16	43	33

Football League Records

Top scorers: Div 1, K.Keegan (Southampton) 26 goals; Div 2, R.Moore (Rotherham United) 22 goals; Div 3, G.Davies (Fulham) 24 goals; Div 4, K.Edwards (Sheffield United & Hull City) 36 goals.

From this season three points were awarded for a win.

DIVISION 1

	ARSENAL	ASTON VILLA	BIRMINGHAM C	BRIGHTON & HA	COVENTRY C	EVERTON	IPSWICH T	LEEDS U	LIVERPOOL	MANCHESTER C	MANCHESTER U	MIDDLESBROUGH	NOTTINGHAM F	NOTTS CO	SOUTHAMPTON	STOKE C	SUNDERLAND	SWANSEA C	TOTTENHAM H	W.B.A.	WEST HAM U	WOLVERHAMPTON W
1 ARSENAL		M27 4-3	S22 1-0	J26 0-0	O31 1-0	N28 1-0	M13 1-0	J30 1-0	m11 1-1	O17 1-0	S26 0-0	F16 1-0	a17 2-0	F13 1-0	m15 4-1	A29 0-1	S12 1-1	F27 0-2	a12 1-3	M16 2-2	m01 2-0	F02 2-1
2 ASTON VILLA	N07 0-2		S26 0-0	a12 3-0	F27 2-1	m15 1-2	O31 0-1	a28 1-4	J30 0-3	m01 0-0	S12 1-1	a17 1-0	N28 3-1	A29 0-1	F10 1-1	S23 2-2	F02 1-0	m21 3-0	F17 1-1	M30 2-1	O17 3-2	M13 3-1
3 BIRMINGHAM C	m04 0-1	F20 0-1		M27 1-0	J26 3-3	a06 0-2	S01 1-1	a10 0-1	m08 0-1	S19 3-0	M06 0-1	F06 0-0	S05 4-3	D05 2-1	O10 4-0	M13 2-1	F16 2-0	a24 2-1	M23 0-0	O31 3-3	O03 2-2	N21 0-3
4 BRIGHTON & H.A.	a10 2-1	D28 0-1	N07 1-1		S19 2-2	F06 3-1	m08 0-1	M02 1-0	O17 3-3	O03 4-1	a24 0-1	S05 2-0	F20 0-1	N21 2-2	a03 1-1	O31 0-0	D05 2-1	S01 1-2	M09 1-3	F27 2-2	J16 1-0	m04 2-0
5 COVENTRY C	M20 1-0	O10 1-1	m15 0-1	J30 0-1		a13 1-0	J16 2-4	S12 4-0	S22 1-2	D12 0-1	A29 2-1	N28 1-1	M09 0-1	F16 1-5	S26 4-2	N24 3-0	a27 6-1	O24 3-1	m01 0-0	D26 0-2	a17 1-0	M27 0-0
6 EVERTON	a24 2-1	D19 2-0	A29 3-1	S12 1-1	D28 3-2		O17 2-1	m04 1-0	M27 1-3	O31 0-1	a10 3-3	M13 2-0	a20 2-1	S22 3-1	J19 1-1	F13 0-0	N21 1-2	D05 3-1	J30 1-1	S26 1-0	F27 0-0	m08 1-1
7 IPSWICH T	O24 2-1	M20 3-1	J05 3-2	M30 3-1	a03 1-0	M06 3-0		S26 2-1	S12 2-0	N28 2-0	a20 2-1	m01 3-1	m15 1-3	J30 1-3	F16 5-2	a17 2-0	A29 3-3	N07 2-3	m17 2-1	S22 1-0	a13 3-2	O10 1-0
8 LEEDS U	S19 0-0	O03 1-1	m12 3-3	m15 2-1	F06 0-0	S02 1-1	F20 0-2		F27 0-2	M10 0-1	a03 0-0	a13 1-1	M20 1-1	N07 1-0	a17 1-3	m01 0-0	O24 1-0	J16 2-0	D12 0-0	O17 3-1	N28 3-3	S05 3-0
9 LIVERPOOL	S05 2-0	S19 0-0	M30 3-1	M06 0-1	F20 4-0	N07 3-1	F06 4-0	O10 3-0		D26 1-3	O24 1-2	S01 1-1	m01 2-0	a02 1-0	N28 0-1	a13 2-0	M20 1-0	O03 2-2	m15 3-1	a17 1-0	J05 3-0	J16 2-1
10 MANCHESTER C	M06 0-0	D05 1-0	J30 4-2	F13 4-0	m08 1-3	M20 1-1	a24 1-1	S23 4-0	a10 0-5		O10 0-0	N07 3-2	O24 0-0	m05 1-0	S12 1-1	J09 1-1	D19 2-3	N21 4-0	S26 0-1	A29 2-1	a03 0-1	D28 2-1
11 MANCHESTER U	F20 0-0	F06 4-1	O17 1-1	N28 2-0	M17 0-1	J06 1-1	S05 1-2	S30 1-0	a07 0-1	F27 1-1		O21 1-0	A31 0-0	O31 2-1	m01 1-0	m15 2-0	M27 0-0	S19 1-0	a17 2-0	a12 1-0	J27 1-0	O03 5-0
12 MIDDLESBROUGH	m08 1-3	N21 3-3	S12 2-1	a20 2-1	a24 0-0	O24 0-2	D05 0-1	a06 0-0	m18 0-0	M27 0-0	S22 0-2		O10 1-1	a10 3-0	J30 0-1	S26 3-2	N14 0-0	F13 1-1	A29 1-3	M09 1-0	M20 2-3	M06 0-0
13 NOTTINGHAM F	N21 1-2	a24 1-1	J09 2-1	S26 2-1	O17 2-1	a03 0-1	M17 1-1	O31 2-1	D05 0-2	M13 1-1	m05 0-1	F27 1-1		J23 0-2	A29 2-1	J30 0-0	S23 2-0	m08 0-2	m12 2-0	S12 0-0	N07 0-0	a10 0-1
14 NOTTS CO	O03 2-1	J16 1-0	m01 1-4	a17 4-1	S05 2-1	N24 2-2	S19 1-4	M27 2-1	J26 0-4	S01 1-1	M20 1-3	m11 0-1	a12 1-2		M06 1-1	a26 3-1	O10 2-0	F06 0-1	N28 2-2	m15 1-2	O24 1-1	F20 4-0
15 SOUTHAMPTON	J23 3-1	a10 0-3	F27 3-1	D08 0-2	m04 5-5	S05 1-0	O03 4-3	N21 4-0	a24 2-3	F06 2-1	D05 3-2	S19 2-0	F13 2-0	O17 3-1		M27 4-3	m08 1-0	D28 3-1	O31 1-2	M13 0-0	F20 2-1	S01 4-1
16 STOKE C	J20 0-1	m05 1-0	O24 1-0	M20 0-0	S02 4-0	O03 3-1	N21 2-0	D05 1-2	M09 1-5	S05 1-3	J23 0-3	F20 2-0	S19 1-2	m08 2-2	N07 0-2		a10 0-1	O17 1-2	F27 0-2	m20 3-0	F06 2-1	a24 2-1
17 SUNDERLAND	F06 0-0	S02 2-1	a12 2-0	m01 3-0	O03 0-0	a17 3-1	a07 1-1	M13 0-1	O31 0-2	m15 1-0	N07 1-5	a03 0-2	N25 2-3	F27 1-1	M10 2-0	F10 0-2		F20 0-1	O17 0-2	N28 1-2	S05 0-2	S19 0-0
18 SWANSEA C	O10 2-0	D15 2-1	N28 1-0	N24 0-0	M13 0-0	m01 1-3	M27 1-2	A29 5-1	F16 2-0	a17 2-0	J30 2-0	m15 1-2	D12 1-2	S12 3-2	a13 1-0	M06 3-0	S26 2-0		S22 2-1	a06 3-1	M30 0-1	O31 0-0
19 TOTTENHAM H	M29 2-2	S05 1-3	a28 1-1	O24 0-1	D05 1-2	S19 3-0	a10 1-0	m08 2-1	m03 2-2	F20 2-0	N21 3-1	J27 1-0	O03 3-0	a24 3-1	M20 3-2	O10 2-0	a14 2-2	m05 2-1		N07 1-2	S02 0-4	F06 6-1
20 W.B.A.	S02 0-2	m08 0-1	M20 1-1	O10 0-0	a10 1-2	F20 0-0	m05 1-2	m18 2-0	N21 1-1	a21 0-1	m12 0-3	O03 2-0	F06 2-1	M24 2-4	O24 1-1	N14 1-2	a24 2-3	S05 4-1	M27 1-0		S19 0-0	D05 3-0
21 WEST HAM U	D05 1-2	M06 2-2	F13 2-2	A29 1-1	N21 5-2	O10 1-1	M02 2-0	a24 4-3	S26 1-1	F02 1-1	m08 1-1	O31 3-2	M27 0-1	M13 1-0	S22 4-2	S12 3-2	m04 1-1	a10 1-1	m10 2-2	J30 3-1		a06 3-1
22 WOLVERHAMPTON W	a03 1-1	O24 0-3	a17 1-1	S22 0-1	N07 1-0	J23 0-3	F27 2-1	M16 1-0	A29 1-0	a12 4-1	F13 0-1	O17 0-0	F16 0-0	S26 3-2	N24 0-0	N28 2-0	J30 0-1	M20 0-1	S12 0-1	m01 1-2	m15 2-1	

Liverpool's goalscoring sensation Ian Rush. In his first full season with the Reds he hit 17 goals in another Championship-winning campaign.

DIVISION 2

	BARNSLEY	BLACKBURN R	BOLTON W	CAMBRIDGE U	CARDIFF C	CHARLTON A	CHELSEA	CRYSTAL P	DERBY CO	GRIMSBY T	LEICESTER C	LUTON T	NEWCASTLE U	NORWICH C	OLDHAM A	ORIENT	Q.P.R.	ROTHERHAM U	SHEFFIELD W	SHREWSBURY T	WATFORD	WREXHAM
1 BARNSLEY		F27 0-1	S12 3-0	J30 0-0	S26 0-1	a24 1-0	M12 2-1	D05 2-0	a10 0-0	M23 3-2	m04 0-2	M16 4-3	O17 1-0	F24 0-1	N07 3-1	O31 1-0	m08 3-0	a02 3-0	S22 1-0	A29 4-0	F09 0-0	N21 2-2
2 BLACKBURN R	O10 2-1		a12 0-2	S23 1-0	J30 1-0	J13 0-2	m15 1-1	M27 1-0	M06 4-1	M13 2-0	S26 0-2	N14 0-1	m01 4-1	N28 3-0	a09 0-0	S12 2-0	F16 2-1	J23 2-0	A29 0-1	N25 0-0	a17. 1-2	O31 0-0
3 BOLTON W	F06 2-1	D28 2-2		O24 3-4	M06 1-0	D19 2-0	J16 2-2	a24 0-0	m04 3-2	O03 1-2	O10 0-3	S05 1-2	S29 1-0	M20 0-1	S19 0-2	N21 1-0	D05 1-0	F20 0-1	m08 3-1	a03 1-1	N07 2-0	a10 2-0
4 CAMBRIDGE U	S19 2-1	m04 1-0	M13 2-1		O31 2-1	m08 4-0	O03 1-0	J26 0-0	S01 1-2	F27 2-2	a24 1-2	a10 1-1	F06 1-0	a03 1-2	F20 0-0	a20 2-0	F09 1-0	S05 3-0	S21 1-2	N07 2-0	O17 1-2	D05 2-3
5 CARDIFF C	F20 0-0	S19 1-3	O17 2-1	M20 5-4		D28 0-1	S05 1-2	m08 0-1	D04 1-0	M30 2-1	N21 3-1	m17 2-3	O03 0-4	N07 1-0	J20 0-1	a10 2-1	a24 1-2	F06 1-2	F27 0-2	O24 1-1	a03 2-0	N04 3-2
6 CHARLTON A	N28 2-1	S05 2-0	a28 1-0	J23 0-0	a13 2-2		N24 3-4	F06 2-1	O03 2-1	S19 2-0	N07 1-4	J19 0-0	a03 0-1	D30 0-0	O20 3-1	M12 5-2	O31 1-2	a17 1-2	O17 3-0	F27 1-0	m01 1-1	F20 1-0
7 CHELSEA	O24 1-2	D19 1-1	A29 2-0	a07 4-1	F17 1-0	S23 2-2		M17 1-2	a24 0-2	N21 1-1	M09 4-1	m08 1-2	N07 2-1	S26 2-1	a03 2-2	m05 2-2	a10 2-1	M20 1-4	D05 2-1	J30 3-1	S12 1-3	O10 2-0
8 CRYSTAL P	m01 1-2	N07 1-2	N28 1-0	A29 2-1	M09 1-0	S12 2-0	a12 0-1		O24 0-1	a03 0-3	M23 0-2	M20 3-3	m15 1-2	N24 2-1	a17 4-0	S22 1-0	J30 0-0	O10 3-1	J19 1-2	S26 0-1	a27 0-3	m11 2-1
9 DERBY CO	a28 0-1	O17 1-1	S23 0-2	N25 2-1	m01 0-0	F13 1-1	N28 1-1	M13 4-1		O31 1-1	S12 3-1	M27 0-0	F27 2-2	a17 0-2	J23 1-0	A29 1-2	S26 3-1	a12 3-1	J30 3-1	M10 1-1	m15 3-2	N14 2-1
10 GRIMSBY T	a09 3-2	O24 1-1	M02 1-1	O10 1-2	m15 0-1	J30 3-3	a17 3-3	a20 0-1	M20 1-0		A29 2-2	M06 0-0	N28 1-1	S22 1-2	m01 2-1	J09 1-2	S12 2-1	F09 1-2	S26 0-1	a27 5-1	M16 0-2	M27 1-1
11 LEICESTER C	S08 1-0	F20 1-0	F27 1-0	N28 4-1	a17 3-1	M27 3-1	O16 1-1	O03 1-1	F06 2-1	m12 1-2		S19 1-2	M02 3-0	m01 1-4	a13 2-1	N14 0-1	M13 3-2	M17 1-0	O31 0-0	m15 0-0	D12 1-1	S05 1-0
12 LUTON T	m15 1-1	a03 2-0	N24 2-0	M02 1-0	S22 2-3	A29 3-0	a20 2-2	O31 1-0	N07 3-2	O17 6-0	J30 2-1		a17 3-2	a12 2-0	F27 2-0	M30 2-0	m11 3-2	N28 3-1	S12 0-3	a30 4-1	S26 4-1	M12 0-0
13 NEWCASTLE U	M06 1-0	D05 0-0	F03 2-0	S12 1-0	F13 2-1	N14 4-1	M27 1-0	M31 0-0	O10 3-0	a24 0-1	a10 0-0	N21 3-2		J30 2-1	M20 2-0	S26 1-0	m05 0-4	O24 1-1	F24 1-0	S23 2-0	A29 0-1	m08 4-2
14 NORWICH C	S05 1-1	a24 2-0	O31 0-0	N14 2-1	M27 2-1	a10 5-0	F20 2-1	S02 1-0	N21 4-1	m05 2-1	D05 0-0	D28 1-3	S19 2-1		O03 1-2	m08 2-0	F27 0-1	J16 2-0	F03 2-3	O17 2-1	M13 4-2	F06 4-0
15 OLDHAM A	M27 1-1	D26 0-3	J30 1-1	S26 2-0	A29 2-2	m04 1-0	N16 1-0	N21 0-0	m08 1-1	D05 3-1	D28 1-1	O10 1-1	O31 3-1	F16 2-0		D19 3-2	S22 2-0	M06 0-3	M13 0-3	S12 1-1	J09 1-1	a24 2-1
16 ORIENT	J23 1-3	F06 0-0	a17 3-0	a12 0-0	a28 1-1	O25 1-1	S28 0-2	F21 0-0	J16 3-2	S05 1-2	m18 3-0	O03 0-3	N24 1-0	M16 1-1	m15 0-3		O18 1-1	m01 1-2	N07 3-0	N28 2-0	F27 1-3	S19 0-0
17 Q.P.R.	D12 1-0	O03 2-0	m01 7-1	m15 2-1	N28 2-0	M20 4-0	D26 0-2	S19 1-0	F20 3-0	F06 1-0	O24 2-0	S01 1-2	S05 3-0	O10 2-0	N24 0-0	a06 3-0		N07 1-1	M29 2-0	a17 2-1	a12 0-0	J16 1-1
18 ROTHERHAM U	N14 2-4	m08 4-1	S26 2-0	F13 1-0	S12 1-0	N21 2-1	O31 6-0	F27 2-0	F02 2-1	a10 2-2	S22 1-1	a24 2-2	M13 0-0	A29 4-1	O17 1-2	D05 1-0	M27 1-0		m04 2-2	F16 3-0	J30 1-2	F23 2-0
19 SHEFFIELD W	N24 2-2	J16 2-2	F16 0-1	a17 2-1	O10 2-1	M06 1-1	m01 0-0	S05 1-0	S19 1-1	F20 1-1	M20 2-0	F06 3-3	a12 2-1	m15 2-1	O24 2-1	M27 2-0	N14 1-3	S08 2-0		M02 0-0	N28 3-1	O03 0-3
20 SHREWSBURY T	F02 0-2	S01 1-2	N14 2-0	M27 1-0	M13 1-1	O10 1-1	S19 1-0	m04 1-0	S05 4-1	m08 2-0	M30 1-1	D05 2-2	F20 0-0	a20 0-2	F06 2-1	a24 2-0	N21 2-1	O03 2-1	a10 0-1		O31 0-2	M16 1-1
21 WATFORD	O03 3-1	N21 3-2	M27 3-0	M06 0-0	N14 0-0	D05 2-2	F06 1-0	a09 1-1	J26 6-1	S01 0-2	m08 3-1	F20 1-1	J16 2-3	O24 3-0	S05 1-1	O10 3-0	M09 4-0	S19 1-0	a24 4-0	M20 3-1		m04 2-0
22 WREXHAM	a17 0-0	M20 1-0	M09 2-1	m01 0-0	N24 3-1	S26 1-0	F27 1-0	O17 0-1	a03 1-1	N07 2-0	a20 0-0	O24 0-2	a06 4-2	S12 2-3	N28 0-3	J30 0-1	A29 1-3	m15 3-2	F13 0-1	a12 1-0	S22 0-1	

Burnley's Welsh international Bryan Flynn, a great servant who sadly missed much of the Clarets' Division Three title-winning season of 1980-81.

Season 1981-82

DIVISION 3

	BRENTFORD	BRISTOL C	BRISTOL R	BURNLEY	CARLISLE U	CHESTER	CHESTERFIELD	DONCASTER R	EXETER C	FULHAM	GILLINGHAM	HUDDERSFIELD T	LINCOLN C	MILLWALL	NEWPORT CO	OXFORD U	PLYMOUTH A	PORTSMOUTH	PRESTON N.E.	READING	SOUTHEND U	SWINDON T	WALSALL	WIMBLEDON
1 BRENTFORD		N07 0-1	M22 1-0	O31 0-0	O03 1-2	N28 1-0	M13 2-0	m01 2-2	F27 2-0	J23 0-1	S21 0-1	J02 0-1	O17 3-1	a09 4-1	F20 2-0	a03 1-2	S19 0-0	F06 2-2	a17 0-0	m15 1-2	O19 0-1	a19 4-2	S05 0-0	a26 2-3
2 BRISTOL C	M27 0-1		a12 1-2	N28 2-3	a06 1-1	m15 1-0	O31 0-0	S05 2-2	F23 3-2	F06 0-0	m01 2-1	J16 0-0	M13 0-1	m12 4-1	S19 2-1	M06 0-2	S22 3-2	F20 0-1	O10 0-0	O20 2-0	N14 0-2	a17 0-3	O03 0-1	J02 1-3
3 BRISTOL R	m03 1-2	D29 1-0		S12 2-1	D19 0-1	A29 2-2	J19 1-0	M20 3-0	F09 3-2	D05 1-2	N07 2-0	O24 3-2	S26 0-2	a03 0-1	N03 2-0	m11 1-0	m08 2-3	a10 1-1	F13 2-0	J30 1-1	F27 2-1	O17 1-4	a24 2-1	S29 2-2
4 BURNLEY	M20 0-0	a24 2-0	F06 4-0		m04 1-0	N03 1-0	m18 1-1	S22 0-1	O17 3-3	O24 2-2	F02 1-0	S19 0-0	a10 1-0	F20 1-1	J16 2-1	D05 2-1	S05 1-0	F27 3-0	m11 2-0	a03 3-0	a20 3-5	O03 0-2	m08 2-1	N07 2-2
5 CARLISLE U	F13 1-0	A29 2-2	m15 1-2	S29 1-0		a13 3-0	F09 3-0	N03 2-0	a20 3-2	N07 1-2	N28 2-0	M09 2-2	J30 1-0	a17 2-1	M20 2-2	S26 2-1	O17 3-1	a03 2-0	F02 1-0	M23 2-1	S12 3-2	F27 1-1	O24 2-1	m01 2-1
6 CHESTER	a24 1-2	a21 0-0	J23 1-1	M17 0-1	m19 0-1		O21 0-2	D02 1-1	N14 0-2	m05 0-2	F06 0-0	F20 3-1	m08 1-2	S19 0-0	a10 0-2	O10 2-2	M13 0-3	J19 3-2	M27 0-1	O31 2-3	D05 1-1	S05 0-0	S23 0-0	M31 1-1
7 CHESTERFIELD	O24 0-2	M20 1-0	S05 2-0	a12 1-2	S22 1-0	M09 3-5		F02 3-1	a17 2-1	S19 3-0	m15 1-3	N03 1-0	a03 0-2	a27 0-1	J23 1-0	N07 2-2	F20 2-2	O03 2-2	J05 0-0	F27 2-1	O17 1-2	m01 2-1	F06 1-0	N28 2-0
8 DONCASTER R	S26 1-0	m18 2-2	O31 4-2	F09 0-1	M16 1-1	F13 4-3	a10 0-0		S11 3-0	m08 2-1	a03 1-1	N06 1-2	O20 4-1	O07 1-0	F27 0-2	M23 1-1	a24 2-2	D05 0-0	S29 1-0	A29 0-1	m04 1-1	M12 0-0	a20 1-0	J29 1-3
9 EXETER C	O10 3-1	a10 4-0	S23 1-3	M06 2-1	S05 2-1	a03 3-0	D05 0-3	F06 2-1		M10 1-0	F20 1-1	m12 1-0	M24 1-2	O03 5-4	a24 1-0	N04 1-2	D28 1-1	m05 3-3	O24 4-3	N07 4-3	m08 1-1	S19 1-2	J16 2-0	M20 2-1
10 FULHAM	A29 1-2	S12 2-1	a17 4-2	M13 1-1	M27 4-1	S26 2-0	J30 1-0	a06 3-1	O20 4-1		m11 0-0	F27 2-2	m18 1-1	N28 0-0	O17 3-1	F23 0-0	M16 1-3	O31 1-1	m15 3-0	m01 2-2	S29 2-1	a13 2-0	N14 1-1	F09 4-1
11 GILLINGHAM	F09 1-1	S29 1-1	M27 2-0	A29 3-1	a24 0-0	S12 0-1	a06 3-2	N14 3-0	S26 2-3	a10 2-0		O17 3-2	m04 1-0	M12 1-1	D28 1-1	m08 2-1	F27 3-2	O20 4-2	J30 0-2	m18 2-1	M16 2-0	O31 1-0	D05 1-4	F13 6-1
12 HUDDERSFIELD T	m08 1-1	m04 5-0	M13 0-2	J30 1-2	O20 2-1	S29 1-2	M23 1-1	M27 1-2	A29 1-1	O10 1-0	M06 2-0		M02 0-2	O31 1-2	M30 2-0	J09 2-0	D05 0-0	a24 0-1	F09 2-3	F13 6-1	S26 3-2	N14 3-0	a10 2-1	S12 1-1
13 LINCOLN C	M06 1-0	O24 1-2	m01 1-0	M31 1-1	S19 0-0	F03 3-0	N14 2-1	M10 5-0	m15 2-0	S05 1-1	J16 2-0	a12 2-0		S23 0-1	O03 2-2	M20 2-1	F06 2-0	J23 1-1	N04 1-2	a17 2-1	M27 1-1	N28 2-0	F20 1-1	O10 5-1
14 MILLWALL	D28 0-1	N03 2-0	N14 0-0	S26 4-3	D05 1-2	J30 2-1	m04 3-2	M06 0-2	F14 5-1	a25 4-3	O24 1-2	a06 1-3	F09 1-1		M09 1-0	S29 1-2	a20 2-1	m08 1-0	A29 2-1	S13 0-1	a12 1-1	M28 0-0	O11 2-0	F24 2-1
15 NEWPORT CO	S29 0-1	J30 1-1	M16 1-1	m01 0-0	O31 2-0	D26 0-1	A29 1-0	O10 1-0	N28 1-1	M07 1-3	a12 4-2	m15 1-0	F13 0-0	O20 1-1		S12 3-2	N14 0-1	M13 1-1	S26 1-1	J02 3-1	m11 3-2	m18 1-0	M27 2-2	a17 0-0
16 OXFORD U	N14 1-2	O17 1-0	O21 1-1	a17 0-0	F20 2-1	F27 3-1	M27 1-1	a12 3-1	M17 0-0	O03 2-0	M31 1-1	S05 1-0	O31 1-1	m01 0-0	F06 1-1		a28 1-0	S23 0-2	N28 3-0	F03 1-0	M13 0-2	a07 5-0	S19 0-1	m15 0-3
17 PLYMOUTH A	J30 1-0	F09 2-1	J02 4-0	J09 1-1	M06 1-0	O24 5-1	S26 0-2	N28 4-2	a09 2-1	N03 3-1	O10 1-2	a17 1-1	S12 0-2	m15 2-1	a02 1-2	A29 0-1		N07 0-0	m01 0-3	S29 1-1	F13 0-0	D26 2-1	M20 4-1	a14 2-0
18 PORTSMOUTH	S12 2-2	S26 2-0	D26 0-0	O10 1-2	N14 1-2	m01 2-0	F13 5-1	a17 0-0	S29 2-0	M20 1-1	M09 1-0	N28 2-1	A29 1-1	m21 2-2	O24 0-0	F09 1-1	M27 1-0		a06 1-1	a12 3-0	J30 0-0	m15 3-0	M06 1-0	N03 1-0
19 PRESTON N.E.	D05 1-3	F27 1-3	O03 0-1	O20 1-1	a10 0-1	N07 0-1	m08 2-0	F20 3-1	M13 1-0	a20 1-3	S19 1-1	S22 1-1	M16 1-1	J23 1-0	m04 2-1	a24 2-2	J16 1-0	S05 1-0		O17 0-0	O31 1-0	F06 0-0	a27 1-0	a03 3-2
20 READING	J27 4-1	M10 3-1	S19 0-3	N14 1-1	m08 2-2	M20 4-1	O10 0-2	F17 3-3	M27 4-0	J20 0-3	S05 3-2	O03 1-2	D05 3-2	F06 4-0	S23 2-1	a10 0-3	J23 2-2	J06 2-1	M06 2-1		a24 0-2	F20 1-1	N04 0-0	O24 2-1
21 SOUTHEND U	M08 1-1	a03 3-0	O09 1-0	m14 1-4	F06 1-1	a17 2-0	M05 0-2	J16 1-1	J01 2-1	F19 0-0	N02 3-0	m01 4-0	N07 0-2	F01 2-2	S04 0-4	O24 0-1	O03 3-0	S19 2-0	M19 2-2	N27 2-0		S21 0-0	J23 3-2	a09 2-0
22 SWINDON T	N03 0-3	D05 0-0	M06 5-2	F13 1-2	O10 2-1	a27 3-0	S29 1-2	O24 2-2	J31 3-2	D30 1-4	M20 0-1	a03 1-5	a24 1-0	N07 1-2	m08 1-1	m04 3-2	a10 0-2	F23 2-0	S12 4-0	S26 0-2	F09 0-0		M09 2-2	A29 4-1
23 WALSALL	J19 3-0	F13 0-1	N28 2-1	M02 1-1	M13 1-1	F09 2-1	S12 1-1	m15 0-0	m01 2-1	a03 1-1	a17 1-0	F16 1-1	S29 2-1	F27 1-1	N07 3-1	J30 1-3	O31 0-1	O17 3-1	a13 0-3	M16 1-2	A29 0-1	O20 5-0		S26 1-0
24 WIMBLEDON	a12 1-2	m08 0-0	F20 1-0	M27 0-0	m11 3-1	O17 1-0	a24 3-1	S19 0-1	O31 1-1	S22 1-3	O03 0-2	F06 2-0	F27 1-1	S05 1-3	D05 2-3	a20 2-3	O20 2-1	m18 3-2	N14 3-2	M13 0-0	M23 3-0	J23 1-1	m04 2-0	

DIVISION 4

	ALDERSHOT	BLACKPOOL	BOURNEMOUTH	BRADFORD C	BURY	COLCHESTER U	CREWE A	DARLINGTON	HALIFAX T	HARTLEPOOL U	HEREFORD U	HULL C	MANSFIELD T	NORTHAMPTON T	PETERBOROUGH U	PORT VALE	ROCHDALE	SCUNTHORPE U	SHEFFIELD U	STOCKPORT CO	TORQUAY U	TRANMERE R	WIGAN A	YORK C
1 ALDERSHOT		O17 3-2	O20 2-0	F28 0-2	N07 1-2	F09 1-1	J31 3-0	A29 0-0	S12 3-1	O31 1-2	a12 2-2	M12 0-3	S26 2-3	F23 2-1	M16 0-1	a03 1-2	F14 2-2	m01 4-0	a17 1-1	a06 1-1	J03 1-1	N28 2-1	m15 2-0	S29 0-1
2 BLACKPOOL	M06 0-2		N14 0-3	M03 1-0	N04 1-1	a17 0-0	S12 5-0	J30 1-0	S30 7-1	m15 2-2	m01 1-0	S26 3-1	F13 2-3	F17 1-0	M27 2-2	N11 2-3	F10 1-1	J09 2-0	M20 0-1	A29 2-0	O10 2-1	J13 1-2	a09 1-2	M10 3-1
3 BOURNEMOUTH	M09 2-2	a03 1-0		F02 0-2	O24 3-2	D26 1-1	A29 2-0	S12 2-0	J30 1-1	a17 5-1	m15 1-1	m01 1-0	F23 1-0	O10 1-1	M06 1-1	N07 1-1	S26 1-0	N03 2-0	N28 0-0	F13 1-0	a13 4-0	M20 1-1	S29 0-0	F09 5-1
4 BRADFORD C	O11 4-1	a24 1-0	m08 2-2		F24 1-1	S26 2-1	m05 4-1	J03 3-0	a10 5-2	N08 1-0	J30 0-0	J09 1-1	J20 3-4	M07 2-1	D05 2-0	N04 1-0	S30 2-0	F14 0-0	O24 0-2	M10 5-1	M21 3-0	a03 1-1	A29 3-3	S12 6-2
5 BURY	M27 1-1	m18 0-1	M13 2-2	a12 1-1		m01 4-3	F09 2-1	S26 2-0	F13 1-1	J19 1-1	a06 1-1	N28 0-2	J30 3-2	O31 7-1	N14 3-1	O17 3-2	A29 3-0	S29 4-0	a27 1-1	S12 2-0	a17 0-1	F27 4-0	O20 5-3	m15 3-1
6 COLCHESTER U	S22 1-1	D04 2-1	a10 1-2	F19 1-2	J16 1-1		M30 1-1	a24 1-0	M12 1-1	J23 3-3	O20 4-0	M26 2-0	M16 0-1	O02 5-1	a27 1-1	m03 1-0	F26 3-2	N13 2-1	F06 5-2	m07 0-1	S18 3-0	S04 4-0	O30 1-2	O16 4-0
7 CREWE A	S18 2-3	F05 1-1	J23 0-0	a26 0-1	S23 1-2	m15 1-3		N04 1-0	O31 0-1	M16 1-2	M23 1-0	a17 1-1	M13 0-2	M27 2-2	F19 0-1	O06 0-2	O21 1-2	O10 3-0	m01 2-3	M06 0-2	S06 0-1	a12 1-1	J26 0-1	N28 1-1
8 DARLINGTON	J23 0-1	S19 2-2	F06 0-1	S22 1-5	F20 2-3	N28 1-2	a04 1-0		O20 1-1	a12 5-2	M14 0-1	M23 2-1	O17 1-0	a17 3-0	O03 0-0	S05 1-1	O31 2-0	F17 4-1	m15 0-2	N07 2-0	m18 1-1	a30 1-2	M16 3-1	F28 3-1
9 HALIFAX T	F06 2-2	F20 0-0	S19 1-1	M23 0-0	O03 2-1	O24 0-2	M20 2-1	M09 3-3		m01 2-0	F27 1-2	m14 2-2	N07 2-1	m04 2-1	S05 1-1	J22 1-1	O17 0-0	N28 1-2	a12 1-5	a02 4-1	N03 1-2	S22 0-2	a17 0-0	m11 0-0
10 HARTLEPOOL U	M20 2-2	a28 2-2	D05 1-1	M27 0-2	m08 1-0	A29 1-3	N04 1-2	F03 1-2	S26 3-2		F13 2-1	S30 3-2	m05 3-0	N14 3-1	O10 0-1	a24 3-1	M31 1-1	F10 3-3	M06 2-3	a10 2-2	O24 0-0	M10 0-0	S12 2-1	J30 3-2
11 HEREFORD U	F03 0-1	a21 2-1	M31 1-2	S19 1-2	S05 3-0	M10 2-2	m08 4-1	O24 1-1	O10 2-2	O03 1-1		N14 2-2	a24 3-1	F20 2-1	m05 2-1	a10 1-0	D05 0-0	M06 2-1	F17 1-1	N04 0-0	S23 0-3	F06 1-1	M27 3-0	M20 2-1
12 HULL C	O24 1-2	m04 1-0	m11 0-0	S05 2-1	a24 3-2	N07 2-3	D05 1-0	a10 1-3	M02 2-0	F20 5-2	a03 2-1		F27 2-0	F06 0-1	S22 1-1	M20 3-1	m08 2-1	M09 2-0	S19 2-1	a20 0-0	J23 1-0	O03 1-2	O17 0-2	N03 2-0
13 MANSFIELD T	F20 1-0	O03 2-2	S05 0-1	m15 0-2	S19 1-1	N02 1-3	O24 0-1	M06 2-3	M27 3-2	J16 3-2	N28 2-1	O10 3-3		S21 4-1	J23 1-2	F06 1-3	N14 4-3	a13 1-1	M08 1-1	M20 2-2	m01 3-1	a17 3-0	J02 1-2	a05 0-2
14 NORTHAMPTON T	a10 0-0	O13 0-1	F27 1-0	O17 0-2	M20 1-0	F14 1-2	N08 3-0	D05 0-1	a20 0-1	a03 2-1	S26 2-3	S12 1-1	F09 1-1		a24 1-0	F02 3-5	M02 2-1	A29 1-1	N03 1-2	S29 0-0	M09 2-0	O24 3-2	J30 2-3	M23 5-0
15 PETERBOROUGH U	N04 7-1	N07 3-1	O17 1-0	a17 2-0	a03 1-0	a13 2-2	S26 3-0	F13 3-1	J26 0-0	F27 4-4	O28 3-1	F10 3-0	A29 1-0	N28 1-0		M10 1-0	S12 5-1	M20 2-1	a21 0-4	J30 2-0	M24 1-0	m15 1-2	m01 0-3	O24 0-1
16 PORT VALE	N14 1-0	M13 2-0	M27 1-1	M15 1-1	M06 0-0	S28 2-1	F13 0-0	J20 2-2	A29 0-0	N28 5-2	a26 1-1	O31 2-1	S12 0-0	a12 1-0	O19 1-3		J30 1-1	a17 2-1	O10 0-2	S26 1-0	m15 2-0	J25 0-0	F08 1-1	m01 0-0
17 ROCHDALE	O04 0-0	S22 0-0	F20 0-1	m01 1-1	J23 1-1	O11 1-2	M09 1-0	M20 3-2	J13 0-1	S05 2-1	a17 0-1	a06 0-1	a03 1-1	m15 5-3	F06 1-1	S19 1-2		a20 1-1	J16 0-1	O24 4-1	N08 1-0	N03 0-0	N28 1-1	a12 2-0
18 SCUNTHORPE U	M23 1-1	S05 1-1	M16 0-2	O03 1-3	m04 2-2	a02 2-1	F28 0-1	m08 1-1	a24 0-0	S22 2-1	O17 2-2	O20 4-4	F02 1-0	J23 2-1	O31 0-1	D05 0-0	a10 1-0		F20 2-1	M30 0-0	F06 0-2	S19 2-1	M12 2-7	N07 0-3
19 SHEFFIELD U	D05 2-0	O31 3-1	a24 0-0	M30 1-1	a10 1-1	S12 1-0	S29 4-0	J26 0-0	J02 2-2	O17 1-1	A29 2-2	J30 0-0	O20 4-1	M16 7-3	m08 4-0	F27 2-1	m04 3-1	S26 1-0		F09 4-0	a03 4-1	N07 2-0	M23 1-0	F13 4-0
20 STOCKPORT CO	S04 4-2	F01 2-3	O03 1-2	O19 2-3	F06 2-1	M22 0-0	O16 2-0	M26 1-0	N13 2-1	J25 0-2	M15 1-1	a12 1-2	O30 3-0	a30 0-0	S18 3-0	F19 1-2	M12 0-4	m14 1-1	S21 1-0		N28 2-1	F15 1-1	F26 0-1	a16 4-1
21 TORQUAY U	m08 2-1	F27 1-1	D28 1-2	O31 2-0	D05 1-1	J30 1-0	F24 1-1	m05 1-2	a27 2-2	M13 1-1	F10 1-2	A29 2-1	S30 2-0	O21 2-2	a10 1-2	D19 0-1	M27 2-1	S12 1-0	N14 1-1	a24 1-0		O17 1-2	F13 0-0	S26 3-2
22 TRANMERE R	a24 1-0	a10 3-1	O31 0-1	N14 1-1	O10 1-3	M02 2-1	J19 3-0	S29 1-1	F09 1-1	O20 1-0	S12 0-0	F13 2-2	D05 2-2	M13 0-2	F23 1-2	m08 1-2	M16 2-0	J30 0-1	M27 2-2	m04 2-0	M06 1-1		S26 0-0	A29 0-2
23 WIGAN A	F17 1-0	M30 2-1	m04 0-0	J23 4-1	M09 3-2	M20 3-2	a10 3-0	N04 2-1	D05 2-0	F06 1-1	N07 1-1	M06 2-1	m08 3-1	S19 3-1	J19 5-0	S23 2-0	a24 1-1	O24 2-1	S05 0-1	O10 2-1	O03 1-0	J05 0-0		a02 4-2
24 YORK C	m04 4-0	O20 0-4	S22 0-1	F06 0-3	F02 0-0	M05 3-0	a23 6-0	O09 2-2	m07 4-0	S18 1-2	O31 3-4	M16 1-3	a10 2-1	S04 2-1	M13 4-3	F22 2-0	a27 1-2	M26 3-1	O03 3-4	D05 2-2	F19 1-1	J23 1-3	N14 0-0	

LEAGUE TABLES

DIVISION 1

	P	W	D	L	F	A	W	D	L	F	A	Pts
Liverpool	42	14	3	4	39	14	12	6	3	41	18	87
Ipswich T	42	17	1	3	47	25	9	4	8	28	28	83
Manchester U	42	12	6	3	27	9	10	6	5	32	20	78
Tottenham H	42	12	4	5	41	26	8	7	6	26	22	71
Arsenal	42	13	5	3	27	15	7	6	8	21	22	71
Swansea C	42	13	3	5	34	16	8	3	10	24	35	69
Southampton	42	15	2	4	49	30	4	7	10	23	37	66
Everton	42	11	7	3	33	21	6	6	9	23	29	64
West Ham U	42	9	10	2	42	29	5	6	10	24	28	58
Manchester C	42	9	7	5	32	23	6	6	9	17	27	58
Aston Villa	42	9	6	6	28	24	6	6	9	27	29	57
Nottingham F	42	7	7	7	19	20	8	5	8	23	28	57
Brighton & H.A.	42	8	7	6	30	24	5	6	10	13	28	52
Coventry C	42	9	4	8	31	24	4	7	10	25	38	50
Notts Co	42	8	5	8	32	33	5	3	13	29	36	47
Birmingham C	42	8	6	7	29	25	2	8	11	24	36	44
W.B.A.	42	6	6	9	24	25	5	5	11	22	32	44
Stoke C	42	9	2	10	27	28	3	6	12	17	35	44
Sunderland	42	6	5	10	19	26	5	6	10	19	32	44
Leeds U	42	6	11	4	23	20	4	1	16	16	41	42
Wolverh'pton W	42	8	5	8	19	20	2	5	14	13	43	40
Middlesbrough	42	5	9	7	20	24	3	6	12	14	28	39

DIVISION 2

	P	W	D	L	F	A	W	D	L	F	A	Pts
Luton T	42	16	3	2	48	19	9	10	2	38	27	88
Watford	42	13	6	2	46	16	10	5	6	30	26	80
Norwich C	42	14	3	4	41	19	8	2	11	23	31	71
Sheffield W	42	10	8	3	31	23	10	2	9	24	28	70
Q.P.R.	42	15	4	2	40	9	6	2	13	25	34	69
Barnsley	42	13	4	4	33	14	6	6	9	26	27	67
Rotherham U	42	13	5	3	42	19	7	2	12	24	35	67
Leicester C	42	12	5	4	31	19	6	7	8	25	29	66
Newcastle U	42	14	4	3	30	14	4	4	13	22	36	62
Blackburn R	42	11	4	6	26	15	5	7	9	21	28	59
Oldham A	42	9	9	3	28	23	6	5	10	22	28	59
Chelsea	42	10	5	6	37	30	5	7	9	23	30	57
Charlton A	42	11	5	5	33	22	2	7	12	17	43	51
Cambridge U	42	11	4	6	31	19	2	5	14	17	34	48
Crystal Palace	42	9	2	10	25	26	4	7	10	9	19	48
Derby Co	42	9	8	4	32	23	3	4	14	21	45	48
Grimsby T	42	5	8	8	29	30	6	5	10	24	35	46
Shrewsbury T	42	10	6	5	26	19	1	7	13	11	38	46
Bolton W	42	10	4	7	28	24	3	3	15	11	37	46
Cardiff C	42	9	2	10	28	32	3	6	12	17	29	44
Wrexham	42	9	4	8	22	22	2	7	12	18	34	44
Orient	42	6	8	7	23	24	4	1	16	13	37	39

DIVISION 3

	P	W	D	L	F	A	W	D	L	F	A	Pts
Burnley	46	13	7	3	37	20	8	10	5	29	25	80
Carlisle U	46	17	4	2	44	21	6	7	10	21	29	80
Fulham	46	12	9	2	44	22	9	6	8	33	29	78
Lincoln C	46	13	7	3	40	16	8	7	8	26	24	77
Oxford U	46	10	8	5	28	18	9	6	8	35	31	71
Gillingham	46	14	5	4	44	26	6	6	11	20	30	71
Southend U	46	11	7	5	35	23	7	8	8	28	28	69
Brentford	46	8	6	9	28	22	11	5	7	28	25	68
Millwall	46	12	4	7	36	28	6	9	8	26	34	67
Plymouth A	46	12	5	6	37	24	6	6	11	27	32	65
Chesterfield	46	12	4	7	33	27	6	6	11	24	31	64
Reading	46	11	6	6	43	35	6	5	12	24	40	62
Portsmouth	46	11	10	2	33	14	3	9	11	23	37	61
Preston N.E.	46	10	7	6	25	22	6	6	11	25	34	61
Bristol R	46	12	4	7	35	28	6	5	12	23	37	*61
Newport Co	46	9	10	4	28	21	5	6	12	26	33	58
Huddersfield T	46	10	5	8	38	25	5	7	11	26	34	57
Exeter C	46	14	4	5	46	33	2	5	16	25	51	57
Doncaster R	46	9	9	5	31	24	4	8	11	24	44	56
Walsall	46	10	7	6	32	23	3	7	13	19	32	53
Wimbledon	46	10	6	7	33	27	4	5	14	28	48	53
Swindon T	46	9	5	9	37	36	4	8	11	18	35	52
Bristol C	46	7	6	10	24	29	4	7	12	16	36	46
Chester C	46	2	10	11	16	30	5	1	17	20	48	32

*Bristol Rovers had two points deducted for fielding an unregistered player.

DIVISION 4

	P	W	D	L	F	A	W	D	L	F	A	Pts
Sheffield U	46	15	8	0	53	15	12	7	4	41	26	96
Bradford C	46	14	7	2	52	23	12	6	5	36	22	91
Wigan A	46	17	5	1	47	18	9	8	6	33	28	91
Bournemouth	46	12	10	1	37	15	11	9	3	25	15	88
Peterborough U	46	16	3	4	46	22	8	7	8	25	35	82
Colchester U	46	12	6	5	47	23	8	6	9	35	34	72
Port Vale	46	9	12	2	26	17	9	4	10	30	32	70
Hull C	46	14	3	6	36	23	5	9	9	34	38	69
Bury	46	13	7	3	53	26	4	10	9	27	33	68
Hereford U	46	10	9	4	36	25	6	10	7	28	33	67
Tranmere R	46	7	9	7	27	25	7	9	7	24	31	60
Blackpool	46	11	5	7	40	26	4	8	11	26	34	58
Darlington	46	10	5	8	36	28	5	8	10	25	34	58
Hartlepool U	46	9	8	6	39	34	4	8	11	34	50	55
Torquay U	46	9	8	6	30	25	5	5	13	17	34	55
Aldershot	46	8	7	8	34	29	5	8	10	23	39	54
York C	46	9	5	9	45	37	5	3	15	24	54	50
Stockport Co	46	10	5	8	34	28	2	8	13	14	39	49
Halifax T	46	6	11	6	28	30	3	11	9	23	42	49
Mansfield T	46	8	6	9	39	39	5	4	14	24	42	*47
Rochdale	46	7	9	7	26	22	3	7	13	24	40	46
Northampton T	46	9	5	9	32	27	2	4	17	25	57	42
Scunthorpe U	46	7	9	7	26	35	2	6	15	17	44	42
Crewe A	46	3	6	14	19	32	3	3	17	10	52	27

*Mansfield Town had two points deducted for fielding an ineligible player.

Football League Records

Top scorers: Div 1, L.Blissett (Watford) 27 goals; Div 2, G.Lineker (Leicester City) 26 goals; Div 3, K.Dixon (Reading) 26 goals; Div 4, S.Cammack (Scunthorpe United) 25 goals.

Graeme Souness, a strong, intelligent midfielder who played a great part in many of Liverpool's triumphs of the 1980s. In 1991 he returned to Anfield as manager.

DIVISION 1

	ARSENAL	ASTON VILLA	BIRMINGHAM C	BRIGHTON & HA	COVENTRY C	EVERTON	IPSWICH T	LIVERPOOL	LUTON T	MANCHESTER C	MANCHESTER U	NORWICH C	NOTTINGHAM F	NOTTS CO	SOUTHAMPTON	STOKE C	SUNDERLAND	SWANSEA C	TOTTENHAM H	WATFORD	W.B.A.	WEST HAM U
1 ARSENAL		D07 2-1	O30 0-0	F05 3-1	a09 2-1	N13 1-1	M22 2-2	S04 0-2	M19 4-1	a23 3-0	m02 3-0	A31 1-1	M05 0-0	S18 2-0	a02 0-0	J15 3-0	m07 0-1	J01 2-1	D27 2-0	N27 2-4	O16 2-0	O02 2-3
2 ASTON VILLA	m14 2-1		a04 1-0	N13 1-0	M19 4-0	F12 2-0	D29 1-1	D18 2-4	S08 4-1	J22 1-1	N20 2-1	M05 3-2	S11 4-1	M08 2-0	J03 2-0	a30 4-0	A28 1-3	S25 2-0	O30 4-0	O16 3-0	a19 1-0	D04 1-0
3 BIRMINGHAM C	M15 2-1	D27 3-0		m02 1-1	S18 1-0	a23 1-0	O23 0-0	A31 0-0	O09 2-3	J01 2-2	J15 1-2	a09 0-4	F26 1-1	M26 3-0	D11 0-2	S04 1-4	N27 2-1	a02 1-1	m07 2-0	O02 1-1	N06 2-1	F05 3-0
4 BRIGHTON & H.A.	S07 1-0	M26 0-0	S25 1-0		a23 1-0	a09 1-2	A28 1-1	M22 2-2	J22 2-4	m07 0-1	N06 1-0	D11 3-0	J03 1-1	N27 0-2	D27 0-1	F26 1-2	S11 3-2	O09 1-1	a02 2-1	J01 1-1	F12 0-0	O23 3-1
5 COVENTRY C	S11 0-2	N06 0-0	a16 0-1	D04 2-0		S25 4-2	N23 1-1	a12 0-0	N20 4-2	F12 4-0	D28 3-0	O30 2-0	a05 1-2	O16 1-0	A28 1-0	D18 2-0	S07 1-0	J22 0-0	M12 1-1	M05 0-1	a30 0-1	m14 2-4
6 EVERTON	M26 2-3	A31 5-0	D04 0-0	O02 2-2	m02 1-0		m14 1-1	N06 0-5	D18 5-0	O09 2-1	a19 2-0	S18 1-1	D28 3-1	F05 3-0	M15 2-0	a04 3-1	O23 3-1	F26 2-2	S04 3-1	J15 1-0	N20 0-0	a30 2-0
7 IPSWICH T	O09 0-1	a02 1-2	M05 3-1	J15 2-0	S04 1-1	D11 0-2		O02 1-0	F26 3-0	N13 1-0	F05 1-1	D27 2-3	M19 2-0	a09 0-0	J01 2-1	S18 2-3	a23 4-1	N27 3-1	A31 1-2	m07 3-1	O30 6-1	m03 1-2
8 LIVERPOOL	J03 3-1	m07 1-1	J22 1-0	O30 3-1	N13 4-0	M19 0-0	F12 1-0		S11 3-3	D27 5-2	O16 0-0	a23 0-2	S07 4-3	J01 5-1	S25 5-0	M05 5-1	a02 1-0	a09 3-0	N27 3-0	D11 3-1	A28 2-0	M12 3-0
9 LUTON T	N06 2-2	a09 2-1	a12 3-1	S18 5-0	J01 1-2	m07 1-5	O16 1-1	F05 1-3		D11 3-1	O02 1-1	a02 0-1	O30 0-2	S04 5-3	N27 3-3	m02 0-0	M26 1-3	a23 3-1	J15 1-1	D27 1-0	M05 0-0	A31 0-2
10 MANCHESTER C	D04 2-1	S18 0-1	N20 0-0	D18 1-1	O02 3-2	M02 0-0	M26 0-1	a04 0-4	m14 0-1		M05 1-2	J15 4-1	a30 1-2	F19 0-1	N06 2-0	S01 1-0	O16 2-2	O30 2-1	F05 2-2	S04 1-0	D28 2-1	a16 2-0
11 MANCHESTER U	S25 0-0	J01 3-1	A28 3-0	M19 1-1	a02 3-0	S08 2-1	S11 3-1	F26 1-1	m09 3-0	O23 2-2		N27 3-0	J22 2-0	D11 4-0	a09 1-1	O09 1-0	D27 0-0	m07 2-1	N13 1-0	a23 2-0	J03 0-0	M22 2-1
12 NORWICH C	a20 3-1	O23 1-0	S08 5-1	m14 2-1	M23 1-1	J22 0-1	a04 0-0	D04 1-0	D28 1-0	A28 1-2	a30 1-1		D18 0-1	N06 1-2	S11 1-1	N20 4-2	a16 2-0	J03 1-0	O16 0-0	M02 3-0	S25 1-3	M26 1-1
13 NOTTINGHAM F	O23 3-0	F05 1-2	O16 1-1	S04 4-0	D27 4-2	a02 2-0	N06 2-1	m02 1-0	M12 0-1	N27 3-0	S01 0-3	m07 2-2		a23 2-1	M26 1-2	O02 1-0	J01 0-0	D11 2-1	a09 2-2	S18 2-0	F19 0-0	J15 1-0
14 NOTTS CO	J22 1-0	O09 4-1	N13 0-0	a30 1-0	F26 5-1	S11 1-0	S25 0-6	N20 1-2	a16 1-1	S07 1-0	m14 3-2	M19 2-2	D04 3-2		F15 1-2	D28 4-0	J03 0-1	A28 0-0	M05 3-0	O30 3-2	a04 2-1	D18 1-2
15 SOUTHAMPTON	D28 2-2	S04 1-0	m14 0-1	a05 0-0	J15 1-1	O30 3-2	N20 0-1	a16 3-2	a30 2-2	M19 4-1	S18 0-1	F05 4-0	N13 1-1	O02 1-0		D04 1-0	F19 2-0	M05 2-1	m03 1-2	A31 1-4	D18 4-1	O16 3-0
16 STOKE C	A28 2-1	N27 0-3	J03 1-1	O16 3-0	m07 0-3	D27 1-0	J22 1-0	O23 1-1	S25 4-4	a09 1-0	M02 1-0	J01 1-0	M16 1-0	a02 1-0	a23 1-1		M12 0-1	S11 4-1	D11 2-0	M26 4-0	S08 0-3	N06 5-2
17 SUNDERLAND	D18 3-0	J15 2-0	a30 1-2	a19 1-1	F05 2-1	M05 2-1	D04 2-3	D28 0-0	N13 1-1	F26 3-2	a04 0-0	O02 4-1	N20 0-1	S01 1-1	O09 1-1	O30 2-2		M19 1-1	S18 0-1	m02 2-2	m14 1-1	S04 1-0
18 SWANSEA C	N20 1-2	m02 2-1	D29 0-0	M01 1-2	A31 2-1	O16 0-3	a30 1-1	S18 0-3	D04 2-0	M12 4-1	D18 0-0	S04 4-0	m14 0-3	J15 2-0	O23 3-2	a16 1-1	N06 3-0		O02 2-0	F06 1-3	M26 2-1	a05 1-5
19 TOTTENHAM H	a04 5-0	M23 2-0	D18 2-1	D28 2-0	O09 4-0	J03 2-1	a16 3-1	a30 2-0	A28 2-2	S11 1-2	m11 2-0	F26 0-0	S25 4-1	O23 4-2	S08 6-0	m14 4-1	J22 1-1	F12 1-0		N06 0-1	D04 1-1	N20 2-1
20 WATFORD	a30 2-1	F26 2-1	M22 2-1	N20 4-1	O23 0-0	A28 2-0	D18 2-1	m14 2-1	a04 5-2	J03 2-0	D04 0-1	O09 2-2	a16 1-3	M12 5-3	J22 2-0	N13 1-0	S25 8-0	S07 2-1	M19 0-1		S11 3-0	D29 2-1
21 W.B.A.	F26 0-0	O02 1-0	M19 2-0	S01 5-0	N27 2-0	J01 2-2	M12 4-1	J15 0-1	O23 1-0	a02 0-2	S04 3-1	m02 1-0	O09 2-1	D27 2-2	m07 1-0	F05 1-1	D11 3-0	N13 3-3	a23 0-1	a09 1-3		S18 1-2
22 WEST HAM U	m10 1-3	a23 2-0	S11 5-0	M05 2-1	D11 0-3	N27 2-0	S07 1-1	O09 3-1	J04 2-3	S25 4-1	O30 3-1	N13 1-0	A28 1-2	m07 2-0	F26 1-1	M19 1-1	a09 2-1	D27 3-2	J01 3-0	a02 2-1	J22 0-1	

Queen's Park Rangers' striker Tony Sealy top-scored with 16 goals when Rangers won the Division Two title in 1982-83.

DIVISION 2

	BARNSLEY	BLACKBURN R	BOLTON W	BURNLEY	CAMBRIDGE U	CARLISLE U	CHARLTON A	CHELSEA	CRYSTAL P	DERBY CO	FULHAM	GRIMSBY T	LEEDS U	LEICESTER C	MIDDLESBROUGH	NEWCASTLE U	OLDHAM A	Q.P.R.	ROTHERHAM U	SHEFFIELD W	SHREWSBURY T	WOLVERHAMPTON W
1 BARNSLEY		a23 2-2	M05 3-1	S18 3-0	a09 2-3	D11 2-2	m07 0-0	N13 1-1	J15 3-1	O19 1-1	O02 4-3	J01 4-0	N27 2-1	a02 1-2	M19 2-0	m04 0-5	S04 1-1	O09 0-1	F26 2-1	D27 0-0	O30 2-2	F05 2-1
2 BLACKBURN R	D04 1-1		N20 1-1	a04 2-1	S04 3-1	N06 3-2	M13 2-0	O16 3-0	a16 3-0	m02 2-0	F19 0-0	F05 2-1	O23 0-0	S18 3-1	a30 1-1	S01 1-2	D29 2-2	M26 1-3	D18 3-0	O02 2-3	m14 1-0	J15 2-2
3 BOLTON W	O23 0-2	J01 1-0		J15 3-0	a23 2-0	D27 1-0	D11 4-1	m07 0-1	O02 1-0	M26 0-2	F05 0-1	m02 0-0	a02 1-2	N27 3-1	F26 3-1	S04 3-1	S28 2-3	M12 3-2	O09 2-2	a09 0-2	N06 1-4	S18 0-1
4 BURNLEY	J22 3-1	D27 0-1	A28 0-0		N13 2-1	S07 4-1	F26 7-1	a23 3-0	O09 2-1	N27 1-1	M05 1-0	m07 1-1	a09 1-2	D11 2-4	J03 1-1	M19 1-0	O30 1-2	m10 2-1	S11 1-2	J01 4-1	S25 1-2	a02 0-1
5 CAMBRIDGE U	S07 1-1	J03 2-0	D04 0-0	M26 2-0		S25 1-1	S11 3-2	A28 0-1	D28 1-0	M15 0-0	a05 1-0	M12 1-0	F12 0-0	N06 3-1	D17 2-0	a30 1-0	m14 1-4	N20 1-4	J22 2-0	O16 2-2	a16 0-0	N02 2-1
6 CARLISLE U	m14 1-1	M19 3-1	a05 5-0	a16 1-1	m03 2-2		O09 4-1	O30 2-1	S18 4-1	J15 3-0	D18 3-2	S04 2-3	F26 2-2	F05 0-1	D28 1-3	N20 2-0	M05 0-0	a30 1-0	N13 2-2	S28 4-2	D04 2-3	O02 0-2
7 CHARLTON A	D18 3-2	O30 3-0	m14 4-1	O16 2-1	F05 2-1	F19 0-0		M05 5-2	a04 2-1	O02 1-1	S28 3-0	S18 0-1	M19 0-1	J15 2-1	N13 2-3	D04 2-0	a17 4-1	D29 1-3	N20 1-5	S04 0-3	a29 0-1	m02 3-3
8 CHELSEA	M26 0-3	F26 2-0	D18 2-1	D04 2-1	J15 6-0	M12 4-2	O23 3-1		N06 0-0	F05 1-3	D28 0-0	O02 5-2	O09 0-0	S04 1-1	m14 0-0	a16 0-2	S18 2-0	a04 0-2	a30 1-1	m02 1-1	N20 1-2	A31 0-0
9 CRYSTAL P	A28 1-1	S11 2-0	F22 3-0	m17 1-0	a02 0-0	a09 2-1	D27 1-1	M19 0-0		m07 4-1	O30 1-1	a23 2-0	N13 1-1	J01 1-0	S25 3-0	M05 0-2	O16 1-0	J22 0-3	J03 1-1	D11 2-0	S07 2-1	N27 3-4
10 DERBY CO	a16 1-1	S25 1-2	N13 0-0	a30 2-0	O09 1-1	A28 0-3	a13 1-1	S08 1-0	D18 1-1		m14 1-0	F26 2-0	J22 3-3	O23 0-4	S11 1-1	a04 2-1	N20 2-2	J03 2-0	D04 3-0	M19 0-0	D29 2-3	M12 1-1
11 FULHAM	a19 1-0	O09 3-1	S11 4-0	O23 3-1	D27 1-1	m07 2-0	a09 2-1	a02 1-1	M12 1-0	D11 2-1		M26 4-0	S25 3-2	a23 0-1	J22 1-0	F26 2-2	N06 0-3	S07 1-1	A28 1-1	N27 1-0	J03 2-1	J01 1-3
12 GRIMSBY T	N20 1-2	S07 5-0	S25 1-0	D18 3-2	O30 1-0	J03 2-1	J22 1-1	F12 2-1	D04 4-1	O16 1-1	N13 0-4		A28 1-1	F19 2-0	a16 0-3	D28 2-2	a30 0-2	m14 1-1	a04 1-2	M05 1-1	S11 2-0	M19 1-1
13 LEEDS U	a30 0-0	M05 2-1	D28 1-1	O20 3-1	O02 2-1	O16 1-1	N06 1-2	F19 3-3	M26 2-1	S18 2-1	a16 1-1	J15 1-0		m02 2-2	N20 0-0	O30 3-1	a05 0-0	D04 0-1	m14 2-2	a27 1-2	D18 1-1	S04 0-0
14 LEICESTER C	D28 1-0	J22 0-1	a30 0-0	m14 0-0	M19 4-0	S11 6-0	A28 1-2	J03 3-0	N20 0-1	M05 1-1	D04 2-0	O09 2-0	S08 0-1		a05 1-0	N13 2-2	D18 2-1	S25 0-1	a16 3-1	O30 0-2	F22 3-2	F26 5-0
15 MIDDLESBROUGH	N06 2-0	N27 1-5	O16 1-0	S04 1-4	m07 0-1	a02 1-0	M26 3-0	D11 3-1	m10 2-0	a09 2-3	S18 1-4	S28 1-4	J01 0-0	D27 1-1		F05 1-1	O02 1-1	O23 2-1	M12 1-1	J15 1-1	M08 2-1	a23 0-0
16 NEWCASTLE U	S25 1-2	a09 3-2	J03 2-2	N06 3-0	N27 2-0	J01 2-2	a23 4-2	S11 1-1	O23 1-0	D27 1-0	O16 1-4	a02 4-0	M12 2-1	M26 2-2	S08 1-1		F19 1-0	A28 1-0	a20 4-0	m07 2-1	J22 4-0	D11 1-1
17 OLDHAM A	J03 1-1	a01 0-0	J22 2-3	a12 3-0	D11 3-0	O23 4-3	S25 2-2	a09 2-2	F26 2-0	J01 2-2	M19 1-0	N27 1-1	D26 2-2	m07 1-2	F12 3-0	O09 2-2		S11 0-1	S07 1-1	a23 1-1	A28 1-0	N13 4-1
18 Q.P.R.	F19 3-0	N13 2-2	O30 1-0	O02 3-2	A31 2-1	N27 1-0	M22 5-1	D27 1-2	S28 0-0	S04 4-1	m02 3-1	D11 4-0	a23 1-0	a09 2-2	M05 6-1	J15 2-0	F05 1-0		M19 4-0	S18 0-2	O16 4-0	m07 2-1
19 ROTHERHAM U	O16 1-0	m07 3-1	F19 1-1	F05 1-1	S18 2-0	M26 1-2	J01 1-0	N27 1-0	S04 2-2	a23 1-1	J15 0-1	D27 3-0	D11 0-1	A31 1-3	O30 1-1	O02 1-5	J29 1-3	N06 0-0		a02 0-3	M05 0-3	a09 1-1
20 SHEFFIELD W	a04 0-1	F15 0-0	S07 3-1	N20 1-1	F26 3-1	J22 1-1	J03 5-4	S25 3-2	m14 2-1	N06 2-0	a30 2-1	O23 2-0	S11 2-3	M22 2-2	A28 3-1	D18 1-1	D04 1-1	a19 0-1	D28 0-1		M26 0-0	O09 0-0
21 SHREWSBURY T	M12 3-1	D11 0-0	M19 1-0	m03 1-2	S28 2-1	a23 2-1	N27 0-0	J01 2-0	F05 1-1	a02 1-1	S04 0-1	a08 0-0	m07 0-0	O02 0-2	O09 2-2	S18 2-1	J15 0-0	F26 0-0	O23 2-0	N13 1-0		D27 0-2
22 WOLVERHAMPTON W	S11 2-0	A28 2-1	a16 0-0	D28 2-0	M05 1-1	F12 2-1	S07 5-0	J22 2-1	a30 1-0	O30 2-1	N20 2-4	N06 3-0	J03 3-0	O16 0-3	D04 4-0	m14 2-2	M26 0-0	D18 4-0	S25 2-0	M01 1-0	a04 2-2	

SEASON 1982-83

DIVISION 3

	BOURNEMOUTH	BRADFORD C	BRENTFORD	BRISTOL R	CARDIFF C	CHESTERFIELD	DONCASTER R	EXETER C	GILLINGHAM	HUDDERSFIELD T	LINCOLN C	MILLWALL	NEWPORT CO	ORIENT	OXFORD U	PLYMOUTH A	PORTSMOUTH	PRESTON N.E.	READING	SHEFFIELD U	SOUTHEND U	WALSALL	WIGAN A	WREXHAM
1 BOURNEMOUTH		N27 2-2	J01 4-3	N02 0-0	O09 3-1	a09 2-1	m02 2-2	S25 2-0	O23 0-1	N06 0-1	a23 1-0	J22 3-0	M26 0-1	a02 2-0	F01 2-0	M15 1-0	F26 0-2	M12 4-0	D27 1-1	S11 0-0	S28 0-2	A28 3-0	m07 2-2	F12 1-1
2 BRADFORD C	a30 2-3		M19 0-1	F12 2-0	F16 4-2	F26 1-0	O23 1-0	N13 3-3	J03 1-1	m14 3-1	M12 1-1	a16 0-0	S11 4-2	J12 2-3	N03 3-2	O09 4-0	D04 2-2	a04 1-2	A28 3-2	m08 2-0	S25 1-0	S29 1-1	J22 0-1	D28 0-0
3 BRENTFORD	m14 2-1	N06 0-2		A28 5-1	J03 1-3	O09 4-2	F26 1-0	D18 4-0	D28 1-1	M26 1-0	O23 2-0	S25 1-1	S28 2-0	J22 5-2	M22 1-1	M11 2-0	a01 1-1	N02 3-1	F12 1-2	a30 2-1	S11 4-2	a16 2-3	J08 1-3	D04 4-1
4 BRISTOL R	N30 1-1	O02 4-1	J15 2-0		m14 1-1	J29 3-0	S04 2-0	D29 4-4	S07 2-1	a30 1-0	S18 1-2	O19 4-0	F19 1-3	M05 2-1	a05 0-1	F05 2-0	N13 5-1	a16 3-2	O30 3-0	M29 2-1	M19 2-2	D04 2-0	O16 4-0	D18 4-0
5 CARDIFF C	F19 1-1	O19 1-0	m02 3-1	J01 3-1		D07 1-1	a09 3-0	S28 2-0	O16 1-0	M15 1-1	M26 1-0	F01 3-0	D27 3-2	m07 2-0	F12 3-0	a02 0-0	O30 1-0	N06 3-1	M01 0-0	S25 2-0	a23 4-1	J22 3-1	S11 3-2	A28 1-2
6 CHESTERFIELD	D04 0-0	O16 3-0	F19 2-1	S11 0-0	a30 0-1		M12 3-3	a16 1-3	N02 1-2	a04 0-1	N06 1-3	m14 0-1	F01 3-1	A28 1-2	S28 1-2	O23 1-2	D18 0-1	M26 1-1	J22 0-0	D28 3-1	M15 0-2	M01 0-0	S25 2-0	J03 5-1
7 DONCASTER R	J03 2-1	M05 1-2	O16 4-4	J08 1-2	D04 2-2	O30 0-0		S10 6-1	M25 0-2	M01 0-4	F19 2-2	D18 2-1	A28 0-0	a12 0-3	a16 0-1	N08 2-2	a30 0-2	D28 2-0	S25 7-5	a05 2-0	J22 0-0	m14 1-3	S28 3-6	O19 1-1
8 EXETER C	F05 4-2	M26 2-1	a23 1-7	a02 0-1	J29 0-2	O02 2-3	m07 3-0		S04 2-2	J15 3-4	M02 3-1	O16 2-1	J01 0-1	N27 2-0	M12 3-1	D27 1-0	S08 1-1	S18 5-1	D11 2-2	O23 0-3	m02 4-3	N06 4-3	N03 2-1	F19 3-3
9 GILLINGHAM	M05 2-5	m03 3-0	a02 2-2	m07 1-0	F26 2-3	F15 3-1	N13 1-1	J08 4-4		O30 1-3	J01 0-2	S11 1-0	a09 2-0	O19 4-0	A28 0-1	a23 2-1	M19 1-0	O09 2-1	S28 1-0	M15 0-2	D27 1-0	S25 3-0	N27 0-2	J22 1-1
10 HUDDERSFIELD T	M19 0-0	J01 6-3	N13 2-0	N27 3-1	O23 4-0	D27 3-1	N02 3-0	A28 1-1	M12 3-2		a02 1-1	F12 5-1	m07 1-0	S28 6-0	S25 2-0	a09 2-0	O09 1-1	F26 1-1	a23 3-1	J22 0-0	O19 2-1	S11 2-2	m10 1-1	M29 4-1
11 LINCOLN C	D18 9-0	O30 1-0	M05 2-1	J22 2-1	N13 2-1	M19 2-0	O09 5-1	O20 4-1	m14 3-1	D28 1-2		D04 3-1	M23 1-4	S25 2-0	a30 1-1	F26 1-2	F16 0-3	J03 3-0	S11 4-0	S29 3-0	F23 0-1	a04 2-1	A28 2-1	a16 2-0
12 MILLWALL	S08 2-0	S18 1-1	m08 1-0	a12 1-1	S05 0-4	J01 1-1	a23 3-0	F26 5-2	J30 4-1	O02 3-0	a09 2-1		m02 3-0	D26 0-1	O09 2-1	N02 2-2	F06 0-2	J15 1-0	N28 1-1	M12 1-2	a02 3-1	O23 2-2	M27 2-0	N06 1-1
13 NEWPORT CO	N13 5-1	J29 1-1	F06 0-0	O09 2-0	a04 1-0	S04 1-0	J15 1-2	m14 1-1	D04 2-1	S18 2-1	O02 1-0	J03 2-2		F26 4-1	D28 1-2	S07 2-2	a16 0-3	F15 3-0	M19 1-0	N02 3-1	O23 1-1	D18 1-1	M12 1-0	a30 4-0
14 ORIENT	D28 5-0	S04 0-1	S18 3-3	O23 1-5	S08 4-0	J15 2-0	O02 1-0	a30 5-1	M01 2-0	a16 1-3	F05 1-1	a04 2-3	O16 1-5		D04 1-5	J29 0-2	J18 2-1	D17 2-1	F20 3-3	m14 4-1	M13 1-1	N02 2-1	N06 1-1	M25 0-0
15 OXFORD U	S04 2-0	M02 5-1	O20 2-2	D27 4-2	O02 2-2	m07 1-0	S08 3-0	O30 1-1	J15 1-1	F05 1-1	M16 1-0	a27 1-0	a02 0-3	a09 2-2		M26 1-1	S18 1-1	J29 3-2	m02 1-2	N06 0-0	J01 1-0	O16 4-2	a20 2-0	M05 2-0
16 PLYMOUTH A	O19 2-0	F19 3-1	O30 2-0	S28 0-4	D28 3-2	M05 2-0	M19 1-2	a01 1-0	D18 2-0	D04 2-1	O16 0-2	M01 3-1	J22 2-4	S11 2-0	N13 2-1		m14 0-1	a30 1-1	F01 3-0	a16 3-1	A28 1-0	F08 0-0	a19 0-2	S25 2-0
17 PORTSMOUTH	O16 0-2	a09 0-1	D27 2-1	M26 1-0	M12 0-0	a23 4-0	N27 2-1	F12 3-2	N06 1-0	F22 3-2	N02 4-1	S28 2-0	S25 1-2	m02 2-2	J22 1-0	J01 2-1		O23 3-1	a02 2-2	A28 4-1	m07 2-0	m10 1-0	M01 0-0	S11 3-0
18 PRESTON N.E.	O30 0-1	D27 0-0	M01 3-0	S25 2-2	M19 2-1	N13 1-1	a02 4-1	J22 2-2	F19 0-0	O16 0-0	m02 1-0	A28 3-2	O19 0-0	a23 2-1	S11 1-2	N27 2-2	M05 0-0		m07 2-0	a12 1-0	a08 1-1	M29 1-0	J01 4-1	S28 3-0
19 READING	a04 2-1	J15 2-1	S08 1-1	M12 1-2	N03 1-2	S18 0-0	F05 2-0	D04 3-1	a16 0-0	D18 1-1	J29 1-1	a30 3-3	N06 4-2	O09 3-0	J03 0-3	S04 3-2	D28 1-2	O02 2-3		F23 2-0	F26 1-1	M25 1-1	O23 2-1	m14 1-0
20 SHEFFIELD U	J29 2-2	a23 2-1	N27 1-2	m02 2-1	F05 2-0	a02 3-1	D27 3-1	M05 3-0	O02 0-2	S07 2-0	m07 0-1	O30 1-1	M01 2-0	J01 3-0	M19 3-2	S18 3-1	J15 2-1	S04 2-1	O19 1-1		N13 0-1	F19 3-1	a09 2-0	O16 2-0
21 SOUTHEND U	a16 0-0	F05 1-1	J29 4-2	N05 1-0	D17 1-2	S06 2-0	S18 3-2	J03 1-1	a01 1-1	F14 0-1	S04 2-0	D28 1-1	M04 1-4	O29 1-1	m13 1-2	J14 3-1	O01 4-0	D03 2-3	O15 4-2	M26 3-1		a29 1-1	F18 2-0	F28 2-2
22 WALSALL	J15 3-1	m07 1-1	O02 2-1	a09 5-0	S18 1-2	O19 0-1	J01 1-0	M19 3-2	F05 0-0	J29 2-0	D27 1-1	M05 4-0	a23 2-1	F15 2-0	F26 1-0	m02 2-0	S04 0-3	S07 2-1	N13 2-1	O09 0-0	N27 1-3		a02 2-0	O30 1-1
23 WIGAN A	S18 1-2	S07 3-2	S04 3-2	F26 0-5	a16 0-0	F05 2-2	J29 0-3	F15 1-0	a30 2-2	J03 2-0	J15 2-1	N13 3-1	O30 0-1	M19 0-1	D18 0-1	O02 3-0	O19 0-1	m14 0-1	M05 2-2	D04 3-2	O09 4-0	D29 1-3		a04 3-1
24 WREXHAM	O02 1-0	a02 0-4	a08 3-4	a22 0-0	J15 0-0	m02 0-0	F15 5-0	O09 1-2	S18 1-0	S04 1-1	S07 0-1	M19 4-3	N27 1-0	N13 1-0	O23 1-1	m07 2-3	J29 0-2	F05 3-1	J01 4-0	F26 4-1	N02 3-2	M12 4-0	D27 1-1	

DIVISION 4

	ALDERSHOT	BLACKPOOL	BRISTOL C	BURY	CHESTER	COLCHESTER U	CREWE A	DARLINGTON	HALIFAX T	HARTLEPOOL U	HEREFORD U	HULL C	MANSFIELD T	NORTHAMPTON T	PETERBOROUGH U	PORT VALE	ROCHDALE	SCUNTHORPE U	STOCKPORT CO	SWINDON T	TORQUAY U	TRANMERE R	WIMBLEDON	YORK C
1 ALDERSHOT		N27 2-1	O30 0-0	a09 1-1	N13 1-2	a02 0-1	O19 2-1	M01 1-6	m07 6-1	M05 0-2	m02 2-1	S25 1-2	J01 2-1	F12 3-0	S11 2-0	S28 1-4	a23 6-4	M15 1-1	O16 2-1	D27 1-1	J22 2-1	A28 1-0	F19 1-1	M19 2-3
2 BLACKPOOL	a30 4-1		a16 1-4	S07 1-1	J29 1-1	F05 1-2	N06 2-0	O02 2-0	O09 0-0	m14 1-2	O23 5-1	D04 1-1	J15 2-1	M26 0-0	J03 0-3	M12 2-0	F26 1-0	D18 3-1	a01 0-0	S04 2-1	N02 1-0	D28 0-2	S18 1-1	O19 1-1
3 BRISTOL C	M12 2-0	S11 0-0		a23 2-1	N02 0-0	N27 0-2	m07 2-1	m02 2-2	F15 3-0	F26 2-0	a02 1-1	A28 2-1	M26 3-1	J22 1-3	F12 1-0	D27 1-3	a09 0-0	S25 0-2	N06 2-2	J01 1-1	S28 0-1	J18 1-0	O23 4-2	O09 2-2
4 BURY	D04 3-1	J22 4-1	D18 2-2		M19 3-2	O30 1-0	S11 0-1	M05 3-0	S25 2-0	D28 4-0	A28 3-2	M01 2-3	F19 1-0	J03 1-1	a16 1-0	J08 0-1	F12 0-0	a30 1-0	O19 3-2	O16 0-0	N13 3-0	S28 3-0	m14 1-3	a04 2-1
5 CHESTER	M26 1-1	S29 1-2	D11 1-0	N06 0-1		M05 1-1	A28 1-0	F19 2-3	F12 2-0	D04 2-1	S25 5-0	a30 0-0	O16 1-3	a16 2-1	O20 1-1	J22 1-0	J08 5-2	m14 1-2	D28 0-2	O30 0-1	S11 0-0	a04 0-0	J04 1-2	D18 0-1
6 COLCHESTER U	D28 0-0	S25 4-1	a29 3-1	M12 2-1	N09 1-0		J21 4-3	O15 2-2	A28 1-0	J03 4-1	J07 3-2	S28 0-0	N05 2-0	M01 3-1	a01 1-0	a12 1-2	S10 4-1	a15 5-1	D17 3-0	F18 1-0	m13 1-0	M25 3-3	N02 3-0	D03 0-0
7 CREWE A	F15 0-0	M19 3-1	S07 4-1	J29 3-3	J15 3-2	S17 0-1		S03 2-5	M11 1-1	a15 3-0	F26 3-1	D17 0-3	O01 1-2	a04 1-0	D28 0-3	O22 1-2	O08 1-1	N12 0-1	J03 3-0	F05 3-0	D03 1-1	m13 0-1	a30 0-2	N02 2-1
8 DARLINGTON	N02 1-1	a12 0-1	J03 2-2	O23 1-2	O09 0-2	F26 1-3	J08 1-1		J22 1-2	a04 2-1	S11 2-1	D28 1-2	M12 0-0	a30 2-0	m17 4-3	S25 0-0	A28 3-0	S28 0-1	M26 3-1	N06 1-0	a16 0-2	F15 1-0	D04 0-2	m14 1-3
9 HALIFAX T	S18 1-3	F18 2-0	O19 2-2	F05 1-0	O01 0-0	J14 4-0	O29 0-3	S07 2-0		a29 1-1	N05 2-2	a04 1-2	S03 0-0	F01 2-0	M01 1-2	O15 0-2	M04 0-0	D28 3-1	m13 1-0	M15 1-0	J03 3-0	D17 1-2	m10 1-1	a15 2-2
10 HARTLEPOOL U	O23 1-1	J01 2-1	O16 3-1	a02 0-1	a09 1-0	m02 1-4	S29 1-0	D27 2-0	N27 1-2		M26 0-1	J22 0-0	N03 0-4	S11 2-1	J12 0-0	M02 2-2	m07 3-0	A28 0-0	F19 3-2	a23 1-2	F12 0-2	S25 4-0	N06 1-0	M12 2-0
11 HEREFORD U	J03 2-1	M05 0-0	D28 1-3	J15 0-2	F05 5-2	S04 0-0	O16 1-0	J29 0-0	M19 2-0	N13 1-0		O20 2-0	S18 0-2	D18 1-1	m14 0-1	F19 0-2	O30 1-0	D04 0-2	M02 0-0	S08 1-2	a05 0-1	a30 1-0	a16 1-4	O02 0-0
12 HULL C	F05 2-2	a09 3-1	J15 1-0	N02 2-1	N27 2-0	D11 3-0	a23 1-0	a02 0-0	D27 1-1	S18 1-1	F15 2-0		m02 2-2	O23 4-0	N06 4-1	M26 1-0	J01 2-1	F26 1-1	J29 7-0	O02 0-0	O09 4-1	M12 0-1	S04 1-1	S07 4-0
13 MANSFIELD T	m14 4-1	A28 2-1	N13 1-1	O09 1-4	F26 2-1	M19 1-1	M28 1-0	O30 0-2	J08 1-2	M14 3-0	J22 0-1	J03 3-1		D28 2-0	S27 0-0	S11 0-2	S25 2-1	O18 0-2	D04 1-0	M05 1-0	D17 2-1	a16 1-1	a05 2-2	a30 2-2
14 NORTHAMPTON T	O02 1-1	N13 2-1	S19 7-1	S21 0-3	S07 1-1	O19 2-1	D27 4-0	N28 3-3	a10 3-1	J29 3-1	a23 2-1	M05 1-2	a02 1-2		O30 0-0	J01 2-2	a19 1-1	M20 2-1	F05 2-3	S28 0-1	F26 2-0	O10 1-0	J15 2-2	S04 1-1
15 PETERBOROUGH U	J29 0-0	m04 3-1	O02 3-0	S18 1-1	F16 0-1	D27 2-1	a02 2-1	a23 1-1	N03 2-1	S04 2-1	J01 4-0	M19 1-1	m07 3-2	M12 2-0		N27 0-0	N13 1-0	O09 0-1	J15 1-0	a09 4-3	O23 1-3	F26 3-0	S08 0-3	F05 2-2
16 PORT VALE	a16 2-1	O30 1-0	a04 1-1	S04 0-0	S18 2-1	S06 0-0	M05 1-1	F05 2-1	F26 2-1	O18 3-0	O09 2-0	N13 1-0	J29 4-1	m14 1-2	a29 2-1		M19 4-0	m09 0-1	O02 2-3	J15 3-0	D28 1-0	D04 0-1	D18 1-0	J03 2-1
17 ROCHDALE	D18 3-1	O16 3-1	D04 1-0	O02 0-0	S04 0-1	a26 2-1	M15 2-0	J15 1-1	O23 2-2	S07 2-0	M12 4-1	m14 1-3	F05 2-2	N02 2-0	M26 1-1	N06 3-3		a04 0-1	a16 1-0	S18 1-1	a30 2-2	J03 4-2	D11 0-2	D28 1-0
18 SCUNTHORPE U	S04 1-1	a23 4-3	F05 1-1	N27 0-1	J01 2-0	O02 2-1	M25 2-0	m07 2-2	a01 2-0	J16 3-0	a08 1-2	O15 0-1	M01 2-2	N06 5-1	a26 3-0	N02 1-0	D27 1-1		S07 3-0	m02 2-0	M12 2-0	O23 2-1	J29 0-0	S19 0-0
19 STOCKPORT CO	F26 2-1	D27 3-0	M18 2-2	F14 2-1	a02 3-3	a22 3-0	D10 3-2	N12 2-1	J01 4-2	O08 1-1	N01 2-1	S10 1-1	a08 1-1	S24 0-1	A28 1-1	m06 0-2	S27 2-2	F12 1-1		N26 1-2	a17 1-0	J21 3-2	M11 1-3	O22 2-1
20 SWINDON T	a04 2-0	a19 3-3	m14 2-0	F26 1-1	M12 2-3	O10 3-0	S25 1-0	M19 1-2	S11 0-1	D18 3-0	F12 3-2	a16 0-1	O23 4-0	m08 1-5	D04 1-0	A28 1-0	J22 4-1	J03 2-2	a30 2-0		a26 2-1	N02 4-2	D28 0-1	N13 3-2
21 TORQUAY U	S08 4-2	M02 1-3	M20 0-2	M26 2-3	m07 0-1	J01 2-0	a09 2-1	S18 1-0	m02 1-3	O02 3-2	D27 2-1	F19 0-0	a23 3-1	O16 3-1	M05 2-1	a02 0-1	N27 3-2	O30 1-1	S04 3-0	O20 1-1		N06 3-0	F05 0-1	J15 1-3
22 TRANMERE R	J25 1-1	a02 1-1	S04 2-2	m07 1-1	D27 2-4	N13 2-4	J01 1-1	O18 2-0	a23 1-2	F05 1-1	N27 2-1	O30 0-1	S06 3-0	F19 2-1	O16 1-0	a08 0-2	m16 0-0	M05 0-4	S18 1-1	F28 2-0	M18 2-0		O02 0-2	J29 3-0
23 WIMBLEDON	O09 6-1	m07 5-0	M05 2-1	J01 2-1	m02 4-0	F15 2-1	a19 3-2	a09 3-1	N13 2-4	M19 2-0	S28 1-0	J08 1-2	D27 1-1	A28 1-1	J22 2-1	a23 1-0	O19 3-0	S11 2-2	O30 2-1	a01 0-0	S25 4-1	M15 4-0		F26 4-3
24 YORK C	N06 4-0	F15 2-0	F19 3-0	D27 3-1	a23 1-0	a09 3-0	M01 2-0	J01 5-2	S28 3-2	O30 5-1	m07 5-1	a19 1-0	N27 6-1	M15 5-2	S25 1-1	m02 0-0	a02 1-0	J23 2-1	M05 3-1	M26 0-0	A28 1-1	S11 2-1	O16 1-4	

LEAGUE TABLES

DIVISION 1

	P	W	D	L	F	A	W	D	L	F	A	Pts
Liverpool	42	16	4	1	55	16	8	6	7	32	21	82
Watford	42	16	2	3	49	20	6	3	12	25	37	71
Manchester U	42	14	7	0	39	10	5	6	10	17	28	70
Tottenham H	42	15	4	2	50	15	5	5	11	15	35	69
Nottingham F	42	12	5	4	34	18	8	4	9	28	32	69
Aston Villa	42	17	2	2	47	15	4	3	14	15	35	68
Everton	42	13	6	2	43	19	5	4	12	23	29	64
West Ham U	42	13	3	5	41	23	7	1	13	27	39	64
Ipswich T	42	11	3	7	39	23	4	10	7	25	27	58
Arsenal	42	11	6	4	36	19	5	4	12	22	37	58
W.B.A.	42	11	5	5	35	20	4	7	10	16	29	57
Southampton	42	11	5	5	36	22	4	7	10	18	36	57
Stoke C	42	13	4	4	34	21	3	5	13	19	43	57
Norwich C	42	10	6	5	30	18	4	6	11	22	40	54
Notts Co	42	12	4	5	37	25	3	3	15	18	46	52
Sunderland	42	7	10	4	30	22	5	4	12	18	39	50
Birmingham C	42	9	7	5	29	24	3	7	11	11	31	50
Luton T	42	7	7	7	34	33	5	6	10	31	51	49
Coventry C	42	10	5	6	29	17	3	4	14	19	42	48
Manchester C	42	9	5	7	26	23	4	3	14	21	47	47
Swansea C	42	10	4	7	32	29	0	7	14	19	40	41
Brighton & H.A.	42	8	7	6	25	22	1	6	14	13	46	40

DIVISION 2

	P	W	D	L	F	A	W	D	L	F	A	Pts
Q.P.R.	42	16	3	2	51	16	10	4	7	26	20	85
Wolverh'pton W	42	14	5	2	42	16	6	10	5	26	28	75
Leicester C	42	11	4	6	36	15	9	6	6	36	29	70
Fulham	42	13	5	3	36	20	7	4	10	28	27	69
Newcastle U	42	13	6	2	43	21	5	7	9	32	32	67
Sheffield W	42	9	8	4	33	23	7	7	7	27	24	63
Oldham A	42	8	10	3	38	24	6	9	6	26	23	61
Leeds U	42	7	11	3	28	22	6	10	5	23	24	60
Shrewsbury T	42	8	9	4	20	15	7	5	9	28	33	59
Barnsley	42	9	8	4	37	28	5	7	9	20	27	57
Blackburn R	42	11	7	3	38	21	4	5	12	20	37	57
Cambridge U	42	11	7	3	26	17	2	5	14	16	43	51
Derby Co	42	7	10	4	27	24	3	9	9	22	34	49
Carlisle U	42	10	6	5	44	28	2	6	13	24	42	48
Crystal Palace	42	11	7	3	31	17	1	5	15	12	35	48
Middlesbrough	42	8	7	6	27	29	3	8	10	19	38	48
Charlton A	42	11	3	7	40	31	2	6	13	23	55	48
Chelsea	42	8	8	5	31	22	3	6	12	20	39	47
Grimsby T	42	9	7	5	32	26	3	4	14	13	44	47
Rotherham U	42	6	7	8	22	29	4	8	9	23	39	45
Burnley	42	10	4	7	38	24	2	4	15	18	42	44
Bolton W	42	10	2	9	30	26	1	9	11	12	35	44

DIVISION 3

	P	W	D	L	F	A	W	D	L	F	A	Pts
Portsmouth	46	16	4	3	43	19	11	6	6	31	22	91
Cardiff C	46	17	5	1	45	14	8	6	9	31	36	86
Huddersfield T	46	15	8	0	56	18	8	5	10	28	31	82
Newport Co	46	13	7	3	40	20	10	2	11	36	34	78
Oxford U	46	12	9	2	41	23	10	3	10	30	30	78
Lincoln C	46	17	1	5	55	22	6	6	11	22	29	76
Bristol R	46	16	4	3	55	21	6	5	12	29	37	75
Plymouth A	46	15	2	6	37	23	4	6	13	24	43	65
Brentford	46	14	4	5	50	28	4	6	13	38	49	64
Walsall	46	14	5	4	38	19	3	8	12	26	44	64
Sheffield U	46	16	3	4	44	20	3	4	16	18	44	64
Bradford C	46	11	7	5	41	27	5	6	12	27	42	61
Gillingham	46	12	4	7	37	29	4	9	10	21	30	61
Bournemouth	46	11	7	5	35	20	5	6	12	24	48	61
Southend U	46	10	8	5	41	28	5	6	12	25	37	59
Preston N.E.	46	11	10	2	35	17	4	3	16	25	52	58
Millwall	46	12	7	4	41	24	2	6	15	23	53	55
Wigan A	46	10	4	9	35	33	5	5	13	25	39	54
Exeter C	46	12	4	7	49	43	2	8	13	32	61	54
Orient	46	10	6	7	44	38	5	3	15	20	50	54
Reading	46	10	8	5	37	28	2	9	12	27	51	53
Wrexham	46	11	6	6	40	26	1	9	13	16	50	51
Doncaster R	46	6	8	9	38	44	3	3	17	19	53	38
Chesterfield	46	6	6	11	28	28	2	7	14	15	40	37

DIVISION 4

	P	W	D	L	F	A	W	D	L	F	A	Pts
Wimbledon	46	17	4	2	57	23	12	7	4	39	22	98
Hull C	46	14	8	1	48	14	11	7	5	27	20	90
Port Vale	46	15	4	4	37	16	11	6	6	30	18	88
Scunthorpe U	46	13	7	3	41	17	10	7	6	30	25	83
Bury	46	15	4	4	43	20	8	8	7	31	26	81
Colchester U	46	17	5	1	51	19	7	4	12	24	36	81
York C	46	18	4	1	59	19	4	9	10	29	39	79
Swindon T	46	14	3	6	45	27	5	8	10	16	27	68
Peterborough U	46	13	6	4	38	23	4	7	12	20	29	64
Mansfield T	46	11	6	6	32	26	5	7	11	29	44	61
Halifax T	46	9	8	6	31	23	7	4	12	28	43	60
Torquay U	46	12	3	8	38	30	5	4	14	18	35	58
Chester C	46	8	6	9	28	24	7	5	11	27	36	56
Bristol C	46	10	8	5	32	25	3	9	11	27	45	56
Northampton T	46	10	8	5	43	29	4	4	15	22	46	54
Stockport Co	46	11	8	4	41	31	3	4	16	19	48	54
Darlington	46	8	5	10	27	30	5	8	10	34	41	52
Aldershot	46	11	5	7	40	35	1	10	12	21	47	51
Tranmere R	46	8	8	7	30	29	5	3	15	19	42	50
Rochdale	46	11	8	4	38	25	0	8	15	17	48	49
Blackpool	46	10	8	5	32	23	3	4	16	23	51	*49
Hartlepool U	46	11	5	7	30	24	2	4	17	16	52	48
Crewe A	46	9	5	9	35	32	2	3	18	18	39	41
Hereford U	46	8	6	9	19	23	3	2	18	23	56	41

*Blackpool had two points deducted for fielding an ineligible player

Football League Records

Top scorers: Div 1, I.Rush (Liverpool) 32 goals; Div 2, K.Dixon (Chelsea) 28 goals; Div 3, K.Edwards (Sheffield United) 33 goals; Div 4, T.Senior (Reading) 36 goals.
Chester became Chester City.

Liverpool's brilliantly eccentric goalkeeper Bruce Grobbelaar, who took over from Ray Clemence at Anfield.

DIVISION 1

	ARSENAL	ASTON VILLA	BIRMINGHAM C	COVENTRY C	EVERTON	IPSWICH T	LEICESTER C	LIVERPOOL	LUTON T	MANCHESTER U	NORWICH C	NOTTINGHAM F	NOTTS CO	Q.P.R.	SOUTHAMPTON	STOKE C	SUNDERLAND	TOTTENHAM H	WATFORD	W.B.A.	WEST HAM U	WOLVERHAMPTON W
1 ARSENAL		F18 1-1	D27 1-1	O15 0-1	N19 2-1	M10 4-1	a28 2-1	S10 0-2	A27 2-1	S06 2-3	S24 3-0	O22 4-1	J21 1-1	F04 0-2	D31 2-2	a07 3-1	N05 1-2	a21 3-2	D17 3-1	D03 0-1	m07 3-3	M24 4-1
2 ASTON VILLA	O29 2-6		O15 1-0	a07 2-0	m07 0-2	D17 4-0	N19 3-1	J20 1-3	F04 0-0	M03 0-3	S10 1-0	M17 1-0	a28 3-1	D31 2-1	S24 1-0	N12 1-1	A29 1-0	D27 0-0	a21 2-1	A27 4-3	D03 1-0	F25 4-0
3 BIRMINGHAM C	a23 1-1	M31 2-1		N05 1-2	J02 0-2	S17 1-0	O01 2-1	m05 0-0	M20 1-1	F07 2-2	D10 0-1	D26 1-2	M24 0-0	a14 0-2	m12 0-0	S06 1-0	N26 0-1	O22 0-1	S03 2-0	F28 2-1	J14 3-0	F11 0-0
4 COVENTRY C	M31 1-4	M13 3-3	M03 0-1		S03 1-1	O01 1-2	S17 2-1	D10 4-0	m05 2-2	D26 1-1	m12 2-1	a17 2-1	S06 2-1	N12 1-0	N26 0-0	F18 2-3	J02 2-1	M24 2-4	J14 1-2	O22 1-2	F11 1-2	a14 2-1
5 EVERTON	a09 0-0	D10 1-1	S24 1-1	D31 0-0		M17 1-0	M20 1-1	M03 1-1	O15 0-1	m05 1-1	N26 0-2	N12 1-0	F04 4-1	m12 3-1	M31 1-0	A27 1-0	D26 0-0	J21 2-1	O22 1-0	S10 0-0	A29 0-1	a23 2-0
6 IPSWICH T	N12 1-0	m12 2-1	J21 1-2	F04 3-1	S06 3-0		O22 0-0	N26 1-1	M31 3-0	D10 0-2	a23 2-0	a14 2-2	D31 1-0	O15 0-2	F21 0-3	S10 5-0	m05 1-0	A27 3-1	M24 0-0	S24 3-4	M03 0-3	D26 3-1
7 LEICESTER C	N26 3-0	a14 2-0	F04 2-3	J21 1-1	O29 2-0	F25 2-0		a18 3-3	A31 0-3	N12 1-1	M31 2-1	m05 2-1	A27 0-4	D26 2-1	N30 2-1	S24 2-2	m12 0-2	S10 0-3	M03 4-1	D31 1-1	M17 4-1	D10 5-1
8 LIVERPOOL	F11 2-1	S17 2-1	D03 1-0	m07 5-0	N06 3-0	a28 2-2	D27 2-2		O29 6-0	J02 1-1	m15 1-1	S03 1-0	D17 5-0	F25 2-0	S06 1-1	N19 1-0	O01 0-1	M10 3-1	F01 3-0	a21 3-0	a07 6-0	J14 0-1
9 LUTON T	J14 1-2	O01 1-0	N12 1-1	D03 2-4	a07 0-3	M13 2-1	M24 0-0	F18 0-0		F12 0-5	S06 2-2	J02 2-3	a21 3-2	M03 0-0	O22 3-1	m07 0-1	S03 4-1	N19 2-4	a28 1-2	D18 2-0	D27 0-1	S17 4-0
10 MANCHESTER U	M17 4-0	N05 1-2	a07 1-0	a21 4-1	D03 0-1	m07 1-2	M10 2-0	S24 1-0	S10 2-0		F04 0-0	A29 1-2	D27 3-3	A27 3-1	J21 3-2	D31 1-0	F25 2-1	D16 4-2	N19 4-1	O15 3-0	a28 0-0	O29 3-0
11 NORWICH C	J02 1-1	F11 3-1	m07 1-1	D17 0-0	a28 1-1	D27 0-0	O19 3-1	A31 0-1	M17 0-0	O01 3-3		S17 2-3	M13 0-1	O29 0-3	N05 1-0	a21 2-2	J14 3-0	D03 2-1	a07 6-1	N19 2-0	F25 1-0	S03 3-0
12 NOTTINGHAM F	F25 0-1	S07 2-2	a21 5-1	D28 3-0	M13 1-0	N19 2-1	D04 3-2	D31 0-1	S24 1-0	m16 2-0	J21 3-0		O16 3-1	S10 3-2	A27 0-1	a28 0-0	O29 1-1	F04 2-2	m07 5-1	a07 3-1	D17 3-0	N05 5-0
13 NOTTS CO	S17 0-4	N26 5-2	A30 2-1	M17 2-1	O01 0-1	S03 0-2	J14 2-5	m12 0-0	D26 0-3	a14 1-0	N12 1-1	M31 0-0		m05 0-3	m17 1-3	O22 1-1	D10 6-1	F21 0-0	F11 3-5	M03 1-1	J02 2-2	m01 4-0
14 Q.P.R.	O01 2-0	S03 2-1	N19 2-1	M10 2-1	D17 2-0	a07 1-0	a21 2-0	O22 0-1	N05 0-1	J13 1-1	F14 2-0	F11 0-1	D03 1-0		M24 4-0	J17 6-0	S17 3-0	a28 2-1	S06 1-1	m07 1-1	F07 1-1	J02 2-1
15 SOUTHAMPTON	S03 1-0	J02 2-2	D17 2-1	a28 8-2	a17 3-1	O29 3-2	a07 2-2	M16 2-0	F25 2-1	S17 3-0	M03 2-1	J23 0-1	N19 0-2	A29 0-0		D03 3-1	F11 1-1	m07 5-0	D27 1-0	N12 1-0	a21 2-0	O01 1-0
16 STOKE C	J28 1-0	M10 1-0	M17 2-1	O29 1-3	J14 1-1	F11 1-0	J02 0-1	a14 2-0	D10 2-4	S03 0-1	D26 2-0	N26 1-1	F25 1-0	a23 1-2	m05 1-1		M31 2-1	N05 1-1	S17 0-4	A29 3-1	O01 3-1	m12 4-0
17 SUNDERLAND	M03 2-2	M24 0-1	a28 2-1	S24 1-0	a21 2-1	D03 1-1	D18 1-1	F04 0-0	D31 2-0	O22 0-1	A27 1-1	F18 1-1	m07 0-0	M07 1-0	S10 0-2	O15 2-2		a07 1-1	N12 3-0	D27 3-0	N19 0-1	S07 3-2
18 TOTTENHAM H	D26 2-4	a18 2-1	F25 0-1	A29 1-1	S17 1-2	J14 2-0	F11 3-2	N12 2-2	a14 2-1	m12 1-1	m05 2-0	O02 2-1	O29 1-0	N26 3-2	D10 0-0	M03 1-0	F08 3-0		J02 2-3	M17 0-1	S03 0-2	M31 1-0
19 WATFORD	m12 2-1	D26 3-2	D31 1-0	A27 2-3	F25 4-4	A30 2-2	N05 3-3	M31 0-2	N26 1-2	a17 0-0	O15 1-3	D10 3-2	S10 3-1	M17 1-0	a24 1-1	J21 2-0	M20 2-1	S24 2-3		F04 3-1	O28 0-0	m05 0-0
20 W.B.A.	m05 1-3	J14 3-1	O29 1-2	F25 1-1	F11 1-1	J02 2-1	S03 1-0	D26 1-2	m12 3-0	M31 2-0	a14 0-0	F08 0-5	N05 2-0	D10 1-2	m14 0-2	M24 3-0	a23 3-1	S07 1-1	O01 2-0		S17 1-0	N26 1-3
21 WEST HAM U	D10 3-1	m05 0-1	A27 4-0	S10 5-2	m14 0-1	N05 2-1	S06 3-1	O15 1-3	a17 3-1	N27 1-1	O22 0-0	m12 1-2	S24 3-0	M31 2-2	D26 0-1	F04 3-0	a14 0-1	D31 4-1	F21 2-4	J21 1-0		M10 1-1
22 WOLVERHAMPTON W	A29 1-2	O23 1-1	S10 1-1	N19 0-0	D27 3-0	a21 0-3	m07 1-0	A27 1-1	J21 1-2	F18 1-1	D31 2-0	M03 1-0	a07 0-1	S24 0-4	F04 0-1	D17 0-0	M17 0-0	O15 2-3	D03 0-5	a28 0-0	N12 0-3	

Former Liverpool idol Kevin Keegan was the toast of Tyneside as Newcastle United clinched the last promotion place to Division One in 1983-84.

DIVISION 2

	BARNSLEY	BLACKBURN R	BRIGHTON & HA	CAMBRIDGE U	CARDIFF C	CARLISLE U	CHARLTON A	CHELSEA	CRYSTAL P	DERBY CO	FULHAM	GRIMSBY T	HUDDERSFIELD T	LEEDS U	MANCHESTER C	MIDDLESBROUGH	NEWCASTLE U	OLDHAM A	PORTSMOUTH	SHEFFIELD W	SHREWSBURY T	SWANSEA C
1 BARNSLEY		a23 0-0	N26 3-1	D26 2-0	F04 2-3	m12 2-1	a14 2-0	D10 0-0	F18 1-1	M31 5-1	A27 3-0	S27 3-1	O15 2-2	O22 0-2	D31 1-1	S10 0-2	S24 1-1	m05 0-1	M17 0-3	M03 0-1	M13 3-0	N12 3-2
2 BLACKBURN R	D28 1-1		S24 2-2	D31 1-0	m07 1-1	M24 4-1	M21 1-1	S07 0-0	D17 2-1	S10 5-1	a29 0-1	D04 1-1	A27 2-2	N12 1-1	J21 2-1	a07 1-0	a20 1-1	O22 3-1	N19 2-1	F04 0-0	O16 1-1	M07 4-1
3 BRIGHTON & H.A.	a28 1-0	J02 1-1		F28 3-0	D03 3-1	S17 1-1	O01 7-0	S03 1-2	a21 3-1	S06 1-0	D27 1-1	a07 2-0	N05 3-1	M24 3-0	M10 1-1	m07 3-0	D17 0-1	J14 4-0	O08 0-1	O22 1-3	N19 2-2	F11 1-1
4 CAMBRIDGE U	a21 0-3	S03 2-0	O29 3-4		M10 0-2	J14 0-2	S17 2-2	F11 0-1	O08 1-3	N05 0-1	D03 1-1	D28 2-2	O18 0-3	a07 2-2	D17 0-0	N19 0-0	a28 1-0	O01 2-1	F25 1-3	M17 1-2	m07 1-0	J02 1-1
5 CARDIFF C	O01 0-3	A29 0-1	m05 2-2	N12 5-0		O08 2-0	J31 2-1	M31 3-3	a17 0-2	a23 1-0	F19 0-4	S03 3-1	N26 3-1	F11 0-1	A29 2-1	M03 2-1	O19 0-2	a14 2-0	S17 0-0	m12 0-2	M17 2-0	D26 3-2
6 CARLISLE U	D17 4-2	D10 0-1	J21 1-2	A27 0-0	a07 1-1		M17 3-0	O22 0-0	m07 2-2	F04 2-1	O15 2-0	a28 1-1	S24 0-0	D03 1-0	N19 2-0	a20 1-1	D27 3-1	F18 2-0	N12 0-0	D31 1-1	S10 1-0	M03 2-0
7 CHARLTON A	N19 3-2	N05 2-0	F04 2-0	J21 5-2	A27 2-0	S06 1-0		N15 1-1	D27 1-0	S24 1-0	m07 3-4	M10 3-3	D31 1-2	D15 2-0	O15 1-0	D03 2-0	a07 1-3	M24 2-1	a21 2-1	S10 1-1	a28 2-4	O22 2-2
8 CHELSEA	m07 3-1	M16 2-1	D31 1-0	S10 2-1	O15 2-0	F25 0-0	O29 3-2		N19 2-2	A27 5-0	a07 4-0	D17 2-3	F04 3-1	a28 5-0	D03 0-1	S24 0-0	N12 4-0	M03 3-0	D27 2-2	J21 3-2	a21 3-0	D06 6-1
9 CRYSTAL P	O29 0-1	m12 0-2	D26 0-2	a01 1-1	N08 1-0	D11 1-2	a23 2-0	a14 0-1		O15 0-1	S11 1-1	F25 0-1	M17 0-0	M03 0-0	A27 0-2	F04 1-0	J21 3-1	N12 2-1	S27 2-1	N26 1-0	D31 1-1	m05 2-0
10 DERBY CO	O08 0-2	F11 1-1	M17 0-3	M03 1-0	D27 2-3	O01 1-4	J02 0-1	J14 1-2	a07 3-0		a21 1-0	O29 1-2	F25 1-1	N19 1-1	a28 1-0	N12 1-0	D03 3-2	S17 2-2	m09 2-0	A29 1-1	D17 1-0	S03 2-1
11 FULHAM	J14 1-0	N26 0-1	a23 3-1	m05 1-0	O31 0-2	M31 0-0	D10 0-1	O08 3-5	F11 1-1	D26 2-2		J02 1-1	a14 0-2	S17 2-1	M17 5-1	S27 2-1	M03 2-2	m12 3-0	S03 0-2	N11 1-1	F25 3-0	O01 5-0
12 GRIMSBY T	a10 1-0	m05 3-2	O15 5-0	a23 0-0	D31 1-0	N26 1-1	N12 2-1	m12 0-1	O22 2-0	F21 2-1	S24 2-1		M31 2-1	S06 2-0	F04 1-1	J21 0-0	S10 1-1	D13 3-0	M03 3-4	D26 1-0	A27 1-1	a14 3-0
13 HUDDERSFIELD T	a07 0-1	J14 0-2	M03 0-1	M24 3-0	a28 4-0	J02 0-0	S03 0-0	O01 2-3	S06 2-1	O22 3-0	N19 2-0	O08 0-0		a21 2-2	D27 1-3	D17 2-2	m07 2-2	F11 0-1	D03 2-1	m01 0-1	N12 1-0	S17 1-0
14 LEEDS U	F25 1-2	M10 1-0	A29 3-2	O14 3-1	S10 1-0	m05 3-0	m12 1-0	N26 1-1	N05 1-1	a14 0-0	J21 1-0	M17 2-1	D26 1-2		S24 1-2	D31 4-1	A27 0-1	a24 2-0	O29 2-1	M31 1-1	F04 3-0	F15 1-0
15 MANCHESTER C	S03 3-2	S17 6-0	N12 4-0	m12 5-0	M24 2-1	a14 3-1	M31 0-1	m04 0-2	J14 3-1	N26 1-1	S07 0-0	O01 2-1	a23 2-3	J02 1-1		O22 2-1	F18 1-2	D26 2-0	F11 2-1	D10 1-2	M03 1-0	O08 2-1
16 MIDDLESBROUGH	F11 2-1	O08 1-2	D10 0-0	a14 1-1	N05 2-0	D26 0-1	m05 1-0	J02 2-1	O01 1-3	M20 0-0	M24 0-2	S17 1-1	m12 0-0	S03 2-2	F25 0-0		S06 3-2	M31 3-2	J14 0-0	a25 2-0	O29 4-0	N26 1-0
17 NEWCASTLE U	J02 1-0	D26 1-1	m12 3-1	N26 2-1	F25 3-1	a23 5-1	O08 2-1	M10 1-1	S17 3-1	m05 4-0	N05 3-2	F11 0-1	D10 5-2	M28 1-0	O29 5-0	M17 3-1		S03 3-0	O01 4-2	a14 0-1	A29 0-1	M31 2-0
18 OLDHAM A	D03 1-0	F25 0-0	A27 1-0	F04 0-0	N19 2-1	O29 2-3	S27 0-0	N05 1-1	M10 3-2	J21 3-0	D17 3-0	m07 2-1	S10 0-3	D27 3-2	a20 2-2	O15 2-1	D31 1-2		a28 3-2	S24 1-3	a07 0-1	M17 3-3
19 PORTSMOUTH	S06 2-1	a14 2-4	M31 5-1	N01 5-0	J21 1-1	M10 0-1	D26 4-0	a24 2-2	M24 0-1	D10 3-0	D31 1-4	N05 4-0	m05 1-1	F18 2-3	S10 1-2	A27 0-1	F04 1-4	N26 3-4		O15 0-1	S24 4-1	m12 5-0
20 SHEFFIELD W	N05 2-0	O01 4-2	F25 2-1	S06 1-0	D17 5-2	S03 2-0	F11 4-1	S17 2-1	a28 1-0	a10 3-1	M07 1-1	a21 1-0	O29 0-0	O08 3-1	m07 0-0	D27 0-2	N19 4-2	J02 3-0	a07 2-0		D03 1-1	J14 6-1
21 SHREWSBURY T	S17 3-2	M30 1-0	a14 2-1	D10 1-0	S06 1-0	F11 0-0	N26 1-1	D26 2-4	S03 1-1	m12 3-0	O22 0-0	J14 1-2	M10 1-0	O01 5-1	N05 1-3	F28 1-0	M24 2-2	O08 2-0	J02 2-0	m05 2-1		a24 2-0
22 SWANSEA C	M10 1-0	O29 0-1	S10 1-3	S24 2-1	a21 3-2	N05 0-0	F25 1-0	N22 1-3	D03 1-0	D31 2-0	F05 0-3	N19 0-1	J18 2-2	m07 2-2	a07 0-2	a27 2-1	O16 1-2	S06 0-0	D17 1-2	A27 0-1	D27 0-2	

SEASON 1983-84

DIVISION 3

	BOLTON W	BOURNEMOUTH	BRADFORD C	BRENTFORD	BRISTOL R	BURNLEY	EXETER C	GILLINGHAM	HULL C	LINCOLN C	MILLWALL	NEWPORT CO	ORIENT	OXFORD U	PLYMOUTH A	PORT VALE	PRESTON N.E.	ROTHERHAM U	SCUNTHORPE U	SHEFFIELD U	SOUTHEND U	WALSALL	WIGAN A	WIMBLEDON
1 BOLTON W		a28 0-1	M27 0-2	D03 1-0	F04 3-0	S27 0-0	M17 1-0	a07 0-1	O18 0-0	F14 0-2	J02 2-0	O15 2-3	N05 3-2	D27 1-0	a16 2-1	F25 2-0	D17 2-2	S24 2-0	J21 0-0	m07 3-1	O29 2-0	S10 8-1	a21 0-1	A27 2-0
2 BOURNEMOUTH	N26 2-2		m12 4-1	F18 0-3	S27 0-1	a09 1-0	D31 3-1	S24 2-0	N05 2-3	F04 3-0	J21 1-1	D26 1-1	a24 3-2	O22 2-1	O08 2-1	m05 1-1	A27 0-1	N01 4-2	a14 1-1	M24 0-1	M10 1-0	M03 3-0	S10 0-1	M31 2-3
3 BRADFORD C	S03 0-2	D17 5-2		a28 1-1	m02 0-1	a21 2-1	O01 1-3	a11 3-2	S07 0-0	m07 0-0	N12 3-3	a25 1-0	J14 4-1	M03 2-2	D03 2-0	F11 2-2	J02 3-2	F18 1-0	O08 2-2	a07 2-1	S17 1-1	O22 0-0	D27 6-2	J07 5-2
4 BRENTFORD	a14 3-0	O29 1-1	N26 1-4		M31 2-2	S24 0-0	a20 3-0	F04 2-3	O15 1-1	S10 3-0	A27 2-2	D31 2-0	M10 1-1	M17 1-2	N05 2-2	O18 3-1	a03 4-1	M20 2-1	m05 3-0	F25 1-3	F14 0-0	m12 1-1	J21 0-1	D24 3-4
5 BRISTOL R	O01 2-1	a07 1-3	O15 1-0	S06 3-1		N12 2-1	S17 2-0	D27 3-0	D17 1-3	a28 3-1	m08 3-2	J14 4-0	F11 0-0	a21 1-1	M03 2-0	J28 0-0	N01 3-1	M06 2-0	O22 4-1	D03 1-1	S03 2-1	F18 4-2	M27 2-1	M17 1-1
6 BURNLEY	M31 2-2	S03 5-1	D26 1-2	F11 2-2	M10 0-0		F14 4-0	O15 2-3	m15 0-2	F25 4-0	M17 1-0	S06 2-0	m05 2-3	M27 1-1	O01 2-1	N26 7-0	N05 2-1	a14 2-2	D31 5-0	N08 2-1	O18 3-0	a23 0-2	O29 3-0	m12 0-2
7 EXETER C	O08 2-2	m07 0-2	F03 0-2	D27 1-2	J21 1-2	N02 1-1		M03 0-0	D03 2-1	S28 0-3	D17 3-2	O22 1-2	F18 3-4	J02 3-1	a21 1-1	N05 1-1	a28 2-1	S10 0-1	a11 1-1	M10 1-2	M23 3-3	A27 0-1	a07 1-1	S24 0-3
8 GILLINGHAM	S06 2-0	F11 2-1	F14 0-0	O01 4-2	a23 1-2	M24 0-1	O18 3-1		S03 1-2	N05 2-0	O29 3-3	m05 4-1	M31 3-1	S17 2-3	m01 2-1	a14 1-1	O08 2-0	N26 4-2	m12 1-1	J14 4-2	D26 5-1	M10 1-3	F25 3-0	D31 0-1
9 HULL C	M03 1-1	M06 3-1	M31 1-0	M24 2-0	m12 0-0	A27 4-1	a14 1-0	a17 0-0		S24 2-0	S10 5-0	N12 0-0	N26 2-1	F28 0-1	O22 1-2	D31 1-0	a10 3-0	a23 5-0	D26 1-0	O08 4-1	m05 2-1	N01 2-2	F04 1-0	S27 1-0
10 LINCOLN C	N02 0-0	O01 3-0	D31 2-3	F01 2-0	N26 4-0	O22 3-1	M31 1-1	M07 4-0	F11 1-3		O15 2-2	M03 2-3	S07 2-0	J14 2-2	S17 3-1	m12 3-2	F18 2-1	m05 0-1	N12 2-1	S03 0-2	a23 1-2	D26 2-1	M17 0-1	a14 1-2
11 MILLWALL	m05 3-0	S17 3-1	M10 0-0	J15 1-2	D30 1-0	O09 2-0	m12 3-0	F19 2-2	J28 1-0	m01 0-2		N01 1-1	D26 4-3	F11 2-1	S03 1-0	S06 3-2	O21 1-0	M03 2-0	N26 2-1	O01 1-2	a18 4-0	a14 2-0	N05 2-0	a23 1-1
12 NEWPORT CO	M24 2-3	a21 2-1	S10 4-3	m07 1-1	A27 2-1	a07 1-0	F25 1-0	M27 1-0	M10 1-1	O18 1-0	F14 1-1		O08 0-0	a28 1-1	D27 2-0	O29 2-1	S27 1-1	F04 1-4	S24 1-1	D17 0-2	N05 1-1	J22 3-1	D03 5-3	M06 1-1
13 ORIENT	M06 2-1	D27 2-0	A27 2-0	N12 2-0	S23 0-1	J02 1-2	O29 2-2	O24 1-1	a28 3-1	a07 1-1	a21 5-3	M17 2-2		m07 1-2	D17 3-2	O14 3-0	D03 2-1	J22 2-1	S09 1-0	O18 2-0	F26 1-0	J07 0-1	J27 0-0	F04 2-6
14 OXFORD U	a20 5-0	F25 3-2	O19 2-0	O08 2-1	D26 3-2	S10 2-2	m05 1-1	M13 0-1	O29 1-1	A27 3-0	S24 4-2	N26 2-0	D31 5-2		M24 5-0	M10 2-0	F04 2-0	m12 3-2	M31 1-0	N05 2-2	a14 2-1	S28 6-3	m02 0-0	F15 2-0
15 PLYMOUTH A	N12 2-0	M17 1-0	m09 3-0	M06 1-1	O18 1-1	F04 1-1	D26 2-2	S10 1-1	F25 2-0	J21 2-2	M20 0-1	a20 0-1	m12 3-1	O15 2-1		F14 3-0	S24 1-0	M30 1-1	S27 4-0	O29 0-1	D31 4-0	m05 3-1	A27 0-0	a10 1-2
16 PORT VALE	O22 1-2	J02 2-1	S24 1-2	M03 4-3	S10 2-0	a28 2-3	M05 2-2	D03 0-1	m07 1-0	D17 0-1	m14 1-0	F18 4-2	a09 2-0	N12 1-3	O31 0-1		a21 1-1	a02 2-3	A27 0-0	D27 2-0	J30 2-1	F04 0-2	S26 1-1	J21 2-0
17 PRESTON N.E.	m12 2-1	J14 2-0	m05 1-2	S03 3-3	F14 1-0	M06 4-2	N26 2-1	M17 2-2	S17 0-0	O29 1-2	F25 0-0	M30 2-0	a14 3-1	O01 1-2	F11 2-1	D26 4-0		N12 1-0	a24 1-0	J31 2-2	S06 4-1	D31 0-1	O15 2-3	O18 2-3
18 ROTHERHAM U	F11 1-1	a17 1-0	O29 1-0	a07 4-0	N05 2-2	D03 1-1	m01 1-0	a28 3-0	D27 0-1	J02 1-1	O18 1-0	O01 0-1	S17 0-1	D17 1-2	S06 2-0	S03 2-1	M10 0-1		m15 3-0	a21 0-1	a10 0-0	O08 0-1	m07 4-1	F25 1-2
19 SCUNTHORPE U	S16 1-0	D03 1-2	M17 2-1	J02 4-4	F25 2-2	m07 4-0	S03 3-1	D17 2-0	a21 2-0	M10 0-0	a27 0-1	F10 3-3	m01 3-1	S07 0-0	a07 3-0	a17 1-1	D27 1-5	O15 1-2		M27 1-1	S30 1-6	N05 0-0	O18 0-0	O29 5-1
20 SHEFFIELD U	D31 5-0	O15 2-0	S27 2-0	O22 0-0	a14 4-0	J21 0-0	N12 2-2	A27 4-0	M17 2-2	F07 0-0	F04 2-0	m12 2-0	M03 6-3	M06 1-2	F28 2-0	a24 3-1	S10 1-1	D26 3-0	N01 5-3		N26 5-0	M31 2-0	S24 2-2	m05 1-2
21 SOUTHEND U	F06 0-1	N11 0-0	a16 2-1	O31 6-0	J09 1-2	M02 2-2	O15 0-3	a20 3-1	J02 2-2	D27 2-0	S19 3-2	a30 3-1	O21 3-0	D02 0-1	m07 1-1	M19 1-2	a06 1-1	A27 2-2	F03 0-0	a28 0-1		S24 0-0	D17 1-0	S10 1-1
22 WALSALL	J28 1-0	O18 3-1	F25 1-2	D17 1-0	O29 2-1	D27 1-1	J14 4-1	N12 3-1	M27 2-1	a21 0-1	D03 1-1	S17 3-2	S03 0-1	a07 0-1	J02 3-2	O01 2-0	m07 2-1	M17 2-2	M06 1-1	S06 1-2	F11 4-0		a28 3-0	O15 4-0
23 WIGAN A	D26 0-1	M20 1-3	a23 0-1	S17 2-1	a17 0-0	F18 1-0	S06 1-1	O22 1-2	O01 1-1	O08 2-0	M06 0-0	a14 1-0	N01 0-1	S03 0-2	a03 1-1	M31 3-0	M24 1-0	D31 2-1	M03 2-0	F11 3-0	m12 1-0	N26 0-1		N12 3-2
24 WIMBLEDON	J14 4-0	S06 3-2	N05 4-1	a21 2-1	O08 1-1	D17 1-4	F11 2-1	m07 1-3	a07 1-4	D03 3-1	D27 4-3	S03 6-0	O01 2-2	N01 3-1	a28 1-0	S17 4-2	M03 2-2	O22 3-1	F18 1-1	J02 3-1	J28 3-2	M24 2-0	M10 2-2	

DIVISION 4

	ALDERSHOT	BLACKPOOL	BRISTOL C	BURY	CHESTER C	CHESTERFIELD	COLCHESTER U	CREWE A	DARLINGTON	DONCASTER R	HALIFAX T	HARTLEPOOL U	HEREFORD U	MANSFIELD T	NORTHAMPTON T	PETERBOROUGH U	READING	ROCHDALE	STOCKPORT CO	SWINDON T	TORQUAY U	TRANMERE R	WREXHAM	YORK C
1 ALDERSHOT		m05 3-2	O22 1-0	S10 1-2	M10 5-2	D31 2-1	a23 5-1	M31 0-0	m12 0-0	M24 2-1	F18 5-2	J07 2-1	A27 1-4	F04 7-1	N01 1-0	N05 3-2	D26 0-0	N26 2-1	D10 1-1	S27 2-1	J21 3-1	O08 1-1	S24 1-1	a14 1-4
2 BLACKPOOL	J02 5-0		N01 1-0	a07 1-1	M24 3-3	O22 1-0	m01 3-2	S24 3-0	N05 3-1	M10 3-1	m07 4-0	D27 1-0	a28 3-1	S27 2-0	S10 2-3	D03 1-2	A27 1-0	O08 0-2	a10 1-1	J21 1-1	D17 1-0	a21 0-1	M03 4-0	F04 3-0
3 BRISTOL C	F25 2-1	F14 1-1		J31 3-2	D31 4-2	N26 2-0	M31 4-1	a17 2-1	M10 1-0	N05 1-2	O08 3-0	S10 2-0	F04 1-0	A27 4-0	a14 4-1	O29 0-1	S27 3-1	M13 1-1	D26 3-1	m05 1-0	S24 5-0	M24 1-1	J21 2-1	O18 1-0
4 BURY	m01 0-3	S06 0-0	S03 2-1		a14 2-1	a23 2-0	M03 1-1	N13 1-1	a01 0-3	F11 2-3	S18 3-0	F18 3-0	M24 1-4	O08 2-2	m05 1-2	N29 2-2	N26 2-3	D26 3-1	N01 2-1	m12 2-1	M06 0-0	F07 0-0	O22 2-0	D31 1-3
5 CHESTER C	N12 1-2	N09 0-2	m07 1-2	D03 2-1		M07 0-2	F04 1-4	S10 0-1	M17 2-1	a28 1-0	N02 1-1	M03 4-1	a07 0-1	D27 0-4	A27 1-1	D17 1-1	S24 2-1	F18 1-0	O22 2-4	F08 0-3	S28 1-2	J02 0-0	a21 1-0	a18 1-1
6 CHESTERFIELD	m07 3-1	F25 1-1	a28 1-1	D27 1-5	N05 1-1		S24 1-1	J07 1-3	O29 1-1	O18 0-0	J02 0-0	a07 4-1	S27 0-0	a21 0-0	F04 2-1	M10 1-0	J21 2-1	M24 3-0	O08 2-0	A27 1-0	M18 3-2	D03 3-3	D17 1-1	S10 2-1
7 COLCHESTER U	D27 4-1	S03 2-1	S06 0-0	O18 1-0	O01 1-0	F11 2-0		O29 2-0	J14 2-1	F14 1-1	D17 4-1	D03 6-0	m07 3-0	M10 1-0	O15 2-2	a21 1-1	N05 3-0	S17 4-0	J28 1-1	F25 0-0	a28 3-0	a07 0-1	J02 1-1	M17 1-3
8 CREWE A	S06 0-0	F11 2-1	D28 2-2	M10 2-1	J28 1-1	S03 2-1	F18 1-1		S17 2-1	D18 1-1	M03 6-1	N01 2-0	a21 1-1	m07 1-3	O22 3-2	a07 0-1	M23 1-1	J14 0-1	S30 0-3	O08 2-0	J02 2-1	a28 3-0	m15 1-1	N05 0-3
9 DARLINGTON	D17 0-1	m15 2-0	N12 0-1	S27 1-2	O08 2-1	F18 2-1	A27 0-2	M27 2-0		D27 1-2	a28 3-2	a21 2-0	M03 0-0	D03 3-0	F28 5-3	J02 1-0	F04 1-1	O22 1-0	m02 1-0	S10 1-0	a07 0-1	N01 1-0	m08 2-2	S24 0-0
10 DONCASTER R	O15 3-1	N12 2-1	M06 1-0	S24 3-1	N26 0-0	M03 2-1	N01 3-3	m12 1-0	a24 3-2		O21 3-2	m15 0-1	S11 3-0	J07 3-1	D26 1-0	M17 1-1	m01 2-3	m05 3-0	D31 2-1	a14 3-0	F04 1-1	F18 1-1	A27 3-0	S27 2-2
11 HALIFAX T	O29 1-0	D31 1-0	M17 1-2	J21 0-0	F14 2-2	m04 2-1	m11 4-1	O18 1-0	N25 0-2	F25 1-2		S23 3-2	J07 2-1	S09 0-0	S27 2-2	O15 2-1	a13 0-1	a23 5-0	M09 2-0	M30 2-1	A27 2-2	N04 1-2	F04 1-1	D26 1-2
12 HARTLEPOOL U	S03 0-1	a20 0-1	J28 2-2	O29 1-3	O19 1-1	S07 2-2	a14 0-0	F15 2-1	D26 2-1	S17 1-0	F11 3-0		N05 0-0	F25 4-1	D31 2-0	M27 1-1	m12 3-3	M31 1-2	m05 1-2	M10 0-1	M17 2-1	O01 0-1	O15 1-1	N26 2-3
13 HEREFORD U	J14 2-1	N26 1-2	O01 0-2	J18 1-2	S07 2-1	M31 3-1	a04 1-1	D26 0-1	O19 1-0	J28 0-3	S03 0-0	M07 5-0		O29 0-0	N12 0-0	S17 2-1	m05 1-1	a14 2-1	a23 2-0	F15 2-1	F25 1-1	F11 0-1	M17 3-0	m12 2-1
14 MANSFIELD T	O01 5-2	M31 1-1	M27 0-1	M17 1-1	a24 3-1	D26 0-1	N12 0-0	D31 3-3	a14 1-0	S03 1-2	a10 7-1	O22 5-0	F18 1-1		m12 3-1	F11 0-0	M03 2-0	N01 3-0	S06 1-2	N26 2-2	O15 1-3	S17 1-0	M06 3-4	m05 0-1
15 NORTHAMPTON T	F14 1-4	M20 1-5	D03 1-0	J02 1-0	J14 2-1	O01 1-1	M24 3-1	F25 2-0	S03 2-0	a21 1-4	a07 1-1	a10 1-1	M10 0-3	D18 2-1		D27 2-1	O09 2-2	F11 1-1	S18 0-0	N05 2-0	O18 2-1	S06 0-0	a28 3-3	O29 1-2
16 PETERBOROUGH U	M07 1-2	a14 4-0	F18 4-1	F04 2-1	m12 1-0	N12 2-0	D26 2-0	S28 1-0	m05 2-2	O08 1-1	M24 4-0	A27 3-1	J21 1-1	S24 3-0	a24 6-0		N02 3-3	M03 2-0	N26 2-0	D31 1-1	S10 5-0	O22 2-0	J07 0-1	a01 0-2
17 READING	a21 1-0	J14 2-0	a07 2-0	a28 1-1	F11 1-0	S17 1-1	M07 1-0	O14 5-0	O01 1-0	S07 3-2	D02 1-0	D17 5-1	J02 3-1	O19 4-0	M17 3-0	F15 1-1		J28 0-0	S03 6-2	O29 2-2	D27 2-2	m07 1-0	N12 4-1	F25 1-0
18 ROCHDALE	a28 3-1	M17 1-0	D17 0-1	a21 0-2	O29 1-1	O15 2-4	a17 0-0	A27 1-0	F25 2-0	J02 3-3	D27 1-1	S27 2-0	D03 3-3	F14 0-0	S24 1-1	O18 2-1	S10 4-1		N05 2-2	F04 3-3	m07 1-0	M10 2-3	a07 1-2	M27 0-2
19 STOCKPORT CO	O17 2-2	O29 1-2	a21 0-0	F13 1-1	F24 2-1	M16 2-0	S09 0-0	F03 2-3	O15 2-0	m07 0-2	N11 4-0	J02 1-0	D27 1-0	a06 0-4	J20 1-0	a27 4-1	J06 3-0	M05 2-1		S23 1-3	D02 2-1	D16 2-1	S26 1-1	A27 0-2
20 SWINDON T	a07 0-2	S17 0-0	J24 1-1	D17 0-0	S03 4-0	J14 1-2	O22 2-1	M18 1-0	a17 1-0	D03 2-1	S06 2-3	N12 3-2	N01 3-0	a29 1-1	M06 0-0	m07 2-0	F18 1-1	O01 2-1	F11 2-1		a21 2-3	M03 1-1	D27 0-1	O15 3-2
21 TORQUAY U	S17 0-1	m12 1-0	F11 1-0	N05 2-0	m02 1-0	N02 1-1	N26 2-1	m05 3-1	S07 0-1	O01 4-1	J14 1-1	O08 0-0	O22 1-1	M24 1-0	M03 2-1	J28 1-0	a23 2-2	D31 4-2	a14 1-1	D26 1-0		S03 1-1	F18 1-0	M10 1-3
22 TRANMERE R	M17 3-0	D26 3-2	O14 2-0	A27 1-1	m05 2-2	a14 0-3	S26 2-1	N26 2-3	F13 0-1	O29 1-1	M05 3-2	F03 0-1	S23 0-1	J30 1-0	M30 1-0	F24 0-0	D30 2-3	N12 2-2	m12 1-0	O17 2-1	J07 3-0		S10 2-1	a23 0-1
23 WREXHAM	F11 1-1	O18 0-1	S16 3-1	F25 3-0	D26 2-0	m12 4-2	m05 0-2	a14 0-1	D31 1-1	J14 1-2	O01 1-0	M24 1-4	O08 0-0	N05 2-3	N26 0-1	S03 2-2	M10 0-3	S06 5-1	M30 1-2	a20 0-3	O29 2-2	m21 5-1		F28 0-0
24 YORK C	D03 2-0	O01 4-0	M03 1-1	m07 3-0	S17 4-1	J31 1-0	O07 3-0	M06 5-2	F11 2-0	a08 1-1	a20 4-1	a28 2-0	D17 4-0	J02 2-1	F18 3-0	S06 2-0	O22 2-2	S03 2-0	J14 3-1	M24 2-0	N12 2-3	D27 1-1	N01 3-2	

LEAGUE TABLES

DIVISION 1

	P	W	D	L	F	A	W	D	L	F	A	Pts
Liverpool	42	14	5	2	50	12	8	9	4	23	20	80
Southampton	42	15	4	2	44	17	7	7	7	22	21	77
Nottingham F	42	14	4	3	47	17	8	4	9	29	28	74
Manchester U	42	14	3	4	43	18	6	11	4	28	23	74
Q.P.R.	42	14	4	3	37	12	8	3	10	30	25	73
Arsenal	42	10	5	6	41	29	8	4	9	33	31	63
Everton	42	9	9	3	21	12	7	5	9	23	30	62
Tottenham H	42	11	4	6	31	24	6	6	9	33	41	61
West Ham U	42	10	4	7	39	24	7	5	9	21	31	60
Aston Villa	42	14	3	4	34	22	3	6	12	25	39	60
Watford	42	9	7	5	36	31	7	2	12	32	46	57
Ipswich T	42	11	4	6	34	23	4	4	13	21	34	53
Sunderland	42	8	9	4	26	18	5	4	12	16	35	52
Norwich C	42	9	8	4	34	20	3	7	11	14	29	51
Leicester C	42	11	5	5	40	30	2	7	12	25	38	51
Luton T	42	7	5	9	30	33	7	4	10	23	33	51
W.B.A.	42	10	4	7	30	25	4	5	12	18	37	51
Stoke C	42	11	4	6	30	23	2	7	12	14	40	50
Coventry C	42	8	5	8	33	33	5	6	10	24	44	50
Birmingham C	42	7	7	7	19	18	5	5	11	20	32	48
Notts Co	42	6	7	8	31	36	4	4	13	19	36	41
Wolverh'pton W	42	4	8	9	15	28	2	3	16	12	52	29

DIVISION 2

	P	W	D	L	F	A	W	D	L	F	A	Pts
Chelsea	42	15	4	2	55	17	10	9	2	35	23	88
Sheffield W	42	16	4	1	47	16	10	6	5	25	18	88
Newcastle U	42	16	2	3	51	18	8	6	7	34	35	80
Manchester C	42	13	3	5	43	21	7	7	7	23	27	70
Grimsby T	42	13	6	2	36	15	6	7	8	24	32	70
Blackburn R	42	9	11	1	35	19	8	5	8	22	27	67
Carlisle U	42	10	9	2	29	13	6	7	8	19	28	64
Shrewsbury T	42	13	5	3	34	18	4	5	12	15	35	61
Brighton & H.A.	42	11	6	4	42	17	6	3	12	27	43	60
Leeds U	42	13	4	4	33	16	3	8	10	22	40	60
Huddersfield T	42	8	6	7	27	20	6	9	6	29	29	57
Fulham	42	9	6	6	35	24	6	6	9	25	29	57
Charlton A	42	13	4	4	40	26	3	5	13	13	38	57
Barnsley	42	9	6	6	33	23	6	1	14	24	30	52
Cardiff C	42	11	3	7	32	27	4	3	14	21	39	51
Portsmouth	42	8	3	10	46	32	6	4	11	27	32	49
Middlesbrough	42	9	8	4	26	18	3	5	13	15	29	49
Crystal Palace	42	8	5	8	18	18	4	6	11	24	34	47
Oldham A	42	10	6	5	33	27	3	2	16	14	46	47
Derby Co	42	9	5	7	26	26	2	4	15	10	46	42
Swansea C	42	7	4	10	20	28	0	4	17	16	57	29
Cambridge U	42	4	7	10	20	33	0	5	16	8	44	24

DIVISION 3

	P	W	D	L	F	A	W	D	L	F	A	Pts
Oxford U	46	17	5	1	58	22	11	6	6	33	28	95
Wimbledon	46	15	5	3	58	35	11	4	8	39	41	87
Hull C	46	16	5	2	42	11	7	9	7	29	27	83
Sheffield U	46	14	7	2	56	18	10	4	9	30	35	83
Bristol R	46	16	5	2	47	21	6	8	9	21	33	79
Walsall	46	14	4	5	44	22	8	5	10	24	39	75
Bradford C	46	11	9	3	46	30	9	2	12	27	35	71
Gillingham	46	13	4	6	50	29	7	6	10	24	40	70
Millwall	46	16	4	3	42	18	2	9	12	29	47	67
Bolton W	46	13	4	6	36	17	5	6	12	20	43	64
Orient	46	13	5	5	40	27	5	4	14	31	54	63
Burnley	46	12	5	6	52	25	4	9	10	24	36	62
Newport Co	46	11	9	3	35	27	5	5	13	23	48	62
Lincoln C	46	11	4	8	42	29	6	6	11	17	33	61
Wigan A	46	11	5	7	26	18	5	8	10	20	38	61
Preston N.E.	46	12	5	6	42	27	3	6	14	24	39	56
Bournemouth	46	11	5	7	38	27	5	2	16	25	46	55
Rotherham U	46	10	5	8	29	17	5	4	14	28	47	54
Plymouth A	46	11	8	4	38	17	2	4	17	18	45	51
Brentford	46	8	9	6	41	30	3	7	13	28	49	49
Scunthorpe U	46	9	9	5	40	31	0	10	13	14	42	46
Southend U	46	8	9	6	34	24	2	5	16	21	52	44
Port Vale	46	10	4	9	33	29	1	6	16	18	54	43
Exeter C	46	4	8	11	27	39	2	7	14	23	45	33

DIVISION 4

	P	W	D	L	F	A	W	D	L	F	A	Pts
York C	46	18	4	1	58	16	13	4	6	38	23	101
Doncaster R	46	15	6	2	46	22	9	7	7	36	32	85
Reading	46	17	6	0	51	14	5	10	8	33	42	82
Bristol C	46	18	3	2	51	17	6	7	10	19	27	82
Aldershot	46	14	6	3	49	29	8	3	12	27	40	75
Blackpool	46	15	4	4	47	19	6	5	12	23	33	72
Peterborough U	46	15	5	3	52	16	3	9	11	20	32	68
Colchester U	46	14	7	2	45	14	3	9	11	24	39	67
Torquay U	46	13	7	3	32	18	5	6	12	27	46	67
Tranmere R	46	11	5	7	33	26	6	10	7	20	27	66
Hereford U	46	11	6	6	31	21	5	9	9	23	32	63
Stockport Co	46	12	5	6	34	25	5	6	12	26	39	62
Chesterfield	46	10	11	2	34	24	5	4	14	25	37	60
Darlington	46	13	4	6	31	19	4	4	15	18	31	59
Bury	46	9	7	7	34	32	6	7	10	27	32	59
Crewe A	46	10	8	5	35	27	6	3	14	21	40	59
Swindon T	46	11	7	5	34	23	4	6	13	24	33	58
Northampton T	46	10	8	5	32	32	3	6	14	21	46	53
Mansfield T	46	9	7	7	44	27	4	6	13	22	43	52
Wrexham	46	7	6	10	34	33	4	9	10	25	41	48
Halifax T	46	11	6	6	36	25	1	6	16	19	64	48
Rochdale	46	8	9	6	35	31	3	4	16	17	49	46
Hartlepool U	46	7	8	8	31	28	3	2	18	16	57	40
Chester C	46	7	5	11	23	35	0	8	15	22	47	34

Football League Records

Top scorers: Div 1, K.Dixon (Chelsea), G.Lineker (Leicester City) 24 goals; Div 2, J.Aldridge (Oxford United) 30 goals; Div 3, T.Tynan (Plymouth Argyle) 31 goals; Div 4, J.Clayton (Tranmere Rovers) 31 goals.

Everton's Graeme Sharp netted 21 times when the League Championship trophy moved across Stanley Park in 1985.

DIVISION 1

	ARSENAL	ASTON VILLA	CHELSEA	COVENTRY C	EVERTON	IPSWICH T	LEICESTER C	LIVERPOOL	LUTON T	MANCHESTER U	NEWCASTLE U	NORWICH C	NOTTINGHAM F	Q.P.R.	SHEFFIELD W	SOUTHAMPTON	STOKE C	SUNDERLAND	TOTTENHAM H	WATFORD	W.B.A.	WEST HAM U
1 ARSENAL		N10 1-1	A25 1-1	F02 2-1	O06 1-0	M19 1-1	M16 2-0	S08 3-1	D01 3-1	F23 0-1	S04 2-0	a06 2-0	a13 1-1	N17 1-0	a27 1-0	m06 1-0	S22 4-0	O20 3-2	J01 1-2	D22 1-1	D15 4-0	M02 2-1
2 ASTON VILLA	M13 0-0		S08 4-2	A25 1-0	M16 1-1	F02 2-1	M02 0-1	D15 0-0	m06 0-1	O06 3-0	D22 4-0	O20 2-2	S05 0-5	a27 5-2	a06 3-0	N17 2-2	M27 2-0	D01 1-0	S22 0-1	a24 1-1	J01 3-1	N03 0-0
3 CHELSEA	J19 1-1	a16 3-1		N03 6-2	A31 0-1	O27 2-0	S29 3-0	D01 3-1	m08 2-0	D29 1-3	F16 1-0	m14 1-2	J01 1-0	a06 1-0	m06 2-1	M09 0-2	D15 1-1	A27 1-0	a27 1-1	O13 2-3	N17 3-1	S15 3-0
4 COVENTRY C	S29 1-2	J19 0-3	F23 1-0		m26 4-1	N10 1-0	S01 2-0	m06 0-2	m23 1-0	S15 0-3	O13 1-1	A28 0-0	N17 1-3	M09 3-0	O27 1-0	D15 2-1	J01 4-0	a13 0-1	D01 1-1	M23 3-1	a27 2-1	D29 1-2
5 EVERTON	M23 2-0	O13 2-1	D22 3-4	S08 2-1		S04 1-1	N03 3-0	m23 1-0	J01 2-1	O27 5-0	J12 4-0	a27 3-0	D15 5-0	m06 2-0	D01 1-1	S22 2-2	N17 4-0	a06 4-1	A25 1-4	F02 4-0	a16 4-1	m08 3-0
6 IPSWICH T	S15 2-1	S29 3-0	M02 2-0	m14 0-0	D29 0-2		a23 2-0	a27 0-0	A28 1-1	S01 1-1	M23 1-1	J01 2-0	a06 1-0	O13 1-1	a13 1-2	D01 0-1	m06 5-1	D15 0-2	N17 0-3	N03 3-3	O20 2-0	m17 0-1
7 LEICESTER C	O13 1-4	O27 5-0	F02 1-1	D23 5-1	F23 1-2	S08 2-1		a06 0-1	D15 2-2	N10 2-3	A25 2-3	N17 2-0	a27 1-0	D01 4-0	M09 3-1	J01 1-2	J12 0-0	m06 2-0	a13 1-2	S05 1-1	S22 2-1	M23 1-0
8 LIVERPOOL	F12 3-0	m11 2-1	m04 4-3	D04 3-1	O20 0-1	N24 2-0	D26 1-2		D29 1-0	M31 0-1	a20 3-1	J19 4-0	M02 1-0	S01 1-1	S29 0-2	N10 1-1	F23 2-0	S15 1-1	M16 0-1	m17 4-3	O06 0-0	A27 3-0
9 LUTON T	m04 3-1	D08 1-0	S22 0-0	D26 2-0	m28 2-0	M30 3-1	m11 4-0	S04 1-2		a21 2-1	N03 2-2	a16 3-1	a24 1-2	M23 2-0	O13 1-2	S08 1-1	A25 2-0	M02 2-1	F02 2-2	O20 3-2	D18 1-2	N24 2-2
10 MANCHESTER U	N02 4-2	M23 4-0	S05 1-1	J12 0-1	M02 1-1	D22 3-0	a03 2-1	S22 1-1	N17 2-0		S08 5-0	D01 2-0	m06 2-0	D15 3-0	J01 1-2	a24 0-0	a06 5-0	a27 2-2	O20 1-0	A25 1-1	F02 2-0	O13 5-1
11 NEWCASTLE U	D29 1-3	S01 3-0	N10 2-1	a17 0-1	S15 2-3	O06 3-0	M20 1-4	N18 0-2	F23 1-0	F09 1-1		D15 1-1	O20 1-1	a13 1-0	A27 2-1	a27 2-1	D01 2-1	J01 3-1	m06 2-3	M02 3-1	a06 1-0	S29 1-1
12 NORWICH C	D26 1-0	M09 2-2	O06 0-0	M30 2-1	N24 4-2	a08 0-2	a20 1-3	A25 3-3	N10 3-0	m04 0-1	m11 0-0		F02 0-1	O27 2-0	a03 1-1	J12 1-0	S19 0-0	M16 1-3	D22 1-2	S22 3-2	S05 2-1	D08 1-0
13 NOTTINGHAM F	A29 2-0	D29 3-2	a10 2-0	a20 2-0	m11 1-0	D26 2-0	N25 2-1	O28 0-2	S16 3-1	D08 3-2	M09 0-0	S29 3-1		F09 2-0	M20 0-0	F23 2-0	O06 1-1	S01 3-1	N10 1-2	m04 1-1	M16 1-2	M30 1-2
14 Q.P.R.	a20 1-0	N24 2-0	D26 2-2	O20 2-1	D08 0-0	M16 3-0	m04 4-3	D21 0-2	O06 2-3	m11 1-3	S22 5-5	M02 2-2	S08 3-0		N10 0-0	F02 0-4	D04 2-0	F23 1-0	J12 2-2	M30 2-0	A25 3-1	a08 4-2
15 SHEFFIELD W	N25 2-1	D26 1-1	D08 1-1	M02 1-0	m04 0-1	S22 2-2	O20 5-0	F02 1-1	M16 1-1	a09 1-0	M30 4-2	N03 1-2	A25 3-1	a23 3-1		S04 2-1	D22 2-1	O06 2-2	S08 2-1	F24 1-1	J12 2-0	m11 2-1
16 SOUTHAMPTON	D08 1-0	a20 2-0	O20 1-0	m11 2-1	M30 1-2	m04 3-0	a09 3-1	m14 1-1	a02 1-0	A28 0-0	N24 1-0	S15 2-1	N03 1-0	S29 1-1	D29 0-3		M16 0-0	J29 1-0	O06 1-0	D26 1-2	M02 4-3	S01 2-3
17 STOKE C	M30 2-0	A27 1-3	m11 0-1	m17 0-1	a20 0-2	D08 0-2	S15 2-2	N03 0-1	a08 0-4	D26 2-1	m04 0-1	a24 2-3	M23 1-4	D29 0-2	S01 2-1	O13 1-3		S29 2-2	M02 0-1	N24 1-3	M12 0-0	O20 2-4
18 SUNDERLAND	M09 0-0	m04 0-4	M30 0-2	S22 0-0	D26 1-2	m11 1-2	D08 0-4	a03 0-3	O27 3-0	N24 3-2	a08 0-0	O13 2-1	D23 0-2	N03 3-0	a16 0-0	A25 3-1	F02 1-0		S04 1-0	M12 1-1	S08 1-1	a20 0-1
19 TOTTENHAM H	a17 0-2	M30 0-2	N24 1-1	m04 4-2	a03 1-2	a20 2-3	A27 2-2	O12 1-0	S29 4-2	M12 1-2	D08 3-1	S01 3-1	m17 1-0	S15 5-0	m14 2-0	M23 5-1	O27 4-0	D29 2-0		m11 1-5	N03 2-3	D26 2-2
20 WATFORD	S01 3-4	S15 3-3	M16 1-3	O06 0-1	S29 4-5	a16 3-1	D29 4-1	J01 1-1	M19 3-0	m13 5-1	O27 3-3	a13 2-0	D01 2-0	A28 1-1	N17 1-0	a06 1-1	a27 2-0	N10 3-1	D15 1-2		m07 0-2	a02 5-0
21 W.B.A.	m11 2-2	a08 1-0	a20 0-1	N24 5-2	A27 2-1	a03 1-2	M30 2-0	M23 0-5	S01 4-0	S29 1-2	D26 2-1	D29 0-1	O13 4-1	J26 0-0	S15 2-2	O27 0-0	N10 2-0	a24 1-0	F23 0-1	D08 2-1		m04 5-1
22 WEST HAM U	O27 3-1	F23 1-2	a13 1-1	S04 3-1	N10 0-1	A25 0-0	O06 3-1	m20 0-3	a27 0-0	M15 2-2	F02 1-1	m06 1-0	S22 0-0	J01 1-3	D15 0-0	D22 2-3	m14 5-1	N17 1-0	a06 1-1	S08 2-0	D01 0-2	

Oxford United's John Aldridge was a key man in their promotion to Division One. Soon, however, Aldridge was sharing in Liverpool's continuing glory.

DIVISION 2

	BARNSLEY	BIRMINGHAM C	BLACKBURN R	BRIGHTON & HA	CARDIFF C	CARLISLE U	CHARLTON A	CRYSTAL P	FULHAM	GRIMSBY T	HUDDERSFIELD T	LEEDS U	MANCHESTER C	MIDDLESBROUGH	NOTTS CO	OLDHAM A	OXFORD U	PORTSMOUTH	SHEFFIELD U	SHREWSBURY T	WIMBLEDON	WOLVERHAMPTON W
1 BARNSLEY		a27 0-1	J01 1-1	M13 0-0	S15 2-0	A27 1-3	O27 1-0	M23 3-1	D01 1-0	a30 0-0	a13 2-1	O13 1-0	a06 0-0	F26 1-0	D29 0-0	S01 0-1	a02 3-0	F09 2-2	N13 1-0	N17 3-1	m06 0-0	S29 5-1
2 BIRMINGHAM C	N24 0-0		O13 0-2	M23 1-1	m04 2-0	S15 2-0	a20 2-1	a16 3-0	D29 2-2	D26 2-1	S29 1-0	m11 1-0	M19 0-0	D08 3-2	M09 2-1	M05 0-1	O27 0-0	S18 0-1	a08 4-1	N03 0-0	S01 4-2	M30 1-0
3 BLACKBURN R	a08 0-0	M16 2-1		N10 2-0	S18 2-1	S01 4-0	N24 3-0	a23 0-1	F09 2-1	S15 3-1	D29 1-3	D26 2-1	M02 0-1	a20 3-0	M30 1-0	O20 1-1	F23 1-1	m04 0-1	D08 3-1	O06 3-1	S29 2-0	m11 3-0
4 BRIGHTON & H.A.	O20 0-0	O06 2-0	M06 3-1		F09 1-0	F05 4-1	a08 2-1	S15 1-0	S29 2-0	D08 0-0	S01 0-1	a20 1-1	N03 0-0	N24 1-2	A28 2-1	M29 2-0	M16 0-0	D26 1-1	m11 1-0	M02 1-0	D29 2-1	m04 5-1
5 CARDIFF C	a23 3-0	D01 1-2	a13 1-2	S08 2-4		N17 2-1	A25 0-3	m06 0-3	M09 0-2	O27 2-4	a27 3-0	S12 2-1	S22 0-3	F02 2-1	M17 1-4	N10 2-2	a06 0-2	O06 1-2	D22 1-3	J01 0-0	D15 1-3	F23 0-0
6 CARLISLE U	M30 2-0	M12 2-1	D23 0-1	A25 0-3	a20 0-1		m03 1-1	O13 1-0	N20 3-0	M09 1-1	O27 0-1	F26 2-2	S08 0-0	D26 0-3	N24 1-0	m11 2-5	F02 0-1	D08 3-0	S22 1-1	S04 2-0	M23 6-1	a08 0-1
7 CHARLTON A	M02 5-3	N17 2-1	a27 1-0	J01 0-1	M05 1-4	N30 1-1		a06 1-1	O13 1-2	D29 4-1	A28 2-2	N03 2-3	D15 1-3	M22 1-0	S01 3-0	S15 2-1	m07 3-3	S29 2-2	a16 0-0	O20 1-1	a13 0-1	M12 1-0
8 CRYSTAL P	O07 0-1	S08 0-2	A25 1-1	a02 1-1	D09 1-1	M17 2-1	D26 2-1		O27 2-2	m11 0-2	N10 1-1	S22 3-1	F02 1-2	m04 1-0	a08 1-0	N25 3-0	F05 1-0	a20 2-1	M30 1-3	N06 2-2	F24 0-5	M09 0-0
9 FULHAM	m04 1-1	S04 0-1	S08 3-2	F02 2-0	O20 3-2	F23 3-2	M16 0-0	M02 2-2		a20 2-1	O06 2-1	M30 0-2	D22 3-2	S22 2-1	m11 1-0	D07 3-1	F19 1-0	a08 1-3	D26 1-0	A25 1-2	N10 3-1	N24 1-2
10 GRIMSBY T	A25 1-0	a05 1-0	J12 1-1	m07 2-4	M02 6-3	O20 1-0	S04 2-1	D15 1-3	N17 2-4		J01 5-1	S08 0-2	a13 4-1	D22 3-1	F23 2-0	O06 4-1	S22 1-2	M16 2-3	F02 0-2	D01 2-1	a27 2-1	N10 5-1
11 HUDDERSFIELD T	S22 1-1	F02 0-1	S04 1-1	D22 1-2	N24 2-1	M02 2-0	M30 2-1	F16 2-0	M23 2-2	a09 0-0		O20 1-0	J12 0-2	N03 3-1	a20 1-2	D26 2-1	A25 0-3	m11 0-2	m13 2-2	S08 1-5	O13 2-1	D08 3-1
12 LEEDS U	M16 2-0	D15 0-1	a06 0-0	N17 1-0	D29 1-1	N10 1-1	F23 1-0	a13 4-1	A27 2-0	F09 0-0	M09 0-0		J01 1-1	O27 2-0	J19 5-0	S29 6-0	a27 1-0	S15 0-1	O06 1-1	m06 1-0	D01 5-2	S01 3-2
13 MANCHESTER C	D26 1-1	N10 1-0	O27 2-1	F23 2-0	M30 2-2	F09 1-3	m11 5-1	S29 2-1	S01 2-3	A27 3-0	S15 1-0	a08 1-2		M09 1-0	D08 2-0	m04 0-0	O06 1-0	N24 2-2	a20 2-0	M16 4-0	J19 3-0	D29 4-0
14 MIDDLESBROUGH	N10 0-0	m06 0-0	N17 1-2	a27 2-1	S29 3-2	a06 1-2	O06 1-0	D01 1-1	a13 2-0	S01 1-5	F23 2-2	M02 0-0	O20 2-1		F09 0-1	F05 1-2	J01 0-1	J19 0-0	M16 1-0	D14 1-1	S18 2-4	S15 1-1
15 NOTTS CO	S04 0-2	O20 1-3	S22 0-3	a14 1-2	O14 0-2	a27 3-0	J19 0-0	J01 0-0	D16 2-1	N03 1-1	N17 0-2	A25 1-2	m06 3-2	S08 3-2		M02 0-0	D01 2-0	a02 1-3	J12 0-0	F02 1-3	a06 2-3	M23 4-1
16 OLDHAM A	D23 2-1	A25 0-1	M09 2-0	S22 1-0	F16 0-1	D15 2-3	J12 2-1	a27 1-0	m06 2-1	M23 2-0	a06 2-2	F02 1-1	D01 0-2	O02 2-0	O27 3-2		N17 0-0	N03 0-2	S08 2-2	a13 0-1	J01 0-1	O13 3-2
17 OXFORD U	m11 4-0	M02 0-3	N03 2-1	O13 2-1	D26 4-0	S29 4-0	D08 5-0	D29 5-0	S15 3-2	M30 1-0	a17 3-0	N24 5-2	M23 3-0	a08 1-0	m04 1-1	a20 5-2		S01 1-1	O20 5-1	a24 1-0	M13 4-0	S19 3-1
18 PORTSMOUTH	S08 0-0	a13 1-3	D01 2-2	a06 1-1	M23 0-0	m06 3-1	F02 0-1	N17 1-1	J01 4-4	O13 3-2	D15 3-2	M12 3-1	a27 1-2	A25 1-0	N10 3-1	F23 5-1	D22 2-1		O02 2-1	S22 3-0	M09 1-0	O27 0-1
19 SHEFFIELD U	F23 3-1	J01 3-4	m06 1-3	D15 1-1	S01 2-1	a13 0-0	N10 1-1	S18 1-2	a06 0-1	S29 2-3	D01 0-2	M23 2-1	N17 0-0	O13 0-3	S15 3-0	F12 2-0	M09 1-1	D29 4-1		a27 0-1	O27 3-0	J26 2-2
20 SHREWSBURY T	a20 2-0	F23 1-0	M23 3-0	O27 0-0	a09 0-0	D29 4-2	M09 1-1	S01 4-1	J26 3-1	m04 4-1	M12 5-1	D08 2-3	O13 1-0	m11 0-2	S29 4-2	S18 3-0	N10 2-2	M30 0-0	N24 3-3		S15 1-2	D26 2-1
21 WIMBLEDON	D08 3-3	D22 1-2	F02 1-1	O02 1-0	m11 2-1	O06 3-0	S22 1-3	N04 3-2	a16 1-1	N24 1-1	a30 0-1	m04 2-2	A25 2-2	M30 1-1	D26 3-2	a09 1-0	S08 1-3	O20 3-2	M02 5-0	M27 4-1		a20 1-1
22 WOLVERHAMPTON W	F02 0-1	S22 0-2	D15 0-3	D01 0-1	N03 3-0	J01 0-2	S08 1-0	O20 2-1	a27 0-4	M05 0-1	m06 2-1	D22 0-2	S04 2-0	J12 0-0	O06 2-3	M16 0-3	a13 1-2	M02 0-0	A25 2-2	a06 0-1	N17 3-3	

SEASON 1984-85

DIVISION 3

	BOLTON W	BOURNEMOUTH	BRADFORD C	BRENTFORD	BRISTOL C	BRISTOL R	BURNLEY	CAMBRIDGE U	DERBY CO	DONCASTER R	GILLINGHAM	HULL C	LINCOLN C	MILLWALL	NEWPORT CO	ORIENT	PLYMOUTH A	PRESTON N.E.	READING	ROTHERHAM U	SWANSEA C	WALSALL	WIGAN A	YORK C
1 BOLTON W		O13 2-1	m06 0-2	a27 1-1	M05 1-4	A25 0-1	M02 1-3	D22 0-0	J12 3-0	F02 3-1	N24 1-2	S08 0-0	N03 1-0	D15 2-0	a13 3-1	J01 0-0	S22 7-2	O20 4-0	M23 1-2	J26 2-0	F16 0-0	O02 3-1	a06 1-0	N06 2-1
2 BOURNEMOUTH	M16 4-0		a26 4-1	N24 1-0	D15 2-1	F02 1-0	O06 1-1	a06 0-0	A25 1-0	S22 1-3	J01 2-0	J12 1-1	M09 3-1	m08 1-2	m13 3-0	D21 1-0	J26 1-0	O27 2-0	F23 0-3	S08 3-0	O02 1-2	a13 4-1	N06 1-0	O23 4-0
3 BRADFORD C	D29 2-1	D01 1-0		M23 5-4	O20 1-1	F13 2-0	a20 3-2	A25 2-0	N10 3-1	D26 0-1	M02 1-1	O03 2-0	m11 0-0	N28 3-1	S22 1-0	F02 4-1	M30 1-0	M06 3-0	m04 2-5	a08 1-1	J26 1-1	S08 1-1	J12 4-2	O13 1-0
4 BRENTFORD	D01 2-1	a20 0-0	O06 0-1		F23 1-2	D26 0-3	M05 2-1	F02 2-0	M30 1-1	O02 1-1	O20 5-2	m11 2-1	N10 2-2	m19 1-1	J26 2-5	A25 0-1	a08 3-1	m04 3-1	D29 2-1	a23 3-0	S22 3-0	M27 3-1	S08 2-0	O27 2-1
5 BRISTOL C	O23 3-2	m04 2-0	M09 2-0	N03 1-1		N10 3-0	D29 1-0	J26 3-0	F26 3-0	M30 1-0	O13 2-0	a08 2-0	D01 2-1	M02 0-1	a30 2-1	S22 3-2	D26 4-3	a20 4-0	m11 2-3	O02 0-1	S08 2-2	F02 1-2	A25 2-0	M23 1-0
6 BRISTOL R	J29 1-2	S29 1-0	S18 2-0	a06 3-0	a13 1-0		a16 4-0	J01 2-1	O06 2-1	O20 1-1	m07 3-2	O27 1-1	a02 0-0	N24 1-1	D15 2-0	a27 0-1	F23 1-0	S01 3-0	S15 1-0	M16 1-0	D22 4-2	a23 0-0	M05 2-0	m14 1-1
7 BURNLEY	O27 3-2	M23 1-1	N24 1-2	O23 3-1	m06 0-1	S08 0-0		a13 2-0	a23 0-1	M12 0-1	N06 0-1	S22 1-1	O13 1-2	a27 1-1	O02 2-0	F16 1-1	A25 1-1	F23 2-0	M09 0-2	F02 7-0	D15 1-1	D22 1-2	J01 1-2	a06 1-1
8 CAMBRIDGE U	m11 2-3	D26 1-0	a23 0-4	S29 1-2	S15 2-3	a08 0-2	N10 2-3		D01 0-2	M05 1-1	a02 1-2	M30 1-3	a30 0-2	S01 1-0	F23 1-2	M16 2-3	m04 1-1	S18 0-3	a20 0-2	D29 0-2	O27 0-2	O06 0-1	O19 1-1	F09 0-4
9 DERBY CO	S01 3-2	J30 2-3	a13 0-0	N07 1-0	S19 1-0	M23 0-0	S15 2-2	a27 1-0		N28 3-1	a06 1-0	O20 3-1	S29 2-0	a03 1-2	D22 3-3	D15 1-0	O13 3-1	M13 2-0	a17 4-1	M02 1-1	m06 1-1	M06 2-0	N24 2-2	J01 1-0
10 DONCASTER R	S29 2-0	F09 3-0	a06 0-3	F16 2-2	N06 1-1	M08 2-2	A31 2-0	O23 3-2	F22 2-1		D22 0-1	M16 1-2	S14 3-2	S18 0-1	a27 3-2	m06 1-1	O26 4-3	M26 1-2	J19 0-4	O07 0-1	N24 4-1	J01 4-1	D14 1-1	a14 3-0
11 GILLINGHAM	a20 2-3	a09 3-2	O27 2-2	M09 2-0	M16 1-3	D29 4-1	M29 1-1	S08 3-0	D26 3-2	m11 2-1		F26 1-0	m04 3-2	O06 1-4	A25 1-1	J12 2-0	O02 3-3	D01 4-0	O23 4-1	N10 2-1	F02 1-1	S22 3-0	m17 5-1	F23 1-0
12 HULL C	a02 2-2	S01 3-0	F16 0-2	D22 4-0	J01 2-1	M02 2-0	F09 2-0	N06 2-1	M09 3-2	O13 3-2	S18 2-0		M19 1-0	a06 2-1	N24 2-0	a13 5-1	M23 2-2	S15 1-2	S29 0-0	N03 0-0	O23 4-1	D15 1-0	a27 3-1	m06 0-2
13 LINCOLN C	F23 2-0	O20 0-0	D22 1-2	a13 1-1	a27 1-1	S22 1-2	M16 3-1	N27 1-1	F02 0-0	a24 0-2	D15 2-0	A25 0-0		M06 0-1	N07 2-2	a06 0-0	S08 2-2	O06 4-0	O27 5-1	M13 3-3	J01 1-0	m06 0-0	F16 1-0	N24 2-1
14 MILLWALL	m04 5-2	D29 2-1	F23 4-0	O13 2-0	O27 1-1	a20 1-0	D01 2-1	a16 2-1	O02 2-1	a30 2-1	M23 2-1	D18 2-2	O23 2-0		F02 2-0	S09 1-0	m11 2-0	N10 3-0	a09 0-0	M29 0-0	A25 2-0	J26 0-0	S22 4-1	M09 1-0
15 NEWPORT CO	N10 3-2	S18 1-1	a16 0-1	N27 2-0	S01 0-0	m04 1-1	a02 2-1	N03 1-2	m11 1-3	D01 2-1	M12 0-3	a20 0-1	M30 2-1	S29 3-2		O20 2-0	D29 1-0	a08 3-3	D26 1-2	D08 0-2	O13 2-0	M02 1-2	M23 1-1	M20 1-1
16 ORIENT	a09 4-3	m11 0-0	S29 1-0	a16 0-1	F09 0-1	N30 1-4	S18 0-2	O13 2-2	m04 2-2	D29 2-1	S01 2-4	N10 4-5	D26 1-0	J29 1-0	M09 1-1		O23 3-0	a30 0-0	M30 0-0	a20 0-1	M23 4-2	N03 0-3	M02 1-1	S15 1-3
17 PLYMOUTH A	F09 2-0	S15 0-0	N06 0-0	J01 1-1	a05 1-0	N03 3-2	M26 2-2	D15 2-0	M16 0-1	M02 2-1	M19 1-1	O06 0-1	a16 2-0	D22 3-1	m06 1-0	M05 1-1		S29 6-4	S01 1-2	O20 1-0	a27 1-2	N24 1-3	a13 1-0	S19 1-1
18 PRESTON N.E.	M09 1-0	M02 2-1	O23 1-4	D15 1-1	N24 3-2	J12 2-2	N03 3-3	F26 3-1	S08 2-1	A25 2-0	a27 0-0	a23 1-4	M23 0-1	a13 2-1	J01 1-1	O02 0-1	F02 1-2		O13 0-2	S22 0-3	N06 3-2	a06 1-0	m06 2-5	D19 2-4
19 READING	O06 3-1	N03 0-2	D15 0-3	m06 0-0	D22 1-0	J26 3-2	O20 5-1	N24 3-1	S22 0-0	S08 1-4	m14 0-2	F02 4-2	M02 1-1	J01 2-2	a06 0-1	N07 1-1	a24 1-1	M16 3-0		A25 1-0	a13 0-1	m01 1-1	O03 0-1	a27 1-2
20 ROTHERHAM U	S15 3-1	J19 1-0	J01 1-2	S18 1-1	F16 2-1	O13 3-3	S29 3-2	m06 0-1	O27 2-0	M23 2-3	a13 1-0	F23 1-1	S01 0-0	M16 0-0	O23 1-0	N24 2-1	M09 0-2	F09 3-0	M26 3-0		a06 0-1	a27 0-1	D22 3-3	D15 4-1
21 SWANSEA C	S18 2-1	F12 0-0	S15 1-2	F09 3-2	m17 0-0	m11 3-2	m04 0-1	M01 2-2	D29 1-5	a19 3-1	S29 0-1	M05 0-2	a09 2-2	M26 1-2	M17 0-3	O06 3-1	D01 0-2	M30 4-1	N10 1-2	D26 1-0		O20 1-2	N03 2-2	S01 1-3
22 WALSALL	M19 1-0	N10 0-0	a02 0-0	S01 0-1	S29 4-1	M30 1-2	m11 2-3	M23 5-0	O23 0-0	a08 1-0	a16 0-1	m04 0-1	D29 0-0	S15 3-3	O27 1-1	F23 4-2	a20 0-3	D26 2-1	S18 3-1	D01 0-2	M09 3-0		O13 0-0	F26 3-0
23 WIGAN A	D26 1-0	M30 1-2	S01 1-0	J19 1-1	a23 2-2	O23 1-0	a08 2-0	M09 3-3	a20 2-0	m03 5-2	S15 0-1	D01 1-1	S18 1-0	F09 0-1	O06 1-1	O27 4-2	N10 1-0	D29 2-0	m13 1-1	m11 2-1	a30 2-0	M17 1-2		S29 1-2
24 YORK C	M29 0-3	M05 4-1	M17 1-2	M02 1-0	O06 0-2	O02 1-0	D26 4-0	S22 3-2	a08 1-1	N11 3-1	N03 7-1	D29 1-2	a20 2-1	O20 1-1	S08 2-0	a02 2-1	F12 0-0	m11 0-1	D01 2-2	m03 3-0	J12 1-0	A25 1-1	F02 2-0	

DIVISION 4

	ALDERSHOT	BLACKPOOL	BURY	CHESTER C	CHESTERFIELD	COLCHESTER U	CREWE A	DARLINGTON	EXETER C	HALIFAX T	HARTLEPOOL U	HEREFORD U	MANSFIELD T	NORTHAMPTON T	PETERBOROUGH U	PORT VALE	ROCHDALE	SCUNTHORPE U	SOUTHEND U	STOCKPORT CO	SWINDON T	TORQUAY U	TRANMERE R	WREXHAM
1 ALDERSHOT		M23 1-0	O13 0-1	S01 1-2	J05 1-1	a23 1-0	D26 1-1	S29 3-4	S15 1-1	a02 2-0	D01 1-0	m11 0-1	O23 0-0	M09 0-0	S18 0-0	N10 1-0	m17 5-0	F23 1-2	O27 6-2	M30 2-1	a20 0-1	a09 1-0	m04 3-2	D29 2-1
2 BLACKPOOL	O06 1-0		O20 0-0	S29 3-1	a02 1-0	M26 1-1	a09 6-1	S15 0-0	S01 3-0	J05 1-1	D29 2-1	a20 2-0	D01 1-0	O27 2-1	M30 4-2	S18 1-1	D26 3-0	M16 1-0	F23 1-0	N10 4-1	F19 1-0	m04 3-3	M05 1-2	m11 0-0
3 BURY	a30 2-1	M09 1-0		a23 4-1	S29 0-0	S15 4-3	N10 2-2	M19 1-0	F09 2-2	S01 3-0	a08 1-0	O23 2-1	a20 0-0	F23 3-1	m11 1-1	D26 4-0	M29 2-2	O27 0-1	O06 2-0	M26 2-1	S18 2-0	D01 3-1	D29 3-0	m04 2-3
4 CHESTER C	M27 2-0	F12 0-0	S08 2-3		O27 1-1	O20 1-2	M06 0-2	F23 5-2	M16 1-3	O06 2-0	m11 1-0	m01 2-1	M30 0-3	S22 1-0	a09 1-3	a20 2-0	D11 0-1	A25 1-1	J26 5-1	m04 2-1	J30 2-0	N10 0-1	O03 2-4	D26 2-1
5 CHESTERFIELD	A25 2-1	S22 2-1	F02 0-1	M02 3-1		N03 1-1	m04 3-1	O06 0-0	O20 5-1	M16 3-0	F12 0-0	O02 3-1	D26 0-0	J12 2-1	D29 2-0	M05 0-0	m11 0-0	J26 1-0	S08 2-1	D01 3-0	a09 1-0	a20 1-0	N10 4-2	M30 2-1
6 COLCHESTER U	S22 2-0	S08 1-1	J26 1-0	M08 1-1	F22 3-1		m10 4-1	M15 1-2	O16 3-4	O26 1-3	N09 1-0	D26 2-2	F26 2-1	F01 4-1	D01 3-1	D28 3-2	a19 1-1	a02 1-1	A25 3-3	O23 3-0	m03 1-1	O02 2-1	M29 2-1	a08 4-1
7 CREWE A	a06 1-1	J01 0-2	a13 1-0	O23 2-0	D15 1-1	D21 1-4		m06 2-2	a27 0-0	N23 0-1	F01 2-0	S08 0-3	J26 1-1	N06 3-2	F23 2-1	M22 0-0	O27 3-1	F16 1-1	O02 0-2	M09 2-1	O13 3-2	A25 3-0	F26 1-3	S22 3-0
8 DARLINGTON	F02 1-1	m01 0-4	A25 1-1	N03 2-1	M23 1-3	O13 4-0	M12 2-1		M02 2-1	M09 2-0	O02 0-1	M29 1-1	a08 3-1	S08 4-0	a20 2-1	m04 1-1	O23 1-0	S22 2-1	a02 3-1	m11 3-1	D02 1-0	m14 1-0	D26 2-1	N10 2-1
9 EXETER C	J26 3-0	a17 1-1	S22 0-2	O13 1-1	M09 0-1	M23 1-5	D01 0-2	O27 1-1		F23 1-0	M30 3-2	D29 0-0	O03 0-0	A25 5-0	D15 0-1	a08 2-1	N10 1-1	S08 2-1	F01 2-1	a20 0-2	O24 1-1	D26 4-3	m11 0-1	F13 2-0
10 HALIFAX T	S08 1-2	A25 0-2	J12 4-1	M22 0-4	O13 1-3	M01 0-0	a19 1-1	O19 0-1	M26 2-3		D26 2-3	m03 2-1	N10 1-0	F26 1-0	M05 0-0	N30 2-1	a08 0-2	F01 1-2	S21 1-0	a23 2-1	m10 2-1	M30 0-1	F12 2-1	F16 1-2
11 HARTLEPOOL U	a27 1-0	m06 0-2	J02 0-1	D22 2-1	S19 1-0	a13 2-1	S29 3-0	F17 1-2	N05 1-1	a06 0-1		O13 2-2	O27 0-0	D15 0-0	F09 0-3	J19 2-2	S15 0-2	N24 3-2	O24 2-1	a03 5-1	S01 2-2	M09 3-1	M23 2-4	F23 2-0
12 HEREFORD U	D23 2-1	N24 2-1	M06 5-3	S19 0-0	M20 0-1	a06 2-1	a24 3-2	N07 0-1	m06 1-2	D15 3-0	M16 2-1		O06 3-0	a27 1-1	S01 1-0	S29 1-0	a03 1-2	a13 1-0	J01 3-0	S15 2-0	a17 0-3	F23 1-0	O20 2-1	O27 2-1
13 MANSFIELD T	M06 1-2	a27 1-1	N24 0-2	N07 2-0	a06 0-0	S19 0-1	S15 0-2	J01 2-0	a03 2-2	a13 2-1	M02 2-0	M23 1-1		D22 2-0	M27 0-0	M13 1-1	S01 5-1	a24 0-1	m06 1-0	a17 1-0	S29 0-0	O13 1-0	N03 0-0	O20 1-0
14 NORTHAMPTON T	O20 4-0	M02 0-1	N03 0-1	M19 0-2	S01 1-3	S29 1-3	M30 1-3	a23 2-1	J05 5-2	S15 0-1	a15 2-0	D01 0-3	a30 1-0		D26 0-3	a17 1-0	S18 0-0	O06 0-2	M17 1-2	a09 4-0	N10 4-0	D29 3-1	a20 2-0	M05 0-4
15 PETERBOROUGH U	a17 1-2	N07 2-0	D19 1-4	J01 3-1	m06 0-0	a27 0-1	N03 2-1	N24 1-1	m04 0-0	O24 2-0	S22 3-1	J12 1-1	S08 1-0	a02 0-0		M02 0-0	M09 1-1	O03 3-1	a13 1-4	O13 3-1	M23 0-1	F02 1-0	A25 1-0	J26 2-1
16 PORT VALE	a13 1-2	a22 1-1	a06 0-0	N23 0-0	O22 0-0	m06 3-2	O06 2-0	D15 0-2	J01 5-1	a27 3-1	S08 1-1	F02 3-1	A25 0-1	O01 0-3	O27 3-1		M16 3-1	D22 1-1	N05 4-1	F22 3-2	M09 2-0	J26 2-2	S22 2-1	M25 0-0
17 ROCHDALE	O02 1-2	a06 1-1	N06 1-1	a27 1-2	D21 3-1	N24 1-1	M02 1-3	M05 1-2	a13 2-0	J01 2-0	a30 4-3	A25 0-1	m14 2-1	F16 3-0	O20 2-1	O13 1-2		m06 3-3	D15 2-2	m08 0-0	N03 0-1	S22 0-0	F02 2-1	S08 0-2
18 SCUNTHORPE U	N03 2-1	O13 1-1	M02 2-2	M12 2-1	S15 2-4	A31 2-2	S18 2-3	F08 0-1	M19 7-1	S28 4-0	a19 2-0	N09 1-1	m04 2-2	M22 2-1	F12 2-1	m10 3-3	F26 4-2		M08 2-1	D26 1-0	M29 6-2	O23 2-0	a09 5-2	N30 5-2
19 SOUTHEND U	M02 1-0	N03 1-4	M23 3-3	S14 1-1	a23 0-1	J29 2-5	D08 3-1	S10 1-1	S28 1-0	F08 2-1	M04 1-1	a08 0-0	D29 1-3	O13 2-1	N10 2-1	M29 1-1	m03 0-2	O19 1-1		S17 1-1	D26 3-2	m11 1-0	D01 2-3	a19 0-1
20 STOCKPORT CO	F25 6-0	D07 1-3	O01 2-0	D14 5-1	a27 0-1	M04 1-0	O19 0-1	D21 0-0	N24 1-0	m06 0-3	A25 4-1	M11 2-1	S22 1-1	J01 4-2	M16 1-1	N03 3-1	O05 1-1	a06 2-0	F15 1-2		M01 2-1	a01 1-2	S07 0-2	F01 2-2
21 SWINDON T	N24 2-1	O02 4-1	M12 1-0	m06 4-4	J01 4-0	D15 2-1	M16 1-1	a28 1-0	M05 2-0	D22 2-1	M31 2-1	S22 0-3	F02 1-0	a13 2-0	O07 1-1	O20 0-1	F23 2-1	N06 0-0	a06 2-0	O27 4-0		S08 1-3	J26 2-1	A25 2-1
22 TORQUAY U	J01 1-3	D15 0-2	a27 0-2	a13 2-0	N24 0-1	a16 1-1	J05 0-0	S18 1-1	a06 1-1	N06 1-1	O20 0-1	N03 1-0	M19 1-0	m06 0-2	S29 0-0	S15 1-3	F09 1-0	M05 0-0	D22 2-2	S01 0-0	F26 0-0		M02 1-1	O06 4-3
23 TRANMERE R	D15 4-3	O23 3-0	m06 3-2	a16 1-0	a13 0-1	N06 3-1	S01 3-1	a06 3-0	D21 3-2	S17 1-0	O06 1-2	M08 0-1	F22 0-0	N23 1-2	J05 4-0	a01 4-1	S29 3-1	J01 2-0	a26 2-0	a29 3-0	S14 0-2	O27 3-1		M16 3-1
24 WREXHAM	m06 1-0	D22 1-2	D15 3-0	a06 2-0	a16 2-0	J01 2-2	a02 1-3	a13 1-1	S11 2-0	M12 0-1	N03 1-1	M02 1-1	M09 2-2	O16 0-3	S15 1-3	S01 1-1	a23 2-0	a27 2-1	N24 1-2	S29 3-4	J05 4-0	M23 2-0	O13 4-0	

LEAGUE TABLES

DIVISION 1

	P	W	D	L	F	A	W	D	L	F	A	Pts
Everton	42	16	3	2	58	17	12	3	6	30	26	90
Liverpool	42	12	4	5	36	19	10	7	4	32	16	77
Tottenham H	42	11	3	7	46	31	12	5	4	32	20	77
Manchester U	42	13	6	2	47	13	9	4	8	30	34	76
Southampton	42	13	4	4	29	18	6	7	8	27	29	68
Chelsea	42	13	3	5	38	20	5	9	7	25	28	66
Arsenal	42	14	5	2	37	14	5	4	12	24	35	66
Sheffield W	42	12	7	2	39	21	5	7	9	19	24	65
Nottingham F	42	13	4	4	35	18	6	3	12	21	30	64
Aston Villa	42	10	7	4	34	20	5	4	12	26	40	56
Watford	42	10	5	6	48	30	4	8	9	33	41	55
W.B.A.	42	11	4	6	36	23	5	3	13	22	39	55
Luton T	42	12	5	4	40	22	3	4	14	17	39	54
Newcastle U	42	11	4	6	33	26	2	9	10	22	44	52
Leicester C	42	10	4	7	39	25	5	2	14	26	48	51
West Ham U	42	7	8	6	27	23	6	4	11	24	45	51
Ipswich T	42	8	7	6	27	20	5	4	12	19	37	50
Coventry C	42	11	3	7	29	22	4	2	15	18	42	50
Q.P.R.	42	11	6	4	41	30	2	5	14	12	42	50
Norwich C	42	9	6	6	28	24	4	4	13	18	40	49
Sunderland	42	7	6	8	20	26	3	4	14	20	36	40
Stoke C	42	3	3	15	18	41	0	5	16	6	50	17

DIVISION 2

	P	W	D	L	F	A	W	D	L	F	A	Pts
Oxford U	42	18	2	1	62	15	7	7	7	22	21	84
Birmingham C	42	12	6	3	30	15	13	1	7	29	18	82
Manchester C	42	14	4	3	42	16	7	7	7	24	24	74
Portsmouth	42	11	6	4	39	25	9	8	4	30	25	74
Blackburn R	42	14	3	4	38	15	7	7	7	28	26	73
Brighton & H.A.	42	13	6	2	31	11	7	6	8	23	23	72
Leeds U	42	12	7	2	37	11	7	5	9	29	32	69
Shrewsbury T	42	12	6	3	45	22	6	5	10	21	31	65
Fulham	42	13	3	5	35	26	6	5	10	33	38	65
Grimsby T	42	13	1	7	47	32	5	7	9	25	32	62
Barnsley	42	11	7	3	27	12	3	9	9	15	30	58
Wimbledon	42	9	8	4	40	29	7	2	12	31	46	58
Huddersfield T	42	9	5	7	28	29	6	5	10	24	35	55
Oldham A	42	10	4	7	27	23	5	4	12	22	44	53
Crystal Palace	42	8	7	6	25	27	4	5	12	21	38	48
Carlisle U	42	8	5	8	27	23	5	3	13	23	44	47
Charlton A	42	8	7	6	34	30	3	5	13	17	33	45
Sheffield U	42	7	6	8	31	28	3	8	10	23	38	44
Middlesbrough	42	6	8	7	22	26	4	2	15	19	31	40
Notts Co	42	6	5	10	25	32	4	2	15	20	41	37
Cardiff C	42	5	3	13	24	42	4	5	12	23	37	35
Wolverh'pton W	42	5	4	12	18	32	3	5	13	19	47	33

DIVISION 3

	P	W	D	L	F	A	W	D	L	F	A	Pts
Bradford C	46	15	6*	2	44	23	13	4	6	33	22	94
Millwall	46	18	5	0	44	12	8	7	8	29	30	90
Hull C	46	16	4	3	46	20	9	8	6	32	29	87
Gillingham	46	15	5	3	54	29	10	3	10	26	33	83
Bristol C	46	17	2	4	46	19	7	7	9	28	28	81
Bristol R	46	15	6	2	37	13	6	6	11	29	35	75
Derby Co	46	14	7	2	40	20	5	6	12	25	34	70
York C	46	13	5	5	42	22	7	4	12	28	35	69
Reading	46	8	7	8	31	29	11	5	7	37	33	69
Bournemouth	46	16	3	4	42	16	3	8	12	15	30	68
Walsall	46	9	7	7	33	22	9	6	8	25	30	67
Rotherham U	46	11	6	6	36	24	7	5	11	19	31	65
Brentford	46	13	5	5	42	27	3	9	11	20	37	62
Doncaster R	46	11	5	7	42	33	6	3	14	30	41	59
Plymouth A	46	11	7	5	33	23	4	7	12	29	42	59
Wigan A	46	12	6	5	36	22	3	8	12	24	42	59
Bolton W	46	12	5	6	38	22	4	1	18	31	53	54
Newport Co	46	9	6	8	30	30	4	7	12	25	37	52
Lincoln C	46	8	11	4	32	20	3	7*	13	18	31	51
Swansea C	46	7	5	11	31	39	5	6	12	22	41	47
Burnley	46	6	8	9	30	24	5	5	13	30	49	46
Orient	46	7	7	9	30	36	4	6	13	21	40	46
Preston N.E.	46	9	5	9	33	41	4	2	17	18	59	46
Cambridge U	46	2	3	18	17	48	2	6	15	20	47	21

*Includes one match abandoned at 0-0 after 40 minutes. Result stands.

DIVISION 4

	P	W	D	L	F	A	W	D	L	F	A	Pts
Chesterfield	46	16	6	1	40	13	10	7	6	24	22	91
Blackpool	46	15	7	1	42	15	9	7	7	31	24	86
Darlington	46	16	4	3	41	22	8	9	6	25	27	85
Bury	46	15	6	2	46	20	9	6	8	30	30	84
Hereford U	46	16	2	5	38	21	6	9	8	27	26	77
Tranmere R	46	17	1	5	50	21	7	2	14	33	45	75
Colchester U	46	13	7	3	49	29	7	7	9	38	36	74
Swindon T	46	16	4	3	42	21	5	5	13	20	37	72
Scunthorpe U	46	14	6	3	61	33	5	8	10	22	29	71
Crewe A	46	10	7	6	32	28	8	5	10	33	41	66
Peterborough U	46	11	7	5	29	21	5	7	11	25	32	62
Port Vale	46	11	8	4	39	24	3	10	10	22	35	60
Aldershot	46	11	6	6	33	20	6	2	15	23	43	59
Mansfield T	46	10	8	5	25	15	3	10	10	16	23	57
Wrexham	46	10	6	7	39	27	5	3	15	28	43	54
Chester C	46	11	3	9	35	30	4	6	13	25	42	54
Rochdale	46	8	7	8	33	30	5	7	11	22	39	53
Exeter C	46	9	7	7	30	27	4	7	12	27	52	53
Hartlepool U	46	10	6	7	34	29	4	4	15	20	38	52
Southend U	46	8	8	7	30	34	5	3	15	28	49	50
Halifax T	46	9	3	11	26	32	6	2	15	16	37	50
Stockport Co	46	11	5	7	40	26	2	3	18	18	53	47
Northampton T	46	10	1	12	32	32	4	4	15	21	42	47
Torquay U	46	5	11	7	18	24	4	3	16	20	39	41

Football League Records

Top scorers: Div 1, G.Lineker (Everton) 30 goals; Div 2, K.Drinkell (Norwich City) 22 goals; Div 3, T.Senior (Reading) 27 goals; Div 4, S.Taylor (Rochdale), R.Cadette (Southend United) 25 goals.

South African-born Craig Johnston, signed from Australian soccer, was an individualist whose style was harnessed to the Reds' team by manager Kenny Dalglish.

DIVISION 1

	ARSENAL	ASTON VILLA	BIRMINGHAM C	CHELSEA	COVENTRY C	EVERTON	IPSWICH T	LEICESTER C	LIVERPOOL	LUTON T	MANCHESTER C	MANCHESTER U	NEWCASTLE U	NOTTINGHAM F	OXFORD U	Q.P.R.	SHEFFIELD W	SOUTHAMPTON	TOTTENHAM H	WATFORD	W.B.A.	WEST HAM U
1 ARSENAL		O05 3-2	N30 0-0	a29 2-0	M22 3-0	a12 0-1	O19 1-0	A31 1-0	D14 2-0	F01 2-1	N02 1-0	A24 1-2	S28 0-0	a08 1-1	N16 2-1	D28 3-1	S14 1-0	A20 3-2	J01 0-0	M31 0-2	a26 2-2	M15 1-0
2 ASTON VILLA	M08 1-4		M22 0-3	a26 3-1	S14 1-1	S28 0-0	a16 1-0	M31 1-0	A21 2-2	A31 3-1	J01 0-1	D14 1-3	O26 1-2	O12 1-2	N02 2-0	A24 1-2	N16 1-1	F01 0-0	N30 1-2	a12 4-1	D28 1-1	M19 2-1
3 BIRMINGHAM C	m03 0-1	S07 0-0		D21 1-2	O26 0-1	J18 0-2	J11 0-1	S21 2-1	N23 0-2	a06 0-2	S03 1-0	M29 1-1	N09 0-1	D26 0-1	A26 3-1	M01 2-0	O05 0-2	a19 0-2	M15 1-2	D07 1-2	F08 0-1	A17 1-0
4 CHELSEA	S21 2-1	N23 2-1	A24 2-0		A20 1-0	O12 2-1	a05 1-1	F01 2-2	m03 0-1	J11 1-0	M08 1-0	O26 1-2	a19 1-1	N09 4-2	F08 1-4	M19 1-1	D14 2-1	S14 2-0	D28 2-0	m05 1-5	A31 3-0	M29 0-4
5 COVENTRY C	S07 0-2	J11 3-3	F16 4-4	D07 1-1		D21 1-3	D26 0-1	O06 3-0	N09 0-3	a19 1-0	A17 1-1	a05 1-3	A26 1-2	M29 0-0	S03 5-2	m03 2-1	M15 0-1	F22 3-2	O20 2-3	J18 0-2	S28 3-0	N23 0-1
6 EVERTON	N09 6-1	M01 2-0	A31 4-1	M16 1-1	A24 1-1		a19 1-0	D14 1-2	S21 2-3	S14 2-0	F11 4-0	D26 3-1	M29 1-0	N23 1-1	O05 2-0	J11 4-3	D28 3-1	m03 6-1	F01 1-0	O19 4-1	A20 2-0	m05 3-1
7 IPSWICH T	M11 1-2	S21 0-3	S14 0-1	N02 0-2	M31 1-0	N16 3-4		a08 0-2	F01 2-1	D28 1-1	a12 0-0	A20 0-1	O12 2-2	M08 1-0	a26 3-2	D14 1-0	N30 2-1	A31 1-1	A24 1-0	J01 0-0	M22 1-0	O26 0-1
8 LEICESTER C	J18 2-2	D26 3-1	M12 4-2	A28 0-0	M08 2-1	A17 3-1	S28 1-0		a30 0-2	M29 0-0	D07 1-1	N23 3-0	m03 2-0	S08 0-3	O02 4-4	a14 1-4	O19 2-3	N09 2-2	a05 1-4	S04 2-2	O12 2-2	J11 0-1
9 LIVERPOOL	A17 2-0	D07 3-0	a26 5-0	N30 1-1	a12 5-0	F22 0-2	A26 5-0	N02 1-0		O26 3-2	M31 2-0	F09 1-1	D21 1-1	S03 2-0	M22 6-0	M08 4-1	J01 2-2	O12 1-0	S28 4-1	S07 3-1	N16 4-1	J18 3-1
10 LUTON T	A27 2-2	J18 2-0	N02 2-0	S07 1-1	N16 0-1	M22 2-1	O01 1-0	J01 3-1	a16 0-1		N30 2-1	O05 1-1	D07 2-0	A17 1-1	M15 1-2	S21 2-0	M01 1-0	O19 7-0	a12 1-1	a26 3-2	a01 3-0	D21 0-0
11 MANCHESTER C	a05 0-1	M29 2-2	D28 1-1	O05 0-1	D14 5-1	O26 1-1	N09 1-1	A21 1-1	D26 1-0	m03 1-1		S14 0-3	N23 1-0	a19 1-2	M01 0-3	F08 2-0	A24 1-3	J11 1-0	A31 2-1	M15 0-1	F01 2-1	S21 2-2
12 MANCHESTER U	D21 0-1	A17 4-0	J01 1-0	a09 1-2	N02 2-0	M31 0-0	D07 1-0	a26 4-0	O19 1-1	M19 2-0	M22 2-2		S04 3-0	J18 2-3	S07 3-0	O12 2-0	a13 0-2	S28 1-0	N16 0-0	N30 1-1	F22 3-0	A26 2-0
13 NEWCASTLE U	M01 1-0	a09 2-2	a12 4-1	N16 1-3	F01 3-2	J01 2-2	M15 3-1	N30 2-1	A24 1-0	A21 2-2	a26 3-1	a16 2-4		O19 0-3	S21 3-0	A31 3-1	M31 4-1	D14 2-1	M22 2-2	N02 1-1	S14 4-1	O05 1-2
14 NOTTINGHAM F	O26 3-2	M15 1-1	M31 3-0	a12 0-0	J01 5-2	a26 0-0	O05 3-1	M22 4-3	D28 1-1	D14 2-0	N16 0-2	A31 1-3	F08 1-2		D01 1-1	F01 4-0	A21 0-1	A24 2-1	S14 0-1	S21 3-2	N03 2-1	a02 2-1
15 OXFORD U	m05 3-0	a05 1-1	F01 0-1	O19 2-1	J25 0-1	a30 1-0	N23 4-3	A24 5-0	S14 2-2	O12 1-1	S28 1-0	J11 1-3	M19 1-2	m03 1-2		M29 3-3	A31 0-1	D26 3-0	A21 1-1	a09 1-1	D14 2-2	N09 1-2
16 Q.P.R.	S03 0-1	D17 0-1	S28 3-1	M31 6-0	N30 0-2	S07 3-0	A17 1-0	N16 2-0	O05 2-1	F22 1-1	O19 0-0	M15 1-0	J18 3-1	A27 2-1	J01 3-1		N02 1-1	M11 0-2	a26 2-5	M22 2-1	a12 1-0	D07 0-1
17 SHEFFIELD W	a16 2-0	a19 2-0	M08 5-1	A17 1-1	O12 2-2	S03 1-5	m03 1-0	M18 1-0	M29 0-0	S28 3-2	D21 3-2	N09 1-0	D26 2-2	D07 2-1	J18 2-1	a08 0-0		N23 2-1	F22 1-2	A26 2-1	O26 1-0	S07 2-2
18 SOUTHAMPTON	D07 3-0	A27 0-0	N16 1-0	M22 0-1	S21 1-1	N30 2-3	J18 1-0	a12 0-0	M15 1-2	F08 1-2	S07 3-0	M01 1-0	A17 1-1	D20 3-1	a01 1-1	O26 3-0	a26 2-3		N02 1-0	O05 3-1	J01 3-1	S03 1-1
19 TOTTENHAM H	M29 1-0	m03 4-2	a16 2-0	S04 4-1	F08 0-1	A26 0-1	D21 2-0	O26 1-3	M02 1-2	N09 1-3	J18 0-2	a19 0-0	S07 5-1	J11 0-3	D07 5-1	N23 1-1	S21 5-1	m05 5-3		A17 4-0	M08 5-0	D26 1-0
20 WATFORD	a01 3-0	N09 1-1	A20 3-0	S28 3-1	A31 3-0	a15 0-2	M29 0-0	D28 2-1	J12 2-3	N23 1-2	O12 3-2	m03 1-1	a05 4-1	a21 1-1	O26 2-2	S14 2-0	F01 2-1	a29 1-1	D14 1-0		A24 5-1	a19 0-2
21 W.B.A.	N23 0-0	S04 0-3	O19 2-1	J18 0-3	M19 0-0	D07 0-3	S07 1-2	M15 2-2	a19 1-2	D26 1-2	A26 2-3	S21 1-5	J11 1-1	a05 1-1	A17 1-1	N09 0-1	a22 1-1	M29 1-0	O05 1-1	D22 3-1		m03 2-3
22 WEST HAM U	O12 0-0	O19 4-1	D14 2-0	a15 1-2	a26 1-0	N02 2-1	a30 2-1	S14 3-0	A31 2-2	A24 0-1	a28 1-0	F02 2-1	a21 8-1	S28 4-2	a12 3-1	A20 3-1	M22 1-0	a08 1-0	M31 2-1	N16 2-1	N30 4-0	

Goalkeeper Chris Woods was ever-present when Norwich City won Division Two in 1985-86. He later signed for Glasgow Rangers and became regarded as England's number-one after the retirement of Peter Shilton.

DIVISION 2

	BARNSLEY	BLACKBURN R	BRADFORD C	BRIGHTON & HA	CARLISLE U	CHARLTON A	CRYSTAL P	FULHAM	GRIMSBY T	HUDDERSFIELD T	HULL C	LEEDS U	MIDDLESBROUGH	MILLWALL	NORWICH C	OLDHAM A	PORTSMOUTH	SHEFFIELD U	SHREWSBURY T	STOKE C	SUNDERLAND	WIMBLEDON
1 BARNSLEY		a12 1-1	M15 2-2	A20 3-2	M22 1-2	D14 2-1	a26 2-4	A31 2-0	S21 1-0	M31 1-3	J01 1-4	O27 3-0	M25 0-0	N30 2-1	F01 2-2	N02 1-0	O05 0-1	a08 2-1	S14 2-0	A24 0-0	N16 1-1	D28 0-1
2 BLACKBURN R	N09 0-3		O05 3-0	M18 1-4	A31 2-0	N23 0-0	F15 1-2	S21 1-0	m05 3-1	a15 0-1	F01 2-2	D26 2-0	a05 0-1	M15 1-2	A20 2-1	O19 0-0	M01 1-0	a19 6-1	A24 1-1	M29 0-1	D14 2-0	S14 2-0
3 BRADFORD C	O12 2-0	M08 3-2		D20 3-2	D13 1-0	M19 1-2	N02 1-0	a02 3-1	M01 0-1	M22 3-0	S14 4-2	a09 0-1	a23 2-1	a30 0-2	a12 0-2	M04 1-0	D03 2-1	O26 1-4	a26 3-1	S01 3-1	J01 2-0	m08 1-1
4 BRIGHTON & H.A.	D07 0-1	S07 3-1	A24 2-1		O05 6-1	O19 3-5	J01 2-0	a16 2-3	A17 2-2	N16 4-3	N30 3-1	S04 0-1	J18 3-3	M22 1-0	N02 1-1	a02 1-1	M31 2-3	A27 0-0	a12 0-2	M15 2-0	a26 3-1	S21 2-0
5 CARLISLE U	S07 1-1	J18 2-1	A17 1-2	a29 2-0		m03 2-3	A27 2-2	a19 2-1	J11 1-2	M18 2-0	M11 2-1	N23 1-2	D26 1-0	D07 1-0	O12 0-4	S17 3-1	D22 0-1	M29 1-0	S28 0-2	N09 3-0	O19 1-2	a06 2-3
6 CHARLTON A	A17 2-1	a26 3-0	O15 1-1	F04 2-2	N30 3-0		S07 3-1	a29 2-0	D21 2-0	a12 3-0	N16 1-2	J18 4-0	A27 2-0	a15 3-3	M31 1-0	M22 1-1	M15 1-2	D07 2-0	N02 4-1	S21 2-0	O05 2-1	m06 0-0
7 CRYSTAL P	N23 1-0	O26 2-0	a05 2-1	M29 1-0	F01 1-1	J11 2-1		S14 0-0	N09 2-1	A31 2-3	O01 0-2	a19 3-0	M08 2-1	S21 2-1	J25 1-2	O12 3-2	a08 2-1	m03 1-1	D15 0-1	M18 0-1	A24 1-0	D26 1-3
8 FULHAM	J18 2-0	M11 3-3	D07 4-1	S28 1-0	a08 0-1	a22 0-3	M22 2-3		A26 2-1	a26 2-1	a12 1-1	A17 3-1	D21 0-3	M31 1-2	J01 0-1	N30 2-2	S07 0-1	S17 2-3	O05 2-1	O19 1-0	N02 1-2	M15 0-2
9 GRIMSBY T	a22 1-2	N30 5-2	S28 2-0	D14 0-2	S13 1-0	A24 2-2	a12 3-0	F01 1-0		A20 1-1	a01 0-1	F08 1-0	O26 3-2	N02 5-1	a26 1-0	M08 1-4	N16 1-0	O12 0-1	J01 3-1	J25 3-3	M22 1-1	A31 0-1
10 HUDDERSFIELD T	D26 1-1	S03 0-0	S07 2-0	a19 1-0	O26 3-3	N09 0-2	J18 0-0	N23 1-3	D07 2-2		F25 2-1	O05 3-1	M29 0-3	A17 4-3	S21 0-0	D21 2-0	A26 1-2	J11 3-1	M15 1-0	a05 2-0	M01 2-0	m03 0-1
11 HULL C	M29 0-1	A26 2-2	J11 1-0	m02 2-0	S21 4-0	a19 1-1	D07 1-2	N09 5-0	D26 2-0	O19 3-1		D22 2-1	S07 0-0	S17 3-0	a29 1-0	J18 4-2	A17 2-2	a05 0-0	M04 4-3	O05 0-2	M15 1-1	N23 1-1
12 LEEDS U	F15 0-2	M31 1-1	S21 2-1	D28 2-3	a26 2-0	A31 1-2	N16 1-3	D14 1-0	O19 1-1	M08 2-0	A24 1-1		O12 1-0	a12 3-1	N30 0-2	J01 3-1	N02 2-1	S28 1-1	M22 1-1	F01 4-0	S14 1-1	A21 0-0
13 MIDDLESBROUGH	S28 0-0	N02 0-0	O19 1-1	A31 0-1	M31 1-3	F01 1-3	O05 0-2	A24 1-0	M04 3-1	J01 0-1	M22 1-2	M15 2-2		a26 3-0	S14 1-1	N16 3-2	a12 1-0	M18 1-2	N30 3-1	S10 1-1	D28 2-0	D14 1-0
14 MILLWALL	m03 2-2	O12 0-1	a19 2-1	S14 0-1	O22 3-1	M29 2-2	a22 3-2	M18 1-1	a05 1-0	D14 2-1	D28 5-0	N09 3-1	N23 3-0		A24 4-2	S28 0-1	O26 0-4	M08 3-0	F01 2-0	J11 2-3	A31 1-0	M11 0-1
15 NORWICH C	A26 1-1	D07 3-0	N09 0-0	a05 3-0	M15 2-1	D26 3-1	S18 4-3	M29 2-1	N23 3-2	M12 4-1	S28 2-0	m03 4-0	J11 2-0	D21 6-1		A17 1-0	J18 2-0	S07 4-0	O19 3-1	a19 1-1	a09 0-0	O05 1-2
16 OLDHAM A	a06 1-1	F08 3-1	D26 0-1	O26 4-0	m05 2-1	S13 2-1	M15 2-0	m03 2-1	O05 2-1	A24 1-1	A31 3-1	M28 3-1	a19 1-0	M01 0-0	D14 1-3		S21 2-0	N09 1-5	A20 4-3	N23 2-4	F01 2-2	J11 2-1
17 PORTSMOUTH	M08 1-1	S28 3-0	m03 4-0	D26 1-2	A24 4-0	O12 1-0	O19 1-0	J11 1-1	a19 3-1	F01 4-1	D14 1-1	a05 2-3	J25 1-0	M25 2-1	A31 2-0	F22 1-2		N23 0-3	D28 4-0	S14 3-0	A20 3-0	M29 1-1
18 SHEFFIELD U	O19 3-1	N16 3-3	M11 3-1	F01 3-0	J01 1-0	O01 1-1	N30 0-0	D28 2-1	M15 1-1	S14 1-1	N02 3-1	a22 3-2	S21 0-1	O05 1-3	M22 2-5	a12 2-0	a26 0-0		A31 1-1	D14 1-2	M31 1-0	A24 4-0
19 SHREWSBURY T	J11 3-0	D20 2-0	N23 2-0	N09 2-1	M01 0-0	a05 2-1	A18 0-2	M08 2-1	M29 0-2	O12 3-0	O26 0-0	S07 1-3	m03 2-1	A27 1-1	F08 0-3	D07 2-0	S03 1-1	J18 3-1		D26 1-0	S21 1-2	a19 1-1
20 STOKE C	D21 0-0	J01 2-2	J18 3-1	O12 1-1	a12 0-0	F22 0-0	S28 0-0	F18 1-0	S04 1-1	N02 3-0	M08 0-1	A26 6-2	D07 3-2	S07 0-0	N16 1-1	a26 2-0	a22 2-0	A17 1-3	M31 2-2		N30 1-0	O25 0-0
21 SUNDERLAND	a19 2-0	A17 0-2	M29 1-1	N23 2-1	F08 2-2	M08 1-2	D22 1-1	a05 4-2	S07 3-3	S28 1-0	O12 1-1	J11 4-2	O22 1-0	J18 1-2	O26 0-2	A26 0-3	D07 1-3	D26 2-1	a29 2-0	m03 2-0		N09 2-1
22 WIMBLEDON	S03 1-0	M22 1-1	A26 1-0	F22 0-0	N03 4-1	S28 3-1	a01 1-1	O12 1-0	J18 3-0	N30 2-2	a26 3-1	D07 0-3	A17 3-0	O19 1-1	M08 2-1	S07 0-0	J01 1-3	D21 5-0	N16 2-1	a29 1-0	a12 3-0	

Season 1985-86

DIVISION 3

	BLACKPOOL	BOLTON W	BOURNEMOUTH	BRENTFORD	BRISTOL C	BRISTOL R	BURY	CARDIFF C	CHESTERFIELD	DARLINGTON	DERBY CO	DONCASTER R	GILLINGHAM	LINCOLN C	NEWPORT CO	NOTTS CO	PLYMOUTH A	READING	ROTHERHAM U	SWANSEA C	WALSALL	WIGAN A	WOLVERHAMPTON W	YORK C
1 BLACKPOOL		D26 1-1	a29 2-0	O26 4-0	M01 2-1	N09 4-2	O19 5-0	S21 3-0	F04 0-1	D28 0-0	F01 0-1	O01 4-0	O05 2-2	F25 2-0	m03 0-0	A24 1-3	N30 1-1	J18 0-0	M29 2-1	A31 2-0	a19 2-1	M15 1-2	a05 0-1	S14 0-2
2 BOLTON W	M31 1-3		N02 1-0	O12 1-2	a26 0-4	F04 0-2	A26 1-4	M22 5-0	D14 2-1	N05 0-3	N23 0-1	D21 2-0	J11 0-1	S17 1-1	F22 4-0	a12 1-0	S28 3-1	M08 2-0	A17 1-1	O19 1-1	J25 3-1	J01 1-2	S07 4-1	M04 1-1
3 BOURNEMOUTH	S17 1-4	M18 2-1		D28 0-0	A24 5-0	O26 6-1	O12 2-1	M08 1-1	J31 3-2	S28 4-2	J18 1-1	a19 1-1	O19 2-3	M04 2-2	A31 0-1	S14 0-0	a05 1-3	D26 0-1	D17 1-2	M29 4-0	m03 0-1	F22 0-2	N09 3-2	F04 2-0
4 BRENTFORD	M22 1-1	M14 1-1	A26 1-0		a13 1-2	D22 1-0	D14 1-0	N02 3-0	N23 1-0	m05 2-1	N06 3-3	J24 1-3	M31 1-2	a22 0-1	O19 0-0	J21 1-1	S07 1-1	S17 1-2	S28 1-1	O05 1-0	F04 1-3	J11 1-3	A17 2-1	a26 3-3
5 BRISTOL C	S28 2-1	N30 2-0	D21 1-3	N09 0-0		M29 2-0	F04 4-1	J25 2-1	O05 0-0	O19 1-0	S17 1-1	J07 4-1	A26 1-2	a05 1-1	M04 3-1	M15 3-0	D26 2-0	m03 3-0	J11 3-1	a19 0-1	A17 2-3	S07 1-0	O26 3-0	F22 2-2
6 BRISTOL R	a12 1-0	O22 2-1	M22 2-3	A24 0-1	a22 1-1		N05 2-1	N23 2-1	a26 1-1	J18 3-1	A31 0-0	F08 1-0	D14 1-0	S14 0-0	F01 2-0	O01 1-1	M08 1-2	D28 0-2	O12 5-2	M01 0-0	S21 0-1	a01 1-1	M25 1-1	N02 0-1
7 BURY	a22 4-1	F25 2-1	M15 3-0	m03 0-0	O22 6-3	a05 1-1		a08 3-0	J18 1-1	F01 0-1	S14 1-1	M29 1-2	S21 1-2	A31 4-0	D26 1-1	M01 2-4	N09 0-1	O26 3-1	a19 2-0	M25 2-2	N30 2-1	O05 0-0	O01 3-1	A24 4-2
8 CARDIFF C	F22 1-0	O26 0-1	O05 0-1	J04 1-0	S14 1-3	a19 2-0	S17 0-0		A24 0-2	F04 0-1	S28 0-2	N08 0-1	M15 1-1	m03 2-1	D28 1-1	J18 1-3	M28 1-2	A31 1-3	M25 2-3	D26 1-0	a05 1-1	O19 3-1	N30 1-1	J31 2-1
9 CHESTERFIELD	O22 1-2	m03 3-0	S07 0-1	a19 1-3	M08 0-0	a15 2-0	A17 4-3	D20 3-4		S17 1-0	F22 1-0	O26 0-0	J25 1-1	D26 2-2	N09 3-1	F08 2-2	M18 1-2	M04 3-4	A27 2-0	a05 4-1	M25 2-3	S28 1-1	M29 3-0	O12 1-0
10 DARLINGTON	A26 2-1	a24 0-1	M01 0-0	O01 3-5	m15 1-1	A18 3-3	O30 1-1	O22 4-1	a22 2-1		m12 2-1	D08 0-2	D20 3-2	M29 1-0	M18 3-2	S22 2-3	m03 0-2	a19 0-0	D26 2-2	N09 6-0	O27 0-3	a29 1-1	a02 2-1	M09 1-0
11 DERBY CO	S07 1-2	a19 2-1	A17 3-0	a05 1-1	M19 2-0	a09 0-2	a30 1-1	M01 2-1	S21 0-0	M15 1-1		m03 1-1	a07 2-0	N09 7-0	M29 1-1	O05 2-0	O26 1-2	N30 1-1	m09 2-1	O02 5-1	M12 3-1	D22 1-0	A26 4-2	O19 2-1
12 DONCASTER R	M04 0-0	A24 1-1	N23 1-1	S13 1-0	N02 1-1	O19 0-2	J01 1-0	a12 0-2	M21 2-0	A31 2-0	D15 0-3		a25 2-3	F01 1-1	J18 1-1	D28 2-1	S17 1-0	S28 0-1	a15 0-0	F04 0-0	O05 1-0	N05 2-2	M15 0-1	M31 1-1
13 GILLINGHAM	M08 2-2	A31 2-1	F08 2-0	M18 1-2	D28 1-1	m03 2-0	F22 1-0	O12 2-0	S14 1-1	A24 1-1	O22 1-2	N30 4-0		J18 2-0	a29 0-1	F01 4-0	M04 1-1	M29 3-0	a04 3-0	O26 5-1	N09 5-2	S17 2-0	a19 2-0	S28 1-2
14 LINCOLN C	N02 0-3	M25 1-1	O02 3-2	S21 3-0	N06 1-1	a30 2-2	J11 2-0	D14 0-4	M31 2-1	J01 1-1	a12 0-1	S08 3-3	A17 1-0		O05 1-1	M22 0-2	a16 1-1	O19 0-1	D22 0-0	M16 4-1	A26 3-2	a26 0-0	m05 2-3	N24 3-4
15 NEWPORT CO	D14 1-1	S21 0-1	J11 2-1	M11 1-2	O01 1-1	S07 3-0	M31 1-0	A26 1-2	a12 3-3	a26 3-0	a22 1-1	A17 2-2	N02 1-1	M08 1-2		N23 1-2	J25 3-1	O12 0-2	O22 0-0	F16 2-0	F28 1-5	M22 3-4	D21 3-1	N06 1-1
16 NOTTS CO	D22 1-2	N09 1-0	a15 3-1	M29 0-4	O12 4-0	M04 0-0	S28 2-2	A17 1-4	O19 2-1	m06 5-0	M08 0-3	A26 1-1	S07 1-1	O27 3-2	a19 1-2		J11 2-0	a05 0-0	m03 1-0	N30 3-0	a08 3-1	F04 1-1	D26 4-0	S17 3-1
17 PLYMOUTH A	a26 3-1	a22 4-1	N05 2-1	F01 2-0	a29 4-0	O05 4-2	a12 3-0	J01 4-4	N02 0-0	D14 4-2	M22 4-1	F15 0-1	O01 3-0	O22 2-1	S14 2-0	A31 0-1		A24 0-1	a08 4-0	D28 2-0	M15 2-0	N23 2-1	S21 3-1	J18 2-2
18 READING	A17 1-0	O05 1-0	M31 1-2	a16 3-1	D14 1-0	A26 3-2	M22 2-0	J11 1-1	O02 4-2	N23 0-2	a26 1-0	m05 2-0	J01 1-2	M12 0-2	M15 2-0	N06 3-1	D21 4-3		M19 2-1	S21 2-0	S07 2-1	N02 1-0	O23 2-2	a12 0-0
19 ROTHERHAM U	J01 4-1	J18 4-0	a26 4-1	M01 1-2	A31 2-0	M15 2-0	N23 2-0	O01 3-0	D28 1-2	M31 1-2	N02 1-1	S21 2-1	N06 1-1	A24 1-0	F04 0-0	D14 1-0	O19 1-1	S14 1-2		F01 4-1	F15 3-0	a12 0-0	O05 1-2	M22 4-1
20 SWANSEA C	J11 2-0	F08 3-1	J01 1-1	M08 2-0	N23 1-3	S28 0-1	N02 1-0	M31 2-0	N05 1-1	a12 2-2	m06 0-3	O22 0-2	M22 2-2	O11 3-1	S17 1-1	a26 0-0	A26 0-2	F22 2-3	S07 1-0		J07 2-1	A17 0-1	J25 0-2	D14 1-0
21 WALSALL	N23 1-1	S14 2-0	D14 4-2	O22 1-2	J18 2-1	M18 6-0	a26 3-2	N05 6-3	A31 3-0	M22 0-0	M31 1-1	M08 1-0	a12 4-1	D28 2-1	S28 2-0	N02 0-0	O12 2-2	F01 6-0	S17 3-1	A24 3-1		a15 3-3	F09 1-1	J01 3-1
22 WIGAN A	O12 1-1	M29 1-3	S21 3-0	A31 4-0	F01 1-1	D26 4-0	M11 1-0	F08 2-0	M01 2-0	S14 5-1	A24 2-1	a05 0-1	F15 3-3	N30 3-2	O26 0-0	O22 3-1	a19 3-0	a22 1-0	N09 2-0	J18 5-0	O01 2-0		m03 5-3	M18 1-0
23 WOLVERHAMPTON W	N05 2-1	F01 0-2	a12 0-3	J18 1-4	M22 2-1	S17 3-4	M18 1-1	a26 3-1	J01 1-0	N02 2-1	D28 0-4	O12 1-2	N23 1-3	S28 1-1	A24 1-2	M31 2-2	M11 0-3	a08 2-3	M08 0-0	S14 1-5	O19 0-0	D14 2-2		A31 3-2
24 YORK C	m06 3-0	O01 3-0	O22 2-1	N30 1-0	S21 1-1	M12 4-0	D20 0-0	S07 1-1	M15 2-0	O05 7-0	F08 1-3	D26 0-1	M01 2-0	a19 2-1	a05 3-1	a22 2-2	A17 3-1	N09 0-1	O26 2-1	m03 3-1	M29 1-0	A26 4-1	J11 2-1	

DIVISION 4

	ALDERSHOT	BURNLEY	CAMBRIDGE U	CHESTER C	COLCHESTER U	CREWE A	EXETER C	HALIFAX T	HARTLEPOOL U	HEREFORD U	MANSFIELD T	NORTHAMPTON T	ORIENT	PETERBOROUGH U	PORT VALE	PRESTON N.E.	ROCHDALE	SCUNTHORPE U	SOUTHEND U	STOCKPORT CO	SWINDON T	TORQUAY U	TRANMERE R	WREXHAM
1 ALDERSHOT		A31 0-2	F01 2-1	D07 1-1	D28 1-1	O26 3-2	A24 4-0	M08 1-2	a05 0-1	a29 2-0	S14 1-2	N09 1-0	F04 1-1	N30 1-0	S17 0-0	m03 4-0	J18 2-1	S28 2-1	O12 1-3	a19 6-1	a22 2-4	M29 1-1	a15 3-1	O19 6-0
2 BURNLEY	M11 1-2		a12 1-1	M08 1-0	O01 0-2	a15 0-1	N23 3-1	M22 1-3	S07 2-0	J25 3-2	N05 2-1	A17 3-2	D14 1-0	M01 1-1	A26 1-2	a22 1-1	S21 1-0	a26 1-2	N02 1-3	A23 0-1	O12 0-2	O22 3-0	M31 3-1	J01 5-2
3 CAMBRIDGE U	S07 0-2	N09 0-4		D26 3-2	a29 1-3	a19 1-0	S20 1-1	a08 4-0	A17 4-2	J11 4-0	O05 4-2	N30 2-5	O19 1-2	O26 3-1	J25 1-3	O02 2-0	M28 1-0	M15 0-1	A27 1-2	D06 1-2	a05 1-1	m03 3-0	D20 3-2	F04 4-3
4 CHESTER C	N02 1-0	O05 4-0	M31 1-1		N06 4-0	S21 4-0	a12 2-1	A17 1-1	A26 1-1	S07 1-0	O02 1-0	F05 2-3	N23 3-0	D21 2-1	J01 4-1	M15 2-0	F15 1-1	D14 1-1	a26 2-0	M01 1-2	O19 0-1	J25 3-1	J11 1-0	M22 2-1
5 COLCHESTER U	A27 4-0	m06 2-2	S17 4-1	a04 2-3		M25 1-2	O04 1-1	S06 3-1	m02 3-1	J03 4-1	M14 0-0	O26 0-2	a08 4-0	a22 5-0	S27 1-0	a18 4-0	N08 0-1	O18 1-1	F04 2-0	A17 3-1	M28 1-1	J11 0-0	J24 1-2	D20 5-2
6 CREWE A	M22 2-0	O19 3-1	N23 0-1	F22 2-2	a26 0-2		D13 0-1	N02 2-2	D20 0-0	A27 2-0	a11 2-1	J25 0-1	N05 1-3	F04 1-1	M31 0-1	O05 3-3	M15 4-2	M04 4-0	A17 1-1	S06 0-1	S17 2-0	S28 1-0	M18 2-1	J11 3-2
7 EXETER C	D21 2-0	a19 0-2	F21 0-0	N09 1-3	M08 2-2	m03 1-2		O23 1-0	O26 1-2	M29 3-2	F08 0-1	A26 1-2	O12 1-1	M19 1-0	A17 1-0	N30 3-0	a04 2-0	S18 2-0	S07 0-2	J11 1-0	M04 0-3	M26 2-2	S28 1-0	J25 0-1
8 HALIFAX T	O05 1-1	O26 2-2	S27 1-1	J17 1-2	J31 2-2	J04 1-0	F04 1-0		M28 3-2	D03 1-0	m05 1-2	a18 2-0	S13 2-1	N09 1-1	a29 2-0	A30 2-1	D26 1-1	A23 2-1	S17 2-3	a04 0-0	m02 1-3	a14 0-0	O18 1-2	M14 5-2
9 HARTLEPOOL U	N06 2-1	F01 3-1	J18 2-1	J08 1-1	D14 4-1	A24 4-1	M22 0-0	J01 3-0		O19 2-1	N02 1-1	S18 2-1	A31 1-2	O05 2-1	M05 1-1	F05 1-0	S13 2-0	a01 0-1	a12 3-2	M14 1-1	S28 1-0	a15 1-0	N23 1-0	a26 3-3
10 HEREFORD U	O02 4-1	S14 2-2	A31 1-0	F01 0-2	N02 2-0	D28 4-1	J01 4-1	a26 2-1	a09 2-2		J18 4-2	M08 3-0	M31 3-2	S21 2-1	N06 1-1	M01 1-1	O23 2-2	M22 1-1	M19 2-1	a16 3-2	A24 4-1	O12 4-1	D14 1-4	a12 3-1
11 MANSFIELD T	J25 2-0	a05 0-0	M08 2-0	M04 0-0	O12 2-1	N09 2-2	O19 2-1	A27 2-0	a22 4-0	A17 4-0		J11 1-0	S18 1-1	m03 0-1	D22 2-1	M29 2-3	N30 3-2	M25 1-1	S28 3-0	D26 4-2	a19 1-1	O26 4-0	a29 0-0	S07 1-1
12 NORTHAMPTON T	a12 2-3	J18 2-0	a26 0-2	O22 2-2	M22 1-0	S14 0-1	a08 2-2	N23 4-0	M11 3-0	O05 1-3	A31 1-0		a15 2-3	M15 2-2	D14 2-2	S10 6-0	M01 1-0	N02 2-2	M31 0-0	S21 3-1	F01 0-1	a29 5-1	N05 2-2	O01 1-2
13 ORIENT	O22 1-1	m03 3-0	F08 3-1	a19 0-0	S21 1-2	a05 0-1	M15 2-2	a22 1-0	J11 1-1	D26 2-2	F15 0-1	M29 0-1		A27 2-2	S07 1-0	N09 2-0	O01 5-0	O05 3-0	D21 3-0	O26 0-1	N30 1-0	M18 4-2	A17 3-1	M01 1-3
14 PETERBOROUGH U	a26 3-0	S28 0-0	M22 0-0	A24 3-0	M31 1-2	O23 0-0	N02 1-1	a12 1-1	M08 3-1	M26 0-0	D14 4-2	O12 0-5	D28 2-2		N23 1-0	J18 1-1	m07 1-1	A31 1-0	J01 1-1	a08 2-0	S14 3-0	S18 2-0	M05 0-1	N06 1-1
15 PORT VALE	M18 3-1	F24 1-1	S14 4-1	M29 1-1	M01 1-1	D26 3-0	J17 0-0	S21 3-2	S30 4-0	a05 1-0	A24 0-0	m03 0-0	F01 2-0	a19 2-0		J04 0-1	A31 1-1	F03 3-1	O19 4-0	N09 1-1	O26 3-0	D17 1-0	M15 0-0	O05 4-0
16 PRESTON N.E.	D14 1-3	S17 1-0	M18 1-2	O12 3-6	N23 3-2	M08 1-2	a26 2-2	J11 0-1	O22 2-1	S28 2-0	J01 0-2	D21 1-1	a12 1-3	A17 2-4	N02 0-1		F08 1-1	N05 0-1	M22 3-2	S13 1-2	F22 0-3	S07 4-0	A26 2-2	M31 1-0
17 ROCHDALE	A17 2-0	M18 1-0	J01 2-1	a29 1-2	a12 3-3	O12 1-0	N05 1-1	M31 1-0	J25 0-2	F04 1-1	a26 1-1	S28 3-2	m05 1-4	S07 2-1	J11 3-3	O19 1-1		N23 1-0	a21 2-1	A26 4-1	M08 1-2	D21 5-0	M22 1-1	N02 3-2
18 SCUNTHORPE U	M01 1-0	N30 1-1	O11 0-0	m03 2-0	a15 1-1	O01 3-1	a22 1-0	D22 3-3	D26 1-0	O25 2-1	S21 0-3	M18 1-0	M08 2-2	J11 2-0	O22 0-0	a04 1-3	a18 3-1		J24 2-0	M28 2-3	N09 0-2	A17 4-0	S06 0-1	A26 1-1
19 SOUTHEND U	M15 2-0	J03 2-3	D28 1-0	N29 1-1	O22 2-4	J18 0-1	J31 2-0	M05 2-1	N09 3-2	a18 3-1	a15 3-1	D06 0-4	A23 5-1	M29 0-1	m05 2-1	O25 2-1	m02 5-0	S14 2-1		O01 0-0	A30 0-0	a04 1-2	O04 2-2	S20 3-0
20 STOCKPORT CO	N23 3-2	D20 1-1	N01 3-1	S28 2-2	J17 1-1	J31 3-0	F24 1-1	N04 2-1	O11 1-3	S16 1-1	M31 0-2	F21 1-0	M21 2-3	O18 2-2	a11 1-2	J24 2-1	D28 3-0	J01 0-0	M03 2-1		F03 0-2	M07 1-1	a25 1-1	D13 2-0
21 SWINDON T	M31 4-1	M15 3-1	N06 1-0	a08 4-2	J01 2-1	m05 1-0	O01 2-1	D14 3-2	M25 3-1	D22 1-0	N23 2-1	S06 3-2	a27 4-1	a15 3-0	M23 0-0	D07 4-1	O05 4-0	a12 1-1	J12 2-1	O22 1-0		A26 2-1	N02 2-1	A17 0-1
22 TORQUAY U	a08 1-2	F04 2-0	D14 1-1	S14 0-3	A31 2-1	M01 0-0	a01 1-2	O01 2-0	S21 1-3	M15 2-1	M22 1-2	O19 1-1	N02 2-2	M11 2-0	a26 0-1	F01 1-0	A24 1-2	J18 1-0	N06 2-2	O05 4-3	D28 0-1		a12 1-2	N23 1-3
23 TRANMERE R	S21 3-0	D26 2-1	A23 6-2	A31 2-3	S14 3-4	M29 0-1	F28 0-1	F07 0-3	a18 4-2	m02 1-2	O22 1-2	a04 1-3	J17 0-3	O29 7-0	O12 1-2	M25 2-3	O26 2-0	J31 2-1	M07 1-1	N29 2-3	J04 3-1	N09 2-0		F15 1-3
24 WREXHAM	M25 4-1	M29 0-1	O15 6-2	O26 1-1	A24 2-1	A31 2-1	S14 1-1	O12 2-1	F25 1-0	N09 0-1	F01 1-2	M04 1-0	S28 1-3	a05 0-1	M08 1-3	D26 1-1	M11 2-0	a29 1-0	a08 0-0	m03 3-0	J18 0-1	a19 3-2	S17 1-1	

LEAGUE TABLES

DIVISION 1

	P	W	D	L	F	A	W	D	L	F	A	Pts
Liverpool	42	16	4	1	58	14	10	6	5	31	23	88
Everton	42	16	3	2	54	18	10	5	6	33	23	86
West Ham U	42	17	2	2	48	16	9	4	8	26	24	84
Manchester U	42	12	5	4	35	12	10	5	6	35	24	76
Sheffield W	42	13	6	2	36	23	8	4	9	27	31	73
Chelsea	42	12	4	5	32	27	8	7	6	25	29	71
Arsenal	42	13	5	3	29	15	7	4	10	20	32	69
Nottingham F	42	11	5	5	38	25	8	6	7	31	28	68
Luton T	42	12	6	3	37	15	6	6	9	24	29	66
Tottenham H	42	12	2	7	47	25	7	6	8	27	27	65
Newcastle U	42	12	5	4	46	31	5	7	9	21	41	63
Watford	42	11	6	4	40	22	5	5	11	29	40	59
Q.P.R.	42	12	3	6	33	20	3	4	14	20	44	52
Southampton	42	10	6	5	32	18	2	4	15	19	44	46
Manchester C	42	7	7	7	25	26	4	5	12	18	31	45
Aston Villa	42	7	6	8	27	28	3	8	10	24	39	44
Coventry C	42	6	5	10	31	35	5	5	11	17	36	43
Oxford U	42	7	7	7	34	27	3	5	13	28	53	42
Leicester C	42	7	8	6	35	35	3	4	14	19	41	42
Ipswich T	42	8	5	8	20	24	3	3	15	12	31	41
Birmingham C	42	5	2	14	13	25	3	3	15	17	48	29
W.B.A.	42	3	8	10	21	36	1	4	16	14	53	24

DIVISION 2

	P	W	D	L	F	A	W	D	L	F	A	Pts
Norwich C	42	16	4	1	51	15	9	5	7	33	22	84
Charlton A	42	14	5	2	44	15	8	6	7	34	30	77
Wimbledon	42	13	6	2	38	16	8	7	6	20	21	76
Portsmouth	42	13	4	4	43	17	9	3	9	26	24	73
Crystal Palace	42	12	3	6	29	22	7	6	8	28	30	66
Hull C	42	11	7	3	39	19	6	6	9	26	36	64
Sheffield U	42	10	7	4	36	24	7	4	10	28	39	62
Oldham A	42	13	4	4	40	28	4	5	12	22	33	60
Millwall	42	12	3	6	39	24	5	5	11	25	41	59
Stoke C	42	8	11	2	29	16	6	4	11	19	34	57
Brighton & H.A.	42	10	5	6	42	30	6	3	12	22	34	56
Barnsley	42	9	6	6	29	26	5	8	8	18	24	56
Bradford C	42	14	1	6	36	24	2	5	14	15	39	54
Leeds U	42	9	7	5	30	22	6	1	14	26	50	53
Grimsby T	42	11	4	6	35	24	3	6	12	23	38	52
Huddersfield T	42	10	6	5	30	23	4	4	13	21	44	52
Shrewsbury T	42	11	5	5	29	20	3	4	14	23	44	51
Sunderland	42	10	5	6	33	29	3	6	12	14	32	50
Blackburn R	42	10	4	7	30	20	2	9	10	23	42	49
Carlisle U	42	10	2	9	30	28	3	5	13	17	43	46
Middlesbrough	42	8	6	7	26	23	4	3	14	18	30	45
Fulham	42	8	3	10	29	32	2	3	16	16	37	36

DIVISION 3

	P	W	D	L	F	A	W	D	L	F	A	Pts
Reading	46	16	3	4	39	22	13	4	6	28	29	94
Plymouth A	46	17	3	3	56	20	9	6	8	32	33	87
Derby Co	46	13	7	3	45	20	10	8	5	35	21	84
Wigan A	46	17	4	2	54	17	6	10	7	28	31	83
Gillingham	46	14	5	4	48	17	8	8	7	33	37	79
Walsall	46	15	7	1	59	23	7	2	14	31	41	75
York C	46	16	4	3	49	17	4	7	12	28	41	71
Notts Co	46	12	6	5	42	26	7	8	8	29	34	71
Bristol C	46	14	5	4	43	19	4	9	10	26	41	68
Brentford	46	8	8	7	29	29	10	4	9	29	32	66
Doncaster R	46	7	10	6	20	21	9	6	8	25	31	64
Blackpool	46	11	6	6	38	19	6	6	11	28	36	63
Darlington	46	10	7	6	39	33	5	6	12	22	45	58
Rotherham U	46	13	5	5	44	18	2	7	14	17	41	57
Bournemouth	46	9	6	8	41	31	6	3	14	24	41	54
Bristol R	46	9	8	6	27	21	5	4	14	24	54	54
Chesterfield	46	10	6	7	41	30	3	8	12	20	34	53
Bolton W	46	10	4	9	35	30	5	4	14	19	38	53
Newport Co	46	7	8	8	35	33	4	10	9	17	32	51
Bury	46	11	7	5	46	26	1	6	16	17	41	49
Lincoln C	46	7	9	7	33	34	3	7	13	22	43	46
Cardiff C	46	7	5	11	22	29	5	4	14	31	54	45
Wolverh'pton W	46	6	6	11	29	47	5	4	14	28	51	43
Swansea C	46	9	6	8	27	27	2	4	17	16	60	43

DIVISION 4

	P	W	D	L	F	A	W	D	L	F	A	Pts
Swindon T	46	20	2	1	52	19	12	4	7	30	24	102
Chester C	46	15	5	3	44	16	8	10	5	39	34	84
Mansfield T	46	13	8	2	43	17	10	4	9	31	30	81
Port Vale	46	13	9	1	42	11	8	7	8	25	26	79
Orient	46	11	6	6	39	21	9	6	8	40	43	72
Colchester U	46	12	6	5	51	22	7	7	9	37	41	70
Hartlepool U	46	15	6	2	41	20	5	4	14	27	47	70
Northampton T	46	9	7	7	44	29	9	3	11	35	29	64
Southend U	46	13	4	6	43	27	5	6	12	26	40	64
Hereford U	46	15	6	2	55	30	3	4	16	19	43	64
Stockport Co	46	9	9	5	35	28	8	4	11	28	43	64
Crewe A	46	10	6	7	35	26	8	3	12	19	35	63
Wrexham	46	11	5	7	34	24	6	4	13	34	56	60
Burnley	46	11	3	9	35	30	5	8	10	25	35	59
Scunthorpe U	46	11	7	5	33	23	4	7	12	17	32	59
Aldershot	46	12	5	6	45	25	5	2	16	21	49	58
Peterborough U	46	9	11	3	31	19	4	6	13	21	45	56
Rochdale	46	12	7	4	41	29	2	6	15	16	48	55
Tranmere R	46	9	1	13	46	41	6	8	9	28	32	54
Halifax T	46	10	8	5	35	27	4	4	15	25	44	54
Exeter C	46	10	4	9	26	25	3	11	9	21	34	54
Cambridge U	46	12	2	9	45	38	3	7	13	20	42	54
Preston N.E.	46	7	4	12	32	41	4	6	13	22	48	43
Torquay U	46	8	5	10	29	32	1	5	17	14	56	37

FOOTBALL LEAGUE RECORDS

Top scorers: Div 1, C.Allen (Tottenham Hotspur) 33 goals; Div 2, M.Quinn (Portsmouth) 22 goals; Div 3, A.Jones (Port Vale) 29 goals; Div 4, R.Hill (Northampton Town) 29 goals.

Play-offs: Div 1, Ipswich Town v Charlton Athletic 0-0, 1-2; Leeds United v Oldham Athletic 1-0, 1-2; Charlton Athletic v Leeds United 1-0, 0-1, 2-1; Div 2, Gillingham v Sunderland 3-2, 3-4; Wigan Athletic v Swindon Town 2-3, 0-0; Gillingham v Swindon Town 1-0, 1-2, 0-2; Div 3, Aldershot v Bolton Wanderers 1-0, 2-2; Colchester United v Wolverhampton Wanderers 0-2, 0-0; Aldershot v Wolverhampton Wanderers 2-0, 1-0.

Aston Villa, Leicester City and Manchester City relegate from Div 1; Derby County and Portsmouth promoted to Di 1; Brighton & Hove Albion, Grimsby Town and Sunderlan

Everton skipper and Welsh international Kevin Ratcliffe holds aloft the League Championship trophy at Goodison Park in 1987.

DIVISION 1

	ARSENAL	ASTON VILLA	CHARLTON A	CHELSEA	COVENTRY C	EVERTON	LEICESTER C	LIVERPOOL	LUTON T	MANCHESTER C	MANCHESTER U	NEWCASTLE U	NORWICH C	NOTTINGHAM F	OXFORD U	Q.P.R.	SHEFFIELD W	SOUTHAMPTON	TOTTENHAM H	WATFORD	WEST HAM U	WIMBLEDON
1 ARSENAL		m02 2-1	a11 2-1	O25 3-1	J18 0-0	M28 0-1	a20 4-1	M10 0-1	D20 3-0	N22 3-0	A23 1-0	a14 0-1	m09 1-2	M17 0-0	S20 0-0	D06 3-1	S02 2-0	D27 1-0	S06 0-0	O11 3-1	N08 0-0	J01 3-1
2 ASTON VILLA	N29 0-4		D26 2-0	N15 0-0	M28 1-0	a18 0-1	N01 2-0	F21 2-2	S03 2-1	a04 0-0	D13 3-3	O25 2-0	S20 1-4	J03 0-0	S06 1-2	F07 0-1	m04 1-2	O11 3-1	A23 0-3	M25 1-1	a25 4-0	M04 0-0
3 CHARLTON A	N01 0-2	a20 3-0		a07 0-0	S20 1-1	O11 3-2	O18 2-0	D20 0-0	m02 0-1	D28 5-0	F07 0-0	D06 1-1	S06 1-2	J31 0-1	M24 0-0	m09 2-1	A23 1-1	N22 1-3	J01 0-2	a04 4-3	M07 2-1	S02 0-1
4 CHELSEA	M07 1-0	D27 4-1	O04 0-1		S02 0-0	a04 1-2	m02 3-1	m09 3-3	S06 1-3	O18 2-1	F21 1-1	N22 1-3	A23 0-0	S20 2-6	F10 4-0	J01 3-1	F07 2-0	a20 1-1	D20 0-2	N01 0-0	M21 1-0	D06 0-4
5 COVENTRY C	A26 2-1	O04 0-1	F28 2-1	F14 3-0		A30 1-1	D06 1-0	m02 1-0	J01 0-1	D21 2-2	m06 1-1	S13 3-0	N22 2-1	N08 1-0	M20 3-0	a20 4-1	M07 1-0	m09 1-1	D27 4-3	S27 1-0	J24 1-3	O19 1-0
6 EVERTON	O04 0-1	J01 3-0	M21 2-1	N08 2-2	F07 3-1		D28 5-1	N23 0-0	m09 3-1	m02 0-0	S21 3-1	a20 3-0	D06 4-0	A23 2-0	S02 3-1	S06 0-0	J17 2-0	M14 3-0	m11 1-0	O25 3-2	a11 4-0	D20 3-0
7 LEICESTER C	D26 1-1	a11 1-1	M14 1-0	N29 2-2	m04 1-1	N15 0-2		S03 2-1	A23 1-1	M28 4-0	S06 1-1	N08 1-1	F21 0-2	O11 3-1	D14 2-0	M25 4-1	J03 6-1	O25 2-3	S20 1-2	a25 1-2	a18 2-0	F07 3-1
8 LIVERPOOL	A30 2-1	S27 3-3	S13 2-0	D14 3-0	N29 2-0	a25 3-1	F14 4-3		M07 2-0	A25 0-0	D26 0-1	J24 2-0	N01 6-2	a18 3-0	O18 4-0	M18 2-1	N16 1-1	F28 1-0	O11 0-1	m04 1-0	J03 1-0	M28 1-2
9 LUTON T	S13 0-0	F14 2-1	N29 1-0	J03 1-0	a18 2-0	D13 1-0	J24 1-0	O25 4-1		S27 1-0	M14 2-1	A30 0-0	O11 0-0	N15 4-2	m05 2-3	N01 1-0	a25 0-0	A26 2-1	M28 3-1	D26 0-2	F28 2-1	a04 0-0
10 MANCHESTER C	a25 3-0	N08 3-1	N15 2-1	M14 1-2	S06 0-1	N29 1-3	O04 1-2	J17 0-1	F21 1-1		O26 1-1	M21 0-0	S03 2-2	m04 1-0	J03 1-0	S20 0-0	D26 1-0	a11 2-4	a15 1-1	a18 1-2	D13 3-1	A23 3-1
11 MANCHESTER U	J24 2-0	m09 3-1	A30 0-1	S28 0-1	N01 1-1	F28 0-0	D20 2-0	a20 1-0	O18 1-0	M07 2-0		J01 4-1	D27 0-1	M28 2-0	a04 3-2	N22 1-0	O11 3-1	S13 5-1	D07 3-3	F14 3-1	A25 2-3	m02 0-1
12 NEWCASTLE U	O18 1-2	M07 2-1	m04 0-3	a25 1-0	J03 1-2	D26 0-4	a04 2-0	A23 0-2	F07 2-2	O11 3-1	a18 2-1		a08 4-1	D13 3-2	N01 0-0	S03 0-2	S06 2-3	M28 2-0	M25 1-1	N15 2-2	N30 4-0	S20 1-0
13 NORWICH C	D13 1-1	F28 1-1	J03 1-1	J24 2-2	a25 1-1	m04 0-1	S17 2-1	a11 2-1	M21 0-0	F14 1-1	N15 0-0	S27 2-0		D26 2-1	N29 2-1	O04 1-0	a18 1-0	A30 4-3	N08 2-1	S13 1-3	O18 1-1	M07 0-0
14 NOTTINGHAM F	S27 1-0	S13 6-0	A27 4-0	F28 0-1	a04 0-0	J25 1-0	M22 2-1	J01 1-1	D28 2-2	D06 2-0	O04 1-1	m09 2-1	a20 1-1		M07 2-0	O18 1-0	N01 3-2	D20 0-0	m02 2-0	A30 1-1	F14 1-1	N22 3-2
15 OXFORD U	F25 0-0	D20 2-2	S27 3-2	A25 1-1	O11 2-0	F14 1-1	m09 0-0	M14 1-3	D06 4-2	S13 0-0	N08 2-0	a11 1-1	m02 0-1	O25 2-1		D27 0-1	M28 2-1	J01 3-1	N22 2-4	J24 1-3	A30 0-0	a20 3-1
16 Q.P.R.	m04 1-4	A30 1-0	D13 0-0	a18 1-1	D26 3-1	J03 0-1	S27 0-1	N08 1-3	a11 2-2	F28 1-0	a25 1-1	F14 2-1	M28 1-1	M14 3-1	N15 1-1		N29 2-2	J24 2-1	O25 2-0	A26 3-2	S13 2-3	O11 2-1
17 SHEFFIELD W	F14 1-1	D06 2-1	J24 1-1	A30 2-0	O25 2-2	A25 2-2	S13 2-2	D27 0-1	N22 1-0	a20 2-1	M21 1-0	D21 2-0	J01 1-1	a14 2-3	O04 6-1	m02 7-1		N08 3-1	a07 0-1	F28 0-1	S27 2-2	m09 0-2
18 SOUTHAMPTON	N15 0-4	M21 5-0	a25 2-2	D26 1-2	F03 2-0	O18 0-2	M07 4-0	S20 2-1	M24 3-0	N01 1-1	J03 1-1	O04 4-1	F07 1-2	S06 1-3	a18 3-0	A23 5-1	a22 1-1		S02 2-0	N29 3-1	m04 1-0	a07 2-2
19 TOTTENHAM H	J04 1-2	J24 3-0	a18 1-0	S13 1-3	N15 1-0	S27 2-0	F25 5-0	M22 1-0	O04 0-0	A30 1-0	m04 4-0	A25 1-1	a04 3-0	N29 2-3	a25 3-1	M07 1-0	O18 1-1	F14 2-0		D13 2-1	D26 4-0	N01 1-2
20 WATFORD	M21 2-0	O18 4-2	N08 4-1	a14 3-1	a30 2-3	M08 2-1	N22 5-1	D06 2-0	a21 2-0	J01 1-1	S16 1-0	D27 1-0	D19 1-1	F07 1-1	A23 3-0	a06 0-3	S20 0-1	m02 1-1	m09 1-0		O04 2-2	S06 0-1
21 WEST HAM U	a08 3-1	N22 1-1	O25 1-3	O11 5-3	A23 1-0	N02 1-0	J01 4-1	S06 2-5	S20 2-0	m09 2-0	a14 0-0	m02 1-1	M14 0-2	S02 1-2	F07 0-1	D20 1-1	M24 0-2	D06 3-1	a20 2-1	M28 1-0		D27 2-3
22 WIMBLEDON	a18 1-2	A26 3-2	F15 2-0	m05 2-1	M24 2-1	S13 1-2	A30 1-0	O04 1-3	N08 0-1	J24 0-0	N29 1-0	F28 3-1	O25 2-0	a25 2-1	D26 1-1	M21 1-1	D13 3-0	S27 2-2	a22 2-2	J03 2-1	N15 0-1	

Derby County's Bobby Davison was the Rams' spearhead in successive promotions from Division Three to Division One.

DIVISION 2

	BARNSLEY	BIRMINGHAM C	BLACKBURN R	BRADFORD C	BRIGHTON & HA	CRYSTAL P	DERBY CO	GRIMSBY T	HUDDERSFIELD T	HULL C	IPSWICH T	LEEDS U	MILLWALL	OLDHAM A	PLYMOUTH A	PORTSMOUTH	READING	SHEFFIELD U	SHREWSBURY T	STOKE C	SUNDERLAND	W.B.A.
1 BARNSLEY		M28 2-2	N01 1-1	O11 2-0	M14 3-1	A23 2-3	N15 0-1	F24 1-0	m04 0-1	a18 1-1	a25 2-1	S02 0-1	F07 1-0	J03 1-1	S20 1-1	S06 0-2	a04 2-0	O25 2-2	M03 2-1	D26 0-2	D13 1-0	N29 2-2
2 BIRMINGHAM C	O04 1-1		D06 1-1	A25 2-1	F14 2-0	O18 4-1	A30 1-1	m02 1-0	S13 1-1	F28 0-0	S27 2-2	N21 2-1	D29 1-1	N08 1-3	J01 3-2	M21 0-1	a20 1-1	D19 2-1	m09 0-2	J24 0-0	M31 2-0	a12 0-1
3 BLACKBURN R	a11 4-2	m05 1-0		M24 2-1	a25 1-1	S20 0-2	a17 3-1	J17 2-2	D26 1-2	N15 0-2	N29 0-0	A23 2-1	F21 1-0	J31 1-0	S30 1-2	J03 1-0	a14 0-0	N08 0-2	F07 2-1	M14 2-1	S06 6-1	O11 0-1
4 BRADFORD C	M21 0-0	J03 0-0	M07 2-0		m04 2-0	S03 1-2	D26 0-1	F07 4-2	N15 4-3	a25 2-0	O18 3-4	S20 2-0	J17 4-0	S06 0-3	A23 2-2	a04 1-0	N01 3-0	O04 1-1	F21 0-0	N29 1-4	a18 3-2	D12 1-3
5 BRIGHTON & H.A.	O18 1-1	S03 2-0	N22 0-2	D06 2-2		a20 2-0	M07 0-1	S06 0-1	a03 1-1	N01 2-1	M21 1-2	m09 0-1	J01 0-1	F21 1-2	a07 1-1	A23 0-0	D27 1-1	m02 2-0	D21 3-0	O04 1-0	F07 0-3	S20 2-0
6 CRYSTAL P	J24 0-1	M14 6-0	F28 2-0	F14 1-1	D26 2-0		J03 1-0	N08 0-3	S09 1-0	D13 5-1	N15 3-3	M21 1-0	O04 2-1	a25 2-1	a11 0-0	m04 1-0	S27 1-3	S13 1-2	O25 2-3	A30 1-0	N29 2-0	a18 1-1
7 DERBY CO	D27 3-2	F07 2-2	M18 3-2	a20 1-0	O25 4-1	S06 1-0		D21 4-0	a08 2-0	O11 1-1	N08 2-1	m02 2-1	S20 1-1	A23 0-1	m09 4-2	M04 0-0	D06 3-0	N22 2-0	M14 3-1	a11 0-0	O01 3-2	F21 1-1
8 GRIMSBY T	S27 0-1	N29 0-1	D02 1-0	A30 0-0	J03 1-2	a04 0-1	S13 0-1		a18 0-1	m05 2-2	J24 1-1	O25 0-0	N01 1-0	D26 2-2	O11 1-1	a25 0-2	F14 3-2	F28 1-0	M28 0-1	D13 1-1	N15 1-1	M14 3-1
9 HUDDERSFIELD T	M31 2-2	M03 2-2	a20 1-2	D27 5-2	N08 2-1	D20 1-2	O04 2-0	J01 0-0		O25 1-3	a11 1-2	S06 1-1	m09 3-0	S20 5-4	N22 1-2	F21 2-0	m02 2-0	M14 1-1	O21 2-1	M21 2-2	A23 0-2	F07 2-1
10 HULL C	J01 3-4	S20 3-2	D27 0-0	N22 2-1	a28 1-0	m09 3-0	M21 1-1	D06 1-1	M07 0-0		O04 2-1	a08 0-0	a14 2-1	F07 1-0	S06 0-3	S02 0-2	O18 0-2	a20 0-0	m02 3-0	N08 0-4	M03 1-0	A23 2-0
11 IPSWICH T	N22 1-0	F21 3-0	m02 3-1	M14 1-0	O11 1-0	D27 3-0	a04 0-2	A23 1-1	N01 3-0	M28 0-0		J01 2-0	a21 0-0	S02 0-1	D19 3-0	F07 0-1	m09 1-1	D06 2-2	S06 1-0	O25 2-0	S20 1-1	M03 1-0
12 LEEDS U	F14 2-2	a25 4-0	J24 0-0	F28 1-0	D13 3-1	O11 3-0	N29 2-0	M07 2-0	J03 1-1	S27 3-0	a18 3-2		a04 2-0	N15 0-2	M28 4-0	O18 3-1	S13 3-2	A30 0-1	N01 1-0	A25 2-1	D26 1-1	m04 3-2
13 MILLWALL	A30 1-0	N15 0-2	S27 2-2	S13 1-2	a18 3-1	M28 0-1	F28 0-1	a11 1-0	N13 4-0	A26 0-1	D26 1-0	N08 1-0		M14 0-0	O25 3-1	N29 1-1	J24 2-1	F14 1-0	O11 4-0	J03 1-1	m05 1-1	a25 0-1
14 OLDHAM A	A25 2-0	a04 2-2	m09 3-0	D21 2-1	S27 1-1	N22 1-0	J24 1-4	a21 1-1	F28 2-0	A30 0-0	F14 2-1	D27 0-1	O17 2-1		m02 2-1	N01 0-0	M06 4-0	J01 3-1	D06 3-0	S13 2-0	O11 1-1	M28 2-1
15 PLYMOUTH A	F28 2-0	a18 0-0	F14 1-1	J24 3-2	S13 2-2	N01 3-1	D13 1-1	M21 5-0	a25 1-1	J03 4-0	O21 2-0	O04 1-1	M07 1-0	N29 3-2		D26 2-3	A30 1-0	O14 1-0	a04 3-2	m04 1-3	O18 2-4	N15 1-0
16 PORTSMOUTH	D20 2-1	O11 2-0	S13 1-0	N08 2-1	J24 1-0	D06 2-0	O21 3-1	N27 2-1	S27 1-0	F14 1-0	A30 1-1	M10 1-1	m02 2-0	a11 3-0	a20 0-1		J01 1-0	m09 1-2	D29 3-0	F28 3-0	M28 3-1	O25 2-1
17 READING	N08 0-0	D26 2-2	O04 4-0	a11 0-1	N15 2-1	F21 1-0	m04 2-0	O01 2-3	F17 3-2	M14 1-0	D13 1-4	a22 2-1	A23 0-1	O25 2-3	F07 2-0	a18 2-2		M21 2-0	S20 3-1	a25 0-1	J31 1-0	S06 1-1
18 SHEFFIELD U	M07 1-0	S06 1-1	a04 4-1	M28 2-2	N29 0-1	M17 1-0	a25 0-1	S20 1-2	O18 0-0	D26 4-2	m04 0-0	F07 0-0	S02 2-1	a18 2-0	F21 2-1	D13 1-0	O11 3-3		A23 1-1	N15 3-1	N01 2-1	J03 1-1
19 SHREWSBURY T	S13 1-0	D13 1-0	A30 0-1	S27 0-1	S16 1-0	M24 0-0	O18 0-1	O04 4-1	F14 1-2	N29 3-0	J03 2-1	a14 0-2	M21 1-2	m05 2-0	N08 1-1	N15 1-0	F28 0-0	J24 1-0		a18 4-1	a25 0-1	D26 1-0
20 STOKE C	a20 1-2	A23 0-2	O18 1-0	m02 2-3	M28 1-1	F07 3-1	N01 0-2	m09 5-1	O11 2-0	a04 1-1	M25 0-0	D21 7-2	S06 2-0	a28 0-2	D06 1-0	S20 1-1	N22 3-0	D27 5-2	J01 1-0		M17 3-0	S02 1-1
21 SUNDERLAND	m09 2-3	O25 2-0	D21 3-0	a28 2-3	A30 1-1	m02 1-0	F14 1-2	D27 0-1	J24 2-1	S13 1-0	F28 1-0	a20 1-1	D06 1-1	M21 0-2	M14 2-1	O04 0-0	O21 1-1	a11 1-2	N22 1-1	S27 2-0		N08 0-3
22 W.B.A.	m02 0-1	N01 3-2	M21 0-1	m09 2-2	F28 0-0	J01 1-2	S27 2-0	O18 1-1	A30 1-0	J24 1-1	S13 3-4	D06 3-0	N22 0-1	O04 2-0	D27 0-0	a29 1-0	D19 1-2	A25 1-0	a20 1-2	F14 4-1	a04 2-2	

SEASON 1986-87

relegated from Div 2; AFC Bournemouth, Middlesbrough and Swindon Town promoted to Div 2; Bolton Wanderers, Carlisle United, Darlington and Newport County relegated from Div 3; Preston North End, Northampton Town, Southend United and Aldershot promoted to Div 3; Lincoln City were relegated from Division Four and replaced by Scarborough.

DIVISION 3

	BLACKPOOL	BOLTON W	BOURNEMOUTH	BRENTFORD	BRISTOL C	BRISTOL R	BURY	CARLISLE U	CHESTER C	CHESTERFIELD	DARLINGTON	DONCASTER R	FULHAM	GILLINGHAM	MANSFIELD T	MIDDLESBROUGH	NEWPORT CO	NOTTS CO	PORT VALE	ROTHERHAM U	SWINDON T	WALSALL	WIGAN A	YORK C
1 BLACKPOOL		M17 1-1	a25 1-3	J03 2-0	N01 1-0	F21 6-1	D13 1-1	S06 1-2	m04 1-0	A23 0-0	a18 2-1	a28 1-1	a07 1-0	a11 0-1	M07 1-2	M21 0-1	N29 1-1	O18 3-1	S30 2-0	N08 1-0	F07 1-1	O04 1-1	S20 5-1	D26 2-1
2 BOLTON W	O21 1-0		J31 0-1	M03 0-2	a25 0-0	J17 2-2	D26 2-3	a18 2-0	O25 1-1	S30 1-2	S06 4-3	m04 0-1	F07 3-2	D13 3-0	J03 0-1	a11 0-1	N08 0-1	O04 1-1	S20 3-0	M14 0-0	A23 1-2	M21 1-0	a07 1-2	N29 3-1
3 BOURNEMOUTH	F03 1-1	S13 2-1		J10 1-1	S27 2-0	a20 2-0	M14 1-0	N08 2-1	S16 2-0	N22 2-0	M28 1-0	O21 3-2	D27 3-2	D02 0-2	F14 4-1	M03 3-1	A30 2-1	J24 3-0	m02 0-0	m09 2-0	J01 1-0	a11 1-0	O25 3-1	F28 3-0
4 BRENTFORD	N22 1-1	N01 1-2	A23 1-1		M17 1-1	D28 1-2	S30 0-2	F07 3-1	a04 3-1	J01 2-2	S20 5-3	a14 1-1	F01 3-3	F21 3-2	M21 3-1	D21 0-1	O04 2-0	N04 1-0	S06 0-2	m02 2-0	a20 1-1	M07 0-1	m09 2-3	O18 3-1
5 BRISTOL C	M03 3-1	D20 4-1	F21 2-0	a28 0-2		J01 0-1	A23 2-2	S20 3-0	M28 1-0	J31 1-0	S30 1-1	F07 5-0	a04 0-0	a22 2-0	N04 0-0	O25 2-2	M14 4-0	m02 3-1	a20 1-0	N22 0-1	m09 1-1	D27 2-1	S06 2-1	O11 3-0
6 BRISTOL R	S27 2-2	A30 1-0	D26 0-3	m04 0-1	a18 0-0		N08 1-1	a22 4-0	a28 3-2	O04 3-2	a30 2-1	m06 2-3	M18 0-0	a25 0-1	S13 0-0	S17 1-2	D14 2-2	F28 0-0	O18 0-0	F14 0-2	a11 3-4	M11 0-3	M21 1-0	J23 1-0
7 BURY	m09 4-1	a20 0-0	O18 0-1	F28 1-1	M31 1-2	a04 1-0		M17 0-0	A30 1-1	m02 1-1	F03 2-0	O11 2-0	M07 2-1	M28 1-0	S16 1-1	J24 0-3	S27 4-3	D27 0-2	N01 2-2	S13 0-2	N22 1-2	D20 4-0	J01 1-3	F14 1-0
8 CARLISLE U	J24 3-1	F03 0-0	a04 0-0	S15 0-0	F14 1-2	O25 2-0	O21 2-1		m06 0-2	m09 3-0	O11 1-0	M28 1-0	N22 1-3	M14 2-4	S27 1-2	a20 0-1	F28 2-2	D21 0-2	N04 2-0	D27 3-5	m02 0-3	S13 0-3	M03 0-2	A30 2-2
9 CHESTER C	D27 1-4	M07 0-0	F07 2-2	N08 1-1	O04 0-3	N22 3-1	M25 0-1	A23 2-2		D19 1-1	F21 6-0	O01 1-0	S06 2-2	O15 1-1	O18 1-1	m02 1-2	M21 2-0	F17 1-2	m09 1-2	a11 1-0	a01 2-0	N01 0-0	a20 1-2	M18 2-1
10 CHESTERFIELD	F17 1-1	F28 0-0	J03 1-1	a18 1-2	S13 0-3	M28 1-1	N29 1-1	D13 3-2	a25 0-1		m04 1-0	D26 4-1	N04 3-1	M03 1-0	J25 0-1	F14 2-1	O25 3-2	S27 1-2	O11 2-4	S16 2-1	M14 1-3	A30 3-2	O21 4-3	a04 1-0
11 DARLINGTON	M10 1-1	F18 0-1	O04 0-3	F15 1-1	F28 0-0	M03 1-1	a11 4-1	M21 0-1	S27 1-0	D27 1-1		M14 2-2	m02 0-1	O21 1-1	A30 2-1	N08 0-1	S16 1-3	S13 2-1	D19 3-2	a20 1-1	O25 0-0	m09 1-3	N22 1-0	F24 2-2
12 DONCASTER R	S14 2-2	D27 3-0	M17 0-3	A30 2-0	S17 1-0	m02 2-0	M21 0-0	O14 2-0	F27 1-1	a20 1-1	O18 0-0		N01 2-1	N07 2-0	F17 1-0	m09 0-2	F14 0-1	M07 1-2	N22 2-1	J01 3-0	D21 2-2	J24 1-1	a22 1-1	S27 3-1
13 FULHAM	A30 0-1	S16 4-2	m04 1-3	S13 1-3	N08 0-3	O21 2-2	O25 2-1	J03 3-0	J24 0-5	a11 3-1	N29 3-1	M03 0-0		D26 2-2	D13 1-1	S27 2-2	a18 2-0	F14 3-1	M28 0-6	F17 1-1	O11 0-2	F28 2-2	a28 2-2	a25 1-0
14 GILLINGHAM	N04 2-1	m09 1-0	M21 2-1	S27 2-0	A30 1-1	D19 4-1	O04 1-0	O18 1-0	F14 1-2	N01 3-0	M17 4-1	a04 2-1	a20 4-1		F28 2-0	S13 0-0	F17 1-1	N22 3-1	M07 0-0	F03 1-0	D27 1-3	J01 4-0	m02 0-0	S16 2-0
15 MANSFIELD T	D06 1-1	N22 2-2	S20 1-1	O11 1-0	a11 2-0	J31 5-0	F07 1-3	F21 2-0	M14 2-3	S07 1-1	a28 1-0	A23 2-1	m09 1-1	S30 1-0		D27 1-1	N25 1-0	a21 1-2	J01 0-1	M03 0-0	N08 0-0	m02 2-0	D21 1-5	M28 1-1
16 MIDDLESBROUGH	O11 1-3	N04 0-0	N01 4-0	a25 2-0	M07 1-0	F07 1-0	S06 3-1	D26 1-0	N29 1-2	S20 2-0	a05 1-1	D13 1-0	F21 3-0	a28 3-0	m04 1-0		J03 2-0	M17 2-0	A23 2-2	M28 0-0	S30 1-0	O18 3-1	m06 0-0	a18 3-1
17 NEWPORT CO	m02 1-1	a04 2-1	F24 0-1	a07 2-2	D02 0-1	m09 0-1	F21 2-2	O28 1-1	O11 2-2	M08 1-0	a14 3-0	S20 3-2	J01 0-0	A23 1-2	M17 0-3	N22 0-1		N01 1-1	D27 0-2	D20 1-2	S06 2-2	a20 2-4	M31 1-2	N04 1-1
18 NOTTS CO	M14 3-2	M28 0-0	S06 1-1	a11 1-1	N29 2-0	S30 3-0	m04 1-2	a26 2-1	a18 1-1	F21 2-1	J31 2-2	O25 3-1	S20 2-3	J03 3-1	D26 0-0	O21 1-0	M03 5-2		F07 4-1	O11 5-0	a28 2-3	N08 2-1	A23 2-0	D13 5-1
19 PORT VALE	F28 1-6	F14 1-1	M31 1-2	J24 4-1	D26 0-0	M14 4-1	M03 2-0	a11 0-1	D14 2-1	M21 2-2	a25 1-2	F03 4-2	O04 0-1	O25 1-2	a18 3-2	F17 0-0	m04 6-1	S16 1-1		A30 1-1	O21 3-4	S27 4-1	N08 0-1	S13 2-3
20 ROTHERHAM U	a04 1-0	O18 1-0	D13 4-2	N30 2-3	J03 2-0	S20 0-1	J31 2-1	m04 2-1	N04 3-0	F07 0-1	D26 0-0	a18 2-0	A23 0-0	S06 0-1	N01 2-2	O04 1-4	a25 3-1	M21 1-1	J27 1-1		F21 1-2	M17 1-0	S30 0-2	M07 0-0
21 SWINDON T	S16 2-6	M24 2-0	a18 1-1	D26 2-0	D14 1-2	N04 1-2	J03 1-0	N29 2-0	S13 1-1	O18 2-1	a22 1-0	a25 1-1	M21 2-0	m04 1-1	a03 3-0	F28 1-0	J25 3-0	A31 1-2	M17 1-0	S27 2-0		m06 0-0	O05 3-1	N01 3-1
22 WALSALL	M28 2-1	O11 3-3	N04 2-0	O25 5-2	m04 1-1	A23 0-3	a25 3-1	a07 3-0	a22 1-0	a14 2-1	D13 4-2	S06 1-3	S30 1-1	a18 1-0	N29 2-0	M14 1-0	D26 2-0	a04 1-1	a28 5-2	O21 4-1	N25 1-0		F07 2-3	M24 3-2
23 WIGAN A	F13 4-1	S26 2-1	a14 0-2	D13 1-1	J24 3-1	O11 4-3	a17 1-0	N01 2-0	D26 2-2	M17 1-1	J03 1-1	N04 1-1	O18 2-0	N29 3-1	a25 3-0	A30 0-2	S13 1-2	M24 1-0	a04 2-1	F28 2-1	M28 3-2	S16 5-1		m04 3-2
24 YORK C	a20 1-1	m02 2-1	S30 2-0	M14 2-1	M21 1-1	S06 1-0	S20 1-0	M31 2-0	O21 1-1	N08 1-1	A23 3-1	F21 1-1	D20 1-1	F07 2-1	O04 1-3	J01 3-1	a11 3-0	m09 1-1	a14 1-4	O25 2-1	M03 0-3	N22 1-5	D27 1-1	

DIVISION 4

	ALDERSHOT	BURNLEY	CAMBRIDGE U	CARDIFF C	COLCHESTER U	CREWE A	EXETER C	HALIFAX T	HARTLEPOOL U	HEREFORD U	LINCOLN C	NORTHAMPTON T	ORIENT	PETERBOROUGH U	PRESTON N.E.	ROCHDALE	SCUNTHORPE U	SOUTHEND U	STOCKPORT CO	SWANSEA C	TORQUAY U	TRANMERE R	WOLVERHAMPTON W	WREXHAM
1 ALDERSHOT		O11 2-0	O21 4-1	m09 1-2	D27 1-0	D20 1-0	m02 2-1	M24 4-1	O25 1-1	M03 1-0	S13 4-0	m06 3-3	a20 1-2	J24 1-1	M14 0-0	N22 2-1	S16 2-1	J01 0-1	N09 3-1	F28 4-1	F14 1-1	S27 0-2	A30 1-2	a11 1-0
2 BURNLEY	M21 0-1		a04 0-2	D19 1-3	N04 2-1	D27 4-0	M07 0-0	S27 3-0	S13 1-1	J24 0-6	N22 3-1	M17 2-1	m09 2-1	N01 0-0	O04 1-4	J01 0-3	A30 1-0	m02 2-1	O18 2-0	S16 1-1	a14 2-2	F28 2-2	F14 2-5	a20 0-0
3 CAMBRIDGE U	M17 0-3	N08 3-1		m01 2-1	a21 0-1	O31 0-3	S13 2-2	A30 1-0	J24 3-0	m09 2-1	S27 1-1	O17 2-3	M10 2-0	N22 1-1	M21 2-0	D20 3-0	F28 1-0	D28 1-2	O03 5-0	a11 1-0	S16 3-3	F14 1-1	J10 0-0	M07 1-0
4 CARDIFF C	D13 2-0	a25 1-0	N29 3-0		M14 0-2	O04 1-1	M31 0-0	M03 0-0	m07 4-0	S27 4-1	S16 1-1	m04 1-1	M24 1-1	F28 0-1	a11 1-1	A30 0-0	O25 1-1	N08 0-2	J03 1-1	D26 0-0	a18 3-1	S13 0-2	J24 0-2	M21 0-0
5 COLCHESTER U	m04 0-1	a10 1-0	D26 1-2	O17 3-1		M17 2-1	A29 1-1	N28 3-1	S16 2-1	F27 2-0	J10 2-0	a17 3-1	N07 0-0	S27 1-3	D13 0-2	F13 2-0	J03 1-0	M20 1-2	M06 5-1	a24 2-1	S12 3-0	J23 1-1	O31 3-0	O03 2-1
6 CREWE A	a25 1-3	m04 1-0	M03 0-0	M28 1-2	O21 1-1		S16 2-2	O25 2-2	F28 1-0	A30 1-2	a11 1-2	N28 0-5	O10 3-2	F14 1-3	D26 2-2	M31 5-1	J24 2-2	M13 2-1	a17 5-0	S27 1-1	D13 1-0	J03 3-2	S13 1-1	N08 1-1
7 EXETER C	N29 4-0	O25 3-0	J31 1-1	S20 0-0	J17 2-0	F07 1-0		a11 2-2	O22 2-0	M14 1-0	O11 2-0	J03 1-1	A23 1-0	N08 1-1	M04 1-2	M28 1-1	a25 0-0	O01 0-0	S06 4-0	a18 2-2	D26 2-2	D13 1-0	m04 1-3	F21 4-2
8 HALIFAX T	A23 1-0	F21 2-2	a14 1-0	O31 1-1	a29 0-0	M07 0-3	N04 2-0		a20 1-0	D19 2-1	F24 1-2	S30 3-6	N21 4-0	m09 1-0	F07 1-3	D27 3-1	a03 1-1	S05 0-1	S19 0-2	O04 1-0	M21 2-4	O17 0-0	M17 3-4	J31 2-1
9 HARTLEPOOL U	M07 1-1	J31 2-2	S06 2-2	A23 1-1	F06 1-0	O01 0-5	M18 1-0	D26 0-0		O11 0-0	M29 2-1	N01 3-3	F21 1-3	O18 1-2	m04 2-2	a04 1-1	a17 0-2	a14 1-0	N28 1-0	J03 1-1	N04 2-1	a24 1-1	D13 0-1	S21 0-1
10 HEREFORD U	N01 1-0	S06 2-0	D13 2-3	F21 0-2	O01 2-3	J28 2-0	O18 1-1	a26 1-0	M21 4-0		N08 0-0	a08 3-2	S20 1-1	O04 2-0	F25 2-3	M18 0-1	N29 2-2	F07 0-1	a11 1-2	m04 2-0	J03 2-2	a18 1-0	D26 2-0	A23 0-0
11 LINCOLN C	M31 0-2	J03 2-1	F22 0-3	F07 0-1	A23 3-1	N04 2-1	M21 1-1	a18 0-0	O05 1-4	a04 0-0		a26 3-1	S30 2-0	M08 1-2	S06 1-1	O18 1-1	m04 1-2	S20 1-3	D26 0-0	D13 4-0	M17 1-1	N01 3-1	N29 3-0	a14 0-1
12 NORTHAMPTON T	O04 4-2	O22 4-2	M14 3-0	D28 4-1	J01 3-2	a29 2-1	D02 4-0	F27 1-0	M04 1-1	O25 3-2	D21 3-1		a12 2-0	S14 2-1	N08 3-1	J24 5-0	M11 1-0	a20 2-1	M21 2-1	F14 0-1	A31 1-0	S17 2-0	S27 2-1	D13 2-2
13 ORIENT	D26 1-3	D13 2-0	a18 3-0	M17 2-0	a03 1-0	M21 1-1	a07 2-0	J03 1-3	S27 2-0	F14 2-0	F28 2-1	N04 0-1		A30 1-0	a25 1-2	S16 3-0	S13 3-1	O04 1-0	O31 1-0	J24 1-4	m04 3-2	N29 2-2	M07 3-1	O18 2-4
14 PETERBOROUGH U	S06 1-1	M04 1-1	J04 2-1	O01 1-2	F21 2-0	S20 1-2	a04 2-2	D13 2-0	M14 3-1	M28 2-1	O25 0-1	J31 0-1	J17 0-1		N29 2-1	O11 1-1	D26 1-1	A23 2-0	m04 0-0	O22 1-1	a25 2-1	N05 2-1	a18 0-1	F07 1-0
15 PRESTON N.E.	O18 1-2	M28 2-1	O11 1-0	N04 0-1	m09 1-0	a20 2-1	N01 2-1	S16 3-2	D27 0-0	S13 2-1	J24 3-0	a03 1-0	D20 1-0	m02 0-0		a14 2-4	F14 2-1	N22 2-0	M17 3-0	A30 2-1	S27 1-1	a28 2-0	F28 2-2	J01 1-0
16 ROCHDALE	F24 3-1	a18 0-2	a25 2-0	M10 0-0	S20 1-0	A23 1-1	O04 0-0	m04 5-3	N08 0-2	O21 2-0	M14 1-1	S06 1-2	F07 0-0	M21 3-2	a07 0-2		D13 1-1	F21 1-2	m06 2-1	a29 2-0	N29 3-3	D26 0-1	a11 0-3	M25 3-3
17 SCUNTHORPE U	F07 2-0	a28 2-1	S30 1-1	M07 1-3	N21 5-2	S07 2-1	D19 3-1	N09 2-1	J01 1-2	m01 3-1	D27 2-1	A23 2-2	F10 0-2	a20 2-0	S19 4-0	m09 2-0		a11 3-0	F21 1-2	M21 3-2	O17 2-0	J31 6-0	O05 0-2	N01 3-3
18 SOUTHEND U	a18 2-0	N28 2-1	m05 3-1	a03 2-0	O10 1-1	O18 3-1	F27 2-1	F03 2-3	A29 1-1	S16 2-0	F14 1-0	D26 0-4	M27 2-1	J10 2-2	J03 1-2	S26 5-3	N04 3-1		D13 0-0	S12 1-2	O31 4-0	M06 3-0	a24 1-0	M17 0-3
19 STOCKPORT CO	a03 0-0	M13 0-1	M27 3-2	N22 2-0	O24 1-1	J01 2-1	J23 0-0	F14 2-0	m01 0-2	N03 1-2	a20 1-0	O27 0-3	M02 2-2	D27 3-1	O20 1-3	S12 1-1	a13 1-0	m08 0-2		a27 3-1	F27 0-0	A29 0-2	S15 0-2	D19 2-1
20 SWANSEA C	S30 2-1	F06 2-2	N04 2-0	a20 2-0	D20 1-2	F21 1-1	J01 1-0	M29 0-2	N22 1-0	D27 1-3	m09 2-0	S20 2-1	S06 4-1	M17 0-1	J17 1-1	N01 1-0	O11 1-2	J31 1-0	A23 3-0		a07 0-1	a03 2-0	O18 1-0	m02 0-3
21 TORQUAY U	S20 2-2	A23 1-1	F07 1-0	a28 1-0	J31 3-1	m09 2-2	a20 1-1	O11 1-0	a11 0-1	N22 1-1	O21 0-1	F24 0-1	D27 2-2	M31 1-0	F21 0-2	m02 2-1	M14 2-2	M03 2-1	S30 0-0	O25 3-5		M28 0-2	N08 1-2	S06 2-1
22 TRANMERE R	F21 1-1	S30 2-1	S20 1-1	F24 2-1	S05 3-4	N22 3-2	m08 1-0	M13 3-4	J10 1-1	J01 3-3	M03 2-0	F06 1-1	m01 1-3	a11 1-1	A23 1-1	a20 1-1	O21 1-0	O24 1-3	a07 0-3	N08 1-1	O03 2-2		M21 0-1	D27 0-2
23 WOLVERHAMPTON W	F17 3-0	S20 0-1	A23 1-2	S06 0-1	M03 2-0	J31 2-3	D27 2-2	O21 1-2	m09 4-1	a20 1-0	m02 3-0	F21 1-1	O25 3-1	J01 0-3	S30 1-0	N04 0-0	M28 1-0	D20 1-2	F07 3-1	M14 4-0	a04 1-0	O11 2-1		N22 0-3
24 WREXHAM	O28 3-0	D26 2-2	D10 2-1	O11 5-1	M28 0-1	a04 2-1	S27 0-0	S12 3-1	F14 1-1	m06 2-2	A30 1-1	m09 1-3	M14 1-1	O14 4-3	a18 1-1	F28 2-2	M03 1-1	a30 4-0	a25 0-0	N29 0-0	J24 2-1	m04 1-1	J03 0-0	

LEAGUE TABLES

DIVISION 1

	P	W	D	L	F	A	W	D	L	F	A	Pts
Everton	42	16	4	1	49	11	10	4	7	27	20	86
Liverpool	42	15	3	3	43	16	8	5	8	29	26	77
Tottenham H	42	14	3	4	40	14	7	5	9	28	29	71
Arsenal	42	12	5	4	31	12	8	5	8	27	23	70
Norwich C	42	9	10	2	27	20	8	7	6	26	31	68
Wimbledon	42	11	5	5	32	22	8	4	9	25	28	66
Luton T	42	14	5	2	29	13	4	7	10	18	32	66
Nottingham F	42	12	8	1	36	14	6	3	12	28	37	65
Watford	42	12	5	4	38	20	6	4	11	29	34	63
Coventry C	42	14	4	3	35	17	3	8	10	15	28	63
Manchester U	42	13	3	5	38	18	1	11	9	14	27	56
Southampton	42	11	5	5	44	24	3	5	13	25	44	52
Sheffield W	42	9	7	5	39	24	4	6	11	19	35	52
Chelsea	42	8	6	7	30	30	5	7	9	23	34	52
West Ham U	42	10	4	7	33	28	4	6	11	19	39	52
Q.P.R.	42	9	7	5	31	27	4	4	13	17	37	50
Newcastle U	42	10	4	7	33	29	2	7	12	14	36	47
Oxford U	42	8	8	5	30	25	3	5	13	14	44	46
Charlton A	42	7	7	7	26	22	4	4	13	19	33	44
Leicester C	42	9	7	5	39	24	2	2	17	15	52	42
Manchester C	42	8	6	7	28	24	0	9	12	8	33	39
Aston Villa	42	7	7	7	25	25	1	5	15	20	54	36

DIVISION 2

	P	W	D	L	F	A	W	D	L	F	A	Pts
Derby Co	42	14	6	1	42	18	11	3	7	22	20	84
Portsmouth	42	17	2	2	37	11	6	7	8	16	17	78
Oldham A	42	13	6	2	36	16	9	3	9	29	28	75
Leeds U	42	15	4	2	43	16	4	7	10	15	28	68
Ipswich T	42	12	6	3	29	10	5	7	9	30	33	64
Crystal Palace	42	12	4	5	35	20	7	1	13	16	33	62
Plymouth A	42	12	6	3	40	23	4	7	10	22	34	61
Stoke C	42	11	5	5	40	21	5	5	11	23	32	58
Sheffield U	42	10	8	3	31	19	5	5	11	19	30	58
Bradford C	42	10	5	6	36	27	5	5	11	26	35	55
Barnsley	42	8	7	6	26	23	6	6	9	23	29	55
Blackburn R	42	11	4	6	30	22	4	6	11	15	33	55
Reading	42	11	4	6	33	23	3	7	11	19	36	53
Hull C	42	10	6	5	25	22	3	8	10	16	33	53
W.B.A.	42	8	6	7	29	22	5	6	10	22	27	51
Millwall	42	10	5	6	27	16	4	4	13	12	29	51
Huddersfield T	42	9	6	6	38	30	4	6	11	16	31	51
Shrewsbury T	42	11	3	7	24	14	4	3	14	17	39	51
Birmingham C	42	8	9	4	27	21	3	8	10	20	38	50
Sunderland	42	8	6	7	25	23	4	6	11	24	36	48
Grimsby T	42	5	8	8	18	21	5	6	10	21	38	44
Brighton & H.A.	42	7	6	8	22	20	2	6	13	15	34	39

DIVISION 3

	P	W	D	L	F	A	W	D	L	F	A	Pts
Bournemouth	46	19	3	1	44	14	10	7	6	32	26	97
Middlesbrough	46	16	5	2	38	11	12	5	6	29	19	94
Swindon T	46	14	5	4	37	19	11	7	5	40	28	87
Wigan A	46	15	5	3	47	26	10	5	8	36	34	85
Gillingham	46	16	5	2	42	14	7	4	12	23	34	78
Bristol C	46	14	6	3	42	15	7	8	8	21	21	77
Notts Co	46	14	6	3	52	24	7	7	9	25	32	76
Walsall	46	16	4	3	50	27	6	5	12	30	40	75
Blackpool	46	11	7	5	35	20	5	9	9	39	39	64
Mansfield T	46	9	9	5	30	23	6	7	10	22	32	61
Brentford	46	9	7	7	39	32	6	8	9	25	34	60
Port Vale	46	8	6	9	43	36	7	6	10	33	34	57
Doncaster R	46	11	8	4	32	19	3	7	13	24	43	57
Rotherham U	46	10	6	7	29	23	5	6	12	19	34	57
Chester C	46	7	9	7	32	28	6	8	9	29	31	56
Bury	46	9	7	7	30	26	5	6	12	24	34	55
Chesterfield	46	11	5	7	36	33	2	10	11	20	36	54
Fulham	46	8	8	7	35	41	4	9	10	24	36	53
Bristol R	46	7	8	8	26	29	6	4	13	23	46	51
York C	46	11	8	4	34	29	1	5	17	21	50	49
Bolton W	46	8	5	10	29	26	2	10	11	17	32	45
Carlisle U	46	7	5	11	26	35	3	3	17	13	43	38
Darlington	46	6	10	7	25	28	1	6	16	20	49	37
Newport Co	46	4	9	10	26	34	4	4	15	23	52	37

DIVISION 4

	P	W	D	L	F	A	W	D	L	F	A	Pts
Northampton T	46	20	2	1	56	20	10	7	6	47	33	99
Preston N.E.	46	16	4	3	36	18	10	8	5	36	29	90
Southend U	46	14	4	5	43	27	11	1	11	25	28	80
Wolverh'pton W	46	12	3	8	36	24	12	4	7	33	26	79
Colchester U	46	15	3	5	41	20	6	4	13	23	36	70
Aldershot	46	13	5	5	40	22	7	5	11	24	35	70
Orient	46	15	2	6	40	25	5	7	11	24	36	69
Scunthorpe U	46	15	3	5	52	27	3	9	11	21	30	66
Wrexham	46	8	13	2	38	24	7	7	9	32	27	65
Peterborough U	46	10	7	6	29	21	7	7	9	28	29	65
Cambridge U	46	12	6	5	37	23	5	5	13	23	39	62
Swansea C	46	13	3	7	31	21	4	8	11	25	40	62
Cardiff C	46	6	12	5	24	18	9	4	10	24	32	61
Exeter C	46	11	10	2	37	17	0	13	10	16	32	56
Halifax T	46	10	5	8	32	32	5	5	13	27	42	55
Hereford U	46	10	6	7	33	23	4	5	14	27	38	53
Crewe A	46	8	9	6	38	35	5	5	13	32	37	53
Hartlepool U	46	6	11	6	24	30	5	7	11	20	35	51
Stockport Co	46	9	6	8	25	27	4	6	13	15	42	51
Tranmere R	46	6	10	7	32	37	5	7	11	22	35	50
Rochdale	46	8	8	7	31	30	3	9	11	23	43	50
Burnley	46	9	7	7	31	35	3	6	14	22	39	49
Torquay U	46	8	8	7	28	29	2	10	11	28	43	48
Lincoln C	46	8	7	8	30	27	4	5	14	15	38	48

FOOTBALL LEAGUE RECORDS

Top scorers: Div 1, J.Aldridge (Liverpool) 26 goals; Div 2, D.Currie (Barnsley) 28 goals; Div 3, D.Crown (Southend United) 26 goals; Div 4, S.Bull (Wolverhampton Wanderers) 34 goals.

Play-offs: Div 1, Blackburn Rovers v Chelsea 0-2, 1-4; Bradford City v Middlesbrough 2-1, 0-2; Middlesbrough v Chelsea 2-0, 1-0; Div 2, Bristol City v Sheffield United 1-0, 1-1; Notts County v Walsall 1-3, 1-1; Bristol City v Walsall 1-3, 2-0, 0-4; Div 3, Swansea City v Rotherham United 1-0, 1-1; Torquay United v Scunthorpe United 2-1, 1-1; Swansea City v Torquay United 2-1, 3-3.

Aston Villa, Millwall and Middlesbrough promoted to Div 1; Chelsea, Oxford United, Portsmouth and Watford relegated to Div 2; Brighton & Hove Albion, Sunderland and Walsall

Peter Beardsley, signed from Newcastle United for £1.9 million, he took a little time to settle at Anfield but eventually proved his worth.

DIVISION 1

	ARSENAL	CHARLTON A	CHELSEA	COVENTRY C	DERBY CO	EVERTON	LIVERPOOL	LUTON T	MANCHESTER U	NEWCASTLE U	NORWICH C	NOTTINGHAM F	OXFORD U	PORTSMOUTH	Q.P.R.	SHEFFIELD W	SOUTHAMPTON	TOTTENHAM H	WATFORD	WEST HAM U	WIMBLEDON
1 ARSENAL		F27 4-0	N03 3-1	m02 1-1	O24 2-1	D19 1-1	A15 1-2	F13 2-1	J24 1-2	M19 1-1	a04 2-0	D26 0-2	O10 2-0	A29 6-0	J02 0-0	D05 3-1	N21 0-1	M06 2-1	a15 0-1	S26 1-0	S19 3-0
2 CHARLTON A	O03 0-3		D20 2-2	N21 2-2	O17 0-1	D05 0-0	J23 0-2	S19 1-0	A29 1-3	a23 2-0	N07 2-0	A15 1-2	M26 0-0	D26 2-1	S05 0-1	F20 3-1	O31 1-1	m02 1-1	a04 1-0	M12 3-0	F13 1-1
3 CHELSEA	a02 1-1	m07 1-1		O17 1-0	a09 1-0	M12 0-0	a30 1-1	A29 3-0	F13 1-2	O03 2-2	S19 1-0	S05 4-3	O31 2-1	J23 0-0	D26 1-1	A15 2-1	M26 0-1	J02 0-0	M29 1-1	D12 1-1	N28 1-1
4 COVENTRY C	D13 0-0	a09 0-0	M05 3-3		M19 0-3	a19 1-2	A29 1-4	M15 4-0	S05 0-0	O24 1-3	F20 0-0	S19 0-3	a02 1-0	a30 1-0	m07 0-0	F13 3-0	O20 2-3	A15 2-1	O03 1-0	N28 0-0	N14 3-3
5 DERBY CO	M26 0-0	M05 1-1	N22 2-0	O31 2-0		m02 0-0	M16 1-1	A15 1-0	F10 1-2	a04 2-1	D26 1-2	O10 0-1	S26 0-1	S05 0-0	a13 0-2	S19 2-2	a23 2-0	D20 1-2	D05 1-1	F27 1-0	A29 0-1
6 EVERTON	m07 1-2	a30 1-1	O10 4-1	S26 1-2	D12 3-0		M20 1-0	D26 2-0	S19 2-1	M05 1-0	A15 1-0	J03 1-0	N28 0-0	a09 2-1	F13 2-0	A29 4-0	F27 1-0	S05 0-0	O24 2-0	N14 3-1	M29 2-2
7 LIVERPOOL	J16 2-0	S15 3-2	D06 2-1	J01 4-0	S29 4-0	N01 2-0		m09 1-1	a04 3-3	D28 4-0	N21 0-0	a13 5-0	S12 2-0	O03 4-0	O17 4-0	D19 1-0	m02 1-1	a23 1-0	N24 4-0	F06 0-0	M26 2-1
8 LUTON T	A31 1-1	D28 1-0	J01 3-0	A18 0-1	J16 1-0	S12 2-1	O24 0-1		O03 1-1	N07 4-0	D05 1-2	m13 1-1	F06 7-4	M29 4-1	a19 2-1	a05 2-2	D18 2-2	N21 2-0	m02 2-1	A22 2-2	O17 2-0
9 MANCHESTER U	A19 0-0	J01 0-0	A31 3-1	F06 1-0	a02 4-1	D28 2-1	N15 1-1	a12 3-0		S12 2-2	O17 2-1	O31 2-2	D12 3-1	m07 4-1	a30 2-1	M12 4-1	J16 0-2	S26 1-0	A22 2-0	M26 3-1	m09 2-1
10 NEWCASTLE U	O31 0-1	N28 2-1	F27 3-1	M26 2-2	N14 0-0	O17 1-1	S20 1-4	a02 4-0	D26 1-0		F13 1-3	A29 0-1	a30 3-1	D12 1-1	a09 1-1	J02 2-2	S26 2-1	J23 2-0	a12 3-0	m07 2-1	S05 1-2
11 NORWICH C	N14 2-4	a02 2-0	D28 3-0	A22 3-1	S12 1-2	J16 0-3	a20 0-0	a30 2-2	M05 1-0	S01 1-1		S26 0-2	M16 4-2	N28 0-1	O31 1-1	M26 0-3	A19 0-1	O10 2-1	F06 0-0	J01 4-1	m07 0-1
12 NOTTINGHAM F	S12 0-1	J16 2-2	F06 3-2	D28 4-1	M30 2-1	A22 0-0	a02 2-1	m15 1-1	M19 0-0	J01 0-2	m04 2-0		m07 5-3	N14 5-0	D13 4-0	O17 3-0	S02 3-3	O24 3-0	A19 1-0	a20 0-0	a30 0-0
13 OXFORD U	M30 0-0	O24 2-1	M19 4-4	N07 1-0	F20 0-0	a23 1-1	D26 0-3	S05 2-5	m02 0-2	D05 1-3	O03 3-0	D19 0-2		A15 4-2	S19 2-0	a13 0-3	a04 0-0	F13 0-0	N21 1-1	O17 1-2	J02 2-5
14 PORTSMOUTH	J01 1-1	S12 1-1	A18 0-3	D05 0-0	F06 2-1	N21 0-1	F27 0-2	O10 3-1	D19 1-2	m02 1-2	a23 2-2	a04 0-1	J16 2-2		M26 0-1	O31 1-2	A22 2-2	N04 0-0	D28 1-1	A31 2-1	S26 2-1
15 Q.P.R.	A22 2-0	F06 2-0	S12 3-1	D18 1-2	A19 1-1	S02 1-0	M05 0-1	S26 2-0	D05 0-2	N21 1-1	M19 3-0	M16 2-1	D28 3-2	O24 2-1		a23 1-1	J01 3-0	a04 2-0	N07 0-0	J16 0-1	F27 1-0
16 SHEFFIELD W	a30 3-3	S26 2-0	J16 3-0	A31 0-3	D28 2-1	J01 1-0	m07 1-5	N14 0-2	O10 2-4	A22 0-1	O24 1-0	M05 0-1	A18 1-1	M19 1-0	N28 3-1		F06 2-1	F27 0-3	S12 2-3	a02 2-1	D12 1-0
17 SOUTHAMPTON	a09 4-2	M19 0-1	O24 3-0	M12 1-2	N28 1-2	O03 0-4	D12 2-2	m07 1-1	A15 2-2	M01 1-1	J23 0-0	F13 1-1	N14 3-0	J03 0-2	A29 0-1	S05 1-1		D26 2-1	O17 1-0	a30 2-1	a02 2-2
18 TOTTENHAM H	O18 1-2	D13 0-1	A22 1-0	J16 2-2	M01 0-0	M09 2-1	N28 0-2	m04 2-1	F23 1-1	A19 3-1	M12 1-3	M26 1-1	S01 3-0	a02 0-1	N14 1-1	O03 2-0	S12 2-1		J01 2-1	D28 2-1	O31 0-3
19 WATFORD	N28 2-0	N14 2-1	S26 0-3	F27 0-1	a30 1-1	M26 1-2	F13 1-4	D12 0-1	J02 0-1	a19 1-1	S05 0-1	J23 0-0	a09 3-0	S19 0-0	a01 0-1	D26 1-3	M05 0-1	A29 1-1		O31 1-2	A15 1-0
20 WEST HAM U	a12 0-1	O10 1-1	m02 4-1	a23 1-1	O03 1-1	a04 0-0	S05 1-1	J02 1-1	O25 1-1	D19 2-1	A29 2-0	N21 3-2	M05 1-1	F13 1-1	A15 0-3	N07 0-1	D05 2-1	S19 0-1	M19 1-0		D26 1-2
21 WIMBLEDON	D28 3-1	S01 4-1	a23 2-2	a05 1-2	J01 2-1	A18 1-1	N04 1-1	M05 2-0	N21 2-1	F06 0-0	D18 1-0	D05 1-1	A22 1-1	a19 2-2	O03 1-2	m03 1-1	N07 2-0	M19 3-0	J16 1-2	S12 1-1	

Teddy Sheringham was Millwall's leading scorer with 22 goals as the Lions won promotion to Division One for the first time.

DIVISION 2

	ASTON VILLA	BARNSLEY	BIRMINGHAM C	BLACKBURN R	BOURNEMOUTH	BRADFORD C	CRYSTAL P	HUDDERSFFIELD T	HULL C	IPSWICH T	LEEDS U	LEICESTER C	MANCHESTER C	MIDDLESBROUGH	MILLWALL	OLDHAM A	PLYMOUTH A	READING	SHEFFIELD U	SHREWSBURY T	STOKE C	SWINDON T	W.B.A.
1 ASTON VILLA		S12 0-0	A22 0-2	S30 1-1	O17 1-1	m02 1-0	O21 4-1	D28 1-1	J01 5-0	J16 1-0	M12 1-2	F06 2-1	A31 1-1	S08 0-1	N07 1-2	a04 1-2	F27 5-2	O31 2-1	S26 1-1	a23 1-0	M26 0-1	D05 2-1	D18 0-0
2 BARNSLEY	J02 1-3		a23 2-2	F13 0-1	M08 2-1	N07 3-0	A29 2-1	a04 1-0	O17 1-3	F27 2-3	A16 1-1	M12 1-1	M26 3-1	m02 0-3	D19 4-1	D26 1-1	S05 2-1	O20 5-2	S29 1-2	N21 2-1	O31 5-2	S15 0-1	D05 3-1
3 BIRMINGHAM C	D12 1-2	N03 2-0		S15 1-0	A29 1-1	M05 1-1	S05 0-6	O03 2-0	a02 1-1	N28 1-0	m06 0-0	N14 2-2	a30 0-3	O24 0-0	F09 1-0	M19 1-3	D26 0-1	O10 2-2	a09 1-0	S19 0-0	A15 2-0	J02 1-1	M08 0-1
4 BLACKBURN R	F20 3-2	A18 0-1	D19 2-0		M12 3-1	D28 1-1	N21 2-0	S12 2-2	J16 2-1	S01 1-0	O03 1-1	M19 3-3	F06 2-1	S26 0-2	D05 2-1	N07 1-0	O24 1-1	m02 1-1	J01 4-1	a04 2-2	O17 2-0	a25 0-0	A22 3-1
5 BOURNEMOUTH	M05 1-2	A31 1-2	J01 4-2	O10 1-1		A22 2-0	N07 2-3	N21 0-2	F06 6-2	O31 1-1	M26 0-0	S26 2-3	D01 0-2	D19 0-0	a19 1-2	D05 2-2	S29 2-2	S12 3-0	J16 1-2	O20 2-0	F27 0-0	m02 2-0	D28 3-2
6 BRADFORD C	N28 2-4	a02 1-1	O17 4-0	S19 2-1	D12 2-0		O31 2-0	M01 0-1	a09 2-0	m07 2-3	A29 0-0	a30 4-1	O21 2-4	O03 2-0	S05 3-1	F13 5-3	S16 3-1	a20 3-0	N14 2-0	D26 1-1	J02 1-4	A15 2-0	M12 4-1
7 CRYSTAL P	a09 1-1	J01 3-2	F06 3-0	a30 2-0	a02 3-0	M19 1-1		J16 2-1	A22 2-2	S26 1-2	N28 3-0	S12 2-1	m07 2-0	S01 3-1	O10 1-0	M05 3-1	N03 5-1	D28 2-3	D13 2-1	F27 1-2	N14 2-0	O24 2-1	S08 4-1
8 HUDDERSFIELD T	S19 0-1	N14 2-2	F27 2-2	J02 1-2	a30 1-2	S29 1-2	A15 2-2		O20 0-2	a08 1-2	S15 0-0	N28 1-0	a02 1-0	O10 1-4	O31 2-1	a19 2-2	D12 2-1	M05 0-2	m07 0-2	A29 0-0	D26 0-3	F13 0-3	M26 1-3
9 HULL C	A29 2-1	M05 1-2	N07 2-0	A15 2-2	S05 2-1	N03 0-0	D19 2-1	a23 4-0		O10 1-0	J03 3-1	O24 2-2	S29 3-1	a04 0-0	m02 0-1	S19 1-0	M19 1-1	D05 2-2	F27 1-2	S15 1-1	F13 0-0	a12 1-4	N21 1-0
10 IPSWICH T	A15 1-1	O03 1-0	m02 1-0	J30 0-2	M19 1-2	D05 4-0	D26 2-3	N03 3-0	M12 2-0		S05 1-0	F20 0-2	O17 3-0	a23 4-0	J02 1-1	N21 2-0	F13 1-2	N07 2-1	O24 1-0	D18 2-0	A29 2-0	S19 3-2	a04 1-1
11 LEEDS U	O10 1-3	J16 0-2	D05 4-1	F27 2-2	O24 3-2	J01 2-0	m02 1-0	D19 3-0	S12 0-2	F06 1-0		A19 1-0	S26 2-0	D28 2-0	a06 1-2	a23 1-1	M05 1-0	A22 0-0	M19 5-0	N07 2-1	S30 0-0	N21 4-2	A31 1-0
12 LEICESTER C	S05 0-2	O10 0-0	a05 2-0	O31 1-2	D26 0-1	N21 0-2	J02 4-4	m02 3-0	M26 2-1	S30 1-1	F13 3-2		F27 1-0	D05 0-0	A29 1-0	S16 4-1	S19 4-0	a23 1-0	M05 1-0	A15 0-1	M16 1-1	N07 3-2	O21 3-0
13 MANCHESTER C	J23 0-2	O24 1-1	N21 3-0	S05 1-2	F13 2-0	a23 2-2	D05 1-3	N07 10-1	M02 2-0	M05 2-0	D26 1-2	O03 4-2		N04 1-1	S16 4-0	D19 1-2	A15 2-1	a04 2-0	O10 2-3	J02 1-3	S19 3-0	M19 1-1	M02 4-2
14 MIDDLESBROUGH	F14 2-1	N28 2-0	M26 1-1	D26 1-1	S15 3-0	F27 1-2	J23 2-1	M12 2-0	N14 1-0	O20 3-1	S19 2-0	m07 1-2	a09 2-1		A15 1-1	A29 1-0	a30 3-1	S29 0-0	a02 6-0	O31 4-0	D12 2-0	S05 2-3	O17 2-1
15 MILLWALL	a02 2-1	A22 3-1	S01 3-1	m07 1-4	N03 1-2	F06 0-1	M12 1-1	M19 4-1	N28 2-0	S12 2-1	N14 3-1	J01 1-0	D12 0-1	J16 2-1		F20 1-1	a09 3-2	D01 3-0	D28 3-1	O17 4-1	a30 2-0	O03 2-2	S26 2-0
16 OLDHAM A	N14 0-1	S26 1-0	O31 1-2	a01 4-2	m07 2-0	A18 0-2	J29 1-0	A31 3-2	D28 1-2	a30 3-1	O20 1-1	D12 2-0	A22 1-1	J01 3-1	S29 0-0		N28 0-1	F06 4-2	S12 3-2	M26 2-2	a09 5-1	M12 4-3	J16 2-1
17 PLYMOUTH A	O03 1-3	a15 0-0	S26 1-1	M26 3-0	a26 1-2	D20 2-1	a23 1-3	A22 6-1	O31 3-1	A18 0-0	O17 6-3	D28 4-0	J16 3-2	N21 0-1	O20 1-2	m02 1-0		J01 1-3	A31 1-0	D05 2-0	M12 3-0	a04 1-0	S12 3-3
18 READING	M19 0-2	a09 2-1	M12 1-1	N28 0-0	a13 0-0	O24 1-1	S19 2-3	O17 3-2	m07 0-0	a02 1-1	D12 0-1	J30 1-2	N14 0-2	F20 0-0	F13 2-3	S05 3-0	A29 0-1		a30 2-1	J23 1-0	S16 0-1	D26 0-1	O03 1-2
19 SHEFFIELD U	D26 1-1	F20 1-0	O20 0-2	A29 3-1	A15 0-1	a04 1-2	S15 1-1	D05 2-2	O03 2-1	M26 4-1	O31 2-2	O17 2-1	M08 1-2	N07 0-2	S19 1-2	J02 0-5	a19 1-0	N21 4-1		F13 0-1	S05 0-0	D20 1-0	a23 0-0
20 SHREWSBURY T	N03 1-2	a30 1-1	D28 0-0	N14 1-2	a08 2-1	S26 2-2	O03 2-0	J01 3-1	D12 2-2	A22 0-0	a02 1-0	J16 0-0	S12 0-0	M19 0-1	M05 0-0	O24 2-3	m07 2-1	S01 0-1	N17 2-0		N28 0-3	F20 2-1	F06 0-1
21 STOKE C	O24 0-0	M19 3-1	J16 3-1	M05 2-1	O03 1-0	S12 1-2	a04 1-1	S26 1-1	A18 1-1	J01 1-2	F23 2-1	A31 2-1	D28 1-3	A22 1-0	N21 1-2	D08 2-2	O10 1-0	D19 4-2	F06 1-0	m02 1-1		a23 1-0	N07 3-0
22 SWINDON T	m07 0-0	M15 3-0	S12 0-2	a09 1-2	N28 4-2	M30 2-2	M27 2-2	D01 4-1	A31 0-0	D28 4-2	a30 1-2	a02 3-2	O31 3-4	F06 1-1	F27 0-1	O10 2-0	N14 1-1	S26 4-0	A22 2-0	S29 1-1	O20 3-0		J01 2-0
23 W.B.A.	S16 0-2	m07 2-2	S30 3-1	D12 0-1	S19 3-0	O10 0-1	F13 1-0	O24 3-2	a30 1-1	N14 2-2	J30 1-4	a09 1-1	N28 1-1	M05 0-0	D26 1-4	A15 0-0	J02 1-0	F27 0-1	N04 4-0	S05 2-1	a02 2-0	A29 1-2	

SEASON 1987-88

promoted to Div 2; Huddersfield Town, Reading and Sheffield United relegated to Div 3; Bolton Wanderers, Cardiff City, Swansea City and Wolverhampton Wanderers promoted to Div 3; Doncaster Rovers, Grimsby Town, Rotherham United and York City relegated to Div 4; Newport County were relegated from Division Four and replaced by Lincoln City. Orient became Leyton Orient.

DIVISION 3

	ALDERSHOT	BLACKPOOL	BRENTFORD	BRIGHTON & HA	BRISTOL C	BRISTOL R	BURY	CHESTER C	CHESTERFIELD	DONCASTER R	FULHAM	GILLINGHAM	GRIMSBY T	MANSFIELD T	NORTHAMPTON T	NOTTS CO	PORT VALE	PRESTON N.E.	ROTHERHAM U	SOUTHEND U	SUNDERLAND	WALSALL	WIGAN A	YORK C
1 ALDERSHOT		M29 0-0	S26 4-1	S12 1-4	N07 2-1	J01 3-0	J16 0-2	F06 4-1	O20 2-0	A31 2-1	M26 0-3	D28 6-0	D19 3-2	a19 3-0	O31 4-4	F23 0-2	a15 3-0	m02 0-0	N28 1-3	a04 0-1	F27 3-2	J09 0-1	S29 3-2	M05 1-2
2 BLACKPOOL	M12 3-2		J16 0-1	F06 1-3	N03 4-2	A31 2-1	J01 5-1	S12 0-1	m02 1-0	a15 4-2	O03 2-1	F20 3-3	a23 3-0	M19 2-0	N28 3-1	D28 1-1	a04 1-2	S26 3-0	N07 3-0	D19 1-1	O17 0-2	A22 1-2	O24 0-0	M01 2-1
3 BRENTFORD	D26 3-0	S19 2-1		M26 1-1	A29 0-2	O31 1-1	M12 0-3	O20 1-1	S15 2-0	a30 1-1	F14 3-1	a09 2-2	F23 0-2	D12 2-2	J09 0-1	a02 1-0	O03 1-0	M01 2-0	S05 1-1	J02 1-0	A15 0-1	O17 0-0	N21 2-1	m07 1-2
4 BRIGHTON & H.A.	J02 1-1	S05 1-3	O24 2-1		F13 3-2	m07 2-1	O03 2-1	D12 1-0	F17 2-2	N04 2-0	A29 2-0	a02 2-0	M19 0-0	a30 3-1	a15 3-0	N28 1-1	M02 2-0	O17 0-0	S16 1-1	D26 0-0	S19 3-1	M12 2-1	a09 1-0	A15 1-0
5 BRISTOL C	a02 2-0	a09 2-1	J01 2-3	D28 5-2		S12 3-3	F06 3-2	N21 2-2	S29 2-1	m07 1-0	D15 4-0	S26 3-3	M05 1-1	F20 1-2	F27 2-2	J16 2-1	A31 1-0	A22 3-1	M26 2-0	O10 3-2	O20 0-1	F09 0-0	a30 4-1	D12 3-2
6 BRISTOL R	A29 3-1	a27 2-0	M19 0-0	D19 1-2	a12 1-0		a04 0-0	O17 2-2	N07 2-0	O24 4-0	D26 3-1	M12 2-0	N28 4-2	O03 2-1	S19 0-2	M02 1-1	a23 1-0	N04 1-2	A15 3-1	F13 0-0	F24 4-0	m02 3-0	S05 2-3	S16 2-1
7 BURY	S19 1-0	A29 3-1	O10 2-2	F27 2-1	S05 1-1	N21 4-1		m07 0-1	J30 2-0	M19 2-1	D12 1-1	a30 2-1	S15 0-2	N03 1-0	F13 0-0	a09 0-1	M05 0-1	O24 4-0	J09 2-2	A15 2-2	J02 2-3	S29 2-2	D26 0-2	a02 0-1
8 CHESTER C	S05 4-1	J02 1-1	a23 1-1	m02 2-2	a04 1-0	M05 0-3	D18 4-4		N28 1-1	D05 1-1	S16 1-2	M02 3-1	S19 1-0	O24 0-2	A15 0-5	O03 1-2	N04 1-0	M19 1-0	J30 1-0	J09 1-1	D26 1-2	N07 1-1	F13 1-0	A29 1-0
9 CHESTERFIELD	a09 1-0	D12 1-1	a19 2-1	A22 0-0	M01 1-4	a02 0-1	A31 1-0	a30 0-0		J16 0-1	m07 1-0	F06 1-4	O10 0-3	J01 3-1	M05 0-2	S26 2-0	S12 1-3	F20 0-0	O03 3-2	O24 3-1	N21 1-1	D28 2-1	N03 0-1	M19 2-1
10 DONCASTER R	J31 0-0	S15 2-1	N28 0-1	a23 0-2	D19 1-2	M25 0-1	O31 1-2	M11 2-2	S18 1-0		J09 2-2	O03 4-2	A15 1-0	M01 0-2	S05 0-2	O17 0-1	N07 1-1	a04 3-2	F13 2-2	m02 0-1	A29 0-2	O20 0-4	J01 3-4	D26 2-0
11 FULHAM	O24 1-2	F27 3-1	D28 2-2	J01 1-2	M19 0-0	S26 3-1	m02 0-1	a15 1-0	D19 1-3	A22 4-0		S12 0-2	N03 5-0	F06 0-0	N07 0-0	S01 0-0	J16 1-2	N28 0-1	a04 3-1	a23 3-1	S29 0-2	F20 2-0	M05 3-2	O10 3-1
12 GILLINGHAM	F13 2-1	A15 0-0	N03 0-1	N07 1-1	D26 1-1	O10 3-0	N28 3-3	S29 0-1	S05 10-0	F27 3-1	J02 2-2		F02 1-1	M05 0-0	a04 1-2	O24 3-1	M19 0-0	a23 4-0	m02 0-2	A29 8-1	S15 0-0	D18 0-1	J23 0-1	S19 3-1
13 GRIMSBY T	m07 1-1	O20 1-1	A31 0-1	O31 0-1	O17 1-4	a30 0-0	J26 2-0	J16 2-1	M12 1-1	F20 0-0	a09 0-2	A22 2-0		S12 2-3	M26 2-2	J01 0-0	D28 3-1	F06 0-1	M08 2-1	O03 1-3	a02 0-1	S26 0-2	D12 0-2	N21 5-1
14 MANSFIELD T	M22 1-0	O31 0-0	m02 2-1	N21 1-1	A15 2-0	F27 1-0	a23 0-0	M26 1-2	A29 0-1	S29 2-0	S04 0-2	O17 2-2	J02 1-0		O20 3-1	M12 1-1	D20 4-0	N07 0-0	D26 0-1	S19 1-0	a26 0-4	a05 1-3	S15 0-1	F13 2-1
15 NORTHAMPTON T	M19 1-1	a30 3-3	S09 2-1	A31 1-1	O03 3-0	J16 2-1	D28 0-0	F20 2-0	O17 4-0	F06 1-0	a02 3-2	N21 2-1	O24 2-1	a10 2-0		S12 0-1	S26 1-0	J27 0-1	M11 0-0	M02 4-0	D12 0-2	J01 2-2	J30 1-1	N04 0-0
16 NOTTS CO	S15 2-1	F13 2-3	N07 3-0	a04 1-2	S19 0-1	S29 1-1	O20 3-0	F27 1-0	D26 2-0	M05 2-0	J30 5-1	M26 0-1	A29 0-0	O11 1-1	J02 3-1		m02 1-2	D19 4-2	a23 4-0	S05 6-2	O31 2-1	N21 3-1	A15 4-4	J09 3-0
17 PORT VALE	A15 4-2	N22 0-0	F27 1-0	S28 2-0	a18 1-1	O19 2-1	O17 1-0	a09 1-1	J02 0-1	a02 5-0	S19 1-1	O31 0-0	F13 2-0	m07 1-1	D26 1-1	D12 1-3		M12 3-2	A29 0-0	S14 4-1	a30 0-1	M26 2-1	a25 2-1	S05 2-1
18 PRESTON N.E.	D12 0-2	D26 2-1	S29 1-2	M05 3-0	J09 2-0	a08 3-1	M26 1-0	O31 1-1	A15 0-1	N21 1-2	a30 2-1	O20 1-1	S05 1-3	a02 1-0	S15 0-0	m07 1-2	O10 3-2		S19 0-0	J30 1-1	F13 2-2	F27 1-0	A29 0-1	J02 3-0
19 ROTHERHAM U	a30 1-0	a02 0-1	F17 2-0	M16 1-0	O24 4-1	F20 1-1	A22 0-1	A31 5-2	F27 1-1	D28 1-0	N21 0-2	D12 1-2	S29 0-0	S26 2-1	O11 2-2	N03 1-1	J01 1-0	J16 2-2		M05 1-1	m07 1-4	S12 0-1	M19 1-1	a08 0-1
20 SOUTHEND U	N21 0-1	m07 4-0	S12 2-3	S26 2-1	M11 2-0	D28 4-2	F20 1-0	A22 2-2	M25 3-0	D11 4-1	O20 0-2	J01 1-3	F26 0-0	J15 2-1	S29 1-1	F05 1-2	J22 3-3	S01 1-2	O16 1-1		a09 1-4	O30 1-1	a01 3-2	a29 3-1
21 SUNDERLAND	O03 3-1	M05 2-2	F20 2-0	J16 1-0	a23 0-1	A22 1-1	S12 1-1	S26 0-2	a04 3-2	J01 3-1	M01 2-0	J30 2-1	N07 1-1	A31 4-1	m02 3-1	M19 1-1	N28 2-1	D28 1-1	D20 3-0	N03 7-0		F06 1-1	O10 4-1	O24 4-2
22 WALSALL	N03 2-0	F23 3-2	M05 4-2	O10 1-1	S15 1-1	D12 0-0	M01 2-1	a02 1-0	F13 0-0	a09 2-1	A15 0-1	m07 0-0	D26 3-2	N28 2-1	A29 1-0	a30 2-1	O24 2-1	O03 1-0	J02 5-2	M19 2-1	S05 2-2		S19 1-2	J30 2-1
23 WIGAN A	M01 4-0	M25 0-0	a04 1-1	O20 3-3	N28 1-1	F06 1-0	S26 0-2	D28 1-0	a23 1-2	S12 2-1	O17 1-3	A31 1-1	m02 0-1	M28 2-1	D19 2-2	F20 2-1	a12 2-0	J01 2-0	O31 3-0	N07 1-0	M12 2-2	J16 3-1		O03 1-1
24 YORK C	O17 2-2	S29 1-3	D18 1-1	F20 0-2	m02 0-1	a15 0-4	N07 1-1	J01 2-0	O31 1-0	S26 1-1	M12 1-3	J16 0-2	a04 0-2	D28 2-2	a23 2-2	A22 3-5	F06 2-3	S12 1-1	O20 1-2	N28 0-3	M26 2-1	A31 1-3	F27 3-1	

DIVISION 4

	BOLTON W	BURNLEY	CAMBRIDGE U	CARDIFF C	CARLISLE U	COLCHESTER U	CREWE A	DARLINGTON	EXETER C	HALIFAX T	HARTLEPOOL U	HEREFORD U	LEYTON O	NEWPORT CO	PETERBOROUGH U	ROCHDALE	SCARBOROUGH	SCUNTHORPE U	STOCKPORT CO	SWANSEA C	TORQUAY U	TRANMERE R	WOLVERHAMPTON W	WREXHAM
1 BOLTON W		a04 2-1	N28 2-2	A22 1-0	O17 5-0	m02 4-0	A15 1-1	M11 1-1	O20 1-0	S12 2-0	S26 1-2	F06 1-0	N07 1-0	a23 6-0	A31 2-0	M26 0-0	J01 3-1	a19 0-0	D28 2-1	O31 1-1	J16 1-2	M01 2-0	O03 1-0	D19 2-0
2 BURNLEY	N21 2-1		S19 0-2	m07 1-2	A29 4-3	A15 0-3	S29 0-0	F13 2-1	M05 3-0	a08 3-1	O10 1-0	D12 0-0	M22 2-0	J09 2-0	a30 1-2	D26 4-0	F27 0-1	O20 1-1	O31 1-1	S05 1-0	m04 1-0	J02 1-1	a02 0-3	S15 1-0
3 CAMBRIDGE U	a29 2-2	J16 2-0		S01 0-0	m07 1-2	O24 0-1	A22 4-1	a01 1-0	F19 2-1	S26 2-1	a19 1-1	N03 0-1	M05 2-0	O10 4-0	J01 1-3	N21 1-2	D28 1-0	S12 3-3	D11 2-0	F27 0-3	F06 1-0	M19 1-1	a10 1-1	S29 0-1
4 CARDIFF C	a15 1-0	D19 2-1	J30 4-0		S19 4-2	F13 1-0	m02 2-0	S15 3-1	N07 3-2	S29 0-0	N28 1-1	O10 0-1	A15 1-1	a04 4-0	M04 0-0	O31 1-0	a23 2-0	M26 0-1	F27 0-0	A29 1-0	O20 2-1	D26 3-0	S05 3-2	M16 1-1
5 CARLISLE U	M05 0-2	J01 3-4	D18 2-1	J16 0-0		a23 4-0	M19 0-1	S29 3-3	J23 0-0	a19 1-1	S12 1-3	A31 3-1	N03 1-2	N07 3-1	F20 0-2	F27 2-0	S26 4-0	A22 3-1	F06 2-0	m02 0-1	N28 3-3	O24 3-2	O10 0-1	a04 0-4
6 COLCHESTER U	D11 3-0	F19 0-1	M25 0-0	D28 2-1	O20 1-0		F05 1-4	O30 2-1	S25 0-2	a01 2-1	J15 0-0	a19 1-0	O09 0-0	F26 0-0	S12 4-1	a08 1-0	A31 1-3	J01 0-3	a29 2-0	S29 2-1	A21 0-1	m07 0-0	N21 0-1	M04 1-2
7 CREWE A	F20 2-1	M01 0-1	a15 0-0	D12 0-0	O31 4-1	S04 0-0		a09 3-1	M26 0-0	a29 0-0	O03 1-1	a01 0-0	S18 3-3	F13 2-1	m07 0-1	J29 0-1	O17 1-0	N21 2-2	O20 3-1	D26 2-2	M11 0-1	S15 0-0	J02 0-2	A29 2-0
8 DARLINGTON	O10 1-0	D28 4-2	N08 0-1	F02 0-0	J09 2-1	M19 2-0	N03 1-0		D08 4-1	F20 4-1	J01 1-1	J17 3-1	a04 2-2	m02 0-2	M15 2-1	M05 2-1	S12 2-1	S26 1-4	A22 1-2	D19 2-0	A31 1-1	O03 0-0	O24 2-2	a23 2-1
9 EXETER C	a09 1-1	O17 1-2	A15 3-0	a02 0-2	S16 1-1	D26 0-2	O24 3-1	a30 4-1		m07 1-2	M02 1-0	M19 2-2	J02 2-3	A29 3-0	M09 0-1	S19 1-1	M12 1-0	D12 1-1	N21 2-1	J09 3-1	O03 0-1	J30 0-1	F13 2-4	S05 1-1
10 HALIFAX T	J12 0-0	N03 2-1	D26 1-1	M01 0-1	a26 1-1	N06 1-2	N27 1-2	A15 2-2	D18 2-0		a23 3-1	O03 2-1	a14 1-0	S05 3-1	O24 0-0	A28 1-2	a04 2-2	M12 2-2	O16 2-0	S16 3-1	m02 2-3	S18 2-1	F16 2-1	F23 2-0
11 HARTLEPOOL U	D26 0-0	M12 2-1	S16 2-1	a30 0-1	J02 0-0	S19 3-1	F27 2-1	A29 2-5	S30 3-1	O21 2-1		m07 1-2	S05 2-2	A15 0-0	a02 0-1	F13 1-1	M26 1-0	O31 1-0	a09 1-3	J30 0-2	O17 0-0	N21 1-2	D12 0-0	J26 1-0
12 HEREFORD U	S05 0-3	m02 2-1	a23 1-0	M13 1-2	J30 2-0	S16 1-0	N07 1-1	S19 1-0	O31 1-1	F27 2-1	D19 4-2		N28 0-3	D26 4-2	S30 0-1	A15 0-0	O21 1-1	O17 2-3	M26 0-1	J02 0-0	a04 0-0	J09 1-1	A29 1-2	F13 0-2
13 LEYTON O	a02 1-2	S01 4-1	O17 0-2	F20 4-1	a09 4-1	M12 0-0	J16 1-1	N20 4-3	S12 2-3	O31 4-1	F06 0-2	a30 4-0		S29 4-1	S26 2-0	O20 8-0	A22 3-1	D28 1-1	J23 1-1	M26 3-0	J01 0-2	D12 3-1	m07 0-2	F27 2-1
14 NEWPORT CO	N03 0-1	A22 0-1	M12 0-0	N21 1-2	a02 1-2	O03 1-2	D28 1-2	J12 2-1	J01 1-1	F05 1-0	F19 2-3	S27 0-0	M01 0-0		a09 0-4	m07 0-1	a12 0-4	J16 1-1	A31 1-2	M05 1-2	S12 3-1	a30 0-3	a26 1-3	O24 2-0
15 PETERBOROUGH U	J30 0-4	N28 5-0	A29 1-0	O17 4-3	A15 1-0	J02 2-0	D18 0-4	S05 1-2	a23 2-1	M26 1-0	N07 0-1	F24 1-2	D26 1-2	O21 3-0		J09 1-1	m02 0-0	O03 1-1	M12 0-0	a04 0-1	O31 0-2	F13 2-1	S16 1-1	S19 1-0
16 ROCHDALE	O24 2-2	S26 2-1	a04 2-1	M29 2-2	O03 1-2	N03 1-4	A31 2-2	O17 1-3	J16 0-0	J01 0-0	D28 0-2	F20 3-1	a23 1-3	D19 3-0	A22 1-1		N28 1-1	F06 2-1	S12 0-1	N07 2-3	J26 1-1	M12 0-0	M01 0-1	m02 1-2
17 SCARBOROUGH	A29 4-0	O03 1-0	F13 0-0	N04 1-1	D26 3-1	J30 3-1	M05 2-0	J02 0-1	O10 3-1	N21 1-1	O24 1-1	a09 2-1	F24 3-1	S16 3-1	D12 1-1	a30 2-1		a02 0-0	m07 1-1	S19 2-0	M02 1-2	S05 2-0	A15 2-2	M19 0-2
18 SCUNTHORPE U	S15 1-1	a23 1-1	J02 3-2	O24 2-1	a12 1-0	A29 2-2	a04 2-1	D26 1-0	m02 1-1	O10 1-0	M19 3-0	M05 3-0	F13 3-2	S19 3-1	F27 5-0	S05 1-0	N07 0-1		S29 0-0	N28 1-2	D18 2-3	A15 3-0	J30 0-1	N03 3-1
19 STOCKPORT CO	F12 1-2	M18 2-0	m02 0-2	O02 0-1	S04 3-0	N27 1-1	a22 1-1	a19 1-1	a04 2-1	M04 1-0	N03 1-0	O23 0-2	S15 1-2	J29 5-1	O10 0-1	J02 1-1	D19 1-1	M01 1-1		A15 0-2	N06 2-1	A28 1-2	S19 0-2	D26 1-1
20 SWANSEA C	M18 1-0	F06 0-0	O03 1-1	J01 2-2	D12 3-1	M01 1-2	S26 2-4	m07 3-0	A22 0-2	J23 1-1	A31 2-1	S12 3-0	O24 3-0	O17 1-2	N21 2-1	a02 0-3	J16 3-0	a30 1-1	F19 1-1		D28 1-1	a09 1-2	N03 1-2	O10 2-1
21 TORQUAY U	S19 2-1	O24 1-3	S05 0-1	a09 2-0	a30 1-0	a15 0-0	O10 1-0	a27 0-0	F27 1-1	D12 1-2	M05 1-1	N21 1-0	A29 1-1	a19 6-1	M19 0-0	S15 5-0	S29 0-1	m07 1-2	a02 3-0	M29 0-1		N03 1-0	F23 0-0	A15 6-1
22 TRANMERE R	D15 2-0	S11 0-1	O30 0-1	S25 0-1	M25 3-0	D18 0-2	a25 2-2	F26 2-1	A31 2-1	J15 2-0	a04 3-1	A21 0-1	m02 2-1	N27 4-0	D28 3-1	O09 6-1	F06 1-0	F20 1-3	J01 4-0	O20 1-2	a22 1-1		M04 3-0	N06 1-0
23 WOLVERHAMPTON W	F27 4-0	N07 3-0	O20 3-0	F06 1-4	M12 3-1	a04 2-0	S12 2-2	M26 5-3	D28 3-0	A22 0-1	m02 2-0	J01 2-0	D19 2-0	O31 2-1	M22 0-1	S29 2-0	F19 0-0	A31 4-1	J16 1-1	a23 2-0	S26 1-2	O17 3-0		N28 0-2
24 WREXHAM	m07 0-1	F02 1-3	M01 3-0	S12 3-0	N21 4-0	O17 0-1	J01 2-1	O20 0-1	M22 3-0	A31 2-2	A22 2-1	D28 0-0	O03 2-2	M26 4-1	J16 3-1	D12 2-3	O31 1-0	a09 2-1	S26 2-1	M12 1-2	F20 2-3	a02 3-0	a30 4-2	

LEAGUE TABLES

DIVISION 1

	P	W	D	L	F	A	W	D	L	F	A	Pts
Liverpool	40	15	5	0	49	9	11	7	2	38	15	90
Manchester U	40	14	5	1	41	17	9	7	4	30	21	81
Nottingham F	40	11	7	2	40	17	9	6	5	27	22	73
Everton	40	14	4	2	34	11	5	9	6	19	16	70
Q.P.R.	40	12	4	4	30	14	7	6	7	18	24	67
Arsenal	40	11	4	5	35	16	7	8	5	23	23	66
Wimbledon	40	8	9	3	32	20	6	6	8	26	27	57
Newcastle U	40	9	6	5	32	23	5	8	7	23	30	56
Luton T	40	11	6	3	40	21	3	5	12	17	37	53
Coventry C	40	6	8	6	23	25	7	6	7	23	28	53
Sheffield W	40	10	2	8	27	30	5	6	9	25	36	53
Southampton	40	6	8	6	27	26	6	6	8	22	27	50
Tottenham H	40	9	5	6	26	23	3	6	11	12	25	47
Norwich C	40	7	5	8	26	26	5	4	11	14	26	45
Derby Co	40	6	7	7	18	17	4	6	10	17	28	43
West Ham U	40	6	9	5	23	21	3	6	11	17	31	42
Charlton A	40	7	7	6	23	21	2	8	10	15	31	42
Chelsea	40	7	11	2	24	17	2	4	14	26	51	42
Portsmouth	40	4	8	8	21	27	3	6	11	15	39	35
Watford	40	4	5	11	15	24	3	6	11	12	27	32
Oxford U	40	5	7	8	24	34	1	6	13	20	46	31

DIVISION 2

	P	W	D	L	F	A	W	D	L	F	A	Pts
Millwall	44	15	3	4	45	23	10	4	8	27	29	82
Aston Villa	44	9	7	6	31	21	13	5	4	37	20	78
Middlesbrough	44	15	4	3	44	16	7	8	7	19	20	78
Bradford C	44	14	3	5	49	26	8	8	6	25	28	77
Blackburn R	44	12	8	2	38	22	9	6	7	30	30	77
Crystal Palace	44	16	3	3	50	21	6	6	10	36	38	75
Leeds U	44	14	4	4	37	18	5	8	9	24	33	69
Ipswich T	44	14	3	5	38	17	5	6	11	23	35	66
Manchester C	44	11	4	7	50	28	8	4	10	30	32	65
Oldham A	44	13	4	5	43	27	5	7	10	29	37	65
Stoke C	44	12	6	4	34	22	5	5	12	16	35	62
Swindon T	44	10	7	5	43	25	6	4	12	30	35	59
Leicester C	44	12	5	5	35	20	4	6	12	27	41	59
Barnsley	44	11	4	7	42	32	4	8	10	19	30	57
Hull C	44	10	8	4	32	22	4	7	11	22	38	57
Plymouth A	44	12	4	6	44	26	4	4	14	21	41	56
Bournemouth	44	7	7	8	36	30	6	3	13	20	38	49
Shrewsbury T	44	7	8	7	23	22	4	8	10	19	32	49
Birmingham C	44	7	9	6	20	24	4	6	12	21	42	48
W.B.A.	44	8	7	7	29	26	4	4	14	21	43	47
Sheffield U	44	8	6	8	27	28	5	1	16	18	46	46
Reading	44	5	7	10	20	25	5	5	12	24	45	42
Huddersfield T	44	4	6	12	20	38	2	4	16	21	62	28

DIVISION 3

	P	W	D	L	F	A	W	D	L	F	A	Pts
Sunderland	46	14	7	2	51	22	13	5	5	41	26	93
Brighton & H.A.	46	15	7	1	37	16	8	8	7	32	31	84
Walsall	46	15	6	2	39	22	8	7	8	29	28	82
Notts Co	46	14	4	5	53	24	9	8	6	29	25	81
Bristol C	46	14	6	3	51	30	7	6	10	26	32	75
Northampton T	46	12	8	3	36	18	6	11	6	34	33	73
Wigan A	46	11	8	4	36	23	9	4	10	34	38	72
Bristol R	46	14	5	4	43	19	4	7	12	25	37	66
Fulham	46	10	5	8	36	24	9	4	10	33	36	66
Blackpool	46	13	4	6	45	27	4	10	9	26	35	65
Port Vale	46	12	8	3	36	19	6	3	14	22	37	65
Brentford	46	9	8	6	27	23	7	6	10	26	36	62
Gillingham	46	8	9	6	45	21	6	8	9	32	40	59
Bury	46	9	7	7	33	26	6	7	10	25	31	59
Chester C	46	9	8	6	29	30	5	8	10	22	32	58
Preston N.E.	46	10	6	7	30	23	5	7	11	18	36	58
Southend U	46	10	6	7	42	33	4	7	12	23	50	55
Chesterfield	46	10	5	8	25	28	5	5	13	16	42	55
Mansfield T	46	10	6	7	25	21	4	6	13	23	38	54
Aldershot	46	12	3	8	45	32	3	5	15	19	42	53
Rotherham U	46	8	8	7	28	25	4	8	11	22	41	52
Grimsby T	46	6	7	10	25	29	6	7	10	23	29	50
York C	46	4	7	12	27	45	4	2	17	21	46	33
Doncaster R	46	6	5	12	25	36	2	4	17	15	48	33

DIVISION 4

	P	W	D	L	F	A	W	D	L	F	A	Pts
Wolverh'pton W	46	15	3	5	47	19	12	6	5	35	24	90
Cardiff C	46	15	6	2	39	14	9	7	7	27	27	85
Bolton W	46	15	6	2	42	12	7	6	10	24	30	78
Torquay U	46	10	7	6	34	16	11	7	5	32	25	77
Scunthorpe U	46	14	5	4	42	20	6	12	5	34	31	77
Swansea C	46	9	7	7	35	28	11	3	9	27	28	70
Peterborough U	46	10	5	8	28	26	10	5	8	24	27	70
Leyton O	46	13	4	6	55	27	6	8	9	30	36	69
Colchester U	46	10	5	8	23	22	9	5	9	24	29	67
Burnley	46	12	5	6	31	22	8	2	13	26	40	67
Wrexham	46	13	3	7	46	26	7	3	13	23	32	66
Scarborough	46	12	8	3	38	19	5	6	12	18	29	65
Darlington	46	13	6	4	39	25	5	5	13	32	44	65
Tranmere R	46	14	2	7	43	20	5	7	11	18	33	*64
Cambridge U	46	10	6	7	32	24	6	7	10	18	28	61
Hartlepool U	46	9	7	7	25	25	6	7	10	25	32	59
Crewe A	46	7	11	5	25	19	6	8	9	32	34	58
Halifax T	46	11	7	5	37	25	3	7	13	17	34	†55
Hereford U	46	8	7	8	25	27	6	5	12	16	32	54
Stockport Co	46	7	7	9	26	26	5	8	10	18	32	51
Rochdale	46	5	9	9	28	34	6	6	11	19	42	48
Exeter C	46	8	6	9	33	29	3	7	13	20	39	46
Carlisle U	46	9	5	9	38	33	3	3	17	19	53	44
Newport Co	46	4	5	14	19	36	2	2	19	16	69	25

*Two points deducted for failing to meet a fixture. †One point deducted for fielding an unregistered player

Top scorers: Div 1, A.Smith (Arsenal) 23 goals; Div 2, K.Edwards (Hull City) 26 goals; Div 3, S.Bull (Wolverhampton Wanderers) 37 goals; Div 4, P.Stant (Hereford United) 28 goals.

Play-offs: Div 1, Blackburn Rovers v Watford 0-0, 1-1; Swindon Town v Crystal Palace 1-0, 0-2; Blackburn Rovers v Crystal Palace 3-1 0-3; Div 2, Bristol Rovers v Fulham 1-0, 4-0; Preston North End v Port Vale 1-1, 1-3; Bristol Rovers v Port Vale 1-1, 0-1; Div 3, Leyton Orient v Scarborough 2-0, 0-1; Wrexham v Scunthorpe United 3-1, 2-0; Wrexham v Leyton Orient 0-0, 1-2.

Chelsea, Crystal Palace and Manchester City promoted to

Alan Smith was Arsenal's top scorer with 23 goals when the Gunners won the Championship from Liverpool in the most dramatic fashion in 1988-89.

DIVISION 1

	ARSENAL	ASTON VILLA	CHARLTON A	COVENTRY C	DERBY CO	EVERTON	LIVERPOOL	LUTON T	MANCHESTER U	MIDDLESBROUGH	MILLWALL	NEWCASTLE U	NORWICH C	NOTTINGHAM F	Q.P.R.	SHEFFIELD W	SOUTHAMPTON	TOTTENHAM H	WEST HAM U	WIMBLEDON
1 ARSENAL		S03 2-3	M21 2-2	O29 2-0	m13 1-2	a08 2-0	D04 1-1	F25 2-0	D17 2-1	N19 3-0	F28 0-0	a15 1-0	m01 5-0	M11 1-3	O22 2-1	J21 1-1	S17 2-2	J02 2-0	F04 2-1	m17 2-2
2 ASTON VILLA	D31 0-3		F25 1-2	m13 1-1	N19 1-2	O22 2-0	S10 1-1	a01 2-1	M12 0-0	a29 1-1	A27 2-2	J14 3-1	D03 3-1	S24 1-1	D26 2-1	F04 2-0	m02 1-2	O29 2-1	M25 0-1	O08 0-1
3 CHARLTON A	D26 2-3	O15 2-2		M25 0-0	m10 3-0	N12 1-2	A27 0-3	J14 3-0	a22 1-0	a01 2-0	S10 0-3	S24 2-2	F04 1-2	N26 0-1	D10 1-1	O29 2-1	M11 2-2	O08 2-2	D31 0-0	m06 1-0
4 COVENTRY C	F21 1-0	N26 2-1	S17 3-0		D17 0-2	S03 0-1	M22 1-3	N12 1-0	D10 1-0	O01 3-4	O15 0-0	F11 1-2	a08 2-1	m15 2-2	a22 0-3	J02 5-0	M27 2-1	M18 1-1	N05 1-1	J21 2-1
5 DERBY CO	N26 2-1	m06 2-1	O22 0-0	a01 1-0		F25 3-2	D26 0-1	D10 0-1	N12 2-2	A27 1-0	D31 0-1	S10 2-0	O08 0-1	M25 0-2	S24 0-1	a22 1-0	F04 3-1	M11 1-1	J14 1-2	O29 4-1
6 EVERTON	J14 1-3	F14 1-1	a10 3-2	D31 3-1	m15 1-0		m03 0-0	S24 0-2	O30 1-1	D26 2-1	M25 1-1	A27 4-0	N19 1-1	S10 1-1	a01 4-1	M11 1-0	O08 4-1	D03 1-0	m13 3-1	F04 1-1
7 LIVERPOOL	m26 0-2	J03 1-0	M01 2-0	O22 0-0	M29 1-0	D11 1-1		M14 5-0	S03 1-0	N05 3-0	N12 1-1	O01 1-2	D17 0-1	m10 1-0	m16 2-0	a08 5-1	J21 2-0	S17 1-1	m23 5-1	N26 1-1
8 LUTON T	O25 1-1	D17 1-1	m02 5-2	a15 2-2	a29 3-0	J21 1-0	O08 1-0		S17 0-2	F18 1-0	M11 1-2	D03 0-0	m13 1-0	F04 2-3	O29 0-0	M18 0-1	J02 6-1	M28 1-3	N19 4-1	S03 2-2
9 MANCHESTER U	a02 1-1	N05 1-1	D03 3-0	a29 0-1	a15 0-2	m10 1-2	J01 3-1	M25 2-0		S10 1-0	J14 3-0	m13 2-0	O26 1-2	D26 2-0	A27 0-0	N23 1-1	N19 2-2	F05 1-0	S24 2-0	m02 1-0
10 MIDDLESBROUGH	m06 0-1	D10 3-3	D17 0-0	F04 1-1	M18 0-1	M27 3-3	M11 0-4	O22 2-1	J02 1-0		O29 4-2	F26 1-1	S03 2-3	a22 3-4	N12 1-0	N26 0-1	a08 3-3	J21 2-2	O08 1-0	S17 1-0
11 MILLWALL	F11 1-2	M18 2-0	J02 1-0	F25 1-0	S03 1-0	S17 2-1	a11 1-2	N05 3-1	a08 0-0	F21 2-0		N19 4-0	J22 2-3	O22 2-2	O01 3-2	D17 1-0	m13 1-1	a29 0-5	D03 0-1	M27 0-1
12 NEWCASTLE U	N12 0-1	a08 1-2	J21 0-2	O08 0-3	J02 0-1	M22 2-0	F04 2-2	a22 0-0	N27 0-0	O26 3-0	m06 1-1		S17 0-2	O29 0-1	M11 1-2	M27 1-3	D17 3-3	S03 2-2	m03 1-2	D10 2-1
13 NORWICH C	D10 0-0	a22 2-2	O01 1-3	J14 1-2	F11 1-0	m06 1-0	a01 0-1	N26 2-2	F25 2-1	D31 0-0	S24 2-2	M25 0-2		A27 2-1	S10 1-0	N12 1-1	O29 1-1	O22 3-1	D27 2-1	M11 1-0
14 NOTTINGHAM F	N06 1-4	J21 4-0	m13 4-0	N19 0-0	S17 1-1	J02 2-0	O26 2-1	O01 0-0	M27 2-0	D03 2-2	m03 4-1	M15 1-1	a05 2-0		F11 0-0	S03 1-1	a12 3-0	M22 1-2	m18 1-2	D18 0-1
15 Q.P.R.	F18 0-0	M27 1-0	a29 1-0	D03 2-1	J21 0-1	D17 0-0	N19 0-1	M21 1-1	m08 3-2	a15 0-0	F04 1-2	N05 3-0	J02 1-1	O08 1-2		S17 2-0	S03 0-1	m13 1-0	O15 2-1	a08 4-3
16 SHEFFIELD W	S24 2-1	O01 1-0	M04 3-1	S10 1-2	D03 1-1	N05 1-1	J14 2-2	A27 1-0	F11 0-2	m13 1-0	a01 3-0	D26 1-2	m17 2-2	D31 0-3	M25 0-2		F18 1-1	N20 0-2	m09 0-2	a05 1-1
17 SOUTHAMPTON	M25 1-3	N12 3-1	N05 2-0	D26 2-2	O01 0-0	F11 1-1	S24 1-3	S10 2-1	m06 2-1	J14 1-3	N26 2-2	a01 1-0	a19 0-0	D10 1-1	D31 1-4	O22 1-2		F25 0-2	A27 4-0	a22 0-0
18 TOTTENHAM H	S10 2-3	M01 2-0	F11 1-1	N23 1-1	N05 1-3	a22 2-1	M26 1-2	D26 0-0	O01 2-2	S24 3-2	D10 2-0	D31 2-0	F21 2-1	J15 1-2	N26 2-2	a12 0-0	O25 1-2		a01 3-0	N12 3-2
19 WEST HAM U	O01 1-4	S17 2-2	S03 1-3	M11 1-1	a08 1-1	N26 0-1	O29 0-2	m06 1-0	J21 1-3	a11 1-2	a22 3-0	O22 2-0	M27 0-2	N12 3-3	F25 0-0	D10 0-0	a15 1-2	D17 0-2		J02 1-2
20 WIMBLEDON	A27 1-5	F11 1-0	N19 1-1	S24 0-1	M01 4-0	O01 2-1	m13 1-2	D31 4-0	O22 1-1	M25 1-1	D26 1-0	a29 4-0	N05 0-2	a01 4-1	J14 1-0	F25 1-0	D03 2-1	a15 1-2	S10 0-1	

Kerry Dixon, the former Reading striker who helped Chelsea back to Division One in 1988-89.

DIVISION 2

	BARNSLEY	BIRMINGHAM C	BLACKBURN R	BOURNEMOUTH	BRADFORD C	BRIGHTON & HA	CHELSEA	CRYSTAL P	HULL C	IPSWICH T	LEEDS U	LEICESTER C	MANCHESTER C	OLDHAM A	OXFORD U	PLYMOUTH A	PORTSMOUTH	SHREWSBURY T	STOKE C	SUNDERLAND	SWINDON T	WALSALL	WATFORD	W.B.A.
1 BARNSLEY		a15 0-0	F25 0-1	N26 5-2	N12 0-0	F04 2-2	S17 1-1	M11 1-1	J02 0-2	O22 2-0	M19 2-2	D17 3-0	S24 1-2	J21 4-3	m01 1-0	O29 3-1	m06 1-0	a08 1-0	S03 1-0	M27 3-0	A29 1-1	D10 1-0	F28 2-2	O08 2-1
2 BIRMINGHAM C	O01 3-5		a22 2-0	F11 0-1	m01 1-0	a08 1-2	D16 1-4	D10 0-1	m06 1-0	N26 1-0	N22 0-0	S03 2-3	F18 0-2	J02 0-0	M04 0-0	O04 0-1	N05 0-0	M27 1-2	O25 0-1	S17 3-2	a18 1-2	M18 1-0	J21 2-3	O15 1-4
3 BLACKBURN R	O15 2-1	S24 3-0		m01 2-0	F04 2-1	N12 2-1	J21 1-1	O08 5-4	M18 4-0	D10 1-0	M27 2-0	a08 0-0	a15 4-0	S03 3-1	F21 3-1	M11 1-2	N26 3-1	N22 0-1	J02 4-3	F28 2-2	S17 0-0	m06 3-0	D17 2-1	O29 1-2
4 BOURNEMOUTH	a29 3-2	O08 0-1	D03 2-1		M11 3-0	J02 2-1	S03 1-0	N12 2-0	N29 5-1	O29 1-0	S17 0-0	M27 2-1	N19 0-1	F28 2-2	S24 2-1	m13 0-0	F25 1-0	O21 0-1	a15 0-1	J21 0-1	M18 2-3	D17 2-1	a08 0-1	F04 2-1
5 BRADFORD C	M04 1-2	D03 2-2	O05 1-1	N15 0-1		J21 0-1	N19 2-2	O15 0-1	M27 1-1	a15 2-2	O26 1-1	a29 2-1	m13 1-1	S17 2-0	M15 0-0	F11 1-1	O01 2-1	S03 1-0	A29 0-0	J02 1-0	D17 2-2	a08 3-1	M18 2-1	F18 2-0
6 BRIGHTON & H.A.	O05 0-1	D31 4-0	M04 3-0	S10 1-2	A27 1-3		M15 0-1	D26 3-1	m01 1-1	m06 0-1	O01 2-1	F11 1-1	a01 2-1	O22 2-0	M25 2-1	J14 2-2	a05 2-1	N05 3-1	D10 1-1	N26 3-0	a22 0-2	O26 2-2	F25 1-0	S21 0-1
7 CHELSEA	a01 5-3	a04 3-1	A27 1-2	M25 2-0	m06 3-1	O29 2-0		J14 1-0	F28 2-1	D26 3-0	a22 1-0	O01 2-1	S20 1-3	F25 2-2	S10 1-1	O22 5-0	D10 3-3	N26 2-0	m01 2-1	N12 1-1	F11 3-2	O04 2-0	M11 2-2	D31 1-1
8 CRYSTAL P	N05 1-1	m13 4-1	F11 2-2	M04 2-3	F25 2-0	M27 2-1	A30 1-1		O22 3-1	O04 2-0	D17 0-0	N19 4-2	D03 0-0	a08 2-0	O25 1-0	O01 4-1	a15 2-0	S17 1-1	m09 1-0	M18 1-0	J21 2-1	J02 4-0	S03 0-2	a29 1-0
9 HULL C	S10 0-0	N19 1-1	S20 1-3	J14 4-0	D26 1-1	D03 5-2	O25 3-0	a11 0-1		D31 1-1	M14 1-2	O04 2-2	A27 1-0	a22 1-1	a04 1-2	M25 3-0	a01 1-1	F11 3-0	M04 1-4	O15 0-0	N05 1-0	O01 0-0	a29 0-3	m13 0-1
10 IPSWICH T	F21 2-0	a29 4-0	m13 2-0	M14 3-1	S24 1-1	N19 2-3	M28 0-1	F04 1-2	a08 1-1		N05 0-1	J02 2-0	O08 1-0	D16 2-1	O15 1-2	D03 2-2	O25 0-1	M18 2-0	J21 5-1	S03 2-0	M04 1-2	N08 3-1	S17 3-2	a22 2-1
11 LEEDS U	S21 2-0	J14 1-0	D26 2-0	a01 3-0	M01 3-3	a15 1-0	S24 0-2	a05 1-2	O29 2-1	M11 2-4		O22 1-1	S10 1-1	m06 0-0	A27 1-1	D31 2-0	M25 1-0	D10 2-3	N26 4-0	F04 2-0	F25 0-0	m01 1-0	O08 0-1	N12 2-1
12 LEICESTER C	a11 0-1	M25 2-0	D31 4-0	D26 0-1	N26 1-0	O08 1-0	a15 2-0	m06 2-2	F04 0-2	S10 0-1	F18 1-2		N05 0-0	m01 1-2	a01 1-0	S21 1-0	J14 2-1	M15 1-1	O15 2-0	D10 3-1	O26 3-3	M04 1-0	S24 2-2	A27 1-1
13 MANCHESTER C	a22 1-2	O22 0-0	O01 1-0	m06 3-3	D10 4-0	S17 2-1	M18 2-3	m01 1-1	J21 4-1	F11 4-0	J02 0-0	M11 4-2		A29 1-4	N26 2-1	F25 2-0	O05 4-1	D17 2-2	M27 2-1	O29 1-1	a08 2-1	S03 2-2	N12 3-1	M01 1-1
14 OLDHAM A	A27 1-1	S10 4-0	M24 1-1	O25 2-0	a01 1-1	F18 2-1	O15 1-4	D30 2-3	S24 2-2	a04 4-0	N19 2-2	D03 1-1	J14 0-1		S20 3-0	a29 2-2	M14 5-3	M03 3-0	O08 2-2	a15 2-2	m13 2-2	N05 3-0	F04 3-1	D26 1-3
15 OXFORD U	D03 2-0	N12 3-0	O22 1-1	a22 3-1	O29 3-4	S03 3-2	J02 2-3	M01 1-0	A29 1-0	F25 1-1	J21 3-2	S17 1-1	a29 2-4	M18 1-1		N19 0-1	F11 1-0	O01 4-1	a08 3-2	N02 2-4	O05 1-1	M27 1-0	m13 0-4	M11 1-1
16 PLYMOUTH A	a25 1-2	F04 0-1	N05 4-3	D10 1-1	O08 3-1	D06 3-0	F18 0-1	a22 0-2	S03 2-0	m01 0-1	a09 1-0	M18 1-1	O15 0-1	N26 3-0	m06 3-1		M04 0-1	O25 0-0	S17 4-0	D18 1-4	M27 4-1	J21 2-0	J02 1-0	S24 1-1
17 PORTSMOUTH	N19 3-0	M11 1-0	a29 1-2	O15 2-1	a22 1-2	D17 2-0	m13 2-3	S24 1-1	S17 1-3	F28 0-1	S03 4-0	A29 3-0	F04 0-1	O29 1-1	O08 2-1	N12 2-0		J21 2-0	M18 0-0	a08 2-0	J02 0-2	F18 1-1	M27 2-2	D03 0-0
18 SHREWSBURY T	D31 2-3	D26 0-0	J14 1-1	a11 1-0	M25 1-3	M11 1-1	a29 1-1	a01 2-1	O08 1-3	S20 1-5	m13 3-3	O29 3-0	a04 0-1	N11 0-0	a15 2-2	F28 2-0	A27 1-2		F04 1-2	S24 0-0	D03 0-1	O15 0-0	N19 1-1	S10 1-1
19 STOKE C	M25 1-1	F28 1-0	S10 0-1	O01 2-1	J14 2-1	m13 2-2	D03 0-3	O29 2-1	N13 4-0	A27 1-1	a29 2-3	F25 2-2	D26 3-1	F11 0-0	D31 1-0	a01 2-2	S20 2-2	O04 0-0		M11 2-0	N19 2-1	a22 0-3	O22 2-0	a04 0-0
20 SUNDERLAND	D26 1-0	a01 2-2	O25 2-0	A27 1-1	S10 0-0	a29 1-0	M21 1-2	S20 1-1	F25 2-0	M25 4-0	O04 2-1	m13 2-2	M14 2-4	O01 3-2	J14 1-0	a04 2-1	D31 4-0	a22 2-1	N05 1-1		O22 4-0	F11 0-3	D03 1-1	N19 1-1
21 SWINDON T	J14 0-0	O29 2-1	a01 1-1	S20 3-1	a04 1-0	S24 3-0	O09 1-1	a25 1-0	M11 1-0	N12 2-3	O16 0-0	F28 2-1	D31 1-2	D10 2-2	F05 3-0	D26 1-0	S11 1-1	m01 1-0	m06 3-0	F18 4-1		N26 1-0	a15 1-1	M25 0-0
22 WALSALL	m13 1-3	S20 5-0	N19 1-2	a04 1-1	D31 0-1	F28 1-0	F04 0-7	S10 0-0	a15 1-1	J14 2-4	D03 0-3	N12 0-1	M25 3-3	M11 2-2	D26 1-5	A27 2-2	O22 1-1	F25 1-1	S24 1-2	O08 2-0	a29 2-2		O29 0-1	a01 0-0
23 WATFORD	O25 4-0	A27 1-0	a04 2-2	D31 1-0	S20 2-0	O15 1-1	N05 1-2	M24 0-1	N26 2-0	a01 3-2	F11 1-1	a22 2-1	M04 1-0	O04 3-1	D10 1-1	S10 3-0	D26 1-0	m06 0-0	a11 3-2	m01 0-1	O01 2-3	a18 5-0		J14 2-0
24 W.B.A.	F11 1-1	F25 0-0	M15 2-0	O05 0-0	O22 1-0	M18 1-0	a08 2-3	N26 5-3	D10 2-0	O01 1-2	M05 2-1	J21 1-1	O26 1-0	M27 3-1	N05 3-2	a15 2-2	m01 3-0	J02 4-0	D18 6-0	m06 0-0	S03 3-1	S17 0-0	A29 0-1	

Season 1988-89

Div 1; Middlesbrough, Newcastle United and West Ham United relegated to Div 2; Port Vale, Sheffield United and Wolverhampton Wanderers promoted to Div 2; Birmingham City Shrewsbury Town and Walsall relegated to Div 3; Crewe Alexandra, Leyton Orient, Rotherham United and Tranmere Rovers promoted to Div 3; Darlington were relegated from Division Four and replaced by Maidstone United.

DIVISION 3

	ALDERSHOT	BLACKPOOL	BOLTON W	BRENTFORD	BRISTOL C	BRISTOL R	BURY	CARDIFF C	CHESTER C	CHESTERFIELD	FULHAM	GILLINGHAM	HUDDERSFIELD T	MANSFIELD T	NORTHAMPTON T	NOTTS CO	PORT VALE	PRESTON N.E.	READING	SHEFFIELD U	SOUTHEND U	SWANSEA C	WIGAN A	WOLVERHAMPTON W
1 ALDERSHOT		a29 1-0	S24 0-3	D18 0-0	F21 0-1	J21 1-3	a08 4-1	J02 0-1	O29 1-1	M18 2-0	a25 1-2	S03 0-2	O22 0-1	m13 0-0	F04 5-1	D03 2-3	M11 2-2	J07 2-1	M27 1-1	N08 1-0	S17 2-2	O09 0-1	O04 3-1	a15 1-2
2 BLACKPOOL	N12 4-0		F18 2-0	M27 0-3	S20 2-2	D17 1-1	J02 2-2	O29 1-0	M18 1-1	a22 1-2	M11 0-1	m01 4-1	m06 2-1	S17 1-1	O04 3-1	S03 0-1	O22 3-2	J21 1-0	a08 2-4	O15 1-2	m09 3-2	N26 0-0	F04 2-0	F28 0-2
3 BOLTON W	a22 1-0	O08 2-2		m06 4-2	M11 2-0	S17 1-1	N12 2-4	S03 4-0	D17 0-1	O29 5-0	S20 3-2	J06 2-1	m01 3-1	J02 0-0	N26 2-1	a08 3-3	a25 1-1	M27 1-0	J21 1-1	O01 2-0	M18 0-0	F11 1-0	m09 1-1	O22 1-2
4 BRENTFORD	a01 2-1	D26 1-0	D03 3-0		a04 3-0	a15 2-1	F25 2-2	m13 1-1	F11 0-1	F28 1-0	M24 0-1	O01 1-0	A27 1-0	a29 1-0	J14 2-0	N08 2-1	O29 2-1	O22 0-2	M11 3-2	S24 1-4	O09 4-0	m09 1-1	S10 1-1	D31 2-2
5 BRISTOL C	O25 1-1	a15 1-2	N05 1-1	a11 0-1		J02 0-1	M27 3-0	D17 2-0	J21 0-1	S03 4-0	O08 1-5	F11 1-0	a18 6-1	M21 2-0	M04 3-1	M18 0-4	S24 0-1	S17 1-1	D03 2-1	m13 2-0	a08 0-2	O01 2-0	a29 0-1	N08 0-1
6 BRISTOL R	S10 2-2	a01 1-0	J28 2-0	S21 1-2	M25 1-1		N26 1-3	F04 0-1	O22 4-1	M11 2-1	m06 0-0	N12 2-0	O29 5-1	F18 0-0	a22 1-1	O15 2-0	a05 2-2	O05 1-0	M01 1-1	J14 1-1	m01 1-1	D31 1-1	A27 3-2	D26 0-0
7 BURY	D31 0-1	M25 0-0	a29 0-0	O15 3-1	D26 2-1	m13 0-0		a15 1-0	N08 2-1	F04 2-1	J28 3-1	M04 1-0	a01 0-6	S24 0-1	a04 0-1	N05 1-1	S10 0-0	F18 1-1	O04 2-1	M14 1-2	O25 3-1	J14 1-0	D03 1-1	A27 3-1
8 CARDIFF C	M25 3-2	m16 0-0	J14 1-0	N25 1-0	a01 1-1	O01 2-2	N01 3-0		m09 2-0	m01 0-1	A27 1-2	N05 1-0	S10 3-0	M04 0-0	N12 1-0	a18 0-1	J28 3-0	m05 0-0	O08 1-2	F11 0-0	a22 2-0	D26 2-2	D30 2-2	a04 1-1
9 CHESTER C	M15 1-1	A27 1-1	a01 0-0	O05 3-2	S10 2-0	M04 0-2	m01 2-0	O15 0-0		N12 3-1	a05 7-0	m06 2-0	S24 3-0	O26 0-0	D31 2-1	F18 1-0	J14 1-2	a22 0-1	F04 3-0	a19 0-1	N26 2-4	N05 3-1	D26 1-0	M25 1-1
10 CHESTERFIELD	A27 2-1	S24 0-2	M14 1-1	O25 2-2	J14 1-0	N05 0-3	O01 1-2	M21 4-0	a29 1-2		D31 4-1	F18 3-1	D26 1-1	D03 1-3	J28 1-1	F11 3-0	a15 1-2	O15 0-3	m13 2-4	M25 2-1	M04 2-1	a01 2-0	a04 1-1	S10 0-3
11 FULHAM	O15 5-1	N05 1-1	a15 1-1	J02 3-3	F18 3-1	D03 0-2	S17 1-0	M18 2-0	J07 4-1	a08 2-1		M27 1-2	F04 1-2	J21 1-1	O25 3-2	M14 2-1	m13 1-2	D17 2-1	N08 2-1	a29 2-2	S03 1-0	M04 1-0	S24 1-1	O05 2-2
12 GILLINGHAM	J14 1-1	N08 1-0	a04 0-1	F04 0-0	O04 0-1	a28 2-3	O22 3-4	M11 1-2	D03 0-2	O08 0-1	D26 0-1		J28 1-2	a15 3-0	a01 1-0	m13 2-1	D30 1-0	F28 1-3	S24 0-1	S10 2-1	F25 1-1	A27 2-3	M24 2-1	O29 1-3
13 HUDDERSFIELD T	M04 2-1	D03 1-1	N08 0-1	a25 1-2	O15 0-1	M14 2-3	D17 3-2	J21 1-0	a15 3-1	M27 1-1	O01 2-0	S17 1-1		a08 2-0	F18 1-2	S20 3-1	F11 0-0	S03 2-0	M07 2-2	N05 3-2	J02 3-2	O25 1-1	m13 1-1	a29 0-0
14 MANSFIELD T	N26 1-1	J28 0-1	M25 1-1	N12 1-0	O29 2-2	O08 2-1	a22 1-1	O22 2-2	F28 2-0	m06 3-1	S10 3-1	S20 2-1	D31 1-0		A27 1-1	O01 1-1	D26 0-1	M11 0-3	F25 2-1	a04 0-1	F11 4-0	m02 0-0	J14 0-1	a01 3-1
15 NORTHAMPTON T	O01 6-0	F11 4-2	m13 2-3	S03 1-0	O22 1-3	S24 1-2	J07 2-0	a29 3-0	a08 0-2	S17 3-0	F28 2-1	D18 1-2	O08 1-3	M18 2-1		J21 1-3	N08 1-3	J02 1-0	O29 1-3	a15 1-2	M27 2-2	F25 1-0	M11 1-1	D04 3-1
16 NOTTS CO	m06 4-1	J14 1-1	D31 2-0	m01 3-0	A27 0-0	F25 1-0	M11 3-0	F28 2-0	O09 2-2	O04 4-0	O29 0-1	N26 1-2	a22 3-0	F04 2-1	S10 0-1		M25 1-4	S24 0-0	O22 3-3	D26 1-4	N12 1-1	a04 1-0	a01 1-0	J29 1-1
17 PORT VALE	F13 3-0	M04 1-0	O15 2-1	M13 3-2	a21 0-1	m09 1-0	J21 1-3	S17 6-1	S03 1-2	S19 5-0	N26 3-0	a08 2-1	O03 2-0	M27 1-2	m01 1-2	J02 1-0		M18 1-1	D17 3-0	O24 3-3	m06 2-0	N12 2-1	F18 2-1	F04 0-0
18 PRESTON N.E.	a04 2-2	S10 1-0	D26 3-1	M04 5-3	J28 2-0	F11 1-1	O08 1-0	D03 3-3	S20 3-3	F25 6-0	a01 1-4	O25 5-0	J14 1-0	N05 2-0	M25 3-2	a15 3-0	A27 1-3		a29 2-1	D31 2-0	O01 3-2	M14 1-1	N08 2-2	m13 3-3
19 READING	D26 3-1	D30 2-1	S10 1-1	N05 2-2	m05 1-2	O26 3-1	F11 1-1	F18 3-1	O01 3-1	N26 0-0	m01 0-1	a22 1-2	a05 2-1	O15 1-0	M15 1-1	M04 1-3	a01 3-0	N12 2-2		A27 1-3	S21 4-0	M25 2-0	a19 0-3	J14 0-2
20 SHEFFIELD U	m01 1-0	F25 4-1	F04 4-0	a22 2-2	N26 3-0	S03 4-1	O29 2-1	a11 0-1	S17 6-1	J02 1-3	N12 1-0	J21 4-2	M11 5-1	a25 1-2	S20 4-0	M27 1-1	F28 0-0	a08 3-1	M18 1-0		D17 1-2	m06 5-1	O22 2-1	O08 2-0
21 SOUTHEND U	J28 1-1	a04 2-1	A27 2-0	a18 1-1	D31 1-2	N08 2-2	F28 1-1	S23 0-0	m13 1-0	O22 3-1	J13 0-0	O15 2-1	M25 2-4	O04 1-1	D26 2-1	a28 1-1	D02 1-1	F03 2-1	a14 2-1	M31 2-1		S10 0-2	O28 1-2	M10 3-1
22 SWANSEA C	F17 1-0	m13 1-2	O04 1-0	S17 1-1	F03 1-1	a08 1-2	S03 1-1	M27 1-1	M11 1-1	D17 2-0	O22 2-0	M19 3-2	M22 1-0	N08 3-1	O15 1-0	J07 2-0	a29 0-0	O29 1-1	J02 2-0	D03 2-2	J21 2-0		a15 1-2	S24 2-5
23 WIGAN A	F11 2-1	S30 2-1	O25 1-1	J21 1-1	N12 0-1	m03 3-0	m06 1-0	a07 1-0	M27 3-0	J07 0-2	a22 0-1	J02 3-0	N26 0-2	S03 0-0	N05 1-3	D18 0-1	O08 0-2	m01 1-1	S17 3-0	M04 1-2	D10 3-0	N01 1-2		m16 1-1
24 WOLVERHAMPTON W	S20 1-0	O25 2-1	M04 1-0	a08 2-0	m01 2-0	M27 0-1	M18 4-0	J10 2-0	J02 3-1	J21 1-0	F11 5-2	M14 6-1	N12 4-1	D17 6-2	m06 3-2	S17 0-0	O01 3-3	N26 6-0	S03 2-1	m09 2-2	N05 3-0	a22 1-1	O15 2-1	

DIVISION 4

	BURNLEY	CAMBRIDGE U	CARLISLE U	COLCHESTER U	CREWE A	DARLINGTON	DONCASTER R	EXETER C	GRIMSBY T	HALIFAX T	HARTLEPOOL U	HEREFORD U	LEYTON O	LINCOLN C	PETERBOROUGH U	ROCHDALE	ROTHERHAM U	SCARBOROUGH	SCUNTHORPE U	STOCKPORT CO	TORQUAY U	TRANMERE R	WREXHAM	YORK C
1 BURNLEY		O29 2-0	M21 0-0	S24 2-0	a04 1-0	a15 0-1	a29 3-0	O08 3-0	D31 1-0	J14 2-1	D03 0-0	a01 3-3	O22 2-2	N08 1-4	F25 1-1	A27 2-1	O04 1-0	m13 0-1	M11 0-1	J28 1-0	F04 1-0	M25 2-2	D26 1-3	S10 6-0
2 CAMBRIDGE U	M14 2-1		S30 3-2	M05 3-1	a22 1-1	m02 1-3	D26 0-0	N04 2-0	A27 4-1	O08 2-1	F11 6-0	J14 2-1	N26 2-2	S20 2-3	M25 2-1	D30 2-0	N12 1-1	O25 2-2	F25 0-3	S10 1-0	m06 3-0	J28 1-1	M31 2-0	a04 1-1
3 CARLISLE U	O25 0-0	a15 1-1		O04 1-2	M25 0-1	N12 1-2	a04 0-1	M04 1-0	N26 2-1	J28 3-1	a01 2-1	F18 3-0	m01 2-1	M14 2-1	A27 2-2	D26 1-0	S24 0-2	N05 0-1	F04 0-3	D31 1-1	O15 2-1	S10 1-1	m06 1-2	J14 0-0
4 COLCHESTER U	F10 2-2	O21 1-2	a21 1-1		M10 2-1	N25 1-2	S09 0-1	m05 4-0	M24 0-0	m01 3-2	D30 1-2	a04 1-1	F24 1-0	O01 1-3	D26 1-2	M31 3-0	F28 1-1	S20 3-1	O08 1-2	O28 1-1	N11 2-2	J13 2-3	a25 2-1	A27 1-0
5 CREWE A	m09 4-0	O04 2-0	J02 1-0	N04 3-1		S17 2-0	O15 0-2	M14 2-1	O25 2-2	m05 2-2	M04 3-0	F04 2-1	J21 2-1	M18 2-0	N25 1-1	a14 3-1	M27 1-3	a08 1-1	S03 3-2	S23 1-1	D16 0-0	N12 2-1	F17 2-2	m01 1-2
6 DARLINGTON	O01 1-1	N08 1-1	m13 2-3	a29 1-2	J28 1-1		N05 1-3	S20 2-2	a04 1-1	D26 0-2	J14 0-0	D31 0-0	F11 1-3	M04 2-1	S10 2-2	M14 1-2	O08 1-1	a22 2-1	D03 3-3	A27 1-4	O25 0-0	a01 1-2	M25 2-1	F25 2-2
7 DONCASTER R	N26 1-0	M27 1-1	J10 1-3	M18 3-1	F24 0-1	M10 1-0		S03 2-1	m01 2-3	O21 1-4	O08 1-0	O04 3-2	O29 1-0	a08 0-1	N12 2-3	F04 1-1	J21 1-0	J02 3-1	D17 2-2	a14 2-2	S16 1-2	m06 0-0	S24 2-2	F28 1-2
8 EXETER C	F18 3-0	M11 0-3	O22 3-0	D03 4-2	O29 1-2	F04 2-1	J14 3-0		O15 2-1	S10 4-1	a29 2-1	D26 3-1	M01 1-1	m13 0-1	a01 3-1	J28 5-1	a15 0-0	N09 1-0	S24 2-2	M25 2-2	O05 3-0	a05 0-1	A27 0-2	D31 2-0
9 GRIMSBY T	a08 1-0	J21 4-0	a29 0-0	J02 2-2	F28 0-0	F14 0-0	N08 5-0	F25 2-1		O29 3-2	m13 3-0	a15 1-1	D17 2-2	M27 1-0	O08 0-0	S24 1-3	S17 0-4	D03 2-1	M18 1-1	M11 2-0	S03 1-0	O04 0-0	F04 0-1	O22 2-0
10 HALIFAX T	S03 1-2	F17 0-0	S16 3-3	N08 3-2	D02 0-1	M27 1-0	M03 2-0	M17 0-3	M14 2-1		N04 1-0	m13 2-2	F14 2-2	a29 0-1	O25 5-0	O14 4-1	a07 1-1	D17 0-2	J02 5-1	F04 2-2	J20 2-0	S23 2-3	O04 4-0	a14 0-0
11 HARTLEPOOL U	m06 2-2	S24 3-2	D17 0-2	a08 2-1	O22 0-3	S03 2-1	F18 2-1	N26 2-2	N12 2-1	M11 2-0		O29 1-1	S17 1-0	J21 3-2	m01 2-1	O04 0-1	J02 1-1	a11 3-1	M27 0-2	F28 2-2	M18 0-1	a15 2-2	O15 1-3	F04 0-1
12 HEREFORD U	D17 0-0	S03 4-2	O08 2-1	a12 1-1	S21 0-1	a08 1-1	a22 3-1	M27 1-0	O01 2-1	N12 3-1	M15 2-0		M18 1-1	F11 3-2	M04 4-0	O26 4-4	N26 1-1	S17 1-3	J21 1-2	F25 2-1	J02 1-1	m01 2-1	N05 0-0	m06 1-2
13 LEYTON O	M04 3-0	a29 1-1	N08 2-0	O15 8-0	A27 0-0	S23 1-0	M14 4-0	O25 4-0	a01 5-0	a04 2-0	M21 4-3	S10 1-3		D03 3-1	N05 1-2	M25 3-0	F04 3-1	F18 2-3	m13 4-1	J14 1-2	a15 3-1	D26 2-0	D31 0-1	O04 4-0
14 LINCOLN C	m01 2-3	F04 3-0	O29 0-2	a15 1-1	S10 2-2	O22 3-2	D28 3-1	N12 2-0	D26 2-2	N26 2-1	A27 0-1	S24 2-0	m06 0-1		J28 1-1	a05 4-1	M11 0-1	O15 2-2	O05 1-0	a01 0-0	F18 1-0	M01 2-1	J14 4-3	M25 2-1
15 PETERBOROUGH U	O15 3-0	J03 1-5	J21 1-4	M27 3-0	a29 3-2	M18 1-1	m13 2-0	D17 0-1	a25 1-2	M01 2-1	N09 0-1	O22 2-1	M11 0-1	S17 1-1		D03 1-0	J07 0-3	S03 1-4	O29 1-2	O05 1-0	a08 3-1	F04 1-1	a15 1-0	S24 0-1
16 ROCHDALE	J21 2-1	a08 2-1	M27 0-0	D16 1-1	O01 2-1	O29 2-2	S20 2-0	S17 2-1	F11 0-2	a25 1-1	a22 0-0	F28 2-2	J02 0-3	J07 2-2	m06 0-0		S03 0-2	M18 2-1	O22 1-0	O08 1-1	m01 2-1	M11 3-1	N12 3-3	N26 2-0
17 ROTHERHAM U	a22 3-1	m13 0-0	F11 2-1	O25 2-0	D26 1-2	F18 1-2	A27 3-0	O01 0-1	M07 1-0	D31 2-0	M25 4-0	a29 6-0	S20 4-1	N05 2-0	a04 1-1	J14 3-1		M14 1-1	N08 3-3	D03 2-1	M04 1-0	O15 0-0	S10 2-2	a01 0-1
18 SCARBOROUGH	N12 1-0	M01 2-1	M11 0-1	F04 0-0	D31 2-1	O05 3-2	M25 2-0	m01 2-1	m06 2-3	a01 3-1	a05 2-0	J28 0-2	O08 0-0	F25 1-1	J14 2-1	S10 3-3	O29 1-0		a15 1-0	O22 1-1	S24 5-2	A27 0-0	N26 0-3	D26 0-0
19 SCUNTHORPE U	N05 2-1	O15 1-0	S20 1-1	F18 2-3	J14 2-2	m06 5-1	a01 2-1	F11 2-0	S10 1-1	M25 0-0	D26 1-1	A27 3-1	N12 2-2	a22 0-0	M14 3-0	M04 4-0	m01 0-0	O01 0-3		a04 1-1	N26 1-0	D31 0-1	O25 3-1	J28 4-2
20 STOCKPORT CO	S16 0-0	M17 0-0	a07 1-1	M13 1-0	F10 0-1	J20 0-0	O01 2-0	J02 4-0	N05 3-1	S19 1-1	O24 3-0	O15 1-2	S03 0-0	D17 1-0	a21 1-2	F17 3-0	m06 1-3	M04 2-2	J07 1-2		M27 0-0	N25 1-1	m01 2-2	N11 3-2
21 TORQUAY U	S20 2-0	D02 3-1	m03 1-0	m13 1-3	M31 2-1	F28 1-0	J28 3-2	a22 0-4	J14 2-2	A27 0-2	S10 2-0	M25 1-0	O01 3-0	O08 1-0	D31 1-0	N08 1-0	O22 1-2	F11 0-1	a28 0-2	D26 2-1		O29 3-2	a04 0-0	a25 2-0
22 TRANMERE R	J02 2-1	S16 1-2	M17 0-0	S02 0-0	m13 1-1	D16 2-0	D02 2-2	M20 2-0	m09 3-2	F10 2-0	S30 2-1	N07 1-0	M27 3-0	O24 1-0	S19 1-0	N04 2-0	F25 0-0	J21 1-1	a07 2-1	a28 1-0	M13 3-0		M03 2-1	O07 0-1
23 WREXHAM	M27 4-2	D16 3-1	D03 2-1	S16 2-2	O08 0-0	J02 3-3	F11 1-1	J21 3-0	S20 1-2	a21 3-0	M07 4-3	M11 1-1	a08 0-1	S03 3-0	O01 1-1	m13 2-1	M18 1-4	a29 0-1	F28 2-0	N08 2-0	m09 1-0	O22 3-3		O29 2-1
24 YORK C	M18 0-0	m09 1-2	S03 1-1	J21 2-0	N08 3-0	O15 4-1	O25 1-1	a08 3-1	M04 0-3	O01 5-3	S20 2-3	D03 4-1	a22 1-1	J02 2-1	F11 5-1	a29 3-3	D16 1-1	M27 0-0	S17 1-2	m13 2-0	N05 1-1	F18 0-1	M14 1-0	

LEAGUE TABLES

DIVISION 1

	P	W	D	L	F	A	W	D	L	F	A	Pts
Arsenal	38	10	6	3	35	19	12	4	3	38	17	76
Liverpool	38	11	5	3	33	11	11	5	3	32	17	76
Nottingham F	38	8	7	4	31	16	9	6	4	33	27	64
Norwich C	38	8	7	4	23	20	9	4	6	25	25	62
Derby Co	38	9	3	7	23	18	8	4	7	17	20	58
Tottenham H	38	8	6	5	31	24	7	6	6	29	22	57
Coventry C	38	9	4	6	28	23	5	9	5	19	19	55
Everton	38	10	7	2	33	18	4	5	10	17	27	54
Q.P.R.	38	9	5	5	23	16	5	6	8	20	21	53
Millwall	38	10	3	6	27	21	4	8	7	20	31	53
Manchester U	38	10	5	4	27	13	3	7	9	18	22	51
Wimbledon	38	10	3	6	30	19	4	6	9	20	27	51
Southampton	38	6	7	6	25	26	4	8	7	27	40	45
Charlton A	38	6	7	6	25	24	4	5	10	19	34	42
Sheffield W	38	6	6	7	21	25	4	6	9	13	26	42
Luton T	38	8	6	5	32	21	2	5	12	10	31	41
Aston Villa	38	7	6	6	25	22	2	7	10	20	34	40
Middlesbrough	38	6	7	6	28	30	3	5	11	16	31	39
West Ham U	38	3	6	10	19	30	7	2	10	18	32	38
Newcastle U	38	3	6	10	19	28	4	4	11	13	35	31

DIVISION 2

	P	W	D	L	F	A	W	D	L	F	A	Pts
Chelsea	46	15	6	2	50	25	14	6	3	46	25	99
Manchester C	46	12	8	3	48	28	11	5	7	29	25	82
Crystal Palace	46	15	6	2	42	17	8	6	9	29	32	81
Watford	46	14	5	4	41	18	8	7	8	33	30	78
Blackburn R	46	16	4	3	50	22	6	7	10	24	37	77
Swindon T	46	13	8	2	35	15	7	8	8	33	38	76
Barnsley	46	12	8	3	37	21	8	6	9	29	37	74
Ipswich T	46	13	3	7	42	23	9	4	10	29	38	73
W.B.A.	46	13	7	3	43	18	5	11	7	22	23	72
Leeds U	46	12	6	5	34	20	5	10	8	25	30	67
Sunderland	46	12	8	3	40	23	4	7	12	20	37	63
Bournemouth	46	13	3	7	32	20	5	5	13	21	42	62
Stoke C	46	10	9	4	33	25	5	5	13	24	47	59
Bradford C	46	8	11	4	29	22	5	6	12	23	37	56
Leicester C	46	11	6	6	31	20	2	10	11	25	43	55
Oldham A	46	9	10	4	49	32	2	11	10	26	40	54
Oxford U	46	11	6	6	40	34	3	6	14	22	36	54
Plymouth A	46	11	4	8	35	22	3	8	12	20	44	54
Brighton & H.A.	46	11	5	7	36	24	3	4	16	21	42	51
Portsmouth	46	10	6	7	33	21	3	6	14	20	41	51
Hull C	46	7	9	7	31	25	4	5	14	21	43	47
Shrewsbury T	46	4	11	8	25	31	4	7	12	15	36	42
Birmingham C	46	6	4	13	21	33	2	7	14	10	43	35
Walsall	46	3	10	10	27	42	2	6	15	14	38	31

DIVISION 3

	P	W	D	L	F	A	W	D	L	F	A	Pts
Wolverh'pton W	46	18	4	1	61	19	8	10	5	35	30	92
Sheffield U	46	16	3	4	57	21	9	6	8	36	33	84
Port Vale	46	15	3	5	46	21	9	9	5	32	27	84
Fulham	46	12	7	4	42	28	10	2	11	27	39	75
Bristol R	46	9	11	3	34	21	10	6	7	33	30	74
Preston N.E.	46	14	7	2	56	31	5	8	10	23	29	72
Brentford	46	14	5	4	36	21	4	9	10	30	40	68
Chester C	46	12	6	5	38	18	7	5	11	26	43	68
Notts Co	46	11	7	5	37	22	7	6	10	27	32	67
Bolton W	46	12	8	3	42	23	4	8	11	16	31	64
Bristol C	46	10	3	10	32	25	8	6	9	21	30	63
Swansea C	46	11	8	4	33	22	4	8	11	18	31	61
Bury	46	11	7	5	27	22	5	6	12	28	45	61
Huddersfield T	46	10	8	5	35	25	7	1	15	28	48	60
Mansfield T	46	10	8	5	32	22	4	9	10	16	30	59
Cardiff C	46	10	9	4	30	16	4	6	13	14	40	57
Wigan A	46	9	5	9	28	22	5	9	9	27	31	56
Reading	46	10	6	7	37	29	5	5	13	31	43	56
Blackpool	46	10	6	7	36	29	4	7	12	20	30	55
Northampton T	46	11	2	10	41	34	5	4	14	25	42	54
Southend U	46	10	9	4	33	26	3	6	14	23	49	54
Chesterfield	46	9	5	9	35	35	5	2	16	16	51	49
Gillingham	46	7	3	13	25	32	5	1	17	22	49	40
Aldershot	46	7	6	10	29	29	1	7	15	19	49	37

DIVISION 4

	P	W	D	L	F	A	W	D	L	F	A	Pts
Rotherham U	46	13	6	4	44	18	9	10	4	32	17	82
Tranmere R	46	15	6	2	34	13	6	11	6	28	30	80
Crewe A	46	13	7	3	42	24	8	8	7	25	24	78
Scunthorpe U	46	11	9	3	40	22	10	5	8	37	35	77
Scarborough	46	12	7	4	33	23	9	7	7	34	29	77
Leyton O	46	16	2	5	61	19	5	10	8	25	31	75
Wrexham	46	12	7	4	44	28	7	7	9	33	35	71
Cambridge U	46	13	7	3	45	25	5	7	11	26	37	68
Grimsby T	46	11	9	3	33	18	6	6	11	32	41	66
Lincoln C	46	12	6	5	39	26	6	4	13	25	34	64
York C	46	10	8	5	43	27	7	5	11	19	36	64
Carlisle U	46	9	6	8	26	25	6	9	8	27	27	60
Exeter C	46	14	4	5	46	23	4	2	17	19	45	60
Torquay U	46	15	2	6	32	23	2	6	15	13	37	59
Hereford U	46	11	8	4	40	27	3	8	12	26	45	58
Burnley	46	12	6	5	35	20	2	7	14	17	41	55
Peterborough U	46	10	3	10	29	32	4	9	10	23	42	54
Rochdale	46	10	10	3	32	26	3	4	16	24	56	53
Hartlepool U	46	10	6	7	33	33	4	4	15	17	45	52
Stockport Co	46	8	10	5	31	20	2	11	10	23	32	51
Halifax T	46	10	7	6	42	27	3	4	16	27	48	50
Colchester U	46	8	7	8	35	30	4	7	12	25	48	50
Doncaster R	46	9	6	8	32	32	4	4	15	17	46	49
Darlington	46	3	12	8	28	38	5	6	12	25	38	42

Football League Records

Top scorers: Div 1, G.Lineker (Tottenham Hotspur) 24 goals; Div 2, M.Quinn (Newcastle United) 32 goals; Div 3, R.Taylor(Bristol City) 27 goals; Div 4, B.Angell (Stockport County) 23 goals.
Play offs Div 1, Blackburn Rovers v Swindon Town 1-2, 2-1; Sunderland v Newcastle United 0-0, 2-0; Sunderland v Swindon Town (Wembley) 0-1; Div 2, Bolton Wanderers v Notts County 1-1, 0-2; Bury v Tranmere Rovers 0-0, 0-2; Notts County v Tranmere Rovers (Wembley) 2-0; Div 3, Cambridge United v Maidstone United 1-1, 2-0; Chesterfield v Stockport County 4-0, 2-0; Cambridge United v Chesterfield (Wembley) 1-0.
Leeds United, Sheffield United and Sunderland promoted to Div 1; Charlton Athletic, Millwall and Sheffield Wednesday relegated to Div 2; Bristol City, Bristol Rovers

John Barnes, whose electrifying displays caught the imagination as Liverpool took the title back from Arsenal in 1989-90.

DIVISION 1

	ARSENAL	ASTON VILLA	CHARLTON A	CHELSEA	COVENTRY C	CRYSTAL P	DERBY CO	EVERTON	LIVERPOOL	LUTON T	MANCHESTER C	MANCHESTER U	MILLWALL	NORWICH C	NOTTINGHAM F	Q.P.R.	SHEFFIELD W	SOUTHAMPTON	TOTENHAM H	WIMBLEDON
1 ARSENAL		a11 0-1	S23 1-0	M17 0-1	A22 2-0	J01 4-1	O28 1-1	M31 1-0	a18 1-1	D16 3-2	O14 4-0	D03 1-0	a28 2-0	N04 4-3	M07 3-0	N18 3-0	S09 5-0	m02 2-1	J20 1-0	A26 0-0
2 ASTON VILLA	D30 2-1		A26 1-1	a14 1-0	N18 4-1	O28 2-1	S30 1-0	N05 6-2	A23 1-1	M10 2-0	a01 1-2	D26 3-0	a21 1-0	a28 3-3	D02 2-1	S23 1-3	F10 1-0	J20 2-1	S09 2-0	F24 0-3
3 CHARLTON A	F27 0-0	J13 0-2		A29 3-0	O28 1-1	D16 1-2	A19 0-0	S16 0-1	a11 0-4	F19 2-0	N25 1-1	N04 2-0	D09 1-1	M03 0-1	M17 1-1	M31 1-0	a28 1-2	J01 2-4	O14 1-3	a17 1-2
4 CHELSEA	S30 0-0	J01 0-3	J20 3-1		S23 1-0	a16 3-0	M31 1-1	a28 2-1	D16 2-5	a07 1-0	O28 1-1	F24 1-0	N04 4-0	M10 0-0	S09 2-2	A22 1-1	A26 4-0	N18 2-2	F10 1-2	D02 2-5
5 COVENTRY C	D09 0-1	M04 2-0	M24 1-2	F03 3-2		J13 1-0	a07 1-0	A19 2-0	m05 1-6	S16 1-0	A30 2-1	O21 1-4	F17 3-1	N25 1-0	O14 0-2	a16 1-1	M17 1-4	N11 1-0	J01 0-0	D16 2-1
6 CRYSTAL P	a14 1-1	M24 1-0	a21 2-0	D26 2-2	A26 0-1		M20 1-1	S30 2-1	J20 0-2	N11 1-1	m05 2-2	A22 1-1	O21 4-3	D30 1-0	S23 1-0	D02 0-3	F24 1-1	F10 3-1	N18 2-3	S09 2-0
7 DERBY CO	M24 1-3	M17 0-1	D02 2-0	O21 0-1	D30 4-1	O14 3-1		D26 0-1	S09 0-3	m05 2-3	N11 6-0	A26 2-0	a14 2-0	a21 0-2	J20 0-2	F10 2-0	N18 2-0	S23 0-1	F24 2-1	A23 1-1
8 EVERTON	O21 3-0	m05 3-3	F10 2-1	N11 0-1	D02 2-0	M17 4-0	a16 2-1		S23 1-3	J01 2-1	D17 0-0	S09 3-2	O14 2-1	M24 3-1	a04 4-0	a07 1-0	J20 2-0	A26 3-0	A22 2-1	N18 1-1
9 LIVERPOOL	N26 2-1	D09 1-1	D30 1-0	a21 4-1	N04 0-1	S12 9-0	m01 1-0	F03 2-1		J13 2-2	A19 3-1	D23 0-0	M03 1-0	S16 0-0	a14 2-2	a28 2-1	D26 2-1	M31 3-2	O29 1-0	a03 2-1
10 LUTON T	a21 2-0	O14 0-1	S09 1-0	D30 0-3	M07 3-2	a28 1-0	N04 1-0	a14 2-2	A26 0-0		M17 1-1	N18 1-3	M24 2-1	O21 4-1	D26 1-1	J20 1-1	A22 2-0	F24 1-1	D02 0-0	S23 1-1
11 MANCHESTER C	M10 1-1	O22 0-2	F24 1-2	M21 1-1	J20 1-0	N04 3-0	a28 0-1	a21 1-0	D02 1-4	S30 3-1		S23 5-1	D30 2-0	D26 1-0	N18 0-3	S09 1-0	a14 2-1	A23 1-2	A26 1-1	F10 1-1
12 MANCHESTER U	A19 4-1	a17 2-0	m05 1-0	N25 0-0	M31 3-0	D09 1-2	J13 1-2	M14 0-0	M18 1-2	M03 4-1	F03 1-1		S16 5-1	A30 0-2	N12 1-0	J01 0-0	O14 0-0	O28 2-1	D16 0-1	a30 0-0
13 MILLWALL	N11 1-2	D16 2-0	A22 2-2	m05 1-3	S09 4-1	M31 1-2	J01 1-1	M21 1-2	N19 1-2	O28 1-1	a07 1-1	F10 1-2		S30 0-1	A26 1-0	F24 1-2	S23 2-0	D02 2-2	a16 0-1	J20 0-0
14 NORWICH C	m05 2-2	N11 2-0	N18 0-0	O14 2-0	M14 0-0	a04 2-0	D16 1-0	O28 1-1	F10 0-0	M31 2-0	a16 0-1	J21 2-0	M17 1-1		A23 1-1	A26 0-0	D02 2-1	S09 4-4	S23 2-2	J01 0-1
15 NOTTINGHAM F	S16 1-2	A19 1-1	S30 2-0	F17 1-1	M10 2-4	F03 3-1	A30 2-1	N25 1-0	J01 2-2	a16 3-0	M03 1-0	m02 4-0	J13 3-1	D09 0-1		O28 2-2	N04 0-1	D17 2-0	a07 1-3	M31 0-1
16 Q.P.R.	M03 2-0	M20 1-1	O21 0-1	D09 4-2	D26 1-1	A19 2-0	S16 0-1	D30 1-0	N11 3-2	A30 0-0	a11 1-3	a14 1-2	N25 0-0	J13 2-1	M24 2-0		a21 1-0	O14 1-4	M17 3-1	m05 2-3
17 SHEFFIELD W	F17 1-0	S16 1-0	N11 3-0	J14 1-1	S30 0-0	N25 2-2	M03 1-0	A30 1-1	N29 2-0	D09 1-1	J01 2-0	M21 1-0	F03 1-1	A19 0-2	m05 0-3	D16 2-0		a07 0-1	M31 2-4	O28 0-1
18 SOUTHAMPTON	D26 1-0	A29 2-1	a14 3-2	M03 2-3	a28 3-0	S16 1-1	M10 2-1	J13 2-2	O21 4-1	N25 6-3	D09 2-1	M24 0-2	A19 1-2	F27 4-1	a21 2-0	a03 0-2	D30 2-2		N04 1-1	S30 2-2
19 TOTTENHAM H	O18 2-1	F21 0-2	M10 3-0	S16 1-4	a14 3-2	M03 0-1	N25 1-2	D09 2-1	M21 1-0	A19 2-1	J13 1-1	a21 2-1	D26 3-1	F04 4-0	D30 2-3	S30 3-2	O21 3-0	m05 2-1		N11 0-1
20 WIMBLEDON	J13 1-0	N25 0-2	D26 3-1	A19 0-1	a21 0-0	m02 0-1	D09 1-1	M03 3-1	O14 1-2	F14 1-2	S16 1-0	D30 2-2	A29 2-2	a14 1-1	O21 1-3	N04 0-0	M24 1-1	M17 3-3	a28 1-0	

Leeds United spent around £5 million to win back their Division One place. Lee Chapman was one signing and his goals helped achieve promotion.

DIVISION 2

	BARNSLEY	BLACKBURN R	BOURNEMOUTH	BRADFORD C	BRIGHTON & HA	HULL C	IPSWICH T	LEEDS U	LEICESTER C	MIDDLESBROUGH	NEWCASTLE U	OLDHAM A	OXFORD U	PLYMOUTH A	PORTSMOUTH	PORT VALE	SHEFFIELD U	STOKE C	SUNDERLAND	SWINDON T	WATFORD	W.B.A.	WEST HAM U	WOLVERHAMPTON W
1 BARNSLEY		a03 0-0	a21 0-1	S23 2-0	A26 1-0	F24 1-1	D02 0-1	D30 1-0	O28 2-2	S09 1-1	N18 1-1	M17 1-0	M31 1-0	J20 1-1	N04 0-1	O14 0-3	O17 1-2	S05 3-2	a10 1-0	F10 0-1	D26 0-1	a28 2-2	a14 1-1	S26 2-2
2 BLACKBURN R	S30 5-0		F03 1-1	J01 2-2	m05 1-1	O31 0-0	N11 2-2	J13 1-2	D09 2-4	N21 2-4	M24 2-0	A19 1-0	S02 2-2	a07 2-0	M20 2-0	F17 1-0	m01 0-0	J27 3-0	S16 1-1	a16 2-1	O21 2-2	M10 2-1	N25 5-4	M03 2-3
3 BOURNEMOUTH	D16 2-1	S23 2-4		F24 1-0	D02 0-2	A26 5-4	J20 3-1	m05 0-1	a17 2-3	F10 2-2	S09 2-1	O14 2-0	M06 0-1	J01 2-2	O21 0-1	S26 1-0	N11 0-1	N18 2-1	M17 0-1	a07 1-2	M24 0-0	A22 1-1	N01 1-1	a03 1-1
4 BRADFORD C	F03 0-0	a14 0-1	N25 1-0		O07 2-0	N11 2-3	O18 1-0	O28 0-1	S16 2-0	D26 0-1	M21 3-2	m07 1-1	F17 1-2	m05 0-1	S02 1-1	A19 2-2	M03 1-4	M10 1-0	M31 0-1	S30 1-1	a21 2-1	D30 2-0	D09 2-1	J13 1-1
5 BRIGHTON & H.A.	J13 1-1	N04 1-2	A19 2-1	M17 2-1		a06 2-0	S27 1-0	a21 2-2	F17 1-0	F28 1-0	O21 0-3	M03 1-1	D30 0-1	M07 2-1	D26 0-0	S02 2-0	M14 2-2	a28 1-4	N25 1-2	N01 1-2	O14 1-0	a14 0-3	S16 3-0	D09 1-1
6 HULL C	N25 1-2	a10 2-0	J13 1-4	a28 2-1	O28 0-2		m01 4-3	S16 0-1	A19 1-1	M10 0-0	S30 1-3	O17 0-0	M03 1-0	a24 3-3	F17 1-2	D09 2-1	F03 0-0	M20 0-0	J01 3-2	O07 2-3	N04 0-0	M31 0-2	S02 1-1	a16 2-0
7 IPSWICH T	A19 3-1	a28 3-1	S02 1-1	M24 1-0	M10 2-1	M21 0-1		F17 2-2	M03 2-2	D30 3-0	O07 2-1	N25 1-1	M13 1-0	O21 3-0	a10 0-1	a14 3-2	J13 1-1	S30 2-2	D09 1-1	M20 1-0	O31 1-0	N04 3-1	D26 1-0	S16 1-3
8 LEEDS U	a25 1-2	A26 1-1	N04 3-0	a07 1-1	D16 3-0	F10 4-3	S09 1-1		a28 2-1	A23 2-1	D02 1-0	J01 1-1	S27 2-1	N01 2-1	M24 2-0	M07 0-0	a16 4-0	J20 2-0	O14 2-0	S23 4-0	N18 2-1	F24 2-2	M17 3-2	O21 1-0
9 LEICESTER C	a07 2-2	A23 0-1	D26 2-1	F10 1-1	S23 1-0	D02 2-1	N18 0-1	N11 4-3		a21 2-1	A26 2-2	a03 3-0	O14 0-0	M24 1-1	a14 1-1	M17 2-0	m05 2-5	F24 2-1	S27 2-3	O21 2-1	J20 1-1	S09 1-3	D30 1-0	N01 0-0
10 MIDDLESBROUGH	m02 0-1	M17 0-3	S16 2-1	a16 2-0	O18 2-2	S27 1-0	a25 1-2	D09 0-2	D16 4-1		m05 4-1	M31 1-0	N25 1-0	O14 0-2	F03 2-0	a11 2-3	S02 3-3	J01 0-1	J14 3-0	N11 0-2	M07 1-2	O28 0-0	M03 0-1	A19 4-2
11 NEWCASTLE U	M03 4-1	O18 2-1	F28 3-0	O14 1-0	M31 2-0	M07 2-0	M17 2-1	A19 5-2	J13 5-4	N04 2-2		S02 2-1	D09 2-3	a03 3-1	S16 1-0	O28 2-2	N25 2-0	a16 3-0	F04 1-1	a25 0-0	S27 2-1	a11 2-1	a28 2-1	J01 1-4
12 OLDHAM A	O07 2-0	D01 2-0	M20 4-0	O31 2-2	N18 1-1	M24 3-2	F24 4-1	a13 3-1	S30 1-0	O21 2-0	J20 1-1		m01 4-1	S09 3-2	D30 3-3	D26 2-1	M28 0-2	F10 2-0	N04 2-1	A26 2-2	A22 1-1	S23 2-1	a21 3-0	m03 1-1
13 OXFORD U	O21 2-3	J20 1-1	S30 1-2	S09 2-1	a25 0-1	N18 0-0	S23 2-2	M10 2-4	M21 4-2	F24 3-1	S13 2-1	N11 0-1		D02 3-2	O07 2-1	m05 0-0	J01 3-0	N01 3-0	a16 0-1	M24 2-2	A26 1-1	F10 0-1	a07 0-2	D16 2-2
14 PLYMOUTH A	S02 2-1	O28 2-2	a14 1-0	N04 1-1	S30 2-1	D29 1-2	M31 1-0	a10 1-1	O17 3-1	M20 1-2	a21 1-1	a18 2-0	A19 2-0		D10 0-2	N25 1-2	S16 0-0	O07 3-0	M03 3-0	M10 0-3	a28 0-0	D26 2-2	J13 1-1	F03 0-1
15 PORTSMOUTH	m05 2-1	O14 1-1	M31 2-1	J20 3-0	a16 3-0	S09 2-2	O28 2-3	O17 3-3	J01 2-3	S23 3-1	F10 1-1	a21 2-1	M17 2-1	S12 0-3		N11 2-0	a07 3-2	A26 0-0	D16 3-3	F24 1-1	D02 1-2	N18 1-1	S26 0-1	M06 1-3
16 PORT VALE	M19 2-1	S09 0-0	M10 1-1	D02 3-2	J20 2-1	S12 1-1	J01 5-0	S30 0-0	O07 2-1	O30 1-1	a07 1-2	a16 2-0	N04 1-2	F24 3-0	a28 1-1		D16 1-1	F03 0-0	m01 1-2	N18 2-0	F10 1-0	A26 2-1	O21 2-2	M24 3-1
17 SHEFFIELD U	M24 1-2	D30 1-2	a28 4-2	N18 1-1	S09 5-4	S23 0-0	A26 2-0	D26 2-2	N04 1-1	J20 1-0	F24 1-1	S26 2-1	a14 2-1	F10 1-0	O31 2-1	a21 2-1		O21 2-1	a03 1-3	S12 2-0	a10 4-1	D02 3-1	O14 0-2	M17 3-0
18 STOKE C	D09 0-1	a21 0-1	M03 0-0	S26 1-1	N11 3-2	O14 1-1	M06 0-0	S02 1-1	N25 0-1	a14 0-0	D26 2-1	S16 1-2	a10 1-2	M17 0-0	J13 1-2	S23 1-1	M31 0-1		O28 0-2	m05 1-1	D30 2-2	O17 2-1	A19 1-1	F17 2-0
19 SUNDERLAND	O31 4-2	F10 0-1	O07 3-2	O21 1-0	F24 2-1	a14 0-1	A22 2-4	M20 0-1	M10 2-2	A27 2-1	S24 0-0	m05 2-3	D26 1-0	N18 3-1	a21 2-2	D30 2-2	S30 1-1	a07 2-1		D02 2-2	S09 4-0	J20 1-1	A24 4-3	N11 1-1
20 SWINDON T	S16 0-0	D26 4-3	D05 2-3	M06 3-1	a10 1-2	M17 1-3	O14 3-0	F04 3-2	M31 1-1	a28 1-1	D30 1-1	J13 3-2	O17 3-0	S26 3-0	N26 2-2	M03 3-0	D10 0-2	N04 6-0	A19 0-2		a14 2-0	a21 2-1	F18 2-2	S03 3-1
21 WATFORD	a17 2-2	M31 3-1	O17 2-2	D16 7-2	M20 4-2	m05 3-1	a07 3-3	M03 1-0	S02 3-1	S30 1-0	M10 0-0	D09 3-0	J13 0-1	N11 1-2	A19 1-0	S16 1-0	O28 1-3	a24 1-1	F17 1-1	J01 0-2		O07 0-2	M13 0-1	N25 3-1
22 W.B.A.	N11 7-0	S27 2-2	D09 2-2	M14 2-0	J01 3-0	O21 1-1	m05 1-3	N25 2-1	F21 0-1	a07 0-0	N01 1-5	F03 2-2	S16 3-2	a16 0-3	M03 0-0	J13 2-3	A19 0-3	M24 1-1	S02 1-1	D17 1-2	M17 2-0		a04 1-3	O15 1-2
23 WEST HAM U	J01 4-2	F24 1-1	a11 4-1	A23 2-0	F10 3-1	J20 1-2	a17 2-0	O07 0-1	m02 3-1	N18 2-0	N11 0-0	D16 0-2	O28 3-2	A26 3-2	M10 2-1	M31 2-2	M21 5-0	D02 0-0	O18 5-0	S09 1-1	S23 1-0	S30 2-3		m05 4-0
24 WOLVERHAMPTON W	M10 1-1	N18 1-2	D30 3-1	A26 1-1	S12 2-4	D26 1-2	F10 2-1	M31 1-0	a10 5-0	D02 2-0	a14 0-1	O28 1-1	a21 2-0	S23 1-0	S30 5-0	O17 2-0	O07 1-2	S09 0-0	a28 0-1	J20 2-1	F24 1-1	M20 2-1	N04 1-0	

SEASON 1989-90

and Notts County promoted to Div 2; AFC Bournemouth, Bradford City and Stoke City relegated to Div 3; Exeter City, Grimsby Town, Cambridge United and Southend United promoted to Div 3; Blackpool, Cardiff City, Northampton Town and Walsall relegated to Div 4; Swindon Town demoted to Div 2, Sunderland took their place in Div 1; Colchester United were relegated from Division Four and replaced by Darlington.

DIVISION 3

	BIRMINGHAM C	BLACKPOOL	BOLTON W	BRENTFORD	BRISTOL C	BRISTOL R	BURY	CARDIFF C	CHESTER C	CREWE A	FULHAM	HUDDERSFIELD T	LEYTON O	MANSFIELD T	NORTHAMPTON T	NOTTS CO	PRESTON N.E.	READING	ROTHERHAM U	SHREWSBURY T	SWANSEA C	TRANMERE R	WALSALL	WIGAN A
1 BIRMINGHAM C		M06 3-1	N25 1-0	M13 0-1	J13 0-4	a16 2-2	a07 0-0	O31 1-1	M24 0-0	A19 3-0	J01 1-1	O21 0-1	N11 0-0	M03 4-1	O14 4-0	a24 1-2	D16 3-1	m05 0-1	M17 4-1	J27 0-1	S02 2-0	S16 2-1	S26 2-0	F17 0-0
2 BLACKPOOL	S30 3-2		a16 2-1	N11 4-0	J13 1-3	m05 0-3	O31 0-1	O21 1-0	a24 1-3	S16 1-3	D16 0-1	J01 2-2	M20 1-0	F03 3-1	M24 1-0	J13 0-0	M10 2-2	O06 0-0	a07 1-2	S02 0-1	a30 2-2	N25 0-3	M03 4-3	A19 0-0
3 BOLTON W	F24 3-1	D26 2-0		M24 0-1	a28 1-0	S09 1-0	D30 3-1	J20 3-1	O21 1-0	M20 0-0	A26 0-0	m01 2-2	S23 2-1	S30 1-1	D02 0-3	M10 3-0	a07 2-1	a03 3-0	F10 0-2	a21 0-1	N04 0-0	a14 1-1	O31 1-1	O07 3-2
4 BRENTFORD	S23 0-1	a28 5-0	O17 1-2		O07 0-2	J20 2-1	S09 0-1	F21 0-1	A26 1-1	M10 0-2	O28 2-0	F10 2-1	D03 4-3	D17 2-1	F25 3-2	a07 0-1	M20 2-2	a16 1-1	J06 4-2	M31 1-1	m02 2-1	N04 2-4	J01 4-0	S30 3-1
5 BRISTOL C	A26 1-0	S09 2-0	N11 1-1	M17 2-0		S23 0-0	J20 1-0	F10 1-0	J30 1-0	a10 4-1	a16 5-1	a24 1-1	D16 2-1	M31 1-1	M27 3-1	O17 2-0	J01 2-1	F24 0-1	D02 0-0	S26 2-1	O14 1-3	M06 1-3	m05 4-0	O28 3-0
6 BRISTOL R	D26 0-0	N04 1-1	J28 1-1	A19 1-0	m02 3-0		M21 2-1	M24 2-1	a07 2-1	a21 1-1	O07 2-0	N01 2-2	M11 0-0	J13 1-1	O21 4-2	S02 3-2	S16 3-0	S30 0-0	a14 2-0	a28 1-0	N25 2-0	D30 2-0	F18 2-0	M03 6-1
7 BURY	O28 0-0	a10 2-0	a24 2-0	J27 0-2	A19 1-1	O14 0-0		m05 2-0	M17 1-0	N25 0-3	M31 0-0	a16 6-0	J01 2-0	S16 3-0	M06 1-0	M03 3-2	J13 1-2	N11 4-0	S26 1-1	F03 0-0	O17 3-2	F17 1-2	D16 0-2	S02 2-2
8 CARDIFF C	a10 0-1	M31 2-2	A19 0-2	S02 2-2	S16 0-3	O17 1-1	N03 3-1		O13 1-1	F17 0-0	a28 3-3	M17 1-5	O28 1-1	M27 1-0	S26 2-3	D16 1-3	N25 3-0	m01 3-2	M06 2-0	M02 0-1	a16 0-2	J13 0-0	a24 3-1	F03 1-1
9 CHESTER C	O17 4-0	D30 2-0	M31 2-0	J12 1-1	J03 0-3	O28 0-0	O07 1-4	M20 1-0		S02 2-1	S30 0-2	N04 2-1	J06 1-0	A19 0-2	a14 0-1	S15 3-3	F03 3-1	M09 1-1	a28 2-0	F17 1-0	J26 1-0	a20 2-2	N24 1-1	D26 0-0
10 CREWE A	J20 0-2	F10 2-0	O14 2-2	S26 2-3	O31 0-1	D15 1-0	F24 2-1	D02 1-1	F13 0-0		S09 2-3	M13 3-0	a24 0-1	N10 2-1	S23 2-1	J01 1-0	M24 1-0	A25 1-1	O21 0-0	M06 1-1	M17 1-1	a06 2-2	a16 3-1	m05 3-2
11 FULHAM	a14 1-2	a21 0-0	J13 2-2	a10 1-0	D26 0-1	M17 1-2	O21 2-2	N11 2-5	M06 1-0	J27 1-1		S26 0-0	m05 1-2	S02 1-0	O31 1-1	F17 5-2	M03 3-1	M24 1-2	O14 1-1	D30 2-1	S16 2-0	A19 1-2	a04 0-0	N25 4-0
12 HUDDERSFIELD T	M31 1-2	a14 2-2	S02 1-1	S16 1-0	D30 2-1	a10 1-1	D26 2-1	O07 2-3	m05 4-1	M03 0-1	M10 0-1		S30 2-0	F17 1-0	N11 2-2	N25 1-2	a03 0-2	M20 0-1	a21 2-1	O28 1-1	A19 1-0	F03 1-0	J13 1-0	O17 2-0
13 LEYTON O	a28 1-2	O14 2-0	M27 0-0	F18 0-1	a21 1-1	S26 0-1	a14 2-3	a07 3-1	O31 0-3	D30 2-1	N05 1-1	M06 1-0		N25 3-1	D26 1-1	A19 0-1	S02 3-1	O21 4-1	M24 1-1	J13 1-0	M03 0-2	M17 0-1	J27 1-1	S16 1-0
14 MANSFIELD T	a03 5-2	S23 0-3	M06 0-1	a21 2-3	O21 1-0	A26 0-1	F10 1-0	S09 1-0	J20 1-0	a28 2-1	F13 3-0	D02 1-2	F24 1-0		D30 1-2	N04 1-3	O31 2-2	a07 1-1	D26 3-1	M17 2-1	O24 4-0	M24 1-0	O14 0-2	a14 1-0
15 NORTHAMPTON T	M20 2-2	O17 4-2	F17 0-2	N25 0-2	S02 2-0	M31 1-2	S30 0-1	M10 1-1	J01 1-0	a30 3-1	a07 2-2	a28 1-0	a16 0-1	a24 1-2		O28 0-0	O07 1-2	D17 2-1	N04 1-2	S16 2-1	J13 1-1	M03 0-4	F20 1-1	M13 1-1
16 NOTTS CO	D30 3-2	A26 0-1	S26 2-1	O31 3-1	M24 0-0	a26 3-1	J06 0-4	a21 2-1	F10 0-0	a14 2-0	D02 2-0	F24 1-0	J20 1-0	m05 4-2	a10 3-2		O21 2-1	S09 0-0	S23 2-0	D26 4-0	M06 2-1	O14 1-0	M17 2-0	N11 1-1
17 PRESTON N.E.	a21 2-2	S26 2-1	O28 1-4	O14 4-2	a14 2-2	F10 0-1	A26 2-3	F24 4-0	S23 5-0	O17 0-0	J06 1-0	S09 3-3	F13 0-3	a10 4-0	M17 0-0	M31 2-4		D02 1-0	J20 0-1	N04 2-1	a28 2-0	D26 2-2	M06 2-0	D30 1-1
18 READING	N04 0-2	M17 1-1	M03 2-0	D26 1-0	N25 1-1	M06 0-1	a28 1-0	a14 0-1	S26 1-1	J13 1-1	O17 3-2	O14 0-0	M31 1-1	O28 1-0	a21 3-2	m03 1-1	F17 6-0		D30 3-2	A19 3-3	F20 1-1	S02 1-0	S16 0-1	a10 2-0
19 ROTHERHAM U	O07 5-1	O28 1-1	S16 1-0	M03 2-1	a03 1-2	J01 3-2	M10 1-3	S30 4-0	N11 5-0	M31 1-3	M20 2-1	D16 0-0	O17 5-2	a16 0-0	m05 2-0	F03 1-2	A19 3-1	a24 1-1		N25 4-2	F17 3-2	J27 0-0	S02 2-2	J13 1-2
20 SHREWSBURY T	S09 2-0	F13 1-1	D16 3-3	O21 1-0	J10 0-1	N11 2-3	S23 3-1	M13 0-0	D02 2-0	S30 0-0	a24 2-0	a07 3-3	A26 4-2	O07 0-1	a03 2-0	a17 2-2	m05 2-0	J20 1-1	F24 1-1		J01 1-1	O31 3-1	M24 2-0	M20 1-3
21 SWANSEA C	F13 1-1	D02 0-0	m05 0-0	D30 2-1	M20 0-5	F24 0-0	M23 0-1	D26 0-1	S09 2-1	O07 3-2	F10 4-2	J21 1-3	a03 0-1	M10 1-0	A26 1-1	S30 0-0	N11 2-1	S23 1-6	O31 1-0	a14 0-1		O20 1-0	a07 2-0	a21 3-0
22 TRANMERE R	F09 5-1	F23 4-2	J06 1-3	m05 2-2	S29 6-0	a23 1-2	D02 2-4	A26 3-0	D15 0-0	O27 1-1	J19 2-1	S22 4-0	O06 3-0	O16 1-1	m02 0-0	M19 2-0	a16 2-1	F12 3-1	S09 2-1	a09 3-1	M30 3-0		N10 2-1	M09 2-0
23 WALSALL	M10 0-1	M27 1-1	a10 2-1	a14 2-1	N04 0-2	D02 1-2	a21 2-2	D30 0-2	F24 1-1	D26 1-1	S23 0-0	A26 2-3	S09 1-3	M20 1-0	A19 1-0	O07 2-2	S30 1-0	F10 1-1	m01 1-1	O17 0-2	O28 0-1	a28 2-1		M31 1-2
24 WIGAN A	D01 1-0	J20 1-1	M16 2-0	M06 2-1	a07 2-3	a04 1-2	F13 0-0	S23 1-1	a16 1-0	N04 1-0	F24 2-1	M24 1-2	F10 0-2	J01 4-0	S09 0-0	a28 1-1	a24 0-1	O31 3-1	A26 0-3	O14 0-0	D16 2-0	S26 1-3	O21 3-0	

DIVISION 4

	ALDERSHOT	BURNLEY	CAMBRIDGE U	CARLISLE U	CHESTERFIELD	COLCHESTER U	DONCASTER R	EXETER C	GILLINGHAM	GRIMSBY T	HALIFAX T	HARTLEPOOL U	HEREFORD U	LINCOLN C	MAIDSTONE U	PETERBOROUGH U	ROCHDALE	SCARBOROUGH	SCUNTHORPE U	SOUTHEND U	STOCKPORT CO	TORQUAY U	WREXHAM	YORK C
1 ALDERSHOT		a06 1-1	m05 0-2	O31 1-0	F10 0-0	O07 4-0	M10 1-1	D26 0-1	J20 1-0	F24 0-0	D02 2-0	N11 6-1	m01 0-2	A26 0-1	a14 0-2	F27 0-1	D30 1-1	a21 1-1	S30 4-2	S09 0-5	S23 2-1	O21 1-2	M27 1-0	M24 2-2
2 BURNLEY	O28 0-0		a14 1-3	D26 2-1	a03 0-0	N04 0-0	M31 0-1	S09 1-0	F10 1-2	D02 1-1	D30 1-0	O14 0-0	S23 3-1	F24 0-0	M17 1-1	O17 1-2	J20 0-1	J09 3-0	a28 0-1	a10 0-0	A26 0-0	M06 1-0	a21 2-3	S26 1-1
3 CAMBRIDGE U	N04 2-2	J01 0-1		S26 1-2	S09 0-1	a29 4-0	O17 1-0	F10 3-2	m01 2-1	J20 2-0	S22 1-0	a10 2-1	A26 0-1	a17 2-1	M06 2-0	D17 3-2	D02 0-3	a02 5-2	O28 5-3	F25 2-1	a23 0-2	O13 5-2	M30 1-1	M16 2-2
4 CARLISLE U	a10 1-3	a16 1-1	a04 3-1		A26 4-3	S30 1-0	M20 1-0	F13 1-0	S23 3-0	S09 1-1	F10 1-1	O28 1-0	J20 2-1	a24 1-2	N04 3-2	D02 0-0	F24 0-1	M31 3-1	O17 0-1	J06 3-0	D17 3-1	a28 2-0	O07 1-0	J01 2-1
5 CHESTERFIELD	S16 2-0	S02 0-1	a25 1-1	J13 3-0		A19 1-1	J01 0-1	M20 2-1	M31 2-0	m05 2-0	O17 4-3	N25 3-1	M10 2-1	O07 0-0	F03 3-1	a16 1-1	S30 2-1	a10 2-2	m01 1-1	O28 1-1	N11 1-1	M03 5-1	F17 3-0	D16 0-0
6 COLCHESTER U	M17 1-0	m05 1-2	N10 1-2	M06 4-0	J20 1-0		a24 2-0	a10 0-1	F23 2-0	F20 1-0	A26 2-2	J01 3-1	S08 1-1	D02 0-1	S26 4-1	O28 0-1	F10 1-2	S23 0-0	M31 1-0	a16 0-2	J05 0-1	D16 0-3	O17 1-3	O13 0-2
7 DONCASTER R	S26 0-1	O21 2-3	M25 2-1	O14 1-1	a14 1-0	D30 2-0		J20 2-1	A26 0-0	J16 0-0	a21 3-4	M06 2-2	F25 0-1	F13 0-1	O31 1-1	S09 0-3	a28 4-0	F10 1-1	N04 1-2	S22 0-1	D02 2-1	M17 2-1	D26 2-2	a07 1-2
8 EXETER C	a16 2-0	m01 2-1	S16 3-2	S02 0-0	O14 2-1	N01 2-1	A19 1-0		D16 3-1	S27 2-1	M07 2-0	J13 3-1	O21 2-0	N04 3-0	F17 2-0	M17 2-0	M24 5-0	a28 3-2	M28 1-0	a25 2-1	a07 1-1	J01 3-0	N25 1-1	M03 3-1
9 GILLINGHAM	A19 0-0	S16 0-0	M03 1-0	F27 2-1	O21 3-0	N24 3-3	J13 3-1	a21 1-1		M24 1-2	M16 3-1	J27 0-0	a14 0-1	a28 1-1	D26 1-2	M06 0-0	O31 1-0	N04 2-0	S02 0-3	S26 5-0	O14 0-3	a07 0-2	D30 1-0	F17 0-0
10 GRIMSBY T	N25 2-1	F17 4-2	A19 0-0	J27 1-0	N04 0-1	S02 4-1	M03 2-1	M10 1-0	O17 2-0		O28 1-1	a24 0-0	S30 0-2	M31 1-0	S16 2-3	a10 1-2	O07 1-2	M20 3-0	a17 2-1	D19 2-0	J01 4-2	J13 0-0	a28 5-1	F03 3-0
11 HALIFAX T	F17 4-1	a24 0-0	F02 0-0	S15 1-1	M24 1-1	J12 1-1	D15 0-2	S30 1-2	O06 0-1	a07 2-2		A19 4-0	O31 1-1	M20 0-1	N25 1-2	J01 2-2	O21 1-0	M10 1-2	M03 0-1	N10 1-2	m05 1-2	S02 3-1	J26 4-2	a16 2-2
12 HARTLEPOOL U	a28 2-0	M20 3-0	O31 1-2	a07 1-0	F24 3-1	a14 0-2	S30 0-6	A26 0-3	S09 1-2	D30 4-2	J20 2-0		D02 1-2	J06 1-1	a21 4-2	S23 2-2	M10 2-1	D26 4-1	O07 3-2	F13 1-1	F10 5-0	M24 1-1	N04 3-0	O21 1-2
13 HEREFORD U	M03 4-1	M28 0-1	J13 0-2	A19 2-2	S27 3-2	M14 2-0	N25 0-1	M31 2-1	J01 1-2	M07 0-1	a11 0-1	F17 4-1		O28 2-2	S02 3-0	a28 1-2	N04 1-3	O18 3-1	D16 1-2	O14 0-3	M17 1-2	a16 0-0	S16 0-0	a25 1-2
14 LINCOLN C	J13 0-1	N25 1-0	D26 4-3	D30 1-3	M17 1-1	F17 2-1	S02 2-1	m05 1-5	N11 1-3	O21 1-1	O14 2-1	M03 4-1	a07 1-0		M25 1-2	S27 1-0	a21 1-2	a14 0-0	A19 1-0	M07 2-0	N01 0-0	a04 2-2	F03 1-0	S16 0-0
15 MAIDSTONE U	J01 5-1	O07 1-2	S30 2-2	m05 5-2	S23 0-1	M10 4-1	a11 1-0	D02 1-0	a16 0-1	F10 2-2	F24 1-2	D16 4-2	F14 2-0	O18 2-0		J20 1-1	a04 2-0	A26 4-1	M21 1-1	M31 3-0	S09 0-1	a25 5-1	O28 2-0	N11 1-0
16 PETERBOROUGH U	S02 1-1	M24 4-1	a21 1-2	F17 3-0	D26 1-1	a07 1-0	J27 2-1	O07 4-3	S30 1-1	N01 1-1	a14 3-0	F07 0-2	N11 1-1	M13 1-0	A19 1-0		M21 0-1	D30 1-2	S16 1-1	m05 1-2	O21 2-0	N25 1-1	M03 3-1	J13 1-1
17 ROCHDALE	a24 2-0	A19 2-1	M27 2-0	N25 1-2	M06 1-0	S16 2-2	N11 1-3	O17 1-0	a10 1-0	M17 0-1	M31 0-2	S26 0-0	m05 5-2	D16 1-0	M03 3-2	O14 1-2		O28 1-0	J13 3-0	J01 0-1	a16 1-1	F03 0-0	S02 0-3	F06 0-1
18 SCARBOROUGH	J06 1-0	M03 4-2	S02 1-1	O21 2-1	N01 2-3	F03 2-2	S16 1-2	N11 1-2	m05 0-1	O14 3-1	S27 2-3	a16 4-1	M24 0-1	J01 2-0	J13 0-1	a25 2-1	a07 2-1		J27 0-0	M17 1-1	D09 2-0	F17 0-0	A19 2-1	N24 1-3
19 SCUNTHORPE U	M06 3-2	N11 3-0	a07 1-1	M24 2-3	D30 0-1	O21 4-0	m05 4-1	S23 5-4	F13 0-0	D26 2-2	J06 1-1	M17 0-1	a21 3-3	J20 1-1	O14 1-0	F10 0-0	A26 0-1	S09 0-1		D02 1-1	F24 5-0	S26 2-0	a14 3-1	O31 1-1
20 SOUTHEND U	J27 5-0	O31 3-2	N24 0-0	M03 2-0	a07 0-2	D26 0-2	F02 2-0	D30 1-2	M09 2-0	a20 0-2	a27 2-0	S01 3-0	M20 2-0	S30 2-0	O21 0-1	N04 0-0	a14 3-2	O07 1-0	F16 0-0		M23 2-0	S15 1-0	J12 2-1	A19 2-0
21 STOCKPORT CO	F03 1-1	J13 3-1	D29 3-1	a20 3-1	a28 3-1	M02 1-1	F16 3-1	O28 2-1	M19 1-0	a14 2-4	N03 0-1	S15 6-0	O07 2-1	a09 1-1	J27 1-2	M30 0-0	D26 2-1	S30 3-2	N25 4-2	O16 1-0		A19 1-1	M09 0-2	S01 2-2
22 TORQUAY U	M31 1-2	S30 0-1	M20 3-0	N11 1-2	M13 1-0	a21 4-1	O07 2-0	a14 0-2	N14 0-2	A26 0-3	M27 1-0	O17 4-3	D26 1-1	S09 0-3	D30 2-1	F24 2-1	S23 1-0	D02 3-2	M10 0-3	F06 3-0	J20 3-0		a10 0-1	m05 1-1
23 WREXHAM	O14 2-2	M13 1-0	O21 2-3	M17 1-0	D02 0-2	M24 3-2	a16 0-0	F24 1-1	a24 2-1	N11 0-1	S09 2-1	m05 1-2	F10 0-0	S23 0-2	a07 4-2	J06 2-1	F13 1-1	J20 0-2	J01 0-0	A26 3-3	S05 0-1	O31 1-1		M06 2-0
24 YORK C	O17 2-2	M10 1-3	O07 4-2	a14 0-1	a21 4-0	J27 3-1	O28 2-1	a02 3-0	D09 1-0	S23 0-1	D26 0-2	M31 1-1	D30 1-2	F10 0-0	a28 0-0	A26 1-0	S09 1-0	F24 1-2	a10 0-1	J20 2-1	F13 0-3	N04 1-1	S30 1-0	

LEAGUE TABLES

DIVISION 1

	P	W	D	L	F	A	W	D	L	F	A	Pts
Liverpool	38	13	5	1	38	15	10	5	4	40	22	79
Aston Villa	38	13	3	3	36	20	8	4	7	21	18	70
Tottenham H	38	12	1	6	35	24	7	5	7	24	23	63
Arsenal	38	14	3	2	38	11	4	5	10	16	27	62
Chelsea	38	8	7	4	31	24	8	5	6	27	26	60
Everton	38	14	3	2	40	16	3	5	11	17	30	59
Southampton	38	10	5	4	40	27	5	5	9	31	36	55
Wimbledon	38	5	8	6	22	23	8	8	3	25	17	55
Nottingham F	38	9	4	6	31	21	6	5	8	24	26	54
Norwich C	38	7	10	2	24	14	6	4	9	20	28	53
Q.P.R.	38	9	4	6	27	22	4	7	8	18	22	50
Coventry C	38	11	2	6	24	25	3	5	11	15	34	49
Manchester U	38	8	6	5	26	14	5	3	11	20	33	48
Manchester C	38	9	4	6	26	21	3	8	8	17	31	48
Crystal Palace	38	8	7	4	27	23	5	2	12	15	43	48
Derby Co	38	9	1	9	29	21	4	6	9	14	19	46
Luton T	38	8	8	3	24	18	2	5	12	19	39	43
Sheffield W	38	8	6	5	21	17	3	4	12	14	34	43
Charlton A	38	4	6	9	18	25	3	3	13	13	32	30
Millwall	38	4	6	9	23	25	1	5	13	16	40	26

DIVISION 2

	P	W	D	L	F	A	W	D	L	F	A	Pts
Leeds U	46	16	6	1	46	18	8	7	8	33	34	85
Sheffield U	46	14	5	4	43	27	10	8	5	35	31	85
Newcastle U	46	17	4	2	51	26	5	10	8	29	29	80
Swindon T	46	12	6	5	49	29	8	8	7	30	30	74
Blackburn R	46	10	9	4	43	30	9	8	6	31	29	74
Sunderland	46	10	8	5	41	32	10	6	7	29	32	74
West Ham U	46	14	5	4	50	22	6	7	10	30	35	72
Oldham A	46	15	7	1	50	23	4	7	12	20	34	71
Ipswich T	46	13	7	3	38	22	6	5	12	29	44	69
Wolverh'pton W	46	12	5	6	37	20	6	8	9	30	40	67
Port Vale	46	11	9	3	37	20	4	7	12	25	37	61
Portsmouth	46	9	8	6	40	34	6	8	9	22	31	61
Leicester C	46	10	8	5	34	29	5	6	12	33	50	59
Hull C	46	7	8	8	27	31	7	8	8	31	34	58
Watford	46	11	6	6	41	28	3	9	11	17	32	57
Plymouth A	46	9	8	6	30	23	5	5	13	28	40	55
Oxford U	46	8	7	8	35	31	7	2	14	22	35	54
Brighton & H.A.	46	10	6	7	28	27	5	3	15	28	45	54
Barnsley	46	7	9	7	22	23	6	6	11	27	48	54
W.B.A.	46	6	8	9	35	37	6	7	10	32	34	51
Middlesbrough	46	10	3	10	33	29	3	8	12	19	34	50
Bournemouth	46	8	6	9	30	31	4	6	13	27	45	48
Bradford C	46	9	6	8	26	24	0	8	15	18	44	41
Stoke C	46	4	11	8	20	24	2	8	13	15	39	37

DIVISION 3

	P	W	D	L	F	A	W	D	L	F	A	Pts
Bristol R	46	15	8	0	43	14	11	7	5	28	21	93
Bristol C	46	15	5	3	40	16	12	5	6	36	24	91
Notts Co	46	17	4	2	40	18	8	8	7	33	35	87
Tranmere R	46	15	5	3	54	22	8	6	9	32	27	80
Bury	46	11	7	5	35	19	10	4	9	35	30	74
Bolton W	46	12	7	4	32	19	6	8	9	27	29	69
Birmingham C	46	10	7	6	33	19	8	5	10	27	40	66
Huddersfield T	46	11	5	7	30	23	6	9	8	31	39	65
Rotherham U	46	12	6	5	48	28	5	7	11	23	34	64
Reading	46	10	9	4	33	21	5	10	8	24	32	64
Shrewsbury T	46	10	9	4	38	24	6	6	11	21	30	63
Crewe A	46	10	8	5	32	24	5	9	9	24	29	62
Brentford	46	11	4	8	41	31	7	3	13	25	35	61
Leyton O	46	9	6	8	28	24	7	4	12	24	32	58
Mansfield T	46	13	2	8	34	25	3	5	15	16	40	55
Chester C	46	11	7	5	30	23	2	8	13	13	32	54
Swansea C	46	10	6	7	25	27	4	6	13	20	36	54
Wigan A	46	10	6	7	29	22	3	8	12	19	42	53
Preston N.E.	46	10	7	6	42	30	4	3	16	23	49	52
Fulham	46	8	8	7	33	27	4	7	12	22	39	51
Cardiff C	46	6	9	8	30	35	6	5	12	21	35	50
Northampton T	46	7	7	9	27	31	4	7	12	24	37	47
Blackpool	46	8	6	9	29	33	2	10	11	20	40	46
Walsall	46	6	8	9	23	30	3	6	14	17	42	41

DIVISION 4

	P	W	D	L	F	A	W	D	L	F	A	Pts
Exeter C	46	20	3	0	50	14	8	2	13	33	34	89
Grimsby T	46	14	4	5	41	20	8	9	6	29	27	79
Southend U	46	15	3	5	35	14	7	6	10	26	34	75
Stockport Co	46	13	6	4	45	27	8	5	10	23	35	74
Maidstone U	46	14	4	5	49	21	8	3	12	28	40	73
Cambridge U	46	14	3	6	45	30	7	7	9	31	36	73
Chesterfield	46	12	9	2	41	19	7	5	11	22	31	71
Carlisle U	46	15	4	4	38	20	6	4	13	23	40	71
Peterborough U	46	10	8	5	35	23	7	9	7	24	23	68
Lincoln C	46	11	6	6	30	27	7	8	8	18	21	68
Scunthorpe U	46	9	9	5	42	25	8	6	9	27	29	66
Rochdale	46	11	4	8	28	23	9	2	12	24	32	66
York C	46	10	5	8	29	24	6	11	6	26	29	64
Gillingham	46	9	8	6	28	21	8	3	12	18	27	62
Torquay U	46	12	2	9	33	29	3	10	10	20	37	57
Burnley	46	6	10	7	19	18	8	4	11	26	37	56
Hereford U	46	7	4	12	31	32	8	6	9	25	30	55
Scarborough	46	10	5	8	35	28	5	5	13	25	45	55
Hartlepool U	46	12	4	7	45	33	3	6	14	21	55	55
Doncaster R	46	7	7	9	29	29	7	2	14	24	31	51
Wrexham	46	8	8	7	28	28	5	4	14	23	39	51
Aldershot	46	8	7	8	28	26	4	7	12	21	43	50
Halifax T	46	5	9	9	31	29	7	4	12	26	36	49
Colchester U	46	9	3	11	26	25	2	7	14	22	50	43

Football League Records

Top scorers: Div 1, L.Chapman (Leeds United) 31 goals; Div 2, E.Sheringham (Millwall) 38 goals; Div 3, B.Angell (Southend United), A.Philliskirk (Bolton Wanderers) 26 goals; Div 4, J.Allon (Hartlepool United), S.Norris (Halifax Town) 35 goals.

Play-offs: Div 1, Brighton & Hove Albion v Millwall 4-1, 2-1; Middlesbrough v Notts County 1-1, 0-1; Brighton & Hove Albion v Notts County (Wembley) 1-3; Div 2, Brentford v Tranmere Rovers 2-2, 0-1; Bury v Bolton Wanderers 1-1, 0-1; Bolton Wanderers v Tranmere Rovers (Wembley) 0-1; Div 3, Scunthorpe United v Blackpool 1-1, 1-2; Torquay United v Burnley 2-0, 0-1; Blackpool v Torquay United (Wembley) 2-2 (4-5 penalties).

Oldham Athletic, West Ham United, Sheffield Wednesday and Notts County promoted to Div 1; Sunderland and Derby

Arsenal's Swedish international midfielder Anders Limpar, scored 11 goals in 34 appearances for the Gunners in their latest title-winning campaign.

DIVISION 1

	ARSENAL	ASTON VILLA	CHELSEA	COVENTRY C	CRYSTAL P	DERBY CO	EVERTON	LEEDS U	LIVERPOOL	LUTON T	MANCHESTER C	MANCHESTER U	NORWICH C	NOTTINGHAM F	Q.P.R.	SHEFFIELD U	SOUTHAMPTON	SUNDERLAND	TOTTENHAM H	WIMBLEDON
1 ARSENAL		a03 5-0	S15 4-1	m11 6-1	F23 4-0	D26 3-0	J19 1-0	M17 2-0	D02 3-0	A29 2-1	a17 2-2	m06 3-1	O06 2-0	M20 1-1	a23 2-0	D29 4-1	N17 4-0	O27 1-0	S01 0-0	D15 2-2
2 ASTON VILLA	D23 0-0		m11 2-2	S08 2-1	J01 2-0	F02 3-2	M30 2-2	O27 0-0	J12 0-0	M09 1-2	a23 1-5	a06 1-1	m08 2-1	N10 1-1	S22 2-2	D01 2-1	A25 1-1	O06 3-0	M16 3-2	a20 1-2
3 CHELSEA	F02 2-1	N03 1-0		D22 2-1	D08 2-1	A25 2-1	J01 1-2	M30 1-2	m04 4-2	a06 3-3	S22 1-1	M09 3-2	N10 1-1	O20 0-0	J12 2-0	S29 2-2	M23 0-2	S08 3-2	D01 3-2	F16 0-0
4 COVENTRY C	N03 0-2	J19 2-1	a01 1-0		M02 3-1	a13 3-0	A29 3-1	N24 1-1	N17 0-1	M13 2-1	M23 3-1	D15 2-2	D29 2-0	S01 2-2	S29 3-1	m04 0-0	O20 1-2	F23 0-0	D26 2-0	S15 0-0
5 CRYSTAL P	N10 0-0	a13 0-0	A28 2-1	D01 2-1		M16 2-1	a20 0-0	O06 1-1	D30 1-0	D16 1-0	a01 1-3	m11 3-0	J19 1-3	S15 2-2	F16 0-0	S01 1-0	M09 2-1	D26 2-1	a17 1-0	O27 4-3
6 DERBY CO	M30 0-2	S15 0-2	D15 4-6	J01 1-1	S29 0-2		m08 2-3	a23 0-1	M23 1-7	N03 2-1	O20 1-1	N10 0-0	F23 0-0	N24 2-1	D23 1-1	A29 1-1	m04 6-2	M02 3-3	J20 0-1	S01 1-1
7 EVERTON	S08 1-1	D26 1-0	a13 2-2	D08 1-0	O20 0-0	D29 2-0		A25 2-3	S22 2-3	m04 1-0	J13 2-0	D01 0-1	a01 1-0	M23 0-0	N03 3-0	F23 1-2	S29 3-0	F02 2-0	N18 1-1	a10 1-2
8 LEEDS U	S29 2-2	m04 5-2	D26 4-1	M09 2-0	M23 1-2	N17 3-0	D16 2-0		a13 4-5	J19 2-1	a10 1-2	A28 0-0	S01 3-0	N03 3-1	O20 2-3	m08 2-1	D01 2-1	a02 5-0	S15 0-2	D29 3-0
9 LIVERPOOL	M03 0-1	S01 2-1	O27 2-0	a09 1-1	a23 3-0	O06 2-0	F09 3-1	J01 3-0		N10 4-0	N24 2-2	S16 4-0	a20 3-0	A28 2-0	M30 1-3	D15 2-0	D22 3-2	M16 2-1	m11 2-0	J19 1-1
10 LUTON T	D08 1-1	N24 2-0	D29 2-0	S22 1-0	A25 1-1	m11 2-0	O27 1-1	S08 1-0	F23 3-1		N17 2-2	S04 0-1	M16 0-1	M02 1-0	F02 1-2	D26 0-1	J12 3-4	a20 1-2	a01 0-0	a13 0-1
11 MANCHESTER C	J01 0-1	S05 2-1	F09 2-1	O06 2-0	D22 0-2	a20 2-1	S01 1-0	N11 2-3	M09 0-3	M05 3-0		O27 3-3	S15 2-1	a06 3-1	D01 2-1	J19 2-0	M30 3-3	m11 3-2	D15 2-1	M16 1-1
12 MANCHESTER U	O20 0-1	D29 1-1	N25 2-3	A25 2-0	N03 2-0	a16 3-1	M02 0-2	D08 1-1	F03 1-1	M23 4-1	m04 1-0		D26 3-0	S29 0-1	S08 3-1	N17 2-0	S22 3-2	J12 3-0	m20 1-1	a02 2-1
13 NORWICH C	M23 0-0	N17 2-0	a17 1-3	a06 2-2	S08 0-3	S22 2-1	D22 1-0	J12 2-0	O20 1-1	S29 1-3	F02 1-2	M30 0-3		J02 2-6	m04 1-0	N03 3-0	D08 3-1	A25 3-2	a10 2-1	D01 0-4
14 NOTTINGHAM F	S22 0-2	F23 2-2	a20 7-0	J12 3-0	F02 0-1	a10 1-0	O07 3-1	m11 4-3	m06 2-1	D01 2-2	D29 1-3	M16 1-1	a24 5-0		A25 1-1	a01 2-0	S08 3-1	N17 2-0	O27 1-2	D26 2-1
15 Q.P.R.	N24 1-3	a10 2-1	S01 1-0	M16 1-0	N17 1-2	a01 1-1	m11 1-1	a17 2-0	D26 1-1	S15 6-1	M02 1-0	J19 1-1	O27 1-3	D15 1-2		a13 1-2	F23 2-1	D29 3-2	O06 0-0	A29 0-1
16 SHEFFIELD U	a06 0-2	M02 2-1	M16 1-0	O27 0-1	J12 0-1	J26 1-0	N10 0-0	S23 0-2	A25 1-3	M30 2-1	S08 1-1	F26 2-1	m11 2-1	D22 3-2	J01 1-0		F02 4-1	N24 0-2	a20 2-2	O06 1-2
17 SOUTHAMPTON	a09 1-1	D15 1-1	O06 3-3	a20 2-1	N24 2-3	O27 0-1	M16 3-4	M02 2-0	a01 1-0	S01 1-2	D26 2-1	M13 1-1	A28 1-0	J19 1-1	N10 3-1	S15 2-0		a13 3-1	D29 3-0	m11 1-1
18 SUNDERLAND	m04 0-0	M23 1-3	J19 1-0	N10 0-0	M30 2-1	D01 1-2	S15 2-2	D23 0-1	S29 0-1	O20 2-0	N03 1-1	S01 2-1	D15 1-2	F16 1-0	a06 0-1	M09 0-1	J01 1-0		A28 0-0	a23 0-0
19 TOTTENHAM H	J12 0-0	S29 2-1	M02 1-1	M30 2-2	S22 1-1	S08 3-0	a24 3-3	F02 0-0	N04 1-3	D22 2-1	A25 3-1	J01 1-2	N24 2-1	m04 1-1	M23 0-0	O20 4-0	a06 2-0	D08 3-3		N10 4-2
20 WIMBLEDON	A25 0-3	O20 0-0	N17 2-1	F02 1-0	m04 0-3	J12 3-1	N24 2-1	a06 0-1	S08 1-2	J01 2-0	S29 1-1	D22 1-3	M02 0-0	M30 3-1	D08 3-0	M23 1-1	N03 1-1	S22 2-2	F23 5-1	

Andy Ritchie, whose goalscoring helped Oldham Athletic into Division One after an absence of 68 years.

DIVISION 2

	BARNSLEY	BLACKBURN R	BRIGHTON & HA	BRISTOL C	BRISTOL R	CHARLTON A	HULL C	IPSWICH T	LEICESTER C	MIDDLESBROUGH	MILLWALL	NEWCASTLE U	NOTTS CO	OLDHAM A	OXFORD U	PLYMOUTH A	PORTSMOUTH	PORT VALE	SHEFFIELD W	SWINDON T	WATFORD	W.B.A.	WEST HAM U	WOLVERHAMPTON W
1 BARNSLEY		a23 0-1	A25 2-1	J01 2-0	F26 1-0	M16 1-1	a06 3-1	O02 5-1	N10 1-1	m11 1-0	J12 1-2	m07 1-1	a09 1-0	S08 0-1	O06 3-0	M30 1-0	M19 4-0	S22 1-1	O23 1-1	O27 5-1	M02 2-1	a20 1-1	D22 1-0	N24 1-1
2 BLACKBURN R	S15 1-2		S29 1-2	D15 0-1	M12 2-2	a13 2-2	A28 2-1	J19 0-1	S18 4-1	a01 1-0	N03 1-0	S01 0-1	D26 0-1	M23 2-0	D29 1-3	O20 0-0	F09 1-1	N23 1-1	N10 1-0	M02 2-1	O13 0-2	F16 0-3	a27 3-1	m04 1-1
3 BRIGHTON & HA	D15 1-0	M16 1-0		a23 0-1	D26 0-1	S15 3-2	O24 3-1	m11 2-1	F20 3-0	O27 2-4	N24 0-0	J16 4-2	a13 0-0	M02 1-2	a20 0-3	N10 3-2	S19 3-2	a03 1-2	O03 0-4	O06 3-3	J19 3-0	M20 2-0	a10 1-0	S01 1-1
4 BRISTOL C	a13 1-0	A25 4-2	S22 3-1		M05 1-0	D01 0-1	N17 4-1	M09 4-2	M12 1-0	D29 3-0	a27 1-4	S29 1-0	a01 3-2	O20 1-2	F23 3-1	S08 1-1	D26 4-1	m04 1-1	D08 1-1	J12 0-4	N03 3-2	F02 2-0	O13 1-1	M23 1-1
5 BRISTOL R	N07 2-1	O03 1-2	M30 1-3	J26 3-2		S01 2-1	S15 1-1	a10 1-0	D15 0-0	a20 2-0	M02 1-0	D22 1-1	M16 1-1	N24 2-0	O24 1-0	a06 0-0	O27 1-2	N10 2-0	O06 0-1	M20 2-1	F16 3-1	m11 1-1	J01 0-1	J19 1-1
6 CHARLTON A	S29 2-1	J01 0-0	F02 1-2	M02 2-1	J12 2-2		D22 2-1	a06 1-1	O13 1-2	F23 0-1	S22 0-0	a27 1-0	J22 3-1	a16 1-1	N17 3-3	N03 0-1	N24 2-1	M23 0-1	S08 0-1	A25 1-2	O20 1-2	M30 2-0	m04 1-1	M12 1-0
7 HULL C	D29 1-2	D08 3-1	a27 0-1	F16 1-2	F02 2-0	a01 2-2		N10 3-3	N23 5-2	M02 0-0	a16 1-1	N03 2-1	A25 1-2	O13 2-2	D26 3-3	m04 2-0	a13 0-2	S29 3-2	J12 0-1	S08 1-1	M12 1-1	S22 1-1	M23 0-0	O20 1-2
8 IPSWICH T	a25 2-0	S08 2-1	N03 1-3	N24 1-1	S22 2-1	D29 4-4	F23 2-0		m04 3-2	D26 0-1	F02 0-3	O20 2-1	N17 0-0	a27 1-2	a13 1-1	M22 3-1	a02 2-2	O13 3-0	A25 0-2	D08 1-1	S29 1-1	J12 1-0	a17 0-1	M02 0-0
9 LEICESTER C	F23 2-1	J26 1-3	a06 3-0	O03 3-0	A25 3-2	M20 1-2	M09 0-1	O27 1-2		M16 4-3	M30 1-2	D01 5-4	O06 2-1	a10 0-0	m11 1-0	F02 3-1	a20 2-1	J12 1-1	S22 2-4	O24 2-2	D23 0-0	J01 2-1	S08 1-2	N17 1-0
10 MIDDLESBROUGH	N03 1-0	D22 0-1	m04 2-0	a06 2-1	O20 1-2	N10 1-2	D01 3-0	M30 1-1	S29 6-0		O13 2-1	M12 3-0	S08 1-0	S22 0-1	M09 0-0	J12 0-0	F26 1-2	a09 4-0	J01 0-2	F02 2-0	M23 1-2	F19 3-2	A25 0-0	a27 2-0
11 MILLWALL	S01 4-1	m11 2-1	M09 3-0	O24 1-2	D01 1-1	a10 3-1	S19 3-3	S15 1-1	D26 2-1	M20 2-2		J19 0-1	a20 1-2	D29 0-0	N07 1-2	F16 4-1	O03 2-0	a13 1-2	O27 4-2	M16 1-0	D15 0-2	O06 4-1	N10 1-1	a03 2-1
12 NEWCASTLE U	N17 0-0	J12 1-0	F27 0-0	M16 0-0	a01 0-2	O24 1-3	m11 1-2	a20 2-2	M02 2-1	O03 0-0	S08 1-2		D29 0-2	a13 3-2	a10 2-2	A25 2-0	O06 2-1	F02 2-0	a17 1-0	D26 1-1	N24 1-0	O27 1-1	S22 1-1	F23 0-0
13 NOTTS CO	S18 2-3	M30 4-1	J01 2-1	D22 3-2	S29 3-2	O30 2-2	D15 2-1	m07 3-1	M23 0-2	J19 3-2	O20 0-1	a06 3-0		m04 2-0	S01 3-1	a27 4-0	S15 2-1	M12 1-1	M02 0-2	N24 0-0	a16 1-0	N10 4-3	N03 0-1	O13 1-1
14 OLDHAM A	J19 2-0	O06 1-1	D01 6-1	a20 2-1	M09 2-0	S18 1-1	M20 1-2	O23 2-0	A28 2-0	m07 2-0	a06 1-1	J01 1-1	O27 2-1		S15 3-0	D21 5-3	S01 3-1	F16 2-0	m11 3-2	O02 3-2	N10 4-1	M16 2-1	M29 1-1	D15 4-1
15 OXFORD U	M23 2-0	a06 0-0	O20 3-0	N10 3-1	a27 3-1	F16 1-1	M30 1-0	J01 2-1	N03 2-2	N24 2-5	F27 0-0	O13 0-0	J12 3-3	F02 5-1		a17 0-0	M02 1-0	A25 5-2	D22 2-2	S22 2-4	m04 0-1	S08 1-3	M13 2-1	S29 1-1
16 PLYMOUTH A	D26 1-1	a20 4-1	F23 2-0	J19 1-0	D29 2-2	m11 2-0	O27 4-1	O06 0-0	S15 2-0	S01 1-1	N17 3-2	D16 0-1	O23 0-0	a01 1-2	S18 2-2		M16 1-1	M02 2-0	M19 1-1	a13 3-3	A28 1-1	O02 2-0	N24 0-1	a09 1-0
17 PORTSMOUTH	O13 0-0	S22 3-2	a16 1-0	M30 4-1	m04 3-1	M09 0-1	J01 5-1	D21 1-1	O20 3-1	N17 0-3	M12 0-0	M23 0-1	F02 2-1	J12 1-4	D01 1-1	S29 3-1		S08 2-4	a06 2-0	F23 2-1	a27 0-1	A25 1-1	D08 0-1	N03 0-0
18 PORT VALE	a15 0-1	M09 3-0	D22 0-1	O27 3-2	F23 3-2	O06 1-1	M16 0-0	M18 1-2	S01 2-0	S17 3-1	J01 0-2	S15 0-1	O01 0-1	N17 1-0	D15 1-0	D01 5-1	J19 3-2		m06 1-1	m11 3-1	M30 0-0	O22 1-2	a06 0-1	A28 1-2
19 SHEFFIELD W	a27 3-1	a10 3-1	M13 1-1	m08 3-1	M23 2-1	J19 0-0	S01 5-1	D15 2-2	a24 0-0	a13 2-0	m04 2-1	S18 2-2	D01 2-2	N03 2-2	a01 0-2	O13 3-0	D29 2-1	O20 1-1		N17 2-1	S15 2-0	M09 1-0	S29 1-1	D26 2-2
20 SWINDON T	m04 1-2	D01 1-1	M23 1-3	S02 0-1	O13 0-2	D15 1-1	J19 3-1	A28 1-0	a27 5-2	S15 1-3	S30 0-0	M30 3-2	a23 1-2	M12 2-2	M05 0-0	J01 1-1	N10 3-0	N03 1-2	F19 2-1		a06 1-2	D22 2-1	O20 0-1	S18 1-0
21 WATFORD	D01 0-0	M19 0-3	S08 0-1	m11 2-3	N17 1-1	a20 2-1	O02 0-1	M16 1-1	a01 1-0	O06 0-3	A25 1-2	M09 1-2	S22 1-3	F23 1-1	O27 1-1	D08 2-0	O23 0-1	D26 2-1	F02 2-2	D29 2-2		a23 1-1	J12 0-1	a13 3-1
22 W.B.A.	O20 1-1	N17 2-0	O13 1-1	S15 2-1	N03 3-1	D26 1-0	a10 1-1	S01 1-2	a13 2-1	N06 0-1	M23 0-1	m04 1-1	F23 2-2	S29 0-0	J19 2-0	M13 1-2	D15 0-0	a27 1-1	N24 1-2	a01 2-1	D05 1-1		M02 0-0	D29 1-1
23 WEST HAM U	a01 3-2	O24 1-0	N17 2-1	M20 1-0	m08 1-0	O27 2-1	O06 7-1	S19 3-1	J19 1-0	D15 0-0	F24 3-1	a24 1-1	m11 1-2	D26 2-0	O03 2-0	M05 2-2	A29 1-1	D29 0-0	M16 1-3	a20 2-0	S01 1-0	D01 3-1		S15 1-1
24 WOLVERHAMPTON W	M09 0-5	O27 2-3	J12 2-3	O06 4-0	S08 1-1	O02 3-0	a20 0-0	D01 2-2	M05 2-1	O23 1-0	D22 4-1	N10 2-1	M19 0-2	A25 2-3	M16 3-3	S22 3-1	m11 3-1	F26 3-1	M30 3-2	a16 1-2	J01 0-0	a06 2-2	F02 2-1	

SEASON 1990-91

County relegated to Div 2; Cambridge United, Southend United, Grimsby Town and Tranmere Rovers promoted to Div 2; West Bromwich Albion and Hull City relegated to Div 3; Darlington, Stockport County, Hartlepool United, Peterborough United and Torquay United promoted to Div 3; Crewe Alexandra, Rotherham United and Mansfield Town relegated to Div 4.

DIVISION 3

	BIRMINGHAM C	BOLTON W	BOURNEMOUTH	BRADFORD C	BRENTFORD	BURY	CAMBRIDGE U	CHESTER C	CREWE A	EXETER C	FULHAM	GRIMSBY T	HUDDERSFIELD T	LEYTON O	MANSFIELD T	PRESTON N.E.	READING	ROTHERHAM U	SHREWSBURY T	SOUTHEND U	STOKE C	SWANSEA C	TRANMERE R	WIGAN A
1 BIRMINGHAM C		D29 1-3	N24 0-0	J05 1-1	D26 0-2	S15 1-0	J19 0-3	F23 1-0	a27 0-2	S18 1-1	M12 2-0	O20 0-0	N03 1-2	S01 3-1	a13 0-0	S29 1-1	M23 1-1	D15 2-1	m04 0-1	O13 1-1	a16 2-1	M02 2-0	a02 1-0	F05 0-0
2 BOLTON W	a07 3-1		J01 4-1	S01 0-1	F05 1-0	M19 1-3	D22 2-2	m11 1-0	S15 3-2	F13 1-0	M09 3-0	F16 0-0	F09 1-1	a20 1-0	O02 1-1	S18 1-2	N10 3-1	O23 0-0	J19 1-0	M30 1-0	O06 0-1	O27 1-0	D01 2-1	M16 2-1
3 BOURNEMOUTH	F16 1-2	a13 1-0		S18 3-1	J19 2-0	S01 1-1	a16 0-1	M02 1-0	O20 1-1	F05 2-1	S29 3-0	a02 2-1	a27 3-1	D29 2-2	D26 0-0	m02 0-0	M12 2-0	N10 4-2	N03 3-2	M23 3-1	S15 1-1	D14 1-0	O30 1-0	M05 0-3
4 BRADFORD C	F13 2-0	J12 1-1	F02 3-0		O06 0-1	J01 3-1	D15 0-1	O03 2-1	M26 2-0	M20 3-0	M30 0-0	J26 0-2	M03 2-2	M16 4-0	a20 1-0	N10 2-1	S08 2-1	m11 1-0	D22 2-4	a06 2-1	O24 1-2	S22 0-1	A25 1-2	O27 2-1
5 BRENTFORD	M30 2-2	S22 4-2	A25 0-0	M23 6-1		N10 2-2	O14 0-3	S08 0-1	a06 1-0	F16 1-0	a16 1-2	S29 1-0	O20 1-0	D02 1-0	J12 0-0	M12 2-0	a27 1-0	F02 1-2	J01 3-0	N04 0-1	M09 0-4	J26 2-0	m04 0-2	D23 1-0
6 BURY	J26 0-1	O13 2-2	J12 2-4	a13 0-0	F23 1-1		M23 3-1	A25 2-1	S29 1-3	D15 3-1	a27 1-1	a09 3-2	a01 2-1	F19 1-0	S22 1-0	D29 3-1	O20 2-1	S08 3-1	M12 2-1	m04 0-1	N24 1-1	F02 1-0	N03 3-0	M02 2-2
7 CAMBRIDGE U	A25 0-1	a02 2-1	a24 4-0	m07 2-1	M19 0-0	O06 2-2		S21 1-1	N30 3-4	M16 1-0	J12 1-0	D29 1-0	F23 0-0	O02 1-0	F01 2-1	a13 1-1	a09 3-0	O27 4-1	N24 3-1	S09 1-4	a20 3-0	m11 2-0	D26 3-1	O23 2-3
8 CHESTER C	N10 0-1	N03 0-2	D01 0-0	M12 4-2	a30 1-2	J19 1-0	M25 0-2		m04 3-1	S01 1-2	a06 1-0	O13 1-2	S29 1-2	S15 2-0	M09 1-0	a27 1-1	M05 1-0	M30 1-2	O20 3-2	D22 1-0	S18 1-1	a23 2-1	M23 0-2	F26 1-2
9 CREWE A	O23 1-1	a16 1-3	a20 0-2	N24 0-0	D29 3-3	M16 2-2	M01 3-1	O27 1-3		a13 1-1	A25 1-1	S08 1-2	D15 1-1	a01 3-3	m11 3-0	D26 2-2	F01 1-0	a30 3-1	F22 1-2	J12 0-2	O02 1-2	M19 3-0	S21 2-3	O06 1-0
10 EXETER C	F02 0-2	M26 2-1	S22 2-0	O13 2-2	N24 1-1	M09 2-0	S29 0-1	J12 1-1	J01 3-0		m04 0-1	N03 0-0	M13 2-2	F23 2-0	J26 2-0	M23 4-0	A25 1-3	D22 2-0	a30 3-0	a27 1-2	D01 2-0	S08 2-0	O20 0-0	M30 1-0
11 FULHAM	O02 2-2	D15 0-1	M16 1-1	D26 0-0	a23 0-1	O23 2-0	S01 0-2	D29 4-1	J19 2-1	O27 3-2		a13 0-0	S15 0-0	m11 1-1	a01 1-0	F05 1-0	M02 1-1	O06 2-0	a09 4-0	F23 0-3	M19 0-1	a20 1-1	N24 1-2	S18 1-2
12 GRIMSBY T	a20 0-0	N24 0-1	D22 5-0	S15 1-1	M16 2-0	J05 0-1	a06 1-0	M20 2-0	a23 0-1	m11 2-1	J01 3-0		S18 4-0	O23 2-2	D01 2-0	J19 4-1	M30 3-0	O02 2-1	F05 1-0	M09 1-0	O27 2-0	O06 1-0	F23 0-1	S01 4-3
13 HUDDERSFIELD T	m11 0-1	S08 4-0	O23 1-3	D02 1-2	a20 1-2	D22 2-1	N10 3-1	M16 1-1	M09 3-1	O02 1-0	J26 1-0	F02 1-1		O06 1-0	O27 2-2	F16 1-0	S22 0-2	M19 4-0	M30 2-1	A25 1-2	a06 3-0	J12 1-2	F26 2-1	J01 1-0
14 LEYTON O	J12 1-1	O20 0-1	a06 2-0	S29 2-1	M03 1-2	M30 1-0	M12 0-3	J26 1-0	D22 3-2	N10 1-0	N04 1-0	a27 0-2	M23 1-0		S08 2-1	D15 1-0	m04 4-0	S22 3-0	O13 3-2	a09 0-1	J01 0-2	A25 3-0	F02 4-0	a23 1-1
15 MANSFIELD T	J01 1-2	M12 4-0	M30 1-1	O20 0-1	S01 0-2	F05 0-1	S18 2-2	D15 1-0	N03 1-3	S15 0-2	D22 1-1	M02 1-1	m04 0-0	a16 3-3		O13 0-1	a06 2-0	a23 1-2	M23 2-1	S29 0-1	M05 0-0	N10 2-0	a27 0-2	J19 1-1
16 PRESTON N.E.	M16 2-0	F02 1-2	O27 0-0	F23 0-3	O02 1-1	a06 1-1	J01 0-2	O23 0-0	M30 5-1	O06 1-0	S22 1-0	A25 1-3	N24 1-1	M09 2-1	M19 3-1		J12 1-2	a20 1-2	D01 4-3	J26 2-1	D22 2-0	M26 2-0	S08 0-4	m11 2-1
17 READING	O06 2-2	F23 0-1	O02 2-1	a30 1-2	O23 1-2	a20 1-0	S15 2-2	a13 2-2	S18 2-1	J19 1-0	D01 1-0	D26 2-0	M26 1-2	O27 1-2	D29 2-1	S01 3-3		M16 2-0	a23 1-2	N24 2-4	m11 1-0	a01 0-0	M09 1-0	J26 3-1
18 ROTHERHAM U	M09 1-1	a27 2-2	F23 1-1	N03 0-2	S18 2-2	M05 0-3	m04 3-2	D26 2-1	a09 1-1	a01 2-4	M23 3-1	M12 1-4	O13 1-3	F05 0-0	N24 1-1	O20 1-0	S29 0-2		S01 2-2	D01 0-1	J19 0-0	a13 2-3	D29 1-1	S15 5-1
19 SHREWSBURY T	O27 4-1	A25 0-1	m11 3-1	a02 1-0	a13 1-1	O02 1-1	a18 1-2	a20 1-0	N09 1-0	D29 2-2	S08 2-2	S22 1-2	F19 0-0	M19 3-0	O06 0-3	M02 0-1	m07 5-1	J12 0-0		F02 0-1	M16 2-0	O23 1-2	M26 0-1	D15 0-0
20 SOUTHEND U	M18 2-1	D26 1-1	O05 2-1	D28 1-1	m11 0-1	O27 2-1	a30 0-0	a02 1-1	S01 3-2	O23 2-1	N10 1-1	D15 2-0	J19 0-1	m07 1-1	M15 2-1	S14 3-2	F19 1-2	M01 2-1	S18 2-1		F05 1-0	O02 4-1	a12 1-0	a19 0-2
21 STOKE C	S08 0-1	M23 2-2	F27 1-3	a27 2-1	D16 2-2	F16 2-2	O20 1-1	F02 2-3	M13 1-0	M02 2-1	O13 2-1	m04 0-0	D29 2-0	a13 1-2	M26 3-1	a01 0-1	N03 0-1	A25 3-1	S29 1-3	S22 4-0		D26 2-2	J12 1-1	N10 2-0
22 SWANSEA C	D01 2-0	m04 1-2	M09 1-2	m09 0-2	S15 2-2	S18 1-2	N03 0-0	N24 1-0	O13 3-1	F26 0-3	O20 2-2	M23 0-0	S01 1-0	a30 0-0	F23 1-2	a16 3-1	D22 3-1	J01 5-0	a27 0-1	M12 1-4	M30 2-1		S28 1-1	a06 1-6
23 TRANMERE R	D21 1-0	M01 1-1	M18 1-0	J18 2-1	O26 2-1	m11 1-2	M29 2-0	O06 1-2	F04 2-0	a20 1-0	F16 1-1	N10 1-2	J05 2-0	S17 3-0	O22 6-2	m07 2-1	D14 0-0	a05 1-2	S14 1-1	J01 3-1	A31 1-2	M15 2-1		O01 1-1
24 WIGAN A	S22 1-1	S28 2-1	S08 2-0	m04 3-0	a01 1-0	D01 1-2	a27 0-1	a16 2-0	M23 1-0	D26 4-1	F02 2-0	J12 2-0	a13 1-1	N24 1-2	A25 0-2	N03 2-1	O13 1-0	M26 2-0	M09 2-2	O20 4-1	F23 4-0	D29 2-4	M12 0-1	

DIVISION 4

	ALDERSHOT	BLACKPOOL	BURNLEY	CARDIFF C	CARLISLE U	CHESTERFIELD	DARLINGTON	DONCASTER R	GILLINGHAM	HALIFAX T	HARTLEPOOL U	HEREFORD U	LINCOLN C	MAIDSTONE U	NORTHAMPTON T	PETERBOROUGH U	ROCHDALE	SCARBOROUGH	SCUNTHORPE U	STOCKPORT CO	TORQUAY U	WALSALL	WREXHAM	YORK C
1 ALDERSHOT		F23 1-4	a16 1-2	S18 0-0	a13 3-0	a23 1-0	F19 0-2	M02 1-1	a27 1-0	N02 2-2	M12 1-5	D15 1-0	M23 0-3	N24 4-3	S14 3-3	D29 5-0	J19 2-2	S29 2-2	S01 3-2	O19 2-2	O12 2-3	m04 0-4	M05 3-2	a01 0-1
2 BLACKPOOL	N10 4-2		S18 1-2	a17 3-0	a02 6-0	F05 3-0	O13 1-2	F16 2-0	O20 2-0	a30 2-0	S29 2-0	M02 3-0	D29 5-0	D15 2-2	m07 2-1	D26 1-1	S01 0-0	M12 3-1	J19 3-1	a27 3-2	M23 1-0	N03 1-2	S15 4-1	a13 1-0
3 BURNLEY	S22 3-0	a23 2-0		D01 2-0	M16 2-1	M30 0-1	J12 3-1	a30 1-0	M09 2-2	N24 2-1	D22 4-0	M19 2-1	A25 2-2	O23 2-1	O02 3-0	a20 4-1	O27 1-0	S08 2-1	J01 1-1	J26 3-2	a06 1-1	F23 2-0	m11 2-0	O06 0-0
4 CARDIFF C	F01 1-3	m02 1-1	M01 3-0		D26 3-1	N10 2-1	a13 0-1	O23 0-2	F15 2-0	D29 1-0	J12 1-0	a20 0-2	J26 0-1	m11 0-0	a01 1-0	O27 1-1	O02 0-1	A25 0-0	M16 1-0	S22 3-3	S08 3-3	D15 0-2	O05 1-0	M19 2-1
5 CARLISLE U	J01 1-2	D23 1-0	S28 1-1	M30 3-2		O20 1-0	F26 0-2	A25 2-3	M12 0-4	O13 0-3	S22 1-0	J26 0-1	N03 0-0	S08 1-0	D15 4-1	J12 3-2	F16 1-1	a27 4-1	a06 0-3	F02 1-0	m04 3-1	M23 0-3	M02 2-0	N10 1-0
6 CHESTERFIELD	a30 1-0	S22 2-2	M05 2-1	F23 0-0	a20 4-1		a01 2-2	O27 2-1	D01 1-1	M09 2-1	A25 2-3	S08 1-0	F02 1-1	a13 1-2	O06 0-0	m11 2-2	M19 1-1	J12 0-1	O23 1-0	D29 1-1	J26 1-1	N25 2-2	M16 2-1	O02 2-2
7 DARLINGTON	M30 3-1	M19 1-1	S01 3-1	J01 4-1	J05 3-1	D22 1-0		M16 1-1	J29 1-1	S15 3-0	N10 0-1	O06 3-1	a09 1-1	a20 1-1	O23 1-1	O02 0-1	m11 2-0	a06 2-1	O27 0-0	M02 1-0	D15 3-0	M05 1-0	F05 1-0	S18 0-0
8 DONCASTER R	D01 3-0	N24 1-0	F26 2-1	a27 1-1	J19 4-0	m04 0-1	S29 0-1		N03 1-1	a23 1-2	O13 2-2	D29 3-1	O20 1-0	D26 3-0	a13 2-1	F22 0-2	J25 1-0	M24 0-2	M08 2-3	a01 1-0	m07 1-1	S18 2-0	S01 3-1	F05 2-2
9 GILLINGHAM	O23 1-1	a20 2-2	D15 3-2	N24 4-0	O02 2-1	M02 0-1	A25 1-0	m11 2-0		F22 1-0	S08 3-0	F02 2-1	a01 2-2	S22 0-2	D29 0-0	F26 2-3	O06 2-2	J25 1-1	M19 1-1	a13 1-3	J11 2-2	D26 1-0	O27 2-3	M16 0-0
10 HALIFAX T	m11 3-0	O27 5-3	F16 1-2	a06 1-2	M19 1-1	D15 2-1	J26 0-0	S08 0-1	N09 1-2		J01 1-2	O23 0-4	J12 1-1	a16 3-2	M15 2-1	F01 1-1	D21 2-0	M30 1-2	O06 0-0	A25 0-0	S21 0-1	M02 5-2	M26 2-0	a19 2-1
11 HARTLEPOOL U	O02 1-0	M16 1-2	a01 0-0	S01 0-2	F05 4-1	J19 2-0	F23 0-0	a16 1-1	a30 1-0	a13 2-1		O27 2-1	D15 2-0	O06 1-0	m11 3-1	O23 2-0	S18 2-2	N24 2-0	a09 2-0	J29 3-1	M02 0-0	M26 2-1	a20 2-1	O16 0-1
12 HEREFORD U	M09 1-0	D01 1-1	O13 3-0	O20 1-1	S15 4-2	a17 2-3	M23 1-1	a06 1-1	S19 1-1	a27 1-0	m04 1-3		M13 0-1	F23 4-0	A25 1-2	N24 0-0	J30 2-0	N03 3-3	D22 2-0	S29 0-0	J01 0-0	F06 0-0	M30 1-0	S01 2-0
13 LINCOLN C	O06 2-2	a06 0-1	J19 1-0	S15 0-0	m11 6-2	S19 1-1	N24 0-3	a20 0-0	D22 1-1	S01 1-0	M09 3-1	O03 1-1		M16 2-1	O27 3-1	M20 0-2	O24 1-2	D01 2-0	a17 1-2	F23 0-3	M30 3-2	J05 2-1	J01 0-0	M26 2-1
14 MAIDSTONE U	m08 1-1	M09 1-1	a27 1-0	N03 3-0	m01 0-0	J01 1-0	O20 2-3	M30 0-1	a24 3-1	F27 5-1	M23 1-4	N10 1-1	S29 4-1		S01 1-3	D01 2-0	a06 0-1	m04 0-1	S15 6-1	M13 2-3	D22 2-2	O13 1-3	O31 0-2	J19 5-4
15 NORTHAMPTON T	J26 2-1	S08 1-0	M12 0-0	D21 0-0	M09 1-1	M23 2-0	a27 0-3	J01 0-0	a06 2-1	S29 1-0	N03 3-2	J19 3-0	a30 1-1	J12 2-0		S22 1-2	D01 3-2	F01 0-2	M30 2-1	O13 1-0	a16 1-4	O19 5-0	N09 1-0	F15 2-1
16 PETERBOROUGH U	a06 3-2	M30 2-0	O20 3-2	m04 3-0	S01 1-1	N03 2-1	M12 2-2	N10 1-1	a16 2-0	S18 2-0	a27 1-1	m07 3-0	O13 2-0	M02 2-0	F05 1-0		J02 1-1	D21 2-0	a23 0-0	M23 0-0	S29 1-2	S15 0-0	J19 2-2	D15 2-0
17 ROCHDALE	A25 4-0	J12 2-1	m04 0-0	M12 0-0	N24 0-1	O13 3-0	N03 1-1	S15 0-3	M23 1-3	a01 1-1	a23 0-0	a30 2-1	a27 0-0	D29 3-2	M02 1-1	a13 0-3		S22 1-1	F23 2-1	S08 1-0	O20 0-0	S29 3-2	D15 2-0	a16 2-1
18 SCARBOROUGH	M16 2-0	O03 0-1	M26 0-1	F19 1-2	O24 1-1	S01 1-0	D29 1-1	O07 2-1	S15 2-1	D26 4-1	F16 2-0	m11 2-1	M02 3-0	O27 0-2	S18 1-1	a03 3-1	F06 0-0		a20 3-1	D16 0-2	N09 1-0	a13 1-0	D07 4-2	J05 2-2
19 SCUNTHORPE U	J12 6-2	A25 2-0	a13 1-3	S29 0-2	D29 2-0	a27 3-0	m04 2-1	D15 1-1	O13 1-0	M23 4-4	F26 2-1	a01 3-0	S22 2-1	J26 2-2	M05 3-0	S08 1-1	N10 2-1	O20 3-0		N03 3-0	F02 3-0	M12 1-0	m07 2-0	M02 2-1
20 STOCKPORT CO	a19 3-2	O22 0-0	S14 2-2	F26 1-1	S17 3-1	a06 3-1	D01 3-1	D21 0-0	J01 1-1	J18 5-1	M29 1-3	M16 4-2	N10 4-0	O01 1-0	a09 2-0	O06 2-1	M26 3-0	M08 2-2	m11 5-0		a23 2-1	S01 3-0	J04 2-0	O26 2-0
21 TORQUAY U	a08 5-0	O06 2-1	D29 2-0	a10 2-1	O27 3-0	S15 2-0	M09 2-1	O02 1-0	A31 3-1	F05 3-1	D01 0-1	a13 1-1	M05 0-1	a02 1-1	M26 0-0	M15 0-0	a20 3-1	a30 2-0	S18 1-1	D07 1-1		J19 0-0	O16 1-0	m11 2-1
22 WALSALL	O27 2-2	m11 2-0	N10 1-0	M09 0-0	O06 1-1	F16 3-0	S08 2-2	F02 1-0	M30 0-0	D01 3-1	a06 0-1	S22 0-0	F19 0-0	M20 0-0	a20 3-3	J26 0-1	M16 0-1	J01 0-0	O02 3-0	J12 0-2	A25 2-2		D21 1-0	O23 1-1
23 WREXHAM	S08 4-2	J26 0-1	N03 2-4	M22 1-0	D01 3-0	S29 1-1	S22 1-1	J12 2-1	m04 3-0	M12 1-2	O20 2-2	D26 1-2	a13 2-2	a09 2-2	F23 0-2	A25 0-0	M09 2-1	O13 1-2	N24 1-0	a16 1-3	a27 2-1	a01 1-1		D29 0-4
24 YORK C	D21 2-0	J01 0-1	M23 2-0	O13 1-2	F23 2-0	M12 0-2	F02 0-1	S22 3-1	S29 1-1	O20 3-3	J26 0-0	J12 1-0	F26 1-0	A25 0-1	N24 0-1	M09 0-4	M30 0-2	a23 2-0	D01 2-2	m04 0-2	N03 0-0	a26 1-0	a06 0-0	

LEAGUE TABLES

DIVISION 1

	P	W	D	L	F	A	W	D	L	F	A	Pts
Arsenal	38	15	4	0	51	10	9	9	1	23	8	*83
Liverpool	38	14	3	2	42	13	9	4	6	35	27	76
Crystal Palace	38	11	6	2	26	17	9	3	7	24	24	69
Leeds U	38	12	2	5	46	23	7	5	7	19	24	64
Manchester C	38	12	3	4	35	25	5	8	6	29	28	62
Manchester U	38	11	4	4	34	17	5	8	6	24	28	†59
Wimbledon	38	8	6	5	28	22	6	8	5	25	24	56
Nottingham F	38	11	4	4	42	21	3	8	8	23	29	54
Everton	38	9	5	5	26	15	4	7	8	24	31	51
Tottenham H	38	8	9	2	35	22	3	7	9	16	28	49
Chelsea	38	10	6	3	33	25	3	4	12	25	44	49
Q.P.R.	38	8	5	6	27	22	4	5	10	17	31	46
Sheffield U	38	9	3	7	23	23	4	4	11	13	32	46
Southampton	38	9	6	4	33	22	3	3	13	25	47	45
Norwich C	38	9	3	7	27	32	4	3	12	14	32	45
Coventry C	38	10	6	3	30	16	1	5	13	12	33	44
Aston Villa	38	7	9	3	29	25	2	5	12	17	33	41
Luton T	38	7	5	7	22	18	3	2	14	20	43	37
Sunderland	38	6	6	7	15	16	2	4	13	23	44	34
Derby Co	38	3	8	8	25	36	2	1	16	12	39	24

*Arsenal had two points deducted for disciplinary reasons.
†Manchester United had one point deducted for disciplinary reasons.

DIVISION 2

	P	W	D	L	F	A	W	D	L	F	A	Pts
Oldham A	46	17	5	1	55	21	8	8	7	28	32	88
West Ham U	46	15	6	2	41	18	9	9	5	19	16	87
Sheffield W	46	12	10	1	43	23	10	6	7	37	28	82
Notts Co	46	14	4	5	45	28	9	7	7	31	27	80
Millwall	46	11	6	6	43	28	9	7	7	27	23	73
Brighton & H.A.	46	12	4	7	37	31	9	3	11	26	38	70
Middlesbrough	46	12	4	7	36	17	8	5	10	30	30	69
Barnsley	46	13	7	3	39	16	6	5	12	24	32	69
Bristol C	46	14	5	4	44	28	6	2	15	24	43	67
Oxford U	46	10	9	4	41	29	4	10	9	28	37	61
Newcastle U	46	8	10	5	24	22	6	7	10	25	34	59
Wolverh'pton W	46	11	6	6	45	35	2	13	8	18	28	58
Bristol R	46	11	7	5	29	20	4	6	13	27	39	58
Ipswich T	46	9	8	6	32	28	4	10	9	28	40	57
Port Vale	46	10	4	9	32	24	5	8	10	24	40	57
Charlton A	46	8	7	8	27	25	5	10	8	30	36	56
Portsmouth	46	10	6	7	34	27	4	5	14	24	43	53
Plymouth A	46	10	10	3	36	20	2	7	14	18	48	53
Blackburn R	46	8	6	9	26	27	6	4	13	25	39	52
Watford	46	5	8	10	24	32	7	7	9	21	27	51
Swindon T	46	8	6	9	31	30	4	8	11	34	43	50
Leicester C	46	12	4	7	41	33	2	4	17	19	50	50
W.B.A.	46	7	11	5	26	21	3	7	13	26	40	48
Hull C	46	6	10	7	35	32	4	5	14	22	53	45

DIVISION 3

	P	W	D	L	F	A	W	D	L	F	A	Pts
Cambridge U	46	14	5	4	42	22	11	6	6	33	23	86
Southend U	46	13	6	4	34	23	13	1	9	33	28	85
Grimsby	46	16	3	4	42	13	8	8	7	24	21	83
Bolton W	46	14	5	4	33	18	10	6	7	31	32	83
Tranmere R	46	13	5	5	38	21	10	4	9	26	25	78
Brentford	46	12	4	7	30	22	9	9	5	29	25	76
Bury	46	13	6	4	39	26	7	7	9	28	30	73
Bradford C	46	13	3	7	36	22	7	7	9	26	32	70
Bournemouth	46	14	6	3	37	20	5	7	11	21	38	70
Wigan A	46	14	3	6	40	20	6	6	11	31	34	69
Huddersfield T	46	13	3	7	37	23	5	10	8	20	28	67
Birmingham C	46	8	9	6	21	21	8	8	7	24	28	65
Leyton O	46	15	2	6	35	19	3	8	12	20	39	64
Stoke C	46	9	7	7	36	29	7	5	11	19	30	60
Reading	46	11	5	7	34	28	6	3	14	19	38	59
Exeter C	46	12	6	5	35	16	4	3	16	23	36	57
Preston N.E.	46	11	5	7	33	29	4	6	13	21	38	56
Shrewsbury T	46	8	7	8	29	22	6	3	14	32	46	52
Chester C	46	10	3	10	27	27	4	6	13	19	31	51
Swansea C	46	8	6	9	31	33	5	3	15	18	39	48
Fulham	46	8	8	7	27	22	2	8	13	14	34	46
Crewe A	46	6	9	8	35	35	5	2	16	27	45	44
Rotherham U	46	5	10	8	31	38	5	2	16	19	49	42
Mansfield T	46	5	8	10	23	27	3	6	14	19	36	38

DIVISION 4

	P	W	D	L	F	A	W	D	L	F	A	Pts
Darlington	46	13	8	2	36	14	9	9	5	32	24	83
Stockport Co	46	16	6	1	54	19	7	7	9	30	28	82
Hartlepool U	46	15	5	3	35	15	9	5	9	32	33	82
Peterborough U	46	13	9	1	38	15	8	8	7	29	30	80
Blackpool	46	17	3	3	55	17	6	7	10	23	30	79
Burnley	46	17	5	1	46	16	6	5	12	24	35	79
Torquay U	46	14	7	2	37	13	4	11	8	27	34	72
Scunthorpe U	46	17	4	2	51	20	3	7	13	20	42	71
Scarborough	46	13	5	5	36	21	6	7	10	23	35	69
Northampton T	46	14	5	4	34	21	4	8	11	23	37	67
Doncaster R	46	12	5	6	36	22	5	9	9	20	24	65
Rochdale	46	10	9	4	29	22	5	8	10	21	31	62
Cardiff C	46	10	6	7	26	23	5	9	9	17	31	60
Lincoln C	46	10	7	6	32	27	4	10	9	18	34	59
Gillingham	46	9	9	5	35	27	3	9	11	22	33	54
Walsall	46	7	12	4	25	17	5	5	13	23	34	53
Hereford	46	9	10	4	32	19	4	4	15	21	39	53
Chesterfield	46	8	12	3	33	26	5	2	16	14	36	53
Maidstone	46	9	5	9	42	34	4	7	12	24	37	51
Carlisle U	46	12	3	8	30	30	1	6	16	17	59	48
York C	46	8	6	9	21	23	3	7	13	24	34	46
Halifax T	46	9	6	8	34	29	3	4	16	25	50	46
Aldershot	46	8	7	8	38	43	2	4	17	23	58	41
Wrexham	46	8	7	8	33	34	2	3	18	15	40	40

Football League Records

Top scorers: Div 1, I.Wright (Arsenal) 29 goals (5 for Crystal Palace); Div 2, A.Shearer, D.Speedie (both Blackburn Rovers) 23 goals; Div 3, D.Holdsworth (Brentford), I.Roberts (Huddersfield Town) 24 goals; Div 4, D.Bamber (Blackpool), P.Stant (Mansfield Town) 28 goals.

Play-offs: Prem Lge, Blackburn Rovers v Derby County 4-2, 1-2; Cambridge United v Leicester City 1-1, 0-5; Blackburn Rovers v Leicester City (Wembley) 1-0; Div 1, Stockport County v Stoke City 1-0, 1-1; Peterborough United v Huddersfield Town 2-2, 2-1; Peterborough United v Stockport County (Wembley) 2-1; Div 2, Barnet v Blackpool 1-0, 0-2; Crewe Alexandra v Scunthorpe United 2-2, 0-2; Blackpool v Scunthorpe United (Wembley) 1-1 (4-3 penalties).

From 1992-93 Division 1 became Premier League, and

Gordon Strachan holds aloft the Premiership trophy won by Leeds United.

DIVISION 1

	ARSENAL	ASTON VILLA	CHELSEA	COVENTRY C	CRYSTAL P	EVERTON	LEEDS U	LIVERPOOL	LUTON T	MANCHESTER C	MANCHESTER U	NORWICH C	NOTTINGHAM F	NOTTS CO	OLDHAM A	Q.P.R.	SHEFFIELD U	SHEFFIELD W	SOUTHAMPTON	TOTTENHAM H	WEST HAM U	WIMBLEDON
1 ARSENAL		J11 0-0	O05 3-2	S07 1-2	a11 4-1	D21 4-2	M22 1-1	a20 4-0	A27 2-0	A31 2-1	F01 1-1	F11 1-1	M31 3-3	O26 2-0	M10 2-1	A17 1-1	S21 5-2	F15 7-1	m02 5-1	D01 2-0	N02 0-1	J01 1-1
2 ASTON VILLA	A24 3-1		a20 3-1	m02 2-0	S04 0-1	F02 0-0	N24 1-4	a11 1-0	O05 4-0	D07 3-1	A21 0-1	M28 1-0	S21 3-1	N16 1-0	F22 1-0	M14 0-1	M31 1-1	J18 0-1	D28 2-1	S07 0-0	D26 3-1	O26 2-1
3 CHELSEA	a25 1-1	S18 2-0		M14 0-1	F08 1-1	S28 2-2	S14 0-1	O19 2-2	A31 4-1	J01 1-1	D15 1-3	N16 0-3	N30 1-0	A28 2-2	D21 4-2	a18 2-1	M21 1-2	F29 0-3	F12 1-1	J11 2-0	a04 2-1	A17 2-2
4 COVENTRY C	a04 0-1	S28 1-0	N02 0-1		O19 1-2	a18 0-1	S18 0-0	F08 0-0	A21 5-0	A17 0-1	F29 0-0	M04 0-0	M11 0-2	S14 1-0	M21 1-1	J11 2-2	A28 3-1	a08 0-0	N30 2-0	J01 1-2	a25 1-0	A31 0-1
5 CRYSTAL P	S14 1-4	M21 0-0	O26 0-0	F01 0-1		a04 2-0	O01 1-0	M14 1-0	F25 1-1	J11 1-1	N30 1-3	F29 3-4	M03 0-0	J01 1-0	a18 0-0	S28 2-2	A31 2-1	a25 1-1	N16 1-0	D22 1-2	S17 2-3	A27 3-2
6 EVERTON	A20 3-1	O19 0-2	m02 2-1	S21 3-0	S07 2-2		F23 1-1	D28 1-1	M14 1-1	a20 1-2	A24 0-0	S03 1-1	J19 1-1	N23 1-0	M07 2-1	F08 0-0	a11 0-2	D26 0-1	a01 0-1	O05 3-1	D07 4-0	N16 2-0
7 LEEDS U	S03 2-2	M03 0-0	a11 3-0	a20 2-0	J18 1-1	N30 1-0		S21 1-0	F29 2-0	S07 3-0	D29 1-1	M02 1-0	A20 1-0	F01 3-0	O26 1-0	N16 2-0	O05 4-3	A24 1-1	D26 3-3	D14 1-1	M28 0-0	M14 5-1
8 LIVERPOOL	J29 2-0	S14 1-1	F01 1-2	O26 1-0	N02 1-2	A31 3-1	a18 0-0		J11 2-1	D21 2-2	a26 2-0	N30 2-1	D14 2-0	M31 4-0	A17 2-1	A27 1-0	J01 2-1	S28 1-1	F29 0-0	M21 2-1	M11 1-0	a08 2-3
9 LUTON T	D26 1-0	a25 2-0	D28 2-0	D20 1-0	M07 1-1	N02 0-1	D07 0-2	A24 0-0		N23 2-2	a18 1-1	F08 2-0	a14 2-1	S28 1-1	S14 2-1	S17 0-1	F22 2-1	O19 2-2	S04 2-1	M11 0-0	J18 0-1	a04 2-1
10 MANCHESTER C	D28 1-0	F29 2-0	M28 0-0	J18 1-0	A24 3-2	S17 0-1	a04 4-0	A21 2-1	F15 4-0		N16 0-0	D26 2-1	S04 2-1	a25 2-0	S28 1-2	D14 2-2	O26 3-2	S14 0-1	M15 0-1	F01 1-0	a18 2-0	N30 0-0
11 MANCHESTER U	O19 1-1	J22 1-0	F26 1-1	D07 4-0	F22 2-0	J11 1-0	A31 1-1	O06 0-0	S21 5-0	a07 1-1		S07 3-0	a20 1-2	A17 2-0	A28 1-0	J01 1-4	N02 2-0	F08 1-1	a16 1-0	m02 3-1	N23 2-1	M21 0-0
12 NORWICH C	a08 1-3	J01 2-1	M11 0-1	N23 3-2	D07 3-3	M21 4-3	S28 2-2	F22 3-0	O26 1-0	A28 0-0	M31 1-3		N02 0-0	a18 0-1	J11 1-2	D21 0-1	A17 2-2	S18 1-0	F01 2-1	A31 0-1	S14 2-1	a25 1-1
13 NOTTINGHAM F	D08 3-2	a18 2-0	F22 1-1	N16 1-0	N23 5-1	A17 2-1	D22 0-0	a22 1-1	J01 1-1	M21 2-0	M18 1-0	M14 2-0		J11 1-1	A31 3-1	a25 1-1	F01 2-5	a04 0-2	O26 1-3	A28 1-3	S28 2-2	S14 4-2
14 NOTTS CO	F08 0-1	M10 0-0	D26 2-0	a11 1-0	M28 2-3	M17 0-0	O19 2-4	S07 1-2	m02 2-1	O06 1-3	J18 1-1	S21 2-2	A24 0-4		N02 2-0	N30 0-1	a20 1-3	S03 2-1	A20 1-0	a07 0-2	D28 3-0	F25 1-1
15 OLDHAM A	N16 1-1	N30 3-2	A21 3-0	S03 2-1	S21 2-3	D14 2-2	F08 2-0	J18 2-3	a11 5-1	m02 2-5	D26 3-6	A24 2-2	D28 2-1	M14 4-3		F15 2-1	S07 2-1	M28 3-0	O05 1-1	a20 1-0	O19 2-2	F29 0-1
16 Q.P.R.	J18 0-0	N02 0-1	S21 2-2	A24 1-1	m02 1-0	O26 3-1	M11 4-1	D26 0-0	a20 2-1	M07 4-0	M28 0-0	A21 0-2	O05 0-2	F22 1-1	N23 1-3		D07 1-0	D28 1-1	S07 2-2	a11 1-2	S04 0-0	F01 1-1
17 SHEFFIELD U	a18 1-1	D14 2-0	S03 0-1	D26 0-3	D28 1-1	S14 2-1	a26 2-3	M28 2-0	N30 1-1	F08 4-2	M14 1-2	J18 1-0	O19 4-2	S17 1-3	a04 2-0	F29 0-0		N17 2-0	A24 0-2	a14 2-0	A20 1-1	S28 0-0
18 SHEFFIELD W	N23 1-1	A17 2-3	D07 3-0	M07 1-1	O05 4-1	A28 2-1	J12 1-6	m02 0-0	F01 3-2	a11 2-0	O26 3-2	a20 2-0	S07 2-1	M21 1-0	J01 1-1	A31 4-1	M11 1-3		S21 2-0	N02 0-0	F22 2-1	D21 2-0
19 SOUTHAMPTON	S28 0-4	A31 1-1	N23 1-0	F22 0-0	M11 1-0	J01 1-2	A28 0-4	D07 1-1	M21 2-1	N02 0-3	S14 0-1	O19 0-0	A08 0-1	D20 1-1	a25 1-0	a04 2-1	J11 2-4	a18 0-1		A17 2-3	M03 1-0	S18 1-0
20 TOTTENHAM H	F22 1-1	a04 2-5	A24 1-3	M28 4-3	F16 0-1	a25 3-3	M07 1-3	D18 1-2	N16 4-1	O19 0-1	S28 1-2	D28 3-0	D26 1-2	D07 2-1	J25 0-0	S14 2-0	N23 0-1	M14 0-2	J18 1-2		a01 3-0	a18 3-2
21 WEST HAM U	M14 0-2	A28 3-1	S07 1-1	O05 0-1	a20 0-2	F29 0-2	J01 1-3	N17 0-0	A17 0-0	S21 1-2	a22 1-0	a11 4-0	m02 3-0	A31 0-2	F01 1-0	M21 2-2	D21 1-1	N30 1-2	a14 0-1	O26 2-1		J11 1-1
22 WIMBLEDON	M28 1-3	F08 2-0	J18 1-2	D28 1-1	D26 1-1	M10 0-0	N02 0-0	N23 0-0	S07 3-0	F22 2-1	S03 1-2	O05 3-1	a02 3-0	M07 2-0	D07 2-1	O19 0-1	m02 3-0	O02 2-1	a20 0-1	S21 3-5	A24 2-0	

Gary Lineker, top-scored for Tottenham before leaving for a new challenge in Japan.

DIVISION 2

	BARNSLEY	BLACKBURN R	BRIGHTON & HA	BRISTOL C	BRISTOL R	CAMBRIDGE U	CHARLTON A	DERBY CO	GRIMSBY T	IPSWICH T	LEICESTER C	MIDDLESBROUGH	MILLWALL	NEWCASTLE U	OXFORD U	PLYMOUTH A	PORTSMOUTH	PORT VALE	SOUTHEND U	SUNDERLAND	SWINDON T	TRANMERE R	WATFORD	WOLVERHAMPTON W
1 BARNSLEY		M28 2-1	A24 1-2	O19 1-2	N09 0-1	F08 0-0	F29 1-0	a04 0-3	D14 4-1	S14 1-0	S17 3-1	N05 2-1	S28 0-2	N30 3-0	M14 1-0	J18 1-3	O12 2-0	D26 0-0	F15 1-0	A20 0-3	D28 1-1	a18 1-1	S03 0-3	a25 2-0
2 BLACKBURN R	N16 3-0		N02 1-0	J11 4-0	D14 3-0	J01 2-1	M21 0-2	F11 2-0	O26 2-1	A31 1-2	a18 0-1	N30 2-1	a25 2-1	F15 3-1	F29 1-1	O12 5-2	A17 1-1	S14 1-0	M10 2-2	a29 2-2	F01 2-1	S28 0-0	S17 1-0	a14 1-2
3 BRIGHTON & HA	J11 3-1	M14 0-3		J01 0-0	S28 3-1	M28 1-1	F01 1-2	a15 1-2	N06 3-0	O12 2-2	O30 1-2	N09 1-1	D21 3-4	D14 2-2	F15 1-2	N30 1-0	a29 2-1	S18 3-1	F29 3-2	a25 2-2	O26 0-2	A17 0-2	S14 0-1	A31 3-3
4 BRISTOL C	F01 0-2	A24 1-0	A20 2-1		S04 1-0	M14 1-2	N30 0-2	a25 1-2	F29 1-1	a18 2-1	a04 2-1	a07 1-1	S17 2-2	O26 1-1	M28 1-1	N05 2-0	S28 0-2	D28 3-0	J18 2-2	N09 1-0	D26 1-1	S14 2-2	O12 1-0	M17 2-0
5 BRISTOL R	M21 0-0	M07 3-0	a20 4-1	D21 3-2		D07 2-2	m02 1-0	N23 2-3	S07 2-3	A17 3-3	J01 1-1	O05 2-1	F22 3-2	A31 1-2	S21 2-1	O19 0-0	J29 1-0	N02 3-3	a01 4-1	F08 2-1	a12 1-1	J11 1-0	N16 1-1	M11 1-1
6 CAMBRIDGE U	O26 2-1	F25 2-1	N16 0-0	N02 0-0	F28 6-1		F15 1-0	S13 0-0	J18 0-1	M21 1-1	S29 5-1	M17 0-0	a04 1-0	M10 0-2	N30 1-1	D26 1-1	a17 2-2	a25 4-2	S03 0-1	O12 3-0	A24 3-2	J31 0-0	D29 0-1	S17 2-1
7 CHARLTON A	D07 1-1	N09 0-2	O19 2-0	F22 2-1	O12 1-0	N23 1-2		S01 0-2	M03 1-3	O30 1-1	a25 2-0	M28 0-0	M07 1-0	A18 2-1	J08 2-2	a04 0-0	S14 3-0	S28 2-0	F08 2-0	S17 1-4	N06 0-0	a28 0-1	a18 1-1	J15 0-2
8 DERBY CO	S07 1-1	S04 0-2	S21 3-1	O05 4-1	F15 1-0	a01 0-0	D28 1-2		D26 0-0	N16 1-0	N30 1-2	A21 2-0	F08 0-2	a20 4-1	a11 2-2	M25 2-0	O19 2-0	M11 3-1	A24 1-2	J18 1-2	m02 2-1	N02 0-1	F29 3-1	M21 1-2
9 GRIMSBY T	M07 0-1	F08 2-3	M10 0-1	D07 3-1	a04 0-1	A17 3-4	N02 1-0	a07 0-1		S28 1-2	M17 0-1	O19 1-0	N23 1-1	M21 1-1	J11 1-0	S14 2-1	S17 1-1	O12 1-2	F18 3-2	a18 2-0	F22 0-0	A31 2-2	a25 0-1	J01 0-2
10 IPSWICH T	M31 2-0	D28 2-1	m02 3-1	S21 4-2	J18 1-0	N09 1-2	D26 2-0	M28 2-1	a21 0-0		M14 0-0	A24 2-1	O19 0-0	a11 3-2	O05 2-1	F29 2-0	F08 5-2	A20 2-1	S07 1-0	N05 0-1	S03 1-4	N30 4-0	M17 1-2	a07 2-1
11 LEICESTER C	a11 3-1	S21 3-0	D26 2-1	S07 2-1	N20 1-1	a21 2-1	O05 0-2	F22 1-2	S04 2-0	N02 2-2		a01 2-1	D07 1-1	m02 1-2	F08 2-1	A24 2-0	M11 2-2	N23 0-1	D28 2-0	a08 3-2	J18 3-1	a15 1-0	M21 1-2	O19 3-0
12 MIDDLESBROUGH	a13 0-1	F22 0-0	M21 4-0	N23 3-1	a25 2-1	M07 1-1	N16 2-0	J01 1-1	a28 2-0	J11 1-0	S14 3-0		A17 1-0	A27 3-0	a15 2-1	a18 2-1	A31 2-0	O26 1-0	N02 1-1	S28 2-1	D07 2-2	S17 1-0	a04 1-2	O12 0-0
13 MILLWALL	a22 1-1	O05 1-3	S04 1-2	a11 2-3	N30 0-1	S07 1-2	F26 1-0	O26 1-2	F15 1-1	F01 2-3	F29 2-0	J18 2-0		S21 2-1	a01 2-1	D28 2-1	N02 1-1	M21 1-0	m02 2-0	A24 4-1	a08 1-1	M11 0-3	D26 0-4	N16 2-1
14 NEWCASTLE U	F22 1-1	N23 0-0	M07 0-1	F08 3-0	D28 2-1	N06 1-1	J18 3-4	S28 2-2	N09 2-0	S17 1-1	O12 2-0	D26 0-1	a18 0-1		O19 4-3	S04 2-2	a25 1-0	D07 2-2	N20 3-2	M29 1-0	M14 3-1	a04 2-3	A24 2-2	S14 1-2
15 OXFORD U	N02 0-1	D07 1-3	N23 3-1	N16 1-1	a18 2-2	F22 1-0	O23 1-2	S18 2-0	A24 1-2	a25 1-1	O26 1-2	S04 1-2	S14 2-2	F01 5-2		S28 3-2	M21 2-1	J18 2-2	D26 0-1	D28 3-0	M07 5-3	O12 1-0	M11 0-0	a04 1-0
16 PLYMOUTH A	A17 2-1	m02 1-3	F22 1-1	M10 1-0	F01 0-0	F11 0-1	S07 0-2	M07 1-1	M31 1-2	D07 1-0	J11 2-2	S21 1-1	A31 3-2	D20 2-0	a20 3-1		J01 3-2	N16 1-0	a11 0-2	N23 1-0	O05 0-4	M21 1-0	O26 0-1	N02 1-0
17 PORTSMOUTH	m02 2-0	J18 2-2	S07 0-0	a20 1-0	D26 2-0	S21 3-0	M31 1-2	F01 0-1	a11 2-0	O26 1-1	N05 1-0	D28 4-0	M14 6-1	O05 3-1	N09 2-1	F04 4-1		A24 1-0	D14 1-1	S03 1-0	M28 1-1	F29 2-0	a22 0-0	N30 1-0
18 PORT VALE	A27 0-0	M31 2-0	a11 2-1	A31 1-1	M14 0-1	O05 1-0	a21 1-1	N06 1-0	m02 0-1	J01 1-2	F15 1-2	F08 1-2	N09 0-2	F29 0-1	A17 2-1	M28 1-0	J11 0-2		S21 0-0	O19 3-3	S07 2-2	D13 1-1	N30 2-1	D21 1-1
19 SOUTHEND U	N23 2-1	N05 3-0	D07 2-1	A17 1-1	S14 2-0	D22 1-1	O26 1-1	J11 1-0	M28 3-1	a04 1-2	A31 1-2	M14 0-1	O12 2-3	J01 4-0	O30 2-3	S17 2-1	M17 2-3	a15 0-0		F22 2-0	N09 3-2	a25 1-1	F01 1-0	S28 0-2
20 SUNDERLAND	J01 2-0	S07 1-1	O05 4-2	M21 1-3	O26 1-1	m02 2-2	a11 1-2	A17 1-1	S21 1-2	a14 3-0	D14 1-0	a20 1-0	J11 6-2	N17 1-1	A31 2-0	a16 0-1	D21 1-0	F01 1-1	N30 1-2		a27 0-0	F11 1-1	N02 3-1	F29 1-0
21 SWINDON T	A31 3-1	O19 2-1	F08 2-1	F04 2-0	S17 1-0	J11 0-2	M10 1-2	O12 1-2	N30 1-1	D20 0-0	A17 0-0	F29 0-1	J01 3-1	N02 2-1	J28 2-1	a25 1-0	N16 2-3	a04 1-0	M21 3-1	S14 5-3		M17 2-0	S28 3-1	a18 1-0
22 TRANMERE R	S21 2-1	a20 2-2	J17 1-1	M31 2-2	A23 2-2	O18 1-2	S03 2-2	M14 4-3	D28 1-1	F21 0-1	M27 1-2	a10 1-2	N05 2-1	S07 3-2	m02 1-2	N08 1-0	a07 2-0	M06 2-1	O04 1-1	D26 1-0	N22 0-0		J24 1-1	F08 4-3
23 WATFORD	D22 1-1	a11 2-1	M31 0-1	m02 5-2	M28 1-0	A31 1-3	S21 2-0	D07 1-2	O05 2-0	M07 0-1	N09 0-1	S07 1-2	O29 0-2	J11 2-2	N06 2-0	F08 1-0	N23 2-1	F22 0-0	O19 1-2	M14 1-0	a20 0-0	J01 0-0		A17 0-2
24 WOLVERHAMPTON W	O05 1-2	D26 0-0	D28 2-0	M07 1-1	N05 2-3	a11 2-1	A24 1-1	N09 2-3	N26 2-1	N23 1-2	F01 0-1	m02 1-2	M28 0-0	M31 6-2	S07 3-1	M14 1-0	F22 0-0	S03 0-2	a20 3-1	D07 1-0	S21 2-1	O26 1-1	J18 3-0	

SEASON 1991-92

Divisions 2, 3 and 4 became Divisions 1, 2 and 3. Ipswich Town Middlesbrough and Blackburn Rovers promoted to Prem Lge; Luton Town, Notts County and West Ham United relegated to Div 1; Brentford, Birmingham City and Peterborough United promoted to Div 1; Plymouth Argyle, Brighton & Hove Albion and Port Vale relegated to Div 2; Burnley, Rotherham United, Mansfield Town and Blackpool promoted to Div 2; Bury, Shrewsbury Town, Torquay United and Darlington relegated to Div 3.

DIVISION 3

	BIRMINGHAM C	BOLTON W	BOURNEMOUTH	BRADFORD C	BRENTFORD	BURY	CHESTER C	DARLINGTON	EXETER C	FULHAM	HARTLEPOOL U	HUDDERSFIELD T	HULL C	LEYTON O	PETERBOROUGH U	PRESTON N.E.	READING	SHREWSBURY T	STOCKPORT CO	STOKE C	SWANSEA C	TORQUAY U	W.B.A.	WIGAN A
1 BIRMINGHAM C		a14 2-1	F15 0-1	N30 2-0	M10 1-0	A17 3-2	S17 3-2	A31 1-0	N23 1-0	D21 3-1	a18 2-1	M21 2-0	J01 2-2	J11 2-2	S14 1-1	S28 3-1	a04 2-0	a25 1-0	O12 3-0	F29 1-1	M03 1-1	N02 3-0	F08 0-3	O19 3-3
2 BOLTON W	M17 1-1		M31 0-2	a11 1-1	a20 1-2	M21 2-1	F08 0-0	J01 2-0	F22 1-2	O19 0-3	J18 2-2	A17 1-1	D14 1-0	A31 1-0	M24 2-1	N23 1-0	N02 1-1	F11 1-0	M10 0-0	m02 3-1	a07 0-0	O05 1-0	S07 3-0	S21 1-1
3 BOURNEMOUTH	D14 2-1	S14 1-2		O26 1-3	N22 0-0	F11 4-0	a03 2-0	A17 1-2	M24 1-0	S27 0-0	O12 2-0	a14 1-1	A31 0-0	F01 0-1	M07 1-2	J01 1-0	a25 3-2	S17 1-0	N01 1-0	D21 1-2	M20 3-0	M10 2-1	F22 2-1	J18 3-0
4 BRADFORD C	F11 1-2	S17 4-4	F08 3-1		N02 0-1	J04 1-1	S14 1-1	M07 0-1	M10 1-1	O12 3-4	A31 1-1	D22 1-1	J18 2-1	J01 1-1	M21 2-1	a04 1-1	a18 1-0	S28 3-0	a25 1-0	A17 1-0	N23 4-6	O19 2-0	D14 1-1	F22 1-1
5 BRENTFORD	N06 2-2	S28 3-2	M29 2-2	M14 3-4		F08 0-3	M03 2-0	a17 4-1	D22 3-0	a26 4-0	J01 1-0	A31 2-3	S17 4-1	A17 4-3	O12 2-1	J25 1-0	S14 1-0	a04 2-0	F29 2-1	J11 2-0	N30 3-2	F15 3-2	O19 1-2	N09 4-0
6 BURY	D28 1-0	N09 1-1	N30 0-1	F29 0-1	O26 0-3		F25 1-2	a25 1-0	a14 3-1	S17 3-1	S28 1-1	S14 4-4	a04 3-2	F15 4-2	S03 3-0	O12 2-3	D26 0-1	A24 0-0	a18 0-0	N05 1-3	J11 1-0	M03 0-0	M14 1-1	M28 1-4
7 CHESTER C	a11 0-1	O26 0-1	S07 0-1	M31 0-0	J18 1-1	M07 3-1		J04 2-5	F11 5-2	A17 2-0	F22 2-0	J01 0-0	M21 1-1	m02 1-0	M10 2-4	N02 3-2	N23 2-2	D14 1-4	M24 3-2	O05 0-0	A31 2-0	a20 2-0	S21 1-2	F18 1-0
8 DARLINGTON	D26 1-1	S03 3-2	D28 0-0	a07 1-3	S21 1-2	O05 0-2	F29 1-1		m02 5-2	N30 3-1	N02 4-0	F15 1-3	F08 0-1	M31 0-1	N23 1-2	M21 0-2	M10 2-4	O19 3-3	M03 1-3	S07 0-1	a11 1-1	J11 3-2	A24 0-1	a20 0-1
9 EXETER C	M28 2-1	J11 2-2	F29 0-3	N06 1-0	A24 1-2	O19 5-2	N30 0-0	O12 4-1		J25 1-1	S14 1-1	a04 0-1	a25 0-3	M14 2-0	a18 2-2	M03 4-1	S28 2-1	D26 1-0	S17 2-1	N09 0-0	F15 2-1	S04 1-0	D28 1-1	F08 0-1
10 FULHAM	A24 0-1	F01 1-1	a20 2-0	m02 2-1	O05 0-1	a11 4-2	D28 2-2	F11 4-0	M07 0-0		M20 1-0	M10 1-0	N02 0-0	S21 2-1	F22 0-1	O26 1-0	a07 1-0	J18 0-1	N23 1-2	M31 1-1	S07 3-0	D26 2-1	S03 0-0	J28 1-1
11 HARTLEPOOL U	S21 1-0	M03 0-4	m02 1-0	D26 1-0	S03 1-0	a20 0-0	J11 1-0	M14 2-0	M31 3-1	N09 2-0		N30 0-0	O19 2-3	S07 2-3	F08 0-1	F15 2-0	A24 2-0	M28 4-2	F18 0-1	a11 1-1	F29 0-1	D28 1-1	N05 0-0	O05 4-3
12 HUDDERSFIELD T	N09 3-2	D28 1-0	S21 0-0	A25 1-0	D26 2-1	M31 3-0	S04 2-0	D14 2-1	S07 0-0	N06 3-1	F11 1-0		F25 1-1	a20 1-0	J18 0-0	F01 1-2	F22 1-2	M07 2-1	O25 0-1	M14 1-2	O05 1-0	m02 4-0	M28 3-0	a11 3-1
13 HULL C	S03 1-2	a29 2-0	D26 0-1	M03 0-0	a11 0-3	S07 0-1	N09 1-0	O26 5-2	O05 1-2	M14 0-0	F01 0-2	F29 1-0		M28 1-0	A24 1-2	N30 2-2	D28 0-1	N05 4-0	J11 0-2	J25 0-1	m02 3-0	S21 4-1	a20 1-0	M31 1-1
14 LEYTON O	F22 0-0	D26 2-1	O19 1-1	S03 1-1	D28 4-2	M24 4-0	O12 1-0	S14 2-1	N02 1-0	a18 0-1	a04 4-0	S28 1-0	N23 1-0		a25 1-2	S17 0-0	M07 1-1	J28 2-0	A24 3-3	F08 0-1	M10 1-2	M21 2-0	J18 1-1	F11 3-1
15 PETERBOROUGH U	M31 2-3	F29 1-0	a08 2-0	N09 2-1	m02 0-1	J01 0-0	N05 2-0	M28 1-1	S21 1-1	J11 4-1	O26 3-2	M03 2-0	D20 3-0	O05 0-2		A17 1-0	F01 5-3	M14 1-0	F15 3-2	A31 1-1	a21 3-1	N30 1-1	a11 0-0	S07 0-0
16 PRESTON N.E.	a21 3-2	M28 2-1	S03 2-2	S07 1-1	M07 3-2	m02 2-0	M14 0-3	N09 2-1	J18 1-3	F08 1-2	D14 1-4	O19 1-0	F11 3-1	a11 2-1	D28 1-1		a14 1-1	F22 2-2	D26 3-2	S21 2-2	M31 1-1	A24 3-0	O01 2-0	N05 3-0
17 READING	S07 1-1	M14 1-0	O05 0-0	S21 1-2	a01 0-0	A31 3-2	M28 0-0	N05 2-2	a20 1-0	F15 0-2	D20 0-1	J11 1-0	A17 0-1	a29 3-2	O19 1-1	F29 2-2		F08 2-1	N30 1-1	M04 3-4	J01 1-0	a11 6-1	N09 1-2	m02 3-2
18 SHREWSBURY T	O05 1-1	N30 1-3	a11 1-2	a21 3-2	S07 1-0	D21 1-1	F15 2-2	F01 0-2	A31 6-1	M03 0-0	N23 1-4	J25 1-1	M10 2-3	F29 0-1	N02 2-0	J11 2-0	O26 1-2		M20 0-1	J01 1-0	S21 0-0	M31 2-2	m02 1-3	A18 1-0
19 STOCKPORT CO	m02 2-0	N05 2-2	M13 5-0	O05 4-1	J04 2-1	S21 2-0	O18 0-4	J18 2-0	a10 4-1	M27 2-0	M06 0-1	F07 0-0	F22 1-1	D20 1-0	D14 3-0	A30 2-0	F11 1-0	N26 1-4		a20 0-0	A17 5-0	S06 2-1	M31 3-0	J01 3-3
20 STOKE C	J04 2-1	O12 2-0	A24 1-1	D28 0-0	D22 2-1	M11 1-2	a25 0-1	a03 3-0	M21 5-2	S14 2-2	S17 3-2	N02 0-2	M07 2-3	O26 2-0	D26 3-3	a18 2-1	J18 3-0	S04 1-0	S28 2-2		F01 2-1	N23 3-0	F12 1-0	D14 3-0
21 SWANSEA C	J18 0-2	A24 1-1	N08 3-1	M28 2-2	F11 1-1	F22 2-1	D26 3-0	J28 4-2	D14 1-0	a04 2-2	a28 1-1	a25 0-1	O11 0-0	N05 2-2	S28 1-0	S14 2-2	S03 1-2	a17 1-2	D28 2-1	O19 2-1		F08 1-0	M06 0-0	M14 3-0
22 TORQUAY U	M24 1-2	a25 2-0	N06 1-0	F01 1-1	D14 1-1	J18 0-2	S28 3-2	F22 3-0	J01 1-0	A31 0-1	A17 3-1	O12 0-1	a14 2-1	N09 1-0	a28 2-2	D20 1-0	S17 1-2	S14 1-2	a04 2-0	M28 1-0	O26 1-0		J04 1-0	M07 0-1
23 W.B.A.	O26 0-1	a04 2-2	J11 4-0	F15 1-1	F01 2-0	N02 1-1	a18 1-1	D22 3-1	A17 6-3	J01 2-3	M11 1-2	N23 2-1	S28 1-0	M03 1-3	S17 4-0	a25 3-0	M21 2-0	O12 2-0	S14 1-0	N30 2-2	J25 2-3	F29 1-0		A31 1-1
24 WIGAN A	a28 3-0	a18 1-1	M03 2-0	J11 2-1	M20 2-1	N22 2-0	A23 2-1	S28 1-2	O26 4-1	F28 0-2	a24 1-1	S17 1-3	S14 0-1	N30 1-1	a03 3-0	M10 3-0	O11 1-1	D28 1-1	S03 1-3	F15 1-0	N01 1-0	a07 0-0	D26 0-1	

DIVISION 4

	ALDERSHOT	BARNET	BLACKPOOL	BURNLEY	CARDIFF C	CARLISLE U	CHESTERFIELD	CREWE A	DONCASTER R	GILLINGHAM	HALIFAX T	HEREFORD U	LINCOLN C	MAIDSTONE U	MANSFIELD T	NORTHAMPTON T	ROCHDALE	ROTHERHAM U	SCARBOROUGH	SCUNTHORPE U	WALSALL	WREXHAM	YORK C
1 ALDERSHOT		J17 0-1	N05 2-5	D21 1-2	N08 1-2	S06 2-2		J01 0-2	D14 0-0	F11 0-0	S20 1-3		M14 0-3	A31 3-0	F21 1-3	M07 1-4	O04 1-1	O18 0-1		J03 0-0	F08 1-1		
2 BARNET	M03 5-0		O19 3-0	M24 0-0	S28 3-1	N05 4-2	N30 1-2	A17 4-7	S14 1-0	a18 2-0	N09 3-0	A31 1-0	J01 1-0	F15 3-2	D21 2-0	a04 3-0	M28 3-0	J11 2-5	F08 5-1	S17 3-2	a25 0-1	M14 2-0	O12 2-0
3 BLACKPOOL	M10 1-0	F18 4-2		J11 5-2	S14 1-1	D21 1-0	M21 3-1	N23 0-2	a14 1-0	S17 2-0	N30 3-0	M03 2-0	O13 3-0	F29 1-1	a04 2-1	a25 1-0	F15 3-0	S28 3-0	N02 1-1	A31 2-1	A17 3-0	N19 4-0	J01 3-1
4 BURNLEY	A24 2-0	M07 3-0	F22 1-1		a22 3-1	O05 2-0	S03 3-0	S07 1-1	D28 2-1	J18 4-1	M14 1-0	M31 2-0	F08 1-0	M28 2-1	N09 3-2	F11 5-0	S21 0-1	D26 1-2	a20 1-1	D14 1-1	O19 2-0	m02 1-2	N05 3-1
5 CARDIFF C	M20 2-0	a20 3-1	M31 1-1	F29 0-2		A31 1-0	J25 4-0	a28 1-1	O26 2-1	M10 2-3	a11 4-0	J11 1-0	A17 1-2	J01 0-5	J31 3-2	N23 3-2	S07 1-2	N30 1-0	S21 2-1	N02 2-2	M03 2-1	O05 5-0	F15 3-0
6 CARLISLE U		M10 1-3	A24 1-2	a25 1-1	D28 2-2		F29 1-2	O26 2-1	D26 1-0	N02 0-0	J25 1-1	N23 1-0	S14 0-2	N30 3-0	S17 1-2	a18 2-1	J11 0-0	S03 1-3	M21 2-2	O12 0-0	S28 3-3	M24 0-1	M03 1-1
7 CHESTERFIELD	S28 2-1	F11 3-2	N09 1-1	J01 0-2	M07 2-2	J04 0-0		M24 2-1	J18 0-0	a25 3-3	a07 4-0	O26 2-0	a18 1-5	A17 3-0	A31 0-2	D21 1-2	M14 0-1	O12 1-1	F22 1-0	S14 0-1	S17 0-1	M28 1-1	a04 1-3
8 CREWE A	S03 4-0	D26 3-0	M28 1-0	a04 1-0	A24 1-1	F07 2-1	F15 3-1		a24 1-0	S28 2-1	F28 3-2	N30 4-2	J11 1-0	N05 1-1	S13 1-2	S17 1-1	M03 1-1	D28 0-1	O19 3-3	a18 1-1	O11 0-1	N09 2-1	F25 1-0
9 DONCASTER R	F15 1-0	M31 1-0	S20 0-2	A31 1-4	F08 1-2	A17 0-3	M03 0-1	O05 1-3		O19 1-1	J11 0-2	F18 2-0	N30 1-5	m02 3-0	M14 0-1	J01 0-3	a20 2-0	N06 1-1	a11 3-2	D20 1-2	F29 0-1	S07 3-1	N08 0-1
10 GILLINGHAM	N30 3-1	S21 3-3	a11 3-2	M03 3-0	N05 0-0	M14 1-2	O05 0-1	a20 0-1	F01 2-1		m02 2-0	J01 2-1	F29 1-3	N09 1-1	M28 2-0	O26 3-1	M17 0-0	F15 5-1	S07 2-0	A17 4-0	J11 4-0	M31 2-1	D21 1-1
11 HALIFAX T		M21 3-1	F12 1-2	N02 0-2	S17 1-1	M06 3-2	O19 2-0	a14 2-1	F22 0-0	O12 0-3		M11 0-2	a25 1-4	D21 1-1	S27 1-3	A17 0-1	F08 1-1	S13 0-4	N22 1-0	J18 1-4	a03 1-0	D13 4-3	A30 0-0
12 HEREFORD U	O12 1-0	D28 2-2	J18 1-2	S14 2-0	F22 2-2	M28 1-0	F08 1-0	F12 1-2	M07 0-1	S04 2-0	N06 0-2		S28 3-0	M14 2-2	F25 0-1	a28 1-2	N09 1-1	a04 1-0	A24 4-1	a25 1-2	a18 1-2	D26 3-1	S17 2-1
13 LINCOLN C	N02 0-0	S04 0-6	m02 2-0	O26 0-3	D26 0-0	a01 1-0	S21 1-2	F22 2-2	F12 2-0	J04 1-0	O05 0-0	a20 3-0		a11 1-0	M07 2-0	M21 1-2	D28 0-3	A24 0-2	D17 0-2	N23 4-2	M11 1-0	J18 0-0	M18 0-0
14 MAIDSTONE U	D28 1-2	J08 1-1	J04 0-0	N23 0-1	S04 1-1	F12 5-1	D26 0-1	M11 2-0	O12 2-2	M21 1-1	A24 0-1	N02 3-2	S17 0-2		a25 0-0	J18 1-1	O19 1-1	a18 0-0	M07 2-1	a04 0-1	S14 2-1	F22 2-4	S28 1-0
15 MANSFIELD T	J11 3-0	A24 1-2	S07 1-1	M21 0-1	O19 3-0	a11 2-1	D28 2-1	M31 4-3	N02 2-2	N23 4-3	a21 3-2	F15 1-1	M24 0-0	O05 2-0		M10 2-0	m02 2-1	M03 1-0	D26 1-2	F08 1-3	N30 3-1	S03 3-0	F29 5-2
16 NORTHAMPTON T	F04 1-0	S07 1-1	O05 1-1	N30 1-2	M28 0-0	S21 2-2	O15 1-1	a11 0-1	S03 3-1	F08 0-0	D26 4-0	F29 0-1	N09 1-0	M03 1-0	N05 1-2		M31 2-2	M14 1-2	D07 3-2	O19 0-1	F15 0-1	D28 1-1	J11 2-2
17 ROCHDALE		N23 1-0	D14 4-2	m05 1-3	a04 2-0	F22 3-1	N02 3-3	J18 1-0	S28 1-1	M07 2-1	O26 1-0	M21 3-1	A31 1-0	a07 1-2	O12 0-2	S14 1-0		S17 1-1	F11 2-2	M10 2-0	J01 1-1	a22 2-1	A17 1-1
18 ROTHERHAM U	F01 2-0	F22 3-0	a20 2-0	A17 2-1	F11 1-2	J01 1-0	m02 1-1	A31 1-2	M10 3-1	D14 1-1	M31 1-0	S07 0-0	D21 1-1	S21 3-3	J18 1-1	N02 1-0	a11 2-0		J04 0-2	M21 5-0	N22 2-1	M07 3-0	O25 4-0
19 SCARBOROUGH	S14 0-2	O26 0-4	M14 1-2	S28 3-1	a14 2-2	N09 2-2	M17 3-2	F18 2-1	S19 1-0	a04 2-1	M28 3-0	a07 1-1	F15 1-1	a29 2-0	A17 0-0	O12 2-1	N30 3-2	F29 0-3		J01 4-1	A31 2-3	N05 4-1	a25 1-0
20 SCUNTHORPE U	F29 1-0	a11 1-1	D28 2-1	F15 2-2	M14 1-0	m02 4-0	M31 2-0	S21 1-0	A24 3-2	D26 2-0	M03 1-0	O05 1-1	M28 0-2	S07 2-0	O26 1-4	a14 3-0	N05 6-2	N09 1-0	S03 1-1		J25 1-1	a20 3-1	N30 1-0
21 WALSALL	O26 3-1	O05 2-0	D26 4-2	F01 2-2	J18 0-0	a21 0-0	a11 2-2	m02 2-3	J04 1-3	F22 0-1	S07 3-0	S21 3-0	N05 0-0	M31 1-1	F11 3-3	J28 1-2	S03 1-3	M28 0-2	D28 0-0	M07 2-1		A24 0-0	M14 1-1
22 WREXHAM	S17 0-0	N02 1-0	F08 1-1	O12 2-6	a25 0-3	O19 3-0	N23 0-1	M21 1-0	a03 1-2	S14 2-1	F15 2-0	A17 0-1	M03 1-1	J11 0-0	J01 3-2	A31 2-2	F29 2-1	a28 0-3	M10 2-0	S28 4-0	D20 2-1		a18 2-1
23 YORK C	N23 1-0	m02 1-4	S03 1-0	a28 1-2	D14 1-3	J18 2-0	S07 0-1	M07 1-1	M21 1-1	A24 1-1	D28 1-1	a11 1-0	O19 1-1	a20 1-1	J04 1-2	F22 0-0	D26 0-1	F08 1-1	O05 4-1	F11 3-0	N02 2-0	S21 2-2	

LEAGUE TABLES

DIVISION 1

	P	W	D	L	F	A	W	D	L	F	A	Pts
Leeds U	42	13	8	0	38	13	9	8	4	36	24	82
Manchester U	42	12	7	2	34	13	9	8	4	29	20	78
Sheffield W	42	13	5	3	39	24	8	7	6	23	25	75
Arsenal	42	12	7	2	51	22	7	8	6	30	24	72
Manchester C	42	13	4	4	32	14	7	6	8	29	34	70
Liverpool	42	13	5	3	34	17	3	11	7	13	23	64
Aston Villa	42	13	3	5	31	16	4	6	11	17	28	60
Nottingham F	42	10	7	4	36	27	6	4	11	24	31	59
Sheffield U	42	9	6	6	29	23	7	3	11	36	40	57
Crystal Palace	42	7	8	6	24	25	7	7	7	29	36	57
Q.P.R.	42	6	10	5	25	21	6	8	7	23	26	54
Everton	42	8	8	5	28	19	5	6	10	24	32	53
Wimbledon	42	10	5	6	32	20	3	9	9	21	33	53
Chelsea	42	7	8	6	31	30	6	6	9	19	30	53
Tottenham H	42	7	3	11	33	35	8	4	9	25	28	52
Southampton	42	7	5	9	17	28	7	5	9	22	27	52
Oldham A	42	11	5	5	46	36	3	4	14	17	31	51
Norwich C	42	8	6	7	29	28	3	6	12	18	35	45
Coventry C	42	6	7	8	18	15	5	4	12	17	29	44
Luton T	42	10	7	4	25	17	0	5	16	13	54	42
Notts Co	42	7	5	9	24	29	3	5	13	16	33	40
West Ham U	42	6	6	9	22	24	3	5	13	15	35	38

DIVISION 2

	P	W	D	L	F	A	W	D	L	F	A	Pts
Ipswich T	46	16	3	4	42	22	8	9	6	28	28	84
Middlesbrough	46	15	6	2	37	13	8	5	10	21	28	80
Derby Co	46	11	4	8	35	24	12	5	6	34	27	78
Leicester C	46	14	4	5	41	24	9	4	10	21	31	77
Cambridge U	46	10	9	4	34	19	9	8	6	31	28	74
Blackburn R	46	14	5	4	41	21	7	6	10	29	32	74
Charlton A	46	9	7	7	25	23	11	4	8	29	25	71
Swindon T	46	15	3	5	38	22	3	12	8	31	33	69
Portsmouth	46	15	6	2	41	12	4	6	13	24	39	69
Watford	46	9	5	9	25	23	9	6	8	26	25	65
Wolverh'pton W	46	11	6	6	36	24	7	4	12	25	30	64
Southend U	46	11	5	7	37	26	6	6	11	26	37	62
Bristol R	46	11	9	3	43	29	5	5	13	17	34	62
Tranmere R	46	9	9	5	37	32	5	10	8	19	24	61
Millwall	46	10	4	9	32	32	7	6	10	32	39	61
Barnsley	46	11	4	8	27	25	5	7	11	19	32	59
Bristol C	46	10	8	5	30	24	3	7	13	25	47	54
Sunderland	46	10	8	5	36	23	4	3	16	25	42	53
Grimsby	46	7	5	11	25	28	7	6	10	22	34	53
Newcastle U	46	9	8	6	38	30	4	5	14	28	54	52
Oxford U	46	10	6	7	39	30	3	5	15	27	43	50
Plymouth A	46	11	5	7	26	26	2	4	17	16	38	48
Brighton & H.A.	46	7	7	9	36	37	5	4	14	20	40	47
Port Vale	46	7	8	8	23	25	3	7	13	19	34	45

DIVISION 3

	P	W	D	L	F	A	W	D	L	F	A	Pts
Brentford	46	17	2	4	55	29	8	5	10	26	26	82
Birmingham C	46	15	6	2	42	22	8	6	9	27	30	81
Huddersfield T	46	15	4	4	36	15	7	8	8	23	23	78
Stoke C	46	14	5	4	45	24	7	9	7	24	25	77
Stockport Co	46	15	5	3	47	19	7	5	11	28	32	76
Peterborough U	46	13	7	3	38	20	7	7	9	27	38	74
W.B.A.	46	12	6	5	45	25	7	8	8	19	24	71
Bournemouth	46	13	4	6	33	18	7	7	9	19	30	71
Fulham	46	11	7	5	29	16	8	6	9	28	37	70
Leyton O	46	12	7	4	36	18	6	4	13	26	34	65
Hartlepool U	46	12	5	6	30	21	6	6	11	27	36	65
Reading	46	9	8	6	33	27	7	5	11	26	35	61
Bolton W	46	10	9	4	26	19	4	8	11	31	37	59
Hull C	46	9	4	10	28	23	7	7	9	26	31	59
Wigan A	46	11	6	6	33	21	4	8	11	25	43	59
Bradford C	46	8	10	5	36	30	5	9	9	26	31	58
Preston N.E.	46	12	7	4	42	32	3	5	15	19	40	57
Chester C	46	10	6	7	34	29	4	8	11	22	30	56
Swansea C	46	10	9	4	35	24	4	5	14	20	41	56
Exeter C	46	11	7	5	34	25	3	4	16	23	55	53
Bury	46	8	7	8	31	31	5	5	13	24	43	51
Shrewsbury T	46	7	7	9	30	31	5	4	14	23	37	47
Torquay U	46	13	3	7	29	19	0	5	18	13	49	47
Darlington	46	5	5	13	31	39	5	2	16	25	51	37

DIVISION 4

	P	W	D	L	F	A	W	D	L	F	A	Pts
Burnley	42	14	4	3	42	16	11	4	6	37	27	83
Rotherham U	42	12	6	3	38	16	10	5	6	32	21	77
Mansfield T	42	13	4	4	43	26	10	4	7	32	27	77
Blackpool	42	17	3	1	48	13	5	7	9	23	32	76
Scunthorpe U	42	14	5	2	39	18	7	4	10	25	41	72
Crewe A	42	12	6	3	33	20	8	4	9	33	31	70
Barnet	42	16	1	4	48	23	5	5	11	33	38	69
Rochdale	42	12	6	3	34	22	6	7	8	23	31	67
Cardiff C	42	13	3	5	42	26	4	12	5	24	27	66
Lincoln C	42	9	5	7	21	24	8	6	7	29	20	62
Gillingham	42	12	5	4	41	19	3	7	11	22	34	57
Scarborough	42	12	5	4	39	28	3	7	11	25	40	57
Chesterfield	42	6	7	8	26	28	8	4	9	23	33	53
Wrexham	42	11	4	6	31	26	3	5	13	21	47	51
Walsall	42	5	10	6	28	26	7	3	11	20	32	49
Northampton T	42	5	9	7	25	23	6	4	11	21	34	46
Hereford	42	9	4	8	31	24	3	4	14	13	33	44
Maidstone	42	6	9	6	24	22	2	9	10	21	34	42
York C	42	6	9	6	26	23	2	7	12	16	35	40
Halifax T	42	7	5	9	23	35	3	3	15	11	40	38
Doncaster	42	6	2	13	21	35	3	6	12	19	30	35
Carlisle U	42	5	9	7	24	27	2	4	15	17	40	34

Aldershot resigned from the League. Record not included.

FOOTBALL LEAGUE RECORDS

Top scorers: Prem Lge, Sheringham (Tottenham Hotspur) 22 goals; Div 1, G.Whittingham (Portsmouth) 42 goals; Div 2, R.Taylor (West Bromwich Albion) 30 goals; Div 3, D.Foreman (Scarborough), C.Griffiths (Shrewsbury Town) 27 goals.

Play-offs: Prem Lge, Leicester City v Portsmouth 1-0, 2-2; Swindon Town v Tranmere Rovers 3-1, 2-3; Leicester City v Swindon Town 3-4; Div 1, Stockport County v Port Vale 1-1, 0-1; Swansea City v West Bromwich Albion 2-1, 0-2; Port Vale v West Bromwich Albion 0-3; Div 2, Bury v York City 0-0, 0-1; Crewe Alexandra v Walsall 5-1, 4-2; Crewe Alexandra v York City 1-1 (3-5 penalties).

Newcastle United, West Ham United and Swindon Town pro-

Teddy Sheringham top-scored in the Premiership with 22 goals for Tottenham Hotspur.

DIVISION PREMIER

		ARSENAL	ASTON VILLA	BLACKBURN	CHELSEA	COVENTRY	C.PALACE	EVERTON	IPSWICH	LEEDS	LIVERPOOL	MANCHESTER C	MANCHESTER U	MIDDLESBROUGH	NORWICH	NOTTINGHAM F	OLDHAM	Q.P.R.	SHEFFIELD U	SHEFFIELD W	SOUTHAMPTON	TOTTENHAM	WIMBLEDON
1	ARSENAL		a12 0-1	S12 0-1	O03 2-1	N07 3-0	m08 3-0	O24 2-0	D26 0-0	F24 0-0	J31 0-1	S28 1-0	N28 0-1	D19 1-1	A15 2-4	a21 1-1	A26 2-0	m04 0-0	J09 1-1	A29 2-1	M20 4-3	m11 1-3	F10 0-1
2	ASTON VILLA	D28 1-0		O19 0-0	S02 1-3	a10 0-0	S05 3-0	F20 2-1	F06 2-0	A19 1-1	S19 4-2	a18 3-1	N07 1-0	J17 5-1	N28 2-3	D12 2-1	m02 0-1	N01 2-0	J27 3-1	M20 2-0	A22 1-1	M10 0-0	F27 1-0
3	BLACKBURN	A18 1-0	a21 3-0		F21 2-0	J26 2-5	F02 1-2	S15 2-3	a12 2-1	D26 3-1	a03 4-1	A22 1-0	O24 0-0	M20 1-1	O03 7-1	S05 4-1	S26 2-0	N28 1-0	D19 1-0	m08 1-0	M09 0-0	N07 0-2	J09 0-0
4	CHELSEA	M01 1-0	F13 0-1	A26 0-0		m01 2-1	N07 3-1	M10 2-1	O17 2-1	N29 1-0	F10 0-0	J09 2-4	D19 1-1	a03 4-0	S12 2-3	S26 0-0	A15 1-1	A29 1-0	O31 1-2	J30 0-2	D26 1-1	M20 1-1	a12 4-2
5	COVENTRY	M13 0-2	D26 3-0	A29 0-2	O24 1-2		O03 2-2	M07 0-1	D05 2-2	m08 3-3	D19 5-1	N21 2-3	a12 0-1	A15 2-1	S26 1-1	J09 0-1	J23 3-0	A26 0-1	M24 1-3	M03 1-0	a03 2-0	S14 1-0	J30 0-2
6	C.PALACE	N02 1-2	F10 1-0	A15 3-3	M15 1-1	F27 0-0		J09 0-2	m01 3-1	D20 1-0	M23 1-1	O17 0-0	a21 0-2	a12 4-1	A29 1-2	N21 1-1	S12 2-2	a03 1-1	D05 2-0	A25 1-1	S26 1-2	J30 1-3	D26 2-0
7	EVERTON	m01 0-0	A25 1-0	M03 2-1	N21 0-1	O17 1-1	S19 0-2		M24 3-0	J16 2-0	D07 2-1	O31 1-3	S12 0-2	D26 2-2	J30 0-1	M13 3-0	F27 2-2	a12 3-5	m04 0-2	A15 1-1	D19 2-1	F10 1-2	A29 0-0
8	IPSWICH	a10 1-2	A15 1-1	D28 2-1	a06 1-1	M20 0-0	O24 2-2	N28 1-0		O03 4-2	A25 2-2	D12 3-1	J30 2-1	M02 0-1	a19 3-1	m08 2-1	J09 1-2	F09 1-1	S26 0-0	M10 0-1	N07 0-0	A30 1-1	S12 2-1
9	LEEDS	N21 3-0	S13 1-1	a10 5-2	M24 1-1	O31 2-2	a17 0-0	S26 2-0	F27 1-0		A29 2-2	M13 1-0	F08 0-0	J30 3-0	D28 0-0	D05 1-4	F13 2-0	m01 1-1	O17 3-1	D12 3-1	J09 2-1	A25 5-0	A15 2-1
10	LIVERPOOL	A23 0-2	J09 1-2	D13 2-1	S05 2-1	a17 4-0	N28 5-0	M20 1-0	F20 0-0	a21 2-0		D28 1-1	M06 1-2	N07 4-1	O25 4-1	F06 0-0	a10 1-0	M10 1-0	A19 2-1	O03 1-0	S01 1-1	m08 6-2	S26 2-3
11	MANCHESTER C	J16 0-1	D19 1-1	J30 3-2	S20 0-1	M10 1-0	m05 0-0	m08 2-5	a03 3-1	N07 4-0	a12 1-1		M20 1-1	S12 0-1	A26 3-1	O03 2-2	A29 3-3	A17 1-1	D26 2-0	F23 1-2	O24 1-0	N28 0-1	a21 1-1
12	MANCHESTER U	M24 0-0	M14 1-1	m03 3-1	a17 3-0	D28 5-0	S02 1-0	A19 0-3	A22 1-1	S06 2-0	O18 2-2	D06 2-1		F27 3-0	D12 1-0	J27 2-0	N21 3-0	S26 0-0	F06 2-1	a10 2-1	F20 2-1	J09 4-1	O31 0-1
13	MIDDLESBROUGH	a06 1-0	S26 2-3	D05 3-2	D11 0-0	F06 0-2	D28 0-1	a10 1-2	S01 2-2	A22 4-1	M13 1-2	A19 2-0	O03 1-1		m08 3-3	F20 1-2	M22 2-3	J09 0-1	S05 2-0	O24 1-1	J26 2-1	a20 3-0	N21 2-0
14	NORWICH	M03 1-1	M24 1-0	F28 0-0	A19 2-1	J16 1-1	J27 4-2	A22 1-1	D21 0-2	a14 4-2	m01 1-0	F20 2-1	A05 1-3	O31 1-1		A31 3-1	M13 1-0	O17 2-1	N21 2-1	S19 1-0	S05 1-0	D26 0-0	D05 2-1
15	NOTTINGHAM F	O17 0-1	a04 0-1	a07 1-3	J16 3-0	S21 1-1	M03 1-1	N07 0-1	O31 0-1	M21 1-1	A16 1-0	F27 0-2	A29 0-2	O21 1-0	M17 0-3		J30 2-0	F24 1-0	m01 0-2	S12 1-2	N28 1-2	a12 2-1	D20 1-1
16	OLDHAM	F20 0-1	O24 1-1	J16 0-1	F06 3-1	S05 0-1	A19 1-1	O04 1-0	S19 4-2	S01 2-2	m05 3-2	J26 0-1	M09 1-0	N28 4-1	N09 2-3	A22 5-3		M20 2-2	a13 1-1	a07 1-1	m08 4-3	D19 2-1	a03 6-2
17	Q.P.R.	S02 0-0	m09 2-1	M24 0-3	J27 1-1	F20 2-0	D12 1-3	D28 4-2	S05 0-0	O24 2-1	N23 0-1	F06 1-1	J18 1-3	S19 3-3	M06 3-1	a10 4-3	D05 3-2		A22 3-2	m11 3-1	A19 3-1	O03 4-1	M13 1-2
18	SHEFFIELD U	S19 1-1	A29 0-2	a17 1-3	m08 4-2	N28 1-1	M20 0-1	D12 1-0	J16 3-0	a06 2-1	S12 1-0	a09 1-1	A15 2-1	F09 2-0	M10 0-1	O24 0-0	F22 2-0	J30 1-2		N08 1-1	O03 2-0	M02 6-0	A25 2-2
19	SHEFFIELD W	m06 1-0	D05 1-2	O31 0-0	A22 3-3	S02 1-2	F20 2-1	F06 3-1	N21 1-1	m04 1-1	F27 1-1	S05 0-3	D26 3-3	m01 2-3	J10 1-0	A19 2-0	O17 2-1	D19 1-0	a21 1-1		a12 5-2	S27 2-0	M24 1-1
20	SOUTHAMPTON	D05 2-0	J30 2-0	N22 1-1	a10 1-0	D12 2-2	J16 1-0	a17 0-0	M13 4-3	S19 1-1	F13 2-1	m01 0-1	A24 0-1	A29 2-1	F10 3-0	M24 1-2	O31 1-0	S12 1-2	F27 3-2	D28 1-2		A15 0-0	O17 2-2
21	TOTTENHAM	D12 1-0	N21 0-0	m05 1-2	D05 1-2	A19 0-2	A22 2-2	S05 2-1	J27 0-2	F20 4-0	O31 2-0	M24 3-1	S19 1-1	O17 2-2	a09 5-1	D28 2-1	a17 4-1	F27 3-2	S02 2-0	J16 0-2	F07 4-2		m01 1-1
22	WIMBLEDON	S05 3-2	O03 2-3	S19 1-1	D28 0-0	A22 1-2	a09 4-0	J26 1-3	A18 0-1	F06 1-0	J16 2-0	S01 0-1	m09 1-2	M09 2-0	M20 3-0	a17 1-0	D12 5-2	N07 0-2	F20 2-0	N28 1-1	M06 1-2	O25 1-1	

DIVISION 1

		BARNSLEY	BIRMINGHAM	BRENTFORD	BRISTOL C	BRISTOL R	CAMBRIDGE	CHARLTON	DERBY	GRIMSBY	LEICESTER	LUTON	MILLWALL	NEWCASTLE	NOTTS CO	OXFORD	PETERBOROUGH	PORTSMOUTH	SOUTHEND	SUNDERLAND	SWINDON	TRANMERE	WATFORD	WEST HAM	WOLVERHAMPTON
1	BARNSLEY		N21 1-0	O24 3-2	J16 2-1	M27 2-1	M09 2-0	N28 1-0	S12 1-1	a10 0-2	M06 2-3	O10 3-0	A29 0-0	D13 1-0	M16 0-0	a24 0-1	S19 1-2	J30 1-1	a17 3-1	M21 2-0	m08 1-0	D28 3-1	N07 0-1	A16 0-1	S01 0-1
2	BIRMINGHAM	M23 3-0		D05 1-3	M13 0-1	O24 2-1	J30 0-2	m08 1-0	a06 1-1	A30 2-1	O10 0-2	J09 2-1	F09 0-0	N04 2-3	A16 1-0	M06 1-0	J22 2-0	F13 2-3	S01 2-0	M16 1-0	a12 4-6	a24 0-0	D19 2-2	a03 1-2	S27 0-4
3	BRENTFORD	m01 3-1	M20 0-2		O31 5-1	J30 0-3	F14 0-1	N07 2-0	D26 2-1	N21 1-3	J09 1-3	S13 1-2	S26 1-1	O04 1-2	a12 2-2	N28 1-0	F27 0-1	S01 4-1	A29 2-1	a06 1-1	M27 0-0	M09 0-1	O17 1-1	D20 0-0	A15 0-2
4	BRISTOL C	S26 2-1	N07 3-0	m08 4-1		a06 2-1	a24 0-0	O10 2-1	a20 0-0	M28 1-0	O24 2-1	J30 0-0	M09 0-1	J09 1-2	N28 1-0	D26 1-1	D19 0-1	A15 3-3	S12 0-1	A29 0-0	N21 2-2	M06 1-3	M20 2-1	S15 1-5	a12 1-0
5	BRISTOL R	N03 1-5	m01 3-3	A22 2-1	D13 4-0		a17 1-1	J27 0-2	N14 1-2	S19 0-3	a03 0-0	D05 2-0	O31 1-0	S05 1-2	O03 3-3	F06 0-1	M24 3-1	a10 1-2	D28 0-2	J16 2-2	A19 3-4	F20 1-0	F27 0-3	O17 0-4	M13 1-1
6	CAMBRIDGE	N14 1-2	A22 0-3	S04 1-0	O17 2-1	D18 0-1		A18 0-1	O03 1-3	J16 2-0	M23 1-3	N03 3-3	F27 1-1	a03 0-3	a06 3-0	J23 2-2	M16 2-2	M13 0-1	m01 3-1	S19 2-1	F20 1-0	F06 0-1	a13 1-1	O31 2-1	D05 1-1
7	CHARLTON	a03 0-0	N01 0-0	M13 1-0	F27 2-1	A25 4-1	S12 0-0		m01 2-1	A15 3-1	N04 2-0	A29 0-0	O18 0-2	N14 1-3	J30 2-1	D19 1-1	a12 0-1	D05 1-0	O03 1-1	F13 0-1	S26 2-0	J09 2-2	a06 3-1	D26 1-1	M23 0-1
8	DERBY	F10 3-0	D12 3-1	a10 3-2	S06 3-4	M10 3-1	M03 0-0	O24 4-3		a17 2-1	F24 2-0	a24 1-1	N07 1-2	A22 1-2	m05 2-0	O11 0-1	F06 2-3	D28 2-4	S26 2-0	N21 0-1	M21 2-1	N28 1-2	F20 1-2	J10 0-2	m08 2-0
9	GRIMSBY	D26 4-2	F20 1-1	M23 0-1	N14 2-1	J09 2-0	S26 1-1	F06 1-0	D20 0-2		D05 1-3	M13 3-1	a06 1-0	m04 0-2	F27 3-3	S05 1-1	O03 1-3	O31 3-0	O17 1-0	a12 1-0	J26 2-1	M16 0-0	A22 3-2	N03 1-1	a03 1-0
10	LEICESTER	O03 2-1	F28 2-1	S19 0-0	m01 0-0	N28 0-1	N21 2-2	M27 3-1	A26 3-2	M20 3-0		A15 2-1	a14 3-0	O31 2-1	J23 1-1	a07 2-1	O18 0-2	A29 1-0	a20 4-1	M10 3-2	D20 4-2	N07 0-1	J16 5-2	J30 1-2	S13 0-0
11	LUTON	F27 2-2	S19 1-1	F09 0-0	A22 0-3	M20 1-1	M27 2-0	F20 1-0	O17 1-3	N07 1-4	F06 2-0		N21 1-1	J27 0-0	J16 0-0	J09 3-1	m01 0-0	O03 1-4	O31 2-2	D19 0-0	M17 0-0	S05 3-3	N29 2-0	a13 2-0	a07 1-1
12	MILLWALL	F20 0-4	S12 0-0	J17 6-1	N04 4-1	m08 0-3	O10 2-2	a24 1-0	M13 1-0	D12 2-1	D28 2-0	M24 1-0		a17 1-2	S19 6-0	A22 3-1	J27 4-0	a03 1-1	D05 1-1	M06 0-0	S05 2-1	a10 0-0	F06 5-2	N15 2-1	O25 2-0
13	NEWCASTLE	a07 6-0	M28 2-2	M06 5-1	S19 5-0	F24 0-0	N28 4-1	M10 2-2	J31 1-1	O24 0-1	m09 7-1	S02 2-0	D20 1-1		M20 4-0	m06 2-1	J16 3-0	S12 3-1	A15 3-2	a25 1-0	N08 0-0	O10 1-0	N21 2-0	A29 2-0	D26 2-1
14	NOTTS CO	S05 1-3	F06 3-1	D28 1-1	a03 0-0	M06 3-0	D12 1-0	a10 2-0	N03 0-2	O10 1-0	A22 1-1	S26 0-0	J09 1-2	D05 0-2		O24 1-1	F21 1-0	a17 0-1	M23 4-0	m08 3-1	a24 1-1	J26 5-1	A25 1-2	M13 1-0	N14 2-2
15	OXFORD	O17 0-0	O03 0-0	a03 0-2	a10 2-0	A15 2-1	S15 3-0	a17 0-1	F27 0-1	F23 0-1	D13 0-0	N14 4-0	J30 3-0	D28 4-2	m01 1-1		a20 2-1	N03 5-5	M13 0-1	S12 0-1	J09 0-1	S26 1-2	O31 1-1	M23 1-0	A29 0-0
16	PETERBOROUGH	J09 1-1	M09 2-1	O10 0-0	a17 1-1	N21 1-1	a10 1-0	D28 1-1	A15 1-0	M06 1-0	a24 3-0	O24 2-3	S15 0-0	S26 0-1	A29 1-3	M20 1-1		D12 1-1	J30 1-0	N07 5-2	N29 3-3	m08 1-1	M27 0-0	S12 1-3	F13 2-3
17	PORTSMOUTH	A22 1-0	S05 4-0	J23 1-0	F06 2-3	D26 4-1	N07 3-0	M20 1-0	a12 3-0	m08 2-1	F20 1-1	M06 2-1	N28 1-0	F09 2-0	D19 0-0	M27 3-0	a06 4-0		J09 2-0	O24 2-0	O10 3-1	N21 4-0	M09 1-0	S27 0-1	a24 2-0
18	SOUTHEND	D19 3-0	J27 4-0	F21 3-0	F10 1-1	a14 3-0	O25 1-1	M06 0-2	J16 0-0	a23 1-0	S05 3-1	m08 2-1	M21 3-3	J20 1-1	N21 3-1	N07 0-3	A22 0-1	S18 0-0		N28 0-1	M10 1-1	M26 1-2	D26 1-2	a07 1-0	O10 1-1
19	SUNDERLAND	D05 2-1	a10 1-2	D12 1-3	F20 0-0	S26 1-1	J09 3-3	S05 0-2	M24 1-0	D28 2-0	N15 1-2	a17 2-2	O03 2-0	O18 1-2	O31 2-2	F09 2-0	M13 3-0	m01 4-1	a03 2-4		F06 0-1	A22 1-0	J27 1-2	F27 0-0	N03 2-0
20	SWINDON	O31 1-0	J12 0-0	N03 0-2	M24 2-1	S12 2-2	A29 4-1	J16 2-2	D06 2-4	S29 1-0	a17 1-1	a10 1-0	F13 3-0	M13 2-1	O17 5-1	S20 2-2	a03 1-0	F27 1-0	N14 3-2	A15 1-0		F23 2-0	O03 3-1	m02 1-3	J30 1-0
21	TRANMERE	a12 2-1	O17 4-0	N14 3-2	O03 3-0	A28 2-1	A15 2-0	S18 0-0	a02 2-1	S12 1-1	M13 2-3	F13 0-2	D26 1-1	F28 0-3	S29 3-1	J15 4-0	O30 1-1	M23 0-2	N03 3-0	m04 2-1	a06 3-1		m01 2-1	D04 5-2	D19 3-0
22	WATFORD	M13 1-2	a17 1-0	a24 1-0	D05 0-0	O10 4-2	D28 2-2	D13 1-1	A29 0-0	J30 2-3	S26 0-3	a03 0-0	A15 3-1	M23 1-0	S12 1-3	m08 0-1	N03 1-2	N14 0-0	a10 0-0	S29 2-1	M06 0-4	O24 3-2		F13 1-2	J09 3-1
23	WEST HAM	F06 1-1	N28 3-1	a17 4-0	J27 2-0	a24 2-1	m08 2-0	A22 0-1	S20 1-1	M09 2-1	a11 3-0	D28 2-2	M28 2-2	F21 0-0	N07 2-0	N21 5-3	F09 2-1	J16 2-0	D12 2-0	O11 6-0	O24 0-1	M20 2-0	S05 2-1		M06 3-1
24	WOLVERHAMPTON	J27 1-0	J17 2-1	F06 1-2	D28 0-0	N07 5-1	M20 1-2	N22 2-1	O31 0-2	N28 2-1	A18 3-0	D12 1-2	m01 3-1	a10 1-0	M09 3-0	F20 0-1	S05 4-3	O17 1-1	F27 1-1	M27 2-1	A22 2-2	a17 0-2	S19 2-2	O04 0-0	

Bob Taylor scored 30 goals for West Brom who won promotion to Division One via the Play-offs.

Season 1992-93

moted to Prem Lge; Crystal Palace, Middlesbrough and Nottingham Forest relegated to Div 1; Stoke City, Bolton Wanderers and West Bromwich Albion promoted to Div 1; Brentford, Cambridge United and Bristol Rovers relegated to Div 2; Cardiff City, Wrexham, Barnet and York City promoted to Div 2; Preston North End, Mansfield Town, Wigan Athletic and Chester City relegated to Div 3; Halifax Town relegated from Div 3, replaced by Wycombe Wanderers.

DIVISION 2

	BLACKPOOL	BOLTON	BOURNEMOUTH	BRADFORD C	BRIGHTON	BURNLEY	CHESTER	EXETER	FULHAM	HARTLEPOOL	HUDDERSFIELD	HULL	LEYTON O	MANSFIELD	PLYMOUTH	PORT VALE	PRESTON	READING	ROTHERHAM	STOCKPORT	STOKE	SWANSEA	W.B.A.	WIGAN
1 BLACKPOOL		F20 1-1	S15 2-0	D26 3-3	S19 2-2	O24 1-3	a13 2-0	A22 2-0	D20 1-1	M06 1-1	N03 2-2	M23 5-1	J26 3-1	S05 1-1	a03 1-1	m08 2-4	O10 2-3	M13 0-1	J16 2-0	a24 2-0	N21 1-3	J05 0-0	F06 2-1	a06 2-1
2 BOLTON	S01 3-0		S19 1-1	D19 5-0	J30 0-1	N28 4-0	a24 5-0	M20 4-1	M27 1-0	O10 1-2	A15 2-0	O24 2-0	M06 1-0	M09 2-1	J16 3-1	N07 1-1	m08 1-0	A29 2-1	M30 2-0	a06 2-1	m04 1-0	a12 3-1	S15 0-2	D26 2-1
3 BOURNEMOUTH	J09 5-1	a27 1-2		a06 1-1	N03 1-1	a13 1-1	a03 0-0	M06 1-3	S12 2-1	S05 0-2	S26 1-1	D19 0-0	a24 3-0	F20 4-1	M22 1-3	A22 2-1	F06 2-1	N21 1-1	O10 0-0	O24 1-0	M13 1-1	D26 0-2	J26 0-1	m08 0-0
4 BRADFORD C	a10 2-0	a17 2-1	D12 0-1		A29 1-1	O10 1-0	A15 3-1	M10 3-1	N07 3-2	m08 0-2	F14 0-1	M06 1-2	O24 1-0	J02 0-0	J30 0-0	D28 3-2	S19 4-0	a24 3-0	N28 0-3	S15 2-3	S02 3-1	J16 0-0	M28 2-2	M20 2-1
5 BRIGHTON	M31 1-1	A22 2-1	M20 1-0	J27 1-1		D26 3-0	m08 3-2	F20 3-0	N28 0-2	O24 1-1	S12 2-1	a14 2-0	F06 1-3	a07 3-1	D19 2-1	M06 0-2	S05 2-0	S26 0-1	a24 1-2	N07 2-0	J09 2-2	M27 0-2	M10 3-1	O10 1-0
6 BURNLEY	m01 2-2	M23 0-1	M16 1-1	F27 2-2	a10 1-3		F13 5-0	a17 3-1	O17 5-2	a03 3-0	N21 2-1	M13 2-0	D12 2-0	S19 1-0	S29 0-0	S15 1-1	F16 2-0	N03 1-1	A29 1-1	J30 1-1	O31 0-2	A15 1-0	O03 2-1	J16 0-1
7 CHESTER	D28 1-2	O17 2-2	M09 1-0	F06 2-5	O31 2-1	S05 3-0		M27 0-3	m01 2-3	F20 1-0	a17 0-2	J30 3-0	J02 1-3	S15 1-2	F27 1-2	J16 1-2	J26 2-4	D12 0-3	M19 1-2	S19 0-3	O03 1-1	N07 3-2	a10 1-3	N28 1-2
8 EXETER	J30 0-1	N03 1-3	O03 1-1	a03 0-1	S01 2-3	D19 2-2	N21 2-0		O31 1-2	M13 3-1	m01 1-2	a06 1-1	S19 1-0	O17 2-0	D26 2-0	m04 1-1	a12 0-1	M23 0-0	A15 0-2	F13 2-2	A29 2-2	F27 0-2	J16 2-3	S15 0-0
9 FULHAM	a17 1-0	N21 1-4	M02 1-1	M13 1-1	M23 2-0	a24 4-0	O24 1-0	m08 1-1		D28 1-3	a02 0-1	O10 3-3	a10 1-0	D05 0-0	S19 3-1	F06 1-2	A22 2-1	M06 0-0	D12 0-1	J16 2-1	N03 0-0	S15 1-1	S05 1-1	F20 1-0
10 HARTLEPOOL	O02 1-0	F27 0-2	F13 0-1	O31 2-0	m01 2-0	M09 0-0	S01 2-0	N07 1-3	a12 0-3		A29 1-0	D26 1-0	S15 0-2	M27 0-1	a05 1-0	S19 1-1	J16 0-0	A15 1-1	J30 0-2	N28 3-2	D19 1-2	O17 0-1	M20 2-2	M02 0-0
11 HUDDERSFIELD	M20 5-2	F06 1-1	J16 0-1	S06 1-2	M03 1-2	M27 1-1	D19 0-2	O24 0-0	M10 1-0	J27 3-0		a24 3-0	F20 1-1	N07 2-1	S15 2-1	N28 1-2	M17 1-0	O10 0-0	M06 1-1	m08 2-1	a07 1-0	S19 1-2	A22 0-1	a12 2-1
12 HULL	N28 3-2	a30 1-2	a17 3-0	O03 0-2	D28 1-0	N07 0-2	A22 1-1	D12 4-0	F27 1-1	a10 3-2	O17 2-3		J16 0-0	M20 1-0	A28 2-0	M27 0-1	S15 2-4	F13 1-1	S19 0-1	a27 0-2	A15 1-0	S01 1-0	O31 1-2	M09 0-0
13 LEYTON O	A29 1-0	O03 1-0	O17 1-0	m01 4-2	A15 3-2	a06 3-2	S12 4-3	J23 5-0	D26 0-0	J09 0-0	S01 4-1	S26 0-0		N28 5-1	F13 2-0	M20 0-1	D18 3-1	J30 1-2	M09 1-1	a12 3-0	F27 1-0	O31 4-2	N07 2-0	M27 1-2
14 MANSFIELD	F13 2-2	a03 1-1	S01 0-2	S12 5-2	D12 1-3	J23 1-1	J09 2-0	a24 0-0	A29 2-3	F16 2-0	M13 1-2	N03 3-1	M23 3-0		A15 0-0	a10 0-1	O24 2-2	D28 1-1	m08 1-3	O10 2-0	S26 0-4	J30 3-3	a17 0-3	M06 2-0
15 PLYMOUTH	M09 2-1	S26 2-1	N28 2-1	A22 3-0	a17 3-2	F20 1-2	O10 2-0	a10 0-3	J23 1-1	D12 2-2	M30 1-3	J26 0-0	S05 2-0	F06 3-2		a24 0-1	M06 4-0	m08 2-2	N07 2-1	M27 3-4	S12 1-1	M20 0-1	D28 0-0	O24 2-0
16 PORT VALE	O31 2-1	M13 0-0	J30 3-0	a13 1-2	O03 3-1	J09 3-0	S26 2-0	S12 2-2	A15 0-0	F09 2-0	M23 1-0	N21 1-1	N03 2-0	a27 3-0	O17 4-0		a06 2-2	a03 3-1	S01 4-2	A29 0-0	M31 0-2	F13 2-0	F27 2-1	D19 2-2
17 PRESTON	F27 3-3	O31 2-2	A15 1-1	J23 3-2	F13 1-0	S12 2-0	A29 4-3	D28 2-2	J30 1-2	S26 0-2	a10 2-1	J09 1-2	a17 1-4	m01 1-5	O03 1-2	D12 2-5		O20 2-0	M27 5-2	M20 2-3	O17 1-2	M09 1-3	N28 1-1	N07 2-0
18 READING	N07 0-0	J27 1-2	M27 3-2	O17 1-1	J16 3-0	M20 1-0	a07 1-0	N28 2-3	O02 3-0	F06 2-0	F27 2-1	S05 1-2	A22 1-1	a12 3-1	O31 3-0	M10 1-0	F20 4-0		S16 3-1	D19 2-4	D26 0-1	m01 2-0	a21 1-1	S19 4-0
19 ROTHERHAM	S26 3-2	S12 2-1	F26 1-2	M23 2-0	O17 1-0	J26 0-1	N03 3-3	F06 1-1	a06 1-1	A22 0-0	O03 1-0	F09 0-1	a03 1-1	O31 2-0	M13 2-2	F20 4-1	N21 1-0	J09 3-2		M02 0-2	a12 0-2	D18 0-0	m01 0-2	S05 2-3
20 STOCKPORT	O16 0-0	F09 2-0	m01 0-0	J09 2-2	M13 0-0	A22 2-1	J22 2-0	S05 2-2	S25 0-0	M23 4-1	O30 5-0	S12 5-3	D28 1-1	F26 0-1	N20 3-0	F16 2-0	N03 3-0	a16 2-2	a09 2-2		a03 1-1	O03 1-1	F20 5-1	F05 3-0
21 STOKE	M27 0-1	S05 0-0	N07 2-0	F20 1-0	S16 1-1	m08 1-1	M06 4-0	J27 1-1	M20 1-0	a17 0-1	D12 3-0	F06 3-0	O10 2-1	J16 4-0	a28 1-0	O24 2-1	a24 1-0	a10 2-0	D28 2-0	M09 2-1		N28 2-1	S19 4-3	A22 2-1
22 SWANSEA	S12 3-0	D28 1-2	a10 2-1	S26 1-1	N20 0-1	F05 1-1	M13 4-2	O10 0-0	J09 2-2	a24 3-0	a20 3-0	F20 1-0	m08 0-1	A22 4-0	N03 0-0	S05 2-0	a27 2-0	O24 2-1	a17 2-0	M05 2-2	M23 1-2		D12 0-0	m04 2-1
23 W.B.A.	A15 3-1	J09 3-1	A29 2-1	N21 1-1	a03 3-1	M06 2-0	D26 2-0	S26 2-0	F13 4-0	N03 3-1	J30 2-2	m08 3-1	M13 2-0	D20 2-0	a12 2-5	O10 0-1	M24 3-2	S09 3-0	O24 2-2	S02 3-0	J23 1-2	a07 3-0		a24 5-1
24 WIGAN	D12 2-1	a10 0-2	O31 0-0	N03 1-2	F27 1-2	S26 1-1	M23 1-2	J09 0-1	S01 1-3	S11 2-2	F16 1-0	a03 2-0	N21 3-1	O03 2-0	M01 0-2	A17 0-4	M12 2-3	J23 1-1	F13 1-1	A15 1-2	J30 1-1	A29 2-3	O17 1-0	

DIVISION 3

	BARNET	BURY	CARDIFF	CARLISLE	CHESTERFIELD	COLCHESTER	CREWE	DARLINGTON	DONCASTER	GILLINGHAM	HALIFAX	HEREFORD	LINCOLN	NORTHAMPTON	ROCHDALE	SCARBOROUGH	SCUNTHORPE	SHREWSBURY	TORQUAY	WALSALL	WREXHAM	YORK
1 BARNET		a20 1-0	N22 2-1	S05 2-0	F06 2-1	A21 3-1	O31 3-2	J02 0-0	F20 2-0	M02 2-0	a03 0-0	S19 2-0	m01 1-1	S15 3-0	D12 2-0	a10 3-1	O17 3-0	O03 2-2	D28 5-4	N03 3-0	J16 3-1	M13 1-5
2 BURY	S12 0-0		M23 1-0	F20 6-0	J26 3-0	S05 3-2	m01 1-2	M13 1-1	F06 3-0	A22 1-0	a17 1-2	N21 2-0	O17 1-2	D12 3-3	M16 2-2	O03 0-2	a03 0-0	M30 0-0	S26 2-0	J09 2-1	F27 3-1	O31 1-1
3 CARDIFF	M27 1-1	N28 3-0		S08 2-2	M20 2-1	N07 3-1	F27 1-1	A15 0-0	a06 1-1	S19 3-1	A29 2-1	J02 2-1	a12 3-1	S01 2-1	O03 1-1	M09 1-0	O31 3-0	m01 2-1	F13 4-0	J30 2-1	D18 1-2	D26 3-3
4 CARLISLE	F13 0-1	S01 5-1	J09 1-2		J23 3-1	M20 0-2	D12 1-3	a10 2-2	M27 1-1	N07 1-0	O03 1-1	a17 0-0	A29 2-0	N28 2-0	F27 3-0	O31 2-2	S26 0-2	M09 1-0	m01 0-1	A15 3-4	O17 0-2	S12 1-2
5 CHESTERFIELD	A15 1-2	A29 2-1	N03 2-1	S19 1-0		J16 4-0	S15 2-1	S01 2-0	D19 0-0	F16 1-1	M23 2-1	M13 1-0	M02 2-1	J30 1-3	O31 2-3	m01 0-3	O03 1-2	O17 2-4	F27 1-0	a03 2-1	a12 2-3	a06 1-1
6 COLCHESTER	J29 1-2	F13 0-0	M12 2-4	N03 2-1	S26 3-0		O16 3-2	A29 0-3	J08 2-0	a16 3-0	F26 2-1	M23 3-1	A15 2-1	a20 2-0	N21 4-4	D29 1-0	m01 1-0	S01 0-2	D11 2-0	S12 3-1	O30 2-4	J22 0-0
7 CREWE	m08 4-1	O24 2-1	O10 2-0	a06 4-0	J09 0-2	a24 7-1		F13 1-0	S12 4-0	M06 3-1	S01 2-1	a02 1-1	N21 1-2	A28 3-2	M12 1-1	J30 2-3	a20 1-0	a12 2-2	A15 4-2	a27 0-1	D26 0-1	M23 3-1
8 DARLINGTON	N28 1-0	N07 0-0	F06 0-2	J12 1-1	F20 1-1	m04 1-0	S05 3-0		a12 1-2	M27 1-1	J09 0-3	A19 0-1	O31 1-3	M20 3-1	J23 0-4	O17 2-3	D19 2-2	F27 0-2	O02 4-1	a06 1-2	M09 1-1	S25 0-1
9 DONCASTER	S01 2-1	A15 2-3	D11 0-1	N21 1-2	a17 2-1	S15 1-0	F16 1-1	D28 0-1		O10 1-0	a10 0-1	O24 2-1	S18 0-0	a24 2-2	J02 1-1	J16 4-3	M13 0-1	J29 0-1	A29 2-3	m08 0-3	F13 1-1	M05 0-1
10 GILLINGHAM	A29 1-1	D26 1-4	J23 0-1	M13 1-0	S12 0-0	D18 0-1	O03 1-2	N21 3-1	F27 1-1		m01 2-0	N03 3-1	M23 3-1	A15 2-3	J08 4-2	F13 3-1	a12 1-1	a06 1-0	O31 0-2	S26 0-1	S01 4-1	a02 1-4
11 HALIFAX	D05 1-2	D19 0-1	J26 0-1	M06 0-2	N28 1-1	O10 2-4	F20 1-2	S15 1-0	D26 2-2	O24 2-0		m08 0-1	F16 2-1	J16 2-2	F06 2-3	S19 3-4	A22 0-0	M20 1-1	N07 0-2	a24 0-4	M26 0-1	a12 0-1
12 HEREFORD	J23 1-1	M27 3-1	S13 1-1	a12 1-0	N07 1-3	N28 3-1	M09 0-1	J30 1-1	m01 0-2	M20 3-1	O31 3-0		S01 0-2	F13 3-2	S26 1-1	A15 1-1	a06 2-2	D26 1-1	O17 3-1	A29 1-3	O03 1-1	J09 1-1
13 LINCOLN	O24 4-1	a24 1-2	D28 3-2	J26 2-1	a10 1-1	F06 1-1	M27 1-1	m08 2-0	J23 2-1	N28 1-1	S12 2-1	F20 2-0		M06 2-0	a17 1-2	M20 3-0	S05 1-0	S26 0-1	M09 2-2	O10 0-2	N07 0-0	A22 0-1
14 NORTHAMPTON	J08 1-1	a06 1-0	F19 1-2	M23 2-0	O13 0-1	D26 1-0	J26 0-2	N03 1-2	O17 0-1	F06 2-2	S26 2-5	S06 1-1	O03 0-2		a02 1-0	F27 1-3	S12 1-0	O31 0-0	J23 0-1	a12 0-0	a27 0-2	N21 4-3
15 ROCHDALE	a06 0-1	a13 1-2	M06 1-2	O10 2-2	m08 2-1	M27 5-2	N07 0-1	S19 3-1	N28 1-1	S15 1-1	A15 2-3	J16 1-3	D19 5-1	M09 0-3		A29 3-0	D26 2-0	F13 2-0	M20 1-0	O24 4-3	J30 1-2	a24 1-0
16 SCARBOROUGH	M30 2-2	M06 1-3	a03 1-3	m08 2-2	O24 2-2	a13 0-1	A22 1-0	a24 0-3	S26 1-1	S05 1-1	J23 2-0	F06 2-0	N03 0-1	O10 4-2	F20 1-1		M23 1-2	a20 1-2	S12 1-0	M13 4-1	a06 1-1	D19 4-2
17 SCUNTHORPE	a24 2-0	M09 2-0	m08 0-3	J16 0-0	M06 0-1	O24 3-1	S19 3-3	a17 1-3	N07 0-1	D28 2-2	J30 4-1	D12 3-1	F13 1-1	M30 5-0	a10 5-1	N28 1-2		A29 1-1	M27 2-2	S01 2-0	M20 0-0	O10 1-2
18 SHREWSBURY	M06 1-0	S19 2-0	O24 3-2	a03 2-3	a24 2-2	F20 4-3	D28 4-1	O10 1-2	A22 2-1	D12 2-1	N03 1-0	a10 1-1	J16 3-2	m08 2-3	S05 1-2	S15 2-0	J26 2-1		a17 0-1	N21 0-3	J02 0-1	F06 1-1
19 TORQUAY	a13 0-1	J16 0-1	S05 2-1	O24 0-2	O10 2-2	a06 2-2	F06 1-2	M06 0-2	J26 1-2	m08 2-1	M13 2-0	a24 0-0	a20 1-2	S19 1-0	N03 0-2	J02 1-3	N21 0-1	D20 1-0		D26 0-1	S15 1-1	F20 1-0
20 WALSALL	M20 2-0	S15 4-3	A22 2-3	F06 2-1	M09 3-2	J02 1-3	a17 1-0	D12 2-2	O31 3-1	J16 1-1	O17 1-2	J26 1-1	F27 1-2	D28 2-0	m01 3-1	N07 3-2	F20 3-2	M27 1-1	a10 2-2		N28 1-1	S05 3-1
21 WREXHAM	S26 2-3	O10 4-2	a17 0-2	a24 3-1	D28 5-4	m08 4-3	a10 2-0	a02 1-1	S05 1-1	F20 2-0	N21 1-1	M06 2-0	M13 2-0	O24 0-1	A22 3-1	D12 4-1	N03 0-2	S12 2-0	J09 4-2	J23 3-1		J26 3-0
22 YORK	N07 2-0	M20 1-2	a10 3-1	J19 2-2	D12 0-0	S19 2-0	N28 3-1	J16 0-0	O03 1-1	M09 1-1	D29 1-1	S15 4-2	J30 2-0	M26 2-1	O17 3-0	a17 1-0	F27 5-1	A15 2-0	S01 2-1	F13 0-1	A29 4-0	

LEAGUE TABLES

PREMIER LEAGUE

	P	W	D	L	F	A	W	D	L	F	A	Pts
Manchester U	42	14	5	2	39	14	10	7	4	28	17	84
Aston Villa	42	13	5	3	36	16	8	6	7	21	24	74
Norwich C	42	13	6	2	31	19	8	3	10	30	46	72
Blackburn R	42	13	4	4	38	18	7	7	7	30	28	71
Q.P.R.	42	11	5	5	41	32	6	7	8	22	23	63
Liverpool	42	13	4	4	41	18	3	7	11	21	37	59
Sheffield W	42	9	8	4	34	26	6	6	9	21	25	59
Tottenham H	42	11	5	5	40	25	5	6	10	20	41	59
Manchester C	42	7	8	6	30	25	8	4	9	26	26	57
Arsenal	42	8	6	7	25	20	7	5	9	15	18	56
Chelsea	42	9	7	5	29	22	5	7	9	22	32	56
Wimbledon	42	9	4	8	32	23	5	8	8	24	32	54
Everton	42	7	6	8	26	27	8	2	11	27	28	53
Sheffield U	42	10	6	5	33	19	4	4	13	21	34	52
Coventry C	42	7	4	10	29	28	6	9	6	23	29	52
Ipswich T	42	8	9	4	29	22	4	7	10	21	33	52
Leeds U	42	12	8	1	40	17	0	7	14	17	45	51
Southampton	42	10	6	5	30	21	3	5	13	24	40	50
Oldham A	42	10	6	5	43	30	3	4	14	20	44	49*
Crystal Palace	42	6	9	6	27	25	5	7	9	21	36	49
Middlesbrough	42	8	5	8	33	27	3	6	12	21	48	44
Nottingham F	42	6	4	11	17	25	4	6	11	24	37	40

DIVISION 1

	P	W	D	L	F	A	W	D	L	F	A	Pts
Newcastle U	46	16	6	1	58	15	13	3	7	34	23	96
West Ham U	46	16	5	2	50	17	10	5	8	31	24	88
Portsmouth	46	19	2	2	48	9	7	8	8	32	37	88
Tranmere R	46	15	4	4	48	24	8	6	9	24	32	79
Swindon T	46	15	5	3	41	23	6	8	9	33	36	76
Leicester C	46	14	5	4	43	24	8	5	10	28	40	76
Millwall	46	14	6	3	46	21	4	10	9	19	32	70
Derby Co	46	11	2	10	40	33	8	7	8	28	24	66
Grimsby	46	12	6	5	33	25	7	1	15	25	32	64
Peterborough U	46	7	11	5	30	26	9	3	11	25	37	62
Wolverh'pton W	46	11	6	6	37	26	5	7	11	20	30	61
Charlton A	46	10	8	5	28	19	6	5	12	21	27	61
Barnsley	46	12	4	7	29	19	5	5	13	27	41	60
Oxford U	46	8	7	8	29	21	6	7	10	24	35	56
Bristol C	46	10	7	6	29	25	4	7	12	20	42	56
Watford	46	8	7	8	27	30	6	6	11	30	41	55
Notts Co	46	10	7	6	33	21	2	9	12	22	49	52
Southend U	46	9	8	6	33	22	4	5	14	21	42	52
Birmingham C	46	10	4	9	30	32	3	8	12	20	40	51
Luton T	46	6	13	4	26	26	4	8	11	22	36	51
Sunderland	46	9	6	8	34	28	4	5	14	16	36	50
Brentford	46	7	6	10	28	30	6	4	13	24	41	49
Cambridge U	46	8	6	9	29	32	3	10	10	19	37	49
Bristol R	46	6	6	11	30	42	4	5	14	25	45	41

DIVISION 2

	P	W	D	L	F	A	W	D	L	F	A	Pts
Stoke C	46	17	4	2	41	13	10	8	5	32	21	93
Bolton W	46	18	2	3	48	14	9	7	7	32	27	90
Port Vale	46	14	7	2	44	17	12	4	7	35	27	89
W.B.A.	46	17	3	3	56	22	8	7	8	32	32	85
Swansea C	46	12	7	4	38	17	8	6	9	27	30	73
Stockport Co	46	11	11	1	47	18	8	4	11	34	39	72
Leyton O	46	16	4	3	49	20	5	5	13	20	33	72
Reading	46	14	4	5	44	20	4	11	8	22	31	69
Brighton & H.A.	46	13	4	6	36	24	7	5	11	27	35	69
Bradford C	46	12	5	6	36	24	6	9	8	33	43	68
Rotherham U	46	9	7	7	30	27	8	7	8	30	33	65
Fulham	46	9	9	5	28	22	7	8	8	29	33	65
Burnley	46	11	8	4	38	21	4	8	11	19	38	61
Plymouth A	46	11	6	6	38	28	5	6	12	21	36	60
Huddersfield T	46	10	6	7	30	22	7	3	13	24	39	60
Hartlepool U	46	8	6	9	19	23	6	6	11	23	37	54
Bournemouth	46	7	10	6	28	24	5	7	11	17	28	53
Blackpool	46	9	9	5	40	30	3	6	14	23	45	51
Exeter C	46	5	8	10	26	30	6	9	8	28	39	50
Hull C	46	9	5	9	28	26	4	6	13	18	43	50
Preston N.E.	46	8	5	10	41	47	5	3	15	24	47	47
Mansfield T	46	7	8	8	34	34	4	3	16	18	46	44
Wigan A	46	6	6	11	26	34	4	5	14	17	38	41
Chester C	46	6	2	15	30	47	2	3	18	19	55	29

DIVISION 3

	P	W	D	L	F	A	W	D	L	F	A	Pts
Cardiff C	42	13	7	1	42	20	12	1	8	35	27	83
Wrexham	42	14	3	4	48	26	9	8	4	27	26	80
Barnet	42	16	4	1	45	19	7	6	8	21	29	79
York C	42	13	6	2	41	15	8	6	7	31	30	75
Walsall	42	11	6	4	42	31	11	1	9	34	30	73
Crewe A	42	13	3	5	47	23	8	4	9	28	33	70
Bury	42	10	7	4	36	19	8	2	11	27	36	63
Lincoln C	42	10	6	5	31	20	8	3	10	26	33	63
Shrewsbury T	42	11	3	7	36	30	6	8	7	21	22	62
Colchester U	42	13	3	5	38	26	5	2	14	29	50	59
Rochdale	42	10	3	8	38	29	6	7	8	32	41	58
Chesterfield	42	11	3	7	32	28	4	8	9	27	35	56
Scarborough	42	7	7	7	32	30	8	2	11	34	41	54
Scunthorpe U	42	8	7	6	38	25	6	5	10	19	29	54
Darlington	42	5	6	10	23	31	7	8	6	25	22	50
Doncaster	42	6	5	10	22	28	5	9	7	20	29	47
Hereford	42	7	9	5	31	27	3	6	12	16	33	45
Carlisle U	42	7	5	9	29	27	4	6	11	22	38	44
Torquay U	42	6	4	11	18	26	6	3	12	27	41	43
Northampton T	42	6	5	10	19	28	5	3	13	29	46	41
Gillingham	42	9	4	8	32	28	0	9	12	16	36	40
Halifax T	42	3	5	13	20	35	6	4	11	25	33	36

Football League Records

Top scorers: Prem Lge, A.Cole (Newcastle United) 34 goals; Div 1, J.McGinlay (Bolton Wanderers) 25 goals; Div 2, J.Quinn (Reading.) 35 goals; Div 3, T.Ellis (Preston North End) 26 goals.

Play-offs: Prem Lge, Derby County v Millwall 2-0, 3-1; Tranmere Rovers v Leicester City 0-0, 1-2; Derby County v Leicester City 1-2; Div 1, Burnley v Plymouth Argyle 0-0, 3-1; York City v Stockport County 0-0, 0-1; Burnley v Stockport County 2-1; Div 2, Carlisle United v Wycombe Wanderers 0-2, 1-2; Torquay United v Preston North End 2-0, 1-4; Preston North End v Wycombe Wanderers 2-4.

Crystal Palace, Nottingham Forest and Leicester City promoted to Prem Lge; Sheffield United, Oldham Athletic and Swindon Town relegated to Div 1; Reading, Port Vale and Burnley promoted to Div 1; Birmingham City, Oxford United

Andy Cole's 34 goals for Newcastle United saw him top the Premiership scorers.

DIVISION PREMIER

	ARSENAL	ASTON VILLA	BLACKBURN	CHELSEA	COVENTRY	EVERTON	IPSWICH	LEEDS	LIVERPOOL	MANCHESTER C	MANCHESTER U	NEWCASTLE	NORWICH	OLDHAM	Q.P.R.	SHEFFIELD U	SHEFFIELD W	SOUTHAMPTON	SWINDON	TOTTENHAM	WEST HAM A	WIMBLEDON
1 ARSENAL		N06 1-2	F25 1-0	a16 1-0	A14 0-3	A28 2-0	S11 4-0	A24 2-1	M26 1-0	O16 0-0	M22 2-2	N27 2-1	O30 0-0	J22 1-1	J03 0-0	D29 3-0	D12 1-0	S25 1-0	a02 1-1	D06 1-1	a30 0-2	a19 1-1
2 ASTON VILLA	a23 1-2		J01 0-1	O23 1-0	S11 0-0	M29 0-0	M12 0-1	F06 1-0	m07 2-1	F22 0-0	A23 1-2	O02 0-2	a04 0-0	M19 1-2	A14 4-1	N20 1-0	D08 2-2	N24 0-2	F12 5-0	A28 1-0	J15 3-1	D11 0-1
3 BLACKBURN	S01 1-1	a11 1-0		D05 2-0	N23 2-1	D29 2-0	m07 0-0	J23 2-1	M05 2-0	D18 2-0	a02 2-0	F19 1-0	A18 2-3	A21 1-0	a24 1-1	O18 0-0	S25 1-1	N20 2-0	M26 3-1	O30 1-0	S18 0-2	F05 3-0
4 CHELSEA	N20 0-2	J22 1-1	A14 1-2		m04 1-2	J03 4-2	D11 1-1	a23 1-1	S25 1-0	N22 0-0	S11 1-0	D28 1-0	O16 1-2	O30 0-1	A25 2-0	m07 3-2	A28 1-1	a02 2-0	a27 2-0	F27 4-3	M26 2-0	M16 2-0
5 COVENTRY	D04 1-0	M06 0-1	m02 2-1	S18 1-1		N06 2-1	F02 1-0	S25 0-2	S01 1-0	F19 4-0	N27 0-1	A18 2-1	M26 2-1	D18 1-1	J22 0-1	O31 0-0	a16 1-1	O16 1-1	J03 1-1	a09 1-0	A21 1-1	a02 1-2
6 EVERTON	F19 1-1	A31 0-1	a04 0-3	F05 4-2	a23 0-0		F12 0-0	N23 1-1	S18 2-0	A17 1-0	O23 0-1	D18 0-2	S25 1-5	M05 2-1	N20 0-3	A21 4-2	D27 0-2	D04 1-0	J15 6-2	M26 0-1	J01 0-1	m07 3-2
7 IPSWICH	M05 1-5	S18 1-2	N27 1-0	A21 1-0	a04 0-2	O30 0-2		O17 0-0	J01 1-2	M29 2-2	m01 1-2	A31 1-1	D18 2-1	D04 0-0	M26 1-3	F22 3-2	N06 1-4	A17 1-0	a16 1-1	S26 2-2	D27 1-1	J22 0-0
8 LEEDS	D18 2-1	M16 2-0	O23 3-3	N06 4-1	M19 1-0	a30 3-0	J15 0-0		F19 2-0	D04 3-2	a27 0-2	a04 1-1	A21 0-4	A30 1-0	D29 1-1	S18 2-1	m03 2-2	M05 0-0	N27 3-0	a17 2-0	A17 1-0	O02 4-0
9 LIVERPOOL	O02 0-0	N28 2-1	S12 0-1	M19 2-1	F25 1-0	M13 2-1	a09 1-0	A28 2-0		J22 2-1	J04 3-3	a16 0-2	a30 0-1	O16 2-1	D08 3-2	a02 1-2	A14 2-0	O30 4-2	D11 2-2	A25 1-2	N06 2-0	D28 1-1
10 MANCHESTER C	J15 0-0	a02 3-0	A24 0-2	a30 2-2	A27 1-1	D08 1-0	F05 2-1	A14 1-1	O23 1-1		N07 2-3	a09 2-1	a16 1-1	O04 1-1	S11 3-0	M19 0-0	N27 1-3	D28 1-1	F25 2-1	D11 0-2	F12 0-0	M12 0-1
11 MANCHESTER U	S19 1-0	D19 3-1	D26 1-1	M05 0-1	m08 0-0	J22 1-0	N24 0-0	J01 0-0	M29 1-0	a23 2-0		A21 1-1	D04 2-2	a04 3-2	O30 2-1	A18 3-0	M16 5-0	m04 2-0	S25 4-2	O16 2-1	S01 3-0	N20 3-1
12 NEWCASTLE	m07 2-0	a27 5-1	A29 1-1	a04 0-0	F23 4-0	A25 1-0	M23 2-0	D22 1-1	N21 3-0	J01 2-0	D11 1-1		M29 3-0	a23 3-2	O16 1-2	N24 4-0	S13 4-2	J22 1-2	M12 7-1	A14 0-1	S25 2-0	O30 4-0
13 NORWICH	F13 1-1	D29 1-2	F22 2-2	J15 1-1	O02 1-0	M21 3-0	A25 1-0	D13 2-1	F05 2-2	N20 1-1	A15 0-2	J04 1-2		m07 1-1	M12 3-4	a23 0-1	F25 1-1	a09 4-5	A28 0-0	a02 1-2	O23 0-0	S11 0-1
14 OLDHAM	O23 0-0	S25 1-1	D11 1-2	F12 2-1	A24 3-3	S11 0-1	A14 0-3	F28 1-1	J15 0-3	M26 0-0	D29 2-5	N08 1-3	N27 2-1		a02 4-1	m03 1-1	a30 0-0	F05 2-1	D07 2-1	m05 0-2	a16 1-2	A28 1-1
15 Q.P.R.	a27 1-1	D04 2-2	N06 1-0	a13 1-1	O23 5-1	a16 2-1	O02 3-0	a04 0-4	A18 1-3	M05 1-1	F05 2-3	J16 1-2	S18 2-2	D27 2-0		S01 2-1	J01 1-2	A21 2-1	a30 1-3	N27 1-1	m03 0-0	M19 1-0
16 SHEFFIELD U	a04 1-1	a16 1-2	J15 1-2	N27 1-0	F12 0-0	D11 0-0	A28 1-1	M13 2-2	D26 0-0	S25 0-1	D07 0-3	a30 2-0	N06 1-2	J01 2-1	M16 1-1		O23 1-1	M26 0-0	A14 3-1	S11 2-2	M28 3-2	A24 2-1
17 SHEFFIELD W	A21 0-1	A18 0-0	M20 1-2	M30 3-1	N20 0-0	a02 5-1	a23 5-0	O30 3-3	D04 3-1	m07 1-1	O02 2-3	M05 0-1	S01 3-3	N24 3-0	a09 3-1	J22 3-1		S18 2-0	D29 3-3	J03 1-0	D18 5-0	O16 2-2
18 SOUTHAMPTON	M19 0-4	a30 4-1	a16 3-1	D27 3-1	J15 1-0	A14 0-2	D08 0-1	S11 0-2	F14 4-2	a04 0-1	A28 1-3	O24 2-1	J01 0-1	M30 1-3	D11 0-1	O02 3-3	M12 1-1		A25 5-1	N06 1-0	N29 0-2	F25 1-0
19 SWINDON	D27 0-4	O30 1-2	O02 1-3	J01 1-3	F05 3-1	O16 1-1	N20 2-2	m07 0-5	A22 0-5	S01 1-3	M19 2-2	S18 2-2	F19 3-3	A18 0-1	N24 1-0	D04 0-0	a04 0-1	D18 2-1		J22 2-1	M05 1-1	a23 2-4
20 TOTTENHAM	A16 0-1	M02 1-1	F12 0-2	S01 1-1	J01 1-2	O03 3-2	M19 1-1	N20 1-1	D18 3-3	A21 1-0	J15 0-1	D04 1-2	D27 1-3	S18 5-0	m07 1-2	M05 2-2	F05 1-3	a23 3-0	O23 1-1		a04 1-4	N24 1-1
21 WEST HAM	N24 0-0	O16 0-0	a27 1-2	O02 1-0	D11 3-2	a09 0-1	a02 2-1	D08 0-1	a23 1-2	N01 3-1	F25 2-2	M19 2-4	J24 3-3	N20 2-0	A28 0-4	J03 0-0	A25 2-0	A25m07 3-3	S11 0-0	D28 1-3		A14 0-2
22 WIMBLEDON	J01 0-3	A21 2-2	M29 4-1	A17 1-1	D26 1-2	N27 1-1	O25 0-2	M26 1-0	a04 1-1	S20 1-0	a16 1-0	F12 4-2	M05 3-1	a26 3-0	S27 1-1	D18 2-0	J15 2-1	A31 1-0	N06 3-0	a30 2-1	D04 1-2	

DIVISION 1

	BARNSLEY	BIRMINGHAM	BOLTON	BRISTOL C	CHARLTON	C.PALACE	DERBY	GRIMSBY	LEICESTER	LUTON	MIDDLESBROUGH	MILLWALL	NOTTINGHAM F	NOTTS CO	OXFORD	PETERBOROUGH	PORTSMOUTH	SOUTHEND	STOKE	SUNDERLAND	TRANMERE	WATFORD	W.B.A.	WOLVERHAMPTON
1 BARNSLEY		A28 2-3	N27 1-1	J15 1-1	O09 0-1	N20 1-3	D27 0-1	N07 1-2	S25 0-1	M26 1-0	A24 1-4	m03 0-1	S11 1-0	a04 0-3	a16 1-0	D11 1-0	J01 2-0	O23 1-3	F12 3-0	M29 4-0	M12 1-0	a12 0-1	A14 1-1	a30 2-0
2 BIRMINGHAM	M05 0-2		O19 2-1	a16 2-2	D18 1-0	A31 2-4	S04 3-0	S18 1-1	M15 0-3	S25 1-1	M26 1-0	O31 1-0	N06 0-3	F19 2-3	J03 1-1	F05 0-0	N20 0-1	a09 3-1	a02 3-1	J22 0-0	N27 0-3	O16 1-0	D28 2-0	A22 2-2
3 BOLTON	m08 2-3	a30 1-1		M26 2-2	M05 3-2	N24 1-0	O30 0-2	D18 1-1	S18 1-2	m05 2-1	a23 4-1	O16 4-0	S26 4-3	J01 4-2	A31 1-0	N02 1-1	a04 1-1	a12 0-2	A21 1-1	D27 0-0	J23 2-1	F05 3-1	D07 1-1	M29 1-3
4 BRISTOL C	O16 0-2	N02 3-0	O02 2-0		S18 0-0	A21 2-0	M05 0-0	a09 1-0	S14 1-3	a19 1-0	D04 0-0	N13 2-2	D28 1-4	J22 0-2	M15 0-1	m08 4-1	M19 1-0	S04 2-1	J03 0-0	O30 2-0	F05 2-0	a23 1-1	a02 0-0	D18 2-1
5 CHARLTON	J22 2-1	A14 1-0	A28 3-0	m03 3-1		S26 0-0	N02 1-2	F05 0-1	O16 2-1	D04 1-0	m08 2-5	S11 0-0	a09 0-1	N13 5-1	O30 1-0	a23 5-1	D12 0-1	a02 4-3	D29 2-0	F22 0-0	A24 3-1	F25 2-1	J03 2-1	M26 0-1
6 C.PALACE	a23 1-0	D11 2-1	F25 1-1	F22 4-1	M20 2-0		F05 1-1	O30 1-0	J22 2-1	N02 3-2	M23 0-1	a09 1-0	A24 2-0	D05 1-2	a02 2-1	F01 3-2	A28 5-1	D29 1-0	O02 4-1	S12 1-0	A14 0-0	m08 0-2	M12 1-0	O17 1-1
7 DERBY	a02 2-0	F25 1-1	F12 2-0	A28 1-0	a16 2-0	O23 3-1		N20 2-1	D28 3-2	O09 2-1	F22 0-1	M12 0-0	a27 0-2	a20 1-1	a30 2-1	S11 2-0	J15 1-0	N27 1-3	a09 4-2	A14 5-0	J03 4-0	J29 1-2	O03 5-3	N07 0-4
8 GRIMSBY	D04 2-2	M12 1-0	A14 0-0	J01 1-0	O23 0-1	F12 1-1	a23 1-1		N02 0-0	a04 2-0	M29 1-1	m08 0-0	m03 0-0	D27 2-2	M26 1-0	M08 3-2	A24 1-1	O09 4-0	J15 0-0	a12 0-1	A28 0-0	S11 2-2	F01 2-2	S25 2-0
9 LEICESTER	M19 0-1	S12 1-1	m03 1-1	D11 3-0	J16 2-1	D08 1-1	a05 3-3	a16 1-1		F12 2-1	M12 2-0	A28 4-0	O24 1-0	O02 3-2	N20 2-3	A14 2-1	M30 0-3	N06 3-0	a30 1-1	J01 2-1	F23 1-1	D27 4-4	J12 4-2	N27 2-2
10 LUTON	O02 5-0	M19 1-1	S11 0-2	O05 0-2	N07 1-0	a16 0-1	J22 2-1	D29 2-1	O30 0-2		M08 1-1	a26 1-1	A28 1-2	O16 1-0	F05 3-0	a02 2-0	F22 4-1	a30 1-1	N27 6-2	F25 2-1	D11 0-1	A14 2-1	m03 3-2	a12 0-2
11 MIDDLESBROUGH	a26 5-0	O02 2-2	N21 0-1	N06 0-1	a19 2-0	m01 2-3	A21 3-0	J03 1-0	S29 2-0	S18 0-0		F06 4-2	a02 2-2	D18 3-0	a09 2-1	O30 1-1	a16 0-2	M15 1-0	S14 1-2	O17 4-1	D29 0-0	J22 1-1	M19 3-0	M05 1-0
12 MILLWALL	S04 2-0	F12 2-1	J15 1-0	a30 0-0	M15 2-1	J01 3-0	S18 0-0	N27 1-0	M06 0-0	M30 2-2	O24 1-1		a17 2-2	O20 2-0	N06 2-2	M22 1-0	D27 0-0	A22 1-4	D19 2-0	a06 2-1	N20 3-1	O02 4-1	O09 2-1	a20 1-0
13 NOTTINGHAM F	M16 2-1	D04 1-0	M19 3-2	a04 0-0	J01 1-1	F19 1-1	A18 1-1	A21 5-3	F06 4-0	M05 2-0	D27 1-1	N03 1-3		O30 1-0	O20 0-0	M02 2-0	O02 1-1	D19 2-0	S19 2-3	m08 2-2	O16 2-1	M30 2-1	a24 2-1	J23 0-0
14 NOTTS CO	M01 3-1	J11 2-1	a09 2-1	O09 2-0	a30 3-3	N06 3-2	S25 4-1	a02 2-1	M26 4-1	J15 1-2	A14 2-3	D11 1-3	F12 2-1		N28 2-1	F22 2-1	O23 1-1	J03 2-1	N20 2-0	A28 1-0	a12 0-0	M12 1-0	S11 1-0	a16 0-2
15 OXFORD	N02 1-1	M29 2-0	D11 0-2	S11 4-2	F12 0-4	D27 1-3	N13 2-0	O02 2-2	a23 2-2	O23 0-1	J01 1-1	D04 0-2	F25 1-0	m08 2-1		M12 1-2	A14 3-2	J15 2-1	O10 1-0	J11 0-3	M19 1-0	A28 2-3	a12 1-1	a04 4-0
16 PETERBOROUGH	A17 4-1	O23 1-0	a16 2-3	N27 0-2	N20 0-1	M29 1-1	M16 2-2	S04 1-2	D19 1-1	D27 0-0	F12 1-0	S25 0-0	a30 2-3	A21 1-1	S18 3-1		O09 2-2	M05 3-1	F19 1-1	M26 1-3	N06 0-0	a05 3-4	J15 2-0	J01 0-1
17 PORTSMOUTH	a09 2-1	a23 0-2	D28 0-0	S25 0-0	A17 1-2	M05 0-1	O16 3-2	F19 3-1	a26 0-1	A21 1-0	N02 2-0	a02 2-2	M26 2-1	F05 0-0	D18 1-1	J22 0-2		S18 2-1	S04 3-3	D04 0-1	O30 2-0	D07 2-0	m08 0-1	M15 3-0
18 SOUTHEND	F05 0-3	J01 3-1	J12 0-2	F25 0-1	D27 4-2	a06 1-2	m08 4-3	J22 1-2	D05 0-0	N13 2-1	S11 1-0	M02 1-1	A15 1-1	M30 1-0	O16 6-1	A28 3-0	M12 2-1		M19 0-0	a23 0-1	O02 1-2	N03 2-0	D11 0-3	O30 1-1
19 STOKE	O30 5-4	D26 2-1	F22 2-0	M30 3-0	a04 1-0	M26 0-2	J01 2-1	O16 1-0	N14 1-0	m08 2-2	D11 3-1	A14 1-2	M12 0-1	a23 0-0	J22 1-1	a13 3-0	F25 2-0	S25 0-1		N03 1-0	S11 1-2	D04 2-0	A28 1-0	F05 1-1
20 SUNDERLAND	J03 1-0	O09 1-0	a02 2-0	F12 0-0	A21 4-0	M16 1-0	D18 1-0	S28 2-2	a09 2-3	O20 2-0	J16 2-1	D28 2-1	N27 2-3	M05 2-0	a26 2-3	O02 2-0	N06 1-2	N20 0-2	a16 0-1		a30 3-2	M19 2-0	O23 1-0	S18 0-2
21 TRANMERE	S18 0-3	m08 1-2	O09 2-1	O22 2-2	a26 2-0	D19 0-1	M29 4-0	M05 1-2	A21 1-0	S14 4-1	a04 4-0	a23 3-2	J16 1-2	S04 3-1	S25 2-0	D03 2-1	F11 3-1	M25 1-1	M15 2-0	N13 4-1		J01 2-1	N02 3-0	D27 1-1
22 WATFORD	A21 0-2	J15 5-2	O23 4-3	N20 1-1	S04 2-2	N28 1-3	F19 3-4	M15 0-3	a02 1-1	D19 2-2	O10 2-0	M26 2-0	J03 1-2	S18 3-1	M05 2-1	D28 2-1	a30 1-0	a16 3-0	N06 1-3	S25 1-1	a09 1-2		F12 0-1	S07 1-0
23 W.B.A.	D19 1-1	a27 2-4	N06 2-2	D27 0-1	M30 2-0	S18 1-4	M26 1-2	a30 1-0	F19 1-2	J01 1-1	S25 1-1	J22 0-0	N21 0-2	M16 3-0	A21 3-1	O16 3-0	N27 4-1	S01 2-2	M05 0-0	F05 2-1	a16 1-3	O30 4-1		S05 3-2
24 WOLVERHAMPTON	N13 1-1	F22 3-0	J03 1-0	A14 3-1	O02 1-1	J15 2-0	D05 2-2	M19 0-0	m08 1-1	a23 1-0	A28 2-3	A25 2-0	N10 1-1	N02 3-0	D28 2-1	a09 1-1	S11 1-1	F12 0-1	O23 1-1	m03 1-1	a02 2-1	D11 2-0	F25 1-2	

Bolton's John McGinlay was the First Division's leading scorer with 25 goals.

SEASON 1993-94

and Peterborough United relegated to Div 2; Shrewsbury Town, Chester City, Crewe Alexandra and Wycombe Wanderers promoted to Div 2; Fulham, Exeter City, Hartlepool United and Barnet relegated to Div 3.

DIVISION 2

	BARNET	BLACKPOOL	BOURNEMOUTH	BRADFORD C	BRENTFORD	BRIGHTON	BRISTOL R	BURNLEY	CAMBRIDGE	CARDIFF	EXETER	FULHAM	HARTLEPOOL	HUDDERSFIELD	HULL	LEYTON O	PLYMOUTH	PORT VALE	READING	ROTHERHAM	STOCKPORT	SWANSEA	WREXHAM	YORK
1 BARNET		F25 0-1	S11 1-2	N06 1-2	J29 0-0	a02 1-1	O02 1-2	D29 1-1	O23 2-3	O10 0-0	M22 2-1	S14 0-2	a26 3-2	J15 0-1	A14 1-2	M12 3-1	F12 0-0	D11 2-3	a12 0-1	N27 2-1	a09 0-0	A28 0-1	M19 1-2	a30 1-3
2 BLACKPOOL	S04 3-1		S25 2-1	M05 1-3	A21 1-1	O30 2-0	J03 0-1	a09 1-2	D19 2-3	S18 1-0	F05 1-0	J08 2-3	D04 2-1	N20 2-1	N02 6-2	m07 4-1	A31 2-1	O16 1-3	a23 0-4	M26 1-2	a02 2-0	J22 1-1	F19 4-1	D28 0-5
3 BOURNEMOUTH	M05 1-1	M19 1-0		A21 1-1	D27 0-3	O16 2-1	D18 3-0	S04 1-0	S18 1-2	M15 3-2	O30 1-1	J22 1-3	F19 0-0	M29 1-2	N20 0-2	F05 1-1	J01 0-1	D07 2-1	m05 2-1	a05 0-0	O02 1-1	a19 0-1	a23 1-2	A31 3-1
4 BRADFORD C	m03 2-1	S11 2-1	D11 0-0		a04 1-0	S14 2-0	J22 0-1	O16 0-1	S25 2-0	m07 2-0	A28 6-0	a13 0-0	F05 2-1	N02 3-0	M26 1-1	J08 0-0	N20 1-5	M29 2-1	S15 2-4	D27 2-1	a26 1-2	M12 2-1	J01 1-0	O30 0-0
5 BRENTFORD	O30 1-0	D11 3-0	a02 1-1	D29 2-0		M12 1-1	J08 3-4	N20 0-0	M26 3-3	N02 1-1	A14 2-1	a09 1-2	J22 1-0	m07 1-2	F22 0-3	S14 0-1	a23 1-1	S25 1-2	A28 1-0	F25 2-2	J03 1-1	S11 1-1	O16 2-1	F05 1-1
6 BRIGHTON	D27 1-0	J29 3-2	J15 3-3	D18 0-1	S18 2-1		S01 0-2	M16 1-1	J01 4-1	a12 3-5	O02 0-0	a23 2-0	A21 1-1	S04 2-2	F12 3-0	M19 2-0	M30 2-1	m07 1-3	N20 0-1	O23 0-2	O09 1-1	a06 4-1	N02 1-1	M05 2-0
7 BRISTOL R	M26 5-2	M30 1-0	A14 0-1	O09 4-3	F12 1-4	F23 1-0		S25 3-1	N27 2-1	J15 2-1	S15 1-1	A28 2-1	N06 1-1	J29 0-0	F25 1-1	D11 1-1	O23 0-0	S11 2-0	J26 1-1	M12 0-2	a30 1-1	J01 1-2	a04 3-1	a16 0-1
8 BURNLEY	a04 5-0	J01 3-1	F25 4-0	J15 0-1	a30 4-1	S14 3-0	M19 3-1		J29 3-0	F12 2-0	N27 3-2	S11 3-1	O02 2-0	O23 1-1	M29 3-1	A28 4-1	O09 4-2	A14 2-1	D11 0-1	a26 0-0	M12 1-1	a16 1-1	D27 2-1	N06 2-1
9 CAMBRIDGE	F05 1-1	A14 3-2	M12 3-2	M19 2-1	O02 1-1	a09 2-1	m07 1-3	O30 0-1		N19 1-1	D29 3-0	J03 3-0	O16 1-0	a26 4-5	A28 3-4	a02 3-1	N02 2-0	F22 1-0	F25 0-1	S11 0-1	D11 0-0	S14 2-0	J22 2-2	J08 0-2
10 CARDIFF	J22 0-0	M12 0-2	a21 2-1	N27 1-1	a16 1-1	A28 2-2	O16 1-2	M01 2-1	a30 2-7		a26 2-0	D11 1-0	O30 2-2	a04 2-2	S11 3-4	A14 2-0	S25 2-3	m03 1-3	J01 3-0	M29 1-0	N06 3-1	D22 1-0	F05 5-1	M26 0-0
11 EXETER	M29 0-0	O23 1-0	J29 0-2	F19 0-0	D18 2-2	M26 1-1	M15 1-0	m07 4-1	a04 0-5	A31 2-2		N02 6-4	S04 2-1	M05 2-3	J01 0-1	a23 1-0	M02 2-3	N20 1-1	O09 4-6	F12 1-1	m02 1-2	S25 1-0	S18 5-0	A21 1-2
12 FULHAM	M15 3-0	F12 1-0	O09 0-2	S04 1-1	J01 0-0	N06 0-1	F19 0-1	M05 3-2	M29 0-2	A21 1-3	a16 0-2		D17 2-0	M19 1-1	J15 0-1	O02 2-3	a04 1-1	D27 0-0	J30 1-0	a30 1-0	O23 0-1	N27 3-1	A31 0-0	S18 0-1
13 HARTLEPOOL	N02 2-1	S14 2-0	A28 1-1	O23 1-2	O09 0-1	D11 2-2	a23 2-1	M26 4-1	J15 0-2	M22 3-0	F25 1-2	A14 0-1		D27 1-4	a04 0-1	M08 1-1	m07 1-8	M12 1-4	F12 1-4	J01 2-0	S11 1-0	M29 1-0	N20 1-2	S25 0-2
14 HUDDERSFIELD	O16 1-2	a30 2-1	J03 1-1	a17 1-1	N27 1-3	F25 1-3	O30 1-0	F05 1-1	N06 1-1	a19 2-0	S11 0-1	S25 1-0	a02 1-1		M12 0-2	a09 1-0	M26 1-0	S14 1-1	A14 0-3	D11 2-1	A28 1-1	F22 1-1	a12 3-0	J22 3-2
15 HULL	D18 4-4	a16 0-0	a30 1-1	O02 3-1	A31 1-0	J08 0-0	S04 3-0	J03 1-2	F19 2-0	M05 1-0	a09 5-1	O16 1-1	D28 1-0	S18 2-1		O30 0-1	A21 2-2	J22 0-0	M19 1-2	N06 4-1	N27 0-1	F05 0-1	M15 0-0	a02 1-1
16 LEYTON O	S18 4-2	N27 2-0	O23 0-0	F12 2-1	M15 1-1	S25 1-3	A21 1-0	F19 3-1	D27 2-1	D18 2-2	N06 1-1	M26 2-2	A31 1-2	J01 1-0	J29 3-1		M05 2-1	a04 2-3	J15 1-1	O09 1-1	a16 0-0	a30 2-1	a29 2-2	S04 2-0
17 PLYMOUTH	M08 1-0	F22 2-1	a09 2-0	a30 3-1	N06 1-1	J03 1-1	F05 3-3	J22 3-2	a16 0-3	M19 1-2	a02 1-0	D28 3-1	N27 2-0	O02 2-0	D11 2-1	S11 3-1		A28 2-0	M12 3-1	S14 4-2	A14 2-3	F25 2-1	O30 1-1	O16 2-1
18 PORT VALE	A21 6-0	J15 2-0	a16 2-1	M01 0-0	M19 1-0	N27 4-0	M05 2-0	D18 1-1	A31 2-2	S04 2-2	a30 3-0	a02 2-2	S18 1-0	M15 1-0	O09 2-1	D29 2-1	F19 2-1		O23 0-4	a12 2-1	F12 1-1	N06 3-0	O02 3-0	a21 2-1
19 READING	S01 4-1	N06 1-1	N27 3-0	M15 1-1	F19 2-1	a30 2-0	a02 2-0	A21 2-1	S04 3-1	a09 1-1	J22 1-0	O30 1-0	J08 4-0	D18 0-0	S25 1-1	O16 2-1	S18 3-2	F05 1-2		a16 0-0	D28 2-0	M26 2-1	M05 0-1	J03 2-1
20 ROTHERHAM	m07 1-1	O02 0-2	M08 1-2	a02 2-1	S04 2-0	F05 0-1	S18 1-1	A31 3-2	M05 3-0	J03 5-2	a19 3-0	N20 1-2	a09 7-0	A21 2-3	a23 1-0	J22 2-1	M15 0-3	O30 0-2	N02 2-2		M19 1-2	O16 1-1	D17 2-1	F19 2-1
21 STOCKPORT	J01 2-1	F01 1-0	F26 0-2	A31 4-1	M29 3-1	J22 3-0	N20 0-2	S18 2-1	A21 3-1	a23 2-2	O16 4-0	F05 2-4	M05 5-0	F19 3-0	m07 0-0	N02 3-0	D17 2-3	a19 2-1	a28 1-1	S25 2-0		O30 4-0	S04 1-0	M15 1-2
22 SWANSEA	F18 2-0	O09 4-4	F12 1-1	S18 2-0	M05 1-1	M08 3-0	a09 2-0	N02 3-1	M15 4-2	a02 1-0	M19 2-0	m07 2-1	J28 1-1	A31 1-0	O23 1-0	N20 1-1	S04 0-1	a26 0-1	O01 1-1	J14 0-0	a12 1-2		A21 3-1	D18 1-2
23 WREXHAM	S25 4-0	A28 2-3	N06 2-1	a09 0-3	J15 1-2	a16 1-3	M22 3-2	a02 1-0	O09 1-1	O23 3-1	M12 1-1	F22 2-0	a30 2-0	F12 3-1	S14 3-0	J03 4-2	a26 0-3	M26 2-1	S11 3-2	A14 3-3	M08 0-1	D11 3-2		N27 1-1
24 YORK	N20 1-1	a04 2-1	M22 2-0	J29 1-1	O23 0-2	S11 3-1	N02 0-1	a23 0-0	F12 2-0	O02 5-0	D11 3-0	M12 2-0	M19 3-0	O09 0-2	D27 0-0	F25 3-0	J15 0-0	J01 1-0	M29 1-0	A28 0-0	S14 1-2	A14 2-1	m07 1-1	

DIVISION 3

	BURY	CARLISLE	CHESTER	CHESTERFIELD	COLCHESTER	CREWE	DARLINGTON	DONCASTER	GILLINGHAM	HEREFORD	LINCOLN	MANSFIELD	NORTHAMPTON	PRESTON	ROCHDALE	SCARBOROUGH	SCUNTHORPE	SHREWSBURY	TORQUAY	WALSALL	WIGAN	WYCOMBE
1 BURY		F12 2-1	a16 1-1	N06 2-1	M19 0-1	A28 1-0	N27 5-1	J15 4-0	a19 0-0	O23 5-3	M12 1-0	O02 2-2	A14 0-0	J04 1-1	a30 0-1	J29 0-2	D11 1-0	F25 2-3	M29 1-1	a02 1-2	O09 3-0	S11 1-2
2 CARLISLE	J25 1-2		M19 1-0	S11 3-0	m07 2-0	D28 1-2	a02 2-0	D11 4-2	O02 1-2	a09 1-2	N02 3-3	O16 1-1	F05 0-1	N20 0-1	A28 0-1	F25 2-0	M12 3-1	m03 2-1	J03 1-1	O30 2-1	a23 3-0	A14 2-2
3 CHESTER	N02 3-0	S25 0-0		A28 3-1	a09 2-1	m07 1-2	J22 0-0	A14 0-1	M01 1-0	a23 3-1	F01 1-1	F05 1-1	N20 1-0	a02 3-2	F25 3-1	M12 4-1	S11 0-2	O16 1-0	O30 1-1	M15 2-1	M26 2-1	D11 3-1
4 CHESTERFIELD	a23 1-1	M05 3-0	F19 1-2		M29 0-0	O30 2-0	S04 1-1	J25 1-1	D18 3-2	A21 3-1	F05 2-2	A31 0-2	m07 4-0	J22 1-1	M19 1-1	N20 1-0	a04 1-1	J01 1-2	O16 3-1	S18 0-1	N02 1-0	O02 2-3
5 COLCHESTER	S25 4-1	N27 2-1	J01 0-0	F12 0-2		D11 2-4	a16 1-2	a30 3-1	J29 1-2	J15 1-0	A14 1-0	D27 0-0	A28 3-2	M26 1-1	S11 2-5	a04 1-2	O09 2-1	A31 3-3	F25 1-2	N06 0-1	O23 3-1	M12 0-2
6 CREWE	F19 2-4	F04 2-3	N27 2-1	J29 0-1	A21 2-1		S18 2-1	J01 2-0	O23 1-0	O09 6-0	O02 2-2	S04 2-1	A31 3-1	D17 4-3	N06 2-1	J15 1-1	F12 3-3	a16 0-0	M19 2-3	M05 1-2	a19 4-1	a30 2-1
7 DARLINGTON	m07 1-0	D27 1-3	O09 1-2	M08 0-0	N02 7-3	M12 1-0		a04 1-3	J15 2-1	F12 1-3	D11 3-2	N20 2-0	M26 0-1	a23 0-2	A14 1-1	A31 0-2	J29 2-1	S11 0-2	A28 1-2	S25 0-0	J25 0-0	O23 0-0
8 DONCASTER	O16 1-3	A21 0-0	D17 3-4	a02 0-0	N20 2-1	a09 0-0	D28 1-3		J03 0-0	m07 1-0	J22 1-0	S17 0-1	O30 2-1	M04 1-1	O02 2-1	a23 0-4	N01 3-1	F05 0-0	J08 0-2	F19 4-0	S04 3-1	M19 0-3
9 GILLINGHAM	J01 1-0	M26 2-0	a04 2-2	A14 0-2	O30 3-0	F05 1-3	O16 2-1	A31 0-0		N02 2-0	m07 1-1	a23 1-0	D27 1-0	a12 2-2	D11 1-2	A28 2-2	S25 1-0	M12 0-2	S11 2-2	J22 1-1	N20 2-2	F25 0-1
10 HEREFORD	F05 3-0	J01 0-0	N06 0-5	M15 0-3	O16 5-0	J22 1-2	J08 1-1	N27 2-1	a16 2-0		A28 1-2	a04 2-3	S11 1-1	O30 2-3	M12 5-1	A14 0-1	M29 1-2	D27 0-1	a30 2-2	M26 0-1	S25 3-0	A31 3-4
11 LINCOLN	S18 2-2	a16 0-0	A31 0-3	O23 1-2	M15 2-0	M26 1-2	A21 1-1	O09 2-1	N27 3-1	F19 3-1		M05 1-2	S25 4-3	S04 0-2	J29 1-1	J01 0-1	D27 2-0	a04 0-1	N06 1-0	a30 1-2	F12 0-1	J15 1-3
12 MANSFIELD	M26 2-2	J15 0-1	O23 0-4	J03 1-2	a02 1-1	F25 1-2	a30 0-3	M12 2-1	N06 2-1	J18 2-1	S11 1-0		D11 1-0	S25 2-2	a16 0-1	O09 4-2	A28 0-1	A14 1-0	a09 2-1	N27 1-2	J29 2-3	F12 3-0
13 NORTHAMPTON	D18 0-1	O23 1-1	a30 1-0	N27 2-2	F19 1-1	J03 2-2	O02 1-0	J29 0-0	a02 1-2	M05 0-1	M19 0-0	O12 5-1		M15 2-0	a09 1-2	F12 3-2	M08 4-0	N06 0-3	a16 0-1	S04 0-1	S18 0-2	O09 1-1
14 PRESTON	A31 3-1	a30 0-3	D27 1-1	O09 4-1	O02 1-0	A14 0-2	N06 3-2	S11 3-1	F12 0-0	M01 3-0	F25 2-0	M19 3-1	a04 1-1		O23 2-1	D11 2-2	J01 2-2	A28 6-1	M12 3-1	a16 2-0	J15 3-0	N27 2-3
15 ROCHDALE	N20 2-1	F19 0-1	S04 2-0	S25 5-1	M05 1-1	a23 2-1	D18 0-0	M26 0-1	A21 3-0	S18 2-0	O30 0-1	N02 1-1	J01 6-2	F05 2-1		M01 2-1	m07 2-3	a12 1-2	J22 4-1	O16 0-0	A31 1-2	a04 2-2
16 SCARBOROUGH	O30 1-0	S04 0-3	S18 0-1	a30 1-1	D28 0-2	O16 1-2	J03 3-0	N06 2-0	F19 1-1	D18 0-1	a09 2-2	J22 1-1	J08 2-1	A21 3-4	a02 2-1		M26 0-1	S25 1-3	N27 1-2	F05 1-0	M05 4-1	a16 3-1
17 SCUNTHORPE	A21 1-1	S18 2-1	M05 1-1	D28 2-2	J22 1-1	M15 2-1	O30 3-0	a16 1-3	M19 1-1	S04 1-2	a02 2-0	F19 2-3	O16 7-0	a09 3-1	N27 2-1	O02 1-1		a30 1-4	F05 1-3	J03 5-0	D18 1-0	N06 0-0
18 SHREWSBURY	S04 1-0	O09 1-0	J15 3-0	a09 0-0	J03 2-1	N02 2-2	M05 1-1	O23 0-1	S18 2-2	a02 2-0	M01 1-2	D17 2-2	a23 2-1	F19 1-0	F12 1-1	M19 2-0	N20 0-0		O02 3-2	A21 1-2	m07 0-0	J29 1-0
19 TORQUAY	a05 0-0	A31 1-1	J29 1-3	J15 1-0	S04 3-3	S25 3-3	F19 2-1	F12 2-1	M05 0-1	N20 1-1	a23 3-2	J01 1-0	N02 2-0	S18 4-3	O09 1-1	m07 2-0	O23 1-1	M26 0-0		D18 0-1	A21 1-1	D27 1-1
20 WALSALL	D27 0-1	J29 0-1	F12 1-1	M12 0-1	a23 1-2	S11 2-2	M19 3-0	A28 1-2	O09 1-0	O02 3-3	N20 5-2	m07 0-2	F25 1-3	N02 2-0	J15 1-0	O23 1-0	A31 0-0	D11 0-1	A14 1-2		a05 1-1	J01 4-2
21 WIGAN	J22 3-1	N06 0-2	O02 6-3	a16 1-0	F05 0-1	a02 2-2	a09 2-0	M22 0-0	a30 2-0	M19 3-4	M29 0-1	O30 4-1	M12 1-1	O16 2-2	J04 0-0	S11 1-2	A14 0-2	N27 2-5	D11 1-3	J11 2-2		A28 1-1
22 WYCOMBE	M05 2-1	D18 2-0	A21 1-0	M26 0-1	S18 2-5	N20 3-1	M29 2-0	S25 1-0	S04 1-1	J03 3-2	O16 2-3	J25 1-0	J22 1-0	M07 1-1	a19 1-1	N02 4-0	a23 2-2	O30 1-1	a02 1-1	a09 3-0	F19 0-1	

LEAGUE TABLES

PREMIER LEAGUE

	P	W	D	L	F	A	W	D	L	F	A	Pts
Manchester U	42	14	6	1	39	13	13	5	3	41	25	92
Blackburn R	42	14	5	2	31	11	11	4	6	32	25	84
Newcastle U	42	14	4	3	51	14	9	4	8	31	27	77
Arsenal	42	10	8	3	25	15	8	9	4	28	13	71
Leeds U	42	13	6	2	37	18	5	10	6	28	21	70
Wimbledon	42	12	5	4	35	21	6	6	9	21	32	65
Sheffield W	42	10	7	4	48	24	6	9	6	28	30	64
Liverpool	42	12	4	5	33	23	5	5	11	26	32	60
Q.P.R.	42	8	7	6	32	29	8	5	8	30	32	60
Aston Villa	42	8	5	8	23	18	7	7	7	23	32	57
Coventry C	42	9	7	5	23	17	5	7	9	20	28	56
Norwich C	42	4	9	8	26	29	8	8	5	39	32	53
West Ham U	42	6	7	8	26	31	7	6	8	21	27	52
Chelsea	42	11	5	5	31	20	2	7	12	18	33	51
Tottenham H	42	4	8	9	29	33	7	4	10	25	26	45
Manchester C	42	6	10	5	24	22	3	8	10	14	27	45
Everton	42	8	4	9	26	30	4	4	13	16	33	44
Southampton	42	9	2	10	30	31	3	5	13	19	35	43
Ipswich T	42	5	8	8	21	32	4	8	9	14	26	43
Sheffield U	42	6	10	5	24	23	2	8	11	18	37	42
Oldham A	42	5	8	8	24	33	4	5	12	18	35	40
Swindon T	42	4	7	10	25	45	1	8	12	22	55	30

DIVISION 1

	P	W	D	L	F	A	W	D	L	F	A	Pts
Crystal Palace	46	16	4	3	39	18	11	5	7	34	28	90
Nottingham F	46	12	9	2	38	22	11	5	7	36	27	83
Millwall	46	14	8	1	36	17	5	9	9	22	32	74
Leicester C	46	11	9	3	45	30	8	7	8	27	29	73
Tranmere R	46	15	3	5	48	23	6	6	11	21	30	72
Derby Co	46	15	3	5	44	25	5	8	10	29	43	71
Notts Co	46	16	3	4	43	26	4	5	14	22	43	68
Wolverh'pton W	46	10	10	3	34	19	7	7	9	26	28	68
Middlesbrough	46	12	6	5	40	19	6	7	10	26	35	67
Stoke C	46	14	4	5	35	19	4	9	10	22	40	67
Charlton A	46	14	3	6	39	22	5	5	13	22	36	65
Sunderland	46	14	2	7	35	22	5	6	12	19	35	65
Bristol C	46	11	7	5	27	18	5	9	9	20	32	64
Bolton W	46	10	8	5	40	31	5	6	12	23	33	59
Southend U	46	10	5	8	34	28	7	3	13	29	39	59
Grimsby	46	7	14	2	26	16	6	6	11	26	31	59
Portsmouth	46	10	6	7	29	22	5	7	11	23	36	58
Barnsley	46	9	3	11	25	26	7	4	12	30	41	55
Watford	46	10	5	8	39	35	5	4	14	27	45	54
Luton T	46	12	4	7	38	25	2	7	14	18	35	53
W.B.A.	46	9	7	7	38	31	4	5	14	22	38	51
Birmingham C	46	9	7	7	28	29	4	5	14	24	40	51
Oxford U	46	10	5	8	33	33	3	5	15	21	42	49
Peterborough U	46	6	9	8	31	30	2	4	17	17	46	37

DIVISION 2

	P	W	D	L	F	A	W	D	L	F	A	Pts
Reading	46	15	6	2	40	16	11	5	7	41	28	89
Port Vale	46	16	6	1	46	18	10	4	9	33	28	88
Plymouth A	46	16	4	3	46	26	9	6	8	42	30	85
Stockport Co	46	15	3	5	50	22	9	10	4	24	22	85
York C	46	12	7	4	33	13	9	5	9	31	27	75
Burnley	46	17	4	2	55	18	4	6	13	24	40	73
Bradford C	46	13	5	5	34	20	6	8	9	27	33	70
Bristol R	46	10	8	5	33	26	10	2	11	27	33	70
Hull C	46	9	9	5	33	20	9	5	9	29	34	68
Cambridge U	46	11	5	7	38	29	8	4	11	41	44	66
Huddersfield T	46	9	8	6	27	26	8	6	9	31	35	65
Wrexham	46	13	4	6	45	33	4	7	12	21	44	62
Swansea C	46	12	7	4	37	20	4	5	14	19	38	60
Brighton & H.A.	46	10	7	6	38	29	5	7	11	22	38	59
Rotherham U	46	11	4	8	42	30	4	9	10	21	30	58
Brentford	46	7	10	6	30	28	6	9	8	27	27	58
Bournemouth	46	8	7	8	26	27	6	8	9	25	32	57
Leyton O	46	11	9	3	38	26	3	5	15	19	45	56
Cardiff C	46	10	7	6	39	33	3	8	12	27	46	54
Blackpool	46	12	2	9	41	37	4	3	16	22	38	53
Fulham	46	7	6	10	20	23	7	4	12	30	40	52
Exeter C	46	8	7	8	38	37	3	5	15	14	46	45
Hartlepool U	46	8	3	12	28	40	1	6	16	13	47	36
Barnet	46	4	6	13	22	32	1	7	15	19	54	28

DIVISION 3

	P	W	D	L	F	A	W	D	L	F	A	Pts
Shrewsbury T	42	10	8	3	28	17	12	5	4	35	22	79
Chester C	42	13	5	3	35	18	8	6	7	34	28	74
Crewe A	42	12	4	5	45	30	9	6	6	35	31	73
Wycombe	42	11	6	4	34	21	8	7	6	33	32	70
Preston N.E.	42	13	5	3	46	23	5	8	8	33	37	67
Torquay U	42	8	10	3	30	24	9	6	6	34	32	67
Carlisle U	42	10	4	7	35	23	8	6	7	22	19	64
Chesterfield	42	8	8	5	32	22	8	6	7	23	26	62
Rochdale	42	10	5	6	38	22	6	7	8	25	29	60
Walsall	42	7	5	9	28	26	10	4	7	20	27	60
Scunthorpe U	42	9	7	5	40	26	6	7	8	24	30	59
Mansfield T	42	9	3	9	28	30	6	7	8	25	32	55
Bury	42	9	6	6	33	22	5	5	11	22	34	53
Scarborough	42	8	4	9	29	28	7	4	10	26	33	53
Doncaster	42	8	6	7	24	26	6	4	11	20	31	52
Gillingham	42	8	8	5	27	23	4	7	10	17	28	51
Colchester U	42	8	4	9	31	33	5	6	10	25	38	49
Lincoln C	42	7	4	10	26	29	5	7	9	26	34	47
Wigan A	42	6	7	8	33	33	5	5	11	18	37	45
Hereford	42	6	4	11	34	33	6	2	13	26	46	42
Darlington	42	7	5	9	24	28	3	6	12	18	36	41
Northampton T	42	6	7	8	25	23	3	4	14	19	43	38

Football League Records

Top scorers: Prem Lge, A.Shearer (Blackburn Rovers) 34 goals; Div 1, J.Aldridge (Tranmere Rovers) 24 goals; Div 2, G.Bennett (Wrexham.) 29 goals; Div 3, P.Stant (Bury 13, Cardiff 13) 26 goals.
Play-offs: Prem Lge, Tranmere Rovers v Reading 1-3, 0-0; Wolverhampton Wanderers v Bolton Wanderers 2-1, 0-2; Bolton Wanderers v Reading 4-3; Div 1, Bristol Rovers v Crewe Alexandra 0-0, 1-1; Huddersfield Town v Brentford 1-1, 1-1 (4-3 penalties); Bristol Rovers v Huddersfield Town 1-2; Div 2, Mansfield Town v Chesterfield 1-1, 2-5; Preston North End v Bury 0-1, 0-1; Bury v Chesterfield 0-2.
Middlesbrough and Bolton Wanderers promoted to Prem Lge; Crystal Palace, Norwich City, Leicester City and Ipswich Town relegated to Div 1; Birmingham City and Huddersfield Town promoted to Div 1; Swindon Town,

Liverpool's Robbie Fowler hit 25 Premiership goals for Liverpool to finish behind Blackburn's Alan Shearer.

DIVISION PREMIER

	ARSENAL	ASTON VILLA	BLACKBURN	CHELSEA	COVENTRY	C.PALACE	EVERTON	IPSWICH	LEEDS	LEICESTER	LIVERPOOL	MANCHESTER C	MANCHESTER U	NEWCASTLE	NORWICH	NOTTINGHAM F	Q.P.R.	SHEFFIELD W	SOUTHAMPTON	TOTTENHAM	WEST HAM	WIMBLEDON
1 ARSENAL		D26 0-0	A31 0-0	O15 3-1	O23 2-1	O01 1-2	J14 1-1	a15 4-1	D17 1-3	F11 1-1	a12 0-1	A20 3-0	N26 0-0	S18 2-3	a01 5-1	F21 1-0	D31 1-3	N06 0-0	J24 1-1	a29 1-1	M05 0-1	m04 0-0
2 ASTON VILLA	a17 0-4		M04 0-1	D28 3-0	M06 0-0	A27 1-1	D10 0-0	S10 2-0	J02 0-0	F22 4-4	m06 2-0	m03 1-1	N06 1-2	O01 0-2	O15 1-1	O22 0-2	J14 2-1	N27 1-1	A24 1-1	J25 1-0	M18 0-2	F11 7-1
3 BLACKBURN	M08 3-1	S24 3-1		M18 2-1	A27 4-0	a20 2-1	S10 3-0	J28 4-1	F01 1-1	A23 3-0	O15 3-2	a17 2-3	O23 2-4	m08 1-0	F25 0-0	J14 3-0	N26 4-0	F12 3-1	D10 3-2	N05 2-0	J02 4-2	F22 2-1
4 CHELSEA	m14 2-1	a15 1-0	S18 1-2		N06 2-2	M05 0-0	N26 0-1	O23 2-0	M11 0-3	O08 4-0	D18 0-0	A31 3-0	D26 2-3	a01 1-1	A20 2-0	J25 0-2	a29 1-0	J14 1-1	a12 0-2	F11 1-1	O02 1-2	D31 1-1
5 COVENTRY	J21 0-1	A29 0-1	M11 1-1	F04 2-2		N02 1-4	m14 0-0	O10 2-0	S17 2-1	F25 4-2	D03 1-1	O29 1-0	m01 2-3	D17 0-0	N19 1-0	D26 0-0	a01 0-1	a15 2-0	S24 1-3	D31 0-4	F18 2-0	A20 1-1
6 C.PALACE	F25 0-3	a04 0-0	D31 0-1	S24 0-1	F11 0-2		O22 1-0	N05 3-0	A30 1-2	J14 2-0	A20 1-6	a01 2-1	J25 1-1	O15 0-1	D17 0-1	a29 1-2	D26 0-0	M14 2-1	N26 0-0	a14 1-1	m06 1-0	S17 0-0
7 EVERTON	O29 1-1	A20 2-2	a01 1-2	m03 3-3	O15 0-2	J21 3-1		D31 4-1	D05 3-0	S24 1-1	N21 2-0	M15 1-1	F25 1-0	a14 2-0	F04 2-1	A30 1-2	S17 2-2	D26 1-4	m06 0-0	D17 0-0	N01 1-0	a29 0-0
8 IPSWICH	D28 0-2	a01 0-1	N19 1-3	J21 2-2	m06 2-0	F04 0-2	m09 0-1		N01 2-0	J02 4-1	O29 1-3	D03 1-2	S24 3-2	F28 0-2	S19 1-2	A20 0-1	a11 0-1	O16 1-2	F25 2-1	A30 1-3	a17 1-1	D16 2-2
9 LEEDS	A23 1-0	a29 1-0	a15 1-1	A27 2-3	M18 3-0	m09 3-1	F22 1-0	a05 4-0		O24 2-1	D31 0-2	O01 2-0	S11 2-1	D26 0-0	m06 2-1	N26 1-0	J24 4-0	M04 0-1	J14 0-0	O15 1-1	D10 2-2	N05 3-1
10 LEICESTER	N23 2-1	D03 1-1	D17 0-0	m06 1-1	O03 2-2	O29 0-1	M04 2-2	a29 2-0	M15 1-3		D26 1-2	N20 0-1	a15 0-4	A21 1-3	a05 1-0	M11 2-4	A31 1-1	D31 0-1	O15 4-3	S17 3-1	F04 1-2	a01 3-4
11 LIVERPOOL	A28 3-0	O08 3-2	m14 2-1	N09 3-1	M14 2-3	D11 0-0	J24 0-0	J14 0-1	a09 0-1	a17 2-0		D28 2-0	M19 2-0	M04 2-0	J02 4-0	N05 1-0	F11 1-1	O01 4-1	a05 3-1	N26 1-1	S10 0-0	O22 3-0
12 MANCHESTER C	D12 1-2	D31 2-2	D26 1-3	M08 1-2	J14 0-0	S10 1-1	A27 4-0	F22 2-0	F25 0-0	J25 0-1	a14 2-1		F11 0-3	a29 0-0	S24 2-0	O08 3-3	m14 2-3	M18 3-2	N05 3-3	O22 5-2	A24 3-0	N26 2-0
13 MANCHESTER U	M22 3-0	F04 1-0	J22 1-0	a17 0-0	J03 2-0	N19 3-0	O01 2-0	M04 9-0	a02 0-0	D28 1-1	S17 2-0	N10 5-0		O29 2-0	D03 1-0	D17 1-2	A20 2-0	m07 1-0	m10 2-1	M15 0-0	O15 1-0	A31 3-0
14 NEWCASTLE	M19 1-0	F25 3-1	O09 1-1	S10 4-2	A24 4-0	m14 3-2	F01 2-0	N26 1-1	a17 1-2	D10 3-1	S24 1-1	J02 0-0	J15 1-1		a08 3-0	F11 2-1	N05 2-1	O22 2-1	A27 5-1	m03 3-3	M08 2-0	J25 2-1
15 NORWICH	S10 0-0	m14 1-1	O01 2-1	D10 3-0	J25 2-2	A24 0-0	N05 0-0	M20 3-0	O08 2-1	N26 2-1	a29 1-2	M04 1-1	F22 0-2	D31 2-1		a12 0-1	O22 4-2	M08 0-0	F11 2-2	D26 0-2	A27 1-0	J14 1-2
16 NOTTINGHAM F	D03 2-2	J21 1-2	O29 0-2	N19 0-1	a17 2-0	J02 1-0	M08 2-1	D10 4-1	M22 3-0	A27 1-0	F04 1-1	m06 1-0	A22 1-1	N07 0-0	D27 1-0		O02 3-2	S10 4-1	M18 3-0	M04 2-2	a08 1-1	O17 3-1
17 Q.P.R.	a08 3-1	O29 2-0	a04 0-1	M22 1-0	S10 2-2	a17 0-1	M18 2-3	A27 1-2	N19 3-2	M08 2-0	O31 2-1	O15 1-2	D10 2-3	F04 3-0	M15 2-0	F26 1-1		A24 3-2	D28 2-2	m06 2-1	D04 2-1	S24 0-1
18 SHEFFIELD W	F04 3-1	F18 1-2	N02 0-1	O29 1-1	D28 5-1	D03 1-0	a17 0-0	m05 4-1	S26 1-1	a08 1-0	F25 1-2	S17 1-1	O08 1-0	J21 0-0	A31 0-0	a01 1-7	D17 0-2		J02 1-1	A20 3-4	N19 1-0	M11 0-1
19 SOUTHAMPTON	N19 1-0	D19 2-1	A20 1-1	D03 0-1	M04 0-0	m03 3-1	O08 2-0	O01 3-1	O29 1-3	m14 2-2	A31 0-2	F04 2-2	D31 2-2	M22 3-1	N02 1-1	S17 1-1	a15 2-1	a29 0-0		a02 4-3	M15 1-1	D26 2-3
20 TOTTENHAM	J02 1-0	N19 3-4	F05 3-1	N23 0-0	m09 1-3	D27 0-0	A24 2-1	M08 3-0	m14 1-1	M18 1-0	M22 0-0	a11 2-1	A27 0-1	D03 4-2	a17 1-0	S24 1-4	O08 1-1	D10 3-1	S12 1-2		O29 3-1	F25 1-2
21 WEST HAM	S25 0-2	S17 1-0	a30 2-0	F25 1-2	N26 0-1	O08 1-0	F13 2-2	D26 1-1	A20 0-0	N05 1-0	m10 3-0	D17 3-0	M14 1-1	A31 1-3	M11 2-2	D31 3-1	m03 0-0	J23 0-2	O22 2-0	J14 1-2		a13 3-0
22 WIMBLEDON	O08 1-3	N09 4-3	D03 0-3	a10 1-1	D10 2-0	M18 2-0	J02 2-1	A23 1-1	F04 0-0	S10 2-1	m02 0-0	M21 2-0	M07 0-1	N19 3-2	O30 1-0	m13 2-2	M04 1-3	A27 0-1	a17 0-2	O01 1-2	D28 1-0	

Twenty-nine goals for Wrexham's Gary Bennett saw him top the Second Division scorers.

DIVISION 1

	BARNSLEY	BOLTON	BRISTOL C	BURNLEY	CHARLTON	DERBY	GRIMSBY	LUTON	MIDDLESBROUGH	MILLWALL	NOTTS CO	OLDHAM	PORT VALE	PORTSMOUTH	READING	SHEFFIELD U	SOUTHEND	STOKE	SUNDERLAND	SWINDON	TRANMERE	WATFORD	W.B.A.	WOLVERHAMPTON
1 BARNSLEY		N26 3-0	D07 2-1	M07 2-0	D10 2-1	A13 2-1	D26 4-1	J14 3-1	a22 1-1	F21 4-1	S13 1-1	m02 1-1	M18 3-1	a15 1-0	A27 0-2	a29 2-1	O08 0-0	N05 2-0	M24 2-0	O01 2-1	F11 2-2	S10 0-0	O22 2-0	D31 1-3
2 BOLTON	F18 2-1		A20 0-2	m07 1-1	J21 5-1	O01 1-0	D217 3-3	a11 0-0	M11 1-0	A30 1-0	N19 2-0	O16 2-2	D06 1-0	S17 1-1	J02 1-0	M22 1-1	M04 3-0	S03 4-0	a17 1-0	N01 3-0	D27 1-0	O29 3-0	a08 1-0	F04 5-1
3 BRISTOL C	F04 3-2	D10 0-1		M18 1-1	M07 2-1	S13 0-2	D03 1-2	F25 2-2	S24 0-1	O08 1-0	S10 2-1	F18 2-2	A27 0-0	O29 1-1	a29 1-2	J21 2-1	M25 0-0	D27 3-1	A13 0-0	N20 3-2	a08 0-1	J02 0-0	a17 1-0	N01 1-5
4 BURNLEY	S03 0-1	O08 2-2	A30 1-1		a04 2-0	a15 3-1	F18 0-2	M21 2-1	D18 0-3	a01 1-2	O29 2-1	M11 2-1	M28 4-3	a22 1-2	J21 1-2	N20 4-2	D31 5-1	A20 1-1	a29 1-1	F04 1-2	O01 1-1	N01 1-1	M04 1-1	S17 0-1
5 CHARLTON	A20 2-2	N05 1-2	S03 3-2	O22 1-2		J14 3-4	M21 2-1	a22 1-0	N26 0-2	J01 1-1	M04 1-0	D17 2-0	a29 1-1	M11 1-0	O08 1-2	A30 1-1	D26 3-1	a01 0-0	F11 1-0	S17 1-0	F21 0-1	O01 3-0	N13 1-1	a15 3-2
6 DERBY	D17 1-0	F26 2-1	a01 3-1	M15 4-0	O29 2-2		S03 2-1	A20 0-0	A31 0-1	M11 3-2	D03 0-0	S17 2-1	N19 2-0	J22 3-0	N02 1-2	F04 2-3	a29 1-2	S25 3-0	a08 0-1	M22 3-1	A17 5-0	O08 1-1	J02 1-1	a12 3-3
7 GRIMSBY	a17 1-0	A13 3-3	O22 1-0	N26 2-2	S10 0-1	M07 0-1		F11 5-0	N05 2-1	N12 1-0	J28 2-1	D27 1-3	S13 4-1	O01 2-0	a08 1-0	O08 0-0	J14 4-1	F21 0-0	M19 3-1	M04 1-1	A27 3-1	D10 0-0	M25 0-2	a29 0-0
8 LUTON	O29 0-1	S13 0-3	O01 0-1	S10 0-1	J02 0-1	D11 0-0	N01 1-2		O15 5-1	M04 1-1	a08 2-0	F04 2-1	M07 2-1	N19 2-0	a17 0-1	D03 3-6	A27 2-2	m07 2-3	D27 3-0	F18 3-0	M18 2-0	M26 1-1	A13 1-1	a04 3-3
9 MIDDLESBROUGH	M14 1-1	A27 1-0	M04 3-0	A13 2-0	F18 1-0	M18 2-4	J21 1-1	a30 2-1		O01 3-0	D28 2-1	N01 2-1	M26 3-0	D03 4-0	F04 0-1	a17 1-1	D10 1-2	a08 2-1	S11 2-2	O29 3-1	O08 0-1	M07 2-0	S14 2-1	N20 1-0
10 MILLWALL	N19 0-1	M19 0-1	m07 1-1	S14 2-3	a08 3-1	A27 4-1	F04 2-0	S24 0-0	F26 0-0		a19 0-0	J03 1-1	a05 1-3	N02 2-2	M08 2-0	O29 2-1	A13 3-1	O15 1-1	D10 2-0	M01 3-1	M25 2-1	D27 2-1	S10 2-2	D04 1-0
11 NOTTS CO	a01 1-3	F07 1-1	M21 1-1	J14 3-0	S24 3-3	O23 0-0	a22 0-2	D31 0-1	a15 1-1	D26 0-1		A30 1-3	O08 2-2	D17 0-1	F25 1-0	M11 2-1	F11 2-2	S17 0-2	N05 3-2	S03 0-1	D06 1-0	a29 1-0	N26 2-0	A21 1-1
12 OLDHAM	S24 1-0	a29 3-1	N26 2-0	A27 3-0	A13 5-2	M25 1-0	a15 1-0	N12 0-0	a05 1-0	a22 0-1	M14 1-1		D10 3-2	O08 3-2	S10 1-3	F25 3-3	M07 0-2	O22 0-0	J14 0-0	D31 1-1	N06 0-0	S13 0-2	F21 1-0	D26 4-1
13 PORT VALE	A30 2-1	O22 1-1	M11 2-1	a17 1-0	O15 0-2	F21 1-0	a01 1-2	S03 0-1	S17 2-1	N26 2-1	m07 1-1	A20 3-1		M21 1-0	D28 0-2	S24 0-2	N05 5-0	M14 1-1	N29 0-0	D17 2-2	J15 2-0	a08 0-1	F11 1-0	F25 2-4
14 PORTSMOUTH	D27 3-0	M25 1-1	J14 0-0	J02 2-0	A27 1-1	N06 0-1	F25 2-1	F21 3-2	O23 0-0	M15 3-2	A13 2-1	m07 1-1	S10 0-2		D10 1-1	a08 1-0	M18 1-1	N30 0-1	N26 1-4	O15 4-3	S14 1-1	a17 2-1	M08 1-2	S24 1-2
15 READING	M11 0-3	a21 2-1	O15 1-0	N05 0-0	m07 2-1	F11 1-0	D31 1-1	D26 0-0	D06 1-1	S03 0-0	O01 2-0	M21 2-1	a15 3-3	A20 0-0		S17 1-0	F21 2-0	A30 4-0	O22 0-2	a01 3-0	N26 1-3	M04 4-1	J14 0-2	D18 4-2
16 SHEFFIELD U	O16 0-0	S10 3-1	N05 3-0	F21 2-0	M18 2-1	N12 2-1	m06 3-1	O22 1-3	D26 1-1	J14 1-1	A27 1-3	O01 2-0	M04 1-1	D31 3-1	M25 1-1		N26 2-0	F11 1-1	S13 0-0	a15 2-2	M07 2-0	A13 3-0	D10 2-0	a22 3-3
17 SOUTHEND	m07 3-1	S24 2-1	S17 2-1	a08 3-1	a18 2-1	O16 1-0	O29 0-0	M11 3-0	A20 0-2	D17 0-1	N01 1-0	S03 1-0	J28 1-2	A30 1-2	N19 4-1	F18 1-3		M21 4-2	F25 0-1	D03 2-0	J02 0-0	F04 0-4	D27 2-1	a01 0-1
18 STOKE	a12 0-0	m03 1-1	a15 2-1	D10 2-0	S14 3-2	M04 0-0	N19 3-0	O09 1-2	D31 1-1	a29 4-3	M25 2-1	D04 0-1	a22 0-1	F04 0-2	M18 0-1	N02 1-1	S10 4-1		A27 0-1	D26 0-0	A13 1-0	a04 1-0	O02 4-1	O30 1-1
19 SUNDERLAND	S17 2-0	D26 1-1	D17 2-0	O15 0-0	N01 1-1	D31 1-1	A30 2-2	a15 1-1	M21 0-1	A20 1-1	J21 1-2	O29 0-0	F04 1-1	F18 2-2	D03 0-1	a01 1-0	O01 0-1	M11 1-0		A22 1-0	M05 0-1	N19 1-3	m07 2-2	S03 1-1
20 SWINDON	F25 0-0	a05 0-1	F15 0-3	N23 1-1	M25 0-1	S11 1-1	S24 3-2	N26 1-2	J15 2-1	N05 1-2	m03 3-0	a08 3-1	A14 2-0	a29 0-2	S13 1-0	D27 1-3	O22 2-2	a17 0-1	M15 1-0		D10 2-2	A27 1-0	A31 0-0	O08 3-2
21 TRANMERE	N01 6-1	a14 1-0	D31 2-0	F25 4-1	N19 1-1	D26 3-1	M11 2-0	A30 4-2	m07 1-1	S17 3-1	F04 3-2	J22 3-1	O29 1-1	a01 4-2	F18 1-0	S03 2-1	a21 0-2	D17 0-1	S24 1-0	A20 3-2		D03 2-1	O15 3-1	m03 1-1
22 WATFORD	M21 3-2	J14 0-0	a22 1-0	F11 2-0	m02 2-0	m07 2-1	A20 0-0	S17 2-4	S03 1-1	a14 1-0	O15 3-1	a01 1-2	D31 3-2	D26 2-0	S24 2-2	D17 0-0	N12 1-0	N26 0-0	F21 0-1	M11 2-0	O22 2-0		N05 1-0	A30 2-1
23 W.B.A.	D03 2-1	D31 1-0	D26 1-0	S24 1-0	F05 0-1	a22 0-0	S17 1-1	D18 1-0	a01 1-3	M22 3-0	F18 3-2	N19 3-1	N02 0-0	S28 0-2	O29 2-0	O18 1-0	a15 2-0	F25 1-3	O08 1-3	M19 2-5	a30 5-1	F01 0-1		M15 2-0
24 WOLVERHAMPTON	a08 0-0	N23 3-1	F11 2-0	M24 2-0	D28 2-0	N27 0-2	O15 2-1	N05 2-3	F21 0-2	O22 3-3	D10 1-0	a17 2-1	O01 2-1	M05 1-0	A13 1-0	J02 2-2	S13 5-0	J14 2-0	M08 1-0	m07 1-1	S10 2-0	M18 1-1	A28 2-0	

SEASON 1994-95

Burnley, Bristol City and Notts County relegated to Div 2; Carlisle United, Walsall and Chesterfield promoted to Div 2; Cambridge United, Plymouth Argyle, Cardiff City, Chester City and Leyton Orient relegated to Div 3.

DIVISION 2

	BIRMINGHAM	BLACKPOOL	BOURNEMOUTH	BRADFORD C	BRENTFORD	BRIGHTON	BRISTOL R	CAMBRIDGE	CARDIFF	CHESTER	CREWE	HUDDERSFIELD	HULL	LEYTON O	OXFORD	PETERBOROUGH	PLYMOUTH	ROTHERHAM	SHREWSBURY	STOCKPORT	SWANSEA	WREXHAM	WYCOMBE	YORK
1 BIRMINGHAM		D31 7-1	N19 0-0	m02 0-0	a26 2-0	a29 3-3	O29 2-0	D26 1-1	a15 2-1	A20 1-0	N01 5-0	O08 1-1	S24 2-2	D17 2-0	M21 3-0	S18 4-0	S03 4-2	a01 2-1	a11 2-0	F04 1-0	M11 0-1	F25 5-2	A30 0-1	F18 4-2
2 BLACKPOOL	a04 1-1		D10 3-1	O15 2-0	M25 1-2	S13 2-2	M18 0-2	J14 2-3	S10 2-1	F21 3-1	M07 0-0	A13 1-4	m06 1-2	N05 2-1	F11 2-1	J02 4-0	J28 5-2	F25 2-2	A27 2-1	D27 1-2	O22 2-1	S24 2-1	N26 0-1	a18 0-5
3 BOURNEMOUTH	F21 2-1	A20 1-2		O22 2-3	O15 0-1	F11 0-3	a18 2-0	N05 1-0	S24 3-2	S17 1-1	D27 1-1	J28 0-2	F25 2-3	a01 2-0	N26 0-2	A30 0-3	J14 0-0	M11 1-1	m02 3-0	M31 2-0	J02 3-2	D16 1-3	a08 2-0	S03 1-4
4 BRADFORD C	J02 1-1	a29 0-1	J07 1-2		N02 1-0	O08 2-1	F07 2-1	F25 1-1	O30 2-3	D17 1-1	N19 0-2	S24 3-4	D28 1-0	A20 2-0	A30 0-2	F18 4-2	M11 2-0	a17 0-3	F04 1-1	a08 1-2	M21 1-3	a01 1-1	S03 2-1	S17 0-0
5 BRENTFORD	O22 1-2	S17 3-2	a29 1-2	F11 4-3		N26 2-1	O08 3-0	J28 6-0	a22 2-0	a15 1-1	M04 2-0	F21 0-0	N05 0-1	D26 3-0	D31 2-0	A20 0-1	D17 7-0	A30 2-0	O01 1-0	M11 1-0	J14 0-0	S03 0-2	M21 0-0	a01 3-0
6 BRIGHTON	O15 0-1	a01 2-2	N02 0-0	m06 1-0	F04 1-1		F14 1-2	S24 2-0	M15 0-0	M22 1-0	F18 0-1	F25 0-0	a08 1-0	S03 1-0	S17 1-1	N19 1-2	A20 1-1	O29 1-1	D27 2-1	J02 2-0	D17 1-1	M11 4-0	a19 1-1	A31 1-0
7 BRISTOL R	M29 1-1	A31 0-0	D26 2-1	N05 4-0	m06 2-2	O22 3-0		M15 2-1	O15 2-2	D31 3-0	O01 2-2	N26 1-1	M01 0-2	a22 1-0	J14 3-2	D17 3-1	a15 2-0	M22 2-0	M04 4-0	S03 2-2	a01 1-0	S17 4-2	M11 1-0	A20 3-1
8 CAMBRIDGE	a17 1-0	F18 0-0	J21 2-2	O01 4-1	O29 0-0	M04 0-2	N01 1-1		J17 2-0	A30 2-1	F04 1-2	a29 1-1	J02 2-2	M21 0-0	M11 1-2	a08 2-0	a01 1-1	S03 2-1	N19 3-1	A20 3-4	S17 1-3	O08 1-2	D16 2-2	D28 1-0
9 CARDIFF	D28 0-1	J07 0-1	M04 1-1	M28 2-4	J02 2-3	N05 3-0	a29 0-1	O22 3-1		a01 2-1	O08 1-2	J14 0-0	N25 0-2	a04 2-1	A20 1-3	O01 1-2	S17 0-1	a08 1-1	a17 1-2	D17 1-1	S03 1-1	A30 0-0	F21 2-0	M11 1-2
10 CHESTER	D10 0-4	N19 2-0	M25 1-1	A13 1-4	D27 1-4	S10 1-2	a08 0-0	M18 1-3	S13 0-2		a17 0-1	A27 1-2	M28 1-2	a29 1-0	O01 2-0	J28 1-1	M04 1-0	F04 4-4	F18 1-3	N02 1-0	O08 2-2	O30 1-1	J31 0-2	J07 0-4
11 CREWE	F11 2-1	S03 4-3	a15 2-0	F21 0-1	S24 0-2	J14 4-0	F25 2-1	N26 4-2	m06 0-0	D26 2-1		O22 3-3	m02 3-2	D31 3-0	a01 3-2	M11 1-3	a22 2-2	A20 3-1	O15 1-0	A30 2-1	N05 1-2	M21 1-3	S17 1-2	D16 2-1
12 HUDDERSFIELD	m06 1-2	D17 1-1	O29 3-1	M04 0-0	N19 1-0	O01 3-0	F04 1-1	O15 3-1	F18 5-1	M11 5-1	J07 1-2		a17 1-1	A30 2-1	S03 3-3	a01 1-2	M21 2-0	D27 1-0	J02 2-1	S17 2-1	a08 2-0	N01 2-1	A20 0-1	F28 3-0
13 HULL	M04 0-0	O08 1-0	O01 3-1	a15 2-0	J21 1-2	D31 2-2	N19 0-2	a22 1-0	F04 4-0	S03 2-0	O29 7-1	D26 1-0		M11 2-0	D17 3-1	M21 1-1	A30 2-0	S17 0-2	J07 2-2	F18 0-0	A20 0-2	a29 3-2	a01 0-0	N01 3-0
14 LEYTON O	A13 2-1	F07 0-1	S13 3-2	D10 0-0	a17 0-2	M07 0-3	a11 1-2	S10 1-1	N01 2-0	O15 2-0	a08 1-4	M18 0-2	A27 1-1		M04 1-1	F04 4-1	O01 0-2	J07 0-0	M25 2-1	O29 0-1	D27 0-1	F18 1-1	m06 0-1	N19 0-1
15 OXFORD	S10 1-1	N01 3-2	F04 0-3	M18 1-0	a08 1-1	M25 0-0	F18 0-0	A27 1-0	D10 1-0	F25 1-0	S13 2-1	M07 3-1	A13 4-0	S24 3-2		a17 1-0	O08 1-0	N19 2-1	O29 0-0	F28 4-0	a30 1-2	a04 0-0	D27 0-2	J02 0-2
16 PETERBOROUGH	M25 1-1	a22 1-0	M18 0-0	J14 0-0	D10 2-2	F21 2-1	A13 0-0	D31 2-2	F25 2-1	N05 2-0	A27 1-5	S13 2-2	S10 2-1	N26 0-0	D26 1-4		F11 1-2	S24 2-2	M07 1-1	O15 0-1	a04 1-0	a15 1-0	O22 1-3	m06 1-1
17 PLYMOUTH	a19 1-3	O29 0-2	F18 0-1	A27 1-5	A13 1-5	D10 0-3	a04 1-1	S13 0-0	M25 0-0	S24 1-0	J02 3-2	S10 0-3	M18 2-1	F25 1-0	m06 1-1	N01 0-1		J21 0-0	a08 1-0	M28 0-2	a17 2-1	N19 4-1	O15 2-2	F04 1-2
18 ROTHERHAM	S13 1-1	O01 0-2	A27 4-0	D26 3-1	M18 0-2	M28 4-3	S10 0-3	M07 1-0	D31 2-0	N26 2-0	D10 2-2	a15 1-1	M25 2-0	O22 2-0	F21 1-1	M04 0-0	N05 3-1		A13 0-4	m06 1-0	F11 3-3	a22 0-1	J14 2-0	O15 2-1
19 SHREWSBURY	N05 0-2	M11 0-0	O08 3-0	N26 1-2	F25 2-1	a15 1-1	S24 1-0	F21 1-1	D26 0-1	J14 1-0	a29 1-2	a22 2-1	O22 2-3	S17 3-0	J28 1-1	S03 2-2	F07 3-2	D16 1-0		a01 1-1	S06 3-3	A20 2-2	F11 2-2	M21 1-0
20 STOCKPORT	N26 0-1	a15 3-2	S10 1-0	D31 1-2	A27 0-1	a22 2-0	M07 2-1	D10 2-1	A13 4-1	F11 2-2	M18 3-1	M25 1-2	J14 4-0	J28 2-1	N05 0-2	a29 1-1	O22 2-4	O08 1-0	S13 2-1		F21 0-1	D26 1-1	S24 4-1	F25 2-3
21 SWANSEA	A27 0-2	F28 1-0	a22 1-0	S10 0-0	F17 0-2	A13 1-1	S13 0-0	M24 1-0	M07 4-1	m06 0-1	a25 0-1	D31 1-1	D10 2-0	a15 2-0	O15 1-3	O29 2-0	D26 3-0	N01 1-0	M17 0-0	N19 2-0		F04 0-0	F25 1-1	S24 0-0
22 WREXHAM	O01 1-1	M04 0-1	A13 2-0	S13 0-1	M07 0-0	A27 2-1	M25 1-1	m06 0-1	M18 0-3	F14 2-2	S10 1-0	F11 1-2	O15 2-2	J14 4-1	O22 3-2	D27 3-3	F21 3-1	M14 3-1	D10 0-1	a17 1-0	N26 4-1		N05 4-1	a08 1-1
23 WYCOMBE	M18 0-3	F04 1-1	D31 1-1	a04 3-1	S10 4-3	D26 0-0	A27 0-0	A13 3-0	N19 3-1	a22 3-1	M25 0-0	D10 2-1	S13 1-2	O08 2-1	a15 1-0	M28 3-1	a29 1-2	F18 2-0	N01 1-0	M04 1-1	O01 1-0	a11 3-0		O29 0-0
24 YORK	J14 2-0	D26 4-0	M07 1-0	M25 0-0	S13 2-1	M18 1-0	D10 0-3	a15 2-0	A27 1-1	O22 2-0	A13 1-2	N05 3-0	a04 3-1	F21 4-1	a22 0-2	O08 1-1	N26 1-0	a29 2-0	S10 3-0	O01 2-4	M04 2-4	F07 0-1	M14 0-0	

DIVISION 3

	BARNET	BURY	CARLISLE	CHESTERFIELD	COLCHESTER	DARLINGTON	DONCASTER	EXETER	FULHAM	GILLINGHAM	HARTLEPOOL	HEREFORD	LINCOLN	MANSFIELD	NORTHAMPTON	PRESTON	ROCHDALE	SCARBOROUGH	SCUNTHORPE	TORQUAY	WALSALL	WIGAN
1 BARNET		N19 1-1	J24 0-2	O29 4-1	F18 0-1	F04 2-3	S10 0-0	F28 1-1	O01 0-0	D27 1-0	M18 4-0	O08 2-2	a04 2-1	a08 2-2	a29 2-3	A27 2-1	S13 6-2	D10 3-1	A13 1-2	M04 2-0	a17 1-3	M25 1-1
2 BURY	M14 3-0		a15 2-0	S24 2-1	F25 4-1	m06 2-1	S13 2-0	D10 0-0	N26 0-0	O22 3-2	A27 2-0	J14 1-1	O15 2-0	M25 2-2	a22 5-0	A30 0-0	A13 0-1	N05 1-0	S10 2-0	F28 3-1	m04 0-0	D26 3-3
3 CARLISLE	O22 4-0	D27 3-0		a04 1-1	O15 0-0	O01 2-1	N26 1-1	S10 1-0	J28 1-1	a08 2-0	a17 0-1	F11 1-0	m06 1-3	S13 2-1	M04 2-1	J14 0-0	N05 4-1	A27 2-0	M25 2-1	D10 1-0	M18 2-1	A13 2-1
4 CHESTERFIELD	F14 2-0	M04 0-0	m02 1-2		m06 2-2	O15 0-0	D26 2-0	S13 2-0	O22 1-1	F11 2-0	M25 2-0	N05 1-0	D31 1-0	A27 0-1	a15 3-0	N26 1-0	D10 2-2	A13 0-1	J14 3-1	O01 1-0	S10 0-0	M18 0-0
5 COLCHESTER	J14 1-1	O01 1-0	a29 0-1	O08 0-3		M04 1-0	A27 0-3	M18 3-1	a15 5-2	N05 2-2	S10 1-0	D31 2-2	a22 1-2	D10 1-1	D26 0-1	O22 3-1	F11 0-0	M25 0-2	N26 4-2	A13 1-3	S13 3-2	J28 0-1
6 DARLINGTON	N26 0-1	O08 0-2	F25 0-2	a29 0-1	S24 2-3		M25 0-2	A27 2-0	J14 0-0	F21 2-0	D10 1-2	O22 3-1	a15 0-0	M18 0-0	D31 4-1	A13 0-0	a22 4-0	D26 1-0	S13 1-3	S10 2-1	N05 2-2	F11 1-3
7 DONCASTER	M11 1-1	a01 1-2	F04 0-0	a17 1-3	D16 1-2	S03 0-0		J31 1-0	A30 0-0	F07 1-2	N19 3-0	S16 3-0	F18 3-0	J10 0-2	A20 1-0	S24 2-1	F25 0-1	a29 1-0	D27 1-1	O29 3-0	a08 0-2	O08 5-3
8 EXETER	a22 1-2	A20 0-4	M11 1-1	a01 1-2	A30 1-0	D17 0-2	N05 1-5		a29 0-1	S03 3-0	O01 2-1	a15 1-1	S17 1-0	M04 2-3	O08 0-0	M21 0-1	J14 0-0	N26 5-2	O22 2-2	D26 1-2	a04 1-3	F21 2-4
9 FULHAM	F25 4-0	F04 1-0	O29 1-3	J08 1-1	D27 1-2	F18 3-1	M18 0-2	O15 4-0		a17 1-0	a08 1-0	S24 1-1	N19 1-1	J02 4-2	F14 4-4	S10 0-1	m06 5-0	S13 1-2	D10 1-0	M25 2-1	A13 1-1	A27 2-0
10 GILLINGHAM	a15 2-1	a04 1-1	D31 0-1	N19 1-1	a11 1-3	O29 2-1	a22 4-2	M25 3-0	D26 4-1		A13 0-0	a29 0-0	F04 0-0	O01 0-2	F18 3-1	S13 2-3	A27 1-1	S10 3-1	M18 2-2	O08 1-0	M04 1-3	D10 0-1
11 HARTLEPOOL	A30 0-1	D17 3-1	D26 1-5	S03 0-2	M11 3-1	A20 1-0	M21 2-1	F25 2-2	D31 1-2	S17 2-0		a22 4-0	S24 0-3	m06 3-2	a01 1-1	O15 3-1	N26 1-0	J14 3-3	J28 1-4	a15 1-1	O22 1-1	N05 0-1
12 HEREFORD	m06 3-2	F18 1-0	N19 0-1	J24 0-2	a08 3-0	J07 0-0	A13 0-1	D27 3-0	M04 1-1	O15 2-1	F21 1-0		O29 0-3	a17 0-0	F04 2-1	A20 0-2	M25 0-0	M18 2-1	O01 2-1	S13 1-1	A27 0-0	S10 1-2
13 LINCOLN	N05 1-2	a29 0-3	O08 1-1	a08 0-1	F21 2-0	D27 3-1	J14 1-0	A13 2-0	a11 2-0	N26 1-1	M04 3-0	J28 2-0		S10 3-2	O01 2-2	M25 1-1	M18 2-2	O22 2-0	a17 3-3	A27 1-2	D10 1-1	S13 1-0
14 MANSFIELD	D31 3-0	S03 0-2	a01 1-2	D18 4-2	A20 2-0	A30 0-1	O22 0-1	S24 1-1	a22 1-1	F25 4-0	O08 2-0	D26 7-1	M11 6-2		S17 1-1	N05 1-2	M07 1-1	a15 3-2	F21 1-0	a29 2-2	N26 1-3	J14 4-3
15 NORTHAMPTON	O15 1-1	M07 0-5	S24 2-1	D27 2-3	a17 1-1	a08 2-1	D10 0-0	m06 2-1	N05 0-1	J14 2-0	S13 1-1	N26 1-3	F25 3-1	O11 0-1		F11 2-1	S10 1-2	J28 0-3	D16 0-1	M18 2-0	M25 2-2	O22 1-0
16 PRESTON	D17 1-0	M18 5-0	F18 1-0	F04 0-0	J10 2-1	S17 1-3	M04 2-2	O29 0-1	M11 3-2	a01 1-1	a29 3-0	D10 4-2	S03 4-0	J21 2-1	N19 2-0		D26 3-0	D31 1-0	O08 0-1	a22 0-1	O01 1-2	a15 1-0
17 ROCHDALE	a01 2-2	S17 0-3	J21 1-1	A20 4-1	N19 0-0	M21 2-0	O01 2-0	F18 0-1	O08 1-2	D17 2-1	F04 1-0	S03 1-3	A30 1-0	O29 3-3	M11 0-0	a17 0-1		a25 1-1	a08 1-2	J07 2-0	D27 0-2	a29 1-0
18 SCARBOROUGH	A20 0-1	M21 1-2	D17 1-2	S17 0-1	S03 0-1	a18 3-1	O15 2-2	F04 0-2	a01 3-1	M11 0-0	F18 2-2	A30 3-1	F07 1-1	D27 2-5	O29 0-0	a08 1-1	S24 2-4		F28 3-0	N19 1-1	m02 1-2	F25 0-1
19 SCUNTHORPE	S17 1-0	M11 3-2	S093 2-3	F18 0-1	F04 3-4	a01 2-1	a15 0-5	J07 3-0	A20 1-2	A30 3-0	O29 0-0	F25 1-0	D26 2-0	N19 3-4	A27 1-1	m06 2-1	D31 4-1	a22 3-1		J21 3-2	O15 0-1	S24 3-1
20 TORQUAY	S24 1-2	a08 2-2	A20 1-1	F25 3-3	S17 3-3	M11 1-0	J28 0-1	a18 0-0	S03 2-1	m06 3-1	D27 2-2	a01 0-1	D17 2-1	O15 2-1	A30 2-1	J02 1-0	O22 4-1	M07 2-1	N05 1-1		J14 3-2	N26 0-0
21 WALSALL	D26 4-0	O29 0-1	A30 1-2	M11 1-3	a01 2-0	M14 2-0	D31 1-0	N19 1-0	S17 5-1	S24 2-1	M07 4-1	D17 4-3	A20 2-1	F04 1-0	S03 1-1	F28 2-2	a15 0-0	O08 4-1	a29 2-1	F18 1-0		a22 2-0
22 WIGAN	S03 1-2	a18 0-3	S17 0-2	A30 2-3	O29 1-2	N19 4-1	m06 3-2	a08 3-1	D17 1-1	A20 0-3	F28 2-0	M29 1-1	a01 0-1	F18 0-4	J07 2-1	J24 1-1	O15 4-0	O01 1-1	a04 0-0	F04 1-1	a11 1-0	

LEAGUE TABLES

PREMIER LEAGUE

	P	W	D	L	F	A	W	D	L	F	A	Pts
Blackburn R	42	17	2	2	54	21	10	6	5	26	18	89
Manchester U	42	16	4	1	42	4	10	6	5	35	24	88
Nottingham F	42	12	6	3	36	18	10	5	6	36	25	77
Liverpool	42	13	5	3	38	13	8	6	7	27	24	74
Leeds U	42	13	5	3	35	15	7	8	6	24	23	73
Newcastle U	42	14	6	1	46	20	6	6	9	21	27	72
Tottenham H	42	10	5	6	32	25	6	9	6	34	33	62
Q.P.R.	42	11	3	7	36	26	6	6	9	25	33	60
Wimbledon	42	9	5	7	26	26	6	6	9	22	39	56
Southampton	42	8	9	4	33	27	4	9	8	28	36	54
Chelsea	42	7	7	7	25	22	6	8	7	25	33	54
Arsenal	42	6	9	6	27	21	7	3	11	25	28	51
Sheffield W	42	7	7	7	26	26	6	5	10	23	31	51
West Ham U	42	9	6	6	28	19	4	5	12	16	29	50
Everton	42	8	9	4	31	23	3	8	10	13	28	50
Coventry C	42	7	7	7	23	25	5	7	9	21	37	50
Manchester C	42	8	7	6	37	28	4	6	11	16	36	49
Aston Villa	42	6	9	6	27	24	5	6	10	24	32	48
Crystal Palace	42	6	6	9	16	23	5	6	10	18	26	45
Norwich C	42	8	8	5	27	21	2	5	14	10	33	43
Leicester C	42	5	6	10	28	37	1	5	15	17	43	29
Ipswich T	42	5	3	13	24	34	2	3	16	12	59	27

DIVISION 1

	P	W	D	L	F	A	W	D	L	F	A	Pts
Middlesbrough	46	15	4	4	41	19	8	9	6	26	21	82
Reading	46	12	7	4	34	21	11	3	9	24	23	79
Bolton W	46	16	6	1	43	13	5	8	10	24	32	77
Wolverh'pton W	46	15	5	3	39	18	6	8	9	38	43	76
Tranmere R	46	17	4	2	51	23	5	6	12	16	35	76
Barnsley	46	15	6	2	42	19	5	6	12	21	33	72
Watford	46	14	6	3	33	17	5	7	11	19	29	70
Sheffield U	46	12	9	2	41	21	5	8	10	33	34	68
Derby Co	46	12	6	5	44	23	6	6	11	22	28	66
Grimsby	46	12	7	4	36	19	5	7	11	26	37	65
Stoke C	46	10	7	6	31	21	6	8	9	19	32	63
Millwall	46	11	8	4	36	22	5	6	12	24	38	62
Southend U	46	13	2	8	33	25	5	6	12	21	48	62
Oldham A	46	12	7	4	34	21	4	6	13	26	39	61
Charlton A	46	11	6	6	33	25	5	5	13	25	41	59
Luton T	46	8	6	9	35	30	7	7	9	26	34	58
Port Vale	46	11	5	7	30	24	4	8	11	28	40	58
Portsmouth	46	9	8	6	31	28	6	5	12	22	35	58
W.B.A.	46	13	3	7	33	24	3	7	13	18	33	58
Sunderland	46	5	12	6	22	22	7	6	10	19	23	54
Swindon T	46	9	6	8	28	27	3	6	14	26	46	48
Burnley	46	8	7	8	36	33	3	6	14	13	41	46
Bristol C	46	8	8	7	26	28	3	4	16	16	35	45
Notts Co	46	7	8	8	26	28	2	5	16	19	38	40

DIVISION 2

	P	W	D	L	F	A	W	D	L	F	A	Pts
Birmingham C	46	15	6	2	53	18	10	8	5	31	19	89
Brentford	46	14	4	5	44	15	11	6	6	37	24	85
Crewe A	46	14	3	6	46	33	11	5	7	34	35	83
Bristol R	46	15	7	1	48	20	7	9	7	22	20	82
Huddersfield T	46	14	5	4	45	21	8	10	5	34	28	81
Wycombe	46	13	7	3	36	19	8	8	7	24	27	78
Oxford U	46	13	6	4	30	18	8	6	9	36	34	75
Hull C	46	13	6	4	40	18	8	5	10	30	39	74
York C	46	13	4	6	37	21	8	5	10	30	30	72
Swansea C	46	10	8	5	23	13	9	6	8	34	32	71
Stockport Co	46	12	3	8	40	29	7	5	11	23	31	65
Blackpool	46	11	4	8	40	36	7	6	10	24	34	64
Wrexham	46	10	7	6	38	27	6	8	9	27	37	63
Bradford C	46	8	6	9	29	32	8	6	9	28	32	60
Peterborough U	46	7	11	5	26	29	7	7	9	28	40	60
Brighton & H.A.	46	9	10	4	25	15	5	7	11	29	38	59
Rotherham U	46	12	6	5	36	26	2	8	13	21	35	56
Shrewsbury T	46	9	9	5	34	27	4	5	14	20	35	53
Bournemouth	46	9	4	10	30	34	4	7	12	19	35	50
Cambridge U	46	8	9	6	33	28	3	6	14	19	41	48
Plymouth A	46	7	6	10	22	36	5	4	14	23	47	46
Cardiff C	46	5	6	12	25	31	4	5	14	21	43	38
Chester C	46	5	6	12	23	42	1	5	17	14	42	29
Leyton O	46	6	6	11	21	29	0	2	21	9	46	26

DIVISION 3

	P	W	D	L	F	A	W	D	L	F	A	Pts
Carlisle U	42	14	5	2	34	14	13	5	3	33	17	91
Walsall	42	15	3	3	42	18	9	8	4	33	22	83
Chesterfield	42	11	7	3	26	10	12	5	4	36	27	81
Bury	42	13	7	1	39	13	10	4	7	34	23	80
Preston N.E.	42	13	3	5	37	17	6	7	8	21	24	67
Mansfield T	42	10	5	6	45	27	8	6	7	39	32	65
Scunthorpe U	42	12	2	7	40	30	6	6	9	28	33	62
Fulham	42	11	5	5	39	22	5	9	7	21	32	62
Doncaster	42	9	5	7	28	20	8	5	8	30	23	61
Colchester U	42	8	5	8	29	30	8	5	8	27	34	58
Barnet	42	8	7	6	37	27	7	4	10	19	36	56
Lincoln C	42	10	7	4	34	22	5	4	12	20	33	56
Torquay U	42	10	8	3	35	25	4	5	12	19	32	55
Wigan A	42	7	6	8	28	30	7	4	10	25	30	52
Rochdale	42	8	6	7	25	23	4	8	9	19	44	50
Hereford	42	9	6	6	22	19	3	7	11	23	43	49
Northampton T	42	8	5	8	25	29	2	9	10	20	38	44
Hartlepool U	42	9	5	7	33	32	2	5	14	10	37	43
Gillingham	42	8	7	6	31	25	2	4	15	15	39	41
Darlington	42	7	5	9	25	24	4	3	14	18	33	41
Scarborough	42	4	7	10	26	31	4	3	14	23	39	34
Exeter C	42	5	5	11	25	36	3	5	13	11	34	34

Football League Records

Top scorers: Prem Lge, A.Shearer (Blackburn Rovers) 31 goals; Div 1, J.Aldridge (Tranmere Rovers) 27 goals; Div 2, M.Stewart (Bristol Rovers), G.Martindale (Notts County) 21 goals; Div 3, S.White (Hereford United), A.Saville (Cardiff City) 29 goals.

Play-offs: Prem Lge, Charlton Athletic v Crystal Palace 1-2, 0-1; Leicester City v Stoke City 0-0, 1-0; Crystal Palace v Leicester City 1-2; Div 1, Bradford City v Blackpool 0-2, 3-0; Crewe Alexandra v Notts County 2-2, 0-1; Bradford City v Notts County 2-0; Div 2, Colchester United v Plymouth Argyle 1-0, 1-3; Hereford United v Darlington 1-2, 1-2; Darlington v Plymouth Argyle 0-1.

Sunderland, Derby County and Leicester City promoted to Prem Lge; Manchester City, Q.P.R and Bolton Wanderers relegated to Div 1; Swindon Town, Oxford United and

Alan Shearer led the way with 31 goals but Blackburn Rovers could not hold on to their Premiership title.

DIVISION PREMIER

	ARSENAL	ASTON VILLA	BLACKBURN	BOLTON	CHELSEA	COVENTRY	EVERTON	LEEDS	LIVERPOOL	MANCHESTER C	MANCHESTER U	MIDDLESBROUGH	NEWCASTLE	NOTTINGHAM F	Q.P.R.	SHEFFIELD W	SOUTHAMPTON	TOTTENHAM	WEST HAM	WIMBLEDON
1 ARSENAL		O21 2-0	N26 0-0	m05 2-1	D16 1-1	F03 1-1	J20 1-2	a06 2-1	m01 0-0	M05 3-1	N04 1-0	A20 1-1	M23 2-0	A29 1-1	D26 3-0	N21 4-2	S23 4-2	a15 0-0	S16 1-0	D30 1-3
2 ASTON VILLA	D02 1-1		F28 2-0	A30 1-0	O14 0-1	D16 4-1	O28 1-0	F03 3-0	J31 0-2	a27 0-1	A19 3-1	M19 0-0	N18 1-1	S23 1-1	M09 4-2	M06 3-2	a08 3-0	J21 2-1	a17 1-1	S16 2-0
3 BLACKBURN	a27 1-1	S09 1-1		F03 3-1	O28 3-0	S23 5-1	M30 0-3	M13 1-0	F24 2-3	D26 2-0	A28 1-2	D16 1-0	a08 2-1	N18 7-0	A19 1-0	J20 3-0	O14 2-1	D30 2-1	D02 4-2	a17 3-2
4 BOLTON	O30 1-0	F10 0-2	A26 2-1		a08 2-1	D30 1-2	O14 1-1	D27 0-2	D09 0-1	M30 1-1	F25 0-6	S09 1-1	A22 1-3	D02 1-1	S30 0-1	M23 2-1	a27 0-1	M20 2-3	N18 0-3	J13 1-0
5 CHELSEA	S30 1-0	a06 1-2	m05 2-3	N22 3-2		A30 2-2	A19 0-0	a13 4-1	D30 2-2	M12 1-1	O21 1-4	F04 5-0	D09 1-0	J20 1-0	M23 1-1	N04 0-0	S16 3-0	N25 0-0	F17 1-2	D26 1-2
6 COVENTRY	A26 0-0	S30 0-3	D09 5-0	M16 0-2	F10 1-0		D23 2-1	m05 0-0	a06 1-0	A23 2-1	N22 0-4	F24 0-0	J14 0-1	S09 1-1	a13 1-0	O21 0-1	J01 1-1	N04 2-3	M02 2-2	N25 3-3
7 EVERTON	A23 0-2	m05 1-0	N05 1-0	a06 3-0	J13 1-1	M09 2-2		D30 2-0	a16 1-1	F10 2-0	S09 2-3	D26 4-0	O01 1-3	F24 3-0	N22 2-0	N25 2-2	A26 2-0	O22 1-1	D11 3-0	M23 2-4
8 LEEDS	O14 0-3	A26 2-0	J01 0-0	M02 0-1	N18 1-0	O28 3-1	M17 2-2		A21 1-0	D02 0-1	D24 3-1	M30 0-1	a29 0-1	a08 1-3	S16 1-3	S30 2-0	a03 1-0	m02 1-3	J13 2-0	D09 1-1
9 LIVERPOOL	D23 3-1	M03 3-0	S16 3-0	S23 5-2	M16 2-0	O14 0-0	N18 1-2	J20 5-0		O28 6-0	D17 2-0	a27 1-0	a03 4-3	J01 4-2	A30 1-0	A19 1-0	D02 1-1	F03 0-0	a08 2-0	M13 2-2
10 MANCHESTER C	S10 0-1	N25 1-0	M02 1-1	N04 1-0	D23 0-1	J20 1-1	A30 0-2	O21 0-0	m05 2-2		a06 2-3	S23 0-1	F24 3-3	D18 1-1	F03 2-0	a13 1-0	M16 2-1	A19 1-1	J01 2-1	N22 1-0
11 MANCHESTER U	M20 1-0	J13 0-0	F10 1-0	S16 3-0	D02 1-1	a08 1-0	F21 2-0	a17 1-0	O01 2-2	O14 1-0		O28 2-0	D27 2-0	a28 5-0	D30 2-1	D09 2-2	N18 4-1	M24 1-0	A23 2-1	A26 3-1
12 MIDDLESBROUGH	J13 2-3	J01 0-2	S30 2-0	F17 1-4	A26 2-0	S16 2-1	M02 0-2	N04 1-1	N25 2-1	D09 4-1	m05 0-3		F10 1-2	M16 1-1	O21 1-0	a05 3-1	S12 0-0	N21 0-1	D23 4-2	a13 1-2
13 NEWCASTLE	J02 2-0	a14 1-0	N08 1-0	J20 2-1	S24 2-0	A19 3-0	D16 1-0	N25 2-1	N04 2-1	S16 3-1	M04 0-1	A30 1-0		D23 3-1	a06 2-1	F03 2-0	a17 1-0	m05 1-1	M18 3-0	O21 6-1
14 NOTTINGHAM F	F10 0-1	D10 1-1	a13 1-5	O21 3-2	A23 0-0	a17 0-0	S17 3-2	J31 2-1	M23 1-0	S30 3-0	N27 1-1	D30 1-0	m02 1-1		m05 3-0	D26 1-0	J13 1-0	a06 2-1	A26 1-1	N06 4-1
15 Q.P.R.	M02 1-1	D23 1-0	J13 0-1	D16 2-1	J02 1-2	N19 1-1	a08 3-1	M06 1-2	F11 1-2	A26 1-0	M16 1-1	D02 1-1	O14 2-3	O28 1-1		S09 0-3	M30 3-0	S25 2-3	a27 3-0	A23 0-3
16 SHEFFIELD W	a08 1-0	M16 2-0	A23 2-1	J01 4-2	a17 0-0	D04 4-3	a27 2-5	D16 6-2	J13 1-1	N18 1-1	S23 0-0	O15 0-1	A27 0-2	M02 1-3	F17 1-3		D23 2-2	S16 1-3	O28 0-1	F10 2-1
17 SOUTHAMPTON	D09 0-0	N20 0-1	a06 1-0	N25 1-0	F24 2-3	M25 1-0	F03 2-2	A30 1-1	O22 1-3	J31 1-1	a13 3-1	J20 2-1	S09 1-0	A19 3-4	N04 2-0	M20 0-1		D26 0-0	O02 0-0	m05 0-0
18 TOTTENHAM	N18 2-1	A23 0-1	M16 2-3	D23 2-2	a27 1-1	M30 3-1	D02 0-0	S09 2-1	A26 1-3	J13 1-0	J01 4-1	a08 1-1	O29 1-1	O14 0-1	D09 1-0	F24 1-0	M02 1-0		F12 0-1	S30 3-1
19 WEST HAM	F24 0-1	N04 1-4	O21 1-1	a13 1-0	S11 1-3	J31 3-2	S23 2-1	A19 1-2	N22 0-0	M23 4-2	J22 0-1	M09 2-0	F21 2-0	F03 1-0	N25 1-0	m05 1-1	D16 2-1	A30 1-1		a06 1-1
20 WIMBLEDON	M16 0-3	F24 3-3	D23 1-1	A19 3-2	M02 1-1	a27 0-2	J01 2-3	S23 2-4	S09 1-0	a08 3-0	F03 2-4	N18 0-0	D03 3-3	M30 1-0	J20 2-1	A30 2-2	O28 1-2	D16 0-1	O16 0-1	

John Aldridge scored 27 goals for Tranmere Rovers, although they still finished mid-table in the First Division.

DIVISION 1

	BARNSLEY	BIRMINGHAM	CHARLTON	C.PALACE	DERBY	GRIMSBY	HUDDERSFIELD	IPSWICH	LEICESTER	LUTON	MILLWALL	NORWICH	OLDHAM	PORTSMOUTH	PORT VALE	READING	SHEFFIELD U	SOUTHEND	STOKE	SUNDERLAND	TRANMERE	WATFORD	W.B.A.	WOLVERHAMPTON
1 BARNSLEY		S02 0-5	D16 1-2	J20 1-1	S23 2-0	m04 1-1	M19 3-0	M09 3-3	O07 2-2	N25 1-0	F27 3-1	a02 2-2	A19 2-1	N21 0-0	O21 1-1	a13 0-1	S17 2-2	M23 1-1	D26 3-1	a06 0-1	A29 2-1	F03 2-1	a30 1-1	N04 1-0
2 BIRMINGHAM	F20 0-0		J14 3-4	S09 0-0	N21 1-4	O21 3-1	M12 2-0	A12 3-1	N26 2-2	a13 4-0	N04 2-2	A26 3-1	S30 0-0	a02 2-0	a06 3-1	m05 1-2	M02 0-1	O08 2-0	S12 1-1	M17 0-2	D23 1-0	D09 1-0	M20 1-1	M05 2-0
3 CHARLTON	S30 1-1	A19 3-1		F04 0-0	a14 0-0	O07 0-1	S02 2-1	D09 0-2	a02 0-1	a05 1-1	M09 2-0	O21 1-1	S16 1-1	D26 2-1	N25 2-2	N21 2-1	F17 1-1	M05 0-3	M23 2-1	N05 1-1	a30 0-0	A29 2-1	J20 4-1	m05 1-1
4 C.PALACE	A12 4-3	F27 3-2	A26 1-1		N25 0-0	M05 5-0	S16 0-0	J13 1-1	a06 0-1	M19 2-0	O22 1-2	m05 0-1	D09 2-2	M23 0-0	a02 2-2	N04 0-2	F10 0-0	a13 2-0	S30 1-1	O07 0-1	M12 2-1	F17 4-0	M09 1-0	N22 3-2
5 DERBY	D09 4-1	a20 1-1	N18 2-0	a28 2-1		A26 1-1	M02 3-2	O14 1-1	S10 0-1	F21 1-1	O01 2-2	J01 2-1	O28 2-1	F24 3-2	A13 0-0	J13 3-0	D02 4-2	S13 1-0	M30 3-1	D23 3-1	a08 6-2	M16 1-1	N11 3-0	F10 0-0
6 GRIMSBY	N11 3-1	M30 2-1	D02 1-2	M16 0-2	F03 1-1		J01 1-1	a08 3-1	D23 2-2	A29 0-0	J20 1-2	S23 2-2	O14 1-1	A19 2-1	S16 1-0	F17 0-0	a20 0-2	D16 1-1	O28 1-0	M03 0-4	a27 1-1	S02 0-0	N18 1-0	M12 3-0
7 HUDDERSFIELD	S12 3-0	A30 4-2	F20 2-2	F24 3-0	D26 0-1	M24 1-3		S09 2-1	N21 3-1	M09 1-0	a13 3-0	N04 3-2	J20 0-0	m05 0-1	O07 0-2	a02 3-1	S24 1-2	a06 3-1	D30 1-1	O21 1-1	F03 1-0	A19 1-0	D16 4-1	N25 2-1
8 IPSWICH	D23 2-2	J20 2-0	S23 1-5	A19 1-0	a02 1-0	N04 2-2	m01 2-1		M03 4-2	O22 0-1	m05 0-0	a14 2-1	M19 2-1	N25 3-2	J01 5-1	a06 1-2	D16 1-1	N22 1-1	A30 4-1	S02 3-0	M16 1-2	S16 4-2	F03 2-1	O07 1-2
9 LEICESTER	D02 2-2	a27 3-0	O14 1-1	O28 2-3	F28 0-0	M09 2-1	a20 2-1	M13 0-2		F03 1-1	M23 2-1	D17 3-2	a17 2-0	A30 4-2	F17 1-1	S16 1-1	M30 0-2	S23 1-3	A19 2-3	J21 0-0	N19 0-1	N11 1-0	a09 1-2	S02 1-0
10 LUTON	a27 1-3	N18 0-0	O29 0-1	M02 0-0	S02 1-2	F10 3-2	D23 2-2	M30 1-2	A26 1-1		F17 1-0	A13 1-3	N11 1-1	S30 3-1	a30 3-2	F27 1-2	J31 1-0	J13 3-1	a09 1-2	S16 0-2	D02 3-2	a20 0-0	O14 1-2	D10 2-3
11 MILLWALL	S09 0-1	a10 2-0	D05 0-2	M30 1-4	D16 0-1	A12 2-1	N18 0-0	N11 2-1	J01 1-1	S13 1-0		F24 2-1	A20 0-1	F27 1-1	J13 1-2	F10 1-1	M16 1-0	A26 0-0	a27 2-3	S23 1-2	O14 2-2	D02 1-2	O28 2-1	M02 0-1
12 NORWICH	O14 3-1	F04 1-1	M30 0-1	N11 1-0	M23 1-0	D09 2-2	a08 2-0	N19 2-1	S30 0-1	J20 0-1	S16 0-0		A30 2-1	M09 1-1	S02 2-1	D30 3-3	F28 0-0	D26 0-1	D02 0-1	A19 0-0	O29 1-1	a27 1-2	a20 2-2	F17 2-3
13 OLDHAM	J13 0-1	D16 4-0	F24 1-1	S23 3-1	a06 0-1	a02 1-0	A12 3-0	S12 1-1	M16 3-1	m05 1-0	N21 2-2	F10 2-0		O07 1-1	N05 2-2	O21 2-1	A26 2-1	N25 0-1	a30 2-0	M12 1-2	M03 1-2	D23 0-0	S09 1-2	a13 0-0
14 PORTSMOUTH	a20 0-0	O14 0-1	M02 2-1	J01 2-3	S16 2-2	J13 3-1	N11 1-1	a27 0-1	F10 2-1	D16 4-0	S02 0-1	D23 1-0	D02 2-1		M27 1-2	A26 0-0	a08 1-2	A12 4-2	N18 3-3	F17 2-2	S23 0-2	O28 4-2	M30 0-2	M16 0-2
15 PORT VALE	M30 3-0	O29 1-2	a27 1-3	O15 1-2	J20 1-1	a16 1-0	D02 1-0	M23 2-1	S12 0-2	a23 1-0	A19 0-1	M20 1-0	a08 1-3	S09 0-2		D09 3-2	N11 2-3	M09 2-1	M12 1-0	A30 1-1	a20 1-1	N18 1-1	D26 3-1	S30 2-2
16 READING	N18 0-0	N11 0-1	a20 0-0	a08 0-2	A19 3-2	S12 0-2	O14 3-1	O28 1-4	F24 1-1	S09 3-1	A29 1-2	M16 0-3	M30 2-0	F04 0-1	S23 2-2		a27 0-3	M19 3-3	J20 1-0	D16 1-1	J01 1-0	M02 0-0	D02 3-1	a30 3-0
17 SHEFFIELD U	F24 1-0	D26 1-1	S12 2-0	A29 2-3	O07 0-2	N21 1-2	D09 0-2	S30 2-2	O21 1-3	M23 1-0	F13 2-0	S09 2-1	F03 2-1	N04 4-1	m04 1-1	N25 0-0		a02 3-0	M09 0-0	a13 0-0	A19 0-2	J20 1-1	F20 1-2	a06 2-1
18 SOUTHEND	J01 0-0	D02 3-1	M16 1-1	N19 1-1	F17 1-2	S30 1-0	O28 0-0	a20 2-1	D09 2-1	A19 0-1	F03 2-0	M02 1-1	a27 1-1	J20 2-1	D20 2-1	S01 0-0	O14 2-1		N11 2-4	F27 0-2	M30 2-0	a08 1-1	A29 2-1	S16 2-1
19 STOKE	M02 2-0	F17 1-0	a17 1-0	D16 1-2	O22 1-1	a06 1-2	M16 1-1	F10 3-1	J13 1-0	N04 5-0	N25 1-0	O07 1-1	S02 0-1	a13 2-1	A27 0-1	A12 1-1	D23 2-2	m05 1-0		N22 1-0	S16 0-0	F28 2-0	S24 2-1	a03 2-0
20 SUNDERLAND	O28 2-1	a16 3-0	a08 0-0	D03 1-0	M09 3-0	J24 1-0	M30 3-2	F20 1-0	A12 1-2	F24 1-0	D09 6-0	J14 0-1	M23 1-0	S12 1-1	F10 0-0	S30 2-2	N18 2-0	S09 1-0	a21 0-0		J30 0-0	O14 1-1	a27 0-0	A26 2-0
21 TRANMERE	F10 1-3	M09 2-2	S09 0-0	F20 2-3	N04 5-1	N25 0-1	A26 3-1	a17 5-2	a13 1-1	O07 1-0	a02 2-2	a06 1-1	D26 2-0	D09 1-2	N22 2-1	M23 2-1	J13 1-1	O21 3-0	F24 0-0	m05 2-0		S30 2-3	S12 2-2	A12 2-2
22 WATFORD	A26 2-3	S23 1-1	F10 1-2	S12 0-0	M05 0-0	a23 6-3	J13 0-1	F24 2-3	m05 0-1	N21 1-1	O07 0-1	N26 0-2	M09 2-1	a06 1-2	a13 5-2	a16 4-2	A12 2-1	N04 2-2	S09 3-0	a02 3-3	D16 3-0		M23 1-1	O21 1-1
23 W.B.A.	M16 2-1	S17 1-0	A12 1-0	D23 2-3	m05 3-2	a13 3-1	S30 1-2	A26 0-0	N05 2-3	a02 0-2	a06 1-0	N21 1-4	F27 1-0	O21 2-1	M02 1-1	O07 2-0	S02 3-1	F10 3-1	D09 0-1	N25 0-1	F17 1-1	M12 4-4		J13 0-0
24 WOLVERHAMPTON	a08 2-2	M23 3-2	N12 0-0	a20 0-2	A30 3-0	S09 4-1	a27 0-0	D03 2-2	F21 2-3	S23 0-0	D26 1-1	S13 0-2	N18 1-3	D30 2-2	D16 0-1	M09 1-1	O28 1-0	F24 2-0	O14 1-4	F03 3-0	J20 2-1	M30 3-0	A20 1-1	

Season 1995-96

Bradford City promoted to Div 1; Millwall, Watford and Luton Town relegated to Div 2; Preston North End, Gillingham, Bury and Plymouth Argyle promoted to Div 2; Carlisle United, Swansea City, Brighton & Hove Albion and Hull Clty relegated to Div 3.

	BLACKPOOL	BOURNEMOUTH	BRADFORD C	BRENTFORD	BRIGHTON	BRISTOL C	BRISTOL R	BURNLEY	CARLISLE	CHESTERFIELD	CREWE	HULL	NOTTS CO	OXFORD	PETERBOROUGH	ROTHERHAM	SHREWSBURY	STOCKPORT	SWANSEA	SWINDON	WALSALL	WREXHAM	WYCOMBE	YORK
1 BLACKPOOL		S12 2-1	D16 4-1	M30 1-0	F24 2-1	J20 3-0	O31 3-0	M12 3-1	M23 3-1	O14 0-0	S23 2-1	F03 1-1	M09 1-0	O28 1-1	A29 2-1	a08 1-2	F20 2-1	S09 0-1	F13 4-0	a20 1-1	a27 1-2	A19 2-0	J23 1-1	N18 1-3
2 BOURNEMOUTH	F17 1-0		J20 3-1	N18 1-0	S24 3-1	J06 1-1	M30 2-1	O14 0-2	O28 2-0	a27 2-0	S16 0-4	D23 2-0	F27 0-2	M02 0-1	A19 3-0	S02 2-1	J02 0-2	D16 3-2	a09 3-1	O31 0-0	a20 0-0	A29 1-1	F03 2-3	M16 2-2
3 BRADFORD C	S30 2-1	A12 1-0		a26 2-1	J13 1-3	S16 3-0	O14 2-3	O28 2-2	a08 3-1	a20 2-1	J31 2-1	N18 1-1	M19 1-0	D23 1-0	D09 2-1	M16 2-0	A26 3-1	F10 0-1	M30 5-1	a30 1-1	O31 1-0	F27 2-0	S02 0-4	M02 2-2
4 BRENTFORD	O07 1-2	m04 2-0	N25 2-1		D26 0-1	F17 2-2	D09 0-0	F03 1-0	M19 1-1	S30 1-2	a06 2-1	A29 1-0	a13 0-0	A19 1-0	O21 3-0	F27 1-1	N04 0-2	a02 1-0	M23 0-0	S02 0-2	S16 1-0	M09 1-0	J30 1-0	J20 2-0
5 BRIGHTON	S16 1-2	D09 2-0	A19 0-0	M02 0-0		F27 0-2	O28 2-0	a09 1-0	a20 1-0	D22 0-2	F17 2-2	M16 4-0	S02 1-0	M12 1-2	J20 1-2	M30 1-1	S30 2-2	J01 1-1	O31 0-2	O14 1-3	N18 0-3	F03 2-2	A29 1-2	m09 1-3
6 BRISTOL C	A12 1-1	F10 3-0	F24 2-1	S12 0-0	S09 0-1		J16 0-2	M09 0-1	N18 1-1	O31 2-1	J13 3-2	O14 4-0	D09 0-2	a20 0-2	F20 0-1	a27 4-3	F13 2-0	A26 1-0	D26 1-0	M30 0-0	O28 0-2	M23 3-1	S30 0-0	a08 1-1
7 BRISTOL R	a13 1-1	O07 0-2	a02 1-0	S23 2-0	a06 1-0	M16 2-4		A29 1-0	J20 1-1	M26 1-0	D23 1-2	J06 2-1	O21 0-3	D16 2-0	N04 1-1	F17 1-0	M02 2-1	N25 1-3	A19 2-2	S16 1-4	F03 2-0	S02 1-2	m04 2-1	F27 1-0
8 BURNLEY	M02 0-1	a02 0-0	a06 2-3	A26 1-0	O21 3-0	D23 0-0	a23 0-1		D02 2-0	D09 2-2	F10 0-1	S16 2-1	N04 3-4	J30 0-2	a13 2-1	A12 2-1	m04 2-1	J13 4-3	S30 3-0	M16 0-0	S06 1-1	N25 2-2	O07 1-1	F17 3-3
9 CARLISLE	J01 1-2	a06 4-0	O21 2-2	F10 2-1	N04 1-0	m04 2-1	A12 1-2	S09 2-0		J13 1-1	a02 1-0	S23 2-0	O07 0-0	F24 1-2	S12 1-1	M26 2-0	M16 1-1	M02 0-1	F20 3-0	A26 0-1	D16 1-1	a13 1-2	N26 4-2	a23 2-0
10 CHESTERFIELD	a02 1-0	N25 3-0	N04 2-1	D16 2-2	M09 1-0	a13 1-1	M23 2-1	S23 4-2	A19 3-0		O07 1-2	S02 0-0	m04 1-0	J20 1-0	D26 1-1	S16 3-0	O21 1-0	a06 1-2	F03 3-2	a23 1-3	a16 1-1	M19 1-1	F17 3-1	A29 2-1
11 CREWE	D09 1-2	F24 2-0	M23 1-2	O28 3-1	S12 3-1	D05 4-2	M09 1-2	M19 3-1	O14 2-1	M30 3-0		O31 1-0	S30 2-2	a27 1-2	a30 2-1	a20 0-2	S09 3-0	F20 0-1	N18 4-1	a08 0-2	A29 1-0	D26 0-0	J20 2-0	M05 1-1
12 HULL	A26 2-1	M09 1-1	m04 2-3	M05 0-1	J23 0-0	a02 2-3	F10 1-3	F24 3-0	D09 2-5	M12 0-0	a13 1-2		M26 0-0	S09 0-0	N25 2-3	J13 1-4	O07 2-3	O21 1-1	S12 0-0	A12 0-1	M23 1-0	N04 1-1	a06 4-2	S30 0-3
13 NOTTS CO	D23 1-1	S09 2-0	A29 0-2	N01 4-0	a23 2-1	S23 2-2	a09 4-2	a20 1-1	M30 3-1	N18 4-1	D16 0-1	M02 1-0		M16 1-1	F03 1-0	O14 2-1	F24 1-1	S12 1-0	a27 4-0	O28 1-3	M06 2-1	J20 1-0	A19 2-0	M12 2-2
14 OXFORD	a06 1-0	D26 2-0	M09 2-0	J13 2-1	F10 1-1	N04 2-0	S30 1-2	M23 5-0	S16 4-0	A12 1-0	N25 1-0	F27 2-0	a16 1-1		m04 4-0	A26 1-1	a23 6-0	O07 2-1	D09 5-1	M19 3-0	F17 3-2	a02 0-0	O21 1-4	S03 2-0
15 PETERBOROUGH	M26 0-0	J13 4-5	S23 3-1	a08 0-1	A12 3-1	S02 1-1	a20 0-0	O31 0-2	F17 6-1	M02 0-1	M16 3-1	a27 3-1	A26 0-1	N18 1-1		D16 1-0	F10 2-2	D19 0-1	O14 1-1	M05 0-2	M30 2-3	S16 1-0	F27 3-0	O28 6-1
16 ROTHERHAM	O21 2-1	F20 1-0	J23 2-0	S09 1-0	O07 1-0	N25 2-3	S12 1-0	J20 1-0	A29 2-2	F24 0-1	N04 2-2	A19 1-1	a02 2-0	F03 1-0	S30 5-1		a06 2-2	a23 2-0	M09 1-1	D09 0-2	D26 0-1	m04 0-1	M23 0-0	J06 2-2
17 SHREWSBURY	S02 0-2	M23 1-2	F03 1-1	a20 2-1	D16 2-1	A29 4-1	D26 1-1	N18 3-0	D30 1-1	a09 0-0	F27 2-3	M30 1-1	S16 0-1	O31 2-0	M19 1-1	O28 3-1		S23 1-2	J20 1-2	a27 1-2	A19 0-2	a17 2-2	M09 1-1	O14 2-1
18 STOCKPORT	F27 1-1	S30 3-1	J10 1-2	O14 1-1	M23 3-1	M19 0-0	a27 2-0	A19 0-0	D26 2-0	O28 0-1	S02 1-1	a08 0-0	F17 2-0	M30 4-2	M09 0-1	O31 1-1	D09 0-2		A29 2-0	N18 1-1	J20 0-1	F13 2-3	S16 1-1	a20 3-0
19 SWANSEA	M16 0-2	O21 1-1	O07 2-0	M12 2-1	a13 2-1	M02 2-1	J13 2-2	D16 2-4	S01 1-1	A26 3-2	m04 2-1	F17 0-0	N25 0-0	S23 1-1	a02 0-0	D02 0-0	A12 3-1	F06 0-3		F10 0-1	F27 2-1	a06 1-3	N04 1-2	S16 0-1
20 SWINDON	N04 1-1	a13 2-2	S13 4-1	F21 2-2	a03 3-2	O07 2-0	F24 2-1	a17 0-0	F03 2-1	S09 1-1	O21 2-1	J20 3-0	a06 1-0	A30 1-1	M23 2-0	S23 1-0	N25 0-1	m04 0-0	J10 3-0		M09 1-1	D16 1-1	D26 0-0	A19 3-0
21 WALSALL	N25 1-1	N04 0-0	a13 2-1	F24 0-1	m04 2-1	a06 2-1	A26 1-1	a30 3-1	S30 2-1	M16 3-0	M12 3-2	a23 3-0	F10 0-0	S12 2-2	O07 1-1	M02 3-1	J13 3-0	A12 0-2	S09 4-1	D23 0-0		O21 1-2	a02 0-1	D09 2-0
22 WREXHAM	J13 1-1	M12 5-0	S09 1-2	D23 2-2	A26 1-1	J23 0-0	F20 3-2	a27 0-2	O31 3-2	M05 3-0	M02 2-3	a20 5-0	A12 1-1	O14 2-1	F24 1-0	N18 7-0	S12 1-1	M16 2-3	O28 1-0	S30 4-3	a08 3-0		D09 1-0	M30 2-3
23 WYCOMBE	F10 0-1	A26 1-2	M26 5-2	M16 2-1	M06 0-2	D16 1-1	N18 1-1	M30 4-1	a27 4-0	S12 1-0	A12 1-1	O28 2-2	J13 1-1	a08 0-3	S09 1-1	a16 1-1	D23 2-0	F24 4-1	a20 0-1	M02 1-2	O14 1-0	S23 1-1		O31 2-1
24 YORK	m04 0-2	M26 3-1	D26 0-3	A12 2-2	N25 3-1	O21 0-1	S09 0-1	S12 1-1	M09 1-1	a30 0-1	A26 2-3	D16 0-1	M23 1-3	F20 1-0	a06 3-1	F10 2-2	a02 1-2	N04 2-2	F24 0-0	J13 2-0	S23 1-0	O07 1-0	a13 2-1	

DIVISION 3

	BARNET	BURY	CAMBRIDGE	CARDIFF	CHESTER	COLCHESTER	DARLINGTON	DONCASTER	EXETER	FULHAM	GILLINGHAM	HARTLEPOOL	HEREFORD	LEYTON O	LINCOLN	MANSFIELD	NORTHAMPTON	PLYMOUTH	PRESTON	ROCHDALE	SCARBOROUGH	SCUNTHORPE	TORQUAY	WIGAN
1 BARNET		D09 0-0	F27 2-0	a02 1-0	M09 1-1	A19 1-1	S30 1-1	N04 1-1	O07 3-2	m04 3-0	A29 0-2	a13 5-1	J20 1-3	N25 3-0	S02 3-1	D26 0-0	a06 2-0	S16 1-2	J06 1-0	O21 0-4	M23 1-0	F03 1-0	M16 4-0	F17 5-0
2 BURY	S23 0-0		S16 1-2	m04 3-0	A19 1-1	D23 0-0	N04 0-0	J06 4-1	N25 2-0	a02 3-0	D16 1-0	J01 0-3	M19 2-0	O07 2-1	F17 7-1	a06 0-2	J20 0-1	S02 0-5	A29 0-0	M16 1-1	O21 0-2	M02 3-0	a13 1-0	F27 2-1
3 CAMBRIDGE	S09 1-1	F24 2-4		O07 4-2	J06 1-1	A29 3-1	O21 0-1	a13 2-2	S12 1-1	F13 0-0	F03 0-0	S30 0-1	A19 2-2	m04 2-0	D09 2-1	M23 0-2	a02 0-1	M09 2-3	a16 2-1	a06 2-1	N04 4-1	J20 1-2	N25 1-1	D26 2-1
4 CARDIFF	O14 1-1	N18 0-1	M30 1-1		D26 0-0	O28 1-2	F20 0-2	F03 3-2	A29 0-1	M09 1-4	F24 2-0	D09 2-0	a27 3-2	J06 0-0	a08 1-1	S30 3-0	A19 0-1	a20 0-1	M23 0-1	J20 1-0	S12 2-1	O31 0-1	S09 0-0	M05 3-0
5 CHESTER	D23 0-2	J13 1-1	M26 1-1	M02 4-0		F27 1-1	N25 4-1	O07 0-3	M16 2-2	O21 1-1	S23 1-1	A12 2-0	S02 2-1	a02 1-1	S16 5-1	m04 2-1	a23 1-0	A26 3-1	D16 1-1	a13 1-2	a06 5-0	F17 3-0	N04 4-1	M19 0-0
6 COLCHESTER	J13 3-2	M09 1-0	M19 2-1	a06 1-0	S09 1-2		F24 1-1	m04 1-0	N04 1-1	a13 2-2	a16 1-1	O07 4-1	S23 2-0	D26 0-0	A26 3-0	N25 1-3	O21 1-0	A12 2-1	S12 2-2	a02 1-0	F06 1-1	D16 2-1	M23 3-1	F10 1-2
7 DARLINGTON	D16 1-1	a20 4-0	a08 0-0	S02 0-1	a27 3-1	S16 2-2		J16 1-2	J20 1-0	A29 1-1	O14 1-0	F27 1-0	M23 1-0	F03 2-0	M30 3-2	F17 1-1	J06 1-2	O28 2-0	J30 1-2	A19 0-1	S23 1-2	N18 0-0	M09 1-2	O31 2-1
8 DONCASTER	a20 1-0	F10 0-1	O30 2-1	A26 0-0	M30 1-2	N18 3-2	M02 1-2		D02 2-0	F26 0-2	a08 0-1	S02 1-0	O14 0-0	D16 4-1	F05 1-1	M25 0-0	S16 1-0	F17 0-0	O28 2-2	S23 0-3	A12 1-0	M16 2-0	J13 1-0	a27 2-1
9 EXETER	M30 1-0	a27 1-1	F17 1-0	M12 2-0	D30 1-2	a20 2-2	A12 0-1	M09 1-0		S16 2-1	O31 0-0	J30 1-0	a08 0-2	S23 2-2	O28 1-1	F13 2-2	F27 1-2	M23 1-1	N18 1-1	D16 2-0	A26 2-0	S02 1-0	D26 0-0	O14 0-4
10 FULHAM	N18 1-1	O14 0-0	M16 0-2	D19 4-2	a08 2-0	O31 1-1	M05 2-2	S09 3-1	F24 2-1		a27 0-0	F10 2-2	O28 0-0	M26 2-1	M02 1-2	A12 4-2	D16 1-3	M30 4-0	S23 2-2	S12 1-1	J13 1-0	J30 1-3	A26 4-0	a20 1-0
11 GILLINGHAM	F13 1-0	S30 3-0	A26 3-0	S16 1-0	J09 3-1	S02 0-1	a02 0-0	O21 4-0	a13 1-0	N25 1-0		a06 2-0	F17 1-1	M23 1-1	J13 2-0	J30 2-0	N04 0-0	D26 1-0	M09 1-1	O07 1-0	m04 1-0	F27 0-0	F10 2-0	A12 2-1
12 HARTLEPOOL	O31 0-0	M23 1-2	D16 1-2	S23 2-1	J20 2-1	M30 2-1	S09 1-1	F20 0-1	A19 0-0	M12 1-0	O28 1-1		M05 0-1	F24 4-1	a20 3-0	M09 1-1	A29 2-1	N18 2-2	a27 0-2	F03 1-1	J06 1-1	O14 2-0	S12 2-2	a08 1-2
13 HEREFORD	A12 4-1	A26 3-4	J13 5-2	N26 1-3	F20 1-0	D09 1-1	a23 0-1	a02 1-0	O21 2-2	a06 1-0	S12 0-0	a30 4-1		a13 3-2	M27 1-0	N04 0-1	M02 1-0	a16 3-0	S09 0-1	m04 2-0	F24 0-0	D19 3-0	O07 2-1	S30 2-2
14 LEYTON O	a27 3-3	M30 0-2	N18 3-1	F10 4-1	O14 0-2	M02 0-1	A26 1-1	S30 3-1	D09 0-3	S02 1-0	J01 0-1	S16 4-1	O31 0-1		M16 2-0	J13 1-0	F17 2-0	F27 0-1	a20 0-2	D22 2-0	M19 1-0	a08 0-0	A12 1-0	O28 1-1
15 LINCOLN	M19 1-2	S12 2-2	S23 1-3	O21 0-1	F24 0-0	F03 0-0	O07 0-2	M23 4-0	a06 0-1	D26 4-0	A19 0-3	N04 1-1	F13 2-1	J16 1-0		a13 2-1	N25 1-0	D16 0-0	J20 0-0	S09 1-2	a02 3-1	A28 2-2	m04 5-0	M09 2-4
16 MANSFIELD	M02 2-1	O28 1-5	J23 2-1	D16 1-1	N18 3-4	a27 1-2	S12 2-2	A29 0-0	J06 1-1	J20 1-0	M16 0-1	D23 0-3	a20 1-2	A19 0-0	N01 1-2		F03 0-0	O14 1-1	a08 0-0	a16 2-2	S09 2-0	S23 1-1	a23 2-0	M30 1-0
17 NORTHAMPTON	O28 0-2	A12 4-1	O14 3-0	J13 1-0	M23 1-0	a08 2-1	F10 1-1	F24 3-3	S09 0-0	S30 2-0	a20 1-1	M19 0-0	D26 1-1	S12 1-2	a27 1-1	A26 3-3		J30 1-0	O31 1-2	F20 2-1	M09 2-0	M30 1-2	D09 1-1	N18 0-0
18 PLYMOUTH	F24 1-1	F20 1-0	D23 1-0	N04 0-0	F03 4-2	J20 1-1	a06 0-1	S12 3-1	J01 2-2	O07 3-0	M02 1-0	m04 3-0	A29 0-1	S09 1-1	S30 3-0	a02 1-0	M16 1-0		A19 0-2	N25 2-0	a13 5-1	J23 1-3	O21 4-3	D09 3-1
19 PRESTON	F10 0-1	M26 0-0	S02 3-3	J01 5-0	S30 2-0	F17 2-0	M16 1-1	a06 1-0	m04 2-0	D09 1-1	D23 0-0	N25 3-0	F27 2-2	N04 4-0	A12 1-2	O21 6-0	a13 0-3	J13 3-2		M02 1-2	O07 3-2	S16 2-2	a02 1-0	A26 1-1
20 ROCHDALE	a08 0-4	F13 1-1	O28 3-1	A12 3-3	O31 1-3	O14 1-1	J13 1-2	D09 1-0	S30 4-2	F17 1-1	M30 2-0	A26 4-0	N18 0-0	M09 1-0	F27 3-3	S16 1-1	S02 1-2	a27 0-1	M12 0-3		F10 0-2	a20 1-1	M19 3-0	M23 0-2
21 SCARBOROUGH	J09 1-1	a09 0-2	a20 2-0	F17 1-0	O28 0-0	M16 0-0	D09 1-2	J20 0-2	F03 0-0	A19 2-2	N18 0-2	M02 1-2	S16 2-2	A30 2-1	O14 0-0	F27 1-1	D23 2-1	O31 2-2	M30 1-2	J23 1-1		a27 1-4	S30 2-1	S02 0-0
22 SCUNTHORPE	A26 2-0	a16 1-2	A12 1-2	a13 1-1	S12 0-2	S30 1-0	m04 3-3	a23 2-2	M26 4-0	M23 3-1	S09 1-1	a02 2-1	M09 0-1	O21 2-0	M05 2-3	D09 1-1	O07 0-0	F10 1-1	F24 1-2	N04 1-3	N25 3-3		a06 1-0	J13 3-1
23 TORQUAY	F06 1-1	O31 0-2	a27 0-3	F27 0-0	a20 1-1	J01 2-3	D23 0-1	A19 1-2	M02 0-2	F03 2-1	M12 0-0	F17 0-0	M30 1-1	J20 2-1	N18 0-2	S02 1-1	S23 3-0	a08 0-2	O14 0-4	A29 1-0	D16 0-0	O28 1-8		S16 1-1
24 WIGAN	S12 1-0	S09 1-2	M02 3-1	M16 3-1	A29 2-1	J30 2-0	a13 1-1	N25 2-0	a02 1-0	N04 1-1	J20 2-1	O21 1-0	D16 2-1	a06 1-0	D23 1-1	O07 2-6	m04 1-2	S23 0-1	F03 0-1	J02 2-0	F20 2-0	A19 2-1	F24 3-0	

LEAGUE TABLES

FA PREMIER LEAGUE

	P	W	D	L	F	A	W	D	L	F	A	Pts
Manchester U	38	15	4	0	36	9	10	3	6	37	26	82
Newcastle U	38	17	1	1	38	9	7	5	7	28	28	78
Liverpool	38	14	4	1	46	13	6	7	6	24	21	71
Aston Villa	38	11	5	3	32	15	7	4	8	20	20	63
Arsenal	38	10	7	2	30	16	7	5	7	19	16	63
Everton	38	10	5	4	35	19	7	5	7	29	25	61
Blackburn R	38	14	2	3	44	19	4	5	10	17	28	61
Tottenham H	38	9	5	5	26	19	7	8	4	24	19	61
Nottingham F	38	11	6	2	29	17	4	7	8	21	37	58
West Ham U	38	9	5	5	25	21	5	4	10	18	31	51
Chelsea	38	7	7	5	30	22	5	7	7	16	22	50
Middlesbrough	38	8	3	8	27	27	3	7	9	8	23	43
Leeds U	38	8	3	8	21	21	4	4	11	19	36	43
Wimbledon	38	5	6	8	27	33	5	5	9	28	37	41
Sheffield W	38	7	5	7	30	31	3	5	11	18	30	40
Coventry C	38	6	7	6	21	23	2	7	10	21	37	38
Southampton	38	7	7	5	21	18	2	4	13	13	34	38
Manchester C	38	7	7	5	21	19	2	4	13	12	39	38
Q.P.R.	38	6	5	8	25	26	3	1	15	13	31	33
Bolton W	38	5	4	10	16	31	3	1	15	23	40	29

DIVISION 1

	P	W	D	L	F	A	W	D	L	F	A	Pts
Sunderland	46	13	8	2	32	10	9	9	5	27	23	83
Derby Co	46	14	8	1	48	22	7	8	8	23	29	79
Crystal Palace	46	9	9	5	34	22	11	6	6	33	26	75
Stoke C	46	13	6	4	32	15	7	7	9	28	34	73
Leicester C	46	9	7	7	32	29	10	7	6	34	31	71
Charlton A	46	8	11	4	28	23	9	9	5	29	22	71
Ipswich T	46	13	5	5	45	30	6	7	10	34	39	69
Huddersfield T	46	14	4	5	42	23	3	8	12	19	35	63
Sheffield U	46	9	7	7	29	25	7	7	9	28	29	62
Barnsley	46	9	10	4	34	28	5	8	10	26	38	60
W.B.A.	46	11	5	7	34	29	5	7	11	26	39	60
Port Vale	46	10	5	8	30	29	5	10	8	29	37	60
Tranmere R	46	9	9	5	42	29	5	8	10	22	31	59
Southend U	46	11	8	4	30	22	4	6	13	22	39	59
Birmingham C	46	11	7	5	37	23	4	6	13	24	41	58
Norwich C	46	7	9	7	26	24	7	6	10	33	31	57
Grimsby	46	8	10	5	27	25	6	4	13	28	44	56
Oldham A	46	10	7	6	33	20	4	7	12	21	30	56
Reading	46	8	7	8	28	30	5	10	8	26	33	56
Wolverh'pton W	46	8	9	6	34	28	5	7	11	22	34	55
Portsmouth	46	8	6	9	34	32	5	7	11	27	37	52
Millwall	46	7	6	10	23	28	6	7	10	20	35	52
Watford	46	7	8	8	40	33	3	10	10	22	37	48
Luton T	46	7	6	10	30	34	4	6	13	10	30	45

DIVISION 2

	P	W	D	L	F	A	W	D	L	F	A	Pts
Swindon T	46	12	10	1	37	16	13	7	3	34	18	92
Oxford U	46	17	4	2	52	14	7	7	9	24	25	83
Blackpool	46	14	5	4	41	20	9	8	6	26	20	82
Notts Co	46	14	6	3	42	21	7	9	7	21	18	78
Crewe A	46	13	3	7	40	24	9	4	10	37	36	73
Bradford C	46	15	4	4	41	25	7	3	13	30	44	73
Chesterfield	46	14	6	3	39	21	6	6	11	17	30	72
Wrexham	46	12	6	5	51	27	6	10	7	25	28	70
Stockport Co	46	8	9	6	30	20	11	4	8	31	27	70
Bristol R	46	12	4	7	29	28	8	6	9	28	32	70
Walsall	46	12	7	4	38	20	7	5	11	22	25	69
Wycombe	46	9	8	6	36	26	6	7	10	27	33	60
Bristol C	46	10	6	7	28	22	5	9	9	27	38	60
Bournemouth	46	12	5	6	33	25	4	5	14	18	45	58
Brentford	46	12	6	5	24	15	3	7	13	19	34	58
Rotherham U	46	11	7	5	31	20	3	7	13	23	42	56
Burnley	46	9	8	6	35	28	5	5	13	21	40	55
Shrewsbury T	46	7	8	8	32	29	6	6	11	26	41	53
Peterborough U	46	9	6	8	40	27	4	7	12	19	39	52
York C	46	8	6	9	28	29	5	7	11	30	44	52
Carlisle U	46	11	6	6	35	20	1	7	15	22	52	49
Swansea C	46	8	8	7	27	29	3	6	14	16	50	47
Brighton & H.A.	46	6	7	10	25	31	4	3	16	21	38	40
Hull C	46	4	8	11	26	37	1	8	14	10	41	31

DIVISION 3

	P	W	D	L	F	A	W	D	L	F	A	Pts
Preston N.E.	46	11	8	4	44	22	12	9	2	34	16	86
Gillingham	46	16	6	1	33	6	6	11	6	16	14	83
Bury	46	11	6	6	33	21	11	7	5	33	27	79
Plymouth A	46	14	5	4	41	20	8	7	8	27	29	78
Darlington	46	10	6	7	30	21	10	12	1	30	21	78
Hereford	46	13	5	5	40	22	7	9	7	25	25	74
Colchester U	46	13	7	3	37	22	5	11	7	24	29	72
Chester C	46	11	9	3	45	22	7	7	9	27	31	70
Barnet	46	13	6	4	40	19	5	10	8	25	26	70
Wigan A	46	15	3	5	36	21	5	7	11	26	35	70
Northampton T	46	9	10	4	32	22	9	3	11	19	22	67
Scunthorpe U	46	8	8	7	36	30	7	7	9	31	31	60
Doncaster	46	11	6	6	25	19	5	5	13	24	41	59
Exeter C	46	9	9	5	25	22	4	9	10	21	31	57
Rochdale	46	7	8	8	32	33	7	5	11	25	28	55
Cambridge U	46	8	8	7	34	30	6	4	13	27	41	54
Fulham	46	10	9	4	39	26	2	8	13	18	37	53
Lincoln C	46	8	7	8	32	26	5	7	11	25	47	53
Mansfield T	46	6	10	7	25	29	5	10	8	29	35	53
Hartlepool U	46	8	9	6	30	24	4	4	15	17	43	49
Leyton O	46	11	4	8	29	22	1	7	15	15	41	47
Cardiff C	46	8	6	9	24	22	3	6	14	17	42	45
Scarborough	46	5	11	7	22	28	3	5	15	17	41	40
Torquay U	46	4	9	10	17	36	1	5	17	13	48	29

FOOTBALL LEAGUE RECORDS

Top scorers: Prem Lge, A.Shearer (Newcastle United) 25 goals; Div 1, J.McGinlay (Bolton Wanderers) 24 goals; Div 2,T.Thorpe (Luton Town) 28 goals; Div 3, G.Jones (Wigan Athletic) 31 goals.
Play-offs: Prem Lge, Crystal Palace v Wolverhampton Wanderers 3-1, 1-2; Sheffield United v Ipswich Town 1-1, 2-2; Crystal Palace v Sheffield United 1-0; Div 1, Bristol City v Brentford 1-2, 1-2; Crewe Alexandra v Luton Town 2-1, 2-2; Brentford v Crewe Alexandra 0-1; Div 2, Cardiff City v Northampton Town 0-1, 2-3; Chester City v Swansea City 0-0, 0-3; Northampton Town v Swansea City 1-0.
Bolton Wanderers, Barnsley and Crystal Palace promoted to Prem Lge; Sunderland, Middlesbrough and Nottingham Forest relegated to Div 1; Bury, Stockport County and

Arsenal's Ian Wright scored 23 Premiership goals to finish second-highest scorer behind Alan Shearer.

DIVISION PREMIER

	ARSENAL	ASTON VILLA	BLACKBURN	CHELSEA	COVENTRY C	DERBY	EVERTON	LEEDS	LEICESTER	LIVERPOOL	MANCHESTER U	MIDDLESBROUGH	NEWCASTLE	NOTTINGHAM F	SHEFFIELD W	SOUTHAMPTON	SUNDERLAND	TOTTENHAM	WEST HAM	WIMBLEDON
1 ARSENAL		D28 22	a19 1-1	S04 3-3	O19 0-0	D07 2-2	J19 3-1	O26 3-0	a12 2-0	M24 1-2	F19 1—2	J01 2-0	m03 0-1	M08 2-0	S16 4-1	D04 3-1	S28 2-0	N24 3-1	A17 2-0	F23 0-1
2 ASTON VILLA	S07 2-2		A21 1-0	D26 0-2	F19 2-1	A24 2-0	a05 3-1	O19 2-0	N16 1-3	M02 1-0	S21 0-0	N30 1-0	J11 2-2	N02 2-0	J29 0-1	m11 1-0	F01 1-0	a19 1-1	M15 0-0	D22 5-0
3 BLACKBURN	O12 0-2	M22 0-2		N16 1-1	J11 4-0	S09 1-2	S21 1-1	S04 0-1	m11 2-4	N03 3-0	a12 2-3	m08 0-0	D26 1'0	M11 1-1	a22 4-1	N30 2-1	M01 1-0	A17 0-2	F01 2-1	M15 3-1
4 CHELSEA	a05 0-3	S15 1-1	M05 1-1		A24 2-0	J18 3-1	D07 2-2	m03 0-0	a19 2-1	J01 1-0	F22 1-1	A21 1-0	N23 1-1	S28 1-1	D28 2-2	M19 1-0	M16 6-2	O26 3-1	D21 3-1	O19 2-4
5 COVENTRY C	a21 1-1	N23 1-2	S28 0-0	a09 3-1		m03 1-2	F22 0-0	S14 2-1	M08 0-0	S04 0-1	J18 0-2	D28 3-0	D17 2-1	A17 0-3	O26 0-0	O13 1-1	J01 2-2	D07 1-2	M22 1-3	M03 1-1
6 DERBY	m11 1-3	a12 2-1	D28 0-0	M01 3-2	N30 2-1		D16 0-1	A17 3-3	N02 2-0	F01 0-1	S04 1-1	N17 2-1	O12 0-1	a23 0-0	F19 2-2	a09 1-1	S14 1-0	M22 4-2	F15 1-0	S28 0-2
7 EVERTON	M01 0-2	S04 0-1	J01 0-2	m11 1-2	N04 1-1	M15 1-0		D12 0-0	a09 1-1	a16 1-1	M22 0-2	S14 1-2	A17 2-0	F01 2-0	S28 2-0	N16 7-1	N30 1-3	a12 1-0	O12 2-1	D28 1-3
8 LEEDS	F01 0-0	a22 0-0	a07 0-0	D01 2-0	D26 1-3	J29 0-0	M08 1-0		J11 3-0	N16 0-2	S07 0-4	m11 1-1	S21 0-1	O12 2-0	A20 0-2	M12 0-0	N02 3-0	D14 0-0	M01 1-0	A26 1-0
9 LEICESTER	A24 0-2	M05 1-0	D07 1-1	O12 1-3	D21 0-2	F22 4-2	N23 1-2	S28 1-0		S15 0-3	m03 2-2	M15 1-3	O26 2-0	D28 2-2	a07 1-0	A21 2-1	J29 1-1	M19 1-1	a23 0-1	J18 1-0
10 LIVERPOOL	A19 2-0	J18 3-0	F22 0-0	S21 5-1	a06 1-2	O27 2-1	N20 1-1	F19 4-0	D26 1-1		a19 1-3	D14 5-1	M10 4-3	D17 4-2	D07 0-1	S07 2-1	A24 0-0	m03 2-1	J11 0-0	N23 1-1
11 MANCHESTER U	N16 1-0	J01 0-0	A25 2-2	N02 1-2	M01 3-1	a05 2-3	A21 2-2	D28 1-0	N30 3-1	O12 1-0		m05 3-3	m08 0-0	S14 4-1	M15 2-0	F01 2-1	D21 5-0	S29 2-0	m11 2-0	J29 2-1
12 MIDDLESBROUGH	S21 0-2	m03 3-2	M19 2-1	M22 1-0	S07 4-0	M05 6-1	D26 4-2	D07 0-0	D03 0-2	A17 3-3	N23 2-2		F22 0-1	M24 1-1	J18 4-2	J11 0-1	a19 0-1	O19 0-3	S04 4-1	O26 0-0
13 NEWCASTLE	N30 1-2	S30 4-3	S14 2-1	a16 3-1	M15 4-0	a19 3-1	J29 4-1	J01 3-0	F02 4-3	D23 1-1	O20 5-0	N03 3-1		m11 5-0	A24 1-2	M01 0-1	a05 1-1	D28 7-1	N16 1-1	A21 2-0
14 NOTTINGHAM F	D21 2-1	F22 0-0	N25 2-2	J11 2-0	J29 0-1	O19 1-1	O28 0-1	a19 1-1	S07 0-0	M15 1-1	D26 0-4	A24 1-1	D09 0-0		M05 0-3	a05 1-3	A21 1-4	J19 2-1	S21 0-2	m03 1-1
15 SHEFFIELD W	D26 0-0	A17 2-1	O19 1-1	S07 0-2	F01 0-0	S21 0-0	J11 2-1	M22 2-2	S02 2-1	m11 1-1	D18 1-1	M01 3-1	a13 1-1	N18 2-0		N02 1-1	M12 2-1	a09 2-1	N30 0-0	a19 3-1
16 SOUTHAMPTON	M15 0-2	D07 0-1	m03 2-0	A18 0-0	a19 2-2	D21 3-1	M05 2-2	N23 0-2	M22 2-2	D29 0-1	O26 6-3	S28 4-0	J18 2-2	S04 2-2	F22 2-3		O19 3-0	S14 0-1	a12 2-0	F26 0-0
17 SUNDERLAND	J11 1-0	O26 1-0	J18 0-0	D15 3-0	S21 1-0	D26 2-0	m03 3-0	F22 0-1	A17 0-0	a13 1-2	M08 2-1	O14 2-2	S04 1-2	M22 1-1	N23 1-1	a22 0-1		M04 0-4	S08 0-0	D07 1-3
18 TOTTENHAM	F15 0-0	O12 1-0	J29 2-1	F01 1-2	m11 1-2	A21 1-1	A24 0-0	M15 1-0	S22 1-2	D02 0-2	J12 1-2	a24 1-0	S07 1-2	M01 0-1	D21 1-1	D26 3-1	N16 2-0		N02 1-0	a05 1-0
19 WEST HAM	J29 1-2	D04 0-2	O26 2-1	M12 3-2	A21 1-1	N23 1-1	a19 2-2	J20 0-2	O19 1-0	S29 1-2	D08 2-2	a09 0-0	m06 0-0	J01 0-1	m03 5-1	A24 2-1	D28 2-0	F24 4-3		S14 0-2
20 WIMBLEDON	N02 2-2	a09 0-2	D14 1-0	a22 0-1	N16 2-2	J11 1-1	S07 4-0	a16 2-0	M01 1-3	m06 2-1	A17 0-3	F01 1-1	M23 1-1	N30 1-0	O12 4-2	S23 3-1	m11 1-0	S04 1-0	M18 1-1	

Steve Bull of Wolves also scored 23 goals this season and he, too, finished in second place, behind Bolton's John McGinlay in the First Division.

DIVISION 1

	BARNSLEY	BIRMINGHAM	BOLTON	BRADFORD C	CHARLTON	C.PALACE	GRIMSBY	HUDDERSFIELD	IPSWICH	MANCHESTER C	NORWICH	OLDHAM	OXFORD	PORT VALE	PORTSMOUTH	Q.P.R.	READING	SHEFFIELD U	SOUTHEND	STOKE	SWINDON	TRANMERE	W.B.A.	WOLVERHAMPTON
1 BARNSLEY		a05 0-1	O25 2-2	a26 2-0	a12 4-0	O12 0-0	S28 1-3	A25 3-1	J18 1-2	D28 2-0	N12 3-1	a15 2-0	O15 0'0	F08 1-0	N23 3-2	S14 1-3	A28 3-0	M07 2-0	D07 3-0	S10 3-0	M04 1-1	D14 3-0	M28 2-0	F22 1-3
2 BIRMINGHAM	D03 0-0		N13 3-1	O12 3-0	M31 0-0	A18 1-0	D07 0-0	a12 1-0	O15 1-0	M11 2-0	O26 2-3	S10 0-0	a26 2-0	F23 1-2	F08 0-3	S28 0-0	J18 4-1	M22 1-1	M08 2-1	S14 3-1	N23 1-0	a15 0-0	F04 2-3	M04 1-2
3 BOLTON	N30 2-2	F01 2-1		J01 2-1	a25 4-1	N16 2-2	S10 6-1	N02 2-0	D14 1-2	A20 1-0	A24 3-1	O12 3-1	a12 4-0	M18 4-2	S14 2-0	a05 2-1	O29 2-1	F15 2-2	D28 3-1	S28 1-1	M08 7-0	O15 1-0	M02 1-0	J18 3-0
4 BRADFORD C	O19 2-2	a19 0-2	S21 2-4		m01 1-0	O29 0-4	M08 3-4	F01 1-1	N16 2-1	M01 1-3	S07 0-2	N02 0-3	J11 2-0	J28 1-0	A17 3-1	m04 3-0	D17 0-0	D26 1-2	O05 0-0	M31 1-0	O02 2-1	A31 1-0	N30 1-1	M22 2-1
5 CHARLTON	F15 2-2	N20 2-1	O19 3-3	N23 0-2		M08 2-1	N26 1-3	a09 2-1	J01 1-1	a05 1-1	F22 4-4	S28 1-0	O26 2-0	D14 1-3	a19 2-1	M04 2-1	S14 1-0	m04 0-0	S10 2-0	J18 1-2	D07 2-0	F07 3-1	A24 1-1	D28 0-0
6 C.PALACE	a19 1-1	M29 0-1	M04 1-1	F08 3-1	D21 1-0		O26 3-0	a05 1-1	S10 0-0	S14 3-1	M15 2-0	A24 3-1	D07 2-2	m04 1-1	J18 1-2	N10 3-0	a23 3-2	D17 0-1	S28 6-1	a15 2-0	O19 1-2	F22 0-1	A27 0-0	N23 2-3
7 GRIMSBY	J28 2-3	M01 1-2	D26 1-2	D21 1-1	F01 2-0	N30 2-1		F15 2-2	M31 2-1	M15 1-1	O01 1-4	O29 0-3	S21 0-2	J11 1-1	A31 0-1	O05 2-0	a19 2-0	N03 2-4	m04 4-0	N16 1-1	S07 2-1	M22 0-0	O19 1-1	A17 1-3
8 HUDDERSFIELD	M22 0-0	O08 3-0	F22 1-2	N08 3-3	A17 2-0	A31 1-1	N23 2-0		D28 2-0	J18 1-1	D07 2-0	S13 3-2	M04 1-0	O26 0-1	M15 1-3	D21 1-2	S28 1-0	M31 2-1	O19 0-0	J01 2-1	m04 0-0	S10 0-1	a19 0-0	F08 0-2
9 IPSWICH	O01 1-1	m04 1-1	M15 0-1	M04 3-2	S20 2-1	D26 3-1	A27 1-1	S07 1-3		a22 1-0	a18 2-0	a05 4-0	F22 2-1	N23 2-1	O19 1-1	F08 2-0	A24 5-2	M18 3-1	N09 1-1	D21 1-1	N19 3-2	O26 0-2	J25 5-0	D07 0-0
10 MANCHESTER C	S07 1-2	S21 1-0	a09 1-2	D07 3-2	S03 2-1	J11 1-1	a16 3-1	N19 0-0	A16 1-0		O19 2-1	M08 1-0	N13 2-3	D26 0-1	M05 1-1	a19 0-3	m03 3-2	J29 0-0	F08 3-0	M22 2-0	F22 3-0	N23 1-2	N27 3-2	O27 0-1
11 NORWICH	F01 1-1	N30 0-1	M22 0-1	D28 2-0	N02 1-2	D14 1-1	J18 2-1	M01 2-0	O11 3-1	a25 0-0		O16 2-0	M31 1-1	M08 1-1	J01 1-0	S11 1-1	N16 1-1	O30 1-1	S14 0-0	a12 2-0	A17 2-0	S28 1-1	F15 2-4	A31 1-0
12 OLDHAM	S21 0-1	a08 2-2	a19 0-0	F22 1-2	M18 1-1	M23 0-1	F08 0-3	J25 1-2	A31 3-3	D21 2-1	m04 3-0		N23 2-1	O05 3-0	N09 0-0	D07 0-2	O19 1-1	S07 0-2	O26 0-0	A17 1-2	M31 5-1	M04 1-2	O01 1-1	M15 3-2
13 OXFORD	m04 5-1	O18 0-0	N19 0-0	S14 2-0	N30 0-2	M01 1-4	M18 3-2	N16 1-0	N02 3-1	F02 1-4	A27 0-1	F15 3-1		a05 0-2	S28 2-0	M29 2-3	D28 2-1	D14 4-1	A24 5-0	O29 4-1	a19 2-0	J18 2-1	M08 1-0	S10 1-1
14 PORT VALE	O29 1-3	N02 3-0	A17 1-1	S29 1-1	M15 2-0	O16 0-2	S14 1-1	N30 0-0	F15 2-2	S10 0-2	D21 6-1	a12 3-2	A31 2-0		D28 0-2	J19 4-4	M01 1-0	N16 0-0	J25 2-1	O13 1-1	M22 1-0	M31 2-1	F01 2-2	a27 1-2
15 PORTSMOUTH	a22 4-2	O29 1-1	J11 0-3	M29 3-1	O12 2-0	O01 2-2	a05 1-0	D14 3-1	a25 0-1	N16 2-1	S21 0-1	F01 1-0	J28 2-1	S07 1-1		A23 1-2	M25 1-0	M01 1-1	A27 1-0	N30 1-0	D26 0-1	a12 1-3	N02 4-0	O15 0-2
16 Q.P.R.	J11 3-1	J29 1-1	S01 1-2	O16 1-0	N16 1-2	F01 0-1	a12 3-0	M08 2-0	O30 0-1	O12 2-2	D26 3-2	M01 0-1	A17 2-1	O02 1-2	M22 2-1		M12 0-2	N30 1-0	D14 4-0	N02 1-1	S21 1-1	a26 2-0	S07 0-2	M31 2-2
17 READING	M31 1-2	N26 0-0	F08 3-2	M15 0-0	J11 2-2	S21 1-6	O12 1-1	J28 4-1	M22 1-0	O15 2-0	M04 2-1	a26 2-0	S08 2-0	D07 0-1	D21 0-0	N23 2-1		A17 1-0	F22 3-2	A31 2-2	O26 2-0	D03 2-0	D26 2-2	a12 2-1
18 SHEFFIELD U	D21 0-1	A24 4-4	N22 1-1	S10 3-0	O15 3-0	a12 3-0	F22 3-1	D03 3-1	S14 1-3	S28 2-0	F09 2-3	D28 2-2	M15 3-1	M04 3-0	D07 1-0	O26 1-1	M29 2-0		J18 3-0	a25 1-0	N26 2-0	O12 0-0	a05 1-2	J24 2-3
19 SOUTHEND	M01 1-2	D20 1-1	S07 5-2	a12 1-1	D26 0-2	J28 2-1	O16 1-0	a26 1-2	F01 0-0	O29 2-3	F25 1-1	N30 1-1	M22 2-2	S21 0-0	M31 2-1	M15 0-1	N02 2-1	O01 3-2		F15 2-1	A31 1-3	A17 1-1	N16 2-3	O13 1-1
20 STOKE	D26 1-0	J10 1-0	J29 1-2	A28 1-0	D04 1-0	S07 2-2	M05 3-1	S22 3-2	M08 0-1	A24 2-1	J22 1-2	M29 2-1	F07 2-1	a20 2-0	O26 3-1	F22 0-0	a05 1-1	O19 0-4	N23 1-2		D14 2-0	D07 2-0	m04 2-1	M18 1-0
21 SWINDON	N16 3-0	F26 3-1	D22 2-2	J18 1-1	M01 1-0	a26 0-2	J25 3-3	O16 6-0	a12 0-4	N02 2-0	M29 0-3	A28 1-0	O12 1-0	A24 1-1	S11 0-1	F05 1-1	N30 3-1	F01 2-1	a05 0-0	M15 1-0		S14 2-1	O30 2-3	S27 1-2
22 TRANMERE	M15 1-1	S07 1-0	m04 2-2	a04 3-0	O29 4-0	N02 1-3	A23 3-2	D26 1-1	N30 3-0	a18 1-1	J28 3-1	N15 1-1	O01 0-0	A27 2-0	O04 4-3	O20 2-3	F01 2-2	a19 1-1	M28 3-0	F28 0-0	J10 2-1		S21 2-3	D21 0-2
23 W.B.A.	A17 1-2	M16 2-0	D08 2-2	O26 0-0	M22 1-2	a09 1-0	a26 2-0	O12 1-1	S28 0-0	a12 1-3	D18 5-1	J18 1-1	D21 3-3	N09 1-1	F22 0-2	D28 4-1	S10 3-2	N13 1-2	M05 4-0	O16 0-2	F08 1-2	J01 1-2		S15 2-4
24 WOLVERHAMPTON	N02 3-3	N17 1-2	O02 1-2	A24 1-0	S06 1-0	F15 0-3	a23 1-1	O30 0-0	M01 0-0	D01 3-0	a05 3-2	D14 0-1	D26 3-1	O19 0-1	m04 0-1	A28 1-1	O05 0-1	S21 1-2	a19 4-1	F01 2-0	J29 1-0	M08 3-2	J12 2-0	

Season 1996-97

Crewe Alexandra promoted to Div 1; Grimsby Town, Oldham Athletic and Southend United relegated to Div 2; Wigan Athletic, Fulham, Carlisle United and Northampton Town promoted to Div 2; Peterborough United, Shrewsbury Town, Rotherham United and Notts County relegated to Div 3; Hereford United relegated from Div 3, replaced by Macclesfield Town.

DIVISION 2

	BLACKPOOL	BOURNEMOUTH	BRENTFORD	BRISTOL C	BRISTOL R	BURNLEY	BURY	CHESTERFIELD	CREWE	GILLINGHAM	LUTON	MILLWALL	NOTTS CO	PETERBOROUGH	PLYMOUTH	PRESTON	ROTHERHAM	SHREWSBURY	STOCKPORT	WALSALL	WATFORD	WREXHAM	WYCOMBE	YORK
1 BLACKPOOL		N09 1-1	a22 1-0	M22 1-0	a26 3-2	F25 1-3	a12 2-0	A17 0-1	J18 1-2	O12 2-0	a15 0-0	J25 3-0	N23 1-0	F08 5-1	D03 2-2	M15 2-1	M31 4-1	S21 1-1	F22 2-1	S07 2-1	O26 1-1	O15 3-3	A31 0-0	D21 3-0
2 BOURNEMOUTH	F01 0-0		N19 2-1	O29 0-2	D26 1-0	F15 0-0	N02 1-1	M11 3-0	S07 0-1	a12 2-2	N30 3-2	D14 1-1	S21 0-1	A31 1-2	O15 1-0	F11 2-0	J11 1-1	M01 0-0	a01 0-0	O01 0-1	A17 1-2	a26 2-1	O12 2-1	M22 1-1
3 BRENTFORD	S14 1-1	F22 1-0		J18 0-0	J21 0-0	M15 0-3	M29 0-2	a15 1-0	a19 0-2	A27 2-0	A24 3-2	O26 0-0	D03 2-0	m03 0-1	S10 3-2	D21 0-0	O05 4-2	a05 0-0	N09 2-2	O19 1-1	F08 1-1	N23 2-0	M04 0-0	S28 3-3
4 BRISTOL C	A24 0-1	J25 0-1	O01 1-2		D15 1-1	J11 2-1	a05 1-0	a30 2-0	F22 3-0	M29 0-1	A27 5-0	N09 1-1	O26 4-0	N23 2-0	a26 3-1	S07 2-1	M18 0-2	D26 3-2	F07 1-1	S21 4-1	D03 1-1	a15 2-1	O15 3-0	O11 2-0
5 BRISTOL R	O19 0-0	S10 3-2	O29 2-1	M16 1-2		N19 1-2	N30 4-3	S28 2-0	O04 2-0	N02 0-0	F15 3-2	a08 1-0	a20 1-0	A17 1-0	F25 2-0	M23 1-0	m03 1-2	F01 2-0	A31 1-1	M01 0-1	S14 0-1	M31 2-0	D21 3-4	J18 1-1
6 BURNLEY	S10 2-0	N23 1-0	D14 1-2	S28 2-3	F22 2-2		J17 3-1	J28 0-0	N09 2-0	D28 5-1	M29 0-2	a05 1-0	O19 1-0	M08 5-0	O26 2-1	J25 1-2	a19 3-3	A27 1-3	O05 5-2	A24 2-1	m03 4-1	D03 2-0	S14 2-1	F08 1-2
7 BURY	O05 1-0	F08 2-1	A17 1-1	A31 4-0	O26 2-1	O01 1-0		M22 1-0	a15 1-0	M15 3-0	S21 0-0	m03 2-0	F22 2-0	a19 1-0	N23 1-0	D03 3-0	S07 3-1	M04 2-0	D21 0-0	a08 2-1	O19 1-1	F25 0-0	M31 2-0	N09 4-1
8 CHESTERFIELD	M29 0-0	D21 1-1	S07 0-2	O05 1-1	J11 1-0	S21 0-0	A24 1-2		O19 1-0	a05 2-2	M04 1-1	a19 1-0	m03 1-0	D03 2-1	F22 1-2	N09 2-1	F18 1-1	O01 2-1	a28 0-1	A27 1-0	a08 0-0	F08 0-0	M15 4-2	O26 2-0
9 CREWE	O01 3-2	D28 2-0	O12 2-0	M25 1-2	a12 1-0	F01 1-1	S10 2-0	a26 1-2		M01 3-2	M15 0-0	M18 0-0	D20 3-0	M22 1-1	S28 3-0	M31 1-0	O29 1-0	N30 5-1	A17 1-0	F15 1-0	A31 0-2	S14 3-1	N02 3-0	O15 0-1
10 GILLINGHAM	a19 2-3	O05 1-1	M31 1-2	A17 3-2	F08 1-0	S07 1-0	D14 2-2	A31 0-1	D03 2-1		D26 1-2	O19 2-3	O01 1-0	F22 2-1	J25 4-1	O26 1-1	S21 3-1	m03 2-0	a16 1-0	a29 2-0	M08 3-1	N09 1-2	M22 1-0	N23 0-1
11 LUTON	S28 1-0	O26 2-0	M21 1-0	a01 2-2	N23 2-1	A17 1-2	a22 0-0	S14 0-1	D14 6-0	S10 2-1		M08 0-2	N09 2-0	O19 3-0	F08 2-2	F22 5-1	A31 1-0	a19 2-0	m03 1-1	O05 3-1	J27 0-0	J18 0-0	a08 0-0	D03 2-0
12 MILLWALL	O30 2-1	M15 0-1	N29 0-0	F01 0-2	S07 2-0	A31 2-1	O16 1-0	O12 2-1	S21 2-0	a26 0-2	D18 0-1		F25 1-0	D26 0-2	a12 0-0	J11 3-2	F15 2-0	N20 2-1	O02 3-4	N02 1-0	M22 0-1	A17 1-1	M01 2-1	a02 1-1
13 NOTTS CO	F15 1-1	F04 0-2	M01 1-1	N30 2-0	O12 1-1	a26 1-1	M25 0-1	O15 0-0	M08 0-1	J18 1-1	F01 1-2	S14 1-2		M31 0-0	a15 2-1	A17 2-1	D14 0-0	N02 1-2	M22 1-2	O29 2-0	S10 2-3	S28 0-0	a12 1-2	A31 0-1
14 PETERBOROUGH	N02 0-0	a05 3-1	O15 0-1	F15 3-1	M29 1-2	D20 3-2	O12 1-2	M01 1-1	A24 2-2	N19 0-1	a26 0-1	S10 3-3	O08 1-3		J18 0-0	a12 2-0	N30 6-2	O29 2-2	M15 0-2	F01 0-1	M04 2-1	F11 0-1	S28 6-3	S14 2-2
15 PLYMOUTH	M01 0-1	m03 0-0	D26 1-4	O19 0-0	S21 0-1	N30 0-0	F15 2-0	N19 0-3	J11 1-0	O29 2-0	N02 3-3	O05 0-0	S07 0-0	O01 1-1		A30 2-1	M08 1-0	D14 2-2	a08 0-0	a19 2-0	M31 0-0	M22 0-1	F01 0-0	A17 2-1
16 PRESTON	D13 3-0	S14 0-1	M08 1-0	D28 0-2	A24 0-0	O29 1-1	M01 3-1	F01 0-1	A27 2-1	N30 1-0	N19 3-2	S28 2-1	M29 2-0	O05 3-4	a05 1-1		N02 0-0	O19 2-1	a19 1-0	m03 2-0	J18 1-1	M18 2-1	F15 2-1	S10 1-0
17 ROTHERHAM	A27 1-2	S28 1-0	a11 0-1	S14 2-2	O15 0-0	O12 1-0	D28 1-1	S10 0-1	J25 1-4	M25 1-2	a05 0-3	N23 0-0	M15 2-2	O26 2-0	D21 1-2	F08 0-1		A24 1-2	D03 0-1	M29 1-2	N09 0-0	F22 0-0	J18 2-1	a26 0-2
18 SHREWSBURY	J01 1-3	D03 1-1	A31 0-3	S10 1-0	N12 2-0	a01 2-1	S14 1-1	J18 2-0	O26 0-1	O15 1-2	O12 0-3	F22 1-1	F08 2-1	J25 2-2	M15 2-3	a26 0-2	M22 0-2		N23 3-2	D20 2-2	S28 1-0	a12 0-1	A18 1-1	D28 2-0
19 STOCKPORT	N19 1-0	A27 0-1	F01 1-2	N02 1-1	a05 1-0	a12 1-0	M08 2-1	O29 1-0	M29 1-0	S28 2-1	O15 1-1	J18 5-1	A24 0-0	D14 0-0	S14 3-1	O12 1-0	M01 0-0	F15 3-1		N30 2-0	a14 1-0	S10 0-2	a26 2-1	a22 2-1
20 WALSALL	M18 1-1	J18 2-1	a26 1-0	M04 2-0	D03 1-0	M22 1-3	S28 3-1	a01 1-1	N23 1-0	S14 1-0	a12 3-2	F08 2-1	J25 3-1	N09 4-0	O12 0-1	O15 1-0	A17 1-1	M08 2-2	O26 1-1		D14 1-1	S24 0-1	S10 2-2	F22 1-1
21 WATFORD	N30 2-2	M29 0-1	N02 2-0	M01 3-0	M18 1-0	O15 2-2	a26 0-0	a24 0-2	a05 0-1	D21 0-0	O29 1-1	A24 0-2	D26 0-0	S21 0-0	A27 0-2	O01 1-0	F01 2-0	F25 2-0	S07 1-0	M15 1-0		O12 1-1	N19 1-0	a12 4-0
22 WREXHAM	m03 2-1	O19 2-0	M25 0-2	D21 2-1	S17 1-0	M01 0-0	O29 1-1	N02 3-2	a22 1-1	F01 1-1	M12 2-1	M28 3-3	J11 3-3	S07 1-1	A24 4-4	S21 1-0	a08 1-0	O08 2-1	D26 2-3	a05 1-2	a19 3-1		N30 1-0	M15 0-0
23 WYCOMBE	a05 1-0	a19 1-1	S21 0-1	m03 2-0	M08 2-0	a15 5-0	A27 0-1	D14 1-0	F08 2-0	A24 1-1	S07 0-1	D03 1-0	O05 1-0	F25 2-0	N09 2-1	N23 0-1	O01 4-2	M29 3-0	O19 0-2	D26 0-2	F22 0-0	O26 0-0		J25 3-1
24 YORK	M08 1-0	A24 1-2	J11 2-4	a19 0-3	O01 2-2	N02 1-0	F01 0-2	N30 0-0	m03 1-1	F15 2-3	M01 1-1	A27 3-2	a05 1-2	a08 1-0	M29 1-1	F25 3-1	O19 2-1	S07 0-0	S21 1-2	F11 0-2	O05 1-2	D14 1-0	O29 2-0	

DIVISION 3

	BARNET	BRIGHTON	CAMBRIDGE	CARDIFF	CARLISLE	CHESTER	COLCHESTER	DARLINGTON	DONCASTER	EXETER	FULHAM	HARTLEPOOL	HEREFORD	HULL	LEYTON O	LINCOLN	MANSFIELD	NORTHAMPTON	ROCHDALE	SCARBOROUGH	SCUNTHORPE	SWANSEA	TORQUAY	WIGAN
1 BARNET		A27 3-0	M29 2-1	a19 3-1	O26 0-0	D21 1-2	m03 2-4	J25 0-0	N23 3-0	S21 3-0	F22 2-2	O19 1-0	F08 2-3	a05 1-0	D03 0-0	F25 1-0	D26 1-1	S07 1-1	N09 3-2	O01 1-3	a08 1-1	M15 0-1	O05 0-0	A24 1-1
2 BRIGHTON	a01 1-0		O12 1-2	M22 2-0	N23 1-3	A17 2-1	D26 1-1	D03 2-3	a26 1-0	F11 1-0	O26 0-0	F08 5-0	O15 0-1	D14 3-0	M08 4-4	O01 1-3	N09 1-1	M04 2-1	J25 3-0	S07 3-2	A31 1-1	F22 3-2	S21 2-2	a12 1-0
3 CAMBRIDGE	A17 1-0	a19 1-1		A31 0-2	F21 1-3	M22 2-2	M07 1-0	O01 5-2	O25 0-1	J21 3-2	m03 0-1	O05 1-0	J25 0-1	F08 1-0	N23 2-0	M31 1-3	D03 2-1	a08 0-0	O19 2-2	S21 2-1	F25 0-2	N09 2-1	S07 2-1	D14 1-1
4 CARDIFF	O12 1-2	A24 1-0	a05 0-0		a26 2-0	a12 1-0	F08 1-2	O15 2-0	M14 0-2	S07 2-1	N09 1-2	F22 2-0	N23 2-0	J25 2-0	O26 3-0	J11 1-3	D21 1-2	S21 2-2	N05 2-1	M18 1-1	a15 0-0	D03 1-3	D26 2-0	A27 0-2
5 CARLISLE	N30 2-1	F15 2-1	N19 3-0	O19 0-2		O29 3-1	O01 3-0	S21 1-0	M29 0-0	m03 2-0	a05 1-2	D26 1-0	M15 2-3	A24 0-0	A27 1-0	M01 1-0	O05 1-1	F01 2-1	a29 3-2	J11 1-0	D21 3-2	S07 4-1	M04 5-1	N02 0-3
6 CHESTER	M08 1-0	M29 2-1	A24 1-1	N26 0-1	F25 1-1		N22 1-2	D14 2-1	F08 6-0	O19 2-1	D03 1-1	J11 0-0	O26 1-3	N09 0-0	m03 0-1	S07 4-1	F22 1-0	O01 2-1	J14 0-0	a19 1-0	S21 1-0	A27 2-0	M11 0-0	a05 1-1
7 COLCHESTER	O15 1-0	S10 2-0	D20 2-2	N02 1-1	J18 1-1	F14 0-0		M31 0-3	S28 2-2	O29 1-0	J14 2-1	A17 0-2	A31 1-1	S14 1-1	F04 2-1	N30 7-1	M14 2-1	a26 0-0	M21 1-0	F28 1-3	N19 1-1	a11 3-1	J31 2-0	O12 3-1
8 DARLINGTON	O29 0-1	M01 2-0	J18 2-0	m03 2-1	a08 2-1	M15 1-1	A27 1-1		a05 0-3	N19 0-1	S28 0-2	a19 1-2	S14 1-0	M29 1-0	D28 1-1	F01 5-2	O19 2-4	N30 3-1	O05 1-1	N02 1-1	F15 2-0	A24 4-1	D21 2-3	S10 3-1
9 DONCASTER	F15 1-1	O19 3-0	N30 2-1	a08 3-3	A17 0-1	N02 0-1	J11 0-0	A31 3-2		M31 1-2	a19 0-0	O01 2-1	M21 1-0	M08 0-0	O05 2-1	O29 1-3	S07 0-0	N19 1-2	M25 3-0	D26 1-2	F01 1-1	S21 0-1	m03 2-1	F28 2-0
10 EXETER	M04 1-1	S14 2-1	S28 0-1	D28 2-0	O15 2-1	a26 1-5	J25 0-3	F22 3-2	A27 1-1		S10 0-1	O26 2-0	D03 1-1	N23 0-0	N09 3-2	a12 3-3	M29 0-0	O12 0-1	F08 0-0	A24 2-2	M15 0-1	D21 1-2	a05 1-1	J18 0-1
11 FULHAM	N19 2-0	N30 2-0	O15 3-0	J31 1-4	A31 1-0	M01 1-1	S07 3-1	J11 6-0	O12 3-1	D26 1-1		M22 1-0	A17 1-0	a26 2-0	D14 1-1	N02 1-2	S21 1-2	a12 0-1	M31 1-1	M08 4-0	O29 2-1	F11 2-1	O01 1-2	F15 1-1
12 HARTLEPOOL	a26 4-0	N02 2-3	a12 0-2	F11 2-3	S10 1-2	S28 2-0	M29 1-0	O12 1-2	J18 2-4	N30 1-1	A24 2-1		D28 2-1	J01 1-1	a05 3-1	D21 2-1	A27 2-2	O29 0-2	M15 1-2	F01 1-0	M01 0-1	O15 1-1	F15 1-1	S14 1-1
13 HEREFORD	N02 1-1	m03 1-1	O29 0-1	F16 1-1	D14 2-3	N30 1-2	a05 1-0	F04 1-1	A24 1-0	M01 1-2	M29 0-0	S07 0-1		A27 0-1	O19 2-0	N19 1-1	J11 0-1	M08 1-2	S21 3-0	O05 2-2	O01 3-2	D26 0-1	a19 1-1	F01 3-1
14 HULL	A31 0-0	M15 3-0	N02 1-3	O29 1-1	M22 0-1	F01 1-0	a15 1-2	A17 3-2	D21 3-1	F15 2-0	O19 0-3	S21 1-0	M31 1-1		a19 3-2	D26 2-1	O01 1-1	M01 1-1	S07 1-1	m03 0-2	O05 0-2	J11 1-1	N20 2-0	N30 1-1
15 LEYTON O	M01 0-1	D22 2-0	F15 1-1	N30 3-0	M31 2-1	O15 0-0	S21 1-1	S07 0-0	a12 2-1	F01 1-1	M16 0-2	A31 2-0	a26 2-1	O12 1-1		M22 2-3	J04 2-1	D26 2-1	F11 2-1	O29 0-1	A17 0-1	O01 1-0	N02 1-0	J21 1-2
16 LINCOLN	S14 1-0	J18 2-1	A27 1-1	S28 2-0	D03 1-1	J28 0-0	O26 3-2	N09 2-0	J25 3-2	O05 2-3	F08 2-0	M08 2-1	F22 3-3	S10 0-1	A24 1-1		N23 0-0	D14 1-1	m03 0-2	O19 1-1	a19 2-0	a05 4-0	M29 1-2	F04 1-3
17 MANSFIELD	S10 0-0	F01 1-1	M01 1-0	M08 1-3	a11 0-0	F04 0-2	D14 1-1	a26 2-1	J21 2-0	A17 0-1	a08 0-0	M31 1-0	S28 3-1	J18 1-0	S14 0-2	F15 2-2		M22 1-0	A31 0-0	N30 2-0	N02 2-0	O12 0-0	O29 1-2	O15 0-1
18 NORTHAMPTON	D28 2-0	S28 3-0	S14 1-2	J01 4-0	N09 1-1	J18 5-1	O19 2-1	O26 3-1	F22 2-0	a19 4-1	O05 0-1	J25 3-0	D20 1-0	D03 2-1	S10 0-1	M15 1-1	A24 3-0		N23 2-2	a05 1-0	m03 1-0	F08 1-2	A27 1-1	M29 0-1
19 ROCHDALE	F01 1-1	O29 3-0	a26 3-0	J18 1-0	O12 2-2	S10 0-1	A24 0-0	a12 2-0	S14 2-1	N02 2-0	A27 1-2	D14 1-3	F18 0-0	F25 1-2	S28 1-0	O15 2-0	a05 0-1	F15 1-1		F04 3-3	N30 1-2	M29 2-3	M01 2-1	M08 3-1
20 SCARBOROUGH	J18 1-1	D28 1-1	J14 1-0	A17 0-0	S14 1-1	O12 0-0	D03 1-1	F08 4-1	S10 2-1	M22 3-4	D21 0-2	N09 2-4	a12 1-1	O15 3-2	J25 2-1	a26 0-2	O26 2-1	A31 1-1	F22 2-2		M31 3-2	N23 0-1	M15 3-1	S28 3-1
21 SCUNTHORPE	S28 1-2	a05 1-0	S10 3-2	S14 0-1	M08 0-0	F18 0-2	F22 2-1	N23 3-2	N09 1-2	D14 4-1	J25 1-4	D03 2-1	J18 5-1	a12 2-2	M29 1-2	O12 2-0	F08 0-2	O15 2-1	O26 2-2	A27 0-2		a26 1-0	A24 1-0	D28 2-3
22 SWANSEA	J14 3-0	N19 1-0	M31 3-1	M02 0-1	D28 0-1	M31 2-1	O04 1-1	M22 1-1	J28 2-0	M08 3-1	S14 1-2	m03 2-2	S10 4-0	S28 0-0	J18 1-0	A30 1-2	a19 3-2	N02 1-0	A17 2-1	F15 1-2	O19 1-1		N30 2-0	O29 2-1
23 TORQUAY	a12 1-2	J01 2-1	D28 0-1	S10 2-0	S28 1-2	S14 0-0	N09 0-2	M08 1-1	O15 1-0	A31 2-0	J18 3-1	N23 0-1	O12 2-1	F22 1-1	F08 0-0	A17 2-1	F18 1-2	M31 1-2	D03 0-1	D14 1-0	M22 1-2	O26 2-0		a26 0-3
24 WIGAN	M22 2-0	O05 1-0	M15 1-1	M31 0-1	F08 1-0	A31 4-2	a08 1-0	F25 3-2	D03 4-1	O01 2-0	N23 1-1	M04 2-2	N09 4-1	O26 1-2	F22 5-1	S21 1-0	m03 2-0	A17 2-1	D21 0-1	M11 7-1	S07 3-0	J25 3-2	O19 3-2	

LEAGUE TABLES

FA PREMIER LEAGUE

	P	W	D	L	F	A	W	D	L	F	A	Pts
Manchester U	38	12	5	2	38	17	9	7	3	38	27	75
Newcastle U	38	13	3	3	54	20	6	8	5	19	20	68
Arsenal	38	10	5	4	36	18	9	6	4	26	14	68
Liverpool	38	10	6	3	38	19	9	5	5	24	18	68
Aston Villa	38	11	5	3	27	13	6	5	8	20	21	61
Chelsea	38	9	8	2	33	22	7	3	9	25	33	59
Sheffield W	38	8	10	1	25	16	6	5	8	25	35	57
Wimbledon	38	9	6	4	28	21	6	5	8	21	25	56
Leicester C	38	7	5	7	22	26	5	6	8	24	28	47
Tottenham H	38	8	4	7	19	17	5	3	11	25	34	46
Leeds U	38	7	7	5	15	13	4	6	9	13	25	46
Derby Co	38	8	6	5	25	22	3	7	9	20	36	46
Blackburn R	38	8	4	7	28	23	1	11	7	14	20	42
West Ham U	38	7	6	6	27	25	3	6	10	12	23	42
Everton	38	7	4	8	24	22	3	8	8	20	35	42
Southampton	38	6	7	6	32	24	4	4	11	18	32	41
Coventry C	38	4	8	7	19	23	5	6	8	19	31	41
Sunderland	38	7	6	6	20	18	3	4	12	15	35	40
Middlesbrough	38	8	5	6	34	25	2	7	10	17	35	*39
Nottingham F	38	3	9	7	15	27	3	7	9	16	32	34

*Middlesbrough deducted 3 points

DIVISION 1

	P	W	D	L	F	A	W	D	L	F	A	Pts
Bolton W	46	18	4	1	60	20	10	10	3	40	33	98
Barnsley	46	14	4	5	43	19	8	10	5	33	36	80
Wolverh'pton W	46	10	5	8	31	24	12	5	6	37	27	76
Ipswich T	46	13	7	3	44	23	7	7	9	24	27	74
Sheffield U	46	13	5	5	46	23	7	8	8	29	29	73
Crystal Palace	46	10	7	6	39	22	9	7	7	39	26	71
Portsmouth	46	12	4	7	32	24	8	4	11	27	29	68
Port Vale	46	9	9	5	36	28	8	7	8	22	27	67
Q.P.R.	46	10	5	8	33	25	8	7	8	31	35	66
Birmingham C	46	11	7	5	30	18	6	8	9	22	30	66
Tranmere R	46	10	9	4	42	27	7	5	11	21	29	65
Stoke C	46	15	3	5	34	22	3	7	13	17	35	64
Norwich C	46	9	10	4	28	18	8	2	13	35	50	63
Manchester C	46	12	4	7	34	25	5	6	12	25	35	61
Charlton A	46	11	8	4	36	28	5	3	15	16	38	59
W.B.A.	46	7	7	9	37	33	7	8	8	31	39	57
Oxford U	46	14	3	6	44	26	2	6	15	20	42	57
Reading	46	13	7	3	37	24	2	5	16	21	43	57
Swindon T	46	11	6	6	36	27	4	3	16	16	44	54
Huddersfield T	46	10	7	6	28	20	3	8	12	20	41	54
Bradford C	46	10	5	8	29	32	2	7	14	18	40	48
Grimsby	46	7	7	9	31	34	4	6	13	29	47	46
Oldham A	46	6	8	9	30	30	4	5	14	21	36	43
Southend U	46	7	9	7	32	32	1	6	16	10	54	39

DIVISION 2

	P	W	D	L	F	A	W	D	L	F	A	Pts
Bury	46	18	5	0	39	7	6	7	10	23	31	84
Stockport Co	46	15	5	3	31	14	8	8	7	28	27	82
Luton T	46	13	7	3	38	14	8	8	7	33	31	78
Brentford	46	8	11	4	26	22	12	3	8	30	21	74
Bristol C	46	14	4	5	43	18	7	6	10	26	33	73
Crewe A	46	15	4	4	38	15	7	3	13	18	32	73
Blackpool	46	13	7	3	41	21	5	8	10	19	26	69
Wrexham	46	11	9	3	37	28	6	9	8	17	22	69
Burnley	46	14	3	6	48	27	5	8	10	23	28	68
Chesterfield	46	10	9	4	25	18	8	5	10	17	21	68
Gillingham	46	13	3	7	37	25	6	7	10	23	34	67
Walsall	46	12	8	3	35	21	7	2	14	19	32	67
Watford	46	10	8	5	24	14	6	11	6	21	24	67
Millwall	46	12	4	7	27	22	4	9	10	23	33	61
Preston N.E.	46	14	5	4	33	19	4	2	17	16	36	61
Bournemouth	46	8	9	6	24	20	7	6	10	19	25	60
Bristol R	46	13	4	6	34	22	2	7	14	13	28	56
Wycombe	46	13	4	6	31	14	2	6	15	20	42	55
Plymouth A	46	7	11	5	19	18	5	7	11	28	40	54
York C	46	8	6	9	27	31	5	7	11	20	37	52
Peterborough U	46	7	7	9	38	34	4	7	12	17	39	47
Shrewsbury T	46	8	6	9	27	32	3	7	13	22	42	46
Rotherham U	46	4	7	12	17	29	3	7	13	22	41	35
Notts Co	46	4	9	10	20	25	3	5	15	13	34	35

DIVISION 3

	P	W	D	L	F	A	W	D	L	F	A	Pts
Wigan A	46	17	3	3	53	21	9	6	8	31	30	87
Fulham	46	13	5	5	41	20	12	7	4	31	18	87
Carlisle U	46	16	3	4	41	21	8	9	6	26	23	84
Northampton T	46	14	4	5	43	17	6	8	9	24	27	72
Swansea C	46	13	5	5	37	20	8	3	12	25	38	71
Chester C	46	11	8	4	30	16	7	8	8	25	27	70
Cardiff C	46	11	4	8	30	23	9	5	9	26	31	69
Colchester U	46	11	9	3	36	23	6	8	9	26	28	68
Lincoln C	46	10	8	5	35	25	8	4	11	35	44	66
Cambridge U	46	11	5	7	30	27	7	6	10	23	32	65
Mansfield T	46	9	8	6	21	17	7	8	8	26	28	64
Scarborough	46	9	9	5	36	31	7	6	10	29	37	63
Scunthorpe U	46	11	3	9	36	33	7	6	10	23	29	63
Rochdale	46	10	6	7	34	24	4	10	9	24	34	58
Barnet	46	9	9	5	32	23	5	7	11	14	28	58
Leyton O	46	11	6	6	28	20	4	6	13	22	38	57
Hull C	46	9	8	6	29	26	4	10	9	15	24	57
Darlington	46	11	5	7	37	28	3	5	15	27	50	52
Doncaster	46	9	7	7	29	23	5	3	15	23	43	52
Hartlepool U	46	8	6	9	33	32	6	3	14	20	34	51
Torquay U	46	9	4	10	24	24	4	7	12	22	38	50
Exeter C	46	6	9	8	25	30	6	3	14	23	43	48
Brighton & H.A.	46	12	6	5	41	27	1	4	18	12	43	*47
Hereford	46	6	8	9	26	25	5	6	12	24	40	47

*Brighton & HA deducted 2 points.

Football League Records

Top scorers: Prem Lge, C.Sutton (Blackburn Rovers), D.Dublin (Coventry City), M.Owen (Liverpool) 18 goals; Div 1, P.Van Hooijdonk (Nottingham Forest), K.Phillips (Sunderland) 29 goals; Div 2, B.Hayles (Bristol Rovers) 23 goals; Div 3, G.Jones (Notts County) 28 goals.

Play-offs: Prem Lge, Ipswich Town v Charlton Athletic 0-1, 0-1; Sheffield United v Sunderland 2-1, 0-2; Charlton Athletic v Sunderland 4-4 (7-6 penalties); Div 1, Bristol Rovers v Northampton Town 3-1, 0-3; Fulham v Grimsby Town 1-1, 0-1; Grimsby Town v Northampton Town 1-0; Div 2, Barnet v Colchester United 1-0, 1-3; Scarborough v Torquay United 1-3, 1-4; Colchester United v Torquay United 1-0.

Nottingham Forest, Middlesbrough and Charlton Athletic promoted to Prem Lge; Bolton Wanderers, Barnsley and

Blackburn's Chris Sutton top-scored with 18 Premiership goals and was joined on that mark by Dion Dublin of Coventry City and Michael Owen of Liverpool.

DIVISION PREMIER

	ARSENAL	ASTON VILLA	BARNSLEY	BLACKBURN	BOLTON	CHELSEA	COVENTRY	C PALACE	DERBY	EVERTON	LEEDS	LEICESTER	LIVERPOOL	MANCHESTER U	NEWCASTLE	SHEFFIELD W	SOUTHAMPTON	TOTTENHAM	WEST HAM	WIMBLEDON
1 ARSENAL		O26 0-0	O04 5-0	D13 1-3	S13 4-1	F08 2-0	A11 2-0	F21 1-0	a25 1-0	m03 4-0	J10 2-1	D26 2-1	N30 0-1	N09 3-2	a11 3-1	M28 1-0	J31 3-0	A30 0-0	S24 4-0	a18 5-0
2 ASTON VILLA	m10 1-0		M11 0-1	A13 0-4	a25 1-3	N01 0-2	D06 3-0	M14 3-1	S20 2-1	N22 2-1	A30 1-0	J10 1-1	F28 2-1	F18 0-2	F01 0-1	S27 2-2	D20 1-1	D26 4-1	a04 2-0	O18 1-2
3 BARNSLEY	a25 0-2	S13 0-3		N01 1-1	A27 2-1	A24 0-6	O20 2-0	J17 1-0	D28 1-0	F07 2-2	N29 2-3	S27 0-2	M28 2-3	m10 0-2	D13 2-2	a11 2-1	M14 4-3	a18 1-1	A09 1-2	F28 2-1
4 BLACKBURN	a13 1-4	J17 5-0	M31 2-1		D06 3-1	N22 1-0	S28 0-0	D28 2-2	A09 1-0	N08 3-2	S14 3-4	F28 5-3	A23 1-1	a06 1-3	m10 1-0	A25 7-2	O18 1-0	F07 0-3	D20 3-0	a25 0-0
5 BOLTON	M31 0-1	O04 0-1	D26 1-1	a11 2-1		O26 1-0	J31 1-5	m02 5-2	D14 3-3	S01 0-0	a18 2-3	M28 2-0	N01 1-1	S20 0-0	D01 1-0	M14 3-2	J10 0-0	S23 1-1	F21 1-1	N29 1-0
6 CHELSEA	S21 2-3	M08 0-1	J31 2-0	a29 0-1	m10 2-0		J10 3-1	M11 6-2	N29 4-0	N26 2-0	D13 0-0	O18 1-0	a25 4-1	F28 0-1	S27 1-0	a19 1-0	A30 4-2	a11 2-0	N09 2-1	D26 1-1
7 COVENTRY	J17 2-2	a11 1-2	F21 1-0	m02 2-0	A23 2-2	A09 3-2		S24 1-1	M28 1-0	O25 0-0	O04 0-0	N29 0-2	a19 1-1	D28 3-2	N08 2-2	F07 1-0	S13 1-0	D13 4-0	A27 1-1	a29 0-0
8 C PALACE	O18 0-0	N08 1-1	A12 0-1	A30 1-2	S27 2-2	S13 0-3	F28 0-3		a18 3-1	J10 1-3	J31 0-2	a11 0-3	D13 0-3	a27 0-3	N29 1-2	m10 1-0	D26 1-1	M28 1-3	m05 3-3	F09 0-3
9 DERBY	N01 3-0	F07 0-1	A30 1-0	J11 3-1	a13 4-0	a05 0-1	N22 3-1	D20 0-0		S13 3-1	M15 0-5	a26 0-4	m10 1-0	O18 2-2	D26 1-0	F28 3-0	S27 4-0	J31 2-1	D06 2-0	O22 1-1
10 EVERTON	S27 2-2	a28 1-4	S20 4-2	M14 1-0	D28 3-2	J18 3-1	m10 1-1	A09 1-2	F14 1-2		a11 2-0	a18 1-1	O18 2-0	A27 0-2	F28 0-0	a25 1-3	N02 0-2	N29 0-2	A23 2-1	D13 0-0
11 LEEDS	A09 1-1	D28 1-1	a04 2-1	M11 4-0	D20 2-0	a08 3-1	a25 3-3	A23 0-2	N08 4-3	D06 0-0		S20 0-1	A26 0-2	S27 1-0	O18 4-1	J17 1-2	F28 0-1	M04 1-0	N23 3-1	m10 1-1
12 LEICESTER	A27 3-3	A09 1-0	m02 1-0	S24 1-1	N22 0-0	F21 2-0	a04 1-1	D06 1-1	O06 1-2	D20 0-1	F07 1-0		J17 0-0	A23 0-0	a29 0-0	D28 1-1	a14 3-3	S13 3-0	O27 2-1	N10 0-1
13 LIVERPOOL	m06 4-0	S22 3-0	N22 0-1	J31 0-0	M07 2-1	O05 4-2	D20 1-0	a13 2-1	O25 4-0	F23 1-1	D26 3-1	A13 1-2		D06 1-3	J20 1-0	S13 2-1	F07 2-3	N08 4-0	m02 5-0	J10 2-0
14 MANCHESTER U	M14 0-1	D15 1-0	O25 7-0	N30 4-0	F07 1-1	S24 2-2	A30 3-0	O04 2-0	F21 2-0	D28 2-0	m04 3-0	J31 0-1	a10 1-1		a18 1-1	N01 6-1	A13 1-0	J10 2-0	S13 2-1	M28 2-0
15 NEWCASTLE	D06 0-1	A23 1-0	a13 2-1	O25 1-1	J17 2-1	m02 3-1	M14 0-0	M18 1-2	D17 0-0	S24 1-0	F22 1-1	N01 3-3	D28 1-2	D21 0-1		A09 2-1	N22 2-1	O04 1-0	F07 0-1	S13 1-3
16 SHEFFIELD W	N22 2-0	m02 1-3	D08 2-1	D26 0-0	N08 5-0	D20 1-4	S20 0-0	O25 1-3	S24 2-5	O04 3-1	A13 1-3	A30 1-0	F14 3-3	M07 2-0	J10 2-1		a04 1-0	F21 1-0	a13 1-1	J31 1-1
17 SOUTHAMPTON	A23 1-3	a18 1-2	N08 4-1	F21 3-0	A09 0-1	D29 1-0	F18 1-2	A27 1-0	m02 0-2	M07 2-1	S24 0-2	D13 2-1	S20 1-1	J19 1-0	M28 2-1	N29 2-3		O25 3-2	O04 3-0	a11 0-1
18 TOTTENHAM	D28 1-1	A27 3-2	D20 3-0	S20 0-0	M01 1-0	D06 1-6	a13 1-1	N24 0-1	A23 1-0	a04 1-1	N01 0-1	F14 1-1	M14 3-3	A10 0-2	a25 2-0	O19 3-2	m10 1-1		J17 1-0	S27 0-0
19 WEST HAM	M02 0-0	N29 2-1	J10 6-0	a18 2-1	O18 3-0	M14 2-1	D26 1-0	D03 4-1	a11 0-0	J31 2-2	M30 3-0	m10 4-3	S27 2-1	M11 1-1	S20 0-1	D13 1-0	a25 2-4	A13 2-1		A30 3-1
20 WIMBLEDON	M11 0-1	F21 2-1	S23 4-1	O04 0-1	a04 0-0	A27 0-2	N01 1-2	S20 0-1	J17 0-0	a13 0-0	O25 1-0	M14 2-1	A09 1-1	N22 2-5	M31 0-0	A23 1-1	D07 1-0	m02 2-6	D28 1-2	

In Division One, Nottingham Forest's controversial star Pierre Van Hooijdonk was joint top scorer with 27 goals, the same number as Sunderland's Kevin Phillips.

DIVISION 1

	BIRMINGHAM	BRADFORD	BURY	CHARLTON	CREWE	HUDDERSFIELD	IPSWICH	MANCHESTER C	MIDDLESBROUGH	NORWICH	NOTTINGHAM F	OXFORD	PORT VALE	PORTSMOUTH	Q.P.R.	READING	SHEFFIELD U	STOCKPORT	STOKE	SUNDERLAND	SWINDON	TRANMERE	W.B.A.	WOLVERHAMPTON
1 BIRMINGHAM		N04 0-0	F25 1-3	m03 0-0	O04 0-1	J17 0-0	O28 1-1	D13 2-1	F07 1-1	N08 1-2	M21 1-2	O25 0-0	a11 1-1	N29 2-1	M07 1-0	A23 3-0	F22 2-0	J27 4-1	A09 2-0	S14 0-1	a18 3-0	D28 0-0	M28 1-0	O12 1-0
2 BRADFORD	M14 0-0		D13 1-0	F07 1-0	O25 1-0	D28 1-1	A23 2-1	M28 2-1	S13 2-2	N29 2-1	a11 0-3	F21 0-0	F24 2-1	m03 1-3	a19 1-1	J27 4-1	N18 1-1	A09 2-1	A15 0-0	S05 0-4	J24 1-1	N15 0-1	N01 0-0	O04 2-0
3 BURY	O18 2-1	a13 2-0		A23 0-0	D28 1-1	a04 2-2	a25 0-1	S12 1-1	D06 0-1	M07 1-0	N04 2-0	M21 1-0	F07 2-2	N08 0-2	O21 1-1	A09 1-1	D20 1-1	J18 0-1	F17 0-0	N22 1-1	F28 1-0	S07 1-0	S27 1-3	J27 1-3
4 CHARLTON	O22 1-1	S21 4-1	J31 0-0		N15 3-2	F28 1-0	N01 3-0	A30 2-1	J10 3-0	D26 2-1	M28 4-2	A16 3-2	D13 1-0	a18 1-0	F17 1-1	a10 3-0	D09 2-1	S27 1-3	O19 1-1	M15 1-1	N28 3-0	a25 2-0	M03 5-0	a07 1-0
5 CREWE	F17 0-2	a25 5-0	S02 1-2	M21 0-3		D06 2-5	O21 0-0	D26 1-0	O18 1-1	J31 1-0	M07 1-4	N08 2-1	S16 0-1	F14 3-1	S20 2-3	F28 1-0	a30 2-1	N22 0-1	a13 2-0	D20 0-3	J11 2-0	S27 2-1	A16 2-3	N04 0-2
6 HUDDERSFIELD	S09 0-1	S02 1-2	N29 2-0	O14 0-3	a11 2-0		S13 2-2	M03 1-3	D26 0-1	D13 1-3	O03 0-2	J10 5-1	m03 0-4	O25 1-1	M28 1-1	N15 1-0	A30 0-0	F07 1-0	N01 3-1	F24 2-3	J31 0-0	M14 3-0	a18 1-0	F21 1-0
7 IPSWICH	D26 0-1	J31 2-1	O25 2-0	M07 3-1	m03 3-2	F14 5-1		O04 1-0	D02 1-1	F21 5-0	N29 0-1	F24 5-2	a18 5-1	D13 2-0	J10 0-0	M28 1-0	N09 2-2	N04 0-2	S20 2-3	a28 2-0	S02 2-1	a11 0-0	A30 1-1	M21 3-0
8 MANCHESTER C	a13 0-1	N22 1-0	F14 0-1	J28 2-2	O29 1-0	N07 0-1	F18 1-2		D20 2-0	S20 1-2	D28 2-3	M07 0-2	N04 2-3	A09 2-2	a25 2-2	O18 0-0	M21 0-0	a04 4-1	O22 0-1	J17 0-1	S27 6-0	A22 1-1	F28 1-0	D06 0-1
9 MIDDLESBROUGH	S20 3-1	F14 1-0	a11 4-0	A09 2-1	F25 1-0	O28 3-0	J17 1-1	a17 1-0		M22 3-0	N26 0-0	m03 4-1	O25 2-1	N05 1-1	N08 3-0	D13 4-0	O05 1-2	D28 3-1	A23 0-1	F21 3-1	M11 6-0	F04 3-0	N29 1-0	a29 1-1
10 NORWICH	M04 3-3	a04 2-3	N01 2-2	S17 0-4	A23 0-2	a13 5-0	S26 2-1	F07 0-0	N15 1-3		J17 1-0	N22 2-1	S13 1-0	D30 2-0	F28 0-0	O21 0-0	D06 2-1	O18 1-1	D20 0-0	J28 2-1	a25 5-0	F18 0-2	M14 1-1	A09 0-2
11 NOTTINGHAM F	N15 1-0	D06 2-2	M14 3-0	N22 5-2	N01 3-1	F17 3-0	a05 2-1	S03 1-3	M01 4-0	A15 4-1		J31 1-3	J10 2-1	S20 1-0	A30 4-0	a26 1-0	a01 3-0	D20 2-1	S27 1-0	M04 0-3	D26 3-0	O18 2-2	O21 1-0	a13 3-0
12 OXFORD	a25 0-2	S27 0-0	N15 1-1	J17 1-2	M03 0-0	A09 2-0	O18 1-0	N01 0-0	O21 1-4	M28 2-0	A23 0-1		N29 2-0	J24 1-0	D12 3-1	M17 3-0	S20 2-4	F28 3-0	M14 5-1	D28 1-1	a11 2-1	a18 1-1	F17 2-1	S07 3-0
13 PORT VALE	D06 0-1	O18 0-0	S20 1-1	a13 0-1	J24 2-3	O21 4-1	D20 1-3	M14 2-1	a24 0-1	F14 2-2	A09 0-1	a04 3-0		J17 2-1	S27 2-0	N01 0-0	N22 0-0	S09 2-1	M01 0-0	A23 3-1	F17 0-1	M04 0-1	N15 1-2	D28 0-2
14 PORTSMOUTH	a04 1-1	O21 1-1	M03 1-1	D20 0-2	S13 2-3	a25 3-0	a13 0-1	J10 0-3	M14 0-0	S02 1-1	F07 0-1	A30 2-1	A16 3-1		D26 3-1	S27 0-2	J31 1-1	F17 1-0	D06 2-0	N15 1-4	O31 0-1	F28 1-0	O18 2-3	D09 3-2
15 Q.P.R.	N01 1-1	D21 1-0	m03 0-1	O04 2-4	F07 3-2	N22 2-1	A09 0-0	O28 2-0	M04 5-0	D03 1-1	J24 0-1	a14 1-1	F21 0-1	S24 1-0		D28 1-1	F25 2-2	A23 2-1	N15 1-1	D06 0-1	M14 1-2	J17 0-0	S13 2-0	a01 0-0
16 READING	J31 2-0	A30 0-3	J10 1-1	D06 2-0	O11 3-3	M21 0-2	N22 0-4	F24 3-0	a13 0-1	m03 0-1	O24 3-3	S13 2-1	M07 0-3	F21 0-1	S02 1-2		N04 0-1	N08 1-0	a04 2-0	O04 4-0	A16 0-1	F07 1-3	D26 2-1	D20 0-0
17 SHEFFIELD U	S27 0-0	F28 2-1	a18 3-0	D28 4-1	N29 1-0	J27 1-1	M03 0-1	N15 1-1	a07 1-0	a11 2-2	S13 1-0	F07 1-0	M28 2-1	A23 2-1	O18 2-2	M14 4-0		O21 5-1	D02 3-2	A10 2-0	D13 2-1	N01 2-1	a25 2-4	J17 1-0
18 STOCKPORT	A29 2-2	J10 1-2	A16 0-0	F21 3-0	M28 0-1	S20 3-0	M14 0-1	N29 3-1	S02 1-1	F24 2-2	a18 2-2	O11 3-2	D26 3-0	O04 3-1	J31 2-0	M03 5-1	m03 1-0		F14 1-0	N01 1-1	N15 4-2	D13 3-1	a11 2-1	O25 1-0
19 STOKE	J10 0-7	J16 2-1	O04 3-2	F25 1-2	D13 0-2	M07 1-2	F07 1-1	m03 2-5	F01 1-2	a18 2-0	F21 1-1	N04 0-0	O12 2-1	a11 2-1	M21 2-1	N29 1-2	D26 2-2	S13 2-1		O25 1-2	A30 1-2	M28 0-3	S03 0-0	N08 3-0
20 SUNDERLAND	M10 1-1	D26 2-0	M28 2-1	N04 0-0	a18 2-1	O18 3-1	F28 2-2	A15 3-1	S28 1-2	A30 0-1	N08 1-1	S02 3-1	J31 4-2	M21 2-1	a10 2-2	F17 4-1	J10 4-2	M07 4-1	a25 3-0		O21 0-0	N29 3-0	D13 2-0	S20 1-1
21 SWINDON	D20 1-1	N08 1-0	O11 3-1	a04 0-1	A09 2-0	A23 1-1	D28 0-2	F21 1-3	N22 1-2	O25 1-0	S07 0-0	D06 4-1	O04 4-2	M07 0-1	N05 3-1	J17 0-2	a13 1-1	M21 1-1	J28 1-0	m03 1-2		S13 2-1	F07 0-2	M18 0-0
22 TRANMERE	S02 0-3	M21 3-1	D26 0-0	O25 2-2	F21 0-3	N04 1-0	D06 1-1	J31 0-0	A30 0-2	O04 2-0	F24 0-0	D20 0-2	N08 1-2	a07 2-2	A15 2-1	S20 6-0	a28 3-3	a13 3-0	N22 3-1	a03 0-2	F10 3-0		J09 0-0	m03 2-1
23 W.B.A.	N23 1-0	M07 1-1	F21 1-1	N08 1-0	J17 0-1	D20 0-2	J27 2-3	D02 0-1	a04 2-1	N04 1-0	m03 1-1	O04 1-2	M21 2-2	F24 0-3	F14 1-1	S07 1-0	O25 2-0	D06 3-2	D28 1-1	a13 3-3	S20 0-0	A09 2-1		A24 1-0
24 WOLVERHAMPTON	F28 1-3	F18 2-1	A30 4-2	S13 3-1	M14 1-0	S27 1-1	N15 1-1	a11 2-2	N01 1-0	J10 5-0	D14 2-1	D26 1-0	S03 1-1	M29 2-0	N29 3-2	a18 3-1	A16 0-0	a25 3-4	M04 1-1	F07 0-1	O18 3-1	O22 2-1	J31 0-1	

Season 1997-98

Crystal Palace relegated to Div 1; Watford, Bristol City and Grimsby Town promoted to Div 1; Manchester City, Stoke City and Reading relegated to Div 2; Notts County, Macclesfield Town, Lincoln City and Colchester United promoted to Div 2; Brentford, Plymouth Argyle, Carlisle United and Southend United relegated to Div 3; Doncaster Rovers relegated from Div 3, replaced by Halifax Town.

DIVISION 2

	BLACKPOOL	BOURNEMOUTH	BRENTFORD	BRISTOL C	BRISTOL R	BURNLEY	CARLISLE	CHESTERFIELD	FULHAM	GILLINGHAM	GRIMSBY	LUTON	MILLWALL	NORTHAMPTON	OLDHAM	PLYMOUTH	PRESTON	SOUTHEND	WALSALL	WATFORD	WIGAN	WREXHAM	WYCOMBE	YORK
1 BLACKPOOL		J17 1-0	a13 1-2	F02 2-2	a25 1-0	N08 2-1	S07 2-1	O21 2-1	F28 2-1	M21 2-1	O18 2-2	A09 1-0	F14 3-0	N04 1-1	S20 2-2	D02 0-0	D20 2-1	S27 3-0	a04 1-0	M07 1-1	J31 0-2	D28 1-2	A23 2-4	N22 1-0
2 BOURNEMOUTH	A30 2-0		N01 0-0	F07 1-0	S02 1-1	a25 2-1	N22 3-2	F14 2-0	O18 2-1	D26 4-0	S27 0-1	S13 1-1	O21 0-0	J10 3-0	J24 0-0	M03 3-3	F28 0-2	N18 2-1	a14 10	D20 0-1	A16 1-0	M14 0-1	a04 0-0	D02 0-0
3 BRENTFORD	D13 3-1	M07 3-2		N08 1-4	O21 2-3	S27 2-1	N04 0-1	A16 0-0	a11 0-2	S02 2-0	A30 3-1	a25 2-2	J10 2-1	M21 0-0	M28 2-1	J31 3-1	F14 0-0	D26 1-1	O18 3-0	J24 1-2	a18 0-2	N29 1-1	S19 1-1	F28 1-2
4 BRISTOL C	A16 2-0	S20 1-1	M03 2-2		M14 2-0	D02 3-1	a04 1-0	D20 1-0	S02 0-2	F14 0-2	J10 4-1	S27 3-0	D26 4-1	J24 0-0	N01 1-0	N18 2-1	O21 2-1	F28 1-0	a25 2-1	a13 1-1	A30 3-0	M31 1-1	N22 3-1	O17 2-1
5 BRISTOL R	O25 0-3	D28 5-3	m02 2-1	N04 1-2		J17 1-0	A23 3-1	F07 3-1	N08 2-3	S13 1-2	D12 0-4	a18 2-1	N29 2-1	M07 0-2	F21 3-1	A09 1-1	M21 2-2	M27 2-0	S09 2-0	O14 1-2	a10 5-0	O04 1-0	F24 3-1	M10 1-2
6 BURNLEY	a07 1-2	O25 2-2	F21 1-1	a11 1-0	A30 0-0		O11 3-1	D26 0-0	a18 2-1	A16 0-0	M28 2-1	M14 1-1	N18 1-2	N29 2-1	S02 0-0	m02 2-1	S20 1-1	J24 1-0	N01 2-1	J10 2-0	D13 0-2	F24 1-2	O04 2-2	J31 7-2
7 CARLISLE	D26 1-1	M28 0-1	M14 1-2	N29 0-3	J24 3-1	F28 2-1		N18 0-2	D13 2-0	S27 2-1	a21 0-1	O21 0-1	M03 1-0	A30 0-2	a11 3-1	S20 2-2	O17 0-2	J10 5-0	F14 1-1	A16 0-2	S02 1-0	N01 2-2	J31 0-0	a25 1-2
8 CHESTERFIELD	m02 1-1	O04 1-1	J03 0-0	a18 1-0	S20 0-0	S07 1-0	M21 2-1		M07 0-2	N04 1-1	N08 1-0	D13 0-0	M28 3-1	a11 2-1	F24 2-1	J17 2-1	A23 3-2	N29 1-0	A09 3-1	J31 0-1	O11 2-3	F21 3-1	O25 1-0	D28 1-1
9 FULHAM	O11 1-0	F24 0-1	D02 1-1	D28 1-0	M03 1-0	D19 1-0	a13 5-0	N01 1-1		N21 3-0	S13 0-2	A23 0-0	M14 1-2	O25 1-1	O04 3-1	S09 2-0	a04 2-1	F07 2-0	a07 1-1	m02 1-2	F21 2-0	A09 1-0	J17 0-0	N18 1-1
10 GILLINGHAM	N18 1-1	S05 2-1	D29 3-1	O04 2-0	J31 1-1	J03 2-0	F21 1-0	M14 1-0	M28 2-0		N29 0-2	a11 2-1	N01 1-3	F24 1-0	M03 2-1	O25 2-1	A09 0-0	D13 1-2	A23 2-1	S20 2-2	m02 0-0	a18 1-1	O11 1-0	J17 0-0
11 GRIMSBY	F24 1-0	F21 2-1	J17 4-0	A09 1-1	a13 1-2	N22 4-1	D20 1-0	M03 0-0	J31 1-1	a04 0-0		a07 0-1	S20 0-1	O11 1-0	m02 0-2	M24 1-0	D28 3-1	N01 5-1	M14 3-0	O25 0-1	O04 2-1	A23 0-0	D02 0-0	S09 0-0
12 LUTON	J10 3-0	J31 1-2	O25 2-0	F21 0-0	D20 2-4	N04 2-3	m02 3-2	a14 3-0	J24 1-4	D02 2-2	M21 2-2		S02 0-2	D26 2-2	A30 1-1	O11 3-0	N08 1-3	A18 1-0	N22 0-1	O04 0-4	F24 1-1	S20 2-5	M07 0-0	a04 3-0
13 MILLWALL	O04 2-1	m02 1-2	A09 3-0	O29 0-2	a04 1-1	M21 1-0	N08 1-1	N22 1-1	N04 1-1	M07 1-0	F07 0-1	D28 0-2		F21 0-0	O11 2-1	a13 1-1	M25 0-1	S13 3-1	D03 0-1	F25 1-1	O25 1-1	J17 0-1	D20 1-0	A23 2-3
14 NORTHAMPTON	M14 2-0	A09 0-2	N18 4-0	A23 2-1	N01 1-1	a04 0-1	J17 2-1	D02 0-0	a25 1-0	O18 2-1	F28 2-1	S09 1-0	S27 2-0		J31 0-0	D20 2-1	a13 2-2	F14 3-1	D28 3-2	N22 0-1	S20 1-0	M03 0-1	F10 2-0	O21 1-1
15 OLDHAM	F07 0-1	A23 2-1	N22 1-1	M31 1-2	S27 4-4	a28 3-3	D02 3-1	O18 2-0	F14 1-0	N07 3-1	O21 2-0	J17 2-1	F28 1-1	S13 2-2		a04 2-0	S09 1-0	a25 2-0	D19 0-0	M21 2-2	N04 3-1	J27 3-0	a13 0-1	A09 3-1
16 PLYMOUTH	a11 3-1	N08 3-0	S13 0-0	M21 2-0	J10 1-2	O21 2-2	F07 2-1	A30 1-1	D26 1-4	a25 0-1	A16 2-2	F28 0-2	D13 3-0	a18 1-3	N29 0-2		M07 2-0	O18 2-3	S27 2-1	S02 0-1	J24 3-2	M28 2-0	N04 4-2	F14 0-0
17 PRESTON	a18 3-3	O11 0-1	O04 2-1	m02 2-1	N18 1-2	F07 2-3	F24 0-3	J24 0-0	N29 3-1	J10 1-3	S02 2-0	M03 1-0	A16 2-1	D13 1-0	D26 1-1	N01 0-1		a11 1-0	S13 0-0	A30 2-0	M28 1-1	O25 0-1	F21 1-1	M14 3-2
18 SOUTHEND	F21 2-1	M21 5-3	S05 3-1	O11 0-2	N22 1-1	A23 1-0	A09 1-1	a03 0-2	S20 1-0	a13 0-0	M07 0-1	J03 1-2	J31 0-0	O04 0-0	O25 1-1	F24 3-0	D02 3-2		J17 0-1	N04 0-3	N08 1-0	m02 1-3	D28 1-2	D19 4-4
19 WALSALL	N29 2-1	D13 2-1	F24 0-0	O25 0-0	D26 0-1	M07 0-0	O04 3-1	J10 3-2	A16 1-1	M31 1-0	N04 0-0	M28 2-3	a11 2-0	S02 0-2	a18 0-0	F21 0-1	J31 1-1	A30 3-1		N08 0-0	M21 1-0	O11 3-0	m02 0-1	S20 2-0
20 WATFORD	N01 4-1	a28 2-1	A23 3-1	D13 1-1	F28 3-2	A09 1-0	M17 2-1	S13 2-1	O21 2-0	F08 0-2	a25 0-0	F14 1-1	O18 0-1	M28 1-1	N18 2-1	D28 1-1	J17 3-1	M14 1-1	M03 1-2		N29 2-1	a11 1-0	S07 2-1	S27 1-1
21 WIGAN	S13 3-0	a07 1-0	D20 4-0	J17 0-3	D02 3-0	a13 5-1	D28 0-2	F28 2-1	S27 2-1	O21 1-4	F14 0-2	O18 1-1	a24 0-0	F07 1-1	M14 1-0	A23 1-1	N22 1-4	M17 1-3	a21 2-0	a04 3-2		S08 3-2	A09 5-2	N01 1-1
22 WREXHAM	S02 3-4	N04 2-1	a04 2-2	S13 2-1	F14 1-0	O18 0-0	M07 2-2	S27 0-0	J10 0-3	D20 0-0	M31 0-0	F07 2-1	M17 1-0	N08 1-0	A16 3-1	N22 1-1	a25 0-0	O21 3-1	F28 2-1	D02 1-1	D26 2-2		M21 2-0	a13 1-2
23 WYCOMBE	J24 2-1	N29 1-1	F07 0-0	M28 1-2	O18 1-0	F14 2-1	S13 1-4	a25 1-1	A30 2-0	F28 1-0	a10 1-1	N01 2-2	a18 0-0	A16 0-0	D13 2-1	M14 5-1	S27 0-0	S02 4-1	O21 4-2	D26 0-0	J10 1-2	N18 0-0		M03 1-0
24 YORK	M28 1-1	a11 0-1	O11 3-1	F24 0-1	A16 0-1	S13 3-1	O25 4-3	S02 0-1	M21 0-1	A30 2-1	D26 0-0	N29 1-2	J24 2-3	m02 0-0	J10 0-0	O04 1-0	N04 1-0	a18 1-1	F07 1-0	F21 1-1	M07 2-2	D13 1-0	N08 2-0	

DIVISION 3

	BARNET	BRIGHTON	CAMBRIDGE	CARDIFF	CHESTER	COLCHESTER	DARLINGTON	DONCASTER	EXETER	HARTLEPOOL	HULL	LEYTON O	LINCOLN	MACCLESFIELD	MANSFIELD	NOTTS CO	PETERBOROUGH	ROCHDALE	ROTHERHAM	SCARBOROUGH	SCUNTHORPE	SHREWSBURY	SWANSEA	TORQUAY
1 BARNET		M14 2-0	J31 2-0	F14 2-2	A30 2-1	J24 3-2	N29 2-0	N08 1-1	A16 1-2	M28 1-1	O18 2-0	a11 1-2	S27 0-0	D13 3-1	a25 0-1	N01 1-2	D26 2-0	O21 3-1	J10 0-0	a18 1-1	S20 0-1	F28 1-1	S02 2-0	N18 3-3
2 BRIGHTON	N05 0-3		M21 0-2	N22 0-1	F28 3-2	D26 4-4	S13 0-0	F14 0-0	O18 1-3	M07 0-0	a25 2-2	A30 0-1	O22 0-1	A16 1-1	a13 1-1	D03 0-1	S03 2-2	S27 2-1	N08 1-2	J24 1-1	a04 2-1	D20 0-0	J10 0-1	F07 1-4
3 CAMBRIDGE	S13 1-3	N18 1-1		S27 2-2	J24 1-2	S02 4-1	M28 1-0	F07 2-1	D12 2-1	N29 2-0	O21 0-1	D26 1-0	F13 1-1	M03 0-0	F28 2-0	a25 2-2	a11 1-0	O18 1-1	A16 2-1	J10 2-3	M14 2-2	A30 4-3	a18 4-1	N01 1-1
4 CARDIFF	O04 1-1	M28 0-0	F21 0-0		S16 0-2	a11 0-2	m02 0-0	M14 7-1	D26 1-1	O25 1-1	N18 2-1	J10 1-0	F07 0-1	a18 1-2	F17 4-1	A30 1-1	D13 0-0	S13 2-1	F24 2-2	N29 1-1	N11 0-0	S02 2-2	N02 0-1	N08 1-1
5 CHESTER	J17 0-1	O11 2-0	A23 1-1	J27 0-0		a18 3-1	D13 2-1	a11 2-1	N29 1-1	O04 3-1	S05 1-0	M03 1-1	A09 2-0	O25 1-1	F07 0-1	M14 0-1	N18 0-0	N01 4-0	F21 4-0	m02 1-1	D28 1-0	S13 2-0	N26 2-0	F24 1-3
6 COLCHESTER	A22 1-1	S08 3-1	D29 3-2	J20 2-1	D19 2-0		A09 2-1	O21 2-1	S27 1-2	J03 1-2	a13 4-3	a25 1-1	N22 0-1	M14 5-1	F13 2-0	N18 2-0	F27 1-0	M03 0-0	a03 2-1	S12 1-0	O31 3-3	O18 1-1	F06 1-2	J16 1-0
7 DARLINGTON	a04 2-3	J31 1-0	N22 1-1	O21 0-0	a13 1-0	J10 4-2		O18 5-1	J24 3-2	S20 1-1	N01 4-3	N18 1-0	a25 2-2	D26 4-2	S27 0-0	F14 0-2	M03 3-1	F28 1-0	A30 1-1	S02 1-2	D20 1-0	M31 3-1	S09 3-2	M14 1-2
8 DONCASTER	M03 0-2	O04 1-3	S20 0-0	N04 1-1	D02 2-1	m02 0-1	F24 0-2		A30 0-1	O11 2-2	a04 1-0	S02 1-4	M21 2-4	J24 0-3	F03 0-3	a13 1-2	A16 0-5	N22 0-3	D19 0-3	M10 1-2	J30 1-2	J10 1-0	O24 0-3	F21 0-1
9 EXETER	J20 0-0	F24 2-1	a13 1-0	S09 1-1	a04 5-0	F21 0-1	A23 1-0	J17 5-1		A09 1-1	M14 3-0	J31 2-2	D02 1-2	m02 1-3	N18 1-0	M03 2-5	N01 0-0	D20 3-0	S20 3-1	O04 1-1	O25 2-3	N22 2-2	O11 1-0	D28 1-1
10 HARTLEPOOL	N22 2-0	N01 0-0	a04 3-3	a25 2-0	F14 0-0	A16 3-2	F07 2-2	F28 3-1	J10 1-1		D02 2-2	O18 2-2	a13 1-1	A30 0-0	D20 2-2	S02 1-1	O21 2-1	N18 2-0	J24 0-0	D26 3-0	M03 0-1	S27 2-1	M14 4-2	S13 3-0
11 HULL	F24 0-2	O25 0-0	m02 1-0	M21 0-1	D26 1-2	D13 3-1	M07 1-1	N29 3-0	N04 3-2	a11 2-1		a18 3-2	S13 0-2	M28 0-0	J10 0-0	A16 0-3	J24 3-1	F07 0-2	S02 0-0	O11 3-0	F21 2-1	N08 1-4	A30 7-4	O04 3-3
12 LEYTON O	D02 2-0	J17 3-1	S05 0-2	A09 0-1	N08 1-0	O25 0-2	M21 2-0	D28 8-0	S13 1-0	F24 2-1	D20 2-1		M07 1-0	O04 1-1	a04 2-2	N22 1-1	F06 1-0	A23 2-0	O11 1-1	N04 3-1	a21 1-0	a13 2-3	F21 2-2	m02 2-1
13 LINCOLN	F21 2-0	m02 2-1	O04 0-0	S20 1-0	J10 1-3	M28 0-1	O25 3-1	N18 2-1	a21 2-1	D13 1-1	J31 1-0	N01 1-0		N29 1-1	S02 0-2	J24 3-5	a18 3-0	M14 2-0	D26 0-1	A30 3-3	F24 1-1	A16 1-0	M03 1-1	O11 1-1
14 MACCLESFIELD	a13 2-0	J27 1-0	N08 3-1	D20 1-0	a25 3-2	N04 0-0	S05 2-1	A23 3-0	O21 2-2	J17 2-1	N22 2-0	F14 1-0	a04 1-0		O18 1-0	F28 2-0	S27 1-1	D28 1-0	M07 0-0	F07 3-1	J20 2-0	M21 2-1	S13 3-0	A09 2-1
15 MANSFIELD	O25 1-2	D13 1-1	O11 3-2	A23 1-2	S20 4-1	O04 1-1	F21 4-0	S05 1-1	M21 3-2	a18 2-2	A09 2-0	N29 0-0	D28 2-2	F24 1-0		J31 0-2	M28 2-0	J03 3-0	N04 3-3	N08 3-2	J17 1-0	M07 1-1	m02 1-0	a11 2-2
16 NOTTS CO	M07 2-0	a11 2-2	O25 1-0	J17 3-1	N04 1-2	M21 0-0	O04 1-1	D13 5-2	N08 1-1	D28 2-0	J20 1-0	M28 1-0	A23 1-2	O11 1-1	S13 1-0		N29 2-2	A09 2-1	m02 5-2	F21 1-0	S07 2-1	F07 1-1	F24 2-1	a18 3-0
17 PETERBOROUGH	S07 5-1	D28 1-2	D02 1-0	a13 2-0	M21 2-1	O11 3-2	N08 1-1	F10 0-1	M07 1-1	m02 0-0	A23 2-0	S20 2-0	D20 5-1	F21 0-1	N22 1-1	a03 1-0		J17 3-1	J31 1-0	F24 0-0	A09 0-1	N04 1-1	O04 3-1	O25 2-0
18 ROCHDALE	m02 2-1	F21 2-0	F24 2-0	J31 0-0	M07 1-1	N08 2-1	O11 5-0	M28 4-1	a18 3-0	M21 2-1	S20 2-1	J24 0-2	N04 0-0	S02 2-0	A16 2-0	J10 1-2	A30 1-2		O25 0-1	a11 4-0	O04 2-0	D26 3-1	D13 3-0	N29 0-1
19 ROTHERHAM	A09 2-3	M03 0-0	J27 2-2	O18 1-1	S27 4-2	N29 3-2	J17 3-0	a18 3-0	F07 1-0	A23 2-1	D28 5-4	F28 2-1	S10 3-1	N01 1-0	M14 2-2	O21 1-1	S13 2-2	a25 2-2		M28 0-0	N18 1-3	F14 0-1	a11 1-1	D13 0-1
20 SCARBOROUGH	D19 1-0	A22 2-1	A09 1-0	a03 3-1	O21 4-1	J31 1-1	J06 2-1	N01 4-0	F14 4-1	S07 1-1	F28 2-1	M14 2-0	J17 2-2	S20 2-1	M03 2-2	S27 1-2	O18 1-3	D06 1-0	N22 1-2		a13 0-0	a25 0-0	N18 3-2	J20 4-1
21 SCUNTHORPE	F07 1-1	N29 0-2	N04 3-3	F28 3-3	S02 2-1	M07 1-0	a18 1-0	S13 1-1	a25 2-1	N08 1-1	S27 2-0	A16 1-0	O18 0-1	a11 1-0	A30 1-0	D26 1-2	J10 1-3	F14 2-0	M21 1-1	D13 1-3		O21 1-1	J24 1-0	M28 2-0
22 SHREWSBURY	O11 2-0	a18 2-1	J17 1-1	D18 3-2	J31 1-1	F24 0-2	a11 3-0	A09 2-1	M28 1-1	F21 1-0	M03 2-0	D13 1-2	M24 0-2	N18 4-3	N01 3-2	S20 1-2	M14 4-1	S09 1-0	O04 2-1	O25 0-1	m02 0-2		N29 0-1	A23 1-2
23 SWANSEA	D28 0-2	A09 1-0	D20 1-1	M08 1-1	M28 2-0	S20 0-1	J27 4-0	a25 0-0	F28 2-1	N04 0-2	J17 2-0	S27 1-1	N08 0-0	J31 1-1	O21 0-1	O18 1-2	F14 0-1	a13 3-0	D02 1-1	M21 0-0	A23 2-0	a04 0-1		S05 2-0
24 TORQUAY	M21 0-0	S20 3-0	M07 0-3	M03 1-0	O18 3-1	A30 1-1	N04 2-1	S27 2-0	S02 1-2	J31 1-0	F14 5-1	O21 1-1	F28 3-2	J10 2-0	D02 2-1	D20 0-2	a25 3-1	a04 0-0	a13 1-2	A16 1-0	N22 2-4	J24 3-0	D26 2-0	

LEAGUE TABLES

FA PREMIER LEAGUE

	P	W	D	L	F	A	W	D	L	F	A	Pts
Arsenal	38	15	2	2	43	10	8	7	4	25	23	78
Manchester U	38	13	4	2	42	9	10	4	5	31	17	77
Liverpool	38	13	2	4	42	16	5	9	5	26	26	65
Chelsea	38	13	2	4	37	14	7	1	11	34	29	63
Leeds U	38	9	5	5	31	21	8	3	8	26	25	59
Blackburn R	38	11	4	4	40	26	5	6	8	17	26	58
Aston Villa	38	9	3	7	26	24	8	3	8	23	24	57
West Ham U	38	13	4	2	40	18	3	4	12	16	39	56
Derby Co	38	12	3	4	33	18	4	4	11	19	31	55
Leicester C	38	6	10	3	21	15	7	4	8	30	26	53
Coventry C	38	8	9	2	26	17	4	7	8	20	27	52
Southampton	38	10	1	8	28	23	4	5	10	22	32	48
Newcastle U	38	8	5	6	22	20	3	6	10	13	24	44
Tottenham H	38	7	8	4	23	22	4	3	12	21	34	44
Wimbledon	38	5	6	8	18	25	5	8	6	16	21	44
Sheffield W	38	9	5	5	30	26	3	3	13	22	41	44
Everton	38	7	5	7	25	27	2	8	9	16	29	40
Bolton W	38	7	8	4	25	22	2	5	12	16	39	40
Barnsley	38	7	4	8	25	35	3	1	15	12	47	35
Crystal Palace	38	2	5	12	15	39	6	4	9	22	32	33

DIVISION 1

	P	W	D	L	F	A	W	D	L	F	A	Pts
Nottingham F	46	18	2	3	52	20	10	8	5	30	22	94
Middlesbrough	46	17	4	2	51	12	10	6	7	26	29	91
Sunderland	46	14	7	2	49	22	12	5	6	37	28	90
Charlton A	46	17	5	1	48	17	9	5	9	32	32	88
Ipswich T	46	14	5	4	47	20	9	9	5	30	23	83
Sheffield U	46	16	5	2	44	20	3	12	8	25	34	74
Birmingham C	46	10	8	5	27	15	9	9	5	33	20	74
Stockport Co	46	14	6	3	46	21	5	2	16	25	48	65
Wolverh'pton W	46	13	6	4	42	25	5	5	13	15	28	65
W.B.A.	46	9	8	6	27	26	7	5	11	23	30	61
Crewe A	46	10	2	11	30	34	8	3	12	28	31	59
Oxford U	46	12	6	5	36	20	4	4	15	24	44	58
Bradford	46	10	9	4	26	23	4	6	13	20	36	57
Tranmere R	46	9	8	6	34	26	5	6	12	20	31	56
Norwich C	46	9	8	6	32	27	5	5	13	20	42	55
Huddersfield T	46	9	5	9	28	28	5	6	12	22	44	53
Bury	46	7	10	6	22	22	4	9	10	20	36	52
Swindon T	46	9	6	8	28	25	5	4	14	14	48	52
Port Vale	46	7	6	10	25	24	6	4	13	31	42	49
Portsmouth	46	8	6	9	28	30	5	4	14	23	33	49
Q.P.R.	46	8	9	6	28	21	2	10	11	23	42	49
Manchester C	46	6	6	11	28	26	6	6	11	28	31	48
Stoke C	46	8	5	10	30	40	3	8	12	14	34	46
Reading	46	8	4	11	27	31	3	5	15	12	47	42

DIVISION 2

	P	W	D	L	F	A	W	D	L	F	A	Pts
Watford	46	13	7	3	36	22	11	9	3	31	19	88
Bristol C	46	16	5	2	41	17	9	5	9	28	22	85
Grimsby	46	11	7	5	30	14	8	8	7	25	23	72
Northampton T	46	14	5	4	33	17	4	12	7	19	20	71
Bristol R	46	13	2	8	43	33	7	8	8	27	31	70
Fulham	46	12	7	4	31	14	8	3	12	29	29	70
Wrexham	46	10	10	3	31	23	8	6	9	24	28	70
Gillingham	46	13	7	3	30	18	6	6	11	22	29	70
Bournemouth	46	11	8	4	28	15	7	4	12	29	37	66
Chesterfield	46	13	7	3	31	19	3	10	10	15	25	65
Wigan A	46	12	5	6	41	31	5	6	12	23	35	62
Blackpool	46	13	6	4	35	24	4	5	14	24	43	62
Oldham A	46	13	7	3	43	23	2	9	12	19	31	61
Wycombe	46	10	10	3	32	20	4	8	11	19	33	60
Preston N.E.	46	10	6	7	29	26	5	8	10	27	30	59
York C	46	9	7	7	26	21	5	10	8	26	37	59
Luton T	46	7	7	9	35	38	7	8	8	25	26	57
Millwall	46	7	8	8	23	23	7	5	11	20	31	55
Walsall	46	10	8	5	26	16	4	4	15	17	36	54
Burnley	46	10	9	4	34	23	3	4	16	21	42	52
Brentford	46	9	7	7	33	29	2	10	11	17	42	50
Plymouth A	46	10	5	8	36	30	2	8	13	19	40	49
Carlisle U	46	8	5	10	27	28	4	3	16	30	45	44
Southend U	46	8	7	8	29	30	3	3	17	18	49	43

DIVISION 3

	P	W	D	L	F	A	W	D	L	F	A	Pts
Notts Co	46	14	7	2	41	20	15	5	3	41	23	99
Macclesfield	46	19	4	0	40	11	4	9	10	23	33	82
Lincoln C	46	11	7	5	32	24	9	8	6	28	27	75
Colchester U	46	14	5	4	41	24	7	6	10	31	36	74
Torquay U	46	14	4	5	39	22	7	7	9	29	37	74
Scarborough	46	14	6	3	44	23	5	9	9	23	35	72
Barnet	46	10	8	5	35	22	9	5	9	26	29	70
Scunthorpe U	46	11	7	5	30	24	8	5	10	26	28	69
Rotherham U	46	10	9	4	41	30	6	10	7	26	31	67
Peterborough U	46	13	6	4	37	16	5	7	11	26	35	67
Leyton O	46	14	5	4	40	20	5	7	11	22	27	*66
Mansfield T	46	11	9	3	42	26	5	8	10	22	29	65
Shrewsbury T	46	12	3	8	35	28	4	10	9	26	34	61
Chester C	46	12	7	4	34	15	5	3	15	26	46	61
Exeter C	46	10	8	5	39	25	5	7	11	29	38	60
Cambridge U	46	11	8	4	39	27	3	10	10	24	30	60
Hartlepool U	46	10	12	1	40	22	2	11	10	21	31	59
Rochdale	46	15	3	5	43	15	2	4	17	13	40	58
Darlington	46	13	6	4	43	28	1	6	16	13	44	54
Swansea C	46	8	8	7	24	16	5	3	15	25	46	50
Cardiff C	46	5	13	5	27	22	4	10	9	21	30	50
Hull C	46	10	6	7	36	32	1	2	20	20	51	41
Brighton & H.A.	46	3	10	10	21	34	3	7	13	17	32	35
Doncaster	46	3	3	17	14	48	1	5	17	16	65	20

* Leyton Orient deducted 3 points.

Football League Records

Top scorers: Prem Lge, J.F.Hasslebank (Leeds United) M.Owen (Liverpool, D.Yorke (Manchester United) 18 goals; Div 1, L.Hughes (West Bromwich Albion) 31 goals; Div 2, J.Cureton (Bristol Rovers) 25 goals; Div 3, M.Gabbiadini (Darlington) 23 goals.

Play-offs: Prem Lge, Bolton Wanderers v Ipswich Town 1-0, 3-4; Watford v Birmingham City 1-0, 0-1 (7-6 penalties); Bolton Wanderers v Watford 0-2; Div 1, Wigan Athletic v Manchester City 1-1, 0-1; Preston North End v Gillingham 1-1, 0-1; Gillingham v Manchester City 2-2 (1-3 penalties); Div 2, Leyton Orient v Rotherham United 0-0, 0-0 (4-2 penalties); Swansea City v Scunthorpe United 1-0, 1-3; Leyton Orient v Scunthorpe United 0-1.

Sunderland, Bradford City and Watford promoted to Prem Lge; Charlton Athletic, Blackburn Rovers and Nottingham

Eighteen goals was enough to top the Premiership list this season. Leeds United's Jimmy Floyld Hasslebank (above) shared the distinction with Michael Owen (Liverpool) and Dwight Yorke (Manchester United).

DIVISION PREMIER

	ARSENAL	ASTON VILLA	BLACKBURN	CHARLTON	CHELSEA	COVENTRY	DERBY	EVERTON	LEEDS	LEICESTER	LIVERPOOL	MANCHESTER U	MIDDLESBROUGH	NEWCASTLE	NOTTINGHAM F	SHEFFIELD W	SOUTHAMPTON	TOTTENHAM	WEST HAM	WIMBLEDON
1 ARSENAL		m16 1-0	a06 1-0	A29 0-0	J31 1-0	M20 2-0	m02 1-0	N08 1-0	D20 3-1	F20 5-0	J09 0-0	S20 3-0	N29 1-1	O04 3-0	A17 2-1	M09 3-0	O17 1-1	N14 0-0	D26 1-0	a19 5-1
2 ASTON VILLA	D13 3-2		F06 1-3	m08 3-4	M21 0-3	F27 1-4	S26 1-0	J18 3-0	F17 1-2	O24 1-1	N21 2-4	D05 1-1	A23 3-1	S09 1-0	a24 2-0	D28 2-1	a10 3-0	N07 3-2	a02 0-0	S12 2-0
3 BLACKBURN	O25 1-2	D26 2-1		D05 1-0	S21 3-4	N07 1-2	A15 0-0	M10 1-2	J09 1-0	A29 1-0	a24 1-3	m12 0-0	a03 0-0	D12 0-0	m08 1-2	F20 1-4	N21 0-2	J30 1-1	O03 3-0	M20 3-1
4 CHARLTON	D28 0-1	D21 0-1	m01 0-0		a03 0-1	S26 1-1	S12 1-2	N28 1-2	a17 1-1	N07 0-0	F13 1-0	J31 0-1	N14 1-1	J17 2-2	F27 0-0	m16 0-1	A22 5-0	a20 1-4	O24 4-2	F08 2-0
5 CHELSEA	S09 0-0	D09 2-1	F17 1-1	O17 2-1		J16 2-1	m16 2-1	m01 3-1	m05 1-0	a18 2-2	F27 2-1	D29 0-0	S26 2-0	A22 1-1	S12 2-1	N28 1-1	F06 1-0	D19 2-0	M13 0-1	N14 3-0
6 COVENTRY	O31 0-1	O03 1-2	M13 1-1	M06 2-1	A15 2-1		D19 1-1	N15 3-0	m16 2-2	N28 1-1	J30 2-1	F20 0-1	a17 1-2	S19 1-5	J09 4-0	O18 1-0	a05 1-0	D26 1-1	A29 0-0	m01 2-1
7 DERBY	D05 0-0	M10 2-1	J16 1-0	F20 0-2	D12 2-2	m08 0-0		F07 2-1	O31 2-2	S19 2-0	M13 3-2	O24 1-1	D28 2-1	a03 3-4	a10 1-0	S09 1-0	a24 0-0	O03 0-1	N22 0-2	A22 0-0
8 EVERTON	M13 0-2	A15 0-0	S26 0-0	a24 4-1	D05 0-0	a11 2-0	D26 0-0		S12 0-0	J09 0-0	O17 0-0	O31 1-4	F17 5-0	N23 1-0	J30 0-1	a05 1-2	D12 1-0	A29 0-1	m08 6-0	F27 1-1
9 LEEDS	m11 1-0	S19 0-0	A24 1-0	N21 4-1	O25 0-0	D14 2-0	M20 4-1	F20 1-0		O03 0-1	a12 0-0	a25 1-1	J16 2-0	F06 0-1	a03 3-1	N08 2-1	S08 3-0	M10 2-0	D05 4-0	D29 2-2
10 LEICESTER	S12 1-1	a06 2-2	D28 1-1	M13 1-1	N21 2-4	a24 1-0	m05 1-2	A22 2-0	M01 1-2		O31 1-0	J16 2-6	S09 0-1	m08 2-0	D12 3-1	F06 0-2	D05 2-0	O19 2-1	a10 0-0	S27 1-1
11 LIVERPOOL	A22 0-0	a17 0-1	N29 2-0	S19 3-3	O04 1-1	S09 2-0	N07 1-2	a03 3-2	N14 1-3	a21 0-1		m05 2-2	F06 3-1	D28 4-2	O24 5-1	D19 2-0	J16 7-1	m01 3-2	F20 2-2	m16 3-0
12 MANCHESTER U	F17 1-1	m01 2-1	N14 3-2	S09 4-1	D16 1-1	S12 2-0	F03 1-0	M21 3-1	N29 3-2	A15 2-2	S24 2-0		D19 2-3	N08 0-0	D26 3-0	a17 3-0	F27 2-1	m16 2-1	J10 4-1	O17 5-1
13 MIDDLESBROUGH	a24 1-6	J09 0-0	O17 2-1	a10 2-0	a14 0-0	N21 2-0	A29 1-1	S19 2-2	A15 0-0	J30 0-0	D26 1-3	m09 0-1		D06 2-2	N01 1-1	O03 4-0	M14 3-0	F20 0-0	D12 1-0	a05 3-1
14 NEWCASTLE	F28 1-1	J30 2-1	m16 1-1	A15 0-0	J09 0-1	F17 4-1	O17 2-1	a17 1-3	D26 0-3	D19 1-0	A30 1-4	M13 1-2	m01 1-1		S26 2-0	N14 1-1	S12 4-0	a05 1-1	O31 0-3	N28 3-1
15 NOTTINGHAM F	J16 0-1	N28 2-2	D19 2-2	O03 0-1	F20 1-3	A22 1-0	N16 2-2	S08 0-2	O17 1-1	m16 1-0	a05 2-2	F06 1-8	M20 1-2	M10 1-2		m01 2-0	D28 1-1	a17 0-1	S19 0-0	N07 0-1
16 SHEFFIELD W	S26 1-0	A29 0-1	S12 3-0	D12 3-0	a25 0-0	a03 1-2	J30 0-1	O24 0-0	M13 0-2	D26 0-1	m08 1-0	N21 3-1	F27 3-1	a21 1-1	D07 3-2		O31 0-0	J09 0-0	A15 0-1	M03 1-2
17 SOUTHAMPTON	a03 0-0	N14 1-4	a17 3-3	J09 3-1	D26 0-2	O24 2-1	N28 0-1	m16 2-0	J30 3-0	m01 2-1	A16 1-2	O03 0-3	N07 3-3	F20 2-1	A29 1-2	M20 1-0		S19 1-1	M06 1-0	D19 3-1
18 TOTTENHAM	m05 1-3	M13 1-0	S09 2-1	N02 2-2	m10 2-2	F06 0-0	F27 1-1	D28 4-1	S26 3-3	a03 0-2	D05 2-1	D12 2-2	S13 0-3	O24 2-0	N21 2-0	A22 0-3	M02 3-0		a24 1-2	J16 0-0
19 WEST HAM	F06 0-4	O17 0-0	F27 2-0	a05 0-1	N08 1-1	D28 2-0	a17 5-1	D19 2-1	m01 1-5	N14 3-2	S12 2-1	A22 0-0	m16 4-0	M20 2-0	F13 2-1	J16 0-4	S28 1-0	N28 2-1		S09 3-4
20 WIMBLEDON	N21 1-0	F21 0-0	O31 1-1	D26 2-1	a11 1-2	D05 2-1	J09 2-1	O03 1-2	A29 1-1	M06 0-1	D13 1-0	a03 1-1	O24 2-2	a24 1-1	M13 1-3	S19 2-1	m08 0-2	A15 3-1	J30 0-0	

Lee Hughes scored 31 goals for West Bromwich Albion but his side still finished in mid-table in Division One.

DIVISION 1

	BARNSLEY	BIRMINGHAM	BOLTON	BRADFORD C	BRISTOL C	BURY	CREWE	C PALACE	GRIMSBY	HUDDERSFIELD	IPSWICH	NORWICH	OXFORD	PORT VALE	PORTSMOUTH	Q.P.R.	SHEFFIELD U	STOCKPORT	SUNDERLAND	SWINDON	TRANMERE	WATFORD	W.B.A.	WOLVERHAMPTON
1 BARNSLEY		J16 0-0	O03 2-2	M03 0-1	M23 2-0	N07 1-1	F06 2-2	S19 4-0	F20 0-0	N27 7-1	N14 0-1	S08 1-3	A31 1-0	O11 0-2	O24 2-1	D28 1-0	a03 2-1	A21 1-1	a16 1-3	D19 1-3	a10 1-1	m01 2-2	A08 2-2	M20 2-3
2 BIRMINGHAM	A29 0-0		F21 0-0	J31 2-1	N28 4-2	S05 1-0	O17 3-1	A16 3-1	S19 0-1	O31 1-1	m02 1-0	M02 0-0	N14 0-1	J09 1-0	M06 4-1	a20 1-0	D26 1-0	S08 2-0	D19 0-0	O20 1-1	O03 2-2	a05 1-2	M13 4-0	a17 0-1
3 BOLTON	M09 3-3	S12 3-1		D26 0-0	a13 1-0	N28 4-0	F27 1-3	J10 3-0	A15 2-0	S26 3-0	a17 2-0	J30 2-0	O17 1-1	N04 3-1	D19 3-1	M13 2-1	A29 2-2	a05 1-2	N01 0-3	S29 2-1	N14 2-2	O20 1-2	F13 2-1	a30 1-1
4 BRADFORD C	S26 2-1	A31 2-1	A23 2-2		O31 5-0	O09 3-0	J16 4-1	J19 2-1	a03 3-0	a17 2-3	F13 0-0	M13 4-1	m01 0-0	S29 4-0	a10 2-1	N28 0-3	S12 2-2	A08 1-2	M09 0-1	N14 3-0	D28 2-0	F06 2-0	F27 1-0	D19 2-1
5 BRISTOL C	S29 1-1	a24 1-2	O23 2-1	M20 2-3		M09 1-1	S26 5-2	D12 1-1	a10 4-1	A31 1-2	F27 0-1	m09 1-0	A08 2-2	a03 2-0	O10 2-2	F05 0-0	D05 2-0	N21 1-1	F13 0-1	D28 3-1	J16 1-1	A22 1-4	S13 1-3	N07 1-6
6 BURY	M13 0-0	D28 2-4	a23 2-1	a05 0-2	O03 0-1		A22 1-0	M06 0-0	N21 1-0	A08 1-0	F06 0-3	F20 0-2	O20 1-0	m09 1-0	S08 2-1	J16 1-1	D11 3-3	O17 1-1	a13 2-5	A31 3-0	S19 0-0	O31 1-3	D05 2-0	M16 0-0
7 CREWE	A15 3-1	a02 0-0	S19 4-4	A28 2-1	a27 1-0	D26 3-1		S08 0-1	M16 0-0	D19 1-2	N28 0-3	J09 3-2	M20 3-1	a10 0-0	m01 3-1	N14 0-2	J30 1-2	F20 0-2	N03 1-4	N07 0-2	O24 1-4	a17 0-1	D08 1-1	O03 0-0
8 C PALACE	F28 1-0	F06 1-1	A08 2-2	M28 1-0	N14 2-1	S30 4-2	F13 1-1		M20 3-1	m01 2-2	M09 3-2	O17 5-1	A22 2-0	S12 0-1	N07 4-1	D19 1-1	S27 1-0	J16 2-2	a05 1-1	a17 0-1	D08 1-1	N28 2-2	D28 1-1	O20 3-2
9 GRIMSBY	S12 1-2	F27 0-3	F06 0-1	O17 2-0	O20 2-1	a17 0-0	S29 1-1	O31 2-0		A22 1-0	A09 0-0	a05 0-1	J16 1-0	S26 2-2	N14 1-1	a13 1-0	a20 1-2	D28 1-0	M13 0-2	N28 1-0	m01 1-0	D19 2-1	A31 5-1	m04 0-0
10 HUDDERSFIELD	a24 0-1	M20 1-1	M02 3-2	N21 2-1	J30 2-2	J09 2-2	m09 0-0	D05 4-0	D26 2-0		N07 2-2	M24 1-1	O03 2-0	A15 2-1	A29 3-3	O17 2-0	S05 1-0	M06 3-0	O21 1-1	a05 1-2	F20 0-0	S08 2-0	D12 0-3	S19 2-1
11 IPSWICH	D12 0-2	D05 1-0	N21 0-1	S08 3-0	S19 3-1	A15 0-0	a24 1-2	O03 3-0	J09 0-1	M13 3-0		O20 0-1	F20 2-1	J30 1-0	D26 3-0	a05 3-1	m09 4-1	a20 1-0	A29 0-2	O17 1-0	M06 1-0	M02 3-2	O31 2-0	N03 2-0
12 NORWICH	F16 0-0	S26 2-0	a20 2-2	N07 2-2	D19 2-1	S13 0-0	A08 2-1	a03 0-1	D02 3-1	O24 4-1	a11 0-0		N29 1-3	M09 3-4	M20 0-0	A22 4-2	F27 1-1	F06 0-2	S29 2-2	m01 2-1	a17 2-2	D29 1-1	J16 1-1	N14 0-0
13 OXFORD	J30 1-0	D12 1-7	a03 0-0	D05 0-1	J09 0-0	a10 0-1	O31 1-1	D26 1-3	A29 0-0	M09 2-2	S12 3-3	a24 2-4		N21 2-1	S06 3-0	S26 4-1	O24 0-2	m09 5-0	F27 0-0	F13 2-0	O10 1-2	M13 0-0	S29 3-0	A15 0-2
14 PORT VALE	a05 1-0	A08 0-2	D28 0-2	a13 1-1	O17 3-2	D19 1-0	O20 1-0	F20 1-0	M23 0-1	F06 2-0	A31 0-3	O03 1-0	a17 1-0		S19 0-2	m01 2-0	O31 2-3	M13 1-1	N14 0-2	J16 0-1	N28 2-2	a27 1-2	A22 0-3	S08 2-1
15 PORTSMOUTH	M28 1-3	S29 0-1	m09 0-2	O20 2-4	a05 0-1	F13 2-1	D05 2-0	M13 1-1	D13 0-1	J16 1-0	A22 0-0	N10 1-2	D28 2-2	F27 4-0		A31 3-0	M09 1-0	a24 3-1	S26 1-1	S12 5-2	F06 1-1	A08 1-2	N21 2-1	O17 1-0
16 Q.P.R.	N04 2-1	O25 0-1	N07 2-0	a24 1-3	A15 1-1	A29 0-0	D12 0-1	m09 6-0	O03 1-2	a03 1-1	D02 1-1	D26 2-0	M03 1-0	D05 3-2	J30 1-1		N21 1-2	S19 2-0	J09 2-2	M20 4-0	S08 0-0	F20 1-2	a10 2-1	M06 0-1
17 SHEFFIELD U	O17 1-1	A22 0-2	J16 1-2	F19 2-2	m01 3-1	N14 3-1	A31 3-1	M02 1-1	S08 3-2	D28 2-1	D20 1-2	S19 2-1	M26 1-2	M20 3-0	O03 2-1	a17 2-0		O20 1-1	N28 0-4	A08 2-1	N07 2-2	M06 3-0	F06 3-0	a05 1-1
18 STOCKPORT	D26 0-1	F13 1-0	N24 0-1	J09 1-2	a17 2-2	a03 0-0	S12 1-1	A29 1-1	S05 2-0	S29 1-1	O24 0-1	A15 0-2	D19 2-0	N08 4-2	N28 2-0	F27 0-0	a10 1-0		m01 0-1	M09 2-1	M20 0-0	N14 1-1	S26 2-2	J30 1-2
19 SUNDERLAND	N21 2-3	m09 2-1	M20 3-1	O03 0-0	S08 1-1	O24 1-0	D23 2-0	D15 2-0	N07 3-1	a10 2-0	J17 2-1	M06 1-0	S19 7-0	D12 2-0	M02 2-0	A08 1-0	a24 0-0	D05 1-0		F06 2-0	A22 5-0	A25 4-1	a03 3-0	F20 2-1
20 SWINDON	m09 1-3	a10 0-1	M06 3-3	D12 1-4	S05 3-2	J30 1-1	M13 1-2	N21 2-0	a24 2-0	O10 3-0	a03 0-6	D05 1-1	S09 4-1	A29 1-1	F20 3-3	O31 3-1	J09 2-2	O03 2-3	A15 1-1		M03 2-3	S19 1-4	O24 2-2	D26 1-0
21 TRANMERE	O20 3-0	M09 0-1	D12 1-1	N10 0-1	A29 1-1	F27 4-0	M26 3-0	J30 3-1	D05 1-2	S11 2-3	S29 0-2	N21 1-3	a05 2-2	a24 1-1	A15 1-1	F13 3-2	M13 2-3	O31 1-1	D26 1-0	S25 0-0		O17 3-2	m09 3-1	J08 1-2
22 WATFORD	D05 0-0	O10 1-1	a10 2-0	A15 1-0	D26 1-0	M20 0-0	N21 4-2	a24 2-1	m09 1-0	F16 1-1	S26 1-0	N03 1-1	N07 2-0	O24 2-2	J09 0-0	S12 2-1	S29 1-1	D12 4-2	J30 2-1	F26 0-1	a03 2-1		J23 0-2	A28 0-2
23 W.B.A.	J09 2-0	N07 1-3	S08 2-3	S20 0-2	F20 2-2	m01 1-0	a05 1-5	N03 3-2	J30 1-1	N14 3-1	M20 0-1	A29 2-0	M06 2-0	D26 3-2	a17 2-2	O21 2-0	A15 4-1	M02 3-1	O18 2-3	a13 1-1	D19 0-2	O04 4-1		N29 2-0
24 WOLVERHAMPTON	O31 1-1	N22 3-1	D05 1-1	m09 2-3	M13 3-0	S26 1-0	M30 3-0	a10 0-0	O24 2-0	F27 2-2	D28 1-0	D12 2-2	F06 1-1	F13 3-1	a03 2-0	S29 1-2	N10 2-1	A31 2-2	S12 1-1	A22 1-0	A08 2-0	J16 0-0	a25 1-1	

SEASON 1998-99

Forest relegated to Div 1; Fulham, Walsall and Manchester City promoted to Div 1; Bury, Oxford United and Bristol City relegated to Div 2; Brentford, Cambridge United, Cardiff City and Scunthorpe United promoted to Div 2; York City, Northampton Town, Lincoln City and Macclesfield Town relegated to Div 3; Scarborough relegated from Div 3, replaced by Cheltenham Town.

DIVISION 2

	BLACKPOOL	BOURNEMOUTH	BRISTOL R	BURNLEY	CHESTERFIELD	COLCHESTER	FULHAM	GILLINGHAM	LINCOLN	LUTON	MACCLESFIELD	MANCHESTER C	MILLWALL	NORTHAMPTON	NOTTS CO	OLDHAM	PRESTON	READING	STOKE	WALSALL	WIGAN	WREXHAM	WYCOMBE	YORK
1 BLACKPOOL		M16 0-0	a24 1-2	a13 0-2	D05 1-1	m08 2-1	O31 2-3	A29 2-2	F20 0-1	S19 1-0	J30 2-1	J09 0-0	O10 2-3	S05 2-1	S08 1-0	A15 3-0	N21 0-0	a10 2-0	M06 0-1	a03 0-2	D26 1-1	M13 1-1	D12 0-0	O03 1-2
2 BOURNEMOUTH	S01 1-1		M09 1-0	N21 5-0	a24 0-0	M27 2-1	M02 1-1	O20 3-3	A08 2-0	D28 1-0	a06 1-0	F13 0-0	A22 3-0	O17 1-1	J16 2-0	S26 2-0	J26 3-1	M13 0-1	F06 4-0	a13 0-1	S12 1-0	m08 0-0	F27 2-0	D12 2-1
3 BRISTOL R	N10 0-2	O03 1-0		J09 3-4	S08 0-0	J30 1-1	M12 2-3	F23 0-1	S19 3-0	F20 1-0	D18 0-0	m01 2-2	a27 3-0	a05 1-1	M27 1-1	N28 2-2	S05 2-2	A15 4-1	O20 1-0	O31 3-4	A29 3-2	O17 0-0	M23 0-2	M06 2-0
4 BURNLEY	N28 1-0	a17 0-0	A08 2-1		J16 1-2	a05 3-1	m01 1-0	F27 0-5	D28 1-1	F06 1-2	M28 4-3	M09 0-6	S01 2-1	D19 0-2	O17 1-1	O20 1-0	M14 0-1	F13 1-1	N10 0-2	J02 0-0	S26 1-1	O31 2-1	S12 1-1	A22 0-1
5 CHESTERFIELD	M27 1-2	N10 3-1	a20 0-0	A15 1-0		J09 3-1	a17 1-0	S05 1-0	N07 3-0	M20 3-1	N28 2-0	F27 1-1	M02 2-1	m03 0-0	O20 3-0	D26 1-3	J23 0-1	A29 1-0	a05 1-1	S12 0-1	D19 1-1	S26 2-1	J30 2-0	O17 2-1
6 COLCHESTER	D18 2-2	a27 2-1	D28 0-3	O09 0-4	A08 1-0		A22 0-1	S12 1-1	m01 1-3	J02 2-2	N06 1-1	M20 0-1	N28 0-0	N10 1-0	a16 2-1	M09 2-2	a02 1-0	F27 1-1	A31 0-1	a10 1-0	F12 2-1	J15 1-3	S26 2-1	F05 2-1
7 FULHAM	M20 4-0	A29 0-0	N07 1-0	D12 4-0	N21 2-1	D26 2-0		a13 3-0	M06 1-0	O03 1-3	J09 1-0	A14 3-0	a21 4-1	J30 2-0	F20 2-1	J26 1-0	m08 3-0	F23 3-1	S08 1-0	O24 4-1	a10 2-0	a24 1-1	S29 2-0	S19 3-3
8 GILLINGHAM	J02 1-0	a09 2-1	A22 0-0	S19 2-1	F06 3-1	F20 1-1	N28 1-0		M20 4-0	O24 1-0	O03 2-2	a17 0-2	D29 1-1	S08 2-3	D19 4-0	N10 2-1	M06 1-1	a01 2-1	m01 4-0	A08 0-1	N07 2-0	S01 4-0	O10 3-0	J16 3-1
9 LINCOLN	S12 1-2	J09 2-1	F27 1-0	J30 1-1	M13 2-0	D12 0-0	S26 1-2	O31 1-2		N21 2-2	D26 1-0	O20 2-1	F13 2-0	J23 1-0	a05 0-1	S05 1-3	A29 3-4	a13 2-2	O17 1-2	a24 0-1	A15 1-0	m04 1-0	m08 0-1	M28 1-2
10 LUTON	F27 1-0	J30 2-2	S12 2-0	S05 1-0	a27 1-0	A29 2-0	M09 0-4	M27 1-0	a17 0-1		m01 1-2	N28 1-1	D19 1-2	O20 1-0	F23 0-1	O17 2-0	A15 1-1	M23 1-1	M13 1-2	S26 0-1	J23 0-4	F13 1-2	J09 3-1	a06 2-1
11 MACCLESFIELD	D28 0-1	O10 2-2	m08 3-4	O24 2-1	a13 2-0	M13 2-0	A08 0-1	M09 1-0	A22 0-0	D12 2-2		S12 0-1	J26 0-2	O31 0-1	A31 0-1	F13 1-0	a10 3-2	S26 2-1	a27 1-2	N21 1-1	F27 0-1	F06 0-2	a03 1-3	a24 1-2
12 MANCHESTER C	A08 3-0	S08 2-1	D12 0-0	O03 2-2	S19 1-1	O31 2-1	J16 3-0	N21 0-0	a10 4-0	a14 2-0	F20 2-0		F06 3-0	M06 0-0	M16 2-1	M13 1-2	O12 0-1	O24 0-1	D28 2-1	S02 3-1	a03 1-0	A22 0-0	a24 1-2	m08 4-0
13 MILLWALL	a05 1-0	D26 1-2	N21 1-1	J23 1-2	O03 0-0	a14 2-0	O17 0-1	J30 3-3	S09 2-0	m08 0-1	A29 0-0	S29 1-1		S19 2-1	M06 1-3	O31 1-1	a24 2-2	D12 1-1	F20 2-0	M13 1-2	J09 3-1	M27 3-0	A15 2-1	O21 3-1
14 NORTHAMPTON	F06 0-0	a02 2-1	O10 3-1	m08 2-2	D12 1-0	a24 3-3	D28 1-1	F13 0-1	A31 0-0	a10 1-0	M20 0-2	S26 2-2	F27 1-2		A22 1-1	S12 1-1	O24 1-1	N21 0-1	A08 1-3	F23 0-1	a29 3-3	M02 0-2	N07 1-1	a13 2-2
15 NOTTS CO	F13 0-1	A15 1-2	O24 1-1	a03 0-0	a10 2-0	N21 1-3	S12 1-0	m08 0-1	O10 2-3	a24 1-2	m04 1-1	S29 1-1	S26 3-1	D26 3-1		J09 0-1	D12 2-3	J30 1-1	O31 1-0	F27 2-1	S05 0-1	a13 1-1	a27 1-0	M13 4-2
16 OLDHAM	J16 3-0	M06 2-3	a13 2-1	a10 1-1	A22 2-0	O03 1-0	A31 1-1	a24 1-4	F06 2-0	a02 1-1	S08 1-2	N07 0-3	M20 0-1	F20 0-1	A08 1-3		S19 0-1	m08 2-0	m04 1-0	D12 0-2	O09 2-3	N21 3-2	O24 0-0	D28 0-2
17 PRESTON	a17 1-2	M20 0-1	F06 2-2	N07 4-1	A31 2-0	O17 2-0	D19 0-1	S26 1-1	F23 5-0	J16 2-1	O20 2-2	a05 1-1	N10 0-1	M27 3-0	m01 1-1	F27 2-1		S12 4-0	A22 3-4	a20 1-0	N28 2-2	D28 3-1	F13 2-1	A08 3-0
18 READING	O21 1-1	N07 3-3	J16 0-6	S09 1-1	J02 1-2	S19 1-1	a05 0-1	O17 0-0	N28 2-1	A22 3-0	M06 1-0	M27 1-3	m01 2-0	a17 0-1	D28 1-0	D19 1-1	F20 2-1		O03 2-1	F06 0-1	N11 0-1	J09 4-0	M20 2-1	N04 1-0
19 STOKE	S26 1-3	S05 2-0	a10 1-4	a24 1-4	O12 0-0	J23 3-3	M16 0-1	D12 0-0	a03 2-0	N07 3-1	A15 2-0	J29 0-1	S12 1-0	J09 3-1	M20 2-3	A29 2-0	D26 0-1	M10 0-4		m08 2-0	O24 2-1	F27 1-3	a14 2-2	N21 2-0
20 WALSALL	O17 1-0	N28 1-0	M20 3-3	A29 3-1	F20 1-1	O20 1-1	m04 2-2	J09 2-1	N10 2-1	M06 1-0	a17 2-0	J23 1-1	N07 3-0	A15 0-0	S18 3-2	m01 3-1	O03 1-0	S30 0-2	D19 1-0		J30 1-2	a06 1-0	D26 2-2	S08 2-3
21 WIGAN	A22 3-0	F20 2-1	M30 1-0	m03 0-0	m08 3-1	S08 1-1	D01 2-0	M13 4-1	a27 3-1	A31 1-3	S19 2-0	O17 0-1	A08 0-1	O03 1-0	F16 3-0	a05 2-0	a13 2-2	a24 4-1	M27 2-3	D28 2-0		D12 1-1	N21 0-0	O31 5-0
22 WREXHAM	N07 1-1	D19 0-1	a03 1-0	M20 1-1	M06 0-0	A15 2-4	N10 0-2	a20 2-1	O03 2-1	S08 1-1	S05 2-1	D26 0-1	O24 0-0	A29 1-0	N28 1-0	a17 1-2	J30 0-5	A08 3-0	S19 0-1	O10 2-1	m01 0-2		a10 0-2	F20 1-1
23 WYCOMBE	m01 2-2	S19 0-2	A31 1-1	F20 2-0	D28 1-0	M06 2-2	F06 1-1	a05 0-2	D19 4-1	A08 0-1	O17 3-0	N10 1-0	J16 0-1	M13 1-2	O03 1-1	M27 3-0	S08 0-1	O31 2-3	N28 0-1	A22 1-2	m05 2-1	O20 3-0		J02 1-2
24 YORK	a27 1-0	m01 0-1	S26 1-0	D26 3-3	a03 1-2	S05 1-2	F27 0-3	A15 1-1	D08 2-1	O10 3-3	N10 0-2	D19 2-1	a10 2-1	N28 1-1	N07 1-1	J30 0-1	J09 0-1	J23 1-1	a17 2-2	F13 1-2	M20 1-3	S12 1-1	A29 3-0	

DIVISION 3

	BARNET	BRENTFORD	BRIGHTON	CAMBRIDGE	CARDIFF	CARLISLE	CHESTER	DARLINGTON	EXETER	HALIFAX	HARTLEPOOL	HULL	MANSFIELD	ORIENT	PETERBOROUGH	PLYMOUTH	ROCHDALE	ROTHERHAM	SCARBOROUGH	SCUNTHORPE	SHREWSBURY	SOUTHEND	SWANSEA	TORQUAY
1 BARNET		A29 0-3	O24 0-1	M13 3-0	F13 1-0	M09 1-0	O11 0-0	J09 3-0	F27 0-1	a03 2-2	A15 0-2	S12 4-1	a17 0-0	D19 3-2	S05 1-9	D26 1-1	O31 0-1	S26 4-2	a10 1-0	N10 1-0	J23 2-2	m01 0-2	J30 0-1	N28 3-1
2 BRENTFORD	J02 3-1		A22 2-0	D18 1-0	D28 1-0	F02 1-1	N28 2-1	S26 3-0	m01 3-0	M16 1-1	O17 3-1	F06 0-2	A08 3-0	a17 0-0	M09 3-0	a05 3-1	A31 2-1	S12 0-3	F27 1-1	O20 2-1	M13 0-0	N10 4-1	m04 4-1	F13 3-2
3 BRIGHTON	M27 0-1	D26 3-1		a06 1-3	M09 0-2	J09 1-3	A15 2-2	M13 0-4	F13 0-1	N21 0-1	O31 3-2	a24 0-0	O17 1-3	F27 1-2	J30 1-0	O20 1-3	m08 1-1	D12 4-1	J23 1-0	S26 1-3	a13 1-0	S12 0-2	S05 1-0	A29 2-0
4 CAMBRIDGE	N07 3-2	m08 0-1	O09 2-3		a03 0-0	J30 1-0	J23 2-1	N21 2-1	S26 1-1	a10 4-0	A29 1-2	M09 2-0	M20 7-2	S12 1-0	a24 1-1	D12 1-0	a13 1-1	D26 3-2	S05 2-3	F13 0-0	O24 0-0	F27 3-0	A15 2-1	J09 2-0
5 CARDIFF	S08 1-0	J30 4-1	O03 2-0	O17 0-1		M27 2-1	M05 0-0	J23 3-2	O31 1-0	F19 1-1	J09 4-1	a05 1-1	D19 4-2	O20 0-0	A15 1-3	S05 1-0	S19 2-1	A29 0-1	N10 1-0	m01 0-0	D26 3-0	N28 2-0	a18 0-0	M13 2-2
6 CARLISLE	O03 2-1	M20 0-1	A08 1-0	D28 1-1	D01 0-1		S19 1-1	a24 3-3	J02 1-3	N07 0-1	D12 2-1	a13 0-0	F20 0-0	F06 1-1	a10 1-1	m08 2-1	A22 0-1	N21 0-0	O09 1-0	J16 0-1	M06 2-1	S01 3-0	S08 1-2	a03 3-0
7 CHESTER	a05 3-0	a13 1-3	J15 1-1	S01 0-3	S26 2-2	F27 2-1		D12 1-0	F06 0-0	a24 2-2	O20 1-1	A23 2-2	D28 1-1	A08 0-2	F13 1-0	M27 3-2	N21 1-1	m08 1-1	M09 1-3	M13 0-2	O31 1-1	J02 1-1	O17 1-1	S12 2-0
8 DARLINGTON	A08 0-2	a27 2-2	N07 1-2	a17 0-0	A31 3-0	M23 1-1	m01 1-2		m04 4-0	A22 2-2	S08 2-0	F16 0-1	F06 5-1	D28 1-1	O10 3-0	F20 1-2	J02 3-0	a03 1-2	N28 3-0	D19 3-1	S19 1-0	M20 2-1	O03 2-2	a10 0-2
9 EXETER	S19 1-0	D12 0-1	S08 1-0	M06 0-3	M20 0-2	A29 2-0	S05 0-1	M26 0-0		m08 2-1	F20 2-1	O20 3-0	O03 2-1	a05 1-1	J23 2-0	J30 1-1	a24 2-1	a13 3-0	A15 1-0	O17 2-2	N21 0-1	N07 2-1	J09 4-0	D26 1-1
10 HALIFAX	O16 1-1	A15 1-0	a17 1-0	O20 3-3	S11 1-2	M13 1-0	N10 3-2	D26 0-0	D19 1-1		S04 2-1	F27 0-1	N27 2-2	M26 1-2	J09 2-2	J23 2-0	a05 0-0	J30 2-4	m01 1-2	a27 1-0	A28 2-0	F13 3-1	O31 2-0	S26 1-1
11 HARTLEPOOL	J16 2-2	a03 0-1	M20 0-0	J02 2-2	A08 1-1	m01 0-0	a10 2-0	F13 2-3	S12 4-3	F06 2-0		A31 1-0	N10 1-2	a27 1-0	S26 1-2	N07 2-0	D28 0-1	F27 0-0	a17 3-0	A22 1-2	O10 1-1	D19 2-4	N28 1-2	O24 4-1
12 HULL	F20 1-1	S05 2-3	N10 0-2	O03 0-3	O09 1-2	N28 1-0	D26 1-2	A15 1-2	a10 2-1	S19 1-2	J23 4-0		M06 0-0	N07 0-1	A29 10	M20 1-0	S08 2-1	J08 1-0	a03 1-1	a17 2-3	J30 1-1	O24 1-1	D19 0-2	m01 1-0
13 MANSFIELD	N20 5-0	J09 3-1	a03 2-0	O31 1-3	m08 3-0	S12 1-1	J30 3-0	S05 0-1	a27 0-1	a13 0-1	a24 2-0	S26 2-0		F13 1-2	D01 1-0	A15 2-0	M13 3-1	J22 0-3	D26 3-2	F27 2-1	D11 1-0	a10 0-0	A29 1-0	O09 2-1
14 ORIENT	m08 2-2	N21 2-1	S19 1-0	F20 2-0	a10 1-1	S05 2-1	J09 2-2	J30 3-2	O09 2-0	O24 1-0	O03 1-1	M13 1-2	S08 1-1		D12 1-2	a13 4-3	M06 3-0	A15 1-4	A29 0-3	O31 1-0	a24 6-1	a03 0-3	D26 1-1	M02 2-0
15 PETERBOROUGH	F06 5-2	O03 2-4	D28 1-2	N10 2-1	J16 2-1	O20 0-1	S08 3-0	a05 0-1	A31 4-1	A08 0-2	M06 1-1	J26 1-1	M28 1-0	m01 3-0		S19 0-2	O17 2-0	O31 2-4	D19 3-1	N28 2-1	F20 2-2	A22 1-1	M13 0-1	a17 4-0
16 PLYMOUTH	A22 2-0	N03 3-0	a10 1-2	m01 2-2	F06 1-1	D19 2-0	F23 2-0	S12 1-2	D28 1-0	A31 1-0	M13 0-0	A31 0-0	J16 3-0	N28 2-4	F27 0-2		A08 2-1	F13 1-0	S26 0-0	M30 5-0	a03 2-0	a17 0-3	N10 1-2	M09 0-0
17 ROCHDALE	M20 0-0	J23 2-0	D19 2-1	a27 0-2	F27 1-1	D26 1-1	a17 3-1	A29 0-0	N10 1-1	O11 1-0	J30 0-1	F12 3-0	N07 1-0	S26 2-1	a03 0-3	J09 1-1		a10 0-0	N17 0-1	S12 2-2	S05 1-0	M30 1-0	m01 0-3	A15 0-2
18 ROTHERHAM	a27 1-1	F20 2-4	m01 2-1	A22 2-0	M16 1-0	a17 3-1	D18 2-4	O17 3-1	N28 0-0	D28 3-1	S19 3-0	A08 3-1	A31 0-0	J16 3-1	M20 2-2	S08 0-2	O20 2-2		N07 4-0	M27 0-0	O03 0-1	F06 2-2	a05 1-0	N10 2-2
19 SCARBOROUGH	O21 0-0	S19 3-1	A31 1-2	F06 1-5	a24 1-2	a05 3-0	O03 2-4	a14 0-2	J16 1-0	D12 1-0	N21 1-2	O17 1-2	A22 2-3	a21 1-3	m08 1-1	m05 3-0	M26 1-0	M13 0-4		D28 1-4	S09 2-0	A08 1-2	F20 2-1	O31 1-1
20 SCUNTHORPE	a24 3-1	a10 0-0	M06 3-1	S08 3-2	D12 0-2	A15 3-1	N07 2-1	m08 0-1	a03 2-0	O03 0-4	D26 1-0	N21 3-2	S19 3-2	M20 2-0	a13 1-1	A29 0-2	F20 0-1	O24 4-3	J30 5-1		J09 3-0	O10 1-1	M23 1-2	S05 2-0
21 SHREWSBURY	A31 0-2	N07 2-0	N28 1-3	M26 1-1	A21 0-3	S26 1-1	M20 2-0	F27 3-0	a17 1-1	J02 2-2	a06 0-1	D28 3-2	m01 1-0	N10 1-1	S12 1-1	O17 2-1	F06 3-2	a20 2-3	F13 3-1	A08 2-1		J16 3-1	O20 1-0	D18 1-2
22 SOUTHEND	D12 2-3	a24 1-4	F20 3-0	S19 0-1	a13 0-1	J23 0-1	A29 0-1	O31 2-1	M13 0-0	S08 0-0	m08 1-1	M26 0-1	O20 1-2	O17 2-2	D26 2-0	N21 1-0	O03 1-1	S05 3-0	J09 1-0	a05 0-1	A15 2-1		M06 2-0	J30 0-0
23 SWANSEA	D28 2-1	F16 2-1	F05 2-2	m06 2-0	N22 2-1	F13 1-1	a03 1-1	M09 2-0	A08 2-0	M20 1-2	a13 1-0	m08 2-0	F23 1-0	A22 1-1	N07 0-0	a24 2-3	D12 1-1	O09 1-1	S12 2-0	A31 1-2	a09 1-1	S26 3-1		F27 0-0
24 TORQUAY	a13 1-1	S08 3-1	J02 1-1	A08 0-1	N07 0-0	O17 2-2	F20 0-3	O20 2-2	A22 1-0	M06 4-0	M27 3-0	D12 2-0	a05 0-0	S01 1-1	N21 0-1	O03 1-1	J16 2-1	a24 2-0	M20 0-1	F06 1-0	m08 0-3	D28 2-0	A19 1-1	

LEAGUE TABLES

FA PREMIER LEAGUE

	P	W	D	L	F	A	W	D	L	F	A	Pts
Manchester U	38	14	4	1	45	18	8	9	2	35	19	79
Arsenal	38	14	5	0	34	5	8	7	4	25	12	78
Chelsea	38	12	6	1	29	13	8	9	2	28	17	75
Leeds U	38	12	5	2	32	9	6	8	5	30	25	67
West Ham U	38	11	3	5	32	26	5	6	8	14	27	57
Aston Villa	38	10	3	6	33	28	5	7	7	18	18	55
Liverpool	38	10	5	4	44	24	5	4	10	24	25	54
Derby Co	38	8	7	4	22	19	5	6	8	18	26	52
Middlesbrough	38	7	9	3	25	18	5	6	8	23	36	51
Leicester C	38	7	6	6	25	25	5	7	7	15	21	49
Tottenham H	38	7	7	5	28	26	4	7	8	19	24	47
Sheffield W	38	7	5	7	20	15	6	2	11	21	27	46
Newcastle U	38	7	6	6	26	25	4	7	8	22	29	46
Everton	38	6	8	5	22	12	5	2	12	20	35	43
Coventry C	38	8	6	5	26	21	3	3	13	13	30	42
Wimbledon	38	7	7	5	22	21	3	5	11	18	42	42
Southampton	38	9	4	6	29	26	2	4	13	8	38	41
Charlton A	38	4	7	8	20	20	4	5	10	21	36	36
Blackburn R	38	6	5	8	21	24	1	9	9	17	28	35
Nottingham F	38	3	7	9	18	31	4	2	13	17	38	30

DIVISION 1

	P	W	D	L	F	A	W	D	L	F	A	Pts
Sunderland	46	19	3	1	50	10	12	9	2	41	18	105
Bradford C	46	15	4	4	48	20	11	5	7	34	27	87
Ipswich T	46	16	1	6	37	15	10	7	6	32	17	86
Birmingham C	46	12	7	4	32	15	11	5	7	34	22	81
Watford	46	12	8	3	30	19	9	6	8	35	37	77
Bolton W	46	13	6	4	44	25	7	10	6	34	34	76
Wolverh'pton W	46	11	10	2	37	19	8	6	9	27	24	73
Sheffield U	46	12	6	5	42	29	6	7	10	29	37	67
Norwich C	46	7	12	4	34	28	8	5	10	28	33	62
Huddersfield T	46	11	9	3	38	23	4	7	12	24	48	61
Grimsby	46	11	6	6	25	18	6	4	13	15	34	61
W.B.A.	46	12	4	7	43	33	4	7	12	26	43	59
Barnsley	46	7	9	7	35	30	7	8	8	24	26	59
Crystal Palace	46	11	10	2	43	26	3	6	14	15	45	58
Tranmere R	46	8	7	8	37	30	4	13	6	26	31	56
Stockport Co	46	7	9	7	24	21	5	8	10	25	39	53
Swindon T	46	7	8	8	40	44	6	3	14	19	37	50
Crewe A	46	7	6	10	27	35	5	6	12	27	43	48
Portsmouth	46	10	5	8	34	26	1	9	13	23	47	47
Q.P.R.	46	9	7	7	34	22	3	4	16	18	39	47
Port Vale	46	10	3	10	22	28	3	5	15	23	47	47
Bury	46	9	7	7	24	27	1	10	12	11	33	47
Oxford U	46	7	8	8	31	30	3	6	14	17	41	44
Bristol C	46	7	8	8	35	36	2	7	14	22	44	42

DIVISION 2

	P	W	D	L	F	A	W	D	L	F	A	Pts
Fulham	46	19	3	1	50	12	12	5	6	29	20	101
Walsall	46	13	7	3	37	23	13	2	8	26	24	87
Manchester C	46	13	6	4	38	14	9	10	4	31	19	82
Gillingham	46	15	5	3	45	17	7	9	7	30	27	80
Preston N.E.	46	12	6	5	46	23	10	7	6	32	27	79
Wigan A	46	14	5	4	44	17	8	5	10	31	31	76
Bournemouth	46	14	7	2	37	11	7	6	10	26	30	76
Stoke C	46	10	4	9	32	32	11	2	10	27	31	69
Chesterfield	46	14	5	4	34	16	3	8	12	12	28	64
Millwall	46	9	8	6	33	24	8	3	12	19	35	62
Reading	46	10	6	7	29	26	6	7	10	25	37	61
Luton T	46	10	4	9	25	26	6	6	11	26	34	58
Bristol R	46	8	9	6	35	28	5	8	10	30	28	56
Blackpool	46	7	8	8	24	24	7	6	10	20	30	56
Burnley	46	8	7	8	23	33	5	9	9	31	40	55
Notts Co	46	8	6	9	29	27	6	6	11	23	34	54
Wrexham	46	8	6	9	21	28	5	8	10	22	34	53
Colchester U	46	9	7	7	25	30	3	9	11	27	40	52
Wycombe	46	8	5	10	31	26	5	7	11	21	32	51
Oldham A	46	8	4	11	26	31	6	5	12	22	35	51
York C	46	6	8	9	28	33	7	3	13	28	47	50
Northampton T	46	4	12	7	26	31	6	6	11	17	26	48
Lincoln C	46	9	4	10	27	27	4	3	16	15	47	46
Macclesfield	46	7	4	12	24	30	4	6	13	19	33	43

DIVISION 3

	P	W	D	L	F	A	W	D	L	F	A	Pts
Brentford	46	16	5	2	45	18	10	2	11	34	38	85
Cambridge U	46	13	6	4	41	21	10	6	7	37	27	81
Cardiff C	46	13	7	3	35	17	9	7	7	25	22	80
Scunthorpe U	46	14	3	6	42	28	8	5	10	27	30	74
Rotherham U	46	11	8	4	41	26	9	5	9	38	35	73
Orient	46	12	6	5	40	30	7	9	7	28	29	72
Swansea C	46	11	9	3	33	19	8	5	10	23	29	71
Mansfield T	46	15	2	6	38	18	4	8	11	22	40	67
Peterborough U	46	11	4	8	41	29	7	8	8	31	27	66
Halifax T	46	10	8	5	33	25	7	7	9	25	31	66
Darlington	46	10	6	7	41	24	8	5	10	28	34	65
Exeter C	46	13	5	5	32	18	4	7	12	15	32	63
Plymouth A	46	11	6	6	32	19	6	4	13	26	35	61
Chester C	46	6	12	5	28	30	7	6	10	29	36	57
Shrewsbury T	46	11	6	6	36	29	3	8	12	16	34	56
Barnet	46	10	5	8	30	31	4	8	11	24	40	55
Brighton & H.A.	46	8	3	12	25	35	8	4	11	24	31	55
Southend U	46	8	6	9	24	21	6	6	11	28	37	54
Rochdale	46	9	8	6	22	21	4	7	12	20	34	54
Torquay U	46	9	9	5	29	20	3	8	12	18	38	53
Hull C	46	8	5	10	25	28	6	6	11	19	34	53
Hartlepool U	46	8	7	8	33	27	5	5	13	19	38	51
Carlisle U	46	8	8	7	25	21	3	8	12	18	32	49
Scarborough	46	8	3	12	30	39	6	3	14	20	38	48

Football League Records

Top scorers: Prem Lge, K.Phillips (Sunderland) 30 goals; Div 1, A.Hunt (Charlton) 24 goals; Div 2, A.Payton (Burnley) 27 goals; Div 3, M.Gabbiadini (Darlington) 24 goals.
Play-offs: Prem Lge, Birmingham City v Barnsley 0-4, 1-2; Bolton W v Ipswich 2-2, 5-3; Barnsley v Ipswich 2-4; Div 1, Millwall v Wigan 0-0, 1-0; Stoke C v Gillingham 3-2, 3-0; Gillingham v Wigan 3-2; Div 2, Barnett v Peterborough 1-2, 3-0; Hartlepool v Darlington 0-2, 1-0; Peterborough v Darlington 1-0.

Charlton, Manchester City and Ipswich Town promoted to Prem Lge; Wimbledon, Sheffield Wednesday and Watford relegated to Div 1; Preston NE, Burnley and Gillingham promoted to Div 1; Walsall, Port Vale and Swindon relegated to Div 2; Swansea, Rotherham, Northampton and Peterbor-

Sunderland's Kevin Phillips topped the 30-goal mark in his first season of Premiership football. It was a remarkable achievement and helped the Wearsiders to a comfortable finishing position.

DIVISION PREMIER

		ARSENAL	ASTON VILLA	BRADFORD C	CHELSEA	COVENTRY	DERBY	EVERTON	LEEDS	LEICESTER	LIVERPOOL	MANCHESTER U	MIDDLESBROUGH	NEWCASTLE	SHEFFIELD W	SOUTHAMPTON	SUNDERLAND	TOTTENHAM	WATFORD	WEST HAM	WIMBLEDON
1	ARSENAL		S11 3-1	A25 2-0	m06 2-1	M26 3-0	N28 2-1	O16 4-1	D28 2-0	A07 2-1	F13 0-1	A22 1-2	N20 5-1	O30 0-0	m09 3-3	F26 3-1	J15 4-1	M19 2-1	S25 1-0	m02 2-1	D18 1-1
2	ASTON VILLA	M03 1-1		S18 1-0	J22 0-0	M11 1-0	M25 2-0	A11 3-0	a09 1-0	a22 2-2	O02 0-0	m14 0-1	A28 1-0	D04 0-1	D18 2-1	N06 0-1	a29 1-1	D29 1-1	F05 4-0	A16 2-2	O23 1-1
3	BRADFORD C	F05 2-1	F26 1-1		J08 1-1	N06 1-1	a21 4-4	D28 0-0	M12 1-2	O23 3-1	m14 1-0	M25 0-4	D04 1-1	D1 2-0	A14 1-1	a08 1-2	O02 0-4	S12 1-1	J22 3-2	A28 0-3	a30 3-0
4	CHELSEA	O23 2-3	A21 1-0	N28 1-0		a12 2-1	m14 4-0	M11 1-1	D19 0-2	J15 1-1	a29 2-0	O03 5-0	a22 1-1	S11 1-0	D29 3-0	M25 1-1	A07 4-0	J12 1-0	F26 2-1	N07 0-0	F12 3-1
5	COVENTRY	D26 3-2	N22 2-1	M18 4-0	J04 2-2		A21 2-0	M15 1-0	S11 3-4	N27 0-1	a01 0-3	A25 1-2	a15 2-1	O16 4-1	m06 4-1	A07 0-1	F12 3-2	F26 0-1	O31 4-0	S25 1-0	J15 2-0
6	DERBY	A10 1-2	D26 0-2	S25 0-1	O30 3-1	J22 0-0		A28 1-0	D05 0-1	a02 3-0	M18 0-2	N20 1-2	A14 1-3	m06 0-0	F05 3-3	a24 2-0	S18 0-5	O16 0-1	J03 2-0	a15 1-2	M04 4-0
7	EVERTON	a29 0-1	N27 0-0	a15 4-0	N20 1-1	O02 1-1	F12 2-1		O24 4-4	J03 2-2	a21 0-0	A08 1-1	m14 0-2	M19 0-2	M04 1-1	A21 4-1	D26 5-0	J15 2-2	a01 4-2	S19 1-0	A25 4-0
8	LEEDS	a16 0-4	J03 1-2	N20 2-1	a01 0-1	M05 3-0	A07 0-0	m08 1-1		D26 2-1	A23 1-2	F20 0-1	S19 2-0	S25 3-2	O16 2-0	N28 1-0	A21 2-1	F12 1-0	m03 3-1	O30 1-0	M19 4-1
9	LEICESTER	D04 0-3	S25 3-1	m06 3-0	A14 2-2	A11 1-0	D18 0-1	a08 1-1	M26 2-1		S18 2-2	M18 0-2	F05 2-1	D28 1-2	O30 3-0	O16 2-1	M05 5-2	a19 0-1	A30 1-0	J22 1-3	N20 2-1
10	LIVERPOOL	A28 2-0	M15 0-0	N01 3-1	O16 1-0	D18 2-0	N06 2-0	S27 0-1	F05 3-1	m03 0-2		S11 2-3	J22 0-0	M25 2-1	D05 4-1	m07 0-0	M11 1-1	a09 2-0	A14 0-1	O27 1-0	D28 3-1
11	MANCHESTER U	J24 1-1	O30 3-0	D26 4-0	a24 3-2	F05 3-2	M11 3-1	D04 5-1	A14 2-0	N06 2-0	M04 1-1		J29 1-0	A30 5-1	A11 4-0	S25 3-3	a15 4-0	m06 3-1	O16 4-1	a01 7-1	S18 1-1
12	MIDDLESBROUGH	M12 2-1	F14 0-4	A07 0-1	S25 0-1	F19 2-0	J15 1-4	O30 2-1	F26 0-0	A24 0-3	A21 1-0	a10 3-4		m02 2-2	M25 1-0	S11 3-2	N06 1-1	D18 2-1	m06 1-1	O17 2-0	N27 0-0
13	NEWCASTLE	m14 4-2	A07 0-1	a01 2-0	M04 0-1	a29 2-0	O25 2-0	N07 1-1	a23 2-2	a15 0-2	D26 2-2	F12 3-0	O03 2-1		S19 8-0	J16 5-0	A25 1-2	N28 2-1	M11 1-0	J03 2-2	A21 3-3
14	SHEFFIELD W	J03 1-1	a05 0-1	J15 2-0	a15 1-0	O23 0-0	A25 0-2	S11 0-2	a30 0-3	m14 4-0	A07 1-2	F02 0-1	D26 1-0	F26 0-2		F12 0-1	a22 0-2	A21 1-2	N06 2-2	M11 3-1	O02 5-1
15	SOUTHAMPTON	S18 0-1	M18 2-0	J03 1-0	D26 1-2	D04 0-0	O04 3-3	J22 2-0	A11 0-3	a29 1-2	O23 1-1	a22 1-3	M04 1-1	A15 4-2	A28 2-0		a01 1-2	N20 0-1	a15 2-0	F05 2-1	m14 2-0
16	SUNDERLAND	A14 0-0	O18 2-1	a24 0-1	D04 4-1	A29 1-1	F26 1-1	M25 2-1	J23 1-2	S11 2-0	N20 0-2	D28 2-2	M18 1-1	F05 2-2	S25 1-0	D18 2-0		O31 2-1	A10 2-0	m06 1-0	a08 2-1
17	TOTTENHAM	N07 2-1	a15 2-4	M04 1-1	F05 0-1	S19 3-2	a29 1-1	A14 3-2	A28 1-2	O03 2-3	J03 1-0	O23 3-1	a03 2-3	A09 3-1	J22 0-1	M11 7-2	m14 3-1		D26 4-0	D06 0-0	a22 2-0
18	WATFORD	a23 2-3	A24 0-1	A21 1-0	S18 1-0	m14 1-0	a08 0-0	D18 1-3	O03 1-2	F12 1-1	J15 2-3	a29 2-3	O24 1-3	N20 1-1	M18 1-0	D28 3-2	N27 2-3	M25 1-1		M04 1-2	A07 2-3
19	WEST HAM	O03 2-1	J15 1-1	F12 5-4	M18 0-0	a22 5-0	D28 1-1	F26 0-4	m14 0-0	A21 2-1	N27 1-0	D18 2-4	a29 0-1	a12 2-1	N21 4-3	M08 2-0	O24 1-1	A07 1-0	S11 1-0		M26 2-1
20	WIMBLEDON	a01 1-3	m06 2-2	O16 3-2	A28 0-1	A14 1-1	S11 2-2	F06 0-3	N07 2-0	M11 2-1	a16 1-2	F26 2-2	A10 2-3	J22 2-0	a12 0-2	O30 1-1	J03 1-0	S26 1-1	D04 5-0	D26 2-2	

Shaun Goater's goals for Manchester City were a major factor in their return to the Premiership as First Division runners-up.

DIVISION 1

		BARNSLEY	BIRMINGHAM	BLACKBURN-	BOLTON	CHARLTON	CREWE	C PALACE	FULHAM	GRIMSBY	HUDDERSFIELD	IPSWICH	MANCHESTER C	NORWICH	NOTTINGHAM F	PORT VALE	PORTSMOUTH	Q.P.R.	SHEFFIELD U	STOCKPORT	SWINDON	TRANMERE	WALSALL	W.B.A.	WOLVERHAMPTON
1	BARNSLEY		N20 2-1	J22 5-1	F26 1-1	D04 1-1	m07 0-2	A14 2-3	M21 1-0	M27 3-0	S25 4-2	F05 0-2	M11 2-1	a24 2-1	O30 1-0	D28 3-1	A28 6-0	F19 1-1	N06 2-0	S10 2-1	O19 1-0	S03 3-0	D18 3-2	a08 2-2	O16 1-2
2	BIRMINGHAM	M18 3-1		F15 1-0	F12 2-1	O30 1-0	A30 5-1	O16 2-0	A07 2-2	m07 0-0	J03 1-0	F27 1-1	O19 0-1	J15 2-0	a15 0-1	A21 4-2	M07 1-0	S25 2-0	D26 0-2	J29 2-1	N27 1-1	N23 3-1	a24 2-0	S11 1-1	a01 1-0
3	BLACKBURN	A21 1-2	M22 1-0		D07 3-1	a24 1-1	M12 0-1	O20 1-1	N20 2-0	O16 1-1	J15 2-0	N06 2-2	m07 1-4	F29 1-1	D26 2-1	A07 0-0	a15 1-1	O30 0-2	a01 5-0	N27 2-0	F12 0-0	S11 2-0	S25 2-0	F26 2-1	J03 1-1
4	BOLTON	S18 2-2	S05 3-3	F05 3-1		M04 0-2	O19 2-2	N06 2-0	M11 3-1	N20 2-0	O16 1-0	J22 1-1	A28 0-1	m07 1-0	S25 3-2	M25 2-1	F22 3-0	A14 2-1	M21 2-0	D18 0-1	O30 2-0	D04 2-3	a08 4-3	D28 1-1	m03 2-1
5	CHARLTON	A07 3-1	O02 1-0	N30 1-2	S11 2-1		J15 1-0	D26 2-1	f15 1-0	M22 4-0	a14 0-1	a29 1-3	N20 0-1	A21 1-0	J03 3-0	N27 2-2	a21 1-1	M07 2-1	F26 1-0	S28 4-0	M11 0-1	O26 3-2	N06 2-1	O23 0-0	F12 2-0
6	CREWE	O23 0-1	F05 2-3	N23 0-0	a29 1-3	N02 0-2		D04 2-0	O26 1-1	A27 1-1	D26 1-1	F19 1-2	J03 1-1	M04 1-0	a01 0-3	M07 2-1	M18 1-3	a15 2-1	O09 1-0	a22 3-2	S18 2-1	O03 0-2	J22 2-3	D07 2-0	D14 1-0
7	C PALACE	J15 0-2	a22 0-2	a29 2-1	M07 0-0	M25 0-1	A07 1-1		D18 0-0	S18 3-0	J29 2-2	D07 2-2	M04 1-1	N23 1-0	N27 2-0	M18 1-1	O02 4-0	N14 3-0	F12 1-1	a08 3-3	A21 1-2	O23 2-2	D28 3-2	O26 0-2	S28 1-1
8	FULHAM	n13 1-3	D04 0-0	M18 2-2	N23 1-1	A28 2-1	S25 3-0	a01 1-0		J22 0-1	m07 3-0	D26 0-0	A14 0-0	O30 1-1	a24 1-1	M04 3-1	N09 1-0	S18 1-0	a15 4-0	M07 4-1	O16 1-0	J03 1-0	F19 2-0	F05 1-0	O19 0-1
9	GRIMSBY	D26 0-3	O23 1-1	a22 0-0	M18 0-1	N12 2-5	J29 1-1	F26 1-0	A21 1-1		a01 0-0	O02 2-1	A15 1-1	N28 2-1	J15 4-3	F12 2-0	O26 1-0	N23 2-1	J03 2-2	A07 0-1	A30 1-0	a29 1-2	S11 1-0	D14 1-1	M07 1-0
10	HUDDERSFIELD	O26 2-1	a08 0-0	A13 3-2	a22 0-3	D28 1-2	M25 3-0	A28 7-1	O23 1-1	D18 3-1		N02 3-1	F18 1-1	S18 1-0	M21 2-1	O09 2-2	F05 0-1	D04 1-0	O02 4-1	a29 0-2	N06 4-0	J22 1-0	M11 1-1	N20 1-0	M04 2-0
11	IPSWICH	A30 6-1	S18 0-1	M07 0-0	A21 1-0	O19 4-2	N27 2-1	a25 1-0	M25 1-0	O30 2-0	F12 2-1		S26 2-1	M19 0-2	A07 3-1	a08 3-0	M04 0-1	O16 1-4	J29 1-1	D28 1-0	J15 3-0	N12 0-0	m07 2-0	D18 3-1	N24 1-0
12	MANCHESTER C	N24 3-1	a28 1-0	O23 2-0	a05 2-0	M19 1-1	a08 4-0	S11 2-1	J16 4-0	D28 2-1	N27 0-1	O27 1-0		F12 3-1	A30 1-0	O02 2-1	N03 4-2	M08 1-3	A21 6-0	D07 1-2	D18 3-0	a22 2-0	F26 1-1	M25 2-1	A08 0-1
13	NORWICH	J08 2-2	A14 0-1	A28 0-2	O24 2-1	J22 0-3	S11 2-1	M11 0-1	O02 1-2	F19 3-0	F26 1-1	N21 0-0	S28 1-0		N06 1-0	a22 0-0	J03 2-1	D26 2-1	a29 2-1	O26 2-0	M22 0-2	a01 1-1	F05 1-1	D04 2-1	a15 1-0
14	NOTTINGHAM F	O01 3-0	D28 1-0	M25 0-1	O27 1-1	a08 1-1	D18 1-0	F19 2-0	D15 0-0	A14 2-1	N14 1-3	D05 0-1	F05 1-3	M08 1-1		a29 2-0	N24 2-0	A28 1-1	a22 0-0	O23 1-1	M04 3-1	M18 1-1	S04 4-1	J22 0-0	S19 1-1
15	PORT VALE	a15 2-2	J22 3-1	D04 0-0	F08 0-1	a04 2-2	N05 1-0	N20 2-2	S11 0-2	S05 3-1	a24 1-2	J03 1-2	O30 1-2	O16 0-1	O19 0-2		a01 2-0	F05 1-1	M11 2-3	F26 1-1	S25 2-0	A28 1-0	M21 1-2	A14 1-2	m07 0-1
16	PORTSMOUTH	J29 3-0	N06 2-2	D28 1-2	N27 0-0	O16 0-2	N20 0-2	O30 3-1	F12 0-1	S25 1-2	A30 0-0	S11 1-1	a24 2-2	a08 2-1	M11 2-1	D18 0-0		m07 1-3	A07 2-0	A21 2-0	M25 4-1	M01 1-2	O19 5-1	M21 2-0	J15 2-3
17	Q.P.R.	N27 2-2	O27 2-2	O02 0-0	J15 0-1	D18 0-0	D28 1-0	M22 0-1	F28 0-0	M11 1-0	A07 3-1	a22 3-1	N06 1-1	M25 2-2	J29 1-1	A31 3-2	O23 0-0		N30 3-1	F12 1-1	a08 2-1	O09 2-1	N20 2-1	a29 0-0	A21 1-1
18	SHEFFIELD U	M07 3-3	M25 1-2	D19 2-1	N14 1-2	S18 1-2	a24 1-1	S04 3-1	D28 2-0	a08 0-0	O30 0-1	A28 2-2	J22 1-0	O19 0-0	O16 2-1	N23 1-3	D04 1-0	M05 1-1		M18 1-0	m07 2-2	F05 3-1	A14 1-1	F19 6-0	S25 3-0
19	STOCKPORT	M03 1-3	A27 2-0	F19 0-1	M14 0-0	F05 1-3	O16 2-1	J03 1-2	N06 2-1	D04 2-1	O19 1-1	a15 0-1	M21 2-2	S25 2-2	m07 2-3	S18 1-0	J22 1-1	N02 3-3	N20 1-1		a24 3-0	A14 2-1	O30 1-1	M11 0-1	D26 3-2
20	SWINDON	a29 1-2	F19 1-4	S28 2-1	O02 0-4	N23 1-2	F26 0-1	J21 2-4	a22 1-0	F05 0-1	M07 2-0	A15 1-4	a01 0-2	N12 0-0	S11 0-0	O26 2-1	D26 1-1	J03 0-1	O23 2-2	O09 1-1		a15 3-1	D04 1-1	A28 1-2	M18 1-2
21	TRANMERE	F11 2-2	M11 2-1	M04 2-1	A07 0-0	S25 2-2	O30 2-0	m07 1-2	a09 1-1	O19 3-2	A21 1-0	M22 0-2	O16 1-1	D17 1-2	N20 3-0	a18 2-1	S18 2-4	a24 1-1	A30 1-3	J15 0-0	D28 3-1		M25 1-1	N06 3-0	N27 1-0
22	WALSALL	a01 1-4	O08 1-0	O26 1-1	J03 2-0	M07 2-4	A21 1-4	a15 2-2	N26 1-3	M04 1-0	N23 2-0	O23 0-1	S18 0-1	A30 2-2	F12 0-2	N12 0-0	a29 1-0	M18 2-3	J15 2-1	O02 1-2	A07 0-0	D26 1-2		a22 2-1	J29 1-1
23	W.B.A.	J03 0-2	M04 0-3	S18 2-2	a15 4-4	m07 2-0	F12 1-0	S25 0-0	A30 0-0	a24 2-1	M18 0-1	a04 1-1	D26 0-2	A07 1-1	A20 1-1	J15 0-0	N14 3-2	O19 0-1	N27 2-2	N23 2-0	J29 1-1	M07 2-0	O16 0-1		O31 1-1
24	WOLVERHAMPTON	a22 2-0	D17 2-1	a08 2-1	O09 1-0	J11 2-3	M21 2-0	F05 2-1	a30 3-0	N06 3-0	S11 0-1	M11 2-1	D03 4-1	D28 1-0	F26 3-0	O23 2-2	A14 1-1	J22 3-2	O26 1-0	M25 2-2	N20 1-1	F16 4-0	A28 1-2	O03 1-1	

SEASON 1999-2000

ugh promoted to Div 2; Cardiff, Blackpool, Scunthorpe and Chesterfield elegated to Div 3; Chester relegated from Div 3, replaced by idderminster Harriers.

DIVISION 2

	BLACKPOOL	BOURNEMOUTH	BRENTFORD	BRISTOL C	BRISTOL R	BURNLEY	BURY	CAMBRIDGE	CARDIFF	CHESTERFIELD	COLCHESTER	GILLINGHAM	LUTON	MILLWALL	NOTTS CO	OXFORD	OLDHAM	PRESTON	READING	SCUNTHORPE	STOKE	WIGAN	WREXHAM	WYCOMBE
BLACKPOOL		S18 0-0	J29 0-1	F12 1-2	a24 2-1	M21 1-1	O16 0-5	N27 2-1	M11 2-2	m06 2-2	J03 1-1	A21 1-1	J15 3-3	N23 1-2	M04 2-1	O19 1-2	A30 1-1	a01 0-0	F08 0-2	a15 0-2	D26 1-2	N06 2-2	A07 2-1	S25 1-2
BOURNEMOUTH	F26 2-0		N23 4-1	J15 2-3	O19 0-1	F12 0-1	S25 1-1	A07 2-1	N06 1-0	a25 1-1	A21 4-0	M21 0-1	A31 1-0	N27 1-2	J08 1-1	a08 3-0	D18 4-0	M11 0-1	S11 3-1	J29 1-1	O16 1-1	m06 2-2	D28 1-0	M25 2-0
BRENTFORD	A28 2-0	M18 0-2		D26 2-1	D04 0-3	a24 2-3	J22 2-1	M04 1-1	S28 2-1	D10 1-1	m06 0-0	O19 1-2	S18 2-0	a15 1-3	F05 0-2	A14 2-0	O16 2-0	S25 2-2	N02 1-1	N12 4-3	J03 0-1	a01 0-2	M07 0-2	F19 0-0
BRISTOL C	S04 5-2	A14 3-1	M25 1-0		O17 0-0	S25 0-0	A28 1-1	N06 1-1	J09 0-0	F05 3-0	O19 1-1	M11 0-1	D28 0-0	S11 0-0	F19 2-2	N23 1-1	a24 2-2	m06 0-2	D04 3-1	F26 2-1	M28 2-2	J22 0-0	a08 4-0	D17 0-0
BRISTOL R	O02 3-1	a29 2-2	A07 0-0	a22 2-0		A30 1-0	N02 0-0	J03 1-0	O09 1-1	M18 3-1	D11 2-1	J15 2-1	N27 3-0	D26 1-0	O23 0-1	S18 3-2	A21 1-0	a15 0-2	a04 0-1	F12 1-1	a01 3-3	M04 1-1	J29 3-1	M07 1-0
BURNLEY	N14 1-0	S03 2-1	O02 2-2	O23 2-0	F05 1-0		M25 2-2	a29 2-0	D18 2-1	A14 2-1	S18 3-0	a18 0-3	M07 0-2	a22 4-3	a08 2-1	J22 3-0	D28 3-2	M04 0-3	M18 3-0	O10 1-2	A28 1-0	F19 0-0	N02 5-0	D04 1-0
BURY	a22 3-2	O23 2-2	A21 2-2	J29 0-0	M11 0-0	D26 4-2		F22 0-2	O02 3-2	a15 1-1	A30 5-2	A07 2-1	F12 1-0	J04 2-2	O09 1-3	M04 2-2	M21 1-2	N27 1-3	a29 1-1	a01 3-0	N06 0-0	N23 2-2	J15 0-2	S18 2-0
CAMBRIDGE	F19 0-2	D04 0-2	S11 2-2	M07 3-0	a08 1-1	O19 0-1	a04 3-0		D28 0-0	J22 2-0	O15 5-2	S25 2-2	N12 3-1	F26 0-2	A28 1-1	D18 2-3	M25 2-0	a24 2-0	A14 3-1	N02 1-3	S04 1-3	F05 1-1	M18 3-4	m06 1-2
CARDIFF	N02 1-1	M07 1-2	F12 1-1	F22 0-0	m06 1-0	a01 1-2	a24 0-2	a15 0-4		N12 2-1	M17 3-2	N27 1-2	J30 1-3	A07 1-1	S18 2-1	O16 1-1	J15 1-1	J03 0-4	D26 1-0	A30 1-1	O19 1-2	S25 0-0	A20 1-1	M03 2-2
CHESTERFIELD	O09 0-0	O02 0-1	J08 1-0	D07 0-2	N20 0-1	J15 1-1	M28 0-1	A21 4-2	M21 1-1		A07 0-1	F01 0-0	M25 1-3	J29 2-0	a29 2-1	N06 0-1	N27 0-0	F12 0-1	F26 2'-0	O23 1-1	S11 0-2	M11 1-1	a22 0-3	a08 1-2
COLCHESTER	a08 1-1	J22 3-1	N19 0-3	a29 3-4	J08 5-4	F26 1-2	F05 1-3	a22 3-1	N23 0-3	D03 1-0		M25 2-1	D17 3-0	O23 1-2	A14 0-3	M21 0-1	M11 1-2	N06 2-2	A28 3-2	S11 0-1	F19 1-0	O26 2-2	O01 2-2	J18 1-0
GILLINGHAM	J22 1-3	N12 4-1	a29 2-0	N02 3-0	A14 0-1	M14 2-2	D04 1-0	O23 2-1	m02 4-1	a01 1-0	D26 2-1		a22 2-0	O02 2-0	M07 0-1	S04 2-1	M04 1-0	S18 0-2	J03 2-2	M18 3-1	F05 3-0	a15 2-1	O09 5-1	A28 2-2
LUTON	A14 3-2	F05 1-2	F26 1-2	a18 1-2	F19 1-4	N06 2-1	S04 1-1	M21 2-2	A28 1-0	D26 1-1	a01 3-2	O16 3-1		M11 0-2	D04 2-2	m06 1-1	S25 4-2	N23 0-2	J22 3-1	J03 4-1	F08 2-1	a24 1-1	S11 3-1	O19 1-1
MILLWALL	M18 1-1	F19 3-1	D28 3-2	M04 4-1	M25 3-0	O16 1-1	a08 3-0	S18 2-1	D04 2-0	A28 1-1	S25 1-0	a24 2-2	N02 1-0		D18 1-0	F05 1-0	m06 1-0	O19 0-2	N16 5-0	M07 1-2	J22 1-0	A14 3-3	N12 0-0	J08 1-1
NOTTS CO	S11 2-1	D11 5-1	O26 0-1	N27 4-4	S25 0-2	J03 2-0	m06 2-2	F15 2-3	F26 2-1	O10 1-0	J15 1-2	N06 1-1	A07 0-0	a01 1-1		a24 0-1	N23 0-1	M21 1-0	a15 1-2	A21 3-0	M11 0-0	D26 0-2	F12 2-1	O16 2-1
OLDHAM	a29 1-1	J03 1-0	J15 3-0	M18 1-1	F26 1-4	A21 0-1	S11 2-0	a01 1-0	a22 1-2	a18 1-2	N14 1-2	F12 1-3	O09 2-1	N09 2-1	O02 1-2		J29 2-0	A07 0-1	O23 1-2	D26 1-1	a04 0-1	a11 2-1	N27 0-0	N02 2-2
OXFORD	F05 0-1	a01 1-0	a22 1-1	O02 3-0	J22 0-5	a15 1-2	N13 1-1	D26 1-0	A14 2-3	F19 2-1	N02 1-1	S11 1-2	O23 0-1	O09 1-3	M18 2-3	A28 1-0		F01 0-4	M07 1-3	a29 2-0	D04 1-1	J03 1-2	F26 1-4	S04 0-0
PRESTON	D18 3-0	N03 3-0	O23 2-1	O09 1-0	D28 2-1	S11 0-0	F19 1-1	O02 2-1	a08 0-0	S04 0-2	M07 2-3	F26 0-2	M18 1-0	a29 3-2	N12 2-0	D04 2-0	M14 3-1		F05 2-2	a22 1-0	A14 2-1	A28 1-4	M25 1-0	J22 3-2
READING	J08 1-1	M04 2-0	M11 1-0	A07 2-1	M22 2-0	N24 0-0	O20 2-0	J15 0-0	M25 0-1	S18 1-0	J29 2-0	a07 2-2	A21 1-2	F12 2-0	D28 0-0	S25 1-1	N07 1-2	S01 2-2		N27 1-1	m06 1-0	O16 0-2	D18 2-2	a24 2-1
SCUTHORPE	D28 1-0	A28 3-1	M21 0-0	S18 1-2	S04 0-2	m06 1-2	D18 0-2	M11 0-3	F05 0-0	S25 0-0	M04 0-0	N23 1-4	a08 1-2	N06 1-4	J22 1-0	M25 1-2	O19 1-0	O16 1-1	F19 2-2		a24 0-2	D04 1-2	F01 0-2	A14 0-1
STOKE	M25 3-0	a22 1-0	a08 1-0	N14 1-1	D18 1-2	J29 2-2	m03 3-0	F12 1-0	a30 2-1	M04 5-1	N27 1-1	A30 1-1	J08 2-1	A22 3-1	N03 0-1	D28 0-0	A07 1-2	J14 2-1	O09 2-1	O02 1-0		S18 1-1	O23 2-0	M18 1-1
WIGAN	M07 5-1	N16 3-1	D18 1-0	A21 2-1	S11 3-1	N27 1-1	M18 1-0	A30 1-1	O23 2-0	N02 3-0	F12 0-1	D28 2-0	O02 1-0	J15 1-1	M25 2-0	J07 0-1	a08 2-0	a04 0-1	a22 1-0	A07 3-0	F26 1-2		a29 0-1	N12 2-1
WREXHAM	D04 1-1	a15 1-0	N06 0-1	J03 0-1	A28 2-1	M11 0-1	A14 1-0	N23 1-1	J22 2-1	O16 1-1	a24 1-0	m06 1-0	M04 1-0	M21 1-1	S03 2-3	F19 0-3	S18 1-0	D26 0-0	a01 0-1	M28 3-1	S25 2-3	O19 1-1		F05 1-3
WYCOMBE	O23 0-2	D26 2-1	N27 2-0	a01 1-2	N06 1-1	A07 1-1	F26 3-0	O09 1-0	S11 3-1	J03 3-0	a15 3-0	M28 1-0	a29 0-1	D11 1-2	a21 2-0	M11 0-0	F12 0-1	A21 1-1	O02 5-3	J15 2-1	N23 0-4	M21 0-2	A31 0-1	

DIVISION 3

	BARNET	BRIGHTON	CARLISLE	CHELTENHAM	CHESTER	DARLINGTON	EXETER	HALIFAX	HARTLEPOOL	HULL	LEYTON O	LINCOLN	MACCLESFIELD	MANSFIELD	NORTHAMPTON	PETERBOROUGH	PLYMOUTH	ROCHDALE	ROTHERHAM	SHREWSBURY	SOUTHEND	SWANSEA	TORQUAY	YORK
BARNET		M25 0-1	N23 3-0	F05 3-2	D04 2-0	N06 1-0	A14 2-2	D28 0-1	M11 1-1	O02 0-0	a29 2-2	J22 5-3	S05 2-1	D18 0-0	S18 2-1	F19 0-2	M21 1-0	O09 1-0	a22 1-0	a08 1-1	J08 2-1	M04 0-1	O23 1-2	A28 6-3
BRIGHTON	D26 1-1		m06 1-0	S25 1-0	S18 2-3	J29 1-1	J03 4-2	M04 2-1	N06 1-0	A31 3-0	J15 0-1	N23 2-2	M21 5-2	A07 6-0	N27 1-3	a26 0-0	F12 1-1	D10 3-4	a15 1-1	O19 1-0	M11 1-0	a01 1-1	A21 0-1	O16 0-1
CARLISLE	M18 3-1	O09 0-1		a04 1-1	J03 4-1	a29 1-1	a22 0-0	O23 1-1	A21 0-3	a01 0-4	A07 2-1	S11 1-0	a15 0-1	J29 0-2	a11 0-1	N12 1-1	A30 4-2	D26 1-2	N27 0-1	F26 1-1	O02 1-1	M28 2-0	D14 0-0	N02 0-1
CHELTENHAM	A30 1-2	O23 0-0	N06 3-1		a29 1-0	a22 0-0	D26 3-1	M11 3-0	J29 2-1	A21 1-0	N27 2-0	J03 0-2	D11 1-1	J15 1-0	M21 2-1	F26 2-1	N23 2-0	A07 0-2	O02 0-2	S12 0-1	O09 2-1	F13 0-0	a01 2-0	A15 0-1
CHESTER	A07 0-2	F26 1-7	a08 0-1	O19 2-1		J08 1-2	S11 1-1	D18 2-1	M21 1-1	F12 0-0	D28 1-5	S25 1-3	O16 1-2	M25 5-0	A18 0-2	m06 0-1	N06 0-1	A30 0-2	J15 0-2	M11 0-0	N23 0-0	N27 0-1	J29 2-1	a24 2-0
DARLINGTON	M07 4-0	A28 1-1	O19 3-1	O16 1-0	D15 3-1		S04 1-0	D04 4-0	a24 1-1	D26 0-0	N02 3-1	m06 2-0	A14 3-0	S18 0-0	a15 0-1	F06 2-0	S25 2-0	M04 4-1	a01 2-2	A05 2-2	F19 1-0	M18 1-1	N12 1-1	J18 2-2
EXETER	J15 0-0	a08 0-0	O16 1-1	M25 1-2	M04 0-2	F12 1-4		M21 1-0	D18 1-2	A07 1-0	J08 1-3	a24 3-0	S25 0-3	A30 1-0	N23 1-2	D28 2-2	M11 1-1	J29 2-0	A21 3-1	m06 1-2	N06 0-1	O19 1-1	N27 3-2	S18 2-1
HALIFAX	a15 1-2	S11 2-1	S25 5-2	N02 1-1	a01 0-1	A07 0-1	N12 1-0		J15 1-1	M18 0-1	J29 0-2	D26 3-0	m06 0-1	N27 0-1	J03 2-2	O16 2-1	A21 0-1	F12 0-2	D11 0-0	a24 2-1	F26 0-0	M07 0-1	A31 2-0	O19 0-2
HARTLEPOOL	N02 3-0	M07 0-0	J22 1-0	A28 0-1	N13 1-0	O02 2-0	a01 2-1	A14 0-2		O09 2-0	O23 1-0	a15 2-0	F19 1-4	a22 1-0	M04 2-1	D04 1-0	S18 3-0	J03 3-2	a29 1-2	F05 1-0	S04 1-2	D11 0-1	M18 2-0	D26 2-1
HULL	a24 1-3	F05 2-0	D18 2-1	J22 1-1	S03 2-1	M25 0-1	D04 4-0	N23 0-1	m06 0-3		a08 2-0	A14 1-1	A28 2-3	D28 2-0	O16 0-1	J08 2-3	O19 0-1	M11 2-2	N06 0-0	F19 0-0	M21 0-0	S18 2-0	M04 0-0	S25 1-1
LEYTON O	O19 0-0	A14 1-2	D04 0-1	F19 1-0	a15 1-2	M11 2-1	F08 4-1	A28 1-0	S25 2-1	J03 0-0		O16 2-3	a01 0-0	M04 1-3	N06 0-0	J22 1-1	A24 3-0	N23 0-0	M21 0-1	S03 1-2	F05 2-1	D26 0-1	S18 0-2	m06 0-0
LINCOLN	A21 0-0	M18 1-3	M04 5-0	a08 1-2	O23 4-1	O09 1-0	O02 1-0	M25 1-1	D28 1-2	J15 2-1	a22 0-0		S18 1-1	M07 3-0	J29 2-2	N02 1-2	F22 3-0	N27 1-1	A07 2-1	D18 1-2	a29 1-0	A30 0-1	F12 2-1	N12 4-2
MACCLESFIELD	F12 2-0	N14 1-1	D28 2-1	J08 1-2	a22 1-1	J15 2-1	O23 1-0	O09 0-2	N27 3-3	J29 0-2	D18 1-0	F26 1-1		N02 5-2	A07 1-0	M18 1-1	A08 4-1	a29 1-2	A30 1-1	M25 4-2	S11 1-2	A21 1-2	O02 1-2	M07 1-1
MANSFIELD	a01 0-1	F01 1-0	A28 1-1	A14 0-1	D26 2-1	F26 1-2	F04 1-1	F19 0-2	O16 2-3	a15 0-1	S11 1-1	N06 5-2	M11 1-0		O19 0-0	S03 3-1	m06 2-2	M28 0-0	N23 1-2	S24 4-0	J22 3-1	a24 0-1	J03 4-3	F08 1-0
NORTHAMPTON	F26 1-0	F19 1-0	S04 0-0	N12 3-2	J22 3-1	D28 0-3	M18 2-1	a08 3-4	S11 2-1	a21 1-0	M07 2-1	A27 1-0	D04 2-0	a29 1-0		A14 0-1	D17 1-1	O02 0-1	O23 0-1	J08 3-0	M25 2-0	N02 2-1	O09 3-0	F05 3-0
PETERBOROUGH	N27 1-2	O02 0-0	M21 0-2	S18 1-0	O09 2-1	A30 4-2	a15 3-1	a22 2-1	A07 2-1	F22 2-1	A21 2-1	M11 2-2	N20 2-2	F12 1-0	J15 1-0		J29 2-0	a01 3-3	D26 0-5	N06 4-1	O23 1-0	J03 2-3	A29 0-2	M04 2-0
PLYMOUTH	N14 4-1	S05 3-3	F05 2-0	M18 1-0	M07 0-0	O23 0-0	N02 1-0	J22 1-1	F26 1-1	a29 0-1	O02 5-0	M14 1-1	J03 3-2	O09 2-1	a01 2-1	A28 2-1		a22 1-1	S11 1-1	A14 0-0	D04 3-1	a15 1-0	D26 2-2	F19 2-0
ROCHDALE	m06 1-1	J08 1-0	M25 3-2	D04 0-0	F05 2-1	S11 0-0	A28 0-2	S03 0-1	a08 2-0	N02 0-2	M18 1-4	F19 1-1	O19 0-1	N14 2-1	a24 0-3	a18 1-2	O16 0-0		F26 0-1	D28 2-1	A14 2-0	S25 0-0	a05 1-1	J22 2-1
ROTHERHAM	O16 2-0	D28 1-3	F19 4-2	a24 2-0	A14 4-0	D18 2-1	J22 5-0	J08 0-1	O19 3-0	M07 3-0	N12 0-1	D04 1-1	F05 2-1	M17 2-3	S25 3-0	M25 1-1	M04 1-1	S18 0-1		A28 4-0	a08 0-0	m06 1-1	N02 1-0	S04 1-0
SHREWSBURY	J03 1-1	a29 1-2	S18 4-1	M04 0-2	N02 0-1	A21 0-1	O09 1-4	O02 0-0	A31 0-0	N27 3-0	F12 1-0	a01 1-2	D26 0-1	O23 1-2	D11 1-0	M07 0-1	J15 0-0	a15 2-4	J29 0-0		a22 2-1	N12 1-1	A07 1-2	M18 0-1
SOUTHEND	D10 1-3	N02 2-1	a24 2-0	m06 2-1	M18 3-1	N27 1-2	M07 1-2	S18 4-1	F12 2-1	N12 1-2	A30 1-1	O19 2-2	M03 1-0	A21 1-0	D26 2-2	S25 0-1	A07 2-1	J15 3-3	J03 1-2	O16 3-2		J29 2-1	m02 0-2	a01 0-0
SWANSEA	S11 1-2	D18 2-0	A14 1-0	N16 0-0	F18 2-1	N23 0-0	a29 3-0	N05 3-1	J08 2-1	F26 0-0	M25 0-0	F04 2-1	J22 1-0	O02 0-1	M10 4-1	a08 0-0	D28 1-0	O22 1-0	O12 2-0	M21 1-1	A28 3-1		a22 2-1	D04 1-0
TORQUAY	S25 0-1	J22 0-0	J08 4-1	M14 1-1	A28 2-2	M21 1-0	F19 1-0	F05 4-0	N23 0-0	S11 0-1	F26 0-0	S04 5-2	a24 3-2	a08 4-0	m06 1-2	O19 2-1	M25 0-4	N06 1-0	M11 2-1	D04 3-1	D28 0-1	O16 1-0		A14 0-0
YORK	J29 1-0	a22 0-0	M11 1-1	D28 1-2	O02 2-2	a08 0-0	F26 0-0	a29 2-0	M25 2-1	O23 1-1	O09 2-1	M21 2-0	N06 0-2	J08 0-1	A30 0-1	S11 0-0	N27 0-0	A21 0-3	F12 1-2	N23 1-0	D17 2-2	A07 1-0	J15 2-2	

LEAGUE TABLES

FA PREMIER LEAGUE

	P	W	D	L	F	A	W	D	L	F	A	Pts
Manchester U	38	15	4	0	59	16	13	3	3	38	29	91
Arsenal	38	14	3	2	42	17	8	4	7	31	26	73
Leeds	38	12	2	5	29	18	9	4	6	29	25	69
Liverpool	38	11	4	4	28	13	8	6	5	23	17	67
Chelsea	38	12	5	2	35	12	6	6	7	18	22	65
Aston Villa	38	8	8	3	23	12	7	5	7	23	23	58
Sunderland	38	10	6	3	28	17	6	4	9	29	39	58
Leicester	38	10	3	6	31	24	6	4	9	24	31	55
West Ham	38	11	5	3	32	23	4	5	10	20	30	55
Tottenham	38	10	3	6	40	26	5	5	9	17	23	53
Newcastle	38	10	5	4	42	20	4	5	10	21	34	52
Middlebrough	38	8	5	6	23	26	6	5	8	23	26	52
Everton	38	7	9	3	36	21	5	5	9	23	28	50
Coventry	38	12	1	6	38	22	0	7	12	9	32	44
Southampton	38	8	4	7	26	22	4	4	11	19	40	44
Derby	38	6	3	10	22	25	3	8	8	22	32	38
Bradford	38	6	8	5	26	29	3	1	15	12	39	36
Wimbledon	38	6	7	6	30	28	1	5	13	16	46	33
Sheffield W	38	6	3	10	21	23	2	4	13	17	47	31
Watford	38	5	4	10	24	31	1	2	16	11	46	24

DIVISION 1

	P	W	D	L	F	A	W	D	L	F	A	Pts
Charlton	46	15	3	5	37	18	12	7	4	42	27	91
Manchester C	46	17	2	4	48	17	9	9	5	30	23	89
Ipswich	46	16	3	4	39	17	9	9	5	32	25	87
Barnsley	46	15	4	4	48	24	9	6	8	40	43	82
Birmingham	46	15	5	3	37	16	7	6	10	28	28	77
Bolton	46	14	5	4	43	26	7	8	8	26	24	76
Wolverhampton	46	15	5	3	45	20	6	6	11	19	28	74
Huddersfield	46	14	5	4	43	21	7	6	10	19	28	74
Fulham	46	13	7	3	33	13	4	9	10	16	28	67
Q.P.R.	46	9	12	2	30	20	7	6	10	32	33	66
Blackburn	46	10	9	4	33	20	5	8	10	22	31	62
Norwich	46	11	6	6	26	22	3	9	11	19	28	57
Tranmere	46	10	8	5	35	27	5	4	14	22	41	57
Nottingham F	46	9	10	4	29	18	5	4	14	24	37	56
C. Palace	46	7	11	5	33	26	6	4	13	24	41	54
Sheffield U	46	10	8	5	38	24	3	7	13	21	47	54
Stockport	46	8	8	7	33	31	5	7	11	22	36	54
Portsmouth	46	9	6	8	36	27	4	6	13	19	39	51
Crewe	46	9	5	9	27	31	5	4	14	19	36	51
Grimsby	46	10	8	5	27	25	3	4	16	14	42	51
W.B.A.	46	6	11	6	25	26	4	8	11	18	34	49
Walsall	46	7	6	10	26	34	4	7	12	26	43	46
Port Vale	46	6	6	11	27	30	1	9	13	21	39	36
Swindon	46	5	6	12	23	37	3	6	14	15	40	36

DIVISION 2

	P	W	D	L	F	A	W	D	L	F	A	Pts
Preston	46	15	4	4	37	23	13	7	3	37	14	95
Burnley	46	16	3	4	42	23	9	10	4	27	24	88
Gillingham	46	16	3	4	46	21	9	7	7	33	27	85
Wigan	46	15	3	5	37	14	7	14	2	35	24	83
Millwall	46	14	7	2	41	18	9	6	8	35	32	82
Stoke	46	13	7	3	37	18	10	6	7	31	24	82
Bristol R	46	13	7	3	34	19	10	4	9	35	26	80
Notts Co	46	9	6	8	32	27	9	5	9	29	28	65
Bristol C	46	7	14	2	31	18	8	5	10	28	39	64
Reading	46	10	9	4	28	18	6	5	12	29	45	62
Wrexham	46	9	6	8	23	24	8	5	10	29	37	62
Wycombe	46	11	4	8	32	24	5	9	9	24	29	61
Luton	46	10	7	6	41	35	7	3	13	20	30	61
Oldham	46	8	5	10	27	28	8	7	8	23	27	60
Bury	46	8	10	5	38	33	5	8	10	23	31	57
Bournemouth	46	11	6	6	37	19	5	3	15	22	43	57
Brentford	46	8	6	9	27	31	5	7	11	20	30	52
Colchester	46	9	4	10	36	40	5	6	12	23	42	52
Cambridge	46	8	6	9	38	33	4	6	13	26	32	48
Oxford	46	6	5	12	24	38	6	4	13	19	35	45
Cardiff	46	5	10	8	23	34	4	7	12	22	33	44
Blackpool	46	4	10	9	26	37	4	7	12	23	40	41
Scunthorpe	46	4	6	13	16	34	5	6	12	24	40	39
Chesterfield	46	5	7	11	17	25	2	8	13	17	38	36

DIVISION 2

	P	W	D	L	F	A	W	D	L	F	A	Pts
Swansea	46	15	6	2	32	11	9	7	7	19	19	85
Rotherham	46	13	5	5	43	17	11	7	5	29	19	84
Northampton	46	16	2	5	36	18	9	5	9	27	27	82
Darlington	46	13	9	1	43	15	8	7	8	23	21	79
Peterborough	46	14	4	5	39	30	8	8	7	24	24	78
Barnet	46	12	6	5	36	24	9	6	8	23	29	75
Hartlepool	46	16	1	6	32	17	5	8	10	28	32	72
Cheltenham	46	13	4	6	28	17	7	6	10	22	25	70
Torquay	46	12	6	5	35	20	7	6	10	27	32	69
Rochdale	46	8	7	8	21	25	10	7	6	36	29	68
Brighton	46	10	7	6	38	25	7	9	7	26	21	67
Plymouth	46	12	10	1	38	18	4	8	11	17	33	66
Macclesfield	46	9	7	7	36	30	9	4	10	30	31	65
Hull	46	7	8	8	26	23	8	6	9	17	20	59
Lincoln	46	11	6	6	38	23	4	8	11	29	46	59
Southend	46	11	5	7	37	31	4	6	13	16	30	56
Mansfield	46	9	6	8	33	26	7	2	14	17	39	56
Halifax	46	7	5	11	22	24	8	4	11	22	34	54
Leyton O	46	7	7	9	22	22	6	6	11	25	30	52
York	46	7	10	6	21	21	5	6	12	18	32	52
Exeter	46	8	6	9	27	30	3	5	15	19	42	44
Shrewbury	46	5	6	12	20	27	4	7	12	20	40	40
Carlisle	46	6	8	9	23	27	3	4	16	19	48	39
Chester	46	5	5	13	20	36	5	4	14	24	43	39

English FA Cup Results 1871-2000

Season 1871-72

1st Round

Date	Team	Score	Team	Score
Nov 11	Barnes	2	Civil Service	0
Nov 11	Crystal Palace	0	Hitchin	0
Nov 11	Maidenhead	2	Great Marlow	0
Nov 11	Royal Engineers	*W*	Reigate Priory	*0*
Nov 11	Upton Park	0	Clapham R	3
Nov 11	Wanderers	*W*	Harrow Chequers	*0*

2nd Round

Date	Team	Score	Team	Score
Dec 23	Barnes	1	Hampstead H	1
Dec 16	Clapham R	1	Wanderers	3
Dec 16	Crystal Palace	3	Maidenhead	0
Jan 10	Hitchin	0	Royal Engineers	5
Dec 16	Queen's Park	*W*	Donington School	*0*

Replay

Date	Team	Score	Team	Score
Jan 06	Hampstead H	1	Barnes	0

3rd Round

Date	Team	Score	Team	Score
Jan 27	Royal Engineers	2	Hampstead H.	0
Jan 20	Wanderers	0	Crystal Palace	0

Semi-finals

Date	Team	Score	Team	Score
Feb 17	Crystal Palace	0	Royal Engineers	0
	played at Kennington Oval			
Mar 05	Wanderers	0	Queen's Park	0
	played at Kennington Oval			

Replays

Date	Team	Score	Team	Score
	Wanderers	*W*	Queen's Park	*0*
Mar 09	Crystal Palace	0	Royal Engineers	3
	played at Kennington Oval			

Final

Date	Team	Score	Team	Score
Mar 16	Royal Engineers	0	Wanderers	1
	played at Kennington Oval			

Season 1872-73

1st Round

Date	Team	Score	Team	Score
Oct 26	1st Surrey Rifles	2	Upton Park	0
Oct 19	Barnes	0	South Norwood	1
Oct 19	Clapham R	*W*	Hitchin	*0*
Oct 26	Maidenhead	1	Marlow	0
Oct 26	Oxford Univ	3	Crystal Palace	2
Oct 26	Royal Engineers	3	Civil Service	0
Oct 26	Windsor Home Park	4	Reigate Priory	2

2nd Round

Date	Team	Score	Team	Score
Nov 23	Clapham R	0	Oxford Univ	3
Nov 23	Maidenhead	3	1st Surrey Rifles	0
Dec 07	Windsor Home Park	3	South Norwood	0

3rd Round

Date	Team	Score	Team	Score
Dec 09	Oxford Univ	1	Royal Engineers	0
Dec 21	Windsor Home Park	0	Maidenhead	1

4th Round

Date	Team	Score	Team	Score
Feb 03	Oxford Univ	4	Maidenhead	0

Semi-final

Date	Team	Score	Team	Score
	Oxford Univ	*W*	Queen's Park	*0*

Final

Date	Team	Score	Team	Score
Mar 29	Oxford Univ	0	Wanderers	2
	played at Lillie Bridge			

Season 1873-74

1st Round

Date	Team	Score	Team	Score
Oct 25	1st Surrey Rifles	0	Barnes	0
Oct 25	Cambridge Univ	1	South Norwood	0
	Clapham R	*W*	Athletic Club	*0*
	High Wycombe	*W*	Old Etonians	*0*
	Maidenhead	*W*	Civil Service	*0*
Oct 29	Oxford Univ	4	Upton Park	0
Oct 09	Pilgrims	1	Great Marlow	0
Oct 11	Royal Engineers	5	Brondesbury	0
Oct 30	Sheffield	0	Shropshire	0
Oct 18	Swifts	1	Crystal Palace	0
	Trojans	*W*	Farningham	*0*
Oct 28	Uxbridge	3	Gitanos	0
	Wanderers	*W*	Southall	*0*
Oct 11	Woodford Wells	3	Reigate Priory	2

Replays

Date	Team	Score	Team	Score
Nov 08	Barnes	1	1st Surrey Rifles	0
Nov 17	Shropshire	0	Sheffield	0
	decided by toss of coin			

2nd Round

Date	Team	Score	Team	Score
Nov 15	Clapham R	1	Cambridge Univ	1
Nov 22	Maidenhead	1	High Wycombe	0
Nov 22	Oxford Univ	2	Barnes	0
Nov 26	Royal Engineers	2	Uxbridge	1
Nov 22	Sheffield	1	Pilgrims	0
Nov 22	Swifts	2	Woodford Wells	1
	Wanderers	*W*	Trojans	*0*

Replays

Date	Team	Score	Team	Score
Nov 29	Cambridge Univ	1	Clapham R	1
Dec 20	Clapham R	4	Cambridge Univ	1
	played at Clapham			

3rd Round

Date	Team	Score	Team	Score
Jan 17	Clapham R	2	Sheffield	1
Dec 10	Royal Engineers	7	Maidenhead	0
Dec 06	Wanderers	1	Oxford Univ	1

Replay

Date	Team	Score	Team	Score
Jan 31	Oxford Univ	1	Wanderers	0

Semi-finals

Date	Team	Score	Team	Score
Jan 28	Royal Engineers	2	Swifts	0
	played at Kennington Oval			
Feb 28	Clapham R	0	Oxford Univ	1
	played at Kennington Oval			

Final

Date	Team	Score	Team	Score
Mar 14	Oxford Univ	2	Royal Engineers	0
	played at Kennington Oval			

Season 1874-75

1st Round

Date	Team	Score	Team	Score
Nov 14	Cambridge Univ	0	Crystal Palace	0
	Civil Service	*W*	Harrow Chequers	
Nov 07	Clapham R	3	Panthers	0
Nov 14	Hitchin	0	Maidenhead	1
Nov 05	Old Etonians	0	Swifts	0
Oct 31	Oxford Univ	6	Brondesbury	0
Oct 10	Pilgrims	3	South Norwood	1
Nov 07	Royal Engineers	3	Great Marlow	0
	Shropshire	*W*	Sheffield	*0*
Nov 14	Southall	0	Leyton	0
Oct 24	Upton Park	0	Barnes	3
Oct 31	Wanderers	16	Farningham	0
	Windsor Home Park	*W*	Uxbridge	*0*
Oct 31	Woodford Wells	1	High Wycombe	0

Replays

Date	Team	Score	Team	Score
Nov 14	Swifts	1	Old Etonians	1
Nov 21	Crystal Palace	1	Cambridge Univ	2
Nov 26	Old Etonians	3	Swifts	0
	played at Old Etonians			
Nov 28	Leyton	0	Southall	5

2nd Round

Date	Team	Score	Team	Score
Dec 05	Clapham R	2	Pilgrims	0
Dec 05	Maidenhead	2	Reigate Priory	1
	Oxford Univ	*W*	Windsor Home Park	*0*
Dec 05	Royal Engineers	5	Cambridge Univ	0
Nov 14	Shropshire	1	Civil Service	0
Nov 21	Wanderers	5	Barnes	0
Dec 05	Woodford Wells	3	Southall	0

3rd Round

Date	Team	Score	Team	Score
Jan 23	Old Etonians	1	Maidenhead	0
Jan 30	Royal Engineers	3	Clapham R	2
Jan 23	Shropshire	1	Woodford Wells	1
Jan 30	Wanderers	1	Oxford Univ	2

Replay

Date	Team	Score	Team	Score
Feb 06	Woodford Wells	0	Shropshire	2

Semi-finals

Date	Team	Score	Team	Score
Feb 27	Old Etonians	1	Shropshire	0
	played at Kennington Oval			
Feb 27	Oxford Univ	1	Royal Engineers	1
	played at Kennington Oval			

Replay

Date	Team	Score	Team	Score
Mar 05	Oxford Univ	0	Royal Engineers	1
	played at Kennington Oval			

Final

Date	Team	Score	Team	Score
Mar 13	Old Etonians	1	Royal Engineers	1
	played at Kennington Oval			

Replay

Date	Team	Score	Team	Score
Mar 16	Old Etonians	0	Royal Engineers	2
	played at Kennington Oval			

Season 1875-76

1st Round

Date	Team	Score	Team	Score
Nov 06	105th Regiment	0	Crystal Palace	0
Oct 30	Barnes	0	Reigate Priory	1
	Cambridge Univ	*W*	Civil Service	*0*
	Clapham R	*W*	Hitchin	*0*
Nov 06	Herts Rangers	4	Rochester	0
	Leyton	*W*	Harrow Chequers	*0*
Oct 23	Maidenhead	2	Ramblers	0
Nov 09	Old Etonians	4	Pilgrims	1
Nov 06	Oxford Univ	6	Forest School	0
Nov 06	Panthers	1	Woodford Wells	0
Nov 10	Royal Engineers	15	High Wycombe	0
	Sheffield	*W*	Shropshire	*0*
	South Norwood	*W*	Clydesdale	*0*
Nov 03	Swifts	2	Great Marlow	0
Oct 23	Upton Park	1	Southall	0
Oct 23	Wanderers	5	1st Surrey Rifles	0

Replay

Date	Team	Score	Team	Score
Nov 20	Crystal Palace	3	105th Regiment	0
	played at Kennington Oval			

2nd Round

Date	Team	Score	Team	Score
Dec 18	Clapham R	12	Leyton	0
Dec 18	Herts Rangers	2	Oxford Univ	8
Dec 11	Old Etonians	8	Maidenhead	0
Dec 11	Reigate Priory	0	Cambridge Univ	8
	Royal Engineers	*W*	Panthers	*0*
	Sheffield	*W*	Upton Park	*0*
Dec 11	Swifts	5	South Norwood	0
	Both Qualified			
Dec 11	Wanderers	3	Crystal Palace	0

3rd Round

Date	Team	Score	Team	Score
Jan 31	Cambridge Univ	0	Oxford Univ	4
Jan 29	Old Etonians	1	Clapham R	0
Jan 29	Royal Engineers	1	Swifts	3
Jan 29	Wanderers	2	Sheffield	0

Semi-finals

Date	Team	Score	Team	Score
Feb 19	Old Etonians	1	Oxford Univ	0
	played at Kennington Oval			
Feb 26	Swifts	1	Wanderers	2
	played at Kennington Oval			

Final

Date	Team	Score	Team	Score
Mar 11	Old Etonians	1	Wanderers	1
	played at Kennington Oval			

Replay

Date	Team	Score	Team	Score
Mar 18	Old Etonians	0	Wanderers	3
	played at Kennington Oval			

Season 1876-77

1st Round

Nov 11	105th Regiment	3	1st Surrey Rifles	0
	Barnes	*W*	Old Etonians	*0*
	Cambridge Univ	*W*	High Wycombe	*0*
Nov 11	Clapham R	5	Reigate Priory	0
Nov 04	Forest School	4	Gresham	1
Nov 04	Great Marlow	2	Herts Rangers	1
	Oxford Univ	*W*	Old Salopians	*0*
Nov 08	Panthers	3	Woodgrange	0
Oct 14	Pilgrims	4	Ramblers	1
Nov 04	Rochester	5	Highbury Union	0
Nov 04	Royal Engineers	2	Old Harrovians	1
	Sheffield	*W*	Trojans	*0*
	Shropshire	*W*	Druids	*0*
Nov 04	South Norwood	4	Saxons	1
	Southall	*W*	Old Wykehamists	*0*
Nov 04	Swifts	2	Reading	0
Oct 28	Upton Park	7	Leyton	0
	Wanderers	*W*	Saffron Walden	*0*

2nd Round

Dec 09	Barnes	0	Upton Park	1
Dec 16	Cambridge Univ	2	Clapham R	1
Nov 29	Great Marlow	1	Forest School	0
Dec 14	Oxford Univ	6	105th Regiment	1
Dec 09	Panthers	0	Pilgrims	1
Dec 16	Rochester	1	Swifts	0
Dec 09	Royal Engineers	3	Shropshire	0
Dec 02	South Norwood	0	Sheffield	7
Dec 16	Southall	0	Wanderers	6

3rd Round

Feb 03	Cambridge Univ	4	Rochester	0
	Oxford Univ	*W*	Queen's Park	*0*
Jan 20	Royal Engineers	1	Sheffield	0
Jan 24	Upton Park	2	Great Marlow	2
Jan 20	Wanderers	3	Pilgrims	0

Replay

Jan 27	Great Marlow	0	Upton Park	1

4th Round

Feb 17	Cambridge Univ	1	Royal Engineers	0
Feb 24	Oxford Univ	0	Upton Park	0
	Both Qualified			

Replay

Mar 10	Upton Park	0	Oxford Univ	1

Semi-final

Mar 20	Cambridge Univ	0	Wanderers	1
	played at Kennington Oval			

Final

Mar 24	Oxford Univ	1	Wanderers	2
	played at Kennington Oval			

Season 1877-78

1st Round

Nov 10	103rd Light Inf	0	Old Harrovians	2
Nov 10	1st Surrey Rifles	1	Forest School	0
	Barnes	*W*	St Marks	*0*
Nov 02	Cambridge Univ	3	Southall	1
Nov 07	Darwen	3	Manchester	0
Oct 27	Grantham	0	Clapham R	2
Nov 03	Hawks	5	Minerva	2
Nov 03	Hendon	0	Great Marlow	2
Oct 27	High Wycombe	4	Woodgrange	0
Oct 27	Maidenhead	10	Reading Hornets	0
Nov 03	Notts Co	1	Sheffield	1
	Old Foresters	*W*	Old Wykehamists	*0*
Nov 03	Oxford Univ	5	Herts Rangers	2
Nov 10	Panthers	1	Wanderers	9
Nov 03	Pilgrims	0	Ramblers	0
Nov 09	Ramblers	0	Pilgrims	1
Nov 07	Reading	2	South Norwood	0
Nov 10	Remnants	4	St Stephens	0
	Royal Engineers	*W*	Union	*0*
Nov 12	Shropshire	0	Druids	1
Nov 10	Swifts	3	Leyton	2
Nov 10	Upton Park	3	Rochester	0

Replay

Dec 01	Sheffield	3	Notts Co	0

2nd Round

Dec 22	1st Surrey Rifles	0	Old Harrovians	6
Dec 15	Barnes	3	Great Marlow	1
Dec 08	Cambridge Univ	4	Maidenhead	2
Dec 22	Clapham R	4	Swifts	0
Dec 29	Darwen	0	Sheffield	1
Dec 15	High Wycombe	0	Wanderers	9
Dec 15	Oxford Univ	1	Old Foresters	0
Dec 08	Reading	0	Upton Park	1
Dec 22	Remnants	2	Hawks	0
Dec 08	Royal Engineers	6	Pilgrims	0

3rd Round

Feb 02	Old Harrovians	2	Cambridge Univ	2
Feb 02	Oxford Univ	3	Clapham R	2
Jan 30	Royal Engineers	8	Druids	0
Jan 19	Upton Park	3	Remnants	0
Jan 12	Wanderers	1	Barnes	1

Replays

Jan 26	Barnes	1	Wanderers	4
Feb 09	Cambridge	2	Old Harrovians	2
Feb 16	Cambridge	0	Old Harrovians	2
	played at Kennington Oval			

4th Round

Mar 09	Old Harrovians	3	Upton Park	1
Feb 15	Royal Engineers	3	Oxford Univ	3
Feb 16	Wanderers	3	Sheffield	0

Replays

Feb 27	Oxford Univ	2	Royal Engineers	2
Mar 12	Oxford Univ	2	Royal Engineers	4
	played at Royal Engineers			

Semi-final

Mar 16	Old Harrovians	1	Royal Engineers	2
	played at Kennington Oval			

Final

Mar 23	Royal Engineers	1	Wanderers	3
	played at Kennington Oval			

Season 1878-79

1st Round

Oct 19	Barnes	1	Maidenhead	1
Nov 09	Brentford	1	Pilgrims	3
Nov 09	Cambridge Univ	2	Herts Rangers	0
	Clapham R	*W*	Finchley	*0*
	Darwen	*W*	Birch Manchester	*0*
Nov 02	Forest School	4	Rochester	2
Nov 09	Grey Friars	2	Great Marlow	1
	Minerva	*W*	105th Regiment	*0*
Nov 16	Notts Co	1	Nottingham F	3
Nov 02	Old Harrovians	8	Southall	0
Nov 02	Oxford Univ	7	Wednesbury	0
	Panthers	*W*	Runnymede	*0*
Nov 09	Reading	1	Hendon	0
	Remnants	*W*	Unity	*0*
Nov 02	Romford	3	Ramblers	1
Nov 09	Royal Engineers	3	Old Foresters	0
Oct 28	Sheffield	1	Grantham	1
	South Norwood	*W*	Leyton	*0*
Nov 09	Swifts	2	Hawks	1
Oct 30	Upton Park	5	Saffron Waldon	0
Nov 09	Wanderers	2	Old Etonians	7

Replays

Nov 09	Maidenhead	0	Barnes	4
Nov 18	Grantham	1	Sheffield	3

2nd Round

Jan 04	Barnes	3	Upton Park	2
Dec 04	Cambridge Univ	3	South Norwood	0
Dec 07	Clapham R	10	Forest School	1
Dec 07	Eagley	0	Darwen	0
Dec 07	Grey Friars	0	Minerva	3
Dec 21	Nottingham F	2	Sheffield	0
Dec 21	Old Harrovians	3	Panthers	0
Dec 18	Reading	0	Old Etonians	1
Dec 21	Remnants	6	Pilgrims	2
Dec 10	Royal Engineers	0	Oxford Univ	4
Dec 21	Swifts	3	Romford	1

Replay

Dec 21	Darwen	4	Eagley	1

3rd Round

Feb 01	Clapham R	1	Cambridge Univ	0
Jan 11	Old Etonians	5	Minerva	2
Jan 28	Old Harrovians	0	Nottingham F	2
Feb 01	Oxford Univ	2	Barnes	1
Jan 30	Remnants	2	Darwen	3

4th Round

Mar 08	Clapham R	8	Swifts	1
Feb 25	Nottingham F	2	Oxford Univ	1
Feb 13	Old Etonians	5	Darwen	5

Replays

Mar 08	Darwen	2	Old Etonians	2
Mar 15	Old Etonians	6	Darwen	2

Semi-final

Mar 22	Nottingham F	1	Old Etonians	2
	played at Kennington Oval			

Final

Mar 29	Clapham R	0	Old Etonians	1
	played at Kennington Oval			

Season 1879-80

1st Round

Nov 08	Acton	0	Old Carthusians	4
	Birmingham	*W*	Panthers	*0*
Nov 01	Blackburn	5	Tyne Assoc	1
Nov 08	Clapham R	7	Romford	0
Nov 01	Eagley	0	Darwen	1
Nov 08	Finchley	0	Old Harrovians	2
Nov 06	Great Marlow	1	Oxford Univ	1
Nov 01	Gresham	3	Kildare	0
Nov 08	Grey Friars	2	Hanover	1
Nov 08	Hendon	1	Old Foresters	1
	Henley	*W*	Reading	*0*
Nov 15	Herts Rangers	2	Minerva	1
Nov 08	Hotspur	1	Argonauts	1
Oct 25	Maidenhead	3	Calthorpe	1
Nov 01	Mosquitoes	3	St Peters Inst	1
Nov 08	Nottingham F	4	Notts Co	0
	Old Etonians	*W*	Barnes	*0*
Nov 01	Pilgrims	5	Clarence	2
Nov 15	Remnants	1	Upton Park	1
Nov 15	Rochester	0	Wanderers	6
Nov 13	Royal Engineers	2	Cambridge Univ	0
	Sheffield	*W*	Queen's Park	*0*
Nov 01	South Norwood	4	Brentwood	2
Nov 08	Stafford Road	2	Wednesbury	0
Nov 01	Turton	7	Brigg	0
	West End	*W*	Swifts	*0*

Replays

Nov 10	Oxford Univ	1	Great Marlow	0
Nov 15	Argonauts	0	Hotspur	1
Nov 15	Old Foresters	2	Hendon	2
Nov 22	Hendon	3	Old Foresters	1
Nov 25	Upton Park	5	Remnants	2
	Later disqualified			

2nd Round

Dec 06	Blackburn	3	Darwen	1
Dec 20	Clapham R	4	South Norwood	0
Dec 20	Gresham	0	Grey Friars	9
Nov 29	Henley	1	Maidenhead	3
Dec 20	Mosquitoes	1	Hendon	7
Jan 19	Oxford Univ	6	Birmingham	0
	Pilgrims	*W*	Herts Rangers	*0*
Dec 23	Royal Engineers	4	Upton Park	1
Dec 15	Sheffield	3	Providence	3
Dec 13	Stafford Road	1	Aston Villa	1
Dec 13	Turton	0	Nottingham F	6
Jan 10	Wanderers	1	Old Carthusians	0
Dec 13	West End	1	Hotspur	0

Replays

Dec 29	Providence	0	Sheffield	3
	played at Sheffield			
Jan 24	Aston Villa	3	Stafford Road	1

3rd Round

Jan 31	Nottingham F	6	Blackburn	0
Jan 24	Old Etonians	3	Wanderers	1
	Oxford Univ	*W*	Aston Villa	*0*
Jan 17	Pilgrims	0	Clapham R	7
Feb 04	Royal Engineers	2	Old Harrovians	0

4th Round

Feb 14	Clapham R	2	Hendon	0
Feb 19	Nottingham F	2	Sheffield	2
	Sheffield disqualified			
Feb 07	Old Etonians	5	West End	1
Feb 14	Oxford Univ	1	Maidenhead	0
Feb 18	Royal Engineers	1	Grey Friars	0

5th Round

Feb 21	Old Etonians	0	Clapham R	1

Mar 05 Oxford Univ 1 Royal Engineers 1
played at Kennington Oval

Replay
Mar 15 Royal Engineers 0 Oxford Univ 1
played at Kennington Oval

Semi-final
Mar 27 Nottingham F 0 Oxford Univ 1
played at Kennington Oval

Final
Apr 10 Clapham R 1 Oxford Univ 0
played at Kennington Oval

Season 1880-81

1st Round
Nov 13 Acton 1 Kildare 1
Oct 30 Astley Bridge 4 Eagley 0
Oct 30 Aston Villa 5 Wednesbury 3
Oct 30 Blackburn 6 Sheffield Prov 2
Nov 06 Brentwood 0 Old Etonians 10
Nov 11 Calthorpe 1 Grantham 2
Nov 13 Clapham R 15 Finchley 0
Nov 13 Darwen 8 Brigg 0
Oct 30 Great Marlow 6 Clarence 0
Nov 13 Grey Friars 0 Windsor Home Parka 0
Nov 06 Herts Rangers 6 Barnes 0
Nov 13 Maidenhead 1 Old Harrovians 1
Nov 13 Mosquitoes 1 Upton Park 8
Nottingham F *W* Caius College *0*
Nov 04 Notts Co 4 Derbyshire 4
Oct 23 Old Carthusians 7 Saffron Walden 0
Pilgrims *W* Old Philberdian *0*
Rangers *W* Wanderers *0*
Nov 13 Reading 5 Hotspur 1
Nov 13 Reading Abbey 1 St Albans 0
Nov 13 Rochester 1 Dreadnought 2
Nov 13 Romford 1 Reading Minster 1
Nov 13 Royal Engineers 0 Remnants 0
Oct 30 Sheffield 5 Blackburn O 4
Sheffield W *W* Queen's Park *0*
Nov 06 Spilsby 0 Stafford Road 7
Nov 06 St Peters 1 Hendon 8
Nov 06 Swifts 1 Old Foresters 1
Oct 16 Turton 5 Briggs Britanni 0
Nov 06 West End 1 Hanover 0
Nov 13 Weybridge 3 Henley 0

Replays
Romford *W* Reading Minster *0*
Nov 20 Kildare 0 Acton 5
Nov 20 Old Foresters 1 Swifts 2
Nov 20 Old Harrovians 0 Maidenhead 1
Nov 20 Remnants 0 Royal Engineers 1
Nov 20 Windsor Home Parka 1 Grey Friars 3
Nov 27 Derbyshire 2 Notts Co 4

2nd Round
Dec 18 Astley Bridge 0 Turton 3
Dec 18 Blackburn 0 Sheffield W 4
Dec 11 Grantham 1 Stafford Road 1
Dec 11 Great Marlow 4 West End 0
Dec 11 Grey Friars 1 Maidenhead 0
Dec 04 Nottingham F 1 Aston Villa 2
Dec 11 Old Carthusians 5 Dreadnought 1
Dec 04 Old Etonians 2 Hendon 0
Dec 18 Reading 0 Swifts 1
Dec 11 Reading Abbey 2 Acton 1
Dec 09 Royal Engineers 1 Pilgrims 0
Dec 18 Sheffield 1 Darwen 5
Dec 18 Weybridge 0 Upton Park 3

Replay
Dec 16 Stafford Road 7 Grantham 1

3rd Round
Jan 08 Clapham R 2 Swifts
Feb 12 Notts Co 1 Aston Villa
Feb 05 Old Etonians 3 Herts Rangers
Feb 12 Romford 2 Reading Abbey
Feb 09 Royal Engineers 6 Rangers
Jan 08 Turton 0 Sheffield W

4th Round
Feb 19 Aston Villa 2 Stafford Road
Feb 12 Clapham R 5 Upton Park
Feb 05 Darwen 5 Sheffield W
Feb 19 Grey Friars 0 Old Etonians
Feb 19 Old Carthusians 2 Royal Engineers
Feb 19 Romford 2 Great Marlow

5th Round
Mar 05 Darwen 15 Romford
Mar 19 Old Carthusians 3 Clapham R
Mar 19 Stafford Road 1 Old Etonians

Semi-final
Mar 26 Darwen 1 Old Carthusians
played at Kennington Oval

Final
Apr 09 Old Carthusians 3 Old Etonians
played at Kennington Oval

Season 1881-82

1st Round
Accrington *W* Queen's Park *0*
Oct 29 Astley Bridge 2 Turton 2
Nov 05 Aston Villa 4 Nottingham F 1
Nov 05 Barnes 3 Rochester 1
Oct 29 Blackburn 9 Blackburn Park 1
Oct 22 Bolton 5 Eagley 5
Nov 05 Bootle 2 Blackburn Law 1
Oct 29 Darwen 3 Blackburn O 1
Dreadnought *W* Caius College *0*
Oct 29 Finchley 0 Acton 0
Nov 05 Grantham 6 Brigg 0
Oct 22 Great Marlow 3 Brentwood 1
Oct 22 Henley 0 Maidenhead 2
Nov 05 Hotspur 1 Union 0
Nov 05 Mosquitoes 1 Pilgrims 1
Notts Co *W* Calthorpe *0*
Nov 05 Old Carthusians 5 Esher Leopold 0
Nov 05 Old Etonians 2 Clapham R 2
Nov 05 Old Foresters 3 Morton 0
Nov 05 Old Harrovians 4 Olympic 2
Oct 29 Reading 5 Hendon 0
Nov 12 Reading Abbey 2 Woodford Bridge 1
Romford *W* Rangers *0*
Nov 05 Royal Engineers 6 Kildare 0
Nov 05 Sheffield 8 Briggs Britanni 0
Oct 17 Sheffield Heele 5 Lockwood 1
Nov 05 Sheffield W 2 Sheffield Prov 0
Nov 05 Small Heath 4 Derby Town 1
St Bartholomew *W* Wanderers *0*
Oct 29 Staveley 5 Spilsby 1
Nov 05 Swifts 4 Herts Rangers 0
Oct 22 Upton Park 3 St Albans 0
Nov 05 Wednesbury Old 9 Birmingham St George's 1
Nov 05 Wednesbury Stro 3 Stafford Road 1
Oct 29 West End 3 Remnants 2
Oct 22 Windsor Home Parka 0 Reading Minster 1

Replays
Oct 22 Woodford Bridge 1 Reading Abbey 1
Nov 05 Acton 4 Finchley 0
Nov 12 Eagley 0 Bolton 1
Nov 12 Pilgrims 5 Mosquitoes 0
Nov 12 Turton 1 Astley Bridge 1
Nov 19 Astley Bridge 3 Turton 3
Nov 19 Clapham R 0 Old Etonians 1
Nov 26 Turton 2 Astley Bridge 0

2nd Round
Nov 19 Blackburn 6 Bolton 2
Nov 26 Darwen 3 Accrington 1
Nov 30 Great Marlow 2 St Bartholomew 0
Nov 26 Hanover 1 Upton Park 3
Dec 03 Maidenhead 2 Acton 1
Nov 24 Notts Co 5 Wednesbury Stro 3
Dec 03 Old Carthusians 7 Barnes 1
Dec 03 Old Foresters 3 Pilgrims 1
Nov 26 Reading 1 West End 1
Nov 26 Reading Abbey 1 Hotspur 4
Dec 03 Reading Minster 3 Romford 1
Nov 26 Sheffield 0 Sheffield Heele 4
Nov 28 Staveley 3 Grantham 1
Dec 03 Swifts 7 Old Harrovians 1
Dec 03 Turton 4 Bootle 0
Dec 03 Wednesbury Old 6 Small Heath 0

Replays
Reading *W* West End *0*
Dec 10 Notts Co 11 Wednesbury Stro 1

3rd Round
Dec 31 Aston Villa 2 Notts Co 2
Dec 17 Darwen 4 Turton 2
Dec 17 Great Marlow 2 Dreadnought 1
Dec 17 Hotspur 0 Reading Minster 0
Dec 20 Old Carthusians 0 Royal Engineers 2
Dec 17 Old Etonians 3 Swifts 0
Dec 28 Sheffield W 2 Staveley

Replays
Dec 26 Reading Minster 0 Hotspur
Jan 07 Notts Co 2 Aston Villa
Jan 07 Staveley 0 Sheffield W
Jan 09 Sheffield W 5 Staveley
played at Lockwood
Jan 14 Aston Villa 4 Notts Co
played at Aston Villa

4th Round
Jan 30 Blackburn 5 Darwen
Great Marlow *W* Reading
Jan 14 Old Etonians 6 Maidenhead
Jan 21 Old Foresters 2 Royal Engineers
Jan 21 Sheffield W 3 Sheffield Heele
Jan 21 Upton Park 5 Hotspur
Jan 21 Wednesbury Old 4 Aston Villa

5th Round
Feb 18 Great Marlow 1 Old Foresters
Feb 07 Old Foresters 0 Great Marlow
Feb 07 Sheffield W 6 Upton Park
Feb 11 Wednesbury Old 1 Blackburn

Semi-finals
Mar 06 Blackburn 0 Sheffield W
played at Huddersfield
Mar 04 Great Marlow 0 Old Etonians
played at Kennington Oval

Replay
Mar 15 Blackburn 5 Sheffield W
played at Manchester

Final
Mar 25 Blackburn 0 Old Etonians
played at Kennington Oval

Season 1882-83

1st Round
Oct 21 Aston Villa 4 Walsall Swifts 1
Oct 28 Barnes 2 Brentwood 4
Oct 28 Birmingham St George's 4 Calthorpe 1
Oct 23 Blackburn 11 Blackpool 1
Nov 04 Blackburn O 6 Accrington 3
Nov 04 Bolton 6 Bootle 1
Nov 04 Bolton Olympic 4 Eagley 7
Sep 02 Church 5 Clitheroe 0
Nov 04 Clapham R 3 Kildare 0
Oct 21 Darwen 4 Blackburn Park 1
Oct 14 Darwen Ramblers 5 South Shore 2
Oct 21 Dreadnought 1 South Reading 2
Nov 04 Druids 1 Oswestry 1
Oct 21 Etonian Rambler 6 Romford 2
Oct 28 Great Marlow 2 Hornchurch 0
Grimsby *W* Queen's Park *0*
Oct 21 Halliwell 3 Great Lever 2
Nov 04 Hanover 1 Mosquitoes 0
Oct 21 Liverpool Ramblers 1 Southport 1
Oct 28 Lower Darwen 5 Irwell Springs 2
Nov 04 Macclesfield 3 Lockwood 4
Nov 04 Maidenhead 0 Old Westminster 2
Oct 28 Northwich V 3 Astley Bridge 2
Nottingham F *W* Brigg Britannia *0*
Nov 04 Notts Co 6 Sheffield 1
Nov 04 Old Etonians 1 Old Foresters 1
Phoenix Bessemer *W* Grantham *0*
Oct 21 Pilgrims 0 Old Carthusians 6
Reading Minster *W* Remnants *0*
Nov 04 Rochester 2 Hotspur 0
Oct 21 Royal Engineers 3 Woodford 1
Nov 04 Sheffield W 12 Spilsby 2
Nov 04 Small Heath 3 Stafford Road 3
Nov 04 Spital 1 Wednesbury Old 7
Nov 04 Swifts 4 Highbury Union 1
Nov 04 United Hospital 3 London Olympic 0
Oct 21 Walsall Town 4 Staveley 1
Nov 04 West End 1 Hendon
Nov 04 Windsor Home Park 3 Acton

Replays
Nov 04 Dreadnought 1 South Reading

Nov 04 Southport 0 Liverpool Rambl
Nov 18 Old Foresters 1 Old Etonians
Nov 18 Oswestry 0 Druids
Nov 18 Stafford Road 6 Small Heath

2nd Round
Dec 02 Aston Unity 3 Birmingham St Georg
Nov 18 Aston Villa 4 Wednesbury Old
Dec 09 Blackburn O 8 Lower Darwen
Dec 02 Bolton 3 Liverpool Ramblers
Dec 02 Brentwood 1 Etonians
Dec 02 Clapham R 7 Hanover
Dec 02 Darwen 1 Blackburn

Nov 25	Darwen Ramblers	3	Haslingden	2
Dec 09	Druids	5	Northwich V	0
Dec 02	Eagley	3	Halliwell	1
Dec 02	Etonian Rambler	0	Old Carthusians	7
	Great Marlow	*W*	Reading Minster	*O*
Dec 02	Hendon	2	Chatham	1
Dec 02	Nottingham F	7	Sheffield Heele	2
Nov 25	Phoenix Besseme	8	Grimsby	1
Nov 29	Royal Engineers	8	Reading	0
Dec 02	Sheffield W	6	Lockwood	0
Dec 02	Stafford Road	1	Walsall Town	4
Nov 30	Swifts	2	Upton Park	2
Nov 30	Windsor Home Park	3	United Hospital	1

Replay

Dec 02	Upton Park	2	Swifts	3

3rd Round

Jan 06	Aston Villa	3	Aston Unity	1
Dec 16	Blackburn O	8	Darwen Ramblers	0
Jan 06	Church	2	Darwen	2
Jan 06	Druids	0	Bolton	0
Jan 06	Hendon	11	South Reading	1
Jan 06	Nottingham F	2	Sheffield W	2
Dec 27	Notts Co	4	Phoenix Besseme	1
Dec 16	Old Carthusians	3	Old Westminster	2
Dec 16	Old Etonians	7	Rochester	0
Jan 06	Windsor Home Park	0	Clapham R	3

Replays

Jan 13	Sheffield W	3	Nottingham F	2
Jan 20	Darwen	0	Church	2
Jan 22	Bolton	1	Druids	1
Jan 29	Bolton	0	Druids	1
	played at Wrexham			

4th Round

Jan 27	Aston Villa	2	Walsall Town	1
Feb 03	Church	0	Blackburn O	2
Feb 10	Eagley	1	Druids	2
Feb 03	Great Marlow	0	Hendon	3
Jan 25	Old Carthusians	6	Royal Engineers	2
Jan 24	Old Etonians	2	Swifts	0
Feb 12	Sheffield W	1	Notts Co	4

5th Round

Feb 24	Blackburn O	4	Druids	1
Mar 03	Hendon	2	Old Etonians	4
Mar 03	Notts Co	4	Aston Villa	3
Feb 20	Old Carthusians	5	Clapham R	3

Semi-final

Mar 17	Blackburn O	4	Old Carthusians	0
	played at Manchester			
Mar 17	Notts Co	1	Old Etonians	2
	played at Kennington Oval			

Final

Mar 31	Blackburn O	2	Old Etonians	1
	played at Kennington Oval			

Season 1883-84

1st Round

Nov 10	Accrington	4	Blackpool	0
Nov 10	Acton	0	Upton Park	2
Oct 20	Blackburn Park	7	Southport	0
Oct 16	Blackburn O	5	Darwen R	1
Oct 27	Blackburn	6	Clitheroe	0
Nov 10	Bolton	9	Bolton O	0
Nov 03	Bolton A	5	Bradshaw	1
Nov 10	Calthorpe	0	Walsall	9
	Clapham	*W*	Kildare	*O*
Nov 10	Clitheroe	3	South Shore	3
Oct 06	Crewe	0	Queen's Park	10
Oct 27	Darwen	2	Church	2
Nov 10	Davenham	2	Macclesfield	0
Nov 10	Druids	0	Northwich	1
Nov 10	Grantham	3	Spilsby	2
Oct 20	Great Lever	4	Astley Bridge	1
Oct 13	Halliwell	2	Eagley	5
Nov 03	Hanover	1	Brentwood	6
Nov 10	Hendon	3	Old Eton	2
Nov 10	Hornchurch	0	Great Marlow	9
Nov 03	Hull	1	Grimsby	3
Oct 20	Hurst	3	Turton	1
Nov 10	Lockwood	4	Sheffield	1
Nov 10	Manchester	2	Stoke	1
Nov 10	Middlesbrough	1	staveley	5
Nov 10	Mosquito	3	Pilgrims	2
	Nottingham	*W*	Redcar	*O*
Nov 10	Notts Co	3	Sheffield	1
Nov 10	Old Foresters	2	Dreadnought	1
Nov 03	Old Westminsters	3	Chatham	0
Nov 10	Oswestry	7	Hartford	0
Nov 03	Padiham	3	Lower Darwen	1
Nov 10	Reading	2	South Reading	2
Nov 10	Reading	1	Old Carthusians	10
Nov 03	Rochester	2	Uxbridge	1
Nov 03	Romford	3	Woodford	0
Nov 17	Rossendale	6	Irwell Springs	2
Oct 20	Small Heath	1	Birmingham Excel	1
Nov 10	Spital	1	Rotherham	1
Nov 10	Stafford	5	Aston Unity	1
Nov 10	Upton Rangers	0	Old Wyke	7
Nov 10	Walsall	1	Aston Villa	5
Nov 10	Wednesbury	5	Mitchell	0
Nov 10	West End	1	Maidenhead	0
Nov 10	Windsor	5	Royal Engineer	3
Oct 27	Wolverhampton	4	Long Eaton	1
	Wrexham	*W*	Liverpool	*O*
Nov 10	W.B.A.	0	Wednesbury	2

Replays

Nov 03	Church	0	Darwen	1
Nov 10	Birmingham	3	Small Heath	2
Nov 17	Rotherham	7	Spital	2
Nov 17	South Reading	0	Reading	4
Nov 24	South Shore	3	Clitheroe	2

2nd Round

Dec 01	Birmingham	1	Derby Midland	1
Nov 24	Blackburn Rark	2	Accrington	3
	Accrington disqualified			
Dec 01	Bolton	3	Bolton A	0
Dec 01	Clapham	7	Rochester	0
Dec 01	Darwen	1	Blackburn O	2
Nov 26	Grantham	4	Grimsby	0
Dec 01	Hurst	3	Irwell S	2
Dec 01	Lockwood	3	Rotherham	1
Nov 24	Northwich	5	Davenham	1
Dec 01	Notts Co	3	Nottingham	0
Nov 24	Old Cart	2	Old Foresters	7
Dec 01	Old Westminsters	2	Hendon	1
Dec 01	Preston	4	Great Lever	1
Dec 01	Queen's	15	Manchester	0
Dec 01	Reading	1	West End	0
Dec 01	Romford	3	Mosquito	1
Dec 01	South Shore	0	Blackburn	7
Dec 01	Stafford	0	Aston Villa	5
Dec 01	Staveley	3	Sheffield	1
Dec 01	Swifts	2	Great Marlow	0
Dec 01	Walsall	2	Wednesbury Town	2
Dec 01	Wednesbury Old A	4	Wolverhampton	2
Dec 01	Windsor	0	Old Wyke	1
Dec 01	Wrexham	3	Oswestry	4

Replays

Dec 08	Wednesbury Town	6	Walsall	0
Dec 15	Derby Midland	2	Birmingham	1

3rd Round

Dec 24	Blackburn	3	Padiham	0
Dec 29	Bolton	8	Irwell Springs	1
Dec 22	Clapham	1	Swifts	2
Dec 20	Grantham	1	Notts Co	4
Dec 29	Oswestry	1	Queen's Park	7
Dec 29	Preston	9	Eagley	1
Dec 22	Reading	1	Upton Park	6
Dec 29	Romford	1	Brentwood	4
Dec 29	Staveley	1	Lockwood	0
Dec 29	Wednesbury Old A	4	Aston Villa	7
Dec 29	Wednesbury Town	1	Derby Midland	0

4th Round

Jan 19	Blackburn	5	Staveley	1
Jan 19	Blackburn O	6	Old Wyke	0
Jan 19	Northwich	3	Brentwood	0
Jan 19	Notts Co	2	Bolton	2
Jan 19	Old Westminsters	5	Wednesbury	0
Jan 19	Preston	1	Upton Park	1
	Preston disqualified			
Jan 19	Queen's	6	Aston Villa	1
Jan 19	Swifts	2	Old Foresters	1

Replay

Feb 02	Bolton	1	Notts Co	2

5th Round

Feb 09	Blackburn O	9	Northwich	1
Feb 09	Notts Co	1	Swifts	1
Feb 09	Old Westminsters	0	Queen's Park	1
Feb 09	Upton Park	0	Blackburn	3

Replay

Feb 14	Swifts	0	Notts Co	1

Semi-finals

Mar 01	Blackburn	1	Notts Co	0
	played at Birmingham			
Mar 01	Blackburn O	0	Queen's Park	4
	played at Nottingham			

Final

Mar 29	Blackburn	2	Queen's Park	1
	played at Kennington Oval			

Season 1884-85

1st Round

Oct 11	Accrington	3	Southport	0
Nov 08	Acton	1	Old Carthusians	7
Nov 03	Aston Villa	4	Wednesbury Town	1
Nov 08	Birmingham Excel	2	Small Heath	0
Nov 01	Birmingham St George's	5	Aston Unity	0
Oct 11	Blackburn	11	Rossendale	0
Oct 04	Blackburn O	12	Oswaldtwistle	0
	Bolton Assoc	*W*	Astley Bridge	*O*
Nov 08	Brentwood	2	Barnes	0
	Chatham	*W*	Windsor Home Parka	*O*
Oct 25	Chirk	4	Davenham	2
Oct 18	Church	3	Hurst	2
Nov 08	Clapham R	3	Hendon	3
Nov 08	Crewe	2	Oswestry	1
Oct 11	Darwen	11	Bradshaw	0
Nov 01	Darwen Ramblers	1	Fishwick	2
Nov 08	Derby	0	Walsall Town	7
Nov 08	Derby Midland	1	Wednesbury Old	2
Nov 08	Druids	6	Liverpool Rambl	1
Nov 08	Dulwich	3	Pilgrims	2
Nov 08	Great Marlow	10	Royal Engineers	1
Nov 10	Grimsby	1	Grantham	0
Nov 08	Hanover	1	Reading Minster	0
Oct 11	Higher Walton	1	Darwen Old Wdrs	1
Nov 01	Hull	1	Lincoln	5
Oct 25	Junction St	1	W.B.A.	7
Nov 08	Leek	4	Northwich V	3
Nov 08	Lockwood	0	Sheffield	3
	Low Moor	*W*	Blackburn Park	*O*
Oct 11	Lower Darwen	4	Halliwell	1
Nov 08	Luton	1	Old Etonians	3
Nov 08	Macclesfield	9	Hartford St J	0
Nov 08	Maidenhead	0	Old Wykehamists	3
	Middlesbrough	*W*	Grimsby Dist	*O*
Nov 08	Newark	7	Spilsby	3
	Newtown	*W*	Stafford Ranger	*O*
Nov 08	Nottingham F	5	Rotherham	0
Nov 08	Notts Co	2	Notts Olympic	0
Nov 01	Old Foresters	8	Hoddesdon	0
Nov 01	Old Westminster	6	Bournemouth	0
	Queen's Park	*W*	Stoke	*O*
Nov 08	Reading	2	Rochester	0
Nov 08	Redcar	3	Sunderland	1
Nov 01	Romford	3	Clapton	2
Nov 08	Sheffield Heele	1	Notts Wanderers	0
Nov 08	Sheffield W	1	Long Eaton	0
Nov 08	South Reading	4	Casuals	1
	South Shore	*W*	Rawtenstall	*O*
Nov 08	Staveley	4	Notts Rangers	1
Nov 08	Swifts	3	Old Brightonian	0
Nov 08	Uxbridge	1	Hotspur	3
Nov 08	Walsall Swifts	0	Stafford Road	0
Nov 08	West End	3	Upton Park	3
	Witton West End	*W*	Clitheroe	*O*
Nov 08	Wolverhampton	0	Derby St Luke's	0
Oct 18	Wrexham O	1	Goldenhill	0

Replays

Nov 08	Darwen Old Wdrs	4	Higher Walton	1
Nov 17	Stafford Road	1	Walsall Swifts	2
Nov 22	Derby St Luke's	4	Wolverhampton	2
Nov 22	Hendon	6	Clapham R	0

2nd Round

Dec 06	Birmingham St George's	2	Birmingham Exce	2
Dec 06	Blackburn	3	Blackburn O	2
Dec 06	Brentwood	2	Old Etonians	2
Dec 06	Chatham	1	Hendon	0
Nov 29	Chirk	4	Wrexham O	1
Nov 29	Darwen Old Wdrs	7	Bolton Assoc	2
Dec 06	Derby St Luke's	0	Walsall Swifts	1
Nov 22	Fishwick	0	Darwen	2
Dec 06	Grimsby	3	Redcar	1
Nov 29	Hanover	2	Old Foresters	1
Dec 06	Hotspur	1	Old Wykehamists	2
Dec 06	Macclesfield	1	Leek	5
Dec 06	Middlesbrough	4	Newark	1
Dec 20	Newtown	1	Druids	1
Dec 06	Nottingham F	4	Sheffield Heele	1
Dec 06	Old Carthusians	5	Great Marlow	3
Dec 06	Old Westminster	7	Henley	0
Dec 06	Queen's Park	2	Crewe	1
Dec 06	Romford	3	Dulwich	0
Dec 06	Sheffield	4	Chesterfield	1
Dec 06	South Shore	2	Church	3
Nov 22	Southport	3	Low Moor	1
Dec 06	Staveley	0	Notts Co	2
Dec 06	Swifts	3	South Reading	2
Dec 06	Upton Park	3	Reading	1
Dec 06	Walsall Town	0	Aston Villa	2
Dec 06	W.B.A.	4	Wednesbury Old	2

Replays

Dec 22	Birmingham Exce	0	Birmingham St George's	2
Dec 23	Old Etonians	6	Brentwood	1
Dec 27	Druids	6	Newtown	0

3rd Round

Jan 03	Aston Villa	0	W.B.A.	0
Jan 10	Birmingham St George's	2	Walsall Swifts	3
Dec 22	Blackburn	5	Witton	1
Jan 03	Church	10	Southport	0
Jan 10	Druids	4	Chirk	1
Jan 03	Grimsby	1	Lincoln	0
Jan 03	Hanover	0	Chatham	2
Jan 03	Leek	2	Queen's Park	3
Dec 20	Lower Darwen	4	Darwen Old Wdrs	2
Jan 03	Notts Co	5	Sheffield	0
Jan 03	Old Wykehamists	2	Upton Park	1
Jan 03	Sheffield W	1	Nottingham F	2

Jan 03 Swifts 1 Old Westminster 1

Replays
Jan 10 W.B.A. 3 Aston Villa 0
Jan 14 Old Westminster 2 Swifts 2
Jan 21 Old Westminster 1 Swifts 2
played at Kennington Oval

4th Round
Jan 17 Blackburn 8 Romford 0
Jan 24 Chatham 1 Lower Darwen 0
Jan 17 Church 3 Darwen 0
Jan 24 Old Carthusians 3 Grimsby 0
Jan 24 Old Etonians 5 Middlesbrough 2
Jan 17 Queen's Park 7 Old Wykehamists 0

Jan 24 Swifts 0 Nottingham F 1
Jan 24 Walsall Swifts 1 Notts Co 4
Jan 24 W.B.A. 1 Druids 0

5th Round
Feb 07 Chatham 0 Old Carthusians 3

6th Round
Feb 14 Church 0 Old Carthusians 1
Feb 21 Notts Co 2 Queen's Park 2
Feb 21 Old Etonians 0 Nottingham F 2
Feb 21 W.B.A. 0 Blackburn 2

Replay
Feb 28 Queen's Park 2 Notts Co 1

Semi-finals
Mar 07 Blackburn 5 Old Carthusians
played at Nottingham
Mar 14 Nottingham F 1 Queen's Park
played at Derby

Replay
Mar 28 Nottingham F 0 Queen's Park
played at Edinburgh

Final
Apr 04 Blackburn 2 Queen's Park
played at Kennington Oval

Season 1885-86

1st Round
Oct 17 Accrington 5 Witton 4
Oct 31 Barnes 1 Lancing Old Boy 7
Nov 28 Blackburn O 1 Church 3
Oct 24 Bollington 0 Oswestry 5
Oct 17 Bolton 6 Eagley 0
Oct 31 Brentwood 3 Maidenhead 0
Oct 24 Burslem Port Vale 3 Chirk 1
Oct 31 Chatham 0 Old Carthusians 2
Oct 31 Clapham R 12 1st Surrey Rifles 0
Oct 24 Clitheroe 0 Blackburn 2
Oct 31 Darwen 2 Derby Junction 2
Oct 17 Darwen Old Wdrs 11 Burnley 0
Oct 31 Davenham 2 Goldenhill 1
Oct 31 Derby 3 Birmingham St George's 0
Oct 31 Derby Midland 2 Birmingham Exce 1
Oct 31 Dulwich 1 South Reading 2
Oct 24 Gainsborough 4 Grantham 1
Oct 31 Great Marlow 3 Luton 0
Oct 31 Halliwell 2 Fishwick 1
Oct 31 Hanover 1 Romford 1
Oct 24 Hendon 0 Clapton 4
Oct 17 Higher Walton 3 South Shore 4
Nov 18 Hurst 3 Bradshaw 1
Oct 31 Leek 6 Wrexham 3
Oct 31 Lincoln 0 Grimsby 2
Oct 17 Lincoln Lindum 4 Grimsby Distric 0
Oct 31 Lockwood 2 Notts Rangers 2
Oct 31 Long Eaton 2 Sheffield W 0
Oct 31 Luton *W* 3 Chesham 2
Oct 31 Macclesfield 4 Northwich V 1
Oct 31 Mexborough 1 Staveley 1
Middlesbrough *W* Horncastle *0*
Oct 31 Newark 0 Sheffield 3
Oct 24 Newtown 3 Hartford St Joh 1
Oct 31 Nottingham F 6 Mellors 2
Oct 24 Notts Co 15 Rotherham 0
Oct 31 Notts *W* 2 Notts Olympic 2
Oct 31 Old Brightonian 2 Acton 1
Old Etonians *W* Bournemouth *0*
Old Harrovians *W* St James *0*
Oct 31 Old Westminster 3 Hotspur 1
Oct 31 Old Wykehamists 5 Uxbridge 0
Oct 31 Oswaldtwistle 3 Lower Darwen 1
Padiham *W* Hearts *0*
Preston *W* Great Lever *0*
Oct 31 Queen's Park 5 Partick 1
Rawtenstall *W* Rangers *0*
Oct 24 Redcar 3 Sunderland 0
Oct 31 Rochester 6 Reading 1
Oct 24 Rossendale 6 Low Moor 2
Oct 31 Royal Engineers 1 Old Foresters 5
Oct 19 Sheffield Heele 2 Eckington 1
Oct 31 Small Heath 9 Burton W 2
Oct 10 Southport 2 Astley Bridge 3
Oct 31 Stafford Ranger 1 Druids 4

Oct 17 Stafford Road 7 Matlock 0
Oct 31 Stoke 2 Crewe 2
Oct 31 Swifts 7 Casuals 1
Oct 17 T. Lanark 4 Blackburn Park 2
Oct 24 Upton Park 4 United Ldn Scot 2
Oct 17 Walsall Town 0 Aston Villa 5
Oct 31 Wednesbury Old 5 Burton S 1
Oct 31 Wolverhampton 7 Derby St Lukes 0
Oct 31 W.B.A. 4 Aston Unity 1

Replays
Staveley *W* Mexborough *0*
Nov 07 Crewe 1 Stoke 0
Nov 07 Derby Junction 0 Darwen 4
Nov 07 Notts Olympic 4 Notts *W* 1
Both Qualified
Nov 07 Notts Rangers 4 Lockwood 0
Nov 07 Romford 3 Hanover 0

2nd Round
Nov 21 Blackburn 1 Oswaldtwistle 0
Nov 14 Brentwood 6 Lancing Old Boy 1
Church *W* T. Lanark *0*
Nov 21 Clapton 1 South Reading 1
Clapton disqualified
Nov 21 Darwen Old Wdrs 2 Accrington 1
Nov 21 Davenham 8 Macclesfield 1
Nov 14 Derby 2 Aston Villa 0
Nov 21 Derby Midland 1 Walsall Swifts 3
Nov 21 Druids 2 Burslem Port Vale 2
Nov 21 Gainsborough 1 Middlesbrough 2
Nov 21 Great Marlow 6 Old Etonians 1
Nov 21 Grimsby 8 Darlington 0
Halliwell *W* Hurst *0*
Leek *W* Newtown *0*
Nov 21 Long Eaton 1 Staveley 4
Nov 21 Nottingham F 4 Notts Olympic 1
Nov 21 Notts Co 8 Sheffield 0
Nov 21 Old Carthusians 8 Upton Park 0
Nov 21 Old Harrovians 2 Old Foresters 1
Nov 21 Old Westminster 3 Old Brightonian 0
Nov 21 Old Wykehamists 10 Luton *W* 0
Nov 21 Oswestry 1 Crewe 1
Oswestry disqualified
Nov 18 Preston 11 Astley Bridge 3
Nov 21 Rawtenstall 3 Bolton 3
Rawtenstall disqualified
Nov 21 Redcar 2 Lincoln Lindum 0
Nov 21 Rossendale 9 Padiham 1
Nov 21 Sheffield Heele 1 Notts R 6
Nov 21 Small Heath 3 Darwen 1
South Shore *W* Queen's Park *0*
Nov 21 Swifts 5 Rochester 1
Nov 21 Wolverhampton 4 Stafford Road 2
Nov 21 W.B.A. 3 Wednesbury Old 2

Replay
Nov 28 Burslem Port Vale 5 Druids

3rd Round
Dec 05 Blackburn 6 Darwen Old Wdrs
Dec 12 Bolton 2 Preston
Dec 12 Church 5 Rossendale
Dec 12 Davenham 2 Crewe
Dec 19 Grimsby 1 Middlesbrough
Dec 19 Halliwell 1 South Shore
Dec 12 Leek 2 Burslem Port Vale
Dec 12 Notts Co 3 Notts R
Dec 12 Old Westminster 5 Romford
Old Wykehamists *W* Great Marlow
Dec 12 Small Heath 4 Derby
South Reading *W* Clapham R
Dec 12 Staveley 2 Nottingham F
Swifts *W* Old Harrovians *0*
Dec 12 Wolverhampton 2 Walsall Swifts

4th Round
Jan 02 South Reading 0 Brentwood
Jan 02 W.B.A. 3 Wolverhampton

5th Round
Jan 23 Blackburn 7 Staveley
Jan 30 Burslem Port Vale 2 Brentwood
B.P.V. Scratched
Jan 16 Church 2 Swifts
Jan 16 Davenham 1 Small Heath
Old Westminster *W* Bolton
Jan 23 Redcar 2 Middlesbrough
Jan 23 South Shore 2 Notts Co
Jan 23 W.B.A. 1 Old Carthusians

6th Round
Feb 27 Brentwood 1 Blackburn
Feb 13 Small Heath 2 Redcar
Feb 13 South Shore 1 Swifts
Feb 13 W.B.A. 6 Old Westminster

Semi-finals
Mar 13 Blackburn 2 Swifts
played at Derby
Mar 06 Small Heath 0 W.B.A.
played at Birmingham

Final
Apr 03 Blackburn 0 W.B.A.
played at Kennington Oval

Replay
Apr 10 Blackburn 2 W.B.A.
played at Derby

Season 1886-87

1st Round
Oct 23 Astley Bridge 0 Burnley 0
Oct 30 Aston Villa 13 Wednesbury Old 0
Oct 30 Birmingham Exce 3 Derby Midland 3
Oct 30 Bishop Auckland 0 Middlesbrough 1
Blackburn *W* Halliwell *0*
Oct 23 Blackburn O 1 Partick 3
Oct 09 Blackburn Park 2 Cliftonville 2
Oct 30 Bollington 2 Oswestry 8
played at Macclesfield
Oct 30 Bolton 5 South Shore 3
Oct 16 Bootle 2 Great Lever 4
Oct 30 Burslem Port Vale 1 Davenham 1
Oct 30 Burton S 0 Crosswells Brew 1
Oct 30 Casuals 2 Dulwich 4
Chatham *W* Bournemouth *0*
Oct 30 Chesham 4 Lyndhurst 2
Oct 23 Chirk 8 Hartford St Joh 1
Oct 30 Church 1 Rawtenstall 1
Oct 30 Clapham R 0 Old Brightonian 6
Oct 23 Clapton 0 Crusaders 5
Oct 30 Cleethorpes 2 Mellors 1
Oct 30 Darwen 7 Hearts 1
Oct 23 Darwen Old Wdrs 1 Cowslairs 4
Oct 30 Derby 4 Aston Unity 1
Oct 30 Derby St Lukes 3 Walsall Town 3
Oct 30 Fleetwood 2 Newton Heath 2
Newton H. disqualified
Oct 30 Goldenhill 4 Macclesfield 2
Oct 30 Grimsby 4 Sheffield Heele 1
Oct 30 Hendon 1 London Cal 2

Oct 30 Horncastle 3 Darlington 1
Oct 23 Leek 2 Druids 1
Oct 23 Lincoln Lindum 0 Grantham 1
Oct 30 Lockwood 1 Long Eaton 0
Oct 23 Luton 1 Hotspur 3
Oct 30 Northwich V 10 Furness Vale 0
Oct 30 Nottingham F 3 Notts Olympics 0
Oct 30 Notts Co 13 Basford 0
Oct 23 Old Carthusians 2 Reading 1
Oct 30 Old Etonians 1 Royal Engineers 0
Old Foresters *W* Cannon *0*
Oct 30 Old Harrovians 0 Old Westminster 4
Oct 30 Old Wykehamists 3 Hanover 0
Oct 23 Oswaldtwistle 2 Witton 2
Oct 30 Queen's Park 0 Preston 3
Rangers *W* Everton *0*
Oct 30 Redcar 4 Tyne Assoc 0
Oct 30 Renton 1 Accrington 0
Oct 23 Rochester 0 Great Marlow 2
Oct 30 Sheffield 0 Notts R 3
Oct 30 Small Heath 1 Birmingham St George's 3
Oct 30 South Bank 0 Gainsborough 4
Oct 30 South Reading 0 Maidenhead 2
Oct 30 Staveley 7 Attercliffe 0
Oct 30 Stoke 10 Caernarvon *W* 1
Oct 30 Sunderland 2 Newcastle 1
Oct 23 Swifts 13 Luton *W* 0
Oct 16 T. Lanark 5 Higher Walton 0
Oct 23 Upton Park 9 1st Surrey Rifles 0
Oct 23 Watford 0 Swindon 1
Oct 30 Wellington Stg 0 Derby Junction 1

Oct 30 Wolverhampton 6 Matlock
Oct 23 Wrexham O 1 Crewe
Oct 30 W.B.A. 6 Burton W

Replays
Oct 23 Cliftonville 7 Blackburn Park
Oct 30 Burnley 2 Astley Bridge
Burnley disqualified
Nov 13 Davenham 0 Burslem Port Vale
Nov 13 Derby Midland 2 Birmingham Exce
Nov 13 Goldenhill 3 Macclesfield
Nov 13 Rawtenstall 1 Church
Nov 13 Walsall Town 6 Derby St Lukes

2nd Round
Nov 20 Aston Villa 6 Derby Midland
Nov 20 Chatham 1 Hotspur
Nov 20 Chesham 1 Old Etonians
Nov 20 Chester 1 Goldenhill
Chester disqualified
Nov 20 Cleethorpes 1 Lockwood
Nov 20 Crewe 6 Stoke
Darwen *W* Astley Bridge
Nov 20 Derby 1 Birmingham St Geor
Nov 20 Grantham 3 Redcar
Nov 13 Great Lever 1 Cliftonville
Nov 20 Great Marlow 4 Upton Park
Nov 20 Leek 4 Oswestry
Nov 20 Maidenhead 2 Dulwich
Nov 20 Middlesbrough 1 Lincoln
Nov 20 Newcastle 2 Gainsborough

Nov 13 Northwich V 0 Chirk 0
Nov 13 Nottingham F 2 Grimsby 2
Nov 13 Notts Co 3 Notts R 3
Nov 16 Old Brightonian 1 Old Westminster 1
Nov 13 Old Carthusians 4 Crusaders 2
Nov 20 Old Wykehamists 0 London Cal 1
Nov 20 Partick 7 Fleetwood 0
Nov 13 Preston 6 Witton 0
Nov 20 Rangers 2 Church 1
Nov 20 Renton 2 Blackburn 2
Nov 20 Rossendale 2 Cowlairs 10
Nov 20 Staveley 4 Rotherham 0
Nov 20 Swifts 7 Swindon 1
Nov 13 T. Lanark 2 Bolton 3
Nov 13 Wolverhampton 14 Crosswell 0
Nov 20 W.B.A. 2 Derby Junction 1

Replays
Nov 20 Chirk 3 Northwich V 0
Nov 20 Grimsby 0 Nottingham F 1
Nov 20 Notts R 0 Notts Co 5
Nov 20 Old Westminster 3 Old Brightonian 1
Nov 27 Lincoln 2 Middlesbrough 0
Dec 04 Blackburn 0 Renton 2

3rd Round
Dec 11 Aston Villa 2 Wolverhampton 2
Dec 11 Chatham 1 Old Foresters 4
Chirk *W* Goldenhill *0*
Dec 04 Cliftonville 1 Partick 11
Dec 11 Darwen 4 Bolton 3
Dec 11 Gainsborough 2 Lincoln 2
Dec 11 Great Marlow 2 Dulwich 0
Dec 09 Horncastle 2 Grantham 0
Dec 11 Leek 2 Burslem Port Vale 2
Dec 11 Lockwood 2 Nottingham F 1
Old Carthusians *W* London Cal *0*
Dec 11 Old Westminster 3 Old Etonians 0
Dec 04 Rangers 3 Cowlairs 2
Jan 22 Renton 0 Preston 2
Dec 11 Staveley 0 Notts Co 3
Dec 11 Walsall Town 2 Birmingham St George's 7

Replays
Jan 15 Wolverhampton 1 Aston Villa 1
Jan 20 Burslem Port Vale 1 Leek 3
played at Stafford
Jan 22 Wolverhampton 3 Aston Villa 3
Jan 24 Lincoln 1 Gainsborough 0
played at Sheffield
Jan 29 Aston Villa 2 Wolverhampton 0

4th Round
Jan 15 Birmingham St George's 0 W.B.A. 1
Jan 29 Crewe 0 Leek 1
Jan 15 Old Foresters 2 Swifts 0

5th Round
Feb 05 Aston Villa 5 Horncastle 0
Jan 22 Chirk 1 Darwen 2
Feb 05 Leek 0 Old Carthusians 2
Jan 29 Lockwood 0 W.B.A. 1
Jan 29 Notts Co 5 Great Marlow 2
Jan 29 Old Foresters 0 Preston 3
Jan 29 Old Westminster 1 Partick 0
Jan 29 Rangers 3 Lincoln 0

Replay
Feb 12 W.B.A. 2 Lockwood 1

6th Round
Feb 12 Aston Villa 3 Darwen 2
Feb 19 Notts Co 1 W.B.A. 4
Mar 02 Old Carthusians 1 Preston 2
Feb 19 Rangers 5 Old Westminster 1

Semi-finals
Mar 05 Aston Villa 3 Rangers 1
played at Crewe
Mar 05 Preston 1 W.B.A. 3
played at Nottingham

Final
Apr 02 Aston Villa 2 W.B.A. 0
played at Kennington Oval

Season 1887-88

1st Round
Oct 15 Accrington 11 Rossendale 0
Oct 15 Aston Shakespeare 2 Burton W 3
Oct 15 Basford 3 Lincoln A 2
Oct 15 Belper 2 Sheffield W 3
Oct 15 Birmingham Exce 4 Warwick County 1
Oct 15 Blackburn 10 Bury 0
Oct 08 Blackburn Park 2 Distillery 1
Blackburn Scratched
Oct 15 Bolton 1 Everton 0
Oct 15 Bootle 6 Workington 0
Oct 15 Burnley 4 Darwen Old Wdrs 0
Oct 15 Burton S 7 Southfield 0
Oct 15 Chatham 5 Luton 1
Oct 15 Chesham 4 Watford R 2
Oct 15 Chester 2 Davenham 3
Oct 15 Chirk 4 Chester St Oswa 1
Church *W* Cliftonville *0*
Oct 15 Cleethorpes 0 Grimsby 4
Oct 15 Crewe 5 Druids 0
Oct 15 Crusaders 9 Lyndhurst 0
played at Tooting
Oct 15 Derby Junction 3 Derby St Lukes 2
Oct 15 Ecclesfield 4 Derby Midland 1
Oct 15 Elswick 3 Bishop Auckland 3
Oct 15 Fleetwood 4 West Manchester 1
Oct 15 Gainsborough 7 Boston 0
Oct 15 Gateshead 0 Darlington 3
Oct 15 Grantham 4 Lincoln Lindrum 0
Oct 15 Great Marlow 4 South Reading 1
Oct 15 Hendon 2 Old Harrovians 4
Oct 15 Higher Walton 8 Heywood 1
Oct 15 Hitchin 2 Old Wykehamists 5
Oct 15 Hurst 5 Astley Bridge 3
Hurst Scratched
Oct 15 Leek 2 Northwich V 2
Oct 15 Lincoln 4 Horncastle 1
Oct 15 Liverpool Stanl 1 Halliwell 5
Oct 15 London Cal 1 Old Foresters 6
Oct 15 Long Eaton 6 Park Grange 3
Oct 15 Macclesfield 1 Shrewsbury 3
Oct 15 Matlock 2 Rotherham 3
Oct 15 Middlesbrough 4 Whitburn 0
Millwall *W* Casuals *0*
Oct 15 Newcastle West 5 Redcar 1
Oct 15 Nottingham F 2 Notts Swifts 1
Oct 15 Notts Co 9 Lincoln Rambler 0
Oct 15 Notts Olympic 3 Mellors 6
Oct 15 Notts R 10 Jardines 1
Oct 08 Old Brightonian 1 Swindon 0
Oct 15 Old Carthusians 5 Hanover 0
Oct 08 Old Etonians 4 Lancing Old Boy 2
Oct 15 Old St Marks 7 East Sheen 2
Oct 15 Old Westminster 4 Clapton 1
Oct 15 Oldbury 0 Aston Villa 4
Oct 08 Oswaldtwistle 1 Witton 4
Oct 15 Over 3 Wellington Stg 1
Oct 15 Owlerton 2 Eckington 1
Oct 15 Preston 2 6hyde 0
Oct 15 Rawtenstall 1 Darwen 3
Oct 15 Reading 0 Dulwich 2
Oct 15 Royal Engineers 3 Rochester 0
Oct 15 Scarborough 3 Shankhouse 5
Oct 15 Sheffield 1 Lockwood 3
Oct 15 Sheffield Heele 9 Attercliffe 0
Oct 15 Small Heath 6 Aston Unity 1
Oct 15 South Bank 3 Newcastle East 2
South Shore *W* Denton *0*
Oct 15 Stafford Road 2 Great Bridge Un 1
Oct 15 Staveley 1 Derby 2
Oct 15 Stoke 1 Burslem Port Vale 0
Oct 15 Sunderland 4 Morpeth 2
Oct 15 Swifts 3 Maidenhead 1
Oct 08 Vale Of Llangol 1 Oswestry 3
Oct 15 Walsall Swifts 1 Wolverhampton 2
Oct 15 Walsall Town 1 Birmingham St George's 2
Oct 15 W.B.A. 7 Wednesbury Old 1

Replays
Aston Shakespeare *W* Burton W *0*
Royal Engineers *W* Rochester *0*
Oct 22 Bishop Auckland 0 Elswick 2
Oct 22 Great Bridge Un 1 Stafford Road 1
Stafford Scratched
Oct 22 Mellors 2 Notts Olympic 1
Oct 22 Morpeth 2 Sunderland 3
Oct 22 Northwich V 4 Leek 2
Oct 22 Oswestry 2 Vale Of Llangol 0
Oct 22 Warwick County 0 Birmingham Exce 5
Oct 22 Watford R 3 Chesham 1
Oct 29 Everton 2 Bolton 2
Nov 12 Bolton 1 Everton 1
played at Bolton
Nov 19 Everton 2 Bolton 1
played at Everton & disqualified

2nd Round
Nov 05 Accrington 3 Burnley 2
Nov 05 Astley Bridge 0 Halliwell 4
Nov 05 Birmingham St George's 0 W.B.A. 1
Nov 05 Blackburn 5 Blackburn O 1
Nov 05 Bootle 1 South Shore 1
Nov 05 Burton S 2 Great Bridge Un 5
Nov 05 Chatham 3 Royal Engineers 1
Nov 05 Chirk 10 Shrewsbury 2
Nov 05 Darlington 4 Elswick 3
Nov 05 Darwen 2 Church 0
Nov 05 Derby 6 Ecclesfield 0
Nov 05 Derby Junction 3 Rotherham 2
Nov 05 Distillery 2 Witton 4
Nov 05 Dulwich 2 Hotspur 1
Nov 05 Fleetwood 1 Higher Walton 3
Nov 05 Grantham 0 Notts R 4
Nov 05 Great Marlow 2 Old Foresters 3
Nov 05 Lincoln 2 Gainsborough 1
Nov 05 Long Eaton 1 Sheffield W 2
Nov 05 Middlesbrough 4 South Bank 1
Nov 05 Northwich V 0 Crewe 1
Nov 05 Nottingham F 2 Mellors 0
Notts Co *W* Basford *0*
Nov 05 Old Etonians 3 Old St Marks 2
Nov 05 Old Harrovians 0 Old Brightonian 4
Nov 05 Old Westminster 8 Millwall 1
Oct 29 Old Wykehamists 2 Crusaders 3
Nov 05 Over 0 Stoke 3
Nov 05 Owlerton 1 Sheffield Heele 0
Preston *W* Everton *0*
Nov 05 Small Heath 0 Aston Villa 4
Nov 05 Sunderland 3 Newcastle West 1
Nov 05 Watford 0 Old Carthusians 3
Nov 05 Wolverhampton 3 Aston Shakespeare 0
Nov 05 Wrexham O 1 Davenham 2

Replay
Nov 12 South Shore 0 Bootle 3

3rd Round
Nov 26 Accrington 1 Blackburn 3
Nov 26 Crusaders 4 Chatham 0
Nov 26 Darlington 0 Shankhouse 2
Nov 26 Darwen 1 Witton 1
Nov 19 Davenham 2 Chirk 2
Nov 26 Derby 6 Owlerton 2
Nov 19 Derby Junction 2 Lockwood 1
Nov 26 Dulwich 1 Swifts 3
Nov 26 Great Bridge Un 2 Birmingham Exce 1
Nov 26 Grimsby 2 Lincoln 0
Nov 26 Higher Walton 1 Bootle 6
Nov 26 Middlesbrough 2 Sunderland 2
Nov 26 Nottingham F 2 Notts Co 1
Nov 24 Old Carthusians 5 Old Brightonian 0
Nov 26 Old Etonians 7 Old Westminster 2
Dec 03 Preston 4 Halliwell 0
Nov 26 Stoke 3 Oswestry 0
Nov 26 W.B.A. 2 Wolverhampton 0

Replays
Nov 26 Chirk 6 Davenham 1
Dec 03 Sunderland 4 Middlesbrough 2
Dec 03 Witton 0 Darwen 2
played at Blackburn

4th Round
Dec 10 Crewe 2 Swifts 2
Dec 17 Crusaders 0 Sheffield W 1
Dec 17 Darwen 3 Notts R 1
Dec 17 Great Bridge Un 1 Bootle 2
Dec 17 Nottingham F 6 Old Etonians 0
Dec 17 Old Foresters 4 Grimsby 2
Dec 10 Preston 9 Bolton 1
Dec 17 Shankhouse 0 Aston Villa 9

Replays
Dec 17 Swifts 3 Crewe 2
Dec 31 Crewe 2 Swifts 1
played at Derby after protest

5th Round
Jan 07 Aston Villa 1 Preston 3
Dec 31 Chirk 1 Derby Junction 1
Jan 07 Crewe 1 Derby 0
Jan 07 Darwen 0 Blackburn 3
Jan 07 Middlesbrough 4 Old Foresters 0
Jan 07 Nottingham F 2 Sheffield W 4
Jan 07 Old Carthusians 2 Bootle 0
Jan 07 W.B.A. 4 Stoke 1

Replay
Jan 07 Derby Junction 1 Chirk 0

6th Round
Jan 28 Derby Junction 2 Blackburn 1
Jan 28 Middlesbrough 0 Crewe 2
Jan 30 Sheffield W 1 Preston 3
Jan 28 W.B.A. 4 Old Carthusians 2

Semi-finals
Feb 18 Crewe 0 Preston 5
played at Liverpool
Feb 18 Derby Junction 0 W.B.A. 3
played at Stoke

Final
Mar 24 Preston 1 W.B.A. 2
played at Kennington Oval

Season 1888-89

1st Round
Feb 02 Accrington 1 Blackburn 1
Feb 02 Aston Villa 3 Witton 2
Feb 02 Birmingham St G 3 Long Eaton 2
Feb 02 Bootle 0 Preston 3
Feb 02 Burnley 4 Old Westminster 3
Feb 02 Chatham 2 South Shore 1
Feb 02 Derby 1 Derby Junction 0
Feb 02 Grimsby 3 Sunderland A 1
Feb 02 Halliwell 2 Crewe 2
Feb 02 Nottingham F 2 Linfield 2
Feb 02 Notts Co 2 Old Brightonian 0
Feb 02 Notts R 1 Sheffield W 1
Feb 02 Small Heath 2 W.B.A. 3
Feb 02 Swift 3 Wrexham 1

Feb 02 Walsall 5 Sheffield Heele 1
Feb 02 Wolverhampton 4 Old Carthusians 3

Replays
Nottingham F *W* Linfield *0*
Feb 09 Black8urn 5 Accrington 0
Feb 09 Crewe 1 Halliwell 5
Feb 09 Sheffield W 3 Notts R 0

2nd Round
Feb 16 Aston Villa 5 Derby 3
Feb 16 Blackburn *W* Swifts *0*
Feb 16 Chatham 1 Nottingham F 1
Feb 16 Grimsby 0 Preston 2
Feb 16 Halliwell 2 Birmingham St George's 3
Feb 16 Sheffield W 3 Notts Co 2
Feb 16 Wolverhampton 6 Walsall 1
Feb 16 W.B.A. 5 Burnley 1

Replays
Feb 23 Nottingham F 2 Chatham 2
Feb 28 Chatham 3 Nottingham F 2
played at Kennington Oval

3rd Round
Mar 02 Blackburn 8 Aston Villa 1
Mar 02 Chatham 1 W.B.A. 10
Mar 02 Preston 2 Birmingham St George's 0
Mar 02 Wolverhampton 3 Sheffield W 0

Semi-finals
Mar 16 Blackburn 1 Wolverhampton
played at Crewe
Mar 16 Preston 1 W.B.A.
played at Sheffield W

Replay
Mar 23 Wolverhampton 3 Blackburn
played at Crewe

Final
Mar 30 Preston 3 Wolverhampton
played at Kennington Oval
Both Qualified

Season 1889-90

1st Round
Jan 18 Accrington 3 W.B.A. 1
Jan 18 Blackburn 4 Sunderland 2
Jan 18 Bolton 10 Belfast Dist 1
Jan 18 Bootle 1 Sunderland A 3
Jan 18 Derby Midland 3 Nottingham F 0
Jan 18 Everton 11 Derby 2
Jan 18 Lincoln 2 Chester 0
Jan 18 Newcastle 1 Grimsby 2
Jan 18 Notts Co 4 Birmingham St George's 4
Jan 18 Preston 6 Newton Heath 1
Jan 18 Sheffield U 2 Burnley 1
Jan 18 Sheffield W 4 Swifts 1
Jan 18 Small Heath 3 Clapton 1
Jan 18 South Shore 2 Aston Villa 4
Jan 18 Stoke 3 Old Westminster 0
Jan 18 Wolverhampton 2 Old Carthusians 0

Replays
Jan 25 Accrington 3 W.B.A. 0
Jan 25 Birmingham St George's 2 Notts Co 6

2nd Round
Feb 01 Blackburn 3 Grimsby 0
Feb 01 Bolton 13 Sheffield U 0
Feb 01 Bootle 2 Derby Midland 1
Feb 01 Notts Co 4 Aston Villa 1
Feb 01 Preston 4 Lincoln 0
Feb 01 Sheffield W 2 Accrington 1
Feb 01 Stoke 4 Everton 2
Feb 01 Wolverhampton 2 Small Heath 1

3rd Round
Feb 15 Bootle 0 Blackburn 7
Feb 13 Preston 2 Bolton 3
Feb 15 Sheffield W 5 Notts Co
Feb 15 Wolverhampton 4 Stoke

Replays
Feb 22 Sheffield W 2 Notts Co
Feb 22 Wolverhampton 8 Stoke
Mar 03 Notts Co 1 Sheffield W

Semi-finals
Mar 08 Blackburn 1 Wolverhampton
played at Derby
Mar 08 Bolton 1 Sheffield W
played at Aston Villa

Final
Mar 29 Blackburn 6 Sheffield W
played at Kennington Oval

Season 1890-91

1st Round
Jan 17 Accrington 2 Bolton 2
Jan 17 Aston Villa 13 Casuals 1
Jan 17 Burnley 4 Crewe 2
Jan 17 Chester 1 Lincoln 0
Jan 17 Clapton 0 Nottingham F 14
Jan 24 Crusaders 0 Birmingham St George's 2
Jan 17 Darwen 3 Kidderminster 1
Jan 17 Long Eaton R 1 Wolverhampton 2
Jan 17 Middlesbrough I 1 Blackburn 2
Jan 17 Royal Arsenal 1 Derby 2
Jan 17 Sheffield U 1 Notts Co 9
Jan 17 Sheffield W 12 Halliwell 0
Jan 17 Stoke 3 Preston 0
Jan 17 Sunderland 1 Everton 0
Jan 17 Sunderland A 2 93rd Highlander 0
Jan 17 W.B.A. *W* Old Westminster

Replays
Jan 24 Bolton 1 Accrington 5
Jan 24 Darwen 13 Kidderminster 0
Jan 24 Middlesbrough I 0 Blackburn 3

2nd Round
Jan 31 Accrington 2 Wolverhampton 3
Jan 31 Birmingham St George's 0 W.B.A. 3
Jan 31 Blackburn 7 Chester 0
Jan 31 Darwen 0 Sunderland 2
Jan 31 Derby 2 Sheffield W 3
Jan 31 Notts Co 2 Burnley 1
Jan 31 Stoke 3 Aston Villa 0
Jan 31 Sunderland A 1 Nottingham F 1

Replays
Feb 07 Nottingham F 3 Sunderland A 3
Feb 11 Nottingham F 5 Sunderland A 0
played at Sheffield U

3rd Round
Feb 14 Blackburn 2 Wolverhampton 0
Feb 14 Notts Co 1 Stoke
Feb 14 Sheffield W 0 W.B.A.
Feb 14 Sunderland 4 Nottingham F

Semi-finals
Feb 28 Blackburn 3 W.B.A.
played at Stoke
Feb 28 Notts Co 3 Sunderland
played at Sheffield U

Replay
Mar 11 Notts Co 2 Sunderland
played at Sheffield U

Final
Mar 21 Blackburn 3 Notts Co
played at Kennington Oval

Season 1891-92

1st Round
Jan 16 Aston Villa 4 Heanor 1
Jan 16 Blackburn 4 Derby 1
Jan 16 Blackpool 0 Sheffield U 3
Jan 16 Bootle 0 Darwen 2
Jan 16 Crusaders 1 Accrington 4
Jan 16 Everton 2 Burnley 4
Jan 16 Luton 0 Middlesbrough 3
Jan 16 Nottingham F 2 Newcastle 1
Jan 16 Old Westminster 2 W.B.A. 3
Jan 16 Preston 2 Middlesbrough 2
Jan 16 Sheffield W 2 Bolton 1
Jan 16 Small Heath 5 Royal Arsenal 1
Jan 16 Stoke 3 Casuals 0
Jan 16 Sunderland 3 Notts Co 0
Jan 23 Sunderland A 4 Birmingham St George's 0
Jan 16 Wolverhampton 2 Crewe 2

Replays
Jan 23 Crewe 1 Wolverhampton 4
Jan 23 Everton 1 Burnley 3
Jan 23 Middlesbrough 0 Preston 6
Jan 23 Sheffield W 4 Bolton 1
Jan 23 Stoke 3 Casuals 0
Jan 23 Sunderland 4 Notts Co 0

2nd Round
Jan 30 Accrington 1 Sunderland 0
Jan 30 Aston Villa 2 Darwen 0
Jan 30 Burnley 1 Stoke 3
Jan 30 Middlesbrough 1 Preston 2
Jan 30 Sheffield W 2 Small Heath 0
Jan 30 Sunderland A 0 Nottingham F 1
Jan 30 Wolverhampton 3 Sheffield U 1
Jan 30 W.B.A. 3 Blackburn 1

Replay
Feb 06 Accrington 1 Sunderland 3

3rd Round
Feb 13 Nottingham F 2 Preston 0
Feb 13 Stoke 2 Sunderland 2
Feb 13 Wolverhampton 1 Aston Villa
Feb 13 W.B.A. 2 Sheffield W

Replay
Feb 20 Sunderland 4 Stoke

Semi-finals
Feb 27 Aston Villa 4 Sunderland
played at Sheffield U
Feb 27 Nottingham F 1 W.B.A.
played at Wolverhampton

Replays
Mar 05 Nottingham F 1 W.B.A.
played at Wolverhampton
Mar 09 Nottingham F 2 W.B.A.
played at Derby

Final
Mar 19 Aston Villa 0 W.B.A.
played at Kennington Oval

Season 1892-93

1st Round
Jan 21 Accrington 2 Stoke 1
Jan 21 Blackburn 4 Newton Heath 0
Jan 21 Blackpool 1 Sheffield U 3
Jan 21 Bolton 1 Wolverhampton 1
Jan 21 Burnley 2 Small Heath 0
Jan 21 Darwen 5 Aston Villa 4
Jan 21 Everton 4 W.B.A. 1
Jan 21 Grimsby 5 Stockton 0
Jan 21 Loughborough 1 Northwich V 2
Jan 21 Marlow 1 Middlesbrough I 3
Jan 21 Newcastle 2 Middlesbrough 3
Jan 21 Nottingham F 4 Casuals 0
Jan 21 Notts Co 4 Shankhouse 0
Jan 21 Preston 9 Burtons 2
Jan 21 Sheffield W 3 Derby 2
Jan 21 Sunderland 6 Royal Arsenal 0

Replay
Jan 28 Wolverhampton 2 Bolton 1

2nd Round
Feb 04 Accrington 1 Preston 4
Feb 04 Blackburn 4 Northwich V 1
Feb 04 Darwen 2 Grimsby 0
Feb 04 Everton 4 Nottingham F 2
Feb 04 Middlesbrough I 3 Notts Co 2
Feb 04 Sheffield U 1 Sunderland 3
Feb 04 Sheffield W 1 Burnley 0
Feb 04 Wolverhampton 2 Middlesbrough 1

3rd Round
Feb 18 Blackburn 3 Sunderland 0
Feb 18 Everton 3 Sheffield W 0
Feb 18 Middlesbrough I 2 Preston 2
Feb 18 Wolverhampton 5 Darwen 0

Replay
Feb 25 Preston 7 Middlesbrough I

Semi-finals
Mar 04 Blackburn 1 Wolverhampton
played at Nottingham F
Mar 04 Everton 2 Preston
played at Sheffield U

Replays
Mar 16 Everton 0 Preston
played at Sheffield U
Mar 20 Everton 2 Preston
played at Blackburn

Final
Mar 25 Everton 0 Wolverhampton
played at Fallowfield

Season 1893-94

1st Round

Date	Home		Away	
Jan 27	Aston Villa	4	Wolverhampton	2
Jan 27	Derby	2	Darwen	0
Jan 27	Leicester	2	South Shore	1
Jan 27	Liverpool	3	Grimsby	0
Jan 27	Middlesbrough I	2	Luton	1
Jan 27	Newcastle	2	Sheffield U	0
Jan 27	Newton Heath	4	Middlesbrough	0
Jan 27	Nottingham F	1	Heanor	0
Jan 27	Notts Co	1	Burnley	0
Jan 27	Preston	1	8reading	0
Jan 27	Small Heath	3	Bolton	4
Jan 27	Stockport	0	Burton W	1
Jan 27	Stoke	1	Everton	0
Jan 27	Sunderland	3	Accrington	0
Jan 27	W.B.A.	2	Blackburn	3
Jan 27	Woolwich A	1	Sheffield W	2

2nd Round

Date	Home		Away	
Feb 10	Burton W	1	Notts Co	2
Feb 10	Leicester	0	Derby	0
Feb 10	Liverpool	3	Preston	2
Feb 10	Middlesbrough I	0	Nottingham F	2
Feb 10	Newcastle	1	Bolton	2
Feb 10	Newton Heath	0	Blackburn	0
Feb 10	Sheffield W	1	Stoke	0
Feb 10	Sunderland	2	Aston Villa	2

Replays

Date	Home		Away	
Feb 17	Blackburn	5	Newton Heath	1
Feb 17	Derby	3	Leicester	0
Feb 21	Aston Villa	3	Sunderland	1

3rd Round

Date	Home		Away	
Feb 24	Bolton	3	Liverpool	0
Feb 24	Derby	1	Blackburn	4
Feb 24	Nottingham F	1	Notts Co	1
Feb 24	Sheffield W	3	Aston Villa	2

Replay

Date	Home		Away	
Mar 03	Notts Co	4	Nottingham F	1

Semi-final

Date	Home		Away	
Mar 10	Blackburn	0	Notts Co	1
	played at Sheffield U			
Mar 10	Bolton	2	Sheffield W	1
	played at Fallowfield			

Final

Date	Home		Away	
Mar 31	Bolton	1	Notts Co	4
	played at Everton			

Season 1894-95

1st Round

Date	Home		Away	
Feb 02	Aston Villa	2	Derby	1
Feb 02	Barnsley	1	Liverpool	2
Feb 02	Bolton	1	Woolwich A	0
Feb 02	Burton W	1	Blackburn	2
Feb 02	Bury	4	Leicester	1
Feb 02	Darwen	0	Wolverhampton	0
Feb 02	Luton	0	Preston	2
Feb 02	Middlesbrough	4	Chesterfield	0
Feb 02	Newcastle	2	Burnley	1
Feb 02	Newton Heath	2	Stoke	3
Feb 02	Sheffield U	3	Millwall	1
Feb 02	Sheffield W	5	Notts Co	1
Feb 02	Small Heath	1	W.B.A.	2
Feb 02	Southampton St Mary's	1	Nottingham F	4
Feb 02	Southport	0	Everton	3
Feb 02	Sunderland	11	Fairfield	1

Replays

Date	Home		Away	
Feb 06	Wolverhampton	2	Darwen	0
Feb 11	Barnsley	0	Liverpool	4

2nd Round

Date	Home		Away	
Feb 16	Aston Villa	7	Newcastle	1
Feb 16	Bolton	1	Bury	0
Feb 16	Everton	1	Blackburn	1
Feb 16	Liverpool	0	Nottingham F	2
Feb 16	Sheffield U	1	W.B.A.	1
Feb 16	Sheffield W	6	Middlesbrough	1
Feb 16	Sunderland	2	Preston	0
Feb 16	Wolverhampton	2	Stoke	0

Replays

Date	Home		Away	
Feb 20	Blackburn	2	Everton	3
Feb 20	W.B.A.	2	Sheffield U	1

3rd Round

Date	Home		Away	
Mar 02	Aston Villa	6	Nottingham F	2
Mar 02	Sheffield W	2	Everton	0
Mar 02	Sunderland	2	Bolton	1
Mar 02	W.B.A.	1	Wolverhampton	0

Semi-finals

Date	Home		Away	
Mar 16	Aston Villa	2	Sunderland	1
	played at Blackburn			
Mar 16	Sheffield W	0	W.B.A.	2
	played at Derby			

Final

Date	Home		Away	
Apr 20	Aston Villa	1	W.B.A.	0
	played at Crystal Palace			

Season 1895-96

1st Round

Date	Home		Away	
Feb 01	Blackburn	1	W.B.A.	2
Feb 01	Blackpool	4	Burton S	1
Feb 01	Burnley	6	Woolwich A	1
Feb 01	Burton W	1	Sheffield U	1
Feb 01	Chesterfield	0	Newcastle	4
Feb 01	Crewe	0	Bolton	4
Feb 01	Darwen	0	Grimsby	2
Feb 01	Derby	4	Aston Villa	2
Feb 01	Liverpool	4	Millwall	1
Feb 01	Newton Heath	2	Kettering	1
Feb 01	Nottingham F	0	Everton	2
Feb 01	Small Heath	1	Bury	4
Feb 01	Southampton St Mary's	2	Sheffield W	3
Feb 01	Stoke	5	Tottenham	0
Feb 01	Sunderland	4	Preston	1
Feb 01	Wolverhampton	2	Notts Co	2

Replays

Date	Home		Away	
Feb 05	Notts Co	3	Wolverhampton	4
Feb 06	Sheffield U	1	Burton W	0

2nd Round

Date	Home		Away	
Feb 15	Blackpool	0	Bolton	2
Feb 15	Burnley	1	Stoke	1
Feb 15	Everton	3	Sheffield U	0
Feb 15	Grimsby	1	W.B.A.	1
Feb 15	Newcastle	1	Bury	3
Feb 15	Newton Heath	1	Derby	1
Feb 15	Sheffield W	2	Sunderland	1
Feb 15	Wolverhampton	2	Liverpool	0

Replays

Date	Home		Away	
Feb 19	Derby	5	Newton Heath	1
Feb 20	Stoke	7	Burnley	1
Feb 20	W.B.A.	3	Grimsby	0

3rd Round

Date	Home		Away	
Feb 29	Bolton	2	Bury	0
Feb 29	Derby	1	W.B.A.	0
Feb 29	Sheffield W	4	Everton	0
Feb 29	Wolverhampton	3	Stoke	0

Semi-finals

Date	Home		Away	
Mar 21	Bolton	1	Sheffield W	1
	played at Everton			
Mar 21	Derby	1	Wolverhampton	2
	played at Aston Villa			

Replay

Date	Home		Away	
Mar 28	Bolton	1	Sheffield W	3
	played at Nottingham F			

Final

Date	Home		Away	
Apr 18	Sheffield W	2	Wolverhampton	1
	played at Crystal Palace			

Season 1896-97

1st Round

Date	Home		Away	
Jan 30	Aston Villa	5	Newcastle	0
Jan 30	Blackburn	2	Sheffield U	1
Jan 30	Burnley	0	Sunderland	1
Jan 30	Derby	8	Barnsley	1
Jan 30	Everton	5	Burton W	2
Jan 30	Grimsby	0	Bolton	0
Jan 30	Liverpool	4	Burton S	3
Jan 30	Luton	0	W.B.A.	1
Jan 30	Millwall	1	Wolverhampton	2
Jan 30	Newton Heath	5	Kettering	1
Jan 30	Preston	6	Manchester C	0
Jan 30	Sheffield W	0	Nottingham F	1
Jan 30	Small Heath	1	Notts Co	2
Jan 30	Southampton St Mary's	1	Heanor	1
Jan 30	Stockton	0	Bury	0
Jan 30	Stoke	5	Glossop	2

Replays

Date	Home		Away	
Feb 02	Bury	12	Stockton	1
Feb 03	Heanor	0	Southampton St Mary's	1
Feb 08	Bolton	3	Grimsby	3
Feb 11	Grimsby	2	Bolton	3
	played at Sheffield U			

2nd Round

Date	Home		Away	
Feb 13	Aston Villa	2	Notts Co	1
Feb 13	Blackburn	2	Wolverhampton	1
Feb 13	Derby	4	Bolton	1
Feb 13	Everton	3	Bury	0
Feb 13	Preston	2	Stoke	1
Feb 13	Southampton St Mary's	1	Newton Heath	1
Feb 13	Sunderland	1	Nottingham F	3
Feb 13	W.B.A.	1	Liverpool	2

Replay

Date	Home		Away	
Feb 17	Newton Heath	3	Southampton St Mary's	1

3rd Round

Date	Home		Away	
Feb 27	Derby	2	Newton Heath	0
Feb 27	Everton	2	Blackburn	0
Feb 27	Liverpool	1	Nottingham F	1
Feb 27	Preston	1	Aston Villa	1

Replays

Date	Home		Away	
Mar 03	Aston Villa	0	Preston	0
Mar 03	Nottingham F	0	Liverpool	1
Mar 10	Aston Villa	3	Preston	2
	played at Sheffield U			

Semi-finals

Date	Home		Away	
Mar 20	Aston Villa	3	Liverpool	0
	played at Sheffield U			
Mar 20	Derby	2	Everton	3
	played at Stoke			

Final

Date	Home		Away	
Apr 10	Aston Villa	3	Everton	2
	played at Crystal Palace			

Season 1897-98

1st Round

Date	Home		Away	
Jan 29	Burnley	3	Woolwich A	1
Jan 29	Bury	1	Stoke	2
Jan 29	Derby	1	Aston Villa	0
Jan 29	Everton	1	Blackburn	0
Jan 29	Liverpool	2	Hucknall St John	2
Jan 29	Long Eaton	0	Gainsborough	1
Jan 29	Luton	0	Bolton	1
Jan 29	Manchester C	1	Wigan	0
Jan 29	Newton Heath	1	Walsall	0
Jan 29	Nottingham F	4	Grimsby	0
Jan 29	Notts Co	0	Wolverhampton	1
Jan 29	Preston	1	Newcastle	2
Jan 29	Sheffield U	1	Burslem Port Vale	1
Jan 29	Southampton St Mary's	2	Leicester	1
Jan 29	Sunderland	0	Sheffield W	1
Jan 29	W.B.A.	2	New Brighton	0

Replay

Date	Home		Away	
Feb 02	Burslem Port Vale	2	Sheffield U	1

2nd Round

Date	Home		Away	
Feb 12	Bolton	1	Manchester C	0
Feb 12	Burnley	3	Burslem Port Vale	0
Feb 12	Newton Heath	0	Liverpool	0
Feb 12	Nottingham F	4	Gainsborough	0
Feb 12	Southampton St Mary's	1	Newcastle	0
Feb 12	Stoke	0	Everton	0
Feb 12	Wolverhampton	0	Derby	1
Feb 12	W.B.A.	1	Sheffield W	0

Replays
Feb 16 Liverpool 2 Newton Heath 1
Feb 17 Everton 5 Stoke 1

3rd Round
Feb 26 Bolton 0 Southampton St Mary's 0
Feb 26 Burnley 1 Everton 3
Feb 26 Derby 1 Liverpool 1
Feb 26 W.B.A. 2 Nottingham F 3

Replays
Mar 02 Liverpool 1 Derby 5
Mar 02 Southampton St Mary's 4 Bolton 0

Semi-finals
Mar 19 Derby 3 Everton 1
played at Wolverhampton
Mar 19 Nottingham F 1 Southampton St Mary's 1
played at Sheffield U

Replay
Mar 24 Nottingham F 2 Southampton St Mary
played at Crystal Palace

Final
Apr 14 Derby 1 Nottingham F
played at Crystal Palace

Season 1898-99

1st Round
Jan 28 Bristol C 2 Sunderland 4
Jan 28 Burnley 2 Sheffield U 2
Jan 28 Everton 3 Jarrow 1
Jan 28 Glossop 0 Newcastle 1
Jan 28 Heanor 0 Bury 3
Jan 28 Liverpool 2 Blackburn 0
Jan 28 New Brompton 0 Southampton 1
Jan 28 Nottingham F 2 Aston Villa 1
Jan 28 Notts Co 2 Kettering 0
Jan 28 Preston 7 Grimsby 0
Jan 28 Sheffield W 2 Stoke 2
Jan 28 Small Heath 3 Manchester C 2
Jan 28 Tottenham 1 Newton Heath 1
Jan 28 Wolverhampton 0 Bolton 0
Jan 28 Woolwich A 0 Derby 6
Jan 28 W.B.A. 8 South Shore 0

Replays
Feb 01 Bolton 0 Wolverhampton 1
Feb 01 Newton Heath 3 Tottenham 5
Feb 02 Sheffield U 2 Burnley 1
Feb 02 Stoke 2 Sheffield W 0

2nd Round
Feb 11 Derby 2 Wolverhampton 1
Feb 11 Everton 0 Nottingham F 1
Feb 11 Liverpool 3 Newcastle 1
Feb 11 Notts Co 0 Southampton 1
Feb 11 Preston 2 Sheffield U 2
Feb 11 Stoke 2 Small Heath 2
Feb 11 Tottenham 2 Sunderland 1
Feb 11 W.B.A. 2 Bury 1

Replays
Feb 15 Small Heath 1 Stoke 2
Feb 16 Sheffield U 2 Preston 1

3rd Round
Feb 25 Nottingham F 0 Sheffield U 1
Feb 25 Southampton 1 Derby
Feb 25 Stoke 4 Tottenham
Feb 25 W.B.A. 0 Liverpool

Semi-finals
Mar 18 Derby 3 Stoke
played at Wolverhampton
Mar 18 Liverpool 2 Sheffield U
played at Nottingham F

Replays
Mar 23 Liverpool 4 Sheffield U
played at Bolton
Mar 27 Liverpool 1 Sheffield U
played at Fallowfield Abd
Mar 30 Liverpool 0 Sheffield U
played at Derby

Final
Apr 13 Derby 1 Sheffield U
played at Crystal Palace

Season 1899-1900

1st Round
Jan 27 Bristol C 2 Stalybridge 1
Jan 27 Burnley 0 Bury 1
Jan 27 Derby 2 Sunderland 2
Jan 27 Jarrow 0 Millwall 2
Jan 27 Manchester C 1 Aston Villa 1
Jan 27 Newcastle 2 Reading 1
Jan 27 Nottingham F 3 Grimsby 0
Jan 27 Notts Co 6 Chorley 0
Jan 27 Portsmouth 0 Blackburn 0
Jan 27 Preston 1 Tottenham 0
Jan 27 Q.P.R. 1 Wolverhampton 1
Jan 27 Sheffield U 1 Leicester 0
Jan 27 Sheffield W 1 Bolton 0
Jan 27 Southampton 3 Everton 0
Jan 27 Stoke 0 Liverpool 0
Jan 27 Walsall 1 W.B.A. 1

Replays
Jan 31 Aston Villa 3 Manchester C 0
Jan 31 Sunderland 3 Derby 0
Jan 31 Wolverhampton 0 Q.P.R. 1
Feb 01 Blackburn 1 Portsmouth 1
Feb 01 Liverpool 1 Stoke 0
Feb 01 W.B.A. 6 Walsall 1
Feb 05 Blackburn 5 Portsmouth 0
played at Aston Villa

2nd Round
Feb 10 Aston Villa 5 Bristol C 1
Feb 17 Liverpool 1 W.B.A. 1
Feb 10 Nottingham F 3 Sunderland 0
Feb 10 Notts Co 0 Bury 0
Feb 17 Preston 1 Blackburn 0
Feb 17 Q.P.R. 0 Millwall 2
Feb 17 Sheffield U 1 Sheffield W 1
Feb 17 Southampton 4 Newcastle 1

Replays
Feb 14 Bury 2 Notts Co 0
Feb 19 Sheffield W 0 Sheffield U 2
Feb 21 W.B.A. 2 Liverpool 1

3rd Round
Feb 24 Millwall 1 Aston Villa 1
Feb 24 Preston 0 Nottingham F 0
Feb 24 Sheffield U 2 Bury 2
Feb 24 Southampton 2 W.B.A. 1

Replays
Feb 28 Aston Villa 0 Millwall
Feb 28 Nottingham F 1 Preston
Mar 01 Bury 2 Sheffield U
Mar 05 Aston Villa 1 Millwall
played at Reading

Semi-final
Mar 24 Bury 1 Nottingham F
played at Stoke
Mar 24 Millwall 0 Southampton
played at Crystal Palace

Replays
Mar 28 Millwall 0 Southampton
played at Reading
Mar 29 Bury 3 Nottingham F
played at Sheffield U

Final
Apr 21 Bury 4 Southampton
played at Crystal Palace

Season 1900-01

1st Round
Feb 09 Aston Villa 5 Millwall 0
Feb 09 Bolton 1 Derby 0
Feb 09 Kettering 1 Chesterfield 1
Feb 09 Middlesbrough 3 Newcastle 1
Feb 09 Newton Heath 0 Burnley 0
Feb 09 Nottingham F 5 Leicester 1
Feb 09 Notts Co 2 Liverpool 0
Feb 09 Reading 2 Bristol R 0
Feb 09 Sheffield W 0 Bury 1
Feb 09 Southampton 1 Everton 3
Feb 09 Stoke 1 Small Heath 1
Feb 09 Sunderland 1 Sheffield U 2
Feb 09 Tottenham 1 Preston 1
Feb 09 Wolverhampton 5 New Brighton 1
Feb 09 Woolwich A 2 Blackburn 0
Feb 09 W.B.A. 1 Manchester C 0

Replays
Feb 13 Burnley 7 Newton Heath 1
Feb 13 Chesterfield 1 Kettering 2
Feb 13 Preston 2 Tottenham 4
Feb 13 Small Heath 2 Stoke 1

2nd Round
Feb 23 Aston Villa 0 Nottingham F 0
Feb 23 Bolton 0 Reading 1
Feb 23 Middlesbrough 5 Kettering 0
Feb 23 Notts Co 2 Wolverhampton 3
Feb 23 Sheffield U 2 Everton 0
Feb 23 Small Heath 1 Burnley 0
Feb 23 Tottenham 2 Bury 1
Feb 23 Woolwich A 0 W.B.A. 1

Replay
Feb 27 Nottingham F 1 Aston Villa 3

3rd Round
Mar 23 Middlesbrough 0 W.B.A. 1
Mar 23 Reading 1 Tottenham 1
Mar 23 Small Heath 0 Aston Villa 0
Mar 23 Wolverhampton 0 Sheffield U 4

Replays
Mar 27 Aston Villa 1 Small Heath
Mar 28 Tottenham 3 Reading

Semi-finals
Apr 06 Aston Villa 2 Sheffield U
played at Nottingham F
Apr 06 Tottenham 4 W.B.A.
played at Aston Villa

Replay
Apr 11 Sheffield U 3 Aston Villa
played at Derby

Final
Apr 20 Sheffield U 2 Tottenham
played at Crystal Palace

Replay
Apr 27 Sheffield U 1 Tottenham
played at Bolton

Season 1901-02

1st Round
Feb 01 Blackburn 0 Derby 2
Jan 25 Bury 5 W.B.A. 1
Jan 25 Glossop 1 Nottingham F 3
Jan 25 Grimsby 1 Portsmouth 1
Jan 25 Liverpool 2 Everton 2
Jan 25 Middlesbrough 1 Bristol R 1
Jan 25 Northampton 0 Sheffield U 2
Jan 25 Notts Co 1 Reading 2
Jan 25 Oxford 0 Lincoln 0
Jan 25 Preston 1 Manchester C 1
Jan 25 Sheffield W 0 Sunderland 1
Jan 25 Stoke 2 Aston Villa 2
Jan 25 Tottenham 1 Southampton 1
Jan 25 Walsall 1 Burnley 0
Jan 25 Wolverhampton 0 Bolton 2
Jan 25 Woolwich A 0 Newcastle 2

Replays
Jan 29 Aston Villa 1 Stoke 2
Jan 29 Bristol R 1 Middlesbrough 0
Jan 29 Lincoln 4 Oxford 0
Jan 29 Manchester C 0 Preston 0
Jan 29 Portsmouth 2 Grimsby 0
Jan 29 Southampton 2 Tottenham 2
Jan 30 Everton 0 Liverpool 2
Feb 03 Manchester C 4 Preston 2
played at Preston
Feb 03 Southampton 2 Tottenham 1
played at Reading

2nd Round
Feb 08 Bristol R 0 Stoke
Feb 08 Lincoln 1 Derby
Feb 08 Manchester C 0 Nottingham F
Feb 12 Newcastle 1 Sunderland
Feb 08 Reading 0 Portsmouth
Feb 08 Sheffield U 2 Bolton
Feb 08 Southampton 4 Liverpool
Feb 08 Walsall 0 Bury

3rd Round
Feb 22 Bury 2 Southampton
Feb 22 Newcastle 1 Sheffield U
Feb 22 Nottingham F 2 Stoke
Feb 22 Portsmouth 0 Derby

Replays
Feb 27 Derby 6 Portsmouth 3
Feb 27 Sheffield U 2 Newcastle 1

Semi-finals
Mar 15 Derby 1 Sheffield U 1
played at W.B.A.
Mar 15 Nottingham F 1 Southampton 3
played at Tottenham

Replays
Mar 20 Derby 1 Sheffield U 1
played at Wolverhampton
Mar 27 Derby 0 Sheffield U 1
played at Nottingham F

Final
Apr 19 Sheffield U 1 Southampton 1
played at Crystal Palace

Replay
Apr 26 Sheffield U 2 Southampton 1
played at Crystal Palace

Season 1902-03

1st Round
Feb 07 Aston Villa 4 Sunderland 1
Feb 07 Barnsley 2 Lincoln 0
Feb 07 Blackburn 0 Sheffield W 0
Feb 07 Bolton 0 Bristol C 5
Feb 07 Bury 1 Wolverhampton 0
Feb 07 Derby 2 Small Heath 1
Feb 07 Everton 5 Portsmouth 0
Feb 07 Glossop 2 Stoke 3
Feb 07 Grimsby 2 Newcastle 1
Feb 07 Manchester U 2 Liverpool 1
Feb 07 Millwall 3 Luton 0
Feb 07 Nottingham F 0 Reading 0
Feb 07 Notts Co 0 Southampton 0
Feb 07 Preston 3 Manchester C 1
Feb 07 Tottenham 0 W.B.A. 0
Feb 07 Woolwich A 1 Sheffield U 3
Feb 11 Reading 3 Nottingham F 6
Feb 11 Southampton 2 Notts Co 2
Feb 11 W.B.A. 0 Tottenham 2
Feb 12 Sheffield W 0 Blackburn 1
Feb 16 Notts Co 2 Southampton 1
played at Aston Villa

2nd Round
Feb 21 Aston Villa 4 Barnsley 1
Feb 21 Derby 2 Blackburn 0
Feb 21 Everton 3 Manchester U 1
Feb 21 Grimsby 0 Notts Co 2
Feb 21 Millwall 4 Preston 1
Feb 21 Nottingham F 0 Stoke 0
Feb 21 Sheffield U 0 Bury 1
Feb 21 Tottenham 1 Bristol C 0

Replay
Feb 26 Stoke 2 Nottingham F 0

3rd Round
Mar 07 Bury 1 Notts Co 0
Mar 07 Derby 3 Stoke 0
Mar 07 Millwall 1 Everton 0
Mar 07 Tottenham 2 Aston Villa 3

Semi-finals
Mar 21 Aston Villa 0 Bury 3
played at Everton
Mar 21 Derby 3 Millwall 0
played at Aston Villa

Final
Apr 18 Bury 6 Derby 0
played at Crystal Palace

Season 1903-04

1st Round
Feb 06 Blackburn 3 Liverpool 1
Feb 06 Bristol C 1 Sheffield U 3
Feb 06 Bury 2 Newcastle 1
Feb 06 Everton 1 Tottenham 2
Feb 06 Manchester C 3 Sunderland 2
Feb 06 Millwall 0 Middlesbrough 2
Feb 06 Notts Co 3 Manchester U 3
Feb 06 Plymouth 2 Sheffield W 2
Feb 06 Portsmouth 2 Derby 5
Feb 06 Preston 1 Grimsby 0
Feb 06 Reading 1 Bolton 1
Feb 06 Southampton 3 Burslem Port Vale 0
Feb 06 Stockton 1 Wolverhampton 4
Feb 06 Stoke 2 Aston Villa 3
Feb 06 Woolwich A 1 Fulham 0
Feb 10 W.B.A. 1 Nottingham F 1

Replays
Feb 10 Bolton 3 Reading 2
Feb 10 Manchester U 2 Notts Co 1
Feb 10 Sheffield W 2 Plymouth 0
Feb 13 Nottingham F 3 W.B.A. 1

2nd Round
Feb 20 Blackburn 3 Nottingham F 1
Feb 20 Bolton 4 Southampton 1
Feb 20 Bury 1 Sheffield U 2
Feb 20 Derby 2 Wolverhampton 2
Feb 20 Preston 0 Middlesbrough 3
Feb 20 Sheffield W 6 Manchester U 0
Feb 25 Tottenham 1 Aston Villa 0
Feb 20 Woolwich A 0 Manchester C 2

Replays
Feb 24 Wolverhampton 2 Derby 2
Feb 29 Derby 1 Wolverhampton 0
played at Aston Villa

3rd Round
Mar 05 Derby 2 Blackburn 1
Mar 05 Manchester C 0 Middlesbrough 0
Mar 05 Sheffield U 0 Bolton 2
Mar 05 Tottenham 1 Sheffield W 1

Replays
Mar 09 Middlesbrough 1 Manchester C 3
Mar 09 Sheffield W 2 Tottenham 0

Semi-finals
Mar 19 Bolton 1 Derby 0
played at Wolverhampton
Mar 19 Manchester C 3 Sheffield W 0
played at Everton

Final
Apr 23 Bolton 0 Manchester C 1
played at Crystal Palace

Season 1904-05

1st Round
Feb 04 Aston Villa 5 Leicester 1
Feb 04 Blackburn 1 Sheffield W 2
Feb 04 Bolton 1 Bristol R 1
Feb 04 Bury 1 Notts Co 0
Feb 04 Derby 0 Preston 2
Feb 04 Fulham 0 Reading 0
Feb 04 Lincoln 1 Manchester C 2
Feb 04 Liverpool 1 Everton 1
Feb 04 Middlesbrough 1 Tottenham 1
Feb 04 Newcastle 1 Plymouth 1
Feb 04 Nottingham F 2 Sheffield U 0
Feb 04 Small Heath 0 Portsmouth 2
Feb 04 Southampton 3 Millwall 1
Feb 04 Stoke 2 Grimsby 0
Feb 04 Sunderland 1 Wolverhampton 1
Feb 04 Woolwich A 0 Bristol C 0

Replays
Feb 08 Bristol C 1 Woolwich A 0
Feb 08 Bristol R 0 Bolton 3
Feb 08 Everton 2 Liverpool 1
Feb 08 Plymouth 1 Newcastle 1
Feb 08 Reading 0 Fulham 0
Feb 08 Wolverhampton 1 Sunderland 0
Feb 09 Tottenham 1 Middlesbrough 0
Feb 13 Fulham 1 Reading 0
played at Tottenham
Feb 13 Newcastle 2 Plymouth 0
played at Woolwich

2nd Round
Feb 18 Aston Villa 3 Bury 2
Feb 18 Bristol C 0 Preston 0
Feb 18 Fulham 1 Nottingham F 0
Feb 18 Manchester C 1 Bolton 2
Feb 18 Sheffield W 2 Portsmouth 1
Feb 18 Stoke 0 Everton 4
Feb 18 Tottenham 1 Newcastle 1
Feb 18 Wolverhampton 2 Southampton 3

Replays
Feb 22 Newcastle 4 Tottenham 0
Feb 23 Preston 1 Bristol C 0

3rd Round
Mar 04 Aston Villa 5 Fulham 0
Mar 04 Bolton 0 Newcastle 2
Mar 04 Everton 4 Southampton 0
Mar 04 Preston 1 Sheffield W 1

Replay
Mar 09 Sheffield W 3 Preston 0

Semi-finals
Mar 25 Aston Villa 1 Everton 1
played at Stoke
Mar 25 Newcastle 1 Sheffield W 0
played at Manchester C

Replay
Mar 29 Aston Villa 2 Everton 1
played at Nottingham F

Final
Apr 15 Aston Villa 2 Newcastle 0
played at Crystal Palace

Season 1905-06

1st Round
Jan 13 Aston Villa 11 Kings Lynn 0
Jan 13 Birmingham 1 Preston 0
Jan 13 Bishop Auckland 0 Wolverhampton 3
Jan 13 Blackpool 1 Crystal Palace 1
Jan 13 Bradford C 3 Barrow 2
Jan 13 Brentford 2 Bristol C 1
Jan 13 Brighton 3 Swindon 0
Jan 13 Burslem Port Vale 0 Gainsborough 3
Jan 13 Bury 1 Nottingham F 1
Jan 13 Clapton O 0 Chesterfield 0
Jan 13 Crewe 1 Barnsley 1
Jan 13 Derby 4 Kettering 0
Jan 13 Everton 3 W.B.A. 1
Jan 13 Fulham 1 Q.P.R. 0
Jan 13 Hull 0 Reading 1
Jan 13 Lincoln 4 Stockport 2
Jan 13 Liverpool 2 Leicester 1
Jan 13 Manchester U 7 Staplehill 2
Jan 13 Middlesbrough 3 Bolton 0
Jan 13 Millwall 1 Burton 0
Jan 13 New Brompton 2 Northampton 1
Jan 13 New Crusaders 3 Plymouth 6
Jan 13 Newcastle 6 Grimsby 0
Jan 13 Norwich 1 Tonbridge Wells 1
Jan 13 Sheffield U 4 Manchester C 1
Jan 13 Sheffield W 1 Bristol R 0
Jan 13 Southampton 5 Portsmouth 1
Jan 13 Stoke 1 Blackburn 0
Jan 13 Sunderland 1 Notts Co 0
Jan 13 Tottenham 2 Burnley 0
Jan 13 Woolwich A 1 West Ham 1
Jan 13 Worcester 0 Watford 6

Replays
Jan 17 Chesterfield 3 Clapton O 0
Jan 17 Crystal Palace 1 Blackpool 1
Jan 17 Nottingham F 6 Bury 2
Jan 17 Tonbridge Wells 0 Norwich 5
Jan 18 Barnsley 4 Crewe 0
Jan 18 West Ham 2 Woolwich A 3
Jan 22 Blackpool 1 Crystal Palace 0
played at Aston Villa

2nd Round
Feb 03 Aston Villa 0 Plymouth 0
Feb 03 Blackpool 2 Sheffield U 1
Feb 03 Bradford C 5 Wolverhampton 0
Feb 03 Brentford 3 Lincoln 0
Feb 03 Brighton 1 Middlesbrough 1
Feb 03 Derby 0 Newcastle 0
Feb 03 Everton 3 Chesterfield 0
Feb 03 Fulham 1 Nottingham F 3
Feb 03 Liverpool 1 Barnsley 0
Feb 03 Manchester U 3 Norwich 0
Feb 03 New Brompton 0 Southampton 0
Feb 03 Sheffield W 1 Millwall 1
Feb 03 Stoke 0 Birmingham 1
Feb 03 Sunderland 1 Gainsborough 1
Feb 03 Tottenham 3 Reading 2

Feb 03	Woolwich A	3	Watford	0

Replays

Feb 07	Gainsborough	0	Sunderland	3
Feb 07	Middlesbrough	1	Brighton	1
Feb 07	Newcastle	2	Derby	1
Feb 07	Plymouth	1	Aston Villa	5
Feb 07	Southampton	1	New Brompton	0
Feb 08	Millwall	0	Sheffield W	3
Feb 12	Brighton	1	Middlesbrough	3
	played at Sheffield U			

3rd Round

Feb 24	Everton	1	Bradford C	0
Feb 24	Liverpool	2	Brentford	0
Feb 24	Manchester U	5	Aston Villa	1
Feb 24	Newcastle	5	Blackpool	0
Feb 24	Sheffield W	4	Nottingham F	1
Feb 24	Southampton	6	Middlesbrough	1
Feb 24	Tottenham	1	Birmingham	1
Feb 24	Woolwich A	5	Sunderland	0

Replay

Feb 28	Birmingham	2	Tottenham	0

4th Round

Mar 10	Birmingham	2	Newcastle	2
Mar 10	Everton	4	Sheffield W	3
Mar 10	Liverpool	3	Southampton	0
Mar 10	Manchester U	2	Woolwich A	3

Replay

Mar 14	Newcastle	3	Birmingham	0

Semi-finals

Mar 31	Everton	2	Liverpool	0
	played at Aston Villa			
Mar 31	Newcastle	2	Woolwich A	0
	played at Stoke			

Final

Apr 21	Everton	1	Newcastle	0
	played at Crystal Palace			

Season 1906-07

1st Round

Jan 12	Blackburn	2	Manchester C	2
Jan 12	Bolton	3	Brighton	1
Jan 12	Bradford C	2	Reading	0
Jan 12	Brentford	2	Glossop	1
Jan 12	Bristol C	4	Leeds	1
Jan 12	Bristol R	0	Q.P.R.	0
Jan 12	Burnley	1	Aston Villa	3
Jan 12	Burslem Port Vale	7	Irthlingborough	1
Jan 12	Burton	0	New Brompton	0
Jan 12	Crewe	1	Accrington	1
Jan 12	Derby	1	Chesterfield	1
Jan 12	Everton	1	Sheffield U	0
Jan 12	Fulham	0	Stockport	0
Jan 12	Gainsborough	0	Luton	0
Jan 12	Grimsby	1	Woolwich A	1
Jan 12	Lincoln	2	Chelsea	2
Jan 12	Liverpool	2	Birmingham	1
Jan 12	Middlesbrough	4	Northampton	2
Jan 12	Millwall	2	Plymouth	0
Jan 12	Newcastle	0	Crystal Palace	1
Jan 12	Norwich	3	Hastings	1
Jan 12	Nottingham F	1	Barnsley	1
Jan 12	Notts Co	1	Preston	0
Jan 12	Oldham	5	Kidderminster	0
Jan 12	Oxford	0	Bury	3
Jan 12	Portsmouth	2	Manchester U	2
Jan 12	Sheffield W	3	Wolverhampton	2
Jan 12	Southampton	2	Watford	1
Jan 12	Sunderland	4	Leicester	1
Jan 12	Tottenham	0	Hull	0
Jan 12	West Ham	2	Blackpool	1
Jan 12	W.B.A.	1	Stoke	1

Replays

Jan 14	Q.P.R.	0	Bristol R	1
Jan 16	Accrington	1	Crewe	0
Jan 16	Chelsea	0	Lincoln	1
Jan 16	Fulham	2	Stockport	1
	played at Fulham			
Jan 16	Luton	2	Gainsborough	1
Jan 16	Manchester C	0	Blackburn	1
Jan 16	Manchester U	1	Portsmouth	2
Jan 16	Woolwich A	3	Grimsby	0
Jan 17	Barnsley	2	Nottingham F	1
Jan 17	Stoke	2	W.B.A.	2
Jan 21	Chesterfield	0	Derby	4
Jan 21	Hull	0	Tottenham	1
Jan 21	New Brompton	2	Burton	0
	played at Fulham			
Jan 21	Stoke	1	W.B.A.	2
	played at Aston Villa			

2nd Round

Feb 02	Barnsley	1	Portsmouth	0
Feb 02	Blackburn	1	Tottenham	1
Feb 02	Bolton	2	Aston Villa	0
Feb 02	Bradford C	1	Accrington	0
Feb 02	Brentford	1	Middlesbrough	0
Feb 02	Bristol R	3	Millwall	0
Feb 02	Burslem Port Vale	2	Notts Co	2
Feb 02	Bury	1	New Brompton	0
Feb 02	Derby	1	Lincoln	0
Feb 02	Fulham	0	Crystal Palace	0
Feb 02	Luton	0	Sunderland	0
Feb 02	Oldham	0	Liverpool	1
Feb 02	Southampton	1	Sheffield W	1
Feb 02	W.B.A.	1	Norwich	0
Feb 02	West Ham	1	Everton	2
Feb 02	Woolwich A	2	Bristol C	1

Replays

Feb 06	Crystal Palace	1	Fulham	0
Feb 06	Notts Co	5	Burslem Port Vale	0
Feb 06	Sunderland	1	Luton	0
Feb 07	Sheffield W	3	Southampton	1
Feb 07	Tottenham	1	Blackburn	1
Feb 11	Blackburn	1	Tottenham	2
	played at Aston Villa			

3rd Round

Feb 23	Barnsley	1	Bury	0
Feb 23	Crystal Palace	1	Brentford	1
Feb 23	Everton	0	Bolton	0
Feb 23	Liverpool	1	Bradford C	0
Feb 23	Notts Co	4	Tottenham	0
Feb 23	Sheffield W	0	Sunderland	0
Feb 23	W.B.A.	2	Derby	0
Feb 23	Woolwich A	1	Bristol R	0

Replays

Feb 27	Bolton	0	Everton	3
Feb 27	Brentford	0	Crystal Palace	1
Feb 27	Sunderland	0	Sheffield W	1

4th Round

Mar 09	Barnsley	1	Woolwich A	2
Mar 09	Crystal Palace	1	Everton	1
Mar 09	Sheffield W	1	Liverpool	0
Mar 09	W.B.A.	3	Notts Co	1

Replay

Mar 13	Everton	4	Crystal Palace	0

Semi-finals

Mar 23	Everton	2	W.B.A.	1
	played at Bolton			
Mar 23	Sheffield W	3	Woolwich A	1
	played at Birmingham			

Final

Apr 20	Everton	1	Sheffield W	2
	played at Crystal Palace			

Season 1907-08

1st Round

Jan 11	Aston Villa	3	Stockport	0
Jan 11	Bolton	5	Woking	0
Jan 11	Bradford C	1	Wolverhampton	1
Jan 11	Brighton	1	Preston	1
Jan 11	Bristol C	0	Grimsby	0
Jan 11	Burnley	1	Southampton	2
Jan 11	Bury	2	Millwall	1
Jan 11	Carlisle	2	Brentford	2
Jan 11	Chelsea	9	Worksop	1
Jan 11	Chesterfield	4	Stockton	0
Jan 11	Coventry	2	Crystal Palace	4
Jan 11	Everton	1	Tottenham	0
Jan 11	Gainsborough	1	Watford	0
Jan 11	Glossop	0	Manchester C	0
Jan 11	Hastings	0	Portsmouth	1
Jan 11	Leicester	2	Blackburn	0
Jan 11	Liverpool	4	Derby	2
Jan 11	Luton	3	Fulham	8
Jan 11	Manchester U	3	Blackpool	1
Jan 11	New Brompton	3	Sunderland	1
Jan 11	Newcastle	2	Nottingham F	0
Jan 11	Northampton	0	Bristol R	1
Jan 11	Norwich	2	Sheffield W	0
Jan 11	Notts Co	2	Middlesbrough	0
Jan 11	Oldham	2	Leeds	1
Jan 11	Plymouth	1	Barnsley	0
Jan 11	Q.P.R.	1	Reading	0
Jan 11	Stoke	5	Lincoln	0
Jan 11	Swindon	0	Sheffield U	0
Jan 11	W.B.A.	1	Birmingham	1
Jan 11	West Ham	1	Rotherham	0
Jan 11	Woolwich A	0	Hull	0

Replays

Jan 15	Birmingham	1	W.B.A.	2
Jan 15	Brentford	1	Carlisle	3
Jan 15	Grimsby	2	Bristol C	1
Jan 15	Manchester C	6	Glossop	0
Jan 15	Wolverhampton	1	Bradford C	0
Jan 16	Hull	4	Woolwich A	1
Jan 16	Preston	1	Brighton	1
Jan 16	Sheffield U	2	Swindon	3
Jan 20	Brighton	1	Preston	0
	played at Chelsea			

2nd Round

Feb 01	Aston Villa	3	Hull	0
Feb 01	Bristol R	2	Chesterfield	0
Feb 01	Fulham	2	Norwich	1
Feb 01	Grimsby	6	Carlisle	2
Feb 01	Liverpool	1	Brighton	1
Feb 01	Manchester C	1	New Brompton	1
Feb 01	Manchester U	1	Chelsea	0
Feb 01	Newcastle	2	West Ham	0
Feb 01	Notts Co	1	Bolton	1
Feb 01	Oldham	0	Everton	0
Feb 01	Plymouth	2	Crystal Palace	3
Feb 01	Portsmouth	1	Leicester	0
Feb 01	Southampton	1	W.B.A.	0
Feb 01	Stoke	1	Gainsborough	1
Feb 01	Swindon	2	Q.P.R.	1
Feb 01	Wolverhampton	2	Bury	0

Replays

Feb 05	Bolton	2	Notts Co	1
Feb 05	Brighton	0	Liverpool	3
Feb 05	Everton	6	Oldham	1
Feb 05	Gainsborough	2	Stoke	2
Feb 05	New Brompton	1	Manchester C	2
Feb 10	Gainsborough	1	Stoke	3
	played at Nottingham F			

3rd Round

Feb 22	Aston Villa	0	Manchester U	2
Feb 22	Bolton	3	Everton	3
Feb 22	Grimsby	1	Crystal Palace	0
Feb 22	Manchester C	1	Fulham	1
Feb 22	Newcastle	3	Liverpool	1
Feb 22	Portsmouth	0	Stoke	1
Feb 22	Southampton	2	Bristol R	0
Feb 22	Wolverhampton	2	Swindon	0

Replays

Feb 26	Everton	3	Bolton	1
Feb 26	Fulham	3	Manchester C	1

4th Round

Mar 07	Everton	0	Southampton	0
Mar 07	Fulham	2	Manchester U	1
Mar 07	Newcastle	5	Grimsby	1
Mar 07	Stoke	0	Wolverhampton	1

Replay

Mar 11	Southampton	3	Everton	2

Semi-finals

Mar 28	Fulham	0	Newcastle	6
	played at Liverpool			
Mar 28	Southampton	0	Wolverhampton	2
	played at Chelsea			

Final

Apr 25	Newcastle	1	Wolverhampton	3
	played at Crystal Palace			

Season 1908-09

1st Round

Jan 16	Birmingham	2	Portsmouth	5
Jan 16	Blackpool	2	Hastings	0
Jan 19	Bradford C	2	Workington	0
Jan 16	Brentford	2	Gainsborough	0
Jan 16	Bristol C	1	Southampton	1
Jan 16	Bristol R	1	Burnley	4
Jan 16	Bury	8	Kettering	0
Jan 16	Chesterfield	0	Glossop	2
Jan 16	Croydon	1	Woolwich A	1
Jan 16	Everton	3	Barnsley	1
Jan 16	Fulham	4	Carlisle	1
Jan 20	Grimsby	0	Stockport	2
Jan 16	Hull	1	Chelsea	1
Jan 16	Liverpool	5	Lincoln	1
Jan 16	Luton	1	Millwall	2
Jan 16	Manchester C	3	Tottenham	4
Jan 16	Manchester U	1	Brighton	0
Jan 16	Newcastle	5	Clapton O	0
Jan 16	Northampton	1	Derby	1
Jan 16	Norwich	0	Reading	0
Jan 16	Nottingham F	2	Aston Villa	0
Jan 16	Notts Co	0	Blackburn	1
Jan 16	Oldham	1	Leeds	1
Jan 16	Plymouth	1	Swindon	0
Jan 16	Preston	1	Middlesbrough	0
Jan 16	Q.P.R.	0	West Ham	0
Jan 16	Sheffield U	2	Sunderland	3
Jan 16	Sheffield W	5	Stoke	0
Jan 16	Watford	1	Leicester	1

Jan 16 Wolverhampton 2 Crystal Palace 2
Jan 16 Wrexham 1 Exeter 1
Jan 16 W.B.A. 3 Bolton 1

Replays
Jan 20 Chelsea 1 Hull 0
Jan 20 Derby 4 Northampton 2
Jan 20 Exeter 2 Wrexham 1
Jan 20 Leeds 2 Oldham 0
Jan 20 Leicester 3 Watford 1
Jan 20 Reading 1 Norwich 1
Jan 20 Southampton 0 Bristol C 2
Jan 20 West Ham 1 Q.P.R. 0
Jan 20 Woolwich A 2 Croydon 0
Jan 21 Crystal Palace 4 Wolverhampton 2
Jan 25 Norwich 3 Reading 2
played at Aston Villa

2nd Round
Feb 06 Blackburn 2 Chelsea 1
Feb 06 Bristol C 2 Bury 2
Feb 06 Crystal Palace 0 Burnley 0
Feb 06 Leeds 1 West Ham 1
Feb 06 Leicester 0 Derby 2
Feb 06 Liverpool 2 Norwich 3
Feb 06 Manchester U 1 Everton 0
Feb 06 Newcastle 2 Blackpool 1

Feb 06 Nottingham F 1 Brentford 0
Feb 06 Plymouth 2 Exeter 0
Feb 06 Portsmouth 2 Sheffield W 2
Feb 06 Preston 1 Sunderland 2
Feb 06 Stockport 1 Glossop 1
Feb 06 Tottenham 1 Fulham 0
Feb 06 W.B.A. 1 Bradford C 2
Feb 06 Woolwich A 1 Millwall 1

Replays
Feb 09 Glossop 1 Stockport 0
Feb 10 Burnley 9 Crystal Palace 0
Feb 10 Bury 0 Bristol C 1
Feb 10 Millwall 1 Woolwich A 0
Feb 11 Sheffield W 3 Portsmouth 0
Feb 11 West Ham 2 Leeds 1

3rd Round
Feb 20 Bradford C 0 Sunderland 1
Feb 20 Bristol C 2 Norwich 0
Feb 20 Derby 1 Plymouth 0
Feb 20 Manchester U 6 Blackburn 1
Feb 20 Nottingham F 3 Millwall 1
Feb 20 Sheffield W 0 Glossop 1
Feb 20 Tottenham 0 Burnley 0
Feb 20 West Ham 0 Newcastle 0

Replays
Feb 24 Burnley 3 Tottenham 1
Feb 24 Newcastle 2 West Ham 1

4th Round
Mar 10 Burnley 2 Manchester U 3
Mar 13 Derby 3 Nottingham F 0
Mar 06 Glossop 0 Bristol C 0
Mar 06 Newcastle 2 Sunderland 2

Replays
Mar 10 Bristol C 1 Glossop 0
Mar 10 Sunderland 0 Newcastle 3

Semi-finals
Mar 27 Bristol C 1 Derby 1
played at Chelsea
Mar 27 Manchester U 1 Newcastle 0
played at Sheffield U

Replay
Mar 31 Bristol C 2 Derby 1
played at Birmingham

Final
Apr 24 Bristol C 0 Manchester U 1
played at Crystal Palace

SEASON 1909-10

1st Round
Jan 15 Birmingham 1 Leicester 4
Jan 15 Blackburn 7 Accrington 1
Jan 15 Blackpool 1 Barnsley 1
Jan 15 Bradford 8 Bishop Auckland 0
Jan 15 Bradford C 4 Notts Co 2
Jan 15 Brighton 0 Southampton 1
Jan 15 Bristol C 2 Liverpool 0
Jan 15 Burnley 2 Manchester U 0
Jan 15 Bury 2 Glossop 1
Jan 15 Crystal Palace 1 Swindon 3
Jan 15 Chelsea 2 Hull 1
Jan 15 Chesterfield 0 Fulham 0
Jan 15 Derby 5 Millwall 0
Jan 15 Gainsborough 1 Southend 1
Jan 15 Grimsby 0 Bristol R 2
Jan 15 Leyton 0 New Brompton 0
Jan 15 Middlesbrough 1 Everton 1
Jan 15 Northampton 0 Sheffield W 0
Jan 15 Norwich 0 Q.P.R. 0
Jan 15 Nottingham F 3 Sheffield U 2
Jan 15 Oldham 1 Aston Villa 2
Jan 15 Plymouth 1 Tottenham 1
Jan 15 Portsmouth 3 Shrewsbury 0
Jan 15 Preston 1 Coventry 2
Jan 15 Reading 0 Wolverhampton 5
Jan 15 Stockport 4 Bolton 1
Jan 15 Stoke 1 Newcastle 1
Jan 15 Sunderland 1 Leeds 0
Jan 15 W.B.A. 2 Clapton O 0
Jan 15 West Ham 1 Carlisle 1
Jan 15 Woolwich A 3 Watford 0
Jan 15 Workington 1 Manchester C 2

Replays
Jan 19 Everton 5 Middlesbrough 3

Jan 19 Fulham 2 Chesterfield 1
Jan 19 New Brompton 2 Leyton 2
Jan 19 Newcastle 2 Stoke 1
Jan 19 Q.P.R. 3 Norwich 0
Jan 19 Southend 1 Gainsborough 0
Jan 19 Tottenham 7 Plymouth 1
Jan 20 Barnsley 6 Blackpool 0
Jan 20 Carlisle 0 West Ham 5
Jan 20 Sheffield W 0 Northampton 1
Jan 24 Leyton 1 New Brompton 0
played at Tottenham

2nd Round
Feb 05 Aston Villa 6 Derby 1
Feb 05 Barnsley 4 Bristol R 0
Feb 05 Bradford C 1 Blackburn 2
Feb 05 Bristol C 1 W.B.A. 1
Feb 05 Chelsea 0 Tottenham 1
Feb 05 Everton 5 Woolwich A 0
Feb 05 Leicester 3 Bury 2
Feb 05 Newcastle 4 Fulham 0
Feb 05 Northampton 0 Nottingham F 0
Feb 05 Portsmouth 0 Coventry 1
Feb 05 Southampton 0 Manchester C 5
Feb 05 Southend 0 Q.P.R. 0
Feb 05 Stockport 0 Leyton 2
Feb 05 Sunderland 3 Bradford 1
Feb 05 Swindon 2 Burnley 0
Feb 05 Wolverhampton 1 West Ham 5

Replays
Feb 09 Nottingham F 1 Northampton 0
Feb 09 Q.P.R. 3 Southend 2
Feb 09 W.B.A. 4 Bristol C 2

3rd Round
Feb 19 Aston Villa 1 Manchester C 2
Feb 19 Barnsley 1 W.B.A. 0
Feb 19 Coventry 3 Nottingham F 1
Feb 19 Everton 2 Sunderland 0
Feb 19 Leicester 1 Leyton 0
Feb 19 Newcastle 3 Blackburn 1
Feb 19 Q.P.R. 1 West Ham 1
Feb 19 Swindon 3 Tottenham 2

Replay
Feb 24 West Ham 0 Q.P.R. 1

4th Round
Mar 05 Barnsley 1 Q.P.R. 0
Mar 05 Coventry 0 Everton 2
Mar 05 Newcastle 3 Leicester 0
Mar 05 Swindon 2 Manchester C 0

Semi-finals
Mar 26 Barnsley 0 Everton 0
played at Leeds
Mar 26 Newcastle 2 Swindon 0
played at Tottenham

Replay
Mar 31 Barnsley 3 Everton 0
played at Manchester U

Final
Apr 23 Barnsley 1 Newcastle 1
played at Crystal Palace

Replay
Apr 28 Barnsley 0 Newcastle 2
played at Everton

SEASON 1910-11

1st Round
Jan 14 Birmingham 1 Oldham 1
Jan 14 Blackburn 5 Southend 1
Jan 14 Bolton 0 Chesterfield 2
Jan 14 Bradford 5 Q.P.R. 3
Jan 14 Brentford 0 Preston 1
Jan 14 Bristol C 0 Crewe 3
Jan 14 Bristol R 0 Hull 0
Jan 14 Burnley 2 Exeter 0
Jan 14 Chelsea 0 Leyton 0
Jan 16 Clapton O 1 Woolwich A 2
Jan 14 Crystal Palace 0 Everton 4
Jan 14 Derby 2 Plymouth 1
Jan 14 Grimsby 3 Croydon 0
Jan 14 Leeds 1 Brighton 3
Jan 14 Leicester 3 Southampton 1
Jan 14 Liverpool 3 Gainsborough 2
Jan 14 Manchester U 2 Blackpool 1
Jan 14 Middlesbrough 1 Glossop 0
Jan 14 New Brompton 0 Bradford C 1
Jan 14 Newcastle 6 Bury 1
Jan 14 Northampton 5 Luton 1
Jan 14 Norwich 3 Sunderland 1
Jan 14 Portsmouth 1 Aston Villa 4
Jan 14 Sheffield U 0 Darlington 1
Jan 14 Sheffield W 1 Coventry 2
Jan 14 Stoke 1 Manchester C 2
Jan 14 Swindon 3 Notts Co 1
Jan 14 Tottenham 2 Millwall 1
Jan 14 Watford 0 Barnsley 2
Jan 14 West Ham 2 Nottingham F 1

Jan 14 Wolverhampton 2 Accrington 0
Jan 14 W.B.A. 4 Fulham 1

Replays
Jan 17 Oldham 2 Birmingham 0
Jan 19 Hull 1 Bristol R 0
Jan 19 Leyton 0 Chelsea 2

2nd Round
Feb 04 Blackburn 0 Tottenham 0
Feb 04 Bradford C 2 Norwich 1
Feb 04 Brighton 0 Coventry 0
Feb 04 Burnley 2 Barnsley 0
Feb 04 Chelsea 4 Chesterfield 1
Feb 04 Crewe 1 Grimsby 5
Feb 04 Darlington 2 Bradford 1
Feb 04 Derby 2 W.B.A. 0
Feb 04 Everton 2 Liverpool 1
Feb 04 Hull 1 Oldham 0
Feb 04 Manchester U 2 Aston Villa 1
Feb 04 Middlesbrough 0 Leicester 0
Feb 04 Newcastle 1 Northampton 1
Feb 04 Swindon 1 Woolwich A 0
Feb 04 West Ham 3 Preston 0
Feb 04 Wolverhampton 1 Manchester C 0

Replays
Feb 08 Northampton 0 Newcastle 1
Feb 09 Coventry 2 Brighton 0
Feb 09 Leicester 1 Middlesbrough 2
Feb 09 Tottenham 0 Blackburn 2

3rd Round
Feb 25 Bradford C 1 Grimsby 0
Feb 25 Burnley 5 Coventry 0
Feb 25 Darlington 0 Swindon 3
Feb 25 Derby 5 Everton 0
Feb 25 Middlesbrough 0 Blackburn 3
Feb 25 Newcastle 3 Hull 2
Feb 25 West Ham 2 Manchester U 1
Feb 25 Wolverhampton 0 Chelsea 2

4th Round
Mar 11 Bradford C 1 Burnley 0
Mar 11 Chelsea 3 Swindon 1
Mar 11 Newcastle 4 Derby 0
Mar 11 West Ham 2 Blackburn 3

Semi-finals
Mar 25 Blackburn 0 Bradford C 3
played at Sheffield U
Mar 25 Chelsea 0 Newcastle 3
played at Birmingham

Final
Apr 22 Bradford C 0 Newcastle 0
played at Crystal Palace

Replay
Apr 26 Bradford C 1 Newcastle 0
played at Manchester U

SEASON 1911-12

1st Round
Jan 13 Aston Villa 6 Walsall 0
Jan 13 Birmingham 0 Barnsley 0
Jan 13 Blackburn 4 Norwich 1

Jan 13 Bolton 1 Woolwich A 0
Jan 13 Brentford 0 Crystal Palace 0
Jan 13 Bristol R 1 Portsmouth 2
Jan 13 Bury 2 Millwall 1

Jan 13 Chelsea 1 Sheffield U 0
Jan 13 Clapton O 1 Everton 2
Jan 13 Crewe 1 Blackpool 1
Jan 13 Croydon 2 Leicester 2

Jan 13	Darlington	2	Brighton	1
Jan 13	Derby	3	Newcastle	0
Jan 13	Fulham	2	Burnley	1
Jan 13	Leeds	1	Glossop	0
Jan 13	Lincoln	2	Stockport	0
Jan 13	Liverpool	1	Leyton	0
Jan 13	Luton	2	Notts Co	4
Jan 13	Manchester U	3	Huddersfield	1
Jan 13	Middlesbrough	0	Sheffield W	0
Jan 13	Northampton	1	Bristol C	0
Jan 13	Nottingham F	0	Bradford	1
Jan 13	Oldham	1	Hull	1
Jan 13	Preston	0	Manchester C	1
Jan 13	Q.P.R.	0	Bradford C	0
Jan 13	Southampton	0	Coventry	2
Jan 13	Southport	0	Reading	2
Jan 13	Sunderland	3	Plymouth	1
Jan 13	Swindon	5	Sutton	0
Jan 13	W.B.A.	3	Tottenham	0
Jan 13	Watford	0	Wolverhampton	0
Jan 13	West Ham	2	Gainsborough	1

Replays

Jan 16	Hull	0	Oldham	1
Jan 17	Crystal Palace	4	Brentford	0
Jan 18	Bradford C	4	Q.P.R.	0
Jan 22	Barnsley	3	Birmingham	0
Jan 22	Blackpool	2	Crewe	2
Jan 22	Leicester	6	Croydon	1
Jan 24	Wolverhampton	10	Watford	0
Jan 25	Blackpool	2	Crewe	1
	played at Manchester C			
Jan 25	Sheffield W	1	Middlesbrough	2

2nd Round

Feb 03	Aston Villa	1	Reading	1
Feb 03	Barnsley	1	Leicester	0
Feb 03	Bolton	1	Blackpool	0
Feb 03	Bradford	2	Portsmouth	0
Feb 03	Bradford C	2	Chelsea	0
Feb 03	Coventry	1	Manchester U	5
Feb 03	Crystal Palace	0	Sunderland	0
Feb 03	Darlington	1	Northampton	1
Feb 03	Derby	1	Blackburn	2
Feb 03	Everton	1	Bury	1
Feb 03	Fulham	3	Liverpool	0
Feb 03	Leeds	0	W.B.A.	1
Feb 03	Manchester C	0	Oldham	1
Feb 03	Middlesbrough	1	West Ham	1
Feb 07	Reading	1	Aston Villa	0
Feb 03	Swindon	2	Notts Co	0
Feb 03	Wolverhampton	2	Lincoln	1

Replays

Feb 03	Swindon	2	Notts Co	0
Feb 07	Sunderland	1	Crystal Palace	0
Feb 08	Bury	0	Everton	6
Feb 08	Northampton	2	Darlington	0
Feb 08	West Ham	2	Middlesbrough	1

3rd Round

Feb 24	Blackburn	3	Wolverhampton	2
Feb 24	Bolton	1	Barnsley	2
Feb 24	Bradford	0	Bradford C	1
Feb 24	Fulham	2	Northampton	1
Feb 24	Oldham	0	Everton	2
Feb 24	Reading	1	Manchester U	1
Feb 24	Sunderland	1	W.B.A.	2
Feb 24	West Ham	1	Swindon	1

Replays

Feb 28	Swindon	4	West Ham	0
Feb 29	Manchester U	3	Reading	0

4th Round

Mar 09	Barnsley	0	Bradford C	0
Mar 09	Manchester U	1	Blackburn	1
Mar 09	Swindon	2	Everton	1
Mar 09	W.B.A.	3	Fulham	0

Replays

Mar 13	Bradford C	0	Barnsley	0
Mar 14	Blackburn	4	Manchester U	2
Mar 18	Barnsley	0	Bradford C	0
	played at Leeds			
Mar 21	Barnsley	3	Bradford C	2
	played at Sheffield U			

Semi-finals

Mar 30	Barnsley	0	Swindon	0
	played at Chelsea			
Mar 30	Blackburn	0	W.B.A.	0
	played at Liverpool			

Replays

Apr 03	Barnsley	1	Swindon	0
	played at Notts Co			
Apr 03	Blackburn	0	W.B.A.	1
	played at Sheffield W			

Final

Apr 20	Barnsley	0	W.B.A.	0
	played at Crystal Palace			

Replay

Apr 24	Barnsley	1	W.B.A.	0
	played at Sheffield U			

Season 1912-13

1st Round

Jan 18	Blackburn	7	Northampton	2
Jan 15	Bradford	1	Barrow	1
Jan 11	Bristol R	2	Notts Co	0
Jan 11	Chelsea	5	Southend	2
Jan 18	Chesterfield	1	Nottingham F	4
Jan 11	Croydon	0	Woolwich A	0
Jan 11	Crystal Palace	2	Glossop	0
Jan 15	Derby	1	Aston Villa	3
Jan 15	Everton	5	Stockport	1
Jan 11	Fulham	0	Hull	2
Jan 11	Gillingham	0	Barnsley	0
Jan 15	Huddersfield	3	Sheffield U	1
Jan 15	Leeds	2	Burnley	3
Jan 16	Leicester	1	Norwich	4
Jan 15	Liverpool	3	Bristol C	0
Jan 11	Manchester C	4	Birmingham	0
Jan 11	Manchester U	1	Coventry	1
Jan 11	Millwall	0	Middlesbrough	0
Jan 16	Newcastle	1	Bradford C	0
Jan 11	Oldham	2	Bolton	0
Jan 11	Plymouth	2	Preston	0
Jan 15	Portsmouth	1	Brighton	2
Jan 11	Q.P.R.	4	Halifax	2
Jan 11	Rochdale	0	Swindon	2
Jan 16	Sheffield W	5	Grimsby	1
Jan 18	South Shields	0	Gainsborough	1
Jan 11	Southampton	1	Bury	1
Jan 16	Stoke	2	Reading	2
Jan 11	Sunderland	6	Clapton O	0
Jan 11	Tottenham	1	Blackpool	1
Jan 18	Wolverhampton	3	London Cal	1
Jan 13	W.B.A.	1	West Ham	1

Replays

Jan 15	Bury	2	Southampton	1
Jan 15	Middlesbrough	4	Millwall	1
Jan 15	Woolwich A	2	Croydon	1
Jan 16	Barnsley	3	Gillingham	1
Jan 16	Blackpool	1	Tottenham	6
Jan 16	Coventry	1	Manchester U	2
Jan 16	West Ham	2	W.B.A.	2
Jan 22	Barrow	0	Bradford	1
Jan 22	Reading	3	Stoke	0
Jan 22	W.B.A.	0	West Ham	3
	played at Chelsea			

2nd Round

Feb 01	Aston Villa	5	West Ham	0
Feb 01	Barnsley	2	Blackburn	3
Feb 01	Bradford	3	Wolverhampton	0
Feb 01	Brighton	0	Everton	0
Feb 01	Bristol R	1	Norwich	1
Feb 01	Burnley	4	Gainsborough	1
Feb 01	Chelsea	1	Sheffield W	1
Feb 01	Crystal Palace	2	Bury	0
Feb 01	Huddersfield	1	Swindon	2
Feb 01	Hull	0	Newcastle	0
Feb 01	Middlesbrough	3	Q.P.R.	2
Feb 01	Oldham	5	Nottingham F	1
Feb 01	Plymouth	0	Manchester U	2
Feb 01	Reading	1	Tottenham	0
Feb 05	Sunderland	2	Manchester C	0
Feb 01	Woolwich A	1	Liverpool	4

Replays

Feb 05	Everton	1	Brighton	0
Feb 05	Newcastle	3	Hull	0
Feb 05	Sheffield W	6	Chelsea	0
Feb 06	Norwich	2	Bristol R	2
Feb 10	Bristol R	1	Norwich	0
	played at Chelsea			

3rd Round

Feb 22	Aston Villa	5	Crystal Palace	0
Feb 22	Bradford	2	Sheffield W	1
Feb 22	Bristol R	0	Everton	4
Feb 22	Burnley	3	Middlesbrough	1
Feb 22	Liverpool	1	Newcastle	1
Feb 22	Oldham	0	Manchester U	0
Feb 22	Reading	1	Blackburn	2
Feb 22	Sunderland	4	Swindon	2

Replays

Feb 26	Manchester U	1	Oldham	2
Feb 26	Newcastle	1	Liverpool	0

4th Round

Mar 08	Blackburn	0	Burnley	1
Mar 08	Bradford	0	Aston Villa	5
Mar 08	Everton	0	Oldham	1
Mar 08	Sunderland	0	Newcastle	0

Replays

Mar 12	Newcastle	2	Sunderland	2
Mar 17	Newcastle	0	Sunderland	3
	played at Newcastle			

Semi-finals

Mar 29	Aston Villa	1	Oldham	0
	played at Blackburn			
Mar 29	Burnley	0	Sunderland	0
	played at Sheffield U			

Replay

Apr 02	Burnley	2	Sunderland	3
	played at Birmingham			

Final

Apr 19	Aston Villa	1	Sunderland	0
	played at Crystal Palace			

Season 1913-14

1st Round

Jan 10	Aston Villa	4	Stoke	0
Jan 10	Birmingham	2	Southend	1
Jan 10	Blackburn	3	Middlesbrough	0
Jan 10	Bolton	3	Port Vale	0
Jan 10	Bradford	5	Reading	1
Jan 10	Bradford C	2	Woolwich A	0
Jan 10	Burnley	3	South Shields	1
Jan 10	Crystal Palace	2	Norwich	1
Jan 10	Clapton O	2	Nottingham F	2
Jan 10	Derby	1	Northampton	0
Jan 10	Gainsborough	2	Leeds	4
	played at Leeds			
Jan 10	Gillingham	1	Blackpool	0
Jan 10	Glossop	2	Everton	1
Jan 10	Huddersfield	3	London Cal	0
Jan 10	Hull	0	Bury	0
Jan 10	Leicester	5	Tottenham	5
Jan 10	Liverpool	1	Barnsley	1
Jan 10	Manchester C	2	Fulham	0
Jan 10	Millwall	0	Chelsea	0
Jan 10	Newcastle	0	Sheffield U	5
Jan 10	Oldham	1	Brighton	1
Jan 10	Plymouth	4	Lincoln	1
Jan 10	Portsmouth	0	Exeter	4
Jan 10	Preston	5	Bristol R	2
Jan 10	Q.P.R.	3	Bristol C	2
Jan 10	Sheffield W	3	Notts Co	2
Jan 10	Sunderland	9	Chatham	0
Jan 10	Swansea	2	Merthyr T	0
Jan 10	Swindon	1	Manchester U	0
Jan 10	W.B.A.	2	Grimsby	0
Jan 10	West Ham	8	Chesterfield	1
Jan 10	Wolverhampton	3	Southampton	0

Replays

Jan 14	Brighton	1	Oldham	0
Jan 14	Bristol C	0	Q.P.R.	2
Jan 14	Bury	2	Hull	1
Jan 14	Chelsea	0	Millwall	1
Jan 14	Nottingham F	0	Clapton O	1
Jan 15	Barnsley	0	Liverpool	1
Jan 15	Tottenham	2	Leicester	0

2nd Round

Jan 31	Birmingham	1	Huddersfield	0
Jan 31	Blackburn	2	Bury	0
Jan 31	Bolton	4	Swindon	2
Jan 31	Brighton	3	Clapton O	1
Jan 31	Burnley	3	Derby	2
Jan 31	Exeter	1	Aston Villa	2
Jan 31	Glossop	0	Preston	1
Jan 31	Leeds	0	W.B.A.	2
Jan 31	Liverpool	2	Gillingham	0
Jan 31	Manchester C	2	Tottenham	1
Jan 31	Millwall	1	Bradford C	0
Jan 31	Sheffield U	3	Bradford	1
Jan 31	Sunderland	2	Plymouth	1
Jan 31	Swansea	1	Q.P.R.	2
Jan 31	West Ham	2	Crystal Palace	0
Jan 31	Wolverhampton	1	Sheffield W	1
	Tynecastle			

Replay

Feb 04	Sheffield W	1	Wolverhampton	0

3rd Round

Feb 21	Aston Villa	2	W.B.A.	1
Feb 21	Birmingham	1	Q.P.R.	2
Feb 21	Blackburn	1	Manchester C	2
Feb 21	Burnley	3	Bolton	0
Feb 21	Millwall	0	Sheffield U	4
Feb 21	Sheffield W	3	Brighton	0
Feb 21	Sunderland	2	Preston	0
Feb 21	West Ham	1	Liverpool	1

Replay

Feb 25	Liverpool	5	West Ham	1

4th Round

Mar 07	Liverpool	2	Q.P.R.	1
Mar 07	Manchester C	0	Sheffield U	0
Mar 07	Sheffield W	0	Aston Villa	1
Mar 07	Sunderland	0	Burnley	0

Replays

Mar 11	Burnley	2	Sunderland	1
Mar 12	Sheffield U	0	Manchester C	0

Mar 16	Manchester C	0	Sheffield U	1
	played at Aston Villa			

Semi-finals

Mar 28	Aston Villa	0	Liverpool	2
	played at Tottenham			
Mar 28	Burnley	0	Sheffield U	0
	played at Manchester U			

Replay

Apr 01	Burnley	1	Sheffield U	0
	played at Everton			

Final

Apr 25	Burnley	1	Liverpool	0
	played at Crystal Palace			

Season 1914-15

1st Round

Jan 09	Arsenal	3	Merthyr T	0
Jan 09	Aston Villa	2	Exeter	0
Jan 09	Birmingham	2	Crystal Palace	2
Jan 09	Blackpool	1	Sheffield U	2
Jan 09	Bolton	2	Notts Co	1
Jan 09	Bradford	1	Portsmouth	0
Jan 09	Brighton	2	Lincoln	1
Jan 09	Bristol C	2	Cardiff	0
Jan 16	Bristol R	0	Southend	0
Jan 09	Burnley	3	Huddersfield	1
Jan 09	Bury	1	Plymouth	1
Jan 09	Chelsea	1	Swindon	1
Jan 09	Croydon	0	Oldham	3
Jan 09	Darlington	0	Bradford C	1
Jan 09	Derby	1	Leeds	2
Jan 09	Everton	3	Barnsley	0
Jan 09	Grimsby	0	Northampton	3
Jan 09	Hull	1	W.B.A.	0
Jan 09	Liverpool	3	Stockport	0
Jan 09	Middlesbrough	9	Goole	3
Jan 09	Millwall	2	Clapton O	1
Jan 09	Nottingham F	1	Norwich	4
Jan 09	Preston	0	Manchester C	0
Jan 09	Q.P.R.	2	Glossop	1
Jan 09	Reading	0	Wolverhampton	1
Jan 09	Rochdale	2	Gillingham	0
Jan 09	Sheffield W	1	Manchester U	0
Jan 09	South Shields	1	Fulham	2
Jan 09	Southampton	3	Luton	0
Jan 09	Swansea	1	Blackburn	0
Jan 09	Tottenham	2	Sunderland	1
Jan 09	West Ham	2	Newcastle	2

Replays

Jan 16	Crystal Palace	0	Birmingham	3
Jan 16	Manchester C	3	Preston	0
Jan 16	Newcastle	3	West Ham	2
Jan 16	Plymouth	1	Bury	2
Jan 16	Swindon	2	Chelsea	5
Jan 23	Southend	3	Bristol R	0

2nd Round

Jan 30	Bolton	0	Millwall	0
Jan 30	Bradford C	1	Middlesbrough	0
Jan 30	Brighton	0	Birmingham	0
Jan 30	Burnley	6	Southend	0
Jan 30	Bury	0	Bradford	1
Jan 30	Chelsea	1	Arsenal	0
Jan 30	Everton	4	Bristol C	0
Jan 30	Fulham	2	Southampton	3
Jan 30	Hull	2	Northampton	1
Jan 30	Manchester C	1	Aston Villa	0
Jan 30	Newcastle	1	Swansea	1
Jan 30	Norwich	3	Tottenham	2
Jan 30	Oldham	3	Rochdale	0
Jan 30	Q.P.R.	1	Leeds	0
Jan 30	Sheffield U	1	Liverpool	0
Jan 30	Sheffield W	2	Wolverhampton	0

Replays

Feb 06	Birmingham	3	Brighton	0
Feb 06	Millwall	2	Bolton	2
Feb 06	Swansea	0	Newcastle	2
Feb 13	Bolton	4	Millwall	1
	played at Bolton			

3rd Round

Feb 20	Birmingham	2	Oldham	3
Feb 20	Bolton	2	Burnley	1
Feb 20	Bradford C	1	Norwich	1
Feb 20	Manchester C	0	Chelsea	1
Feb 20	Q.P.R.	1	Everton	2
Feb 20	Sheffield U	1	Bradford	0
Feb 20	Sheffield W	1	Newcastle	2
Feb 20	Southampton	2	Hull	2

Replays

Feb 27	Hull	4	Southampton	0
Feb 27	Norwich	0	Bradford C	0
Mar 03	Bradford C	2	Norwich	0
	played at Lincoln			

4th Round

Mar 06	Bolton	4	Hull	2
Mar 06	Bradford C	0	Everton	2
Mar 06	Chelsea	1	Newcastle	1
Mar 06	Oldham	0	Sheffield U	0

Replays

Mar 13	Newcastle	0	Chelsea	1
Mar 13	Sheffield U	3	Oldham	0

Semi-finals

Mar 27	Bolton	1	Sheffield U	2
	played at Blackburn			
Mar 27	Chelsea	2	Everton	0
	played at Aston Villa			

Final

Apr 24	Chelsea	0	Sheffield U	3
	played at Manchester U			

Season 1919-20

1st Round

Jan 10	Arsenal	4	Rochdale	2
Jan 10	Aston Villa	2	Q.P.R.	1
Jan 10	Birmingham	2	Everton	0
Jan 10	Blackburn	2	Wolverhampton	2
Jan 10	Blackpool	0	Derby	0
Jan 10	Bolton	0	Chelsea	1
Jan 10	Bradford	3	Nottingham F	0
Jan 10	Bradford C	2	Portsmouth	2
Jan 10	Bristol R	1	Tottenham	4
Jan 10	Bury	2	Stoke	0
Jan 10	Cardiff	2	Oldham	0
Jan 10	Castleford	2	Hednesford	0
Jan 14	Darlington	0	Sheffield W	0
Jan 10	Fulham	1	Swindon	2
Jan 10	Grimsby	1	Bristol C	2
Jan 10	Huddersfield	5	Brentford	1
Jan 10	Luton	2	Coventry	2
Jan 10	Manchester C	4	Clapton O	1
Jan 14	Middlesbrough	4	Lincoln	1
Jan 10	Newcastle	2	Crystal Palace	0
Jan 10	Newport	0	Leicester	0
Jan 10	Notts Co	2	Millwall	0
Jan 10	Plymouth	2	Reading	0
Jan 10	Port Vale	0	Manchester U	1
Jan 10	Preston	3	Stockport	1
Jan 10	Sheffield U	3	Southend	0
Jan 10	South Shields	1	Liverpool	1
Jan 10	Southampton	0	West Ham	0
Jan 14	Sunderland	6	Hull	2
Jan 10	Thornycroft	0	Burnley	0
Jan 17	West Stanley	3	Gillingham	1
Jan 10	W.B.A.	0	Barnsley	1

Replays

Jan 13	Burnley	5	Thornycroft	0
	played at Portsmouth			
Jan 14	Derby	1	Blackpool	4
Jan 14	Liverpool	2	South Shields	0
Jan 15	Coventry	0	Luton	1
Jan 15	Leicester	2	Newport	0
Jan 15	West Ham	3	Southampton	1
Jan 15	Wolverhampton	1	Blackburn	0
Jan 17	Portsmouth	0	Bradford C	2
Jan 19	Sheffield W	0	Darlington	2

2nd Round

Jan 31	Birmingham	4	Darlington	0
Jan 31	Bradford	3	Castleford	2
Jan 31	Bradford C	2	Sheffield U	1
Jan 31	Bristol C	1	Arsenal	0
Jan 31	Burnley	1	Sunderland	1
Jan 31	Chelsea	4	Swindon	0
Jan 31	Leicester	3	Manchester C	0
Jan 31	Luton	0	Liverpool	2
Jan 31	Manchester U	1	Aston Villa	2
Jan 31	Newcastle	0	Huddersfield	1
Jan 31	Notts Co	1	Middlesbrough	0
Jan 31	Plymouth	4	Barnsley	1
Jan 31	Preston	2	Blackpool	1
Jan 31	Tottenham	4	West Stanley	0
Jan 31	West Ham	6	Bury	0
Jan 31	Wolverhampton	1	Cardiff	2

Replay

Feb 04	Sunderland	2	Burnley	0

3rd Round

Feb 21	Aston Villa	1	Sunderland	0
Feb 21	Bristol C	2	Cardiff	1
Feb 21	Chelsea	3	Leicester	0
Feb 21	Huddersfield	3	Plymouth	1
Feb 21	Liverpool	2	Birmingham	0
Feb 21	Notts Co	3	Bradford	4
Feb 21	Preston	0	Bradford C	3
Feb 21	Tottenham	3	West Ham	0

4th Round

Mar 06	Bristol C	2	Bradford C	0
Mar 06	Chelsea	4	Bradford	1
Mar 06	Huddersfield	2	Liverpool	1
Mar 06	Tottenham	0	Aston Villa	1

Semi-finals

Mar 27	Aston Villa	3	Chelsea	1
	played at Sheffield U			
Mar 27	Bristol C	1	Huddersfield	2
	played at Chelsea			

Final

Apr 24	Aston Villa	1	Huddersfield	0
	played at Chelsea			

Season 1920-21

1st Round

Jan 08	Aston Villa	2	Bristol C	0
Jan 08	Blackburn	1	Fulham	1
Jan 08	Bradford	1	Clapton O	0
Jan 08	Bradford C	3	Barnsley	1
Jan 08	Brentford	1	Huddersfield	2
Jan 08	Brighton	4	Oldham	1
Jan 08	Crystal Palace	2	Manchester C	0
Jan 08	Darlington	2	Blackpool	2
Jan 08	Derby	2	Middlesbrough	0
Jan 08	Everton	1	Stockport	0
Jan 08	Grimsby	1	Norwich	0
Jan 08	Hull	3	Bath	0
Jan 08	Leicester	3	Burnley	7
Jan 08	Liverpool	1	Manchester U	1
Jan 08	Luton	2	Birmingham	1
Jan 08	Millwall	0	Lincoln	3
Jan 08	Newcastle	1	Nottingham F	1
Jan 08	Northampton	0	Southampton	0
Jan 08	Notts Co	3	W.B.A.	0
Jan 08	Plymouth	2	Rochdale	0
Jan 08	Preston	2	Bolton	0
Jan 08	Q.P.R.	2	Arsenal	0
Jan 08	Reading	0	Chelsea	0
Jan 08	Sheffield W	1	West Ham	0
Jan 08	South Shields	3	Portsmouth	0
Jan 08	Southend	5	Eccles	1
Jan 08	Sunderland	0	Cardiff	1
Jan 08	Swansea	3	Bury	0
Jan 08	Swindon	1	Sheffield U	0
Jan 08	Tottenham	6	Bristol R	2
Jan 08	Watford	3	Exeter	0
Jan 08	Wolverhampton	3	Stoke	2

Replays

Jan 12	Blackpool	2	Darlington	1
Jan 12	Chelsea	2	Reading	2
Jan 12	Manchester U	1	Liverpool	2
Jan 12	Nottingham F	0	Newcastle	2
	played at Newcastle			
Jan 12	Southampton	4	Northampton	1
Jan 13	Fulham	1	Blackburn	0
Jan 17	Chelsea	3	Reading	1
	played at Chelsea			

2nd Round

Jan 29	Bradford	0	Huddersfield	1
Jan 29	Brighton	0	Cardiff	0
Jan 29	Burnley	4	Q.P.R.	2
Jan 29	Crystal Palace	0	Hull	2
Jan 29	Derby	1	Wolverhampton	1
Jan 29	Everton	1	Sheffield W	1
Jan 29	Grimsby	1	Southampton	3
Jan 29	Lincoln	0	Fulham	0
Jan 29	Newcastle	1	Liverpool	0
Jan 29	Notts Co	0	Aston Villa	0
Jan 29	Preston	4	Watford	1
Jan 29	South Shields	0	Luton	4
Jan 29	Southend	1	Blackpool	0
Jan 29	Swansea	1	Plymouth	2
Jan 29	Swindon	0	Chelsea	2
Jan 29	Tottenham	4	Bradford C	0

Replays

Feb 02	Aston Villa	1	Notts Co	0
Feb 02	Cardiff	1	Brighton	0
Feb 03	Sheffield W	0	Everton	1

Feb 03 Wolverhampton 1 Derby 0
Feb 07 Fulham 1 Lincoln 0

3rd Round
Feb 19 Aston Villa 2 Huddersfield 0
Feb 19 Everton 3 Newcastle 0
Feb 19 Fulham 0 Wolverhampton 1
Feb 19 Hull 3 Burnley 0
Feb 19 Luton 2 Preston 3
Feb 19 Plymouth 0 Chelsea 0
Feb 19 Southampton 0 Cardiff 1
Feb 19 Southend 1 Tottenham 4

Replays
Feb 24 Chelsea 0 Plymouth 0
Feb 28 Chelsea 2 Plymouth 1
played at Bristol C

4th Round
Mar 05 Cardiff 1 Chelsea 0
Mar 05 Everton 0 Wolverhampton 1
Mar 05 Hull 0 Preston 0
Mar 05 Tottenham 1 Aston Villa 0

Replay
Mar 10 Preston 1 Hull 0

Semi-final
Mar 19 Cardiff 0 Wolverhampton 0
played at Liverpool
Mar 19 Preston 1 Tottenham 2
played at Sheffield W

Replay
Mar 23 Cardiff 1 Wolverhampton 3
played at Manchester U

Final
Apr 23 Tottenham 1 Wolverhampton 0
played at Chelsea

Season 1921-22

1st Round
Jan 07 Arsenal 0 Q.P.R. 0
Jan 07 Aston Villa 6 Derby 1
Jan 07 Barnsley 1 Norwich 1
Jan 07 Blackburn 1 Southport 1
Jan 07 Blackpool 1 Watford 2
Jan 07 Bolton 1 Bury 0
Jan 07 Bradford 1 Sheffield W 0
Jan 07 Brentford 0 Tottenham 2
Jan 07 Brighton 1 Sheffield U 0
Jan 07 Bristol C 0 Nottingham F 0
Jan 07 Burnley 2 Huddersfield 2
Jan 07 Chelsea 2 W.B.A. 4
Jan 07 Everton 0 Crystal Palace 6
Jan 07 Gillingham 1 Oldham 3
Jan 07 Grimsby 1 Notts Co 1
Jan 07 Hull 5 Middlesbrough 0
Jan 07 Leicester 2 Clapton O 0
Jan 07 Manchester C 3 Darlington 1
Jan 07 Manchester U 1 Cardiff 4
Jan 07 Millwall 4 Ashington 2
Jan 07 Newcastle 6 Newport 0
Jan 07 Northampton 3 Reading 0
Jan 07 Plymouth 1 Fulham 1
Jan 07 Port Vale 2 Stoke 4
Jan 07 Portsmouth 1 Luton 1
Jan 07 Preston 3 Wolverhampton 0
Jan 07 Southampton 3 South Shields 1
Jan 07 Sunderland 1 Liverpool 1
Jan 07 Swansea 0 West Ham 0
Jan 07 Swindon 2 Leeds 1
Jan 07 Walsall 3 Bradford C 3
Jan 07 Worksop 1 Southend 2

Replays
Jan 11 Bradford C 4 Walsall 0
Jan 11 Fulham 1 Plymouth 0
Jan 11 Huddersfield 3 Burnley 2
Jan 11 Liverpool 5 Sunderland 0
Jan 11 Luton 2 Portsmouth 1
Jan 11 Nottingham F 3 Bristol C 1
Jan 11 Q.P.R. 1 Arsenal 2
Jan 11 West Ham 1 Swansea 1
Jan 12 Norwich 1 Barnsley 2
Jan 12 Notts Co 3 Grimsby 0
Jan 12 Southport 0 Blackburn 2
Jan 16 Swansea 1 West Ham 0
played at Bristol C

2nd Round
Jan 28 Aston Villa 1 Luton 0
Jan 28 Barnsley 3 Oldham 1
Jan 28 Bolton 1 Manchester C 3
Jan 28 Bradford 2 Arsenal 3
Jan 28 Bradford C 1 Notts Co 1
Jan 28 Brighton 0 Huddersfield 0
Jan 28 Crystal Palace 0 Millwall 0
Jan 28 Leicester 2 Fulham 0
Jan 28 Liverpool 0 W.B.A. 1
Jan 28 Northampton 2 Stoke 2
Jan 28 Nottingham F 3 Hull 0
Jan 28 Preston 3 Newcastle 1
Jan 28 Southampton 1 Cardiff 1
Jan 28 Southend 0 Swansea 1
Jan 28 Swindon 0 Blackburn 1
Jan 28 Tottenham 1 Watford 0

Replays
Feb 01 Cardiff 2 Southampton 0
Feb 01 Huddersfield 2 Brighton 0
Feb 01 Millwall 2 Crystal Palace 0
Feb 01 Notts Co 1 Bradford C 1
Feb 02 Stoke 3 Northampton 0
Feb 06 Bradford C 0 Notts Co 1
played at Sheffield U

3rd Round
Feb 18 Arsenal 3 Leicester 0
Feb 18 Barnsley 1 Preston 1
Feb 18 Blackburn 1 Huddersfield 1
Feb 18 Cardiff 4 Nottingham F 1
Feb 18 Millwall 4 Swansea 0
Feb 18 Stoke 0 Aston Villa 0
Feb 18 Tottenham 2 Manchester C 1
Feb 18 W.B.A. 1 Notts Co 1

Replays
Feb 22 Aston Villa 4 Stoke 0
Feb 22 Huddersfield 5 Blackburn 0
Feb 22 Notts Co 2 W.B.A. 0
Feb 23 Preston 3 Barnsley 0

4th Round
Mar 04 Arsenal 1 Preston 1
Mar 04 Cardiff 1 Tottenham 1
Mar 04 Huddersfield 3 Millwall 0
Mar 04 Notts Co 2 Aston Villa 2

Replays
Mar 08 Aston Villa 3 Notts Co 4
Mar 08 Preston 2 Arsenal 1
Mar 09 Tottenham 2 Cardiff 1

Semi-finals
Mar 25 Huddersfield 3 Notts Co 1
played at Burnley
Mar 25 Preston 2 Tottenham 1
played at Sheffield W

Final
Apr 29 Huddersfield 1 Preston 0
played at Stamford Bridge

Season 1922-23

1st Round
Jan 13 Aberdare 1 Preston 3
Jan 13 Aston Villa 0 Blackburn R 1
Jan 13 Blyth 0 Stoke 3
Jan 13 Bradford C 1 Manchester U 1
Jan 13 Brighton & HA 1 Corinthians 1
Jan 13 Bristol C 5 Wrexham 1
Jan 13 Bury 2 Luton 1
Jan 13 Cardiff 1 Watford 1
Jan 13 Chelsea 1 Rotherham 0
Jan 13 Clapton O 0 Millwall 2
Jan 13 Derby 2 Blackpool 0
Jan 13 Everton 1 Bradford 1
Jan 13 Huddersfield 2 Birmingham 1
Jan 13 Hull 2 West Ham 3
Jan 13 Leicester 4 Fulham 0
Jan 13 Liverpool 0 Arsenal 0
Jan 13 Manchester C 1 Charlton 2
Jan 13 Merthyr T 0 Wolverhampton 1
Jan 13 Newcastle 0 Southampton 0
Jan 13 Norwich 0 Bolton 2
Jan 13 Nottingham F 0 Sheffield U 0
Jan 13 Oldham 0 Middlesbrough 1
Jan 13 Plymouth 0 Notts Co 0
Jan 13 Portsmouth 0 Leeds 0
Jan 13 Q.P.R. 1 Crystal Palace 0
Jan 13 Sheffield W 3 New Brighton 0
Jan 13 South Shields 3 Halifax 1
Jan 13 Sunderland 3 Burnley 1
Jan 13 Swindon 0 Barnsley 0
Jan 13 Tottenham 0 Worksop 0
Jan 13 Wigan 4 Bath 1
Jan 13 W.B.A. 0 Stalybridge 0

Replays
Jan 15 Worksop 0 Tottenham 9
played at Tottenham
Jan 17 Arsenal 1 Liverpool 4
Jan 17 Bradford 1 Everton 0
Jan 17 Corinthians 1 Brighton 1
played at Crystal Palace
Jan 17 Leeds 3 Portsmouth 1
Jan 17 Manchester U 2 Bradford C 0
Jan 17 Notts Co 0 Plymouth 1
Jan 17 Southampton 3 Newcastle 1
Jan 17 Stalybridge 0 W.B.A. 2
Jan 17 Watford 2 Cardiff 2
Jan 18 Barnsley 2 Swindon 0
Jan 18 Sheffield U 0 Nottingham F 0
Jan 22 Brighton 1 Corinthians 0
played at Chelsea
Jan 22 Cardiff 2 Watford 1
played at Aston Villa
Jan 22 Nottingham F 1 Sheffield U 1
played at Notts Co
Jan 25 Nottingham F 0 Sheffield U 1
played at Sheffield W

2nd Round
Feb 03 Bolton 3 Leeds 1
Feb 03 Brighton 1 West Ham 1
Feb 03 Bristol 0 Derby 3
Feb 03 Bury 3 Stoke 1
Feb 03 Charlton 2 Preston 0
Feb 03 Chelsea 0 Southampton 0
Feb 03 Leicester 0 Cardiff 1
Feb 03 Middlesbrough 1 Sheffield U 1
Feb 03 Millwall 0 Huddersfield 0
Feb 03 Plymouth 4 Bradford C 1
Feb 03 Sheffield W 2 Barnsley 1
Feb 03 South Shields 0 Blackburn 0
Feb 03 Tottenham 4 Manchester U 0
Feb 03 W.B.A. 2 Sunderland 1
Feb 03 Wigan 2 Q.P.R. 4
Feb 03 Wolverhampton 0 Liverpool 2

Replays
Feb 07 Huddersfield 3 Millwall 0
Feb 07 Southampton 1 Chelsea 0
Feb 07 West Ham 1 Brighton 0
Feb 08 Blackburn 0 South Shields 1
Feb 08 Sheffield U 3 Middlesbrough 0

3rd Round
Feb 24 Bury 0 Southampton 0
Feb 24 Cardiff 2 Tottenham 3
Feb 24 Charlton 1 W.B.A. 0
Feb 24 Derby 1 Sheffield W 0
Feb 24 Huddersfield 1 Bolton 1
Feb 24 Liverpool 1 Sheffield U 2
Feb 24 Q.P.R. 3 South Shields 0
Feb 24 West Ham 2 Plymouth 0

Replays
Feb 28 Bolton 1 Huddersfield 0
Feb 28 Southampton 1 Bury 0

4th Round
Mar 10 Charlton 0 Bolton 1
Mar 10 Q.P.R. 0 Sheffield U 1
Mar 10 Southampton 1 West Ham 1
Mar 10 Tottenham 0 Derby 1

Replays
Mar 14 West Ham 1 Southampton 1
Mar 19 Southampton 0 West Ham 1
played at Aston Villa

Semi-finals
Mar 24 Bolton 1 Sheffield U 0
played at Manchester U
Mar 24 Derby 2 West Ham 5
played at Chelsea

Final
Apr 28 Bolton 2 West Ham 0
played at Wembley

Season 1923-24

1st Round

Jan 12	Accrington	0	Charlton	0
Jan 12	Arsenal	4	Luton	1
Jan 12	Ashington	1	Aston Villa	5
Jan 12	Barnsley	0	Brighton	0
Jan 12	Blackpool	1	Sheffield U	0
Jan 12	Burnley	3	South Shields	2
Jan 12	Crystal Palace	2	Tottenham	0
Jan 12	Cardiff	0	Gillingham	0
Jan 12	Chelsea	1	Southampton	1
Jan 12	Corinthians	1	Blackburn	0
	played at Crystal Palace			
Jan 12	Derby	2	Bury	1
Jan 12	Everton	3	Preston	1
Jan 12	Exeter	1	Grimsby	0
Jan 12	Fulham	2	Llanelly	0
Jan 12	Huddersfield	1	Birmingham	0
Jan 12	Hull	2	Bolton	2
Jan 12	Leeds	1	Stoke	0
Jan 12	Liverpool	2	Bradford C	1
Jan 12	Manchester C	2	Nottingham F	0
Jan 12	Manchester U	1	Plymouth	0
Jan 12	Middlesbrough	0	Watford	1
Jan 12	Millwall	0	W.B.A.	1
Jan 12	Northampton	1	Halifax	1
Jan 12	Norwich	0	Bristol C	1
Jan 12	Oldham	2	Sunderland	1
Jan 12	Portsmouth	2	Newcastle	4
Jan 12	Q.P.R.	1	Notts Co	2
Jan 12	Sheffield W	4	Leicester	1
Jan 12	Swansea	1	Clapton O	1
Jan 12	Swindon	4	Bradford	0
Jan 12	West Ham	5	Aberdare	0
Jan 12	Wolverhampton	3	Darlington	1

Replays

Jan 16	Bolton	4	Hull	0
Jan 16	Brighton	1	Barnsley	0
Jan 16	Gillingham	0	Cardiff	2
Jan 16	Southampton	2	Chelsea	0
Jan 17	Charlton	1	Accrington	0
Jan 17	Clapton O	1	Swansea	1
Jan 17	Halifax	1	Northampton	1
Jan 21	Clapton O	1	Swansea	2
	played at Tottenham			
Jan 21	Halifax	4	Northampton	2
	played at Sheffield U			

2nd Round

Feb 02	Bolton	1	Liverpool	4
Feb 02	Brighton	5	Everton	2
Feb 02	Burnley	0	Fulham	0
Feb 02	Crystal Palace	0	Notts Co	0
Feb 02	Cardiff	1	Arsenal	0
Feb 02	Charlton	0	Wolverhampton	0
Feb 02	Derby	2	Newcastle	2
Feb 02	Exeter	0	Watford	0
Feb 02	Manchester C	2	Halifax	2
Feb 02	Manchester U	0	Huddersfield	3
Feb 02	Sheffield W	1	Bristol C	1
Feb 02	Southampton	3	Blackpool	1
Feb 02	Swansea	0	Aston Villa	2
Feb 02	Swindon	2	Oldham	0
Feb 02	W.B.A.	5	Corinthians	0
Feb 02	West Ham	1	Leeds	1

Replays

Feb 06	Bristol C	2	Sheffield W	0
Feb 06	Halifax	0	Manchester C	0
Feb 06	Leeds	1	West Ham	0
Feb 06	Newcastle	2	Derby	2
Feb 06	Notts Co	0	Crystal Palace	0
Feb 06	Watford	1	Exeter	0
Feb 07	Fulham	0	Burnley	1
Feb 07	Wolverhampton	1	Charlton	0
Feb 11	Crystal Palace	0	Notts Co	0
	played at Aston Villa			
Feb 11	Derby	2	Newcastle	2
	played at Bolton			
Feb 11	Halifax	0	Manchester C	3
	played at Manchester U			
Feb 13	Derby	3	Newcastle	5
	played at Newcastle			
Feb 18	Crystal Palace	2	Notts Co	1
	played at Aston Villa			

3rd Round

Feb 23	Aston Villa	3	Leeds	0
Feb 23	Brighton	1	Manchester C	5
Feb 23	Burnley	1	Huddersfield	0
Feb 23	Crystal Palace	1	Swindon	2
Feb 23	Cardiff	3	Bristol C	0
Feb 23	Southampton	0	Liverpool	0
Feb 23	W.B.A.	1	Wolverhampton	1
Feb 23	Watford	0	Newcastle	1

Replays

Feb 27	Liverpool	2	Southampton	0
Feb 27	Wolverhampton	0	W.B.A.	2

4th Round

Mar 08	Manchester C	0	Cardiff	0
Mar 08	Newcastle	1	Liverpool	0
Mar 08	Swindon	1	Burnley	1
Mar 08	W.B.A.	0	Aston Villa	2

Replays

Mar 12	Burnley	3	Swindon	1
Mar 12	Cardiff	0	Manchester C	1

Semi-finals

Mar 29	Aston Villa	3	Burnley	0
	played at Sheffield U			
Mar 29	Manchester C	0	Newcastle	2
	played at Birmingham			

Final

Apr 26	Aston Villa	0	Newcastle	2
	played at Wembley			

Goalmouth action during the 1924 FA Cup Final at Wembley.

Season 1924-25

1st Round

Jan 10	Accrington	2	Portsmouth	5
Jan 10	Aston Villa	7	Port Vale	2
Jan 10	Birmingham	2	Chelsea	0
Jan 10	Blackburn	1	Oldham	0
Jan 10	Blackpool	0	Barrow	0
Jan 10	Bolton	3	Huddersfield	0
Jan 10	Bradford	1	Middlesbrough	0
Jan 10	Bristol R	0	Bristol C	1
Jan 10	Bury	0	Sunderland	3
Jan 10	Cardiff	0	Darlington	0
Jan 10	Coventry	2	Notts Co	2
Jan 10	Crystal Palace	2	South Shields	1
Jan 10	Derby	0	Bradford C	1
Jan 10	Doncaster	1	Norwich	2
Jan 10	Everton	2	Burnley	1
Jan 10	Hull	1	Wolverhampton	1
Jan 10	Leicester	3	Stoke	0
Jan 10	Liverpool	3	Leeds	0
Jan 10	Millwall	0	Barnsley	0
Jan 10	Newcastle	4	Hartlepool	1
Jan 10	Nottingham F	1	Clapton O	0
Jan 10	Preston	4	Manchester C	1
Jan 10	Q.P.R.	1	Stockport	3
Jan 10	Sheffield U	5	Corinthians	0
Jan 10	Sheffield W	2	Manchester U	0
Jan 14	Southampton	3	Exeter	1

Jan 10	Swansea	3	Plymouth	0
Jan 10	Swindon	1	Fulham	2
Jan 10	Tottenham	3	Northampton	0
Jan 10	Watford	1	Brighton	1
Jan 10	West Ham	0	Arsenal	0
Jan 10	W.B.A.	4	Luton	0

Replays

Jan 14	Arsenal	2	West Ham	2
Jan 14	Barrow	0	Blackpool	2
Jan 14	Brighton	4	Watford	3
Jan 14	Darlington	0	Cardiff	0
Jan 15	Barnsley	2	Millwall	1
Jan 15	Wolverhampton	0	Hull	1
Jan 19	Cardiff	2	Darlington	0
	played at Liverpool			
Jan 21	Arsenal	0	West Ham	1
	played at Chelsea			

2nd Round

Jan 31	Barnsley	0	Bradford C	3
Jan 31	Birmingham	1	Stockport	0
Jan 31	Blackburn	0	Portsmouth	0
Jan 31	Bradford	1	Blackpool	1
Jan 31	Bristol C	0	Liverpool	1
Jan 31	Cardiff	1	Fulham	0
Jan 31	Hull	3	Crystal Palace	2
Jan 31	Newcastle	2	Leicester	2
Jan 31	Nottingham F	0	West Ham	2
Jan 31	Notts Co	4	Norwich	0
Jan 31	Sheffield U	3	Sheffield W	2
Jan 31	Southampton	1	Brighton	0
Jan 31	Sunderland	0	Everton	0
Jan 31	Swansea	1	Aston Villa	3
Jan 31	Tottenham	1	Bolton	1
Jan 31	W.B.A.	2	Preston	0

Replays

Feb 04	Blackpool	2	Bradford	1
Feb 04	Bolton	0	Tottenham	1
Feb 04	Everton	2	Sunderland	1
Feb 04	Portsmouth	0	Blackburn	0
Feb 05	Leicester	1	Newcastle	0
Feb 09	Blackburn	1	Portsmouth	0
	played at Arsenal			

3rd Round

Feb 21	Hull	1	Leicester	1
Feb 21	Liverpool	2	Birmingham	1
Feb 21	Notts Co	0	Cardiff	2
Feb 21	Sheffield U	1	Everton	0
Feb 21	Southampton	2	Bradford C	0
Feb 21	Tottenham	2	Blackburn	2
Feb 21	W.B.A.	1	Aston Villa	1
Feb 21	West Ham	1	Blackpool	1

Replays

Feb 25	Aston Villa	1	W.B.A.	2
Feb 25	Blackpool	3	West Ham	0
Feb 26	Blackburn	3	Tottenham	1
Feb 26	Leicester	3	Hull	1

4th Round

Mar 07	Blackburn	1	Blackpool	0
Mar 07	Cardiff	2	Leicester	1
Mar 07	Sheffield U	2	W.B.A.	0
Mar 07	Southampton	1	Liverpool	0

Semi-final

Mar 28	Blackburn	1	Cardiff	3
	played at Notts Co			
Mar 28	Sheffield U	2	Southampton	0
	played at Chelsea			

Final

Apr 25	Cardiff	0	Sheffield U	1
	played at Wembley			

Season 1925-26

1st Round

Nov 28	Aberdare	4	Bristol R	1
Nov 28	Accrington	4	Wrexham	0
Nov 28	Blyth	2	Hartlepool	2
Nov 28	Boston	5	Mansfield	2
Nov 28	Bournemouth	3	Merthyr T	0
Nov 28	Bradford	2	Lincoln	2
Nov 28	Brentford	3	Barnet	1
Nov 28	Brighton	1	Watford	1
Nov 28	Carlisle	0	Chilton Coll	2
Nov 28	Charlton	4	Windsor & Eton	2
Nov 28	Chatham	0	Sittingbourne	3
Nov 28	Clapton	3	Norwich	1
Nov 28	Doncaster	2	Wellington	0
Dec 02	Durham	4	Ashington	1
Nov 28	Exeter	1	Swansea	3
Nov 28	Farnham	1	Swindon	10
Nov 28	Gillingham	6	Southall	0
Nov 28	Halifax	0	Rotherham	3
Nov 28	Horden	2	Darlington	3
Nov 28	Leyton	1	St Albans	0
Nov 28	London Cal	1	Ilford	2
Nov 28	Luton	3	Folkestone	0
Nov 28	New Brighton	2	Barrow	0
Nov 28	Northampton	3	Barnsley	1
Nov 28	Northfleet	2	Q.P.R.	2
Nov 28	Oldham	10	Lytham	1
Dec 01	Rochdale	4	West Stanley	0
Dec 03	Southbank	1	Stockton	4
Nov 28	Southend	5	DulwichH	1
Nov 28	Southport	1	Mold	0
Nov 28	Torquay	1	Reading	1
Nov 28	Tranmere	0	Crewe	0
Nov 28	Walsall	0	Grimsby	1
Nov 28	Wath	0	Chesterfield	5
Nov 28	Weymouth	0	Newport	1
Dec 02	Wigan	3	Nelson	0
Nov 28	Worcester	0	Kettering	0
Nov 28	Worksop	1	Coventry	0

Replays

Dec 02	Crewe	2	Tranmere	1
Dec 02	Hartlepool	1	Blyth	1
Dec 02	Lincoln	1	Bradford	1
Dec 02	Reading	1	Torquay	1
Dec 02	Watford	2	Brighton	0
Dec 03	Kettering	0	Worcester	0
Dec 03	Q.P.R.	2	Northfleet	0
Dec 07	Blyth	1	Hartlepool	1
	played at Newcastle			
Dec 07	Bradford	2	Lincoln	1
	played at Sheffield U			
Dec 07	Kettering	2	Worcester	0
	played at Birmingham			
Dec 07	Reading	2	Torquay	0
	played at Bristol C			
Dec 09	Blyth	2	Hartlepool	1
	played at Sunderland			

2nd Round

Dec 12	Aberdare	1	Luton	0
Dec 12	Accrington	5	Blyth	0
Dec 12	Boston	1	Bradford	0
Dec 12	Brentford	1	Bournemouth	2
Dec 12	Chilton Coll	1	Rochdale	1
Dec 12	Clapton	1	Ilford	0
Dec 12	Crewe	2	Wigan	2
Dec 12	Doncaster	0	Rotherham	2
Dec 12	Durham	0	Southport	3
Dec 12	Kettering	1	Grimsby	1
Dec 12	New Brighton	2	Darlington	0
Dec 12	Northampton	3	Newport	1
Dec 12	Q.P.R.	1	Charlton	1
Dec 12	Reading	6	Leyton	0
Dec 12	Southend	1	Gillingham	0
Dec 12	Stockton	4	Oldham	6
Dec 12	Swansea	3	Watford	2
Dec 12	Swindon	7	Sittingbourne	0
Dec 12	Worksop	1	Chesterfield	2

Replays

Dec 15	Grimsby	3	Kettering	1
Dec 16	Wigan	2	Crewe	1
Dec 17	Charlton	1	Q.P.R.	0
Dec 17	Rochdale	1	Chilton Coll	2

3rd Round

Jan 09	Birmingham	2	Grimsby	0
Jan 09	Blackburn	1	Preston	1
Jan 09	Blackpool	0	Swansea	2
Jan 09	Bolton	1	Accrington	0
Jan 09	Bournemouth	2	Reading	0
Jan 09	Cardiff	2	Burnley	2
Jan 09	Charlton	0	Huddersfield	1
Jan 09	Chesterfield	0	Clapton O	1
Jan 09	Clapton	2	Swindon	3
Jan 09	Corinthians	3	Manchester C	3
Jan 09	Derby	0	Portsmouth	0
Jan 09	Everton	1	Fulham	1
Jan 09	Hull	0	Aston Villa	3
Jan 09	Middlesbrough	5	Leeds	1
Jan 09	Millwall	1	Oldham	1
Jan 09	New Brighton	2	Sheffield W	1
Jan 09	Newcastle	4	Aberdare	1
Jan 09	Northampton	3	Crystal Palace	3
Jan 09	Nottingham F	1	Bradford C	0
Jan 09	Notts Co	2	Leicester	0
Jan 09	Plymouth	1	Chelsea	2
Jan 09	Port Vale	2	Manchester U	3
Jan 09	Rotherham	2	Bury	3
Jan 09	Sheffield U	2	Stockport	0
Jan 09	South Shields	3	Chilton Coll	0
Jan 09	Southampton	0	Liverpool	0
Jan 09	Southend	5	Southport	2
Jan 09	Sunderland	8	Boston	1
Jan 09	Tottenham	5	West Ham	0
Jan 09	Wigan	2	Stoke	5
Jan 09	Wolverhampton	1	Arsenal	1
Jan 09	W.B.A.	4	Bristol C	1

Replays

Jan 12	Oldham	0	Millwall	1
Jan 13	Arsenal	1	Wolverhampton	0
Jan 13	Burnley	0	Cardiff	2
Jan 13	Crystal Palace	2	Northampton	1
Jan 13	Liverpool	1	Southampton	0
Jan 13	Manchester C	4	Corinthians	0
Jan 13	Portsmouth	1	Derby	1
Jan 14	Fulham	1	Everton	0
Jan 14	Preston	1	Blackburn	4
Jan 18	Derby	2	Portsmouth	0
	played at Leicester			

4th Round

Jan 30	Arsenal	3	Blackburn	1
Jan 30	Bournemouth	2	Bolton	2
Jan 30	Bury	3	Millwall	3
Jan 30	Cardiff	0	Newcastle	2
Jan 30	Clapton O	4	Middlesbrough	2
Jan 30	Crystal Palace	2	Chelsea	1
Jan 30	Fulham	3	Liverpool	1
Jan 30	Manchester C	4	Huddersfield	0
Jan 30	Nottingham F	2	Swindon	0
Jan 30	Notts Co	2	New Brighton	0
Jan 30	Sheffield U	1	Sunderland	2
Jan 30	South Shields	2	Birmingham	1
Jan 30	Southend	4	Derby	1
Jan 30	Swansea	6	Stoke	3
Jan 30	Tottenham	2	Manchester U	2
Jan 30	W.B.A.	1	Aston Villa	2

Replays

Feb 03	Bolton	6	Bournemouth	2
Feb 03	Manchester U	2	Tottenham	0
Feb 04	Millwall	2	Bury	0

5th Round

Feb 20	Aston Villa	1	Arsenal	1
Feb 20	Bolton	3	South Shields	0
Feb 20	Clapton O	2	Newcastle	0
Feb 20	Manchester C	11	Crystal Palace	4
Feb 20	Millwall	0	Swansea	1
Feb 20	Notts Co	0	Fulham	1
Feb 20	Southend	0	Nottingham F	1
Feb 20	Sunderland	3	Manchester U	3

Replays

Feb 24	Arsenal	2	Aston Villa	0
Feb 24	Manchester U	2	Sunderland	1

6th Round

Mar 06	Clapton O	1	Manchester C	6
Mar 06	Fulham	1	Manchester U	2
Mar 06	Nottingham F	2	Bolton	2
Mar 06	Swansea	2	Arsenal	1

Replays

Mar 10	Bolton	0	Nottingham F	0
Mar 15	Bolton	1	Nottingham F	0
	played at Manchester U			

Semi-finals

Mar 27	Bolton	3	Swansea	0
	played at Tottenham			
Mar 27	Manchester C	3	Manchester U	0
	played at Sheffield U			

Final

Apr 24	Bolton	1	Manchester C	0
	played at Wembley			

Season 1926-27

1st Round

Nov 27	Accrington	4	Rochdale	3
Nov 27	Annfield	2	Chilton Coll	4
Nov 27	Barking	0	Gillingham	0
Nov 27	Bishop Auckland	0	Bedlington	1
Nov 27	Boston	1	Northampton	1
Nov 27	Bournemouth	1	Swindon	1
Nov 27	Brighton	3	Barnet	0
Nov 27	Carlisle	6	Hartlepool	2
Nov 27	Chatham	3	St Albans	1
Dec 01	Chesterfield	2	Mexborough	1
Nov 27	Clapton	1	Brentford	1
Dec 01	Crewe	4	Nomads	1
Nov 27	Crystal Palace	0	Norwich	0
Dec 02	Doncaster	3	Desborough	0
Nov 27	DulwichH	1	Southend	4
Nov 27	Exeter	3	Aberdare	0
Nov 27	Grimsby	3	Halifax	2
Nov 27	Kettering	2	Coventry	3
Nov 27	Lincoln	2	Rotherham	0
Nov 27	Luton	4	London Cal	2
Nov 27	Merthyr T	0	Bristol C	2
Nov 27	Nelson	4	Stockport	1
Nov 27	Nunhead	9	Kingstonian	0
Nov 27	Poole	1	Newport	0
Nov 27	Reading	4	Weymouth	4
Nov 27	Rhyl	1	Stoke	1
Nov 27	Sittingbourne	1	Northfleet	3
Nov 27	Southport	1	Tranmere	1
Nov 27	Stockton	1	Ashington	2
Nov 27	Torquay	1	Bristol R	1
Nov 27	Walsall	1	Bradford	0
Nov 27	Watford	10	Lowestoft	1
Nov 27	Wellington	1	Mansfield	2
Dec 02	Wigan	2	Barrow	2
Nov 27	Woking	1	Charlton	3
Nov 27	Workington	1	Crook	2
Nov 27	Wrexham	1	New Brighton	1
Dec 01	York	4	Worksop	1

Replays

Nov 29	Swindon	3	Bournemouth	4
Dec 01	Brentford	7	Clapton	3
Dec 01	Bristol R	1	Torquay	0
Dec 01	Gillingham	2	Barking	0
Dec 01	New Brighton	2	Wrexham	2
Dec 01	Reading	5	Weymouth	0
Dec 02	Northampton	2	Boston	1
Dec 02	Norwich	1	Crystal Palace	0
Dec 02	Stoke	1	Rhyl	1
Dec 02	Tranmere	1	Southport	2
Dec 06	Barrow	0	Wigan	1
Dec 06	New Brighton	1	Wrexham	3
	played at Liverpool			
Dec 06	Rhyl	2	Stoke	1
	played at Manchester U			

2nd Round

Dec 11	Ashington	2	Nelson	1
Dec 11	Bristol C	1	Bournemouth	1
Dec 11	Bristol R	4	Charlton	1
Dec 11	Carlisle	4	Bedlington	0
Dec 11	Chilton Coll	0	Accrington	3
Dec 11	Coventry	1	Lincoln	1
Dec 11	Crewe	4	Wigan	1
Dec 11	Doncaster	0	Chesterfield	1
Dec 11	Exeter	1	Northampton	0
Dec 11	Gillingham	1	Brentford	1
Dec 11	Grimsby	2	York	1
Dec 11	Luton	6	Northfleet	2
Dec 11	Norwich	5	Chatham	0
Dec 11	Nunhead	1	Poole	2
Dec 11	Reading	3	Southend	2
Dec 11	Rhyl	3	Wrexham	1
Dec 11	Southport	2	Crook	0
Dec 11	Walsall	2	Mansfield	0
Dec 11	Watford	0	Brighton	1

Replays

Dec 15	Bournemouth	2	Bristol C	0
Dec 15	Brentford	1	Gillingham	0
Dec 15	Lincoln	2	Coventry	1

3rd Round

Jan 08	Ashington	0	Nottingham F	2
Jan 08	Barnsley	6	Crewe	1
Jan 08	Birmingham	4	Manchester C	1
Jan 08	Blackpool	1	Bolton	3
Jan 08	Bournemouth	1	Liverpool	1
Jan 08	Bradford C	2	Derby	6
Jan 08	Bristol R	3	Portsmouth	3
Jan 08	Burnley	3	Grimsby	1
Jan 08	Cardiff	2	Aston Villa	1
Jan 08	Carlisle	0	Wolverhampton	2
Jan 08	Chelsea	4	Luton	0
Jan 08	Clapton O	1	Port Vale	1
Jan 08	Darlington	2	Rhyl	1
Jan 08	Everton	3	Poole	1
Jan 08	Exeter	0	Accrington	2
Jan 08	Fulham	4	Chesterfield	3
Jan 08	Hull	2	W.B.A.	1
Jan 08	Leeds	3	Sunderland	2
Jan 08	Lincoln	2	Preston	4
Jan 08	Middlesbrough	5	Leicester	3
Jan 08	Millwall	3	Huddersfield	1
Jan 08	Newcastle	8	Notts Co	1
Jan 10	Oldham	2	Brentford	4
Jan 08	Reading	1	Manchester U	1
Jan 08	Sheffield U	2	Arsenal	3
Jan 08	Sheffield W	2	Brighton	0
Jan 08	South Shields	3	Plymouth	1
Jan 08	Southampton	3	Norwich	0
Jan 08	Southport	2	Blackburn	0
Jan 08	Swansea	4	Bury	1
Jan 08	Walsall	0	Corinthians	4
Jan 08	West Ham	3	Tottenham	2

Replays

Jan 12	Liverpool	4	Bournemouth	1
Jan 12	Manchester U	2	Reading	2
Jan 12	Port Vale	5	Clapton O	1
Jan 12	Portsmouth	4	Bristol R	0
Jan 17	Manchester U	1	Reading	2
	played at Aston Villa			

4th Round

Jan 29	Barnsley	1	Swansea	3
Jan 29	Chelsea	7	Accrington	2
Jan 29	Corinthians	1	Newcastle	3
Jan 29	Darlington	0	Cardiff	2
Jan 29	Derby	0	Millwall	2
Jan 29	Fulham	0	Burnley	4
Jan 29	Hull	1	Everton	1
Jan 29	Leeds	0	Bolton	0
Jan 29	Liverpool	3	Southport	1
Jan 29	Port Vale	2	Arsenal	2
Jan 29	Preston	0	Middlesbrough	3
Jan 29	Reading	3	Portsmouth	1
Jan 29	Sheffield W	1	South Shields	1
Jan 29	Southampton	4	Birmingham	1
Jan 29	West Ham	1	Brentford	1
Jan 29	Wolverhampton	2	Nottingham F	0

Replays

Feb 02	Arsenal	1	Port Vale	0
Feb 02	Bolton	3	Leeds	0
Feb 02	Brentford	2	West Ham	0
Feb 02	Everton	2	Hull	2
Feb 02	South Shields	1	Sheffield W	0
Feb 07	Everton	2	Hull	3
	played at Aston Villa			

5th Round

Feb 19	Arsenal	2	Liverpool	0
Feb 19	Bolton	0	Cardiff	2
Feb 19	Chelsea	2	Burnley	1
Feb 19	Millwall	3	Middlesbrough	2
Feb 19	Reading	1	Brentford	0
Feb 19	South Shields	2	Swansea	2
Feb 19	Southampton	2	Newcastle	1
Feb 19	Wolverhampton	1	Hull	0

Replays

Feb 24	Swansea	2	South Shields	1

6th Round

Mar 05	Arsenal	2	Wolverhampton	1
Mar 05	Chelsea	0	Cardiff	0
Mar 05	Millwall	0	Southampton	0
Mar 05	Swansea	1	Reading	3

Replays

Mar 09	Cardiff	3	Chelsea	2
Mar 09	Southampton	2	Millwall	0

Semi-finals

Mar 26	Arsenal	2	Southampton	1
	played at Chelsea			
Mar 26	Cardiff	3	Reading	0
	played at Wolverhampton			

Final

Apr 23	Arsenal	0	Cardiff	1
	played at Wembley			

Cardiff City's goal under seige in the 1927 Final against Arsenal. But the Bluebirds took the Cup out of England for the first time.

SEASON 1927-28

1st Round

Nov 26	Accrington	2	Lincoln	5
Nov 30	Aldershot	2	Q.P.R.	1
Nov 26	Bath	2	Southall	0
Nov 30	Botwell Mission	3	Peterborough	4
Nov 26	Bradford C	6	Workington	0
Nov 26	Bristol R	4	Walsall	2
Nov 26	Carlisle	2	Doncaster	1
Nov 26	Coventry	2	Bournemouth	2
Nov 26	Crewe	2	Ashington	2
Nov 26	Darlington	4	Chesterfield	1
Nov 26	Dartford	1	Crystal Palace	3
Nov 26	Denaby	2	Southport	3
Nov 26	Durham	1	Wrexham	1
Nov 26	Exeter	9	Aberdare	1
Nov 26	Gainsborough	6	Stockton	0
Nov 26	Gillingham	2	Plymouth	1
Nov 26	Halifax	3	Hartlepool	0
Nov 26	Ilford	4	Dulwich H	0
Nov 26	Kettering	2	Chatham	0
Nov 30	Luton	9	Clapton	0
Nov 26	Merthyr T	0	Charlton	0
Nov 26	Nelson	0	Bradford	3
Nov 26	Newport	0	Swindon	1
Nov 26	Northampton	8	Leyton	0
Nov 26	Northfleet	0	London Cal	1
Nov 26	Poole	1	Norwich	1
Nov 26	Rhyl	4	Wigan	3
Nov 26	Rochdale	8	Crook	2
Nov 26	Shildon	1	New Brighton	3
Nov 26	Shirebrook	1	Tranmere	3
Nov 26	Southend	1	Wellington	0
Nov 26	Spennymoor	1	Rotherham	1
Nov 26	Stockport	5	Oswestry	2
Nov 30	Watford	1	Brighton	2

Replays

Nov 30	Ashington	0	Crewe	2
Nov 30	Bournemouth	2	Coventry	0
Nov 30	Charlton	2	Merthyr T	1
Nov 30	Wrexham	4	Durham	0
Dec 01	Norwich	5	Poole	0
Dec 01	Rotherham	4	Spennymoor	2

2nd Round

Dec 10	Bournemouth	6	Bristol R	1
Dec 10	Bradford	0	Southport	2
Dec 10	Bradford C	2	Rotherham	3

Dec 10 Charlton 1 Kettering 1
Dec 10 Crewe 2 Stockport 0
Dec 10 Darlington 2 Rochdale 1
Dec 10 Exeter 5 Ilford 3
Dec 10 Gainsborough 0 Lincoln 2
Dec 10 Gillingham 2 Southend 0
Dec 10 London Cal 1 Bath 0
Dec 10 Luton 6 Norwich 0
Dec 10 New Brighton 7 Rhyl 2
Dec 10 Northampton 1 Brighton 0
Dec 10 Peterborough 2 Aldershot 1
Dec 10 Swindon 0 Crystal Palace 0
Dec 10 Tranmere 3 Halifax 1
Dec 10 Wrexham 1 Carlisle 0

Replays
Dec 14 Crystal Palace 1 Swindon 2
Dec 15 Kettering 1 Charlton 2

3rd Round
Jan 14 Arsenal 2 W.B.A. 0
Jan 14 Birmingham 4 Peterborough 3
Jan 14 Blackburn 4 Newcastle 1
Jan 14 Blackpool 1 Oldham 4
Jan 14 Bolton 2 Luton 1
Jan 14 Bristol C 1 Tottenham 2
Jan 14 Burnley 0 Aston Villa 2
Jan 14 Cardiff 2 Southampton 1
Jan 14 Charlton 1 Bury 1
Jan 14 Huddersfield 4 Lincoln 2
Jan 14 Hull 0 Leicester 1
Jan 14 Liverpool 1 Darlington 0
Jan 14 London Cal 2 Crewe 3
played at Chelsea
Jan 14 Manchester C 1 Leeds 0
Jan 14 Manchester U 7 Brentford 1
Jan 14 Middlesbrough 3 South Shields 0
Jan 14 Millwall 1 Derby 2
Jan 14 New Brighton 2 Corinthians 1
Jan 14 Nottingham F 1 Tranmere 0
Jan 14 Notts Co 2 Sheffield U 3
Jan 14 Port Vale 3 Barnsley 0
Jan 14 Portsmouth 0 West Ham 2
Jan 14 Preston 0 Everton 3
Jan 14 Reading 4 Grimsby 0
Jan 14 Rotherham 3 Exeter 3
Jan 14 Sheffield W 3 Bournemouth 0
Jan 14 Southport 3 Fulham 0
Jan 14 Stoke 6 Gillingham 1
Jan 14 Sunderland 3 Northampton 3
Jan 14 Swindon 2 Clapton O 1
Jan 14 Wolverhampton 2 Chelsea 1
Jan 14 Wrexham 2 Swansea 1

Replays
Jan 18 Bury 4 Charlton 3
Jan 18 Exeter 3 Rotherham 1
Jan 19 Northampton 0 Sunderland 3

4th Round
Jan 28 Arsenal 4 Everton 3
Jan 28 Aston Villa 3 Crewe 0
Jan 28 Bury 1 Manchester U 1
Jan 28 Cardiff 2 Liverpool 1
Jan 28 Derby 0 Nottingham F 0
Jan 28 Exeter 2 Blackburn 2
Jan 28 Huddersfield 2 West Ham 1
Jan 28 Port Vale 3 New Brighton 0
Jan 28 Reading 0 Leicester 1
Jan 28 Sheffield U 3 Wolverhampton 1
Jan 28 Southport 0 Middlesbrough 3
Jan 28 Stoke 4 Bolton 2
Jan 28 Sunderland 1 Manchester C 2
Jan 28 Swindon 1 Sheffield W 2
Jan 28 Tottenham 3 Oldham 0
Jan 28 Wrexham 1 Birmingham 3

Replays
Feb 01 Manchester U 1 Bury 0
Feb 01 Nottingham F 2 Derby 0
Feb 02 Blackburn 3 Exeter 1

5th Round
Feb 18 Arsenal 4 Aston Villa 1
Feb 18 Blackburn 2 Port Vale 1
Feb 18 Huddersfield 4 Middlesbrough 0
Feb 18 Leicester 0 Tottenham 3
Feb 18 Manchester C 0 Stoke 1
Feb 18 Manchester U 1 Birmingham 0
Feb 18 Nottingham F 2 Cardiff 1
Feb 18 Sheffield W 1 Sheffield U 1

Replays
Feb 22 Sheffield U 4 Sheffield W 1

6th Round
Mar 03 Arsenal 4 Stoke 1
Mar 03 Blackburn 2 Manchester U 0
Mar 03 Huddersfield 6 Tottenham 1
Mar 03 Sheffield U 3 Nottingham F 0

Semi-finals
Mar 24 Arsenal 0 Blackburn 1
played at Leicester
Mar 24 Huddersfield 2 Sheffield U 2
played at Manchester U

Replays
Mar 26 Huddersfield 0 Sheffield U 0
played at Everton
Apr 02 Huddersfield 1 Sheffield U 0
played at Manchester C

Final
Apr 21 Blackburn 3 Huddersfield 1
played at Wembley

Season 1928-29

1st Round
Nov 24 Accrington 2 South Shields 1
Nov 24 Annfield 1 Southport 4
Nov 24 Bradford C 4 Doncaster 1
Nov 24 Brentford 4 Broughton 1
Nov 24 Bristol R 2 Wellingborough 1
Nov 24 Chesterfield 3 Rochdale 2
Nov 24 Coventry 1 Fulham 4
Nov 24 Crystal Palace 2 Kettering 0
Nov 24 Darlington 3 New Brighton 0
Nov 24 Exeter 6 Barking 0
Nov 24 Gainsborough 3 Crewe 1
Nov 24 Gillingham 0 Torquay 0
Nov 24 Grantham 1 Rhyl 0
Nov 24 Guildford 4 Q.P.R. 2
Nov 24 Horwich 1 Scarborough 2
Nov 24 Lancaster 1 Lincoln 3
Nov 24 Leyton 0 Watford 2
Nov 24 Luton 5 Southend 1
Nov 24 Merthyr T 4 DulwichH 2
Nov 24 Newport 7 Woking 0
Nov 24 Northfleet 5 Ilford 2
Nov 24 Norwich 6 Chatham 1
Nov 24 Peterborough 0 Charlton 2
Nov 24 Poole 1 Bournemouth 4
Nov 24 Shirebrook 2 Mansfield 4
Nov 24 Sittingbourne 2 Southall 1
Nov 24 Spennymoor 5 Hartlepool 2
Nov 24 Stockport 1 Halifax 0
Nov 24 Tranmere 2 Rotherham 1
Nov 24 Walsall 3 Worcester 1
Nov 24 Wigan 2 Ashington 0
Nov 24 Wrexham 0 Carlisle 1
Nov 24 Yeovil 1 Plymouth 4
Nov 24 York 0 Barrow 1

Replays
Nov 28 Torquay 5 Gillingham 1

2nd Round
Dec 08 Accrington 7 Spennymoor 0
Dec 08 Barrow 1 Mansfield 2
Dec 08 Brentford 0 Plymouth 1
Dec 08 Carlisle 0 Lincoln 1
Dec 08 Crystal Palace 3 Bristol R 1
Dec 08 Fulham 0 Luton 0
Dec 08 Gainsborough 2 Chesterfield 3
Dec 08 Guildford 1 Bournemouth 5
Dec 08 Northfleet 1 Charlton 5
Dec 08 Norwich 6 Newport 0
Dec 08 Scarborough 2 Darlington 2
Dec 08 Stockport 3 Southport 0
Dec 08 Torquay 0 Exeter 1
Dec 08 Tranmere 0 Bradford C 1
Dec 08 Walsall 2 Sittingbourne 1
Dec 08 Watford 2 Merthyr T 0
Dec 08 Wigan 2 Grantham 1

Replays
Dec 12 Darlington 2 Scarborough 1
Dec 13 Luton 4 Fulham 1

3rd Round
Jan 12 Accrington 1 Bournemouth 1
Jan 12 Arsenal 2 Stoke 1
Jan 12 Aston Villa 6 Cardiff 1
Jan 12 Birmingham 3 Manchester C 1
Jan 12 Blackburn 1 Barnsley 0
Jan 12 Bolton 2 Oldham 0
Jan 12 Bradford C 2 Stockport 0
Jan 12 Bristol C 0 Liverpool 2
Jan 12 Burnley 2 Sheffield U 1
Jan 12 Chelsea 1 Everton 0
Jan 12 Chesterfield 1 Huddersfield 7
Jan 12 Darlington 2 Bury 6
Jan 12 Derby 4 Notts Co 3
Jan 12 Exeter 2 Leeds 2
Jan 12 Grimsby 1 W.B.A. 1
Jan 12 Hull 1 Bradford 1
Jan 12 Lincoln 0 Leicester 1
Jan 12 Luton 0 Crystal Palace 0
Jan 12 Millwall 1 Northampton 1
Jan 12 Norwich 0 Corinthians 5
Jan 12 Nottingham F 1 Swansea 2
Jan 12 Plymouth 3 Blackpool 0
Jan 12 Port Vale 0 Manchester U 3
Jan 12 Portsmouth 2 Charlton 1
Jan 12 Reading 2 Tottenham 0
Jan 12 Southampton 0 Clapton O 0
Jan 12 Swindon 2 Newcastle 0
Jan 12 Walsall 1 Middlesbrough 1
Jan 12 Watford 1 Preston 0
Jan 12 West Ham 1 Sunderland 0
Jan 12 Wigan 1 Sheffield W 3
Jan 12 Wolverhampton 0 Mansfield 1

Replays
Jan 16 Bournemouth 2 Accrington 0
Jan 16 Bradford 3 Hull 1
Jan 16 Crystal Palace 7 Luton 0
Jan 16 Leeds 5 Exeter 1
Jan 16 W.B.A. 2 Grimsby 0
Jan 17 Clapton O 2 Southampton 1
Jan 17 Northampton 2 Millwall 2
Jan 21 Middlesbrough 5 Walsall 1
Jan 21 Millwall 2 Northampton 0
played at Arsenal

4th Round
Jan 26 Arsenal 2 Mansfield 0
Jan 26 Aston Villa 0 Clapton O 0
Jan 26 Blackburn 1 Derby 1
Jan 26 Bournemouth 6 Watford 4
Jan 26 Burnley 3 Swindon 3
Jan 26 Chelsea 1 Birmingham 0
Jan 26 Huddersfield 3 Leeds 0
Jan 26 Leicester 1 Swansea 0
Jan 26 Liverpool 0 Bolton 0
Jan 26 Manchester U 0 Bury 1
Jan 26 Millwall 0 Crystal Palace 0
Jan 26 Plymouth 0 Bradford 1
Jan 26 Portsmouth 2 Bradford C 0
Jan 26 Reading 1 Sheffield W 0
Jan 26 West Ham 3 Corinthians 0
Jan 26 W.B.A. 1 Middlesbrough 0

Replays
Jan 31 Bolton 5 Liverpool 2
Jan 31 Clapton O 0 Aston Villa 8
Jan 31 Crystal Palace 5 Millwall 3
Jan 31 Derby 0 Blackburn 3
Jan 31 Swindon 3 Burnley 2

5th Round
Feb 16 Blackburn 1 Bury 0
Feb 16 Bournemouth 1 West Ham 1
Feb 16 Chelsea 1 Portsmouth 1
Feb 16 Huddersfield 5 Crystal Palace 2
Feb 16 Leicester 1 Bolton 2
Feb 16 Reading 1 Aston Villa 3
Feb 16 Swindon 0 Arsenal 0
Feb 16 W.B.A. 6 Bradford 0

Replays
Feb 20 Arsenal 1 Swindon 0
Feb 20 Portsmouth 1 Chelsea 0
Feb 20 West Ham 3 Bournemouth 1

6th Round
Mar 02 Aston Villa 1 Arsenal 0
Mar 02 Blackburn 1 Bolton 1
Mar 02 Portsmouth 3 West Ham 2
Mar 02 W.B.A. 1 Huddersfield 1

Replays
Mar 06 Bolton 2 Blackburn 1
Mar 06 Huddersfield 2 W.B.A. 1

Semi-finals
Mar 23 Aston Villa 0 Portsmouth 1
played at Arsenal
Mar 23 Bolton 3 Huddersfield 1
played at Liverpool

Final
Apr 27 Bolton 2 Portsmouth 0
played at Wembley

Season 1929-30

1st Round
Nov 30 Accrington 3 Rochdale 1
Nov 30 Aldershot 0 Northampton 1
Nov 30 Barrow 1 Newark 0
Nov 30 Barry 0 Dagenham 0
Nov 30 Bournemouth 2 Torquay 0
Nov 30 Brighton 4 Peterborough 0
Nov 30 Caernarvon 4 Darlington 2
Nov 30 Carlisle 2 Halifax 0
Nov 30 Clapton 0 Folkestone 0
Nov 30 Doncaster 0 Shildon 0
Nov 30 Dulwich 0 Plymouth 3
Nov 30 Fulham 4 Thames 0
Nov 30 Gainsborough 0 Port Vale 0
Nov 30 Gillingham 0 Margate 2
Nov 30 Ilford 0 Watford 3
Nov 30 Leyton 4 Merthyr 1
Nov 30 Lincoln 3 Wigan 1
Nov 30 Luton 2 Q.P.R. 3
Nov 30 Mansfield 0 Manchester Central 2
Nov 30 Nelson 0 Crewe 3
Nov 30 New Brighton 4 Lancaster 1
Nov 30 Newport 3 Kettering 2
Nov 30 Norwich 3 Coventry 3

Date	Home		Away	
Nov 30	Nunhead	0	Bristol R	2
Nov 30	Rotherham	3	Ashington	0
Nov 30	Scunthorpe	1	Hartlepool	0
Nov 30	South Shields	2	Wrexham	4
Nov 30	Southend	1	Brentford	0
Nov 30	Southport	0	Chesterfield	0
Nov 30	Tunbridge	1	Bath	3
Nov 30	Walsall	1	Exeter	0
Nov 30	Wellington	1	Stockport	4
Nov 30	Wimbledon	1	Northfleet	4
Nov 30	York	2	Tranmere	2

Replays

Date	Home		Away	
Dec 04	Chesterfield	3	Southport	2
Dec 04	Dagenham	0	Barry	1
Dec 04	Folkestone	2	Clapton	2
Dec 04	Port Vale	5	Gainsborough	0
Dec 04	Shildon	1	Doncaster	1
Dec 05	Coventry	2	Norwich	0
Dec 05	Tranmere	0	York	1
Dec 09	Clapton O	4	Folkestone	1
	played at Arsenal			
Dec 09	Doncaster	3	Shildon	0
	played at York			

2nd Round

Date	Home		Away	
Dec 14	Brighton	4	Barry	1
Dec 14	Bristol R	4	Accrington	1
Dec 14	Caernarvon	1	Bournemouth	1
Dec 14	Carlisle	4	Crewe	2
Dec 14	Chesterfield	2	Port Vale	0
Dec 14	Clapton O	2	Northfleet	0
Dec 14	Coventry	7	Bath	1
Dec 14	Doncaster	1	New Brighton	0
Dec 14	Leyton O	1	Fulham	4
Dec 14	Manchester Central	0	Wrexham	1
Dec 14	Newport	2	Walsall	3
Dec 14	Northampton	6	Margate	0
Dec 14	Q.P.R.	2	Lincoln	1
Dec 14	Scunthorpe	3	Rotherham	3
Dec 14	Southend	1	York	4
Dec 14	Stockport	4	Barrow	0
Dec 14	Watford	1	Plymouth	1

Replays

Date	Home		Away	
Dec 18	Bournemouth	5	Caernarvon	2
Dec 18	Plymouth	3	Watford	0
Dec 19	Rotherham	5	Scunthorpe	4

3rd Round

Date	Home		Away	
Jan 11	Arsenal	2	Chelsea	0
Jan 11	Aston Villa	5	Reading	1
Jan 11	Barnsley	0	Bradford	1
Jan 11	Birmingham	1	Bolton	0
Jan 11	Blackburn	4	Northampton	1
Jan 11	Blackpool	2	Stockport	1
Jan 11	Bradford	4	Southampton	1
Jan 11	Brighton	1	Grimsby	1
Jan 11	Bury	0	Huddersfield	0
Jan 11	Carlisle	2	Everton	4
Jan 11	Charlton	1	Q.P.R.	1
Jan 11	Chesterfield	1	Middlesbrough	1
Jan 11	Clapton	1	Bristol R	0
Jan 11	Corinthians	2	Millwall	2
Jan 11	Coventry	1	Sunderland	2
Jan 11	Derby	5	Bristol C	1
Jan 16	Doncaster	1	Stoke C	0
Jan 11	Fulham	1	Bournemouth	1
Jan 11	Leeds	8	Crystal Palace	1
Jan 11	Liverpool	1	Cardiff	2
Jan 11	Manchester U	0	Swindon	2
Jan 11	Newcastle	1	York	1
Jan 11	Oldham	1	Wolverhampton	0
Jan 11	Plymouth	3	Hull	4
Jan 11	Portsmouth	2	Preston	0
Jan 11	Rotherham	0	Nottingham F	5
Jan 11	Sheffield U	2	Leicester	1
Jan 11	Sheffield W	1	Burnley	0
Jan 11	Tottenham	2	Manchester C	2
Jan 11	Walsall	2	Swansea	0
Jan 11	West Ham	4	Notts Co	0
Jan 11	Wrexham	1	W.B.A.	0

Replays

Date	Home		Away	
Jan 14	Grimsby	0	Brighton	1
Jan 15	Bournemouth	0	Fulham	2
Jan 15	Huddersfield	3	Bury	1
Jan 15	Manchester C	4	Tottenham	1
Jan 15	Middlesbrough	4	Chesterfield	3
Jan 15	Millwall	1	Corinthians	1
Jan 15	York	1	Newcastle	2
Jan 16	Q.P.R.	0	Charlton	3
Jan 20	Corinthians	1	Millwall	5
	played at Chelsea			

4th Round

Date	Home		Away	
Jan 25	Arsenal	2	Birmingham	2
Jan 25	Aston Villa	3	Walsall	1
Jan 25	Blackburn	4	Everton	1
Jan 25	Derby	1	Bradford	1
Jan 25	Huddersfield	2	Sheffield U	1
Jan 25	Hull	3	Blackpool	1
Jan 25	Middlesbrough	1	Charlton	1
Jan 25	Millwall	4	Doncaster	0
Jan 25	Newcastle	3	Clapton	1
Jan 25	Nottingham F	2	Fulham	1
Jan 25	Oldham	3	Sheffield W	4
Jan 25	Portsmouth	0	Brighton	1
Jan 25	Sunderland	2	Cardiff	1
Jan 25	Swindon	1	Manchester C	1
Jan 25	West Ham	4	Leeds	1
Jan 25	Wrexham	0	Bradford C	0

Replays

Date	Home		Away	
Jan 27	Bradford	2	Wrexham	1
Jan 29	Birmingham	0	Arsenal	1
Jan 29	Bradford	2	Derby	1
Jan 29	Charlton	1	Middlesbrough	1
Jan 29	Manchester C	10	Swindon	1
Feb 03	Charlton	0	Middlesbrough	1
	played at Manchester C			

5th Round

Date	Home		Away	
Feb 15	Aston Villa	4	Blackburn	1
Feb 15	Huddersfield	2	Bradford C	1
Feb 15	Manchester C	1	Hull	2
Feb 15	Middlesbrough	0	Arsenal	2
Feb 15	Newcastle	3	Brighton	0
Feb 15	Sheffield W	5	Bradford	1
Feb 15	Sunderland	2	Nottingham F	2
Feb 15	West Ham	4	Millwall	1

Replay

Date	Home		Away	
Feb 19	Nottingham	3	Sunderland	1

6th Round

Date	Home		Away	
Mar 01	Aston Villa	1	Huddersfield	2
Mar 01	Newcastle	1	Hull	1
Mar 01	Nottingham F	2	Sheffield W	2
Mar 01	West Ham	0	Arsenal	3

Replays

Date	Home		Away	
Mar 05	Sheffield W	3	Nottingham F	1
Mar 06	Hull	1	Newcastle	0

Semi-finals

Date	Home		Away	
Mar 22	Arsenal	2	Hull	2
	played at Leeds			
Mar 22	Huddersfield	2	Sheffield W	1
	played at Manchester U			

Replays

Date	Home		Away	
Mar 26	Arsenal	1	Hull	0
	played at Aston Villa			

Final

Date	Home		Away	
Apr 26	Arsenal	2	Huddersfield	0
	played at Wembley			

Season 1930-31

1st Round

Date	Home		Away	
Nov 29	Accrington	3	Lancaster	1
Nov 29	Aldershot	4	Peterborough	1
Nov 29	Bristol R	4	Merthyr T	1
Nov 29	Carlisle	3	New Brighton	1
Nov 29	Chesterfield	1	Notts Co	2
Nov 29	Crewe	1	Jarrow	0
Nov 29	Crystal Palace	6	Taunton	0
Nov 29	DulwichH	2	Newport	2
Nov 29	Folkestone	5	Sittingbourne	3
Nov 29	Fulham	1	Wimbledon	1
Nov 29	Gainsborough	1	Scunthorpe	0
Nov 29	Gillingham	7	Guildford	2
Nov 29	Halifax	2	Mansfield	2
Nov 29	Hartlepool	2	Stockport	3
Nov 29	Ilford	1	Brentford	6
Nov 29	Lincoln	8	Barrow	3
Nov 29	Luton	2	Clapton O	2
Nov 29	Nelson	4	Workington	0
Nov 29	Newark	2	Rotherham	1
Nov 29	Northampton	1	Coventry	2
Nov 29	Northfleet	0	Exeter	3
Nov 29	Norwich	2	Swindon	0
Nov 29	Q.P.R.	5	Thames	0
Nov 29	Rochdale	1	Doncaster	2
Nov 29	Scarborough	6	Rhyl	0
Nov 29	Southend	0	Torquay	1
Nov 29	Southport	4	Darlington	2
Nov 29	Tranmere	4	Gateshead	4
Nov 29	Tunbridge Wells	3	Kingstonians	0
Nov 29	Walsall	1	Bournemouth	0
Nov 29	Walthamstow	1	Watford	5
Nov 29	Wellington	0	Wombwell	0
Nov 29	Wrexham	2	Wigan	0
Nov 29	York	3	Gresley	1

Replays

Date	Home		Away	
Dec 03	Gateshead	3	Tranmere	2
Dec 03	Mansfield	1	Halifax	2
Dec 03	Wimbledon	0	Fulham	6
Dec 04	Clapton O	2	Luton	4
Dec 04	Newport	4	DulwichH	1
Dec 04	Wombwell	0	Wellington	3

2nd Round

Date	Home		Away	
Dec 13	Accrington	0	Torquay	1
Dec 13	Brentford	1	Norwich	0
Dec 13	Bristol R	4	Stockport	2
Dec 13	Carlisle	4	Tunbridge Wells	2
Dec 13	Crystal Palace	6	Newark	0
Dec 13	Doncaster	0	Notts Co	1
Dec 13	Exeter	1	Coventry	1
Dec 13	Fulham	4	Halifax	0
Dec 13	Gainsborough	0	Southport	4
Dec 13	Gateshead	3	Folkestone	2
Dec 13	Gillingham	1	Aldershot	3
Dec 13	Nelson	1	York	1
Dec 13	Q.P.R.	4	Crewe	2
Dec 13	Scarborough	6	Lincoln	4
Dec 13	Walsall	4	Newport	0
Dec 13	Watford	3	Luton	1
Dec 13	Wellington	2	Wrexham	4

Replays

Date	Home		Away	
Dec 18	Coventry	1	Exeter	2
Dec 18	York	3	Nelson	2

3rd Round

Date	Home		Away	
Jan 10	Aldershot	0	Bradford	1
Jan 10	Arsenal	2	Aston Villa	2
Jan 10	Barnsley	4	Bristol C	1
Jan 10	Blackburn	1	Walsall	1
Jan 10	Bolton	1	Carlisle	0
Jan 10	Brentford	2	Cardiff	2
Jan 10	Bristol R	3	Q.P.R.	1
Jan 10	Burnley	3	Manchester C	0
Jan 10	Bury	1	Torquay	1
Jan 10	Corinthians	1	Port Vale	3
Jan 10	Crystal Palace	1	Reading	1
Jan 10	Exeter	3	Derby	2
Jan 10	Fulham	0	Portsmouth	2
Jan 10	Gateshead	2	Sheffield W	6
Jan 10	Hull	1	Blackpool	2
Jan 10	Leeds	2	Huddersfield	0
Jan 10	Leicester	1	Brighton	2
Jan 10	Liverpool	0	Birmingham	2
Jan 10	Newcastle	4	Nottingham F	0
Jan 10	Notts Co	3	Swansea	1
Jan 10	Oldham	1	Watford	3
Jan 10	Plymouth	0	Everton	2
Jan 10	Scarborough	1	Grimsby	2
Jan 10	Sheffield U	1	York	1
Jan 10	Southport	3	Millwall	1
Jan 10	Stoke	3	Manchester U	3
Jan 10	Sunderland	2	Southampton	0
Jan 10	Tottenham	3	Preston	1
Jan 10	West Ham	1	Chelsea	3
Jan 10	Wolverhampton	9	Wrexham	1
Jan 10	W.B.A.	2	Charlton	2
Jan 14	Middlesbrough	1	Bradford C	1

Replays

Date	Home		Away	
Jan 14	Aston Villa	1	Arsenal	3
Jan 14	Cardiff	1	Brentford	2
Jan 14	Charlton	1	W.B.A.	1
Jan 14	Manchester U	0	Stoke	0
Jan 14	Reading	1	Crystal Palace	1
Jan 14	Torquay	1	Bury	2
Jan 14	York	0	Sheffield U	2
Jan 15	Walsall	0	Blackburn	3
Jan 19	Bradford C	2	Middlesbrough	1
Jan 19	Charlton	1	W.B.A.	3
	played at Aston Villa			
Jan 19	Crystal Palace	2	Reading	0
	played at Chelsea			
Jan 19	Manchester U	4	Stoke	2
	played at Liverpool			

4th Round

Date	Home		Away	
Jan 24	Barnsley	2	Sheffield W	1
Jan 24	Birmingham	2	Port Vale	0
Jan 24	Blackburn	5	Bristol R	1
Jan 24	Bolton	1	Sunderland	1
Jan 24	Bradford	0	Wolverhampton	0
Jan 24	Bradford	2	Burnley	0
Jan 24	Brentford	0	Portsmouth	1
Jan 24	Bury	1	Exeter	2
Jan 24	Chelsea	2	Arsenal	1
Jan 24	Crystal Palace	0	Everton	6
Jan 24	Grimsby	1	Manchester U	0
Jan 24	Leeds	4	Newcastle	1
Jan 24	Sheffield U	4	Notts Co	1
Jan 24	Southport	2	Blackpool	1
Jan 24	Watford	2	Brighton	0
Jan 24	W.B.A.	1	Tottenham	0

Replays

Date	Home		Away	
Jan 28	Sunderland	3	Bolton	1
Jan 28	Wolverhampton	4	Bradford	2

5th Round

Date	Home		Away	
Feb 14	Barnsley	1	Wolverhampton	3
Feb 14	Birmingham	3	Watford	0
Feb 14	Chelsea	3	Blackburn	0
Feb 14	Everton	5	Grimsby	3
Feb 14	Exeter	3	Leeds	1
Feb 14	Portsmouth	0	W.B.A.	1
Feb 14	Southport	1	Bradford	0
Feb 14	Sunderland	2	Sheffield U	1

6th Round

Date	Home		Away	
Feb 28	Birmingham	2	Chelsea	2
Feb 28	Everton	9	Southport	1
Feb 28	Sunderland	1	Exeter	1
Feb 28	W.B.A.	1	Wolverhampton	1

Replays

Date	Home		Away	
Mar 04	Chelsea	0	Birmingham	3
Mar 04	Exeter	2	Sunderland	4
Mar 04	Wolverhampton	1	W.B.A.	2

Semi-finals

Date	Home		Away	
Mar 14	Birmingham	2	Sunderland	0
	played at Leeds			
Mar 14	Everton	0	W.B.A.	1
	played at Manchester U			

Final

Date	Home		Away	
Apr 25	Birmingham	1	W.B.A.	2
	played at Wembley			

Season 1931-32

1st Round

Date	Home		Away	
Nov 28	Aldershot	7	Chelmsford	0
Nov 28	Barnet	3	Q.P.R.	7
Nov 28	Barrow	3	Doncaster	3
Nov 28	Bath	9	Nunhead	0
Nov 28	Bournemouth	1	Northfleet	1
Nov 28	Bristol R	5	Gillingham	1
	Burton	W	Wigan	0
Nov 28	Cardiff	8	Enfield	0
Nov 28	Chester	4	Hartlepool	1
Nov 28	Coventry	2	Clapton O	2
Nov 28	Crewe	2	Gainsborough	2
Nov 28	Crook	3	Stockport	1
Nov 28	Darlington	1	Walsall	0
Nov 28	Darwen	4	Peterborough	1
Nov 28	Folkestone	2	Brighton	5
Nov 28	Fulham	2	Guildford	0
Nov 28	Gateshead	3	Wrexham	2
Nov 28	Hull	4	Mansfield	1
Nov 28	Lancaster	0	Blyth S	3
Nov 28	Manchester Cen	0	Lincoln	3
Nov 28	New Brighton	3	York	1
Nov 28	Newark	1	Halifax	1
Nov 28	Northampton	9	Metropolitan Po	0
Nov 28	Reading	0	Crystal Palace	1
Nov 28	Rotherham	0	Accrington	0
Nov 28	Scunthorpe	2	Rochdale	1
Nov 28	Swindon	0	Luton	5
Nov 28	Thames	2	Watford	2
Nov 28	Torquay	1	Southend	3
Nov 28	Tranmere	3	West Stanley	0
Nov 28	Tunbridge Wells	1	Brentford	1
Nov 28	Wimbledon	1	Norwich	3
Nov 28	Yeovil	3	Hayes	1
Nov 28	York Amateurs	1	Carlisle	3

Replays

Date	Home		Away	
Dec 02	Accrington	5	Rotherham	0
Dec 02	Brentford	2	Tunbridge Wells	1
Dec 02	Gainsborough	1	Crewe	0
Dec 02	Halifax	2	Newark	1
Dec 02	Northfleet	0	Bournemouth	1
Dec 02	Watford	3	Thames	2
Dec 03	Clapton O	2	Coventry	0
Dec 03	Doncaster	1	Barrow	1
Dec 07	Barrow	1	Doncaster	1
	played at Manchester C			
Dec 09	Barrow	0	Doncaster	1
	played at Leeds			

2nd Round

Date	Home		Away	
Dec 12	Aldershot	1	Crook	1
Dec 12	Bath	2	Crystal Palace	1
Dec 12	Bournemouth	1	Blyth S	0
Dec 12	Brentford	4	Norwich	1
Dec 12	Brighton	5	Doncaster	0
Dec 12	Burton	4	Gateshead	1
Dec 12	Cardiff	4	Clapton O	0
Dec 12	Carlisle	0	Darlington	2
Dec 12	Darwen	2	Chester	1
Dec 12	Fulham	0	Yeovil	0
Dec 12	Gainsborough	2	Watford	5
Dec 12	Halifax	3	Accrington	0
Dec 12	Lincoln	2	Luton	2
Dec 12	New Brighton	0	Hull	4
Dec 12	Northampton	3	Southend	0
Dec 12	Scunthorpe	1	Q.P.R.	4
Dec 12	Tranmere	2	Bristol R	0

Replays

Date	Home		Away	
Dec 16	Crook	1	Aldershot	0
Dec 16	Luton	4	Lincoln	1
Dec 17	Yeovil	2	Fulham	5

3rd Round

Date	Home		Away	
Jan 09	Arsenal	11	Darwen	1
Jan 09	Barnsley	0	Southport	0
Jan 09	Birmingham	1	Bradford C	0
Jan 09	Blackpool	1	Newcastle	1
Jan 09	Bradford	2	Cardiff	0
Jan 09	Brentford	2	Bath	0
Jan 09	Brighton	1	Port Vale	2
Jan 09	Burnley	0	Derby	4
Jan 09	Burton	0	Blackburn	4
Jan 09	Bury	2	Swansea	1
Jan 09	Charlton	1	West Ham	2
Jan 09	Chesterfield	5	Nottingham F	2
Jan 09	Darlington	1	Northampton	1
Jan 09	Everton	1	Liverpool	2
Jan 09	Grimsby	4	Exeter	1
Jan 09	Halifax	1	Bournemouth	3
Jan 09	Leicester	7	Crook	0
Jan 09	Luton	1	Wolverhampton	2
Jan 09	Middlesbrough	1	Portsmouth	1
Jan 09	Millwall	2	Manchester C	3
Jan 09	Notts Co	2	Bristol C	2
Jan 09	Oldham	1	Huddersfield	1
Jan 09	Plymouth	4	Manchester U	1
Jan 09	Preston	0	Bolton	0
Jan 09	Q.P.R.	3	Leeds	1
Jan 09	Sheffield U	2	Corinthians	1
Jan 09	Stoke	3	Hull	0
Jan 09	Sunderland	0	Southampton	0
Jan 09	Tottenham	2	Sheffield W	2
Jan 09	Tranmere	2	Chelsea	2
Jan 09	Watford	1	Fulham	1
Jan 09	W.B.A.	1	Aston Villa	2

Replays

Date	Home		Away	
Jan 12	Southport	4	Barnsley	1
Jan 13	Bolton	2	Preston	5
Jan 13	Bristol C	3	Notts Co	2
Jan 13	Chelsea	5	Tranmere	3
Jan 13	Huddersfield	6	Oldham	0
Jan 13	Newcastle	1	Blackpool	0
Jan 13	Portsmouth	3	Middlesbrough	0
Jan 13	Sheffield W	3	Tottenham	1
Jan 13	Southampton	2	Sunderland	4
Jan 14	Fulham	0	Watford	3
Jan 14	Northampton	2	Darlington	0

4th Round

Date	Home		Away	
Jan 23	Arsenal	4	Plymouth	2
Jan 23	Bradford	4	Northampton	2
Jan 23	Bury	3	Sheffield U	1
Jan 23	Chelsea	3	West Ham	1
Jan 23	Chesterfield	2	Liverpool	4
Jan 23	Derby	3	Blackburn	2
Jan 23	Grimsby	2	Birmingham	1
Jan 23	Huddersfield	5	Q.P.R.	0
Jan 23	Manchester C	6	Brentford	1
Jan 23	Newcastle	1	Southport	1
Jan 23	Port Vale	1	Leicester	2
Jan 23	Portsmouth	1	Aston Villa	1
Jan 23	Preston	2	Wolverhampton	0
Jan 23	Sheffield W	7	Bournemouth	0
Jan 23	Sunderland	1	Stoke	1
Jan 23	Watford	2	Bristol C	1

Replays

Date	Home		Away	
Jan 26	Southport	1	Newcastle	1
Jan 27	Aston Villa	0	Portsmouth	1
Jan 28	Stoke	1	Sunderland	1
Feb 01	Newcastle	9	Southport	0
	played at Sheffield W			
Feb 01	Stoke	2	Sunderland	1
	played at Manchester C			

5th Round

Date	Home		Away	
Feb 13	Bury	3	Stoke	0
Feb 13	Huddersfield	4	Preston	0
Feb 13	Liverpool	1	Grimsby	0
Feb 13	Manchester C	3	Derby	0
Feb 13	Newcastle	3	Leicester	1
Feb 13	Portsmouth	0	Arsenal	2
Feb 13	Sheffield W	1	Chelsea	1
Feb 13	Watford	1	Bradford	0

Replays

Date	Home		Away	
Feb 17	Chelsea	2	Sheffield W	0

6th Round

Date	Home		Away	
Feb 27	Bury	3	Manchester C	4
Feb 27	Huddersfield	0	Arsenal	1
Feb 27	Liverpool	0	Chelsea	2
Feb 27	Newcastle	5	Watford	0

Semi-finals

Date	Home		Away	
Mar 12	Arsenal	1	Manchester C	0
	played at Aston Villa			
Mar 12	Chelsea	1	Newcastle	2
	played at Huddersfield			

Final

Date	Home		Away	
Apr 23	Arsenal	1	Newcastle	2
	played at Wembley			

Season 1932-33

1st Round

Date	Home		Away	
Nov 26	Accrington	2	Hereford	1
Nov 26	Barrow	0	Gateshead	1
Nov 26	Bristol C	4	Romford	0
Nov 26	Cardiff	1	Bristol R	1
Nov 26	Carlisle	1	Denaby	0
Nov 26	Chester	4	Rotherham	0
Nov 26	Clapton	0	Aldershot	1
Nov 26	Crewe	4	Crook	0
Nov 26	Crystal Palace	1	Brighton	2
Nov 26	Darlington	1	Boston	0
Nov 26	Dartford	0	Yeovil	0
Nov 26	Doncaster	4	Gainsborough	1
Nov 26	Folkestone	1	Norwich	0
Nov 26	Gillingham	1	Wycombe	1
Nov 26	Guildford	1	Coventry	2
Nov 26	Halifax	2	Darwen	0
Nov 26	Luton	2	Kingston	2
Nov 26	Margate	5	Ryde	0
Nov 26	Marine	2	Hartlepool	5
Nov 26	Merthyr	1	Q.P.R.	1
Nov 26	Newport	4	Ilford	2
Nov 26	Northampton	8	Lloyds	1
Nov 26	Reading	3	Brentford	2
Nov 26	Rochdale	0	Stockport	2
Nov 26	Southend	1	Exeter	1
Nov 26	Southport	3	Nelson	3
Nov 26	Stalybridge	2	Hull	8
Nov 26	Swindon	4	Dulwich	1
Nov 26	Torquay	0	Bournemouth	0
Nov 26	Tranmere	3	New Brighton	0
Nov 26	Walsall	4	Mansfield	1
Nov 26	Workington	5	Scunthorpe	1
Nov 26	Wrexham	3	Spennymoor	0
Nov 26	York	1	Scarborough	3

Replays

Date	Home		Away	
Nov 29	Nelson	0	Southport	4
Nov 30	Bournemouth	2	Torquay	2
Nov 30	Bristol R	4	Cardiff	1
Nov 30	Exeter	0	Southend	1
Nov 30	Kingston	2	Luton	3
Nov 30	Wycombe	2	Gillingham	4
Dec 01	Q.P.R.	5	Merthyr	1
Dec 01	Yeovil	4	Dartford	2
Dec 05	Bournemouth	2	Torquay	3
	played at Bristol C			

2nd Round

Date	Home		Away	
Dec 10	Accrington	1	Aldershot	2
Dec 10	Brighton	0	Wrexham	0
Dec 10	Bristol C	2	Tranmere	2
Dec 10	Bristol R	1	Gillingham	1
Dec 10	Carlisle	1	Hull	1
Dec 10	Chester	2	Yeovil	1
Dec 10	Crewe	0	Darlington	2
Dec 10	Folkestone	2	Newport	1
Dec 10	Gateshead	5	Margate	2
Dec 10	Halifax	2	Workington	1
Dec 10	Northampton	0	Doncaster	1
Dec 10	Reading	2	Coventry	2
Dec 10	Southend	4	Scarborough	1
Dec 10	Southport	1	Swindon	2
Dec 10	Stockport	2	Luton	3
Dec 10	Torquay	1	Q.P.R.	1
Dec 10	Walsall	2	Hartlepool	1

Replays

Date	Home		Away	
Dec 14	Gillingham	1	Bristol R	3
Dec 14	Tranmere	3	Bristol C	2
Dec 14	Wrexham	2	Brighton	3
Dec 15	Coventry	3	Reading	3
Dec 15	Hull	2	Carlisle	1
Dec 15	Q.P.R.	3	Torquay	1
Dec 19	Coventry	0	Reading	1
	played at Chelsea			

3rd Round

Date	Home		Away	
Jan 14	Aldershot	1	Bristol R	0
Jan 14	Barnsley	0	Luton	0
Jan 14	Birmingham	2	Preston	1
Jan 14	Blackpool	2	Port Vale	1
Jan 14	Bradford	5	Plymouth	1
Jan 14	Bradford C	2	Aston Villa	2
Jan 14	Brighton	2	Chelsea	1
Jan 14	Bury	2	Nottingham	2
Jan 14	Charlton	1	Bolton	5
Jan 14	Chester	5	Fulham	0
Jan 14	Corinthians	0	West Ham	2
Jan 14	Darlington	2	Q.P.R.	0
Jan 14	Doncaster	0	Halifax	3
Jan 14	Gateshead	1	Manchester C	1
Jan 14	Grimsby	3	Portsmouth	2
Jan 14	Huddersfield	2	Folkestone	0
Jan 14	Hull	0	Sunderland	2
Jan 14	Leicester	2	Everton	3
Jan 14	Lincoln	1	Blackburn	5
Jan 14	Manchester U	1	Middlesbrough	4
Jan 18	Millwall	1	Reading	1
Jan 14	Newcastle	0	Leeds	3
Jan 14	Oldham	0	Tottenham	6
Jan 14	Sheffield W	2	Chesterfield	2
Jan 14	Stoke	1	Southampton	0
Jan 14	Swansea	2	Sheffield U	3
Jan 14	Swindon	1	Burnley	2
Jan 14	Tranmere	2	Notts Co	1
Jan 14	Walsall	2	Arsenal	0
Jan 14	Watford	1	Southend	1
Jan 14	Wolverhampton	3	Derby	6
Jan 14	W.B.A.	2	Liverpool	0

Replays

Date	Home		Away	
Jan 18	Aston Villa	2	Bradford C	1
Jan 18	Chesterfield	4	Sheffield W	2
Jan 18	Luton	2	Barnsley	0
Jan 18	Manchester C	9	Gateshead	0
Jan 18	Nottingham	1	Bury	2
Jan 18	Southend	2	Watford	0
Jan 23	Reading	0	Millwall	2

4th Round

Date	Home		Away	
Jan 28	Aldershot	1	Millwall	0
Jan 28	Aston Villa	0	Sunderland	3
Jan 28	Birmingham	3	Blackburn	0
Jan 28	Blackpool	2	Huddersfield	0
Jan 28	Bolton	2	Grimsby	1
Jan 28	Brighton	2	Bradford	1
Jan 28	Burnley	3	Sheffield U	1
Jan 28	Chester	0	Halifax	0
Jan 28	Darlington	0	Chesterfield	2
Jan 28	Everton	3	Bury	1
Jan 28	Luton	2	Tottenham	0
Jan 28	Manchester C	2	Walsall	0
Jan 28	Middlesbrough	4	Stoke	1
Jan 28	Southend	2	Derby	3
Jan 28	Tranmere	0	Leeds	0
Jan 28	West Ham	2	W.B.A.	0

Replays

Date	Home		Away	
Feb 01	Leeds	4	Tranmere	0
Feb 02	Halifax	3	Chester	2

5th Round

Feb 18 Bolton 2 Manchester C 4
Feb 18 Brighton 2 West Ham 2
Feb 18 Burnley 1 Chesterfield 0
Feb 18 Derby 2 Aldershot 0
Feb 18 Everton 2 Leeds 0
Feb 18 Halifax 0 Luton 2
Feb 18 Middlesbrough 0 Birmingham 0
Feb 18 Sunderland 1 Blackpool 0

Replays
Feb 22 Birmingham 3 Middlesbrough 0
Feb 22 West Ham 1 Brighton 0

6th Round
Mar 04 Burnley 0 Manchester C 1
Mar 04 Derby 4 Sunderland 4
Mar 04 Everton 6 Luton 0
Mar 04 West Ham 4 Birmingham 0

Replays
Mar 08 Sunderland 0 Derby 1

Semi-finals
Mar 18 Derby 2 Manchester C 3
played at Huddersfield
Mar 18 Everton 2 West Ham 1
played at Wolverhampton

Final
Apr 29 Everton 3 Manchester C 0
played at Wembley

Dixie Dean (9) and Langford in City's net as Everton score their second goal in the 3-0 victory at Wembley in 1933.

SEASON 1933-34

1st Round
Nov 25 Barrow 4 Doncaster 2
Nov 25 Bath 0 Charlton 0
Nov 25 Bournemouth 3 Hayes 0
Nov 25 Cardiff 0 Aldershot 0
Nov 25 Carlisle 2 Wrexham 1
Nov 25 Cheltenham 5 Barnet 1
Nov 25 Chester 6 Darlington 1
Nov 25 Clapton O 4 Epsom 2
Nov 25 Coventry 3 Crewe 0
Nov 25 Crystal Palace 3 Norwich 0
Nov 25 Dulwich H 2 Newport 2
Nov 25 Folkestone 0 Bristol R 0
Nov 25 Gainsborough 1 Altrincham 0
Nov 25 Gateshead 5 Darwen 2
Nov 25 Halifax 3 Barnsley 2
Nov 25 Ilford 2 Swindon 4
Nov 25 Kingstonians 1 Bristol C 7
Nov 25 Lancaster 0 Stockport 1
Nov 25 London Paper M 0 Southend 1
Nov 25 New Brighton 0 Mansfield 0
Nov 25 North Shields 3 Scarborough 0
Nov 25 Northampton 2 Exeter 0
Nov 25 Northfleet 0 Dartford 2
Nov 25 Oxford 1 Gillingham 5
Nov 25 Q.P.R. 6 Kettering 0
Nov 25 Rotherham 3 South Bank 2
Nov 25 Scunthorpe 1 Accrington 1
Nov 25 Sutton 2 Rochdale 1
Nov 25 Torquay 1 Margate 1
Nov 25 Tranmere 7 Newark 0
Nov 25 Walsall 4 Spennymoor 0
Nov 25 Watford 0 Reading 3
Nov 25 Workington 1 Southport 0
Nov 25 York 2 Hartlepool 3

Replays
Nov 29 Accrington 3 Scunthorpe 0
Nov 29 Aldershot 3 Cardiff 1
Nov 29 Bristol R 3 Folkestone 1
Nov 29 Charlton 3 Bath 1
Nov 29 Mansfield 3 New Brighton 4
Nov 30 Margate 0 Torquay 2
Nov 30 Newport 6 DulwichH 2

2nd Round
Dec 09 Accrington 1 Bristol R 0
Dec 09 Bournemouth 2 Tranmere 4
Dec 09 Bristol C 2 Barrow 1
Dec 09 Carlisle 1 Cheltenham 2
Dec 09 Charlton 1 Gillingham 0
Dec 09 Gainsborough 0 Aldershot 2
Dec 09 Gateshead 1 North Shields 0
Dec 09 Halifax 1 Hartlepool 1
Dec 09 Northampton 3 Torquay 0
Dec 09 Q.P.R. 1 New Brighton 1
Dec 09 Rotherham 2 Coventry 1
Dec 09 Southend 2 Chester 1
Dec 09 Stockport 1 Crystal Palace 2
Dec 09 Sutton 1 Reading 2
Dec 09 Swindon 1 Dartford 0
Dec 09 Walsall 0 Clapton O 0
Dec 09 Workington 3 Newport 1

Replays
Dec 13 New Brighton 0 Q.P.R. 4
Dec 13 Hartlepool 1 Halifax 2
Dec 14 Clapton O 2 Walsall 0

3rd Round
Jan 13 Birmingham 2 Sheffield U 1
Jan 13 Bolton 3 Halifax 1
Jan 13 Brighton 3 Swindon 1
Jan 13 Bristol C 1 Derby 1
Jan 13 Burnley 0 Bury 0
Jan 13 Charlton 2 Port Vale 0
Jan 13 Chelsea 1 W.B.A. 1
Jan 13 Cheltenham 1 Blackpool 3
Jan 13 Chesterfield 2 Aston Villa 2
Jan 13 Crystal Palace 1 Aldershot 0
Jan 13 Grimsby 1 Clapton O 0
Jan 13 Hull 1 Brentford 0
Jan 13 Leeds 0 Preston 1
Jan 13 Leicester 3 Lincoln 0
Jan 13 Liverpool 1 Fulham 1
Jan 13 Luton 0 Arsenal 1
Jan 13 Manchester C 3 Blackburn 1
Jan 13 Manchester U 1 Portsmouth 1
Jan 13 Millwall 3 Accrington 0
Jan 13 Nottingham F 4 Q.P.R. 0
Jan 13 Plymouth 1 Huddersfield 1
Jan 13 Reading 1 Oldham 2
Jan 13 Rotherham 0 Sheffield W 3
Jan 13 Southampton 1 Northampton 1
Jan 13 Stoke 3 Bradford 0
Jan 13 Sunderland 1 Middlesbrough 1
Jan 13 Swansea 1 Notts Co 0
Jan 13 Tottenham 3 Everton 0
Jan 13 Tranmere 3 Southend 0
Jan 13 West Ham 3 Bradford C 2
Jan 13 Wolverhampton 1 Newcastle 0
Jan 13 Workington 4 Gateshead 1

Replays
Jan 17 Aston Villa 2 Chesterfield 0
Jan 17 Bury 3 Burnley 2
Jan 17 Derby 1 Bristol C 0
Jan 17 Fulham 2 Liverpool 3
Jan 17 Huddersfield 6 Plymouth 2
Jan 17 Middlesbrough 1 Sunderland 2
Jan 17 Portsmouth 4 Manchester U 1
Jan 17 W.B.A. 0 Chelsea 1
Jan 18 Northampton 1 Southampton 0

4th Round
Jan 27 Arsenal 7 Crystal Palace 0
Jan 27 Aston Villa 7 Sunderland 2
Jan 27 Birmingham 1 Charlton 0
Jan 27 Brighton 1 Bolton 1
Jan 27 Bury 1 Swansea 1
Jan 27 Chelsea 1 Nottingham F 1
Jan 27 Derby 3 Wolverhampton 0
Jan 27 Huddersfield 0 Northampton 2
Jan 27 Hull 2 Manchester C 2
Jan 27 Liverpool 3 Tranmere 1
Jan 27 Millwall 3 Leicester 6
Jan 27 Oldham 1 Sheffield W 1
Jan 27 Portsmouth 2 Grimsby 0
Jan 27 Stoke 3 Blackpool 0
Jan 27 Tottenham 4 West Ham 1
Jan 27 Workington 1 Preston 2

Replays
Jan 31 Bolton 6 Brighton 1
Jan 31 Manchester C 4 Hull 1
Jan 31 Nottingham F 0 Chelsea 3
Jan 31 Sheffield W 6 Oldham 1
Feb 01 Swansea 3 Bury 0

5th Round
Feb 17 Arsenal 1 Derby 0
Feb 17 Birmingham 1 Leicester 2
Feb 17 Liverpool 0 Bolton 3
Feb 17 Preston 4 Northampton 0
Feb 17 Sheffield W 2 Manchester C 2
Feb 17 Stoke 3 Chelsea 1
Feb 17 Swansea 0 Portsmouth 1
Feb 17 Tottenham 0 Aston Villa 1

Replays
Feb 21 Manchester C 2 Sheffield W 0

6th Round
Mar 03 Arsenal 1 Aston Villa 2
Mar 03 Bolton 0 Portsmouth 3
Mar 03 Manchester C 1 Stoke 0
Mar 03 Preston 0 Leicester 1

Semi-finals
Mar 17 Aston Villa 1 Manchester C 6
played at Huddersfield
Mar 17 Leicester 1 Portsmouth 4
played at Birmingham

Final
Apr 28 Manchester C 2 Portsmouth 1
played at Wembley

SEASON 1934-35

1st Round
Nov 24 Aldershot 4 Bournemouth 0
Nov 24 Ashford 1 Clapton O 4
Nov 24 Barry 0 Northampton 1
Nov 24 Bedford 2 Dartford 3
Nov 24 Blyth S 1 Stockport 1
Nov 24 Brighton 3 Folkestone 1
Nov 24 Bristol C 2 Gillingham 0
Nov 24 Bristol R 3 Harwich 0
Nov 24 Burton 2 York 3
Nov 24 Cardiff 1 Reading 2
Nov 24 Carlisle 1 Wigan 6
Nov 24 Charlton 2 Exeter 2
Nov 24 Chester 3 Dinnington 1
Nov 24 Coventry 7 Scunthorpe 0
Nov 24 Crewe 1 Walsall 2
Nov 24 Darwen 1 Boston 2
Nov 24 Doncaster 0 Barrow 2
Nov 24 DulwichH 1 Torquay 2
Nov 24 Gateshead 1 Darlington 4
Nov 24 Guildford 1 Bath 2
Nov 24 Halifax 1 Hartlepool 1
Nov 24 Mansfield 6 Accrington 1
Nov 24 Q.P.R. 2 Walthamstow 0

Nov 24 Rotherham ..... 2 Spennymoor 0
Nov 24 Shildon Col ..... 2 Lincoln 2
Nov 24 Southend ..... 10 Golders Green 1
Nov 24 Southport ..... 1 New Brighton 1
Nov 24 Swindon ..... 4 Newport 0
Nov 24 Tranmere ..... 3 Stalybridge 1
Nov 24 Watford ..... 2 Corinthians 0
Nov 24 Wimbledon ..... 1 Leyton 1
Nov 24 Workington ..... 2 Birmingham Ct 0
Nov 24 Wrexham ..... 4 Rochdale 1
Nov 24 Yeovil ..... 3 Crystal Palace 0

Replays
Nov 28 Exeter ..... 5 Charlton 2
Nov 28 Hartlepool ..... 2 Halifax 0
Nov 28 Lincoln ..... 4 Shildon Col 0
Nov 28 New Brighton ..... 1 Southport 1
Nov 28 Stockport ..... 4 Blyth S 1
Nov 29 Leyton ..... 0 Wimbledon 1
Dec 03 New Brighton ..... 2 Southport 1
played at Everton

2nd Round
Dec 08 Barrow ..... 0 Aldershot 2
Dec 08 Bath ..... 2 Boston 1
Dec 08 Clapton O ..... 1 Chester 3
Dec 08 Dartford ..... 0 Bristol R 1
Dec 08 Hartlepool ..... 0 Coventry 4
Dec 08 Mansfield ..... 4 Tranmere 2
Dec 08 Northampton ..... 0 Workington 0
Dec 08 Q.P.R. ..... 1 Brighton 2
Dec 08 Reading ..... 3 Wrexham 0
Dec 08 Rotherham ..... 1 Bristol C 2
Dec 08 Stockport ..... 3 Darlington 2
Dec 08 Swindon ..... 4 Lincoln 3
Dec 08 Watford ..... 1 Walsall 1
Dec 08 Wigan ..... 3 Torquay 2
Dec 08 Wimbledon ..... 1 Southend 5
Dec 08 Yeovil ..... 4 Exeter 1
Dec 08 York ..... 1 New Brighton 0

Replays
Dec 13 Walsall ..... 1 Watford 0
Dec 13 Workington ..... 0 Northampton 1

3rd Round
Jan 12 Aldershot ..... 0 Reading 0
Jan 12 Aston Villa ..... 1 Bradford C 3
Jan 12 Birmingham ..... 5 Coventry 1
Jan 12 Brentford ..... 0 Plymouth 1
Jan 12 Brighton ..... 0 Arsenal 2
Jan 12 Bristol C ..... 1 Bury 1
Jan 12 Bristol R ..... 1 Manchester U 3
Jan 12 Burnley ..... 4 Mansfield 2
Jan 12 Chelsea ..... 1 Luton 1
Jan 12 Chester ..... 0 Nottingham F 4
Jan 12 Everton ..... 6 Grimsby 3
Jan 12 Hull ..... 1 Newcastle 5
Jan 12 Leeds ..... 4 Bradford 1
Jan 12 Leicester ..... 2 Blackpool 1
Jan 12 Middlesbrough ..... 1 Blackburn 1
Jan 12 Northampton ..... 0 Bolton 2
Jan 12 Norwich ..... 2 Bath 0
Jan 12 Portsmouth ..... 1 Huddersfield 1
Jan 12 Preston ..... 0 Barnsley 0
Jan 12 Sheffield W ..... 3 Oldham 1
Jan 12 Southend ..... 0 Sheffield U 4
Jan 12 Sunderland ..... 3 Fulham 2
Jan 12 Swansea ..... 4 Stoke 1
Jan 12 Swindon ..... 2 Chesterfield 1
Jan 12 Tottenham ..... 1 Manchester C 0
Jan 12 Walsall ..... 1 Southampton 2
Jan 12 West Ham ..... 1 Stockport 1
Jan 12 Wigan ..... 1 Millwall 4
Jan 12 Wolverhampton ..... 4 Notts Co 0
Jan 12 W.B.A. ..... 2 Port Vale 1
Jan 12 Yeovil ..... 2 Liverpool 6
Jan 12 York ..... 0 Derby 1

Replays
Jan 16 Barnsley ..... 0 Preston 1
Jan 16 Bury ..... 2 Bristol C 2
Jan 16 Huddersfield ..... 2 Portsmouth 3
Jan 16 Luton ..... 2 Chelsea 0
Jan 16 Reading ..... 3 Aldershot 1
Jan 16 Stockport ..... 1 West Ham 0
Jan 17 Blackburn ..... 1 Middlesbrough 0
Jan 21 Bristol C ..... 2 Bury 1
played at Aston Villa

4th Round
Jan 26 Blackburn ..... 1 Liverpool 0
Jan 26 Bradford C ..... 0 Stockport 0
Jan 26 Burnley ..... 3 Luton 1
Jan 26 Derby ..... 3 Swansea 0
Jan 26 Leicester ..... 0 Arsenal 1
Jan 26 Norwich ..... 3 Leeds 3
Jan 26 Nottingham F ..... 0 Manchester U 0
Jan 26 Plymouth ..... 1 Bolton 4
Jan 26 Portsmouth ..... 0 Bristol C 0
Jan 26 Reading ..... 1 Millwall 0
Jan 26 Southampton ..... 0 Birmingham 3
Jan 26 Sunderland ..... 1 Everton 1
Jan 26 Swindon ..... 0 Preston 2
Jan 26 Tottenham ..... 2 Newcastle 0
Jan 26 Wolverhampton ..... 1 Sheffield W 2
Jan 26 W.B.A. ..... 7 Sheffield U 1

Replays
Jan 30 Bristol C ..... 2 Portsmouth 0
Jan 30 Everton ..... 6 Sunderland 4
Jan 30 Leeds ..... 1 Norwich 2
Jan 30 Manchester U ..... 0 Nottingham F 3
Jan 31 Stockport ..... 3 Bradford C 2

5th Round
Feb 21 Blackburn ..... 1 Birmingham 2
Feb 16 Bristol C ..... 0 Preston 0
Feb 16 Everton ..... 3 Derby 1
Feb 16 Norwich ..... 0 Sheffield W 1
Feb 16 Nottingham F ..... 0 Burnley 0
Feb 16 Reading ..... 0 Arsenal 1
Feb 16 Tottenham ..... 1 Bolton 1
Feb 16 W.B.A. ..... 5 Stockport 0

Replays
Feb 19 Burnley ..... 3 Nottingham F 0
Feb 20 Bolton ..... 1 Tottenham 1
Feb 25 Bolton ..... 2 Tottenham 0
played at Aston Villa
Feb 25 Preston ..... 5 Bristol C 0

6th Round
Mar 02 Burnley ..... 3 Birmingham 2
Mar 02 Everton ..... 1 Bolton 2
Mar 02 Sheffield W ..... 2 Arsenal 1
Mar 02 W.B.A. ..... 1 Preston 0

Semi-finals
Mar 16 Bolton ..... 1 W.B.A. 1
played at Leeds
Mar 16 Burnley ..... 0 Sheffield W 3
played at Aston Villa

Replay
Mar 20 Bolton ..... 0 W.B.A. 2
played at Stoke

Final
Apr 27 Sheffield W ..... 4 W.B.A. 2
played at Wembley

Season 1935-36

1st Round
Nov 30 Barrow ..... 4 Wrexham 1
Nov 30 Brighton ..... 0 Cheltenham 0
Nov 30 Bristol C ..... 0 Crystal Palace 1
Nov 30 Cardiff ..... 0 Dartford 3
Nov 30 Chester ..... 1 Gateshead 0
Nov 30 Chesterfield ..... 3 Southport 0
Nov 30 Clapton O ..... 0 Aldershot 0
Nov 30 Coventry ..... 1 Scunthorpe 1
Nov 30 Crewe ..... 4 Boston 2
Nov 30 Darlington ..... 4 Accrington 2
Nov 30 DulwichH ..... 2 Torquay 3
Nov 30 Exeter ..... 0 Gillingham 4
Nov 30 Gainsborough ..... 3 Blyth S 1
Nov 30 Grantham ..... 0 Notts Co 2
Nov 30 Halifax ..... 4 Rochdale 0
Nov 30 Kidderminster ..... 4 Bishop Auckland 1
Nov 30 Mansfield ..... 2 Hartlepool 3
Nov 30 Margate ..... 3 Q.P.R. 1
Nov 30 New Brighton ..... 1 Workington 3
Nov 30 Newport ..... 0 Southend 1
Nov 30 Northampton ..... 0 Bristol R 0
Nov 30 Nunhead ..... 2 Watford 4
Nov 30 Oldham ..... 6 Ferryhill 1
Nov 30 Reading ..... 8 Corinthians 3
Nov 30 Romford ..... 3 Folkestone 3
Nov 30 Scarborough ..... 2 Darwen 0
Nov 30 Southall ..... 3 Swindon 1
Nov 30 Stalybridge ..... 4 Kells 0
Nov 30 Tranmere ..... 3 Carlisle 0
Nov 30 Walsall ..... 2 Lincoln 0
Nov 30 Walthamstow ..... 1 Bournemouth 1
Nov 30 Wigan ..... 1 Rotherham 2
Nov 30 Yeovil ..... 0 Newport (IOW) 1
Nov 30 York ..... 1 Burton 5

Replays
Dec 04 Aldershot ..... 0 Clapton O 1
Dec 04 Bournemouth ..... 8 Walthamstow 1
Dec 04 Bristol R ..... 3 Northampton 1
Dec 04 Cheltenham ..... 0 Brighton 6
Dec 04 Folkestone ..... 2 Romford 1
Dec 09 Scunthorpe ..... 4 Coventry 2

2nd Round
Dec 14 Bournemouth ..... 5 Barrow 2
Dec 14 Chester ..... 3 Reading 3
Dec 14 Chesterfield ..... 0 Walsall 0
Dec 14 Crewe ..... 2 Gillingham 1
Dec 14 Dartford ..... 4 Gainsborough 0
Dec 14 Folkestone ..... 1 Clapton O 2
Dec 14 Halifax ..... 1 Hartlepool 1
Dec 14 Margate ..... 3 Crystal Palace 1
Dec 14 Notts Co ..... 3 Torquay 0
Dec 14 Oldham ..... 1 Bristol R 1
Dec 14 Rotherham ..... 1 Watford 1
Dec 14 Scarborough ..... 1 Brighton 1
Dec 14 Southall ..... 8 Newport (IOW) 0
Dec 14 Southend ..... 5 Burton 0
Dec 14 Stalybridge ..... 0 Darlington 1
Dec 14 Tranmere ..... 6 Scunthorpe 2
Dec 14 Workington ..... 5 Kidderminster 1

Replays
Dec 18 Brighton ..... 3 Scarborough 0
Dec 18 Bristol R ..... 4 Oldham 1
Dec 18 Hartlepool ..... 0 Halifax 0
Dec 18 Reading ..... 3 Chester 0
Dec 18 Watford ..... 1 Rotherham 0
Dec 19 Walsall ..... 2 Chesterfield 1
Dec 23 Halifax ..... 1 Hartlepool 4
played at Newcastle

3rd Round
Jan 11 Aston Villa ..... 0 Huddersfield 1
Jan 11 Barnsley ..... 3 Birmingham 3
Jan 11 Blackburn ..... 1 Bolton 1
Jan 11 Blackpool ..... 3 Margate 1
Jan 11 Bradford ..... 3 Workington 2
Jan 11 Bradford C ..... 1 Bournemouth 0
Jan 11 Bristol R ..... 1 Arsenal 5
Jan 11 Burnley ..... 0 Sheffield U 0
Jan 11 Clapton O ..... 3 Charlton 0
Jan 11 Crewe ..... 1 Sheffield W 1
Jan 11 Darlington ..... 2 Bury 3
Jan 11 Derby ..... 3 Dartford 2
Jan 11 Doncaster ..... 1 Nottingham F 2
Jan 11 Everton ..... 1 Preston 3
Jan 11 Fulham ..... 2 Brighton 1
Jan 11 Hartlepool ..... 0 Grimsby 0
Jan 11 Leicester ..... 1 Brentford 0
Jan 11 Liverpool ..... 1 Swansea 0
Jan 11 Manchester C ..... 3 Portsmouth 1
Jan 11 Middlesbrough ..... 1 Southampton 0
Jan 11 Millwall ..... 0 Stoke 0
Jan 11 Norwich ..... 1 Chelsea 1
Jan 11 Notts Co ..... 0 Tranmere 0
Jan 11 Reading ..... 1 Manchester U 3
Jan 11 Southall ..... 1 Watford 4
Jan 11 Stockport ..... 2 Plymouth 3
Jan 11 Sunderland ..... 2 Port Vale 2
Jan 11 Tottenham ..... 4 Southend 4
Jan 11 Walsall ..... 0 Newcastle 2
Jan 11 West Ham ..... 2 Luton 2
Jan 11 Wolverhampton ..... 1 Leeds 1
Jan 11 W.B.A. ..... 2 Hull 0

Replays
Jan 13 Port Vale ..... 2 Sunderland 0
Jan 14 Grimsby ..... 4 Hartlepool 1
Jan 15 Birmingham ..... 0 Barnsley 2
Jan 15 Bolton ..... 0 Blackburn 1
Jan 15 Chelsea ..... 3 Norwich 1
Jan 15 Leeds ..... 3 Wolverhampton 1
Jan 15 Luton ..... 4 West Ham 0
Jan 15 Sheffield W ..... 3 Crewe 1
Jan 15 Southend ..... 1 Tottenham 2
Jan 15 Stoke ..... 4 Millwall 0
Jan 15 Tranmere ..... 4 Notts Co 3
Jan 16 Sheffield U ..... 2 Burnley 1

4th Round
Jan 29 Bradford ..... 1 W.B.A. 1
Feb 03 Bradford C ..... 3 Blackburn 1
Jan 25 Chelsea ..... 4 Plymouth 1
Jan 25 Derby ..... 2 Nottingham F 0
Jan 25 Fulham ..... 5 Blackpool 2
Jan 29 Leeds ..... 3 Bury 2
Jan 25 Leicester ..... 6 Watford 3
Jan 25 Liverpool ..... 0 Arsenal 2
Jan 25 Manchester C ..... 2 Luton 1
Jan 25 Middlesbrough ..... 3 Clapton O 0
Jan 25 Port Vale ..... 0 Grimsby 4
Jan 25 Preston ..... 0 Sheffield U 0
Jan 27 Sheffield W ..... 1 Newcastle 1
Jan 25 Stoke ..... 0 Manchester U 0
Jan 25 Tottenham ..... 1 Huddersfield 0
Jan 25 Tranmere ..... 2 Barnsley 4

Replays
Jan 29 Manchester U ..... 0 Stoke 2
Jan 29 Newcastle ..... 3 Sheffield W 1
Jan 30 Sheffield U ..... 2 Preston 0
Feb 03 W.B.A. ..... 1 Bradford 1
Feb 10 Bradford ..... 2 W.B.A. 0
played at Manchester U

5th Round
Feb 15 Barnsley ..... 2 Stoke 1
Feb 15 Bradford ..... 0 Tottenham 0
Feb 15 Bradford C ..... 0 Derby 1
Feb 19 Chelsea ..... 0 Fulham 0
Feb 15 Grimsby ..... 3 Manchester C 2
Feb 15 Middlesbrough ..... 2 Leicester 1
Feb 15 Newcastle ..... 3 Arsenal 3
Feb 15 Sheffield U ..... 3 Leeds 1

Replays
Feb 17 Tottenham ..... 2 Bradford 1
Feb 19 Arsenal ..... 3 Newcastle 0

Feb 24 Fulham 3 Chelsea 2

6th Round
Feb 29 Arsenal 4 Barnsley 1
Feb 29 Fulham 3 Derby 0
Feb 29 Grimsby 3 Middlesbrough 1
Feb 29 Sheffield U 3 Tottenham 1

Semi-finals
Mar 21 Arsenal 1 Grimsby 0
played at Huddersfield
Mar 21 Fulham 1 Sheffield U 2
played at Wolverhampton

Final
Apr 25 Arsenal 1 Sheffield U 0
played at Wembley

SEASON 1936-37

1st Round
Nov 28 Accrington 3 Wellington 1
Nov 28 Aldershot 1 Millwall 6
Nov 28 Barrow 0 Mansfield 4
Nov 28 Bath 1 Tunbridge Wells 2
Nov 28 Blyth S 0 Wrexham 2
Nov 28 Boston 1 Spennymoor 1
Nov 28 Bournemouth 5 Harwich 1
Nov 28 Burton 5 Wigan 1
Nov 28 Cardiff 3 Southall 1
Nov 28 Carlisle 2 Stockport 1
Nov 28 Clapton O 2 Torquay 1
Nov 28 Corinthians 0 Bristol R 2
Nov 28 Crewe 5 Rochdale 1
Nov 28 Crystal Palace 1 Southend 1
Nov 28 Dartford 3 Peterborough 0
Nov 28 Exeter 3 Folkestone 0
Nov 28 Frickley 0 Southport 2
Nov 28 Gateshead 2 Notts Co 0
Nov 28 Halifax 1 Darlington 2
Nov 28 Ilford 2 Reading 4
Nov 28 Ipswich 2 Watford 1
Nov 28 Lincoln 1 New Brighton 1
Nov 28 Newport 3 Bristol C 0
Nov 28 Oldham 1 Tranmere 0
Nov 28 Q.P.R. 5 Brighton 1
Nov 28 Rotherham 4 Hartlepool 4
Nov 28 Ryde 1 Gillingham 5
Nov 28 Shildon 4 Stalybridge 2
Nov 28 South Liverpool 1 Morecambe 0
Nov 28 Swindon 6 DulwichH 0
Nov 28 Walsall 3 Scunthorpe 0
Nov 28 Walthamstow 6 Northampton 1
Nov 28 Yeovil 4 Worthing 3
Nov 28 York 5 Hull 2

Replays
Dec 02 Hartlepool 2 Rotherham 0
Dec 02 New Brighton 2 Lincoln 3
Dec 02 Southend 2 Crystal Palace 0
Dec 02 Spennymoor 2 Boston 0

2nd Round
Dec 12 Accrington 1 Tunbridge Wells 0
Dec 12 Bristol R 2 Southport 1
Dec 12 Burton 1 Darlington 2
Dec 12 Cardiff 2 Swindon 1
Dec 12 Carlisle 4 Clapton O 1
Dec 12 Crewe 1 Hartlepool 1
Dec 12 Ipswich 1 Spennymoor 2
Dec 12 Lincoln 2 Oldham 3
Dec 12 Mansfield 0 Bournemouth 3
Dec 12 Millwall 7 Gateshead 0
Dec 12 Reading 7 Newport 2
Dec 12 Shildon 0 Dartford 3
Dec 12 South Liverpool 0 Q.P.R. 1
Dec 12 Southend 3 York 3
Dec 12 Walsall 1 Yeovil 1
Dec 17 Walthamstow 2 Exeter 3
Dec 12 Wrexham 2 Gillingham 0

Replays
Dec 16 Hartlepool 1 Crewe 2
Dec 16 Yeovil 0 Walsall 1
Dec 16 York 2 Southend 1

3rd Round
Jan 16 Aston Villa 2 Burnley 3
Jan 16 Blackburn 2 Accrington 2
Jan 16 Bradford 0 Derby 4
Jan 16 Bradford C 2 York 2
Jan 16 Brentford 5 Huddersfield 0
Jan 16 Bristol R 2 Leicester 5
Jan 16 Bury 1 Q.P.R. 0
Jan 16 Cardiff 1 Grimsby 3
Jan 16 Chelsea 4 Leeds 0
Jan 16 Chester 4 Doncaster 0
Jan 16 Chesterfield 1 Arsenal 5
Jan 16 Coventry 2 Charlton 0
Jan 16 Crewe 0 Plymouth 2
Jan 16 Dartford 0 Darlington 1
Jan 16 Everton 5 Bournemouth 0
Jan 16 Exeter 3 Oldham 0
Jan 16 Luton 3 Blackpool 3
Jan 16 Manchester U 1 Reading 0
Jan 16 Millwall 2 Fulham 0
Jan 16 Norwich 3 Liverpool 0
Jan 16 Nottingham F 2 Sheffield U 4
Jan 16 Portsmouth 0 Tottenham 5
Jan 16 Preston 2 Newcastle 0
Jan 16 Sheffield W 2 Port Vale 0
Jan 16 Southampton 2 Sunderland 3
Jan 16 Stoke 4 Birmingham 1
Jan 16 Swansea 1 Carlisle 0
Jan 16 Walsall 3 Barnsley 1
Jan 14 West Ham 0 Bolton 0
Jan 16 Wolverhampton 6 Middlesbrough 1
Jan 16 Wrexham 1 Manchester C 3
Jan 16 W.B.A. 7 Spennymoor 1

Replays
Jan 20 Accrington 3 Blackburn 1
Jan 20 Blackpool 1 Luton 2
Jan 20 Bolton 1 West Ham 0
Jan 20 York 1 Bradford C 0

4th Round
Jan 30 Arsenal 5 Manchester U 0
Jan 30 Bolton 1 Norwich 1
Jan 30 Burnley 4 Bury 1
Jan 30 Coventry 2 Chester 0
Jan 30 Derby 3 Brentford 0
Jan 30 Everton 3 Sheffield W 0
Jan 30 Exeter 3 Leicester 1
Jan 30 Grimsby 5 Walsall 1
Jan 30 Luton 2 Sunderland 2
Jan 30 Manchester C 2 Accrington 0
Jan 30 Millwall 3 Chelsea 0
Jan 30 Preston 5 Stoke 1
Jan 30 Swansea 0 York 0
Jan 30 Tottenham 1 Plymouth 0
Jan 30 Wolverhampton 2 Sheffield U 2
Jan 30 W.B.A. 3 Darlington 2

Replays
Feb 03 Sunderland 3 Luton 1
Feb 03 York 1 Swansea 3
Feb 04 Norwich 1 Bolton 2
Feb 04 Sheffield U 1 Wolverhampton 2

5th Round
Feb 20 Bolton 0 Manchester C 5
Feb 20 Burnley 1 Arsenal 7
Feb 20 Coventry 2 W.B.A. 3
Feb 20 Everton 1 Tottenham 1
Feb 20 Grimsby 1 Wolverhampton 1
Feb 20 Millwall 2 Derby 1
Feb 20 Preston 5 Exeter 3
Feb 20 Sunderland 3 Swansea 0

Replays
Feb 22 Tottenham 4 Everton 3
Feb 24 Wolverhampton 6 Grimsby 2

6th Round
Mar 06 Millwall 2 Manchester C 0
Mar 06 Tottenham 1 Preston 3
Mar 06 W.B.A. 3 Arsenal 1
Mar 06 Wolverhampton 1 Sunderland 1

Replays
Mar 10 Sunderland 2 Wolverhampton 2
Mar 15 Sunderland 4 Wolverhampton 0
played at Sheffield W

Semi-finals
Apr 10 Millwall 1 Sunderland 2
played at Huddersfield
Apr 10 Preston 4 W.B.A. 1
played at Arsenal

Final
May 01 Preston 1 Sunderland 3
played at Wembley

SEASON 1937-38

1st Round
Nov 27 Accrington 1 Lancaster 1
Nov 27 Barrow 0 Crewe 1
Nov 27 Bournemouth 0 Dartford 0
Nov 27 Brighton 5 Tunbridge Wells 1
Nov 27 Bristol C 3 Enfield 0
Nov 27 Bristol R 1 Q.P.R. 8
Nov 27 Burton 1 Rotherham 1
Nov 27 Corinthians 0 Southend 2
Nov 27 Crystal Palace 2 Kettering 2
Nov 27 Darlington 0 Scarborough 2
Nov 27 Doncaster 7 Blyth S 0
Nov 27 DulwichH 1 Aldershot 2
Nov 27 Exeter 1 Folkestone 0
Nov 27 Gillingham 3 Swindon 4
Nov 27 Guildford 1 Reading 0
Nov 27 Hartlepool 3 Southport 1
Nov 27 Hull 4 Scunthorpe 0
Nov 27 Kidderminster 2 Newport 2
Nov 27 Kings Lynn 0 Bromley 4
Nov 27 New Brighton 5 Workington 0
Nov 27 Northampton 1 Cardiff 2
Nov 27 Port Vale 1 Gainsborough 1
Nov 27 Rochdale 1 Lincoln 1
Nov 27 Torquay 1 Clapton O 2
Nov 27 Tranmere 2 Carlisle 1
Nov 27 Walker Celtic 1 Bradford C 1
Nov 27 Walsall 4 Gateshead 0
Nov 27 Watford 3 Cheltenham 0
Nov 27 Wellington 1 Mansfield 2
Nov 27 Westbury 1 Walthamstow 3
Nov 27 Wigan 1 South Liverpool 4
Nov 27 Wrexham 2 Oldham 1
Nov 27 Yeovil 2 Ipswich 1
Nov 27 York 1 Halifax 1

Replays
Nov 29 Rotherham 3 Burton 0
Dec 01 Bradford C 11 Walker Celtic 3
Dec 01 Dartford 0 Bournemouth 6
Dec 01 Gainsborough 2 Port Vale 1
Dec 01 Halifax 0 York 1
Dec 01 Lancaster 1 Accrington 1
Dec 01 Lincoln 2 Rochdale 0
Dec 02 Kettering 0 Crystal Palace 4
Dec 02 Newport 4 Kidderminster 1
Dec 06 Accrington 4 Lancaster 0
played at Preston

2nd Round
Dec 11 Accrington 0 Crystal Palace 1
Dec 11 Cardiff 1 Bristol C 1
Dec 11 Clapton O 2 York 2
Dec 15 Crewe 2 New Brighton 2
Dec 11 Doncaster 4 Guildford 0
Dec 11 Exeter 1 Hull 2
Dec 15 Mansfield 2 Lincoln 1
Dec 11 Newport 2 Bournemouth 1
Dec 11 Rotherham 1 Aldershot 3
Dec 11 Scarborough 4 Bromley 1
Dec 11 South Liverpool 1 Brighton 1
Dec 11 Swindon 2 Q.P.R. 1
Dec 11 Tranmere 3 Hartlepool 1
Dec 11 Walthamstow 0 Southend 1
Dec 11 Watford 3 Walsall 0
Dec 11 Wrexham 1 Bradford C 2
Dec 11 Yeovil 2 Gainsborough 1

Replays
Dec 15 Brighton 6 South Liverpool 0
Dec 15 Bristol C 0 Cardiff 2
Dec 15 York 1 Clapton O 0
Dec 20 New Brighton 4 Crewe 1

3rd Round
Jan 08 Aldershot 1 Notts Co 3
Jan 08 Arsenal 3 Bolton 1
Jan 08 Birmingham 0 Blackpool 1
Jan 08 Bradford 7 Newport 4
Jan 08 Bradford C 1 Chesterfield 1
Jan 08 Brentford 3 Fulham 1
Jan 08 Bury 2 Brighton 0
Jan 08 Charlton 5 Cardiff 0
Jan 08 Chelsea 0 Everton 1
Jan 08 Crystal Palace 0 Liverpool 0
Jan 08 Derby 1 Stoke 2
Jan 08 Doncaster 0 Sheffield U 2
Jan 08 Grimsby 1 Swindon 1
Jan 08 Huddersfield 3 Hull 1
Jan 08 Leeds 3 Chester 1
Jan 08 Manchester U 3 Yeovil 0
Jan 08 Mansfield 1 Leicester 2
Jan 08 Middlesbrough 2 Stockport 0
Jan 08 Millwall 2 Manchester C 2
Jan 08 New Brighton 1 Plymouth 0
Jan 08 Norwich 2 Aston Villa 3
Jan 08 Nottingham F 3 Southampton 1
Jan 08 Preston 3 West Ham 0
Jan 08 Scarborough 1 Luton 1
Jan 08 Sheffield W 1 Burnley 1
Jan 08 Southend 2 Barnsley 2
Jan 08 Sunderland 1 Watford 0
Jan 08 Swansea 0 Wolverhampton 4
Jan 08 Tottenham 3 Blackburn 2
Jan 08 Tranmere 1 Portsmouth 2
Jan 08 W.B.A. 1 Newcastle 0
Jan 08 York 3 Coventry 2

Replays
Jan 11 Burnley 3 Sheffield W 1
Jan 12 Barnsley 2 Southend 1
Jan 12 Chesterfield 1 Bradford C 1
Jan 12 Liverpool 3 Crystal Palace 1
Jan 12 Luton 5 Scarborough 1
Jan 12 Manchester C 3 Millwall 1
Jan 12 Swindon 2 Grimsby 1
Jan 17 Bradford C 0 Chesterfield 2
played at Sheffield U

4th Round
Jan 22 Aston Villa 4 Blackpool 0
Jan 22 Barnsley 2 Manchester U 2
Jan 22 Bradford 1 Stoke 1
Jan 22 Brentford 2 Portsmouth 1
Jan 22 Charlton 2 Leeds 1
Jan 22 Chesterfield 3 Burnley 2
Jan 22 Everton 0 Sunderland 1
Jan 22 Huddersfield 1 Notts Co 0
Jan 22 Luton 2 Swindon 1
Jan 22 Manchester C 3 Bury 1
Jan 22 New Brighton 0 Tottenham 0
Jan 22 Nottingham F 1 Middlesbrough 3
Jan 22 Preston 2 Leicester 0
Jan 22 Sheffield U 1 Liverpool 1
Jan 22 Wolverhampton 1 Arsenal 2
Jan 22 York 3 W.B.A. 2

Replays
Jan 26 Liverpool 1 Sheffield U 0
Jan 26 Manchester U 1 Barnsley 0
Jan 26 Stoke 1 Bradford 2
Jan 26 Tottenham 5 New Brighton 2

5th Round
Feb 12 Arsenal 0 Preston 1
Feb 12 Brentford 2 Manchester U 0
Feb 12 Charlton 1 Aston Villa 1
Feb 12 Chesterfield 2 Tottenham 2
Feb 12 Liverpool 0 Huddersfield 1
Feb 12 Luton 1 Manchester C 3
Feb 12 Sunderland 1 Bradford 0
Feb 12 York 1 Middlesbrough 0

Replays
Feb 16 Aston Villa 2 Charlton 2
Feb 16 Tottenham 2 Chesterfield 1
Feb 21 Aston Villa 4 Charlton 1
played at Arsenal

6th Round
Mar 05 Aston Villa 3 Manchester C 2
Mar 05 Brentford 0 Preston 3
Mar 05 Tottenham 0 Sunderland 1
Mar 05 York 0 Huddersfield 0

Replays
Mar 09 Huddersfield 2 York 1

Semi-finals
Mar 26 Aston Villa 1 Preston 2
played at Sheffield U
Mar 26 Huddersfield 3 Sunderland 1
played at Blackburn

Final
Apr 30 Huddersfield 0 Preston 1
played at Wembley

Season 1938-39

1st Round
Nov 26 Aldershot 1 Guildford 1
Nov 26 Bournemouth 2 Bristol C 1
Nov 26 Bristol R 4 Peterborough 1
Nov 26 Bromley 2 Aspley 1
Nov 26 Chelmsford 4 Kidderminster 0
Nov 26 Cheltenham 1 Cardiff 1
Nov 26 Chester 3 Bradford C 1
Nov 26 Clapton O 3 Hayes 1
Nov 26 Crystal Palace 1 Q.P.R. 1
Nov 26 Darlington 4 Stalybridge 0
Nov 26 Doncaster 4 New Brighton 2
Nov 26 Folkestone 2 Colchester 1
Nov 26 Gainsborough 2 Gateshead 1
Nov 26 Halifax 7 Rochdale 3
Nov 26 Hartlepool 2 Accrington 1
Nov 26 Horden 1 Chorley 1
Nov 26 Hull 4 Rotherham 1
Nov 26 Ipswich 7 Street 0
Nov 26 Lincoln 4 Barrow 1
Nov 26 North Shields 1 Stockport 4
Nov 26 Oldham 2 Crewe 2
Nov 26 Reading 3 Newport 3
Nov 26 Runcorn 3 Wellington 0
Nov 26 Scarborough 0 Southport 0
Nov 26 Scunthorpe 4 Lancaster 2
Nov 26 Southend 3 Corinthians 0
Nov 26 Swindon 6 Lowestoft 0
Nov 26 Torquay 3 Exeter 1
Nov 26 Walsall 4 Carlisle 1
Nov 26 Walthamston 4 Tunbridge Wells 1
Nov 26 Watford 4 Northampton 1
Nov 26 Workington 1 Mansfield 1
Nov 26 Wrexham 1 Port Vale 2
Nov 26 Yeovil 2 Brighton 1

Replays
Nov 28 Q.P.R. 3 Crystal Palace 0
Nov 29 Southport 5 Scarborough 3
Nov 30 Cardiff 1 Cheltenham 0
Nov 30 Chorley 1 Horden 2
Nov 30 Crewe 1 Oldham 0
Nov 30 Guildford 3 Aldershot 4
Nov 30 Mansfield 2 Workington 1
Dec 05 Newport 3 Reading 1

2nd Round
Dec 10 Bristol R 0 Bournemouth 3
Dec 10 Cardiff 1 Crewe 0
Dec 10 Chelmsford 3 Darlington 1
Dec 10 Chester 1 Hull 2
Dec 10 Folkestowe 1 Yeovil 1
Dec 10 Gainsborough 0 Doncaster 1
Dec 10 Halifax 1 Mansfield 1
Dec 10 Hartlepool 0 Q.P.R. 2
Dec 10 Horden 2 Newport 3
Dec 10 Ipswich 4 Torquay 1
Dec 10 Lincoln 8 Bromley 1
Dec 10 Port Vale 0 Southend 1
Dec 10 Runcorn 3 Aldershot 1
Dec 10 Scunthorpe 1 Watford 2
Dec 10 Southport 2 Swindon 0
Dec 10 Stockport 0 Walthamstow 0
Dec 10 Walsall 4 Clapton O 2

Replays
Dec 14 Mansfield 3 Halifax 3
Dec 15 Hull 0 Chester 1
Dec 15 Walthamstow 1 Stockport 3
Dec 15 Yeovil 1 Folkestowe 0
Dec 19 Halifax 0 Mansfield 0
played at Doncaster
Dec 21 Halifax 2 Mansfield 1
played at Manchester U

3rd Round
Jan 07 Aston Villa 1 Ipswich 1
Jan 07 Barnsley 1 Stockport 2
Jan 07 Birmingham 2 Halifax 0
Jan 07 Blackburn 2 Swansea 0
Jan 07 Blackpool 1 Sheffield U 2
Jan 07 Brentford 0 Newcastle 2
Jan 07 Cardiff 1 Charlton 0
Jan 07 Chelmsford 4 Southampton 1
Jan 07 Chelsea 2 Arsenal 1
Jan 07 Chester 1 Coventry 0
Jan 11 Chesterfield 1 Southend 1
Jan 07 Derby 0 Everton 1
Jan 07 Fulham 6 Bury 0
Jan 10 Grimsby 6 Tranmere 0
Jan 11 Huddersfield 0 Nottingham F 0
Jan 11 Leeds 3 Bournemouth 1
Jan 07 Leicester 1 Stoke 1
Jan 07 Liverpool 3 Luton 0
Jan 07 Middlesbrough 1 Bolton 0
Jan 07 Newport 0 Walsall 2
Jan 12 Norwich 0 Manchester C 5
Jan 07 Notts Co 3 Burnley 1
Jan 07 Portsmouth 4 Lincoln 0
Jan 07 Q.P.R. 1 West Ham 2
Jan 07 Runcorn 2 Preston 4
Jan 07 Sheffield W 1 Yeovil 1
Jan 10 Southport 1 Doncaster 1
Jan 07 Sunderland 3 Plymouth 0
Jan 07 Tottenham 7 Watford 1
Jan 07 Wolverhampton 3 Bradford 1
Jan 07 W.B.A. 0 Manchester U 0
Jan 11 York 0 Millwall 5

Replays
Jan 11 Bolton 0 Middlesbrough 0
Jan 11 Ipswich 1 Aston Villa 2
Jan 11 Manchester U 1 W.B.A. 5
Jan 11 Stoke 1 Leicester 2
Jan 12 Doncaster 2 Southport 1
Jan 12 Yeovil 1 Sheffield W 2
Jan 16 Bolton 0 Middlesbrough 1
played at Leeds
Jan 16 Nottingham F 0 Huddersfield 3
Jan 16 Southend 4 Chesterfield 3

4th Round
Jan 21 Birmingham 6 Chelmsford 0
Jan 21 Blackburn 4 Southend 2
Jan 21 Cardiff 0 Newcastle 0
Jan 21 Chelsea 3 Fulham 0
Jan 21 Everton 8 Doncaster 0
Jan 21 Leeds 2 Huddersfield 4
Jan 21 Liverpool 5 Stockport 1
Jan 21 Middlesbrough 0 Sunderland 2
Jan 21 Millwall 2 Grimsby 2
Jan 21 Notts Co 0 Walsall 0
Jan 21 Portsmouth 2 W.B.A. 0
Jan 21 Preston 2 Aston Villa 0
Jan 21 Sheffield U 2 Manchester C 0
Jan 21 Sheffield W 1 Chester 1
Jan 21 West Ham 3 Tottenham 3
Jan 21 Wolverhampton 5 Leicester 1

Replays
Jan 24 Grimsby 3 Millwall 2
Jan 25 Chester 1 Sheffield W 1
Jan 25 Newcastle 4 Cardiff 1
Jan 26 Walsall 4 Notts Co 0
Jan 30 Chester 0 Sheffield W 2
played at Manchester C
Jan 30 Tottenham 1 West Ham 1
Feb 02 Tottenham 1 West Ham 2
played at Arsenal

5th Round
Feb 11 Birmingham 2 Everton 2
Feb 11 Chelsea 1 Sheffield W 1
Feb 11 Huddersfield 3 Walsall 0
Feb 11 Newcastle 1 Preston 2
Feb 11 Portsmouth 2 West Ham 0
Feb 11 Sheffield U 0 Grimsby 0
Feb 11 Sunderland 1 Blackburn 1
Feb 11 Wolverhampton 4 Liverpool 1

Replays
Feb 13 Sheffield W 0 Chelsea 0
Feb 14 Grimsby 1 Sheffield U 0
Feb 15 Everton 2 Birmingham 1
Feb 16 Blackburn 0 Sunderland 0
Feb 20 Blackburn 1 Sunderland 0
played at Sheffield W
Feb 20 Chelsea 3 Sheffield W 1
played at Arsenal

6th Round
Mar 04 Chelsea 0 Grimsby 1
Mar 04 Huddersfield 1 Blackburn 1
Mar 04 Portsmouth 1 Preston 0
Mar 04 Wolverhampton 2 Everton 0

Replay
Mar 09 Blackburn 1 Huddersfield 2

Semi-finals
Mar 25 Grimsby 0 Wolverhampton 5
played at Manchester U
Mar 25 Huddersfield 1 Portsmouth 2
played at Arsenal

Final
Apr 29 Portsmouth 4 Wolverhampton 1
played at Wembley

Season 1945-46

1st Round
Nov 17 Barnet 2 Q.P.R. 6
Nov 27 Q.P.R. 2 Barnet 1 8-3
Nov 17 Barrow 1 Netherfield 0
Nov 24 Netherfield 2 Barrow 2 2-3
Nov 17 Bath 3 Cheltenham 2
Nov 24 Cheltenham 0 Bath 2 2-5
Nov 17 Brighton 3 Romford 1
Nov 24 Romford 1 Brighton 1 2-4
Nov 21 Bromley 6 Slough 1
Nov 24 Slough 1 Bromley 0 2-6
Nov 17 Carlisle 5 North Shields 1
Nov 24 North Shields 2 Carlisle 3 3-8
Nov 17 Chorley 2 Accrington 1
Nov 24 Accrington 2 Chorley 0 3-2
Nov 17 Clapton O 2 Newport (IOW) 1
Nov 24 Newport (IOW) 2 Clapton O 0 3-2
Nov 17 Crewe 4 Wrexham 2
Nov 24 Wrexham 3 Crewe 0 5-4
Nov 17 Darlington 2 Stockton 0
Nov 24 Stockton 1 Darlington 4 1-6
Nov 17 Doncaster 0 Rotherham 1
Nov 24 Rotherham 2 Doncaster 1 3-1
Nov 17 Halifax 1 York 0
Nov 24 York 4 Halifax 2 4-3
Nov 17 Hartlepool 1 Gateshead 2
Nov 24 Gateshead 6 Hartlepool 2 8-3
Nov 17 Kettering 1 Grantham 5
Nov 24 Grantham 2 Kettering 2 7-3
Nov 17 Lovell's A 4 Bournemouth 1
Nov 24 Bournemouth 3 Lovell's A 2 4-6
Nov 17 Mansfield 3 Gainsborough 0
Nov 24 Gainsborough 4 Mansfield 2 4-5
Nov 17 Marine 4 Stalybridge 0
Nov 24 Stalybridge 3 Marine 3 3-7
Nov 17 Northampton 5 Chelmsford 1
Nov 24 Chelmsford 0 Northampton 5 1-10
Nov 17 Notts Co 2 Bradford C 2
Nov 24 Bradford C 1 Notts Co 2 3-4
Nov 17 Port Vale 4 Wellington 0
Nov 24 Wellington 0 Port Vale 2 0-6
Nov 17 Reading 3 Aldershot 1
Nov 24 Aldershot 7 Reading 3 8-6
Nov 17 Shrewsbury 5 Walsall 0
Nov 24 Walsall 4 Shrewsbury 1 4-6
Nov 17 South Liverpool 1 Tranmere 1
Nov 24 Tranmere 6 South Liverpool 1 7-2
Nov 17 Southport 1 Oldham 2
Nov 24 Oldham 3 Southport 1 5-2
Nov 17 Stockport 1 Rochdale 2
Nov 24 Rochdale 1 Stockport 1 3-2
Nov 17 Sutton 1 Walthamstow 4
Nov 24 Walthamstow 7 Sutton 2 11-3
Nov 17 Swindon 1 Bristol R 0
Nov 24 Bristol R 4 Swindon 1 4-2
Nov 17 Torquay 0 Newport 1
Nov 24 Newport 1 Torquay 1 2-1
Nov 17 Trowbridge 1 Exeter 3
Nov 24 Exeter 7 Trowbridge 2 10-3
Nov 17 Watford 1 Southend 1

Date	Home		Away		Agg
Nov 24	Southend	0	Watford	3	1-4
Nov 17	Willington	0	Bishop Auckland	5	
Nov 24	Bishop Auckland	0	Willington	2	5-2
Nov 17	Wisbech	0	Ipswich	3	
Nov 24	Ipswich	5	Wisbech	0	8-0
Nov 17	Yeovil	2	Bristol C	2	
Nov 24	Bristol C	3	Yeovil	0	5-2
Nov 17	Yorkshire Amtr	1	Lincoln	0	
Nov 24	Lincoln	5	Yorkshire Amtr	1	5-2

2nd Round

Date	Home		Away		Agg
Dec 08	Aldershot	7	Newport (IOW)	0	
Dec 15	Newport (IOW)	0	Aldershot	5	0-12
Dec 08	Barrow	4	Carlisle	2	
Dec 15	Carlisle	3	Barrow	4	5-8
Dec 08	Bishop Auckland	1	York	2	
Dec 15	York	3	Bishop Auckland	0	5-1
Dec 08	Bristol C	4	Bristol R	2	
Dec 15	Bristol R	0	Bristol C	2	2-6
Dec 08	Bromley	1	Watford	3	
Dec 15	Watford	1	Bromley	1	4-2
Dec 08	Darlington	2	Gateshead	4	
Dec 15	Gateshead	1	Darlington	2	5-4
Dec 08	Grantham	1	Mansfield	2	
Dec 15	Mansfield	2	Grantham	1	4-2
Dec 08	Lovell's A	2	Bath	1	
Dec 15	Bath	2	Lovell's A	5	3-7
Dec 08	Newport	5	Exeter	1	
Dec 15	Exeter	1	Newport	3	2-8
Dec 08	Northampton	3	Notts Co	1	
Dec 15	Notts Co	1	Northampton	0	2-3
Dec 08	Oldham	2	Accrington	1	
Dec 15	Accrington	3	Oldham	1	4-3
Dec 08	Port Vale	3	Marine	1	
Dec 15	Marine	1	Port Vale	1	2-4
Dec 08	Q.P.R.	4	Ipswich	0	
Dec 15	Ipswich	0	Q.P.R.	2	0-6
Dec 08	Rotherham	2	Lincoln	1	
Dec 15	Lincoln	1	Rotherham	1	2-3
Dec 08	Shrewsbury	0	Wrexham	1	
Dec 15	Wrexham	1	Shrewsbury	1	2-1
Dec 08	Tranmere	3	Rochdale	1	
Dec 15	Rochdale	3	Tranmere	0	4-3
Dec 08	Walthamstow	1	Brighton	1	
Dec 15	Brighton	4	Walthamstow	2	5-3

3rd Round

Date	Home		Away		Agg
Jan 05	Accrington	2	Manchester U	2	
Jan 09	Manchester U	5	Accrington	1	7-3
Jan 05	Aldershot	2	Plymouth	0	
Jan 09	Plymouth	0	Aldershot	1	0-3
Jan 05	Birmingham	1	Portsmouth	0	
Jan 09	Portsmouth	0	Birmingham	0	0-1
Jan 05	Bolton	1	Blackburn	0	
Jan 09	Blackburn	1	Bolton	3	1-4
Jan 05	Bradford	2	Port Vale	1	
Jan 07	Port Vale	1	Bradford	1	2-3
Jan 05	Bristol C	5	Swansea	1	
Jan 10	Swansea	2	Bristol C	2	3-7
Jan 05	Bury	3	Rochdale	3	
Jan 08	Rochdale	2	Bury	4	5-7
Jan 05	Cardiff	1	W.B.A.	1	
Jan 09	W.B.A.	4	Cardiff	0	5-1
Jan 05	Charlton	3	Fulham	1	
Jan 07	Fulham	2	Charlton	1	3-4
Jan 05	Chelsea	1	Leicester	1	
Jan 10	Leicester	0	Chelsea	2	1-3
Jan 05	Chester	0	Liverpool	2	
Jan 09	Liverpool	2	Chester	1	4-1
Jan 05	Chesterfield	1	York	1	
Jan 09	York	3	Chesterfield	2	4-3
Jan 05	Coventry	2	Aston Villa	1	
Jan 08	Aston Villa	2	Coventry	0	3-2
Jan 05	Grimsby	1	Sunderland	3	
Jan 09	Sunderland	2	Grimsby	1	5-2
Jan 05	Huddersfield	1	Sheffield U	1	
Jan 07	Sheffield U	2	Huddersfield	0	3-1
Jan 05	Leeds	4	Middlesbrough	4	
Jan 09	Middlesbrough	7	Leeds	2	11-6
Jan 05	Lovell's A	2	Wolverhampton	4	
Jan 09	Wolverhampton	8	Lovell's A	1	12-3
Jan 05	Luton	0	Derby	6	
Jan 09	Derby	3	Luton	0	9-0
Jan 05	Manchester C	6	Barrow	2	
Jan 10	Barrow	2	Manchester C	2	4-8
Jan 05	Mansfield	0	Sheffield W	0	
Jan 10	Sheffield W	5	Mansfield	0	5-0
Jan 05	Newcastle	4	Barnsley	2	
Jan 09	Barnsley	3	Newcastle	0	5-4
Jan 05	Northampton	2	Millwall	2	
Jan 07	Millwall	3	Northampton	0	5-2
Jan 05	Norwich	1	Brighton	2	
Jan 09	Brighton	4	Norwich	1	6-2
Jan 05	Nottingham F	1	Watford	1	
Jan 09	Watford	1	Nottingham F	1	
Jan 16	Nottingham F	0	Watford	1	2-3
	played at Chelsea				
Jan 05	Preston	2	Everton	1	
Jan 09	Everton	2	Preston	2	3-4
Jan 05	Q.P.R.	0	Crystal Palace	0	
Jan 09	Crystal Palace	0	Q.P.R.	0	E/t
Jan 16	Crystal Palace	0	Q.P.R.	1	0-1
	played at Fulham				
Jan 05	Rotherham	2	Gateshead	2	
Jan 09	Gateshead	0	Rotherham	2	2-4
Jan 05	Southampton	4	Newport	3	
Jan 10	Newport	1	Southampton	2	4-6
Jan 05	Stoke	3	Burnley	1	
Jan 07	Burnley	2	Stoke	1	3-4
Jan 05	Tottenham	2	Brentford	2	
Jan 10	Brentford	2	Tottenham	0	4-2
Jan 05	West Ham	6	Arsenal	0	
Jan 09	Arsenal	1	West Ham	0	1-6
Jan 05	Wrexham	1	Blackpool	4	
Jan 09	Blackpool	4	Wrexham	1	8-2

4th Round

Date	Home		Away		Agg
Jan 26	Barnsley	3	Rotherham	0	
Jan 31	Rotherham	2	Barnsley	1	2-4
Jan 26	Birmingham	5	Watford	0	
Jan 30	Watford	1	Birmingham	1	1-6
Jan 26	Blackpool	3	Middlesbrough	2	
Jan 30	Middlesbrough	3	Blackpool	2	
Feb 04	Blackpool	0	Middlesbrough	1	5-6
	played at Leeds				
Jan 26	Bolton	5	Liverpool	0	
Jan 30	Liverpool	2	Bolton	0	2-5
Jan 26	Bradford	1	Manchester C	3	
Jan 30	Manchester C	2	Bradford	8	5-9
Jan 26	Brighton	3	Aldershot	0	
Jan 30	Aldershot	1	Brighton	4	1-7
Jan 26	Bristol C	2	Brentford	1	
Jan 31	Brentford	5	Bristol C	0	6-2
Jan 26	Charlton	5	Wolverhampton	2	
Jan 30	Wolverhampton	1	Charlton	1	3-6
Jan 26	Chelsea	2	West Ham	0	
Jan 30	West Ham	1	Chelsea	0	1-2
Jan 26	Derby	1	W.B.A.	0	
Jan 30	W.B.A.	1	Derby	3	1-4
Jan 26	Manchester U	1	Preston	0	
Jan 30	Preston	3	Manchester U	1	3-2
Jan 26	Millwall	2	Aston Villa	4	
Jan 28	Aston Villa	9	Millwall	11	3-3
Jan 26	Sheffield W	5	York	1	
Jan 30	York	1	Sheffield W	6	2-11
Jan 26	Southampton	0	Q.P.R.	1	
Jan 30	Q.P.R.	4	Southampton	3	5-3
Jan 26	Stoke	2	Sheffield U	0	
Jan 28	Sheffield U	3	Stoke	2	3-4
Jan 26	Sunderland	3	Bury	1	
Jan 29	Bury	5	Sunderland	4	6-7

5th Round

Date	Home		Away		Agg
Feb 09	Barnsley	0	Bradford	1	
Feb 13	Bradford	1	Barnsley	1	2-1
Feb 09	Bolton	1	Middlesbrough	0	
Feb 13	Middlesbrough	1	Bolton	1	1-2
Feb 09	Brighton	1	Derby	4	
Feb 13	Derby	6	Brighton	0	10-1
Feb 09	Chelsea	0	Aston Villa	1	
Feb 12	Aston Villa	1	Chelsea	0	2-0
Feb 09	Preston	1	Charlton	1	
Feb 13	Charlton	6	Preston	0	7-1
Feb 09	Q.P.R.	1	Brentford	3	
Feb 14	Brentford	0	Q.P.R.	0	3-1
Feb 09	Stoke	2	Sheffield W	0	
Feb 11	Sheffield W	0	Stoke	0	0-2
Feb 09	Sunderland	1	Birmingham	0	
Feb 13	Birmingham	3	Sunderland	1	3-2

6th Round

Date	Home		Away		Agg
Mar 02	Aston Villa	3	Derby	4	
Mar 09	Derby	1	Aston Villa	1	5-4
Mar 02	Bradford	2	Birmingham	2	
Mar 09	Birmingham	6	Bradford	0	8-2
Mar 02	Charlton	6	Brentford	3	
Mar 09	Brentford	1	Charlton	3	4-9
Mar 02	Stoke	0	Bolton	2	
Mar 09	Bolton	0	Stoke	0	2-0

Semi-finals

Date	Home		Away	
Mar 23	Bolton	0	Charlton	2
	played at Aston Villa			
Mar 23	Birmingham	1	Derby	1
	played at Sheffield W			

Replay

Date	Home		Away	
Mar 27	Birmingham	0	Derby	4
	played at Manchester C			

Final

Date	Home		Away	
Apr 27	Charlton	1	Derby	4
	played at Wembley			

SEASON 1946-47

1st Round

Date	Home		Away	
Nov 30	Aldershot	4	Cheltenham	2
Nov 30	Barnet	3	Sutton	0
Nov 30	Barrow	0	Halifax	0
Nov 30	Bournemouth	4	Exeter	2
Nov 30	Bristol C	9	Heyes	3
Nov 30	Brush Sports	1	Southend	6
Nov 30	Carlisle	4	Runcorn	0
Nov 30	Doncaster	2	Accrington	2
Nov 30	Gainsborough	1	Darlington	2
Nov 30	Gateshead	3	Bradford C	1
Nov 30	Gillingham	4	Gravesend	1
Nov 30	Hartlepool	6	North Shields	0
Nov 30	Hull	0	New Brighton	0
Nov 30	Ipswich	2	Torquay	0
Nov 30	Lancaster	1	Spennymoor	0
Nov 30	Leyton O	1	Notts Co	2
Nov 30	Leytonstone	1	Walsall	6
Nov 30	Merthyr T	3	Bristol o??? R	1
Nov 30	Northampton	2	Mansfield	0
Nov 30	Norwich	7	Brighton	2
Nov 30	Oldham	1	Tranmere	0
Nov 30	Port Vale	5	Finchley	0
Nov 30	Q.P.R.	2	Poole	2
Nov 30	Reading	5	Colchester	0
Nov 30	Rochdale	6	Bishop Auckland	1
Nov 30	Rotherham	2	Crewe	0
Nov 30	South Liverpool	2	Workington	1
Nov 30	Stockport	2	Southport	0
Nov 30	Stockton	2	Lincoln	4
Nov 30	Swindon	4	Cambridge	1
Nov 30	Wellington	1	Watford	1
Nov 30	Wrexham	5	Marine	0
Nov 30	Yeovil	2	Peterborough	2
Nov 30	York	0	Scunthorpe	1

Replays

Date	Home		Away	
Dec 04	Accrington	0	Doncaster	5
Dec 04	Halifax	1	Barrow	0
Dec 04	New Brighton	1	Hull	2
Dec 04	Poole	0	Q.P.R.	6
Dec 04	Watford	1	Wellington	0
Dec 05	Peterborough	1	Yeovil	0

2nd Round

Date	Home		Away	
Dec 14	Barnet	2	Southend	9
Dec 14	Bournemouth	4	Aldershot	2
Dec 14	Bristol C	1	Gillingham	2
Dec 14	Darlington	1	Hull	2
Dec 14	Gateshead	4	Lancaster	0
Dec 14	Halifax	1	Stockport	1
Dec 14	Lincoln	1	Wrexham	1
Dec 14	Merthyr T	1	Reading	3
Dec 14	Norwich	4	Q.P.R.	4
Dec 14	Notts Co	2	Swindon	1
Dec 14	Oldham	1	Doncaster	2
Dec 14	Peterborough	1	Northampton	1
Dec 14	Rochdale	6	Hartlepool	1
Dec 14	Rotherham	4	Scunthorpe	1
Dec 14	South Liverpool	2	Carlisle	3
Dec 14	Walsall	0	Ipswich	0
Dec 14	Watford	1	Port Vale	1

Replays

Date	Home		Away	
Dec 16	Port Vale	2	Watford	1
Dec 18	Ipswich	0	Walsall	1
Dec 18	Q.P.R.	2	Norwich	0
Dec 18	Stockport	2	Halifax	1
Dec 18	Wrexham	3	Lincoln	3
Dec 19	Northampton	1	Peterborough	1
Dec 23	Lincoln	2	Wrexham	1
	played at Manchester C			
Dec 23	Northampton	8	Peterborough	1
	played at Coventry			

3rd Round

Date	Home		Away	
Jan 11	Blackburn	1	Hull	1
Jan 11	Bolton	5	Stockport	1
Jan 11	Bournemouth	0	Derby	2
Jan 11	Bradford	0	Manchester U	3
Jan 11	Brentford	1	Cardiff	0
Jan 11	Burnley	5	Aston Villa	1
Jan 11	Charlton	3	Rochdale	1
Jan 11	Chelsea	1	Arsenal	1
Jan 11	Chester	2	Plymouth	0
Jan 11	Chesterfield	2	Sunderland	1
Jan 11	Coventry	5	Newport	2
Jan 11	Doncaster	2	Portsmouth	3
Jan 11	Everton	4	Southend	2
Jan 11	Fulham	1	Birmingham	2
Jan 11	Huddersfield	3	Barnsley	4
Jan 11	Lincoln	0	Nottingham F	1
Jan 11	Luton	6	Notts Co	0
Jan 11	Manchester C	3	Gateshead	0
Jan 11	Millwall	0	Port Vale	3
Jan 11	Newcastle	6	Crystal Palace	2
Jan 11	Northampton	1	Preston	2
Jan 11	Q.P.R.	1	Middlesbrough	1
Jan 11	Reading	2	Grimsby	2
Jan 11	Sheffield U	3	Carlisle	0
Jan 11	Sheffield W	4	Blackpool	1
Jan 11	Southampton	5	Bury	1
Jan 11	Swansea	4	Gillingham	1
Jan 11	Tottenham	2	Stoke	2
Jan 11	Walsall	2	Liverpool	5
Jan 11	West Ham	1	Leicester	2
Jan 11	Wolverhampton	3	Rotherham	0
Jan 11	W.B.A.	2	Leeds	1

Replays

Date	Home		Away	
Jan 14	Grimsby	3	Reading	1
Jan 15	Arsenal	1	Chelsea	1
Jan 15	Middlesbrough	3	Q.P.R.	1
Jan 15	Stoke	1	Tottenham	0
Jan 16	Hull	0	Blackburn	3
Jan 20	Arsenal	0	Chelsea	2
	played at Tottenham			

4th Round

Date	Home		Away	
Jan 25	Birmingham	1	Portsmouth	0
Jan 25	Blackburn	2	Port Vale	0
Jan 25	Bolton	3	Manchester C	3
Jan 25	Brentford	0	Leicester	0
Jan 25	Burnley	2	Coventry	0
Jan 25	Chelsea	2	Derby	2
Jan 25	Chester	0	Stoke	0
Jan 25	Liverpool	2	Grimsby	0
Jan 25	Luton	2	Swansea	0
Jan 25	Manchester U	0	Nottingham F	2
Jan 25	Middlesbrough	2	Chesterfield	1
Jan 25	Newcastle	3	Southampton	1
Jan 25	Preston	2	Barnsley	0
Jan 25	Sheffield W	2	Everton	1
Jan 25	Wolverhampton	0	Sheffield U	0
Jan 25	W.B.A.	1	Charlton	2

Replays

Date	Home		Away	
Jan 29	Derby	1	Chelsea	0

Date	Home		Away	
Jan 29	Manchester C	1	Bolton	0
Jan 29	Sheffield U	2	Wolverhampton	0
Jan 29	Stoke	3	Chester	2
Jan 30	Leicester	0	Brentford	0
Feb 03	Brentford	1	Leicester	4
	played at Aston Villa			

5th Round

Date	Home		Away	
Feb 08	Birmingham	5	Manchester C	0
Feb 08	Charlton	1	Blackburn	0
Feb 08	Liverpool	1	Derby	0
Feb 08	Luton	0	Burnley	0
Feb 08	Newcastle	1	Leicester	1
Feb 08	Nottingham F	2	Middlesbrough	2
Feb 20	Sheffield W	0	Preston	2
Feb 08	Stoke	0	Sheffield U	1

Replays

Date	Home		Away	
Feb 11	Burnley	3	Luton	0
Feb 12	Middlesbrough	6	Nottingham F	2
Feb 20	Leicester	1	Newcastle	2

6th Round

Date	Home		Away	
Mar 01	Charlton	2	Preston	1
Mar 01	Liverpool	4	Birmingham	1
Mar 01	Middlesbrough	1	Burnley	1
Mar 01	Sheffield U	0	Newcastle	2

Replays

Date	Home		Away	
Mar 04	Burnley	1	Middlesbrough	0

Semi-finals

Date	Home		Away	
Mar 29	Burnley	0	Liverpool	0
	played at Blackburn			
Mar 29	Charlton	4	Newcastle	0
	played at Leeds			

Replays

Date	Home		Away	
Apr 12	Burnley	1	Liverpool	0
	played at Manchester C			

Final

Date	Home		Away	
Apr 26	Burnley	0	Charlton	1
	played at Wembley			

SEASON 1947-48

1st Round

Date	Home		Away	
Nov 29	Aldershot	2	Bromsgrove	1
Nov 29	Barrow	3	Carlisle	2
Nov 29	Bournemouth	2	Guildford	0
Nov 29	Bristol R	3	Leytonstone	2
Nov 29	Bromley	3	Reading	3
Nov 29	Cheltenham	5	Street	0
Nov 29	Chester	3	Bishop Auckland	1
Nov 29	Colchester	2	Banbury	1
Nov 29	Crewe	4	South Shields	1
Nov 29	Crystal Palace	2	Port Vale	1
Nov 29	Dartford	0	Bristol C	0
Nov 29	Exeter	1	Northampton	1
Nov 29	Gateshead	1	Bradford C	3
Nov 29	Gillingham	1	Leyton O	0
Nov 29	Great Yarmouth	1	Shrewsbury	4
Nov 29	Hartlepool	1	Darlington	0
Nov 29	Hull	1	Southport	1
Nov 29	Lincoln	0	Workington	2
Nov 29	New Brighton	4	Marine	0
Nov 29	Newport	3	Southend	2
Nov 29	Norwich	3	Merthyr T	0
Nov 29	Notts Co	9	Horsham	1
Nov 29	Oldham	6	Lancaster	0
Nov 29	Runcorn	4	Scunthorpe	2
Nov 29	Stockport	3	Accrington	1
Nov 29	Stockton	2	Grantham	1
Nov 29	Swindon	4	Ipswich	2
Nov 29	Tranmere	2	Stalybridge	0
Nov 29	Trowbridge	1	Brighton	1
Nov 29	Vauxhall	1	Walsall	2
Nov 29	Watford	1	Torquay	1
Nov 29	Wimbledon	0	Mansfield	1
Nov 29	Wrexham	5	Halifax	0
Nov 29	York	0	Rochdale	1

Replays

Date	Home		Away	
Dec 06	Brighton	5	Trowbridge	0
Dec 06	Bristol C	9	Dartford	2
Dec 06	Northampton	2	Exeter	0
Dec 06	Reading	3	Bromley	0
Dec 06	Southport	2	Hull	3
Dec 06	Torquay	3	Watford	0

2nd Round

Date	Home		Away	
Dec 13	Aldershot	0	Swindon	0
Dec 13	Bournemouth	1	Bradford C	0
Dec 13	Bristol C	0	Crystal Palace	1
Dec 13	Bristol R	4	New Brighton	0
Dec 13	Colchester	1	Wrexham	0
Dec 13	Hartlepool	1	Brighton	1
Dec 13	Hull	4	Cheltenham	2
Dec 13	Northampton	1	Torquay	1
Dec 13	Norwich	2	Walsall	2
Dec 13	Notts Co	1	Stockton	1
Dec 13	Oldham	0	Mansfield	1
Dec 13	Reading	3	Newport	0
Dec 13	Rochdale	1	Gillingham	1
Dec 13	Runcorn	0	Barrow	1
Dec 13	Stockport	1	Shrewsbury	1
Dec 13	Tranmere	0	Chester	1
Dec 13	Workington	1	Crewe	2

Replays

Date	Home		Away	
Dec 20	Brighton	2	Hartlepool	1
Dec 20	Gillingham	3	Rochdale	0
Dec 20	Shrewsbury	2	Stockport	2
Dec 20	Stockton	1	Notts Co	4
	played at Middlesbrough			
Dec 20	Swindon	2	Aldershot	0
Dec 20	Torquay	2	Northampton	0
Dec 20	Walsall	3	Norwich	2
Dec 22	Shrewsbury	2	Stockport	3
	played at Manchester C			

3rd Round

Date	Home		Away	
Jan 10	Arsenal	0	Bradford	1
Jan 10	Aston Villa	4	Manchester U	6
Jan 10	Birmingham	0	Notts Co	2
Jan 10	Blackburn	0	West Ham	0
Jan 10	Blackpool	4	Leeds	0
Jan 10	Bolton	0	Tottenham	2
Jan 10	Bournemouth	1	Wolverhampton	2
Jan 10	Bristol R	3	Swansea	0
Jan 10	Burnley	0	Swindon	2
Jan 10	Cardiff	1	Sheffield W	2
Jan 10	Charlton	2	Newcastle	1
Jan 10	Chelsea	5	Barrow	0
Jan 10	Colchester	1	Huddersfield	0
Jan 10	Coventry	2	Walsall	1
Jan 10	Crewe	3	Sheffield U	1
Jan 10	Crystal Palace	0	Chester	1
Jan 10	Derby	2	Chesterfield	0
Jan 10	Fulham	2	Doncaster	0
Jan 10	Gillingham	1	Q.P.R.	1
Jan 10	Grimsby	1	Everton	4
Jan 10	Hull	1	Middlesbrough	3
Jan 10	Leicester	1	Bury	0
Jan 10	Liverpool	4	Nottingham F	1

HM The King shaking hands with the Manchester United team before the start of the FA Cup Final at Wembley Stadium against Blackpool.

Jan 10 Manchester C 2 Barnsley 1
Jan 10 Mansfield 2 Stoke 4
Jan 10 Millwall 1 Preston 2
Jan 10 Plymouth 2 Luton 4
Jan 10 Portsmouth 4 Brighton 1
Jan 10 Rotherham 0 Brentford 3
Jan 10 Southampton 1 Sunderland 0
Jan 10 Stockport 3 Torquay 0
Jan 10 W.B.A. 2 Reading 0

Replays
Jan 17 Q.P.R. 3 Gillingham 1
Jan 17 West Ham 2 Blackburn 4

4th Round
Jan 24 Blackpool 4 Chester 0
Jan 24 Brentford 1 Middlesbrough 2
Jan 24 Charlton 3 Stockport 0
Jan 24 Colchester 3 Bradford 2
Jan 24 Crewe 0 Derby 3
Jan 24 Fulham 5 Bristol R 2
Jan 24 Leicester 2 Sheffield W 1
Jan 24 Luton 3 Coventry 2
Jan 24 Manchester C 2 Chelsea 0
Jan 24 Manchester U 3 Liverpool 0
played at Everton
Jan 24 Portsmouth 1 Preston 3
Jan 24 Q.P.R. 3 Stoke 0
Jan 24 Southampton 3 Blackburn 2
Jan 24 Swindon 1 Notts Co 0
Jan 24 Tottenham 3 W.B.A. 1
Jan 24 Wolverhampton 1 Everton 1

Replay
Jan 31 Everton 3 Wolverhampton 2

5th Round
Feb 07 Blackpool 5 Colchester 0
Feb 07 Fulham 1 Everton 1
Feb 07 Manchester C 0 Preston 1
Feb 07 Manchester U 2 Charlton 0
played at Huddersfield
Feb 07 Middlesbrough 1 Derby 2
Feb 07 Q.P.R. 3 Luton 1
Feb 07 Southampton 3 Swindon 0
Feb 07 Tottenham 5 Leicester 2

Replays
Feb 14 Everton 0 Fulham 1

6th Round
Feb 28 Fulham 0 Blackpool 2
Feb 28 Manchester U 4 Preston 1
Feb 28 Q.P.R. 1 Derby 1
Feb 28 Southampton 0 Tottenham 1

Replays
Mar 06 Derby 5 Q.P.R. 0

Semi-finals
Mar 13 Blackpool 3 Tottenham 1
played at Sheffield W
Mar 13 Derby 1 Manchester U 3
played at Aston Villa

Final
Apr 24 Blackpool 2 Manchester U 4
played at Wembley

Season 1948-49

1st Round
Dec 04 Barnet 2 Exeter 6
Dec 04 Bradford C 4 Doncaster 3
Dec 04 Colchester 2 Reading 4
Nov 27 Crewe 5 Billingham 0
Nov 27 Crystal Palace 0 Bristol c 1
Nov 27 Dartford 2 Leyton O 3
Nov 27 Gainsborough 1 Witton 0
Nov 27 Gateshead 3 Netherfield 0
Dec 04 Halifax 0 Scunthorpe 0
Nov 27 Hartlepool 1 Chester 3
Nov 27 Hull 3 Accrington 1
Dec 04 Ipswich 0 Aldershot 3
Nov 27 Kidderminster 0 Hereford 3
Dec 04 Leytonstone 2 Watford 1
Nov 27 Mansfield 4 Gloucester 0
Nov 27 Millwall 1 Tooting 0
Nov 27 New Brighton 1 Carlisle 0
Nov 27 Newport 3 Brighton 1
Nov 27 Northampton 2 Dulwich 1
Nov 27 Norwich 1 Wellington 0
Nov 27 Notts Co 2 Port Vale 1
Nov 27 Peterborough 0 Torquay 1
Dec 04 Rhyl 0 Scarborough 2
Nov 27 Rochdale 1 Barrow 1
played at Oldham
Dec 04 Southend 1 Swansea 2
Nov 27 Southport 2 Horden 1
Nov 27 Tranmere 1 Darlington 3
Nov 27 Walsall 2 Bristol R 1
Nov 27 Walthamstow 3 Cambridge 2
Nov 27 Weymouth 2 Chelmsford 1
Nov 27 Workington 0 Stockport 3
Nov 27 Wrexham 0 Oldham 3
Nov 27 Yeovil 4 Romford 0
Nov 27 York 2 Runcorn 1

Replays
Dec 04 Barrow 2 Rochdale 0
Dec 06 Scunthorpe 1 Halifax 0

2nd Round
Dec 11 Aldershot 1 Chester 0
Dec 11 Bradford C 0 New Brighton 0
Dec 11 Bristol C 3 Swansea 1
Dec 11 Crewe 3 Millwall 2
Dec 11 Darlington 1 Leyton O 0
Dec 11 Exeter 2 Hereford 1
Dec 11 Gateshead 3 Scarborough 0
Dec 11 Hull 0 Reading 0
Dec 11 Leytonstone 3 Newport 4
Dec 11 Mansfield 2 Northampton 1
Dec 11 Notts Co 3 Barrow 2
Dec 11 Scunthorpe 0 Stockport 1
Dec 11 Southport 2 York 2
Dec 11 Torquay 3 Norwich 1
Dec 11 Walsall 4 Gainsborough 3
Dec 11 Walthamstow 2 Oldham 2
Dec 11 Weymouth 0 Yeovil 4

Replays
Dec 18 New Brighton 1 Bradford C 0
Dec 18 Oldham 3 Walthamstow 1
Dec 18 Reading 1 Hull 2
Dec 18 York 0 Southport 2

3rd Round
Jan 08 Arsenal 3 Tottenham 0
Jan 08 Aston Villa 1 Bolton 1
Jan 08 Barnsley 0 Blackpool 1
Jan 08 Blackburn 1 Hull 2
Jan 08 Brentford 3 Middlesbrough 2
Jan 08 Bristol C 1 Chelsea 3
Jan 08 Burnley 2 Charlton 1
Jan 08 Crewe 0 Sunderland 2
Jan 08 Derby 4 Southport 1
Jan 08 Everton 1 Manchester C 0
Jan 08 Fulham 0 Walsall 1
Jan 08 Gateshead 3 Aldershot 1
Jan 08 Grimsby 2 Exeter 1
Jan 08 Leeds 1 Newport 3
Jan 08 Leicester 1 Birmingham 1
Jan 08 Lincoln 0 W.B.A. 1
Jan 08 Luton 3 West Ham 1
Jan 08 Manchester U 6 Bournemouth 0
Jan 08 Newcastle 0 Bradford 2
Jan 08 Nottingham F 2 Liverpool 2
Jan 08 Oldham 2 Cardiff 3
Jan 08 Plymouth 0 Notts Co 1
Jan 08 Portsmouth 7 Stockport 0
Jan 08 Preston 2 Mansfield 1
Jan 08 Q.P.R. 0 Huddersfield 0
Jan 08 Rotherham 4 Darlington 2
Jan 08 Sheffield U 5 New Brighton 2
Jan 08 Sheffield W 2 Southampton 1
Jan 08 Swindon 1 Stoke 3
Jan 08 Torquay 1 Coventry 0
Jan 08 Wolverhampton 6 Chesterfield 0
Jan 08 Yeovil 3 Bury 1

Replays
Jan 15 Birmingham 1 Leicester 1
Jan 15 Bolton 0 Aston Villa 0
Jan 15 Huddersfield 5 Q.P.R. 0
Jan 15 Liverpool 4 Nottingham F 0
Jan 17 Aston Villa 2 Bolton 1
played at Aston Villa
Jan 17 Birmingham 1 Leicester 2
played at Birmingham

4th Round
Jan 29 Aston Villa 1 Cardiff 2
Jan 29 Brentford 1 Torquay 0
Jan 29 Chelsea 2 Everton 0
Jan 29 Derby 1 Arsenal 0
Jan 29 Gateshead 1 W.B.A. 3
Jan 29 Grimsby 2 Hull 3
Jan 29 Leicester 2 Preston 0
Jan 29 Liverpool 1 Notts Co 0
played at Manchester C
Jan 29 Luton 4 Walsall 0
Jan 29 Manchester U 1 Bradford 1
Jan 29 Newport 3 Huddersfield 3
Jan 29 Portsmouth 2 Sheffield W 1
Jan 29 Rotherham 0 Burnley 1
Jan 29 Sheffield U 0 Wolverhampton 3
Jan 29 Stoke 1 Blackpool 1
Jan 29 Yeovil 2 Sunderland 1

Replays
Feb 05 Blackpool 0 Stoke 1
Feb 05 Bradford 1 Manchester U 1
Feb 05 Huddersfield 1 Newport 3
Feb 07 Bradford 0 Manchester U 5
played at Manchester C

5th Round
Feb 12 Brentford 4 Burnley 2
Feb 12 Derby 2 Cardiff 1
Feb 12 Luton 5 Leicester 5
Feb 12 Manchester U 8 Yeovil 0
Feb 12 Portsmouth 3 Newport 2
Feb 12 Stoke 0 Hull 2
Feb 12 Wolverhampton 3 Liverpool 1
Feb 12 W.B.A. 3 Chelsea 0

Replay
Feb 19 Leicester 5 Luton 3

6th Round
Feb 26 Brentford 0 Leicester 2
Feb 26 Hull 0 Manchester U 1
Feb 26 Portsmouth 2 Derby 1
Feb 26 Wolverhampton 1 W.B.A. 0

Semi-finals
Mar 26 Leicester 3 Portsmouth 1
played at Arsenal
Mar 26 Manchester U 1 Wolverhampton 1
played at Sheffield W

Replay
Apr 02 Manchester U 0 Wolverhampton 1
played at Everton

Final
Apr 30 Leicester 1 Wolverhampton 3
played at Wembley

Season 1949-50

1st Round
Nov 26 Accrington 0 Hartlepool 1
Nov 26 Bradford C 9 Fleetwood 0
Nov 26 Bromley 1 Watford 2
Nov 26 Carlisle 1 Lincoln 0
Nov 26 Chester 4 Goole 1
Nov 26 Crystal Palace 0 Newport 3
Nov 26 Darlington 2 Crewe 2
Nov 26 Doncaster 5 New Brighton 1
Nov 26 Gateshead 3 York 1
Nov 26 Gloucester 2 Norwich 3
Nov 26 Gravesend 1 Torquay 3
Nov 26 Hastings 1 Gillingham 3
Nov 26 Hereford 3 Bromsgrove 0
Nov 26 Ipswich 2 Brighton 1
Nov 26 Leyton O 0 Southend 2
Nov 26 Leytonstone 1 Chelmsford 2
Nov 26 Mansfield 4 Walsall 1
Nov 26 Millwall 3 Exeter 5
Nov 26 Netherfield 4 North Shields 3
Nov 26 Northampton 4 Walthamstow 1
Nov 26 Nottingham F 1 Bristol C 0
Nov 26 Notts Co 4 Tilbury 0
Nov 26 Nuneaton 2 Kings Lynn 1
Nov 26 Oldham 4 Stockton 0
Nov 26 Port Vale 1 Wealdstone 0
Nov 26 Rhyl 0 Rochdale 3
Nov 26 Southport 1 Barrow 1
Nov 26 Stockport 3 Billingham 0
Nov 26 Swindon 1 Bristol R 0
Nov 26 Tranmere 2 Halifax 1
Nov 26 Weymouth 2 Aldershot 2
Nov 26 Witton 0 Mossley 1
Nov 26 Wrexham 4 Grantham 1
Nov 26 Yeovil 4 Romford 1

Replays
Nov 30 Aldershot 2 Weymouth 3
Nov 30 Crewe 1 Darlington 0
Dec 01 Barrow 0 Southport 1

2nd Round
Dec 10 Carlisle 2 Swindon 0
Dec 10 Chelmsford 1 Ipswich 1
Dec 10 Crewe 1 Oldham 1
Dec 10 Doncaster 1 Mansfield 0
Dec 10 Exeter 2 Chester 0
Dec 10 Hartlepool 1 Norwich 1
Dec 10 Newport 1 Gateshead 1
Dec 10 Northampton 4 Torquay 2
Dec 10 Nottingham F 0 Stockport 2
Dec 10 Nuneaton 0 Mossley 0
Dec 10 Port Vale 1 Tranmere 0
Dec 10 Rochdale 1 Notts Co 2
Dec 10 Southport 2 Bradford C 1
Dec 10 Watford 6 Netherfield 0
Dec 10 Weymouth 2 Hereford 1
Dec 10 Wrexham 2 Southend 2
Dec 10 Yeovil 3 Gillingham 1

Replays
Dec 13 Oldham 0 Crewe 0
Dec 15 Gateshead 1 Newport 2
Dec 15 Ipswich 1 Chelmsford 0
Dec 15 Southend 2 Wrexham 0
Dec 16 Norwich 5 Hartlepool 1
Dec 17 Mossley 0 Nuneaton 3
Dec 19 Crewe 0 Oldham 3
played at Manchester C

3rd Round
Jan 07 Arsenal 1 Sheffield W 0

Jan 07 Aston Villa 2 Middlesbrough 2
Jan 07 Blackburn 0 Liverpool 0
Jan 07 Blackpool 4 Southend 0
Jan 07 Bradford 0 Bournemouth 1
Jan 07 Brentford 0 Chelsea 1
Jan 07 Bury 5 Rotherham 4
Jan 07 Cardiff 2 W.B.A. 2
Jan 07 Carlisle 2 Leeds 5
Jan 07 Charlton 2 Fulham 2
Jan 07 Chesterfield 3 Yeovil 1
Jan 07 Coventry 1 Bolton 2
Jan 07 Exeter 3 Nuneaton 0
Jan 07 Luton 3 Grimsby 4
Jan 07 Manchester C 3 Derby 5
Jan 07 Manchester U 4 Weymouth 0
Jan 07 Newport 1 Port Vale 2
Jan 07 Northampton 1 Southampton 1
Jan 07 Notts Co 1 Burnley 4
Jan 07 Oldham 2 Newcastle 7
Jan 07 Plymouth 1 Wolverhampton 1
Jan 07 Portsmouth 1 Norwich 1
Jan 07 Q.P.R. 0 Everton 2
Jan 07 Reading 2 Doncaster 3
Jan 07 Sheffield U 3 Leicester 1
Jan 07 Southport 0 Hull 0
Jan 07 Stockport 4 Barnsley 2
Jan 07 Stoke 0 Tottenham 1
Jan 07 Sunderland 6 Huddersfield 0
Jan 07 Swansea 3 Birmingham 0
Jan 07 Watford 2 Preston 2
Jan 07 West Ham 5 Ipswich 1

Replays
Jan 11 Fulham 1 Charlton 2
Jan 11 Liverpool 2 Blackburn 1
Jan 11 Middlesbrough 0 Aston Villa 0
Jan 11 Preston 0 Watford 1
Jan 11 Southampton 2 Northampton 3
Jan 11 Wolverhampton 3 Plymouth 0
Jan 11 W.B.A. 0 Cardiff 1
Jan 12 Hull 5 Southport 0
Jan 12 Norwich 0 Portsmouth 2
Jan 16 Aston Villa 0 Middlesbrough 3
played at Leeds

4th Round
Jan 28 Arsenal 2 Swansea 1
Jan 28 Blackpool 2 Doncaster 1
Jan 28 Bournemouth 1 Northampton 1
Jan 28 Burnley 2 Port Vale 1
Jan 28 Bury 2 Derby 2
Jan 28 Charlton 1 Cardiff 1
Jan 28 Chelsea 3 Newcastle 0
Jan 28 Chesterfield 3 Middlesbrough 2
Jan 28 Leeds 1 Bolton 1
Jan 28 Liverpool 3 Exeter 1
Jan 28 Portsmouth 5 Grimsby 0
Jan 28 Stockport 0 Hull 0
Jan 28 Tottenham 5 Sunderland 1
Jan 28 Watford 0 Manchester U 1
Jan 28 West Ham 1 Everton 2
Jan 28 Wolverhampton 0 Sheffield U 0

Replays
Feb 01 Bolton 2 Leeds 3
Feb 01 Cardiff 2 Charlton 0
Feb 01 Derby 5 Bury 2
Feb 01 Sheffield U 3 Wolverhampton 4
Feb 02 Hull 0 Stockport 2
Feb 02 Northampton 2 Bournemouth 1

5th Round
Feb 11 Arsenal 2 Burnley 0
Feb 11 Chesterfield 1 Chelsea 1
Feb 11 Derby 4 Northampton 2
Feb 11 Everton 1 Tottenham 0
Feb 11 Leeds 3 Cardiff 1
Feb 11 Manchester U 3 Portsmouth 3
Feb 11 Stockport 1 Liverpool 2
Feb 11 Wolverhampton 0 Blackpool 0

Replays
Feb 15 Blackpool 1 Wolverhampton 0
Feb 15 Chelsea 3 Chesterfield 0
Feb 15 Portsmouth 1 Manchester U 3

6th Round
Mar 04 Arsenal 1 Leeds 0
Mar 04 Chelsea 2 Manchester U 0
Mar 04 Derby 1 Everton 2
Mar 04 Liverpool 2 Blackpool 1

Semi-finals
Mar 18 Arsenal 2 Chelsea 2
played at Tottenham
Mar 25 Everton 0 Liverpool 2
played at Manchester C

Replay
Mar 22 Arsenal 1 Chelsea 0
played at Tottenham

Final
Apr 29 Arsenal 2 Liverpool 0
played at Wembley

Season 1950-51

1st Round
Nov 25 Aldershot 2 Bromley 2
Nov 25 Bishop Auckland 2 York 2
Nov 25 Bournemouth 1 Colchester 0
Nov 25 Bradford C 2 Oldham 2
Nov 25 Bristol C 4 Gloucester 0
Nov 25 Bristol R 1 Llanelly 1
Nov 25 Bromsgrove 1 Hereford 3
Nov 25 Carlisle 2 Barrow 1
Nov 25 Chelmsford 2 Tonbridge 2
Nov 25 Chester 1 Bradford 2
Nov 25 Cleator Moor 0 Tranmere 5
played at Workington
Nov 25 Crewe 4 North Shields 0
Nov 29 Crystal Palace 1 Millwall 4
Nov 25 Darlington 2 Rotherham 7
Nov 25 Gainsborough 0 Plymouth 3
Nov 25 Glastonbury 1 Exeter 2
Nov 25 Guildford 1 Dartford 5
Nov 25 Halifax 2 Ashington 3
Nov 25 Leyton O 1 Ipswich 2
Nov 25 Linby 1 Gillingham 4
Nov 25 Lincoln 1 Southport 1
Nov 25 Mansfield 1 Walthamstow 0
Nov 25 Newport 4 Walsall 2
Nov 25 Norwich 2 Watford 0
Nov 25 Nottingham F 6 Torquay 1
Nov 25 Port Vale 3 New Brighton 2
Nov 25 Reading 3 Cheltenham 1
Nov 25 Rochdale 3 Willington 1
Nov 25 Scarborough 1 Rhyl 2
Nov 29 Southend 0 Swindon 3
Nov 25 Tooting & M 2 Brighton 3
Nov 25 Witton 1 Nelson 2
Nov 25 Worcester 1 Hartlepool 4
Nov 25 Wrexham 1 Accrington 0

Replays
Nov 28 Llanelly 1 Bristol R 1
Nov 28 Oldham 2 Bradford C 1
Nov 28 Southport 3 Lincoln 2
Nov 29 Bromley 0 Aldershot 1
Nov 29 Tonbridge 0 Chelmsford 1
Nov 29 York 2 Bishop Auckland 1
Dec 04 Bristol R 3 Llanelly 1
played at Cardiff

2nd Round
Dec 09 Aldershot 3 Bournemouth 0
Dec 09 Ashington 1 Rochdale 2
Dec 09 Brighton 2 Ipswich 0
Dec 09 Bristol C 2 Wrexham 1
Dec 09 Bristol R 2 Gillingham 2
Dec 09 Chelmsford 1 Mansfield 4
Dec 09 Crewe 2 Plymouth 2
Dec 09 Exeter 3 Swindon 0
Dec 09 Hartlepool 1 Oldham 2
Dec 09 Hereford 0 Newport 3
Dec 09 Millwall 1 Bradford 1
Dec 09 Port Vale 3 Nelson 2
Dec 09 Reading 4 Dartford 0
Dec 09 Rhyl 0 Norwich 1
Dec 09 Rotherham 3 Nottingham F 1
Dec 09 Southport 1 Carlisle 3
Dec 09 York 2 Tranmere 1

Replays
Dec 13 Bradford 0 Millwall 1
Dec 13 Gillingham 1 Bristol R 1
Dec 13 Plymouth 3 Crewe 0
Dec 18 Bristol R 2 Gillingham 1
played at Tottenham

3rd Round
Jan 06 Arsenal 0 Carlisle 0
Jan 06 Aston Villa 2 Burnley 0
Jan 06 Birmingham 2 Manchester C 0
Jan 06 Bolton 2 York 0
Jan 06 Brighton 2 Chesterfield 1
Jan 06 Bristol C 2 Blackburn 1
Jan 10 Bristol R 5 Aldershot 1
Jan 06 Charlton 2 Blackpool 2
Jan 06 Derby 2 W.B.A. 2
Jan 06 Fulham 1 Sheffield W 0
Jan 06 Grimsby 3 Exeter 3
Jan 06 Huddersfield 2 Tottenham 0
Jan 06 Hull 2 Everton 0
Jan 06 Leeds 1 Middlesbrough 0
Jan 06 Leicester 0 Preston 3
Jan 06 Luton 2 Portsmouth 0
Jan 06 Manchester U 4 Oldham 1
Jan 06 Mansfield 2 Swansea 0
Jan 06 Newcastle 4 Bury 1
Jan 06 Newport 3 Reading 2
Jan 06 Northampton 3 Barnsley 1
Jan 06 Norwich 3 Liverpool 1
Jan 06 Notts Co 3 Southampton 4
Jan 06 Plymouth 1 Wolverhampton 2
Jan 06 Q.P.R. 3 Millwall 4
Jan 09 Rochdale 2 Chelsea 3
Jan 06 Rotherham 2 Doncaster 1
Jan 06 Sheffield U 1 Gateshead 0
Jan 06 Stockport 2 Brentford 1
Jan 06 Stoke 2 Port Vale 2
Jan 06 Sunderland 2 Coventry 0
Jan 06 West Ham 2 Cardiff 1

Replays
Jan 08 Port Vale 0 Stoke 1
played at Stoke
Jan 10 Blackpool 3 Charlton 0
Jan 10 Exeter 4 Grimsby 2
Jan 10 W.B.A. 0 Derby 1
Jan 11 Carlisle 1 Arsenal 4

4th Round
Jan 27 Arsenal 3 Northampton 2
Jan 27 Blackpool 2 Stockport 1
Jan 27 Bristol C 1 Brighton 0
Jan 27 Derby 1 Birmingham 3
Jan 27 Exeter 1 Chelsea 1
Jan 27 Hull 2 Rotherham 0
Jan 27 Luton 1 Bristol R 2
Jan 27 Manchester U 4 Leeds 0
Jan 27 Millwall 0 Fulham 1
Jan 27 Newcastle 3 Bolton 2
Jan 27 Newport 0 Norwich 2
Jan 27 Preston 0 Huddersfield 2
Jan 27 Sheffield U 0 Mansfield 0
Jan 27 Stoke 1 West Ham 0
Jan 27 Sunderland 2 Southampton 0
Jan 27 Wolverhampton 3 Aston Villa 1

Replays
Jan 31 Chelsea 2 Exeter 0
Jan 31 Mansfield 2 Sheffield U 1

5th Round
Feb 10 Birmingham 2 Bristol C 0
Feb 10 Blackpool 2 Mansfield 0
Feb 10 Bristol R 3 Hull 0
Feb 10 Chelsea 1 Fulham 1
Feb 10 Manchester U 1 Arsenal 0
Feb 10 Stoke 2 Newcastle 4
Feb 10 Sunderland 3 Norwich 1
Feb 10 Wolverhampton 2 Huddersfield 0

Replay
Feb 14 Fulham 3 Chelsea 0

6th Round
Feb 24 Birmingham 1 Manchester U 0
Feb 24 Blackpool 1 Fulham 0
Feb 24 Newcastle 0 Bristol R 0
Feb 24 Sunderland 1 Wolverhampton 1

Replays
Feb 28 Bristol R 1 Newcastle 3
Feb 28 Wolverhampton 3 Sunderland 1

Semi-finals
Mar 10 Birmingham 0 Blackpool 0
played at Manchester C
Mar 10 Newcastle 0 Wolverhampton 0
played at Sheffield W

Replays
Mar 14 Birmingham 1 Blackpool 2
played at Everton
Mar 14 Newcastle 2 Wolverhampton 1
played at Huddersfield

Final
Apr 28 Blackpool 0 Newcastle 2
played at Wembley

Season 1951-52

1st Round
Nov 24 Accrington 1 Chester 2
Nov 24 Aylesbury 0 Watford 5
Nov 24 Bangor 2 Southport 2
Nov 24 Barnstaple 2 Folkestone 2
Nov 24 Barrow 0 Chesterfield 2
Nov 24 Blackhall 2 Workington 5
Nov 24 Blyth 2 Bishop Auckland 1
Nov 24 Bradford C 6 Carlisle 1
Nov 24 Brighton 1 Bristol C 2
Nov 24 Bristol R 3 Kettering 0
Nov 24 Brush Sports 2 Weymouth 3
Nov 24 Colchester 3 Port Vale 1
Nov 24 Crewe 2 Lincoln 4
Nov 24 Crystal Palace 0 Gillingham 1
Nov 24 Grimsby 4 Darlington 0
Nov 24 Guildford 4 Hereford 1
Nov 24 Hartlepool 2 Rhyl 0
Nov 24 Ilkeston 0 Rochdale 2
Nov 24 Kings Lynn 1 Exeter 3
Nov 24 Leyton 3 Chippenham 0
Nov 24 Leyton O 2 Gorleston 2
Nov 24 Leytonstone 2 Shrewsbury 0
Nov 24 Merthyr T 2 Ipswich 2
Nov 24 Millwall 1 Plymouth 0
Nov 24 Nelson 0 Oldham 4
Nov 24 Newport 4 Barry 0

Nov 24 Norwich 3 Northampton 2
Nov 24 Rawmarsh 1 Buxton 4
Nov 24 Reading 1 Walsall 0
Nov 24 Scunthorpe 5 Billingham 0
Nov 24 Southend 6 Bournemouth 1
Nov 24 Stockport 2 Gateshead 2
Nov 24 Stockton 1 Mansfield 1
Nov 24 Swindon 2 Bedford 0
Nov 24 Tonbridge 0 Aldershot 0
Nov 24 Torquay 3 Bromley 2
Nov 24 Tranmere 4 Goole 2
Nov 24 Witton 2 Gainsborough 1
Nov 24 Wrexham 3 Halifax 0
Nov 24 York 1 Bradford 1

Replays
Nov 27 Southport 3 Bangor 0
Nov 28 Aldershot 3 Tonbridge 2
Nov 28 Bradford 1 York 1
Nov 28 Folkestone 5 Barnstaple 2
Nov 28 Gateshead 1 Stockport 1
Nov 28 Mansfield 0 Stockton 2
Nov 29 Gorleston 0 Leyton O 0
Dec 03 Bradford 4 York 0
played at Leeds
Dec 03 Gateshead 2 Stockport 1
played at Sheffield W
Dec 03 Gorleston 4 Leyton O 5
played at Arsenal
Dec 05 Ipswich 1 Merthyr T 0

2nd Round
Dec 15 Bradford 3 Bradford C 2
Dec 15 Bristol R 2 Weymouth 0
Dec 15 Buxton 4 Aldershot 3
Dec 15 Chester 5 Leyton 2
Dec 15 Colchester 2 Bristol C 1
Dec 15 Gateshead 2 Guildford 0
Dec 15 Gillingham 0 Rochdale 3
Dec 15 Ipswich 4 Exeter 0
Dec 15 Leytonstone 2 Newport 2
Dec 15 Lincoln 3 Grimsby 1
Dec 15 Millwall 0 Scunthorpe 0
Dec 15 Norwich 3 Chesterfield 1
Dec 15 Reading 1 Southport 1
Dec 15 Southend 5 Oldham 0
Dec 15 Stockton 2 Folkestone 1
Dec 15 Swindon 3 Torquay 3
Dec 15 Tranmere 1 Blyth 1
Dec 15 Watford 1 Hartlepool 2
Dec 15 Witton 3 Workington 3
Dec 15 Wrexham 1 Leyton O 1

Replays
Dec 18 Southport 1 Reading 1
Dec 19 Blyth 1 Tranmere 1
Dec 19 Leyton O 3 Wrexham 2
Dec 19 Torquay 1 Swindon 1
Dec 20 Newport 3 Leytonstone 0
Dec 20 Scunthorpe 3 Millwall 0
Dec 20 Workington 1 Witton 0
Jan 01 Reading 2 Southport 0
played at Aston Villa
Jan 02 Swindon 3 Torquay 1
played at Bristol C
Jan 03 Blyth 2 Tranmere 2
played at Carlisle
Jan 07 Blyth 1 Tranmere 5
played at Everton

3rd Round
Jan 12 Barnsley 3 Colchester 0
Jan 12 Bradford 2 Sheffield W 1
Jan 12 Brentford 3 Q.P.R. 1
Jan 12 Bristol R 2 Preston 0
Jan 12 Burnley 1 Hartlepool 0
Jan 12 Cardiff 1 Swindon 1
Jan 12 Chelsea 2 Chester 2
Jan 12 Doncaster 2 Buxton 0
Jan 12 Fulham 0 Birmingham 1
Jan 12 Huddersfield 1 Tranmere 2
Jan 12 Ipswich 2 Gateshead 2
Jan 12 Leicester 1 Coventry 1
Jan 12 Leyton O 0 Everton 0
Jan 12 Liverpool 1 Workington 0
Jan 12 Luton 1 Charlton 0
Jan 12 Manchester C 2 Wolverhampton 2
Jan 12 Manchester U 0 Hull 2
Jan 12 Middlesbrough 2 Derby 2
Jan 12 Newcastle 4 Aston Villa 2
Jan 12 Norwich 0 Arsenal 5
Jan 12 Nottingham F 2 Blackburn 2
Jan 12 Notts Co 4 Stockton 0
Jan 12 Portsmouth 4 Lincoln 0
Jan 12 Reading 0 Swansea 3
Jan 12 Rochdale 0 Leeds 2
Jan 12 Rotherham 2 Bury 1
Jan 12 Scunthorpe 0 Tottenham 3
Jan 12 Sheffield U 2 Newport 0
Jan 12 Southend 3 Southampton 0
Jan 12 Sunderland 0 Stoke 0
Jan 12 West Ham 2 Blackpool 1
Jan 12 W.B.A. 4 Bolton 0

Replays
Jan 14 Coventry 4 Leicester 1
Jan 14 Stoke 3 Sunderland 1
Jan 16 Blackburn 2 Nottingham F 0
Jan 16 Chester 2 Chelsea 3
Jan 16 Derby 0 Middlesbrough 2
Jan 16 Everton 1 Leyton O 3
Jan 16 Gateshead 3 Ipswich 3
Jan 16 Swindon 1 Cardiff 0
Jan 16 Wolverhampton 4 Manchester C 1
Jan 21 Gateshead 2 Ipswich 1
played at Sheffield U

4th Round
Feb 02 Arsenal 4 Barnsley 0
Feb 02 Birmingham 0 Leyton O 1
Feb 02 Blackburn 2 Hull 0
Feb 02 Burnley 2 Coventry 0
Feb 02 Chelsea 4 Tranmere 0
Feb 06 Gateshead 0 W.B.A. 2
played at Newcastle
Feb 02 Leeds 2 Bradford 0
Feb 02 Liverpool 2 Wolverhampton 1
Feb 02 Luton 2 Brentford 2
Feb 06 Middlesbrough 1 Doncaster 4
Feb 02 Notts Co 1 Portsmouth 3
Feb 02 Southend 2 Bristol R 1
Feb 02 Swansea 3 Rotherham 0
Feb 02 Swindon 1 Stoke 1
Feb 02 Tottenham 0 Newcastle 3
Feb 02 West Ham 0 Sheffield U 0

Replays
Feb 04 Stoke 0 Swindon 1
Feb 06 Brentford 0 Luton 0
Feb 06 Sheffield U 4 West Ham 2
Feb 11 Brentford 2 Luton 3
played at Arsenal

5th Round
Feb 23 Blackburn 1 W.B.A. 0
Feb 23 Burnley 2 Liverpool 0
Feb 23 Leeds 1 Chelsea 1
Feb 23 Leyton O 0 Arsenal 3
Feb 23 Luton 3 Swindon 1
Feb 23 Portsmouth 4 Doncaster 0
Feb 23 Southend 1 Sheffield U 2
Feb 23 Swansea 0 Newcastle 1

Replays
Feb 27 Chelsea 1 Leeds 1
Mar 03 Chelsea 5 Leeds 1
played at Aston Villa

6th Round
Mar 08 Blackburn 3 Burnley 1
Mar 08 Luton 2 Arsenal 3
Mar 08 Portsmouth 2 Newcastle 4
Mar 08 Sheffield U 0 Chelsea 1

Semi-finals
Apr 05 Arsenal 1 Chelsea 1
played at Tottenham
Mar 29 Blackburn 0 Newcastle 0
played at Sheffield W

Replays
Apr 02 Blackburn 1 Newcastle 2
played at Leeds
Apr 07 Arsenal 3 Chelsea 0
played at Tottenham

Final
May 03 Arsenal 0 Newcastle 1
played at Wembley

SEASON 1952-53

1st Round
Nov 22 Aldershot 0 Millwall 0
Nov 22 Bath 3 Southend 1
Nov 22 Beighton 0 Wrexham 3
Nov 22 Boston 1 Oldham 2
Nov 22 Bradford 2 Rochdale 1
Nov 22 Bradford C 4 Rhyl 0
Nov 22 Chester 0 Hartlepool 1
Nov 22 Chesterfield 1 Workington 0
Nov 22 Coventry 2 Bristol C 0
Nov 22 Crystal Palace 1 Reading 1
Nov 22 Darlington 2 Grimsby 3
Nov 22 Gainsborough 1 Netherfield 1
Nov 22 Gateshead 2 Crewe 0
Nov 22 Greys 0 Llanelly 5
Nov 22 Guildford 1 Gt Yarmouth 2
Nov 22 Halifax 1 Ashton 1
Nov 22 Hendon 0 Northampton 0
Nov 22 Horden 1 Accrington 2
Nov 22 Ipswich 2 Bournemouth 2
Nov 22 Kidderminster 0 Finchley 1
Nov 22 Leyton 0 Hereford 0
Nov 22 Leyton O 1 Bristol R 1
Nov 22 Leytonstone 0 Watford 2
Nov 22 Newport 2 Walsall 1
Nov 22 North Shields 3 Stockport 6
Nov 22 Peterborough 2 Torquay 1
Nov 22 Port Vale 2 Exeter 1
Nov 22 Q.P.R. 2 Shrewsbury 2
Nov 22 Scarborough 0 Mansfield 8
Nov 22 Scunthorpe 1 Carlisle 0
Nov 22 Selby 1 Bishop Auckland 5
Nov 22 Southport 3 Bangor 1
Nov 22 Swindon 5 Newport (IOW) 0
Nov 22 Tonbridge 2 Norwich 2
Nov 22 Tranmere 8 Ashington 1
Nov 22 Walthamstow 2 Wimbledon 2
Nov 22 Wellington 1 Gillingham 1
Nov 22 Weymouth 1 Colchester 1
Nov 22 Yeovil 1 Brighton 4
Nov 22 York 1 Barrow 2

Replays
Nov 24 Bristol R 1 Leyton O 0
Nov 25 Ashton 1 Halifax 2
Nov 26 Bournemouth 2 Ipswich 2
Nov 26 Gillingham 3 Wellington 0
Nov 26 Reading 1 Crystal Palace 3
Nov 26 Wimbledon 0 Walthamstow 3
Nov 27 Colchester 4 Weymouth 0
Nov 27 Gt Yarmouth 1 Guildford 0
Nov 27 Hereford 3 Leyton 2
Nov 27 Millwall 7 Aldershot 1
Nov 27 Netherfield 0 Gainsborough 3
Nov 27 Northampton 2 Hendon 0
Nov 27 Norwich 1 Tonbridge 0
Nov 27 Shrewsbury 2 Q.P.R. 2
Dec 01 Bournemouth 2 Ipswich 3
played at Arsenal
Dec 01 Q.P.R. 1 Shrewsbury 4
played at Aston Villa

2nd Round
Dec 06 Accrington 0 Mansfield 2
Dec 06 Barrow 2 Millwall 2
Dec 06 Bishop Auckland 1 Coventry 4
Dec 06 Bradford 1 Gateshead 2
Dec 06 Bradford C 1 Ipswich 1
Dec 06 Brighton 2 Norwich 0
Dec 06 Colchester 3 Llanelly 2
Dec 10 Finchley 3 Crystal Palace 1
Dec 06 Grimsby 1 Bath 0
Dec 06 Gt Yarmouth 1 Wrexham 2
Dec 06 Halifax 4 Southport 2
Dec 06 Hereford 0 Scunthorpe 0
Dec 06 Newport 2 Gainsborough 1
Dec 06 Peterborough 0 Bristol R 1
Dec 06 Port Vale 0 Oldham 3
Dec 06 Shrewsbury 0 Chesterfield 0
Dec 06 Stockport 3 Gillingham 1
Dec 06 Swindon 2 Northampton 0
Dec 06 Tranmere 2 Hartlepool 1
Dec 06 Walthamstow 1 Watford 1

Replays
Dec 10 Chesterfield 2 Shrewsbury 4
Dec 10 Ipswich 5 Bradford C 1
Dec 10 Millwall 4 Barrow 1
Dec 10 Watford 1 Walthamstow 2
Dec 11 Scunthorpe 2 Hereford 1

3rd Round
Jan 10 Arsenal 4 Doncaster 0
Jan 10 Aston Villa 3 Middlesbrough 1
Jan 10 Barnsley 4 Brighton 3
Jan 14 Bolton 3 Fulham 1
Jan 10 Brentford 2 Leeds 1
Jan 10 Derby 4 Chelsea 4
Jan 10 Everton 3 Ipswich 2
Jan 10 Gateshead 1 Liverpool 0
Jan 10 Grimsby 1 Bury 3
Jan 10 Halifax 3 Cardiff 1
Jan 10 Huddersfield 2 Bristol R 0
Jan 10 Hull 3 Charlton 1
Jan 10 Leicester 2 Notts Co 4
Jan 10 Lincoln 1 Southampton 1
Jan 10 Luton 6 Blackburn 1
Jan 10 Manchester C 7 Swindon 0
Jan 10 Mansfield 0 Nottingham F 1
Jan 10 Millwall 0 Manchester U 1
Jan 14 Newcastle 3 Swansea 0
Jan 10 Newport 1 Sheffield U 4
Jan 10 Oldham 1 Birmingham 3
Jan 10 Plymouth 4 Coventry 1
Jan 10 Portsmouth 1 Burnley 1
Jan 10 Preston 5 Wolverhampton 2
Jan 10 Rotherham 2 Colchester 2
Jan 10 Sheffield W 1 Blackpool 2
Jan 10 Shrewsbury 2 Finchley 0
Jan 10 Stoke 2 Wrexham 1
Jan 10 Sunderland 1 Scunthorpe 1
Jan 10 Tranmere 1 Tottenham 1
Jan 10 Walthamstow 2 Stockport 1
Jan 10 West Ham 1 W.B.A. 4

Replays
Jan 12 Tottenham 9 Tranmere 1
Jan 13 Burnley 3 Portsmouth 1
Jan 14 Chelsea 1 Derby 0
Jan 14 Southampton 2 Lincoln 1
Jan 15 Colchester 0 Rotherham 2
Jan 15 Scunthorpe 1 Sunderland 2

4th Round
Jan 31 Arsenal 6 Bury 2
Jan 31 Aston Villa 0 Brentford 0
Jan 31 Blackpool 1 Huddersfield 0
Jan 31 Bolton 1 Notts Co 1
Jan 31 Burnley 2 Sunderland 0
Jan 31 Chelsea 1 W.B.A. 1
Jan 31 Everton 4 Nottingham F 1
Jan 31 Halifax 1 Stoke 0
Jan 31 Hull 1 Gateshead 2
Jan 31 Manchester C 1 Luton 1
Jan 31 Manchester U 1 Walthamstow 1
Jan 31 Newcastle 1 Rotherham 3
Jan 31 Plymouth 1 Barnsley 0
Jan 31 Preston 2 Tottenham 2
Jan 31 Sheffield U 1 Birmingham 1
Jan 31 Shrewsbury 1 Southampton 4

Replays
Feb 04 Birmingham 3 Sheffield U 1
Feb 04 Brentford 1 Aston Villa 2
Feb 04 Luton 5 Manchester C 1
Feb 04 Tottenham 1 Preston 0
Feb 04 W.B.A. 0 Chelsea 0
Feb 05 Notts Co 2 Bolton 2
Feb 05 Walthamstow 2 Manchester U 5
played at Arsenal
Feb 09 Bolton 1 Notts Co 0
played at Sheffield W
Feb 09 Chelsea 1 W.B.A. 1
played at Aston Villa
Feb 11 Chelsea 4 W.B.A. 0
played at Arsenal

5th Round
Feb 14 Blackpool 1 Southampton 1
Feb 14 Burnley 0 Arsenal 2
Feb 14 Chelsea 0 Birmingham 4
Feb 14 Everton 2 Manchester U 1
Feb 14 Halifax 0 Tottenham 3
Feb 14 Luton 0 Bolton 1
Feb 14 Plymouth 0 Gateshead 1
Feb 14 Rotherham 1 Aston Villa 3

Replay
Feb 18 Southampton 1 Blackpool 2

6th Round
Feb 28 Arsenal 1 Blackpool 2
Feb 28 Aston Villa 0 Everton 1
Feb 28 Birmingham 1 Tottenham 1
Feb 28 Gateshead 0 Bolton 1

Replays
Mar 04 Tottenham 2 Birmingham 2
Mar 09 Birmingham 0 Tottenham 1
played at Wolverhampton

Semi-finals
Mar 21 Blackpool 2 Tottenham 1
played at Aston Villa
Mar 21 Bolton 4 Everton 3
played at Manchester C

Final
May 02 Blackpool 4 Bolton 3
played at Wembley

Season 1953-54

1st Round
Nov 21 Aldershot 5 Wellington 3
Nov 21 Barnsley 5 York 2
Nov 21 Bath 0 Walsall 3
Nov 21 Blyth 0 Accrington 1
Nov 21 Brighton 5 Coventry 1
Nov 21 Cambridge 2 Newport 2
Nov 21 Colchester 1 Millwall 1
Nov 21 Crewe 0 Bradford C 0
Nov 21 Darlington 1 Port Vale 3
Nov 21 Exeter 1 Hereford 1
Nov 21 Finchley 1 Southend 3
Nov 21 Gainsborough 1 Chesterfield 4
Nov 21 Gateshead 1 Tranmere 2
Nov 21 Grimsby 2 Rochdale 0
Nov 21 Gt Yarmouth 1 Crystal Palace 0
Nov 21 Halifax 0 Rhyl 0
Nov 21 Hartlepool 1 Mansfield 1
Nov 21 Harwich 2 Headington 3
Nov 21 Hastings 1 Guildford 0
Nov 21 Hitchin 1 Peterborough 3
Nov 21 Horden 0 Wrexham 1
Nov 21 Ipswich 4 Reading 1
Nov 21 Leyton O 3 Kettering 0
Nov 21 Northampton 3 Llanelly 0
Nov 21 Nuneaton 3 Watford 0
Nov 21 Q.P.R. 2 Shrewsbury 0
Nov 21 Scunthorpe 9 Boston 0
Nov 21 Selby 0 Bradford 2
Nov 21 Southampton 1 Bournemouth 1
Nov 21 Southport 1 Carlisle 0
Nov 21 Spennymoor 0 Barrow 3
Nov 21 Stockport 4 Chester 2
Nov 21 Swindon 2 Newport (IOW) 1
Nov 21 Torquay 1 Bristol C 3
Nov 21 Walthamstow 1 Gillingham 0
Nov 21 Weymouth 2 Bedford 0
Nov 21 Wigan 4 Scarborough 0
Nov 21 Witton 4 Nelson 1
Nov 21 Workington 3 Ferryhill 0
Nov 21 Yeovil 0 Norwich 2

Replays
Nov 23 Millwall 4 Colchester 0
Nov 25 Bournemouth 3 Southampton 1
Nov 25 Bradford C 0 Crewe 1
Nov 25 Mansfield 0 Hartlepool 3
Nov 26 Hereford 2 Exeter 0
Nov 26 Newport 1 Cambridge 2
Nov 26 Rhyl 4 Halifax 3

2nd Round
Dec 12 Accrington 2 Tranmere 2
Dec 12 Barrow 5 Gt Yarmouth 2
Dec 12 Cambridge 1 Bradford 2
Dec 12 Hastings 4 Swindon 1
Dec 12 Ipswich 2 Walthamstow 2
Dec 12 Leyton O 4 Weymouth 0
Dec 12 Millwall 3 Headington 3
Dec 12 Northampton 1 Hartlepool 1
Dec 12 Norwich 2 Barnsley 1
Dec 12 Peterborough 2 Aldershot 1
Dec 12 Q.P.R. 1 Nuneaton 1
Dec 12 Rhyl 0 Bristol C 3
Dec 12 Scunthorpe 1 Bournemouth 0
Dec 12 Southend 1 Chesterfield 2
Dec 12 Southport 1 Port Vale 1
Dec 12 Stockport 2 Workington 1
Dec 12 Walsall 3 Crewe 0
Dec 12 Wigan 4 Hereford 1
Dec 12 Witton 1 Grimsby 1
Dec 12 Wrexham 1 Brighton 1

Replays
Dec 14 Port Vale 2 Southport 0
Dec 15 Grimsby 6 Witton 1
Dec 16 Brighton 1 Wrexham 1
Dec 16 Hartlepool 1 Northampton 0
Dec 16 Tranmere 5 Accrington 1
Dec 16 Walthamstow 0 Ipswich 1
Dec 17 Headington 1 Millwall 0
Dec 17 Nuneaton 1 Q.P.R. 2
Dec 21 Brighton 1 Wrexham 3
played at Crystal Palace

3rd Round
Jan 09 Arsenal 5 Aston Villa 1
Jan 09 Barrow 2 Swansea 2
Jan 09 Blackpool 1 Luton 1
Jan 09 Bolton 1 Liverpool 0
Jan 09 Bradford 2 Manchester C 5
Jan 09 Brentford 0 Hull 0
Jan 09 Bristol C 1 Rotherham 3
Jan 09 Bristol R 0 Blackburn 1
Jan 09 Burnley 5 Manchester U 3
Jan 09 Cardiff 3 Peterborough 1
Jan 09 Chesterfield 2 Bury 0
Jan 09 Derby 0 Preston 2
Jan 09 Everton 2 Notts Co 1
Jan 09 Grimsby 5 Fulham 5
Jan 09 Hastings 3 Norwich 3
Jan 09 Ipswich 3 Oldham 3
Jan 09 Leeds 3 Tottenham 3
Jan 09 Lincoln 1 Walsall 1
Jan 09 Middlesbrough 0 Leicester 0
Jan 09 Newcastle 2 Wigan 2
Jan 09 Plymouth 2 Nottingham F 0
Jan 09 Portsmouth 3 Charlton 3
Jan 09 Q.P.R. 0 Port Vale 1
Jan 09 Sheffield W 1 Sheffield U 1
Jan 09 Stockport 0 Headington 0
Jan 09 Stoke 6 Hartlepool 2
Jan 09 Sunderland 0 Doncaster 2
Jan 09 Tranmere 2 Leyton O 2
Jan 09 West Ham 4 Huddersfield 0
Jan 09 Wolverhampton 1 Birmingham 2
Jan 09 Wrexham 3 Scunthorpe 3
Jan 09 W.B.A. 1 Chelsea 0

Replays
Jan 12 Oldham 0 Ipswich 1
Jan 13 Luton 0 Blackpool 0
Jan 13 Norwich 3 Hastings 0
Jan 13 Sheffield U 1 Sheffield W 3
Jan 13 Tottenham 1 Leeds 0
Jan 13 Wigan 2 Newcastle 3
Jan 14 Charlton 2 Portsmouth 3
Jan 14 Headington 1 Stockport 0
Jan 14 Hull 2 Brentford 2
Jan 14 Leicester 3 Middlesbrough 2
Jan 14 Leyton O 4 Tranmere 1
Jan 14 Scunthorpe 3 Wrexham 1
Jan 14 Swansea 4 Barrow 2
Jan 14 Walsall 1 Lincoln 1
Jan 18 Blackpool 1 Luton 1
played at Aston Villa
Jan 18 Brentford 2 Hull 5
played at Doncaster
Jan 18 Fulham 3 Grimsby 1
Jan 18 Lincoln 2 Walsall 1
played at Nottingham F
Jan 25 Blackpool 2 Luton 0
played at Wolverhampton

4th Round
Jan 30 Arsenal 1 Norwich 2
Jan 30 Blackburn 2 Hull 2
Jan 30 Burnley 1 Newcastle 1
Jan 30 Cardiff 0 Port Vale 2
Jan 30 Everton 3 Swansea 0
Jan 30 Headington 2 Bolton 4
Jan 30 Ipswich 1 Birmingham 0
Jan 30 Leyton O 2 Fulham 1
Jan 30 Lincoln 0 Preston 2
Jan 30 Manchester C 0 Tottenham 1
Jan 30 Plymouth 0 Doncaster 2
Jan 30 Scunthorpe 1 Portsmouth 1
Jan 30 Sheffield W 0 Chesterfield 0
Jan 30 Stoke 0 Leicester 0
Jan 30 West Ham 1 Blackpool 1
Jan 30 W.B.A. 4 Rotherham 0

Replays
Feb 02 Leicester 3 Stoke 1
Feb 03 Blackpool 3 West Ham 1
Feb 03 Chesterfield 2 Sheffield W 4
Feb 03 Newcastle 1 Burnley 0
Feb 03 Portsmouth 2 Scunthorpe 2
Feb 04 Hull 2 Blackburn 1
Feb 08 Portsmouth 4 Scunthorpe 0
played at Arsenal

5th Round
Feb 20 Bolton 0 Portsmouth 0
Feb 20 Hull 1 Tottenham 1
Feb 20 Leyton O 3 Doncaster 1
Feb 20 Norwich 1 Leicester 2
Feb 20 Port Vale 2 Blackpool 0
Feb 20 Preston 6 Ipswich 1
Feb 20 Sheffield W 3 Everton 1
Feb 20 W.B.A. 3 Newcastle 2

Replays
Feb 24 Portsmouth 1 Bolton 2
Feb 24 Tottenham 2 Hull 0

6th Round
Mar 13 Leicester 1 Preston 1
Mar 13 Leyton O 0 Port Vale 1
Mar 13 Sheffield W 1 Bolton 1
Mar 13 W.B.A. 3 Tottenham 0

Replays
Mar 17 Bolton 0 Sheffield W 2
Mar 17 Preston 2 Leicester 2
Mar 22 Leicester 1 Preston 3
played at Sheffield W

Semi-finals
Mar 27 Port Vale 1 W.B.A. 2
played at Aston Villa
Mar 27 Preston 2 Sheffield W 0
played at Manchester C

Final
May 01 Preston 2 W.B.A. 3
played at Wembley

Season 1954-55

1st Round
Nov 20 Accrington 7 Cresswell 1
Nov 20 Aldershot 3 Chelmsford 1
Nov 20 Barnet 1 Southampton 4
Nov 20 Barnsley 3 Wigan 2
Nov 20 Barnstaple 1 Bournemouth 4
Nov 20 Barrow 1 Darlington 1
Nov 20 Bishop Auckland 5 Kettering 1
Nov 20 Boston 1 Blyth 1
Nov 20 Bradford 2 Southport 0
Nov 20 Bradford C 3 Mansfield 1
Nov 20 Brentford 2 Nuneaton 1
Nov 20 Brighton 5 Tunbridge Wells 0
Nov 20 Bristol C 1 Southend 2
Nov 20 Corby 0 Watford 2
Nov 20 Crook 5 Stanley 3
Nov 20 Dorchester 2 Bedford 0
Nov 20 Frome 0 Leyton O 3
Nov 20 Gateshead 6 Chester 0
Nov 20 Gillingham 2 Newport 0
Nov 20 Grimsby 2 Halifax 1
Nov 20 Hartlepool 1 Chesterfield 0
Nov 20 Hinckley 4 Newport (IOW) 3
Nov 20 Hordern 0 Scunthorpe 1
Nov 20 Hounslow 2 Hastings 4
Nov 20 Merthyr T 1 Wellington 1
Nov 20 Millwall 3 Exeter 2
Nov 20 Netherfield 3 Wrexham 3
Nov 20 Northampton 0 Coventry 1
Nov 20 Norwich 4 Headington 2
Nov 20 Oldham 1 Crewe 0
Nov 20 Q.P.R. 2 Walthamstow 2
Nov 20 Reading 3 Colchester 3
Nov 20 Selby 2 Rhyl 1
Nov 20 Stockport 0 Carlisle 1
Nov 20 Swindon 0 Crystal Palace 2
Nov 20 Torquay 4 Cambridge 0
Nov 20 Tranmere 3 Rochdale 3
Nov 20 Walsall 5 Shrewsbury 2
Nov 20 Workington 5 Hyde 1
Nov 20 York 3 Scarborough 2

Replays
Nov 23 Rochdale 1 Tranmere 0
Nov 24 Blyth 5 Boston 4
Nov 24 Darlington 2 Barrow 1
Nov 24 Wellington 1 Merthyr T 6
Nov 24 Wrexham 4 Netherfield 0
Nov 25 Colchester 1 Reading 2
Nov 25 Walthamstow 2 Q.P.R. 2
Nov 29 Q.P.R. 0 Walthamstow 4
played at Arsenal

2nd Round

Date	Home		Away	
Dec 11	Blyth	1	Torquay	3
Dec 11	Bournemouth	1	Oldham	0
Dec 11	Bradford	2	Southend	3
Dec 11	Bradford C	7	Merthyr T	1
Dec 11	Brentford	4	Crook	1
Dec 11	Carlisle	2	Watford	2
Dec 11	Coventry	4	Scunthorpe	0
Dec 11	Crystal Palace	2	Bishop Auckland	4
Dec 11	Dorchester	2	York	5
Dec 11	Gateshead	3	Barnsley	3
Dec 11	Gillingham	1	Reading	1
Dec 11	Grimsby	4	Southampton	1
Dec 11	Hartlepool	4	Aldershot	0
Dec 11	Leyton O	0	Workington	1
Dec 11	Millwall	3	Accrington	2
Dec 11	Norwich	0	Brighton	0
Dec 11	Rochdale	2	Hinckley	1
Dec 11	Selby	0	Hastings	2
Dec 11	Walthamstow	0	Darlington	3
Dec 11	Wrexham	1	Walsall	2

Replays

Date	Home		Away	
Dec 13	Reading	5	Gillingham	3
Dec 15	Brighton	5	Norwich	1
Dec 15	Watford	4	Carlisle	1
Dec 16	Barnsley	0	Gateshead	1

3rd Round

Date	Home		Away	
Jan 08	Arsenal	1	Cardiff	0
Jan 08	Blackburn	0	Swansea	2
Jan 08	Blackpool	0	York	2
Jan 08	Bolton	3	Millwall	1
Jan 08	Bournemouth	0	W.B.A.	1
Jan 08	Brentford	1	Bradford C	1
Jan 08	Brighton	2	Aston Villa	2
Jan 08	Bristol R	2	Portsmouth	1
Jan 08	Bury	1	Stoke	1
Jan 08	Chelsea	2	Walsall	0
Jan 08	Derby	1	Manchester C	3
Jan 08	Everton	3	Southend	1
Jan 08	Fulham	2	Preston	3
Jan 08	Gateshead	0	Tottenham	2
Jan 08	Grimsby	2	Wolverhampton	5
Jan 08	Hartlepool	1	Darlington	1
Jan 08	Huddersfield	3	Coventry	3
Jan 08	Hull	0	Birmingham	2
Jan 08	Ipswich	2	Bishop Auckland	2
Jan 08	Leeds	2	Torquay	2
Jan 08	Lincoln	1	Liverpool	1
Jan 08	Luton	5	Workington	0
Jan 08	Middlesbrough	1	Notts Co	4
Jan 08	Plymouth	0	Newcastle	1
Jan 08	Reading	1	Manchester U	1
Jan 08	Rochdale	1	Charlton	3
Jan 08	Rotherham	1	Leicester	0
Jan 08	Sheffield U	1	Nottingham F	3
Jan 08	Sheffield W	2	Hastings	1
Jan 08	Sunderland	1	Burnley	0
Jan 08	Watford	1	Doncaster	2
Jan 08	West Ham	2	Port Vale	2

Replays

Date	Home		Away	
Jan 10	Aston Villa	4	Brighton	2
Jan 10	Port Vale	3	West Ham	1
Jan 12	Bishop Auckland	3	Ipswich	0
Jan 12	Bradford C	2	Brentford	2
Jan 12	Darlington	2	Hartlepool	2
Jan 12	Liverpool	1	Lincoln	0
Jan 12	Manchester U	4	Reading	1
Jan 12	Stoke	1	Bury	1
Jan 12	Torquay	4	Leeds	0
Jan 13	Coventry	1	Huddersfield	2
Jan 17	Bury (played at Everton)	3	Stoke	3
Jan 17	Darlington (played at Middlesbrough)	0	Hartlepool	2
Jan 19	Bury (played at Liverpool)	2	Stoke	2
Jan 20	Bradford C (played at Arsenal)	0	Brentford	1
Jan 24	Bury (played at Manchester U)	2	Stoke	3

4th Round

Date	Home		Away	
Jan 29	Birmingham	2	Bolton	1
Jan 29	Bishop Auckland	1	York	3
Jan 29	Bristol R	1	Chelsea	3
Jan 29	Doncaster	0	Aston Villa	0
Jan 29	Everton	0	Liverpool	4
Jan 29	Hartlepool	1	Nottingham F	1
Jan 29	Manchester C	2	Manchester U	0
Jan 29	Newcastle	3	Brentford	2
Jan 29	Preston	3	Sunderland	3
Jan 29	Rotherham	1	Luton	5
Jan 29	Sheffield W	1	Notts Co	1
Jan 29	Swansea	3	Stoke	1
Jan 29	Torquay	0	Huddersfield	1
Jan 29	Tottenham	4	Port Vale	2
Jan 29	Wolverhampton	1	Arsenal	0
Jan 29	W.B.A.	2	Charlton	4

Replays

Date	Home		Away	
Feb 02	Aston Villa	2	Doncaster	2
Feb 02	Nottingham F	2	Hartlepool	1
Feb 02	Sunderland	2	Preston	0
Feb 03	Notts Co	1	Sheffield W	0
Feb 07	Aston Villa (played at Manchester C)	1	Doncaster	1
Feb 14	Aston Villa (played at Sheffield W)	0	Doncaster	0
Feb 15	Aston Villa (played at W.B.A.)	1	Doncaster	3

5th Round

Date	Home		Away	
Feb 19	Birmingham	2	Doncaster	1
Feb 19	Liverpool	0	Huddersfield	2
Feb 19	Luton	0	Manchester C	2
Feb 19	Nottingham F	1	Newcastle	1
Feb 19	Notts Co	1	Chelsea	0
Feb 19	Swansea	2	Sunderland	2
Feb 19	Wolverhampton	4	Charlton	1
Feb 19	York	3	Tottenham	1

Replays

Date	Home		Away	
Feb 23	Sunderland	1	Swansea	0
Feb 28	Newcastle	2	Nottingham F	2
Mar 02	Newcastle (played at Newcastle)	2	Nottingham F	1

6th Round

Date	Home		Away	
Mar 12	Birmingham	0	Manchester C	1
Mar 12	Huddersfield	1	Newcastle	1
Mar 12	Notts Co	0	York	1
Mar 12	Sunderland	2	Wolverhampton	0

Replay

Date	Home		Away	
Mar 16	Newcastle	2	Huddersfield	0

Semi-finals

Date	Home		Away	
Mar 26	Manchester C (played at Aston Villa)	1	Sunderland	0
Mar 26	Newcastle (played at Sheffield W)	1	York	1

Replay

Date	Home		Away	
Mar 30	Newcastle (played at Sunderland)	2	York	0

Final

Date	Home		Away	
May 07	Manchester C (played at Wembley)	1	Newcastle	3

SEASON 1955-56

1st Round

Date	Home		Away	
Nov 19	Accrington	3	Wrexham	1
Nov 19	Barrow	0	Crewe	0
Nov 19	Bedford	3	Leyton	0
Nov 19	Bishop Auckland	3	Durham	1
Nov 19	Boston	3	Northwich	2
Nov 19	Bradford C	3	Oldham	1
Nov 19	Brentford	4	March	0
Nov 19	Brighton	8	Newport	1
Nov 19	Chesterfield	1	Chester	0
Nov 19	Coventry	0	Exeter	1
Nov 19	Crook	2	Derby	2
Nov 19	Crystal Palace	0	Southampton	0
Nov 19	Darlington	0	Carlisle	0
Nov 19	Easington	0	Tranmere	2
Nov 19	Gillingham	1	Shrewsbury	1
Nov 19	Goole	1	Halifax	2
Nov 19	Halesowen	2	Hendon	4
Nov 19	Hartlepool	3	Gateshead	0
Nov 19	Hastings	6	Southall	1
Nov 19	Leyton O	7	Lovell's	1
Nov 19	Mansfield	2	Stockport	0
Nov 19	Margate	2	Walsall	2
Nov 19	Netherfield	1	Grimsby	5
Nov 19	Northampton	4	Millwall	1
Nov 19	Norwich	4	Dorchester	0
Nov 19	Peterborough	3	Ipswich	1
Nov 19	Reading	1	Bournemouth	0
Nov 19	Rhyl	0	Bradford	3
Nov 19	Rochdale	0	York	1
Nov 19	Scunthorpe	3	Shildon	0
Nov 19	Skegness	0	Worksop	4
Nov 19	Southend	2	Q.P.R.	0
Nov 19	Southport	6	Ashton	1
Nov 19	Swindon	4	Hereford	0
Nov 19	Torquay	2	Colchester	0
Nov 19	Watford	5	Ramsgate	3
Nov 19	Weymouth	3	Salisbury	2
Nov 19	Workington	4	Scarborough	2
Nov 19	Wycombe	1	Burton	3
Nov 19	Yeovil	1	Aldershot	1

Replays

Date	Home		Away	
Nov 22	Carlisle	0	Darlington	0
Nov 23	Aldershot	1	Yeovil	1
Nov 23	Crewe	2	Barrow	3
Nov 23	Derby	5	Crook	1
Nov 23	Southampton	2	Crystal Palace	0
Nov 23	Shrewsbury	4	Gillingham	1
Nov 24	Walsall	6	Margate	1
Nov 28	Aldershot (played at Southampton)	3	Yeovil	0
Nov 28	Carlisle (played at Newcastle)	1	Darlington	3

2nd Round

Date	Home		Away	
Dec 10	Bedford	3	Watford	2
Dec 10	Bishop Auckland	0	Scunthorpe	0
Dec 10	Bradford	4	Workington	3
Dec 10	Bradford C	2	Worksop	2
Dec 10	Brighton	1	Norwich	2
Dec 10	Chesterfield	1	Hartlepool	2
Dec 10	Darlington	0	Accrington	1
Dec 10	Derby	1	Boston	6
Dec 10	Exeter	6	Hendon	2
Dec 10	Halifax	0	Burton	0
Dec 10	Leyton O	4	Brentford	1
Dec 10	Northampton	4	Hastings	1
Dec 10	Reading	2	Aldershot	2
Dec 10	Shrewsbury	0	Torquay	0
Dec 10	Southport	0	Grimsby	0
Dec 10	Swindon	1	Peterborough	1
Dec 10	Tranmere	0	Barrow	3
Dec 10	Walsall	2	Southampton	1
Dec 10	Weymouth	0	Southend	1
Dec 10	York	2	Mansfield	1

Replays

Date	Home		Away	
Dec 14	Aldershot	3	Reading	0
Dec 14	Burton	1	Halifax	0
Dec 14	Grimsby	3	Southport	2
Dec 14	Torquay	5	Shrewsbury	1
Dec 15	Peterborough	1	Swindon	2
Dec 15	Scunthorpe	2	Bishop Auckland	0
Dec 15	Worksop	1	Bradford C	0

3rd Round

Date	Home		Away	
Jan 07	Aldershot	1	Barnsley	2
Jan 07	Arsenal	2	Bedford	2
Jan 07	Aston Villa	1	Hull	1
Jan 07	Bradford	0	Middlesbrough	4
Jan 07	Bristol R	4	Manchester U	0
Jan 07	Charlton	7	Burton	0
Jan 07	Doncaster	3	Nottingham F	0
Jan 07	Everton	3	Bristol C	1
Jan 07	Exeter	0	Stoke	0
Jan 07	Hartlepool	0	Chelsea	1
Jan 07	Leeds	1	Cardiff	2
Jan 07	Leyton O	1	Plymouth	0
Jan 07	Lincoln	2	Southend	3
Jan 07	Liverpool	2	Accrington	0
Jan 07	Northampton	1	Blackburn	2
Jan 07	Notts Co	0	Fulham	1
Jan 07	Portsmouth	3	Grimsby	1
Jan 07	Rotherham	1	Scunthorpe	1
Jan 07	Sheffield U	5	Barrow	0
Jan 07	Sheffield W	1	Newcastle	3
Jan 07	Sunderland	4	Norwich	2
Jan 07	Swansea	1	York	2
Jan 07	Swindon	1	Worksop	0
Jan 07	Torquay	1	Birmingham	7
Jan 07	Tottenham	4	Boston	0
Jan 07	Walsall	0	Port Vale	1
Jan 07	West Ham	5	Preston	2
Jan 07	Wolverhampton	1	W.B.A.	2
Jan 10	Bury	0	Burnley	1
Jan 11	Bolton	3	Huddersfield	0
Jan 11	Luton	0	Leicester	4
Jan 11	Manchester C	2	Blackpool	1

Replays

Date	Home		Away	
Jan 09	Stoke	3	Exeter	0
Jan 12	Bedford	1	Arsenal	2
Jan 12	Hull	1	Aston Villa	2
Jan 12	Scunthorpe	4	Rotherham	2

4th Round

Date	Home		Away	
Jan 28	Arsenal	4	Aston Villa	1
Jan 28	Barnsley	0	Blackburn	1
Jan 28	Bolton	1	Sheffield U	2
Jan 28	Bristol R	1	Doncaster	1
Jan 28	Burnley	1	Chelsea	1
Jan 28	Charlton	2	Swindon	1
Jan 28	Fulham	4	Newcastle	5
Jan 28	Leicester	3	Stoke	3
Jan 28	Leyton O	0	Birmingham	4
Jan 28	Liverpool	3	Scunthorpe	3
Jan 28	Port Vale	2	Everton	3
Jan 28	Southend	0	Manchester C	1
Jan 28	Tottenham	3	Middlesbrough	1
Jan 28	West Ham	2	Cardiff	1
Jan 28	W.B.A.	2	Portsmouth	0
Jan 28	York	0	Sunderland	0

Replays

Date	Home		Away	
Jan 30	Stoke	2	Leicester	1
Jan 31	Doncaster	1	Bristol R	0
Feb 01	Chelsea	1	Burnley	1
Feb 01	Sunderland	2	York	1
Feb 06	Burnley (played at Birmingham)	2	Chelsea	2
Feb 06	Scunthorpe	1	Liverpool	2
Feb 13	Burnley (played at Arsenal)	0	Chelsea	0
Feb 15	Burnley (played at Tottenham)	0	Chelsea	2

5th Round

Date	Home		Away	
Feb 18	Charlton	0	Arsenal	2
Feb 18	Doncaster	0	Tottenham	2
Feb 18	Everton	1	Chelsea	0
Feb 18	Manchester C	0	Liverpool	0
Feb 18	Newcastle	2	Stoke	1
Feb 18	Sheffield U	0	Sunderland	0
Feb 18	West Ham	0	Blackburn	0
Feb 18	W.B.A.	0	Birmingham	1

Replays

Date	Home		Away	
Feb 22	Liverpool	1	Manchester C	2
Feb 22	Sunderland	1	Sheffield U	0
Feb 23	Blackburn	2	West Ham	3

6th Round

Date	Home		Away	
Mar 03	Arsenal	1	Birmingham	3
Mar 03	Manchester C	2	Everton	1
Mar 03	Newcastle	0	Sunderland	2
Mar 03	Tottenham	3	West Ham	3

Replay

Date	Home		Away	
Mar 08	West Ham	1	Tottenham	2

Semi-finals

Date	Home		Away	
Mar 17	Birmingham	3	Sunderland	0
	played at Sheffield W			
Mar 17	Manchester C	1	Tottenham	0
	played at Aston Villa			

Final

Date	Home		Away	
May 05	Birmingham	1	Manchester C	3
	played at Wembley			

Season 1956-57

1st Round

Date	Home		Away	
Nov 17	Accrington	4	Morecambe	1
Nov 17	Bishop Auckland	2	Tranmere	1
Nov 17	Boston	0	Bradford	2
Nov 17	Bournemouth	8	Burton	0
Nov 17	Brentford	3	Guildford	0
Nov 17	Brighton	1	Millwall	1
Nov 17	Carlisle	6	Billingham	1
Nov 17	Cheltenham	1	Reading	2
Nov 17	Chester	0	Barrow	0
Nov 17	Colchester	1	Southend	4
Nov 17	Crewe	2	Wrexham	2
Nov 17	Crystal Palace	2	Walthamstow	0
Nov 17	Darlington	7	Evenwood	2
Nov 17	Derby	2	Bradford C	1
Nov 17	Ely	2	Torquay	6
Nov 17	Exeter	0	Plymouth	2
Nov 17	Halifax	2	Oldham	3
Nov 17	Hartlepool	3	Selby	1
Nov 17	Hereford	3	Aldershot	2
Nov 17	Hull	4	Gateshead	0
Nov 17	Ilkeston	1	Blyth	5
Nov 17	Ipswich	4	Hastings	0
Nov 17	Mansfield	1	Workington	1
Nov 17	Margate	3	Dunstable	1
Nov 17	New Brighton	3	Stockport	3
Nov 17	Newport (IOW)	0	Watford	6
Nov 17	Norwich	2	Bedford	4
Nov 17	Q.P.R.	4	Dorchester	0
Nov 17	Rhyl	3	Scarborough	2
Nov 17	Scunthorpe	1	Rochdale	0
Nov 17	South Shields	2	Chesterfield	2
Nov 17	Southampton	2	Northampton	0
Nov 17	Southport	0	York	0
Nov 17	Swindon	2	Coventry	1
Nov 17	Tooting & M	2	Bromsgrove	1
Nov 17	Walsall	0	Newport	1
Nov 17	Weymouth	1	Shrewsbury	0
Nov 17	Wigan	1	Goole	2
Nov 17	Yeovil	1	Peterborough	3
Nov 17	Yiewsley	2	Gillingham	2

Replays

Date	Home		Away	
Nov 19	Millwall	3	Brighton	1
Nov 21	Chesterfield	4	South Shields	0
Nov 21	Gillingham	2	Yiewsley	0
Nov 21	Stockport	2	New Brighton	3
Nov 21	Workington	2	Mansfield	1
Nov 21	Wrexham	2	Crewe	1
Nov 21	York	2	Southport	1
Nov 22	Barrow	3	Chester	1

2nd Round

Date	Home		Away	
Dec 08	Accrington	2	Oldham	1
Dec 08	Blyth	0	Hartlepool	1
Dec 08	Brentford	1	Crystal Palace	1
Dec 08	Carlisle	2	Darlington	1
Dec 08	Chesterfield	4	Barrow	1
Dec 08	Derby	1	New Brighton	3
Dec 08	Gillingham	1	Newport	2
Dec 08	Goole	2	Workington	2
Dec 08	Hereford	2	Southend	3
Dec 08	Hull	2	York	1
Dec 08	Millwall	4	Margate	0
Dec 08	Peterborough	3	Bradford	0
Dec 08	Reading	1	Bedford	0
Dec 08	Rhyl	3	Bishop Auckland	1
Dec 08	Scunthorpe	0	Wrexham	0
Dec 08	Southampton	3	Weymouth	2
Dec 08	Swindon	0	Bournemouth	1
Dec 08	Tooting & M	0	Q.P.R.	2
Dec 08	Torquay	1	Plymouth	0
Dec 08	Watford	1	Ipswich	3

Replays

Date	Home		Away	
Dec 12	Crystal Palace	3	Brentford	2
Dec 12	Workington	0	Goole	1
Dec 12	Wrexham	6	Scunthorpe	2

3rd Round

Date	Home		Away	
Jan 05	Arsenal	4	Stoke	2
Jan 05	Barnsley	3	Port Vale	3
Jan 05	Bolton	2	Blackpool	3
Jan 05	Bournemouth	2	Accrington	0
Jan 05	Bristol C	4	Rotherham	1
Jan 05	Burnley	7	Chesterfield	0
Jan 05	Bury	1	Portsmouth	3
Jan 05	Carlisle	3	Birmingham	3
Jan 05	Doncaster	1	W.B.A.	1
Jan 05	Everton	1	Blackburn	0
Jan 05	Hartlepool	3	Manchester U	4
Jan 05	Huddersfield	0	Sheffield U	0
Jan 05	Hull	3	Bristol R	4
Jan 05	Ipswich	2	Fulham	3
Jan 05	Leeds	1	Cardiff	2
Jan 05	Leyton O	0	Chelsea	2
Jan 05	Luton	2	Aston Villa	2
Jan 05	Middlesbrough	1	Charlton	1
Jan 05	Millwall	2	Crystal Palace	0
Jan 05	New Brighton	2	Torquay	1
Jan 05	Newcastle	1	Manchester C	1
Jan 05	Newport	3	Southampton	3
Jan 05	Nottingham F	6	Goole	0
Jan 05	Notts Co	1	Rhyl	3
Jan 05	Peterborough	2	Lincoln	2
Jan 05	Preston	0	Sheffield W	0
Jan 05	Southend	2	Liverpool	1
Jan 05	Sunderland	4	Q.P.R.	0
Jan 05	Tottenham	2	Leicester	0
Jan 05	West Ham	5	Grimsby	3
Jan 05	Wolverhampton	5	Swansea	3
Jan 05	Wrexham	1	Reading	1

Replays

Date	Home		Away	
Jan 07	Aston Villa	2	Luton	0
Jan 07	Port Vale	0	Barnsley	1
Jan 07	Sheffield U	1	Huddersfield	1
Jan 09	Birmingham	4	Carlisle	0
Jan 09	Lincoln	4	Peterborough	5
Jan 09	Manchester C	4	Newcastle	5
Jan 09	Reading	1	Wrexham	2
Jan 09	Sheffield W	2	Preston	2
Jan 09	Southampton	0	Newport	1
Jan 09	W.B.A.	2	Doncaster	0
Jan 10	Charlton	2	Middlesbrough	3
Jan 14	Huddersfield	2	Sheffield U	1
	played at Manchester C			
Jan 14	Preston	5	Sheffield W	1
	played at Everton			

4th Round

Date	Home		Away	
Jan 26	Blackpool	6	Fulham	2
Jan 26	Bristol C	3	Rhyl	0
Jan 26	Bristol R	1	Preston	4
Jan 26	Burnley	9	New Brighton	0
Jan 26	Cardiff	0	Barnsley	1
Jan 26	Everton	2	West Ham	1
Jan 26	Huddersfield	3	Peterborough	1
Jan 26	Middlesbrough	2	Aston Villa	3
Jan 26	Millwall	2	Newcastle	1
Jan 26	Newport	0	Arsenal	2
Jan 26	Portsmouth	1	Nottingham F	3
Jan 26	Southend	1	Birmingham	6
Jan 26	Tottenham	4	Chelsea	0
Jan 26	Wolverhampton	0	Bournemouth	1
Jan 26	Wrexham	0	Manchester U	5
Jan 26	W.B.A.	4	Sunderland	2

5th Round

Date	Home		Away	
Feb 16	Aston Villa	2	Bristol C	1
Feb 16	Barnsley	1	Nottingham F	2
Feb 16	Blackpool	0	W.B.A.	0
Feb 16	Bournemouth	3	Tottenham	1
Feb 16	Huddersfield	1	Burnley	2
Feb 16	Manchester U	1	Everton	0
Feb 16	Millwall	1	Birmingham	4
Feb 16	Preston	3	Arsenal	3

Replays

Date	Home		Away	
Feb 19	Arsenal	2	Preston	1
Feb 20	W.B.A.	2	Blackpool	1

6th Round

Date	Home		Away	
Mar 02	Birmingham	0	Nottingham F	0
Mar 02	Bournemouth	1	Manchester U	2
Mar 02	Burnley	1	Aston Villa	1
Mar 02	W.B.A.	2	Arsenal	2

Replays

Date	Home		Away	
Mar 05	Arsenal	1	W.B.A.	2
Mar 06	Aston Villa	2	Burnley	0
Mar 07	Nottingham F	0	Birmingham	1

Semi-finals

Date	Home		Away	
Mar 23	Aston Villa	2	W.B.A.	2
	played at Wolverhampton			
Mar 23	Birmingham	0	Manchester U	2
	played at Sheffield W			

Replay

Date	Home		Away	
Mar 28	Aston Villa	1	W.B.A.	0
	played at Birmingham			

Final

Date	Home		Away	
May 04	Aston Villa	2	Manchester U	1
	played at Wembley			

Season 1957-58

1st Round

Date	Home		Away	
Nov 16	Aldershot	0	Worcester	0
Nov 16	Bath	2	Exeter	1
Nov 16	Bishop Auckland	0	Bury	0
Nov 16	Boston	5	Billingham	2
Nov 16	Bradford C	6	Scarborough	0
Nov 16	Brighton	2	Walsall	1
Nov 16	Carlisle	5	Rhyl	1
Nov 16	Chester	4	Gateshead	3
Nov 16	Clapton	1	Q.P.R.	1
Nov 16	Coventry	1	Walthamstow	0
Nov 16	Dorchester	3	Wycombe	2
Nov 16	Durham	3	Spalding	1
Nov 16	Gillingham	10	Gorleston	1
Nov 16	Guildford	2	Yeovil	2
Nov 16	Hartlepool	5	Prescot	0
Nov 16	Hull	2	Crewe	1
Nov 16	Mansfield	2	Halifax	0
Nov 16	Margate	2	Crystal Palace	3
Nov 16	Millwall	1	Brentford	0
Nov 16	Newport (IOW)	0	Hereford	3
Nov 16	Northampton	3	Newport	0
Nov 16	Norwich	6	Redhill	1
Nov 16	Oldham	2	Bradford	0
Nov 16	Oswestry	1	Bournemouth	5
Nov 16	Peterborough	3	Torquay	3
Nov 16	Plymouth	6	Watford	2
Nov 16	Port Vale	2	Shrewsbury	1
Nov 16	Reading	1	Swindon	0
Nov 16	Rochdale	0	Darlington	2
Nov 16	Scunthorpe	2	Goole	1
Nov 16	South Shields	3	Frickley	2
Nov 16	Southport	1	Wigan	2
Nov 16	Stockport	2	Barrow	1
Nov 16	Tranmere	2	Witton	1
Nov 16	Trowbridge	0	Southend	2
Nov 16	Walton &H	1	Southampton	6
Nov 16	Wisbech	1	Colchester	0
Nov 16	Workington	8	Crook	1
Nov 16	Wrexham	0	Accrington	1
Nov 16	York	1	Chesterfield	0

Replays

Date	Home		Away	
Nov 18	Q.P.R.	3	Clapton	1
Nov 19	Bury	4	Bishop Auckland	1
Nov 20	Torquay	1	Peterborough	0
Nov 21	Worcester	2	Aldershot	2
Nov 21	Yeovil	1	Guildford	0
Nov 25	Aldershot	3	Worcester	2
	played at Birmingham			

2nd Round

Date	Home		Away	
Dec 07	Aldershot	4	Coventry	1
Dec 07	Carlisle	1	Accrington	1
Dec 07	Chester	3	Bradford C	3
Dec 07	Crystal Palace	1	Southampton	0
Dec 07	Darlington	5	Boston	3
Dec 07	Durham	0	Tranmere	3
Dec 07	Hereford	6	Q.P.R.	1
Dec 07	Millwall	1	Gillingham	1
Dec 07	Northampton	4	Bournemouth	1
Dec 07	Norwich	1	Brighton	1
Dec 07	Oldham	1	Workington	5
Dec 07	Plymouth	5	Dorchester	2
Dec 07	Port Vale	2	Hull	2
Dec 07	Reading	2	Wisbech	1
Dec 07	Scunthorpe	2	Bury	0
Dec 07	South Shields	1	York	3
Dec 07	Stockport	2	Hartlepool	1
Dec 07	Torquay	1	Southend	1
Dec 07	Wigan	1	Mansfield	1
Dec 07	Yeovil	2	Bath	0

Replays

Date	Home		Away	
Dec 09	Hull	4	Port Vale	3
Dec 11	Accrington	3	Carlisle	2
Dec 11	Bradford C	3	Chester	1
Dec 11	Brighton	1	Norwich	2
Dec 11	Gillingham	6	Millwall	1
Dec 11	Mansfield	3	Wigan	1
Dec 11	Southend	2	Torquay	1

3rd Round

Date	Home		Away	
Jan 04	Accrington	2	Bristol C	2
Jan 04	Bristol R	5	Mansfield	0
Jan 04	Burnley	4	Swansea	2
Jan 04	Crystal Palace	0	Ipswich	1
Jan 04	Doncaster	0	Chelsea	2
Jan 04	Fulham	4	Yeovil	0
Jan 04	Hereford	0	Sheffield W	3
Jan 04	Huddersfield	2	Charlton	2
Jan 04	Hull	1	Barnsley	1
Jan 04	Leeds	1	Cardiff	2
Jan 04	Leyton O	1	Reading	0
Jan 04	Lincoln	0	Wolverhampton	1
Jan 04	Liverpool	1	Southend	1
Jan 04	Middlesbrough	5	Derby	0
Jan 04	Northampton	3	Arsenal	1
Jan 04	Norwich	1	Darlington	2
Jan 04	Nottingham F	2	Gillingham	0
Jan 04	Notts Co	2	Tranmere	0
Jan 04	Plymouth	1	Newcastle	6

Jan 04 Portsmouth 5 Aldershot 1
Jan 04 Preston 0 Bolton 3
Jan 04 Rotherham 1 Blackburn 4
Jan 04 Scunthorpe 1 Bradford C 0
Jan 04 Sheffield U 5 Grimsby 1
Jan 04 Stockport 3 Luton 0
Jan 04 Stoke 1 Aston Villa 1
Jan 04 Sunderland 2 Everton 2
Jan 04 Tottenham 4 Leicester 0
Jan 04 West Ham 5 Blackpool 1
Jan 04 Workington 1 Manchester U 3
Jan 04 W.B.A. 5 Manchester C 1
Jan 08 York 3 Birmingham 0

Replays

Jan 07 Bristol C 3 Accrington 1
Jan 08 Aston Villa 3 Stoke 3
Jan 08 Barnsley 0 Hull 2
Jan 08 Charlton 1 Huddersfield 0
Jan 08 Everton 3 Sunderland 1
Jan 08 Southend 2 Liverpool 3
Jan 13 Aston Villa 0 Stoke 2
played at Wolverhampton

4th Round

Jan 25 Bristol R 2 Burnley 2
Jan 25 Cardiff 4 Leyton O 1
Jan 25 Chelsea 3 Darlington 3
Jan 29 Everton 1 Blackburn 2
Jan 25 Fulham 1 Charlton 1
Jan 25 Liverpool 3 Northampton 1
Jan 25 Manchester U 2 Ipswich 0
Jan 25 Newcastle 1 Scunthorpe 3
Jan 25 Notts Co 1 Bristol C 2
Jan 29 Sheffield W 4 Hull 3
Jan 25 Stoke 3 Middlesbrough 1
Jan 25 Tottenham 0 Sheffield U 3
Jan 25 West Ham 3 Stockport 2
Jan 25 Wolverhampton 5 Portsmouth 1
Jan 25 W.B.A. 3 Nottingham F 3
Jan 25 York 0 Bolton 0

Replays

Jan 28 Burnley 2 Bristol R 3
Jan 29 Bolton 3 York 0
Jan 29 Charlton 0 Fulham 2
Jan 29 Darlington 4 Chelsea 1
Jan 29 Nottingham F 1 W.B.A. 5

5th Round

Feb 15 Bolton 3 Stoke 1
Feb 15 Bristol C 3 Bristol R 4
Feb 15 Cardiff 0 Blackburn 0
Feb 19 Manchester U 3 Sheffield W 0
Feb 15 Scunthorpe 0 Liverpool 1
Feb 15 Sheffield U 1 W.B.A. 1
Feb 15 West Ham 2 Fulham 3
Feb 15 Wolverhampton 6 Darlington 1

Replays

Feb 19 W.B.A. 4 Sheffield U 1
Feb 20 Blackburn 2 Cardiff 1

6th Round

Mar 01 Blackburn 2 Liverpool 1
Mar 01 Bolton 2 Wolverhampton 1
Mar 01 Fulham 3 Bristol R 1
Mar 01 W.B.A. 2 Manchester U 2

Replay

Mar 05 Manchester U 1 W.B.A. 0

Semi-finals

Mar 22 Blackburn 1 Bolton 2
played at Manchester C
Mar 22 Fulham 2 Manchester U 2
played at Aston Villa

Replay

Mar 26 Fulham 3 Manchester U 5
played at Arsenal

Final

May 03 Bolton 2 Manchester U 0
played at Wembley

SEASON 1958-59

1st Round

Nov 15 Accrington 5 Workington 1
Nov 15 Ashford 0 Crystal Palace 1
Nov 15 Brentford 3 Exeter 2
Nov 18 Bury 1 York 0
Nov 15 Buxton 4 Crook 1
Nov 15 Chelmsford 0 Worcester 0
Nov 15 Chester 3 Boston 2
Nov 15 Chesterfield 3 Rhyl 0
Nov 15 Colchester 2 Bath 0
Nov 15 Crewe 2 South Shields 2
Nov 15 Denaby 0 Oldham 2
Nov 15 Doncaster 5 Consett 0
Nov 15 Gateshead 1 Bradford 4
Nov 15 Guildford 1 Hereford 2
Nov 15 Hartlepool 1 Rochdale 1
Nov 15 Headington 3 Margate 2
Nov 15 Heanor 1 Carlisle 5
Nov 15 Hitchin 1 Millwall 1
Nov 15 Hull 0 Stockport 1
Nov 15 Kings Lynn 2 Merthyr T 1
Nov 15 Mansfield 3 Bradford C 4
Nov 15 Morecambe 1 Blyth 2
Nov 15 Newport (IOW) 0 Shrewsbury 0
Nov 15 Northampton 2 Wycombe 0
Nov 15 Norwich 3 Ilford 1
Nov 15 Notts Co 1 Barrow 2
Nov 15 Peterborough 2 Kettering 2
Nov 15 Plymouth 2 Gillingham 2
Nov 15 Southampton 4 Woking 1
Nov 15 Southend 0 Yeovil 0
Nov 15 Southport 0 Halifax 2
Nov 15 Swindon 5 Aldershot 0
Nov 15 Tooting & M 3 Bournemouth 1
Nov 15 Torquay 1 Port Vale 0
Nov 15 Tranmere 8 Bishop Auckland 1
Nov 15 Walsall 0 Q.P.R. 1
Nov 15 Watford 1 Reading 1
Nov 15 Weymouth 2 Coventry 5
Nov 15 Wisbech 2 Newport 2
Nov 15 Wrexham 1 Darlington 2

Replays

Nov 17 Millwall 2 Hitchin 1
Nov 17 Newport 4 Wisbech 1
Nov 19 Gillingham 1 Plymouth 4
Nov 19 Reading 0 Watford 2
Nov 19 Rochdale 3 Hartlepool 3
Nov 19 South Shields 5 Crewe 0
Nov 20 Kettering 2 Peterborough 3
Nov 20 Shrewsbury 5 Newport (IOW) 0
Nov 21 Worcester 3 Chelmsford 1
Nov 21 Yeovil 1 Southend 0
Nov 27 Hartlepool 2 Rochdale 1
played at Manchester U

2nd Round

Dec 06 Accrington 6 Buxton 1
Dec 06 Barrow 2 Hartlepool 0
Dec 06 Blyth 3 Stockport 4
Dec 06 Bradford 0 Bradford C 2
Dec 06 Brentford 3 Kings Lynn 1
Dec 06 Carlisle 0 Chesterfield 0
Dec 06 Chester 1 Bury 1
Dec 06 Colchester 1 Yeovil 1
Dec 06 Coventry 1 Plymouth 3
Dec 06 Crystal Palace 2 Shrewsbury 2
Dec 06 Halifax 1 Darlington 1
Dec 06 Hereford 0 Newport 2
Dec 06 Oldham 2 South Shields 0
Dec 06 Peterborough 4 Headington 2
Dec 06 Q.P.R. 0 Southampton 1
Dec 06 Swindon 1 Norwich 1
Dec 06 Tooting & M 2 Northampton 1
Dec 06 Torquay 2 Watford 0
Dec 06 Tranmere 1 Doncaster 2
Dec 06 Worcester 5 Millwall 2

Replays

Dec 09 Bury 2 Chester 1
Dec 10 Chesterfield 1 Carlisle 0
Dec 10 Darlington 3 Halifax 0
Dec 11 Norwich 1 Swindon 0
Dec 11 Shrewsbury 2 Crystal Palace 2
Dec 11 Yeovil 1 Colchester 7
Dec 15 Crystal Palace 4 Shrewsbury 1
played at Wolverhampton

3rd Round

Jan 10 Accrington 3 Darlington 0
Jan 10 Aston Villa 2 Rotherham 1
Jan 10 Barrow 2 Wolverhampton 4
Jan 10 Blackburn 4 Leyton O 2
Jan 10 Brentford 2 Barnsley 0
Jan 10 Brighton 0 Bradford C 2
Jan 10 Bristol R 0 Charlton 4
Jan 10 Bury 0 Arsenal 1
Jan 10 Colchester 2 Chesterfield 0
Jan 10 Derby 2 Preston 2
Jan 19 Doncaster 0 Bristol C 2
Jan 10 Everton 4 Sunderland 0
Jan 10 Fulham 0 Peterborough 0
Jan 10 Grimsby 2 Manchester C 2
Jan 10 Ipswich 1 Huddersfield 0
Jan 10 Leicester 1 Lincoln 1
Jan 10 Luton 5 Leeds 1
Jan 24 Middlesbrough 0 Birmingham 1
Jan 19 Newcastle 1 Chelsea 4
Jan 10 Newport 0 Torquay 0
Jan 10 Norwich 3 Manchester U 0
Jan 10 Plymouth 0 Cardiff 3
Jan 10 Portsmouth 3 Swansea 1
Jan 10 Scunthorpe 0 Bolton 2
Jan 10 Sheffield U 2 Crystal Palace 0
Jan 19 Sheffield W 0 W.B.A. 2
Jan 10 Southampton 1 Blackpool 2
Jan 14 Stockport 1 Burnley 3
Jan 10 Stoke 5 Oldham 1
Jan 10 Tooting & M 2 Nottingham F 2
Jan 10 Tottenham 2 West Ham 0
Jan 15 Worcester 2 Liverpool 1

Replays

Jan 14 Lincoln 0 Leicester 2
Jan 14 Torquay 0 Newport 1
Jan 19 Preston 4 Derby 2
Jan 24 Manchester C 1 Grimsby 2
Jan 24 Nottingham F 3 Tooting & M 0
Jan 24 Peterborough 0 Fulham 1

4th Round

Jan 24 Accrington 0 Portsmouth 0
Jan 28 Birmingham 1 Fulham 1
Jan 28 Blackburn 1 Burnley 2
Jan 24 Bristol C 1 Blackpool 1
Jan 24 Charlton 2 Everton 2
Jan 24 Chelsea 1 Aston Villa 2
Jan 24 Colchester 2 Arsenal 2
Jan 24 Leicester 1 Luton 1
Jan 24 Norwich 3 Cardiff 2
Jan 28 Nottingham F 4 Grimsby 1
Jan 24 Preston 3 Bradford C 2
Jan 24 Stoke 0 Ipswich 1
Jan 24 Tottenham 4 Newport 1
Jan 24 Wolverhampton 1 Bolton 2
Jan 24 Worcester 0 Sheffield U 2
Jan 24 W.B.A. 2 Brentford 0

Replays

Jan 28 Arsenal 4 Colchester 0
Jan 28 Blackpool 1 Bristol C 0
Jan 28 Everton 4 Charlton 1
Jan 28 Luton 4 Leicester 1
Jan 28 Portsmouth 4 Accrington 1
Feb 04 Fulham 2 Birmingham 3

5th Round

Feb 14 Arsenal 2 Sheffield U 2
Feb 14 Birmingham 1 Nottingham F 1
Feb 14 Blackpool 3 W.B.A. 1
Feb 14 Bolton 2 Preston 2
Feb 14 Burnley 1 Portsmouth 0
Feb 14 Everton 1 Aston Villa 4
Feb 14 Ipswich 2 Luton 5
Feb 14 Tottenham 1 Norwich 1

Replays

Feb 18 Norwich 1 Tottenham 0
Feb 18 Nottingham F 1 Birmingham 1
Feb 18 Preston 1 Bolton 1
Feb 18 Sheffield U 3 Arsenal 0
Feb 23 Birmingham 0 Nottingham F 5
played at Leicester
Feb 23 Bolton 1 Preston 0
played at Blackburn

6th Round

Feb 28 Aston Villa 0 Burnley 0
Feb 28 Blackpool 1 Luton 1
Feb 28 Nottingham F 2 Bolton 1
Feb 28 Sheffield U 1 Norwich 1

Replays

Mar 03 Burnley 0 Aston Villa 2
Mar 04 Luton 1 Blackpool 0
Mar 04 Norwich 3 Sheffield U 2

Semi-finals

Mar 14 Aston Villa 0 Nottingham F 1
played at Sheffield W
Mar 14 Luton 1 Norwich 1
played at Tottenham

Replay

Mar 18 Luton 1 Norwich 0
played at Birmingham

Final

May 02 Luton 1 Nottingham F 2
played at Wembley

SEASON 1959-60

1st Round

Nov 14 Accrington 1 Mansfield 2
Nov 14 Barnsley 3 Bradford C 3
Nov 14 Bath 3 Millwall 1
Nov 14 Bedford 0 Gillingham 4
Nov 14 Bradford 6 Scarborough 1
Nov 14 Brentford 5 Ashford 0
Nov 14 Burscough 1 Crewe 3
Nov 14 Bury 5 Hartlepool 0
Nov 14 Cheltenham 0 Watford 0
Nov 14 Colchester 2 Q.P.R. 3
Nov 14 Coventry 1 Southampton 1
Nov 14 Crook 2 Matlock 2
Nov 14 Crystal Palace 5 Chelmsford 1
Nov 14 Darlington 4 Prescot 0
Nov 14 Doncaster 3 Gainsborough 3
Nov 14 Dorchester 1 Port Vale 2
Nov 14 Enfield 4 Headington 3
Nov 14 Exeter 4 Barnstaple 0
Nov 14 Gateshead 3 Halifax 4
Nov 14 Hastings 1 Notts Co 2

Nov 14 Kettering 1 Margate 1
Nov 14 Kings Lynn 3 Aldershot 1
Nov 14 Newport 4 Hereford 2
Nov 14 Norwich 1 Reading 1
Nov 14 Peterborough 4 Shrewsbury 3
Nov 14 Rhyl 1 Grimsby 2
Nov 14 Rochdale 2 Carlisle 2
Nov 14 Salisbury 1 Barnet 0
Nov 14 Shildon 1 Oldham 1
Nov 14 South Shields 2 Chesterfield 1
Nov 14 Southend 6 Oswestry 0
Nov 14 Southport 2 Workington 2
Nov 14 Swindon 2 Walsall 3
Nov 14 Torquay 7 Northampton 1
Nov 14 Tranmere 0 Chester 1
Nov 14 Walthamstow 2 Bournemouth 3
Nov 14 West Auckland 2 Stockport 6
Nov 14 Wrexham 2 Blyth 1
Nov 14 Wycombe 4 Wisbech 2
Nov 14 York 3 Barrow 1

Replays
Nov 17 Carlisle 1 Rochdale 3
Nov 17 Oldham 3 Shildon 0
Nov 17 Watford 3 Cheltenham 0
Nov 18 Bradford C 2 Barnsley 1
Nov 18 Gainsborough 0 Doncaster 1
Nov 18 Reading 2 Norwich 1
Nov 18 Southampton 5 Coventry 1
Nov 18 Workington 3 Southport 0
Nov 19 Margate 3 Kettering 2
Nov 19 Matlock 0 Crook 1

2nd Round
Dec 05 Bury 2 Oldham 1
Dec 05 Crook 0 York 1
Dec 05 Doncaster 3 Darlington 2
Dec 05 Enfield 1 Bournemouth 5
Dec 05 Exeter 3 Brentford 1
Dec 05 Gillingham 2 Torquay 2
Dec 05 Grimsby 2 Wrexham 3
Dec 05 Mansfield 2 Chester 0
Dec 05 Margate 0 Crystal Palace 0
Dec 05 Notts Co 0 Bath 1
Dec 05 Q.P.R. 3 Port Vale 3
Dec 05 Reading 4 Kings Lynn 2
Dec 05 Rochdale 1 Bradford C 1
Dec 05 Salisbury 0 Newport 1
Dec 05 South Shields 1 Bradford 5
Dec 05 Southampton 3 Southend 0
Dec 05 Stockport 0 Crewe 0
Dec 05 Walsall 2 Peterborough 3
Dec 05 Watford 5 Wycombe 1
Dec 05 Workington 1 Halifax 0

Replays
Dec 07 Port Vale 2 Q.P.R. 1
Dec 09 Bradford C 2 Rochdale 1
Dec 09 Crewe 2 Stockport 0
Dec 09 Crystal Palace 3 Margate 0
Dec 09 Torquay 1 Gillingham 2

3rd Round
Jan 09 Aston Villa 2 Leeds 1
Jan 09 Bath 0 Brighton 1
Jan 09 Blackpool 3 Mansfield 0
Jan 09 Bournemouth 1 York 0
Jan 09 Bradford C 3 Everton 0
Jan 09 Bristol C 2 Charlton 3
Jan 09 Bristol R 0 Doncaster 0
Jan 09 Bury 1 Bolton 1
Jan 09 Cardiff 0 Port Vale 2
Jan 09 Chelsea 5 Bradford 1
Jan 09 Crewe 2 Workington 0
Jan 09 Derby 2 Manchester U 4
Jan 09 Exeter 1 Luton 2
Jan 09 Fulham 5 Hull 0
Jan 09 Gillingham 1 Swansea 4
Jan 09 Huddersfield 1 West Ham 1
Jan 09 Ipswich 2 Peterborough 3
Jan 09 Lincoln 1 Burnley 1
Jan 09 Liverpool 2 Leyton O 1
Jan 09 Manchester C 1 Southampton 5
Jan 09 Newcastle 2 Wolverhampton 2
Jan 09 Newport 0 Tottenham 4
Jan 09 Nottingham F 1 Reading 0
Jan 09 Rotherham 2 Arsenal 2
Jan 09 Scunthorpe 1 Crystal Palace 0
Jan 09 Sheffield U 3 Portsmouth 0
Jan 09 Sheffield W 2 Middlesbrough 1
Jan 09 Stoke 1 Preston 1
Jan 09 Sunderland 1 Blackburn 1
Jan 09 Watford 2 Birmingham 1
Jan 09 Wrexham 1 Leicester 2
Jan 09 W.B.A. 3 Plymouth 2

Replays
Jan 12 Burnley 2 Lincoln 0
Jan 12 Doncaster 1 Bristol R 2
Jan 12 Preston 3 Stoke 1
Jan 13 Arsenal 1 Rotherham 1
Jan 13 Blackburn 4 Sunderland 1
Jan 13 Bolton 4 Bury 2
Jan 13 West Ham 1 Huddersfield 5
Jan 13 Wolverhampton 4 Newcastle 2
Jan 18 Arsenal 0 Rotherham 2
played at Sheffield W

4th Round
Jan 30 Blackburn 1 Blackpool 1
Jan 30 Bradford C 3 Bournemouth 1
Jan 30 Bristol R 3 Preston 3
Jan 30 Chelsea 1 Aston Villa 2
Jan 30 Crewe 2 Tottenham 2
Jan 30 Huddersfield 0 Luton 1
Jan 30 Leicester 2 Fulham 1
Jan 30 Liverpool 1 Manchester U 3
Jan 30 Rotherham 1 Brighton 1
Jan 30 Scunthorpe 0 Port Vale 1
Jan 30 Sheffield U 3 Nottingham F 0
Jan 30 Sheffield W 2 Peterborough 0
Jan 30 Southampton 2 Watford 2
Jan 30 Swansea 0 Burnley 0
Jan 30 Wolverhampton 2 Charlton 1
Jan 30 W.B.A. 2 Bolton 0

Replays
Feb 02 Burnley 2 Swansea 1
Feb 02 Preston 5 Bristol R 1
Feb 02 Watford 1 Southampton 0
Feb 03 Blackpool 0 Blackburn 3
Feb 03 Brighton 1 Rotherham 1
Feb 03 Tottenham 13 Crewe 2
Feb 08 Brighton 6 Rotherham 0
played at Arsenal

5th Round
Feb 20 Bradford C 2 Burnley 2
Feb 20 Leicester 2 W.B.A. 1
Feb 20 Luton 1 Wolverhampton 4
Feb 20 Manchester U 0 Sheffield W 1
Feb 20 Port Vale 1 Aston Villa 2
Feb 20 Preston 2 Brighton 1
Feb 20 Sheffield U 3 Watford 2
Feb 20 Tottenham 1 Blackburn 3

Replay
Feb 23 Burnley 5 Bradford C 0

6th Round
Mar 12 Aston Villa 2 Preston 0
Mar 12 Burnley 3 Blackburn 3
Mar 12 Leicester 1 Wolverhampton 2
Mar 12 Sheffield U 0 Sheffield W 2

Replay
Mar 16 Blackburn 2 Burnley 0

Semi-finals
Mar 26 Aston Villa 0 Wolverhampton 1
played at W.B.A.
Mar 26 Blackburn 2 Sheffield W 1
played at Manchester C

Final
May 07 Blackburn 0 Wolverhampton 3
played at Wembley

Season 1960-61

1st Round
Nov 05 Accrington 2 Barrow 1
Nov 05 Aldershot 2 Notts Co 0
Nov 05 Ashford 1 Gillingham 2
Nov 05 Bangor 1 Wrexham 0
Nov 05 Bishop Auckland 3 Bridlington 2
Nov 05 Bradford C 0 Scarborough 0
Nov 05 Bridgwater 3 Hereford 0
Nov 05 Bristol C 11 Chichester 0
Nov 05 Chelmsford 2 Port Vale 3
Nov 05 Chester 0 Carlisle 1
Nov 05 Chesterfield 3 Doncaster 3
Nov 05 Clacton 1 Southend 3
Nov 05 Colchester 5 Maidenhead 0
Nov 05 Crewe 1 Rochdale 1
Nov 05 Crystal Palace 6 Hitchin 2
Nov 05 Darlington 2 Grimsby 0
Nov 05 Dover 1 Peterborough 4
Nov 05 Exeter 1 Bournemouth 1
Nov 05 Gateshead 0 Barnsley 0
Nov 05 Halifax 5 Hartlepool 1
Nov 05 Hendon 2 Oxford 2
Nov 05 Hull 3 Sutton T 0
Nov 05 Loughborough 0 Kings Lynn 0
Nov 05 Mansfield 3 Blyth 1
Nov 05 Northampton 2 Hastings 1
Nov 05 Q.P.R. 3 Walthamstow 2
Nov 05 Reading 6 Millwall 2
Nov 05 Rhyl 0 Oldham 1
Nov 05 Shrewsbury 4 Newport 1
Nov 05 Southport 7 Macclesfield 2
Nov 05 Stockport 1 Workington 0
Nov 05 Sutton U 2 Romford 2
Nov 05 Swindon 2 Bath 2
Nov 05 Tranmere 1 Bury 0
Nov 05 Walsall 0 Yeovil 1
Nov 05 Watford 2 Brentford 2
Nov 05 Weymouth 1 Torquay 3
Nov 05 Worcester 1 Coventry 4
Nov 05 Wycombe 1 Kettering 2
Nov 05 York 0 Bradford 0

Replays
Nov 08 Brentford 0 Watford 2
Nov 08 Rochdale 1 Crewe 2
Nov 09 Barnsley 2 Gateshead 0
Nov 09 Bath 4 Swindon 6
Nov 09 Bournemouth 3 Exeter 1
Nov 09 Bradford 0 York 2
Nov 09 Doncaster 0 Chesterfield 1
Nov 09 Kings Lynn 3 Loughborough 0
Nov 09 Oxford 3 Hendon 2
Nov 09 Romford 5 Sutton U 0
Nov 09 Scarborough 1 Bradford C 3

2nd Round
Nov 30 Accrington 3 Mansfield 0
Nov 26 Aldershot 3 Colchester 1
Nov 26 Bangor 1 Southport 1
Nov 26 Bournemouth 3 Yeovil 1
Nov 26 Bradford C 1 Barnsley 2
Nov 26 Chesterfield 4 Oldham 4
Nov 26 Crystal Palace 0 Watford 0
Nov 26 Darlington 1 Hull 1
Nov 26 Gillingham 3 Southend 2
Nov 29 Halifax 2 Crewe 2
Nov 26 Kings Lynn 2 Bristol C 2
Nov 26 Oxford 2 Bridgwater 1
Nov 26 Port Vale 2 Carlisle 1
Nov 26 Q.P.R. 1 Coventry 2
Nov 26 Reading 4 Kettering 2
Nov 26 Romford 1 Northampton 5
Nov 26 Stockport 2 Bishop Auckland 0
Nov 26 Swindon 0 Shrewsbury 1
Nov 26 Torquay 1 Peterborough 3
Nov 30 Tranmere 1 York 1

Replays
Nov 28 Hull 1 Darlington 1
Nov 29 Bristol C 3 Kings Lynn 0
Nov 29 Oldham 0 Chesterfield 3
Nov 29 Southport 3 Bangor 1
Nov 29 Watford 1 Crystal Palace 0
Dec 05 Crewe 3 Halifax 0
Dec 05 Darlington 1 Hull 1
played at Leeds
Dec 05 York 2 Tranmere 1
Dec 12 Darlington 0 Hull 0
played at Doncaster
Dec 15 Darlington 0 Hull 3
played at Middlesbrough

3rd Round
Jan 07 Aldershot 1 Shrewsbury 1
Jan 07 Brighton 3 Derby 1
Jan 07 Bristol R 1 Aston Villa 1
Jan 07 Burnley 1 Bournemouth 0
Jan 07 Cardiff 1 Manchester C 1
Jan 07 Chelsea 1 Crewe 2
Jan 07 Chesterfield 0 Blackburn 0
Jan 07 Everton 0 Sheffield U 1
Jan 07 Gillingham 2 Leyton O 6
Jan 07 Hull 0 Bolton 1
Jan 07 Leicester 3 Oxford 1
Jan 07 Lincoln 3 W.B.A. 1
Jan 07 Liverpool 3 Coventry 2
Jan 07 Luton 4 Northampton 0
Jan 07 Manchester U 3 Middlesbrough 0
Jan 07 Newcastle 5 Fulham 0
Jan 07 Nottingham F 0 Birmingham 2
Jan 07 Plymouth 0 Bristol C 1
Jan 07 Portsmouth 1 Peterborough 2
Jan 07 Preston 1 Accrington 1
Jan 07 Reading 1 Barnsley 1
Jan 07 Rotherham 1 Watford 0
Jan 07 Scunthorpe 6 Blackpool 2
Jan 07 Sheffield W 2 Leeds 0
Jan 07 Southampton 7 Ipswich 1
Jan 07 Stockport 3 Southport 1
Jan 07 Sunderland 2 Arsenal 1
Jan 07 Swansea 3 Port Vale 0
Jan 07 Tottenham 3 Charlton 2
Jan 07 West Ham 2 Stoke 2
Jan 07 Wolverhampton 1 Huddersfield 1
Jan 07 York 1 Norwich 1

Replays
Jan 09 Accrington 0 Preston 4
Jan 09 Aston Villa 4 Bristol R 0
Jan 11 Barnsley 3 Reading 1
Jan 11 Blackburn 3 Chesterfield 0
Jan 11 Huddersfield 2 Wolverhampton 1
Jan 11 Manchester C 0 Cardiff 0
Jan 11 Norwich 1 York 0
Jan 11 Shrewsbury 2 Aldershot 2
Jan 11 Stoke 1 West Ham 0
Jan 16 Aldershot 2 Shrewsbury 0
played at Aston Villa
Jan 16 Cardiff 0 Manchester C 2
played at Arsenal

4th Round
Jan 28 Birmingham 4 Rotherham 0
Jan 28 Bolton 3 Blackburn 3
Jan 28 Brighton 3 Burnley 3
Feb 01 Huddersfield 1 Barnsley 1
Jan 31 Leicester 5 Bristol C 1
Jan 28 Liverpool 0 Sunderland 2
Feb 01 Luton 3 Manchester C 1
Feb 01 Newcastle 4 Stockport 0
Jan 28 Peterborough 1 Aston Villa 1
Jan 28 Scunthorpe 1 Norwich 4
Jan 28 Sheffield U 3 Lincoln 1
Jan 28 Sheffield W 1 Manchester U 1
Jan 28 Southampton 0 Leyton O 1
Jan 28 Stoke 0 Aldershot 0
Jan 28 Swansea 2 Preston 1
Jan 28 Tottenham 5 Crewe 1

Replays
Jan 31 Burnley 2 Brighton 0
Feb 01 Aldershot 0 Stoke 0
Feb 01 Aston Villa 2 Peterborough 1
Feb 01 Blackburn 4 Bolton 0
Feb 01 Manchester U 2 Sheffield W 7

Danny Blanchflower and Bill Brown collect the trophy and medals as Spurs complete the first modern League and Cup double with victory over Leicester City in 1961.

Feb 06 Aldershot 0 Stoke 3
played at Wolverhampton
Feb 06 Barnsley 1 Huddersfield 0

5th Round
Feb 18 Aston Villa 0 Tottenham 2
Feb 18 Barnsley 1 Luton 0
Feb 18 Birmingham 1 Leicester 1
Feb 18 Burnley 4 Swansea 0
Feb 18 Leyton O 0 Sheffield W 2
Feb 18 Newcastle 3 Stoke 1
Feb 18 Norwich 0 Sunderland 1
Feb 18 Sheffield U 2 Blackburn 1

Replay
Feb 22 Leicester 2 Birmingham 1

6th Round
Mar 04 Leicester 0 Barnsley 0
Mar 04 Newcastle 1 Sheffield U 3
Mar 04 Sheffield W 0 Burnley 0
Mar 04 Sunderland 1 Tottenham 1

Replays
Mar 07 Burnley 2 Sheffield W 0
Mar 08 Barnsley 1 Leicester 2
Mar 08 Tottenham 5 Sunderland 0

Semi-finals
Mar 18 Burnley 0 Tottenham 3
played at Aston Villa
Mar 18 Leicester 0 Sheffield U 0
played at Leeds

Replays
Mar 23 Leicester 0 Sheffield U 0
played at Nottingham F
Mar 27 Leicester 2 Sheffield U 0
played at Birmingham

Final
May 06 Leicester 0 Tottenham 2
played at Wembley

SEASON 1961-62

1st Round
Nov 04 Aldershot 3 Tunbridge 1
Nov 04 Barry 1 Q.P.R. 1
Nov 04 Bournemouth 0 Margate 3
Nov 04 Bradford 0 Port Vale 1
Nov 04 Bradford C 1 York 0
Nov 04 Brentford 3 Oxford 0
Nov 04 Bridgwater 0 Weston-s-Mare 0
Nov 04 Brierley 3 Grantham 0
Nov 04 Bristol C 1 Hereford 1
Nov 04 Chelmsford 1 Kings Lynn 2
Nov 04 Chester 4 Ashington 1
Nov 04 Coventry 2 Gillingham 0
Nov 04 Crewe 2 Lincoln 0
Nov 04 Crystal Palace 3 Portsmouth 0
Nov 04 Darlington 0 Carlisle 4
Nov 04 Doncaster 0 Chesterfield 4
Nov 04 Exeter 3 Dartford 3
Nov 04 Hartlepool 5 Blyth 1
Nov 04 Hull 5 Rhyl 0
Nov 04 Mansfield 3 Grimsby 2
Nov 04 Morecambe 2 South Shields 1
Nov 04 Northampton 2 Millwall 0
Nov 04 Notts Co 4 Yeovil 2
Nov 04 Oldham 5 Shildon 2
Nov 04 Peterborough 3 Colchester 3
Nov 04 Reading 1 Newport 1
Nov 04 Rochdale 2 Halifax 0
Nov 04 Shrewsbury 7 Banbury 1
Nov 04 Southend 0 Watford 2
Nov 04 Southport 1 Northwich 0
Nov 04 Stockport 0 Accrington 1
Nov 04 Swindon 2 Kettering 2
Nov 04 Torquay 5 Harwich 1
Nov 04 Tranmere 2 Gateshead 3
Nov 04 Walthamstow 2 Romford 3
Nov 04 West Auckland 3 Barnsley 3
Nov 04 Weymouth 1 Barnet 0
Nov 04 Workington 2 Worksop 0
Nov 04 Wrexham 3 Barrow 2
Nov 04 Wycombe 0 Ashford 0

Replays
Nov 06 Colchester 2 Peterborough 2
Nov 06 Newport 1 Reading 0
Nov 06 Q.P.R. 7 Barry 0
Nov 08 Ashford 3 Wycombe 0
Nov 08 Barnsley 2 West Auckland 0
Nov 08 Dartford 2 Exeter 1
Nov 08 Hereford 2 Bristol C 5
Nov 08 Kettering 3 Swindon 0
Nov 09 Weston-s-Mare 0 Bridgwater 1
Nov 13 Colchester 0 Peterborough 3
played at Norwich

2nd Round
Nov 25 Aldershot 2 Brentford 2
Nov 25 Ashford 0 Q.P.R. 3
Nov 25 Barnsley 1 Carlisle 2
Nov 25 Bridgwater 0 Crystal Palace 3
Nov 25 Bristol C 8 Dartford 2
Nov 25 Chester 0 Morecambe 1
Nov 25 Chesterfield 2 Oldham 2
Nov 25 Coventry 1 Kings Lynn 2
Nov 25 Crewe 1 Port Vale 1
Nov 25 Gateshead 0 Workington 2
Nov 25 Hartlepool 2 Accrington 1
Nov 25 Hull 0 Bradford C 2
Nov 25 Margate 1 Notts Co 1
Nov 25 Northampton 3 Kettering 0
Nov 25 Rochdale 1 Wrexham 2
Nov 25 Romford 1 Watford 3
Nov 25 Shrewsbury 3 Brierley 0
Nov 25 Southport 4 Mansfield 2
Nov 25 Torquay 1 Peterborough 4
Nov 25 Weymouth 1 Newport 0

Replays
Nov 27 Port Vale 3 Crewe 0
Nov 28 Brentford 2 Aldershot 0
Nov 29 Oldham 4 Chesterfield 2
Nov 30 Notts Co 3 Margate 1

3rd Round
Jan 06 Arsenal 3 Bradford C 0
Jan 06 Aston Villa 4 Crystal Palace 3
Jan 06 Birmingham 3 Tottenham 3
Jan 06 Blackpool 0 W.B.A. 0
Jan 06 Brentford 1 Leyton O 1
Jan 06 Brighton 0 Blackburn 3
Jan 06 Bristol C 0 Walsall 0
Jan 08 Bristol R 1 Oldham 1
Jan 06 Burnley 6 Q.P.R. 1
Jan 06 Bury 0 Sheffield U 0
Jan 06 Charlton 1 Scunthorpe 0
Jan 06 Everton 4 Kings Lynn 0
Jan 06 Fulham 3 Hartlepool 1
Jan 09 Huddersfield 4 Rotherham 3
Jan 06 Ipswich 1 Luton 1
Jan 06 Leeds 2 Derby 2
Jan 10 Leicester 1 Stoke 1
Jan 06 Liverpool 4 Chelsea 3

Jan 06	Manchester U	2	Bolton	1
Jan 10	Middlesbrough	1	Cardiff	0
Jan 06	Morecambe	0	Weymouth	1
Jan 06	Newcastle	0	Peterborough	1
Jan 10	Norwich	3	Wrexham	1
Jan 06	Notts Co	0	Manchester C	1
Jan 06	Plymouth	3	West Ham	0
Jan 06	Port Vale	3	Northampton	1
Jan 06	Preston	3	Watford	2
Jan 09	Sheffield W	1	Swansea	0
Jan 06	Southampton	2	Sunderland	2
Jan 09	Southport	1	Shrewsbury	3
Jan 08	Wolverhampton	3	Carlisle	1
Jan 06	Workington	1	Nottingham F	2

Replays

Jan 08	Leyton O	2	Brentford	1
Jan 09	Walsall	4	Bristol C	1
Jan 10	Derby	3	Leeds	1
Jan 10	Luton	1	Ipswich	1
Jan 10	Oldham	2	Bristol R	0
Jan 10	Sheffield U	2	Bury	2
Jan 10	Sunderland	3	Southampton	0
Jan 10	Tottenham	4	Birmingham	2
Jan 10	W.B.A.	2	Blackpool	1
Jan 15	Bury	0	Sheffield U	2
	played at Sheffield W			
Jan 15	Ipswich	5	Luton	1
	played at Arsenal			
Jan 15	Stoke	5	Leicester	2

4th Round

Jan 27	Aston Villa	2	Huddersfield	1
Jan 30	Burnley	1	Leyton O	1
Jan 27	Charlton	2	Derby	1
Jan 27	Everton	2	Manchester C	0
Jan 27	Fulham	2	Walsall	2
Jan 31	Manchester U	1	Arsenal	0
Jan 27	Norwich	1	Ipswich	1
Jan 27	Nottingham F	0	Sheffield W	2
Jan 27	Oldham	1	Liverpool	2
Jan 27	Peterborough	1	Sheffield U	3
Jan 27	Plymouth	1	Tottenham	5
Jan 29	Preston	2	Weymouth	0
Jan 27	Shrewsbury	2	Middlesbrough	2
Jan 27	Stoke	0	Blackburn	1
Jan 27	Sunderland	0	Port Vale	0
Jan 27	Wolverhampton	1	W.B.A.	2

Replays

Jan 30	Ipswich	1	Norwich	2
Jan 30	Walsall	0	Fulham	2
Jan 31	Middlesbrough	5	Shrewsbury	1
Jan 31	Port Vale	3	Sunderland	1
Feb 06	Leyton O	0	Burnley	1

5th Round

Feb 17	Aston Villa	2	Charlton	1
Feb 17	Blackburn	2	Middlesbrough	1
Feb 17	Burnley	3	Everton	1
Feb 17	Fulham	1	Port Vale	0
Feb 17	Liverpool	0	Preston	0
Feb 17	Manchester U	0	Sheffield W	0
Feb 17	Sheffield U	3	Norwich	
Feb 17	W.B.A.	2	Tottenham	

Replays

Feb 20	Preston	0	Liverpool	
Feb 21	Sheffield W	0	Manchester U	
Feb 26	Liverpool	0	Preston	
	played at Manchester U			

6th Round

Mar 10	Fulham	2	Blackburn	
Mar 10	Preston	0	Manchester U	
Mar 10	Sheffield U	0	Burnley	
Mar 10	Tottenham	2	Aston Villa	

Replays

Mar 14	Blackburn	0	Fulham	
Mar 14	Manchester U	2	Preston	

Semi-finals

Mar 31	Burnley	1	Fulham	
	played at Aston Villa			
Mar 31	Manchester U	1	Tottenham	
	played at Sheffield W			

Replay

Apr 09	Burnley	2	Fulham	
	played at Leicester			

Final

May 05	Burnley	1	Tottenham	
	played at Wembley			

SEASON 1962-63

1st Round

Nov 03	Aldershot	1	Brentford	0
Nov 03	Andover	0	Gillingham	1
Nov 03	Barnsley	4	Rhyl	0
Nov 03	Bedford	2	Cambridge	1
Nov 03	Blyth	2	Morecambe	1
Nov 03	Boston	1	Kings Lynn	2
Nov 03	Bristol C	4	Wellington	2
Nov 03	Bristol R	0	Port Vale	2
Nov 03	Buxton	2	Barrow	2
Nov 03	Carlisle	2	Hartlepool	1
Nov 03	Chelmsford	2	Shrewsbury	6
Nov 03	Cheltenham	3	Enfield	6
Nov 03	Chester	0	Tranmere	2
Nov 03	Chesterfield	4	Stockport	1
Nov 03	Coventry	1	Bournemouth	0
Nov 03	Crewe	1	Scarborough	1
Nov 03	Crystal Palace	2	Hereford	0
Nov 03	Falmouth	1	Oxford	2
Nov 03	Gateshead	2	Wigan	1
Nov 03	Gravesend	3	Exeter	2
Nov 03	Halifax	1	Bradford	0
Nov 03	Hinckley	3	Sittingbourne	0
Nov 03	Hounslow	3	Mansfield	3
Nov 03	Hull	5	Crook	4
Nov 03	Lincoln	1	Darlington	1
Nov 03	Maidenhead	0	Wycombe	3
Nov 03	Millwall	3	Margate	1
Nov 03	North Shields	2	Workington	2
Nov 03	Northampton	1	Torquay	2
Nov 03	Notts Co	0	Peterborough	3
Nov 03	Oldham	2	Bradford C	5
Nov 03	Q.P.R.	3	Newport	2
Nov 03	South Shields	0	Doncaster	0
Nov 03	Southend	2	Brighton	1
Nov 03	Southport	1	Wrexham	1
Nov 03	Swindon	4	Reading	2
Nov 03	Watford	2	Poole	2
Nov 03	Wimbledon	2	Colchester	1
Nov 03	Yeovil	3	Dartford	2
Nov 03	York	0	Rochdale	0

Replays

Nov 05	Barrow	3	Buxton	1
Nov 05	Mansfield	9	Hounslow	2
Nov 06	Poole	1	Watford	2
Nov 06	Rochdale	1	York	2
Nov 07	Darlington	1	Lincoln	2
Nov 07	Scarborough	2	Crewe	3
Nov 07	Wrexham	3	Southport	2
Nov 08	Doncaster	2	South Shields	1
Nov 08	Workington	7	North Shields	2

2nd Round

Nov 24	Barnsley	2	Chesterfield	1
Nov 24	Blyth	0	Carlisle	2
Nov 24	Bradford C	3	Gateshead	2
Nov 24	Bristol C	2	Wimbledon	1
Nov 24	Crystal Palace	2	Mansfield	2
Nov 24	Doncaster	1	Tranmere	4
Nov 24	Gillingham	3	Bedford	0
Nov 24	Gravesend	3	Wycombe	1
Nov 24	Hull	2	Workington	0
Nov 24	Kings Lynn	1	Oxford	2
Nov 24	Lincoln	1	Halifax	0
Nov 24	Millwall	0	Coventry	0
Nov 24	Peterborough	1	Enfield	0
Nov 24	Port Vale	2	Aldershot	0
Nov 24	Q.P.R.	7	Hinckley	2
Nov 24	Shrewsbury	2	Torquay	1
Nov 24	Southend	0	Watford	2
Nov 24	Wrexham	5	Barrow	2
Nov 24	Yeovil	0	Swindon	2
Nov 24	York	2	Crewe	1

Replays

Nov 26	Mansfield	7	Crystal Palace	2
Nov 27	Coventry	2	Millwall	1

3rd Round

Jan 30	Arsenal	5	Oxford	1
Jan 15	Barnsley	0	Everton	3
Mar 05	Birmingham	3	Bury	3
Mar 05	Blackburn	1	Middlesbrough	1
Mar 07	Bradford C	1	Newcastle	6
Jan 16	Bristol C	1	Aston Villa	1
Jan 29	Carlisle	0	Gravesend	1
Feb 18	Charlton	1	Cardiff	0
Feb 04	Derby	2	Peterborough	0
Feb 27	Gillingham	2	Port Vale	4
Jan 08	Grimsby	1	Leicester	3
Mar 06	Leeds	3	Stoke	1
Feb 11	Leyton O	1	Hull	1
Mar 06	Lincoln	1	Coventry	5
Jan 26	Luton	0	Swindon	2
Mar 04	Manchester U	5	Huddersfield	0
Jan 09	Mansfield	2	Ipswich	3
Mar 04	Norwich	1	Blackpool	1
Jan 29	Nottingham F	4	Wolverhampton	3
Jan 05	Plymouth	1	W.B.A.	5
Jan 26	Portsmouth	1	Scunthorpe	1
Jan 05	Preston	1	Sunderland	4
Mar 06	Sheffield U	3	Bolton	1
Feb 21	Shrewsbury	1	Sheffield W	1
Feb 13	Southampton	5	York	0
Jan 26	Swansea	2	Q.P.R.	0
Jan 16	Tottenham	0	Burnley	3
Jan 05	Tranmere	2	Chelsea	2
Mar 06	Walsall	0	Manchester C	1
Feb 20	Watford	2	Rotherham	0
Feb 04	West Ham	0	Fulham	0
Jan 09	Wrexham	0	Liverpool	3

Replays

Feb 19	Hull	0	Leyton O	2
Feb 20	Fulham	1	West Ham	2
Jan 30	Chelsea	3	Tranmere	1
Mar 06	Blackpool	1	Norwich	3
Mar 07	Aston Villa	3	Bristol C	2
Mar 07	Bury	2	Birmingham	0
Mar 07	Scunthorpe	1	Portsmouth	2
Mar 07	Sheffield W	2	Shrewsbury	1
Mar 11	Middlesbrough	3	Blackburn	

4th Round

Mar 12	Arsenal	2	Sheffield W	
Jan 26	Burnley	1	Liverpool	
Mar 06	Charlton	0	Chelsea	
Feb 12	Gravesend	1	Sunderland	
Jan 30	Leicester	3	Ipswich	
Mar 04	Leyton O	3	Derby	
Mar 13	Manchester C	1	Bury	
Mar 11	Manchester U	1	Aston Villa	
Mar 16	Middlesbrough	0	Leeds	
Mar 13	Norwich	5	Newcastle	
Mar 13	Port Vale	1	Sheffield U	
Mar 13	Portsmouth	1	Coventry	
Feb 27	Southampton	3	Watford	
Jan 29	Swindon	1	Everton	
Mar 04	West Ham	1	Swansea	
Mar 06	W.B.A.	0	Nottingham F	

Replays

Feb 18	Sunderland	5	Gravesend	2
Feb 20	Liverpool	2	Burnley	1
Mar 11	Nottingham F	2	W.B.A.	1
Mar 16	Coventry	2	Portsmouth	2
Mar 19	Coventry	2	Portsmouth	1
	played at Tottenham			

5th Round

Mar 16	Arsenal	1	Liverpool	2
Mar 25	Coventry	2	Sunderland	1
Mar 16	Leyton O	0	Leicester	1
Mar 16	Manchester C	1	Norwich	2
Mar 16	Manchester U	2	Chelsea	1
Mar 19	Nottingham F	3	Leeds	0
Mar 16	Southampton	1	Sheffield U	0
Mar 16	West Ham	1	Everton	0

6th Round

Mar 30	Coventry	1	Manchester U	3
Mar 30	Liverpool	1	West Ham	0
Mar 30	Norwich	0	Leicester	2
Mar 30	Nottingham F	1	Southampton	1

Replays

Apr 03	Southampton	3	Nottingham F	3
Apr 08	Nottingham F	0	Southampton	5
	played at Tottenham			

Semi-finals

Apr 27	Leicester	1	Liverpool	0
	played at Sheffield W			
Apr 27	Manchester U	1	Southampton	0
	played at Aston Villa			

Final

May 25	Leicester	1	Manchester U	3
	played at Wembley			

SEASON 1962-63

1st Round

Nov 20	Altrincham	0	Wrexham	0
Nov 16	Barnsley	1	Stockport	0
Nov 16	Barrow	3	Bangor	2
Nov 16	Bexley	1	Wimbledon	5
Nov 16	Bournemouth	1	Bristol R	3
Nov 16	Bradford	3	Heanor	1
Nov 16	Bradford C	1	Port Vale	2
Nov 16	Brentford	2	Margate	2
Nov 16	Bridgwater	0	Luton	3
Nov 16	Brighton	0	Colchester	1
Nov 16	Cambridge	0	Chelmsford	1
Nov 16	Chester	3	Blyth	2
Nov 16	Corby	1	Bristol C	3
Nov 16	Crook	1	Chesterfield	2
Nov 16	Crystal Palace	8	Harwich	2
Nov 16	Darlington	1	Gateshead	4
Nov 16	Doncaster	3	Tranmere	0
Nov 16	Exeter	2	Shrewsbury	1
Nov 16	Hartlepool	0	Lincoln	1
Nov 16	Hereford	1	Newport	1
Nov 16	Hull	2	Crewe	2
Nov 16	Kettering	1	Millwall	1
Nov 16	Maidenhead	0	Bath	2
Nov 16	Netherfield	6	Loughborough	1
Nov 16	Notts Co	2	Frickley	1
Nov 20	Oldham	3	Mansfield	2
Nov 16	Oxford	2	Folkestone	0
Nov 16	Peterborough	1	Watford	1
Nov 16	Q.P.R.	4	Gillingham	1

Nov 16 Reading 2 Enfield 2
Nov 18 Rochdale 2 Chorley 1
Nov 16 Southport 2 Walsall 1
Nov 16 Sutton 0 Aldershot 4
Nov 16 Tooting & M 1 Gravesend 2
Nov 16 Torquay 6 Barnet 2
Nov 16 Trowbridge 1 Coventry 6
Nov 16 Weymouth 1 Bedford 1
Nov 16 Workington 4 Halifax 1
Nov 16 Yeovil 1 Southend 0
Nov 16 York 2 Carlisle 5

Replays
Nov 18 Newport 4 Hereford 0
Nov 19 Enfield 2 Reading 4
Nov 19 Watford 2 Peterborough 1
Nov 20 Crewe 0 Hull 3
Nov 20 Margate 0 Brentford 2
Nov 21 Bedford 1 Weymouth 0
Nov 25 Millwall 2 Kettering 3
Nov 27 Wrexham 3 Altrincham 0

2nd Round
Dec 07 Barnsley 3 Rochdale 1
Dec 07 Brentford 1 Gravesend 0
Dec 07 Carlisle 4 Gateshead 3
Dec 07 Chelmsford 0 Bedford 1
Dec 07 Chester 0 Barrow 2
Dec 07 Colchester 0 Q.P.R. 1
Dec 07 Coventry 1 Bristol R 2
Dec 07 Doncaster 1 Notts Co 1
Dec 07 Exeter 0 Bristol C 2
Dec 07 Lincoln 2 Southport 0
Dec 07 Luton 2 Reading 1
Dec 07 Netherfield 1 Chesterfield 1
Dec 07 Newport 2 Watford 0
Dec 07 Oldham 2 Bradford 0
Dec 07 Oxford 2 Kettering 1
Dec 07 Port Vale 2 Workington 1
Dec 07 Torquay 2 Aldershot 3
Dec 07 Wimbledon 2 Bath 2
Dec 07 Wrexham 0 Hull 2
Dec 07 Yeovil 3 Crystal Palace 1

Replays
Dec 10 Notts Co 1 Doncaster 2
Dec 11 Chesterfield 4 Netherfield 1
Dec 12 Bath 4 Wimbledon 0

3rd Round
Jan 04 Arsenal 2 Wolverhampton 1
Jan 04 Aston Villa 0 Aldershot 0
Jan 04 Bath 1 Bolton 1
Jan 04 Birmingham 1 Port Vale 2
Jan 04 Blackburn 4 Grimsby 0
Jan 04 Brentford 2 Middlesbrough 1
Jan 04 Bristol R 2 Norwich 1
Jan 04 Burnley 1 Rotherham 1
Jan 04 Cardiff 0 Leeds 1
Jan 04 Carlisle 2 Q.P.R. 0
Jan 04 Doncaster 2 Bristol C 2
Jan 04 Fulham 4 Luton 1
Jan 04 Hull 1 Everton 1
Jan 04 Ipswich 6 Oldham 3
Jan 04 Leicester 2 Leyton O 3
Jan 04 Lincoln 0 Sheffield U 4
Jan 04 Liverpool 5 Derby 0
Jan 04 Newcastle 1 Bedford 2
Jan 04 Newport 3 Sheffield W 2
Jan 04 Nottingham F 0 Preston 0
Jan 04 Oxford 1 Chesterfield 0
Jan 04 Plymouth 0 Huddersfield 1
Jan 04 Scunthorpe 2 Barnsley 2
Jan 04 Southampton 2 Manchester U 3
Jan 04 Stoke 4 Portsmouth 1
Jan 04 Sunderland 2 Northampton 0
Jan 04 Swansea 4 Barrow 1
Jan 04 Swindon 2 Manchester C 1
Jan 04 Tottenham 1 Chelsea 1
Jan 04 West Ham 3 Charlton 0
Jan 04 W.B.A. 2 Blackpool 2
Jan 04 Yeovil 0 Bury 2

Replays
Jan 07 Barnsley 3 Scunthorpe 2
Jan 07 Bristol C 2 Doncaster 0
Jan 07 Everton 2 Hull 1
Jan 07 Rotherham 2 Burnley 3
Jan 08 Aldershot 2 Aston Villa 1
Jan 08 Blackpool 0 W.B.A. 1
Jan 08 Bolton 3 Bath 0
Jan 08 Chelsea 2 Tottenham 0
Jan 13 Preston 1 Nottingham F 0

4th Round
Jan 25 Aldershot 1 Swindon 2
Jan 25 Barnsley 2 Bury 1
Jan 25 Bedford 0 Carlisle 3
Jan 25 Blackburn 2 Fulham 0
Jan 25 Bolton 2 Preston 2
Jan 25 Burnley 2 Newport 1
Jan 25 Chelsea 1 Huddersfield 2
Jan 25 Ipswich 1 Stoke 1
Jan 25 Leeds 1 Everton 1
Jan 25 Leyton O 1 West Ham 1
Jan 25 Liverpool 0 Port Vale 0
Jan 25 Manchester U 4 Bristol R 1
Jan 25 Oxford 2 Brentford 2
Jan 25 Sheffield U 1 Swansea 1
Jan 25 Sunderland 6 Bristol C 1
Jan 25 W.B.A. 3 Arsenal 3

Replays
Jan 27 Port Vale 1 Liverpool 2
Jan 27 Preston 2 Bolton 1
Jan 28 Brentford 1 Oxford 2
Jan 28 Everton 2 Leeds 0
Jan 28 Swansea 4 Sheffield U 0
Jan 29 Arsenal 2 W.B.A. 0
Jan 29 Stoke 1 Ipswich 0
Jan 29 West Ham 3 Leyton O 0

5th Round
Feb 15 Arsenal 0 Liverpool 1
Feb 15 Barnsley 0 Manchester U 4
Feb 15 Burnley 3 Huddersfield 0
Feb 15 Oxford 3 Blackburn 1
Feb 15 Preston 1 Carlisle 0
Feb 15 Stoke 2 Swansea 2
Feb 15 Sunderland 3 Everton 1
Feb 15 Swindon 1 West Ham 3

Replay
Feb 18 Swansea 2 Stoke 0

6th Round
Feb 29 Liverpool 1 Swansea 2
Feb 29 Manchester U 3 Sunderland 3
Feb 29 Oxford 1 Preston 2
Feb 29 West Ham 3 Burnley 2

Replays
Mar 04 Sunderland 2 Manchester U 2
Mar 09 Manchester U 5 Sunderland 1
played at Huddersfield

Semi-finals
Mar 14 Manchester U 1 West Ham 3
played at Sheffield W
Mar 14 Preston 2 Swansea 1
played at Aston Villa

Final
May 02 Preston 2 West Ham 3
played at Wembley

SEASON 1964-65

1st Round
Nov 14 Barnet 2 Cambridge 1
Nov 14 Barrow 1 Grimsby 1
Nov 14 Bournemouth 7 Gravesend 0
Nov 14 Bradford 2 Doncaster 3
Nov 14 Bristol C 1 Brighton 0
Nov 14 Canterbury 0 Torquay 6
Nov 14 Chester 5 Crewe 0
Nov 14 Chesterfield 2 South Shields 0
Nov 14 Colchester 3 Bideford 3
Nov 14 Corby 1 Hartlepool 3
Nov 14 Crook 1 Carlisle 0
Nov 14 Dartford 1 Aldershot 1
Nov 14 Exeter 1 Hayes 0
Nov 14 Guildford 2 Gillingham 2
Nov 14 Halifax 2 South Liverpool 2
Nov 14 Kidderminster 1 Hull 4
Nov 14 Kings Lynn 0 Shrewsbury 1
Nov 14 Luton 1 Southend 0
Nov 14 Macclesfield 1 Wrexham 2
Nov 14 Millwall 2 Kettering 0
Nov 14 Netherfield 1 Barnsley 3
Nov 14 Newport 5 Spalding 3
Nov 14 Notts Co 2 Chelmsford 0
Nov 14 Oldham 4 Hereford 0
Nov 14 Oxford 0 Mansfield 1
Nov 14 Peterborough 5 Salisbury 1
Nov 14 Port Vale 2 Hendon 1
Nov 14 Q.P.R. 2 Bath 0
Nov 14 Reading 3 Watford 1
Nov 14 Romford 0 Enfield 0
Nov 14 Scarborough 1 Bradford C 0
Nov 14 Scunthorpe 1 Darlington 2
Nov 14 Southport 6 Anfield P 1
Nov 14 Stockport 2 Wigan 1
Nov 14 Tranmere 0 Lincoln 0
Nov 14 Walsall 0 Bristol R 2
Nov 14 Welton 1 Weymouth 1
Nov 14 Wisbech 0 Brentford 2
Nov 14 Workington 2 Rochdale 0
Nov 14 York 5 Bangor 1

Replays
Nov 17 Enfield 0 Romford 0
Nov 17 Grimsby 2 Barrow 2
Nov 18 Aldershot 1 Dartford 0
Nov 18 Bideford 1 Colchester 2
Nov 18 Gillingham 1 Guildford 0
Nov 18 Lincoln 1 Tranmere 0
Nov 18 South Liverpool 4 Halifax 2
Nov 18 Weymouth 4 Welton 3
Nov 23 Barrow 0 Grimsby 2
played at Manchester U
Nov 23 Enfield 4 Romford 2
played at Arsenal

2nd Round
Dec 05 Aldershot 1 Reading 3
Dec 05 Barnsley 2 Chester 5
Dec 05 Bournemouth 0 Bristol C 3
Dec 05 Brentford 4 Notts Co 0
Dec 05 Bristol R 4 Weymouth 1
Dec 05 Chesterfield 2 York 1
Dec 05 Crook 0 Oldham 1
Dec 05 Doncaster 0 Scarborough 0
Dec 05 Enfield 4 Barnet 4
Dec 05 Exeter 1 Shrewsbury 2
Dec 05 Hartlepool 0 Darlington 0
Dec 05 Hull 0 Lincoln 1
Dec 05 Luton 1 Gillingham 0
Dec 05 Millwall 4 Port Vale 0
Dec 05 Newport 3 Mansfield 0
Dec 05 Q.P.R. 3 Peterborough 3
Dec 05 South Liverpool 0 Workington 2
Dec 07 Stockport 1 Grimsby 0
Dec 05 Torquay 2 Colchester 0
Dec 05 Wrexham 2 Southport 3

Replays
Dec 08 Barnet 3 Enfield 0
Dec 09 Darlington 4 Hartlepool 1
Dec 09 Lincoln 3 Hull 1
Dec 09 Peterborough 2 Q.P.R. 1
Dec 09 Scarborough 1 Doncaster 2

3rd Round
Jan 09 Aston Villa 3 Coventry 0
Jan 09 Barnet 2 Preston 3
Jan 09 Bolton 4 Workington 1
Jan 09 Bristol C 1 Sheffield U 1
Jan 09 Bristol R 0 Stockport 0
Jan 09 Burnley 1 Brentford 1
Jan 09 Cardiff 1 Charlton 2
Jan 09 Chelsea 4 Northampton 1
Jan 09 Chesterfield 0 Peterborough 3
Jan 09 Crystal Palace 5 Bury 1
Jan 09 Darlington 0 Arsenal 2
Jan 09 Doncaster 0 Huddersfield 1
Jan 09 Everton 2 Sheffield W 2
Jan 09 Fulham 3 Millwall 3
Jan 09 Leeds 3 Southport 0
Jan 09 Leicester 2 Blackburn 2
Jan 09 Luton 0 Sunderland 3
Jan 09 Manchester C 1 Shrewsbury 1
Jan 09 Manchester U 2 Chester 1
Jan 09 Middlesbrough 6 Oldham 2
Jan 09 Nottingham F 1 Norwich 0
Jan 09 Plymouth 4 Derby 2
Jan 09 Portsmouth 0 Wolverhampton 0
Jan 09 Reading 2 Newport 2
Jan 09 Rotherham 5 Lincoln 1
Jan 09 Southampton 3 Leyton O 1
Jan 11 Stoke 4 Blackpool 1
Jan 09 Swansea 1 Newcastle 0
Jan 09 Swindon 1 Ipswich 2
Jan 09 Torquay 3 Tottenham 3
Jan 09 West Ham 4 Birmingham 2
Jan 09 W.B.A. 1 Liverpool 2

Replays
Jan 11 Millwall 2 Fulham 0
Jan 11 Newport 0 Reading 1
Jan 11 Sheffield U 3 Bristol C 0
Jan 11 Stockport 3 Bristol R 2
Jan 12 Brentford 0 Burnley 2
Jan 12 Wolverhampton 3 Portsmouth 2
Jan 13 Sheffield W 0 Everton 3
Jan 13 Shrewsbury 3 Manchester C 1
Jan 14 Blackburn 1 Leicester 2
Jan 18 Tottenham 5 Torquay 1

4th Round
Jan 30 Charlton 1 Middlesbrough 1
Jan 30 Leeds 1 Everton 1
Jan 30 Leicester 5 Plymouth 0
Jan 30 Liverpool 1 Stockport 1
Jan 30 Millwall 1 Shrewsbury 2
Jan 30 Peterborough 2 Arsenal 1
Jan 30 Preston 1 Bolton 2
Jan 30 Reading 1 Burnley 1
Jan 30 Sheffield U 0 Aston Villa 2
Jan 30 Southampton 1 Crystal Palace 2
Jan 30 Stoke 0 Manchester U 0
Jan 30 Sunderland 1 Nottingham F 3
Jan 30 Swansea 1 Huddersfield 0
Jan 30 Tottenham 5 Ipswich 0
Jan 30 West Ham 0 Chelsea 1
Jan 30 Wolverhampton 2 Rotherham 2

Replays
Feb 01 Middlesbrough 2 Charlton 1
Feb 02 Burnley 1 Reading 0
Feb 02 Everton 1 Leeds 2
Feb 02 Rotherham 0 Wolverhampton 3
Feb 03 Manchester U 1 Stoke 0
Feb 03 Stockport 0 Liverpool 2

5th Round
Feb 20 Aston Villa 1 Wolverhampton 1
Feb 20 Bolton 0 Liverpool 1
Feb 20 Chelsea 1 Tottenham 0
Feb 20 Crystal Palace 3 Nottingham F 1
Feb 20 Leeds 2 Shrewsbury 0
Feb 20 Manchester U 2 Burnley 1
Feb 20 Middlesbrough 0 Leicester 3
Feb 20 Peterborough 0 Swansea 0

Replays
Feb 23 Swansea 0 Peterborough 2
Feb 24 Wolverhampton 0 Aston Villa 0
Mar 01 Aston Villa 1 Wolverhampton 3
played at W.B.A.

6th Round
Mar 06 Chelsea 5 Peterborough 1
Mar 10 Crystal Palace 0 Leeds 3
Mar 06 Leicester 0 Liverpool 0
Mar 10 Wolverhampton 3 Manchester U 5

Replay

Mar 10	Liverpool	1	Leicester	0

Semi-finals

Mar 27	Chelsea	0	Liverpool	2
	played at Aston Villa			
Mar 27	Leeds	0	Manchester U	0
	played at Sheffield W			

Replay

Mar 31	Leeds	1	Manchester U	0
	played at Nottingham F			

Final

May 01	Leeds	1	Liverpool	2
	played at Wembley			

Season 1965-66

Wednesday's Ron Springett is beaten by Trebilcock as Everton equalise in the 1966 FA Cup Final.

1st Round

Nov 13	Aldershot	2	Wellingborough	1
Nov 13	Altrincham	6	Scarborough	0
Nov 13	Barnet	0	Dartford	2
Nov 13	Barrow	1	Grimsby	2
Nov 13	Bath	2	Newport	0
Nov 13	Bournemouth	0	Weymouth	0
Nov 13	Bradford	2	Hull	3
Nov 13	Brentford	2	Yeovil	1
Nov 13	Brighton	10	Wisbech	1
Nov 13	Chesterfield	0	Chester	2
Nov 13	Colchester	3	Q.P.R.	3
Nov 13	Corby	6	Burton	3
Nov 13	Corinthian C	1	Watford	5
Nov 13	Crewe	3	Scunthorpe	0
Nov 13	Darlington	3	Bradford C	2
Nov 13	Doncaster	2	Wigan	2
Nov 13	Exeter	1	Bedford	2
Nov 13	Fleetwood	2	Rochdale	2
Nov 13	Gateshead	4	Crook	2
Nov 13	Gillingham	1	Folkestone	2
Nov 13	Grantham	4	Hendon	1
Nov 13	Guildford	2	Wycombe	2
Nov 13	Hartlepool	3	Workington	1
Nov 13	Leytonstone	0	Hereford	1
Nov 13	Lincoln	1	Barnsley	3
Nov 13	Mansfield	1	Oldham	3
Nov 13	Millwall	3	Wealdstone	1
Nov 13	Oxford	2	Port Vale	2
Nov 13	Peterborough	2	Kidderminster	1
Nov 13	Reading	3	Bristol R	2
Nov 13	Romford	1	Luton	1
Nov 13	Shrewsbury	2	Torquay	1
Nov 13	South Shields	3	York	1
Nov 13	Southend	3	Notts Co	1
Nov 13	Southport	2	Halifax	0
Nov 13	Swindon	5	Merthyr T	1
Nov 13	Tranmere	0	Stockport	1
Nov 13	Walsall	6	Swansea	3
Nov 13	Wimbledon	4	Gravesend	1
Nov 13	Wrexham	4	South Liverpool	1

Replays

Nov 15	Port Vale	3	Oxford	2
Nov 17	Q.P.R.	4	Colchester	0
Nov 17	Rochdale	5	Fleetwood	0
Nov 17	Weymouth	1	Bournemouth	4
Nov 17	Wigan	3	Doncaster	1
Nov 17	Wycombe	0	Guildford	1
Nov 18	Luton	1	Romford	0

2nd Round

Dec 04	Aldershot	0	Walsall	2
Dec 04	Barnsley	1	Grimsby	1
Dec 04	Bournemouth	5	Bath	3
Dec 04	Brighton	1	Bedford	1
Dec 04	Chester	2	Wigan	1
Dec 04	Corby	2	Luton	2
Dec 04	Crewe	3	South Shields	1
Dec 04	Darlington	0	Oldham	1
Dec 08	Gateshead	0	Hull	4
Dec 04	Grantham	1	Swindon	6
Dec 04	Hartlepool	2	Wrexham	0
Dec 04	Hereford	1	Millwall	0
Dec 04	Port Vale	1	Dartford	0
Dec 04	Q.P.R.	3	Guildford	0
Dec 04	Reading	5	Brentford	0
Dec 08	Rochdale	1	Altrincham	3
Dec 04	Shrewsbury	3	Peterborough	2
Dec 04	Southend	2	Watford	1
Dec 04	Southport	3	Stockport	3
Dec 04	Wimbledon	0	Folkestone	1

Replays

Dec 06	Bedford	2	Brighton	1
Dec 07	Luton	0	Corby	1
Dec 08	Grimsby	2	Barnsley	0
Dec 13	Stockport	0	Southport	2

3rd Round

Jan 22	Aston Villa	1	Leicester	2
Jan 22	Bedford	2	Hereford	1
Jan 22	Birmingham	3	Bristol C	2
Jan 22	Blackburn	3	Arsenal	0
Jan 22	Blackpool	1	Manchester C	1
Jan 22	Bolton	3	W.B.A.	0
Jan 22	Bournemouth	1	Burnley	1
Jan 26	Cardiff	2	Port Vale	1
Jan 22	Carlisle	3	Crystal Palace	0
Jan 22	Charlton	2	Preston	3
Jan 22	Chester	1	Newcastle	3
Jan 22	Derby	2	Manchester U	5
Jan 22	Everton	3	Sunderland	0
Jan 22	Folkestone	1	Crewe	5
Jan 22	Grimsby	0	Portsmouth	0
Jan 24	Huddersfield	3	Hartlepool	1
Jan 22	Hull	1	Southampton	0
Jan 22	Leeds	6	Bury	0
Jan 22	Leyton O	1	Norwich	3
Jan 22	Liverpool	1	Chelsea	2
Jan 22	Northampton	1	Nottingham F	2
Jan 22	Oldham	2	West Ham	2
Jan 22	Plymouth	6	Corby	0
Jan 22	Q.P.R.	0	Shrewsbury	0
Jan 22	Reading	2	Sheffield W	3
Jan 22	Rotherham	3	Southend	2
Jan 22	Sheffield U	3	Fulham	1
Jan 22	Southport	0	Ipswich	0
Jan 22	Stoke	0	Walsall	2
Jan 22	Swindon	1	Coventry	2
Jan 22	Tottenham	4	Middlesbrough	0
Jan 22	Wolverhampton	5	Altrincham	0

Replays

Jan 24	Manchester C	3	Blackpool	1
Jan 24	West Ham	2	Oldham	1
Jan 25	Burnley	7	Bournemouth	0
Jan 25	Ipswich	2	Southport	3

Jan 26 Portsmouth 1 Grimsby 3
Jan 26 Shrewsbury 1 Q.P.R. 0

4th Round
Feb 12 Bedford 0 Evrton 3
Feb 12 Birmingham 1 Leicester 2
Feb 12 Bolton 1 Preston 1
Feb 12 Chelsea 1 Leeds 0
Feb 12 Crewe 1 Coventry 1
Feb 12 Hull 2 Nottingham F 0
Feb 12 Manchester C 2 Grimsby 0
Feb 12 Manchester U 0 Rotherham 0
Feb 12 Newcastle 1 Sheffield W 2
Feb 12 Norwich 3 Walsall 2
Feb 12 Plymouth 0 Huddersfield 2
Feb 12 Shrewsbury 0 Carlisle 0
Feb 12 Southport 2 Cardiff 0
Feb 12 Tottenham 4 Burnley 3
Feb 12 West Ham 3 Blackburn 3
Feb 12 Wolverhampton 3 Sheffield U 0

Replays
Feb 14 Coventry 4 Crewe 1
Feb 14 Preston 3 Bolton 2
Feb 15 Carlisle 1 Shrewsbury 1
Feb 15 Rotherham 0 Manchester U 1
Feb 16 Blackburn 4 West Ham 1
Feb 21 Carlisle 3 Shrewsbury 4
played at Preston

5th Round
Mar 05 Chelsea 3 Shrewsbury 2
Mar 05 Everton 3 Coventry 0
Mar 05 Huddersfield 1 Sheffield W 2
Mar 05 Hull 2 Southport 0
Mar 05 Manchester C 2 Leicester 2
Mar 05 Norwich 2 Blackburn 2
Mar 05 Preston 2 Tottenham 1
Mar 05 Wolverhampton 2 Manchester U 4

Replays
Mar 09 Blackburn 3 Norwich 2
Mar 09 Leicester 0 Manchester C 1

6th Round
Mar 26 Blackburn 1 Sheffield W 2
Mar 26 Chelsea 2 Hull 2
Mar 26 Manchester C 0 Everton 0
Mar 26 Preston 1 Manchester U 1

Replays
Mar 29 Everton 0 Manchester C 0
Mar 30 Manchester U 3 Preston 1
Mar 31 Hull 1 Chelsea 3
Apr 05 Everton 2 Manchester C 0
played at Wolverhampton

Semi-finals
Apr 23 Chelsea 0 Sheffield W 2
played at Aston Villa
Apr 23 Everton 1 Manchester U 0
played at Bolton

Final
May 14 Everton 3 Sheffield W 2
played at Wembley

Season 1966-67

1st Round
Nov 26 Aldershot 2 Torquay 1
Nov 26 Ashford 4 Cambridge 1
Nov 26 Barnsley 3 Southport 1
Nov 26 Bath 1 Sutton 0
Nov 26 Bishop Auckland 1 Blyth 1
Nov 26 Bournemouth 3 Welton 0
Nov 26 Bradford 3 Witton 2
Nov 26 Bradford C 1 Port Vale 2
Nov 26 Brentford 1 Chelmsford 0
Nov 26 Chester 2 Middlesbrough 5
Nov 26 Crewe 1 Grimsby 1
Nov 26 Darlington 0 Stockport 0
Nov 26 Enfield 6 Chesham 0
Nov 26 Exeter 1 Luton 1
Nov 26 Folkestone 2 Swansea 2
Nov 26 Gainsborough 0 Colchester 1
Nov 26 Gillingham 4 Tamworth 1
Nov 26 Grantham 2 Wimbledon 1
Nov 26 Halifax 2 Doncaster 2
Nov 26 Hendon 1 Reading 3
Nov 26 Horsham 0 Swindon 3
Nov 26 Leyton O 2 Lowestoft 1
Nov 26 Lincoln 3 Scunthorpe 4
Nov 26 Mansfield 4 Bangor 1
Nov 26 Newport 1 Brighton 2
Nov 26 Oldham 3 Notts Co 1
Nov 26 Oxford 2 Bristol R 2
Nov 26 Peterborough 4 Hereford 1
Nov 26 Q.P.R. 3 Poole 2
Nov 26 Rochdale 1 Barrow 3
Nov 26 Shrewsbury 5 Hartlepool 2
Nov 26 South Shields 1 Workington 4
Nov 26 Tranmere 1 Wigan 1
Nov 26 Walsall 2 St Neots 0
Nov 26 Watford 1 Southend 0
Nov 26 Wealdstone 0 Nuneaton 2
Nov 26 Wrexham 3 Chesterfield 2
Nov 26 Wycombe 1 Bedford 1
Nov 26 Yeovil 1 Oxford 3
Nov 26 York 0 Morecambe 0

Replays
Nov 28 Wigan 0 Tranmere 1
Nov 29 Bristol R 4 Oxford 0
Nov 29 Doncaster 1 Halifax 3
Nov 29 Stockport 1 Darlington 1
Nov 29 Swansea 7 Folkestone 2
Nov 30 Bedford 3 Wycombe 3
Nov 30 Blyth 0 Bishop Auckland 0
Nov 30 Grimsby 0 Crewe 1
Dec 01 Luton 2 Exeter 0
Dec 05 Bishop Auckland 3 Blyth 3
played at Sunderland
Dec 05 Darlington 4 Stockport 2
played at Leeds
Dec 05 Morecambe 1 York 1
Dec 05 Wycombe 1 Bedford 1
Dec 08 Bedford 3 Wycombe 2
Dec 08 Bishop Auckland 4 Blyth 1
played at Sunderland
Dec 08 Morecambe 0 York 1
played at Manchester C

2nd Round
Jan 16 Aldershot 1 Reading 0
Jan 07 Barnsley 1 Port Vale 1
Jan 07 Barrow 2 Tranmere 1
Jan 07 Bath 0 Brighton 5
Jan 07 Bishop Auckland 0 Halifax 0
Jan 11 Bradford 3 Workington 0
Jan 07 Bristol R 3 Luton 2
Jan 07 Colchester 0 Peterborough 3
Jan 07 Crewe 2 Darlington 1
Jan 07 Enfield 2 Watford 4
Jan 07 Grantham 0 Oldham 4
Jan 07 Leyton O 0 Brentford 0
Jan 07 Mansfield 2 Scunthorpe 1
Jan 07 Middlesbrough 1 York 1
Jan 07 Nuneaton 2 Swansea 0
Jan 11 Oxford 1 Bedford 1
Jan 07 Q.P.R. 2 Bournemouth 0
Jan 07 Shrewsbury 5 Wrexham 1
Jan 10 Swindon 5 Ashford 0
Jan 07 Walsall 3 Gillingham 1

Replays
Jan 10 Brentford 3 Leyton O 1
Jan 10 Halifax 7 Bishop Auckland 0
Jan 11 York 0 Middlesbrough 0
Jan 16 Bedford 1 Oxford 0
Jan 16 Middlesbrough 4 York 1
played at Newcastle
Jan 16 Port Vale 0 Barnsley 3

3rd Round
Jan 28 Aldershot 0 Brighton 0
Jan 28 Barnsley 1 Cardiff 1
Jan 28 Barrow 2 Southampton 2
Jan 28 Bedford 2 Peterborough 6
Jan 28 Birmingham 2 Blackpool 1
Jan 28 Blackburn 1 Carlisle 2
Jan 28 Bolton 1 Crewe 0
Jan 28 Bradford 1 Fulham 3
Jan 28 Bristol R 0 Arsenal 3
Jan 28 Burnley 0 Everton 0
Jan 28 Bury 2 Walsall 0
Jan 28 Charlton 0 Sheffield U 1
Jan 28 Coventry 3 Newcastle 4
Jan 28 Halifax 1 Bristol C 1
Jan 28 Huddersfield 1 Chelsea 2
Jan 28 Hull 1 Portsmouth 1
Jan 28 Ipswich 4 Shrewsbury 1
Jan 28 Leeds 3 Crystal Palace 0
Jan 28 Manchester C 2 Leicester 1
Jan 28 Manchester U 2 Stoke 0
Jan 28 Mansfield 2 Middlesbrough 0
Jan 28 Millwall 0 Tottenham 0
Jan 28 Northampton 1 W.B.A. 3
Jan 28 Norwich 3 Derby 0
Jan 28 Nottingham F 2 Plymouth 1
Jan 28 Nuneaton 1 Rotherham 1
Jan 28 Oldham 2 Wolverhampton 2
Jan 28 Preston 0 Aston Villa 1
Jan 28 Sheffield W 3 Q.P.R. 0
Jan 28 Sunderland 5 Brentford 2
Jan 28 Watford 0 Liverpool 0
Jan 28 West Ham 3 Swindon 3

Replays
Jan 31 Bristol C 4 Halifax 1
Jan 31 Cardiff 2 Barnsley 1
Jan 31 Everton 2 Burnley 1
Jan 31 Rotherham 1 Nuneaton 0
Jan 31 Swindon 3 West Ham 1
Feb 01 Brighton 3 Aldershot 1
Feb 01 Liverpool 3 Watford 1
Feb 01 Portsmouth 2 Hull 2
Feb 01 Southampton 3 Barrow 0
Feb 01 Tottenham 1 Millwall 0
Feb 01 Wolverhampton 4 Oldham 1
Feb 06 Hull 1 Portsmouth 3
played at Coventry

4th Round
Feb 18 Bolton 0 Arsenal 0
Feb 18 Brighton 1 Chelsea 1
Feb 18 Bristol C 1 Southampton 0
Feb 18 Cardiff 1 Manchester C 1
Feb 18 Fulham 1 Sheffield U 1
Feb 18 Ipswich 2 Carlisle 0
Feb 18 Leeds 5 W.B.A. 0
Feb 18 Liverpool 1 Aston Villa 0
Feb 18 Manchester U 1 Norwich 2
Feb 18 Nottingham F 3 Newcastle 0
Feb 18 Rotherham 0 Birmingham 0
Feb 18 Sheffield W 4 Mansfield 0
Feb 18 Sunderland 7 Peterborough 1
Feb 18 Swindon 2 Bury 1
Feb 18 Tottenham 3 Portsmouth 1
Feb 18 Wolverhampton 1 Everton 1

Replays
Feb 21 Birmingham 2 Rotherham 1
Feb 21 Everton 3 Wolverhampton 1
Feb 22 Arsenal 3 Bolton 0
Feb 22 Chelsea 4 Brighton 0
Feb 22 Manchester C 3 Cardiff 1
Mar 01 Sheffield U 3 Fulham 1

5th Round
Mar 11 Birmingham 1 Arsenal 0
Mar 11 Chelsea 2 Sheffield U 0
Mar 11 Everton 1 Liverpool 0
Mar 11 Manchester C 1 Ipswich 1
Mar 11 Norwich 1 Sheffield W 3
Mar 11 Nottingham F 0 Swindon 0
Mar 11 Sunderland 1 Leeds 1
Mar 11 Tottenham 2 Bristol C 0

Replays
Mar 14 Ipswich 0 Manchester C 3
Mar 14 Swindon 1 Nottingham F 1
Mar 15 Leeds 1 Sunderland 1
Mar 20 Leeds 2 Sunderland 1
played at Hull
Mar 20 Nottingham F 3 Swindon 0
played at Aston Villa

6th Round
Apr 08 Birmingham 0 Tottenham 0
Apr 08 Chelsea 1 Sheffield W 0
Apr 08 Leeds 1 Manchester C 0
Apr 08 Nottingham F 3 Everton 2

Replay
Apr 12 Tottenham 6 Birmingham 0

Semi-finals
Apr 29 Chelsea 1 Leeds 0
played at Aston Villa
Apr 29 Nottingham F 1 Tottenham 2
played at Sheffield W

Final
May 20 Chelsea 1 Tottenham 2
played at Wembley

Season 1967-68

1st Round
Dec 09 Arnold 0 Bristol R 3
Dec 09 Barrow 2 Oldham 0
Dec 09 Bournemouth 2 Northampton 0
Dec 09 Bradford C 7 Wrexham 1
Dec 14 Brentford 2 Guildford 2
Dec 13 Brighton 1 Southend 0
Dec 09 Chelmsford 3 Oxford U 3
Dec 09 Chesterfield 2 Barnsley 0
Dec 09 Corby 0 Boston 3
Dec 09 Dagenham 1 Tonbridge 0
Dec 09 Goole 0 Spennymoor 0
Dec 09 Grantham 0 Altrincham 3
Dec 09 Grimsby 1 Bradford 1
Dec 13 Halifax 3 Crewe 2
Dec 09 Hartlepool 2 Bury 3
Dec 13 Hereford 3 Barnet 2
Dec 09 Leytonstone 0 Walsall 1
Dec 09 Lowestoft 0 Watford 1
Dec 18 Newport 3 Gillingham 0
Dec 09 Nuneaton 0 Exeter 0
Dec 14 Oxford C 1 Luton 2
Dec 11 Peterborough 5 Falmouth 2
Dec 09 Port Vale 1 Chester 2
Dec 13 Reading 6 Aldershot 2
Dec 09 Runcorn 1 Notts Co 0
Dec 09 Ryhope 0 Workington 1
Dec 09 Scunthorpe 2 Skelmersdale 0
Dec 13 Shrewsbury 3 Darlington 0
Dec 09 Southport 3 Lincoln 1
Dec 09 Stockport 1 Macclesfield 1
Dec 18 Swansea 2 Enfield 0
Dec 12 Swindon 4 Salisbury 0
Dec 12 Torquay 1 Colchester 1
Dec 13 Tow Law 5 Mansfield 1
Dec 09 Tranmere 5 Rochdale 1

Dec 09 Walthamstow 2 Kidderminster 1
Dec 09 Weymouth 0 Leyton O 2
Dec 09 Wimbledon 3 Romford 0
Dec 13 Yeovil 1 Margate 3
Dec 09 York 0 Doncaster 1

Replays
Dec 11 Bradford 4 Grimsby 1
Dec 13 Exeter 0 Nuneaton 0
Dec 13 Macclesfield 2 Stockport 1
Dec 13 Oxford U 3 Chelmsford 3
Dec 13 Spennymoor 3 Goole 1
Dec 18 Chelmsford 1 Oxford U 0
played at Brentford
Dec 18 Colchester 2 Torquay 1
Dec 18 Exeter 1 Nuneaton 0
played at Bristol C
Dec 18 Guildford 2 Brentford 1

2nd Round
Jan 06 Altrincham 1 Barrow 2
Jan 06 Boston 1 Leyton O 1
Jan 06 Bradford 2 Tranmere 3
Jan 06 Bradford C 2 Bury 3
Jan 06 Chelmsford 0 Colchester 2
Jan 06 Chester 0 Chesterfield 1
Jan 06 Doncaster 1 Workington 1
Jan 06 Exeter 1 Walsall 3
Jan 06 Guildford 0 Newport 1
Jan 06 Halifax 1 Scunthorpe 0
Jan 06 Macclesfield 2 Spennymoor 0
Jan 06 Margate 0 Peterborough 4
Jan 06 Reading 1 Dagenham 1
Jan 06 Southport 4 Runcorn 2
Jan 06 Swansea 2 Brighton 1
Jan 06 Swindon 3 Luton 2
Jan 15 Tow Law 1 Shrewsbury 1
Jan 06 Walthamstow 1 Bournemouth 3
Jan 06 Watford 3 Hereford 0
Jan 06 Wimbledon 0 Bristol R 4

Replays
Jan 10 Workington 1 Doncaster 2
Jan 15 Dagenham 0 Reading 1
Jan 15 Leyton O 2 Boston 1
Jan 18 Shrewsbury 6 Tow Law 2

3rd Round
Jan 27 Aston Villa 3 Millwall 0
Jan 27 Barrow 1 Leicester 2
Jan 27 Blackpool 2 Chesterfield 1
Jan 27 Bournemouth 0 Liverpool 0
Jan 27 Bristol C 0 Bristol R 0
Jan 27 Burnley 1 West Ham 3
Jan 27 Chelsea 3 Ipswich 0
Jan 27 Colchester 1 W.B.A. 1
Jan 27 Coventry 3 Charlton 0
Jan 27 Doncaster 0 Swansea 2
Jan 27 Fulham 4 Macclesfield 2
Jan 27 Halifax 2 Birmingham 4
Jan 27 Leeds 2 Derby 0
Jan 27 Leyton O 1 Bury 0
Jan 27 Manchester C 0 Reading 0
Jan 27 Manchester U 2 Tottenham 2
Jan 27 Middlesbrough 1 Hull 1
Jan 27 Newcastle 0 Carlisle 1
Jan 27 Norwich 1 Sunderland 1
Jan 27 Nottingham F 4 Bolton 2
Jan 27 Peterborough 0 Portsmouth 1
Jan 27 Q.P.R. 1 Preston 3
Jan 27 Rotherham 1 Wolverhampton 0
Jan 27 Sheffield W 3 Plymouth 0
Jan 27 Shrewsbury 1 Arsenal 1
Jan 27 Southampton 1 Newport 1
Jan 27 Southport 0 Everton 1
Jan 27 Stoke 4 Cardiff 1
Jan 27 Swindon 1 Blackburn 0
Jan 27 Tranmere 2 Huddersfield 1
Jan 27 Walsall 1 Crystal Palace 1
Jan 27 Watford 0 Sheffield U 1

Replays
Jan 30 Arsenal 2 Shrewsbury 0
Jan 30 Bristol R 1 Bristol C 2
Jan 30 Liverpool 4 Bournemouth 1
Jan 30 Newport 2 Southampton 3
Jan 31 Crystal Palace 1 Walsall 2
Jan 31 Hull 2 Middlesbrough 2
Jan 31 Reading 0 Manchester C 7
Jan 31 Sunderland 0 Norwich 1
Jan 31 Tottenham 1 Manchester U 0
Jan 31 W.B.A. 4 Colchester 0
Feb 07 Hull 0 Middlesbrough 1
played at York

4th Round
Feb 17 Aston Villa 0 Rotherham 1
Feb 17 Birmingham 3 Leyton O 0
Feb 17 Carlisle 0 Everton 2
Feb 17 Chelsea 1 Norwich 0
Feb 17 Coventry 1 Tranmere 1
Feb 17 Fulham 0 Portsmouth 0
Feb 17 Leeds 2 Nottingham F 1
Feb 17 Manchester C 0 Leicester 0
Feb 17 Middlesbrough 1 Bristol C 1
Feb 17 Sheffield U 2 Blackpool 1
Feb 17 Sheffield W 2 Swindon 1
Feb 17 Stoke 0 West Ham 3
Feb 17 Swansea 0 Arsenal 1
Feb 17 Tottenham 3 Preston 1
Feb 17 Walsall 0 Liverpool 0
Feb 17 W.B.A. 1 Southampton 1

Replays
Feb 19 Leicester 4 Manchester C 3
Feb 19 Liverpool 5 Walsall 2
Feb 20 Bristol C 2 Middlesbrough 1
Feb 21 Portsmouth 1 Fulham 0
Feb 21 Southampton 2 W.B.A. 3
Feb 21 Tranmere 2 Coventry 0

5th Round
Mar 09 Arsenal 1 Birmingham 1
Mar 09 Everton 2 Tranmere 0
Mar 09 Leeds 2 Bristol C 0
Mar 09 Portsmouth 1 W.B.A. 2
Mar 09 Rotherham 1 Leicester 1
Mar 09 Sheffield W 2 Chelsea 2
Mar 09 Tottenham 1 Liverpool 1
Mar 09 West Ham 1 Sheffield U 2

Replays
Mar 12 Birmingham 2 Arsenal 1
Mar 12 Chelsea 2 Sheffield W 0
Mar 12 Liverpool 2 Tottenham 1
Mar 13 Leicester 2 Rotherham 0

6th Round
Mar 30 Birmingham 1 Chelsea 0
Mar 30 Leeds 1 Sheffield U 0
Mar 30 Leicester 1 Everton 3
Mar 30 W.B.A. 0 Liverpool 0

Replays
Apr 08 Liverpool 1 W.B.A. 1
Apr 18 Liverpool 1 W.B.A. 2
played at Manchester C

Semi-finals
Apr 27 Birmingham 0 W.B.A. 2
played at Aston Villa
Apr 27 Everton 1 Leeds 0
played at Manchester U

Final
May 18 Everton 0 W.B.A. 1
played at Wembley

Season 1968-69

1st Round
Nov 16 Altrincham 0 Crewe 1
Nov 16 Bangor 2 Morecambe 3
Nov 16 Barnet 1 Brentwood 1
Nov 16 Barnsley 0 Rochdale 0
Nov 16 Bilston 1 Halifax 3
Nov 16 Bradford C 1 Chester 2
Nov 16 Brentford 2 Woking 0
Nov 16 Brighton 2 Kidderminster 2
Nov 16 Bristol R 3 Peterborough 1
Nov 16 Bury 0 Bournemouth 0
Nov 16 Canterbury 0 Swindon 1
Nov 16 Cheltenham 0 Watford 4
Nov 16 Chesterfield 2 Skelmersdale 0
Nov 16 Colchester 5 Chesham 0
Nov 16 Darlington 2 Grimsby 0
Nov 16 Dartford 3 Aldershot 1
Nov 16 Doncaster 1 Notts Co 0
Nov 16 Exeter 0 Newport 0
Nov 16 Goole 1 Barrow 3
Nov 16 Grantham 2 Chelmsford 1
Nov 16 Hartlepool 1 Rotherham 1
Nov 16 Hereford 0 Torquay 0
Nov 16 Leytonstone 0 Walsall 1
Nov 16 Luton 6 Ware 1
Nov 16 Macclesfield 1 Lincoln 3
Nov 16 Mansfield 4 Tow Law 1
Nov 16 Northampton 3 Margate 1
Nov 16 Orient 1 Gillingham 1
Nov 16 Oxford 2 Swansea 3
Nov 16 Reading 1 Plymouth 0
Nov 16 Shrewsbury 1 Port Vale 1
Nov 16 South Shields 0 York 6
Nov 16 Southend 9 Kings Lynn 0
Nov 16 Stockport 3 Bradford 0
Nov 16 Tranmere 0 Southport 1
Nov 16 Waterlooville 1 Kettering 2
Nov 16 Wealdstone 1 St Albans 1
Nov 16 Weymouth 2 Yeovil 1
Nov 16 Workington 2 Scunthorpe 0
Nov 16 Wrexham 4 Oldham 2

Replays
Nov 18 Brentwood 1 Barnet 0
Nov 18 Newport 1 Exeter 3
Nov 18 Port Vale 3 Shrewsbury 1
Nov 18 Rochdale 0 Barnsley 1
Nov 19 Rotherham 3 Hartlepool 0
Nov 19 St Albans 1 Wealdstone 0
Nov 20 Bournemouth 3 Bury 0
Nov 20 Gillingham 2 Orient 1
Nov 20 Kidderminster 0 Brighton 1
Nov 20 Torquay 4 Hereford 2

2nd Round
Dec 07 Bournemouth 0 Bristol R 0
Dec 07 Brighton 1 Northampton 2
Dec 07 Chester 1 Lincoln 1
Dec 07 Chesterfield 2 Wrexham 1
Dec 07 Colchester 0 Exeter 1
Dec 07 Darlington 0 Barnsley 0
Dec 07 Doncaster 2 Southport 1
Dec 07 Grantham 0 Swindon 2
Dec 07 Halifax 1 Crewe 1
Dec 07 Kettering 5 Dartford 0
Dec 07 Luton 3 Gillingham 1
Dec 07 Port Vale 0 Workington 0
Dec 07 Reading 0 Torquay 0
Dec 07 Rotherham 2 Mansfield 2
Dec 07 Southend 10 Brentwood 1
Dec 07 St Albans 1 Walsall 1
Dec 07 Stockport 2 Barrow 0
Dec 07 Watford 1 Brentford 0
Dec 07 Weymouth 1 Swansea 1
Dec 07 York 2 Morecambe 0

Replays
Dec 09 Mansfield 1 Rotherham 0
Dec 10 Barnsley 1 Darlington 0
Dec 10 Bristol R 1 Bournemouth 0
Dec 10 Swansea 2 Weymouth 0
Dec 10 Walsall 3 St Albans 1
Dec 11 Crewe 1 Halifax 3
Dec 11 Lincoln 2 Chester 1
Dec 11 Torquay 1 Reading 2
Dec 11 Workington 1 Port Vale 2

3rd Round
Jan 04 Aston Villa 2 Q.P.R. 1
Jan 04 Barnsley 1 Leicester 1
Jan 04 Birmingham 2 Lincoln 1
Jan 04 Blackburn 2 Stockport 0
Jan 04 Bolton 2 Northampton 1
Jan 04 Bristol R 1 Kettering 1
Jan 04 Burnley 3 Derby 1
Jan 04 Bury 1 Huddersfield 2
Jan 04 Cardiff 0 Arsenal 0
Jan 04 Charlton 0 Crystal Palace 0
Jan 04 Chelsea 2 Carlisle 0
Jan 04 Coventry 3 Blackpool 1
Jan 04 Everton 2 Ipswich 1
Jan 04 Exeter 1 Manchester U 3
Jan 04 Hull 1 Wolverhampton 3
Jan 04 Liverpool 2 Doncaster 0
Jan 04 Manchester C 1 Luton 0
Jan 04 Mansfield 2 Sheffield U 1
Jan 04 Middlesbrough 1 Millwall 1
Jan 04 Newcastle 4 Reading 0
Jan 04 Oxford 1 Southampton 1
Jan 04 Portsmouth 3 Chesterfield 0
Jan 04 Preston 3 Nottingham F 0
Jan 04 Sheffield W 1 Leeds 1
Jan 04 Sunderland 1 Fulham 4
Jan 04 Swansea 0 Halifax 1
Jan 04 Swindon 0 Southend 2
Jan 04 Walsall 0 Tottenham 1
Jan 04 Watford 2 Port Vale 0
Jan 04 West Ham 3 Bristol C 2
Jan 04 W.B.A. 3 Norwich 0
Jan 04 York 0 Stoke 2

Replays
Jan 06 Millwall 1 Middlesbrough 0
Jan 07 Arsenal 2 Cardiff 0
Jan 08 Crystal Palace 0 Charlton 2
Jan 08 Kettering 1 Bristol R 2
Jan 08 Leeds 1 Sheffield W 3
Jan 08 Leicester 2 Barnsley 1
Jan 08 Southampton 2 Oxford 0

4th Round
Jan 25 Arsenal 2 Charlton 0
Jan 25 Blackburn 4 Portsmouth 0
Jan 25 Bolton 1 Bristol R 2
Jan 25 Everton 2 Coventry 0
Jan 25 Fulham 1 W.B.A. 2
Jan 25 Huddersfield 0 West Ham 2
Jan 25 Liverpool 2 Burnley 1
Jan 25 Manchester U 1 Watford 1
Jan 25 Mansfield 2 Southend 1
Jan 25 Millwall 0 Leicester 1
Jan 25 Newcastle 0 Manchester C 0
Jan 25 Preston 0 Chelsea 0
Jan 25 Sheffield W 2 Birmingham 2
Jan 25 Southampton 2 Aston Villa 2
Jan 25 Stoke 1 Halifax 1
Jan 25 Tottenham 2 Wolverhampton 1

Replays
Jan 28 Birmingham 2 Sheffield W 1
Jan 28 Halifax 0 Stoke 3
Jan 29 Aston Villa 2 Southampton 1
Jan 29 Manchester C 2 Newcastle 0
Feb 03 Chelsea 2 Preston 1
Feb 03 Watford 0 Manchester U 2

5th Round
Feb 11 Birmingham 2 Manchester U 2
Feb 24 Blackburn 1 Manchester C 4
Feb 12 Chelsea 3 Stoke 2
Feb 12 Everton 1 Bristol R 0
Mar 01 Leicester 0 Liverpool 0
Feb 26 Mansfield 3 West Ham 0
Feb 12 Tottenham 3 Aston Villa 2
Feb 12 W.B.A. 1 Arsenal 0

Replays
Feb 24 Manchester U 6 Birmingham 2
Mar 03 Liverpool 0 Leicester 1

6th Round
Mar 01 Chelsea 1 W.B.A. 2
Mar 01 Manchester C 1 Tottenham 0
Mar 01 Manchester U 0 Everton 1

Mar 08 Mansfield 0 Leicester 1

Semi-finals
Mar 22 Everton 0 Manchester C 1
played at Aston Villa
Mar 29 Leicester 1 W.B.A. 0
played at Sheffield W

Final
Apr 26 Leicester 0 Manchester C 1
played at Wembley

SEASON 1969-70

1st Round
Nov 15 Alfreton 1 Barrow 1
Nov 15 Bangor 6 Kirkby 0
Nov 15 Bournemouth 1 Luton 1
Nov 15 Bradford C 2 Grimsby 1
Nov 15 Brentford 0 Plymouth 0
Nov 15 Brentwood 1 Reading 0
Nov 15 Brighton 2 Enfield 1
Nov 15 Bury 2 Mansfield 2
Nov 15 Chelmsford 1 Hereford 2
Nov 15 Cheltenham 0 Oxford C 2
Nov 15 Dagenham 0 Sutton 1
Nov 15 Darlington 0 Barnsley 0
Nov 15 Doncaster 1 Crewe 1
Nov 15 Exeter 2 Fulham 0
Nov 15 Falmouth 1 Peterborough 4
Nov 15 Halifax 3 Chester 3
Nov 15 Hartlepool 3 North Shields 0
Nov 15 Hendon 5 Carshalton 3
Nov 15 Hillingdon 2 Wimbledon 0
Nov 15 Kettering 0 Swansea 2
Nov 15 Lincoln 2 Southport 0
Nov 15 Macclesfield 1 Scunthorpe 1
Nov 15 Margate 2 Aldershot 7
Nov 15 Newport 2 Colchester 1
Nov 15 Northampton 0 Weymouth 0
Nov 15 Notts Co 0 Rotherham 3
Nov 15 Oldham 3 Grantham 1
Nov 15 South Shields 2 Bradford 1
Nov 15 Southend 0 Gillingham 0
Nov 15 Spennymoor 1 Wrexham 4
Nov 15 Stockport 1 Mossley 1
Nov 15 Tamworth 2 Torquay 1
Nov 15 Telford 0 Bristol R 3
Nov 15 Tranmere 3 Chesterfield 0
Nov 15 Walsall 0 Orient 0
Nov 15 Walton & H 0 Barnet 1
Nov 15 Wigan 1 Port Vale 1
Nov 15 Workington 2 Rochdale 1
Nov 15 Yeovil 2 Shrewsbury 3
Nov 15 York 2 Whitby 0

Replays
Nov 17 Barrow 0 Alfreton 0
Nov 17 Orient 0 Walsall 2
Nov 18 Barnsley 2 Darlington 0
Nov 18 Luton 3 Bournemouth 1
Nov 18 Mossley 0 Stockport 1
Nov 18 Port Vale 2 Wigan 2
Nov 18 Scunthorpe 4 Macclesfield 2
Nov 19 Chester 1 Halifax 0
Nov 19 Crewe 0 Doncaster 1
Nov 19 Gillingham 2 Southend 0
Nov 19 Mansfield 2 Bury 0
Nov 19 Plymouth 2 Brentford 0
Nov 19 Weymouth 1 Northampton 3
Nov 20 Alfreton 2 Barrow 2
played at Chesterfield
Nov 24 Alfreton 0 Barrow 2
played at Preston
Nov 24 Port Vale 1 Wigan 0
played at Manchester U

2nd Round
Dec 06 Aldershot 3 Bristol R 1
Dec 06 Bangor 0 York 0
Dec 06 Barnet 0 Sutton 2
Dec 06 Barnsley 3 Barrow 0
Dec 06 Bradford C 3 Lincoln 0
Dec 06 Brighton 1 Walsall 1
Dec 06 Chester 1 Doncaster 1
Dec 06 Gillingham 6 Tamworth 0
Dec 06 Hartlepool 0 Wrexham 1
Dec 06 Hendon 0 Brentwood 2
Dec 06 Hillingdon 2 Luton 1
Dec 06 Newport 2 Hereford 1
Dec 06 Northampton 1 Exeter 1
Dec 06 Oxford C 1 Swansea 5
Dec 06 Peterborough 2 Plymouth 0
Dec 06 Port Vale 2 Tranmere 2
Dec 06 Rotherham 3 Workington 0
Dec 06 Shrewsbury 1 Mansfield 2
Dec 06 South Shields 0 Oldham 0
Dec 06 Stockport 0 Scunthorpe 0

Replays
Dec 08 Tranmere 3 Port Vale 1
Dec 09 Doncaster 0 Chester 2
Dec 09 Exeter 0 Northampton 0
Dec 09 Oldham 1 South Shields 2
Dec 09 Scunthorpe 4 Stockport 0
Dec 09 Walsall 1 Brighton 1
Dec 09 York 2 Bangor 0
Dec 15 Brighton 0 Walsall 0
played at Fulham
Dec 15 Exeter 1 Northampton 2
played at Swindon
Dec 17 Brighton 1 Walsall 2
played at Coventry

3rd Round
Jan 03 Arsenal 1 Blackpool 1
Jan 03 Aston Villa 1 Charlton 1
Jan 03 Blackburn 0 Swindon 4
Jan 03 Bolton 1 Watford 2
Jan 03 Bradford C 2 Tottenham 2
Jan 12 Brentwood 0 Northampton 1
Jan 03 Burnley 3 Wolverhampton 0
Jan 03 Chelsea 3 Birmingham 0
Jan 03 Chester 2 Bristol C 1
Jan 07 Coventry 1 Liverpool 1
Jan 03 Crystal Palace 2 Walsall 0
Jan 03 Gillingham 1 Newport 0
Jan 06 Hillingdon 0 Sutton 0
Jan 03 Huddersfield 1 Aldershot 1
Jan 03 Hull 0 Manchester C 1
Jan 03 Ipswich 0 Manchester U 1
Jan 03 Leeds 2 Swansea 1
Jan 03 Leicester 1 Sunderland 0
Jan 03 Mansfield 3 Barnsley 2
Jan 03 Middlesbrough 2 West Ham 1
Jan 03 Norwich 1 Wrexham 2
Jan 03 Nottingham F 0 Carlisle 0
Jan 03 Oxford 0 Stoke 0
Jan 03 Portsmouth 1 Tranmere 2
Jan 03 Preston 1 Derby 1
Jan 03 Q.P.R. 4 South Shields 1
Jan 03 Rotherham 0 Peterborough 1
Jan 03 Scunthorpe 2 Millwall 1
Jan 03 Sheffield U 2 Everton 1
Jan 03 Sheffield W 2 W.B.A. 1
Jan 03 Southampton 3 Newcastle 0
Jan 03 York 1 Cardiff 1

Replays
Jan 06 Carlisle 2 Nottingham F 1
Jan 07 Derby 4 Preston 1
Jan 07 Stoke 3 Oxford 2
Jan 07 Tottenham 5 Bradford C 0
Jan 12 Aldershot 3 Huddersfield 1
Jan 12 Cardiff 1 York 1
Jan 12 Charlton 1 Aston Villa 0
Jan 12 Liverpool 3 Coventry 0
Jan 12 Sutton 4 Hillingdon 1
Jan 15 Blackpool 3 Arsenal 2
Jan 15 Cardiff 1 York 3
played at Birmingham

4th Round
Jan 24 Blackpool 0 Mansfield 2
Jan 24 Carlisle 2 Aldershot 2
Jan 24 Charlton 2 Q.P.R. 3
Jan 24 Chelsea 2 Burnley 2
Jan 24 Derby 3 Sheffield U 0
Jan 24 Gillingham 5 Peterborough 1
Jan 24 Liverpool 3 Wrexham 1
Jan 24 Manchester U 3 Manchester C 0
Jan 24 Middlesbrough 4 York 1
Jan 24 Sheffield W 1 Scunthorpe 2
Jan 24 Southampton 1 Leicester 1
Jan 24 Sutton 0 Leeds 6
Jan 24 Swindon 4 Chester 2
Jan 24 Tottenham 0 Crystal Palace 0
Jan 24 Tranmere 0 Northampton 0
Jan 24 Watford 1 Stoke 0

Replays
Jan 27 Burnley 1 Chelsea 3
Jan 27 Northampton 2 Tranmere 1
Jan 28 Aldershot 1 Carlisle 4
Jan 28 Crystal Palace 1 Tottenham 0
Jan 28 Leicester 4 Southampton 2

5th Round
Feb 07 Carlisle 1 Middlesbrough 2
Feb 07 Crystal Palace 1 Chelsea 4
Feb 07 Leeds 2 Mansfield 0
Feb 07 Liverpool 0 Leicester 0
Feb 07 Northampton 2 Manchester U 8
Feb 07 Q.P.R. 1 Derby 0
Feb 07 Swindon 3 Scunthorpe 1
Feb 07 Watford 2 Gillingham 1

Replay
Feb 11 Leicester 0 Liverpool 2

6th Round
Feb 21 Middlesbrough 1 Manchester U 1
Feb 21 Q.P.R. 2 Chelsea 4
Feb 21 Swindon 0 Leeds 2
Feb 21 Watford 1 Liverpool 0

Replay
Feb 25 Manchester U 2 Middlesbrough 1

Semi-finals
Mar 14 Chelsea 5 Watford 1
played at Tottenham
Mar 14 Leeds 0 Manchester U 0
played at Sheffield W

Replays
Mar 23 Leeds 0 Manchester U 0
played at Aston Villa
Mar 26 Leeds 1 Manchester U 0
played at Bolton

Final
Apr 11 Chelsea 2 Leeds 2
played at Wembley

Replay
Apr 29 Chelsea 2 Leeds 1
played at Manchester U

SEASON 1970-71

1st Round
Nov 21 Barnet 6 Newport 1
Nov 21 Barnsley 1 Bradford 0
Nov 21 Bradford 3 Macclesfield 2
Nov 21 Brentford 2 Gillingham 1
Nov 21 Brighton 4 Cheltenham 0
Nov 21 Chesterfield 2 Halifax 0
Nov 21 Colchester 3 Ringmer 0
Nov 21 Crawley 1 Chelmsford 1
Nov 21 Crewe 0 Doncaster 0
Nov 21 Dagenham 2 Margate 0
Nov 21 Darlington 5 Bangor 1
Nov 21 Enfield 0 Cambridge 1
Nov 21 Fulham 1 Bristol R 2
Nov 21 Grantham 2 Stockport 1
Nov 24 Great Harwood 2 Rotherham 6
Nov 21 Grimsby 0 Bury 1
Nov 21 Hendon 0 Aldershot 2
Nov 21 Hereford 2 Northampton 2
Nov 21 Lincoln 2 Barrow 1
Nov 21 Mansfield 2 Wrexham 0
Nov 21 Minehead 1 Shrewsbury 2
Nov 21 Notts Co 1 Port Vale 0
Nov 21 Oxford C 1 Bournemouth 1
Nov 21 Peterborough 3 Wimbledon 1
Nov 21 Preston 1 Chester 1
Nov 21 Reading 6 Bishop's Stortford 1
Nov 21 Rhyl 1 Hartlepool 0
Nov 21 Rochdale 2 Oldham 0
Nov 21 Scarborough 2 Workington 3
Nov 21 South Shields 1 Wigan 1
Nov 21 Southend 7 Weymouth 0
Nov 21 Southport 0 Boston 2
Nov 21 Swansea 4 Exeter 1
Nov 21 Tamworth 0 York 0
Nov 21 Torquay 3 Aston Villa 1
Nov 21 Tranmere 1 Scunthorpe 1
Nov 21 Walsall 3 Plymouth 0
Nov 21 Walton & H 2 Telford 5
Nov 21 Wycombe 1 Slough 1
Nov 21 Yeovil 1 Aveley 0

Replays
Nov 23 Chelmsford 6 Crawley 1
Nov 23 Wigan 2 South Shields 0
Nov 23 York 5 Tamworth 0
Nov 24 Doncaster 1 Crewe 3
Nov 24 Northampton 1 Hereford 2
Nov 24 Scunthorpe 0 Tranmere 0
Nov 25 Bournemouth 8 Oxford C 1
Nov 25 Chester 1 Preston 0
Nov 25 Slough 1 Wycombe 0
Nov 30 Scunthorpe 1 Tranmere 0
played at Everton

2nd Round
Dec 12 Aldershot 1 Bristol R 1
Dec 12 Boston 1 York 2
Dec 12 Bournemouth 0 Yeovil 1
Dec 12 Brentford 1 Walsall 0
Dec 12 Bury 1 Notts Co 1
Dec 12 Chelmsford 0 Torquay 1
Dec 12 Chester 1 Crewe 0
Dec 12 Chesterfield 0 Workington 0
Dec 12 Colchester 3 Cambridge 0
Dec 12 Darlington 0 Rochdale 2
Dec 12 Grantham 1 Rotherham 4
Dec 12 Hereford 1 Brighton 2
Dec 12 Lincoln 2 Bradford 2
Dec 12 Rhyl 0 Barnsley 0
Dec 12 Scunthorpe 3 Mansfield 0
Dec 12 Shrewsbury 2 Reading 2
Dec 12 Slough 0 Barnet 1
Dec 12 Southend 1 Dagenham 0
Dec 12 Swansea 6 Telford 2
Dec 12 Wigan 2 Peterborough 1

Replays
Dec 15 Barnsley 1 Rhyl 1
Dec 15 Bristol R 1 Aldershot 3
Dec 16 Bradford 2 Lincoln 2
Dec 16 Workington 3 Chesterfield 2

Date	Home		Away	
Dec 21	Barnsley	0	Rhyl	2
	played at Manchester U			
Dec 21	Bradford	1	Lincoln	4
	played at Doncaster			
Dec 21	Notts Co	3	Bury	0
Dec 21	Reading	1	Shrewsbury	0

3rd Round

Date	Home		Away	
Jan 05	Barnet	0	Colchester	1
Jan 02	Blackpool	4	West Ham	0
Jan 02	Cardiff	1	Brighton	0
Jan 02	Chester	1	Derby	2
Jan 02	Crystal Palace	2	Chelsea	2
Jan 02	Everton	2	Blackburn	0
Jan 02	Huddersfield	1	Birmingham	1
Jan 02	Hull	3	Charlton	0
Jan 02	Leicester	2	Notts Co	0
Jan 02	Liverpool	1	Aldershot	0
Jan 02	Manchester C	1	Wigan	0
Jan 02	Manchester U	0	Middlesbrough	0
Jan 11	Newcastle	1	Ipswich	1
Jan 02	Nottingham	1	Luton	1
Jan 11	Oxford U	3	Burnley	0
Jan 02	Portsmouth	2	Sheffield	0
Jan 02	Q.P.R.	1	Swindon	2
Jan 11	Rochdale	2	Coventry	1
Jan 11	Rotherham	0	Leeds	0
Jan 11	Southampton	3	Bristol C	0
Jan 11	Southend	0	Carlisle	3
Jan 02	Stoke	2	Millwall	1
Jan 11	Sunderland	0	Orient	3
Jan 02	Swansea	6	Rhyl	1
Jan 02	Torquay	4	Lincoln	3
Jan 02	Tottenham	4	Sheffield	1
Jan 06	Watford	5	Reading	0
Jan 02	Wolverhampton	5	Norwich	1
Jan 02	Workington	0	Brentford	1
Jan 02	W.B.A.	0	Scunthorpe	0
Jan 06	Yeovil	0	Arsenal	3
Jan 02	York	2	Bolton	0

Replays

Date	Home		Away	
Jan 05	Birmingham	0	Huddersfield	2
Jan 05	Middlesbrough	2	Manchester U	1
Jan 06	Chelsea	2	Crystal Palace	0
Jan 11	Luton	3	Nottingham	4
Jan 11	Scunthorpe	1	W.B.A.	3
Jan 13	Ipswich	2	Newcastle	1
Jan 18	Leeds	3	Rotherham	2

4th Round

Date	Home		Away	
Jan 23	Cardiff	0	Brentford	2
Jan 23	Carlisle	2	Tottenham	3
Jan 23	Chelsea	0	Manchester C	3
Jan 23	Derby	2	Wolverhampton	1
Jan 23	Everton	3	Middlesbrough	0
Jan 23	Hull	2	Blackpool	0
Jan 23	Leeds	4	Swindon	0
Jan 25	Leicester	3	Torquay	0
Jan 23	Liverpool	3	Swansea	0
Jan 23	Nottingham F	1	Orient	1
Jan 23	Oxford U	1	Watford	1
Jan 23	Portsmouth	1	Arsenal	1
Jan 23	Rochdale	3	Colchester	3
Jan 23	Stoke	3	Huddersfield	3
Jan 23	W.B.A.	1	Ipswich	1
Jan 23	York	3	Southampton	3

Replays

Date	Home		Away	
Jan 25	Colchester	5	Rochdale	0
Jan 26	Huddersfield	0	Stoke	0
Jan 26	Ipswich	3	W.B.A.	0
Jan 27	Watford	1	Oxford U	2
Feb 01	Arsenal	3	Portsmouth	2
Feb 01	Orient	0	Nottingham F	1
Feb 01	Southampton	3	York	2
Feb 08	Huddersfield	0	Stoke	1
	played at Manchester U			

5th Round

Date	Home		Away	
Feb 13	Colchester	3	Leeds	2
Feb 13	Everton	1	Derby	0
Feb 13	Hull	2	Brentford	1
Feb 13	Leicester	1	Oxford	1
Feb 13	Liverpool	1	Southampton	0
Feb 17	Manchester C	1	Arsenal	2
Feb 13	Stoke	0	Ipswich	0
Feb 13	Tottenham	2	Nottingham F	1

Replays

Date	Home		Away	
Feb 16	Ipswich	0	Stoke	1
Feb 17	Oxford	1	Leicester	3

6th Round

Date	Home		Away	
Mar 06	Everton	5	Colchester	0
Mar 06	Hull	2	Stoke	3
Mar 06	Leicester	0	Arsenal	0
Mar 06	Liverpool	0	Tottenham	0

Replays

Date	Home		Away	
Mar 15	Arsenal	1	Leicester	0
Mar 16	Tottenham	0	Liverpool	1

Semi-finals

Date	Home		Away	
Mar 27	Arsenal	2	Stoke	2
	played at Sheffield W			
Mar 27	Everton	1	Liverpool	2
	played at Manchester U			

Replay

Date	Home		Away	
Mar 31	Arsenal	2	Stoke	0
	played at Aston Villa			

Final

Date	Home		Away	
May 08	Arsenal	2	Liverpool	1
	played at Wembley			

Season 1971-72

1st Round

Date	Home		Away	
Nov 24	Aldershot	4	Alvechurch	2
Nov 20	Barrow	0	Darlington	2
Nov 20	Basingstoke	1	Northampton	5
Nov 20	Blackburn	1	Port Vale	1
Nov 20	Bolton	3	Bangor	0
Nov 20	Bournemouth	11	Margate	0
Nov 20	Bridgwater	0	Reading	3
Nov 20	Brighton	7	Hillingdon	1
Nov 20	Bristol R	3	Telford	0
Nov 20	Cambridge	2	Weymouth	1
Nov 20	Chester	1	Mansfield	1
Nov 20	Chesterfield	3	Oldham	0
Nov 20	Colchester	1	Shrewsbury	4
Nov 20	Crawley	0	Exeter	0
Nov 20	Crewe	0	Blyth	1
Nov 20	Doncaster	1	Stockport	2
Nov 20	Ellesmere	0	Boston	3
Nov 20	Enfield	2	Maidenhead	0
Nov 20	Frickley	2	Rotherham	2
Nov 20	Gillingham	3	Plymouth	2
Nov 20	Guildford	0	Dover	0
Nov 20	Hartlepool	6	Scarborough	1
Nov 20	Kettering	2	Barnet	4
Nov 20	Kings Ly	0	Hereford	0
Nov 20	Lincoln	1	Bury	2
Nov 20	Notts Co	6	Newport	0
Nov 20	Redditch	1	Peterborough	1
Nov 20	Rochdale	1	Barnsley	3
Nov 23	Rossendale	1	Altrincham	0
Nov 20	Skelmersdale	0	Tranmere	4
Nov 20	South Shields	3	Scunthorpe	3
Nov 20	Southend	1	Aston Villa	0
Nov 20	Southport	1	Workington	3
Nov 20	Swansea	1	Brentford	1
Nov 20	Torquay	1	Nuneaton	0
Nov 20	Walsall	4	Dagenham	1
Nov 20	Wigan	2	Halifax	1
Nov 20	Witney	0	Romford	3
Nov 20	Wrexham	5	Bradford	1
Nov 20	York	4	Grimsby	2

Replays

Date	Home		Away	
Nov 22	Brentford	2	Swansea	3
Nov 22	Mansfield	4	Chester	3
Nov 22	Peterborough	6	Redditch	0
Nov 22	Port Vale	3	Blackburn	1
Nov 23	Rotherham	4	Frickley	0
Nov 24	Dover	0	Guildford	2
Nov 24	Exeter	2	Crawley	0
Nov 24	Hereford	1	Kings Lynn	0
Nov 29	Scunthorpe	2	South Shields	3

2nd Round

Date	Home		Away	
Dec 11	Barnet	1	Torquay	4
Dec 11	Barnsley	0	Chesterfield	0
Dec 11	Blyth	1	Stockport	0
Dec 11	Boston	2	Hartlepool	1
Dec 11	Bournemouth	2	Southend	0
Dec 11	Brighton	1	Walsall	1
Dec 11	Bristol R	3	Cambridge	0
Dec 11	Hereford	0	Northampton	0
Dec 11	Mansfield	2	Tranmere	2
Dec 11	Peterborough	4	Enfield	0
Dec 11	Port Vale	1	Darlington	0
Dec 11	Reading	1	Aldershot	0
Dec 11	Romford	0	Gillingham	1
Dec 11	Rossendale	1	Bolton	4
Dec 11	Rotherham	1	York	1
Dec 11	Shrewsbury	2	Guildford	1
Dec 11	South Shields	1	Notts Co	3
Dec 11	Swansea	0	Exeter	0
Dec 11	Workington	1	Bury	3
Dec 11	Wrexham	4	Wigan	0

Replays

Date	Home		Away	
Dec 13	York	2	Rotherham	3
Dec 14	Northampton	2	Hereford	2
Dec 14	Walsall	2	Brighton	1
Dec 15	Chesterfield	1	Barnsley	0
Dec 15	Exeter	0	Swansea	1
Dec 15	Tranmere	4	Mansfield	2
Dec 20	Hereford	2	Northampton	1
	played at W.B.A.			

3rd Round

Date	Home		Away	
Jan 15	Birmingham	3	Port Vale	0
Jan 15	Blackpool	0	Chelsea	1
Jan 15	Blyth	2	Reading	2
Jan 15	Bolton	2	Torquay	1
Jan 15	Boston	0	Portsmouth	1
Jan 15	Burnley	0	Huddersfield	1
Jan 15	Bury	1	Rotherham	1
Jan 15	Charlton	0	Tranmere	0
Jan 15	Crystal Palace	2	Everton	2
Jan 15	Derby	2	Shrewsbury	0
Jan 15	Leeds	4	Bristol R	1
Jan 15	Manchester C	1	Middlesbrough	1
Jan 15	Millwall	3	Nottingham F	1
Jan 24	Newcastle	2	Hereford	2
Jan 15	Norwich	0	Hull	3
Jan 15	Orient	3	Wrexham	0
Jan 15	Oxford	0	Liverpool	3
Jan 15	Peterborough	0	Ipswich	2
Jan 15	Preston	4	Bristol C	2
Jan 15	Q.P.R.	1	Fulham	1
Jan 15	Sheffield U	1	Cardiff	3
Jan 15	Southampton	1	Manchester U	1
Jan 15	Stoke	2	Chesterfield	1
Jan 15	Sunderland	3	Sheffield	0
Jan 15	Swansea	1	Gillingham	0
Jan 15	Swindon	0	Arsenal	2
Jan 15	Tottenham	1	Carlisle	1
Jan 15	Walsall	1	Bournemouth	0
Jan 15	Watford	1	Notts Co	4
Jan 15	West Ham	2	Luton	1
Jan 15	Wolverhampton	1	Leicester	1
Jan 15	W.B.A.	1	Coventry	2

Replays

Date	Home		Away	
Jan 17	Tranmere	4	Charlton	2
Jan 18	Carlisle	1	Tottenham	3
Jan 18	Everton	3	Crystal Palace	2
Jan 18	Fulham	2	Q.P.R.	1
Jan 18	Middlesbrough	1	Manchester C	0
Jan 19	Leicester	2	Wolverhampton	0
Jan 19	Manchester U	4	Southampton	1
Jan 19	Reading	6	Blyth	1
Jan 24	Rotherham	2	Bury	1
Feb 05	Hereford	2	Newcastle	1

4th Round

Date	Home		Away	
Feb 05	Birmingham	1	Ipswich	0
Feb 05	Cardiff	1	Sunderland	1
Feb 05	Chelsea	3	Bolton	0
Feb 09	Coventry	0	Hull	1
Feb 05	Derby	6	Notts Co	0
Feb 05	Everton	2	Walsall	1
Feb 09	Hereford	0	West Ham	0
Feb 05	Huddersfield	3	Fulham	0
Feb 05	Leicester	0	Orient	2
Feb 05	Liverpool	0	Leeds	0
Feb 05	Millwall	2	Middlesbrough	2
Feb 05	Portsmouth	2	Swansea	0
Feb 05	Preston	0	Manchester U	2
Feb 05	Reading	1	Arsenal	2
Feb 05	Tottenham	2	Rotherham	0
Feb 05	Tranmere	2	Stoke	2

Replays

Date	Home		Away	
Feb 08	Middlesbrough	2	Millwall	1
Feb 09	Leeds	2	Liverpool	0
Feb 09	Stoke	2	Tranmere	0
Feb 14	Sunderland	1	Cardiff	1
Feb 14	West Ham	3	Hereford	1
Feb 16	Cardiff	3	Sunderland	1
	played at Manchester C			

5th Round

Date	Home		Away	
Feb 26	Birmingham	3	Portsmouth	1
Feb 26	Cardiff	0	Leeds	2
Feb 26	Derby	2	Arsenal	2
Feb 26	Everton	0	Tottenham	2
Feb 26	Huddersfield	4	West Ham	2
Feb 26	Manchester U	0	Middlesbrough	0
Feb 26	Orient	3	Chelsea	2
Feb 26	Stoke	4	Hull	1

Replays

Date	Home		Away	
Feb 29	Arsenal	0	Derby	0
Feb 29	Middlesbrough	0	Manchester U	3
Mar 13	Arsenal	1	Derby	0
	played at Leicester			

6th Round

Date	Home		Away	
Mar 18	Birmingham	3	Huddersfield	1
Mar 18	Leeds	2	Tottenham	1
Mar 18	Manchester	1	Stoke	1
Mar 18	Orient	0	Arsenal	1

Replay

Date	Home		Away	
Mar 22	Stoke	2	Manchester U	1

Semi-finals

Date	Home		Away	
Apr 15	Arsenal	1	Stoke	1
	played at Aston Villa			
Apr 15	Birmingham	0	Leeds	3
	played at Sheffield W			

Replay

Date	Home		Away	
Apr 19	Arsenal	2	Stoke	1
	played at Everton			

Final

Date	Home		Away	
May 06	Arsenal	0	Leeds	1
	played at Wembley			

SEASON 1972-73

1st Round

Date	Home		Away	
Nov 18	Altrincham	0	Notts Co	1
Nov 18	Barbury	0	Barnet	2
Nov 18	Barnsley	1	Halifax	1
Nov 18	Barnstaple	0	Bilston	2
Nov 18	Bolton	1	Chester	1
Nov 18	Boston	1	Lancaster	2
Nov 18	Bournemouth	5	Cambridge	1
Nov 18	Bradford C	3	Grantham	0
Nov 18	Chelmsford	2	Hillingdon	0
Nov 18	Chesterfield	4	Rhyl	2
Nov 18	Colchester	6	Bognor Regis	0
Nov 18	Crewe	1	Stafford	0
Nov 18	Darlington	1	Wrexham	1
Nov 18	Doncaster	3	Bury	1
Nov 18	Enfield	1	Bishop's Stortford	1
Nov 18	Gillingham	1	Reading	2
Nov 18	Grimsby	2	Wigan	1
Nov 18	Hartlepool	0	Scunthorpe	0
Nov 18	Hayes	1	Bristol R	0
Nov 18	Lincoln	2	Blackburn	2
Nov 18	Margate	1	Swansea	0
Nov 18	Newport	5	Alton	1
Nov 18	Oldham	1	Scarborough	1
Nov 18	Peterborough	1	Northampton	0
Nov 18	Plymouth	1	Hendon	0
Nov 18	Port Vale	2	Southport	1
Nov 18	Rochdale	1	Bangor	2
Nov 18	Rotherham	4	South Shields	0
Nov 18	South Liverpool	0	Tranmere	2
Nov 18	Southend	0	Aldershot	2
Nov 18	Spennymoor	1	Shrewsbury	1
Nov 18	Stockport	1	Workington	0
Nov 18	Telford	3	Nuneaton	2
Nov 18	Tonbridge	0	Charlton	5
Nov 18	Torquay	3	Hereford	0
Nov 18	Walsall	3	Kettering	3
Nov 18	Walton & H	2	Exeter	1
Nov 18	Watford	4	Guildford	2
Nov 18	Yeovil	2	Brentford	1
Nov 18	York	2	Mansfield	1

Replays

Date	Home		Away	
Nov 21	Bishop's Stortford	1	Enfield	0
Nov 21	Halifax	2	Barnsley	1
Nov 21	Scunthorpe	0	Hartlepool	0
Nov 21	Shrewsbury	3	Spennymoor	1
Nov 22	Chester	0	Bolton	1
Nov 22	Kettering	1	Walsall	2
Nov 22	Scarborough	2	Oldham	1
Nov 22	Wrexham	5	Darlington	0
Nov 27	Blackburn	4	Lincoln	1
Nov 27	Hartlepool	1	Scunthorpe	2
	played at Sunderland			

2nd Round

Date	Home		Away	
Dec 09	Bangor	2	York	3
Dec 09	Barnet	1	Bilston	1
Dec 09	Blackburn	0	Crewe	1
Dec 09	Bolton	3	Shrewsbury	0
Dec 09	Bournemouth	0	Colchester	0
Dec 09	Bradford C	2	Tranmere	1
Dec 09	Bishop's Stortford	2	Peterborough	2
Dec 09	Chelmsford	5	Telford	0
Dec 09	Grimsby	2	Chesterfield	2
Dec 09	Notts Co	2	Lancaster	1
Dec 09	Port Vale	1	Wrexham	0
Dec 09	Reading	0	Hayes	0
Dec 09	Rotherham	0	Stockport	1
Dec 09	Scarborough	1	Doncaster	2
Dec 09	Scunthorpe	3	Halifax	2
Dec 09	Torquay	0	Newport	1
Dec 12	Walsall	1	Charlton	2
Dec 09	Walton & H	0	Margate	1
Dec 09	Watford	2	Aldershot	0
Dec 09	Yeovil	0	Plymouth	2

Replays

Date	Home		Away	
Dec 11	Colchester	0	Bournemouth	2
Dec 11	Peterborough	3	Bishop's Stortford	1
Dec 12	Bilston	0	Barnet	1
Dec 12	Hayes	0	Reading	1
Dec 13	Chesterfield	0	Grimsby	1

3rd Round

Date	Home		Away	
Jan 13	Arsenal	2	Leicester	2
Jan 13	Bradford C	2	Blackpool	1
Jan 13	Brighton	0	Chelsea	2
Jan 13	Burnley	0	Liverpool	0
Jan 13	Carlisle	2	Huddersfield	2
Jan 13	Charlton	1	Bolton	1
Jan 13	Chelmsford	1	Ipswich	3
Jan 13	Crystal Palace	2	Southampton	0
Jan 13	Everton	3	Aston Villa	2
Jan 13	Grimsby	0	Preston	0
Jan 13	Luton	2	Crewe	0
Jan 13	Manchester C	3	Stoke	2
Jan 13	Margate	0	Tottenham	6
Jan 13	Millwall	3	Newport	0
Jan 13	Newcastle	2	Bournemouth	0
Jan 13	Norwich	1	Leeds	1
Jan 13	Notts Co	1	Sunderland	1
Jan 13	Orient	1	Coventry	4
Jan 13	Peterborough	0	Derby	1
Jan 13	Plymouth	1	Middlesbrough	0
Jan 13	Port Vale	0	West Ham	1
Jan 13	Portsmouth	1	Bristol C	1
Jan 13	Q.P.R.	0	Barnet	0
Jan 17	Reading	2	Doncaster	0
Jan 13	Scunthorpe	2	Cardiff	3
Jan 13	Sheffield W	2	Fulham	0
Jan 13	Stockport	0	Hull	0
Jan 13	Swindon	2	Birmingham	0
Jan 13	Watford	0	Sheffield U	1
Jan 13	Wolverhampton	1	Manchester U	0
Jan 13	W.B.A.	1	Nottingham F	1
Jan 13	York	0	Oxford	1

Replays

Date	Home		Away	
Jan 15	Preston	0	Grimsby	1
Jan 16	Barnet	0	Q.P.R.	3
Jan 16	Bristol C	4	Portsmouth	1
Jan 16	Huddersfield	0	Carlisle	1
Jan 16	Liverpool	3	Burnley	0
Jan 16	Sunderland	2	Notts Co	0
Jan 17	Bolton	4	Charlton	0
Jan 17	Leeds	1	Norwich	1
Jan 17	Leicester	1	Arsenal	2
Jan 22	Nottingham F	0	W.B.A.	0
Jan 23	Hull	2	Stockport	0
Jan 29	Leeds	5	Norwich	0
	played at Aston Villa			
Jan 29	Nottingham F	1	W.B.A.	3
	played at Leicester			

4th Round

Date	Home		Away	
Feb 03	Arsenal	2	Bradford C	0
Feb 03	Bolton	2	Cardiff	2
Feb 03	Carlisle	2	Sheffield U	1
Feb 03	Chelsea	2	Ipswich	0
Feb 03	Coventry	1	Grimsby	0
Feb 03	Derby	1	Tottenham	1
Feb 03	Everton	0	Millwall	2
Feb 03	Hull	1	West Ham	0
Feb 03	Leeds	2	Plymouth	1
Feb 03	Liverpool	0	Manchester C	0
Feb 03	Newcastle	0	Luton	2
Feb 03	Oxford	0	Q.P.R.	2
Feb 03	Sheffield W	1	Crystal Palace	1
Feb 03	Sunderland	1	Reading	1
Feb 03	Wolverhampton	1	Bristol C	0
Feb 03	W.B.A.	2	Swindon	0

Replays

Date	Home		Away	
Feb 06	Crystal Palace	1	Sheffield W	1
Feb 07	Cardiff	1	Bolton	1
Feb 07	Manchester C	2	Liverpool	0
Feb 07	Reading	1	Sunderland	3
Feb 07	Tottenham	3	Derby	5
Feb 12	Bolton	1	Cardiff	0
	played at W.B.A.			
Feb 19	Crystal Palace	2	Sheffield W	3
	played at Aston Villa			

5th Round

Date	Home		Away	
Feb 24	Bolton	0	Luton	1
Feb 24	Carlisle	1	Arsenal	2
Feb 24	Coventry	3	Hull	0
Feb 24	Derby	4	Q.P.R.	2
Feb 24	Leeds	2	W.B.A.	0
Feb 24	Manchester C	2	Sunderland	2
Feb 24	Sheffield W	1	Chelsea	2
Feb 24	Wolverhampton	1	Millwall	0

Replay

Date	Home		Away	
Feb 27	Sunderland	3	Manchester C	1

6th Round

Date	Home		Away	
Mar 17	Chelsea	2	Arsenal	2
Mar 17	Derby	0	Leeds	1
Mar 17	Sunderland	2	Luton	0
Mar 17	Wolverhampton	2	Coventry	0

Replay

Date	Home		Away	
Mar 20	Arsenal	2	Chelsea	1

Semi-finals

Date	Home		Away	
Apr 07	Arsenal	1	Sunderland	2
	played at Sheffield W			
Apr 07	Leeds	1	Wolverhampton	0
	played at Manchester C			

Final

Date	Home		Away	
May 05	Leeds	0	Sunderland	1
	played at Wembley			

Sunderland's Ian Porterfield smashes home the only goal of the 1973 Final to give the Division Two side a sensational victory over Leeds.

Season 1973-74

1st Round

Date	Home		Away	
Nov 24	Alfreton	0	Blyth	0
Nov 24	Altrincham	2	Hartlepool	0
Nov 24	Banbury	0	Northampton	0
Nov 24	Bideford	0	Bristol R	2
Nov 24	Boston	0	Hayes	0
Nov 24	Bournemouth	1	Charlton	0
Nov 24	Bradford C	2	Workington	0
Nov 24	Cambridge	3	Gillingham	2
Nov 24	Chester	1	Telford	0
Nov 24	Chesterfield	0	Barnsley	0
Nov 24	Colchester	2	Peterborough	3
Nov 24	Crewe	0	Scarborough	0
Nov 24	Dagenham	0	Aldershot	4
Nov 24	Doncaster	1	Lincoln	0
Nov 24	Exeter	0	Alvechurch	1
Nov 24	Formby	0	Oldham	2
Nov 24	Halifax	6	Frickley	1
Nov 24	Hendon	3	Leytonstone	0
Nov 24	Hereford	3	Torquay	1
Nov 24	Hillingdon	0	Grantham	4
Nov 24	Hitchin	1	Guildford	1
Nov 24	Huddersfield	2	Wigan	0
Nov 24	Kings Lynn	1	Wimbledon	0
Nov 24	Plymouth	2	Brentford	1
Nov 24	Reading	3	Slough	0
Nov 24	Rochdale	2	South Shields	0
Nov 24	Rotherham	2	Southport	1
Nov 24	Runcorn	0	Grimsby	1
Nov 24	Scunthorpe	1	Darlington	0
Nov 24	Southend	3	Boreham Wood	0
Nov 24	Stockport	0	Port Vale	1
Nov 24	Tranmere	2	Bury	1
Nov 24	Walsall	1	Swansea	0
Nov 24	Walton & H	0	Brighton	0
Nov 24	Watford	1	Chelmsford	0
Nov 24	Weymouth	0	Merthyr T	1
Nov 24	Willington	0	Blackburn	0
Nov 24	Wrexham	1	Shrewsbury	1
Nov 24	Wycombe	3	Newport	1
Nov 24	York	0	Mansfield	0

Replays

Date	Home		Away	
Nov 27	Shrewsbury	0	Wrexham	1
Nov 28	Barnsley	2	Chesterfield	1
Nov 28	Blyth	2	Alfreton	1
Nov 28	Brighton	0	Walton & H	4
Nov 28	Guildford	1	Hitchin	4
Nov 28	Hayes	1	Boston	2
Nov 28	Scarborough	2	Crewe	1
Nov 29	Northampton	3	Banbury	2
Dec 03	Blackburn	6	Willington	1
Dec 10	Mansfield	5	York	3

2nd Round

Date	Home		Away	
Dec 15	Aldershot	1	Cambridge	2
Dec 15	Alvechurch	6	Kings Lynn	1
Dec 15	Barnsley	1	Bradford C	1
Dec 15	Blackburn	0	Altrincham	0
Dec 15	Boston	1	Hitchin	0
Dec 15	Chester	3	Huddersfield	2
Dec 15	Doncaster	3	Tranmere	0
Dec 15	Grantham	1	Rochdale	1
Dec 15	Grimsby	1	Blyth	1
Dec 15	Halifax	0	Oldham	1
Dec 15	Hereford	3	Walton & H	0
Dec 15	Mansfield	1	Scunthorpe	1
Dec 15	Merthyr T	0	Hendon	3
Dec 15	Northampton	1	Bristol R	2
Dec 15	Plymouth	1	Walsall	0
Dec 15	Port Vale	2	Scarborough	1
Dec 15	Southend	2	Reading	0
Dec 15	Watford	0	Bournemouth	1
Dec 15	Wrexham	3	Rotherham	0
Dec 15	Wycombe	1	Peterborough	3

Replays

Date	Home		Away	
Dec 18	Rochdale	3	Grantham	5
Dec 18	Scunthorpe	1	Mansfield	0
Dec 19	Altrincham	0	Blackburn	2
Dec 19	Blyth	0	Grimsby	2
Dec 19	Bradford C	2	Barnsley	1

3rd Round

Date	Home		Away	
Jan 05	Aston Villa	3	Chester	1
Jan 05	Birmingham	5	Cardiff	2
Jan 05	Bolton	3	Stoke	2
Jan 05	Bradford C	4	Alvechurch	2
Jan 05	Bristol C	1	Hull	1
Jan 05	Cambridge	2	Oldham	2
Jan 05	Carlisle	0	Sunderland	0
Jan 05	Chelsea	0	Q.P.R.	0
Jan 05	Crystal Palace	0	Wrexham	2
Jan 05	Derby	0	Boston	0
Jan 05	Everton	3	Blackburn	0
Jan 05	Fulham	1	Preston	0
Jan 05	Grantham	0	Middlesbrough	2
Jan 05	Grimsby	0	Burnley	2
Jan 05	Ipswich	3	Sheffield U	2
Jan 05	Leicester	1	Tottenham	0
Jan 05	Liverpool	2	Doncaster	2
Jan 05	Manchester U	1	Plymouth	0
Jan 05	Millwall	1	Scunthorpe	1
Jan 05	Newcastle	1	Hendon	1
Jan 05	Norwich	0	Arsenal	1
Jan 05	Nottingham F	4	Bristol R	3
Jan 05	Orient	2	Bournemouth	1
Jan 05	Oxford	2	Manchester C	5
Jan 05	Peterborough	3	Southend	1
Jan 05	Port Vale	1	Luton	1
Jan 05	Portsmouth	3	Swindon	3
Jan 05	Sheffield W	0	Coventry	0
Jan 05	Southampton	2	Blackpool	1
Jan 05	West Ham	1	Hereford	1
Jan 05	Wolverhampton	1	Leeds	1
Jan 05	W.B.A.	4	Notts Co	0

Replays

Date	Home		Away	
Jan 08	Coventry	3	Sheffield W	1
Jan 08	Doncaster	0	Liverpool	2
Jan 08	Hull	0	Bristol C	1
Jan 08	Oldham	3	Cambridge	3
Jan 08	Scunthorpe	1	Millwall	0
Jan 09	Boston	1	Derby	6
Jan 09	Hendon	0	Newcastle	4
Jan 09	Hereford	2	West Ham	1
Jan 09	Leeds	1	Wolverhampton	0
Jan 09	Luton	4	Port Vale	2
Jan 09	Sunderland	0	Carlisle	1
Jan 09	Swindon	0	Portsmouth	1
Jan 14	Cambridge played at Nottingham F	1	Oldham	2
Jan 15	Q.P.R.	1	Chelsea	0

4th Round

Date	Home		Away	
Jan 26	Arsenal	1	Aston Villa	1
Jan 27	Coventry	0	Derby	0
Jan 27	Everton	0	W.B.A.	0
Jan 26	Fulham	1	Leicester	1
Jan 26	Hereford	0	Bristol C	1
Jan 26	Liverpool	0	Carlisle	0
Jan 26	Luton	3	Bradford C	0
Jan 26	Manchester U	0	Ipswich	1
Jan 26	Newcastle	1	Scunthorpe	1
Jan 27	Nottingham F	4	Manchester C	1
Jan 26	Oldham	1	Burnley	4
Jan 26	Peterborough	1	Leeds	4
Jan 27	Portsmouth	0	Orient	0
Jan 26	Q.P.R.	2	Birmingham	0
Jan 26	Southampton	3	Bolton	3
Jan 26	Wrexham	1	Middlesbrough	0

Replays

Date	Home		Away	
Jan 29	Carlisle	0	Liverpool	2
Jan 29	Orient	1	Portsmouth	1
Jan 30	Aston Villa	2	Arsenal	0
Jan 30	Bolton	0	Southampton	2
Jan 30	Derby	0	Coventry	1
Jan 30	Leicester	2	Fulham	1
Jan 30	Scunthorpe	0	Newcastle	3
Jan 30	W.B.A.	1	Everton	0
Feb 05	Orient played at Crystal Palace	0	Portsmouth	2

5th Round

Date	Home		Away	
Feb 16	Bristol C	1	Leeds	1
Feb 16	Burnley	1	Aston Villa	0
Feb 16	Coventry	0	Q.P.R.	0
Feb 16	Liverpool	2	Ipswich	0
Feb 16	Luton	0	Leicester	4
Feb 16	Southampton	0	Wrexham	1
Feb 16	W.B.A.	0	Newcastle	3
Feb 17	Nottingham F	1	Portsmouth	0

Replays

Date	Home		Away	
Feb 19	Leeds	0	Bristol C	1
Feb 19	Q.P.R.	3	Coventry	2

6th Round

Date	Home		Away	
Mar 09	Bristol C	0	Liverpool	1
Mar 09	Burnley	1	Wrexham	0
Mar 09	Newcastle	4	Nottingham F	3
Abandoned				
Mar 09	Q.P.R.	0	Leicester	2

Replays

Date	Home		Away	
Mar 18	Nottingham F played at Everton	0	Newcastle	0
Mar 21	Newcastle played at Everton	1	Nottingham F	0

Semi-finals

Date	Home		Away	
Mar 30	Burnley played at Sheffield W	0	Newcastle	2
Mar 30	Leicester played at Manchester U	0	Liverpool	0

Replay

Date	Home		Away	
Apr 03	Leicester played at Aston Villa	1	Liverpool	3

Final

Date	Home		Away	
May 04	Liverpool played at Wembley	3	Newcastle	0

Season 1974-75

1st Round

Date	Home		Away	
Nov 27	Ashford	1	Walsall	3
Nov 23	Barnsley	1	Halifax	2
Nov 23	Bishop Auckland	5	Morecambe	0
Nov 23	Blyth	1	Preston	1
Nov 23	Bournemouth	5	Southwick	0
Nov 23	Brighton	3	Aldershot	1
Nov 23	Bury	4	Southport	2
Nov 23	Bishop's Stortford	0	Leatherhead	0
Nov 23	Chelmsford	0	Charlton	1
Nov 23	Chesterfield	3	Boston	1
Nov 23	Crewe	2	Gateshead	2
Nov 23	Darlington	1	Workington	0
Nov 23	Dartford	2	Plymouth	3
Nov 23	Exeter	1	Newport	2
Nov 23	Farsley	0	Tranmere	2
Nov 23	Grimsby	1	Huddersfield	0
Nov 23	Hartlepool	1	Bradford C	0
Nov 26	Hereford	1	Gillingham	0
Nov 23	Hitchin	0	Cambridge	0
Nov 23	Leamington	1	Southend	2
Nov 23	Mansfield	3	Wrexham	1
Nov 23	Matlock	1	Blackburn	4
Nov 23	Nuneaton	2	Maidstone	2
Nov 23	Oswestry	1	Doncaster	3
Nov 23	Peterborough	0	Weymouth	0
Nov 23	Port Vale	2	Lincoln	2
Nov 23	Rochdale	0	Marine	0
Nov 23	Romford	0	Ilford	2
Nov 23	Rotherham	1	Chester	0
Nov 23	Scunthorpe	1	Altrincham	1
Nov 23	Shrewsbury	1	Wigan	1
Nov 23	Slough	1	Brentford	4
Nov 23	Stockport	0	Stafford	0
Nov 26	Swansea	1	Kettering	1
Nov 23	Swindon	4	Reading	0
Nov 27	Tooting & M	1	Crystal Palace	2
Nov 23	Torquay	0	Northampton	1
Nov 23	Watford	0	Colchester	1
Nov 23	Wimbledon	1	Bath	0
Nov 23	Wycombe	3	Cheltenham	1

Replays

Date	Home		Away	
Nov 25	Altrincham	3	Scunthorpe	1
Nov 25	Gateshead	1	Crewe	0
Nov 25	Wigan	2	Shrewsbury	1
Nov 26	Cambridge	3	Hitchin	0
Nov 26	Leatherhead	2	Bishop's Stortford	0
Nov 26	Maidstone	2	Nuneaton	0
Nov 26	Preston	5	Blyth	1
Nov 26	Stafford	1	Stockport	0
Nov 27	Lincoln	2	Port Vale	0
Nov 27	Marine	1	Rochdale	2
Dec 02	Kettering	3	Swansea	1
Dec 04	Weymouth	3	Peterborough	3
Dec 09	Peterborough	3	Weymouth	0

2nd Round

Date	Home		Away	
Dec 14	Altrincham	3	Gateshead	0
Dec 14	Bishop Auckland	0	Preston	2
Dec 14	Blackburn	1	Darlington	0
Dec 14	Brighton	1	Brentford	0
Dec 14	Cambridge	2	Hereford	0
Dec 14	Chesterfield	1	Doncaster	0
Dec 14	Grimsby	1	Bury	1
Dec 14	Hartlepool	0	Lincoln	0
Dec 14	Ilford	0	Southend	2
Dec 14	Leatherhead	1	Colchester	0
Dec 14	Newport	1	Walsall	3
Dec 14	Peterborough	3	Charlton	0
Dec 14	Plymouth	2	Crystal Palace	1
Dec 14	Rochdale	1	Tranmere	1
Dec 14	Rotherham	2	Northampton	1
Dec 14	Stafford	2	Halifax	1
Dec 14	Swindon	3	Maidstone	1
Dec 14	Wigan	1	Mansfield	1
Dec 14	Wimbledon	2	Kettering	0
Dec 14	Wycombe	0	Bournemouth	0

Replays

Date	Home		Away	
Dec 16	Mansfield	3	Wigan	1
Dec 16	Tranmere	1	Rochdale	0
Dec 17	Bury	2	Grimsby	1
Dec 17	Lincoln	1	Hartlepool	0
Dec 18	Bournemouth	1	Wycombe	2

3rd Round

Date	Home		Away	
Jan 04	Arsenal	1	York	1
Jan 04	Blackburn	1	Bristol R	2
Jan 04	Bolton	0	W.B.A.	0
Jan 04	Brighton	0	Leatherhead	1
Jan 04	Burnley	0	Wimbledon	1
Jan 04	Bury	2	Millwall	2
Jan 04	Chelsea	3	Sheffield W	2
Jan 04	Coventry	2	Norwich	0
Jan 04	Everton	1	Altrincham	1
Jan 04	Fulham	1	Hull	1
Jan 04	Leeds	4	Cardiff	1
Jan 04	Leicester	3	Oxford	1
Jan 04	Liverpool	2	Stoke	0
Jan 04	Luton	0	Birmingham	1
Jan 04	Manchester C	0	Newcastle	2
Jan 04	Manchester U	0	Walsall	0
Jan 04	Mansfield	1	Cambridge	0
Jan 04	Nottingham F	1	Tottenham	1
Jan 03	Notts Co	3	Portsmouth	1
Jan 04	Oldham	0	Aston Villa	3
Jan 04	Orient	2	Derby	2
Jan 04	Peterborough	1	Tranmere	0
Jan 04	Plymouth	2	Blackpool	0
Jan 04	Preston	0	Carlisle	1

Date	Home		Away	
Jan 04	Sheffield U	2	Bristol C	0
Jan 04	Southampton	1	West Ham	2
Jan 04	Southend	2	Q.P.R.	2
Jan 04	Stafford	0	Rotherham	0
Jan 04	Sunderland	2	Chesterfield	0
Jan 04	Swindon	2	Lincoln	0
Jan 04	Wolverhampton	1	Ipswich	2
Jan 04	Wycombe	0	Middlesbrough	0

Replays

Date	Home		Away	
Jan 07	Altrincham	0	Everton	2
	played at Manchester U			
Jan 07	Hull	2	Fulham	2
Jan 07	Middlesbrough	1	Wycombe	0
Jan 07	Millwall	1	Bury	1
Jan 07	Q.P.R.	2	Southend	0
Jan 07	Rotherham	0	Stafford	2
Jan 07	Walsall	3	Manchester U	2
Jan 07	York	1	Arsenal	3
Jan 08	Derby	2	Orient	1
Jan 08	Tottenham	0	Nottingham F	1
Jan 08	W.B.A.	4	Bolton	0
Jan 13	Bury	2	Millwall	0
	played at W.B.A.			
Jan 13	Fulham	1	Hull	0
	played at Leicester			

4th Round

Date	Home		Away	
Jan 25	Aston Villa	4	Sheffield U	1
Jan 25	Bury	1	Mansfield	2
Jan 25	Carlisle	3	W.B.A.	2
Jan 25	Chelsea	0	Birmingham	1
Jan 25	Coventry	1	Arsenal	1
Jan 27	Derby	2	Bristol R	0
Jan 28	Fulham	0	Nottingham F	0
Jan 25	Ipswich	1	Liverpool	0
Jan 25	Leatherhead	2	Leicester	3
Jan 25	Leeds	0	Wimbledon	0
Jan 25	Middlesbrough	3	Sunderland	1
Jan 25	Plymouth	1	Everton	3
Jan 24	Q.P.R.	3	Notts Co	0
Jan 25	Stafford	1	Peterborough	2
Jan 25	Walsall	1	Newcastle	0
Jan 25	West Ham	1	Swindon	1

Replays

Date	Home		Away	
Jan 28	Swindon	1	West Ham	2
Jan 29	Arsenal	3	Coventry	0
Feb 03	Nottingham F	1	Fulham	1
Feb 05	Fulham	1	Nottingham F	1
Feb 10	Nottingham F	1	Fulham	2
Feb 10	Wimbledon	0	Leeds	1
	played at Crystal Palace			

5th Round

Date	Home		Away	
Feb 15	Arsenal	0	Leicester	0
Feb 15	Birmingham	2	Walsall	1
Feb 18	Derby	0	Leeds	1
Feb 15	Everton	1	Fulham	2
Feb 15	Ipswich	3	Aston Villa	2
Feb 15	Mansfield	0	Carlisle	1
Feb 15	Peterborough	1	Middlesbrough	1
Feb 15	West Ham	2	Q.P.R.	1

Replays

Date	Home		Away	
Feb 18	Middlesbrough	2	Peterborough	0
Feb 19	Leicester	1	Arsenal	1
Feb 24	Leicester	0	Arsenal	1

6th Round

Date	Home		Away	
Mar 08	Arsenal	0	West Ham	2
Mar 08	Birmingham	1	Middlesbrough	0
Mar 08	Carlisle	0	Fulham	1
Mar 08	Ipswich	0	Leeds	0

Replays

Date	Home		Away	
Mar 11	Leeds	1	Ipswich	1
Mar 25	Ipswich	0	Leeds	0
	played at Leicester			
Mar 27	Ipswich	3	Leeds	2
	played at Leicester			

Semi-finals

Date	Home		Away	
Apr 05	Birmingham	1	Fulham	1
	played at Sheffield W			
Apr 05	Ipswich	0	West Ham	0
	played at Aston Villa			

Replays

Date	Home		Away	
Apr 09	Birmingham	0	Fulham	1
	played at Manchester C			
Apr 09	Ipswich	1	West Ham	2
	played at Chelsea			

Final

Date	Home		Away	
May 03	Fulham	0	West Ham	2
	played at Wembley			

SEASON 1975-76

1st Round

Date	Home		Away	
Nov 22	Aldershot	4	Wealdstone	3
Nov 22	Boston	0	Lincoln	1
Nov 22	Bradford C	1	Chesterfield	0
Nov 22	Brentford	2	Northampton	0
Nov 22	Bury	4	Doncaster	2
Nov 22	Cardiff	6	Exeter	2
Nov 22	Colchester	3	Dover	3
Nov 22	Coventry S	2	Tranmere	0
Nov 22	Crystal Palace	1	Walton	0
Nov 22	Darlington	0	Chester	0
Nov 22	Dartford	1	Bishop's Stortford	4
Nov 22	Grantham	2	Port Vale	2
Nov 22	Grimsby	1	Gateshead	3
Nov 22	Halifax	3	Altrincham	1
Nov 22	Hartlepool	3	Stockport	0
Nov 22	Hendon	1	Reading	0
Nov 22	Hereford	2	Torquay	0
Nov 22	Leamington	2	Stafford	3
Nov 22	Leatherhead	2	Cambridge	0
Nov 22	Mansfield	1	Wrexham	1
Nov 22	Marine	3	Barnsley	1
Nov 22	Newport	2	Swindon	2
Nov 22	Nuneaton	0	Wimbledon	1
Nov 22	Peterborough	4	Winsford	1
Nov 22	Preston	2	Scunthorpe	1
Nov 22	Romford	0	Tooting & M	1
Nov 22	Rossendale	0	Shrewsbury	1
Nov 22	Rotherham	2	Crewe	1
Nov 22	Scarborough	2	Morecambe	0
Nov 22	Sheffield W	3	Macclesfield	1
Nov 22	Southend	2	Swansea	0
Nov 22	Spennymoor	4	Southport	1
Nov 22	Sutton	1	Bournemouth	1
Nov 22	Walsall	0	Huddersfield	1
Nov 22	Watford	0	Brighton	3
Nov 22	Weymouth	0	Gillingham	2
Nov 22	Wigan	4	Matlock	1
Nov 22	Workington	1	Rochdale	1
Nov 22	Wycombe	0	Bedford	0
Nov 22	Yeovil	1	Millwall	1

Replays

Date	Home		Away	
Nov 24	Bedford	2	Wycombe	2
Nov 24	Port Vale	4	Grantham	1
Nov 24	Wrexham	1	Mansfield	1
Nov 25	Millwall	2	Yeovil	2
Nov 25	Rochdale	2	Workington	1
Nov 25	Swindon	3	Newport	0
Nov 26	Bournemouth	1	Sutton	0
Nov 26	Chester	2	Darlington	0
Nov 26	Dover	4	Colchester	1
Dec 01	Wycombe	2	Bedford	1
Dec 02	Millwall	1	Yeovil	0
	played at Aldershot			
Dec 08	Mansfield	2	Wrexham	1
	played at Aston Villa			

2nd Round

Date	Home		Away	
Dec 13	Aldershot	2	Bishop's Stortford	0
Dec 13	Bournemouth	2	Hereford	2
Dec 13	Bury	3	Spennymoor	0
Dec 13	Cardiff	1	Wycombe	0
Dec 13	Coventry	0	Peterborough	4
Dec 13	Gateshead	1	Rochdale	1
Dec 13	Gillingham	0	Brighton	1
Dec 13	Hendon	0	Swindon	1
Dec 13	Huddersfield	2	Port Vale	1
Dec 13	Leatherhead	0	Tooting & M	0
Dec 13	Mansfield	1	Lincoln	2
Dec 13	Marine	1	Hartlepool	1
Dec 13	Millwall	1	Crystal Palace	1
Dec 13	Rotherham	0	Bradford C	3
Dec 13	Scarborough	3	Preston	2
Dec 13	Sheffield W	2	Wigan	0
Dec 13	Shrewsbury	3	Chester	1
Dec 13	Southend	4	Dover	1
Dec 13	Stafford	1	Halifax	3
Dec 13	Wimbledon	0	Brentford	2

Replays

Date	Home		Away	
Dec 15	Hartlepool	6	Marine	3
Dec 16	Crystal Palace	2	Millwall	1
Dec 16	Rochdale	3	Gateshead	1
Dec 17	Hereford	2	Bournemouth	0
Dec 22	Tooting & M	2	Leatherhead	1

3rd Round

Date	Home		Away	
Jan 03	Aldershot	1	Lincoln	2
Jan 03	Blackpool	1	Burnley	0
Jan 03	Brentford	0	Bolton	0
Jan 03	Charlton	2	Sheffield W	1
Jan 01	Chelsea	1	Bristol R	1
Jan 03	Coventry	2	Bristol C	1
Jan 03	Derby	2	Everton	1
Jan 03	Fulham	2	Huddersfield	3
Jan 03	Hull	1	Plymouth	1
Jan 03	Ipswich	3	Halifax	1
Jan 03	Leicester	3	Sheffield U	0
Jan 03	Luton	2	Blackburn	0
Jan 03	Manchester C	6	Hartlepool	0
Jan 03	Manchester U	2	Oxford	1
Jan 03	Middlesbrough	0	Bury	0
Jan 03	Norwich	1	Rochdale	1
Jan 01	Nottingham F	0	Peterborough	0
Jan 03	Notts Co	0	Leeds	1
Jan 03	Orient	0	Cardiff	1
Jan 03	Portsmouth	1	Birmingham	1
Jan 03	Q.P.R.	0	Newcastle	0
Jan 03	Scarborough	1	Crystal Palace	2
Jan 03	Shrewsbury	1	Bradford C	2
Jan 03	Southampton	1	Aston Villa	1
Jan 03	Southend	2	Brighton	1
Jan 03	Sunderland	2	Oldham	0
Jan 03	Swindon	2	Tooting & M	2
Jan 03	Tottenham	1	Stoke	1
Jan 03	West Ham	0	Liverpool	2
Jan 03	Wolverhampton	3	Arsenal	0
Jan 03	W.B.A.	3	Carlisle	1
Jan 03	York	2	Hereford	1

Replays

Date	Home		Away	
Jan 03	Bristol R	0	Chelsea	1
Jan 06	Birmingham	0	Portsmouth	1
Jan 06	Bolton	2	Brentford	0
Jan 06	Bury	3	Middlesbrough	2
Jan 06	Plymouth	1	Hull	4
Jan 06	Rochdale	0	Norwich	0
Jan 06	Tooting & M	2	Swindon	1
Jan 07	Aston Villa	1	Southampton	2
Jan 07	Newcastle	2	Q.P.R.	1
Jan 07	Peterborough	1	Nottingham F	0
Jan 13	Norwich	2	Rochdale	1
Jan 24	Stoke	2	Tottenham	1

4th Round

Date	Home		Away	
Jan 24	Bradford C	3	Tooting & M	1
Jan 24	Charlton	1	Portsmouth	1
Jan 24	Coventry	1	Newcastle	1
Jan 24	Derby	1	Liverpool	0
Jan 24	Huddersfield	0	Bolton	1
Jan 24	Ipswich	0	Wolverhampton	0
Jan 24	Leeds	0	Crystal Palace	1
Jan 24	Leicester	1	Bury	0
Jan 24	Manchester U	3	Peterborough	1
Jan 24	Norwich	2	Luton	0
Jan 24	Southampton	3	Blackpool	1
Jan 24	Southend	2	Cardiff	1
Jan 28	Stoke	1	Manchester C	0
Feb 02	Sunderland	1	Hull	0
Jan 24	W.B.A.	3	Lincoln	2
Jan 24	York	0	Chelsea	2

Replays

Date	Home		Away	
Jan 27	Portsmouth	0	Charlton	3
Jan 27	Wolverhampton	1	Ipswich	0
Jan 28	Newcastle	5	Coventry	0

5th Round

Date	Home		Away	
Feb 14	Bolton	3	Newcastle	3
Feb 14	Chelsea	2	Crystal Palace	3
Feb 14	Derby	1	Southend	0
Feb 14	Leicester	1	Manchester U	2
Feb 23	Norwich	1	Bradford C	2
Feb 14	Stoke	0	Sunderland	0
Feb 14	Wolverhampton	3	Charlton	0
Feb 14	W.B.A.	1	Southampton	1

Replays

Date	Home		Away	
Feb 17	Southampton	4	W.B.A.	0
Feb 17	Sunderland	2	Stoke	1
Feb 18	Newcastle	0	Bolton	0
Feb 23	Bolton	1	Newcastle	2
	played at Leeds			

6th Round

Date	Home		Away	
Mar 06	Bradford C	0	Southampton	1
Mar 06	Derby	4	Newcastle	2
Mar 06	Manchester U	1	Wolverhampton	1
Mar 06	Sunderland	0	Crystal Palace	1

Replay

Date	Home		Away	
Mar 09	Wolverhampton	2	Manchester U	3

Semi-finals

Date	Home		Away	
Apr 03	Crystal Palace	0	Southampton	2
	played at Chelsea			
Apr 03	Derby	0	Manchester U	2
	played at Sheffield W			

Final

Date	Home		Away	
May 01	Manchester U	0	Southampton	1
	played at Wembley			

SEASON 1976-77

1st Round

Date	Home		Away	
Nov 20	Aldershot	1	Portsmouth	1
Nov 20	Barnsley	3	Boston	1
Nov 20	Barrow	0	Goole	2
Nov 20	Bournemouth	0	Newport	0
Nov 20	Brentford	2	Chesham	0
Nov 20	Brighton	2	Crystal Palace	2
Nov 20	Bury	6	Workington	0
Nov 20	Cambridge	1	Colchester	1
Nov 20	Chester	1	Hartlepool	0
Nov 20	Crewe	1	Preston	1
Nov 20	Crook	1	Nuneaton	4
Nov 20	Doncaster	2	Shrewsbury	2
Nov 20	Droylsden	0	Grimsby	0
Nov 20	Dudley	1	York	1
Nov 20	Enfield	0	Harwich	0
Nov 20	Exeter	1	Southend	1
Nov 20	Gillingham	0	Watford	1
Nov 20	Huddersfield	0	Mansfield	0
Nov 20	Kettering	1	Oxford	1
Nov 20	Leatherhead	2	Northampton	0

Date	Home		Away	
Nov 20	Lincoln	1	Morecambe	0
Nov 20	Matlock	2	Wigan	0
Nov 20	Reading	1	Wealdstone	0
Nov 20	Rochdale	1	Northwich	1
Nov 20	Rotherham	5	Altrincham	0
Nov 20	Scarborough	0	Darlington	0
Nov 20	Scunthorpe	1	Chesterfield	2
Nov 20	Sheffield W	2	Stockport	0
Nov 20	Southport	1	Port Vale	2
Nov 20	Stafford	0	Halifax	0
Nov 20	Swansea	0	Minehead	1
Nov 20	Swindon	7	Bromley	0
Nov 20	Tooting & M	4	Dartford	2
Nov 20	Torquay	1	Hillingdon	2
Nov 20	Tranmere	0	Peterborough	4
Nov 20	Walsall	0	Bradford C	0
Nov 20	Waterlooville	1	Wycombe	2
Nov 20	Weymouth	1	Hitchin	1
Nov 20	Wimbledon	1	Workington	0
Nov 20	Wrexham	6	Gateshead	0

Replays

Date	Home		Away	
Nov 22	Darlington	4	Scarborough	1
Nov 22	Mansfield	2	Huddersfield	1
Nov 22	Northwich	0	Rochdale	0
Nov 22	Southend	2	Exeter	1
Nov 23	Crystal Palace	1	Brighton	1
Nov 23	Grimsby	5	Droylsden	3
Nov 23	Halifax	1	Stafford	0
Nov 23	Harwich	0	Enfield	3
Nov 23	Hitchin	2	Weymouth	2
Nov 23	Newport	3	Bournemouth	0
Nov 23	Oxford	0	Kettering	1
Nov 23	Portsmouth	2	Aldershot	1
Nov 23	Preston	2	Crewe	2
Nov 23	Shrewsbury	4	Doncaster	3
Nov 23	York	4	Dudley	1
Nov 24	Bradford C	0	Walsall	2
Nov 24	Colchester	2	Cambridge	0
Nov 29	Crewe	0	Preston	3
	played at Liverpool			
Nov 29	Hitchin	3	Weymouth	3
	played at Aldershot			
Nov 29	Northwich	2	Rochdale	1
	played at Manchester C			
Dec 02	Hitchin	3	Weymouth	1
	played at Salisbury			
Dec 06	Brighton	0	Crystal Palace	1
	played at Chelsea			

2nd Round

Date	Home		Away	
Dec 14	Bury	0	Shrewsbury	0
Dec 11	Chesterfield	1	Walsall	1
Dec 20	Colchester	3	Brentford	2
Dec 15	Darlington	1	Sheffield W	0
Dec 11	Enfield	0	Crystal Palace	4
Dec 11	Grimsby	0	Chester	1
Dec 14	Halifax	1	Preston	0
Dec 11	Hillingdon	2	Watford	3
Dec 11	Hitchin	1	Swindon	1
Dec 11	Kettering	1	Tooting & M	0
Dec 14	Leatherhead	1	Wimbledon	3
Dec 11	Lincoln	6	Nuneaton	0
Dec 15	Mansfield	2	Matlock	5
Dec 14	Northwich	4	Peterborough	0
Dec 11	Port Vale	3	Barnsley	0
Dec 11	Portsmouth	2	Minehead	1
Dec 11	Rotherham	0	York	0
Dec 11	Southend	3	Newport	0
Dec 11	Wrexham	1	Goole	1
Dec 11	Wycombe	1	Reading	2

Replays

Date	Home		Away	
Dec 14	Goole	0	Wrexham	1
Dec 14	Walsall	0	Chesterfield	0
Dec 14	York	1	Rotherham	1
Dec 21	Chesterfield	0	Walsall	1
	played at Derby			
Dec 21	Rotherham	2	York	1
Dec 21	Shrewsbury	2	Bury	1
Dec 21	Swindon	3	Hitchin	1

3rd Round

Date	Home		Away	
Jan 08	Birmingham	1	Portsmouth	0
Jan 08	Blackpool	0	Derby	0
Jan 08	Burnley	2	Lincoln	2
Jan 08	Cardiff	1	Tottenham	0
Jan 08	Carlisle	5	Matlock	1
Jan 08	Charlton	1	Blackburn	1
Jan 08	Coventry	1	Millwall	0
Jan 08	Darlington	2	Orient	2
Jan 08	Everton	2	Stoke	0
Jan 08	Fulham	3	Swindon	3
Jan 08	Halifax	0	Luton	1
Jan 08	Hereford	1	Reading	0
Jan 08	Hull	1	Port Vale	1
Jan 08	Ipswich	4	Bristol C	1
Jan 08	Kettering	2	Colchester	3
Jan 08	Leeds	5	Norwich	2
Jan 08	Leicester	0	Aston Villa	1
Jan 08	Liverpool	0	Crystal Palace	0
Jan 08	Manchester C	1	W.B.A.	1
Jan 08	Manchester U	1	Walsall	0
Jan 08	Northwich	3	Watford	2
Jan 08	Nottingham F	1	Bristol R	1
Jan 08	Notts Co	0	Arsenal	1
Jan 08	Oldham	3	Plymouth	0
Jan 08	Q.P.R.	2	Shrewsbury	1
Jan 08	Sheffield U	0	Newcastle	0
Jan 08	Southampton	1	Chelsea	1
Jan 08	Southend	0	Chester	4
Jan 08	Sunderland	2	Wrexham	2
Jan 08	West Ham	2	Bolton	1
Jan 08	Wimbledon	0	Middlesbrough	0
Jan 08	Wolverhampton	3	Rotherham	2

Replays

Date	Home		Away	
Jan 10	Port Vale	3	Hull	1
Jan 11	Bristol R	1	Nottingham F	1
Jan 11	Crystal Palace	2	Liverpool	3
Jan 11	Middlesbrough	1	Wimbledon	0
Jan 11	Orient	0	Darlington	0
Jan 11	Swindon	5	Fulham	0
Jan 11	W.B.A.	0	Manchester C	1
Jan 12	Blackburn	2	Charlton	0
Jan 12	Chelsea	0	Southampton	3
Jan 12	Lincoln	0	Burnley	1
Jan 12	Wrexham	1	Sunderland	0
Jan 17	Darlington	0	Orient	3
	played at Tottenham			
Jan 18	Bristol R	0	Nottingham F	6
	played at Aston Villa			
Jan 19	Derby	3	Blackpool	2
Jan 24	Newcastle	3	Sheffield U	1

4th Round

Date	Home		Away	
Jan 29	Arsenal	3	Coventry	1
Jan 29	Aston Villa	3	West Ham	0
Jan 29	Birmingham	1	Leeds	2
Jan 29	Blackburn	3	Orient	0
Jan 29	Cardiff	3	Wrexham	2
Jan 29	Chester	1	Luton	0
Jan 29	Colchester	1	Derby	1
Jan 29	Ipswich	2	Wolverhampton	2
Jan 29	Liverpool	3	Carlisle	0
Jan 29	Manchester U	1	Q.P.R.	0
Jan 29	Middlesbrough	4	Hereford	0
Jan 29	Newcastle	1	Manchester C	3
Jan 29	Northwich	1	Oldham	3
	played at Manchester C			
Jan 29	Nottingham F	3	Southampton	3
Jan 29	Port Vale	2	Burnley	1
Jan 29	Swindon	2	Everton	2

Replays

Date	Home		Away	
Feb 01	Everton	2	Swindon	1
Feb 01	Southampton	2	Nottingham F	1
Feb 02	Derby	1	Colchester	0
Feb 02	Wolverhampton	1	Ipswich	0

5th Round

Date	Home		Away	
Feb 26	Aston Villa	3	Port Vale	0
Feb 26	Cardiff	1	Everton	2
Feb 26	Derby	3	Blackburn	1
Feb 26	Leeds	1	Manchester C	0
Feb 26	Liverpool	3	Oldham	1
Feb 26	Middlesbrough	4	Arsenal	1
Feb 26	Southampton	2	Manchester U	2
Feb 26	Wolverhampton	1	Chester	0

Replays

Date	Home		Away	
Mar 08	Manchester U	2	Southampton	1

6th Round

Date	Home		Away	
Mar 19	Everton	2	Derby	0
Mar 19	Liverpool	2	Middlesbrough	0
Mar 19	Manchester U	2	Aston Villa	1
Mar 19	Wolverhampton	0	Leeds	1

Semi-finals

Date	Home		Away	
Apr 23	Everton	2	Liverpool	2
	played at Manchester C			
Apr 23	Leeds	1	Manchester U	2
	played at Sheffield W			

Replay

Date	Home		Away	
Apr 27	Everton	0	Liverpool	3
	played at Manchester C			

Final

Date	Home		Away	
May 21	Liverpool	1	Manchester U	2
	played at Wembley			

Stuart Pearson nets Manchester United's first goal against Liverpool in 1997.

Season 1977-78

1st Round

Nov 26	Arnold	0	Port Vale	0
Nov 26	Barnet	1	Peterborough	2
Nov 26	Barnsley	1	Huddersfield	0
Nov 26	Bath	0	Plymouth	0
Nov 26	Blyth	1	Burscough	0
Nov 26	Borehamwood	0	Swindon	0
Nov 26	Bradford C	0	Crewe	1
Nov 26	Brentford	2	Folkestone	0
Nov 26	Carlisle	2	Stafford	0
Nov 26	Chester	4	Darlington	1
Nov 26	Chesterfield	1	Halifax	0
Nov 26	Colchester	1	Bournemouth	1
Nov 26	Doncaster	0	Shrewsbury	1
Nov 26	Enfield	3	Wimbledon	0
Nov 26	Gillingham	1	Weymouth	1
Nov 26	Leamington	6	Enderby	1
Nov 26	Leatherhead	0	Swansea	0
Nov 26	Lowestoft	0	Cambridge	2
Nov 26	Minehead	2	Wycombe	0
Nov 26	Newport	1	Exeter	1
Nov 26	Nuneaton	2	Oxford	0
Nov 26	Portsmouth	3	Bideford	1
Nov 26	Preston	3	Lincoln	2
Nov 26	Reading	3	Aldershot	1
Nov 26	Rotherham	3	Mossley	0
Nov 26	Scarborough	4	Rochdale	2
Nov 26	Sheffield W	1	Bury	0
Nov 26	Southport	2	Runcorn	2
Nov 26	Spennymoor	3	Goole	1
Nov 26	Stockport	3	Scunthorpe	0
Dec 05	Tilbury	2	Kettering	2
Nov 26	Tooting	1	Northampton	2
Nov 26	Torquay	1	Southend	2
Nov 26	Tranmere	1	Hartlepool	1
Nov 26	Walsall	1	Dagenham	0
Nov 26	Watford	2	Hendon	0
Nov 26	Wealdstone	0	Hereford	0
Nov 26	Wigan	1	York	0
Nov 26	Workington	0	Grimsby	2
Nov 26	Wrexham	2	Burton	0

Replays

Nov 28	Port Vale	5	Arnold	2
Nov 28	Runcorn	1	Southport	0
Nov 29	Bournemouth	0	Colchester	0
Nov 29	Hartlepool	3	Tranmere	1
Nov 29	Plymouth	2	Bath	0
Nov 29	Swansea	2	Leatherhead	1
Nov 29	Swindon	2	Borehamwood	0
Nov 30	Exeter	4	Newport	2
Nov 30	Hereford	2	Wealdstone	3
Nov 30	Weymouth	0	Gillingham	1
Dec 05	Bournemouth played at Watford	1	Colchester	4
Dec 07	Kettering	2	Tilbury	3

2nd Round

Dec 17	Blyth	1	Chesterfield	0
Dec 17	Carlisle	3	Chester	1
Dec 17	Crewe	0	Scarborough	0
Dec 17	Gillingham	1	Peterborough	1
Dec 17	Grimsby	2	Barnsley	0
Dec 17	Hartlepool	4	Runcorn	2
Dec 17	Leamington	0	Southend	0
Dec 17	Minehead	0	Exeter	3
Dec 17	Northampton	0	Enfield	2
Dec 17	Nuneaton	1	Tilbury	2
Dec 17	Plymouth	1	Cambridge	0
Dec 17	Portsmouth	2	Swansea	2
Dec 17	Preston	0	Wrexham	2
Dec 17	Rotherham	6	Spennymoor	0
Dec 17	Shrewsbury	1	Stockport	1
Dec 17	Swindon	2	Brentford	1
Dec 17	Walsall	1	Port Vale	1
Dec 17	Watford	2	Colchester	0
Dec 17	Wealdstone	2	Reading	1
Dec 17	Wigan	1	Sheffield W	0

Replays

Dec 19	Port Vale	1	Walsall	3
Dec 19	Southend	4	Leamington	0
Dec 19	Stockport	1	Shrewsbury	2
Dec 20	Peterborough	2	Gillingham	0
Dec 20	Swansea	2	Portsmouth	1
Dec 21	Scarborough	2	Crewe	0

3rd Round

Jan 07	Birmingham	4	Wigan	0
Jan 07	Blackburn	2	Shrewsbury	1
Jan 07	Blyth	1	Enfield	0
Jan 07	Brighton	3	Scarborough	0
Jan 07	Bristol C	4	Wrexham	4
Jan 07	Burnley	1	Fulham	0
Jan 07	Cardiff	0	Ipswich	2
Jan 07	Carlisle	1	Manchester U	1
Jan 07	Charlton	0	Notts Co	2
Jan 07	Chelsea	4	Liverpool	2
Jan 07	Derby	3	Southend	2
Jan 07	Everton	4	Aston Villa	1
Jan 07	Exeter	2	Wolverhampton	2
Jan 07	Grimsby	0	Southampton	0
Jan 07	Hartlepool	2	Crystal Palace	1
Jan 07	Hull	0	Leicester	1
Jan 07	Leeds	1	Manchester C	2
Jan 07	Luton	1	Oldham	1
Jan 07	Mansfield	1	Plymouth	0
Jan 07	Middlesbrough	3	Coventry	0
Jan 07	Nottingham F	4	Swindon	1
Jan 06	Orient	1	Norwich	1
Jan 07	Peterborough	1	Newcastle	1
Jan 07	Q.P.R.	4	Wealdstone	0
Jan 07	Rotherham	1	Millwall	1
Jan 07	Sheffield U	0	Arsenal	5
Jan 07	Stoke	4	Tilbury	0
Jan 07	Sunderland	0	Bristol R	1
Jan 07	Tottenham	2	Bolton	2
Jan 07	Walsall	4	Swansea	1
Jan 07	West Ham	1	Watford	0
Jan 07	W.B.A.	4	Blackpool	1

Replays

Jan 09	Wrexham	3	Bristol C	0
Jan 10	Bolton	2	Tottenham	1
Jan 10	Millwall	2	Rotherham	0
Jan 10	Oldham	1	Luton	2
Jan 10	Southampton	0	Grimsby	0
Jan 10	Wolverhampton	3	Exeter	1
Jan 11	Manchester U	4	Carlisle	2
Jan 11	Newcastle	2	Peterborough	0
Jan 16	Grimsby played at Leicester	1	Southampton	4
Jan 16	Norwich	0	Orient	1

4th Round

Jan 28	Arsenal	2	Wolverhampton	1
Feb 06	Bolton	1	Mansfield	0
Jan 31	Brighton	1	Notts Co	2
Jan 28	Bristol R	2	Southampton	0
Jan 31	Chelsea	6	Burnley	2
Feb 01	Derby	2	Birmingham	1
Jan 28	Ipswich	4	Hartlepool	1
Jan 28	Manchester U	1	W.B.A.	1
Jan 28	Middlesbrough	3	Everton	2
Jan 31	Millwall	4	Luton	0
Jan 28	Newcastle	2	Wrexham	2
Jan 31	Nottingham F	2	Manchester C	1
Jan 28	Orient	3	Blackburn	1
Feb 06	Stoke	2	Blyth	3
Jan 28	Walsall	1	Leicester	0
Jan 28	West Ham	1	Q.P.R.	1

Replays

Jan 31	Q.P.R.	6	West Ham	1
Feb 01	W.B.A.	3	Manchester U	2
Feb 06	Wrexham	4	Newcastle	1

5th Round

Feb 18	Arsenal	4	Walsall	1
Feb 18	Bristol R	2	Ipswich	2
Feb 18	Millwall	2	Notts Co	1
Feb 18	Orient	0	Chelsea	0
Feb 18	Q.P.R.	1	Nottingham F	1
Feb 18	Wrexham	1	Blyth	1
Feb 22	Derby	2	W.B.A.	3
Feb 27	Middlesbrough	2	Bolton	0

Replays

Feb 27	Blyth	1	Wrexham	2
Feb 27	Chelsea	1	Orient	2
Feb 27	Nottingham F	1	Q.P.R.	1
Feb 28	Ipswich	3	Bristol R	0
Mar 02	Nottingham F	3	Q.P.R.	1

6th Round

Mar 11	Middlesbrough	0	Orient	0
Mar 11	Millwall	1	Ipswich	6
Mar 11	Wrexham	2	Arsenal	3
Mar 11	W.B.A.	2	Nottingham F	0

Replay

Mar 14	Orient	2	Middlesbrough	1

Semi-final

Apr 08	Arsenal played at Chelsea	3	Orient	0
Apr 08	Ipswich played at Arsenal	3	W.B.A.	1

Final

May 06	Arsenal played at Wembley	0	Ipswich	1

Season 1978-79

1st Round

Nov 25	Aldershot	1	Weymouth	1
Nov 25	Altrincham	4	Southport	3
Nov 25	Barnet	3	Woking	3
Nov 25	Barnsley	5	Worksop	1
Nov 25	Blackpool	2	Lincoln	1
Nov 25	Bournemouth	2	Hitchin	1
Nov 25	Bradford C	1	Port Vale	0
Nov 25	Carlisle	1	Halifax	0
Nov 25	Chester	1	Runcorn	1
Nov 25	Chorley	0	Scarborough	1
Nov 25	Colchester	4	Oxford	2
Nov 25	Darlington	1	Chesterfield	1
Nov 25	Dartford	1	Leamington	2
Nov 25	Doncaster	2	Huddersfield	1
Nov 25	Exeter	1	Brentford	0
Nov 25	Gravesend	1	Wimbledon	1
Nov 25	Hartlepool	1	Grimsby	0
Nov 25	Hereford	0	Newport	1
Nov 25	Hull	2	Stafford	1
Nov 25	Leatherhead	2	Merthyr T	1
Nov 25	Maidstone	1	Wycombe	0
Nov 25	Mansfield	0	Shrewsbury	2
Nov 25	Nuneaton	0	Crewe	2
Nov 25	Portsmouth	2	Northampton	0
Nov 25	Reading	0	Gillingham	0
Nov 25	Rochdale	0	Droylsden	1
Nov 25	Rotherham	3	Workington	0
Nov 25	Scunthorpe	1	Sheffield W	1
Nov 25	Southend	3	Peterborough	2
Nov 25	Stockport	5	Morecambe	1
Nov 25	Swansea	4	Hillingdon	1
Nov 25	Swindon	2	March	0
Nov 25	Tranmere	2	Boston	1
Nov 25	Walsall	0	Torquay	2
Nov 25	Watford	3	Dagenham	0
Nov 25	Wealdstone	0	Enfield	5
Nov 25	Wigan	2	Bury	2
Nov 25	Worcester	2	Plymouth	0
Nov 25	Yeovil	0	Barking	1
Nov 25	York	1	Blyth	1

Replays

Nov 28	Blyth	3	York	5
Nov 28	Bury	4	Wigan	1
Nov 28	Gillingham	1	Reading	2
Nov 28	Runcorn	0	Chester	5
Nov 28	Sheffield W	1	Scunthorpe	0
Nov 28	Wimbledon	1	Gravesend	0
Nov 28	Woking	3	Barnet	3
Nov 29	Weymouth	0	Aldershot	2
Dec 05	Barnet played at Brentford	0	Woking	3
Dec 06	Chesterfield	0	Darlington	1

2nd Round

Dec 16	Barking	1	Aldershot	2
Dec 16	Barnsley	1	Rotherham	1
Dec 16	Bury	3	Blackpool	1
Dec 16	Carlisle	3	Hull	0
Dec 16	Crewe	0	Hartlepool	1
Dec 16	Darlington	2	Chester	1
Dec 16	Doncaster	0	Shrewsbury	3
Dec 16	Droylsden	0	Altrincham	2
Dec 16	Leamington	0	Torquay	1
Dec 16	Leatherhead	1	Colchester	1
Dec 16	Maidstone	1	Exeter	0
Dec 16	Newport	0	Worcester	0
Dec 16	Portsmouth	0	Reading	1
Dec 16	Stockport	4	Bradford C	2
Dec 16	Swansea	2	Woking	2
Dec 16	Swindon	3	Enfield	0
Dec 16	Tranmere	1	Sheffield W	1
Dec 16	Watford	1	Southend	1
Dec 16	Wimbledon	1	Bournemouth	1
Dec 16	York	3	Scarborough	0

Replays

Dec 18	Southend	1	Watford	0
Dec 18	Worcester	1	Newport	2
Dec 19	Colchester	4	Leatherhead	0
Dec 19	Sheffield W	4	Tranmere	0
Dec 19	Woking	3	Swansea	5
Dec 28	Bournemouth	1	Wimbledon	2
Jan 09	Rotherham	2	Barnsley	1

3rd Round

Jan 09	Birmingham	0	Burnley	2
Jan 09	Brighton	2	Wolverhampton	3
Jan 09	Bristol C	3	Bolton	1
Jan 09	Charlton	1	Maidstone	1
Jan 09	Coventry	2	W.B.A.	2
Jan 09	Darlington	0	Colchester	1
Jan 09	Fulham	2	Q.P.R.	0
Jan 18	Hartlepool	2	Leeds	6
Jan 10	Ipswich	3	Carlisle	2
Jan 06	Leicester	3	Norwich	0
Jan 15	Manchester C	0	Rotherham	0
Jan 15	Manchester U	3	Chelsea	0
Jan 09	Middlesbrough	1	Crystal Palace	1
Jan 10	Millwall	1	Blackburn	2
Jan 16	Newcastle	3	Torquay	1
Jan 09	Newport	2	West Ham	1
Jan 10	Nottingham F	2	Aston Villa	0
Jan 09	Notts Co	4	Reading	2
Jan 09	Orient	3	Bury	2
Jan 16	Preston	3	Derby	0
Jan 09	Sheffield U	0	Aldershot	0
Jan 06	Sheffield W	1	Arsenal	1
Jan 06	Shrewsbury	3	Cambridge	1
Jan 10	Southend	0	Liverpool	0
Jan 17	Stoke	0	Oldham	1
Jan 10	Sunderland	2	Everton	1
Jan 08	Swansea	0	Bristol R	1
Jan 09	Swindon	3	Cardiff	0
Jan 10	Tottenham	1	Altrincham	1
Jan 09	Wimbledon	0	Southampton	2
Feb 01	Wrexham	6	Stockport	2
Jan 09	York	2	Luton	0

Replays
Jan 09 Arsenal 1 Sheffield W 1
Jan 15 Aldershot 1 Sheffield U 0
Jan 15 Arsenal 2 Sheffield W 2
played at Leicester
Jan 15 Crystal Palace 1 Middlesbrough 0
Jan 15 Maidstone 1 Charlton 2
Jan 15 W.B.A. 4 Coventry 0
Jan 16 Altrincham 0 Tottenham 3
Jan 17 Arsenal 3 Sheffield W 3
played at Leicester
Jan 17 Liverpool 3 Southend 0
Jan 17 Rotherham 2 Manchester C 4
Jan 22 Arsenal 2 Sheffield W 0
played at Leicester

4th Round
Jan 30 Aldershot 2 Swindon 1
Jan 27 Arsenal 2 Notts Co 0
Feb 05 Bristol R 1 Charlton 0
Feb 21 Burnley 1 Sunderland 1
Jan 29 Crystal Palace 3 Bristol C 0
Jan 31 Fulham 1 Manchester U 1
Jan 27 Ipswich 0 Orient 0
Feb 26 Leeds 3 W.B.A. 3
Jan 30 Liverpool 1 Blackburn 0
Jan 27 Newcastle 1 Wolverhampton 1
Jan 30 Newport 0 Colchester 0
Jan 27 Nottingham F 3 York 1
Feb 26 Oldham 3 Leicester 1
Feb 12 Preston 0 Southampton 1
Jan 27 Shrewsbury 2 Manchester C 0
Feb 12 Tottenham 3 Wrexham 3

Replays
Feb 05 Colchester 1 Newport 0
Feb 12 Manchester U 1 Fulham 0
Feb 21 Wrexham 2 Tottenham 3
Feb 22 Wolverhampton 1 Newcastle 0
Feb 26 Sunderland 0 Burnley 3
Jan 30 Orient 0 Ipswich 2
Mar 01 W.B.A. 2 Leeds 0

5th Round
Feb 20 Aldershot 2 Shrewsbury 2
Feb 20 Colchester 0 Manchester U 1
Feb 26 Crystal Palace 0 Wolverhampton 1
Feb 26 Ipswich 6 Bristol R 1
Feb 28 Liverpool 3 Burnley 0
Feb 26 Nottingham F 0 Arsenal 1
Feb 28 Oldham 0 Tottenham 1
Mar 10 W.B.A. 1 Southampton 1

Replays
Feb 26 Shrewsbury 3 Aldershot 1
Mar 12 Southampton 2 W.B.A. 1

6th Round
Mar 10 Ipswich 0 Liverpool 1
Mar 19 Southampton 1 Arsenal 1
Mar 10 Tottenham 1 Manchester U 1
Mar 10 Wolverhampton 1 Shrewsbury 1

Replays
Mar 13 Shrewsbury 1 Wolverhampton 3
Mar 14 Manchester U 2 Tottenham 0
Mar 21 Arsenal 2 Southampton 0

Semi-finals
Mar 31 Arsenal 2 Wolverhampton 0
played at Aston Villa
Mar 31 Liverpool 2 Manchester U 2
played at Manchester C

Replay
Apr 04 Liverpool 0 Manchester U 1
played at Everton

Final
May 12 Arsenal 3 Manchester U 2
played at Wembley

Season 1979-80

1st Round
Nov 24 Aldershot 4 Exeter 1
Nov 24 Altrincham 3 Crewe 0
Nov 24 Barking 1 Oxford 0
Nov 24 Barnsley 5 Hartlepool 2
Nov 24 Blackpool 1 Wigan 1
Nov 24 Blyth 0 Mansfield 2
Nov 24 Brandon 0 Bradford 3
Nov 24 Burton 0 Bury 2
Nov 24 Carlisle 3 Hull 3
Nov 24 Chester 5 Workington 1
Nov 24 Colchester 1 Plymouth 1
Nov 24 Darlington 1 Huddersfield 1
Nov 24 Enfield 0 Yeovil 1
Nov 24 Fareham 2 Merthyr 3
Nov 24 Gillingham 0 Wimbledon 0
Nov 24 Gravesend 0 Torquay 1
Nov 24 Grimsby 1 Chesterfield 1
Nov 24 Halifax 2 Scarborough 0
Nov 24 Harlow 2 Leytonstone 1
Nov 24 Hereford 1 Northampton 0
Nov 24 Kidderminster 0 Blackburn 2
Nov 24 Minehead 1 Chesham 2
Nov 24 Morecambe 1 Rotherham 1
Nov 24 Nuneaton 3 Northwich 3
Nov 24 Peterborough 1 Bournemouth 2
Nov 23 Port Vale 1 Doncaster 3
Nov 24 Portsmouth 1 Newport 0
Nov 24 Reading 4 Kettering 2
Nov 24 Rochdale 2 Scunthorpe 1
Nov 24 Salisbury 1 Millwall 2
Nov 24 Sheffield U 3 Burscough 0
Nov 24 Sheffield W 3 Lincoln 0
Nov 24 Slough 3 Hungerford 1
Nov 24 Stafford 3 Moor Green 2
Nov 24 Swindon 4 Brentford 1
Nov 24 Tranmere 9 Leamington 0
Nov 24 Walsall 2 Stockport 0
Nov 24 Wealdstone 0 Southend 1
Nov 24 Wycombe 0 Croydon 3
Nov 24 York 5 Mossley 2

Replays
Nov 26 Northwich 3 Nuneaton 0
Nov 27 Chesterfield 2 Grimsby 3
Nov 27 Huddersfield 0 Darlington 1
Nov 27 Plymouth 0 Colchester 1
Nov 27 Rotherham 2 Morecambe 0
Nov 27 Wimbledon 4 Gillingham 2
Nov 28 Hull 0 Carlisle 2
Nov 28 Wigan 2 Blackpool 0

2nd Round
Dec 17 Blackburn 2 Stafford 0
Dec 15 Bury 0 York 0
Dec 15 Carlisle 3 Sheffield W 0
Dec 19 Chesham 1 Merthyr 1
Dec 18 Chester 1 Barnsley 0
Dec 15 Colchester 1 Bournemouth 0
Dec 15 Croydon 1 Millwall 1
Dec 15 Darlington 0 Bradford 1
Dec 15 Doncaster 1 Mansfield 2
Dec 15 Grimsby 2 Sheffield U 0
Dec 15 Hereford 1 Aldershot 2
Jan 05 Northwich 2 Wigan 2
Dec 15 Reading 3 Barking 1
Dec 15 Rotherham 0 Altrincham 2
Dec 15 Southend 1 Harlow 1
Dec 15 Torquay 3 Swindon 3
Dec 15 Tranmere 2 Rochdale 2
Dec 15 Walsall 1 Halifax 1
Dec 18 Wimbledon 0 Portsmouth 0
Dec 15 Yeovil 1 Slough 0

Replays
Dec 18 Halifax 1 Walsall 1
Dec 18 Harlow 1 Southend 0
Dec 18 Millwall 3 Croydon 2
Dec 18 Rochdale 2 Tranmere 1
Dec 18 York 0 Bury 2
Dec 22 Merthyr 1 Chesham 3
Dec 22 Swindon 3 Torquay 2
Dec 24 Halifax 2 Walsall 0
Dec 24 Portsmouth 3 Wimbledon 3
Jan 05 Wimbledon 0 Portsmouth 1
Jan 07 Wigan 1 Northwich 0

3rd Round
Jan 05 Altrincham 1 Orient 1
Jan 05 Birmingham 2 Southampton 1
Jan 08 Blackburn 1 Fulham 1
Jan 05 Bristol C 6 Derby 2
Jan 04 Bristol R 1 Aston Villa 2
Jan 05 Burnley 1 Stoke 0
Jan 05 Cardiff 0 Arsenal 0
Jan 05 Carlisle 3 Bradford 2
Jan 14 Chelsea 0 Wigan 1
Jan 05 Chesham 0 Cambridge 2
Jan 05 Everton 4 Aldershot 1
Jan 05 Halifax 1 Manchester C 0
Jan 05 Leeds 1 Nottingham F 4
Jan 05 Leicester 1 Harlow 1
Jan 05 Liverpool 5 Grimsby 0
Jan 05 Luton 0 Swindon 2
Jan 05 Mansfield 0 Brighton 2
Jan 05 Millwall 5 Shrewsbury 1
Jan 05 Newcastle 0 Chester 2
Jan 05 Notts Co 1 Wolverhampton 3
Jan 05 Oldham 0 Coventry 1
Jan 09 Portsmouth 1 Middlesbrough 1
Jan 05 Preston 0 Ipswich 3
Jan 05 Q.P.R. 1 Watford 2
Jan 05 Reading 2 Colchester 0
Jan 08 Rochdale 1 Bury 1
Jan 05 Sunderland 0 Bolton 1
Jan 05 Swansea 2 Crystal Palace 2
Jan 05 Tottenham 1 Manchester U 1
Jan 05 Wrexham 6 Charlton 0
Jan 05 W.B.A. 1 West Ham 1
Jan 05 Yeovil 0 Norwich 3

Replays
Jan 08 Arsenal 2 Cardiff 1
Jan 08 Crystal Palace 3 Swansea 3
Jan 08 Harlow 1 Leicester 0
Jan 08 West Ham 2 W.B.A. 1
Jan 09 Manchester U 0 Tottenham 1
Jan 09 Orient 2 Altrincham 1
Jan 14 Crystal Palace 1 Swansea 2
played at Cardiff
Jan 14 Middlesbrough 3 Portsmouth 0
Jan 15 Fulham 0 Blackburn 1
Jan 21 Bury 3 Rochdale 2

4th Round
Jan 26 Arsenal 2 Brighton 0
Jan 26 Birmingham 2 Middlesbrough 1
Jan 26 Blackburn 1 Coventry 0
Jan 26 Bolton 2 Halifax 0
Jan 26 Bristol C 1 Ipswich 2
Jan 26 Bury 1 Burnley 0
Jan 26 Cambridge 1 Aston Villa 1
Jan 26 Carlisle 0 Wrexham 0
Jan 26 Chester 2 Millwall 0
Jan 26 Everton 3 Wigan 0
Jan 26 Nottingham F 0 Liverpool 2
Jan 26 Orient 2 West Ham 3
Jan 26 Swansea 4 Reading 1
Jan 26 Swindon 0 Tottenham 0
Jan 26 Watford 4 Harlow 3
Jan 26 Wolverhampton 1 Norwich 1

Replays
Jan 29 Wrexham 3 Carlisle 1
Jan 30 Aston Villa 4 Cambridge 1
Jan 30 Norwich 2 Wolverhampton 3
Jan 30 Tottenham 2 Swindon 1

5th Round
Feb 16 Blackburn 1 Aston Villa 1
Feb 16 Bolton 1 Arsenal 1
Feb 16 Everton 5 Wrexham 2
Feb 16 Ipswich 2 Chester 1
Feb 16 Liverpool 2 Bury 0
Feb 16 Tottenham 3 Birmingham 1
Feb 16 West Ham 2 Swansea 0
Feb 16 Wolverhampton 0 Watford 3

Replays
Feb 19 Arsenal 3 Bolton 0
Feb 20 Aston Villa 1 Blackburn 0

6th Round
Mar 08 Everton 2 Ipswich 1
Mar 08 Tottenham 0 Liverpool 1
Mar 08 Watford 1 Arsenal 2
Mar 08 West Ham 1 Aston Villa 0

Semi-finals
Apr 12 Arsenal 0 Liverpool 0
played at Sheffield W
Apr 12 Everton 1 West Ham 1
played at Aston Villa

Replays
Apr 16 Arsenal 1 Liverpool 1
played at Aston Villa
Apr 16 Everton 1 West Ham 2
played at Leeds
Apr 28 Arsenal 1 Liverpool 1
played at Aston Villa
May 01 Arsenal 1 Liverpool 0
played at Coventry

Final
May 10 Arsenal 0 West Ham 1
played at Wembley

Season 1980-81

1st Round
Nov 22 Addlestone 2 Brentford 2
Nov 22 Barnet 0 Minehead 2
Nov 22 Blyth 2 Burton 1
Nov 22 Boston 0 Rotherham 4
Nov 22 Burnley 1 Scarborough 0
Nov 22 Burscough 1 Altrincham 2
Nov 22 Chester 1 Barnsley 2
Nov 22 Colchester 3 Portsmouth 0
Nov 22 Darlington 0 Bury 2
Nov 22 Enfield 3 Wembley 0
Nov 22 Exeter 5 Leatherhead 0
Nov 22 Fleetwood 0 Blackpool 4
Nov 22 Gillingham 2 Dagenham 1
Nov 22 Gravesend 1 St Albans 2
Nov 22 Harlow 0 Charlton 2
Nov 22 Hull 2 Halifax 1
Nov 22 Kettering 1 Maidstone 1
Nov 22 Kidderminster 1 Millwall 1
Nov 22 Lincoln 1 Gateshead 0
Nov 22 Mansfield 3 Rochdale 1
Nov 22 Mossley 1 Crewe 0
Nov 22 Northampton 1 Peterborough 4
Nov 22 Northwich 1 Huddersfield 1
Nov 22 Oxford 1 Aldershot 0
Nov 22 Plymouth 2 Newport 0
Nov 22 Port Vale 4 Bradford C 2

Nov 22 Reading 1 Fulham 2
Nov 22 Scunthorpe 3 Hartlepool 1
Nov 22 Southend 0 Hereford 1
Nov 22 Stockport 0 Sheffield U 0
Nov 22 Sutton Coldfield 0 Doncaster 2
Nov 22 Swindon 3 Weymouth 2
Nov 22 Torquay 2 Barton 0
Nov 22 Tranmere 0 York 0
Nov 22 Walsall 3 Stafford 0
Nov 22 Wigan 2 Chesterfield 2
Nov 22 Wimbledon 7 Windsor & Eton 2
Nov 22 Workington 0 Carlisle 0
Nov 22 Wycombe 0 Bournemouth 3
Nov 22 Yeovil 2 Farnborough 1

Replays
Nov 25 Brentford 2 Addlestone 0
Nov 25 Chesterfield 2 Wigan 0
Nov 25 Huddersfield 6 Northwich 0
Nov 25 Millwall 1 Kidderminster 0
Nov 25 Minehead 1 Barnet 2
Nov 25 Sheffield U 3 Stockport 2
Nov 25 York 1 Tranmere 2
Nov 26 Maidstone 0 Kettering 0
Dec 01 Carlisle 4 Workington 1
Dec 01 Maidstone 3 Kettering 1

2nd Round
Dec 13 Barnet 0 Peterborough 1
Dec 13 Burnley 1 Port Vale 1
Dec 13 Bury 2 Lincoln 0
Dec 13 Carlisle 3 Walsall 0
Dec 13 Charlton 2 Bournemouth 1
Dec 13 Colchester 1 Yeovil 1
Dec 13 Doncaster 2 Blackpool 1
Dec 13 Enfield 2 Hereford 0
Dec 13 Fulham 1 Brentford 0
Dec 13 Gillingham 0 Maidstone 0
Dec 13 Hull 1 Blyth 1
Dec 13 Millwall 0 Exeter 1
Dec 13 Mossley 1 Mansfield 3
Dec 13 Plymouth 3 Oxford 0
Dec 13 Rotherham 0 Barnsley 1
Dec 13 Scunthorpe 0 Altrincham 0
Dec 13 Sheffield U 1 Chesterfield 1
Dec 13 St Albans 1 Torquay 1
Dec 13 Tranmere 0 Huddersfield 3
Dec 13 Wimbledon 2 Swindon 0

Replays
Dec 15 Altrincham 1 Scunthorpe 0
Dec 16 Blyth 2 Hull 2
Dec 16 Chesterfield 1 Sheffield U 0
Dec 16 Maidstone 0 Gillingham 0
Dec 16 Port Vale 2 Burnley 0
Dec 17 Torquay 4 St Albans 1
Dec 17 Yeovil 0 Colchester 2
Dec 22 Gillingham 0 Maidstone 2
Dec 22 Hull 2 Blyth 1

3rd Round
Jan 03 Barnsley 2 Torquay 1
Jan 03 Birmingham 1 Sunderland 1
Jan 03 Bury 1 Fulham 1
Jan 03 Colchester 0 Watford 1
Jan 03 Derby 0 Bristol C 0
Jan 03 Everton 2 Arsenal 0
Jan 03 Huddersfield 0 Shrewsbury 3
Jan 03 Hull 1 Doncaster 0
Jan 03 Ipswich 1 Aston Villa 0
Jan 03 Leeds 1 Coventry 1
Jan 03 Leicester 3 Cardiff 0
Jan 03 Liverpool 4 Altrincham 1
Jan 03 Maidstone 2 Exeter 4
Jan 03 Manchester C 4 Crystal Palace 0
Jan 03 Manchester U 2 Brighton 2
Jan 03 Mansfield 2 Carlisle 2
Jan 03 Newcastle 2 Sheffield W 1
Jan 03 Norwich 1 Cambridge 0
Jan 03 Nottingham F 3 Bolton 3
Jan 03 Notts Co 2 Blackburn 1
Jan 03 Orient 1 Luton 3
Jan 03 Peterborough 1 Chesterfield 1
Jan 03 Plymouth 1 Charlton 2
Jan 03 Port Vale 1 Enfield 1
Jan 03 Preston 3 Bristol R 4
Jan 03 Q.P.R. 0 Tottenham 0
Jan 03 Southampton 3 Chelsea 1
Jan 03 Stoke 2 Wolverhampton 2
Jan 03 Swansea 0 Middlesbrough 5
Jan 03 West Ham 1 Wrexham 1
Jan 03 Wimbledon 0 Oldham 0
Jan 03 W.B.A. 3 Grimsby 0

Replays
Jan 06 Bolton 0 Nottingham F 1
Jan 06 Carlisle 2 Mansfield 1
Jan 06 Chesterfield 1 Peterborough 2
Jan 06 Coventry 1 Leeds 0
Jan 06 Enfield 3 Port Vale 0
Jan 06 Fulham 0 Bury 0
Jan 06 Oldham 0 Wimbledon 1
Jan 06 Wolverhampton 2 Stoke 1
Jan 06 Wrexham 0 West Ham 0
Jan 07 Brighton 0 Manchester U 2
Jan 07 Bristol C 2 Derby 0
Jan 07 Sunderland 1 Birmingham 2
Jan 07 Tottenham 3 Q.P.R. 1
Jan 12 Bury 0 Fulham 1
played at W.B.A.
Jan 19 Wrexham 1 West Ham 0

4th Round
Jan 24 Barnsley 1 Enfield 1
Jan 24 Carlisle 1 Bristol C 1
Jan 24 Coventry 3 Birmingham 2
Jan 24 Everton 2 Liverpool 1
Jan 24 Fulham 1 Charlton 2
Jan 24 Leicester 1 Exeter 1
Jan 24 Manchester C 6 Norwich 0
Jan 24 Middlesbrough 1 W.B.A. 0
Jan 24 Newcastle 2 Luton 1
Jan 24 Nottingham F 1 Manchester U 0
Jan 24 Notts Co 0 Peterborough 1
Jan 24 Shrewsbury 0 Ipswich 0
Jan 24 Southampton 3 Bristol R 1
Jan 24 Tottenham 2 Hull 0
Jan 24 Watford 1 Wolverhampton 1
Jan 24 Wrexham 2 Wimbledon 1

Replays
Jan 27 Ipswich 3 Shrewsbury 0
Jan 27 Wolverhampton 2 Watford 1
Jan 28 Bristol C 5 Carlisle 0
Jan 28 Enfield 0 Barnsley 3
played at Tottenham
Jan 28 Exeter 3 Leicester 1

5th Round
Feb 14 Ipswich 2 Charlton 0
Feb 14 Middlesbrough 2 Barnsley 1
Feb 14 Newcastle 1 Exeter 1
Feb 14 Nottingham F 2 Bristol C 1
Feb 14 Peterborough 0 Manchester C 1
Feb 14 Southampton 0 Everton 0
Feb 14 Tottenham 3 Coventry 1
Feb 14 Wolverhampton 3 Wrexham 1

Replays
Feb 17 Everton 1 Southampton 0
Feb 18 Exeter 4 Newcastle 0

6th Round
Mar 07 Everton 2 Manchester C 2
Mar 07 Middlesbrough 1 Wolverhampton 1
Mar 07 Nottingham F 3 Ipswich 3
Mar 07 Tottenham 2 Exeter 0

Replays
Mar 10 Ipswich 1 Nottingham F 0
Mar 10 Wolverhampton 3 Middlesbrough 1
Mar 11 Manchester C 3 Everton 1

Semi-finals
Apr 11 Ipswich 0 Manchester C 1
played at Aston Villa
Apr 11 Tottenham 2 Wolverhampton 2
played at Sheffield W

Replay
Apr 15 Tottenham 3 Wolverhampton 0
played at Arsenal

Final
May 09 Manchester C 1 Tottenham 1
played at Wembley

Replay
May 14 Manchester C 2 Tottenham 3
played at Wembley

Season 1981-82

1st Round
Nov 21 Aldershot 2 Leytonstone 0
Nov 21 Bedford 0 Wimbledon 2
Nov 21 Bideford 1 Barking 2
Nov 21 Bishop Auckland 4 Nuneaton 1
Nov 21 Blyth 1 Walsall 2
Nov 21 Boston 0 Kettering 1
Nov 21 Bournemouth 1 Reading 0
Nov 21 Brentford 2 Exeter 0
Nov 20 Bristol C 0 Torquay 0
Nov 21 Bristol R 1 Fulham 2
Nov 21 Burnley 0 Runcorn 0
Nov 21 Bishop's Stortford 2 Sutton 2
Nov 21 Chesterfield 4 Preston 1
Nov 21 Colchester 2 Newport 0
Nov 21 Dagenham 2 Yeovil 2
Nov 21 Darlington 2 Carlisle 2
Nov 21 Dorchester 3 Minehead 3
Nov 21 Dover 0 Oxford 2
Nov 21 Enfield 2 Hastings 0
Nov 21 Halifax 0 Peterborough 3
Nov 21 Harlow 0 Barnet 0
Nov 21 Hendon 1 Wycombe 1
Nov 21 Hereford 3 Southend 1
Nov 21 Horden 0 Blackpool 1
Nov 21 Lincoln 2 Port Vale 2
Nov 21 Mansfield 0 Doncaster 1
Nov 21 Penrith 1 Chester 0
Nov 21 Plymouth 0 Gillingham 0
Nov 21 Portsmouth 1 Millwall 1
Nov 21 Rochdale 2 Hull 2
Nov 21 Scunthorpe 1 Bradford C 0
Nov 21 Sheffield U 2 Altrincham 2
Nov 21 Stafford 1 York 2
Nov 21 Stockport 3 Mossley 1
Nov 21 Swindon 2 Taunton 1
Nov 21 Tranmere 1 Bury 1
Nov 21 Weymouth 0 Northampton 0
Nov 21 Wigan 2 Hartlepool 2
Nov 21 Willenhall 0 Crewe 1
Nov 21 Workington 1 Huddersfield 1

Replays
Nov 23 Altrincham 3 Sheffield U 0
Nov 23 Minehead 0 Dorchester 4
Nov 24 Barnet 1 Harlow 0
Nov 24 Bury 3 Tranmere 1
Nov 24 Carlisle 3 Darlington 1
Nov 24 Gillingham 1 Plymouth 0
Nov 24 Huddersfield 5 Workington 0
Nov 24 Hull 2 Rochdale 2
Nov 24 Northampton 6 Weymouth 2
Nov 24 Runcorn 1 Burnley 2
Nov 24 Sutton 2 Bishop's Stortford 1
Nov 24 Wycombe 2 Hendon 0
Nov 25 Hartlepool 1 Wigan 0
Nov 25 Millwall 3 Portsmouth 2
Nov 25 Torquay 1 Bristol C 2
Nov 25 Yeovil 0 Dagenham 1
Nov 30 Hull 1 Rochdale 0
played at Leeds
Nov 30 Port Vale 0 Lincoln 0
Dec 02 Port Vale 2 Lincoln 0

2nd Round
Dec 15 Aldershot 2 Oxford 2
Dec 15 Barnet 2 Wycombe 0
Jan 09 Bishop Auckland 0 Carlisle 1
played at Workington
Dec 16 Brentford 1 Colchester 1
Dec 15 Bristol C 3 Northampton 0
Jan 02 Bury 1 Burnley 1
Dec 12 Chesterfield 0 Huddersfield 1
Jan 02 Crewe 1 Scunthorpe 3
Dec 30 Dagenham 1 Millwall 2
Dec 12 Doncaster 3 Penrith 0
Dec 12 Dorchester 1 Bournemouth 1
Dec 15 Enfield 4 Wimbledon 1
Dec 15 Gillingham 1 Barking 1
Jan 02 Hereford 1 Fulham 0
Jan 04 Hull 2 Hartlepool 0
Jan 02 Kettering 0 Blackpool 3
Jan 02 Peterborough 2 Walsall 1
Jan 02 Port Vale 4 Stockport 1
Dec 15 Swindon 2 Sutton 1
Dec 12 York 0 Altrincham 0

Replays
Dec 15 Bournemouth 2 Dorchester 1
Dec 30 Colchester 1 Brentford 0
Dec 30 Oxford 4 Aldershot 2
Jan 02 Altrincham 4 York 3
Jan 02 Barking 3 Gillingham 3
Jan 04 Burnley 2 Bury 1

3rd Round
Jan 02 Barnet 0 Brighton 0
Jan 05 Barnsley 0 Blackpool 2
Jan 02 Birmingham 2 Ipswich 3
Jan 02 Bolton 3 Derby 1
Jan 02 Bournemouth 0 Oxford 2
Jan 18 Burnley 6 Altrincham 1
Jan 23 Carlisle 2 Huddersfield 3
Jan 18 Chelsea 0 Hull 0
Jan 02 Coventry 3 Sheffield W 1
Jan 02 Doncaster 2 Cambridge 1
Jan 02 Enfield 2 Crystal Palace 3
Jan 05 Gillingham 2 Oldham 1
Jan 02 Leicester 3 Southampton 1
Jan 02 Luton 2 Swindon 1
Jan 02 Manchester C 3 Cardiff 1
Jan 05 Millwall 1 Grimsby 6
Jan 04 Newcastle 1 Colchester 1
Jan 02 Nottingham F 1 Wrexham 3
Jan 05 Notts Co 0 Aston Villa 6
Jan 02 Orient 1 Charlton 0
Jan 06 Peterborough 0 Bristol C 1
Jan 02 Q.P.R. 1 Middlesbrough 1
Jan 02 Rotherham 1 Sunderland 1
Jan 06 Scunthorpe 1 Hereford 1
Jan 05 Shrewsbury 1 Port Vale 0
Jan 02 Stoke 0 Norwich 1
Jan 02 Swansea 0 Liverpool 4
Jan 02 Tottenham 1 Arsenal 0
Jan 02 Watford 1 Manchester U 0
Jan 02 West Ham 2 Everton 1
Jan 02 Wolverhampton 1 Leeds 3
Jan 02 W.B.A. 3 Blackburn 2

Replays
Jan 05 Brighton 3 Barnet 1
Jan 18 Colchester 3 Newcastle 4
Jan 18 Middlesbrough 2 Q.P.R. 3
Jan 18 Sunderland 1 Rotherham 0
Jan 20 Hereford 4 Scunthorpe 1
Jan 21 Hull 0 Chelsea 2

4th Round
Jan 23 Blackpool 0 Q.P.R. 0
Jan 23 Brighton 0 Oxford 3
Jan 23 Bristol C 0 Aston Villa 1
Jan 23 Chelsea 0 Wrexham 0
Jan 23 Crystal Palace 1 Bolton 0
Jan 23 Gillingham 0 W.B.A. 1
Jan 23 Hereford 0 Leicester 1
Jan 26 Huddersfield 1 Orient 1
Jan 23 Luton 0 Ipswich 3
Jan 23 Manchester C 1 Coventry 3
Jan 23 Newcastle 1 Grimsby 2
Jan 23 Norwich 2 Doncaster 1

Jan 23 Shrewsbury 1 Burnley 0
Jan 23 Sunderland 0 Liverpool 3
Jan 23 Tottenham 1 Leeds 0
Jan 23 Watford 2 West Ham 0

Replays
Jan 26 Q.P.R. 5 Blackpool 1
Jan 26 Wrexham 1 Chelsea 1
Feb 01 Orient 2 Huddersfield 0
Feb 01 Wrexham 1 Chelsea 2

5th Round
Feb 13 Chelsea 2 Liverpool 0
Feb 13 Coventry 4 Oxford 0
Feb 13 Crystal Palace 0 Orient 0
Feb 13 Leicester 2 Watford 0
Feb 13 Q.P.R. 3 Grimsby 1
Feb 13 Shrewsbury 2 Ipswich 1
Feb 13 Tottenham 1 Aston Villa 0
Feb 13 W.B.A. 1 Norwich 0

Replay
Feb 16 Orient 0 Crystal Palace 1

6th Round
Mar 06 Chelsea 2 Tottenham 3
Mar 06 Leicester 5 Shrewsbury 2
Mar 06 Q.P.R. 1 Crystal Palace 0
Mar 06 W.B.A. 2 Coventry 0

Semi-finals
Apr 03 Leicester 0 Tottenham 2
played at Aston Villa
Apr 03 Q.P.R. 1 W.B.A. 0
played at Arsenal

Final
May 22 Q.P.R. 1 Tottenham 1
played at Wembley

Replay
May 27 Q.P.R. 0 Tottenham 1
played at Wembley

Season 1982-83

1st Round
Nov 20 Aldershot 4 Wimborne 0
Nov 20 Altrincham 2 Rochdale 1
Nov 20 Blackpool 3 Horwich Rmi 0
Nov 20 Boston 3 Crewe 1
Nov 20 Bournemouth 0 Southend 2
Nov 20 Bristol R 1 Wycombe 0
Nov 20 Carshalton 4 Barnet 0
Nov 20 Chesham 0 Yeovil 1
Nov 20 Chester 1 Northwich 1
Nov 20 Chesterfield 2 Peterborough 2
Nov 20 Colchester 0 Torquay 2
Nov 20 Darlington 0 Scunthorpe 1
Nov 20 Enfield 0 Newport 0
Nov 20 Gillingham 1 Dagenham 0
Nov 20 Halifax 0 North Shields 1
Nov 20 Hartlepool 3 Lincoln 0
Nov 20 Holbeach 0 Wrexham 4
Nov 20 Huddersfield 1 Mossley 0
Nov 20 Hull 1 Sheffield U 1
Nov 20 Macclesfield 1 Worcester 5
Nov 20 Mansfield 3 Stockport 2
Nov 20 Northampton 2 Wimbledon 2
Nov 20 Orient 4 Bristol C 1
Nov 20 Oxford 5 Folkestone 2
Nov 20 Plymouth 2 Exeter 0
Nov 20 Port Vale 0 Bradford C 1
Nov 20 Portsmouth 4 Hereford 1
Nov 20 Preston 5 Shepshed 1
Nov 20 Reading 1 Bishop's Stortford 2
Nov 20 Slough 1 Millwall 0
Nov 20 Swindon 2 Wealdstone 0
Nov 20 Tranmere 4 Scarborough 2
Nov 20 Walsall 3 Kettering 0
Nov 20 Weymouth 4 Maidstone 3
Nov 21 Wigan 0 Telford 0
Nov 20 Windsor & Eton 0 Brentford 7
Nov 20 Wokingham 1 Cardiff 1
Nov 20 Workington 1 Doncaster 2
Nov 20 Worthing 2 Dartford 1
Nov 20 York 3 Bury 1

Replays
Nov 22 Northwich 3 Chester 1
Nov 23 Cardiff 3 Wokingham 0
Nov 23 Newport 4 Enfield 2
Nov 23 Sheffield U 2 Hull 0
Nov 23 Telford 2 Wigan 1
Nov 23 Wimbledon 0 Northampton 2
Nov 24 Peterborough 2 Chesterfield 1

2nd Round
Dec 11 Altrincham 0 Huddersfield 1
Dec 11 Boston 1 Sheffield U 1
Dec 11 Bristol R 2 Plymouth 2
Dec 11 Cardiff 2 Weymouth 3
Dec 11 Gillingham 1 Northampton 1
Dec 11 Hartlepool 1 York 1
Dec 11 Mansfield 1 Bradford C 1
Dec 11 Newport 1 Orient 0
Dec 11 North Shields 0 Walsall 3
Dec 11 Oxford 4 Worthing 0
Dec 11 Peterborough 5 Doncaster 2
Dec 11 Portsmouth 1 Aldershot 3
Dec 11 Preston 2 Blackpool 1
Abandoned In Et
Dec 11 Scunthorpe 2 Northwich 1
Dec 11 Slough 1 Bishop's Stortford 4
Dec 11 Southend 3 Yeovil 0
Dec 11 Swindon 2 Brentford 2
Dec 11 Telford 1 Tranmere 1
Dec 11 Torquay 4 Carshalton 1
Dec 11 Worcester 2 Wrexham 1

Replays
Dec 14 Brentford 1 Swindon 3
Dec 14 Northampton 3 Gillingham 2
Dec 14 Sheffield U 5 Boston 1
Dec 14 Tranmere 2 Telford 1
Dec 14 York 4 Hartlepool 0
Dec 15 Bradford C 3 Mansfield 2
Dec 20 Plymouth 1 Bristol R 0

3rd Round
Jan 08 Arsenal 2 Bolton 1
Jan 08 Blackburn 1 Liverpool 2
Jan 08 Bradford C 0 Barnsley 1
Jan 08 Brighton 1 Newcastle 1
Jan 08 Cambridge 1 Weymouth 0
Jan 08 Carlisle 2 Burnley 2
Jan 08 Charlton 2 Ipswich 3
Jan 08 Coventry 3 Worcester 1
Jan 08 Crystal Palace 2 York 1
Jan 08 Derby 2 Nottingham F 0
Jan 08 Huddersfield 1 Chelsea 1
Jan 08 Leeds 3 Preston 0
Jan 08 Leicester 2 Notts Co 3
Jan 08 Luton 3 Peterborough 0
Jan 08 Manchester U 2 West Ham 0
Jan 08 Middlesbrough 2 Bishop's Stortford 2
Jan 08 Newport 1 Everton 1
Jan 08 Northampton 0 Aston Villa 1
Jan 08 Norwich 2 Swansea 1
Jan 08 Oldham 0 Fulham 2
Jan 08 Oxford 1 Torquay 1
Jan 08 Scunthorpe 0 Grimsby 0
Jan 08 Sheffield U 0 Stoke 0
Jan 08 Shrewsbury 2 Rotherham 1
Jan 08 Southend 0 Sheffield W 0
Jan 08 Sunderland 0 Manchester C 0
Jan 08 Swindon 7 Aldershot 0
Jan 08 Tottenham 1 Southampton 0
Jan 08 Tranmere 0 Wolverhampton 1
Jan 08 Walsall 0 Birmingham 0
Jan 08 Watford 2 Plymouth 0
Jan 08 W.B.A. 3 Q.P.R. 2

Replays
Jan 11 Birmingham 1 Walsall 0
Jan 11 Burnley 3 Carlisle 1
Jan 11 Bishop's Stortford 1 Middlesbrough 2
Jan 11 Everton 2 Newport 1
Jan 11 Grimsby 2 Scunthorpe 0
Jan 11 Sheffield W 2 Southend 2
Jan 12 Chelsea 2 Huddersfield 0
Jan 12 Manchester C 2 Sunderland 1
Jan 12 Newcastle 0 Brighton 1
Jan 12 Stoke 3 Sheffield U 2
Jan 12 Torquay 2 Oxford 1
Jan 24 Sheffield W 2 Southend 1

4th Round
Jan 29 Arsenal 1 Leeds 1
Jan 29 Aston Villa 1 Wolverhampton 0
Jan 29 Brighton 4 Manchester C 0
Jan 29 Burnley 3 Swindon 1
Jan 29 Cambridge 1 Barnsley 0
Jan 29 Coventry 2 Norwich 2
Jan 29 Crystal Palace 1 Birmingham 0
Jan 29 Derby 2 Chelsea 1
Jan 30 Everton 2 Shrewsbury 1
Jan 29 Ipswich 2 Grimsby 0
Jan 29 Liverpool 2 Stoke 0
Jan 29 Luton 0 Manchester U 2
Jan 29 Middlesbrough 2 Notts Co 0
Jan 29 Torquay 2 Sheffield W 3
Jan 29 Tottenham 2 W.B.A. 1
Jan 29 Watford 1 Fulham 1

Replays
Feb 01 Fulham 1 Watford 2
Feb 02 Leeds 1 Arsenal 1
Feb 02 Norwich 2 Coventry 1
Feb 09 Arsenal 2 Leeds 1

5th Round
Feb 19 Aston Villa 4 Watford 1
Feb 19 Cambridge 1 Sheffield W 2
Feb 19 Crystal Palace 0 Burnley 0
Feb 19 Derby 0 Manchester U 1
Feb 19 Everton 2 Tottenham 0
Feb 20 Liverpool 1 Brighton 2
Feb 19 Middlesbrough 1 Arsenal 1
Feb 19 Norwich 1 Ipswich 0

Replays
Feb 28 Arsenal 3 Middlesbrough 2
Feb 28 Burnley 1 Crystal Palace 0

6th Round
Mar 12 Arsenal 2 Aston Villa 0
Mar 12 Brighton 1 Norwich 0
Mar 12 Burnley 1 Sheffield W 1
Mar 12 Manchester U 1 Everton 0

Replay
Mar 16 Sheffield W 5 Burnley 0

Semi-finals
Apr 16 Arsenal 1 Manchester U 2
played at Aston Villa
Apr 16 Brighton 2 Sheffield W 1
played at Arsenal

Final
May 21 Brighton 2 Manchester U 2
played at Wembley

Replay
May 26 Brighton 0 Manchester U 4
played at Wembley

Season 1983-84

1st Round
Nov 19 Aldershot 1 Worcester 1
Nov 19 Barking 2 Farnborough 1
Nov 19 Barnet 0 Bristol R 0
Nov 19 Boston 0 Bury 3
Nov 19 Bournemouth 4 Walsall 0
Nov 19 Bradford C 0 Wigan 0
Nov 19 Hyde 0 Burnley 2
Nov 19 Burton 1 Windsor & Eton 2
Nov 19 Chelmsford 0 Wycombe 0
Nov 19 Chester 1 Chesterfield 2
Nov 19 Corinthians 0 Bristol C 0
Nov 19 Dagenham 2 Brentford 2
Nov 19 Darlington 5 Mossley 0
Nov 19 Exeter 1 Maidstone 1
Nov 19 Frickley 0 Altrincham 1
Nov 19 Gainsborough 0 Blackpool 2
Nov 19 Halifax 2 Whitby 3
Nov 19 Kettering 0 Swindon 7
Nov 19 Leamington 0 Gillingham 1
Nov 19 Macclesfield 0 York 0
Nov 19 Mansfield 3 Doncaster 0
Nov 19 Millwall 2 Dartford 1
Nov 19 Northampton 1 Waterlooville 1
Nov 19 Northwich 1 Bangor 1
Nov 19 Oxford 2 Peterborough 0
Nov 19 Penrith 0 Hull 2
Nov 20 Poole 0 Newport 0
Nov 19 Port Vale 1 Lincoln 2
Nov 19 Reading 2 Hereford 0
Nov 19 Rochdale 1 Crewe 0
Nov 19 Rotherham 0 Hartlepool 0
Nov 19 Scunthorpe 1 Preston 0
Nov 19 Southend 0 Plymouth 0
Nov 19 Telford 3 Stockport 0
Nov 19 Torquay 1 Colchester 2
Nov 19 Tranmere 2 Bolton 2
Nov 19 Wealdstone 1 Enfield 1
Nov 19 Wimbledon 2 Orient 1
Nov 19 Wrexham 1 Sheffield U 5
Nov 19 Yeovil 0 Harrow 1

Replays
Nov 21 Worcester 2 Aldershot 1
Nov 22 Bangor 1 Northwich 0
Nov 22 Bolton 4 Tranmere 1
Nov 22 Brentford 2 Dagenham 1
Nov 22 Bristol R 3 Barnet 1
Nov 22 Enfield 2 Wealdstone 2
Nov 22 Newport 3 Poole 1
Nov 22 Plymouth 2 Southend 0
Nov 22 Wycombe 1 Chelmsford 2
Nov 22 York 2 Macclesfield 0
Nov 23 Bristol C 4 Corinthians 0
Nov 23 Hartlepool 0 Rotherham 1
Nov 23 Maidstone 2 Exeter 1
Nov 23 Waterlooville 1 Northampton 1
Nov 28 Northampton 2 Waterlooville 0
Nov 28 Wealdstone 2 Enfield 0
Nov 28 Wigan 4 Bradford C 2

2nd Round
Dec 10 Bangor 1 Blackpool 1
Dec 10 Bolton 2 Mansfield 0
Dec 10 Brentford 3 Wimbledon 2
Dec 10 Bristol R 1 Bristol C 2
Dec 10 Chesterfield 2 Burnley 2
Dec 10 Colchester 4 Wealdstone 0
Dec 10 Darlington 0 Altrincham 0
Dec 10 Gillingham 6 Chelmsford 1
Dec 10 Harrow 1 Newport 3
Dec 10 Lincoln 0 Sheffield U 0

Date	Home		Away	
Dec 10	Maidstone	3	Worcester	2
Dec 10	Millwall	2	Swindon	3
Dec 10	Northampton	1	Telford	1
Dec 10	Plymouth	2	Barking	1
Dec 10	Reading	1	Oxford	1
Dec 10	Rotherham	2	Hull	1
Dec 10	Scunthorpe	2	Bury	0
Dec 10	Wigan	1	Whitby	0
Dec 13	Windsor & Eton	0	Bournemouth	0
Dec 13	York	0	Rochdale	2

Replays

Date	Home		Away	
Dec 13	Blackpool	2	Bangor	1
Dec 14	Altrincham	0	Darlington	2
Dec 14	Oxford	3	Reading	0
Dec 14	Telford	3	Northampton	2
Dec 19	Bournemouth	2	Windsor & Eton	0
Dec 19	Burnley	3	Chesterfield	2
Dec 19	Sheffield U	1	Lincoln	0

3rd Round

Date	Home		Away	
Jan 07	Aston Villa	1	Norwich	1
Jan 07	Blackburn	1	Chelsea	0
Jan 07	Blackpool	2	Manchester C	1
Jan 07	Bolton	0	Sunderland	3
Jan 07	Bournemouth	2	Manchester U	0
Jan 07	Brighton	2	Swansea	0
Jan 07	Burnley	0	Oxford	0
Jan 07	Cambridge	0	Derby	3
Jan 07	Cardiff	0	Ipswich	3
Jan 07	Carlisle	1	Swindon	1
Jan 07	Colchester	0	Charlton	1
Jan 07	Coventry	1	Wolverhampton	1
Jan 07	Crystal Palace	1	Leicester	0
Jan 07	Darlington	4	Maidstone	1
Jan 07	Fulham	0	Tottenham	0
Jan 07	Gillingham	5	Brentford	3
Jan 07	Huddersfield	2	Q.P.R.	1
Jan 07	Leeds	1	Scunthorpe	1
Jan 06	Liverpool	4	Newcastle	0
Jan 07	Luton	2	Watford	2
Jan 07	Middlesbrough	3	Arsenal	2
Jan 07	Nottingham F	1	Southampton	2
Jan 07	Plymouth	2	Newport	2
Jan 07	Portsmouth	2	Grimsby	1
Jan 07	Rochdale	1	Telford	4
Jan 07	Rotherham	0	W.B.A.	0
Jan 07	Sheffield U	1	Birmingham	1
Jan 07	Sheffield W	1	Barnsley	0
Jan 07	Shrewsbury	3	Oldham	0
Jan 07	Stoke	0	Everton	2
Jan 07	West Ham	1	Wigan	0
Jan 08	Notts Co	2	Bristol C	2

Replays

Date	Home		Away	
Jan 10	Birmingham	2	Sheffield U	0
Jan 10	Bristol C	0	Notts Co	2
Jan 10	Newport	0	Plymouth	1
Jan 10	Scunthorpe	1	Leeds	1
Jan 10	Swindon	3	Carlisle	1
Jan 10	Watford	4	Luton	3
Jan 10	Wolverhampton	1	Coventry	1
Jan 11	Norwich	3	Aston Villa	0
Jan 11	Oxford	2	Burnley	1
Jan 11	Tottenham	2	Fulham	0
Jan 11	W.B.A.	3	Rotherham	0
Jan 16	Coventry	3	Wolverhampton	0
Jan 16	Scunthorpe	4	Leeds	2

4th Round

Date	Home		Away	
Jan 29	Brighton	2	Liverpool	0
Jan 28	Charlton	0	Watford	2
Jan 28	Crystal Palace	1	West Ham	1
Feb 01	Derby	3	Telford	2
Jan 28	Everton	0	Gillingham	0
Feb 01	Huddersfield	1	Notts Co	2
Jan 31	Middlesbrough	2	Bournemouth	0
Jan 28	Oxford	2	Blackpool	1
Jan 28	Plymouth	2	Darlington	1
Jan 28	Portsmouth	0	Southampton	1
Jan 30	Sheffield W	3	Coventry	2
Jan 28	Shrewsbury	2	Ipswich	0
Jan 28	Sunderland	1	Birmingham	2
Jan 28	Swindon	1	Blackburn	2
Jan 28	Tottenham	0	Norwich	0
Feb 01	W.B.A.	1	Scunthorpe	0

Replays

Date	Home		Away	
Jan 31	Gillingham	0	Everton	0
Jan 31	West Ham	2	Crystal Palace	0
Feb 01	Norwich	2	Tottenham	1
Feb 06	Gillingham	0	Everton	3

5th Round

Date	Home		Away	
Feb 18	Birmingham	3	West Ham	0
Feb 17	Blackburn	0	Southampton	1
Feb 18	Derby	2	Norwich	1
Feb 18	Everton	3	Shrewsbury	0
Feb 18	Notts Co	1	Middlesbrough	0
Feb 18	Oxford	0	Sheffield W	3
Feb 18	Watford	3	Brighton	1
Feb 18	W.B.A.	0	Plymouth	1

6th Round

Date	Home		Away	
Mar 10	Birmingham	1	Watford	3
Mar 10	Notts Co	1	Everton	2
Mar 10	Plymouth	0	Derby	0
Mar 11	Sheffield W	0	Southampton	0

Replays

Date	Home		Away	
Mar 14	Derby	0	Plymouth	1
Mar 20	Southampton	5	Sheffield W	1

Semi-finals

Date	Home		Away	
Apr 14	Everton	1	Southampton	0
	played at Arsenal			
Apr 14	Plymouth	0	Watford	1
	played at Aston Villa			

Final

Date	Home		Away	
May 19	Everton	2	Watford	0
	played at Wembley			

Season 1984-85

1st Round

Date	Home		Away	
Nov 17	Bangor	1	Tranmere	1
Nov 17	Barry	1	Reading	2
Nov 17	Blackpool	0	Altrincham	1
Nov 17	Bradford C	7	Tow Law	2
Nov 17	Brentford	4	Bishop's Stortford	0
Nov 17	Bristol R	2	Kings Lynn	1
Nov 17	Buckingham	0	Orient	2
Nov 17	Burton	2	Staines	0
Nov 17	Cambridge	0	Peterborough	2
Nov 19	Dagenham	0	Swindon	0
Nov 17	Darlington	3	Chester	2
Nov 17	Exeter	2	Enfield	2
Nov 17	Fisher	0	Bristol C	1
Nov 17	Frickley	2	Stalybridge	1
Nov 17	Gillingham	2	Windsor & Eton	1
Nov 17	Halifax	2	Goole	0
Nov 17	Hartlepool	2	Derby	1
Nov 17	Hereford	3	Farnborough	0
Nov 17	Hull	2	Bolton	1
Nov 17	Kettering	0	Bournemouth	0
Nov 17	Lincoln	1	Telford	1
Nov 17	Macclesfield	1	Port Vale	2
Nov 17	Mansfield	2	Rotherham	1
Nov 17	Met. Police	0	Dartford	3
Nov 17	Newport	1	Aldershot	1
Nov 17	Northampton	2	Rugby	2

Manchester United's Whiteside, Moran and Bailey parade the trophy after defeating Everton in the 1985 Final.

Nov 17 Northwich 3 Crewe 1
Nov 17 Nuneaton 1 Scunthorpe 1
Nov 17 Penrith 0 Burnley 9
Nov 17 Plymouth 3 Barnet 0
Nov 17 Preston 4 Bury 3
Nov 17 Rochdale 1 Doncaster 2
Nov 17 Southend 2 Colchester 2
Nov 17 Stockport 1 Walsall 2
Nov 17 Swansea 1 Bognor Regis 1
Nov 17 Torquay 2 Yeovil 0
Nov 17 Weymouth 0 Millwall 3
Nov 17 Whitby 1 Chesterfield 3
Nov 17 Wrexham 0 Wigan 2
Nov 17 York 2 Blue Star 0

Replays
Nov 20 Aldershot 4 Newport 0
Nov 20 Bournemouth 3 Kettering 2
Nov 20 Enfield 3 Exeter 0
Nov 20 Scunthorpe 2 Nuneaton 1
Nov 20 Telford 2 Lincoln 1
Nov 20 Tranmere 7 Bangor 0
Nov 21 Bognor Regis 3 Swansea 1
Nov 21 Colchester 3 Southend 2
Nov 21 Rugby 0 Northampton 1
Nov 26 Swindon 1 Dagenham 2

2nd Round
Dec 08 Aldershot 0 Burton 2
Dec 08 Altrincham 1 Doncaster 3
Dec 08 Bradford C 2 Mansfield 1
Dec 08 Brentford 2 Northampton 2
Dec 08 Bristol C 1 Bristol R 3
Dec 08 Burnley 3 Halifax 1
Dec 08 Colchester 0 Gillingham 5
Dec 08 Dagenham 1 Peterborough 0
Dec 08 Darlington 1 Frickley 0
Dec 08 Dartford 1 Bournemouth 1
Dec 08 Hartlepool 0 York 2
Dec 08 Millwall 1 Enfield 0
Dec 08 Orient 3 Torquay 0
Dec 08 Plymouth 0 Hereford 0
Dec 07 Port Vale 4 Scunthorpe 1
Dec 08 Preston 1 Telford 4
Dec 08 Reading 6 Bognor Regis 2
Dec 08 Tranmere 0 Hull 3
Dec 08 Walsall 1 Chesterfield 0
Dec 08 Wigan 2 Northwich 1

Replays
Dec 11 Bournemouth 4 Dartford 1
Dec 12 Hereford 2 Plymouth 0
Dec 17 Northampton 0 Brentford 2

3rd Round
Jan 05 Barnsley 4 Reading 3
Jan 05 Birmingham 0 Norwich 0
Jan 05 Brighton 1 Hull 0
Jan 05 Bristol R 1 Ipswich 2
Jan 05 Burton 1 Leicester 6
played at Derby, replayed
Jan 05 Carlisle 1 Dagenham 0
Jan 05 Chelsea 2 Wigan 2
Jan 05 Coventry 2 Manchester C 1
Jan 05 Doncaster 1 Q.P.R. 0
Jan 05 Fulham 2 Sheffield W 3
Jan 21 Gillingham 2 Cardiff 1
Jan 05 Hereford 1 Arsenal 1
Jan 04 Leeds 0 Everton 2
Jan 05 Liverpool 3 Aston Villa 0
Jan 05 Luton 1 Stoke 1
Jan 05 Manchester U 3 Bournemouth 0
Jan 05 Middlesbrough 0 Darlington 0
Jan 05 Millwall 1 Crystal Palace 1
Jan 06 Nottingham F 1 Newcastle 1
Jan 05 Notts Co 2 Grimsby 2
Jan 05 Oldham 2 Brentford 1
Jan 05 Orient 2 W.B.A. 1
Jan 05 Portsmouth 0 Blackburn 0
Jan 05 Shrewsbury 0 Oxford 2
Jan 05 Southampton 4 Sunderland 0
Jan 05 Telford 2 Bradford C 1
Jan 05 Tottenham 1 Charlton 1
Jan 05 Watford 5 Sheffield U 0
Jan 05 West Ham 4 Port Vale 1
Jan 05 Wimbledon 3 Burnley 1
Jan 05 Wolverhampton 1 Huddersfield 1
Jan 05 York 3 Walsall 0

Replays
Jan 08 Darlington 2 Middlesbrough 1
Jan 08 Grimsby 4 Notts Co 2
Jan 09 Newcastle 1 Nottingham F 3
Jan 09 Stoke 2 Luton 3
Jan 16 Burton 0 Leicester 1
played at Coventry
Jan 21 Arsenal 7 Hereford 2
Jan 23 Charlton 1 Tottenham 2
Jan 23 Crystal Palace 1 Millwall 2
Jan 23 Huddersfield 3 Wolverhampton 1
Jan 23 Norwich 1 Birmingham 1
Jan 26 Birmingham 1 Norwich 1
Jan 26 Blackburn 2 Portsmouth 1
Jan 26 Wigan 0 Chelsea 5
Jan 28 Norwich 1 Birmingham 0

4th Round
Jan 26 Barnsley 2 Brighton 1
Feb 04 Chelsea 2 Millwall 3
Jan 29 Darlington 1 Telford 1
Jan 26 Everton 2 Doncaster 0
Jan 26 Grimsby 1 Watford 3
Jan 26 Ipswich 3 Gillingham 2
Jan 26 Leicester 1 Carlisle 0
Jan 27 Liverpool 1 Tottenham 0
Jan 26 Luton 2 Huddersfield 0
Jan 26 Manchester U 2 Coventry 1
Jan 26 Nottingham F 0 Wimbledon 0
Jan 26 Orient 0 Southampton 2
Jan 30 Oxford 0 Blackburn 1
Jan 26 Sheffield W 5 Oldham 1
Feb 04 West Ham 2 Norwich 1
Jan 26 York 1 Arsenal 0

Replays
Jan 30 Wimbledon 1 Nottingham F 0
Feb 04 Telford 3 Darlington 0

5th Round
Feb 15 Blackburn 0 Manchester U 2
Feb 16 Everton 3 Telford 0
Mar 04 Ipswich 3 Sheffield W 2
Mar 04 Luton 0 Watford 0
Feb 19 Millwall 2 Leicester 0
Mar 04 Southampton 1 Barnsley 2
Mar 04 Wimbledon 1 West Ham 1
Feb 16 York 1 Liverpool 1

Replays
Feb 20 Liverpool 7 York 0
Mar 06 Watford 2 Luton 2
Mar 06 West Ham 5 Wimbledon 1
Mar 09 Luton 1 Watford 0

6th Round
Mar 10 Barnsley 0 Liverpool 4
Mar 09 Everton 2 Ipswich 2
Mar 13 Luton 1 Millwall 0
Mar 09 Manchester U 4 West Ham 2

Replay
Mar 13 Ipswich 0 Everton 1

Semi-finals
Apr 13 Everton 2 Luton 1
played at Aston Villa
Apr 13 Liverpool 2 Manchester U 2
played at Everton

Replay
Apr 17 Liverpool 1 Manchester U 2
played at Manchester C

Final
May 18 Everton 0 Manchester U 1
played at Wembley

Season 1985-86

1st Round
Nov 16 Bournemouth 0 Dartford 0
Nov 16 Brentford 1 Bristol R 3
Nov 16 Bury 2 Chester 0
Nov 16 Bishop's Stortford 2 Peterborough 2
Nov 16 Chelmsford 1 Weymouth 0
Nov 16 Chorley 0 Altrincham 2
Nov 16 Dagenham 2 Cambridge 1
Nov 16 Derby 5 Crewe 1
Nov 16 Enfield 0 Bognor Regis 2
Nov 16 Exeter 1 Cardiff 1
Nov 16 Fareham 0 Maidstone 3
Nov 16 Farnborough 0 Bath 4
Nov 16 Frickley 1 Halesowen 1
Nov 16 Gillingham 3 Northampton 0
Nov 16 Halifax 1 Scunthorpe 3
Nov 16 Lincoln 0 Blackpool 1
Nov 16 Macclesfield 1 Hartlepool 2
Nov 16 Mansfield 1 Port Vale 1
Nov 17 Notts Co 6 Scarborough 1
Nov 16 Nuneaton 2 Burnley 3
Nov 16 Plymouth 1 Aldershot 0
Nov 16 Reading 1 Wealdstone 0
Nov 16 Rochdale 2 Darlington 1
Nov 16 Rotherham 6 Wolverhampton 0
Nov 16 Rugby 2 Orient 2
Nov 16 Runcorn 2 Boston 2
Nov 16 Slough 2 Aylesbury 2
Nov 16 Southend 0 Newport 1
Nov 16 Stockport 0 Telford 1
Nov 16 Swansea 2 Leyton Wingate 0
Nov 17 Swindon 0 Bristol C 0
Nov 16 Tranmere 2 Chesterfield 2
Nov 16 Walsall 7 Preston 3
Nov 16 Whitby 1 South Liverpool 0
Nov 16 Wigan 4 Doncaster 1
Nov 16 Windsor & Eton 1 Torquay 1
Nov 16 Wrexham 3 Bolton 1
Nov 16 Wycombe 2 Colchester 0
Nov 16 Yeovil 2 Hereford 4
Nov 16 York 0 Morecambe 0

Replays
Nov 18 Port Vale 1 Mansfield 0
Nov 19 Aylesbury 2 Slough 5
Nov 19 Chesterfield 0 Tranmere 1
Nov 19 Dartford 0 Bournemouth 2
Nov 19 Halesowen 1 Frickley 3
Nov 19 Morecambe 0 York 2
Nov 19 Orient 4 Rugby 1
Nov 19 Torquay 3 Windsor & Eton 0
Nov 20 Boston 1 Runcorn 1
Nov 20 Bristol C 4 Swindon 2
Nov 20 Peterborough 3 Bishop's Stortford 1
Nov 25 Runcorn 4 Boston 1

2nd Round
Dec 07 Blackpool 1 Altrincham 2
Dec 07 Bournemouth 4 Dagenham 1
Dec 07 Bristol C 1 Exeter 2
Dec 09 Derby 6 Telford 1
Dec 07 Gillingham 6 Bognor Regis 1
Dec 07 Hartlepool 0 Frickley 1
Dec 07 Newport 1 Torquay 1
Dec 07 Notts Co 2 Wrexham 2
Dec 07 Orient 2 Slough 2
Dec 07 Peterborough 1 Bath 0
Dec 07 Plymouth 3 Maidstone 0
Dec 08 Port Vale 0 Walsall 0
Dec 07 Reading 2 Hereford 0
Dec 07 Rotherham 4 Burnley 1
Dec 07 Runcorn 1 Wigan 1
Dec 07 Scunthorpe 2 Rochdale 2
Dec 07 Swansea 1 Bristol R 2
Dec 07 Tranmere 1 Bury 1
Dec 07 Wycombe 2 Chelmsford 0
Dec 07 York 3 Whitby 1

Replays
Dec 10 Bury 2 Tranmere 1
Dec 10 Rochdale 2 Scunthorpe 1
Dec 10 Slough 2 Orient 3
Dec 10 Torquay 2 Newport 3
Dec 10 Walsall 2 Port Vale 1
Dec 10 Wigan 4 Runcorn 0
Dec 10 Wrexham 0 Notts Co 3

3rd Round
Jan 14 Birmingham 1 Altrincham 2
Jan 04 Bristol R 3 Leicester 1
Jan 13 Bury 2 Barnsley 0
Jan 13 Carlisle 1 Q.P.R. 0
Jan 05 Charlton 0 West Ham 1
Jan 04 Coventry 1 Watford 3
Jan 06 Crystal Palace 1 Luton 2
Jan 05 Everton 1 Exeter 0
Jan 04 Frickley 1 Rotherham 3
Jan 04 Gillingham 1 Derby 1
Jan 04 Grimsby 3 Arsenal 4
Jan 04 Huddersfield 0 Reading 0
Jan 04 Hull 2 Plymouth 2
Jan 04 Ipswich 4 Bradford C 4
Jan 04 Liverpool 5 Norwich 0
Jan 09 Manchester U 2 Rochdale 0
Jan 13 Middlesbrough 1 Southampton 3
Jan 04 Millwall 3 Wimbledon 1
Jan 04 Newcastle 0 Brighton 2
Jan 04 Nottingham F 1 Blackburn 1
Jan 06 Oldham 1 Orient 2
Jan 04 Oxford 1 Tottenham 1
Jan 04 Peterborough 1 Leeds 0
Jan 04 Portsmouth 2 Aston Villa 2
Jan 13 Sheffield U 2 Fulham 0
Jan 13 Sheffield W 2 W.B.A. 2
Jan 04 Shrewsbury 0 Chelsea 1
Jan 13 Stoke 0 Notts Co 2
Jan 04 Sunderland 2 Newport 0
Jan 04 Walsall 1 Manchester C 3
Jan 04 Wigan 3 Bournemouth 0
Jan 04 York 2 Wycombe 0

Replays
Jan 07 Plymouth 0 Hull 1
Jan 08 Tottenham 2 Oxford 1
Jan 13 Aston Villa 3 Portsmouth 2
Jan 13 Blackburn 3 Nottingham F 2
Jan 13 Bradford C 0 Ipswich 1
Jan 13 Derby 3 Gillingham 1
Jan 13 Reading 2 Huddersfield 1
Jan 16 W.B.A. 2 Sheffield W 3

4th Round
Jan 25 Arsenal 5 Rotherham 1
Jan 25 Aston Villa 1 Millwall 1
Jan 26 Chelsea 1 Liverpool 2
Jan 25 Everton 3 Blackburn 1
Jan 25 Hull 2 Brighton 3
Jan 25 Luton 4 Bristol R 0
Jan 25 Manchester C 1 Watford 1
Jan 25 Notts Co 1 Tottenham 1
Jan 25 Peterborough 1 Carlisle 0
Jan 25 Reading 1 Bury 1
Jan 25 Sheffield U 0 Derby 1
Jan 25 Sheffield W 5 Orient 0
Jan 25 Southampton 3 Wigan 0
Jan 25 Sunderland 0 Manchester U 0
Jan 25 West Ham 0 Ipswich 0

Jan 25 York 2 Altrincham 0

Replays

Jan 28 Bury 3 Reading 0
Jan 29 Manchester U 3 Sunderland 0
Jan 29 Millwall 1 Aston Villa 0
Jan 29 Tottenham 5 Notts Co 0
Feb 03 Watford 0 Manchester C 0
Feb 04 Ipswich 1 West Ham 1
Feb 06 Ipswich 0 West Ham 1
Feb 06 Manchester C 1 Watford 3

5th Round

Feb 26 Derby 1 Sheffield W 1
Feb 15 Luton 2 Arsenal 2
Feb 15 Peterborough 2 Brighton 2
Feb 15 Southampton 0 Millwall 0
Mar 04 Tottenham 1 Everton 2
Mar 05 Watford 1 Bury 1
Mar 05 West Ham 1 Manchester U 1
Feb 15 York 1 Liverpool 1

Replays

Feb 18 Liverpool 3 York 1
Mar 03 Arsenal 0 Luton 0
Mar 03 Brighton 1 Peterborough 0
Mar 05 Luton 3 Arsenal 0
Mar 05 Millwall 0 Southampton 1
Mar 05 Sheffield W 2 Derby 0
Mar 08 Bury 0 Watford 3
Mar 09 Manchester U 0 West Ham 2

6th Round

Mar 08 Brighton 0 Southampton 2
Mar 11 Liverpool 0 Watford 0
Mar 08 Luton 2 Everton 2
Mar 12 Sheffield W 2 West Ham 1

Replays

Mar 12 Everton 1 Luton 0
Mar 17 Watford 1 Liverpool 2

Semi-finals

Apr 05 Everton 2 Sheffield W 1
played at Aston Villa
Apr 05 Liverpool 2 Southampton 0
played at Tottenham

Final

May 10 Everton 1 Liverpool 3
played at Wembley

Season 1986-87

1st Round

Nov 15 Aldershot 1 Torquay 0
Nov 15 Bath 3 Aylesbury 2
Nov 15 Bournemouth 7 Fareham 2
Nov 15 Bristol C 3 Rugby 1
Dec 03 Bristol R 0 Brentford 0
Nov 15 Bromsgrove 0 Newport 1
Nov 15 Bishop's Stortford 1 Colchester 1
Nov 15 Caernarfon 1 Stockport 0
Nov 15 Chester 1 Rotherham 1
Nov 15 Chorley 1 Wolverhampton 1
played at Bolton
Nov 16 Darlington 2 Mansfield 1
Nov 15 Dartford 1 Enfield 1
Nov 15 Exeter 1 Cambridge 1
Nov 15 Farnborough 0 Swindon 4
Nov 15 Frickley 0 Altrincham 0
Nov 15 Halifax 1 Bolton 1
Nov 15 Hereford 3 Fulham 3
Nov 15 Kettering 0 Gillingham 3
Nov 15 Middlesbrough 3 Blackpool 0
Nov 16 Northampton 3 Peterborough 0
Nov 15 Notts Co 1 Carlisle 1
Nov 15 Nuneaton 0 Rochdale 3
Nov 15 Port Vale 1 Stafford 0
Nov 15 Preston 5 Bury 1
Nov 15 Runcorn 1 Boston 1
Nov 15 Scunthorpe 2 Southport 0
Nov 15 Slough 1 Bognor 1
Nov 15 Southend 4 Halesowen 1
Nov 15 Spennymoor 2 Tranmere 3
Nov 15 Telford 3 Burnley 0
Nov 15 Ton Pentre 1 Cardiff 4
Nov 15 Walsall 2 Chesterfield 0
Nov 15 Wealdstone 1 Swansea 1
Nov 15 Welling 1 Maidstone 1
Nov 15 Whitby 2 Doncaster 2
Nov 15 Wigan 3 Lincoln 1
Nov 15 Woking 1 Chelmsford 1
Nov 15 Woodford 0 Orient 1
Nov 15 Wrexham 2 Hartlepool 1
Nov 15 York 3 Crewe 1

Replays

Nov 17 Chelmsford 2 Woking 1
Nov 18 Altrincham 4 Frickley 0
Nov 18 Bognor 0 Slough 1
Nov 18 Bolton 1 Halifax 1
Nov 18 Carlisle 0 Notts Co 3
Nov 18 Colchester 2 Bishop's Stortford 0
Nov 18 Doncaster 3 Whitby 2
Nov 18 Enfield 3 Dartford 0
Nov 18 Rotherham 1 Chester 1
Nov 18 Wolverhampton 1 Chorley 1
Nov 19 Boston 1 Runcorn 2
Nov 19 Cambridge 2 Exeter 0
Nov 24 Chester 1 Rotherham 0
Nov 24 Chorley 3 Wolverhampton 0
played at Bolton
Nov 24 Fulham 4 Hereford 0
Nov 24 Halifax 1 Bolton 3
Nov 24 Maidstone 4 Welling 1
Nov 24 Swansea 4 Wealdstone 1
Dec 06 Brentford 2 Bristol R 0

2nd Round

Dec 06 Aldershot 3 Colchester 2
Dec 06 Bolton 2 Tranmere 0
Dec 06 Bournemouth 0 Orient 1
Dec 06 Bristol C 1 Bath 1
Dec 06 Caernarfon 0 York 0
Dec 09 Cardiff 2 Brentford 0
Dec 06 Chester 3 Doncaster 1
Dec 06 Chorley 0 Preston 0
Dec 06 Darlington 0 Wigan 5
Dec 06 Fulham 2 Newport 0
Dec 06 Gillingham 2 Chelmsford 0
Dec 06 Maidstone 1 Cambridge 0
Dec 06 Notts Co 0 Middlesbrough 1
Dec 06 Rochdale 1 Wrexham 4
Dec 06 Scunthorpe 1 Runcorn 0
Dec 05 Southend 4 Northampton 4
Dec 06 Swansea 3 Slough 0
Dec 06 Swindon 3 Enfield 0
Dec 06 Telford 1 Altrincham 0
Dec 06 Walsall 5 Port Vale 0

Replays

Dec 09 Bath 0 Bristol C 3
Dec 09 Preston 5 Chorley 0
Dec 09 York 1 Caernarfon 2
Dec 10 Northampton 3 Southend 2

3rd Round

Jan 10 Aldershot 3 Oxford 0
Jan 10 Aston Villa 2 Chelsea 2
Jan 10 Bristol C 1 Plymouth 1
Jan 10 Caernarfon 0 Barnsley 0
Jan 10 Charlton 1 Walsall 2
Jan 10 Coventry 3 Bolton 0
Jan 11 Crystal Palace 1 Nottingham F 0
Jan 10 Everton 2 Southampton 1
Jan 10 Fulham 0 Swindon 1
Jan 10 Grimsby 1 Stoke 1
Jan 10 Ipswich 0 Birmingham 1
Jan 11 Luton 0 Liverpool 0
Jan 10 Manchester U 1 Manchester C 0
Jan 10 Middlesbrough 0 Preston 1
Jan 10 Millwall 0 Cardiff 0
Jan 21 Newcastle 2 Northampton 1
Jan 10 Norwich 1 Huddersfield 1
Jan 10 Oldham 1 Bradford C 1
Jan 10 Orient 1 West Ham 1
Jan 10 Portsmouth 2 Blackburn 0
Jan 10 Q.P.R. 5 Leicester 2
Jan 10 Reading 1 Arsenal 3
Jan 10 Sheffield U 0 Brighton 0
Jan 26 Sheffield W 1 Derby 0
Jan 31 Shrewsbury 1 Hull 2
Jan 10 Swansea 3 W.B.A. 2
Jan 11 Telford 1 Leeds 2
Jan 10 Tottenham 3 Scunthorpe 2
Jan 10 Watford 3 Maidstone 1
Jan 19 Wigan 2 Gillingham 1
Jan 10 Wimbledon 2 Sunderland 1
Jan 10 Wrexham 1 Chester 2

Replays

Jan 19 Bradford C 5 Oldham 1
Jan 19 Plymouth 3 Bristol C 1
Jan 20 Cardiff 2 Millwall 2
Jan 21 Brighton 1 Sheffield U 2
Jan 21 Chelsea 2 Aston Villa 1
Jan 21 Huddersfield 2 Norwich 4
Jan 26 Barnsley 1 Caernarfon 0
Jan 26 Cardiff 1 Millwall 0
Jan 26 Liverpool 0 Luton 0
Jan 26 Stoke 1 Grimsby 1
Jan 28 Luton 3 Liverpool 0
Jan 28 Stoke 6 Grimsby 0
Jan 31 West Ham 4 Orient 1

4th Round

Jan 31 Aldershot 1 Barnsley 1
Jan 31 Arsenal 6 Plymouth 1
Jan 31 Bradford C 0 Everton 1
Jan 31 Chester 1 Sheffield W 1
Jan 31 Luton 1 Q.P.R. 1
Jan 31 Manchester U 0 Coventry 1
Jan 31 Newcastle 2 Preston 0
Jan 31 Stoke 2 Cardiff 1
Feb 03 Swansea 0 Hull 1
Feb 03 Swindon 1 Leeds 2
Jan 31 Tottenham 4 Crystal Palace 0
Jan 31 Walsall 1 Birmingham 0
Feb 01 Watford 1 Chelsea 0
Feb 09 West Ham 4 Sheffield U 0
Jan 31 Wigan 1 Norwich 0
Jan 31 Wimbledon 4 Portsmouth 0

Replays

Feb 03 Barnsley 3 Aldershot 0
Feb 04 Q.P.R. 2 Luton 1
Feb 04 Sheffield W 3 Chester 1

5th Round

Feb 21 Arsenal 2 Barnsley 0
Feb 21 Leeds 2 Q.P.R. 1
Feb 21 Sheffield W 1 West Ham 1
Feb 21 Stoke 0 Coventry 1
Feb 21 Tottenham 1 Newcastle 0
Feb 21 Walsall 1 Watford 1
Feb 21 Wigan 3 Hull 0
Feb 22 Wimbledon 3 Everton 1

Replays

Feb 24 Watford 4 Walsall 4
Feb 25 West Ham 0 Sheffield W 2
Mar 02 Walsall 0 Watford 1

6th Round

Mar 14 Arsenal 1 Watford 3
Mar 14 Sheffield W 0 Coventry 3
Mar 15 Wigan 0 Leeds 2
Mar 15 Wimbledon 0 Tottenham 2

Semi-finals

Apr 12 Coventry 3 Leeds 2
played at Sheffield W
Apr 11 Tottenham 4 Watford 1
played at Aston Villa

Final

May 16 Coventry 3 Tottenham 2
played at Wembley

Season 1987-88

1st Round

Nov 14 Altrincham 0 Wigan 2
Nov 14 Barnet 0 Hereford 1
Nov 14 Billingham 2 Halifax 4
Nov 14 Bishop Auckland 1 Blackpool 4
Nov 14 Bognor Regis 0 Torquay 3
Nov 14 Brentford 0 Brighton 2
Nov 14 Bristol C 1 Aylesbury 0
Nov 14 Bristol R 6 Merthyr T 0
Nov 14 Burnley 0 Bolton 1
Nov 14 Cambridge 2 Farnborough 1
Nov 14 Chelmsford 1 Bath 2
Nov 14 Chester 0 Runcorn 1
Nov 14 Chorley 0 Hartlepool 2
Nov 14 Colchester 3 Tamworth 0
Nov 14 Dagenham 0 Maidstone 2
Nov 14 Doncaster 1 Rotherham 1
Nov 14 Gillingham 2 Fulham 1
Nov 14 Halesowen 2 Kidderminster 2
Nov 14 Hayes 0 Swansea 1
Nov 14 Leyton O 2 Exeter 0
Nov 14 Lincoln 2 Crewe 1
Nov 14 Macclesfield 4 Carlisle 2
Nov 14 Northampton 2 Newport 1
Nov 14 Northwich 1 Colwyn Bay 0
Nov 15 Notts Co 3 Chesterfield 3
Nov 14 Peterborough 2 Cardiff 1
Nov 14 Preston 1 Mansfield 1
Nov 14 Rochdale 0 Wrexham 2
Nov 14 Rugby 0 Atherstone 0
Nov 14 Scarborough 1 Grimsby 2
Nov 14 Scunthorpe 3 Bury 1
Nov 14 Southend 0 Walsall 0
Nov 14 Sunderland 2 Darlington 0
Nov 14 Sutton 3 Aldershot 0
Nov 14 Telford 1 Stockport 1
Nov 14 Tranmere 2 Port Vale 2
Nov 23 Welling 3 Carshalton 2
Nov 14 Wolverhampton 5 Cheltenham 1
Nov 14 Worcester 1 Yeovil 1
Nov 14 York 0 Burton 0

Replays

Nov 16 Kidderminster 4 Halesowen 0
Nov 16 Port Vale 3 Tranmere 1
Nov 17 Atherstone 0 Rugby 2
Nov 17 Chesterfield 0 Notts Co 1
Nov 17 Mansfield 4 Preston 2
Nov 17 Rotherham 2 Doncaster 0
Nov 17 Stockport 2 Telford 0
Nov 17 Walsall 2 Southend 1
Nov 18 Burton 1 York 2
Nov 18 Yeovil 1 Worcester 0

2nd Round

Dec 05 Bristol C 0 Torquay 1
Dec 05 Cambridge 0 Yeovil 1
Dec 05 Colchester 3 Hereford 2
Dec 05 Gillingham 2 Walsall 1
Dec 05 Grimsby 0 Halifax 0
Dec 05 Leyton O 2 Swansea 0
Dec 06 Macclesfield 4 Rotherham 0
Dec 05 Maidstone 1 Kidderminster 1

Dec 05 Mansfield 4 Lincoln 3
Dec 05 Northampton 1 Brighton 2
Dec 06 Northwich 0 Blackpool 2
Dec 05 Peterborough 1 Sutton 3
Dec 05 Port Vale 2 Notts Co 0
Dec 05 Rugby 1 Bristol R 1
Dec 05 Runcorn 0 Stockport 1
Dec 05 Scunthorpe 2 Sunderland 1
Dec 05 Welling 0 Bath 1
Dec 05 Wigan 1 Wolverhampton 3
Dec 05 Wrexham 1 Bolton 2
Dec 05 York 1 Hartlepool 1

Replays
Dec 07 Kidderminster 2 Maidstone 2
Dec 08 Halifax 2 Grimsby 0
Dec 09 Hartlepool 3 York 1
Dec 14 Kidderminster 0 Maidstone 0
Dec 16 Maidstone 2 Kidderminster 1
Dec 17 Bristol R 4 Rugby 0

3rd Round
Jan 09 Arsenal 2 Millwall 0
Jan 09 Barnsley 3 Bolton 1
Jan 09 Blackburn 1 Portsmouth 2
Jan 09 Bradford C 2 Wolverhampton 1
Jan 09 Brighton 2 Bournemouth 0
Jan 09 Coventry 2 Torquay 0
Jan 09 Derby 1 Chelsea 3
Jan 09 Gillingham 0 Birmingham 3
Jan 09 Halifax 0 Nottingham F 4
Jan 09 Hartlepool 1 Luton 2
Jan 09 Huddersfield 2 Manchester C 2
Jan 10 Ipswich 1 Manchester U 2
Jan 09 Leeds 1 Aston Villa 2
Jan 09 Mansfield 4 Bath 0
Jan 09 Newcastle 1 Crystal Palace 0
Jan 09 Oldham 2 Tottenham 4
Jan 09 Oxford 2 Leicester 0
Jan 11 Plymouth 2 Colchester 0
Jan 10 Port Vale 1 Macclesfield 0
Jan 09 Reading 0 Southampton 1
Jan 09 Scunthorpe 0 Blackpool 0
Jan 09 Sheffield U 1 Maidstone 0
Jan 09 Sheffield W 1 Everton 1
Jan 09 Shrewsbury 2 Bristol R 1
Jan 09 Stockport 1 Leyton O 2
Jan 09 Stoke 0 Liverpool 0
Jan 09 Sutton 1 Middlesbrough 1
Jan 09 Swindon 0 Norwich 0
Jan 09 Watford 1 Hull 1
Jan 09 West Ham 2 Charlton 0
Jan 09 Wimbledon 4 W.B.A. 1
Jan 09 Yeovil 0 Q.P.R. 3

Replays
Jan 12 Blackpool 1 Scunthorpe 0
Jan 12 Hull 2 Watford 2
Jan 12 Liverpool 1 Stoke 0
Jan 12 Manchester C 0 Huddersfield 0
Jan 12 Middlesbrough 1 Sutton 0
Jan 13 Everton 1 Sheffield W 1
Jan 13 Norwich 0 Swindon 2
Jan 18 Watford 1 Hull 0
Jan 25 Everton 1 Sheffield W 1
Jan 25 Huddersfield 0 Manchester C 3
Jan 27 Sheffield W 0 Everton 5

4th Round
Jan 31 Aston Villa 0 Liverpool 2
Jan 30 Barnsley 0 Birmingham 2
Jan 30 Blackpool 1 Manchester C 1
Jan 30 Bradford C 4 Oxford 2
Jan 30 Brighton 1 Arsenal 2
Jan 30 Coventry 0 Watford 1
Jan 30 Everton 1 Middlesbrough 1
Jan 30 Leyton O 1 Nottingham F 2
Jan 30 Luton 2 Southampton 1
Jan 30 Manchester U 2 Chelsea 0
Jan 30 Mansfield 1 Wimbledon 2
Jan 30 Newcastle 5 Swindon 0
Jan 30 Plymouth 1 Shrewsbury 0
Jan 30 Port Vale 2 Tottenham 1
Feb 01 Portsmouth 2 Sheffield U 1
Jan 30 Q.P.R. 3 West Ham 1

Replays
Feb 03 Manchester C 2 Blackpool 1
Feb 03 Middlesbrough 2 Everton 2
Feb 09 Everton 2 Middlesbrough 1

5th Round
Feb 20 Arsenal 2 Manchester U 1
Feb 20 Birmingham 0 Nottingham F 1
Feb 21 Everton 0 Liverpool 1
Feb 20 Manchester C 3 Plymouth 1
Feb 20 Newcastle 1 Wimbledon 3
Feb 20 Port Vale 0 Watford 0
Feb 20 Portsmouth 3 Bradford C 0
Feb 20 Q.P.R. 1 Luton 1

Replay
Feb 23 Watford 2 Port Vale 0
Feb 24 Luton 1 Q.P.R. 0

6th Round
Mar 12 Arsenal 1 Nottingham F 2
Mar 12 Luton 3 Portsmouth 1
Mar 13 Manchester C 0 Liverpool 4
Mar 12 Wimbledon 2 Watford 1

Semi-finals
Apr 09 Liverpool 2 Nottingham F 1
played at Sheffield W
Apr 09 Luton 1 Wimbledon 2
played at Tottenham

Final
May 14 Liverpool 0 Wimbledon 1
played at Wembley

SEASON 1988-89

1st Round
Nov 19 Aldershot 1 Hayes 0
Nov 19 Altrincham 3 Lincoln 2
Nov 19 Bath 2 Grays 0
Nov 19 Blackpool 2 Scunthorpe 1
Nov 19 Bognor Regis 2 Exeter 1
Nov 19 Bolton 0 Chesterfield 0
Nov 19 Brentford 2 Halesowen 0
Nov 19 Bristol C 3 Southend 1
Nov 20 Bristol R 3 Fisher 0
Nov 19 Burnley 0 Chester 2
Nov 19 Cardiff 3 Hereford 0
Nov 19 Dagenham 0 Sutton 4
Nov 19 Darlington 1 Notts Co 2
Nov 19 Doncaster 0 Brandon 0
Nov 19 Enfield 1 Leyton O 1
Nov 19 Frickley 0 Northwich 2
Nov 19 Fulham 0 Colchester 1
Nov 19 Gillingham 3 Peterborough 3
Nov 19 Grimsby 1 Wolverhampton 0
Nov 19 Guisborough 0 Bury 1
Nov 19 Halifax 1 York 0
Nov 19 Hartlepool 2 Wigan 0
Nov 19 Huddersfield 1 Rochdale 1
Nov 19 Kettering 2 Dartford 1
Nov 19 Mansfield 1 Sheffield U 1
Nov 19 Newport 1 Maidstone 2
Nov 19 Preston 1 Tranmere 1
Nov 19 Reading 4 Hendon 2
Nov 19 Rotherham 3 Barrow 1
Nov 19 Runcorn 2 Wrexham 2
Nov 19 Scarborough 2 Stockport 1
Nov 19 Southport 0 Port Vale 2
Nov 19 Stafford 2 Crewe 2
Nov 19 Swansea 3 Northampton 1
Nov 19 Telford 1 Carlisle 1
Nov 19 Torquay 2 Fareham 2
Nov 19 Waterlooville 1 Aylesbury 4
Nov 19 Welling 3 Bromsgrove 0
Nov 19 Woking 1 Cambridge 4
Nov 19 Yeovil 3 Merthyr T 2

Replays
Nov 22 Brandon 1 Doncaster 2
Nov 22 Carlisle 4 Telford 1
Nov 22 Crewe 3 Stafford 2
Nov 22 Sheffield U 2 Mansfield 1
Nov 22 Tranmere 3 Preston 0
Nov 22 Wrexham 2 Runcorn 3
Nov 23 Fareham 2 Torquay 3
Nov 23 Leyton O 2 Enfield 2
Nov 23 Peterborough 1 Gillingham 0
Nov 28 Chesterfield 2 Bolton 3
Nov 28 Leyton O 0 Enfield 1
Nov 28 Rochdale 3 Huddersfield 4

2nd Round
Dec 10 Aldershot 1 Bristol C 1
Dec 10 Altrincham 0 Halifax 3
Dec 10 Aylesbury 0 Sutton 1
Dec 10 Bath 0 Welling 0
Dec 10 Blackpool 3 Bury 0
Dec 10 Bognor Regis 0 Cambridge 1
Dec 10 Bolton 1 Port Vale 2
Dec 10 Colchester 2 Swansea 2
Dec 11 Doncaster 1 Sheffield U 3
Dec 11 Enfield 1 Cardiff 4
Dec 10 Grimsby 3 Rotherham 2
Dec 10 Hartlepool 1 Notts Co 0
Dec 10 Huddersfield 1 Chester 0
Dec 10 Kettering 2 Bristol R 1
Dec 10 Northwich 1 Tranmere 2
Dec 10 Peterborough 0 Brentford 0
Dec 10 Reading 1 Maidstone 1
Dec 10 Runcorn 0 Crewe 3
Dec 10 Scarborough 0 Carlisle 1
Dec 10 Yeovil 1 Torquay 1

Replays
Dec 13 Bristol C 0 Aldershot 0
Dec 13 Swansea 1 Colchester 3
Dec 14 Brentford 3 Peterborough 2
Dec 14 Maidstone 1 Reading 2
Dec 14 Torquay 1 Yeovil 0
Dec 14 Welling 3 Bath 2
Dec 20 Aldershot 2 Bristol C 2
Dec 22 Bristol C 1 Aldershot 0

3rd Round
Jan 07 Barnsley 4 Chelsea 0
Jan 07 Birmingham 0 Wimbledon 1
Jan 07 Blackpool 0 Bournemouth 1
Jan 07 Bradford C 1 Tottenham 0
Jan 07 Brighton 1 Leeds 2
Jan 07 Cardiff 1 Hull 2
Jan 07 Carlisle 0 Liverpool 3
Jan 07 Charlton 2 Oldham 1
Jan 07 Crewe 2 Aston Villa 3
Jan 07 Derby 1 Southampton 1
Jan 07 Hartlepool 1 Bristol C 0
Jan 07 Huddersfield 0 Sheffield U 1
Jan 07 Kettering 1 Halifax 1
Jan 07 Manchester C 1 Leicester 0
Jan 07 Manchester U 0 Q.P.R. 0
Jan 07 Middlesbrough 1 Grimsby 2
Jan 07 Millwall 3 Luton 2
Jan 07 Newcastle 0 Watford 0
Jan 07 Nottingham F 3 Ipswich 0
Jan 07 Plymouth 2 Cambridge 0
Jan 08 Port Vale 1 Norwich 3
Jan 07 Portsmouth 1 Swindon 1
Jan 07 Sheffield W 5 Torquay 1
Jan 07 Shrewsbury 0 Colchester 3
Jan 07 Stoke 1 Crystal Palace 0
Jan 07 Sunderland 1 Oxford 1
Jan 07 Sutton 2 Coventry 1
Jan 07 Tranmere 1 Reading 1
Jan 07 Walsall 1 Brentford 1
Jan 07 Welling 0 Blackburn 1
Jan 08 West Ham 2 Arsenal 2
Jan 07 W.B.A. 1 Everton 1

Replays
Jan 10 Brentford 1 Walsall 0
Jan 10 Halifax 2 Kettering 3
Jan 10 Southampton 1 Derby 2
Jan 10 Swindon 2 Portsmouth 0
Jan 10 Watford 2 Newcastle 2
Jan 11 Arsenal 0 West Ham 1
Jan 11 Everton 1 W.B.A. 0
Jan 11 Oxford 2 Sunderland 0
Jan 11 Q.P.R. 2 Manchester U 2
Jan 11 Reading 2 Tranmere 1
Jan 16 Newcastle 0 Watford 0
Jan 18 Watford 1 Newcastle 0
Jan 23 Manchester U 3 Q.P.R. 0

4th Round
Jan 28 Aston Villa 0 Wimbledon 1
Jan 28 Blackburn 2 Sheffield W 1
Jan 28 Bradford C 1 Hull 2
Jan 28 Brentford 3 Manchester C 1
Jan 28 Charlton 2 Kettering 1
Jan 28 Grimsby 1 Reading 1
Jan 28 Hartlepool 1 Bournemouth 1
Jan 28 Manchester U 4 Oxford 0
Jan 29 Millwall 0 Liverpool 2
Jan 28 Norwich 8 Sutton 0
Jan 28 Nottingham F 2 Leeds 0
Jan 28 Plymouth 1 Everton 1
Jan 28 Sheffield U 3 Colchester 3
Jan 28 Stoke 3 Barnsley 3
Jan 28 Swindon 0 West Ham 0
Jan 28 Watford 2 Derby 1

Replays
Jan 31 Barnsley 2 Stoke 1
Jan 31 Bournemouth 5 Hartlepool 2
Jan 31 Colchester 0 Sheffield U 2
Jan 31 Everton 4 Plymouth 0
Feb 01 Reading 1 Grimsby 2
Feb 01 West Ham 1 Swindon 0

5th Round
Feb 18 Barnsley 0 Everton 1
Feb 18 Blackburn 0 Brentford 2
Feb 18 Bournemouth 1 Manchester U 1
Feb 18 Charlton 0 West Ham 1
Feb 18 Hull 2 Liverpool 3
Feb 18 Norwich 3 Sheffield U 2
Feb 19 Watford 0 Nottingham F 3
Feb 18 Wimbledon 3 Grimsby 1

Replay
Feb 22 Manchester U 1 Bournemouth 0

6th Round
Mar 19 Everton 1 Wimbledon 0
Mar 18 Liverpool 4 Brentford 0
Mar 18 Manchester U 0 Nottingham F 1
Mar 18 West Ham 0 Norwich 0

Replay
Mar 22 Norwich 3 West Ham 1

Semi-finals
Apr 15 Everton 1 Norwich 0
played at Aston Villa
May 07 Liverpool 3 Nottingham F 1
played at Manchester U

Final
May 20 Everton 2 Liverpool 3
played at Wembley

Season 1989-90

1st Round

Nov 17 Aldershot 0 Cambridge 1
Nov 18 Aylesbury 1 Southend 0
Nov 18 Basingstoke 3 Bromsgrove 0
Nov 19 Bath 2 Fulham 2
Nov 18 Bishop Auckland 2 Tow Law 0
Nov 18 Blackpool 2 Bolton 1
Nov 18 Brentford 0 Colchester 1
Nov 18 Bristol C 2 Barnet 0
Nov 18 Bristol R 1 Reading 1
Nov 18 Burnley 1 Stockport 1
Nov 18 Cardiff 1 Halesowen 0
Nov 18 Carlisle 3 Wrexham 0
Nov 18 Crewe 2 Congleton 0
Nov 18 Darlington 6 Northwich 2
Nov 18 Dartford 1 Exeter 1
Nov 18 Doncaster 1 Notts Co 0
Nov 18 Farnborough 0 Hereford 1
Nov 18 Gillingham 0 Welling 0
Nov 18 Gloucester 1 Dorchester 0
Nov 18 Hartlepool 0 Huddersfield 2
Nov 18 Kettering 0 Northampton 1
Nov 18 Kidderminster 2 Swansea 3
Nov 18 Leyton O 0 Birmingham 1
Nov 18 Lincoln 1 Billingham 0
Nov 18 Macclesfield 1 Chester 1
Nov 19 Maidstone 2 Yeovil 1
Nov 17 Marine 0 Rochdale 1
Nov 18 Peterborough 1 Hayes 1
Nov 18 Preston 1 Tranmere 0
Nov 18 Redditch 1 Merthyr 3
Nov 18 Rotherham 0 Bury 0
Nov 18 Scarborough 0 Whitley Bay 1
Nov 18 Scunthorpe 4 Matlock 1
Nov 18 Shrewsbury 2 Chesterfield 3
Nov 18 Slough 1 Woking 2
Nov 18 Stafford 2 Halifax 3
Nov 18 Sutton 1 Torquay 1
Nov 18 Telford 0 Walsall 3
Nov 19 Wigan 2 Mansfield 0
Nov 18 York 1 Grimsby 2

Replays

Nov 21 Bury 1 Rotherham 2
Nov 21 Chester 3 Macclesfield 2
Nov 21 Hayes 0 Peterborough 1
Nov 21 Reading 1 Bristol R 1
Nov 22 Exeter 4 Dartford 1
Nov 22 Fulham 2 Bath 1
Nov 22 Stockport 1 Burnley 2
Nov 22 Torquay 4 Sutton 0
Nov 22 Welling 1 Gillingham 0
Nov 27 Bristol R 0 Reading 1

2nd Round

Dec 09 Basingstoke 2 Torquay 3
Dec 09 Blackpool 3 Chester 0
Dec 09 Bristol C 2 Fulham 1
Dec 09 Cambridge 3 Woking 1
Dec 09 Cardiff 2 Gloucester 2
Dec 09 Chesterfield 0 Huddersfield 2
Dec 09 Colchester 0 Birmingham 2
Dec 09 Crewe 1 Bishop Auckland 1
Dec 09 Darlington 3 Halifax 0
Dec 09 Grimsby 1 Doncaster 0
Dec 09 Hereford 3 Merthyr T 2
Dec 09 Maidstone 1 Exeter 1
Dec 09 Northampton 0 Aylesbury 0
Dec 09 Reading 0 Welling 0
Dec 09 Rochdale 3 Lincoln 0
Dec 09 Scunthorpe 2 Burnley 2
Dec 09 Swansea 3 Peterborough 1
Dec 09 Walsall 1 Rotherham 0
Dec 09 Whitley Bay 2 Preston 0
Dec 09 Wigan 2 Carlisle 0

Replays

Dec 12 Burnley 1 Scunthorpe 1
Dec 12 Gloucester 0 Cardiff 1
Dec 13 Aylesbury 0 Northampton 1
Dec 13 Bishop Auckland 0 Crewe 2
Dec 13 Exeter 3 Maidstone 2
Dec 13 Welling 1 Reading 1
Dec 18 Burnley 5 Scunthorpe 0
Dec 19 Reading 0 Welling 0
Dec 22 Welling 1 Reading 2

3rd Round

Jan 06 Birmingham 1 Oldham 1
Jan 06 Blackburn 2 Aston Villa 2
Jan 06 Blackpool 1 Burnley 0
Jan 06 Brighton 4 Luton 1
Jan 06 Bristol C 2 Swindon 1
Jan 06 Cambridge 0 Darlington 0
Jan 06 Cardiff 0 Q.P.R. 0
Jan 07 Charlton 1 Bradford C 1
Jan 06 Chelsea 1 Crewe 1
Jan 06 Crystal Palace 2 Portsmouth 1
Jan 06 Exeter 1 Norwich 1
Jan 06 Hereford 2 Walsall 1
Jan 06 Huddersfield 3 Grimsby 1
Jan 06 Hull 0 Newcastle 1
Jan 06 Leeds 0 Ipswich 1
Jan 06 Leicester 1 Barnsley 2
Jan 06 Manchester C 0 Millwall 0
Jan 06 Middlesbrough 0 Everton 0
Jan 06 Northampton 1 Coventry 0
Jan 07 Nottingham F 0 Manchester U 1
Jan 06 Plymouth 0 Oxford 1
Jan 07 Port Vale 1 Derby 1
Jan 06 Reading 2 Sunderland 1
Jan 06 Rochdale 1 Whitley Bay 0
Jan 06 Sheffield U 2 Bournemouth 0
Jan 06 Stoke 0 Arsenal 1
Jan 06 Swansea 0 Liverpool 0
Jan 06 Torquay 1 West Ham 0
Jan 06 Tottenham 1 Southampton 3
Jan 06 Watford 2 Wigan 0
Jan 06 Wolverhampton 1 Sheffield W 2
Jan 06 W.B.A. 2 Wimbledon 0

Replays

Jan 09 Darlington 1 Cambridge 3
Jan 09 Liverpool 8 Swansea 0
Jan 09 Millwall 1 Manchester C 1
Jan 10 Aston Villa 3 Blackburn 1
Jan 10 Bradford C 0 Charlton 3
Jan 10 Crewe 0 Chelsea 2
Jan 10 Derby 2 Port Vale 3
Jan 10 Everton 1 Middlesbrough 1
Jan 10 Norwich 2 Exeter 0
Jan 10 Oldham 1 Birmingham 0
Jan 10 Q.P.R. 2 Cardiff 0
Jan 15 Millwall 3 Manchester C 1
Jan 17 Everton 1 Middlesbrough 0

4th Round

Jan 27 Arsenal 0 Q.P.R. 0
Jan 27 Aston Villa 6 Port Vale 0
Jan 27 Barnsley 2 Ipswich 0
Jan 27 Blackpool 1 Torquay 0
Jan 27 Bristol C 3 Chelsea 1
Jan 27 Crystal Palace 4 Huddersfield 0
Jan 28 Hereford 0 Manchester U 1
Jan 27 Millwall 1 Cambridge 1
Jan 28 Norwich 0 Liverpool 0
Jan 27 Oldham 2 Brighton 1
Jan 27 Reading 3 Newcastle 3
Jan 27 Rochdale 3 Northampton 0
Jan 27 Sheffield U 1 Watford 1
Jan 28 Sheffield W 1 Everton 2
Jan 27 Southampton 1 Oxford 0
Jan 27 W.B.A. 1 Charlton 0

Replays

Jan 30 Cambridge 1 Millwall 0
Jan 30 Watford 1 Sheffield U 2
Jan 31 Liverpool 3 Norwich 1
Jan 31 Newcastle 4 Reading 1
Jan 31 Q.P.R. 2 Arsenal 0

5th Round

Feb 18 Blackpool 2 Q.P.R. 2
Feb 17 Bristol C 0 Cambridge 0
Feb 17 Crystal Palace 1 Rochdale 0
Feb 17 Liverpool 3 Southampton 0
Feb 18 Newcastle 2 Manchester U 3
Feb 17 Oldham 2 Everton 2
Feb 17 Sheffield U 2 Barnsley 2
Feb 17 W.B.A. 0 Aston Villa 2

Replays

Feb 23 Barnsley 0 Sheffield U 0
Feb 23 Cambridge 1 Bristol C 1
Feb 23 Everton 1 Oldham 1
Feb 23 Q.P.R. 0 Blackpool 0
Feb 26 Q.P.R. 3 Blackpool 0
Feb 27 Cambridge 5 Bristol C 1
Mar 05 Barnsley 0 Sheffield U 1
Mar 10 Oldham 2 Everton 1

6th Round

Mar 10 Cambridge 0 Crystal Palace 1
Mar 14 Oldham 3 Aston Villa 0
Mar 11 Q.P.R. 2 Liverpool 2
Mar 11 Sheffield U 0 Manchester U 1

Replay

Mar 14 Liverpool 1 Q.P.R. 0

Semi-finals

Apr 08 Crystal Palace 4 Liverpool 3
played at Aston Villa
Apr 08 Manchester U 3 Oldham 3
played at Manchester C

Replay

Apr 11 Manchester U 2 Oldham 1
played at Manchester C

Final

May 12 Crystal Palace 3 Manchester U 3
played at Wembley

Replay

May 17 Crystal Palace 0 Manchester U 1
played at Wembley

Season 1990-91

1st Round

Nov 17 Aldershot 6 Tiverton 2
Nov 18 Altrincham 1 Huddersfield 2
Nov 17 Atherstone 3 Fleetwood 1
Nov 17 Aylesbury 0 Walsall 1
Nov 17 Barnet 2 Chelmsford 2
Nov 17 Birmingham 1 Cheltenham 0
Nov 17 Bishop Auckland 0 Barrow 1
Nov 17 Blackpool 2 Grimsby 0
Nov 17 Boston 1 Wycombe 1
Nov 17 Bournemouth 2 Gillingham 1
Nov 17 Bradford C 0 Shrewsbury 0
Nov 17 Brentford 5 Yeovil 0
Nov 17 Cardiff 0 Hayes 0
Nov 17 Chester 2 Doncaster 2
Nov 17 Chesterfield 3 Spennymoor 2
Nov 17 Chorley 2 Bury 1
Nov 17 Colchester 2 Reading 1
Nov 17 Darlington 1 York 1
Nov 17 Exeter 1 Cambridge 2
Nov 17 Fulham 2 Farnborough 1
Nov 17 Halesowen 1 Tranmere 2
Nov 17 Halifax 3 Wrexham 2
Nov 17 Hereford 1 Peterborough 1
Nov 17 Leyton O 3 Southend 2
Nov 17 Lincoln 1 Crewe 4
Nov 17 Littlehampton 0 Northampton 4
Nov 17 Maidstone 4 Torquay 1
Nov 17 Merthyr T 1 Sutton 1
Nov 17 Preston 0 Mansfield 1
Nov 17 Rochdale 1 Scunthorpe 1
Nov 17 Rotherham 1 Stockport 0
Nov 17 Runcorn 0 Hartlepool 3
Nov 17 Scarborough 0 Leek 2
Nov 17 Stafford 1 Burnley 3
Nov 17 Swansea 5 Welling 2
Nov 17 Tamworth 4 Whitley Bay 6
Nov 17 Telford 0 Stoke 0
Nov 17 Wigan 5 Carlisle 0
Nov 17 Witton 1 Bolton 2
Nov 17 Woking 0 Kidderminster 0

Replays

Nov 19 York 1 Darlington 0
Nov 20 Doncaster 1 Chester 2
Nov 20 Peterborough 2 Hereford 1
Nov 20 Scunthorpe 2 Rochdale 1
Nov 21 Chelmsford 1 Barnet 2
Nov 21 Hayes 1 Cardiff 0
Nov 21 Kidderminster 1 Woking 1
Nov 21 Shrewsbury 2 Bradford C 1
Nov 21 Stoke 1 Telford 0
Nov 21 Sutton 0 Merthyr T 1
Nov 21 Wycombe 4 Boston 0
Nov 26 Kidderminster 1 Woking 2

2nd Round

Dec 08 Aldershot 2 Maidstone 1
Dec 08 Barnet 0 Northampton 0
Dec 12 Birmingham 1 Brentford 3
Dec 08 Bournemouth 1 Hayes 0
Dec 12 Burnley 2 Stoke 0
Dec 11 Chesterfield 3 Bolton 4
Dec 12 Colchester 0 Leyton O 0
Dec 12 Crewe 1 Atherstone 0
Dec 07 Fulham 0 Cambridge 0
Dec 10 Huddersfield 0 Blackpool 2
Dec 12 Leek 1 Chester 1
Dec 17 Mansfield 0 Barnet 1
Dec 11 Rotherham 1 Halifax 1
Dec 08 Scunthorpe 3 Tranmere 2
Dec 11 Shrewsbury 1 Chorley 0
Dec 08 Swansea 2 Walsall 1
Dec 12 Whitley Bay 0 Barrow 1
Dec 08 Wigan 2 Hartlepool 0
Dec 08 Woking 5 Merthyr T 1
Dec 12 Wycombe 1 Peterborough 1

Replays

Dec 11 Cambridge 2 Fulham 1
Dec 12 Northampton 0 Barnet 1
Dec 17 Chester 4 Leek 0
Dec 17 Halifax 1 Rotherham 2
Dec 17 Leyton O 4 Colchester 1
Dec 17 Peterborough 2 Wycombe 0

3rd Round

Jan 05 Aldershot 0 West Ham 0
Jan 05 Arsenal 2 Sunderland 1
Jan 05 Aston Villa 1 Wimbledon 1
Jan 05 Barnet 0 Portsmouth 5
Jan 06 Barnsley 1 Leeds 1
Jan 05 Blackburn 1 Liverpool 1
Jan 05 Blackpool 0 Tottenham 1
Jan 05 Bolton 1 Barrow 0
Jan 05 Brighton 3 Scunthorpe 2
Jan 05 Bristol R 0 Crewe 2
Jan 06 Burnley 0 Manchester C 1
Jan 05 Charlton 1 Everton 2

Jan 05 Chelsea 1 Oxford 3
Jan 05 Chester 2 Bournemouth 3
Jan 05 Coventry 1 Wigan 1
Jan 06 Crystal Palace 0 Nottingham F 0
Jan 05 Hull 2 Notts Co 5
Jan 05 Leyton O 1 Swindon 1
Jan 07 Manchester U 2 Q.P.R. 1
Jan 05 Mansfield 0 Sheffield W 2
Jan 05 Middlesbrough 0 Plymouth 0
Jan 05 Millwall 2 Leicester 1
Jan 05 Newcastle 2 Derby 0
Jan 05 Norwich 2 Bristol C 1
Jan 05 Oldham 3 Brentford 1
Jan 05 Port Vale 2 Peterborough 1
Jan 05 Sheffield U 1 Luton 3
Jan 05 Shrewsbury 4 Watford 1
Jan 05 Southampton 3 Ipswich 2
Jan 05 Swansea 0 Rotherham 0
Jan 05 Wolverhampton 0 Cambridge 1
Jan 05 W.B.A. 2 Woking 4

Replays
Jan 08 Liverpool 3 Blackburn 0
Jan 09 Leeds 4 Barnsley 0
Jan 09 Wigan 0 Coventry 1
Jan 09 Wimbledon 1 Aston Villa 0
Jan 14 Plymouth 1 Middelsbrough 2
Jan 16 West Ham 6 Aldershot 1
Jan 21 Nottingham F 2 Crystal Palace 2
Jan 21 Rotherham 4 Swansea 0
Jan 21 Swindon 1 Leyton O 0

Jan 28 Nottingham F 3 Crystal Palace 0

4th Round
Jan 27 Arsenal 0 Leeds 0
Jan 26 Cambridge 2 Middlesbrough 0
Jan 26 Coventry 1 Southampton 1
Jan 26 Crewe 1 Rotherham 0
Jan 26 Liverpool 2 Brighton 2
Jan 26 Luton 1 West Ham 1
Jan 26 Manchester U 1 Bolton 0
Jan 26 Millwall 4 Sheffield W 4
Feb 13 Newcastle 2 Nottingham F 2
Jan 26 Norwich 3 Swindon 1
Jan 26 Notts Co 2 Oldham 0
Jan 26 Port Vale 1 Manchester C 2
Jan 26 Portsmouth 5 Bournemouth 1
Jan 26 Shrewsbury 1 Wimbledon 0
Jan 26 Tottenham 4 Oxford 2
Jan 27 Woking 0 Everton 1

Replays
Jan 29 Southampton 2 Coventry 0
Jan 30 Brighton 2 Liverpool 3
Jan 30 Leeds 1 Arsenal 1
Jan 30 Sheffield W 2 Millwall 0
Jan 30 West Ham 5 Luton 0
Feb 13 Arsenal 0 Leeds 0
Feb 16 Leeds 1 Arsenal 2
Feb 18 Nottingham F 3 Newcastle 0

5th Round
Feb 16 Cambridge 4 Sheffield W 0
Feb 17 Liverpool 0 Everton 0
Feb 18 Norwich 2 Manchester U 1
Feb 16 Notts Co 1 Manchester C 0
Feb 16 Portsmouth 1 Tottenham 2
Feb 27 Shrewsbury 0 Arsenal 1
Feb 25 Southampton 1 Nottingham F 1
Feb 16 West Ham 1 Crewe 0

Replays
Feb 20 Everton 4 Liverpool 4
Feb 27 Everton 1 Liverpool 0
Mar 04 Nottingham F 3 Southampton 1

6th Round
Mar 09 Arsenal 2 Cambridge 1
Mar 09 Norwich 0 Nottingham F 1
Mar 10 Tottenham 2 Notts Co 1
Mar 11 West Ham 2 Everton 1

Semi-finals
Apr 14 Arsenal 1 Tottenham 3
played at Wembley
Apr 14 Nottingham F 4 West Ham 0
played at Villa Park

Final
May 18 Nottingham F 1 Tottenham 2
played at Wembley

SEASON 1991-92

1st Round
Nov 16 Aldershot 0 Enfield 1
Nov 16 Atherstone U 0 Hereford U 0
Nov 16 Barnet 5 Tiverton T 0
Nov 16 Blackpool 2 Grimsby T 1
Nov 16 Bournemouth 3 Bromsgrove R 1
Nov 18 Brentford 3 Gillingham 3
Nov 16 Bridlington T 1 York C 2
Nov 16 Burnley 1 Doncaster R 1
Nov 16 Bury 0 Bradford C 1
Nov 16 Carlisle U 1 Crewe A 1
Nov 16 Chester C 1 Guiseley 0
Nov 16 Colchester U 0 Exeter C 0
Nov 16 Crawley T 4 Northampton T 2
Nov 16 Darlington 2 Chesterfield 1
Nov 17 Emley 0 Bolton W 3
played at Huddersfield
Nov 15 Fulham 0 Hayes 2
Nov 16 Gretna 0 Rochdale 0
Nov 16 Halesowen T 2 Farnborough T 2
Nov 16 Hartlepool U 3 Shrewsbury T 2
Nov 16 Huddersfield T 6 Lincoln U 0
Nov 16 Kettering T 1 Wycombe *W* 1
Nov 16 Kidderminster H 0 Aylesbury U 1
Nov 16 Leyton O 2 Welling U 1
Nov 16 Maidstone U 1 Sutton U 0
Nov 27 Mansfield T 0 Preston N.E. 1
Nov 16 Morecambe 0 Hull C 1
Nov 16 Peterborough U 7 Harlow T 0
Nov 16 Scarborough 0 Wigan 2
Nov 16 Scunthorpe U 1 Rotherham U 1
Nov 16 Slough T 3 Reading 3
Nov 16 Stockport Co 3 Lincoln C 1
Nov 16 Stoke C 0 Telford U 0
Nov 16 Swansea C 2 Cardiff C 1
Nov 16 Torquay U 3 Birmingham C 0
Nov 16 Tranmere R 3 Runcorn 0
Nov 26 Windsor & Eton 2 Woking 4
Nov 16 Witton A 1 Halifax T 1
Nov 16 Wrexham 5 Winsford U 2
Nov 16 W.B.A. 6 Marlow 0
Nov 16 Yeovil T 1 Walsall 1

Replays
Nov 26 Crewe A 5 Carlisle U 3
Nov 26 Farnborough T 4 Halesowen T 0
Nov 26 Gillingham 1 Brentford 3
Nov 26 Hereford U 3 Atherstone U 0
Nov 26 Rotherham U 3 Scunthorpe U 3
Penalties 7-6
Nov 26 Telford U 2 Stoke C 1
Nov 27 Doncaster R 1 Burnley 3
Nov 27 Exeter C 0 Colchester U 0
Penalties 4-2
Nov 27 Halifax T 1 Witton A 2
Nov 27 Reading 2 Slough T 1
Nov 27 Rochdale 3 Gretna 1
Nov 27 Walsall 0 Yeovil T 1
Nov 27 Wycombe W 0 Kettering T 2

2nd Round
Dec 07 Aylesbury T 2 Hereford U 3
Dec 07 Blackpool 0 Hull C 1
Dec 07 Bolton W 3 Bradford C 1
Dec 07 Bournemouth 2 Brentford 1
Dec 07 Burnley 2 Rotherham U 0
Dec 07 Crewe A 2 Chester C 0
Dec 17 Darlington 1 Hartlepool U 2
Dec 07 Enfield 1 Barnet 4
Dec 07 Exeter C 0 Swansea T 0
Dec 07 Hayes 0 Crawley T 2
Dec 09 Leyton O 2 W.B.A. 1
Dec 07 Maidstone U 1 Kettering T 2
Dec 07 Peterborough U 0 Reading 0
Dec 07 Preston N.E. 5 Witton A 1
Dec 07 Rochdale 1 Huddersfield T 2
Dec 07 Torquay U 1 Farnborough T 1
Dec 07 Wigan A 2 Stockport Co 0
Dec 07 Woking 3 Yeovil T 0
Dec 07 Wrexham 1 Telford U 0
Dec 07 York C 1 Tranmere R 1

Replays
Dec 17 Farnborough T 4 Torquay U 3
Dec 17 Reading 1 Peterborough 0
Dec 17 Swansea T 1 Exeter C 2
Dec 17 Tranmere R 2 York C 1

3rd Round
Jan 05 Aston Villa 0 Tottenham 0
Jan 04 Blackburn R 4 Kettering T 1
Jan 04 Bolton W 2 Reading 0
Jan 04 Bournemouth 0 Newcastle U 0
Jan 04 Brighton & HA 5 Crawley T 0
Jan 04 Bristol C 1 Wimbledon 1
Jan 05 Bristol R 5 Plymouth A 0
Jan 04 Burnley 2 Derby Co 2
Jan 05 Charlton A 3 Barnet 1
Jan 04 Coventry C 1 Cambridge U 1
Jan 06 Crewe A 0 Liverpool 4
Jan 04 Everton 1 Southend U 0
Jan 04 Exeter C 1 Portsmouth 2
Jan 04 Huddersfield T 0 Millwall 4
Jan 04 Hull C 0 Chelsea 2
Jan 04 Ipswich T 1 Hartlepool U 1
Jan 15 Leeds U 0 Manchester U 1
Jan 04 Leicester C 1 Crystal P 0
Jan 04 Middlesbrough 2 Manchester C 1
Jan 04 Norwich C 1 Barnsley 0
Jan 04 Nottingham F 1 Wolverhampton *W* 0
Jan 05 Notts Co 2 Wigan A 0
Jan 04 Oldham A 1 Leyton O 1
Jan 04 Oxford U 3 Tranmere R 1
Jan 04 Preston N.E. 0 Sheffield W 2
Jan 04 Sheffield U 4 Luton T 0
Jan 04 Southampton 2 Q.P.R. 0
Jan 04 Sunderland 3 Port Vale 0
Jan 04 Swindon T 3 Watford 2
Jan 04 West Ham U 1 Farnborough T 1
Jan 04 Woking 0 Hereford U 0
Jan 04 Wrexham 2 Arsenal 1

Replays
Jan 14 Hereford U 2 Woking 1
Jan 14 Cambridge U 1 Coventry C 0
Jan 14 Tottenham 0 Aston Villa 1
Jan 14 West Ham U 1 Farnborough T 0
Jan 14 Wimbledon 0 Bristol C 1
Jan 15 Hartlepool U 0 Ipswich T 2
Jan 15 Leyton O 4 Oldham A 3
Jan 22 Newcastle U 2 Bournemouth 2
Penalties 3-4
Jan 25 Derby Co 2 Burnley 0

4th Round
Jan 25 Bolton W 2 Brighton & HA 1
Feb 05 Bristol R 1 Liverpool 1
Jan 25 Cambridge U 0 Swindon T 3
Jan 26 Charlton A 0 Sheffield U 0
Jan 26 Chelsea 1 Everton 0
Jan 25 Derby Co 3 Aston Villa 4
Feb 05 Ipswich T 3 Bournemouth 0
Jan 25 Leicester C 1 Bristol C 2
Feb 05 Norwich C 2 Millwall 1
Jan 26 Nottingham F 2 Hereford U 0
Feb 04 Notts Co 2 Blackburn R 1
Feb 05 Oxford U 2 Sunderland 3
Jan 25 Portsmouth 2 Leyton O 1
Feb 04 Sheffield W 1 Middlesbrough 2
Jan 27 Southampton 0 Manchester U 0
Jan 25 West Ham U 2 Wrexham 2

Replays
Feb 04 Wrexham 0 West Ham U 1
Feb 05 Manchester U 2 Southampton 0
Penalties 2-4
Feb 05 Sheffield U 3 Charlton A 1
Feb 11 Liverpool 2 Bristol R 1

5th Round
Feb 16 Bolton W 2 Southampton 2
Feb 15 Chelsea 1 Sheffield U 0
Feb 16 Ipswich T 0 Liverpool 0
Feb 15 Norwich C 3 Notts Co 0
Feb 15 Nottingham F 4 Bristol C 1
Feb 15 Portsmouth 1 Middlesbrough 1
Feb 15 Sunderland 1 West Ham U 1
Feb 16 Swindon T 1 Aston Villa 2

Replays
Feb 26 Liverpool 3 Ipswich T 2
Feb 26 Middlesbrough 2 Portsmouth 4
Feb 26 Southampton 3 Bolton W 2
Feb 26 West Ham U 2 Sunderland 3

6th Round
Mar 10 Chelsea 1 Sunderland 1
Mar 08 Liverpool 1 Aston Villa 0
Mar 07 Portsmouth 1 Nottingham F 0
Mar 07 Southampton 0 Norwich C 0

Replays
Mar 18 Norwich 2 Southampton 1
Mar 18 Sunderland 2 Chelsea 1

Semi-finals
Apr 05 Liverpool 1 Portsmouth 1
played at Arsenal
Apr 05 Norwich C 0 Sunderland 1
played at Sheffield W

Replay
Apr 13 Liverpool 0 Portsmouth 0
played at Villa. Penalties 3-1

Final
Apr 09 Liverpool 2 Sunderland 0
played at Wembley

SEASON 1992-93

1st Round
Nov 14 Accrington 3 Gateshead 2
Nov 14 Blackpool 1 Rochdale 1
Nov 14 Blyth S 1 Southport 2
Nov 14 Bolton 2 Sutton 1
Nov 14 Bournemouth 0 Barnet 0
Nov 14 Bradford C 1 Preston 1
Nov 14 Brighton 2 Hayes 1
Nov 14 Burnley 2 Scarborough 1
Nov 14 Bury 2 Witton 0
Nov 14 Cardiff 2 Bath 3
Nov 14 Chester 1 Altrincham 1
Nov 14 Colchester 4 Slough 0
Nov 14 Crewe 6 Wrexham 1
Nov 14 Dagenham & R 4 Leyton O 5
Nov 14 Darlington 1 Hull 2
Nov 14 Doncaster 1 Hartlepool 2
Nov 15 Dorking 2 Plymouth 3

Date	Home		Away	
Nov 14	Exeter	1	Kidderminster	0
Nov 14	Gillingham	3	Kettering	2
Nov 14	Kingstonian	1	Peterborough	1
Nov 14	Lincoln	0	Stafford	0
Nov 14	Macclesfield	0	Chesterfield	0
Nov 14	Marine	4	Halifax	1
Nov 14	Marlow	3	Salisbury	3
Nov 14	Northampton	3	Fulham	1
Nov 15	Reading	1	Birmingham	0
Nov 14	Rotherham	4	Walsall	0
Nov 14	Scunthorpe	0	Huddersfield	0
Nov 14	Shrewsbury	3	Mansfield	1
Nov 14	Solihull	2	Rugby	2
Nov 14	St Albans	1	Cheltenham	2
Nov 16	Stoke	0	Port Vale	0
Nov 14	Sutton	1	Hereford	2
Nov 14	Torquay	2	Yeovil	5
Nov 14	Wigan	3	Carlisle	1
Nov 14	Woking	3	Nuneaton	2
Nov 14	Wycombe	3	Merthyr	1
Nov 14	W.B.A.	8	Aylesbury	0
Nov 14	York	1	Stockport	3

Replays

Date	Home		Away	
Nov 24	Port Vale	3	Stoke	1
Nov 25	Altrincham	2	Chester	0
Nov 25	Barnet	1	Bournemouth	2
Nov 25	Chesterfield	2	Macclesfield	2
	Penalties 2-3			
Nov 25	Huddersfield	2	Scunthorpe	1
Nov 25	Preston	4	Bradford C	5
Nov 25	Rochdale	1	Blackpool	0
Nov 25	Rugby	2	Solihull	1
Nov 25	Stafford	2	Lincoln	1
Dec 04	Peterborough	1	Kingstonian	0
Dec 05	Salisbury	2	Marlow	2
	Penalties 3-4			

2nd Round

Date	Home		Away	
Dec 05	Accrington	1	Crewe	6
Dec 05	Altrincham	1	Port Vale	4
Dec 06	Bath	2	Northampton	2
Dec 05	Bolton	4	Rochdale	0
Dec 06	Bradford C	0	Huddersfield	2
Dec 05	Brighton	1	Woking	1
Dec 05	Burnley	1	Shrewsbury	1
Dec 05	Cheltenham	1	Bournemouth	1
Dec 05	Exeter	1	Swansea	2
Dec 15	Exeter	2	Swansea	5
Dec 05	Gillingham	1	Colchester	1
Dec 06	Hartlepool	4	Southport	0
Dec 05	Macclesfield	0	Stockport	2
Dec 05	Marine	3	Stafford	2
Dec 09	Plymouth	3	Peterborough	2
Dec 05	Reading	3	Leyton O	0
Dec 05	Rotherham	1	Hull	0
Dec 09	Rugby	0	Marlow	0
Dec 15	Wigan	1	Bury	1
Dec 06	Wycombe	2	W.B.A.	2
Dec 05	Yeovil	0	Hereford	0

Replays

Date	Home		Away	
Dec 15	Northampton	3	Bath	0
Dec 15	Shrewsbury	1	Barnsley	2
Dec 15	W.B.A.	1	Wycombe	0
Dec 16	Bournemouth	3	Cheltenham	0
Dec 16	Colchester	2	Gillingham	3
Dec 16	Hereford	1	Yeovil	2
Dec 16	Marlow	2	Rugby	0
Dec 16	Woking	1	Brighton	2
Jan 02	Bury	1	Wigan	0

3rd Round

Date	Home		Away	
Jan 02	Aston Villa	1	Bristol R	1
Jan 02	Blackburn	3	Bournemouth	1
Jan 03	Bolton	2	Liverpool	2
Jan 02	Brentford	0	Grimsby	2
Jan 02	Brighton	1	Portsmouth	0
Jan 13	Cambridge	1	Sheffield W	2
Jan 12	Crewe	3	Marine	1
Jan 02	Derby	2	Stockport	1
Jan 02	Gillingham	0	Huddersfield	0
Jan 02	Hartlepool	1	Crystal Palace	0
Jan 12	Ipswich	3	Plymouth	1
Jan 02	Leeds	1	Charlton	1
Jan 13	Leicester	2	Barnsley	2
Jan 19	Luton	2	Bristol C	0
Jan 02	Manchester C	1	Reading	1
Jan 05	Manchester U	2	Bury	0
Jan 02	Marlow	1	Tottenham	5
Jan 13	Middlesbrough	2	Chelsea	1
Jan 02	Newcastle	4	Port Vale	0
Jan 12	Northampton	0	Rotherham	1
Jan 13	Norwich	1	Coventry	0
Jan 03	Nottingham F	2	Southampton	1
Jan 12	Notts Co	0	Sunderland	2
Jan 02	Oldham	2	Tranmere	2
Jan 04	Q.P.R.	3	Swindon	0
Jan 02	Sheffield U	2	Burnley	2
Jan 13	Southend	1	Millwall	0
Jan 02	Swansea	1	Oxford	1
Jan 02	Watford	1	Wolverhampton	4
Jan 02	Wimbledon	0	Everton	0
Jan 02	W.B.A.	0	West Ham	2
Jan 02	Yeovil	1	Arsenal	3

Replays

Date	Home		Away	
Jan 12	Burnley	2	Sheffield U	4
Jan 12	Everton	1	Wimbledon	2
Jan 12	Oxford	2	Swansea	2
	Penalties 4-5			
Jan 12	Tranmere	3	Oldham	0
Jan 13	Charlton	1	Leeds	3
Jan 13	Huddersfield	2	Gillingham	1
Jan 13	Liverpool	0	Bolton	2
Jan 13	Reading	0	Manchester C	4
Jan 20	Barnsley	1	Leicester	1
	Penalties 5-4			
Jan 20	Bristol R	0	Aston Villa	3

4th Round

Date	Home		Away	
Jan 25	Arsenal	2	Leeds	2
Jan 23	Aston Villa	1	Wimbledon	1
Jan 24	Barnsley	4	West Ham	1
Jan 23	Crewe	0	Blackburn	3
Jan 23	Huddersfield	1	Southend	2
Jan 23	Luton	1	Derby	5
Jan 23	Manchester U	1	Brighton	0
Jan 24	Norwich	0	Tottenham	2
Jan 23	Nottingham F	1	Middlesbrough	1
Jan 23	Q.P.R.	1	Manchester C	2
Jan 23	Rotherham	1	Newcastle	1
Jan 23	Sheffield U	1	Hartlepool	0
Jan 24	Sheffield W	1	Sunderland	0
Feb 02	Swansea	0	Grimsby	0
Jan 23	Tranmere	1	Ipswich	2
Jan 24	Wolverhampton	0	Bolton	2

Replays

Date	Home		Away	
Feb 03	Leeds	2	Arsenal	3
Feb 03	Middlesbrough	0	Nottingham F	3
Feb 03	Newcastle	2	Rotherham	0
Feb 03	Wimbledon	0	Aston Villa	0
	Penalties 6-5			
Feb 09	Grimsby	2	Swansea	0

5th Round

Date	Home		Away	
Feb 13	Arsenal	2	Nottingham F	0
Feb 13	Blackburn	1	Newcastle	0
Feb 13	Derby	3	Bolton	1
Feb 13	Ipswich	4	Grimsby	0
Feb 13	Manchester C	2	Barnsley	0
Feb 14	Sheffield U	2	Manchester U	1
Feb 13	Sheffield W	2	Southend	0
Feb 14	Tottenham	3	Wimbledon	2

6th Round

Date	Home		Away	
Mar 06	Blackburn	0	Sheffield U	0
Mar 06	Ipswich	2	Arsenal	4
Mar 07	Manchester C	2	Tottenham	4
Mar 08	Derby	3	Sheffield W	3

Replays

Date	Home		Away	
Mar 16	Sheffield U	2	Blackburn	2
	Penalties 5-3			
Mar 17	Sheffield W	1	Derby	0

Semi-finals

Date	Home		Away	
Apr 04	Arsenal	1	Tottenham	0
	played at Wembley			
Apr 03	Sheffield U	1	Sheffield W	2
	played at Wembley			

Final

Date	Home		Away	
May 15	Arsenal	1	Sheffield W	1
	played at Wembley			

Replay

Date	Home		Away	
May 20	Arsenal	2	Sheffield W	1

Season 1993-94

1st Round

Date	Home		Away	
Nov 14	Accrington	2	Scunthorpe	3
Nov 13	Barnet	2	Carshalton	1
Nov 13	Bournemouth	4	Brighton	2
Nov 13	Bradford C	0	Chester	0
Nov 14	Bristol R	1	Wycombe	2
Nov 13	Burnley	0	York	0
Nov 14	Cambridge C	0	Hereford	1
Nov 13	Cambridge U	0	Reading	0
Nov 13	Chesterfield	0	Rochdale	1
Nov 13	Colchester	3	Sutton	4
Nov 13	Crewe	4	Darlington	2
Nov 13	Enfield	0	Cardiff	0
Nov 13	Farnborough	1	Exeter	3
Nov 13	Gretna	2	Bolton	3
Nov 14	Halifax	2	W.B.A.	1
Nov 13	Kidderminster	3	Kettering	0
Nov 13	Knowsley	1	Carlisle	4
Nov 12	Leek	2	Wigan	2
Nov 13	Leyton O	2	Gravesend	1
Nov 13	Macclesfield	2	Hartlepool	0
Nov 13	Mansfield	1	Preston	2
Nov 13	Marlow	0	Plymouth	2
Nov 13	Met Police	0	Crawley	2
Nov 13	Moseley	0	Bath	4
Nov 13	Northampton	1	Bromesgrove	2
Nov 13	Port Vale	2	Blackpool	0
Nov 13	Rotherham	1	Stockport	2
Nov 23	Runcorn	0	Hull	2
Nov 13	Scarborough	1	Bury	0
Nov 13	Shrewsbury	1	Doncaster	1
Nov 13	Slough	1	Torquay	2
Nov 13	Stalybridge	1	Marine	1
Nov 13	Swansea	1	Nuneaton	1
Nov 13	Telford	1	Huddersfield	1
Nov 13	Vs Rugby	0	Brentford	3
Nov 13	Witton	0	Lincoln	2
Nov 13	Woking	2	Weston Spr Mare	2
Nov 13	Wrexham	1	Walsall	1
Nov 13	Yeading	0	Gillingham	0
Nov 15	Yeovil	1	Fulham	0

Replays

Date	Home		Away	
Nov 23	Huddersfield	1	Telford	0
Nov 23	Nuneaton	2	Swansea	1
Nov 23	Walsall	2	Wrexham	0
Nov 23	Weston Spr Mare	0	Woking	1
Nov 24	Reading	1	Cambridge U	2
Nov 29	Marine	4	Stalybridge	4
	Penalties .2-4			
Nov 30	Cardiff	1	Enfield	0
Nov 30	Chester	1	Bradford C	0
Nov 30	Gillingham	3	Yeading	1
Nov 30	Wigan	3	Leek	0
Nov 30	York	2	Burnley	3
Dec 01	Doncaster	1	Shrewsbury	2

2nd Round

Date	Home		Away	
Dec 05	Bath	2	Hereford	1
Dec 04	Bournemouth	1	Nuneaton	1
Dec 04	Brentford	1	Cardiff	3
Dec 04	Burnley	4	Rochdale	1
Dec 04	Carlisle	3	Stalybridge	1
Dec 04	Chester	2	Hull	0
Dec 04	Crawley	1	Barnet	2
Dec 04	Crewe	2	Macclesfield	1
Dec 04	Kidderminster	1	Woking	0
Dec 04	Leyton O	1	Exeter	1
Dec 04	Lincoln	1	Bolton	3
Dec 04	Plymouth	2	Gillingham	0
Dec 03	Port Vale	1	Huddersfield	0
Dec 04	Shrewsbury	0	Preston	1
Dec 04	Stockport	5	Halifax	1
Dec 04	Torquay	0	Sutton	1
Dec 04	Walsall	1	Scunthorpe	1
Dec 04	Wigan	1	Scarborough	0
Dec 04	Wycombe	1	Cambridge U	0
Dec 04	Yeovil	0	Bromsgrove	2

Replays

Date	Home		Away	
Dec 14	Exeter	2	Leyton O	0
	Penalties 5-4			
Dec 14	Scunthorpe	0	Walsall	0
	Penalties 7-6			
Dec 15	Nuneaton	0	Bournemouth	1

3rd Round

Date	Home		Away	
Jan 08	Barnet	0	Chelsea	0
Jan 08	Birmingham	1	Kidderminster	2
Jan 08	Blackburn	3	Portsmouth	3
Jan 08	Bolton	1	Everton	1
Jan 19	Bristol C	1	Liverpool	1
Jan 08	Bromsgrove	1	Barnsley	2
Jan 08	Cardiff	2	Middlesbrough	2
Jan 08	Charlton	3	Burnley	0
Jan 08	Exeter	0	Aston Villa	1
Jan 08	Grimsby	1	Wigan	0
Jan 08	Leeds	3	Crewe	1
Jan 18	Luton	1	Southend	0
Jan 08	Manchester C	4	Leicester	1
Jan 10	Millwall	0	Arsenal	1
Jan 08	Newcastle	2	Coventry	0
Jan 08	Notts Co	3	Sutton	2
Jan 08	Oldham	2	Derby	1
Jan 08	Oxford	2	Tranmere	0
Jan 08	Peterborough	1	Tottenham	1
Jan 08	Plymouth	1	Chester	0
Jan 08	Preston	2	Bournemouth	1
Jan 09	Sheffield U	0	Manchester U	1
Jan 08	Sheffield W	1	Nottingham F	1
Jan 08	Southampton	1	Port Vale	1
Jan 08	Stockport	2	Q.P.R.	1
Jan 08	Stoke	0	Bath	0
Jan 08	Sunderland	1	Carlisle	1
Jan 08	Swindon	1	Ipswich	1
Jan 08	West Ham	2	Watford	1
Jan 08	Wimbledon	3	Scunthorpe	0
Jan 08	Wolverhampton	1	Crystal P	0
Jan 08	Wycombe	0	Norwich	2

Replays

Date	Home		Away	
Jan 18	Bath	1	Stoke	4
Jan 18	Carlisle	0	Sunderland	1
Jan 18	Ipswich	2	Swindon	1
Jan 18	Port Vale	1	Southampton	0
Jan 19	Chelsea	4	Barnet	0
Jan 19	Everton	2	Bolton	3
Jan 19	Middlesbrough	1	Cardiff	2
Jan 19	Nottingham F	0	Sheffield W	2
Jan 19	Portsmouth	1	Blackburn	3
Jan 19	Tottenham	1	Peterborough	1
	Penalties 5-4			
Jan 25	Liverpool	0	Bristol C	1

4th Round

Date	Home		Away	
Jan 31	Bolton	2	Arsenal	2
Jan 29	Cardiff	1	Manchester C	0
Jan 29	Charlton	0	Blackburn	0
Jan 29	Chelsea	1	Sheffield W	1
Jan 29	Grimsby	1	Aston Villa	2
Jan 29	Ipswich	3	Tottenham	0
Jan 29	Kidderminster	1	Preston	0
Jan 29	Newcastle	1	Luton	1
Jan 30	Norwich	0	Manchester U	2
Jan 29	Notts Co	1	West Ham	1
Jan 29	Oldham	0	Stoke	0
Jan 29	Oxford	2	Leeds	2
Jan 29	Plymouth	2	Barnsley	2
Jan 29	Port Vale	0	Wolverhampton	2
Feb 09	Stockport	0	Bristol C	4

Jan 29	Wimbledon	2	Sunderland	1

Replays

Feb 08	Blackburn	0	Charlton	1
Feb 09	Arsenal	1	Bolton	3
Feb 09	Barnsley	1	Plymouth	0
Feb 09	Leeds	2	Oxford	3
Feb 09	Luton	2	Newcastle	0
Feb 09	Sheffield W	1	Chelsea	3
Feb 09	Stoke	0	Oldham	1
Feb 09	West Ham	1	Notts Co	0

5th Round

Feb 20	Bolton	1	Aston Villa	0
Feb 19	Bristol C	1	Charlton	1
Feb 20	Cardiff	1	Luton	2
Feb 19	Kidderminster	0	West Ham	1
Feb 19	Oldham	1	Barnsley	0
Feb 19	Oxford	1	Chelsea	2
Feb 20	Wimbledon	0	Manchester U	3
Feb 19	Wolverhampton	1	Ipswich	1

Replays

Mar 02	Charlton	2	Bristol C	0
Mar 02	Ipswich	1	Wolverhampton	2

6th Round

Mar 12	Bolton	0	Oldham	1
Mar 13	Chelsea	1	Wolverhampton	0
Mar 12	Manchester U	3	Charlton	1
Mar 14	West Ham	0	Luton	0

Replay

Mar 23	Luton	3	West Ham	2

Semi-finals

Apr 09	Chelsea	2	Luton	0
	played at Wembley			
Apr 10	Manchester U	1	Oldham	1
	played at Wembley			

Replay

Apr 13	Manchester U	4	Oldham	1
	played at Manchester C			

Final

May 14	Chelsea	0	Manchester U	4
	played at Wembley			

Season 1994-95

1st Round

Nov 12	Altrincham	3	Southport	2
Nov 12	Ashford	2	Fulham	2
Nov 12	Barnet	4	Woking	4
Nov 12	Bath	0	Bristol R	5
Nov 12	Bishop Auckland	0	Bury	0
Nov 12	Bournemouth	3	Worthing	1
Nov 12	Bradford C	1	Scunthorpe	1
Nov 12	Burnley	2	Shrewsbury	1
Nov 12	Cambridge	2	Brentford	2
Nov 12	Chesham	0	Bashley	1
Nov 12	Chester	2	Witton	0
Nov 12	Chesterfield	0	Scarborough	0
Nov 12	Crewe	7	Gresley	1
Nov 12	Doncaster	1	Huddersfield	4
Nov 12	Enfield	1	Cardiff	0
Nov 12	Exeter	1	Crawley	4
Nov 13	Guiseley	1	Carlisle	4
Nov 12	Halifax	1	Runcorn	1
Nov 12	Hereford	2	Hitchin	2
Nov 11	Heybridge	0	Gillingham	2
Nov 12	Hull	0	Lincoln	1
Nov 12	Hyde	1	Darlington	3
Nov 12	Kettering	0	Plymouth	1
Nov 12	Kidderminster	1	Torquay	1
Nov 12	Kingstonian	2	Brighton	1
Nov 22	Mansfield	3	Northwich	1
Nov 13	Marlow	2	Oxford	0
Nov 12	Newport low	2	Aylesbury	3
Nov 12	Peterborough	4	Northampton	0
Nov 12	Port Vale	6	Hartlepool	0
Nov 14	Preston	1	Blackpool	0
Nov 12	Slough	0	Birmingham	4
Nov 12	Tiverton	1	Leyton O	3
Nov 12	Walsall	3	Rochdale	0
Nov 21	Walton & H	0	Swansea	2
Nov 12	Wigan	4	Spennymoor	0
Nov 12	Wrexham	1	Stockport	0
Nov 12	Wycombe	4	Chelmsford	0
Nov 12	Yeading	2	Colchester	2
Nov 12	York	3	Rotherham	3

Replays

Nov 21	Runcorn	1	Halifax	3
Nov 22	Brentford	1	Cambridge	2
Nov 22	Bury	1	Bishop Auckland	1
	Penalties 4-2			
Nov 22	Colchester	7	Yeading	1
Nov 22	Fulham	5	Ashford	3
Nov 22	Hitchin	4	Hereford	2
Nov 22	Rotherham	3	York	0
Nov 22	Scarborough	2	Chesterfield	0
Nov 22	Scunthorpe	3	Bradford C	2
Nov 22	Woking	1	Barnet	0
Nov 23	Torquay	1	Kidderminster	0

2nd Round

Dec 03	Altrincham	1	Wigan	0
Dec 04	Bashley	0	Swansea	1
Dec 02	Birmingham	0	Scunthorpe	0
Dec 04	Carlisle	2	Darlington	0
Dec 04	Chester	1	Burnley	2
Dec 03	Crewe	1	Bury	2
Dec 03	Enfield	1	Torquay	1
Dec 03	Exeter	1	Colchester	2
Dec 03	Gillingham	1	Fulham	1
Dec 03	Halifax	0	Mansfield	0
Dec 03	Hitchin	0	Wycombe	5
Dec 03	Kingstonian	1	Aylesbury	4
Dec 03	Leyton O	0	Bristol R	2
Dec 03	Lincoln	1	Huddersfield	0
Dec 04	Marlow	2	Woking	1
Dec 03	Peterborough	0	Cambridge	2
Dec 03	Plymouth	2	Bournemouth	1
Dec 03	Preston	1	Walsall	1
Dec 03	Scarborough	1	Port Vale	0
Dec 03	Wrexham	5	Rotherham	2

Replays

Dec 13	Fulham	1	Gillingham	2
Dec 13	Mansfield	2	Halifax	1
Dec 13	Torquay	0	Enfield	1
Dec 13	Walsall	4	Preston	0
Dec 14	Scunthorpe	1	Birmingham	2

3rd Round

Jan 07	Aylesbury	0	Q.P.R.	4
Jan 07	Barnsley	0	Aston Villa	2
Jan 07	Birmingham	0	Liverpool	0
Jan 07	Bristol C	0	Stoke	0
Jan 07	Bury	2	Tranmere	2
Jan 07	Cambridge	2	Burnley	4
Jan 07	Chelsea	3	Charlton	0
Jan 07	Coventry	1	W.B.A.	1
Jan 08	Crystal Palace	5	Lincoln	1
Jan 07	Everton	1	Derby	0
Jan 07	Gillingham	1	Sheffield W	2
Jan 07	Grimsby	0	Norwich	1
Jan 07	Leicester	2	Enfield	0
Jan 07	Luton	1	Bristol R	1
Jan 07	Mansfield	2	Wolverhampton	3
Jan 07	Millwall	0	Arsenal	0
Jan 08	Newcastle	1	Blackburn	1
Jan 07	Nottingham F	2	Plymouth	0
Jan 08	Notts Co	2	Manchester C	2
Jan 07	Portsmouth	3	Bolton	1
Jan 07	Reading	1	Oldham	3
Jan 07	Scarborough	0	Watford	0
Jan 09	Sheffield U	0	Manchester U	2
Jan 07	Southampton	2	Southend	0
Jan 07	Sunderland	1	Carlisle	1
Jan 07	Swansea	1	Middlesbrough	1
Jan 07	Swindon	2	Marlow	0
Jan 07	Tottenham	3	Altrincham	0
Jan 07	Walsall	1	Leeds	1
Jan 07	Wimbledon	1	Colchester	0
Jan 07	Wrexham	2	Ipswich	1
Jan 07	Wycombe	0	West Ham	2

Replays

Jan 17	Carlisle	1	Sunderland	3
Jan 17	Leeds	5	Walsall	2
Jan 17	Middlesbrough	1	Swansea	2
Jan 17	Watford	2	Scarborough	0
Jan 18	Arsenal	0	Millwall	2
Jan 18	Blackburn	1	Newcastle	2
Jan 18	Bristol R	0	Luton	1
Jan 18	Liverpool	1	Birmingham	1
	Penalties .2-0			
Jan 18	Manchester C	5	Notts Co	2
Jan 18	Stoke	1	Bristol C	3
Jan 18	Tranmere	3	Bury	0
Jan 18	W.B.A.	1	Coventry	2

4th Round

Jan 29	Bristol C	0	Everton	1
Jan 28	Burnley	0	Liverpool	0
Jan 28	Coventry	0	Norwich	0
Jan 28	Leeds	3	Oldham	2
Jan 28	Luton	1	Southampton	1
Jan 28	Manchester C	1	Aston Villa	0
Jan 28	Manchester U	5	Wrexham	1
Jan 28	Millwall	0	Chelsea	0
Jan 28	Newcastle	3	Swansea	0
Jan 28	Nottingham F	1	Crystal Palace	2
Jan 28	Portsmouth	0	Leicester	1
Jan 28	Q.P.R.	1	West Ham	0
Jan 30	Sheffield W	0	Wolverhampton	0
Jan 29	Sunderland	1	Tottenham	4
Jan 29	Tranmere	0	Wimbledon	2
Jan 28	Watford	1	Swindon	0

Replays

Feb 07	Liverpool	1	Burnley	0
Feb 08	Chelsea	1	Millwall	1
	Penalties .4-5			
Feb 08	Norwich	3	Coventry	1
Feb 08	Southampton	6	Luton	0
Feb 08	Wolverhampton	1	Sheffield W	1

5th Round

Feb 18	Everton	5	Norwich	0
Feb 19	Liverpool	1	Wimbledon	1
Feb 19	Manchester U	3	Leeds	1
Feb 19	Newcastle	3	Manchester C	1
Feb 18	Q.P.R.	1	Millwall	0
Feb 18	Tottenham	1	Southampton	1
Feb 18	Watford	0	Crystal Palace	0
Feb 18	Wolverhampton	1	Leicester	0

Replays

Feb 28	Wimbledon	0	Liverpool	2
Mar 01	Crystal Palace	1	Watford	0
Mar 01	Southampton	2	Tottenham	6

6th Round

Mar 11	Crystal Palace	1	Wolverhampton	1
Mar 12	Everton	1	Newcastle	0
Mar 11	Liverpool	1	Tottenham	2
Mar 12	Manchester U	2	Q.P.R.	0

Replay

Mar 22	Wolverhampton	1	Crystal Palace	4

Semi-finals

Apr 09	Crystal Palace	2	Manchester U	2
	played at Aston Villa			
Apr 09	Everton	4	Tottenham	1
	played at Leeds			

Replay

Apr 12	Crystal Palace	0	Manchester U	2
	played at Aston Villa			

Final

May 20	Everton	1	Manchester U	0
	played at Wembley			

Season 1995-96

1st Round

Nov 22	Altrincham	0	Crewe	2
Nov 11	Barnet	2	Woking	2
Nov 11	Barrow	2	Nuneaton	1
Nov 11	Blackpool	2	Chester	1
Nov 11	Bognor Regis	1	Ashford	1
Nov 11	Bournemouth	0	Bristol C	0
Nov 11	Bradford C	4	Burton A	3
Nov 11	Brentford	1	Farnborough	1
Nov 10	Burnley	1	Walsall	3
Nov 11	Bury	0	Blyth Spartans	2
Nov 12	Canvey Is	2	Brighton	2
Nov 11	Carlisle	1	Preston	2
Nov 11	Cinderford	2	Bromsgrove	1
Nov 11	Exeter	0	Peterborough	1
Nov 11	Fulham	7	Swansea	0
Nov 11	Gravesend	2	Colchester	0
Nov 11	Hartlepool	2	Darlington	4
Nov 11	Hereford	2	Stevenage	1
Nov 11	Hitchin	2	Bristol R	1
Nov 11	Hull	0	Wrexham	0
Nov 11	Kidderminster	2	Sutton	2
Nov 11	Kingstonan	5	Wisbech	0
Nov 11	Mansfield	4	Doncaster	2
Nov 11	Newport (IOW)	1	Enfield	1
Nov 11	Northampton	1	Hayes	0
Nov 11	Northwich	1	Scunthorpe	3
Nov 11	Oxford	9	Dorchester	1
Nov 11	Rochdale	5	Rotherham	3
Nov 11	Runcorn	1	Wigan	1
Nov 11	Rushden	1	Cardiff	3
Nov 11	Scarborough	0	Chesterfield	2
Nov 11	Shrewsbury	11	Marine	2
Nov 11	Slough	0	Plymouth	2
Nov 11	Spennymoor	0	Colwyn Bay	1
Nov 11	Stockport	5	Lincoln	0
Nov 11	Swindon	4	Cambridge	1
Nov 11	Telford	2	Witton	1
Nov 11	Torquay	1	Leyton O	0
Nov 13	Wycombe	1	Gillingham	1
Nov 12	York	0	Notts Co	1

Replays

Nov 21	Ashford	0	Bognor Regis	1
Nov 21	Brighton	4	Canvey Is	1
Nov 21	Bristol C	0	Bournemouth	1
Nov 21	Enfield	2	Newport (IOW)	1
Nov 21	Gillingham	1	Wycombe	0
Nov 21	Sutton	1	Kidderminster	1
	Penalties 3-2			
Nov 21	Wigan	4	Runcorn	2
Nov 21	Woking	2	Barnet	1
Nov 21	Wrexham	0	Hull	0
	Penalties 3-1			
Nov 22	Farnborough	0	Brentford	4

2nd Round

Dec 02	Barrow	0	Wigan	4
Dec 02	Blackpool	2	Colwyn Bay	0
Dec 02	Bournemouth	0	Brentford	1

Dec 02 Bradford C 2 Preston 1
Dec 02 Cinderford 1 Gravesend 1
Dec 02 Crewe 2 Mansfield 2
Dec 02 Enfield 1 Woking 1
Dec 02 Fulham 0 Brighton 0
Dec 02 Gillingham 3 Hitchin 0
Dec 02 Hereford 2 Sutton 0
Dec 03 Kingstonian 1 Plymouth 2
Dec 02 Oxford 2 Northampton 0
Dec 02 Peterborough 4 Bognor Regis 0
Dec 02 Rochdale 5 Darlington 2
Dec 02 Scunthorpe 1 Shrewsbury 1
Dec 02 Stockport 2 Blyth Spartans 0
Dec 02 Swindon 2 Cardiff 0
Dec 02 Telford 2 Oxford 0
Dec 02 Torquay 1 Walsall 1
Dec 02 Wrexham 3 Chesterfield 2

Replays
Dec 12 Darlington 0 Rochdale 1
Dec 12 Shrewsbury 2 Scunthorpe 1
Dec 12 Walsall 8 Torquay 4
Dec 12 Woking 2 Enfield 1
Dec 14 Brighton 0 Fulham 0
Penalties 1-4
Dec 14 Gravesend 3 Cinderford 0

3rd Round
Jan 06 Arsenal 1 Sheffield U 1
Jan 06 Barnsley 0 Oldham 0
Jan 06 Birmingham 1 Wolverhampton 1
Jan 06 Bradford C 0 Bolton 3
Jan 06 Crystal Palace 0 Port Vale 0
Jan 06 Charlton 2 Sheffield W 0
Jan 07 Chelsea 1 Newcastle 1
Jan 06 Crewe 4 W.B.A. 3
Jan 07 Derby 2 Leeds 4
Jan 07 Everton 2 Stockport 2
Jan 06 Fulham 1 Shrewsbury 1
Jan 06 Gravesend 0 Aston Villa 3
Jan 06 Grimsby 7 Luton 1
Jan 06 Hereford 1 Tottenham 1
Jan 06 Huddersfield 2 Blackpool 1
Jan 06 Ipswich 0 Blackburn 0
Jan 06 Leicester 0 Manchester C 0
Jan 06 Liverpool 7 Rochdale 0
Jan 06 Manchester U 2 Sunderland 2
Jan 06 Millwall 3 Oxford 3
Jan 06 Norwich 1 Brentford 2
Jan 06 Notts Co 1 Middlesbrough 2
Jan 06 Peterborough 1 Wrexham 0
Jan 06 Plymouth 1 Coventry 3
Jan 06 Reading 3 Gillingham 1
Jan 07 Southampton 3 Portsmouth 0
Jan 06 Stoke 1 Nottingham F 1
Jan 06 Swindon 2 Woking 0
Jan 06 Tranmere 0 Q.P.R. 2
Jan 06 Walsall 1 Wigan 0
Jan 06 Watford 1 Wimbledon 1
Jan 06 West Ham 2 Southend 0

Replays
Jan 16 Blackburn 0 Ipswich 1
Jan 16 Oxford 1 Millwall 0
Jan 16 Port Vale 4 Crystal Palace 3
Jan 16 Shrewsbury 2 Fulham 1
Jan 16 Sunderland 1 Manchester U 2
Jan 17 Manchester C 5 Leicester 0
Jan 17 Newcastle 2 Chelsea 2
Penalties 2-4
Jan 17 Nottingham F 2 Stoke 0
Jan 17 Sheffield U 1 Arsenal 0
Jan 17 Stockport 2 Everton 3
Jan 17 Tottenham 5 Hereford 1
Jan 17 Wimbledon 1 Watford 0
Jan 17 Wolverhampton 2 Birmingham 1
Jan 23 Oldham 2 Barnsley 1

4th Round
Feb 14 Bolton 0 Leeds 1
Feb 07 Charlton 3 Brentford 2
Feb 07 Coventry 2 Manchester C 2
Jan 27 Everton 2 Port Vale 2
Feb 06 Huddersfield 2 Peterborough 0
Feb 13 Ipswich 1 Walsall 0
Feb 07 Middlesbrough 0 Wimbledon 0
Feb 07 Nottingham F 1 Oxford 1
Jan 29 Q.P.R. 1 Chelsea 2
Jan 27 Reading 0 Manchester U 3
Jan 28 Sheffield U 0 Aston Villa 1
Feb 18 Shrewsbury 0 Liverpool 4
Feb 07 Southampton 1 Crewe 1
Feb 12 Swindon 1 Oldham 0
Jan 27 Tottenham 1 Wolverhampton 1
Feb 07 West Ham 1 Grimsby 1

Replays
Feb 07 Wolverhampton 0 Tottenham 2
Feb 13 Crewe 2 Southampton 3
Feb 13 Oxford 0 Nottingham F 3
Feb 08 Wimbledon 1 Middlesbrough 0
Feb 14 Grimsby 3 West Ham 0
Feb 14 Manchester C 2 Coventry 1
Feb 14 Port Vale 2 Everton 1

5th Round
Feb 21 Grimsby 0 Chelsea 0
Feb 17 Huddersfield 2 Wimbledon 2
Feb 17 Ipswich 1 Aston Villa 3
Feb 21 Leeds 0 Port Vale 0
Feb 28 Liverpool 2 Charlton 1
Feb 18 Manchester U 2 Manchester C 1
Feb 28 Nottingham F 2 Tottenham 2
Feb 17 Swindon 1 Southampton 1

Replays
Feb 27 Port Vale 1 Leeds 2
Feb 28 Chelsea 4 Grimsby 1
Feb 28 Southampton 2 Swindon 0
Feb 28 Wimbledon 3 Huddersfield 1
Mar 09 Tottenham 1 Nottingham F 1
Penalties 1-3

6th Round
Mar 09 Chelsea 2 Wimbledon 2
Mar 10 Leeds 0 Liverpool 0
Mar 11 Manchester U 2 Southampton 0
Mar 13 Nottingham F 0 Aston Villa 1

Replays
Mar 20 Liverpool 3 Leeds 0
Mar 20 Wimbledon 1 Chelsea 3

Semi-finals
Mar 31 Aston Villa 0 Liverpool 3
played at Manchester U
Mar 31 Chelsea 1 Manchester U 2
played at Aston Villa

Final
May 11 Liverpool 0 Manchester U 1
played at Wembley

SEASON 1996-97

1st Round
Nov 16 Ashford 2 Dagenham 2
Nov 16 Blackpool 1 Wigan 0
Nov 16 Boreham Wood 1 Rushden 1
Nov 16 Boston 3 Morecambe 0
Nov 16 Brentford 2 Bournemouth 0
Nov 16 Bristol R 1 Exeter 2
Nov 16 Bromley 1 Enfield 3
Nov 16 Burnley 2 Lincoln 1
Nov 16 Cambridge 3 Welling 0
Nov 16 Cardiff 2 Hendon 0
Nov 16 Carlisle 6 Shepshed 0
Nov 16 Chester 3 Stalybridge 0
Nov 16 Chesterfield 1 Bury 0
Nov 16 Colchester 1 Wycombe 2
Nov 16 Colwyn Bay 1 Wrexham 1
Nov 16 Crewe 4 Kidderminster 1
Nov 16 Farnborough 2 Barnet 2
Nov 16 Gillingham 1 Hereford 0
Nov 16 Hartlepool 0 York 0
Nov 16 Hednesford 2 Southport 1
Nov 16 Leyton O 2 Merthyr T 1
Nov 16 Macclesfield 0 Rochdale 2
Nov 16 Mansfield 4 Consett 0
Nov 17 Newcastle 0 Notts Co 2
Nov 17 Northampton 0 Watford 1
Nov 16 Northwich 2 Walsall 2
Nov 16 Peterborough 0 Cheltenham 0
Nov 16 Plymouth 5 Fulham 0
Nov 16 Preston 4 Altrincham 1
Nov 16 Runcorn 1 Darlington 4
Nov 16 Scunthorpe 4 Rotherham 1
Nov 16 Shrewsbury 1 Scarborough 1
Nov 16 Stevenage 2 Hayes 2
Nov 16 Stockport 2 Doncaster 1
Nov 16 Sudbury 0 Brighton 0
Nov 16 Swansea 1 Bristol C 1
Nov 16 Torquay 0 Luton 1
Nov 17 Whitby 0 Hull 0
Nov 16 Wisbech 1 St Albans 2
Nov 15 Woking 2 Millwall 2

Replays
Nov 25 Dagenham 1 Ashford 1
Penalties 3-4
Nov 26 Barnet 1 Farnborough 0
Nov 26 Brighton 1 Sudbury 1
Penalties 3-4
Nov 26 Bristol C 1 Swansea 0
Nov 26 Hayes 0 Stevenage 2
Nov 26 Hull 8 Whitby 4
Nov 26 Millwall 0 Woking 1
Nov 26 Rushden 2 Boreham Wood 3
Nov 26 Scarborough 1 Shrewsbury 0
Nov 26 Walsall 3 Norwich 1
Nov 26 Wrexham 2 Colwyn Bay 0
Nov 26 York 3 Hartlepool 0
Nov 27 Cheltenham 1 Peterborough 3

2nd Round
Dec 07 Barnet 3 Wycombe 3
Dec 07 Blackpool 0 Hednesford 1
Dec 07 Bristol C 9 St Albans 2
Dec 07 Cambridge 0 Woking 2
Dec 07 Cardiff 0 Gillingham 2
Dec 07 Carlisle 1 Darlington 0
Dec 07 Chester 1 Boston 0
Dec 07 Chesterfield 2 Scarborough 0
Dec 07 Enfield 1 Peterborough 1
Dec 07 Hull 1 Crewe 5
Dec 07 Leyton O 1 Stevenage 2
Dec 07 Luton 2 Boreham Wood 1
Dec 07 Mansfield 0 Stockport 3
Dec 07 Notts Co 3 Rochdale 1
Dec 06 Plymouth 4 Exeter 1
Dec 07 Preston 2 York 3
Dec 07 Sudbury 1 Brentford 3
Dec 07 Walsall 1 Burnley 1
Dec 07 Watford 5 Ashford 0
Dec 07 Wrexham 2 Scunthorpe 2

Replays
Dec 17 Peterborough 4 Enfield 1
Dec 17 Scunthorpe 2 Wrexham 3
Dec 17 Wycombe 3 Barnet 2
Dec 23 Burnley 1 Walsall 1
Penalties 4-2

3rd Round
Jan 04 Arsenal 1 Sunderland 1
Jan 14 Barnsley 2 Oldham 0
Jan 04 Blackburn 1 Port Vale 0
Jan 25 Brentford 0 Manchester C 1
Jan 14 Carlisle 1 Tranmere 0
Jan 05 Charlton 1 Newcastle 1
Jan 04 Chelsea 3 W.B.A. 0
Jan 14 Chesterfield 2 Bristol C 0
Jan 25 Coventry 1 Woking 1
Jan 14 Crewe 1 Wimbledon 1
Jan 14 Crystal Palace 2 Leeds 2
Jan 05 Everton 3 Swindon 0
Jan 21 Gillingham 0 Derby 2
Jan 13 Hednesford 1 York 0
Jan 15 Leicester 2 Southend 0
Jan 04 Liverpool 1 Burnley 0
Jan 21 Luton 1 Bolton 1
Jan 05 Manchester U 2 Tottenham 0
Jan 04 Middlesbrough 6 Chester 0
Jan 04 Norwich 1 Sheffield U 0
Jan 04 Nottingham F 3 Ipswich 0
Jan 14 Notts Co 0 Aston Villa 0
Jan 04 Plymouth 0 Peterborough 1
Jan 04 Q.P.R. 1 Huddersfield 1
Jan 04 Reading 3 Southampton 1
Jan 04 Sheffield W 7 Grimsby 1
Jan 04 Stevenage 0 Birmingham 2
Jan 15 Stoke 0 Stockport 2
Jan 21 Watford 2 Oxford 0
Jan 04 Wolverhampton 1 Portsmouth 2
Jan 04 Wrexham 1 West Ham 1
Jan 05 Wycombe 0 Bradford C 2

Replays
Jan 14 Huddersfield 1 Q.P.R. 2
Jan 15 Newcastle 2 Charlton 1
Jan 15 Sunderland 0 Arsenal 2
Jan 21 Wimbledon 2 Crewe 0
Jan 22 Aston Villa 3 Notts Co 0
Jan 25 Leeds 1 Crystal Palace 0
Jan 25 Bolton 6 Luton 2
Jan 25 West Ham 0 Wrexham 1
Feb 04 Woking 1 Coventry 2

4th Round
Feb 04 Arsenal 0 Leeds 1
Jan 25 Birmingham 3 Stockport 1
Feb 15 Blackburn 1 Coventry 2
Feb 04 Bolton 2 Chesterfield 3
Jan 25 Carlisle 0 Sheffield W 2
Jan 26 Chelsea 4 Liverpool 2
Jan 25 Derby 3 Aston Villa 1
Jan 25 Everton 2 Bradford C 3
Jan 25 Hednesford 2 Middlesbrough 3
Jan 25 Leicester 2 Norwich 1
Feb 05 Manchester C 3 Watford 1
Jan 25 Manchester U 1 Wimbledon 1
Jan 26 Newcastle 1 Nottingham F 2
Feb 04 Peterborough 2 Wrexham 4
Jan 25 Portsmouth 3 Reading 0
Jan 25 Q.P.R. 3 Barnsley 2

Replays
Feb 04 Wimbledon 1 Manchester U 0

5th Round
Feb 15 Birmingham 1 Wrexham 3
Feb 16 Bradford C 0 Sheffield W 1
Feb 15 Chesterfield 1 Nottingham F 0
Feb 26 Derby 3 Coventry 2
Feb 15 Leeds 2 Portsmouth 3
Feb 16 Leicester 2 Chelsea 2
Feb 15 Manchester C 0 Middlesbrough 1
Feb 15 Wimbledon 2 Q.P.R. 1

Replays
Feb 26 Chelsea 1 Leicester 0

6th Round
Mar 09 Chesterfield 1 Wrexham 0
Mar 08 Derby 0 Middlesbrough 2
Mar 09 Portsmouth 1 Chelsea 4
Mar 09 Sheffield W 0 Wimbledon 2

Semi-finals
Apr 13 Chelsea 3 Wimbledon 0
played at Arsenal
Apr 13 Chesterfield 3 Middlesbrough 3
played at Manchester U

Replay
Apr 22 Chesterfield 0 Middlesbrough 3
played at Sheffield W

Final
May 17 Chelsea 2 Middlesbrough 0
played at Wembley

Season 1997-98

1st Round
Nov 15 Barnet 1 Watford 2
Nov 15 Billericay 2 Wisbech 3
Nov 15 Blackpool 4 Blyth S 3
Nov 15 Bournemouth 3 Heybridge 0
Nov 15 Brentford 2 Colchester 2
Nov 15 Bristol C 1 Millwall 0
Nov 14 Bristol R 2 Gillingham 2
Nov 15 Carlisle 0 Wigan 1
Nov 15 Carshalton 0 Stevenage 0
Nov 15 Cheltenham 2 Tiverton 1
Nov 15 Chester 2 Winsford 1
Nov 15 Chesterfield 1 Northwich 0
Nov 15 Darlington 1 Solihull 1
Nov 15 Exeter 1 Northampton 1
Nov 15 Farnborough 0 Dagenham 1
Nov 15 Hartlepool 2 Macclesfield 4
Nov 15 Hayes 0 Boreham Wood 1
Nov 15 Hendon 2 Leyton O 2
Nov 15 Hereford 2 Brighton 1
Nov 15 Hull 0 Hednesford 2
Nov 15 Ilkeston 2 Boston 1
Nov 15 Kings Lynn 1 Bromsgrove 0
Nov 15 Lincoln 1 Gainsborough 1
Nov 15 Luton 0 Torquay 1
Nov 16 Margate 1 Fulham 2
Nov 15 Morecambe 1 Emley 1
Nov 16 Notts Co 2 Colwyn Bay 0
Nov 15 Oldham 1 Mansfield 1
Nov 15 Plymouth 0 Cambridge 0
Nov 15 Preston 3 Doncaster 2
Nov 15 Rochdale 0 Wrexham 2
Nov 15 Rotherham 3 Burnley 3
Nov 15 Scunthorpe 2 Scarborough 1
Nov 15 Shrewsbury 1 Grimsby 1
Nov 15 Slough 1 Cardiff 1
Nov 15 Southport 0 York 4
Nov 14 Swansea 1 Peterborough 4
Nov 15 Walsall 2 Lincoln 0
Nov 15 Woking 0 Southend 2
Nov 15 Wycombe 2 Basingstoke 2

Replays
Nov 24 Stevenage 5 Carshalton 0
Nov 25 Basingstoke 2 Wycombe 2
Penalties 5-4
Nov 25 Burnley 0 Rotherham 3
Nov 25 Cambridge 3 Plymouth 2
Nov 25 Cardiff 3 Slough 2
Nov 25 Colchester 0 Brentford 0
Penalties 4-2
Nov 25 Emley 3 Morecambe 3
Penalties 3-1
Nov 25 Gainsborough 2 Lincoln 3
Nov 25 Gillingham 0 Bristol R 2
Nov 25 Grimsby 4 Shrewsbury 0
Nov 25 Leyton O 0 Hendon 1
Nov 25 Mansfield 0 Oldham 1
Nov 25 Northampton 2 Exeter 1
Nov 26 Solihull 3 Darlington 3
Penalties 2-4

2nd Round
Dec 07 Bournemouth 3 Bristol C 1
Dec 06 Cambridge 1 Stevenage 1
Dec 06 Cardiff 3 Hendon 1
Dec 06 Cheltenham 1 Boreham Wodd 1
Dec 05 Chester 0 Wrexham 2
Dec 06 Colchester 1 Hereford 1
Dec 06 Fulham 1 Southend 0
Dec 06 Grimsby 2 Chesterfield 2
Dec 06 Hednesford 0 Darlington 1
Dec 06 Lincoln 2 Emley 2
Dec 06 Macclesfield 0 Walsall 7
Dec 06 Northampton 1 Basingstoke 1
Dec 06 Oldham 2 Blackpool 1
Dec 06 Peterborough 3 Dagenham 2
Dec 06 Preston 2 Notts Co 2
Dec 06 Rotherham 6 Kings Lynn 0
Dec 06 Scunthorpe 1 Ilkeston 1
Dec 06 Torquay 1 Watford 1
Dec 06 Wigan 2 York 1
Dec 06 Wisbech 0 Bristol R 2

Replays
Dec 15 Stevenage 2 Cambridge 1
Dec 16 Basingstoke 0 Northampton 0
Penalties 3-4
Dec 16 Boreham Wood 0 Cheltenham 2
Dec 16 Chesterfield 0 Grimsby 2
Dec 16 Hereford 1 Colchester 1
Penalties 5-4
Dec 16 Notts Co 1 Preston 2
Dec 16 Watford 2 Torquay 1
Dec 17 Emley 3 Lincoln 3
Penalties 4-3
Dec 17 Ilkeston 1 Scunthorpe 2

3rd Round
Jan 03 Arsenal 0 Port Vale 0
Jan 03 Barnsley 1 Bolton 0
Jan 03 Blackburn 4 Wigan 2
Jan 13 Bournemouth 0 Huddersfield 1
Jan 03 Bristol R 1 Ipswich 1
Jan 03 Cardiff 1 Oldham 0
Jan 03 Charlton 4 Nottingham F 1
Jan 04 Chelsea 3 Manchester U 5
Jan 13 Cheltenham 1 Reading 1
Jan 03 Crewe 1 Birmingham 2
Jan 03 Crystal Palace 2 Scunthorpe 0
Jan 14 Darlington 0 Wolverhampton 4
Jan 03 Derby 2 Southampton 0
Jan 04 Everton 0 Newcastle 1
Jan 03 Grimsby 3 Norwich 0
Jan 13 Hereford 0 Tranmere 3
Jan 03 Leeds 4 Oxford 0
Jan 03 Leicester 4 Northampton 0
Jan 03 Liverpool 1 Coventry 3
Jan 03 Manchester C 2 Bradford C 0
Jan 13 Peterborough 0 Walsall 2
Jan 03 Portsmouth 2 Aston Villa 2
Jan 03 Preston 1 Stockport 2
Jan 03 Q.P.R. 2 Middlesbrough 2
Jan 03 Rotherham 1 Sunderland 5
Jan 03 Sheffield U 1 Bury 1
Jan 03 Swindon 1 Stevenage 2
Jan 05 Tottenham 3 Fulham 1
Jan 03 Watford 1 Sheffield W 1
Jan 03 West Ham 2 Emley 1
Jan 04 Wimbledon 0 Wrexham 0
Jan 13 W.B.A. 3 Stoke 1

Replays
Jan 13 Bury 1 Sheffield U 2
Jan 13 Ipswich 1 Bristol R 0
Jan 13 Middlesbrough 2 Q.P.R. 0
Jan 13 Wrexham 2 Wimbledon 3
Jan 14 Aston Villa 1 Portsmouth 0
Jan 14 Port Vale 1 Arsenal 1
Penalties 3-4
Jan 14 Sheffield W 0 Watford 0
Penalties 5-3
Jan 20 Reading 2 Cheltenham 1

4th Round
Jan 24 Aston Villa 4 W.B.A. 0
Jan 24 Birmingham 2 Stockport 1
Jan 24 Cardiff 1 Reading 1
Jan 24 Charlton 1 Wolverhampton 1
Jan 24 Coventry 2 Derby 0
Jan 24 Crystal Palace 3 Leicester 0
Jan 24 Huddersfield 0 Wimbledon 1
Jan 24 Ipswich 1 Sheffield U 1
Jan 24 Leeds 2 Grimsby 0
Jan 25 Manchester C 1 West Ham 2
Jan 24 Manchester U 5 Walsall 1
Jan 24 Middlesbrough 1 Arsenal 2
Jan 26 Sheffield W 0 Blackburn 3
Jan 25 Stevenage 1 Newcastle 1
Jan 24 Tottenham 1 Barnsley 1
Jan 24 Tranmere 1 Sunderland 0

Replays
Feb 03 Reading 1 Cardiff 1
Penalties 4-3
Feb 03 Sheffield U 1 Ipswich 0
Feb 03 Wolverhampton 3 Charlton 0
Feb 04 Barnsley 3 Tottenham 1
Feb 04 Newcastle 2 Stevenage 1

5th Round
Feb 15 Arsenal 0 Crystal Palace 0
Feb 14 Aston Villa 0 Coventry 1
Feb 14 Leeds 3 Birmingham 2
Feb 15 Manchester U 1 Barnsley 1
Feb 14 Newcastle 1 Tranmere 0
Feb 13 Sheffield U 1 Reading 0
Feb 14 West Ham 2 Blackburn 2
Feb 14 Wimbledon 1 Wolverhampton 1

Replays
Feb 25 Barnsley 3 Manchester U 2
Feb 25 Blackburn 1 West Ham 1
Penalties 4-5
Feb 25 Crystal Palace 1 Arsenal 2
Feb 25 Wolverhampton 2 Wimbledon 1

6th Round
Mar 08 Arsenal 1 West Ham 1
Mar 07 Coventry 1 Sheffield U 1
Mar 07 Leeds 0 Wolverhampton 1
Mar 08 Newcastle 3 Barnsley 1

Replays
Mar 17 Sheffield U 1 Coventry 1
Penalties 3-1
Mar 17 West Ham 1 Arsenal 1
Penalties 3-4

Semi-finals
Apr 05 Arsenal 1 Wolverhampton 0
played at Aston Villa
Apr 05 Newcastle 1 Sheffield U 0
played at Manchester U

Final
May 16 Arsenal 2 Newcastle 0
played at Wembley

Season 1998-99

1st Round
Nov 14 Basingstoke 1 Bournemouth 2
Nov 14 Bedlington 4 Colchester 1
Nov 15 Boreham Wood 2 Luton 3
Nov 14 Brentford 5 Camerley 0
Nov 14 Bristol R 3 Welling 0
Nov 14 Cardiff 6 Chester 0
Nov 14 Cheltenham 0 Lincoln 1
Nov 17 Darlington 3 Burnley 2
Nov 14 Dulwich 0 Southport 1
Nov 15 Emley 1 Rotherham 1
Nov 14 Enfield 2 York 2
Nov 15 Fulham 1 Leigh 1
Nov 14 Hartlepool 2 Carlisle 1
Nov 14 Hednesford 3 Barnet 1
Nov 15 Hendon 0 Notts Co 0
Nov 14 Kingstonian 1 Burton 0
Nov 14 Leyton O 4 Brighton 2
Nov 14 Macclesfield 2 Slough 2
Nov 13 Manchester C 3 Halifax 0
Nov 14 Mansfield 2 Hayes 1
Nov 14 Northampton 2 Lancaster 1
Nov 14 Oldham 2 Gillingham 0
Nov 14 Plymouth 0 Kidderminster 0
Nov 14 Preston 3 Ford 0
Nov 14 Reading 0 Stoke 1
Nov 14 Runcorn 1 Stevenage 1
Nov 14 Rushden 1 Shrewsbury 0
Nov 14 Salisbury 0 Hull 2
Nov 14 Scarborough 1 Rochdale 1
Nov 14 Southend 0 Doncaster 1
Nov 13 Swansea 3 Millwall 0
Nov 14 Tamworth 2 Exeter 2
Nov 14 Telford 0 Cambridge 2
Nov 14 Walsall 1 Gresley 0
Nov 14 Wigan 4 Blackpool 3
Nov 14 Woking 0 Scunthorpe 1
Nov 14 Worcester 0 Torquay 1
Nov 14 Wrexham 1 Peterborough 0
Nov 14 Wycombe 1 Chesterfield 0
Nov 14 Yeovil 2 West Auckland 2

Replays
Nov 23 Stevenage 2 Runcorn 0
Nov 24 Exeter 4 Tamworth 1
Nov 24 Leigh 0 Fulham 2
Nov 24 Rochdale 2 Scarborough 0
Nov 24 Rotherham 3 Emley 1
Nov 24 Slough 1 Macclesfield 1
Penalties 8-9
Nov 24 West Auckland 1 Yeovil 1
Penalties 3-5
Nov 24 York 2 Enfield 1
Dec 01 Kidderminster 0 Plymouth 0
Penalties 4-5
Dec 01 Notts Co 3 Hendon 0

2nd Round
Dec 05 Cardiff 3 Hednesford 1
Dec 04 Darlington 1 Manchester C 1
Dec 05 Doncaster 0 Rushden 0
Dec 05 Exeter 2 Bristol R 2
Dec 05 Fulham 4 Hartlepool 2
Dec 06 Kingstonian 0 Leyton O 0
Dec 05 Lincoln 4 Stevenage 1
Dec 05 Luton 1 Hull 2
Dec 05 Macclesfield 4 Cambridge 1
Dec 05 Mansfield 1 Southport 2
Dec 05 Notts Co 1 Wigan 1
Dec 05 Oldham 1 Brentford 1
Dec 05 Preston 2 Walsall 0
Dec 05 Rochdale 0 Rotherham 0
Dec 05 Scunthorpe 2 Bedlington 0
Dec 05 Swansea 1 Stoke 0
Dec 05 Torquay 0 Bournemouth 1
Dec 05 Wrexham 2 York 1
Dec 05 Wycombe 1 Plymouth 1
Dec 05 Yeovil 2 Northampton 0

Replays
Dec 15 Brentford 2 Oldham 2
Penalties 2-4
Dec 15 Bristol R 5 Exeter 0
Dec 15 Leyton O 2 Kingstonian 1
Dec 15 Manchester C 1 Darlington 0
Dec 15 Plymouth 3 Wycombe 2
Dec 15 Rotherham 4 Rochdale 0
Dec 15 Rushden 4 Doncaster 2
Dec 15 Wigan 0 Notts Co 0
Penalties 2-4

3rd Round
Jan 02 Aston Villa 3 Hull 0
Jan 02 Blackburn 2 Charlton 0
Jan 02 Bolton 1 Wolverhampton 2
Jan 02 Bournemouth 1 W.B.A. 0
Jan 02 Bradford C 2 Grimsby 1
Jan 02 Bristol C 0 Everton 2
Jan 02 Bury 0 Stockport 3
Jan 02 Cardiff 1 Yeovil 1
Jan 02 Coventry 7 Macclesfield 0
Jan 02 Crewe 1 Oxford 3
Jan 02 Leicester 4 Birmingham 2
Jan 02 Lincoln 0 Sunderland 1
Jan 03 Manchester U 3 Middlesbrough 1

Jan 02	Newcastle	2	Crystal Palace	1
Jan 02	Nottingham F	0	Portsmouth	1
Jan 02	Oldham	0	Chelsea	2
Jan 02	Plymouth	0	Derby	3
Jan 03	Port Vale	0	Liverpool	3
Jan 04	Preston	2	Arsenal	4
Jan 02	Q.P.R.	0	Huddersfield	1
Jan 02	Rotherham	0	Bristol R	1
Jan 02	Rushden	0	Leeds	0
Jan 02	Sheffield U	1	Notts Co	1
Jan 03	Sheffield W	4	Norwich	1
Jan 02	Southampton	1	Fulham	1
Jan 02	Southport	0	Leyton O	2
Jan 02	Swindon	0	Barnsley	0
Jan 02	Tottenham	5	Watford	2
Jan 02	Tranmere	0	Ipswich	1
Jan 02	Wimbledon	1	Manchester C	0
Jan 02	West Ham	1	Swansea	1
Jan 02	Wrexham	4	Scunthorpe	3

Replays

Jan 12	Yeovil	1	Cardiff	2
Jan 13	Fulham	1	Southampton	0
Jan 13	Leeds	3	Rushden	1
Jan 13	Swansea	1	West Ham	0
Jan 19	Barnsley	3	Swindon	1
Jan 23	Notts Co	3	Sheffield U	4

4th Round

Jan 23	Aston Villa	0	Fulham	2
Jan 23	Barnsley	3	Bournemouth	1
Jan 23	Blackburn	1	Sunderland	0
Jan 23	Bristol R	3	Leyton O	0
Jan 23	Everton	1	Ipswich	0
Jan 23	Leicester	0	Coventry	3
Jan 24	Manchester U	2	Liverpool	1
Jan 23	Newcastle	3	Bradford C	0
Jan 25	Oxford	1	Chelsea	1
Jan 23	Portsmouth	1	Leeds	5
Jan 27	Sheffield U	4	Cardiff	1
Jan 23	Sheffield W	2	Stockport	0
Jan 23	Swansea	0	Derby	1
Jan 23	Wimbledon	1	Tottenham	1
Jan 24	Wolverhampton	1	Arsenal	2
Jan 23	Wrexham	1	Huddersfield	1

Replays

Feb 02	Tottenham	3	Wimbledon	0
Feb 03	Chelsea	4	Oxford	2
Feb 03	Huddersfield	2	Wrexham	1

5th Round

Feb 13	Arsenal	2	Sheffield U	1
Feb 13	Barnsley	4	Bristol R	1
Feb 13	Everton	2	Coventry	1
Feb 13	Huddersfield	2	Derby	2
Feb 13	Leeds	1	Tottenham	1
Feb 14	Manchester U	1	Fulham	0
Feb 14	Newcastle	0	Blackburn	0
Feb 13	Sheffield W	0	Chelsea	1

Replays

Feb 24	Blackburn	0	Newcastle	1
Feb 24	Derby	3	Huddersfield	1
Feb 24	Tottenham	2	Leeds	0

6th Round

Mar 06	Arsenal	1	Derby	0
Mar 16	Barnsley	0	Tottenham	1
Mar 07	Manchester U	0	Chelsea	0
Mar 07	Newcastle	4	Everton	1

Replay

Mar 10	Chelsea	0	Manchester U	2

Semi-finals

Apr 11	Arsenal	0	Manchester U	0
	played at Aston Villa			
Apr 11	Newcastle	2	Tottenham	0
	played at Old Trafford			

Replay

Apr 14	Arsenal	1	Manchester U	2
	played at Aston Villa			

Final

May 22	Manchester U	2	Newcastle	0
	played at Wembley			

Season 1999-2000

1st Round

Oct 30	Aldershot	1	Hednesford	1
Oct 31	Barnet	0	Burnley	1
Oct 30	Bath	0	Hendon	2
Oct 30	Blackpool	2	Stoke	0
Oct 30	Brentford	2	Plymouth	2
Oct 30	Bristol C	3	Mansfield	2
Oct 31	Bristol R	0	Preston	1
Oct 30	Burton A	0	Rochdale	0
Oct 30	Cambridge C	0	Wigan	2
Oct 30	Cambridge U	1	Gateshead	0
Oct 30	Cheltenham	1	Gillingham	1
Oct 30	Chesterfield	1	Enfield	2
Oct 30	Darlington	2	Southport	1
Oct 30	Doncaster	0	Halifax	2
Oct 30	Exeter	2	Eastwood	1
Oct 30	Forest Green	6	Guiseley	0
Oct 31	Hartlepool	1	Millwall	0
Oct 30	Hayes	2	Runcorn	1
Oct 30	Hereford	1	York	0
Oct 30	Ilkeston	2	Carlisle	1
Oct 30	Leyton O	1	Cardiff	1
Oct 30	Lincoln	1	Welling	0
Oct 30	Luton	4	Kingstonian	2
Oct 30	Macclesfield	0	Hull	0
Nov 02	Merthyr T	2	Stalybridge	2
Oct 30	Notts Co	1	Bournemouth	1
Oct 30	Oldham	4	Chelmsford	0
Oct 30	Oxford U	3	Morecambe	2
Oct 30	Peterborough	1	Brighton	1
Oct 30	Reading	4	Yeovil	2
Oct 30	Rotherham	3	Worthing	0
Oct 29	Rushden & Diamonds	2	Scunthorpe	0
Oct 30	Shrewsbury	2	Northampton	1
Oct 30	St Albans	0	Bamber Bridge	2
Oct 30	Swansea	2	Colchester	1
Oct 30	Tamworth	2	Bury	2
Oct 30	Torquay	1	Southend	0
Oct 30	Whyteleafe	0	Chester	0
Oct 30	Wrexham	1	Kettering	1
Oct 30	Wycombe	1	Oxford C	1

Replays

Nov 08	Hednesford		Aldershot	
Nov 09	Bournemouth	4	Notts Co	2
Nov 09	Brighton	3	Peterborough	0
Nov 09	Bury	2	Tamworth	1
Nov 09	Cardiff	3	Leyton O	1
Nov 09	Chester	3	Whyteleafe	1
Nov 09	Gillingham	3	Cheltenham	2
Nov 09	Hull	4	Macclesfield	0
Nov 09	Plymouth	2	Brentford	1
Nov 09	Rochdale	3	Burton A	0
Nov 09	Stalybridge	3	Merthyr T	1
Nov 10	Kettering	0	Wrexham	2
Nov 16	Oxford C	0	Wycombe	1

2nd Round

Nov 20	Blackpool	2	Hendon	0
Nov 20	Bournemouth	0	Bristol C	2
Nov 20	Burnley	2	Rotherham	0
Nov 20	Bury	0	Cardiff	0
Nov 20	Cambridge	1	Bamber Bridge	0
Nov 20	Exeter	2	Aldershot	0
Nov 21	Forest Green	0	Torquay	3
Nov 20	Gillingham	3	Darlington	1
Nov 20	Hayes	2	Hull	2
Nov 21	Hereford	1	Hartlepool	0
Nov 20	Ilkeston	1	Rushden & Diamonds	1
Nov 19	Luton	2	Lincoln	2
Nov 20	Oldham	1	Swansea	0
Nov 20	Plymouth	0	Brighton	0
Nov 20	Preston	0	Enfield	0
Nov 20	Reading	1	Halifax	1
Nov 20	Shrewsbury	2	Oxford U	2
Nov 20	Stalybridge	1	Chester	2
Nov 20	Wrexham	2	Rochdale	1
Nov 20	Wycombe	2	Wigan	2

Replays

Nov 30	Brighton	1	Plymouth	2
Nov 30	Cardiff	1	Bury	0
Nov 30	Enfield	0	Preston	3
Nov 30	Halifax	0	Reading	1
Nov 30	Hull	3	Hayes	2
Nov 30	Lincoln	0	Luton	1
Nov 30	Oxford U	2	Shrewsbury	1
Nov 30	Rushden & Diamonds	3	Ilkeston	0
Nov 30	Wigan	2	Wycombe	1

3rd Round

Dec 13	Arsenal	3	Blackpool	1
Dec 11	Aston Villa	2	Darlington	1
Dec 21	Bolton	1	Cardiff	0
Dec 10	Cambridge	2	C Palace	0
Dec 11	Charlton	2	Swindon	1
Dec 12	Chester	1	Manchester C	4
Dec 11	Crewe	1	Bradford	2
Dec 11	Derby	0	Burnley	1
Dec 11	Exeter	0	Everton	0
Dec 11	Fulham	2	Luton	2
Dec 11	Grimsby	3	Stockport	2
Dec 11	Hereford	0	Leicester	0
Dec 12	Huddersfield	0	Liverpool	2
Dec 11	Hull	1	Chelsea	6
Dec 13	Ipswich	0	Southampton	1
Dec 12	Leeds	2	Port vale	0
Dec 11	Norwich	1	Coventry	3
Dec 10	Nottingham F	1	Oxford U	1
Dec 11	Preston	2	Oldham	1
Dec 11	Q.P.R.	1	Torquay	1
Dec 11	Reading	1	Plymouth	1
Dec 12	Sheffield U	1	Rushden & Diamonds	1
Dec 11	Sheffield W	1	Bristol C	0
Dec 11	Sunderland	1	Portsmouth	0
Dec 12	Tottenham	1	Newcastle	1
Dec 11	Tranmere	1	West Ham	0
Dec 11	W.B.A.	2	Blackburn	2
Dec 11	Watford	0	Birmingham	1
Dec 11	Walsall	1	Gillingham	1
Dec 11	Wigan	0	Wolverhampton	1
Dec 11	Wimbledon	1	Barnsley	0
Dec 11	Wrexham	2	Middlesbrough	1

Replays

Dec 21	Everton	1	Exeter	0
Dec 21	Luton	0	Fulham	3
Dec 21	Plymouth	1	Reading	0
Dec 21	Rushden & Diamonds	1	Sheffield U	1
	Penalties 5-6			
Dec 21	Torquay	2	Q.P.R.	3
Dec 22	Blackburn	2	W.B.A.	0
Dec 22	Leicester	2	Hereford	1
Dec 22	Newcastle	6	Tottenham	1
Jan 08	Gillingham	2	Walsall	1
Jan 08	Oxford U	1	Nottingham F	3

4th Round

Jan 09	Arsenal	0	Leicester	0
Jan 08	Aston Villa	1	Southampton	0
Jan 08	Charlton	1	Q.P.R.	0
Jan 19	Chelsea	2	Nottingham F	0
Jan 08	Coventry	3	Burnley	0
Jan 08	Everton	2	Birmingham	0
Jan 08	Fulham	3	Wimbledon	0
Jan 11	Gillingham	3	Bradford C	1
Jan 08	Grimsby	0	Bolton	2
Jan 10	Liverpool	0	Blackburn	1
Jan 09	Manchester C	2	Leeds	5
Jan 08	Newcastle	4	Sheffield U	1
Jan 08	Plymouth	0	Preston	3
Jan 08	Sheffield W	1	Wolverhampton	1
Jan 08	Tranmere	1	Sunderland	0
Jan 08	Wrexham	1	Cambridge	2

Replays

Jan 18	Wolverhampton	0	Sheffield W	0
	Penalties 3-4			
Jan 19	Leicester	0	Arsenal	0
	Penalties 6-5			

5th Round

Jan 30	Aston Villa	3	Leeds	2
Jan 31	Blackburn	1	Newcastle	2
Jan 29	Cambridge	1	Bolton	3
Jan 30	Chelsea	2	Leicester	1
Jan 29	Coventry	2	Charlton	3
Jan 29	Everton	2	Preston	0
Jan 29	Fulham	1	Tranmere	2
Jan 29	Gillingham	3	Sheffield W	1

6th Round

Feb 19	Bolton	1	Charlton	0
Feb 20	Chelsea	5	Gillingham	0
Feb 20	Everton	1	Aston Villa	2
Feb 20	Tranmere	2	Newcastle	3

Semi-finals

Apr 02	Aston Villa	0	Bolton	0
	Penalties 4-1			
Apr 09	Chelsea	2	Newcastle	1

Final

May 20	Aston Villa	0	Chelsea	1

English League Cup Results 1960-2000

Season 1960-61

1st Round				
Sep 26	Bristol R	2	Fulham	1
Oct 12	Chester	2	Leyton O	2
Oct 10	Colchester	4	Newcastle	1
Oct 10	Coventry	4	Barrow	2
Oct 12	Darlington	2	Crystal Palace	0
Oct 12	Everton	3	Accrington	1
Oct 19	Exeter	1	Manchester U	1
Oct 10	Hull	0	Bolton	0
Oct 11	Ipswich	0	Barnsley	2
Oct 12	Leicester	4	Mansfield	0
Oct 12	Lincoln	2	Bradford	2
Oct 03	Middlesbrough	3	Cardiff	4
Oct 10	Millwall	1	Chelsea	7
Oct 10	Newport	2	Southampton	2
Oct 11	Oldham	2	Hartlepool	1
Oct 12	Plymouth	2	Southport	0
Oct 11	Preston	4	Peterborough	1
Oct 17	Q.P.R.	2	Port Vale	2
Oct 10	Rochdale	1	Scunthorpe	1
Oct 10	Stockport	2	Carlisle	0
Oct 11	Watford	2	Derby	5
Sep 26	West Ham	3	Charlton	1
Oct 10	York	1	Blackburn	3

Replays				
Oct 17	Leyton O	1	Chester	0
Oct 17	Southampton	2	Newport	2
Oct 19	Bolton	5	Hull	1
Oct 19	Bradford	1	Lincoln	0
Oct 19	Port Vale	3	Q.P.R.	1
Oct 20	Scunthorpe	0	Rochdale	1
Oct 26	Manchester U	4	Exeter	1
Oct 26	Southampton	5	Newport	3

2nd Round				
Oct 10	Aldershot	1	Bristol C	1
Oct 12	Aston Villa	4	Huddersfield	1
Oct 26	Bolton	6	Grimsby	2
Oct 12	Bournemouth	1	Crewe	1
Oct 31	Bradford	0	Birmingham	1
Nov 02	Bradford C	2	Manchester U	1
Oct 25	Brentford	4	Sunderland	3
Oct 11	Bury	3	Sheffield U	1
Oct 24	Cardiff	0	Burnley	4
Oct 24	Chelsea	4	Workington	2
Oct 31	Colchester	0	Southampton	2
Oct 24	Darlington	3	West Ham	2
Oct 19	Derby	3	Barnsley	0
Oct 18	Doncaster	3	Stoke	1
Oct 31	Everton	3	Walsall	1
Oct 19	Gillingham	1	Preston	1
Sep 28	Leeds	0	Blackpool	0
Oct 26	Leicester	1	Rotherham	2
Nov 14	Leyton O	0	Chesterfield	1
Oct 19	Liverpool	1	Luton	1
Oct 18	Manchester C	3	Stockport	0
Oct 18	Northampton	1	Wrexham	1
Oct 26	Norwich	6	Oldham	2
Oct 06	Nottingham F	2	Halifax	0
Oct 20	Notts Co	1	Brighton	3
Nov 02	Plymouth	1	Torquay	1
Oct 24	Port Vale	0	Tranmere	2
Nov 02	Portsmouth	2	Coventry	0
Oct 12	Reading	3	Bristol R	5
Oct 25	Rochdale	5	Southend	2
Oct 18	Swansea	1	Blackburn	2
Oct 12	Swindon	1	Shrewsbury	1

Replays				
Oct 05	Blackpool	1	Leeds	3
Oct 19	Crewe	2	Bournemouth	0
Oct 24	Luton	2	Liverpool	5
Oct 24	Shrewsbury	2	Swindon	2
Oct 25	Bristol C	3	Aldershot	0
Oct 25	Preston	3	Gillingham	0
Oct 25	Wrexham	2	Northampton	0
Oct 26	Swindon	0	Shrewsbury	2
Nov 07	Torquay	1	Plymouth	2

3rd Round				
Nov 14	Birmingham	0	Plymouth	0
Nov 21	Blackburn	2	Rochdale	1
Nov 22	Brentford	1	Burnley	1
Nov 16	Brighton	0	Wrexham	2
Nov 23	Chesterfield	0	Leeds	4
Nov 14	Darlington	1	Bolton	2
Nov 14	Derby	1	Norwich	4
Nov 16	Doncaster	0	Chelsea	7
Nov 23	Everton	3	Bury	1
Nov 16	Liverpool	1	Southampton	2
Nov 15	Nottingham F	2	Bristol C	1
Nov 21	Portsmouth	2	Manchester C	0
Nov 15	Preston	3	Aston Villa	3
Nov 23	Rotherham	2	Bristol R	0
Nov 16	Shrewsbury	2	Bradford C	1
Nov 16	Tranmere	2	Crewe	0

Replays				
Nov 16	Plymouth	3	Birmingham	1
Nov 23	Aston Villa	3	Preston	1
Dec 06	Burnley	2	Brentford	1

4th Round				
Dec 13	Aston Villa	3	Plymouth	3
Dec 05	Blackburn	1	Wrexham	1
Dec 20	Bolton	0	Rotherham	2
Jan 10	Burnley	2	Nottingham F	1
Dec 14	Portsmouth	1	Chelsea	0
Dec 14	Shrewsbury	1	Norwich	0
Dec 05	Southampton	5	Leeds	4
Dec 21	Tranmere	0	Everton	4

Replays				
Dec 14	Wrexham	3	Blackburn	1
Dec 19	Plymouth	0	Aston Villa	0
Feb 06	Plymouth	3	Aston Villa	5

5th Round				
Feb 22	Aston Villa	3	Wrexham	0
Feb 13	Rotherham	3	Portsmouth	0
Feb 15	Shrewsbury	2	Everton	1
Feb 06	Southampton	2	Burnley	4

Semi-finals				
Apr 10	Burnley	1	Aston Villa	1
Apr 26	Aston Villa	2	Burnley	2
May 02	Aston Villa	2	Burnley	1
	Aggregate 5-4			
Mar 21	Rotherham	3	Shrewsbury	2
Mar 29	Shrewsbury	1	Rotherham	1
	Aggregate 3-4			

Final				
Aug 08	Rotherham	2	Aston Villa	0
Sep 05	Aston Villa	3	Rotherham	0
	Aggregate 3-2			

Season 1961-62

1st Round				
Sep 13	Barnsley	3	Southport	2
Sep 13	Barrow	0	Portsmouth	2
Sep 13	Birmingham	1	Swindon	1
Sep 13	Blackpool	2	Port Vale	1
Sep 13	Bolton	1	Sunderland	1
Sep 13	Bournemouth	2	Torquay	2
Sep 13	Bradford C	3	Aston Villa	4
Sep 11	Bristol R	2	Hartlepool	1
Sep 12	Bury	5	Brighton	1
Sep 13	Cardiff	2	Wrexham	0
Sep 12	Carlisle	1	Huddersfield	1
Sep 13	Chesterfield	2	Norwich	3
Sep 13	Colchester	1	Crewe	2
Sep 11	Darlington	0	Rotherham	1
Sep 13	Doncaster	3	Grimsby	2
Sep 13	Fulham	1	Sheffield U	1
Sep 11	Hull	4	Bradford	2
Sep 11	Ipswich	4	Manchester C	2
Sep 13	Leeds	4	Brentford	1
Sep 13	Lincoln	1	Accrington	0
Sep 13	Luton	2	Northampton	1
Sep 11	Mansfield	5	Exeter	2
Sep 13	Millwall	1	Walsall	2
Sep 13	Newcastle	2	Scunthorpe	0
Sep 11	Newport	0	Shrewsbury	0
Sep 11	Nottingham F	4	Gillingham	1
Sep 14	Notts Co	2	Derby	2
Sep 12	Oldham	1	Charlton	4
Sep 11	Peterborough	1	Blackburn	3
Sep 13	Preston	3	Aldershot	1
Sep 13	Q.P.R.	5	Crystal Palace	2
Sep 13	Reading	4	Chester	2
Sep 13	Southampton	0	Rochdale	0
Sep 13	Southend	0	Stoke	1
Sep 11	Stockport	0	Leyton O	1
Sep 13	Tranmere	3	Middlesbrough	6
Sep 11	Watford	3	Halifax	0
Sep 11	West Ham	3	Plymouth	2
Sep 13	Workington	3	Coventry	0
Sep 13	York	3	Bristol C	0

Replays				
Sep 25	Huddersfield	3	Carlisle	0
Sep 25	Sheffield U	4	Fulham	0
Sep 25	Sunderland	1	Bolton	0
Sep 25	Swindon	2	Birmingham	0
Sep 25	Torquay	0	Bournemouth	1
Sep 27	Derby	3	Notts Co	2
Sep 27	Rochdale	2	Southampton	1
Sep 28	Shrewsbury	3	Newport	1

2nd Round				
Oct 09	Barnsley	1	Workington	3
Oct 02	Bristol R	1	Blackburn	1
Oct 03	Bury	3	Hull	4
Oct 04	Charlton	4	Stoke	1
Oct 04	Leeds	3	Huddersfield	2
Oct 04	Leyton O	0	Blackpool	1
Oct 04	Luton	0	Rotherham	0
Oct 05	Mansfield	1	Cardiff	1
Oct 04	Middlesbrough	3	Crewe	1
Oct 04	Norwich	3	Lincoln	2
Oct 04	Portsmouth	1	Derby	1
Oct 05	Preston	3	Swindon	1
Oct 11	Q.P.R.	1	Nottingham F	2
Oct 04	Rochdale	4	Doncaster	0
Oct 02	Sheffield U	2	Newcastle	2
Oct 09	Shrewsbury	1	Bournemouth	3
Oct 04	Sunderland	5	Walsall	2
Oct 03	Swansea	3	Ipswich	3
Oct 16	Watford	3	Reading	1
Oct 09	West Ham	1	Aston Villa	3
Oct 09	York	2	Leicester	1

Replays				
Oct 10	Rotherham	2	Luton	0
Oct 11	Newcastle	0	Sheffield U	2
Oct 16	Blackburn	4	Bristol R	0
Oct 23	Cardiff	2	Mansfield	1
Oct 24	Ipswich	3	Swansea	2
Oct 30	Blackpool	5	Leyton O	1
Nov 01	Derby	2	Portsmouth	4

3rd Round				
Nov 21	Aston Villa	2	Ipswich	3
Nov 15	Bournemouth	3	Cardiff	0
Nov 15	Norwich	3	Middlesbrough	2
Nov 14	Nottingham F	1	Blackburn	2
Nov 14	Preston	0	Rotherham	0
Nov 14	Rochdale	1	Charlton	0
Nov 13	Sheffield U	1	Portsmouth	0
Nov 15	Sunderland	2	Hull	1
Nov 15	Workington	0	Blackpool	1
Nov 15	York	1	Watford	1

Replays				
Nov 21	Watford	2	York	2
Nov 28	Rotherham	3	Preston	0
Dec 04	York	3	Watford	2

4th Round				
Dec 11	Blackburn	4	Ipswich	1
Dec 12	Rotherham	1	Leeds	1
Dec 13	York	1	Bournemouth	0

Replay				
Jan 15	Leeds	1	Rotherham	2

5th Round				
Feb 06	Blackpool	0	Sheffield U	0
Feb 07	Rochdale	2	York	1
Feb 06	Rotherham	0	Blackburn	1
Feb 07	Sunderland	1	Norwich	4

Replay				
Mar 27	Sheffield U	0	Blackpool	2

Semi-finals				
Apr 11	Norwich	4	Blackpool	1
Apr 16	Blackpool	2	Norwich	0
	Aggregate 3-4			
Mar 19	Rochdale	3	Blackburn	1
Apr 04	Blackburn	2	Rochdale	1
	Aggregate 3-4			

Final				
Apr 26	Rochdale	0	Norwich	3
May 01	Norwich	1	Rochdale	0
	Aggregate 4-0			

Season 1962-63

st Round
ep 05 Aldershot 2 Exeter 0
ep 05 Barrow 3 Workington 2
ep 05 Bradford C 2 Doncaster 2
ep 04 Brentford 3 Wrexham 0
ep 05 Chester 2 Stockport 0
ep 05 Crewe 2 Oldham 3
ep 05 Darlington 1 Chesterfield 0
ep 13 Halifax 2 Mansfield 3
ep 06 Hartlepool 1 Barnsley 1
ep 05 Newport 2 Gillingham 1
ep 05 Shrewsbury 3 Millwall 1
ep 05 Southport 0 Rochdale 0
ep 03 Torquay 2 Oxford 0
ep 03 Tranmere 2 Carlisle 3
ep 06 Watford 1 Colchester 2
ep 05 York 2 Lincoln 2

eplays
ep 13 Barnsley 2 Hartlepool 1
ep 18 Doncaster 2 Bradford C 0
ep 18 Rochdale 1 Southport 2
ep 19 Lincoln 2 York 0

nd Round
ep 26 Aldershot 0 Newport 3
ep 24 Aston Villa 6 Peterborough 1
ep 25 Barnsley 3 Grimsby 2
ep 24 Barrow 3 Shrewsbury 1
ep 26 Birmingham 5 Doncaster 0
ep 26 Bradford 3 Huddersfield 1
ep 26 Brentford 1 Sheffield U 4
ep 25 Brighton 1 Portsmouth 5
ep 25 Bristol C 1 Rotherham 2
ep 27 Bristol R 2 Port Vale 0
ep 24 Bury 2 Lincoln 2
ep 26 Cardiff 5 Reading 1
ep 26 Chester 1 Mansfield 2
ep 26 Coventry 3 Swansea 2
ep 26 Derby 1 Blackburn 1
ep 26 Fulham 4 Bournemouth 0
ep 24 Hull 2 Middlesbrough 2

Sep 26 Leeds 2 Crystal Palace 1
Sep 26 Leicester 4 Charlton 4
Sep 24 Manchester C 0 Blackpool 0
Sep 26 Newcastle 1 Leyton O 1
Sep 26 Northampton 2 Colchester 0
Sep 26 Norwich 4 Bolton 0
Sep 24 Q.P.R. 1 Preston 2
Sep 24 Southampton 1 Scunthorpe 1
Sep 26 Southend 2 Notts Co 3
Sep 24 Southport 1 Luton 3
Sep 24 Sunderland 7 Oldham 1
Sep 25 Swindon 4 Darlington 0
Sep 26 Torquay 1 Carlisle 2
Sep 25 Walsall 1 Stoke 2
Sep 26 West Ham 6 Plymouth 0

Replays
Oct 01 Leyton O 4 Newcastle 2
Oct 02 Blackburn 3 Derby 1
Oct 02 Charlton 2 Leicester 1
Oct 02 Scunthorpe 2 Southampton 2
Oct 08 Blackpool 3 Manchester C 3
Oct 08 Lincoln 2 Bury 3
Oct 08 Middlesbrough 1 Hull 1
Oct 09 Scunthorpe 3 Southampton 0
Oct 10 Hull 3 Middlesbrough 0
Oct 10 Mansfield 0 Chester 1
Oct 15 Manchester C 4 Blackpool 2

3rd Round
Oct 17 Aston Villa 3 Stoke 1
Oct 16 Barnsley 1 Luton 2
Oct 15 Barrow 1 Birmingham 1
Oct 17 Blackburn 4 Leeds 0
Oct 16 Bradford 2 Charlton 2
Oct 23 Bristol R 2 Cardiff 0
Oct 23 Bury 3 Sheffield U 1
Oct 16 Carlisle 1 Norwich 1
Oct 17 Hull 1 Fulham 2
Oct 17 Leyton O 9 Chester 2
Oct 24 Newport 1 Manchester C 2
Oct 16 Northampton 1 Preston 1

Oct 17 Notts Co 5 Swindon 0
Oct 17 Portsmouth 5 Coventry 1
Oct 16 Rotherham 3 West Ham 1
Oct 17 Sunderland 2 Scunthorpe 0

Replays
Oct 23 Charlton 1 Bradford 0
Oct 24 Norwich 5 Carlisle 0
Oct 29 Birmingham 5 Barrow 1
Oct 29 Preston 2 Northampton 1

4th Round
Nov 12 Aston Villa 6 Preston 2
Nov 14 Birmingham 3 Notts Co 2
Nov 14 Blackburn 4 Rotherham 1
Nov 13 Bury 3 Bristol R 1
Nov 12 Leyton O 3 Charlton 2
Nov 14 Manchester C 1 Luton 0
Nov 14 Norwich 1 Fulham 0
Nov 14 Portsmouth 0 Sunderland 0

Replay
Nov 21 Sunderland 2 Portsmouth 1

5th Round
Dec 03 Aston Villa 4 Norwich 1
Dec 11 Birmingham 6 Manchester C 0
Dec 03 Leyton O 0 Bury 2
Dec 05 Sunderland 3 Blackburn 2

Semi-finals
Mar 27 Birmingham 3 Bury 2
Apr 08 Bury 1 Birmingham 1
Aggregate 3-4
Jan 12 Sunderland 1 Aston Villa 3
Apr 22 Aston Villa 0 Sunderland 0
Aggregate 3-1

Final
May 23 Birmingham 3 Aston Villa 1
May 27 Aston Villa 0 Birmingham 0
Aggregate 1-3

Season 1963-64

st round
Sep 04 Aldershot 3 Q.P.R. 1
Sep 04 Bradford 7 Bradford C 3
Sep 04 Carlisle 3 Crewe 2
Sep 04 Chesterfield 0 Halifax 1
Sep 04 Darlington 2 Barnsley 2
Sep 04 Doncaster 0 York 0
Sep 04 Gillingham 4 Bristol C 2
Sep 04 Lincoln 3 Hartlepool 2
Sep 04 Mansfield 2 Watford 1
Sep 04 Newport 3 Millwall 4
Sep 04 Oldham 3 Workington 5
Sep 04 Oxford 0 Exeter 1
Sep 04 Reading 1 Brentford 1
Sep 04 Rochdale 1 Chester 1
Sep 04 Shrewsbury 1 Bristol R 1
Sep 04 Southport 2 Barrow 1
Sep 04 Torquay 1 Brighton 2
Sep 04 Tranmere 2 Stockport 0

Replays
Sep 11 Barnsley 6 Darlington 2
Sep 18 Chester 2 Rochdale 5
Sep 23 Brentford 2 Reading 0
Sep 23 Bristol R 6 Shrewsbury 2
Sep 23 York 3 Doncaster 0

2nd Round
Sep 25 Aston Villa 3 Barnsley 1
Sep 25 Blackpool 7 Charlton 1
Sep 25 Bradford 2 Middlesbrough 2
Sep 25 Brentford 0 Bournemouth 0
Sep 25 Brighton 1 Northampton 1
Sep 25 Bristol R 2 Crystal Palace 0
Sep 25 Cardiff 2 Wrexham 2
Sep 25 Colchester 5 Fulham 3
Sep 2 Gillingham 3 Bury 0
Sep 25 Grimsby 1 Rotherham 3
Sep 25 Halifax 4 Rochdale 2
Sep 25 Hull 1 Exeter 0
Sep 25 Ipswich 0 Walsall 0
Sep 25 Leeds 5 Mansfield 1
Sep 25 Leicester 2 Aldershot 0

Sep 25 Luton 3 Coventry 4
Sep 25 Manchester C 2 Carlisle 0
Sep 25 Millwall 3 Peterborough 2
Sep 25 Newcastle 3 Preston 0
Sep 25 Norwich 2 Birmingham 0
Sep 25 Notts Co 2 Blackburn 1
Sep 25 Plymouth 2 Huddersfield 2
Sep 25 Portsmouth 3 Derby 2
Sep 25 Scunthorpe 2 Stoke 2
Sep 25 Sheffield U 1 Bolton 2
Sep 25 Southend 2 Port Vale 1
Sep 25 Swansea 3 Sunderland 1
Sep 25 Swindon 3 Chelsea 0
Sep 25 Tranmere 2 Southampton 0
Sep 25 West Ham 2 Leyton O 1
Sep 25 Workington 3 Southport 0
Sep 25 York 1 Lincoln 1

Replays
Oct 02 Middlesbrough 2 Bradford 3
Oct 03 Walsall 1 Ipswich 0
Oct 07 Wrexham 1 Cardiff 1
Oct 14 Lincoln 2 York 0
Oct 14 Northampton 3 Brighton 2
Oct 16 Stoke 3 Scunthorpe 3
Oct 21 Huddersfield 3 Plymouth 3
Oct 21 Wrexham 3 Cardiff 0
Oct 22 Scunthorpe 0 Stoke 1
Oct 28 Huddersfield 2 Plymouth 1
Nov 04 Bournemouth 2 Brentford 0

3rd Round
Oct 16 Aston Villa 0 West Ham 2
Nov 06 Bournemouth 2 Newcastle 1
Nov 04 Bristol R 1 Gillingham 1
Nov 04 Colchester 4 Northampton 1
Oct 16 Halifax 2 Walsall 0
Oct 16 Hull 0 Manchester C 3
Oct 22 Leeds 2 Swansea 0
Nov 04 Millwall 1 Lincoln 1
Oct 30 Norwich 1 Blackpool 0
Nov 05 Notts Co 3 Bradford 2
Nov 04 Rotherham 4 Coventry 2

Oct 29 Stoke 3 Bolton 0
Oct 16 Swindon 3 Southend 0
Oct 16 Tranmere 1 Leicester 2
Nov 04 Workington 1 Huddersfield 0
Nov 04 Wrexham 3 Portsmouth 5

Replays
Nov 06 Gillingham 3 Bristol R 1
Nov 12 Lincoln 1 Millwall 2

4th Round
Nov 27 Halifax 1 Norwich 7
Nov 27 Leicester 3 Gillingham 1
Nov 27 Manchester C 3 Leeds 1
Nov 13 Notts Co 3 Portsmouth 2
Nov 27 Rotherham 5 Millwall 2
Nov 27 Stoke 2 Bournemouth 1
Nov 19 Swindon 3 West Ham 3
Nov 26 Workington 2 Colchester 1

Replay
Nov 25 West Ham 4 Swindon 1

5th Round
Dec 18 Norwich 1 Leicester 1
Dec 17 Notts co 0 Manchester C 1
Dec 16 Stoke 3 Rotherham 2
Dec 16 West Ham 6 Workington 0

Replay
Jan 15 Leicester 2 Norwich 1

Semi-finals
Feb 05 Leicester 4 West Ham 3
Mar 23 West Ham 0 Leicester 2
Aggregate 3-6
Jan 15 Stoke 2 Manchester C 0
Feb 05 Manchester C 1 Stoke 0
Aggregate 1-2

Final
Apr 15 Stoke 1 Leicester 1
Apr 22 Leicester 3 Stoke 2
Aggregate 4-3

Season 1964-65

1st Round
Sep 02 Barnsley 2 Lincoln 1
Sep 02 Bradford C 2 York 0
Sep 02 Brentford 0 Southend 2
Sep 02 Brighton 2 Millwall 2
Sep 02 Chester 3 Wrexham 0
Sep 02 Chesterfield 3 Hartlepool 0
Sep 02 Colchester 1 Torquay 1
Sep 02 Doncaster 1 Bradford 0
Sep 02 Exeter 2 Gillingham 0

Sep 02 Halifax 1 Darlington 3
Sep 02 Notts Co 3 Newport 2
Sep 07 Port Vale 0 Luton 1
Sep 02 Q.P.R. 5 Aldershot 2
Sep 02 Southport 0 Carlisle 0
Sep 02 Stockport 1 Rochdale 3
Sep 02 Tranmere 2 Crewe 0
Sep 02 Walsall 1 Oxford 1
Sep 02 Workington 9 Barrow 1

Replays
Sep 07 Oxford 6 Walsall 1
Sep 09 Millwall 1 Brighton 0
Sep 10 Torquay 3 Colchester 0
Sep 14 Carlisle 1 Southport 0

2nd Round
Sep 23 Birmingham 0 Chelsea 3
Sep 23 Blackpool 3 Newcastle 0
Sep 23 Bolton 1 Blackburn 5

Sep 23 Bournemouth 0 Northampton 2
Sep 22 Bristol R 0 Chesterfield 2
Sep 23 Bury 1 Darlington 0
Sep 23 Carlisle 4 Bristol C 1
Sep 23 Charlton 2 Middlesbrough 1
Sep 23 Chester 5 Derby 4
Sep 23 Coventry 4 Ipswich 1
Sep 23 Doncaster 1 Preston 0
Sep 23 Exeter 3 Bradford C 5
Sep 23 Fulham 2 Oxford 0
Sep 23 Grimsby 3 Oldham 1
Sep 22 Hull 0 Southend 0
Sep 23 Leeds 3 Huddersfield 2
Sep 23 Leicester 0 Peterborough 0
Sep 23 Leyton O 3 Barnsley 0
Sep 23 Luton 0 Aston Villa 1
Sep 23 Manchester C 3 Mansfield 5
Sep 23 Millwall 1 Norwich 2
Sep 23 Plymouth 2 Sheffield U 1
Sep 23 Reading 4 Q.P.R. 0
Sep 23 Rotherham 2 Rochdale 0
Sep 23 Scunthorpe 0 Workington 1
Sep 23 Southampton 3 Cardiff 2
Sep 23 Stoke 1 Shrewsbury 1
Sep 30 Sunderland 4 West Ham 1
Sep 23 Swansea 3 Swindon 1
Sep 23 Torquay 1 Notts Co 2
Sep 23 Tranmere 0 Crystal Palace 2
Sep 22 Watford 2 Portsmouth 2

Replays
Sep 28 Southend 3 Hull 1

Sep 29 Shrewsbury 0 Stoke 1
Oct 08 Peterborough 0 Leicester 2
Oct 12 Portsmouth 2 Watford 1

3rd Round
Oct 14 Bury 0 Plymouth 1
Oct 14 Charlton 2 Leyton O 1
Oct 26 Chelsea 4 Notts Co 0
Oct 14 Chesterfield 3 Carlisle 1
Oct 14 Coventry 3 Mansfield 2
Oct 26 Crystal Palace 2 Southampton 0
Oct 14 Doncaster 2 Bradford C 3
Oct 19 Grimsby 0 Leicester 5
Oct 14 Leeds 2 Aston Villa 3
Oct 20 Northampton 2 Portsmouth 1
Oct 21 Norwich 5 Chester 3
Oct 14 Reading 1 Fulham 1
Oct 14 Rotherham 2 Swansea 2
Oct 14 Stoke 3 Southend 1
Oct 26 Sunderland 4 Blackpool 1
Oct 14 Workington 0 Blackburn 0

Replays
Oct 19 Fulham 1 Reading 3
Oct 22 Blackburn 1 Workington 5
Oct 28 Swansea 2 Rotherham 0

4th Round
Nov 04 Aston Villa 3 Reading 1
Nov 04 Charlton 0 Bradford C 1
Nov 11 Chelsea 3 Swansea 2
Nov 10 Coventry 4 Sunderland 2
Nov 04 Leicester 0 Crystal Palace [illegible]
Nov 04 Northampton 4 Chesterfield [illegible]
Nov 04 Stoke 1 Plymouth [illegible]
Nov 04 Workington 3 Norwich [illegible]

Replays
Nov 11 Crystal Palace 1 Leicester 2
Nov 11 Plymouth 3 Stoke [illegible]

5th Round
Nov 23 Aston Villa 7 Bradford C [illegible]
Dec 01 Coventry 1 Leicester 8
Nov 25 Plymouth 1 Northampton [illegible]
Nov 25 Workington 2 Chelsea 2

Replay
Dec 16 Chelsea 2 Workington 0

Semi-finals
Jan 20 Aston Villa 2 Chelsea 3
Feb 10 Chelsea 1 Aston Villa 1
Aggregate 4-3
Jan 20 Leicester 3 Plymouth 2
Feb 10 Plymouth 0 Leicester 1
Aggregate 2-4

Final
Mar 15 Chelsea 3 Leicester 2
Apr 05 Leicester 0 Chelsea 0
Aggregate 2-3

Season 1965-66

1st Round
Sep 01 Bradford 1 Halifax 0
Sep 01 Barrow 1 Rochdale 1
Sep 01 Bournemouth 0 Aldershot 0
Sep 01 Colchester 2 Exeter 1
Sep 01 Crewe 2 Scunthorpe 0
Sep 01 Doncaster 2 Barnsley 2
Sep 01 Hartlepool 1 Bradford C 0
Sep 01 Lincoln 2 York 2
Sep 01 Luton 1 Brighton 1
Sep 01 Newport 2 Southend 2
Sep 01 Notts Co 0 Chesterfield 0
Sep 01 Oldham 3 Tranmere 2
Sep 01 Oxford 0 Millwall 1
Sep 01 Port Vale 2 Reading 2
Sep 01 Q.P.R. 1 Walsall 1
Sep 01 Scunthorpe 0 Darlington 2
Sep 01 Shrewsbury 3 Torquay 0
Sep 01 Stockport 2 Workington 3
Sep 01 Wrexham 5 Chester 2

Replays
Sep 06 Southend 3 Newport 1
Sep 07 Barnsley 1 Doncaster 2
Sep 07 Brighton 2 Luton 0
Sep 07 Walsall 3 Q.P.R. 2
Sep 07 York 4 Lincoln 2
Sep 08 Aldershot 2 Bournemouth 1
Sep 08 Chesterfield 2 Notts Co 1
Sep 08 Reading 1 Port Vale 0
Sep 08 Rochdale 3 Barrow 1

2nd Round
Sep 21 Blackburn 0 Northampton 1
Sep 22 Blackpool 5 Gillingham 2
Sep 22 Bolton 3 Aldershot 0
Sep 21 Brighton 1 Ipswich 2
Sep 21 Bristol R 3 West Ham 3
Sep 21 Bury 0 Huddersfield 2
Sep 21 Charlton 4 Carlisle 1
Sep 22 Chesterfield 3 Bradford 0
Sep 22 Colchester 2 Middlesbrough 4
Sep 22 Crewe 1 Cardiff 1
Sep 22 Crystal Palace 0 Grimsby 1

Sep 22 Darlington 2 Swindon 1
Sep 22 Doncaster 0 Burnley 4
Sep 22 Hull 2 Derby 2
Sep 22 Leeds 4 Hartlepool 2
Sep 22 Leyton O 0 Coventry 3
Sep 22 Manchester C 3 Leicester 1
Sep 22 Mansfield 2 Birmingham 1
Sep 22 Millwall 4 York 1
Sep 22 Newcastle 3 Peterborough 4
Sep 22 Oldham 1 Portsmouth 2
Sep 22 Preston 1 Plymouth 0
Sep 22 Reading 5 Southend 1
Sep 22 Rotherham 2 Watford 0
Sep 22 Shrewsbury 1 Bristol C 0
Sep 22 Southampton 3 Rochdale 0
Sep 22 Stoke 2 Norwich 1
Sep 22 Sunderland 2 Sheffield U 1
Sep 21 Swansea 2 Aston Villa 3
Sep 22 Workington 0 Brentford 0
Sep 22 Wrexham 1 Fulham 2
Sep 22 W.B.A. 3 Walsall 1

Replays
Sep 29 Cardiff 3 Crewe 0
Sep 29 Derby 4 Hull 3
Sep 29 West Ham 3 Bristol R 2
Sep 30 Brentford 1 Workington 2

3rd Round
Oct 13 Blackpool 1 Darlington 2
Oct 13 Burnley 3 Southampton 2
Oct 13 Cardiff 2 Portsmouth 0
Oct 13 Chesterfield 2 Stoke 2
Oct 13 Derby 1 Reading 1
Oct 13 Fulham 5 Northampton 0
Oct 13 Grimsby 4 Bolton 2
Oct 13 Huddersfield 0 Preston 1
Oct 13 Leeds 2 W.B.A. 4
Oct 13 Manchester C 2 Coventry 3
Oct 13 Middlesbrough 0 Millwall 0
Oct 13 Peterborough 4 Charlton 3
Oct 13 Shrewsbury 2 Rotherham 5
Oct 13 Sunderland 1 Aston Villa 2
Oct 13 West Ham 4 Mansfield 0

Oct 13 Workington 1 Ipswich 1

Replays
Oct 18 Millwall 3 Middlesbrough 1
Oct 20 Ipswich 3 Workington 1
Oct 20 Reading 2 Derby 0
Oct 20 Stoke 2 Chesterfield 1

4th Round
Nov 03 Cardiff 5 Reading 1
Nov 03 Coventry 1 W.B.A. 1
Nov 03 Fulham 1 Aston Villa 1
Nov 03 Grimsby 4 Preston 0
Nov 03 Ipswich 2 Darlington 0
Nov 03 Millwall 1 Peterborough 4
Nov 03 Rotherham 1 West Ham 2
Nov 03 Stoke 0 Burnley 0

Replays
Nov 08 Aston Villa 2 Fulham 0
Nov 09 Burnley 2 Stoke 1
Nov 10 W.B.A. 6 Coventry 1

5th Round
Nov 17 Cardiff 2 Ipswich 1
Nov 17 Grimsby 2 West Ham 2
Nov 17 Peterborough 4 Burnley 0
Nov 17 W.B.A. 3 Aston Villa 1

Replay
Dec 15 West Ham 1 Grimsby 0

Semi-finals
Dec 01 W.B.A. 2 Peterborough 1
Dec 15 Peterborough 2 W.B.A. 4
Aggregate 3-6
Dec 20 West Ham 5 Cardiff 2
Feb 02 Cardiff 1 West Ham 5
Aggregate 3-10

Final
Mar 09 West Ham 2 W.B.A. 1
Mar 23 W.B.A. 4 West Ham 1
Aggregate 5-3

Season 1966-67

1st Round
Aug 24 Aldershot 2 Luton 2
Aug 24 Barnsley 1 Grimsby 2
Aug 24 Barrow 2 Oldham 1
Aug 24 Bradford 2 Hartlepool 2
Aug 24 Bradford C 1 Doncaster 1
Aug 24 Brentford 0 Millwall 0
Aug 24 Brighton 1 Leyton O 0
Aug 23 Bury 2 Rochdale 0
Aug 24 Cardiff 1 Bristol R 0
Aug 24 Chester 2 Tranmere 5
Aug 24 Chesterfield 2 Scunthorpe 1
Aug 24 Crewe 1 Stockport 0
Aug 24 Exeter 2 Torquay 2
Aug 23 Halifax 0 Darlington 0
Aug 24 Lincoln 1 Hull 0
Aug 24 Middlesbrough 0 York 0
Aug 24 Newport 1 Swansea 2
Aug 24 Notts Co 1 Mansfield 1
Aug 24 Peterborough 2 Oxford 1
Aug 23 Port Vale 1 Walsall 3
Aug 23 Q.P.R. 5 Colchester 0
Aug 24 Shrewsbury 6 Wrexham 1
Aug 24 Southend 0 Gillingham 0
Aug 24 Southport 0 Workington 1
Aug 24 Swindon 2 Bournemouth 1
Aug 23 Watford 1 Reading 1

Replays
Aug 29 Darlington 4 Halifax 0
Aug 29 Luton 1 Aldershot 2
Aug 29 Mansfield 3 Notts Co 0
Aug 29 Millwall 0 Brentford 1
Aug 29 Reading 1 Watford 0
Aug 29 York 2 Middlesbrough 1
Aug 30 Doncaster 5 Bradford C 2
Aug 31 Gillingham 2 Southend 0
Aug 31 Hartlepool 1 Bardford 2
Aug 31 Torquay 1 Exeter 2

2nd Round
Sep 14 Aldershot 1 Q.P.R. 1
Sep 13 Arsenal 1 Gillingham 1
Sep 14 Blackburn 4 Barrow 1
Sep 14 Blackpool 5 Manchester U 1
Sep 14 Bradford 0 Grimsby 0
Sep 13 Brentford 2 Ipswich 4
Sep 13 Bristol C 1 Swansea 1
Sep 14 Bury 2 Workington 3
Sep 14 Cardiff 0 Exeter 1
Sep 14 Carlisle 1 Tranmere 1
Sep 14 Chelsea 5 Charlton 2
Sep 13 Coventry 2 Derby 1
Sep 14 Darlington 1 Doncaster 1
Sep 13 Fulham 2 Crystal Palace 0

Sep 13 Leeds 1 Newcastle 0
Sep 14 Leicester 5 Reading 0
Sep 14 Lincoln 2 Huddersfield 1
Sep 14 Manchester C 3 Bolton 1
Sep 14 Northampton 2 Peterborough 2
Sep 14 Norwich 0 Brighton 1
Sep 13 Nottingham F 1 Birmingham 1
Sep 14 Preston 2 Crewe 0
Sep 14 Sheffield W 0 Rotherham 1
Sep 14 Shrewsbury 1 Burnley 1
Sep 14 Southampton 4 Plymouth 3
Sep 14 Sunderland 1 Sheffield U 1
Sep 13 Swindon 4 Portsmouth 1
Sep 13 Walsall 2 Stoke 1
Sep 14 West Ham 1 Tottenham 0
Sep 13 Wolverhampton 2 Mansfield 1
Sep 14 W.B.A. 6 Aston Villa 1
Sep 13 York 3 Chesterfield 2

Replays
Sep 19 Doncaster 2 Darlington 0
Sep 19 Swansea 2 Bristol C 1
Sep 20 Birmingham 2 Nottingham F 1
Sep 20 Q.P.R. 2 Aldershot 0
Sep 20 Sheffield U 1 Sunderland 0
Sep 21 Gillingham 1 Arsenal 1
Sep 21 Grimsby 3 Bradford 1

Sep 21	Tranmere	0	Carlisle	2
Sep 26	Peterborough	0	Northampton	2
Sep 28	Arsenal	5	Gillingham	0
Sep 29	Burnley	5	Shrewsbury	0

3rd Round

Oct 05	Arsenal	1	West Ham	3
Oct 04	Birmingham	2	Ipswich	1
Oct 05	Blackpool	1	Chelsea	1
Oct 05	Brighton	1	Coventry	1
Oct 04	Doncaster	1	Swindon	1
Oct 05	Exeter	1	Walsall	2
Oct 05	Fulham	5	Wolverhampton	0
Oct 05	Grimsby	3	Workington	0
Oct 05	Leicester	5	Lincoln	0
Oct 05	Northampton	2	Rotherham	1
Oct 04	Preston	1	Leeds	1
Oct 12	Q.P.R.	2	Swansea	1
Oct 05	Sheffield U	2	Burnley	0
Oct 05	Southampton	3	Carlisle	3
Oct 05	W.B.A.	4	Manchester C	2
Oct 04	York	0	Blackburn	2

Replays

Oct 11	Coventry	1	Brighton	3
Oct 11	Swindon	4	Doncaster	2
Oct 12	Carlisle	2	Southampton	1
Oct 12	Leeds	3	Preston	0
Oct 17	Chelsea	1	Blackpool	3

4th Round

Oct 26	Blackpool	4	Fulham	2
Oct 26	Brighton	1	Northampton	1
Oct 26	Carlisle	4	Blackburn	0
Oct 26	Grimsby	2	Birmingham	4
Oct 25	Q.P.R.	4	Leicester	2
Oct 26	Sheffield U	2	Walsall	1
Oct 25	Swindon	0	W.B.A.	2
Nov 07	West Ham	7	Leeds	0

Replay

Nov 01	Northampton	8	Brighton	0

5th Round

Dec 07	Blackpool	1	West Ham	3
Dec 07	Northampton	1	W.B.A.	3
Dec 07	Q.P.R.	2	Carlisle	1
Dec 07	Sheffield U	2	Birmingham	3

Semi-finals

Jan 17	Birmingham	1	Q.P.R.	4
Feb 07	Q.P.R.	3	Birmingham	1
	Aggregate 7-2			
Jan 18	W.B.A.	4	West Ham	0
Feb 08	West Ham	2	W.B.A.	2
	Aggregate 2-6			

Final

Mar 04	Q.P.R.	3	W.B.A.	2
	played at Wembley			

Third Division Queen's Park Rangers lift the League Cup after defeating First Division West Bromwich Albion in the 1967 League Cup Final.

SEASON 1967-68

1st Round

Aug 23	Aldershot	2	Cardiff	3
Aug 23	Barrow	1	Southport	0
Aug 22	Bournemouth	1	Watford	1
Aug 23	Brighton	4	Colchester	0
Aug 23	Crewe	1	Stockport	1
Aug 23	Darlington	1	York	0
Aug 23	Doncaster	1	Scunthorpe	2
Aug 23	Grimsby	1	Chesterfield	0
Aug 23	Halifax	5	Bradford	0
Aug 23	Hartlepool	2	Bradford C	0
Aug 22	Leyton O	1	Gillingham	3
Aug 23	Luton	1	Charlton	1
Aug 23	Mansfield	2	Lincoln	3
Aug 22	Middlesbrough	4	Barnsley	1
Aug 23	Northampton	3	Peterborough	2
Aug 23	Notts Co	0	Rotherham	1
Aug 23	Oxford	3	Swansea	1
Aug 22	Port Vale	3	Chester	0
Aug 23	Reading	3	Bristol R	0
Aug 23	Rochdale	0	Bury	1
Aug 23	Southend	1	Brentford	0
Aug 22	Swindon	1	Newport	1
Aug 22	Torquay	0	Exeter	0
Aug 23	Tranmere	2	Wrexham	1
Aug 22	Walsall	4	Shrewsbury	2
Aug 23	Workington	1	Oldham	1

Replays

Aug 28	Exeter	0	Torquay	3
Aug 28	Stockport	3	Crewe	0
Aug 29	Newport	2	Swindon	0
Aug 29	Oldham	1	Workington	1
Aug 29	Watford	0	Bournemouth	0
Aug 30	Charlton	1	Luton	2
Aug 31	Oldham	1	Workington	2
	played at Carlisle			
Sep 06	Bournemouth	1	Watford	2
	played at Swindon			

2nd Round

Sep 13	Barrow	1	Crystal Palace	0
Sep 13	Blackburn	3	Brighton	1
Sep 13	Bristol C	0	Everton	5
Sep 12	Burnley	2	Cardiff	1
Sep 13	Carlisle	0	Workington	2
Sep 12	Coventry	1	Arsenal	2
Sep 13	Derby	4	Hartlepool	0
Sep 13	Fulham	1	Tranmere	0
Sep 13	Gillingham	2	Torquay	2
Sep 12	Grimsby	2	Bury	2
Sep 12	Huddersfield	1	Wolverhampton	0
Sep 12	Ipswich	5	Southampton	2
Sep 13	Leeds	3	Luton	1
Sep 13	Lincoln	2	Newcastle	1
Sep 13	Liverpool	1	Bolton	1
Sep 13	Manchester C	4	Leicester	0
Sep 13	Middlesbrough	2	Chelsea	1
Sep 13	Millwall	3	Sheffield U	2
Sep 12	Newport	0	Blackpool	1
Sep 13	Northampton	3	Aston Villa	1
Sep 13	Norwich	1	Rotherham	1
Sep 13	Oxford	2	Preston	1
Sep 13	Plymouth	0	Birmingham	2
Sep 13	Portsmouth	3	Port Vale	1
Sep 12	Q.P.R.	2	Hull	1
Sep 13	Reading	3	W.B.A.	1
Sep 13	Scunthorpe	0	Nottingham F	1
Sep 13	Southend	1	Darlington	2
Sep 13	Stockport	3	Sheffield W	5
Sep 13	Stoke	2	Watford	0
Sep 13	Sunderland	3	Halifax	2
Sep 13	Walsall	1	West Ham	5

Replays

Sep 19	Bury	2	Grimsby	0
Sep 19	Rotherham	0	Norwich	2
Sep 20	Torquay	2	Gillingham	0

Sep 27 Bolton 3 Liverpool 2

3rd Round
Oct 11 Arsenal 1 Reading 0
Oct 11 Blackburn 3 Middlesbrough 2
Oct 10 Burnley 3 Nottingham F 0
Oct 11 Darlington 4 Portsmouth 1
Oct 11 Derby 3 Birmingham 1
Oct 11 Everton 2 Sunderland 3
Oct 11 Leeds 3 Bury 0
Oct 11 Lincoln 4 Torquay 2
Oct 11 Manchester C 1 Blackpool 1
Oct 11 Northampton 0 Millwall 0
Oct 11 Norwich 0 Huddersfield 1
Oct 10 Q.P.R. 5 Oxford 1
Oct 11 Sheffield W 3 Barrow 1
Oct 11 Stoke 2 Ipswich 1
Oct 11 West Ham 4 Bolton 1
Oct 11 Workington 2 Fulham 2

Replays
Oct 16 Fulham 6 Workington 2
Oct 16 Millwall 5 Northampton 1
Oct 18 Blackpool 0 Manchester C 2

4th Round
Nov 01 Arsenal 2 Blackburn 1
Oct 31 Darlington 2 Millwall 0
Nov 01 Derby 1 Lincoln 1
Nov 01 Fulham 3 Manchester C 2
Nov 01 Huddersfield 2 West Ham 0
Oct 31 Q.P.R. 1 Burnley 2
Nov 01 Sheffield W 0 Stoke 0
Nov 15 Sunderland 0 Leeds 2

Replays
Nov 15 Lincoln 0 Derby 3
Nov 15 Stoke 2 Sheffield W 1

5th Round
Nov 29 Burnley 3 Arsenal
Nov 29 Derby 5 Darlington
Nov 29 Fulham 1 Huddersfield
Dec 13 Leeds 2 Stoke

Replays
Dec 05 Arsenal 2 Burnley
Dec 12 Huddersfield 2 Fulham

Semi-finals
Jan 17 Arsenal 3 Huddersfield
Feb 06 Huddersfield 1 Arsenal
Aggregate 3-6
Jan 17 Derby 0 Leeds
Feb 07 Leeds 3 Derby
Aggregate 4-2

Final
Mar 02 Arsenal 0 Leeds
played at Wembley

SEASON 1968-69

1st Round
Aug 14 Aldershot 2 Brentford 4
Aug 13 Bournemouth 1 Southend 6
Aug 13 Bradford 0 Darlington 3
Aug 14 Bradford C 3 Hartlepool 2
Aug 14 Brighton 2 Oxford 0
Aug 13 Bristol C 2 Newport 0
Aug 13 Bristol R 0 Swansea 2
Aug 13 Bury 1 Stockport 1
Aug 13 Chester 0 Tranmere 0
Aug 13 Colchester 2 Reading 0
Aug 13 Derby 3 Chesterfield 0
Aug 14 Doncaster 0 Peterborough 0
Aug 14 Gillingham 2 Leyton O 2
Aug 14 Grimsby 0 Notts Co 0
Aug 14 Halifax 0 Hull 3
Aug 14 Lincoln 2 Mansfield 1
Aug 14 Luton 3 Watford 0
Aug 14 Northampton 1 Crewe 1
Aug 14 Plymouth 0 Exeter 0
Aug 14 Preston 1 Oldham 1
Aug 13 Scunthorpe 2 Rotherham 1
Aug 14 Southport 2 Barrow 2
Aug 13 Swindon 2 Torquay 1
Aug 13 Walsall 2 Shrewsbury 0
Aug 14 Workington 2 Rochdale 1
Aug 14 Wrexham 2 Port Vale 0
Aug 14 York 3 Barnsley 4

Replays
Aug 19 Barrow 1 Southport 3
Aug 19 Peterborough 1 Doncaster 0
Aug 19 Stockport 1 Bury 0
Aug 20 Leyton O 3 Gillingham 0
Aug 21 Crewe 1 Northampton 0
Aug 21 Exeter 0 Plymouth 0
Aug 21 Notts Co 0 Grimsby 1
Aug 21 Oldham 0 Preston 1
Aug 21 Tranmere 2 Chester 2
Aug 26 Exeter 1 Plymouth 0
played at Torquay
Aug 26 Tranmere 1 Chester 1
Aug 28 Chester 1 Tranmere 2

2nd Round
Sep 04 Arsenal 1 Sunderland 0
Sep 04 Aston Villa 1 Tottenham 4
Sep 03 Barnsley 1 Millwall 1
Sep 03 Birmingham 0 Chelsea 1
Sep 04 Blackburn 1 Stoke 1
Sep 04 Bradford C 1 Swindon 1
Sep 04 Brentford 3 Hull 0
Sep 04 Brighton 1 Luton 1
Sep 04 Bristol C 1 Middlesbrough 0
Sep 04 Carlisle 2 Cardiff 0
Sep 04 Colchester 0 Workington 1
Sep 03 Coventry 2 Portsmouth 0
Sep 04 Crystal Palace 3 Preston 1
Sep 04 Darlington 1 Leicester 2
Sep 04 Derby 5 Stockport 1
Sep 03 Everton 4 Tranmere 0
Sep 04 Exeter 3 Sheffield W 1
Sep 04 Grimsby 1 Burnley 1
Sep 03 Huddersfield 0 Manchester C 0
Sep 03 Ipswich 2 Norwich 4
Sep 04 Leeds 1 Charlton 0
Sep 03 Leyton O 1 Fulham 0
Sep 04 Liverpool 4 Sheffield U 0
Sep 03 Nottingham F 2 W.B.A. 3
Sep 04 Peterborough 4 Q.P.R. 2
Sep 03 Scunthorpe 2 Lincoln 1
Sep 04 Southampton 3 Crewe 1
Sep 02 Southport 0 Newcastle 2
Sep 03 Walsall 1 Swansea 1
Sep 04 West Ham 7 Bolton 2
Sep 04 Wolverhampton 1 Southend 0
Sep 04 Wrexham 1 Blackpool 1

Replays
Sep 09 Blackpool 3 Wrexham 0
Sep 09 Millwall 3 Barnsley 1
Sep 10 Burnley 6 Grimsby 0
Sep 10 Swansea 3 Walsall 2
Sep 10 Swindon 4 Bradford C 3
Sep 11 Luton 4 Brighton 2
Sep 11 Manchester C 4 Huddersfield 0
Sep 11 Stoke 0 Blackburn 1

3rd Round
Sep 25 Blackpool 1 Manchester C 0
Sep 24 Brentford 0 Norwich 2
Sep 24 Carlisle 0 Leicester 3
Sep 25 Chelsea 0 Derby 0
Sep 24 Everton 5 Luton 1
Sep 25 Leeds 2 Bristol C 1
Sep 24 Leyton O 0 Crystal Palace 1
Sep 25 Liverpool 2 Swansea
Sep 25 Peterborough 2 W.B.A.
Sep 25 Scunthorpe 1 Arsenal
Sep 25 Southampton 4 Newcastle
Sep 24 Swindon 1 Blackburn 0
Sep 25 Tottenham 6 Exeter 3
Sep 25 West Ham 0 Coventry
Sep 25 Wolverhampton 5 Millwall
Sep 25 Workington 0 Burnley

Replays
Oct 01 Coventry 3 West Ham 2
Oct 02 Derby 3 Chelsea 1

4th Round
Oct 15 Arsenal 2 Liverpool 1
Oct 16 Blackpool 2 Wolverhampton 1
Oct 16 Burnley 4 Leicester 0
Oct 16 Coventry 2 Swindon 2
Oct 16 Crystal Palace 2 Leeds 1
Oct 16 Everton 0 Derby 0
Oct 16 Norwich 0 Southampton 4
Oct 16 Tottenham 1 Peterborough

Replays
Oct 21 Swindon 3 Coventry 0
Oct 23 Derby 1 Everton 0

5th Round
Oct 29 Arsenal 5 Blackpool 1
Oct 30 Burnley 2 Crystal Palace 0
Oct 30 Derby 0 Swindon 0
Oct 30 Tottenham 1 Southampton 0

Replay
Nov 05 Swindon 1 Derby 0

Semi-finals
Nov 20 Arsenal 1 Tottenham 0
Dec 04 Tottenham 1 Arsenal 1
Aggregate 1-2
Nov 20 Burnley 1 Swindon 2
Dec 04 Swindon 1 Burnley 2
Dec 18 Burnley 2 Swindon 3
Aggregate 5-6 played at W.B.A.

Final
Mar 15 Arsenal 1 Swindon 3
played at Wembley

SEASON 1969-70

1st Round
Aug 13 Aldershot 0 Gillingham 1
Aug 13 Barnsley 0 Halifax 1
Aug 13 Bolton 6 Rochdale 3
Aug 13 Bournemouth 3 Bristol R 0
Aug 12 Bradford 0 Rotherham 2
Aug 13 Bradford C 1 Chesterfield 1
Aug 13 Brighton 1 Portsmouth 0
Aug 13 Chester 1 Aston Villa 2
Aug 13 Colchester 1 Reading 1
Aug 13 Crewe 0 Wrexham 0
Aug 13 Darlington 3 York 0
Aug 13 Exeter 1 Bristol C 1
Aug 13 Grimsby 0 Doncaster 2
Aug 13 Mansfield 3 Notts Co 1
Aug 12 Newport 2 Swansea 3
Aug 13 Orient 0 Fulham 1
Aug 13 Oxford 2 Northampton 0
Aug 13 Peterborough 1 Luton 1
Aug 13 Plymouth 2 Torquay 2
Aug 13 Port Vale 0 Tranmere 1
Aug 13 Preston 0 Bury 1
Aug 12 Scunthorpe 0 Hartlepool 2
Aug 13 Shrewsbury 1 Walsall 0
Aug 12 Southend 2 Brentford 2
Aug 13 Southport 5 Oldham 1
Aug 13 Stockport 0 Blackburn 2
Aug 13 Watford 2 Lincoln 1
Aug 13 Workington 0 Barrow 0

Replays
Aug 18 Barrow 3 Workington 1
Aug 18 Brentford 0 Southend 0
Aug 18 Fulham 3 Orient 1
Aug 18 Wrexham 1 Crewe 0
Aug 19 Bristol C 3 Exeter 2
Aug 19 Luton 5 Peterborough 2
Aug 20 Chesterfield 0 Bradford C 1
Aug 20 Reading 0 Colchester 3
Aug 20 Torquay 1 Plymouth 0
Aug 21 Brentford 2 Southend 3
played at Millwall

2nd Round
Sep 03 Aston Villa 1 W.B.A. 2
Sep 03 Barrow 1 Nottingham F 2
Sep 03 Blackburn 4 Doncaster 2
Sep 03 Blackpool 3 Gillingham 1
Sep 03 Bolton 0 Rotherham 0
Sep 03 Brighton 2 Birmingham 0
Sep 02 Bristol C 0 Leicester 0
Sep 02 Carlisle 2 Huddersfield 0
Sep 02 Charlton 0 Wrexham 2
Sep 02 Coventry 0 Chelsea 1
Sep 03 Crystal Palace 3 Cardiff 1
Sep 03 Darlington 0 Everton 1
Sep 03 Fulham 0 Leeds 1
Sep 03 Hartlepool 1 Derby 3
Sep 03 Hull 1 Norwich 0
Sep 03 Ipswich 4 Colchester 0
Sep 02 Luton 2 Millwall 2
Sep 03 Manchester U 1 Middlesbrough 0
Sep 03 Mansfield 2 Q.P.R. 2
Sep 03 Oxford 4 Bury 1
Sep 02 Sheffield U 2 Newcastle 0
Sep 03 Sheffield W 1 Bournemouth 1
Sep 02 Shrewsbury 2 Southend 2
Sep 02 Southampton 1 Arsenal 1
Sep 03 Southport 0 Manchester C 3
Sep 03 Stoke 0 Burnley 2
Sep 03 Sunderland 1 Bradford C 2
Sep 02 Swansea 1 Swindon 3
Sep 03 Tranmere 2 Torquay 1
Sep 03 Watford 1 Liverpool 2
Sep 03 West Ham 4 Halifax 2
Sep 03 Wolverhampton 1 Tottenham 0

Replays
Sep 04 Arsenal 2 Southampton 0
Sep 08 Millwall 0 Luton 1
Sep 08 Southend 2 Shrewsbury 0
Sep 09 Bournemouth 1 Sheffield W 0
Sep 09 Q.P.R. 4 Mansfield 0
Sep 09 Rotherham 3 Bolton 3
Sep 10 Leicester 0 Bristol C 0
Sep 11 Rotherham 1 Bolton 0
Sep 15 Leicester 3 Bristol C 1

3rd Round
Sep 24 Arsenal 0 Everton 0
Sep 24 Bournemouth 0 Leicester 2
Sep 24 Bradford C 2 Southend 1
Sep 24 Brighton 2 Wolverhampton 3
Sep 24 Carlisle 2 Blackburn 1
Sep 24 Crystal Palace 2 Blackpool 2
Sep 24 Derby 3 Hull 1
Sep 24 Ipswich 1 W.B.A. 1
Sep 24 Leeds 1 Chelsea 1
Sep 24 Manchester C 3 Liverpool 2
Sep 23 Manchester U 2 Wrexham 0
Sep 23 Nottingham F 1 West Ham 0
Sep 24 Oxford 1 Swindon 0
Sep 23 Q.P.R. 6 Tranmere 0
Sep 24 Rotherham 1 Burnley 1
Sep 23 Sheffield U 3 Luton 0

Replays
Sep 30 Blackpool 0 Crystal Palace 1
Sep 30 Burnley 2 Rotherham 0
Sep 30 Everton 1 Arsenal 0
Sep 30 W.B.A. 2 Ipswich 0

Oct 06	Chelsea	2	Leeds	0

4th Round

Oct 15	Burnley	0	Manchester U	0
Oct 15	Carlisle	1	Chelsea	0
Oct 15	Crystal Palace	1	Derby	1
Oct 15	Leicester	2	Sheffield U	0
Oct 15	Manchester C	2	Everton	0
Oct 15	Nottingham F	0	Oxford	1
Oct 15	Q.P.R.	3	Wolverhampton	1
Oct 15	W.B.A.	4	Bradford C	0

Replays

Oct 20	Manchester U	1	Burnley	0
Oct 29	Derby	3	Crystal Palace	0

5th Round

Nov 12	Derby	0	Manchester U	0
Oct 29	Leicester	0	W.B.A.	0
Oct 29	Manchester C	3	Q.P.R.	0
Oct 29	Oxford	0	Carlisle	0

Replays

Nov 04	Carlisle	1	Oxford	0
Nov 05	W.B.A.	2	Leicester	1
Nov 19	Manchester U	1	Derby	0

Semi-finals

Nov 19	Carlisle	1	W.B.A.	0
Dec 03	W.B.A.	4	Carlisle	1
	Aggregate 4-2			
Dec 03	Manchester C	2	Manchester U	1
Dec 17	Manchester U	2	Manchester C	2
	Aggregate 3-4			

Final

Mar 07	Manchester City	2	W.B.A.	1
	played at Wembley			

Season 1970-71

1st Round

Aug 19	Aldershot	1	Brentford	0
Aug 19	Aston Villa	4	Notts Co	0
Aug 19	Barnsley	0	Rotherham	1
Aug 18	Birmingham	3	Wrexham	3
Aug 18	Bristol R	1	Brighton	0
Aug 18	Bury	1	Oldham	3
Aug 18	Charlton	3	Southend	0
Aug 19	Chester	2	Shrewsbury	1
Aug 19	Colchester	5	Cambridge	0
Aug 18	Crewe	2	Tranmere	2
Aug 19	Doncaster	1	Darlington	1
Aug 18	Exeter	0	Swansea	0
Aug 19	Fulham	1	Orient	0
Aug 19	Gillingham	0	Luton	1
Aug 19	Halifax	3	Bradford C	2
Aug 19	Hartlepool	2	York	3
Aug 19	Lincoln	2	Grimsby	1
Aug 19	Mansfield	6	Chesterfield	2
Aug 19	Newport	2	Reading	1
Aug 18	Port Vale	0	Walsall	1
Aug 19	Portsmouth	2	Plymouth	0
Aug 19	Rochdale	1	Southport	0
Aug 19	Scunthorpe	2	Northampton	3
Aug 19	Stockport	0	Preston	1
Aug 19	Torquay	1	Bournemouth	1
Aug 19	Watford	2	Peterborough	0
Aug 19	Workington	2	Barrow	0

Replays

Aug 24	Darlington	3	Doncaster	1
Aug 24	Tranmere	4	Crewe	0
Aug 25	Swansea	4	Exeter	2
Aug 26	Bournemouth	1	Torquay	2
Aug 26	Wrexham	2	Birmingham	3

2nd Round

Sep 09	Aldershot	1	Manchester U	3
Sep 09	Aston Villa	2	Burnley	0
Sep 09	Blackpool	4	Newport	1
Sep 09	Bolton	1	Blackburn	0
Sep 08	Bristol R	2	Newcastle	1
Sep 09	Carlisle	2	Manchester C	1
Sep 09	Colchester	1	Birmingham	1
Sep 09	Crystal Palace	3	Rochdale	3
Sep 09	Darlington	0	Fulham	4
Sep 08	Derby	3	Halifax	1
Sep 09	Huddersfield	0	Nottingham F	0
Sep 08	Ipswich	0	Arsenal	0
Sep 09	Leicester	3	Southampton	2
Sep 09	Lincoln	2	Sunderland	1
Sep 08	Luton	3	Workington	0
Sep 08	Mansfield	0	Liverpool	0
Sep 09	Norwich	0	Chester	0
Sep 08	Oldham	2	Middlesbrough	4
Sep 09	Oxford	1	Wolverhampton	0
Sep 09	Portsmouth	1	Walsall	0
Sep 08	Q.P.R.	4	Cardiff	0
Sep 08	Rotherham	0	Bristol C	0
Sep 08	Sheffield U	1	Leeds	0
Sep 09	Sheffield W	1	Chelsea	1
Sep 09	Stoke	0	Millwall	0
Sep 08	Swindon	4	Watford	2
Sep 09	Torquay	1	Preston	3
Sep 09	Tottenham	3	Swansea	0
Sep 09	Tranmere	1	Coventry	1
Sep 09	West Ham	2	Hull	0
Sep 08	W.B.A.	3	Charlton	1
Sep 09	York	0	Northampton	0

Replays

Sep 14	Rochdale	1	Crystal Palace	3
Sep 15	Birmingham	2	Colchester	1
Sep 15	Bristol C	4	Rotherham	0
Sep 15	Northampton	1	York	1
Sep 16	Chester	1	Norwich	2
Sep 21	Millwall	2	Stoke	1
Sep 21	Nottingham F	2	Huddersfield	0
Sep 22	Chelsea	2	Sheffield W	1
Sep 22	Coventry	2	Tranmere	1
Sep 22	Liverpool	3	Mansfield	2
Sep 28	Arsenal	4	Ipswich	0
Sep 28	Northampton	2	York	1
	played at Aston Villa			

3rd Round

Oct 06	Birmingham	2	Nottingham F	1
Oct 07	Blackpool	0	Bristol C	1
Oct 07	Bolton	1	Leicester	1
Oct 06	Carlisle	3	Oxford	1
Oct 07	Chelsea	3	Middlesbrough	2
Oct 06	Coventry	3	West Ham	1
Oct 07	Crystal Palace	4	Lincoln	0
Oct 07	Derby	4	Millwall	2
Oct 06	Fulham	2	Q.P.R.	0
Oct 06	Luton	0	Arsenal	1
Oct 07	Manchester U	1	Portsmouth	0
Oct 06	Northampton	1	Aston Villa	1
Oct 07	Norwich	1	Bristol R	1
Oct 06	Preston	0	W.B.A.	1
Oct 06	Swindon	2	Liverpool	0
Oct 07	Tottenham	2	Sheffield U	1

Replays

Oct 12	Leicester	1	Bolton	0
Oct 13	Aston Villa	3	Northampton	0
Oct 13	Bristol R	3	Norwich	1

4th Round

Oct 28	Aston Villa	1	Carlisle	0
Oct 27	Bristol R	3	Birmingham	0
Oct 27	Coventry	1	Derby	0
Oct 28	Crystal Palace	0	Arsenal	0
Oct 27	Fulham	1	Swindon	0
Oct 28	Leicester	2	Bristol C	2
Oct 28	Manchester U	2	Chelsea	1
Oct 28	Tottenham	5	W.B.A.	0

Replays

Nov 03	Bristol C	2	Leicester	1
Nov 09	Arsenal	0	Crystal Palace	2

5th Round

Nov 17	Bristol R	1	Aston Villa	1
Nov 17	Fulham	0	Bristol C	0
Nov 18	Manchester U	4	Crystal Palace	2
Nov 18	Tottenham	4	Coventry	1

Replays

Nov 24	Bristol C	1	Fulham	0
Nov 25	Aston Villa	1	Bristol R	0

Semi-finals

Dec 16	Bristol C	1	Tottenham	1
Dec 23	Tottenham	2	Bristol C	0
	Aggregate 3-1			
Dec 16	Manchester U	1	Aston Villa	1
Dec 23	Aston Villa	2	Manchester U	1
	Aggregate 3-2			

Final

Feb 27	Aston Villa	0	Tottenham	2
	played at Wembley			

Tottenham's Martin Chivers (left) steers the second goal wide of Villa goalkeeper John Dunn.

Season 1971-72

1st Round

Aug 18	Aldershot	1	Southend	1
Aug 18	Aston Villa	2	Wrexham	2
Aug 18	Barnsley	0	Hartlepool	0
Aug 18	Barrow	0	Preston	2
Aug 18	Blackburn	2	Workington	0
Aug 17	Bournemouth	2	Portsmouth	1
Aug 18	Bradford C	1	Bolton	1
Aug 17	Charlton	5	Peterborough	1
Aug 18	Chesterfield	0	Mansfield	0
Aug 18	Colchester	3	Brentford	1
Aug 18	Crewe	0	Southport	1
Aug 18	Darlington	0	York	1
Aug 18	Exeter	0	Bristol R	3
Aug 17	Fulham	4	Cambridge	0
Aug 18	Gillingham	4	Reading	0
Aug 17	Grimsby	4	Doncaster	3
Aug 18	Halifax	1	Rochdale	1
Aug 17	Newport	1	Torquay	2
Aug 17	Oldham	1	Bury	0
Aug 17	Orient	1	Notts Co	1
Aug 17	Plymouth	1	Bristol C	0
Aug 18	Port Vale	0	Shrewsbury	2
Aug 17	Rotherham	0	Sheffield W	2
Aug 18	Scunthorpe	0	Lincoln	1
Aug 18	Stockport	1	Walsall	0
Aug 17	Swansea	0	Brighton	1
Aug 18	Tranmere	1	Chester	1
Aug 18	Watford	2	Northampton	0

Replays

Aug 23	Hartlepool	0	Barnsley	1
Aug 23	Mansfield	0	Chesterfield	5
Aug 23	Southend	1	Aldershot	2
Aug 23	Wrexham	1	Aston Villa	1
Aug 24	Rochdale	2	Halifax	2
Aug 25	Bolton	2	Bradford C	1
Aug 25	Chester	1	Tranmere	3
Aug 25	Notts Co	3	Orient	1
Aug 31	Aston Villa	4	Wrexham	3
	played at W.B.A.			
Aug 31	Rochdale	0	Halifax	2

2nd Round

Sep 08	Arsenal	1	Barnsley	0
Sep 08	Blackburn	0	Lincoln	0
Sep 08	Bournemouth	0	Blackpool	2
Sep 07	Bristol R	3	Sunderland	1
Sep 07	Carlisle	5	Sheffield W	0
Sep 07	Charlton	3	Leicester	1
Sep 08	Chelsea	2	Plymouth	0
Sep 08	Chesterfield	2	Aston Villa	3
Sep 08	Colchester	4	Swindon	1
Sep 07	Coventry	0	Burnley	1
Sep 07	Crystal Palace	2	Luton	0
Sep 08	Derby	0	Leeds	0
Sep 07	Grimsby	2	Shrewsbury	1
Sep 07	Huddersfield	0	Bolton	2
Sep 07	Ipswich	1	Manchester U	3
Sep 07	Liverpool	3	Hull	0
Sep 08	Manchester C	4	Wolverhampton	3
Sep 08	Newcastle	2	Halifax	1
Sep 08	Norwich	2	Brighton	0
Sep 07	Nottingham F	5	Aldershot	1
Sep 08	Notts Co	1	Gillingham	2
Sep 08	Oxford	1	Millwall	0
Sep 07	Q.P.R.	2	Birmingham	0
Sep 07	Sheffield U	3	Fulham	0
Sep 07	Southampton	2	Everton	1
Sep 08	Southport	1	Stoke	2
Sep 07	Stockport	0	Watford	1
Sep 08	Torquay	2	Oldham	1
Sep 08	Tranmere	0	Preston	1
Sep 08	West Ham	1	Cardiff	1
Sep 08	W.B.A.	0	Tottenham	1
Sep 08	York	2	Middlesbrough	2

Replays

Sep 14	Middlesbrough	1	York	2
Sep 15	Lincoln	4	Blackburn	1
Sep 22	Cardiff	1	West Ham	2
Sep 27	Leeds	2	Derby	0

3rd Round

Oct 06	Arsenal	4	Newcastle	0
Oct 05	Blackpool	4	Colchester	0
Oct 05	Bolton	3	Manchester C	0
Oct 05	Bristol R	2	Charlton	1
Oct 05	Crystal Palace	2	Aston Villa	2
Oct 06	Gillingham	1	Grimsby	1
Oct 05	Liverpool	1	Southampton	0
Oct 06	Manchester U	1	Burnley	1
Oct 06	Norwich	4	Carlisle	1
Oct 06	Nottingham F	1	Chelsea	1
Oct 06	Oxford	1	Stoke	1
Oct 05	Q.P.R.	4	Lincoln	2
Oct 05	Sheffield U	3	York	2
Oct 06	Torquay	1	Tottenham	4
Oct 06	Watford	1	Preston	1
Oct 06	West Ham	0	Leeds	0

Replays

Oct 11	Chelsea	2	Nottingham F	1
Oct 11	Preston	2	Watford	1
Oct 12	Grimsby	1	Gillingham	0
Oct 13	Aston Villa	2	Crystal Palace	0
Oct 18	Burnley	0	Manchester U	1
Oct 18	Stoke	2	Oxford	0
Oct 20	Leeds	0	West Ham	1

4th Round

Oct 26	Arsenal	0	Sheffield U	0
Oct 26	Blackpool	4	Aston Villa	1
Oct 27	Chelsea	1	Bolton	1
Oct 26	Grimsby	1	Norwich	1
Oct 27	Manchester U	1	Stoke	1
Oct 26	Q.P.R.	1	Bristol R	1
Oct 27	Tottenham	1	Preston	1
Oct 27	West Ham	2	Liverpool	1

Replays

Nov 02	Bristol R	1	Q.P.R.	0
Nov 03	Norwich	3	Grimsby	1
Nov 08	Bolton	0	Chelsea	6
Nov 08	Preston	1	Tottenham	2
Nov 08	Sheffield U	2	Arsenal	0
Nov 08	Stoke	0	Manchester U	0
Nov 15	Stoke	2	Manchester U	1

5th Round

Nov 23	Bristol R	2	Stoke	4
Nov 17	Norwich	0	Chelsea	1
Nov 17	Tottenham	2	Blackpool	0
Nov 17	West Ham	5	Sheffield U	0

Semi-finals

Dec 22	Chelsea	3	Tottenham	2
Jan 05	Tottenham	2	Chelsea	2
	Aggregate 4-5			
Dec 08	Stoke	1	West Ham	2
Dec 15	West Ham	0	Stoke	1
Jan 05	Stoke	0	West Ham	0
	played at Sheffield W			
Jan 26	Stoke	3	West Ham	2
	Aggregate 5-4 played at Manchester U			

Final

Mar 04	Chelsea	1	Stoke	2
	played at Wembley			

Season 1972-73

1st Round

Aug 16	Aston Villa	4	Hereford	1
Aug 16	Barnsley	0	Grimsby	0
Aug 16	Blackburn	0	Rochdale	1
Aug 16	Bolton	3	Oldham	0
Aug 16	Bradford C	1	Stockport	1
Aug 16	Brentford	1	Cambridge	0
Aug 16	Brighton	2	Exeter	1
Aug 16	Cardiff	2	Bristol R	2
Aug 16	Chester	4	Shrewsbury	3
Aug 16	Darlington	0	Rotherham	1
Aug 16	Gillingham	1	Colchester	0
Aug 15	Halifax	1	Bury	2
Aug 16	Hartlepool	1	Doncaster	0
Aug 16	Mansfield	3	Lincoln	1
Aug 15	Northampton	0	Charlton	3
Aug 16	Notts Co	3	York	1
Aug 16	Orient	2	Watford	0
Aug 16	Oxford	4	Peterborough	0
Aug 15	Plymouth	0	Bournemouth	2
Aug 16	Reading	1	Fulham	1
Aug 15	Scunthorpe	0	Chesterfield	0
Aug 16	Southend	2	Aldershot	1
Aug 16	Southport	4	Walsall	1
Aug 15	Swansea	1	Newport	1
Aug 16	Torquay	1	Portsmouth	2
Aug 16	Tranmere	0	Port Vale	1
Aug 16	Workington	1	Preston	0
Aug 16	Wrexham	4	Crewe	0

Replays

Aug 21	Stockport	1	Bradford C	1
Aug 22	Bristol R	3	Cardiff	1
Aug 22	Grimsby	2	Barnsley	0
Aug 22	Newport	3	Swansea	0
Aug 23	Chesterfield	5	Scunthorpe	0
Aug 23	Fulham	1	Reading	1
Aug 28	Bradford C	0	Stockport	2
	played at Bolton			
Aug 28	Reading	0	Fulham	1

2nd Round

Sep 05	Arsenal	1	Everton	0
Sep 05	Birmingham	1	Luton	1
Sep 06	Bournemouth	0	Blackpool	0
Sep 05	Bristol R	4	Brighton	0
Sep 05	Bury	1	Grimsby	0
Sep 05	Carlisle	1	Liverpool	1
Sep 05	Charlton	4	Mansfield	3
Sep 05	Coventry	1	Hartlepool	0
Sep 05	Crystal Palace	0	Stockport	1
Sep 05	Gillingham	0	Millwall	2
Sep 05	Hull	1	Fulham	0
Sep 06	Leeds	4	Burnley	0
Sep 06	Manchester C	4	Rochdale	0
Sep 05	Middlesbrough	2	Wrexham	0
Sep 05	Newport	0	Ipswich	3
Sep 06	Norwich	2	Leicester	1
Sep 05	Nottingham F	0	Aston Villa	1
Sep 06	Notts Co	3	Southport	2
Sep 06	Oxford	2	Manchester U	2
Sep 05	Port Vale	1	Newcastle	3
Sep 06	Portsmouth	0	Chesterfield	1
Sep 05	Rotherham	2	Brentford	0
Sep 06	Sheffield W	2	Bolton	0
Sep 05	Southampton	0	Chester	0
Sep 06	Southend	0	Chelsea	1
Sep 06	Stoke	3	Sunderland	0
Sep 05	Swindon	0	Derby	1
Sep 06	Tottenham	2	Huddersfield	1
Sep 06	West Ham	2	Bristol C	1
Sep 05	Wolverhampton	2	Orient	1
Sep 06	Workington	0	Sheffield U	1
Sep 06	W.B.A.	2	Q.P.R.	1

Replays

Sep 11	Blackpool	1	Bournemouth	1
Sep 12	Manchester U	3	Oxford	1
Sep 13	Chester	2	Southampton	2
Sep 13	Luton	1	Birmingham	1
Sep 18	Blackpool	2	Bournemouth	1
	played at Aston Villa			
Sep 19	Birmingham	1	Luton	0
Sep 19	Liverpool	5	Carlisle	1
Sep 20	Chester	0	Southampton	2
	played at W.B.A.			

3rd Round

Oct 03	Arsenal	5	Rotherham	0
Oct 04	Aston Villa	1	Leeds	1
Oct 03	Birmingham	2	Coventry	1
Oct 03	Bristol R	1	Manchester U	1
Oct 03	Bury	2	Manchester C	0
Oct 04	Derby	0	Chelsea	0
Oct 03	Hull	1	Norwich	2
Oct 03	Ipswich	1	Stoke	2
Oct 03	Middlesbrough	1	Tottenham	1
Oct 03	Millwall	2	Chesterfield	0
Oct 04	Newcastle	0	Blackpool	3
Oct 03	Sheffield U	0	Charlton	0
Oct 03	Southampton	1	Notts Co	3
Oct 04	Stockport	2	West Ham	1
Oct 04	Wolverhampton	3	Sheffield W	1
Oct 03	W.B.A.	1	Liverpool	1

Replays

Oct 09	Chelsea	3	Derby	2
Oct 10	Charlton	2	Sheffield U	2
Oct 10	Liverpool	2	W.B.A.	1
Oct 11	Leeds	2	Aston Villa	0
Oct 11	Manchester U	1	Bristol R	2
Oct 11	Tottenham	0	Middlesbrough	0
Oct 23	Sheffield U	1	Charlton	0
Oct 30	Tottenham	2	Middlesbrough	1

4th Round

Oct 31	Blackpool	2	Birmingham	0
Oct 31	Bury	0	Chelsea	1
Oct 31	Liverpool	2	Leeds	2
Oct 31	Notts Co	3	Stoke	1
Oct 31	Sheffield U	1	Arsenal	2
Nov 01	Stockport	1	Norwich	5
Nov 01	Tottenham	2	Millwall	0
Oct 31	Wolverhampton	4	Bristol R	0

Replay

Nov 22	Leeds	0	Liverpool	1

5th Round

Nov 21	Arsenal	0	Norwich	3
Nov 22	Chelsea	3	Notts Co	1
Dec 04	Liverpool	1	Tottenham	1
Nov 21	Wolverhampton	1	Blackpool	1

Replays

Nov 28	Blackpool	0	Wolverhampton	1
Dec 06	Tottenham	3	Liverpool	1

Semi-finals

Dec 13	Chelsea	0	Norwich	2
Jan 03	Norwich	1	Chelsea	0
	Aggregate 3-0			
Dec 20	Wolverhampton	1	Tottenham	2
Dec 30	Tottenham	2	Wolverhampton	2
	Aggregate 4-3			

Final

Mar 03	Norwich	0	Tottenham	1
	played at Wembley			

Season 1973-74

1st Round

Date	Team	Score	Team	Score
Aug 29	Aldershot	1	Cambridge	1
Aug 28	Bolton	1	Preston	1
Aug 29	Bournemouth	1	Bristol R	0
Aug 28	Brentford	1	Orient	2
Aug 29	Brighton	1	Charlton	2
Aug 28	Bury	0	Oldham	0
Aug 29	Cardiff	2	Hereford	0
Aug 28	Carlisle	2	Workington	2
Aug 29	Chester	0	Wrexham	2
Aug 29	Chesterfield	1	Mansfield	1
Aug 29	Darlington	2	Bradford C	1
Aug 29	Gillingham	4	Colchester	2
Aug 28	Grimsby	2	Northampton	1
Aug 28	Halifax	1	Barnsley	1
Aug 28	Notts Co	3	Doncaster	4
Aug 29	Peterborough	2	Scunthorpe	2
Aug 28	Portsmouth	2	Southend	1
Aug 29	Reading	2	Watford	2
Aug 29	Rochdale	5	Hartlepool	3
Aug 28	Rotherham	2	Lincoln	1
Aug 29	Southport	1	Blackburn	1
Aug 29	Stockport	2	Port Vale	0
Aug 28	Swansea	1	Exeter	1
Aug 28	Swindon	3	Newport	3
Aug 29	Torquay	0	Plymouth	2
Aug 29	Tranmere	3	Crewe	3
Aug 29	Walsall	6	Shrewsbury	1
Aug 29	York	1	Huddersfield	0

Replays

Date	Team	Score	Team	Score
Sep 03	Mansfield	0	Chesterfield	1
Sep 03	Preston	0	Bolton	2
Sep 04	Barnsley	0	Halifax	1
Sep 04	Newport	1	Swindon	2
Sep 04	Oldham	2	Bury	3
Sep 04	Scunthorpe	2	Peterborough	1
Sep 05	Blackburn	3	Southport	1
Sep 05	Cambridge	3	Aldershot	0
Sep 05	Crewe	0	Tranmere	1
Sep 05	Exeter	2	Swansea	1
Sep 05	Watford	2	Reading	3
Sep 05	Workington	0	Carlisle	1

2nd Round

Date	Team	Score	Team	Score
Oct 02	Arsenal	0	Tranmere	1
Oct 09	Blackpool	1	Birmingham	1
Oct 10	Bournemouth	0	Sheffield W	0
Oct 09	Bury	2	Cambridge	0
Oct 10	Cardiff	2	Burnley	2
Oct 10	Chesterfield	1	Swindon	0
Oct 08	Coventry	5	Darlington	1
Oct 08	Derby	2	Sunderland	2
Oct 08	Everton	1	Reading	0
Oct 10	Gillingham	1	Carlisle	2
Oct 08	Halifax	0	Wolverhampton	3
Oct 08	Ipswich	2	Leeds	0
Oct 08	Leicester	3	Hull	3
Oct 10	Luton	1	Grimsby	1
Oct 08	Manchester U	0	Middlesbrough	1
Oct 10	Millwall	0	Nottingham F	0
Oct 08	Newcastle	6	Doncaster	0
Oct 10	Norwich	6	Wrexham	2
Oct 09	Orient	2	Blackburn	0
Oct 10	Oxford	1	Fulham	1
Oct 09	Plymouth	4	Portsmouth	0
Oct 08	Q.P.R.	1	Tottenham	0
Oct 10	Rochdale	0	Bolton	4
Oct 10	Rotherham	1	Exeter	4
Oct 09	Scunthorpe	0	Bristol C	0
Oct 08	Southampton	3	Charlton	0
Oct 09	Stockport	1	Crystal Palace	0
Oct 08	Stoke	1	Chelsea	0
Oct 02	Walsall	0	Manchester C	0
Oct 08	West Ham	2	Liverpool	2
Oct 08	W.B.A.	2	Sheffield U	1
Oct 09	York	1	Aston Villa	0

Replays

Date	Team	Score	Team	Score
Oct 15	Sheffield W	2	Bournemouth	2
Oct 16	Birmingham	4	Blackpool	2
Oct 16	Bristol C	2	Scunthorpe	1
Oct 16	Burnley	3	Cardiff	2
Oct 16	Fulham	3	Oxford	0
Oct 16	Grimsby	0	Luton	0
Oct 16	Nottingham F	1	Millwall	3
Oct 22	Manchester C	0	Walsall	0
Oct 23	Grimsby	0	Luton	2
Oct 29	Liverpool	1	West Ham	0
Oct 29	Sheffield W	2	Bournemouth	1
Oct 29	Sunderland	1	Derby	1
Oct 30	Manchester C	4	Walsall	0
Oct 31	Hull	3	Leicester	2
Oct 31	Sunderland	3	Derby	0

3rd Round

Date	Team	Score	Team	Score
Oct 30	Birmingham	2	Newcastle	2
Oct 30	Bristol C	2	Coventry	2
Oct 30	Burnley	1	Plymouth	2
Nov 06	Carlisle	0	Manchester C	1
Oct 30	Everton	0	Norwich	1
Oct 31	Fulham	2	Ipswich	2
Nov 06	Hull	4	Stockport	1
Oct 31	Luton	0	Bury	0
Oct 31	Millwall	1	Bolton	1
Oct 31	Orient	1	York	1
Nov 06	Q.P.R.	8	Sheffield W	2
Oct 30	Southampton	3	Chesterfield	0
Oct 31	Stoke	1	Middlesbrough	1
Nov 21	Sunderland	0	Liverpool	2
Oct 31	Tranmere	1	Wolverhampton	1
Oct 31	W.B.A.	1	Exeter	3

Replays

Date	Team	Score	Team	Score
Nov 06	Bolton	1	Millwall	2
Nov 06	Bury	2	Luton	3
Nov 06	Coventry	2	Bristol C	1
Nov 06	Middlesbrough	1	Stoke	2
Nov 06	York	2	Orient	1
Nov 07	Newcastle	0	Birmingham	1
Nov 13	Wolverhampton	2	Tranmere	1
Nov 14	Ipswich	2	Fulham	1

4th Round

Date	Team	Score	Team	Score
Nov 20	Coventry	2	Stoke	1
Nov 27	Hull	0	Liverpool	0
Nov 21	Ipswich	1	Birmingham	3
Nov 21	Millwall	3	Luton	1
Nov 20	Q.P.R.	0	Plymouth	3
Nov 21	Southampton	0	Norwich	2
Nov 20	Wolverhampton	5	Exeter	1
Nov 21	York	0	Manchester C	0

Replays

Date	Team	Score	Team	Score
Dec 04	Liverpool	3	Hull	1
Dec 05	Manchester C	4	York	1

5th Round

Date	Team	Score	Team	Score
Dec 19	Birmingham	1	Plymouth	2
Dec 19	Coventry	2	Manchester C	2
Dec 19	Millwall	1	Norwich	1
Dec 19	Wolverhampton	1	Liverpool	0

Replays

Date	Team	Score	Team	Score
Jan 16	Manchester C	4	Coventry	2
Jan 16	Norwich	2	Millwall	1

Semi-finals

Date	Team	Score	Team	Score
Jan 23	Norwich	1	Wolverhampton	1
Jan 26	Wolverhampton	1	Norwich	0
	Aggregate 2-1			
Jan 23	Plymouth	1	Manchester C	1
Jan 30	Manchester C	2	Plymouth	0
	Aggregate 3-1			

Final

Date	Team	Score	Team	Score
Mar 02	Manchester C	1	Wolverhampton	2
	played at Wembley			

Season 1974-75

1st Round

Date	Team	Score	Team	Score
Aug 20	Barnsley	0	Halifax	1
Aug 20	Bradford C	2	Darlington	1
Aug 21	Brentford	3	Aldershot	0
Aug 19	Bristol C	2	Cardiff	1
Aug 20	Bristol R	0	Plymouth	0
Aug 20	Bury	2	Oldham	0
Aug 20	Charlton	4	Peterborough	0
Aug 21	Chester	2	Walsall	1
Aug 21	Chesterfield	3	Grimsby	0
Aug 20	Colchester	1	Oxford	0
Aug 20	Doncaster	2	Mansfield	1
Aug 21	Exeter	3	Swansea	1
Aug 21	Gillingham	1	Bournemouth	1
Aug 21	Hereford	1	Shrewsbury	1
Aug 20	Newport	1	Torquay	0
Aug 20	Northampton	1	Port Vale	0
Aug 20	Preston	1	Rochdale	0
Aug 21	Reading	0	Brighton	0
Aug 20	Rotherham	1	Lincoln	1
Aug 20	Scunthorpe	1	Sheffield W	0
Aug 21	Southend	2	Cambridge	0
Aug 21	Southport	0	Tranmere	2
Aug 21	Stockport	0	Blackburn	2
Aug 20	Swindon	0	Portsmouth	1
Aug 21	Watford	1	Crystal Palace	1
Aug 21	Workington	1	Hartlepool	2
Aug 20	Wrexham	1	Crewe	2
Aug 21	York	0	Huddersfield	2

Replays

Date	Team	Score	Team	Score
Aug 27	Crystal Palace	5	Watford	1
Aug 27	Plymouth	0	Bristol R	1
Aug 27	Shrewsbury	0	Hereford	1
Aug 28	Bournemouth	1	Gillingham	1
Aug 28	Brighton	2	Reading	2
Aug 28	Lincoln	1	Rotherham	1
Sep 03	Bournemouth	2	Gillingham	1
	played at Brentford			
Sep 03	Reading	0	Brighton	0
Sep 03	Rotherham	2	Lincoln	1
Sep 05	Brighton	2	Reading	3

2nd Round

Date	Team	Score	Team	Score
Sep 10	Arsenal	1	Leicester	1
Sep 11	Aston Villa	1	Everton	1
Sep 10	Bolton	0	Norwich	0
Sep 11	Bournemouth	1	Hartlepool	1
Sep 11	Bradford C	0	Carlisle	1
Sep 10	Bury	2	Doncaster	0
Sep 11	Chelsea	4	Newport	2
Sep 11	Chester	3	Blackpool	1
Sep 10	Coventry	1	Ipswich	2
Sep 11	Crewe	2	Birmingham	1
Sep 10	Crystal Palace	1	Bristol C	4
Sep 11	Exeter	0	Hereford	1
Sep 10	Huddersfield	1	Leeds	1
Sep 11	Hull	1	Burnley	2
Sep 10	Liverpool	2	Brentford	1
Sep 11	Luton	1	Bristol R	0
Sep 10	Manchester C	6	Scunthorpe	0
Sep 11	Manchester U	5	Charlton	1
Sep 10	Northampton	2	Blackburn	2
Sep 10	Nottingham F	1	Newcastle	1
Sep 11	Portsmouth	1	Derby	5
Sep 10	Preston	2	Sunderland	0
Sep 10	Q.P.R.	4	Orient	1
Sep 11	Reading	4	Rotherham	2
Sep 10	Sheffield U	3	Chesterfield	1
Sep 10	Southampton	1	Notts Co	0
Sep 11	Southend	0	Colchester	2
Sep 11	Stoke	3	Halifax	0
Sep 11	Tottenham	0	Middlesbrough	4
Sep 11	Tranmere	0	West Ham	0
Sep 11	Wolverhampton	1	Fulham	3
Sep 10	W.B.A.	1	Millwall	0

Replays

Date	Team	Score	Team	Score
Sep 17	Norwich	3	Bolton	1
Sep 17	Orient	0	Q.P.R.	3
Sep 18	Blackburn	1	Northampton	0
Sep 18	Everton	0	Aston Villa	3
Sep 18	Hartlepool	2	Bournemouth	2
Sep 18	Leicester	2	Arsenal	1
Sep 18	West Ham	6	Tranmere	0
Sep 23	Bournemouth	1	Hartlepool	1
Sep 24	Leeds	1	Huddersfield	1
Sep 25	Newcastle	3	Nottingham F	0
Sep 26	Hartlepool	1	Bournemouth	0
Oct 07	Leeds	2	Huddersfield	1

3rd Round

Date	Team	Score	Team	Score
Oct 08	Bristol C	0	Liverpool	0
Oct 09	Bury	1	Leeds	2
Oct 09	Chelsea	2	Stoke	2
Oct 09	Chester	1	Preston	0
Oct 09	Colchester	2	Carlisle	0
Oct 09	Crewe	2	Aston Villa	2
Oct 08	Fulham	2	West Ham	1
Oct 09	Hartlepool	1	Blackburn	1
Oct 08	Ipswich	4	Hereford	1
Oct 09	Manchester U	1	Manchester C	0
Oct 08	Middlesbrough	1	Leicester	0
Oct 08	Q.P.R.	0	Newcastle	4
Oct 09	Reading	1	Burnley	2
Oct 08	Sheffield U	2	Luton	0
Oct 08	Southampton	5	Derby	0
Oct 09	W.B.A.	1	Norwich	1

Replays

Date	Team	Score	Team	Score
Oct 16	Aston Villa	1	Crewe	0
Oct 16	Blackburn	1	Hartlepool	2
Oct 16	Liverpool	4	Bristol C	0
Oct 16	Norwich	2	W.B.A.	0
Oct 16	Stoke	1	Chelsea	1
Oct 22	Stoke	6	Chelsea	2

4th Round

Date	Team	Score	Team	Score
Nov 13	Chester	3	Leeds	0
Nov 13	Colchester	0	Southampton	0
Nov 12	Hartlepool	1	Aston Villa	1
Nov 12	Ipswich	2	Stoke	1
Nov 12	Liverpool	0	Middlesbrough	1
Nov 13	Manchester U	3	Burnley	2
Nov 13	Newcastle	3	Fulham	0
Nov 12	Sheffield U	2	Norwich	2

Replays

Date	Team	Score	Team	Score
Nov 25	Aston Villa	6	Hartlepool	1
Nov 25	Southampton	0	Colchester	1
Nov 27	Norwich	2	Sheffield U	1

5th Round

Date	Team	Score	Team	Score
Dec 03	Colchester	1	Aston Villa	2
Dec 04	Middlesbrough	0	Manchester U	0
Dec 04	Newcastle	0	Chester	0
Dec 04	Norwich	1	Ipswich	1

Replays

Date	Team	Score	Team	Score
Dec 10	Ipswich	1	Norwich	2
Dec 18	Chester	1	Newcastle	0
Dec 18	Manchester U	3	Middlesbrough	0

Semi-finals

Date	Team	Score	Team	Score
Jan 15	Chester	2	Aston Villa	2
Jan 22	Aston Villa	3	Chester	2
	Aggregate 5-4			
Jan 15	Manchester U	2	Norwich	2
Jan 22	Norwich	1	Manchester U	0
	Aggregate 3-2			

Final

Date	Team	Score	Team	Score
Mar 01	Aston Villa	1	Norwich	0
	played at Wembley			

Season 1975-76

1st Round

Aldershot	v Portsmouth	Aug 20	1-1	Aug 26	1-2	2-3
Bradford C	v York	Aug 20	2-0	Aug 26	0-3	2-3
Brentford	v Brighton	Aug 19	2-1	Aug 27	1-1	3-2
Bury	v Rochdale	Aug 19	2-0	Aug 26	2-0	4-0
Cambridge	v Charlton	Aug 19	1-1	Aug 26	0-3	1-4
Cardiff	v Bristol R	Aug 20	1-2	Aug 26	1-1	2-3
Crewe	v Tranmere	Aug 20	2-1	Aug 26	1-2	3-3
Crystal Palace	v Colchester	Aug 19	3-0	Aug 25	1-3	4-3
Darlington	v Sheffield W	Aug 19	0-2	Aug 27	2-0	2-2
Doncaster	v Grimsby	Aug 19	3-1	Aug 25	0-0	3-1
Halifax	v Hartlepool	Aug 19	4-1	Aug 25	1-2	5-3
Huddersfield	v Barnsley	Aug 19	2-1	Aug 27	1-1	3-2
Lincoln	v Chesterfield	Aug 20	4-2	Aug 25	2-3	6-5
Mansfield	v Scunthorpe	Aug 20	4-0	Aug 26	2-0	6-0
Newport	v Exeter	Aug 19	1-1	Aug 26	0-2	1-3
Oldham	v Workington	Aug 19	3-0	Aug 26	3-1	6-1
Plymouth	v Bournemouth	Aug 19	2-0	Aug 26	2-1	4-1
Port Vale	v Hereford	Aug 18	4-2	Aug 27	0-2	4-4
Preston	v Blackburn	Aug 19	2-0	Aug 27	0-0	2-0
Reading	v Gillingham	Aug 20	0-1	Aug 25	1-1	1-2
Rotherham	v Nottingham F	Aug 19	1-2	Aug 27	1-5	2-7
Southend	v Peterborough	Aug 20	2-0	Aug 27	0-3	2-3
Southport	v Stockport	Aug 20	3-1	Aug 25	2-1	5-2
Swansea	v Torquay	Aug 19	1-2	Aug 27	3-5	4-7
Swindon	v Millwall	Aug 19	2-1	Aug 25	1-0	3-1
Walsall	v Shrewsbury	Aug 19	0-0	Aug 26	1-2	1-2
Watford	v Northampton	Aug 19	2-0	Aug 27	1-1	3-1
Wrexham	v Chester	Aug 20	3-0	Aug 27	0-0	3-0

Replays

Sep 02 Crewe 2 Tranmere 1
Sep 01 Hereford 1 Port Vale 0
played at Shrewsbury
Sep 03 Sheffield W 0 Darlington 0
Penalties 3-5

2nd Round

Sep 10 Aston Villa 2 Oldham 0
Sep 09 Birmingham 4 Orient 0
Sep 10 Bolton 1 Coventry 3
Sep 09 Bury 1 Middlesbrough 2
Sep 09 Carlisle 2 Gillingham 0
Sep 09 Charlton 3 Oxford 3
Sep 10 Crewe 1 Chelsea 0
Sep 09 Darlington 2 Luton 1
Sep 10 Derby 2 Huddersfield 1
Sep 09 Doncaster 2 Crystal Palace 1
Sep 09 Everton 2 Arsenal 2
Sep 10 Halifax 2 Sheffield U 4
Sep 10 Hereford 1 Burnley 4
Sep 09 Hull 4 Preston 2
Sep 09 Leeds 3 Ipswich 2
Sep 10 Lincoln 2 Stoke 1
Sep 10 Manchester U 2 Brentford 1
Sep 10 Newcastle 6 Southport 0
Sep 10 Norwich 1 Manchester C 1
Sep 10 Nottingham F 1 Plymouth 0
Sep 09 Notts Co 2 Sunderland 1
Sep 10 Peterborough 2 Blackpool 0
Sep 09 Portsmouth 1 Leicester 1
Sep 09 Shrewsbury 1 Q.P.R. 4
Sep 09 Southampton 0 Bristol R 1
Sep 09 Swindon 2 Wolverhampton 2
Sep 10 Torquay 1 Exeter 1
Sep 09 Watford 0 Tottenham 1
Sep 09 West Ham 0 Bristol C 0
Sep 10 Wrexham 1 Mansfield 2
Sep 09 W.B.A. 1 Fulham 1
Sep 10 York 0 Liverpool 1

Replays

Sep 16 Wolverhampton 3 Swindon 2
Sep 17 Exeter 1 Torquay 2
Sep 17 Leicester 1 Portsmouth 0
Sep 17 Manchester C 2 Norwich 2
Sep 17 Oxford 1 Charlton 1
Sep 23 Arsenal 0 Everton 1
Sep 24 Bristol C 1 West Ham 3
Sep 24 Fulham 1 W.B.A. 0
Sep 29 Manchester C 6 Norwich 1
played at Chelsea
Sep 29 Oxford 2 Charlton 3

3rd Round

Oct 08 Aston Villa 1 Manchester U 2
Oct 07 Birmingham 0 Wolverhampton 2
Oct 07 Bristol R 1 Newcastle 1
Oct 08 Crewe 0 Tottenham 2
Oct 08 Everton 2 Carlisle 0
Oct 08 Fulham 0 Peterborough 1
Oct 07 Hull 2 Sheffield U 0
Oct 08 Leeds 0 Notts Co 1
Oct 08 Leicester 2 Lincoln 1
Oct 07 Liverpool 1 Burnley 1
Oct 08 Manchester C 2 Nottingham F 1
Oct 08 Mansfield 2 Coventry 0
Oct 07 Middlesbrough 1 Derby 0
Oct 07 Q.P.R. 1 Charlton 1
Oct 07 Torquay 1 Doncaster 1
Oct 08 West Ham 3 Darlington 0

Replays

Oct 13 Doncaster 3 Torquay 0
Oct 14 Burnley 1 Liverpool 0
Oct 14 Charlton 0 Q.P.R. 3
Oct 15 Newcastle 2 Bristol R 0

4th Round

Nov 11 Burnley 2 Leicester 0
Nov 11 Doncaster 2 Hull 1
Nov 11 Everton 2 Notts Co 2
Nov 12 Manchester C 4 Manchester U 0
Nov 12 Mansfield 1 Wolverhampton 0
Nov 11 Middlesbrough 3 Peterborough 0
Nov 11 Q.P.R. 1 Newcastle 3
Nov 12 Tottenham 0 West Ham 0

Replays

Nov 24 West Ham 0 Tottenham 2
Nov 25 Notts Co 2 Everton 0

5th Round

Dec 03 Burnley 0 Middlesbrough 2
Dec 03 Manchester C 4 Mansfield 2
Dec 03 Newcastle 1 Notts Co 0
Dec 03 Tottenham 7 Doncaster 2

Semi-finals

Jan 13 Middlesbrough 1 Manchester C 0
Jan 21 Manchester C 4 Middlesbrough 0
Aggregate 4-1
Jan 14 Tottenham 1 Newcastle 0
Jan 21 Newcastle 3 Tottenham 1
Aggregate 3-2

Final

Feb 28 Manchester C 2 Newcastle 1
played at Wembley

Season 1976-77

1st Round

Aldershot	v Gillingham	Aug 14	1-1	Aug 18	0-2	1-3
Bournemouth	v Torquay	Aug 14	0-0	Aug 17	0-1	0-1
Bradford C	v Oldham	Aug 14	1-1	Aug 17	3-1	4-2
Bury	v Preston	Aug 14	2-1	Aug 17	1-1	3-2
Cardiff	v Bristol R	Aug 14	2-1	Aug 17	4-4	6-5
Chester	v Hereford	Aug 14	2-0	Aug 18	3-4	5-4
Chesterfield	v Rotherham	Aug 14	3-1	Aug 17	0-3	3-4
Crewe	v Tranmere	Aug 14	2-1	Aug 18	1-3	3-4
Crystal Palace	v Portsmouth	Aug 14	2-2	Aug 17	1-0	3-2
Doncaster	v Lincoln	Aug 14	1-1	Aug 18	1-1	2-2
Grimsby	v Sheffield W	Aug 14	0-3	Aug 18	0-0	0-3
Halifax	v Darlington	Aug 14	0-0	Aug 18	1-1	1-1
Huddersfield	v Hartlepool	Aug 14	2-0	Aug 18	2-1	4-1
Mansfield	v Scunthorpe	Aug 14	2-0	Aug 17	0-2	2-2
Millwall	v Colchester	Aug 14	2-1	Aug 17	1-2	3-3
Oxford	v Cambridge	Aug 14	1-0	Aug 17	0-2	1-2
Plymouth	v Exeter	Aug 14	0-1	Aug 18	0-1	0-2
Port Vale	v Wrexham	Aug 14	1-1	Aug 18	0-1	1-2
Reading	v Peterborough	Aug 14	2-3	Aug 18	1-0	3-3
Rochdale	v Blackburn	Aug 14	0-1	Aug 18	1-4	1-5
Shrewsbury	v Walsall	Aug 16	0-1	Aug 18	0-1	0-2
Southend	v Brighton	Aug 14	1-1	Aug 17	1-2	2-3
Southport	v Carlisle	Aug 14	1-2	Aug 17	1-0	2-2
Swansea	v Newport	Aug 14	4-1	Aug 17	0-1	4-2
Swindon	v Northampton	Aug 14	3-2	Aug 18	0-2	3-4
Watford	v Brentford	Aug 14	1-1	Aug 17	2-0	3-1
Workington	v Stockport	Aug 14	0-0	Aug 18	0-0	0-0
York	v Barnsley	Aug 14	0-0	Aug 17	0-0	0-0

Replays

Aug 24 Carlisle 3 Southport 2
Aug 30 Colchester 4 Millwall 4
Penalties
Aug 24 Doncaster 2 Lincoln 2
Penalties 2-4
played at Nottingham F
Aug 30 Halifax 1 Darlington 2
Aug 25 Peterborough 3 Reading 1
Aug 24 Scunthorpe 2 Mansfield 1
Aug 30 Workington 0 Stockport 2
Aug 24 York 1 Barnsley 2

2nd Round

Aug 31 Arsenal 3 Carlisle 2
Sep 01 Aston Villa 3 Manchester C 0
Sep 01 Blackburn 1 Stockport 3
Aug 31 Blackpool 2 Birmingham 1
Sep 01 Bradford C 1 Bolton 2
Aug 31 Bristol C 0 Coventry 1
Sep 01 Bury 2 Darlington 1
Sep 01 Cardiff 1 Q.P.R. 3
Sep 01 Chelsea 3 Sheffield U 1
Aug 31 Chester 2 Swansea 3
Aug 31 Crystal Palace 1 Watford 3
Aug 31 Doncaster 1 Derby 2
Aug 30 Everton 3 Cambridge 0
Aug 31 Exeter 1 Norwich 3
Aug 31 Fulham 1 Peterborough 1
Sep 01 Gillingham 1 Newcastle 2
Aug 31 Ipswich 0 Brighton 0
Aug 31 Liverpool 1 W.B.A. 1
Sep 01 Manchester U 5 Tranmere 0
Aug 31 Middlesbrough 1 Tottenham 2
Aug 31 Northampton 0 Huddersfield 1
Aug 31 Orient 1 Hull 0
Sep 01 Rotherham 1 Millwall 2
Aug 31 Scunthorpe 0 Notts Co 2
Aug 31 Southampton 1 Charlton 1
Sep 01 Stoke 2 Leeds 1
Aug 31 Sunderland 3 Luton 1
Sep 01 Torquay 1 Burnley 0
Aug 31 Walsall 2 Nottingham F 4
Sep 01 West Ham 3 Barnsley 0
Aug 31 Wolverhampton 1 Sheffield W 2
Sep 01 Wrexham 1 Leicester 0

Replays

Sep 06 W.B.A. 1 Liverpool 0
Sep 07 Brighton 2 Ipswich 1
Sep 07 Charlton 2 Southampton 1
Sep 07 Peterborough 1 Fulham 2

3rd Round

Sep 21 Aston Villa 2 Norwich 1
Sep 21 Blackpool 1 Arsenal 1
Sep 21 Charlton 0 West Ham 1
Sep 20 Chelsea 2 Huddersfield 0
Sep 22 Derby 1 Notts Co 1
Sep 22 Fulham 2 Bolton 2
Sep 22 Manchester U 2 Sunderland 2
Sep 21 Millwall 0 Orient 0
Sep 22 Newcastle 3 Stoke 0
Sep 21 Nottingham F 0 Coventry 3
Sep 21 Q.P.R. 2 Bury 1
Sep 21 Sheffield W 3 Watford 1
Sep 20 Stockport 0 Everton 1
Sep 22 Torquay 1 Swansea 2
Sep 22 Tottenham 2 Wrexham 3
Sep 22 W.B.A. 0 Brighton 2

Replays

Sep 28 Arsenal 0 Blackpool 0
Oct 04 Notts Co 1 Derby 2
Oct 04 Sunderland 2 Manchester U 2
Oct 05 Arsenal 2 Blackpool 0
Oct 05 Bolton 2 Fulham 2
Oct 06 Manchester U 1 Sunderland 0
Oct 12 Orient 0 Millwall 0
Oct 18 Bolton 2 Fulham 1
played at Birmingham
Oct 19 Millwall 3 Orient 0
played at Arsenal

4th Round

Oct 26 Arsenal 2 Chelsea 1
Oct 27 Aston Villa 5 Wrexham 1
Oct 26 Brighton 1 Derby 1
Oct 26 Everton 3 Coventry 0
Oct 27 Manchester U 7 Newcastle 2
Oct 27 Millwall 3 Sheffield U 0
Oct 26 Swansea 1 Bolton 1
Oct 27 West Ham 0 Q.P.R. 2

Replays

Nov 02 Bolton 5 Swansea 1
Nov 08 Derby 2 Brighton 1

5th Round

Dec 01 Aston Villa 2 Millwall 0
Dec 01 Derby 1 Bolton 2
Dec 01 Manchester U 0 Everton 3
Dec 01 Q.P.R. 2 Arsenal 1

Semi-finals

Jan 18 Everton 1 Bolton 1
Feb 15 Bolton 0 Everton 1
Aggregate 1-2
Feb 01 Q.P.R. 0 Aston Villa 0
Feb 16 Aston Villa 2 Q.P.R. 2
Feb 22 Aston Villa 3 Q.P.R. 0
Aggregate 5-2 played at Arsenal

Final

Mar 12 Aston Villa 0 Everton 0
played at Wembley

Replays

Mar 16 Aston Villa 1 Everton 1
played at Sheffield W
Apr 13 Aston Villa 3 Everton 2
played at Manchester U

Season 1977-78

1st Round

Aldershot	v Colchester	Aug 13	1-1	Aug 16	1-4	2-5
Brentford	v Crystal Palace	Aug 13	2-1	Aug 16	1-5	3-6
Bristol R	v Walsall	Aug 13	1-2	Aug 16	0-1	1-3
Burnley	v Chester	Aug 13	2-0	Aug 17	0-1	2-1
Bury	v Crewe	Aug 13	3-0	Aug 17	1-1	4-1
Cambridge	v Brighton	Aug 13	0-0	Aug 16	0-0	0-0
Chesterfield	v Barnsley	Aug 13	4-1	Aug 16	0-3	4-4
Darlington	v Scunthorpe	Aug 13	0-0	Aug 16	1-3	1-3
Exeter	v Plymouth	Aug 13	2-2	Aug 16	0-0	2-2
Fulham	v Orient	Aug 13	0-2	Aug 16	2-1	2-3
Gillingham	v Wimbledon	Aug 13	1-1	Aug 16	1-3	2-4
Grimsby	v Hartlepool	Aug 13	3-0	Aug 16	2-1	5-1
Hereford	v Bournemouth	Aug 13	2-0	Aug 16	2-4	4-4
Huddersfield	v Carlisle	Aug 13	1-1	Aug 16	2-2	3-3
Mansfield	v Lincoln	Aug 13	0-1	Aug 17	0-0	0-1
Oxford	v Shrewsbury	Aug 13	3-0	Aug 16	2-2	5-2
Peterborough	v Bradford C	Aug 13	4-1	Aug 17	1-1	5-2
Port Vale	v Preston	Aug 13	2-1	Aug 16	1-2	3-3
Portsmouth	v Newport	Aug 13	3-1	Aug 16	2-3	5-4
Rochdale	v Halifax	Aug 13	1-1	Aug 16	2-1	3-2
Rotherham	v York	Aug 13	3-0	Aug 16	0-3	3-3
Sheffield W	v Doncaster	Aug 13	5-2	Aug 16	3-0	8-2
Southend	v Northampton	Aug 13	2-3	Aug 16	1-2	3-5
Swansea	v Swindon	Aug 13	1-3	Aug 16	1-2	2-5
Torquay	v Cardiff	Aug 13	1-0	Aug 17	2-3	3-3
Tranmere	v Southport	Aug 13	0-1	Aug 16	2-2	2-3
Watford	v Reading	Aug 13	2-1	Aug 17	0-1	2-2
Wrexham	v Stockport	Aug 13	1-0	Aug 17	1-1	2-1

Replays

Aug 23	Barnsley	0	Chesterfield	2
Aug 23	Brighton	3	Cambridge	0
Aug 24	Cardiff	2	Torquay	1
Aug 23	Hereford	1	Bournemouth	2
Aug 23	Huddersfield	2	Carlisle	1
Aug 23	Plymouth	0	Exeter	1
Aug 23	Port Vale played at Stockport	1	Preston	2
Aug 23	Watford	5	Reading	0
Aug 23	York Penalties 5-6	1	Rotherham	1

2nd Round

Aug 30	Arsenal	3	Manchester U	2
Aug 30	Birmingham	0	Notts Co	2
Aug 31	Blackburn	1	Colchester	1
Aug 30	Blackpool	2	Sheffield W	2
Aug 30	Bolton	1	Lincoln	0
Aug 30	Brighton	0	Oldham	0
Aug 29	Bristol C	1	Stoke	0
Aug 30	Burnley	3	Norwich	1
Aug 30	Charlton	1	Wrexham	2
Aug 31	Chesterfield	0	Manchester C	1
Aug 30	Crystal Palace	0	Southampton	0
Aug 31	Derby	3	Orient	1
Aug 31	Exeter	1	Aston Villa	3
Aug 30	Grimsby	1	Watford	2
Aug 30	Huddersfield	0	Coventry	2
Aug 30	Ipswich	5	Northampton	0
Aug 30	Liverpool	2	Chelsea	0
Aug 31	Newcastle	0	Millwall	2
Aug 30	Nottingham F	5	West Ham	0
Aug 31	Oxford	1	Bury	1
Aug 30	Peterborough	1	Scunthorpe	1
Aug 30	Portsmouth	2	Leicester	0
Aug 31	Q.P.R.	2	Bournemouth	0
Aug 31	Rochdale	0	Leeds	3
Aug 30	Sheffield U	0	Everton	3
Aug 31	Southport	2	Hull	2
Aug 30	Sunderland	2	Middlesbrough	2
Aug 30	Swindon	5	Cardiff	1
Aug 31	Tottenham	4	Wimbledon	0
Aug 30	Walsall	0	Preston	0
Aug 30	Wolverhampton	1	Luton	3
Aug 31	W.B.A.	4	Rotherham	0

Replays

Sep 05	Bury	1	Oxford	0
Sep 05	Sheffield W	3	Blackpool	1
Sep 06	Preston	0	Walsall	1
Sep 06	Scunthorpe	0	Peterborough	1
Sep 07	Colchester	4	Blackburn	0
Sep 13	Middlesbrough	1	Sunderland	0
Sep 13	Oldham	2	Brighton	2
Sep 13	Southampton	2	Crystal Palace	1
Sep 14	Hull	1	Southport	0
Sep 17	Brighton played at Leicester	1	Oldham	2

3rd Round

Oct 25	Arsenal	2	Southampton	0
Oct 26	Aston Villa	1	Q.P.R.	0
Oct 25	Bolton	3	Peterborough	1
Oct 25	Burnley	1	Ipswich	2
Oct 25	Everton	2	Middlesbrough	2
Oct 25	Hull	2	Oldham	0
Oct 26	Leeds	4	Colchester	0
Oct 26	Liverpool	2	Derby	0
Oct 25	Luton	1	Manchester C	1
Oct 25	Millwall	1	Bury	1
Oct 25	Nottingham F	4	Notts Co	0
Oct 25	Portsmouth	1	Swindon	1
Oct 25	Sheffield W	2	Walsall	1
Oct 26	Tottenham	2	Coventry	3
Oct 26	Wrexham	1	Bristol C	0
Oct 25	W.B.A.	1	Watford	0

Replays

Oct 31	Middlesbrough	1	Everton	2
Nov 01	Bury	2	Millwall	0
Nov 01	Manchester C	0	Luton	0
Nov 01	Swindon	4	Portsmouth	3
Nov 09	Manchester C played at Manchester U	3	Luton	2

4th Round

Nov 29	Arsenal	5	Hull	1
Nov 30	Bolton	1	Leeds	3
Nov 29	Bury	1	W.B.A.	0
Nov 29	Ipswich	1	Manchester C	2
Nov 29	Liverpool	2	Coventry	2
Nov 29	Nottingham F	4	Aston Villa	2
Nov 29	Sheffield W	1	Everton	3
Dec 07	Wrexham	2	Swindon	0

Replay

Dec 20	Coventry	0	Liverpool	2

5th Round

Jan 17	Bury	0	Nottingham F	3
Jan 18	Leeds	4	Everton	1
Jan 18	Manchester C	0	Arsenal	0
Jan 17	Wrexham	1	Liverpool	3

Replay

Jan 24	Arsenal	1	Manchester C	0

Semi-finals

Feb 08	Leeds	1	Nottingham F	3
Feb 22	Nottingham F Aggregate 7-3	4	Leeds	2
Feb 07	Liverpool	2	Arsenal	1
Feb 14	Arsenal Aggregate 1-2	0	Liverpool	0

Final

Mar 18	Liverpool played at Wembley	0	Nottingham F	0

Replay

Mar 22	Liverpool played at Manchester U	0	Nottingham F	1

Season 1978-79

1st Round

Aldershot	v Millwall	Aug 12	0-1	Aug 16	0-1	0-2
Barnsley	v Chesterfield	Aug 12	1-2	Aug 16	0-0	1-2
Bournemouth	v Exeter	Aug 12	0-1	Aug 15	1-1	1-2
Bradford C	v Lincoln	Aug 12	2-0	Aug 16	1-1	3-1
Bristol R	v Hereford	Aug 12	2-1	Aug 16	0-4	2-5
Cambridge	v Northampton	Aug 12	2-2	Aug 16	1-2	3-4
Cardiff	v Oxford	Aug 12	1-2	Aug 16	1-2	2-4
Carlisle	v Blackpool	Aug 12	2-2	Aug 16	1-2	3-4
Colchester	v Charlton	Aug 12	2-3	Aug 15	0-0	2-3
Crewe	v Rochdale	Aug 12	1-0	Aug 14	4-2	5-2
Doncaster	v Sheffield W	Aug 12	0-1	Aug 15	1-0	1-1
Grimsby	v York	Aug 12	2-0	Aug 15	3-0	5-0
Hull	v Peterborough	Aug 12	0-1	Aug 15	2-1	2-2
Mansfield	v Darlington	Aug 12	0-1	Aug 15	2-2	2-3
Newport	v Swansea	Aug 12	2-1	Aug 15	0-5	2-6
Plymouth	v Torquay	Aug 12	1-1	Aug 16	2-1	3-2
Port Vale	v Chester	Aug 12	0-3	Aug 16	1-1	1-4
Portsmouth	v Swindon	Aug 12	0-0	Aug 15	2-4	2-4
Preston	v Huddersfield	Aug 12	3-0	Aug 15	2-2	5-2
Reading	v Gillingham	Aug 12	3-1	Aug 15	2-1	5-2
Rotherham	v Hartlepool	Aug 12	5-0	Aug 15	1-1	6-1
Scunthorpe	v Notts Co	Aug 12	0-1	Aug 15	0-3	0-4
Shrewsbury	v Stockport	Aug 14	1-0	Aug 16	1-3	2-3
Southend	v Wimbledon	Aug 12	1-0	Aug 15	1-4	2-4
Tranmere	v Wigan	Aug 12	1-1	Aug 16	1-2	2-3
Walsall	v Halifax	Aug 12	2-1	Aug 15	2-0	4-1
Watford	v Brentford	Aug 12	4-0	Aug 15	3-1	7-1
Wrexham	v Bury	Aug 12	2-0	Aug 15	2-1	4-1

Replays

Aug 22	Doncaster	0	Sheffield W	1
Aug 22	Peterborough	1	Hull	0

2nd Round

Aug 30	Aston Villa	1	Sheffield W	0
Aug 29	Birmingham	2	Southampton	5
Aug 30	Blackpool	2	Ipswich	0
Aug 29	Bolton	2	Chelsea	1
Aug 29	Brighton	1	Millwall	0
Aug 29	Bristol C	1	Crystal Palace	2
Aug 29	Burnley	1	Bradford C	1
Aug 30	Chester	2	Coventry	1
Aug 30	Crewe	2	Notts Co	0
Aug 29	Everton	8	Wimbledon	0
Aug 29	Exeter	2	Blackburn	1
Aug 29	Fulham	2	Darlington	2
Aug 30	Leicester	0	Derby	1

Forest's Gary Birtles with Tony Woodcock and John Robertson after netting the winner against Southampton in 1979.

Aug 29	Luton	2	Wigan	0
Aug 29	Manchester C	2	Grimsby	0
Aug 29	Middlesbrough	0	Peterborough	0
Aug 29	Northampton	0	Hereford	0
Aug 29	Oldham	0	Nottingham F	0
Aug 29	Orient	1	Chesterfield	2
Aug 30	Oxford	1	Plymouth	1
Aug 29	Preston	1	Q.P.R.	3
Aug 30	Reading	1	Wolverhampton	0
Aug 29	Rotherham	3	Arsenal	1
Aug 28	Sheffield U	1	Liverpool	0
Aug 30	Stockport	2	Manchester U	3
Aug 30	Sunderland	0	Stoke	2
Aug 29	Swansea	2	Tottenham	2
Aug 29	Walsall	1	Charlton	2
Aug 29	Watford	2	Newcastle	1
Aug 30	West Ham	1	Swindon	2
Aug 29	Wrexham	1	Norwich	3
Aug 29	W.B.A.	0	Leeds	0

Replays

Sep 05	Bradford C	2	Burnley	3
Sep 05	Darlington	1	Fulham	0
Sep 05	Peterborough	1	Middlesbrough	0
Sep 05	Plymouth	1	Oxford	2
Sep 06	Hereford	0	Northampton	1
Sep 06	Leeds	0	W.B.A.	0
Sep 06	Nottingham F	4	Oldham	2
Sep 06	Tottenham	1	Swansea	3
Oct 02	Leeds	1	W.B.A.	0
	played at Manchester C			

3rd Round

Oct 04	Aston Villa	1	Crystal Palace	1
Oct 04	Blackpool	1	Manchester C	1
Oct 03	Burnley	1	Brighton	3
Oct 04	Chester	0	Norwich	2
Oct 04	Chesterfield	4	Charlton	5
Oct 03	Everton	1	Darlington	0
Oct 04	Exeter	2	Bolton	1
Oct 03	Luton	2	Crewe	1
Oct 04	Manchester U	1	Watford	2
Oct 03	Northampton	1	Stoke	3
Oct 04	Oxford	0	Nottingham F	5
Oct 03	Peterborough	1	Swindon	1
Oct 03	Q.P.R.	2	Swansea	0
Oct 03	Rotherham	2	Reading	2
Oct 10	Sheffield U	1	Leeds	4
Oct 03	Southampton	1	Derby	0

Replays

Oct 10	Crystal Palace	0	Aston Villa	0
Oct 10	Manchester C	3	Blackpool	0
Oct 10	Reading	1	Rotherham	0
Oct 10	Swindon	0	Peterborough	2
Oct 16	Aston Villa	3	Crystal Palace	0
	played at Coventry			

4th Round

Nov 08	Aston Villa	0	Luton	2
Nov 07	Brighton	1	Peterborough	0
Nov 07	Charlton	2	Stoke	3
Nov 07	Everton	2	Nottingham F	3
Nov 08	Exeter	0	Watford	2
Nov 08	Norwich	1	Manchester C	3
Nov 07	Q.P.R.	0	Leeds	2
Nov 08	Reading	0	Southampton	0

Replay

Nov 14	Southampton	2	Reading	0

5th Round

Dec 13	Leeds	4	Luton	1
Dec 13	Nottingham F	3	Brighton	1
Dec 12	Southampton	2	Manchester C	1
Dec 13	Stoke	0	Watford	0

Replay

Jan 09	Watford	3	Stoke	1

Semi-finals

Jan 24	Leeds	2	Southampton	2
Jan 30	Southampton	1	Leeds	0
	Aggregate 3-2			
Jan 17	Nottingham F	3	Watford	1
Jan 30	Watford	0	Nottingham F	0
	Aggregate 1-3			

Final

Mar 17	Nottingham F	3	Southampton	2
	played at Wembley			

Season 1979-80

1st Round

Blackpool	v Rochdale	Aug 11	1-1	Aug 14	1-0	2-1
Bradford C	v Darlington	Aug 11	0-2	Aug 14	3-0	3-2
Bury	v Blackburn	Aug 11	0-3	Aug 14	2-3	2-6
Chester	v Walsall	Aug 11	2-1	Aug 14	0-0	2-1
Chesterfield	v Hartlepool	Aug 11	5-1	Aug 14	1-2	6-3
Colchester	v Watford	Aug 11	2-0	Aug 14	1-2	3-2
Gillingham	v Luton	Aug 11	3-0	Aug 14	1-1	4-1
Grimsby	v Scunthorpe	Aug 11	2-0	Aug 14	0-0	2-0
Halifax	v Shrewsbury	Aug 11	2-2	Aug 14	0-1	2-3
Hereford	v Exeter	Aug 11	1-3	Aug 15	1-2	2-5
Huddersfield	v Crewe	Aug 11	2-1	Aug 15	3-1	5-2
Leicester	v Rotherham	Aug 11	1-2	Aug 14	0-3	1-5
Lincoln	v Barnsley	Aug 11	2-1	Aug 14	1-2	3-3
Mansfield	v York	Aug 11	1-0	Aug 14	2-3	3-3
Newport	v Plymouth	Aug 11	1-0	Aug 14	0-2	1-2
Northampton	v Millwall	Aug 13	2-1	Aug 15	2-2	4-3
Oxford	v Reading	Aug 11	1-5	Aug 15	1-2	2-7
Peterborough	v Charlton	Aug 11	3-1	Aug 14	1-1	4-2
Port Vale	v Tranmere	Aug 11	1-2	Aug 15	0-1	1-3
Portsmouth	v Swindon	Aug 11	1-1	Aug 14	0-2	1-3
Sheffield U	v Doncaster	Aug 11	1-1	Aug 14	1-3	2-4
Sheffield W	v Hull	Aug 11	1-1	Aug 14	2-1	3-2
Southend	v Brentford	Aug 15	2-1	Aug 21	4-1	6-2
Stockport	v Wigan	Aug 11	2-1	Aug 15	0-0	2-1
Swansea	v Bournemouth	Aug 11	4-1	Aug 14	0-0	4-1
Torquay	v Bristol R	Aug 11	1-2	Aug 14	3-1	4-3
Wimbledon	v Aldershot	Aug 11	4-1	Aug 14	2-1	6-2
Wrexham	v Carlisle	Aug 11	1-1	Aug 14	2-1	3-2

2nd Round

Birmingham	v Preston	Aug 28	2-1	Sep 04	1-0	3-1
Blackburn	v Nottingham F	Aug 29	1-1	Sep 05	1-6	2-7
Bolton	v Southend	Aug 28	1-2	Sep 03	0-0	1-2
Brighton	v Cambridge	Aug 28	2-0	Sep 04	2-1	4-1
Bristol C	v Rotherham	Aug 28	1-0	Sep 04	1-1	2-1
Burnley	v Wolverhampton	Aug 28	1-1	Sep 04	0-2	1-3
Chesterfield	v Shrewsbury	Aug 28	3-0	Sep 04	0-0	3-0
Colchester	v Aston Villa	Aug 28	0-2	Sep 05	2-0	2-2
Derby	v Middlesbrough	Aug 29	0-1	Sep 04	1-1	1-2
Doncaster	v Exeter	Aug 28	3-1	Sep 05	1-5	4-6
Everton	v Cardiff	Aug 28	2-0	Sep 05	0-1	2-1
Gillingham	v Norwich	Aug 28	1-1	Sep 05	2-4	3-5
Grimsby	v Huddersfield	Aug 28	1-0	Sep 04	4-1	5-1
Ipswich	v Coventry	Aug 29	0-1	Sep 04	0-0	0-1
Leeds	v Arsenal	Aug 29	1-1	Sep 04	0-7	1-8
Northampton	v Oldham	Aug 28	3-0	Sep 04	1-3	4-3
Notts Co	v Torquay	Aug 28	0-0	Sep 05	1-0	1-0
Orient	v Wimbledon	Aug 29	2-2	Sep 04	2-2	4-4
Peterborough	v Blackpool	Aug 29	0-0	Sep 05	1-0	1-0
Plymouth	v Chelsea	Aug 28	2-2	Sep 04	2-1	4-3
Q.P.R.	v Bradford C	Aug 28	2-1	Sep 05	2-0	4-1
Reading	v Mansfield	Aug 29	4-3	Sep 04	2-4	6-7
Sheffield W	v Manchester C	Aug 28	1-1	Sep 04	1-2	2-3
Southampton	v Wrexham	Aug 28	5-0	Sep 05	3-0	8-0
Stockport	v Crystal Palace	Aug 29	1-1	Sep 04	0-7	1-8
Stoke	v Swansea	Aug 29	1-1	Sep 04	3-1	4-2
Sunderland	v Newcastle	Aug 29	2-2	Sep 05	2-2	4-4
Swindon	v Chester	Aug 28	1-0	Sep 05	1-1	2-1
Tottenham	v Manchester U	Aug 29	2-1	Sep 05	1-3	3-4
Tranmere	v Liverpool	Aug 29	0-0	Sep 04	0-4	0-4
West Ham	v Barnsley	Aug 28	3-1	Sep 04	2-0	5-1
W.B.A.	v Fulham	Aug 29	1-1	Sep 05	1-0	2-1

3rd Round

Sep 25	Arsenal	2	Southampton	1
Sep 25	Aston Villa	0	Everton	0
Sep 26	Birmingham	1	Exeter	2
Sep 25	Crystal Palace	1	Wolverhampton	2
Sep 25	Grimsby	3	Notts Co	1
Sep 25	Liverpool	3	Chesterfield	1
Sep 26	Manchester C	1	Sunderland	1
Sep 25	Mansfield	0	Q.P.R.	3
Sep 25	Middlesbrough	1	Nottingham F	3
Sep 25	Northampton	0	Brighton	1
Sep 26	Norwich	4	Manchester U	1
Sep 26	Peterborough	1	Bristol C	1
Sep 25	Plymouth	0	Wimbledon	0
Sep 26	Stoke	2	Swindon	2
Sep 25	West Ham	1	Southend	1
Sep 26	W.B.A.	2	Coventry	1

Replays

Oct 01	Southend	0	West Ham	0
Oct 02	Bristol C	4	Peterborough	0
Oct 02	Swindon	2	Stoke	1
Oct 02	Wimbledon	1	Plymouth	0
Oct 03	Sunderland	1	Manchester C	0
Oct 08	West Ham	5	Southend	1
Oct 09	Everton	4	Aston Villa	1

4th Round

Oct 30	Brighton	0	Arsenal	0
Oct 30	Bristol C	1	Nottingham F	1
Oct 30	Grimsby	2	Everton	1
Oct 30	Liverpool	2	Exeter	0
Oct 30	Q.P.R.	1	Wolverhampton	1
Oct 31	Sunderland	1	West Ham	1
Oct 30	Wimbledon	1	Swindon	2
Oct 31	W.B.A.	0	Norwich	0

Replays

Nov 05	West Ham	2	Sunderland	1
Nov 06	Wolverhampton	1	Q.P.R.	0
Nov 07	Norwich	3	W.B.A.	0
Nov 13	Arsenal	4	Brighton	0
Nov 14	Nottingham F	3	Bristol C	0

5th Round

Dec 04	Arsenal	1	Swindon	1
Dec 04	Grimsby	0	Wolverhampton	0
Dec 05	Norwich	1	Liverpool	3
Dec 04	West Ham	0	Nottingham F	0

Replays

Dec 11	Swindon	4	Arsenal	3
Dec 11	Wolverhampton	1	Grimsby	1
Dec 12	Nottingham F	3	West Ham	0
Dec 18	Grimsby	0	Wolverhampton	2
	played at Derby			

Semi-finals

Jan 22	Nottingham F	1	Liverpool	0
Feb 12	Liverpool	1	Nottingham F	1
	Aggregate 1-2			
Jan 22	Swindon	2	Wolverhampton	1
Feb 12	Wolverhampton	3	Swindon	1
	Aggregate 4-3			

Final

Mar 15	Nottingham F	0	Wolverhampton	1
	played at Wembley			

Season 1980-81

1st Round

Aldershot	v Wimbledon	Aug 09	2-0	Aug 12	1-4	3-4
Blackburn	v Huddersfield	Aug 09	0-0	Aug 12	1-1	1-1
Bournemouth	v Swindon	Aug 09	1-1	Aug 12	0-2	1-3
Brentford	v Charlton	Aug 09	3-1	Aug 12	0-5	3-6
Bury	v Halifax	Aug 09	2-2	Aug 12	1-0	3-2
Carlisle	v Rochdale	Aug 09	2-0	Aug 12	1-1	3-1
Chester	v Stockport	Aug 09	1-1	Aug 11	0-1	1-2
Chesterfield	v Darlington	Aug 09	1-0	Aug 12	2-1	3-1
Colchester	v Gillingham	Aug 09	0-2	Aug 12	1-2	1-4
Doncaster	v Mansfield	Aug 09	1-1	Aug 12	1-2	2-3
Exeter	v Bristol R	Aug 09	1-1	Aug 12	1-1	2-2
Grimsby	v Notts Co	Aug 09	1-0	Aug 12	0-3	1-3
Hereford	v Newport	Aug 09	1-0	Aug 12	0-5	1-5
Lincoln	v Hull	Aug 09	5-0	Aug 12	2-0	7-0
Northampton	v Reading	Aug 08	0-2	Aug 13	3-2	3-4
Peterborough	v Fulham	Aug 09	3-2	Aug 12	1-1	4-3
Plymouth	v Portsmouth	Aug 09	0-1	Aug 12	1-2	1-3
Port Vale	v Tranmere	Aug 09	2-3	Aug 12	1-0	3-3
Rotherham	v Bradford C	Aug 09	1-3	Aug 13	0-0	1-3
Scunthorpe	v Barnsley	Aug 09	0-1	Aug 12	1-2	1-3
Sheffield W	v Sheffield U	Aug 09	2-0	Aug 12	1-1	3-1
Southend	v Oxford	Aug 09	1-0	Aug 13	0-2	1-2
Torquay	v Cardiff	Aug 09	0-0	Aug 13	1-2	1-2
Walsall	v Blackpool	Aug 09	2-3	Aug 13	1-3	3-6
Watford	v Millwall	Aug 09	2-1	Aug 12	2-0	4-1
Wigan	v Crewe	Aug 09	2-1	Aug 13	2-2	4-3
Wrexham	v Burnley	Aug 09	1-3	Aug 12	1-2	2-5
York	v Hartlepool	Aug 09	2-1	Aug 12	0-0	2-1

2nd Round

Aston Villa	v Leeds	Aug 27	1-0	Sep 03	3-1	4-1
Birmingham	v Bristol C	Aug 26	2-1	Sep 02	0-0	2-1
Blackburn	v Gillingham	Aug 27	0-0	Sep 02	2-1	2-1
Bolton	v Crystal Palace	Aug 26	0-3	Sep 02	1-2	1-5
Bradford C	v Liverpool	Aug 27	1-0	Sep 02	0-4	1-4
Brighton	v Tranmere	Aug 26	3-1	Sep 03	4-2	7-3
Burnley	v West Ham	Aug 26	0-2	Sep 02	0-4	0-6
Cambridge	v Wolverhampton	Aug 26	3-1	Sep 02	1-0	4-1
Cardiff	v Chelsea	Aug 27	1-0	Sep 03	1-1	2-1
Carlisle	v Charlton	Aug 26	1-2	Sep 02	1-2	2-4
Chesterfield	v Oxford	Aug 26	3-1	Sep 03	0-3	3-4
Everton	v Blackpool	Aug 26	3-0	Sep 03	2-2	5-2
Lincoln	v Swindon	Aug 27	1-1	Sep 02	0-2	1-3
Manchester U	v Coventry	Aug 27	0-1	Sep 02	0-1	0-2
Mansfield	v Barnsley	Aug 26	0-0	Sep 02	2-4	2-4
Middlesbrough	v Ipswich	Aug 26	3-1	Sep 02	0-3	3-4
Newcastle	v Bury	Aug 27	3-2	Sep 02	0-1	3-3
Newport	v Notts Co	Aug 26	1-1	Sep 02	0-2	1-3
Nottingham F	v Peterborough	Aug 27	3-0	Sep 03	1-1	4-1
Oldham	v Portsmouth	Aug 26	3-2	Sep 02	0-1	3-3
Orient	v Tottenham	Aug 27	0-1	Sep 03	1-3	1-4
Preston	v Wigan	Aug 26	1-0	Sep 03	2-1	3-1
Q.P.R.	v Derby	Aug 26	0-0	Sep 03	0-0	0-0
Reading	v Luton	Aug 27	0-2	Sep 02	1-1	1-3
Shrewsbury	v Norwich	Aug 26	1-1	Sep 03	0-2	1-3
Southampton	v Watford	Aug 26	4-0	Sep 02	1-7	5-7
Stockport	v Sunderland	Aug 27	1-1	Sep 03	2-1	3-2
Stoke	v Manchester C	Aug 27	1-1	Sep 03	0-3	1-4
Swansea	v Arsenal	Aug 26	1-1	Sep 02	1-3	2-4
Wimbledon	v Sheffield W	Aug 26	2-1	Sep 02	1-3	3-4
W.B.A.	v Leicester	Aug 26	1-0	Sep 03	1-0	2-0
York	v Bristol R	Aug 27	2-1	Sep 03	0-1	2-2

3rd Round

Sep 23	Barnsley	3	Cardiff	2
Sep 23	Birmingham	1	Blackburn	0
Sep 23	Brighton	1	Coventry	2
Sep 23	Bristol R	0	Portsmouth	0
Sep 23	Bury	0	Nottingham F	7
Sep 23	Cambridge	2	Aston Villa	1
Sep 23	Charlton	1	West Ham	2
Sep 24	Everton	1	W.B.A.	2
Sep 23	Ipswich	1	Norwich	1
Sep 23	Liverpool	5	Swindon	0
Sep 23	Luton	1	Manchester C	2
Sep 23	Notts Co	4	Q.P.R.	1
Sep 23	Preston	1	Oxford	0
Sep 23	Sheffield W	1	Watford	2
Sep 22	Stockport	1	Arsenal	3
Sep 24	Tottenham	0	Crystal Palace	0

Replays

Sep 30	Crystal Palace	1	Tottenham	3
Sep 30	Portsmouth	2	Bristol R	0
Oct 08	Norwich	1	Ipswich	3

4th Round

Oct 28	Birmingham	2	Ipswich	1
Oct 28	Coventry	1	Cambridge	1
Oct 28	Liverpool	4	Portsmouth	1
Oct 29	Manchester C	5	Notts Co	1
Nov 04	Tottenham	1	Arsenal	0
Oct 28	Watford	4	Nottingham F	1
Oct 28	West Ham	2	Barnsley	1
Oct 29	W.B.A.	0	Preston	0

Replays

Nov 04	Cambridge	0	Coventry	1
Nov 04	Preston	1	W.B.A.	1
Nov 12	W.B.A.	2	Preston	1

5th Round

Dec 02	Liverpool	3	Birmingham	1
Dec 03	Manchester C	2	W.B.A.	1
Dec 02	Watford	2	Coventry	2
Dec 02	West Ham	1	Tottenham	0

Replay

Dec 09	Coventry	5	Watford	0

Semi-finals

Jan 27	Coventry	3	West Ham	2
Feb 10	West Ham	2	Coventry	0
	Aggregate 4-3			
Jan 14	Manchester C	0	Liverpool	1
Feb 10	Liverpool	1	Manchester C	1
	Aggregate 2-1			

Final

Mar 14	Liverpool	1	West Ham	1
	played at Wembley			

Replay

Apr 01	Liverpool	2	West Ham	1
	played at Aston Villa			

Season 1981-82

1st Round

Aldershot	v Wimbledon	Sep 01	0-0	Sep 15	3-1	3-1
Bolton	v Oldham	Sep 01	2-1	Sep 15	2-4	4-5
Bournemouth	v Fulham	Sep 01	0-1	Sep 15	0-2	0-3
Bradford C	v Blackpool	Sep 02	3-1	Sep 16	0-0	3-1
Bristol C	v Walsall	Sep 01	2-0	Sep 15	0-1	2-1
Bury	v Carlisle	Sep 01	3-3	Sep 15	1-2	4-5
Cardiff	v Exeter	Sep 02	2-1	Sep 16	1-3	3-4
Chester	v Plymouth	Sep 08	1-1	Sep 15	0-1	1-2
Colchester	v Gillingham	Sep 01	2-0	Sep 15	1-1	3-1
Crewe	v Bristol R	Sep 02	1-1	Sep 15	0-1	1-2
Darlington	v Rotherham	Sep 01	1-3	Sep 15	1-2	2-5
Doncaster	v Chesterfield	Sep 01	0-0	Sep 15	1-1	1-1
Halifax	v Preston	Sep 01	1-2	Sep 15	0-0	1-2
Hereford	v Port Vale	Sep 02	1-1	Sep 14	0-2	1-3
Huddersfield	v Rochdale	Sep 01	3-1	Sep 15	4-2	7-3
Lincoln	v Hull	Sep 02	3-0	Sep 15	1-1	4-1
Northampton	v Hartlepool	Sep 01	2-0	Sep 16	1-2	3-2
Orient	v Millwall	Sep 01	1-1	Sep 16	2-3	3-4
Oxford	v Brentford	Sep 02	1-0	Sep 15	2-0	3-0
Peterborough	v Barnsley	Sep 02	2-3	Sep 15	0-6	2-9
Reading	v Charlton	Sep 02	2-2	Sep 15	1-3	3-5
Scunthorpe	v Mansfield	Sep 01	0-0	Sep 14	0-2	0-2
Sheffield U	v York	Sep 01	1-0	Sep 15	1-1	2-1
Southend	v Portsmouth	Sep 02	0-0	Sep 16	1-4	1-4
Torquay	v Newport	Sep 02	2-3	Sep 15	0-0	2-3
Tranmere	v Burnley	Sep 01	4-2	Sep 15	3-3	7-5
Wigan	v Stockport	Aug 31	3-0	Sep 14	2-1	5-1
Wrexham	v Swindon	Sep 01	3-2	Sep 15	2-0	5-2

2nd Round

Aldershot	v Wigan	Oct 06	2-2	Oct 27	0-1	2-3
Aston Villa	v Wolverhampton	Oct 07	3-2	Oct 27	2-1	5-3
Barnsley	v Swansea	Oct 06	2-0	Oct 27	2-3	4-3
Birmingham	v Nottingham F	Oct 06	2-3	Oct 28	1-2	3-5
Blackburn	v Sheffield W	Oct 07	1-1	Oct 27	2-1	3-2
Bradford C	v Mansfield	Oct 07	3-4	Oct 26	2-0	5-4
Bristol R	v Northampton	Oct 06	1-2	Oct 27	1-3	2-5
Carlisle	v Bristol C	Oct 06	0-0	Oct 27	1-2	1-2
Colchester	v Cambridge	Oct 06	3-1	Oct 27	2-3	5-4
Derby	v West Ham	Oct 07	2-3	Oct 27	0-2	2-5
Doncaster	v Crystal Palace	Oct 06	1-0	Oct 27	0-2	1-2
Everton	v Coventry	Oct 06	1-1	Oct 27	1-0	2-1
Grimsby	v Watford	Oct 06	1-0	Oct 27	1-3	2-3
Huddersfield	v Brighton	Oct 06	1-0	Oct 27	0-2	1-2
Leeds	v Ipswich	Oct 07	0-1	Oct 27	0-3	0-4
Lincoln	v Notts Co	Oct 07	1-1	Oct 27	3-2	4-3
Liverpool	v Exeter	Oct 07	5-0	Oct 28	6-0	11-0
Luton	v Wrexham	Oct 06	0-2	Oct 27	1-0	1-2
Manchester C	v Stoke	Oct 07	2-0	Oct 28	0-2	2-2
Middlesbrough	v Plymouth	Oct 06	2-1	Oct 27	0-0	2-1
Millwall	v Oxford	Oct 06	3-3	Oct 28	0-1	3-4
Newcastle	v Fulham	Oct 07	1-2	Oct 27	0-2	1-4
Norwich	v Charlton	Oct 07	1-0	Oct 28	1-0	2-0
Oldham	v Newport	Oct 06	1-0	Oct 27	0-0	1-0
Preston	v Leicester	Oct 06	1-0	Oct 28	0-4	1-4
Q.P.R.	v Portsmouth	Oct 06	5-0	Oct 27	2-2	7-2
Sheffield U	v Arsenal	Oct 06	1-0	Oct 27	0-2	1-2
Shrewsbury	v W.B.A.	Oct 06	3-3	Oct 28	1-2	4-5
Southampton	v Chelsea	Oct 06	1-1	Oct 28	1-2	2-3
Sunderland	v Rotherham	Oct 07	2-0	Oct 27	3-3	5-3
Tottenham	v Manchester U	Oct 07	1-0	Oct 28	1-0	2-0
Tranmere	v Port Vale	Oct 05	2-0	Oct 28	2-1	4-1

3rd Round

Nov 10	Arsenal	1	Norwich	0
Nov 10	Barnsley	4	Brighton	1
Nov 11	Blackburn	0	Nottingham F	1
Nov 11	Everton	1	Oxford	0
Nov 10	Ipswich	1	Bradford C	1
Nov 11	Leicester	0	Aston Villa	0
Nov 10	Liverpool	4	Middlesbrough	1
Nov 11	Manchester C	3	Northampton	1
Nov 10	Oldham	1	Fulham	1
Nov 10	Q.P.R.	3	Bristol C	0
Nov 11	Sep sunderland	0	Crystal Palace	1
Nov 11	Tottenham	2	Wrexham	0
Nov 10	Tranmere	1	Colchester	0
Nov 10	Watford	2	Lincoln	2
Nov 10	West Ham	2	W.B.A.	2
Nov 11	Wigan	4	Chelsea	2

Replays

Nov 17	Fulham	3	Oldham	0
Nov 24	W.B.A.	1	West Ham	1
Nov 25	Aston Villa	2	Leicester	0
Nov 25	Lincoln	2	Watford	3
Dec 01	West Ham	0	W.B.A.	1
Dec 02	Bradford C	2	Ipswich	3

4th Round

Dec 01	Arsenal	0	Liverpool	0
Dec 02	Barnsley	1	Manchester C	0
Dec 15	Crystal Palace	1	W.B.A.	3
Dec 15	Everton	2	Ipswich	3
Dec 02	Nottingham F	2	Tranmere	0
Dec 02	Tottenham	1	Fulham	0
Dec 01	Watford	4	Q.P.R.	1
Dec 01	Wigan	1	Aston Villa	2

Replay

Dec 08	Liverpool	3	Arsenal	0

5th Round

Jan 19	Aston Villa	0	W.B.A.	1
Jan 18	Ipswich	2	Watford	1
Jan 12	Liverpool	0	Barnsley	0
Jan 18	Tottenham	1	Nottingham F	0

Replay

Jan 19	Barnsley	1	Liverpool	3

Semi-finals

Feb 02	Ipswich	0	Liverpool	2
Feb 09	Liverpool	2	Ipswich	2
	Aggregate 4-2			
Feb 03	W.B.A.	0	Tottenham	0
Feb 10	Tottenham	1	W.B.A.	0
	Aggregate 1-0			

Final

Mar 13	Liverpool	3	Tottenham	1
	played at Wembley			

Season 1982-83

1st Round

Bradford C	v Mansfield	Sep 01	1-0	Sep 13	2-0	3-0
Bristol R	v Torquay	Aug 31	2-2	Sep 15	4-0	6-2
Bury	v Burnley	Aug 31	3-5	Sep 14	1-3	4-8
Cardiff	v Hereford	Aug 31	2-1	Sep 15	2-1	4-2
Carlisle	v Bolton	Aug 31	3-3	Sep 14	0-4	3-7
Chester	v Blackpool	Sep 01	1-2	Sep 14	1-5	2-7
Chesterfield	v Hartlepool	Aug 31	2-1	Sep 15	0-2	2-3
Colchester	v Aldershot	Aug 31	2-0	Sep 14	1-0	3-0
Crewe	v Tranmere	Aug 31	1-1	Sep 13	0-0	1-1
Crystal Palace	v Portsmouth	Aug 31	2-0	Sep 14	1-1	3-1
Darlington	v Peterborough	Aug 31	0-2	Sep 15	2-4	2-6
Exeter	v Newport	Sep 01	1-2	Sep 14	0-6	1-8
Gillingham	v Orient	Aug 31	3-0	Sep 14	0-2	3-2
Halifax	v Derby	Aug 31	2-1	Sep 15	2-5	4-6
Huddersfield	v Doncaster	Aug 31	1-1	Sep 14	1-0	2-1
Millwall	v Northampton	Aug 31	0-2	Sep 14	2-2	2-4
Plymouth	v Bournemouth	Aug 31	2-0	Sep 14	0-3	2-3
Port Vale	v Rochdale	Aug 30	1-0	Sep 14	0-2	1-2
Reading	v Oxford	Sep 01	0-2	Sep 15	0-2	0-4
Scunthorpe	v Grimsby	Aug 31	1-2	Sep 14	0-0	1-2
Sheffield U	v Hull	Aug 31	3-1	Sep 14	0-1	3-2
Southend	v Fulham	Sep 01	1-0	Sep 14	2-4	3-4
Stockport	v Wigan	Aug 30	1-1	Sep 14	1-1	2-2
Swindon	v Bristol C	Aug 31	2-1	Sep 14	0-2	2-3
Walsall	v Preston	Aug 31	0-1	Sep 14	1-1	1-2
Wimbledon	v Brentford	Aug 30	1-1	Sep 14	0-2	1-3
Wrexham	v Shrewsbury	Aug 31	1-0	Sep 14	0-2	1-2
York	v Lincoln	Aug 31	2-1	Sep 15	1-3	3-4

2nd Round

Arsenal	v Cardiff	Oct 05	2-1	Oct 26	3-1	5-2
Aston Villa	v Notts Co	Oct 06	1-2	Oct 26	0-1	1-3
Barnsley	v Cambridge	Oct 12	2-1	Oct 26	3-1	5-2
Bolton	v Watford	Oct 05	1-2	Oct 26	1-2	2-4
Brentford	v Blackburn	Oct 05	3-2	Oct 27	0-0	3-2
Bristol C	v Sheffield W	Oct 04	1-2	Oct 26	1-1	2-3
Bristol R	v Swansea	Oct 05	1-0	Oct 26	0-3	1-3
Burnley	v Middlesbrough	Oct 05	3-2	Oct 26	1-1	4-3
Chelsea	v Tranmere	Oct 06	3-1	Oct 27	2-1	5-2
Colchester	v Southampton	Oct 06	0-0	Oct 26	2-4	2-4
Derby	v Hartlepool	Oct 06	2-0	Oct 25	2-4	4-4
Fulham	v Coventry	Oct 05	2-2	Oct 26	0-0	2-2
Gillingham	v Oldham	Oct 05	2-0	Oct 26	0-1	2-1
Grimsby	v Sheffield U	Oct 12	3-3	Oct 26	1-5	4-8
Huddersfield	v Oxford	Oct 05	2-0	Oct 27	0-1	2-1
Ipswich	v Liverpool	Oct 05	1-2	Oct 26	0-2	1-4
Leeds	v Newcastle	Oct 06	0-1	Oct 27	4-1	4-2
Lincoln	v Leicester	Oct 06	2-0	Oct 27	1-0	3-0
Luton	v Charlton	Oct 05	3-0	Oct 26	0-2	3-2
Manchester U	v Bournemouth	Oct 06	2-0	Oct 26	2-2	4-2
Newport	v Everton	Oct 05	0-2	Oct 27	2-2	2-4
Northampton	v Blackpool	Oct 05	1-1	Oct 26	1-2	2-3
Norwich	v Preston	Oct 06	2-1	Oct 26	2-1	4-2
Nottingham F	v W.B.A.	Oct 06	6-1	Oct 27	1-3	7-4
Peterborough	v Crystal Palace	Oct 06	0-2	Oct 26	1-2	1-4
Rochdale	v Bradford C	Oct 05	0-1	Oct 27	0-4	0-5
Rotherham	v Q.P.R.	Oct 05	2-1	Oct 26	0-0	2-1
Shrewsbury	v Birmingham	Oct 05	1-1	Oct 26	1-4	2-5
Stoke	v West Ham	Oct 06	1-1	Oct 26	1-2	2-3
Tottenham	v Brighton	Oct 06	1-1	Oct 26	1-0	2-1
Wigan	v Manchester C	Oct 05	1-1	Oct 27	0-2	1-3
Wolverhampton	v Sunderland	Oct 05	1-1	Oct 27	0-5	1-6

3rd Round

Nov 09	Birmingham	3	Derby	1
Nov 10	Bradford C	0	Manchester U	0
Nov 09	Brentford	1	Swansea	1
Nov 09	Coventry	1	Burnley	2
Nov 09	Crystal Palace	1	Sheffield W	2
Nov 09	Everton	1	Arsenal	1
Nov 09	Gillingham	2	Tottenham	4
Nov 10	Leeds	0	Huddersfield	1
Nov 10	Lincoln	1	West Ham	1
Nov 10	Liverpool	1	Rotherham	0
Nov 09	Luton	4	Blackpool	2
Nov 10	Manchester C	1	Southampton	1
Nov 10	Nottingham F	7	Watford	3
Nov 09	Notts Co	2	Chelsea	0
Nov 09	Sheffield U	1	Barnsley	3
Nov 10	Sunderland	0	Norwich	0

Replays

Nov 17	Swansea	1	Brentford	2
Nov 23	Arsenal	3	Everton	0
Nov 24	Manchester U	4	Bradford C	1
Nov 24	Norwich	3	Sunderland	1
Nov 24	Southampton	4	Manchester C	0
Nov 29	West Ham	2	Lincoln	1

4th Round

Nov 30	Arsenal	1	Huddersfield	0
Nov 30	Burnley	3	Birmingham	2
Nov 30	Liverpool	2	Norwich	0
Dec 01	Manchester U	2	Southampton	0
Dec 01	Nottingham F	2	Brentford	0
Dec 07	Notts Co	3	West Ham	3
Nov 30	Sheffield W	1	Barnsley	0
Dec 01	Tottenham	1	Luton	0

Replay

Dec 21	West Ham	3	Notts Co	0

5th Round

Jan 18	Arsenal	1	Sheffield W	0
Jan 18	Liverpool	2	West Ham	1
Jan 19	Manchester U	4	Nottingham F	0
Jan 19	Tottenham	1	Burnley	4

Semi-finals

Feb 15	Arsenal	2	Manchester U	4
Feb 22	Manchester U	2	Arsenal	1
	Aggregate 6-3			
Feb 08	Liverpool	3	Burnley	0
Feb 15	Burnley	1	Liverpool	0
	Aggregate 1-3			

Final

Mar 26	Liverpool	2	Manchester U	1
	played at Wembley			

Season 1983-84

Round 1

Aldershot	v Orient	Aug 30	3-1	Sep 13	3-3	6-4
Blackpool	v Walsall	Aug 30	2-1	Sep 13	1-3	3-4
Bolton	v Chester	Aug 30	3-0	Sep 14	0-3	3-3
Bournemouth	v Bristol R	Aug 30	1-2	Sep 13	2-2	3-4
Bradford C	v Sheffield U	Aug 29	0-1	Sep 13	1-1	1-2
Brentford	v Charlton	Aug 30	3-0	Sep 13	1-2	4-2
Colchester	v Reading	Aug 30	3-2	Sep 14	3-4	6-6
Crewe	v Burnley	Aug 30	1-0	Sep 13	4-3	5-3
Crystal Palace	v Peterborough	Aug 30	3-0	Sep 14	0-3	3-3
Exeter	v Cardiff	Aug 31	2-3	Sep 13	1-2	3-5
Gillingham	v Chelsea	Aug 30	1-2	Sep 13	0-4	1-6
Halifax	v Darlington	Aug 30	0-1	Sep 13	2-3	2-4
Hereford	v Portsmouth	Aug 31	3-2	Sep 13	1-3	4-5
Hull	v Lincoln	Aug 30	0-0	Sep 14	1-3	1-3
Mansfield	v Huddersfield	Aug 30	1-2	Sep 13	1-5	2-7
Middlesbrough	v Chesterfield	Aug 30	0-1	Sep 13	1-0	1-1
Millwall	v Northampton	Aug 29	3-0	Sep 13	2-1	5-1
Newport	v Torquay	Aug 30	2-3	Sep 14	0-1	2-4
Oxford	v Bristol C	Aug 31	1-1	Sep 12	1-0	2-1
Port Vale	v Wrexham	Aug 31	3-1	Sep 13	5-1	8-2
Preston	v Tranmere	Aug 30	1-0	Sep 12	0-0	1-0
Rochdale	v Stockport	Aug 30	0-3	Sep 12	2-2	2-5
Rotherham	v Hartlepool	Aug 30	0-0	Sep 14	1-0	1-0
Scunthorpe	v Doncaster	Aug 30	1-1	Sep 13	0-3	1-4
Southend	v Wimbledon	Aug 29	1-0	Sep 13	4-6	5-6
Swindon	v Plymouth	Aug 30	1-0	Sep 13	1-4	2-4
Wigan	v Bury	Aug 30	1-2	Sep 13	0-2	1-4
York	v Grimsby	Aug 30	2-1	Sep 13	0-2	2-3

2nd Round

Aldershot	v Notts Co	Oct 04	2-4	Oct 25	1-4	3-8
Brentford	v Liverpool	Oct 05	1-4	Oct 25	0-4	1-8
Brighton	v Bristol R	Oct 04	4-2	Oct 25	1-2	5-4
Bury	v West Ham	Oct 04	1-2	Oct 25	0-10	1-12
Cambridge	v Sunderland	Oct 04	2-3	Oct 26	3-4	5-7
Cardiff	v Norwich	Oct 04	0-0	Oct 26	0-3	0-3
Carlisle	v Southampton	Oct 04	2-0	Oct 25	0-3	2-3
Chesterfield	v Everton	Oct 04	0-1	Oct 26	2-2	2-3
Derby	v Birmingham	Oct 05	0-3	Oct 25	0-4	0-7
Doncaster	v Fulham	Oct 05	1-3	Oct 26	1-3	2-6
Grimsby	v Coventry	Oct 04	0-0	Oct 25	1-2	1-2
Huddersfield	v Watford	Oct 04	2-1	Oct 25	2-2	4-3
Ipswich	v Blackburn	Oct 05	4-3	Oct 26	2-1	6-4
Leeds	v Chester	Oct 05	0-1	Oct 26	4-1	4-2
Leicester	v Chelsea	Oct 05	0-2	Oct 25	2-0	2-2
Millwall	v W.B.A.	Oct 04	3-0	Oct 25	1-5	4-5
Newcastle	v Oxford	Oct 05	1-1	Oct 26	1-2	2-3
Plymouth	v Arsenal	Oct 04	1-1	Oct 25	0-1	1-2
Port Vale	v Manchester U	Oct 03	0-1	Oct 26	0-2	0-3
Portsmouth	v Aston Villa	Oct 04	2-2	Oct 26	2-3	4-5
Q.P.R.	v Crewe	Oct 04	8-1	Oct 25	0-3	8-4
Rotherham	v Luton	Oct 04	2-3	Oct 25	2-0	4-3
Sheffield W	v Darlington	Oct 04	3-0	Oct 25	4-2	7-2
Shrewsbury	v Sheffield U	Oct 04	2-1	Oct 25	2-2	4-3
Stockport	v Oldham	Oct 03	0-2	Oct 25	2-2	2-4
Stoke	v Peterborough	Oct 05	0-0	Oct 26	2-1	2-1
Swansea	v Colchester	Oct 04	1-1	Oct 25	0-1	1-2
Torquay	v Manchester C	Oct 05	0-0	Oct 25	0-6	0-6
Tottenham	v Lincoln	Oct 05	3-1	Oct 26	1-2	4-3
Walsall	v Barnsley	Oct 04	1-0	Oct 25	2-0	3-0
Wimbledon	v Nottingham F	Oct 04	2-0	Oct 26	1-1	3-1
Wolverhampton	v Preston	Oct 04	2-3	Oct 25	0-1	2-4

3rd Round

Nov 09	Aston Villa	3	Manchester C	0
Nov 08	Birmingham	2	Notts Co	2
Nov 09	Chelsea	0	W.B.A.	1
Nov 08	Colchester	0	Manchester U	2
Nov 09	Everton	2	Coventry	1
Nov 08	Fulham	1	Liverpool	1
Nov 09	Ipswich	3	Q.P.R.	2
Nov 09	Leeds	1	Oxford	1
Nov 09	Norwich	0	Sunderland	0
Nov 08	Preston	0	Sheffield W	2
Nov 08	Rotherham	2	Southampton	1
Nov 08	Stoke	0	Huddersfield	0
Nov 09	Tottenham	1	Arsenal	2
Nov 08	Walsall	2	Shrewsbury	1
Nov 08	West Ham	1	Brighton	0
Nov 08	Wimbledon	3	Oldham	1

Replays

Nov 22	Huddersfield	0	Stoke	2
Nov 22	Liverpool	1	Fulham	1
Nov 22	Notts Co	0	Birmingham	0
Nov 22	Sunderland	1	Norwich	2
Nov 23	Oxford	4	Leeds	1
Nov 29	Birmingham	0	Notts Co	0
Nov 29	Fulham	0	Liverpool	1
Dec 05	Notts Co	1	Birmingham	3

4th Round

Nov 29	Arsenal	1	Walsall	2
Dec 20	Birmingham	1	Liverpool	1
Nov 30	Ipswich	0	Norwich	1
Nov 30	Oxford	1	Manchester U	1
Nov 29	Rotherham	1	Wimbledon	0
Nov 30	Stoke	0	Sheffield W	1
Nov 30	West Ham	2	Everton	2
Nov 30	W.B.A.	1	Aston Villa	2

Replays

Dec 06	Everton	2	West Ham	0
Dec 07	Manchester U	1	Oxford	1
Dec 19	Oxford	2	Manchester U	1
Dec 22	Liverpool	3	Birmingham	0

5th Round

Jan 17	Norwich	0	Aston Villa	2
Jan 18	Oxford	1	Everton	1
Jan 18	Rotherham	2	Walsall	4
Jan 17	Sheffield W	2	Liverpool	2

Replays

Jan 24	Everton	4	Oxford	1
Jan 25	Liverpool	3	Sheffield W	0

Semi-finals

Feb 15	Everton	2	Aston Villa	0
Feb 22	Aston Villa	1	Everton	0
	Aggregate 1-2			
Feb 07	Liverpool	2	Walsall	2
Feb 14	Walsall	0	Liverpool	2
	Aggregate 2-4			

Final

Mar 25	Everton	0	Liverpool	0
	played at Wembley			

Replay

Mar 28	Everton	0	Liverpool	1
	played at Manchester C			

Season 1984-85

1st Round

Aldershot	v Bournemouth	Aug 28	4-0	Sep 04	1-0	5-0
Blackpool	v Chester	Aug 28	1-0	Sep 05	3-0	4-0
Bolton	v Oldham	Aug 28	2-1	Sep 04	4-4	6-5
Bradford C	v Middlesbrough	Aug 29	2-0	Sep 04	2-2	4-2
Brentford	v Cambridge	Aug 28	2-0	Sep 04	0-1	2-1
Bristol C	v Newport	Aug 28	2-1	Sep 04	3-0	5-1
Burnley	v Crewe	Aug 28	1-2	Sep 04	3-0	4-2
Crystal Palace	v Northampton	Aug 27	1-0	Sep 04	0-0	1-0
Darlington	v Rotherham	Aug 28	1-2	Sep 04	0-4	1-6
Derby	v Hartlepool	Aug 29	5-1	Sep 05	1-0	6-1
Doncaster	v York	Aug 28	2-3	Sep 04	0-5	2-8
Exeter	v Cardiff	Aug 29	1-0	Sep 04	0-2	1-2
Gillingham	v Colchester	Aug 28	3-2	Sep 04	2-0	5-2
Halifax	v Chesterfield	Aug 28	1-1	Sep 05	2-1	3-2
Hereford	v Oxford	Aug 29	2-2	Sep 05	3-5	5-7
Lincoln	v Hull	Aug 29	0-2	Sep 04	1-4	1-6
Orient	v Southend	Aug 28	2-1	Sep 05	0-0	2-1
Plymouth	v Torquay	Aug 27	1-0	Sep 04	1-0	2-0
Port Vale	v Bury	Aug 28	1-0	Sep 04	1-2	2-2
Portsmouth	v Wimbledon	Aug 28	3-0	Sep 04	0-1	3-1
Reading	v Millwall	Aug 29	1-1	Sep 04	3-4	4-5
Scunthorpe	v Mansfield	Aug 28	0-1	Sep 05	2-1	2-2
Sheffield U	v Peterborough	Aug 28	1-0	Sep 05	2-2	3-2
Stockport	v Rochdale	Aug 27	3-1	Sep 04	2-1	5-2
Swansea	v Walsall	Aug 28	0-2	Sep 04	1-3	1-5
Swindon	v Bristol R	Aug 27	1-5	Sep 04	1-0	2-5
Tranmere	v Preston	Aug 28	2-3	Sep 04	2-2	4-5
Wrexham	v Wigan	Aug 28	0-3	Sep 04	0-2	0-0

2nd Round

Arsenal	v Bristol R	Sep 25	4-0	Oct 09	1-1	5-1
Birmingham	v Plymouth	Sep 25	4-1	Oct 09	1-0	5-1
Blackburn	v Oxford	Sep 25	1-1	Oct 10	1-3	2-4
Brighton	v Aldershot	Sep 25	3-1	Oct 09	0-3	3-4
Bristol C	v West Ham	Sep 25	2-2	Oct 09	1-6	3-8
Charlton	v Notts Co	Sep 25	0-1	Oct 09	0-2	0-3
Chelsea	v Millwall	Sep 26	3-1	Oct 09	1-1	4-2
Fulham	v Carlisle	Sep 25	2-0	Oct 09	2-1	4-1
Gillingham	v Leeds	Sep 25	1-2	Oct 10	2-3	3-5
Grimsby	v Barnsley	Sep 25	3-0	Oct 09	1-1	4-1
Halifax	v Tottenham	Sep 26	1-5	Oct 09	0-4	1-9
Ipswich	v Derby	Sep 25	4-2	Oct 10	1-1	5-3
Leicester	v Brentford	Sep 26	4-2	Oct 09	2-0	6-2
Manchester C	v Blackpool	Sep 25	4-2	Oct 09	3-1	7-3
Manchester U	v Burnley	Sep 26	4-0	Oct 09	3-0	7-0
Newcastle	v Bradford C	Sep 26	3-1	Oct 10	1-0	4-1
Orient	v Luton	Sep 25	1-4	Oct 09	1-3	2-7
Port Vale	v Wolverhampton	Sep 24	1-2	Oct 09	0-0	1-2
Portsmouth	v Nottingham F	Sep 25	1-0	Oct 10	0-3	1-3
Preston	v Norwich	Sep 25	3-3	Oct 10	1-6	4-9
Scunthorpe	v Aston Villa	Sep 24	2-3	Oct 10	1-3	3-6
Sheffield U	v Everton	Sep 26	2-2	Oct 10	0-4	2-6
Sheffield W	v Huddersfield	Sep 25	3-0	Oct 09	1-2	4-2
Shrewsbury	v Bolton	Sep 25	2-2	Oct 09	1-2	3-4
Southampton	v Hull	Sep 25	3-2	Oct 09	2-2	5-4
Stockport	v Liverpool	Sep 24	0-0	Oct 09	0-2	0-2
Stoke	v Rotherham	Sep 26	1-2	Oct 09	1-1	2-3
Sunderland	v Crystal Palace	Sep 25	2-1	Oct 10	0-0	2-1
Walsall	v Coventry	Sep 25	1-2	Oct 09	3-0	4-2
Watford	v Cardiff	Sep 25	3-1	Oct 09	0-1	3-2
Wigan	v W.B.A.	Sep 25	0-0	Oct 10	1-3	1-3
York	v Q.P.R.	Sep 25	2-4	Oct 09	1-4	3-8

3rd Round

Oct 30	Birmingham	0	W.B.A.	0
Oct 30	Ipswich	1	Newcastle	1
Oct 31	Leeds	0	Watford	4
Oct 30	Luton	3	Leicester	1
Oct 31	Manchester C	0	West Ham	0
Oct 30	Manchester U	1	Everton	2
Oct 31	Norwich	0	Aldershot	0
Oct 31	Nottingham F	1	Sunderland	1
Oct 30	Notts Co	6	Bolton	1
Oct 31	Oxford	3	Arsenal	2
Oct 30	Q.P.R.	1	Aston Villa	0
Oct 30	Rotherham	0	Grimsby	0
Oct 30	Sheffield W	3	Fulham	2
Oct 30	Southampton	2	Wolverhampton	2
Oct 31	Tottenham	1	Liverpool	0
Oct 30	Walsall	2	Chelsea	2

Replays

Nov 06	Aldershot	0	Norwich	4
Nov 06	Chelsea	3	Walsall	0
Nov 06	Grimsby	6	Rotherham	1
Nov 06	Sunderland	1	Nottingham F	0
Nov 06	West Ham	1	Manchester C	2
Nov 06	Wolverhampton	0	Southampton	2
Nov 07	Newcastle	1	Ipswich	2
Nov 07	W.B.A.	3	Birmingham	1

4th Round

Nov 21	Chelsea	4	Manchester C	1
Nov 20	Everton	0	Grimsby	1
Nov 20	Ipswich	2	Oxford	1
Nov 21	Norwich	3	Notts Co	0
Nov 20	Sheffield W	4	Luton	2
Nov 20	Southampton	1	Q.P.R.	1
Nov 21	Sunderland	0	Tottenham	0
Nov 20	Watford	4	W.B.A.	1

Replays

Nov 27	Q.P.R.	0	Southampton	0
Dec 05	Tottenham	1	Sunderland	2
Dec 12	Q.P.R.	4	Southampton	0

5th Round

Jan 28	Chelsea	1	Sheffield W	1
Jan 16	Grimsby	0	Norwich	1
Jan 23	Ipswich	0	Q.P.R.	0
Jan 23	Watford	0	Sunderland	1

Replays

Jan 28	Q.P.R.	1	Ipswich	2
Jan 30	Sheffield W	4	Chelsea	4
Feb 06	Chelsea	2	Sheffield W	1

Semi-finals

Feb 23	Ipswich	1	Norwich	0
Mar 06	Norwich	2	Ipswich	0
	Aggregate 2-1			
Feb 13	Sunderland	2	Chelsea	0
Mar 04	Chelsea	2	Sunderland	3
	Aggregate 2-5			

Final

Mar 24	Norwich	1	Sunderland	0
	played at Wembley			

Season 1985-86

1st Round

Aldershot	v Orient	Aug 20	1-3	Sep 03	2-2	3-5
Bolton	v Stockport	Aug 20	4-1	Sep 03	1-1	5-2
Bradford C	v Chesterfield	Aug 21	2-2	Sep 03	4-3	6-5
Bristol R	v Newport	Aug 20	2-0	Sep 03	0-1	2-1
Burnley	v Bury	Aug 20	2-1	Sep 03	3-5	5-6
Cambridge	v Brentford	Aug 20	1-1	Sep 03	0-2	1-3
Cardiff	v Swansea	Aug 20	2-1	Sep 03	1-3	3-4
Charlton	v Crystal Palace	Aug 20	1-2	Sep 03	1-1	2-3
Colchester	v Millwall	Aug 21	2-3	Sep 03	1-4	3-7
Crewe	v Carlisle	Aug 20	3-3	Sep 03	4-3	7-6
Darlington	v Scunthorpe	Aug 20	3-2	Sep 10	0-0	3-2
Derby	v Hartlepool	Aug 21	3-0	Sep 04	0-2	3-2
Halifax	v Hull	Aug 20	1-1	Sep 03	0-3	1-4
Hereford	v Bristol C	Aug 21	5-1	Sep 03	0-2	5-3
Mansfield	v Middlesbrough	Aug 21	2-0	Sep 03	4-4	6-4
Notts Co	v Doncaster	Aug 20	1-0	Sep 03	1-2	2-2
Peterborough	v Northampton	Aug 21	0-0	Sep 03	0-2	0-2
Plymouth	v Exeter	Aug 20	2-1	Sep 04	0-2	2-3
Preston	v Blackpool	Aug 20	2-1	Sep 03	3-1	5-2
Reading	v Bournemouth	Aug 21	1-3	Sep 03	0-2	1-5
Rotherham	v Sheffield U	Aug 20	1-3	Sep 03	1-5	2-8
Southend	v Gillingham	Aug 20	1-1	Sep 03	0-2	1-3
Torquay	v Swindon	Aug 20	1-2	Sep 03	2-2	3-4
Tranmere	v Chester	Aug 28	1-3	Sep 04	0-0	1-3
Walsall	v Wolverhampton	Aug 20	1-1	Sep 03	1-0	2-1
Wigan	v Port Vale	Aug 20	2-1	Sep 02	0-2	2-3
Wrexham	v Rochdale	Aug 20	4-0	Sep 03	1-2	5-2
York	v Lincoln	Aug 20	2-1	Sep 04	2-1	4-2

2nd Round

Brentford	v Sheffield W	Sep 25	2-2	Oct 15	0-2	2-4
Brighton	v Bradford C	Sep 25	5-2	Oct 07	2-0	7-2
Bristol R	v Birmingham	Sep 24	2-3	Oct 07	1-2	3-5
Bury	v Manchester C	Sep 25	1-2	Oct 07	1-2	2-4
Chester	v Coventry	Sep 25	1-2	Oct 08	2-7	3-9
Crewe	v Watford	Sep 24	1-3	Oct 07	2-3	3-6
Crystal Palace	v Manchester U	Sep 24	0-1	Oct 08	0-1	0-2
Derby	v Leicester	Sep 25	2-0	Oct 08	1-1	3-1
Everton	v Bournemouth	Sep 25	3-2	Oct 07	2-0	5-2
Exeter	v Aston Villa	Sep 25	1-4	Oct 08	1-8	2-12
Fulham	v Notts Co	Sep 24	1-1	Oct 07	4-2	5-3
Gillingham	v Portsmouth	Sep 24	1-3	Oct 07	1-2	2-5
Grimsby	v York	Sep 24	1-1	Oct 07	3-2	4-3
Hereford	v Arsenal	Sep 25	0-0	Oct 07	1-2	1-2
Ipswich	v Darlington	Sep 24	3-1	Oct 07	4-1	7-2
Leeds	v Walsall	Sep 25	0-0	Oct 07	3-0	3-0
Liverpool	v Oldham	Sep 24	3-0	Oct 08	5-2	8-2
Mansfield	v Chelsea	Sep 25	2-2	Oct 08	0-2	2-4
Millwall	v Southampton	Sep 25	0-0	Oct 07	0-0	0-0
Newcastle	v Barnsley	Sep 25	0-0	Oct 07	1-1	1-1
Nottingham F	v Bolton	Sep 25	4-0	Oct 07	3-0	7-0
Orient	v Tottenham	Sep 23	2-0	Oct 30	0-4	2-4
Oxford	v Northampton	Sep 25	2-1	Oct 07	2-0	4-1
Preston	v Norwich	Sep 30	1-1	Oct 08	1-2	2-3
Q.P.R.	v Hull	Sep 24	3-0	Oct 07	5-1	8-1
Sheffield U	v Luton	Sep 24	1-2	Oct 07	1-3	2-5
Shrewsbury	v Huddersfield	Sep 24	2-3	Oct 07	2-0	4-3
Sunderland	v Swindon	Sep 24	3-2	Oct 07	1-3	4-5
West Ham	v Swansea	Sep 24	3-0	Oct 07	3-2	6-2
Wimbledon	v Blackburn	Sep 24	5-0	Oct 07	1-2	6-2
Wrexham	v Stoke	Sep 24	0-1	Oct 08	0-1	0-2
W.B.A.	v Port Vale	Sep 24	1-0	Oct 07	2-2	3-2

3rd Round

Oct 30	Birmingham	1	Southampton	1
Oct 29	Chelsea	1	Fulham	1
Oct 29	Coventry	0	W.B.A.	0
Oct 30	Derby	1	Nottingham F	2
Oct 29	Grimsby	0	Ipswich	2
Oct 30	Leeds	0	Aston Villa	3
Oct 29	Liverpool	4	Brighton	0
Oct 29	Luton	0	Norwich	2
Oct 30	Manchester C	1	Arsenal	2
Oct 29	Manchester U	1	West Ham	0
Oct 30	O oxford	3	Newcastle	1
Oct 29	Portsmouth	2	Stoke	0
Oct 29	Shrewsbury	1	Everton	4
Oct 29	Swindon	1	Sheffield W	0
Nov 06	Tottenham	2	Wimbledon	0
Oct 29	Watford	0	Q.P.R.	1

Replays

Nov 06	Fulham	0	Chelsea	1
Nov 06	Southampton	3	Birmingham	0
Nov 06	W.B.A.	4	Coventry	3

4th Round

Nov 19	Arsenal	0	Southampton	0
Nov 19	Aston Villa	2	W.B.A.	2
Nov 26	Chelsea	2	Everton	2
Nov 26	Ipswich	6	Swindon	1
Nov 26	Liverpool	2	Manchester U	1
Nov 19	Oxford	3	Norwich	1
Nov 25	Q.P.R.	3	Nottingham F	1
Nov 19	Tottenham	0	Portsmouth	0

Replays

Nov 26	Portsmouth	0	Tottenham	0
Nov 26	Southampton	1	Arsenal	3
Nov 26	W.B.A.	1	Aston Villa	2
Dec 10	Everton	1	Chelsea	2
Dec 10	Portsmouth	1	Tottenham	0

5th Round

Jan 22	Aston Villa	1	Arsenal	1
Jan 21	Liverpool	3	Ipswich	0
Jan 22	Oxford	3	Portsmouth	1
Jan 22	Q.P.R.	1	Chelsea	1

Replays

Jan 29	Chelsea	0	Q.P.R.	2
Feb 04	Arsenal	1	Aston Villa	2

Semi-finals

Feb 12	Aston Villa	2	Oxford	2
Mar 12	Oxford	2	Aston Villa	1
	Aggregate 4-3			
Feb 12	Q.P.R.	1	Liverpool	0
Mar 05	Liverpool	2	Q.P.R.	2
	Aggregate 2-3			

Final

Apr 20	Oxford	3	Q.P.R.	0
	played at Wembley			

SEASON 1986-87

1st Round

Aldershot	v Fulham	Aug 26	1-3	Sep 03	0-2	1-5
Blackpool	v Preston	Aug 26	0-0	Sep 02	1-2	1-2
Bournemouth	v Bristol C	Aug 26	0-1	Sep 02	1-1	1-2
Bristol R	v Reading	Aug 27	1-2	Sep 03	0-4	1-6
Bury	v Bolton	Aug 26	2-1	Sep 02	0-0	2-1
Cardiff	v Plymouth	Aug 26	5-4	Sep 02	1-0	6-4
Carlisle	v Grimsby	Sep 02	1-0	Sep 09	0-2	1-2
Chesterfield	v Wrexham	Aug 26	0-2	Sep 02	2-2	2-4
Colchester	v Peterborough	Aug 26	0-0	Sep 03	0-2	0-2
Derby	v Chester	Aug 27	0-1	Sep 03	2-1	2-2
Doncaster	v Rotherham	Aug 26	1-1	Sep 02	1-4	2-5
Exeter	v Newport	Aug 27	0-0	Sep 02	0-1	0-1
Gillingham	v Northampton	Aug 25	1-0	Sep 03	2-2	3-2
Hartlepool	v Middlesbrough	Aug 26	1-1	Sep 02	0-2	1-3
Hereford	v Swansea	Aug 27	3-3	Sep 02	1-5	4-8
Huddersfield	v Halifax	Aug 26	3-1	Sep 02	2-2	5-3
Notts Co	v Port Vale	Aug 26	1-3	Sep 03	1-4	2-7
Orient	v Cambridge	Aug 26	2-2	Sep 02	0-1	2-3
Rochdale	v Burnley	Aug 26	1-1	Sep 02	3-1	4-2
Scunthorpe	v Darlington	Aug 26	2-0	Sep 02	2-1	4-1
Shrewsbury	v Crewe	Aug 26	0-0	Sep 02	4-0	4-0
Southend	v Brentford	Aug 26	1-0	Sep 02	3-2	4-2
Stockport	v Tranmere	Aug 26	2-1	Sep 02	3-3	5-4
Sunderland	v York	Aug 26	2-4	Sep 02	3-1	5-5
Swindon	v Torquay	Aug 26	3-0	Sep 02	3-2	6-2
Walsall	v Mansfield	Aug 26	1-0	Sep 02	4-2	5-2
Wigan	v Blackburn	Aug 26	1-3	Sep 02	0-2	1-5
Wolverhampton	v Lincoln	Aug 26	1-2	Sep 02	1-0	2-2

2nd Round

Arsenal	v Huddersfield	Sep 23	2-0	Oct 07	1-1	3-1
Barnsley	v Tottenham	Sep 23	2-3	Oct 08	3-5	5-8
Bradford C	v Newcastle	Sep 23	2-0	Oct 08	0-1	2-1
Brighton	v Nottingham F	Sep 24	0-0	Oct 08	0-3	0-3
Bristol C	v Sheffield U	Sep 23	2-2	Oct 07	0-3	2-5
Cambridge	v Wimbledon	Sep 23	1-1	Oct 07	2-2	3-3
Charlton	v Lincoln	Sep 23	3-1	Oct 08	1-0	4-1
Coventry	v Rotherham	Sep 23	3-2	Oct 07	1-0	4-2
Crystal Palace	v Bury	Sep 24	0-0	Oct 07	1-0	1-0
Derby	v W.B.A.	Sep 24	4-1	Oct 07	1-0	5-1
Everton	v Newport	Sep 24	4-0	Oct 07	5-1	9-1
Hull	v Grimsby	Sep 23	1-0	Oct 07	1-1	2-1
Liverpool	v Fulham	Sep 23	10-0	Oct 07	3-2	13-2
Luton	v Cardiff	Luton Disqualified				
Manchester U	v Port Vale	Sep 24	2-0	Oct 07	5-2	7-2
Middlesbrough	v Birmingham	Sep 23	2-2	Oct 07	2-3	4-5
Oldham	v Leeds	Sep 23	3-2	Oct 08	1-0	4-2
Oxford	v Gillingham	Sep 24	6-0	Oct 07	1-1	7-1
Peterborough	v Norwich	Sep 24	0-0	Oct 08	0-1	0-1
Preston	v West Ham	Sep 23	1-1	Oct 07	1-4	2-5
Q.P.R.	v Blackburn	Sep 23	2-1	Oct 07	2-2	4-3
Reading	v Aston Villa	Sep 24	1-1	Oct 08	1-4	2-5
Scunthorpe	v Ipswich	Sep 23	1-2	Oct 07	0-2	1-4
Sheffield W	v Stockport	Sep 23	3-0	Oct 06	7-0	10-0
Shrewsbury	v Stoke	Sep 23	2-1	Oct 08	0-0	2-1
Southampton	v Swindon	Sep 23	3-0	Oct 08	0-0	3-0
Southend	v Manchester C	Sep 23	0-0	Oct 08	1-2	1-2
Swansea	v Leicester	Sep 23	0-2	Oct 08	2-4	2-6
Walsall	v Millwall	Oct 07	0-1	Oct 14	2-3	2-4
Watford	v Rochdale	Sep 23	1-1	Oct 07	2-1	3-2
Wrexham	v Portsmouth	Sep 24	1-2	Oct 07	0-2	1-4
York	v Chelsea	Sep 23	1-0	Oct 08	0-3	1-3

3rd Round

Oct 28	Arsenal	3	Manchester C	1
Nov 04	Aston Villa	2	Derby	1
Oct 29	Bradford C	3	Portsmouth	1
Oct 28	Cambridge	1	Ipswich	0
Oct 28	Cardiff	2	Chelsea	1
Oct 28	Charlton	1	Q.P.R.	0
Oct 28	Coventry	2	Oldham	1
Oct 29	Crystal Palace	2	Nottingham F	2
Oct 29	Derby	1	Aston Villa	1
Oct 28	Everton	4	Sheffield W	0
Oct 29	Liverpool	4	Leicester	1
Oct 29	Manchester U	0	Southampton	0
Oct 29	Norwich	4	Millwall	1
Oct 29	Oxford	3	Sheffield U	1
Oct 28	Shrewsbury	1	Hull	0
Oct 29	Tottenham	5	Birmingham	0
Oct 29	Watford	2	West Ham	3

Replays

Nov 04	Southampton	4	Manchester U	1
Nov 05	Nottingham F	1	Crystal Palace	0

4th Round

Nov 18	Arsenal	2	Charlton	0
Nov 19	Bradford C	0	Nottingham F	5
Nov 26	Cambridge	1	Tottenham	3
Nov 19	Coventry	0	Liverpool	0
Nov 19	Norwich	1	Everton	4
Nov 18	Shrewsbury	1	Cardiff	0
Nov 18	Southampton	2	Aston Villa	1
Nov 18	West Ham	1	Oxford	0

Replay

Nov 26	Liverpool	3	Coventry	1

5th Round

Jan 21	Arsenal	2	Nottingham F	0
Jan 21	Everton	0	Liverpool	1
Jan 27	Southampton	1	Shrewsbury	0
Jan 27	West Ham	1	Tottenham	1

Replay

Feb 02	Tottenham	5	West Ham	0

Semi-finals

Feb 08	Arsenal	0	Tottenham	1
Mar 01	Tottenham	1	Arsenal	2
Mar 04	Tottenham	1	Arsenal	2
	Aggregate 3-4			
Feb 11	Southampton	0	Liverpool	0
Feb 25	Liverpool	3	Southampton	0
	Aggregate 3-0			

Final

Apr 05	Arsenal	2	Liverpool	1
	played at Wembley			

SEASON 1987-88

1st Round

Blackpool	v Chester	Aug 18	2-0	Aug 26	0-1	2-1
Bournemouth	v Exeter	Aug 18	1-1	Aug 26	3-1	4-2
Brentford	v Southend	Aug 18	2-1	Aug 25	2-4	4-5
Bristol R	v Hereford	Aug 19	1-0	Aug 26	0-2	1-2
Bury	v Preston	Aug 18	2-2	Aug 25	3-2	5-4
Cambridge	v Aldershot	Aug 18	1-1	Aug 25	4-1	5-2
Chesterfield	v Peterborough	Aug 18	2-1	Aug 26	0-2	2-3
Crewe	v Shrewsbury	Aug 25	3-3	Sep 08	1-4	4-7
Fulham	v Colchester	Aug 18	3-1	Aug 25	2-0	5-1
Gillingham	v Brighton	Aug 18	1-0	Aug 26	0-1	1-1
Grimsby	v Darlington	Aug 18	3-2	Aug 26	1-2	4-4
Halifax	v York	Aug 18	1-1	Aug 25	0-1	1-2
Leyton O	v Millwall	Aug 18	1-1	Aug 25	0-1	1-2
Mansfield	v Birmingham	Aug 18	2-2	Aug 25	1-0	3-2
Newport	v Cardiff	Aug 18	2-1	Aug 25	2-2	4-3
Port Vale	v Northampton	Aug 17	0-1	Sep 02	0-4	0-5
Rochdale	v Tranmere	Aug 18	3-1	Aug 25	0-1	3-2
Rotherham	v Huddersfield	Aug 18	4-4	Aug 25	3-1	7-5
Scarborough	v Doncaster	Aug 19	1-0	Aug 25	1-3	2-3
Scunthorpe	v Hartlepool	Aug 18	3-1	Aug 26	1-0	4-1
Stockport	v Carlisle	Aug 18	0-1	Aug 25	0-3	0-4
Sunderland	v Middlesbrough	Aug 18	1-0	Aug 25	0-2	1-2
Swindon	v Bristol C	Aug 18	3-0	Aug 25	2-3	5-3
Torquay	v Swansea	Aug 18	2-1	Aug 25	1-1	3-2
Wigan	v Bolton	Aug 18	2-3	Aug 25	3-1	5-4
Wolverhampton	v Notts Co	Aug 18	3-0	Aug 25	2-1	5-1
Wrexham	v Burnley	Aug 18	1-0	Aug 25	0-3	1-3
W.B.A.	v Walsall	Aug 19	2-3	Aug 25	0-0	2-3

2nd Round

Barnsley	v West Ham	Sep 22	0-0	Oct 06	5-2	5-2
Blackburn	v Liverpool	Sep 23	1-1	Oct 06	0-1	1-2
Blackpool	v Newcastle	Sep 23	1-0	Oct 07	1-4	2-4
Bournemouth	v Southampton	Sep 22	1-0	Oct 06	2-2	3-2
Burnley	v Norwich	Sep 22	1-1	Oct 07	0-1	1-2
Bury	v Sheffield U	Sep 22	2-1	Oct 07	1-1	3-2
Cambridge	v Coventry	Sep 22	0-1	Oct 06	1-2	1-3
Carlisle	v Oldham	Sep 22	4-3	Oct 06	1-4	5-7
Charlton	v Walsall	Sep 23	3-0	Oct 06	0-2	3-2
Crystal Palace	v Newport	Sep 22	4-0	Oct 06	2-0	6-0
Darlington	v Watford	Sep 22	0-3	Oct 06	0-8	0-11
Doncaster	v Arsenal	Sep 23	0-3	Oct 06	0-1	0-4
Everton	v Rotherham	Sep 22	3-2	Oct 06	0-0	3-2
Fulham	v Bradford C	Sep 22	1-5	Oct 07	1-2	2-7
Ipswich	v Northampton	Sep 22	1-1	Oct 07	4-2	5-3
Leeds	v York	Sep 23	1-1	Oct 06	4-0	5-1
Leicester	v Scunthorpe	Sep 23	2-1	Oct 06	2-1	4-2
Manchester C	v Wolverhampton	Sep 22	1-2	Oct 06	2-0	3-2
Manchester U	v Hull	Sep 23	5-0	Oct 07	1-0	6-0
Middlesbrough	v Aston Villa	Sep 23	0-1	Oct 07	0-1	0-2
Nottingham F	v Hereford	Sep 23	5-0	Oct 07	1-1	6-1
Oxford	v Mansfield	Sep 23	1-1	Oct 06	2-0	3-1
Peterborough	v Plymouth	Sep 23	4-1	Oct 06	1-1	5-2
Q.P.R.	v Millwall	Sep 23	2-1	Oct 06	0-0	2-1
Reading	v Chelsea	Sep 23	3-1	Oct 07	2-3	5-4
Rochdale	v Wimbledon	Sep 22	1-1	Oct 06	1-2	2-3
Shrewsbury	v Sheffield W	Sep 22	1-1	Oct 06	1-2	2-3
Southend	v Derby	Sep 22	1-0	Oct 07	0-0	1-0
Stoke	v Gillingham	Sep 22	2-0	Oct 06	1-0	3-0
Swindon	v Portsmouth	Sep 22	3-1	Oct 07	3-1	6-2
Torquay	v Tottenham	Sep 23	1-0	Oct 07	0-3	1-3
Wigan	v Luton	Sep 22	0-1	Oct 06	2-4	2-5

3rd Round

Oct 27	Arsenal	3	Bournemouth	0
Oct 28	Aston Villa	2	Tottenham	1
Oct 27	Barnsley	1	Sheffield W	2
Oct 27	Bury	1	Q.P.R.	0
Oct 27	Charlton	0	Bradford C	1
Oct 27	Ipswich	1	Southend	0
Oct 28	Leeds	2	Oldham	2
Oct 28	Liverpool	0	Everton	1
Oct 27	Luton	3	Coventry	1
	played at Leicester			
Oct 27	Manchester C	3	Nottingham F	0
Oct 28	Manchester U	2	Crystal Palace	1
Oct 28	Oxford	0	Leicester	0
Oct 28	Peterborough	0	Reading	0
Oct 27	Stoke	2	Norwich	1
Oct 28	Swindon	1	Watford	1
Oct 28	Wimbledon	2	Newcastle	1

Replays

Nov 03	Watford	4	Swindon	2
Nov 04	Leicester	2	Oxford	3
Nov 04	Oldham	4	Leeds	2
Nov 04	Reading	1	Peterborough	0

4th Round

Nov 17	Arsenal	3	Stoke	0
Nov 18	Aston Villa	1	Sheffield W	2
Nov 18	Bury	1	Manchester U	2
Nov 17	Everton	2	Oldham	1
Nov 17	Ipswich	0	Luton	1
Nov 17	Manchester C	3	Watford	1
Nov 18	Oxford	2	Wimbledon	1
Nov 18	Reading	0	Bradford C	0

Replay

Nov 24	Bradford C	1	Reading	0

5th Round

Jan 20	Everton	2	Manchester C	0
Jan 19	Luton	2	Bradford C	0
Jan 20	Oxford	2	Manchester U	0
Jan 20	Sheffield W	0	Arsenal	1

Semi-finals

Feb 07	Everton	0	Arsenal	1
Feb 24	Arsenal	3	Everton	1
	Aggregate 4-1			
Feb 10	Oxford	1	Luton	1
Feb 28	Luton	2	Oxford	0
	Aggregate 3-1			

Final

Apr 24	Arsenal	2	Luton	3
	played at Wembley			

Season 1988-89

1st Round

Bolton	v Chester	Aug 30	1-0	Sep 07	1-3	2-3
Bournemouth	v Bristol R	Aug 30	1-0	Sep 07	0-0	1-0
Bristol C	v Exeter	Aug 30	1-0	Sep 07	1-0	2-0
Bury	v Wrexham	Aug 30	2-1	Sep 06	2-2	4-3
Cambridge	v Gillingham	Aug 30	1-2	Sep 06	1-3	2-5
Cardiff	v Swansea	Aug 30	0-1	Sep 20	2-0	2-1
Carlisle	v Blackpool	Aug 30	1-1	Sep 06	0-3	1-4
Colchester	v Northampton	Aug 30	0-0	Sep 06	0-5	0-5
Crewe	v Lincoln	Aug 30	1-1	Sep 07	1-2	2-3
Doncaster	v Darlington	Aug 30	1-1	Sep 06	0-2	1-3
Fulham	v Brentford	Aug 30	2-2	Sep 06	0-1	2-3
Grimsby	v Rotherham	Aug 30	0-1	Sep 06	0-1	0-2
Hartlepool	v Sheffield U	Aug 30	2-2	Sep 06	0-2	2-4
Hereford	v Plymouth	Aug 29	0-3	Sep 06	2-3	2-6
Leyton O	v Aldershot	Aug 30	2-0	Sep 06	0-0	2-0
Notts Co	v Mansfield	Aug 30	5-0	Sep 06	0-1	5-1
Port Vale	v Chesterfield	Aug 30	3-2	Sep 06	1-1	4-3
Rochdale	v Burnley	Aug 30	3-3	Sep 06	1-2	4-5
Scarborough	v Halifax	Aug 31	1-1	Sep 06	2-2	3-3
Scunthorpe	v Huddersfield	Aug 30	3-2	Sep 06	2-2	5-4
Shrewsbury	v Walsall	Aug 30	2-2	Sep 06	0-3	2-5
Southend	v Brighton	Aug 30	2-0	Sep 07	1-0	3-0
Stockport	v Tranmere	Aug 29	0-1	Sep 05	1-1	1-2
Torquay	v Reading	Aug 30	0-1	Sep 07	1-3	1-4
Wigan	v Preston	Aug 29	0-0	Sep 06	0-1	0-1
Wolverhampton	v Birmingham	Aug 30	3-2	Sep 06	0-1	3-3
W.B.A.	v Peterborough	Aug 31	0-3	Sep 07	2-0	2-3
York	v Sunderland	Aug 30	0-0	Sep 06	0-4	0-4

2nd Round

Barnsley	v Wimbledon	Sep 27	0-2	Oct 12	1-0	1-2
Birmingham	v Aston Villa	Sep 27	0-2	Oct 12	0-5	0-7
Blackburn	v Brentford	Sep 27	3-1	Oct 12	3-4	6-5
Blackpool	v Sheffield W	Sep 27	2-0	Oct 12	1-3	3-3
Bournemouth	v Coventry	Sep 27	0-4	Oct 11	1-3	1-7
Darlington	v Oldham	Sep 27	2-0	Oct 11	0-4	2-4
Derby	v Southend	Sep 28	1-0	Oct 11	2-1	3-1
Everton	v Bury	Sep 27	3-0	Oct 11	2-2	5-2
Hull	v Arsenal	Sep 28	1-2	Oct 12	0-3	1-5
Leicester	v Watford	Sep 28	4-1	Oct 11	2-2	6-3
Leyton O	v Stoke	Sep 27	1-2	Oct 11	2-1	3-3
Lincoln	v Southampton	Sep 28	1-1	Oct 11	1-3	2-4
Liverpool	v Walsall	Sep 28	1-0	Oct 12	3-1	4-1
Luton	v Burnley	Sep 27	1-1	Oct 11	1-0	2-1
Manchester C	v Plymouth	Sep 28	1-0	Oct 12	6-3	7-3
Middlesbrough	v Tranmere	Sep 28	0-0	Oct 11	0-1	0-1
Millwall	v Gillingham	Sep 27	3-0	Oct 11	3-1	6-1
Northampton	v Charlton	Sep 27	1-1	Oct 11	1-2	2-3
Norwich	v Preston	Sep 28	2-0	Oct 11	3-0	5-0
Nottingham F	v Chester	Sep 28	6-0	Oct 12	4-0	10-0
Notts Co	v Tottenham	Sep 27	1-1	Oct 11	1-2	2-3
Oxford	v Bristol C	Sep 28	2-4	Oct 11	0-2	2-6
Peterborough	v Leeds	Sep 27	1-2	Oct 12	1-3	2-5
Port Vale	v Ipswich	Sep 26	1-0	Oct 11	0-3	1-3
Portsmouth	v Scarborough	Sep 27	2-2	Oct 12	1-3	3-5
Q.P.R.	v Cardiff	Sep 28	3-0	Oct 11	4-1	7-1
Reading	v Bradford C	Sep 28	1-1	Oct 12	1-2	2-3
Rotherham	v Manchester U	Sep 28	0-1	Oct 12	0-5	0-6
Scunthorpe	v Chelsea	Sep 27	4-1	Oct 12	2-2	6-3
Sheffield U	v Newcastle	Sep 27	3-0	Oct 12	0-2	3-2
Sunderland	v West Ham	Sep 27	0-3	Oct 12	1-2	1-5
Swindon	v Crystal Palace	Sep 27	1-2	Oct 12	0-2	1-4

3rd Round

Nov 02	Aston Villa	3	Millwall	1
Nov 02	Bradford C	1	Scunthorpe	1
Nov 01	Bristol C	4	Crystal Palace	1
Nov 08	Everton	1	Oldham	1
Nov 01	Ipswich	2	Leyton O	0
Nov 02	Leeds	0	Luton	2
Nov 02	Leicester	2	Norwich	0
Nov 02	Liverpool	1	Arsenal	1
Nov 02	Manchester C	4	Sheffield U	2
Nov 02	Nottingham F	3	Coventry	2
Nov 02	Q.P.R.	2	Charlton	1
Nov 02	Scarborough	2	Southampton	2
Nov 01	Tottenham	0	Blackburn	0
Nov 01	Tranmere	1	Blackpool	0
Nov 01	West Ham	5	Derby	0
Nov 02	Wimbledon	2	Manchester U	1

Replays

Nov 09	Arsenal	0	Liverpool	0
Nov 09	Blackburn	1	Tottenham	2
Nov 22	Scunthorpe	0	Bradford C	1
Nov 22	Southampton	1	Scarborough	0
Nov 23	Arsenal	1	Liverpool	2
	played at Aston Villa			
Nov 29	Oldham	0	Everton	2

4th Round

Nov 30	Aston Villa	6	Ipswich	2
Dec 14	Bradford C	3	Everton	1
Nov 29	Bristol C	1	Tranmere	0
Nov 30	Leicester	0	Nottingham F	0
Nov 29	Luton	3	Manchester C	1
Nov 30	Q.P.R.	0	Wimbledon	0
Nov 29	Southampton	2	Tottenham	1
Nov 30	West Ham	4	Liverpool	1

Replays

Dec 14	Nottingham F	2	Leicester	1
Dec 14	Wimbledon	0	Q.P.R.	1

5th Round

Jan 18	Bradford C	0	Bristol C	1
Jan 18	Luton	1	Southampton	1
Jan 18	Nottingham F	5	Q.P.R.	2
Jan 18	West Ham	2	Aston Villa	1

Replay

Jan 25	Southampton	1	Luton	2

Semi-finals

Feb 15	Nottingham F	1	Bristol C	1
Feb 26	Bristol C	0	Nottingham F	1
	Aggregate 1-2			
Feb 12	West Ham	0	Luton	3
Mar 01	Luton	2	West Ham	0
	Aggregate 5-0			

Final

Apr 09	Luton	1	Nottingham F	3
	played at Wembley			

Season 1989-90

1st Round

Birmingham	v Chesterfield	Aug 22	2-1	Aug 29	1-1	3-2
Blackpool	v Burnley	Aug 22	2-2	Aug 29	1-0	3-2
Brighton	v Brentford	Aug 23	0-3	Aug 29	1-1	1-4
Bristol C	v Reading	Aug 22	2-3	Aug 29	2-2	4-5
Bristol R	v Portsmouth	Aug 23	1-0	Aug 29	0-2	1-2
Cambridge	v Maidstone	Aug 22	3-1	Aug 30	1-0	4-1
Cardiff	v Plymouth	Aug 22	0-3	Aug 29	2-0	2-3
Colchester	v Southend	Aug 22	3-4	Aug 29	1-2	4-6
Crewe	v Chester	Aug 22	4-0	Aug 29	2-0	6-0
Exeter	v Swansea	Aug 23	3-0	Aug 29	1-1	4-1
Fulham	v Oxford	Aug 23	0-1	Aug 30	5-3	5-4
Gillingham	v Leyton O	Aug 22	1-4	Aug 29	0-3	1-7
Halifax	v Carlisle	Aug 22	3-1	Aug 29	0-1	3-2
Hartlepool	v York	Aug 23	3-3	Aug 29	1-4	4-7
Huddersfield	v Doncaster	Aug 22	1-1	Aug 29	2-1	3-2
Hull	v Grimsby	Aug 22	1-0	Aug 29	0-2	1-2
Mansfield	v Northampton	Aug 22	1-1	Sep 05	2-0	3-1
Peterborough	v Aldershot	Aug 23	2-0	Aug 29	2-6	4-6
Preston	v Tranmere	Aug 22	3-4	Aug 29	1-3	4-7
Rochdale	v Bolton	Aug 22	2-1	Aug 29	1-5	3-6
Scarborough	v Scunthorpe	Aug 23	2-0	Aug 29	1-1	3-1
Sheffield U	v Rotherham	Aug 22	1-1	Aug 29	0-1	1-2
Shrewsbury	v Notts Co	Aug 22	3-0	Aug 29	1-3	4-3
Stockport	v Bury	Aug 21	1-0	Aug 29	1-1	2-1
Torquay	v Hereford	Aug 22	0-1	Aug 30	0-3	0-4
Walsall	v Port Vale	Aug 22	1-2	Aug 28	0-1	1-3
Wolverhampton	v Lincoln	Aug 22	1-0	Aug 30	2-0	3-0
Wrexham	v Wigan	Aug 22	0-0	Aug 29	0-5	0-5

2nd Round

Arsenal	v Plymouth	Sep 19	2-0	Oct 03	6-1	8-1
Aston Villa	v Wolverhampton	Sep 20	2-1	Oct 04	1-1	3-2
Barnsley	v Blackpool	Sep 19	1-1	Oct 03	1-1	2-2
Birmingham	v West Ham	Sep 19	1-2	Oct 04	1-1	2-3
Bolton	v Watford	Sep 19	2-1	Oct 03	1-1	3-2
Brentford	v Manchester C	Sep 19	2-1	Oct 04	1-4	3-5
Cambridge	v Derby	Sep 19	2-1	Oct 04	0-5	2-6
Charlton	v Hereford	Sep 20	3-1	Oct 04	1-0	4-1
Chelsea	v Scarborough	Sep 19	1-1	Oct 04	2-3	3-4
Crewe	v Bournemouth	Sep 19	0-1	Oct 03	0-0	0-1
Crystal Palace	v Leicester	Sep 19	1-2	Oct 04	3-2	4-4
Exeter	v Blackburn	Sep 20	3-0	Oct 03	1-2	4-2
Grimsby	v Coventry	Sep 19	3-1	Oct 04	0-3	3-4
Ipswich	v Tranmere	Sep 19	0-1	Oct 03	0-1	0-2
Leyton O	v Everton	Sep 19	0-2	Oct 03	2-2	2-4
Liverpool	v Wigan	Sep 19	5-2	Oct 04	3-0	8-2
Mansfield	v Luton	Sep 19	3-4	Oct 03	2-7	5-11
Middlesbrough	v Halifax	Sep 20	4-0	Oct 03	1-0	5-0
Norwich	v Rotherham	Sep 20	1-1	Oct 03	2-0	3-1
Nottingham F	v Huddersfield	Sep 20	1-1	Oct 03	3-3	4-4
Oldham	v Leeds	Sep 19	2-1	Oct 03	2-1	4-2
Port Vale	v Wimbledon	Sep 18	1-2	Oct 04	0-3	1-5
Portsmouth	v Manchester U	Sep 20	2-3	Oct 03	0-0	2-3
Q.P.R.	v Stockport	Sep 20	2-1	Oct 02	0-0	2-1
Reading	v Newcastle	Sep 19	3-1	Oct 04	0-4	3-5
Sheffield W	v Aldershot	Sep 20	0-0	Oct 03	8-0	8-0
Shrewsbury	v Swindon	Sep 19	0-3	Oct 03	1-3	1-6
Stoke	v Millwall	Sep 19	1-0	Oct 03	0-2	1-2
Sunderland	v Fulham	Sep 19	1-1	Oct 03	3-0	4-1
Tottenham	v Southend	Sep 20	1-0	Oct 04	2-3	3-3
W.B.A.	v Bradford C	Sep 20	1-3	Oct 04	5-3	6-6
York	v Southampton	Sep 20	0-1	Oct 03	0-2	0-3

3rd Round

Oct 25	Arsenal	1	Liverpool	0
Oct 25	Aston Villa	0	West Ham	0
Oct 24	Crystal Palace	0	Nottingham F	0
Oct 25	Derby	2	Sheffield W	1
Oct 24	Everton	3	Luton	0
Oct 25	Exeter	3	Blackpool	0
Oct 25	Manchester C	3	Norwich	1
Oct 25	Manchester U	0	Tottenham	3
Oct 25	Middlesbrough	1	Wimbledon	1
Oct 25	Newcastle	0	W.B.A.	1
Oct 25	Oldham	7	Scarborough	0
Oct 25	Q.P.R.	1	Coventry	2
Oct 24	Southampton	1	Charlton	0
Oct 24	Sunderland	1	Bournemouth	1
Oct 24	Swindon	3	Bolton	3
Oct 23	Tranmere	3	Millwall	2

Replays

Nov 01	Nottingham F	5	Crystal Palace	0
Nov 07	Bolton	1	Swindon	1
Nov 07	Bournemouth	0	Sunderland	1
Nov 08	West Ham	1	Aston Villa	0
Nov 08	Wimbledon	1	Middlesbrough	0
Nov 14	Bolton	1	Swindon	1
Nov 21	Swindon	2	Bolton	1

4th Round

Nov 22	Derby	2	W.B.A.	0
Nov 29	Exeter	2	Sunderland	2
Nov 22	Manchester C	0	Coventry	1
Nov 22	Nottingham F	1	Everton	0
Nov 22	Oldham	3	Arsenal	1
Nov 29	Swindon	0	Southampton	0
Nov 22	Tranmere	2	Tottenham	2
Nov 22	West Ham	1	Wimbledon	0

Replays

Nov 29	Tottenham	4	Tranmere	0
Dec 05	Sunderland	5	Exeter	2
Jan 16	Southampton	4	Swindon	2

5th Round

Jan 17	Nottingham F	2	Tottenham	2
Jan 24	Southampton	2	Oldham	2
Jan 17	Sunderland	0	Coventry	0
Jan 17	West Ham	1	Derby	1

Replays

Jan 24	Coventry	5	Sunderland	0
Jan 24	Derby	0	West Ham	0
Jan 24	Tottenham	2	Nottingham F	3
Jan 31	Oldham	2	Southampton	0
Jan 31	West Ham	2	Derby	1

Semi-finals

Feb 11	Nottingham F	2	Coventry	1
Feb 25	Coventry	0	Nottingham F	0
	Aggregate 1-2			
Feb 14	Oldham	6	West Ham	0
Mar 07	West Ham	3	Oldham	0
	Aggregate 3-6			

Final

Apr 29	Nottingham F	1	Oldham	0
	played at Wembley			

Season 1990-91

1st Round

Birmingham	v Bournemouth	Aug 28	0-1	Sep 04	1-1	1-2
Bradford C	v Bury	Aug 29	2-0	Sep 04	2-3	4-3
Brentford	v Hereford	Aug 28	2-0	Sep 05	0-1	2-1
Brighton	v Northampton	Aug 29	0-2	Sep 04	1-1	1-3
Bristol R	v Torquay	Aug 29	1-2	Sep 04	1-1	2-3
Carlisle	v Scunthorpe	Aug 28	1-0	Sep 04	1-1	2-1
Chesterfield	v Hartlepool	Aug 28	1-2	Sep 11	2-2	3-4
Darlington	v Blackpool	Aug 28	0-0	Sep 04	1-1	1-1
Doncaster	v Rotherham	Aug 28	2-6	Sep 04	1-2	3-8
Exeter	v Notts Co	Aug 29	1-1	Sep 04	0-1	1-2
Fulham	v Peterborough	Aug 28	1-2	Sep 04	0-2	1-3
Gillingham	v Shrewsbury	Aug 28	1-0	Sep 04	0-2	1-2
Grimsby	v Crewe	Aug 28	2-1	Sep 04	0-1	2-2
Halifax	v Lincoln	Aug 28	2-0	Sep 05	0-1	2-1
Huddersfield	v Bolton	Aug 29	0-3	Sep 04	1-2	1-5
Maidstone	v Leyton O	Aug 29	2-2	Sep 04	1-4	3-6
Mansfield	v Cardiff	Aug 28	1-1	Sep 04	0-3	1-4
Middlesbrough	v Tranmere	Aug 28	1-1	Sep 03	2-1	3-2
Preston	v Chester	Aug 28	2-0	Sep 04	1-5	3-5
Reading	v Oxford	Aug 28	0-1	Sep 05	1-2	1-3
Rochdale	v Scarborough	Aug 28	4-0	Sep 05	3-3	7-3
Southend	v Aldershot	Aug 28	2-1	Sep 04	2-2	4-3
Stockport	v Burnley	Aug 27	0-2	Sep 04	1-0	1-2
Stoke	v Swansea	Aug 29	0-0	Sep 04	1-0	1-0
Walsall	v Cambridge	Aug 28	4-2	Sep 04	1-2	5-4
Wigan	v Barnsley	Aug 28	0-1	Sep 04	1-0	1-1
W.B.A.	v Bristol C	Aug 29	2-2	Sep 05	0-1	2-3
York	v Wrexham	Aug 28	0-1	Sep 04	0-2	0-3

2nd Round

Aston Villa	v Barnsley	Sep 26	1-0	Oct 09	1-0	2-0
Bournemouth	v Millwall	Sep 25	0-0	Oct 10	1-2	1-2
Cardiff	v Portsmouth	Sep 25	1-1	Oct 09	1-3	2-4
Carlisle	v Derby	Sep 25	1-1	Oct 10	0-1	1-2
Charlton	v Leyton O	Sep 26	2-2	Oct 09	0-1	2-3
Chester	v Arsenal	Sep 25	0-1	Oct 09	0-5	0-6
Coventry	v Bolton	Sep 26	4-2	Oct 09	3-2	7-4
Crystal Palace	v Southend	Sep 25	8-0	Oct 09	2-1	10-1
Darlington	v Swindon	Sep 25	3-0	Oct 09	0-4	3-4
Halifax	v Manchester U	Sep 26	1-3	Oct 10	1-2	2-5
Hull	v Wolverhampton	Sep 25	0-0	Oct 09	1-1	1-1
Leicester	v Leeds	Sep 26	1-0	Oct 10	0-3	1-3
Liverpool	v Crewe	Sep 25	5-1	Oct 09	4-1	9-2
Luton	v Bradford C	Sep 25	1-1	Oct 10	1-1	2-2
Middlesbrough	v Newcastle	Sep 25	2-0	Oct 10	0-1	2-1
Northampton	v Sheffield U	Sep 25	0-1	Oct 10	0-2	0-3
Norwich	v Watford	Sep 26	2-0	Oct 09	3-0	5-0
Nottingham F	v Burnley	Sep 26	4-1	Oct 10	1-0	5-1
Notts Co	v Oldham	Sep 25	1-0	Oct 10	2-5	3-5
Plymouth	v Wimbledon	Sep 25	1-0	Oct 10	2-0	3-0
Port Vale	v Oxford	Sep 24	0-2	Oct 10	0-0	0-2
Q.P.R.	v Peterborough	Sep 26	3-1	Oct 09	1-1	4-2
Rochdale	v Southampton	Sep 25	0-5	Oct 09	0-3	0-8
Rotherham	v Blackburn	Sep 25	1-1	Oct 09	0-1	1-2
Sheffield W	v Brentford	Sep 26	2-1	Oct 09	2-1	4-2
Shrewsbury	v Ipswich	Sep 25	1-1	Oct 09	0-3	1-4
Sunderland	v Bristol C	Sep 25	0-1	Oct 09	6-1	6-2
Torquay	v Manchester C	Sep 26	0-4	Oct 10	0-0	0-4
Tottenham	v Hartlepool	Sep 26	5-0	Oct 09	2-1	7-1
Walsall	v Chelsea	Sep 26	0-5	Oct 10	1-4	1-9
West Ham	v Stoke	Sep 26	3-0	Oct 10	2-1	5-1
Wrexham	v Everton	Sep 25	0-5	Oct 09	0-6	0-11

3rd Round

Oct 31	Aston Villa	2	Millwall	0
Oct 31	Chelsea	0	Portsmouth	0
Oct 31	Coventry	3	Hull	0
Oct 30	Crystal Palace	0	Leyton O	0
Oct 31	Derby	6	Sunderland	0
Oct 30	Ipswich	0	Southampton	2
Oct 31	Leeds	2	Oldham	0
Oct 30	Manchester C	1	Arsenal	2
Oct 31	Manchester U	3	Liverpool	1
Oct 30	Middlesbrough	2	Norwich	0
Oct 31	Oxford	2	West Ham	1
Oct 31	Plymouth	1	Nottingham F	2
Oct 31	Q.P.R.	2	Blackburn	1
Oct 30	Sheffield U	2	Everton	1
Oct 31	Sheffield W	0	Swindon	0
Oct 30	Tottenham	2	Bradford C	1

Replays

Nov 06	Portsmouth	2	Chelsea	3
Nov 06	Swindon	0	Sheffield W	1
Nov 07	Leyton O	0	Crystal Palace	1

4th Round

Nov 28	Arsenal	2	Manchester U	6
Nov 28	Aston Villa	3	Middlesbrough	2
Nov 28	Coventry	5	Nottingham F	4
Nov 28	Oxford	1	Chelsea	2
Nov 27	Q.P.R.	0	Leeds	3
Nov 27	Sheffield U	0	Tottenham	2
Nov 28	Sheffield W	1	Derby	1
Nov 27	Southampton	2	Crystal Palace	0

Replays

Dec 12	Derby	1	Sheffield W	2

5th Round

Jan 16	Chelsea	0	Tottenham	0
Jan 23	Coventry	0	Sheffield W	1
Jan 16	Leeds	4	Aston Villa	1
Jan 16	Southampton	1	Manchester U	1

Replays

Jan 23	Manchester U	3	Southampton	2
Jan 23	Tottenham	0	Chelsea	3

Semi-finals

Feb 24	Chelsea	0	Sheffield W	2
Feb 27	Sheffield W	3	Chelsea	1
	Aggregate 5-1			
Feb 10	Manchester U	2	Leeds	1
Feb 24	Leeds	0	Manchester U	1
	Aggregate 1-3			

Final

Apr 21	Manchester U	0	Sheffield W	1
	played at Wembley			

Season 1991-92

1st Round

Barnet	v Brentford	Aug 20	5-5	Aug 27	1-3	6-8
Blackburn	v Hull	Aug 20	1-1	Aug 27	0-1	1-2
Bolton	v York	Aug 20	2-2	Aug 27	2-1	4-3
Cambridge	v Reading	Aug 21	1-0	Aug 28	3-0	4-0
Cardiff	v Bournemouth	Aug 21	3-2	Aug 27	1-4	4-6
Charlton	v Fulham	Aug 21	4-2	Aug 27	1-1	5-3
Chester	v Lincoln	Aug 20	1-0	Aug 28	3-4	4-4
Crewe	v Doncaster	Aug 20	5-2	Aug 27	4-2	9-4
Darlington	v Huddersfield	Aug 20	1-0	Aug 27	0-4	1-4
Exeter	v Birmingham	Aug 21	0-1	Aug 27	0-4	0-5
Halifax	v Tranmere	Aug 20	3-4	Aug 27	3-4	6-8
Hartlepool	v Bury	Aug 20	1-0	Aug 27	2-2	3-2
Leicester	v Maidstone	Aug 21	3-0	Aug 28	1-0	4-0
Leyton O	v Northampton	Aug 20	5-0	Sep 10	0-2	5-2
Mansfield	v Blackpool	Aug 20	0-3	Aug 27	2-4	2-7
Peterborough	v Aldershot	Aug 20	3-1	Aug 27	2-1	5-2
Portsmouth	v Gillingham	Aug 20	2-1	Aug 27	4-3	6-4
Preston	v Scarborough	Aug 20	5-4	Aug 28	1-3	6-7
Rochdale	v Carlisle	Aug 20	5-1	Aug 27	1-1	6-2
Rotherham	v Grimsby	Aug 20	1-3	Aug 27	0-1	1-4
Shrewsbury	v Plymouth	Aug 20	1-1	Aug 27	2-2	3-3
Stockport	v Bradford	Aug 20	1-1	Aug 28	1-3	2-4
Stoke	v Chesterfield	Aug 21	1-0	Aug 27	2-1	3-1
Swansea	v Walsall	Aug 20	2-2	Aug 27	1-0	3-2
Swindon	v W.B.A.	Aug 20	2-0	Aug 28	2-2	4-2
Torquay	v Hereford	Aug 20	2-0	Aug 28	1-2	3-2
Watford	v Southend	Aug 20	2-0	Aug 28	1-1	3-1
Wigan	v Burnley	Aug 20	3-1	Aug 27	3-2	6-3
Wrexham	v Scunthorpe	Aug 20	1-0	Aug 27	0-3	1-3

2nd Round

Blackpool	v Barnsley	Sep 24	1-0	Oct 08	0-2	1-2
Bradford	v Wrexham	Sep 24	1-1	Oct 09	0-4	1-5
Brentford	v Brighton	Sep 24	4-1	Oct 09	2-4	6-5
Bristol R	v Bristol C	Sep 25	1-3	Oct 08	4-2	5-5
Charlton	v Norwich	Sep 25	0-2	Oct 09	0-3	0-5
Chelsea	v Tranmere	Sep 25	1-1	Oct 08	1-3	2-4
Coventry	v Rochdale	Sep 25	4-0	Oct 08	0-1	4-1
Crewe	v Newcastle	Sep 24	3-4	Oct 09	0-1	3-5
Derby	v Ipswich	Sep 25	0-0	Oct 08	2-0	2-0
Everton	v Watford	Sep 24	1-0	Oct 08	2-1	3-1
Grimsby	v Aston Villa	Sep 25	0-0	Oct 09	1-1	1-1
Hartlepool	v Crystal Palace	Sep 25	1-1	Oct 08	1-6	2-7
Hull	v Q.P.R.	Sep 24	0-3	Oct 09	1-5	1-8
Leicester	v Arsenal	Sep 25	1-1	Oct 08	0-2	1-3
Leyton O	v Sheffield W	Sep 24	0-0	Oct 09	1-4	1-4
Liverpool	v Stoke	Sep 25	2-2	Oct 09	3-2	5-4
Luton	v Birmingham	Sep 25	2-2	Oct 08	2-3	4-5
Manchester C	v Chester	Sep 25	3-1	Oct 08	3-0	6-1
Manchester U	v Cambridge	Sep 25	3-0	Oct 09	1-1	4-1
Middlesbrough	v Bournemouth	Sep 24	1-1	Oct 08	2-1	3-2
Millwall	v Swindon	Sep 25	2-2	Oct 08	1-3	3-5
Nottingham F	v Bolton	Sep 25	4-0	Oct 08	5-2	9-2
Oldham	v Torquay	Sep 24	7-1	Oct 09	2-0	9-1
Port Vale	v Notts Co	Sep 24	2-1	Oct 09	2-3	4-4
Portsmouth	v Oxford	Sep 24	0-0	Oct 09	1-0	1-0
Scarborough	v Bolton	Sep 24	1-3	Oct 09	2-2	3-5
Scunthorpe	v Leeds	Sep 24	0-0	Oct 08	0-3	0-3
Sunderland	v Huddersfield	Sep 24	1-2	Oct 09	0-4	1-6
Swansea	v Tottenham	Sep 25	1-0	Oct 09	1-5	2-5
Wigan	v Sheffield U	Sep 24	2-2	Oct 08	0-1	2-3
Wimbledon	v Peterborough	Sep 24	1-2	Oct 08	2-2	3-4
Wolverhampton	v Shrewsbury	Sep 24	6-1	Oct 08	1-3	7-4

3rd Round

Oct 29	Birmingham	1	Crystal Palace	1
Oct 30	Coventry	1	Arsenal	0
Oct 30	Everton	4	Wolverhampton	1
Oct 29	Grimsby	0	Tottenham	3
Oct 29	Huddersfield	1	Swindon	4
Oct 29	Leeds	3	Tranmere	1
Oct 29	Liverpool	2	Port Vale	2
Oct 29	Manchester C	0	Q.P.R.	0
Oct 30	Manchester U	3	Portsmouth	1
Oct 29	Middlesbrough	1	Barnsley	0
Oct 30	Norwich	4	Brentford	1
Oct 30	Nottingham F	2	Bristol R	0
Oct 29	Oldham	2	Derby	1
Oct 29	Peterborough	1	Newcastle	0
Oct 29	Sheffield U	0	West Ham	2
Oct 30	Sheffield W	1	Southampton	1

Replays

Nov 19	Crystal Palace	5	Birmingham	0
Nov 20	Port Vale	1	Liverpool	4
Nov 20	Q.P.R.	1	Manchester C	3
Nov 20	Southampton	1	Sheffield W	0
Dec 03	Crystal Palace	2	Birmingham	1

4th Round

Dec 04	Coventry	1	Tottenham	2
Dec 04	Everton	1	Leeds	4
Dec 04	Manchester U	2	Oldham	0
Dec 03	Middlesbrough	2	Manchester C	1
Dec 04	Norwich	2	West Ham	1
Dec 04	Nottingham F	0	Southampton	0
Dec 03	Peterborough	1	Liverpool	0
Dec 17	Swindon	0	Crystal Palace	1

Replays

Dec 17	Southampton	0	Nottingham F	1

5th Round

Jan 08	Crystal Palace	1	Nottingham F	1
Jan 08	Leeds	1	Manchester U	3
Jan 08	Peterborough	0	Middlesbrough	0
Jan 08	Tottenham	2	Norwich	1

Replays

Feb 05	Nottingham F	4	Crystal Palace	2
Feb 12	Middlesbrough	1	Peterborough	0

Semi-finals

Feb 09	Nottingham F	1	Tottenham	1
Mar 01	Tottenham	1	Nottingham F	2
	Aggregate 2-3			
Mar 04	Middlesbrough	0	Manchester U	0
Mar 11	Manchester U	2	Middlesbrough	1
	Aggregate 2-1			

Final

Apr 12	Manchester U	1	Nottingham F	0
	played at Wembley			

Season 1992-93

1st Round

Bolton	v Port Vale	Aug 18	2-1	Aug 25	1-1	3-2
Cardiff	v Bristol C	Aug 18	1-1	Aug 25	1-5	2-6
Carlisle	v Burnley	Aug 18	4-1	Aug 25	1-1	5-2
Chesterfield	v York	Aug 18	2-0	Aug 25	0-0	2-0
Colchester	v Brighton	Aug 18	1-1	Aug 26	0-1	1-2
Crewe	v Rochdale	Aug 18	4-1	Aug 25	2-1	6-2
Darlington	v Scunthorpe	Aug 18	1-1	Aug 25	0-2	1-3
Doncaster	v Lincoln	Aug 18	0-3	Aug 25	1-1	1-4
Exeter	v Birmingham	Aug 18	0-0	Aug 25	4-1	4-1
Fulham	v Brentford	Aug 18	0-2	Aug 25	0-2	0-4
Gillingham	v Northampton	Aug 18	2-1	Sep 09	2-0	4-1
Grimsby	v Barnsley	Aug 19	1-1	Aug 25	1-1	2-2
Halifax	v Hartlepool	Aug 18	1-2	Aug 25	2-3	3-5
Hereford	v Torquay	Aug 18	2-2	Aug 25	0-5	2-7
Hull	v Rotherham	Aug 18	2-2	Aug 25	0-1	2-3
Leyton O	v Millwall	Aug 18	2-2	Aug 26	0-3	2-5
Newcastle	v Mansfield	Aug 19	2-1	Aug 25	0-0	2-1
Oxford	v Swansea	Aug 18	3-0	Aug 25	0-1	3-1
Peterborough	v Barnet	Aug 18	4-0	Aug 25	2-2	6-2
Preston	v Stoke	Aug 18	2-1	Aug 26	0-4	2-5
Scarborough	v Bradford C	Aug 19	3-0	Aug 26	5-3	8-3
Shrewsbury	v Wigan	Aug 18	1-2	Aug 25	1-0	2-2
Stockport	v Chester	Aug 18	1-1	Aug 25	2-1	3-2
Sunderland	v Huddersfield	Aug 18	2-3	Aug 26	1-0	3-3
Tranmere	v Blackpool	Aug 19	3-0	Aug 25	0-4	3-4
Walsall	v Bournemouth	Aug 19	1-1	Aug 25	1-0	2-1
Wrexham	v Bury	Aug 18	1-1	Aug 25	3-4	4-5
W.B.A.	v Plymouth	Aug 19	1-0	Aug 25	0-2	1-2

2nd Round

Arsenal	v Millwall	Sep 22	1-1	Oct 07	1-1	2-2
Blackpool	v Portsmouth	Sep 23	0-4	Oct 06	0-2	0-6
Bolton	v Wimbledon	Sep 22	1-3	Oct 06	1-0	2-3
Brighton	v Manchester U	Sep 23	1-1	Oct 07	0-1	1-2
Bristol C	v Sheffield U	Sep 22	2-1	Oct 07	1-4	3-5
Bury	v Charlton	Sep 22	0-0	Oct 07	1-0	1-0
Cambridge	v Stoke	Sep 22	2-2	Oct 07	2-1	4-3
Carlisle	v Norwich	Sep 22	2-2	Oct 07	0-2	2-4
Coventry	v Scarborough	Sep 23	2-0	Oct 07	0-3	2-3
Crystal Palace	v Lincoln	Sep 22	3-1	Oct 06	1-1	4-2
Exeter	v Oldham	Sep 22	0-1	Oct 07	0-0	0-1
Gillingham	v Southampton	Sep 23	0-0	Oct 07	0-3	0-3
Huddersfield	v Blackburn	Sep 23	1-1	Oct 06	3-4	4-5
Leeds	v Scunthorpe	Sep 22	4-1	Oct 27	2-2	6-3
Leicester	v Peterborough	Sep 23	2-0	Oct 06	1-2	3-2
Liverpool	v Chesterfield	Sep 22	4-4	Oct 06	4-1	8-5
Luton	v Plymouth	Sep 23	2-2	Oct 06	2-3	4-5
Manchester C	v Bristol R	Sep 23	0-0	Oct 07	2-1	2-1
Newcastle	v Middlesbrough	Sep 23	0-0	Oct 07	3-1	3-1
Notts Co	v Wolverhampton	Sep 22	3-2	Oct 07	1-0	4-2

Oxford v Aston Villa Sep 23 1-2 Oct 07 1-2 2-4
Q.P.R. v Grimsby Sep 23 2-1 Oct 06 1-2 3-3
Rotherham v Everton Sep 23 1-0 Oct 07 0-3 1-3
Sheffield W v Hartlepool Sep 23 3-0 Oct 06 2-2 5-2
Southend v Derby Sep 23 1-0 Oct 07 0-7 1-7
Stockport v Nottingham F Sep 23 2-3 Oct 07 1-2 3-5
Torquay v Swindon Sep 23 0-6 Oct 06 2-3 2-9
Tottenham v Brentford Sep 21 3-1 Oct 07 4-2 7-3
Walsall v Chelsea Sep 23 0-3 Oct 07 0-1 0-4
Watford v Reading Sep 22 2-2 Oct 07 2-0 4-2
West Ham v Crewe Sep 23 0-0 Oct 07 0-2 0-2
Wigan v Ipswich Sep 22 2-2 Oct 06 0-4 2-6

3rd Round
Oct 28 Aston Villa 1 Manchester U 0
Oct 28 Blackburn 2 Norwich 0
Oct 27 Bury 0 Q.P.R. 2
Oct 28 Chelsea 2 Newcastle 1
Oct 28 Crewe 0 Nottingham F 1
Oct 28 Derby 1 Arsenal 1
Oct 28 Everton 0 Wimbledon 0
Oct 28 Manchester C 0 Tottenham 1
Oct 27 Notts Co 2 Cambridge 3
Oct 27 Plymouth 3 Scarborough 3
Oct 27 Portsmouth 0 Ipswich 1
Oct 28 Sheffield U 0 Liverpool 0
Oct 27 Sheffield W 7 Leicester 1
Oct 28 Southampton 0 Crystal Palace 2
Oct 27 Swindon 0 Oldham 1
Nov 10 Watford 2 Leeds 1

Replays
Nov 10 Wimbledon 0 Everton 1
Nov 11 Liverpool 3 Sheffield U 0
Nov 11 Scarborough 2 Plymouth 1
Dec 01 Arsenal 2 Derby 1

4th Round
Dec 02 Aston Villa 2 Ipswich 2
Dec 09 Blackburn 6 Watford 1
Dec 01 Cambridge 1 Oldham 0
Dec 02 Everton 2 Chelsea 2
Dec 01 Liverpool 1 Crystal Palace 1
Dec 02 Nottingham F 2 Tottenham 0
Jan 06 Scarborough 0 Arsenal 1
Dec 02 Sheffield W 4 Q.P.R. 0

Replays
Dec 15 Ipswich 1 Aston Villa 0
Dec 16 Chelsea 1 Everton 0
Dec 16 Crystal Palace 2 Liverpool 1

5th Round
Jan 06 Blackburn 3 Cambridge 2
Jan 06 Crystal Palace 3 Chelsea 1
Jan 12 Arsenal 2 Nottingham F 0
Jan 19 Ipswich 1 Sheffield W 1

Replays
Feb 03 Sheffield W 1 Ipswich 0

Semi-finals
Feb 10 Blackburn 2 Sheffield W 4
Mar 14 Sheffield W 2 Blackburn 1
Aggregate 6-3
Feb 07 Crystal Palace 1 Arsenal 3
Mar 10 Arsenal 2 Crystal Palace 0
Aggregate 1-5

Final
Apr 18 Arsenal 2 Sheffield W 1
played at Wembley

Season 1993-94

1st Round
Birmingham v Plymouth Aug 17 3-0 Aug 24 0-2 3-2
Bolton v Bury Aug 17 0-2 Aug 24 2-0 2-2
Bournemouth v Cardiff Aug 17 3-1 Aug 24 1-1 4-2
Brentford v Watford Aug 17 2-2 Aug 24 1-3 3-5
Bristol R v W.B.A. Aug 18 1-4 Aug 25 0-0 1-4
Cambridge v Luton Aug 17 1-0 Aug 24 1-0 2-0
Chesterfield v Carlisle Aug 17 3-1 Aug 24 1-1 4-2
Crewe v Wrexham Aug 17 0-1 Aug 24 3-3 3-4
Darlington v Bradford C Aug 17 1-5 Aug 25 0-6 1-11
Doncaster v Blackpool Aug 16 0-1 Aug 24 3-3 3-4
Fulham v Colchester Aug 17 2-1 Aug 24 2-1 4-2
Gillingham v Brighton Aug 17 1-0 Aug 25 0-2 1-2
Hereford v Torquay Aug 17 0-2 Aug 24 2-0 2-2
Huddersfield v Scarborough Aug 17 0-0 Aug 24 3-0 3-0
Leyton O v Wycombe Aug 17 0-2 Aug 24 0-1 0-3
Notts Co v Hull Aug 17 2-0 Aug 24 1-3 3-3
Port Vale v Lincoln Aug 17 2-2 Aug 24 0-0 2-2
Preston v Burnley Aug 17 1-2 Aug 25 1-4 2-6
Reading v Northampton Aug 18 3-0 Sep 07 2-0 5-0
Rochdale v York Aug 17 2-0 Aug 24 0-0 2-0
Shrewsbury v Scunthorpe Aug 17 1-0 Aug 24 1-1 2-1
Southend v Barnet Aug 18 0-2 Aug 24 1-1 1-3
Stockport v Hartlepool Aug 17 1-1 Aug 24 1-2 2-3
Stoke v Mansfield Aug 18 2-2 Aug 24 3-1 5-3
Sunderland v Chester Aug 17 3-1 Aug 24 0-0 3-1
Swansea v Bristol C Aug 17 0-1 Aug 24 2-0 2-1
Walsall v Exeter Aug 17 0-0 Aug 25 1-2 1-2
Wigan v Rotherham Aug 17 0-1 Aug 24 2-4 2-5

2nd Round
Barnet v Q.P.R. Sep 21 1-2 Oct 06 0-4 1-6
Barnsley v Peterborough Sep 21 1-1 Oct 05 1-3 2-4
Birmingham v Aston Villa Sep 21 0-1 Oct 06 0-1 0-2
Blackburn v Bournemouth Sep 21 1-0 Oct 05 0-0 1-0
Blackpool v Sheffield U Sep 21 3-0 Oct 05 0-2 3-2
Bolton v Sheffield W Sep 21 1-1 Oct 06 0-1 1-2
Bradford C v Norwich Sep 22 2-1 Oct 06 0-3 2-4
Burnley v Tottenham Sep 22 0-0 Oct 06 1-3 1-3
Coventry v Wycombe Sep 22 3-0 Oct 05 2-4 5-4
Crystal P v Charlton Sep 21 3-1 Oct 05 1-0 4-1
Exeter v Derby Sep 22 1-3 Oct 06 0-2 1-5
Fulham v Liverpool Sep 22 1-3 Oct 05 0-5 1-8
Grimsby v Hartlepool Sep 21 3-0 Oct 05 2-0 5-0
Hereford v Wimbledon Sep 22 0-1 Oct 05 1-4 1-5
Huddersfield v Arsenal Sep 21 0-5 Oct 05 1-1 1-6
Ipswich v Cambridge Sep 21 2-1 Oct 05 2-0 4-1
Lincoln v Everton Sep 21 3-4 Oct 06 2-4 5-8
Manchester C v Reading Sep 22 1-1 Oct 06 2-1 3-2
Middlesbrough v Brighton Sep 21 5-0 Oct 06 3-1 8-1
Newcastle v Notts Co Sep 22 4-1 Oct 05 7-1 11-2
Rochdale v Leicester Sep 21 1-6 Oct 06 1-2 2-8
Rotherham v Portsmouth Sep 21 0-0 Oct 05 0-5 0-5
Southampton v Shrewsbury Sep 22 1-0 Oct 06 0-2 1-2
Stoke v Manchester U Sep 22 2-1 Oct 06 0-2 2-3
Sunderland v Leeds Sep 21 2-1 Oct 06 2-1 4-2
Swansea v Oldham Sep 21 2-1 Oct 06 0-2 2-3
Swindon v Wolverhampton Sep 22 2-0 Oct 05 1-2 3-2
Tranmere v Oxford Sep 21 5-1 Oct 05 1-1 6-2
Watford v Millwall Sep 21 0-0 Oct 06 3-4 3-4
West Ham v Chesterfield Sep 22 5-1 Oct 05 2-0 7-1
Wrexham v Nottingham F Sep 21 3-3 Oct 06 1-3 4-6
W.B.A. v Chelsea Sep 22 1-1 Oct 06 1-2 2-3

3rd Round
Oct 26 Arsenal 1 Norwich 1
Oct 26 Blackburn 0 Shrewsbury 0
Oct 26 Blackpool 2 Peterborough 2
Oct 27 Derby 0 Tottenham 1
Oct 26 Everton 2 Crystal P 2
Oct 27 Liverpool 3 Ipswich 2
Oct 26 Manchester C 1 Chelsea 0
Oct 27 Manchester U 5 Leicester 1
Oct 27 Middlesbrough 1 Sheffield W 1
Oct 27 Nottingham F 2 West Ham 1
Oct 26 Oldham 2 Coventry 0
Oct 26 Portsmouth 2 Swindon 0
Oct 27 Q.P.R. 3 Millwall 0
Oct 26 Sunderland 1 Aston Villa 4
Oct 26 Tranmere 4 Grimsby 1
Oct 27 Wimbledon 2 Newcastle 1

Replays
Nov 09 Peterborough 2 Blackpool 1
Nov 09 Shrewsbury 3 Blackburn 4
Nov 10 Crystal P 1 Everton 4
Nov 10 Norwich 0 Arsenal 3
Nov 10 Sheffield W 2 Middlesbrough 1

4th Round
Nov 30 Arsenal 0 Aston Villa 1
Nov 30 Everton 0 Manchester U 2
Dec 01 Liverpool 1 Wimbledon 1
Dec 01 Nottingham F 0 Manchester C 0
Nov 30 Peterborough 0 Portsmouth 0
Dec 01 Q.P.R. 1 Sheffield W 2
Dec 01 Tottenham 1 Blackburn 0
Nov 30 Tranmere 3 Oldham 0

Replays
Dec 14 Wimbledon 2 Liverpool 2
Penalties 4-3
Dec 15 Manchester C 1 Nottingham F 2
Dec 15 Portsmouth 1 Peterborough 0

5th Round
Jan 12 Manchester U 2 Portsmouth 2
Jan 26 Nottingham F 1 Tranmere 1
Jan 12 Tottenham 1 Aston Villa 2
Jan 11 Wimbledon 1 Sheffield W 2

Replays
Jan 26 Portsmouth 0 Manchester U 1
Jan 29 Tranmere 2 Nottingham F 0

Semi-finals
Feb 13 Manchester U 1 Sheffield W 0
Mar 02 Sheffield W 1 Manchester U 4
Aggregate 1-5
Feb 16 Tranmere 3 Aston Villa 1
Feb 27 Aston Villa 3 Tranmere 1
Penalties 5-4

Final
Mar 27 Aston Villa 3 Manchester U 1
played at Wembley

Season 1994-95

1st Round
Barnet v Leyton O Aug 16 4-0 Aug 23 1-1 5-1
Blackpool v Chesterfield Aug 16 1-2 Aug 23 2-4 3-6
Bournemouth v Northampton Aug 16 2-0 Sep 06 1-0 3-0
Bradford C v Grimsby Aug 16 2-1 Aug 23 2-1 4-2
Brighton v Wycombe Aug 17 2-1 Aug 23 3-1 5-2
Bristol R v Port Vale Aug 17 1-3 Aug 23 1-1 2-4
Burnley v York Aug 16 1-0 Aug 23 2-2 3-2
Bury v Hartlepool Aug 16 2-0 Aug 23 1-5 3-5
Cardiff v Torquay Aug 16 1-0 Aug 23 2-4 3-4
Colchester v Brentford Aug 16 0-2 Aug 23 0-2 0-4
Crewe v Wigan Aug 16 2-1 Aug 23 0-3 2-4
Darlington v Barnsley Aug 17 2-2 Aug 23 0-0 2-2
Doncaster v Wrexham Aug 15 2-4 Aug 23 1-1 3-5
Exeter v Swansea Aug 17 2-2 Aug 23 0-2 2-4
Gillingham v Reading Aug 16 0-1 Aug 23 0-3 0-4
Hereford v W.B.A. Aug 16 0-0 Sep 07 1-0 1-0
Hull v Scarborough Aug 16 2-1 Aug 23 0-2 2-3
Lincoln v Chester Aug 16 2-0 Aug 23 3-2 5-2
Luton v Fulham Aug 16 1-1 Aug 23 1-1 2-2
Oxford v Peterborough Aug 16 3-1 Aug 23 1-0 4-1
Portsmouth v Cambridge Aug 17 2-0 Aug 23 3-2 5-2
Preston v Stockport Aug 17 1-1 Aug 23 1-4 2-5
Rochdale v Mansfield Aug 16 1-2 Aug 23 0-1 1-3
Rotherham v Carlisle Aug 16 1-0 Aug 23 1-3 2-3
Scunthorpe v Huddersfield Aug 16 2-1 Aug 23 0-3 2-4
Shrewsbury v Birmingham Aug 16 2-1 Aug 23 0-2 2-3
Southend v Watford Aug 16 0-0 Aug 23 0-1 0-1
Walsall v Plymouth Aug 16 4-0 Aug 23 1-2 5-2

2nd Round
Aston Villa v Wigan Sep 21 5-0 Oct 05 3-0 8-0
Barnet v Manchester C Sep 20 1-0 Oct 05 1-4 2-4
Blackburn v Birmingham Sep 20 2-0 Oct 04 1-1 3-1
Brighton v Leicester Sep 21 1-0 Oct 05 2-0 3-0
Bristol C v Notts Co Sep 20 0-1 Sep 27 0-3 0-4
Carlisle v Q.P.R. Sep 20 0-1 Oct 05 0-2 0-3
Chelsea v Bournemouth Sep 21 1-0 Oct 04 1-0 2-0
Chesterfield v Wolverhampton Sep 20 1-3 Sep 27 1-1 2-4
Everton v Portsmouth Sep 20 2-3 Oct 05 1-1 3-4
Fulham v Stoke Sep 20 3-2 Sep 28 0-1 3-3
Hartlepool v Arsenal Sep 21 0-5 Oct 05 0-2 0-7
Huddersfield v Southampton Sep 20 0-1 Oct 05 0-4 0-5
Ipswich v Bolton Sep 21 0-3 Oct 05 0-1 0-4
Leeds v Mansfield Sep 21 0-1 Oct 04 0-0 0-1
Lincoln v Crystal Palace Sep 20 1-0 Oct 04 0-3 1-3
Liverpool v Burnley Sep 21 2-0 Oct 05 4-1 6-1
Millwall v Sunderland Sep 21 2-1 Oct 04 1-1 3-2
Newcastle v Barnsley Sep 21 2-1 Oct 05 1-0 3-1
Norwich v Swansea Sep 21 3-0 Oct 04 0-1 3-1
Nottingham F v Hereford Sep 21 2-1 Oct 04 0-0 2-1
Oxford v Oldham Sep 20 1-1 Oct 04 0-1 1-2
Port Vale v Manchester U Sep 21 1-2 Oct 05 0-2 1-4
Reading v Derby Sep 20 3-1 Sep 28 0-2 3-3
Scarborough v Middlesbrough Sep 20 1-4 Sep 27 1-4 2-8
Sheffield W v Bradford C Sep 21 2-1 Oct 04 1-1 3-2
Stockport v Sheffield U Sep 20 1-5 Sep 27 0-1 1-6
Swindon v Charlton Sep 21 1-3 Sep 27 4-1 5-4
Tranmere v Brentford Sep 20 1-0 Sep 27 0-0 1-0
Walsall v West Ham Sep 20 2-1 Oct 05 0-2 2-3
Watford v Tottenham Sep 21 3-6 Oct 04 3-2 6-8
Wimbledon v Torquay Sep 20 2-0 Oct 05 1-0 3-0
Wrexham v Coventry Sep 20 1-2 Oct 05 2-3 3-5

3rd Round
Oct 26 Aston Villa 1 Middlesbrough 0
Oct 26 Blackburn 2 Coventry 0
Oct 26 Brighton 1 Swindon 1
Oct 25 Liverpool 2 Stoke 1
Oct 25 Mansfield 0 Millwall 2
Oct 26 Newcastle 2 Manchester U 0
Oct 26 Notts Co 3 Tottenham 0
Oct 26 Oldham 0 Arsenal 0
Oct 26 Portsmouth 0 Derby 1
Oct 25 Q.P.R. 3 Manchester C 4
Oct 25 Sheffield U 1 Bolton 2
Oct 26 Sheffield W 1 Southampton 0
Oct 26 Tranmere 1 Norwich 1
Oct 26 West Ham 1 Chelsea 0
Oct 25 Wimbledon 0 Crystal Palace 1
Oct 26 Wolverhampton 2 Nottingham F 3

Replays

Nov 09	Arsenal	2	Oldham	0
Nov 09	Norwich	4	Tranmere	2
Nov 09	Swindon	4	Brighton	1

4th Round

Nov 30	Arsenal	2	Sheffield W	0
Nov 30	Blackburn	1	Liverpool	3
Nov 30	Crystal Palace	4	Aston Villa	1
Nov 30	Manchester C	1	Newcastle	1
Nov 30	Norwich	1	Notts Co	0
Nov 30	Nottingham F	0	Millwall	2
Nov 30	Swindon	2	Derby	1
Nov 30	West Ham	1	Bolton	3

Replays

Dec 21	Newcastle	0	Manchester C	2

5th Round

Jan 11	Bolton	1	Norwich	0
Jan 11	Crystal Palace	4	Manchester C	0
Jan 11	Liverpool	1	Arsenal	0
Jan 11	Swindon	3	Millwall	1

Semi-finals

Feb 15	Liverpool	1	Crystal Palace	0
Mar 08	Crystal Palace	0	Liverpool	1
	Aggregate 0-2			
Feb 12	Swindon	2	Bolton	1
Mar 08	Bolton	3	Swindon	1
	Aggregate 4-3			

Final

Apr 02	Bolton	1	Liverpool	2
	played at Wembley			

Season 1995-96

1st Round

Barnet	v Charlton	Aug 15	0-0	Aug 22	0-2	0-2
Birmingham	v Plymouth	Aug 15	1-0	Aug 22	2-1	3-1
Bradford C	v Blackpool	Aug 15	2-1	Aug 22	3-2	5-3
Cambridge	v Swindon	Aug 15	2-1	Aug 23	0-2	2-3
Chester	v Wigan	Aug 15	4-1	Aug 22	3-1	7-2
Chesterfield	v Bury	Aug 15	0-1	Sep 05	1-2	1-3
Colchester	v Bristol C	Aug 15	2-1	Aug 22	1-2	3-3
Crewe	v Darlington	Aug 23	4-0	Sep 05	1-1	5-1
Doncaster	v Shrewsbury	Aug 14	1-1	Aug 22	0-0	1-1
Fulham	v Brighton	Aug 15	3-0	Aug 22	2-0	5-0
Gillingham	v Bristol R	Aug 15	1-1	Aug 23	2-4	3-5
Hereford	v Oxford	Aug 15	0-2	Aug 22	2-3	2-5
Huddersfield	v Port Vale	Aug 15	1-2	Aug 22	3-1	4-3
Hull	v Carlisle	Aug 15	1-2	Aug 22	4-2	5-4
Luton	v Bournemouth	Aug 15	1-1	Aug 22	1-2	2-3
Mansfield	v Burnley	Aug 15	0-1	Aug 22	1-3	1-4
Notts Co	v Lincoln	Aug 15	2-0	Aug 22	2-0	4-0
Portsmouth	v Cardiff	Aug 16	0-2	Aug 22	0-1	0-3
Preston	v Sunderland	Aug 15	1-1	Aug 23	2-3	3-4
Rochdale	v York	Aug 15	2-1	Aug 22	1-5	3-6
Scarborough	v Hartlepool	Aug 15	1-0	Aug 22	0-1	1-1
Scunthorpe	v Rotherham	Aug 15	4-1	Aug 22	0-5	4-6
Stockport	v Wrexham	Aug 15	1-0	Sep 05	2-2	3-2
Swansea	v Peterborough	Aug 15	4-1	Aug 22	0-3	4-4
Torquay	v Exeter	Aug 15	0-0	Aug 23	1-1	1-1
Walsall	v Brentford	Aug 15	2-2	Aug 22	2-3	4-5
Wycombe	v Leyton O	Aug 15	3-0	Aug 22	0-2	3-2
W.B.A.	v Northampton	Aug 15	1-1	Aug 22	4-2	5-3

2nd Round

Aston Villa	v Peterborough	Sep 20	6-0	Oct 03	1-1	7-1
Birmingham	v Grimsby	Sep 20	3-1	Oct 03	1-1	4-2
Bolton	v Brentford	Sep 19	1-0	Oct 03	3-2	4-2
Bradford C	v Nottingham F	Sep 19	3-2	Oct 04	2-2	5-4
Bristol C	v Newcastle	Sep 19	0-5	Oct 04	1-3	1-8
Bristol R	v West Ham	Sep 20	0-1	Oct 04	0-3	0-4
Cardiff	v Southampton	Sep 19	0-3	Oct 04	1-2	1-5
Coventry	v Hull	Sep 20	2-0	Oct 04	1-0	3-0
Crewe	v Sheffield W	*Sep* 19	2-2	Oct 04	2-5	4-7
Hartlepool	v Arsenal	Sep 19	0-3	Oct 03	0-5	0-8
Huddersfield	v Barnsley	Sep 19	2-0	Oct 03	0-4	2-4
Leeds	v Notts Co	Sep 19	0-0	Oct 03	3-2	3-2
Leicester	v Burnley	Sep 20	2-1	Oct 03	2-0	4-1
Liverpool	v Sunderland	Sep 20	2-0	Oct 04	1-0	3-0
Manchester U	v York	Sep 20	0-3	Oct 03	3-1	3-4
Middlesbrough	v Rotherham	Sep 20	2-1	Oct 03	1-0	3-1
Millwall	v Everton	Sep 20	0-0	Oct 04	4-2	4-2
Norwich	v Torquay	Sep 20	6-1	Oct 04	3-2	9-3
Oxford	v Q.P.R.	Sep 19	1-1	Oct 03	1-2	2-3
Reading	v W.B.A	Sep 20	1-1	Oct 03	4-2	5-3
Sheffield U	v Bury	Sep 20	2-1	Oct 03	2-4	4-5
Shrewsbury	v Derby	Sep 19	1-3	Oct 04	1-1	2-4
Southend	v Crystal Palace	Sep 19	2-2	Oct 03	0-2	2-4
Stockport	v Ipswich	Sep 19	1-1	Oct 03	2-1	3-2
Stoke	v Chelsea	Sep 20	0-0	Oct 04	1-0	1-0
Swindon	v Blackburn	Sep 20	2-3	Oct 04	0-2	2-5
Tottenham	v Chester	Sep 20	4-0	Oct 04	3-1	7-1
Tranmere	v Oldham	Sep 19	1-0	Oct 04	3-1	4-1
Watford	v Bournemouth	Sep 19	1-1	Oct 03	1-1	2-2
Wimbledon	v Charlton	Sep 19	4-5	Oct 03	3-3	7-8
Wolverhampton	v Fulham	Sep 20	2-0	Oct 03	5-1	7-1
Wycombe	v Manchester C	Sep 19	0-0	Oct 04	0-4	0-4

3rd Round

Oct 25	Aston Villa	2	Stockport	0
Oct 24	Barnsley	0	Arsenal	3
Oct 24	Birmingham	1	Tranmere	1
Oct 24	Bolton	0	Leicester	0
Oct 25	Crystal Palace	3	Middlesbrough	2
Oct 25	Coventry	3	Tottenham	2
Oct 25	Derby	0	Leeds	1
Oct 25	Liverpool	4	Manchester C	0
Oct 25	Millwall	0	Sheffield W	2
Oct 25	Norwich	0	Bradford C	0
Oct 25	Q.P.R.	3	York	1
Nov 07	Reading	2	Bury	1
Oct 25	Southampton	2	West Ham	1
Oct 25	Stoke	0	Newcastle	4
Oct 24	Watford	1	Blackburn	1
Oct 25	Wolverhampton	0	Charlton	0

Replays

Nov 07	Bradford C	3	Norwich	5
Nov 08	Charlton	1	Wolverhampton	2
Nov 08	Leicester	2	Bolton	3
Nov 08	Middlesbrough	2	Crystal Palace	0
Nov 08	Tranmere	1	Birmingham	3

4th Round

Nov 29	Arsenal	2	Sheffield W	1
Nov 29	Aston Villa	1	Q.P.R.	0
Nov 29	Leeds	2	Blackburn	1
Nov 29	Liverpool	0	Newcastle	1
Nov 29	Middlesbrough	0	Birmingham	0
Nov 29	Norwich	0	Bolton	0
Nov 28	Reading	2	Southampton	1
Nov 29	Wolverhampton	2	Coventry	1

Replays

Dec 20	Birmingham	2	Middlesbrough	0
Dec 20	Bolton	0	Norwich	0
	Penalties 2-3			

5th Round

Jan 10	Arsenal	2	Newcastle	0
Jan 10	Aston Villa	1	Wolverhampton	0
Jan 10	Leeds	2	Reading	1
Jan 10	Norwich	1	Birmingham	1

Replay

Jan 24	Birmingham	2	Norwich	1

Semi-finals

Feb 14	Arsenal	2	Aston Villa	2
Feb 21	Aston Villa	0	Arsenal	0
	Aggregate 2-2			
Feb 11	Birmingham	1	Leeds	2
Feb 25	Leeds	3	Birmingham	0
	Aggregate 5-1			

Final

Mar 24	Aston Villa	3	Leeds	0
	played at Wembley			

Season 1996-97

1st Round

Brentford	v Plymouth	Aug 20	1-0	Sep 03	0-0	1-0
Brighton	v Birmingham	Aug 21	0-1	Sep 04	0-2	0-3
Cardiff	v Northampton	Aug 20	1-0	Sep 03	0-2	1-2
Carlisle	v Chester	Aug 20	1-0	Sep 03	3-1	4-1
Colchester	v W.B.A.	Aug 20	2-3	Sep 03	3-1	5-4
Darlington	v Rotherham	Aug 20	1-0	Sep 03	1-0	2-0
Doncaster	v York	Aug 20	1-1	Sep 03	0-2	1-3
Exeter	v Barnet	Aug 20	0-4	Sep 03	0-2	0-6
Hartlepool	v Lincoln	Aug 20	2-2	Sep 03	2-3	4-5
Hereford	v Cambridge	Aug 20	3-0	Sep 03	1-1	4-1
Huddersfield	v Wrexham	Aug 20	3-0	Sep 03	2-1	5-1
Hull	v Scarborough	Aug 20	2-2	Sep 03	2-3	4-5
Ipswich	v Bournemouth	Aug 20	2-1	Sep 03	3-0	5-1
Luton	v Bristol R	Aug 20	3-0	Sep 04	1-2	4-2
Mansfield	v Burnley	Aug 20	0-3	Sep 03	0-2	0-5
Millwall	v Peterborough	Aug 21	1-0	Sep 03	0-2	1-2
Notts Co	v Bury	Aug 20	1-1	Sep 03	0-1	1-2
Oldham	v Grimsby	Aug 20	0-1	Sep 03	1-0	1-1
Oxford	v Norwich	Aug 20	1-1	Sep 04	3-2	4-3
Port Vale	v Crewe	Aug 20	1-0	Sep 03	5-1	6-1
Portsmouth	v Leyton O	Aug 20	2-0	Sep 04	0-1	2-1
Reading	v Wycombe	Aug 20	1-1	Sep 03	0-2	1-3
Rochdale	v Barnsley	Aug 20	2-1	Sep 03	0-2	2-3
Scunthorpe	v Blackpool	Aug 20	2-1	Sep 03	0-2	2-3
Sheffield U	v Bradford C	Aug 20	3-0	Sep 03	2-1	5-1
Shrewsbury	v Tranmere	Aug 21	0-2	Sep 03	1-1	1-3
Southend	v Fulham	Aug 20	0-2	Sep 03	2-1	2-3
Stockport	v Chesterfield	Aug 20	2-1	Sep 03	2-1	4-2
Swansea	v Gillingham	Aug 20	0-1	Sep 03	0-2	0-3
Swindon	v Wolverhampton	Aug 20	2-0	Sep 04	0-1	2-1
Torquay	v Bristol C	Aug 20	3-3	Sep 03	0-1	3-4
Walsall	v Watford	Aug 20	1-0	Sep 03	0-2	1-2
Wigan	v Preston	Aug 20	2-3	Sep 03	4-4	6-7

2nd Round

Barnet	v West Ham	Sep 18	1-1	Sep 25	0-1	1-2
Barnsley	v Gillingham	Sep 17	1-1	Sep 24	0-1	1-2
Blackpool	v Chelsea	Sep 18	1-4	Sep 25	3-1	4-5
Brentford	v Blackburn	Sep 17	1-2	Sep 24	0-2	1-4
Bristol C	v Bolton	Sep 18	0-0	Sep 24	1-3	1-3
Bury	v Crystal Palace	Sep 17	1-3	Sep 24	0-4	1-7
Charlton	v Burnley	Sep 17	4-1	Sep 24	2-1	6-2
Coventry	v Birmingham	Sep 18	1-1	Sep 24	1-0	2-1
Everton	v York	Sep 18	1-1	Sep 24	2-3	3-4
Fulham	v Ipswich	Sep 17	1-1	Sep 24	2-4	3-5
Huddersfield	v Colchester	Sep 17	1-1	Sep 24	2-0	3-1
Leeds	v Darlington	Sep 18	2-2	Sep 24	2-0	4-2
Lincoln	v Manchester C	Sep 17	4-1	Sep 24	1-0	5-1
Luton	v Derby	Sep 17	1-0	Sep 25	2-2	3-2
Middlesbrough	v Hereford	Sep 18	7-0	Sep 24	3-0	10-0
Nottingham F	v Wycombe	Sep 18	1-0	Sep 24	1-1	2-1
Oldham	v Tranmere	Sep 17	2-2	Sep 24	1-0	3-2
Port Vale	v Carlisle	Sep 17	1-0	Sep 24	2-2	3-2
Preston	v Tottenham	Sep 17	1-1	Sep 25	0-3	1-4
Scarborough	v Leicester	Sep 17	0-2	Sep 25	1-2	1-4
Sheffield W	v Oxford	Sep 18	1-1	Sep 24	0-1	1-2
Southampton	v Peterborough	Sep 18	2-0	Sep 25	4-1	6-1
Stockport	v Sheffield U	Sep 17	2-1	Sep 24	5-2	7-3
Stoke	v Northampton	Sep 18	1-0	Sep 24	2-1	3-1
Swindon	v Q.P.R.	Sep 18	1-2	Sep 25	3-1	4-3
Watford	v Sunderland	Sep 17	0-2	Sep 24	0-1	0-3
Wimbledon	v Portsmouth	Sep 18	1-0	Sep 25	1-1	2-1

3rd Round

Oct 22	Blackburn	0	Stockport	1
Oct 22	Bolton	2	Chelsea	1
Oct 23	Charlton	1	Liverpool	1
Oct 22	Gillingham	2	Coventry	2
Oct 22	Ipswich	4	Crystal Palace	1
Oct 23	Leeds	1	Aston Villa	2
Oct 23	Manchester U	2	Swindon	1
Oct 23	Middlesbrough	5	Huddersfield	1
Oct 23	Newcastle	1	Oldham	0
Oct 22	Port Vale	0	Oxford	0
Oct 23	Southampton	2	Lincoln	2
Oct 23	Stoke	1	Arsenal	1
Oct 23	Tottenham	2	Sunderland	1
Oct 23	West Ham	4	Nottingham F	1
Oct 22	Wimbledon	1	Luton	1
Oct 22	York	0	Leicester	2

Replays

Nov 05	Oxford	2	Port Vale	0
Nov 12	Lincoln	1	Southampton	3
Nov 12	Luton	1	Wimbledon	2
Nov 13	Arsenal	5	Stoke	2
Nov 13	Coventry	0	Gillingham	1
Nov 13	Liverpool	4	Charlton	1

4th Round

Nov 27	Bolton	6	Tottenham	1
Nov 26	Ipswich	1	Gillingham	0
Nov 27	Leicester	2	Manchester U	0
Nov 27	Liverpool	4	Arsenal	2
Nov 27	Middlesbrough	3	Newcastle	1
Nov 26	Oxford	1	Southampton	1
Nov 27	West Ham	1	Stockport	1
Nov 26	Wimbledon	1	Aston Villa	0

Replays

Dec 18	Southampton	3	Oxford	2
Dec 18	Stockport	2	West Ham	1

5th Round

Jan 08	Bolton	0	Wimbledon	2
Jan 21	Ipswich	0	Leicester	1
Jan 08	Middlesbrough	2	Liverpool	1
Jan 22	Stockport	2	Southampton	2

Replay

Jan 29	Southampton	1	Stockport	2

Semi-finals

Feb 18	Leicester	0	Wimbledon	0
Mar 11	Wimbledon	1	Leicester	1
	Aggregate 1-1			
Feb 26	Stockport	0	Middlesbrough	2
Mar 12	Middlesbrough	0	Stockport	1
	Aggregate 2-1			

Final

Apr 06	Leicester	1	Middlesbrough	1
	played at Wembley			

Replay

Apr 16	Leicester	1	Middlesbrough	0
	played at Wembley			

SEASON 1997-98

1st Round

Blackpool	v Manchester C	Aug 12	1-0	Aug 26	0-1	1-1
Bournemouth	v Torquay	Aug 12	0-1	Aug 26	1-1	1-2
Brentford	v Shrewsbury	Aug 12	1-1	Aug 26	5-3	6-4
Brighton	v Leyton O	Aug 13	1-1	Aug 26	1-3	2-4
Bristol C	v Bristol R	Aug 12	0-0	Aug 26	2-1	2-1
Cambridge	v W.B.A.	Aug 12	1-1	Aug 27	1-2	2-3
Cardiff	v Southend	Aug 12	1-1	Aug 26	1-3	2-4
Charlton	v Ipswich	Aug 13	0-1	Aug 26	1-3	1-4
Chester	v Carlisle	Aug 12	1-2	Aug 26	0-3	1-5
Colchester	v Luton	Aug 12	0-1	Aug 26	1-1	1-2
Crewe	v Bury	Aug 12	2-3	Aug 26	3-3	5-6
Darlington	v Notts Co	Aug 12	1-1	Aug 26	1-2	2-3
Doncaster	v Nottingham F	Aug 11	0-8	Aug 27	1-2	1-10
Gillingham	v Birmingham	Aug 12	0-1	Aug 26	0-3	0-4
Huddersfield	v Bradford C	Aug 12	2-1	Aug 26	1-1	3-2
Lincoln	v Burnley	Aug 12	1-1	Aug 26	1-2	2-3
Macclesfield	v Hull	Aug 12	0-0	Aug 26	1-2	1-2
Mansfield	v Stockport	Aug 12	4-2	Aug 26	3-6	7-8
Northampton	v Millwall	Aug 12	2-1	Aug 27	1-2	3-3
Norwich	v Barnet	Aug 12	2-1	Aug 26	1-3	3-4
Oldham	v Grimsby	Aug 12	1-0	Aug 26	0-5	1-5
Oxford	v Plymouth	Aug 12	2-0	Aug 26	5-3	7-3
Peterborough	v Portsmouth	Aug 11	2-2	Aug 26	2-1	4-3
Port Vale	v York	Aug 12	1-2	Aug 26	1-1	2-3
Q.P.R.	v Wolverhampton	Aug 12	0-2	Aug 27	2-1	2-3
Reading	v Swansea	Aug 12	2-0	Aug 26	1-1	3-1
Rochdale	v Stoke	Aug 12	1-3	Aug 27	1-1	2-4
Rotherham	v Preston	Aug 12	1-3	Aug 26	0-2	1-5
Scarborough	v Scunthorpe	Aug 12	0-2	Aug 26	1-2	1-4
Swindon	v Watford	Aug 13	0-2	Aug 26	1-1	1-3
Tranmere	v Hartlepool	Aug 12	3-1	Aug 26	1-2	4-3
Walsall	v Exeter	Aug 12	2-0	Aug 26	1-0	3-0
Wigan	v Chesterfield	Aug 12	1-2	Aug 26	0-1	1-3
Wrexham	v Sheffield U	Aug 12	1-1	Aug 26	1-3	2-4
Wycombe	v Fulham	Aug 12	1-2	Aug 26	4-4	5-6

2nd Round

Birmingham	v Stockport	Sep 17	4-1	Sep 23	1-2	5-3
Blackburn	v Preston	Sep 17	6-0	Sep 30	0-1	6-1
Blackpool	v Coventry	Sep 16	1-0	Oct 01	1-3	2-3
Burnley	v Stoke	Sep 16	0-4	Sep 24	0-2	0-6
Chesterfield	v Barnsley	Sep 16	1-2	Sep 30	1-4	2-6
Fulham	v Wolverhampton	Sep 16	0-1	Sep 24	0-1	0-2
Grimsby	v Sheffield W	Sep 17	2-0	Oct 01	2-3	4-3
Huddersfield	v West Ham	Sep 16	1-0	Sep 29	0-3	1-3
Hull	v Crystal Palace	Sep 16	1-0	Sep 30	1-2	2-2
Ipswich	v Torquay	Sep 16	1-1	Sep 23	3-0	4-1
Leeds	v Bristol C	Sep 17	3-1	Sep 30	1-2	4-3
Leyton O	v Bolton	Sep 16	1-3	Sep 30	4-4	5-7
Luton	v W.B.A.	Sep 16	1-1	Sep 23	2-4	3-5
Middlesbrough	v Barnet	Sep 16	1-0	Sep 23	2-0	3-0
Nottingham F	v Walsall	Sep 17	0-1	Sep 24	2-2	2-3
Notts Co	v Tranmere	Sep 16	0-2	Sep 23	1-0	1-3
Oxford	v York	Sep 16	4-1	Sep 23	2-1	6-2
Reading	v Peterborough	Sep 16	0-0	Sep 23	2-0	2-0
Scunthorpe	v Everton	Sep 16	0-1	Oct 01	0-5	0-6
Southampton	v Brentford	Sep 17	3-1	Sep 30	2-0	5-1
Southend	v Derby	Sep 16	0-1	Oct 01	0-5	0-6
Sunderland	v Bury	Sep 16	2-1	Sep 23	2-1	4-2
Tottenham	v Carlisle	Sep 17	3-2	Sep 30	2-0	5-2
Watford	v Sheffield U	Sep 16	1-1	Sep 23	0-4	1-5
Wimbledon	v Millwall	Sep 16	5-1	Oct 01	4-1	9-2

3rd Round

Oct 14	Arsenal	4	Birmingham	1
Oct 14	Barnsley	1	Southampton	2
Oct 14	Bolton	2	Wimbledon	0
Oct 15	Chelsea	1	Blackburn	1
	Penalties 4-1			
Oct 15	Coventry	4	Everton	1
Oct 14	Grimsby	3	Leicester	1
Oct 14	Ipswich	2	Manchester U	0
Oct 15	Middlesbrough	2	Sunderland	0
Oct 15	Newcastle	2	Hull	0
Oct 14	Oxford	1	Tranmere	1
Oct 14	Reading	4	Wolverhampton	2
Oct 15	Stoke	1	Leeds	3
Oct 15	Tottenham	1	Derby	2
Oct 14	Walsall	2	Sheffield U	1
Oct 15	West Ham	3	Aston Villa	0
Oct 15	W.B.A.	0	Liverpool	2

4th Round

Nov 18	Arsenal	1	Coventry	0
Nov 19	Chelsea	2	Southampton	1
Nov 18	Derby	0	Newcastle	1
Nov 18	Leeds	2	Reading	3
Nov 18	Liverpool	3	Grimsby	0
Nov 18	Middlesbrough	2	Bolton	1
Nov 18	Oxford	1	Ipswich	2
Nov 19	West Ham	4	Walsall	1

5th Round

Jan 07	Ipswich	2	Chelsea	2
	Penalties 1-4			
Jan 07	Newcastle	0	Liverpool	2
Jan 06	Reading	0	Middlesbrough	1
Jan 06	West Ham	1	Arsenal	2

Semi-finals

Jan 28	Arsenal	2	Chelsea	1
Feb 18	Chelsea	3	Arsenal	1
	Aggregate 4-3			
Jan 27	Liverpool	2	Middlesbrough	1
Feb 18	Middlesbrough	2	Liverpool	0
	Aggregate 3-2			

Final

Mar 29	Chelsea	2	Middlesbrough	0
	played at Wembley			

SEASON 1998-99

1st Round

Barnet	v Wolverhampton	Aug 11	2-1	Aug 18	0-5	2-6
Birmingham	v Millwall	Aug 11	2-0	Aug 19	1-1	3-1
Blackpool	v Scunthorpe	Aug 11	1-0	Aug 18	1-1	2-1
Bolton	v Hartlepool	Aug 11	1-0	Aug 25	3-0	4-0
Bournemouth	v Colchester	Aug 11	2-0	Aug 18	2-3	4-3
Bradford C	v Lincoln	Aug 11	1-1	Aug 18	1-0	2-1
Bristol C	v Shrewsbury	Aug 11	4-0	Aug 18	3-4	7-4
Bury	v Burnley	Aug 11	1-1	Aug 18	4-1	5-2
Cambridge	v Watford	Aug 11	1-0	Aug 18	1-1	2-1
Exeter	v Ipswich	Aug 11	1-1	Aug 18	1-5	2-6
Fulham	v Cardiff	Aug 11	2-1	Aug 18	2-1	4-2
Grimsby	v Preston	Aug 12	0-0	Aug 18	0-0	0-0
Huddersfield	v Mansfield	Aug 11	3-2	Aug 18	1-1	4-3
Leyton O	v Bristol R	Aug 11	1-1	Aug 18	2-1	3-2
Luton	v Oxford	Aug 11	2-3	Aug 18	3-1	5-4
Macclesfield	v Stoke	Aug 11	3-1	Aug 19	0-1	3-2
Northampton	v Brighton	Aug 11	2-1	Aug 19	1-1	3-2
Notts Co	v Manchester C	Aug 11	0-2	Aug 19	1-7	1-9
Oldham	v Crewe	Aug 11	3-2	Aug 18	0-2	3-4
Peterborough	v Reading	Aug 11	1-1	Aug 26	0-2	1-3
Plymouth	v Portsmouth	Aug 11	1-3	Aug 18	2-3	3-6
Port Vale	v Chester	Aug 11	1-2	Aug 18	2-2	3-4
Rotherham	v Chesterfield	Aug 11	0-1	Aug 18	0-2	0-3
Scarborough	v Barnsley	Aug 12	0-1	Aug 18	0-3	0-4
Sheffield U	v Darlington	Aug 11	3-1	Aug 18	2-2	5-3
Southend	v Gillingham	Aug 11	1-0	Aug 18	1-0	2-0
Stockport	v Hull	Aug 11	2-2	Aug 18	0-0	2-2
Swansea	v Norwich	Aug 11	1-1	Aug 18	0-1	1-2
Swindon	v Wycombe	Aug 12	2-1	Aug 18	0-2	2-3
Torquay	v Crystal Palace	Aug 11	1-1	Aug 25	1-2	2-3
Tranmere	v Carlisle	Aug 11	3-0	Aug 18	1-0	4-0
Walsall	v Q.P.R.	Aug 11	0-0	Aug 26	1-3	1-3
Wigan	v Rochdale	Aug 11	1-0	Aug 18	1-0	2-0
Wrexham	v Halifax	Aug 11	0-2	Aug 18	2-0	2-2
W.B.A.	v Brentford	Aug 11	2-1	Aug 18	0-3	2-4
York	v Sunderland	Aug 11	0-2	Aug 18	1-2	1-4

2nd Round

Barnsley	v Reading	Sep 15	3-0	Sep 23	1-1	4-1
Blackpool	v Tranmere	Sep 15	2-1	Sep 22	1-3	3-4
Bolton	v Hull	Sep 15	3-1	Sep 22	3-2	6-3
Bournemouth	v Wolverhampton	Sep 15	1-1	Sep 22	2-1	3-2
Brentford	v Tottenham	Sep 15	2-3	Sep 23	2-3	4-6
Bristol C	v Crewe	Sep 16	1-1	Sep 22	0-2	1-3
Bury	v Crystal Palace	Sep 15	3-0	Sep 23	1-2	4-2
Coventry	v Southend	Sep 16	1-0	Sep 22	4-0	5-0
Derby	v Manchester C	Sep 16	1-1	Sep 23	1-0	2-1
Fulham	v Southampton	Sep 15	1-1	Sep 23	1-0	2-1
Halifax	v Bradford C	Sep 15	1-2	Sep 22	1-3	2-5
Huddersfield	v Everton	Sep 15	1-1	Sep 23	1-2	2-3
Ipswich	v Luton	Sep 15	2-1	Sep 22	2-4	4-5
Leicester	v Chesterfield	Sep 16	3-0	Sep 22	3-1	6-1
Leyton O	v Nottingham F	Sep 15	1-5	Sep 22	0-0	1-5
Macclesfield	v Birmingham	Sep 15	0-3	Sep 22	0-6	0-9
Middlesbrough	v Wycombe	Sep 16	2-0	Sep 22	1-1	3-1
Northampton	v West Ham	Sep 15	2-0	Sep 22	0-1	2-1
Norwich	v Wigan	Sep 16	1-0	Sep 22	3-2	4-2
Portsmouth	v Wimbledon	Sep 15	2-1	Sep 22	1-4	3-5
Q.P.R.	v Charlton	Sep 16	0-2	Sep 22	0-1	0-3
Sheffield U	v Grimsby	Sep 15	2-1	Sep 22	0-2	2-3
Sheffield W	v Cambridge	Sep 16	0-1	Sep 22	1-1	1-2
Sunderland	v Chester	Sep 15	3-0	Sep 22	1-0	4-0

3rd Round

Oct 27	Barnsley	2	Bournemouth	1
Oct 28	Birmingham	1	Wimbledon	2
Oct 27	Charlton	1	Leicester	2
Oct 28	Chelsea	4	Aston Villa	1
Oct 28	Crewe	0	Blackburn	1
Oct 28	Derby	1	Arsenal	2
Oct 28	Leeds	1	Bradford C	0
Oct 27	Liverpool	3	Fulham	1
Oct 27	Luton	2	Coventry	0
Oct 28	Manchester U	2	Bury	0
Oct 28	Middlesbrough	2	Everton	3
Oct 27	Northampton	1	Tottenham	3
Oct 27	Norwich	1	Bolton	1
	Penalties 1-3			
Oct 27	Nottingham F	3	Cambridge	3
	Penalties 4-3			
Oct 27	Sunderland	2	Grimsby	1
Oct 27	Tranmere	0	Newcastle	1

4th Round

Nov 11	Arsenal	0	Chelsea	5
Nov 10	Bolton	1	Wimbledon	2
Nov 11	Everton	1	Sunderland	1
	Penalties 4-5			
Nov 11	Leicester	2	Leeds	1
Nov 10	Liverpool	1	Tottenham	3
Nov 10	Luton	1	Barnsley	0
Nov 11	Manchester U	2	Nottingham F	1
Nov 11	Newcastle	1	Blackburn	1
	Penalties 2-4			

5th Round

Dec 02	Leicester	1	Blackburn	0
Dec 01	Sunderland	3	Luton	0
Dec 02	Tottenham	3	Manchester U	1
Dec 01	Wimbledon	2	Chelsea	1

Semi-finals

Jan 26	Sunderland	1	Leicester	2
Feb 17	Leicester	1	Sunderland	1
	Aggregate 3-2			
Jan 27	Tottenham	0	Wimbledon	0
Feb 16	Wimbledon	0	Tottenham	1
	Aggregate 0-1			

Final

Mar 21	Leicester	0	Tottenham	1
	played at Wembley			

SEASON 1999-2000

1st Round

Birmingham	v Exeter	Aug 10	3-0	Aug 24	2-1	5-1
Blackpool	v Tranmere	Aug 10	2-1	Aug 24	1-3	3-4
Bournemouth	v Barnet	Aug 10	2-0	Aug 24	2-3	4-3
Brentford	v Ipswich	Aug 11	0-2	Aug 24	0-2	0-4
Brighton	v Gillingham	Aug 11	0-2	Aug 24	0-2	0-4
Bury	v Notts Co	Aug 10	1-0	Aug 24	0-2	1-2
Cambridge	v Bristol C	Aug 10	2-2	Aug 24	1-2	3-4
Cardiff	v Q.P.R.	Aug 10	1-2	Aug 25	2-1	3-3
Carlisle	v Grimsby	Aug 10	0-0	Aug 24	0-6	0-6
Chester	v Port Vale	Aug 10	2-1	Aug 24	4-4	6-5
Colchester	v C Palace	Aug 10	2-2	Aug 24	1-3	3-5
Darlington	v Bolton	Aug 10	1-1	Aug 24	3-5	4-6
Halifax	v W.B.A.	Aug 10	0-0	Aug 24	1-5	1-5
Hartlepool	v Crewe	Aug 10	3-3	Aug 24	0-1	3-4
Lincoln	v Barnsley	Aug 10	2-4	Aug 24	2-2	4-6
Luton	v Bristol R	Aug 10	0-2	Aug 25	2-2	2-4
Macclesfield	v Stoke	Aug 10	1-1	Aug 25	0-3	1-4
Manchester C	v Burnley	Aug 11	5-0	Aug 24	1-0	6-0
Northampton	v Fulham	Aug 10	1-2	Aug 24	1-3	2-5
Norwich	v Cheltenham	Aug 10	2-0	Aug 24	1-2	3-2
Nottingham F	v Mansfield	Aug 11	3-0	Aug 24	0-1	3-1
Preston	v Wrexham	Aug 10	1-0	Aug 24	2-0	3-0
Reading	v Peterborough	Aug 11	0-0	Aug 24	2-1	2-1
Rochdale	v Chesterfield	Aug 10	1-2	Aug 24	1-2	2-4
Rotherham	v Hull	Aug 10	0-1	Aug 24	0-2	0-3
Scunthorpe	v Huddersfield	Aug 10	0-2	Aug 24	0-0	0-2
Sheffield U	v Shrewsbury	Aug 10	3-0	Aug 24	3-0	6-0
Southend	v Oxford	Aug 10	0-2	Aug 24	0-1	0-3
Stockport	v Oldham	Aug 10	2-0	Aug 24	1-1	3-1
Swansea	v Millwall	Aug 11	2-0	Aug 24	1-1	3-1
Swindon	v Leyton O	Aug 10	0-1	Aug 24	1-1	1-2
Torquay	v Portsmouth	Aug 17	0-0	Aug 24	0-3	0-3
Walsall	v Plymouth	Aug 10	4-1	Aug 24	4-1	8-2
Wycombe	v Wolverhampton	Aug 10	0-1	Aug 24	4-2	4-3
York	v Wigan	Aug 10	0-1	Aug 24	1-2	1-3

2nd Round

Barnsley	v Stockport	Sep 14	1-1	Sep 21	3-3	4-4
Birmingham	v Bristol R	Sep 14	2-0	Sep 21	1-0	3-0
Bradford	v Reading	Sep 14	1-1	Sep 22	2-2	3-3
C Palace	v Leicester	Sep 14	3-3	Sep 22	2-4	5-7
Cardiff	v Wimbledon	Sep 14	1-1	Sep 21	1-3	2-4
Charlton	v Bournemouth	Sep 14	0-0	Sep 21	0-0	0-0
Chester	v Aston Villa	Sep 14	0-1	Sep 21	0-5	0-6
Chesterfield	v Middlesbrough	Sep 14	0-0	Sep 21	1-2	1-2
Crewe	v Ipswich	Sep 14	2-1	Sep 21	1-1	3-2
Gillingham	v Bolton	Sep 14	1-4	Sep 21	0-2	1-6
Grimsby	v Leyton O	Sep 14	4-1	Sep 21	0-1	4-2
Hudderfield	v Notts Co	Sep 14	2-1	Sep 21	2-2	4-3
Hull	v Liverpool	Sep 14	1-5	Sep 21	2-4	3-9
Manchester C	v Southampton	Sep 15	0-0	Sep 21	3-4	3-4
Norwich	v Fulham	Sep 14	0-4	Sep 21	0-2	0-6
Nottingham F	v Bristol C	Sep 15	2-1	Sep 22	0-0	2-1
Oxford	v Everton	Sep 14	1-1	Sep 22	1-0	2-1
Portsmouth	v Blackburn	Sep 14	0-3	Sep 22	1-3	1-6
Sheffield U	v Preston	Sep 14	2-0	Sep 21	0-3	2-3
Stoke	v Sheffield W	Sep 14	0-0	Sep 22	1-3	1-3
Sunderland	v Walsall	Sep 14	3-2	Sep 21	5-0	8-2
Swansea	v Derby	Sep 14	0-0	Sep 22	1-3	1-3
Tranmere	v Coventry	Sep 14	5-1	Sep 22	1-3	6-4
W.B.A.	v Wycombe	Sep 14	1-1	Sep 21	4-3	5-4
Watford	v Wigan	Sep 14	2-0	Sep 21	1-3	3-3

3rd Round

Oct 12	Arsenal	2	Preston	1
Oct 13	Aston Villa	3	Manchester U	0
Oct 12	Birmingham	2	Newcastle	0
Oct 12	Bradford C	2	Barnsley	3
Oct 13	Chelsea	0	Huddersfield	1
Oct 13	Derby	1	Bolton	2
Oct 13	Leeds	1	Blackburn	0

Oct 13	Leicester	2	Grimsby	0
Oct 13	Middlesbrough	1	Watford	0
Oct 13	Sheffield W	4	Nottingham F	1
Oct 13	Southampton	2	Liverpool	1
Oct 13	Tottenham	3	Crewe	1
Oct 12	Tranmere	2	Oxford	0
Oct 12	W.B.A.	1	Fulham	2
Oct 13	West Ham	2	Bournemouth	0
Oct 12	Wimbledon	3	Sunderland	2

4th Round

Dec 01	Aston Villa	4	Southampton	0
Nov 30	Birmingham	2	West Ham	3
Nov 30	Bolton	1	Sheffield W	0
Dec 01	Fulham	3	Tottenham	1
Nov 30	Huddersfield	1	Wimbledon	2
Dec 15	Leicester	0	Leeds	0
	Penalties 4-2			
Nov 30	Middlesbrough	2	Arsenal	2
	Penalties 3-1			
Nov 30	Tranmere	4	Barnsley	0

5th Round

Dec 14	Bolton	2	Wimbledon	1
Jan 12	Leicester	3	Fulham	3
	Penalties 3-0			
Dec 14	Tranmere	2	Middlesbrough	1
Jan 11	West Ham	1	Aston Villa	3

Semi Final

Jan 25	Aston Villa	0	Leicester	0
Feb 02	Leicester	1	Aston Villa	0
	Aggregate 1-0			
Jan 12	Bolton	0	Tranmere	1
Jan 26	Tranmere	3	Bolton	0
	Aggregate 4-0			

F inal

Feb 27	Leicester	2	Tranmere	1

Looking For The Right Result

WHAT follows is a complete record of Scottish first-class football results. Add in the intonation of a voice, picture the scenes at the final whistle, recollect an image of where the news was first heard, and football results turn into vivid memories. Somewhere in this book you may be able to trace the first top-class game you ever saw, the moment you realised your team was relegated or promoted, the day of the wedding when you missed a game, the time you were on holiday and telephoned from a public call-box, and, if you've been really lucky, the eighth draw that brought your fortune.

When people are a long way from home, hearing a score takes on special significance. The bare details of 'the result' can spark such speculation, such pride, such longing and such identification. I often think of soldiers overseas. During World War Two, men of the 15th Scottish Division huddled round their Tam o' Shanter newsletters in France, Belgium, Holland and Germany. They read aloud the results of the Scottish Southern League – "Clyde five Hearts one, Motherwell two Celtic one" – and made them stretch as far as they possibly could.

Part of football's history concerns the various ways that results have been sprung upon us. In the early part of the century it was done by telegraph, newspapers and pigeon post. Pigeon fanciers would take three or four birds to the match and let them off at regular intervals in order to relay the score to a waiting village or newspaper offices. The results service has come a long way from those days, to Teletext, club calls and Internet. Successive generations of fans have relied on wirelesses, transistors, televisions, teleprinters and frantic telephone calls to friends. Or they have stopped their car at a set of traffic-lights, rolled down a window and asked a passer-by who is wearing the right scarf, "What was the score?" Sometimes there was no need – the result was written across faces.

The story of official Scottish results begins in 1873, when 15 clubs subscribed towards the purchase of the Scottish Cup. The trophy and a full set of medals cost £56 12s 11d. Queen's Park won the Cup that year, and went on to dominate the early years with ten Scottish Cup wins in the first 20 seasons.

The Scottish Cup was soon providing us with some wonderful statistics. There is the well-chronicled tie on 5 September 1885 when Arbroath beat Bon Accord 36-0 with Petrie scoring thirteen. On the same day Dundee Harp thrashed Aberdeen Rovers 35-0 in the same competition, a result that has not been accorded the glamour it deserves. It must have been like Elisha Gray and Alexander Graham Bell turning up on the same day to file patent accounts dealing with the invention of the telephone.

Aside from Scottish Cup matches, clubs in the 1880s relied on friendlies and matches in minor competitions. The games could hardly be called 'fixtures' – there were too many late cancellations for that. Inevitably, the idea of a more organised fixture list was discussed, and this led to the formation of the Scottish League, on 30 April 1890. The League was based on the English model and had 11 founder members: Abercorn, Celtic, Cowlairs, Cambuslang, Dumbarton, Hearts, Rangers, St Mirren, Renton, Third Lanark and Vale of Leven. Reporters were quick to analyse the motivation behind the organisation. Said Scottish Sport: "Our first and last objection to them is that they exist. The entire rules stink of finance – money making and money grabbing."

Unlike clubs in the English League, their Scottish counterparts were bound to amateur status. In the League's first season, Celtic, Third Lanark and Cowlairs each had four points deducted for infringements of registration rules, and Renton were banned by the Scottish FA after only five League matches. Renton's crime was playing a friendly against a new club called Edinburgh Saints (which was really a hastily reformed St Bernard's after the latter had been banned by the authorities for 'concealed professionalism'). Renton and Edinburgh Saints were turfed out of the Scottish FA and both sets of players suspended.

That first season, 1890-91, was a wonderful start for the statistically minded. Dumbarton and Rangers finished level on points and drew 2-2 in their play-off match. In the absence of goal average – it wasn't introduced until 1922 – they were declared joint champions, the only time it has happened.

The Renton case was not an isolated instance of clubs violating the amateur rules. Many players were being paid, and the authorisation of professionalism, in 1893, was a sign that the Scottish Football Association had accepted the inevitable. When Celtic's John McLaughlin, secretary of the League, spoke at the 1893 Scottish FA annual meeting, he put it succinctly: "You might as well attempt to stop the flow of Niagara with a kitchen chair as to endeavour to stem the tide of professionalism."

Queen's Park had initially declined the opportunity for League soccer, but when their major fixtures disappeared they accepted the necessity of progress and joined the Scottish League in 1900. Although they won the Scottish Cup for the tenth (and last) time in 1893, Queen's Park were slipping away as a national force. Thereafter, the history of top-class Scottish soccer became irretrievably linked with the history of 'the Old Firm' – Rangers and Celtic. Rangers first qualified for a Scottish Cup Final in 1877, but, two years later, failed to turn up for the replay with Vale of Leven after being incensed at a decision in the first game. Celtic were formed later, in 1887, but had the edge in the period before the World War One.

In 1893, the year professionalism was legitimised, Division Two was formed. There was no automatic promotion and relegation between the two divisions – that wasn't introduced until 1921 – and clubs in the lower division relied on the First Division 'electing' new members. Hence, in 1905, Falkirk (second) and Aberdeen (seventh) were elected to Division One, whereas Clyde (Division Two's champions) had to stay down. Meanwhile, clubs like Port Glasgow and Queen's Park retained their Division One status despite poor placings in the higher division in the 1900s and 1910s.

There are some startling statistics from those early years: Celtic's unbeaten season of 1897-98; Rangers' 100 per cent record of 1898-99; Kilmarnock's unbeaten Division Two season of 1898-99; Third Lanark's championship of 1904 and Scottish Cup win of 1905; Celtic's astonishing defensive record of 1913-14 when they conceded only 14 goals in 38 games; Celtic's two games in a day at the end of 1915-16 season (against Raith Rovers in the afternoon and Motherwell in the evening); and 76 points out of 84 for Rangers in 1920-21. In other instances, however, statistics disappear from the records, like the abandoned Scottish Cup tie of 1905, when Rangers led ten-men Celtic 2-0 and fans invaded the pitch.

Already, Celtic and Rangers had begun their dominance, and the Scottish League became near enough an Old Firm monopoly. Between 1904, when Third Lanark were champions, and 1948 (Hibernian), only Motherwell, in 1931-32, wrested the League flag from the two premier Glasgow teams. That period began with Celtic winning six consecutive League titles (1904-05 to 1909-10). Manager Willie Maley shrewdly satisfied the first golden rule of management – get good players. He had Alec McNair at full-back, a half-back line of Young, Loney and Hay, the powerful Jimmy Quinn at centre-forward, the zippy Alex Bennett on one wing and Jimmy McMenemy and Peter Somers orchestrating from inside-forward.

During World War One, football was largely insignificant when compared with the brutal conflict which brought the deaths of many footballers. Players of some teams, like Queen's Park and Hearts, had enlisted en bloc. The Scottish Cup was abandoned, and, although the Scottish League continued, it was a shadow of itself, some of the events resembling those of local amateur soccer. In November 1915, for instance, Rangers fielded nine players against Falkirk; and, on 20 January 1917, Partick Thistle fielded a substitute against Rangers.

After World War One a rebel Central League caused disruption, and a number of clubs broke away from Division Two. These clubs were lured back with the promise of automatic relegation and promotion. The Second Division was reformed in 1921 after a gap of seven years, and it included 11 new clubs. A First Division of 22 clubs was deemed to be too large, which led to three clubs being relegated and only one promoted at the end of 1921-22. Alloa Athletic were the first Scottish team to be automatically promoted on merit.

The following season 'goal-average' was introduced to separate teams on the same number of points. It was a curious name to describe 'the number of goals scored divided by the number of goals conceded' but the calculation managed to reach parts of the brain that whole education systems have sometimes failed to reach. Another dramatic change came with the new offside law, in 1925, when the Scots put forth a proposal at a meeting of the International Football Federation. With only two defenders, rather than three, needed behind the ball when it was last played, the game became easier for attackers, and 1925-26 saw the return of high scores.

If Celtic came out on top in the period leading up to World War One, Rangers were undoubtedly the more successful during the inter-war period, winning the League 15 times in 20 seasons under the stewardship of manager Willie Struth. This was during the heyday of players like Alan Morton, Davie Meiklejohn and Bob McPhail. Surprisingly, Rangers did not win the Cup between 1903 and 1928, although that did not stop Bob McPhail ending up with seven Scottish Cup winners' medals (including one for Airdrie in 1924). It was a man associated with Celtic, however, who set goalscoring standards that will never be equalled. Jimmy McGrory scored a British record 550 goals in first-class football, including eight in one match against Dunfermline in 1928.

Although Rangers dominated the inter-war years, there was enough excitement and competition to sustain interest outside Glasgow. Airdrieonians, for instance, were runners-up in four consecutive seasons (1922-23 to 1925-26) and Motherwell finished in the top three eight times in succession (1926-27 to 1933-34). A number of new names appeared on the Scottish Cup in the 1920s – Kilmarnock (1920), Partick Thistle (1921), Morton (1922), Airdrie (1924) and St Mirren (1926). Then, after the Old Firm had seemingly regained its grip on the competition, there came two more surprises – Second Division East Fife (1938) and Clyde (1939).

In the League, the most bizarre 'achievements' came from Edinburgh City, an all-amateur team known as 'the Queen's Park of the east'. Elected to Division Two in 1931, they showed remarkable consistency over the next eight seasons, conceding 981 goals in 276 games, an average of 3.62 per game. They finished bottom of Division Two no fewer than six times, and were responsible for one unenviable statistic: East Fife 13 Edinburgh City 2. On a clear day City could see no higher than 15th place in the League table.

After a few games of 1939-40, the Scottish League was suspended for the duration of World War Two. The following season, the Southern League began as a separate organisation, and clubs in the north and the east followed suit in 1941-42 with their own league. The North-Eastern League was unusual in awarding extra points for draws and victories away from home.

When football returned to something more normal, in 1945-46, the divisions were lettered 'A' and 'B' rather than numbered '1' and '2'. Soon, in 1946-47, a 'C' Division arrived, and Stirling Albion made an immediate impact, racing through the three divisions in three seasons. This third division, however, like its three-year predecessor in the early 1920s, was not to prove a permanent addition to the League's structure. It lasted from 1946 to 1955.

The wartime period also saw the birth of the League Cup model. It began with four sections, each section consisting of four teams playing each other home and away on a league basis. The winners of each mini-league qualified for the semi-finals. These additional fixtures served to extend the meagre wartime programme. The League Cup became an official competition in 1946-47, and this brought a new target for Scottish clubs – 'the treble'.

The first club to achieve the treble were Rangers, in 1948-49. The Ibrox club had maintained their pre-war momentum with a team known for their 'Iron Curtain' defence – Bobby Brown, George Young, Jock 'Tiger' Shaw, Ian McColl, Willie Woodburn and Sammy Cox – and two magnificent attackers in Willie Waddell and Willie Thornton. But, in those post-war years, clubs other than Rangers and Celtic showed that they, too, could attract large attendances. Good players stayed longer than usual with provincial clubs and teams were settled enough to challenge the Glasgow duo. Between 1946-47 and 1952-53, Hibernian won the League three times and were runners-up on three other occasions. In the late 1950s and the early 1960s, other clubs reached new heights of League success – Aberdeen, Hearts, Dundee and Kilmarnock – and the Cup competitions proved to be exciting and unpredictable.

Hibernian's great post-war team had Tommy Younger in goal and the 'Famous Five' forward line of Gordon Smith, Bobby Johnstone, Lawrie Reilly, Eddie Turnbull and Willie Ormond. Gordon Smith went on to win League winners' medals with three different clubs (Hibernian, Hearts and Dundee), an astonishing achievement for someone who didn't play with either Rangers or Celtic. The Hearts team of 1957-58, scorers of 132 goals to win the League, could field the 'Terrible Trio' of Alfie Conn, Willie Bauld and Jimmy Wardhaugh.

By the time Dundee won the League, in 1962, provincial clubs were beginning to sense the impact of the removal of the maximum wage in England. It became very difficult for clubs other than Rangers and Celtic to hang on to good players, and a succession of stars left Scotland at the start of the 1960s – George Mulhall (Aberdeen), Jim Storrie (Airdrie), Eddie Connachan (Dunfermline), George Herd (Clyde), John McLeod and Joe Baker (Hibs), Bobby Kennedy (Kilmarnock), Alex Young, Gordon Marshall and Bobby Blackwood (Hearts), Jimmy Gabriel and Ian Ure (Dundee), Ian St John and Pat Quinn (Motherwell), Dave Hilley, Matt Gray and Alex Harley (Third Lanark), Tommy Bryceland and Gerry Baker (St Mirren), Ron Yeats (Dundee United) and Bertie Auld (Celtic).

After this exodus, power reverted almost exclusively to the Old Firm, with the exception of 1964-65, when Kilmarnock won the title on goal-average after beating nearest-rivals Hearts by the required 2-0 on the final day of the season. In 1963-64 Rangers launched their new strength by winning the treble again. Manager Scot Symon's team included Bobby Shearer, Ron McKinnon and John Greig in defence, Willie Henderson and Davie Wilson on the wings, Jim Forrest and Ralph Brand up front and Jim Baxter all over the place. At the other end of the spectrum, Third Lanark faded into obscurity. They folded in 1967 and were lost to the League.

The most dramatic watershed came in February 1965 when Jock Stein took over as Celtic manager. Captained mainly by Billy McNeill, Celtic won the championship for nine successive seasons from 1965-66 to 1973-74, and became the first British team to win the European Cup. The 'Lisbon Lions', who beat Internazionale 2-1 in Lisbon to take the European Cup, are indelibly etched on many a mind: Simpson, Craig, Gemmell, Murdoch, McNeill, Clark, Johnstone, Wallace, Chalmers, Auld, Lennox.

The advent of the 1970s brought more changes to the Scottish soccer scene – the Texaco Cup, the Drybrough Cup, goal-difference, two substitutes – but Jock Stein's Celtic just went on and on. Without paying transfer fees of any great note, Stein was able to call on a new generation of players – McBride, Hughes, Hay, Williams, Hood, Macari, Connelly, McGrain, Dalglish, Deans, etc – and his team became hungry for more and more trophies. The stranglehold was finally broken in 1974-75, when Jock Stein was incapacitated after a horrific car accident and Rangers won the treble.

Between 1970-71 and 1978-79, every Scottish League and Scottish Cup competition was won by one of the Old Firm. Fortunately, for lesser mortals, the League Cup retained some of its unpredictability, especially in 1972 when Partick Thistle smacked four early goals past Celtic in the Final. And to prove there was still open competition, Hibernian and Dundee won the next two League Cup Finals.

In 1975 the Scottish League was restructured – a ten-club Premier Division, a 14-club Division One and a 14-club Division Two. The new structure gave a chance to Ferranti Thistle (later known as Meadowbank Thistle), an Edinburgh works team called in to extend the numbers to a more manageable 38. However, the new structure was to benefit clubs at the top rather than those at the bottom. Premier Division clubs played each other four times a season, a better prospect for high attendances, especially with four Rangers-Celtic derbies instead of two. But the Premier League, like so many Premier Leagues, initially created a fear of relegation rather than a quest for winning championships.

The new system's first casualty was the Spring Cup, which lasted only one season. This competition was open to First and Second clubs, who were split into seven groups of four for the qualifying competition. Sixteen teams – the top two in each group plus the two third-placed teams with the best records – went forward to the knockout stage. When Airdrie beat Clydebank 4-2 in the Final at Firhill Park, after extra-time, there were only 5,000 present, so the competition was doomed. Thereafter, to make up for the loss of fixtures, the First and Second Division teams played each other three times a season instead of twice.

The first four seasons of the Premier League brought a familiar ring to the names on the trophy – Rangers, Celtic, Rangers, Celtic – and a Rangers team managed by Jock Wallace twice won the treble (1975-76 and 1977-78). Wallace's team was built around John Greig, Tom Forsyth, Colin Jackson, Alec MacDonald, Derek Johnstone and Tommy McLean. But Celtic, with the likes of Kenny Dalglish, Danny McGrain and a young Roy Aitken, were always in contention.

Then, in the 1980s, came a big challenge from the east of the country. In that decade, Aberdeen won the League championship three times, the Scottish Cup four times and the League Cup twice. Managed by Alex Ferguson, the club could field players like Alex McLeish and Willie Miller in defence, and Gordon Strachan, Mark McGhee and Peter Weir in attack. In 1982-83 Aberdeen won the European Cup-winners' Cup by beating Real Madrid 2-1 in Gothenburg. Their team that night was: Leighton, Rougvie, Miller, McLeish, McMaster, Cooper, Strachan, Simpson, Weir, McGhee, Black (Hewitt).

That same season, 1982-83, Dundee United took the League title, and the balance of power continued to shift eastwards. It didn't last for long, though. After Hearts had failed on goal-difference to win the League in 1985-86 – on the last day of the season they lost at Dundee while Celtic were scoring five against St Mirren at Love Street – the next run of League champions had that familiar Old Firm ring.

The arrival at Rangers of Graeme Souness, as player-manager in 1986, began a sustained period of success for the Ibrox club. The traditional Scotland-England exodus was now reversed. Star players like Terry Butcher, Trevor Steven, Gary Stevens, Mark Hateley, Trevor Francis and Chris Woods moved across the border, but this time it was from England to Rangers. The most sensational signing was that of Maurice Johnston from Nantes in 1989, when Rangers broke with its Protestant tradition by signing a Catholic.

Meanwhile, the authorities were still experimenting with the structure of Scottish soccer. In 1986-87, a League system with two 12-club divisions at the top created an arduous programme of 44 Premier League games. This lasted only two seasons before a return to the 10-14-14 divisional structure. Another three seasons and a mid-season decision increased the Premier League from ten to 12 again, saving two clubs from relegation. In 1994-95, the next format – four ten-club divisions – came in. This provided opportunities for two Highland League clubs, Ross County and Caledonian Thistle (themselves an amalgam of two clubs), who were elected to the new Division Three.

And through all this Rangers marched on. When they took the Premier League title in 1999-2000 they had finished at the top of Scottish football for all but two of the last 14 seasons. Celtic had poked their noses in just twice – once to prevent Rangers achieving ten consecutive Championships – but by 2000 the Parkhead club was riven with internal problems as they suffered a humiliating exit from the Cup, sacked their coach and finished a country mile behind their bitter rivals.

While Rangers carried all before them for a decade and more there were other developments. Penalty competitions arrived in the Skol Cup (the sponsored League Cup) and the Scottish Cup. It wasn't too long before the Finals were settled by such means, spectacularly so in 1990, when Aberdeen won the Scottish Cup by beating Celtic 9-8 on the 20th penalty. And then, in 1994-95, Raith Rovers stressed the uncertainty of the Skol Cup by winning on penalties from Celtic. Raith Rovers were the first team outside the top flight to win a major trophy since East Fife won the League Cup in 1947-48.

The success of Raith Rovers is a reminder that the Scottish League stretches far beyond the confines of the Old Firm, or even the Premier League. The section which follows captures not only moments of brilliant success but also times of glorious failure. Not only can you trace how Rangers won the treble in 1992-93, but you can relive the last 13 League games of Stirling Albion's 1980-81 season, when they failed to score a goal. They played 1,293 goalless minutes, and 500 or so fans still turned up to watch the last game of the season. Like all fans – and managers and players – they were still looking for 'the right result'. This book has thousands of them.

Scottish Football League Records
Season 1890-91

DIVISION 1

	ABERCORN	CAMBUSLANG	CELTIC	COWLAIRS	DUMBARTON	HEARTS	RANGERS	ST MIRREN	T LANARK	VALE OF LEVEN	RENTON
ABERCORN		Dec06 2-5	Oct25 1-5	Mar21 1-0	Dec27 1-2	Apr25 1-0	Feb07 1-1	Jan24 5-1	Oct04 2-4	Mar07 6-0	Sep13 4-2
CAMBUSLANG	Apr11 4-5		Mar07 3-1	Jan17 4-0	Mar21 2-2	May02 2-0	Aug23 2-6	Sep13 3-2	Feb28 2-2	Aug16 8-2	
CELTIC	May12 2-0	Aug30 5-2		Mar14 2-0	Apr11 1-0	Feb28 1-0	Mar21 2-2	Feb07 3-2	Apr25 1-1	May05 9-1	Aug16 1-4
COWLAIRS	Feb28 7-5	Apr18 1-1	Apr29 0-5		Oct25 1-6	Mar07 1-2	Mar28 0-2	Apr25 4-2	Apr11 2-2	Aug23 3-2	
DUMBARTON	Oct11 5-1	Jan24 5-0	Feb21 2-2	Aug16 1-1		Aug30 3-1	Sep13 5-1	Mar07 5-1	Mar28 5-1	Feb28 4-0	
HEARTS	Mar28 1-1	Feb14 2-2	Aug23 0-5	Sep13 4-0	Apr20 0-4		Jan24 0-1	Feb21 1-0	Mar21 4-1	Oct25 8-1	
RANGERS	Mar14 2-0	Feb21 2-1	May02 1-2	Oct18 1-1	Apr25 4-2	Aug16 5-2		Oct04 8-2	May09 4-1	Apr04 4-0	Aug30 4-1
ST MIRREN	Sep20 4-2	Mar28 2-3	Apr04 1-0	Aug30 5-2	May02 2-4	Apr11 3-2	Feb28 3-7		Mar14 3-2	Oct11 1-1	
T LANARK	Apr28 2-1	Apr04 1-2	Sep13 2-1	May06 3-0	Aug23 1-3	Apr18 4-0	Mar07 0-4	Oct25 5-3		Feb21 4-1	
VALE OF LEVEN	Aug30 2-1	Apr25 2-1	Jan24 3-1	Feb07 2-1	Oct04 1-3	May09 2-4	Jan17 1-3	Mar21 5-2	May02 1-2		
RENTON								Aug23 2-2		Sep20 1-2	

LEAGUE TABLES
DIVISION 1

	P	W	D	L	F	A	W	D	L	F	A	Pts
Dumbarton	18	7	2	0	35	8	6	1	2	26	13	†29
Rangers	18	7	1	1	31	11	6	2	1	27	14	†29
Celtic	18	7	2	0	26	8	4	1	4	22	13	*21
Cambusling	18	5	2	2	30	20	3	2	4	17	22	20
T. Lanark	18	6	0	3	22	15	2	3	4	16	24	*15
Hearts	18	4	2	3	20	15	2	0	7	11	22	14
Abercorn	18	4	1	4	20	18	1	1	7	16	29	12
St Mirren	18	5	1	3	24	23	0	0	9	15	39	11
Vale of Leven	18	5	0	4	19	18	0	1	8	8	47	11
Cowlairs	18	3	2	4	19	27	0	2	7	5	23	*6

† Dumbarton and Rangers drew 2-2 in a play-off and were declared joint Champions.
* Each had four points deducted for infringements.

Scottish Football League Records
Season 1891-92

DIVISION 1

	ABERCORN	CAMBUSLANG	CELTIC	CLYDE	DUMBARTON	HEARTS	LEITH A	RANGERS	RENTON	ST MIRREN	T LANARK	VALE OF LEVEN
ABERCORN		Feb06 3-1	Sep12 2-5	Dec26 3-3	May07 1-1	Mar12 1-3	Aug29 3-2	Mar26 0-1	Nov14 3-3	Sep19 1-1	Oct24 2-4	Oct10 6-3
CAMBUSLANG	Oct03 0-2		Jan30 0-4	Jan23 3-5	Aug15 0-2	Sep05 3-3	Sep26 1-3	Feb27 0-6	Apr30 1-1	Aug29 1-1	Apr09 1-1	Nov21 1-0
CELTIC	Apr30 3-1	Apr16 3-1		Mar19 0-0	Sep26 2-0	Oct17 3-1	May14 2-0	Aug22 3-0	Sep05 3-0	Dec26 2-1	Feb27 5-1	Oct24 6-1
CLYDE	Jan30 7-2	Dec19 2-0	Aug29 2-7		Apr30 4-1	Oct03 3-101-2	May07 1-3	May21 1-3	Apr04 4-1	Sep12 3-3	Apr23 10-3	Aug15
DUMBARTON	Aug22 8-1	Mar26 5-2	Apr23 1-0	Nov14 8-2		Sep19 5-1	Sep12 6-0	May04 6-0	Dec26 2-1	Oct24 4-2	Oct17 2-0	Dec12 8-0
HEARTS	Sep21 2-1	Dec26 1-0	Aug15 3-1	Apr16 2-1	Aug29 3-1		Oct24 3-1	Apr23 3-2	Sep12 4-2	Oct10 2-2	Sep26 2-0	Mar19 7-0
LEITH A	Oct17 3-2	May05 3-0	Apr18 2-1	Sep05 1-0	Oct31 1-3	Apr30 2-2		Oct03 3-1	Aug22 2-3	Sep21 4-2	Nov14 3-1	Sep19 10-0
RANGERS	Sep26 6-2	Oct17 2-1	May07 1-1	Oct24 1-5	Sep05 1-3	Nov21 0-1	Apr16 3-2		Mar19 5-2	May10 2-3	Aug29 2-3	Feb13 7-0
RENTON	Dec05 2-1	Oct24 1-1	May05 0-4	Sep26 2-1	Nov07 1-2	Apr09 0-3	Oct10 3-0	Aug15 1-4		Mar12 5-2	Nov21 1-0	Aug29 3-0
ST MIRREN	Feb27 0-3	Apr23 2-2	Oct03 1-2	Apr02 1-4	Mar19 2-3	Aug22 2-5	Nov07 3-1	Dec05 3-4	Oct17 2-1		Sep05 1-2	Sep26 6-4
T LANARK	Mar19 1-1	Sep12 3-1	May24 1-3	Feb13 3-2	Dec05 2-5	May07 3-2	Aug15 0-3	Oct10 2-2	Oct03 1-1	Jan23 2-3		Dec26 9-2
VALE OF LEVEN	Sep05 0-3	Aug22 0-1	Apr02 2-2	Oct17 2-2	Oct03 1-2	Oct31 2-2	Jan30 0-3	Sep12 1-6	May07 1-1	Nov14 2-2	Feb06 0-2	

LEAGUE TABLES
DIVISION 1

	P	W	D	L	F	A	W	D	L	F	A	Pts
Dumbarton	22	11	0	0	55	9	7	1	3	23	18	37
Celtic	22	10	1	0	32	6	6	2	3	30	15	35
Hearts	22	10	1	0	32	11	5	3	3	33	24	34
Leith A	22	8	1	2	34	15	4	0	7	17	25	25
Rangers	22	5	1	5	30	23	6	1	4	29	23	24
T. Lanark	22	4	3	4	27	25	4	2	5	17	22	21
Renton	22	6	1	4	19	18	2	4	5	18	25	21
Clyde	22	5	1	5	38	35	3	3	5	25	26	20
Abercorn	22	3	4	4	25	27	3	1	7	19	32	17
St Mirren	22	3	1	7	23	31	2	4	5	20	29	15
Cambusling	22	1	4	6	11	28	1	2	8	10	25	10
Vale of Leven	22	0	5	6	11	26	0	0	11	13	73	5

SCOTTISH FOOTBALL LEAGUE RECORDS
SEASON 1892-93

DIVISION 1

	ABERCORN	CELTIC	CLYDE	DUMBARTON	HEARTS	LEITH A	RANGERS	RENTON	ST MIRREN	T LANARK
ABERCORN		Feb11 4-2	Nov05 5-1	Apr29 4-0	Sep03 3-4	Sep24 1-0	Aug20 0-4	Oct15 1-2	Mar04 1-2	May06 5-2
CELTIC	Sep10 3-2		Oct01 3-1	Mar18 5-1	Nov05 5-0	May09 3-1	Apr29 3-0	Aug20 4-3	May02 4-1	May18 2-5
CLYDE	Aug27 5-2	May06 1-2		Feb18 1-2	Oct15 2-3	Apr22 1-2	Mar11 0-3	Sep24 2-2	Feb11 1-2	Sep03 1-4
DUMBARTON	Oct22 5-1	Oct15 0-3	Apr15 3-1		Apr01 5-1	Sep10 2-1	Apr22 3-0	Mar04 1-1	Aug20 1-2	Sep24 1-2
HEARTS	Mar11 3-1	Aug27 3-1	Apr29 2-3	Oct08 1-3		Apr15 3-1	Mar18 1-2	Sep10 2-2	Sep24 4-0	May04 2-2
LEITH A	Mar25 1-1	Jan28 0-1	Aug20 3-0	Nov19 3-0	Sep17 1-3		Oct01 1-2	Apr01 6-2	Nov05 5-1	Oct15 2-1
RANGERS	Feb04 4-3	Sep24 2-2	Oct22 4-2	Sep03 3-2	May06 2-1	Aug27 3-2		Apr15 2-0	Oct15 0-0	Apr01 2-1
RENTON	Feb18 2-1	Mar25 0-2	Mar18 1-1	May20 0-4	Oct01 4-1	Oct08 2-3	Nov05 2-2		Sep03 3-2	Feb04 3-1
ST MIRREN	Sep17 4-0	Oct22 1-3	Sep10 8-1	Oct01 3-2	Feb18 3-1	Feb04 4-1	Mar25 2-2	Mar11 3-0		Aug27 1-4
T LANARK	Oct01 8-0	Apr22 0-6	Jan28 4-1	Nov05 3-0	Aug20 1-4	Mar18 1-2	Sep10 2-4	Oct22 6-2	Apr29 6-1	

LEAGUE TABLES
DIVISION 1

	P	W	D	L	F	A	W	D	L	F	A	Pts
Celtic	18	8	0	1	32	14	6	1	2	22	11	29
Rangers	18	7	2	0	22	13	5	2	2	19	14	28
St Mirren	18	6	1	2	29	14	3	1	5	11	25	20
T. Lanark	18	5	0	4	31	20	4	1	4	22	19	19
Hearts	18	4	2	3	21	15	4	0	5	18	26	18
Leith A	18	5	1	3	22	11	3	0	6	13	20	17
Dumbarton	18	5	1	3	21	12	3	0	6	14	23	17
Renton	18	4	2	3	17	17	1	3	5	14	27	15
Abercorn	18	5	0	4	24	17	0	1	8	11	35	*11
Clyde	18	1	1	7	14	22	1	1	7	11	33	*6

* Abercorn and Clyde relegated to new Division Two.

SCOTTISH FOOTBALL LEAGUE RECORDS
SEASON 1893-94

DIVISION 1

	CELTIC	DUMBARTON	DUNDEE	HEARTS	LEITH A	RANGERS	RENTON	ST BERNARD'S	ST MIRREN	T LANARK
CELTIC		Aug26 0-0	Nov04 3-1	Mar10 2-3	Aug23 4-1	Feb24 3-2	Dec02 3-2	Oct14 5-2	Feb10 5-1	Aug12 5-0
DUMBARTON	Dec23 4-5		Sep16 1-1	Sep30 2-2	Feb03 3-1	Jan20 2-0	Nov18 2-0	Sep02 1-5	Oct21 3-3	Mar17 2-1
DUNDEE	Aug19 1-4	Dec09 4-0		Oct21 2-5	Nov11 4-3	Aug12 3-3	Feb10 8-1	Sep30 1-3	Sep23 0-3	Feb24 1-1
HEARTS	Sep09 2-4	Apr28 2-1	Dec16 3-0		Aug19 0-2	Oct14 4-2	Mar03 5-1	Apr07 2-4	Nov18 1-1	Sep23 2-2
LEITH A	Mar17 5-0	Oct28 2-4	Sep09 3-5	Dec02 2-2		Sep30 2-2	Oct21 2-1	Sep18 4-2	Sep02 2-5	Apr14 2-3
RANGERS	Sep02 5-0	Sep23 4-0	Mar10 7-2	Apr14 1-2	Nov04 1-0		Aug19 5-3	May02 1-2	Apr21 5-0	Dec23 0-3
RENTON	Nov11 0-3	Oct07 1-1	Aug26 2-3	Nov04 2-3	Feb17 2-1	Sep09 1-2		Oct28 0-1	Dec09 0-4	Jan27 0-3
ST BERNARD'S	Jan20 1-2	Nov04 2-1	Jan27 3-5	Oct07 1-2	Mar10 3-2	Aug26 0-0	Sep23 4-2		Mar31 8-3	Oct21 6-2
ST MIRREN	Sep30 1-2	Nov11 1-2	Feb17 10-3	Aug26 2-3	Oct14 3-1	Jan27 2-2	Sep16 4-2	Sep09 1-3		Nov04 4-2
T LANARK	Dec30 1-3	Sep09 1-3	Oct14 4-3	Sep02 1-3	Aug26 2-1	Nov11 1-2	Sep30 3-3	Aug19 5-3	Jan20 3-1	

DIVISION 2

	ABERCORN	CLYDE	COWLAIRS	HIBERNIAN	MORTON	MOTHERWELL	NORTHERN	PARTICK T	PORT GLASGOW A	THISTLE
ABERCORN		Sep23 0-2	Dec02 0-4	Mar03 3-3	Feb03 2-1	Aug19 2-3	Oct21 4-2	Feb10 2-3	Mar31 0-3	Apr14 5-2
CLYDE	Nov11 5-4		Dec23 1-1	Sep09 0-4	Oct21 5-0	Apr21 3-2	Mar17 2-1	Sep30 3-2	Aug19 2-2	Oct07 6-1
COWLAIRS	Feb24 7-1	Mar31 2-1		Mar17 2-3	Apr14 7-3	May05 4-1	Sep09 7-0	Nov11 8-1	May12 5-1	Aug12 4-2
HIBERNIAN	Sep16 7-2	Mar10 4-3	Oct07 3-4		Aug26 9-2	Nov25 8-2	Apr07 6-0	Feb03 6-1	May19 10-1	Nov04 4-0
MORTON	Mar24 0-2	Apr07 1-3	Sep30 4-2	Dec02 0-1		Nov11 2-3	Feb17 7-1	Aug19 2-3	Sep16 1-0	Apr21 1-1
MOTHERWELL	Feb17 5-3	Aug12 4-1	Aug26 3-2	Apr14 2-1	May26 4-1		May19 2-0	Nov04 2-3	Sep30 7-2	Dec16 6-2
NORTHERN	Mar10 5-2	Aug26 1-3	Mar03 1-4	Sep30 2-2	Apr28 2-7	Dec02 2-2		Dec23 2-1	Apr21 3-1	Feb03 3-3
PARTICK T	Aug26 0-3	Feb24 5-4	Jan13 5-3	Mar31 1-7	Oct14 5-2	Oct07 4-2	Nov25 4-3		Mar24 0-1	Mar10 13-1
PORT GLASGOW A	Sep09 5-4	Feb03 1-4	Apr07 1-3	Oct21 3-3	May05 10-1	Apr28 5-3	Aug12 6-1	Jan20 4-1		Aug26 4-3
THISTLE	Sep30 3-3	Sep02 1-3	Feb10 1-3	Aug19 1-2	Sep09 2-1	Mar24 1-8	Oct14 3-0	Oct21 3-4	Dec02 1-2	

LEAGUE TABLES

DIVISION 1

	P	W	D	L	F	A	W	D	L	F	A	Pts
Celtic	18	7	1	1	30	12	7	0	2	23	20	29
Hearts	18	4	2	3	21	17	7	2	0	25	15	26
St Bernard's	18	5	1	3	28	19	6	0	3	25	20	23
Rangers	18	6	0	3	29	12	2	4	3	15	18	20
Dumbarton	18	4	3	2	20	18	3	2	4	12	17	19
St Mirren	18	4	1	4	28	20	3	2	4	21	27	17
T. Lanark	18	4	1	4	21	22	3	2	4	17	22	17
Dundee	18	3	2	4	24	23	3	1	5	23	36	15
Leith A	18	3	2	4	24	24	1	0	8	12	22	10
Renton	18	1	1	7	8	21	0	1	8	15	36	4

Dundee and St Bernard's joined Division One

DIVISION 2

	P	*W*	*D*	*L*	*F*	*A*	*Pts*
Hibernian	18	13	3	2	83	29	29
Cowlairs	18	13	1	4	72	32	27
Clyde†	18	11	2	5	51	36	24
Motherwell	18	11	1	6	61	46	23
Partick T	18	10	0	8	56	58	20
Port Glasgow A*	18	9	2	7	52	52	13
Abercorn	18	5	2	11	42	60	12
Morton	18	4	1	13	36	62	9
Northern	18	3	3	12	29	66	9
Thistle	18	2	3	13	31	72	7

* Port Glasgow Athletic had 7 points deducted for fielding an ineligible player
† Clyde promoted to Division One

Scottish Football League Records
Season 1894-95

DIVISION 1

	CELTIC	CLYDE	DUMBARTON	DUNDEE	HEARTS	LEITH A	RANGERS	ST BERNARD'S	ST MIRREN	T LANARK
CELTIC		Apr27 2-0	Oct20 6-0	May04 2-1	Nov03 0-2	Mar16 4-0	Sep22 5-3	Aug18 5-2	Dec22 2-2	Feb23 4-4
CLYDE	Oct13 2-4		Mar16 3-1	May18 2-0	Mar23 3-2	Aug25 5-2	Dec08 1-5	Sep08 1-4	May11 0-2	Sep29 4-3
DUMBARTON	Mar09 0-2	Nov03 2-3		Oct13 2-4	Sep29 1-4	Sep01 3-2	Dec01 1-0	Sep15 3-4	Mar30 4-1	Mar02 2-4
DUNDEE	Aug11 1-1	Aug18 4-1	Sep08 3-0		Dec22 0-2	Dec01 4-1	Jan26 2-1	Sep29 2-2	Mar16 0-1	Nov03 1-2
HEARTS	Feb16 4-0	Dec01 2-4	Oct27 3-1	Mar30 4-0		Sep15 3-1	Jan19 0-0	Oct06 4-3	Sep01 1-0	Aug18 6-3
LEITH A	Mar30 5-6	Mar02 2-1	Apr06 1-1	Oct20 3-2	Nov17 1-4		Sep08 3-4	Oct13 0-2	Aug18 1-2	Sep22 3-2
RANGERS	Mar23 1-1	Feb22 4-1	Aug18 3-0	Sep01 1-0	Oct20 0-1	Nov03 5-1		Apr27 2-1	Sep29 4-3	Feb16 0-1
ST BERNARD'S	Nov10 0-2	Sep22 0-3	Dec22 5-0	Dec08 2-0	Apr06 0-3	Sep17 6-3	Aug25 1-4		Nov03 2-0	Oct20 2-4
ST MIRREN	Sep08 0-3	Oct20 4-2	Sep22 4-3	Sep15 5-1	Oct13 1-2	Nov10 3-2	Mar09 4-2	Mar23 0-1		Dec01 2-0
T LANARK	Aug25 2-1	Apr06 4-2	Nov10 6-3	Apr27 1-3	Sep08 0-3	Dec22 7-1	Oct13 0-2	May11 4-0	Apr04 4-0	

DIVISION 2

	ABERCORN	AIRDRIE	COWLAIRS	DUNDEE W	HIBERNIAN	MORTON	MOTHERWELL	PARTICK T	PORT GLASGOW A	RENTON
ABERCORN		Apr27 3-1	Aug25 3-0	Apr13 9-2	Sep01 1-5	Mar23 5-3	May04 4-3	Jan19 3-3	Mar16 3-3	Nov10 3-2
AIRDRIE	Apr20 4-0		May11 4-3	Dec01 15-1	May25 2-4	Sep08 6-1	Dec29 2-2	Mar30 9-0	Aug25 4-2	Oct06 4-1
COWLAIRS	Mar30 3-3	Nov10 4-4		Apr27 2-1	Mar16 2-8	Feb23 2-4	Sep29 4-3	Dec15 3-4	Dec01 3-3	Apr13 0-3
DUNDEE W	Mar02 3-4	Oct20 1-2	Apr06 6-3		Nov10 0-6	Apr08 0-1	Aug25 2-2	Mar09 6-5	Sep15 9-1	Mar16 4-5
HIBERNIAN	Nov03 4-2	Sep15 6-1	Dec22 8-2	Sep08 8-2		Oct20 6-3	Feb02 5-0	Aug18 5-1	Apr06 3-3	May04 9-1
MORTON	Sep15 5-1	Apr06 3-1	Apr20 6-0	Dec15 7-3	Oct13 1-7		Mar16 3-5	Nov24 4-2	Feb02 4-3	Aug25 5-1
MOTHERWELL	Sep08 7-0	Aug11 4-2	May18 4-0	Mar30 5-0	Oct06 2-0	Mar09 6-4		Apr06 3-0	Apr20 2-0	Dec01 0-2
PARTICK T	Feb23 5-1	Dec22 3-2	Jan05 4-2	Aug11 5-2	Apr13 0-4	Sep29 4-4	Nov17 5-3		May25 5-0	Mar23 0-1
PORT GLASGOW A	Oct20 5-1	May04 5-4	Aug11 5-3	Mar23 6-2	Mar09 2-2	Nov10 9-1	Aug18 3-1	Sep08 6-2		Mar30 4-3
RENTON	Dec29 8-2	Aug18 2-1	Oct13 4-1	Aug29	Nov17 3-2	Dec22 2-0	Sep15 3-4	May18 1-3	May11 4-2	

LEAGUE TABLES

DIVISION 1

	P	W	D	L	F	A	W	D	L	F	A	Pts
Hearts	18	7	1	1	27	12	8	0	1	23	6	31
Celtic	18	6	2	1	30	14	5	2	2	20	15	26
Rangers	18	6	1	2	20	9	4	1	4	21	17	22
T. Lanark	18	6	0	3	28	15	4	1	4	23	24	21
St Mirren	18	6	0	3	23	16	3	1	5	11	18	19
St Bernard's	18	4	0	5	18	19	4	1	4	19	21	17
Clyde	18	5	0	4	21	23	3	0	6	17	24	16
Dundee	18	4	2	3	17	11	2	0	7	11	22	14
Leith A	18	3	1	5	19	24	0	0	9	13	40	*7
Dumbarton	18	3	0	6	18	24	0	1	8	9	34	7

* Leith relegated to Division Two

DIVISION 2

	P	W	D	L	F	A	W	D	L	F	A	Pts
Hibernian	18	8	1	0	54	15	6	1	2	38	13	†30
Motherwell	18	8	0	1	33	8	2	2	5	23	31	22
Port Glasgow A	18	8	1	0	45	19	0	3	6	17	37	20
Renton	18	6	0	2	27	15	4	0	5	19	29	*20
Morton	18	7	0	2	38	23	2	1	6	21	40	19
Airdrie	18	7	1	1	50	14	1	1	7	18	31	18
Partick T	18	6	1	2	31	19	2	1	6	20	40	18
Abercorn	18	6	2	1	34	22	1	1	7	14	44	17
Dundee W	18	3	1	5	31	29	0	0	8	13	57	*9
Cowlairs	18	2	3	4	23	33	0	0	9	14	44	7

† Hibernian elected to Division One

* Dundee Wanderers and Renton played each other only once. Dundee were awarded two points when Renton failed to turn up for the return fixture.

Cowlairs and Dundee W left the League and were replaced by Kilmarnock and Linthouse.

Scottish Football League Records
Season 1895-96

DIVISION 1

	CELTIC	CLYDE	DUMBARTON	DUNDEE	HEARTS	HIBERNIAN	RANGERS	ST BERNARD'S	ST MIRREN	T LANARK
CELTIC		Aug17 3-0	Dec21 3-0	Oct26 11-0	Sep14 0-5	Oct05 3-1	Dec14 6-2	Dec07 2-1	Aug31 4-0	Nov09 7-0
CLYDE	Oct12 1-5		Nov30 5-1	Sep07 0-1	Aug24 1-2	Feb01 0-3	Feb08 2-2	Sep28 5-0	Nov23 1-3	Feb22 2-7
DUMBARTON	Sep28 2-3	Aug31 5-4		Dec07 1-2	Oct19 2-9	Nov09 1-3	Aug17 3-5	Oct26 4-3	Sep14 4-2	Dec14 2-4
DUNDEE	Aug10 1-2	Dec14 1-2	Aug24 4-1		Oct12 5-0	Aug31 2-2	Nov30 1-3	Oct05 4-1	Sep21 1-1	Nov23 2-0
HEARTS	Nov23 1-4	Oct05 9-1	Feb15 7-0	Nov02 2-0		Sep28 4-3	Aug31 1-2	Dec14 6-0	Oct26 5-1	Sep07 3-0
HIBERNIAN	Aug24 4-2	Sep14 4-3	Sep21 7-2	Jan18 3-1	Dec21 3-2		Oct26 1-1	Nov30 2-3	Oct12 5-1	Dec07 2-5
RANGERS	Sep07 2-4	Nov09 4-4	Jan04 3-1	Feb29 3-1	Dec07 7-2	Nov23 4-0		Oct12 2-0	Feb22 3-3	Aug24 0-4
ST BERNARD'S	Sep16 3-0	Feb15 1-4	Sep07 4-3	Aug17 4-2	Sep21 0-5	Oct19 2-5	Sep14 3-4		Nov09 4-3	Feb01 4-1
ST MIRREN	Nov30 1-3	Dec07 2-2	Nov02 1-2	Sep28 3-1	Aug17 2-1	Sep07 1-3	Oct05 1-7	Aug24 1-3		Mar07 3-2
T LANARK	Feb29 1-2	Oct26 6-2	Oct05 5-2	Sep14 3-4	Nov30 5-4	Aug17 2-7	Dec21 2-3	Aug31 0-0	Apr04 0-2	

DIVISION 2

	ABERCORN	AIRDRIE	KILMARNOCK	LEITH A	LINTHOUSE	MORTON	MOTHERWELL	PARTICK T	PORT GLASGOW A	RENTON
ABERCORN		Oct12 5-1	Apr18 3-2	Dec21 4-0	Apr11 2-1	Feb08 4-2	Sep21 1-0	Feb15 3-4	Aug24 3-0	Mar21 4-2
AIRDRIE	Jan25 3-3		Nov09 5-3	Aug24 1-4	Jan18 2-1	Feb01 5-1	Oct19 0-0	Mar07 4-2	Oct05 4-1	Apr18 2-2
KILMARNOCK	May07 2-4	Feb22 6-4		Mar21 1-0	Feb01 3-2	Aug31 5-1	Aug24 7-1	Apr11 2-3	Mar14 2-1	Sep14 4-2
LEITH A	Oct05 3-1	Mar28 5-2	Aug17 3-1		Oct19 4-1	Nov23 2-1	Feb15 6-1	Dec14 7-0	Sep07 6-1	Aug31 0-4
LINTHOUSE	Feb29 1-6	Aug17 2-1	Dec21 1-2	Mar14 3-2		Nov30 1-0	Oct26 0-3	Oct05 1-3	Mar28 2-4	Dec14 1-3
MORTON	Sep07 2-3	Apr11 1-1	Oct26 2-3	Sep21 2-2	Aug24 1-2		Oct05 4-1	Mar14 7-1	Nov02 1-1	Nov09 2-1
MOTHERWELL	Mar28 1-4	Mar14 3-6	Nov16 2-4	Jan25 2-4	Oct12 1-3	Feb22 2-2		Jan11 3-3	Aug10 2-1	Aug17 1-0
PARTICK T	Feb01 4-2	Nov16 0-6	Sep07 2-2	Feb22 3-5	Feb08 5-1	Apr18 2-1	Nov30 1-2		Nov09 2-1	Nov23 1-2
PORT GLASGOW A	Feb22 2-2	Nov30 3-1	Sep28 6-1	Dec07 6-2	Feb15 2-2	Sep14 1-2	Dec21 3-4	Aug17 3-2		Oct12 2-1
RENTON	Nov30 1-1	Feb29 2-0	Oct19 3-0	Oct26 3-0	Nov02 4-0	Sep28 3-0	Jan18 3-2	Aug24 2-6	Sep21 2-2	

LEAGUE TABLES
DIVISION 1

	P	W	D	L	F	A	W	D	L	F	A	Pts
Celtic	18	8	0	1	39	9	7	0	2	25	16	30
Rangers	18	5	2	2	28	19	6	2	1	29	20	26
Hibernian	18	6	1	2	31	20	5	1	3	27	19	24
Hearts	18	7	0	2	38	11	4	0	5	30	25	22
Dundee	18	4	2	3	21	12	3	0	6	12	30	16
T. Lanark	18	3	1	5	24	26	4	0	5	23	25	15
St Bernard's	18	5	0	4	25	27	2	1	6	11	26	15
St Mirren	18	3	1	5	15	24	2	2	5	16	27	13
Clyde	18	2	1	6	17	24	2	2	5	22	35	11
Dumbarton	18	3	0	6	24	35	1	0	8	12	39	*8

* Dumbarton relegated to Division Two.

DIVISION 2

	P	W	D	L	F	A	W	D	L	F	A	Pts
Abercorn	18	8	0	1	29	12	4	3	2	26	19	*27
Leith A	18	8	0	1	36	12	3	1	5	19	25	23
Renton	18	6	2	1	23	11	3	1	5	17	17	21
Kilmarnock	18	7	0	2	32	18	3	1	5	18	27	21
Airdrie	18	5	3	1	26	17	2	1	6	22	27	18
Partick T	18	4	1	4	20	22	4	1	4	24	32	18
Port Glasgow A	18	5	2	2	28	17	1	2	6	12	24	16
Motherwell	18	2	2	5	17	27	3	1	5	14	25	13
Morton	18	3	3	3	22	15	1	1	7	10	25	12
Linthouse	18	3	0	6	12	24	2	1	6	13	24	11

* Abercorn elected to Division One

Season 1896-97

DIVISION 1

	ABERCORN	CELTIC	CLYDE	DUNDEE	HEARTS	HIBERNIAN	RANGERS	ST BERNARD'S	ST MIRREN	T LANARK
ABERCORN		Aug29 0-6	Nov28 1-3	Jan16 1-7	Oct31 0-1	Sep12 2-2	Sep26 2-9	Oct10 2-3	Oct24 3-2	Nov14 1-2
CELTIC	Nov07 5-0		Dec12 4-1	Feb20 0-1	Sep05 3-0	Nov28 1-1	Oct10 1-1	Aug22 2-0	Sep26 2-1	Oct17 2-0
CLYDE	Oct03 6-2	Aug17 2-7		Oct24 0-2	Feb13 1-5	Aug29 0-7	Dec05 2-7	Aug15 1-2	Sep12 3-1	Dec19 3-2
DUNDEE	Oct17 3-0	Oct03 2-2	Nov07 1-0		Aug15 0-5	Aug22 3-0	Nov28 3-2	Sep26 4-1	Dec12 3-2	Sep12 2-0
HEARTS	Aug22 6-1	Oct24 1-1	Feb20 5-0	Sep19 2-2		Dec05 1-0	Sep21 2-1	Nov07 3-1	Aug29 2-1	Nov21 2-1
HIBERNIAN	Nov21 9-0	Aug15 3-1	Nov14 5-1	Oct31 3-1	Sep26 2-0		Sep05 4-3	Sep19 2-0	Jan16 3-0	Aug19 2-0
RANGERS	Dec12 6-1	Dec19 2-0	Oct17 2-1	Aug29 3-1	Sep12 5-0	Oct03 4-3		Feb20 3-2	Aug15 5-1	Oct24 6-1
ST BERNARD'S	Dec19 6-0	Sep12 1-2	Sep05 4-1	Nov14 2-1	Oct03 2-5	Oct17 0-1	Dec26 3-2		Oct31 0-2	Aug29 2-3
ST MIRREN	Sep19 4-2	Mar13 2-0	Aug22 5-0	Sep05 4-1	Oct17 0-2	Feb13 2-0	Nov07 2-2	Nov21 4-0		Oct03 2-0
T LANARK	Sep05 8-3	Dec05 0-3	Sep26 3-2	Oct10 3-1	Dec12 1-5	Nov07 1-3	Aug22 1-1	Nov28 2-3	Feb20 1-3	

DIVISION 2

	AIRDRIE	DUMBARTON	KILMARNOCK	LEITH A	LINTHOUSE	MORTON	MOTHERWELL	PARTICK T	PORT GLASGOW	RENTON
AIRDRIE		Oct03 3-2	Jan02 4-5	Oct31 2-1	Oct24 3-0	Sep19 4-1	Mar20 3-5	Nov28 1-2	Sep26 3-1	Nov14 3-0
DUMBARTON	Dec05 1-3		Apr10 0-6	Sep26 1-2	Mar06 4-5	Aug29 0-3	May15 3-1	Aug15 2-2	May08 4-1	Nov07 1-3
KILMARNOCK	Mar13 1-2	Sep05 5-1		Oct17 1-0	May08 0-3	May15 3-2	May06 2-0	Mar27 1-3	May11 3-0	Aug15 5-1
LEITH A	Jan16 3-1	Oct24 7-1	Aug22 4-1		Oct03 4-0	Sep12 4-2	Mar06 6-3	Dec12 3-1	May03 5-0	Aug29 4-1
LINTHOUSE	Nov07 1-4	Nov28 2-2	Apr27 1-1	Sep05 4-2		Dec26 2-5	Aug22 2-1	Feb27 3-5	Feb20 2-1	Feb06 6-2
MORTON	Nov21 3-1	Oct17 3-1	Oct10 3-2	Nov07 0-0	Dec05 4-0		May08 3-4	Apr24 3-4	Sep05 3-2	Sep26 0-1
MOTHERWELL	Sep05 2-3	Apr17 5-1	May01 1-2	Aug15 2-4	Mar13 4-5	Oct31 1-0		Feb13 0-6	Oct03 3-3	Feb27 4-2
PARTICK T	Oct10 4-3	Nov14 6-1	Apr17 2-0	Mar20 5-0	Nov21 3-2	Aug22 2-2	Feb20 6-2		Dec05 4-1	Sep05 2-1
PORT GLASGOW A	Aug15 4-4	Aug22 3-2	Mar20 5-2	Sep19 0-3	Dec12 6-3	May01 5-1	Apr03 0-2	Jan16 2-2		Oct31 1-1
RENTON	Aug22 3-2	Sep12 4-0	Mar06 1-2	Oct10 2-3	Feb13 2-3	Oct24 4-0	Sep19 2-0	Jan23 1-2	Nov28 3-3	

LEAGUE TABLES

DIVISION 1

	P	W	D	L	F	A	W	D	L	F	A	Pts
Hearts	18	7	2	0	24	8	6	0	3	23	14	28
Hibernian	18	9	0	0	33	6	3	2	4	17	14	26
Rangers	18	9	0	0	36	10	2	3	4	28	20	25
Celtic	18	6	2	1	20	5	4	2	3	22	13	24
Dundee	18	7	1	1	21	12	3	1	5	17	18	22
St Mirren	18	7	1	1	25	7	2	0	7	13	22	19
St Bernard's	18	4	0	5	20	17	3	0	6	12	23	14
T. Lanark	18	3	1	5	20	24	2	0	7	9	22	11
Clyde	18	3	0	6	18	35	1	0	8	9	30	8
Abercorn	18	1	1	7	12	35	0	0	9	9	53	*3

* Abercorn relegated

DIVISION 2

	P	W	D	L	F	A	W	D	L	F	A	Pts
Partick T	18	8	1	0	34	12	6	2	1	27	16	†31
Leith A	18	9	0	0	40	10	4	1	4	15	17	27
Kilmarnock	18	6	0	3	21	12	4	1	4	21	21	21
Airdrie	18	6	0	3	26	17	4	1	4	23	22	21
Morton	18	5	1	3	22	15	2	1	6	16	25	16
Linthouse	18	4	2	3	23	23	4	0	5	21	30	*14
Renton	18	4	1	4	22	15	2	1	6	12	26	14
Port Glasgow A	18	4	3	2	26	20	0	2	7	12	30	13
Motherwell	18	3	1	5	22	26	3	0	6	18	27	13
Dumbarton	18	2	1	6	16	26	0	1	8	11	38	6

* Four points deducted for fielding an ineligible player.
† Partick elected to Division One

Scottish Football League Records
Season 1897-98

DIVISION 1

	CELTIC	CLYDE	DUNDEE	HEARTS	HIBERNIAN	PARTICK T	RANGERS	ST BERNARD'S	ST MIRREN	T LANARK
CELTIC		Sep25 6-1	Jan15 2-1	Oct23 3-2	Sep04 4-1	Jan29 3-1	Apr11 0-0	Dec18 5-1	Feb12 3-0	Dec04 4-0
CLYDE	Dec25 1-9		Nov27 1-5	Nov06 2-2	Jan03 2-4	Nov13 2-3	Oct16 1-8	Oct02 4-2	Dec11 2-3	Sep11 1-1
DUNDEE	Nov06 1-2	Sep04 6-0		Oct16 1-6	Dec04 1-1	Oct23 5-0	Feb12 2-1	Sep11 0-0	Nov20 0-0	Oct02 4-2
HEARTS	Sep11 0-0	Dec04 8-1	Oct30 2-0		Dec18 3-2	Dec25 6-2	Sep20 2-2	Oct09 5-1	Sep25 2-4	Nov13 2-3
HIBERNIAN	Nov27 1-2	Oct09 5-0	Nov13 2-0	Sep18 1-1		Oct02 4-2	Dec11 0-5	Oct16 6-1	Dec25 3-1	Nov06 6-0
PARTICK T	Dec11 3-6	Oct30 1-1	Sep25 3-1	Sep04 3-2	Nov20 0-3		Oct09 1-5	Nov06 5-3	Oct16 1-0	Jan01 5-2
RANGERS	Sep27 0-4	Oct23 7-0	Dec25 5-0	Oct02 2-0	Sep11 1-0	Jan03 6-1		Mar19 8-1	Dec04 9-0	Apr09 0-0
ST BERNARD'S	Sep20 0-2	Jan01 3-1	Dec11 4-1	Nov20 1-5	Sep25 3-2	Dec04 9-1	Sep04 2-4		Oct30 1-2	Oct23 1-3
ST MIRREN	Oct02 0-0	Feb05 4-0	Oct09 2-1	Nov27 3-1	Oct23 2-3	Sep11 1-0	Nov06 1-5	Sep18 7-2		Dec18 0-1
T LANARK	Oct09 0-1	Nov20 6-1	Jan29 3-0	Dec11 2-5	Sep27 1-3	Feb12 5-2	Sep25 0-3	Dec25 6-0	Sep04 2-0	

DIVISION 2

	ABERCORN	AIRDRIE	AYR U	HAMILTON A	KILMARNOCK	LEITH A	LINTHOUSE	MORTON	MOTHERWELL	PORT GLASGOW A	RENTON
ABERCORN		Sep04 2-0	Feb12 1-1	Nov20 3-0	Oct30 4-1	Sep25 3-1	Dec04 3-3	Nov13 2-3	Feb19 0-1	Mar19 1-4	
AIRDRIE	Feb05 2-1		Oct30 5-1	Dec04 2-4	Feb12 2-1	Mar05 3-1	Jan08 5-2	Sep18 1-2	Apr30 7-2	Jan15 2-2	
AYR U	Nov27 2-3	Jan22 4-1		Jan15 3-0	Mar12 0-3	Nov13 5-3	Sep04 1-4	Mar26 6-1	Jan29 3-3	Sep25 3-0	
HAMILTON A	Dec18 1-2	Feb19 3-2	Jan08 3-0		Nov06 2-3		Nov27 1-0	Dec11 3-3		Jan29 5-1	
KILMARNOCK	Sep11 7-1	Nov27 5-2	Oct16 5-2	Mar05 5-0		Oct09 3-1	Nov13 5-0	Oct23 5-2	Dec18 6-2	Apr02 2-1	
LEITH A	Oct23 2-1	Apr23 6-3	Dec04 1-0		Nov20 2-2		Mar26 2-1	Sep11 3-3	Feb12 1-0	Apr25 3-1	Sep04 4-0
LINTHOUSE	Nov06 1-1	Oct23 7-3	Dec25 0-1	Feb12 2-1	Mar19 0-3	Dec11 5-1		Oct02 2-5	Mar05 4-0	Feb05 5-2	
MORTON	Oct09 1-1	Nov06 3-2	Dec18 4-0	Feb05 3-0	Sep25 3-4	Nov27 2-0	Oct30 0-0		Jan15 6-1	Sep04 3-4	
MOTHERWELL	Oct02 3-2	Apr09 2-2	Feb05 2-3	Dec25 3-3	Sep04 1-2	Nov06 2-4	Nov20 1-1	Dec04 1-3		Apr16 0-4	
PORT GLASGOW A	Dec11 8-2	Mar26 8-1	Apr30 4-1		Apr09 4-2	Apr18 4-2	Mar12 4-1	Oct16 3-0	Jan22 4-3		Oct02 8-0
RENTON						Oct16 1-3			Sep18 1-4		

LEAGUE TABLES

DIVISION 1

	P	W	D	L	F	A	W	D	L	F	A	Pts
Celtic	18	8	1	0	30	7	7	2	0	26	6	33
Rangers	18	7	1	1	38	6	6	2	1	33	9	29
Hibernian	18	6	1	2	28	12	4	1	4	19	17	22
Hearts	18	5	2	2	30	15	3	2	4	24	18	20
T. Lanark	18	5	0	4	25	15	3	2	4	12	23	18
St Mirren	18	5	1	3	20	13	3	1	5	10	23	18
Dundee	18	4	3	2	20	12	1	0	8	9	24	13
Partick T	18	5	1	3	22	23	1	0	8	12	41	13
St Bernard's	18	4	0	5	24	21	0	1	8	11	46	9
Clyde	18	1	2	6	16	37	0	1	8	5	46	5

DIVISION 2

	P	W	D	L	F	A	W	D	L	F	A	Pts
Kilmarnock	18	9	0	0	43	11	5	1	3	21	18	29
Port Glasgow A	18	9	0	0	47	12	3	1	5	19	24	25
Morton	18	5	2	2	25	12	4	2	3	22	26	22
Leith A	18	7	2	0	24	11	2	0	7	16	28	20
Linthouse	18	5	1	3	26	17	1	3	5	12	22	16
Ayr U	18	5	1	3	27	18	2	1	6	9	25	16
Abercorn	18	4	2	3	19	14	2	2	5	14	27	16
Airdrie	18	6	1	2	29	16	0	1	8	16	40	14
Hamilton A*	18	4	1	4	20	18	1	1	7	8	33	12
Motherwell	18	1	3	5	15	24	2	1	6	16	32	10

* Took the place of Renton, who resigned

Scottish Football League Records
Season 1898-99

DIVISION 1

	CELTIC	CLYDE	DUNDEE	HEARTS	HIBERNIAN	PARTICK T	RANGERS	ST BERNARD'S	ST MIRREN	T LANARK
CELTIC		Nov05 9-2	Jan07 4-1	Dec17 3-2	Sep26 1-2	Nov26 4-0	Sep24 0-4	Oct08 1-0	Sep03 4-1	Aug20 2-1
CLYDE	Aug27 0-0		Sep10 1-0	Oct22 3-3	Oct01 2-2	Oct29 3-1	Jan07 0-3	Nov19 1-2	Dec03 0-1	Dec24 2-3
DUNDEE	Nov19 1-4	Nov12 1-3		Dec03 2-5	Sep17 2-4	Oct01 5-1	Oct08 1-2	Sep03 1-1	Nov05 1-7	Oct22 1-3
HEARTS	Sep19 2-2	Sep24 4-0	Nov26 6-3		Oct08 4-0	Oct15 5-1	Sep03 2-3	Nov05 3-1	Dec24 4-2	Nov12 2-1
HIBERNIAN	Sep10 2-1	Dec17 2-1	Oct15 5-0	Oct29 1-5		Dec10 1-1	Nov19 3-4	Sep24 4-3	Oct22 4-3	Dec03 1-1
PARTICK T	Dec03 3-8	Oct08 0-1	Dec31 2-0	Jan07 0-1	Sep03 1-4		Nov05 0-5	Sep10 0-3	Sep24 1-4	Dec17 1-3
RANGERS	Jan02 4-1	Nov26 8-0	Dec17 7-0	Oct01 3-1	Dec24 10-0	Aug20 6-2		Dec03 5-2	Dec31 3-2	Sep10 4-1
ST BERNARD'S	Oct29 2-3	Dec10 4-1	Dec24 2-2	Sep17 1-3	Nov12 1-3	Oct22 2-3	Sep19 0-2		Dec17 0-0	Oct01 4-2
ST MIRREN	Oct01 4-0	Aug20 2-2	Oct29 5-1	Sep10 2-3	Nov26 2-0	Nov12 2-2	Aug27 1-3	Oct15 2-1		Nov19 4-1
T LANARK	Dec31 2-4	Sep03 3-1	Sep24 3-1	Dec10 2-1	Nov05 1-4	Aug27 1-0	Sep26 2-3	Nov26 1-1	Oct08 2-2	

DIVISION 2

	ABERCORN	AIRDRIE	AYR U	HAMILTON A	KILMARNOCK	LEITH A	LINTHOUSE	MORTON	MOTHERWELL	PORT GLASGOW A
ABERCORN		Feb11 3-1	Apr08 3-3	Oct08 4-2	Sep03 1-2	Dec03 2-3	Dec24 7-1	Dec10 2-1	Dec31 1-5	Oct22 2-5
AIRDRIE	Aug20 3-2		Apr22 4-0	Nov19 2-0	Oct22 4-4	Oct29 0-2	Dec03 4-0	Sep03 1-2	Dec24 2-2	Sep24 6-2
AYR U	Oct15 7-3	Feb25 0-1		Nov26 3-0	Nov19 1-1	Dec17 2-2	Aug20 4-0	Dec31 1-0	Sep03 1-0	Dec24 2-3
HAMILTON A	Dec17 6-1	Sep17 7-1	Jan14 6-4		Dec03 1-7	Apr22 4-1	Oct01 5-2	Aug20 3-2	Jan21 4-1	Nov05 4-5
KILMARNOCK	Nov26 3-0	Aug27 5-0	Jan07 5-1	Dec10 7-1		Oct08 5-3	Nov05 8-0	Oct15 2-0	Apr22 5-0	Sep10 4-1
LEITH A	Nov12 8-1	Oct01 3-2	Nov05 4-1	Sep03 3-1	Apr15 3-3		Apr01 2-1	Nov26 3-2	Sep17 5-0	Dec10 5-1
LINTHOUSE	Aug27 4-2	Mar18 2-1	Apr15 6-2	Nov12 3-2	Apr08 0-2	Jan21 3-4		Oct29 0-1	Oct08 2-4	Feb11 2-2
MORTON	Nov19 4-2	Oct08 3-1	Aug27 4-0	Dec24 6-1	Sep24 1-2	Sep10 0-5	Oct22 1-2		Nov05 2-4	Dec03 2-4
MOTHERWELL	Oct29 3-2	Jan07 1-1	Dec03 3-1	Aug27 1-1	Mar18 3-3	Oct22 2-2	Dec10 6-1	Oct01 2-2		Nov19 4-3
PORT GLASGOW A	Oct01 4-3	Nov26 8-2	Apr01 6-2	Oct29 5-0	Dec17 4-5	Oct15 8-5	Sep03 5-0	Sep17 7-3	Aug20 2-0	

LEAGUE TABLES

DIVISION 1

	P	W	D	L	F	A	W	D	L	F	A	Pts
Rangers	18	9	0	0	50	9	9	0	0	29	9	36
Hearts	18	7	1	1	32	13	5	1	3	24	17	26
Celtic	18	7	0	2	28	13	4	2	3	23	20	24
Hibernian	18	5	2	2	23	19	5	1	3	19	24	23
St Mirren	18	5	2	2	24	13	3	2	4	22	19	20
T. Lanark	18	4	2	3	17	17	3	1	5	16	21	17
St Bernard's	18	2	2	5	16	19	2	2	5	14	18	12
Clyde	18	2	3	4	12	15	2	1	6	11	33	12
Partick T	18	1	0	8	8	29	1	2	6	11	29	*6
Dundee	18	1	1	7	15	30	0	1	8	8	35	4

* Partick Thistle relegated

DIVISION 2

	P	W	D	L	F	A	W	D	L	F	A	Pts
Kilmarnock	18	9	0	0	44	6	5	4	0	29	18	*32
Leith A	18	8	1	0	36	12	4	2	3	27	26	27
Port Glasgow A	18	8	0	1	49	20	4	1	4	26	31	25
Motherwell	18	4	5	0	25	16	3	1	5	16	24	20
Hamilton A	18	7	0	2	40	24	0	1	8	8	34	15
Airdrie	18	5	2	2	26	14	1	1	7	10	32	15
Morton	18	4	0	5	23	21	2	1	6	13	21	13
Ayr U	18	5	2	2	21	10	0	1	8	14	41	13
Linthouse	18	4	1	4	22	20	1	0	8	7	42	11
Abercorn	18	4	1	4	25	23	0	0	9	16	42	9

* Kilmarnock promoted

Scottish Football League Records
Season 1899-1900

DIVISION 1

	CELTIC	CLYDE	DUNDEE	HEARTS	HIBERNIAN	KILMARNOCK	RANGERS	ST BERNARD'S	ST MIRREN	T LANARK
CELTIC		Aug19 3-2	Dec23 1-1	Sep30 0-2	Sep09 2-1	Dec16 3-3	Jan01 3-2	Oct28 5-0	Dec09 3-1	Sep02 5-2
CLYDE	Sep23 0-5		Dec02 0-7	Oct21 1-2	Nov04 3-4	Dec30 2-3	Aug26 2-6	Dec16 2-4	Nov25 3-1	Jan20 4-2
DUNDEE	Nov25 1-2	Sep02 3-1		Dec16 1-1	Sep16 2-2	Jan06 3-3	Jan20 2-3	Sep23 3-0	Oct14 5-2	Oct28 0-0
HEARTS	Nov04 3-2	Dec09 4-1	Nov11 4-1		Nov25 1-3	Sep23 1-0	Sep18 1-1	Oct14 5-0	Sep16 3-0	Oct07 2-0
HIBERNIAN	Sep18 1-1	Dec23 5-0	Nov18 3-3	Oct28 1-0		Sep02 3-1	Oct21 0-2	Jan06 1-1	Sep23 5-1	Dec16 3-2
KILMARNOCK	Aug26 2-2	Oct07 3-1	Oct21 2-1	Mar17 2-1	Oct14 0-3		Sep09 2-4	Sep16 2-1	Nov11 2-2	Sep30 1-1
RANGERS	Oct07 3-3	Oct14 7-0	Nov04 6-0	Sep02 4-3	Sep25 3-2	Dec09 6-1		Nov25 4-3	Dec16 4-1	Jan06 2-1
ST BERNARD'S	Dec02 1-1	Nov18 3-2	Oct07 2-0	Sep09 2-4	Nov11 0-4	Nov04 1-1	Feb03 1-4		Dec30 3-3	Dec09 4-0
ST MIRREN	Oct21 2-2	Sep30 3-0	Sep09 4-0	Nov18 2-2	Oct07 1-1	Aug19 0-1	Dec02 1-3	Sep02 4-3		Nov04 1-1
T LANARK	Sep25 0-3	Sep09 5-0	Dec30 3-3	Dec23 3-2	Dec02 1-1	Nov25 2-1	Aug19 1-5	Oct21 2-0	Aug26 5-1	

DIVISION 2

	ABERCORN	AIRDRIE	AYR U	HAMILTON A	LEITH A	LINTHOUSE	MORTON	MOTHERWELL	PARTICK T	PORT GLASGOW A
ABERCORN		Jan20 4-1	Nov25 3-3	Dec23 5-0	Aug26 3-0	Oct28 3-4	Feb17 2-3	Mar17 1-2	Dec30 2-2	Sep16 2-0
AIRDRIE	Sep02 2-1		Aug26 5-2	Sep30 2-1	Jan27 2-2	Nov25 3-3	Sep23 0-5	Dec09 1-3	Nov04 0-2	Oct28 2-1
AYR U	Dec09 1-2	Dec30 5-0		Oct07 2-1	Oct14 0-1	Sep02 1-5	Dec23 1-4	Feb17 2-1	Oct21 2-1	Aug19 1-3
HAMILTON A	Jan06 5-3	Mar17 4-0	Dec16 0-4		Feb17 3-0	Aug26 1-1	Jan27 3-4	Mar03 4-2	Mar31 2-4	Mar10 2-0
LEITH A	Feb03 4-1	Sep16 3-2	Dec02 3-1	Aug19 3-1		Jan06 4-1	Mar24 0-1	Dec30 0-1	Sep09 2-1	Oct07 4-1
LINTHOUSE	Dec02 0-6	Aug19 1-1	Nov11 2-2	Dec30 2-4	Oct21 2-4		Nov04 0-5	Mar10 2-2	Sep30 1-5	Dec16 0-4
MORTON	Aug19 3-2	Dec02 2-0	Sep16 7-1	Sep02 7-0	Sep30 4-0	Jan20 5-0		Apr07 3-0	Oct28 2-3	Oct21 3-1
MOTHERWELL	Mar31 1-3	Jan06 4-2	Nov04 4-2	Jan20 1-2	Sep02 2-1	Dec23 4-0	Nov25 4-3		Aug19 1-3	Dec02 4-2
PARTICK T	Mar24 5-3	Oct07 3-2	Sep23 4-1	Dec02 2-0	Nov11 4-0	Dec09 8-1	Aug26 2-1	Feb03 2-1		Sep02 3-1
PORT GLASGOW A	Feb24 3-0	Dec23 3-2	Jan06 2-8	Dec09 3-0	Sep23 7-1	Mar03 6-3	Sep09 6-4	Aug26 3-1	Oct14 4-1	

LEAGUE TABLES

DIVISION 1

	P	W	D	L	F	A	W	D	L	F	A	Pts
Rangers	18	8	1	0	39	14	7	1	1	30	13	32
Celtic	18	6	2	1	25	14	3	5	1	21	13	25
Hibernian	18	5	3	1	22	11	4	3	2	21	13	24
Hearts	18	7	1	1	24	8	3	2	4	17	16	23
Kilmarnock	18	4	3	2	16	16	2	3	4	14	21	18
Dundee	18	3	4	2	20	14	1	3	5	16	25	15
T. Lanark	18	5	2	2	22	16	0	3	6	9	22	15
St Mirren	18	3	4	2	18	13	0	2	7	12	33	12
St Bernard's	18	3	3	3	17	19	1	1	7	12	28	*12
Clyde	18	2	0	7	17	34	0	0	9	7	36	*4

* St Bernard's and Clyde relegated.
Queen's Park joined Division One.

DIVISION 2

	P	W	D	L	F	A	W	D	L	F	A	Pts
Partick T	18	9	0	0	33	10	5	1	3	22	16	*29
Morton	18	8	0	1	36	7	6	0	3	30	18	*28
Port Glasgow A	18	8	0	1	37	20	2	0	7	13	21	20
Motherwell	18	6	0	3	25	18	3	1	5	13	18	19
Leith A	18	7	0	2	23	10	2	1	6	9	27	19
Abercorn	18	4	2	3	25	15	3	0	6	21	24	16
Hamilton A	18	5	1	3	24	18	2	0	7	9	27	15
Ayr U	18	4	0	5	15	18	2	2	5	24	30	14
Airdrie	18	4	2	3	17	20	0	1	8	10	29	11
Linthouse	18	0	3	6	10	33	2	2	5	18	35	9

* Partick Thistle and Morton were elected to Division One.
Linthouse left League replaced by East Stirling.

Scottish Football League Records
Season 1900-01

DIVISION 1

	CELTIC	DUNDEE	HEARTS	HIBERNIAN	KILMARNOCK	MORTON	PARTICK T	QUEEN'S PARK	RANGERS	ST MIRREN	T LANARK
CELTIC		Dec22 1-2	Nov17 1-3	Aug25 3-1	Oct27 1-0	Nov24 4-2	Aug15 3-3	Oct13 2-0	Oct06 2-1	Dec15 3-0	Sep24 5-1
DUNDEE	Nov10 1-1		Sep29 1-2	Dec01 1-3	Sep15 3-0	Oct13 5-2	Dec29 4-0	Sep01 4-0	Dec15 1-5	Feb02 1-1	Nov24 0-0
HEARTS	Sep17 0-2	Sep08 0-4		Oct13 0-0	Dec08 7-0	Oct27 1-2	Oct06 1-3	Sep22 1-2	Aug25 0-1	Dec01 0-0	Nov03 0-0
HIBERNIAN	Sep29 2-2	Oct27 2-1	Sep01 3-0		Nov24 2-2	Dec22 1-1	Jan19 2-0	Oct20 0-1	Sep17 4-1	Sep15 1-0	Dec15 2-0
KILMARNOCK	Nov03 2-1	Aug25 2-0	Nov10 1-3	Sep08 2-2		Oct20 4-1	Sep22 2-1	Oct06 2-1	Dec01 1-2	Dec22 2-2	Jan01 2-1
MORTON	Aug18 2-3	Jan19 5-1	Sep15 2-2	Mar30 1-0	Dec29 3-2		Dec08 2-3	Dec01 6-2	Nov17 1-3	Sep01 1-0	Nov10 1-0
PARTICK T	Dec01 2-6	Nov17 1-1	Dec15 0-1	Sep24 0-1	Aug18 1-2	Jan05 1-2		Dec22 1-4	Sep08 1-2	Feb09 5-3	Sep29 3-1
QUEEN'S PARK	Sep08 0-2	Jan05 1-0	Jan19 4-0	Apr27 1-1	Dec15 5-5	Nov03 3-0	Nov24 2-0		Sep29 2-3	Oct27 0-0	Nov17 0-2
RANGERS	Jan01 2-1	Oct20 4-2	Sep24 1-0	Jan26 6-0	Sep01 5-1	Feb16 3-2	Nov03 4-1	Dec29 3-2		Nov24 5-2	Aug18 4-0
ST MIRREN	Jan19 3-4	Mar30 3-3	Oct20 2-1	Nov17 0-2	Oct13 3-1	Sep22 0-2	Aug25 5-2	Nov10 4-3	Jan05 1-4		Sep08 2-1
T LANARK	Sep01 1-2	Oct06 2-1	Dec22 1-0	Sep22 0-0	Aug22 3-2	Aug25 2-2	Oct20 1-0	Dec08 1-0	Oct13 1-1	Dec29 2-2	

DIVISION 2

	ABERCORN	AIRDRIE	AYR U	CLYDE	E STIRLING	HAMILTON A	LEITH A	MOTHERWELL	PORT GLASGOW A	ST BERNARD'S
ABERCORN		Sep01 3-2	Mar16 2-1	Feb16 3-3	Mar09 3-0	Feb23 5-1	Dec22 5-1	Aug18 2-2	Dec01 3-0	Dec29 1-1
AIRDRIE	Nov24 5-1		Dec15 5-4	Aug25 2-3	Feb16 2-1	Dec29 1-1	Dec08 2-0	Oct20 2-0	Nov17 6-2	Oct13 3-1
AYR U	Sep15 1-0	Nov10 5-1		Jan01 3-2	Apr06 3-2	Aug25 4-2	Feb23 1-0	Dec08 3-1	Oct13 1-0	Nov17 1-0
CLYDE	Dec08 3-4	Sep22 2-0	Apr13 2-1		Apr22 3-3	Nov24 4-2	Sep01 3-1	Dec29 4-0	Sep29 0-1	Oct27 1-2
E STIRLING	Sep29 2-0	Aug18 2-3	Sep01 2-1	Feb23 2-1		May04 5-2	Dec29 1-1	Dec22 2-1	Sep15 3-4	Dec01 1-1
HAMILTON A	Jan05 5-0	Oct27 1-2	May11 3-1	Nov17 2-4	Jan12 5-0		Nov10 1-1	Sep01 1-1	Aug18 2-4	Sep29 2-3
LEITH A	Oct13 1-0	Sep08 1-0	Jan05 4-1	Oct20 1-2	Apr27 1-3	Dec01 1-3		Nov17 1-2	Nov24 3-1	Oct06 1-2
MOTHERWELL	Jan12 1-2	Dec01 0-2	Mar09 2-1	Nov03 2-3	Aug25 0-3	Oct13 4-2	Sep29 0-2		Nov10 5-1	Dec15 2-2
PORT GLASGOW A	Aug25 2-3	Nov03 1-2	Dec29 5-0	Jan19 3-2	Mar23 3-2	Dec15 6-3	Sep22 3-2	Oct27 5-0		Oct20 3-2
ST BERNARD'S	Nov10 2-0	Dec22 4-3	Apr27 1-0	Sep08 3-1	Jan19 5-0	Nov03 3-3	Sep15 2-0	Nov24 4-3	Sep01 4-1	

LEAGUE TABLES

DIVISION 1

	P	W	D	L	F	A	W	D	L	F	A	Pts
Rangers	20	10	0	0	37	11	7	1	2	23	14	35
Celtic	20	7	1	2	25	13	6	2	2	24	15	29
Hibernian	20	6	3	1	19	8	3	4	3	10	14	25
Morton	20	6	1	3	24	16	3	2	5	16	24	21
Kilmarnock	20	6	2	2	20	14	1	2	7	15	33	18
T. Lanark	20	5	4	1	14	10	1	2	7	6	19	18
Dundee	20	4	3	3	21	14	2	2	6	15	21	17
Queen's Park	20	4	3	3	18	13	3	0	7	15	24	17
St Mirren	20	5	1	4	23	23	0	5	5	10	20	16
Hearts	20	1	3	6	10	14	4	1	5	12	16	14
Partick T	20	2	1	7	15	23	2	1	7	13	26	*10

* Partick Thistle relegated.

DIVISION 2

	P	W	D	L	F	A	W	D	L	F	A	Pts
St Bernard's	18	8	1	0	28	11	3	3	3	14	15	26
Airdrie	18	7	1	1	28	13	4	0	5	15	19	23
Abercorn	18	6	3	0	27	11	3	0	6	10	22	21
Clyde	18	5	1	3	22	14	4	1	4	21	21	20
Port Glasgow A	18	7	0	2	31	16	3	0	6	14	27	20
Ayr U	18	9	0	0	22	8	0	0	9	10	26	18
E. Stirling	18	5	2	2	20	14	2	1	6	14	25	17
Hamilton A	18	3	2	4	22	16	1	2	6	19	33	12
Leith A	18	4	0	5	14	14	1	2	6	8	18	12
Motherwell	18	3	1	5	16	18	1	2	6	10	24	11

Arthurlie joined Division Two.

Scottish Football League Records
Season 1901-02

DIVISION 1

	CELTIC	DUNDEE	HEARTS	HIBERNIAN	KILMARNOCK	MORTON	QUEEN'S PARK	RANGERS	ST MIRREN	T LANARK
CELTIC		Aug17 1-1	Nov30 1-2	Dec14 2-2	Dec28 4-2	Sep21 2-1	Oct19 1-0	Jan01 2-4	Nov09 3-1	Aug31 3-2
DUNDEE	Nov16 2-3		Dec07 2-0	Sep21 1-0	Aug24 0-0	Nov02 0-0	Mar01 2-0	Aug31 0-3	Sep14 1-2	Oct19 1-1
HEARTS	Nov02 2-2	Oct12 4-0		Aug17 2-1	Sep21 3-0	Aug31 3-1	Sep28 1-1	Sep16 0-2	Nov23 2-0	Nov09 4-1
HIBERNIAN	Sep16 1-2	Nov30 5-0	Sep14 1-2		Nov16 5-0	Oct26 1-2	Sep07 8-1	Oct19 2-3	Aug24 1-2	Oct05 2-2
KILMARNOCK	Sep28 0-1	Nov09 4-0	Oct19 1-0	Aug31 0-0		Sep14 3-2	Jan18 1-1	Aug17 4-2	Oct12 1-2	Dec07 1-2
MORTON	Aug24 1-2	Sep07 1-4	Nov16 1-3	Oct12 0-2	Oct05 1-1		Nov30 2-2	Nov09 2-3	Sep28 1-3	Nov23 1-4
QUEEN'S PARK	Dec07 3-2	Oct05 1-0	Oct26 2-1	Nov09 2-0	Mar15 0-1	Mar08 1-1		Jan04 0-1	Aug31 3-0	Dec21 0-1
RANGERS	Oct05 2-2	Mar29 3-1	Aug24 2-1	Sep23 0-2	Sep07 3-2	Dec07 2-1	Nov02 2-1		Jan18 3-2	Nov16 1-4
ST MIRREN	Sep07 2-3	Oct26 3-0	Oct05 1-2	Nov02 1-1	Dec21 1-1	Oct19 1-1	Dec28 4-0	Sep21 1-5		Jan04 2-0
T LANARK	Sep23 0-2	Dec28 0-0	Sep07 2-0	Mar01 1-2	Nov02 0-0	Dec14 4-1	Aug24 4-3	Sep28 2-2	Nov30 0-1	

DIVISION 2

	ABERCORN	AIRDRIE	ARTHURLIE	AYR U	CLYDE	E STIRLING	HAMILTON A	LEITH A	MOTHERWELL	PARTICK T	PORT GLASGOW A	ST BERNARD'S
ABERCORN		Mar08 0-3	Oct12 1-1	Aug17 5-2	Nov09 2-2	Feb22 5-4	Sep14 2-3	Nov30 3-1	Aug31 0-3	Aug24 2-2	Sep28 1-1	Jan18 1-0
AIRDRIE	Sep07 4-0		Jan04 3-0	Mar29 3-2	Oct19 3-2	Sep28 3-0	Oct26 1-3	Jan25 3-0	Nov09 0-3	Aug17 2-1	Oct05 0-2	Mar01 3-1
ARTHURLIE	Dec07 2-0	Apr12 3-3		Nov02 0-1	Oct26 3-1	Oct19 3-3	Nov30 1-4	Oct05 2-0	Mar01 2-1	Feb22 1-5	Aug24 3-1	Apr05 0-1
AYR U	Mar15 3-0	Nov16 1-1	Sep14 1-0		Nov30 1-0	Mar01 0-1	Aug24 2-0	Jan04 3-1	Apr19 1-2	Nov09 2-2	Feb22 1-1	Jan02 1-0
CLYDE	Oct05 3-1	Dec07 1-1	Sep28 1-0	Jan25 1-0		Jan18 0-2	Nov02 0-0	Feb08 0-1	Jan04 0-4	Nov16 1-0	Sep07 1-2	Aug24 0-1
E STIRLING	Nov16 4-1	Nov30 3-1	Dec21 1-1	Mar22 0-1	Aug17 2-4		Oct05 4-1	Jan11 2-1	Aug24 1-3	Nov02 1-3	Oct12 1-4	Sep14 0-0
HAMILTON A	Jan04 3-0	Apr19 1-1	Aug31 1-3	Dec07 4-1	Mar01 2-1	Nov09 2-3		Oct19 5-2	Apr12 2-0	Apr05 2-2	Aug17 3-1	Sep28 4-1
LEITH A	Dec21 5-0	Nov02 0-0	Nov16 2-1	Oct12 1-1	Nov23 3-1	Sep21 1-0	Dec14 4-1		Sep28 3-0	Jan18 0-1	Nov09 3-3	Feb01 2-1
MOTHERWELL	Oct26 3-1	Sep14 1-2	Aug17 2-2	Apr05 2-2	Mar15 6-2	Jan25 2-3	Oct12 3-0	Mar08 4-2		Nov30 3-2	Mar29 4-2	Mar22 2-1
PARTICK T	Oct19 5-0	Sep21 2-1	Jan25 5-2	Mar08 2-0	Dec28 1-0	Aug31 2-0	Nov23 3-1	Dec07 1-0	Dec21 4-1		Jan04 1-6	Sep07 5-1
PORT GLASGOW A	Nov02 4-1	Aug31 4-2	Feb15 3-1	Feb01 3-0	Sep21 6-0	Nov23 6-2	Dec28 5-2	Sep14 6-1	Dec07 8-1	Oct26 1-1		Oct19 5-0
ST BERNARD'S	Sep21 1-1	Oct12 2-1	Mar08 2-1	Aug31 4-1	Dec21 4-0	Dec07 2-1	Nov16 0-1	Oct26 0-1	Nov02 4-0	Oct05 2-0	Nov30 2-1	

LEAGUE TABLES

DIVISION 1

	P	W	D	L	F	A	W	D	L	F	A	Pts
Rangers	18	6	1	2	18	16	7	1	1	25	13	28
Celtic	18	5	2	2	19	15	6	2	1	19	13	26
Hearts	18	6	2	1	21	8	4	0	5	11	13	22
T. Lanark	18	3	3	3	13	11	4	2	3	17	15	19
St Mirren	18	3	3	3	16	13	5	0	4	13	15	19
Hibernian	18	3	1	5	26	14	3	3	3	10	9	16
Kilmarnock	18	4	2	3	15	10	1	4	4	7	17	16
Queen's Park	18	5	1	3	12	7	0	3	6	9	25	14
Dundee	18	3	3	3	9	9	1	2	6	6	22	13
Morton	18	0	2	7	10	24	1	3	5	10	17	7

DIVISION 2

	P	W	D	L	F	A	W	D	L	F	A	Pts
Port Glasgow A	22	10	1	0	51	11	4	3	4	24	20	*32
Partick T	22	10	0	1	31	12	3	4	4	19	17	*30
Motherwell	22	7	2	2	32	19	5	0	6	18	25	26
Airdrie	22	8	0	3	25	14	2	5	4	16	18	25
Hamilton A	22	7	2	2	29	15	4	1	6	16	25	25
St Bernard's	22	8	1	2	23	8	2	1	8	7	23	22
Leith A	22	7	3	1	24	9	2	0	9	10	29	21
Ayr U	22	6	3	2	16	8	2	2	7	11	25	21
E. Stirling	22	4	2	5	19	20	4	1	6	19	26	19
Arthurlie	22	5	2	4	20	20	1	3	7	12	22	17
Clyde	22	4	2	5	8	12	1	1	9	13	33	13
Abercorn	22	4	4	3	22	22	0	1	10	5	37	13

* Port Glasgow A & Partick Thistle promoted to Division One.

Falkirk & Raith Rovers joined Division Two.

Scottish Football League Records
Season 1902-03

DIVISION 1

	CELTIC	DUNDEE	HEARTS	HIBERNIAN	KILMARNOCK	MORTON	PARTICK T	PORT GLASGOW A	QUEEN'S PARK	RANGERS	ST MIRREN	T LANARK
CELTIC		Nov29 2-2	Sep29 2-2	Jan02 0-4	Nov01 3-1	Dec20 1-1	Nov15 4-1	Nov22 3-0	Sep06 1-1	Oct18 1-1	Aug23 2-2	Sep27 1-0
DUNDEE	Mar21 2-0		Oct18 0-1	Oct25 0-3	Aug30 2-0	Nov15 3-0	Dec27 3-0	Sep13 2-1	Aug16 2-0	Dec06 3-1	Sep20 2-1	Oct04 0-0
HEARTS	Sep15 1-2	Aug23 0-2		Oct11 1-1	Dec06 1-1	Dec27 3-0	Nov29 4-2	Oct25 3-1	Sep20 4-0	Sep06 2-1	Nov08 1-3	Jan03 3-1
HIBERNIAN	Aug16 1-1	Sep27 1-0	Sep13 0-0		Nov15 2-1	Oct18 3-1	Nov01 2-2	Jan31 5-1	Aug30 3-2	Sep15 1-0	Oct04 4-3	Nov22 1-0
KILMARNOCK	Sep20 1-3	Dec13 0-2	Nov22 1-3	Sep06 1-4		Aug23 4-2	Oct25 2-0	Oct04 1-0	Oct11 1-1	Dec20 0-0	Dec27 2-3	Nov08 2-2
MORTON	Mar14 0-2	Nov22 0-2	Aug16 3-2	Dec06 0-1	Sep13 0-1		Oct04 3-3	Nov08 4-3	Feb14 1-2	Oct11 0-4	Sep06 2-3	Dec13 0-3
PARTICK T	Dec06 0-0	Sep06 0-2	Sep27 2-2	Dec20 0-2	Aug16 2-1	Aug30 1-1		Jan03 4-2	Nov22 4-2	Nov08 2-4	Oct18 2-2	Feb28 1-0
PORT GLASGOW A	Mar07 1-1	Nov01 0-0	Dec20 0-3	Aug23 0-1	Feb14 0-1	Sep27 3-0	Sep20 0-3		Oct18 4-0	Aug30 0-3	Nov15 3-2	Nov29 0-0
QUEEN'S PARK	Oct04 2-1	Dec20 0-0	Nov01 2-5	Nov08 1-3	Jan31 2-3	Nov29 4-0	Dec13 4-1	Feb28 2-2		Sep27 0-2	Feb21 1-1	Aug23 2-1
RANGERS	Jan01 3-3	Jan17 1-1	Oct04 2-1	Sep29 2-5	Nov29 5-0	Sep20 4-1	Aug23 9-0	Dec13 4-2	Nov15 3-2		Jan03 2-2	Nov01 2-0
ST MIRREN	Dec13 3-1	Oct11 1-0	Aug30 1-1	Nov29 1-1	Sep27 4-0	Nov01 1-1	Jan01 0-3	Aug16 2-2	Oct25 3-1	Nov22 0-1		Dec20 1-2
T LANARK	Aug30 1-2	Apr04 0-1	Nov15 0-3	Sep20 1-0	Oct18 2-0	Mar28 2-2	Sep29 1-1	Sep06 5-1	Dec27 3-2	Aug16 4-2	Dec06 6-0	

DIVISION 2

	ABERCORN	AIRDRIE	ARTHURLIE	AYR U	CLYDE	E STIRLING	FALKIRK	HAMILTON A	LEITH A	MOTHERWELL	RAITH R	ST BERNARD'S
ABERCORN		Sep13 2-4	Feb14 0-1	May11 1-2	May06 0-6	Nov15 3-2	Apr04 2-1	Dec27 0-2	Feb21 1-1	Aug23 0-1	Oct04 3-1	Nov08 3-5
AIRDRIE	Feb28 3-1		Jan03 3-1	Nov22 2-0	Nov29 1-1	Nov01 2-0	Oct11 0-0	Aug30 4-0	Aug16 3-0	Sep27 4-2	Dec20 4-3	Sep06 1-0
ARTHURLIE	Nov01 3-3	Aug23 0-3		Sep13 1-1	Dec13 2-2	Oct18 2-1	Nov22 2-3	Apr25 2-1	Nov29 3-1	Feb21 0-2	Nov08 3-3	Dec20 1-2
AYR U	Oct11 1-0	Dec27 2-1	Aug16 2-0		Sep27 2-0	Dec13 1-0	Mar07 2-0	Dec06 3-0	Nov15 3-0	Feb28 1-0	Aug30 5-0	Jan03 1-2
CLYDE	Aug30 1-5	Nov08 1-2	Oct25 1-1	Dec20 1-1		Oct04 0-1	Aug16 0-2	Nov22 1-1	Oct18 0-2	Jan03 1-2	Jan24 2-1	Sep20 0-1
E STIRLING	Dec20 6-4	Dec06 0-0	Sep27 1-2	Oct25 5-2	Dec27 3-2		Aug30 0-2	Nov08 2-5	Jan03 5-1	Oct11 2-1	Aug16 4-1	Nov22 4-1
FALKIRK	Nov29 4-1	Nov15 0-0	Dec27 0-0	Jan31 2-0	Nov01 1-1	Feb28 2-2		Apr18 4-2	Sep13 2-3	Apr11 4-2	Feb21 4-2	Aug23 0-1
HAMILTON A	Sep27 2-3	Dec13 4-0	Apr11 2-3	Aug23 4-1	Nov15 3-1	Nov29 3-1	Dec20 1-0		Nov01 5-1	Sep13 0-1	Jan03 2-0	Oct11 3-2
LEITH A	Dec13 4-1	Sep20 1-1	Oct11 4-2	Nov08 1-1	Sep06 2-0	Aug23 1-4	Dec06 4-1	Mar21 2-1		Dec20 4-3	Nov22 4-1	Sep27 1-0
MOTHERWELL	Nov22 1-0	Mar14 1-3	Aug30 2-2	Mar28 2-0	Feb14 3-0	Apr18 2-2	Nov08 2-2	Aug16 1-0	Oct04 3-3		Mar07 2-1	Oct25 4-3
RAITH R	Mar14 3-1	Oct18 0-1	Sep20 7-1	Nov29 0-3	Aug23 1-1	Jan31 1-0	Jan01 2-2	Oct25 1-3	Dec27 2-2	Mar21 2-5		Dec13 1-2
ST BERNARD'S	Aug16 4-1	Oct04 0-1	Nov15 2-2	Feb14 2-0	Dec06 3-0	Sep13 3-1	Oct18 8-3	Apr04 2-1	Aug30 0-1	Nov29 1-2	Nov01 1-1	

LEAGUE TABLES

DIVISION 1

	P	W	D	L	F	A	W	D	L	F	A	Pts
Hibernian	22	8	3	0	23	11	8	2	1	25	7	37
Dundee	22	8	1	2	19	7	5	4	2	12	5	31
Rangers	22	7	3	1	37	17	5	2	4	19	13	29
Hearts	22	6	2	3	23	14	5	4	2	23	13	28
Celtic	22	4	6	1	20	15	4	4	3	16	15	26
St Mirren	22	4	4	3	17	13	3	4	4	22	27	22
T. Lanark	22	6	2	3	25	14	2	3	6	9	13	21
Partick T	22	4	4	3	18	18	2	3	6	16	32	19
Kilmarnock	22	3	3	5	15	20	3	1	7	9	23	16
Queen's Park	22	4	3	4	20	19	1	2	8	13	29	15
Port Glasgow A	22	3	3	5	11	14	0	2	9	15	35	11
Morton	22	2	1	8	13	26	0	4	7	9	29	9

DIVISION 2

	P	W	D	L	F	A	W	D	L	F	A	Pts
Airdrie	22	9	2	0	27	8	6	3	2	16	11	*35
Motherwell	22	6	4	1	23	16	6	0	5	21	19	*28
Ayr U	22	10	0	1	23	3	2	3	6	11	21	27
Leith A	22	8	2	1	28	15	3	3	5	15	27	27
St Bernard's	22	6	2	3	26	13	6	0	5	19	19	26
Hamilton A	22	8	0	3	29	13	3	1	7	16	22	23
Falkirk	22	5	4	2	23	14	3	3	5	16	23	23
E. Stirling	22	7	1	3	32	21	2	2	7	14	20	21
Arthurlie	22	3	4	4	19	22	3	4	4	15	24	20
Abercorn	22	3	1	7	15	26	2	1	8	20	32	12
Raith R	22	3	3	5	20	21	0	2	9	14	34	11
Clyde	22	1	3	7	8	19	1	4	6	14	21	11

* Airdrie & Motherwell promoted to Division One.

Albion & Ayr Parkhouse joined Division Two.

Scottish Football League Records
Season 1903-04

DIVISION 1

	AIRDRIE	CELTIC	DUNDEE	HEARTS	HIBERNIAN	KILMARNOCK	MORTON	MOTHERWELL	PARTICK T	PORT GLASGOW A	QUEEN'S PARK	RANGERS	ST MIRREN	T LANARK
AIRDRIE		Jan09 4-3	Dec19 2-1	Dec26 1-2	Aug29 0-2	Oct10 1-2	Nov07 1-3	Sep26 2-1	Feb20 2-2	Dec05 1-0	Oct24 0-1	Aug22 1-3	Sep12 3-1	Mar05 0-4
CELTIC	Dec12 3-0		Oct10 4-2	Oct24 4-0	Sep26 1-0	Apr23 6-1	Jan23 5-1	Jan16 6-0	Aug15 2-1	Dec26 4-1	Oct03 3-0	Jan01 2-2	Mar12 3-1	Aug29 1-3
DUNDEE	Nov14 4-3	Jan30 2-1		Oct17 2-1	Dec12 1-2	Sep05 4-0	Aug15 6-0	Dec05 7-1	Jan16 3-0	Sep12 3-1	Aug22 3-0	Nov21 3-1	Oct24 1-1	Oct03 0-1
HEARTS	Feb27 5-0	Apr02 2-1	Aug29 4-2		Oct10 2-0	Sep26 2-1	Dec19 1-0	Sep12 5-0	Oct31 4-1	Nov14 2-0	Jan02 3-1	Jan30 2-1	Aug15 5-1	Feb13 4-1
HIBERNIAN	Oct03 4-0	Sep05 0-2	Nov28 0-1	Feb20 2-4		Mar12 2-2	Nov21 2-0	Aug22 2-1	Feb27 2-2	Oct24 4-1	Dec19 1-1	Dec26 1-2	Sep19 2-1	Oct17 0-2
KILMARNOCK	Nov28 0-2	Nov14 1-6	Nov07 1-2	Mar05 2-3	Sep12 0-0		Sep19 1-1	Jan09 2-1	Aug29 1-3	Oct03 0-4	Aug15 2-1	Dec05 2-2	Oct17 2-0	Oct31 1-2
MORTON	Sep05 3-1	Dec05 0-1	Jan02 1-1	Jan09 1-2	Oct31 3-1	Aug22 4-2		Dec26 2-3	Sep12 1-3	Sep26 0-1	Nov14 2-1	Nov28 0-5	Oct03 1-0	Jan30 1-2
MOTHERWELL	Aug15 1-2	Mar26 1-2	Sep19 1-3	Nov28 0-4	Jan30 1-0	Oct24 2-0	Oct17 0-0		Oct03 2-0	Oct31 1-0	Aug29 2-4	Sep05 2-5	Nov14 1-0	Dec19 0-2
PARTICK T	Mar12 3-0	Dec19 0-4	Feb06 6-1	Sep05 1-1	Jan09 3-1	Nov21 4-0	Oct10 2-1	Mar05 2-2		Aug22 1-0	Dec05 2-0	Sep28 1-4	Jan01 1-1	Oct24 2-2
PORT GLASGOW A	Oct17 2-2	Feb06 2-3	Mar26 1-0	Nov21 1-1	Aug15 3-1	Dec12 4-1	Aug29 2-0	Oct10 4-3	Sep19 1-2		Jan16 2-1	Dec19 1-1	Jan30 0-1	Feb20 0-1
QUEEN'S PARK	Jan30 1-1	Oct31 1-0	Jan09 2-1	Feb06 2-2	Feb13 3-1	Dec26 1-1	Mar19 1-1	Nov21 1-0	Oct17 1-1	Nov28 0-0		Nov07 2-3	Feb27 0-0	Dec12 2-8
RANGERS	Mar26 5-0	Oct17 0-0	Oct31 6-1	Sep19 5-1	Nov14 1-1	Jan16 3-0	Oct24 3-1	Dec12 3-0	Jan02 2-0	Feb13 8-1	Sep26 5-0		Aug29 2-2	Aug15 4-3
ST MIRREN	Oct31 5-2	Aug22 0-1	Sep26 2-0	Jan16 3-0	Nov07 3-0	Dec19 3-0	Dec12 3-2	Jan02 0-0	Nov28 1-0	Sep05 5-1	Oct10 3-1	Jan09 5-4		Jan04 1-2
T LANARK	Sep19 1-1	Sep28 3-1	Apr23 4-1	Aug22 2-1	Apr30 2-0	Mar26 3-2	Jan16 1-2	Mar12 3-0	Nov14 1-0	Jan02 3-0	Sep05 0-0	Oct10 1-0	Dec05 4-2	

DIVISION 2

	ABERCORN	ALBION	ARTHURLIE	AYR PARKHOUSE	AYR U	CLYDE	E STIRLING	FALKIRK	HAMILTON A	LEITH A	RAITH R	ST BERNARD'S
ABERCORN		Dec05 2-1	Mar12 1-3	Nov21 4-1	May07 1-1	Sep12 2-2	Nov14 3-2	May03 2-5	Mar26 2-2	Aug29 1-1	Oct24 7-3	Mar05 0-2
ALBION	Jan02 3-0		Jan16 3-3	Mar12 5-1	Mar26 2-3	Dec12 1-2	Apr23 2-0	Oct17 1-1	Jan30 1-1	Aug15 2-2	Feb06 3-2	Sep26 4-0
ARTHURLIE	Oct10 2-1	Apr16 1-3		Nov14 5-2	Aug22 0-1	Jan02 2-2	Oct24 2-2	Dec26 1-2	Aug29 1-3	Sep19 3-2	Jan09 3-1	Dec12 1-2
AYR PARKHOUSE	Dec19 1-3	Aug22 2-5	Feb06 1-1		Feb13 1-3	Oct31 0-3	Nov07 2-1	Sep19 2-2	Nov28 0-3	Oct17 1-0	Jan16 0-0	Oct03 1-2
AYR U	Feb27 0-1	Apr09 2-1	Mar07 2-1	Jan09 2-2		Aug29 2-2	Sep26 2-1	Jan30 1-0	Dec26 0-2	Jan02 1-0	Mar12 2-1	Aug15 2-0
CLYDE	Feb20 5-2	Dec26 2-1	Dec19 4-1	Aug15 3-1	Mar19 2-0		Nov28 5-1	Mar05 1-1	Feb06 0-3	Feb27 3-1	Aug22 0-1	Jan09 1-2
E STIRLING	Oct31 2-0	Apr30 4-2	Sep12 3-3	Jan30 1-0	Feb06 1-1	Mar26 1-3		Jan09 2-1	Oct17 0-0	Mar19 3-2	Dec26 3-0	Aug22 3-1
FALKIRK	Nov07 4-2	Dec19 0-1	Dec05 2-1	Oct10 6-1	Nov28 4-1	Nov14 3-4	Aug29 2-1		Aug15 1-5	Sep26 5-1	Jan02 2-0	Oct24 3-1
HAMILTON A	Aug22 3-1	Jan09 2-1	Nov07 5-0	Oct24 5-1	Jan16 3-1	Nov21 3-0	Jan23 3-1	Dec12 2-2		Dec19 2-1	Nov14 1-4	Sep12 5-1
LEITH A	Jan09 4-3	Sep12 3-2	Jan30 4-1	Dec26 4-0	Nov07 3-4	Jan16 2-2	Oct10 4-0	Aug22 2-0	Oct31 0-1		Mar05 0-2	Nov14 3-2
RAITH R	Dec12 4-0	Nov07 2-2	Jan23 2-1	Aug29 2-3	Dec19 2-2	Feb13 5-1	Aug15 1-2	Oct31 3-1	Dec05 1-1	Nov21 1-1		Oct10 1-2
ST BERNARD'S	Dec26 4-2	Aug29 2-1	Oct31 2-1	Jan02 2-1	Sep19 1-1	Mar12 1-4	Dec19 1-1	Nov21 1-3	Jan01 0-1	Sep05 1-2	Oct17 1-2	

LEAGUE TABLES

DIVISION 1

	P	W	D	L	F	A	W	D	L	F	A	Pts
T. Lanark	26	10	2	1	28	10	10	1	2	33	16	43
Hearts	26	13	0	0	41	9	5	3	5	22	26	39
Celtic	26	11	1	1	44	12	7	1	5	25	16	38
Rangers	26	10	3	0	47	10	6	3	4	33	23	38
Dundee	26	10	1	2	39	12	3	1	9	16	34	28
St Mirren	26	10	1	2	34	13	1	4	8	11	25	27
Partick T	26	7	4	2	28	17	3	3	7	15	23	27
Queen's Park	26	4	7	2	17	19	2	2	9	11	28	21
Port Glasgow A	26	6	3	4	23	17	2	1	10	10	32	20
Hibernian	26	5	3	5	22	19	2	2	9	9	23	19
Morton	26	5	1	7	19	23	2	3	8	12	28	18
Airdrie	26	5	1	7	18	25	2	3	8	14	37	18
Motherwell	26	5	1	7	14	22	1	2	10	12	39	15
Kilmarnock	26	3	3	7	15	27	1	2	10	12	39	13

DIVISION 2

	P	W	D	L	F	A	W	D	L	F	A	Pts
Hamilton	22	9	1	1	34	13	7	4	0	22	6	37
Clyde	22	7	1	3	26	14	5	4	2	25	22	29
Ayr	22	7	2	2	16	11	4	4	3	18	20	28
Falkirk	22	8	0	3	32	18	3	4	4	18	18	26
Raith	22	4	4	3	24	16	4	1	6	16	22	21
E. Stirling	22	7	3	1	23	13	1	2	8	12	27	21
Leith	22	7	1	3	29	17	1	3	7	13	23	20
St Bernard's	22	4	2	5	16	19	5	0	6	15	24	20
Albion	22	5	4	2	27	15	3	1	7	20	22	*19
Abercorn	22	4	4	3	25	23	2	0	9	15	32	16
Arthurlie	22	4	2	5	21	21	1	3	7	16	29	15
Ayr Parkhouse	22	2	3	6	11	23	1	1	9	13	39	†10

* Albion had 2pts deducted.

† Ayr Parkhouse left the League, replaced in Division Two by Aberdeen.

Scottish Football League Records
Season 1904-05

DIVISION 1

	AIRDRIE	CELTIC	DUNDEE	HEARTS	HIBERNIAN	KILMARNOCK	MORTON	MOTHERWELL	PARTICK T	PORT GLASGOW A	QUEEN'S PARK	RANGERS	ST MIRREN	T LANARK
AIRDRIE		Nov26 1-3	Nov05 2-0	Sep24 3-2	Sep10 1-1	Oct22 1-1	Aug27 3-2	Aug20 3-2	Dec24 3-0	Oct01 2-0	Jan21 0-1	Dec31 2-2	Nov19 1-3	Feb04 1-1
CELTIC	Jan03 2-3		Nov19 3-0	Sep03 1-1	Jan21 2-0	Dec31 3-1	Feb04 5-2	Dec03 4-2	Dec17 2-2	Jan07 3-0	Oct29 1-1	Oct15 2-2	Dec24 1-0	Sep26 2-1
DUNDEE	Sep03 0-1	Jan14 2-1		Nov12 2-0	Dec03 4-1	Sep24 3-0	Oct15 6-1	Jan07 0-0	Oct22 0-1	Dec31 4-0	Apr01 3-0	Sep10 0-3	Aug20 2-0	Dec10 0-0
HEARTS	Dec03 6-0	Sep19 2-0	Feb25 3-1		Jan02 1-0	Jan07 1-3	Mar04 2-0	Dec31 4-1	Oct01 0-1	Nov19 2-0	Mar11 2-0	Nov05 0-5	Oct22 3-1	Aug27 4-1
HIBERNIAN	Dec10 3-2	Nov12 2-2	Sep17 1-1	Oct29 3-0		Nov26 2-1	Jan14 4-0	Oct15 2-0	Mar18 4-0	Feb18 1-1	Aug20 1-1	Sep19 1-2	Sep03 2-0	Dec24 1-1
KILMARNOCK	Jan14 1-0	Nov05 0-3	Feb11 2-1	Aug20 3-2	Oct01 2-1		Dec24 1-0	Aug27 0-2	Jan02 3-2	Sep03 1-1	Oct08 2-1	Dec03 0-4	Oct29 1-0	Sep17 0-0
MORTON	Nov12 2-0	Dec10 0-1	Dec17 5-1	Feb18 1-0	Nov19 2-2	Sep10 2-1		Sep03 1-0	Oct29 0-1	Aug20 1-0	Dec31 1-1	Apr29 0-2	Jan07 1-3	Oct01 0-0
MOTHERWELL	Oct29 1-0	Mar04 2-6	Oct01 0-2	Sep17 2-4	Dec17 1-2	Nov19 2-1	Oct08 0-3		Apr08 1-0	Jan21 0-2	Nov12 1-1	Dec10 0-2	Mar25 3-2	Mar18 0-1
PARTICK T	Oct08 0-3	Aug20 0-5	Jan21 2-1	Oct15 2-1	Sep26 0-1	Dec10 2-0	Sep17 3-1	Nov05 1-0		Nov12 3-0	Jan07 3-1	Jan03 1-4	Dec31 0-1	Dec03 3-2
PORT GLASGOW A	Sep17 1-3	Aug27 1-4	Mar25 1-0	Dec24 3-0	Oct22 1-1	Oct15 1-1	Nov05 2-1	Sep24 2-1	Jan14 6-1		Mar04 4-2	Feb04 0-3	Dec03 0-2	Oct08 1-1
QUEEN'S PARK	Oct15 1-1	Oct01 2-3	Aug27 0-1	Feb04 2-0	Sep24 4-2	Dec17 1-1	Dec03 1-1	Dec24 2-0	Nov19 1-4	Dec10 2-0		Sep17 0-4	Jan14 2-1	Nov05 0-1
RANGERS	Dec17 4-1	Feb18 1-4	Oct29 2-1	Sep26 1-1	Aug27 4-0	Jan21 6-2	Apr01 5-0	Jan14 3-2	Sep03 8-1	Mar18 5-1	Oct22 5-0		Oct01 2-3	Nov19 3-1
ST MIRREN	Mar11 0-1	Sep17 2-3	Oct08 1-1	Dec10 1-1	Nov05 2-0	Feb18 1-0	Sep24 1-0	Jan02 1-2	Aug27 2-2	Sep10 1-2	Mar18 1-1	Nov12 3-0		Oct15 1-2
T LANARK	Jan07 6-0	Oct22 1-2	Dec26 2-2	Nov26 7-1	Dec31 4-1	Nov12 3-1	Jan21 5-0	Sep10 4-3	Feb18 6-1	Oct29 3-0	Sep03 2-0	Aug20 2-1	Apr01 3-0	

DIVISION 2

	ABERCORN	ABERDEEN	ALBION R	ARTHURLIE	AYR U	CLYDE	E STIRLING	FALKIRK	HAMILTON A	LEITH A	RAITH R	ST BERNARD'S
ABERCORN		Feb04 3-1	Nov19 3-0	Dec03 1-2	Dec31 2-1	Jan07 2-2	Oct22 1-0	Dec24 0-2	Oct01 1-0	Oct29 1-4	Aug20 3-1	Dec17 3-2
ABERDEEN	Sep24 3-1		Mar04 7-2	Apr08 0-0	Mar25 2-0	Aug27 0-1	Dec31 3-0	Aug20 1-2	Dec10 1-2	Apr15 0-0	Oct22 3-1	Jan21 1-1
ALBION R	Sep10 5-1	Jan14 1-0		Oct15 1-2	Oct29 3-2	Dec03 2-1	Nov12 4-4	Jan07 2-2	Oct08 0-1	Dec10 5-3	Sep17 1-1	Oct22 3-2
ARTHURLIE	Aug27 1-2	Mar11 2-0	Dec24 2-2		Sep10 5-2	Feb25 1-1	Jan21 3-1	Nov19 1-0	Oct29 3-1	Feb18 0-2	Dec31 3-0	Sep03 1-1
AYR U	Nov12 3-1	Nov19 3-3	Aug27 0-1	Aug20 4-0		Feb18 5-1	Jan14 1-0	Oct01 5-3	Jan21 1-0	Dec24 4-1	Nov05 4-0	Jan07 5-1
CLYDE	Jan21 2-1	Dec17 1-0	Aug20 2-1	Oct01 4-4	Feb11 4-1		Sep24 1-0	Dec31 1-0	Dec24 3-1	Mar04 2-0	Dec10 1-0	Jan14 5-0
E STIRLING	Jan28 3-1	Nov05 1-4	Dec17 5-2	Jan07 5-2	Oct15 2-0	Mar11 2-2		Sep10 2-0	Dec03 0-1	Aug20 0-0	Dec24 1-3	Nov19 4-0
FALKIRK	Dec10 2-1	Apr01 0-0	Sep24 3-1	Jan14 2-0	Nov26 2-1	Oct08 0-0	Oct29 3-1		Oct22 1-3	Nov12 1-0	Feb04 1-0	Aug27 2-1
HAMILTON A	Nov05 5-1	Sep10 3-3	Dec31 3-0	Nov12 4-1	Sep24 1-2	Oct15 0-1	Feb04 1-1	Dec17 3-1		Jan07 2-0	Nov19 1-0	Aug20 4-0
LEITH A	Jan14 2-1	Mar18 1-1	Jan21 7-0	Nov05 2-0	Oct22 0-1	Nov19 0-2	Feb11 1-3	Dec03 0-0	Aug27 3-1		Sep24 4-1	Dec31 4-1
RAITH R	Nov26 2-1	Jan07 1-0	Oct01 1-0	Dec17 4-1	Dec03 3-0	Jan02 1-0	Aug20 4-1	Oct15 1-3	Jan14 0-2	Oct08 0-1		Oct29 1-2
ST BERNARD'S	Oct15 2-0	Dec24 0-3	Nov05 1-2	Dec10 2-3	Oct08 2-1	Feb04 1-1	Feb18 1-1	Jan28 1-2	Feb25 1-1	Nov26 0-1	Nov12 1-5	

LEAGUE TABLES

DIVISION 1

	P	W	D	L	F	A	W	D	L	F	A	Pts
Rangers	26	10	1	2	49	17	9	2	2	34	11	41
Celtic	26	8	4	1	31	15	10	1	2	37	16	*41
T. Lanark	26	11	1	1	48	12	3	6	4	12	16	35
Airdrie	26	6	4	3	23	18	5	1	7	15	27	27
Hibernian	26	7	5	1	27	11	2	3	8	12	28	26
Partick T	26	8	0	5	20	20	4	2	7	16	36	26
Dundee	26	8	2	3	26	8	2	3	8	12	24	25
Hearts	26	10	0	3	30	13	1	3	9	13	31	25
Kilmarnock	26	8	2	3	16	17	1	3	9	13	28	23
St Mirren	26	4	4	5	17	15	5	0	8	16	21	22
Port Glasgow A	26	6	3	4	23	20	2	2	9	7	28	21
Queen's Park	26	5	3	5	18	19	1	5	7	10	26	20
Morton	26	6	3	4	16	12	1	1	11	11	38	18
Motherwell	26	4	1	8	13	26	2	1	10	15	27	14

* Celtic won a deciding match against Rangers.

DIVISION 2

	P	W	D	L	F	A	W	D	L	F	A	Pts
Clyde	22	10	1	0	26	8	3	5	3	12	14	32
Falkirk	22	8	2	1	17	8	4	2	5	15	17	*28
Hamilton A	22	7	2	2	27	10	5	1	5	13	14	27
Leith A	22	6	2	3	24	11	4	2	5	12	15	24
Ayr U	22	9	1	1	35	11	2	0	9	11	26	23
Arthurlie	22	6	3	2	22	12	3	2	6	15	29	23
Aberdeen	22	5	3	3	21	10	2	4	5	15	16	*21
Albion R	22	6	3	2	27	19	2	1	8	11	34	20
E. Stirling	22	6	2	3	25	15	1	3	7	12	23	19
Raith R	22	7	0	4	18	11	2	1	8	12	23	19
Abercorn	22	7	1	3	20	15	1	0	10	11	30	17
St Bernard's	22	2	3	6	12	20	1	2	8	11	33	11

* Aberdeen and Falkirk were promoted to Division One.

Scottish Football League Records
Season 1905-06

DIVISION 1

	ABERDEEN	AIRDRIE	CELTIC	DUNDEE	FALKIRK	HEARTS	HIBERNIAN	KILMARNOCK	MORTON	MOTHERWELL	PARTICK T	PORT GLASGOW A	QUEEN'S PARK	RANGERS	ST MIRREN	T LANARK
ABERDEEN		Feb17 1-2	Mar03 1-0	Jan06 1-2	Dec23 2-0	Dec02 2-1	Sep16 2-1	Sep02 2-0	Nov04 3-0	Feb24 2-2	Aug19 0-1	Oct21 2-2	Sep25 2-2	Dec16 1-1	Oct07 1-0	Nov25 1-2
AIRDRIE	Sep23 2-0		Jan13 2-5	Nov25 1-2	Oct07 4-1	Jan06 1-1	Aug19 2-0	Oct28 1-1	Dec02 4-2	Mar17 2-1	Sep16 3-2	Oct14 0-1	Mar24 4-1	Sep02 5-1	Dec16 0-0	Dec23 0-0
CELTIC	Dec09 1-0	Sep30 2-1		Oct28 3-1	Jan06 7-0	Apr21 1-0	Sep02 1-0	Jan02 2-0	Dec23 4-0	Aug19 3-1	Jan20 4-1	Nov11 0-1	Oct14 5-1	Jan01 1-0	Nov25 2-1	May07 0-1
DUNDEE	Nov18 6-0	Mar10 0-0	Feb03 1-0		Dec09 3-0	Oct21 1-1	Dec23 1-1	Oct07 2-1	Sep02 3-1	Jan20 2-0	Sep09 1-1	Dec30 1-1	Sep23 1-0	Feb17 1-1	Aug19 1-2	Nov04 2-0
FALKIRK	Sep09 1-1	Jan01 0-0	Sep16 0-5	Nov11 2-0		Jan20 2-2	Oct14 2-1	Mar17 7-3	Jan13 4-0	Dec02 6-1	Sep30 1-1	Feb03 3-3	Aug26 3-5	Oct28 1-6	Apr07 2-0	Feb24 2-0
HEARTS	Oct28 1-1	Nov11 2-1	Sep11 1-1	Jan13 4-0	Nov25 1-0		Nov04 1-0	Sep16 3-0	Mar10 2-0	Sep02 4-0	Oct14 2-0	Dec09 4-0	Feb17 4-1	Apr07 2-2	Dec23 1-0	Aug19 3-2
HIBERNIAN	Jan02 1-0	Jan20 0-4	Dec30 0-1	Aug26 2-1	Dec16 4-1	Sep18 0-3		Mar31 2-1	Sep30 1-2	Feb03 2-3	Dec02 1-1	Mar24 3-1	Nov18 4-0	Sep11 1-2	Jan06 0-1	Oct21 2-1
KILMARNOCK	Dec30 2-1	Feb03 0-0	Aug26 2-4	Dec16 2-2	Nov04 2-1	Nov18 1-1	Dec09 0-2		Sep09 3-1	Sep30 1-0	Oct21 1-2	Apr28 3-2	Nov11 7-0	Jan06 1-3	Oct14 5-3	Jan20 2-0
MORTON	Feb03 2-2	Aug26 0-2	Nov18 0-4	Feb24 0-0	Oct21 4-2	Dec16 2-1	Nov11 0-1	Apr07 3-0		Oct14 1-1	Mar31 0-1	Sep23 2-2	Dec30 1-0	Dec09 0-3	Jan20 1-0	Sep16 1-1
MOTHERWELL	Jan13 3-3	Nov04 2-1	Dec16 0-4	Sep16 4-1	Sep23 2-3	Dec30 2-1	Nov25 0-2	Mar10 5-1	Feb17 1-1		Jan01 2-3	Aug26 2-0	Oct07 4-2	Nov18 3-3	Oct21 1-1	Mar03 2-1
PARTICK T	Mar10 1-2	Dec09 1-0	Nov04 0-3	Mar03 1-0	Sep02 2-0	Feb03 4-1	Sep25 1-0	Jan13 2-1	Oct07 2-1	Oct28 2-2		Apr14 3-0	Dec16 2-1	Mar17 1-1	Mar24 1-1	Jan06 2-5
PORT GLASGOW A	Mar17 3-1	Apr21 2-2	Dec02 0-1	Sep30 1-1	Aug19 2-1	Sep09 2-5	Oct28 0-0	Nov25 3-2	Jan06 1-3	Apr07 1-2	Dec23 1-2		Jan13 3-2	Oct07 1-4	Nov04 1-2	Sep02 2-5
QUEEN'S PARK	Jan20 3-0	Oct21 1-3	Mar10 0-6	Mar31 0-0	Mar03 0-5	Sep30 0-3	Mar17 2-2	Dec23 4-1	Aug19 2-3	Jan06 2-1	Nov25 1-2	Sep16 2-2		Nov04 1-2	Sep02 3-1	Dec09 0-5
RANGERS	Aug26 1-0	Dec30 1-3	Oct21 3-2	Oct14 1-1	Mar24 3-1	Sep25 0-5	Mar03 1-1	Aug19 3-2	Nov25 1-2	Dec23 2-1	Jan02 1-0	Jan20 4-0	Dec02 3-1		Sep16 1-0	Nov11 2-4
ST MIRREN	Sep30 4-2	Sep09 0-1	Feb17 1-3	Dec02 1-1	Mar10 2-1	Aug26 0-1	Sep23 2-0	May12 2-1	Oct28 3-1	Dec09 1-1	Apr28 2-1	May05 3-0	Feb03 3-1	Jan13 3-2		Mar17 2-0
T LANARK	Oct14 1-0	May10 1-2	Sep25 0-1	Dec25 1-2	Apr09 2-0	Jan02 1-3	Jan13 3-1	Dec02 5-0	Mar24 0-1	Sep09 6-1	Aug26 2-1	Dec16 3-0	Oct28 6-3	Feb03 3-0	Dec30 1-0	

DIVISION 2

	ABERCORN	ALBION R	ARTHURLIE	AYR U	CLYDE	COWDENBEATH	E STIRLING	HAMILTON A	LEITH A	RAITH R	ST BERNARD'S	VALE OF LEVEN
ABERCORN		Nov25 2-2	Dec23 4-2	Dec30 2-0	Jan01 1-0	Jan20 4-0	Jan06 1-1	Aug26 0-1	Oct21 0-3	Aug19 2-2	Jan27 2-1	Nov04 1-1
ALBION R	Dec16 1-0		Nov04 2-0	Aug26 2-4	Dec09 1-2	Sep09 0-2	Jan27 5-1	Dec30 3-1	Mar10 0-1	Oct21 3-1	Oct28 4-0	Nov11 5-3
ARTHURLIE	Oct28 5-2	Jan13 3-0		Nov25 2-4	Mar10 0-3	Nov11 3-2	Dec30 4-0	Apr07 1-3	Aug26 6-2	Jan06 2-0	Dec16 4-0	Feb03 1-1
AYR U	Sep09 4-1	Jan06 1-1	Aug19 3-0		Dec02 1-1	Dec16 3-0	Nov11 2-4	Oct21 1-2	Nov04 1-5	Jan13 2-1	Sep30 0-0	Oct14 5-1
CLYDE	Nov11 3-1	Oct07 1-4	Feb17 2-0	Jan20 3-1		Dec30 2-0	Jan13 1-1	Dec16 2-2	Mar03 0-0	Feb03 1-1	Jan06 2-0	Sep30 2-0
COWDENBEATH	Sep23 1-1	Feb03 2-1	Dec09 2-3	Nov18 3-5	Nov04 0-1		Aug26 2-1	Oct07 1-3	Aug19 1-0	Jan27 2-1	Sep16 2-2	Jan06 2-0
E STIRLING	Nov18 1-3	Oct14 1-4	Mar03 1-2	Oct07 1-2	Oct21 4-4	Dec23 2-2		Sep23 0-1	Dec09 1-1	Dec16 1-1	Nov04 1-1	Aug19 1-1
HAMILTON A	Mar03 3-0	Feb24 0-2	Dec02 6-4	Feb03 6-0	Aug19 1-2	Mar24 1-0	Mar10 4-0		Apr14 0-1	Dec09 3-0	Sep09 0-4	Dec23 5-3
LEITH A	Jan13 5-2	Mar31 3-1	Mar24 4-1	Feb17 4-1	Dec23 0-0	Nov25 3-1	Feb03 0-0	Jan06 2-1		Nov18 1-0	Mar17 1-0	Dec16 3-1
RAITH R	Dec02 5-1	Sep02 0-3	Feb24 1-1	Oct28 5-2	Aug26 2-2	Oct14 0-1	Sep09 2-2	Jan01 1-1	Dec30 2-1		Dec23 4-3	Nov25 3-2
ST BERNARD'S	Feb03 1-0	Aug19 1-2	Feb10 4-1	Dec09 5-1	Nov25 0-0	Jan13 1-0	Dec02 3-2	Nov11 4-0	Feb24 2-3	Jan20 5-2		Dec30 3-0
VALE OF LEVEN	Dec09 4-1	Dec02 2-2	Sep09 0-1	Jan27 2-1	Feb10 1-3	Oct21 3-2	Oct28 1-0	Jan13 2-1	Oct07 1-3	Sep23 1-2	Aug26 3-2	

LEAGUE TABLES

DIVISION 1

	P	W	D	L	F	A	W	D	L	F	A	Pts
Celtic	30	13	0	2	36	8	11	1	3	40	11	49
Hearts	30	12	3	0	35	8	6	4	5	29	19	43
Airdrie	30	8	4	3	31	18	7	4	4	22	13	38
Rangers	30	9	2	4	27	23	6	5	4	31	25	37
Partick T	30	9	3	3	25	18	6	3	6	19	22	36
T. Lanark	30	10	0	5	35	15	6	2	7	27	23	34
Dundee	30	8	6	1	26	9	3	6	6	14	24	34
St Mirren	30	10	2	3	29	16	3	3	9	12	21	31
Motherwell	30	7	4	4	33	27	2	4	9	17	37	26
Morton	30	5	5	5	17	20	5	1	9	18	34	26
Hibernian	30	7	1	7	23	22	3	4	8	12	18	25
Aberdeen	30	7	4	4	23	16	1	4	10	13	32	24
Falkirk	30	7	5	3	36	28	2	0	13	16	40	23
Kilmarnock	30	8	3	4	32	22	0	1	14	14	46	20
Port Glasgow A	30	4	3	8	23	33	2	5	8	15	35	20
Queen's Park	30	4	3	8	21	36	1	1	13	20	52	14

DIVISION 2

	P	W	D	L	F	A	W	D	L	F	A	Pts
Leith A	22	9	2	0	26	8	6	2	3	20	14	34
Clyde	22	6	4	1	19	10	5	5	1	18	11	*31
Albion R	22	7	0	4	26	15	5	3	3	22	16	27
Hamilton A	22	7	0	4	29	16	5	2	4	16	17	*26
St Bernard's	22	8	1	2	29	11	1	3	7	13	23	22
Arthurlie	22	7	1	3	31	17	3	1	7	15	29	22
Ayr U	22	5	3	3	23	16	4	0	7	21	35	21
Raith R	22	5	4	2	25	19	1	3	7	11	23	19
Cowdenbeath	22	5	2	4	18	18	2	1	8	10	22	17
Abercorn	22	5	4	2	19	13	1	1	9	12	33	17
Vale of Leven	22	6	1	4	20	18	0	3	8	13	31	16
E. Stirling	22	0	6	5	14	22	1	4	6	12	25	12

* Clyde & Hamilton A promoted to Division One.

Ayr Parkhouse & Dumbarton joined Division Two.

Scottish Football League Records
Season 1906-07

DIVISION 1

	ABERDEEN	AIRDRIE	CELTIC	CLYDE	DUNDEE	FALKIRK	HAMILTON A	HEARTS	HIBERNIAN	KILMARNOCK	MORTON	MOTHERWELL	PARTICK T	PORT GLASGOW A	QUEEN'S PARK	RANGERS	ST MIRREN	T LANARK
ABERDEEN		Sep22 0-0	Mar02 2-2	Apr13 3-0	Dec08 0-3	Oct06 0-0	Feb16 2-1	Nov03 2-3	May06 1-1	Jan19 3-0	Mar09 2-0	Feb23 2-2	Oct20 0-0	Nov24 1-0	Sep24 2-1	Dec22 0-3	Sep08 4-2	Aug25 0-2
AIRDRIE	Mar23 0-2		Sep29 0-2	Aug25 4-0	Nov24 1-2	Nov03 4-2	Feb23 1-0	Oct20 3-2	Mar16 3-2	Dec22 1-0	Apr13 3-2	Jan05 0-0	Mar02 1-0	Sep15 5-0	Nov10 3-2	Jan19 2-3	Oct06 1-0	Sep08 4-1
CELTIC	Oct13 2-1	Dec31 2-1		Nov24 3-3	Mar23 0-0	Jan05 3-2	Jan02 2-0	Sep15 3-0	Nov10 2-1	Aug25 5-0	Jan19 2-1	May15 1-1	Dec01 4-1	Dec22 4-0	Apr01 2-1	Oct27 2-1	Apr27 1-1	Sep24 2-0
CLYDE	Nov17 1-3	Apr06 2-0	Jan12 0-2		Sep24 1-1	Oct20 1-0	Aug15 2-0	Aug18 1-3	Oct06 3-1	Feb09 2-0	Nov03 0-0	Mar30 1-0	Dec29 3-1	Dec15 3-1	Mar16 2-2	Dec08 1-5	Apr24 3-1	Mar09 1-2
DUNDEE	Nov10 0-0	Mar30 1-1	Oct20 0-0	Jan01 0-2		Sep01 3-2	Mar16 1-0	Apr08 2-0	Apr20 0-0	Nov03 4-2	Oct06 1-0	Jan19 1-0	Dec15 5-0	Aug18 0-1	Apr13 0-0	Sep22 2-0	Dec29 2-1	Mar02 2-1
FALKIRK	Jan01 3-2	Dec29 3-0	Nov17 2-3	Mar02 3-0	Apr06 4-2		Oct27 5-2	Sep29 2-1	Aug25 2-1	Apr13 2-1	Jan12 2-2	Sep08 2-1	Sep22 1-1	Oct13 2-2	Apr20 6-1	Mar16 2-1	Feb16 1-1	Dec01 3-2
HAMILTON A	Dec01 4-2	Dec08 1-2	Nov03 2-5	Sep03 1-1	Aug25 1-3	Jan19 3-1		May06 5-1	Dec15 2-4	Mar30 0-2	Sep08 0-2	Oct06 0-3	Mar23 3-1	Mar02 0-2	Jan05 3-1	Feb09 0-3	Oct20 2-3	Jan01 0-1
HEARTS	Apr15 1-1	Jan12 0-1	May11 3-3	May04 0-1	Sep08 0-0	May01 2-1	Oct13 3-1		Sep22 4-1	Mar16 1-0	Dec01 1-0	Apr06 1-1	Apr27 5-1	Nov10 2-0	Oct27 2-2	Apr13 0-1	Aug25 1-1	Dec15 1-1
HIBERNIAN	Aug18 2-1	Nov17 4-0	May08 0-1	Dec22 2-0	Sep29 0-4	Feb09 1-2	May04 0-1	Jan01 0-0		Sep15 1-0	Dec08 2-1	Oct20 1-1	Apr15 2-2	Jan05 1-0	Sep01 2-1	Nov24 1-3	Jan19 2-2	Nov03 1-1
KILMARNOCK	Oct27 1-3	Aug18 0-1	Dec29 2-2	Sep08 1-2	Mar09 1-3	Nov24 1-4	Sep22 1-0	Nov17 2-2	Dec01 1-3		Apr06 3-0	Mar23 3-2	Sep01 3-1	Apr27 2-1	Mar02 3-1	Oct13 1-5	Jan01 1-0	Jan12 3-3
MORTON	Sep15 2-1	Oct27 1-1	Sep01 0-2	Apr27 1-0	Dec22 1-2	Nov10 3-1	Feb02 3-0	Mar02 0-0	Oct13 2-1	Dec15 2-2		Mar16 1-1	Mar30 0-2	Jan03 3-0	Aug18 3-0	Jan05 2-1	Nov24 2-0	Sep29 0-1
MOTHERWELL	Sep29 3-2	Sep01 1-1	Aug18 0-6	Oct27 0-1	Oct13 0-3	Mar09 4-0	Dec22 0-2	Dec08 2-0	Dec29 0-0	Nov10 3-0	Nov17 4-1		Jan12 2-2	Apr13 1-0	Feb16 0-5	Mar02 1-0	Sep22 1-2	Nov24 3-2
PARTICK T	Apr06 2-0	Oct13 0-4	Apr24 0-2	Sep19 0-2	Oct27 0-0	Dec08 0-3	Nov10 1-1	Nov24 1-0	Sep24 3-0	Jan05 3-0	Aug25 5-0	Sep15 3-2		Mar16 0-1	Dec22 0-1	Jan02 2-2	Apr13 1-4	Feb23 1-0
PORT GLASGOW A	Jan12 2-2	Mar09 0-3	May04 1-1	Feb16 3-3	Dec01 1-1	Feb23 2-3	Nov17 0-0	Jan19 0-0	Sep08 1-2	Oct20 3-2	Sep22 2-1	Nov03 0-1	Oct06 1-0		Dec08 3-1	Aug25 0-2	Apr06 0-2	Dec29 1-3
QUEEN'S PARK	May04 2-0	Apr27 1-3	Dec15 0-4	Dec01 0-3	Jan12 1-2	Mar23 3-1	Nov24 3-1	Apr24 1-2	May09 3-0	Oct06 1-1	Dec29 2-3	Aug25 2-1	Nov03 3-2	Sep29 4-0		Apr06 1-2	May11 0-3	Oct20 0-1
RANGERS	Sep01 6-2	Dec01 2-1	Jan01 2-1	Mar23 4-0	Apr01 2-2	Aug18 2-2	Dec29 0-1	Sep24 1-1	Jan12 1-0	Apr20 3-0	Oct20 2-0	Dec15 0-1	Sep29 1-2	Mar30 5-0	Nov17 3-2		Nov03 1-1	Feb02 0-0
ST MIRREN	Mar16 2-2	May04 4-2	Dec08 0-3	Nov10 1-0	Nov17 1-1	Mar30 1-1	Jan12 1-1	Dec22 0-2	Oct27 1-1	Sep29 3-0	Apr20 2-1	Dec01 1-0	Aug18 1-1	Sep01 4-1	Oct13 1-1	Feb23 0-0		Sep15 0-2
T LANARK	Mar30 2-0	Feb16 2-2	Mar16 2-1	Oct13 4-2	Dec25 2-0	Dec22 2-3	Aug18 2-2	Sep01 2-2	Jan02 0-0	Dec08 2-1	Mar23 2-1	Dec31 2-3	Aug15 3-1	Oct27 3-1	Jan19 2-2	Nov10 0-2	Jan05 2-3	

DIVISION 2

	ABERCORN	ALBION R	ARTHURLIE	AYR PARKHOUSE	AYR U	COWDENBEATH	DUMBARTON	E STIRLING	LEITH A	RAITH R	ST BERNARD'S	VALE OF LEVEN
ABERCORN		Nov24 2-3	Dec29 2-2	Feb23 1-1	Feb16 1-1	Apr13 2-0	Oct20 0-5	Aug25 4-3	Jan19 3-1	Nov03 1-1	Mar02 0-0	Sep08 1-2
ALBION R	Oct27 4-0		Aug18 3-0	Sep22 2-1	Mar09 1-2	Dec08 4-1	Nov17 2-2	Feb16 7-3	Dec29 6-2	Jan12 4-1	Mar30 0-0	Dec01 3-1
ARTHURLIE	Jan12 3-4	Mar16 1-1		Jan19 3-1	Mar23 3-1	Nov17 2-2	Oct13 3-0	Oct27 1-0	Nov24 3-2	Feb23 3-2	Jan05 5-1	Aug25 5-4
AYR PARKHOUSE	Aug18 2-1	Dec22 1-0	Feb09 1-3		Nov24 3-3	Mar23 2-3	Dec08 2-5	Sep29 2-0	Oct27 1-4	Oct13 0-4	Jan12 0-3	Nov10 3-1
AYR U	Nov17 1-2	Feb02 1-0	Dec01 3-1	Nov03 2-1		Dec15 0-0	Jan05 5-0	Dec29 4-2	Feb23 1-1	Jan19 3-1	Aug25 0-3	Sep22 1-2
COWDENBEATH	Mar30 3-1	Feb23 4-0	Mar09 2-5	Dec01 3-1	Jan12 2-2		Oct27 3-2	Sep08 2-1	Aug18 1-1	Apr06 3-0	Feb16 3-2	Dec22 1-2
DUMBARTON	Dec01 1-1	Nov03 1-0	Nov10 3-2	Aug25 6-0	Dec22 6-1	Dec29 4-0		Jan12 0-2	Sep01 1-2	Feb02 4-0	Feb23 0-2	Sep29 2-1
E STIRLING	Dec22 1-1	Nov10 2-0	Dec08 1-0	Mar09 6-2	Aug18 1-1	Nov24 0-1	Oct06 3-4		Feb09 2-1	Mar02 3-3	Sep15 1-3	Oct20 2-1
LEITH A	Nov10 3-1	Aug25 2-1	Feb16 1-2	Nov17 2-0	Oct13 1-0	Mar16 0-0	Sep22 1-0	Dec01 4-0		Jan05 4-1	Dec15 1-0	Jan12 2-3
RAITH R	Mar16 4-0	Sep08 0-1	Mar30 1-2	Feb16 4-3	Dec08 3-1	Aug25 1-2	Dec15 0-4	Nov17 3-1	Dec22 3-3		Apr01 1-1	Dec29 5-0
ST BERNARD'S	Dec08 2-0	Jan19 3-1	Dec22 3-2	Apr06 3-5	Oct06 2-1	Apr20 2-0	Aug18 3-0	Mar23 1-1	Oct20 2-1	Apr13 3-2		Nov03 1-0
VALE OF LEVEN	Oct13 4-1	Jan05 6-0	Sep15 2-0	Oct06 5-2	Oct27 3-1	Jan19 6-0	Nov24 2-2	Dec15 3-1	Dec08 4-1	Aug18 2-0	Mar16 0-1	

LEAGUE TABLES

DIVISION 1

	P	W	D	L	F	A	W	D	L	F	A	Pts
Celtic	34	13	4	0	40	14	10	5	2	40	16	55
Dundee	34	10	5	2	24	10	8	7	2	29	16	48
Rangers	34	9	5	3	35	16	10	2	5	34	17	45
Airdrle	34	12	1	4	36	20	6	5	6	23	24	42
Falkirk	34	12	4	1	45	23	5	3	9	28	35	41
T. Lanark	34	8	5	4	34	26	7	4	6	23	22	39
St Mirren	34	6	8	3	23	19	6	5	6	27	25	37
Clyde	34	9	3	5	27	22	6	3	8	20	30	36
Hearts	34	7	7	3	27	16	4	6	7	19	27	35
Motherwell	34	8	3	6	25	27	4	6	7	20	21	33
Aberdeen	34	7	6	4	24	20	3	4	10	24	35	30
Hibernian	34	7	5	5	22	20	3	5	9	18	29	30
Morton	34	9	4	4	26	15	2	2	13	15	35	28
Partick	34	7	3	7	22	22	2	5	10	18	38	26
Queen's Park	34	7	1	9	27	29	2	5	10	24	37	24
Hamilton	34	5	1	11	27	37	3	4	10	13	27	21
Kilmarnock	34	7	3	7	29	33	1	2	14	11	39	21
Port Glasgow	34	4	6	7	20	27	3	1	13	10	40	21

DIVISION 2

	P	W	D	L	F	A	W	D	L	F	A	Pts
St Bernard's	22	9	1	1	25	13	5	3	3	16	11	32
Vale of Leven	22	9	1	1	37	9	4	0	7	17	26	27
Arthurlie	22	8	2	1	32	18	4	1	6	19	22	27
Dumbarton	22	7	1	3	28	11	4	2	5	24	24	25
Leith A	22	8	1	2	21	8	2	3	6	19	27	24
Albion R	22	8	2	1	36	13	2	1	8	7	23	23
Cowdenbeath	22	7	2	2	27	17	3	3	5	9	23	*23
Ayr U	22	6	2	3	21	13	1	4	6	14	26	20
Abercorn	22	3	5	3	17	19	2	2	7	12	28	17
Raith R	22	5	2	4	25	18	1	2	8	15	30	16
E. Stirling	22	5	3	3	22	17	1	1	9	14	31	16
Ayr Parkhouse	22	4	1	6	17	27	1	1	9	17	37	12

* Two points deducted for an irregularity.

Scottish Football League Records
Season 1907-08

DIVISION 1

	ABERDEEN	AIRDRIE	CELTIC	CLYDE	DUNDEE	FALKIRK	HAMILTON A	HEARTS	HIBERNIAN	KILMARNOCK	MORTON	MOTHERWELL	PARTICK T	PORT GLASGOW A	QUEEN'S PARK	RANGERS	ST MIRREN	T LANARK
ABERDEEN		Mar28 0-1	Sep23 2-1	Aug17 3-1	Dec07 1-1	Jan11 1-1	Nov02 3-0	Dec21 1-0	Apr18 1-1	Oct05 1-0	Aug31 1-2	Mar07 2-1	Sep28 1-0	Nov23 3-1	Apr20 3-0	Jan18 0-0	Sep14 1-3	Oct19 1-1
AIRDRIE	Jan01 0-1		Dec28 0-0	Aug31 2-0	Jan11 0-2	Sep28 2-2	Jan18 5-2	Nov09 2-3	Sep14 0-2	Mar14 1-0	Dec07 3-0	Oct26 1-1	Dec14 7-2	Feb22 3-1	Aug17 2-0	Jan04 3-0	Nov23 3-0	Oct05 3-0
CELTIC	Jan02 3-0	Sep21 1-1		Jan11 5-1	Aug31 3-2	Sep07 3-2	Aug15 3-0	Apr20 6-0	Mar07 4-0	Dec21 4-1	Apr04 2-0	Aug17 3-0	Feb01 4-1	Nov02 5-0	Nov16 4-1	Jan01 2-1	Dec07 4-0	Feb29 1-1
CLYDE	Apr25 2-2	Feb08 0-3	Nov09 0-2		Dec28 2-3	Feb15 1-2	Aug21 3-2	Aug24 1-1	Oct26 1-1	Nov30 0-0	Jan18 1-2	Mar28 2-0	Sep30 0-1	Oct19 0-4	Dec14 5-4	Mar14 0-2	Feb01 1-4	Nov23 2-1
DUNDEE	Sep21 1-0	Sep07 3-1	Mar28 2-0	Oct12 6-1		Feb29 2-2	Nov30 3-0	Jan04 0-0	Jan02 0-1	Nov23 4-0	Sep24 5-2	Feb01 0-0	Aug24 1-0	Jan01 3-1	Oct19 5-0	Feb21 1-2	Oct26 6-0	Nov09 1-0
FALKIRK	Oct12 4-0	Mar07 1-2	Apr27 1-1	Nov16 2-0	Aug17 1-2		Feb08 5-1	Oct19 3-0	Mar14 3-1	Jan02 5-0	Jan01 4-1	Dec07 2-1	Oct05 3-1	Sep21 9-0	Nov30 5-1	Aug31 4-4	Dec21 5-2	Nov02 1-0
HAMILTON A	Feb01 3-0	Feb29 1-1	Feb14 2-4	Apr20 1-0	Mar07 2-1	Nov23 1-3		Mar28 2-1	Aug17 1-1	Apr04 3-3	Jan04 1-0	Nov09 2-3	Oct26 4-1	Dec28 4-1	Oct12 2-2	Feb15 2-2	Aug31 1-1	Jan01 0-1
HEARTS	Oct26 3-1	Apr11 2-0	Nov23 1-0	Apr18 1-0	Sep14 1-0	Dec14 2-3	Sep28 4-3		Apr04 1-2	Aug17 1-0	Feb15 2-2	Mar14 0-3	Dec28 1-3	Jan02 5-0	Aug31 7-2	Dec07 1-2	Jan11 0-1	Mar07 1-2
HIBERNIAN	Sep07 1-0	Feb01 4-0	Oct05 1-2	Mar21 2-1	Nov02 0-1	Aug24 0-4	Apr29 2-5	Nov16 2-3		Oct19 3-1	Nov30 3-0	Sep21 1-1	Nov09 6-0	Feb29 2-1	Jan18 4-1	Mar28 0-3	Apr27 2-1	Jan04 2-0
KILMARNOCK	Feb29 1-0	Nov16 0-1	Sep14 0-0	Sep28 2-2	Mar21 1-1	Oct26 1-6	Dec07 2-0	Feb01 2-0	Dec14 3-0		Oct12 1-2	Dec28 2-0	Jan11 0-1	Nov09 1-1	Feb15 2-2	Mar07 0-2	Jan01 2-2	Aug24 2-2
MORTON	Dec28 2-0	Nov02 0-2	Aug24 2-3	Mar07 1-1	Dec14 2-2	Nov09 0-2	Mar14 3-2	Sep07 1-1	Jan11 0-3	Apr22 2-2		Oct19 1-1	Dec31 2-0	Oct05 2-0	Apr18 3-2	Sep21 2-3	Feb29 1-1	Mar28 0-2
MOTHERWELL	Nov16 2-3	Jan02 2-0	Jan18 2-2	Jan01 3-0	Oct05 0-1	Sep14 1-5	Jan11 2-1	Nov30 3-0	Sep28 0-0	Nov02 1-2	Nov23 4-0		Feb29 3-4	Aug24 6-0	Sep07 6-1	Apr04 1-2	Aug15 2-3	Dec21 2-1
PARTICK T	Apr04 0-6	Oct19 0-1	Mar14 0-3	Dec21 3-1	Jan18 1-3	Mar21 1-1	Apr11 1-1	Nov02 1-1	Apr30 1-1	Aug31 2-2	Aug17 2-2	Apr18 2-0		Mar07 1-1	Mar28 0-3	Nov16 1-2	Apr25 1-2	Dec07 2-0
PORT GLASGOW A	Mar14 1-1	Nov30 1-3	Feb15 0-3	Dec07 2-3	Nov16 0-5	Mar28 1-3	Sep14 1-0	Jan18 1-1	Aug31 1-3	Jan04 4-1	Dec21 2-4	Mar21 2-2	Oct12 0-5		Oct26 3-2	Aug17 1-6	Sep28 1-2	Feb01 0-0
QUEEN'S PARK	Nov09 2-2	Dec21 3-2	Apr11 0-2	Feb29 4-1	Mar14 1-3	Apr08 2-4	Aug24 0-3	Apr29 6-3	Dec07 1-2	Sep21 1-1	Sep14 1-1	Apr25 1-2	Nov23 0-0	Jan11 1-1		Nov02 3-1	Mar07 2-0	Mar21 0-1
RANGERS	Aug24 4-0	Oct05 1-2	Apr25 0-1	Apr11 1-1	Apr20 2-0	Dec28 2-2	Mar21 1-0	Feb29 2-1	Nov23 1-1	Sep07 1-0	Aug15 3-0	Dec14 4-2	Jan02 3-2	Apr18 5-1	Sep30 1-1		Nov09 2-2	Jan11 2-0
ST MIRREN	Nov30 0-3	Aug24 3-1	Apr30 2-2	Nov02 1-1	Apr28 0-0	Apr04 3-2	Oct19 2-2	Sep21 3-1	Dec28 0-1	Jan18 0-0	Nov16 2-1	Oct12 2-1	Sep07 2-2	Dec14 1-3	Oct05 2-0	Apr13 0-2		Mar14 1-2
T LANARK	Dec14 1-1	Feb15 3-0	Sep30 1-3	Jan02 2-1	Dec25 1-1	Jan18 2-1	Nov16 0-1	Oct05 2-1	Apr11 0-0	Apr25 6-3	Oct26 2-0	Aug31 1-3	Apr20 2-1	Sep07 3-2	Dec28 1-4	Nov30 3-5	Aug17 1-2	

DIVISION 2

	ABERCORN	ALBION R	ARTHURLIE	AYR PARKHOUSE	AYR U	COWDENBEATH	DUMBARTON	E STIRLING	LEITH A	RAITH R	ST BERNARD'S	VALE OF LEVEN
ABERCORN		Oct26 1-2	Nov09 3-3	Aug17 2-0	Sep14 2-1	Feb08 1-1	Feb01 2-4	Dec21 2-1	Dec07 2-2	Sep28 2-0	Aug31 2-1	Feb29 0-0
ALBION R	Mar07 2-3		Feb08 5-2	Jan18 3-2	Aug24 1-1	Mar28 2-1	Oct05 3-3	Mar21 1-2	Nov16 0-2	Feb01 0-1	Feb22 1-3	Feb15 1-1
ARTHURLIE	Nov30 0-1	Aug17 0-1		Aug31 2-1	Feb15 1-3	Mar21 3-2	Oct26 0-0	Mar14 2-1	Nov02 3-1	Dec14 3-1	Sep28 1-4	Oct12 2-1
AYR PARKHOUSE	Nov02 2-0	Oct12 0-3	Dec28 2-1		Jan02 2-1	Feb15 4-3	Dec14 3-1	Dec07 5-1	Aug24 3-2	Jan11 3-2	Jan04 2-1	Sep14 1-2
AYR U	Nov23 2-1	Nov09 4-1	Oct19 2-2	Nov16 1-0		Jan18 3-0	Dec21 1-2	Apr04 1-1	Oct26 2-0	Aug31 2-0	Aug17 3-2	Nov30 2-1
COWDENBEATH	Dec14 1-2	Aug31 5-0	Oct05 1-0	Dec21 3-1	Nov02 1-3		Dec07 3-1	Apr25 0-1	Dec28 1-0	Aug17 0-1	Nov23 0-1	Nov16 0-0
DUMBARTON	Nov16 2-1	Dec28 1-1	Aug24 6-2	Nov30 1-0	Sep28 2-3	Sep14 3-1		Oct19 2-2	Aug17 2-1	Mar14 3-1	Oct12 4-0	Nov02 4-1
E STIRLING	Aug24 0-3	Sep14 1-1	Apr11 2-2	Feb01 2-1	Dec14 2-2	Oct26 3-0	Nov23 2-1		Feb29 3-0	Apr30 0-1	Nov09 2-0	Sep28 2-0
LEITH A	Jan04 1-0	Dec14 5-3	Feb01 2-1	Nov23 2-3	Oct12 5-1	Nov30 3-3	Nov09 2-4	Aug31 2-1		Apr11 0-1	Oct05 1-1	Dec21 5-2
RAITH R	Jan18 1-0	Dec07 1-2	Nov23 4-2	Mar07 2-0	Dec28 4-0	Nov09 2-0	Jan04 2-1	Apr06 2-0	Mar28 2-2		Dec21 2-0	Aug24 3-0
ST BERNARD'S	Feb15 2-2	Jan11 5-2	Mar07 1-0	Feb08 3-2	Dec07 1-1	Aug24 1-0	Jan18 1-1	Dec28 0-1	Sep14 0-1	Feb29 2-3		Oct26 2-1
VALE OF LEVEN	Dec28 2-1	Nov23 4-1	Dec07 1-1	Nov09 0-1	Oct05 2-1	Feb01 0-0	Aug31 0-1	Aug17 4-0	Oct19 2-2	Mar21 1-1	Dec14 0-0	

LEAGUE TABLES

DIVISION 1

	P	W	D	L	F	A	W	D	L	F	A	Pts
Celtic	34	15	2	0	57	11	9	5	3	29	16	55
Falkirk	34	13	2	2	58	17	9	5	3	45	25	51
Rangers	34	10	5	2	35	16	11	3	3	39	24	50
Dundee	34	12	3	2	43	10	8	5	4	28	18	48
Hibernian	34	10	1	6	35	24	7	7	3	20	18	42
Airdrie	34	10	3	4	37	16	8	2	7	21	25	41
St Mirren	34	6	6	5	24	24	7	4	6	26	35	36
Aberdeen	34	9	5	3	25	14	4	4	9	20	30	35
T. Lanark	34	8	3	6	31	29	5	4	8	14	21	33
Motherwell	34	8	2	7	40	25	4	5	8	21	28	31
Hamilton A	34	7	6	4	32	25	3	2	12	23	40	28
Hearts	34	9	1	7	33	24	2	5	10	17	38	28
Morton	34	5	6	6	24	27	4	3	10	19	39	27
Partick T	34	3	7	7	19	30	5	2	10	24	39	25
Kilmarnock	34	5	7	5	22	22	1	6	10	16	39	25
Queen's Park	34	5	5	7	28	29	2	3	12	26	55	22
Clyde	34	4	4	9	21	34	1	4	12	15	41	18
Port Glasgow A	34	3	4	10	21	44	2	3	12	18	54	17

DIVISION 2

	P	W	D	L	F	A	W	D	L	F	A	Pts
Raith R	22	9	1	1	25	7	5	1	5	12	16	30
Dumbarton	22	8	2	1	30	13	4	3	4	19	19	*27
Ayr U	22	8	2	1	23	10	3	3	5	17	23	27
Abercorn	22	5	4	2	19	15	4	1	6	14	15	23
E. Stirling	22	6	3	2	19	11	3	2	6	11	21	23
Ayr Parkhouse	22	9	0	2	27	17	2	0	9	11	21	22
Leith A	22	6	2	3	28	20	2	3	6	13	20	21
St Bernard's	22	5	3	3	18	14	3	2	6	13	18	21
Albion R	22	3	3	5	19	21	4	2	5	17	27	19
Vale of Leven	22	4	5	2	16	9	1	3	7	9	22	18
Arthurlie	22	6	1	4	17	16	0	4	7	16	29	17
Cowdenbeath	22	5	1	5	15	10	0	3	8	11	25	14

* Two points deducted for a registration irregularity.

Scottish Football League Records
Season 1908-09

DIVISION 1

	ABERDEEN	AIRDRIE	CELTIC	CLYDE	DUNDEE	FALKIRK	HAMILTON A	HEARTS	HIBERNIAN	KILMARNOCK	MORTON	MOTHERWELL	PARTICK T	PORT GLASGOW A	QUEEN'S PARK	RANGERS	ST MIRREN	T LANARK
ABERDEEN		Sep12 2-0	Dec19 0-2	Jan01 2-4	Oct24 1-1	Nov07 3-1	Oct17 4-2	Feb13 1-0	Apr03 4-0	Sep26 2-0	Aug22 2-0	Nov28 1-3	Oct10 3-2	Jan02 3-1	Sep28 1-1	Sep05 0-2	Aug15 4-2	Jan30 6-1
AIRDRIE	Dec05 4-2		Nov21 1-2	Jan09 1-2	Aug22 2-5	Sep19 1-1	Jan02 0-1	Apr10 2-1	Mar20 2-1	Feb13 1-1	Oct03 4-1	Sep05 3-0	Apr03 4-0	Dec26 1-1	Feb27 3-3	Oct10 4-3	Nov07 3-2	Mar13 2-2
CELTIC	Feb24 2-0	Apr24 0-0		Dec26 0-1	Oct10 2-0	Jan30 2-0	Apr21 1-1	Jan09 1-1	Dec12 2-0	Aug22 5-1	Apr22 5-1	Apr26 4-0	Nov07 3-0	Nov14 2-1	Nov28 4-0	Mar13 2-3	Sep05 0-1	Sep28 1-0
CLYDE	Aug29 2-1	Oct17 0-0	Oct31 0-2		Mar06 0-2	Jan02 6-3	Aug15 1-0	Mar13 1-0	Apr17 2-0	Aug19 5-2	Apr03 4-1	Feb13 1-1	Apr24 2-0	Aug25 3-2	Dec19 1-0	Nov21 0-1	Apr21 2-1	Jan20 2-0
DUNDEE	Dec12 2-2	Nov28 1-0	Aug29 2-1	Jan30 1-0		Sep12 1-1	Apr03 3-0	Aug15 2-1	Oct17 3-0	Nov14 5-0	Feb27 1-2	Oct31 3-1	Jan16 3-2	Jan01 1-0	Sep26 7-1	Jan09 4-0	Dec19 4-1	Mar27 1-0
FALKIRK	Oct03 0-1	Dec19 0-2	Mar06 1-1	Feb27 1-0	Nov21 3-3		Oct10 5-3	Apr24 4-1	Sep05 0-0	Apr03 3-1	Feb13 7-0	Aug22 4-1	Jan01 3-1	Mar27 2-0	Dec12 1-3	Dec05 1-0	Oct24 1-1	Nov14 1-0
HAMILTON A	Sep19 1-2	Oct31 2-2	Apr30 1-2	Apr10 1-3	Oct03 0-1	Nov28 3-4		Nov14 1-1	Aug22 1-1	Sep05 0-0	Dec19 3-1	Mar06 2-0	Mar13 4-2	Feb20 1-1	Jan09 1-1	Dec12 0-7	Feb13 1-0	Feb27 1-1
HEARTS	Oct31 1-1	Sep26 2-6	Apr19 1-2	Aug22 1-1	Mar20 1-0	Apr17 1-0	Dec26 1-0		Sep19 1-1	Oct10 0-0	Dec05 5-0	Jan16 3-2	Apr28 1-0	Oct17 3-0	Sep05 3-0	Apr03 0-0	Nov21 1-2	Jan02 1-2
HIBERNIAN	Nov14 2-1	Aug15 2-0	Apr29 1-0	Sep12 1-1	Feb20 0-1	Mar13 2-0	Apr24 2-0	Nov07 0-1		Jan09 2-1	Oct24 4-1	Dec19 3-0	Nov28 1-1	Jan30 1-1	Feb13 1-0	Apr19 1-0	Mar27 2-1	Aug29 3-0
KILMARNOCK	Mar13 3-2	Aug29 0-1	Jan02 3-1	Nov07 2-1	Dec26 2-0	Oct17 3-1	Mar20 3-1	Feb20 2-5	Nov21 0-1		Dec12 2-1	Sep19 4-1	Feb27 1-0	Oct31 1-0	Oct24 1-1	Sep12 0-5	Jan01 1-1	Nov28 4-2
MORTON	Feb20 2-3	Mar27 3-1	Aug15 0-5	Nov14 2-4	Sep19 0-0	Oct31 1-1	Sep26 3-3	Jan30 4-1	Jan02 1-0	Feb06 1-1		Mar13 1-1	Aug29 1-0	Nov28 1-2	Oct17 0-2	Apr28 1-7	Apr17 2-0	Dec26 1-1
MOTHERWELL	Feb27 3-2	Jan01 2-4	Dec05 1-2	Oct24 0-1	Jan02 1-4	Dec26 3-1	Nov07 2-2	Sep12 1-6	Sep26 3-0	Mar27 2-1	Oct10 2-1		Feb20 3-3	Aug29 1-0	Nov21 3-3	Jan30 2-5	Mar20 1-0	Aug15 1-0
PARTICK T	Jan09 0-1	Nov14 0-6	Mar29 0-1	Sep28 2-3	Sep05 1-1	Sep26 1-2	Mar27 2-4	Oct24 3-2	Apr10 1-5	Aug15 1-4	Nov21 5-1	Dec12 0-2		Mar20 1-3	Apr08 1-2	Jan02 0-6	Dec05 2-3	Feb13 1-7
PORT GLASGOW A	Nov21 1-1	Jan16 0-1	Feb13 1-4	Apr29 0-1	Nov07 2-3	Jan09 2-1	Oct24 0-0	Dec12 1-0	Oct10 1-2	Apr17 2-0	Sep12 0-2	Apr03 0-0	Dec19 2-2		Aug22 2-1	Feb27 2-0	Apr24 3-0	Apr05 1-1
QUEEN'S PARK	Dec26 2-2	Apr15 0-3	Apr28 0-5	Apr22 0-3	Apr24 0-2	Aug15 0-2	Aug29 1-1	Mar27 2-2	Dec05 0-1	Mar06 0-2	Mar20 4-0	Oct03 0-1	Oct31 5-2	Mar13 1-2		Nov14 1-1	Jan02 1-1	Apr03 1-1
RANGERS	Mar27 3-1	Oct24 2-0	Jan01 1-3	Apr12 2-2	Sep28 2-0	Aug29 4-1	Mar30 4-0	Nov28 4-3	Mar06 0-0	Dec19 1-1	Nov07 8-0	Oct17 3-1	Aug22 2-0	Aug15 7-0	Apr26 2-3		Sep19 1-1	Oct31 2-2
ST MIRREN	Mar06 1-0	Dec12 1-1	Apr03 0-1	Nov28 4-1	Mar13 1-2	Apr10 2-1	Sep12 5-0	Aug29 2-0	Oct31 1-0	Oct03 3-0	Jan09 1-2	Nov14 3-1	Oct17 4-2	Sep26 4-1	Oct10 1-1	Dec26 1-3		Apr19 1-0
T LANARK	Mar20 2-0	Mar31 1-2	Apr12 1-1	Dec12 1-1	Dec25 2-1	Apr29 3-1	Nov21 6-1	Dec19 1-3	Apr27 1-0	Jan04 4-0	Sep05 1-1	Jan09 3-1	Oct03 7-0	Mar06 0-4	Nov07 2-2	Apr24 1-0	Aug22 0-1	

DIVISION 2

	ABERCORN	ALBION R	ARTHURLIE	AYR PARKHOUSE	AYR U	COWDENBEATH	DUMBARTON	E STIRLING	LEITH A	RAITH R	ST BERNARD'S	VALE OF LEVEN
ABERCORN		Aug22 3-1	Oct31 5-2	Mar20 4-0	Feb13 1-0	Dec19 6-0	Oct24 1-0	Nov21 1-1	Nov07 3-1	Oct03 1-0	Jan02 2-1	Feb06 1-1
ALBION R	Nov28 1-2		Aug15 3-3	Dec19 1-2	Dec12 2-0	Oct31 3-1	Sep26 2-4	Nov14 0-1	Aug29 1-0	Sep12 1-0	Oct17 2-0	Apr24 5-0
ARTHURLIE	Jan16 1-2	Jan30 1-2		Dec26 1-0	Nov21 3-5	Nov14 2-0	Jan23 2-0	Oct10 3-2	Sep26 4-0	Oct24 1-3	Oct03 0-4	Aug22 0-1
AYR PARKHOUSE	Oct10 1-1	Oct24 4-0	Aug29 2-1		Apr30 0-0	Feb13 1-0	Mar27 2-2	Apr03 3-0	Mar13 4-2	Nov28 2-2	Dec12 1-0	Sep19 1-2
AYR U	Nov14 2-1	Dec05 5-1	Sep12 3-0	Jan02 1-2		Feb06 3-0	Oct31 5-0	Dec19 4-1	Dec26 4-1	Jan09 2-1	Aug22 1-4	Mar20 2-1
COWDENBEATH	Dec26 0-2	Oct03 1-4	Jan09 2-0	Mar06 2-1	Nov07 2-2		Jan02 2-2	Nov28 0-1	Jan30 0-1	Aug22 0-0	Oct24 2-1	Dec12 0-2
DUMBARTON	Dec12 1-0	Nov07 1-3	Oct17 2-0	Jan09 3-2	Jan30 4-3	Nov21 0-0		Aug22 4-1	Oct10 1-1	Dec26 2-1	Nov28 1-0	Sep12 3-1
E STIRLING	Aug29 0-0	Feb06 4-1	Dec12 3-1	Sep12 3-0	Mar27 3-1	Sep26 2-1	Feb20 1-0		Aug15 1-3	Nov07 0-1	Jan09 1-4	Apr10 1-0
LEITH A	Jan09 1-2	Jan02 6-2	Feb06 5-1	Aug22 1-0	Apr03 2-0	Feb20 2-0	Dec19 2-0	Feb27 1-0		Dec12 0-3	Sep12 3-0	Mar06 2-2
RAITH R	Oct17 0-0	Oct10 3-1	Dec19 6-2	Apr10 3-0	Aug29 4-0	Dec05 4-1	Aug15 1-1	Jan02 2-0	Feb13 0-0		Oct31 4-1	Sep26 4-2
ST BERNARD'S	Sep26 2-1	Nov21 1-1	Nov07 1-0	Jan30 1-0	Oct10 0-0	Aug15 2-5	Aug29 4-2	Feb13 2-0	Dec05 3-2	Nov14 3-3		Dec26 0-2
VALE OF LEVEN	Feb27 1-0	Jan09 5-0	Jan02 4-1	Apr17 1-1	Aug15 3-0	Aug29 1-0	Feb13 0-1	Mar13 1-1	Mar27 2-1	Feb20 2-1	Dec19 4-0	

LEAGUE TABLES

DIVISION 1

	P	W	D	L	F	A	W	D	L	F	A	Pts
Celtic	34	11	3	3	36	10	12	2	3	35	14	51
Dundee	34	14	2	1	44	12	8	4	5	26	20	50
Clyde	34	12	2	3	32	16	9	4	4	29	21	48
Rangers	34	10	5	2	48	18	9	2	6	43	20	45
Airdrie	34	8	5	4	38	28	8	4	5	29	18	41
Hibernian	34	12	3	2	28	9	4	4	9	12	23	39
St Mirren	34	11	2	4	35	16	4	4	9	18	29	36
Aberdeen	34	11	2	4	39	22	4	4	9	22	31	36
Falkirk	34	10	4	3	37	18	3	3	11	21	38	33
Kilmarnock	34	11	2	4	32	24	2	5	10	15	37	33
T. Lanark	34	9	4	4	36	19	2	6	9	20	30	32
Hearts	34	8	5	4	26	17	4	3	10	28	32	32
Port Glasgow A	34	6	5	6	20	19	4	3	10	19	33	28
Motherwell	34	8	3	6	31	35	3	3	11	16	38	28
Queen's Park	34	2	6	9	18	31	4	7	6	24	34	25
Hamilton A	34	4	7	6	23	29	2	5	10	19	43	24
Morton	34	5	6	6	24	32	3	1	13	15	58	23
Partick T	34	2	1	14	21	53	0	3	14	17	49	8

DIVISION 2

	P	W	D	L	F	A	W	D	L	F	A	Pts
Abercorn	22	9	2	0	28	7	4	3	4	11	10	31
Raith R	22	8	3	0	31	8	3	3	5	15	14	28
Vale of Leven	22	8	2	1	24	6	4	2	5	14	19	28
Dumbarton	22	8	2	1	22	12	2	3	6	12	22	25
Ayr U	22	9	0	2	32	12	1	3	7	11	24	23
Leith A	22	8	1	2	25	10	2	2	7	12	23	23
Ayr Parkhouse	22	6	4	1	21	10	2	1	8	8	21	21
St Bernard's	22	6	3	2	19	16	3	0	8	15	21	21
E. Stirling	22	7	1	3	19	12	2	2	7	8	21	21
Albion R	22	6	1	4	21	13	3	1	7	16	34	20
Cowdenbeath	22	3	3	5	11	16	1	1	9	8	26	12
Arthurlie	22	5	0	6	18	19	0	1	10	11	36	11

Scottish Football League Records
Season 1909-10

DIVISION 1

	ABERDEEN	AIRDRIE	CELTIC	CLYDE	DUNDEE	FALKIRK	HAMILTON A	HEARTS	HIBERNIAN	KILMARNOCK	MORTON	MOTHERWELL	PARTICK T	PORT GLASGOW A	QUEEN'S PARK	RANGERS	ST MIRREN	T LANARK
ABERDEEN		Oct09 1-0	Nov27 0-1	Jan15 1-1	Apr23 3-1	Dec04 0-1	Apr20 1-0	Mar12 3-0	Sep25 1-0	Mar26 0-1	Apr02 1-0	Oct23 2-2	Jan03 1-1	Nov06 3-0	Sep27 3-1	Mar05 1-1	Oct02 2-0	Aug28 2-1
AIRDRIE	Dec25 1-3		Jan08 0-2	Dec11 2-0	Apr19 3-0	Sep04 2-1	Jan03 2-1	Mar26 3-1	Apr27 0-2	Nov27 2-2	Nov13 3-2	Mar12 2-2	Oct16 1-3	Sep25 1-1	Oct02 3-4	Aug21 2-1	Oct30 0-0	Feb19 1-1
CELTIC	Apr09 2-0	Nov20 3-1		Mar28 2-1	Oct02 1-0	Aug21 2-0	Aug17 3-1	Nov06 1-0	Apr25 0-0	Dec04 2-1	Apr06 3-0	Sep04 2-2	Mar26 3-1	Jan15 4-0	Oct23 6-0	Jan01 1-1	Dec11 1-1	Mar16 2-0
CLYDE	Oct16 2-1	Sep18 1-1	Jan03 0-1		Apr27 2-0	Dec18 0-0	Dec25 1-0	Apr13 2-2	Oct30 2-1	Apr02 0-0	Apr21 1-0	Aug16 3-1	Sep27 5-0	Aug28 0-1	Oct09 0-1	Nov13 1-0	Apr30 2-1	Mar19 2-1
DUNDEE	Jan01 0-0	Dec18 3-0	Apr30 0-0	Dec04 1-1		Jan15 1-0	Mar05 2-1	Nov13 4-1	Apr13 4-2	Oct16 2-2	Feb12 2-1	Aug21 2-0	Apr06 1-1	Nov20 4-0	Apr02 3-0	Sep04 4-2	Sep18 2-1	Oct30 2-0
FALKIRK	Oct30 1-0	Jan01 4-1	Apr23 2-0	Mar26 6-1	Dec11 6-1		Aug28 2-1	Jan29 2-1	Nov27 2-0	Nov13 4-0	Oct02 2-0	Sep25 3-1	Apr02 2-0	Sep11 0-0	Apr20 1-1	Dec25 3-1	Apr09 1-1	Oct16 3-1
HAMILTON A	Nov13 1-0	Feb26 1-1	Sep18 1-5	Oct23 2-1	Jan08 3-3	Mar12 1-3		Apr23 2-1	Dec11 1-1	Feb12 1-7	Aug21 2-2	Oct30 3-1	Mar19 1-0	Oct09 3-1	Sep04 4-2	Jan15 2-3	Mar26 3-1	Nov27 4-2
HEARTS	Sep04 0-0	Jan15 0-1	Sep20 1-2	Aug21 2-0	Jan03 1-0	Apr16 4-2	Nov20 1-2		Jan01 1-0	Oct02 3-0	Oct16 5-1	Dec11 5-1	Oct30 2-2	Mar19 6-0	Dec25 3-2	Apr18 1-3	Nov27 0-1	Apr02 2-2
HIBERNIAN	Apr18 1-2	Dec04 3-0	Aug28 1-0	Feb12 0-1	Nov06 0-0	Mar05 1-1	Apr30 1-0	Oct23 1-4		Sep18 2-1	Jan03 2-1	Apr23 1-0	Apr09 3-1	Dec18 2-1	Jan08 1-0	Sep20 1-0	Nov13 0-0	Oct09 0-0
KILMARNOCK	Feb26 0-2	Aug28 3-3	Dec25 0-1	Nov06 6-3	Apr26 2-1	Mar19 0-2	Sep25 1-0	Apr30 1-1	Nov20 4-0		Dec11 2-0	Oct09 2-1	Feb19 2-1	Mar12 4-0	Sep11 6-1	Oct23 0-2	Jan01 2-1	Jan15 0-0
MORTON	Nov20 0-1	Oct23 0-1	Sep11 2-1	Sep25 2-1	Aug28 1-0	Oct09 0-1	Nov06 2-0	Dec18 3-3	Jan15 2-0	Mar05 4-0		Mar19 0-1	Aug16 2-1	Jan29 2-0	Mar26 0-2	Dec04 1-4	Mar12 1-0	Apr09 0-2
MOTHERWELL	Jan08 2-1	Sep11 0-1	Dec18 1-3	Nov20 0-0	Apr25 1-1	Nov06 2-2	Jan01 2-2	Apr09 1-0	Oct02 3-1	Jan03 3-1	Dec25 5-0		Aug28 2-2	Mar05 6-3	Dec04 3-0	Jan29 2-3	Oct16 5-2	Sep18 1-3
PARTICK T	Dec11 1-1	Feb05 1-1	Nov13 1-3	Oct02 1-1	Mar28 1-0	Oct23 2-2	Jan05 2-3	Mar05 1-3	Dec25 3-1	Jan08 3-0	Aug25 0-1	Feb12 2-1		Feb26 3-1	Apr16 0-2	Nov06 0-0	Jan15 3-2	Mar12 0-0
PORT GLASGOW A	Aug21 0-3	Apr02 1-2	Oct18 2-3	Jan08 0-5	Mar26 0-3	Feb12 0-1	Feb05 2-1	Sep18 0-2	Sep04 0-2	Oct30 1-1	Jan01 1-1	Nov13 0-1	Nov27 2-4		Dec11 3-0	Oct02 1-1	Feb19 0-2	Apr23 2-4
QUEEN'S PARK	Apr30 2-2	Apr13 2-4	Mar19 0-1	Mar05 2-2	Nov27 3-0	Sep18 1-4	Dec18 2-0	Aug28 2-2	Oct16 1-2	Apr09 1-1	Oct30 5-2	Jan15 3-1	Jan01 2-0	Apr26 6-1		Mar12 3-2	Apr23 2-1	Nov13 0-0
RANGERS	Sep18 2-1	Mar19 3-0	Oct30 0-0	Apr23 1-0	Sep27 2-1	Apr30 0-1	Oct16 5-1	Jan08 1-0	Mar26 1-0	Aug16 3-0	Feb19 2-1	Nov27 4-1	Dec18 2-1	Jan03 4-0	Nov20 7-1		Aug28 1-1	Mar28 1-0
ST MIRREN	Mar19 1-2	Mar05 2-1	Jan29 2-1	Sep04 0-2	Oct23 3-2	Nov20 1-5	Sep11 2-0	Oct09 1-0	Apr02 3-0	Aug21 2-1	Jan08 0-2	Apr16 1-2	Sep25 3-2	Dec04 4-1	Nov06 2-0	Feb26 1-6		Dec18 3-1
T LANARK	Apr16 2-0	Nov06 3-0	Sep27 0-1	Jan01 1-3	Dec25 0-2	Jan08 1-1	Oct02 2-2	Apr20 3-1	Aug21 0-1	Sep04 7-0	Feb26 6-2	Mar26 0-2	Nov20 3-1	Oct23 5-0	Apr06 4-0	Dec11 2-1	Jan03 5-2	

DIVISION 2

	ABERCORN	ALBION R	ARTHURLIE	AYR PARKHOUSE	AYR U	COWDENBEATH	DUMBARTON	E STIRLING	LEITH A	RAITH R	ST BERNARD'S	VALE OF LEVEN
ABERCORN		Nov13 3-2	Sep18 2-3	Sep11 2-1	Oct16 2-0	Oct30 1-0	Feb12 5-2	Oct02 2-1	Jan01 3-1	Dec11 1-1	Nov27 3-3	Oct09 2-2
ALBION R	Feb05 5-2		Nov20 4-1	Oct09 1-3	Dec18 2-0	Aug28 1-1	Nov06 3-1	Jan01 2-1	Feb26 1-2	Sep11 0-0	Oct23 3-2	Mar05 2-1
ARTHURLIE	Aug28 1-1	Sep25 2-2		Oct02 1-4	Apr30 1-0	Oct16 2-1	Dec04 1-2	Nov13 1-2	Feb19 3-3	Dec18 1-2	Oct30 1-2	Oct23 2-1
AYR PARKHOUSE	Dec18 2-2	Nov27 2-2	Apr27 1-3		Jan01 1-3	Mar26 4-0	Feb26 4-2	Sep25 1-2	Aug28 1-1	Nov06 0-2	Nov20 2-3	Oct30 0-2
AYR U	Dec25 2-1	Aug21 4-3	Apr02 2-2	Nov13 2-0		Feb19 1-1	Mar19 3-1	Sep11 2-1	Dec11 1-3	Dec04 2-3	Oct09 3-0	Jan15 4-3
COWDENBEATH	Sep25 2-1	Oct02 1-0	Dec11 1-2	Aug21 1-0	Nov06 2-2		Dec25 1-3	Nov27 2-1	Feb12 2-0	Oct23 0-1	Sep11 3-0	Sep18 2-1
DUMBARTON	Oct23 1-1	Dec11 0-0	Sep11 3-2	Feb05 5-0	Nov27 3-1	Apr02 1-0		Apr23 5-2	Jan15 1-1	Jan01 4-1	Feb19 1-0	Aug21 1-1
E STIRLING	Nov06 3-1	Apr09 1-0	Oct09 2-2	Oct23 3-0	Nov20 2-5	Dec04 3-0	Feb18 3-2		Apr30 2-2	Apr16 1-2	Aug21 3-1	Apr02 2-0
LEITH A	Nov20 3-0	Dec25 1-0	Aug21 3-0	Dec04 2-0	Jan08 3-0	Apr09 4-0	Mar12 2-1	Mar26 3-0		Feb05 0-0	Dec18 1-0	Sep11 3-0
RAITH R	Aug21 2-0	Oct30 3-0	Apr09 4-2	Mar12 1-0	Feb26 2-0	Nov20 3-2	Aug28 2-1	Oct16 1-0	Mar05 2-2		Dec25 2-1	Nov27 0-0
ST BERNARD'S	Jan15 1-1	Feb12 4-0	Jan01 2-1	Jan29 1-0	Aug28 3-0	Nov13 1-0	Sep25 2-1	Dec11 6-2	Oct16 1-1	Apr02 2-1		Oct02 6-1
VALE OF LEVEN	Feb26 2-2	Oct16 4-1	Nov06 3-0	Dec11 2-1	Sep25 1-0	Dec18 2-0	Nov20 3-3	Aug28 3-1	Mar19 1-3	Nov13 2-1	Dec04 1-2	

LEAGUE TABLES

DIVISION 1

	P	W	D	L	F	A	W	D	L	F	A	Pts
Celtic	34	13	4	0	38	9	11	2	4	25	13	54
Falkirk	34	14	3	0	44	10	8	5	4	27	18	52
Rangers	34	14	2	1	39	9	6	4	7	31	26	46
Aberdeen	34	10	4	3	25	11	6	4	7	19	18	40
Clyde	34	10	4	3	24	11	4	5	8	23	29	37
Dundee	34	12	5	0	37	12	2	3	12	15	32	36
T. Lanark	34	10	2	5	44	19	3	6	8	18	25	34
Hibernian	34	10	4	3	20	12	4	2	11	13	28	34
Airdrie	34	7	5	5	28	26	5	4	8	18	31	33
Motherwell	34	8	5	4	39	25	4	3	10	20	35	32
Kilmarnock	34	10	3	4	35	19	2	5	10	18	40	32
Hearts	34	9	3	5	37	19	3	4	10	22	31	31
St Mirren	34	11	0	6	31	28	2	5	10	17	30	31
Queen's Park	34	8	5	4	37	25	4	1	12	17	49	30
Hamilton A	34	9	4	4	35	34	2	2	13	15	33	28
Partick T	34	6	6	5	24	22	2	4	11	21	37	26
Morton	34	9	1	7	22	18	2	2	13	16	42	25
Port Glasgow A	34	2	3	12	15	36	1	2	14	10	57	*11

* Port Glasgow A relegated.

DIVISION 2

	P	W	D	L	F	A	W	D	L	F	A	Pts
Leith A	22	10	1	0	25	1	3	6	2	19	18	33
Raith R	22	9	2	0	22	8	5	3	3	14	13	*33
St Bernard's	22	9	2	0	29	8	3	1	7	14	23	27
Dumbarton	22	7	4	0	25	9	2	1	8	19	29	23
Abercorn	22	7	3	1	26	16	0	5	6	12	24	22
Vale of Leven	22	7	2	2	24	14	1	3	7	12	24	21
Ayr U	22	7	2	2	26	18	2	1	8	11	22	21
E. Stirling	22	7	2	2	25	15	2	0	9	13	28	20
Albion R	22	7	2	2	24	14	0	3	8	10	25	19
Arthurlie	22	3	3	5	16	20	3	2	6	18	27	17
Cowdenbeath	22	7	1	3	17	11	0	2	9	5	23	17
Ayr Parkhouse	22	2	3	6	18	22	2	0	9	9	21	11

* Raith Rovers promoted to Division One.

Ary Parkhouse left League, replaced by Dundee H.

SCOTTISH FOOTBALL LEAGUE RECORDS
SEASON 1910-11

DIVISION 1

	ABERDEEN	AIRDRIE	CELTIC	CLYDE	DUNDEE	FALKIRK	HAMILTON A	HEARTS	HIBERNIAN	KILMARNOCK	MORTON	MOTHERWELL	PARTICK T	QUEEN'S PARK	RAITH R	RANGERS	ST MIRREN	T LANARK
ABERDEEN		Oct22 1-0	Jan14 1-0	Jan02 1-0	Dec24 0-0	Sep24 1-0	Sep03 2-2	Nov05 3-2	Apr08 1-1	Feb18 1-1	Mar04 3-1	Oct08 3-0	Apr01 1-1	Sep26 5-1	Aug20 2-0	Dec03 1-0	Nov19 2-1	Feb04 3-1
AIRDRIE	Mar18 1-3		Nov12 0-0	Aug27 2-2	Oct15 3-1	Nov26 3-1	Feb04 0-1	Mar11 4-1	Oct29 3-0	Jan07 3-1	Apr08 2-1	Sep10 1-1	Dec10 2-0	Mar04 5-2	Jan14 3-3	Jan21 1-4	Oct01 3-2	Dec17 0-1
CELTIC	Apr29 0-0	Aug17 3-0		Jan03 2-0	Sep17 2-1	Jan21 0-0	Apr26 3-0	Oct15 0-0	Mar25 2-0	Dec17 2-0	Aug27 0-1	Dec03 3-0	Jan07 2-0	Feb18 2-0	Dec31 5-0	Oct29 0-1	Nov05 5-0	Nov19 0-0
CLYDE	Oct01 0-0	Apr15 2-0	Dec10 0-2		Sep26 1-1	Oct22 2-1	Dec24 1-0	Aug20 4-0	Oct08 2-0	Aug15 0-0	Apr01 0-0	Jan14 2-0	Nov12 1-2	Nov26 3-0	Apr17 0-0	Apr22 0-1	Mar11 1-1	Sep03 2-0
DUNDEE	Nov12 2-0	Apr10 1-0	Nov26 1-0	Dec17 1-0		Jan02 1-1	Dec31 2-0	Dec10 4-1	Aug27 1-1	Oct08 2-1	Apr29 1-2	Apr15 3-1	Nov05 2-1	Sep24 5-0	Jan21 3-1	Apr08 0-2	Jan14 5-1	Oct22 2-1
FALKIRK	Jan07 1-1	Dec31 2-1	Aug20 2-1	Feb18 4-1	Oct01 0-1		Apr01 4-0	Mar04 3-1	Mar18 2-1	Oct29 2-2	Oct15 3-2	Dec17 3-1	Sep03 3-0	Sep17 3-0	Nov19 0-0	Apr15 2-2	Dec03 3-2	Feb25 4-2
HAMILTON A	Mar25 1-0	Sep24 1-1	Oct22 0-1	Jan21 1-1	Apr19 1-2	Aug27 3-2		Nov12 1-2	Dec03 1-1	Apr10 0-2	Nov26 2-1	Apr22 1-0	Apr24 0-1	Jan07 2-1	Dec17 3-1	Sep10 2-4	Oct29 2-0	Oct08 1-4
HEARTS	Dec17 0-3	Nov19 2-2	Apr01 1-1	Dec03 1-1	Oct29 2-3	Mar25 1-1	Mar18 2-0		Oct22 2-0	Feb11 5-0	Sep24 2-0	Jan07 1-0	Jan14 3-1	Aug27 4-1	Oct08 0-0	Sep19 1-4	Jan21 0-0	Dec31 0-1
HIBERNIAN	Dec10 2-1	Dec24 2-0	Sep19 0-4	Mar04 1-1	Feb18 4-1	Nov05 1-2	Oct01 2-1	Jan02 1-0		Nov26 0-1	Nov12 3-3	Feb25 2-1	Sep17 1-0	Oct15 1-0	Apr22 2-0	Mar11 1-3	Sep03 2-0	Aug20 2-1
KILMARNOCK	Oct15 0-1	Aug20 0-1	Sep03 1-0	Nov19 5-2	Dec03 2-0	Apr08 2-2	Nov05 3-0	Sep17 3-1	Jan14 3-1		Feb04 2-3	Oct22 1-0	Mar04 1-1	Dec24 2-1	Mar25 1-0	Dec31 0-2	Jan02 2-2	Oct01 1-5
MORTON	Apr15 1-1	Dec03 0-1	Dec24 1-1	Nov05 0-2	Nov19 1-1	Apr22 0-1	Jan02 2-1	Feb25 2-2	Jan21 2-2	Sep10 0-0		Oct29 3-0	Aug20 1-1	Oct08 4-1	Aug17 1-0	Mar25 2-2	Jan07 2-3	Jan14 2-3
MOTHERWELL	Jan21 0-1	Jan02 2-2	Feb04 2-1	Oct15 0-2	Aug20 3-0	Mar11 0-3	Sep17 2-2	Sep03 3-2	Nov19 1-2	Apr01 1-0	Dec31 3-2		Dec24 2-3	Dec10 3-3	Mar18 0-1	Oct01 1-2	Apr08 2-0	Nov05 0-1
PARTICK T	Oct29 1-0	Oct08 2-1	Sep26 1-1	Mar25 0-0	Feb04 3-2	Apr29 3-1	Nov19 1-0	Oct01 2-1	Dec31 2-1	Sep24 1-0	Dec17 1-0	Aug27 2-1		Jan21 3-0	Dec03 3-0	Jan03 2-2	Oct15 2-2	Jan02 1-0
QUEEN'S PARK	Apr22 2-4	Sep03 0-1	Oct01 0-1	Dec31 1-3	Apr01 1-2	Jan14 0-2	Aug20 2-1	Apr29 2-0	Dec17 0-1	Feb25 1-1	Mar11 0-0	Mar25 1-0	Oct22 0-3		Nov05 2-1	Nov19 0-4	Feb04 2-0	Dec03 1-4
RAITH R	Nov26 0-1	Feb25 1-1	Oct03 2-1	Oct29 1-2	Jan07 2-1	Dec24 2-2	Oct15 2-0	Feb18 3-2	Sep24 1-3	Dec10 1-1	Aug31 2-0	Nov12 0-1	Mar11 2-2	Apr08 1-1		Aug27 0-2	Mar04 4-0	Feb11 2-2
RANGERS	Sep17 2-4	Nov05 7-1	Jan02 1-1	Jan07 6-1	Sep03 1-2	Dec10 1-1	Jan14 4-0	Dec24 2-0	Sep26 4-0	Nov12 3-0	Oct22 1-5	Nov26 7-1	Feb18 2-0	Mar18 4-0	Feb04 4-1		Aug20 1-0	Apr20 3-1
ST MIRREN	Dec31 2-0	Feb18 3-1	Mar18 1-1	Sep17 0-2	Mar25 1-0	Oct08 1-3	Apr29 1-0	Nov26 3-0	Feb11 2-0	Aug27 1-1	Dec10 1-2	Sep24 4-1	Feb25 2-1	Nov12 3-1	Oct22 2-1	Dec17 2-1		Sep10 1-2
T LANARK	Aug27 2-2	Sep17 0-0	Apr17 1-1	Mar18 2-4	Dec26 2-0	Nov12 3-1	Dec10 3-1	Sep26 1-0	Jan07 0-3	Jan21 0-2	Feb18 3-2	Aug15 2-4	Nov26 4-3	Oct29 2-1	Apr15 2-1	Oct15 1-1	Dec24 2-2	

DIVISION 2

	ABERCORN	ALBION R	ARTHURLIE	AYR U	COWDENBEATH	DUMBARTON	DUNDEE H	E STIRLING	LEITH A	PORT GLASGOW A	ST BERNARD'S	VALE OF LEVEN
ABERCORN		Apr08 1-0	Nov19 2-0	Oct15 3-3	Apr15 1-3	Dec03 3-2	Nov05 1-2	Oct29 3-2	Mar11 1-4	Sep10 3-0	Apr01 1-0	Jan07 1-2
ALBION R	Aug20 2-1		Dec03 3-2	Feb11 1-2	Aug27 1-0	Oct22 3-0	Sep24 0-0	Dec31 1-0	Nov05 2-2	Oct08 0-1	Feb25 2-1	Nov19 1-1
ARTHURLIE	Aug27 2-1	Oct01 1-1		Apr08 1-4	Feb11 2-0	Nov12 1-3	Dec17 3-1	Feb25 0-0	Oct22 5-1	Jan07 3-0	Nov26 1-0	Nov05 2-0
AYR U	Nov26 3-4	Oct29 1-2	Oct08 2-0		Oct22 3-0	Apr01 5-1	Nov12 3-0	Dec17 4-0	Dec31 3-1	Aug20 2-0	Dec10 5-1	Sep10 2-2
COWDENBEATH	Sep24 2-1	Dec24 0-0	Aug20 1-0	Nov19 5-1		Feb04 2-3	Dec31 3-0	Jan07 1-0	Apr22 2-0	Nov05 4-0	Dec17 3-1	Oct29 1-2
DUMBARTON	Dec17 4-1	Dec10 2-0	Dec31 4-1	Nov05 3-2	Mar25 2-0		Apr15 3-1	Apr29 4-0	Jan07 2-0	Oct29 2-1	Feb11 8-2	Sep24 1-0
DUNDEE H	Sep17 4-1	Jan07 1-0	Oct29 2-0	Dec03 1-1	Oct01 2-0	Nov19 0-3		Apr01 0-0	Aug20 2-3	Mar18 4-1	Dec24 1-2	Oct08 1-1
E STIRLING	Mar18 5-1	Mar11 0-1	Mar25 1-1	Sep24 2-0	Dec10 1-1	Apr08 2-0	Jan02 3-1		Jan14 3-3	Dec24 3-0	Apr22 2-0	Jan21 1-0
LEITH A	Mar25 4-2	Mar04 1-0	Dec24 1-1	Aug27 4-6	Nov26 1-1	Feb25 1-3	Dec10 1-1	Feb11 3-1		Dec17 1-0	Jan21 2-3	Mar18 3-2
PORT GLASGOW A	Dec12 2-3	Nov26 3-1	Oct15 3-0	Oct01 1-0	Sep17 5-1	Aug27 2-0	Oct22 1-2	Feb04 4-0	Feb18 1-1		Sep24 0-0	Dec10 1-1
ST BERNARD'S	Oct08 3-2	Nov12 0-3	Feb18 3-0	Jan07 4-1	Mar11 0-0	Sep17 2-1	Sep10 4-3	Aug20 5-1	Dec03 1-3	Nov19 0-1		Dec31 2-0
VALE OF LEVEN	Oct22 1-2	Oct15 1-2	Mar11 0-0	Dec24 0-1	Nov12 1-1	Aug20 1-1	Nov26 2-0	Oct01 1-1	Apr08 1-2	Dec03 1-0	Aug27 1-2	

LEAGUE TABLES

DIVISION 1

	P	W	D	L	F	A	W	D	L	F	A	Pts
Rangers	34	12	2	3	53	18	11	4	2	37	16	52
Aberdeen	34	12	5	0	31	11	7	5	5	22	17	48
Falkirk	34	12	4	1	41	18	5	6	6	24	24	44
Partick T	34	13	4	0	30	12	4	4	9	20	29	42
Celtic	34	11	4	2	31	3	4	7	6	17	15	41
Dundee	34	13	2	2	36	13	5	3	9	18	29	41
Clyde	34	8	6	3	21	8	6	5	6	24	28	39
T. Lanark	34	8	5	4	30	28	8	2	7	29	25	39
Hibernian	34	11	2	4	27	19	4	4	9	17	29	36
Kilmarnock	34	9	3	5	29	22	3	7	7	13	23	34
Airdrie	34	9	4	4	36	24	3	5	9	13	29	33
St Mirren	34	11	2	4	30	17	1	5	11	16	40	31
Morton	34	4	8	5	24	22	5	3	9	25	29	29
Hearts	34	7	6	4	27	18	1	2	14	15	41	24
Raith R	34	6	6	5	26	22	1	4	12	10	33	24
Hamilton A	34	7	3	7	22	24	1	2	14	9	36	21
Motherwell	34	6	3	8	25	27	2	1	14	12	39	20
Queen's Park	34	5	2	10	15	28	0	2	15	13	52	14

DIVISION 2

	P	W	D	L	F	A	W	D	L	F	A	Pts
Dumbarton	22	11	0	0	35	8	4	1	6	17	22	31
Ayr U	22	8	1	2	33	11	4	2	5	21	25	27
Albion R	22	6	3	2	16	10	4	2	5	10	11	25
Leith A	22	5	3	3	22	20	4	3	4	20	23	24
Cowdenbeath	22	8	1	2	24	8	1	4	6	7	19	23
St Bernard's	22	7	1	3	24	15	3	1	7	12	26	22
E. Stirling	22	7	3	1	23	8	0	3	8	5	26	20
Port Glasgow A	22	6	3	2	23	9	2	0	9	4	23	*19
Dundee H	22	5	3	3	18	12	2	2	7	11	24	19
Arthurlie	22	7	2	2	21	11	0	3	8	5	22	19
Abercorn	22	6	1	4	20	18	3	0	8	19	32	19
Vale of Leven	22	2	4	5	10	12	2	4	5	11	16	16

* Port Glasgow left League, replaced by St Johnstone.

Scottish Football League Records
Season 1911-12

DIVISION 1

	ABERDEEN	AIRDRIE	CELTIC	CLYDE	DUNDEE	FALKIRK	HAMILTON A	HEARTS	HIBERNIAN	KILMARNOCK	MORTON	MOTHERWELL	PARTICK T	QUEEN'S PARK	RAITH R	RANGERS	ST MIRREN	T LANARK
ABERDEEN		Nov04 3-0	Mar23 1-1	Mar30 0-0	Dec16 2-1	Apr17 1-0	Jan06 2-0	Mar16 1-0	Mar02 1-1	Sep30 1-2	Apr06 1-1	Dec02 0-1	Oct21 3-1	Sep25 3-0	Aug19 3-1	Sep16 1-2	Dec30 2-1	Aug26 1-2
AIRDRIE	Apr20 3-0		Dec30 0-0	Sep09 0-1	Nov11 0-0	Oct28 2-1	Sep23 1-1	Apr06 2-0	Jan13 1-0	Aug19 1-0	Nov25 0-1	Jan01 1-0	Jan20 1-2	Dec16 4-2	Mar02 5-1	Oct14 2-2	Feb17 1-2	Oct07 1-1
CELTIC	Oct14 1-0	Aug15 3-0		Sep02 3-2	Mar02 2-0	Aug19 3-1	Nov11 2-1	Jan06 1-1	Oct28 3-1	Apr13 2-0	Dec23 1-1	Jan13 2-0	Sep25 3-0	Feb17 2-1	Apr20 1-1	Jan01 3-0	Dec02 3-1	Feb03 3-1
CLYDE	Oct07 0-1	Mar16 2-1	Jan02 1-1		Dec30 3-0	Sep16 1-2	Dec09 3-0	Apr13 1-2	Nov25 1-0	Aug16 3-1	Nov04 1-0	Nov18 1-2	Dec16 2-1	Apr27 0-1	Oct21 2-0	Aug26 0-2	Apr08 3-0	Jan20 1-0
DUNDEE	Jan13 4-0	Sep30 1-1	Sep16 3-1	Dec02 2-0		Dec09 1-1	Dec23 2-0	Oct07 1-1	Nov04 3-2	Mar23 5-2	Oct21 0-3	Aug19 3-1	Mar09 0-2	Sep23 4-0	Feb10 2-2	Mar16 2-1	Nov18 4-0	Mar30 3-1
FALKIRK	Sep23 3-0	Apr27 2-1	Nov04 1-1	Mar23 2-1	Jan01 0-0		Aug26 1-0	Dec02 2-2	Apr20 1-0	Apr06 2-0	Nov18 2-1	Oct21 1-3	Feb24 0-1	Jan13 3-1	Apr13 0-3	Dec23 0-2	Oct07 3-1	Mar02 7-0
HAMILTON A	Sep02 1-1	Nov18 1-2	Oct07 1-0	Jan01 0-0	Apr20 0-1	Mar30 1-3		Mar02 1-1	Sep30 3-0	Jan13 4-0	Mar23 3-1	Nov04 1-0	Dec30 0-3	Aug19 2-1	Sep16 0-1	Feb03 1-1	Oct21 1-0	Dec02 1-1
HEARTS	Nov25 1-2	Sep02 2-1	Sep30 2-1	Aug19 1-0	Oct28 1-4	Oct14 0-2	Apr24 2-0		Jan01 3-0	Sep16 1-1	Jan20 2-0	Apr22 2-1	Apr27 2-1	Mar23 0-0	Nov04 2-0	Apr15 2-1	Jan13 1-2	Dec30 4-0
HIBERNIAN	Dec23 1-1	Oct21 2-1	Nov18 1-1	Feb17 1-2	Aug26 2-1	Nov11 5-0	Mar09 1-0	Dec09 0-4		Dec02 0-1	Dec16 1-2	Oct07 1-0	Apr06 4-0	Mar16 2-0	Sep23 3-0	Jan06 5-0	Mar30 0-0	Sep18 3-2
KILMARNOCK	Apr27 3-0	Jan06 2-1	Sep23 0-2	Dec23 1-3	Nov25 1-0	Dec16 1-0	Sep09 2-3	Nov18 1-3	Jan20 1-2		Mar16 1-0	Mar09 1-1	Nov04 0-1	Oct21 1-2	Oct07 3-1	Mar30 3-2	Jan01 1-1	Dec09 0-0
MORTON	Jan01 2-1	Apr13 1-0	Aug26 1-1	Mar02 1-3	Apr27 4-2	Jan06 2-1	Oct28 3-1	Sep23 2-2	Feb24 2-1	Oct14 2-0		Feb03 0-2	Jan13 2-0	Oct07 2-2	Dec09 0-1	Dec02 2-1	Sep09 1-0	Nov11 0-1
MOTHERWELL	Apr13 2-0	Dec09 0-0	Nov25 3-2	Oct14 2-3	Jan06 0-0	Jan20 2-0	Feb17 0-2	Dec23 0-3	Mar23 0-2	Oct28 0-1	Dec30 0-1		Aug26 1-2	Aug23 1-0	Mar16 3-0	Nov11 1-2	Sep23 3-2	Sep09 2-1
PARTICK T	Dec09 3-1	Dec02 1-2	Mar16 1-1	Sep30 1-0	Feb17 2-0	Sep02 0-0	Oct14 0-0	Nov11 2-2	Sep16 3-0	Mar02 3-1	Aug15 1-1	Apr20 1-0		Dec23 2-1	Mar30 2-2	Oct28 0-1	Aug19 0-0	Jan01 2-2
QUEEN'S PARK	Nov11 2-5	Mar30 2-1	Dec09 1-4	Oct28 2-2	Jan20 1-0	Dec30 0-2	Feb24 0-0	Aug26 0-3	Oct14 2-0	Feb03 1-0	Apr20 1-1	Aug16 1-1	Feb10 0-1		Dec02 2-1	Mar02 0-0	Apr13 2-0	Jan06 1-1
RAITH R	Nov18 1-1	Aug26 0-1	Oct02 1-2	Jan06 0-5	Oct14 1-1	Sep30 1-0	Jan20 1-2	Feb17 3-1	Dec30 2-2	Nov11 3-2	Sep02 1-1	Dec16 3-0	Nov25 3-2	Mar09 0-0		Mar23 0-1	Feb24 1-1	Oct28 4-0
RANGERS	Jan20 2-0	Feb24 4-1	Oct21 3-1	Jan13 1-2	Sep02 2-1	Mar09 4-0	Nov25 7-0	Dec16 2-1	Sep25 2-0	Dec30 6-1	Aug19 6-1	Apr27 3-1	Jan02 4-1	Nov18 1-0	Aug16 5-0		Nov04 4-0	Sep30 4-0
ST MIRREN	Oct28 1-3	Sep16 1-1	Jan20 1-1	Nov11 0-2	Apr06 1-1	Mar16 1-1	Dec16 0-1	Apr20 2-0	Sep02 2-1	Aug26 2-4	Sep30 1-1	Mar02 1-0	Jan06 0-3	Nov25 2-0	Dec23 2-0	Dec09 1-5		Oct14 1-1
T LANARK	Apr08 0-2	Dec23 0-1	Dec16 1-0	Sep25 1-5	Dec25 1-0	Nov25 1-2	Mar16 1-0	Oct21 3-0	Aug19 2-0	Sep02 2-0	Sep16 3-1	Apr06 1-1	Nov18 1-2	Nov04 2-0	Jan13 2-0	Feb17 1-3	Apr27 4-2	

DIVISION 2

	ABERCORN	ALBION R	ARTHURLIE	AYR U	COWDENBEATH	DUMBARTON	DUNDEE H	E STIRLING	LEITH A	ST BERNARD'S	ST JOHNSTONE	VALE OF LEVEN
ABERCORN		Sep09 3-1	Dec30 1-1	Jan13 0-1	Nov04 2-2	Oct21 2-1	Feb10 3-1	Feb24 3-0	Dec02 3-0	Mar23 3-0	Oct07 2-1	Nov18 3-2
ALBION R	Dec23 1-4		Oct21 0-1	Nov04 0-2	Dec02 2-5	Mar02 2-1	Sep16 1-0	Nov18 4-1	Jan06 1-0	Dec09 2-3	Aug26 0-1	Sep30 1-0
ARTHURLIE	Aug26 0-1	Nov11 5-0		Feb03 0-1	Dec23 1-0	Sep23 4-2	Sep30 1-1	Dec02 0-1	Oct07 3-4	Oct28 2-2	Feb10 4-1	Sep16 4-2
AYR U	Aug19 4-2	Feb17 4-0	Jan06 3-0		Apr13 4-0	Dec02 2-1	Oct21 6-0	Oct07 2-0	Dec23 4-2	Jan01 3-2	Jan20 1-1	Dec09 4-0
COWDENBEATH	Nov25 2-0	Oct28 2-1	Oct14 0-1	Aug26 1-2		Jan06 0-3	Nov18 2-0	Mar30 1-0	Sep23 3-1	Nov11 5-0	Dec16 3-1	Aug19 1-3
DUMBARTON	Sep30 1-5	Dec30 2-0	Dec09 1-0	Feb10 6-1	Sep09 2-0		Jan02 1-0	Jan27 2-1	Jan13 5-2	Aug19 3-0	Feb24 4-1	Dec16 2-0
DUNDEE H	Oct28 1-1	Oct07 0-1	Nov25 0-0	Dec16 2-2	Apr08 5-2	Feb17 4-2		Jan06 1-0	Aug26 1-0	Oct14 2-2	Nov11 1-0	Dec30 0-1
E STIRLING	Dec16 0-0	Sep23 0-0	Sep09 2-0	Mar16 1-0	Dec09 0-1	Mar09 1-0	Aug19 3-1		Sep16 0-1	Dec30 2-4	Feb17 2-2	Mar02 2-0
LEITH A	Nov11 2-1	Aug19 1-0	Feb17 1-0	Nov25 1-3	Dec30 2-2	Oct14 2-2	Dec09 3-0	Mar23 2-0		Sep30 2-0	Mar09 0-0	Sep09 0-0
ST BERNARD'S	Jan06 0-1	Dec16 1-0	Jan27 1-1	Mar30 2-2	Oct21 0-1	Dec23 2-1	Nov04 7-1	Aug26 1-3	Nov18 2-1		Dec02 2-0	Oct07 5-0
ST JOHNSTONE	Dec09 1-0	Nov25 3-1	Aug19 4-1	Dec30 1-0	Mar23 0-3	Nov04 0-1	Sep23 1-0	Jan13 3-1	Jan01 2-0	Sep09 0-0		Oct28 2-0
VALE OF LEVEN	Jan20 0-3	Oct14 2-1	Nov04 2-1	Sep23 2-3	Feb17 1-3	Aug26 2-4	Dec02 2-0	Dec23 3-1	Oct21 2-4	Nov25 1-2	Jan06 1-4	

LEAGUE TABLES

DIVISION 1

	P	W	D	L	F	A	W	D	L	F	A	Pts
Rangers	34	16	0	1	60	10	8	3	6	26	24	51
Celtic	34	14	3	0	38	11	3	8	6	20	22	45
Clyde	34	10	1	6	25	14	9	3	5	31	18	42
Hearts	34	11	2	4	28	16	5	6	6	26	24	40
Partick T	34	7	8	2	24	14	9	0	8	23	26	40
Morton	34	10	3	4	27	19	4	6	7	17	25	37
Falkirk	34	10	3	4	30	17	5	3	9	16	26	36
Dundee	34	11	4	2	40	18	2	5	10	12	23	35
Aberdeen	34	9	4	4	26	14	5	3	9	18	30	35
Airdrie	34	8	5	4	25	14	4	3	10	15	27	32
T. Lanark	34	10	1	6	26	19	2	6	9	14	38	31
Hamilton A	34	7	5	5	21	16	4	3	10	11	28	30
Hibernian	34	10	3	4	32	15	2	2	13	12	32	29
Motherwell	34	7	2	8	20	21	4	3	10	14	23	27
Raith R	34	6	6	5	25	22	3	3	11	14	37	27
Kilmarnock	34	7	3	7	22	22	4	1	12	16	38	26
Queen's Park	34	6	6	5	18	22	2	3	12	11	31	25
St Mirren	34	5	6	6	19	25	2	4	11	13	34	24

DIVISION 2

	P	W	D	L	F	A	W	D	L	F	A	Pts
Ayr U	22	10	1	0	37	8	6	2	3	17	16	35
Abercorn	22	8	2	1	25	10	5	2	4	18	12	30
Dumbarton	22	10	0	1	29	10	3	1	7	18	21	27
Cowdenbeath	22	7	0	4	20	12	5	2	4	19	19	26
St Johnstone	22	8	1	2	17	7	2	3	6	12	20	24
St Bernard's	22	6	2	3	23	11	3	3	5	15	25	23
Leith A	22	6	4	1	16	8	3	0	8	15	26	22
Arthurlie	22	5	2	4	24	15	2	3	6	6	15	19
E. Stirling	22	5	3	3	13	9	2	0	9	8	22	17
Dundee H	22	5	4	2	17	11	0	1	10	4	30	15
Vale of Leven	22	4	0	7	18	26	2	1	8	8	24	13
Albion R	22	5	0	6	14	18	1	1	9	5	23	13

Scottish Football League Records
Season 1912-13

DIVISION 1

	ABERDEEN	AIRDRIE	CELTIC	CLYDE	DUNDEE	FALKIRK	HAMILTON A	HEARTS	HIBERNIAN	KILMARNOCK	MORTON	MOTHERWELL	PARTICK T	QUEEN'S PARK	RAITH R	RANGERS	ST MIRREN	T LANARK
ABERDEEN		Jan18 4-1	Feb15 3-0	Sep23 0-1	Jan01 1-0	Oct26 2-2	Sep21 2-0	Oct19 0-1	Dec21 1-3	Nov09 0-0	Dec07 0-0	Mar29 2-2	Nov16 3-1	Sep30 4-0	Aug17 2-0	Oct05 1-3	Mar01 4-0	Feb22 2-0
AIRDRIE	Oct12 1-1		Sep14 1-4	Aug24 2-3	Nov02 1-1	Mar15 5-1	Mar22 4-0	Nov23 1-0	Apr26 1-0	Dec07 3-2	Mar08 5-1	Sep28 1-1	Sep21 2-0	Jan04 4-3	Nov16 0-1	Dec21 3-0	Mar29 2-2	Mar01 3-2
CELTIC	Sep07 2-0	Jan25 1-1		Jan02 3-0	Dec21 2-0	Mar22 1-2	Dec07 2-1	Nov09 1-0	Aug24 1-1	Mar29 4-1	Oct05 1-0	Nov23 1-2	Jan04 1-0	Jan11 1-0	Mar24 4-1	Oct26 3-2	Apr05 2-1	Feb01 2-0
CLYDE	Nov02 0-1	Dec14 0-0	Nov30 1-1		Apr12 2-2	Dec31 0-0	Nov16 2-1	Aug17 0-0	Apr29 2-0	Oct12 0-0	Sep21 0-1	Dec28 3-2	Apr22 1-0	Oct19 3-0	Aug31 1-0	Apr15 0-1	Mar24 2-2	Sep30 1-1
DUNDEE	Aug24 1-3	Jan11 1-1	Sep21 3-1	Sep07 1-3		Oct12 2-2	Apr05 2-1	Dec14 3-0	Nov30 2-2	Feb01 0-0	Nov16 0-1	Mar01 0-0	Dec28 1-0	Sep28 1-0	Nov09 1-0	Apr19 0-0	Apr07 0-0	Oct26 1-0
FALKIRK	Dec14 3-1	Aug31 2-3	Aug17 0-0	Jan25 0-2	Jan04 2-0		Apr19 6-0	Oct05 2-0	Apr05 0-2	Nov23 0-0	Oct19 2-1	Apr16 1-1	Jan11 2-0	Mar01 3-1	Apr28 0-1	Nov30 2-0	Nov02 2-0	Dec28 2-2
HAMILTON A	Mar15 3-0	Oct26 1-3	Apr26 0-1	Mar01 0-1	Nov23 1-0	Sep28 0-0		Jan11 4-2	Oct12 3-1	Sep07 3-1	Feb22 3-1	Jan01 0-0	Dec14 2-0	Mar29 2-1	Dec28 4-0	Aug24 0-2	Nov30 3-1	Nov09 0-0
HEARTS	Feb01 4-1	Sep07 1-1	Apr21 0-0	Jan04 3-2	Mar22 4-3	Apr23 0-2	Dec21 0-0		Sep28 1-0	Oct26 5-0	Apr12 4-2	Apr26 0-1	Nov02 4-0	Aug24 10-3	Nov30 2-0	Mar15 1-1	Nov16 2-0	Oct12 1-2
HIBERNIAN	Nov23 3-1	Dec28 2-2	Jan18 1-0	Dec07 3-1	Jan25 4-0	Nov09 3-3	Apr21 3-1	Apr16 0-3		Apr19 4-0	Jan11 3-1	Mar08 1-2	Aug31 1-0	Oct05 3-0	Dec14 1-2	Oct19 0-1	Sep21 1-1	Aug17 1-4
KILMARNOCK	Mar08 3-1	Oct19 0-1	Aug31 0-2	Jan11 3-2	Oct05 2-0	Apr30 1-1	Jan18 1-1	Dec28 2-2	Nov16 0-1		Sep14 1-1	Dec14 0-1	Aug17 2-1	Nov02 2-1	Mar15 4-3	Mar01 2-3	Jan01 2-1	Sep21 2-0
MORTON	Sep28 0-1	Jan01 2-0	Dec14 1-2	Mar22 3-0	Mar29 1-1	Jan18 1-1	Aug31 3-1	Mar01 1-2	Oct26 0-3	Jan04 1-3		Nov09 2-2	Oct12 3-1	Sep07 2-1	Apr19 1-0	Jan25 0-3	Aug17 3-2	Nov30 4-0
MOTHERWELL	Nov30 1-1	Apr05 2-1	Mar15 1-0	Oct05 0-1	Aug17 0-0	Nov16 1-4	Oct19 0-0	Aug31 1-2	Nov02 5-1	Apr12 0-1	Dec21 2-0		Jan25 4-1	Dec07 6-3	Sep21 1-1	Sep14 1-2	Jan04 3-1	Jan18 0-0
PARTICK T	Apr19 0-1	Feb15 1-1	Sep30 2-3	Nov09 2-2	Oct19 2-0	Sep07 2-1	Oct05 2-1	Dec07 1-3	Mar29 1-2	Nov30 4-1	Mar15 5-3	Aug24 1-1		Dec21 1-0	Oct26 2-0	Jan02 2-3	Jan18 2-1	Jan01 3-1
QUEEN'S PARK	Jan25 0-1	Nov30 0-4	Nov16 0-1	Apr26 3-0	Jan18 1-3	Sep21 2-1	Aug17 0-1	Feb15 1-6	Apr12 3-5	Mar22 1-1	Dec28 3-0	Oct26 1-1	Feb01 0-0		Apr30 1-0	Nov09 2-3	Aug31 2-3	Dec14 0-2
RAITH R	Jan04 0-0	Apr23 2-4	Oct19 2-1	Dec21 5-1	Feb15 0-0	Aug24 0-1	Nov02 3-5	Jan18 3-3	Sep07 4-2	Sep28 0-0	Nov23 2-2	Mar22 2-0	Apr07 0-2	Oct12 5-0		Dec07 2-2	Oct05 2-2	Jan25 1-3
RANGERS	Dec28 3-1	Aug17 4-2	Jan01 0-1	Nov23 3-1	Aug31 3-3	Apr26 2-1	Mar08 3-2	Sep21 2-4	Jan04 5-3	Sep30 3-0	Nov02 1-1	Jan11 3-1	Mar22 2-0	Apr05 4-0	Feb01 4-0		Dec14 2-1	Nov16 2-1
ST MIRREN	Jan11 2-2	Nov09 1-0	Dec28 1-3	Oct26 1-0	Dec07 2-0	Dec21 1-4	Sep14 0-0	Jan25 2-1	Mar22 0-3	Aug24 4-0	Feb01 3-2	Oct12 2-1	Nov23 2-1	Mar15 5-0	Apr26 4-4	Sep07 0-3		Sep28 2-2
T LANARK	Aug31 0-0	Oct05 0-0	Nov02 0-1	Apr19 0-3	Dec25 4-1	Dec07 1-1	Jan04 0-0	Apr05 1-0	Mar15 3-0	Dec21 0-0	Aug24 1-5	Sep07 0-1	Mar08 1-0	Nov23 0-1	Jan11 0-0	Mar24 0-1	Oct19 0-0	

DIVISION 2

	ABERCORN	ALBION R	ARTHURLIE	AYR U	COWDENBEATH	DUMBARTON	DUNDEE H	DUNFERMLINE A	E STIRLING	JOHNSTONE	LEITH A	ST BERNARD'S	ST JOHNSTONE	VALE OF LEVEN
ABERCORN		Jan04 1-0	Nov02 1-0	Dec14 0-0	Mar08 3-1	Feb15 1-2	Mar29 2-0	Apr21 0-1	Mar01 2-2	Jan18 2-0	Aug31 1-1	Apr26 3-0	Apr08 2-1	Oct05 2-0
ALBION R	Apr19 0-0		Feb15 4-2	Oct19 0-1	Aug31 0-3	Dec28 1-0	Oct26 5-1	Jan18 2-1	Jan25 0-0	Aug17 3-1	Dec14 3-0	Feb08 3-2	Jan11 2-1	Feb22 5-0
ARTHURLIE	Aug24 2-3	Feb01 3-1		Nov09 1-2	Oct12 0-2	Mar22 0-2	Sep28 4-1	Apr12 2-2	Dec28 1-1	Oct26 2-0	Jan11 4-1	Dec07 2-1	Nov30 3-0	Nov23 1-0
AYR U	Aug17 0-2	Nov02 3-0	Jan25 1-1		Nov23 1-0	Feb01 1-1	Nov16 0-0	Mar29 1-0	Jan11 3-0	Dec28 5-0	Dec07 3-0	Jan01 3-0	Mar08 3-1	Aug31 6-0
COWDENBEATH	Apr12 0-1	Mar01 2-0	Dec14 1-1	Aug24 1-1		Apr19 2-1	Feb15 1-1	Aug17 2-2	Nov02 1-2	Jan04 2-0	Oct26 3-1	Jan11 2-0	Sep14 2-2	Nov30 1-0
DUMBARTON	Apr16 3-0	Dec21 3-2	Jan04 4-0	Apr12 1-0	Mar29 0-1		Nov30 2-0	Aug31 2-1	Nov23 0-1	Nov09 1-1	Mar01 2-1	Mar15 0-2	Jan25 1-0	Aug17 1-1
DUNDEE H	Feb22 3-0	Mar15 2-1	Aug31 3-1	Jan18 1-0	Dec21 0-0	Jan01 3-3		Mar22 1-1	Aug17 2-3	Jan25 7-1	Nov23 2-1	Jan02 1-1	Dec07 1-1	Sep14 1-2
DUNFERMLINE A	Apr30 3-0	Sep14 5-2	Mar08 5-1	Nov30 0-0	Jan01 1-0	Jan11 3-0	Mar01 0-0		Apr05 1-0	Apr19 2-1	Feb15 1-1	Aug24 2-0	Apr26 1-0	Jan04 4-0
E STIRLING	Apr28 5-1	Mar22 0-1	Jan18 4-2	Dec21 0-0	Feb22 0-1	Dec07 3-1	Mar08 1-1	Mar15 4-2		Jan01 1-1	Nov09 1-1	Nov16 2-0	Aug24 2-0	Oct12 1-2
JOHNSTONE	Sep14 1-1	Dec07 3-0	Nov16 1-0	Mar15 2-1	Feb08 4-2	Aug24 2-1	Jan11 4-1	Dec14 1-1	Oct05 0-2		Oct19 1-0	Oct12 1-2	Nov23 1-0	Dec21 2-0
LEITH A	Mar15 1-1	Oct12 0-0	Oct05 4-1	Feb22 1-4	Nov16 0-3	Jan18 2-2	Aug24 2-0	Jan25 0-2	Jan04 0-3	Nov30 1-0		Sep14 3-0	Dec21 0-1	Feb08 1-1
ST BERNARD'S	Apr05 3-0	Nov23 3-2	Dec21 0-0	Mar22 3-0	Dec28 2-1	Sep28 1-3	Dec14 3-0	Feb22 4-1	Aug31 2-1	Feb15 1-1	Aug17 1-2		Jan18 1-0	Nov09 2-0
ST JOHNSTONE	Jan01 1-1	Nov16 2-1	Aug17 3-2	Jan04 3-3	Nov09 1-2	Apr05 1-0	Oct12 2-0	Dec28 1-2	Feb01 1-3	Aug31 2-2	Sep28 2-2	Mar01 1-0		Oct26 1-1
VALE OF LEVEN	Mar22 1-3	Aug24 1-0	Oct19 2-1	Mar01 1-3	Jan18 3-0	Nov16 0-2	Feb01 2-2	Dec07 2-1	Dec14 1-1	Nov02 3-0	Dec28 5-0	Mar08 0-2	Feb15 0-1	

LEAGUE TABLES

DIVISION 1

	P	W	D	L	F	A	W	D	L	F	A	Pts
Rangers	34	13	2	2	46	22	11	3	3	30	19	53
Celtic	34	13	2	2	32	12	9	3	5	21	16	49
Hearts	34	10	4	3	42	18	7	3	7	29	25	41
Airdrie	34	10	4	3	39	22	5	7	5	25	24	41
Falkirk	34	9	4	4	29	14	5	8	4	27	24	40
Motherwell	34	7	5	5	28	19	5	8	4	19	20	37
Aberdeen	34	9	4	4	31	14	5	5	7	16	26	37
Hibernian	34	9	3	5	34	22	7	2	8	29	32	37
Clyde	34	6	8	3	18	12	7	1	9	23	32	35
Hamilton A	34	10	3	4	29	14	2	5	10	15	33	32
Kilmarnock	34	8	4	5	27	22	2	7	8	10	32	31
St Mirren	34	9	4	4	32	26	1	6	10	18	34	30
Morton	34	8	3	6	28	23	3	4	10	22	36	29
Dundee	34	7	7	3	19	14	1	6	10	14	32	29
T. Lanark	34	4	7	6	11	14	4	5	8	20	27	28
Raith R	34	5	7	5	33	28	3	3	11	13	32	26
Partick T	34	9	3	5	33	24	1	1	15	7	31	24
Queen's Park	34	4	3	10	20	32	1	0	16	14	56	13

DIVISION 2

	P	W	D	L	F	A	W	D	L	F	A	Pts
Ayr U	26	9	3	1	30	5	4	5	4	15	14	*34
Dunfermline A	26	10	3	0	28	5	3	4	6	17	22	*33
E. Stirling	26	6	4	3	24	13	6	4	3	19	14	32
Abercorn	26	8	3	2	20	8	4	4	5	13	23	31
Cowdenbeath	26	6	5	2	20	12	6	1	6	16	15	30
Dumbarton	26	8	2	3	20	10	4	3	6	18	20	29
St Bernard's	26	9	2	2	26	11	3	1	9	10	23	27
Johnstone	26	9	2	2	23	11	0	4	9	8	32	24
Albion R	26	9	2	2	28	12	1	1	11	10	28	23
Dundee H	26	6	5	2	27	15	0	5	8	7	28	22
St Johnstone	26	5	5	3	21	19	2	2	9	8	19	21
Vale of Leven	26	6	2	5	21	16	2	3	8	7	28	21
Arthurlie	26	7	2	4	25	16	0	3	10	12	33	19
Leith A	26	4	4	5	15	18	1	4	8	11	29	18

* Ayr United & Dumbarton were promoted to Division One. No clubs were demoted from Division One.

Dunfermline & Johnstone joined Division Two.

Scottish Football League Records
Season 1913-14

DIVISION 1

	AIRDRIE	AYR U	CELTIC	CLYDE	DUMBARTON	DUNDEE	FALKIRK	HAMILTON A	HEARTS	HIBERNIAN	KILMARNOCK	MORTON	MOTHERWELL	PARTICK T	QUEEN'S PARK	RAITH R	RANGERS	ST MIRREN	T LANARK	
ABERDEEN		Aug30 0-0	Oct25 2-2	Oct11 0-1	Aug16 1-2	Dec20 2-3	Mar28 2-2	Sep13 0-0	Jan24 5-0	Jan10 0-1	Mar21 1-2	Dec06 1-2	Mar07 2-1	Apr11 0-0	Nov15 0-0	Nov22 2-1	Jan03 1-0	Sep22 0-0	Sep27 2-1	Mar18 0-0
AIRDRIE	Apr04 4-1		Mar07 1-1	Nov29 0-1	Apr11 1-1	Oct18 4-1	Dec13 3-0	Oct04 0-0	Nov08 3-2	Dec27 2-2	Apr25 4-3	Sep20 3-1	Jan31 7-1	Jan03 3-1	Sep06 0-0	Nov01 3-3	Aug23 5-2	Feb14 0-3	Mar21 3-1	Jan17 0-0
AYR U	Apr18 2-1	Dec06 0-2		Dec27 0-6	Nov22 2-0	Sep17 1-2	Feb14 1-3	Nov01 3-2	Apr04 3-1	Aug23 0-4	Dec20 1-2	Mar14 0-0	Jan05 0-2	Oct18 4-0	Nov08 2-1	Oct11 2-2	Mar21 0-0	Jan10 1-2	Nov29 2-0	Jan24 2-0
CELTIC	Oct04 2-1	Jan24 1-0	Aug16 5-1		Sep29 2-0	Jan10 4-0	Oct18 1-0	Aug30 4-0	Nov22 1-0	Mar24 0-0	Apr18 3-0	Nov01 4-0	Feb14 3-0	Dec20 0-0	Apr25 1-1	Apr13 5-0	Apr29 2-1	Jan01 4-0	Sep13 0-2	Dec06 3-0
CLYDE	Dec13 1-0	Oct25 0-0	Mar17 1-2	Jan05 0-1		Dec27 0-0	Aug23 2-1	Mar03 1-1	Jan31 0-2	Sep20 2-2	Feb28 4-0	Jan03 0-0	Apr25 3-0	Nov15 5-0	Jan17 2-1	Mar21 3-1	Sep06 0-1	Nov29 0-1	Oct11 0-3	Nov08 3-1
DUMBARTON	Jan31 0-1	Apr18 1-0	Sep01 2-1	Nov15 0-4	Feb21 1-3		Mar07 2-3	Jan03 0-4	Nov29 1-1	Jan17 2-1	Oct11 0-3	Aug23 1-1	Mar28 2-6	Sep27 1-1	Oct25 1-0	Aug16 4-0	Apr06 2-2	Mar14 0-3	Dec13 2-1	Apr23 2-0
DUNDEE	Jan01 0-1	Sep13 2-0	Aug30 2-0	Jan17 0-1	Mar14 2-0	Dec06 5-1		Oct06 4-1	Oct11 1-0	Nov22 2-2	Jan03 2-2	Apr11 3-1	Nov15 1-2	Apr04 2-1	Jan31 4-1	Sep27 5-2	Oct25 2-1	Dec20 0-2	Aug16 1-0	Apr29 3-1
FALKIRK	Mar14 2-0	Mar28 1-1	Sep08 1-3	Feb28 1-0	Jan01 1-0	Nov22 3-1	Nov08 4-0		Jan10 2-1	Sep06 0-0	Apr04 3-2	Jan31 4-1	Oct11 1-1	Apr22 2-0	Aug23 4-3	Dec20 3-2	Dec06 4-0	Apr01 4-1	Oct25 3-1	Sep20 1-1
HAMILTON A	Nov01 3-0	Mar25 2-4	Sep27 4-0	Apr24 1-2	Oct04 1-1	Apr11 3-1	Feb21 1-1	Aug16 1-1		Oct18 1-3	Sep13 0-1	Dec20 6-0	Jan03 1-1	Apr15 1-0	Dec06 2-1	Feb14 2-3	Jan17 1-0	Aug30 0-1	Apr18 1-0	Nov15 0-1
HEARTS	Nov29 4-0	Aug16 3-1	Jan03 2-1	Sep15 2-0	Dec20 1-0	Apr04 5-1	Jan24 3-0	Mar21 1-0	Feb28 1-0		Feb14 3-1	Mar07 0-1	Sep27 4-0	Dec06 2-1	Oct11 1-0	Aug30 1-0	Apr18 2-0	Sep13 2-1	Nov15 6-0	Oct25 0-0
HIBERNIAN	Aug23 1-0	Nov22 1-4	Jan31 0-5	Sep06 1-2	Nov01 1-1	Apr15 1-1	Oct04 4-1	Oct18 0-3	Dec13 6-0	Nov08 1-2		Jan17 0-1	Mar25 1-2	Apr28 2-0	Sep20 0-2	Mar14 2-3	Jan10 0-3	Sep15 0-3	Mar18 5-3	Dec27 1-0
KILMARNOCK	Apr22 1-2	Feb28 3-2	Sep13 0-1	Apr08 0-1	Aug30 2-2	Jan24 6-0	Nov29 0-0	Nov15 2-3	Oct25 5-2	Dec13 0-3	Sep27 0-3		Apr18 0-1	Apr25 2-0	Dec27 2-0	Mar28 3-0	Oct11 3-1	Aug16 1-6	Jan01 3-1	Jan10 1-1
MORTON	Nov08 3-1	Jan01 0-2	Jan17 2-1	Sep20 0-4	Apr04 2-0	Mar21 3-1	Jan10 3-0	Dec27 6-0	Sep06 4-2	Feb21 3-0	Nov29 2-1	Oct18 2-0		Nov01 3-1	Dec13 1-0	Apr11 2-1	Feb28 2-1	Oct04 0-1	Mar14 4-0	Aug23 3-1
MOTHERWELL	Sep20 3-2	Oct11 0-1	Mar28 2-0	Aug23 1-1	Jan10 2-1	Feb28 4-3	Sep06 0-1	Nov29 1-2	Jan01 3-1	Apr01 0-2	Oct25 2-3	Nov08 4-0	Jan24 2-3		Mar21 1-1	Dec13 1-3	Mar14 3-2	Nov22 1-0	Dec27 3-0	Jan31 1-2
PARTICK T	Feb28 0-1	Sep27 0-1	Apr11 0-3	Jan03 0-0	Oct18 1-1	Feb14 2-1	Nov01 2-1	Apr18 1-2	Mar14 0-2	Mar28 2-1	Jan24 3-0	Nov22 4-2	Aug30 1-3	Aug16 2-1		Oct04 1-1	Dec20 2-1	Apr13 1-1	Jan10 2-1	Jan01 1-0
QUEEN'S PARK	Dec27 2-2	Jan10 0-2	Apr15 3-3	Nov08 0-2	Dec06 0-2	Mar31 3-0	Apr18 0-4	Jan17 3-1	Aug23 0-0	Jan31 1-1	Nov15 4-2	Sep06 3-1	Oct25 1-3	Mar23 4-2	Apr28 1-0		Sep20 2-0	Feb28 0-6	Apr22 0-0	Nov29 2-2
RAITH R	Oct18 4-1	Oct06 1-1	Nov15 5-1	Dec13 1-2	Jan24 2-0	Jan01 1-2	Dec27 4-1	Sep27 0-1	Mar07 5-2	Oct04 0-0	Aug30 1-1	Feb14 1-1	Aug16 1-2	Sep13 0-3	Nov29 3-0	Apr25 1-0		Nov01 0-3	Apr04 5-1	Mar25 3-0
RANGERS	Sep06 5-1	Nov15 2-0	Mar25 5-2	Oct25 0-2	Mar07 2-1	Nov08 3-2	Sep20 0-1	Dec13 3-2	Dec27 3-0	Apr25 3-2	Apr07 1-1	Mar21 1-0	Dec06 1-0	Jan17 0-0	Jan05 0-0	Sep29 3-0	Jan31 4-0		Aug23 2-1	Apr18 2-0
ST MIRREN	Jan17 0-2	Dec20 1-4	Apr25 1-1	Jan31 0-3	Feb14 3-2	Aug30 1-1	Feb28 0-3	Apr11 1-1	Sep20 1-0	Nov01 1-0	Dec06 3-3	Jan06 1-1	Nov22 0-2	Oct04 4-0	Mar31 1-0	Oct18 3-1	Nov08 0-1	Jan03 0-1		Sep06 1-2
T LANARK	Apr25 0-0	Mar14 1-1	Dec13 4-2	Apr01 1-3	Apr13 0-0	Nov01 1-0	Dec25 2-1	Feb14 2-1	Apr21 1-2	Apr11 2-1	Aug16 2-1	Oct04 1-1	Dec20 3-1	Aug30 0-1	Sep29 2-1	Jan03 5-0	Nov22 0-2	Oct18 2-4	Apr08 1-0	

DIVISION 2

	ABERCORN	ALBION R	ARTHURLIE	COWDENBEATH	DUNDEE H	DUNFERMLINE A	E STIRLING	JOHNSTONE	LEITH A	ST BERNARD'S	ST JOHNSTONE	VALE OF LEVEN
ABERCORN		Feb21 1-0	Dec27 2-1	Dec13 0-0	Sep13 2-0	Feb07 1-6	Mar21 2-1	Aug16 3-1	Mar28 1-1	Oct11 3-3	Nov15 0-1	Sep27 4-0
ALBION R	Nov22 4-1		Aug16 1-1	Jan03 3-1	Oct11 2-1	Feb28 1-0	Jan10 1-1	Sep13 5-1	Mar14 6-4	Aug30 2-1	Dec06 2-2	Oct25 2-1
ARTHURLIE	Jan31 0-2	Jan17 3-0		Aug30 1-0	Nov22 3-2	Oct04 3-2	Mar14 2-2	Mar07 4-1	Mar21 5-0	Dec06 3-3	Jan03 2-0	Dec13 2-0
COWDENBEATH	Oct04 2-1	Nov08 0-0	Feb21 1-0		Mar14 7-0	Aug16 0-0	Aug23 2-1	Dec20 2-0	Jan31 2-0	Oct25 3-0	Sep13 2-0	Nov15 3-1
DUNDEE H	Jan24 2-1	Feb14 2-2	Aug23 1-0	Mar07 3-0		Feb21 2-1	Nov08 3-1	Oct04 5-0	Jan10 1-1	Jan03 1-3	Apr27 3-2	Sep20 2-0
DUNFERMLINE A	Nov01 2-0	Nov29 3-2	Dec20 6-1	Jan01 0-0	Nov15 1-0		Jan31 1-1	Jan03 7-1	Aug23 1-0	Dec13 2-1	Aug30 4-3	Oct11 2-3
E STIRLING	Aug30 2-1	Mar07 2-0	Apr11 3-2	Nov29 3-0	Jan17 1-3	Dec27 4-1		Nov01 5-0	Feb21 2-1	Nov15 1-1	Dec13 2-2	Aug16 1-1
JOHNSTONE	Nov08 1-3	Aug23 0-0	Sep27 2-1	Oct11 0-0	Jan31 1-0	Nov22 1-2	Dec06 1-1		Dec13 0-1	Jan24 1-1	Mar21 3-1	Feb07 4-0
LEITH A	Dec06 3-0	Jan24 1-1	Feb28 2-0	Sep27 0-1	Aug30 1-1	Oct25 1-1	Dec20 1-1	Nov15 5-1		Aug16 1-1	Oct11 1-1	Nov29 1-0
ST BERNARD'S	Aug23 0-1	Mar28 0-1	Apr04 1-0	Sep20 1-2	Apr11 1-2	Nov08 1-0	Apr28 5-2	Oct18 3-0	Nov22 4-0		Nov01 1-1	Dec27 4-2
ST JOHNSTONE	Dec20 2-1	Jan31 5-0	Nov08 6-0	Nov22 2-3	Aug16 0-0	Oct18 0-3	Jan24 5-3	Nov29 4-2	Jan01 4-3	Sep27 1-3		Aug23 4-0
VALE OF LEVEN	Oct18 0-2	Apr11 2-3	Jan24 1-1	Nov01 1-3	Apr04 1-2	Dec06 2-1	Nov22 1-0	Aug30 2-0	Nov08 3-3	Dec20 2-1	Oct04 0-2	

LEAGUE TABLES

DIVISION 1

	P	W	D	L	F	A	W	D	L	F	A	Pts
Celtic	38	15	3	1	45	6	15	2	2	36	8	65
Rangers	38	14	3	2	40	15	13	2	4	39	16	59
Hearts	38	17	1	1	43	7	6	7	6	27	22	54
Morton	38	16	0	3	45	17	10	2	7	31	34	54
Falkirk	38	14	4	1	44	18	6	5	8	25	33	49
Airdrie	38	10	7	2	46	24	8	5	6	26	19	48
Dundee	38	13	2	4	41	19	6	3	10	23	34	43
T. Lanark	38	10	4	5	30	22	3	6	10	12	29	36
Clyde	38	8	5	6	27	17	3	6	10	17	27	33
Ayr U	38	8	3	8	26	30	5	4	10	30	42	33
Raith R	38	9	4	6	38	22	4	2	13	18	35	32
Kilmarnock	38	8	3	8	34	29	3	6	10	14	39	31
Hibernian	38	6	2	11	27	36	6	4	9	31	39	30
Aberdeen	38	5	8	6	21	18	5	2	12	17	37	30
Partick T	38	9	4	6	25	23	1	5	13	12	28	29
Queen's Park	38	7	6	6	29	33	3	3	13	23	51	29
Hamilton A	38	8	4	7	31	21	3	2	14	18	45	28
Motherwell	38	9	2	8	34	28	2	4	13	12	37	28
Dumbarton	38	7	4	8	24	35	3	3	13	21	52	27
St Mirren	38	6	5	8	22	28	2	1	16	16	45	22

DIVISION 2

	P	W	D	L	F	A	W	D	L	F	A	Pts
Cowdenbeath	22	9	2	0	24	3	4	3	4	10	14	31
Albion R	22	8	3	0	29	14	2	4	5	9	19	27
Dunfermline A	22	8	2	1	29	12	3	2	6	17	16	26
Dundee H	22	8	2	1	25	11	3	2	6	11	20	26
St Johnstone	22	7	1	3	33	18	2	4	5	15	20	23
Abercorn	22	6	3	2	19	14	4	0	7	13	18	23
St Bernard's	22	6	1	4	21	11	2	5	4	18	20	22
E. Stirling	22	7	3	1	26	12	0	5	6	14	24	22
Arthurlie	22	8	2	1	28	12	0	2	9	7	26	20
Leith A	22	4	6	1	17	8	1	3	7	14	29	19
Vale of Leven	22	4	2	5	15	18	1	1	9	8	29	13
Johnstone	22	4	4	3	14	10	0	0	11	7	45	12

Scottish Football League Records
Season 1914-15

DIVISION 1

	ABERDEEN	AIRDRIE	AYR U	CELTIC	CLYDE	DUMBARTON	DUNDEE	FALKIRK	HAMILTON A	HEARTS	HIBERNIAN	KILMARNOCK	MORTON	MOTHERWELL	PARTICK T	QUEEN'S PARK	RAITH R	RANGERS	ST MIRREN	T LANARK
ABERDEEN		Mar20 3-0	Jan09 1-1	Dec05 0-1	Sep05 2-0	Nov21 0-0	Jan01 2-1	Jan23 1-2	Apr17 1-0	Apr03 0-0	Feb20 0-0	Dec19 3-0	Feb06 2-0	Sep19 3-1	Mar06 0-0	Sep28 1-1	Nov07 1-3	Aug22 0-2	Oct03 0-0	Oct17 1-2
AIRDRIE	Oct10 3-0		Apr17 1-2	Dec19 0-1	Feb20 2-1	Feb06 4-1	Oct24 3-4	Dec05 3-2	Sep12 3-2	Mar13 2-2	Jan09 1-3	Sep26 0-2	Jan01 0-0	Nov07 4-1	Mar27 0-0	Aug22 2-1	Apr10 3-3	Nov21 1-2	Jan23 2-1	Aug15 1-0
AYR U	Sep12 1-0	Aug29 0-0		Oct10 1-0	Apr24 3-1	Dec19 2-1	Apr10 0-0	Mar06 1-2	Mar27 2-0	Oct31 0-2	Jan04 2-1	Feb20 2-0	Nov14 2-1	Mar13 1-1	Aug15 4-0	Feb06 2-1	Dec05 3-0	Oct17 2-0	Sep26 0-2	Jan02 1-0
CELTIC	Apr10 1-0	Apr03 3-0	Nov21 4-0		Sep28 3-0	Feb20 1-0	Oct03 6-0	Oct17 1-0	Dec26 3-1	Jan30 1-1	Mar06 5-1	Jan04 2-0	Sep05 6-2	Aug22 1-0	Jan09 6-1	Dec12 5-1	Mar27 3-1	Oct31 2-1	Feb06 2-1	Nov14 1-0
CLYDE	Jan16 3-0	Sep19 0-0	Mar20 3-1	Jan02 0-2		Oct24 2-1	Feb13 1-1	Jan01 4-2	Feb27 2-2	Nov07 1-2	Aug15 1-0	Jan23 1-0	Dec05 2-3	Apr03 0-0	Dec19 1-3	Apr17 2-1	Aug29 1-0	Mar13 1-2	Nov28 1-2	Apr05 1-2
DUMBARTON	Jan30 3-2	Oct17 1-4	Sep05 1-2	Nov28 1-4	Dec26 2-1		Sep19 1-1	Apr24 0-1	Feb13 0-1	Oct03 3-2	Mar20 1-0	Apr03 1-0	Feb27 3-2	Apr10 1-1	Dec05 0-2	Jan09 3-0	Jan01 3-1	Nov14 1-1	Aug22 2-4	Oct31 2-1
DUNDEE	Aug15 1-3	Feb27 2-0	Dec12 2-3	Sep26 1-3	Apr12 3-0	Oct05 0-0		Jan09 1-0	Aug29 1-0	Oct17 1-2	Dec26 2-4	Oct31 0-1	Jan23 1-1	Nov14 1-0	Feb06 1-2	Apr03 2-0	Apr17 2-0	Sep12 1-1	Feb20 2-1	Dec05 0-0
FALKIRK	Oct24 1-1	Jan30 2-1	Nov07 1-1	Jan16 0-1	Nov21 3-1	Aug15 1-3	Oct10 0-1		Sep26 2-0	Jan02 1-1	Mar27 0-0	Apr10 3-2	Dec19 2-0	Nov28 5-1	Aug29 2-1	Feb13 1-0	Feb27 3-1	Sep05 1-3	Apr03 2-0	Mar13 1-1
HAMILTON A	Nov14 3-0	Mar06 0-1	Aug22 2-1	Oct24 0-1	Oct03 3-2	Oct10 4-1	Dec19 2-0	Mar20 0-1		Nov28 1-3	Feb06 2-2	Mar13 0-0	Sep19 1-1	Jan01 0-3	Nov07 2-2	Jan23 3-0	Sep05 1-1	Apr03 4-3	Jan09 5-2	Feb20 4-2
HEARTS	Sep26 2-0	Dec12 3-1	Sep21 1-0	Aug15 2-0	Mar27 2-0	Mar06 4-1	Jan16 3-2	Nov14 2-0	Jan04 3-0		Dec05 3-1	Feb06 3-1	Jan09 1-0	Oct10 2-0	Mar20 3-1	Oct24 2-2	Dec26 4-0	Feb20 3-4	Sep12 5-0	Aug29 2-0
HIBERNIAN	Oct31 1-2	Sep05 1-0	Oct03 0-4	Sep19 1-1	Sep21 3-1	Nov07 2-2	Nov21 2-0	Aug22 1-1	Oct17 0-2	Feb27 2-2		Jan02 3-1	Mar13 1-1	Jan23 1-2	Nov28 4-1	Apr10 4-0	Feb13 2-1	Jan30 1-2	Dec19 3-2	Apr03 4-2
KILMARNOCK	Nov28 5-2	Dec26 2-1	Sep19 1-2	Nov07 1-3	Aug22 0-3	Jan16 4-0	Mar20 3-2	Oct03 1-0	Jan30 1-0	Sep05 0-2	Oct24 5-1		Apr24 2-2	Mar06 2-2	Feb13 2-0	Feb27 3-0	Jan09 3-1	Dec12 0-1	Jan01 2-1	Mar27 2-1
MORTON	Aug29 1-1	Nov28 4-1	Dec26 3-0	Feb13 0-2	Dec12 2-0	Sep12 3-2	Nov07 2-0	Jan04 1-0	Jan02 4-0	Apr10 2-0	Sep26 0-0	Aug15 3-1		Mar20 2-0	Oct24 2-2	Oct10 6-2	Nov21 1-0	Jan16 0-1	Mar06 3-3	Jan30 4-2
MOTHERWELL	Dec26 1-1	Jan02 4-2	Jan16 1-1	Apr24 1-1	Oct31 0-2	Sep26 2-3	Jan30 1-1	Dec12 4-1	Dec05 2-4	Feb13 0-1	Aug29 3-0	Sep12 3-2	Oct17 1-1		Apr17 1-0	Nov21 1-0	Aug15 1-2	Feb27 2-4	Mar27 0-2	Oct03 3-2
PARTICK T	Dec12 3-0	Oct31 4-0	Jan30 2-0	Feb27 0-2	Nov14 0-0	Mar13 1-2	Aug22 4-1	Feb20 2-0	Apr10 1-4	Nov21 0-2	Jan16 3-1	Oct17 0-0	Apr03 1-5	Sep05 4-1		Dec26 5-0	Jan05 2-1	Jan02 3-1	Apr24 0-1	Jan01 1-1
QUEEN'S PARK	Mar13 3-1	Jan16 0-1	Nov28 1-1	Apr05 0-3	Oct17 0-1	Aug29 2-2	Jan02 0-3	Sep12 1-2	Oct31 0-2	Dec19 0-4	Nov14 0-2	Dec05 1-0	Mar27 0-2	Feb20 0-3	Oct03 0-2		Jan30 1-3	Apr24 0-4	Aug15 4-1	Mar06 1-2
RAITH R	Jan02 5-1	Oct03 3-0	Apr03 0-0	Oct05 2-2	Mar06 2-0	Dec12 1-2	Nov28 1-1	Oct31 1-3	Jan16 1-3	Aug22 1-3	Sep12 1-1	Nov14 3-0	Feb20 1-1	Feb06 2-1	Jan23 2-2	Sep19 1-2		Oct10 1-2	Oct17 2-2	Dec19 1-1
RANGERS	Mar27 1-1	Jan04 0-5	Feb13 1-3	Jan01 2-1	Jan09 1-2	Jan23 1-0	Mar06 2-0	Feb06 3-0	Aug15 1-0	Sep19 1-2	Sep28 4-2	Aug29 2-1	Oct03 0-2	Dec19 5-0	Apr05 0-1	Nov07 4-1	Oct24 1-2		Dec05 5-0	Nov28 3-0
ST MIRREN	Feb13 0-2	Nov14 0-0	Feb27 1-3	Aug29 3-3	Jan30 3-1	Jan02 1-1	Sep05 0-1	Dec26 2-0	Dec12 1-0	Apr17 1-0	Oct10 4-2	Nov21 2-3	Oct31 2-4	Oct24 1-1	Sep19 2-0	Mar20 3-0	Mar13 3-2	Apr10 0-2		Jan16 2-0
T LANARK	Feb27 0-1	Feb13 0-2	Oct24 2-1	Apr17 0-4	Feb06 1-1	Apr13 1-0	Dec25 7-0	Sep19 0-0	Apr27 1-2	Jan23 2-2	Dec12 2-2	Oct10 3-2	Aug22 3-3	Jan09 1-0	Sep28 4-0	Sep05 1-1	Sep26 3-0	Dec26 1-1	Nov07 0-0	

DIVISION 2

	ABERCORN	ALBION R	ARTHURLIE	CLYDEBANK	COWDENBEATH	DUNDEE H	DUNFERMLINE A	E STIRLING	JOHNSTONE	LEITH A	LOCHGELLY U	ST BERNARD'S	ST JOHNSTONE	VALE OF LEVEN
ABERCORN		Sep12 1-0	Feb20 1-2	Oct03 4-2	Sep26 2-2	Oct17 4-2	Feb06 1-2	Nov07 3-3	Aug22 1-1	Mar06 1-1	Dec05 0-1	Aug15 1-3	Jan09 3-1	Nov28 3-1
ALBION R	Nov14 0-0		Oct17 2-0	Nov28 2-2	Dec12 0-1	Oct31 3-0	Sep19 3-0	Jan02 4-2	Aug29 2-2	Oct03 0-4	Jan16 2-1	Dec26 1-1	Feb27 4-1	Mar06 4-1
ARTHURLIE	Aug29 1-1	Feb06 0-3		Dec26 0-3	Feb13 0-2	Jan09 2-1	Dec05 2-0	Sep26 0-1	Dec12 1-3	Jan23 0-2	Apr03 5-3	Oct24 1-2	Oct10 2-2	Feb27 5-1
CLYDEBANK	Oct31 6-1	Sep26 1-1	Jan16 6-0		Jan01 1-0	Nov14 2-3	Nov21 3-0	Aug15 3-1	Oct10 5-1	Dec05 9-2	Mar06 4-0	Feb06 1-4	Dec19 2-2	Aug22 3-1
COWDENBEATH	Nov21 5-0	Oct24 2-0	Nov07 5-1	Feb20 2-1		Sep12 3-0	Aug22 3-1	Dec19 2-1	Jan02 3-0	Jan30 0-1	Feb06 2-0	Sep05 2-0	Oct17 1-0	Dec05 3-0
DUNDEE H	Jan16 2-1	Dec19 6-1	Aug22 3-3	Sep19 1-3	Nov28 2-2		Nov07 0-2	Oct24 1-3	Jan01 3-0	Nov21 1-3	Oct03 4-3	Oct10 1-0	Jan02 3-1	Feb13 4-1
DUNFERMLINE A	Oct10 3-0	Jan09 4-0	Jan02 3-2	Dec12 1-0	Jan23 0-1	Aug15 3-1		Aug29 2-2	Nov28 3-1	Oct31 2-3	Jan01 1-3	Sep26 2-1	Oct24 3-2	Nov14 7-2
E STIRLING	Dec12 3-2	Aug22 0-0	Apr17 3-0	Mar27 3-1	Jan09 0-0	Feb06 4-3	Mar06 2-0		Dec26 4-1	Oct17 3-0	Jan23 3-2	Sep12 3-0	Feb20 2-1	Oct31 3-2
JOHNSTONE	Jan30 4-1	Nov07 2-2	Oct03 2-1	Jan23 1-0	Oct31 2-1	Dec05 2-1	Oct17 1-0	Jan16 3-1		Jan09 0-0	Feb20 3-1	Mar20 2-1	Aug15 3-4	Feb06 2-0
LEITH A	Oct24 3-3	Feb20 3-0	Aug15 3-2	Aug29 0-2	Oct10 0-0	Sep26 4-2	Sep12 1-0	Apr03 1-0	Nov14 3-0		Jan02 5-0	Nov28 5-0	Feb06 3-0	Dec26 4-1
LOCHGELLY U	Mar20 4-0	Oct10 1-0	Mar13 2-2	Jan30 1-3	Aug15 0-4	Dec26 2-1	Mar27 1-4	Feb27 6-1	Apr17 6-0	Dec12 0-0		Aug29 1-3	Sep26 1-1	Jan09 1-0
ST BERNARD'S	Feb27 4-0	Nov21 3-1	Jan30 6-0	Oct17 2-1	Mar13 1-0	Jan23 5-1	Dec19 2-1	Feb13 3-2	Mar06 4-2	Aug22 2-0	Apr10 6-0		Mar27 3-1	Sep19 2-1
ST JOHNSTONE	Dec26 4-0	Jan23 4-1	Apr24 2-3	Nov07 4-3	Mar20 2-1	Aug29 3-1	Oct03 2-2	Jan30 3-2	Feb13 2-2	Jan01 2-2	Aug22 5-1	Nov14 3-1		Mar13 2-0
VALE OF LEVEN	Jan23 5-1	Aug15 0-1	Dec19 4-1	Jan02 0-0	Aug29 2-2	Dec12 1-1	Jan16 0-3	Oct10 1-1	Apr24 2-1	Nov07 1-1	Apr24 1-2	Feb20 1-7	Sep12 4-2	

LEAGUE TABLES

DIVISION 1

	P	W	D	L	F	A	W	D	L	F	A	Pts
Celtic	38	18	1	0	56	10	12	4	3	35	15	65
Hearts	38	17	1	1	50	13	10	6	3	33	19	61
Rangers	38	11	1	7	37	23	12	3	4	37	24	50
Morton	38	13	4	2	43	17	5	8	6	31	31	48
Ayr U	38	13	3	3	29	12	7	5	7	26	28	48
Falkirk	38	10	5	4	31	19	6	2	11	17	29	39
Hamilton A	38	9	5	5	37	26	7	1	11	23	29	38
Partick T	38	10	3	6	36	22	5	5	9	20	36	38
St Mirren	38	9	4	6	31	25	5	4	10	25	40	36
Airdrie	38	9	4	6	35	28	5	3	11	19	32	35
Hibernian	38	9	5	5	36	27	3	6	10	23	39	35
Kilmarnock	38	12	2	5	39	24	3	2	14	16	35	34
Dumbarton	38	9	3	7	29	30	4	5	10	22	36	34
Aberdeen	38	7	7	5	21	14	4	4	11	18	38	33
Dundee	38	8	4	7	24	21	4	5	10	19	40	33
T. Lanark	38	7	8	4	32	22	3	4	12	19	35	32
Clyde	38	8	4	7	27	24	4	2	13	17	35	30
Motherwell	38	7	5	7	31	30	3	5	11	18	36	30
Raith R	38	5	8	6	31	27	4	2	13	22	41	28
Queen's Park	38	3	2	14	14	39	1	3	15	13	51	13

DIVISION 2

	P	W	D	L	F	A	W	D	L	F	A	Pts
Cowdenbeath	26	12	0	1	33	5	4	5	4	16	12	37
St Bernard's	26	13	0	0	43	10	5	1	7	23	24	37
Leith A	26	10	2	1	35	10	5	5	3	19	21	37
E. Stirling	26	11	2	0	33	12	2	3	8	20	32	31
Clydebank	26	9	2	2	46	16	4	2	7	21	21	30
Dunfermline A	26	9	1	3	34	18	4	1	8	15	21	28
Johnstone	26	10	2	1	27	13	1	3	9	14	39	27
St Johnstone	26	9	3	1	38	19	1	3	9	18	34	26
Albion R	26	7	4	2	27	15	2	3	8	10	27	25
Lochgelly U	26	6	3	4	26	19	3	0	10	17	41	21
Dundee H	26	7	2	4	31	23	1	1	11	17	38	19
Abercorn	26	5	4	4	25	21	0	3	10	10	44	17
Arthurlie	26	4	2	7	19	24	2	2	9	17	42	16
Vale of Leven	26	4	5	4	22	23	0	0	13	11	43	13

Clydebank & Lochgelly joined Division Two.

Scottish Football League Records
Season 1915-16 & 1916-17

1915-16
DIVISION 1

	ABERDEEN	AIRDRIE	AYR U	CELTIC	CLYDE	DUMBARTON	DUNDEE	FALKIRK	HAMILTON A	HEARTS	HIBERNIAN	KILMARNOCK	MORTON	MOTHERWELL	PARTICK T	QUEEN'S PARK	RAITH R	RANGERS	ST MIRREN	T LANARK
ABERDEEN		Dec11 2-1	Sep25 1-1	Feb05 0-4	Oct09 1-1	Aug28 2-2	Nov20 2-0	Feb26 2-0	Oct30 1-3	Mar11 1-1	Oct23 1-1	Jan08 2-0	Apr08 0-1	Apr01 5-0	Jan22 1-1	Sep27 5-1	Nov13 2-1	Apr30 0-0	Dec25 2-1	Sep11 1-1
AIRDRIE	Sep18 1-1		Nov13 3-1	Aug28 0-5	Dec04 4-1	Jan29 2-1	Sep11 1-2	Jan08 2-3	Jan15 1-1	Feb26 0-0	Dec18 1-0	Oct16 0-0	Nov20 0-0	Feb12 4-0	Apr22 0-2	Oct30 3-0	Mar11 2-1	Oct02 0-1	Apr15 0-0	Apr01 1-0
AYR U	Feb12 2-1	Apr08 2-0		Dec11 0-4	Jan04 2-0	Jan03 3-1	Mar11 1-2	Apr30 4-1	Sep11 1-0	Jan08 3-1	Aug28 2-3	Dec25 2-0	Nov06 1-1	Oct16 3-2	Nov27 0-0	Jan22 4-1	Oct02 1-1	Feb26 1-0	Feb05 1-1	Mar25 6-0
CELTIC	Nov06 3-1	Dec25 6-0	Jan29 3-1		Sep27 5-0	Feb12 6-0	Feb26 3-0	Sep04 2-1	Mar11 5-1	Apr22 0-0	Jan15 3-1	Nov20 2-0	Apr01 0-0	Aug21 3-1	Apr30 5-0	Dec04 6-2	Apr15 6-0	Jan01 2-2	Oct23 0-2	Apr24 4-1
CLYDE	Mar04 3-2	Feb05 1-2	Mar18 1-3	Jan03 1-3		Apr15 3-1	Oct16 2-0	Nov27 3-2	Dec11 1-2	Sep18 1-4	Feb19 2-1	Apr18 1-1	Jan08 2-3	Jan22 1-2	Apr08 1-2	Nov13 0-1	Aug28 1-0	Dec18 0-2	Oct30 4-1	Oct02 2-2
DUMBARTON	Apr25 2-1	Oct23 3-1	Sep04 0-3	Jan08 1-2	Nov06 2-1		Oct02 1-1	Sep18 3-1	Feb26 7-0	Feb05 1-1	Apr08 2-1	Apr30 1-1	Jan22 1-1	Dec25 0-0	Dec11 2-0	Oct09 2-4	Dec04 1-0	Aug21 1-3	Mar04 2-0	Nov20 1-1
DUNDEE	Jan01 1-1	Jan03 4-0	Aug21 2-0	Sep18 0-2	Jan29 1-0	Mar18 0-1		Mar04 3-3	Nov27 3-1	Nov06 1-0	Feb12 2-1	Apr08 2-0	Apr22 0-1	Sep04 1-3	Feb19 3-0	Sep25 7-1	Dec18 3-0	Jan15 2-0	Oct09 1-0	Oct23 1-0
FALKIRK	Dec18 0-3	Mar25 3-2	Dec04 1-0	Apr08 0-2	Jan01 1-2	Feb19 1-2	Oct30 2-0		Sep25 2-1	Oct02 1-1	Sep11 1-1	Aug28 0-0	Jan03 0-0	Dec31 0-1	Mar11 1-0	Feb12 3-2	Oct16 0-0	Nov20 2-0	Jan29 2-1	Jan15 1-1
HAMILTON A	Mar18 2-0	Apr30 2-1	Mar04 2-3	Oct16 2-3	Aug21 3-1	Dec18 1-1	Feb05 4-4	Apr15 0-1		Jan22 3-2	Dec04 3-2	Oct02 5-2	Sep04 5-2	Nov20 3-1	Jan08 1-0	Dec25 5-2	Sep18 2-0	Apr01 0-1	Feb19 4-1	Nov06 2-1
HEARTS	Dec04 1-2	Sep25 1-1	Oct09 0-5	Nov13 2-0	Apr01 3-1	Nov27 3-1	Apr30 1-0	Mar18 0-2	Aug28 3-0		Apr17 1-3	Sep11 0-1	Oct23 2-0	Dec18 4-0	Mar04 1-0	Apr08 5-3	Jan29 2-1	Feb12 1-2	Jan15 3-1	Feb19 2-0
HIBERNIAN	Apr15 0-0	Jan22 3-0	Apr22 3-1	Oct02 0-4	Sep04 0-1	Oct30 1-1	Dec25 0-2	Feb05 2-1	Apr26 1-3	Sep20 1-2		Feb26 1-0	Sep18 0-2	Nov06 1-2	Oct16 0-4	Aug21 3-0	Jan08 1-0	Mar11 2-3	Nov20 2-1	Dec11 0-1
KILMARNOCK	Aug21 5-0	Feb19 4-0	Oct23 0-1	Mar04 0-3	Jan15 0-1	Sep25 5-1	Nov13 2-0	Apr01 1-3	Jan29 3-0	Apr15 3-1	Oct09 0-0		Mar18 1-1	Sep18 1-0	Oct30 1-1	Nov27 4-0	Jan03 2-0	Sep04 0-3	Jan01 1-1	Dec18 1-1
MORTON	Oct16 3-0	Jan01 8-2	Jan15 0-1	Sep11 0-1	Sep25 3-0	Nov13 3-1	Aug28 3-1	Oct09 6-0	Feb12 8-1		Jan29 5-1	Dec11 2-0		Apr30 1-0	Dec25 0-1	Feb26 5-0	Oct30 4-0	Dec04 2-0	Mar11 3-0	Apr15 2-0
MOTHERWELL	Nov27 2-2	Oct09 3-2	Apr15 0-3	Apr15 1-3	Oct23 2-2	Sep11 4-2	Dec11 3-0	Nov13 1-1	Jan01 0-3	Oct30 1-3	Mar04 1-1	Mar11 1-1	Feb19 2-3		Aug28 2-2	Apr22 2-1	Jan15 1-4	Jan29 2-2	Sep25 3-1	Feb05 3-4
PARTICK T	Oct02 3-0	Nov06 4-1	Apr01 1-1	Dec18 0-4	Apr24 2-3	Jan15 0-0	Dec04 2-0	Oct23 5-2	Oct09 0-1	Sep04 0-2	Mar18 4-1	Feb12 4-0	Aug21 3-2	Feb26 3-1		Jan29 5-0	Nov20 2-0	Apr15 5-2	Apr19 4-0	Jan01 1-0
QUEEN'S PARK	Jan15 0-1	Mar18 3-0	Jan01 2-2	Feb19 0-1	Mar11 2-2	Apr01 0-2	Apr15 2-0	Dec11 2-1	Oct23 2-1	Nov20 0-3	Jan03 4-2	Feb05 1-2	Dec18 4-4	Oct02 1-4	Sep18 1-1		Apr30 4-1	Nov06 0-6	Aug28 2-1	Mar04 0-0
RAITH R	Apr22 3-1	Aug21 1-1	Feb19 0-4	Nov27 0-2	Dec25 2-0	Jan01 1-0	Apr01 0-2	Jan22 3-1	Jan04 2-0	Dec11 1-2	Sep25 1-1	Nov06 1-1	Mar04 2-1	Mar18 1-0	Feb05 2-0	Sep04 0-3		Oct23 1-3	Sep11 0-1	Oct09 0-1
RANGERS	Feb19 4-0	Mar04 3-0	Sep18 5-2	Oct30 3-0	Apr22 2-2	Apr20 2-2	Apr10 3-2	Dec25 1-0	Nov13 3-0	Oct16 0-4	Nov27 4-2	Jan22 3-1	Feb05 1-0	Jan08 4-1	Jan03 0-1	Apr24 6-0	Apr08 3-0		Dec11 4-0	Aug28 4-0
ST MIRREN	Sep04 3-2	Nov27 2-4	Dec18 1-0	Mar18 0-5	Feb12 1-0	Oct16 1-2	Jan22 1-2	Nov06 2-1	Apr22 5-0	Aug21 4-1	Apr01 3-1	Dec04 3-0	Oct02 1-3	Apr08 5-0	Nov13 0-2	Jan08 1-2	Feb26 2-0	Apr17 1-1		Sep18 1-0
T LANARK	Jan29 6-2	Sep04 0-1	Oct30 1-1	Jan22 0-4	Feb26 1-1	Mar11 4-0	Jan08 2-1	Aug21 0-0	Apr08 0-1	Dec25 1-3	Nov13 3-0	Apr22 1-2	Nov27 1-3	Dec04 1-3	Sep27 0-0	Oct16 0-0	Feb12 2-0	Mar18 0-1	Apr30 3-0	

LEAGUE TABLES

DIVISION 1

	P	W	D	L	F	A	W	D	L	F	A	Pts
Celtic	38	15	3	1	64	13	17	0	2	52	10	67
Rangers	38	15	2	2	55	17	10	4	5	32	22	56
Morton	37	15	0	3	58	9	7	7	5	28	26	*51
Ayr U	38	12	4	3	39	19	8	4	7	33	26	48
Partick T	38	13	2	4	48	20	6	6	7	17	21	46
Hearts	37	12	1	6	35	23	8	5	5	31	22	*46
Hamilton A	38	13	2	4	49	28	6	1	12	19	48	41
Dundee	38	13	2	4	37	14	5	2	12	19	35	40
Dumbarton	38	9	6	4	33	22	4	5	10	21	42	37
Kilmarnock	38	9	5	5	34	17	3	6	10	12	32	35
Aberdeen	38	8	8	3	31	20	3	4	12	20	44	34
Falkirk	38	8	6	5	21	19	4	3	12	24	42	33
St Mirren	38	11	1	7	37	26	2	3	14	13	41	30
Motherwell	38	5	7	7	34	40	6	1	12	21	42	30
Airdrie	38	8	6	5	25	19	3	2	14	19	55	30
T. Lanark	38	6	5	8	26	23	3	6	10	14	33	29
Clyde	38	7	2	10	30	34	4	5	10	19	37	29
Queen's Park	38	7	5	7	30	34	4	1	14	23	66	28
Hibernian	38	7	2	10	21	28	2	5	12	23	43	25
Raith R	38	8	3	8	21	24	1	2	16	9	41	23

* Morton and Hearts only played each other once.

1916-17
DIVISION 1

	ABERDEEN	AIRDRIE	AYR U	CELTIC	CLYDE	DUMBARTON	DUNDEE	FALKIRK	HAMILTON A	HEARTS	HIBERNIAN	KILMARNOCK	MORTON	MOTHERWELL	PARTICK T	QUEEN'S PARK	RAITH R	RANGERS	ST MIRREN	T LANARK
ABERDEEN		Oct07 1-2	Jan06 1-0	Mar24 0-0	Jan20 0-1	Mar10 2-4	Jan01 5-1	Dec16 0-1	Nov04 0-1	Nov18 2-0	Apr21 2-1	Oct21 1-1	Sep23 1-1	Dec02 0-1	Aug19 2-0	Sep16 2-4	Feb17 1-2	Feb03 3-1	Sep02 1-1	Dec23 0-1
AIRDRIE	Feb24 3-1		Apr14 1-0	Mar17 1-2	Feb03 3-0	Sep16 2-1	Dec23 2-3	Apr28 1-0	Nov25 2-2	Sep02 3-2	Mar31 3-1	Feb17 3-2	Jan01 2-1	Aug26 3-1	Mar03 3-1	Jan06 3-0	Nov11 2-0	Dec09 2-0	Oct14 7-0	Oct28 1-0
AYR U	Sep30 1-0	Oct21 1-1		Sep02 0-1	Feb17 1-1	Nov04 3-1	Feb03 1-2	Jan02 2-2	Dec30 1-1	Sep16 2-0	Nov25 2-1	Dec16 0-2	Mar03 0-3	Jan13 1-2	Dec02 0-0	Apr07 1-1	Apr21 2-1	Oct07 1-3	Mar17 2-1	Aug19 0-1
CELTIC	Nov25 1-0	Sep09 3-1	Dec09 5-0		Jan02 0-0	Jan20 1-1	Feb17 2-0	Dec30 2-0	Mar10 6-1	Sep30 1-0	Aug26 3-1	Apr21 0-2	Oct21 0-0	Jan06 1-0	Nov18 0-0	Mar03 3-2	Feb03 5-0	Oct28 0-0	Mar31 3-0	Apr09 2-0
CLYDE	Oct14 2-0	Dec02 1-1	Nov11 1-4	Apr28 0-5		Dec23 2-2	Mar24 2-0	Jan01 1-1	Aug19 1-1	Mar17 0-1	Feb10 1-2	Sep02 1-1	Dec16 1-0	Apr07 0-1	Jan27 2-1	Nov04 1-1	Sep16 2-0	Jan13 0-1	Apr14 2-1	Feb24 1-1
DUMBARTON	Oct28 1-1	Apr21 1-1	Feb24 3-1	Apr07 1-3	Jan06 5-1		Nov11 4-3	Mar31 1-1	Mar03 0-0	Feb03 4-1	Sep09 2-1	Nov25 1-1	Oct07 1-4	Sep23 3-1	Dec16 2-1	Dec30 0-2	Jan01 2-2	Feb17 0-3	Aug26 2-1	Dec09 2-3
DUNDEE	Sep09 1-1	Sep23 2-2	Jan20 2-1	Nov04 1-2	Aug26 0-1	Mar17 4-1		Oct07 1-2	Oct21 3-1	Jan27 2-3	Jan02 3-1	Dec30 0-2	Feb24 3-1	Apr14 0-2	Feb10 5-1	Mar31 2-1	Dec09 6-2	Apr28 2-1	Nov18 0-2	Dec02 0-1
FALKIRK	Apr07 4-2	Nov04 0-0	Mar10 1-2	Oct14 1-1	Dec09 3-3	Sep30 2-3	Jan06 2-0		Jan20 4-0	Mar24 2-1	Oct21 0-1	Aug19 2-0	Feb17 2-1	Nov18 3-1	Sep16 0-1	Jan27 1-2	Feb24 1-1	Mar17 0-2	Dec23 0-2	Sep02 1-1
HAMILTON A	Mar17 4-1	Jan13 1-0	Mar24 2-1	Dec16 0-4	Mar31 2-1	Nov18 3-1	Apr07 2-4	Sep09 1-1		Oct28 1-0	Feb24 4-1	Feb03 3-0	Jan06 0-1	Jan01 2-4	Sep23 0-1	Aug26 2-0	Apr28 3-1	Apr21 3-1	Dec02 1-1	Feb17 1-1
HEARTS	Feb10 2-0	Mar10 1-4	Dec23 1-2	Jan13 0-1	Oct21 0-3	Dec02 0-1	Dec16 1-0	Sep23 1-6	Jan02 3-1		Sep18 2-1	Apr07 0-0	Mar31 4-1	Feb24 1-3	Nov04 1-0	Nov25 2-0	Oct07 2-1	Aug26 1-3	Mar03 1-2	Sep09 2-1
HIBERNIAN	Dec09 3-3	Aug19 1-1	Oct14 1-4	Apr14 0-1	Oct28 1-1	Jan27 3-1	Sep16 1-2	Feb03 1-2	Sep02 4-3	Apr16 0-2		Jan20 2-1	Dec30 2-4	Feb17 2-3	Mar24 1-0	Mar17 5-1	Nov18 3-3	Nov11 0-0	Jan06 2-1	Sep30 1-1
KILMARNOCK	Jan27 7-0	Nov18 1-3	Sep09 1-2	Feb24 2-2	Mar03 2-0	Mar24 0-0	Oct28 3-0	Apr14 4-1	Dec09 4-0	Oct14 3-0	Sep23 1-3		Aug26 3-2	Mar10 3-0	Jan06 0-1	Feb10 4-2	Dec23 3-0	Mar31 4-1	Jan01 1-4	Nov11 2-1
MORTON	Apr28 2-0	Jan27 2-1	Nov18 2-0	Feb10 0-1	Sep30 3-1	Apr14 3-1	Oct14 1-0	Nov11 2-0	Dec23 3-0	Aug19 3-2	Dec02 1-1	Jan02 2-1		Oct28 2-1	Sep02 3-2	Jan20 4-2	Mar17 7-0	Mar10 1-0	Sep16 0-3	Jan13 3-0
MOTHERWELL	Nov11 1-2	Jan02 1-0	Jan27 2-1	Sep16 0-4	Nov25 3-3	Feb10 3-0	Sep02 4-2	Mar03 1-0	Oct07 2-2	Dec09 2-0	Nov04 1-1	Sep30 0-1	Apr21 0-2		Dec30 2-3	Oct21 4-1	Aug19 2-2	Dec23 2-1	Jan20 2-1	Mar24 0-2
PARTICK T	Mar31 4-0	Sep30 0-0	Aug26 3-0	Dec23 0-2	Apr09 1-0	Oct21 6-0	Nov25 3-0	Jan13 1-0	Oct14 5-0	Feb17 0-0	Mar10 0-3	Oct07 1-1	Feb03 0-0	Mar17 1-1		Apr21 0-2	Oct28 2-0	Jan02 0-1	Dec09 0-1	Jan01 1-0
QUEEN'S PARK	Jan13 2-1	Mar24 0-5	Jan01 3-2	Nov11 1-3	Mar10 2-2	Aug19 1-0	Sep30 2-2	Oct28 1-1	Apr14 4-2	Apr28 1-1	Dec23 4-1	Dec02 0-1	Dec09 3-4	Feb03 0-0	Feb24 2-1		Sep02 3-1	Apr09 1-4	Feb17 1-2	Oct14 3-4
RAITH R	Jan02 3-0	Feb10 0-2	Sep23 1-3	Dec02 1-4	Dec30 1-1	Oct14 0-3	Mar03 3-2	Aug26 0-6	Sep30 0-1	Jan20 1-4	Jan13 2-1	Nov04 0-4	Sep09 1-2	Mar31 2-1	Apr14 3-1	Dec16 2-0		Nov25 1-4	Jan27 1-1	Mar10 0-1
RANGERS	Mar03 1-0	Dec30 3-0	Feb10 1-0	Jan01 0-0	Nov18 1-0	Sep02 6-0	Aug19 3-0	Dec02 3-1	Jan27 2-0	Jan06 1-0	Dec16 5-1	Sep16 3-0	Nov04 0-1	Oct14 2-1	Jan20 3-0	Apr21 1-0	Mar24 4-3		Sep30 1-0	Apr07 0-2
ST MIRREN	Dec30 1-0	Dec16 1-0	Oct28 0-0	Aug19 1-5	Apr21 0-1	Apr28 0-0	Mar10 2-0	Nov25 5-0	Feb10 2-2	Nov11 0-1	Oct07 1-1	Jan13 2-1	Mar24 0-0	Sep09 3-1	Apr07 1-2	Sep23 3-0	Oct21 0-0	Feb24 1-1		Feb03 2-0
T LANARK	Aug26 2-0	Jan20 1-0	Mar31 4-3	Jan27 0-0	Apr14 1-0	Jan02 1-1	Apr21 0-0	Feb10 5-4	Sep16 3-1	Dec30 1-1	Mar03 1-1	Mar17 3-0	Nov25 0-0	Dec16 2-1	Apr28 2-0	Oct07 4-1	Jan06 0-1	Oct21 1-1	Nov04 1-0	

LEAGUE TABLES

DIVISION 1

	P	W	D	L	F	A	W	D	L	F	A	Pts
Celtic	38	13	5	1	38	8	14	5	0	41	9	64
Morton	38	16	1	2	44	16	8	5	6	28	23	54
Rangers	38	16	1	2	40	9	8	4	7	28	23	53
Airdrie	38	16	1	2	47	17	5	7	7	24	21	50
T. Lanark	38	11	7	1	32	15	8	4	7	21	22	49
Kilmarnock	38	12	2	5	48	22	6	5	8	21	24	43
St Mirren	38	8	7	4	25	15	7	3	9	24	28	40
Motherwell	38	9	4	6	32	28	7	2	10	25	31	38
Partick T	38	9	5	5	28	11	5	2	12	16	32	35
Dumbarton	38	8	6	5	35	31	4	5	10	21	42	35
Hamilton A	38	11	3	5	35	24	2	6	11	18	48	35
Falkirk	38	7	5	7	29	24	5	5	9	29	33	34
Clyde	38	6	7	6	20	23	4	7	8	20	29	34
Hearts	38	9	1	9	25	30	5	3	11	19	29	32
Ayr U	38	6	6	7	21	24	6	1	12	26	35	31
Dundee	38	9	2	8	37	28	4	2	13	21	43	30
Hibernian	38	6	6	7	33	34	4	4	11	24	38	30
Queen's Park	38	7	5	7	34	37	4	2	13	22	44	29
Raith R	38	6	2	11	22	41	2	5	12	20	50	23
Aberdeen	38	6	4	9	24	23	1	3	15	12	45	21

Aberdeen, Dundee & Raith Rovers left League.
Clydebank joined Division One.

Scottish Football League Records
Season 1917-18 & 1918-19

1917-18

DIVISION 1

	AIRDRIE	AYR U	CELTIC	CLYDE	CLYDEBANK	DUMBARTON	FALKIRK	HAMILTON A	HEARTS	HIBERNIAN	KILMARNOCK	MORTON	MOTHERWELL	PARTICK T	QUEEN'S PARK	RANGERS	ST MIRREN	T LANARK
AIRDRIE		Dec22 4-1	Nov03 2-0	Dec08 3-0	Jan12 1-2	Mar16 0-0	Sep15 3-1	Oct13 2-1	Mar09 0-1	Feb16 3-0	Nov10 0-1	Oct20 1-1	Sep29 3-1	Feb02 0-1	Aug18 2-4	Mar23 1-2	Sep01 1-0	Nov24 0-3
AYR U	Sep08 1-2		Dec29 1-2	Sep22 1-3	Mar09 1-2	Nov10 0-1	Oct13 4-0	Aug25 2-0	Mar23 1-1	Oct27 2-2	Nov24 0-3	Dec08 0-1	Mar02 1-3	Dec15 0-0	Feb16 2-3	Jan26 0-2	Jan12 2-1	Feb02 2-2
CELTIC	Jan26 3-3	Aug18 4-0		Sep01 3-2	Dec08 3-0	Dec22 3-0	Jan12 0-0	Nov10 1-0	Feb09 3-0	Nov24 2-0	Oct13 2-3	Feb23 2-0	Apr13 1-1	Sep15 2-1	Oct27 3-0	Jan01 0-0	Mar16 1-0	Mar23 1-3
CLYDE	Aug25 3-1	Mar30 4-0	Jan02 1-4		Dec29 0-3	Nov03 0-4	Mar02 1-0	Mar09 1-3	Dec01 3-0	Oct20 2-5	Dec15 1-2	Jan05 0-2	Feb02 0-2	Sep24 0-0	Sep29 1-1	Feb16 0-3	Nov17 1-2	Apr20 2-0
CLYDEBANK	Oct06 3-3	Sep29 3-1	Mar02 1-2	Aug18 0-4		Dec31 1-2	Sep01 1-1	Feb09 2-1	Nov03 3-1	Mar16 2-0	Mar23 1-0	Apr13 1-2	Sep15 1-2	Oct20 1-2	Dec01 3-1	Jan05 1-1	Dec15 4-1	Nov17 2-2
DUMBARTON	Dec15 2-0	Feb23 1-0	Nov17 0-2	Jan26 3-1	Oct13 2-3		Aug18 4-1	Mar23 1-2	Dec29 1-1	Dec08 1-0	Oct27 1-4	Sep01 0-3	Nov24 4-3	Apr06 1-1	Sep15 2-1	Sep29 2-4	Mar02 5-2	Feb09 0-1
FALKIRK	Dec01 4-3	Nov17 3-0	Aug25 1-3	Jan01 4-0	Feb02 0-4	Apr20 1-1		Feb23 2-1	Sep22 4-0	Dec22 2-2	Sep08 1-0	Nov03 0-3	Jan05 1-1	Feb16 1-1	Apr06 1-1	Mar09 2-0	Oct20 1-0	Oct06 1-1
HAMILTON A	Dec29 1-1	Jan05 0-3	Feb16 1-2	Sep15 2-0	Nov24 3-3	Oct20 2-0	Sep29 1-1		Nov17 3-0	Aug18 1-0	Apr06 4-1	Dec22 2-1	Sep01 3-3	Apr13 2-2	Mar02 1-2	Dec08 1-2	Feb02 2-1	Nov03 4-0
HEARTS	Oct27 1-0	Oct20 2-0	Sep29 0-1	Mar16 3-0	Feb16 1-0	Apr13 1-2	Nov24 0-2	Jan26 3-2		Sep01 1-0	Dec08 3-0	Sep15 1-0	Dec22 0-1	Mar30 1-1	Jan05 2-1	Nov10 0-3	Aug18 2-1	Feb23 3-1
HIBERNIAN	Sep22 3-1	Apr20 1-1	Apr06 0-2	Jan12 2-0	Sep08 0-1	Oct06 0-3	Mar23 2-1	Dec15 1-1	Feb02 1-3		Aug25 0-3	Nov17 2-2	Nov03 2-2	Dec29 2-1	Oct13 4-2	Feb09 0-1	Dec01 3-1	Mar09 4-1
KILMARNOCK	Apr13 3-0	Sep01 2-0	Mar30 1-3	Feb23 4-0	Dec22 4-2	Feb02 0-0	Feb09 3-0	Dec01 2-3	Oct06 4-3	Jan05 3-1		Sep29 4-0	Nov17 4-0	Nov03 0-0	Mar16 3-1	Aug18 0-1	Sep15 5-1	Oct20 3-1
MORTON	Jan01 0-3	Apr06 1-0	Dec01 1-1	Oct27 2-0	Aug25 2-1	Feb16 2-2	Dec29 1-0	Sep22 3-0	Dec15 1-1	Jan26 1-1	Jan12 2-2		Mar09 2-0	Mar02 1-3	Nov10 2-1	Oct13 1-1	Feb09 3-1	Sep08 2-0
MOTHERWELL	Feb09 2-0	Dec01 5-1	Dec15 3-4	Nov10 1-3	Jan26 4-1	Aug25 0-0	Oct27 2-1	Jan01 3-0	Sep08 4-0	Mar30 2-1	Sep22 1-1	Oct06 1-3		Mar16 4-1	Jan12 6-3	Feb23 0-0	Oct13 2-1	Dec29 3-1
PARTICK T	Jan05 2-1	Feb09 1-3	Mar09 0-0	Nov24 3-0	Feb23 2-0	Sep08 0-0	Nov10 1-0	Oct27 5-0	Oct13 4-1	Sep29 2-2	Jan26 0-3	Aug18 3-3	Dec08 1-0		Dec22 5-1	Sep01 2-0	Mar23 2-0	Jan01 3-5
QUEEN'S PARK	Mar30 3-0	Jan01 0-0	Feb02 0-2	Feb09 4-2	Sep22 3-1	Mar09 2-0	Dec08 5-0	Oct06 2-1	Aug25 4-0	Feb23 2-0	Dec29 3-0	Mar23 3-0	Oct20 2-2	Nov17 2-0		Nov24 2-3	Nov03 1-1	Dec15 3-3
RANGERS	Nov17 4-0	Nov03 0-0	Oct20 1-2	Apr13 2-1	Mar30 1-0	Dec01 2-1	Dec15 4-1	Mar16 4-2	Jan12 2-0	Sep15 3-0	Mar02 3-0	Feb02 4-2	Apr06 2-1	Jan02 1-0	Sep24 3-0		Dec29 2-0	Aug25 4-2
ST MIRREN	Feb23 2-0	Oct06 1-1	Jan05 0-0	Dec22 0-1	Nov10 3-1	Sep22 2-1	Mar30 1-0	Sep08 5-1	Apr20 3-2	Apr13 1-1	Jan01 2-0	Nov24 0-1	Feb16 1-1	Aug25 0-0	Jan26 3-1	Oct27 0-0		Dec08 3-1
T LANARK	Mar02 2-2	Sep15 1-1	Sep24 0-2	Oct13 3-0	Oct27 0-1	Jan05 4-1	Jan26 4-0	Jan12 2-1	Apr06 2-3	Nov10 1-0	Feb16 1-1	Mar16 1-2	Aug18 2-4	Dec01 0-1	Sep01 5-0	Dec22 0-1	Sep29 1-2	

LEAGUE TABLES

DIVISION 1

	P	W	D	L	F	A	W	D	L	F	A	Pts
Rangers	34	15	1	1	42	12	10	5	2	24	12	56
Celtic	34	11	4	2	34	13	13	3	1	32	13	55
Kilmarnock	34	12	2	3	45	16	7	3	7	24	25	43
Morton	34	9	6	2	27	17	8	3	6	26	25	43
Motherwell	34	11	3	3	43	21	5	6	6	27	30	41
Partick T	34	10	4	3	36	19	4	8	5	15	18	40
Queen's Park	34	11	4	2	41	15	3	2	12	23	48	34
Dumbarton	34	8	2	7	30	29	5	6	6	18	20	34
Clydebank	34	7	4	6	30	26	7	1	9	25	30	33
Hearts	34	11	1	5	24	15	3	3	11	17	43	32
St Mirren	34	9	6	2	27	12	2	1	14	15	38	29
Hamilton A	34	8	5	4	33	22	3	1	13	19	41	28
T. Lanark	34	6	3	8	29	22	4	4	9	27	40	27
Falkirk	34	8	6	3	29	21	1	3	13	9	37	27
Airdrie	34	8	2	7	26	19	2	4	11	20	39	26
Hibernian	34	7	4	6	27	26	1	5	11	15	31	25
Clyde	34	5	2	10	20	32	4	0	13	17	40	20
Ayr U	34	3	4	10	20	28	2	5	10	12	33	19

1918-19

DIVISION 1

	AIRDRIE	AYR U	CELTIC	CLYDE	CLYDEBANK	DUMBARTON	FALKIRK	HAMILTON A	HEARTS	HIBERNIAN	KILMARNOCK	MORTON	MOTHERWELL	PARTICK T	QUEEN'S PARK	RANGERS	ST MIRREN	T LANARK
AIRDRIE		Dec21 0-1	Feb08 1-2	Oct05 1-2	Apr26 2-1	Oct19 1-1	Dec07 1-1	Sep14 0-2	Aug31 1-0	May10 3-3	Jan18 2-2	Jan01 2-1	Nov02 1-1	Aug17 1-1	Apr05 1-2	Nov16 0-0	Nov23 3-1	Jan11 1-6
AYR U	Nov09 1-4		May10 0-2	Feb15 4-1	Feb01 2-0	Dec28 5-0	Feb22 2-0	Nov23 4-1	Jan04 1-2	Nov02 5-0	Dec14 3-1	Sep21 1-5	Oct05 1-2	Aug31 0-1	Oct19 2-0	Mar22 1-1	Jan25 2-0	Aug17 0-2
CELTIC	Apr21 3-0	Sep07 1-0		Jan02 2-0	Jan11 3-1	Dec14 2-0	Apr19 4-0	Feb15 4-1	Nov09 1-1	Dec28 2-0	Feb01 2-1	Aug24 1-1	Jan25 0-0	Feb22 2-1	Mar22 2-0	Oct19 0-3	Nov02 1-0	Sep30 3-1
CLYDE	Mar08 3-5	Sep14 3-1	Aug31 0-3		Mar29 0-2	Aug17 4-1	Jan01 2-4	Jan18 0-1	Oct26 4-2	Oct12 2-1	Nov23 1-1	Apr12 0-2	Feb08 1-2	Jan04 1-1	Dec21 0-1	May10 0-4	Dec07 1-1	Sep28 1-1
CLYDEBANK	Oct12 2-2	Nov30 1-3	Apr12 0-2	Nov02 3-1		Sep14 3-1	Oct19 3-2	Sep28 3-3	Feb08 1-3	Apr05 2-1	Aug31 3-1	Jan04 2-3	Feb15 2-1	Mar08 1-3	Dec28 3-2	Dec14 0-5	Aug17 1-1	Oct05 1-1
DUMBARTON	Feb15 0-0	Dec07 0-0	Oct26 0-5	Feb22 1-0	Dec31 1-1		Nov02 1-2	Nov09 1-2	Sep21 1-2	Nov23 4-0	Mar08 0-1	Jan18 0-1	Aug24 2-0	Dec21 1-1	Oct05 0-0	Feb01 0-2	Jan11 0-0	Apr05 4-3
FALKIRK	Sep07 1-0	Oct26 4-4	Sep28 1-2	Aug24 1-3	Jan18 0-0	Jan04 5-1		Oct12 3-1	Dec21 0-0	Feb01 1-1	Nov09 0-1	Nov30 1-2	Mar22 2-3	Apr05 2-2	Mar08 2-3	Apr12 0-4	Feb08 1-2	Sep14 4-5
HAMILTON A	Jan25 3-1	Feb08 2-2	Dec21 1-2	Apr19 4-2	Mar22 1-3	Mar29 0-3	Jan11 1-2		Oct05 1-4	Aug24 1-0	Apr05 2-0	Nov02 1-1	Jan01 1-3	Sep21 1-2	Apr12 0-1	Sep07 0-3	Oct26 3-2	Nov16 1-0
HEARTS	Dec28 0-0	Oct12 2-3	Apr28 2-3	Mar22 3-0	Dec07 2-1	May03 2-0	Nov16 5-0	Feb01 4-1		Jan11 3-1	Nov02 1-4	Apr05 1-1	Sep07 0-0	Sep28 1-0	Feb15 2-2	Aug24 1-4	Sep14 0-0	Nov23 2-0
HIBERNIAN	Oct26 2-1	Mar08 0-1	Aug17 0-3	Nov30 3-1	Sep21 1-2	Feb08 1-0	Dec14 2-1	Feb22 1-2	Oct19 1-3		Jan04 1-4	Oct05 0-3	Dec21 0-3	Jan18 0-2	Apr26 1-0	Jan25 1-2	Nov09 1-2	Aug31 1-5
KILMARNOCK	Sep21 3-1	Nov16 2-3	Oct12 1-1	Jan25 5-3	Mar15 2-3	Sep28 0-0	Dec28 0-0	Dec07 5-0	Feb22 2-2	Sep07 7-1		Mar22 0-1	Nov30 0-2	Oct26 0-3	Aug24 1-0	Jan11 1-0	Jan01 1-3	Feb08 0-1
MORTON	Sep28 3-2	Mar29 1-1	Mar08 0-0	Dec28 3-0	Oct26 2-2	Aug31 3-1	Jan25 4-0	Dec14 3-3	Aug17 2-0	Feb15 9-2	Sep14 2-2		Jan11 6-2	Dec07 3-0	Nov09 3-3	Nov23 1-0	Jan02 3-1	Oct12 1-1
MOTHERWELL	Feb01 1-3	Jan18 4-0	Dec07 3-1	Dec14 3-2	Nov09 1-1	Apr26 3-0	Nov23 2-1	Aug31 1-1	Mar08 1-2	Sep14 0-0	Aug17 1-2	Oct19 2-0		Oct12 1-1	Jan04 3-1	Dec28 0-1	Sep28 1-2	Feb22 1-1
PARTICK T	Mar22 0-1	Jan11 1-3	Nov23 0-1	Sep30 1-1	Aug24 3-1	Jan25 1-3	Oct05 4-2	Oct19 6-3	Dec14 3-1	Apr21 2-0	Feb15 4-0	Feb01 2-1	Apr12 2-0		Nov02 2-1	Jan02 1-0	Dec28 5-1	Jan01 1-2
QUEEN'S PARK	Dec14 1-0	Jan01 2-2	Sep14 0-3	Jan11 3-1	Nov23 3-4	Apr19 1-0	Aug31 2-0	Aug17 3-2	Jan25 4-0	Sep28 3-0	Mar29 1-2	Feb22 4-2	Apr21 1-3	Feb08 4-3		Sep30 0-2	Oct12 4-1	Oct26 3-4
RANGERS	Jan04 2-1	Sep28 6-2	Jan01 1-1	Nov09 3-0	Feb22 3-0	Oct12 3-0	Aug17 1-0	Mar08 3-0	Mar01 3-2	Dec07 5-1	Dec21 8-0	Feb08 1-0	Oct26 0-0	Sep14 2-0	Jan18 4-0		Aug31 2-0	Apr21 4-0
ST MIRREN	Feb22 1-2	Aug24 1-1	Jan18 0-4	Oct19 1-1	Dec21 2-1	Mar22 2-0	Sep21 3-1	Jan04 2-0	May10 3-3	May03 3-1	Oct05 1-5	Sep07 2-2	Apr05 1-0	Apr19 1-1	Feb01 1-1	Feb15 2-2		Dec14 0-0
T LANARK	Aug24 1-1	Mar01 1-1	Jan04 2-3	Feb01 1-4	Jan02 2-0	Apr12 2-4	Feb15 2-2	Dec28 1-3	Jan18 3-1	Mar22 4-2	Oct19 3-4	Dec21 0-1	Sep21 1-1	Nov09 1-2	Dec07 1-3	Nov02 1-2	Mar08 1-0	

LEAGUE TABLES

DIVISION 1

	P	W	D	L	F	A	W	D	L	F	A	Pts
Celtic	34	13	3	1	33	10	13	3	1	38	12	58
Rangers	34	15	2	0	51	7	11	3	3	35	9	57
Morton	34	10	7	0	49	20	8	4	5	27	20	47
Partick T	34	11	1	5	38	21	6	6	5	24	22	41
Motherwell	34	7	5	5	28	19	7	5	5	23	21	38
Ayr U	34	9	1	7	34	22	6	7	4	28	31	38
Hearts	34	8	5	4	31	20	6	4	7	28	32	37
Queen's Park	34	10	1	6	39	29	5	4	8	20	28	35
Kilmarnock	34	6	4	7	30	24	8	3	6	31	35	35
Clydebank	34	7	4	6	31	35	5	4	8	23	30	32
St Mirren	34	6	8	3	26	25	4	4	9	17	30	32
T. Lanark	34	4	4	9	27	34	7	5	5	33	28	31
Airdrie	34	4	7	6	21	27	5	4	8	24	27	29
Hamilton A	34	6	2	9	23	31	5	3	9	26	44	27
Dumbarton	34	4	6	7	16	20	3	2	12	15	38	22
Falkirk	34	3	5	9	28	34	3	3	11	18	39	20
Clyde	34	4	4	9	23	33	3	2	12	22	42	20
Hibernian	34	5	0	12	16	35	0	3	14	14	56	13

Scottish Football League Records
Season 1919-20

DIVISION 1

	ABERDEEN	AIRDRIE	ALBION R	AYR U	CELTIC	CLYDE	CLYDEBANK	DUMBARTON	DUNDEE	FALKIRK	HAMILTON A	HEARTS	HIBERNIAN	KILMARNOCK	MORTON	MOTHERWELL	PARTICK T	QUEEN'S PARK	RAITH R	RANGERS	ST MIRREN	T LANARK
ABERDEEN		Nov01 2-1	Aug16 2-0	Sep13 2-1	Nov29 0-1	Aug30 1-0	Apr17 0-2	Apr24 3-4	Sep22 2-0	Dec06 1-1	Jan03 2-0	Jan17 1-1	Dec20 1-1	Nov15 1-0	Sep27 0-0	May01 1-1	Apr19 0-0	Jan05 1-1	Mar13 3-1	Mar20 0-2	Oct18 0-1	Mar27 0-1
AIRDRIE	Dec27 2-0		Jan01 2-1	Aug30 1-0	Dec13 0-0	Sep20 0-0	Feb14 1-0	Nov22 1-1	Sep03 1-2	Jan17 1-0	Oct25 2-0	Apr21 4-1	Sep13 2-0	Nov08 0-0	Mar20 0-0	Jan05 0-1	Feb28 2-0	Oct11 3-0	Apr10 3-1	Aug16 0-1	Dec06 1-1	Mar13 1-2
ALBION R	Apr05 1-1	Apr24 0-2		Nov01 2-1	Apr14 0-5	Jan10 0-2	Sep06 2-1	Feb07 1-2	Jan03 1-2	Dec20 2-1	Apr28 1-1	Apr03 6-2	Sep29 1-2	May01 0-2	Apr19 2-4	Oct18 1-1	Aug23 2-0	Nov15 2-0	Apr26 0-0	Nov29 0-4	Dec25 0-2	May05 3-2
AYR U	Apr03 0-0	Mar06 1-1	Sep17 4-0		Nov15 1-1	Dec06 3-1	Jan31 1-1	Jan01 2-1	Apr10 5-3	Sep06 5-1	Nov08 4-0	Aug23 1-2	Oct25 1-0	Sep20 5-0	Dec13 2-0	Jan10 0-0	Apr28 3-0	Mar20 2-2	Sep03 1-1	Dec27 0-3	Mar27 1-2	Oct04 2-0
CELTIC	Apr10 5-0	Apr28 1-0	Feb14 3-0	Apr24 4-0		Sep27 3-1	Aug16 3-1	Aug18 3-1	Apr26 1-1	Nov08 1-1	Feb28 2-0	May01 3-0	Oct11 7-3	Aug27 1-0	Jan10 1-1	Dec06 5-0	Nov22 0-0	Oct25 3-1	Aug30 3-0	Jan01 1-1	Apr22 2-2	Dec27 2-1
CLYDE	Jan31 2-0	Dec20 0-2	Apr10 2-2	Apr17 4-0	Jan05 0-2		Mar23 0-3	Nov01 1-2	Jan17 3-2	Mar02 4-0	Sep03 2-2	Oct18 0-1	Feb17 2-0	Apr03 2-1	Aug19 4-2	Aug23 4-1	Sep29 3-2	Dec13 4-2	Nov29 4-3	Sep13 0-0	Mar06 3-3	Apr05 0-1
CLYDEBANK	Nov08 3-0	Aug23 1-2	Oct04 5-2	Nov22 4-3	Jan24 2-0	Feb07 2-3		Dec31 1-1	Nov01 3-3	Mar06 3-1	Apr24 3-0	Mar27 0-1	Mar20 3-3	Apr10 1-0	Sep13 1-0	Feb21 5-1	Jan08 2-1	Jan17 1-1	Dec27 4-1	Dec13 0-0	Sep29 3-1	Oct18 0-0
DUMBARTON	Jan10 4-0	Sep10 1-1	Dec06 2-1	Aug16 1-1	Dec20 0-0	Feb21 1-0	Aug30 1-0		Oct11 0-3	Apr03 0-0	Sep27 4-1	Nov29 2-0	Feb14 2-0	Sep01 2-2	Apr12 0-1	Jan31 2-3	May01 1-1	Feb28 1-5	Oct25 1-1	Apr28 0-0	Mar13 1-3	Sep06 0-0
DUNDEE	Jan01 1-3	Oct04 1-1	Nov22 3-2	Nov29 7-1	Jan31 2-1	Nov08 3-0	Apr12 1-0	Mar20 3-1		Feb21 1-0	Apr03 2-1	Sep20 1-0	Dec27 3-1	Jan10 3-2	Apr21 2-0	Oct06 3-0	Apr17 2-1	Mar27 1-1	Dec13 5-4	Oct25 0-2	Sep06 1-2	Aug23 3-1
FALKIRK	Feb28 3-1	Sep27 0-2	Oct25 1-1	Sep08 1-2	Mar27 1-2	Oct04 1-1	Oct11 1-0	Dec27 3-2	Sep13 2-1		Feb14 3-2	Dec13 3-3	Jan10 3-0	Jan05 1-0	Apr17 1-1	Aug27 1-2	Mar13 2-2	Aug30 2-0	Aug16 4-1	Jan31 0-3	Nov15 3-1	Nov29 0-0
HAMILTON A	Sep20 2-1	Feb07 1-0	Dec13 0-2	May01 2-1	Aug23 1-2	Dec27 2-2	Dec06 2-0	Mar27 1-3	Oct18 0-1	Nov01 3-1		Mar13 2-2	Feb21 3-2	Sep06 5-2	Jan31 2-2	Sep10 0-3	Mar06 3-2	Apr14 3-0	Oct04 5-5	Jan10 1-2	Apr16 2-1	Jan05 0-0
HEARTS	Oct25 1-1	Nov15 3-1	Oct11 0-0	Jan05 0-1	Sep13 0-1	Mar20 0-3	Sep27 4-2	Apr17 1-2	Feb14 2-1	Apr19 3-0	Aug30 2-0		Jan01 1-3	Apr28 0-1	Dec27 3-6	Nov01 2-0	Dec06 3-1	Aug16 3-1	Feb28 1-1	Apr10 0-0	Dec20 1-2	Jan10 1-1
HIBERNIAN	Sep06 2-1	Mar27 1-4	Mar13 0-1	Jan17 1-2	Apr19 1-2	Nov22 1-0	Jan03 2-0	Oct04 3-3	May01 0-0	Sep20 2-0	Aug20 3-0	Sep15 2-4		Dec13 4-1	Nov29 1-0	Mar06 0-1	Oct18 6-2	Apr24 3-2	Nov08 2-0	Apr21 1-1	Aug23 2-1	Apr03 1-2
KILMARNOCK	Apr21 0-3	Jan31 3-2	Aug30 1-0	Jan03 2-1	Jan17 2-3	Aug16 2-1	Nov29 2-4	Sep13 3-1	Mar13 4-2	Oct18 3-0	Mar20 2-1	Nov22 2-1	Feb28 4-1		Oct11 0-1	Apr19 0-1	Dec20 2-0	Apr07 1-0	Jan24 2-0	Sep15 1-7	Nov01 3-2	Feb14 1-0
MORTON	Sep08 3-1	Sep06 0-2	Jan17 1-1	Mar13 3-1	Nov01 1-2	Jan01 2-0	Apr14 1-1	Oct18 4-0	Dec06 0-0	Aug23 3-0	Nov22 4-0	Oct04 2-0	Apr10 1-1	Apr26 4-0		Sep20 0-1	Jan03 0-0	Nov08 0-1	Apr24 0-0	Feb14 0-2	Jan05 3-1	Dec20 5-1
MOTHERWELL	Oct04 3-3	Nov29 2-1	Feb28 2-0	Oct11 1-1	Apr17 0-0	Feb14 5-1	Dec20 3-2	Nov08 1-1	Aug16 3-1	Nov22 4-0	Jan01 1-0	Jan03 4-1	Aug30 3-2	Oct25 1-1	Apr03 4-3		Jan17 1-0	Apr10 4-1	Sep13 4-1	Sep27 1-0	Apr24 3-0	Mar20 3-3
PARTICK T	Oct11 0-1	Jan10 3-1	Dec27 2-0	Feb14 2-2	Apr05 1-2	Mar27 2-2	Oct25 3-2	Apr10 1-0	Aug30 1-0	Apr24 1-1	Sep13 4-3	Jan31 0-2	Apr14 1-0	Sep09 1-0	Aug16 1-1	Dec13 2-1		Sep27 2-0	Aug26 3-0	Nov08 1-2	Nov29 3-3	Jan01 2-1
QUEEN'S PARK	Feb14 3-0	May01 1-0	Apr21 2-1	Oct18 6-3	Mar13 1-2	Aug26 4-1	Aug19 0-2	Aug23 2-1	Dec20 3-2	Sep29 2-0	Nov29 3-1	Mar06 2-2	Nov01 2-2	Dec27 1-3	Apr05 4-3	Sep06 1-1	Apr03 0-1		Jan10 1-2	Nov22 0-0	Oct04 1-1	Jan31 2-0
RAITH R	Nov22 2-2	Oct18 3-2	Mar20 3-0	Dec20 2-1	Jan03 0-3	Oct06 3-1	Apr03 1-3	Mar06 2-0	Nov15 1-3	Jan01 0-0	Jan17 1-0	Sep06 0-1	Apr17 1-0	Aug23 5-1	Apr28 1-1	Mar27 0-2	Nov01 2-0	Dec06 2-5		Oct11 1-2	Sep20 3-0	May01 0-2
RANGERS	Aug23 3-2	Apr03 3-2	Aug26 3-0	Apr13 2-1	Oct18 3-0	Feb28 1-0	Apr05 1-2	Sep20 4-0	Apr24 6-1	Jan03 3-1	Dec20 4-1	Sep29 3-0	Dec06 7-0	Oct04 5-0	May01 3-1	Mar16 0-0	Jan05 2-2	Apr17 3-1	Sep09 3-2		Jan17 3-1	Nov01 6-1
ST MIRREN	Apr12 3-1	Feb21 4-2	Sep13 1-2	Sep27 1-4	Apr03 0-2	Oct11 0-0	Jan10 0-3	Dec13 1-5	Feb28 1-3	May01 1-0	Aug16 2-0	Nov08 4-1	Sep22 2-1	Jan01 1-2	Oct25 1-3	Dec27 2-1	Mar20 2-0	Sep02 3-1	Jan31 1-1	Aug30 0-4		Nov22 2-2
T LANARK	Dec13 2-2	Jan03 1-1	Nov08 1-0	Apr08 2-1	Sep29 1-4	Oct25 4-1	Feb28 1-2	Jan17 1-0	Dec25 2-0	Sep02 4-1	Oct11 1-3	Apr24 2-1	Aug16 2-0	Dec06 0-1	Aug30 0-4	Apr14 2-0	Aug19 0-0	Sep13 1-1	Sep27 4-3	Apr27 0-2	Apr10 4-1	

LEAGUE TABLES

DIVISION 1

	P	W	D	L	F	A	W	D	L	F	A	Pts
Rangers	42	18	2	1	68	18	13	7	1	38	7	71
Celtic	42	15	6	0	54	14	14	4	3	35	17	68
Motherwell	42	15	6	0	53	22	8	5	8	21	31	57
Dundee	42	16	2	3	48	24	6	4	11	31	41	50
Clydebank	42	12	6	3	47	24	8	2	11	31	30	48
Morton	42	10	6	5	37	15	6	7	8	34	33	45
Airdrie	42	11	6	4	27	11	6	4	11	30	32	44
T. Lanark	42	11	4	6	35	28	5	7	9	21	34	43
Kilmarnock	42	15	0	6	40	31	5	3	13	19	43	43
Ayr U	42	11	7	3	44	19	4	3	14	28	50	40
Dumbarton	42	7	9	5	26	23	6	4	11	31	42	39
Queen's Park	42	11	5	5	41	28	3	5	13	26	45	38
Partick T	42	12	5	4	36	24	1	7	13	15	38	38
St Mirren	42	9	3	9	32	38	6	5	10	31	43	38
Clyde	42	11	4	6	44	31	3	5	13	20	40	37
Hearts	42	8	5	8	31	28	6	4	11	26	44	37
Aberdeen	42	8	7	6	23	19	3	6	12	23	45	35
Hibernian	42	11	3	7	38	27	2	4	15	22	52	33
Raith R	42	10	3	8	33	29	1	7	13	28	54	32
Falkirk	42	10	6	5	36	27	0	5	16	9	47	31
Hamilton A	42	10	5	6	40	34	1	2	18	16	52	29
Albion R	42	7	4	10	27	37	3	4	14	16	40	28

Aberdeen, Albion, Dundee & Raith Rovers joined Division One.

Scottish Football League Records
Season 1920-21

DIVISION 1

	ABERDEEN	AIRDRIE	ALBION R	AYR U	CELTIC	CLYDE	CLYDEBANK	DUMBARTON	DUNDEE	FALKIRK	HAMILTON A	HEARTS	HIBERNIAN	KILMARNOCK	MORTON	MOTHERWELL	PARTICK T	QUEEN'S PARK	RAITH R	RANGERS	ST MIRREN	T LANARK
ABERDEEN		Dec04 1-0	Apr30 1-0	Sep11 0-0	Aug28 1-2	Sep07 3-0	Jan22 4-0	Mar26 2-0	Jan01 0-0	Jan15 1-1	Sep15 3-1	Apr09 5-2	Oct09 0-1	Mar12 1-1	Feb26 0-1	Dec18 1-1	Dec25 0-3	Sep27 2-2	Oct23 1-0	Sep25 1-1	Nov20 3-1	Nov06 0-1
AIRDRIE	Feb19 5-2		Aug28 5-1	Feb09 1-2	Apr30 2-3	Sep11 5-1	Apr09 2-1	Oct30 1-1	Apr16 1-1	Sep08 1-1	Mar26 1-3	Nov06 0-1	Sep25 5-1	Jan03 3-0	Dec25 3-2	Dec11 1-1	Nov20 1-2	Sep22 4-1	Oct09 3-1	Jan29 0-3	Jan08 1-1	Mar05 1-3
ALBION R	Sep04 0-2	Jan01 1-1		Oct23 1-2	Aug21 0-1	Dec18 5-2	Jan15 1-1	Apr23 3-0	Apr02 2-3	Sep18 3-1	Feb28 3-4	Aug23 1-1	Feb12 0-2	Oct16 2-0	Dec04 3-2	Oct02 1-1	Aug30 0-0	Mar12 2-1	Aug16 0-1	Nov27 1-2	Nov13 1-2	Sep20 1-2
AYR U	Jan03 2-2	Sep04 1-2	Apr16 3-0		Mar12 3-1	Jan29 1-3	Feb26 5-1	Sep16 3-0	Dec04 1-1	Apr30 2-2	Oct30 1-1	Sep18 0-0	Nov13 2-1	Oct02 0-0	Aug18 0-2	Nov27 0-0	Aug21 2-1	Jan08 3-0	Feb12 1-0	Dec18 1-1	Oct16 4-2	Apr27 5-1
CELTIC	Jan29 3-1	Dec18 2-1	Oct26 0-2	Sep25 3-1		Jan03 1-0	Apr20 1-1	Apr02 1-1	Mar09 2-0	Oct12 4-1	Sep11 2-1	Mar19 3-2	Apr23 3-0	Nov13 2-0	Sep01 1-1	Sep07 1-0	Dec11 1-0	Oct09 5-1	Nov27 5-0	Oct23 1-2	Feb12 6-0	Sep27 3-0
CLYDE	Oct30 2-0	Feb26 3-0	Apr04 2-0	Nov06 3-1	Nov20 2-1		Aug16 4-0	Aug31 2-1	Apr30 5-2	Oct16 1-1	Sep21 1-0	Aug21 2-1	Jan08 2-0	Dec04 1-2	Aug28 0-0	Apr11 1-0	Feb22 2-1	Feb05 2-0	Apr23 2-1	Dec25 1-3	Mar12 3-1	Mar28 2-2
CLYDEBANK	Oct02 1-1	Sep18 1-2	Oct30 4-1	Nov20 2-0	Jan08 0-2	Sep04 1-0		Jan05 1-2	Feb09 0-1	Feb19 1-2	Jan29 1-1	Sep14 1-2	Dec25 2-2	Sep01 2-2	Mar12 3-1	Apr23 1-2	Aug24 1-1	Apr02 2-0	Dec11 1-1	Nov13 2-4	Mar26 3-4	Oct16 3-0
DUMBARTON	Nov27 0-1	Feb12 1-2	Sep11 0-4	Jan01 0-1	Nov06 1-3	Sep25 0-2	Aug21 1-0		Aug28 1-1	Mar07 4-1	Apr16 3-0	Apr11 0-3	Mar12 1-0	Dec18 1-0	Aug25 1-2	Feb26 2-0	Dec04 0-1	Oct23 4-0	Jan15 2-0	Oct09 2-5	Apr08 1-0	Mar19 0-1
DUNDEE	Aug21 1-1	Nov13 0-1	Dec11 3-0	Mar26 2-0	Oct16 1-2	Nov27 2-1	Apr11 2-0	Jan29 2-1		Sep04 2-0	Dec25 4-0	Oct04 3-0	Jan03 1-1	Oct30 3-1	Jan08 0-0	Apr09 2-1	Mar12 1-0	Sep25 1-1	Feb26 0-0	Feb12 1-2	Apr23 2-0	Sep18 2-1
FALKIRK	Apr23 0-0	Oct02 2-3	Apr09 0-0	Oct09 2-2	Dec04 1-3	Feb12 2-1	Aug28 3-1	Jan08 5-1	Aug16 2-2		Nov06 1-2	Nov20 2-2	Sep11 0-3	Feb09 2-0	Oct23 1-0	Mar12 1-0	Apr26 1-2	Mar26 1-2	Jan01 2-2	Mar02 0-2	Sep13 4-0	Dec18 1-3
HAMILTON A	Oct16 0-2	Oct23 0-0	Mar19 0-0	Aug25 3-0	Aug18 1-1	Dec11 2-1	Nov27 0-0	Sep04 1-1	Sep08 1-0	Feb26 2-0		Oct02 3-1	Dec18 1-1	Feb12 2-0	Apr23 4-2	Jan01 1-4	Apr08 1-0	Nov13 0-1	Mar12 0-0	Jan15 0-1	Sep18 3-0	Aug21 1-1
HEARTS	Nov13 0-0	Mar12 2-1	Oct09 1-1	Sep08 4-1	Oct30 0-1	Apr02 6-0	Sep11 2-0	Dec25 6-2	Oct23 3-1	Jan03 0-2	Apr30 3-0		Aug28 5-1	Nov27 4-1	Jan29 0-1	Feb12 1-0	Jan08 1-0	Apr23 4-0	Sep25 2-0	Sep20 0-4	Dec18 1-0	Feb26 3-0
HIBERNIAN	Mar05 2-3	Sep01 0-2	Nov06 5-2	Jan15 3-2	Sep20 0-3	Mar19 0-1	Dec04 1-1	Sep18 2-0	Nov20 2-0	Aug25 0-0	Feb23 0-1	Jan01 3-0		Sep04 0-0	Mar26 4-0	Oct16 2-3	Apr27 2-0	Dec11 0-2	Apr16 1-1	Apr09 1-1	Aug21 1-0	Oct02 2-1
KILMARNOCK	Dec11 1-0	Apr23 2-0	Feb09 3-1	Mar05 2-1	Mar26 3-2	Apr09 0-1	Sep25 2-2	Feb23 4-1	Mar19 5-0	Dec25 2-0	Oct09 5-0	Jan15 1-2	Apr02 1-3		Sep22 3-1	Oct23 0-3	Nov06 0-1	Sep11 1-1	Aug25 1-0	Aug28 1-2	Jan01 3-2	Nov20 3-2
MORTON	Sep18 6-1	Oct16 0-0	Jan22 1-3	Dec11 0-0	Jan15 1-1	Jan01 2-1	Dec18 1-1	Oct02 4-1	Apr04 1-0	Mar05 2-0	Feb09 0-1	Sep04 1-1	Nov27 1-1	Aug21 9-2		Nov13 4-1	Oct30 4-0	Apr08 4-3	Sep15 1-3	Apr02 0-0	Feb19 1-0	Apr16 1-1
MOTHERWELL	Apr16 4-0	Jan05 1-0	Jan08 1-1	Dec25 6-1	Jan22 1-1	Mar23 3-1	Nov06 0-0	Nov20 8-2	Oct09 1-2	Sep25 4-2	Aug28 2-0	Dec04 2-2	Aug16 4-2	Apr30 0-1	Jan03 2-2		Sep11 0-4	Apr20 2-1	Mar26 2-1	Sep01 0-2	Oct30 2-0	Jan29 1-3
PARTICK T	Apr02 2-2	Jan15 0-0	Jan29 0-0	Apr23 0-0	Mar28 0-1	Sep27 2-1	Oct09 2-2	Aug19 1-0	Dec18 2-1	Nov13 2-1	Sep25 1-1	Jan22 0-0	Oct23 3-2	Feb26 1-1	Feb12 4-0	Mar19 0-0		Nov27 5-0	Aug28 3-1	Jan03 0-2	Sep04 5-1	Jan01 1-0
QUEEN'S PARK	Mar19 0-2	Aug21 1-3	Nov20 1-1	Sep01 3-0	Feb26 0-2	Apr26 1-0	Jan01 2-0	Sep07 3-0	Jan15 0-0	Oct30 0-0	Mar05 3-1	Oct16 1-1	Jan29 0-2	Apr16 1-2	Nov06 1-1	Sep18 0-6	Oct02 1-1		Dec18 3-2	Mar28 1-1	Aug17 2-2	Feb12 0-1
RAITH R	Jan08 1-0	Mar19 3-2	Dec25 2-4	Apr02 2-1	Apr09 2-0	Nov13 0-1	Mar05 3-0	Oct16 3-1	Oct02 1-2	Aug21 1-3	Dec04 1-0	Feb23 2-1	Oct30 2-0	Sep18 2-0	Nov20 2-0	Sep04 1-2	Sep08 1-0	Oct04 5-0		Apr30 0-1	Jan29 3-1	Jan03 1-2
RANGERS	Aug24 2-1	Aug17 4-1	Sep07 2-1	Mar09 7-2	Jan01 0-2	Apr19 3-1	Mar19 1-0	Jan22 2-0	Nov06 5-0	Dec11 2-0	Nov20 4-0	Apr27 0-0	Sep27 1-0	Jan08 2-0	Sep11 2-0	Aug21 2-1	Oct16 3-0	Dec04 3-1	Feb09 1-0		Oct02 2-0	Oct30 2-1
ST MIRREN	Feb08 1-1	Feb05 0-1	Feb22 1-2	Mar19 1-4	Dec25 0-2	Oct09 3-2	Oct23 3-0	Dec11 4-1	Sep11 0-1	Nov27 2-3	Jan03 1-0	Apr15 0-4	Feb26 0-2	Sep07 1-2	Sep25 2-2	Sep21 1-2	Jan04 0-2	Aug28 1-2	Nov06 3-2	Apr21 0-1		Jan15 1-3
T LANARK	Aug30 3-1	Nov27 7-3	Sep25 2-2	Aug28 3-1	Feb23 1-2	Oct23 3-0	Apr30 1-3	Nov13 4-0	Aug25 0-1	Feb05 5-0	Jan08 1-1	Dec11 3-0	Feb19 0-2	Aug18 4-4	Oct09 1-2	Apr02 0-1	Apr19 1-0	Dec25 1-2	Sep11 3-0	Apr23 0-1	Dec04 2-1	

LEAGUE TABLES

DIVISION 1

	P	W	D	L	F	A	W	D	L	F	A	Pts
Rangers	42	19	1	1	50	11	16	5	0	41	13	76
Celtic	42	16	3	2	50	15	14	3	4	36	20	66
Hearts	42	15	2	4	48	16	5	8	8	26	33	50
Dundee	42	13	5	3	35	13	6	6	9	19	35	49
Motherwell	42	11	5	5	46	28	8	5	8	29	23	48
Partick T	42	10	9	2	34	16	7	3	11	19	23	46
Clyde	42	16	3	2	43	17	5	0	16	20	45	45
T. Lanark	42	10	3	8	45	27	9	3	9	29	34	44
Morton	42	10	8	3	44	21	5	6	10	22	37	44
Airdrie	42	9	5	7	46	32	8	4	9	25	32	43
Aberdeen	42	9	7	5	30	18	5	7	9	23	36	42
Kilmarnock	42	13	2	6	43	25	4	6	11	19	43	42
Hibernian	42	9	5	7	31	23	7	4	10	27	34	41
Ayr U	42	10	8	3	40	21	4	4	13	22	48	40
Hamilton A	42	9	8	4	26	16	5	4	12	18	41	40
Raith R	42	14	0	7	38	21	2	5	14	16	37	37
Albion R	42	6	5	10	31	31	5	7	9	26	37	34
Falkirk	42	7	6	8	33	31	4	6	11	21	41	34
Queen's Park	42	6	8	7	24	28	5	3	13	21	52	33
Clydebank	42	6	6	9	33	31	1	8	12	14	41	28
Dumbarton	42	9	1	11	25	27	1	3	17	16	62	24
St Mirren	42	5	2	14	25	39	2	2	17	18	53	18

SCOTTISH FOOTBALL LEAGUE RECORDS
SEASON 1921-22

DIVISION 1

	ABERDEEN	AIRDRIE	ALBION R	AYR U	CELTIC	CLYDE	CLYDEBANK	DUMBARTON	DUNDEE	FALKIRK	HAMILTON A	HEARTS	HIBERNIAN	KILMARNOCK	MORTON	MOTHERWELL	PARTICK T	QUEEN'S PARK	RAITH R	RANGERS	ST MIRREN	T LANARK
ABERDEEN		Nov12 3-0	Mar22 2-0	Aug30 1-0	Sep10 1-1	Oct15 4-2	Dec31 2-0	Jan14 3-0	Sep03 1-2	Sep14 1-1	Feb04 0-0	Apr29 0-1	Oct01 1-2	Apr08 0-1	Feb18 2-2	Dec17 2-0	Nov26 2-1	Sep26 2-1	Jan03 1-2	Apr05 0-0	Dec10 0-1	Oct29 3-0
AIRDRIE	Jan07 4-0		Jan02 1-1	Mar11 2-1	Aug24 0-2	Aug20 1-1	Nov19 2-3	Feb04 3-1	Oct01 0-2	Oct29 3-0	Sep17 1-1	Feb18 3-0	Sep03 2-1	Nov26 2-0	Dec31 3-2	Apr08 2-0	Dec10 0-1	Apr29 1-1	Sep19 0-2	Oct15 1-2	Jan14 4-1	Mar25 0-1
ALBION R	Nov05 0-2	Sep10 2-0		Dec03 2-3	Apr15 0-2	Jan21 1-1	Aug27 2-0	Dec24 1-0	Mar04 1-0	Mar11 4-0	Nov12 1-0	Mar01 2-0	Feb22 2-1	Aug15 4-0	Jan03 1-2	Sep24 0-0	Oct08 0-1	Oct22 1-1	Sep05 2-0	Dec17 0-5	Apr22 0-0	Mar18 1-0
AYR U	Mar25 1-1	Sep24 1-2	Feb04 2-1		Dec10 0-0	Dec24 3-2	Sep14 1-0	Jan02 2-0	Apr29 0-2	Sep10 1-1	Jan14 2-0	Oct22 2-1	Apr08 2-2	Feb18 4-2	Nov26 0-0	Oct08 2-1	Aug27 2-1	Nov05 1-0	Feb25 0-0	Jan07 0-1	Mar18 2-3	Aug24 2-0
CELTIC	Jan21 2-0	Dec03 1-0	Oct15 3-1	Oct29 2-1		Feb18 1-0	Dec17 6-0	Sep06 4-0	Apr08 4-0	Dec24 0-0	Mar01 4-0	Nov05 3-0	Aug20 3-1	Mar11 1-0	Sep26 1-0	Mar15 2-0	Apr17 3-0	Nov19 3-1	Aug15 4-0	Jan02 0-0	Oct04 2-0	Jan07 2-0
CLYDE	Feb21 2-0	Mar04 1-1	Nov26 1-1	Sep20 2-1	Jan03 1-1		Oct22 2-1	Apr01 5-0	Dec31 3-1	Nov12 1-2	Dec10 1-1	Aug23 3-2	Jan14 2-0	Aug27 3-0	Sep24 1-0	Sep13 1-0	Apr15 4-0	Oct08 0-2	Mar25 1-1	Apr29 0-0	Sep10 1-1	Feb04 1-0
CLYDEBANK	Sep21 1-1	Mar18 2-0	Feb18 0-3	Sep03 2-0	Jan14 0-2	Mar01 1-2		Apr26 0-1	Oct29 0-3	Aug24 0-0	Oct01 1-1	Nov26 1-1	Oct15 0-2	Dec24 1-1	Dec03 2-1	Jan03 2-0	Nov12 1-3	Apr15 0-0	Feb04 0-3	Aug20 1-7	Apr08 3-2	Apr01 0-4
DUMBARTON	Aug27 1-1	Oct08 1-0	Mar25 1-2	Feb13 3-1	Sep24 0-5	Nov19 4-1	Sep17 2-0		Dec17 2-0	Dec10 0-0	Aug31 1-2	Apr22 3-2	Mar04 1-1	Jan07 5-3	Oct22 2-1	Apr19 3-2	Dec31 1-4	Oct01 2-3	Nov05 1-2	Apr08 0-4	Feb27 0-2	Sep10 3-3
DUNDEE	Jan02 1-0	Aug17 1-1	Nov19 2-0	Sep17 1-0	Oct08 0-0	Dec03 2-1	Apr22 1-1	Feb18 2-0		Apr15 3-0	Dec24 2-0	Mar18 2-0	Jan03 0-0	Oct22 5-0	Jan14 2-1	Oct03 1-1	Mar01 0-0	Sep24 3-1	Apr19 1-0	Nov05 0-0	Feb04 2-2	Aug27 2-0
FALKIRK	Nov19 2-1	Sep07 2-0	Sep17 0-1	Jan03 1-1	Mar18 1-1	Apr08 0-0	Oct08 3-1	Apr29 0-0	Aug20 1-0		Feb22 0-0	Feb04 1-0	Aug31 3-1	Jan14 2-1	Dec17 7-0	Nov05 1-0	Mar29 3-0	Mar04 2-0	Sep03 1-1	Dec03 1-0	Oct22 3-1	Dec31 1-2
HAMILTON A	Oct22 2-2	Mar08 0-0	Jan07 5-3	Dec17 2-2	Dec31 1-3	Mar22 1-0	Mar04 3-1	Jan03 1-1	Mar25 1-2	Aug27 1-1		Aug17 1-0	Nov19 1-2	Oct08 7-1	Nov05 1-1	Sep10 3-1	Sep07 3-2	Apr08 1-1	Dec03 1-2	Jan21 0-0	Sep24 2-3	Apr22 0-1
HEARTS	Dec03 2-1	Dec17 4-0	Aug20 2-2	Mar04 6-2	Mar25 1-2	Sep17 0-1	Mar11 3-0	Oct29 2-0	Oct15 0-0	Oct01 4-1	Sep03 0-0		Jan02 0-2	Dec26 1-0	Apr08 0-0	Mar29 0-0	Apr01 1-3	Jan14 0-1	Nov19 1-1	Sep19 1-2	Jan03 3-2	Jan21 3-1
HIBERNIAN	Apr22 0-1	Apr15 0-0	Dec10 0-1	Dec31 1-1	Sep19 2-1	Nov05 2-1	Apr29 6-0	Nov26 0-0	Nov12 1-1	Sep24 1-1	Mar18 1-0	Sep10 2-1		Feb04 3-0	Oct08 2-1	Jan07 2-0	Oct22 2-0	Sep07 3-0	Feb18 2-1	Dec24 0-0	Aug27 1-1	Mar01 0-1
KILMARNOCK	Sep17 2-3	Jan03 2-1	Sep03 1-1	Oct01 2-2	Nov12 4-3	Mar18 1-0	Jan21 3-2	Aug20 1-0	Feb15 5-3	Feb25 1-2	Apr01 1-1	Dec31 3-0	Oct29 1-1		Aug23 2-1	Nov19 4-0	Mar04 2-1	Dec03 2-0	Dec17 2-2	Apr24 1-2	Sep21 1-1	Oct15 3-0
MORTON	Dec24 2-1	Mar01 3-0	Oct29 2-1	Jan21 2-1	Apr29 1-1	Jan02 0-3	Mar25 3-0	Mar18 1-0	Sep10 2-1	Jan07 2-0	Apr19 1-0	Aug27 1-1	Apr05 2-2	Dec10 5-1		Aug17 0-0	Feb22 4-0	Sep17 1-0	Oct15 3-1	Nov19 1-2	Nov12 2-1	Oct01 1-1
MOTHERWELL	Apr12 3-0	Dec24 1-2	Apr29 1-1	Apr15 2-1	Nov26 1-1	Oct01 2-0	Dec10 5-2	Oct15 5-0	Sep21 2-1	Apr22 0-1	Jan02 2-1	Nov12 3-1	Sep17 4-1	Mar01 3-0	Sep03 2-0		Jan14 2-1	Mar18 5-1	Aug20 2-1	Feb04 2-0	Oct29 1-1	Feb18 1-3
PARTICK T	Aug30 2-0	Apr04 1-1	Apr08 0-1	Apr22 1-1	Feb04 0-0	Dec17 2-1	Aug16 1-0	Sep03 4-2	Jan07 4-1	Oct15 0-0	Oct29 1-0	Sep24 1-1	Mar15 2-0	Nov05 2-0	Aug20 3-2	Dec03 0-2		Dec24 1-0	Oct01 2-1	Feb18 0-1	Nov19 3-1	Jan02 2-2
QUEEN'S PARK	Mar01 3-1	Aug27 1-1	Sep20 0-4	Aug17 1-6	Apr01 1-3	Apr22 0-3	Jan07 2-2	Feb25 1-0	Jan21 0-3	Nov26 2-1	Oct15 1-5	Dec10 1-1	Dec17 1-3	Mar25 1-1	Feb04 1-3	Dec31 2-1	Sep10 0-1		Aug31 1-3	Oct29 2-4	Feb18 1-0	Nov12 0-0
RAITH R	Oct08 2-1	Oct22 1-0	Dec31 3-0	Nov12 5-0	Aug27 1-1	Oct29 1-1	Sep10 5-0	Feb11 1-1	Dec10 0-0	Jan02 2-1	Apr29 1-0	Jan07 3-1	Jan21 0-0	Sep24 4-0	Apr22 1-0	Mar04 4-1	Mar18 2-0	Feb22 1-1		Apr03 0-3	Dec24 2-3	Nov26 2-2
RANGERS	Sep24 1-0	Apr22 3-0	Aug23 3-1	Apr01 2-0	Oct22 1-1	Sep26 3-0	Feb21 6-1	Nov12 1-1	Dec26 2-1	Feb27 0-0	Nov26 5-0	Oct08 0-2	Mar28 2-0	Sep10 1-0	Mar04 3-0	Aug27 2-1	Jan03 2-2	Apr17 2-1	Jan14 0-1		Dec31 4-1	Dec10 2-1
ST MIRREN	Mar04 2-1	Apr01 1-0	Oct01 2-1	Oct15 1-1	Feb14 0-2	Jan07 6-3	Nov05 4-1	Dec03 4-2	Nov26 2-1	Jan21 0-0	Aug23 5-0	Apr15 2-1	Sep13 1-1	Jan02 1-1	Mar21 1-1	Mar25 2-1	Apr29 1-2	Aug20 5-0	Sep17 1-1	Sep03 1-2		Dec17 1-2
T LANARK	Apr19 2-0	Nov05 2-2	Jan14 2-2	Nov19 2-0	Mar04 0-0	Apr17 1-1	Sep24 4-1	Oct04 1-1	Mar11 1-0	Feb16 1-1	Aug20 2-2	Dec24 2-0	Dec03 2-1	Apr29 2-0	Dec26 3-1	Oct22 4-3	Sep26 1-2	Jan03 0-1	Apr08 1-0	Aug16 1-3	Oct08 0-1	

DIVISION 2

	ALLOA	ARBROATH	ARMADALE	BATHGATE	BO'NESS	BROXBURN U	CLACKMANNAN	COWDENBEATH	DUNDEE H	DUNFERMLINE A	EAST FIFE	E STIRLING	FORFAR A	JOHNSTONE	KING'S PARK	LOCHGELLY U	ST BERNARD'S	ST JOHNSTONE	STENHOUSEMUIR	VALE OF LEVEN
ALLOA		Nov26 2-1	Oct29 2-2	Sep03 3-2	Feb21 5-1	Oct15 3-0	Jan02 2-0	Apr01 2-0	Mar18 3-0	Feb18 2-0	Nov12 1-1	Dec17 3-1	Oct01 3-1	Sep17 1-1	Apr15 1-1	Mar04 2-0	Apr29 2-1	Jan07 1-0	Aug20 1-0	Jan21 4-0
ARBROATH	Dec24 0-1		Jan14 3-1	Mar04 2-0	Sep03 1-0	Sep24 0-0	Feb18 2-0	Dec03 0-1	Jan03 2-0	Feb04 0-0	Apr22 2-1	Oct01 2-1	Oct29 2-2	Aug20 3-1	Mar18 2-5	Oct15 1-0	Apr08 2-2	Nov05 3-1	Nov19 0-1	Jan02 1-1
ARMADALE	Dec03 2-0	Mar25 4-2		Sep21 1-0	Jan21 2-1	Mar04 4-3	Apr04 8-1	Oct22 2-1	Sep17 3-1	Oct01 1-0	Nov19 1-2	Feb18 0-1	Sep03 1-0	Oct15 1-2	Jan07 3-2	Apr15 3-1	Aug20 3-0	Dec24 4-0	Nov05 2-2	Feb22 3-1
BATHGATE	Jan03 0-0	Sep10 2-0	Aug27 0-0		Nov12 2-0	Dec17 1-1	Mar18 1-0	Apr22 0-0	Sep24 4-2	Nov26 3-1	Mar11 2-3	Jan14 2-2	Feb04 2-1	Apr08 4-0	Mar01 3-1	Dec10 1-2	Oct29 2-2	Apr29 0-0	Dec31 4-0	Oct08 0-0
BO'NESS	Sep24 1-1	Apr29 3-1	Oct08 1-0	Feb18 2-0		Aug27 3-1	Apr15 2-0	Nov19 0-2	Jan14 1-0	Sep17 2-1	Mar04 5-0	Feb04 4-2	Nov05 1-1	Mar25 2-0	Nov26 2-0	Dec31 3-4	Dec17 0-1	Oct22 5-1	Jan03 2-1	Apr01 2-1
BROXBURN U	Mar11 0-1	Jan21 0-0	Dec10 1-0	Nov05 0-1	Jan02 2-0		Jan07 1-0	Oct08 2-1	Oct22 3-0	Aug20 3-2	Mar01 0-0	Dec03 4-1	Mar18 2-2	Dec24 2-1	Apr29 1-2	Oct01 2-0	Sep17 1-2	Feb25 1-1	Sep03 0-0	Nov19 2-1
CLACKMANNAN	Aug27 1-2	Oct08 2-2	Sep24 0-1	Nov19 1-3	Dec03 2-1	Apr08 2-2		Dec24 0-1	Apr22 1-1	Nov05 2-0	Sep10 0-4	Jan03 3-1	Dec31 2-0	Feb25 2-1	Dec10 1-0	Jan14 1-3	Mar25 2-3	Mar11 0-0	Apr05 3-2	Oct22 0-0
COWDENBEATH	Nov05 1-2	Apr15 2-2	Feb04 2-0	Sep17 2-0	Mar18 0-0	Mar22 0-1	Oct29 4-0		Feb18 3-0	Sep03 1-0	Nov26 1-0	Dec31 0-0	Mar04 0-0	Dec17 4-0	Oct15 3-0	Aug20 4-3	Jan03 3-0	Apr08 2-0	Oct01 4-1	Dec10 1-0
DUNDEE H	Dec10 0-4	Nov12 1-2	Apr29 4-1	Feb15 1-2	Aug20 2-2	Mar25 1-0	Oct01 7-1	Jan07 2-6		Apr08 1-0	Apr10 0-1	Sep03 2-0	Oct15 1-0	Feb11 0-1	Oct29 0-1	Nov26 4-0	Mar04 2-0	Sep10 3-1	Dec17 1-1	Dec31 0-2
DUNFERMLINE A	Sep10 0-1	Apr17 5-1	Mar11 4-0	Mar25 1-1	Dec24 4-1	Apr01 0-0	Jan21 2-0	Jan02 2-2	Oct08 4-1		Sep24 2-0	Mar04 4-0	Apr15 1-0	Nov12 2-0	Aug27 3-1	Dec03 3-1	Feb22 1-1	Nov19 1-2	Apr29 0-0	Jan07 1-1
EAST FIFE	Jan14 0-2	Dec10 2-1	Jan03 0-2	Aug20 1-2	Oct29 2-1	Dec31 2-0	Apr29 2-2	Feb25 2-0	Nov05 0-0	Dec17 0-2		Sep17 4-2	Feb18 0-1	Oct01 2-2	Feb11 5-4	Sep03 1-0	Oct15 4-2	Mar25 2-2	Dec03 4-0	Apr08 1-2
E STIRLING	Mar25 1-2	Mar01 2-0	Nov26 2-2	Dec24 2-1	Sep10 1-1	Nov12 0-2	Oct15 1-0	Jan21 0-1	Apr01 3-2	Oct29 2-1	Jan07 2-2		Apr19 1-0	Feb15 1-2	Jan02 1-1	Apr08 2-0	Mar11 1-0	Sep24 1-0	Dec10 0-0	Aug27 3-1
FORFAR A	Apr22 2-1	Feb11 1-1	Apr08 1-2	Jan07 2-1	Mar11 1-0	Sep10 1-1	Sep17 2-2	Aug27 1-1	Feb25 0-0	Dec10 2-3	Oct08 0-2	Oct22 0-0		Nov26 1-1	Nov12 2-0	Dec17 1-0	Jan02 3-2	Apr13 1-0	Mar25 3-1	Jan03 0-0
JOHNSTONE	Dec31 2-5	Apr01 4-0	Apr22 1-0	Oct22 0-3	Dec10 1-1	Feb04 1-0	Mar04 1-1	Sep24 0-0	Aug27 2-2	Jan03 2-0	Mar18 1-0	Nov19 3-1	Jan14 1-3		Sep10 4-1	Nov05 2-0	Dec03 1-0	Apr26 0-0	Oct08 1-1	Feb18 2-1
KING'S PARK	Nov19 1-8	Dec17 3-2	Jan04 0-1	Oct01 0-0	Apr08 1-1	Jan03 0-2	Sep03 2-1	Feb22 3-1	Dec03 0-2	Apr22 0-2	Oct22 2-3	Aug20 1-1	Apr01 2-1	Mar11 3-0		Sep17 1-0	Jan14 0-0	Oct08 2-2	Mar04 2-1	Nov05 0-0
LOCHGELLY U	Oct22 1-3	Mar11 0-0	Sep10 1-1	Apr01 0-2	Jan07 0-3	Apr22 1-1	Feb10 4-0	Mar25 2-1	Dec24 1-1	Feb25 1-1	Jan02 3-1	Oct08 4-1	Nov19 4-1	Apr29 0-1	Jan21 0-0		Nov12 0-0	Aug27 2-1	Feb18 4-0	Sep24 2-0
ST BERNARD'S	Oct08 2-0	Aug27 0-0	Feb11 1-0	Apr15 1-2	Feb25 1-2	Feb18 4-0	Nov26 1-0	Sep10 0-2	Nov19 2-0	Dec31 1-0	Jan21 2-0	Nov05 0-1	Sep24 1-5	Jan07 6-0	Dec24 0-0	Feb04 1-1		Dec10 1-0	Oct22 3-1	Apr22 2-1
ST JOHNSTONE	Mar01 4-3	Dec31 1-0	Dec17 3-0	Oct15 1-1	Apr22 1-0	Oct29 1-2	Aug20 1-3	Nov12 1-0	Jan02 3-1	Jan14 0-0	Apr01 0-0	Mar18 2-0	Dec03 2-1	Sep03 1-0	Mar08 2-2	Jan03 1-1	Oct01 1-3		Sep17 1-0	Mar04 2-1
STENHOUSEMUIR	Feb04 1-1	Jan07 2-1	Feb25 2-1	Apr19 2-1	Oct15 1-0	Nov26 1-0	Nov12 1-2	Apr12 2-0	Mar11 3-0	Mar22 5-2	Aug27 2-0	Apr15 1-1	Dec24 4-0	Jan02 2-2	Sep24 1-1	Oct29 1-0	Apr01 4-1	Feb11 3-1		Sep10 0-1
VALE OF LEVEN	Mar07 1-1	Sep17 2-1	Nov12 0-2	Dec03 4-1	Oct01 3-0	Apr15 3-0	Dec17 4-2	Mar11 0-0	Feb04 2-2	Oct15 1-1	Dec24 1-0	Apr29 3-1	Aug20 3-0	Oct29 3-2	Feb25 3-2	Mar18 2-0	Sep03 2-1	Nov26 2-1	Jan14 1-0	

LEAGUE TABLES

DIVISION 1

	P	W	D	L	F	A	W	D	L	F	A	Pts
Celtic	42	19	2	0	51	4	8	11	2	32	16	67
Rangers	42	15	4	2	45	14	13	6	2	38	12	66
Raith R	42	12	7	2	41	16	7	6	8	25	27	51
Dundee	42	13	8	0	33	8	6	3	12	24	32	49
Falkirk	42	13	6	2	35	11	3	11	7	13	27	49
Partick T	42	12	6	3	32	17	8	2	11	25	36	48
Hibernian	42	11	7	3	31	12	5	7	9	24	32	46
St Mirren	42	11	6	4	43	24	6	6	9	28	37	46
T. Lanark	42	10	7	4	34	22	7	5	9	24	30	46
Clyde	42	12	7	2	36	15	4	5	12	24	36	44
Albion R	42	11	4	6	27	18	6	6	9	28	33	44
Morton	42	14	5	2	39	17	2	5	14	19	40	42
Motherwell	42	15	3	3	49	19	1	4	16	14	39	39
Ayr U	42	11	6	4	30	20	2	6	13	25	43	38
Aberdeen	42	10	5	6	31	17	3	4	14	17	37	35
Airdrie	42	10	4	7	35	23	2	7	12	11	33	35
Kilmarnock	42	12	6	3	44	26	1	3	17	12	57	35
Hamilton A	42	7	8	6	37	29	2	8	11	14	33	34
Hearts	42	9	6	6	34	21	2	4	15	16	39	32
Dumbarton	42	9	4	8	36	39	1	6	14	10	42	*30
Queen's Park	42	5	5	11	22	46	4	5	12	16	36	*28
Clydebank	42	5	6	10	18	37	1	2	18	16	66	*20

* Dumbarton, Queen's Park & Clydebank relegated to Division Two.

DIVISION 2

	P	W	D	L	F	A	W	D	L	F	A	Pts
Alloa	38	15	4	0	43	12	11	4	4	38	20	*60
Cowdenbeath	38	13	4	2	37	9	6	5	8	20	21	47
Armadale	38	15	1	3	48	20	5	4	10	16	28	45
Vale of Leven	38	14	4	1	40	17	3	6	10	14	26	44
Bathgate	38	9	8	2	33	15	7	3	9	23	26	43
Bo'ness	38	14	2	3	41	17	2	5	12	15	32	39
Broxburn U	38	10	5	4	27	15	4	6	9	16	28	39
Dunfermline A	38	11	6	2	40	13	3	4	12	16	29	38
St Bernard's	38	11	3	5	29	15	4	5	10	21	34	38
East Fife	38	9	4	6	34	27	6	4	9	20	27	38
Stenhousemuir	38	13	4	2	38	15	1	6	12	12	36	38
Johnstone	38	10	6	3	29	19	4	4	11	17	40	38
St Johnstone	38	11	5	3	28	18	1	6	12	13	34	35
Forfar A	38	8	8	3	24	18	3	4	12	19	33	34
E. Stirling	38	10	5	4	26	18	2	5	12	17	42	34
Arbroath	38	10	5	4	28	18	1	6	12	17	38	33
King's Park	38	7	6	6	23	28	3	6	10	24	37	32
Lochgelly U	38	8	7	4	30	18	3	2	14	16	36	31
Dundee H	38	9	2	8	32	25	1	6	12	15	40	28
Clackmannan	38	7	5	7	25	27	2	3	14	15	48	26

* Alloa promoted.

Clackmannan & Dundee H left the League.

Scottish Football League Records
Season 1922-23

DIVISION 1

	ABERDEEN	AIRDRIE	ALBION R	ALLOA	AYR U	CELTIC	CLYDE	DUNDEE	FALKIRK	HAMILTON A	HEARTS	HIBERNIAN	KILMARNOCK	MORTON	MOTHERWELL	PARTICK T	RAITH R	RANGERS	ST MIRREN	T LANARK
ABERDEEN		Dec23 0-1	Apr14 1-2	Dec02 1-0	Feb03 4-1	Sep25 3-1	Dec09 1-0	Jan01 0-0	Feb28 1-1	Oct28 1-0	Nov11 0-1	Sep09 2-0	Nov18 5-0	Jan20 1-1	Apr28 2-1	Feb17 0-0	Aug26 1-0	Oct14 0-0	Sep30 4-2	Mar24 1-1
AIRDRIE	Oct07 2-0		Aug26 2-0	Sep23 0-2	Dec30 2-1	Nov18 1-0	Oct28 1-1	Feb17 1-1	Apr21 5-1	Jan02 3-1	Nov25 2-2	Mar24 2-1	Mar03 4-1	Sep09 1-0	Mar17 4-1	Feb07 3-3	Aug30 4-0	Feb10 1-0	Oct21 2-1	Dec13 1-0
ALBION R	Sep02 0-2	Jan01 1-2		Nov04 2-1	Feb24 2-1	Dec02 2-3	Jan06 3-0	Sep30 0-0	Sep16 1-2	Aug23 2-0	Dec23 1-2	Mar14 1-2	Aug19 1-1	Feb03 3-0	Nov11 1-1	Apr28 0-1	Dec16 1-2	Mar31 2-1	Jan20 2-0	Oct14 0-1
ALLOA	Oct02 0-2	Mar31 0-3	Jan27 2-0		Nov25 1-1	Aug19 2-3	Nov11 0-0	Oct14 1-3	Jan02 1-2	Nov18 0-2	Sep30 0-3	Oct28 2-1	Dec27 3-3	Apr14 1-1	Sep16 1-1	Feb10 1-0	Feb27 0-1	Dec23 0-2	Feb24 1-1	Mar13 0-0
AYR U	Mar10 2-1	Sep02 2-1	Nov18 2-2	Apr07 1-1		Apr25 0-1	Dec23 4-1	Mar03 1-0	Oct14 1-0	Mar24 4-0	Sep16 1-1	Dec02 1-1	Jan02 2-1	Oct28 1-0	Jan31 2-0	Mar31 2-1	Feb14 2-0	Dec16 1-1	Aug19 1-1	Sep30 1-2
CELTIC	Jan06 1-2	Apr28 1-1	Feb14 1-1	Mar03 1-0	Nov11 1-4		Jan02 0-0	Mar17 2-1	Dec09 1-1	Aug26 2-1	Apr07 2-1	Jan31 0-0	Dec23 1-2	Mar24 3-1	Oct14 1-0	Oct07 4-3	Sep09 3-0	Oct28 1-3	Feb27 1-0	Nov25 3-0
CLYDE	Apr21 0-1	Feb03 2-0	Sep23 3-0	Jan01 1-0	Oct21 1-0	Nov04 0-1		Aug29 4-3	Sep02 0-1	Dec16 1-2	Aug19 1-1	Nov18 0-0	Mar10 2-0	Feb17 0-0	Mar31 3-0	Dec30 2-0	Jan20 0-0	Sep25 1-2	Dec02 2-1	Apr02 1-0
DUNDEE	Aug19 1-1	Nov04 1-0	Dec30 4-0	Dec16 2-1	Oct07 1-0	Sep23 0-1	Apr07 1-0		Apr09 3-0	Oct21 3-0	Jan20 0-0	Jan02 1-0	Sep02 2-0	Mar10 0-1	Apr14 3-1	Sep16 1-0	Dec02 0-4	Mar24 1-2	Nov18 2-0	Oct02 2-0
FALKIRK	Sep23 2-2	Dec16 1-1	Apr07 1-0	Aug26 0-0	Jan06 0-0	Feb17 0-0	Mar24 0-0	Dec23 1-0		Jan20 3-1	Mar03 1-0	Nov04 5-0	Apr28 0-0	Oct07 3-0	Dec02 1-0	Oct21 1-1	Aug19 1-1	Sep09 2-0	Feb03 1-1	Apr14 4-0
HAMILTON A	Apr07 0-0	Aug19 0-1	Jan31 1-0	Apr28 2-0	Nov04 0-1	Mar14 1-1	Apr13 1-2	Mar31 0-0	Sep30 0-1		Sep02 3-1	Feb28 2-1	Sep16 3-3	Dec02 1-1	Jan01 3-0	Jan06 6-1	Mar17 1-1	Nov11 0-3	Oct14 2-0	Dec23 3-1
HEARTS	Mar31 0-0	Feb24 1-1	Sep09 2-2	Mar24 1-1	Apr21 1-1	Dec16 0-3	Feb07 2-1	Aug26 2-1	Oct28 1-1	Dec30 1-2		Sep23 2-2	Feb10 5-0	Nov18 3-1	Mar14 1-2	Dec02 3-0	Oct07 0-0	Sep18 0-0	Nov04 2-2	Jan06 2-0
HIBERNIAN	Mar03 2-0	Oct14 1-0	Nov25 3-0	Feb17 2-1	Jan20 3-0	Sep18 1-0	Mar17 1-2	Nov11 3-3	Aug16 1-0	Dec09 2-0	Jan01 2-1		Sep30 1-1	Dec23 0-1	Sep02 2-1	Aug19 1-0	Oct21 2-0	Apr07 2-0	Sep16 0-3	Feb03 2-0
KILMARNOCK	Aug16 1-0	Nov11 0-1	Mar17 7-0	Oct07 2-2	Aug26 2-0	Feb03 4-3	Sep09 4-1	Jan06 2-0	Nov25 1-0	Feb17 3-0	Oct21 1-2	Dec30 1-0		Mar31 3-2	Nov04 0-6	Dec16 1-3	Sep23 1-2	Jan20 1-2	Jan01 1-2	Mar21 2-0
MORTON	Sep16 2-1	Jan06 3-1	Dec09 3-0	Dec30 1-0	Jan01 0-0	Oct21 0-1	Oct11 1-0	Nov25 2-3	Jan31 1-1	Mar03 3-1	Mar17 0-1	Feb14 1-0	Oct14 1-4		Aug19 2-0	Apr07 1-2	Nov04 4-0	Feb24 1-1	Apr21 0-1	Sep02 2-3
MOTHERWELL	Oct21 3-1	Jan20 0-0	Mar03 1-0	Feb03 2-0	Sep23 4-0	Apr21 0-0	Nov25 5-3	Sep09 3-4	Dec30 3-2	Oct07 0-0	Dec09 4-1	Dec16 0-2	Apr07 4-1	Jan02 4-3		Nov18 1-1	Mar24 2-0	Aug26 0-4	Feb17 1-1	Oct28 1-1
PARTICK T	Nov25 2-1	Sep30 0-0	Oct28 3-0	Jan20 2-0	Sep09 2-1	Apr02 0-2	Aug26 0-0	Feb03 2-0	Mar10 0-1	Sep23 5-3	Oct14 2-2	Apr21 1-0	Mar24 1-1	Nov11 0-1	Feb28 3-0		Dec23 3-0	Jan02 0-1	Dec12 4-1	Jan01 3-0
RAITH R	Jan02 1-1	Sep16 0-0	Feb17 1-1	Jan06 1-0	Dec09 0-0	Dec30 0-3	Oct14 1-0	Oct28 0-3	Jan01 0-0	Nov25 1-0	Feb03 2-1	Apr02 2-2	Feb07 1-1	Apr28 1-1	Sep30 1-1	Apr14 1-0		Mar10 2-0	Sep02 2-1	Nov11 1-0
RANGERS	Dec30 1-1	Dec02 4-1	Oct21 2-2	Aug15 2-0	Mar14 2-1	Jan01 2-0	Mar03 2-1	Dec09 4-1	Mar26 2-0	Feb03 3-0	Apr28 3-0	Oct07 2-0	Apr21 1-0	Sep23 0-0	Jan06 2-1	Nov04 4-1	Nov18 1-0		Apr02 1-1	Aug19 5-1
ST MIRREN	Dec16 0-1	Mar10 4-0	Oct07 1-1	Sep09 0-1	Apr28 0-0	Apr10 1-0	Feb10 2-0	Feb06 4-0	Nov11 2-2	Aug15 2-1	Jan02 2-1	Jan06 2-1	Oct28 2-0	Aug26 1-1	Dec23 3-3	Mar03 1-0	Apr07 1-1	Nov25 1-0		Sep23 3-1
T LANARK	Nov04 2-1	Apr07 1-3	Jan02 2-2	Oct21 0-1	Mar17 3-0	Jan20 1-0	Oct07 3-0	Dec25 2-0	Nov18 1-1	Sep09 2-0	Feb17 3-1	Aug26 0-1	Dec02 1-2	Dec16 1-1	Feb13 1-2	Sep25 1-1	Mar03 2-1	Feb06 2-2	Dec30 1-3	

DIVISION 2

	ARBROATH	ARMADALE	BATHGATE	BO'NESS	BROXBURN U	CLYDEBANK	COWDENBEATH	DUMBARTON	DUNFERMLINE A	EAST FIFE	E STIRLING	FORFAR A	JOHNSTONE	KING'S PARK	LOCHGELLY U	QUEEN'S PARK	ST BERNARD'S	ST JOHNSTONE	STENHOUSEMUIR	VALE OF LEVEN
ARBROATH		Jan06 1-2	Aug26 0-0	Apr07 0-0	Sep16 0-3	Feb24 0-0	Oct07 1-3	Jan27 1-1	Feb03 1-1	Feb07 3-1	Dec16 4-1	Mar17 1-2	Nov25 2-0	Dec23 0-1	Oct21 3-1	Sep25 2-1	Nov18 3-2	Oct28 1-1	Apr28 1-1	Jan01 1-0
ARMADALE	Sep23 3-0		Sep09 2-2	Apr21 3-0	Feb10 2-1	Oct28 2-0	Mar31 1-1	Mar03 1-0	Nov18 1-0	Jan02 0-0	Oct07 2-2	Apr07 5-0	Dec23 7-2	Dec13 2-3	Jan20 5-1	Nov04 2-0	Mar10 3-0	Feb17 2-0	Aug26 3-2	Apr18 2-2
BATHGATE	Mar24 2-1	Jan01 4-2		Nov25 3-3	Aug19 2-2	Jan06 1-0	Feb24 0-1	Feb03 4-1	Sep30 1-1	Sep02 2-1	Nov04 3-2	Sep16 5-1	Apr07 3-0	Mar17 3-0	Dec02 5-0	Dec30 0-0	Apr28 2-0	Oct14 0-1	Dec16 4-0	Mar10 4-1
BO'NESS	Nov11 1-1	Aug19 0-0	Feb14 2-1		Jan01 2-0	Sep16 1-1	Jan06 2-0	Oct21 0-2	Dec02 2-1	Mar24 0-0	Apr28 2-1	Dec30 5-0	Sep02 0-0	Feb28 1-4	Oct14 2-2	Mar31 2-1	Apr09 2-2	Mar17 2-0	Oct07 6-2	Dec16 1-0
BROXBURN U	Jan20 1-1	Oct21 2-0	Apr21 2-0	Sep23 1-2		Mar10 1-0	Aug26 0-0	Feb17 1-1	Nov04 0-2	Nov25 2-0	Mar03 1-0	Nov18 3-2	Mar24 2-0	Jan02 3-0	Apr14 4-1	Oct06 0-0	Sep09 1-0	Dec09 0-0	Feb03 0-2	Dec23 1-1
CLYDEBANK	Nov04 3-1	Dec30 1-0	Jan20 5-0	Mar03 4-0	Nov11 3-0		Mar17 2-0	Sep09 1-1	Feb17 3-0	Apr28 3-2	Apr07 5-0	Feb03 1-0	Jan02 1-0	Oct21 2-0	Oct07 3-1	Aug26 1-2	Dec16 1-1	Nov25 3-1	Sep23 4-1	Dec02 2-2
COWDENBEATH	Apr14 7-4	Sep16 0-1	Oct21 3-1	Nov18 1-1	Dec30 2-1	Dec09 1-1		Jan20 1-0	Sep02 0-1	Oct14 1-2	Feb17 1-0	Jan02 3-1	Apr28 1-2	Feb03 3-2	Mar03 4-0	Dec02 0-1	Mar24 2-1	Sep30 1-1	Nov04 4-0	Aug19 1-0
DUMBARTON	Aug19 3-0	Sep02 3-0	Nov18 2-0	Dec23 2-0	Sep30 1-1	Jan01 1-1	Dec16 1-0		Sep25 2-0	Mar10 1-2	Jan06 3-0	Feb24 1-1	Jan29 6-1	Oct14 2-0	Apr28 5-0	Apr09 0-2	Oct28 2-1	Mar24 0-0	Dec02 1-0	Sep16 3-0
DUNFERMLINE A	Apr21 1-2	Feb24 2-2	Apr09 0-2	Apr14 2-1	Dec16 1-1	Dec23 2-2	Jan01 2-0	Aug26 3-0		Nov11 0-1	Sep09 5-1	Mar10 0-1	Oct07 1-1	Nov25 2-0	Sep23 0-1	Mar17 0-0	Feb14 4-1	Jan06 3-1	Apr07 1-0	Oct28 0-0
EAST FIFE	Dec02 2-1	Dec16 3-0	Feb17 1-1	Nov04 1-1	Mar31 0-1	Nov18 0-0	Mar15 0-2	Oct07 2-1	Mar03 1-0		Sep23 2-0	Jan20 4-1	Apr14 1-0	Apr21 3-1	Jan01 1-2	Oct21 0-2	Aug26 0-0	Dec23 1-3	Sep09 4-0	Jan06 2-0
E STIRLING	Oct14 3-0	Apr14 5-2	Jan02 1-2	Oct28 1-1	Sep02 0-1	Sep30 1-2	Nov11 3-1	Dec20 2-1	Mar24 1-1	Dec30 0-3		Mar31 2-0	Feb24 3-2	Jan01 2-2	Nov18 1-0	Feb07 3-3	Dec02 2-0	Sep16 1-1	Mar10 1-1	Apr21 1-0
FORFAR A	Sep30 2-1	Oct14 1-1	Mar03 3-1	Sep09 1-1	Jan27 2-0	Sep02 0-1	Oct28 0-1	Nov25 0-3	Dec09 0-2	Aug19 2-1	Dec23 2-0		Mar15 5-2	Jan06 4-2	Mar24 3-1	Sep23 2-0	Jan01 2-2	Apr21 2-0	Feb17 2-2	Apr14 3-3
JOHNSTONE	Feb17 2-2	Mar17 2-1	Dec09 1-1	Feb03 2-0	Jan06 0-2	Oct14 1-0	Sep23 4-1	Nov04 2-0	Jan20 1-0	Sep30 1-3	Oct21 2-0	Dec02 0-2		Mar31 1-0	Dec30 0-1	Sep09 0-2	Apr21 1-1	Aug19 1-0	Jan01 4-2	Nov18 3-0
KING'S PARK	Mar10 2-0	Apr28 3-1	Oct07 2-1	Jan20 0-0	Dec02 3-2	Feb10 2-3	Sep09 3-2	Apr07 2-2	Dec30 2-1	Oct28 2-0	Aug19 1-0	Aug26 1-1	Nov11 0-1		Feb17 0-1	Dec16 0-1	Sep23 1-0	Jan31 1-3	Mar03 3-1	Mar24 0-0
LOCHGELLY U	Feb10 1-0	Nov11 1-0	Dec23 2-3	Mar10 1-1	Oct28 1-1	Apr02 0-5	Nov25 3-2	Jan02 3-2	Mar31 2-0	Sep16 1-0	Jan27 3-0	Dec16 2-1	Aug26 0-0	Sep02 0-1		Apr21 2-4	Feb24 1-0	Apr07 0-1	Jan06 3-1	Sep30 2-1
QUEEN'S PARK	Mar03 6-1	Feb03 3-0	Oct28 2-1	Sep30 2-1	Feb24 5-0	Mar24 1-1	Apr02 2-0	Nov11 3-2	Aug19 1-1	Apr07 4-1	Nov25 2-1	Apr28 2-1	Mar10 4-0	Sep20 1-0	Dec09 3-0		Jan06 1-1	Sep12 2-0	Dec23 4-1	Oct14 2-1
ST BERNARD'S	Jan02 2-2	Sep30 0-0	Nov11 1-1	Dec09 1-1	Apr07 0-0	Aug19 1-2	Dec23 0-0	Mar17 0-1	Oct14 2-1	Feb03 2-2	Jan20 0-1	Oct21 2-1	Sep16 1-0	Apr14 3-0	Nov04 1-0	Feb17 1-0		Mar03 4-4	Nov25 1-0	Sep02 3-1
ST JOHNSTONE	Dec30 6-3	Dec02 2-0	Mar31 3-1	Aug26 0-0	Apr28 1-1	Apr14 1-0	Mar10 3-2	Sep23 1-0	Oct21 1-0	Feb24 1-0	Feb03 2-2	Nov04 6-1	Dec16 3-1	Nov18 0-0	Sep09 1-0	Jan02 1-1	Oct07 1-1		Jan20 3-0	Feb10 4-2
STENHOUSEMUIR	Dec13 3-0	Jan27 1-1	Apr14 2-0	Jan02 0-1	Oct14 5-0	Mar31 1-1	Jan31 4-2	Apr21 4-1	Sep16 1-1	Mar17 1-0	Feb10 2-1	Nov11 4-1	Oct28 2-1	Sep30 2-1	Aug19 0-1	Nov18 1-1	Dec30 2-1	Sep02 0-2		Feb24 2-1
VALE OF LEVEN	Sep09 0-0	Nov25 2-2	Sep23 4-1	Feb17 3-1	Mar17 3-0	Aug23 2-1	Apr07 1-2	Dec30 0-3	Jan02 5-4	Dec09 0-1	Aug26 4-3	Oct07 2-0	Mar03 2-0	Nov04 5-1	Feb03 0-0	Jan20 1-2	Mar31 2-0	Nov11 0-1	Oct21 1-0	

LEAGUE TABLES

DIVISION 1

	P	W	D	L	F	A	W	D	L	F	A	Pts
Rangers	38	15	4	0	43	11	8	5	6	24	18	55
Airdrie	38	14	4	1	41	16	6	6	7	17	22	50
Celtic	38	10	5	4	29	21	9	3	7	23	18	46
Falkirk	38	9	10	0	27	7	5	7	7	17	25	45
Aberdeen	38	10	6	3	28	12	5	6	8	18	22	42
St Mirren	38	11	6	2	32	14	4	6	9	22	30	42
Dundee	38	13	2	4	28	11	4	5	10	23	34	41
Hibernian	38	14	2	3	31	13	3	5	11	14	27	41
Raith R	38	9	8	2	18	14	4	5	10	13	29	39
Ayr U	38	11	6	2	31	15	2	6	11	12	29	38
Partick T	38	11	4	4	33	14	3	5	11	18	34	37
Hearts	38	6	10	3	29	20	5	5	9	22	30	37
Motherwell	38	10	6	3	38	24	3	4	12	21	36	36
Morton	38	9	3	7	28	20	3	8	8	16	27	35
Kilmarnock	38	11	1	7	37	26	3	6	10	20	40	35
Clyde	38	10	4	5	24	12	2	5	12	12	32	33
T. Lanark	38	8	5	6	29	22	3	3	13	11	37	30
Hamilton A	38	8	6	5	29	18	3	1	15	14	41	29
Albion R	38	7	3	9	25	22	1	7	11	13	42	26
Alloa	38	3	7	9	16	29	3	4	12	11	23	23

DIVISION 2

	P	W	D	L	F	A	W	D	L	F	A	Pts
Queen's Park	38	16	3	0	50	13	8	6	5	23	18	57
Clydebank	38	16	2	1	48	10	5	8	6	21	19	52
St Johnstone	38	13	6	0	40	15	6	6	7	20	24	*48
Dumbarton	38	13	4	2	39	9	4	4	11	22	31	42
Bathgate	38	13	4	2	48	17	3	5	11	19	38	41
Armadale	38	13	5	1	48	16	2	6	11	15	36	41
Bo'ness	38	10	7	2	33	18	2	10	7	15	28	41
Broxburn U	38	10	6	3	25	12	4	6	9	17	33	40
East Fife	38	10	4	5	28	16	6	3	10	20	26	39
Lochgelly U	38	11	3	5	28	23	5	2	12	13	41	37
Cowdenbeath	38	11	3	5	36	20	5	3	11	20	32	*36
King's Park	38	10	4	5	28	20	4	2	13	18	39	34
Dunfermline A	38	8	6	5	29	17	3	5	11	17	27	33
Stenhousemuir	38	12	4	3	37	17	1	3	15	16	50	33
Forfar A	38	10	5	4	36	24	3	2	14	17	49	33
Johnstone	38	11	3	5	28	18	2	3	14	13	44	32
Vale of Leven	38	11	3	5	37	22	0	5	14	13	37	30
St Bernard's	38	8	8	3	25	17	0	7	12	14	33	*29
E. Stirling	38	9	6	4	33	23	1	2	16	15	46	28
Arbroath	38	7	7	5	25	21	1	5	13	20	50	28

* Two points deducted for fielding an ineligible player.

Scottish Football League Records
Season 1923-24

DIVISION 1

	ABERDEEN	AIRDRIE	AYR U	CELTIC	CLYDE	CLYDEBANK	DUNDEE	FALKIRK	HAMILTON A	HEARTS	HIBERNIAN	KILMARNOCK	MORTON	MOTHERWELL	PARTICK T	QUEEN'S PARK	RAITH R	RANGERS	ST MIRREN	T LANARK
ABERDEEN		Mar01 1-2	Jan12 1-0	Sep29 0-2	Dec29 3-0	Aug18 3-1	Sep01 0-0	Dec15 0-0	Oct13 2-0	Jan05 2-1	Jan02 1-1	Apr19 2-0	Sep15 0-2	Oct27 3-1	Nov10 2-1	Sep24 1-1	Dec01 1-0	Mar19 1-0	Feb02 2-0	Feb13 2-2
AIRDRIE	Dec22 2-1		Sep01 4-0	Mar29 2-0	Sep29 6-1	Oct27 3-2	Feb27 4-2	Jan01 4-1	Aug18 3-2	Nov17 3-0	Sep15 1-1	Dec01 2-2	Oct13 1-1	Nov10 2-0	Mar15 1-1	Mar26 2-2	Dec29 1-0	Apr26 0-0	Jan12 4-0	Feb02 3-1
AYR U	Sep08 1-1	Jan19 2-3		Sep22 4-2	Feb27 2-1	Mar15 3-1	Dec15 2-0	Apr05 2-0	Dec01 0-0	Mar22 2-1	Nov10 2-2	Aug25 0-0	Jan01 1-0	Oct06 0-0	Feb16 1-1	Nov24 2-1	Apr12 1-0	Jan05 2-1	Oct20 2-2	Mar29 3-0
CELTIC	Jan19 4-0	Nov03 2-2	Apr05 3-0		Oct06 4-0	Mar04 1-2	Nov17 0-0	Aug18 2-1	Jan05 1-0	Feb26 4-1	Apr26 1-1	Mar08 2-1	Sep24 3-0	Dec15 2-1	Sep01 1-2	Feb16 1-0	Oct20 0-0	Jan01 2-2	Apr12 0-1	Dec01 3-1
CLYDE	Nov24 1-0	Aug15 1-1	Dec08 1-0	Jan02 0-0		Oct13 2-0	Feb02 0-2	Mar29 2-1	Feb13 0-0	Apr21 2-2	Mar01 2-0	Sep08 1-1	Nov10 3-0	Jan12 2-3	Dec22 4-4	Mar22 0-1	Aug25 2-1	Apr18 3-1	Sep22 0-3	Oct27 0-1
CLYDEBANK	Apr12 2-1	Feb16 0-1	Dec22 1-0	Aug25 0-0	Jan05 2-1		Apr19 0-0	Sep08 0-1	Oct20 1-0	Jan19 2-1	Feb20 2-4	Sep22 1-2	Mar22 0-1	Apr05 0-2	Nov24 2-0	Nov03 2-1	Jan02 2-1	Dec01 1-2	Oct06 2-2	Mar01 1-5
DUNDEE	Jan01 1-1	Oct20 3-1	Feb20 2-1	Dec22 2-1	Apr05 3-1	Nov10 4-1		Dec01 4-2	Mar15 1-1	Aug25 5-1	Oct27 7-2	Jan19 4-2	Mar01 1-1	Mar08 4-1	Dec08 0-0	Sep22 3-0	Jan05 1-1	Oct06 1-4	Mar29 1-1	Sep08 1-0
FALKIRK	Oct06 0-0	Aug25 0-3	Sep15 2-0	Mar15 3-1	Nov03 1-0	Feb02 2-0	Jan02 4-1		Mar26 1-2	Oct20 0-0	Dec08 1-1	Apr12 2-1	Dec22 2-0	Nov24 2-0	Sep29 0-1	Apr19 1-3	Feb20 3-0	Nov17 0-1	Mar01 0-0	Mar12 4-1
HAMILTON A	Mar12 3-0	Jan02 5-1	Dec29 0-0	Nov10 2-5	Dec15 1-2	Apr26 3-2	Nov24 0-0	Sep22 1-2		Feb16 1-3	Apr23 2-1	Mar29 2-1	Oct27 4-1	Aug25 2-1	Mar05 3-1	Oct06 2-1	Sep08 0-2	Jan19 2-3	Dec08 2-0	Apr05 2-0
HEARTS	Dec08 0-1	Feb13 4-2	Sep29 2-3	Oct13 0-0	Aug18 6-0	Sep15 2-0	Dec29 1-0	Apr05 3-1	Sep01 4-0		Jan01 1-1	Nov10 4-1	Dec01 3-1	Mar29 2-1	Oct27 2-1	Jan12 5-2	Mar01 1-2	Sep17 0-0	Jan02 0-0	Mar15 3-1
HIBERNIAN	Aug25 0-1	Apr12 2-0	Feb02 3-0	Sep17 0-0	Nov17 3-1	Dec15 3-2	Feb16 2-0	Jan05 1-0	Nov03 1-3	Sep08 1-1		Feb27 3-1	Nov24 2-1	Sep22 2-4	Apr16 3-1	Dec22 4-0	Oct06 4-0	Oct20 1-3	Apr02 1-1	Jan19 5-2
KILMARNOCK	Nov03 2-1	Apr02 1-2	Jan02 1-1	Dec08 1-1	Mar15 3-0	Jan12 2-3	Sep29 1-3	Oct13 2-1	Sep15 1-0	Dec22 2-1	Sep01 2-1		Feb13 1-3	Apr26 1-0	Feb02 3-1	Aug18 1-4	Nov17 1-2	Mar05 1-1	Oct27 2-0	Dec29 0-0
MORTON	Feb27 1-1	Apr05 2-1	Nov17 4-0	Feb02 1-0	Mar08 1-2	Dec08 1-0	Nov03 2-1	Feb16 2-1	Jan12 0-0	Sep22 1-0	Dec29 1-0	Oct06 0-2		Jan02 3-2	Aug25 1-2	Oct20 3-1	Apr19 2-0	Sep08 0-1	Mar15 4-0	Dec15 2-2
MOTHERWELL	Apr05 1-1	Jan05 2-1	Mar01 1-0	Feb13 0-1	Sep15 1-1	Sep29 3-2	Oct13 4-2	Jan19 3-1	Jan01 3-1	Nov03 3-2	Mar15 2-1	Oct20 4-0	Sep01 3-1		Apr12 1-1	Nov17 2-1	Dec22 1-3	Aug18 0-3	Dec01 0-2	Apr19 2-2
PARTICK T	Mar29 1-0	Oct06 2-1	Aug18 3-0	Mar01 1-1	Oct20 6-1	Aug16 1-1	Mar22 5-2	Dec29 0-1	Nov17 0-1	Apr19 0-1	Dec01 1-0	Dec15 2-2	Jan05 2-0	Sep08 0-2		Apr21 3-0	Jan19 2-0	Nov03 0-6	Feb12 1-2	Dec31 2-2
QUEEN'S PARK	Apr05 1-0	Dec15 0-2	Apr26 0-0	Sep08 0-2	Dec01 0-0	Mar29 1-1	Apr12 1-1	Oct27 4-2	Mar01 2-1	Feb02 1-1	Sep29 1-1	Jan05 3-1	Jan19 3-1	Dec29 2-2	Oct13 0-2		Sep15 2-1	Feb12 0-2	Nov10 0-1	Aug25 1-0
RAITH R	Feb16 1-0	Dec08 2-0	Oct27 4-1	Mar22 1-0	Jan01 2-1	Sep01 1-0	Aug18 3-0	Nov10 3-0	Feb02 0-1	Nov24 1-1	Jan12 0-2	Apr05 4-1	Sep29 4-0	Feb27 1-1	Sep22 4-1	Mar15 2-0		Dec15 0-1	Apr26 1-1	Oct13 6-1
RANGERS	Sep22 2-0	Nov24 0-0	Oct13 5-0	Oct27 0-0	Sep24 2-1	Feb26 3-0	Jan12 1-1	Aug21 2-2	Dec22 4-0	Mar11 1-0	Apr05 2-1	Feb19 2-0	Apr12 2-1	Feb02 3-0	Jan02 1-0	Dec08 1-0	Mar29 0-1		Aug25 5-0	Nov10 2-0
ST MIRREN	Nov17 2-0	Sep08 0-1	Apr19 4-0	Nov24 0-1	Jan19 3-1	Mar08 6-2	Sep15 2-2	Sep01 1-0	Sep29 4-1	Dec15 0-0	Oct13 1-1	Jan01 0-1	Aug18 3-1	Feb16 4-0	Apr05 1-2	Mar04 2-0	Nov03 1-1	Dec29 0-0		Jan05 3-1
T LANARK	Oct20 2-1	Sep22 0-0	Nov03 3-0	Jan12 1-3	Feb16 0-0	Nov17 2-1	Dec25 3-5	Mar04 2-1	Apr21 3-2	Oct06 2-1	Aug18 1-4	Nov24 2-1	Aug22 0-2	Dec08 2-1	Sep24 2-4	Jan02 2-3	Mar08 1-1	Mar22 1-3	Dec22 3-0	

DIVISION 2

	ALBION R	ALLOA	ARBROATH	ARMADALE	BATHGATE	BO'NESS	BROXBURN U	COWDENBEATH	DUMBARTON	DUNDEE U	DUNFERMLINE A	EAST FIFE	FORFAR A	JOHNSTONE	KING'S PARK	LOCHGELLY U	ST BERNARD'S	ST JOHNSTONE	STENHOUSEMUIR	VALE OF LEVEN
ALBION R		Mar22 2-0	Dec08 7-1	Oct06 4-0	Dec15 2-2	Nov03 4-0	Apr26 1-3	Nov24 2-1	Jan02 1-0	Apr05 1-2	Sep08 1-2	Mar01 1-1	Apr19 3-1	Jan19 3-1	Jan05 3-0	Oct20 5-1	Sep22 2-1	Aug25 0-0	Feb25 2-2	Mar08 5-0
ALLOA	Sep29 0-1		Oct13 3-2	Dec29 1-0	Apr05 1-0	Feb16 0-0	Jan12 1-0	Nov10 1-0	Sep08 0-2	Aug25 0-1	Jan01 1-1	Aug28 2-1	Sep22 1-1	Mar29 3-3	Mar01 1-1	Dec01 3-1	Dec04 4-2	Oct27 1-0	Mar15 2-1	Feb02 4-0
ARBROATH	Feb02 1-1	Apr19 1-0		Sep08 2-1	Mar15 2-1	Nov24 0-0	Oct20 0-0	Feb16 0-0	Apr05 3-0	Sep22 2-1	Nov17 0-1	Dec15 3-0	Oct06 0-1	Aug18 1-2	Apr26 5-1	Mar22 3-0	Jan02 0-3	Jan12 0-0	Nov03 0-1	Jan01 3-0
ARMADALE	Apr12 3-1	Sep01 2-1	Jan19 2-2		Jan01 4-4	Mar01 1-0	Dec22 3-1	Mar15 1-4	Nov03 4-1	Dec01 1-1	Jan05 3-1	Aug18 2-1	Dec15 0-1	Dec05 0-0	Oct13 2-4	Feb13 1-0	Mar22 3-2	Apr26 1-3	Sep29 1-0	Sep15 2-0
BATHGATE	Jan12 2-0	Dec22 4-1	Oct27 2-1	Aug25 0-0		Mar29 2-0	Sep08 2-1	Oct06 1-1	Sep22 2-1	Dec08 3-0	Mar08 1-0	Feb23 0-0	Jan02 4-2	Nov24 3-0	Apr19 2-0	Dec29 4-1	Feb02 0-1	Feb16 1-1	Oct20 1-1	Nov10 1-1
BO'NESS	Dec29 1-1	Oct20 2-1	Apr12 3-0	Sep22 3-1	Nov17 2-3		Aug25 3-0	Oct27 1-1	Mar22 0-2	Mar15 1-1	Feb23 2-1	Dec08 2-1	Sep08 2-0	Feb13 2-1	Nov10 1-1	Mar08 0-2	Jan12 2-0	Oct06 1-2	Jan02 2-0	Apr26 1-1
BROXBURN U	Oct13 4-2	Nov03 1-2	Mar01 0-0	Feb16 3-1	Jan19 0-0	Jan01 1-3		Feb02 0-1	Jan05 3-0	Nov24 1-2	Mar29 1-1	Sep29 1-0	Dec29 3-0	Mar15 0-0	Aug18 0-3	Apr19 3-2	Dec15 3-1	Dec01 2-2	Sep15 0-0	Sep01 1-3
COWDENBEATH	Feb23 4-0	Mar08 1-0	Dec29 2-1	Oct20 0-1	Feb13 2-0	Aug15 3-1	Sep22 3-0		Apr12 4-1	Dec31 4-4	Mar22 3-2	Jan12 3-0	Nov03 4-1	Sep29 2-0	Dec01 5-0	Mar29 2-1	Aug25 1-1	Sep08 1-1	Nov17 2-2	Dec15 3-1
DUMBARTON	Aug18 0-1	Feb23 5-0	Sep15 1-0	Mar29 0-2	Apr26 6-2	Sep29 1-1	Nov17 2-0	Sep01 2-2		Oct27 3-0	Dec29 1-0	Feb02 1-1	Feb20 5-1	Apr19 2-1	Jan01 0-5	Dec15 3-0	Mar12 1-0	Nov10 1-4	Dec08 0-1	Oct13 1-0
DUNDEE U	Sep01 2-0	Jan02 0-1	Feb23 2-0	Jan12 4-0	Apr12 2-0	Dec15 0-0	Mar22 0-2	Aug18 0-0	Feb16 0-1		Apr19 2-2	Oct13 0-0	Apr26 2-0	Sep15 1-1	Feb06 0-0	Nov17 1-0	Nov03 3-2	Feb02 1-1	Apr16 0-1	Sep29 3-1
DUNFERMLINE A	Feb16 1-1	Aug18 2-2	Dec22 2-1	Oct27 1-2	Oct13 1-0	Sep01 2-1	Nov10 1-3	Sep15 1-2	Nov24 2-0	Oct06 1-0		Apr05 2-0	Feb02 0-0	Mar01 2-1	Jan19 3-2	Jan02 6-1	Aug22 1-1	Mar15 0-1	Apr26 4-2	Dec08 2-2
EAST FIFE	Nov17 1-2	Sep15 1-0	Mar29 2-0	Jan02 2-1	Dec01 0-1	Jan05 2-0	Feb20 2-1	Dec22 3-2	Oct06 2-0	Jan19 0-0	Oct20 1-2		Mar22 7-0	Nov03 2-1	Mar08 2-2	Aug25 1-0	Sep08 2-0	Apr19 1-1	Apr12 6-0	Dec29 0-1
FORFAR A	Sep15 3-1	Feb28 2-0	Jan05 0-5	Mar08 1-5	Sep01 2-2	Jan19 2-0	Dec08 2-1	Mar01 1-0	Dec01 2-1	Nov10 0-0	Aug25 1-0	Oct27 0-1		Oct13 3-2	Sep29 0-0	Apr12 3-1	Jan01 1-0	Mar29 1-2	Dec22 2-4	Feb23 1-0
JOHNSTONE	Nov10 3-3	Dec08 2-1	Mar08 1-3	Feb02 3-2	Mar22 3-3	Dec01 4-1	Oct06 2-0	Jan02 2-1	Oct20 0-1	Dec22 2-1	Jan17 1-0	Feb16 3-1	Apr05 4-2		Oct27 1-0	Feb23 2-0	Apr26 0-2	Sep22 1-0	Aug25 1-1	Apr12 4-1
KING'S PARK	Dec22 1-1	Oct06 1-0	Feb13 2-2	Aug15 1-2	Nov03 3-0	Feb02 4-0	Jan02 1-2	Apr05 0-3	Aug25 2-0	Oct20 2-3	Sep22 1-0	Nov24 2-2	Mar15 1-1	Dec15 3-1		Sep08 4-0	Feb27 1-0	Apr12 1-0	Jan12 2-1	Nov17 1-0
LOCHGELLY U	Mar15 1-0	Apr26 0-2	Nov10 0-2	Dec08 1-0	Aug18 1-0	Sep15 1-2	Oct27 1-1	Oct13 0-1	Mar01 0-2	Jan05 0-0	Sep29 1-1	Jan01 0-4	Nov24 0-2	Sep01 0-1	Feb16 3-8		Apr05 1-1	Dec22 0-3	Feb02 0-1	Feb20 1-2
ST BERNARD'S	Mar29 1-1	Jan19 2-1	Sep01 2-0	Nov10 0-0	Sep29 0-2	Oct13 2-3	Apr12 1-2	Dec08 0-1	Dec22 3-0	Mar05 0-0	Dec01 2-2	Mar15 4-3	Aug18 2-2	Jan05 2-1	Sep15 1-1	Oct06 1-0		Mar01 0-1	Nov24 1-1	Oct27 3-1
ST JOHNSTONE	Jan01 6-1	Dec15 2-1	Sep29 2-1	Nov24 5-0	Sep15 0-0	Apr05 3-0	Feb23 3-1	Jan05 0-4	Feb13 4-4	Mar08 4-1	Nov03 1-0	Sep01 3-0	Nov17 2-0	Dec29 2-1	Dec08 5-1	Jan19 6-0	Oct20 4-1		Mar22 1-1	Aug18 2-1
STENHOUSEMUIR	Oct27 1-1	Jan05 3-1	Dec01 2-0	Feb23 2-0	Mar01 5-1	Aug18 1-1	Mar08 4-3	Apr19 1-2	Jan19 1-2	Sep08 3-0	Dec15 0-0	Nov10 3-0	Feb16 1-0	Jan01 2-0	Sep01 3-5	Sep22 3-0	Dec29 3-0	Oct13 0-0		Mar29 0-1
VALE OF LEVEN	Dec01 0-0	Nov24 3-1	Aug25 3-2	Apr19 3-2	Jan05 1-2	Dec22 1-1	Apr05 3-0	Jan19 0-3	Mar15 2-2	Mar01 1-1	Feb13 1-2	Sep22 1-1	Oct20 1-0	Sep08 0-4	Mar22 2-0	Nov03 2-0	Feb16 0-4	Jan02 2-2	Oct06 1-0	

DIVISION 3

	ARTHURLIE	BEITH	BRECHIN C	CLACKMANNAN	DUMBARTON H	DYKEHEAD	E STIRLING	GALSTON	HELENSBURGH	MID ANNANDALE	MONTROSE	NITHSDALE W	PEEBLES	QUEEN OF SOUTH	ROYAL ALBERT	SOLWAY STAR
ARTHURLIE		Feb09 0-1	Sep22 4-0	Dec01 2-0	Jan12 3-0	Mar08 3-0	Aug25 2-3	Feb16 3-2	Jan02 5-0	Nov10 3-2	Feb02 3-0	Dec08 2-1	Jan26 1-1	Dec22 3-2	Oct20 2-0	Oct06 3-2
BEITH	Nov24 0-1		Apr12 2-1	Mar29 3-2	Mar08 6-2	Feb16 0-3	Jan02 2-0	Sep22 4-1	Oct06 3-4	Dec15 2-1	Oct20 1-1	Feb02 3-0	Apr05 2-0	Dec08 4-0	Aug25 1-0	Apr21 4-0
BRECHIN C	Nov17 2-0	Mar22 1-0		Sep08 0-1	Apr05 1-3	Apr19 1-0	Mar01 1-1	Nov10 2-8	Mar08 1-1	Jan05 2-3	Aug18 0-4	Jan01 3-3	Dec01 1-1	Feb02 0-0	Jan12 0-1	Dec08 0-2
CLACKMANNAN	Nov03 0-1	Jan05 2-2	Feb09 2-1		Dec31 1-1	Jan19 3-0	Sep15 5-1	Nov24 1-1	Sep22 3-0	Feb23 1-0	Dec15 1-2	Aug18 1-3	Oct06 0-0	Oct20 0-1	Dec08 3-2	Apr19 2-1
DUMBARTON H	Mar15 0-2	Sep08 0-0	Feb23 0-2	Aug25 2-3		Nov24 1-0	Oct20 0-0	Mar01 4-1	Nov03 1-1	Feb16 0-0	Oct06 4-3	Dec22 1-0	Feb02 1-0	Jan19 0-5	Jan02 2-0	Sep22 3-1
DYKEHEAD	Feb23 1-2	Apr28 5-1	Mar29 4-0	Jan12 3-0	Dec15 3-2		Nov03 4-0	Aug25 3-1	Oct20 1-0	Feb02 3-2	Apr05 1-0	Mar15 2-0	Sep22 4-1	Jan02 2-2	Apr26 4-0	Mar01 1-0
E STIRLING	Jan01 1-1	Aug18 2-1	Jan19 4-1	Sep01 5-0	Dec01 4-1	Jan05 1-0		Mar29 3-1	Apr26 2-0	Sep08 2-0	Sep22 3-0	Nov10 4-0	Dec15 2-1	Apr05 2-1	Oct27 1-1	Feb16 1-1
GALSTON	Mar22 0-3	Feb23 3-0	Mar15 2-0	Feb02 1-1	Nov17 3-1	Jan01 2-3	Mar08 1-4		Jan05 1-0	Apr23 1-4	Nov03 3-1	Sep08 2-3	Oct20 5-3	Oct06 2-0	Dec15 2-0	Aug18 2-0
HELENSBURGH	Aug18 0-2	Nov10 1-2	Nov24 3-2	Dec22 1-2	Feb09 1-3	Sep08 2-4	Dec08 3-3	Oct13 2-1		Jan01 3-3	Mar01 4-0	Oct27 0-0	Feb23 2-4	Apr19 2-2	Mar29 6-1	Feb02 1-1
MID ANNANDALE	Mar01 2-2	Mar15 2-3	Apr26 6-1	Nov17 6-1	Dec08 2-1	Apr12 1-0	Oct06 0-1	Dec01 4-1	Aug25 4-3		Apr19 1-1	Nov24 2-0	Jan02 3-2	Nov03 1-3	Sep22 4-1	Mar29 0-1
MONTROSE	Mar29 1-1	Dec22 2-1	Jan02 4-2	Sep29 1-0	Jan05 1-1	Dec08 6-2	Mar22 2-1	Apr12 5-0	Feb16 4-1	Oct27 2-0		Oct13 2-1	Mar15 1-0	Aug25 1-1	Nov10 2-1	Nov24 5-1
NITHSDALE W	Jan19 0-1	Apr19 2-0	Aug25 5-0	Mar01 1-1	Mar22 0-4	Feb09 1-0	Jan12 0-0	Apr05 4-0	Dec15 2-0	Mar08 2-0	Dec01 3-0		Nov03 3-2	Sep22 1-1	Oct06 3-1	Oct20 2-1
PEEBLES	Oct13 1-3	Mar01 0-0	Feb16 2-0	Nov10 4-0	Dec29 0-0	Dec22 2-1	Sep29 2-6	Oct27 1-3	Jan19 5-2	Aug18 1-2	Sep08 3-1	Jan05 0-0		Nov17 1-1	Feb09 3-0	Jan01 2-2
QUEEN OF SOUTH	Sep08 0-0	Apr26 2-0	Dec15 7-2	Mar08 5-0	Mar29 5-2	Aug18 2-0	Nov24 1-0	Nov15 6-1	Dec29 4-0	Mar20 3-0	Jan01 3-3	Feb16 0-0	Mar22 4-0		Mar01 0-1	Jan05 1-1
ROYAL ALBERT	Jan05 0-1	Dec01 2-1	Nov03 2-0	Feb16 3-0	Aug18 3-0	Oct13 2-1	Feb02 1-3	Dec22 1-1	Nov17 4-2	Mar22 1-1	Feb23 2-4	Sep29 2-1	Nov24 4-0	Mar15 2-0		Mar08 3-3
SOLWAY STAR	Dec15 2-0	Oct13 1-0	Dec29 1-1	Oct27 1-1	Nov10 0-0	Mar22 3-0	Nov17 3-3	Jan02 4-1	Dec01 2-1	Apr05 1-3	Jan12 3-1	Feb23 0-1	Aug25 2-1	Apr12 0-2	Sep08 2-3	

DIVISION 1

	P	W	D	L	F	A	W	D	L	F	A	Pts
Rangers	38	14	4	1	38	7	11	5	3	34	15	59
Airdrie	38	13	6	0	48	17	7	4	8	24	29	50
Celtic	38	11	5	3	36	15	6	7	6	20	18	46
Raith R	38	13	3	3	40	12	5	4	10	16	26	43
Dundee	38	12	6	1	48	22	3	7	9	22	35	43
St Mirren	38	10	5	4	37	15	5	7	7	16	30	42
Hibernian	38	12	3	4	41	21	3	8	8	25	31	41
Partick T	38	9	4	6	32	23	6	5	8	26	32	39
Hearts	38	12	4	3	43	17	2	6	11	18	33	38
Motherwell	38	11	4	4	36	26	4	3	12	22	37	37
Morton	38	12	3	4	31	16	4	2	13	17	38	37
Hamilton A	38	11	2	6	37	26	4	4	11	15	31	36
Aberdeen	38	11	5	3	27	14	2	5	12	10	27	36
Ayr U	38	11	7	1	32	16	1	3	15	6	44	34
Falkirk	38	10	4	5	28	15	3	2	14	18	38	32
Kilmarnock	38	9	4	6	28	25	3	4	12	20	40	32
Queen's Park	38	7	7	5	22	21	4	2	13	21	39	31
T. Lanark	38	9	3	7	32	33	2	5	12	22	45	30
Clyde	38	8	6	5	26	21	2	3	14	14	49	29
Clydebank	38	8	3	8	21	25	2	2	15	21	46	25

DIVISION 2

	P	W	D	L	F	A	W	D	L	F	A	Pts
St Johnstone	38	15	3	1	55	18	7	9	3	24	15	56
Cowdenbeath	38	14	4	1	49	17	9	5	5	29	16	55
Bathgate	38	12	6	1	35	12	4	6	9	23	37	44
Stenhousemuir	38	11	4	4	38	17	5	7	7	20	28	43
Albion R	38	12	4	3	49	18	3	8	8	18	35	42
King's Park	38	11	4	4	33	18	5	6	8	34	39	42
Dunfermline A	38	10	5	4	34	22	4	6	9	18	24	39
Johnstone	38	13	3	3	39	23	3	4	12	21	33	39
Dundee U	38	8	7	4	23	12	4	8	7	18	29	39
Dumbarton	38	11	3	5	35	21	6	2	11	20	35	39
Armadale	38	11	4	4	36	27	5	2	12	20	36	38
East Fife	38	12	3	4	37	14	2	6	11	17	33	37
Bo'ness	38	10	5	4	31	19	3	6	10	14	34	37
Forfar A	38	11	3	5	27	25	3	4	12	15	42	35
Alloa	38	11	5	3	29	17	3	1	15	15	36	34
Vale of Leven	38	8	6	5	27	27	4	3	12	16	38	33
Arbroath	38	9	5	5	26	13	3	3	13	23	38	32
St Bernard's	38	7	7	5	27	22	4	3	12	22	32	32
Broxburn U	38	7	6	6	27	23	5	2	12	21	35	32
Lochgelly U	38	3	4	12	11	33	1	0	18	10	53	12

DIVISION 3

	P	W	D	L	F	A	W	D	L	F	A	Pts
Arthurlie	30	12	1	2	39	14	9	4	2	20	10	47
E. Stirling	30	12	3	0	37	9	5	5	5	26	27	42
Queen of South	30	10	4	1	43	10	4	6	5	21	21	38
Montrose	30	12	3	0	39	13	3	3	9	21	35	36
Dykehead	30	13	1	1	41	11	3	0	12	14	30	33
Nithsdale W	30	10	3	2	29	11	3	4	8	13	24	33
Beith	30	11	1	3	37	16	3	3	9	12	25	32
Mid Annandale	30	9	2	4	38	21	4	3	8	21	27	31
Royal Albert	30	9	3	3	32	18	3	1	11	12	35	28
Dumbarton H	30	7	4	4	19	18	3	4	8	21	33	28
Solway Star	30	7	4	4	25	18	2	5	8	17	30	27
Clackmannan	30	7	4	4	25	16	3	3	9	12	38	27
Galston	30	9	1	5	30	23	2	2	11	23	47	25
Peebles	30	6	5	4	27	21	1	3	11	16	35	22
Helensburgh	30	4	5	6	31	30	1	2	12	15	42	17
Brechin C	30	3	5	7	15	28	1	1	13	13	48	14

Scottish Football League Records
Season 1924-25

DIVISION 1

	ABERDEEN	AIRDRIE	AYR U	CELTIC	COWDENBEATH	DUNDEE	FALKIRK	HAMILTON A	HEARTS	HIBERNIAN	KILMARNOCK	MORTON	MOTHERWELL	PARTICK T	QUEEN'S PARK	RAITH R	RANGERS	ST JOHNSTONE	ST MIRREN	T LANARK
ABERDEEN		Oct04 1-2	Mar18 0-1	Sep06 0-4	Sep20 3-0	Oct18 0-0	Jan03 1-1	Apr01 2-0	Apr04 0-0	Jan05 0-1	Nov29 0-0	Sep22 0-1	Apr25 2-0	Jan17 2-0	Sep29 3-1	Feb28 2-3	Aug23 0-1	Nov01 2-1	Nov15 2-3	Dec20 3-1
AIRDRIE	Feb14 0-0		Nov01 3-0	Jan03 3-1	Dec27 2-0	Apr22 1-1	Nov15 1-1	Jan05 2-0	Mar07 2-2	Apr18 2-0	Feb11 4-2	Jan17 6-2	Mar28 5-0	Dec13 4-1	Nov22 3-0	Oct11 1-0	Sep27 1-0	Sep13 6-0	Aug16 2-0	Aug30 3-0
AYR U	Aug30 3-3	Aug20 0-1		Feb11 1-2	Jan17 1-2	Nov08 1-0	Apr04 0-0	Nov29 3-1	Jan03 2-1	Feb28 2-2	Oct18 0-1	Jan05 4-0	Apr11 1-0	Nov15 0-1	Oct25 1-1	Mar14 3-2	Sep13 0-4	Sep27 5-3	Dec13 1-1	Aug16 0-0
CELTIC	Jan10 3-1	Aug23 1-1	Dec06 2-0		Sep29 3-1	Feb28 4-0	Apr01 6-1	Dec20 0-2	Oct11 1-0	Jan31 1-1	Nov08 6-0	Mar24 2-1	Sep27 4-0	Nov29 1-2	Apr18 1-1	Mar28 2-0	Oct25 0-1	Feb14 2-1	Sep13 5-0	Jan05 7-0
COWDENBEATH	Mar28 2-1	Nov08 2-1	Dec20 4-0	Mar14 3-0		Jan31 2-0	Feb11 1-0	Apr04 3-1	Aug16 1-2	Nov29 1-1	Oct25 5-2	Sep13 5-0	Mar04 4-0	Apr25 3-0	Dec13 4-0	Jan01 1-1	Oct11 2-2	Aug30 1-2	Sep27 5-4	Jan10 3-4
DUNDEE	Jan01 2-0	Dec20 3-2	Feb25 1-0	Aug16 0-0	Nov15 1-1		Jan17 1-0	Feb14 2-0	Aug30 6-0	Apr04 3-0	Sep13 3-1	Oct11 0-0	Mar14 1-0	Jan03 0-2	Sep27 2-4	Nov29 2-0	Dec06 0-0	Mar28 2-0	Apr15 0-2	Nov01 1-2
FALKIRK	Aug16 2-0	Jan01 0-2	Nov22 0-3	Aug30 1-2	Dec06 5-1	Dec13 1-2		Oct11 2-1	Sep13 2-1	Jan10 0-0	Sep27 0-0	Aug20 3-0	Oct25 2-1	Apr11 1-0	Nov08 7-0	Jan31 1-1	Feb18 1-1	Feb25 2-0	Mar28 2-1	Dec27 1-2
HAMILTON A	Sep13 2-1	Oct25 1-2	Dec27 1-0	Feb24 0-4	Oct04 5-1	Nov22 4-1	Apr25 1-2		Sep27 0-2	Nov08 0-2	Mar11 2-1	Apr11 1-0	Jan05 1-1	Mar28 1-1	Mar14 3-1	Aug30 1-0	Jan31 1-0	Aug16 3-2	Jan10 1-3	Dec06 1-2
HEARTS	Nov08 1-1	Sep20 2-0	Aug23 2-3	Dec13 3-1	Aug20 3-3	Apr18 1-0	Nov29 3-2	Feb28 3-2		Oct18 2-0	Mar14 1-1	Sep06 5-1	Oct04 2-2	Feb11 2-1	Mar28 3-1	Jan10 2-2	Sep15 1-2	Jan31 1-1	Dec27 5-2	Nov15 2-3
HIBERNIAN	Nov22 4-1	Dec06 1-1	Oct11 7-0	Sep15 2-3	Feb21 4-1	Oct25 4-2	Nov01 1-2	Jan17 2-1	Jan01 2-1		Jan03 2-0	Sep27 2-0	Aug29 1-0	Aug15 3-2	Sep13 2-0	Feb25 3-0	Mar11 4-1	Dec20 5-0	Mar24 2-0	Feb07 5-1
KILMARNOCK	Jan31 0-1	Sep06 2-3	Jan01 4-1	Apr15 2-1	Mar21 0-0	Jan10 4-1	Feb28 1-0	Sep20 1-3	Nov22 2-1	Aug23 0-1		Feb25 3-1	Dec06 0-2	Dec27 1-1	Oct11 3-1	Dec20 3-0	Mar28 0-0	Apr22 4-0	Nov01 3-2	Oct04 2-2
MORTON	Dec13 1-1	Oct18 0-1	Sep20 3-1	Nov01 1-0	Mar07 1-3	Dec27 1-1	Oct04 2-0	Nov15 2-0	Feb14 2-0	Mar28 2-2	Aug16 2-2		Jan31 0-0	Aug30 1-6	Feb21 4-0	Apr18 2-3	Jan10 1-1	Apr04 1-1	Jan01 2-1	Nov29 1-0
MOTHERWELL	Oct11 1-2	Nov29 1-5	Sep06 1-1	Jan17 1-0	Nov01 0-3	Sep20 4-1	Jan05 4-1	Oct18 3-3	Dec20 0-0	Feb11 1-1	Apr04 2-1	Aug23 3-0		Feb28 1-3	Jan03 4-1	Dec13 2-1	Apr18 1-1	Nov15 4-1	Apr01 1-2	Mar21 8-0
PARTICK T	Sep27 1-4	Jan10 2-1	Jan31 2-0	Aug19 2-2	Nov22 6-1	Aug23 1-1	Dec20 2-0	Sep06 3-0	Oct25 3-3	Mar14 3-1	Feb14 2-1	Dec06 2-2	Nov08 2-2		Feb24 3-1	Sep13 0-0	Jan05 0-1	Oct11 0-1	Apr18 1-3	Jan01 0-3
QUEEN'S PARK	Apr13 4-1	Jan31 1-2	Jan10 4-1	Nov15 3-1	Feb14 1-1	Mar10 0-1	Mar25 2-0	Nov01 1-3	Dec06 2-0	Dec27 1-0	Aug20 1-2	Dec20 0-2	Aug16 2-1	Oct04 0-0		Apr25 2-0	Aug26 1-3	Nov29 2-2	Apr03 2-1	Oct18 1-1
RAITH R	Dec06 2-2	Apr11 0-2	Oct04 2-1	Dec27 2-2	Oct18 3-1	Nov05 4-3	Sep06 2-0	Jan03 0-1	Nov01 2-0	Sep20 1-3	Nov15 3-1	Nov22 2-0	Feb14 1-0	Mar21 5-1	Aug23 1-1		Mar25 0-4	Jan17 0-0	Feb18 2-0	Mar07 2-0
RANGERS	Mar07 2-0	Feb25 1-1	Apr25 1-0	Jan01 4-1	Apr01 1-0	Feb10 2-0	Oct18 3-1	Dec13 2-0	Sep29 4-1	Nov15 3-0	Aug30 1-1	Jan03 2-0	Dec27 1-0	Nov01 4-0	Jan17 1-1	Aug16 3-0		Aug20 3-1	Nov29 3-1	Apr11 5-2
ST JOHNSTONE	Dec27 1-1	Apr25 1-0	Mar21 2-2	Oct18 0-0	Sep03 2-2	Oct04 1-2	Aug23 0-0	Feb11 4-1	Apr11 4-3	Sep06 2-3	Dec13 4-2	Nov08 1-3	Jan10 2-1	Mar07 1-1	Dec25 2-1	Oct25 4-2	Nov22 1-3		Feb28 2-2	Sep24 4-0
ST MIRREN	Mar03 1-3	Mar07 1-0	Feb14 1-0	Apr25 2-1	Jan03 2-2	Sep06 2-1	Sep20 1-0	Aug23 0-1	Jan17 3-1	Oct04 2-2	Jan05 3-0	Oct25 3-1	Nov22 4-1	Oct18 3-1	Apr03 1-2	Nov08 3-0	Dec20 1-4	Dec06 0-1		Jan31 3-1
T LANARK	Oct25 4-0	Mar11 1-7	Mar28 0-1	Nov22 1-1	Aug23 1-1	Dec25 3-0	Apr18 4-0	Aug19 2-1	Feb21 2-2	Dec13 1-2	Jan17 2-0	Feb28 2-3	Sep13 1-1	Sep29 1-2	Feb11 1-3	Sep27 2-4	Nov08 1-1	Jan03 0-2	Oct11 0-1	

DIVISION 3

	BEITH	BRECHIN C	CLACKMANNAN	DYKEHEAD	GALSTON	HELENSBURGH	LEITH A	LOCHGELLY U	MID ANNANDALE	MONTROSE	NITHSDALE W	PEEBLES	QUEEN OF SOUTH	ROYAL ALBERT	SOLWAY STAR	VALE OF LEVEN	DUMBARTON H
BEITH		Jan10 7-1	Dec27 3-0	Nov01 1-1	Jan01 4-2	Sep27 4-4	Apr25 5-0	Oct18 1-3	Oct04 8-3	Apr29 3-2	Apr11 3-0	Sep13 1-1	Dec13 2-1	Nov22 1-1	Aug23 2-3	Mar21 2-0	
BRECHIN C	Feb28 5-0		Dec13 3-0	Mar14 3-1	Dec27 0-0	Aug23 3-2	Jan03 2-1	Apr04 0-1	Nov22 5-0	Oct11 0-1	Sep13 1-1	Feb21 4-1	Sep27 1-3	Mar28 2-2	Sep20 0-2	Nov08 4-2	Oct25 4-2
CLACKMANNAN	Aug16 1-0	Nov15 2-1		Apr21 1-1	Oct11 3-2	Feb07 0-0	Jan17 2-1	Mar14 2-0	Jan10 3-1	Nov29 1-0	Apr04 0-1	Feb14 3-2	Sep13 2-2	Oct25 2-0	Sep27 0-2	Jan03 3-0	Dec20 4-1
DYKEHEAD	Mar07 2-2		Nov22 2-1		Feb28 2-1	Mar21 0-0	Dec06 0-2	Apr25 2-0	Jan17 1-1	Apr28 2-0	Dec27 1-1	Aug16 1-1	Apr04 0-1	Sep27 3-1	Oct25 1-1	Aug30 4-1	Jan05 3-1
GALSTON	Mar14 1-0	Aug30 3-0	Apr24 2-1	Dec20 0-2		Nov29 4-2	Oct25 1-1	Sep13 3-2	Feb21 3-2	Apr25 1-1	Jan03 1-1	Apr11 2-5	Oct18 2-1	Nov08 2-0	Dec06 1-0	Jan17 1-0	Aug16 5-0
HELENSBURGH	Dec06 8-4	Dec20 2-1	Sep20 3-1	Apr08 1-0	Apr18 5-0		Apr04 3-2	Feb21 2-1	Jan01 2-1	Feb28 5-0	Mar28 4-0	Mar07 3-1	Nov22 3-4	Aug30 1-1	Jan10 0-0	Aug16 1-4	
LEITH A	Nov08 3-1	Mar07 1-1	Aug23 2-1	Apr15 2-0	Jan31 5-0	Mar14 2-1		Jan10 0-0	Apr11 2-0	Nov15 3-2	Nov29 0-0	Dec13 2-3	Mar28 2-1	Dec27 4-0	Feb28 2-3	Apr18 2-0	
LOCHGELLY U	Sep20 4-1	Nov01 3-1	Dec06 3-1	Aug23 5-1	Mar07 6-0	Apr15 3-2	Nov22 0-1		Mar21 2-0	Dec27 4-1	Nov15 0-2	Feb28 2-1	Jan17 3-3	Apr11 4-0	Feb14 2-1	Sep06 1-3	Oct04 6-0
MID ANNANDALE	Mar28 2-1	Jan31 3-1	Nov08 1-1	Oct11 1-1	Feb07 2-2	Sep13 4-4	Dec20 1-0	Sep27 1-2		Aug23 2-2	Dec06 4-2	Jan03 3-2	Nov29 1-2	Mar14 4-1	Apr04 0-2	Oct25 2-3	
MONTROSE	Aug30 3-0	Jan01 3-1	Apr11 1-0	Mar28 0-0	Jan10 2-0	Dec13 2-3	Feb14 1-2	Nov08 2-4	Mar07 2-1		Oct25 0-2	Nov22 2-1	Mar14 2-0	Aug16 0-3	Jan17 1-2	Oct04 0-1	
NITHSDALE W	Dec20 3-1	Jan17 5-3	Jan01 3-1	Sep20 4-0	Nov22 4-2	Oct11 4-3	Aug16 3-2	Aug30 1-1	Feb28 3-1	Apr18 8-0		Jan10 7-1	Feb07 2-0	Jan31 6-2	Nov08 3-0	Feb21 6-1	Sep27 0-0
PEEBLES	Apr18 7-1	Dec06 3-1	Sep06 4-3	Nov29 2-0	Apr29 4-0	Jan17 5-0	Apr20 1-1	Oct25 1-1	Aug30 4-0	Dec20 4-3	Mar21 3-2		Nov08 0-1	Jan01 1-1	Mar14 1-1	Mar28 1-0	
QUEEN OF SOUTH	Oct25 0-0	Oct04 3-1	Mar07 2-0	Nov15 3-1	Mar21 8-0	Apr11 2-0	Feb21 3-0	Aug16 3-1	Nov01 1-1	Dec06 4-2	Oct02 2-1	Jan31 6-0		Jan10 5-1	Dec20 4-0	Sep20 0-1	Aug30 1-0
ROYAL ALBERT	Jan17 3-2	Feb14 1-5	Feb28 0-0	Dec13 7-0	Apr27 1-1	Jan03 3-1	Mar21 4-2	Dec20 2-0	Apr18 2-3	Apr04 2-1	Mar07 1-4	Oct11 2-2	Aug23 1-1		Nov29 2-0	Apr25 3-0	
SOLWAY STAR	Jan03 5-0	Aug16 4-1	Mar21 0-0	Apr11 1-1	Nov01 3-2	Oct18 2-1	Aug30 1-0	Mar28 1-0	Nov15 2-1	Sep13 1-1	Dec13 0-0	Dec27 2-1	Oct11 1-1	Apr13 1-0		Mar07 0-0	Nov22 7-1
VALE OF LEVEN	Oct11 5-2	Apr11 4-0	Nov01 6-0	Jan10 3-0	Aug23 3-0	Dec27 2-2	Sep13 2-1	Nov29 2-1	Dec13 4-1	Sep27 6-2	Mar14 2-2	Nov15 2-1	Feb28 1-0	Oct18 3-1	Jan31 0-0		
DUMBARTON H	Nov15 2-2	Nov29 1-0		Sep13 0-3	Dec13 3-2			Oct11 1-1	Oct18 3-1		Aug23 1-4		Dec27 6-3			Dec31 3-1	

DIVISION 2

	ALBION R	ALLOA	ARBROATH	ARMADALE	ARTHURLIE	BATHGATE	BO'NESS	BROXBURN U	CLYDE	CLYDEBANK	DUMBARTON	DUNDEE U	DUNFERMLINE A	EAST FIFE	E STIRLING	FORFAR A	JOHNSTONE	KING'S PARK	ST BERNARD'S	STENHOUSEMUIR
ALBION R		Mar14 3-6	Jan01 1-1	Dec06 3-1	Feb14 3-1	Sep20 3-2	Jan31 2-1	Oct18 1-2	Jan10 1-1	Apr03 0-0	Apr11 3-1	Nov29 1-0	Dec20 2-1	Oct04 5-2	Oct25 3-0	Apr25 1-3	Feb21 4-1	Sep06 1-1	Aug23 2-1	Nov08 4-1
ALLOA	Dec13 1-0		Feb14 1-1	Apr18 1-0	Sep06 0-0	Aug23 2-2	Feb28 1-1	Nov22 3-0	Mar21 1-0	Sep20 2-3	Mar28 2-1	Mar07 2-0	Jan01 1-0	Apr11 1-1	Nov08 2-0	Oct04 1-0	Oct18 4-1	Dec06 2-0	Jan10 2-0	Jan31 1-0
ARBROATH	Nov01 1-4	Aug16 2-2		Jan05 1-3	Dec06 2-1	Dec20 2-0	Nov08 2-0	Mar11 3-0	Sep13 2-1	Jan03 1-0	Sep27 0-0	Oct11 0-1	Feb25 3-2	Jan17 2-1	Jan31 3-1	Nov22 2-2	Mar21 2-0	Mar28 2-1	Dec13 2-0	Aug29 2-0
ARMADALE	Mar07 0-1	Nov29 3-2	Oct04 2-1		Jan10 1-0	Nov08 1-2	Sep20 2-2	Mar14 2-3	Oct25 1-1	Apr25 0-0	Dec13 0-2	Mar28 1-0	Oct11 4-1	Sep06 2-1	Dec27 2-1	Aug23 1-0	Jan03 3-2	Apr11 3-0	Jan31 5-1	Feb21 1-1
ARTHURLIE	Sep27 3-0	Jan03 0-0	Apr11 2-2	Sep13 4-2		Oct25 2-0	Feb21 3-0	Oct11 3-0	Mar28 3-1	Aug16 1-1	Jan05 2-1	Jan17 1-2	Aug30 1-2	Nov22 3-1	Mar14 2-2	Dec13 1-0	Nov08 4-5	Feb10 1-2	Sep22 5-2	Dec27 3-0
BATHGATE	Feb28 3-1	Jan17 2-1	Apr24 0-0	Jan01 0-1	Mar21 1-1		Nov15 4-1	Aug30 2-2	Jan05 3-2	Mar18 0-3	Nov01 1-0	Sep27 2-2	Feb07 1-4	Oct18 4-1	Aug16 4-4	Dec06 2-0	Mar27 1-0	Dec13 4-3	Nov22 5-2	Sep13 0-0
BO'NESS	Sep13 2-1	Sep27 3-1	Feb18 1-1	Jan17 3-0	Dec20 2-0	Sep03 0-0		Nov01 3-0	Oct11 4-1	Aug30 4-1	Mar07 1-1	Aug16 2-2	Apr25 3-1	Dec27 3-0	Feb14 2-4	Jan05 5-0	Nov22 6-1	Jan03 3-1	Oct18 6-0	Mar28 2-0
BROXBURN U	Mar27 2-1	Apr03 2-1	Sep20 2-1	Nov15 0-1	Jan31 1-1	Jan10 3-0	Jan01 3-1		Feb28 0-0	Feb25 2-2	Nov29 1-2	Dec20 0-1	Nov08 1-1	Apr25 2-1	Dec06 1-1	Apr11 2-0	Aug23 3-0	Oct04 1-0	Sep06 3-1	Oct25 2-1
CLYDE	Aug16 1-0	Aug30 2-1	Dec27 2-0	Feb17 1-0	Nov01 5-0	Oct04 2-0	Apr10 2-1	Dec13 6-0		Sep16 1-1	Nov15 3-2	Jan03 3-0	Mar14 1-1	Mar07 1-2	Feb21 5-1	Sep20 4-0	Jan17 3-2	Oct18 1-0	Jan07 1-0	Nov22 0-0
CLYDEBANK	Nov15 3-0	Dec27 2-1	Aug23 0-1	Nov01 3-0	Feb28 3-0	Oct11 4-1	Apr18 0-0	Sep27 1-0	Jan31 1-0		Jan01 1-0	Dec13 5-0	Nov29 2-1	Feb07 3-0	Sep13 3-2	Oct18 4-0	Apr11 4-1	Mar14 3-2	Mar28 3-2	Jan10 3-0
DUMBARTON	Nov22 2-0	Dec20 1-1	Apr04 0-0	Mar21 1-0	Sep20 2-0	Feb21 1-0	Dec06 1-0	Jan17 0-1	Apr25 0-4	Nov08 1-0		Aug30 3-3	Oct25 2-0	Jan03 2-1	Sep01 1-1	Sep06 2-0	Oct04 2-1	Aug16 1-1	Feb11 0-1	Mar14 3-2
DUNDEE U	Feb11 3-2	Oct25 1-2	Mar14 1-1	Nov22 5-2	Oct18 4-1	Dec27 2-1	Jan10 0-0	Apr18 2-2	Aug23 1-0	Jan05 1-0	Jan31 0-0		Mar21 2-3	Sep20 1-0	Apr11 2-1	Nov08 2-1	Sep06 3-1	Feb28 2-0	Oct04 3-0	Dec25 3-0
DUNFERMLINE A	Apr18 3-0	Nov01 1-1	Oct18 4-1	Feb28 2-1	Mar07 1-2	Sep06 1-4	Oct04 1-0	Mar28 1-1	Dec06 1-0	Jan17 4-0	Feb14 1-2	Nov15 0-0		Aug23 0-4	Nov22 4-0	Jan03 5-2	Dec27 5-1	Sep20 0-0	Oct06 1-2	Apr11 3-1
EAST FIFE	Mar28 5-0	Oct11 2-1	Nov29 0-1	Apr04 4-1	Apr18 3-0	Jan31 4-1	Oct25 2-1	Aug16 0-0	Nov08 0-3	Dec20 1-1	Sep13 2-1	Feb14 0-1	Jan10 1-1		Sep27 4-1	Feb21 3-2	Dec13 3-1	Aug30 2-1	Mar14 3-0	Jan01 5-1
E STIRLING	Jan17 1-0	Jan05 1-2	Sep06 1-2	Oct18 1-1	Oct04 3-0	Jan03 3-0	Dec13 2-4	Feb11 0-1	Dec20 2-4	Mar07 1-0	Aug23 2-2	Nov01 2-3	Apr04 2-0	Feb28 5-2		Mar28 1-2	Sep20 1-1	Nov15 2-1	Apr18 2-0	Mar21 1-1
FORFAR A	Aug30 2-2	Feb12 1-3	Jan10 2-0	Feb14 1-3	Apr04 1-1	Mar14 5-0	Nov29 1-1	Sep13 0-1	Apr18 1-3	Mar21 2-1	Dec27 3-1	Jan01 0-0	Aug16 1-0	Nov15 2-0	Oct11 1-0		Oct25 1-1	Dec20 0-2	Feb28 0-1	Sep27 4-0
JOHNSTONE	Oct11 1-2	Apr25 2-2	Nov15 1-0	Aug30 2-1	Jan13 1-0	Nov29 3-1	Mar14 3-1	Feb14 3-1	Sep27 1-3	Dec06 4-0	Feb28 0-1	Apr03 0-2	Sep13 2-1	Jan05 1-2	Jan10 3-0	Jan31 3-2		Nov01 1-0	Dec20 1-1	Aug16 0-3
KING'S PARK	Jan05 2-1	Feb21 2-0	Oct25 3-0	Sep27 2-1	Nov29 2-3	Apr04 1-1	Aug23 2-0	Dec27 3-0	Feb14 2-1	Nov22 2-2	Jan10 3-1	Sep13 1-1	Jan31 2-1	Mar21 0-0	Jan14 1-0	Mar07 1-1	Aug20 5-1		Nov08 2-0	Oct11 2-0
ST BERNARD'S	Dec27 2-0	Sep13 1-0	Apr25 2-0	Aug16 3-2	Nov15 0-1	Apr11 2-2	Mar21 1-2	Jan03 3-2	Nov29 2-2	Oct25 1-2	Oct11 2-1	Feb21 1-2	Sep27 3-0	Dec06 1-2	Aug30 3-4	Nov01 2-1	Mar07 5-1	Jan17 1-0		Feb18 2-0
STENHOUSEMUIR	Jan03 1-0	Nov15 0-0	Feb28 2-0	Dec20 4-1	Aug23 2-0	Mar07 5-2	Sep06 1-0	Jan05 2-1	Apr04 2-1	Oct04 3-0	Oct18 1-1	Apr25 3-0	Dec13 1-4	Nov01 2-1	Nov29 0-2	Jan17 5-2	Feb07 3-0	Apr18 2-1	Sep20 1-1	

DIVISION 1

	P	W	D	L	F	A	W	D	L	F	A	Pts
Rangers	38	16	3	0	46	10	9	7	3	30	16	60
Airdrie	38	15	4	0	51	10	10	3	6	34	21	57
Hibernian	38	16	1	2	56	16	6	7	6	22	27	52
Celtic	38	13	3	3	51	13	5	5	9	26	31	44
Cowdenbeath	38	13	3	3	52	21	3	7	9	24	44	42
St Mirren	38	12	2	5	36	22	6	2	11	29	41	40
Partick T	38	8	6	5	35	27	6	4	9	25	34	38
Dundee	38	11	4	4	30	14	3	4	12	17	40	36
Raith R	38	11	4	4	34	22	3	4	12	19	39	36
Hearts	38	10	6	3	44	28	2	5	12	20	40	35
St Johnstone	38	8	7	4	38	29	4	4	11	19	43	35
Kilmarnock	38	10	4	5	35	21	2	5	12	18	43	33
Hamilton A	38	10	2	7	29	26	5	1	13	21	37	33
Morton	38	8	7	4	29	23	4	2	13	17	46	33
Aberdeen	38	7	4	8	23	20	4	6	9	23	36	32
Falkirk	38	10	4	5	33	18	2	4	13	11	36	32
Queen's Park	38	9	4	6	30	22	3	4	12	20	49	32
Motherwell	38	9	5	5	42	27	1	5	13	12	36	30
Ayr U	38	7	6	6	28	25	4	2	13	15	40	30
T. Lanark	38	5	5	9	29	32	6	3	10	24	52	30

DIVISION 2

	P	W	D	L	F	A	W	D	L	F	A	Pts
Dundee U	38	13	4	2	38	17	7	6	6	20	27	50
Clydebank	38	17	1	1	48	11	3	7	9	17	31	48
Clyde	38	15	3	1	44	11	5	4	10	28	28	47
Alloa	38	13	5	1	30	10	4	6	9	27	31	45
Arbroath	38	13	3	3	34	19	3	7	9	13	27	42
Bo'ness	38	14	4	1	55	15	2	5	12	16	33	41
Broxburn U	38	11	5	3	31	16	5	4	10	17	38	41
Dumbarton	38	11	5	3	25	16	4	5	10	20	28	40
East Fife	38	13	3	3	44	18	4	2	13	22	40	39
King's Park	38	13	5	1	38	14	2	3	14	16	32	38
Stenhousemuir	38	14	3	2	40	17	1	4	14	11	41	37
Arthurlie	38	11	4	4	44	23	3	4	12	12	37	36
Dunfermline A	38	10	4	5	38	22	4	3	12	24	35	35
Albion R	38	12	4	3	43	26	3	1	15	15	38	35
Armadale	38	11	4	4	34	21	4	1	14	21	41	35
Bathgate	38	10	6	3	39	28	2	4	13	19	46	34
St Bernard's	38	11	2	6	37	24	3	2	14	15	47	32
E. Stirling	38	8	4	7	33	26	3	4	12	25	46	30
Johnstone	38	11	2	6	32	23	1	2	16	21	62	28
Forfar A	38	8	5	6	28	20	2	2	15	18	47	27

DIVISION 3

	P	W	D	L	F	A	W	D	L	F	A	Pts
Nithsdale W	30	14	1	0	62	18	4	6	5	19	22	43
Queen of South	30	12	2	1	46	9	5	4	6	21	23	40
Solway Star	30	9	6	0	24	9	6	4	5	17	19	40
Vale of Leven	30	12	3	0	45	13	5	1	9	16	30	38
Lochgelly U	30	11	1	3	42	18	4	3	8	17	23	34
Leith A	30	10	3	2	32	13	3	2	10	16	29	31
Helensburgh	30	11	2	2	43	20	1	5	9	25	40	31
Peebles	30	10	4	1	41	15	2	3	10	23	42	31
Royal Albert	30	8	4	3	34	22	1	4	10	14	39	26
Clackmannan	30	10	3	2	25	13	0	3	12	10	35	26
Galston	30	10	3	2	27	18	0	3	12	12	52	26
Dykehead	30	6	6	2	21	13	1	5	9	9	34	25
Beith	30	9	4	2	47	22	0	2	13	15	52	24
Brechin C	30	8	3	4	33	17	1	1	12	18	44	24
Mid Annandale	30	6	5	4	31	26	1	2	12	16	44	21
Montrose	30	7	1	7	21	20	1	3	11	18	46	20
Dumbarton H	17	5	2	2	20	17	0	1	7	5	30	13

Scottish Football League Records
Season 1925-26

DIVISION 1

	ABERDEEN	AIRDRIE	CELTIC	CLYDEBANK	COWDENBEATH	DUNDEE	DUNDEE U	FALKIRK	HAMILTON A	HEARTS	HIBERNIAN	KILMARNOCK	MORTON	MOTHERWELL	PARTICK T	QUEEN'S PARK	RAITH R	RANGERS	ST JOHNSTONE	ST MIRREN
ABERDEEN		Feb27 3-1	Nov07 2-4	Dec19 4-1	Aug29 2-1	Jan01 2-1	Apr03 1-0	Jan16 0-0	Aug15 3-3	Dec05 0-2	Oct10 5-0	Oct31 3-2	Sep26 1-2	Mar13 1-0	Feb17 0-0	Jan04 3-1	Apr17 1-1	Sep12 3-1	Nov21 0-1	Sep28 1-2
AIRDRIE	Aug22 4-1		Oct03 5-1	Nov07 2-0	Jan04 3-2	Nov14 4-1	Dec26 0-1	Jan01 1-1	Oct24 2-1	Feb13 2-2	Mar27 5-1	Apr17 3-2	Dec05 1-2	Mar10 2-0	Jan16 1-3	Mar13 1-1	Feb24 6-0	Sep05 2-1	Sep19 7-1	Nov28 2-1
CELTIC	Mar30 4-1	Dec19 3-2		Dec05 1-1	Sep12 6-1	Oct31 0-0	Apr24 6-2	Sep26 3-1	Aug29 2-0	Nov25 3-0	Aug15 5-0	Apr03 0-0	Apr14 3-1	Jan30 3-1	Jan04 3-0	Oct13 4-1	Jan09 1-0	Jan01 2-2	Mar23 4-1	Mar09 6-1
CLYDEBANK	Sep19 0-0	Dec12 0-1	Aug22 1-2		Oct31 4-3	Jan30 1-2	Oct03 6-1	Nov14 2-3	Dec26 1-3	Apr17 1-5	Mar13 0-1	Feb20 5-1	Feb13 2-1	Jan09 1-1	Oct17 3-2	Nov28 3-0	Oct24 2-3	Apr10 2-2	Jan02 2-0	Sep05 1-2
COWDENBEATH	Jan09 2-1	Apr10 1-0	Dec26 1-1	Feb06 5-2		Sep19 5-0	Aug22 5-1	Dec05 3-0	Feb27 4-0	Jan02 1-2	Nov07 3-1	Mar13 1-0	Nov21 5-1	Oct03 2-2	Apr17 3-1	Dec23 7-3	Oct17 2-1	Jan30 2-3	Sep05 1-0	Oct24 1-1
DUNDEE	Oct17 3-2	Apr03 0-1	Mar17 1-2	Sep26 3-1	Apr24 4-3		Nov21 0-0	Feb17 1-0	Sep12 2-2	Oct03 1-0	Dec26 1-4	Dec12 1-0	Aug15 3-0	Oct05 1-2	Nov07 3-1	Apr10 2-1	Jan02 1-1	Feb27 1-5	Aug22 0-1	Jan09 1-1
DUNDEE U	Nov14 2-0	Mar20 1-2	Sep19 1-0	Mar27 5-0	Jan16 1-2	Jan04 0-1		Aug29 1-2	Oct10 2-5	Feb24 2-3	Nov28 2-2	Oct24 3-1	Oct31 2-2	Sep05 1-1	Dec05 1-0	Sep09 1-2	Mar06 3-1	Dec19 2-1	Apr17 0-0	Feb13 1-2
FALKIRK	Oct03 2-1	Oct17 2-1	Feb13 1-1	Apr24 2-2	Mar20 1-1	Mar06 1-0	Jan09 1-1		Nov21 1-0	Jan30 3-3	Apr17 1-1	Sep05 6-1	Nov07 2-0	Jan02 3-3	Dec26 2-2	Dec12 1-1	Sep19 3-0	Feb24 1-1	Oct24 2-1	Aug22 0-1
HAMILTON A	Jan30 1-1	Jan02 3-4	Apr17 1-3	Apr03 2-0	Nov28 2-1	Feb13 0-0	Dec12 3-1	Mar13 1-1		Aug22 3-0	Nov14 1-0	Sep19 2-2	Feb24 2-5	Oct17 0-2	Mar06 2-1	Oct31 1-0	Sep05 3-1	Jan09 3-3	Oct03 7-2	Dec19 3-2
HEARTS	Sep21 1-0	Aug29 0-2	Mar03 1-2	Sep12 7-0	Oct10 4-3	Mar27 2-2	Nov07 1-0	Aug15 1-1	Feb10 4-0		Jan01 1-4	Nov28 1-0	Mar13 6-1	Nov14 3-1	Oct24 3-0	Jan09 4-2	Apr03 5-1	Sep26 3-0	Dec12 4-2	Dec26 1-0
HIBERNIAN	Jan02 0-0	Jan30 1-4	Jan16 4-4	Nov21 5-1	Mar06 1-2	Sep05 2-1	Apr10 3-5	Oct31 3-1	Dec05 8-4	Oct17 0-0		Aug22 8-0	Jan13 4-1	Feb13 3-1	Sep19 3-4	Feb20 1-2	Mar20 2-0	Sep21 0-2	Jan04 0-3	Oct03 0-2
KILMARNOCK	Mar17 3-0	Oct10 3-2	Feb10 2-1	Aug29 2-2	Sep26 1-1	Jan16 5-2	Jan02 2-3	Dec19 2-3	Jan04 4-1	Mar20 5-1	Apr24 2-1		Sep12 2-0	Apr10 1-2	Feb13 3-3	Aug15 2-1	Nov21 3-0	Dec05 2-2	Nov07 3-2	Oct17 2-3
MORTON	Dec30 2-0	Apr24 3-2	Oct24 0-5	Mar10 2-2	Dec12 3-4	Nov28 3-0	Jan30 3-1	Feb27 3-1	Mar20 3-1	Sep05 1-1	Feb10 2-5	Jan09 1-2		Sep19 1-1	Aug22 1-1	Nov14 2-0	Oct03 1-0	Apr03 1-3	Oct17 3-1	Jan02 0-0
MOTHERWELL	Oct24 1-1	Sep26 2-1	Mar27 2-1	Aug15 2-1	Feb20 2-1	Mar20 2-0	Feb06 4-0	Oct10 3-0	Jan01 1-0	Dec19 3-1	Sep12 2-1	Feb27 1-2	Jan04 4-1		Apr03 1-0	Aug29 1-0	Nov07 5-0	Nov25 1-3	Jan16 4-1	Dec05 0-1
PARTICK T	Dec12 2-2	Oct31 2-3	Apr05 0-0	Jan01 2-2	Aug15 3-1	Feb23 0-1	Feb27 2-0	Sep12 2-3	Sep26 3-3	Apr24 1-4	Jan09 2-1	Nov14 2-4	Mar27 3-3	Nov28 2-1		Jan30 3-3	Dec19 2-1	Oct10 2-0	Mar20 3-1	Apr13 3-2
QUEEN'S PARK	Sep05 0-1	Nov24 1-5	Jan02 1-4	Mar20 4-1	Feb13 3-4	Dec05 1-3	Oct17 2-1	Apr03 3-1	Jan16 6-2	Sep19 3-4	Oct24 2-0	Mar27 2-2	Apr17 3-1	Dec26 0-3	Oct03 2-1		Aug22 4-0	Nov07 3-6	Feb27 2-0	Feb16 1-0
RAITH R	Nov28 0-1	Sep12 2-1	Nov14 1-2	Feb27 2-0	Jan01 2-1	Oct10 1-0	Aug15 4-2	Mar27 1-4	Apr10 0-2	Jan04 1-3	Sep26 1-0	Dec26 4-5	Jan16 3-0	Dec12 2-1	Aug29 1-1	Apr24 1-2		Oct31 1-0	Feb10 2-2	Mar13 1-3
RANGERS	Mar27 0-1	Feb10 1-2	Oct17 1-0	Jan04 3-1	Nov14 3-0	Oct24 1-2	Apr05 2-1	Nov28 2-3	Apr24 2-0	Jan16 2-2	Dec12 3-1	Oct03 3-0	Aug29 4-1	Aug22 1-0	Jan02 2-1	Mar10 1-2	Feb13 4-2		Dec26 0-1	Sep19 4-1
ST JOHNSTONE	Feb13 1-1	Jan09 3-7	Nov28 0-3	Oct10 3-1	Mar10 1-1	Dec19 0-0	Sep12 0-1	Apr10 2-1	Mar27 1-1	Mar06 1-1	Aug29 0-0	Jan30 0-2	Jan01 1-0	Oct31 2-2	Mar13 2-2	Sep26 1-4	Dec05 3-1	Aug15 0-3		Nov14 1-0
ST MIRREN	Apr24 3-0	Aug15 1-1	Dec12 0-2	Jan16 3-0	Mar27 2-1	Aug29 2-2	Sep26 2-0	Jan04 2-0	Nov07 1-0	Oct31 2-1	Feb27 2-1	Jan01 1-4	Oct10 3-0	Feb23 2-2	Nov21 2-2	Sep12 3-1	Jan30 0-3	Mar23 3-2	Apr03 3-1	

DIVISION 3

	BEITH	BRECHIN C	CLACKMANNAN	DYKEHEAD	FORFAR A	GALSTON	HELENSBURGH	JOHNSTONE	LEITH A	LOCHGELLY U	MID ANNANDALE	MONTROSE	PEEBLES	ROYAL ALBERT	SOLWAY STAR	VALE OF LEVEN
BEITH		Jan01 7-3	Jan09 2-0	Feb27 2-2	Nov07 2-2		Jan30 2-2	Aug29 3-1	Apr21 2-4	Nov21 5-1	Mar27 2-0	Mar13 4-1	Aug15 1-2	Oct17 2-1	Sep12 2-5	Feb20 3-1
BRECHIN C	Apr03 3-0		Aug29 3-1	Jan16 2-3	Feb13 2-0	Jan02 9-2	Mar06 2-2	Dec05 0-1	Apr19 0-4	Nov07 4-0	Aug15 4-2	Apr26 4-1		Mar27 4-2	Apr17 3-2	Sep26 4-5
CLACKMANNAN	Nov14 7-3	Mar13 1-1			Oct03 2-2		Jan23 2-2	Mar27 1-1	Apr24 3-3	Aug22 3-0	Nov28 3-2	Dec05 2-2	Sep12 2-4		Jan01 4-3	Oct24 1-7
DYKEHEAD	Sep26 3-1	Nov28 3-0	Jan30 5-1		Jan02 2-3		Dec19 2-0	Aug15 2-1	Sep12 2-0	Oct24 1-0	Jan09 2-1	Aug29 3-1	Nov07 4-1	Feb13 8-2	Apr10 2-2	Mar20 1-1
FORFAR A		Oct31 3-1	Sep26 5-0	Aug22 2-1		Nov14 1-1	Aug15 3-1	Sep19 4-1	Mar13 3-0	Oct17 1-0	Oct10 3-1	Mar06 2-0	Jan30 5-2	Dec12 3-2	Jan09 4-1	Jan01 6-2
GALSTON	Oct24 3-3	Sep12 6-1		Jan01 2-2			Oct31 0-3	Jan09 8-2			Dec12 2-0		Nov28 1-2	Aug22 1-5		
HELENSBURGH	Oct10 2-1	Nov14 4-3	Nov07 2-0	Feb20 0-1	Feb27 3-0	Dec05 6-0		Sep12 4-1	Mar20 3-2	Mar13 1-1	Feb13 1-1	Apr17 5-1	Aug22 1-0	Jan09 5-1	Sep26 1-1	Jan16 1-5
JOHNSTONE	Oct03 3-0	Apr10 2-3	Oct17 2-2	Dec12 1-3	Sep05 4-0		Nov28 2-4		Aug22 2-2	Jan02 2-2	Oct24 6-2	Mar20 1-1	Mar13 3-1	Jan30 1-1	Feb20 3-2	Oct10 3-4
LEITH A	Mar06 4-0	Dec12 0-2	Oct10 4-0	Apr14 3-0	Oct24 2-1	Aug29 3-5	Nov21 5-3	Apr17 4-1		Jan30 2-2	Apr10 4-0	Aug15 6-1	Jan09 2-0	Sep26 2-0	Mar27 2-0	Feb13 2-1
LOCHGELLY U	Jan16 5-2	Jan09 7-2	Dec12 5-0	Feb06 4-4	Mar20 1-0	Aug15 2-2	Aug29 1-2	Sep26 2-1	Apr03 2-2		Mar06 0-1	Mar27 3-3	Oct10 5-3	Feb20 6-0	Apr24 1-1	Nov28 1-0
MID ANNANDALE	Oct31 4-0	Mar20 1-1	Feb06 5-2	Oct17 4-1	Dec19 2-1		Jan01 1-0	Jan16 3-2	Feb27 3-1	Sep12 0-3		Nov14 1-0	Dec26 3-1	Mar13 2-0	Aug22 1-3	Dec05 3-1
MONTROSE	Dec12 4-3	Aug22 5-2	Feb13 2-1	Apr24 4-1	Sep12 0-2		Jan02 1-2	Feb27 4-1	Feb20 1-0	Jan01 2-1	Jan30 4-0		Sep26 5-3	Apr03 4-0	Nov21 4-2	
PEEBLES	Jan02 0-4	Oct24 3-0		Mar27 3-1	Apr10 2-1		Apr03 2-3	Feb13 2-1	Jan01 0-6	Oct31 5-0	Nov21 2-4			Apr17 1-4	Oct17 5-0	Aug29 2-4
ROYAL ALBERT		Feb27 6-1	Aug15 7-1	Oct10 2-1	Nov21 5-2	Nov07 5-4	Feb06 3-1	Jan01 2-0	Jan04 2-0	Dec05 5-0	Aug29 3-0	Apr16 3-0	Mar20 5-3		Jan16 4-1	Sep12 3-1
SOLWAY STAR	Mar20 2-1	Jan30 0-3	Dec26 0-0	Mar13 2-1	Aug29 2-1	Oct10 2-1	Dec12 0-2	Apr03 2-3	Nov28 0-0	Feb13 1-1	Jan02 0-1	Sep05 1-2	Mar06 7-1	Oct24 5-2		Aug15 1-6
VALE OF LEVEN	Aug22 3-1		Oct31 2-3	Nov21 2-1	Mar27 0-1		Oct17 3-0	Feb06 6-3	Sep19 2-4	Dec19 8-2	Apr03 2-2	Jan09 5-3	Dec12 4-2	Nov14 2-0	Feb27 1-2	

DIVISION 2

	ALBION R	ALLOA	ARBROATH	ARMADALE	ARTHURLIE	AYR U	BATHGATE	BO'NESS	BROXBURN U	CLYDE	DUMBARTON	DUNFERMLINE A	EAST FIFE	E STIRLING	KING'S PARK	NITHSDALE W	QUEEN OF SOUTH	ST BERNARD'S	STENHOUSEMUIR	T LANARK
ALBION R		Mar27 1-2	Aug15 2-0	Jan25 0-1	Feb27 3-2	Aug29 0-0	Mar13 3-2	Dec19 2-0	Dec12 5-2	Jan09 1-3	Jan30 11-1	Jan02 1-0	Sep12 2-0	Apr10 3-1	Oct10 4-1	Feb17 3-0	Oct31 3-4	Sep26 2-4	Oct17 4-4	Apr14 0-0
ALLOA	Nov07 1-2		Sep26 2-2	Feb27 4-0	Aug29 1-2	Feb09 0-1	Feb13 4-2	Jan30 6-0	Oct05 0-3	Oct13 0-0	Dec12 0-2	Oct17 1-1	Dec26 2-1	Mar20 1-0	Jan02 0-1	Sep12 2-4	Jan09 2-3	Apr10 3-3	Mar06 1-2	Nov21 2-1
ARBROATH	Feb24 4-2	Apr17 2-3		Mar27 2-2	Nov21 4-3	Jan02 1-3	Dec05 4-0	Mar13 4-1	Mar06 5-1	Apr10 0-1	Sep19 6-0	Oct03 5-0	Aug29 2-4	Nov07 2-1	Jan09 0-1	Dec23 4-1	Sep12 5-2	Nov14 4-1	Jan30 3-0	Oct24 2-1
ARMADALE	Apr03 3-1	Dec05 1-2	Dec12 3-0		Aug15 2-2	Mar13 1-0	Jan01 5-1	Sep26 1-3	Nov07 4-3	Jan30 1-3	Oct31 6-2	Dec19 0-5	Oct10 4-5	Feb19 2-2	Sep12 4-1	Aug29 2-4	Oct17 4-3	Jan09 5-1	Apr17 3-1	Feb13 3-0
ARTHURLIE	Sep05 4-2	Mar13 3-1	Apr03 3-1	Dec26 7-4		Dec05 2-2	Oct17 2-1	Nov14 3-0	Sep19 4-0	Dec19 1-0	Jan02 1-2	Jan09 2-6	Nov28 5-0	Oct03 4-1	Apr17 1-0	Feb13 6-6	Jan30 2-0	Nov07 2-3	Oct24 1-2	Aug22 1-2
AYR U	Jan01 2-2	Aug15 2-1	Aug22 5-0	Sep05 2-0	Mar06 1-0		Apr17 4-1	Feb20 4-0	Oct03 4-1	Feb24 1-0	Dec26 1-2	Nov14 2-2	Oct31 0-0	Jan09 5-0	Oct24 0-2	Nov28 6-1	Mar27 3-0	Jan30 2-0	Dec12 1-1	Sep19 0-0
BATHGATE	Sep19 3-1	Sep05 3-1	Mar03 4-0	Aug22 3-1	Jan04 1-3	Nov21 2-1		Feb24 0-4	Jan16 2-2	Mar20 3-7	Mar27 5-0	Apr10 2-4	Apr05 1-1	Jan13 1-1	Nov28 1-2	Oct24 1-1	Nov14 1-2	Mar06 1-3	Jan02 1-4	Oct03 2-1
BO'NESS	Oct24 4-1	Oct03 0-0	Sep05 1-3	Mar20 2-1	Apr10 1-0	Jan04 1-3	Nov07 4-0		Jan01 2-0	Nov21 4-3	Feb27 1-0	Aug22 3-1	Dec12 1-2	Apr17 0-4	Mar27 3-1	Jan16 4-1	Nov28 5-0	Dec26 6-3	Sep19 3-1	Feb17 1-1
BROXBURN U	Feb13 4-3	Feb03 0-5	Oct31 1-2	Apr24 3-4	Mar20 1-2	Feb27 3-3	Sep26 1-1	Aug29 3-2		Sep12 1-1	Nov14 1-1	Jan30 0-2	Mar27 1-2	Oct17 6-5	Aug15 0-1	Oct10 0-2	Apr17 2-2	Jan02 4-7	Jan09 1-2	Dec05 0-1
CLYDE	Aug22 1-0	Jan16 1-0	Nov28 2-1	Oct03 4-1	Mar27 2-1	Oct17 0-2	Dec12 3-1	Jan02 4-0	Feb17 3-2		Apr17 6-0	Feb27 0-1	Mar13 1-3	Sep19 7-1	Nov14 3-1	Nov07 2-0	Dec26 5-0	Oct24 4-2	Feb13 2-1	Dec25 1-0
DUMBARTON	Dec05 0-1	Apr24 0-0	Jan01 1-0	Feb17 2-0	Sep12 0-0	Sep26 1-1	Oct10 4-1	Aug15 3-0	Feb24 5-1	Aug29 1-1		Mar10 1-3	Jan16 2-1	Oct24 3-0	Dec19 4-1	Jan04 2-2	Apr03 1-1	Mar20 1-0	Nov21 1-1	Nov07 1-1
DUNFERMLINE A	Apr17 1-1	Jan01 5-0	Dec26 3-0	Oct24 7-1	Oct10 0-0	Mar20 2-1	Sep12 4-0	Apr03 4-1	Nov21 6-1	Sep26 5-0	Nov28 1-0		Sep17 5-3	Feb13 2-1	Feb20 6-2	Aug15 4-1	Dec12 4-0	Aug29 3-0	Nov07 1-1	Jan16 1-1
EAST FIFE	Mar06 1-3	Oct24 1-0	Mar20 4-0	Apr10 4-1	Feb20 7-1	Feb13 2-2	Dec19 7-3	Jan09 4-1	Sep05 2-1	Dec05 1-1	Oct17 6-1	Sep19 3-3		Jan30 3-1	Nov07 4-3	Apr24 4-2	Oct03 1-0	Nov21 4-0	Aug22 1-1	Jan02 3-1
E STIRLING	Nov28 0-1	Oct31 1-1	Jan16 2-1	Nov14 2-3	Feb17 3-1	Oct10 2-4	Aug15 2-2	Sep12 0-2	Apr03 8-2	Jan04 1-3	Mar13 3-1	Dec05 1-5	Sep26 2-1		Aug29 0-0	Mar06 3-2	Jan02 4-2	Apr24 2-0	Dec19 0-3	Mar27 2-1
KING'S PARK	Dec26 1-2	Sep19 2-0	Oct17 2-3	Mar06 2-2	Oct31 1-3	Jan16 0-0	Apr03 4-2	Feb13 1-3	Jan04 7-1	Apr24 4-3	Aug22 1-1	Sep05 2-0	Feb27 7-3	Jan01 0-0		Nov21 2-2	Dec05 0-0	Dec12 2-0	Oct03 0-0	Mar20 3-3
NITHSDALE W	Oct03 3-0	Feb20 0-3	Feb27 2-3	Jan02 4-2	Dec12 3-1	Feb06 1-3	Jan09 2-1	Oct31 0-0	Dec26 4-0	Apr03 0-2	Sep05 5-1	Mar13 0-1	Nov14 3-3	Aug22 3-1	Jan30 2-5		Sep19 3-2	Dec05 2-1	Mar20 5-1	Oct17 1-0
QUEEN OF SOUTH	Mar20 3-3	Aug22 4-0	Jan04 2-2	Jan16 2-2	Sep26 2-0	Nov07 1-3	Feb27 4-2	Mar06 1-1	Oct24 2-1	Aug15 3-4	Feb13 1-3	Apr24 1-2	Feb06 3-4	Nov21 3-0	Apr10 4-1	Jan01 0-3		Oct10 2-0	Sep05 2-2	Dec19 0-2
ST BERNARD'S	Jan04 3-1	Nov28 2-1	Feb13 0-0	Sep19 6-2	Jan16 5-3	Feb13 1-2	Oct31 4-0	Oct17 1-1	Aug22 8-0	Jan01 1-2	Oct03 3-2	Feb06 1-4	Apr17 2-2	Sep05 6-1	Mar13 4-0	Mar27 1-1	Feb20 4-1		Apr03 0-2	Feb27 3-2
STENHOUSEMUIR	Jan16 3-0	Nov14 1-1	Oct10 3-1	Jan04 3-1	Apr24 2-3	Sep12 5-0	Aug29 1-0	Dec05 2-1	Nov28 6-2	Oct31 1-1	Apr10 4-0	Mar27 1-3	Jan01 1-1	Feb27 2-0	Feb10 1-2	Sep26 3-0	Mar13 3-2	Aug15 2-1		Dec26 1-0
T LANARK	Nov14 3-2	Jan04 4-1	Apr24 4-2	Nov28 3-0	Jan01 3-0	Apr03 1-1	Jan30 4-3	Oct10 2-0	Mar13 2-0	Mar17 4-1	Jan09 1-2	Oct31 3-2	Aug15 4-0	Dec12 1-1	Sep26 4-1	Apr09 3-2	Aug29 1-0	Sep12 4-2	Feb24 3-0	

DIVISION 1

	P	W	D	L	F	A	W	D	L	F	A	Pts
Celtic	38	15	4	0	59	15	10	4	5	38	25	58
Airdrie	38	13	3	3	53	22	10	1	8	42	32	50
Hearts	38	14	2	3	52	21	7	6	6	35	35	50
St Mirren	38	12	4	3	37	23	8	3	8	25	29	47
Motherwell	38	15	1	3	41	15	4	7	8	26	31	46
Rangers	38	12	1	6	39	21	7	5	7	40	34	44
Cowdenbeath	38	14	3	2	54	20	4	3	12	33	48	42
Falkirk	38	8	10	1	35	21	6	4	9	26	36	42
Kilmarnock	38	11	4	4	49	30	6	3	10	30	47	41
Dundee	38	9	4	6	29	27	5	5	9	18	32	37
Aberdeen	38	10	4	5	35	23	3	6	10	14	31	36
Hamilton A	38	10	5	4	40	29	3	4	12	28	50	35
Queen's Park	38	10	1	8	43	39	5	3	11	27	42	34
Partick T	38	8	6	5	39	35	2	7	10	25	38	33
Morton	38	9	5	5	35	30	3	2	14	22	54	31
Hibernian	38	8	3	8	48	37	4	3	12	24	40	30
Dundee U	38	7	4	8	31	27	4	2	13	21	47	28
St Johnstone	38	5	8	6	22	31	4	2	13	21	47	28
Raith R	38	9	2	8	30	30	2	2	15	16	51	26
Clydebank	38	7	3	9	37	33	0	5	14	18	59	22

DIVISION 2

	P	W	D	L	F	A	W	D	L	F	A	Pts
Dunfermline A	38	15	4	0	64	14	11	3	5	45	29	59
Clyde	38	16	0	3	51	17	8	5	6	36	33	53
Ayr U	38	12	5	2	45	13	8	7	4	32	26	52
East Fife	38	14	4	1	62	25	6	5	8	36	48	49
Stenhousemuir	38	13	3	3	45	19	6	7	6	29	33	48
T. Lanark	38	16	2	1	54	20	3	6	10	18	27	46
Arthurlie	38	12	2	5	54	33	5	3	11	27	42	39
Bo'ness	38	13	2	4	46	25	4	3	12	20	45	39
Albion R	38	11	3	5	50	27	5	3	11	28	44	38
Arbroath	38	13	1	5	59	27	4	3	12	21	46	38
Dumbarton	38	9	8	2	33	15	5	2	12	21	63	38
Nithsdale W	38	11	2	6	43	30	4	5	10	35	52	37
King's Park	38	7	8	4	41	28	7	1	11	26	45	37
St Bernard's	38	11	4	4	55	27	4	1	14	31	55	35
Armadale	38	11	2	6	54	39	3	3	13	28	62	33
Alloa	38	6	4	9	32	30	5	4	10	22	33	30
Queen of South	38	7	5	7	40	35	3	3	13	24	53	28
E. Stirling	38	9	3	7	38	35	1	4	14	21	54	27
Bathgate	38	7	4	8	37	39	0	2	17	23	66	20
Broxburn U	38	3	5	11	32	48	1	1	17	23	79	*14

*Broxburn U left the League.

DIVISION 3

	P	W	D	L	F	A	W	D	L	F	A	Pts
Helensburgh	30	10	2.5	2	39	18	6	2.5	6	27	29	38
Leith A	29	12	0.5	2	45	16	4	4	6	28	25	37
Forfar A	28	13	1	0	45	13	3	2	9	16	29	35
Dykehead	28	11	1.5	1	40	14	3	3	8	22	33	33
Royal Albert	28	14	0	0	55	15	2	1	11	20	46	33
Mid Annandale	29	11	1	2	33	16	3	1.5	10	17	38	31
Vale of Leven	26	8	1	4	40	24	6	1	6	38	31	30
Montrose	26	11	0	2	40	18	1	3	9	16	40	27
Lochgelly U	29	8	4.5	2	45	23	1	4	9	13	40	27
Brechin C	28	9	1	4	44	25	3	2	9	23	48	27
Solway Star	29	6	2.5	6	25	25	3	3	8	25	37	24
Beith	27	8	3	3	39	25	1	1	11	19	43	22
Johnstone	29	5	4.5	4	35	27	2	0.5	12	20	47	20
Peebles	26	6	0	6	27	28	3	0	11	25	48	18
Clackmannan	25	4	6	2	31	30	1	2	10	11	44	18
Galston	15	3	2	3	23	18	1	2	4	15	28	12

Scottish Football League Records Season 1926-27

DIVISION 1

	ABERDEEN	AIRDRIE	CELTIC	CLYDE	COWDENBEATH	DUNDEE	DUNDEE U	DUNFERMLINE A	FALKIRK	HAMILTON A	HEARTS	HIBERNIAN	KILMARNOCK	MORTON	MOTHERWELL	PARTICK T	QUEEN'S PARK	RANGERS	ST JOHNSTONE	ST MIRREN
ABERDEEN		Apr16 1-1	Mar09 0-0	Aug21 5-2	Dec25 0-0	Oct30 2-1	Mar26 2-2	Dec11 3-1	Jan15 3-0	Oct02 3-3	Nov20 6-5	Jan03 2-5	Sep27 5-1	Sep18 6-1	Apr30 2-0	Nov06 1-4	Sep04 2-0	Feb16 2-2	Oct16 3-1	Nov27 1-0
AIRDRIE	Dec04 2-1		Nov06 2-2	Dec25 1-1	Sep18 5-2	Jan15 3-1	Mar09 7-2	Apr09 6-2	Oct30 2-1	Jan03 7-1	Apr23 0-0	Sep04 3-0	Oct02 2-0	Feb09 4-0	Oct16 1-3	Mar30 3-1	Feb19 5-0	Aug21 3-3	Dec18 6-1	Nov20 2-2
CELTIC	Oct23 6-2	Mar16 2-1		Jan15 7-0	Aug21 2-0	Oct02 0-0	Nov27 7-2	Apr02 2-1	Feb23 3-1	Sep18 2-2	Nov13 1-0	Feb02 2-3	Dec25 4-0	Sep04 3-0	Apr20 3-2	Apr30 2-1	Jan03 2-3	Apr18 0-1	Dec11 4-0	Feb26 6-2
CLYDE	Mar12 5-1	Aug14 2-1	Sep11 2-2		Mar26 0-2	Dec04 2-2	Jan29 1-0	Feb12 1-1	Oct16 2-1	Apr23 0-0	Oct09 2-3	Mar05 2-0	Nov20 1-1	Dec18 6-0	Jan08 1-4	Jan01 0-5	Nov06 5-0	Apr09 0-0	Aug28 1-1	Sep25 1-2
COWDENBEATH	Aug14 0-0	Jan29 6-0	Mar12 2-1	Nov13 1-0		Feb26 0-1	Sep11 4-1	Jan01 1-2	Dec04 3-2	Oct23 5-1	Aug28 2-1	Apr30 2-0	Dec11 3-1	Apr02 3-2	Sep25 1-1	Oct09 1-2	Apr09 1-1	Mar23 1-0	Feb12 0-1	Jan08 5-1
DUNDEE	Jan01 1-1	Sep11 1-0	Feb12 1-2	Apr16 1-2	Oct16 1-2		Aug28 5-0	Sep25 1-1	Mar16 2-3	Apr02 1-0	Aug14 4-1	Nov06 3-0	Mar26 1-2	Nov27 6-1	Jan29 3-1	Jan08 4-2	Apr30 3-0	Dec11 1-1	Mar12 4-1	Oct09 2-1
DUNDEE U	Nov13 2-2	Oct23 2-4	Apr09 3-3	Sep18 3-1	Jan15 0-2	Jan03 1-0		Feb26 4-4	Feb09 0-2	Mar02 1-2	Dec04 5-3	Aug21 0-2	Sep04 1-2	Oct30 0-0	Nov20 0-1	Apr23 2-1	Oct02 2-2	Dec25 2-0	Mar19 1-2	Dec18 2-1
DUNFERMLINE A	Apr23 1-0	Nov27 0-2	Nov20 0-6	Oct02 3-1	Oct30 0-3	Feb16 4-3	Oct16 2-0		Sep04 0-1	Aug21 0-1	Dec18 0-2	Sep18 4-2	Jan03 2-3	Dec25 1-1	Nov06 0-4	Mar09 1-1	Jan15 3-3	Feb23 1-3	Apr16 4-0	Mar26 3-1
FALKIRK	Sep11 1-1	Jan01 2-1	Apr06 4-1	Feb26 3-3	Apr16 2-2	Oct23 3-1	Sep25 5-3	Oct09 2-0		Dec18 8-2	Feb12 2-1	Nov27 2-0	Mar19 0-1	Nov13 6-1	Aug28 1-1	Aug14 1-1	Dec11 6-0	Apr02 3-3	Jan29 4-0	Mar12 1-1
HAMILTON A	Feb12 2-0	Aug28 4-2	Feb16 3-3	Dec11 4-2	Mar05 4-2	Nov20 1-4	Oct09 1-1	Mar12 2-2	Apr30 3-1		Jan08 2-1	Oct16 0-1	Apr09 2-0	Nov06 1-1	Jan01 0-3	Sep11 0-2	Mar26 1-5	Apr16 1-1	Sep25 1-4	Aug14 2-3
HEARTS	Apr02 2-2	Dec11 1-3	Mar30 3-0	Feb23 5-0	Jan03 4-3	Dec25 0-0	Apr16 1-2	Apr30 1-2	Oct02 0-0	Sep04 1-1		Oct30 2-2	Feb19 1-1	Jan15 3-0	Feb05 1-3	Oct16 1-0	Aug21 4-1	Sep18 0-2	Nov27 0-0	Nov06 4-3
HIBERNIAN	Aug28 2-3	Jan08 2-1	Sep25 3-2	Oct23 3-0	Dec18 2-0	Mar19 0-1	Mar12 3-2	Jan29 2-2	Apr09 1-0	Feb26 3-1	Jan01 2-2		Dec04 5-1	Apr23 1-1	Oct09 1-1	Feb12 3-2	Nov20 2-0	Nov13 2-2	Aug14 1-5	Sep11 2-1
KILMARNOCK	Oct09 0-0	Feb12 4-2	Aug14 2-3	Apr02 4-1	Apr23 1-4	Nov13 3-2	Jan08 3-0	Aug28 2-3	Nov06 1-1	Nov27 0-1	Sep25 1-4	Apr20 4-0		Oct16 2-0	Mar12 1-4	Jan29 2-0	Mar05 2-2	Dec18 0-0	Sep11 2-0	Jan01 2-2
MORTON	Jan29 3-4	Sep25 2-1	Jan08 2-6	Apr30 0-2	Nov20 3-2	Apr09 3-1	Jan01 3-1	Aug14 3-0	Mar30 4-1	Mar19 3-0	Sep11 1-3	Dec11 3-0	Feb26 3-2		Feb12 0-3	Mar12 3-0	Dec04 2-0	Oct23 2-8	Oct09 0-2	Aug28 0-2
MOTHERWELL	Dec18 1-0	Feb26 1-5	Dec04 0-1	Sep04 2-0	Feb09 0-0	Sep18 2-5	Apr02 6-0	Mar19 2-1	Jan03 3-3	Oct30 3-1	Oct23 5-1	Feb19 2-1	Aug21 1-0	Oct02 6-0		Nov27 3-1	Dec25 2-1	Jan15 1-4	Nov13 5-2	Apr23 1-0
PARTICK T	Mar19 4-0	Nov13 5-1	Dec18 0-3	Oct30 3-0	Feb23 5-3	Sep04 3-3	Dec11 2-2	Oct23 5-1	Dec25 0-1	Jan15 2-3	Feb26 2-2	Oct02 5-1	Sep18 5-0	Aug21 4-5	Apr09 3-0		Feb08 1-7	Jan03 1-4	Apr02 3-1	Dec04 5-2
QUEEN'S PARK	Jan08 1-1	Oct13 3-3	Aug28 1-6	Mar19 4-0	Nov27 3-1	Apr18 1-4	Feb12 5-3	Sep11 4-1	Apr23 1-2	Nov13 4-0	Mar12 2-0	Apr05 3-4	Oct23 1-0	Apr20 2-1	Aug14 1-2	Sep25 4-3		Mar01 1-2	Jan01 5-2	Jan29 1-0
RANGERS	Sep25 3-2	Mar12 1-1	Jan01 2-1	Nov27 6-0	Nov06 4-1	Apr23 0-0	Aug14 2-0	Aug17 2-0	Nov20 2-1	Dec04 1-4	Jan29 1-0	Mar29 2-0	Apr30 1-0	Mar16 2-1	Sep11 2-0	Aug28 2-1	Oct16 0-1		Jan08 4-2	Feb12 4-0
ST JOHNSTONE	Feb26 1-1	Apr30 1-1	Apr23 1-0	Jan03 1-3	Oct02 1-3	Aug21 0-1	Nov06 4-1	Dec04 1-0	Sep18 4-0	Feb09 3-2	Apr09 1-1	Dec25 0-0	Jan15 3-3	Feb19 4-0	Mar26 0-1	Nov20 1-1	Oct30 1-0	Sep04 2-1		Oct23 0-0
ST MIRREN	Apr09 6-3	Apr02 1-3	Oct16 3-1	Feb08 3-2	Sep04 5-1	Feb22 2-2	Apr30 4-3	Nov13 4-0	Aug21 3-0	Dec25 0-1	Mar19 0-1	Jan15 3-1	Oct30 1-0	Jan03 3-1	Dec11 5-1	Apr16 1-3	Sep18 5-1	Oct02 3-7	Mar05 2-1	

DIVISION 2

	ALBION R	ALLOA	ARBROATH	ARMADALE	ARTHURLIE	AYR U	BATHGATE	BO'NESS	CLYDEBANK	DUMBARTON	EAST FIFE	E STIRLING	FORFAR A	KING'S PARK	NITHSDALE W	QUEEN OF SOUTH	RAITH R	ST BERNARD'S	STENHOUSEMUIR	T LANARK
ALBION R		Jan08 1-1	Mar19 2-2	Sep11 1-3	Oct23 3-0	Jan01 5-1	Dec11 1-0	Mar12 1-0	Nov13 2-3	Aug14 4-0	Nov27 4-2	Oct09 2-2	Aug28 1-1	Apr30 6-1	Apr02 2-2	Jan29 3-2	Feb26 1-1	Apr16 2-1	Sep25 1-3	Feb12 0-1
ALLOA	Sep04 4-3		Jan15 3-1	Nov13 2-0	Sep18 1-2	Nov27 1-3	Feb15 2-3	Mar01 0-1	Oct02 0-2	Dec04 1-1	Dec25 1-0	Oct23 1-1	Apr23 2-0	Jan03 2-2	Oct16 5-2	Nov06 3-2	Dec18 3-2	Aug21 2-3	Apr02 1-0	Mar12 2-2
ARBROATH	Nov06 1-2	Sep11 1-1		Jan08 4-3	Mar12 3-0	Jan29 1-1	Mar26 3-1	Dec18 0-0	Oct23 2-3	Oct09 1-3	Nov20 2-0	Aug14 5-0	Jan01 0-3	Apr16 3-0	Dec11 2-0	Feb12 1-0	Aug28 1-3	Apr09 1-2	Feb26 2-1	Sep25 1-0
ARMADALE	Jan15 1-1	Mar26 2-6	Sep04 3-1		Mar02 2-2	Nov20 4-1	Aug21 2-0	Dec25 1-2	Sep18 3-3	Nov06 3-4	Oct16 5-1	Mar12 1-1	Apr09 1-1	Oct02 4-0	Jan03 5-1	Apr30 2-1	Oct23 2-0	Feb09 2-2	Dec11 3-1	Apr16 2-1
ARTHURLIE	Mar08 1-4	Jan29 4-0	Oct30 4-1	Oct09 2-0		Jan08 0-0	Apr30 4-0	Apr02 1-1	Nov27 3-1	Sep11 2-1	Apr19 4-0	Sep25 0-1	Aug14 3-1	Mar19 4-3	Nov13 7-1	Feb26 2-4	Feb12 3-2	Dec11 3-2	Aug28 7-2	Jan01 2-3
AYR U	Aug21 3-0	Apr09 3-2	Sep18 3-1	Apr02 1-1	Sep04 1-1		Dec25 2-2	Oct02 2-1	Jan15 0-0	Apr30 0-5	Jan03 1-1	Nov13 3-2	Nov06 2-0	Feb09 5-2	Feb19 4-0	Dec04 1-2	Dec11 2-1	Oct16 1-1	Mar12 0-2	Oct23 1-1
BATHGATE	Apr23 1-0	Sep25 3-3	Nov13 5-5	Jan01 2-1	Dec18 5-2	Aug14 4-2		Mar19 2-3	Apr02 2-2	Aug28 2-1	Mar09 5-3	Feb12 0-2	Feb26 4-3	Nov27 2-1	Apr16 3-0	Jan08 8-3	Sep11 1-3	Oct30 2-1	Oct09 2-2	Jan29 0-5
BO'NESS	Oct30 5-3	Oct09 1-1	Apr30 1-1	Aug14 4-2	Nov20 2-1	Feb12 1-1	Nov06 7-0		Apr16 3-2	Jan29 3-1	Dec11 3-2	Feb26 3-1	Jan08 6-0	Mar09 1-1	Nov27 3-0	Aug28 3-0	Sep25 2-0	Mar26 2-1	Jan01 1-1	Sep11 2-0
CLYDEBANK	Mar26 3-1	Feb12 5-1	Mar05 6-1	Jan29 4-1	Apr09 5-2	Sep11 1-1	Nov20 5-1	Dec04 0-2		Dec31 6-2	Oct30 2-4	Aug28 1-4	Sep25 2-2	Apr23 2-1	Dec18 4-1	Aug14 1-1	Oct09 2-0	Nov06 4-1	Jan08 4-1	Feb26 2-2
DUMBARTON	Dec25 3-0	Apr16 3-1	Feb19 1-0	Mar19 2-0	Jan15 4-1	Dec18 3-5	Jan03 1-1	Sep18 1-0	Aug21 1-1		Sep04 1-3	Nov27 3-2	Mar12 1-3	Oct16 0-1	Feb16 6-2	Apr23 0-3	Apr02 1-3	Oct02 3-0	Oct23 2-1	Nov13 1-1
EAST FIFE	Apr09 8-2	Aug14 4-1	Apr02 4-1	Feb26 3-2	Dec04 7-1	Aug28 4-3	Oct23 5-4	Apr23 2-1	Mar12 3-2	Jan08 5-3		Sep11 3-3	Jan29 4-2	Nov13 5-2	Mar19 5-3	Sep25 2-0	Jan01 0-1	Dec18 3-2	Feb12 6-0	Oct09 3-0
E STIRLING	Feb19 4-4	Mar05 5-2	Dec25 3-1	Oct30 1-1	Feb09 4-5	Mar26 2-0	Oct02 1-0	Oct16 2-3	Jan03 4-1	Apr09 3-2	Jan15 4-2		Apr30 5-2	Aug21 2-2	Sep04 7-2	Nov20 2-1	Dec04 3-0	Sep18 5-2	Nov06 3-0	Apr23 1-1
FORFAR A	Jan03 1-0	Dec11 3-2	Aug21 2-0	Nov27 4-3	Dec25 1-3	Mar19 2-2	Oct16 1-2	Sep04 1-3	Apr07 5-4	Oct30 4-2	Sep18 3-1	Dec18 3-2		Jan15 3-2	Oct02 2-0	Mar05 2-0	Nov13 2-2	Feb19 1-0	Apr16 1-1	Apr02 0-1
KING'S PARK	Dec18 4-1	Aug28 3-2	Dec04 2-1	Feb12 1-1	Nov06 2-4	Sep25 1-1	Apr09 4-1	Oct23 1-3	Dec11 4-1	Feb26 2-0	Mar30 5-0	Jan01 3-0	Sep11 2-2		Mar12 2-2	Oct09 2-2	Aug14 3-2	Nov20 5-0	Jan29 5-0	Jan08 2-0
NITHSDALE W	Nov20 2-2	Feb26 0-3	Apr23 2-3	Aug28 2-2	Mar26 3-1	Oct09 2-2	Dec04 2-0	Apr09 1-1	Apr30 3-4	Sep25 3-0	Nov06 3-1	Jan08 1-2	Feb12 2-0	Oct30 3-3		Aug21 1-1	Jan29 2-4	Mar05 2-3	Sep11 2-2	Aug14 2-1
QUEEN OF SOUTH	Sep18 5-3	Mar19 1-0	Oct02 7-4	Dec18 6-0	Oct16 4-1	Feb05 1-2	Sep04 2-1	Jan03 0-2	Dec25 2-3	Dec11 3-2	Mar17 3-0	Apr02 1-4	Oct23 2-1	Feb19 3-2	Jan01 2-1		Mar12 1-1	Jan15 1-0	Nov13 2-0	Nov27 1-2
RAITH R	Oct16 7-1	Apr30 2-3	Jan03 4-2	Mar05 3-0	Oct02 1-2	Apr23 3-1	Jan15 1-0	Apr04 3-3	Feb19 0-0	Nov20 4-2	Aug21 4-2	Apr16 6-3	Mar26 5-0	Dec25 2-0	Sep18 1-0	Oct30 7-2		Sep04 5-1	Nov27 4-0	Nov06 3-0
ST BERNARD'S	Dec04 4-1	Jan01 3-3	Nov27 1-2	Sep25 1-2	Apr23 3-2	Feb26 2-4	Mar12 6-3	Nov13 2-5	Mar19 4-1	Feb12 1-1	Apr30 2-1	Jan29 2-0	Oct09 3-0	Apr02 3-0	Oct23 1-0	Sep11 4-1	Jan08 1-2		Aug14 3-3	Aug28 2-0
STENHOUSEMUIR	Feb05 1-1	Nov20 2-2	Oct16 1-3	Apr23 4-0	Jan03 3-3	Oct30 1-1	Feb19 5-2	Aug21 2-1	Sep04 4-0	Mar05 7-0	Oct02 3-3	Mar19 3-1	Dec04 2-1	Sep18 1-0	Jan15 3-4	Mar26 3-0	Apr09 0-0	Dec25 0-0		Dec18 3-1
T LANARK	Oct02 3-3	Nov02 1-0	Feb05 6-0	Dec04 2-0	Aug21 2-1	Mar05 5-1	Sep18 2-2	Jan15 1-1	Oct16 1-2	Mar26 2-2	Feb22 3-1	Dec11 3-1	Nov20 2-3	Sep04 1-0	Dec25 1-0	Apr09 4-0	Mar19 0-0	Jan03 2-0	Apr30 4-1	

LEAGUE TABLES

DIVISION 1

	P	W	D	L	F	A	W	D	L	F	A	Pts
Rangers	38	15	2	2	41	15	8	8	3	44	26	56
Motherwell	38	13	2	4	46	26	10	3	6	35	26	51
Celtic	38	14	2	3	58	21	7	5	7	43	34	49
Airdrie	38	13	5	1	64	23	5	4	10	33	41	45
Dundee	38	11	3	5	45	21	6	6	7	32	30	43
Falkirk	38	11	7	1	56	23	5	3	11	21	37	42
Cowdenbeath	38	12	3	4	41	18	6	3	10	33	42	42
Aberdeen	38	11	6	2	49	29	2	8	9	24	43	40
Hibernian	38	11	5	3	40	27	5	2	12	22	44	39
St Mirren	38	13	1	5	54	32	3	4	12	24	44	37
Partick T	38	10	3	6	58	39	5	3	11	31	35	36
Queen's Park	38	11	2	6	47	35	4	4	11	27	49	36
Hearts	38	7	7	5	34	25	5	4	10	31	39	35
St Johnstone	38	8	7	4	29	19	5	2	12	26	50	35
Hamilton A	38	7	5	7	34	38	6	4	9	26	47	35
Kilmarnock	38	8	5	6	36	29	4	3	12	18	42	32
Clyde	38	7	7	5	34	26	3	2	14	20	59	29
Dunfermline A	38	7	3	9	29	37	3	5	11	24	48	28
Morton	38	11	0	8	40	38	1	4	14	16	63	28
Dundee U	38	6	5	8	31	34	1	3	15	25	67	22

DIVISION 2

	P	W	D	L	F	A	W	D	L	F	A	Pts
Bo'ness	38	14	5	0	53	18	9	5	5	33	23	56
Raith R	38	15	2	2	65	22	6	5	8	27	30	49
Clydebank	38	12	4	3	59	29	6	5	8	35	46	45
T. Lanark	38	12	5	2	45	18	5	5	9	22	30	44
E. Stirling	38	13	4	2	61	31	5	4	10	32	44	44
East Fife	38	17	1	1	76	33	2	2	15	27	58	41
Arthurlie	38	13	2	4	56	27	5	3	11	34	56	41
Ayr U	38	9	7	3	35	25	4	8	7	32	43	41
Forfar A	38	12	3	4	41	30	3	4	12	25	49	37
Stenhousemuir	38	10	7	2	48	23	2	5	12	21	53	36
Queen of South	38	13	1	5	47	29	3	3	13	25	51	36
King's Park	38	12	5	2	53	23	1	4	14	23	52	35
St Bernard's	38	11	3	5	48	31	3	3	13	22	46	34
Alloa	38	9	4	6	36	30	3	6	10	34	47	34
Armadale	38	10	6	3	48	29	2	4	13	22	49	34
Albion R	38	9	6	4	42	26	2	5	12	32	61	33
Bathgate	38	11	4	4	53	42	2	3	14	23	56	33
Dumbarton	38	10	3	6	37	28	3	3	13	32	56	32
Arbroath	38	10	3	6	34	23	3	3	13	30	60	32
Nithsdale W	38	6	7	6	38	35	1	2	16	21	65	23

Nithsdale W left the League, were replaced by Leith A.

Scottish Football League Records
Season 1927-28

DIVISION 1

	ABERDEEN	AIRDRIE	BO'NESS	CELTIC	CLYDE	COWDENBEATH	DUNDEE	DUNFERMLINE A	FALKIRK	HAMILTON A	HEARTS	HIBERNIAN	KILMARNOCK	MOTHERWELL	PARTICK T	QUEEN'S PARK	RAITH R	RANGERS	ST JOHNSTONE	ST MIRREN
ABERDEEN		Dec03 0-0	Nov12 0-1	Oct22 3-1	Jan14 6-0	Apr14 3-0	Jan02 3-1	Oct08 2-1	Sep24 2-1	Feb08 2-0	Mar24 2-0	Sep10 4-2	Aug27 1-2	Dec17 2-0	Mar10 3-0	Dec31 2-1	Mar03 3-0	Aug13 2-3	Sep26 4-0	Mar31 3-2
AIRDRIE	Apr07 2-1		Oct22 4-2	Apr09 3-1	Oct08 1-2	Nov26 1-2	Sep24 1-1	Mar07 3-1	Jan02 0-1	Sep10 2-0	Dec10 2-0	Dec31 2-2	Feb08 0-2	Feb22 0-2	Nov12 2-0	Aug27 0-0	Aug13 2-4	Jan14 2-7	Apr21 2-0	Mar24 2-3
BO'NESS	Mar17 0-0	Feb25 2-2		Nov26 0-1	Mar03 0-0	Oct29 0-3	Sep10 2-0	Sep24 4-2	Aug13 2-1	Aug27 2-2	Apr07 2-2	Jan14 2-1	Oct08 2-1	Mar24 1-1	Dec10 1-4	Feb08 2-0	Jan02 1-1	Apr28 1-1	Nov05 1-2	Apr21 2-3
CELTIC	Feb25 1-1	Nov05 3-2	Mar31 4-1		Sep24 3-0	Nov19 1-1	Feb14 3-1	Jan14 9-0	Aug27 3-0	Mar06 4-0	Mar17 2-1	Aug13 3-0	Aug16 6-1	Dec03 1-2	Dec17 0-0	Sep10 3-0	Apr23 0-3	Jan02 1-0	Apr18 3-0	Oct29 6-0
CLYDE	Sep17 3-2	Jan28 2-2	Aug20 3-0	Feb11 0-1		Oct01 2-3	Apr07 0-0	Nov12 4-0	Feb29 1-1	Dec10 3-1	Jan07 2-2	Oct22 0-2	Mar24 1-1	Sep03 1-2	Oct15 0-2	Mar10 2-1	Apr21 1-1	Nov26 1-4	Jan03 1-0	Dec24 1-0
COWDENBEATH	Dec10 2-2	Mar31 2-1	Feb18 2-3	Mar26 0-2	Feb08 1-1		Aug13 1-0	Jan02 1-1	Dec31 0-2	Jan14 3-1	Apr21 0-1	Mar07 3-1	Sep10 1-1	Mar21 3-4	Oct22 2-1	Sep24 1-0	Oct08 3-1	Aug27 1-4	Dec03 4-2	Nov12 2-4
DUNDEE	Oct15 3-2	Feb11 3-0	Jan03 3-2	Oct01 1-4	Dec03 4-3	Dec24 3-1		Feb22 3-2	Oct22 1-0	Nov19 3-1	Jan28 2-7	Mar10 4-1	Nov12 7-0	Aug20 0-3	Sep03 4-2	Dec17 1-3	Mar31 1-2	Apr18 0-1	Sep17 1-2	Jan07 2-1
DUNFERMLINE A	Jan28 2-3	Aug20 1-4	Feb11 1-2	Sep17 1-1	Mar17 2-3	Oct15 3-2	Oct29 3-1		Apr07 1-0	Feb25 1-2	Jan03 0-2	Dec17 0-2	Apr14 0-4	Dec24 0-5	Jan07 1-7	Nov26 3-1	Nov19 0-4	Nov05 0-5	Oct01 2-3	Sep03 1-2
FALKIRK	Feb11 5-1	Oct15 3-1	Dec24 3-2	Jan07 1-3	Nov29 4-2	Sep03 1-3	Feb25 5-1	Dec03 5-1		Apr21 1-2	Oct01 1-3	Mar31 2-2	Nov05 6-0	Jan03 2-1	Jan28 2-1	Apr14 1-2	Mar17 4-1	Nov19 1-2	Aug20 5-1	Sep17 3-0
HAMILTON A	Oct01 2-3	Jan03 0-2	Jan07 7-0	Aug20 0-0	Apr13 1-1	Sep17 5-1	Mar24 3-3	Oct22 6-3	Dec17 3-0		Sep03 1-6	Feb29 4-1	Nov26 3-1	Oct15 1-3	Feb11 0-2	Nov12 2-1	Mar10 4-1	Dec03 1-1	Dec24 2-1	Jan28 1-2
HEARTS	Nov19 3-0	Apr14 1-1	Dec03 5-0	Nov12 2-2	Aug27 5-0	Dec17 2-3	Oct08 1-0	Sep10 6-0	Feb08 9-3	Dec31 2-1		Jan02 2-2	Aug13 0-1	Oct22 0-0	Feb22 1-2	Jan14 4-2	Sep24 2-0	Mar07 0-0	Mar31 0-2	Mar10 2-1
HIBERNIAN	Jan03 0-0	Sep03 2-3	Sep17 3-0	Dec24 2-2	Feb25 0-1	Aug20 3-0	Nov05 4-0	Apr21 3-3	Nov26 3-1	Oct29 5-1	Oct15 2-1		Apr07 3-1	Jan07 2-2	Oct01 4-1	Mar26 6-2	Dec10 3-2	Mar17 2-1	Jan28 2-2	Feb11 1-1
KILMARNOCK	Jan07 2-1	Oct01 2-2	Sep03 3-1	Jan28 2-2	Nov19 3-0	Jan03 2-1	Mar17 1-2	Dec10 2-1	Mar10 1-1	Mar31 3-1	Dec24 5-0	Dec03 2-1		Sep17 1-3	Aug20 2-3	Oct22 1-1	Feb29 1-0	Dec17 1-1	Feb11 1-7	Oct15 6-2
MOTHERWELL	Apr16 2-1	Oct29 1-1	Nov19 3-2	Apr07 3-1	Dec31 5-0	Nov05 2-1	Mar07 2-2	Aug13 4-0	Sep10 2-3	Jan02 5-1	Feb25 0-3	Aug27 2-1	Jan14 3-3		Mar31 1-3	Oct08 4-1	Feb15 6-0	Sep24 1-1	Mar17 1-0	Dec10 4-0
PARTICK T	Nov05 7-0	Mar17 0-2	Apr14 2-1	Apr21 3-3	Jan02 2-1	Apr09 2-4	Dec31 2-2	Aug27 2-1	Oct08 1-1	Sep24 5-2	Oct29 1-3	Feb08 3-0	Mar07 2-0	Nov26 1-1		Aug13 2-0	Jan14 5-0	Sep10 0-6	Nov19 2-2	Dec03 6-2
QUEEN'S PARK	Sep03 4-3	Jan07 1-1	Oct01 1-0	Jan03 1-3	Nov05 2-2	Feb11 1-1	Apr21 1-2	Mar31 4-0	Dec10 0-1	Mar17 4-1	Sep17 0-2	Nov19 6-2	Feb25 5-3	Jan28 3-1	Dec24 4-2		Dec03 8-1	Oct29 3-1	Oct15 1-1	Aug20 3-4
RAITH R	Aug20 2-3	Dec24 5-0	Oct15 3-2	Sep03 0-3	Dec17 2-0	Jan28 0-1	Nov26 1-1	Mar24 5-1	Nov12 2-2	Nov05 3-3	Feb11 0-5	Apr14 3-0	Oct29 1-3	Oct01 2-4	Sep17 4-2	Apr07 1-0		Apr02 0-0	Jan07 0-0	Jan03 1-2
RANGERS	Dec24 5-0	Sep17 2-1	Jan28 3-1	Oct15 1-0	Mar31 3-1	Jan07 2-2	Dec10 5-1	Apr09 4-0	Mar26 4-0	Apr07 3-1	Aug20 4-1	Nov12 4-1	Apr21 5-1	Feb11 0-2	Jan03 2-1	Feb28 4-0	Oct22 7-0		Sep03 5-1	Oct01 4-2
ST JOHNSTONE	Oct29 1-0	Dec17 6-1	Mar10 4-1	Dec10 3-5	Sep10 0-0	Apr07 0-3	Jan14 5-1	Feb08 1-1	Mar03 2-1	Aug13 2-1	Nov26 2-3	Oct08 2-0	Sep24 1-1	Nov12 1-4	Mar24 1-2	Jan02 5-1	Aug27 2-1	Dec31 0-1		Feb25 0-0
ST MIRREN	Nov26 0-1	Nov19 2-2	Dec17 5-0	Feb21 0-2	Aug13 3-1	Mar17 3-2	Aug27 0-0	Dec31 5-1	Jan14 3-2	Oct08 1-0	Nov05 2-0	Sep24 3-2	Jan02 1-1	Apr14 1-1	Apr07 2-2	Mar06 5-1	Sep10 4-3	Feb14 3-3	Oct22 3-2	

DIVISION 2

	ALBION R	ALLOA	ARBROATH	ARMADALE	ARTHURLIE	AYR U	BATHGATE	CLYDEBANK	DUMBARTON	DUNDEE U	EAST FIFE	E STIRLING	FORFAR A	KING'S PARK	LEITH A	MORTON	QUEEN OF SOUTH	ST BERNARD'S	STENHOUSEMUIR	T LANARK
ALBION R		Nov05 3-1	Jan07 3-1	Sep03 3-0	Feb25 0-1	Jan03 1-1	Apr14 2-1	Mar17 4-2	Sep17 2-3	Feb11 2-0	Dec24 3-0	Oct01 2-3	Dec17 1-2	Oct29 0-1	Aug20 0-0	Nov19 0-0	Dec03 3-1	Mar31 6-2	Oct15 4-0	Jan28 0-3
ALLOA	Mar10 4-3		Sep03 4-0	Aug20 3-3	Nov26 2-2	Jan07 1-3	Mar24 4-0	Dec10 0-1	Oct01 3-3	Oct15 0-0	Jan03 1-1	Jan28 6-3	Feb21 3-2	Nov12 2-1	Feb11 1-1	Apr07 3-3	Apr21 4-0	Oct22 3-0	Dec24 3-3	Sep17 1-0
ARBROATH	Aug27 4-2	Dec31 4-1		Feb18 5-0	Sep24 2-3	Oct22 0-2	Oct08 5-0	Jan14 1-3	Apr14 3-0	Dec03 3-2	Nov12 2-1	Mar31 2-2	Jan02 1-2	Feb08 2-1	Nov05 5-3	Aug13 1-1	Sep10 4-1	Mar03 3-2	Nov19 3-0	Apr21 4-0
ARMADALE	Dec31 2-3	Mar03 1-0	Oct29 4-5		Feb08 2-0	Mar31 3-1	Jan02 0-0	Oct08 1-3	Dec03 2-0	Dec17 4-2	Feb25 1-5	Apr14 0-0	Aug27 1-3	Jan14 1-1	Mar17 1-0	Sep24 2-1	Aug13 1-4	Sep10 2-1	Nov05 2-2	Nov19 2-2
ARTHURLIE	Oct22 6-4	Mar31 1-0	Feb11 4-1	Oct01 10-0		Sep03 4-1	Dec17 1-1	Nov05 5-1	Dec24 0-1	Sep17 1-3	Aug20 2-1	Jan07 4-3	Nov19 3-0	Apr07 1-1	Jan28 1-1	Dec10 4-2	Mar17 4-1	Feb18 3-4	Jan03 4-1	Oct15 2-0
AYR U	Sep10 5-3	Aug27 3-0	Feb25 7-3	Nov26 5-0	Dec31 6-1		Jan14 7-2	Feb08 3-1	Mar24 0-1	Apr14 7-1	Oct29 3-0	Apr07 2-1	Sep24 7-0	Mar03 2-2	Dec17 3-1	Jan02 4-1	Oct08 3-1	Aug13 4-4	Mar17 2-2	Nov05 6-2
BATHGATE	Dec10 3-1	Nov19 2-0	Jan28 3-3	Oct15 1-1	Apr21 2-3	Sep17 1-1		Feb18 5-0	Sep03 2-3	Dec24 1-2	Feb11 2-3	Aug20 3-1	Oct22 3-3	Nov26 0-0	Jan03 3-2	Mar17 1-1	Nov05 2-1	Dec03 1-1	Jan07 1-0	Oct01 3-2
CLYDEBANK	Nov12 0-2	Apr13 4-1	Sep17 1-2	Jan28 1-0	Mar21 2-0	Oct01 1-4	Oct29 2-3		Oct15 1-2	Aug20 2-1	Jan07 2-3	Jan03 4-1	Dec03 5-1	Mar24 5-0	Sep03 2-2	Feb25 2-1	Nov26 6-3	Dec17 7-1	Feb11 3-1	Dec24 1-1
DUMBARTON	Jan14 0-1	Feb08 2-1	Dec10 2-0	Apr07 6-2	Aug13 0-1	Nov19 2-0	Dec31 2-1	Jan02 0-2		Mar31 3-0	Nov05 1-3	Mar17 6-1	Oct08 2-0	Sep24 4-5	Oct29 2-2	Sep10 5-0	Mar03 1-0	Aug27 3-3	Apr21 4-1	Feb25 0-0
DUNDEE U	Sep24 3-2	Jan02 2-1	Apr07 1-0	Apr21 1-1	Jan14 9-2	Dec10 1-3	Aug13 4-2	Mar03 2-2	Nov26 3-1		Mar24 2-3	Nov05 3-1	Dec31 4-0	Sep10 1-1	Feb25 3-1	Feb15 3-2	Aug27 1-1	Oct08 5-3	Oct29 5-3	Mar17 4-3
EAST FIFE	Aug13 2-0	Sep10 2-4	Mar17 2-1	Oct22 4-1	Mar03 6-1	Feb18 2-0	Sep24 2-3	Aug27 2-1	Mar10 4-1	Nov19 2-1		Apr21 2-2	Jan14 4-3	Dec31 1-1	Dec10 3-4	Oct08 5-0	Jan02 5-1	Feb04 2-2	Mar31 1-3	Dec03 2-2
E STIRLING	Feb08 3-1	Oct08 2-3	Nov26 3-0	Dec10 4-1	Aug27 8-0	Dec03 2-3	Mar03 1-0	Sep10 2-1	Nov12 5-0	Mar10 3-1	Dec17 4-1		Aug13 4-0	Jan02 2-2	Mar24 1-1	Jan14 2-2	Dec31 2-2	Sep24 1-2	Feb25 0-1	Oct29 0-0
FORFAR A	Apr21 4-1	Oct29 4-0	Oct15 2-2	Jan07 3-0	Mar24 4-1	Feb11 1-2	Feb25 2-0	Apr07 2-1	Jan28 3-2	Sep03 0-0	Sep17 4-0	Dec24 1-1		Mar10 3-1	Oct01 2-2	Nov26 5-2	Dec10 4-1	Nov12 9-2	Aug20 3-1	Jan03 3-2
KING'S PARK	Dec22 0-4	Mar17 2-2	Oct01 5-1	Sep17 5-2	Dec03 5-1	Aug20 2-1	Mar31 1-0	Nov19 5-1	Feb11 4-0	Jan03 0-1	Sep03 1-1	Oct15 2-2	Nov05 1-1		Dec24 1-0	Dec17 3-1	Oct26 4-3	Apr14 8-1	Jan28 4-2	Jan07 4-2
LEITH A	Mar06 4-1	Sep24 2-1	Mar10 4-2	Nov12 5-0	Oct08 3-4	Apr21 2-1	Sep10 2-2	Dec31 4-0	Feb04 2-1	Oct22 0-2	Apr14 2-3	Nov19 2-3	Feb08 3-1	Aug13 4-1		Aug27 2-3	Jan14 3-1	Oct15 2-1	Dec03 1-2	Mar31 2-3
MORTON	Mar24 0-2	Dec03 2-1	Dec24 1-0	Feb11 2-1	Apr14 3-1	Oct15 0-2	Nov12 2-2	Oct22 5-6	Jan03 2-0	Oct01 1-1	Jan28 1-1	Sep17 3-1	Mar31 2-1	Apr21 2-3	Jan07 3-1		Feb18 2-0	Mar10 3-1	Sep03 1-0	Aug20 1-2
QUEEN OF SOUTH	Apr07 2-4	Dec17 2-2	Jan03 3-2	Dec24 8-5	Nov12 1-0	Jan28 2-4	Mar10 4-3	Feb04 3-2	Aug20 6-2	Jan07 2-2	Oct15 2-4	Sep03 5-3	Apr14 2-1	Feb25 2-2	Sep17 5-2	Oct29 4-1		Nov19 6-3	Oct01 4-3	Feb11 2-2
ST BERNARD'S	Nov26 3-1	Feb25 2-2	Aug20 1-2	Jan03 2-1	Oct29 3-2	Dec24 0-4	Apr07 2-0	Apr21 1-0	Jan07 2-0	Jan28 3-2	Oct01 2-1	Feb11 1-2	Mar17 3-0	Dec10 2-1	Jan02 1-0	Nov05 2-5	Mar24 8-2		Sep17 3-1	Sep03 0-1
STENHOUSEMUIR	Jan02 0-3	Aug13 2-4	Mar24 6-2	Mar10 1-0	Sep10 4-1	Nov12 6-2	Aug27 4-2	Sep24 2-0	Dec17 1-0	Feb18 2-2	Nov26 4-1	Oct22 2-5	Mar03 2-3	Oct08 3-2	Apr07 0-0	Dec31 5-2	Feb08 1-2	Jan14 2-0		Dec10 1-0
T LANARK	Oct05 2-2	Jan14 5-0	Dec17 4-3	Mar24 10-3	Jan02 2-1	Apr09 3-3	Feb07 6-1	Aug13 4-0	Oct22 4-1	Nov12 5-1	Apr07 3-2	Feb18 5-0	Sep10 1-1	Aug27 5-1	Nov26 2-4	Mar03 3-1	Sep24 1-2	Dec31 6-1	Apr17 3-1	

LEAGUE TABLES

DIVISION 1

	P	W	D	L	F	A	W	D	L	F	A	Pts
Rangers	38	17	1	1	67	16	9	7	3	42	20	60
Celtic	38	14	3	2	56	13	9	6	4	37	26	55
Motherwell	38	12	4	3	51	24	11	5	3	41	22	55
Hearts	38	10	5	4	47	20	10	2	7	42	30	47
St Mirren	38	11	6	2	46	26	7	2	10	31	50	44
Partick T	38	10	5	4	48	31	8	2	9	37	36	43
Aberdeen	38	15	1	3	47	15	4	4	11	24	46	43
Kilmarnock	38	10	5	4	41	30	5	5	9	27	48	40
Cowdenbeath	38	8	4	7	32	32	8	3	8	34	36	39
Falkirk	38	12	1	6	55	29	4	4	11	21	40	37
St Johnstone	38	9	4	6	38	27	5	4	10	28	40	36
Hibernian	38	11	6	2	50	24	2	3	14	23	51	35
Airdrie	38	8	3	8	31	31	4	8	7	28	38	35
Dundee	38	12	0	7	46	37	2	7	10	19	43	35
Clyde	38	7	6	6	28	25	3	5	11	18	47	31
Queen's Park	38	10	4	5	52	31	2	2	15	17	49	30
Raith R	38	7	5	7	35	32	4	2	13	25	57	29
Hamilton A	38	9	4	6	46	32	2	2	15	21	54	28
Bo'ness	38	6	8	5	27	27	3	0	16	21	59	26
Dunfermline A	38	4	1	14	22	53	0	3	16	19	73	12

DIVISION 2

	P	W	D	L	F	A	W	D	L	F	A	Pts
Ayr U	38	15	3	1	79	26	9	3	7	38	34	54
T. Lanark	38	14	3	2	74	28	4	6	9	27	38	45
King's Park	38	13	4	2	57	26	3	8	8	27	42	44
East Fife	38	11	4	4	53	31	7	3	9	34	42	43
Forfar A	38	14	4	1	59	21	4	3	12	24	52	43
Dundee U	38	13	4	2	57	32	4	5	10	24	41	43
Arthurlie	38	13	3	3	60	26	5	1	13	25	64	40
Albion R	38	10	3	6	39	22	7	1	11	40	47	38
E. Stirling	38	10	5	4	49	21	4	5	10	35	55	38
Arbroath	38	13	2	4	54	26	3	2	14	30	60	36
Dumbarton	38	11	3	5	45	23	5	1	13	21	49	36
Queen of South	38	12	4	3	65	47	3	2	14	27	59	36
Leith A	38	11	1	7	49	32	2	8	9	27	39	35
Clydebank	38	11	2	6	51	29	5	1	13	27	51	35
Alloa	38	9	8	2	48	29	3	3	13	24	47	35
Stenhousemuir	38	12	2	5	48	31	3	3	13	27	51	35
St Bernard's	38	13	1	5	41	27	2	4	13	34	76	35
Morton	38	11	3	5	36	26	2	5	12	29	56	34
Bathgate	38	8	7	4	39	28	2	4	13	23	53	31
Armadale	38	8	5	6	32	33	0	3	16	21	79	24

Scottish Football League Records
Season 1928-29

DIVISION 1

	ABERDEEN	AIRDRIE	AYR U	CELTIC	CLYDE	COWDENBEATH	DUNDEE	FALKIRK	HAMILTON A	HEARTS	HIBERNIAN	KILMARNOCK	MOTHERWELL	PARTICK T	QUEEN'S PARK	RAITH R	RANGERS	ST JOHNSTONE	ST MIRREN	T LANARK
ABERDEEN		Oct13 2-1	Mar09 2-1	Nov10 2-2	Sep22 3-1	Aug11 4-2	Mar23 4-0	Dec15 5-3	Dec01 4-1	Oct27 1-3	Jan05 0-1	Sep24 2-1	Feb23 1-1	Mar30 5-0	Aug18 3-0	Sep29 3-1	Apr20 2-2	Sep08 2-0	Jan12 6-0	Jan01 4-0
AIRDRIE	Mar12 5-0		Feb27 3-0	Dec22 0-1	Apr20 2-2	Sep08 3-2	Nov03 1-1	Oct20 2-3	Mar02 1-0	Sep22 1-1	Oct06 0-2	Aug25 2-1	Aug11 0-1	Nov17 1-0	Dec25 2-2	Mar16 3-1	Dec15 2-5	Mar30 5-1	Feb11 3-0	Jan12 2-1
AYR U	Nov03 3-3	Sep29 2-0		Aug25 0-2	Mar02 3-1	Oct06 3-1	Jan02 0-3	Apr13 2-0	Feb09 1-1	Jan12 2-4	Mar30 4-1	Nov17 2-4	Sep08 2-0	Mar16 1-3	Oct20 4-2	Dec15 0-1	Dec01 1-3	Apr20 1-2	Aug11 2-2	Dec22 3-0
CELTIC	Mar16 2-2	Aug18 4-1	Jan05 3-0		Nov17 4-0	Feb12 1-0	Dec29 2-1	Apr20 3-0	Feb19 3-0	Dec15 1-0	Apr13 1-4	Sep08 3-0	Mar19 2-0	Apr01 1-0	Apr17 1-2	Nov03 3-1	Oct20 1-2	Dec01 0-0	Sep22 0-3	Mar30 3-1
CLYDE	Feb09 2-1	Dec08 3-1	Oct13 1-0	Mar26 0-1		Dec22 2-3	Nov10 2-1	Aug11 2-1	Apr27 2-3	Aug25 1-1	Sep15 0-1	Sep29 1-1	Jan12 1-1	Jan01 0-4	Dec25 2-2	Apr06 2-0	Nov24 2-3	Oct27 2-1	Feb23 4-0	Mar09 3-2
COWDENBEATH	Dec29 1-1	Apr27 2-1	Feb23 3-1	Sep15 0-1	Aug18 1-2		Nov24 4-2	Nov03 3-1	Dec08 2-0	Mar02 1-2	Sep01 2-0	Jan02 2-0	Apr06 1-3	Jan26 2-0	Sep22 0-1	Oct20 2-0	Jan05 0-2	Mar16 1-0	Sep29 0-0	Nov17 1-1
DUNDEE	Nov17 1-1	Mar09 2-2	Oct27 2-3	Aug11 0-1	Mar16 1-2	Mar30 4-0		Feb09 1-2	Sep15 0-1	Sep29 5-3	Jan26 1-0	Jan12 1-3	Dec08 3-0	Dec22 0-0	Apr06 0-0	Feb23 0-3	Sep08 2-3	Jan01 0-2	Aug25 2-3	Oct13 2-2
FALKIRK	Jan26 2-0	Jan01 2-1	Sep15 5-2	Dec08 3-0	Dec29 2-1	Mar09 2-2	Sep22 1-3		Sep01 4-2	Feb23 3-3	Apr27 2-1	Dec01 2-2	Oct27 0-7	Aug25 0-0	Mar23 1-0	Nov24 4-1	Nov10 1-4	Dec22 2-0	Oct13 2-2	Feb20 3-1
HAMILTON A	Apr06 3-2	Oct27 1-3	Sep22 2-0	Sep29 1-1	Sep08 2-0	Apr20 0-0	Apr12 3-3	Jan12 2-2		Dec22 3-2	Nov10 2-1	Dec15 0-2	Jan01 0-3	Feb23 2-2	Nov24 3-3	Mar05 5-1	Mar27 3-1	Aug25 2-1	Mar09 3-0	Aug11 1-4
HEARTS	Jan02 3-2	Feb09 3-0	Sep01 7-3	Jan26 2-1	Jan05 4-0	Oct13 4-1	Mar06 1-1	Oct06 6-2	Aug18 5-0		Oct20 1-1	Mar30 3-3	Nov10 5-1	Dec08 2-1	Dec29 4-1	Apr27 1-1	Sep15 0-1	Mar09 0-3	Dec25 1-0	Dec01 4-1
HIBERNIAN	Aug25 4-1	Apr06 1-1	Nov24 2-2	Feb23 2-1	Feb20 3-0	Jan12 1-2	Dec15 2-0	Sep08 3-2	Mar16 0-1	Jan01 1-0		Dec22 1-1	Sep22 1-1	Sep29 3-1	Mar02 1-2	Nov17 2-0	Nov03 1-2	Aug11 2-2	Apr20 3-5	Oct27 6-1
KILMARNOCK	Sep15 0-1	Jan05 0-2	Apr24 1-2	Apr27 2-3	Apr01 3-1	Oct27 4-2	Sep01 3-1	Apr09 1-1	Jan26 0-0	Nov24 3-2	Aug18 1-0		Mar09 4-2	Oct13 2-2	Nov10 7-4	Dec08 7-1	Dec29 1-3	Feb23 1-1	Jan01 2-4	Sep22 3-0
MOTHERWELL	Oct06 1-0	Dec29 4-2	Apr27 5-0	Oct13 3-3	Sep01 1-0	Dec01 5-1	Apr20 1-1	Jan02 2-1	Oct20 4-3	Mar16 3-2	Feb09 3-1	Nov03 2-3		Sep15 5-4	Jan05 0-5	Aug18 3-1	Apr17 2-4	Nov17 1-1	Mar30 1-1	Dec15 3-2
PARTICK T	Nov24 3-2	Mar23 1-1	Nov10 4-8	Jan12 3-0	Oct20 2-0	Dec15 2-1	Aug18 4-2	Mar02 5-2	Oct06 8-0	Apr20 2-0	Feb16 3-0	Mar12 2-1	Feb06 1-3		Nov03 2-2	Dec29 6-1	Apr24 1-1	Sep22 6-2	Dec01 2-4	Sep08 3-4
QUEEN'S PARK	Dec22 6-2	Feb23 2-0	Jan01 3-0	Oct27 4-4	Dec15 2-1	Feb09 6-1	Dec01 2-4	Nov17 1-3	Mar30 5-0	Aug11 1-3	Oct13 6-1	Mar20 2-0	Aug25 2-3	Mar09 3-2		Sep15 5-0	Jan12 0-4	Feb16 6-0	Sep08 5-0	Apr20 8-3
RAITH R	Feb20 2-2	Nov10 3-2	Oct01 4-2	Mar09 1-4	Dec01 3-0	Jan01 0-2	Oct06 0-3	Mar30 2-0	Oct13 3-1	Sep08 0-2	Mar23 1-0	Apr20 5-3	Dec22 2-2	Aug11 2-4	Apr24 1-1		Feb09 1-3	Jan12 3-3	Oct27 1-5	Aug25 0-0
RANGERS	Dec08 2-0	Jan26 2-0	Apr09 0-0	Jan01 3-0	Mar30 0-0	Aug25 3-1	Apr27 3-0	Mar16 1-1	Nov17 4-0	Mar12 2-0	Mar09 3-0	Aug11 4-2	Sep29 0-0	Jan02 1-0	Apr01 2-1	Sep22 7-1		Oct13 8-0	Dec22 1-1	Feb26 5-1
ST JOHNSTONE	Apr27 2-1	Nov24 1-0	Dec08 0-0	Apr06 1-1	Jan02 5-0	Nov10 3-1	Oct20 2-2	Aug18 3-1	Jan05 2-2	Nov03 0-3	Dec29 4-0	Oct06 1-0	Mar23 2-3	Feb09 1-3	Sep29 1-0	Sep01 3-1	Mar06 1-3		Dec15 1-0	Mar02 2-1
ST MIRREN	Sep01 5-2	Sep15 2-0	Dec29 2-3	Feb09 0-1	Oct06 1-0	Feb19 1-4	Apr22 2-2	Mar12 5-0	Nov03 1-3	Nov17 2-2	Dec08 1-0	Oct20 5-4	Nov24 2-3	Apr06 3-0	Apr27 1-2	Apr09 5-2	Aug18 1-5	Jan26 2-2		Mar16 5-0
T LANARK	Oct20 1-3	Sep01 4-0	Aug18 2-2	Nov24 0-2	Nov03 2-4	Mar23 3-1	Dec25 1-2	Sep29 5-2	Dec29 3-2	Apr01 2-2	Jan02 2-1	Feb09 2-3	Jan26 2-2	Apr27 2-5	Dec08 3-1	Jan05 5-1	Oct06 2-5	Sep15 4-1	Nov10 1-2	

DIVISION 2

	ALBION R	ALLOA	ARBROATH	ARMADALE	ARTHURLIE	BATHGATE	BO'NESS	CLYDEBANK	DUMBARTON	DUNDEE U	DUNFERMLINE A	EAST FIFE	E STIRLING	FORFAR A	KING'S PARK	LEITH A	MORTON	QUEEN OF SOUTH	ST BERNARD'S	STENHOUSEMUIR
ALBION R		Jan05 3-1	Feb09 2-1	Mar09 9-1	Sep01 4-1	Dec08 2-1	Oct27 4-0	Sep15 3-0	Mar23 6-4	Oct13 2-0	Dec29 3-4	Dec01 4-1	Feb23 3-1	Apr27 6-2	Mar20 0-0	Sep29 6-2	Nov10 2-2	Nov24 2-0	Aug18 3-2	Jan01 2-0
ALLOA	Aug25 0-0		Mar09 1-2	Nov10 5-2	Jan26 3-0	Sep01 1-2	Sep29 2-2	Apr06 3-1	Dec22 0-2	Apr13 3-0	Nov24 1-1	Oct27 2-4	Sep22 5-0	Feb02 2-4	Apr27 1-0	Aug11 2-4	Mar23 1-3	Dec08 0-4	Oct13 0-3	Feb23 7-1
ARBROATH	Sep22 5-3	Nov03 6-3		Mar02 6-1	Dec29 4-1	Dec01 3-1	Jan26 3-0	Aug18 4-2	Feb20 7-1	Mar30 1-2	Apr27 2-1	Mar23 1-0	Nov10 5-2	Oct20 1-0	Apr20 0-0	Apr13 3-2	Jan05 1-1	Jan02 1-0	Oct06 1-1	Sep01 5-2
ARMADALE	Nov03 0-0	Mar16 1-1	Oct13 1-1		Feb23 1-1	Oct20 2-1	Sep15 0-1	Sep01 2-2	Mar30 1-1	Sep29 0-2	Jan09 3-1	Feb09 4-2	Dec08 2-1	Jan26 3-1	Dec01 2-0	Dec15 1-0	Aug18 1-3	Nov17 2-3	Apr12 0-3	Dec29 3-2
ARTHURLIE	Jan12 2-1	Sep08 1-2	Aug11 1-1	Oct06 3-1		Nov03 4-3		Mar16 1-0	Sep22 3-3	Nov17 3-1	Oct20 1-0		Dec01 2-3		Dec22 1-4	Mar02 2-2	Feb02 1-2	Aug25 4-0	Mar30 1-1	
BATHGATE		Jan12 3-1					Nov24 3-5	Dec15 0-2	Oct06 2-3	Aug11 0-4	Sep22 1-1	Aug25 4-1			Feb16 1-3	Oct27 0-5	Sep08 1-3	Dec22 1-3	Nov10 0-0	
BO'NESS	Jan02 2-2	Feb16 2-3	Sep08 2-3	Feb06 2-0	Dec08 0-2			Nov03 2-0	Mar02 6-0	Dec22 1-0	Mar16 2-1	Aug11 4-1	Aug25 2-0	Oct06 4-3	Nov17 1-3	Sep22 3-0	Oct20 2-2	Jan12 5-1	Apr27 1-0	Dec01 5-1
CLYDEBANK	Feb06 2-4	Dec01 1-3	Dec22 4-3	Jan12 4-0	Nov10 5-1		Mar09 3-0		Dec31 1-6	Aug25 4-1	Dec08 5-2	Mar30 0-3	Oct27 1-3	Mar23 1-1	Mar02 5-1	Sep08 3-1	Feb13 3-3	Oct06 3-1	Feb16 1-3	Sep22 2-0
DUMBARTON	Nov17 1-0	Aug18 4-1	Sep29 0-2	Nov24 5-2	Feb09 2-0	Feb23 3-0	Oct13 0-3	Oct20 1-1		Apr06 1-1	Sep15 3-1	Apr27 2-2	Apr08 3-2	Jan05 0-0	Sep01 3-3	Mar16 1-4	Jan02 1-0	Nov03 4-2	Dec08 2-1	Jan26 0-1
DUNDEE U	Mar06 8-1	Oct20 5-0	Nov24 4-3	Feb27 5-0	Mar23 4-3	Dec29 6-1	Aug18 4-1	Jan05 2-1	Dec01 3-1		Sep01 1-0	Apr08 4-3	Apr27 3-1	Apr20 0-1	Jan02 4-0	Nov03 5-3	Oct06 3-0	Sep22 3-2	Oct01 3-1	Nov10 8-0
DUNFERMLINE A	Aug11 1-5	Mar30 0-1	Dec15 3-3	Aug25 3-2	Jan01 5-1	Feb09 8-0	Nov10 1-0	Apr20 2-1	Apr01 3-2	Jan12 1-1		Oct13 2-3	Mar09 3-1	Dec01 4-0	Oct06 2-2	Dec22 3-1	Feb16 0-0	Sep08 2-1	Mar23 3-1	Oct27 4-3
EAST FIFE	Apr06 3-4	Jan02 1-1	Nov17 2-3	Sep22 1-1	Sep29 2-2	Jan05 6-2	Dec29 4-2	Nov24 4-0	Dec15 6-3	Sep15 4-5	Mar02 5-1		Jan26 3-1	Aug18 4-2	Mar16 1-2	Feb23 3-1	Nov03 2-1	Oct20 6-1	Sep01 2-1	Dec08 2-1
E STIRLING	Oct06 5-3	Feb09 1-1	Mar16 3-0	Apr20 0-1	Apr06 2-1	Nov17 5-0	Jan05 1-2	Jan02 4-2	Aug11 1-0	Dec15 2-3	Nov03 3-1	Sep08 4-2		Sep29 2-2	Oct20 5-2	Jan12 0-2	Mar30 0-2	Mar02 4-5	Sep15 2-1	Aug18 0-1
FORFAR A	Dec15 3-3	Sep15 4-1	Jan01 2-2	Sep08 3-1	Oct27 1-1	Oct13 8-2	Feb23 5-1	Nov17 3-2	Aug25 1-1	Dec08 2-1	Apr06 2-0	Dec22 3-1	Mar14 3-1		Aug11 2-1	Nov24 1-0	Jan12 0-2	Mar16 4-4	Feb09 3-1	Mar09 4-1
KING'S PARK	Sep08 1-1	Dec15 1-1	Dec08 2-2	Apr06 4-0	Aug18 2-1	Sep29 3-1	Mar23 0-0	Oct13 4-3	Jan12 1-1	Oct27 0-2	Feb23 5-1	Nov10 2-2	Jan01 3-5	Apr13 1-1		Aug25 1-3	Sep22 4-3	Feb06 2-3	Mar09 2-4	Nov24 3-3
LEITH A	Apr15 3-1	Dec29 4-2	Sep15 4-2	Apr27 5-1	Oct13 6-1	Jan02 1-2	Feb09 2-0	Jan26 0-0	Nov10 3-0	Mar09 3-2	Aug18 1-1	Oct06 5-2	Sep01 1-1	Mar30 5-0	Jan05 4-0		Dec08 1-0	Apr06 2-0	Oct20 0-0	Mar23 1-0
MORTON	Mar16 3-1	Nov17 3-4	Aug25 3-0	Dec22 4-2	Sep15 2-0	Jan26 2-0	Jan01 4-0	Aug11 3-2	Oct27 3-1	Feb23 2-0	Sep29 1-1	Mar09 3-2	Nov24 2-2	Sep01 4-0	Feb09 5-0	Apr20 4-1		Dec15 0-0	Apr06 4-1	Oct13 3-0
QUEEN OF SOUTH	Mar30 2-0	Apr20 2-1	Oct27 0-3	Mar23 7-3	Jan05 3-6	Aug18 3-4	Sep01 2-0	Feb23 7-2	Mar09 3-0	Feb09 2-3	Jan26 2-1	Jan01 1-1	Oct13 1-4	Nov10 9-2	Sep15 6-1	Dec01 4-1	Apr27 2-3		Dec29 3-1	Sep29 1-0
ST BERNARD'S	Dec22 1-1	Mar02 2-0	Feb23 3-2	Oct27 5-1	Nov24 5-1		Dec15 2-2	Sep29 1-2	Apr20 3-0	Sep08 2-2	Nov17 3-0	Jan12 2-1	Feb06 2-0	Sep22 2-1	Nov03 4-1	Jan01 1-1	Dec01 7-3	Aug11 1-1		Aug25 2-2
STENHOUSEMUIR	Oct20 3-1	Oct06 3-0	Jan12 1-1	Aug11 3-1	Dec15 1-2	Sep15 4-1	Apr06 3-2	Feb09 3-1	Sep08 1-0	Mar16 1-4	Jan02 1-7	Apr20 2-3	Dec22 0-4	Nov03 3-3	Mar30 2-2	Nov17 0-0	Mar02 1-2	Feb16 2-1	Jan05 3-4	

LEAGUE TABLES

DIVISION 1

	P	W	D	L	F	A	W	D	L	F	A	Pts
Rangers	38	14	5	0	51	8	16	2	1	56	24	67
Celtic	38	13	2	4	38	17	9	5	5	29	27	51
Motherwell	38	12	4	3	49	35	8	6	5	36	31	50
Hearts	38	13	4	2	56	23	6	5	8	35	34	47
Queen's Park	38	13	1	5	69	31	5	6	8	31	38	43
Partick T	38	12	3	4	60	34	5	4	10	31	36	41
Aberdeen	38	14	3	2	55	20	2	5	12	26	48	40
St Mirren	38	9	3	7	46	35	7	5	7	32	40	40
St Johnstone	38	11	4	4	35	22	3	6	10	22	48	38
Kilmarnock	38	9	4	6	45	32	5	4	10	34	42	36
Falkirk	38	11	5	3	41	32	3	3	13	27	54	36
Hamilton A	38	9	6	4	38	31	4	3	12	20	52	35
Cowdenbeath	38	10	3	6	28	18	4	2	13	27	51	33
Hibernian	38	9	5	5	39	25	4	1	14	15	37	32
Airdrie	38	10	4	5	38	24	2	3	14	18	41	31
Ayr U	38	8	3	8	36	33	4	4	11	29	51	31
Clyde	38	9	4	6	32	27	3	2	14	15	44	30
Dundee	38	4	5	10	27	31	5	6	8	32	38	29
T. Lanark	38	8	3	8	46	41	2	3	14	25	61	26
Raith R	38	7	5	7	34	39	2	1	16	18	66	24

DIVISION 2

	P	W	D	L	F	A	W	D	L	F	A	Pts
Dundee U	36	17	0	1	69	21	7	3	8	30	34	51
Morton	36	14	3	1	53	17	7	5	6	32	32	50
Arbroath	36	14	3	1	56	22	5	6	7	34	38	47
Albion R	36	15	2	1	64	22	3	6	9	31	45	44
Leith A	36	14	4	0	50	13	4	3	11	28	43	43
St Bernard's	36	11	6	1	48	21	5	3	10	29	34	41
Forfar A	35	12	5	1	46	24	2	5	10	23	51	38
East Fife	35	11	3	4	55	32	4	3	10	33	45	36
Queen of South	36	12	1	5	57	32	4	3	11	29	47	36
Bo'ness	35	12	2	4	46	22	3	3	11	16	40	35
Dunfermline A	36	11	4	3	42	28	2	3	13	24	44	33
E. Stirling	36	9	2	7	39	31	5	2	11	32	44	32
Alloa	36	7	3	8	38	33	5	4	9	26	44	31
Dumbarton	36	9	5	4	33	26	2	4	12	26	52	31
King's Park	36	5	8	5	38	36	3	5	10	22	48	29
Clydebank	36	10	2	6	48	36	1	3	14	22	49	27
Arthurlie	32	6	4	4	26	21	3	3	12	25	52	25
Stenhousemuir	35	7	4	7	33	38	2	2	13	18	52*	24
Armadale	36	7	6	5	27	25	1	1	16	20	74	23
Bathgate	28	2	2	8	16	31	3	0	13	21	61†	12

*Arthurlie resigned towards the end of the season – but their record was allowed to stand.

†Bathgate resigned, record shown but not recognised by League.

Brechin & Montrose joined Division Two.

Scottish Football League Records
Season 1929-30

DIVISION 1

	ABERDEEN	AIRDRIE	AYR U	CELTIC	CLYDE	COWDENBEATH	DUNDEE	DUNDEE U	FALKIRK	HAMILTON A	HEARTS	HIBERNIAN	KILMARNOCK	MORTON	MOTHERWELL	PARTICK T	QUEEN'S PARK	RANGERS	ST JOHNSTONE	ST MIRREN
ABERDEEN		Jan11 3-1	Oct12 4-1	Jan04 3-1	Sep23 5-2	Nov09 2-0	Oct26 1-0	Mar29 2-2	Dec21 1-0	Nov30 4-2	Jan02 2-2	Dec07 2-0	Mar08 4-3	Sep21 5-3	Aug17 2-2	Sep28 2-1	Apr19 3-0	Sep07 1-1	Feb22 1-0	Mar22 3-3
AIRDRIE	Aug31 0-2		Nov02 2-0	Sep14 0-1	Oct05 2-4	Mar12 4-1	Mar22 3-2	Jan25 3-4	Jan01 4-1	Oct19 1-0	Apr12 3-2	Dec21 3-0	Nov09 2-2	Nov23 2-2	Feb08 2-0	Apr26 2-0	Nov30 1-2	Apr19 1-0	Aug17 5-1	Mar05 2-2
AYR U	Mar01 5-1	Mar08 3-1		Sep28 1-3	Mar22 2-2	Oct05 3-1	Nov30 2-2	Oct19 6-1	Feb08 0-0	Mar29 3-3	Nov09 3-1	Aug31 3-2	Jan25 1-1	Dec07 2-0	Sep14 3-2	Aug17 2-4	Jan01 2-5	Mar26 0-3	Dec21 4-0	Jan04 1-0
CELTIC	Aug24 3-4	Feb05 1-2	Feb18 4-0		Apr21 0-2	Nov16 2-1	Sep21 1-1	Mar01 7-0	Oct05 7-0	Apr15 3-0	Aug10 2-1	Nov02 4-0	Apr19 4-0	Dec28 0-1	Mar15 0-4	Apr05 2-0	Oct19 2-1	Jan01 1-2	Mar29 6-2	Dec07 3-0
CLYDE	Sep14 1-3	Feb22 2-0	Dec14 3-1	Jan25 2-3		Apr11 4-1	Mar08 1-1	Dec21 3-2	Sep28 1-2	Mar26 3-1	Nov30 3-3	Feb08 0-2	Jan04 1-1	Oct12 2-1	Aug31 1-2	Oct26 2-3	Nov09 2-1	Nov23 3-3	Jan02 2-0	Aug17 1-2
COWDENBEATH	Mar15 0-1	Sep28 2-0	Feb22 7-1	Mar22 1-2	Dec07 4-0		Nov23 2-1	Jan01 4-1	Apr05 3-0	Apr19 3-0	Aug24 0-1	Jan25 0-0	Oct19 2-3	Aug10 2-0	Oct12 0-0	Sep14 0-2	Dec28 1-1	Apr26 3-2	Aug31 2-1	Feb08 2-3
DUNDEE	Jan01 0-3	Nov16 3-0	Apr05 3-0	Feb08 2-2	Nov02 0-1	Mar29 3-0		Aug31 1-0	Aug17 0-0	Mar12 3-2	Dec14 3-0	Oct19 4-0	Sep28 2-2	Mar15 3-2	Jan04 0-3	Dec21 2-4	Oct05 1-0	Apr23 1-3	Sep14 0-1	Jan25 1-3
DUNDEE U	Nov23 2-4	Sep07 0-3	Jan02 1-2	Oct23 2-2	Aug10 3-3	Oct26 2-1	Jan11 0-1		Dec07 2-2	Dec28 1-2	Apr02 2-3	Apr19 2-2	Mar22 6-4	Aug24 3-1	Mar08 1-1	Nov09 3-2	Sep21 2-1	Feb19 0-1	Nov30 1-1	Feb22 0-2
FALKIRK	Aug10 3-2	Oct26 3-2	Sep21 1-1	Feb22 0-1	Mar05 1-1	Nov30 2-2	Dec28 5-2	Apr12 5-2		Apr26 1-0	Oct12 2-3	Nov16 1-1	Mar29 1-0	Sep07 3-0	Jan02 4-1	Mar08 0-0	Aug24 1-2	Apr30 2-1	Dec14 4-0	Mar15 1-0
HAMILTON A	Apr05 4-2	Jan02 0-1	Nov23 6-2	Aug31 2-3	Nov16 1-1	Dec14 5-1	Oct12 2-0	Aug17 5-2	Sep14 0-2		Mar08 2-1	Jan04 3-2	Dec21 1-1	Feb22 4-2	Oct26 2-3	Jan25 2-1	Apr11 4-2	Mar15 1-1	Feb08 3-0	Sep28 2-0
HEARTS	Oct19 2-2	Dec07 1-0	Mar15 1-2	Dec21 1-3	Apr05 0-1	Jan04 2-2	Apr19 1-0	Sep14 3-1	Mar12 0-2	Nov02 6-4		Jan01 1-1	Aug17 1-1	Nov16 4-0	Jan25 3-2	Feb08 0-0	Mar29 0-3	Oct05 2-0	Sep28 2-2	Aug31 5-0
HIBERNIAN	Apr12 0-1	Aug10 3-1	Jan11 1-0	Mar08 0-2	Sep21 1-1	Sep07 1-1	Jan02 0-1	Dec14 3-0	Mar22 1-0	Aug24 1-2	Oct26 1-1		Nov30 0-0	Apr26 0-1	Feb22 1-1	Oct12 3-0	Mar01 6-3	Dec28 0-2	Nov09 3-1	Nov23 2-2
KILMARNOCK	Nov02 4-2	Mar15 7-1	Sep07 2-0	Dec14 1-1	Aug24 2-1	Jan02 3-2	Apr21 0-2	Nov16 0-2	Nov23 3-2	Aug10 3-0	Dec28 2-1	Apr05 3-1		Feb15 7-2	Apr12 2-3	Feb22 1-1	Jan11 1-5	Sep21 1-0	Oct12 3-1	Oct26 2-3
MORTON	Feb08 1-2	Mar29 1-1	Apr12 3-4	Aug17 1-2	Mar01 1-2	Dec21 3-4	Nov09 2-1	Jan04 6-1	Jan25 1-1	Oct05 4-4	Mar26 3-2	Sep28 3-2	Sep14 4-2		Dec14 1-3	Aug31 2-2	Feb01 2-4	Nov30 2-2	Oct26 4-1	Jan02 2-0
MOTHERWELL	Dec28 4-1	Sep21 2-0	Apr21 4-1	Nov09 2-1	Jan11 2-1	Mar01 7-2	Aug24 3-0	Nov02 6-1	Oct19 4-3	Jan01 5-1	Sep07 0-2	Oct05 3-0	Dec07 2-0	Apr19 3-0		Mar29 4-0	Apr26 9-0	Aug10 0-2	Mar22 5-0	Nov30 3-0
PARTICK T	Feb19 2-1	Aug24 4-0	Dec28 2-3	Nov30 3-2	Jan01 3-3	Apr30 3-4	Aug10 0-2	Mar15 1-1	Nov02 5-0	Sep07 2-2	Sep21 2-1	Mar05 0-0	Oct05 3-2	Jan11 4-1	Nov23 6-1		Dec25 1-0	Oct19 0-1	Apr23 2-1	Apr19 3-2
QUEEN'S PARK	Dec14 2-2	Apr05 1-3	Oct26 2-3	Jan02 2-1	Feb15 1-1	Aug17 1-2	Feb22 2-1	Feb11 1-0	Jan04 2-0	Dec07 2-0	Nov23 6-2	Sep14 2-0	Aug31 1-4	Nov02 2-4	Sep28 0-3	Nov16 4-1		Mar04 1-3	Jan25 3-0	Dec21 1-6
RANGERS	Jan25 3-1	Dec14 2-0	Nov16 9-0	Oct26 1-0	Mar29 3-0	Mar08 5-0	Dec07 4-1	Sep28 3-1	Aug31 4-0	Nov09 5-2	Feb22 1-3	Aug17 3-0	Feb08 4-0	Apr21 3-0	Dec21 4-2	Jan02 2-1	Sep03 1-0		Jan04 6-1	Sep14 2-1
ST JOHNSTONE	Oct05 0-1	Dec28 2-1	Aug10 2-3	Nov23 1-6	Oct19 3-1	Jan11 1-1	Dec25 0-1	Apr05 6-1	Apr19 3-4	Sep21 2-2	Feb19 0-3	Mar15 4-3	Mar01 1-3	Jan01 1-1	Nov16 1-1	Dec07 1-1	Sep07 4-0	Aug24 0-1		Nov02 1-3
ST MIRREN	Nov16 1-0	Oct12 0-1	Aug24 3-0	Apr12 0-0	Dec28 3-0	Sep21 2-0	Sep07 3-0	Oct05 6-1	Nov09 2-3	Feb18 2-0	Jan11 6-2	Mar29 1-2	Jan01 3-1	Oct19 5-0	Apr05 0-2	Dec14 0-3	Aug10 1-1	Feb11 0-1	Mar08 3-2	

DIVISION 2

	ALBION R	ALLOA	ARBROATH	ARMADALE	BO'NESS	BRECHIN C	CLYDEBANK	DUMBARTON	DUNFERMLINE A	EAST FIFE	E STIRLING	FORFAR A	KING'S PARK	LEITH A	MONTROSE	QUEEN OF SOUTH	RAITH R	ST BERNARD'S	STENHOUSEMUIR	T LANARK
ALBION R		Aug24 4-2	Feb22 3-2	Nov16 2-1	Jan02 6-1	Oct12 7-1	Mar08 3-0	Apr05 2-0	Mar15 3-5	Jan11 3-0	Sep21 2-1	Aug10 2-1	Sep07 6-1	Dec28 3-1	Apr30 5-2	Mar29 1-1	Dec14 7-0	Dec07 2-1	Oct26 5-2	Sep28 4-2
ALLOA	Jan04 0-0		Aug31 2-4	Sep14 0-1	Jan01 2-1	Dec21 0-2	Nov16 1-0	Jan25 2-1	Feb08 1-3	Jan02 3-4	Feb22 1-1	Nov30 2-6	Aug17 1-2	Oct12 1-3	Apr19 1-3	Dec07 0-0	Mar15 2-3	Sep28 0-1	Mar29 1-2	Nov02 2-4
ARBROATH	Oct05 3-3	Jan11 3-0		Mar01 3-2	Sep07 4-0	Mar29 4-2	Aug10 6-1	Apr12 4-3	Aug24 2-2	Feb15 1-4	Apr21 5-2	Oct26 0-5	Mar15 2-1	Nov30 2-2	Sep21 1-1	Apr19 1-1	Nov02 0-2	Nov16 1-0	Dec28 2-1	Jan02 1-4
ARMADALE	Mar22 1-3	Feb01 2-3	Oct12 0-1		Sep21 0-4	Nov02 3-1	Feb15 1-1	Nov23 2-1	Jan01 3-3	Dec14 3-2	Dec28 4-2	Mar15 3-2	Apr02 4-2	Aug24 2-2	Sep07 6-0	Nov30 3-0	Apr12 1-1	Oct19 1-0	Aug10 2-1	Feb22 0-1
BO'NESS	Oct19 1-1	Oct26 2-0	Jan25 2-1	Feb08 4-3		Sep14 4-2	Nov09 1-0	Feb22 3-1	Mar22 4-2	Mar01 1-4	Nov30 0-1	Dec14 1-1	Dec21 2-2	Mar08 3-3	Nov23 5-1	Sep28 2-1	Aug31 2-1	Aug17 1-0	Apr12 2-0	Jan04 1-3
BRECHIN C	Mar01 1-0	Aug10 2-2	Nov23 2-3	Mar08 3-1	Feb01 1-2		Aug24 3-2	Mar15 1-0	Apr19 2-3	Sep07 3-4	Jan11 2-1	Sep21 3-6	Nov16 1-1	Jan02 2-2	Oct26 3-1	Oct05 0-3	Dec28 0-3	Apr05 0-1	Feb15 2-3	Dec07 0-1
CLYDEBANK	Nov02 1-3	Mar22 2-2	Dec21 4-1	Sep28 0-1	Mar15 3-1	Jan04 6-2		Oct26 1-2	Aug31 0-1	Aug17 1-1	Jan02 4-1	Nov23 5-5	Dec14 2-1	Feb22 0-0	Dec07 3-3	Feb08 1-2	Jan25 1-1	Sep14 1-1	Oct12 5-2	Apr26 0-2
DUMBARTON	Nov30 1-2	Sep07 1-2	Dec07 1-4	Mar29 6-0	Oct05 2-5	Nov09 4-1	Jan01 1-3		Dec28 1-3	Feb01 6-3	Feb15 5-3	Aug24 1-2	Sep21 4-2	Aug10 2-3	Jan11 3-1	Mar01 4-0	Oct19 2-3	Apr19 3-0	Mar08 5-1	Nov16 4-3
DUNFERMLINE A	Nov09 2-3	Sep21 4-1	Jan04 6-4	Oct26 7-1	Nov16 5-0	Dec14 10-1	Jan11 4-2	Aug17 2-3		Oct05 0-6	Mar29 3-1	Apr16 3-0	Mar01 2-5	Sep07 0-1	Mar12 3-2	Mar08 0-2	Nov30 2-2	Dec21 1-2	Jan02 5-1	Feb01 3-5
EAST FIFE	Aug31 0-1	Oct19 3-1	Sep28 3-0	Apr19 3-0	Oct12 5-0	Jan25 7-2	Dec28 4-2	Sep14 4-1	Feb22 3-0		Aug24 2-1	Apr12 5-2	Nov02 5-4	Nov23 1-3	Aug10 2-0	Mar22 4-1	Jan01 0-2	Feb08 3-1	Nov30 7-0	Mar15 2-0
E STIRLING	Feb08 2-6	Oct05 2-4	Sep14 3-1	Aug17 6-0	Apr05 4-1	Aug31 7-0	Oct19 3-1	Sep28 1-0	Nov23 4-1	Jan04 3-3		Mar01 4-2	Jan01 3-2	Apr12 2-3	Apr16 2-0	Dec21 0-2	Mar22 3-1	Nov02 4-0	Mar15 5-0	Jan25 2-1
FORFAR A	Dec21 4-0	Apr05 5-4	Jan01 4-3	Nov09 1-1	Apr19 5-2	Feb08 2-0	Mar29 5-2	Jan04 1-2	Sep14 1-4	Dec07 1-4	Oct12 1-0		Oct19 2-3	Mar22 1-2	Nov02 5-2	Aug17 2-1	Sep28 2-0	Jan25 3-2	Feb22 4-1	Aug31 1-1
KING'S PARK	Jan25 4-0	Dec28 9-0	Nov09 3-3	Aug31 4-0	Aug10 3-1	Mar22 5-2	Apr19 5-3	Feb08 1-1	Dec07 3-3	Mar08 2-3	Oct26 0-1	Jan02 12-2		Mar12 2-2	Mar05 5-1	Sep14 3-0	Nov23 2-2	Oct05 3-2	Aug24 7-3	Apr05 2-1
LEITH A	Aug17 2-1	Mar01 7-1	Apr05 1-2	Jan04 2-0	Nov02 5-1	Oct19 4-0	Oct05 5-0	Dec21 6-2	Jan25 1-1	Mar29 0-0	Dec07 2-0	Nov16 3-2	Sep28 4-0		Mar15 2-2	Aug31 3-1	Feb08 4-1	Jan01 0-0	Apr19 5-1	Sep14 2-0
MONTROSE	Sep14 2-1	Dec14 5-1	Feb08 2-2	Jan25 2-1	Mar29 4-2	Jan01 1-1	Nov30 2-1	Aug31 6-0	Sep28 1-1	Dec21 1-1	Apr26 2-2	Mar08 5-2	Oct12 3-2	Nov09 1-2		Oct19 4-1	Feb22 1-2	Jan04 5-3	Nov16 6-6	Aug17 1-0
QUEEN OF SOUTH	Nov23 1-1	Apr12 1-2	Dec14 3-1	Apr05 2-0	Feb15 4-1	Feb22 3-1	Sep21 2-2	Oct12 5-0	Nov02 4-1	Nov16 2-4	Aug10 4-2	Dec28 2-2	Apr26 3-1	Jan11 1-0	Jan02 0-1		Aug24 1-3	Mar15 2-1	Sep07 3-1	Oct26 0-4
RAITH R	Apr19 6-2	Nov09 7-2	Mar08 3-1	Dec07 8-0	Jan11 4-2	Aug17 6-1	Sep07 6-0	Jan02 1-2	Apr05 3-1	Oct26 0-2	Nov16 4-1	Feb15 1-4	Mar29 1-3	Sep21 1-2	Oct05 1-1	Jan04 0-1		Mar01 2-1	Feb01 6-2	Dec21 1-1
ST BERNARD'S	Apr12 1-1	Feb15 1-2	Mar22 5-2	Jan02 5-1	Dec28 4-2	Nov30 3-1	Apr14 3-2	Dec14 5-0	Aug10 1-0	Sep21 1-2	Mar08 4-2	Sep07 1-2	Feb22 0-0	Oct26 0-1	Aug24 0-1	Nov09 1-2	Oct12 2-2		Jan11 3-3	Nov23 3-2
STENHOUSEMUIR	Jan01 0-3	Nov23 2-3	Aug17 0-1	Dec21 1-2	Dec07 5-0	Sep28 4-3	Mar01 3-2	Nov02 5-0	Oct19 3-2	Apr05 5-3	Nov09 1-1	Oct05 3-2	Jan04 0-1	Dec14 1-1	Mar22 6-1	Jan25 0-1	Sep14 2-2	Aug31 4-2		Feb08 0-2
T LANARK	Apr21 4-0	Mar08 1-1	Oct19 4-2	Oct05 2-0	Aug24 2-0	Apr12 6-3	Dec25 2-2	Mar22 2-2	Oct12 3-1	Nov09 1-1	Sep07 1-0	Jan11 5-0	Nov30 5-1	Apr23 2-1	Dec28 3-2	Jan01 6-2	Aug10 4-2	Mar29 1-4	Sep21 1-0	

LEAGUE TABLES

DIVISION 1

	P	W	D	L	F	A	W	D	L	F	A	Pts
Rangers	38	18	0	1	65	13	10	4	5	29	19	60
Motherwell	38	17	0	2	68	15	8	5	6	36	33	55
Aberdeen	38	14	5	0	50	24	9	2	8	35	37	53
Celtic	38	12	1	6	52	21	10	4	5	36	25	49
St Mirren	38	11	2	6	41	19	7	3	9	32	37	41
Partick T	38	11	4	4	46	27	5	5	9	26	34	41
Falkirk	38	11	5	3	40	21	5	4	10	22	43	41
Kilmarnock	38	12	2	5	47	30	3	7	9	30	43	39
Ayr U	38	10	5	4	46	32	6	1	12	24	60	38
Hearts	38	8	6	5	35	26	6	3	10	34	43	37
Clyde	38	8	4	7	37	32	5	7	7	27	37	37
Airdrie	38	11	3	5	42	26	5	1	13	18	40	36
Hamilton A	38	12	3	4	49	27	2	4	13	27	54	35
Dundee	38	9	3	7	32	26	5	3	11	19	32	34
Queen's Park	38	9	2	8	36	36	6	2	11	31	44	34
Cowdenbeath	38	10	3	6	38	19	3	4	12	26	55	33
Hibernian	38	7	6	6	27	20	2	5	12	18	42	29
Morton	38	7	5	7	46	40	3	2	14	21	55	27
Dundee U	38	5	6	8	33	38	2	2	15	23	71	22
St Johnstone	38	5	5	9	33	37	1	2	16	15	59	19

DIVISION 2

	P	W	D	L	F	A	W	D	L	F	A	Pts
Leith A	38	14	4	1	58	15	9	7	3	34	27	57
East Fife	38	16	0	3	63	21	10	5	4	51	37	57
Albion R	38	17	1	1	70	24	7	5	7	31	36	54
T. Lanark	38	14	4	1	55	24	9	2	8	37	29	52
Raith R	38	11	2	6	61	29	7	6	6	33	38	44
King's Park	38	12	5	2	75	30	5	3	11	34	50	42
Queen of South	38	11	3	5	43	28	7	3	9	22	35	42
Forfar A	38	12	2	5	50	34	6	3	10	48	61	41
Arbroath	38	10	5	4	45	36	6	2	11	38	51	39
Dunfermline A	38	10	1	8	62	42	6	5	8	37	43	38
Montrose	38	11	6	2	54	31	3	4	12	25	56	38
E. Stirling	38	14	1	4	60	28	2	3	14	23	47	36
Bo'ness	38	12	4	3	41	27	3	0	16	26	68	34
St Bernard's	38	9	4	6	43	28	4	2	13	22	37	32
Armadale	38	10	4	5	41	30	3	1	15	15	61	31
Dumbarton	38	10	0	9	56	41	4	2	13	21	54	30
Stenhousemuir	38	9	3	7	45	32	2	2	15	30	76	27
Clydebank	38	6	7	6	40	32	1	3	15	26	60	24
Alloa	38	3	3	13	22	41	6	3	10	33	63	24
Brechin C	38	6	3	10	31	39	1	1	17	26	86	18

Scottish Football League Records
Season 1930-31

DIVISION 1

	ABERDEEN	AIRDRIE	AYR U	CELTIC	CLYDE	COWDENBEATH	DUNDEE	EAST FIFE	FALKIRK	HAMILTON A	HEARTS	HIBERNIAN	KILMARNOCK	LEITH A	MORTON	MOTHERWELL	PARTICK T	QUEEN'S PARK	RANGERS	ST MIRREN
ABERDEEN		Aug30 2-0	Feb07 3-1	Jan24 1-1	Apr18 8-1	Jan03 1-1	Jan01 6-1	Feb21 4-1	Apr04 2-1	Sep22 0-2	Sep27 2-1	Nov15 7-0	Nov08 2-0	Aug16 2-1	Nov29 4-0	Sep13 2-4	Dec20 3-1	Oct25 3-1	Mar07 1-3	Oct11 0-0
AIRDRIE	Jan10 2-0		Nov01 2-1	Dec06 1-2	Sep06 2-1	Nov29 2-1	Nov15 2-0	Apr06 0-3	Sep20 1-3	Feb14 3-1	Apr25 2-2	Feb18 4-1	Aug23 4-3	Feb28 4-1	Dec27 2-0	Oct18 0-5	Mar14 0-2	Aug09 1-3	Oct04 3-3	Apr04 3-0
AYR U	Oct04 2-1	Mar07 0-0		Nov22 2-6	Oct11 0-2	Apr25 5-1	Nov08 2-6	Jan05 3-1	Aug23 2-5	Jan10 4-2	Oct25 1-1	Sep06 1-3	Apr29 1-0	Mar21 2-0	Aug09 2-2	Nov29 2-3	Feb21 1-1	Mar28 3-1	Feb18 2-2	Apr18 2-0
CELTIC	Sep06 1-0	Apr18 3-1	Apr04 4-1		Feb18 0-1	Mar21 6-0	Mar25 2-2	Jan10 9-1	Dec27 3-0	Feb24 2-1	Nov08 2-1	Aug23 6-0	Aug09 3-1	Dec13 4-0	Oct04 4-1	Mar04 4-1	Nov01 5-1	Apr28 1-1	Sep20 2-0	Oct18 3-1
CLYDE	Dec06 2-5	Jan24 2-1	Aug16 1-1	Apr06 0-2		Aug30 5-2	Dec20 2-2	Mar07 3-0	Nov15 0-1	Feb21 3-1	Sep13 1-2	Mar14 3-2	Apr25 0-3	Sep27 2-2	Oct25 1-0	Feb07 0-6	Jan01 1-2	Nov22 2-4	Feb14 0-8	Jan03 3-0
COWDENBEATH	Aug23 2-0	Apr11 2-1	Dec13 1-1	Nov15 1-1	Jan10 0-1		Feb21 3-0	Sep20 2-1	Sep06 3-0	Apr01 3-1	Mar07 2-2	Oct04 2-1	Jan05 3-1	Nov22 7-1	Mar28 3-0	Apr18 1-0	Oct25 0-3	Dec27 1-3	Aug09 1-3	Mar18 3-1
DUNDEE	Sep20 4-2	Mar21 0-1	Mar18 5-2	Apr22 0-0	Aug09 2-1	Oct18 2-0		Dec27 2-0	Oct04 3-1	Sep06 4-2	Nov22 1-3	Jan05 1-0	Mar28 0-2	Dec06 6-0	Jan10 3-0	Nov01 2-1	Dec13 0-0	Feb28 3-0	Aug23 0-1	Mar09 2-0
EAST FIFE	Oct18 1-3	Sep13 1-5	Sep27 4-1	Aug30 2-6	Nov01 1-4	Jan01 0-0	Aug16 1-2		Nov29 4-4	Apr04 2-0	Jan03 1-0	Feb28 1-0	Mar21 4-1	Oct11 0-0	Nov08 2-3	Dec20 1-1	Jan24 0-2	Apr18 3-2	Apr25 0-4	Feb07 3-2
FALKIRK	Nov22 5-3	Jan01 1-3	Jan03 2-0	Aug16 3-2	Mar21 4-0	Jan24 4-0	Feb07 4-1	Apr11 1-0		Dec06 1-4	Oct11 0-3	Apr25 2-2	Oct25 4-2	Dec20 2-3	Mar07 3-1	Sep27 0-1	Aug30 2-4	Feb21 3-0	Nov08 1-3	Sep13 1-3
HAMILTON A	Dec13 3-0	Sep27 1-1	Aug30 3-1	Sep13 0-0	Oct18 4-0	Oct11 0-1	Jan24 1-0	Nov22 4-1	Apr18 5-1		Dec20 3-2	Nov29 1-0	Mar07 0-0	Jan03 2-3	Mar21 1-1	Jan01 1-0	Feb07 2-0	Nov08 3-1	Feb28 0-3	Aug16 1-0
HEARTS	Jan05 3-2	Dec13 6-3	Feb28 9-0	Mar18 1-1	Mar28 0-3	Nov01 1-1	Apr04 2-0	Aug23 6-1	Feb18 4-2	Aug09 0-4		Sep20 4-1	Jan10 1-4	Oct18 5-2	Sep06 2-4	Nov15 5-1	Apr18 1-2	Oct04 2-1	Dec27 3-0	Nov29 3-1
HIBERNIAN	Mar21 1-2	Oct11 2-0	Jan24 2-0	Jan03 0-0	Nov08 1-2	Feb07 1-0	Sep27 2-3	Oct25 2-1	Dec13 5-2	Apr11 1-0	Jan01 2-2		Nov22 3-2	Aug30 0-1	Feb21 1-1	Aug16 2-2	Sep13 0-3	Mar11 4-2	Dec06 1-2	Dec20 2-3
KILMARNOCK	Mar18 1-1	Jan03 1-0	Sep13 2-1	Dec20 0-3	Dec13 2-1	Sep27 0-1	Oct11 1-2	Nov15 5-1	Mar11 1-1	Nov01 3-1	Aug30 0-1	Apr04 4-0		Feb07 2-1	Apr18 3-0	Jan24 1-4	Aug16 2-0	Nov29 2-1	Oct18 1-0	Jan01 2-3
LEITH A	Dec27 0-0	Oct25 0-1	Nov15 1-1	Apr25 0-3	Jan05 2-4	Apr04 2-2	Apr18 3-1	Jan31 6-1	Aug09 2-2	Aug23 1-2	Feb21 2-1	Jan10 1-1	Oct04 0-1		Sep20 2-3	Mar17 2-5	Nov29 2-1	Sep06 2-0	Mar14 1-3	Nov01 1-1
MORTON	Apr11 1-2	Aug16 5-0	Dec20 1-1	Feb07 0-1	Feb28 0-1	Sep13 1-2	Aug30 2-1	Mar14 3-0	Nov01 5-3	Nov15 1-0	Jan24 2-4	Oct18 5-4	Dec06 2-2	Jan01 1-1		Oct11 0-3	Jan03 3-1	Dec13 1-3	Apr04 1-2	Dec25 4-2
MOTHERWELL	Feb09 5-0	Feb21 4-0	Apr22 1-1	Oct25 3-3	Oct04 4-4	Dec06 3-1	Mar07 2-0	Aug09 4-1	Mar30 6-1	Sep20 3-0	Mar21 2-0	Dec27 6-0	Sep06 1-1	Nov08 4-1	Feb18 3-0		Apr04 0-0	Aug23 2-1	Jan10 1-0	Apr25 3-1
PARTICK T	Aug09 2-1	Nov08 2-0	Oct18 5-1	Mar07 1-0	Sep20 2-0	Mar10 4-1	Apr25 4-1	Sep06 8-0	Jan10 3-2	Oct04 1-1	Dec06 2-1	Feb10 1-0	Dec27 3-1	Apr11 2-0	Aug23 2-1	Dec25 0-3		Oct11 5-1	Apr22 1-1	Nov15 2-1
QUEEN'S PARK	Mar03 2-2	Dec20 0-0	Dec25 4-1	Sep27 3-3	Apr04 4-1	Aug16 0-3	Sep13 2-2	Dec06 5-1	Oct18 2-0	Mar17 5-0	Feb11 1-2	Nov01 2-2	Apr21 2-0	Jan24 1-1	Apr25 5-2	Jan03 1-3	Feb14 2-1		Nov15 0-2	Aug30 4-1
RANGERS	Nov01 4-0	Feb07 0-1	Apr06 5-1	Jan01 1-0	Nov29 5-1	Dec20 7-0	Jan03 3-0	Dec13 4-0	Mar18 1-0	Sep02 1-0	Aug16 4-1	Apr18 1-0	Feb21 1-0	Sep13 4-1	Nov22 7-1	Aug30 1-1	Sep27 3-1	Apr01 2-0		Jan24 1-1
ST MIRREN	Feb23 2-2	Nov22 2-3	Dec06 0-0	Feb21 1-3	Aug23 2-1	Nov08 0-1	Oct25 3-1	Oct04 2-0	Apr14 0-5	Dec27 4-2	Apr11 0-3	Aug09 1-0	Sep20 4-2	Mar07 2-2	Apr20 0-0	Dec13 2-1	Mar21 0-1	Jan10 2-1	Sep06 1-1	

DIVISION 2

	ALBION R	ALLOA	ARBROATH	ARMADALE	BO'NESS	BRECHIN C	CLYDEBANK	DUMBARTON	DUNDEE U	DUNFERMLINE A	E STIRLING	FORFAR A	KING'S PARK	MONTROSE	QUEEN OF SOUTH	RAITH R	ST BERNARD'S	ST JOHNSTONE	STENHOUSEMUIR	T LANARK
ALBION R		Sep27 0-0	Apr29 3-1	Feb07 5-2	Dec13 4-0	Oct25 3-0	Oct11 5-2	Apr11 1-1	Mar18 0-5	Mar07 3-0	Aug30 3-1	Aug16 4-2	Apr18 2-4	Jan03 4-0	Nov08 4-2	Dec20 2-0	Feb21 4-4	Sep13 1-3	Jan01 2-2	Jan24 0-0
ALLOA	Jan02 3-3		Oct04 5-2	Oct25 2-0	Sep20 3-1	Sep06 3-0	Apr11 0-2	Feb14 2-0	Dec27 1-4	Mar28 2-1	Mar07 1-3	Apr21 3-0	Jan10 0-4	Apr25 8-1	Aug09 2-1	Mar21 3-2	Aug23 2-0	Nov08 2-2	Feb21 3-2	Dec06 2-1
ARBROATH	Mar28 3-2	Feb11 5-3		Aug16 5-1	Nov22 5-0	Apr11 3-0	Jan24 2-1	Oct25 3-1	Apr13 1-2	Feb21 2-0	Sep13 2-2	Jan01 5-3	Nov15 5-2	Oct11 4-2	Mar07 1-4	Jan03 0-1	Dec13 4-4	Dec20 4-0	Aug30 1-0	Sep27 1-2
ARMADALE	Oct04 4-0	Feb28 5-1	Dec27 2-1		Aug23 4-0	Feb14 0-0	Oct18 3-3	Sep06 3-4	Aug09 1-4	Sep20 0-2	Apr11 5-2	Nov01 3-0	Mar28 2-1	Mar18 5-1	Jan10 2-1	Apr04 4-3	Jan05 2-1	Apr25 3-0	Dec06 3-5	Nov15 1-2
BO'NESS	Nov15 1-4	Jan01 2-1	Apr04 3-1	Jan03 1-2		Apr22 4-0	Aug30 6-3	Feb21 4-4	Dec06 1-3	Oct25 1-2	Jan24 0-6	Sep13 3-2	Mar18 2-4	Dec20 3-3	Apr11 4-0	Sep27 3-2	Nov01 0-1	Feb07 2-0	Aug16 1-1	Oct11 0-3
BRECHIN C	Feb28 1-2	Jan24 1-0	Nov29 1-0	Oct11 3-0	Mar28 4-1		Jan03 4-2	Apr04 2-2	Oct18 2-4	Nov15 1-4	Aug16 2-3	Apr29 1-1	Nov01 1-1	Jan01 2-1	Dec13 2-1	Sep13 2-2	Mar18 1-4	Sep27 3-5	Dec20 4-1	Aug30 2-2
CLYDEBANK	Feb14 4-1	Nov29 3-0	Sep06 0-2	Feb21 5-2	Jan10 1-0	Aug23 1-2		Sep20 1-4	Apr06 1-2	Oct04 1-2	Oct25 1-4	Apr18 3-2	Aug09 1-2	Mar07 1-0	Jan31 0-1	Apr25 1-5	Dec27 2-1	Nov15 1-3	Nov08 1-3	Apr04 3-3
DUMBARTON	Nov29 1-0	Oct11 1-0	Feb28 3-1	Jan24 6-2	Oct18 3-1	Apr13 0-1	Jan01 0-2		Nov01 4-1	Jan31 0-0	Sep27 5-0	Dec20 2-2	Dec13 3-2	Sep13 4-1	Mar21 1-2	Aug16 3-1	Apr18 0-3	Aug30 3-2	Feb07 4-1	Jan03 2-4
DUNDEE U	Apr04 4-0	Aug16 1-1	Nov08 4-0	Dec20 4-0	Apr18 0-1	Feb21 6-0	Sep27 5-2	Mar07 1-1		Apr25 2-1	Feb07 1-1	Jan24 4-3	Nov29 2-0	Aug30 4-1	Oct25 5-2	Oct11 1-2	Nov15 5-3	Jan01 1-1	Jan03 5-2	Sep13 1-2
DUNFERMLINE A	Nov01 6-0	Sep13 4-0	Oct18 1-1	Jan01 1-0	Mar25 3-0	Mar21 8-0	Feb07 2-1	Nov08 2-1	Dec13 4-4		Dec20 2-1	Jan03 3-0	Apr04 0-2	Jan24 3-3	Apr18 1-2	Aug30 3-1	Nov29 1-2	Oct11 1-0	Sep27 11-2	Aug16 1-3
E STIRLING	Jan10 3-0	Nov01 3-2	Apr22 0-3	Nov29 5-0	Sep06 2-1	Dec27 1-1	Feb28 6-1	Jan05 7-1	Oct04 3-1	Aug09 0-2		Mar14 3-3	Sep20 1-5	Nov15 3-2	Aug23 1-1	Apr18 1-1	Mar28 0-1	Apr04 1-2	Dec13 3-2	Oct18 2-1
FORFAR A	Dec27 4-4	Apr04 1-3	Sep20 5-3	Mar26 4-3	Apr16 2-1	Oct04 6-1	Dec06 3-1	Aug09 3-0	Sep06 2-2	Aug23 1-4	Nov08 4-1		Jan05 5-1	Oct25 0-1	Feb14 1-1	Nov29 1-0	Jan10 1-0	Feb21 2-1	Mar21 3-2	Apr25 4-1
KING'S PARK	Dec06 5-3	Aug30 1-1	Mar21 5-1	Sep13 3-2	Nov08 5-1	Mar07 0-1	Dec20 1-2	Apr25 0-2	Apr11 1-2	Apr15 0-1	Jan01 2-3	Sep27 0-1		Aug16 2-3	Feb21 3-0	Jan24 5-1	Oct25 3-1	Jan03 1-1	Oct11 0-1	Feb07 1-3
MONTROSE	Aug23 3-2	Dec13 3-2	Feb18 1-0	Nov08 5-3	Aug09 2-1	Sep20 1-0	Nov01 1-0	Mar28 2-1	Jan10 2-1	Sep06 3-0	Mar21 4-3	Feb28 4-2	Dec27 2-1		Jan05 3-1	Oct18 2-1	Oct04 1-3	Apr18 4-1	Nov22 2-2	Apr11 1-2
QUEEN OF SOUTH	Mar14 3-3	Dec20 7-0	Nov01 4-2	Aug30 3-2	Nov29 5-0	Apr25 4-1	Sep13 5-0	Nov15 3-0	Feb28 0-0	Dec06 5-1	Jan03 1-3	Oct11 3-0	Oct18 1-1	Sep27 1-6		Feb07 4-1	Apr04 0-4	Aug16 3-2	Jan24 4-1	Jan01 1-3
RAITH R	Aug09 3-3	Nov15 7-0	Aug23 3-2	Nov22 4-0	Jan02 2-0	Jan31 2-1	Dec13 5-0	Dec27 2-0	Feb14 0-0	Jan10 1-1	Dec06 2-1	Apr11 4-3	Sep06 5-6	Feb21 2-1	Oct04 2-0		Sep20 4-2	Mar07 4-2	Oct25 5-2	Mar14 3-1
ST BERNARD'S	Oct18 2-4	Jan03 5-0	Apr25 8-0	Sep27 3-1	Mar07 2-2	Nov08 2-3	Aug16 6-1	Dec06 2-2	Mar21 2-1	Apr11 2-2	Oct11 1-1	Aug30 0-2	Feb28 3-0	Feb25 7-2	Nov22 1-2	Jan01 1-1		Jan24 1-1	Sep13 2-2	Dec20 0-1
ST JOHNSTONE	Apr06 3-0	Mar14 2-1	Aug09 6-1	Dec13 3-0	Oct04 2-0	Dec25 1-0	Mar21 3-2	Jan10 4-1	Sep20 2-0	Feb14 1-0	Nov22 3-1	Oct18 1-0	Aug23 1-1	Dec06 4-0	Dec27 1-1	Nov01 2-3	Sep06 5-1		Apr11 4-1	Mar18 0-3
STENHOUSEMUIR	Sep20 0-0	Oct18 2-3	Jan10 7-3	Apr18 3-1	Dec27 6-2	Aug09 1-2	Mar14 3-2	Oct04 3-3	Aug23 0-1	Jan05 0-1	Jan31 1-2	Nov15 3-2	Feb14 3-2	Apr04 1-0	Sep06 0-3	Feb28 3-6	Apr15 1-0	Nov29 6-2		Nov01 0-6
T LANARK	Sep06 2-2	Apr18 5-0	Jan02 3-3	Sep17 3-1	Mar21 3-1	Jan10 2-0	Nov22 9-3	Aug23 1-0	Feb10 4-0	Dec27 2-2	Feb21 4-2	Dec13 5-0	Oct04 1-1	Apr06 6-1	Sep20 2-1	Nov08 6-0	Aug09 2-0	Oct25 2-0	Mar07 2-0	

LEAGUE TABLES

DIVISION 1

	P	W	D	L	F	A	W	D	L	F	A	Pts
Rangers	38	16	2	1	55	9	11	4	4	41	20	60
Celtic	38	16	2	1	64	14	8	8	3	37	20	58
Motherwell	38	14	5	0	57	15	10	3	6	45	27	56
Partick T	38	16	2	1	50	16	8	3	8	26	27	53
Hearts	38	12	2	5	58	33	7	4	8	32	30	44
Aberdeen	38	13	3	3	53	20	4	4	11	26	43	41
Cowdenbeath	38	12	3	4	40	21	5	4	10	18	44	41
Dundee	38	13	2	4	40	16	4	3	12	25	47	39
Airdrie	38	11	2	6	38	32	6	3	10	21	34	39
Hamilton A	38	12	4	3	35	15	4	1	14	24	42	37
Kilmarnock	38	11	2	6	33	22	4	3	12	26	38	35
Clyde	38	7	3	9	31	44	8	1	10	29	43	34
Queen's Park	38	9	6	4	45	27	4	1	14	26	45	33
Falkirk	38	10	1	8	43	35	4	3	12	34	52	32
St Mirren	38	8	5	6	28	29	3	3	13	21	43	30
Morton	38	8	3	8	38	33	3	4	12	20	50	29
Leith A	38	5	6	8	30	33	3	5	11	21	52	27
Ayr U	38	8	5	6	37	37	0	6	13	16	55	27
Hibernian	38	8	4	7	32	28	1	3	15	17	53	25
East Fife	38	7	4	8	31	40	1	0	18	14	73	20

DIVISION 2

	P	W	D	L	F	A	W	D	L	F	A	Pts
T. Lanark	38	15	4	0	64	17	12	3	4	43	25	61
Dundee U	38	12	4	3	56	23	9	4	6	37	31	50
Dunfermline A	38	12	3	4	57	23	8	4	7	26	27	47
Raith R	38	15	3	1	60	25	5	3	11	33	47	46
St Johnstone	38	15	2	2	48	16	4	4	11	28	45	44
Queen of South	38	12	3	4	57	30	6	3	10	26	36	42
E. Stirling	38	10	4	5	45	30	7	3	9	40	44	41
Montrose	38	16	1	2	46	26	3	2	14	29	64	41
Albion R	38	11	5	3	50	29	3	6	10	33	55	39
Dumbarton	38	12	2	5	45	26	3	6	10	28	46	38
St Bernard's	38	7	7	5	50	28	7	2	10	35	38	37
Forfar A	38	13	3	3	52	30	2	3	14	28	54	36
Alloa	38	13	2	4	47	29	2	3	14	18	58	35
King's Park	38	7	2	10	38	30	7	4	8	40	40	34
Arbroath	38	13	2	4	56	30	2	2	15	27	64	34
Brechin C	38	8	5	6	39	36	5	2	12	13	48	33
Stenhousemuir	38	9	2	8	43	41	3	4	12	32	60	30
Armadale	38	12	2	5	52	31	1	0	18	22	68	28
Clydebank	38	7	1	11	31	39	3	1	15	30	69	*22
Bo'ness	38	8	3	8	41	42	1	1	17	13	58	22

* Clydebank left the League, replaced by Edinburgh.

Scottish Football League Records
Season 1931-32

DIVISION 1

	ABERDEEN	AIRDRIE	AYR U	CELTIC	CLYDE	COWDENBEATH	DUNDEE	DUNDEE U	FALKIRK	HAMILTON A	HEARTS	KILMARNOCK	LEITH A	MORTON	MOTHERWELL	PARTICK T	QUEEN'S PARK	RANGERS	ST MIRREN	T LANARK
ABERDEEN		Dec26 2-2	Sep19 5-1	Aug22 1-1	Aug26 1-0	Aug08 2-0	Sep05 1-1	Oct17 5-2	Sep28 3-1	Mar19 5-0	Jan02 1-2	Nov14 1-1	Sep02 1-0	Oct31 1-0	Jan23 0-1	Oct03 2-0	Mar05 1-1	Dec12 0-0	Feb20 0-2	Feb06 1-0
AIRDRIE	Aug15 2-4		Feb27 2-2	Apr09 1-1	Jan09 3-0	Nov14 2-1	Nov07 2-2	Aug29 4-2	Jan01 2-1	Sep12 2-0	Dec05 3-1	Dec19 0-2	Oct10 8-2	Sep26 5-1	Aug26 2-2	Aug19 0-3	Feb13 2-0	Apr25 3-0	Oct24 0-2	Mar12 2-2
AYR U	Jan30 3-2	Oct17 5-1		Mar05 2-3	Apr02 5-0	Mar19 5-0	Dec05 1-0	Sep26 2-0	Dec19 2-0	Aug15 1-3	Nov14 1-2	Sep12 1-1	Jan09 6-1	Oct10 2-1	Aug19 1-3	Oct31 0-2	Jan01 0-1	Aug29 1-3	Sep09 2-5	Nov28 3-4
CELTIC	Jan09 2-0	Dec12 6-1	Oct24 4-2		Oct10 1-1	Aug26 7-0	Feb27 0-2	Aug15 3-2	Sep26 4-1	Aug29 6-1	Aug19 3-0	Apr23 4-1	Dec19 6-0	Apr02 6-3	Mar12 2-4	Nov14 1-2	Sep12 2-2	Jan01 1-2	Mar28 1-0	Dec05 5-0
CLYDE	Nov28 0-1	Aug22 3-2	Oct03 3-3	Feb20 2-1		Dec26 1-1	Feb06 0-1	Aug31 4-1	Sep14 1-0	Oct31 1-1	Jan23 6-2	Oct17 0-0	Nov21 3-2	Apr19 3-0	Sep19 2-3	Sep05 2-1	Apr27 1-0	Apr23 1-1	Aug08 2-0	Jan02 2-4
COWDENBEATH	Dec19 3-1	Apr23 1-0	Nov07 1-1	Nov28 1-2	Aug15 3-0		Mar12 2-1	Jan01 1-1	Jan09 2-1	Oct10 1-0	Sep09 2-1	Apr09 7-1	Sep12 3-0	Aug29 2-2	Oct24 1-5	Dec05 2-0	Sep26 2-2	Apr02 1-7	Nov21 1-3	Feb27 2-0
DUNDEE	Jan01 0-0	Mar19 4-1	Sep02 2-2	Oct17 2-0	Sep26 1-1	Oct31 0-4		Sep12 1-1	Feb13 2-0	Jan09 0-3	Mar05 1-0	Oct10 1-1	Apr02 2-2	Aug15 2-1	Nov14 2-2	Dec12 3-1	Aug29 4-0	Dec19 4-2	Aug26 1-2	Sep28 6-3
DUNDEE U	Feb27 0-4	Jan23 2-7	Feb06 1-2	Dec26 1-0	Dec05 1-1	Sep05 0-0	Jan02 0-3		Nov07 2-2	Apr16 0-5	Aug08 0-2	Sep09 0-0	Oct24 0-0	Nov28 3-4	Feb20 1-6	Aug22 3-1	Nov21 0-5	Mar12 0-5	Sep19 1-0	Oct03 3-2
FALKIRK	Nov21 3-0	Sep05 3-0	Aug08 2-2	Feb06 2-0	Dec12 4-3	Aug22 2-2	Oct03 5-2	Mar19 4-0		Nov28 2-1	Feb20 0-2	Apr02 4-1	Mar26 9-1	Oct17 2-2	Jan02 2-3	Dec26 1-2	Oct31 4-1	Sep02 1-2	Jan23 1-4	Sep19 1-3
HAMILTON A	Nov07 4-1	Jan02 3-1	Dec26 1-3	Jan23 1-0	Mar12 6-1	Feb20 1-1	Aug22 6-2	Nov14 4-2	Aug26 2-2		Oct03 1-4	Aug19 1-3	Feb27 7-0	Dec12 5-0	Sep05 2-2	Sep19 3-1	Apr02 2-1	Oct24 1-2	Feb06 2-0	Aug08 2-3
HEARTS	Sep12 0-0	Sep01 0-2	Mar26 1-1	Nov21 2-1	Aug29 2-0	Dec12 3-2	Oct24 3-1	Dec19 5-0	Oct10 2-0	Apr09 4-2		Aug15 3-0	Jan01 4-2	Jan09 0-0	Feb27 0-1	Aug25 0-1	Apr16 2-0	Sep26 0-0	Mar12 2-2	Nov07 2-3
KILMARNOCK	Apr06 0-2	Aug08 4-2	Jan02 5-1	Oct03 2-3	Feb27 1-0	Sep19 3-2	Feb20 0-0	Dec12 8-0	Oct24 2-1	Nov21 1-1	Dec26 2-1		Mar12 6-3	Sep02 1-0	Aug22 1-0	Feb06 3-4	Aug26 4-1	Apr30 2-4	Sep05 3-0	Jan23 2-1
LEITH A	Dec05 1-2	Feb20 0-3	Aug22 4-1	Aug08 0-3	Apr16 1-4	Jan02 1-2	Sep19 1-0	Mar05 1-5	Nov14 2-1	Oct17 1-4	Sep05 2-0	Oct31 3-1		Mar19 0-2	Feb06 0-5	Jan23 1-3	Sep09 1-3	Nov28 2-5	Oct03 0-4	Dec26 2-1
MORTON	Mar12 1-1	Feb06 2-1	Feb13 4-2	Sep19 3-3	Oct24 0-1	Jan23 1-3	Dec26 4-1	Aug26 4-2	Feb27 4-3	Sep09 1-0	Aug22 1-2	Dec05 3-1	Nov07 9-1		Oct03 2-2	Aug08 1-2	Mar26 6-2	Nov21 1-2	Jan02 2-2	Sep05 5-0
MOTHERWELL	Aug29 3-0	Nov28 3-0	Nov21 6-0	Oct31 2-2	Apr30 3-0	Apr16 3-0	Mar26 4-0	Oct10 5-0	Sep12 4-1	Jan01 3-1	Oct17 2-0	Jan09 4-0	Sep26 7-1	Feb17 4-2		Mar19 1-0	Dec19 4-1	Aug15 4-2	Dec05 4-1	Sep16 6-0
PARTICK T	Feb13 1-0	Nov21 3-1	Mar12 2-1	Apr30 0-2	Jan01 3-1	Sep02 5-1	Sep16 1-3	Jan09 3-0	Aug15 1-2	Apr23 1-6	Nov28 1-0	Sep26 4-2	Aug29 2-2	Dec19 1-0	Apr02 0-0		Mar28 2-1	Sep12 1-3	Feb27 2-1	Oct24 0-0
QUEEN'S PARK	Oct24 1-3	Oct03 3-1	Sep05 3-2	Jan02 0-3	Nov07 2-3	Feb06 2-1	Jan23 0-1	Aug18 1-2	Mar12 2-1	Sep01 1-1	Sep19 5-2	Nov28 2-0	Dec12 3-3	Nov14 4-1	Aug08 1-5	Feb20 2-0		Feb27 1-6	Dec26 2-0	Aug22 1-3
RANGERS	Sep15 4-1	Aug11 2-1	Jan23 6-1	Sep05 0-0	Nov14 2-2	Oct03 6-1	Aug08 4-1	Oct31 5-0	Dec05 4-0	Apr27 1-0	Feb06 4-2	Mar19 3-0	Aug25 4-0	Aug18 7-3	Dec26 1-0	Jan02 4-0	Oct17 0-1		Aug22 4-0	Feb20 6-1
ST MIRREN	Oct10 4-2	Apr02 2-1	Dec12 4-0	Mar19 1-2	Dec19 3-1	Aug18 1-4	Nov28 6-1	Apr09 5-1	Aug29 3-1	Sep26 1-0	Oct31 5-1	Jan01 2-0	Feb13 6-3	Sep12 2-0	Sep01 0-1	Oct17 1-1	Aug15 2-0	Jan09 0-2		Nov14 1-1
T LANARK	Sep26 2-0	Oct31 5-2	Aug25 2-0	Sep02 3-3	Sep12 4-2	Oct17 5-3	Nov21 6-1	Apr02 4-1	Jan30 1-0	Dec19 4-1	Mar19 3-4	Aug29 1-3	Aug15 2-0	Jan01 6-2	Dec12 0-2	Apr09 3-1	Jan09 2-1	Mar28 4-3	Mar26 4-0	

DIVISION 2

	ALBION R	ALLOA	ARBROATH	ARMADALE	BO'NESS	BRECHIN C	DUMBARTON	DUNFERMLINE A	EAST FIFE	E STIRLING	EDINBURGH C	FORFAR A	HIBERNIAN	KING'S PARK	MONTROSE	QUEEN OF SOUTH	RAITH R	ST BERNARD'S	ST JOHNSTONE	STENHOUSEMUIR
ALBION R		Jan02 6-2	Nov28 2-2	Sep19 5-3	Oct17 1-3	Mar05 4-1	Oct31 5-0	Dec12 1-2	Nov21 2-1	Dec26 3-2	Feb06 5-2	Feb20 1-4	Mar26 1-0	Sep02 0-3	Aug08 0-1	Mar19 4-0	Oct03 1-3	Aug22 2-1	Jan23 3-4	Sep05 1-3
ALLOA	Sep12 4-2		Apr16 2-0	Oct24 3-2	Aug29 1-1	Jan09 2-0	Sep26 1-1	Jan01 1-4	Oct10 0-2	Dec12 1-2	Nov07 8-2	Nov21 6-1	Dec19 1-2	Aug15 2-2	Feb27 1-4	Feb13 3-4	Mar12 0-0	Aug18 1-3	Mar26 1-0	Nov28 2-1
ARBROATH	Apr09 6-4	Sep19 2-3		Feb20 1-0	Oct31 3-1	Mar26 0-2	Oct17 5-0	Nov21 1-0	Mar19 2-0	Jan23 3-1	Aug22 6-2	Sep05 2-0	Dec05 3-3	Dec12 6-3	Feb06 3-2	Mar05 4-0	Aug08 3-1	Jan02 3-0	Oct03 2-3	Dec26 4-1
ARMADALE	Apr16 3-2	Mar05 1-1	Oct10 0-1		Jan01 7-1	Sep26 3-1	Jan09 0-0	Dec19 1-4	Feb13 5-4	Mar19 1-0	Mar26 3-3	Oct17 0-0	Sep12 1-1	Aug29 0-1	Apr02 5-1	Aug15 1-3	Dec05 1-2	Nov28 2-0	Aug27 1-3	Oct31 1-4
BO'NESS	Feb27 4-3	Jan23 3-3	Mar12 1-4	Sep05 2-1		Nov21 3-0	Apr09 1-3	Mar26 1-3	Aug19 1-0	Aug22 2-5	Dec26 3-2	Aug08 3-1	Oct24 2-2	Nov07 3-2	Oct03 2-0	Dec12 1-1	Jan02 4-3	Feb06 1-2	Sep19 1-0	Feb20 3-1
BRECHIN C	Oct24 1-1	Aug22 2-5	Nov14 2-0	Feb06 3-4	Apr02 4-2		Dec12 1-1	Nov07 3-0	Nov28 2-5	Feb20 0-1	Aug08 4-3	Sep19 1-1	Mar12 3-3	Feb27 0-5	Sep05 1-0	Aug19 0-2	Jan23 0-1	Dec26 2-2	Jan02 0-1	Oct03 1-7
DUMBARTON	Mar12 3-1	Feb06 3-1	Feb27 2-2	Aug22 3-1	Nov28 6-2	Aug25 2-2		Oct24 2-1	Apr16 3-2	Jan02 2-3	Sep05 1-1	Oct03 1-3	Nov07 0-2	Mar26 3-2	Jan23 5-1	Apr02 5-0	Feb20 6-1	Aug08 1-1	Dec26 3-0	Sep19 4-0
DUNFERMLINE A	Aug26 2-0	Sep05 1-2	Apr02 6-0	Aug08 3-0	Nov14 3-1	Mar19 0-1	Apr04 2-0		Oct31 4-3	Feb06 2-1	Sep19 0-0	Jan23 4-2	Apr16 1-1	Nov28 8-3	Aug22 2-2	Oct17 5-2	Dec26 0-3	Oct03 1-1	Feb20 2-2	Jan02 0-0
EAST FIFE	Apr02 6-2	Feb20 2-1	Nov07 4-1	Oct03 4-1	Dec05 4-0	Apr09 5-1	Sep03 4-1	Mar12 5-2		Sep19 2-0	Jan02 6-0	Aug22 3-3	Feb27 1-1	Oct24 7-1	Dec26 4-1	Nov14 3-1	Sep05 1-4	Jan23 0-2	Feb06 2-4	Aug08 3-3
E STIRLING	Aug15 5-1	Aug26 2-1	Aug29 1-0	Nov07 6-1	Jan09 5-2	Oct10 2-0	Sep12 3-0	Sep26 4-1	Jan30 5-1		Feb27 6-4	Nov14 5-0	Feb13 4-1	Jan01 3-1	Oct24 4-1	Dec19 5-0	Apr09 5-1	Apr02 5-1	Mar12 0-1	Apr16 1-1
EDINBURGH C	Sep26 1-4	Mar19 2-4	Jan09 4-2	Nov14 4-6	Aug15 2-3	Dec19 1-1	Dec25 4-2	Apr30 4-1	Sep12 0-7	Oct17 0-2		Oct31 2-2	Oct10 2-1	Feb13 3-4	Apr23 4-4	Aug29 4-8	Dec12 2-4	Mar05 1-6	Apr09 1-7	Nov21 2-5
FORFAR A	Oct10 4-3	Apr02 1-1	Jan01 3-2	Feb27 1-3	Dec19 4-2	Jan30 2-1	Feb13 3-0	Aug29 3-2	Jan09 6-1	Mar26 6-3	Mar12 2-2		Aug15 1-0	Sep12 4-2	Nov28 7-0	Sep26 2-1	Nov07 2-1	Dec12 5-3	Oct24 3-1	Apr23 2-3
HIBERNIAN	Nov14 4-1	Aug08 1-0	Aug18 3-1	Jan02 1-0	Mar05 2-1	Oct31 4-0	Mar19 0-1	Sep02 6-2	Oct17 3-2	Oct03 1-1	Feb20 3-1	Dec26 5-1		Apr02 2-1	Sep19 0-0	Nov28 1-4	Feb06 0-1	Sep05 2-4	Aug22 6-0	Jan23 0-2
KING'S PARK	Dec05 1-2	Dec26 1-0	Aug26 5-2	Jan23 9-0	Mar19 5-0	Oct17 5-1	Nov14 2-2	Apr09 3-1	Mar05 2-2	Sep05 2-3	Oct03 3-2	Jan02 3-2	Nov21 1-4		Feb20 9-2	Oct31 2-3	Aug22 1-1	Sep19 2-2	Aug08 0-2	Feb06 7-1
MONTROSE	Dec19 0-3	Oct17 4-1	Sep26 1-1	Nov21 4-3	Feb13 5-1	Jan01 1-2	Aug29 1-0	Jan09 0-1	Aug15 3-2	Mar05 0-3	Dec05 0-1	Apr09 2-2	Jan30 0-1	Oct10 2-0		Sep12 4-2	Nov14 3-4	Oct31 1-2	Sep02 2-3	Mar19 3-2
QUEEN OF SOUTH	Nov07 4-0	Oct03 0-3	Oct24 2-2	Dec26 4-2	Aug27 3-4	Dec05 7-2	Nov21 2-1	Feb27 2-4	Mar26 3-3	Aug08 5-1	Jan23 5-4	Feb06 2-1	Apr09 2-3	Mar12 4-2	Jan02 5-1		Sep19 3-1	Feb20 2-2	Sep05 4-1	Aug22 2-4
RAITH R	Feb13 4-0	Oct31 2-1	Dec19 5-1	Aug19 5-1	Sep12 3-1	Aug29 1-3	Oct10 4-2	Aug15 0-2	Jan01 2-1	Nov28 4-2	Aug26 7-2	Mar19 0-2	Sep26 1-2	Jan09 2-0	Mar26 2-2	Apr16 2-0		Oct17 4-3	Nov21 1-1	Mar05 0-0
ST BERNARD'S	Jan09 3-2	Dec05 3-0	Sep12 3-1	Apr09 3-1	Sep26 1-3	Aug15 5-1	Dec19 0-0	Apr23 4-0	Aug29 2-3	Nov21 0-4	Oct24 4-2	Aug26 1-2	Jan01 1-0	Apr16 4-0	Mar12 1-2	Oct10 1-0	Feb27 2-0		Nov07 2-2	Mar26 3-1
ST JOHNSTONE	Aug29 7-0	Nov14 4-1	Feb13 4-1	Dec12 6-1	Apr23 6-1	Sep12 3-1	Aug15 3-0	Oct10 3-1	Sep26 3-0	Oct31 2-2	Nov28 4-1	Mar05 3-0	Jan09 2-1	Dec19 5-0	Apr16 4-0	Jan01 2-2	Apr02 2-0	Mar19 0-2		Oct17 2-2
STENHOUSEMUIR	Jan01 5-3	Apr09 1-3	Aug15 2-0	Mar12 3-2	Oct10 2-0	Feb13 3-2	Jan30 1-1	Sep12 5-1	Dec19 0-2	Sep08 1-4	Apr02 3-1	Dec05 4-2	Aug29 2-1	Sep26 3-2	Nov07 3-0	Jan09 1-5	Oct24 3-3	Nov14 3-1	Feb27 2-2	

LEAGUE TABLES

DIVISION 1

	P	W	D	L	F	A	W	D	L	F	A	Pts
Motherwell	38	18	1	0	72	11	12	5	2	47	20	66
Rangers	38	16	2	1	67	14	12	3	4	51	28	61
Celtic	38	13	2	4	64	24	7	6	6	30	26	48
T. Lanark	38	15	1	3	61	29	6	3	10	31	52	46
St Mirren	38	13	2	4	49	22	7	2	10	28	34	44
Partick T	38	11	3	5	33	26	8	1	10	25	33	42
Aberdeen	38	10	6	3	33	15	6	3	10	24	34	41
Hearts	38	10	5	4	35	18	7	0	12	28	43	39
Kilmarnock	38	13	2	4	50	26	3	5	11	18	44	39
Hamilton A	38	11	3	5	54	29	5	3	11	30	36	38
Dundee	38	9	7	3	38	26	5	3	11	23	46	38
Cowdenbeath	38	11	4	4	38	28	4	4	11	28	50	38
Clyde	38	10	5	4	37	24	3	4	12	21	46	35
Airdrie	38	10	5	4	45	28	3	1	15	29	53	32
Morton	38	10	4	5	54	31	2	3	14	24	56	31
Queen's Park	38	9	2	8	36	38	4	3	12	23	41	31
Ayr U	38	9	1	9	43	32	2	6	11	27	58	29
Falkirk	38	10	3	6	52	31	1	2	16	18	45	27
Dundee U	38	4	5	10	18	49	2	2	15	22	69	19
Leith A	38	6	0	13	23	49	0	4	15	23	88	16

DIVISION 2

	P	W	D	L	F	A	W	D	L	F	A	Pts
E. Stirling	38	17	1	1	71	18	9	2	8	40	37	55
St Johnstone	38	15	3	1	65	16	9	4	6	37	36	55
Raith R	38	12	3	4	49	26	8	3	8	34	39	46
Stenhousemuir	38	12	3	4	47	35	7	5	7	41	41	46
St Bernard's	38	12	2	5	43	24	7	5	7	38	38	45
Forfar A	38	15	2	2	61	31	4	5	10	29	48	45
Hibernian	38	12	2	5	44	23	6	6	7	29	29	44
East Fife	38	13	3	3	66	29	5	2	12	41	48	41
Queen of South	38	11	3	5	61	41	7	2	10	38	50	41
Dunfermline A	38	10	6	3	46	24	7	0	12	32	49	40
Arbroath	38	15	1	3	59	26	2	4	13	23	52	39
Dumbarton	38	12	4	3	55	26	2	6	11	15	42	38
Alloa	38	8	4	7	40	33	6	3	10	33	41	35
Bo'ness	38	11	3	5	41	36	4	1	14	29	67	34
King's Park	38	10	4	5	63	32	4	1	14	34	61	33
Albion R	38	10	1	8	47	37	3	1	15	34	67	28
Montrose	38	8	2	9	36	34	3	4	12	24	62	28
Armadale	38	7	5	7	36	32	3	0	16	32	70	25
Brechin C	38	5	5	9	30	44	4	2	13	22	53	25
Edinburgh	38	4	3	12	43	73	1	4	14	35	73	17

Scottish Football League Records
Season 1932-33

DIVISION 1

	ABERDEEN	AIRDRIE	AYR U	CELTIC	CLYDE	COWDENBEATH	DUNDEE	E STIRLING	FALKIRK	HAMILTON A	HEARTS	KILMARNOCK	MORTON	MOTHERWELL	PARTICK T	QUEEN'S PARK	RANGERS	ST JOHNSTONE	ST MIRREN	T LANARK
ABERDEEN		Sep03 2-0	Jan07 5-0	Dec24 1-0	Nov19 8-1	Feb25 6-2	Jan02 3-2	Sep17 1-3	Sep14 8-2	Oct29 2-1	Sep26 3-0	Aug24 7-1	Mar11 6-0	Aug20 1-1	Jan28 0-0	Dec17 3-4	Apr15 1-1	Nov26 0-0	Oct15 5-1	Oct01 1-0
AIRDRIE	Jan14 2-0		Dec10 3-2	Dec03 0-3	Aug13 5-2	Aug24 1-2	Mar18 3-0	Apr08 8-1	Sep10 1-0	Jan03 2-1	Dec31 2-7	Oct08 2-1	Mar04 2-1	Nov19 1-4	Nov12 0-1	Sep24 1-1	Aug27 1-2	Feb11 1-1	Apr29 1-3	Oct22 1-2
AYR U	Aug27 3-1	Apr22 4-2		Dec17 0-1	Sep24 3-1	Oct29 3-2	Apr08 6-0	Aug24 4-2	Oct08 0-1	Feb11 0-1	Jan14 1-1	Jan03 2-3	Sep10 0-1	Nov12 2-6	Mar11 2-0	Aug13 4-3	Dec31 3-3	Mar04 2-0	Dec03 1-0	Mar25 1-0
CELTIC	Aug13 3-0	Apr18 2-1	Aug30 4-1		Apr10 2-1	Nov19 3-0	Dec10 3-2	Nov12 3-0	Jan14 0-1	Dec31 0-3	Feb11 3-2	Sep24 0-0	Aug27 7-1	Oct22 4-1	Aug24 1-2	Dec26 2-0	Sep10 1-1	Oct08 5-0	Apr03 0-0	Aug16 4-2
CLYDE	Mar25 2-0	Dec24 6-0	Jan28 2-0	Oct15 0-2		Oct01 2-1	Sep03 0-3	Aug20 4-3	Dec03 3-1	Mar11 7-2	Nov26 0-1	Apr22 0-1	Dec17 2-1	Jan07 2-3	Jan02 1-0	Oct29 6-2	Nov05 0-5	Sep12 2-3	Feb25 2-1	Sep17 1-0
COWDENBEATH	Oct08 0-3	Nov05 6-1	Mar18 6-2	Mar25 1-5	Feb11 5-2		Oct22 4-1	Dec03 4-3	Aug13 4-3	Mar04 1-2	Sep10 0-0	Aug27 4-1	Dec31 0-0	Apr29 1-4	Apr08 0-0	Jan14 0-2	Sep24 2-3	Jan03 3-2	Sep14 1-3	Dec10 2-1
DUNDEE	Sep10 0-2	Oct29 4-2	Nov26 1-1	Apr22 3-0	Jan14 2-1	Mar11 4-2		Dec17 3-0	Sep24 3-0	Aug13 1-5	Jan03 2-2	Mar29 3-0	Feb11 2-2	Aug24 0-3	Apr15 1-0	Dec31 2-1	Oct08 0-3	Aug27 0-0	Nov19 1-1	Nov12 2-2
E STIRLING	Jan03 2-1	Nov26 1-0	Nov05 4-0	Sep14 1-3	Dec31 2-2	Apr15 1-1	Apr29 3-2		Mar04 1-2	Sep24 1-5	Oct08 1-3	Feb11 2-3	Aug13 0-3	Dec10 1-4	Apr01 2-7	Aug27 1-1	Jan14 2-3	Sep10 1-3	Oct22 2-1	Mar18 2-0
FALKIRK	Nov12 2-0	Jan02 3-1	Feb25 1-2	Sep03 1-1	Feb18 2-1	Dec24 6-0	Jan28 0-0	Oct15 3-0		Mar25 5-0	Oct29 3-1	Dec17 2-2	Apr22 2-1	Sep17 2-2	Oct01 1-2	Mar11 2-3	Nov26 1-4	Aug24 1-1	Aug20 2-3	Jan07 7-1
HAMILTON A	Mar18 1-0	Sep17 7-0	Oct01 3-0	Aug20 1-1	Oct22 1-1	Oct15 10-2	Dec24 1-2	Jan28 4-3	Nov19 2-0		Aug24 3-2	Nov12 0-0	Apr14 2-2	Jan02 2-3	Jan07 4-3	Nov26 3-2	Apr29 2-4	Dec10 1-1	Sep03 4-3	Feb25 3-2
HEARTS	Dec10 3-1	Aug20 4-0	Sep03 4-2	Oct01 1-1	Apr08 1-1	Jan02 3-1	Sep17 1-0	Feb25 3-1	Apr01 3-2	Nov05 6-1		Dec03 1-0	Mar25 5-2	Oct15 2-0	Dec24 1-2	Sep13 5-0	Oct22 1-0	Apr29 2-1	Jan07 0-0	Jan28 3-1
KILMARNOCK	Nov05 4-3	Feb25 2-4	Sep17 3-5	Jan28 2-2	Dec10 1-2	Jan07 4-1	Oct15 2-2	Oct01 2-1	Apr29 1-1	Sep14 3-2	Apr12 0-0		Nov26 1-1	Dec24 1-3	Sep03 3-0	Nov19 3-1	Mar18 2-6	Oct22 5-4	Jan02 0-1	Aug20 6-0
MORTON	Oct22 0-1	Oct15 4-2	Feb18 1-1	Jan07 0-1	Apr29 0-0	Aug20 2-2	Oct01 1-4	Dec24 3-1	Dec10 3-4	Dec03 2-5	Nov19 1-5	Apr08 5-2		Jan28 1-2	Feb25 2-3	Nov05 0-2	Aug17 1-3	Mar18 2-0	Sep17 0-1	Sep03 1-3
MOTHERWELL	Dec31 2-3	Mar25 4-1	Sep14 3-1	Mar11 4-2	Aug27 1-0	Dec17 2-0	Nov05 6-1	Apr22 4-1	Jan03 2-0	Sep10 4-1	Mar29 5-1	Aug13 3-3	Sep24 7-0		Oct29 1-2	Oct08 7-2	Feb11 1-3	Jan14 1-0	Apr08 3-0	Dec03 6-3
PARTICK T	Sep24 1-2	Dec26 3-0	Oct22 7-0	Nov05 3-0	Sep10 2-3	Nov26 4-1	Dec03 4-0	Mar25 6-3	Feb11 2-1	Aug27 1-2	Aug13 1-2	Jan14 1-3	Oct08 2-1	Apr03 0-1		Mar04 3-4	Jan03 0-0	Dec31 2-2	Dec10 3-1	Apr29 2-2
QUEEN'S PARK	Apr29 4-0	Feb18 0-0	Dec24 4-1	Sep17 4-1	Apr19 1-4	Sep03 5-0	Aug20 2-0	Jan07 6-2	Oct22 1-3	Apr10 1-0	Nov12 2-1	Apr26 1-2	Aug23 1-1	Feb25 4-2	Mar15 2-1		Dec10 0-0	Apr03 3-3	Oct01 4-2	Jan02 1-1
RANGERS	Dec03 3-1	Jan07 5-1	Aug20 4-1	Jan02 0-0	Aug23 2-2	Jan28 4-1	Feb25 6-4	Sep03 4-0	Apr08 5-1	Dec17 4-4	Mar11 4-4	Oct29 2-0	Nov12 6-1	Oct01 2-2	Sep17 3-0	Apr22 1-0		Nov19 3-0	Dec24 4-0	Aug31 5-0
ST JOHNSTONE	Apr08 2-2	Oct01 1-0	Oct15 4-0	Feb25 1-0	Nov12 2-1	Sep17 3-1	Jan07 2-1	Jan02 2-0	Nov05 1-0	Apr22 2-0	Dec17 2-1	Mar11 6-1	Oct29 7-1	Sep03 0-1	Aug20 2-1	Dec03 5-2	Mar25 0-2		Jan28 3-1	Dec24 2-2
ST MIRREN	Mar04 2-2	Dec17 7-1	Apr15 3-1	Oct29 3-1	Oct08 2-1	Nov12 7-1	Mar25 2-1	Mar11 3-0	Dec31 1-2	Jan14 3-0	Aug27 0-1	Sep10 3-2	Jan03 1-1	Nov26 2-5	Apr22 1-1	Feb11 1-2	Aug13 2-0	Sep24 2-0		Aug23 3-1
T LANARK	Feb11 3-0	Mar11 3-2	Nov19 5-1	Nov26 0-4	Jan03 4-1	Apr22 3-1	Dec26 1-1	Oct29 4-1	Aug27 4-0	Oct08 2-1	Sep24 2-1	Dec31 3-2	Jan14 2-0	Apr25 1-1	Dec17 0-3	Sep10 6-0	Mar04 1-3	Aug13 2-2	Nov05 1-3	

DIVISION 2

	ALBION R	ALLOA	ARBROATH	BRECHIN C	DUMBARTON	DUNDEE U	DUNFERMLINE A	EAST FIFE	EDINBURGH C	FORFAR A	HIBERNIAN	KING'S PARK	LEITH A	MONTROSE	QUEEN OF SOUTH	RAITH R	ST BERNARD'S	STENHOUSEMUIR	ARMADALE	BO'NESS
ALBION R		Sep17 5-2	Nov05 4-0	Nov26 5-1	Jan02 3-1	Dec17 4-2	Sep07 5-0	Sep14 3-2	Oct29 0-1	Sep03 4-1	Aug20 2-0	Apr22 3-4	Mar11 5-1	Feb25 5-1	Oct15 0-3	Oct01 1-2	Dec24 3-1	Jan28 0-1		
ALLOA	Jan03 0-2		Aug27 2-0	Aug13 1-3	Nov26 4-1	Jan14 1-0	Sep10 2-1	Oct08 1-2	Sep24 4-1	Mar18 9-2	Oct22 0-3	Dec31 4-3	Feb11 4-1	Mar25 1-0	Apr15 3-2	Dec10 4-1	Apr29 2-1	Nov12 0-0	Aug23 6-0	
ARBROATH	Aug24 1-2	Jan07 0-0		Dec03 2-0	Dec24 3-1	Nov12 0-0	Mar18 1-4	Apr29 3-2	Apr08 4-0	Jan02 5-1	Oct01 0-3	Nov19 4-1	Apr22 3-1	Sep03 3-2	Aug20 4-0	Oct15 1-3	Sep17 1-2	Feb25 2-1		Oct22 3-3
BRECHIN C	Apr08 1-4	Dec24 3-1	Apr15 3-1		Apr01 2-1	Apr22 1-3	Apr04 2-2	Oct22 2-3	Dec17 2-1	Jan07 0-1	Sep17 2-4	Nov05 2-2	Nov19 8-2	Jan02 5-2	Jan28 2-2	Aug20 2-4	Oct15 3-1	Oct01 1-2	Sep03 3-2	
DUMBARTON	Sep10 3-0	Apr08 3-1	Sep24 2-1	Oct08 2-0		Jan03 2-0	Mar04 1-2	Feb11 2-1	Aug27 6-2	Nov19 2-2	Dec03 3-2	Jan14 2-0	Dec31 3-0	Apr22 6-2	Nov12 1-1	Feb18 3-2	Mar18 6-0	Aug24 2-0	Oct22 3-1	Aug13 5-1
DUNDEE U	Dec03 2-0	Sep03 1-1	Sep14 2-1	Dec10 3-1	Sep17 5-2		Oct22 2-4	Nov05 3-3	Mar25 5-0	Feb25 4-1	Dec24 0-2	Mar18 7-3	Apr08 4-3	Oct15 3-1	Jan02 1-2	Jan07 2-1	Oct01 1-0	Aug20 2-1		
DUNFERMLINE A	Apr01 3-1	Jan02 3-0	Oct29 2-2	Nov12 4-2	Oct15 3-0	Mar11 5-1		Feb18 7-3	Aug24 4-0	Aug20 6-1	Sep03 2-2	Dec17 4-1	Dec03 6-0	Dec24 4-1	Jan07 4-1	Jan28 1-0	Apr22 4-0	Sep17 1-1	Oct01 9-1	
EAST FIFE	Nov12 6-1	Apr01 5-0	Dec17 4-2	Mar11 3-4	Oct01 1-1	Aug24 1-0	Nov19 0-1		Dec03 3-1	Dec24 3-0	Jan07 0-5	Apr08 4-2	Oct29 6-1	Jan28 2-0	Sep17 3-3	Jan02 2-1	Aug20 4-0	Sep03 6-2	Oct15 8-1	
EDINBURGH C	Mar18 0-7	Jan28 0-2	Nov26 0-7	Apr29 4-3	Jan07 1-1	Nov19 1-1	Nov05 1-3	Apr15 2-4		Oct01 4-3	Oct15 0-4	Oct22 4-4	Sep06 1-0	Aug20 2-4	Sep03 1-2	Feb25 2-5	Dec26 2-8	Dec24 0-3	Sep17 4-3	Sep13 1-2
FORFAR A	Jan14 1-1	Oct29 2-1	Sep10 2-4	Aug27 3-0	Mar25 8-3	Oct08 1-4	Dec31 0-3	Aug13 3-0	Feb11 4-1		Apr29 3-3	Jan03 1-1	Mar04 5-0	Nov12 3-2	Mar11 1-3	Aug25 4-1	Apr15 4-0	Dec10 1-2		Sep24 3-2
HIBERNIAN	Dec31 2-1	Mar11 1-0	Feb11 2-0	Jan03 3-1	Apr15 1-0	Aug13 2-0	Jan14 3-1	Aug27 2-1	Feb18 7-1	Dec17 2-0		Sep24 0-1	Sep10 3-0	Aug24 4-1	Apr22 1-2	Oct29 2-1	Mar25 4-1	Nov26 4-1	Nov12 8-2	Oct08 7-0
KING'S PARK	Dec10 2-3	Oct15 2-1	Mar25 1-1	Aug24 2-3	Sep03 3-3	Oct29 7-2	Apr29 2-1	Nov26 2-1	Mar11 7-1	Sep17 3-0	Jan28 0-0		Nov12 4-0	Oct01 3-1	Feb25 4-0	Dec24 6-0	Jan07 2-4	Jan02 3-1	Aug20 1-1	
LEITH A	Oct22 1-2	Oct01 1-0	Dec10 1-2	Mar25 4-0	Aug20 3-1	Nov26 2-1	Apr15 0-0	Mar18 1-1	Apr01 3-0	Oct15 2-1	Jan02 0-1	Sep14 4-2		Sep17 1-1	Dec24 2-2	Sep03 1-0	Jan28 1-1	Jan07 2-1		
MONTROSE	Oct08 2-3	Nov19 1-3	Jan14 2-4	Sep10 0-1	Dec10 3-1	Mar04 3-0	Aug13 1-1	Sep24 4-3	Dec31 2-2	Sep14 2-3	Nov05 1-3	Feb11 3-3	Jan03 3-1		Oct29 3-1	Mar11 4-2	Nov26 1-1	Apr29 1-2		Aug27 3-1
QUEEN OF SOUTH	Feb18 4-1	Dec03 1-1	Dec31 3-1	Sep24 9-1	Sep29 2-0	Sep10 1-0	Aug27 3-1	Jan03 5-3	Jan14 4-1	Oct22 5-1	Dec10 0-0	Oct08 4-2	Aug13 5-2	Mar18 4-3		Apr08 2-2	Nov05 2-2	Nov19 5-3		Oct01 10-0
RAITH R	Feb11 2-1	Apr22 4-3	Mar04 4-0	Dec31 5-3	Apr29 2-2	Aug27 4-1	Sep24 1-1	Sep10 3-1	Oct08 5-0	Nov05 2-1	Mar18 1-2	Aug13 9-1	Jan14 3-0	Oct22 4-2	Nov26 1-3		Sep14 4-2	Apr15 1-1		
ST BERNARD'S	Aug13 4-1	Dec17 2-2	Jan03 0-0	Mar04 8-0	Oct29 4-0	Feb11 3-2	Oct08 2-0	Dec31 2-1	Sep10 8-1	Dec03 0-1	Nov19 0-1	Aug27 1-0	Sep24 0-1	Apr08 1-3	Aug23 2-2	Nov12 3-2		Mar11 3-2		
STENHOUSEMUIR	Sep24 0-0	Sep13 1-0	Oct08 5-2	Feb11 1-1	Nov05 3-2	Dec31 3-1	Jan03 2-1	Jan14 2-1	Aug13 4-1	Apr22 5-3	Apr08 3-2	Sep10 2-2	Aug27 2-1	Dec17 4-1	Mar25 2-5	Dec03 3-1	Oct22 1-0			
ARMADALE	Aug27 2-3	Nov05 0-2	Aug13 1-4			Sep24 5-3					Sep15 2-4		Oct08 2-2			Nov19 1-5		Oct29 2-4		Sep10 1-3
BO'NESS		Aug20 2-2		Oct29 4-3									Aug24 2-1			Sep17 1-2	Sep03 3-6	Oct15 2-3		

LEAGUE TABLES

DIVISION 1

	P	W	D	L	F	A	W	D	L	F	A	Pts
Rangers	38	14	5	0	67	22	12	5	2	46	21	62
Motherwell	38	15	1	3	66	24	12	4	3	48	29	59
Hearts	38	15	3	1	49	16	6	5	8	35	35	50
Celtic	38	13	3	3	47	18	7	5	7	28	26	48
St Johnstone	38	15	2	2	47	17	2	8	9	23	38	44
Aberdeen	38	13	4	2	63	19	5	2	12	22	39	42
St Mirren	38	12	3	4	48	23	6	3	10	25	37	42
Hamilton A	38	11	5	3	54	31	7	1	11	36	47	42
Queen's Park	38	11	5	3	46	24	6	2	11	32	55	41
Partick T	38	9	3	7	47	28	8	3	8	28	27	40
Falkirk	38	9	5	5	46	25	6	1	12	24	45	36
Clyde	38	12	0	7	42	29	3	5	11	27	46	35
T. Lanark	38	12	3	4	47	27	2	4	13	23	53	35
Kilmarnock	38	8	5	6	45	39	5	4	10	27	47	35
Dundee	38	9	6	4	34	27	3	3	13	26	50	33
Ayr U	38	11	2	6	41	28	2	2	15	21	67	30
Cowdenbeath	38	9	3	7	44	38	1	2	16	21	73	25
Airdrie	38	9	2	8	37	34	1	1	17	18	68	23
Morton	38	4	3	12	29	42	2	6	11	20	55	21
E. Stirling	38	6	3	10	30	44	1	0	18	25	71	17

DIVISION 2

	P	W	D	L	F	A	W	D	L	F	A	Pts
Hibernian	34	15	0	2	43	12	10	4	3	37	17	54
Queen of South	34	13	4	0	59	24	7	5	5	34	35	49
Dunfermline A	34	14	3	0	63	16	6	4	7	26	28	47
Stenhousemuir	34	13	3	1	43	24	5	3	9	24	34	42
Albion R	34	12	0	5	52	23	7	2	8	30	34	40
Raith R	34	12	3	2	55	24	4	1	12	28	43	36
East Fife	34	12	2	3	53	24	3	2	12	32	47	34
King's Park	34	11	3	3	53	22	2	5	10	32	58	34
Dumbarton	34	14	2	1	49	16	0	4	13	20	51	34
Arbroath	34	10	2	5	37	23	4	3	10	28	39	33
Alloa	34	12	1	4	42	23	2	4	11	18	35	33
St Bernard's	34	10	3	4	43	19	3	3	11	24	45	32
Dundee U	34	12	2	3	47	26	2	2	13	18	41	32
Forfar A	34	9	3	5	46	29	3	1	13	22	58	28
Brechin C	34	7	3	7	41	36	4	1	12	24	59	26
Leith A	34	9	5	3	29	16	1	0	16	14	65	25
Montrose	34	6	4	7	36	34	2	1	14	27	55	21
Edinburgh	34	3	3	11	25	61	1	1	15	14	72	12

Armadale & Boness did not complete their fixtures and their records were expunged.

Scottish Football League Records
Season 1933-34

DIVISION 1

	ABERDEEN	AIRDRIE	AYR U	CELTIC	CLYDE	COWDENBEATH	DUNDEE	FALKIRK	HAMILTON A	HEARTS	HIBERNIAN	KILMARNOCK	MOTHERWELL	PARTICK T	QUEEN OF SOUTH	QUEEN'S PARK	RANGERS	ST JOHNSTONE	ST MIRREN	T LANARK
ABERDEEN		Dec30 4-0	Aug12 8-0	Oct07 3-0	Mar24 4-0	Jan02 5-0	Sep09 1-3	Nov11 5-0	Feb10 5-1	Apr21 0-1	Sep23 2-1	Nov04 2-0	Sep25 1-1	Aug26 3-0	Oct21 5-0	Apr28 2-2	Dec02 1-2	Nov25 1-1	Apr14 0-0	Jan13 3-0
AIRDRIE	Aug19 0-1		Apr28 1-1	Apr07 2-4	Feb24 1-0	Dec09 2-0	Oct28 2-1	Jan01 2-2	Sep30 3-4	Apr14 3-2	Nov25 0-3	Jan27 3-1	Mar24 3-6	Sep13 2-1	Oct14 2-5	Jan06 3-4	Dec23 2-7	Sep02 1-1	Nov04 4-1	Mar10 1-2
AYR U	Dec23 1-2	Dec16 1-1		Nov18 3-1	Jan06 4-2	Mar17 6-2	Nov25 3-3	Jan27 1-0	Sep02 3-1	Aug19 4-3	Apr07 4-1	Sep30 1-1	Apr21 2-3	Oct21 3-1	Jan01 0-3	Feb24 2-6	Sep16 0-2	Oct14 3-2	Sep13 2-2	Nov04 5-1
CELTIC	Feb24 2-2	Dec02 4-2	Mar24 0-3		Apr02 2-1	Sep19 7-0	Apr21 3-2	Aug19 2-2	Apr23 5-1	Sep02 0-0	Oct28 2-1	Jan06 4-1	Mar10 3-0	Nov04 2-0	Dec23 0-1	Sep30 3-1	Jan01 2-2	Jan27 0-0	Apr11 3-0	Nov25 3-1
CLYDE	Nov18 2-2	Oct07 4-2	Aug26 5-2	Apr18 1-1		Jan13 2-3	Dec30 3-0	Apr07 2-0	Oct21 0-2	Mar27 1-2	Apr14 1-0	Dec09 0-1	Aug12 0-1	Sep09 3-3	Apr28 3-1	Mar17 1-1	Aug22 1-6	Nov11 3-0	Sep23 0-0	Jan02 4-2
COWDENBEATH	Sep30 2-4	Apr21 1-3	Oct28 2-2	Nov11 0-1	Sep02 5-1		Mar10 1-1	Feb24 0-3	Oct14 4-0	Jan27 1-5	Aug23 2-4	Dec23 0-1	Dec16 0-4	Nov25 1-1	Sep16 1-3	Aug19 0-2	Jan06 3-4	Jan01 1-5	Apr30 6-0	Nov18 3-1
DUNDEE	Jan01 1-1	Mar17 4-0	Mar31 2-1	Dec09 3-2	Aug19 1-1	Oct21 4-2		Jan06 1-3	Feb24 1-1	Sep30 0-1	Apr28 1-0	Oct14 0-2	Nov04 2-3	Dec02 1-2	Sep02 8-0	Sep16 1-0	Jan27 0-6	Dec23 3-0	Mar24 3-0	Sep13 3-0
FALKIRK	Sep13 6-5	Sep09 0-2	Sep23 2-3	Dec30 2-0	Dec02 2-2	Oct07 4-3	Aug26 2-1		Nov18 2-0	Mar17 2-1	Mar03 3-1	Apr28 2-2	Jan02 1-3	Jan13 3-0	Dec09 3-0	Oct21 5-1	Apr25 1-3	Nov04 4-0	Aug17 2-1	Aug12 3-3
HAMILTON A	Oct28 2-1	Jan02 4-2	Jan13 1-1	Apr14 1-1	Mar10 1-0	Mar03 1-0	Oct07 3-2	Mar24 2-1		Nov04 1-1	Aug25 4-1	Sep13 2-2	Sep09 1-2	Aug12 3-7	Dec02 0-2	Mar31 1-0	Mar14 1-2	Apr21 4-1	Dec30 1-2	Sep23 2-2
HEARTS	Dec09 0-0	Dec25 8-1	Dec30 1-1	Jan13 2-1	Nov25 1-1	Sep23 5-4	Jan02 6-1	Oct28 3-1	Aug22 4-2		Sep09 0-0	Apr07 1-1	Apr16 1-3	Oct07 1-0	Nov18 1-3	Nov11 4-0	Mar10 1-2	Apr28 2-1	Aug12 6-0	Aug26 5-1
HIBERNIAN	Jan27 3-2	Mar31 0-2	Dec02 0-0	Mar17 1-2	Sep16 3-0	Nov04 6-1	Dec16 2-1	Oct14 1-3	Jan06 1-2	Jan01 1-4		Sep02 4-1	Sep13 0-2	Mar24 0-2	Feb24 0-2	Dec23 2-1	Aug19 0-0	Sep30 2-6	Oct21 2-1	Apr21 3-1
KILMARNOCK	Aug23 2-0	Sep23 7-1	Jan02 4-2	Aug26 4-3	Feb17 2-2	Aug12 4-1	Mar03 1-3	Dec16 1-1	Nov11 1-1	Dec02 2-5	Jan13 2-0		Oct07 1-3	Dec30 2-0	Mar31 3-0	Apr18 3-1	Oct28 1-3	Mar10 1-0	Sep09 3-0	Aug16 1-2
MOTHERWELL	Sep16 4-1	Nov18 3-1	Dec09 5-2	Oct21 1-1	Dec23 1-2	Apr11 6-1	Aug23 1-0	Sep30 2-1	Jan01 2-1	Oct14 2-1	Nov11 2-1	Feb24 2-0		Mar17 2-3	Jan06 1-2	Jan27 3-0	Sep02 2-1	Aug19 1-0	Nov25 1-0	Apr07 2-2
PARTICK T	Jan06 4-0	Nov11 1-0	Mar10 5-1	Aug23 0-3	Jan01 2-0	Mar31 5-3	Apr07 1-1	Sep02 0-3	Dec23 1-2	Feb24 7-2	Nov18 3-2	Aug19 2-3	Oct28 1-4		Jan27 1-1	Oct14 5-2	Sep30 3-4	Sep16 0-3	Apr24 2-3	Apr14 3-0
QUEEN OF SOUTH	Mar10 4-1	Apr26 1-1	Sep09 2-4	Aug12 3-2	Dec16 2-2	Feb10 4-0	Jan13 3-1	Apr21 2-1	Apr07 3-1	Mar24 3-1	Oct07 1-0	Nov25 4-1	Aug26 0-5	Sep23 4-3		Aug23 1-4	Nov11 0-4	Oct28 2-3	Jan02 0-1	Dec30 5-1
QUEEN'S PARK	Mar28 1-5	Aug26 2-1	Oct07 4-5	Dec25 2-3	Oct28 1-2	Dec30 1-0	Feb17 2-4	Apr14 1-0	Nov25 2-4	Sep12 1-1	Aug12 2-1	Nov18 3-4	Sep23 1-5	Mar03 0-1	Nov04 4-2		Apr30 1-1	Apr07 1-0	Jan13 0-0	Jan01 4-2
RANGERS	Apr07 2-1	Aug12 5-1	Aug15 9-1	Sep09 2-2	Nov04 3-1	Aug26 3-1	Sep23 1-0	Nov25 3-1	Apr28 4-2	Oct21 3-1	Dec30 6-0	Mar17 2-2	Jan13 4-2	Jan02 2-2	Sep13 5-1	Dec09 4-0		Mar24 3-0	Oct07 3-0	Mar21 1-0
ST JOHNSTONE	Apr11 5-1	Jan13 4-0	Feb17 0-2	Sep23 1-1	Sep13 1-0	Sep09 3-3	Aug12 0-1	Aug23 3-0	Dec09 5-1	Dec16 3-1	Jan02 0-1	Oct21 0-3	Dec30 1-2	Feb10 4-0	Mar17 4-0	Dec02 1-0	Nov18 3-1		Aug26 1-1	Oct07 4-1
ST MIRREN	Oct14 2-3	Aug22 1-1	Nov11 1-1	Apr28 1-2	Jan27 2-0	Dec02 0-0	Nov18 0-3	Sep16 3-1	Aug19 2-3	Dec23 1-1	Mar10 0-3	Jan01 3-1	Mar20 1-3	Dec09 2-0	Sep30 0-3	Sep02 1-2	Feb24 1-2	Jan06 1-4		Oct28 7-2
T LANARK	Sep02 2-3	Oct21 3-1	Aug22 3-7	Mar31 1-1	Sep30 3-3	Mar24 5-1	Nov11 4-1	Dec23 3-1	Jan27 1-1	Jan06 1-1	Dec09 1-0	Sep16 1-1	Dec02 2-2	Apr28 3-1	Aug19 1-2	Sep08 2-5	Apr02 0-1	Feb24 1-4	Mar17 1-5	

LEAGUE TABLES

DIVISION 1

	P	W	D	L	F	A	W	D	L	F	A	Pts
Rangers	38	16	3	0	65	18	14	3	2	53	23	66
Motherwell	38	14	2	3	43	20	15	2	2	54	25	62
Celtic	38	12	5	2	47	20	6	6	7	31	33	47
Queen of South	38	11	2	6	44	36	10	1	8	31	42	45
Aberdeen	38	12	4	3	55	12	6	4	9	35	45	44
Hearts	38	11	5	3	52	23	6	5	8	34	36	44
Kilmarnock	38	11	3	5	45	28	6	6	7	28	36	43
Ayr U	38	10	4	5	48	37	6	6	7	39	55	42
St Johnstone	38	11	3	5	43	19	6	3	10	31	34	40
Falkirk	38	12	3	4	49	31	4	3	12	24	37	38
Hamilton A	38	9	5	5	35	30	6	3	10	30	49	38
Dundee	38	10	3	6	39	25	5	3	11	29	39	36
Partick T	38	9	2	8	46	37	5	3	11	27	41	33
Clyde	38	8	5	6	36	29	2	6	11	20	41	31
Queen's Park	38	7	3	9	33	41	6	2	11	32	44	31
Hibernian	38	8	2	9	31	33	4	1	14	20	36	27
St Mirren	38	5	4	10	29	35	4	5	10	17	40	27
Airdrie	38	7	3	9	37	46	3	3	13	22	57	26
T. Lanark	38	6	6	7	38	41	2	3	14	24	62	25
Cowdenbeath	38	4	3	12	33	45	1	2	16	25	73	15

DIVISION 2

	P	W	D	L	F	A	W	D	L	F	A	Pts
Albion R	34	14	3	0	55	19	6	2	9	19	28	45
Dunfermline A	34	14	1	2	53	18	6	3	8	37	34	44
Arbroath	34	15	0	2	56	20	5	4	8	27	33	44
Stenhousemuir	34	13	2	2	47	27	5	2	10	23	46	40
Morton	34	12	2	3	42	24	5	3	9	25	40	39
Dumbarton	34	15	0	2	43	15	2	3	12	24	53	37
King's Park	34	11	6	0	54	22	3	2	12	24	48	36
Raith R	34	11	3	3	46	16	4	2	11	25	39	35
E. Stirling	34	9	4	4	41	29	5	3	9	24	45	35
St Bernard's	34	12	3	2	50	13	3	1	13	25	43	34
Forfar A	34	10	5	2	51	24	3	2	12	26	47	33
Leith A	34	8	3	6	36	23	4	5	8	27	37	32
East Fife	34	8	3	6	42	35	4	5	8	29	41	32
Brechin C	34	10	3	4	37	21	3	2	12	23	49	31
Alloa	34	8	4	5	36	27	3	5	9	19	41	31
Montrose	34	9	1	7	34	30	2	3	12	19	51	26
Dundee U	34	7	3	7	53	39	3	1	13	28	49	24
Edinburgh	34	4	4	9	22	37	0	2	15	15	74	14

DIVISION 2

	ALBION R	ALLOA	ARBROATH	BRECHIN C	DUMBARTON	DUNDEE U	DUNFERMLINE A	EAST FIFE	E STIRLING	EDINBURGH C	FORFAR A	KING'S PARK	LEITH A	MONTROSE	MORTON	RAITH R	ST BERNARD'S	STENHOUSEMUIR
ALBION R		Jan03 2-1	Mar10 4-0	Apr14 3-0	Sep09 2-0	Nov04 4-3	Jan13 3-2	Oct07 1-1	Aug26 3-1	Oct14 8-1	Dec02 3-2	Mar31 4-2	Oct21 2-0	Aug12 6-2	Dec30 3-1	Feb10 2-2	Sep23 1-1	Jan06 4-0
ALLOA	Sep02 1-1		Mar31 2-2	Mar03 3-1	Nov11 2-0	Aug19 1-2	Jan01 2-1	Feb10 2-2	Dec02 4-1	Apr14 4-0	Dec09 2-1	Sep30 1-2	Sep16 3-1	Oct14 1-2	Mar17 1-1	Dec23 3-1	Jan27 1-3	Oct28 3-6
ARBROATH	Oct28 4-1	Aug12 5-0		Mar17 2-3	Aug26 4-1	Jan27 4-2	Dec23 3-2	Sep23 5-1	Oct07 6-1	Apr07 2-0	Sep09 3-1	Dec02 4-1	Oct14 2-1	Mar03 2-0	Jan06 1-4	Nov11 1-0	Apr21 5-2	Feb10 3-0
BRECHIN C	Nov25 3-1	Oct07 1-2	Dec30 2-0		Sep23 4-0	Oct21 4-2	Feb24 0-4	Apr07 2-1	Feb10 2-1	Nov04 0-0	Aug12 1-4	Nov18 4-0	Dec16 4-4	Sep09 5-0	Aug26 0-1	Jan06 0-0	Dec09 2-1	Mar31 3-0
DUMBARTON	Jan01 2-0	Feb24 3-2	Nov18 2-0	Dec23 3-1		Sep02 4-2	Sep30 3-1	Oct14 3-4	Mar17 2-0	Dec16 4-1	Nov04 3-0	Aug19 2-1	Jan13 1-2	Mar31 2-0	Apr21 3-1	Sep16 2-0	Mar03 2-0	Dec02 2-0
DUNDEE U	Apr28 2-3	Nov25 2-0	Dec16 4-4	Jan13 0-1	Dec30 4-4		Oct28 4-2	Aug12 1-3	Sep23 2-2	Nov18 9-3	Aug26 0-3	Mar03 8-1	Mar10 5-2	Nov11 1-2	Sep09 0-2	Apr21 5-2	Jan06 4-1	Oct07 2-4
DUNFERMLINE A	Mar17 1-2	Sep09 1-1	Oct21 3-0	Dec02 2-1	Feb10 3-0	Mar24 1-0		Aug26 4-0	Dec30 10-3	Mar10 7-0	Sep23 2-1	Nov04 3-1	Nov18 2-1	Jan06 3-2	Aug12 3-2	Mar31 1-3	Oct07 4-1	Dec09 3-0
EAST FIFE	Dec09 0-2	Oct21 1-1	Nov04 2-4	Sep30 6-3	Jan06 3-3	Dec23 5-1	Jan27 1-2		Mar31 0-2	Sep02 3-0	Mar03 4-3	Sep16 2-3	Aug19 2-1	Feb24 1-1	Nov25 3-0	Jan01 2-6	Apr14 3-2	Nov11 4-1
E STIRLING	Mar24 1-3	Apr27 3-0	Dec09 2-1	Sep16 3-1	Nov25 3-1	Apr07 1-1	Sep02 1-4	Oct28 4-3		Sep30 2-2	Apr14 5-1	Jan01 3-3	Dec23 4-4	Jan27 1-0	Feb24 0-2	Aug19 5-1	Nov11 2-0	Oct14 1-2
EDINBURGH C	Mar28 0-1	Aug26 1-2	Nov25 1-3	Jan27 3-2	Aug12 2-1	Feb10 2-1	Nov11 1-6	Dec25 2-2	Jan06 1-2		Apr21 2-2	Dec09 1-0	Mar31 0-2	Oct07 2-2	Dec02 1-2	Oct21 1-2	Sep09 0-5	Sep23 2-2
FORFAR A	Aug19 3-1	Jan13 4-1	Jan01 0-3	Oct14 1-1	Mar24 4-0	Mar31 4-1	Nov25 3-3	Mar17 1-3	Nov18 4-1	Sep16 5-2		Sep02 3-3	Sep30 4-0	Dec16 2-2	Nov11 2-2	Mar10 3-0	Oct28 2-1	Dec23 6-0
KING'S PARK	Nov11 2-0	Jan06 1-1	Apr14 3-3	Mar10 7-1	Oct28 3-1	Oct14 5-2	Apr07 0-0	Dec16 2-0	Sep09 2-2	Mar24 4-2	Dec30 6-1		Feb10 1-1	Sep23 5-2	Oct07 2-2	Nov25 3-1	Aug12 3-2	Aug26 5-1
LEITH A	Jan27 0-1	Dec30 0-1	Feb24 1-1	Nov11 2-2	Oct07 0-1	Dec09 1-5	Mar03 4-1	Apr21 4-4	Aug12 1-2	Oct28 3-1	Jan06 3-0	Mar17 2-0		Nov25 5-0	Sep23 3-1	Nov04 2-0	Aug26 4-1	Sep09 1-2
MONTROSE	Apr07 2-1	Apr21 4-1	Aug19 2-1	Jan01 1-2	Oct21 2-4	Sep30 0-2	Sep16 1-4	Dec02 2-0	Nov04 1-2	Dec23 3-1	Feb10 3-0	Jan13 2-4	Sep02 1-3		Mar10 4-2	Dec09 2-1	Mar17 4-2	Dec30 0-0
MORTON	Sep16 1-0	Nov18 3-3	Sep30 3-0	Mar24 4-2	Dec09 3-1	Jan01 4-3	Apr14 0-2	Jan13 3-1	Oct21 3-1	Aug19 4-0	Jan27 2-4	Dec23 1-0	Apr07 2-2	Oct28 4-1		Sep02 2-1	Feb10 0-2	Mar03 3-1
RAITH R	Nov18 2-0	Sep23 2-2	Jan13 0-1	Oct28 5-1	Apr07 1-1	Dec02 4-1	Oct14 1-1	Sep09 0-1	Mar03 3-0	Feb24 6-0	Oct07 3-0	Jan27 4-2	Mar24 3-1	Aug26 5-0	Dec16 3-1		Dec30 3-1	Aug12 1-3
ST BERNARD'S	Dec23 2-0	Nov04 5-1	Sep02 1-0	Aug19 2-1	Mar10 7-2	Sep16 3-0	Dec16 4-1	Nov18 2-2	Jan13 1-1	Jan01 5-0	Feb24 1-1	Oct21 2-0	Dec02 0-1	Mar24 2-0	Oct14 10-10-1	Sep30	3-1	Apr07
STENHOUSEMUIR	Sep30 2-2	Mar24 3-0	Sep16 1-4	Sep02 2-0	Jan27 6-4	Mar17 2-0	Aug19 3-1	Mar10 3-1	Apr21 0-2	Jan13 5-2	Oct21 4-2	Feb24 2-1	Jan01 1-1	Nov18 4-3	Nov04 1-0	Apr14 5-4	Nov25 3-0	

Scottish Football League Records
Season 1934-35

DIVISION 1

	ABERDEEN	AIRDRIE	ALBION R	AYR U	CELTIC	CLYDE	DUNDEE	DUNFERMLINE A	FALKIRK	HAMILTON A	HEARTS	HIBERNIAN	KILMARNOCK	MOTHERWELL	PARTICK T	QUEEN OF SOUTH	QUEEN'S PARK	RANGERS	ST JOHNSTONE	ST MIRREN
ABERDEEN		Sep29 1-3	Mar16 1-1	Feb16 7-1	Jan19 2-0	Nov03 2-1	Jan01 3-0	Sep01 3-0	Aug18 1-0	Dec15 3-3	Nov24 1-0	Jan05 2-0	Sep24 1-3	Sep15 2-2	Dec22 3-0	Aug22 1-0	Dec01 5-0	Apr13 1-3	Nov10 2-0	Oct13 1-0
AIRDRIE	Feb02 4-1		Sep08 3-0	Apr27 3-2	Nov17 0-2	Sep22 0-0	Sep12 0-3	Apr20 2-3	Dec08 2-1	Jan02 2-2	Jan12 4-7	Mar29 7-0	Aug25 3-2	Nov03 2-0	Mar16 0-2	Mar02 3-1	Aug11 4-2	Oct06 1-2	Dec29 1-1	Oct20 1-0
ALBION R	Oct27 1-1	Jan01 0-3		Jan05 8-0	Sep29 2-1	Apr13 4-1	Dec22 1-2	Jan19 1-2	Feb16 0-0	Mar23 4-1	Dec15 2-2	Oct13 2-0	Dec01 1-0	Sep01 2-3	Aug18 2-0	Nov24 3-2	Aug22 0-0	Nov10 1-5	Mar13 2-4	Sep15 2-3
AYR U	Oct06 0-3	Dec01 2-1	Aug25 0-1		Mar23 1-0	Aug11 2-3	Mar30 3-2	Dec15 1-3	Apr10 3-1	Dec29 1-2	Feb02 0-3	Nov17 1-1	Jan02 2-1	Nov24 1-0	Aug22 3-2	Sep08 1-1	Sep22 5-1	Jan12 2-4	Mar02 3-0	Oct27 1-0
CELTIC	Sep22 4-1	Apr13 2-0	Feb02 5-1	Nov03 7-0		Mar02 0-2	Nov24 4-0	Oct27 3-0	Apr17 7-3	Jan12 3-1	Dec29 4-2	Sep11 4-0	Aug11 4-1	Dec08 3-2	Feb23 3-1	Oct06 1-2	Dec25 4-1	Sep08 1-1	Aug25 0-0	Apr27 2-1
CLYDE	Mar23 1-1	Jan19 3-0	Nov17 1-1	Dec22 5-1	Oct13 0-3		Sep29 2-2	Aug18 2-1	Sep01 3-0	Aug21 3-3	Nov10 0-1	Sep15 3-2	Mar09 1-1	Feb16 3-3	Jan01 3-4	Dec01 1-2	Dec15 3-0	Oct20 2-1	Mar16 4-1	Jan05 5-2
DUNDEE	Sep08 0-0	Dec15 2-0	Aug11 3-2	Nov10 5-4	Oct01 0-0	Feb02 2-2		Aug22 1-1	Oct27 1-0	Sep22 2-1	Jan02 1-5	Dec01 0-2	Mar02 0-2	Feb23 3-1	Mar09 2-0	Dec29 5-0	Jan12 4-1	Aug25 3-2	Oct06 1-2	Mar23 0-2
DUNFERMLINE A	Jan02 1-1	Nov24 1-1	Sep22 1-3	Sep12 1-2	Mar16 1-3	Dec29 4-2	Dec08 2-5		Mar23 2-1	Mar02 4-1	Aug25 1-2	Oct20 2-1	Oct06 2-2	Apr27 1-0	Mar30 2-1	Jan12 3-1	Feb02 2-2	Aug11 1-7	Sep08 1-2	Nov17 3-2
FALKIRK	Dec29 3-2	Aug22 2-4	Oct06 3-0	Oct20 8-1	Nov10 1-2	Jan02 2-4	Mar16 1-1	Nov03 2-0		Aug25 1-2	Aug11 0-2	Apr20 5-2	Jan12 5-2	Apr13 0-3	Dec01 1-2	Feb02 3-1	Sep08 1-1	Mar02 0-3	Sep22 3-0	Dec15 1-1
HAMILTON A	Sep12 6-1	Aug31 5-0	Nov03 4-2	Aug18 3-2	Sep15 4-2	Dec08 4-3	Jan19 1-1	Oct13 3-0	Jan05 1-2		Apr05 2-0	Dec22 2-1	Oct27 4-2	Jan01 6-1	Mar20 2-1	Apr13 1-1	Nov10 2-2	Apr27 2-1	Nov24 2-2	Sep29 4-0
HEARTS	Apr20 2-1	Sep15 1-0	Sep12 4-0	Sep29 5-0	Aug18 0-0	Apr15 2-0	Sep01 1-1	Jan05 0-1	Dec22 4-1	Oct24 1-1		Jan01 5-2	Nov17 2-2	Oct13 2-1	Jan19 1-2	Mar23 4-2	Mar16 2-1	Dec08 4-1	Dec01 2-2	Feb16 0-1
HIBERNIAN	Aug25 2-3	Nov10 2-2	Mar02 3-3	Apr13 1-1	Dec15 3-2	Jan12 4-0	Aug27 2-1	Mar09 3-1	Nov24 2-0	Aug11 3-1	Sep08 1-0		Dec29 1-0	Oct27 1-1	Nov03 2-0	Sep22 1-1	Oct06 5-1	Feb02 1-2	Jan02 1-1	Aug22 0-0
KILMARNOCK	Oct20 1-3	Jan05 0-0	Apr27 2-1	Sep01 6-3	Dec22 2-3	Nov24 2-0	Oct13 2-0	Feb16 1-3	Sep15 4-1	Mar16 4-1	Apr13 3-3	Aug18 0-1		Jan19 3-3	Sep29 2-0	Nov10 3-1	Nov03 5-0	Sep04 1-3	Dec08 1-0	Jan01 1-4
MOTHERWELL	Jan12 1-2	Mar23 3-2	Jan02 5-2	Apr20 2-3	Aug22 1-0	Oct06 1-1	Oct20 5-3	Dec01 9-3	Nov17 5-2	Sep08 0-0	Mar02 2-2	Mar16 4-1	Sep22 3-2		Dec15 4-1	Aug11 4-0	Aug25 3-0	Dec29 2-2	Feb02 0-1	Mar30 3-0
PARTICK T	Aug11 2-1	Oct27 4-1	Dec29 1-0	Dec08 1-1	Oct20 1-3	Sep08 0-0	Nov17 1-4	Nov10 7-1	Apr27 2-2	Oct06 0-1	Sep22 1-3	Mar23 3-1	Feb02 4-2	Sep12 1-1		Aug25 2-1	Mar02 2-2	Jan02 1-0	Jan12 3-0	Nov24 2-1
QUEEN OF SOUTH	Dec08 2-1	Oct13 1-1	Apr20 1-0	Jan01 7-1	Feb16 3-4	Feb23 1-0	Aug18 1-0	Sep15 2-0	Sep29 1-1	Nov17 4-1	Nov03 1-3	Jan19 0-2	Mar30 0-1	Dec22 2-3	Jan05 2-4		Oct20 1-0	Oct27 2-3	Sep12 0-2	Sep01 2-0
QUEEN'S PARK	Apr27 1-1	Dec22 4-2	Dec08 1-1	Jan19 5-4	Sep01 1-0	Sep11 0-1	Sep15 4-0	Sep29 1-0	Jan01 4-0	Apr08 3-4	Oct27 3-3	Apr15 3-1	Feb23 1-4	Jan05 1-1	Apr22 3-1	Mar09 2-1		Nov24 0-4	Apr13 2-1	Aug18 4-1
RANGERS	Nov17 2-2	Feb16 3-1	Apr24 2-2	Sep15 2-0	Jan01 2-1	Mar20 4-2	Jan05 3-1	Dec22 8-1	Dec25 1-0	Dec01 1-1	Aug22 2-1	Sep29 4-2	Dec15 2-3	Aug18 1-0	Sep01 4-0	Mar16 5-0	Apr30 0-1		Nov03 3-1	Jan19 1-0
ST JOHNSTONE	Apr03 1-1	Aug18 4-1	Oct20 2-0	Oct13 4-0	Jan05 0-1	Oct27 5-2	Feb16 0-1	Jan01 5-1	Jan19 4-0	Apr10 3-1	Apr27 2-2	Sep01 2-0	Aug22 2-1	Sep29 2-1	Sep15 2-1	Dec15 1-1	Nov17 0-0	Mar23 2-0		Dec22 4-0
ST MIRREN	Mar02 3-0	Mar12 1-0	Jan12 5-4	Mar16 3-3	Dec01 2-4	Aug25 1-2	Nov03 0-1	Apr13 3-0	Sep11 2-1	Feb02 1-2	Oct06 2-4	Dec08 1-2	Sep08 0-2	Nov10 1-0	Apr20 2-1	Jan02 1-1	Dec29 2-3	Sep22 0-2	Aug11 1-1	

DIVISION 2

	ALLOA	ARBROATH	BRECHIN C	COWDENBEATH	DUMBARTON	DUNDEE U	EAST FIFE	E STIRLING	EDINBURGH C	FORFAR A	KING'S PARK	LEITH A	MONTROSE	MORTON	RAITH R	ST BERNARD'S	STENHOUSEMUIR	T LANARK
ALLOA		Apr06 0-0	Mar02 5-1	Sep22 5-2	Mar16 4-1	Dec29 3-3	Aug25 5-2	Sep08 1-2	Aug11 5-0	Oct27 5-2	Jan19 4-0	Oct06 1-2	Dec01 3-0	Dec15 2-1	Feb16 5-2	Nov03 2-1	Nov17 1-1	Jan05 0-2
ARBROATH	Sep15 1-0		Jan12 1-1	Dec29 1-0	Mar30 4-0	Feb02 2-2	Apr13 5-0	Mar16 1-0	Jan05 1-0	Jan01 0-3	Mar02 3-1	Nov24 3-1	Sep29 6-0	Sep01 6-2	Dec15 2-0	Aug18 2-5	Oct27 3-1	Oct20 2-1
BRECHIN C	Sep01 3-0	Nov17 0-1		Jan19 1-2	Oct20 1-4	Oct27 0-8	Nov03 2-1	Nov24 3-0	Dec29 7-1	Sep15 1-1	Aug18 2-1	Feb02 3-2	Jan01 3-2	Mar23 0-3	Mar09 0-0	Apr20 2-3	Dec15 3-5	Sep29 1-1
COWDENBEATH	Apr13 2-2	Mar09 1-3	Oct13 2-2		Jan01 8-1	Nov24 1-0	Feb16 1-1	Nov17 0-0	Oct27 7-0	Aug18 1-2	Dec15 7-2	Nov10 5-2	Apr06 3-2	Jan05 4-0	Sep29 3-3	Sep01 1-10	Feb09 5-3	Sep15 1-3
DUMBARTON	Oct13 0-0	Aug11 2-1	Aug25 2-0	Oct06 4-2		Jan12 5-1	Mar02 4-2	Sep22 2-2	Dec22 2-0	Nov24 1-1	Mar23 4-2	Oct27 1-2	Nov10 1-1	Feb02 2-5	Apr13 3-4	Dec15 1-4	Dec29 2-1	Apr05 0-1
DUNDEE U	Sep29 2-0	Nov03 3-2	Dec22 9-2	Oct20 0-2	Aug18 5-2		Jan05 4-0	Mar30 4-0	Nov28 9-6	Jan19 5-3	Dec08 2-1	Nov17 2-2	Sep15 4-3	Jan01 4-1	Sep01 4-0	Feb16 3-3	Mar16 8-0	Oct13 0-2
EAST FIFE	Mar09 0-1	Oct13 1-2	Apr06 1-2	Dec22 3-2	Sep29 9-1	Nov10 1-1		Oct27 2-0	Jan19 3-1	Feb02 5-0	Sep01 2-1	Dec29 5-2	Dec15 4-2	Aug18 1-0	Oct06 4-2	Sep15 1-1	Apr20 6-1	Mar30 1-3
E STIRLING	Nov07 0-0	Dec01 1-2	Jan05 0-1	Dec08 2-1	Jan19 6-2	Mar09 0-8	Mar23 1-2		Apr06 2-4	Sep01 5-1	Jan01 0-3	Jan12 1-1	Oct20 3-1	Dec22 3-1	Sep15 2-1	Sep29 0-0	Feb16 1-3	Aug18 2-2
EDINBURGH C	Oct31 2-2	Nov10 0-4	Jan05 1-1	Mar23 1-6	Sep08 3-2	Dec15 2-8	Nov17 0-5	Sep10 1-3		Apr13 0-5	Feb02 1-4	Oct13 1-2	Sep01 3-1	Sep17 1-2	Jan12 1-3	Dec25 2-6	Dec05 1-3	Feb23 0-2
FORFAR A	Mar23 1-1	Oct06 1-3	Dec08 5-1	Mar02 2-2	Jan05 4-1	Aug11 0-2	Sep22 1-3	Dec15 5-2	Aug25 4-1		Oct13 0-3	Sep08 4-2	Jan12 5-1	Dec01 1-1	Dec22 3-1	Mar16 4-4	Mar30 6-4	Nov10 3-1
KING'S PARK	Mar30 4-1	Aug25 2-1	Feb16 8-1	Aug11 1-0	Nov03 3-2	Sep08 3-1	Dec01 5-1	Oct06 2-1	Sep29 9-4	Mar09 1-2		Sep22 2-1	Mar16 5-1	Apr13 2-1	Nov17 2-1	Oct20 4-2	Jan12 2-3	Dec22 2-4
LEITH A	Jan01 4-4	Dec08 0-4	Dec01 2-1	Mar16 3-1	Sep15 2-1	Apr20 4-0	Oct20 1-3	Mar02 1-5	Mar30 6-0	Feb16 2-1	Jan05 3-1		Aug18 5-4	Sep29 2-2	Jan19 3-0	Dec22 2-1	Nov03 3-1	Sep01 1-2
MONTROSE	Dec22 2-2	Jan19 0-5	Oct06 1-5	Aug25 5-3	Feb16 5-0	Mar23 2-1	Sep08 1-4	Aug11 2-3	Mar09 3-2	Nov03 2-1	Nov24 3-3	Apr13 0-0		Nov17 2-1	Oct13 3-2	Jan05 0-4	Sep22 1-1	Dec08 2-4
MORTON	Nov24 4-1	Feb16 0-1	Sep22 7-0	Sep08 2-1	Mar09 3-2	Oct06 3-3	Jan12 8-1	Aug25 9-2	Sep15 3-1	Dec29 3-1	Nov10 4-2	Apr06 5-1	Mar30 4-1		Oct27 5-1	Oct13 3-4	Aug11 0-1	Jan19 1-0
RAITH R	Dec08 3-0	Sep22 3-4	Aug11 7-0	Nov03 2-3	Dec01 4-2	Mar02 0-3	Jan01 0-3	Feb02 3-0	Aug18 2-1	Oct20 2-2	Apr06 2-0	Aug25 1-0	Dec29 1-0	Mar16 6-0		Mar30 3-0	Sep08 3-1	Nov24 0-1
ST BERNARD'S	Jan12 2-1	Mar23 0-0	Sep08 5-1	Feb02 2-0	Dec08 5-0	Sep22 1-0	Nov24 6-1	Apr13 7-0	Oct06 6-2	Nov17 0-0	Dec29 4-1	Aug11 0-1	Oct27 1-1	Mar02 0-1	Nov10 6-2		Aug25 4-1	Mar09 3-2
STENHOUSEMUIR	Aug18 2-0	Dec22 6-0	Nov10 3-0	Sep11 2-3	Sep01 6-1	Apr12 3-2	Dec08 2-1	Oct13 3-2	Nov24 2-1	Sep29 4-2	Sep15 2-2	Mar09 1-4	Feb02 9-4	Oct20 3-1	Jan05 2-1	Jan19 1-2		Jan01 2-2
T LANARK	Feb02 6-1	Sep08 5-2	Mar16 4-0	Jan12 3-2	Nov17 4-2	Aug25 5-0	Aug11 3-0	Dec29 3-3	Sep22 3-0	Apr27 3-1	Oct27 1-2	Dec15 5-0	Mar02 4-0	Nov03 2-2	Jan02 5-3	Dec01 2-1	Oct06 3-3	

LEAGUE TABLES

DIVISION 1

	P	W	D	L	F	A	W	D	L	F	A	Pts
	P	W	D	L	F	A	W	D	L	F	A	Pts
Rangers	38	14	3	2	50	19	11	2	6	46	27	55
Celtic	38	15	2	2	61	19	9	2	8	31	26	52
Hearts	38	11	5	3	42	19	9	5	5	45	32	50
Hamilton A	38	14	4	1	58	24	5	6	8	29	43	48
St Johnstone	38	13	4	2	45	14	5	6	8	21	32	46
Aberdeen	38	13	3	3	42	17	4	7	8	26	37	44
Motherwell	38	12	4	3	57	27	3	6	10	26	37	40
Dundee	38	10	4	5	35	27	6	4	9	28	36	40
Kilmarnock	38	10	3	6	43	30	6	3	10	33	38	38
Clyde	38	9	6	4	45	29	5	4	10	26	40	38
Hibernian	38	10	7	2	38	20	4	1	14	21	50	36
Queen's Park	38	11	4	4	43	30	2	6	11	18	50	36
Partick T	38	10	5	4	38	25	5	0	14	23	43	35
Airdrie	38	10	3	6	42	31	3	4	12	22	41	33
Dunfermline A	38	8	4	7	35	39	5	1	13	21	57	31
Albion R	38	8	4	7	38	30	2	5	12	24	47	29
Queen of South	38	9	2	8	33	27	2	5	12	19	45	29
Ayr U	38	10	2	7	32	29	2	3	14	29	83	29
St Mirren	38	7	3	9	31	33	4	2	13	18	37	27
Falkirk	38	8	3	8	42	33	1	3	15	16	49	24

DIVISION 2

	P	W	D	L	F	A	W	D	L	F	A	Pts
T. Lanark	34	13	3	1	61	22	10	3	4	33	21	52
Arbroath	34	13	2	2	43	17	10	2	5	35	25	50
St Bernard's	34	12	3	2	52	14	8	4	5	51	33	47
Dundee U	34	13	2	2	68	29	5	4	8	37	36	42
Stenhousemuir	34	12	2	3	53	28	5	3	9	33	52	39
Morton	34	13	1	3	64	23	4	3	10	24	41	38
King's Park	34	14	0	3	57	27	4	2	11	29	44	38
Leith A	34	11	2	4	44	31	5	3	9	25	40	37
East Fife	34	11	2	4	49	22	5	1	11	30	51	35
Alloa	34	11	3	3	51	22	1	7	9	16	38	34
Forfar A	34	9	4	4	49	33	4	4	9	28	40	34
Cowdenbeath	34	8	5	4	52	36	5	1	11	32	39	32
Raith R	34	11	1	5	42	20	2	2	13	26	53	29
E. Stirling	34	7	4	6	32	27	4	3	10	25	49	29
Brechin C	34	7	3	7	32	35	3	3	11	19	63	26
Dumbarton	34	8	4	5	36	29	1	0	16	24	76	22
Montrose	34	7	4	6	34	41	0	2	15	24	64	20
Edinburgh	34	2	2	13	20	59	1	0	16	24	74	8

Scottish Football League Records
Season 1935-36

DIVISION 1

	ABERDEEN	AIRDRIE	ALBION R	ARBROATH	AYR U	CELTIC	CLYDE	DUNDEE	DUNFERMLINE A	HAMILTON A	HEARTS	HIBERNIAN	KILMARNOCK	MOTHERWELL	PARTICK T	QUEEN OF SOUTH	QUEEN'S PARK	RANGERS	ST JOHNSTONE	T LANARK
ABERDEEN		Jan18 2-2	Apr11 6-1	Feb29 1-2	Sep07 3-0	Aug10 3-1	Aug28 3-1	Sep21 4-1	Jan02 3-3	Sep23 3-0	Nov30 2-1	Aug24 3-1	Mar14 2-1	Dec28 1-1	Oct05 4-0	Nov02 4-3	Oct19 2-1	Nov23 1-0	Mar28 3-0	Feb01 2-0
AIRDRIE	Sep14 3-4		Jan01 1-2	Nov30 3-3	Nov09 3-0	Mar07 2-3	Apr04 5-3	Aug28 2-0	Feb22 6-2	Aug31 2-4	Aug17 3-1	Dec14 3-2	Jan04 1-4	Apr11 1-1	Apr18 3-0	Oct12 1-0	Feb15 1-1	Jan11 0-2	Sep28 3-3	Oct26 1-2
ALBION R	Nov16 1-3	Sep21 4-1		Dec28 5-2	Aug24 5-1	Jan18 0-3	Apr08 4-4	Oct05 1-1	Aug10 1-3	Dec07 4-0	Mar14 1-2	Feb29 0-1	Nov02 2-3	Jan02 0-2	Feb01 5-2	Oct19 2-0	Apr25 2-1	Aug14 1-2	Nov23 1-2	Sep07 2-0
ARBROATH	Oct12 0-1	Apr25 1-1	Aug17 1-2		Sep11 3-1	Apr11 0-2	Jan04 2-1	Nov23 1-0	Oct26 2-1	Sep14 0-1	Jan11 1-3	Dec07 3-2	Jan01 0-0	Mar28 1-1	Nov02 1-1	Aug31 3-1	Sep28 0-1	Dec21 0-0	Feb15 2-2	Mar11 1-3
AYR U	Jan11 1-1	Mar28 3-1	Jan04 4-1	Dec14 0-2		Nov23 0-2	Feb15 4-3	Mar14 1-2	Apr11 1-2	Sep28 1-0	Sep14 1-3	Nov02 3-0	Aug31 1-3	Aug28 1-0	Oct19 3-1	Jan01 1-3	Dec21 1-0	Aug17 2-2	Oct12 1-2	Nov30 1-3
CELTIC	Dec21 5-3	Oct19 4-0	Sep14 4-0	Nov16 5-0	Apr18 6-0		Apr13 2-1	Nov02 4-2	Sep16 5-3	Aug17 1-0	Sep28 2-1	Mar28 4-1	Feb15 4-0	Mar14 5-0	Nov30 1-1	Jan11 5-0	Aug31 3-0	Jan01 3-4	Jan04 2-0	Aug28 6-0
CLYDE	Dec07 0-3	Aug10 1-1	Nov09 5-2	Aug24 1-3	Oct05 2-0	Feb29 0-4		Jan18 2-1	Feb01 4-2	Mar21 1-2	Apr11 1-0	Dec28 7-4	Nov23 1-0	Sep07 1-2	Sep21 1-0	Apr25 3-0	Dec14 1-3	Oct26 1-4	Mar17 3-1	Jan02 0-1
DUNDEE	Jan01 2-2	Dec07 1-0	Feb15 2-0	Apr18 3-0	Oct26 6-1	Mar21 0-2	Sep14 4-3		Nov09 2-3	Dec21 3-0	Aug31 2-5	Mar07 2-1	Oct12 0-0	Nov30 2-2	Nov16 3-3	Sep28 1-1	Aug17 6-4	Jan04 0-3	Jan11 0-2	Oct07 3-2
DUNFERMLINE A	Aug31 0-2	Nov02 2-0	Dec21 5-5	Mar14 1-2	Nov16 2-1	Dec14 1-0	Sep28 1-1	Mar28 2-2		Oct12 2-2	Jan04 2-0	Apr25 0-1	Jan11 0-1	Oct19 1-3	Aug28 1-1	Aug17 4-1	Sep14 2-2	Feb15 2-6	Jan01 2-6	Nov23 1-0
HAMILTON A	Dec14 2-3	Jan02 3-1	Aug28 7-2	Feb08 2-2	Feb01 4-2	Dec28 0-2	Nov02 0-0	Aug10 2-2	Feb29 6-1		Nov23 3-4	Oct05 2-3	Oct19 3-2	Sep21 3-3	Sep07 5-1	Mar14 3-1	Mar28 4-1	Apr11 1-0	Apr04 5-1	Aug24 1-0
HEARTS	Apr25 1-2	Dec28 3-0	Oct26 4-2	Sep07 2-1	Jan18 3-0	Feb01 1-0	Nov16 3-3	Jan02 3-0	Aug24 1-1	Feb22 4-1		Sep21 8-3	Apr01 4-2	Feb29 2-2	Aug10 2-0	Dec14 2-0	Dec07 4-1	Apr22 1-1	Nov02 6-1	Oct05 2-0
HIBERNIAN	Jan04 1-4	Sep18 2-3	Oct12 3-0	Aug28 0-2	Mar21 0-1	Nov09 0-5	Aug17 1-1	Oct19 2-1	Nov30 2-3	Feb15 3-2	Jan01 1-1		Sep28 3-1	Nov23 2-3	Mar14 2-0	Dec21 3-0	Jan11 0-1	Sep14 1-1	Aug31 0-2	Apr11 3-0
KILMARNOCK	Oct26 2-5	Aug24 2-2	Mar21 2-2	Sep21 5-0	Jan02 7-2	Oct05 1-1	Apr29 2-0	Feb29 4-1	Sep07 1-2	Mar07 4-3	Nov09 2-0	Apr08 0-1		Aug10 2-3	Feb22 2-1	Dec07 4-2	Nov16 1-1	Apr25 0-3	Sep18 4-1	Dec28 1-0
MOTHERWELL	Aug17 2-2	Nov16 6-2	Aug31 2-0	Nov09 4-0	Dec07 4-1	Oct26 1-2	Jan11 1-1	Apr25 3-0	Apr22 2-3	Jan01 2-1	Oct12 4-2	Apr18 1-1	Apr04 3-2		Dec14 5-3	Feb15 0-2	Jan04 1-0	Sep28 0-2	Sep14 3-0	Mar21 2-1
PARTICK T	Feb15 3-3	Nov23 3-1	Sep28 5-3	Mar21 1-1	Mar07 2-2	Apr25 1-3	Dec31 4-1	Apr11 1-1	Dec07 2-0	Jan11 3-0	Feb08 1-0	Oct26 2-1	Sep14 2-0	Sep17 4-1		Jan04 2-1	Oct12 7-0	Aug31 1-3	Aug17 3-1	Nov09 0-0
QUEEN OF SOUTH	Mar21 1-1	Feb29 3-3	Mar07 1-0	Jan02 3-2	Sep21 2-1	Sep07 1-3	Nov30 2-2	Feb01 3-4	Dec28 3-1	Oct26 1-2	Sep18 2-0	Aug10 1-1	Aug28 2-1	Oct05 1-1	Aug24 1-0		Apr18 4-0	Nov09 0-2	Apr11 1-1	Jan18 2-1
QUEEN'S PARK	Apr04 0-1	Oct05 3-2	Nov30 0-1	Feb01 0-0	Aug10 1-2	Feb22 2-3	Sep17 4-1	Dec28 3-2	Jan18 2-1	Nov09 1-1	Aug27 2-2	Sep07 6-1	Apr11 1-0	Aug24 2-2	Feb29 1-1	Nov23 1-1		Mar21 1-3	Oct26 5-1	Jan01 1-0
RANGERS	Apr29 2-3	Sep07 5-3	Dec14 5-1	Aug10 6-0	Dec28 6-1	Sep21 1-2	Mar14 4-1	Aug24 4-3	Oct05 6-2	Nov16 3-1	Oct19 1-1	Mar18 3-0	Nov30 2-1	Feb01 0-0	Jan02 3-1	Apr08 2-1	Nov02 3-3		Aug28 7-0	Feb29 4-2
ST JOHNSTONE	Nov09 0-0	Apr13 4-1	Apr18 2-3	Oct05 2-1	Feb29 2-3	Aug24 2-3	Oct19 2-1	Sep07 2-0	Sep21 4-2	Apr25 1-1	Mar21 3-1	Jan02 2-2	Dec14 0-0	Jan18 2-3	Dec28 3-0	Nov16 3-1	Mar07 5-2	Dec07 1-2		Aug10 3-1
T LANARK	Sep28 5-1	Mar14 2-0	Jan11 0-1	Oct19 1-1	Apr24 6-4	Dec07 1-3	Aug31 3-0	Dec14 2-2	Apr27 3-1	Jan04 4-0	Feb15 1-5	Nov16 1-1	Aug17 3-2	Nov02 2-1	Apr01 4-1	Sep14 2-2	Sep21 3-0	Apr13 1-3	Dec21 3-1	

DIVISION 2

	ALLOA	BRECHIN C	COWDENBEATH	DUMBARTON	DUNDEE U	EAST FIFE	E STIRLING	EDINBURGH C	FALKIRK	FORFAR A	KING'S PARK	LEITH A	MONTROSE	MORTON	RAITH R	ST BERNARD'S	ST MIRREN	STENHOUSEMUIR
ALLOA		Oct19 3-1	Mar21 5-1	Nov16 5-0	Aug17 2-3	Nov23 2-1	Dec21 0-0	Apr04 2-0	Jan04 2-2	Aug31 1-1	Dec07 4-0	Jan01 2-1	Sep14 1-2	Jan18 1-5	Feb15 1-0	Nov02 4-3	Feb29 1-1	Sep28 4-2
BRECHIN C	Mar28 3-1		Jan11 3-2	Mar07 6-1	Aug31 2-1	Feb08 1-1	Feb29 3-2	Sep14 1-2	Oct12 0-4	Aug17 2-2	Nov23 2-2	Sep28 0-2	Jan01 1-2	Mar14 1-4	Dec07 2-1	Oct26 2-8	Nov02 2-3	Dec21 1-2
COWDENBEATH	Aug10 1-2	Sep07 3-0		Oct05 6-2	Oct26 7-0	Feb29 1-4	Apr04 1-1	Nov30 2-1	Feb01 2-7	Mar07 1-0	Sep21 8-0	Jan04 5-1	Dec07 3-1	Aug24 1-3	Dec28 2-0	Jan18 3-4	Apr18 2-3	Nov09 2-1
DUMBARTON	Jan11 0-3	Nov30 1-5	Jan01 3-3		Sep28 3-5	Aug17 4-2	Feb15 3-3	Feb08 1-2	Dec14 2-7	Oct19 1-2	Oct12 6-1	Aug31 1-1	Nov23 4-4	Nov09 1-3	Apr11 3-4	Apr25 2-0	Mar14 1-2	Sep14 2-0
DUNDEE U	Feb01 4-0	Dec14 2-2	Mar14 6-1	Dec28 8-0		Oct19 4-2	Apr13 12-1	Nov23 4-1	Sep07 3-1	Nov02 4-1	Aug24 1-1	Apr04 8-2	Feb29 2-3	Oct05 1-1	Jan18 4-3	Aug10 2-2	Sep21 1-2	Mar28 6-1
EAST FIFE	Sep07 0-2	Aug24 4-3	Dec21 2-0	Jan18 4-2	Jan04 4-3		Oct26 3-3	Feb22 5-1	Sep21 0-0	Feb15 1-4	Mar14 9-2	Nov09 3-2	Oct12 6-1	Dec07 3-1	Oct05 3-1	Dec28 5-2	Aug10 1-6	Nov30 4-1
E STIRLING	Aug24 1-2	Sep21 5-1	Nov02 2-0	Aug10 1-1	Dec07 2-3	Feb01 4-2		Oct12 2-0	Jan11 0-5	Mar28 1-2	Oct05 4-0	Nov23 1-1	Apr11 4-1	Sep07 2-1	Jan04 4-2	Dec14 2-2	Nov16 3-2	Dec28 3-0
EDINBURGH C	Sep21 3-1	Dec28 4-0	Mar28 3-3	Aug24 0-0	Mar07 3-6	Nov16 2-2	Jan18 1-1		Aug10 1-3	Dec07 2-2	Nov02 5-0	Feb01 2-3	Oct26 5-3	Jan11 1-4	Feb29 2-3	Oct05 1-6	Sep07 3-2	Apr18 1-1
FALKIRK	Oct26 3-0	Apr04 4-0	Aug31 1-0	Apr18 3-1	Nov09 4-2	Mar21 8-0	Sep28 3-1	Oct19 3-0		Dec21 1-2	Jan18 10-2	Sep14 3-0	Aug17 8-0	Feb15 2-1	Mar14 5-0	Feb29 7-1	Nov30 5-0	Jan01 5-1
FORFAR A	Dec28 1-2	Jan04 1-1	Oct12 0-0	Sep21 3-1	Apr11 3-4	Dec14 1-2	Nov09 0-4	Mar21 2-2	Aug24 1-4		Sep07 3-0	Nov30 1-2	Feb08 7-3	Feb29 7-3	Aug10 3-2	Nov16 2-2	Oct05 2-5	Oct26 2-3
KING'S PARK	Apr11 1-1	Nov09 5-4	Oct19 1-4	Feb29 5-2	Feb15 2-1	Sep14 2-1	Jan01 0-1	Aug17 2-0	Dec28 3-5	Jan11 3-1		Dec21 1-0	Sep28 1-0	Oct26 2-2	Nov30 3-0	Mar28 2-4	Apr25 1-1	Aug31 1-5
LEITH A	Oct05 1-2	Jan18 4-0	Feb15 4-2	Oct26 6-0	Nov16 3-1	Mar07 4-2	Apr18 5-2	Dec14 1-2	Dec07 2-5	Apr25 4-1	Aug10 0-1		Nov02 1-1	Dec28 2-0	Sep07 2-1	Sep21 2-6	Aug24 0-5	Feb29 2-1
MONTROSE	Mar14 0-2	Oct05 4-1	Nov16 1-1	Sep07 3-0	Nov30 3-2	Mar28 1-3	Oct19 3-1	Nov09 4-2	Apr25 0-4	Feb01 1-2	Dec14 3-0	Jan11 1-3		Aug10 1-3	Sep21 3-1	Aug24 1-3	Dec28 1-0	Feb15 2-1
MORTON	Mar11 2-2	Nov16 3-1	Dec14 8-4	Apr04 5-1	Jan01 4-1	Sep28 4-1	Nov30 4-2	Aug31 1-1	Nov02 2-2	Sep14 3-0	Mar21 5-3	Aug17 2-0	Jan04 4-0		Apr18 11-2	Apr11 6-2	Oct19 1-0	Apr06 9-2
RAITH R	Oct12 1-3	Feb01 2-2	Aug17 4-0	Nov02 1-3	Sep14 1-1	Jan01 1-2	Aug31 1-6	Sep28 4-2	Nov16 2-3	Nov23 4-0	Apr04 1-2	Oct19 2-4	Mar21 2-0	Mar28 2-2		Mar07 4-1	Dec14 1-3	Jan11 3-1
ST BERNARD'S	Nov30 1-2	Feb15 2-3	Sep14 2-3	Mar21 7-0	Jan11 3-1	Aug31 2-2	Aug17 4-0	Jan01 2-0	Nov23 2-3	Sep28 3-0	Jan04 5-3	Mar14 5-2	Dec21 2-1	Oct12 3-2	Nov09 6-2		Apr04 2-0	Oct19 1-2
ST MIRREN	Nov09 4-0	Mar21 7-0	Sep28 1-0	Jan04 8-0	Dec21 6-2	Jan11 3-1	Sep14 4-1	Feb15 5-0	Apr11 0-2	Jan01 6-0	Mar07 8-1	Oct12 6-0	Aug31 1-0	Nov23 5-4	Oct26 6-0	Dec07 4-2		Aug17 2-0
STENHOUSEMUIR	Dec14 2-0	Aug10 2-1	Nov23 1-2	Dec07 3-0	Oct12 5-0	Nov02 1-1	Mar07 3-0	Jan04 2-2	Oct05 1-0	Mar14 3-1	Nov16 3-2	Mar21 2-0	Apr04 1-4	Sep21 1-4	Aug24 1-2	Sep07 3-6	Jan18 1-3	

LEAGUE TABLES

DIVISION 1

	P	W	D	L	F	A	W	D	L	F	A	Pts
Celtic	38	17	1	1	71	16	15	1	3	44	17	66
Rangers	38	14	3	2	67	26	13	4	2	43	17	61
Aberdeen	38	15	3	1	52	19	11	6	2	44	31	61
Motherwell	38	12	3	4	46	25	6	9	4	31	33	48
Hearts	38	14	4	1	56	20	6	3	10	32	35	47
Hamilton A	38	11	4	4	56	31	4	3	12	21	43	37
St Johnstone	38	10	4	5	43	27	5	3	11	27	54	37
Kilmarnock	38	10	4	5	46	30	4	3	12	23	34	35
T. Lanark	38	11	4	4	47	29	4	1	14	16	36	35
Partick T	38	12	5	2	47	22	0	5	14	17	50	34
Arbroath	38	6	6	7	22	24	5	5	9	24	45	33
Dundee	38	9	5	5	42	34	2	5	12	25	46	32
Queen's Park	38	8	6	5	36	25	3	4	12	22	50	32
Dunfermline A	38	6	6	7	31	36	6	2	11	36	56	32
Queen of South	38	9	6	4	34	26	2	3	14	20	46	31
Albion R	38	8	2	9	41	33	5	2	12	28	59	30
Hibernian	38	7	3	9	29	31	4	4	11	27	51	29
Clyde	38	10	1	8	35	33	0	7	12	28	51	28
Airdrie	38	8	4	7	44	37	1	5	13	24	54	27
Ayr U	38	8	2	9	30	31	3	1	15	23	67	25

DIVISION 2

	P	W	D	L	F	A	W	D	L	F	A	Pts
Falkirk	34	16	0	1	75	11	12	3	2	57	23	59
St Mirren	34	16	0	1	76	13	9	2	6	38	28	52
Morton	34	14	3	0	74	24	7	3	7	43	36	48
Alloa	34	10	4	3	40	23	9	2	6	25	28	44
St Bernard's	34	11	1	5	52	26	7	3	7	54	52	40
East Fife	34	12	2	3	57	34	4	4	9	29	45	38
Dundee U	34	11	4	2	72	24	5	1	11	36	57	37
E. Stirling	34	10	3	4	41	25	3	5	9	29	50	34
Leith A	34	10	1	6	43	32	5	2	10	24	45	33
Cowdenbeath	34	10	1	6	50	30	3	4	10	26	47	31
Stenhousemuir	34	9	2	6	35	28	4	1	12	24	50	29
Montrose	34	9	1	7	32	29	4	2	11	26	53	29
Forfar A	34	5	4	8	39	40	5	3	9	21	41	27
King's Park	34	9	3	5	35	32	2	2	13	20	77	27
Edinburgh	34	5	6	6	39	40	3	3	11	18	43	25
Brechin C	34	6	3	8	32	40	2	3	12	25	56	22
Raith R	34	6	3	8	36	35	3	0	14	24	61	21
Dumbarton	34	4	4	9	38	47	1	2	14	14	74	16

Scottish Football League Records
Season 1936-37

DIVISION 1

	ABERDEEN	ALBION R	ARBROATH	CELTIC	CLYDE	DUNDEE	DUNFERMLINE A	FALKIRK	HAMILTON A	HEARTS	HIBERNIAN	KILMARNOCK	MOTHERWELL	PARTICK T	QUEEN OF SOUTH	QUEEN'S PARK	RANGERS	ST JOHNSTONE	ST MIRREN	T LANARK
ABERDEEN		Oct31 4-1	Aug15 4-0	Jan23 1-0	Nov21 3-0	Jan01 3-1	Oct10 3-1	Aug29 4-0	Nov28 3-0	Mar27 4-0	Aug19 1-1	Dec12 2-0	Sep26 2-0	Jan09 4-2	Feb20 1-1	Sep28 2-1	Mar20 1-1	Oct24 4-1	Dec19 5-4	Sep12 2-2
ALBION R	Mar24 1-5		Sep12 2-0	Aug29 1-3	Oct24 1-1	Jan09 1-1	Jan23 4-0	Jan01 1-4	Apr03 2-3	Dec12 1-3	Aug15 4-0	Feb20 1-3	Oct10 1-4	Sep26 2-4	Jan04 4-0	Nov14 2-3	Nov28 2-3	Mar20 0-4	Aug19 2-6	Dec19 0-4
ARBROATH	Sep09 1-4	Jan16 4-2		Oct31 2-3	Aug08 2-1	Mar20 3-0	Apr24 1-1	Nov14 1-2	Dec26 1-2	Aug22 0-3	Apr03 1-0	Feb06 0-0	Oct24 0-0	Feb20 2-1	Jan02 4-0	Oct03 2-0	Sep05 0-0	Sep19 3-1	Nov28 2-2	Dec05 4-1
CELTIC	Oct03 3-2	Dec26 4-0	Apr16 5-1		Sep09 3-1	Feb20 1-2	Nov28 3-1	Mar29 1-0	Jan16 3-3	Feb06 3-2	Oct24 5-1	Sep05 2-4	Dec12 3-2	Mar27 1-1	Aug22 5-0	Jan02 4-0	Sep19 1-1	Aug08 3-2	Nov07 3-0	Nov21 6-3
CLYDE	Apr07 0-0	Mar06 4-1	Aug18 4-2	Aug15 1-1		Aug29 1-2	Sep12 2-1	Jan23 2-2	Oct17 4-3	Mar23 2-1	Sep26 1-3	Mar20 2-0	Dec19 1-2	Jan01 1-0	Nov14 2-1	Apr10 0-2	Apr23 3-2	Dec05 2-0	Jan09 1-1	Oct10 2-4
DUNDEE	Sep19 2-2	Sep05 1-0	Nov07 6-1	Oct17 0-0	Dec26 2-2		Mar06 2-2	Apr03 1-1	Oct03 1-2	Jan02 1-0	Dec05 3-1	Sep09 2-2	Mar27 0-0	Apr12 2-2	Jan16 1-3	Feb06 2-2	Aug08 0-0	Aug22 3-1	Apr24 4-0	Nov28 3-2
DUNFERMLINE A	Jan02 2-2	Oct03 3-3	Dec12 1-4	Apr10 3-4	Jan16 1-3	Oct24 3-4		Feb20 0-2	Sep09 4-2	Aug08 2-5	Nov14 2-3	Aug22 0-5	Jan04 2-2	Nov21 1-1	Sep19 5-0	Dec26 2-2	Feb06 2-3	Sep05 0-0	Mar17 1-0	Mar20 0-0
FALKIRK	Dec26 1-2	Sep19 3-2	Mar27 0-1	Dec05 0-3	Oct03 6-0	Nov21 5-0	Oct17 6-4		Aug08 3-2	Jan16 3-0	Apr10 4-1	Jan02 5-0	Oct31 1-1	Nov07 4-1	Sep08 5-2	Sep05 1-2	Aug22 0-2	Feb06 3-0	Mar06 5-1	Feb27 5-2
HAMILTON A	Apr10 3-2	Nov21 2-3	Aug29 1-4	Sep12 1-2	Feb20 2-1	Jan23 5-1	Aug15 4-2	Aug19 3-2		Mar20 5-1	Jan09 4-1	Apr16 2-2	Jan01 2-3	Dec19 3-2	Dec12 1-1	Oct24 5-2	Apr07 1-5	Mar27 5-2	Oct10 2-1	Sep26 3-1
HEARTS	Nov14 2-0	Apr24 5-0	Dec19 4-1	Sep26 0-1	Apr19 2-1	Oct10 4-0	Aug19 3-2	Sep12 3-1	Nov07 6-0		Jan01 3-2	Oct24 5-0	Aug15 3-4	Jan23 5-1	Apr10 4-2	Apr03 3-1	Dec05 5-2	Feb20 3-1	Aug29 2-1	Jan09 5-2
HIBERNIAN	Aug08 1-3	Sep09 1-1	Nov21 4-1	Mar06 2-2	Feb06 0-1	Apr19 0-0	Mar27 0-0	Nov28 2-2	Sep05 5-4	Sep19 3-3		Jan16 0-0	Mar20 1-2	Dec12 2-2	Oct03 2-2	Aug22 2-3	Dec26 1-4	Jan02 3-3	Oct17 0-0	Oct31 0-1
KILMARNOCK	Apr29 1-2	Oct17 3-1	Sep26 2-0	Jan09 3-3	Nov07 3-1	Aug15 1-1	Dec19 3-3	Oct10 3-2	Dec05 2-2	Mar06 3-0	Sep12 3-2		Jan23 0-1	Aug29 1-0	Apr03 1-0	Apr23 0-0	Nov14 1-2	Nov28 4-2	Jan01 2-1	Aug19 0-3
MOTHERWELL	Feb06 1-0	Jan02 9-1	Mar31 3-1	Apr30 8-0	Aug22 4-1	Nov14 2-1	Apr14 6-0	Apr19 4-2	Sep19 5-2	Sep09 1-3	Nov07 3-4	Oct03 2-1		Apr10 4-2	Sep05 4-1	Aug08 3-1	Jan16 1-4	Dec26 2-2	Apr03 4-1	Oct17 1-2
PARTICK T	Sep05 0-2	Feb06 6-1	Oct17 3-1	Nov14 1-1	Sep19 6-0	Oct31 1-1	Apr03 0-4	Mar20 2-2	Aug22 2-3	Oct03 2-2	Apr21 3-1	Dec26 4-0	Nov28 1-0		Aug08 4-1	Sep08 5-1	Jan02 0-1	Jan16 1-1	Dec25 1-1	Mar06 1-3
QUEEN OF SOUTH	Oct17 2-3	Dec05 5-2	Oct10 2-3	Dec19 1-0	Mar27 1-2	Sep12 2-3	Jan01 2-1	Aug15 1-4	Apr24 3-3	Nov28 0-4	Jan23 1-0	Nov21 1-0	Jan09 0-2	Aug19 3-3		Nov07 1-1	Mar06 0-1	Oct31 1-1	Sep26 1-2	Aug29 1-0
QUEEN'S PARK	Dec05 1-1	Apr07 3-3	Jan23 2-1	Oct10 0-2	Nov28 1-3	Sep26 0-2	Aug29 0-2	Jan09 3-6	Mar06 0-1	Nov21 0-2	Dec19 2-0	Oct31 2-1	Aug18 0-0	Aug15 2-2	Mar20 2-3		Oct17 1-1	Feb27 2-2	Sep12 2-2	Jan01 1-2
RANGERS	Nov07 2-1	Apr10 1-0	Jan09 4-0	Jan01 1-0	Dec12 2-0	Aug19 3-0	Sep26 5-3	Dec19 3-0	Mar24 4-0	Jan04 0-1	Aug29 4-0	Feb27 8-0	Sep12 3-2	Mar29 3-1	Oct24 1-1	Feb20 1-1		Nov21 0-0	Jan23 2-0	Aug15 3-1
ST JOHNSTONE	Mar29 2-1	Nov07 4-0	Jan01 6-1	Aug19 2-1	Jan04 2-1	Dec19 3-3	Jan09 1-0	Sep26 1-0	Nov14 6-1	Oct17 3-0	Oct10 3-1	Apr10 1-3	Aug29 1-3	Sep12 0-2	Mar24 4-0	Dec12 4-1	Apr03 1-2		Aug15 4-2	Jan23 2-3
ST MIRREN	Aug22 1-4	Aug08 3-0	Apr10 5-0	Mar20 1-2	Sep05 1-3	Dec12 4-0	Oct31 2-1	Oct24 3-3	Jan02 1-2	Dec26 2-2	Feb20 1-3	Sep19 3-2	Nov21 3-0	Dec05 1-3	Feb06 6-2	Jan16 1-2	Oct03 1-4	Sep08 2-1		Mar27 2-1
T LANARK	Jan16 2-0	Aug22 0-0	Jan04 3-2	Apr06 4-2	Jan02 0-2	Apr10 4-0	Nov07 6-3	Dec12 2-3	Feb06 3-2	Sep05 3-0	Mar29 1-1	Aug08 2-1	Feb20 1-1	Oct24 1-0	Dec26 4-1	Sep19 1-2	Sep09 0-0	Oct03 2-0	Nov14 3-0	

DIVISION 2

	AIRDRIE	ALLOA	AYR U	BRECHIN C	COWDENBEATH	DUMBARTON	DUNDEE U	EAST FIFE	E STIRLING	EDINBURGH C	FORFAR A	KING'S PARK	LEITH A	MONTROSE	MORTON	RAITH R	ST BERNARD'S	STENHOUSEMUIR
AIRDRIE		Nov07 3-1	Oct17 1-1	Feb06 7-5	Dec26 2-2	Mar27 5-0	Aug22 4-0	Sep19 2-2	Jan16 4-1	Oct03 4-0	Aug08 2-3	Oct31 5-2	Nov21 2-1	Jan02 8-2	Mar06 1-1	Apr10 3-2	Apr23 4-2	Sep05 2-1
ALLOA	Apr03 3-0		Mar06 1-4	Mar13 2-2	Oct03 2-0	Oct31 2-0	Dec26 2-0	Aug22 0-2	Aug08 0-2	Sep19 3-2	Nov28 2-1	Nov14 2-3	Sep05 2-0	Jan16 3-1	Dec12 4-3	Feb06 1-3	Oct10 0-0	Jan02 3-3
AYR U	Feb20 5-2	Oct24 4-0		Oct31 8-1	Feb06 2-0	Dec12 4-1	Sep19 4-1	Oct03 4-1	Jan02 7-2	Aug22 3-2	Sep05 6-1	Mar27 5-0	Aug08 2-1	Dec26 8-1	Mar20 1-1	Jan16 1-0	Feb13 5-2	Nov21 8-3
BRECHIN C	Nov14 0-0	Dec05 4-3	Jan23 2-3		Aug22 1-1	Jan16 3-2	Jan02 4-3	Aug08 0-0	Sep19 2-5	Mar20 4-0	Feb20 1-1	Oct17 0-3	Apr03 1-2	Sep05 1-1	Dec26 1-3	Nov28 3-1	Nov07 1-1	Oct03 2-0
COWDENBEATH	Aug15 4-0	Jan23 1-1	Sep12 2-1	Jan09 1-1		Jan01 1-0	Oct17 5-3	Oct10 3-1	Mar06 3-1	Dec19 2-2	Dec05 7-1	Nov28 4-0	Oct31 0-2	Apr03 3-3	Nov21 0-0	Sep26 4-1	Aug29 2-0	Mar27 1-0
DUMBARTON	Dec19 2-3	Apr10 1-1	Nov07 1-3	Oct10 2-1	Sep05 3-2		Nov28 4-5	Jan02 2-1	Oct03 2-1	Aug08 2-0	Sep19 1-1	Jan23 6-3	Mar06 1-1	Aug22 3-1	Oct24 0-4	Mar20 3-1	Nov14 1-4	Feb27 3-4
DUNDEE U	Oct10 2-1	Sep26 0-1	Dec19 1-2	Aug15 3-3	Feb20 1-1	Sep12 1-1		Dec12 0-0	Oct31 4-6	Nov21 2-2	Nov14 5-0	Jan09 3-3	Mar20 4-2	Oct24 5-1	Jan01 1-4	Aug29 2-4	Apr10 0-3	Jan23 3-2
EAST FIFE	Jan09 3-0	Oct17 2-0	Apr16 4-1	Dec19 7-0	Mar20 0-4	Sep26 1-2	Feb06 4-4		Dec05 5-1	Nov28 3-0	Mar27 3-1	Aug29 3-0	Jan16 2-1	Nov14 1-1	Sep12 0-0	Jan01 3-4	Aug15 6-1	Oct31 1-2
E STIRLING	Sep12 1-3	Dec19 2-2	Aug29 2-0	Dec12 5-4	Oct24 3-1	Jan09 4-1	Apr03 2-1	Jan23 0-2		Apr17 4-1	Mar20 4-2	Jan01 2-0	Nov28 3-0	Feb20 5-2	Nov14 5-3	Aug15 0-3	Sep26 1-1	Mar13 7-2
EDINBURGH C	Jan23 3-2	Jan09 2-8	Nov14 1-4	Aug29 1-4	Nov07 2-2	Feb20 2-5	Mar27 2-3	Apr03 2-8	Oct17 1-3		Apr10 0-1	Sep26 2-1	Dec26 1-4	Dec05 2-3	Aug15 0-1	Sep12 1-3	Jan01 0-3	Feb13 1-3
FORFAR A	Oct24 2-2	Aug15 4-3	Jan01 0-5	Sep26 3-1	Apr24 4-2	Apr03 3-4	Jan16 3-3	Nov21 3-3	Nov07 1-2	Dec12 4-1		Feb27 5-0	Feb06 3-0	Oct10 4-1	Aug29 2-2	Jan09 1-1	Sep12 1-8	Dec26 8-1
KING'S PARK	Mar13 1-3	Mar20 1-4	Dec05 2-6	Apr10 2-1	Sep19 3-8	Nov21 1-1	Aug08 2-4	Dec26 3-2	Sep05 3-1	Jan02 4-1	Aug22 1-1		Oct03 6-4	Nov07 2-4	Apr24 2-1	Oct10 5-1	Oct24 3-2	Jan16 1-3
LEITH A	Aug29 1-1	Jan01 4-2	Jan09 3-2	Sep12 2-5	Apr10 3-0	Aug15 2-1	Dec05 2-2	Oct24 1-2	Mar27 3-0	Oct10 2-1	Dec19 2-0	Feb20 4-1		Apr24 2-2	Sep26 2-1	Nov14 3-0	Jan23 2-4	Nov07 1-3
MONTROSE	Sep26 0-5	Aug29 1-1	Aug15 2-3	Jan01 4-3	Dec12 2-1	Feb06 2-1	Mar06 5-0	Apr10 0-1	Nov21 2-1	Oct31 4-2	Jan23 4-0	Sep12 3-0	Oct17 2-1		Jan09 1-3	Mar27 0-2	Dec19 1-3	Mar20 1-2
MORTON	Nov28 0-1	Feb20 2-0	Oct10 3-2	Mar27 6-0	Aug08 6-1	Apr21 5-0	Sep05 4-1	Nov07 2-1	Aug22 3-0	Jan16 7-2	Oct31 4-2	Dec19 6-0	Jan02 5-3	Oct03 8-3		Feb13 5-1	Apr14 4-1	Sep19 6-1
RAITH R	Dec12 0-0	Nov21 4-3	Apr03 2-2	Oct24 3-2	Jan02 1-3	Oct17 3-0	Nov07 2-3	Sep05 2-2	Dec26 5-0	Mar06 6-0	Oct03 1-6	Apr17 3-1	Aug22 1-0	Sep19 3-0	Jan23 0-2		Feb20 0-1	Aug08 2-1
ST BERNARD'S	Mar20 6-1	Mar27 3-0	Nov28 2-5	Nov21 6-0	Jan16 2-2	Dec26 4-0	Oct03 3-0	Mar06 3-0	Feb06 4-3	Sep05 4-1	Jan02 3-1	Dec12 6-1	Sep19 2-0	Aug08 7-1	Oct17 2-1	Oct31 3-0		Aug22 3-2
STENHOUSEMUIR	Jan01 1-2	Sep12 1-2	Sep26 1-1	Mar06 7-1	Nov14 5-2	Aug29 4-1	Apr16 9-2	Feb20 2-0	Oct10 1-2	Oct24 4-2	Oct17 4-0	Aug15 0-1	Dec12 1-1	Nov28 4-4	Apr10 1-4	Dec19 2-7	Jan09 2-1	

LEAGUE TABLES

DIVISION 1

	P	W	D	L	F	A	W	D	L	F	A	Pts
Rangers	38	15	3	1	50	11	11	6	2	38	21	61
Aberdeen	38	15	4	0	53	16	8	4	7	36	28	54
Celtic	38	14	3	2	59	26	8	5	6	30	32	52
Motherwell	38	14	1	4	67	29	8	6	5	29	25	51
Hearts	38	17	0	2	67	22	7	3	9	32	38	51
T. Lanark	38	12	4	3	42	20	8	2	9	37	41	46
Falkirk	38	13	1	5	60	26	6	5	8	38	40	44
Hamilton A	38	12	2	5	54	38	6	3	10	37	58	41
Dundee	38	7	10	2	36	23	5	5	9	22	46	39
Clyde	38	10	4	5	35	28	6	2	11	24	42	38
Kilmarnock	38	10	5	4	36	26	4	4	11	24	44	37
St Johnstone	38	13	1	5	50	25	1	7	11	24	43	36
Partick T	38	8	6	5	43	26	3	6	10	30	42	34
Arbroath	38	9	5	5	33	23	4	0	15	24	61	31
Queen's Park	38	3	7	9	24	36	6	5	8	27	41	30
St Mirren	38	9	2	8	43	35	2	5	12	25	46	29
Hibernian	38	2	11	6	29	34	4	2	13	25	49	25
Queen of South	38	6	4	9	28	35	2	4	13	21	60	24
Dunfermline A	38	3	7	9	34	45	2	4	13	31	53	21
Albion R	38	4	2	13	32	51	1	4	14	21	65	16

DIVISION 2

	P	W	D	L	F	A	W	D	L	F	A	Pts
Ayr U	34	16	1	0	77	19	9	3	5	45	30	54
Morton	34	16	0	1	76	19	7	5	5	34	23	51
St Bernard's	34	15	1	1	63	18	7	3	7	37	33	48
Airdrie	34	12	4	1	59	26	6	4	7	26	34	44
East Fife	34	10	3	4	48	22	5	5	7	28	29	38
Cowdenbeath	34	11	5	1	43	17	3	5	9	32	42	38
E. Stirling	34	12	2	3	50	28	6	0	11	31	50	38
Raith R	34	9	3	5	38	26	7	1	9	34	40	36
Alloa	34	9	3	5	32	26	4	4	9	32	39	33
Stenhousemuir	34	8	3	6	49	33	6	1	10	33	53	32
Leith A	34	10	3	4	39	27	3	2	12	23	38	31
Forfar A	34	8	5	4	51	39	3	3	11	22	50	30
Montrose	34	9	1	7	34	29	2	5	10	31	69	28
Dundee U	34	5	6	6	37	36	4	3	10	35	61	27
Dumbarton	34	8	3	6	37	36	3	2	12	20	47	27
Brechin C	34	6	6	5	30	29	2	3	12	34	69	25
King's Park	34	8	2	7	42	47	3	1	13	19	59	25
Edinburgh	34	2	1	14	23	58	0	2	15	19	62	7

Scottish Football League Records
Season 1937-38

DIVISION 1

	ABERDEEN	ARBROATH	AYR U	CELTIC	CLYDE	DUNDEE	FALKIRK	HAMILTON A	HEARTS	HIBERNIAN	KILMARNOCK	MORTON	MOTHERWELL	PARTICK T	QUEEN OF SOUTH	QUEEN'S PARK	RANGERS	ST JOHNSTONE	ST MIRREN	T LANARK
ABERDEEN		Sep27 3-0	Jan03 4-0	Sep25 1-1	Sep01 5-2	Sep11 2-3	Sep15 1-2	Mar26 1-0	Nov06 0-0	Oct09 5-0	Apr09 2-1	Feb19 4-1	Jan08 4-0	Aug28 3-1	Dec11 2-3	Nov27 1-1	Apr13 0-3	Jan29 4-0	Aug14 4-0	Sep08 1-0
ARBROATH	Dec18 3-3		Aug28 4-0	Oct09 2-0	Nov27 1-2	Aug14 0-3	Jan08 0-1	Mar12 2-0	Apr16 3-5	Jan03 3-3	Nov20 2-1	Feb26 2-2	Sep15 2-1	Jan05 1-1	Oct23 2-2	Mar05 2-2	Nov13 1-1	Sep11 2-0	Jan29 2-1	Sep25 3-2
AYR U	Oct16 4-1	Dec25 0-1		Nov20 1-1	Sep04 3-3	Apr30 0-0	Dec11 2-3	Oct02 2-3	Feb05 2-4	Mar12 1-1	Aug25 4-2	Jan15 6-2	Nov27 3-3	Apr27 1-1	Jan01 1-0	Aug21 6-2	Sep18 1-1	Apr09 3-1	Oct23 1-1	Oct30 1-1
CELTIC	Jan15 5-2	Feb05 4-0	Mar26 1-1		Oct02 3-1	Apr18 3-0	Nov27 2-0	Sep04 4-2	Sep18 2-1	Apr30 3-0	Dec25 8-0	Aug21 4-0	Apr09 4-1	Nov06 6-0	Aug25 2-2	Oct16 4-3	Jan01 3-0	Oct23 6-0	Feb26 5-1	Mar19 1-1
CLYDE	Nov13 2-1	Apr02 6-1	Dec31 0-0	Jan29 1-6		Sep14 3-2	Sep25 2-4	Apr16 2-0	Feb19 1-3	Jan08 1-1	Oct30 2-2	Mar16 7-1	Aug14 2-2	Sep11 1-1	Mar12 0-0	Nov20 5-0	Dec04 1-1	Oct09 1-2	Aug28 1-1	Jan03 3-3
DUNDEE	Jan01 0-1	Aug25 1-0	Apr11 5-1	Apr16 2-3	Aug21 4-1		Nov13 1-4	Jan15 3-0	Oct16 0-2	Apr02 1-2	Oct02 1-2	Dec25 2-2	Nov06 2-2	Oct23 5-3	Sep04 4-1	Sep18 2-0	Feb05 6-1	Feb26 6-1	Mar05 0-0	Oct04 2-1
FALKIRK	Aug21 4-1	Sep18 2-2	Apr16 1-1	Apr02 3-0	Jan15 1-2	Apr23 5-0		Feb05 4-5	Sep04 4-2	Nov20 0-0	Oct16 2-2	Jan01 6-1	Feb19 0-1	Feb26 2-1	Oct02 1-4	Dec25 2-0	Aug25 0-1	Nov06 3-1	Mar23 0-2	Dec04 3-1
HAMILTON A	Nov20 0-1	Nov06 2-2	Jan29 0-3	Aug18 1-2	Apr23 3-1	Sep25 4-0	Oct09 1-2		Oct30 2-3	Aug27 4-0	Nov27 4-2	Mar19 5-0	Sep11 1-3	Aug14 4-2	Apr09 3-1	Apr30 1-1	Feb19 2-2	Sep15 8-3	Jan03 0-1	Jan08 3-1
HEARTS	Mar12 2-1	Dec11 4-1	Oct09 7-0	Jan08 2-4	Oct23 0-0	Jan03 2-1	Jan04 1-0	Feb26 2-1		Sep11 3-2	Apr30 5-1	Dec04 2-1	Jan29 2-0	Sep25 3-0	Nov20 0-0	Nov13 2-0	Apr23 3-2	Aug14 2-1	Sep15 4-0	Aug28 2-1
HIBERNIAN	Feb05 1-1	Oct16 5-0	Nov06 3-0	Dec18 0-3	Sep18 6-3	Nov27 2-1	Mar26 2-4	Dec25 1-1	Jan01 2-2		Sep04 1-1	Oct02 4-2	Oct30 1-1	Apr09 2-1	Jan15 2-0	Aug25 0-2	Aug21 0-0	Mar19 2-2	Apr16 2-1	Feb19 2-2
KILMARNOCK	Dec04 3-3	Mar26 2-1	Aug14 2-1	Aug28 2-1	Feb26 2-1	Jan29 3-1	Jan03 2-2	Apr13 2-2	Feb12 3-1	Dec29 0-3		Apr29 3-0	Sep25 0-2	Sep15 1-3	Nov13 1-1	Oct23 1-3	Mar12 2-1	Jan08 2-2	Sep11 0-3	Oct09 4-2
MORTON	Oct23 3-5	Oct30 4-5	Sep25 7-3	Sep15 2-3	Apr30 1-3	Aug28 0-2	Sep11 1-1	Nov13 2-6	Apr13 1-2	Jan29 2-4	Dec11 4-2		Jan03 4-1	Jan08 1-2	Apr02 2-5	Apr20 1-2	Mar26 2-3	Dec31 3-2	Oct09 3-1	Aug14 1-3
MOTHERWELL	Sep18 2-1	Aug21 5-1	Apr02 4-3	Dec04 1-2	Aug25 1-0	Mar12 1-1	Oct23 3-2	Jan01 0-1	Oct02 3-3	Feb26 1-0	Jan15 4-3	Oct16 4-1		Nov20 1-1	Dec25 5-1	Feb05 3-0	Sep04 1-1	Mar23 3-1	Nov13 3-2	Apr16 4-4
PARTICK T	Dec25 3-1	Sep04 0-0	Nov13 6-2	Mar12 1-6	Oct16 4-1	Feb19 1-0	Oct30 2-1	Aug24 4-3	Jan15 3-1	Dec04 4-0	Aug21 3-0	Sep18 1-3	Mar26 3-0		Feb05 1-2	Oct02 3-2	Apr18 1-1	Apr16 1-4	Apr02 3-2	Apr12 1-3
QUEEN OF SOUTH	Mar19 1-0	Feb19 0-1	Sep11 0-1	Aug14 2-2	Nov06 1-1	Sep30 2-2	Jan29 2-3	Dec04 3-1	Mar26 2-3	Sep25 3-2	Apr16 3-1	Nov27 1-0	Aug28 0-3	Oct09 0-0		Feb26 1-3	Mar05 0-2	Jan03 2-3	Jan08 1-0	Sep15 2-4
QUEEN'S PARK	Apr05 1-1	Dec04 1-1	Sep14 1-1	Jan03 0-3	Mar26 1-1	Jan08 3-1	Aug28 1-5	Mar30 2-1	Mar19 1-4	Aug14 1-1	Feb19 1-1	Nov06 5-1	Oct09 1-3	Jan29 1-1	Oct30 3-3		Apr16 0-3	Sep25 2-0	Sep27 4-0	Jan01 4-1
RANGERS	Feb26 2-2	Mar23 3-1	Jan08 2-2	Sep11 3-1	Apr09 1-0	Oct09 6-0	Aug14 0-0	Oct23 2-2	Nov27 0-3	Sep15 2-0	Nov06 4-1	Nov20 3-1	Aug18 2-1	Jan03 1-3	Apr30 2-3	Dec11 2-1		Aug28 2-2	Sep25 4-0	Jan29 3-0
ST JOHNSTONE	Oct02 1-1	Jan01 2-2	Apr20 4-1	Feb19 1-2	Feb05 2-1	Oct30 4-2	Mar12 0-0	Aug21 6-3	Aug25 1-2	Nov13 2-0	Sep18 6-2	Sep04 3-2	Apr30 2-2	Apr23 3-1	Oct16 3-1	Jan15 1-2	Dec25 1-5		Nov20 3-0	Apr02 2-0
ST MIRREN	Aug24 2-1	Oct02 4-1	Feb19 1-2	Apr23 1-3	Dec25 6-1	Mar19 2-1	Apr30 0-3	Oct16 3-1	Aug21 1-1	Dec11 1-0	Jan01 0-2	Feb05 7-0	Apr12 3-0	Nov27 1-0	Sep18 4-2	Sep04 4-1	Jan15 1-1	Mar26 0-1		Nov06 1-4
T LANARK	Sep04 2-0	Jan15 1-1	Feb26 2-2	Nov13 1-1	Mar05 2-3	Nov20 4-3	Apr09 2-2	Sep18 1-1	Dec25 3-0	Oct23 1-0	Feb05 2-4	Aug25 3-0	Dec11 5-3	Apr30 1-1	Aug21 1-1	Sep11 1-1	Oct02 1-2	Nov27 0-5	Mar12 1-0	

DIVISION 2

	AIRDRIE	ALBION R	ALLOA	BRECHIN C	COWDENBEATH	DUMBARTON	DUNDEE U	DUNFERMLINE A	EAST FIFE	E STIRLING	EDINBURGH C	FORFAR A	KING'S PARK	LEITH A	MONTROSE	RAITH R	ST BERNARD'S	STENHOUSEMUIR
AIRDRIE		Sep11 2-1	Aug28 4-1	Feb12 10-0	Oct30 4-4	Sep25 1-3	Nov06 4-3	Aug14 5-3	Nov20 1-1	Apr02 4-2	Dec25 4-2	Mar12 7-2	Jan29 2-0	Apr16 1-0	Oct09 1-1	Jan03 2-3	Jan08 3-0	Feb05 3-0
ALBION R	Jan01 0-2		Dec04 7-1	Jan15 10-0	Sep04 4-3	Mar19 3-0	Sep18 4-1	Oct16 2-2	Feb19 2-2	Apr20 7-0	Nov13 5-3	Aug21 3-0	Apr09 3-3	Feb26 2-1	Apr30 1-1	Nov27 1-5	Oct23 5-0	Oct02 1-1
ALLOA	Jan15 4-3	Feb05 1-2		Aug21 3-2	Sep18 2-4	Nov13 2-1	Feb26 2-4	Nov06 2-4	Mar12 2-1	Oct02 3-0	Apr23 6-0	Apr30 3-3	Nov27 3-2	Jan01 5-2	Oct23 1-2	Apr02 3-8	Dec25 0-1	Sep04 2-5
BRECHIN C	Feb19 0-4	Sep25 1-4	Mar19 5-6		Apr16 1-1	Aug14 3-4	Mar05 3-0	Dec25 0-4	Nov13 1-2	Oct16 3-3	Nov27 2-7	Jan08 2-1	Jan03 3-4	Apr02 0-3	Sep11 2-3	Aug28 2-8	Oct09 2-3	Nov06 3-4
COWDENBEATH	Mar05 1-1	Dec25 2-3	Jan08 5-3	Nov20 10-0		Jan03 4-1	Feb05 3-1	Sep11 5-2	Dec04 2-3	Mar19 6-0	Sep25 3-1	Nov06 8-1	Aug28 2-6	Oct16 3-6	Aug14 6-1	Oct09 4-3	Mar12 2-2	Apr02 5-0
DUMBARTON	Apr09 2-0	Nov06 3-2	Apr16 2-2	Dec04 7-0	Oct02 4-4		Sep04 5-1	Mar12 4-1	Dec18 3-2	Jan15 3-1	Feb05 8-1	Jan01 2-0	Feb26 4-1	Sep18 3-0	Nov20 4-0	Oct16 2-2	Mar26 2-1	Aug21 5-1
DUNDEE U	Apr30 5-5	Apr23 1-4	Sep25 2-2	Mar12 3-4	Feb19 2-3	Jan29 1-4		Oct09 4-2	Oct30 0-2	Nov20 6-1	Sep11 5-2	Nov27 2-0	Jan08 2-0	Jan03 3-4	Aug28 2-1	Dec25 4-4	Aug14 1-7	Mar19 0-4
DUNFERMLINE A	Feb26 0-4	Jan08 3-3	Jan29 0-3	Oct02 3-0	Jan01 1-1	Oct23 4-1	Apr16 2-0		Apr09 1-1	Sep04 3-1	Oct30 4-2	Sep18 5-1	Mar26 4-4	Aug21 1-0	Nov27 3-0	Apr30 1-4	Nov13 2-1	Feb19 3-1
EAST FIFE	Oct16 2-0	Aug28 1-2	Aug14 3-1	Feb05 4-2	Mar26 1-2	Oct09 4-1	Apr29 7-0	Sep25 5-4		Nov06 4-1	Dec11 13-2	Apr28 3-0	Dec25 4-0	Nov27 3-1	Jan03 6-2	Sep11 3-5	Jan15 3-3	Feb26 5-1
E STIRLING	Nov27 0-3	Aug14 1-4	Mar26 3-1	Feb26 2-1	Apr30 2-3	Aug28 2-2	Oct23 1-1	Jan03 4-2	Apr25 2-1		Oct09 3-2	Nov13 2-0	Sep11 6-0	Apr09 1-2	Jan29 4-1	Jan08 1-8	Sep25 1-1	Oct30 0-0
EDINBURGH C	Aug21 0-4	Mar26 0-2	Nov20 2-4	Sep18 6-1	Oct23 2-1	Apr02 4-0	Jan01 0-2	Dec18 3-5	Sep04 3-3	Feb19 3-4		Jan29 2-8	Apr16 5-4	Oct02 2-4	Jan08 5-4	Nov06 1-6	Dec04 0-4	Oct16 5-2
FORFAR A	Apr23 1-5	Jan03 2-2	Oct09 4-2	Oct30 3-4	Feb26 0-5	Sep11 4-3	Jan15 4-3	Feb05 1-3	Oct23 3-5	Dec25 5-0	Aug28 4-4		Aug14 3-1	Mar05 2-2	Sep25 3-3	Mar26 2-3	Apr16 1-2	Nov20 1-1
KING'S PARK	Sep18 2-3	Nov20 0-2	Oct16 4-2	Sep04 2-1	Nov13 0-4	Oct30 1-0	Oct02 4-4	Dec04 1-3	Aug21 0-2	Jan01 2-1	Jan15 5-4	Apr02 1-0		Feb05 2-0	Mar12 4-3	Apr13 1-4	Feb19 0-1	Mar05 1-4
LEITH A	Nov13 0-2	Oct09 1-0	Sep11 3-0	Oct23 3-4	Apr23 1-1	Jan08 2-0	Mar26 5-0	Nov20 3-0	Jan29 4-2	Dec04 3-1	Mar12 1-1	Feb19 3-1	Sep25 1-1		Dec25 3-2	Aug14 3-4	Aug28 1-1	Jan15 5-2
MONTROSE	Mar19 3-1	Oct30 0-1	Feb19 1-1	Jan01 2-0	Jan15 3-3	Feb12 0-0	Dec04 1-3	Apr02 0-1	Oct02 3-0	Aug21 2-2	Feb26 4-1	Oct16 2-4	Nov06 4-2	Sep04 1-3		Feb05 2-2	Apr23 1-2	Sep18 2-3
RAITH R	Sep04 2-0	Mar12 4-1	Dec18 6-3	Apr23 3-0	Jan29 6-2	Feb19 7-0	Aug21 4-2	Jan15 4-1	Jan01 1-3	Sep18 1-1	Apr09 3-1	Oct02 3-0	Oct23 5-1	Oct30 3-1	Nov13 6-0		Nov20 4-2	Dec04 6-2
ST BERNARD'S	Oct02 3-2	Jan29 1-1	Oct30 6-1	Apr09 2-1	Aug21 3-2	Nov27 1-0	Oct16 3-0	Apr20 4-0	Sep18 3-1	Feb05 3-0	Jan03 4-0	Sep04 0-1	Apr30 3-4	Nov06 1-0	Mar05 2-1	Feb26 0-3		Jan01 4-2
STENHOUSEMUIR	Oct23 2-3	Apr16 2-3	Jan03 5-1	Jan29 5-0	Nov27 1-1	Dec25 4-2	Nov13 3-1	Aug28 2-5	Jan08 3-2	Mar12 5-2	Aug14 3-1	Apr09 4-2	Oct09 4-1	Apr30 1-0	Mar26 6-0	Sep25 2-2	Sep11 2-1	

LEAGUE TABLES

DIVISION 1

	P	W	D	L	F	A	W	D	L	F	A	Pts
Celtic	38	16	3	0	70	15	11	4	4	44	27	61
Hearts	38	16	2	1	48	16	10	4	5	42	34	58
Rangers	38	11	5	3	44	23	7	8	4	31	26	49
Falkirk	38	9	4	6	43	27	10	5	4	39	25	47
Motherwell	38	12	5	2	49	28	5	5	9	29	41	44
Aberdeen	38	12	3	4	47	18	3	6	10	27	41	39
Partick T	38	12	2	5	45	32	3	7	9	23	38	39
St Johnstone	38	11	4	4	47	29	5	3	11	31	52	39
T. Lanark	38	7	8	4	34	30	4	5	10	34	43	35
Hibernian	38	8	8	3	38	27	3	5	11	19	38	35
Arbroath	38	8	7	4	37	30	3	6	10	21	49	35
Queen's Park	38	6	8	5	33	32	5	4	10	26	42	34
Hamilton A	38	9	3	7	48	30	4	4	11	33	46	33
St Mirren	38	11	2	6	42	25	3	3	13	16	41	33
Clyde	38	6	9	4	41	31	4	4	11	27	47	33
Queen of South	38	6	4	9	26	32	5	7	7	32	39	33
Ayr U	38	6	9	4	42	31	3	6	10	24	54	33
Kilmarnock	38	9	5	5	35	33	3	4	12	30	58	33
Dundee	38	10	3	6	47	27	3	3	13	23	47	32
Morton	38	5	1	13	44	55	1	2	16	20	72	15

DIVISION 2

	P	W	D	L	F	A	W	D	L	F	A	Pts
Raith R	34	15	1	1	68	20	12	4	1	74	34	59
Albion R	34	10	5	2	60	25	10	3	4	37	25	48
Airdrie	34	12	3	2	58	26	9	2	6	42	27	47
St Bernard's	34	13	1	3	43	19	7	4	6	32	30	45
East Fife	34	13	1	3	71	27	6	4	7	33	34	43
Cowdenbeath	34	11	2	4	71	34	6	7	4	44	37	43
Dumbarton	34	14	3	0	63	19	3	2	12	22	47	39
Stenhousemuir	34	12	2	3	54	27	5	3	9	33	51	39
Dunfermline A	34	10	4	3	40	27	7	1	9	42	49	39
Leith A	34	10	4	3	42	22	6	1	10	29	34	37
Alloa	34	8	1	8	44	44	3	3	11	34	62	26
King's Park	34	8	1	8	30	38	3	3	11	34	58	26
E. Stirling	34	8	4	5	35	32	1	3	13	20	63	25
Dundee U	34	6	3	8	43	49	3	2	12	26	55	23
Forfar A	34	5	5	7	43	48	3	1	13	24	52	22
Montrose	34	5	5	7	31	29	2	3	12	25	59	22
Edinburgh	34	6	1	10	43	58	1	2	14	34	77	17
Brechin C	34	2	2	13	33	61	3	0	14	20	78	12

Scottish Football League Records
Season 1938-39

DIVISION 1

	ABERDEEN	ALBION R	ARBROATH	AYR U	CELTIC	CLYDE	FALKIRK	HAMILTON A	HEARTS	HIBERNIAN	KILMARNOCK	MOTHERWELL	PARTICK T	QUEEN OF SOUTH	QUEEN'S PARK	RAITH R	RANGERS	ST JOHNSTONE	ST MIRREN	T LANARK
ABERDEEN		Dec10 2-1	Jan02 4-0	Oct15 5-2	Dec24 3-1	Oct29 1-2	Oct01 4-1	Nov05 5-0	Feb25 4-3	Jan07 6-1	Nov19 1-2	Sep03 0-0	Aug24 3-0	Apr01 4-3	Mar18 2-1	Dec03 6-3	Apr29 2-0	Sep17 3-0	Jan28 3-2	Aug20 6-1
ALBION R	Apr22 1-0		Aug24 3-2	Dec28 3-3	Oct01 1-8	Dec03 3-0	Jan02 0-3	Mar04 5-0	Nov19 0-1	Sep17 0-1	Apr01 6-1	Oct15 3-4	Sep03 3-1	Nov12 2-1	Oct22 1-3	Apr29 2-1	Nov05 2-7	Aug20 2-3	Jan11 2-1	Jan28 2-4
ARBROATH	Sep10 0-2	Aug13 3-2		Apr08 3-0	Nov26 0-2	Jan14 3-0	Mar04 1-2	Aug27 4-1	Jan03 1-1	Nov12 2-4	Feb11 4-1	Feb25 2-0	Apr22 4-0	Sep14 1-1	Dec31 3-1	Oct08 0-4	Sep24 3-3	Dec17 3-1	Mar25 2-1	Nov05 0-5
AYR U	Jan03 3-3	Aug27 1-1	Dec03 4-1		Mar11 1-4	Sep14 2-4	Apr01 3-0	Feb11 1-1	Sep24 3-1	Oct22 3-1	Oct08 2-2	Mar18 6-1	Oct29 3-0	Sep10 2-3	Jan25 2-0	Aug13 2-1	Dec31 3-4	Nov19 0-0	Apr22 2-3	Apr29 3-3
CELTIC	Aug27 1-2	Jan25 4-1	Apr01 2-0	Nov05 3-3		Feb11 3-1	Mar18 1-2	Sep14 1-2	Dec31 2-2	Dec03 5-4	Aug13 9-1	Nov19 1-3	Feb25 3-1	Oct08 5-1	Jan03 0-1	Sep24 6-1	Sep10 6-2	Apr22 1-1	Dec17 3-2	Oct29 6-1
CLYDE	Mar07 1-1	Apr08 0-0	Oct01 2-0	Aug20 3-1	Sep17 1-4		Dec26 2-4	Nov26 4-3	Dec10 2-6	Sep03 3-0	Apr29 5-1	Jan28 4-0	Jan02 4-1	Oct22 1-1	Mar15 2-3	Nov12 2-3	Mar28 1-1	Jan10 3-1	Aug23 2-0	Apr10 4-1
FALKIRK	Jan14 1-3	Sep10 4-3	Oct29 2-0	Nov26 3-1	Nov12 1-1	Aug27 0-2		Sep24 4-0	Sep13 0-1	Mar11 1-1	Jan03 4-0	Dec10 2-1	Dec17 2-5	Feb11 2-1	Aug13 1-0	Dec31 6-1	Oct08 2-2	Feb25 1-1	Apr08 2-1	Mar25 4-0
HAMILTON A	Mar11 1-0	Oct29 2-1	Dec24 1-1	Sep17 2-0	Aug20 0-1	Apr01 1-2	Jan11 1-3		Apr29 4-1	Aug24 4-1	Mar18 3-1	Jan02 2-1	Jan28 4-0	Nov19 1-0	Dec03 3-1	Feb25 1-3	Dec10 2-1	Oct01 2-1	Oct15 1-2	Sep03 4-3
HEARTS	Oct22 5-2	Mar29 2-0	Oct15 1-1	Jan11 2-0	Sep03 1-5	Apr26 2-0	Aug20 6-2	Dec17 2-3		Jan02 0-1	Dec03 2-1	Sep17 4-0	Dec24 5-0	Mar11 1-2	Mar04 8-3	Apr01 2-1	Nov12 1-3	Jan28 8-2	Oct01 5-2	Aug24 4-2
HIBERNIAN	Sep24 5-0	Feb11 1-2	Mar18 1-1	Feb25 2-3	Apr08 1-0	Dec31 1-1	Nov05 3-0	Aug13 2-2	Sep10 4-0		Sep14 0-1	Apr29 2-1	Nov19 1-2	Aug27 2-3	Oct08 3-1	Jan03 2-1	Jan14 1-1	Oct29 5-2	Nov26 6-1	Dec10 1-1
KILMARNOCK	Apr05 0-3	Nov26 4-2	Sep17 1-1	Jan28 2-2	Aug24 0-0	Dec17 1-4	Oct15 1-1	Nov12 2-2	Apr08 4-1	Aug20 0-1		Dec28 1-3	Oct01 4-2	Mar08 1-1	Apr22 3-0	Nov05 4-2	Oct22 3-1	Sep03 1-0	Jan02 3-2	Jan07 5-2
MOTHERWELL	Dec31 2-2	Jan03 3-1	Oct22 4-0	Nov12 1-2	Apr05 2-3	Oct08 3-2	Apr14 1-3	Sep10 2-3	Feb11 4-2	Dec17 3-2	Aug27 5-2		Mar11 4-3	Aug13 8-5	Sep24 2-0	Jan14 2-4	Sep14 0-5	Apr08 3-1	Mar08 2-1	Nov26 5-1
PARTICK T	Aug13 2-1	Dec31 1-3	Dec10 3-1	Mar04 2-3	Oct22 0-0	Sep10 2-1	Apr29 2-0	Oct08 3-1	Aug27 3-1	Mar28 4-0	Feb18 4-3	Nov05 4-2		Sep24 1-2	Feb11 2-2	Sep13 2-1	Jan03 2-4	Nov26 1-4	Nov12 3-0	Apr08 4-1
QUEEN OF SOUTH	Nov26 1-1	Mar18 3-3	Aug20 2-0	Jan02 6-1	Jan28 1-1	Feb25 3-2	Sep17 2-0	Feb18 3-0	Nov05 0-1	Dec24 2-1	Oct29 2-0	Aug24 4-3	Jan11 0-0		Dec17 3-2	Dec10 4-2	Apr08 1-1	Oct15 1-1	Sep03 1-0	Oct01 1-2
QUEEN'S PARK	Nov12 2-1	Feb25 1-2	Sep03 1-0	Oct01 1-3	Apr10 1-2	Nov05 4-2	Aug23 1-1	Apr08 1-2	Oct29 4-1	Jan28 3-2	Dec10 1-5	Jan11 0-0	Sep17 1-1	Apr29 2-0		Mar25 3-0	Nov26 2-3	Dec24 2-3	Aug20 0-0	Jan02 1-4
RAITH R	Apr08 3-2	Dec17 1-1	Jan28 1-3	Aug24 3-1	Jan07 4-0	Mar18 0-2	Sep03 0-1	Oct22 2-1	Nov26 1-2	Oct15 1-2	Mar11 2-3	Oct01 0-1	Aug20 2-4	Apr22 1-3	Nov19 4-5		Mar04 0-2	Jan02 5-6	Sep17 1-3	Dec24 2-2
RANGERS	Dec17 5-2	Mar11 5-0	Jan11 4-0	Sep03 4-1	Jan02 2-1	Nov19 2-0	Jan28 2-1	Apr21 3-2	Mar18 1-1	Oct01 5-2	Feb25 2-2	Aug20 2-2	Oct15 4-1	Dec03 4-1	Apr01 1-0	Oct29 4-0		Aug24 4-2	Dec26 3-0	Sep17 5-1
ST JOHNSTONE	Feb11 1-0	Sep14 4-0	Feb04 4-3	Mar25 0-1	Dec10 1-1	Sep24 3-2	Oct22 6-3	Jan14 0-2	Oct08 1-7	Mar08 2-1	Dec31 1-3	Dec03 2-1	Apr01 7-0	Jan25 3-0	Aug27 4-1	Sep10 1-2	Aug13 3-3		Mar11 6-2	Nov12 4-0
ST MIRREN	Oct08 3-1	Sep24 1-1	Nov19 1-1	Dec10 2-1	Apr29 2-1	Aug13 2-4	Dec03 1-3	Jan03 2-1	Jan24 1-1	Apr01 0-0	Sep10 0-1	Oct29 2-2	Mar18 1-4	Dec31 2-0	Sep13 2-1	Feb11 1-2	Aug27 1-5	Nov05 4-0		Feb25 3-2
T LANARK	Sep14 1-1	Oct08 4-0	Mar11 3-0	Dec17 3-2	Mar08 0-2	Jan03 3-1	Nov19 2-2	Dec31 2-2	Aug13 1-4	Apr21 2-0	Sep24 3-3	Apr01 3-1	Dec03 2-4	Jan14 0-1	Sep10 5-1	Aug27 5-0	Feb11 1-2	Mar18 1-3	Oct22 3-3	

DIVISION 2

	AIRDRIE	ALLOA	BRECHIN C	COWDENBEATH	DUMBARTON	DUNFERMLINE A	DUNDEE	DUNDEE U	EAST FIFE	E STIRLING	EDINBURGH C	FORFAR A	KING'S PARK	LEITH A	MONTROSE	MORTON	ST BERNARD'S	STENHOUSEMUIR
AIRDRIE		Oct29 2-1	Apr08 6-1	Mar25 1-4	Feb11 6-1	Dec31 4-3	Jan14 3-6	Aug27 1-0	Nov26 1-2	Dec10 8-1	Oct08 3-0	Mar18 4-0	Feb25 2-0	Sep24 2-1	Mar11 2-1	Sep10 3-1	Dec17 4-3	Aug13 1-5
ALLOA	Jan07 3-1		Apr29 1-1	Oct15 2-1	Apr08 2-1	Aug13 4-1	Nov19 2-1	Jan28 3-0	Apr15 1-4	Mar11 5-0	Aug27 5-1	Feb11 5-1	Nov05 2-3	Sep10 4-0	Dec10 2-1	Oct08 1-1	Dec24 6-1	Sep24 4-0
BRECHIN C	Sep03 1-1	Sep17 3-3		Mar11 2-5	Aug20 0-3	Dec17 2-2	Feb11 2-1	Nov26 2-2	Oct01 2-2	Jan14 4-4	Dec31 4-3	Dec03 6-0	Mar25 5-2	Oct29 3-2	Jan02 1-4	Apr22 4-2	Oct22 4-1	Nov12 4-2
COWDENBEATH	Dec03 7-2	Nov26 4-2	Oct08 3-3		Jan14 3-1	Sep10 4-0	Oct22 3-1	Dec31 2-2	Apr08 2-2	Feb11 4-0	Dec17 6-1	Aug13 6-2	Apr22 3-2	Aug27 5-1	Nov12 5-3	Sep24 3-1	Mar18 3-1	Feb25 7-1
DUMBARTON	Nov12 0-0	Dec03 2-3	Feb04 1-3	Nov19 1-4		Feb25 2-2	Oct29 4-4	Sep24 1-0	Jan28 2-0	Aug13 4-0	Apr22 5-1	Sep10 2-0	Oct15 2-1	Dec31 1-1	Dec17 2-2	Aug27 1-3	Apr01 1-2	Oct08 2-2
DUNFERMLINE A	Aug20 0-0	Oct22 1-4	Nov19 8-3	Jan02 1-4	Oct01 2-2		Sep03 4-1	Oct15 3-0	Sep17 1-1	Oct29 7-1	Apr08 2-1	Mar25 4-1	Apr29 7-1	Nov05 3-2	Mar04 4-3	Jan07 5-2	Jan28 4-1	Dec10 7-1
DUNDEE	Nov05 1-2	Dec17 1-4	Aug13 5-0	Jan28 5-0	Apr15 1-1	Apr01 7-1		Mar18 2-0	Oct15 1-1	Oct08 5-6	Sep10 2-2	Sep24 10-2	Feb18 3-0	Feb25 7-0	Nov26 5-0	Dec31 2-1	Dec03 3-0	Aug27 3-1
DUNDEE U	Nov19 1-2	Sep03 1-0	Dec24 1-0	Aug20 1-4	Dec10 4-2	Jan14 1-0	Sep17 3-0		Jan02 2-5	Mar25 10-0	Feb11 1-3	Mar04 6-0	Oct01 2-1	Mar11 6-1	Apr22 3-5	Oct22 1-0	Nov12 5-2	Oct29 2-1
EAST FIFE	Apr01 3-1	Nov12 3-1	Feb25 6-0	Oct29 0-1	Oct22 5-1	Feb11 3-7	Mar11 0-2	Sep10 3-2		Aug27 7-5	Sep24 7-1	Jan03 2-1	Dec03 2-0	Oct08 3-1	Dec31 4-0	Aug13 6-5	Mar25 3-4	Dec17 2-4
E STIRLING	Oct01 1-1	Aug20 1-3	Oct15 3-2	Sep17 2-2	Feb18 6-4	Dec03 2-5	Mar04 3-5	Nov05 3-3	Mar18 2-3		Apr29 2-3	Nov19 2-3	Jan02 2-3	Apr15 5-2	Jan28 1-2	Apr01 3-1	Sep03 5-2	Apr22 0-2
EDINBURGH C	Mar04 1-2	Mar18 3-1	Dec10 1-5	Sep03 0-4	Sep17 2-2	Nov26 2-3	Jan03 1-4	Feb25 3-2	Nov05 2-5	Nov12 2-7		Apr15 2-3	Oct22 2-5	Mar25 0-2	Aug20 4-2	Jan28 4-1	Oct01 0-4	Feb18 3-3
FORFAR A	Sep17 2-3	Oct01 2-6	Jan28 4-4	Apr01 1-8	Jan02 6-6	Nov12 4-2	Dec10 2-1	Dec17 2-1	Sep03 1-4	Feb25 3-2	Oct29 5-3		Apr08 5-6	Nov26 1-0	Oct22 4-3	Mar11 6-5	Aug20 2-2	Dec31 1-0
KING'S PARK	Jan28 2-5	Dec31 0-4	Sep24 6-0	Dec10 1-3	Sep26 2-2	Aug27 1-2	Nov12 3-1	Apr01 3-2	Jan14 2-3	Sep10 3-4	Aug13 2-2	Oct08 11-3		Feb11 1-3	Oct29 7-1	Feb04 6-5	Mar04 5-0	Nov26 1-0
LEITH A	Oct22 1-7	Jan02 2-3	Apr01 3-1	Apr29 0-2	Sep03 1-2	Mar18 2-3	Oct01 3-1	Dec03 0-2	Mar04 1-1	Dec17 6-3	Oct15 3-0	Apr22 4-0	Aug20 3-2		Sep17 5-2	Nov12 1-1	Apr19 1-1	Jan28 1-4
MONTROSE	Feb18 0-1	Mar25 1-2	Sep10 2-5	Jan07 0-1	Nov05 2-2	Oct08 2-3	Apr29 5-5	Aug13 4-5	Nov19 3-2	Sep24 4-5	Dec03 4-0	Aug27 7-3	Mar18 1-0	Jan14 2-0		Feb25 5-1	Oct15 2-2	Apr08 4-3
MORTON	Jan02 1-1	Jan14 0-0	Nov05 3-2	Mar04 2-4	Mar18 2-1	Apr14 3-1	Aug20 2-1	Apr08 3-4	Dec24 0-2	Nov26 6-4	Nov19 4-1	Oct15 3-1	Sep03 4-1	Dec10 2-0	Oct01 2-2		Sep17 2-2	Feb11 5-3
ST BERNARD'S	Apr15 0-1	Feb25 2-0	Aug27 7-1	Nov05 1-2	Nov26 2-4	Sep24 3-1	Apr08 1-1	Oct08 5-3	Dec10 0-1	Dec31 3-2	Mar11 4-3	Feb18 6-2	Nov19 5-4	Aug13 2-1	Feb11 2-1	Oct29 5-0		Sep10 1-0
STENHOUSEMUIR	Oct15 3-2	Feb04 0-2	Mar18 7-2	Oct01 0-1	Mar04 2-0	Mar11 4-0	Dec24 1-1	Apr29 3-0	Aug20 2-2	Oct22 3-2	Apr01 5-1	Nov05 2-1	Sep17 2-0	Nov19 1-3	Sep03 3-2	Dec03 2-0	Jan02 2-2	

LEAGUE TABLES

DIVISION 1

	P	W	D	L	F	A	W	D	L	F	A	Pts
Rangers	38	16	3	0	62	19	9	6	4	50	36	59
Celtic	38	11	3	5	62	31	9	5	5	37	22	48
Aberdeen	38	16	1	2	64	23	4	5	10	27	38	46
Hearts	38	13	1	5	61	30	7	4	8	37	40	45
Falkirk	38	11	4	4	42	24	8	3	8	31	39	45
Queen of South	38	11	6	2	40	21	6	3	10	29	43	43
Hamilton A	38	13	1	5	39	23	5	4	10	28	48	41
St Johnstone	38	12	2	5	53	32	5	4	10	32	50	40
Clyde	38	10	4	5	46	31	7	1	11	32	39	39
Kilmarnock	38	9	6	4	40	30	6	3	10	33	56	39
Partick T	38	12	2	5	45	30	5	2	12	29	57	38
Motherwell	38	12	1	6	56	42	4	4	11	26	44	37
Hibernian	38	9	5	5	43	23	5	2	12	25	46	35
Ayr U	38	8	6	5	46	33	5	3	11	30	50	35
T. Lanark	38	8	5	6	44	32	4	3	12	36	64	32
Albion R	38	9	1	9	41	44	3	5	11	24	46	30
Arbroath	38	10	3	6	39	31	1	5	13	15	44	30
St Mirren	38	8	5	6	31	30	3	2	14	26	50	29
Queen's Park	38	7	4	8	31	32	4	1	14	26	51	27
Raith R	38	4	2	13	33	44	6	0	13	32	55	22

DIVISION 2

	P	W	D	L	F	A	W	D	L	F	A	Pts
Cowdenbeath	34	14	3	0	70	25	14	1	2	50	20	60
Alloa	34	13	2	2	52	18	9	2	6	39	28	48
East Fife	34	12	0	5	59	36	9	6	2	40	25	48
Airdrie	34	13	0	4	53	30	8	5	4	32	27	47
Dunfermline A	34	12	3	2	63	28	6	2	9	36	50	41
Dundee	34	11	3	3	63	21	4	4	9	36	42	37
St Bernard's	34	12	1	4	49	27	3	5	9	30	52	36
Stenhousemuir	34	11	3	3	42	21	4	2	11	32	48	35
Dundee U	34	12	0	5	50	26	3	3	11	28	43	33
Brechin C	34	8	6	3	49	39	3	3	11	33	67	31
Dumbarton	34	6	6	5	33	28	3	6	8	35	48	30
Morton	34	10	4	3	44	30	1	2	14	30	58	28
King's Park	34	8	2	7	56	40	4	0	13	31	52	26
Montrose	34	7	3	7	48	40	3	2	12	34	56	25
Forfar A	34	9	3	5	51	56	2	0	15	23	82	25
Leith A	34	7	3	7	37	35	3	1	13	20	48	24
E. Stirling	34	5	3	9	43	46	4	1	12	46	84	22
Edinburgh	34	4	2	11	32	55	2	2	13	26	64	16

Scottish Football League Records
Season 1939-40

LEAGUE TABLES
DIVISION A

	P	W	D	L	F	A	Pts
Rangers	5	4	1	0	14	3	9
Falkirk	5	4	0	1	20	10	8
Aberdeen	5	3	0	2	9	9	6
Celtic	5	3	0	2	7	7	6
Hearts	5	2	2	1	13	9	6
Partick T	5	2	2	1	7	7	6
Motherwell	5	2	1	2	14	12	5
Hamilton A	5	2	1	1	7	11	5
T Lanark	5	2	1	2	9	8	5
Queen of South	5	2	1	2	10	9	5
Albion R	5	2	1	2	12	7	5
St Mirren	5	1	3	1	8	8	5
Kilmarnock	5	2	1	2	10	9	5
Hibernian	5	2	0	3	11	13	4
Alloa	5	2	0	3	8	13	4
Arbroath	5	2	0	3	9	9	4
St Johnstone	5	2	0	3	7	8	4
Ayr U	5	2	0	3	10	17	4
Clyde	5	1	0	4	10	14	2
Cowdenbeath	5	1	0	4	6	14	2

DIVISION B

	P	W	D	L	F	A	Pts
Dundee	4	3	1	0	13	5	7
Dunfermline A	4	2	2	0	10	5	6
King's Park	4	2	2	0	11	7	6
East Fife	4	2	1	1	12	6	5
Queen's Park	4	1	3	0	7	5	5
Stenhousemuir	4	2	1	1	6	5	5
Dundee U	4	2	1	1	8	7	5
Dumbarton	4	2	1	1	9	9	5
E Stirling	4	1	2	1	7	7	4
St Bernard's	4	1	2	1	7	7	4
Airdrie	4	2	0	2	7	8	4
Edinburgh C	4	1	1	2	9	8	3
Montrose	4	1	1	2	7	8	3
Raith R	4	1	1	2	8	12	3
Morton	4	1	1	2	4	7	3
Leith A	4	1	0	3	4	7	2
Brechin C	4	0	2	2	3	8	2
Forfar A	4	0	0	4	7	18	0

DIVISION A

Saturday, 12 August 1939

Aberdeen	3	Celtic	1
Albion R	5	Ayr U	0
Alloa	3	St Johnstone	0
Clyde	4	Falkirk	6
Cowdenbeath	2	T Lanark	1
Hamilton A	2	Arbroath	0
Hearts	1	Partick T	1
Kilmarnock	3	Motherwell	3
Queen of South	2	Hibernian	1
Rangers	5	St Mirren	1

Saturday, 19 August 1939

Arbroath	5	Alloa	2
Ayr U	0	Rangers	4
Celtic	2	Hearts	0
Falkirk	7	Cowdenbeath	1
Hibernian	3	Clyde	2
Motherwell	3	Aberdeen	0
Partick T	2	Albion R	1
St Johnstone	0	Kilmarnock	3
St Mirren	3	Queen of South	3
T Lanark	2	Hamilton A	2

Tuesday, 22 August 1959

Partick T	2	Hearts	2
St Mirren	0	Rangers	0
T Lanark	4	Cowdenbeath	2

Wednesday, 23 August 1939

Arbroath	2	Hamilton A	0
Ayr U	2	Albion R	1
Celtic	1	Aberdeen	3
Falkirk	4	Clyde	2
Hibernian	3	Queen of South	1
Motherwell	4	Kilmarnock	2
St Johnstone	4	Alloa	0

Saturday, 26 August 1939

Aberdeen	3	Hibernian	1
Albion R	0	St Mirren	0
Alloa	3	Motherwell	2
Clyde	2	St Johnstone	0
Cowdenbeath	1	Celtic	2
Hamilton A	2	Falkirk	1
Hearts	6	Ayr U	2
Kilmarnock	0	T Lanark	1
Queen of South	3	Partick T	0
Rangers	3	Arbroath	1

Saturday, 2 September 1939

Arbroath	1	Kilmarnock	2
Ayr U	6	Hamilton A	1
Celtic	1	Clyde	0
Falkirk	2	Queen of South	1
Hibernian	3	Albion R	5
Motherwell	2	Hearts	4
Partick T	2	Alloa	0
St Johnstone	3	Aberdeen	0
St Mirren	4	Cowdenbeath	0
T Lanark	1	Rangers	2

DIVISION B

Saturday, 12 August 1939

Brechin C	0	St Bernard's	0
Dundee	5	Raith R	1
East Fife	3	Morton	0
E Stirling	4	Montrose	1
Edinburgh C	2	Dundee U	3
Forfar A	3	King's Park	5
Leith A	1	Dumbarton	2
Queen's Park	2	Airdrie	0
Stenhousemuir	0	Dunfermline A	0

Saturday, 19 August 1939

Airdrie	2	Dundee	4
Dumbarton	3	East Fife	3
Dundee U	4	Stenhousemuir	2
Dunfermline A	3	Queen's Park	3
King's Park	3	Leith A	1
Montrose	2	Edinburgh C	2
Morton	3	E Stirling	0
Raith R	2	Brechin C	0
St Bernard's	6	Forfar A	2

Saturday, 26 August 1939

Brechin C	1	King's Park	1
Dundee	3	Dumbarton	1
East Fife	5	St Bernard's	1
E Stirling	1	Dundee U	1
Edinburgh C	3	Morton	0
Forfar A	1	Airdrie	3
Leith A	0	Dunfermline A	2
Queen's Park	2	Raith R	1
Stenhousemuir	1	Montrose	0

Saturday, 2 September 1939

Airdrie	2	East Fife	1
Dumbarton	3	Edinburgh C	2
Dundee U	0	Leith A	2
Dunfermline A	5	Brechin C	2
King's Park	2	E Stirling	2
Montrose	4	Forfar A	1
Morton	1	Dundee	1
Raith R	1	Stenhousemuir	3
St Bernard's	0	Queen's Park	0

Curtailment of Season 1939-40 due to war.

Scottish Football League Records
Season 1945-46

DIVISION A

	ABERDEEN	CELTIC	CLYDE	FALKIRK	HAMILTON A	HEARTS	HIBERNIAN	KILMARNOCK	MORTON	MOTHERWELL	PARTICK T	QUEEN OF SOUTH	QUEEN'S PARK	RANGERS	ST MIRREN	T LANARK
ABERDEEN		Dec15 1-1	Oct20 1-2	Sep08 2-0	Nov17 4-0	Feb09 2-1	Dec22 2-1	Dec01 2-0	Nov03 3-1	Sep22 4-1	Jan03 3-0	Jan26 7-1	Jan05 5-0	Jan12 4-1	Aug25 6-1	Aug11 3-0
CELTIC	Sep01 1-1		Aug18 2-2	Oct27 2-1	Sep15 2-0	Dec29 3-5	Feb02 0-1	Feb16 1-1	Nov24 2-1	Nov10 3-0	Oct06 4-1	Sep29 2-0	Dec08 3-3	Jan01 0-1	Oct20 2-2	Jan12 3-2
CLYDE	Jan19 0-0	Dec01 3-3		Feb13 6-2	Jan26 3-2	Nov03 3-1	Sep22 2-2	Dec22 3-0	Feb09 4-3	Jan02 3-0	Sep08 0-2	Nov17 2-2	Aug25 4-4	Jan05 0-1	Aug11 2-3	Sep05 1-2
FALKIRK	Jan01 3-1	Jan26 4-2	Sep01 4-1		Aug18 7-0	Nov24 3-5	Oct06 2-1	Oct20 3-4	Sep15 3-2	Jan12 3-3	Nov17 2-1	Dec08 3-2	Sep29 1-1	Dec29 0-3	Feb09 1-3	Nov03 3-1
HAMILTON A	Feb16 3-3	Dec22 0-1	Oct27 2-4	Dec01 3-1		Jan12 2-0	Aug25 1-1	Sep22 4-4	Oct20 2-2	Sep08 3-6	Aug11 0-1	Oct06 2-2	Nov10 3-4	Feb02 1-4	Dec15 0-3	Jan02 0-1
HEARTS	Nov10 1-2	Sep22 2-2	Feb02 1-1	Aug11 4-1	Oct13 4-1		Sep08 0-2	Jan02 1-4	Oct06 6-0	Aug25 0-0	Dec01 4-1	Apr15 0-3	Oct27 3-3	Feb16 2-0	Dec22 2-2	Dec15 2-1
HIBERNIAN	Sep15 1-1	Nov03 1-1	Dec29 3-2	Jan05 4-1	Dec08 1-2	Jan01 1-0		Jan12 4-1	Sep29 5-0	Oct20 0-0	Feb09 3-1	Nov24 6-1	Sep01 4-0	Aug18 2-1	Nov17 3-2	Jan26 4-0
KILMARNOCK	Aug18 1-4	Nov17 2-1	Sep15 0-0	Apr06 6-2	Dec29 0-2	Sep29 2-2	Oct13 3-4		Dec08 1-1	Oct06 2-5	Jan26 2-1	Jan01 1-1	Nov24 2-2	Sep01 0-7	Nov03 6-4	Feb09 1-3
MORTON	Feb02 3-2	Aug11 1-1	Nov10 1-1	Dec22 3-3	Jan19 3-1	Jan05 4-2	Jan02 4-1	Aug25 6-1		Dec01 3-3	Dec15 1-1	Oct13 7-1	Feb16 1-2	Oct27 2-2	Sep08 0-1	Sep22 4-4
MOTHERWELL	Dec29 1-3	Feb09 1-3	Sep29 3-2	Oct13 1-1	Jan01 0-0	Dec08 5-4	Jan19 0-0	Jan05 2-2	Aug18 2-1		Nov03 2-1	Sep01 2-1	Sep15 1-2	Nov24 1-2	Jan26 5-1	Nov17 1-3
PARTICK T	Sep29 1-1	Jan05 0-3	Jan01 2-1	Feb16 4-3	Nov24 5-1	Aug18 1-3	Nov10 0-2	Oct27 5-3	Sep01 2-2	Feb02 3-0		Sep15 2-1	Dec29 1-3	Dec08 1-5	Jan12 1-0	Oct20 6-2
QUEEN OF SOUTH	Oct27 3-2	Jan02 0-0	Feb16 1-2	Aug25 0-2	Jan05 5-1	Oct20 3-3	Aug11 3-0	Sep08 2-1	Jan12 2-3	Dec15 1-4	Dec22 5-3		Feb02 3-3	Nov10 2-4	Sep22 5-1	Dec01 5-3
QUEEN'S PARK	Dec25 3-1	Aug16 2-0	Jan12 1-2	Jan02 2-0	Feb09 3-2	Jan26 0-1	Apr23 2-4	Aug11 2-3	Nov17 3-4	Dec22 4-0	Sep22 1-1	Nov03 2-3		Oct20 0-2	Dec01 3-0	Jan01 1-1
RANGERS	Oct13 3-1	Sep08 5-3	Dec25 3-1	Sep22 1-0	Nov03 5-1	Nov17 1-1	Dec01 3-2	Dec15 5-1	Jan26 4-4	Aug11 0-3	Aug16 4-2	Feb09 5-2	Jan19 2-1		Jan02 3-1	Dec22 1-0
ST MIRREN	Dec08 4-1	Jan19 1-2	Nov24 2-1	Nov10 0-0	Sep01 2-3	Sep15 3-1	Feb16 0-3	Feb02 4-1	Jan01 2-4	Oct27 0-0	Oct13 0-2	Dec29 4-1	Aug18 2-3	Sep29 2-2		Oct06 3-4
T LANARK	Nov24 3-1	Oct13 0-2	Dec08 1-6	Feb02 2-3	Sep29 7-2	Sep01 1-2	Oct27 2-1	Nov10 4-1	Dec29 2-1	Feb16 0-2	Jan19 4-2	Aug18 5-1	Sep08 1-0	Sep15 1-5	Jan05 3-1	

DIVISION B

	AIRDRIE	ALBION R	ALLOA	ARBROATH	AYR U	COWDENBEATH	DUMBARTON	DUNDEE	DUNDEE U	DUNFERMLINE A	EAST FIFE	RAITH R	ST JOHNSTONE	STENHOUSEMUIR
AIRDRIE		Jan01 2-5	Jan12 3-0	Nov03 5-0	Nov17 3-2	Oct13 5-2	Jan19 3-2	Sep01 3-3	Dec22 1-1	Sep15 1-1	Dec29 2-0	Nov24 4-2	Sep22 5-5	Aug18 6-0
ALBION R	Sep08 3-2		Aug11 6-2	Dec15 1-1	Dec08 3-2	Dec01 4-0	Nov10 3-0	Oct20 0-2	Aug25 1-0	Jan05 2-0	Sep29 3-2	Jan02 3-0	Oct27 1-6	Oct06 0-0
ALLOA	Oct20 2-3	Nov17 0-2		Oct06 4-4	Aug18 1-3	Oct27 2-0	Sep29 2-1	Sep15 0-1	Dec08 3-1	Sep01 1-5	Nov03 1-1	Jan05 6-0	Nov24 3-1	Jan01 4-0
ARBROATH	Jan02 0-5	Sep15 1-0	Dec29 1-2		Jan19 2-4	Sep29 4-1	Dec08 0-3	Aug18 1-4	Oct13 4-1	Nov24 3-1	Jan12 2-6	Nov17 2-1	Jan01 0-1	Sep01 0-3
AYR U	Aug11 0-3	Sep22 3-1	Nov10 2-6	Oct27 4-1		Aug25 3-1	Sep08 4-1	Dec29 2-1	Dec01 1-1	Dec22 2-1	Dec15 1-1	Oct20 1-1	Jan02 1-0	Jan05 10-1
COWDENBEATH	Jan05 2-3	Sep01 1-0	Jan19 1-1	Dec22 4-2	Nov24 1-1		Oct20 1-5	Jan02 2-2	Oct06 4-2	Jan01 1-0	Sep22 1-3	Aug18 2-1	Sep15 3-3	Nov17 5-1
DUMBARTON	Oct27 1-2	Aug18 4-0	Dec22 4-1	Sep22 2-0	Jan01 1-3	Jan12 3-1		Nov24 0-1	Nov03 2-1	Oct06 2-1	Oct13 3-0	Sep01 6-3	Nov17 3-5	Sep15 1-1
DUNDEE	Dec01 4-1	Jan12 2-0	Dec15 5-1	Nov10 8-0	Oct06 1-4	Nov03 5-0	Aug25 5-2		Sep08 1-0	Jan19 3-1	Aug11 2-1	Dec22 7-0	Oct13 5-1	Dec08 6-1
DUNDEE U	Sep29 4-2	Nov24 2-3	Sep22 2-5	Jan05 4-1	Sep01 3-2	Dec29 0-2	Jan02 4-1	Jan01 2-3		Nov17 1-2	Oct27 5-2	Sep15 0-7	Aug18 3-4	Oct20 7-0
DUNFERMLINE A	Dec15 5-2	Oct13 5-2	Dec01 2-3	Aug25 6-1	Sep29 2-3	Sep08 4-1	Dec29 1-1	Oct27 0-6	Aug11 7-0		Nov10 0-4	Dec08 8-1	Jan12 0-1	Nov03 5-1
EAST FIFE	Oct06 2-1	Dec22 1-0	Jan02 1-1	Oct20 8-0	Sep15 2-0	Dec08 0-1	Jan05 6-2	Nov17 1-4	Jan19 2-0	Aug18 0-0		Jan01 4-0	Sep01 2-1	Nov24 7-2
RAITH R	Aug25 4-0	Nov03 0-1	Oct13 1-2	Aug11 3-2	Jan12 2-3	Nov10 3-2	Dec01 1-4	Sep29 0-5	Dec15 5-0	Sep22 3-2	Sep08 0-2		Dec29 4-5	Oct27 1-2
ST JOHNSTONE	Dec08 0-0	Jan19 3-0	Aug25 0-4	Sep08 4-6	Nov03 3-2	Dec15 1-1	Aug11 3-3	Jan05 4-1	Nov10 3-0	Oct20 1-1	Dec01 1-4	Oct06 5-3		Sep29 4-1
STENHOUSEMUIR	Nov10 0-2	Dec29 0-1	Sep08 3-2	Dec01 3-2	Oct13 0-6	Aug11 4-3	Dec15 2-2	Sep22 1-5	Jan12 2-2	Jan02 1-3	Aug25 1-2	Jan19 2-2	Dec22 4-1	

LEAGUE TABLES

DIVISION A

	P	W	D	L	F	A	W	D	L	F	A	Pts
Rangers	30	12	2	1	45	23	10	2	3	40	18	48
Hibernian	30	11	3	1	42	13	6	3	6	25	24	40
Aberdeen	30	13	1	1	49	10	3	5	7	24	31	38
Celtic	30	7	5	3	30	21	5	6	4	25	23	35
Clyde	30	6	5	4	36	27	5	4	6	28	27	31
Motherwell	30	6	4	5	27	26	5	5	5	27	29	31
Hearts	30	6	5	4	32	23	5	3	7	31	34	30
Queen's Park	30	6	2	7	29	24	5	6	4	31	36	30
T. Lanark	30	9	0	6	36	30	5	2	8	27	38	30
Morton	30	6	7	2	43	26	3	4	8	29	43	29
Falkirk	30	9	2	4	42	30	2	3	10	20	40	27
Partick T	30	8	2	5	34	30	3	2	10	20	35	26
Queen of South	30	7	3	5	40	32	2	3	10	22	50	24
St Mirren	30	5	3	7	29	28	4	2	9	25	42	23
Kilmarnock	30	4	5	6	29	39	3	3	9	27	48	22
Hamilton A	30	2	5	8	26	37	3	1	11	18	51	16

DIVISION B

	P	W	D	L	F	A	W	D	L	F	A	Pts
Dundee	26	12	0	1	54	12	9	2	2	38	16	44
East Fife	26	9	2	2	36	12	6	2	5	28	22	34
Ayr U	26	8	3	2	34	19	7	1	5	35	24	34
Airdrie	26	8	4	1	43	23	6	1	6	26	27	33
St Johnstone	26	6	4	3	32	26	6	2	5	34	34	30
Albion R	26	9	2	2	30	17	5	0	8	15	24	30
Alloa	26	6	2	5	29	22	6	2	5	30	31	28
Dumbarton	26	8	1	4	32	19	3	3	7	27	35	26
Dunfermline A	26	7	1	5	45	26	3	3	7	18	21	24
Cowdenbeath	26	6	4	3	28	24	2	1	10	15	38	21
Stenhousemuir	26	4	3	6	23	33	2	2	9	13	56	17
Dundee U	26	6	0	7	37	34	0	3	10	9	36	15
Raith R	26	5	0	8	27	30	1	2	10	21	50	14
Arbroath	26	5	0	8	20	32	1	2	10	20	56	14

Scottish Football League Records
Season 1946-47

DIVISION A

DIVISION A	ABERDEEN	CELTIC	CLYDE	FALKIRK	HAMILTON A	HEARTS	HIBERNIAN	KILMARNOCK	MORTON	MOTHERWELL	PARTICK T	QUEEN OF SOUTH	QUEEN'S PARK	RANGERS	ST MIRREN	T LANARK
ABERDEEN		Aug17 6-2	Feb01 2-1	Jan01 0-4	May14 3-0	Nov23 2-1	Aug28 2-1	Aug14 1-0	May05 2-2	Dec21 3-1	Sep14 2-2	Nov02 0-0	Nov16 3-1	Sep04 1-0	May03 4-2	Dec07 1-0
CELTIC	Jan02 1-5		Dec14 3-3	Apr26 0-0	Dec28 2-1	Aug21 2-3	Nov09 4-1	Nov30 4-2	Aug10 1-2	May03 3-2	Mar22 2-0	Jan04 2-0	Dec25 1-0	Sep07 2-3	Feb22 2-1	Sep04 1-4
CLYDE	Aug31 0-2	Aug14 2-2		Aug17 4-0	Nov02 2-1	Feb08 0-2	Dec21 2-2	Aug28 3-3	Nov23 2-1	Sep14 3-1	Jan01 2-4	Mar08 1-1	Jan18 2-5	Nov16 2-4	Dec07 2-2	Jan11 0-3
FALKIRK	Sep07 2-0	Nov02 1-4	Jan02 1-2		Dec14 6-0	Aug10 3-3	May17 2-3	Feb01 3-3	Dec28 1-1	Sep04 5-2	Apr19 6-1	Aug24 2-3	Jan04 3-1	Aug21 0-5	Nov23 2-3	Mar29 2-2
HAMILTON A	Nov30 2-5	Aug28 2-2	Feb15 1-2	Aug14 1-4		Sep04 3-1	Jan11 0-0	Dec21 2-2	Feb01 2-2	Jan01 2-2	Dec07 1-3	Mar22 2-3	Apr19 1-2	Nov09 0-6	Aug17 1-4	Sep14 2-2
HEARTS	May17 4-0	Dec21 2-1	Nov09 2-1	Dec07 1-1	Jan18 4-3		Jan01 2-3	Sep14 2-0	Apr05 2-0	Jan11 2-1	Aug14 1-4	Aug31 1-1	Mar29 1-3	Nov30 0-3	Aug28 2-2	Aug17 4-1
HIBERNIAN	Dec28 1-1	Apr12 2-0	Aug21 1-0	Nov16 2-2	Aug24 3-2	Sep07 0-1		Sep04 6-0	Jan04 1-1	Feb01 1-2	Nov23 5-1	Aug10 9-1	Jan02 3-1	Dec14 1-1	Apr26 1-0	Nov02 4-1
KILMARNOCK	Dec14 2-1	Mar29 1-2	Dec28 2-2	Aug31 2-1	Aug21 1-1	Jan04 0-0	Jan18 3-5		Aug24 2-3	Mar22 2-0	Nov02 3-1	Sep07 1-3	Aug10 2-2	Jan02 0-2	Apr05 1-5	Nov23 0-2
MORTON	Nov09 0-0	Dec07 2-1	Mar15 2-2	Aug28 3-3	Aug31 5-1	Nov16 0-1	Sep14 0-2	Feb08 0-0		Aug14 3-1	Aug17 3-4	Jan18 4-1	Nov30 5-4	Feb15 0-1	Jan01 4-0	Dec21 2-0
MOTHERWELL	Aug21 2-2	Nov23 1-2	Jan04 3-3	Jan18 2-0	Sep07 4-0	Aug24 0-2	Aug31 2-1	Nov16 2-1	Dec14 0-1		Apr26 3-3	Jan02 5-1	Dec28 1-0	Aug10 2-4	Nov02 4-2	Apr19 2-1
PARTICK T	Jan04 4-0	Nov16 4-1	Sep07 1-3	Nov30 4-1	Aug10 4-1	Dec14 1-2	May03 0-2	Apr12 5-2	Jan02 3-1	Nov09 0-2		Dec28 1-2	Aug21 4-0	Sep30 3-2	Sep04 3-0	Mar08 3-1
QUEEN OF SOUTH	Apr28 1-5	Sep14 3-1	Nov30 2-0	Jan11 2-2	Nov16 2-3	Feb01 0-1	Dec07 1-3	Jan01 1-1	Sep04 2-2	Aug17 1-6	Aug28 0-0		Nov09 1-4	Feb08 0-2	Dec21 3-2	Aug14 4-1
QUEEN'S PARK	Apr26 0-0	Jan11 1-3	Sep04 1-3	Sep14 0-1	Nov23 2-1	Nov02 2-2	Aug17 0-1	Dec07 0-1	May03 2-3	Aug28 1-1	Dec21 2-6	Apr12 4-1		Feb01 0-0	Aug14 3-2	Jan01 0-0
RANGERS	Jan18 1-0	Jan01 1-1	Mar29 5-0	Dec21 2-1	Apr12 4-1	Apr07 1-2	Aug14 1-2	Aug17 3-2	Nov02 2-1	Dec07 2-1	Jan11 4-0	Nov23 2-1	Aug31 2-0		Sep14 4-0	Aug28 8-1
ST MIRREN	Aug24 4-2	Aug31 0-1	Aug10 1-3	Apr12 1-1	Jan02 1-0	Dec28 1-0	Nov30 0-1	Nov09 3-1	Sep07 1-1	Apr21 1-2	Jan18 1-4	Aug20 1-2	Dec14 3-2	Jan04 1-0		Mar22 2-4
T LANARK	Aug10 0-3	Jan18 0-0	Dec25 5-3	Nov09 4-2	Apr07 2-1	Jan02 4-1	May10 0-2	Mar15 1-4	Aug21 1-4	Nov30 2-1	Aug31 4-1	Dec14 1-1	Sep07 3-4	Dec28 1-1	Nov16 5-1	

DIVISION B

DIVISION B	AIRDRIE	ALBION R	ALLOA	ARBROATH	AYR U	COWDENBEATH	DUMBARTON	DUNDEE	DUNDEE U	DUNFERMLINE A	EAST FIFE	RAITH R	ST JOHNSTONE	STENHOUSEMUIR
AIRDRIE		Aug24 1-2	Nov30 3-2	Jan04 3-1	Aug10 2-1	Jan18 7-2	Mar22 5-4	Dec28 2-1	Apr19 5-0	Mar08 6-4	Apr26 2-2	Sep07 1-1	Nov09 2-1	Jan02 3-1
ALBION R	Jan01 0-1		Dec21 1-6	Sep14 3-1	Jan11 2-1	Aug17 1-1	Aug31 3-0	Feb01 2-2	May03 5-1	Dec07 5-1	Nov02 1-4	Nov16 2-1	Nov23 1-1	Dec14 1-1
ALLOA	Apr05 1-0	Aug10 2-2		Dec14 1-1	Jan02 3-2	Nov23 3-2	Nov02 0-2	Mar08 0-10	Nov09 4-1	Dec28 4-1	Jan04 1-1	Dec07 4-1	Sep07 1-0	Aug24 2-0
ARBROATH	Nov16 2-5	Mar08 3-3	Apr19 1-1		Mar22 2-5	Nov02 1-0	Apr26 2-3	Jan02 1-4	Jan18 5-4	Sep07 1-2	Nov30 3-2	Aug10 2-3	Aug24 2-1	Dec28 3-3
AYR U	Dec21 2-5	Nov09 1-3	Aug31 4-1	Nov23 4-0		Apr26 6-1	Jan01 2-1	Dec14 2-6	Aug17 3-3	Feb15 3-1	Sep14 2-1	Feb01 0-1	Jan04 2-0	Dec07 4-2
COWDENBEATH	Dec07 2-1	Dec28 2-4	Apr23 2-0	Apr05 2-2	Sep07 2-1		Apr12 2-1	Nov16 2-8	Mar29 1-1	Aug24 3-2	Nov09 3-3	Jan02 3-4	Apr19 2-2	Aug10 1-2
DUMBARTON	Nov23 2-3	Jan02 1-1	Feb15 2-2	Nov09 0-1	Aug24 2-2	Nov30 5-1		Sep07 2-1	Jan04 0-2	Dec14 1-2	Jan18 1-0	Dec28 1-1	Aug10 2-3	Mar08 4-1
DUNDEE	Aug17 1-1	Nov30 6-2	Sep14 6-2	Aug31 5-0	May03 6-2	Jan04 6-2	Apr05 4-0		Jan01 2-0	Mar22 10-0	Dec21 2-0	Apr23 5-2	Jan18 2-0	Nov09 4-1
DUNDEE U	Nov02 1-2	Sep07 1-3	Jan11 6-2	Dec07 1-3	Dec28 5-1	Dec14 3-2	Nov16 2-1	Aug24 1-2		Aug10 3-0	Nov23 2-1	Apr14 3-0	Jan02 2-4	Apr12 2-2
DUNFERMLINE A	Sep14 0-5	Jan18 5-1	Aug17 0-3	Mar29 3-1	Nov02 4-0	Jan01 2-2	Apr19 3-2	Nov23 2-5	Dec21 4-3		Aug31 0-2	Jan11 4-1	Nov30 0-4	Jan04 2-2
EAST FIFE	Dec14 2-2	Apr19 2-1	Nov16 3-1	May03 2-1	Mar08 6-2	Jan11 5-0	Dec07 1-0	Aug10 2-6	Feb01 1-2	Jan02 1-1		Aug24 4-4	Dec28 1-0	Sep07 7-1
RAITH R	Apr07 1-2	Jan04 2-0	Jan18 3-2	Dec21 1-0	Nov30 4-1	Aug31 3-0	Aug17 5-1	Nov02 1-4	Sep14 1-1	Nov09 1-4	Jan01 0-0		Mar29 2-1	Nov23 1-1
ST JOHNSTONE	Jan11 2-4	Mar22 3-0	Apr07 0-3	Jan01 1-1	Nov16 7-2	Sep14 0-2	Dec21 5-2	Dec07 1-5	Aug31 3-1	Apr12 2-1	Aug17 1-4	Dec14 2-0		Nov02 1-1
STENHOUSEMUIR	Aug31 0-5	Apr23 4-1	Jan01 3-0	Aug17 1-2	Jan18 3-1	Dec21 4-2	Sep14 0-1	Jan11 0-0	Nov30 3-2	Nov16 1-2	Mar29 0-1	Mar22 4-1	Apr26 2-0	

LEAGUE TABLES
DIVISION A

	P	W	D	L	F	A	W	D	L	F	A	Pts
Rangers	30	12	1	2	42	13	9	3	3	34	13	46
Hibernian	30	9	4	2	40	14	10	2	3	29	19	44
Aberdeen	30	11	3	1	32	17	5	4	6	26	24	39
Hearts	30	8	3	4	30	24	8	3	4	22	19	38
Partick T	30	10	0	5	40	20	6	3	6	34	39	35
Morton	30	7	4	4	33	21	5	6	4	25	24	34
Celtic	30	8	2	5	30	27	5	4	6	23	28	32
Motherwell	30	8	3	4	33	23	4	2	9	25	31	29
T. Lanark	30	7	3	5	33	29	4	3	8	23	35	28
Clyde	30	4	5	6	27	33	5	4	6	28	32	27
Falkirk	30	5	4	6	39	33	3	6	6	23	28	26
Queen of South	30	4	4	7	23	33	5	4	6	21	36	26
Queen's Park	30	3	5	7	18	25	5	1	9	29	35	22
St Mirren	30	6	2	7	21	24	3	2	10	26	41	22
Kilmarnock	30	4	4	7	22	30	2	5	8	22	36	21
Hamilton A	30	1	6	8	22	40	1	1	13	16	45	11

DIVISION B

	P	W	D	L	F	A	W	D	L	F	A	Pts
Dundee	26	12	1	0	59	12	9	2	2	54	18	45
Airdrie	26	10	2	1	42	22	9	2	2	36	16	42
East Fife	26	8	3	2	37	21	4	4	5	21	18	31
Albion R	26	6	4	3	27	21	4	3	6	23	33	27
Alloa	26	8	3	2	26	23	3	2	8	25	34	27
Raith R	26	7	3	3	25	17	3	3	7	20	35	26
Stenhousemuir	26	7	1	5	25	18	1	6	6	18	35	23
Dunfermline A	26	6	2	5	29	31	4	1	8	21	41	23
St Johnstone	26	6	2	5	28	26	3	2	8	17	21	22
Dundee U	26	7	1	5	32	23	2	3	8	21	37	22
Ayr U	26	8	1	4	35	25	1	1	11	21	48	20
Arbroath	26	4	3	6	28	36	3	3	7	14	27	20
Dumbarton	26	4	4	5	23	20	3	0	10	18	34	18
Cowdenbeath	26	5	4	4	27	31	1	2	10	17	46	18

Scottish Football League Records
Season 1947-48

DIVISION A

	ABERDEEN	AIRDRIE	CELTIC	CLYDE	DUNDEE	FALKIRK	HEARTS	HIBERNIAN	MORTON	MOTHERWELL	PARTICK T	QUEEN OF SOUTH	QUEEN'S PARK	RANGERS	ST MIRREN	T LANARK
ABERDEEN		Feb28 3-0	Oct04 2-0	Dec06 3-1	Sep20 3-2	Oct18 1-2	Nov15 1-1	Aug13 0-2	Mar20 2-1	Jan03 2-1	Feb14 0-1	Nov01 2-2	Nov22 6-0	Apr03 1-1	Dec27 5-0	Jan17 2-2
AIRDRIE	Nov08 2-1		Aug13 3-2	Mar13 1-3	Oct18 2-0	Jan03 3-1	Nov29 1-1	Dec27 0-3	Dec06 0-3	Sep20 1-5	Jan17 1-0	Apr03 6-1	Nov15 2-5	May01 1-2	Oct04 1-4	Feb14 2-1
CELTIC	Jan10 1-0	Dec20 0-0		Jan31 0-0	Dec06 1-1	Nov08 0-3	Dec25 4-2	Apr03 2-4	Oct11 3-2	Sep27 0-1	Jan24 1-2	Oct25 4-3	Aug27 4-0	Jan02 0-4	Mar13 0-0	Apr10 1-3
CLYDE	Mar26 1-3	Nov22 5-1	Oct18 2-0		Oct04 1-4	Aug13 1-1	Dec13 2-1	Jan03 2-2	Nov01 3-2	Feb14 3-2	Sep20 2-4	Mar20 5-2	Jan24 2-0	Nov15 1-2	Jan17 3-2	Dec27 1-1
DUNDEE	Jan01 0-0	Sep27 6-0	Apr17 2-3	Jan10 7-0		Feb21 4-0	Oct06 2-1	May01 3-1	Dec20 0-4	Mar13 2-0	Dec13 2-2	Aug27 1-0	Oct25 2-1	Dec25 1-3	Nov08 6-1	Nov29 5-2
FALKIRK	Jan31 3-1	Jan05 0-0	Feb28 0-1	Dec20 1-1	Mar06 3-2		Apr17 0-2	Nov22 3-1	Aug27 4-1	Apr03 2-2	Mar20 1-2	Jan01 1-1	Apr10 3-0	Jan10 1-5	Apr24 1-1	Dec06 8-1
HEARTS	Mar06 1-1	Mar20 2-2	Jan03 1-0	Apr03 1-1	Jan17 0-1	Feb14 3-2		Sep20 2-1	Feb28 3-0	Dec27 0-1	Oct18 1-2	Nov22 1-0	Nov01 1-0	Dec06 1-2	Aug13 3-2	Oct04 1-3
HIBERNIAN	Dec20 4-0	Aug27 7-1	Dec13 1-1	Sep27 2-1	Nov15 2-1	Mar13 2-0	Jan01 3-1		Oct25 1-1	Apr19 5-0	Apr17 1-0	Oct11 6-0	Jan10 4-0	Jan31 1-0	Nov29 5-0	Nov08 8-0
MORTON	Nov29 0-1	May05 1-1	Jan17 4-0	May03 0-1	Aug13 3-0	Dec27 2-1	Nov08 1-1	Feb14 1-2		Oct18 2-3	Oct04 0-2	Apr24 0-1	Dec13 0-1	Mar13 0-1	Sep20 2-2	Jan03 2-2
MOTHERWELL	Apr17 2-1	Jan01 2-0	Mar20 0-3	Oct25 4-1	Nov22 0-2	Dec13 0-0	Aug27 3-1	Nov01 0-2	Apr09 0-1		Feb28 2-0	Jan10 3-1	Dec20 0-2	Apr24 1-1	Mar27 0-1	Oct11 2-1
PARTICK T	Oct25 2-1	Oct11 8-2	Nov15 3-5	Jan01 1-2	Apr03 6-2	Nov29 0-2	Jan31 1-1	Dec06 1-1	Jan10 1-2	Nov08 2-1		Dec20 4-0	Sep27 5-1	Aug27 0-1	Apr09 3-1	Mar13 2-2
QUEEN OF SOUTH	Apr09 0-0	Dec13 3-3	Feb14 2-0	Nov29 3-0	Dec27 5-2	Sep20 6-6	Mar13 0-1	Jan17 0-3	Nov15 4-3	Oct04 3-0	Aug13 0-1		Mar27 3-1	Nov08 0-3	Jan03 2-3	Oct18 2-1
QUEEN'S PARK	Mar13 3-1	Apr20 2-1	Dec27 3-2	Nov08 2-4	Feb14 0-1	Jan17 1-4	Apr24 0-0	Oct04 2-3	Apr03 0-3	Aug13 2-5	Jan03 1-2	Dec06 7-0		Nov29 1-4	Oct18 3-0	Jan01 2-2
RANGERS	Dec13 4-0	Nov01 3-0	Sep20 2-0	Apr26 2-1	Jan03 2-1	Mar29 1-1	May03 1-2	Oct18 2-1	Nov22 1-1	Jan17 2-0	Dec27 2-1	Feb28 2-3	Mar20 1-2		Feb14 3-2	Aug13 5-2
ST MIRREN	Aug26 3-0	Jan10 2-1	Nov22 1-2	Oct11 1-1	Feb28 4-1	Nov15 1-1	Dec20 1-0	Mar20 2-4	Jan01 0-4	Dec06 4-2	Nov01 3-1	Sep27 0-1	Jan31 6-1	Oct25 2-1		Apr03 1-0
T LANARK	Dec25 3-2	Jan24 2-2	Mar29 5-1	Aug27 2-1	Mar20 1-4	Mar26 2-0	Jan10 4-1	Feb28 1-4	Sep27 2-1	Nov15 0-3	Nov22 1-2	Jan31 5-1	Sep20 4-2	D20 0-1	Dec13 1-4	

DIVISION A

	ALBION R	ALLOA	ARBROATH	AYR U	COWDENBEATH	DUMBARTON	DUNDEE U	DUNFERMLINE A	EAST FIFE	HAMILTON A	KILMARNOCK	LEITH A	RAITH R	ST JOHNSTONE	STENHOUSEMUIR	STIRLING A
ALBION R		Dec13 3-1	Nov01 2-1	Dec20 2-0	Mar27 3-1	Feb28 5-3	Aug27 1-0	Sep27 2-0	Apr24 1-4	Jan01 1-2	Nov22 2-1	Jan10 2-0	Oct11 1-1	Oct25 3-2	Jan31 2-2	Mar20 2-0
ALLOA	Apr03 1-3		Feb28 3-1	Jan10 4-4	Nov15 1-2	Nov01 4-1	Dec20 3-1	Aug27 3-1	Dec06 1-3	Dec25 3-3	Mar20 4-1	Oct25 2-2	Jan31 5-2	Oct11 0-7	Apr10 4-2	Nov22 3-1
ARBROATH	Feb21 1-3	Nov08 1-1		Sep27 2-2	Mar13 3-1	Apr03 2-3	Jan10 6-0	Dec20 2-1	Nov29 1-4	Aug27 2-4	Mar06 5-1	Jan05 3-2	Oct25 1-6	Jan01 2-0	Oct11 1-0	Dec06 1-2
AYR U	Aug13 0-2	Oct04 2-0	Oct18 1-0		Jan17 2-1	Feb14 1-1	Dec13 3-3	Nov01 6-2	Jan03 3-3	Feb28 0-0	Sep20 2-3	Mar27 5-1	Nov22 2-4	Mar06 2-1	Feb07 6-0	Dec27 2-0
COWDENBEATH	Dec06 1-3	Sep27 0-0	Nov22 2-1	Oct11 0-0		Mar20 2-1	Oct25 6-2	Jan01 3-0	Apr03 0-3	Dec20 0-1	Nov01 1-0	Aug27 1-2	Jan10 1-1	Jan31 3-1	Dec25 0-3	Feb28 5-2
DUMBARTON	Nov08 1-1	Apr24 3-1	Dec13 3-3	Oct25 3-1	Nov29 1-1		Jan31 3-2	Oct11 4-2	Mar13 2-4	Jan10 0-4	Mar26 1-2	Jan24 5-1	Dec20 4-2	Sep27 2-4	Aug27 2-2	Nov15 5-1
DUNDEE U	Dec27 3-0	Aug13 5-3	Oct04 4-3	Apr03 4-2	Feb14 3-3	Oct18 0-1		Feb28 0-4	Jan17 3-2	Nov22 3-2	Jan03 2-3	Nov15 2-1	Mar20 3-0	Dec06 3-4	Nov01 4-2	Sep20 2-3
DUNFERMLINE A	Jan03 4-0	Dec27 0-2	Aug13 4-3	Apr17 2-1	Sep20 3-4	Jan17 5-1	Nov08 5-3		Oct04 1-1	Mar27 2-1	Feb14 3-1	Nov29 6-1	Dec13 2-4	Mar13 4-3	Mar06 5-2	Oct18 3-5
EAST FIFE	Nov15 3-0	Mar27 6-0	Mar20 3-0	Dec24 3-2	Dec13 3-0	Nov22 6-3	Apr14 5-1	Jan10 4-2		Apr17 5-0	Feb28 1-3	Dec20 5-1	Jan01 3-2	Aug27 2-0	Apr07 4-0	Apr10 6-4
HAMILTON A	Sep20 3-0	Jan03 3-2	Dec27 3-0	Nov08 5-0	Aug13 1-1	Oct04 6-5	Mar13 6-0	Dec06 1-2	Oct18 2-2		Jan17 3-1	Feb21 3-0	Nov15 1-2	Nov29 1-3	Apr03 5-2	Feb14 2-0
KILMARNOCK	Mar13 1-4	Nov29 5-1	Nov15 2-1	Jan01 4-4	Feb21 1-3	Dec06 2-2	Sep27 5-2	Oct25 3-0	Nov08 0-2	Oct11 3-0		Jan31 6-2	Aug27 7-1	Dec20 1-0	Jan10 7-2	Apr03 2-2
LEITH A	Oct04 1-3	Feb14 3-0	Jan03 2-4	Dec06 1-1	Dec27 2-2	Sep20 4-2	Mar06 1-0	Mar20 3-1	Aug13 0-1	Nov01 0-4	Oct18 3-1		Feb28 1-1	Apr03 1-1	Nov22 4-4	Jan17 2-3
RAITH R	Jan17 2-3	Oct18 7-1	Feb14 2-0	Mar13 2-0	Oct04 3-5	Aug13 2-1	Nov29 5-1	Apr03 1-3	Sep20 0-4	Mar06 3-3	Dec27 4-3	Nov08 5-1		Apr24 6-1	Dec06 6-2	Jan03 0-1
ST JOHNSTONE	Feb14 0-1	Jan24 5-2	Sep20 1-0	Nov15 4-1	Oct18 3-4	Jan03 4-0	Mar27 0-1	Nov22 2-2	Dec27 0-2	Mar20 2-3	Aug13 2-2	Dec13 2-0	Nov01 2-5		Feb28 2-2	Oct04 3-2
STENHOUSEMUIR	Oct18 3-3	Sep20 0-0	Jan17 0-3	Nov29 0-3	Jan03 2-1	Dec27 4-2	Apr24 3-0	Nov15 3-3	Feb14 1-5	Dec13 1-1	Oct04 1-0	Mar13 2-2	Mar27 1-1	Nov08 2-6		Aug13 0-0
STIRLING A	Nov29 7-0	Mar13 0-1	Mar27 0-2	Aug27 4-1	Nov08 2-2	Mar06 1-1	Jan24 3-1	Jan31 2-0	Apr21 3-4	Oct25 0-2	Dec13 2-1	Oct11 7-1	Sep27 3-3	Jan10 4-4	Dec20 1-5	

LEAGUE TABLES
DIVISION A

	P	W	D	L	F	A	W	D	L	F	A	Pts
Hibernian	30	13	2	0	52	6	9	2	4	34	21	48
Rangers	30	10	2	3	33	17	11	2	2	31	11	46
Partick T	30	7	3	5	39	24	9	1	5	22	18	36
Dundee	30	10	2	3	43	18	5	1	9	24	33	33
St Mirren	30	9	2	4	31	20	4	3	8	23	38	31
Clyde	30	8	3	4	34	27	4	4	7	18	30	31
Falkirk	30	6	5	4	31	21	4	5	6	24	27	30
Motherwell	30	7	2	6	19	17	6	1	8	26	30	29
Hearts	30	7	3	5	21	18	3	5	7	16	24	28
Aberdeen	30	8	4	3	33	16	2	3	10	12	29	27
T. Lanark	30	8	1	6	33	29	2	5	8	23	44	26
Celtic	30	5	4	6	21	25	5	1	9	20	31	25
Queen of South	30	7	3	5	33	27	3	2	10	16	47	25
Morton	30	3	4	8	18	19	6	2	7	29	24	24
Airdrie	30	7	1	7	26	32	0	6	9	14	46	21
Queen's Park	30	5	2	8	29	32	4	0	11	16	43	20

DIVISION B

	P	W	D	L	F	A	W	D	L	F	A	Pts
East Fife	30	14	0	1	59	18	11	3	1	44	18	53
Albion R	30	11	2	2	32	18	8	2	5	26	31	42
Hamilton A	30	10	2	3	45	20	7	4	4	30	25	40
Raith R	30	9	1	5	48	29	5	5	5	35	37	34
Cowdenbeath	30	7	3	5	25	20	5	5	5	31	33	32
Kilmarnock	30	9	3	3	49	26	4	1	10	23	36	30
Dunfermline A	30	10	1	4	49	32	3	2	10	23	39	29
Stirling A	30	6	4	5	39	28	5	2	8	26	38	28
St Johnstone	30	6	3	6	32	27	5	2	8	37	36	27
Ayr U	30	8	4	3	37	21	1	5	9	22	40	27
Dumbarton	30	7	4	4	39	31	2	3	10	27	48	25
Alloa	30	8	3	4	41	34	2	3	10	15	43	*24
Arbroath	30	7	2	6	33	30	3	1	11	22	32	23
Stenhousemuir	30	4	7	4	23	30	2	4	9	30	53	23
Dundee U	30	9	1	5	41	33	1	1	13	17	55	22
Leith A	30	5	5	5	28	28	1	2	12	17	56	†19

* Two points deducted for fielding unregistered players.
† Leith A left the League, replaced by East Stirling.

Scottish Football League Records
Season 1948-49

DIVISION A

	ABERDEEN	ALBION R	CELTIC	CLYDE	DUNDEE	EAST FIFE	FALKIRK	HEARTS	HIBERNIAN	MORTON	MOTHERWELL	PARTICK T	QUEEN OF SOUTH	RANGERS	ST MIRREN	T LANARK
ABERDEEN		Mar12 4-0	Aug18 1-0	Oct23 4-4	Jan01 1-3	Nov20 3-1	Nov06 1-4	Dec04 2-2	Sep04 1-2	Apr02 0-0	Aug28 2-0	Feb26 4-2	Dec11 1-2	Feb12 0-2	Jan29 0-2	Jan08 2-2
ALBION R	Mar05 2-1		Sep04 3-3	Apr15 1-2	Nov06 0-6	Feb12 0-3	Aug28 2-0	Dec18 1-5	Jan29 0-3	Oct23 2-1	Jan01 1-3	Jan08 2-3	Dec04 1-3	Apr30 1-4	Aug18 1-2	Feb26 1-5
CELTIC	Dec25 3-0	Jan15 3-0		Apr18 2-1	Oct23 0-1	Nov13 0-1	Nov27 4-4	Jan03 2-0	Feb12 1-2	Aug14 0-0	Dec18 3-2	Mar19 3-0	Sep01 2-2	Aug21 0-1	Mar26 2-1	Apr16 1-2
CLYDE	Apr09 0-0	Dec11 1-0	Nov06 0-4		Aug18 3-3	Apr02 2-4	Sep04 3-3	Oct30 3-3	Aug28 3-5	Nov20 0-3	Feb26 1-0	Jan01 0-1	Mar12 4-0	Dec04 1-3	Jan08 4-1	Jan29 2-0
DUNDEE	Aug21 3-0	Feb19 5-0	Apr11 3-2	Dec25 3-1		Sep01 2-5	Apr20 3-1	Aug14 2-1	Mar19 4-3	Jan15 3-1	Apr27 2-1	Apr23 4-2	Nov13 2-1	Jan03 3-1	Nov27 1-0	Dec18 1-1
EAST FIFE	Apr20 1-4	Apr23 5-1	Feb26 3-2	Dec18 1-2	Jan29 3-0		Jan01 1-1	Apr29 5-1	Jan08 2-3	Dec04 3-1	Aug18 0-1	Sep04 2-0	Apr16 4-0	Nov27 1-2	Aug28 3-1	Nov06 4-0
FALKIRK	Feb19 1-2	Jan03 7-1	Mar12 1-1	Jan15 3-2	Apr30 4-1	Aug21 1-2		Nov13 5-3	Dec11 1-1	Sep01 5-1	Feb12 3-0	Apr02 1-3	Aug14 3-2	Dec25 2-2	Mar19 2-1	Oct23 5-1
HEARTS	Mar19 1-1	Apr02 7-1	Aug28 1-2	Feb12 3-0	Jan08 0-1	Dec11 4-0	Feb26 3-1		Jan01 3-2	Mar12 2-4	Jan29 5-1	Nov06 1-3	Nov20 1-1	Oct23 2-0	Sep04 1-3	Aug18 3-2
HIBERNIAN	Jan15 4-1	Sep01 4-4	Oct30 1-2	Jan03 3-0	Dec04 2-1	Aug14 5-2	Apr23 2-0	Aug21 3-1		Nov13 3-4	Apr16 5-1	Apr09 2-1	Dec25 1-1	Feb19 0-1	Dec18 1-1	Nov27 1-0
MORTON	Dec18 1-1	Apr09 3-0	Jun08 0-0	Apr13 2-2	Aug16 2-2	Mar19 2-0	Mar05 0-1	Nov27 0-2	Feb26 2-3		Nov06 1-1	Aug18 2-1	Oct30 2-1	Apr25 0-1	Jan01 1-4	Aug28 3-3
MOTHERWELL	Apr30 1-1	Aug21 5-1	Apr02 0-1	Nov13 2-3	Dec11 0-2	Dec25 1-2	Oct30 0-3	Sep01 3-0	Nov20 5-1	Apr23 1-0		Mar12 3-1	Jan15 2-3	Aug14 1-1	Apr09 4-1	Mar19 1-0
PARTICK T	Nov13 0-0	Aug14 3-0	Dec04 1-2	Aug21 3-2	Feb12 4-4	Jan15 0-0	Dec18 3-3	Apr20 1-1	Oct23 2-6	Dec25 1-0	Nov27 1-1		Jan03 1-1	Sep01 1-1	Apr13 3-0	Oct30 1-3
QUEEN OF SOUTH	Mar26 0-0	Mar19 4-0	Jan29 1-0	Nov27 4-1	Feb26 0-1	Oct23 0-3	Jan08 0-0	Apr23 1-4	Aug18 1-1	Feb12 2-1	Sep04 2-1	Aug28 8-2		Dec18 0-2	Nov06 3-2	Jan01 2-1
RANGERS	Apr16 1-1	Apr18 3-1	Jan01 4-0	Mar19 4-1	Aug28 1-1	Apr13 3-1	Aug18 4-3	Apr05 2-1	Nov06 2-4	Dec11 4-1	Jan08 2-0	Jan29 2-2	Apr02 3-0		Feb26 2-1	Sep04 2-1
ST MIRREN	Aug31 3-1	Dec25 3-2	Dec11 1-1	Aug14 2-1	Mar12 6-1	Jan03 2-0	Dec04 2-0	Jan15 1-2	Apr02 2-0	Aug21 2-1	Oct23 0-0	Nov20 4-2	Feb19 1-1	Nov13 0-2		Feb12 1-2
T LANARK	Aug14 1-0	Nov13 4-1	Nov20 3-2	Sep01 0-1	Apr02 2-3	Feb19 2-2	Apr09 3-2	Dec25 1-1	Apr19 3-2	Jan03 1-0	Dec04 1-3	Dec11 1-2	Aug21 6-1	Jan15 2-1	Apr22 3-1	

DIVISION B

	AIRDRIE	ALLOA	ARBROATH	AYR U	COWDENBEATH	DUMBARTON	DUNDEE U	DUNFERMLINE A	E STIRLING	HAMILTON A	KILMARNOCK	QUEEN'S PARK	RAITH R	ST JOHNSTONE	STENHOUSEMUIR	STIRLING A
AIRDRIE		Apr23 3-0	Nov13 4-1	Sep01 2-2	Aug14 3-1	Mar19 3-1	Jan03 1-1	Apr02 2-2	Dec25 3-0	Aug21 2-1	Nov20 5-0	Jan15 2-2	Apr16 0-3	Dec11 7-1	Feb19 3-0	Mar12 4-1
ALLOA	Oct23 4-5		Aug14 1-1	Jan15 1-2	Nov13 4-2	Feb12 2-4	Sep01 3-3	Dec11 0-6	Apr30 1-0	Dec25 2-1	Apr02 1-0	Feb19 2-6	Dec04 1-5	Mar12 2-1	Aug21 1-0	Nov20 1-0
ARBROATH	Feb26 3-3	Jan08 2-1		Oct30 1-0	Mar19 2-2	Jan29 3-0	Apr09 1-0	Nov06 1-1	Apr02 5-1	Dec11 5-1	Aug28 1-1	Mar12 1-2	Sep04 1-2	Aug18 3-2	Nov20 4-1	Jan01 2-1
AYR U	Jan29 1-1	Sep04 1-4	Feb12 0-1		Oct23 2-1	Aug18 3-2	Mar19 8-0	Aug28 1-3	Dec11 1-1	Apr02 1-1	Jan01 1-1	Nov20 3-2	Feb26 2-3	Jan08 0-2	Mar12 3-1	Nov06 1-2
COWDENBEATH	Jan08 5-1	Feb26 3-0	Dec04 0-3	Apr09 9-2		Sep04 1-2	Oct30 2-3	Jan01 4-0	Mar12 4-2	Apr16 0-0	Nov06 1-0	Apr02 1-0	Aug18 2-1	Aug28 0-3	Dec11 1-1	Jan29 0-2
DUMBARTON	Dec04 0-4	Apr16 5-3	Sep01 1-1	Dec25 0-0	Jan15 1-3		Aug14 3-2	Nov20 3-3	Oct30 2-2	Nov13 5-3	Mar12 2-2	Aug21 5-2	Apr09 0-1	Apr02 1-0	Jan03 2-2	Dec11 1-5
DUNDEE U	Aug28 1-3	Jan29 5-1	Oct23 5-5	Dec04 1-2	Feb12 2-1	Jan08 4-0		Aug18 0-1	Nov20 1-1	Mar12 2-2	Sep04 4-1	Dec11 5-2	Nov06 1-4	Jan01 4-3	Apr02 2-0	Feb26 0-1
DUNFERMLINE A	Dec18 2-4	Mar26 2-2	Feb19 4-2	Jan03 5-0	Aug21 4-2	Mar05 3-2	Dec25 2-0		Nov13 5-2	Jan15 3-4	Feb12 3-2	Sep01 5-2	Nov27 2-0	Oct23 0-2	Aug14 1-1	Mar19 3-3
E STIRLING	Aug17 1-1	Aug28 1-2	Dec18 2-1	Mar26 0-4	Nov27 2-0	Nov06 2-3	Mar05 3-0	Feb26 2-2		Apr23 1-0	Jan08 3-0	Apr09 0-1	Jan01 1-5	Jan29 3-1	Dec04 2-4	Sep04 1-2
HAMILTON A	Jan01 2-0	Aug18 1-2	Mar26 3-2	Dec18 2-2	Mar05 4-0	Feb26 4-0	Nov27 2-4	Sep04 2-4	Feb12 2-1		Jan29 3-1	Dec04 1-1	Aug28 1-4	Nov06 0-3	Oct23 2-0	Jan08 3-1
KILMARNOCK	Mar05 3-3	Dec18 6-0	Jan03 8-0	Aug21 1-2	Feb19 2-2	Nov27 4-2	Jan15 3-3	Oct30 1-2	Aug14 3-2	Sep01 3-1		Dec25 1-1	Mar26 3-1	Dec04 3-1	Nov13 1-0	Feb05 0-2
QUEEN'S PARK	Sep04 1-0	Nov06 3-0	Nov27 3-1	Mar05 4-1	Dec18 2-1	Jan01 2-0	Apr20 0-0	Jan29 4-4	Oct23 4-0	Mar19 0-0	Aug18 2-3		Jan08 1-1	Feb26 5-0	Feb12 1-0	Aug28 2-3
RAITH R	Feb12 0-3	Mar19 5-0	Jan15 3-1	Nov13 6-0	Dec25 3-2	Oct23 4-3	Feb19 1-3	Apr30 4-0	Aug21 5-1	Jan03 3-0	Dec11 3-2	Aug14 3-1		Apr23 1-0	Sep01 3-0	Apr02 0-0
ST JOHNSTONE	Mar26 1-1	Nov27 5-0	Dec25 2-2	Aug14 2-4	Nov20 3-0	Dec18 3-1	Aug21 3-0	Feb05 1-2	Sep01 2-0	Feb19 1-1	Mar19 1-0	Nov13 3-2	Mar05 5-3		Jan15 1-1	Oct30 2-1
STENHOUSEMUIR	Nov06 1-3	Jan01 2-0	Apr16 1-0	Nov27 7-1	Mar26 2-2	Aug28 5-0	Dec18 3-2	Jan08 3-3	Mar19 0-0	Apr09 1-1	Feb26 6-2	Oct30 1-3	Jan29 3-1	Sep04 2-3		Aug18 2-5
STIRLING A	Nov27 1-0	Mar05 5-1	Aug21 1-6	Feb19 4-1	Aug31 2-1	Mar26 3-1	Nov13 5-2	Dec04 2-3	Jan15 3-1	Aug14 3-0	Oct23 3-1	Jan03 2-5	Dec18 5-2	Feb12 2-1	Dec25 1-0	

LEAGUE TABLES

DIVISION A

	P	W	D	L	F	A	W	D	L	F	A	Pts
Rangers	30	11	3	1	39	18	9	3	3	24	14	46
Dundee	30	13	1	1	41	20	7	4	4	30	28	45
Hibernian	30	9	3	3	37	20	8	2	5	38	32	39
East Fife	30	9	1	5	38	19	7	2	6	26	27	35
Falkirk	30	9	3	3	44	23	3	5	7	26	31	32
Celtic	30	7	3	5	26	17	5	4	6	22	23	31
T. Lanark	30	9	2	4	33	22	4	3	8	23	30	31
Hearts	30	8	2	5	37	22	4	4	7	27	32	30
St Mirren	30	9	3	3	30	16	4	1	10	21	31	30
Queen of South	30	8	3	4	28	19	3	5	7	19	34	30
Partick T	30	4	8	3	25	24	5	1	9	25	39	27
Motherwell	30	7	2	6	29	20	3	3	9	15	29	25
Aberdeen	30	5	4	6	26	26	2	7	6	13	22	25
Clyde	30	5	4	6	27	30	4	2	9	23	37	24
Morton	30	4	6	5	21	22	3	2	10	18	29	22
Albion R	30	3	1	11	18	44	0	1	14	12	61	8

DIVISION B

	P	W	D	L	F	A	W	D	L	F	A	Pts
Raith R	30	12	1	2	44	16	8	1	6	36	28	42
Stirling A	30	12	0	3	42	25	8	2	5	29	22	42
Airdrie	30	10	4	1	44	16	6	5	4	32	26	41
Dunfermline A	30	9	3	3	44	28	7	6	2	36	30	41
Queen's Park	30	9	4	2	34	14	5	3	7	32	35	35
St Johnstone	30	9	4	2	35	18	5	0	10	23	33	32
Arbroath	30	9	4	2	35	18	3	4	8	27	38	32
Dundee U	30	7	3	5	37	27	3	4	8	23	40	27
Ayr U	30	5	4	6	28	25	5	3	7	23	45	27
Hamilton A	30	8	2	5	32	25	1	6	8	16	32	26
Kilmarnock	30	8	4	3	42	22	1	3	11	16	39	25
Stenhousemuir	30	7	4	4	39	26	1	4	10	11	28	24
Cowdenbeath	30	8	2	5	33	20	1	3	11	20	38	23
Alloa	30	7	2	6	26	36	3	1	11	16	49	23
Dumbarton	30	5	6	4	31	33	3	0	12	21	46	22
E. Stirling	30	6	2	7	24	26	0	4	11	14	41	*18

* East Stirling left the League, replaced by Forfar A.

Scottish Football League Records
Season 1949-50

DIVISION A

	ABERDEEN	CELTIC	CLYDE	DUNDEE	EAST FIFE	FALKIRK	HEARTS	HIBERNIAN	MOTHERWELL	PARTICK T	QUEEN OF SOUTH	RAITH R	RANGERS	ST MIRREN	STIRLING A	T LANARK
ABERDEEN		Jan14 4-0	Sep17 1-1	Sep24 2-2	Dec31 1-2	Apr01 1-2	Apr08 0-5	Jan03 0-3	Dec17 5-0	Nov12 3-1	Mar18 2-0	Nov26 3-0	Oct29 1-3	Sep10 2-3	Apr22 6-2	Oct08 2-1
CELTIC	Oct15 4-2		Nov05 4-1	Jan21 2-0	Mar25 4-1	Mar04 4-3	Sep17 3-2	Oct29 2-2	Jan07 3-1	Dec03 1-0	Dec24 3-0	Oct01 2-2	Jan02 1-1	Dec10 0-0	Feb18 2-1	Nov19 2-1
CLYDE	Oct22 0-1	Apr15 2-2		Jan14 1-0	Nov12 0-1	Jan03 2-2	Feb04 3-4	Dec31 0-1	Feb25 1-0	Sep24 4-1	Nov26 3-2	Mar18 1-1	Apr10 1-2	Oct08 2-0	Dec17 6-0	Sep10 0-2
DUNDEE	Jan02 1-1	Oct22 3-0	Oct15 2-3		Dec10 1-0	Nov19 2-0	Jan07 3-1	Dec03 1-2	Oct01 3-1	Feb04 1-0	Sep17 3-0	Nov05 2-1	Apr17 0-1	Mar04 2-0	Dec24 4-1	Mar25 1-4
EAST FIFE	Apr15 3-1	Dec17 5-1	Feb18 4-1	Mar18 1-0		Feb04 1-2	Dec24 0-1	Feb25 1-1	Nov05 2-1	Nov26 1-1	Oct01 4-1	Jan02 3-0	Jan07 0-2	Oct22 3-3	Oct15 0-2	Dec03 3-1
FALKIRK	Nov05 1-0	Nov26 1-1	Oct01 7-4	Feb25 2-2	May01 0-2		Feb18 1-1	Mar18 1-2	Dec24 2-4	Dec17 0-3	Jan07 3-3	Sep17 1-1	Oct15 0-2	Dec03 2-2	Jan02 1-1	Jan21 2-1
HEARTS	Dec03 4-1	Dec31 4-2	Oct29 6-2	Apr22 6-2	Sep10 0-1	Nov12 9-0		Sep24 5-2	Nov26 2-0	Apr17 3-3	Feb25 3-0	Dec17 2-0	Jan21 0-1	Jan03 5-0	Mar18 5-2	Jan14 1-0
HIBERNIAN	Oct01 2-0	Feb04 4-1	Apr08 6-3	Mar11 4-2	Nov19 4-1	Dec10 5-1	Jan02 1-2		Feb18 6-1	Oct22 2-0	Oct15 2-0	Dec24 4-2	Nov05 1-0	Mar25 5-0	Jan07 4-1	Mar04 0-1
MOTHERWELL	Mar25 5-1	Oct08 1-2	Nov19 5-2	Jan03 0-2	Apr17 3-4	Sep10 2-2	Mar04 2-3	Nov12 1-3		Jan14 0-2	Feb04 1-0	Oct22 1-1	Dec10 4-0	Sep24 2-2	Dec03 2-1	Dec31 4-0
PARTICK T	Feb18 0-2	Apr10 1-0	Jan02 1-0	Oct29 2-3	Mar04 1-2	Mar25 3-1	Nov05 0-1	Jan21 2-2	Oct15 0-2		Apr08 5-2	Jan07 1-0	Dec24 1-3	Nov19 4-0	Oct01 4-1	Dec10 5-1
QUEEN OF SOUTH	Dec10 1-0	Sep10 0-2	Mar04 2-3	Nov12 1-1	Jan03 0-5	Oct08 2-2	Nov19 0-4	Jan14 2-2	Oct29 2-0	Dec31 3-1		Dec03 0-0	Mar25 1-2	Apr17 1-1	Jan21 3-1	Sep24 4-1
RAITH R	Mar04 1-2	Jan03 1-1	Dec10 7-1	Apr08 4-1	Sep24 4-4	Dec31 6-4	Mar25 2-0	Sep10 0-6	Jan21 0-2	Oct08 1-3	Apr22 2-0		Nov19 1-3	Jan14 2-1	Oct29 2-0	Nov12 1-1
RANGERS	Feb04 2-2	Sep24 4-0	Dec03 5-4	Dec31 2-2	Apr08 2-2	Jan14 3-0	Oct22 1-0	Apr29 0-0	Mar18 2-0	Sep10 2-0	Dec17 1-0	Feb25 2-0		Nov12 1-0	Nov26 2-1	Jan03 3-1
ST MIRREN	Dec24 4-0	Mar18 0-1	Jan07 2-0	Nov26 1-1	Jan21 0-0	Mar11 0-1	Oct01 3-3	Dec17 1-3	Jan02 1-1	Feb25 0-2	Nov05 3-0	Oct15 2-0	Feb18 1-2		Sep17 2-0	Oct29 6-1
STIRLING A	Nov19 0-1	Nov12 2-1	Mar25 1-2	Sep10 2-2	Jan14 1-1	Sep24 3-2	Dec10 2-4	Apr01 3-5	Apr08 1-4	Apr29 2-1	Oct22 1-0	Feb04 1-2	Mar04 0-2	Dec31 1-3		Apr15 0-2
T LANARK	Jan07 3-1	Mar11 1-0	Dec24 1-3	Dec17 1-0	Apr29 4-1	Oct22 0-2	Oct15 3-0	Nov26 0-2	Sep17 3-3	Mar18 2-7	Jan02 2-1	Feb18 0-1	May01 2-2	Feb04 2-1	Nov05 2-4	

DIVISION B

	AIRDRIE	ALBION R	ALLOA	ARBROATH	AYR U	COWDENBEATH	DUMBARTON	DUNDEE U	DUNFERMLINE A	FORFAR A	HAMILTON A	KILMARNOCK	MORTON	QUEEN'S PARK	ST JOHNSTONE	STENHOUSEMUIR
AIRDRIE		Jan02 4-1	Oct22 3-2	Feb18 8-3	Dec24 5-1	Jan07 7-1	Dec03 5-2	Apr08 2-0	Dec17 4-2	Nov26 0-1	Feb04 3-2	Feb25 2-0	Oct15 0-1	Oct01 2-0	Mar18 3-0	Nov05 3-1
ALBION R	Sep24 2-2		Jan14 3-2	Dec10 0-1	Mar25 3-5	Nov19 3-1	Nov12 2-1	Mar04 2-0	Jan03 1-3	Oct08 6-1	Dec31 1-3	Sep10 3-1	Oct29 0-0	Mar11 3-3	Apr01 3-0	Jan21 1-1
ALLOA	Jan21 2-4	Oct15 0-0		Jan07 2-2	Oct01 2-0	Feb18 4-2	Oct29 1-0	Dec24 3-3	Mar18 2-3	Feb25 4-1	Dec03 1-2	Dec17 2-3	Sep17 1-5	Nov05 3-7	Nov26 0-2	Jan02 1-3
ARBROATH	Nov12 2-2	Mar18 1-3	Oct08 1-2		Feb04 0-0	Dec03 2-1	Sep10 1-1	Oct22 3-3	Apr01 2-1	Sep24 2-3	Jan03 2-3	Dec31 1-2	Dec17 1-1	Nov26 1-2	Jan14 1-3	Apr22 3-1
AYR U	Sep10 2-3	Dec17 0-0	Jan03 4-1	Oct29 3-2		Jan21 1-2	Jan14 4-2	Dec03 0-4	Dec31 1-1	Feb11 5-0	Nov12 3-3	Sep24 2-1	Mar18 2-2	Feb25 3-2	Oct08 4-0	Nov26 3-3
COWDENBEATH	Oct08 1-2	Feb25 3-0	Nov12 3-1	Mar11 2-1	Oct22 4-2		Jan03 3-2	Feb04 2-1	Sep24 2-0	Sep10 4-2	Jan14 3-2	Apr01 3-2	Nov26 0-1	Apr15 1-1	Dec31 5-1	Mar18 6-1
DUMBARTON	Mar11 0-1	Feb18 0-3	Feb04 4-0	Dec24 4-2	Oct15 2-0	Oct01 1-2		Jan07 3-0	Apr08 2-4	Mar18 1-1	Oct22 0-1	Nov26 0-1	Nov05 3-4	Jan02 1-3	Dec17 0-2	Sep17 3-0
DUNDEE U	Dec31 0-1	Nov26 2-5	Sep10 6-1	Jan21 3-4	Mar11 4-1	Oct29 2-2	Oct08 5-0		Jan14 1-1	Nov12 0-2	Oct03 4-1	Jan03 3-0	Feb25 2-2	Apr22 7-1	Sep24 3-1	Dec17 5-1
DUNFERMLINE A	Mar25 2-5	Oct01 4-1	Dec10 6-2	Nov05 4-0	Apr22 3-0	Jan02 1-0	Nov19 5-0	Oct15 1-3		Dec03 1-0	Mar04 2-1	Apr29 2-0	Feb18 3-2	Dec24 1-6	Jan21 4-1	Jan07 0-2
FORFAR A	Mar04 4-4	Jan07 6-1	Nov19 6-2	Jan02 3-2	Nov05 5-1	Dec24 2-2	Dec10 2-1	Feb18 0-3	Mar11 1-2		Mar25 0-2	Jan21 1-0	Oct01 1-3	Apr01 3-0	Oct29 2-1	Oct15 1-1
HAMILTON A	Oct29 2-2	Sep17 1-1	Mar11 4-0	Oct01 2-1	Feb18 2-1	Oct15 2-0	Jan21 1-1	Nov05 4-1	Nov26 1-1	Dec17 2-0		Mar18 1-0	Jan02 0-2	Jan07 3-0	Feb25 2-2	Dec24 5-1
KILMARNOCK	Nov19 1-1	Dec24 2-1	Mar25 3-0	Sep17 2-2	Jan02 4-0	Nov05 2-0	Mar04 1-1	Oct01 2-3	Feb04 3-2	Oct22 3-1	Dec10 2-0		Jan07 2-0	Oct15 3-3	Mar11 1-1	Feb18 3-2
MORTON	Jan14 1-0	Feb04 2-0	Dec31 3-1	Mar25 3-1	Dec10 7-0	Mar04 5-3	Apr01 1-0	Nov19 5-2	Nov12 2-2	Jan03 1-1	Sep24 2-0	Oct08 3-1		Oct22 4-2	Sep10 5-0	Dec03 4-0
QUEEN'S PARK	Jan03 2-0	Dec03 1-0	Apr19 4-2	Apr08 2-2	Nov19 4-1	Mar25 1-2	Sep24 4-1	Apr29 0-1	Sep10 2-0	Dec31 0-0	Apr10 3-2	Jan14 1-3	Jan21 2-4		Nov12 2-2	Apr24 2-0
ST JOHNSTONE	Dec10 1-0	Nov05 5-0	Mar04 5-2	Oct15 2-1	Jan07 5-2	Apr08 4-2	Mar25 2-1	Jan02 5-0	Oct22 3-4	Feb04 2-2	Nov19 2-1	Dec03 2-0	Dec24 1-1	Sep17 2-1		Oct01 2-2
STENHOUSEMUIR	Apr01 1-1	Oct22 6-0	Sep24 4-1	Nov19 1-1	Mar04 4-2	Dec10 0-1	Dec31 1-2	Mar25 1-5	Apr15 7-6	Jan14 1-1	Sep10 3-2	Nov12 0-2	Apr08 2-1	Oct08 2-2	Jan03 2-5	

LEAGUE TABLES

DIVISION A

	P	W	D	L	F	A	W	D	L	F	A	Pts
Rangers	30	11	4	0	32	12	11	2	2	26	14	50
Hibernian	30	13	0	2	50	15	9	5	1	36	19	49
Hearts	30	12	1	2	55	16	8	2	5	31	24	43
East Fife	30	8	3	4	31	18	7	4	4	27	25	37
Celtic	30	11	4	0	37	17	3	3	9	14	33	35
Dundee	30	10	1	4	29	15	2	6	7	20	31	31
Partick T	30	8	1	6	30	20	5	2	8	25	25	29
Aberdeen	30	7	2	6	33	25	4	2	9	15	31	26
Raith R	30	7	3	5	34	29	2	5	8	11	25	26
Motherwell	30	6	3	6	33	25	4	2	9	20	33	25
St Mirren	30	6	4	5	26	15	2	5	8	16	34	25
T. Lanark	30	7	2	6	26	28	4	1	10	18	34	25
Clyde	30	6	3	6	26	19	4	1	10	30	54	24
Falkirk	30	3	7	5	24	29	4	3	8	24	43	24
Queen of South	30	5	5	5	22	25	0	1	14	9	38	16
Stirling A	30	4	2	9	20	32	2	1	12	18	45	15

DIVISION B

	P	W	D	L	F	A	W	D	L	F	A	Pts
Morton	30	13	2	0	48	13	7	5	3	29	20	47
Airdrie	30	13	0	2	51	17	6	6	3	28	23	44
Dunfermline A	30	11	0	4	39	23	5	4	6	32	34	36
St Johnstone	30	11	3	1	43	19	4	3	8	21	37	36
Cowdenbeath	30	12	1	2	42	19	4	2	9	21	37	35
Hamilton A	30	9	5	1	32	13	5	1	9	25	31	34
Dundee U	30	8	3	4	45	23	6	2	7	29	33	33
Kilmarnock	30	9	5	1	34	17	5	0	10	16	26	33
Queen's Park	30	8	3	4	30	20	4	4	7	33	39	31
Forfar A	30	8	3	4	37	24	3	5	7	16	32	30
Albion R	30	7	4	4	33	24	3	3	9	16	37	27
Stenhousemuir	30	6	4	5	35	32	2	4	9	19	40	24
Ayr U	30	7	5	3	37	26	1	1	13	16	54	22
Arbroath	30	3	5	7	23	28	2	4	9	24	41	19
Dumbarton	30	5	1	9	24	24	1	3	11	15	38	16
Alloa	30	4	3	8	28	37	1	0	14	19	59	13

Scottish Football League Records
Season 1950-51

DIVISION A

	ABERDEEN	AIRDRIE	CELTIC	CLYDE	DUNDEE	EAST FIFE	FALKIRK	HEARTS	HIBERNIAN	MORTON	MOTHERWELL	PARTICK T	RAITH R	RANGERS	ST MIRREN	T LANARK
ABERDEEN		Dec23 1-1	Oct14 2-1	Oct21 5-3	Jan01 1-0	Apr07 1-2	Nov18 5-1	Dec02 2-0	Sep30 2-1	Mar24 3-0	Dec09 4-2	Feb17 4-1	Mar03 1-2	Feb03 2-4	Jan06 1-1	Nov04 1-2
AIRDRIE	Sep09 2-5		Nov18 2-4	Oct07 3-3	Mar24 2-0	Dec02 2-2	Apr28 1-1	Apr14 2-3	Mar03 2-1	Dec30 2-0	Sep23 2-3	Dec09 1-2	Nov11 2-5	Mar31 2-1	Oct28 2-0	Jan20 2-1
CELTIC	Jan13 3-4	Apr11 0-1		Apr28 1-0	Oct21 0-0	Dec16 6-2	Nov11 3-0	Dec30 2-2	Feb03 0-1	Sep09 3-4	Apr25 3-1	Apr16 0-3	Oct07 2-3	Sep23 3-2	Mar17 2-1	Nov25 1-1
CLYDE	Jan20 0-2	Jan06 2-2	Nov04 1-3		Oct14 2-1	Feb17 1-1	Mar24 3-1	Oct28 2-2	Apr11 0-4	Nov18 1-1	Mar03 1-2	Jan01 1-0	Dec09 1-0	Dec02 2-1	Dec23 2-1	Sep30 0-2
DUNDEE	Sep23 2-0	Dec16 3-0	Jan20 3-1	Mar31 1-1		Mar17 2-4	Oct07 2-0	Sep09 1-0	Apr07 2-2	Jan02 2-1	Nov11 0-0	Oct28 3-2	Apr02 2-0	Dec30 2-0	Nov25 5-0	Feb24 2-1
EAST FIFE	Dec30 0-0	Apr21 4-1	Mar24 3-0	Nov11 2-1	Dec09 1-3		Feb10 2-1	Oct07 1-4	Nov18 1-2	Apr14 3-3	May08 3-2	Mar03 1-1	Sep23 3-1	Sep09 0-3	Jan20 1-1	Oct28 3-1
FALKIRK	Feb24 1-1	Nov04 4-1	Feb17 0-2	Dec16 1-0	Jan06 2-1	Oct14 1-1		Mar17 5-4	Dec23 1-5	Dec02 0-1	Jan20 2-4	Sep30 2-1	Oct28 2-3	Nov25 1-1	Sep16 0-2	Jan01 2-0
HEARTS	Apr18 4-1	Oct14 2-0	Apr07 1-1	Feb03 4-0	Dec23 1-1	Sep16 5-1	Dec09 4-2		Jan01 2-1	Mar03 8-0	Nov18 3-3	Nov04 4-5	Mar24 3-1	Apr21 0-1	Sep30 1-0	Feb17 4-0
HIBERNIAN	Jan02 6-2	Nov25 5-0	Apr30 3-1	Dec30 1-0	Dec02 2-0	Feb24 2-0	Sep09 6-0	Sep23 0-1		Nov11 2-0	Jan13 3-1	Jan20 1-1	Apr25 3-0	Apr28 4-1	Dec16 3-1	Mar17 3-1
MORTON	Dec16 1-2	Sep16 4-1	Sep28 0-2	Apr21 1-4	Sep30 2-3	Nov04 4-2	Mar10 0-1	Nov25 0-1	Feb17 2-4		Apr28 5-0	Oct14 3-2	Jan20 2-0	Mar17 0-2	Jan01 5-2	Jan06 1-3
MOTHERWELL	Mar17 1-1	Jan01 1-2	Jan06 2-1	Nov25 1-1	Feb17 0-2	Sep30 4-2	Oct21 4-0	May05 2-4	Oct14 2-6	Feb24 1-1		Apr11 4-1	May02 3-2	Apr07 2-3	Nov04 4-0	Dec23 4-1
PARTICK T	Nov11 1-4	Mar17 2-0	Dec02 0-1	Sep23 2-1	Apr28 1-1	Mar10 4-0	Mar31 4-1	Oct21 5-2	Apr21 0-0	Apr07 1-0	Apr14 1-1		Sep09 5-2	Oct07 2-1	Feb24 1-1	Dec16 1-0
RAITH R	Nov25 1-0	Feb17 0-1	Sep30 1-2	Mar17 4-1	Nov04 0-1	Jan01 3-0	Feb03 3-0	Dec16 2-0	Jan06 1-3	Oct21 1-1	Dec02 3-4	Dec23 2-2		Feb24 3-1	Oct14 2-0	Sep16 4-0
RANGERS	Oct28 1-2	Sep30 4-1	Jan01 1-0	Mar10 4-0	Sep16 0-0	Dec23 5-0	Mar03 5-2	Jan20 2-1	Nov04 1-1	Dec09 2-0	Mar24 3-0	Jan06 1-3	Nov18 4-1		Feb17 1-1	Oct14 2-1
ST MIRREN	Oct07 4-2	Apr07 3-2	Dec09 0-0	Sep09 3-1	Mar03 2-2	Oct21 1-2	Dec30 0-0	Jan02 1-0	Mar24 0-1	Sep23 1-3	Apr17 3-0	Nov18 2-1	Apr28 2-0	Nov11 0-2		Dec02 0-4
T LANARK	Apr28 2-0	Oct21 1-0	Mar03 2-0	Jan02 1-2	Nov18 2-0	Mar30 1-1	Sep23 2-1	Nov11 1-2	Dec09 1-2	Oct07 0-2	Sep09 2-0	Mar24 4-2	Dec30 1-2	Apr25 1-5	Mar10 1-2	

DIVISION B

	ALBION R	ALLOA	ARBROATH	AYR U	COWDENBEATH	DUMBARTON	DUNDEE U	DUNFERMLINE A	FORFAR A	HAMILTON A	KILMARNOCK	QUEEN OF SOUTH	QUEEN'S PARK	ST JOHNSTONE	STENHOUSEMUIR	STIRLING A
ALBION R		Mar10 4-2	Mar17 4-0	Apr21 2-1	Feb24 1-0	Feb17 3-1	Nov25 0-4	Sep30 1-2	Dec23 3-2	Jan01 3-1	Apr07 1-3	Apr18 1-4	Oct21 3-2	Nov04 4-4	Oct14 2-0	Sep16 1-3
ALLOA	Dec02 3-3		Feb24 2-0	Nov25 3-5	Mar17 7-4	Mar31 3-4	Dec16 1-2	Apr25 2-0	Oct14 3-2	Nov04 2-4	Feb17 1-4	Oct21 0-2	Oct28 0-2	Sep30 1-0	Jan01 3-3	Jan06 1-4
ARBROATH	Dec09 0-3	Nov18 3-4		Oct28 0-2	Mar10 2-1	Jan06 3-2	Jan20 1-3	Nov04 1-1	Jan01 2-1	Feb17 0-0	Sep16 0-2	Mar24 1-3	Mar03 2-2	Oct14 1-6	Dec23 5-1	Sep30 3-3
AYR U	Mar24 0-0	Mar03 4-1	Feb03 4-1		Oct21 0-0	Oct14 3-1	Apr28 2-2	Apr07 8-0	Nov04 4-1	Jan06 0-0	Jan01 1-0	Dec09 2-0	Nov18 2-2	Dec23 3-1	Sep30 4-2	Feb17 2-0
COWDENBEATH	Nov18 1-0	Dec09 6-3	Dec02 3-2	Jan20 1-4		Sep30 1-1	Oct28 6-0	Jan01 3-0	Apr21 8-2	Apr07 4-3	Nov04 3-0	Mar03 1-3	Mar24 3-0	Sep16 0-0	Feb17 2-0	Oct14 1-2
DUMBARTON	Nov11 1-5	Dec30 2-2	Oct07 0-2	Jan13 2-0	Jan02 1-0		Sep09 1-1	Nov18 1-2	Dec09 4-1	Mar10 2-1	Mar03 2-1	Feb10 0-1	Sep23 0-1	Mar24 2-1	Oct28 3-3	Jan20 4-0
DUNDEE U	Mar03 2-1	Mar24 10-1	Oct21 3-4	Dec02 3-1	Feb03 1-5	Dec23 3-2		Oct14 5-1	Feb17 2-1	Oct02 1-3	Sep30 5-3	Nov18 5-0	Dec09 3-2	Jan01 2-0	Jan06 6-0	Nov04 1-3
DUNFERMLINE A	Apr02 0-1	Sep09 4-0	Feb10 5-1	Dec30 3-1	Sep23 3-1	Feb24 2-2	Mar31 1-0		Mar10 2-4	Dec16 1-3	Feb03 4-2	Nov11 3-1	Oct07 4-3	Oct21 2-7	Mar17 5-2	Nov25 2-4
FORFAR A	Sep09 1-0	Feb10 2-4	Sep23 2-1	Mar31 3-2	Oct07 2-0	Mar17 1-4	Nov11 1-3	Dec02 4-2		Nov25 2-2	Oct21 0-0	Apr28 0-2	Dec30 3-2	Feb03 1-3	Feb24 3-1	Dec16 0-1
HAMILTON A	Sep23 5-1	Apr21 5-1	Nov11 8-2	Apr14 2-3	Sep09 3-2	Dec02 0-1	Dec30 1-2	Mar24 2-0	Mar03 6-1		Nov18 2-3	Apr25 0-0	Jan02 0-0	Dec09 2-0	Jan20 4-0	Oct28 1-5
KILMARNOCK	Oct07 3-2	Nov11 2-2	Dec30 1-1	Sep23 0-1	Feb10 4-0	Nov25 1-3	Jan02 2-0	Oct28 1-1	Jan20 1-1	Feb24 1-1		Sep09 0-1	Jan13 3-4	Dec02 2-2	Dec16 1-2	Mar17 1-1
QUEEN OF SOUTH	Oct28 2-0	Jan20 5-1	Dec16 3-1	Mar17 2-1	Nov25 3-0	Nov04 1-2	Feb24 3-3	Feb17 3-0	Sep30 4-1	Oct14 4-1	Dec23 0-1		Mar10 2-1	Jan06 2-1	Mar31 5-2	Apr21 1-0
QUEEN'S PARK	Jan20 1-1	Apr14 2-1	Nov25 2-1	Feb24 2-0	Dec16 2-0	Jan01 2-1	Mar17 4-2	Jan06 3-3	Sep16 0-1	Sep30 1-1	Oct14 2-1	Dec02 1-1		Feb17 4-3	Nov04 4-1	Dec23 0-2
ST JOHNSTONE	Mar31 0-3	Apr28 3-1	Apr21 1-3	Sep09 2-1	Dec30 2-1	Dec16 3-0	Sep23 2-2	Jan20 2-1	Oct28 3-0	Oct07 1-1	Mar10 1-0	Apr07 0-6	Nov11 6-1		Nov25 7-1	Feb24 4-2
STENHOUSEMUIR	Apr28 0-1	Sep23 3-1	Sep09 2-3	Jan02 3-2	Nov11 4-0	Apr07 3-1	Oct07 3-1	Dec09 4-1	Nov18 3-0	Oct21 1-2	Mar24 4-1	Apr14 1-3	Apr20 0-3	Mar03 0-2		Mar10 0-1
STIRLING A	Dec30 3-2	Oct07 4-2	Jan02 4-0	Nov11 1-1	Jan13 2-4	Oct21 3-2	Feb10 3-1	Mar03 1-3	Mar24 4-0	Mar31 5-1	Dec09 1-0	Sep23 5-2	Sep09 3-1	Nov18 4-1	Dec02 4-2	

LEAGUE TABLES
DIVISION A

	P	W	D	L	F	A	W	D	L	F	A	Pts
Hibernian	30	13	1	1	44	9	9	3	3	34	17	48
Rangers	30	10	3	2	36	13	7	1	7	28	24	38
Dundee	30	11	3	1	32	12	4	5	6	15	18	38
Hearts	30	10	3	2	46	17	6	2	7	26	28	37
Aberdeen	30	9	2	4	35	21	6	3	6	26	29	35
Partick T	30	9	4	2	30	15	4	3	8	27	33	33
Celtic	30	6	3	6	29	25	6	2	7	19	21	29
Raith R	30	8	2	5	30	16	5	0	10	22	36	28
Motherwell	30	7	3	5	35	27	4	3	8	23	38	28
East Fife	30	7	4	4	28	24	3	4	8	20	42	28
St Mirren	30	7	3	5	22	20	2	4	9	13	31	25
Morton	30	6	0	9	30	29	4	4	7	17	30	24
T. Lanark	30	7	1	7	22	21	4	1	10	18	30	24
Airdrie	30	7	2	6	39	31	3	2	10	13	36	24
Clyde	30	6	4	5	19	23	2	3	10	18	34	23
Falkirk	30	6	3	6	24	27	1	1	13	11	54	18

DIVISION B

	P	W	D	L	F	A	W	D	L	F	A	Pts
Queen of South	30	12	1	2	40	15	9	2	4	29	20	45
Stirling A	30	12	1	2	47	22	9	2	4	31	22	45
Ayr U	30	10	5	0	39	11	5	1	9	25	29	36
Dundee U	30	11	0	4	52	27	5	4	6	26	31	36
St Johnstone	30	10	2	3	37	23	4	3	8	31	30	33
Queen's Park	30	9	4	2	30	19	4	3	8	26	34	33
Hamilton A	30	8	2	5	41	21	4	6	5	24	28	32
Albion R	30	9	1	5	33	29	5	3	7	23	22	32
Dumbarton	30	7	3	5	25	21	5	2	8	27	32	29
Dunfermline A	30	9	1	5	41	32	3	3	9	17	41	28
Cowdenbeath	30	10	2	3	43	20	2	1	12	18	37	27
Kilmarnock	30	3	7	5	23	22	5	1	9	21	27	24
Arbroath	30	4	4	7	24	34	4	1	10	22	44	21
Forfar A	30	7	2	6	25	27	2	1	12	18	49	21
Stenhousemuir	30	8	0	7	31	22	1	2	12	20	58	20
Alloa	30	5	2	8	32	39	2	2	11	26	59	18

Scottish Football League Records
Season 1951-52

DIVISION A

	ABERDEEN	AIRDRIE	CELTIC	DUNDEE	EAST FIFE	HEARTS	HIBERNIAN	MORTON	MOTHERWELL	PARTICK T	QUEEN OF SOUTH	RAITH R	RANGERS	ST MIRREN	STIRLING A	T LANARK
ABERDEEN		Oct06 1-4	Dec29 3-4	Sep22 3-1	Jan02 2-1	Jan26 3-0	Jan12 1-2	Dec15 3-1	Mar15 2-2	Nov10 4-2	Nov03 1-1	Nov24 2-2	Apr19 1-1	Sep08 3-0	Mar12 6-0	Jan19 2-3
AIRDRIE	Jan05 3-0		Feb27 2-1	Dec15 4-3	Apr19 3-1	Sep15 2-0	Nov24 0-2	Sep29 3-5	Apr23 1-2	Mar15 2-2	Oct20 3-0	Oct13 2-1	Feb16 0-1	Feb02 2-2	Nov03 2-2	Dec22 2-4
CELTIC	Mar29 2-0	Nov17 3-1		Jan19 1-1	Mar22 2-1	Sep29 1-3	Oct27 1-1	Mar05 2-2	Dec22 2-2	Dec01 2-1	Mar01 6-1	Feb23 0-1	Jan01 1-4	Dec08 2-1	Feb16 3-1	Nov03 2-2
DUNDEE	Jan01 3-2	Mar22 0-1	Oct20 2-1		Dec08 3-4	Jan05 3-3	Dec01 1-4	Apr02 2-2	Feb16 1-2	Apr12 0-2	Nov17 0-0	Nov03 2-0	Sep29 1-0	Mar01 3-0	Dec22 4-1	Apr26 6-0
EAST FIFE	Sep29 2-1	Dec01 3-1	Dec15 3-1	Mar15 3-1		Dec22 2-4	Feb23 3-1	Nov03 4-1	Apr26 6-1	Nov24 1-1	Feb02 5-0	Jan01 0-1	Jan05 2-1	Oct20 3-3	Sep15 4-0	Oct13 3-2
HEARTS	Dec01 2-2	Dec29 6-1	Jan02 2-1	Oct06 4-2	Sep08 3-1		Sep22 1-1	Nov24 4-1	Apr30 2-2	Feb13 1-2	Nov10 4-3	Dec15 4-2	Jan19 2-2	Jan12 2-1	Mar15 5-2	Oct27 2-2
HIBERNIAN	Sep15 4-4	Mar01 4-0	Feb02 3-1	Apr09 3-1	Nov17 4-2	Jan01 2-3		Oct13 1-0	Apr21 3-1	Oct20 5-0	Dec08 5-0	Dec22 5-0	Nov03 1-1	Feb16 5-0	Jan05 8-0	Sep29 5-2
MORTON	Mar22 3-2	Feb13 2-3	Oct10 0-1	Jan12 3-0	Oct06 0-2	Mar01 3-1	Nov10 2-1		Apr12 0-2	Dec29 1-2	Sep08 2-2	Oct20 1-4	Dec08 0-1	Sep22 3-0	Dec01 7-1	Nov17 3-1
MOTHERWELL	Dec08 3-3	Sep22 4-1	Sep08 2-2	Nov10 2-1	Jan12 2-1	Nov17 0-5	Dec29 3-1	Oct27 1-2		Jan02 1-1	Oct06 4-0	Dec01 1-3	Mar22 2-1	Feb13 2-0	Jan19 5-2	Mar01 1-1
PARTICK T	Feb16 1-4	Dec08 5-2	Mar08 2-4	Dec25 1-3	Mar01 2-0	Nov03 2-0	Jan19 1-2	Sep15 1-1	Sep29 2-1		Mar22 3-0	Jan09 1-1	Dec22 1-3	Nov17 0-0	Oct13 2-1	Jan01 4-2
QUEEN OF SOUTH	Oct13 1-2	Jan19 4-2	Nov24 4-0	Feb27 1-0	Oct27 2-3	Feb16 1-1	Mar15 5-2	Dec22 4-1	Jan09 4-1	Dec15 2-1		Sep29 2-2	Mar29 2-2	Dec01 3-1	Jan01 2-0	Sep15 1-0
RAITH R	Mar01 2-1	Nov10 1-1	Jan12 1-0	Feb13 1-2	Sep22 2-3	Mar22 2-1	Sep08 0-2	Jan19 2-0	Apr28 2-0	Oct06 1-2	Jan02 0-0		Nov17 3-1	Dec29 2-1	Oct27 3-0	Dec08 1-0
RANGERS	Feb02 3-2	Jan12 1-0	Sep22 1-1	Jan02 1-2	Oct10 1-1	Oct20 2-0	Feb13 2-2	Mar15 1-0	Dec15 3-0	Sep08 4-1	Dec29 3-2	Feb27 1-0		Nov10 5-1	Nov24 3-0	Dec01 1-1
ST MIRREN	Dec22 3-1	Oct27 2-0	Mar15 3-1	Nov24 1-1	Jan19 0-2	Oct13 1-0	Dec15 0-4	Jan01 1-1	Nov03 3-0	Feb23 1-2	Mar08 3-1	Sep15 3-0	Jan26 0-5		Sep29 4-1	Jan15 3-0
STIRLING A	Nov17 0-4	Jan26 3-6	Nov10 2-1	Sep08 2-2	Dec29 3-2	Dec08 0-4	Oct06 1-4	Mar08 1-1	Oct20 2-1	Jan12 2-1	Sep22 1-1	Feb02 1-2	Mar01 1-5	Jan23 0-3		Mar22 3-3
T LANARK	Oct20 2-0	Sep08 4-0	Apr12 3-3	Dec29 0-2	Nov10 1-3	Apr14 4-0	Jan02 0-5	Feb27 3-1	Nov24 0-1	Sep22 0-0	Jan12 2-1	Mar15 3-1	Apr16 1-1	Oct06 4-2	Dec15 1-3	

DIVISION B

	ALBION R	ALLOA	ARBROATH	AYR U	CLYDE	COWDENBEATH	DUMBARTON	DUNDEE U	DUNFERMLINE A	FALKIRK	FORFAR A	HAMILTON A	KILMARNOCK	QUEEN'S PARK	ST JOHNSTONE	STENHOUSEMUIR
ALBION R		Mar05 1-1	Nov17 3-1	Mar01 2-0	Mar22 0-3	Jan12 0-0	Oct27 1-1	Dec08 3-0	Dec01 1-3	Oct06 1-1	Dec29 5-2	Sep22 0-1	Jan09 0-0	Sep08 1-1	Nov10 1-0	Apr12 2-6
ALLOA	Nov03 2-1		Oct13 2-2	Sep15 1-2	Feb16 3-3	Jan19 1-0	Jan01 4-1	Dec22 2-3	Apr26 5-4	Mar12 0-1	Dec15 4-2	Oct27 3-2	Feb23 1-2	Apr23 2-0	Nov24 2-0	Sep29 2-0
ARBROATH	Jan26 2-2	Jan12 2-1		Oct27 0-2	Jan19 1-3	Sep08 3-3	Nov24 1-2	Dec01 1-3	Dec15 5-3	Nov10 2-4	Sep22 1-2	Dec29 3-1	Feb13 2-1	Jan02 0-2	Oct06 4-3	Mar15 0-2
AYR U	Nov24 3-2	Oct06 2-0	Feb02 4-1		Dec01 1-1	Nov10 2-1	Feb27 4-1	Oct20 2-0	Mar15 3-1	Jan12 3-1	Jan09 4-0	Sep08 2-1	Sep22 3-2	Feb13 1-0	Dec29 3-3	Dec15 2-1
CLYDE	Sep15 5-1	Nov10 4-3	Oct20 2-1	Mar08 1-1		Oct06 11-1	Mar15 3-3	Mar11 3-0	Mar04 4-0	Dec29 1-1	Feb12 5-1	Jan12 0-2	Sep08 1-3	Sep22 5-2	Jan02 6-0	Nov24 3-1
COWDENBEATH	Oct13 3-1	Oct20 2-2	Dec22 8-1	Feb16 2-0	Jan05 3-2		Nov03 2-2	Sep29 2-2	Jan01 1-0	Apr12 5-0	Feb23 6-2	Dec01 3-1	Nov24 3-1	Dec15 2-3	Mar15 2-2	Sep15 1-0
DUMBARTON	Apr21 1-4	Sep22 1-2	Mar01 0-1	Nov17 4-2	Dec08 2-2	Jan26 1-5		Mar22 2-1	Oct20 0-0	Sep08 0-1	Nov10 3-1	Jan02 2-2	Dec29 4-2	Oct06 1-0	Jan12 3-1	Dec01 4-1
DUNDEE U	Mar15 0-0	Sep08 4-1	Mar08 3-1	Jan19 2-2	Oct27 3-5	Jan02 5-1	Dec15 4-1		Nov24 2-1	Apr14 2-3	Jan12 8-1	Oct06 3-2	Nov10 1-0	Dec29 5-0	Sep22 4-3	Mar05 3-0
DUNFERMLINE A	Mar08 5-1	Dec29 1-0	Mar22 5-0	Dec08 2-0	Nov17 3-7	Sep22 3-0	Jan19 3-2	Mar01 1-2		Jan02 0-6	Sep08 7-2	Nov10 3-0	Oct06 5-2	Jan12 2-1	Jan26 4-1	Oct27 2-2
FALKIRK	Jan16 3-1	Dec01 1-1	Feb16 5-1	Oct13 5-1	Apr05 2-1	Oct27 0-1	Dec22 1-1	Nov03 6-0	Sep29 5-1		Mar15 6-0	Jan19 0-1	Dec15 3-3	Nov24 6-0	Feb27 3-0	Jan01 5-2
FORFAR A	Apr19 2-0	Mar22 4-1	Jan01 4-1	Sep29 2-1	Nov03 1-2	Nov17 4-2	Feb16 1-3	Oct13 3-3	Dec22 3-2	Dec08 2-2		Mar01 1-6	Oct20 1-0	Feb20 2-1	Mar08 4-5	Jan05 4-1
HAMILTON A	Jan01 0-0	Feb02 0-1	Sep15 1-0	Dec22 1-1	Oct13 0-5	Mar08 3-2	Sep29 3-2	Jan05 1-1	Feb16 0-3	Oct20 0-1	Nov24 3-3		Mar15 2-1	Feb23 1-0	Dec15 4-2	Nov03 3-1
KILMARNOCK	Sep29 3-1	Nov17 1-0	Nov03 4-0	Jan01 4-0	Dec22 1-2	Mar01 5-1	Sep15 2-1	Feb16 2-6	Jan05 5-3	Mar22 2-1	Jan19 3-0	Dec08 3-2		Mar08 3-1	Oct27 3-0	Oct13 0-2
QUEEN'S PARK	Dec22 2-1	Dec08 0-2	Sep29 3-1	Nov03 0-1	Jan01 5-1	Mar22 2-2	Jan05 0-1	Sep15 1-2	Dec25 0-2	Jan26 0-3	Apr26 1-1	Nov17 1-3	Dec01 1-0		Jan19 4-5	Feb16 4-2
ST JOHNSTONE	Feb16 3-0	Mar01 2-2	Jan05 2-2	Feb23 2-0	Sep29 0-1	Dec08 6-0	Oct13 2-1	Jan01 4-1	Nov03 2-3	Nov17 1-3	Dec01 6-2	Mar22 1-1	Feb20 0-2	Oct20 1-1		Dec22 4-1
STENHOUSEMUIR	Oct20 3-3	Jan02 1-4	Dec08 3-0	Mar22 2-3	Mar01 0-8	Dec29 2-2	Mar08 1-1	Nov17 6-2	Apr19 3-2	Sep22 1-1	Oct06 5-2	Feb20 3-0	Jan12 1-2	Nov10 3-4	Sep08 1-1	

LEAGUE TABLES

DIVISION A

	P	W	D	L	F	A	W	D	L	F	A	Pts
Hibernian	30	12	2	1	58	15	8	3	4	34	21	45
Rangers	30	10	4	1	32	13	6	5	4	29	18	41
East Fife	30	11	2	2	44	19	6	1	8	27	30	37
Hearts	30	9	5	1	44	25	5	2	8	25	28	35
Raith R	30	9	2	4	23	14	5	3	7	20	28	33
Partick T	30	7	3	5	28	24	5	4	6	20	27	31
Motherwell	30	8	4	3	33	24	4	3	8	18	33	31
Dundee	30	7	3	5	31	22	4	3	8	22	30	28
Celtic	30	7	5	3	30	22	3	3	9	22	33	28
Queen of South	30	10	3	2	38	18	0	5	10	12	42	28
Aberdeen	30	7	4	4	37	24	3	3	9	28	34	27
T. Lanark	30	7	3	5	28	23	2	5	8	23	39	26
Airdrie	30	7	3	5	31	26	4	1	10	23	43	26
St Mirren	30	9	2	4	28	19	1	3	11	15	39	25
Morton	30	7	1	7	30	23	2	5	8	19	33	24
Stirling A	30	4	4	7	22	40	1	1	13	14	59	15

DIVISION B

	P	W	D	L	F	A	W	D	L	F	A	Pts
Clyde	30	10	3	2	54	20	9	3	3	46	25	44
Falkirk	30	10	3	2	51	14	8	4	3	29	20	43
Ayr U	30	13	2	0	39	15	4	3	8	16	30	39
Dundee U	30	11	2	2	49	21	5	3	7	26	39	37
Kilmarnock	30	12	0	3	41	20	4	2	9	21	28	34
Dunfermline A	30	11	1	3	46	26	4	1	10	28	39	32
Alloa	30	9	2	4	34	23	4	4	7	21	26	32
Cowdenbeath	30	10	4	1	45	19	2	4	9	21	48	32
Hamilton A	30	7	4	4	22	23	5	2	8	25	28	30
Dumbarton	30	7	3	5	28	25	3	5	7	23	32	28
St Johnstone	30	7	4	4	36	20	2	3	10	26	48	25
Forfar A	30	9	2	4	38	30	1	2	12	21	67	24
Stenhousemuir	30	5	5	5	35	35	3	1	11	22	39	22
Albion R	30	5	6	4	21	20	1	4	10	18	37	22
Queen's Park	30	5	2	8	24	27	3	2	10	16	35	20
Arbroath	30	5	2	8	27	34	1	2	12	13	49	16

Scottish Football League Records
Season 1952-53

DIVISION A

	ABERDEEN	AIRDRIE	CELTIC	CLYDE	DUNDEE	EAST FIFE	FALKIRK	HEARTS	HIBERNIAN	MOTHERWELL	PARTICK T	QUEEN OF SOUTH	RAITH R	RANGERS	ST MIRREN	T LANARK
ABERDEEN		Sep13 1-2	Sep27 2-2	Dec13 3-2	Jan01 2-2	Oct25 6-3	Nov22 7-2	Nov15 3-0	Apr11 1-1	Nov01 5-1	Dec20 4-2	Mar21 4-0	Feb28 0-2	Mar28 2-2	Jan10 1-2	Oct11 4-3
AIRDRIE	Oct18 4-7		Nov22 0-0	Oct04 4-4	Mar21 2-1	Nov15 3-1	Jan17 1-1	Jan03 1-2	Feb28 3-7	Sep20 1-2	Nov01 1-0	Apr11 1-2	Sep06 3-1	Dec27 2-2	Dec06 3-1	Apr27 4-2
CELTIC	Apr15 1-3	Mar18 0-1		Jan17 2-4	Dec13 5-0	Apr18 1-1	Sep06 5-3	Feb14 1-1	Mar28 1-3	Oct04 3-0	Mar07 3-1	Oct18 1-1	Dec27 0-1	Sep20 2-1	Apr11 3-2	Nov08 5-4
CLYDE	Jan24 3-0	Jan10 6-1	Oct11 1-2		Sep27 1-1	Dec20 1-2	Mar21 1-4	Dec06 3-2	Oct25 2-3	Feb28 3-2	Jan01 2-2	Nov22 5-0	Nov01 3-2	Nov15 4-6	Jan31 3-1	Apr22 5-2
DUNDEE	Sep20 3-1	Nov29 0-2	Apr04 4-0	Jan03 4-1		Feb21 1-1	Mar14 2-1	Oct18 2-1	Mar07 2-0	Sep06 0-0	Dec06 6-0	Dec27 0-0	Jan17 2-3	Feb14 1-1	Nov08 0-0	Mar18 3-0
EAST FIFE	Feb14 4-1	Mar07 3-1	Mar21 4-1	Sep06 7-1	Nov01 3-2		Jan03 3-1	Oct04 3-1	Nov22 3-5	Dec27 2-2	Feb28 2-3	Jan17 0-0	Sep20 2-0	Oct18 3-2	Apr04 7-0	Dec06 3-1
FALKIRK	Apr20 4-1	Oct11 2-2	Dec20 2-3	Nov29 2-1	Jan10 2-1	Sep27 0-1		Apr18 2-4	Jan31 1-3	Apr04 2-1	Sep13 0-4	Nov15 2-0	Dec06 3-2	Nov08 1-2	Oct25 1-2	Jan01 5-1
HEARTS	Mar07 3-1	Sep27 4-0	Oct25 1-0	Mar28 7-0	Jan31 1-1	Apr28 4-2	Nov01 0-1		Jan01 1-2	Nov22 3-1	Oct11 2-1	Feb28 3-0	Mar21 1-2	Dec13 2-2	Sep13 1-2	Dec20 3-3
HIBERNIAN	Dec27 3-0	Nov08 3-1	Dec06 1-1	Feb14 5-1	Nov15 3-0	Apr20 2-1	Oct18 4-2	Sep20 3-1		Jan03 7-2	Apr04 1-1	Sep06 1-3	Apr29 4-1	Jan17 1-1	Nov29 0-2	Apr25 7-1
MOTHERWELL	Apr18 4-1	Jan01 4-1	Jan10 4-2	Nov08 3-6	Dec20 2-1	Sep13 3-3	Dec13 2-1	Jan24 1-3	Sep27 3-7		Oct25 1-2	Mar28 3-2	Mar07 2-1	Apr20 0-3	Oct11 1-1	Jan31 1-5
PARTICK T	Sep06 1-1	Apr25 3-2	Nov15 3-0	Sep20 1-5	Mar28 0-3	Nov08 1-3	Dec27 0-3	Jan17 2-2	Dec13 5-4	Feb14 4-2		Apr06 2-2	Oct18 4-1	Apr11 1-2	Feb21 5-3	Mar21 0-0
QUEEN OF SOUTH	Nov29 4-0	Oct25 1-2	Jan31 2-1	Sep13 3-1	Apr18 1-0	Oct11 0-1	Mar07 2-2	Nov08 4-2	Dec20 2-7	Dec06 3-1	Sep27 0-1		Apr04 1-1	May07 1-1	Jan01 4-3	Jan10 3-1
RAITH R	Nov08 2-1	Mar14 3-0	Sep13 1-1	Apr11 3-2	Oct11 1-1	Jan01 0-0	Mar28 0-2	Nov29 1-1	Jan10 4-2	Nov15 1-1	Jan31 2-2	Dec13 1-1		Mar18 3-1	Sep27 0-1	Oct25 3-4
RANGERS	Dec06 4-0	Apr15 8-2	Jan01 1-0	Mar07 1-2	May02 3-1	Jan31 4-0	Feb28 4-0	Apr06 3-0	Oct11 1-2	Mar21 4-1	Jan10 2-2	Nov01 3-1	Nov22 3-2		Dec20 4-0	Sep27 4-1
ST MIRREN	Oct04 2-1	Mar28 2-2	Nov01 1-2	Oct18 2-2	Feb28 0-0	Dec13 1-1	Feb14 3-0	Dec27 1-0	Mar21 2-2	Jan17 2-5	Nov22 1-1	Sep20 6-0	Apr25 3-2	Sep06 2-3		Nov15 1-0
T LANARK	Jan17 0-1	Dec13 2-1	Feb28 1-3	Dec27 1-3	Nov22 0-0	Mar28 0-3	Sep20 1-1	Sep06 2-3	Nov01 2-0	Oct18 1-2	Dec25 3-1	Oct04 5-0	Feb14 2-1	Jan03 0-2	Mar07 4-3	

DIVISION B

	ALBION R	ALLOA	ARBROATH	AYR U	COWDENBEATH	DUMBARTON	DUNDEE U	DUNFERMLINE A	FORFAR A	HAMILTON A	KILMARNOCK	MORTON	QUEEN'S PARK	ST JOHNSTONE	STENHOUSEMUIR	STIRLING A
ALBION R		Mar07 1-2	Jan31 1-2	Jan24 5-6	Sep13 2-2	Dec20 3-1	Nov08 2-4	Mar14 2-2	Apr18 1-1	Jan01 0-6	Jan10 2-1	Mar28 4-1	Dec13 1-1	Oct11 3-0	Sep27 0-1	Oct25 0-1
ALLOA	Nov15 4-2		Sep27 2-0	Nov08 3-6	Jan31 2-2	Oct25 4-1	Nov29 6-2	Feb21 3-3	Mar14 4-1	Oct11 0-5	Dec20 1-2	Dec13 3-0	Mar28 1-1	Jan24 2-0	Jan01 2-2	Apr11 1-3
ARBROATH	Oct18 3-0	Jan03 2-0		Jan17 1-1	Nov15 2-2	Feb21 2-1	Sep06 2-1	Oct04 4-1	Sep20 0-0	Nov08 3-2	Dec13 2-2	Dec27 1-0	Oct25 0-2	Mar28 1-3	Mar14 6-2	Nov29 3-1
AYR U	Mar21 4-3	Feb28 2-4	Oct11 7-2		Oct25 1-0	Sep27 5-0	Mar07 2-1	Dec13 1-2	Mar28 8-1	Jan10 0-2	Jan01 0-2	Nov01 4-1	Nov22 4-0	Jan31 5-2	Sep13 2-4	Dec20 2-4
COWDENBEATH	Dec27 3-2	Oct18 1-4	Mar07 3-0	Apr18 0-1		Mar14 2-2	Jan03 0-0	Sep20 4-3	Jan17 3-0	Nov29 2-0	Mar28 2-3	Sep06 1-2	Oct04 1-4	Dec13 3-3	Feb21 2-0	Nov08 0-3
DUMBARTON	Sep06 1-0	Feb14 4-2	Nov01 5-5	Jan03 2-2	Nov22 4-0		Oct18 1-3	Dec27 1-1	Oct04 2-1	Mar07 1-2	Feb28 4-2	Jan17 4-2	Sep20 2-1	Mar21 2-2	Dec06 1-0	Apr04 4-1
DUNDEE U	Feb28 2-1	Sep13 4-2	Dec20 1-2	Nov15 0-4	Sep27 0-0	Jan31 2-3		Mar28 1-1	Dec13 4-1	Oct25 2-3	Apr18 5-4	Nov22 0-4	Nov01 2-1	Jan01 1-0	Jan10 3-1	Oct11 2-3
DUNFERMLINE A	Nov22 2-1	Nov01 2-2	Jan10 0-0	Apr04 0-1	Jan01 2-1	Sep13 2-2	Dec06 1-1		Nov15 5-0	Jan31 2-1	Oct11 2-1	Feb28 0-1	Apr11 1-2	Oct25 2-0	Dec20 3-5	Sep27 5-1
FORFAR A	Nov01 4-2	Nov22 5-2	Jan01 0-0	Dec06 1-2	Oct11 2-0	Jan10 5-2	Apr04 1-3	Mar07 2-1		Dec20 1-3	Apr22 6-0	Mar21 5-1	Feb28 3-6	Sep27 1-3	Apr11 5-0	Jan24 1-3
HAMILTON A	Sep20 3-2	Jan17 2-0	Feb28 2-1	Oct04 4-0	Mar21 0-1	Nov15 3-1	Feb14 3-1	Oct18 7-1	Sep06 2-0		Nov22 2-2	Jan03 3-0	Dec27 4-2	Nov01 1-0	Apr04 2-1	Dec06 2-1
KILMARNOCK	Apr11 4-0	Sep06 1-2	Apr04 4-0	Sep20 0-1	Dec06 2-0	Nov08 2-1	Dec27 1-0	Jan17 2-3	Apr25 4-0	Mar14 6-1		Oct18 3-2	Jan03 0-1	Nov15 2-3	Nov29 4-1	Feb21 6-0
MORTON	Dec06 5-0	Apr04 4-1	Apr18 4-0	Apr11 6-1	Dec20 1-0	Oct11 6-1	Mar14 1-2	Nov08 2-1	Nov29 7-1	Sep27 5-3	Jan31 1-4		Apr25 2-2	Jan10 1-1	Oct25 4-1	Jan01 2-2
QUEEN'S PARK	Apr22 4-0	Dec06 1-2	Apr06 5-1	Mar14 2-0	Jan10 4-0	Jan01 1-0	Feb21 3-0	Apr14 3-0	Nov08 6-2	Sep13 1-1	Sep27 2-3	Nov15 2-7		Dec20 4-1	Oct11 2-2	Jan31 1-1
ST JOHNSTONE	Jan17 1-3	Dec27 3-0	Dec06 0-4	Oct18 1-4	Apr04 1-2	Nov29 3-2	Sep20 1-1	Feb14 1-0	Jan03 2-2	Apr11 0-2	Mar07 1-2	Oct04 3-1	Sep06 0-2		Nov08 2-2	Mar14 4-2
STENHOUSEMUIR	Jan03 3-1	Sep20 4-1	Nov22 1-2	Dec27 2-0	Nov01 3-0	Mar28 1-2	Oct04 0-4	Sep06 3-3	Oct18 5-0	Dec13 4-1	Mar21 0-4	Feb14 2-5	Jan17 2-2	Feb28 3-0		Mar07 0-0
STIRLING A	Apr25 3-0	Oct04 2-1	Mar21 4-1	Sep06 1-0	Feb28 1-0	Dec13 2-1	Jan17 2-0	Jan03 3-0	Dec27 7-2	Mar28 0-0	Nov01 3-1	Sep20 2-1	Oct18 3-2	Nov22 3-0	Nov15 2-1	

LEAGUE TABLES

DIVISION A

	P	W	D	L	F	A	W	D	L	F	A	Pts
Rangers	30	12	1	2	49	14	6	6	3	31	25	43
Hibernian	30	10	3	2	45	18	9	2	4	48	33	43
East Fife	30	11	2	2	49	21	5	5	5	23	27	39
Hearts	30	8	3	4	36	18	4	3	8	23	32	30
Clyde	30	8	2	5	43	30	5	2	8	35	48	30
St Mirren	30	6	6	3	29	21	5	2	8	23	37	30
Dundee	30	8	5	2	30	11	1	6	8	14	26	29
Celtic	30	7	3	5	33	26	4	4	7	18	28	29
Partick T	30	6	4	5	32	33	4	5	6	23	30	29
Queen of South	30	8	3	4	31	24	2	5	8	12	37	28
Aberdeen	30	8	4	3	45	26	3	1	11	19	42	27
Raith R	30	5	7	3	25	20	4	1	10	22	33	26
Falkirk	30	7	1	7	29	28	4	3	8	24	35	26
Airdrie	30	6	4	5	33	33	4	2	9	20	42	26
Motherwell	30	7	2	6	34	39	3	3	9	23	41	25
T. Lanark	30	6	2	7	24	24	2	2	11	28	51	20

DIVISION B

	P	W	D	L	F	A	W	D	L	F	A	Pts
Stirling A	30	14	1	0	38	10	6	3	6	26	33	44
Hamilton A	30	13	1	1	40	13	7	2	6	32	27	43
Queen's Park	30	9	3	3	41	20	6	4	5	29	26	37
Kilmarnock	30	10	0	5	41	15	7	2	6	33	33	36
Ayr U	30	9	0	6	47	28	8	2	5	29	28	36
Morton	30	10	3	2	51	20	5	0	10	28	37	33
Arbroath	30	9	4	2	32	18	4	3	8	20	39	33
Dundee U	30	7	2	6	29	30	5	3	7	23	26	29
Alloa	30	7	4	4	38	30	5	1	9	25	38	29
Dumbarton	30	9	4	2	38	24	2	2	11	20	43	28
Dunfermline A	30	7	4	4	29	19	2	5	8	22	39	27
Stenhousemuir	30	7	3	5	33	25	3	3	9	23	40	26
Cowdenbeath	30	6	3	6	27	27	2	4	9	10	27	23
St Johnstone	30	5	3	7	23	29	3	3	9	18	34	22
Forfar A	30	8	1	6	42	28	0	3	12	12	60	20
Albion R	30	4	4	7	27	31	1	0	14	17	46	14

Scottish Football League Records
Season 1953-54

DIVISION A

	ABERDEEN	AIRDRIE	CELTIC	CLYDE	DUNDEE	EAST FIFE	FALKIRK	HAMILTON A	HEARTS	HIBERNIAN	PARTICK T	QUEEN OF SOUTH	RAITH R	RANGERS	ST MIRREN	STIRLING A
ABERDEEN		Oct17 5-0	Jan02 2-0	Feb20 5-3	Sep19 1-1	Feb06 1-0	Mar17 0-1	Oct10 5-1	Mar20 1-0	Jan16 1-3	Oct03 2-1	Nov14 2-0	Dec05 2-0	Nov07 1-1	Sep05 0-3	Dec26 8-0
AIRDRIE	Jan23 1-3		Mar17 0-6	Dec19 3-4	Nov14 2-2	Mar20 3-2	Sep12 2-2	Jan01 5-0	Sep26 2-1	Dec05 2-2	Mar31 3-6	Oct24 1-1	Jan09 1-2	Apr24 2-0	Feb27 1-3	Oct31 1-1
CELTIC	Sep26 3-0	Nov21 4-1		Sep12 1-0	Feb20 5-1	Mar06 4-1	Jan09 1-0	Apr26 1-0	Oct24 2-0	Nov07 2-2	Nov28 2-1	Jan23 3-1	Oct10 3-0	Jan01 1-0	Dec12 4-0	Mar29 4-0
CLYDE	Oct31 2-4	Sep05 4-1	Dec26 1-7		Jan02 2-0	Oct03 3-1	Nov14 4-1	Apr14 4-1	Apr17 0-1	Feb06 3-6	Sep19 0-4	Mar13 2-0	Apr03 4-2	Mar20 2-5	Oct17 4-2	Jan16 1-1
DUNDEE	Jan01 4-2	Mar10 1-0	Oct31 1-1	Sep26 2-0		Dec12 1-1	Dec19 1-0	Jan09 3-2	Jan23 2-4	Nov28 1-0	Apr17 6-0	Oct10 4-1	Sep12 0-0	Oct24 1-0	Mar27 2-0	Nov21 2-1
EAST FIFE	Apr14 2-0	Nov28 1-0	Nov14 4-1	Jan09 3-1	Apr03 1-1		Sep26 4-1	Apr21 4-0	Dec19 2-2	Mar13 1-3	Dec05 4-1	Apr24 4-0	Jan01 1-1	Jan23 2-1	Oct31 2-0	Apr10 2-1
FALKIRK	Nov21 2-2	Dec26 4-1	Apr14 0-3	Feb27 1-1	Sep05 4-0	Jan02 3-3		Oct31 2-2	Dec12 1-3	Oct17 2-4	Jan16 2-2	Mar20 0-4	Apr10 0-3	Mar27 4-3	Feb06 4-0	Sep19 2-0
HAMILTON A	Dec12 3-2	Sep19 0-1	Sep05 2-0	Mar27 1-3	Oct03 2-3	Jan16 0-1	Feb20 2-1		Nov21 1-5	Jan02 2-6	Feb06 1-3	Nov07 0-5	Nov28 2-1	Mar06 1-1	Dec26 0-2	Oct17 0-1
HEARTS	Nov28 3-2	Jan02 4-3	Feb06 3-2	Nov07 1-2	Oct17 2-1	Sep05 2-2	Jan30 0-0	Mar17 3-0		Sep19 4-0	Dec26 0-2	Sep12 1-4	Nov14 5-1	Feb20 3-3	Jan16 5-1	Oct03 6-1
HIBERNIAN	Apr19 3-0	Mar27 8-1	Apr17 0-3	Oct24 4-0	Mar20 2-0	Nov21 2-1	Jan23 2-3	Sep26 4-1	Jan01 1-2		Oct31 1-2	Jan09 1-0	Dec19 5-0	Apr26 2-2	Mar06 2-1	Dec12 1-2
PARTICK T	Jan09 6-3	Dec12 9-0	Mar20 1-3	Jan01 3-4	Nov07 1-0	Mar27 0-1	Apr24 5-1	Apr10 4-0	Apr19 2-1	Feb20 0-2		Sep26 1-2	Jan23 5-3	Dec19 0-1	Nov21 2-0	Mar06 3-1
QUEEN OF SOUTH	Mar06 2-4	Apr10 6-2	Oct17 2-1	Nov21 1-2	Jan16 5-1	Dec26 5-0	Nov28 5-3	Apr17 2-2	Dec05 2-2	Oct03 3-2	Jan02 2-6		Oct31 5-1	Dec12 2-1	Sep19 4-0	Sep05 4-1
RAITH R	Mar27 3-1	Oct03 5-1	Jan16 2-0	Dec12 3-4	Dec26 1-2	Sep19 2-2	Nov07 0-2	Mar20 5-0	Mar06 4-2	Sep05 4-0	Oct17 4-1	Feb20 1-1		Nov21 1-2	Jan02 1-2	Feb06 1-1
RANGERS	Apr17 1-3	Jan16 3-0	Sep19 1-1	Nov28 1-1	Feb06 2-0	Oct17 2-0	Apr21 3-0	Nov14 8-1	Oct31 0-1	Dec26 3-0	Sep05 3-0	Apr03 2-0	Mar17 2-2		Apr14 1-1	Jan02 3-1
ST MIRREN	Dec19 1-4	Nov07 1-0	Apr07 1-3	Jan23 0-1	Apr10 3-0	Feb13 1-1	Oct24 1-0	Sep12 3-2	Oct10 1-1	Nov14 3-3	Mar24 1-3	Jan01 5-3	Sep26 3-0	Jan09 0-1		Mar20 3-0
STIRLING A	Sep12 1-0	Feb20 2-1	Dec05 2-1	Oct10 2-2	Mar13 2-3	Nov07 3-2	Jan01 0-1	Jan23 6-0	Jan09 0-3	Apr07 2-1	Nov14 1-2	Dec19 3-0	Oct24 1-3	Sep26 2-0	Nov28 0-2	

DIVISION B

	ALBION R	ALLOA	ARBROATH	AYR U	COWDENBEATH	DUMBARTON	DUNDEE U	DUNFERMLINE A	FORFAR A	KILMARNOCK	MORTON	MOTHERWELL	QUEEN'S PARK	ST JOHNSTONE	STENHOUSEMUIR	T LANARK
ALBION R		Feb20 1-3	Feb06 1-1	Nov21 4-2	Jan16 3-2	Dec26 4-1	Dec12 3-3	Nov28 3-1	Jan30 1-2	Jan02 1-1	Nov07 3-2	Sep19 2-3	Apr21 2-0	Oct03 3-2	Oct17 1-0	Sep05 1-0
ALLOA	Oct31 2-2		Jan16 3-3	Dec12 1-1	Jan02 2-1	Feb06 2-2	Nov21 1-3	Feb27 4-1	Mar06 3-3	Oct17 1-0	Mar20 1-2	Dec26 2-3	Apr28 5-1	Sep05 2-3	Sep19 1-2	Oct03 1-4
ARBROATH	Oct24 3-1	Oct10 1-1		Jan30 1-0	Mar27 2-1	Nov21 2-3	Jan09 4-3	Jan23 5-0	Jan01 2-3	Feb20 0-1	Sep26 2-3	Dec12 1-4	Dec19 3-2	Nov07 3-4	Mar06 1-1	Mar20 2-2
AYR U	Mar13 2-2	Apr03 2-4	Dec26 3-0		Sep05 4-0	Jan16 0-0	Nov28 2-1	Nov14 1-2	Nov07 3-1	Sep19 1-0	Dec05 2-1	Jan02 0-3	Feb20 0-0	Oct17 3-4	Oct03 1-2	Feb06 0-6
COWDENBEATH	Oct10 4-3	Sep26 6-1	Dec05 2-1	Dec19 5-2		Oct31 6-1	Oct24 4-2	Jan01 1-1	Jan09 2-3	Jan30 6-0	Sep12 1-2	Nov28 1-5	Jan23 1-1	Apr24 3-1	Feb27 3-3	Nov14 1-3
DUMBARTON	Sep12 5-1	Oct24 0-0	Mar13 1-0	Oct10 3-1	Feb20 2-2		Dec19 2-2	Sep26 4-4	Jan23 0-1	Nov14 2-5	Jan01 2-4	Nov07 1-4	Jan09 1-1	Apr17 3-2	Mar20 1-2	Apr28 3-2
DUNDEE U	Mar31 6-2	Mar13 0-1	Oct03 2-2	Mar20 4-0	Feb06 3-3	Sep05 2-1		Dec05 1-0	Feb20 0-1	Jan16 0-2	Nov14 1-5	Oct17 1-0	Nov07 4-0	Sep19 1-2	Dec26 1-1	Jan04 1-1
DUNFERMLINE A	Mar20 2-0	Nov07 2-1	Oct17 2-0	Mar10 0-0	Sep19 5-3	Jan02 6-1	Mar27 0-1		Dec12 1-1	Sep05 1-0	Feb20 1-3	Oct03 4-3	Nov21 3-1	Dec26 0-4	Feb06 3-2	Jan16 0-3
FORFAR A	Dec05 1-2	Nov14 2-2	Sep19 0-3	Feb27 0-1	Oct03 1-0	Oct17 1-2	Oct31 3-2	Apr24 0-1		Feb06 2-3	Mar13 3-2	Sep05 0-5	Nov28 1-0	Jan02 3-1	Jan16 1-2	Dec26 1-4
KILMARNOCK	Sep26 0-3	Jan23 2-0	Oct31 4-0	Jan01 0-3	Nov21 1-0	Mar06 7-2	Oct10 3-2	Dec19 2-2	Oct24 6-0		Jan09 2-0	Mar31 4-2	Apr24 2-0	Mar20 5-0	Dec12 6-2	Apr17 1-1
MORTON	Apr10 0-1	Nov28 3-0	Jan02 5-2	Mar27 2-2	Dec26 5-0	Sep19 8-0	Mar06 4-1	Oct31 3-3	Nov21 4-0	Oct03 4-6		Feb06 2-5	Dec12 0-3	Jan16 4-3	Sep05 3-3	Oct17 0-3
MOTHERWELL	Jan01 6-0	Sep12 6-0	Apr07 2-1	Sep26 3-4	Mar20 5-2	Apr10 6-6	Jan23 12-1	Jan09 3-0	Dec19 5-0	Dec05 0-2	Oct24 3-2		Oct10 4-0	Nov14 3-1	Oct31 4-0	Mar24 1-1
QUEEN'S PARK	Nov14 2-2	Apr14 4-1	Sep05 3-4	Oct31 2-4	Oct17 7-1	Oct03 6-0	Feb27 3-1	Mar13 4-0	Mar20 2-2	Dec26 1-1	Apr17 4-2	Jan16 0-0		Feb06 2-4	Jan02 4-0	Jan01 1-1
ST JOHNSTONE	Jan09 3-3	Dec19 7-0	Feb27 3-1	Jan23 1-2	Dec12 6-1	Mar27 3-1	Jan01 4-1	Apr10 0-0	Sep26 5-1	Nov28 1-4	Oct10 1-2	Mar06 2-6	Oct24 0-0		Nov21 5-1	Oct31 6-1
STENHOUSEMUIR	Jan23 3-0	Jan01 2-2	Nov14 5-1	Jan09 2-2	Nov07 2-4	Nov28 6-0	Sep12 4-3	Oct24 2-2	Oct10 2-1	Apr03 0-1	Dec19 4-1	Feb20 2-1	Sep26 2-1	Mar13 3-0		Dec05 5-3
T LANARK	Dec19 1-0	Jan09 3-3	Nov28 2-2	Apr21 2-2	Mar06 4-1	Dec12 2-1	Sep26 9-1	Apr19 1-1	Apr12 3-0	Nov07 2-0	Jan23 3-7	Nov21 1-2	Sep19 0-1	Feb20 9-2	Mar30 1-1	

LEAGUE TABLES

DIVISION A

	P	W	D	L	F	A	W	D	L	F	A	Pts
Celtic	30	14	1	0	40	7	6	2	7	32	22	43
Hearts	30	9	3	3	42	24	7	3	5	28	21	38
Partick T	30	9	0	6	42	22	8	1	6	34	32	35
Rangers	30	9	4	2	35	11	4	4	7	21	24	34
Hibernian	30	9	1	5	38	18	6	3	6	34	33	34
East Fife	30	11	3	1	37	13	2	5	8	18	32	34
Dundee	30	11	3	1	31	12	3	3	9	15	35	34
Clyde	30	8	1	6	36	36	7	3	5	28	31	34
Aberdeen	30	10	2	3	36	14	5	1	9	30	37	33
Queen of South	30	10	2	3	50	28	4	2	9	22	30	32
St Mirren	30	7	3	5	27	22	5	1	9	17	32	28
Raith R	30	7	3	5	37	21	3	3	9	19	39	26
Falkirk	30	5	5	5	31	31	4	2	9	16	30	25
Stirling A	30	8	1	6	27	21	2	3	10	12	41	24
Airdrie	30	4	5	6	29	35	1	0	14	12	57	15
Hamilton A	30	4	1	10	17	35	0	2	13	12	59	11

DIVISION B

	P	W	D	L	F	A	W	D	L	F	A	Pts
Motherwell	30	11	2	2	63	20	10	1	4	46	23	45
Kilmarnock	30	11	2	2	45	17	8	2	5	26	22	42
T. Lanark	30	7	5	3	43	24	6	5	4	35	24	36
Stenhousemuir	30	10	3	2	44	22	4	5	6	22	36	36
Morton	30	7	3	5	47	32	8	0	7	38	33	33
St Johnstone	30	8	3	4	47	24	6	0	9	33	47	31
Albion R	30	9	3	3	33	23	3	4	8	22	40	31
Dunfermline A	30	9	2	4	30	23	2	7	6	18	34	31
Ayr U	30	6	3	6	24	26	5	5	5	26	30	30
Queen's Park	30	7	5	3	45	23	2	4	9	11	28	27
Alloa	30	4	5	6	31	31	3	5	7	19	41	24
Forfar A	30	5	1	9	19	30	5	3	7	19	39	24
Cowdenbeath	30	8	3	4	46	29	1	2	12	21	52	23
Arbroath	30	6	3	6	32	29	2	4	9	21	38	23
Dundee U	30	6	4	5	27	21	2	2	11	27	58	22
Dumbarton	30	5	5	5	30	31	2	3	10	21	61	22

Dumbarton left the League, replaced by Brechin.

Scottish Football League Records
Season 1954-55

DIVISION A

	ABERDEEN	CELTIC	CLYDE	DUNDEE	EAST FIFE	FALKIRK	HEARTS	HIBERNIAN	KILMARNOCK	MOTHERWELL	PARTICK T	QUEEN OF SOUTH	RAITH R	RANGERS	ST MIRREN	STIRLING A
ABERDEEN		Oct09 0-2	Dec18 3-0	Jan01 1-0	Oct23 4-1	Nov27 1-0	Nov20 1-0	Sep25 3-1	Mar30 4-1	Jan08 4-1	Feb12 4-0	Nov06 2-0	Apr23 3-2	Apr02 4-0	Jan22 2-1	Sep11 5-0
CELTIC	Apr16 2-1		Dec25 2-2	Dec18 4-1	Dec04 2-2	Oct30 3-1	Jan29 2-0	Apr02 1-2	Oct02 6-3	Mar19 1-0	Mar12 0-0	Oct16 1-1	Jan03 4-1	Sep18 2-0	Feb26 5-2	Nov13 7-0
CLYDE	Apr09 0-1	Sep11 2-2		Oct09 2-0	Feb12 3-0	Mar30 2-0	Dec11 0-3	Oct23 6-3	Nov27 1-1	Jan22 2-2	Jan01 2-2	Mar09 2-2	Nov06 3-0	Nov20 1-1	Jan08 2-2	Sep25 5-1
DUNDEE	Sep18 0-2	Apr09 0-1	Apr11 2-1		Mar09 1-1	Oct16 2-0	Oct02 3-2	Mar12 2-2	Jan03 2-5	Dec04 4-1	Dec11 3-1	Oct30 3-1	Dec25 4-1	Jan29 2-1	Nov13 0-1	Mar19 4-1
EAST FIFE	Jan29 1-1	Mar30 3-4	Oct30 0-3	Nov06 4-1		Apr16 2-0	Oct16 0-2	Nov27 1-5	Dec25 1-5	Mar12 4-2	Mar05 0-2	Jan03 0-1	Sep18 3-1	Oct02 2-7	Apr09 6-1	Dec11 5-0
FALKIRK	Mar19 1-2	Feb12 1-1	Dec04 2-1	Apr30 2-2	Apr23 2-2		Feb26 2-2	Jan08 3-1	Nov20 5-3	Sep11 1-1	Sep25 3-1	Apr09 1-1	Dec11 2-1	Nov13 0-3	Oct23 0-1	Jan01 3-1
HEARTS	Mar12 2-0	Apr30 0-3	Apr02 3-0	Jan08 2-1	Apr13 1-3	Nov06 5-3		Jan01 5-1	Apr06 2-2	Apr18 3-2	Sep11 5-4	Nov27 3-1	Mar26 2-0	Dec18 3-4	Apr22 1-1	Feb12 3-0
HIBERNIAN	Jan03 0-1	Dec11 0-5	Jan29 2-3	Nov20 3-1	Mar19 0-0	Oct02 0-1	Sep18 2-3		Oct30 3-2	Nov13 4-1	Apr09 3-1	Apr16 1-1	Oct16 2-1	Dec25 2-1	Dec04 2-1	Mar23 4-1
KILMARNOCK	Dec04 0-4	Jan08 1-2	Mar19 2-1	Sep25 0-2	Sep11 0-0	Mar12 2-0	Nov24 1-3	Feb12 0-3		Apr13 1-2	Oct09 1-2	Dec11 4-1	Apr09 2-2	Feb26 1-0	Jan01 1-1	Apr30 2-1
MOTHERWELL	Oct02 1-3	Nov27 2-2	Oct16 2-0	Mar26 0-2	Nov20 3-5	Dec25 0-3	Apr16 1-1	Mar09 1-5	Jan29 0-1		Nov06 1-2	Sep18 2-1	Oct30 3-2	Jan03 2-0	Dec11 2-3	Apr09 3-1
PARTICK T	Oct30 1-0	Nov20 4-2	Sep18 2-3	Apr02 2-1	Nov13 1-0	Jan03 2-2	Dec25 4-4	Dec18 0-3	Apr16 0-3	Feb26 0-1		Jan29 1-0	Oct02 1-1	Oct16 2-5	Mar19 1-1	Dec04 3-3
QUEEN OF SOUTH	Feb26 2-6	Jan22 0-2	Nov13 2-1	Feb12 1-1	Apr30 1-0	Dec18 3-2	Mar19 1-1	Oct09 0-2	Mar05 1-0	Jan01 1-0	Oct23 2-3		Mar12 2-0	Dec04 1-2	Sep11 2-7	Jan08 3-2
RAITH R	Nov13 1-2	Sep25 1-3	Feb26 2-3	Sep11 3-0	Jan01 4-1	Apr02 3-0	Dec04 0-6	Apr30 2-1	Dec18 0-0	Feb12 3-2	Jan08 2-3	Nov20 3-1		Mar19 1-0	Oct09 4-0	Oct23 5-1
RANGERS	Dec11 3-1	Jan01 4-1	Mar12 1-0	Oct23 3-0	Jan08 2-0	Mar09 4-1	Apr09 2-1	Sep11 1-1	Nov06 6-0	Apr30 2-0	Apr11 3-1	Mar26 1-0	Nov27 1-0		Feb12 1-1	Oct09 6-1
ST MIRREN	Oct16 0-4	Nov06 1-1	Oct02 4-4	Mar05 0-2	Dec18 3-0	Jan29 1-0	Jan03 1-1	Mar26 4-2	Sep18 2-0	Mar29 0-1	Nov27 3-2	Dec25 3-2	Apr16 0-2	Oct30 2-1		Nov20 7-1
STIRLING A	Dec25 3-4	Mar09 2-3	Jan03 1-4	Nov27 0-2	Apr02 0-4	Sep18 1-1	Oct30 0-5	Nov06 2-4	Oct16 1-2	Dec18 1-3	Mar26 0-1	Oct02 0-3	Jan29 2-1	Mar05 0-2	Mar12 2-1	

DIVISION B

	AIRDRIE	ALBION R	ALLOA	ARBROATH	AYR U	BRECHIN C	COWDENBEATH	DUNDEE U	DUNFERMLINE A	FORFAR A	HAMILTON A	MORTON	QUEEN'S PARK	ST JOHNSTONE	STENHOUSEMUIR	T LANARK
AIRDRIE		Sep18 3-3	Dec25 5-1	Nov06 3-1	Dec11 5-4	Nov27 6-1	Nov20 3-1	Oct02 2-1	Oct30 6-2	Oct16 6-2	Jan29 6-3	Jan03 6-2	Apr23 4-2	Mar30 4-1	Apr09 2-1	Apr16 1-1
ALBION R	Jan01 2-2		Apr20 0-2	Oct09 4-4	Sep11 4-5	Apr27 2-0	Apr30 2-3	May02 3-2	Mar12 2-1	Nov13 1-1	Apr11 3-2	Dec04 3-3	Mar19 1-3	Feb12 4-2	Jan08 2-3	Oct23 1-1
ALLOA	Sep11 2-2	Apr09 1-2		Sep25 3-3	Apr16 3-0	Feb12 4-6	Oct09 4-1	Mar19 0-0	Dec11 2-1	Dec04 2-3	Nov20 2-2	Nov13 2-3	May04 0-0	Jan22 2-4	Jan01 1-1	Jan08 1-3
ARBROATH	Feb26 3-3	Apr23 1-0	Jan03 0-2		Mar19 5-1	Mar12 1-1	Nov13 2-2	Jan29 3-1	Oct02 2-2	Sep18 4-3	Oct30 0-3	Oct16 2-4	Dec25 1-4	Apr02 1-2	Dec04 1-0	Dec18 2-0
AYR U	Apr02 3-2	Dec25 2-2	Jan29 3-0	Nov27 2-0		Nov06 4-0	Dec18 2-1	Oct16 5-1	Apr23 1-1	Oct02 3-3	Sep18 3-5	Apr20 2-0	Jan03 3-1	Mar05 1-0	Nov20 0-4	Mar26 2-0
BRECHIN C	Mar19 2-3	Oct16 1-1	Oct30 4-2	Nov20 4-5	Apr13 0-3		Dec04 3-6	Feb05 2-3	Jan03 1-5	Dec25 2-4	Oct02 2-1	Sep18 3-5	Jan29 1-2	Dec18 1-0	Nov13 0-3	Apr23 2-1
COWDENBEATH	Mar12 1-1	Jan03 4-2	Feb19 2-5	Mar05 3-5	Apr09 1-2	Mar26 1-1		Apr23 3-1	Sep18 3-1	Jan29 2-3	Dec25 2-5	Oct02 0-2	Oct16 0-4	Nov06 2-3	Dec11 3-2	Nov27 2-4
DUNDEE U	Jan08 3-4	Nov06 1-1	Nov27 5-4	Apr16 6-1	Jan22 3-0	Oct09 2-3	Feb12 0-0		Mar05 1-4	Dec18 3-4	Mar26 1-2	Apr02 5-0	Nov20 1-3	Jan01 1-5	Sep11 1-1	Sep25 2-0
DUNFERMLINE A	Feb12 2-2	Nov20 7-0	Apr02 5-0	Jan08 2-1	Oct09 2-0	Sep25 2-1	Jan01 3-1	Nov13 3-1		Apr27 5-1	Dec18 3-2	Mar19 2-0	Dec04 2-1	Sep11 4-3	Oct23 3-4	Apr30 0-0
FORFAR A	Jan22 2-4	Apr13 4-1	Mar26 3-1	Jan01 1-1	Jan08 6-1	Sep11 2-4	Apr16 3-1	Apr09 1-4	Nov06 2-1		Nov27 0-3	Nov20 5-3	Dec11 1-0	Oct09 0-2	Sep25 2-2	Feb12 3-3
HAMILTON A	Oct23 3-3	Dec11 5-0	Mar12 2-1	Feb12 3-2	Jan01 5-1	Jan08 3-1	Sep11 2-1	Dec04 1-1	Apr09 0-1	Mar19 3-0		Feb26 1-0	Nov13 0-5	Apr30 4-2	Apr23 1-1	Oct09 5-1
MORTON	Apr30 3-2	Mar26 2-0	Mar05 3-2	Feb19 1-1	Feb12 1-3	Jan01 1-3	Jan08 3-1	Dec11 5-0	Nov27 0-1	Mar12 2-2	Nov06 2-1		Apr13 3-1	Oct23 1-1	Oct09 2-4	Sep11 2-2
QUEEN'S PARK	Apr11 1-1	Nov27 2-0	Nov06 6-0	Sep11 2-0	Apr30 2-2	Apr16 5-2	Apr26 0-1	Mar12 1-1	Mar30 0-1	Apr02 4-0	Mar23 1-2	Dec18 1-2		Jan08 4-1	May02 1-1	Jan01 3-1
ST JOHNSTONE	Dec04 2-2	Oct30 0-1	Oct16 0-1	Dec11 3-0	Nov13 2-1	Apr09 3-0	Feb26 0-4	Sep18 4-0	Dec25 1-2	Apr23 2-0	Jan03 3-1	Jan29 6-1	Oct02 1-4		Mar19 3-1	Mar12 1-3
STENHOUSEMUIR	Dec18 3-6	Oct02 1-1	Sep18 4-1	Mar26 4-1	Mar12 5-2	Mar05 5-0	Apr02 2-2	Dec25 3-4	Jan29 0-3	Jan03 6-1	Oct16 2-3	Apr16 3-1	Apr20 0-1	Nov27 0-1		Nov06 2-2
T LANARK	Nov13 3-4	Jan29 1-2	Oct02 2-0	Apr09 3-2	Dec04 9-0	Dec11 4-2	Mar19 2-1	Jan03 2-0	Oct16 2-1	Oct30 4-1	Apr20 1-1	Dec25 4-1	Sep18 3-1	Nov20 1-2	Feb26 0-2	

LEAGUE TABLES

DIVISION A

	P	W	D	L	F	A	W	D	L	F	A	Pts
Aberdeen	30	14	0	1	41	9	10	1	4	32	17	49
Celtic	30	10	4	1	42	16	9	4	2	34	21	46
Rangers	30	13	2	0	40	8	6	1	8	27	25	41
Hearts	30	10	2	3	40	25	6	5	4	34	20	39
Hibernian	30	8	2	5	28	23	7	2	6	36	31	34
St Mirren	30	8	3	4	31	23	4	5	6	24	31	32
Clyde	30	6	7	2	33	20	5	2	8	26	30	31
Dundee	30	9	2	4	32	21	4	2	9	16	27	30
Partick T	30	5	5	5	24	29	6	2	7	25	32	29
Kilmarnock	30	5	3	7	18	24	5	3	7	28	34	26
East Fife	30	6	1	8	32	35	3	5	7	19	27	24
Falkirk	30	6	6	3	28	23	2	2	11	14	31	24
Queen of South	30	7	2	6	22	29	2	4	9	16	27	24
Raith R	30	9	1	5	34	23	1	2	12	15	34	23
Motherwell	30	5	2	8	23	31	4	2	9	19	31	22
Stirling A	30	2	1	12	15	40	0	1	14	14	65	6

DIVISION B

	P	W	D	L	F	A	W	D	L	F	A	Pts
Airdrie	30	13	2	0	62	26	5	8	2	41	35	*46
Dunfermline A	30	12	2	1	45	17	7	2	6	27	23	*42
Hamilton A	30	10	3	2	38	20	7	2	6	36	31	39
Queen's Park	30	7	4	4	33	15	8	1	6	32	21	35
T. Lanark	30	10	1	4	41	20	3	6	6	22	29	33
Stenhousemuir	30	6	3	6	40	29	6	5	4	30	22	32
St Johnstone	30	8	1	6	31	21	7	1	7	29	30	32
Ayr U	30	10	3	2	36	20	4	1	10	25	53	32
Morton	30	7	4	4	31	24	5	1	9	27	45	29
Forfar A	30	7	3	5	35	31	4	3	8	28	49	28
Albion R	30	5	5	5	34	34	3	5	7	16	35	26
Arbroath	30	6	4	5	28	28	2	4	9	27	44	24
Dundee U	30	5	3	7	35	32	3	3	9	20	38	22
Cowdenbeath	30	4	2	9	29	41	4	3	8	26	31	21
Alloa	30	3	6	6	29	31	4	0	11	22	44	20
Brechin C	30	4	1	10	28	44	4	2	9	25	45	19

* Airdrie & Dunfermline A promoted.

Berwick, Dumbarton, East Striling, Montrose & Stranraer joined Division Two.

Scottish Football League Records
Season 1955-56

DIVISION A

	ABERDEEN	AIRDRIE	CELTIC	CLYDE	DUNDEE	DUNFERMLINE A	EAST FIFE	FALKIRK	HEARTS	HIBERNIAN	KILMARNOCK	MOTHERWELL	PARTICK T	QUEEN OF SOUTH	RAITH R	RANGERS	ST MIRREN	STIRLING A
ABERDEEN		Dec24 7-2	Jan07 1-0	Nov05 1-4	Sep24 2-0	Mar17 1-0	Mar03 7-3	Feb18 2-2	Apr07 4-1	Sep10 6-2	Apr21 3-2	Nov19 1-1	Apr28 0-4	Oct08 3-2	Mar31 3-5	Dec10 0-0	Feb11 4-1	Jan03 7-0
AIRDRIE	Apr25 2-2		Nov26 1-2	Mar17 1-8	Nov05 3-3	Oct15 1-2	Apr07 1-0	Sep17 4-2	Oct01 1-4	Mar07 3-1	Jan14 3-2	Jan02 3-0	Apr18 3-3	Dec17 3-3	Feb25 4-3	Jan28 0-4	Apr28 4-2	Nov19 4-0
CELTIC	Apr10 1-1	Mar31 3-1		Feb25 4-1	Mar17 1-0	Oct29 4-2	Nov05 0-0	Apr30 1-0	Jan28 1-1	Apr25 0-3	Dec10 0-2	Oct15 2-2	Dec17 5-1	Apr28 1-3	Oct01 2-0	Jan02 0-1	Nov19 3-0	Sep17 3-0
CLYDE	Mar10 0-5	Nov12 2-3	Oct22 1-3		Jan21 4-1	Dec03 1-2	Feb11 0-1	Dec24 1-2	Apr11 2-2	Sep17 2-2	Nov26 1-3	Apr18 1-3	Sep24 1-1	Sep10 1-3	Apr21 1-3	Dec31 0-4	Apr02 1-1	Mar07 2-1
DUNDEE	Jan02 2-4	Mar10 1-3	Nov12 1-2	Oct01 2-1		Sep17 3-0	Nov26 1-0	Oct29 0-0	Jan14 0-2	Apr23 3-2	Feb25 1-1	Dec31 2-1	Mar24 3-0	Dec03 3-0	Oct15 6-3	Apr02 0-3	Dec17 5-1	Apr13 2-1
DUNFERMLINE A	Nov12 2-2	Feb11 3-7	Mar07 1-1	Apr07 4-1	Oct08 2-1		Mar24 2-3	Dec17 1-5	Nov26 1-5	Oct22 2-1	Dec31 0-3	Nov05 1-0	Sep10 1-1	Sep24 0-1	Apr18 3-2	Apr25 1-0	Jan07 2-3	Jan21 0-0
EAST FIFE	Oct29 1-1	Dec03 8-1	Mar10 3-0	Oct15 1-1	Mar31 5-4	Nov19 3-1		Jan28 6-1	Feb25 1-4	Mar17 1-2	Sep17 2-1	Jan14 0-2	Oct01 1-0	Apr18 3-1	Jan02 3-0	Apr09 2-1	Dec24 1-1	Apr21 2-0
FALKIRK	Dec31 3-6	Jan07 1-4	Sep10 3-1	Apr25 1-2	Mar03 3-1	Apr21 0-1	Oct08 6-3		Dec10 1-1	Feb11 2-0	Apr07 0-0	Mar17 3-4	Oct22 2-1	Jan21 1-0	Nov19 3-1	Nov05 1-2	Nov26 5-1	Sep24 2-0
HEARTS	Dec03 3-0	Jan21 4-1	Oct08 2-1	Nov19 5-1	Sep10 4-0	Mar31 5-0	Oct22 3-1	Apr16 8-3		Sep24 0-1	Apr25 0-2	Dec17 7-1	Jan07 5-0	Feb11 2-2	Apr28 7-2	Mar17 1-1	Mar07 4-1	Nov05 5-0
HIBERNIAN	Jan14 1-3	Oct29 3-3	Dec24 2-3	Jan03 1-5	Dec10 6-3	Feb25 7-1	Nov12 3-1	Oct15 2-0	Jan02 2-2		Oct01 2-1	Jan28 7-0	Nov26 5-1	Mar21 4-1	Mar10 2-2	Apr21 2-2	Apr07 2-0	Dec31 6-1
KILMARNOCK	Dec17 1-0	Sep10 2-1	Apr13 0-0	Mar31 1-0	Oct22 0-0	Apr28 3-0	Jan07 3-0	Dec03 4-4	Dec24 2-4	Jan21 0-1		Mar03 2-1	Oct08 0-1	Nov05 2-2	Mar17 1-1	Nov19 1-2	Sep24 1-1	Feb11 3-2
MOTHERWELL	Mar24 1-1	Sep24 0-2	Feb11 2-2	Dec10 2-2	Apr28 1-2	Mar10 2-1	Sep10 5-2	Nov12 0-0	Apr23 1-0	Apr16 1-1	Oct29 2-1		Dec03 3-1	Oct22 1-2	Dec24 5-1	Mar31 1-2	Jan21 1-1	Jan07 2-0
PARTICK T	Apr30 0-2	Dec10 1-3	Apr23 2-0	Jan02 1-0	Nov19 1-2	Apr11 1-1	Dec31 2-2	Feb25 3-2	Apr02 2-0	Mar31 1-1	Jan28 1-1	Apr07 2-1		Apr25 9-1	Oct29 1-2	Oct15 1-3	Nov05 2-0	Mar17 6-1
QUEEN OF SOUTH	Jan28 2-2	Apr21 5-3	Dec31 1-3	Jan14 5-2	Apr07 2-1	Jan02 3-0	Dec10 2-1	Oct01 6-0	Oct15 4-3	Nov19 1-3	Mar10 2-0	Feb25 0-0	Dec24 3-2		Sep17 0-1	Oct29 2-1	Mar17 4-1	Nov26 4-0
RAITH R	Nov26 1-1	Oct22 3-3	Jan21 1-1	Dec17 1-3	Feb11 1-1	Dec10 1-1	Sep24 4-0	Apr02 2-0	Dec31 1-1	Nov05 0-4	Nov12 2-1	Apr26 4-3	Mar07 2-3	Jan07 3-1		Apr07 0-5	Sep10 2-2	Oct08 2-0
RANGERS	Apr18 1-0	Oct08 4-4	Sep24 0-0	Apr28 0-1	Jan07 3-1	Dec24 6-0	Jan21 3-0	Mar10 4-0	Nov12 4-1	Dec17 4-1	Mar24 3-2	Nov26 2-2	Feb11 1-0	Mar07 8-0	Dec03 4-0		Mar21 4-1	Sep10 0-0
ST MIRREN	Oct15 0-3	Dec31 7-2	Mar28 0-2	Jan28 3-0	Apr21 3-1	Mar03 4-2	Apr25 4-0	Mar31 2-0	Oct29 3-1	Dec03 0-1	Jan02 2-2	Apr09 1-1	Mar10 1-3	Nov12 4-1	Apr13 0-1	Feb25 0-1		Dec10 5-2
STIRLING A	Feb25 0-2	Mar24 1-1	Dec03 0-3	Oct29 1-2	Dec24 0-0	Oct01 1-2	Dec17 2-1	Jan02 1-0	Mar10 0-2	Apr28 0-3	Oct15 1-2	Apr11 0-1	Nov12 2-4	Mar31 2-0	Apr30 0-1	Oct22 2-2	Apr18 2-1	

DIVISION B

	ALBION R	ALLOA	ARBROATH	AYR U	BERWICK R	BRECHIN C	COWDENBEATH	DUMBARTON	DUNDEE U	E STIRLING	FORFAR A	HAMILTON A	MONTROSE	MORTON	QUEEN'S PARK	ST JOHNSTONE	STENHOUSEMUIR	STRANRAER	T LANARK
ALBION R		Nov12 1-1	Mar31 1-0	Oct08 4-2	Dec10 1-2	Mar24 1-3	Aug24 5-1	Mar10 0-1	Dec03 1-1	Sep14 2-2	Sep21 4-0	Sep24 3-2	Dec24 4-0	Apr23 0-2	Jan07 0-6	Feb11 2-2	Jan21 3-1	Dec31 2-3	Apr02 2-1
ALLOA	Mar17 5-1		Oct08 3-1	Sep10 1-2	Nov19 1-1	Feb11 0-1	Jan07 5-2	Aug24 3-3	Feb25 1-0	Apr21 3-0	Dec31 4-3	Jan21 3-3	Nov26 6-0	Feb18 5-1	Sep28 0-4	Mar03 2-0	Sep24 2-1	Apr07 2-1	Dec10 2-4
ARBROATH	Nov26 2-2	Jan28 2-1		Dec03 2-0	Oct15 4-0	Mar10 2-2	Nov12 0-2	Oct29 0-1	Oct01 2-4	Mar24 0-0	Jan02 0-4	Sep21 2-3	Jan14 2-1	Aug24 2-1	Apr18 0-1	Apr16 1-0	Dec31 0-1	Sep17 2-2	Dec17 1-0
AYR U	Jan28 3-2	Jan14 5-0	Apr07 5-0		Sep14 4-1	Apr30 2-0	Dec31 4-1	Nov12 5-1	Mar24 1-0	Nov26 8-1	Aug24 3-1	Apr21 3-4	Sep17 7-0	Jan02 3-1	Oct22 1-2	Dec10 4-3	Apr25 1-0	Oct15 3-0	Oct01 1-0
BERWICK R	Apr18 1-1	Mar24 0-0	Feb11 3-0	Sep28 3-4		Jan21 2-0	Sep24 2-1	Feb25 2-2	Dec17 3-2	Sep10 0-6	Nov12 0-0	Apr28 1-2	Apr07 3-1	Dec31 1-2	Nov26 0-2	Nov05 5-3	Jan07 0-4	Jan28 3-0	Oct29 3-1
BRECHIN C	Nov19 1-0	Oct15 4-2	Nov05 1-2	Mar03 1-0	Oct01 2-1		Oct08 5-4	Jan28 0-2	Aug24 2-2	Dec10 2-2	Jan14 1-1	Dec24 3-1	Jan02 3-1	Sep17 0-0	Dec31 2-0	Mar17 2-1	Nov26 1-3	Apr21 2-5	Feb25 3-1
COWDENBEATH	Apr28 3-1	Sep17 3-1	Mar17 2-1	Sep07 4-0	Jan02 1-1	Dec03 2-1		Jan14 2-6	Mar10 3-2	Feb25 1-1	Oct15 3-2	Dec10 4-0	Oct01 0-0	Sep14 3-1	Dec24 1-1	Feb18 1-1	Nov19 4-3	Oct29 4-3	Mar31 1-4
DUMBARTON	Nov05 3-2	Apr28 4-2	Mar03 1-1	Mar17 3-3	Sep21 3-2	Apr13 1-4	Sep10 3-1		Dec31 2-0	Sep24 5-1	Feb18 5-1	Jan03 2-1	Dec10 4-1	Nov26 2-0	Oct15 0-2	Jan07 0-2	Apr21 2-1	Nov19 5-2	Apr07 2-3
DUNDEE U	Apr07 2-0	Sep21 6-2	Jan21 2-1	Nov19 3-3	Apr21 8-1	Dec26 3-1	Nov05 4-4	Apr25 1-1		Jan07 4-0	Sep14 2-2	Feb11 3-3	Mar17 6-3	Dec10 4-2	Sep10 2-2	Sep24 1-1	Mar03 1-0	Mar31 2-2	Oct08 1-0
E STIRLING	Sep28 4-1	Dec17 2-1	Dec24 3-2	Mar31 0-4	Jan14 0-0	Apr18 0-2	Sep21 2-3	Jan02 3-1	Sep17 5-5		Oct29 3-3	Mar10 2-1	Jan28 3-0	Nov12 3-3	Dec03 1-1	Sep07 1-0	Jan03 2-4	Oct01 2-3	Feb11 1-4
FORFAR A	Feb25 2-2	Sep07 1-0	Sep24 1-4	Apr28 0-3	Mar17 3-0	Sep10 0-1	Feb11 4-1	Dec24 1-5	Sep28 1-1	Mar03 5-1		Mar31 3-3	Nov05 4-0	Apr07 4-3	Apr21 2-4	Apr11 0-1	Oct08 0-1	Dec10 3-2	Nov19 3-1
HAMILTON A	Jan02 2-2	Oct01 3-0	Feb25 2-0	Dec17 1-2	Aug24 3-3	Apr25 4-1	Apr18 3-3	Sep28 0-2	Oct15 3-0	Nov05 4-2	Nov26 5-0		Nov19 8-1	Jan28 5-1	Mar03 0-1	Apr07 2-2	Mar17 1-0	Jan14 6-1	Oct22 1-3
MONTROSE	Apr25 2-2	Mar31 2-4	Sep10 1-6	Jan07 2-4	Dec03 0-1	Sep24 1-2	Jan21 2-4	Apr18 1-4	Nov12 2-2	Feb18 5-1	Mar10 1-2	Mar24 2-1		Oct29 1-2	Sep21 1-2	Apr28 0-6	Feb11 1-5	Sep14 4-1	Sep07 2-0
MORTON	Dec17 2-2	Dec24 1-1	Apr28 2-0	Sep24 0-2	Apr25 4-0	Jan07 2-1	Sep28 4-0	Mar31 1-2	Apr18 3-2	Mar17 5-1	Dec03 2-1	Oct08 3-2	Mar03 5-1		Jan21 2-5	Nov19 2-2	Sep10 3-0	Feb25 3-2	Nov05 6-1
QUEEN'S PARK	Sep17 2-0	Sep14 1-0	Nov19 2-0	Nov05 4-2	Mar31 1-2	Sep07 1-1	Apr25 3-0	Feb11 7-0	Jan14 0-0	Apr07 1-0	Dec17 3-2	Oct29 3-0	Feb25 7-1	Apr02 1-1		Oct08 0-2	Dec10 2-0	Mar17 0-1	Jan02 3-1
ST JOHNSTONE	Oct15 7-2	Dec26 4-1	Sep28 3-0	Apr18 0-0	Mar10 2-1	Nov12 3-1	Dec17 4-2	Apr02 2-1	Jan02 2-0	Dec31 2-1	Oct01 3-1	Dec03 7-3	Aug24 3-0	Mar24 4-1	Apr30 0-0		Oct22 5-2	Apr25 3-2	Jan14 2-0
STENHOUSEMUIR	Oct01 1-1	Jan02 2-2	Sep06 5-1	Dec24 4-1	Sep17 5-1	Mar31 2-0	Mar24 3-0	Dec17 2-3	Oct29 4-1	Aug24 2-2	Jan28 1-0	Nov12 6-1	Oct15 4-3	Jan14 1-0	Apr28 2-1	Feb25 2-1		Mar10 4-1	Sep13 1-1
STRANRAER	Sep07 3-1	Dec03 2-1	Jan07 3-3	Feb11 3-6	Feb18 1-0	Dec17 1-2	Mar03 2-4	Mar24 2-1	Nov26 2-0	Jan21 6-5	Jan03 2-2	Sep10 4-2	Sep28 6-1	Sep21 1-0	Nov12 1-1	Dec24 0-2	Nov05 1-3		Apr28 4-2
T LANARK	Mar03 7-0	Apr24 2-0	Feb18 2-1	Jan21 3-2	Dec24 3-3	Sep21 1-2	Nov26 1-5	Dec03 1-0	Jan28 0-1	Oct15 1-3	Mar24 0-0	Jan07 6-1	Dec31 9-0	Mar10 4-0	Sep24 0-2	Sep10 2-1	Sep28 5-2	Aug24 6-2	

LEAGUE TABLES

DIVISION A

	P	W	D	L	F	A	W	D	L	F	A	Pts
Rangers	34	12	4	1	51	13	10	4	3	34	14	52
Aberdeen	34	11	3	3	52	29	7	7	3	35	21	46
Hearts	34	13	2	2	65	17	6	5	6	34	30	45
Hibernian	34	11	4	2	57	24	8	3	6	29	26	45
Celtic	34	9	4	4	31	18	7	5	5	24	21	41
Queen of South	34	12	2	3	46	23	4	3	10	23	50	37
Airdrie	34	8	4	5	41	41	6	4	7	44	55	36
Kilmarnock	34	7	6	4	26	20	5	4	8	26	25	34
Partick T	34	8	4	5	36	22	5	3	9	26	38	33
Motherwell	34	7	6	4	30	21	4	5	8	23	38	33
Raith R	34	6	7	4	30	30	6	2	9	28	45	33
East Fife	34	11	3	3	43	21	2	2	13	18	48	31
Dundee	34	10	2	5	35	24	2	4	11	21	41	30
Falkirk	34	9	2	6	37	28	2	4	11	21	47	28
St Mirren	34	9	2	6	39	23	1	5	11	18	47	27
Dunfermline A	34	6	4	7	26	36	4	2	11	16	46	26
Clyde	34	2	4	11	21	40	6	2	9	29	34	22
Stirling A	34	4	3	10	15	27	0	2	15	8	55	13

DIVISION B

	P	W	D	L	F	A	W	D	L	F	A	Pts
Queen's Park	36	12	3	3	41	13	11	5	2	37	15	54
Ayr U	36	16	0	2	63	17	8	3	7	40	38	51
St Johnstone	36	16	2	0	56	18	5	5	8	30	27	49
Dumbarton	36	12	2	4	47	29	9	3	6	36	33	47
Stenhousemuir	36	13	4	1	51	20	7	0	11	31	34	44
Brechin C	36	10	4	4	35	28	8	2	8	25	28	42
Cowdenbeath	36	11	5	2	42	29	5	2	11	38	56	39
Dundee U	36	10	8	0	55	28	2	6	10	23	37	38
Morton	36	12	3	3	50	25	3	3	12	21	44	36
T. Lanark	36	11	2	5	53	25	5	1	12	27	39	35
Hamilton A	36	10	4	4	53	24	3	3	12	33	60	33
Stranraer	36	10	3	5	44	36	4	2	12	33	56	33
Alloa	36	11	3	4	48	28	1	4	13	19	45	31
Berwick R	36	8	4	6	32	31	3	5	10	20	46	31
Forfar A	36	8	3	7	37	33	2	6	10	25	42	29
E. Stirling	36	7	5	6	37	38	2	5	11	29	56	28
Albion R	36	8	4	6	36	30	0	7	11	22	52	27
Arbroath	36	7	4	7	24	25	3	2	13	23	42	26
Montrose	36	4	2	12	30	49	0	1	17	14	84	11

Scottish Football League Records
Season 1956-57

DIVISION 1

	ABERDEEN	AIRDRIE	AYR U	CELTIC	DUNDEE	DUNFERMLINE A	EAST FIFE	FALKIRK	HEARTS	HIBERNIAN	KILMARNOCK	MOTHERWELL	PARTICK T	QUEEN OF SOUTH	QUEEN'S PARK	RAITH R	RANGERS	ST MIRREN
ABERDEEN		Oct13 2-3	Feb09 2-2	Apr22 0-1	Jan01 2-1	Nov17 3-2	Jan19 1-0	Apr13 3-1	Dec29 2-3	Sep29 3-1	Nov10 1-3	Dec22 2-3	Apr24 2-0	Dec01 5-1	Sep15 2-1	Mar06 1-0	Mar23 1-2	Jan05 4-0
AIRDRIE	Jan26 1-5		Mar27 4-1	Dec22 3-7	Mar23 3-2	Apr27 3-1	Mar16 5-2	Oct06 2-3	Oct20 3-4	Dec08 5-3	Apr13 0-1	Sep22 1-4	Nov10 0-1	Mar06 4-0	Jan12 2-0	Jan02 2-2	Sep08 3-3	Dec01 4-1
AYR U	Oct20 1-6	Oct27 4-1		Nov17 1-3	Feb16 0-1	Mar23 2-1	Dec08 2-2	Jan02 6-1	Oct06 0-2	Mar30 2-3	Jan26 0-2	Mar02 1-2	Dec29 2-1	Sep22 0-1	Apr19 4-4	Sep08 0-3	Jan12 1-0	Nov10 1-2
CELTIC	Feb23 2-1	Apr20 3-0	Mar16 4-0		Mar06 1-1	Dec15 3-1	Nov10 4-0	Jan26 4-0	Dec01 1-1	Apr27 2-1	Jan02 1-1	Jan12 2-1	Nov24 1-1	Apr29 0-0	Sep08 2-0	Oct20 1-1	Sep22 0-2	Apr17 2-3
DUNDEE	Sep22 4-2	Nov24 2-1	Dec15 5-0	Nov03 2-1		Dec08 2-0	Apr20 0-1	Mar30 1-2	Jan12 0-3	Mar09 0-3	Sep08 1-1	Apr08 3-1	Feb23 5-1	Jan26 5-2	Oct20 3-1	Apr27 3-0	Jan02 1-3	Mar16 1-1
DUNFERMLINE A	Mar16 1-3	Dec29 3-3	Nov24 1-3	Apr13 0-1	Mar02 1-1		Feb23 1-4	Sep22 2-1	Sep08 2-3	Dec22 1-3	Oct06 2-1	Jan26 3-1	Dec01 2-1	Nov10 4-3	Jan02 3-0	Jan12 2-2	Apr29 3-4	Nov03 0-2
EAST FIFE	Oct06 4-3	Nov17 4-2	Apr06 2-2	Mar09 2-0	Dec22 2-0	Oct27 3-4		Oct20 1-1	Jan26 1-3	Nov24 1-6	Jan12 0-0	Jan02 1-2	Dec15 2-1	Sep08 3-1	Mar02 0-1	Sep22 2-3	Mar30 0-3	Apr27 5-2
FALKIRK	Dec15 2-5	Jan19 4-1	Sep15 2-3	Oct13 0-1	Dec01 1-1	Jan01 0-1	Feb09 4-3		Oct27 0-2	Jan05 0-1	Mar06 2-0	Apr27 1-2	Apr29 4-1	Apr10 3-2	Nov10 1-1	Dec22 0-4	Nov17 0-2	Sep29 4-5
HEARTS	Apr27 3-0	Feb09 2-0	Jan19 2-2	Mar30 3-1	Sep29 2-1	Jan05 5-1	Oct13 2-5	Feb23 1-1		Jan01 0-2	Nov17 3-2	Dec08 3-2	Nov03 1-0	Dec22 3-1	Nov24 6-1	Mar09 2-1	Apr13 0-1	Sep15 2-2
HIBERNIAN	Jan12 4-1	Apr06 6-0	Dec01 3-0	Dec29 3-3	Nov10 1-1	Apr20 0-0	Mar23 4-0	Sep08 6-1	Sep22 2-3		Oct27 0-0	Oct20 1-1	Mar16 2-0	Jan02 1-1	Oct06 1-1	Jan26 1-4	Mar02 2-3	Dec15 1-1
KILMARNOCK	Mar09 2-1	Dec15 3-4	Oct13 4-1	Apr26 0-0	Jan05 4-0	Jan19 0-0	Sep29 1-1	Nov03 1-1	Mar16 4-1	Feb23 2-1		Dec01 2-2	Feb09 1-1	Apr03 1-3	Apr27 1-0	Nov24 3-0	Dec22 3-2	Jan01 3-2
MOTHERWELL	Apr20 2-5	Jan01 2-0	Nov03 4-2	Sep29 1-0	Jan19 4-2	Oct13 3-2	Sep15 2-2	Dec29 1-3	Apr06 1-3	Feb09 3-0	Mar30 0-2		Jan05 2-2	Oct27 7-0	Dec15 4-2	Nov17 0-2	Mar09 2-5	Nov24 3-0
PARTICK T	Jan02 1-2	Mar09 2-1	Apr27 5-1	Apr10 3-1	Apr22 5-0	Mar30 3-0	Apr13 2-1	Dec08 2-1	Mar02 2-2	Nov17 3-0	Oct20 2-1	Sep08 2-3		Jan12 2-1	Sep22 0-0	Dec25 1-1	Jan26 0-3	Dec22 2-0
QUEEN OF SOUTH	Mar30 2-2	Nov03 3-3	Jan01 5-1	Jan19 4-3	Oct13 3-1	Mar09 3-2	Jan05 4-2	Nov24 1-2	Apr20 0-2	Sep15 2-0	Dec08 0-3	Apr24 2-2	Sep29 3-0		Mar16 1-6	Oct06 1-5	Apr27 0-3	Feb09 2-0
QUEEN'S PARK	Dec08 0-2	Sep29 0-2	Dec25 2-0	Jan05 2-0	Feb09 2-0	Apr16 1-3	Nov03 3-0	Mar09 1-1	Mar25 0-1	Jan19 2-1	Dec29 1-2	Apr13 1-0	Jan01 1-1	Nov17 7-0		Apr30 1-0	Apr22 4-6	Oct13 5-0
RAITH R	Nov03 3-2	Sep15 4-6	Jan05 5-2	Feb09 3-1	Dec29 1-2	Sep29 2-2	Jan01 4-1	Apr26 2-3	Nov10 2-3	Oct13 1-1	Apr15 4-2	Mar16 3-2	Jan19 0-3	Apr13 3-1	Dec01 3-0		Dec08 5-1	Feb23 7-0
RANGERS	Nov24 3-1	Apr17 3-2	Sep29 3-1	Jan01 2-0	Mar20 4-0	Feb09 2-1	Dec01 6-1	Mar16 1-1	Dec15 5-3	Nov03 5-3	Sep15 0-1	Nov10 2-3	Oct13 4-1	Dec29 4-0	Feb23 3-3	Apr02 3-1		Jan19 1-0
ST MIRREN	Sep08 0-2	Mar30 2-3	Mar09 1-0	Dec08 0-2	Nov17 2-3	Mar06 3-2	Dec29 3-1	Jan12 0-0	Jan02 0-2	Apr13 4-2	Sep22 2-0	Mar23 4-0	Apr20 1-1	Oct20 7-1	Jan26 4-1	Oct27 3-3	Oct06 1-2	

DIVISION 2

	ALBION R	ALLOA	ARBROATH	BERWICK R	BRECHIN C	CLYDE	COWDENBEATH	DUMBARTON	DUNDEE U	E STIRLING	FORFAR A	HAMILTON A	MONTROSE	MORTON	ST JOHNSTONE	STENHOUSEMUIR	STIRLING A	STRANRAER	T LANARK
ALBION R		Mar09 1-2	Jan19 2-0	Dec15 6-3	Oct27 2-3	Nov24 1-1	Dec29 5-1	Apr20 3-1	Mar30 5-1	Jan05 7-1	Mar02 3-1	Jan01 2-1	Sep19 6-1	Apr29 3-2	Oct13 4-1	Nov17 6-1	Sep05 1-1	Sep15 2-1	Feb09 5-0
ALLOA	Nov10 2-1		Apr27 0-6	Feb16 2-2	Mar02 2-3	Dec01 1-2	Apr06 3-2	Dec15 2-3	Aug22 2-2	Sep29 2-2	Mar23 5-3	Nov17 3-0	Sep12 7-0	Feb09 2-4	Jan19 1-4	Jan01 0-4	Jan05 2-3	Oct13 2-1	Sep15 1-1
ARBROATH	Feb16 5-3	Dec29 2-0		Jan02 5-1	Dec01 1-1	Jan12 0-1	Jan26 3-0	Oct27 3-2	Apr08 2-2	Nov17 5-0	Feb02 5-1	Apr06 6-1	Feb09 3-2	Sep19 2-1	Oct20 1-0	Mar23 1-1	Mar02 4-2	Apr15 2-3	Dec22 2-0
BERWICK R	Apr13 1-2	Feb23 4-2	Sep15 2-1		Apr24 1-2	Apr17 0-2	Mar16 1-1	Jan12 1-0	Dec25 0-6	Mar23 5-2	Nov10 4-3	Nov03 6-2	Oct13 1-2	Dec08 1-3	Dec29 1-5	Dec22 1-4	Dec01 1-2	Jan05 3-4	Aug22 2-5
BRECHIN C	Jan12 1-1	Nov03 2-4	Mar30 2-1	Feb09 2-2		Sep08 1-1	Oct06 0-2	Mar09 4-1	Jan02 0-0	Feb16 4-1	Apr13 2-2	Sep19 3-1	Apr29 2-0	Dec29 3-2	Mar23 0-2	Oct20 2-1	Nov17 2-0	Dec22 6-0	Dec08 1-3
CLYDE	Mar23 5-0	Mar30 4-0	Sep29 2-1	Jan19 6-0	Jan05 2-2		Nov03 4-0	Dec29 5-3	Mar09 7-1	Apr03 6-1	Dec22 3-1	Feb09 4-1	Dec08 9-0	Nov17 4-1	Oct27 5-1	Oct31 3-2	Oct13 5-2	Apr13 3-1	Jan01 2-1
COWDENBEATH	Apr27 5-2	Dec08 5-2	Oct13 2-0	Nov17 3-1	Jan19 3-3	Apr01 0-0		Aug22 2-1	Dec15 6-2	Jan01 4-1	Feb09 2-1	Jan05 4-0	Oct27 6-0	Mar09 1-2	Apr20 3-2	Sep29 3-0	Apr17 3-2	Mar30 1-1	Feb16 3-4
DUMBARTON	Dec22 8-1	Apr13 5-0	Mar06 3-1	Sep29 4-0	Nov10 2-2	Oct20 2-3	Sep19 2-3		Dec08 3-2	Sep15 3-2	Apr10 5-1	Sep05 2-0	Nov17 7-0	Mar23 2-2	Feb09 4-1	Jan05 6-2	Jan01 1-3	Jan19 4-1	Oct13 0-1
DUNDEE U	Dec01 7-0	Sep19 4-3	Jan05 1-0	Oct01 6-1	Apr22 2-1	Nov10 2-4	Apr13 4-1	Apr17 3-1		Dec22 3-1	Nov17 2-1	Oct13 2-1	Mar23 2-2	Mar02 0-7	Jan01 1-2	Jan19 2-0	Feb09 2-0	Sep29 2-2	Oct27 0-1
E STIRLING	Sep08 1-5	Jan12 1-2	Apr24 1-3	Nov24 1-1	Feb23 2-2	Sep05 2-6	Sep22 2-3	Jan02 3-2	Apr30 3-2		Jan26 2-0	Dec29 0-5	Feb02 4-4	Mar30 0-2	Apr13 1-1	Dec08 0-2	Sep19 5-3	Mar09 1-1	Nov03 1-4
FORFAR A	Dec08 3-3	Nov24 3-0	Jan01 2-1	Mar09 6-1	Dec15 2-3	Apr20 4-1	Apr24 4-0	Nov03 0-2	Mar16 3-1	Oct13 3-4		Jan19 2-4	Mar30 6-1	Sep12 3-2	Jan05 3-3	Apr27 1-1	Feb23 0-4	Aug22 1-2	Sep29 2-1
HAMILTON A	Apr22 2-1	Mar16 5-0	Dec08 2-1	Mar02 4-0	Aug22 4-1	Apr24 0-0	Sep08 1-4	Sep12 1-1	Jan26 4-1	Apr27 4-0	Sep22 3-2		Jan12 4-1	Jan02 1-1	Dec01 4-0	Nov10 2-1	Dec22 1-2	Feb23 1-1	Mar23 1-1
MONTROSE	Aug22 3-0	Sep05 3-4	Dec15 2-1	Jan26 1-2	Jan01 2-4	Apr22 1-5	Feb23 1-0	Mar16 1-6	Nov24 2-2	Jan19 5-4	Dec01 3-3	Sep29 1-1		Feb16 1-2	Sep15 0-2	Mar02 2-3	Nov10 2-1	Apr27 4-4	Jan05 1-1
MORTON	Apr08 2-5	Apr24 3-1	Aug22 4-3	Apr06 2-2	Apr27 6-3	Mar16 0-0	Nov10 0-1	Nov24 1-1	Nov03 4-1	Dec01 4-3	Sep05 5-1	Sep15 3-1	Dec22 1-0		Sep29 2-3	Oct13 1-0	Jan19 0-0	Jan01 5-3	Apr13 1-5
ST JOHNSTONE	Jan26 1-1	Oct06 1-2	Mar16 2-2	Apr27 2-2	Nov24 1-2	Apr29 2-3	Dec22 4-1	Apr24 0-6	Sep22 3-2	Dec15 5-0	Sep08 4-2	Mar30 4-1	Jan02 5-1	Jan12 1-1		Aug22 5-2	Feb16 1-3	Nov03 1-3	Mar09 3-6
STENHOUSEMUIR	Mar16 4-3	Sep22 1-1	Nov24 2-3	Apr19 2-1	Sep05 2-0	Jan02 0-4	Jan12 2-4	Sep08 1-3	Oct06 3-1	Apr17 4-0	Dec29 4-1	Mar09 2-2	Nov03 7-2	Jan26 1-2	Sep19 4-2		Dec15 4-3	Apr23 0-0	Mar30 2-3
STIRLING A	Sep12 1-1	Sep08 5-1	Nov03 1-3	Mar30 7-1	Mar16 2-1	Jan26 2-4	Jan02 0-4	Sep22 3-1	Apr24 2-1	Aug22 3-1	Oct27 4-1	Apr19 1-2	Oct20 3-0	Oct06 6-0	Dec08 1-0	Sep15 1-1		Nov24 3-3	Dec29 3-0
STRANRAER	Jan02 3-5	Jan26 3-0	Sep12 3-0	Sep08 5-3	Apr19 3-1	Dec15 2-3	Dec01 2-2	Oct06 5-4	Jan12 1-0	Nov10 1-1	Sep19 4-2	Oct27 2-2	Dec29 0-2	Sep22 1-2	Mar02 4-3	Feb09 3-1	Mar23 4-2		Nov17 2-0
T LANARK	Apr23 4-0	Jan02 4-3	Apr29 3-0	Sep19 2-0	Apr06 5-1	Sep22 1-3	Sep05 3-2	Jan26 7-0	Apr15 2-3	Mar02 5-2	Jan12 6-1	Nov24 3-0	Oct06 6-1	Dec15 5-1	Nov10 1-2	Dec01 7-0	Apr27 1-0	Mar16 3-0	

LEAGUE TABLES

DIVISION 1

	P	W	D	L	F	A	W	D	L	F	A	Pts
Rangers	34	13	2	2	51	22	13	1	3	45	26	55
Hearts	34	11	3	3	40	23	13	2	2	41	25	53
Kilmarnock	34	9	6	2	35	20	7	4	6	22	19	42
Raith R	34	10	2	5	52	32	6	5	6	32	26	39
Celtic	34	9	6	2	33	14	6	2	9	25	29	38
Aberdeen	34	10	1	6	36	24	8	1	8	43	35	38
Motherwell	34	9	2	6	41	32	7	3	7	31	34	37
Partick T	34	11	3	3	37	18	2	5	10	16	33	34
Hibernian	34	6	8	3	38	20	6	1	10	31	36	33
Dundee	34	10	2	5	38	23	3	4	10	17	38	32
Airdrie	34	8	2	7	45	40	5	2	10	32	49	30
St Mirren	34	8	3	6	37	25	4	3	10	21	47	30
Queen's Park	34	9	2	6	33	19	2	5	10	22	40	29
Falkirk	34	5	2	10	28	35	5	6	6	23	35	28
East Fife	34	7	3	7	33	34	3	3	11	26	48	26
Queen of South	34	8	3	6	36	37	2	2	13	18	59	25
Dunfermline A	34	6	3	8	31	36	3	3	11	23	38	24
Ayr U	34	5	2	10	27	35	2	3	12	21	54	19

DIVISION 2

	P	W	D	L	F	A	W	D	L	F	A	Pts
Clyde	36	17	1	0	79	18	12	5	1	43	21	64
T.lanark	36	15	0	3	68	19	9	3	6	37	32	51
Cowdenbeath	36	13	3	2	56	24	7	2	9	31	41	45
Morton	36	10	4	4	44	33	8	3	7	37	37	43
Albion R	36	14	2	2	64	22	4	4	10	34	58	42
Brechin C	36	9	5	4	37	24	6	5	7	35	44	40
Stranraer	36	11	3	4	48	33	4	7	7	31	44	40
Stirling A	36	11	3	4	48	25	6	2	10	33	39	39
Dumbarton	36	12	2	4	63	25	5	2	11	38	45	38
Arbroath	36	13	3	2	52	21	4	1	13	27	36	38
Hamilton A	36	11	5	2	44	18	3	3	12	25	50	36
St Johnstone	36	7	4	7	45	40	7	2	9	34	40	34
Dundee U	36	12	2	4	45	28	2	4	12	30	52	34
Stenhousemuir	36	9	3	6	45	35	4	3	11	26	46	32
Alloa	36	6	4	8	39	43	5	1	12	27	56	27
Forfar A	36	9	3	6	48	34	0	2	16	27	66	23
Montrose	36	5	5	8	35	45	2	2	14	19	79	21
Berwick R	36	6	1	11	35	48	1	5	12	23	66	20
E. Stirling	36	4	5	9	30	48	1	2	15	26	73	17

Scottish Football League Records
Season 1957-58

DIVISION 1

	ABERDEEN	AIRDRIE	CELTIC	CLYDE	DUNDEE	EAST FIFE	FALKIRK	HEARTS	HIBERNIAN	KILMARNOCK	MOTHERWELL	PARTICK T	QUEEN OF SOUTH	QUEEN'S PARK	RAITH R	RANGERS	ST MIRREN	T LANARK
ABERDEEN		Oct05 5-1	Apr05 0-1	Dec07 2-1	Sep21 3-0	Jan02 6-2	Feb22 1-2	Apr16 0-4	Sep07 0-1	Nov23 1-2	Apr09 4-3	Oct26 1-3	Apr12 3-4	Nov09 5-2	Mar22 3-2	Dec28 1-2	Jan11 3-1	Mar08 2-4
AIRDRIE	Oct12 2-6		Nov30 2-5	Apr21 2-2	Dec28 7-1	Nov02 2-1	Apr05 6-2	Sep14 2-7	Nov16 1-4	Jan04 2-1	Jan01 4-1	Mar15 4-1	Apr30 2-1	Apr02 2-2	Dec21 2-1	Jan18 3-4	Mar01 2-3	Oct19 2-3
CELTIC	Jan18 1-1	Mar22 4-2		Apr09 6-2	Dec07 0-0	Mar05 4-0	Jan04 2-2	Dec28 0-2	Mar19 4-0	Nov02 4-0	Apr21 2-2	Dec21 2-3	Dec25 1-2	Apr07 5-1	Oct12 1-1	Jan01 0-1	Nov16 2-2	Apr30 4-1
CLYDE	Mar29 5-1	Jan11 3-1	Dec14 3-6		Oct05 3-1	Sep07 2-1	Nov09 5-0	Nov23 2-1	May03 2-1	Apr16 3-2	Nov30 4-1	Sep21 6-1	Apr28 3-1	Apr12 2-3	Feb22 6-2	Mar08 1-3	Oct26 2-1	May10 1-1
DUNDEE	Jan01 1-2	Apr26 1-3	Mar29 5-3	Jan18 2-0		Apr30 2-0	Dec21 2-4	Jan04 0-5	Oct19 3-0	Dec25 2-0	Oct12 3-0	Nov16 5-0	Nov02 2-1	Nov30 1-0	Sep14 0-2	Dec14 1-2	Mar15 0-0	Mar05 2-0
EAST FIFE	Apr21 3-2	Feb22 0-6	Nov09 0-3	Jan04 1-3	Oct26 3-1		Apr16 2-1	Jan18 0-3	Dec14 2-3	Oct12 1-2	Dec21 2-1	Sep14 2-2	Mar08 1-2	Sep28 4-0	Jan01 2-2	Mar22 0-1	Mar29 1-2	Nov23 0-6
FALKIRK	Nov02 4-4	Dec14 3-0	Sep07 0-1	Mar05 1-1	Apr12 0-2	Oct19 4-1		Mar22 0-4	Oct05 1-3	Dec07 1-1	Apr30 1-1	Mar31 1-2	Sep21 1-1	Dec28 3-2	Mar08 3-2	Nov23 0-4	Jan02 3-1	Jan11 4-2
HEARTS	Oct19 4-0	Jan02 4-0	Mar14 5-3	Mar19 2-2	Sep07 6-0	Oct05 9-0	Nov30 9-1		Sep21 3-1	Dec14 2-1	Nov02 2-2	Jan11 4-1	Mar10 3-1	Nov16 8-0	Mar29 4-1	Apr30 2-1	Dec21 5-1	Jan25 7-2
HIBERNIAN	Jan04 0-1	Sep28 4-0	Nov23 0-1	Dec28 1-3	Apr16 1-1	Apr18 0-1	Jan18 3-3	Jan01 0-2		Apr12 1-2	Sep14 2-1	Nov09 5-1	Mar22 1-2	Oct12 2-0	Oct26 2-2	Apr21 3-1	Feb22 5-5	Dec07 4-0
KILMARNOCK	Mar19 2-0	Sep07 3-1	Feb22 1-1	Oct19 3-2	Jan11 1-1	Mar15 4-0	Mar29 1-1	Apr05 1-1	Dec21 1-4		Nov16 0-1	Nov30 4-1	Jan02 2-0	Oct26 3-1	Apr26 1-1	Mar10 3-3	Sep21 4-2	Oct05 2-4
MOTHERWELL	Dec14 4-1	Sep21 1-2	Jan11 1-3	Mar22 1-1	Apr28 1-0	Apr12 2-0	Oct26 2-5	Feb22 0-4	Jan02 3-1	Mar08 2-2		Oct05 4-1	Nov23 4-2	Apr16 4-1	Nov09 0-2	Dec07 2-2	Sep07 4-2	Apr26 1-2
PARTICK T	Feb01 1-0	Nov23 2-0	Apr12 0-1	Jan01 2-2	Mar08 2-0	Dec28 5-1	Oct12 3-0	Nov11 1-3	Mar05 2-0	Mar22 2-0	Jan18 3-2		Dec07 4-3	Jan04 1-4	Dec14 3-2	May05 1-2	Oct19 3-2	Nov02 2-3
QUEEN OF SOUTH	Dec21 1-2	Oct26 3-2	Apr16 4-3	Oct12 0-3	Feb22 4-0	Nov16 0-3	Jan01 2-2	Nov09 1-4	Nov30 3-0	Feb01 1-2	Mar19 1-2	Mar29 1-3		Sep14 2-1	Sep28 1-1	Jan04 1-1	Apr26 2-2	Apr05 6-1
QUEEN'S PARK	Mar05 2-5	Dec07 1-3	Jan02 0-3	Dec21 1-4	Mar22 2-7	Jan11 1-4	Apr21 0-2	Mar08 1-4	Jan25 1-2	Apr30 1-2	Apr23 0-7	Sep07 0-6	Oct05 3-0		Nov23 2-3	Nov02 2-4	Apr14 0-1	Jan01 1-3
RAITH R	Nov30 0-1	Apr12 4-0	Jan25 1-2	Nov02 5-0	Jan02 4-0	Sep21 0-2	Nov16 4-1	Dec07 0-3	Apr30 2-0	Dec28 1-1	Mar05 1-1	Apr05 3-2	Oct19 3-1	Mar15 3-1		Apr23 1-3	Oct05 1-0	Sep07 4-2
RANGERS	Apr26 5-0	May03 1-2	Sep21 2-3	Nov16 2-0	May10 0-1	Nov30 3-3	Mar19 3-2	Oct26 2-3	Jan11 3-1	Nov09 3-4	Mar29 2-2	Jan02 2-0	Sep07 4-2	Feb22 5-1	Apr16 4-1		Apr28 1-0	Dec21 5-1
ST MIRREN	Sep28 3-1	Nov09 5-0	Mar08 1-1	Apr30 1-0	Nov23 1-1	Dec07 3-0	Sep14 2-1	Apr12 2-3	Nov02 2-3	Jan01 2-1	Jan04 1-3	Apr18 1-1	Dec28 1-2	Dec14 3-1	Jan18 0-4	Oct12 1-3		Mar22 2-2
T LANARK	Nov16 3-1	Apr16 3-1	Oct26 0-2	Jan02 2-5	Nov09 5-1	Mar19 1-2	Sep28 3-5	Oct12 0-0	Mar29 1-1	Jan18 2-1	Dec28 4-2	Feb22 1-4	Dec14 2-3	Sep21 1-3	Jan04 2-0	Apr12 1-5	Nov30 1-3	

DIVISION 2

	ALBION R	ALLOA	ARBROATH	AYR U	BERWICK R	BRECHIN C	COWDENBEATH	DUMBARTON	DUNDEE U	DUNFERMLINE A	E STIRLING	FORFAR A	HAMILTON A	MONTROSE	MORTON	ST JOHNSTONE	STENHOUSEMUIR	STIRLING A	STRANRAER
ALBION R		Nov09 2-3	Apr26 2-4	Sep18 2-1	Oct26 1-0	Sep07 2-2	Apr28 1-3	Aug21 3-1	Dec14 3-1	Nov23 1-0	Oct05 3-1	Apr12 1-3	Sep21 1-1	Feb22 0-3	Mar08 2-2	Mar22 2-1	Jan11 6-1	Jan02 0-2	Dec07 3-0
ALLOA	Mar01 4-1		Sep07 2-3	Feb22 2-2	Nov02 5-3	Jan02 5-3	Dec07 4-2	Sep18 4-3	Oct19 2-2	Mar08 2-4	Feb15 2-2	Apr30 2-3	Jan11 1-1	Dec28 4-2	Mar22 4-1	Oct05 2-0	Sep21 1-1	Aug21 0-2	Nov23 2-1
ARBROATH	Dec28 1-3	Jan04 2-2		Nov16 4-3	Jan18 4-0	Dec14 1-2	Oct19 4-2	Feb22 3-5	Sep04 3-1	Sep14 0-5	Dec07 4-1	Jan01 2-1	Apr12 2-3	Sep11 2-2	Nov23 2-3	Nov09 2-0	Feb01 2-0	Mar22 3-2	Sep28 3-2
AYR U	Sep04 4-0	Oct12 4-3	Mar08 3-3		Apr16 0-0	Nov09 5-3	Apr12 3-0	Feb15 4-0	Jan04 1-1	Jan18 0-3	Sep10 3-2	Sep28 7-4	Dec07 2-3	Mar22 2-1	Sep14 4-1	Dec28 4-1	Nov23 4-3	Dec14 2-1	Jan01 0-0
BERWICK R	Apr23 2-1	Sep14 1-2	Oct05 1-2	Oct19 0-6		Jan11 1-3	Sep07 0-2	Jan25 2-2	Nov16 1-2	Nov09 1-5	Dec28 2-2	Mar22 4-5	Dec26 3-0	Dec07 1-1	Mar01 2-6	Nov23 2-0	Aug21 0-1	Sep21 0-3	Dec14 2-1
BRECHIN C	Jan04 2-1	Apr21 2-2	Apr05 2-1	Mar01 3-5	Apr30 4-1		Feb15 3-2	Oct19 5-2	Oct12 1-1	Sep04 1-4	Nov23 3-2	Apr23 3-2	Feb22 3-0	Jan01 0-2	Jan18 4-2	Apr12 0-2	Dec28 1-2	Dec07 1-1	Mar22 2-1
COWDENBEATH	Oct12 3-2	Mar29 2-4	Apr16 3-2	Dec21 6-5	Jan04 3-2	Oct26 2-2		Apr26 3-2	Sep11 1-1	Jan01 0-4	Mar22 6-0	Sep14 5-2	Nov23 1-1	Apr23 4-2	Dec14 6-0	Feb22 3-4	Mar08 2-2	Nov09 3-0	Jan18 8-1
DUMBARTON	Sep11 6-0	Sep04 4-0	Nov02 4-0	Oct26 4-2	Oct12 4-1	Apr18 5-1	Dec28 6-1		Sep28 2-0	Dec14 2-0	Mar01 1-3	Nov23 1-1	Mar08 0-1	Jan18 3-1	Jan01 4-0	Dec07 6-0	Mar22 6-1	Apr12 2-2	Sep14 1-0
DUNDEE U	Apr05 2-1	Apr16 1-7	Sep18 5-5	Sep07 3-4	May03 7-0	Apr28 1-2	Aug21 0-4	Jan11 1-2		Feb22 3-3	Jan02 7-0	Nov09 5-2	Mar22 3-0	Apr12 2-1	Dec07 4-1	Sep21 2-1	Oct05 1-2	Nov23 1-2	Dec28 0-0
DUNFERMLINE A	Mar15 8-1	Nov16 8-1	Jan02 0-1	Oct05 5-2	Apr18 4-0	Sep18 1-2	Sep21 5-5	Apr05 3-0	Nov02 6-1		Jan11 1-2	Oct19 4-2	Apr09 5-0	Apr30 5-1	Dec28 2-1	Aug21 7-1	Dec07 5-2	Sep07 2-1	Apr12 9-1
E STIRLING	Jan18 2-1	Dec21 0-2	Mar29 1-2	Aug21 3-2	Apr26 5-0	Mar15 1-1	Nov30 2-0	Nov09 1-2	Sep14 2-0	Sep28 0-1		Oct12 2-1	Apr16 3-1	Nov16 2-0	Jan04 1-1	Oct26 0-5	Apr05 4-2	Sep18 1-4	Feb22 2-0
FORFAR A	Dec21 0-1	Oct26 1-1	Sep21 2-3	Jan11 1-1	Nov30 3-1	Aug21 3-0	Jan02 1-2	May03 2-0	Mar01 1-1	Apr16 0-1	Apr28 3-1		Apr26 2-0	Apr05 3-0	Nov02 2-1	Sep18 1-3	Sep07 4-2	Oct05 4-1	Mar08 2-1
HAMILTON A	Jan01 1-4	Sep28 2-0	Dec21 2-2	Mar29 4-5	Apr21 3-1	Nov02 4-2	Mar15 3-2	Nov16 0-3	Nov30 1-2	Oct12 3-1	Oct19 4-2	Dec28 3-1		Jan04 2-2	Apr18 5-1	Apr05 1-2	Mar01 7-2	Apr30 3-5	Apr23 3-3
MONTROSE	Nov02 0-0	Apr26 3-2	Aug21 1-3	Nov30 3-1	Mar29 1-2	Sep21 2-3	Sep18 1-3	Oct05 2-0	Dec21 3-2	Oct26 1-1	Mar08 2-1	Dec14 2-1	Sep07 1-0		Apr16 1-2	Apr28 1-0	Jan02 3-2	Jan11 3-1	Nov09 2-2
MORTON	Nov16 4-0	Nov30 4-3	Mar15 1-3	Jan02 1-2	Dec21 8-0	Oct05 5-6	Apr05 2-2	Sep21 0-0	Mar29 3-2	Apr26 0-0	Sep07 3-0	Feb22 2-2	Aug21 1-1	Oct19 3-1		Jan11 6-1	Sep18 0-4	Apr23 2-2	Oct26 2-1
ST JOHNSTONE	Nov30 1-1	Jan18 2-2	Mar01 0-4	Apr26 4-2	Mar15 4-0	Dec21 3-3	Nov02 3-3	Mar29 2-3	Jan01 3-3	Sep11 2-2	Apr30 3-1	Sep04 1-0	Dec14 3-3	Oct12 1-3	Feb01 1-5		Oct19 2-2	Mar08 2-2	Jan04 2-1
STENHOUSEMUIR	Sep28 2-1	Jan01 1-5	Oct26 2-3	Mar15 0-1	Sep10 1-1	Apr26 3-2	Nov16 2-2	Nov30 2-4	Jan18 1-6	Mar29 0-2	Dec14 2-1	Jan04 3-2	Nov09 3-2	Sep14 2-1	Sep04 4-1	Apr23 1-2		Feb22 2-4	Oct12 3-0
STIRLING A	Sep14 4-0	Sep11 1-0	Nov30 2-1	Apr05 4-0	Jan01 5-0	Mar29 3-2	Mar01 7-1	Dec21 4-1	Mar15 5-3	Jan04 2-1	Sep04 4-1	Jan18 3-3	Oct26 3-0	Sep28 7-0	Oct12 2-1	Nov16 4-1	Nov02 4-0		Apr16 2-1
STRANRAER	Mar29 4-0	Mar15 2-1	Jan11 2-3	Sep21 3-2	Apr05 3-0	Nov30 1-1	Oct05 2-3	Jan02 2-1	Apr26 1-4	Dec21 0-3	Nov02 1-1	Nov16 1-0	Sep18 2-2	Mar01 3-0	Apr30 3-1	Sep07 1-4	Apr28 6-5	Oct19 1-4	

LEAGUE TABLES

DIVISION 1

	P	W	D	L	F	A	W	D	L	F	A	Pts
Hearts	34	15	2	0	79	17	14	2	1	53	12	62
Rangers	34	10	2	5	47	26	12	3	2	42	23	49
Celtic	34	7	6	4	42	22	12	2	3	42	25	46
Clyde	34	13	1	3	53	27	5	5	7	31	34	42
Kilmarnock	34	8	6	3	36	24	6	3	8	24	31	37
Partick T	34	11	1	5	37	25	6	2	9	32	46	37
Raith R	34	10	2	5	37	20	4	5	8	29	36	35
Motherwell	34	8	3	6	36	31	4	5	8	32	36	32
Hibernian	34	6	4	7	34	26	7	1	9	25	34	31
Falkirk	34	6	5	6	30	32	5	4	8	34	50	31
Dundee	34	10	1	6	32	22	3	4	10	17	43	31
Aberdeen	34	8	0	9	40	35	6	2	9	28	41	30
St Mirren	34	7	4	6	31	27	4	4	9	28	39	30
T. Lanark	34	6	2	9	32	39	7	2	8	37	49	30
Queen of South	34	6	4	7	33	32	6	1	10	28	40	29
Airdrie	34	8	2	7	47	45	5	0	12	24	47	28
East Fife	34	5	2	10	24	40	5	1	11	21	48	23
Queen's Park	34	1	0	16	18	60	3	1	13	23	54	9

DIVISION 2

	P	W	D	L	F	A	W	D	L	F	A	Pts
Stirling A	36	17	1	0	66	16	8	4	6	39	32	55
Dunfermline A	36	14	1	3	80	24	10	4	4	40	18	53
Arbroath	36	10	2	6	44	37	11	3	4	45	35	47
Dumbarton	36	14	2	2	61	14	6	2	10	31	43	44
Ayr U	36	12	4	2	52	29	6	2	10	46	52	42
Cowdenbeath	36	11	4	3	61	36	6	4	8	39	49	42
Brechin C	36	10	3	5	40	33	6	5	7	40	48	40
Alloa	36	9	5	4	48	36	6	4	8	40	42	39
Dundee U	36	8	3	7	48	37	4	6	8	33	40	33
Hamilton A	36	9	3	6	51	40	3	6	9	19	39	33
St Johnstone	36	5	9	4	39	40	7	0	11	28	45	33
Forfar A	36	10	3	5	35	20	3	3	12	35	51	32
Morton	36	8	6	4	47	30	4	2	12	30	53	32
Montrose	36	10	3	5	32	26	3	3	12	23	46	32
E. Stirling	36	10	2	6	32	25	2	3	13	23	54	29
Stenhousemuir	36	8	2	8	34	40	4	3	11	34	58	29
Albion R	36	9	3	6	35	29	3	2	13	18	50	29
Stranraer	36	9	3	6	38	35	0	4	14	16	48	25
Berwick R	36	4	3	11	25	44	1	2	15	12	65	15

Scottish Football League Records
Season 1958-59

DIVISION 1

	ABERDEEN	AIRDRIE	CELTIC	CLYDE	DUNDEE	DUNFERMLINE A	FALKIRK	HEARTS	HIBERNIAN	KILMARNOCK	MOTHERWELL	PARTICK T	QUEEN OF SOUTH	RAITH R	RANGERS	ST MIRREN	STIRLING A	T LANARK
ABERDEEN		Aug20 0-1	Sep27 3-1	Mar21 1-2	Jan01 1-1	Sep13 4-0	Oct25 5-0	Apr15 2-4	Oct18 4-0	Mar04 2-2	Dec13 0-4	Jan24 3-4	Nov29 5-0	Nov15 2-2	Dec20 1-3	Mar07 2-1	Feb07 4-1	Mar11 3-3
AIRDRIE	Dec27 2-1		Oct18 1-4	Jan17 2-1	Apr18 1-1	Nov22 2-1	Mar28 2-2	Jan03 2-3	Feb21 4-3	Oct04 3-0	Sep06 1-5	Mar07 1-2	Feb07 0-1	Dec06 4-0	Sep20 5-4	Dec13 4-2	Nov01 0-1	Mar18 1-1
CELTIC	Mar25 4-0	Mar10 1-2		Dec27 3-1	Mar04 1-1	Mar07 3-1	Oct11 3-4	Apr18 2-1	Mar28 3-0	Jan21 2-0	Jan02 3-3	Mar21 2-0	Oct04 3-1	Sep20 3-1	Sep06 2-2	Nov15 3-3	Dec13 7-3	Oct25 3-1
CLYDE	Nov22 4-0	Sep27 0-2	Aug20 2-1		Oct18 3-2	Nov01 2-5	Apr04 3-2	Mar14 2-2	Feb07 4-1	Dec20 2-4	Feb21 2-0	Jan01 0-3	Mar31 3-0	Nov29 4-1	Nov08 1-4	Jan24 2-3	Jan10 2-2	Sep13 1-2
DUNDEE	Sep06 2-1	Dec20 1-1	Nov01 1-1	Feb28 2-1		Apr13 2-2	Dec27 3-2	Oct11 3-3	Dec06 2-1	Sep20 1-0	Oct04 1-1	Mar28 3-2	Mar14 2-1	Jan03 2-0	Jan28 1-3	Feb21 4-6	Nov08 3-0	Nov22 3-0
DUNFERMLINE A	Jan03 1-1	Mar21 2-1	Nov08 1-0	Mar04 2-4	Dec13 2-1		Jan17 4-1	Dec27 3-3	Nov15 1-2	Feb07 0-3	Sep20 0-4	Apr18 10-14-2	Feb21 3-3	Sep29 1-7	Oct04 2-3	Oct18 3-2	Dec06 2-3	Dec03
FALKIRK	Feb21 5-1	Nov29 1-2	Feb07 3-2	Dec06 1-4	Aug20 2-5	Sep27 0-2		Mar21 0-2	Jan24 1-0	Nov08 0-0	Oct18 1-1	Jan10 0-2	Nov01 4-0	Apr18 2-2	Mar14 5-5	Sep13 3-4	Jan05 2-1	Dec13 2-0
HEARTS	Dec06 5-1	Sep13 4-3	Dec20 1-1	Nov15 2-2	Feb07 1-0	Aug20 6-2	Nov22 5-1		Jan01 1-3	Mar28 3-1	Nov01 0-2	Oct18 2-0	Mar07 2-1	Feb21 2-1	Apr11 2-0	Mar09 4-0	Jan24 1-4	Sep27 8-3
HIBERNIAN	Feb18 1-0	Oct25 2-3	Nov29 3-2	Oct11 2-1	Apr04 1-2	Mar18 3-1	Oct04 2-3	Sep06 0-4		Dec27 4-3	Jan03 2-2	Dec13 4-0	Sep20 4-0	Jan21 4-2	Mar04 2-2	Mar21 0-1	Apr18 0-1	Nov08 4-4
KILMARNOCK	Nov01 2-0	Jan24 4-2	Sep13 1-4	Apr18 4-1	Jan10 1-0	Oct11 1-1	Mar07 4-1	Nov29 3-2	Aug20 1-1		Mar18 1-3	Feb21 1-2	Oct18 5-0	Dec13 2-0	Nov22 0-3	Jan01 1-0	Sep27 3-3	Apr21 4-0
MOTHERWELL	Apr11 2-0	Jan01 5-2	Apr08 2-0	Oct25 1-0	Jan24 2-0	Jan21 1-0	Jan31 1-0	Mar04 0-1	Sep13 2-5	Nov15 1-1		Aug20 3-1	Dec20 6-1	Nov08 3-3	Nov29 2-2	Sep27 2-2	Mar21 3-0	Oct11 8-1
PARTICK T	Oct04 2-3	Nov08 1-3	Nov22 2-0	Sep06 1-0	Nov29 3-0	Dec20 3-3	Sep20 3-1	Feb18 2-1	Apr11 2-2	Oct29 1-1	Dec27 4-0		Jan20 2-3	Feb07 1-3	Jan03 2-0	Dec06 3-1	Mar18 1-5	Mar04 1-1
QUEEN OF SOUTH	Mar28 2-1	Oct11 0-2	Jan24 2-2	Dec13 2-1	Nov15 1-3	Oct25 2-3	Feb28 2-1	Nov08 0-5	Jan10 1-4	Feb18 2-2	Apr18 0-5	Sep27 1-0		Mar21 1-1	Dec06 3-6	Aug20 2-2	Sep13 1-1	Jan01 2-5
RAITH R	Mar18 0-1	Feb28 3-0	Apr06 3-1	Mar28 1-0	Sep13 4-1	Jan01 2-2	Dec20 1-2	Oct29 0-5	Sep27 5-2	Oct25 1-0	Mar07 3-0	Oct11 2-2	Nov22 2-1		Feb18 2-2	Nov01 2-1	Aug20 0-1	Jan24 2-4
RANGERS	Apr18 1-2	Jan21 2-1	Jan01 2-1	Mar07 3-1	Sep27 1-2	Jan24 1-0	Nov15 3-0	Dec13 5-0	Nov01 4-0	Mar21 1-0	Mar28 2-1	Sep13 2-1	Apr06 3-1	Oct18 4-4		Oct11 2-1	Feb21 3-0	Aug20 2-2
ST MIRREN	Nov08 1-5	Mar25 3-3	Mar18 1-0	Oct04 1-3	Oct25 2-2	Feb18 6-2	Jan03 1-2	Sep20 1-1	Nov22 2-1	Sep06 0-2	Feb23 4-1	Apr08 4-3	Dec27 1-1	Mar04 3-1	Feb07 1-3		Nov29 3-2	Apr18 4-1
STIRLING A	Oct11 3-2	Mar04 0-0	Apr11 0-1	Sep20 2-1	Mar07 0-1	Apr04 1-1	Sep10 1-1	Oct04 1-2	Dec20 0-3	Jan17 3-1	Nov26 2-5	Nov15 1-1	Jan03 4-0	Dec27 2-1	Oct25 2-2	Mar28 3-0		Jan31 2-3
T LANARK	Sep20 0-2	Nov15 1-1	Feb21 1-1	Jan20 2-2	Mar21 0-3	Mar28 7-1	Apr11 3-3	Feb25 0-4	Mar07 2-2	Mar24 2-0	Feb07 5-2	Nov01 0-1	Sep06 7-1	Oct04 3-2	Dec27 2-3	Dec20 2-3	Oct18 3-0	

DIVISION 2

	ALBION R	ALLOA	ARBROATH	AYR U	BERWICK R	BRECHIN C	COWDENBEATH	DUMBARTON	DUNDEE U	EAST FIFE	E STIRLING	FORFAR A	HAMILTON A	MONTROSE	MORTON	QUEEN'S PARK	ST JOHNSTONE	STENHOUSEMUIR	STRANRAER
ALBION R		Apr04 2-0	Jan24 3-4	Oct11 1-4	Apr22 2-2	Oct25 4-3	Feb28 1-3	Nov29 1-2	Apr11 3-1	Aug20 1-1	Nov08 8-0	Apr25 3-0	Apr27 2-0	Nov15 3-0	Mar21 2-5	Dec20 5-2	Sep13 3-2	Jan10 6-2	Apr29 4-0
ALLOA	Dec06 5-2		Sep13 2-3	Feb21 1-2	Dec20 2-2	Nov08 2-0	Feb07 2-0	Aug20 3-5	Nov01 3-1	Apr25 3-0	Mar14 4-2	Oct18 5-1	Apr29 2-4	Nov29 4-1	Sep17 2-3	Mar21 3-1	Sep27 2-1	Apr15 2-3	Apr11 1-0
ARBROATH	Oct04 1-1	Jan03 3-3		Mar14 1-3	Sep20 2-0	Feb28 2-0	Jan17 2-0	Nov08 5-4	Mar28 2-0	Oct25 3-2	Feb07 3-0	Sep06 6-1	Apr25 6-0	Dec27 3-0	Apr11 4-1	Dec06 2-1	Apr29 3-1	Oct18 4-1	Nov22 2-0
AYR U	Feb07 6-2	Oct25 6-2	Nov15 5-2		Jan03 2-0	Jan31 1-4	Sep20 1-2	Apr27 3-1	Nov08 6-2	Mar28 2-0	Dec06 4-1	Apr11 3-0	Mar21 4-1	Jan17 8-2	Sep06 3-0	Oct04 3-2	Dec20 4-2	Apr29 2-2	Dec27 4-4
BERWICK R	Oct18 3-2	Apr18 2-1	Jan10 1-1	Sep13 0-4		Jan24 3-1	Mar21 2-0	Sep27 0-3	Feb21 8-2	Sep17 1-0	Jan01 2-0	Feb07 4-2	Nov08 2-3	Dec13 2-1	Dec06 2-1	Apr25 1-1	Aug20 1-1	Mar14 1-4	Nov01 3-0
BRECHIN C	Feb21 3-2	Mar07 3-2	Nov01 3-0	Oct18 0-4	Oct04 3-2		Apr18 4-7	Sep16 2-1	Sep10 1-0	Apr04 2-2	Dec13 4-0	Dec27 3-3	Nov15 0-0	Sep06 2-3	Jan17 3-0	Jan03 5-0	Mar21 0-0	Nov29 0-3	Sep20 2-2
COWDENBEATH	Nov01 4-0	Oct11 1-2	Sep27 3-1	Jan10 1-5	Feb14 2-3	Dec20 1-1		Apr20 2-2	Mar14 6-0	Jan01 4-2	Apr29 2-3	Oct25 1-2	Aug20 0-6	Apr04 1-1	Mar28 2-2	Apr11 4-2	Jan24 1-0	Apr25 1-2	Mar07 4-2
DUMBARTON	Mar28 2-0	Dec27 1-1	Mar07 2-0	Nov01 1-2	Apr29 0-2	Sep03 2-3	Oct18 4-2		Sep20 4-3	Feb28 5-0	Apr25 2-1	Dec06 1-1	Dec20 6-3	Jan03 3-1	Oct04 6-1	Sep06 1-0	Feb07 1-1	Mar21 5-1	Feb21 4-1
DUNDEE U	Dec13 3-4	Apr22 1-1	Nov29 2-3	Mar07 2-3	Oct25 4-1	Apr25 1-2	Nov15 2-0	Jan10 1-1		Jan24 1-1	Aug20 2-5	Sep03 3-2	Sep13 3-1	Mar21 3-0	Apr18 4-1	Feb07 1-1	Jan01 2-3	Sep27 5-2	Apr04 1-0
EAST FIFE	Dec27 5-1	Sep10 3-1	Feb21 1-1	Nov29 1-3	Sep03 5-0	Dec06 2-7	Sep06 4-0	Dec13 2-6	Oct04 5-1		Mar21 6-2	Jan17 4-3	Apr08 2-2	Apr18 3-2	Sep20 1-2	Oct18 3-1	Nov15 6-2	Feb07 2-1	Jan03 5-2
E STIRLING	Mar07 1-0	Nov15 2-2	Oct11 0-1	Apr04 1-0	Sep06 3-2	Apr11 0-0	Sep03 5-2	Sep10 3-2	Dec27 1-1	Nov22 0-0		Sep20 1-3	Apr20 4-2	Oct04 3-1	Apr22 1-1	Feb28 1-2	Oct25 1-0	Dec20 2-2	Mar28 1-1
FORFAR A	Sep10 4-1	Apr27 4-1	Jan01 1-4	Apr22 1-2	Oct11 2-1	Aug20 2-2	Feb21 2-3	Apr04 3-1	Sep17 2-2	Sep27 4-4	Jan10 1-1		Jan24 0-5	Nov01 2-1	Nov15 5-1	Mar07 4-2	Nov29 4-1	Sep13 2-3	Dec20 2-1
HAMILTON A	Sep06 2-2	Sep20 1-0	Apr22 4-0	Nov22 0-0	Mar07 1-2	Mar14 3-4	Dec27 0-0	Apr18 4-1	Jan03 1-0	Nov01 5-1	Oct18 5-0	Oct04 7-1		Feb21 5-2	Feb07 1-2	Mar28 1-3	Dec13 0-1	Dec06 0-3	Apr15 1-1
MONTROSE	Mar14 1-1	Mar28 3-3	Aug20 1-4	Sep27 2-4	Apr11 1-2	Jan01 2-4	Dec06 2-0	Sep13 1-6	Nov22 1-1	Dec20 1-2	Jan24 1-0	Feb28 0-4	Oct25 4-0		Jan31 1-2	Sep03 4-0	Apr25 0-1	Nov08 0-5	Oct11 1-1
MORTON	Nov22 4-3	Sep03 4-1	Dec13 3-4	Mar25 3-3	Apr04 2-1	Sep27 3-3	Nov29 2-4	Jan24 1-1	Dec20 2-1	Apr29 0-1	Sep13 2-1	Mar14 4-1	Oct11 0-1	Oct18 5-2		Nov01 1-1	Mar07 1-3	Feb21 1-3	Sep10 2-2
QUEEN'S PARK	Apr18 1-2	Nov22 4-2	Mar30 1-0	Jan24 0-4	Sep10 1-2	Sep13 4-2	Dec13 2-3	Jan01 2-4	Oct11 2-1	Apr22 1-2	Sep27 3-2	Nov08 1-1	Nov29 0-1	Sep17 2-2	Apr27 1-3		Apr15 1-2	Aug20 2-1	Mar14 3-2
ST JOHNSTONE	Jan03 1-1	Apr20 3-0	Apr04 1-1	Apr18 1-0	Dec27 2-0	Nov22 1-0	Oct04 1-0	Oct11 1-1	Sep06 3-4	Mar14 6-1	Feb21 3-0	Mar28 2-0	Jan31 1-1	Sep10 0-1	Nov08 1-1	Sep20 0-0		Nov01 3-0	Apr22 0-0
STENHOUSEMUIR	Sep20 2-6	Sep06 5-4	Apr20 7-0	Sep03 1-2	Nov15 2-2	Mar28 0-0	Apr22 3-1	Nov22 2-0	Jan17 1-0	Oct11 3-2	Apr18 3-1	Jan03 2-2	Apr04 2-2	Mar07 2-0	Oct25 5-1	Dec27 3-2	Apr11 1-0		Oct04 4-1
STRANRAER	Sep17 0-0	Dec13 2-2	Mar21 1-3	Aug20 2-3	Feb28 3-1	Jan10 1-3	Nov08 4-0	Oct25 2-3	Dec06 4-1	Sep13 2-2	Nov29 2-1	Apr18 1-1	Sep27 1-3	Feb07 5-3	Apr25 5-1	Nov15 2-1	Oct18 2-3	Jan24 4-1	

LEAGUE TABLES

DIVISION 1

	P	W	D	L	F	A	W	D	L	F	A	Pts
Rangers	34	13	2	2	41	17	8	6	3	51	34	50
Hearts	34	12	2	3	49	25	9	4	4	43	26	48
Motherwell	34	11	4	2	44	19	7	4	6	39	31	44
Dundee	34	10	5	2	36	25	6	4	7	25	26	41
Airdrie	34	8	3	6	35	32	7	4	6	29	30	37
Celtic	34	11	4	2	48	24	3	4	10	22	29	36
St Mirren	34	8	4	5	38	33	6	3	8	33	41	35
Kilmarnock	34	10	3	4	38	23	3	5	9	20	28	34
Partick T	34	8	4	5	34	27	6	2	9	25	39	34
Hibernian	34	8	3	6	38	31	5	3	9	30	39	32
T. Lanark	34	6	5	6	40	31	5	5	7	34	52	32
Stirling A	34	6	5	6	27	25	5	3	9	27	39	30
Aberdeen	34	7	4	6	42	29	5	1	11	21	37	29
Raith R	34	9	3	5	33	25	1	6	10	27	45	29
Clyde	34	8	2	7	37	34	4	2	11	25	32	28
Dunfermline A	34	7	3	7	41	41	3	5	9	27	46	28
Falkirk	34	6	4	7	32	33	4	3	10	26	46	27
Queen of South	34	4	5	8	24	44	2	1	14	14	57	18

DIVISION 2

	P	W	D	L	F	A	W	D	L	F	A	Pts
Ayr U	36	14	2	2	67	29	14	2	2	48	19	60
Arbroath	36	15	2	1	54	18	8	3	7	32	41	51
Stenhousemuir	36	12	4	2	48	26	8	2	8	39	42	46
Dumbarton	36	12	3	3	50	23	7	4	7	44	38	45
Brechin C	36	9	5	4	40	31	7	5	6	39	34	42
St Johnstone	36	9	7	2	30	11	6	3	9	24	33	40
Hamilton A	36	8	4	6	41	23	7	4	7	35	39	38
East Fife	36	12	2	4	60	37	3	6	9	23	44	38
Berwick R	36	11	3	4	38	27	5	3	10	25	39	38
Albion R	36	11	2	5	54	31	3	5	10	30	48	35
Morton	36	7	5	6	40	36	6	3	9	28	49	34
Forfar A	36	9	4	5	45	36	3	5	10	28	51	33
Alloa	36	11	1	6	48	31	1	6	11	28	50	31
Cowdenbeath	36	7	4	7	40	36	6	1	11	27	43	31
E. Stirling	36	8	7	3	30	22	2	1	15	20	57	28
Stranraer	36	8	4	6	43	32	0	7	11	20	44	27
Dundee U	36	8	4	6	41	31	1	3	14	21	55	25
Queen's Park	36	7	2	9	31	36	2	4	12	22	44	24
Montrose	36	4	4	10	26	40	2	2	14	23	56	18

Scottish Football League Records
Season 1959-60

DIVISION 1

	ABERDEEN	AIRDRIE	ARBROATH	AYR U	CELTIC	CLYDE	DUNDEE	DUNFERMLINE A	HEARTS	HIBERNIAN	KILMARNOCK	MOTHERWELL	PARTICK T	RAITH R	RANGERS	ST MIRREN	STIRLING A	T LANARK
ABERDEEN		Jan16 2-2	Dec12 0-0	Apr30 2-0	Feb06 3-2	Mar08 0-2	Sep05 0-3	Jan02 1-1	Nov21 1-3	Dec26 6-4	Mar22 0-1	Mar12 2-2	Sep19 5-2	Apr02 4-2	Oct24 0-5	Oct03 3-1	Dec05 3-1	Nov14 3-1
AIRDRIE	Sep26 1-0		Jan09 2-1	Oct31 1-2	Apr18 2-5	Feb20 2-4	Apr02 3-3	Dec05 6-3	Oct10 2-5	Oct24 1-11	Sep12 1-3	Jan01 0-1	Nov21 3-0	Aug19 1-2	Dec19 0-5	Mar19 1-3	Mar12 2-4	Jan23 3-2
ARBROATH	Apr23 1-3	Sep19 1-1		Jan16 1-1	Oct03 0-5	Mar26 2-3	Mar05 1-1	Feb06 2-2	Oct17 1-4	Dec05 2-3	Oct24 0-3	Dec19 3-1	Dec26 2-2	Mar12 1-2	Nov14 0-4	Jan02 6-2	Sep05 4-3	Nov28 2-1
AYR U	Dec19 2-1	Mar05 1-0	Sep26 1-0		Mar16 1-1	Aug19 1-2	Mar09 1-0	Oct24 3-3	Jan23 1-1	Apr22 2-1	Mar26 1-3	Sep12 5-2	Dec05 4-1	Oct10 4-0	Jan09 2-4	Apr02 4-3	Nov14 1-1	Jan01 2-3
CELTIC	Oct10 1-1	Dec12 0-0	Jan23 4-0	Nov07 2-3		Sep26 1-1	Dec05 2-3	Nov14 4-2	Sep12 3-4	Mar07 1-0	Aug19 2-0	Oct24 5-1	Apr12 2-4	Jan09 1-0	Jan01 0-1	Apr30 3-3	Mar26 1-1	Mar28 4-0
CLYDE	Oct31 7-2	Oct17 1-2	Nov21 2-1	Dec26 3-0	Jan16 3-3		Sep19 1-1	Apr23 1-3	Nov28 2-2	Oct03 2-1	Dec19 1-2	Mar19 1-4	Sep05 1-0	Feb27 6-1	Apr25 4-1	Mar22 2-2	Jan02 2-2	Apr16 2-3
DUNDEE	Jan01 4-1	Nov28 1-2	Oct31 5-0	Oct17 3-1	Apr16 2-0	Jan09 2-0		Nov07 3-2	Aug19 1-3	Mar26 6-3	Jan23 0-4	Sep26 1-1	Mar19 3-0	Sep12 0-2	Oct10 1-3	Feb27 3-1	Apr23 4-1	Dec19 2-1
DUNFERMLINE A	Sep12 1-3	Apr16 1-0	Oct10 5-1	Mar01 3-4	Mar19 3-2	Dec12 4-5	Mar12 2-2		Jan09 2-2	Feb27 2-2	Apr04 1-0	Aug19 6-0	Oct31 3-3	Jan01 0-2	Jan23 0-5	Nov21 2-1	Dec19 1-1	Sep26 3-1
HEARTS	Mar26 3-0	Feb06 3-2	Mar09 4-1	Oct03 5-3	Jan02 3-1	Apr05 5-2	Dec26 3-0	Sep19 3-1		Sep05 2-2	Nov14 3-1	Jan30 1-1	Nov07 5-3	Dec19 4-1	Mar05 2-0	Dec05 0-2	Jan16 4-0	Oct28 6-2
HIBERNIAN	Aug19 2-1	Mar30 3-3	Apr16 5-0	Dec12 5-1	Oct31 3-3	Jan23 5-5	Nov21 4-2	Oct17 7-4	Jan01 1-5		Sep26 4-2	Oct10 1-3	Apr30 2-2	Mar19 0-3	Sep12 0-1	Mar16 1-3	Nov28 3-1	Jan09 6-0
KILMARNOCK	Oct17 2-0	Jan02 1-0	Mar01 3-2	Nov21 2-0	Dec26 2-1	Apr30 0-2	Oct03 2-2	Nov28 3-2	Mar19 2-1	Jan16 3-1		Oct31 2-0	Feb06 5-1	Dec12 1-0	Apr16 1-1	Sep05 0-5	Sep19 2-0	Nov07 3-2
MOTHERWELL	Nov07 3-1	Sep05 4-1	Apr30 6-0	Jan02 3-3	Mar21 1-2	Nov14 3-2	Jan16 0-0	Dec26 1-1	Dec12 3-0	Feb06 3-4	Mar05 1-2		Oct03 4-0	Apr16 2-1	Nov28 2-1	Sep19 1-4	Oct17 2-1	Mar26 3-3
PARTICK T	Jan09 1-0	Mar26 0-3	Aug19 2-0	Apr16 3-1	Nov28 3-1	Jan01 0-1	Nov14 0-5	Mar05 2-0	Mar15 1-2	Dec19 2-10	Oct10 3-2	Jan23 1-2		Feb20 1-0	Sep26 0-3	Dec12 4-2	Oct24 1-0	Sep12 2-0
RAITH R	Nov28 5-1	Dec26 2-3	Nov07 5-0	Feb06 2-0	Sep19 0-3	Oct24 3-1	Jan02 1-1	Sep05 3-2	Apr30 2-2	Nov14 4-2	Apr27 0-2	Dec05 1-1	Oct17 1-2		Mar26 1-2	Jan16 6-1	Oct03 0-1	Mar05 2-3
RANGERS	Mar01 2-2	Apr30 0-0	Mar19 1-1	Sep19 0-3	Sep05 3-1	Nov07 6-0	Feb09 0-0	Oct03 4-1	Oct31 0-2	Jan02 1-1	Dec05 5-0	Apr18 0-2	Jan16 1-1	Nov21 2-3		Oct17 1-3	Dec26 3-0	May07 1-2
ST MIRREN	Jan23 3-0	Nov14 1-2	Sep12 8-1	Nov28 4-3	Dec19 0-3	Oct10 2-2	Oct24 2-3	Mar26 0-2	Apr16 4-4	Nov07 2-3	Jan01 0-3	Jan09 5-1	Apr23 2-4	Sep26 3-2	Apr25 1-1		Mar05 0-7	Aug19 1-3
STIRLING A	Apr16 0-2	Nov07 1-2	Jan01 5-0	Mar19 3-4	Nov21 2-2	Sep12 1-1	Dec12 0-1	Apr30 1-4	Sep26 2-2	Apr02 2-3	Jan09 0-1	Feb20 0-3	Mar02 2-1	Jan23 4-2	Aug19 2-3	Oct31 3-2		Oct10 0-3
T LANARK	Mar19 2-1	Oct03 4-2	Apr05 7-1	Sep05 5-0	Oct17 4-2	Dec05 2-3	Apr30 2-2	Jan16 2-0	Feb27 1-4	Sep19 5-3	Mar14 3-4	Nov21 1-4	Jan02 1-2	Oct31 1-3	Dec12 0-2	Jan06 2-2	Feb09 3-3	

DIVISION 2

	ALBION R	ALLOA	BERWICK R	BRECHIN C	COWDENBEATH	DUMBARTON	DUNDEE U	EAST FIFE	E STIRLING	FALKIRK	FORFAR A	HAMILTON A	MONTROSE	MORTON	QUEEN OF SOUTH	QUEEN'S PARK	ST JOHNSTONE	STENHOUSEMUIR	STRANRAER
ALBION R		Dec12 2-2	Oct03 1-3	Sep16 6-3	Apr16 1-1	Nov28 0-0	Feb27 1-4	Sep19 1-1	Jan16 2-1	Oct17 2-2	Jan02 7-1	Sep05 0-3	Sep23 5-1	Nov14 3-2	Mar26 0-3	Apr30 4-1	Mar05 2-1	Dec26 2-0	Apr27 3-1
ALLOA	Apr23 2-3		Mar05 0-3	Dec19 1-7	Apr13 4-2	Sep16 1-1	Mar26 3-2	Nov14 4-0	Jan02 4-2	Nov28 3-0	Sep19 5-1	Dec26 2-1	Dec05 5-1	Oct24 3-1	Sep23 2-1	Oct03 1-2	Jan16 0-1	Sep05 0-2	Mar12 4-2
BERWICK R	Jan23 4-1	Oct31 1-1		Oct10 4-0	Sep26 1-0	Jan09 0-0	Dec19 1-2	Feb13 2-0	Sep23 5-3	Aug19 2-1	Dec05 2-1	Nov14 1-1	Sep12 0-1	Jan01 4-3	Sep02 2-2	Mar12 3-1	Apr27 0-2	Oct24 3-0	Apr02 2-1
BRECHIN C	Sep02 2-2	Apr30 3-0	Feb06 5-2		Apr02 1-2	Sep26 3-1	Jan23 1-1	Mar05 3-1	Mar12 1-1	Jan09 1-0	Oct17 2-1	Sep23 1-3	Jan01 1-0	Sep12 4-0	Dec12 1-1	Nov21 2-1	Nov14 1-1	Dec05 2-1	Oct24 0-3
COWDENBEATH	Dec05 2-6	Oct17 2-1	Jan16 1-0	Nov28 1-5		Apr23 0-4	Nov07 1-2	Sep05 1-2	Oct24 0-3	Apr25 0-3	Oct03 2-4	Sep19 3-2	Mar05 1-3	Mar26 2-5	Apr30 0-4	Feb06 1-9	Dec26 0-2	Nov14 1-2	Jan02 0-1
DUMBARTON	Mar12 6-0	Sep02 2-1	Sep19 0-4	Jan16 2-0	Dec12 6-0		Sep09 3-2	Apr13 4-2	Dec05 4-2	Mar19 1-0	Oct24 4-1	Apr30 2-1	Nov21 0-1	Feb13 1-1	Oct17 1-3	Sep05 3-2	Jan02 1-0	Oct03 0-1	Dec26 4-1
DUNDEE U	Oct24 0-0	Nov21 2-1	Apr30 1-0	Oct03 3-1	Jan30 2-3	Sep23 2-1		Dec26 6-0	Feb06 6-1	Dec12 1-0	Apr02 4-0	Mar05 5-1	Nov14 1-2	Feb20 3-3	Dec05 4-3	Jan02 3-1	Sep05 0-1	Jan16 1-2	Sep19 2-1
EAST FIFE	Jan09 4-1	Mar19 4-7	Nov21 4-3	Oct31 1-0	Jan01 4-1	Oct10 2-2	Aug19 1-3		Apr06 1-3	Feb27 1-1	Sep23 1-1	Apr16 0-2	Apr02 0-0	Sep26 4-0	Sep12 1-2	Dec12 2-3	Mar12 0-1	Feb20 1-6	Dec19 7-1
E STIRLING	Sep26 3-0	Sep12 6-3	Sep08 0-0	Nov07 0-1	Apr20 4-1	Apr16 2-2	Oct10 1-0	Sep02 2-2		Jan01 1-5	Mar26 1-4	Oct17 2-3	Jan09 2-3	Aug19 3-1	Jan23 4-3	Mar19 2-0	Dec12 3-5	Nov28 0-1	Oct31 2-3
FALKIRK	Apr13 2-1	Apr02 5-0	Dec26 4-0	Sep19 1-3	Apr06 8-1	Nov14 0-0	Apr23 1-2	Oct24 5-0	Sep05 2-3		Dec19 7-2	Jan16 4-2	Mar12 2-0	Sep23 4-1	Mar04 3-2	Dec16 0-1	Feb06 1-1	Jan02 4-1	Oct03 3-1
FORFAR A	Sep12 1-0	Jan09 4-0	Apr16 4-1	Feb20 1-0	Jan23 1-2	Feb27 1-0	Nov28 1-3	Apr20 2-1	Nov21 2-2	Apr30 1-0		Nov07 1-6	Aug19 2-4	Dec12 2-2	Sep26 2-5	Oct31 1-1	Sep16 1-2	Oct10 1-4	Mar05 0-0
HAMILTON A	Jan01 0-3	Aug19 2-2	Mar19 3-0	Sep08 4-1	Jan09 2-0	Dec19 5-0	Oct31 2-0	Dec05 2-0	Apr27 2-2	Sep26 2-0	Mar12 3-2		Sep02 0-0	Jan23 7-3	Oct10 0-3	Apr02 2-1	Oct24 4-3	Apr23 5-1	Nov21 5-2
MONTROSE	Sep09 4-1	Jan30 2-2	Jan02 2-1	Sep05 3-1	Oct31 2-0	Mar26 1-2	Mar19 1-3	Nov28 2-0	Sep19 5-0	Nov07 2-2	Dec26 2-1	Sep05 1-1		Oct10 1-0	Apr27 1-2	Jan16 3-1	Oct03 3-0	Dec19 0-3	Apr23 1-0
MORTON	Mar19 1-3	Feb27 3-0	Sep05 1-2	Jan02 2-2	Nov21 7-1	Nov07 3-2	Oct17 1-1	Jan16 1-0	Dec26 1-1	Apr20 1-1	Apr23 0-1	Oct03 5-1	Apr16 3-4		Nov28 3-1	Sep19 2-3	Apr30 1-1	Mar05 3-2	Sep16 2-0
QUEEN OF SOUTH	Nov21 4-1	Sep09 2-1	Sep16 2-1	Apr23 2-1	Dec19 5-0	Apr06 1-0	Apr16 4-4	Jan02 5-1	Oct03 2-2	Oct31 1-1	Jan16 0-0	Feb06 3-3	Oct24 3-1	Apr02 2-0		Dec26 7-1	Sep19 1-2	Mar12 2-0	Sep05 4-2
QUEEN'S PARK	Dec19 0-2	Jan23 2-0	Nov07 3-1	Apr27 2-1	Oct10 4-2	Jan01 2-3	Sep12 1-8	Apr23 1-0	Nov14 1-0	Apr16 0-3	Apr13 2-2	Nov28 2-1	Sep26 2-1	Jan09 2-0	Aug19 3-4		Sep23 3-0	Sep15 3-2	Apr20 0-1
ST JOHNSTONE	Oct31 4-1	Sep26 5-0	Oct17 2-0	Feb13 6-2	Aug19 7-3	Sep12 7-2	Jan01 1-1	Nov07 3-1	Apr23 3-2	Oct10 1-0	Sep02 2-2	Feb27 2-3	Jan23 3-0	Dec19 2-0	Jan09 2-1	Sep09 4-1		Mar26 3-2	Dec05 3-2
STENHOUSEMUIR	Aug19 3-3	Jan01 5-3	Apr12 2-1	Apr16 3-2	Mar19 4-4	Jan23 1-2	Sep26 0-3	Oct17 4-0	Apr02 2-1	Sep12 1-1	Feb06 3-1	Dec12 4-5	Apr30 2-1	Oct31 4-2	Nov07 2-1	Sep02 6-0	Nov21 3-2		Sep07 0-0
STRANRAER	Oct10 6-1	Nov07 1-2	Nov28 0-3	Feb27 3-2	Sep12 3-1	Aug19 0-1	Jan09 0-3	Mar26 2-1	Apr08 2-1	Jan23 1-1	Nov14 4-0	Feb13 1-2	Dec12 0-1	Sep02 2-3	Jan01 0-3	Oct17 2-3	Apr16 0-2	Sep23 4-7	

LEAGUE TABLES

DIVISION 1

	P	W	D	L	F	A	W	D	L	F	A	Pts
Hearts	34	14	2	1	56	22	9	6	2	46	29	54
Kilmarnock	34	13	2	2	34	20	11	0	6	33	25	50
Rangers	34	5	6	6	30	22	12	2	3	42	16	42
Dundee	34	11	1	5	41	25	5	9	3	29	24	42
Motherwell	34	9	4	4	42	26	7	4	6	29	35	40
Clyde	34	7	5	5	41	30	8	4	5	36	39	39
Hibernian	34	8	4	5	52	39	6	3	8	54	46	35
Ayr U	34	9	4	4	36	26	5	2	10	29	47	34
Celtic	34	7	5	5	36	24	5	4	8	37	35	33
Partick T	34	10	0	7	26	32	4	4	9	28	46	32
Raith R	34	7	3	7	38	27	7	0	10	26	35	31
T. Lanark	34	7	3	7	45	38	6	1	10	30	45	30
Dunfermline A	34	7	5	5	39	34	3	4	10	33	46	29
St Mirren	34	5	3	9	38	44	6	3	8	40	42	28
Aberdeen	34	8	4	5	35	32	3	2	12	19	40	28
Airdrie	34	5	1	11	31	54	6	5	6	25	26	28
Stirling A	34	4	3	10	28	36	3	5	9	27	36	22
Arbroath	34	4	5	8	29	41	0	2	15	9	65	15

DIVISION 2

	P	W	D	L	F	A	W	D	L	F	A	Pts
St Johnstone	36	15	2	1	60	23	9	3	6	27	24	53
Dundee U	36	12	2	4	46	21	10	4	4	44	24	50
Queen of South	36	12	5	1	50	21	9	2	7	44	31	49
Hamilton A	36	13	3	2	50	23	8	3	7	41	39	48
Stenhousemuir	36	11	4	3	49	32	9	0	9	37	35	44
Dumbarton	36	13	1	4	44	22	5	6	7	23	31	43
Montrose	36	11	3	4	36	20	8	2	8	24	32	43
Falkirk	36	12	2	4	56	21	3	7	8	21	22	39
Berwick R	36	11	4	3	37	20	5	1	12	25	35	37
Albion R	36	9	5	4	42	30	5	3	10	29	48	36
Queen's Park	36	11	1	6	33	31	6	1	11	32	48	36
Brechin C	36	10	5	3	34	21	4	1	13	32	45	34
Alloa	36	11	1	6	44	32	2	4	12	26	53	31
Morton	36	8	5	5	40	26	2	3	13	27	53	28
E. Stirling	36	7	3	8	38	37	3	5	10	30	45	28
Forfar A	36	7	4	7	28	33	3	4	11	25	51	28
Stranraer	36	6	1	11	31	37	4	2	12	22	42	23
East Fife	36	6	4	8	38	37	1	2	15	12	50	20
Cowdenbeath	36	3	0	15	18	58	3	2	13	24	66	14

Scottish Football League Records
Season 1960-61

DIVISION 1

	ABERDEEN	AIRDRIE	AYR U	CELTIC	CLYDE	DUNDEE	DUNDEE U	DUNFERMLINE A	HEARTS	HIBERNIAN	KILMARNOCK	MOTHERWELL	PARTICK T	RAITH R	RANGERS	ST JOHNSTONE	ST MIRREN	T LANARK
ABERDEEN		Oct29 1-1	Jan21 3-1	Jan14 1-3	Feb18 4-2	Jan02 2-1	Nov26 1-3	Aug24 1-4	Mar14 0-2	Mar25 1-4	Dec10 3-2	Nov12 3-3	Dec17 2-1	Mar01 0-1	Apr08 6-1	Sep17 4-2	Apr29 1-0	Oct08 5-3
AIRDRIE	Mar04 3-1		Dec03 4-2	Oct01 2-0	Dec24 0-2	Apr12 2-4	Feb04 4-4	Apr10 0-1	Sep24 2-2	Oct22 4-3	Nov05 1-1	Sep10 4-2	Mar25 2-3	Apr22 1-0	Jan07 1-1	Feb18 3-0	Nov12 2-1	Dec31 4-1
AYR U	Oct01 1-1	Apr08 2-2		Mar04 1-3	Jan07 2-2	Nov19 2-4	Apr22 3-0	Feb04 4-1	Oct15 1-0	Mar18 0-1	Sep24 2-2	Dec31 0-0	Mar01 2-0	Dec10 1-1	Dec24 1-0	Nov05 0-1	Nov26 0-5	Sep10 2-3
CELTIC	Sep24 0-0	Jan21 4-0	Oct29 2-0		Feb27 6-1	Dec26 2-1	Dec10 1-1	Mar25 2-1	May02 1-3	Feb18 2-0	Dec31 3-2	Dec24 1-0	Nov12 0-1	Mar20 1-1	Sep10 1-5	Apr05 1-1	Oct08 4-2	Jan07 2-3
CLYDE	Oct15 1-1	Apr29 3-1	Sep17 2-2	Oct22 0-3		Jan14 0-0	Mar04 3-1	Apr12 6-0	Nov19 1-1	Dec17 3-3	Feb04 1-3	Oct01 1-0	Jan02 3-3	Mar18 0-2	Nov05 1-3	Feb11 0-0	Aug24 4-2	Nov26 2-4
DUNDEE	Sep10 3-3	Dec10 2-1	Mar25 6-1	Apr08 0-1	Sep24 4-1		Jan07 3-0	Mar04 4-1	Dec24 2-2	Nov05 0-1	Oct15 1-0	Apr22 2-2	Nov26 1-2	Dec31 2-3	Feb08 4-2	Oct01 2-1	Mar08 2-0	Nov12 0-2
DUNDEE U	Apr01 3-3	Oct08 1-2	Dec17 2-1	Apr10 1-1	Oct29 2-1	Sep17 3-1		Apr29 5-0	Jan21 3-0	Aug24 3-1	Nov19 2-4	Oct22 0-1	Jan14 3-0	Feb18 4-1	Mar18 1-1	Jan02 0-2	Dec03 2-0	Mar11 1-2
DUNFERMLINE A	Dec31 2-6	Nov26 6-4	Oct08 2-2	Nov19 2-2	Dec10 2-2	Oct29 4-2	Dec24 3-2		Jan07 2-1	Apr08 4-2	May01 2-4	Sep24 1-6	Mar13 2-1	Sep10 3-2	Feb18 0-0	Mar18 5-1	Jan21 1-2	Mar06 2-3
HEARTS	Nov05 3-4	Jan14 3-1	Feb18 2-1	Dec17 2-1	Mar25 4-2	Apr29 2-1	Oct01 1-1	Sep17 1-1		Jan02 1-2	Mar18 0-1	Mar04 1-5	Oct08 0-1	Nov26 1-0	Oct26 1-3	Aug24 3-1	Apr15 0-0	Apr08 1-0
HIBERNIAN	Nov19 2-2	Feb27 3-3	Nov12 3-1	Oct15 0-6	Apr22 4-0	Mar20 1-0	Dec31 2-0	Dec03 2-1	Sep10 1-4		Jan07 4-0	Apr01 2-1	Jan21 1-1	Sep24 0-1	Dec10 1-2	Feb08 3-1	Oct29 4-3	Dec24 8-4
KILMARNOCK	Mar11 4-1	Mar15 1-0	Jan14 5-1	Aug24 2-2	Oct08 1-0	Feb18 2-1	Mar25 1-1	Dec17 1-1	Nov12 2-1	Sep17 3-2		Dec03 5-3	Apr29 4-1	Jan21 6-0	Apr01 2-0	Oct22 2-2	Jan02 1-2	Nov02 3-1
MOTHERWELL	Mar18 1-0	Jan02 2-2	Aug24 2-2	Apr29 2-2	Jan21 2-1	Dec17 2-0	Mar07 4-3	Jan14 2-4	Oct29 1-1	Nov26 4-1	Apr08 1-3		Sep17 2-0	Oct08 2-1	Dec26 1-2	Dec10 2-0	Mar15 0-3	Oct15 4-5
PARTICK T	Apr22 3-4	Nov19 2-2	Oct22 3-3	Mar18 1-2	Sep10 3-1	Apr01 2-2	Sep24 1-0	Nov05 1-0	Feb04 4-1	Oct01 3-1	Dec24 2-3	Jan07 1-3		Apr08 2-2	Dec31 0-3	Mar04 3-0	Feb18 3-2	Dec10 2-1
RAITH R	Oct22 0-3	Dec17 2-0	Apr12 3-1	Nov05 2-2	Nov12 1-0	Aug24 2-1	Oct15 0-2	Jan02 1-1	Apr01 1-1	Jan14 0-2	Oct01 1-1	Feb04 1-3	Dec03 1-3		Mar04 2-3	Apr29 1-3	Sep17 5-2	Mar25 3-6
RANGERS	Dec03 4-0	Sep17 3-0	Apr29 7-3	Jan02 2-1	Mar11 2-1	Oct08 0-1	Nov12 4-0	Oct15 3-1	Mar08 3-0	Apr11 1-0	Nov26 2-3	Mar25 2-2	Aug24 6-3	Nov02 3-0		Jan14 1-0	Dec17 5-1	Jan21 4-3
ST JOHNSTONE	Jan07 2-1	Oct15 2-2	Mar11 4-1	Nov26 2-1	Dec03 2-2	Jan21 1-1	Sep10 0-2	Nov12 2-1	Dec31 2-3	Oct08 2-0	Feb25 1-1	Apr19 2-1	Oct29 2-1	Dec24 0-2	Sep24 2-5		Mar25 1-1	Apr22 3-4
ST MIRREN	Dec24 1-3	Mar18 1-1	Apr17 2-2	Feb04 2-1	Dec31 2-2	Oct22 1-2	Apr08 0-3	Oct01 0-2	Dec10 2-0	Mar04 2-1	Sep10 0-1	Nov05 2-3	Oct15 5-0	Jan09 3-0	Jan28 1-1	Nov19 0-0		Sep24 1-0
T LANARK	Feb04 5-1	Aug24 5-2	Jan02 3-3	Sep17 2-0	Apr03 7-4	Mar18 2-1	Nov05 6-1	Oct22 4-2	Dec03 0-3	Apr29 6-1	Mar04 0-1	Feb18 1-1	Apr12 3-2	Nov19 4-3	Oct01 2-4	Dec17 4-2	Jan14 1-2	

DIVISION 2

	ALBION R	ALLOA	ARBROATH	BERWICK R	BRECHIN C	COWDENBEATH	DUMBARTON	EAST FIFE	E STIRLING	FALKIRK	FORFAR A	HAMILTON A	MONTROSE	MORTON	QUEEN OF SOUTH	QUEEN'S PARK	STENHOUSEMUIR	STIRLING A	STRANRAER
ALBION R		Apr26 3-1	Sep17 0-1	Feb11 1-2	Jan14 0-2	Jan21 4-2	Nov26 5-0	Sep07 2-0	Oct15 2-4	Dec17 0-0	Apr19 1-1	Jan02 5-3	Oct08 0-3	Oct29 3-3	Apr05 1-4	Aug24 1-0	Apr08 2-5	Nov19 2-4	Mar18 2-2
ALLOA	Nov05 4-1		Nov19 4-0	Apr01 5-0	Oct15 2-2	Apr19 5-3	Dec10 1-2	Aug24 4-1	Mar04 4-1	Sep21 1-1	Sep07 4-0	Apr08 2-3	Mar18 4-2	Apr22 4-2	Dec24 0-1	Jan14 4-1	Jan02 2-3	Apr05 2-4	Oct01 1-0
ARBROATH	Jan07 1-0	Mar25 3-3		Oct15 2-0	Sep19 3-2	Apr22 5-3	Dec24 1-3	Mar04 1-2	Apr08 0-0	Nov12 1-3	Sep10 2-1	Apr19 2-2	Dec31 2-2	Nov26 2-1	Sep24 1-2	Oct01 4-0	Sep07 0-3	Nov05 1-1	Feb04 3-0
BERWICK R	Dec24 1-1	Nov26 1-1	Feb18 2-2		Apr22 2-1	Mar18 0-4	Oct29 2-2	Jan14 4-0	Aug24 3-2	Mar11 0-1	Dec10 5-2	Sep28 0-1	Nov19 1-0	Oct22 4-0	Apr19 1-1	Feb04 3-1	Sep17 1-2	Oct01 2-0	Apr08 2-2
BRECHIN C	Sep24 2-6	Feb18 2-0	Sep28 2-1	Dec17 1-1		Nov26 1-1	Apr08 3-2	Apr29 1-2	Sep14 3-2	Jan21 0-2	Dec31 3-4	Oct08 1-2	Sep10 2-3	Jan07 2-1	Oct22 1-5	Nov05 2-0	Mar18 0-2	Dec10 6-2	Mar04 0-2
COWDENBEATH	Oct01 2-1	Oct22 2-1	Dec17 3-1	Nov12 1-3	Apr01 3-3		Apr04 3-2	Jan03 1-2	Apr26 3-0	Apr15 0-3	Mar04 3-1	Jan28 2-2	Apr29 2-0	Dec03 5-1	Mar25 1-0	Sep17 2-1	Aug24 3-1	Oct15 0-3	Nov05 3-2
DUMBARTON	Apr01 2-0	Apr10 3-1	Apr29 4-2	Mar04 4-3	Dec03 2-0	Sep28 0-2		Sep17 1-0	Nov19 3-3	Oct22 1-2	Oct01 7-2	Aug24 5-1	Nov05 2-4	Oct12 2-4	Feb18 3-1	Jan02 3-2	Jan14 2-4	Mar18 2-4	Dec17 1-2
EAST FIFE	Sep14 4-2	Dec31 3-1	Oct29 1-2	Sep24 4-0	Dec24 3-3	Sep10 1-4	Jan07 4-2		Dec10 8-1	Oct08 3-1	Apr22 4-2	Jan21 4-0	Nov26 2-4	Feb18 3-1	Mar11 0-2	Sep28 2-2	Feb25 1-2	Apr08 0-1	Nov19 1-1
E STIRLING	Feb18 0-4	Oct29 1-1	Apr12 3-1	Dec31 2-4	Sep07 3-2	Oct08 2-1	Mar25 2-4	Apr15 2-3		Sep10 0-0	Nov12 4-2	Dec17 1-2	Jan21 1-3	Sep24 4-1	Jan07 4-1	Oct22 2-2	Apr04 1-2	Apr29 1-4	Nov26 1-4
FALKIRK	Apr22 8-2	Sep28 4-3	Mar18 3-0	Nov05 4-0	Oct01 0-0	Dec10 3-3	Feb25 7-1	Feb15 3-0	Jan02 6-0		Apr08 2-1	Oct15 4-4	Sep14 2-1	Dec24 3-0	Apr01 2-1	Nov19 8-0	Mar04 1-2	Jan14 2-1	Sep17 1-2
FORFAR A	Oct22 2-2	Sep14 1-1	Jan02 1-3	Apr15 4-1	Aug24 5-2	Oct29 0-0	Jan21 1-0	Dec17 4-1	Mar18 1-0	Dec03 1-6		Sep17 5-3	Sep28 1-3	Mar11 5-0	Oct08 1-3	Apr29 2-4	Nov19 1-4	Apr01 0-3	Jan14 2-3
HAMILTON A	Sep10 4-3	Dec03 0-3	Oct22 2-1	Apr26 3-3	Feb04 2-2	Apr12 4-3	Dec31 1-0	Oct01 5-2	Apr22 2-1	Feb18 1-3	Jan07 3-2		Sep24 5-1	Mar25 3-0	Nov12 5-1	Apr01 2-3	Nov05 6-1	Mar04 0-1	Apr15 1-1
MONTROSE	Feb04 2-1	Nov12 3-2	Aug24 4-0	Mar25 2-2	Jan02 0-1	Dec24 0-2	Mar11 4-1	Apr01 1-2	Oct01 6-0	Sep07 2-3	Sep21 2-1	Jan14 4-1		Apr15 3-2	Oct29 3-1	Dec03 2-1	Oct15 4-0	Sep17 1-0	Feb25 0-2
MORTON	Mar04 4-0	Dec17 3-1	Apr01 2-2	Feb25 1-2	Sep17 3-3	Apr08 0-0	Jan28 2-3	Oct15 1-1	Jan14 2-2	Apr29 1-5	Nov05 1-4	Nov19 4-4	Dec10 1-0		Sep28 1-1	Apr17 1-4	Feb04 2-3	Jan02 2-2	Aug24 2-2
QUEEN OF SOUTH	Apr15 1-2	Apr29 2-1	Feb25 4-1	Sep07 0-1	Apr12 3-1	Nov19 3-1	Oct15 0-2	Nov05 5-0	Sep17 5-1	Nov26 1-0	Feb04 4-1	Mar18 1-0	Mar04 4-1	Apr26 4-1		Dec17 4-2	Oct01 1-2	Aug24 1-1	Jan02 5-0
QUEEN'S PARK	Dec31 2-1	Sep24 0-2	Jan21 1-2	Oct08 1-2	Mar11 2-2	Jan07 2-3	Sep10 1-1	Sep21 2-1	Feb25 4-4	Mar25 2-1	Dec24 0-2	Nov26 1-4	Apr08 2-1	Nov12 3-1	Apr24 3-2		Dec10 4-2	Sep07 1-1	Oct15 2-4
STENHOUSEMUIR	Dec03 3-0	Sep10 6-1	Apr26 0-2	Jan07 7-2	Nov12 4-1	Dec31 3-0	Sep24 4-4	Oct22 3-2	Sep28 0-1	Oct29 2-3	Mar25 5-0	Mar11 1-2	Feb18 5-2	Oct08 0-3	Jan21 3-2	Apr15 3-2		Dec17 3-3	Apr29 4-1
STIRLING A	Feb25 6-0	Oct08 2-0	Mar11 7-0	Jan21 2-1	Mar25 1-0	Feb18 3-0	Nov12 0-0	Dec03 3-1	Dec24 5-0	Sep24 1-0	Nov26 5-1	Oct29 2-1	Jan07 1-2	Sep10 2-2	Dec31 4-0	Sep14 2-1	Apr22 6-2		Sep21 1-0
STRANRAER	Nov12 4-0	Jan21 2-2	Oct08 5-1	Dec03 2-1	Oct29 2-1	Mar11 2-0	Apr22 4-2	Mar25 6-2	Apr01 2-3	Jan07 2-3	Sep24 4-1	Dec10 5-0	Oct22 6-0	Dec31 2-0	Sep10 0-1	Apr19 4-2	Dec24 1-3	Sep28 0-1	

LEAGUE TABLES

DIVISION 1

	P	W	D	L	F	A	W	D	L	F	A	Pts
Rangers	34	14	1	2	52	19	9	4	4	36	27	51
Kilmarnock	34	12	4	1	45	19	9	4	4	32	26	50
T. Lanark	34	11	2	4	55	33	9	0	8	45	47	42
Celtic	34	9	4	4	33	22	6	5	6	31	24	39
Motherwell	34	9	3	5	34	28	6	5	6	36	29	38
Aberdeen	34	9	2	6	38	34	5	6	6	34	38	36
Hearts	34	8	3	6	26	25	5	5	7	25	28	34
Hibernian	34	10	3	4	41	30	5	1	11	25	39	34
Dundee U	34	9	3	5	36	21	4	4	9	24	37	33
Dundee	34	9	3	5	38	23	4	3	10	23	30	32
Partick T	34	8	4	5	36	30	5	2	10	23	39	32
Dunfermline A	34	8	4	5	43	42	4	3	10	22	39	31
Airdrie	34	9	4	4	39	28	1	6	10	22	43	30
St Mirren	34	6	5	6	25	22	5	2	10	28	36	29
St Johnstone	34	7	5	5	30	29	3	4	10	17	34	29
Raith R	34	5	4	8	26	34	5	3	9	20	33	27
Clyde	34	5	7	5	31	29	1	4	12	24	48	23
Ayr U	34	5	6	6	24	26	0	6	11	27	55	22

DIVISION 2

	P	W	D	L	F	A	W	D	L	F	A	Pts
Stirling A	36	15	2	1	53	11	9	5	4	36	26	55
Falkirk	36	13	3	2	63	21	11	3	4	37	19	54
Stenhousemuir	36	11	2	5	56	31	13	0	5	43	38	50
Stranraer	36	12	1	5	53	23	7	5	6	30	32	44
Queen of South	36	13	1	4	48	18	7	2	9	29	34	43
Hamilton A	36	11	3	4	49	31	6	4	8	35	49	41
Montrose	36	12	1	5	43	22	7	1	10	32	43	40
Cowdenbeath	36	12	2	4	39	27	5	4	9	32	38	40
Berwick R	36	8	6	4	34	23	6	3	9	28	46	37
Dumbarton	36	10	1	7	47	37	5	4	9	31	45	35
Alloa	36	11	2	5	53	27	2	5	11	25	41	33
Arbroath	36	8	5	5	34	28	5	2	11	22	48	33
East Fife	36	9	3	6	48	31	5	1	12	22	49	32
Brechin C	36	7	2	9	32	38	2	7	9	28	40	27
Queen's Park	36	7	4	7	33	36	3	2	13	28	51	26
E. Stirling	36	6	3	9	34	41	3	4	11	25	59	25
Albion R	36	6	4	8	34	37	3	2	13	26	52	24
Forfar A	36	7	3	8	37	39	3	1	14	28	59	24
Morton	36	3	9	6	33	39	2	2	14	23	54	21

Scottish Football League Records
Season 1961-62

DIVISION 1

	ABERDEEN	AIRDRIE	CELTIC	DUNDEE	DUNDEE U	DUNFERMLINE A	FALKIRK	HEARTS	HIBERNIAN	KILMARNOCK	MOTHERWELL	PARTICK T	RAITH R	RANGERS	ST JOHNSTONE	ST MIRREN	STIRLING A	T LANARK
ABERDEEN		Jan13 1-1	Nov25 0-0	Sep16 3-1	Dec16 1-3	Mar17 1-4	Mar28 2-2	Oct14 0-2	Mar03 1-2	Mar31 3-3	Oct28 3-0	Sep30 1-3	Jan23 3-3	Apr25 1-0	Jan10 1-1	Feb03 3-1	Aug23 7-0	Nov11 2-1
AIRDRIE	Sep23 7-1		Mar17 1-0	Apr07 1-2	Nov04 3-3	Mar14 3-1	Nov25 2-3	Jan20 2-3	Feb10 4-2	Sep09 0-2	Jan17 2-1	Apr28 1-0	Dec02 2-4	Jan31 2-5	Oct28 2-2	Mar19 3-1	Dec27 0-1	Jan06 0-2
CELTIC	Mar24 2-0	Nov18 3-0		Mar03 2-1	Sep23 3-1	Oct28 2-1	Jan20 3-0	Feb21 2-2	Dec16 4-3	Jan06 2-2	Jan22 1-1	Dec02 5-1	Apr21 0-1	Apr09 1-1	Feb03 3-1	Nov15 7-1	Oct14 5-0	Sep09 1-0
DUNDEE	Jan17 2-1	Dec16 5-1	Nov04 2-1		Sep09 4-1	Mar06 1-2	Jan06 2-1	Sep23 2-0	Mar24 1-0	Oct07 5-3	Feb10 1-3	Oct28 3-2	Nov18 5-4	Mar14 0-0	Jan24 2-1	Apr25 2-0	Dec02 2-2	Jan20 2-1
DUNDEE U	Apr07 2-2	Mar03 3-3	Jan13 4-5	Apr09 1-2		Aug23 3-2	Mar31 4-1	Apr28 0-1	Sep30 4-0	Oct21 1-2	Mar17 1-1	Dec23 3-5	Feb24 4-2	Nov25 2-3	Sep16 3-0	Oct14 3-1	Nov11 2-0	Feb03 3-0
DUNFERMLINE A	Nov18 4-0	Nov11 6-2	Feb24 0-3	Oct21 1-2	Jan06 4-1		Sep23 2-1	Sep09 2-1	Mar19 4-0	Mar24 2-0	Jan20 2-1	Feb03 4-2	Jan15 3-0	Dec16 1-0	Oct14 0-1	Dec30 7-0	Mar03 3-0	Dec02 1-1
FALKIRK	Oct21 0-1	Mar24 1-0	Sep30 3-1	Aug23 1-3	Dec02 1-2	Jan13 1-2		Dec23 0-2	Feb03 1-4	Feb24 0-1	Apr07 4-2	Oct14 1-1	Mar03 3-0	Mar17 1-7	Nov11 0-1	Jan10 3-3	Sep16 1-0	Apr28 2-0
HEARTS	Feb10 1-1	Sep30 4-1	Oct21 2-1	Jan13 0-2	Jan24 2-1	Jan31 3-2	Apr21 2-3		Sep16 4-2	Dec16 3-3	Dec02 2-6	Nov11 2-0	Mar24 0-1	Feb24 0-1	Mar03 1-1	Aug23 2-2	Feb03 0-0	Feb07 2-1
HIBERNIAN	Nov04 1-1	Oct14 2-2	Apr07 1-1	Nov25 1-3	Jan20 3-2	Dec23 1-2	Oct07 2-2	Jan17 1-4		Sep23 3-2	Mar14 1-2	Feb12 3-0	Sep09 3-2	Jan06 0-0	Mar17 3-2	Apr04 2-1	Apr28 3-1	Oct28 1-3
KILMARNOCK	Dec02 4-2	Jan10 4-2	Aug23 3-2	Feb03 1-1	Feb21 5-3	Nov25 2-2	Oct28 2-0	Apr07 2-0	Jan13 4-2		Dec23 1-2	Mar03 1-1	Nov11 2-3	Dec30 0-1	Sep30 2-0	Sep16 4-3	Mar17 2-1	Oct14 2-2
MOTHERWELL	Feb24 1-3	Sep16 5-2	Apr23 0-4	Oct14 2-4	Nov18 2-1	Sep30 1-1	Dec16 3-0	Apr02 1-2	Nov11 5-1	Apr21 0-2		Aug23 1-3	Feb03 3-0	Oct21 2-2	Jan13 2-2	Mar03 2-1	Jan10 5-3	Mar24 0-3
PARTICK T	Jan20 4-2	Dec30 1-0	Apr04 1-2	Feb24 3-0	Apr23 4-2	Oct07 1-0	Feb10 1-2	Mar10 3-1	Oct21 4-1	Nov04 2-4	Jan06 1-0		Sep23 3-2	Sep09 1-4	Dec16 3-0	Mar17 0-1	Nov25 2-0	Jan01 2-0
RAITH R	Apr28 3-1	Mar31 1-1	Dec23 0-4	Mar17 2-3	Oct28 0-0	Sep16 2-2	Nov04 1-2	Nov25 0-1	Jan02 0-2	Mar14 2-2	Oct07 0-3	Jan13 1-0		Feb10 1-3	Aug23 1-1	Sep30 4-0	Apr07 2-1	Feb28 4-3
RANGERS	Dec23 2-4	Feb03 4-0	Sep16 2-2	Nov11 1-5	Mar24 0-1	Apr07 1-0	Nov18 4-0	Jan10 2-1	Aug23 3-0	Apr28 1-1	Feb28 2-1	Jan24 2-1	Oct14 6-0		Dec02 2-0	Jan13 4-0	Sep30 4-1	Mar03 3-1
ST JOHNSTONE	Sep09 4-1	Oct07 0-3	Oct18 0-3	Apr28 0-3	Jan17 1-2	Feb10 2-5	Mar10 2-1	Nov04 0-2	Nov18 0-2	Jan20 0-2	Sep23 1-1	Apr07 1-0	Jan06 0-0	Apr04 0-4		Nov25 0-3	Oct21 2-0	Dec23 1-2
ST MIRREN	Oct07 3-2	Oct21 0-2	Mar26 0-5	Dec23 1-1	Feb10 1-1	Apr28 4-1	Sep09 2-0	Jan06 0-1	Dec02 2-3	Jan17 2-1	Nov04 2-1	Nov18 1-3	Jan20 5-1	Sep23 1-1	Mar24 1-3		Feb24 3-1	Apr07 1-2
STIRLING A	Jan06 3-0	Apr20 2-2	Feb10 1-0	Mar31 2-3	Mar14 0-1	Nov04 2-3	Jan01 3-0	Oct07 3-1	Dec30 0-1	Nov18 2-2	Sep09 2-4	Mar24 0-0	Dec16 0-3	Jan20 0-6	Feb21 0-3	Oct28 0-3		Sep23 2-0
T LANARK	Mar20 3-5	Aug23 3-0	Jan10 1-1	Sep30 1-3	Oct07 7-2	Apr13 1-1	Feb13 1-4	Mar17 1-0	Feb24 1-2	Feb10 3-1	Nov25 2-1	Sep16 4-2	Oct21 2-1	Nov04 0-3	Apr20 1-2	Dec16 5-2	Jan13 1-1	

DIVISION 2

	ALBION R	ALLOA	ARBROATH	AYR U	BERWICK R	BRECHIN C	CLYDE	COWDENBEATH	DUMBARTON	EAST FIFE	E STIRLING	FORFAR A	HAMILTON A	MONTROSE	MORTON	QUEEN OF SOUTH	QUEEN'S PARK	STENHOUSEMUIR	STRANRAER
ALBION R		Mar31 1-2	Feb03 2-3	Aug23 1-1	Oct21 0-4	Oct14 0-2	Nov11 2-3	Mar03 0-4	Dec16 2-1	Jan13 1-0	Mar24 1-2	Apr20 1-0	Sep16 2-1	Sep27 4-1	Apr13 1-0	Nov18 0-3	Apr04 1-1	Feb24 3-2	Sep30 2-2
ALLOA	Dec02 2-1		Sep06 4-1	Jan13 7-2	Mar17 5-4	Mar03 4-1	Feb03 2-7	Oct14 3-0	Apr28 1-1	Apr13 4-3	Aug23 2-3	Apr07 2-2	Feb24 3-2	Dec23 2-0	Nov11 2-1	Mar24 0-0	Sep30 7-5	Sep16 6-1	Oct21 1-1
ARBROATH	Oct07 3-1	Sep13 2-0		Nov25 2-2	Dec02 3-4	Mar17 4-1	Jan06 0-2	Dec30 1-4	Feb10 1-0	Sep27 2-1	Oct21 4-0	Jan01 1-0	Apr21 1-2	Sep09 2-0	Jan20 1-2	Sep23 2-1	Nov04 2-3	Apr07 4-2	Feb24 1-1
AYR U	Jan06 1-3	Sep23 2-3	Mar24 3-5		Nov04 5-1	Dec16 5-1	Nov18 1-2	Oct21 5-1	Oct07 3-0	Mar31 1-1	Feb24 0-0	Jan20 6-3	Sep06 1-0	Apr28 1-2	Jan01 4-1	Sep09 1-0	Feb10 1-0	Nov11 1-0	Apr25 4-1
BERWICK R	Feb17 1-1	Nov18 4-2	Mar31 0-1	Mar03 4-2		Sep06 2-5	Oct28 2-2	Jan06 1-0	Sep09 2-1	Sep30 3-1	Jan13 4-0	Jan27 4-1	Apr04 4-4	Mar24 0-0	Apr21 2-3	Oct14 0-2	Dec16 2-0	Sep20 5-1	Feb03 6-0
BRECHIN C	Feb10 1-2	Nov04 0-3	Nov18 0-2	Apr07 3-4	Sep13 1-3		Sep23 1-5	Feb24 1-4	Jan20 0-2	Oct07 2-1	Apr25 3-3	Sep09 2-3	Sep25 3-0	Apr18 1-1	Apr28 1-9	Jan06 0-1	Oct21 0-4	Dec23 0-3	Mar10 1-3
CLYDE	Mar10 2-1	Oct07 5-1	Aug23 1-0	Mar17 5-0	Feb24 7-1	Jan13 5-0		Sep06 4-1	Sep20 2-2	Nov25 4-1	Dec23 4-1	Nov04 0-0	Apr11 6-2	Oct21 2-3	Feb10 3-1	Apr25 1-0	Sep16 2-1	Sep30 4-1	Mar31 4-1
COWDENBEATH	Nov04 3-0	Feb10 4-2	Apr28 3-3	Feb17 1-0	Aug23 0-3	Oct28 3-1	Sep13 1-0		Mar10 0-1	Sep16 4-4	Mar17 2-5	Sep27 2-0	Jan13 7-1	Oct07 0-4	Mar31 1-2	Apr07 0-3	Apr25 2-0	Apr13 2-2	Dec23 1-1
DUMBARTON	Apr07 2-1	Apr25 2-2	Oct14 2-2	Feb03 1-3	Apr13 0-0	Sep30 2-5	Sep27 1-3	Nov11 1-0		Mar17 3-0	Sep16 4-1	Oct21 2-2	Mar24 2-0	Dec02 0-2	Feb24 2-2	Mar03 0-2	Apr20 0-0	Aug23 2-3	Sep06 3-0
EAST FIFE	Sep23 3-0	Sep09 3-2	Apr18 2-4	Dec02 0-0	Jan20 2-0	Feb03 2-1	Mar24 1-0	Jan01 5-3	Nov18 3-0		Nov11 4-1	Apr04 2-1	Mar03 1-2	Feb24 0-0	Oct21 2-2	Apr21 0-3	Apr09 1-0	Oct14 2-1	Dec16 0-1
E STIRLING	Nov25 1-2	Apr04 1-2	Feb17 1-1	Oct28 2-1	Sep23 1-5	Mar31 8-2	Apr21 3-5	Nov18 4-1	Apr09 1-0	Mar10 1-4		Feb10 2-1	Dec16 0-2	Jan20 4-2	Oct07 1-3	Sep13 2-3	Sep20 5-1	Apr27 2-2	Nov04 2-1
FORFAR A	Dec23 5-1	Dec16 2-3	Sep16 1-2	Sep30 1-1	Nov11 2-2	Jan02 4-2	Mar03 3-2	Sep20 3-1	Feb17 4-4	Apr28 1-2	Oct14 3-1		Feb03 2-5	Nov18 1-1	Mar24 1-2	Oct28 1-0	Aug23 1-3	Sep06 1-3	Jan13 5-1
HAMILTON A	Apr23 5-1	Oct28 2-2	Dec23 5-0	Apr18 1-3	Apr28 3-5	Feb17 5-2	Sep09 1-3	Sep23 3-3	Nov25 3-1	Nov04 2-1	Apr07 3-4	Oct07 3-0		Feb10 0-2	Jan06 4-0	Jan20 2-2	Mar10 2-4	Dec02 3-0	Mar17 5-1
MONTROSE	Sep20 3-0	Apr21 2-2	Jan02 2-0	Dec30 1-1	Nov25 2-1	Sep16 6-0	Feb17 2-2	Feb03 1-1	Mar31 4-0	Oct28 2-0	Sep30 1-2	Mar17 3-4	Oct14 2-1		Dec16 1-3	Nov11 2-3	Jan13 1-0	Mar03 2-2	Aug23 2-1
MORTON	Sep13 2-0	Mar10 6-5	Sep30 1-1	Sep16 1-1	Dec23 1-0	Dec30 2-0	Oct14 2-5	Dec02 2-1	Oct28 1-3	Apr25 0-1	Feb03 1-0	Nov25 3-0	Aug23 3-1	Apr07 2-1		Sep27 2-2	Apr16 1-3	Jan13 4-2	Jan02 0-1
QUEEN OF SOUTH	Dec09 2-1	Nov25 2-1	Jan13 2-0	Jan02 2-1	Feb10 3-2	Aug23 5-0	Apr28 3-0	Dec16 7-1	Nov04 4-1	Dec23 3-1	Sep06 2-1	Feb24 0-3	Sep30 0-1	Mar10 1-1	Sep20 2-2		Mar31 3-1	Oct21 4-1	Sep16 3-1
QUEEN'S PARK	Sep09 1-1	Jan20 2-1	Mar07 1-1	Oct14 1-2	Apr07 2-1	Mar24 4-0	Jan17 2-1	Jan27 1-1	Dec23 3-0	Jan31 2-2	Sep27 1-2	Jan06 2-3	Nov22 1-1	Sep23 4-0	Nov18 2-5	Dec01 1-0		Feb03 2-3	Apr28 2-2
STENHOUSEMUIR	Oct28 3-1	Jan01 2-1	Dec16 3-2	Mar10 2-1	Sep27 3-1	Apr21 5-1	Jan20 1-4	Sep09 2-2	Jan06 2-1	Feb10 1-2	Dec30 0-2	Sep11 4-3	Mar31 4-1	Nov04 2-3	Sep23 3-4	Mar17 0-2	Oct07 3-3		Nov25 0-1
STRANRAER	Jan20 2-1	Apr18 1-1	Oct28 0-2	Sep27 4-1	Oct07 4-0	Nov11 4-0	Dec02 2-1	Apr21 1-1	Sep13 2-2	Apr07 2-2	Mar03 4-1	Sep23 1-1	Nov18 3-0	Jan06 1-1	Sep09 4-2	Jan01 0-3	Dec30 2-1	Mar24 4-0	

LEAGUE TABLES

DIVISION 1

	P	W	D	L	F	A	W	D	L	F	A	Pts
Dundee	34	13	2	2	41	23	12	2	3	39	23	54
Rangers	34	12	2	3	43	18	10	5	2	41	13	51
Celtic	34	12	4	1	46	16	7	4	6	35	21	46
Dunfermline A	34	13	1	3	46	15	6	4	7	31	31	43
Kilmarnock	34	10	4	3	41	27	6	6	5	33	31	42
Hearts	34	7	5	5	30	28	9	1	7	24	21	38
Partick T	34	12	0	5	36	21	4	3	10	24	34	35
Hibernian	34	7	5	5	31	30	7	0	10	27	42	33
Motherwell	34	7	3	7	35	34	6	3	8	30	28	32
Dundee U	34	8	3	6	43	30	5	3	9	27	41	32
T. Lanark	34	8	3	6	37	31	5	2	10	22	29	31
Aberdeen	34	6	6	5	33	27	4	3	10	27	46	29
Raith R	34	5	5	7	24	29	5	2	10	27	44	27
Falkirk	34	6	2	9	23	30	5	2	10	22	38	26
Airdrie	34	7	2	8	35	33	2	5	10	22	45	25
St Mirren	34	7	3	7	29	29	3	2	12	23	51	25
St Johnstone	34	4	2	11	14	34	5	5	7	21	27	25
Stirling A	34	5	3	9	22	32	1	3	13	12	44	18

DIVISION 2

	P	W	D	L	F	A	W	D	L	F	A	Pts
Clyde	36	15	2	1	61	17	10	2	6	47	30	54
Queen of South	36	14	2	2	48	19	10	3	5	30	14	53
Morton	36	10	3	5	34	27	9	3	6	44	37	44
Alloa	36	12	4	2	57	35	5	4	9	35	43	42
Montrose	36	9	5	4	39	23	6	6	6	24	27	41
Arbroath	36	10	2	6	36	26	7	5	6	30	33	41
Stranraer	36	10	6	2	41	20	4	5	9	20	42	39
Berwick R	36	10	4	4	46	26	6	2	10	37	44	38
Ayr U	36	11	2	5	45	24	4	6	8	26	39	38
East Fife	36	11	3	4	33	21	4	4	10	27	38	37
E. Stirling	36	8	2	8	41	38	7	2	9	29	43	34
Queen's Park	36	7	6	5	34	26	5	3	10	30	36	33
Hamilton A	36	9	3	6	52	34	5	2	11	26	45	33
Cowdenbeath	36	8	4	6	36	32	3	5	10	29	45	31
Stenhousemuir	36	9	2	7	40	35	4	3	11	29	51	31
Forfar A	36	7	4	7	41	36	4	4	10	27	40	30
Dumbarton	36	6	6	6	29	28	3	4	11	20	38	28
Albion R	36	7	3	8	24	32	3	2	13	18	42	25
Brechin C	36	2	2	14	20	53	3	0	15	24	70	12

Scottish Football League Records
Season 1962-63

DIVISION 1

	ABERDEEN	AIRDRIE	CELTIC	CLYDE	DUNDEE	DUNDEE U	DUNFERMLINE A	FALKIRK	HEARTS	HIBERNIAN	KILMARNOCK	MOTHERWELL	PARTICK T	QUEEN OF SOUTH	RAITH R	RANGERS	ST MIRREN	T LANARK
ABERDEEN		Aug22 2-1	Jan05 1-5	Apr06 0-2	Jan01 1-0	May07 1-2	Sep15 4-0	Nov24 1-0	Mar09 2-1	Nov10 3-0	Dec22 1-0	Mar23 1-1	Dec15 1-1	Mar26 4-1	Oct13 10-02-3	Oct27 0-1	Feb16 4-1	Sep29
AIRDRIE	Apr10 2-0		Oct27 1-6	Oct06 3-1	Mar09 1-0	Apr27 4-2	Dec08 0-1	Oct20 2-1	May13 4-2	Nov24 2-1	Apr24 0-3	Sep08 1-4	Apr06 2-0	Dec15 1-3	Sep22 8-1	May06 0-2	Mar23 4-2	Nov10 1-4
CELTIC	Sep22 1-2	Mar02 3-1		May06 2-0	Mar23 4-1	Oct20 1-0	Dec26 2-1	Dec29 2-1	Dec08 2-2	Apr06 2-0	Oct06 1-1	May13 6-0	Nov24 0-2	Nov10 0-1	Mar19 4-1	Sep08 0-1	Mar09 1-1	Apr20 2-1
CLYDE	Dec01 1-3	Mar20 2-0	Sep15 1-3		Jan05 3-2	Nov17 1-3	Sep29 0-1	Apr13 0-1	Mar16 0-6	Aug22 3-1	Nov03 0-5	Apr27 2-3	Jan01 1-2	Oct13 1-1	Mar27 4-2	May22 1-3	Dec15 2-0	Oct27 3-2
DUNDEE	Sep08 2-2	Nov03 2-1	Nov17 0-0	Sep22 2-0		Apr17 1-2	May15 1-0	Oct06 2-1	May06 2-2	Apr08 1-3	Oct20 1-0	Dec15 2-2	Mar16 2-1	Dec01 10-21-1	Apr27 0-0	May25 5-1	Apr13 5-2	May13
DUNDEE U	Dec08 3-3	Dec22 3-1	May11 3-0	Mar23 4-1	Sep15 1-1		Aug22 0-4	Apr06 1-0	Apr20 0-0	Sep29 5-0	Nov24 3-3	Mar09 2-1	May18 2-2	Jan01 2-1	Oct27 8-1	Nov10 2-1	Oct13 1-1	Apr29 1-0
DUNFERMLINE A	Apr17 3-0	Apr13 2-0	Apr27 1-1	Apr24 2-2	Oct27 2-0	Mar25 1-2		Sep22 2-1	Oct06 2-2	Dec15 3-2	Apr06 1-1	Nov24 4-3	May11 1-1	Mar23 2-0	Sep08 6-0	Mar09 1-2	Nov10 1-3	Oct13 3-0
FALKIRK	Apr03 2-1	May11 0-1	Aug22 1-3	Dec08 7-3	May18 0-2	Dec01 4-1	Apr10 2-0		Oct30 2-0	Mar27 3-1	Apr20 0-5	Nov10 3-2	Oct13 0-2	Sep15 2-2	Mar09 2-3	Mar23 0-2	Sep29 4-2	Jan01 3-5
HEARTS	Nov03 1-1	Sep15 6-1	Apr29 4-3	Nov10 1-1	Aug22 3-1	Dec15 2-2	May18 2-0	Mar13 5-0		May04 3-3	Mar18 2-3	Oct20 2-1	Apr10 2-4	Sep29 3-0	Apr06 2-1	Mar27 0-5	Nov24 5-0	Mar23 2-0
HIBERNIAN	Mar16 2-3	Mar30 0-2	Dec01 1-1	Dec29 1-2	Oct13 2-2	Apr24 1-1	Apr20 1-1	Apr27 0-3	Sep08 0-4		Nov17 0-2	Apr17 1-0	Dec08 0-2	Oct27 3-0	Oct06 1-0	Sep22 1-5	May11 2-1	Mar09 1-1
KILMARNOCK	Apr27 2-2	Sep29 8-0	Mar27 6-0	Mar09 3-2	May11 1-0	May01 2-2	Dec01 3-0	Dec15 3-1	Oct13 2-2	Mar23 2-0		Oct31 7-1	Aug22 1-2	Jan05 7-0	Nov10 3-1	May13 1-0	Jan01 2-1	Sep15 2-2
MOTHERWELL	Nov21 0-2	Jan01 3-0	Oct13 0-2	Dec22 6-2	Apr20 2-1	Nov03 0-0	Mar30 0-0	Mar16 4-1	May11 1-3	Sep15 2-2	Apr13 2-1		Sep29 1-1	Aug22 1-2	May15 5-1	Dec01 1-1	Jan05 1-1	Mar20 3-3
PARTICK T	Apr20 2-3	Dec01 3-0	Apr02 1-5	Sep08 5-1	Nov10 1-0	Oct06 3-0	Oct20 2-1	May01 2-0	Sep22 3-4	Apr13 2-2	Dec29 3-2	Apr24 2-0		Mar09 0-1	Mar23 4-1	Apr17 1-4	Oct27 2-1	Mar30 3-1
QUEEN OF SOUTH	Oct20 2-1	Apr20 1-1	Mar16 2-5	May04 2-2	Apr05 1-0	Sep08 1-0	Nov17 1-0	Jan02 0-1	Apr24 0-3	May15 0-4	Sep22 1-1	Dec29 0-2	Nov03 0-1		Nov24 5-1	Oct06 0-4	Dec22 2-3	Dec08 2-1
RAITH R	May04 0-4	Jan05 0-1	Sep29 0-2	Oct20 1-1	Dec22 2-4	Mar02 2-7	May01 1-2	Nov03 1-3	Dec01 0-3	May18 0-4	Mar16 1-4	Dec08 2-5	Nov17 2-3	May11 1-1		Apr20 2-2	Sep15 0-1	Aug22 1-1
RANGERS	May27 2-2	Oct13 5-2	Jan01 4-0	Nov24 3-1	Sep29 1-1	Mar16 5-0	Nov03 1-1	Nov17 4-0	Apr27 5-1	Apr10 3-1	Dec08 6-1	Apr29 1-1	Sep15 2-1	May18 3-1	Dec15 4-2		Aug22 3-0	May11 1-0
ST MIRREN	Oct06 2-1	Nov17 1-1	Nov03 0-7	Apr20 1-2	Dec08 0-3	May03 2-1	Mar16 3-1	Mar06 2-2	Apr02 7-3	Oct20 2-2	Sep08 2-4	Sep22 2-0	Mar02 1-1	Apr27 4-0	Jan02 1-2	Dec29 0-2		Dec01 2-4
T LANARK	Apr24 1-2	Mar16 2-3	Dec15 2-0	Mar02 2-1	Nov24 4-3	Sep22 1-1	May03 4-0	Sep08 3-3	Nov17 1-2	Nov03 1-4	Jan02 0-1	Oct06 2-2	Apr27 0-1	Apr13 1-0	Dec29 2-1	Oct23 1-4	Apr05 1-1	

DIVISION 2

	ALBION R	ALLOA	ARBROATH	AYR U	BERWICK R	BRECHIN C	COWDENBEATH	DUMBARTON	EAST FIFE	E STIRLING	FORFAR A	HAMILTON A	MONTROSE	MORTON	QUEEN'S PARK	ST JOHNSTONE	STENHOUSEMUIR	STIRLING A	STRANRAER
ALBION R		May15 0-2	Sep15 2-0	Sep29 0-3	Nov03 3-1	Apr20 5-2	Apr13 3-3	Jan05 1-0	Aug22 4-2	May01 2-0	May11 4-1	Jan01 0-2	Dec22 2-1	Mar16 3-0	Apr03 4-2	Apr29 1-0	Dec01 4-1	Oct13 3-2	Sep26 1-0
ALLOA	Oct27 4-2		Sep29 1-3	Sep15 1-1	Nov17 3-2	Apr17 3-0	Oct13 0-1	Aug22 2-0	Mar30 2-1	May11 0-0	Nov10 6-1	Dec01 1-3	May18 1-2	Apr20 0-2	Sep19 2-1	Dec08 0-0	Apr03 1-0	Apr10 3-0	Sep05 4-0
ARBROATH	Apr17 3-0	Apr24 2-0		Oct27 4-1	Sep22 4-0	Mar30 2-0	Sep03 1-1	Dec08 4-2	Nov17 3-0	Sep19 5-2	Sep08 1-2	Feb23 3-1	Apr03 0-0	Apr27 1-0	Dec15 2-1	Oct06 1-2	Nov10 4-1	Mar09 4-4	Apr06 6-1
AYR U	Apr24 5-0	May04 2-2	Mar02 3-5		May06 4-1	Sep05 3-2	Sep22 2-0	Apr06 2-0	Oct20 1-1	Mar30 1-4	Apr27 4-2	Mar16 2-2	Nov17 4-3	Sep08 2-1	Oct06 0-3	Apr17 3-1	Apr20 2-3	Sep19 0-1	Dec08 0-2
BERWICK R	Mar09 1-5	Mar23 1-0	Jan05 0-2	Oct13 1-1		Dec08 3-2	Nov10 0-0	Sep29 1-0	Dec01 2-4	Apr03 1-1	Sep19 5-1	Feb02 3-6	Oct27 0-0	Mar30 2-3	Apr10 4-4	Apr27 1-3	Feb23 4-0	Sep15 2-0	May01 1-1
BRECHIN C	Dec15 2-3	Oct06 1-2	Nov24 0-1	Sep12 2-1	Apr13 1-2		Apr24 0-4	Oct13 0-3	Sep26 1-3	Oct27 1-3	Dec29 1-1	Dec22 0-0	Sep08 0-3	Nov17 3-5	Jan02 3-0	Apr06 1-2	May04 0-0	Mar16 3-6	Sep22 1-3
COWDENBEATH	Dec08 4-1	May01 1-2	Sep12 3-2	Apr29 1-1	Mar16 2-4	Sep29 5-2		Apr10 5-2	Apr01 3-3	Dec01 2-1	Apr15 3-2	Aug22 1-2	Sep26 3-1	Oct20 2-0	Nov03 6-2	May15 1-2	Mar30 5-0	Apr20 0-1	May18 1-1
DUMBARTON	Sep22 1-3	Dec29 1-0	Apr13 3-1	Dec01 3-1	Apr24 3-0	Apr03 4-3	Apr27 1-0		Nov03 5-2	Mar27 2-2	Jan26 1-0	Nov17 0-1	Apr17 3-0	Oct06 0-3	Sep08 1-2	Mar16 2-3	Mar20 2-1	Mar30 3-0	Oct27 5-1
EAST FIFE	Mar27 2-0	Nov24 1-1	Mar23 1-3	Feb23 0-1	Apr06 2-1	Sep19 3-0	Sep08 3-0	Mar09 3-0		Nov10 2-2	Sep05 2-1	Apr13 4-0	Apr24 1-0	Sep22 0-0	Apr27 2-1	Dec15 2-2	Oct13 2-0	Oct27 1-4	Apr17 1-0
E STIRLING	Oct06 4-2	Oct20 1-0	Sep26 3-0	Nov24 3-1	Sep08 2-1	Apr29 2-1	Apr06 3-0	Mar13 3-1	Mar16 2-1		Sep22 4-1	Nov03 3-1	Apr13 2-2	May04 2-0	Apr24 5-1	May06 0-0	Nov17 2-2	Apr27 2-0	Dec15 6-0
FORFAR A	Oct20 4-1	Mar16 1-1	Jan01 2-1	Dec22 2-6	Sep26 6-0	Aug22 7-1	Mar23 2-1	Apr20 3-4	Sep12 4-2	Apr10 3-1		Sep15 2-2	Nov24 2-4	May15 2-3	Apr13 0-4	Nov03 3-3	Sep29 4-1	Apr29 0-2	Oct13 0-3
HAMILTON A	Sep08 4-3	Jan12 1-2	Oct20 1-0	Nov10 2-2	Oct06 4-1	Apr27 1-0	Dec29 1-0	Mar23 4-2	Dec08 2-1	Mar09 1-3	Jan02 2-2		Dec15 5-1	Jan19 0-1	Sep22 2-2	May01 2-0	Oct27 1-0	Sep05 2-2	Nov24 3-3
MONTROSE	Apr27 2-0	Nov03 4-2	Aug22 2-1	Mar23 3-1	Mar02 0-1	Jan12 1-2	Sep19 2-4	Sep15 0-2	Sep29 2-0	Dec08 3-1	Mar30 3-0	Apr20 4-2		Sep04 2-1	May08 1-3	Oct20 1-3	Feb02 0-1	Dec01 2-6	Nov10 3-3
MORTON	Nov10 5-2	Mar27 5-3	Dec22 3-2	Apr03 6-1	Nov24 2-1	Mar23 7-0	May11 6-1	Feb02 0-0	Apr10 5-0	Oct13 2-3	Oct27 8-2	Sep29 1-0	Mar13 6-0		Apr15 4-1	Sep26 0-1	Sep15 4-0	Aug22 3-2	Mar09 3-1
QUEEN'S PARK	Mar23 1-3	Sep26 3-1	Apr20 1-1	Mar27 4-1	Sep12 2-4	Sep15 6-1	Mar09 1-3	Jan01 2-2	Apr29 1-3	Sep29 1-1	Dec08 3-2	Jan05 0-1	Oct13 2-0	Dec01 1-2		Mar30 1-0	Aug22 0-3	Nov10 5-2	May11 1-0
ST JOHNSTONE	Sep05 7-1	Apr13 4-0	May18 1-0	Aug22 1-2	Dec22 1-0	Dec01 7-0	Oct27 1-0	Nov10 2-0	Apr20 6-0	Sep15 5-2	Mar09 2-1	Oct13 4-1	May11 1-0	Apr24 2-1	May04 1-0		Apr10 1-3	Apr03 2-0	Mar23 1-0
STENHOUSEMUIR	Apr06 3-0	Sep08 2-1	Mar16 3-2	Dec15 2-0	Oct20 2-2	Nov03 3-1	Nov24 1-2	Aug28 1-0	Feb16 1-2	Mar23 1-2	Apr24 1-0	Apr29 2-5	Oct06 1-2	Apr17 0-5	Dec29 3-0	Sep22 5-5		Dec08 3-1	Apr27 1-3
STIRLING A	Mar13 3-3	Sep22 1-2	Nov03 2-0	Sep26 2-2	Jan02 0-3	Oct20 7-2	Dec15 2-1	Nov24 3-1	Mar20 3-2	May13 2-1	Oct06 4-3	Sep12 0-2	Apr06 2-1	Dec29 4-2	May06 0-2	Sep08 1-4	Apr13 4-1		Apr24 1-3
STRANRAER	Sep19 2-1	Sep12 6-2	Dec01 2-0	Apr13 7-2	Aug22 3-1	Jan05 2-0	Oct06 3-3	Mar02 5-5	Sep15 6-1	Apr20 2-2	May04 5-4	Mar30 1-0	Mar16 2-2	Nov03 3-1	Oct20 2-2	Nov17 1-3	Dec22 2-2	Sep29 2-0	

LEAGUE TABLES

DIVISION 1

	P	W	D	L	F	A	W	D	L	F	A	Pts
Rangers	34	13	4	0	53	15	12	3	2	41	13	57
Kilmarnock	34	12	4	1	55	16	8	4	5	37	24	48
Partick T	34	11	1	5	39	26	9	5	3	27	18	46
Celtic	34	10	3	4	33	16	9	3	5	43	28	44
Hearts	34	10	4	3	45	26	7	5	5	40	33	43
Aberdeen	34	10	2	5	38	19	7	5	5	32	28	41
Dundee U	34	10	6	1	41	20	5	5	7	26	32	41
Dunfermline A	34	9	5	3	37	20	4	3	10	13	27	34
Dundee	34	9	6	2	39	20	3	3	11	21	29	33
Motherwell	34	6	7	4	32	23	4	4	9	28	40	31
Airdrie	34	10	0	7	36	33	4	2	11	16	43	30
St Mirren	34	6	4	7	32	36	4	4	9	20	36	28
Falkirk	34	8	1	8	35	35	4	2	11	19	34	27
T. Lanark	34	6	4	7	28	29	3	4	10	28	39	26
Queen of South	34	6	3	8	20	30	4	3	10	16	45	26
Hibernian	34	4	5	8	17	30	4	4	9	30	37	25
Clyde	34	6	1	10	25	38	3	4	10	24	45	23
Raith R	34	0	4	13	16	48	2	1	14	19	70	9

DIVISION 2

	P	W	D	L	F	A	W	D	L	F	A	Pts
St Johnstone	36	16	0	2	49	11	9	5	4	34	26	55
E. Stirling	36	15	3	0	49	14	5	6	7	31	36	49
Morton	36	15	1	2	70	20	8	1	9	30	29	48
Hamilton A	36	10	5	3	38	25	8	3	7	31	31	44
Stranraer	36	11	6	1	56	31	5	4	9	25	39	42
Arbroath	36	13	3	2	50	18	5	1	12	24	33	40
Albion R	36	14	1	3	42	22	4	1	13	30	57	38
Cowdenbeath	36	10	3	5	48	29	5	4	9	24	32	37
Alloa	36	10	3	5	34	19	5	3	10	23	37	36
Stirling A	36	10	2	6	41	35	6	2	10	33	40	36
East Fife	36	11	4	3	32	16	4	2	12	28	53	36
Dumbarton	36	12	1	5	40	23	3	3	12	24	41	34
Ayr U	36	9	3	6	40	33	4	5	9	28	44	34
Queen's Park	36	8	3	7	35	30	5	3	10	31	42	32
Montrose	36	9	1	8	35	33	4	4	10	22	37	31
Stenhousemuir	36	9	2	7	35	33	4	3	11	19	42	31
Berwick R	36	6	6	6	32	33	5	1	12	25	44	29
Forfar A	36	8	3	7	47	40	1	2	15	26	59	23
Brechin C	36	2	3	13	20	42	1	0	17	19	71	9

Scottish Football League Records
Season 1963-64

DIVISION 1

	ABERDEEN	AIRDRIE	CELTIC	DUNDEE	DUNDEE U	DUNFERMLINE A	E STIRLING	FALKIRK	HEARTS	HIBERNIAN	KILMARNOCK	MOTHERWELL	PARTICK T	QUEEN OF SOUTH	RANGERS	ST JOHNSTONE	ST MIRREN	T LANARK
ABERDEEN		Jan18 2-2	Feb08 0-3	Sep07 2-4	Apr18 0-0	Apr08 0-1	Dec07 4-1	Oct26 3-0	Feb29 1-2	Mar28 3-1	Feb19 0-0	Nov16 6-2	Dec28 0-5	Mar21 3-0	Mar11 1-1	Jan02 0-1	Sep21 0-2	Oct05 1-1
AIRDRIE	Sep28 1-7		Feb22 0-2	Mar18 3-1	Feb01 3-1	Nov30 0-0	Mar21 5-2	Nov16 2-5	Aug21 0-2	Dec07 5-3	Sep14 4-5	Jan01 1-1	Dec21 2-0	Apr10 2-1	Nov02 0-4	Oct19 3-3	Apr18 2-4	Oct12 1-0
CELTIC	Oct12 3-0	Oct26 9-0		Apr01 2-1	Feb19 1-0	Oct05 2-2	Feb29 5-2	Jan04 7-0	Apr18 1-1	Mar14 5-0	Nov23 5-0	Dec21 2-1	Nov09 5-3	Aug21 4-0	Jan01 0-1	Dec07 3-1	Jan18 3-0	Sep14 4-4
DUNDEE	Jan01 1-4	Nov09 4-0	Nov30 1-1		Sep14 1-1	Oct26 2-1	Sep28 3-1	Dec21 4-3	Mar21 2-4	Feb19 3-0	Apr04 2-1	Oct12 1-3	Apr18 5-2	Feb01 6-2	Aug21 1-1	Apr13 2-1	Feb29 9-2	Jan04 6-0
DUNDEE U	Dec14 1-2	Oct05 9-1	Oct19 0-3	Jan02 2-1		Jan18 1-2	Sep21 2-0	Nov02 3-1	Nov16 0-0	Apr24 1-1	Mar11 2-1	Feb22 4-1	Feb08 1-2	Mar28 2-1	Dec07 2-3	Sep07 3-1	Dec28 6-2	Nov23 4-1
DUNFERMLINE A	Apr24 3-1	Mar30 5-1	Feb01 1-0	Feb22 1-2	Sep28 4-2		Mar14 4-1	Mar09 1-0	Sep14 2-2	Oct12 3-0	Jan04 2-3	Aug21 2-0	Oct19 0-0	Jan01 0-0	Nov23 1-4	Nov02 4-0	Dec07 5-0	Dec14 3-0
E STIRLING	Apr04 2-1	Nov26 1-2	Nov02 1-5	Jan18 1-5	Jan04 1-1	Nov16 0-2		Jan01 1-2	Dec21 2-3	Dec14 1-3	Aug21 0-2	Mar17 0-0	Oct26 1-0	Sep14 4-0	Feb19 0-5	Feb08 0-1	Oct05 2-1	Mar28 2-3
FALKIRK	Feb22 2-3	Mar14 2-1	Sep21 1-0	Apr29 0-2	Feb29 2-1	Nov09 2-2	Sep07 1-0		Sep28 1-2	Jan02 1-4	Oct12 1-1	Mar21 0-4	Nov30 3-0	Apr18 3-2	Feb01 0-1	Dec28 1-1	Oct19 2-0	Dec07 2-2
HEARTS	Nov02 0-0	Dec28 4-0	Dec14 1-1	Nov23 1-3	Mar14 0-4	Jan02 2-1	Jan11 4-0	Jan17 4-1		Sep07 4-2	Feb22 1-1	Dec07 1-1	Sep21 4-1	Oct12 0-1	Apr01 1-2	Oct05 3-3	Nov09 5-1	Mar04 4-1
HIBERNIAN	Nov30 2-0	Apr04 2-1	Nov16 1-1	Oct19 0-4	Dec21 2-3	Feb08 0-0	Apr18 5-2	Sep14 2-2	Jan01 1-1		Sep28 0-2	Feb01 3-1	Feb29 2-1	Mar07 5-2	Jan04 0-1	Oct26 4-1	Mar21 1-0	Aug21 3-0
KILMARNOCK	Oct19 2-0	Jan02 4-1	Mar21 4-0	Dec07 1-1	Nov09 2-0	Sep21 0-3	Dec28 4-1	Feb08 9-2	Oct26 3-1	Jan18 2-1		Nov30 5-2	Oct05 3-0	Feb29 2-1	Nov16 1-1	Apr18 4-1	Sep07 2-0	Apr25 2-0
MOTHERWELL	Mar14 0-1	Sep07 3-0	Mar28 1-1	Feb08 2-2	Oct26 0-3	Dec28 1-1	Nov09 4-1	Nov23 3-0	Apr04 0-1	Oct05 4-3	Apr01 2-0		Jan18 2-1	Jan11 0-0	Dec14 3-3	Sep21 1-3	Jan02 3-0	Feb29 1-1
PARTICK T	Aug21 1-1	Apr24 1-0	Mar11 2-2	Dec14 2-0	Oct12 1-0	Feb19 0-1	Feb22 3-2	Mar27 4-1	Jan04 2-1	Nov02 2-1	Feb01 2-0	Sep28 0-0		Dec07 6-1	Sep14 0-3	Nov23 2-1	Nov16 2-1	Jan01 0-1
QUEEN OF SOUTH	Nov23 2-3	Sep21 3-1	Dec28 0-2	Oct05 0-5	Nov30 1-1	Sep07 1-2	Jan02 2-1	Dec14 3-6	Feb08 1-4	Nov09 3-2	Nov02 0-4	Oct19 2-2	Apr04 1-2		Feb22 1-4	Jan18 0-3	Apr25 1-1	Mar14 2-4
RANGERS	Nov09 0-0	Feb29 4-1	Sep07 2-1	Dec28 2-1	Apr04 2-0	Mar21 2-1	Oct19 3-1	Oct05 4-0	Nov30 0-3	Sep21 5-0	Mar14 2-0	Apr18 5-1	Jan02 4-3	Oct30 2-0		Dec21 2-3	Feb08 2-3	Jan18 2-1
ST JOHNSTONE	Sep14 3-1	Feb19 0-1	Apr04 1-1	Nov16 1-6	Jan01 2-2	Feb29 3-2	Oct12 3-0	Aug21 5-0	Feb01 1-4	Feb22 0-4	Dec14 0-2	Jan04 1-1	Mar21 2-3	Sep28 2-3	Apr29 1-0		Nov30 2-1	Nov09 0-1
ST MIRREN	Jan04 3-1	Dec14 2-4	Sep28 2-1	Nov02 2-1	Aug21 2-1	Apr04 1-1	Feb01 2-1	Feb19 0-0	Mar07 0-2	Nov23 1-1	Jan01 1-3	Sep14 2-1	Mar14 0-0	Dec21 3-2	Oct12 0-3	Mar28 2-1		Oct24 1-0
T LANARK	Feb01 1-2	Feb08 1-2	Jan02 1-1	Sep21 1-2	Mar21 2-2	Apr18 0-1	Nov30 1-2	Apr04 3-7	Oct19 0-2	Dec28 1-0	Dec21 1-2	Nov02 3-1	Sep07 3-2	Nov16 1-1	Sep28 0-5	Mar07 4-2	Feb25 4-2	

DIVISION 2

	ALBION R	ALLOA	ARBROATH	AYR U	BERWICK R	BRECHIN C	CLYDE	COWDENBEATH	DUMBARTON	EAST FIFE	FORFAR A	HAMILTON A	MONTROSE	MORTON	QUEEN'S PARK	RAITH R	STENHOUSEMUIR	STIRLING A	STRANRAER
ALBION R		Nov23 4-3	Oct05 1-1	Oct26 3-1	Mar28 1-2	Sep21 3-1	Apr29 2-2	Mar14 1-1	Sep25 3-3	Feb08 1-1	Apr24 1-1	Sep07 3-3	Dec14 1-0	Apr04 0-0	Dec28 1-0	Sep11 1-0	Nov09 1-3	Feb29 2-2	Jan02 4-1
ALLOA	Mar21 2-2		Dec28 0-2	Jan02 5-1	Sep28 1-2	Mar14 4-2	Oct12 1-4	Apr24 0-0	Apr18 2-1	Feb29 2-3	Dec07 6-1	Nov09 2-0	Oct19 2-4	Nov30 0-3	Sep18 1-2	Feb22 0-6	Sep07 1-2	Feb01 4-2	Sep21 4-0
ARBROATH	Feb01 4-0	Aug21 3-0		Feb29 0-1	Mar07 2-2	Mar28 3-1	Jan04 0-0	Oct12 2-0	Nov16 4-0	Apr18 2-3	Jan01 5-1	Apr25 2-0	Sep14 2-4	Nov23 1-2	Sep11 2-1	Sep24 8-1	Dec07 2-6	Sep28 3-0	Oct26 2-0
AYR U	Feb22 4-3	Sep14 0-2	Nov02 1-2		Aug21 5-1	Oct12 1-0	Mar14 0-2	Jan04 0-1	Apr29 1-0	Dec21 1-1	Nov23 2-1	Apr04 1-4	Sep23 2-5	Jan01 1-3	Sep28 1-3	Feb01 1-1	Nov30 3-2	Apr22 4-1	Apr06 0-2
BERWICK R	Nov30 2-2	Jan18 4-0	Nov09 1-3	Dec28 6-1		Apr25 2-2	Feb29 2-3	Sep23 1-2	Dec07 2-3	Mar21 4-0	Oct26 1-1	Jan02 1-2	Apr01 3-1	Feb15 1-3	Apr18 4-2	Apr08 1-1	Sep21 2-2	Oct12 6-0	Sep07 0-3
BRECHIN C	Jan04 2-4	Nov16 5-1	Nov30 1-1	Feb08 3-4	Apr29 5-2		Oct05 2-2	Nov02 2-1	Mar07 2-1	Jan18 0-6	Sep14 3-0	Dec14 0-2	Jan01 1-2	Sep25 3-7	Apr04 2-2	Aug21 2-1	Oct19 3-2	Feb22 4-2	Sep11 2-2
CLYDE	Oct19 3-2	Feb08 0-1	Sep21 2-0	Nov16 6-0	Nov02 3-1	Feb01 5-0		Mar21 2-1	Apr23 4-2	Nov30 1-3	Sep11 5-2	Dec28 1-0	Apr04 2-0	Sep28 1-2	Sep07 1-0	Mar07 3-3	Sep18 2-2	Jan02 0-0	Dec14 1-1
COWDENBEATH	Nov16 2-2	Dec21 8-2	Feb08 0-2	Sep21 2-1	Apr22 1-1	Feb29 2-3	Oct26 2-3		Nov30 0-1	Jan02 0-0	Apr29 0-0	Jan18 2-2	Nov09 1-1	Apr18 1-5	Apr20 1-1	Apr04 0-3	Sep04 2-1	Dec28 3-3	Oct05 2-2
DUMBARTON	Sep18 0-2	Dec14 2-1	Mar14 1-0	Nov09 3-2	Apr04 1-1	Nov23 1-1	Dec21 0-1	Mar28 8-0		Sep21 1-3	Sep28 3-1	Feb29 2-0	Feb22 2-1	Apr13 0-2	Jan02 1-4	Oct19 4-0	Feb01 3-2	Sep07 5-2	Oct12 4-1
EAST FIFE	Oct12 2-0	Nov02 8-0	Dec14 3-0	Apr25 3-3	Nov23 6-0	Sep28 0-0	Mar28 1-1	Sep14 0-2	Jan04 2-2		Sep24 2-2	Jan11 2-1	Aug21 1-1	Feb01 3-1	Mar07 3-0	Jan01 3-0	Feb22 3-4	Oct19 5-1	Mar14 6-0
FORFAR A	Dec21 3-0	Apr04 3-3	Sep07 1-2	Apr15 3-3	Feb22 3-3	Jan02 2-4	Sep04 0-5	Oct19 2-1	Jan18 0-2	Apr22 5-4		Oct05 1-2	Nov30 2-8	Nov02 4-6	Sep21 2-2	Dec14 0-1	Dec28 4-3	Apr08 2-0	Nov09 0-1
HAMILTON A	Jan01 5-2	Mar07 3-4	Dec21 2-2	Dec07 2-4	Sep14 2-0	Apr18 3-3	Aug21 2-3	Sep28 3-2	Nov02 1-3	Sep04 2-2	Feb01 1-0		Jan04 3-4	Feb22 1-3	Oct19 1-2	Oct12 1-5	Mar21 3-0	Apr15 6-1	Nov30 3-3
MONTROSE	Apr18 3-4	Feb15 4-1	Jan02 1-3	Sep18 4-2	Apr15 1-1	Sep07 4-0	Dec07 1-2	Mar07 4-1	Oct26 2-1	Dec28 3-0	Mar28 5-0	Sep21 2-0		Oct12 0-2	Feb01 2-1	Sep28 1-0	Mar14 2-2	Nov23 4-1	Apr25 2-1
MORTON	Dec07 3-1	Mar28 2-2	Mar21 2-2	Sep07 2-0	Oct19 7-1	Oct01 8-1	Jan18 3-0	Dec14 2-0	Sep04 5-1	Oct05 6-1	Feb29 6-1	Nov04 8-0	Feb08 2-0		Nov16 4-0	Apr24 4-2	Jan02 7-2	Nov09 5-1	Dec28 4-0
QUEEN'S PARK	Aug21 4-2	Sep24 1-0	Sep04 3-2	Jan18 3-2	Dec18 1-2	Dec04 3-0	Jan01 2-4	Nov23 0-1	Sep14 2-1	Nov09 2-0	Jan04 2-0	Feb15 2-0	Oct05 0-0	Mar14 0-3		Apr01 2-3	Oct12 2-0	Apr29 2-1	Apr15 2-0
RAITH R	Sep04 3-0	Oct26 1-2	Sep18 2-3	Oct05 0-1	Nov16 2-0	Dec28 2-0	Nov09 1-2	Dec07 2-0	Feb15 2-1	Sep07 1-1	Apr18 1-4	Feb08 4-0	Jan18 6-1	Dec21 0-3	Nov30 2-3		Feb29 2-2	Sep21 7-0	Mar21 2-1
STENHOUSEMUIR	Mar07 1-2	Jan01 2-1	Apr04 0-4	Mar28 1-2	Jan04 8-2	Feb15 4-0	Sep24 1-3	Sep09 5-1	Oct05 0-1	Oct26 3-3	Aug20 4-2	Nov23 2-0	Nov16 0-1	Sep14 4-5	Apr10 1-0	Nov02 1-0		Dec14 3-1	Jan18 4-0
STIRLING A	Nov02 2-1	Oct05 2-2	Jan18 0-1	Sep04 2-2	Feb08 1-2	Oct26 5-1	Sep14 1-1	Aug21 2-1	Jan01 1-1	Feb15 2-5	Nov16 2-1	Sep23 2-3	Mar21 1-1	Apr07 1-2	Dec21 2-1	Jan04 3-0	Apr18 0-2		Apr04 0-2
STRANRAER	Sep14 1-5	Jan04 3-2	Feb22 3-2	Oct19 1-0	Jan01 3-2	Sep04 4-0	Apr18 3-1	Feb01 3-2	Feb08 2-2	Nov16 3-3	Mar07 5-2	Mar28 1-2	Dec21 4-0	Aug21 1-3	Nov02 2-0	Nov23 2-3	Sep28 5-2	Dec07 5-0	

LEAGUE TABLES

DIVISION 1

	P	W	D	L	F	A	W	D	L	F	A	Pts
Rangers	34	13	1	3	43	19	12	4	1	42	12	55
Kilmarnock	34	14	2	1	50	15	8	3	6	27	25	49
Celtic	34	13	3	1	61	16	6	6	5	28	18	47
Hearts	34	8	5	4	39	23	11	4	2	35	17	47
Dunfermline A	34	11	3	3	41	16	7	6	4	23	17	45
Dundee	34	11	3	3	53	27	9	2	6	41	23	45
Partick T	34	11	3	3	30	16	4	2	11	25	38	35
Dundee U	34	10	2	5	43	23	3	6	8	22	26	34
Aberdeen	34	5	5	7	26	26	7	3	7	27	27	32
Hibernian	34	9	4	4	33	22	3	2	12	26	44	30
Motherwell	34	7	5	5	29	24	2	6	9	22	38	29
St Mirren	34	9	4	4	24	23	3	1	13	20	51	29
St Johnstone	34	6	3	8	27	32	5	3	9	27	38	28
Falkirk	34	7	4	6	24	26	4	2	11	30	58	28
Airdrie	34	7	3	7	34	41	4	1	12	18	56	26
T. Lanark	34	5	3	9	27	36	4	4	9	20	38	25
Queen of South	34	3	3	11	23	47	2	3	12	17	45	16
E. Stirling	34	4	2	11	19	36	1	0	16	18	55	12

DIVISION 2

	P	W	D	L	F	A	W	D	L	F	A	Pts
Morton	36	16	2	0	80	15	16	1	1	55	22	67
Clyde	36	11	4	3	42	20	11	5	2	39	24	53
Arbroath	36	11	2	5	47	22	9	4	5	32	24	46
East Fife	36	10	6	2	53	18	6	7	5	39	39	45
Montrose	36	12	2	4	45	22	7	4	7	34	35	44
Dumbarton	36	11	2	5	41	24	5	4	9	26	35	38
Queen's Park	36	12	1	5	33	21	5	3	10	24	33	38
Stranraer	36	12	2	4	51	31	4	4	10	20	42	38
Albion R	36	7	9	2	33	25	5	3	10	34	46	36
Raith R	36	9	2	7	40	24	6	3	9	30	37	35
Stenhousemuir	36	10	1	7	44	28	5	4	9	39	47	35
Berwick R	36	6	5	7	43	31	4	5	9	25	53	30
Hamilton A	36	6	4	8	44	43	6	2	10	21	38	30
Ayr U	36	7	2	9	28	34	5	3	10	30	49	29
Brechin C	36	8	4	6	42	42	2	4	12	19	56	28
Alloa	36	7	2	9	37	37	4	3	11	27	55	27
Cowdenbeath	36	3	9	6	29	33	4	2	12	17	39	25
Forfar A	36	5	4	9	37	50	1	4	13	20	54	20
Stirling A	36	6	5	7	29	29	0	3	15	18	70	20

Scottish Football League Records
Season 1964-65

DIVISION 1

	ABERDEEN	AIRDRIE	CELTIC	CLYDE	DUNDEE	DUNDEE U	DUNFERMLINE A	FALKIRK	HEARTS	HIBERNIAN	KILMARNOCK	MORTON	MOTHERWELL	PARTICK T	RANGERS	ST JOHNSTONE	ST MIRREN	T LANARK
ABERDEEN		Mar24 5-2	Oct10 1-3	Dec19 0-3	Jan01 1-1	Apr03 1-0	Feb27 2-2	Oct31 2-1	Apr17 0-3	Jan09 1-1	Nov21 1-1	Nov14 2-1	Oct17 0-1	Sep26 5-1	Mar13 2-0	Sep12 5-5	Aug19 2-1	Jan27 3-1
AIRDRIE	Apr10 2-4		Mar10 0-6	Feb17 3-5	Apr24 2-2	Oct24 3-3	Oct17 3-4	Oct03 2-2	Dec26 1-2	Dec12 0-1	Jan02 2-1	Sep19 0-2	Sep05 0-3	Apr03 0-5	Jan16 0-4	Nov21 1-2	Mar20 5-1	Nov07 2-1
CELTIC	Jan30 8-0	Oct31 2-1		Jan02 1-1	Nov14 0-2	Sep19 1-1	Dec19 1-2	Nov21 3-0	Jan16 1-2	Mar22 2-4	Feb27 2-0	Oct12 1-0	Dec26 2-0	Apr17 1-2	Sep05 3-1	Mar13 0-1	Oct17 4-1	Apr03 1-0
CLYDE	Apr24 4-0	Oct10 4-3	Sep12 1-1		Feb20 1-0	Nov07 2-0	Jan09 1-0	Mar20 6-1	Mar27 2-5	Aug19 1-3	Nov28 1-2	Feb13 1-0	Apr07 1-1	Jan01 4-1	Mar10 0-3	Oct24 4-1	Dec12 1-1	Sep26 1-0
DUNDEE	Sep05 3-1	Dec19 4-0	Mar20 3-3	Oct03 1-2		Mar24 2-4	Nov07 3-1	Feb10 3-2	Oct24 1-2	Apr03 2-1	Oct17 1-3	Dec26 1-1	Jan16 4-2	Nov21 3-3	Sep19 4-1	Dec05 4-4	Mar06 2-1	Apr17 6-1
DUNDEE U	Nov28 0-3	Feb27 3-2	Jan09 3-1	Mar13 6-0	Sep12 1-4		Nov14 2-0	Feb13 4-1	Apr10 1-1	Sep26 0-1	Oct31 0-1	Mar27 3-2	Apr24 3-1	Aug19 1-2	Dec12 1-3	Jan01 4-1	Jan23 2-0	Oct10 4-1
DUNFERMLINE A	Oct24 2-0	Feb13 3-1	Apr28 5-1	Sep19 7-2	Mar13 3-3	Mar20 0-1		Sep05 5-1	Jan02 3-2	Nov21 1-0	Jan16 1-0	Feb10 6-0	Oct03 3-0	Oct31 2-0	Apr14 3-1	Apr17 1-1	Apr03 2-1	Mar22 8-0
FALKIRK	Mar06 0-1	Mar02 4-1	Apr14 6-2	Nov14 0-0	Oct10 4-2	Oct17 0-0	Jan01 0-4		Nov07 2-2	Sep12 0-1	Apr07 0-1	Dec19 0-2	Dec12 1-1	Jan09 2-2	Nov28 0-5	Aug19 3-2	Sep26 2-0	Oct24 3-0
HEARTS	Dec12 6-3	Aug19 8-1	Sep26 4-2	Nov21 3-0	Feb27 1-7	Dec05 3-1	Sep12 1-1	Mar13 5-2		Jan01 0-1	Apr24 0-2	Oct31 4-1	Mar20 2-0	Jan23 1-0	Oct17 1-1	Apr03 4-1	Oct10 0-0	Jan09 3-1
HIBERNIAN	Sep19 4-2	Apr17 5-1	Apr07 0-4	Dec26 4-3	Nov28 2-2	Jan16 3-4	Mar31 1-0	Jan02 6-0	Sep05 3-5		Oct03 1-2	Oct24 2-1	Mar10 2-0	Dec19 2-1	Jan30 1-0	Feb13 2-0	Nov07 1-1	Nov14 5-0
KILMARNOCK	Mar27 2-1	Sep12 2-0	Oct28 5-2	Apr03 2-1	Feb13 1-4	Mar10 4-2	Sep26 1-0	Dec05 2-0	Dec19 3-1	Feb16 4-3		Apr17 3-0	Nov07 1-1	Oct10 0-0	Nov14 1-1	Jan09 0-0	Jan01 4-0	Aug19 3-1
MORTON	Mar20 1-1	Jan09 5-0	Jan23 3-3	Oct17 0-0	Aug19 3-2	Nov21 2-0	Oct10 2-0	Apr24 4-0	Mar10 2-3	Feb27 3-2	Dec12 5-1		Apr03 0-2	Nov07 0-3	Apr07 1-3	Sep26 3-1	Sep12 0-0	Jan01 4-0
MOTHERWELL	Apr14 2-2	Jan01 1-2	Aug19 1-3	Mar22 0-1	Sep26 2-1	Dec19 1-1	Jan23 1-3	Apr17 1-0	Nov14 1-3	Oct31 0-2	Mar13 0-2	Nov28 4-1		Feb27 0-2	Apr21 1-3	Oct10 2-2	Jan09 4-0	Sep12 3-3
PARTICK T	Jan16 2-1	Nov28 3-1	Dec12 2-4	Sep05 0-3	Mar27 4-4	Apr19 0-0	Mar08 1-2	Sep19 4-1	Oct03 1-3	Apr23 4-2	Jan30 1-0	Mar13 1-1	Oct24 1-2		Jan02 1-1	Nov14 2-2	Apr07 1-2	Oct17 0-1
RANGERS	Nov07 2-2	Sep26 9-2	Jan01 1-0	Oct31 6-1	Jan09 4-0	Apr17 0-1	Aug19 0-0	Apr03 6-1	Feb13 1-1	Oct10 2-4	Mar20 1-1	Mar30 0-1	Nov21 1-0	Sep12 1-1		Mar24 2-1	Feb27 1-0	Dec19 5-0
ST JOHNSTONE	Feb17 2-4	Mar27 1-1	Nov07 3-0	Feb27 1-0	Apr07 2-2	Sep05 2-0	Dec12 1-3	Mar10 2-2	Nov28 0-3	Oct17 1-3	Sep19 0-1	Jan16 3-0	Feb10 1-1	Mar20 2-2	Oct07 0-1		Apr24 5-1	Mar06 5-0
ST MIRREN	Dec26 4-0	Nov14 3-0	Feb13 1-5	Apr17 2-3	Oct31 0-2	Oct03 2-1	Nov28 1-4	Jan16 3-0	Jan30 2-1	Mar13 0-0	Sep05 0-2	Jan02 1-1	Sep19 1-4	Dec05 4-1	Oct27 0-7	Dec19 1-0		Mar27 2-1
T LANARK	Oct03 4-1	Mar13 0-4	Nov28 0-3	Jan16 0-4	Dec12 0-1	Feb17 1-2	Apr10 1-2	Feb27 1-2	Sep19 1-5	Mar20 0-2	Dec26 0-4	Sep05 1-2	Apr28 0-2	Feb13 0-3	Apr23 0-1	Oct31 0-2	Nov21 2-1	

DIVISION 2

	ALBION R	ALLOA	ARBROATH	AYR U	BERWICK R	BRECHIN C	COWDENBEATH	DUMBARTON	EAST FIFE	E STIRLING	FORFAR A	HAMILTON A	MONTROSE	QUEEN OF SOUTH	QUEEN'S PARK	RAITH R	STENHOUSEMUIR	STIRLING A	STRANRAER
ALBION R		Apr28 2-3	Feb20 0-0	Aug19 2-0	Sep26 2-1	Oct31 4-2	Apr17 0-3	Nov28 0-3	Feb27 2-2	Sep12 3-1	Mar13 3-1	Jan01 3-1	Dec19 3-0	Mar27 1-2	Sep16 1-2	Feb13 3-0	Nov14 1-1	Sep09 3-1	Oct10 5-0
ALLOA	Apr07 3-2		Sep09 0-1	Jan09 2-1	Feb06 4-3	Nov28 6-0	Apr23 0-1	Oct17 2-2	Sep26 2-7	Aug19 1-4	Mar27 3-2	Nov14 2-2	Sep30 4-4	Nov07 1-1	Dec12 0-3	Sep16 4-2	Jan01 3-2	Apr21 0-0	Oct24 2-1
ARBROATH	Oct03 2-1	Sep19 2-1		Sep23 1-1	Nov14 4-0	Feb13 2-1	Dec26 3-2	Apr24 1-1	Apr10 4-1	Oct24 0-1	Sep05 1-1	Mar13 1-1	Jan02 2-2	Oct31 2-0	Jan16 1-2	Jan30 0-1	Mar27 0-0	Nov28 1-1	Dec12 2-1
AYR U	Dec26 1-3	Oct03 1-2	Sep30 1-4		Feb27 0-1	Mar13 5-1	Jan30 2-1	Sep19 3-0	Nov28 3-3	Mar20 1-1	Jan16 3-2	Apr14 0-1	Nov21 2-1	Jan02 3-1	Sep05 1-2	Oct31 0-4	Dec12 3-0	Apr07 1-2	Apr24 2-0
BERWICK R	Jan16 3-0	Oct10 2-4	Mar20 4-1	Oct24 3-0		Sep09 5-1	Oct03 4-1	Jan23 3-2	Apr24 2-2	Mar06 2-1	Apr21 1-2	Sep23 1-4	Dec12 2-2	Dec26 1-1	Feb13 1-1	Nov21 2-3	Sep12 2-1	Nov07 0-3	Apr03 0-1
BRECHIN C	Apr21 0-1	Apr03 2-3	Oct17 4-3	Nov07 2-2	Sep19 2-3		Mar20 1-1	Sep16 1-1	Jan23 4-1	Oct10 0-1	Apr19 2-3	Dec19 3-6	Sep05 2-2	Sep26 3-3	Nov21 1-4	Dec26 3-3	Sep28 1-0	Feb27 1-3	Feb06 0-7
COWDENBEATH	Dec12 3-1	Dec19 2-0	Aug19 2-0	Oct10 0-2	Feb20 4-1	Nov14 1-2		Mar27 1-0	Sep12 1-3	Sep26 1-1	Nov28 1-2	Apr21 2-5	Feb27 4-2	Sep02 0-0	Apr10 2-1	Sep23 1-1	Mar06 1-1	Jan01 0-1	Oct17 1-2
DUMBARTON	Apr03 2-1	Feb13 3-1	Dec19 1-1	Sep09 2-1	Dec05 4-4	Sep01 1-3	Nov21 3-0		Nov07 5-0	Jan01 3-0	Oct24 1-3	Sep12 0-4	Oct10 6-2	Sep23 1-3	Jan09 0-0	Apr17 2-1	Aug19 0-1	Sep26 0-1	Feb20 4-1
EAST FIFE	Oct24 2-0	Jan16 3-4	Dec05 4-0	Apr03 1-0	Dec19 3-4	Oct03 1-0	Jan02 4-2	Mar13 3-1		Apr17 0-0	Apr28 5-2	Feb13 3-0	Dec26 2-5	Sep19 2-3	Oct31 2-1	Sep05 2-1	Mar23 0-1	Sep23 3-3	Nov14 5-2
E STIRLING	Jan02 2-1	Apr26 2-2	Feb27 3-1	Nov14 0-0	Oct31 2-1	Feb20 6-1	Jan16 3-3	Sep05 3-0	Dec12 1-2		Apr23 3-2	Nov28 1-2	Sep16 5-0	Oct03 1-1	Sep19 1-2	Mar13 2-2	Oct17 1-0	Mar27 1-2	Sep30 3-1
FORFAR A	Nov07 4-0	Nov21 1-3	Jan01 2-2	Sep26 4-2	Sep16 3-3	Sep12 2-3	Apr03 2-2	Feb27 0-2	Oct10 1-2	Dec19 2-2		Feb20 0-1	Oct17 3-2	Apr17 0-3	Sep30 1-2	Dec05 2-3	Sep09 1-3	Aug19 0-4	Mar06 1-4
HAMILTON A	Sep05 2-2	Mar20 3-3	Nov07 0-3	Sep02 1-0	Sep30 0-1	Apr24 2-1	Sep19 1-1	Jan02 5-0	Oct17 4-3	Apr03 5-0	Oct03 3-0		Mar06 5-1	Jan30 3-3	Dec26 0-2	Oct24 2-2	Apr10 4-0	Dec12 1-4	Nov21 2-2
MONTROSE	Apr24 0-0	Sep23 5-3	Sep12 2-2	Mar27 4-2	Apr17 2-3	Jan01 3-1	Oct24 4-3	Apr27 5-0	Aug19 4-1	Sep02 1-4	Feb13 1-2	Oct31 0-1		Dec05 3-7	Mar13 2-2	Oct03 8-3	Nov28 7-1	Nov14 1-3	Jan16 0-2
QUEEN OF SOUTH	Nov21 2-1	Mar13 2-1	Apr14 2-3	Sep12 4-3	Aug19 1-1	Jan16 5-1	Sep16 1-1	Sep30 4-0	Jan09 3-2	Jan23 1-0	Dec12 2-2	Oct10 1-2	Feb20 6-1		Apr24 4-0	Nov14 1-1	Oct24 7-1	Feb13 1-1	Jan01 5-1
QUEEN'S PARK	Sep02 1-0	Apr17 5-0	Sep26 1-1	Jan01 2-1	Oct17 1-2	Apr14 2-2	Dec05 3-0	Nov14 0-1	Mar06 3-0	Sep09 0-0	Sep23 2-1	Aug19 2-3	Nov07 2-0	Dec19 1-0		Apr20 0-0	Mar10 1-1	Oct10 0-1	Sep12 2-0
RAITH R	Oct17 1-2	Sep02 0-0	Oct10 1-1	Apr28 1-1	Mar27 3-0	Aug19 2-1	Sep30 0-1	Dec12 0-3	Jan01 1-1	Nov07 3-0	Apr07 5-2	Feb27 0-2	Jan09 0-0	Mar20 1-1	Nov28 4-2		Sep26 1-2	Sep12 0-1	Sep09 0-4
STENHOUSEMUIR	Mar20 2-3	Sep05 2-1	Nov21 1-3	Apr17 2-1	Jan02 2-2	Sep23 3-0	Oct31 3-4	Apr13 4-0	Apr20 1-1	Apr27 2-1	Sep19 2-3	Dec05 2-5	Apr03 0-2	Feb27 2-1	Oct03 2-2	Jan16 0-0		Apr24 0-1	Mar13 3-2
STIRLING A	Sep19 3-0	Oct31 2-1	Apr03 3-1	Dec05 5-0	Mar13 2-2	Oct24 3-0	Sep05 2-2	Jan16 1-0	Sep30 4-0	Nov21 1-4	Apr14 4-0	Apr17 2-3	Mar20 2-1	Oct17 2-1	Jan30 2-0	Jan02 2-1	Dec19 5-1		Sep16 1-1
STRANRAER	Jan30 4-0	Feb27 4-0	Apr17 2-0	Dec19 2-0	Nov28 1-3	Dec05 2-1	Feb13 1-0	Oct03 4-1	Mar20 3-2	Sep23 1-3	Oct31 4-4	Mar27 2-0	Sep26 1-1	Sep05 1-1	Jan02 3-1	Sep19 3-3	Nov07 4-0	Sep02 0-6	

LEAGUE TABLES

DIVISION 1

	P	W	D	L	F	A	W	D	L	F	A	Pts
Kilmarnock	34	12	4	1	38	17	10	2	5	24	16	50
Hearts	34	11	3	3	46	24	11	3	3	44	25	50
Dunfermline A	34	14	2	1	55	14	8	3	6	28	22	49
Hibernian	34	11	2	4	44	26	10	2	5	31	21	46
Rangers	34	9	5	3	42	16	9	3	5	36	19	44
Dundee	34	9	4	4	47	32	6	6	5	39	31	40
Clyde	34	10	3	4	35	22	7	3	7	29	36	40
Celtic	34	9	2	6	33	18	7	3	7	43	39	37
Dundee U	34	10	1	6	38	24	5	5	7	21	27	36
Morton	34	9	4	4	38	21	4	3	10	16	33	33
Partick T	34	5	5	7	28	30	6	5	6	29	28	32
Aberdeen	34	8	5	4	33	27	4	3	10	26	48	32
St Johnstone	34	6	5	6	31	24	3	6	8	26	38	29
Motherwell	34	4	4	9	24	31	6	4	7	21	23	28
St Mirren	34	8	2	7	27	32	1	4	12	11	38	24
Falkirk	34	6	5	6	27	26	1	2	14	16	59	21
Airdrie	34	3	3	11	26	48	2	1	14	22	62	14
T. Lanark	34	2	0	15	11	41	1	1	15	11	58	7

DIVISION 2

	P	W	D	L	F	A	W	D	L	F	A	Pts
Stirling A	36	13	3	2	46	18	13	4	1	38	13	59
Hamilton A	36	8	6	4	43	28	13	2	3	43	25	50
Queen of South	36	11	5	2	52	22	5	8	5	32	28	45
Queen's Park	36	9	5	4	28	13	8	4	6	29	28	43
E. Stirling	36	9	5	4	40	23	6	5	7	24	27	40
Stranraer	36	11	4	3	42	26	6	2	10	32	38	40
Arbroath	36	8	7	3	29	18	5	6	7	27	33	39
Berwick R	36	8	4	6	38	30	7	5	6	35	40	39
East Fife	36	11	2	5	45	29	4	5	9	33	48	37
Alloa	36	8	5	5	39	38	6	3	9	32	43	36
Albion R	36	10	3	5	38	23	4	2	12	18	37	33
Cowdenbeath	36	7	4	7	27	25	4	6	8	28	37	32
Raith R	36	5	6	7	23	24	4	8	6	31	37	32
Dumbarton	36	9	3	6	38	27	4	3	11	17	40	32
Stenhousemuir	36	7	4	7	33	32	4	4	10	16	42	30
Montrose	36	8	3	7	52	40	2	6	10	28	51	29
Forfar A	36	3	4	11	29	43	6	3	9	34	46	25
Ayr U	36	8	2	8	32	29	1	4	13	17	38	24
Brechin C	36	3	6	9	32	47	3	1	14	21	55	19

Scottish Football League Records
Season 1965-66

DIVISION 1

	ABERDEEN	CELTIC	CLYDE	DUNDEE	DUNDEE U	DUNFERMLINE A	FALKIRK	HAMILTON A	HEARTS	HIBERNIAN	KILMARNOCK	MORTON	MOTHERWELL	PARTICK T	RANGERS	ST JOHNSTONE	ST MIRREN	STIRLING A
ABERDEEN		Jan15 3-1	Mar02 2-0	Sep18 2-3	Dec11 0-0	Oct16 2-2	Nov20 2-0	Jan29 5-2	Feb26 0-1	Dec25 1-3	Nov06 1-0	Apr04 5-3	Apr23 1-2	Mar12 2-1	Apr13 1-2	Jan03 2-3	Oct02 4-1	Aug25 2-2
CELTIC	Sep25 7-1		Sep11 2-1	Feb28 5-0	Jan08 1-0	May04 2-1	Feb12 6-0	Nov20 5-0	Oct09 5-2	Dec11 2-0	Nov27 2-1	Dec25 8-1	Jan22 1-0	Nov06 1-1	Jan03 5-1	Mar12 3-2	Apr09 5-0	Oct30 6-1
CLYDE	Oct23 2-2	Jan01 1-3		Aug25 0-2	Mar26 4-1	Mar19 6-1	Apr06 3-2	Apr30 4-1	Apr16 0-1	Oct02 1-2	Feb26 1-4	Nov13 2-0	Mar05 1-3	Sep18 3-1	Dec18 2-2	Jan29 3-2	Oct16 0-1	Jan15 0-1
DUNDEE	Apr20 1-2	Oct27 1-2	Jan08 1-4		Sep11 0-5	Apr27 0-2	Oct09 2-0	Mar09 2-1	Apr13 1-0	Nov13 4-3	Feb12 0-2	Mar05 5-1	Dec25 4-0	Apr23 1-1	Sep25 1-1	Nov20 3-1	Feb26 3-2	Mar26 6-2
DUNDEE U	Apr16 3-0	Aug25 0-4	Nov27 0-2	Jan03 2-1		Jan29 0-4	Mar12 2-3	Oct16 7-0	Nov06 2-2	Apr09 5-4	Dec18 0-0	Oct30 4-2	Mar19 5-1	Oct02 5-2	Mar21 1-0	Sep18 5-1	Jan15 3-0	Apr30 1-1
DUNFERMLINE A	Mar21 2-3	Dec18 0-2	Nov20 6-4	Apr09 2-2	Oct09 2-4		Apr13 6-1	Mar12 1-0	Sep11 1-1	Apr06 3-2	Sep25 1-0	Jan01 2-1	Jan08 6-1	Oct23 4-3	Apr30 1-2	Feb26 5-1	Nov06 5-1	Dec11 5-1
FALKIRK	Mar19 3-0	Oct16 3-4	Apr09 0-1	Jan29 3-1	Nov13 1-4	Oct02 0-3		Jan03 0-0	Nov27 0-1	Jan15 3-2	Dec11 3-2	Apr23 3-2	Oct30 2-0	Dec25 2-0	Mar09 3-2	Mar23 2-1	Aug25 2-3	Sep18 2-0
HAMILTON A	Oct09 0-4	Mar19 1-7	Dec25 1-4	Apr16 1-2	Feb12 0-4	Nov13 1-6	Sep11 1-4		Jan08 0-1	Mar05 1-2	Jan22 1-4	Sep25 1-2	Jan01 1-4	Mar26 4-3	Oct30 1-7	Apr20 1-1	Apr23 1-0	Oct23 3-1
HEARTS	Oct30 1-1	Jan29 3-2	Dec11 4-1	Oct02 0-0	Mar16 0-1	Jan03 0-0	Mar26 1-2	Aug25 2-0		Sep18 0-4	Apr09 2-3	Nov20 2-1	Oct23 5-2	Feb12 3-1	Nov13 0-2	Jan15 0-0	Dec25 4-0	Apr23 1-1
HIBERNIAN	Apr30 0-1	Apr16 0-0	Mar23 3-1	Mar12 1-1	Apr20 3-3	Nov27 1-1	Sep25 5-1	Nov06 11-12-3	Jan01	3-3	Sep11 4-1	Jan08 2-2	Oct09 2-0	Feb26 1-2	Oct16 3-0	Dec18 3-2	Mar02 1-0	Mar19
KILMARNOCK	Mar09 1-3	Mar29 0-2	Oct30 1-2	Oct16 5-3	Apr23 1-0	Jan15 1-0	Apr16 1-0	Oct02 3-1	Apr04 2-2	Jan03 1-0		Feb28 4-0	Nov13 5-0	Aug25 2-1	Mar19 1-1	Dec25 3-1	Sep18 3-1	Jan29 2-1
MORTON	Nov27 1-3	Apr30 0-2	Mar15 1-1	Nov06 2-2	Feb26 2-0	Sep18 1-1	Dec18 0-1	Jan15 3-0	Mar19 0-3	Aug25 1-5	Oct23 1-4		Mar09 3-1	Jan29 0-0	Apr16 0-5	Oct02 1-2	Jan03 0-0	Feb12 2-1
MOTHERWELL	Dec18 1-0	May07 0-1	Nov06 0-1	Apr30 2-0	Nov20 0-3	Aug25 1-3	Feb26 3-0	Sep18 4-2	Mar23 4-2	Jan29 4-0	Mar12 0-3	Apr09 3-0		Jan15 0-3	Nov27 0-3	Oct16 5-3	Dec11 4-1	Jan03 0-1
PARTICK T	Nov13 0-3	Mar21 2-2	Apr11 2-1	Dec18 2-0	Jan22 4-1	Apr20 2-6	Apr30 3-0	Apr28 1-0	Oct16 3-3	Oct30 3-2	Jan08 1-0	Oct09 1-2	Sep25 1-1		Sep11 1-1	Apr16 3-1	Mar19 4-1	Mar05 1-1
RANGERS	Apr09 1-0	Sep18 2-1	May04 4-0	Apr06 1-0	Oct27 2-0	Dec25 2-3	Nov06 3-0	Feb26 4-0	Mar12 1-1	Feb12 2-0	Nov20 5-0	Dec11 3-1	Apr19 2-1	Jan01 4-0		Aug25 3-2	Jan29 4-1	Oct02 6-0
ST JOHNSTONE	Sep11 2-2	Nov13 1-4	Oct09 3-3	Mar19 1-0	Mar30 1-2	Oct30 1-5	Oct23 2-1	Apr09 5-0	Sep25 3-2	Apr23 1-3	Apr30 1-1	Apr13 4-2	Feb12 3-3	Apr06 2-2	Jan08 0-3		Nov27 3-2	Mar09 1-1
ST MIRREN	Jan22 1-0	Apr05 0-3	Feb12 2-1	Oct30 2-5	Sep25 1-2	Mar09 4-3	Jan08 6-0	Dec18 1-0	Apr30 1-1	Oct23 0-2	Jan01 4-7	Sep11 0-1	Apr16 0-0	Nov20 2-0	Oct09 1-6	Mar26 2-3		Nov13 0-0
STIRLING A	Jan08 2-1	Feb26 1-0	Sep25 3-2	Nov27 1-4	Dec25 2-4	Apr16 2-1	Mar30 0-1	Mar24 3-0	Dec18 2-2	Nov20 1-2	Oct09 2-3	Oct16 2-4	Sep11 1-0	Apr09 2-2	Jan22 0-2	Nov06 1-0	Mar12 0-1	

DIVISION 2

	AIRDRIE	ALBION R	ALLOA	ARBROATH	AYR U	BERWICK R	BRECHIN C	COWDENBEATH	DUMBARTON	EAST FIFE	E STIRLING	FORFAR A	MONTROSE	QUEEN OF SOUTH	QUEEN'S PARK	RAITH R	STENHOUSEMUIR	STRANRAER	T LANARK
AIRDRIE		Jan01 7-2	Mar26 4-2	Mar31 5-1	Nov13 1-0	Mar28 3-0	Apr25 7-3	Sep25 4-1	Mar23 3-1	Apr16 1-3	Mar05 1-0	Oct23 6-1	Feb12 2-0	Apr23 0-0	Oct09 2-1	Sep11 1-2	Oct30 7-1	Sep08 5-2	Dec25 3-3
ALBION R	Sep18 2-1		Feb26 0-4	Apr13 1-1	Jan15 0-2	Nov06 0-0	Oct16 4-0	Mar12 2-1	Apr27 0-0	Jan03 0-1	Oct02 4-1	Sep29 2-3	Apr09 3-0	Sep14 1-0	Apr30 1-0	Dec11 1-0	Apr20 2-2	Dec18 2-0	Jan29 1-1
ALLOA	Nov27 3-0	Oct30 1-3		Aug25 2-2	Mar19 2-1	Apr27 3-3	Apr13 0-2	Apr09 1-2	Apr23 1-0	Oct16 0-2	Mar22 1-0	Nov13 4-0	Sep08 2-3	Mar05 2-1	Apr16 1-0	Dec25 1-2	Sep18 1-1	Oct02 3-3	Mar29 3-0
ARBROATH	Sep29 2-2	Oct23 2-2	Jan08 2-2		Apr23 1-1	Sep25 2-1	Apr16 1-1	Apr27 0-2	Feb26 2-0	Mar05 2-1	Dec25 3-1	Jan01 5-0	Sep11 3-1	Feb12 3-3	Sep15 6-2	Oct09 3-1	Nov13 4-1	Nov20 3-1	Mar26 5-2
AYR U	Mar12 1-1	Sep25 2-0	Nov20 2-2	Dec18 2-1		Oct09 4-2	Sep29 1-0	Jan01 1-0	Nov06 2-0	Apr27 2-0	Dec11 5-2	Apr11 4-1	Jan08 2-2	Sep11 1-3	Feb12 2-0	Oct23 2-2	Apr09 3-0	Apr20 2-2	Feb26 2-0
BERWICK R	Oct02 3-0	Mar05 4-1	Sep27 6-3	Feb05 2-1	Jan29 2-2		Oct30 1-3	Dec11 2-0	Sep15 0-1	Aug25 2-1	Sep18 2-2	Dec25 8-1	Nov27 2-1	Nov13 3-1	Mar19 0-1	Apr09 2-2	Jan03 2-0	Apr13 0-2	Apr23 4-0
BRECHIN C	Apr09 2-2	Mar30 1-4	Oct23 1-1	Dec11 2-2	Apr06 0-2	Feb26 1-2		Apr20 1-4	Sep25 1-5	Mar19 1-3	Nov27 2-1	Sep11 3-1	Jan01 2-0	Oct09 2-2	Apr27 0-4	Feb05 1-8	Sep08 4-1	Apr30 3-1	Nov06 1-3
COWDENBEATH	Jan15 3-0	Nov13 1-2	Apr06 0-3	Oct02 2-1	Sep18 3-1	Apr25 3-1	Aug25 2-1		Dec25 1-2	Apr13 3-3	Jan29 2-2	Apr23 2-1	Sep22 3-1	Nov27 0-0	Oct30 2-2	Sep08 0-0	Mar19 0-1	Jan03 4-1	Oct16 3-3
DUMBARTON	Aug25 1-3	Mar19 2-0	Dec18 3-0	Oct30 1-2	Mar30 1-3	Sep08 1-1	Jan15 7-1	Apr30 2-4		Oct02 1-0	Oct16 3-1	Apr25 1-3	Nov13 0-0	Apr16 4-1	Mar09 2-3	Mar26 0-2	Jan29 5-2	Sep22 2-0	Jan03 3-1
EAST FIFE	Dec11 6-3	Sep11 1-2	Mar31 3-1	Nov06 0-0	Mar09 2-1	Mar02 3-2	Nov20 3-1	Oct23 1-3	Apr20 6-1		Apr09 2-1	Oct09 2-0	Apr23 3-0	Sep25 3-1	Sep22 3-1	Mar29 1-1	Dec25 3-1	Feb26 2-1	Mar12 1-0
E STIRLING	Nov06 2-3	Mar31 2-4	Sep11 2-3	Apr30 4-2	Apr16 0-1	Apr20 1-1	Mar26 1-5	Oct09 5-4	Feb12 3-1	Jan08 1-1		Apr06 4-3	Feb26 3-2	Oct23 3-2	Dec18 1-3	Apr27 0-0	Sep22 2-1	Mar12 2-0	Nov20 2-3
FORFAR A	Apr27 2-3	Sep22 1-2	Mar12 2-3	Sep18 2-3	Oct02 1-4	Apr30 3-2	Jan03 1-2	Dec18 2-3	Apr09 2-2	Jan29 4-1	Jan15 4-2		Mar30 3-0	Mar19 1-2	Nov27 3-3	Nov06 1-1	Aug25 0-2	Oct16 2-4	Apr13 1-2
MONTROSE	Oct16 0-6	Dec04 4-0	Apr20 1-1	Jan03 0-0	Aug25 2-3	Mar26 3-2	Sep18 3-0	Sep29 3-1	Mar12 2-1	Dec18 4-1	Oct30 6-2	Apr16 5-2		Dec25 1-1	Mar05 3-1	Nov20 1-2	Apr13 3-1	Jan29 4-2	Oct02 3-0
QUEEN OF SOUTH	Dec18 2-1	Sep08 1-0	Nov06 2-0	Oct16 2-2	Jan03 2-2	Mar12 2-1	Jan29 4-2	Mar26 4-4	Dec11 3-3	Jan15 4-3	Mar30 6-0	Nov20 4-1	Apr30 1-1		Apr09 3-0	Feb26 1-2	Oct02 5-1	Sep18 4-1	Aug25 4-1
QUEEN'S PARK	Jan29 2-2	Dec25 3-4	Jan12 1-3	Sep07 1-2	Oct16 0-3	Nov20 0-0	Oct02 5-0	Mar23 4-2	Apr05 2-3	Sep29 2-0	Apr12 1-0	Apr19 4-1	Nov06 1-0	Mar02 1-2		Mar15 1-1	Jan15 3-2	Aug25 2-2	Sep18 0-2
RAITH R	Jan03 0-8	Apr16 1-1	Apr30 1-1	Jan29 0-3	Apr13 0-2	Mar09 1-0	Dec18 1-1	Mar31 4-0	Nov27 4-0	Sep18 1-3	Aug25 3-1	Mar05 6-0	Mar19 3-0	Oct30 0-1	Nov13 5-1		Oct16 2-0	Jan15 5-0	Sep29 6-1
STENHOUSEMUIR	Feb26 0-3	Mar26 0-1	Jan01 2-3	Mar12 1-0	Apr25 0-4	Sep11 2-2	Sep13 0-1	Nov20 2-3	Oct09 1-1	Apr30 1-2	Sep28 3-2	Feb05 5-7	Oct23 1-4	Jan22 1-5	Sep25 1-4	Feb12 1-1		Nov06 4-1	Apr16 2-0
STRANRAER	Apr06 2-5	Apr23 2-3	Apr25 1-1	Mar19 0-0	Mar26 1-5	Oct23 3-3	Dec25 5-1	Sep11 4-1	Sep29 1-1	Oct30 2-1	Nov13 4-1	Feb12 5-0	Oct09 2-2	Jan01 1-3	Jan08 1-1	Sep25 2-1	Mar05 2-2		Dec04 2-1
T LANARK	Apr30 0-2	Oct09 2-1	Sep25 7-1	Apr20 1-0	Oct30 1-1	Dec18 1-1	Mar05 0-0	Feb12 1-0	Sep11 0-2	Nov13 4-1	Mar19 0-2	Sep15 9-1	Apr28 1-2	Jan08 1-1	Jan01 0-2	Apr06 1-0	Dec11 1-1	Apr09 2-1	

LEAGUE TABLES

DIVISION 1

	P	W	D	L	F	A	W	D	L	F	A	Pts
Celtic	34	16	1	0	66	12	11	2	4	40	18	57
Rangers	34	15	1	1	49	10	10	4	3	42	19	55
Kilmarnock	34	12	2	3	36	18	8	3	6	37	28	45
Dunfermline A	34	11	2	4	52	29	8	4	5	42	26	44
Dundee U	34	10	3	4	45	27	9	2	6	34	24	43
Hibernian	34	8	6	3	45	22	8	0	9	36	33	38
Hearts	34	7	5	5	28	21	6	7	4	28	27	38
Aberdeen	34	8	3	6	35	26	7	3	7	26	28	36
Dundee	34	9	2	6	35	29	5	4	8	26	32	34
Falkirk	34	10	1	6	32	26	5	0	12	16	46	31
Clyde	34	7	2	8	33	29	6	2	9	29	35	30
Partick T	34	9	5	3	34	25	1	5	11	21	39	30
Motherwell	34	9	0	8	31	26	3	4	10	21	43	28
St Johnstone	34	6	6	5	34	36	3	2	12	24	45	26
Stirling A	34	7	2	8	25	29	2	6	9	15	39	26
St Mirren	34	6	3	8	27	34	3	1	13	17	48	22
Morton	34	4	5	8	18	31	4	0	13	24	53	21
Hamilton A	34	3	1	13	19	56	0	1	16	8	61	8

DIVISION 2

	P	W	D	L	F	A	W	D	L	F	A	Pts
Ayr U	36	12	5	1	40	18	10	4	4	38	19	53
Airdrie	36	14	2	2	62	23	8	4	6	45	33	50
Queen of South	36	12	5	1	54	25	6	6	6	29	28	47
East Fife	36	14	2	2	45	20	6	2	10	27	35	44
Raith R	36	10	3	5	43	23	6	8	4	28	20	43
Arbroath	36	11	6	1	49	24	4	7	7	23	28	43
Albion R	36	9	5	4	26	17	9	2	7	32	37	43
Alloa	36	8	4	6	31	25	6	6	6	34	40	38
Montrose	36	12	3	3	48	26	3	4	11	19	37	37
Cowdenbeath	36	8	6	4	34	25	7	1	10	35	43	37
Berwick R	36	11	3	4	45	22	1	8	9	24	36	35
Dumbarton	36	9	2	7	39	27	5	5	8	24	34	35
Queen's Park	36	7	4	7	33	29	6	3	9	29	36	33
T. Lanark	36	8	5	5	32	19	4	3	11	23	46	32
Stranraer	36	7	7	4	40	32	2	3	13	24	51	28
Brechin C	36	5	4	9	28	46	5	3	10	24	46	27
E. Stirling	36	8	3	7	38	39	1	2	15	21	52	23
Stenhousemuir	36	4	3	11	27	44	2	4	12	20	49	19
Forfar A	36	4	3	11	35	41	3	0	15	26	79	17

Scottish Football League Records
Season 1966-67

DIVISION 1

	ABERDEEN	AIRDRIE	AYR U	CELTIC	CLYDE	DUNDEE	DUNDEE U	DUNFERMLINE A	FALKIRK	HEARTS	HIBERNIAN	KILMARNOCK	MOTHERWELL	PARTICK T	RANGERS	ST JOHNSTONE	ST MIRREN	STIRLING A
ABERDEEN		Feb11 7-0	Oct15 2-0	Dec24 1-1	Oct01 1-1	Jan02 5-2	Mar25 0-1	Jan21 1-2	Apr08 6-1	Nov05 3-1	Oct29 2-1	Dec31 4-0	Dec03 2-1	Nov19 5-2	Jan18 1-2	Sep17 3-2	Mar27 0-0	Apr15 1-0
AIRDRIE	Oct22 1-2		Mar25 3-1	Feb04 0-3	Mar18 2-3	Apr22 1-4	Nov05 2-2	Jan14 0-3	Sep24 1-0	Apr26 1-2	Dec31 0-1	Feb25 1-4	Sep10 2-0	Dec10 3-1	Mar07 0-1	Dec03 2-0	Oct08 1-0	Nov12 7-0
AYR U	Feb04 2-5	Nov26 0-1		Feb11 0-5	Apr19 0-1	Nov12 1-1	Sep24 0-7	Sep10 0-0	Jan14 0-1	Oct08 0-1	Dec17 0-2	Jan03 2-3	Mar01 3-3	Dec31 1-2	Mar18 1-4	Apr08 1-0	Apr22 0-0	Mar04 0-1
CELTIC	Apr19 0-0	Oct15 3-0	Oct24 5-1		Jan11 5-1	Jan07 5-1	May03 2-3	Mar18 3-2	Mar20 5-0	Nov26 3-0	Jan21 2-0	May15 2-0	Dec10 4-2	Dec17 6-2	Sep17 2-0	Oct01 6-1	Nov05 1-1	Nov02 7-3
CLYDE	Jan14 0-0	Nov19 1-0	Dec03 0-0	Sep10 0-3		Apr08 1-3	Feb04 2-0	Mar04 1-0	Oct22 4-0	Feb25 2-1	Nov12 5-1	Sep24 1-3	Oct08 3-1	Apr26 4-1	Feb08 1-5	Apr11 2-0	Mar25 2-1	Dec31 0-1
DUNDEE	Sep10 2-1	Dec24 0-0	Mar10 3-0	Sep24 1-2	Dec10 3-4		Jan03 2-3	Apr12 3-1	Feb04 4-1	Jan14 1-1	Nov19 2-1	Oct08 1-1	Oct22 3-0	Feb25 0-0	Apr29 1-1	Nov05 4-0	Dec03 2-0	Mar25 2-0
DUNDEE U	Nov26 1-3	Mar04 3-1	Jan07 4-0	Dec31 3-2	Oct15 4-3	Sep17 1-4		Oct29 2-4	Apr05 4-4	Apr08 2-0	Feb11 1-3	Nov12 1-1	Mar18 1-1	Apr22 2-2	Oct01 2-3	Jan02 1-0	Dec17 2-2	Jan21 2-0
DUNFERMLINE A	Oct08 1-1	Oct01 0-1	Jan02 6-0	Nov19 4-5	Nov05 4-0	Dec17 0-1	Feb25 3-3		Apr29 4-0	Mar22 1-0	Sep17 5-6	Apr08 1-1	Mar25 2-1	Oct22 3-2	Dec03 3-2	Apr05 4-1	Feb04 2-0	Apr22 3-3
FALKIRK	Dec10 1-0	Apr19 2-1	Oct01 5-3	Nov12 0-3	Feb11 0-2	Oct15 3-2	Dec03 0-3	Dec31 1-0		Apr12 2-1	Mar04 0-2	Mar18 0-1	Apr22 0-1	Mar25 1-0	Jan21 0-1	Oct29 0-3	Sep17 2-0	Jan02 1-1
HEARTS	Mar04 0-3	Sep17 1-1	Jan21 1-0	Mar25 0-3	Oct29 0-1	Oct01 3-1	Dec10 2-1	Nov12 1-1	Dec17 1-1		Jan02 0-0	Apr22 1-0	Dec31 1-2	Apr01 0-0	Oct15 1-1	Feb11 1-0	Nov19 4-0	Apr19 5-1
HIBERNIAN	Feb25 1-0	Apr29 0-2	Apr15 4-1	Oct08 3-5	Mar28 1-1	Mar18 2-1	Oct22 2-2	Jan03 2-0	Nov05 3-1	Sep10 3-1		Feb04 3-1	Jan14 2-1	Sep24 7-0	Nov26 1-2	Dec24 2-5	Apr08 1-1	Dec03 6-0
KILMARNOCK	May01 1-1	Oct29 1-0	Sep17 1-0	Dec03 0-0	Jan07 1-3	Jan21 4-4	Mar20 4-0	Dec10 1-1	Nov19 3-0	Dec24 1-2	Oct15 2-1		Apr12 3-0	Nov05 0-0	Feb11 1-2	Mar25 5-3	Jan02 3-0	Oct01 2-1
MOTHERWELL	Apr04 3-2	Jan02 2-2	Oct29 0-0	Apr08 0-2	Jan21 1-1	Feb11 5-3	Nov19 1-1	Nov26 6-2	Apr01 1-2	Apr29 1-0	Oct01 1-2	Dec17 2-0		Mar11 5-0	Mar04 1-5	Oct15 3-3	Apr19 4-0	Sep17 1-1
PARTICK T	Mar18 1-1	Apr08 2-2	Apr27 4-1	Mar27 1-4	Sep17 0-1	Oct29 0-0	May06 3-0	Feb11 0-0	Nov26 1-0	Dec03 1-1	Jan07 1-4	Mar04 1-2	Nov12 2-2		Jan02 1-1	Jan21 3-0	Oct01 2-2	Oct15 2-0
RANGERS	Sep24 3-0	Dec17 3-0	Nov19 4-0	May06 2-2	Apr22 1-1	Dec31 2-2	Jan14 3-1	Apr01 0-1	Oct08 5-0	Feb04 5-1	Mar25 1-0	Nov09 3-0	Nov05 5-1	Sep10 6-1		Mar29 4-3	Feb25 3-0	Dec10 4-0
ST JOHNSTONE	Jan03 1-0	Apr01 1-0	Apr26 3-0	Jan14 0-4	Dec17 2-4	Mar04 0-3	Sep10 2-0	Sep24 3-3	Feb25 2-1	Oct22 3-2	Apr22 1-2	Nov26 1-3	Feb04 1-1	Oct08 3-5	Nov12 1-1		Dec31 3-0	Mar18 4-1
ST MIRREN	Nov12 1-3	Jan21 0-3	Dec24 3-1	Mar04 0-5	Nov26 1-3	Apr01 0-5	Apr12 0-1	Oct15 0-5	Mar11 1-2	Mar18 3-0	Dec10 1-3	Sep10 3-2	Sep24 0-5	Jan14 0-3	Nov02 1-6	Apr27 0-0		Feb11 4-0
STIRLING A	Dec17 2-6	Mar11 0-0	Nov05 1-1	Feb25 1-1	Apr29 2-5	Nov26 2-3	Oct08 1-4	Mar29 1-1	Sep10 1-1	Sep24 0-3	Apr01 1-0	Jan14 1-4	Jan03 0-0	Feb04 1-3	Apr08 0-1	Nov19 2-1	Oct22 2-0	

DIVISION 2

	ALBION R	ALLOA	ARBROATH	BERWICK R	BRECHIN C	CLYDEBANK	COWDENBEATH	DUMBARTON	EAST FIFE	E STIRLING	FORFAR A	HAMILTON A	MONTROSE	MORTON	QUEEN OF SOUTH	QUEEN'S PARK	RAITH R	STENHOUSEMUIR	STRANRAER	T LANARK
ALBION R		Mar11 0-2	Feb18 0-4	Nov26 2-3	Oct15 4-2	Jan21 0-2	Apr29 0-0	Apr01 2-2	Dec24 5-1	Oct01 5-1	Nov19 1-0	Jan02 1-0	Apr08 4-1	Feb11 0-1	Sep14 2-0	Aug24 1-0	Oct29 1-1	Sep17 4-1	Dec17 1-1	Jan28 1-0
ALLOA	Nov12 1-4		Oct01 3-3	Sep07 1-0	Apr26 2-1	Mar04 1-1	Sep21 3-0	Apr22 2-1	Apr12 3-2	Dec31 2-2	Mar25 4-3	Sep17 1-3	Dec03 3-2	Oct29 0-1	Mar18 1-1	Dec10 0-2	Feb11 2-3	Jan02 2-0	Feb18 0-1	Oct15 1-0
ARBROATH	Sep24 1-1	Jan14 3-0		Oct22 1-0	Apr29 4-1	Sep21 3-0	Nov05 2-1	Mar11 1-1	Feb04 2-0	Apr12 3-0	Sep10 9-2	Nov19 3-2	Jan03 3-0	Dec24 0-0	Oct08 2-1	Feb25 2-1	Dec10 5-1	Mar25 1-0	Apr01 1-0	Sep07 2-1
BERWICK R	Mar25 2-1	Sep14 2-1	Feb11 3-1		Oct29 3-0	Oct15 1-1	Sep17 2-0	Dec10 0-1	Apr19 4-1	Jan02 2-1	Apr11 6-0	Oct01 0-1	Mar04 1-1	Nov12 1-4	Aug24 1-1	Dec03 0-2	Mar18 2-0	Dec31 6-0	Apr22 3-1	Jan21 2-0
BRECHIN C	Feb04 2-3	Oct08 4-1	Dec31 1-2	Feb25 2-1		Mar18 3-1	Dec17 1-2	Sep24 0-0	Aug24 2-3	Mar04 1-1	Jan03 2-1	Apr08 1-2	Sep10 4-2	Apr17 0-4	Jan14 1-5	Oct22 3-3	Nov12 1-2	Dec03 4-5	Nov26 5-1	Apr22 3-3
CLYDEBANK	Oct08 3-5	Nov05 0-2	Aug24 0-3	Feb04 2-4	Nov19 4-2		Mar25 2-3	Sep10 1-3	Sep14 2-3	Dec10 3-1	Mar11 3-0	Apr01 0-4	Sep24 0-4	Jan14 0-1	Oct22 3-3	Dec31 4-2	Jan03 3-2	Apr22 2-3	Feb25 4-0	Feb18 0-2
COWDENBEATH	Dec31 0-2	Aug24 1-2	Mar04 0-2	Jan03 0-1	Apr15 2-2	Nov26 4-0		Jan14 6-1	Jan21 2-2	Nov12 3-1	Dec24 3-1	Feb11 3-3	Feb18 4-2	Sep10 0-1	Dec10 3-0	Sep24 1-2	Apr01 0-1	Oct29 7-0	Oct15 2-1	Mar18 2-1
DUMBARTON	Dec03 3-0	Dec24 1-2	Nov12 1-1	Apr08 3-1	Feb18 0-2	Jan02 2-2	Oct01 2-2		Sep17 0-3	Oct15 4-1	Sep21 1-2	Jan21 1-3	Mar18 2-0	Nov26 0-1	Oct29 1-1	Apr11 4-0	Sep07 2-3	Mar04 3-1	Feb11 1-0	Apr28 5-1
EAST FIFE	Apr22 1-2	Dec17 1-0	Oct15 0-1	Sep24 2-1	Sep21 4-0	Sep07 3-1	Oct08 2-1	Jan03 2-1		Mar18 0-0	Dec10 2-4	Oct29 2-1	Nov12 3-1	Apr01 0-1	Mar04 1-2	Jan14 1-1	Sep10 1-2	Feb11 4-3	Dec31 2-2	Nov26 3-1
E STIRLING	Jan14 2-0	Apr29 2-1	Apr17 1-0	Sep10 1-1	Nov05 3-1	Apr08 1-5	Mar11 2-3	Feb04 4-0	Nov19 0-4		Oct22 2-4	Nov26 1-4	Feb25 0-0	Jan03 1-2	Dec24 2-2	Oct08 0-0	Sep24 1-2	Sep07 1-3	Sep21 0-5	Apr01 1-0
FORFAR A	Mar18 4-2	Nov26 2-3	Jan02 0-2	Apr26 4-0	Sep17 0-2	Nov12 4-1	Apr22 0-3	Aug24 1-0	Apr08 0-2	Feb11 2-1		Apr19 3-3	Dec31 5-2	Mar04 1-2	Dec03 3-4	Sep14 2-2	Oct15 1-5	Oct01 2-2	Jan21 3-4	Oct29 5-3
HAMILTON A	Sep10 2-1	Jan03 4-3	Mar18 0-2	Jan14 1-1	Dec10 0-0	Dec03 0-0	Oct22 1-0	Oct08 4-2	Feb25 3-0	Mar25 3-1	Sep24 3-0		Feb04 2-1	Dec31 1-2	Apr15 1-0	Nov05 3-3	Apr22 1-3	Nov12 0-0	Sep07 0-2	Sep21 1-1
MONTROSE	Dec10 1-2	Apr01 3-0	Sep17 2-1	Nov05 1-0	Jan02 2-0	Jan28 1-1	Sep07 5-1	Nov19 3-1	Mar11 1-2	Oct29 2-2	Apr29 1-3	Oct15 0-2		Apr15 2-0	Mar25 2-0	Dec24 1-1	Apr26 1-1	Jan21 1-0	Oct01 0-0	Feb11 4-1
MORTON	Oct22 2-1	Feb25 6-0	Apr22 0-0	Mar11 4-0	Sep28 4-1	Oct01 6-0	Jan02 0-2	Mar25 4-0	Dec03 2-1	Sep17 4-0	Nov05 3-0	Apr29 6-1	Dec17 7-0		Feb04 3-1	Nov22 5-0	Oct08 1-0	Oct04 9-1	Apr08 5-0	Dec26 6-0
QUEEN OF SOUTH	Sep07 7-4	Nov19 2-1	Jan21 2-3	Sep21 1-1	Oct01 6-0	Feb11 2-0	Apr08 0-1	Feb25 2-3	Nov05 2-3	Apr22 0-2	Apr01 2-1	Dec17 4-2	Nov26 6-2	Oct15 2-5		Apr19 1-2	Dec31 2-0	Feb18 2-2	Jan02 1-0	Sep17 3-2
QUEEN'S PARK	Sep21 5-1	Apr08 4-1	Mar28 0-0	Apr13 2-1	Feb11 2-1	Mar22 4-2	Feb28 2-2	Dec17 1-1	Oct01 4-1	Jan21 1-1	Sep07 7-2	Mar04 1-3	Apr22 2-3	Apr24 1-2	Nov12 3-4		Nov26 1-2	Oct15 4-1	Sep17 4-0	Jan02 3-1
RAITH R	Feb25 2-1	Oct22 3-1	Apr08 0-1	Nov19 4-2	Mar11 5-1	Sep17 3-0	Dec03 2-1	Sep14 2-0	Jan02 1-0	Feb18 6-1	Feb04 5-1	Dec24 3-1	Aug24 1-1	Jan21 0-1	Apr29 7-2	Mar25 4-0		Apr12 1-1	Nov05 2-1	Oct01 4-1
STENHOUSEMUIR	Jan03 0-0	Sep10 1-2	Nov26 3-0	Apr29 2-1	Apr01 3-0	Dec24 4-4	Feb25 1-1	Nov05 1-1	Oct22 2-3	Sep12 6-3	Jan14 0-5	Apr25 5-3	Oct08 1-3	Aug24 1-4	Sep24 2-6	Feb04 1-2	Apr18 0-4		Nov19 3-2	Apr08 0-2
STRANRAER	Apr15 0-2	Sep24 2-1	Dec03 2-1	Dec24 2-4	Mar25 2-1	Oct29 2-2	Feb04 2-3	Oct22 2-1	Apr29 0-3	Aug24 3-0	Oct08 3-1	Sep14 0-4	Jan14 4-1	Dec10 1-3	Sep10 1-1	Jan03 2-1	Mar04 1-2	Mar18 2-2		Nov12 2-2
T LANARK	Nov05 2-0	Feb04 3-0	Sep14 2-0	Oct08 3-0	Dec24 1-1	Apr15 1-0	Nov19 1-1	Dec31 0-1	Mar25 3-2	Dec03 0-0	Feb25 6-2	Aug24 3-2	Oct22 7-4	Sep24 1-1	Apr25 3-3	Sep10 4-3	Jan14 1-6	Dec10 3-1	Mar11 1-3	

LEAGUE TABLES

DIVISION 1

	P	W	D	L	F	A	W	D	L	F	A	Pts
Celtic	34	14	2	1	61	17	12	4	1	50	16	58
Rangers	34	13	3	1	54	13	11	4	2	38	18	55
Clyde	34	10	2	5	29	20	10	4	3	35	28	46
Aberdeen	34	11	3	3	44	17	6	5	6	28	21	42
Hibernian	34	10	3	4	43	24	9	1	7	29	25	42
Dundee	34	9	5	3	34	16	7	4	6	40	35	41
Kilmarnock	34	9	5	3	33	18	7	3	7	26	28	40
Dunfermline A	34	9	4	4	46	27	5	6	6	26	25	38
Dundee U	34	7	5	5	36	33	7	4	6	32	29	37
Motherwell	34	7	6	4	37	26	3	5	9	22	34	31
Hearts	34	7	6	4	22	16	4	2	11	17	32	30
Partick T	34	5	8	4	25	21	4	4	9	24	47	30
Airdrie	34	7	1	9	27	27	4	5	8	14	26	28
Falkirk	34	8	1	8	18	24	3	3	11	15	46	26
St Johnstone	34	8	3	6	31	30	2	2	13	22	43	25
Stirling A	34	3	6	8	18	34	2	3	12	13	51	19
St Mirren	34	4	1	12	18	47	0	6	11	7	34	15
Ayr U	34	1	4	12	11	37	0	3	14	9	49	9

DIVISION 2

	P	W	D	L	F	A	W	D	L	F	A	Pts
Morton	38	17	1	1	77	8	16	2	1	36	12	69
Raith R	38	15	2	2	55	17	12	2	5	40	27	58
Arbroath	38	16	3	0	48	12	9	4	6	27	20	57
Hamilton A	38	9	6	4	30	22	9	2	8	44	38	44
East Fife	38	10	3	6	34	25	9	1	9	36	38	42
Cowdenbeath	38	9	3	7	43	25	7	5	7	27	30	40
Queen's Park	38	10	4	5	51	29	5	6	8	27	39	40
Albion R	38	10	4	5	34	22	7	2	10	32	40	40
Queen of South	38	10	2	7	47	34	5	7	7	37	42	39
Berwick R	38	12	3	4	41	17	4	3	12	22	38	38
T. Lanark	38	11	5	3	45	30	2	3	14	22	48*	34
Montrose	38	10	5	4	33	18	3	3	13	30	59	34
Alloa	38	9	4	6	32	30	6	0	13	23	44	34
Dumbarton	38	8	4	7	36	26	4	5	10	20	38	33
Stranraer	38	8	4	7	33	35	5	3	11	24	38	33
Forfar A	38	7	3	9	42	43	5	0	14	32	63	27
Stenhousemuir	38	6	4	9	36	46	3	5	11	26	58	27
Clydebank	38	6	1	12	36	47	2	7	10	23	45	24
E. Stirling	38	6	4	9	25	37	1	6	12	19	50	24
Brechin C	38	6	4	9	40	42	2	3	14	18	51	23

* Third Lanark left the League, replaced by Clydebank.

Scottish Football League Records
Season 1967-68

DIVISION 1

	ABERDEEN	AIRDRIE	CELTIC	CLYDE	DUNDEE	DUNDEE U	DUNFERMLINE A	FALKIRK	HEARTS	HIBERNIAN	KILMARNOCK	MORTON	MOTHERWELL	PARTICK T	RAITH R	RANGERS	ST JOHNSTONE	STIRLING A
ABERDEEN		Apr20 3-2	Apr10 0-1	Sep23 1-2	Sep09 4-2	Oct14 6-0	Oct07 0-1	Mar30 2-0	Feb10 2-0	Mar16 5-0	Apr06 1-1	Feb12 1-0	Nov25 2-1	Mar02 0-1	Nov11 6-2	Dec30 1-4	Apr17 1-0	Dec16 1-0
AIRDRIE	Dec23 1-0		Nov11 0-2	Oct21 1-2	Nov04 0-0	Sep30 2-0	Mar20 1-2	Sep16 1-1	Apr13 2-2	Mar06 1-2	Feb21 3-2	Feb03 2-0	Jan01 2-2	Apr27 0-0	Jan20 4-1	Mar30 1-2	Mar16 2-1	Nov25 3-1
CELTIC	Mar06 4-1	Mar13 4-0		Sep09 3-0	Apr13 5-2	Dec02 1-1	Dec30 3-2	Nov18 3-0	Dec09 3-1	Oct07 4-0	Nov15 3-0	Apr20 2-1	Oct24 4-2	Feb03 4-1	Mar23 5-0	Jan02 2-2	Sep23 1-1	Feb14 2-0
CLYDE	Mar27 1-0	Feb10 0-0	Jan01 2-3		Nov25 1-0	Dec16 5-0	Mar02 4-3	Sep30 0-2	Jan20 6-3	Apr06 2-2	Oct28 2-1	Mar16 2-2	Dec23 2-3	Sep16 4-2	Apr30 5-0	Oct14 1-3	Apr10 0-1	Nov11 2-0
DUNDEE	Jan01 0-2	Mar02 6-2	Dec16 4-5	Mar23 3-0		Sep16 2-2	Nov18 4-0	Apr27 1-1	Apr17 1-0	Nov11 1-4	Jan20 6-5	Apr24 0-3	Sep30 2-1	Dec02 3-4	Dec23 4-0	Feb10 2-4	Oct14 1-4	Nov08 4-2
DUNDEE U	Feb03 2-3	Mar25 1-0	Mar30 0-5	Apr13 2-1	Jan02 0-0		Apr20 1-4	Mar06 3-2	Mar20 2-1	Sep23 2-2	Nov25 3-2	Oct07 3-2	Nov04 1-1	Oct21 2-2	Mar16 3-3	Apr02 0-0	Sep09 2-2	Dec30 9-0
DUNFERMLINE A	Jan20 4-2	Apr06 0-2	Apr30 1-2	Nov04 1-0	Mar16 2-0	Dec23 2-2		Oct21 1-2	Sep16 1-3	Feb03 0-1	Sep30 1-2	Mar23 4-0	Jan06 3-0	Dec16 4-0	Jan01 6-0	Mar06 1-2	Nov11 1-0	Dec02 6-0
FALKIRK	Dec02 2-2	Jan02 3-1	Mar16 0-3	Jan13 0-1	Dec30 0-2	Oct28 1-2	Feb10 1-1		Mar02 4-1	Apr20 2-3	Oct14 1-1	Dec16 1-1	Nov11 1-0	Nov25 2-3	Apr06 0-2	Sep23 0-1	Oct07 1-1	Sep09 0-0
HEARTS	Oct21 2-1	Dec16 3-1	Apr06 0-2	Oct07 2-3	Sep23 1-0	Nov11 1-0	Jan02 1-2	Nov04 1-0		Sep09 1-4	Apr10 1-0	Dec30 3-0	Feb28 3-2	Mar16 0-1	Mar04 0-2	Jan13 2-3	Nov25 1-1	Apr20 2-1
HIBERNIAN	Nov18 1-0	Oct28 5-0	Jan20 0-2	Apr24 2-1	Mar09 2-0	Jan06 3-0	Oct14 2-0	Dec23 1-1	Jan01 1-0		Apr27 3-3	Dec02 0-1	Apr13 2-1	Sep30 5-1	Sep16 3-0	Mar23 1-3	Feb10 4-2	Mar02 5-2
KILMARNOCK	Dec09 3-0	Sep23 2-2	Mar02 0-6	Feb28 5-1	Oct07 0-0	Apr17 4-0	Feb06 1-1	Feb03 3-0	Dec02 3-2	Dec30 1-0		Sep09 3-1	Mar16 1-1	Nov11 0-3	Oct21 1-2	Apr20 1-2	Apr13 1-0	Jan02 5-2
MORTON	Sep30 3-3	Oct14 4-0	Dec23 0-4	Nov18 3-1	Dec09 0-0	Jan20 5-2	Nov25 0-3	Apr13 2-1	Apr29 1-0	Apr10 2-0	Jan01 3-2		Sep16 2-1	Jan06 2-0	Nov04 3-3	Apr17 3-3	Oct28 0-2	Feb10 2-0
MOTHERWELL	Mar23 0-3	Sep09 1-2	Feb10 0-1	Apr20 0-1	Mar13 2-4	Mar02 1-3	Sep23 1-1	Mar09 1-1	Oct28 2-5	Dec16 0-1	Nov18 1-2	Jan02 2-1		Apr06 2-1	Dec02 2-2	Oct07 0-2	Dec30 2-1	Oct14 3-1
PARTICK T	Nov04 2-2	Dec30 3-1	Oct14 1-5	Jan02 2-0	Mar30 1-1	Feb10 1-0	Apr13 1-2	Mar23 2-2	Nov18 3-3	Jan13 1-2	Mar13 1-0	Sep23 0-1	Dec09 2-2		Feb28 3-0	Sep09 0-2	Apr20 0-4	Oct07 2-1
RAITH R	Mar09 3-1	Oct07 1-1	Nov25 0-2	Dec30 1-1	Apr20 0-2	Nov18 0-1	Sep09 1-2	Dec09 1-1	Oct14 2-4	Jan02 2-2	Feb10 1-2	Mar02 3-1	Mar30 3-1	Oct28 2-3		Apr13 2-3	Mar20 3-2	Sep23 7-1
RANGERS	Apr27 2-3	Dec02 2-1	Sep16 1-0	Feb03 1-0	Oct23 2-0	Apr06 4-1	Oct28 0-0	Jan06 2-0	Sep30 1-1	Nov25 2-0	Dec23 4-1	Nov11 1-0	Jan20 2-0	Jan01 5-2	Dec16 10-2	6-2	Mar02 5-0	Mar16
ST JOHNSTONE	Sep16 1-1	Nov18 0-0	Mar25 1-6	Dec02 0-2	Feb03 0-2	Apr24 2-1	Mar13 0-1	Jan20 0-1	Mar23 3-2	Oct21 2-3	Dec16 0-1	Mar06 1-2	Apr27 1-0	Dec23 2-1	Sep30 1-0	Nov04 2-3		Apr06 3-0
STIRLING A	Apr13 0-3	Mar23 0-4	Sep30 0-4	Mar09 3-0	Mar06 0-3	Apr27 2-2	Apr10 2-1	Mar13 1-2	Dec23 1-4	Nov04 4-1	Sep16 0-0	Oct21 0-6	Feb03 1-2	Jan20 2-1	Feb17 0-7	Nov18 2-4	Dec09 0-0	

DIVISION 2

	ALBION R	ALLOA	ARBROATH	AYR U	BERWICK R	BRECHIN C	CLYDEBANK	COWDENBEATH	DUMBARTON	EAST FIFE	E STIRLING	FORFAR A	HAMILTON A	MONTROSE	QUEEN OF SOUTH	QUEEN'S PARK	ST MIRREN	STENHOUSEMUIR	STRANRAER
ALBION R		Sep25 2-0	Mar09 1-1	Oct07 0-2	Nov18 5-2	Dec30 3-1	Jan13 0-0	Dec02 0-2	Apr10 3-1	Sep23 1-2	Mar02 3-2	Oct14 4-1	Sep09 2-0	Oct28 2-0	Sep13 3-0	Feb10 3-5	Apr24 0-5	Apr20 6-0	Apr06 3-0
ALLOA	Sep20 1-1		Dec30 0-2	Dec02 1-3	Aug23 1-5	Mar16 3-1	Mar02 0-1	Nov11 1-1	Apr24 2-0	Oct07 3-1	Jan02 2-0	Nov25 3-2	Apr20 0-2	Feb10 2-1	Oct28 2-1	Mar30 0-1	Oct14 0-1	Sep09 4-3	Apr17 4-1
ARBROATH	Nov11 1-0	Apr27 3-2		Apr20 2-0	Apr10 1-0	Sep27 8-1	Feb10 4-0	Dec16 3-0	Apr06 4-0	Oct28 6-3	Mar27 5-0	Jan01 0-4	Oct14 4-0	Sep16 1-1	Jan20 1-0	Dec02 2-0	Sep30 1-1	Nov25 8-0	Mar16 1-0
AYR U	Jan20 5-2	Feb17 2-1	Dec23 3-1		Apr27 1-0	Apr06 0-0	Aug23 3-1	Nov04 1-0	Nov18 3-0	Feb10 2-0	Nov25 4-0	Sep30 1-2	Dec16 1-0	Apr17 4-0	Sep16 2-3	Mar09 1-3	Jan01 0-3	Oct14 3-0	Sep20 5-2
BERWICK R	Mar16 0-1	Sep13 0-1	Sep23 0-2	Dec30 1-0		Dec02 1-0	Oct28 1-1	Apr06 2-0	Apr20 2-1	Jan13 0-1	Sep09 2-1	Apr24 2-1	Mar02 1-1	Oct14 0-2	Feb10 0-1	Apr01 0-3	Nov25 1-3	Jan02 2-0	Nov11 2-1
BRECHIN C	Apr27 2-0	Nov18 1-1	Sep20 1-2	Apr10 5-1	Mar30 0-1		Nov11 2-4	Mar23 1-1	Jan20 0-4	Apr20 1-2	Oct14 4-1	Sep16 2-1	Oct28 2-2	Jan01 0-0	Mar02 1-0	Sep30 1-1	Dec16 0-4	Feb10 2-2	Apr24 1-2
CLYDEBANK	Sep30 2-2	Nov04 4-1	Oct21 2-3	Feb23 2-2	Feb17 1-0	Mar09 2-2		Sep16 2-0	Jan01 2-1	Sep27 3-1	Apr20 5-5	Apr06 2-3	Apr02 3-2	Jan20 0-2	Mar20 2-4	Oct14 2-0	Nov18 0-2	Jan27 2-0	Dec02 5-1
COWDENBEATH	Mar30 2-3	Mar09 1-0	Sep13 0-3	Apr24 0-3	Dec09 2-0	Nov25 2-2	Jan02 0-2		Sep27 6-2	Sep09 1-2	Apr17 4-3	Oct28 2-0	Sep23 2-1	Apr20 4-2	Oct14 0-0	Nov18 1-3	Feb10 1-2	Oct07 3-0	Dec30 2-0
DUMBARTON	Nov25 1-0	Apr13 3-0	Dec09 3-4	Apr29 1-1	Apr17 0-0	Oct07 2-0	Sep09 5-4	Sep20 2-2		Jan02 1-1	Oct28 2-0	Feb10 3-6	Jan13 0-1	Nov11 2-0	Mar30 1-1	Dec30 0-2	Aug23 0-4	Mar02 1-1	Sep23 4-0
EAST FIFE	Jan06 1-0	Jan20 4-0	Apr02 2-0	Oct21 1-0	Sep30 2-1	Dec23 3-0	Apr10 6-0	Jan01 3-3	Sep16 3-3		Apr06 6-0	Aug23 3-1	Dec02 0-0	Mar23 2-2	Apr27 2-1	Dec16 2-2	Nov04 2-1	Nov11 3-0	Feb03 2-1
E STIRLING	Nov04 2-2	Sep16 3-0	Apr13 1-2	Apr22 2-0	Jan01 4-0	Feb03 0-0	Dec23 0-2	Sep30 1-1	Feb17 2-2	Dec09 1-2		Apr10 2-1	Nov18 1-4	Mar30 4-0	Mar09 2-2	Jan20 2-3	Apr27 1-1	Aug23 5-0	Oct21 2-2
FORFAR A	Feb03 2-1	Mar23 1-1	Sep09 1-0	Mar30 2-1	Apr13 1-1	Jan02 1-1	Dec16 2-2	Feb17 2-0	Oct21 3-3	Apr17 1-1	Sep23 2-1		Mar09 3-2	Sep13 1-1	Nov18 0-3	Nov04 2-2	Dec23 0-5	Dec30 0-1	Oct07 1-1
HAMILTON A	Jan01 1-2	Dec23 0-0	Feb03 1-0	Apr13 0-4	Nov04 1-2	Feb17 1-3	Nov25 1-0	Jan06 2-1	Sep30 3-3	Mar30 0-1	Mar16 1-0	Nov11 2-1		Apr27 2-2	Dec09 2-1	Sep16 1-1	Jan20 1-3	Sep20 1-0	Aug23 3-0
MONTROSE	Feb17 3-0	Oct21 1-2	Jan02 2-2	Sep23 2-2	Feb03 3-0	Sep09 1-0	Oct07 3-2	Dec23 2-1	Mar09 1-3	Nov25 2-0	Dec02 1-1	Sep20 1-2	Dec30 3-5		Apr13 1-1	Jan27 2-3	Apr10 0-0	Mar16 4-1	Nov04 1-2
QUEEN OF SOUTH	Aug23 1-0	Mar27 4-1	Oct07 1-0	Jan02 4-0	Oct21 4-1	Nov04 0-3	Sep23 5-0	Feb03 3-5	Dec02 5-2	Dec30 2-1	Nov11 2-4	Mar16 1-2	Apr06 4-1	Dec16 4-4		Apr20 1-3	Sep20 1-1	Apr02 1-2	Sep09 4-0
QUEEN'S PARK	Oct21 2-2	Dec09 3-1	Mar20 2-1	Nov11 1-1	Sep20 4-0	Feb28 1-1	Feb03 4-0	Mar12 4-1	Jan24 2-3	Apr13 3-0	Oct07 4-5	Apr29 0-0	Jan02 2-1	Aug23 1-2	Dec23 3-0		Feb17 1-4	Sep23 2-0	Nov25 2-1
ST MIRREN	Apr13 2-2	Feb03 6-1	Apr17 1-1	Sep09 3-3	Apr29 4-0	Sep23 3-0	Mar16 3-0	Oct21 2-2	Sep13 4-0	Mar02 2-0	Dec30 1-0	Apr20 7-0	Oct07 3-1	Dec09 2-0	Sep27 2-1	Oct28 1-0		Dec02 7-1	Jan02 2-0
STENHOUSEMUIR	Apr16 1-1	Jan01 1-1	Mar23 0-3	Feb03 1-5	Sep16 0-1	Oct21 1-4	Apr13 2-1	Jan20 1-3	Nov04 1-1	Mar09 2-3	Sep11 1-1	Apr27 0-3	Sep27 2-1	Nov18 3-1	Sep30 1-3	Apr24 1-0	Mar30 2-4		Feb17 3-1
STRANRAER	Dec09 2-2	Sep30 3-0	Nov18 1-5	Apr02 2-0	Mar09 0-3	Apr13 1-0	Mar30 1-1	Apr27 2-1	Jan06 1-3	Oct14 1-3	Feb10 1-2	Jan20 1-2	Sep13 1-2	Mar02 3-1	Jan01 2-4	Mar23 2-3	Sep16 0-1	Oct28 2-0	

LEAGUE TABLES

DIVISION 1

	P	W	D	L	F	A	W	D	L	F	A	Pts
Celtic	34	14	3	0	53	14	16	0	1	53	10	63
Rangers	34	14	2	1	50	13	14	3	0	43	21	61
Hibernian	34	12	2	3	40	17	8	3	6	27	32	45
Dunfermline A	34	9	1	7	38	18	8	4	5	26	23	39
Aberdeen	34	11	1	5	36	17	5	4	8	27	31	37
Morton	34	10	4	3	35	25	5	2	10	22	28	36
Kilmarnock	34	9	4	4	34	23	4	4	9	25	34	34
Clyde	34	9	3	5	39	25	6	1	10	16	30	34
Dundee	34	8	2	7	44	39	5	5	7	18	20	33
Partick T	34	6	5	6	25	28	6	2	9	26	39	31
Dundee U	34	7	7	3	36	30	3	4	10	17	42	31
Hearts	34	9	1	7	24	23	4	3	10	32	38	30
Airdrie	34	7	5	5	26	20	3	4	10	19	38	29
St Johnstone	34	6	2	9	19	26	4	5	8	24	26	27
Falkirk	34	3	6	8	19	25	4	6	7	17	25	26
Raith R	34	5	4	8	32	30	4	3	10	26	56	25
Motherwell	34	4	3	10	20	32	2	4	11	20	34	19
Stirling A	34	4	3	10	18	44	0	1	16	11	61	12

DIVISION 2

	P	W	D	L	F	A	W	D	L	F	A	Pts
St Mirren	36	14	4	0	55	12	13	4	1	45	11	62
Arbroath	36	15	2	1	55	12	9	3	6	32	22	53
East Fife	36	13	5	0	47	15	8	2	8	24	32	49
Queen's Park	36	10	4	4	41	23	10	4	4	35	24	48
Ayr U	36	13	1	4	41	18	5	5	8	28	30	42
Queen of South	36	10	2	6	47	30	6	4	8	26	27	38
Forfar A	36	6	9	3	25	27	8	1	9	32	36	38
Albion R	36	11	2	5	41	24	3	7	8	21	31	37
Clydebank	36	9	4	5	41	31	4	4	10	21	42	34
Dumbarton	36	7	6	5	31	27	4	5	9	32	47	33
Hamilton A	36	8	4	6	23	24	5	3	10	26	34	33
Cowdenbeath	36	9	2	7	33	28	3	6	9	24	34	32
Montrose	36	7	5	6	33	27	3	6	9	21	37	31
Berwick R	36	8	2	8	17	20	5	2	11	17	34	30
E. Stirling	36	6	7	5	35	24	3	3	12	26	50	28
Brechin C	36	5	6	7	26	29	3	6	9	19	33	28
Alloa	36	9	2	7	29	27	2	4	12	13	42	28
Stranraer	36	6	2	10	26	33	2	2	14	15	47	20
Stenhousemuir	36	5	4	9	23	37	2	2	14	11	56	20

Scottish Football League Records
Season 1968-69

DIVISION 1

	ABERDEEN	AIRDRIE	ARBROATH	CELTIC	CLYDE	DUNDEE	DUNDEE U	DUNFERMLINE A	FALKIRK	HEARTS	HIBERNIAN	KILMARNOCK	MORTON	PARTICK T	RAITH R	RANGERS	ST JOHNSTONE	ST MIRREN
ABERDEEN		Apr05 3-1	Nov16 2-2	Jan11 1-3	Oct19 0-1	Jan01 0-0	Sep21 0-1	Mar24 2-2	Dec21 2-0	Oct05 1-2	Dec07 2-6	Apr19 0-1	Apr02 6-3	Feb01 1-1	Nov02 2-1	Apr09 0-0	Sep14 2-0	Nov23 2-0
AIRDRIE	Dec14 2-0		Sep07 2-0	Dec28 0-0	Mar05 1-0	Sep28 0-3	Apr23 1-0	Nov23 2-2	Jan02 1-1	Sep21 2-1	Jan18 3-1	Dec07 0-2	Oct12 2-2	Mar10 2-1	Apr12 2-0	Mar24 3-2	Nov16 3-0	Oct26 1-1
ARBROATH	Mar08 2-1	Apr30 0-2		Nov09 0-5	Apr19 1-1	Oct19 1-2	Jan11 3-1	Feb15 0-1	Mar22 3-0	Dec21 2-3	Nov23 3-4	Oct05 1-2	Jan04 3-1	Dec14 2-2	Feb01 0-1	Nov02 1-5	Mar29 1-2	Sep14 1-1
CELTIC	Sep28 2-1	Apr19 2-2	Mar05 7-1		Jan01 5-0	Nov02 3-1	Oct05 2-0	Jan04 3-1	Apr09 5-2	Feb01 5-0	Mar24 1-1	Dec21 1-1	Apr28 2-4	Mar15 1-0	Nov16 2-0	Sep14 2-4	Oct19 2-1	Dec07 5-0
CLYDE	Apr23 1-1	Nov09 1-0	Mar18 3-1	Sep07 0-3		Jan18 0-0	Mar11 2-2	Mar08 3-0	Oct26 2-0	Mar29 0-1	Oct12 1-1	Nov30 2-1	Dec14 0-0	Jan02 1-2	Sep21 3-2	Nov23 1-1	Jan11 0-3	Apr12 0-0
DUNDEE	Sep07 4-4	Jan11 1-1	Feb08 3-0	May01 1-2	Oct05 2-3		Jan02 1-2	Nov09 1-0	Mar08 0-0	Oct26 3-1	Dec14 0-0	Mar15 0-0	Mar29 0-2	Nov30 1-1	Mar26 2-2	Apr22 3-2	Sep21 2-3	Oct12 0-0
DUNDEE U	Jan04 1-4	Oct19 2-1	Sep28 4-2	Jan18 1-3	Nov02 1-0	Sep14 3-1		Apr19 2-2	Dec07 2-1	Nov16 4-2	Mar31 3-0	Feb01 2-2	Nov23 2-0	Dec21 2-1	Mar05 3-1	Apr05 2-1	Jan01 4-2	Mar22 2-2
DUNFERMLINE A	Nov30 5-1	Mar15 1-0	Oct26 2-0	Sep21 1-1	Nov16 2-1	Mar05 2-0	Dec28 2-2		Feb01 2-0	Jan02 4-2	Apr28 1-1	Jan11 1-1	Nov02 5-3	Mar29 2-0	Sep07 3-2	May01 0-3	Oct05 3-1	Dec14 6-2
FALKIRK	Apr12 1-0	Sep14 2-1	Nov30 2-2	Dec14 0-0	Feb15 3-3	Nov16 0-1	Mar29 2-2	Oct12 0-1		Oct19 1-3	Jan04 0-1	Mar12 1-1	Jan01 4-1	Apr19 2-2	Mar15 1-3	Jan18 0-3	Nov02 2-1	Sep28 0-2
HEARTS	Jan18 3-2	Jan04 1-1	Apr12 2-2	Oct12 0-1	Dec07 2-3	Mar12 2-2	Mar08 1-0	Sep14 3-1	Apr02 2-1		Jan01 0-0	Nov02 0-1	Mar24 2-2	Nov09 2-0	Dec14 1-0	Sep28 1-1	Nov23 2-2	Apr19 2-1
HIBERNIAN	Mar29 1-1	Oct05 5-1	Mar15 1-2	Nov30 2-5	Feb01 2-1	Apr08 1-3	Oct26 1-1	Dec21 3-1	Sep21 3-2	Sep07 1-3		Oct19 1-0	Nov16 5-0	Jan11 1-2	Jan02 3-0	Mar05 1-2	May01 4-0	Mar01 3-0
KILMARNOCK	Dec28 2-1	Mar29 2-1	Jan18 1-0	Apr21 2-2	Mar22 0-0	Nov23 1-0	Oct12 3-0	Sep28 0-1	Nov09 5-1	Feb22 1-0	Feb19 2-1		Sep14 1-0	Mar08 1-1	Oct26 4-4	Jan04 3-3	Dec14 2-0	Jan01 0-0
MORTON	Nov09 1-0	Feb01 1-1	Sep21 5-1	Oct26 1-1	Apr05 1-1	Dec07 2-1	Mar15 1-2	Feb22 0-2	Sep07 2-0	Nov30 0-2	Mar08 4-3	Jan02 3-2		Oct05 3-3	Jan11 3-2	Dec28 0-2	Apr12 4-4	Mar18 3-0
PARTICK T	Oct12 1-0	Nov02 1-1	Apr05 2-1	Nov23 0-4	Sep14 4-0	Mar22 0-4	Apr12 0-0	Dec07 0-1	Mar04 1-2	Mar01 5-1	Sep28 2-1	Nov16 0-2	Jan18 2-1		Feb11 2-1	Jan01 0-2	Apr09 1-1	Jan04 0-2
RAITH R	Mar19 3-2	Dec21 1-2	Oct12 3-1	Mar08 1-3	Jan04 1-1	Apr19 4-0	Nov09 1-2	Jan01 0-3	Nov23 3-1	Apr05 0-3	Sep14 2-0	Mar04 0-0	Sep28 0-1	Oct19 3-0		Dec07 0-3	Mar22 1-5	Jan18 0-2
RANGERS	Oct26 2-3	Nov30 1-1	Mar11 2-0	Jan02 1-0	Mar15 6-0	Apr28 1-1	Dec14 2-1	Oct19 3-0	Oct05 2-1	Jan11 2-0	Nov09 6-1	Sep21 3-3	Apr19 3-0	Sep07 2-0	Mar29 2-1		Feb01 3-0	Mar08 6-0
ST JOHNSTONE	Jan02 3-1	Mar08 3-1	Dec07 5-1	Apr01 2-3	Sep28 0-0	Jan04 3-1	Sep07 1-4	Jan18 2-1	Apr23 4-0	Mar15 2-1	Apr19 2-1	Apr05 1-0	Dec21 2-3	Oct26 2-2	Nov30 3-0	Oct12 2-0		Nov09 2-3
ST MIRREN	Mar15 1-2	Feb15 1-2	Jan02 2-1	Mar29 0-3	Dec21 1-0	Feb01 2-3	Nov30 1-1	Apr05 1-2	Jan11 3-0	Dec28 1-1	Nov02 3-0	Sep07 1-1	Oct19 2-1	Sep21 1-0	Oct05 2-2	Nov16 1-0	Mar05 1-2	

DIVISION 2

	ALBION R	ALLOA	AYR U	BERWICK R	BRECHIN C	CLYDEBANK	COWDENBEATH	DUMBARTON	EAST FIFE	E STIRLING	FORFAR A	HAMILTON A	MONTROSE	MOTHERWELL	QUEEN OF SOUTH	QUEEN'S PARK	STENHOUSEMUIR	STIRLING A	STRANRAER
ALBION R		Mar08 2-0	Apr19 0-1	Apr05 2-1	Jan25 2-1	Nov30 3-1	Jan11 1-0	Feb01 1-2	Dec21 4-1	Nov02 2-1	Sep14 2-1	Jan01 5-0	Sep18 5-4	Apr29 0-1	Nov09 1-0	Oct05 0-0	Apr26 4-2	Mar15 2-1	Oct19 1-1
ALLOA	Nov16 1-2		Sep04 1-2	Sep11 1-0	Sep28 2-0	Jan18 3-3	Nov30 0-1	Mar29 0-1	Apr19 1-2	Mar15 2-0	Jan25 0-3	Apr26 3-1	Mar01 1-2	Oct12 0-2	Apr12 1-2	Apr15 2-2	Jan01 4-4	Nov02 1-2	Sep14 0-2
AYR U	Dec28 3-0	Aug21 3-0		Jan11 2-0	Dec21 6-1	Apr05 0-0	Feb01 4-0	Mar01 4-0	Feb15 2-1	Nov30 6-1	Nov02 4-1	Dec07 1-0	Jan02 4-0	Apr23 1-1	Oct05 2-2	Sep21 1-5	Oct19 7-1	Nov16 1-2	Mar15 3-0
BERWICK R	Dec14 0-0	Sep18 3-2	Sep28 1-1		Jan18 0-0	Apr26 5-0	Mar29 0-4	Oct19 2-0	Sep14 2-0	Jan01 3-0	Apr19 0-0	Nov02 0-0	Nov16 3-1	Mar01 1-3	Sep04 0-2	Apr12 1-1	Mar15 2-4	Oct12 0-1	Feb15 1-5
BRECHIN C	Sep21 1-4	Jan11 1-3	Apr12 0-3	Oct05 2-1		Aug21 3-1	Nov02 5-1	Apr09 1-0	Apr05 0-3	Nov16 1-2	Nov23 0-3	Sep18 0-2	Sep07 2-1	Mar22 0-0	Apr23 1-1	Dec07 4-1	Mar01 4-4	Oct19 0-2	Feb01 0-1
CLYDEBANK	Mar22 2-0	Oct05 0-2	Apr28 0-1	Sep21 1-1	Sep04 0-0		Sep18 1-1	Sep07 0-1	Nov23 1-4	Oct19 0-4	Jan04 3-0	Mar04 5-0	Feb15 5-0	Nov16 0-4	Jan11 3-3	Jan02 1-3	Mar29 2-2	Apr19 2-2	Nov02 2-2
COWDENBEATH	Sep28 0-2	Mar22 2-3	Oct12 1-1	Dec07 1-1	Apr14 3-0	Sep11 3-3		Nov23 3-1	Apr07 0-4	Sep14 1-3	Oct19 1-3	Dec21 1-2	Apr05 2-3	Jan18 0-5	Mar08 1-2	Nov09 3-2	Apr19 6-0	Sep04 0-1	Apr26 4-1
DUMBARTON	Oct12 3-1	Dec07 4-1	Nov09 0-3	Feb08 3-1	Oct26 2-1	Jan01 3-3	Mar15 0-3		Dec14 1-1	Apr25 4-1	Mar08 2-3	Nov30 1-0	Aug21 1-2	Apr12 2-4	Feb22 0-2	Dec28 0-2	Jan18 5-1	Sep14 1-3	Sep28 1-3
EAST FIFE	Apr12 2-0	Dec28 5-0	Oct26 1-0	Jan02 4-1	Mar26 6-1	Mar15 1-1	Sep07 1-0	Sep18 1-1		Mar29 4-2	Oct05 1-2	Jan11 5-0	Nov02 6-1	Feb08 3-1	Sep21 1-1	Aug21 0-0	Nov30 5-0	Mar01 3-2	Nov16 2-1
E STIRLING	Apr23 1-0	Nov23 5-1	Mar22 2-1	Sep07 7-3	Mar08 0-1	Apr14 1-0	Jan02 1-0	Sep21 4-1	Dec07 3-0		Nov09 2-4	Apr05 1-0	Oct05 5-1	Dec28 0-4	Oct26 0-1	Feb01 2-1	Sep11 6-0	Dec21 0-1	Aug21 2-2
FORFAR A	Jan02 4-1	Sep21 1-1	May01 0-1	Apr23 3-3	Apr28 3-3	Apr12 1-0	Feb08 1-3	Nov16 2-0	Apr26 3-2	Mar01 2-4		Aug21 1-1	Nov30 3-1	Sep07 1-0	Apr05 1-0	Oct26 1-2	Oct12 9-1	Sep28 3-2	Dec07 3-1
HAMILTON A	Sep07 3-5	Oct26 3-2	Mar29 2-2	Apr09 2-0	May01 2-1	Oct12 1-2	Apr12 2-2	Mar22 0-0	Sep28 0-1	Dec14 0-0	Sep04 1-3		Sep21 4-4	Jan02 0-1	Feb08 0-3	Nov23 0-2	Nov16 2-1	Jan18 1-1	Mar01 1-3
MONTROSE	Sep11 1-3	Nov09 2-1	Sep14 0-2	Mar08 1-0	Apr02 6-1	Oct26 5-3	May01 3-0	Sep04 2-0	Feb22 3-1	Jan18 2-2	Mar22 0-0	Apr16 1-2		Nov23 0-2	Oct12 1-0	Apr23 3-1	Sep28 3-0	Mar29 0-2	Apr19 2-0
MOTHERWELL	Aug21 7-0	Feb01 4-0	Sep18 4-1	Nov09 7-1	Nov30 2-0	Mar08 2-1	Oct05 4-1	Dec21 1-1	Oct19 4-0	Apr19 4-0	Jan01 3-1	Sep14 2-1	Mar15 4-1		Dec07 2-2	Jan11 5-1	Apr14 7-1	Apr26 3-0	Apr05 3-0
QUEEN OF SOUTH	Mar01 3-0	Dec21 3-0	Apr26 3-2	Aug21 1-0	Apr19 1-2	Sep28 1-1	Nov16 4-0	Nov02 4-1	Jan04 4-2	Apr02 3-3	Apr14 5-0	Oct19 1-2	Feb01 1-0	Mar29 1-2		Sep11 3-1	Sep14 5-1	Nov30 0-1	Jan01 0-2
QUEEN'S PARK	Jan18 1-1	Feb08 4-0	Jan04 0-3	Dec21 3-1	Mar12 2-1	Sep14 2-4	Mar01 0-1	Apr19 2-0	Sep04 0-2	Oct12 3-2	Feb15 2-2	Mar05 1-0	Oct19 1-0	Sep28 1-2	Sep18 0-4		Nov02 2-0	Jan01 0-2	Nov30 1-1
STENHOUSEMUIR	Oct26 2-3	Sep07 4-4	Apr08 1-2	Nov23 1-3	Nov09 2-1	Dec07 0-0	Dec28 1-3	Oct05 3-2	Mar22 1-4	Sep18 0-2	Feb01 1-2	Mar08 3-1	Jan11 2-2	Sep21 1-6	Jan02 3-4	Apr21 2-1		Apr05 2-0	Dec21 1-2
STIRLING A	Nov23 1-1	Feb22 1-1	Mar08 0-0	Feb01 3-1	Feb08 3-0	Dec28 2-0	Aug21 2-1	Jan02 3-0	Nov09 1-2	Apr12 1-1	Jan11 2-1	Oct05 7-1	Dec07 2-0	Oct26 0-4	Mar22 2-3	Sep07 3-0	Dec14 5-1		Sep18 3-2
STRANRAER	Apr14 3-0	Jan02 1-1	Nov23 0-2	Oct26 2-0	Oct12 3-1	Feb22 1-1	Sep21 0-1	Jan11 1-2	Mar08 1-1	Apr28 3-0	Mar29 1-0	Nov09 1-0	Dec28 0-1	Dec14 0-2	Sep07 2-0	Mar22 2-0	Apr12 5-2	Apr21 2-1	

LEAGUE TABLES

DIVISION 1

	P	W	D	L	F	A	W	D	L	F	A	Pts
Celtic	34	12	3	2	50	19	11	5	1	39	13	54
Rangers	34	13	3	1	47	12	8	4	5	34	20	49
Dunfermline A	34	12	4	1	42	20	7	3	7	21	25	45
Kilmarnock	34	10	6	1	30	15	5	8	4	20	17	44
Dundee U	34	12	3	2	40	25	5	6	6	21	24	43
St Johnstone	34	11	2	4	39	22	5	3	9	27	37	37
Airdrie	34	10	5	2	27	16	3	6	8	19	28	37
Hearts	34	7	7	3	26	20	7	1	9	26	34	36
Dundee	34	4	8	5	24	23	6	4	7	23	25	32
Morton	34	8	5	4	34	27	4	3	10	24	41	32
St Mirren	34	7	4	6	24	21	4	6	7	16	33	32
Hibernian	34	9	2	6	38	24	3	5	9	22	35	31
Clyde	34	6	7	4	20	18	3	6	8	15	32	31
Partick T	34	7	3	7	21	24	2	7	8	18	29	28
Aberdeen	34	6	5	6	26	24	3	3	11	24	35	26
Raith R	34	6	2	9	23	29	2	3	12	22	38	21
Falkirk	34	4	6	7	21	27	1	2	14	12	42	18
Arbroath	34	4	3	10	24	34	1	3	13	17	48	16

DIVISION 2

	P	W	D	L	F	A	W	D	L	F	A	Pts
Motherwell	36	16	2	0	68	12	14	2	2	44	11	64
Ayr U	36	13	3	2	54	15	10	4	4	28	16	53
East Fife	36	13	4	1	51	14	8	2	8	31	31	48
Stirling A	36	11	4	3	41	19	10	2	6	26	21	48
Queen of South	36	11	2	5	43	20	9	5	4	32	21	47
Forfar A	36	10	4	4	42	26	8	3	7	29	30	43
Albion R	36	13	2	3	37	18	6	3	9	23	38	43
Stranraer	36	10	3	5	28	15	7	4	7	29	30	41
E. Stirling	36	12	1	5	42	21	5	4	9	28	41	39
Montrose	36	11	2	5	35	20	4	2	12	24	51	34
Queen's Park	36	8	3	7	25	26	5	4	9	25	33	33
Cowdenbeath	36	5	3	10	32	37	7	2	9	22	30	29
Clydebank	36	4	7	7	28	30	2	8	8	24	37	27
Dumbarton	36	7	2	9	33	35	4	3	11	13	34	27
Hamilton A	36	4	6	8	24	33	4	2	12	13	39	24
Berwick R	36	6	6	6	24	24	1	3	14	18	46	23
Brechin C	36	6	3	9	25	33	2	3	13	15	45	22
Alloa	36	4	3	11	23	31	3	4	11	22	48	21
Stenhousemuir	36	5	3	10	30	42	1	3	14	25	83	18

Scottish Football League Records
Season 1969-70

DIVISION 1

	ABERDEEN	AIRDRIE	AYR U	CELTIC	CLYDE	DUNDEE	DUNDEE U	DUNFERMLINE A	HEARTS	HIBERNIAN	KILMARNOCK	MORTON	MOTHERWELL	PARTICK T	RAITH R	RANGERS	ST JOHNSTONE	ST MIRREN
ABERDEEN		Jan31 0-1	Feb25 1-0	Oct29 2-3	Aug30 6-0	Sep27 1-1	Nov08 0-0	Mar21 2-0	Apr04 0-1	Mar09 0-2	Apr06 2-2	Sep13 2-2	Nov22 4-1	Oct11 2-1	Jan10 5-1	Dec20 2-3	Mar02 0-0	Mar18 1-1
AIRDRIE	Sep06 3-4		Apr08 0-0	Oct11 0-2	Nov24 4-4	Feb25 0-1	Jan17 6-3	Apr04 3-0	Sep03 1-2	Mar07 3-2	Apr01 1-0	Mar21 1-1	Mar11 1-0	Nov29 2-3	Mar04 3-0	Nov08 1-3	Oct29 3-1	Sep20 1-0
AYR U	Oct04 1-2	Dec06 1-3		Nov01 2-4	Mar14 1-0	Jan31 3-2	Feb28 2-3	Dec20 1-0	Oct18 0-0	Aug30 3-0	Jan03 3-2	Sep27 1-0	Dec27 1-0	Apr18 2-1	Nov15 2-1	Sep13 2-1	Feb14 0-0	Mar28 1-1
CELTIC	Mar25 1-2	Feb28 4-2	Mar21 3-0		Sep27 2-1	Dec06 1-0	Dec17 7-2	Jan31 3-1	Nov08 0-2	Sep13 1-2	Dec20 3-1	Mar10 4-0	Apr04 6-1	Dec27 8-1	Oct04 7-1	Jan03 0-0	Aug30 2-2	Dec01 2-0
CLYDE	Dec13 2-1	Apr18 1-2	Oct25 0-1	Jan01 0-2		Mar07 1-1	Sep03 2-2	Feb21 2-1	Dec16 2-1	Mar28 1-0	Nov01 2-3	Nov15 0-0	Sep06 0-2	Sep20 2-1	Feb07 1-1	Mar31 1-0	Oct11 3-0	Jan17 1-0
DUNDEE	Jan01 2-0	Oct04 4-2	Sep06 1-0	Apr06 1-2	Oct18 3-0		Sep20 1-2	Nov08 1-1	Nov22 2-0	Dec27 1-0	Feb28 3-0	Mar25 2-1	Sep03 1-3	Apr01 4-1	Jan17 0-0	Mar21 2-1	Apr04 0-2	Nov29 1-0
DUNDEE U	Mar28 2-0	Sep13 5-2	Oct11 3-1	Mar07 0-2	Mar11 3-1	Jan03 4-1		Apr22 1-3	Jan10 2-3	Nov15 0-1	Dec06 2-2	Jan31 5-4	Feb25 0-0	Nov01 1-0	Apr18 4-2	Aug30 0-0	Sep27 1-0	Oct25 3-1
DUNFERMLINE A	Nov01 2-1	Nov15 4-2	Sep03 0-0	Sep06 2-1	Oct04 1-0	Mar28 3-2	Dec10 2-3		Sep20 1-0	Apr18 1-2	Oct18 2-1	Feb28 1-2	Mar25 2-1	Jan17 1-1	Jan01 3-0	Mar14 2-1	Apr10 3-0	Dec13 2-0
HEARTS	Nov15 2-2	Dec20 5-0	Mar07 3-0	Mar28 0-0	Apr11 1-1	Apr18 1-3	Dec27 2-2	Jan03 2-0		Sep27 0-2	Sep13 4-1	Aug30 0-1	Oct11 2-2	Oct25 1-1	Nov01 3-2	Dec06 1-2	Jan31 0-0	Feb21 1-0
HIBERNIAN	Apr13 1-2	Nov11 3-1	Dec13 4-3	Jan17 1-2	Nov08 1-0	Feb16 4-1	Apr04 3-1	Nov25 3-0	Jan01 0-0		Mar25 2-1	Oct04 1-0	Nov29 1-1	Sep06 5-1	Sep20 3-1	Feb28 2-2	Mar21 4-1	Sep03 2-0
KILMARNOCK	Nov29 0-2	Apr11 1-0	Sep20 4-1	Sep03 2-4	Mar21 2-1	Oct11 3-0	Feb11 3-1	Mar07 1-0	Jan17 0-0	Oct25 2-2		Nov08 5-2	Dec13 2-2	Feb25 4-2	Sep06 1-0	Apr04 2-2	Dec02 4-1	Jan01 1-1
MORTON	Jan17 3-2	Nov01 3-3	Jan01 1-0	Nov29 0-3	Apr04 1-0	Oct25 0-1	Sep06 6-0	Oct11 3-1	Dec13 2-3	Feb21 1-1	Mar28 1-1		Sep20 1-0	Apr14 4-1	Sep03 2-1	Nov22 2-2	Mar07 1-1	Jan10 2-1
MOTHERWELL	Apr18 0-2	Sep27 2-2	Apr13 3-0	Nov15 1-2	Jan31 1-0	Dec20 1-1	Oct04 0-2	Dec06 0-0	Feb28 0-2	Apr01 2-1	Aug30 1-0	Mar02 1-0		Mar28 3-1	Mar14 1-2	Oct29 2-2	Sep13 4-1	Nov01 3-0
PARTICK T	Feb28 0-3	Feb14 1-3	Nov22 1-3	Feb16 1-5	Mar03 1-2	Aug30 1-0	Mar21 1-2	Sep13 1-2	Mar14 1-0	Jan31 3-1	Oct04 2-2	Apr08 1-2	Nov08 2-2		Oct18 1-1	Sep27 1-2	Feb07 4-3	Apr04 0-0
RAITH R	Dec27 0-1	Aug30 1-0	Apr04 1-1	Feb25 0-2	Dec06 1-1	Sep13 0-0	Nov22 0-1	Sep27 1-1	Mar21 0-3	Jan03 0-3	Jan31 2-3	Dec20 2-1	Oct25 2-2	Mar07 1-1		Mar11 2-1	Nov08 1-0	Oct11 1-3
RANGERS	Sep03 2-0	Mar28 1-1	Jan17 3-0	Sep20 0-1	Dec27 3-0	Nov01 3-1	Dec13 2-1	Oct25 2-0	Mar25 3-2	Oct11 1-3	Nov15 5-3	Apr18 0-2	Mar07 2-1	Jan01 3-1	Nov29 3-0		Feb25 3-1	Sep06 2-0
ST JOHNSTONE	Sep20 3-1	Mar25 1-1	Dec10 2-0	Dec13 1-4	Feb28 3-2	Nov15 1-4	Jan01 1-0	Dec27 1-0	Sep06 3-3	Nov01 1-0	Apr18 1-1	Oct18 4-0	Jan17 4-3	Sep03 5-2	Mar28 1-1	Oct04 1-3		Apr13 2-3
ST MIRREN	Nov05 2-0	Jan03 1-1	Nov08 2-1	Apr18 2-3	Sep13 4-0	Mar10 2-1	Mar14 3-1	Aug30 1-3	Oct04 0-0	Mar03 3-3	Sep27 0-2	Dec27 1-1	Mar21 2-3	Nov15 1-0	Feb28 3-3	Jan31 0-4	Dec06 1-2	

DIVISION 2

	ALBION R	ALLOA	ARBROATH	BERWICK R	BRECHIN C	CLYDEBANK	COWDENBEATH	DUMBARTON	EAST FIFE	E STIRLING	FALKIRK	FORFAR A	HAMILTON A	MONTROSE	QUEEN OF SOUTH	QUEEN'S PARK	STENHOUSEMUIR	STIRLING A	STRANRAER
ALBION R		Feb28 1-0	Apr18 2-2	Sep13 1-3	Apr14 3-2	Sep24 1-4	Mar14 0-2	Nov01 0-0	Aug30 1-0	Apr07 2-0	Oct04 0-4	Dec06 3-2	Sep27 0-0	Nov15 1-3	Apr27 3-1	Mar28 4-1	Jan31 2-0	Sep09 1-1	Mar31 2-1
ALLOA	Oct11 1-0		Nov15 1-0	Jan24 3-1	Aug30 0-1	Sep13 2-0	Nov01 1-3	Feb21 0-0	Jan03 0-1	Feb14 2-1	Apr28 1-1	Sep10 5-2	Jan31 3-0	Mar28 1-0	Mar07 0-1	Oct25 3-0	Sep27 5-0	Sep24 0-2	Apr11 1-1
ARBROATH	Nov22 3-1	Apr04 1-0		Apr22 4-0	Jan03 3-0	Jan31 2-0	Jan10 2-1	Mar07 5-0	Dec06 1-1	Sep24 3-1	Nov08 3-1	Sep27 1-0	Aug30 2-1	Oct25 4-0	Feb21 3-1	Oct11 1-2	Sep10 6-0	Dec20 0-1	Sep13 3-1
BERWICK R	Jan17 0-2	Sep03 3-0	Sep17 2-1		Dec27 2-0	Apr18 0-2	Dec13 1-3	Oct01 0-1	Oct25 4-0	Nov01 4-1	Nov29 1-3	Feb21 4-1	Mar28 5-1	Feb07 2-2	Sep20 3-0	Sep06 3-0	Oct11 6-1	Mar07 3-0	Nov15 1-0
BRECHIN C	Oct01 5-0	Dec13 1-2	Sep20 1-5	Apr28 2-0		Nov15 2-2	Sep06 1-1	Jan17 1-4	Apr01 2-0	Mar07 2-0	Apr11 2-2	Oct11 2-1	Apr18 3-0	Jan01 0-2	Feb07 1-5	Nov29 1-0	Mar28 1-3	Oct25 1-3	Nov01 1-0
CLYDEBANK	Nov29 3-0	Jan17 3-4	Sep06 0-2	Nov22 1-1	Apr04 1-1		Sep03 1-3	Jan01 0-0	Oct11 4-1	Oct25 2-0	Sep20 0-7	Mar07 0-1	Nov01 2-1	Dec13 1-3	Sep17 1-1	Oct01 1-1	Feb21 0-0	Apr27 0-2	Mar28 2-1
COWDENBEATH	Oct25 1-1	Mar21 0-2	Dec27 2-2	Aug30 3-0	Jan31 1-0	Apr22 3-2		Oct11 1-0	Sep27 2-0	Sep10 3-1	Mar31 2-1	Feb14 5-1	Sep13 0-1	Mar25 3-1	Apr04 0-0	Jan24 4-0	Jan03 7-2	Dec06 0-0	Sep24 3-1
DUMBARTON	Mar21 2-0	Oct04 1-3	Oct18 0-3	Apr13 2-1	Sep13 1-2	Sep27 5-1	Feb28 1-2		Feb14 2-0	Apr21 0-2	Mar14 1-2	Jan31 2-1	Oct29 1-0	Apr18 0-2	Nov08 2-0	Nov15 3-0	Nov12 5-1	Jan03 1-0	Aug30 1-0
EAST FIFE	Dec13 2-4	Sep20 4-0	Oct01 2-0	Mar14 2-1	Oct04 6-3	Feb28 1-1	Jan01 0-1	Sep17 2-1		Mar28 2-1	Sep06 1-2	Jan10 4-1	Nov15 4-0	Nov29 1-0	Apr15 0-2	Sep03 1-2	Apr18 4-2	Nov01 3-1	Oct18 1-1
E STIRLING	Sep20 2-1	Sep17 0-0	Apr01 3-2	Mar21 2-0	Oct18 3-3	Mar14 2-1	Feb07 0-6	Apr28 2-1	Nov08 3-1		Dec13 1-6	Apr04 1-0	Oct04 2-2	Oct01 4-2	Jan17 1-3	Jan01 1-1	Dec27 4-2	Nov22 0-1	Feb28 4-0
FALKIRK	Mar03 4-1	Apr07 1-0	Mar28 3-0	Mar24 1-0	Mar17 5-0	Jan03 1-2	Apr18 2-0	Oct25 0-0	Jan31 1-1	Aug30 3-0		Sep13 3-2	Mar10 6-1	Mar07 5-0	Oct11 7-5	Nov01 3-1	Dec20 2-1	Sep27 0-3	Apr21 0-0
FORFAR A	Sep03 3-2	Apr21 1-2	Jan01 2-1	Oct04 0-3	Feb28 2-0	Oct18 3-1	Sep17 1-2	Sep06 1-4	Dec27 4-1	Nov15 2-4	Apr14 0-3		Mar14 3-1	Sep20 5-2	Nov29 1-2	Dec13 2-1	Nov01 3-3	Mar28 0-1	Apr18 2-3
HAMILTON A	Jan01 2-6	Sep06 2-4	Dec13 2-4	Nov08 2-1	Nov22 2-0	Mar21 0-2	Jan17 2-3	Feb07 1-3	Apr04 3-2	Feb21 3-0	Sep17 1-4	Oct25 2-3		Sep03 1-1	Oct01 0-1	Sep20 1-0	Mar07 3-2	Oct11 1-1	Dec27 3-2
MONTROSE	Apr04 1-0	Nov08 1-4	Mar14 2-1	Sep10 1-1	Sep27 2-0	Aug30 4-1	Oct04 0-1	Nov22 0-2	Sep24 1-2	Apr11 2-1	Oct18 1-1	Jan03 2-1	Apr22 6-0		Mar21 2-1	Dec27 2-1	Feb14 0-1	Sep13 1-1	Jan31 0-0
QUEEN OF SOUTH	Dec27 1-0	Oct18 3-3	Oct04 2-1	Jan03 4-2	Apr22 1-0	Feb14 1-1	Nov15 2-2	Mar28 3-2	Sep10 3-4	Sep13 2-1	Feb28 0-2	Sep24 1-0	Dec06 3-0	Nov01 4-1		Apr18 3-0	Aug30 2-0	Jan31 1-0	Sep27 1-1
QUEEN'S PARK	Nov08 2-1	Mar11 3-2	Mar04 2-1	Jan31 1-2	Sep24 1-2	Mar25 0-0	Oct18 2-2	Apr04 0-2	Mar18 0-2	Sep27 3-3	Dec06 0-3	Aug30 3-0	Jan03 3-0	Apr28 0-0	Nov22 0-3		Sep13 1-0	Feb25 0-3	Sep10 0-1
STENHOUSEMUIR	Sep06 0-3	Jan01 2-1	Feb07 1-0	Feb28 2-1	Nov08 4-2	Oct04 1-1	Sep20 1-6	Nov29 2-2	Nov22 2-0	Jan24 3-4	Sep30 0-1	Mar21 2-1	Oct18 3-1	Sep16 1-6	Dec13 1-2	Jan17 1-0		Apr04 2-2	Mar14 1-1
STIRLING A	Apr10 6-0	Nov29 0-2	Sep03 1-1	Oct18 3-3	Mar14 1-1	Dec27 5-2	Oct01 3-1	Sep20 2-2	Mar21 3-1	Apr18 1-2	Jan01 0-3	Nov08 6-0	Feb28 3-1	Jan17 2-1	Sep06 0-2	Sep17 1-1	Nov15 2-0		Oct04 5-1
STRANRAER	Sep17 0-4	Oct01 0-4	Jan17 0-3	Apr04 3-3	Mar21 6-1	Nov08 1-2	Nov29 0-2	Dec13 6-1	Mar07 4-2	Oct11 4-1	Sep03 3-1	Nov22 1-3	Jan10 4-1	Sep06 1-3	Jan01 4-5	Feb07 0-4	Oct25 2-0	Feb21 2-4	

LEAGUE TABLES

DIVISION 1

	P	W	D	L	F	A	W	D	L	F	A	Pts
Celtic	34	12	2	3	54	18	15	1	1	42	15	57
Rangers	34	13	1	3	38	17	6	6	5	29	23	45
Hibernian	34	12	3	2	40	17	7	3	7	25	23	44
Hearts	34	6	7	4	28	19	7	5	5	22	17	38
Dundee U	34	10	3	4	36	23	6	3	8	26	41	38
Dundee	34	11	2	4	29	15	4	4	9	20	29	36
Kilmarnock	34	10	5	2	37	21	3	5	9	25	36	36
Aberdeen	34	6	6	5	30	19	8	1	8	25	26	35
Morton	34	9	5	3	33	21	4	4	9	19	31	35
Dunfermline A	34	12	2	3	32	17	3	3	11	13	28	35
Motherwell	34	8	4	5	25	18	3	6	8	24	33	32
Airdrie	34	8	3	6	33	26	4	5	8	26	38	32
St Johnstone	34	9	4	4	35	28	2	5	10	15	34	31
Ayr U	34	10	3	4	26	20	2	3	12	11	32	30
St Mirren	34	6	5	6	28	28	2	4	11	11	26	25
Clyde	34	8	4	5	21	18	1	3	13	13	38	25
Raith R	34	4	6	7	15	24	1	5	11	17	43	21
Partick T	34	4	4	9	22	33	1	3	13	19	49	17

DIVISION 2

	P	W	D	L	F	A	W	D	L	F	A	Pts
Falkirk	36	13	3	2	47	17	12	3	3	47	17	56
Cowdenbeath	36	12	4	2	40	15	12	3	3	41	20	55
Queen of South	36	12	4	2	37	20	10	2	6	35	29	50
Stirling A	36	9	5	4	44	24	9	5	4	26	16	46
Arbroath	36	15	1	2	47	11	5	3	10	29	28	44
Alloa	36	10	3	5	29	14	9	2	7	33	27	43
Dumbarton	36	11	0	7	30	20	6	6	6	25	26	40
Montrose	36	9	4	5	28	19	6	3	9	29	36	37
Berwick R	36	12	1	5	44	18	3	4	11	23	37	35
East Fife	36	11	2	5	40	23	4	2	12	19	40	34
Albion R	36	9	4	5	27	26	5	1	12	26	38	33
E. Stirling	36	10	4	4	35	32	4	1	13	23	43	33
Clydebank	36	5	5	8	22	31	5	5	8	25	34	30
Brechin C	36	8	3	7	29	30	3	3	12	18	44	28
Queen's Park	36	6	4	8	21	27	4	2	12	17	35	26
Stenhousemuir	36	8	4	6	29	34	2	2	14	18	55	26
Stranraer	36	7	1	10	41	44	2	6	10	15	31	25
Forfar A	36	8	1	9	35	36	3	0	15	20	47	23
Hamilton A	36	7	2	9	31	39	1	2	15	11	53	20

SCOTTISH FOOTBALL LEAGUE RECORDS
SEASON 1970-71

DIVISION 1

	ABERDEEN	AIRDRIE	AYR U	CELTIC	CLYDE	COWDENBEATH	DUNDEE	DUNDEE U	DUNFERMLINE A	FALKIRK	HEARTS	HIBERNIAN	KILMARNOCK	MORTON	MOTHERWELL	RANGERS	ST JOHNSTONE	ST MIRREN
ABERDEEN		Aug29 1-1	Mar24 4-1	Apr17 1-1	Nov07 3-0	Dec05 7-0	Jan01 3-0	Oct31 4-0	Oct10 3-2	Dec19 1-0	Nov21 1-0	Sep26 3-0	Jan09 3-0	Jan30 3-1	Apr03 0-0	Feb20 0-0	Sep12 0-0	Feb27 1-1
AIRDRIE	Dec26 0-4		Sep19 2-0	Oct17 1-3	Oct24 1-2	Oct03 2-1	Mar20 2-6	Feb06 1-2	Apr24 1-0	Apr26 7-1	Jan16 0-0	Dec05 2-0	Apr14 1-1	Nov07 0-2	Sep05 3-0	Mar10 4-3	Nov21 5-0	Apr17 1-1
AYR U	Nov14 0-1	Jan09 0-0		Dec19 1-2	Sep26 4-0	Apr17 1-2	Oct10 0-1	Mar13 1-0	Aug29 4-1	Feb27 1-1	Apr03 1-0	Feb20 2-0	Sep12 1-1	Jan01 2-1	Dec05 0-0	Nov21 2-1	Jan30 1-3	Oct31 1-1
CELTIC	Dec12 0-1	Feb20 4-1	Apr29 2-0		May01 6-1	Nov07 3-0	Sep26 3-0	Apr10 1-1	Jan30 1-0	Mar27 4-0	Oct28 3-2	Jan09 2-1	Nov14 3-0	Aug29 2-0	Apr12 3-0	Sep12 2-0	Oct10 1-0	Nov28 3-0
CLYDE	Mar13 1-2	Feb27 1-1	Jan16 0-0	Sep05 0-5		Oct17 1-3	Apr03 0-0	Oct03 1-2	Oct31 3-1	Dec26 3-2	Sep19 1-0	Dec19 0-0	Apr17 0-1	Nov21 1-0	Apr21 1-2	Mar20 2-2	Dec05 3-0	Feb06 1-2
COWDENBEATH	Apr10 1-2	Jan30 1-3	Dec12 1-3	Mar13 1-5	Feb20 1-1		Aug29 0-1	Nov28 0-2	Jan01 2-1	Nov14 0-1	Apr24 0-4	Sep12 1-4	Sep26 1-2	Oct10 0-2	Oct24 0-1	Apr14 1-3	Nov02 2-2	Mar27 1-2
DUNDEE	Sep05 1-2	Nov14 3-0	Feb06 2-1	Jan16 1-8	Nov28 1-3	Dec26 5-1		Apr05 2-3	Mar27 0-0	Oct03 1-2	Oct17 1-0	Mar13 1-0	Oct31 3-0	Dec12 2-0	Apr24 4-0	Apr10 1-0	Feb27 0-1	Sep19 2-2
DUNDEE U	Mar10 0-2	Oct10 2-2	Nov07 4-2	Dec05 1-2	Apr14 1-0	Apr03 4-2	Sep12 3-2		Oct24 2-2	Apr17 3-1	Mar20 4-1	Aug29 1-1	Feb20 3-2	Jan09 2-3	Nov21 2-2	Sep26 0-2	Jan01 0-2	Dec19 2-1
DUNFERMLINE A	Feb06 1-0	Dec19 4-1	Dec26 5-0	Oct03 0-2	Mar06 0-0	Sep05 1-2	Nov21 0-0	Feb27 3-1		Sep19 2-4	Mar24 1-2	Apr17 3-3	Dec05 0-1	Mar20 3-0	Oct17 0-1	Nov07 1-1	Apr03 1-1	Jan16 1-0
FALKIRK	Apr24 1-0	Sep12 0-2	Oct24 2-0	Nov21 0-0	Aug29 1-1	Mar20 1-2	Jan30 2-2	Dec12 1-1	Jan09 3-2		Mar06 2-4	Nov28 0-0	Oct10 3-0	Feb20 2-1	Nov07 1-0	Jan01 3-1	Sep26 0-3	Apr10 2-1
HEARTS	Mar27 1-3	Sep26 5-2	Nov28 2-1	Feb27 1-1	Jan09 3-1	Dec19 1-0	Feb20 0-0	Nov14 1-0	Sep12 3-0	Nov11 1-1		Jan01 0-0	Jan30 2-0	Dec05 2-2	Apr17 0-1	Oct10 0-1	Aug29 1-3	Mar13 1-0
HIBERNIAN	Jan16 2-1	Apr10 3-1	Oct17 4-0	Sep19 2-0	Apr24 5-1	Jan02 2-2	Nov07 1-2	Dec26 0-1	Dec12 2-2	Apr03 1-3	Sep05 0-0		Nov21 1-0	Mar10 2-4	Feb06 1-0	Nov25 3-2	Mar20 1-2	Oct03 3-3
KILMARNOCK	Sep19 0-4	Nov28 2-3	Jan02 1-1	Mar20 1-4	Dec12 1-1	Jan16 2-1	Mar09 1-1	Oct17 2-1	Apr10 0-0	Feb06 3-2	Oct03 3-0	Mar27 4-1		Oct24 2-2	Dec26 0-0	Apr24 1-4	Nov07 2-4	Sep05 1-2
MORTON	Oct03 2-0	Mar13 1-4	Sep05 3-2	Dec26 0-3	Mar27 0-0	Feb06 1-0	Apr17 1-0	Sep19 3-0	Nov14 1-1	Oct17 0-0	Apr10 3-0	Nov18 2-1	Feb27 3-0		Jan16 0-2	Nov28 1-2	Dec19 3-1	Jan02 1-1
MOTHERWELL	Nov28 0-2	Jan01 1-1	Apr10 1-1	Oct31 0-5	Sep12 2-1	Feb27 1-3	Dec19 1-1	Mar27 1-2	Feb20 4-3	Mar13 1-1	Dec12 1-2	Oct10 4-0	Aug29 4-1	Sep26 2-0		Jan30 1-2	Jan09 4-1	Nov14 2-1
RANGERS	Oct17 0-2	Oct31 5-0	Mar27 2-0	Jan02 1-1	Nov14 5-0	Sep19 5-0	Dec05 0-0	Jan16 1-1	Mar13 2-0	Sep05 2-0	Feb06 1-0	Feb27 1-1	Dec19 4-2	Apr03 0-0	Oct03 3-1		Apr17 0-2	Dec26 1-0
ST JOHNSTONE	Jan02 0-1	Mar27 4-1	Oct03 4-1	Feb06 3-2	Apr10 2-1	Mar06 0-1	Oct24 3-3	Sep05 1-1	Nov28 5-2	Feb13 1-0	Dec26 2-1	Nov14 0-1	Mar13 2-3	Apr24 0-0	Sep19 2-1	Dec12 2-1		Oct17 2-0
ST MIRREN	Oct24 1-3	Dec12 2-4	Mar06 0-2	Apr27 2-2	Oct10 0-1	Nov21 1-0	Jan09 2-4	Apr24 2-1	Sep26 1-1	Dec05 2-3	Nov07 0-1	Jan30 3-1	Jan01 2-3	Sep12 2-1	Mar20 0-2	Aug29 0-0	Feb20 0-1	

DIVISION 2

	ALBION R	ALLOA	ARBROATH	BERWICK R	BRECHIN C	CLYDEBANK	DUMBARTON	EAST FIFE	E STIRLING	FORFAR A	HAMILTON A	MONTROSE	PARTICK T	QUEEN OF SOUTH	QUEEN'S PARK	RAITH R	STENHOUSEMUIR	STIRLING A	STRANRAER
ALBION R		Dec19 1-0	Nov28 1-2	Apr21 1-0	Oct10 4-1	Feb10 0-1	Apr27 2-6	Aug29 1-3	Jan30 4-2	Mar27 1-1	Jan01 3-0	Apr10 0-1	Nov14 1-0	Sep09 4-0	Mar13 2-1	Feb27 2-0	Jan09 0-2	Sep26 1-1	Sep12 2-1
ALLOA	Apr24 1-1		Oct24 3-6	Nov28 1-1	Apr14 2-2	Dec12 1-3	Oct10 3-1	Sep12 1-2	Apr29 2-2	Nov07 2-1	Jan09 4-1	Mar20 2-5	Mar27 1-4	Apr10 1-1	Sep23 2-1	Apr21 2-1	Jan01 2-1	Aug29 1-1	Sep26 2-1
ARBROATH	Apr03 2-0	Feb27 6-2		Sep12 4-0	Sep09 2-2	Jan30 0-1	Feb13 1-0	Jan09 1-1	Sep26 5-1	Jan01 5-0	Mar27 7-3	Mar06 3-1	Dec05 0-2	Nov14 2-0	Apr17 1-0	Sep23 4-0	Nov07 2-0	Oct10 0-3	Oct17 3-1
BERWICK R	Oct17 1-2	Apr03 1-1	Jan02 2-0		Mar13 0-0	Nov14 1-1	Jan16 0-1	Apr24 2-1	Oct24 2-2	Aug29 2-4	Dec12 2-1	Sep19 4-3	Feb13 1-1	Oct03 1-1	Mar27 1-1	Dec05 0-2	Sep09 6-2	Mar06 0-0	Feb06 1-2
BRECHIN C	Feb06 0-2	Oct03 3-2	Sep16 1-4	Nov07 0-2		Apr28 2-0	Jan02 0-2	Nov28 1-1	Apr24 3-1	Mar06 1-1	Apr10 2-2	Sep05 0-1	Oct17 1-0	Oct24 1-1	Dec26 0-7	Jan16 1-4	Mar20 1-2	Dec12 0-2	Feb13 2-0
CLYDEBANK	Mar06 2-0	Apr17 1-1	Oct03 1-2	Mar20 1-2	Mar27 2-0		Sep05 2-1	Feb20 3-0	Feb24 0-0	Apr14 3-0	Sep23 1-4	Jan02 3-0	Sep19 3-1	Dec26 0-0	Mar10 7-1	Sep09 3-0	Oct10 2-0	Oct24 6-5	Nov07 1-3
DUMBARTON	Sep02 1-1	Feb06 5-1	Apr24 3-0	Sep26 6-2	Sep12 3-1	Jan01 3-1		Sep16 1-1	Apr10 6-0	Jan30 5-1	Mar22 4-1	Nov21 4-0	Feb27 2-2	Mar13 2-1	Apr29 4-1	Oct17 2-0	Dec12 3-2	Apr21 7-0	Aug29 2-0
EAST FIFE	Dec26 3-0	Jan02 3-1	Sep19 4-0	Feb10 4-0	Apr03 1-0	Oct17 2-0	Dec05 3-2		Mar20 6-2	Sep23 3-0	Feb27 5-0	Jan16 3-1	Oct03 0-0	Apr17 2-0	Feb17 5-1	Sep05 5-1	Mar06 3-1	Nov07 5-1	Nov21 0-1
E STIRLING	Oct03 1-2	Oct17 1-1	Jan16 2-1	Feb27 0-1	Apr21 2-1	Apr27 0-1	Jan23 3-1	Nov14 3-5		Apr17 3-1	Mar13 2-1	Dec26 1-1	Jan02 0-2	Sep19 0-3	Sep05 1-2	Feb06 4-2	Sep23 2-2	Sep09 2-5	Apr27 4-0
FORFAR A	Nov21 1-0	Mar13 8-1	Sep05 2-2	Dec26 1-1	Oct31 2-0	Apr24 1-1	Oct03 1-0	Sep02 3-3	Dec12 1-1		Nov28 5-6	Sep16 1-1	Feb06 1-2	Feb20 3-0	Jan16 1-2	Sep19 3-3	Oct24 6-1	Apr10 1-3	Mar20 1-0
HAMILTON A	Sep05 1-3	Sep19 0-4	Nov21 4-1	Apr17 0-2	Apr26 4-1	Apr21 0-0	Mar06 0-3	Oct24 1-1	Nov07 3-1	Apr03 3-1		Feb06 2-3	Jan16 1-1	Jan02 3-1	Oct03 3-0	Dec26 0-1	Feb20 2-2	Mar20 0-2	Sep16 0-0
MONTROSE	Jan23 1-1	Nov14 4-2	Oct31 3-3	Jan09 4-0	Jan01 1-0	Sep12 0-1	Mar27 3-1	Sep26 0-1	Aug29 2-0	Sep09 3-4	Oct10 4-1		Apr17 2-2	Sep23 4-1	Dec05 2-1	Apr03 6-2	Jan30 2-2	Feb20 2-5	Feb27 4-0
PARTICK T	Mar20 3-0	Nov21 3-0	Apr10 1-1	Apr05 4-1	Feb20 5-0	Jan09 1-0	Oct24 1-1	Jan30 4-0	Sep12 5-0	Oct10 6-2	Sep26 2-0	Dec12 3-2		Nov28 3-1	Apr19 2-1	Nov07 1-0	Aug29 4-0	Jan01 2-0	Apr24 3-0
QUEEN OF SOUTH	Sep16 1-1	Dec05 1-1	Mar20 3-1	Jan30 2-1	Feb27 2-1	Aug29 3-1	Nov07 1-0	Dec12 2-3	Jan09 4-5	Oct17 2-0	Sep12 2-1	Sep02 1-3	Apr03 0-1		Oct31 3-2	Nov21 0-1	Sep26 1-2	Apr24 2-1	Jan01 1-1
QUEEN'S PARK	Nov07 2-3	Sep02 3-0	Dec12 2-4	Nov21 1-0	Aug29 1-0	Apr10 1-1	Nov28 2-1	Oct10 2-0	Apr13 2-1	Sep26 0-0	Jan30 1-0	Apr21 0-4	Sep15 1-1	Mar06 1-2		Mar20 0-1	Apr26 0-2	Sep12 0-6	Jan09 4-2
RAITH R	Oct24 2-2	Oct31 4-1	Sep02 1-1	Apr10 2-1	Sep26 2-0	Sep16 1-1	Feb20 3-0	Jan01 2-1	Oct10 1-1	Jan09 3-2	Apr24 0-0	Nov28 2-2	Mar13 0-2	Mar27 1-1	Nov14 6-4		Sep12 4-1	Jan30 1-2	Dec12 0-1
STENHOUSEMUIR	Sep19 3-3	Sep05 1-4	Mar13 0-2	Sep16 1-0	Nov14 4-0	Feb06 2-3	Apr17 2-0	Oct31 4-3	Sep02 2-2	Feb27 2-1	Jan23 4-2	Oct03 5-0	Dec26 0-0	Jan16 0-3	Oct17 0-1	Jan02 3-3		Mar27 5-1	Apr20 0-0
STIRLING A	Jan16 1-1	Dec26 5-0	Feb06 1-1	Apr29 0-1	Apr17 1-2	Feb27 2-0	Sep19 2-2	Mar13 1-1	Sep16 1-3	Apr26 3-1	Nov14 2-0	Oct17 0-1	Sep05 2-2	Dec19 1-2	Jan02 0-2	Oct03 0-1	Nov21 1-2		Apr03 0-1
STRANRAER	Jan02 4-1	Jan16 1-1	Feb20 1-1	Oct10 3-0	Sep23 1-0	Mar13 3-0	Dec26 2-2	Mar27 1-2	Mar06 5-2	Nov14 1-1	Sep09 2-0	Oct24 3-2	Apr14 1-2	Sep05 1-1	Sep19 4-0	Apr17 3-5	Apr10 1-2	Nov28 3-0	

LEAGUE TABLES

DIVISION 1

	P	W	D	L	F	A	W	D	L	F	A	Pts
Celtic	34	15	1	1	43	7	10	5	2	46	16	56
Aberdeen	34	11	6	0	38	7	13	0	4	30	11	54
St Johnstone	34	10	3	4	33	20	9	3	5	26	24	44
Rangers	34	10	5	2	33	10	6	4	7	25	24	41
Dundee	34	9	2	6	30	23	5	8	4	23	22	38
Dundee U	34	8	4	5	34	29	6	4	7	19	25	36
Falkirk	34	8	5	4	24	20	5	4	8	22	33	35
Morton	34	9	4	4	25	17	4	4	9	19	27	34
Airdrie	34	8	3	6	33	26	5	5	7	27	39	34
Motherwell	34	7	4	6	30	27	6	4	7	13	20	34
Hearts	34	8	5	4	24	16	5	2	10	17	24	33
Hibernian	34	8	4	5	33	24	2	6	9	14	29	30
Kilmarnock	34	5	6	6	26	31	5	2	10	17	36	28
Ayr U	34	7	5	5	22	15	2	3	12	15	39	26
Clyde	34	5	5	7	19	23	3	5	9	14	36	26
Dunfermline A	34	6	5	6	26	19	0	6	11	18	37	23
St Mirren	34	4	3	10	20	30	3	6	8	18	26	23
Cowdenbeath	34	1	2	14	13	39	6	1	10	20	38	17

DIVISION 2

	P	W	D	L	F	A	W	D	L	F	A	Pts
Partick T	36	16	2	0	53	9	7	8	3	25	17	56
East Fife	36	16	1	1	57	11	6	6	6	29	33	51
Arbroath	36	13	2	3	48	17	6	6	6	32	35	46
Dumbarton	36	15	3	0	63	15	4	3	11	24	31	44
Clydebank	36	11	3	4	41	20	6	5	7	16	23	42
Montrose	36	10	4	4	47	27	7	3	8	31	37	41
Albion R	36	10	2	6	30	22	5	7	6	23	30	39
Raith R	36	8	7	3	35	23	7	2	9	27	39	39
Stranraer	36	9	5	4	40	22	5	3	10	14	30	36
Stenhousemuir	36	8	5	5	38	28	6	3	9	26	42	36
Queen of South	36	9	3	6	31	26	4	6	8	19	30	35
Stirling A	36	4	5	9	23	23	8	3	7	38	38	32
Queen's Park	36	8	3	7	23	28	5	1	12	28	44	30
Berwick R	36	5	8	5	27	25	5	2	11	15	35	30
Forfar A	36	7	7	4	42	27	2	4	12	21	48	29
Alloa	36	7	6	5	33	35	2	5	11	23	51	29
E. Stirling	36	7	3	8	31	32	2	6	10	26	54	27
Hamilton A	36	6	5	7	27	27	2	2	14	23	52	23
Brechin C	36	5	4	9	19	34	1	3	14	11	39	19

Scottish Football League Records
Season 1971-72

DIVISION 1

	ABERDEEN	AIRDRIE	AYR U	CELTIC	CLYDE	DUNDEE	DUNDEE U	DUNFERMLINE A	EAST FIFE	FALKIRK	HEARTS	HIBERNIAN	KILMARNOCK	MORTON	MOTHERWELL	PARTICK T	RANGERS	ST JOHNSTONE
ABERDEEN		Sep18 5-0	Apr08 7-0	Mar11 1-1	Dec11 4-1	Sep04 3-0	Dec18 3-0	Oct02 2-0	Nov13 5-0	Apr29 0-0	Nov27 2-3	Oct16 2-1	Jan29 4-2	Feb19 1-0	Mar25 4-1	Oct30 7-2	Jan15 0-0	Jan03 4-2
AIRDRIE	Jan08 1-2		Oct09 3-4	Sep25 0-5	Dec25 1-1	Apr08 4-2	Mar29 1-1	Mar04 1-0	Oct23 1-1	Mar11 2-0	Feb12 1-1	Nov13 2-2	Mar25 0-4	Dec11 2-4	Jan01 0-2	Sep11 1-1	Apr22 0-3	Nov27 5-4
AYR U	Dec04 1-5	Jan29 1-1		Oct30 0-1	Oct16 0-1	Oct02 0-0	Apr15 4-2	Sep18 1-1	Mar11 4-0	Dec18 0-3	Mar25 1-0	Jan15 1-2	Jan03 0-0	Sep04 1-0	Nov13 1-1	Apr29 4-0	Nov27 1-2	Feb19 0-0
CELTIC	Nov06 1-1	Jan15 2-0	Mar04 2-0		Sep04 9-1	Oct16 3-1	Apr25 3-0	Feb19 1-0	Dec11 2-1	Nov20 2-0	Dec25 3-2	Jan29 2-1	Dec04 5-1	Sep18 3-1	Apr22 5-2	Apr01 3-1	Jan03 2-1	Oct02 0-1
CLYDE	Apr15 0-0	Apr29 0-0	Feb12 3-0	Jan01 0-7		Mar25 1-1	Oct23 0-3	Dec18 2-1	Sep25 0-1	Jan22 3-1	Oct09 0-1	Oct30 2-1	Mar11 0-3	Nov27 1-2	Sep11 2-0	Jan08 0-2	Apr08 1-1	Nov13 1-2
DUNDEE	Jan01 1-1	Dec04 4-1	Jan22 5-1	May01 1-1	Nov20 0-0		Sep11 6-4	Apr01 1-0	Jan08 0-0	Oct09 4-0	Sep25 0-0	Apr17 1-2	Dec18 2-0	Nov06 0-1	Mar04 2-0	Oct27 0-0	Apr10 2-0	Apr29 1-3
DUNDEE U	Apr22 2-0	Oct02 5-0	Dec11 2-2	Nov13 1-5	Feb19 3-3	Jan03 1-1		Dec25 3-2	Mar15 2-2	Oct30 3-5	Apr08 3-2	Sep18 1-4	Jan15 1-2	Jan29 2-1	Nov27 2-0	Mar11 1-0	Oct16 1-5	Sep04 3-3
DUNFERMLINE A	Jan22 1-0	Oct30 1-0	Jan08 1-1	Oct27 1-2	Apr22 2-2	Nov27 1-2	Apr29 0-1		Jan01 2-2	Mar29 0-1	Sep11 1-4	Mar11 2-1	Nov13 0-1	Apr18 2-1	Sep25 1-1	Oct09 2-2	Dec11 0-2	Mar25 2-1
EAST FIFE	Mar21 0-1	Feb19 1-1	Nov06 2-2	Apr15 0-3	Jan15 2-2	Sep18 2-5	Nov20 0-1	Sep04 0-1		Apr01 2-2	Mar04 2-2	Jan03 2-1	Oct16 2-0	Oct02 0-6	Dec25 1-1	Dec04 1-3	Jan29 0-1	Dec18 2-2
FALKIRK	Dec25 0-3	Nov06 1-2	Apr22 3-0	Mar25 0-1	Oct02 3-1	Jan29 1-1	Mar04 1-1	Oct16 2-1	Nov27 1-1		Dec11 2-0	Feb19 2-3	Sep04 3-1	Jan03 2-1	Apr08 3-0	Nov13 0-0	Sep18 0-3	Jan15 2-4
HEARTS	Apr01 1-0	Oct16 1-1	Nov20 1-0	Apr29 4-1	Jan29 2-0	Jan15 2-5	Dec04 3-2	Jan03 1-1	Oct30 1-1	Apr15 1-0		Sep04 0-2	Feb19 2-1	Nov13 6-1	Mar11 0-0	Dec18 0-0	Oct02 2-1	Sep18 2-1
HIBERNIAN	Feb12 2-2	Mar21 1-3	Sep25 1-0	Oct09 0-1	Mar04 1-0	Dec11 1-0	Jan08 3-0	Nov06 2-0	Sep11 2-1	Oct23 6-0	Jan01 0-0		Nov27 3-2	Apr22 1-0	Jan22 1-2	Mar25 3-0	Dec25 0-1	Apr08 7-1
KILMARNOCK	Oct09 0-3	Nov20 5-2	Sep11 1-2	Apr08 1-3	Nov06 2-1	Apr22 0-3	Sep25 2-0	Mar21 0-0	Feb12 2-3	Jan01 2-0	Oct23 2-2	Apr03 1-1		Dec25 4-2	Jan08 1-0	Jan22 1-4	Mar04 1-2	Dec11 2-0
MORTON	Oct23 0-1	Apr15 2-2	Jan01 0-3	Jan08 1-1	Apr12 4-0	Mar11 2-2	Oct09 1-2	Dec04 1-0	Jan22 0-0	Sep11 3-1	Mar21 1-1	Dec18 1-1	Apr29 1-1		Apr05 3-2	Sep25 2-0	Nov20 1-2	Oct30 0-1
MOTHERWELL	Nov20 0-4	Sep04 0-1	Mar21 2-2	Dec18 1-5	Jan03 4-1	Oct30 1-3	Apr01 0-1	Jan15 4-1	Apr29 1-1	Dec04 2-1	Nov06 5-3	Oct02 1-1	Sep18 3-0	Oct16 3-1		Apr15 2-1	Feb19 2-0	Jan29 2-0
PARTICK T	Mar04 2-0	Jan03 4-2	Dec25 0-1	Nov27 1-5	Sep18 2-2	Feb19 0-0	Nov06 3-1	Jan29 2-0	Apr08 1-0	Mar18 1-1	Apr22 2-2	Dec01 0-1	Oct02 2-2	Jan15 2-0	Dec11 8-3		Sep04 3-2	Oct16 2-1
RANGERS	Sep25 0-2	Dec18 3-0	May01 4-2	Sep11 2-3	Dec04 1-0	Nov13 2-3	Feb12 1-0	Apr27 3-4	Oct09 3-0	Jan08 3-1	Jan22 6-0	Apr29 1-2	Oct30 3-1	Mar25 1-2	Oct23 4-0	Jan01 2-1		Mar11 2-0
ST JOHNSTONE	Sep11 1-1	Apr01 3-3	Oct23 2-0	Jan22 0-3	Mar18 0-1	Dec25 0-0	Jan01 2-0	Nov20 0-0	Apr22 0-1	Sep25 3-2	Jan08 1-1	Dec04 0-2	Apr15 5-1	Mar04 1-0	Oct09 5-1	Feb12 2-1	Nov06 1-4	

DIVISION 2

	ALBION R	ALLOA	ARBROATH	BERWICK R	BRECHIN C	CLYDEBANK	COWDENBEATH	DUMBARTON	E STIRLING	FORFAR A	HAMILTON A	MONTROSE	QUEEN OF SOUTH	QUEEN'S PARK	RAITH R	ST MIRREN	STENHOUSEMUIR	STIRLING A	STRANRAER
ALBION R		Dec04 0-1	Dec18 0-3	Sep08 1-3	Feb19 1-1	Oct02 2-0	Apr29 1-2	Mar18 0-1	Oct16 1-1	Sep22 2-0	Sep04 1-0	Nov20 4-1	Nov06 0-1	Apr11 1-2	Jan03 3-1	Apr15 1-2	Jan29 1-1	Apr25 0-1	Sep18 4-0
ALLOA	Apr08 3-1		Mar25 0-3	Nov06 0-2	Sep18 1-3	Oct16 1-1	Nov27 0-4	Apr22 0-1	Apr26 0-2	Jan29 2-3	Feb19 2-2	Dec25 0-3	Dec11 1-2	Mar04 3-0	Sep22 3-2	Nov13 1-3	Sep04 2-0	Jan03 0-1	Oct02 1-3
ARBROATH	Apr22 2-0	Apr18 1-0		Dec04 2-1	Sep22 3-3	Jan15 1-2	Dec11 2-2	Mar04 3-2	Oct02 2-1	Sep04 3-0	Oct16 3-0	Nov06 2-0	Dec25 2-2	Mar18 1-0	Sep08 4-0	Apr01 3-2	Feb19 3-0	Sep18 4-3	Jan29 3-1
BERWICK R	Sep29 3-1	Mar11 2-0	Apr08 0-1		Feb05 3-0	Sep18 1-1	Jan22 2-0	Oct09 2-2	Nov27 0-1	Jan03 4-1	Feb26 1-1	Apr15 2-1	Sep15 0-3	Apr29 0-2	Oct16 0-1	Mar25 1-2	Nov13 3-0	Oct30 1-3	Feb19 0-1
BRECHIN C	Oct23 2-2	Jan08 1-1	Sep15 2-1	Apr22 3-1		Apr15 1-2	Sep25 0-2	Apr26 1-2	Nov06 1-3	Mar18 2-4	Apr01 4-1	Jan01 1-3	Oct09 0-0	Sep11 1-0	Nov20 0-4	Feb12 1-2	Mar04 1-1	Dec25 2-1	Dec04 1-4
CLYDEBANK	Jan22 3-1	Feb12 3-1	Sep25 0-0	Jan08 0-0	Dec11 1-2		Oct23 1-4	Jan01 2-3	Mar04 3-4	Nov06 2-0	Nov20 7-1	Oct09 1-2	Sep11 1-3	Sep15 1-1	Apr11 3-1	Sep29 1-3	Dec25 2-1	Apr22 0-0	Apr01 3-0
COWDENBEATH	Dec25 1-0	Apr24 3-0	Apr15 0-2	Oct02 3-2	Feb26 6-0	Feb19 0-0		Nov06 0-1	Sep22 5-0	Sep08 7-0	Jan03 1-1	Mar18 2-0	Mar04 1-1	Nov20 4-1	Sep04 1-1	Dec04 2-0	Sep18 1-0	Jan29 3-2	Oct16 0-1
DUMBARTON	Nov13 3-0	Dec18 7-1	Oct30 1-2	May03 4-2	Oct02 4-0	Sep04 2-3	Mar11 2-1		Feb19 4-0	Sep18 2-2	Sep08 2-0	Dec04 3-2	Mar25 2-0	Apr15 3-0	Apr18 5-0	Apr29 1-2	Oct16 3-2	Apr11 2-1	Jan03 2-4
E STIRLING	Feb12 4-1	Sep29 1-2	Jan22 5-0	Apr01 0-4	Mar11 2-1	Oct30 0-1	Sep15 0-0	Oct23 1-3		Dec04 1-1	Apr18 1-4	Sep11 2-1	Sep25 4-2	Jan01 3-1	Apr15 2-1	Jan08 3-1	Mar25 1-0	Nov13 0-3	Apr29 3-1
FORFAR A	Sep15 0-2	Oct09 2-1	Jan01 0-4	Sep11 0-4	Nov13 1-0	Mar11 2-1	Sep28 1-4	Jan08 1-1	Apr08 1-2		Apr29 0-0	Oct23 1-5	Feb12 0-0	Apr27 1-1	Dec18 0-1	Sep25 0-3	Nov27 2-1	Mar25 0-4	Oct30 1-1
HAMILTON A	Jan01 1-0	Oct23 0-5	Feb12 1-1	Sep25 0-2	Nov27 3-0	Mar25 0-1	Sep11 1-1	Sep29 2-6	Apr22 1-1	Dec25 2-1		Sep15 1-6	Jan08 0-3	Oct09 0-1	Mar04 1-1	Jan22 1-5	Dec11 1-3	Apr08 0-2	Nov13 1-5
MONTROSE	Mar25 2-0	Apr29 4-0	Mar11 0-0	Dec11 1-2	Sep04 2-0	Jan29 1-2	Nov13 0-2	Apr08 2-3	Jan03 2-2	Feb19 0-0	Sep22 5-0		Nov27 0-2	Feb26 4-2	Oct02 3-1	Oct30 3-1	Jan15 1-1	Oct16 2-4	Sep08 0-0
QUEEN OF SOUTH	Mar11 1-0	Apr15 4-0	Apr29 1-1	Sep22 4-1	Jan29 0-0	Jan03 2-0	Oct30 0-2	Nov20 2-4	Feb26 4-2	Oct16 3-2	Sep18 2-0	Apr01 2-1		Dec04 0-1	Feb19 1-1	Apr26 0-1	Oct02 0-1	Apr18 0-1	Sep04 5-1
QUEEN'S PARK	Nov27 2-2	Oct30 0-2	Nov13 2-1	Dec25 2-0	Jan03 5-3	Apr18 4-4	Mar20 0-2	Dec11 0-1	Sep04 0-0	Oct02 4-1	Jan29 2-0	Apr22 1-6	Apr08 0-0		Sep18 1-0	Mar11 2-1	Sep08 4-0	Feb19 0-2	Mar28 1-2
RAITH R	Sep11 3-1	Sep15 1-1	Sep29 1-1	Feb12 3-1	Mar25 0-1	Nov13 1-3	Jan01 1-1	Sep25 6-1	Dec11 3-1	Apr22 4-2	Oct30 2-1	Jan22 4-0	Oct23 1-2	Jan08 1-1		Oct09 2-0	Apr08 4-0	Nov27 2-5	Mar11 0-0
ST MIRREN	Dec11 4-0	Mar18 0-1	Nov27 4-3	Nov20 2-0	Oct16 2-0	Dec27 1-1	Apr08 3-1	Dec25 2-2	Sep18 1-2	Apr17 2-0	Oct02 6-2	Mar04 3-1	Apr22 3-0	Nov06 6-2	Jan29 2-0		Jan03 0-1	Sep04 3-2	Oct20 2-0
STENHOUSEMUIR	Oct09 2-0	Jan01 2-1	Oct23 0-1	Mar18 0-1	Oct30 2-0	Apr29 3-1	Jan08 0-0	Feb12 0-3	Nov20 1-1	Apr01 2-1	Apr15 3-1	Sep25 2-2	Jan22 1-3	Sep29 3-0	Dec04 0-1	Sep11 2-4		Mar11 0-0	Feb05 3-4
STIRLING A	Sep25 2-0	Sep11 3-2	Jan08 1-2	Mar04 2-1	Apr29 6-1	Dec18 1-1	Oct09 1-1	Sep15 2-0	Mar18 2-1	Feb26 1-1	Dec04 3-0	Feb12 1-2	Sep29 2-0	Oct23 1-1	Apr01 3-0	Jan01 3-2	Nov06 2-2		Apr15 3-0
STRANRAER	Jan08 2-2	Feb26 5-2	Oct09 4-1	Oct23 2-1	Apr08 3-2	Nov27 2-2	Feb12 1-0	Sep11 3-1	Dec25 0-3	Mar04 6-0	Mar18 4-1	Sep29 0-5	Jan01 1-1	Sep25 1-1	Nov06 2-1	Sep15 2-4	Apr22 3-1	Dec11 1-1	

LEAGUE TABLES

DIVISION 1

	P	W	D	L	F	A	W	D	L	F	A	Pts
Celtic	34	15	1	1	48	14	13	3	1	48	14	60
Aberdeen	34	13	3	1	54	13	8	5	4	26	13	50
Rangers	34	11	0	6	41	21	10	2	5	30	17	44
Hibernian	34	11	2	4	34	13	8	4	5	28	21	44
Dundee	34	8	6	3	30	14	6	7	4	29	24	41
Hearts	34	10	5	2	29	17	3	8	6	24	32	39
Partick T	34	9	5	3	35	23	3	5	9	18	31	34
St Johnstone	34	7	5	5	26	21	5	3	9	26	37	32
Dundee U	34	7	5	5	36	37	5	2	10	19	33	31
Motherwell	34	9	3	5	33	26	2	4	11	16	43	29
Kilmarnock	34	7	3	7	27	28	4	3	10	22	36	28
Ayr U	34	5	6	6	20	19	4	4	9	20	39	28
Morton	34	5	7	5	23	20	5	0	12	23	32	27
Falkirk	34	7	4	6	26	23	3	3	11	18	37	27
Airdrie	34	4	6	7	25	37	3	6	8	19	39	26
East Fife	34	2	7	8	19	34	3	8	6	15	27	25
Clyde	34	5	4	8	16	26	2	6	9	17	40	24
Dunfermline A	34	5	5	7	19	24	2	4	11	12	26	23

DIVISION 2

	P	W	D	L	F	A	W	D	L	F	A	Pts
Dumbarton	36	13	1	4	52	22	11	3	4	37	29	52
Arbroath	36	14	3	1	44	19	8	5	5	27	22	52
Stirling A	36	11	5	2	39	17	10	3	5	36	20	50
St Mirren	36	13	2	3	46	18	11	0	7	38	29	50
Cowdenbeath	36	11	4	3	40	12	8	6	4	29	16	48
Stranraer	36	10	5	3	42	29	8	3	7	28	33	44
Queen of South	36	9	3	6	31	19	8	6	4	25	19	43
E. Stirling	36	10	2	6	33	27	7	5	6	27	31	41
Clydebank	36	7	4	7	34	27	7	7	4	26	25	39
Montrose	36	7	5	6	32	22	8	1	9	41	32	36
Raith R	36	9	5	4	39	22	4	3	11	17	34	34
Queen's Park	36	8	4	6	30	27	4	5	9	17	34	33
Berwick R	36	7	3	8	25	21	7	1	10	28	29	32
Stenhousemuir	36	7	4	7	26	24	3	4	11	15	34	28
Brechin C	36	5	4	9	24	34	3	3	12	17	45	23
Alloa	36	4	2	12	20	36	5	2	11	21	39	22
Forfar A	36	4	5	9	13	35	2	4	12	19	49	21
Albion R	36	6	3	9	23	21	1	3	14	13	40	20
Hamilton A	36	3	4	11	16	44	1	4	13	15	49	16

Scottish Football League Records
Season 1972-73

DIVISION 1

	ABERDEEN	AIRDRIE	ARBROATH	AYR U	CELTIC	DUMBARTON	DUNDEE	DUNDEE U	EAST FIFE	FALKIRK	HEARTS	HIBERNIAN	KILMARNOCK	MORTON	MOTHERWELL	PARTICK T	RANGERS	ST JOHNSTONE
ABERDEEN		Apr07 5-1	Dec09 0-0	Feb17 1-0	Oct28 2-3	Feb20 6-0	Jan01 3-1	Mar31 0-0	Nov11 4-3	Oct14 2-2	Jan27 3-1	Sep02 1-0	Nov18 3-0	Dec23 3-0	Sep30 7-2	Mar10 0-0	Apr21 2-2	Sep16 0-0
AIRDRIE	Dec02 1-1		Nov18 3-1	Apr28 0-1	Jan27 2-1	Oct21 2-3	Sep30 0-1	Dec30 2-2	Apr14 1-1	Mar12 0-0	Dec16 0-2	Feb10 0-4	Mar03 0-1	Nov04 0-3	Sep09 1-2	Sep23 1-3	Mar20 2-6	Mar31 1-3
ARBROATH	Apr14 1-1	Mar24 2-1		Sep23 1-1	Dec16 1-2	Jan20 2-1	Nov11 2-1	Dec02 2-4	Sep09 1-0	Dec30 5-1	Mar03 3-0	Nov25 2-3	Oct07 3-3	Feb10 0-1	Apr28 0-1	Jan06 2-1	Oct21 1-2	Mar10 3-0
AYR U	Oct21 2-3	Dec23 3-2	Jan13 2-0		Jan20 1-3	Dec09 2-0	Nov25 2-1	Mar03 2-1	Feb10 3-2	Nov18 1-1	Mar21 2-0	Apr21 1-1	Jan01 1-1	Sep16 1-1	Nov04 3-2	Oct07 2-1	Sep02 2-1	Apr07 3-1
CELTIC	Mar03 2-0	Oct07 1-1	Apr21 4-0	Sep30 1-0		Apr18 5-0	Jan13 2-1	Nov04 3-1	Oct21 3-0	Mar31 4-0	Nov18 4-2	Dec23 1-1	Sep02 6-2	M06 1-0	Apr03 2-0	Feb10 1-1	Sep16 3-1	F28 4-0
DUMBARTON	Sep23 1-2	Mar07 3-5	Sep30 0-0	Apr14 1-1	Dec02 1-6		Oct14 2-2	Apr28 4-1	Mar10 0-0	Sep09 0-0	Jan06 0-2	Oct28 2-2	Mar17 4-2	Nov18 2-2	Dec16 0-0	Dec30 4-2	Mar31 1-2	Jan27 1-1
DUNDEE	Sep09 0-0	Feb19 1-1	Mar21 6-0	Mar31 2-1	Sep23 2-0	Feb10 2-1		Jan06 3-0	Dec02 4-0	Apr14 5-3	Apr28 2-2	Oct07 1-0	Oct21 1-0	Mar03 6-0	Dec30 2-0	Dec16 4-1	Nov04 1-1	Nov18 3-0
DUNDEE U	Nov25 3-2	Sep02 3-1	Apr07 1-1	Oct28 2-1	Mar10 2-2	Dec23 3-2	Sep16 2-1		Mar24 1-1	Mar07 1-0	Oct14 3-2	Jan13 1-0	Apr21 2-1	Sep30 1-0	Jan27 1-2	Nov11 0-3	Dec09 1-4	Jan01 5-1
EAST FIFE	Mar27 0-1	Dec09 3-0	Jan01 2-0	Oct14 2-2	Feb17 2-2	Nov04 2-1	Apr18 0-1	Nov18 1-0		Jan27 1-2	Sep30 1-0	Sep16 0-1	Jan13 3-0	Sep02 4-3	Mar31 3-1	Oct28 0-1	Dec23 0-4	Apr21 2-2
FALKIRK	Feb10 0-0	Sep16 1-1	Sep02 3-1	Mar24 1-2	Nov25 2-3	Feb06 2-0	Dec09 2-2	Oct21 1-0	Oct07 3-4		Nov04 1-3	Apr07 1-0	Dec23 3-2	Apr21 2-0	Mar03 0-1	Jan20 0-3	Jan13 2-4	Nov11 0-0
HEARTS	Oct07 2-1	Apr21 0-1	Oct28 3-0	Nov11 3-0	Mar24 0-2	Sep16 1-0	Dec23 1-2	Feb10 0-2	Jan20 1-1	Mar10 1-0		Jan01 0-7	Dec09 0-0	Mar12 0-0	Oct21 0-0	Nov25 2-0	Apr07 0-1	Sep02 1-0
HIBERNIAN	Dec30 3-2	Oct14 5-2	Mar31 0-0	Dec16 8-1	Apr28 0-3	Mar03 5-0	Jan27 1-1	Sep23 3-1	Jan06 1-0	Dec02 3-0	Sep09 2-0		Nov04 4-1	Mar17 2-1	Apr14 0-1	Mar13 2-0	Nov18 1-2	Sep30 3-2
KILMARNOCK	Mar24 0-2	Oct28 3-1	Jan27 2-0	Sep09 0-1	Feb07 0-4	Nov11 2-2	Feb27 1-2	Dec16 0-1	Sep23 1-3	Apr28 2-2	Apr14 2-1	Mar10 2-2		Mar31 2-1	Jan06 1-0	Dec02 2-3	Sep30 2-1	Oct14 1-4
MORTON	Apr28 1-2	Mar10 4-0	Oct14 1-1	Jan06 1-1	Sep09 0-2	Mar24 1-1	Oct28 5-2	Feb21 2-0	Dec30 3-1	Dec16 1-1	Sep23 2-4	Nov11 0-3	Nov25 2-1		Dec02 1-0	Apr14 5-0	Jan27 1-2	Feb17 3-0
MOTHERWELL	Feb07 2-0	Jan01 2-0	Dec23 2-0	Mar10 1-2	Nov11 0-5	Apr21 0-2	Sep02 2-2	Oct07 1-4	Nov25 0-1	Oct28 1-1	Feb19 2-2	Apr10 1-1	Sep16 2-0	Apr07 3-0		Mar24 0-0	Oct14 0-2	Jan13 1-1
PARTICK T	Nov04 0-2	Jan13 2-0	Sep16 1-2	Jan27 1-2	Oct14 0-4	Sep02 4-1	Apr21 1-1	Mar21 0-3	Mar03 1-1	Sep30 0-0	Mar31 3-0	Oct21 1-3	Apr07 1-1	Dec09 1-0	Nov18 0-3		Jan01 0-1	Dec23 1-1
RANGERS	Dec16 0-0	Nov11 1-0	Feb19 5-0	Dec30 2-1	Jan06 2-1	Nov25 3-1	Mar10 3-1	Apr14 2-1	Apr28 2-0	Sep23 1-0	Dec02 0-1	Mar24 1-0	Jan20 4-0	Oct07 1-1	Feb10 2-1	Sep09 2-1		Oct28 5-1
ST JOHNSTONE	Mar07 1-0	Nov25 1-1	Nov04 5-2	Dec02 3-0	Apr14 1-3	Oct07 0-2	Mar24 4-1	Sep09 1-3	Dec16 4-2	Mar17 2-1	Dec30 3-2	Feb21 1-3	Feb10 2-2	Oct21 3-1	Sep23 2-2	Apr28 1-3	Mar03 1-2	

DIVISION 2

	ALBION R	ALLOA	BERWICK R	BRECHIN C	CLYDE	CLYDEBANK	COWDENBEATH	DUNFERMLINE A	E.STIRLING	FORFAR A	HAMILTON A	MONTROSE	QUEEN OF SOUTH	QUEEN'S PARK	RAITH R	ST MIRREN	STENHOUSEMUIR	STIRLING A	STRANRAER
ALBION R		Feb21 2-2	Oct14 0-2	Sep16 2-1	Jan13 0-3	Oct28 4-1	Mar24 2-2	Sep27 1-5	Sep13 3-2	Nov25 2-2	Jan01 2-2	Jan20 1-3	Oct07 1-2	Nov11 1-1	Sep02 0-2	Mar10 1-3	Dec23 0-2	Apr21 1-1	Dec09 0-2
ALLOA	Oct21 4-0		Oct28 0-2	Apr10 1-0	Dec09 0-0	Mar10 2-4	Nov25 1-1	Dec23 1-1	Sep16 2-0	Feb03 1-1	Apr07 4-0	Oct07 0-2	Feb10 3-0	Mar24 0-0	Sep27 0-1	Nov11 0-0	Jan01 4-1	Sep13 0-2	Sep02 2-1
BERWICK R	Feb10 1-0	Mar03 3-1		Dec09 3-1	Sep30 0-2	Mar17 1-0	Dec30 1-0	Apr07 1-1	Nov04 2-0	Apr28 1-0	Oct07 3-0	Mar24 1-1	Sep06 0-2	Mar28 2-0	Feb24 1-3	Sep20 0-1	Oct21 0-0	Sep16 0-2	Nov25 0-3
BRECHIN C	Jan06 5-1	Apr28 0-0	Apr14 0-3		Oct21 1-3	Sep06 3-1	Sep20 0-2	Mar03 0-5	Oct07 2-0	Dec02 2-0	Nov25 1-4	Sep09 1-4	Apr23 2-3	Sep23 2-2	Nov04 4-6	Dec30 3-3	Jan20 2-4	Feb10 1-2	Mar24 2-2
CLYDE	Sep23 3-1	Apr14 1-0	Jan20 1-0	Feb20 4-1		Feb24 1-0	Dec02 2-1	Jan27 1-2	Mar24 1-1	Sep20 3-2	Mar10 0-0	Dec30 2-2	Jan06 4-1	Sep09 1-1	Oct14 3-0	Apr28 5-1	Nov11 1-3	Nov25 1-1	Oct28 3-0
CLYDEBANK	Mar03 1-2	Nov04 2-3	Nov11 1-2	Sep27 2-1	Apr21 0-1		Apr18 3-0	Jan13 0-4	Jan01 1-1	Oct07 4-1	Apr25 1-2	Feb10 0-4	Oct21 1-0	Nov25 1-2	Sep16 1-1	Mar24 1-1	Sep13 1-2	Sep02 0-3	Apr07 4-2
COWDENBEATH	Nov18 2-1	Feb24 0-2	Sep02 5-0	Sep13 2-1	Apr07 1-1	Sep30 2-0		Jan01 1-0	Dec09 2-1	Mar03 4-1	Sep16 3-2	Nov04 1-3	Mar17 0-2	Oct14 3-0	Apr21 1-1	Jan27 0-2	Sep27 3-1	Jan13 1-1	Dec23 4-1
DUNFERMLINE A	Feb07 3-0	Dec16 5-0	Dec02 1-2	Oct28 8-0	Oct07 1-2	Apr28 3-3	Sep09 0-2		Nov25 3-2	Sep23 3-1	Nov11 7-2	Apr14 4-1	Dec30 6-1	Sep20 5-1	Apr25 1-0	Jan06 1-1	Mar24 1-0	Apr11 1-1	Mar10 3-0
E.STIRLING	Sep19 0-2	Jan06 2-0	Mar10 1-2	Jan27 2-0	Nov18 0-5	Sep09 4-2	Apr14 1-0	Mar31 0-2		Sep06 2-2	Feb20 0-4	Dec02 1-5	Sep23 3-2	Dec30 2-1	Sep30 0-3	Mar20 2-1	Oct28 2-1	Mar17 4-3	Oct14 2-2
FORFAR A	Mar31 1-0	Sep30 2-1	Dec23 0-1	Apr07 2-1	Sep12 0-2	Jan27 0-3	Oct28 1-1	Feb24 0-6	Sep26 1-0		Sep02 1-0	Apr04 1-1	Nov18 1-1	Feb17 1-2	Jan01 1-0	Oct14 1-2	Sep16 2-0	Dec09 0-4	Apr21 1-0
HAMILTON A	Sep09 3-3	Dec02 0-3	Jan27 4-1	Mar31 5-1	Nov04 2-2	Sep23 1-4	Jan06 3-0	Mar17 2-1	Oct21 5-2	Dec30 4-0		Apr28 2-0	Sep20 1-0	Sep06 2-0	Nov18 3-3	Apr14 1-2	Feb10 0-0	Mar03 3-2	Sep30 3-0
MONTROSE	Sep30 4-0	Jan27 3-0	Nov18 2-2	Jan01 3-2	Sep02 0-1	Oct14 1-3	Mar10 2-2	Dec09 3-2	Apr07 3-5	Nov11 1-1	Dec23 2-0		Mar31 2-1	Oct28 2-2	Sep13 3-2	Feb17 1-4	Apr21 2-0	Sep27 0-2	Apr18 4-1
QUEEN OF SOUTH	Jan27 0-0	Oct14 3-1	Sep27 1-1	Apr21 1-0	Sep16 0-0	Apr11 2-0	Nov11 4-1	Sep02 1-0	Feb24 0-2	Mar24 0-1	Sep13 2-1	Nov25 4-3		Dec16 0-1	Dec23 1-1	Oct28 4-2	Dec09 1-2	Apr07 0-0	Jan01 2-2
QUEEN'S PARK	Mar20 3-2	Nov18 3-3	Apr21 1-0	Feb24 4-1	Jan01 1-3	Mar31 2-2	Feb10 2-2	Sep11 1-3	Sep02 2-2	Oct21 1-1	Sep27 1-2	Apr09 0-1	Nov04 0-2		Apr14 0-1	Sep30 2-3	Apr06 0-0	Dec23 2-1	Sep16 1-0
RAITH R	Dec27 4-0	Mar28 1-1	Sep23 8-1	Mar10 3-1	Feb10 0-0	Feb28 2-0	Dec16 2-2	Oct21 1-2	Jan20 2-2	Sep09 3-2	Mar24 2-0	Sep20 1-0	Apr28 2-0	Dec08 2-1		Dec02 3-0	Nov25 0-2	Oct07 1-1	Nov11 5-1
ST MIRREN	Nov04 4-0	Mar17 4-2	Sep13 3-1	Sep02 5-1	Dec23 0-1	Nov18 4-0	Oct07 6-3	Sep16 0-1	Apr21 1-3	Feb10 0-0	Dec09 7-1	Oct21 2-2	Mar03 2-1	Feb20 0-1	Apr07 3-1		Feb24 1-1	Jan01 4-1	Sep27 5-1
STENHOUSEMUIR	Apr28 3-0	Sep09 0-0	Apr17 2-1	Sep30 3-0	Mar17 1-2	Feb03 1-1	Sep06 0-1	Nov18 0-2	Mar03 0-0	Jan06 3-1	Oct14 0-2	Apr24 1-4	Apr14 1-1	Dec02 3-0	Mar31 2-0	Sep23 1-0		Nov04 3-1	Jan27 1-2
STIRLING A	Mar28 3-0	Apr18 0-1	Jan06 2-0	Oct14 3-0	Mar31 3-1	Sep20 3-0	Sep23 1-0	Sep30 0-0	Nov11 0-0	Apr14 3-4	Oct28 2-1	Sep06 3-2	Dec02 4-0	Apr28 2-2	Jan27 1-2	Sep09 3-1	Mar10 1-0		Mar14 4-2
STRANRAER	Apr14 1-0	Dec30 2-0	Mar31 5-4	Nov18 1-3	Mar03 1-2	Dec02 4-0	Apr28 2-2	Nov04 0-2	Feb10 2-1	Dec16 4-2	Apr11 1-0	Sep23 3-6	Sep09 1-0	Jan06 3-1	Mar17 1-4	Sep06 0-1	Oct07 2-0	Oct21 1-4	

LEAGUE TABLES

DIVISION 1

	P	W	D	L	F	A	W	D	L	F	A	Pts
Celtic	34	14	3	0	47	10	12	2	3	46	18	57
Rangers	34	14	2	1	36	10	12	2	3	38	20	56
Hibernian	34	12	2	3	43	17	7	5	5	31	16	45
Aberdeen	34	10	6	1	42	15	6	5	6	19	19	43
Dundee	34	13	4	0	45	10	4	5	8	23	33	43
Ayr U	34	11	4	2	33	21	5	4	8	17	30	40
Dundee U	34	11	3	3	32	24	6	2	9	24	27	39
Motherwell	34	5	6	6	20	23	6	3	8	18	25	31
East Fife	34	8	3	6	26	21	3	5	9	20	33	30
Hearts	34	7	4	6	15	17	5	2	10	24	33	30
St Johnstone	34	8	3	6	35	30	2	6	9	17	37	29
Morton	34	8	4	5	33	21	2	4	11	14	32	28
Partick T	34	4	5	8	17	25	6	3	8	23	28	28
Falkirk	34	6	4	7	24	26	1	8	8	14	30	26
Arbroath	34	8	3	6	31	23	1	5	11	8	40	26
Dumbarton	34	3	9	5	26	30	3	2	12	17	42	23
Kilmarnock	34	6	3	8	23	30	1	5	11	17	41	22
Airdrie	34	2	4	11	16	35	2	4	11	18	40	16

DIVISION 2

	P	W	D	L	F	A	W	D	L	F	A	Pts
Clyde	36	11	5	2	37	17	12	5	1	31	11	56
Dunfermline A	36	12	3	3	56	19	11	3	4	39	13	52
Stirling A	36	12	3	3	38	16	7	6	5	32	23	47
Raith R	36	11	5	2	42	16	8	4	6	31	26	47
St Mirren	36	11	3	4	51	21	8	4	6	28	29	45
Montrose	36	9	4	5	38	30	9	4	5	44	28	44
Cowdenbeath	36	11	3	4	35	20	3	7	8	22	33	38
Hamilton A	36	11	4	3	44	24	5	2	11	23	39	38
Berwick R	36	9	3	6	20	17	7	2	9	25	37	37
Stenhousemuir	36	8	4	6	25	18	6	4	8	19	23	36
Queen of South	36	8	6	4	26	18	5	2	11	19	34	34
Alloa	36	7	6	5	25	16	4	5	9	20	33	33
E. Stirling	36	9	2	7	28	37	3	6	9	24	32	32
Queen's Park	36	5	6	7	26	29	4	6	8	18	32	30
Stranraer	36	10	1	7	34	32	3	3	12	22	46	30
Forfar A	36	8	3	7	16	25	2	6	10	22	41	29
Clydebank	36	5	3	10	24	32	4	3	11	24	40	24
Albion R	36	3	6	9	23	38	2	2	14	12	45	18
Brechin C	36	4	4	10	31	45	1	0	17	15	54	14

Scottish Football League Records
Season 1973-74

DIVISION 1

	ABERDEEN	ARBROATH	AYR U	CELTIC	CLYDE	DUMBARTON	DUNDEE	DUNDEE U	DUNFERMLINE A	EAST FIFE	FALKIRK	HEARTS	HIBERNIAN	MORTON	MOTHERWELL	PARTICK T	RANGERS	ST JOHNSTONE
ABERDEEN		Apr27 2-2	Apr24 2-1	Apr29 0-0	Jan19 1-1	Feb09 3-0	Sep08 0-0	Oct27 3-1	Oct20 0-0	Mar30 2-0	Mar16 6-0	Nov17 3-1	Oct06 1-1	Mar09 0-0	Dec29 0-0	Apr13 2-0	Apr17 1-1	Jan05 0-1
ARBROATH	Dec22 1-3		Nov17 1-1	Dec01 1-2	Feb09 1-2	Sep22 2-1	Oct20 2-4	Apr20 1-2	Jan05 3-1	Mar16 1-2	Mar02 0-0	Nov03 2-3	Apr13 3-2	Jan19 2-1	Sep08 0-2	Mar30 0-3	Oct06 1-2	Dec29 3-1
AYR U	Apr06 0-0	Mar23 1-2		Nov10 0-1	Sep22 2-2	Jan05 0-1	Mar02 4-2	Nov24 1-1	Feb10 3-1	Dec22 1-0	Dec08 1-0	Apr20 2-1	Jan19 1-1	Sep08 2-1	Oct20 1-0	Apr03 1-0	Dec29 0-1	Oct06 3-2
CELTIC	Apr20 2-0	Apr06 1-0	Mar16 4-0		Sep08 5-0	Mar30 3-3	Feb10 1-2	Dec08 3-3	Dec29 6-0	Nov03 4-2	Dec22 6-0	Mar02 1-0	Oct20 1-1	Apr30 1-1	Oct06 2-0	Nov17 7-0	Jan05 1-0	Jan19 3-0
CLYDE	Sep29 1-3	Oct13 3-2	Jan12 1-3	Jan01 0-2		Oct27 0-3	Apr17 0-2	Feb02 1-2	Nov10 1-0	Sep01 2-0	Sep15 0-0	Apr24 2-0	May01 1-1	Mar23 0-2	Apr13 0-3	Feb23 1-0	Nov24 0-2	Apr27 0-1
DUMBARTON	Oct13 0-1	Jan12 5-2	Sep15 0-2	Nov24 0-2	Mar09 1-1		May10 2-0	Sep01 1-2	Apr24 1-0	Feb16 1-1	Jan02 1-5	Feb23 0-1	Apr06 3-3	Apr20 1-0	Nov03 3-0	Sep29 2-0	Dec22 0-2	Nov17 2-1
DUNDEE	Jan01 1-1	Feb23 5-2	Oct27 2-1	Oct13 0-1	Apr20 6-1	Nov10 2-1		Sep15 0-1	Nov24 1-5	Sep29 0-1	Sep01 4-0	May06 0-0	Apr10 1-3	Apr06 2-1	Dec22 0-1	Feb03 4-1	Apr29 2-3	Apr22 2-2
DUNDEE U	Mar03 0-3	Apr17 3-1	Mar30 2-1	Apr13 0-2	Oct06 4-0	Dec29 6-0	Jan05 1-2		Apr27 0-1	Nov17 0-0	Nov21 2-1	Mar16 3-3	May08 1-4	May10 4-2	Jan19 0-1	Apr24 1-1	Oct20 1-3	Sep08 2-0
DUNFERMLINE A	Feb24 0-0	Sep15 1-1	Oct13 0-4	Sep01 2-3	Mar16 2-3	Apr13 3-2	Mar30 1-5	Dec22 2-3		Jan01 0-1	Sep29 4-0	Apr17 2-3	Dec15 2-3	Mar03 1-1	Nov17 2-4	Jan12 1-1	Nov03 2-2	Apr10 3-1
EAST FIFE	Nov24 2-2	Nov10 0-2	Apr27 0-1	Apr17 1-6	Dec29 1-0	Oct06 0-1	Jan19 0-3	Mar23 0-2	Sep08 0-1		Apr06 1-2	Dec08 0-0	Jan05 0-3	Oct20 0-1	Apr20 1-0	Oct27 2-1	Feb09 0-3	Sep22 1-2
FALKIRK	Nov10 1-3	Oct27 2-2	Apr13 1-1	Apr27 1-1	Jan05 3-0	Sep08 2-3	Dec29 3-3	Apr02 0-1	Jan19 0-1	Apr24 1-1		Mar30 0-2	Feb09 0-0	Oct06 1-1	Sep22 1-1	Mar09 0-0	Mar23 0-0	Oct20 1-1
HEARTS	Mar23 0-0	Apr02 4-0	Dec15 0-1	Oct27 1-3	May04 0-0	Oct20 0-0	Sep22 2-2	Nov10 1-1	Oct06 3-0	Apr13 2-2	Nov24 2-1		Sep08 4-1	Dec29 0-2	Jan05 2-0	Apr27 3-1	Jan19 2-4	Feb09 0-2
HIBERNIAN	Feb02 3-1	Apr23 2-1	Sep29 4-2	Feb23 2-4	Nov03 5-0	Apr17 3-0	Nov17 2-1	Jan12 3-1	Apr20 1-1	Sep15 2-1	Oct13 2-0	Jan01 3-1		Dec22 5-0	Apr15 1-0	Sep01 2-1	Mar02 3-1	Mar30 3-3
MORTON	Nov03 2-0	Sep29 1-1	Jan01 1-2	May06 0-0	Nov17 2-2	Dec15 3-1	May03 0-1	Oct13 0-2	Oct27 1-2	Feb23 1-0	Feb02 0-3	Sep01 2-3	Apr27 0-3		Mar30 4-3	Sep15 0-0	Mar16 2-3	Apr13 1-1
MOTHERWELL	Sep01 0-0	Jan02 3-4	Feb24 2-0	Feb02 3-2	Dec12 0-0	Apr09 2-0	Apr27 2-2	Sep29 4-0	Mar23 1-0	Dec15 3-1	Apr17 2-1	Sep15 2-2	Nov10 1-1	Nov24 1-0		Oct13 1-2	Apr06 1-4	Oct27 0-1
PARTICK T	Apr08 2-0	Nov24 2-3	Nov03 3-0	Mar23 2-0	Oct20 1-3	Jan19 0-0	Oct06 1-0	Apr29 2-1	Sep22 1-1	Mar02 0-1	Apr20 2-2	Dec22 1-3	Dec29 1-0	Jan05 0-0	Feb09 1-0		Sep08 0-1	Mar16 0-1
RANGERS	Jan12 1-1	Feb02 2-3	Sep01 0-0	Sep15 0-1	Mar30 4-0	Apr27 3-1	Apr13 1-2	Feb24 3-1	Apr02 3-0	Oct13 0-1	Nov17 2-1	Sep29 0-3	Oct27 4-0	Nov10 1-0	Apr24 2-1	Jan01 1-1		Dec15 5-1
ST JOHNSTONE	Sep15 1-2	Sep01 0-0	Feb02 1-1	Sep29 2-1	Dec22 1-1	Mar23 3-3	Nov03 1-4	Jan02 1-1	Apr06 3-1	Mar09 1-3	Feb23 2-0	Oct13 0-2	Nov24 0-2	Apr03 1-4	Mar02 0-1	Nov10 2-2	Apr20 1-3	

DIVISION 2

	AIRDRIE	ALBION R	ALLOA	BERWICK R	BRECHIN C	CLYDEBANK	COWDENBEATH	E.STIRLING	FORFAR A	HAMILTON A	KILMARNOCK	MONTROSE	QUEEN OF SOU'	QUEEN'S PARK	RAITH R	ST MIRREN	STENHOUSEMU	STIRLING A	STRANRAER
AIRDRIE		Sep19 0-0	Apr20 5-2	Mar02 2-0	Jan19 8-0	Dec22 4-1	Nov03 5-0	Oct06 2-0	Sep08 4-0	Apr06 4-1	Feb09 0-0	Apr29 2-0	Nov17 3-0	Sep22 4-0	Dec29 4-0	Mar16 6-1	Sep05 1-0	Jan05 3-0	Oct20 3-1
ALBION R	Apr01 0-1		Sep29 2-2	Sep01 0-1	Apr27 3-1	Feb24 3-0	Feb03 0-0	Mar09 3-3	Apr09 1-2	Jan01 1-3	Nov21 3-4	Apr17 1-4	Oct13 0-2	May01 0-1	Mar23 0-1	Sep25 2-3	Oct27 1-1	Nov10 2-0	Apr06 0-2
ALLOA	Apr16 0-1	Jan19 1-0		Nov17 1-1	Sep19 2-1	Apr29 0-1	Mar30 0-2	Dec29 2-2	Apr24 2-0	Apr27 0-1	Oct06 0-1	Oct27 3-1	Apr13 0-1	Mar09 2-1	Feb09 0-4	Apr02 3-1	Sep08 2-0	Sep22 1-0	Mar23 3-2
BERWICK R	Oct27 3-1	Dec29 1-0	Jan26 1-0		Sep22 2-2	Nov24 0-0	Apr13 3-3	Jan05 1-1	Oct06 0-0	Mar10 0-0	Sep05 4-1	Nov10 1-1	Apr27 2-1	Jan19 2-0	Oct20 1-0	Apr17 3-2	Sep19 2-1	Sep08 2-0	Feb09 0-1
BRECHIN C	Sep29 0-3	Dec22 0-0	Sep12 0-4	Jan12 2-0		Oct13 0-1	Sep01 2-4	Nov10 0-3	Apr20 2-1	Feb23 0-1	Apr06 0-4	Jan01 0-4	Sep24 0-3	Oct27 1-5	Nov24 0-4	Sep15 2-4	Mar09 2-1	Mar23 2-5	Apr24 2-2
CLYDEBANK	Apr27 2-1	Oct20 0-1	Nov10 1-2	Mar30 1-2	Feb09 2-0		Apr24 2-2	Sep08 1-3	Feb16 3-3	Oct27 1-1	Dec29 1-2	Mar09 3-0	Apr17 0-1	Mar23 2-0	Sep22 1-1	Apr13 1-1	Jan19 1-1	Sep19 2-0	Oct06 5-0
COWDENBEATH	Mar09 0-1	Oct06 3-4	Nov24 2-1	Apr30 1-1	Dec29 2-1	Apr06 0-2		Sep19 3-5	Feb09 3-2	Nov10 2-3	Jan19 2-4	Mar23 4-3	Oct27 1-1	Apr02 1-1	Sep08 2-2	Apr27 0-0	Oct20 3-0	Sep05 1-4	Sep22 2-2
E.STIRLING	Feb02 0-2	Nov03 1-2	Sep01 2-3	Sep15 1-0	Mar16 1-3	Jan01 2-0	Sep12 5-1		Mar02 0-1	Sep29 1-1	Apr20 1-3	Sep25 3-1	Feb23 0-1	Nov24 1-2	Feb16 0-1	Oct13 1-0	Nov17 1-2	Apr06 1-0	Dec22 1-3
FORFAR A	Jan01 0-7	Apr13 4-0	Sep25 1-1	Feb02 1-1	Dec15 1-2	Sep15 0-2	Oct13 1-2	Oct27 2-1		Sep01 1-2	Mar23 3-5	Feb23 2-3	Jan12 1-2	May06 3-1	Nov10 1-4	Jan19 0-1	Apr27 0-2	Mar09 1-7	Nov24 1-1
HAMILTON A	Dec01 0-0	Sep08 2-0	Dec22 2-0	Nov03 0-4	Oct20 3-1	Mar03 3-0	Mar16 4-1	Jan19 1-0	Dec29 2-1		Apr30 2-2	Apr20 2-0	Mar30 2-0	Apr13 3-2	Sep05 2-1	Nov17 4-2	Jan26 2-1	Oct06 1-2	Sep19 1-1
KILMARNOCK	Oct13 4-0	Mar30 3-1	Feb02 8-2	Oct02 2-3	Dec01 3-1	Sep01 3-2	Sep29 4-3	Apr09 4-0	Nov17 5-1	Jan12 3-1		Sep15 2-1	Apr24 1-0	Apr16 5-0	Oct27 1-1	Jan01 1-1	Apr13 3-1	Apr27 2-1	Mar16 4-1
MONTROSE	Apr13 2-1	Sep22 3-1	Mar02 4-0	Mar16 1-0	Sep08 3-2	Apr03 1-3	Nov17 4-1	Apr23 4-2	Oct20 5-1	Feb16 1-0	Jan05 0-2		Dec01 2-2	Apr27 2-0	Oct06 1-3	Mar30 5-0	Feb09 0-0	Dec29 2-2	Jan19 2-2
QUEEN OF SOUTH	Mar23 1-1	Feb09 5-2	May04 1-0	Dec22 3-3	Sep05 2-1	Apr20 0-1	Mar02 5-0	Oct20 3-1	Sep22 3-2	Nov24 1-2	Sep19 1-0	Apr06 5-0		Dec29 2-0	Apr10 3-0	Nov03 3-3	Oct06 5-1	Jan19 3-1	Sep08 1-2
QUEEN'S PARK	Jan12 1-3	Apr20 3-1	Nov03 0-2	Sep29 1-0	Mar02 2-0	Nov17 2-1	Sep15 1-0	Mar30 1-1	Apr29 6-0	Apr11 0-3	Oct20 0-2	Dec22 0-2	Sep01 0-3		Sep19 1-0	Feb02 2-1	Mar16 0-1	Feb09 0-0	Sep05 1-3
RAITH R	Sep01 0-4	Nov17 3-0	Oct13 3-2	Feb23 1-1	Mar30 1-1	May01 2-2	Jan01 1-2	Apr13 5-0	Mar16 4-1	Sep25 0-3	Mar02 3-1	Feb02 2-2	Sep15 3-0	Apr23 3-1		Sep29 2-4	Apr02 3-0	Apr16 5-4	Nov03 1-0
ST MIRREN	Nov10 3-5	Apr23 3-1	Apr06 0-1	Apr20 1-1	Feb16 3-0	Mar27 2-0	Dec22 0-2	Feb09 3-1	Sep19 3-1	Mar23 2-2	Sep08 1-3	Nov24 2-0	Mar09 0-0	Oct06 3-4	Jan05 0-0		Sep22 4-1	Oct20 3-3	Dec29 1-2
STENHOUSEMUIR	Sep25 2-3	Mar03 1-0	Jan01 4-0	Sep12 2-1	Nov03 4-2	Sep29 1-2	Feb23 0-1	Mar23 3-2	Dec22 1-1	Sep15 0-1	Feb16 0-1	Oct13 3-3	Feb02 0-4	Nov10 3-0	Apr06 0-1	Jan12 3-1		Nov24 0-3	Apr16 4-1
STIRLING A	Sep15 0-2	Mar16 7-1	Jan12 1-0	Jan01 0-2	Nov17 5-0	Apr09 3-0	Sep25 6-1	May01 6-0	Nov03 2-0	Feb02 1-3	Dec22 1-1	Sep01 4-3	Sep29 1-0	Oct13 3-2	Apr20 1-1	Feb23 1-1	Mar30 1-0		Apr02 1-0
STRANRAER	Feb23 1-6	Dec01 1-2	Sep15 1-3	Oct13 1-4	Apr13 3-0	Feb02 1-0	Jan12 5-2	Apr27 3-0	Mar30 4-2	Sep12 2-4	Nov10 2-2	Sep29 3-1	Jan01 5-5	Sep25 1-1	Mar09 2-3	Sep01 0-2	Apr20 1-0	Oct27 2-0	

LEAGUE TABLES

DIVISION 1

	P	W	D	L	F	A	W	D	L	F	A	Pts
Celtic	34	12	4	1	51	12	11	3	3	31	15	53
Hibernian	34	14	2	1	46	18	6	7	4	29	24	49
Rangers	34	9	3	5	32	17	12	3	2	35	17	48
Aberdeen	34	7	9	1	26	9	6	7	4	20	17	42
Dundee	34	7	3	7	32	25	9	4	4	35	23	39
Hearts	34	6	6	5	26	20	8	4	5	28	23	38
Ayr U	34	9	4	4	23	16	6	4	7	21	24	38
Dundee U	34	7	3	7	30	25	8	4	5	25	26	37
Motherwell	34	8	5	4	28	20	6	2	9	17	20	35
Dumbarton	34	7	3	7	23	23	4	4	9	20	35	29
Partick T	34	7	4	6	19	16	2	6	9	14	30	28
St Johnstone	34	3	6	8	20	31	6	4	7	21	29	28
Arbroath	34	5	2	10	24	32	5	5	7	28	37	27
Morton	34	4	5	8	20	27	4	5	8	17	22	26
Clyde	34	5	2	10	13	26	3	7	7	16	39	25
Dunfermline A	34	3	5	9	28	37	5	3	9	15	28	24
East Fife	34	3	2	12	9	30	6	4	7	17	21	24
Falkirk	34	1	11	5	17	21	3	3	11	16	37	22

DIVISION 2

	P	W	D	L	F	A	W	D	L	F	A	Pts
Airdrie	36	16	2	0	60	6	12	2	4	42	19	60
Kilmarnock	36	15	2	1	58	20	11	4	3	38	24	58
Hamilton A	36	13	3	2	36	18	11	4	3	32	20	55
Queen of South	36	12	3	3	47	20	8	4	6	26	21	47
Berwick R	36	10	7	1	28	14	6	6	6	25	21	45
Raith R	36	10	4	4	42	28	8	5	5	27	20	45
Stirling A	36	12	3	3	44	17	5	3	10	32	33	40
Montrose	36	11	4	3	42	22	4	3	11	29	42	37
Stranraer	36	8	3	7	38	37	6	5	7	26	33	36
Clydebank	36	6	6	6	29	21	7	2	9	18	27	34
St Mirren	36	7	5	6	34	27	5	5	8	28	39	34
Alloa	36	9	2	7	22	20	6	2	10	25	38	34
Cowdenbeath	36	5	6	7	32	37	6	3	9	27	48	31
Queen's Park	36	8	2	8	21	23	4	2	12	21	41	28
Stenhousemuir	36	8	2	8	31	27	3	3	12	13	32	27
E. Stirling	36	6	1	11	22	26	3	4	11	25	47	23
Albion R	36	3	4	11	22	31	4	2	12	16	41	20
Forfar A	36	3	3	12	23	44	2	3	13	19	50	16
Brechin C	36	3	2	13	15	49	2	2	14	18	50	14

Scottish Football League Records
Season 1974-75

DIVISION 1

	ABERDEEN	AIRDRIE	ARBROATH	AYR U	CELTIC	CLYDE	DUMBARTON	DUNDEE	DUNDEE U	DUNFERMLINE A	HEARTS	HIBERNIAN	KILMARNOCK	MORTON	MOTHERWELL	PARTICK T	RANGERS	ST JOHNSTONE
ABERDEEN		Sep28 1-0	Oct26 5-1	Oct12 3-0	Mar12 3-2	Apr19 4-1	Feb22 1-1	Jan01 4-0	Mar29 2-0	Dec21 1-1	Feb01 2-2	Aug31 2-3	Jan11 4-0	Nov16 3-3	Apr23 2-2	Nov09 1-1	Dec07 1-2	Sep14 3-1
AIRDRIE	Mar04 2-2		Nov09 1-0	Oct26 1-2	Mar22 1-0	Oct12 0-3	Mar18 1-1	Aug31 0-1	Oct05 1-1	Apr15 5-2	Feb22 1-1	Dec07 0-0	Apr19 2-2	Sep14 3-1	Jan01 2-0	Nov23 1-0	Dec21 4-3	Feb10 1-1
ARBROATH	Mar01 1-2	Mar15 3-1		Mar29 1-3	Feb08 2-2	Sep14 2-0	Sep28 0-3	Jan11 2-2	Nov02 1-3	Jan01 1-3	Nov16 3-1	Dec21 0-2	Apr05 0-0	Aug31 0-2	Oct05 1-1	Oct19 2-0	Apr19 1-2	Dec07 0-0
AYR U	Feb08 2-0	Mar01 1-0	Nov23 1-0		Jan18 1-5	Jan11 1-0	Mar22 1-3	Dec07 2-1	Oct19 1-1	Apr19 3-2	Nov02 3-3	Apr05 2-2	Jan01 3-2	Dec21 1-1	Sep14 0-4	Oct05 5-2	Aug31 1-1	Nov09 1-0
CELTIC	Nov02 1-0	Nov16 6-0	Oct12 1-0	Sep28 5-3		Jan01 5-1	Feb11 2-2	Apr19 1-2	Mar15 0-1	Dec07 2-1	Mar29 4-1	Oct19 5-0	Aug31 5-0	Apr05 1-1	Jan11 2-3	Mar01 3-2	Sep14 1-2	Dec21 3-1
CLYDE	Dec14 1-1	Feb08 2-1	Jan04 3-1	Sep21 1-0	Sep07 2-4		Dec28 1-3	Mar18 0-1	Apr12 1-2	Oct05 2-2	Nov30 2-2	Mar22 0-3	Nov23 4-2	Feb18 1-2	Nov09 0-0	Apr26 2-2	Feb22 1-2	Oct26 2-2
DUMBARTON	Oct19 2-3	Nov02 2-0	Feb19 5-1	Nov16 1-2	Oct05 1-3	Aug31 2-0		Nov23 0-0	Mar01 1-2	Sep14 1-1	Mar15 0-1	Apr19 2-3	Feb26 1-1	Jan01 0-0	Dec21 0-1	Feb08 0-1	Jan11 1-5	Apr05 0-0
DUNDEE	Sep07 0-1	Dec28 1-0	Sep21 0-1	Apr12 2-3	Dec14 0-6	Nov02 4-1	Mar29 2-1		Jan04 2-0	Mar01 2-0	Apr23 2-0	Oct05 0-0	Feb08 4-1	Oct19 3-0	Feb10 4-1	Nov30 1-0	Mar15 1-2	Nov16 4-0
DUNDEE U	Nov27 4-0	Feb01 1-0	Mar19 3-1	Mar05 3-1	Nov09 0-0	Dec07 3-3	Oct26 3-3	Sep14 3-0		Sep28 1-0	Oct12 5-0	Jan11 1-3	Dec21 3-4	Apr19 1-0	Aug31 5-0	Mar22 2-1	Apr05 2-2	Jan02 1-1
DUNFERMLINE A	Apr26 1-3	Nov30 2-2	Sep07 3-1	Mar08 0-2	Apr12 1-3	Feb01 1-1	Jan04 3-0	Oct26 3-1	Feb11 1-2		Sep21 2-2	Nov09 1-1	Mar22 1-1	Nov23 1-1	Mar12 0-1	Dec28 1-2	Oct12 1-6	Feb26 2-3
HEARTS	Oct05 1-4	Oct19 2-1	Mar22 0-0	Mar19 1-0	Nov23 1-1	Apr05 0-1	Nov09 2-1	Dec21 0-0	Feb08 3-1	Jan11 1-0		Jan01 0-0	Sep14 1-1	Dec07 3-1	Apr19 4-1	Jan18 3-1	Oct26 1-1	Aug31 1-2
HIBERNIAN	Dec28 0-1	Apr12 6-1	Apr26 2-1	Nov30 2-1	Feb22 2-1	Nov16 1-0	Dec14 2-0	Feb01 2-1	Sep21 3-0	Mar15 5-1	Sep07 2-1		Mar01 0-2	Nov02 5-0	Oct12 6-2	Jan04 2-2	Mar29 1-1	Sep28 0-1
KILMARNOCK	Sep21 1-0	Dec14 3-3	Nov30 2-2	Sep07 3-0	Dec28 0-1	Mar29 2-0	Apr12 1-2	Oct12 1-1	Apr26 2-4	Nov16 2-4	Jan04 1-1	Nov13 1-1		Mar15 2-1	Feb22 3-1	Mar08 1-1	Sep28 0-6	Feb01 1-1
MORTON	Mar22 0-3	Jan04 3-0	Dec28 3-2	Apr26 1-1	Nov30 0-1	Sep28 1-0	Sep07 1-1	Feb22 1-2	Dec14 0-6	Mar29 0-2	Apr12 0-0	Mar08 0-1	Nov09 2-3		Oct26 0-3	Sep21 3-1	Feb01 1-1	Oct12 1-1
MOTHERWELL	Nov30 2-1	Sep07 1-3	Feb01 3-1	Jan04 5-1	Sep21 1-2	Mar15 1-1	Apr26 3-1	Sep28 0-1	Dec28 0-1	Nov02 1-2	Dec14 1-3	Feb08 4-1	Oct19 2-0	Mar01 3-0		Apr12 0-0	Nov16 0-5	Mar29 3-0
PARTICK T	Mar15 1-0	Mar29 1-3	Feb22 1-0	Feb01 2-2	Nov06 1-2	Dec21 2-2	Oct12 2-1	Apr05 2-2	Nov16 0-5	Aug31 3-0	Sep28 4-1	Sep14 1-5	Nov02 2-2	Jan11 3-1	Dec07 2-1		Jan01 0-4	Apr19 0-0
RANGERS	Apr12 3-2	Apr26 0-1	Dec14 3-0	Dec28 3-0	Jan04 3-0	Oct19 3-1	Sep21 3-2	Nov09 1-0	Nov30 4-2	Feb08 2-0	Mar01 2-1	Nov23 0-1	Feb15 3-3	Oct05 2-0	Mar22 3-0	Sep07 3-2		Mar08 1-0
ST JOHNSTONE	Jan04 1-1	Sep21 0-1	Apr12 3-2	Mar15 0-0	Apr26 2-1	Mar01 1-0	Nov30 3-0	Mar22 3-1	Sep07 2-0	Oct19 2-1	Dec28 2-3	Jan18 2-2	Oct05 2-2	Feb08 2-0	Nov23 0-1	Dec14 1-3	Nov02 1-2	

DIVISION 2

	ALBION R	ALLOA	BERWICK R	BRECHIN C	CLYDEBANK	COWDENBEATH	EAST FIFE	E.STIRLING	FALKIRK	FORFAR A	HAMILTON A	MEADOWBANK T	MONTROSE	QUEEN OF SOUTH	QUEEN'S PARK	RAITH R	ST MIRREN	STENHOUSEMUIR	STIRLING A	STRANRAER
ALBION R		Apr16 3-2	Feb08 3-2	Apr21 3-0	Nov16 1-3	Apr09 2-0	Mar25 2-1	Sep17 6-2	Sep21 4-1	Oct19 5-3	Sep07 1-2	Apr12 0-1	Apr26 3-0	Mar29 1-1	Nov02 1-2	Mar15 2-1	Nov30 2-4	Sep28 0-0	Apr28 1-4	Mar01 4-0
ALLOA	Aug31 1-1		Apr05 0-0	Mar29 1-0	Apr19 1-0	Oct12 0-0	Oct26 0-1	Feb22 2-1	Nov16 0-1	Dec21 3-1	Sep28 0-0	Sep18 8-1	Sep04 0-2	Mar08 0-4	Feb01 3-0	Dec07 0-2	Nov09 3-1	Jan01 0-0	Sep14 2-2	Jan11 1-3
BERWICK R	Oct12 2-0	Nov30 3-0		Aug31 2-1	Sep14 2-0	Oct26 4-1	Mar08 2-0	Jan01 1-0	Mar29 1-2	Jan11 1-1	Sep18 0-1	Nov09 3-0	Mar22 2-2	Apr12 0-3	Apr26 0-2	Sep28 2-1	Sep04 1-5	Feb22 4-2	Feb01 2-1	Dec14 3-0
BRECHIN C	Apr19 3-2	Nov23 2-2	Dec28 0-1		Oct05 0-0	Mar08 3-1	Jan04 3-2	Mar22 1-0	Jan18 0-3	Sep11 4-1	Apr26 1-3	Oct12 0-1	Sep07 1-2	Feb22 0-4	Dec07 2-1	Apr05 1-1	Sep21 2-6	Sep04 4-5	Oct26 1-2	Nov09 2-2
CLYDEBANK	Mar22 2-0	Dec14 4-1	Apr30 2-1	Feb01 3-1		Nov30 2-1	Sep21 0-1	Nov09 0-3	Apr26 2-0	Sep28 2-2	Apr12 1-0	Sep07 3-0	Oct12 1-1	Dec28 3-1	Feb22 2-1	Mar29 3-2	Oct26 0-0	Sep18 1-1	Mar08 0-0	Sep04 0-3
COWDENBEATH	Sep14 1-5	Feb08 1-1	Mar01 0-0	Nov02 1-2	Apr05 0-3		Apr02 0-2	Feb15 1-1	Mar15 1-4	Jan01 2-1	Oct19 1-1	Sep28 5-0	Sep11 1-0	Nov16 0-2	Apr19 2-0	Aug31 0-2	Mar29 1-4	Dec21 0-3	Dec07 4-5	Oct05 0-0
EAST FIFE	Oct05 5-0	Mar01 3-2	Nov02 2-1	Sep14 3-0	Jan11 1-0	Sep25 2-2		Sep28 1-1	Oct19 1-0	Aug31 2-1	Mar15 0-0	Mar29 4-1	Apr05 0-4	Sep11 1-1	Nov16 1-0	Jan01 2-1	Feb08 1-2	Dec07 1-1	Apr19 1-1	Dec21 4-1
E.STIRLING	Sep11 1-0	Oct19 4-0	Sep07 0-2	Nov16 1-2	Mar15 1-0	Sep21 2-2	Jan18 1-0		Oct05 2-0	Mar01 4-0	Feb08 0-3	Sep13 2-0	Dec28 3-1	Apr15 2-4	Sep23 1-0	Nov02 1-1	Apr26 5-0	Nov30 1-0	Mar29 1-1	Apr12 0-2
FALKIRK	Jan11 3-1	Mar22 2-0	Nov23 3-0	Sep28 3-1	Dec21 0-1	Nov09 5-0	Feb22 4-0	Feb01 6-1		Dec07 2-0	Apr23 2-1	Mar08 2-0	Oct26 3-2	Oct12 1-2	Aug31 5-1	Apr19 1-0	Sep18 4-0	Sep14 2-0	Jan01 1-2	Apr05 3-0
FORFAR A	Feb22 0-5	Apr26 0-3	Sep21 2-3	Sep18 1-3	Jan18 0-2	Sep07 1-1	Dec28 1-2	Oct26 2-3	Apr12 0-2		Mar19 0-2	Nov30 1-3	Mar08 0-4	Feb01 2-3	Nov23 2-2	Sep25 2-0	Dec14 1-1	Oct12 0-3	Nov09 0-4	Mar22 1-4
HAMILTON A	Jan01 0-0	Apr30 1-0	Jan04 1-0	Dec21 1-1	Dec07 0-1	Feb22 5-0	Nov09 0-1	Oct12 3-4	Apr16 0-2	Sep14 3-0		Dec14 8-0	Apr19 2-1	Oct26 0-2	Apr05 2-0	Oct05 2-0	Mar08 0-1	Aug31 1-1	Jan11 3-1	Nov23 6-2
MEADOWBANK T	Dec07 3-1	Sep11 0-1	Mar15 1-1	Feb08 0-0	Dec30 1-0	Jan18 1-6	Nov22 2-1	Mar25 0-2	Nov02 1-0	Apr05 0-0	Nov16 0-4		Oct05 1-2	Sep25 0-2	Mar01 0-3	Jan11 1-0	Oct19 2-4	Apr19 0-2	Dec21 1-1	Dec28 1-0
MONTROSE	Dec21 0-1	Sep25 2-1	Nov16 2-0	Jan01 3-0	Feb08 1-1	Sep18 3-0	Nov30 3-1	Aug31 4-3	Mar01 0-0	Nov02 2-1	Apr07 2-1	Feb01 2-0		Mar15 2-0	Jan11 0-0	Sep14 0-0	Apr12 2-1	Mar29 2-1	Sep28 3-1	Oct19 1-2
QUEEN OF SOUTH	Nov23 1-1	Nov02 1-1	Dec07 1-3	Oct19 3-0	Aug31 3-0	Mar22 2-1	Sep18 2-0	Apr19 2-0	Feb08 1-0	Oct05 7-0	Mar01 0-0	Sep04 3-0	Nov09 1-0		Sep14 0-2	Dec21 1-1	Jan18 0-1	Jan11 2-1	Apr05 3-0	Jan01 4-2
QUEEN'S PARK	Mar08 1-4	Oct05 0-2	Dec21 1-2	Apr12 3-0	Oct19 1-0	Dec14 1-1	Mar22 0-0	Sep04 1-2	Dec28 0-2	Mar29 4-0	Nov30 0-3	Apr14 1-1	Sep21 1-2	Apr21 0-3		Feb08 1-1	Sep07 0-0	Nov09 1-1	Sep18 1-2	Mar11 2-1
RAITH R	Nov09 1-2	Apr12 3-1	Jan18 2-0	Nov30 5-2	Nov23 1-2	Dec28 1-0	Sep07 0-2	Mar08 1-1	Dec14 1-0	Apr23 2-0	Feb01 1-0	Jan04 3-1	Feb15 0-4	Apr26 2-2	Oct12 2-2		Mar22 1-2	Oct26 2-0	Feb22 3-0	Sep18 2-1
ST MIRREN	Apr05 1-1	Mar15 5-1	Sep25 1-0	Jan11 6-1	Mar01 2-0	Nov23 1-1	Oct12 0-3	Dec21 2-0	Apr30 0-0	Apr19 2-0	Nov02 0-1	Feb22 4-0	Dec07 1-2	Sep28 0-5	Jan01 0-3	Nov16 0-1		Feb01 4-1	Aug31 3-0	Sep14 4-0
STENHOUSEMUIR	Apr01 6-1	Sep07 0-0	Oct19 2-0	Sep24 2-0	Sep11 1-2	Apr26 1-0	Apr12 0-1	Apr05 0-0	Jan04 0-1	Feb08 5-0	Dec28 2-3	Feb15 1-0	Nov23 0-1	Sep21 1-0	Mar15 1-3	Mar01 1-0	Oct05 4-4		Nov16 2-1	Nov02 0-0
STIRLING A	Sep25 3-2	Feb15 2-2	Oct05 2-0	Mar01 5-0	Nov02 3-3	Apr12 2-0	Dec14 1-3	Nov23 0-0	Sep07 0-2	Mar15 2-0	Sep21 1-2	Apr26 4-1	Jan18 1-4	Nov30 3-0	Sep11 3-0	Oct19 2-1	Dec28 1-1	Mar22 0-1		Feb08 2-0
STRANRAER	Oct26 1-1	Sep21 0-4	Apr19 2-2	Mar15 0-0	Sep25 2-1	Feb01 2-1	Apr26 2-1	Dec07 1-0	Nov30 3-4	Nov16 0-0	Mar29 1-4	Aug31 3-1	Feb22 2-2	Sep07 2-1	Sep28 0-0	Sep11 0-0	Jan25 2-1	Mar08 0-0	Oct12 1-2	

LEAGUE TABLES

DIVISION 1

	P	W	D	L	F	A	W	D	L	F	A	Pts
Rangers	34	14	1	2	39	15	11	5	1	47	18	56
Hibernian	34	12	2	3	41	16	8	7	2	28	21	49
Celtic	34	11	2	4	47	20	9	3	5	34	21	45
Dundee U	34	10	5	2	41	19	9	2	6	31	24	45
Aberdeen	34	9	6	2	42	20	7	3	7	24	23	41
Dundee	34	11	1	5	32	17	5	5	7	16	25	38
Ayr U	34	9	5	3	29	27	5	3	9	21	34	36
Hearts	34	8	6	3	24	16	3	7	7	23	36	35
St Johnstone	34	8	4	5	27	20	3	8	6	14	24	34
Motherwell	34	8	2	7	30	23	6	3	8	22	34	33
Airdrie	34	7	7	3	26	20	4	2	11	17	35	31
Kilmarnock	34	5	7	5	26	29	3	8	6	26	39	31
Partick T	34	7	5	5	27	31	3	5	9	21	31	30
Dumbarton	34	3	5	9	19	24	4	5	8	25	31	24
Dunfermline A	34	3	6	8	24	32	4	3	10	22	34	23
Clyde	34	4	6	7	25	30	2	4	11	15	33	22
Morton	34	4	5	8	17	28	2	5	10	14	34	22
Arbroath	34	4	5	8	20	27	1	2	14	14	39	17

DIVISION 2

	P	W	D	L	F	A	W	D	L	F	A	Pts
Falkirk	38	16	0	3	52	12	10	2	7	24	17	54
Queen of South	38	12	4	3	37	13	11	3	5	40	20	53
Montrose	38	13	4	2	34	14	10	3	6	36	23	53
Hamilton A	38	10	3	6	38	17	11	4	4	31	13	49
East Fife	38	11	6	2	35	19	9	1	9	22	23	47
St Mirren	38	10	3	6	36	20	9	5	5	38	32	46
Clydebank	38	11	5	3	31	19	7	3	9	19	21	44
Stirling A	38	10	4	5	37	22	7	5	7	30	33	43
Berwick R	38	12	2	5	35	22	5	4	10	18	27	40
E. Stirling	38	11	3	5	32	18	5	5	9	24	34	40
Stenhousemuir	38	9	4	6	29	17	5	7	7	23	25	39
Albion R	38	11	2	6	44	29	5	5	9	28	35	39
Raith R	38	11	3	5	33	22	3	6	10	15	22	37
Stranraer	38	7	8	4	24	25	5	3	11	23	40	35
Alloa	38	7	6	6	25	20	4	5	10	24	36	33
Queen's Park	38	4	6	9	19	27	6	4	9	22	27	30
Brechin C	38	6	4	9	30	39	3	3	13	14	46	25
Meadowbank T	38	6	4	9	15	30	3	1	15	11	57	23
Cowdenbeath	38	4	5	10	21	36	1	6	12	18	40	21
Forfar A	38	1	3	15	16	50	0	4	15	11	52	9

Meadowbank elected to Division Two.

Scottish Football League Records
Season 1975-76

PREMIER

	ABERDEEN	AYR U	CELTIC	DUNDEE	DUNDEE U	HEARTS	HIBERNIAN	MOTHERWELL	RANGERS	ST JOHNSTONE
ABERDEEN		Sep27 3-1 Jan31 2-1	Oct11 1-2 Feb21 0-1	Nov01 2-0 Mar13 0-1	Sep13 1-3 Jan10 5-3	Nov22 0-0 Apr07 0-3	Dec27 2-2 Apr24 3-0	Sep06 2-2 Jan03 0-0	Dec06 1-0 Apr14 0-0	Oct18 2-0 Feb28 3-0
AYR U	Nov29 1-0 Apr10 1-1		Nov12 2-7 May01 3-5	Sep20 2-1 Jan17 3-1	Dec06 2-2 Apr14 1-0	Dec20 1-1 Apr21 0-1	Nov15 1-3 Mar27 2-0	Nov01 2-0 May03 2-1	Oct11 3-0 Feb21 0-1	Sep06 1-0 Jan03 2-0
CELTIC	Dec13 0-2 Apr17 1-1	Dec27 3-1 Apr24 1-2		Sep06 4-0 Jan03 3-3	Sep27 2-1 Jan31 2-1	Oct04 3-1 Feb07 2-0	Dec10 1-1 Feb28 4-0	Nov15 0-2 Mar27 4-0	Nov01 1-1 Apr26 0-0	Nov22 3-2 Apr03 1-0
DUNDEE	Aug30 3-2 Jan01 1-3	Nov22 2-2 Apr03 1-2	Nov08 1-0 Mar20 0-1		Dec20 0-0 Apr21 2-1	Sep13 2-3 Jan10 4-1	Dec06 2-0 Apr14 1-1	Oct25 3-6 May01 1-0	Sep27 0-0 Jan31 1-1	Oct11 4-3 Feb21 3-0
DUNDEE U	Nov15 1-2 Mar27 1-0	Oct04 3-2 Mar03 5-0	Nov29 1-3 Apr10 3-2	Oct18 1-2 Feb28 1-0		Dec13 0-1 Apr17 2-0	Sep06 1-0 Apr28 2-0	Sep20 1-1 Jan17 1-4	Dec27 0-0 Apr24 0-1	Nov01 3-1 Mar31 1-1
HEARTS	Sep20 2-2 Jan17 3-3	Oct18 2-1 Feb28 1-0	Dec06 0-1 May03 1-0	Nov15 1-1 Mar27 3-0	Oct11 1-0 Feb21 0-1		Nov01 1-1 Mar13 0-1	Nov29 3-3 Apr10 1-2	Sep06 0-2 Jan03 1-2	Dec27 2-0 Apr24 1-0
HIBERNIAN	Oct25 3-1 Mar31 3-2	Sep13 1-0 Jan10 3-0	Dec20 1-3 Apr21 2-0	Oct04 1-1 Feb07 4-0	Nov08 1-1 Mar20 0-1	Aug30 1-0 Jan01 3-0		Dec13 1-0 Apr17 2-0	Nov22 2-1 Apr03 0-3	Sep27 4-2 Jan31 5-0
MOTHERWELL	Nov08 3-0 Mar20 2-1	Aug30 1-1 Jan01 1-0	Sep13 1-1 Jan10 1-3	Dec27 3-2 Apr24 1-1	Nov22 2-1 Apr03 3-2	Sep27 1-1 Jan31 2-0	Oct11 2-1 Feb21 0-1		Oct18 2-1 Feb28 0-1	Dec06 2-1 Apr14 2-0
RANGERS	Oct04 1-0 Feb07 2-1	Dec13 3-0 Apr17 2-1	Aug30 2-1 Jan01 1-0	Nov29 2-1 Apr10 3-0	Nov12 4-1 May04 0-0	Nov08 1-2 Mar20 3-1	Sep20 1-1 Jan17 2-0	Dec20 3-2 Apr21 2-1		Sep13 2-0 Jan10 4-0
ST JOHNSTONE	Dec20 1-1 Apr21 2-0	Nov08 0-1 Mar20 1-2	Sep20 1-2 Jan17 3-4	Dec13 1-3 Apr17 1-1	Aug30 1-0 Jan01 1-1	Oct25 0-1 Apr26 0-0	Nov29 3-4 Apr10 0-2	Oct04 2-1 Feb07 1-3	Nov15 1-5 Mar27 0-3	

DIVISION 1

	AIRDRIE	ARBROATH	CLYDE	DUMBARTON	DUNFERMLINE A	EAST FIFE	FALKIRK	HAMILTON A	KILMARNOCK	MONTROSE	MORTON	PARTICK T	QUEEN OF SOUTH	ST MIRREN
AIRDRIE		Nov29 2-2	Dec13 2-1	Oct04 3-0	Feb07 1-1	Oct25 1-0	Sep20 2-0	Nov08 2-2	Sep06 3-4	Nov15 2-2	Jan17 2-1	Dec20 2-4	Jan03 2-2	Feb21 1-3
ARBROATH	Sep27 3-0		Feb28 3-0	Nov01 1-5	Jan17 1-0	Dec06 3-1	Feb07 0-1	Oct11 2-1	Dec20 2-0	Sep06 1-2	Jan03 0-1	Oct25 0-0	Sep20 3-2	Nov15 4-1
CLYDE	Oct11 2-2	Nov08 5-2		Aug30 1-2	Sep20 0-2	Dec20 0-2	Dec06 3-4	Feb21 0-0	Nov29 0-2	Oct25 3-0	Feb14 1-2	Jan01 1-2	Jan17 1-3	Sep13 3-0
DUMBARTON	Dec06 0-0	Feb21 3-2	Feb07 1-0		Nov08 2-0	Sep27 5-5	Sep06 1-4	Nov15 5-1	Jan17 3-0	Jan03 0-6	Oct11 4-0	Sep20 2-3	Oct25 2-1	Dec20 2-0
DUNFERMLINE A	Aug30 3-3	Nov22 0-1	Feb18 5-1	Feb28 0-3		Jan01 1-1	Oct25 2-2	Sep13 0-4	Nov15 1-0	Dec20 1-0	Dec06 1-0	Feb21 0-3	Oct11 2-2	Sep27 2-2
EAST FIFE	Dec27 1-1	Oct04 3-1	Oct18 4-3	Nov29 2-1	Sep06 5-1		Jan03 2-1	Jan17 0-0	Sep20 2-4	Feb07 1-7	Nov08 2-2	Jan10 1-1	Feb21 2-0	Dec13 0-2
FALKIRK	Jan31 1-1	Aug30 1-0	Oct04 1-2	Jan01 3-2	Dec27 4-1	Sep13 0-1		Oct21 1-0	Nov01 0-1	Jan17 2-0	Nov29 3-3	Dec13 0-0	Nov15 1-0	Feb28 1-1
HAMILTON A	Feb28 2-1	Dec13 0-1	Nov01 0-0	Mar15 2-3	Jan03 1-1	Nov22 3-2	Dec20 1-0		Feb07 1-1	Feb23 3-3	Sep20 2-0	Oct04 1-2	Sep06 2-0	Oct25 0-1
KILMARNOCK	Jan01 2-1	Oct18 2-1	Sep27 3-0	Nov22 1-0	Jan10 4-0	Jan31 2-1	Feb21 1-0	Aug30 4-2		Dec13 1-1	Dec27 3-2	Sep13 0-1	Nov08 2-0	Oct04 3-1
MONTROSE	Jan10 1-0	Jan01 3-5	Dec27 4-3	Sep13 3-2	Oct18 2-2	Aug30 3-0	Nov22 2-1	Sep27 1-1	Oct11 2-0		Feb21 1-1	Nov08 2-1	Dec06 2-1	Jan31 2-1
MORTON	Nov22 1-0	Sep13 2-2	Nov15 1-1	Dec13 1-1	Oct04 1-1	Feb28 3-0	Sep27 2-3	Jan31 1-4	Oct25 1-3	Nov01 2-1		Aug30 0-0	Dec20 0-1	Jan01 1-0
PARTICK T	Oct18 0-1	Dec27 2-0	Sep06 1-0	Jan31 0-0	Nov01 1-1	Nov15 5-0	Oct11 3-2	Dec06 2-0	Jan03 2-0	Feb28 4-1	Feb07 2-0		Sep27 2-1	Nov22 2-1
QUEEN OF SOUTH	Sep13 1-7	Jan31 2-1	Nov22 1-3	Dec27 4-2	Dec13 5-2	Nov01 1-1	Jan10 3-2	Jan01 2-2	Feb28 2-1	Oct04 2-1	Oct18 0-1	Nov29 1-1		Aug30 2-2
ST MIRREN	Nov01 2-2	Feb14 0-0	Jan03 3-0	Oct18 3-2	Nov29 2-0	Oct11 2-0	Nov08 1-0	Dec27 2-2	Dec06 0-0	Sep20 3-1	Sep06 2-2	Jan17 2-3	Feb07 0-2	

DIVISION 2

	ALBION R	ALLOA	BERWICK R	BRECHIN C	CLYDEBANK	COWDENBEATH	E STIRLING	FORFAR A	MEADOWBANK T	QUEEN'S PARK	RAITH R	STENHOUSEMUIR	STIRLING A	STRANRAER
ALBION R		Sep27 0-1	Dec06 2-2	Apr26 4-0	Oct11 0-4	Feb25 1-1	Sep13 2-1	Nov01 4-0	Nov22 4-0	Feb28 0-0	Dec27 1-2	Aug30 2-2	Oct18 1-1	Jan01 2-1
ALLOA	Nov29 2-0		Oct18 1-0	Jan31 0-0	Apr06 0-0	Feb28 4-0	Oct04 1-0	Nov15 2-1	Aug30 1-1	Nov01 3-3	Mar31 0-1	Jan01 4-2	Dec27 1-2	Sep13 3-3
BERWICK R	Oct04 0-1	Feb18 0-3		Sep13 2-1	Sep27 0-4	Feb21 0-1	Aug30 1-2	Oct25 3-3	Jan01 1-0	Feb14 1-1	Nov15 1-3	Jan31 1-1	Nov22 3-2	Nov08 1-2
BRECHIN C	Nov15 2-0	Sep20 2-3	Apr24 1-0		Feb07 1-2	Oct25 1-2	Nov29 2-2	Sep06 2-1	Feb14 0-3	Oct04 1-0	Jan17 0-4	Nov01 1-1	Feb28 2-3	Apr17 0-4
CLYDEBANK	Feb14 2-2	Nov22 3-1	Nov29 0-1	Aug30 3-0		Sep13 3-0	Nov01 3-0	Feb28 2-0	Dec13 2-0	Oct25 1-1	Oct04 1-1	Oct18 2-1	Jan01 1-0	Jan31 2-1
COWDENBEATH	Sep20 3-0	Nov08 0-1	Nov01 3-2	Dec27 5-2	Jan03 1-1		Oct18 0-1	Feb07 2-2	Nov29 2-0	Jan17 2-2	Sep06 1-1	Mar09 3-1	Apr17 2-1	Oct04 2-1
E STIRLING	Jan03 0-0	Dec06 0-3	Feb07 1-1	Sep27 1-0	Feb21 0-1	Dec20 4-2		Oct11 1-1	Oct25 3-0	Sep06 2-1	Nov08 1-1	Nov22 1-3	Jan31 0-0	Jan24 3-1
FORFAR A	Feb21 1-0	Feb24 3-3	Dec27 1-3	Jan01 0-1	Nov08 0-2	Aug30 1-1	Feb14 2-2		Jan31 1-1	Oct18 4-1	Nov29 0-0	Oct04 3-1	Sep13 0-0	Nov22 0-3
MEADOWBANK T	Jan17 4-1	Feb07 1-2	Sep16 2-6	Oct11 0-4	Nov15 0-0	Sep27 1-1	Dec27 0-4	Sep20 1-0		Jan03 1-0	Oct18 0-1	Nov08 1-1	Dec06 1-0	Feb21 2-3
QUEEN'S PARK	Nov08 2-2	Feb21 3-1	Oct11 1-0	Dec06 1-0	Dec27 0-2	Nov22 4-1	Jan01 1-0	Dec20 4-0	Sep13 1-1		Sep20 2-3	Feb24 0-3	Aug30 3-1	Nov29 2-0
RAITH R	Oct25 1-1	Oct11 1-0	Mar17 3-0	Nov22 1-1	Dec06 1-0	Jan01 2-1	Feb28 0-0	Sep27 2-2	Dec20 3-2	Jan31 0-2		Sep13 2-0	Nov01 2-2	Aug30 3-3
STENHOUSEMUIR	Feb07 4-2	Sep06 0-1	Sep20 2-1	Feb21 4-1	Dec20 2-1	Oct11 0-2	Jan17 2-1	Dec06 1-2	Feb28 2-1	Nov15 2-2	Jan03 0-3		Sep27 0-1	Oct25 1-2
STIRLING A	Dec20 1-1	Oct25 2-2	Jan17 2-0	Nov08 1-1	Sep06 0-1	Nov15 5-2	Sep20 3-2	Dec13 2-0	Oct04 5-0	Feb07 1-3	Mar06 0-1	Nov29 1-2		Oct11 3-0
STRANRAER	Sep06 1-2	Jan03 0-1	Feb28 1-2	Oct18 4-2	Sep20 0-1	Dec06 2-4	Nov15 2-1	Jan17 4-0	Nov01 5-1	Sep27 1-1	Feb07 1-3	Dec27 3-1	Apr24 1-0	

LEAGUE TABLES

PREMIER DIVISION

	P	W	D	L	F	A	W	D	L	F	A	Pts
Rangers	36	15	2	1	38	12	8	6	4	22	12	54
Celtic	36	10	5	3	35	18	11	1	6	36	24	48
Hibernian	36	13	2	3	37	15	5	5	8	18	28	43
Motherwell	36	11	4	3	29	18	5	4	9	28	31	40
Hearts	36	7	5	6	23	20	6	4	8	16	25	35
Ayr U	36	10	3	5	29	24	4	2	12	17	35	33
Aberdeen	36	8	5	5	27	19	3	5	10	22	31	32
Dundee U	36	9	3	6	27	20	3	5	10	19	28	32
Dundee	36	8	5	5	31	26	3	5	10	18	36	32
St Johnstone	36	3	4	11	19	34	0	1	17	10	45	11

Restructured into 3 Divisions.

The top 10 clubs in Division One formed the Premier Division. The bottom 8 clubs in Division One and the top 6 clubs in Division Two formed the new Division One. The bottom 14 clubs in Division Two formed the new Division Two.

DIVISION 1

	P	W	D	L	F	A	W	D	L	F	A	Pts
Partick T	26	10	2	1	26	7	7	5	1	21	12	41
Kilmarnock	26	11	1	1	28	10	5	2	6	16	19	35
Montrose	26	9	3	1	28	18	3	3	7	25	25	30
Dumbarton	26	8	2	3	30	22	4	2	7	23	24	28
Arbroath	26	8	1	4	23	14	3	3	7	18	25	26
St Mirren	26	6	5	2	22	14	3	3	7	15	23	26
Falkirk	26	6	4	3	18	12	4	1	8	20	23	25
Airdrie	26	5	5	3	25	22	2	6	5	19	19	25
Hamilton A	26	5	4	4	18	15	2	6	5	19	22	24
Queen of South	26	6	4	3	26	26	3	2	8	15	21	24
Morton	26	4	5	4	16	17	3	4	6	15	23	23
East Fife	26	6	4	3	25	24	2	3	8	14	29	23
Dunfermline A	26	4	5	4	18	22	1	5	7	12	29	20
Clyde	26	3	2	8	20	23	2	2	9	14	29	14

DIVISION 2

	P	W	D	L	F	A	W	D	L	F	A	Pts
Clydebank	26	9	3	1	25	8	8	3	2	19	5	40
Raith R	26	6	6	1	21	14	9	4	0	24	8	40
Alloa	26	6	5	2	22	13	8	2	3	22	15	35
Queen's Park	26	8	2	3	24	14	2	7	4	17	19	29
Cowdenbeath	26	7	4	2	26	15	4	3	6	18	28	29
Stirling A	26	6	3	4	26	15	3	4	6	13	17	25
Stranraer	26	6	1	6	25	19	5	2	6	24	24	25
E. Stirling	26	5	5	3	17	14	3	3	7	16	19	24
Albion R	26	5	5	3	23	15	2	5	6	12	23	24
Stenhousemuir	26	6	1	6	20	20	3	4	6	19	24	23
Berwick R	26	3	3	7	14	24	4	2	7	18	20	19
Forfar A	26	3	6	4	16	18	1	4	8	12	30	18
Brechin C	26	4	2	7	15	25	2	3	8	13	26	17
Meadowbank T	26	4	3	6	14	23	1	3	9	10	30	16

Scottish Football League Records
Season 1976-77

PREMIER

	ABERDEEN	AYR U	CELTIC	DUNDEE U	HEARTS	HIBERNIAN	KILMARNOCK	MOTHERWELL	PARTICK T	RANGERS
ABERDEEN		Nov24 1-0 Mar26 0-2	Oct23 2-1 Mar05 2-0	Oct30 3-2 Mar12 0-1	Sep04 2-2 Jan03 4-1	Nov27 1-0 Apr09 0-0	Sep18 2-0 Feb07 2-0	Nov02 3-1 Mar23 2-1	Jan12 1-1 Apr16 0-2	Jan19 3-3 Apr30 2-1
AYR U	Sep11 0-5 Jan08 0-0		Oct16 0-2 Feb19 2-4	Sep18 1-4 Feb07 1-4	Dec11 0-1 Apr23 1-1	Oct23 2-3 Mar05 1-2	Jan01 3-1 Apr13 1-1	Nov27 4-1 Apr09 3-2	Nov06 2-1 Mar19 1-1	Oct02 1-1 Feb05 0-2
CELTIC	Dec26 2-2 Apr20 4-1	Dec18 3-0 Apr30 2-0		Oct20 5-1 Mar26 2-0	Sep18 2-2 Feb07 5-1	Oct02 1-1 Feb05 4-2	Nov27 2-1 Apr09 1-0	Oct30 2-0 Mar16 2-2	Feb12 2-0 Mar09 2-1	Sep04 2-2 Jan11 1-0
DUNDEE U	Mar16 3-2 Apr13 2-3	Nov20 2-2 Apr02 0-1	Sep11 1-0 Jan08 1-2		Dec27 1-1 Apr20 1-2	Nov06 2-1 Mar19 1-0	Nov03 3-0 Feb19 4-0	Oct02 2-0 Feb16 1-1	Sep25 2-1 Mar01 0-0	Mar08 0-0 Apr23 0-1
HEARTS	Nov10 2-1 Mar19 1-1	Oct09 2-2 Apr06 1-2	Nov20 3-4 Apr02 0-3	Oct23 1-2 Mar05 1-1		Jan26 0-1 Apr13 2-2	Oct02 2-2 Feb05 4-0	Dec18 2-1 Apr30 3-2	Sep11 0-0 Jan08 1-0	Nov27 0-1 Apr09 1-3
HIBERNIAN	Sep25 0-0 Jan22 0-0	Dec24 1-0 Apr20 2-0	Mar30 1-1 Apr16 0-1	Sep04 1-2 Jan05 0-0	Oct30 1-1 Mar23 3-1		Mar09 2-0 Apr23 0-0	Nov24 0-2 Mar26 1-2	Oct16 0-0 Feb19 1-1	Sep18 1-1 Feb16 0-0
KILMARNOCK	Nov20 1-2 Apr02 1-2	Oct30 6-1 Mar12 0-1	Sep25 0-4 Jan22 1-3	Dec18 1-0 Apr30 1-2	Feb15 2-1 Apr16 2-2	Oct26 1-1 Feb12 0-1		Sep04 1-1 Jan03 2-2	Dec27 0-0 Apr20 1-3	Nov13 0-4 Mar26 1-0
MOTHERWELL	Apr05 1-1 Apr23 1-3	Sep25 4-1 Jan22 2-4	Apr13 3-0 May10 2-2	Apr17 4-0 May04 1-1	Oct16 1-1 Feb19 2-1	Sep11 2-2 Jan08 1-1	Nov06 5-4 Mar19 2-0		Nov20 3-0 Apr02 1-1	Oct23 3-1 Mar05 0-2
PARTICK T	Oct02 2-2 Feb05 2-1	Sep04 0-2 Feb16 0-1	Feb22 2-4 Apr23 1-1	Nov27 1-5 Apr09 0-0	Nov30 2-1 Mar26 2-0	Dec18 1-1 Apr30 1-0	Oct23 2-1 Mar05 3-1	Sep18 2-0 Mar30 0-0		Oct30 2-1 Mar15 4-3
RANGERS	Oct16 1-0 Feb19 1-0	Mar23 1-1 Apr16 5-1	Nov24 0-1 Mar19 2-2	Nov09 3-0 Feb12 2-3	Sep25 4-2 Jan22 3-2	Nov20 1-1 Apr02 2-1	Sep11 0-0 Jan08 3-0	Dec26 1-0 Apr20 4-1	Jan01 1-0 Apr13 2-1	

LEAGUE TABLES

PREMIER DIVISION

	P	W	D	L	F	A	W	D	L	F	A	Pts
Celtic	36	13	5	0	44	16	10	4	4	35	23	55
Rangers	36	12	4	2	36	16	6	6	6	26	21	46
Aberdeen	36	11	4	3	30	18	5	7	6	26	24	43
Dundee U	36	8	5	5	26	17	8	4	6	28	28	41
Partick T	36	9	5	4	27	24	2	8	8	13	20	35
Hibernian	36	4	10	4	14	12	4	8	6	20	23	34
Motherwell	36	8	7	3	38	25	2	5	11	19	35	32
Ayr U	36	4	5	9	23	36	7	3	8	21	32	30
Hearts	36	5	6	7	26	28	2	7	9	23	38	27
Kilmarnock	36	4	5	9	21	30	0	4	14	11	41	17

DIVISION 1

	P	W	D	L	F	A	W	D	L	F	A	Pts
St Mirren	39	15	4	0	46	13	10	8	2	45	25	62
Clydebank	39	16	1	2	49	14	8	9	3	40	24	58
Dundee	39	13	3	3	48	23	8	6	6	42	32	51
Morton	39	11	4	5	39	25	9	6	4	38	27	50
Montrose	39	10	6	4	36	27	6	3	10	25	35	41
Airdrie	39	7	8	5	36	31	6	4	9	27	27	38
Dumbarton	39	6	8	6	37	34	8	1	10	26	34	37
Arbroath	39	11	3	5	27	19	6	0	14	19	43	37
Queen of South	39	7	5	8	32	35	4	8	7	26	30	35
Hamilton A	39	6	5	9	26	31	5	5	9	18	28	32
St Johnstone	39	5	7	7	22	28	3	6	11	20	36	29
East Fife	39	6	6	7	20	32	2	7	11	20	39	29
Raith R	39	7	7	6	29	27	1	4	14	16	41	27
Falkirk	39	5	4	10	19	40	1	4	15	17	45	20

DIVISION 2

	P	W	D	L	F	A	W	D	L	F	A	Pts
Stirling A	39	10	7	2	27	15	12	4	4	32	14	55
Alloa	39	10	7	2	44	18	9	6	5	29	27	51
Dunfermline A	39	14	4	2	32	12	6	6	7	20	24	50
Stranraer	39	15	3	2	49	15	5	3	11	25	38	46
Queen's Park	39	11	4	4	35	21	6	7	7	30	30	45
Albion R	39	9	7	3	44	28	6	5	9	30	33	42
Clyde	39	9	6	4	38	25	6	5	9	30	39	41
Berwick R	39	9	4	7	23	23	4	6	9	14	28	36
Stenhousemuir	39	10	1	9	22	21	5	4	10	16	28	35
E. Stirling	39	8	5	6	26	25	4	3	13	21	38	32
Meadowbank T	39	6	9	5	27	26	2	7	10	14	31	32
Cowdenbeath	39	7	3	9	26	28	6	2	12	20	36	31
Brechin C	39	4	7	9	27	33	3	5	11	24	44	26
Forfar A	39	4	3	13	23	35	3	7	9	20	33	24

DIVISION 1

	AIRDRIE	ARBROATH	CLYDEBANK	DUMBARTON	DUNDEE	EAST FIFE	FALKIRK	HAMILTON A	MONTROSE	MORTON	QUEEN OF SOUTH	RAITH R	ST JOHNSTONE	ST MIRREN
AIRDRIE		Sep29 3-0 Apr30 2-0	Sep11 1-1 Mar02 0-2	Mar26 1-2	Sep21 2-2 Apr02 2-2	Mar30 0-0	Dec18 4-3	Mar16 2-1	Oct02 0-2 Feb05 1-2	Sep18 3-2 Feb09 1-1	Nov06 3-3	Oct23 1-0 Mar05 3-3	Nov27 3-0	Oct12 2-3 Apr23 2-2
ARBROATH	Oct06 1-0		Nov06 0-2	Sep08 1-0 Apr23 1-2	Mar19 1-0	Sep22 1-1 Apr09 1-2	Dec11 4-0	Sep11 1-1 Jan08 2-1	Jan01 2-1	Dec18 2-1	Oct02 2-0 Feb05 1-1	Nov20 2-1	Oct23 2-1 Mar05 2-1	Sep25 0-2 Jan22 1-2
CLYDEBANK	Nov13 1-0	Sep04 3-0 Jan03 8-1		Oct30 2-0 Mar12 4-2	Oct16 2-1 Feb19 3-0	Oct02 2-1 Feb05 3-1	Sep29 4-1	Mar07 2-0	Nov27 1-2	Apr02 2-3	Mar26 2-0	Sep07 3-0 Apr23 2-0	Sep18 1-0 Feb16 2-0	Dec25 2-2
DUMBARTON	Sep14 1-3 Mar19 2-1	Apr16 2-3	Jan01 1-1		Nov10 1-1	Oct05 5-1 Apr30 3-3	Oct20 2-2 Apr09 4-0	Sep25 1-2 Jan22 1-1	Sep11 2-1 Jan08 2-2	Oct09 1-1 Feb12 0-4	Oct23 3-3 Mar05 2-0	Feb23 2-0	Apr06 2-4	Nov20 0-1
DUNDEE	Apr09 3-1	Sep15 2-1 Mar26 5-2	Apr12 2-3	Sep04 2-1 Mar23 4-0		Apr16 2-2	Nov27 2-0	Sep29 5-1	Oct23 6-1 Mar05 3-2	Nov13 1-1	Sep18 1-1 Feb15 0-2	Oct09 3-1 Feb12 4-0	Oct30 1-0 Mar15 2-0	Apr19 0-4
EAST FIFE	Oct09 0-4 Feb23 2-1	Apr02 1-0	Dec04 0-6	Sep29 2-3	Sep08 2-4 Apr23 0-2		Oct23 1-1 Mar05 1-0	Nov20 1-1	Dec18 1-0	Sep25 0-1 Jan22 0-2	Sep11 1-0 Jan08 1-1	Jan01 2-1	Sep15 1-1 Mar26 1-1	Nov06 3-3
FALKIRK	Oct16 1-0 Feb19 1-1	Oct09 1-3 Feb12 1-0	Oct12 0-4 Apr30 2-4	Apr02 1-3	Sep25 1-6 Jan22 0-8	Dec22 1-1		Mar23 1-0	Nov20 0-1	Sep15 3-5 Mar19 0-1	Mar02 2-0	Nov06 1-2	Apr16 0-0	Sep11 2-0 Jan08 1-1
HAMILTON A	Oct30 0-4 Mar12 0-0	Nov13 0-1	Oct09 3-2 Feb12 0-2	Nov27 0-1	Oct06 4-2 Apr30 0-3	Sep18 3-1 Feb16 1-2	Oct02 1-2 Feb05 2-2		Apr16 0-2	Dec26 1-0	Sep22 2-2 Apr09 0-3	Dec18 0-0	Sep04 3-2 Feb27 6-0	Mar26 0-0
MONTROSE	Feb26 3-1	Oct30 1-2 Mar16 3-2	Sep25 2-2 Jan22 3-3	Nov13 2-1	Dec27 0-1	Oct16 2-0 Feb19 1-1	Sep18 3-2 Feb09 1-0	Sep08 1-0 Apr23 3-0		Sep04 0-0 Jan03 1-3	Mar30 2-2	Sep15 2-0 Mar26 2-1	Apr09 2-2	Oct06 2-4
MORTON	Nov20 1-3	Oct16 4-1 Feb19 1-0	Oct27 0-0 Apr09 2-2	Feb26 3-0	Sep11 2-2 Jan08 2-3	Nov27 2-0	Mar26 1-0	Oct23 0-2 Mar05 1-1	Nov06 3-0		Sep08 0-2 Apr23 3-1	Sep29 3-1	Oct02 3-1 Feb05 2-0	Jan01 3-6 Mar12 3-0
QUEEN OF SOUTH	Sep04 2-2 Mar23 3-0	Dec04 0-1	Sep15 1-2 Mar19 2-2	Dec27 1-2	Nov20 2-2	Nov13 3-1	Oct30 3-0 Mar16 3-2	Apr02 0-1	Oct09 4-2 Feb12 2-1	Apr16 0-4		Sep25 1-0 Jan22 3-3	Sep29 0-1 Apr30 1-4	Oct16 1-1 Feb19 0-4
RAITH R	Feb16 2-2	Sep18 1-0 Feb08 0-1	Apr16 2-1	Oct02 1-1 Feb05 3-1	Dec15 1-2	Oct30 1-0 Mar23 2-1	Sep04 1-1 Feb26 3-0	Oct16 0-2 Feb19 1-1	Mar19 1-0	Oct06 3-3 Apr30 3-4	Nov27 1-2		Nov13 1-1	Sep22 1-1 Apr09 1-3
ST JOHNSTONE	Sep25 0-2 Jan22 1-2	Dec27 2-1	Nov20 0-0	Oct16 1-2 Feb19 0-2	Mar30 0-0	Mar19 3-1	Sep08 2-1 Apr23 1-0	Nov06 0-1	Sep22 1-1 Apr02 2-3	Feb23 1-1	Oct06 2-2	Sep11 2-0 Jan25 3-3		Oct09 1-1 Feb12 0-5
ST MIRREN	Apr16 3-0	Nov27 3-0	Oct23 0-0 Mar05 3-1	Sep18 2-1 Feb07 3-2	Oct02 4-0 Feb05 3-1	Sep04 1-1 Mar02 2-0	Nov13 2-0	Sep14 5-2 Mar19 1-0	Sep29 2-0 Apr30 2-2	Oct30 5-1	Dec18 2-1	Apr02 2-0	Mar08 1-1	

DIVISION 2

	ALBION R	ALLOA	BERWICK R	BRECHIN C	CLYDE	COWDENBEATH	DUNFERMLINE A	E STIRLING	FORFAR A	MEADOWBANK T	QUEEN'S PARK	STENHOUSEMUIR	STIRLING A	STRANRAER
ALBION R		Nov13 2-2	Nov20 0-1	Sep25 2-2 Apr18 4-0	Sep04 1-4 Mar23 3-1	Apr20 4-2	Apr11 2-2	Feb12 3-2	Sep28 1-1 Apr16 1-1	Mar19 3-0	Sep15 1-1 Apr09 4-1	Oct16 0-1 Feb19 2-0	Dec27 4-4	Oct30 5-2 Mar12 2-1
ALLOA	Sep11 2-2 Apr30 2-2		Sep25 5-1 Jan22 0-0	Apr20 6-0	Apr16 2-0	Dec25 2-1	Nov20 3-3	Nov06 4-1	Sep22 5-0 Mar19 2-2	Oct06 2-0	Oct16 1-1 Mar29 0-1	Mar12 2-1 Apr25 2-1	Feb12 3-0 Apr06 0-1	Apr09 1-1
BERWICK R	Sep18 1-3 Jan15 1-0	Nov27 2-0		Nov13 3-1 Apr30 4-1	Apr20 1-1	Sep04 0-0 Jan03 1-0	Oct23 0-2 Feb26 0-1	Apr02 1-0	Oct09 2-2	Oct30 2-3 Mar12 0-0	Oct02 0-3 Feb05 3-2	Apr23 1-0	Mar19 0-3 Apr27 1-0	Sep08 0-1
BRECHIN C	Nov27 1-3	Oct02 1-2 Feb05 1-3	Sep11 1-1		Sep08 1-1 Mar26 1-2	Apr02 4-1	Nov06 2-3	Sep22 0-0 Mar05 0-1	Mar12 1-2	Oct23 3-1 Feb26 1-1	Nov20 3-2 Apr05 1-1	Oct09 3-3 Apr13 0-1	Sep15 0-4 Apr23 0-0	Apr27 3-1
CLYDE	Nov06 3-2	Mar16 1-3 Apr02 2-0	Oct16 1-0 Feb19 2-3	Oct06 2-1		Jan08 4-1	Mar19 3-2	Sep11 2-2 Apr30 4-0	Nov20 0-1	Sep14 1-1 Apr23 3-0	Jan01 3-3	Sep25 1-2 Jan22 0-0	Apr13 0-0	Oct23 4-2 Feb26 2-2
COWDENBEATH	Mar26 2-4 Mar30 3-1	Oct23 0-2 Mar09 2-3	Nov06 0-1	Sep29 2-1 Apr16 1-4	Oct09 4-3 Feb12 2-0		Apr06 1-0	Sep15 2-1 Apr23 1-2	Sep11 0-0	Jan29 3-0	Mar19 1-2	Nov20 0-1	Sep25 1-1 Feb26 0-1	Apr13 1-1
DUNFERMLINE A	Oct02 2-1 Feb05 3-1	Sep18 0-2 Mar23 1-2	Jan08 1-0	Sep04 1-1 Jan03 1-0	Sep22 4-0 Mar05 0-0	Oct30 1-1 Mar12 2-0		Oct16 1-0 Feb19 3-2	Apr09 3-1	Nov27 1-1	Apr27 1-0	Apr02 1-0	Apr20 1-0	Nov13 2-0 Apr30 3-0
E STIRLING	Oct09 1-1 Apr06 3-1	Sep04 2-2 Apr27 0-1	Sep29 0-0 Apr16 2-2	Mar19 1-1	Nov13 1-3	Apr09 2-0	Mar30 0-1		Oct23 1-0 Feb26 2-1	Feb05 3-2	Sep25 3-0 Nov27 1-3	Sep07 2-1	Oct30 0-3 Mar12 0-2	Sep18 2-1
FORFAR A	Apr02 2-1	Mar05 1-2	Jan29 1-0 Apr11 1-2	Oct30 1-2 Feb01 0-4	Sep18 1-3 Apr05 1-2	Nov13 1-3 Apr30 1-2	Sep15 1-1 Apr23 0-2	Dec27 4-1		Sep04 0-0 Apr20 0-0	Sep08 1-2	Mar29 4-0	Oct16 0-2 Feb19 1-2	Sep25 2-4
MEADOWBANK T	Dec18 1-3 Mar05 0-0	Sep08 1-1 Mar26 1-1	Jan26 2-0	Dec22 1-1	Apr09 3-3	Oct16 3-1 Feb19 1-2	Sep25 1-1 Jan22 0-0	Oct02 3-1 Mar16 1-4	Nov06 3-2		Apr16 1-1	Sep10 1-2 Apr06 0-0	Nov20 1-2	Oct09 2-1 Mar23 1-0
QUEEN'S PARK	Apr23 3-0	Apr12 1-1	Feb23 1-0	Sep18 3-1	Oct30 0-4 Mar12 4-0	Sep22 0-1 Mar05 1-0	Oct09 0-0 Feb12 3-0	Jan22 3-2	Oct06 3-0 Mar26 2-2	Sep29 1-0 Apr02 2-3		Apr20 1-1	Nov13 2-1	Sep04 1-3 Jan03 4-2
STENHOUSEMUIR	Apr28 1-3	Oct30 3-0	Sep15 2-1 Apr09 0-0	Mar16 3-1	Nov27 3-0	Sep18 0-2 Jan15 0-1	Sep29 2-1 Apr16 0-1	Oct12 1-0 Mar26 0-1	Oct02 2-1 Feb05 0-1	Nov13 1-0	Oct23 1-0 Feb26 2-1		Sep04 0-2 Feb22 0-3	Mar19 1-2
STIRLING A	Oct23 2-1 Mar16 0-0	Oct09 2-1	Mar05 0-0	Apr09 1-1	Oct02 3-2 Feb05 3-0	Nov27 4-1	Sep08 2-0 Mar26 1-0	Mar09 1-1	Feb15 0-0	Sep18 2-2 Mar30 1-0	Sep11 0-3 Apr30 1-1	Nov06 2-1		Sep29 2-0 Apr02 0-1
STRANRAER	Jan01 0-1	Sep15 3-0 Apr23 1-1	Oct06 4-1 Mar26 5-1	Oct16 3-1 Feb19 5-1	Dec27 1-1	Oct02 2-0 Feb05 3-1	Sep11 3-0	Nov20 3-0 Jan15 1-0	Nov27 2-1 Jan22 3-2	Dec11 2-0	Nov06 2-2	Sep22 2-1 Mar05 4-0	Apr16 0-1	

Scottish Football League Records
Season 1977-78

PREMIER

	ABERDEEN	AYR U	CELTIC	CLYDEBANK	DUNDEE U	HIBERNIAN	MOTHERWELL	PARTICK T	RANGERS	ST MIRREN
ABERDEEN		Nov12 0-0 Mar25 4-1	Sep17 2-1 Jan14 2-1	Oct29 1-1 Mar21 2-0	Aug27 0-0 Jan02 1-0	Oct15 1-2 Feb25 3-0	Dec03 4-1 Apr15 5-0	Sep24 2-1 Apr04 2-1	Aug13 3-1 Dec24 4-0	Dec10 3-1 Apr22 4-2
AYR U	Sep10 0-1 Jan07 1-1		Aug20 2-1 Dec31 2-1	Oct15 2-0 Feb25 0-0	Oct01 0-2 Feb04 0-1	Dec10 0-1 Apr22 2-0	Nov19 1-1 Apr01 0-1	Oct22 1-2 Mar15 1-3	Nov26 0-5 Apr08 2-5	Nov05 3-2 Mar18 0-1
CELTIC	Nov19 3-2 Apr01 2-2	Oct29 3-2 Mar11 3-0		Sep24 1-0 Apr17 5-2	Aug13 0-0 Dec24 1-0	Oct01 3-1 Apr05 2-1	Aug27 0-1 Jan02 0-1	Dec10 3-0 Apr22 5-2	Nov12 1-1 Mar25 2-0	Oct15 1-2 Feb25 1-2
CLYDEBANK	Aug20 1-3 Dec21 0-1	Dec17 0-2 Apr29 0-2	Apr08 3-2 Apr26 1-1		Sep17 0-3 May02 2-0	Nov05 1-0 Mar18 0-3	Oct08 2-1 Mar11 0-2	Sep10 0-4 Jan07 2-0	Feb19 0-3 Apr15 0-2	Oct22 2-2 Mar04 2-2
DUNDEE U	Nov05 0-1 Mar18 0-0	Apr15 1-0 Apr26 3-1	Oct22 1-2 Mar04 0-1	Nov19 4-0 Apr12 1-0		Sep10 2-0 Jan07 1-1	Sep24 3-2 Mar29 1-1	Dec17 2-2 Apr29 5-2	Oct08 0-1 Apr19 0-1	Aug20 2-1 Oct31 2-1
HIBERNIAN	Dec17 2-0 Apr29 1-1	Oct08 1-2 Mar22 4-2	Apr12 1-1 Apr15 4-1	Aug27 2-0 Jan02 2-0	Nov12 0-0 Mar25 3-1		Aug13 0-0 Dec24 2-1	Nov19 2-3 Apr01 3-1	Oct29 0-1 Mar29 1-1	Sep24 2-0 Mar11 5-1
MOTHERWELL	Oct01 1-1 Feb04 0-0	Sep17 5-0 Jan14 3-0	Nov05 2-3 Mar22 2-1	Dec10 2-1 Apr22 0-1	Nov26 0-0 Apr08 0-1	Oct22 1-0 Mar15 2-4		Aug20 3-0 Dec31 2-0	Oct15 1-4 Feb25 3-5	Sep10 0-3 Jan07 1-0
PARTICK T	Nov26 1-0 Apr08 0-2	Aug13 2-2 Dec24 4-1	Oct08 1-0 Mar29 0-4	Nov12 1-0 Mar25 0-0	Oct15 2-1 Feb25 0-2	Sep17 1-0 Apr19 2-1	Oct29 1-0 Mar18 2-3		Aug27 0-4 Jan02 1-2	Apr15 2-1 Apr26 5-0
RANGERS	Oct22 3-1 May04 0-3	Sep24 2-0 Aug12 1-1	Sep10 3-2 Jan07 3-1	Oct01 4-1 Feb04 1-0	Dec10 2-0 Apr22 3-0	Aug20 0-2 Dec31 0-0	Dec17 3-1 Apr29 2-0	Nov05 3-3 Mar21 2-1		Nov19 2-1 Apr01 1-1
ST MIRREN	Oct08 0-4 Mar29 1-2	Aug27 2-0 Jan02 2-3	Dec17 3-3 Apr29 3-1	Aug13 1-1 Dec24 2-0	Oct29 0-1 Mar15 1-2	Nov26 3-0 Apr08 3-0	Nov12 1-0 Mar25 1-1	Oct01 2-1 Feb04 1-1	Sep17 3-3 Jan14 0-2	

LEAGUE TABLES

PREMIER DIVISION

	P	W	D	L	F	A	W	D	L	F	A	Pts
Rangers	36	12	4	2	35	18	12	3	3	41	21	55
Aberdeen	36	14	3	1	43	13	8	6	4	25	16	53
Dundee U	36	9	4	5	28	17	7	4	7	14	15	40
Hibernian	36	10	5	3	35	16	5	2	11	16	27	37
Celtic	36	11	3	4	36	19	4	3	11	27	35	36
Motherwell	36	8	3	7	28	24	5	4	9	17	28	33
Partick T	36	10	2	6	25	23	4	3	11	27	41	33
St Mirren	36	7	5	6	29	25	4	3	11	23	38	30
Ayr U	36	5	3	10	17	28	4	3	11	19	40	24
Clydebank	36	5	3	10	16	33	1	4	13	7	31	19

DIVISION 1

	P	W	D	L	F	A	W	D	L	F	A	Pts
Morton	39	12	3	5	45	23	13	5	1	40	19	58
Hearts	39	13	4	2	37	18	11	6	3	40	24	58
Dundee	39	14	2	3	52	20	11	5	4	39	24	57
Dumbarton	39	11	8	1	38	20	5	9	5	27	28	49
Stirling A	39	7	6	7	32	27	8	6	5	28	25	42
Kilmarnock	39	8	7	4	29	16	6	5	9	23	30	40
Hamilton A	39	10	5	5	40	27	2	7	10	14	29	36
St Johnstone	39	7	2	10	19	21	8	4	8	33	43	36
Arbroath	39	7	7	6	26	30	4	6	9	16	25	35
Airdrie	39	8	5	7	31	30	4	5	10	19	34	34
Montrose	39	7	5	7	27	25	3	4	13	28	46	29
Queen of South	39	6	7	6	28	31	2	6	12	16	37	29
Alloa	39	4	6	9	28	41	4	2	14	16	43	24
East Fife	39	4	7	9	22	27	0	4	15	17	47	19

DIVISION 2

	P	W	D	L	F	A	W	D	L	F	A	Pts
Clyde	39	14	3	2	48	13	7	8	5	23	19	53
Raith R	39	10	7	2	36	15	9	8	3	27	19	53
Dunfermline A	39	11	6	2	41	14	7	6	7	23	27	48
Berwick R	39	10	9	1	41	22	6	7	6	27	29	48
Falkirk	39	7	8	5	26	26	8	6	5	25	20	44
Forfar A	39	12	3	4	40	24	5	5	10	21	31	42
Queen's Park	39	6	8	6	19	22	7	7	5	33	29	41
Albion R	39	8	5	6	36	26	8	3	9	32	42	40
E. Stirling	39	9	4	7	28	31	6	4	9	27	34	38
Cowdenbeath	39	8	2	10	38	36	5	6	8	37	42	34
Stranraer	39	9	3	8	33	29	4	4	11	21	34	33
Stenhousemuir	39	7	7	6	26	28	3	3	13	17	39	30
Meadowbank T	39	2	6	11	20	35	4	4	12	23	54	22
Brechin C	39	5	3	11	28	32	2	3	15	17	41	20

DIVISION 1

	AIRDRIE	ALLOA	ARBROATH	DUMBARTON	DUNDEE	EAST FIFE	HAMILTON A	HEARTS	KILMARNOCK	MONTROSE	MORTON	QUEEN OF SOUTH	ST JOHNSTONE	STIRLING A
AIRDRIE		Oct19 3-1 Mar18 2-1	Sep28 1-1 Apr15 2-1	Apr04 0-2	Oct22 3-0 Mar04 3-3	Nov05 2-1 Dec31 0-0	Sep10 1-1	Dec17 2-4	Nov26 1-2	Aug20 0-3 Jan07 4-3	Oct01 0-1 Feb28 2-3	Apr08 2-1 Apr29 2-0	Dec10 1-1	Sep17 0-1
ALLOA	Mar25 3-3		Aug13 1-1 Mar04 0-0	Dec24 2-3 Apr08 3-0	Sep14 3-5 Apr15 1-5	Nov26 3-2	Dec10 2-2	Mar11 0-2	Oct15 1-2	Oct01 1-3 Apr05 3-0	Oct29 1-3 Jan07 0-5	Sep17 2-2	Aug27 1-3 Jan02 0-0	Nov12 1-0
ARBROATH	Mar11 1-0	Oct22 2-0		Aug20 2-2 Jan07 1-1	Mar18 0-0	Oct01 2-2 Feb04 1-0	Nov05 2-1 Dec31 3-0	Dec24 0-7 Apr29 0-1	Nov19 2-2 Apr01 1-0	Sep10 0-3	Oct15 1-2 Feb25 2-2	Sep24 3-1	Sep14 2-2 Apr22 0-1	Dec10 1-3
DUMBARTON	Sep14 2-1 Apr22 2-1	Apr29 2-0	Oct29 1-0		Nov19 0-0 Apr12 2-1	Mar22 3-0	Oct15 1-0 Feb25 1-1	Aug13 2-2	Dec10 2-2	Sep24 4-0 Apr19 2-2	Nov12 1-1 Jan02 1-4	Aug27 2-0 Dec31 1-1	Oct01 5-1 Feb04 2-1	Mar25 2-2
DUNDEE	Aug13 3-0	Jan14 6-0	Oct19 2-3 Mar25 2-0	Sep17 2-1		Oct15 2-1 Feb25 2-0	Nov26 3-0	Oct19 1-1	Oct01 2-1 Mar22 5-2	Dec10 4-1	Dec24 3-1 Apr08 1-1	Mar11 3-0 Apr22 3-0	Nov12 5-3 Jan02 3-4	Aug27 0-1
EAST FIFE	Aug27 2-3	Sep24 2-2 Mar08 1-2	Dec03 0-0	Sep28 3-1 Apr15 0-0	Dec17 0-3		Mar18 0-0	Nov12 2-0 Jan02 1-2	Dec24 2-3 Apr08 0-0	Sep03 1-1	Nov19 2-3	Oct08 1-0 Mar12 2-0	Oct29 1-2 Jan07 1-3	Aug13 0-1 Mar04 1-1
HAMILTON A	Nov12 4-0 Jan02 0-0	Oct08 4-1 Feb28 0-1	Aug27 3-1	Dec17 3-3	Sep24 1-1 Mar08 0-1	Oct19 5-3 Mar25 3-2		Apr02 0-2	Sep14 2-1 Apr22 1-3	Nov19 4-1 Apr01 2-1	Mar21 0-0	Oct29 4-3	Aug13 0-1	Dec24 1-1 Apr29 3-1
HEARTS	Oct15 3-2 Feb25 3-0	Sep28 1-0 Apr22 2-1	Apr08 3-2	Oct22 2-1 Mar04 1-1	Aug20 2-1 Jan07 2-2	Sep10 4-1	Oct01 0-2 Feb04 1-0		Nov05 1-2 Dec31 3-0	Mar18 2-2	Dec10 1-1	Jan14 1-0	Sep17 3-0	Nov26 2-0
KILMARNOCK	Sep24 0-0 Jan21 1-1	Dec17 3-1 Feb25 4-0	Sep17 3-0	Oct08 2-2 Feb11 0-1	Dec03 1-0	Apr29 0-0	Jan14 1-1	Aug27 1-1		Mar15 5-1 Apr15 1-0	Aug13 0-3	Nov12 1-1 Jan02 2-0	Oct19 0-1 Mar25 2-0	Oct29 2-3
MONTROSE	Oct29 1-2	Dec03 1-2	Nov12 2-1 Jan02 1-0	Nov26 2-2	Oct08 1-2 Mar01 0-3	Jan14 2-0 Apr22 2-1	Sep17 1-2	Oct19 3-1 Mar25 0-0	Sep28 0-0		Aug27 0-1	Aug13 0-0 Mar04 5-2	Dec24 1-2 Apr08 3-2	Oct15 2-2
MORTON	Apr26 3-1	Aug13 4-2	Dec17 1-2	Sep10 0-0	Apr29 2-3	Sep17 1-0 Apr12 5-0	Sep28 4-1 Apr15 3-0	Oct08 5-3 Mar08 0-1	Oct22 0-2 Mar04 2-0	Nov05 2-2 Dec31 2-1		Oct19 0-1 Mar25 1-1	Apr05 4-1	Sep14 4-2 Jan14 2-0
QUEEN OF SOUTH	Dec24 2-2	Nov19 1-0 Apr01 1-0	Nov26 1-2 Feb15 0-1	Nov05 1-0	Sep28 0-2	Dec10 3-3	Aug20 2-1 Jan07 1-1	Sep14 3-3 Apr15 1-1	Sep10 1-0	Oct22 2-1	Mar18 2-3		Oct15 2-2 Feb25 2-2	Oct01 2-3 Mar08 1-4
ST JOHNSTONE	Oct08 2-1 Mar07 0-1	Nov05 0-1 Dec31 3-0	Mar22 2-1	Dec03 0-2	Sep10 1-2	Aug20 3-0	Oct22 1-0 Mar04 1-1	Nov19 0-1 Apr12 0-2	Mar18 2-0	Apr29 1-0	Sep24 1-3 Apr19 0-1	Dec17 1-2		Sep28 0-0 Apr15 1-3
STIRLING A	Nov19 0-1 Apr01 2-0	Sep10 1-1	Oct08 0-0 Feb28 0-0	Oct19 2-3 Mar18 2-2	Nov05 0-2 Dec31 2-3	Oct22 4-1	Apr08 1-0	Sep24 2-4 Mar15 1-2	Aug20 2-1 Jan07 0-0	Dec17 2-1 Feb25 4-2	Apr22 1-2	Mar22 1-1	Mar11 5-1	

DIVISION 2

	ALBION R	BERWICK R	BRECHIN C	CLYDE	COWDENBEATH	DUNFERMLINE A	E STIRLING	FALKIRK	FORFAR A	MEADOWBANK T	QUEEN'S PARK	RAITH R	STENHOUSEMUIR	STRANRAER
ALBION R		Apr05 3-3	Oct29 2-0	Aug13 0-0	Feb25 4-3	Oct08 3-0 Apr25 0-1	Sep13 0-1	Oct15 0-2 Dec24 1-1	Sep24 2-0 Apr18 1-1	Nov12 3-2	Oct22 3-3 Apr22 3-4	Mar18 1-2	Nov19 3-1 Apr27 2-0	Aug27 1-2 Jan02 4-0
BERWICK R	Oct01 2-0 Feb04 3-3		Dec10 3-2 Apr26 5-3	Nov12 0-0	Oct19 4-0 Mar18 1-1	Aug13 2-2	Nov19 1-1 Apr01 2-0	Oct29 1-1	Oct22 4-1 Apr22 2-1	Aug27 2-1 Jan02 3-0	Dec24 1-0	Sep14 0-0 Apr15 1-2	Sep24 2-2	Mar04 2-2
BRECHIN C	Aug20 1-2 Mar11 0-1	Oct08 2-3		Nov19 1-2 Apr17 0-2	Dec31 1-2	Sep14 0-1 Apr15 1-2	Feb25 3-2	Apr12 3-1	Nov05 0-0	Sep24 3-5 Apr19 0-1	Sep10 3-1 Mar29 2-2	Oct22 4-0	Apr29 2-1	Oct01 0-2 Apr05 2-2
CLYDE	Dec31 3-0 Apr08 4-0	Sep10 3-1 Mar22 3-1	Sep17 2-0		Sep14 3-2 Mar29 4-1	Sep28 2-0 Mar04 4-2	Oct22 2-2	Jan07 2-1	Jan14 2-1 Mar18 0-0	Apr05 7-0	Nov05 0-1	Oct08 0-0 Apr26 0-1	Aug20 3-0	Apr29 4-0
COWDENBEATH	Sep28 3-4 Mar04 7-1	Apr12 2-1	Aug13 2-1 Apr08 0-2	Apr15 1-2		Aug27 3-1 Jan02 1-1	Sep24 1-2 Apr18 1-2	Mar25 2-1	Nov19 1-4	Oct15 1-1 Dec24 4-0	Oct08 4-3 Apr26 1-3	Oct29 1-2	Mar08 1-2	Nov12 1-0 Dec17 1-3
DUNFERMLINE A	Dec10 2-1	Dec31 0-0 Apr08 1-1	Mar22 6-1	Feb25 1-1	Nov05 3-3		Oct19 1-0	Sep17 0-1 May02 2-0	Oct01 2-0 Apr10 1-1	Oct22 3-0 Apr22 7-1	Aug20 4-0 Apr18 0-0	Apr29 0-2	Sep10 2-1 Mar15 4-1	Nov26 2-0
E STIRLING	Jan14 1-0 Apr15 2-1	Sep17 2-7	Sep28 1-0 Mar04 1-0	Mar25 1-1 Apr22 2-1	Nov26 3-1	Mar18 1-0 Apr12 2-2		Aug27 0-2 Jan02 0-2	Oct15 0-1 Dec24 3-4	Aug13 1-2	Oct01 1-1	Nov12 1-2 Jan28 2-2	Apr25 2-1	Oct29 2-1
FALKIRK	Apr29 1-2	Aug20 2-1 Mar11 0-0	Oct19 1-0 Mar18 2-0	Sep24 2-1 Jan28 1-0	Oct22 2-2 Apr22 2-2	Nov19 0-0	Nov05 2-3		Sep10 1-2	Dec10 1-1 Apr25 2-4	Feb25 0-3	Oct01 2-2 Apr04 2-2	Dec31 1-1 Apr08 1-0	Apr18 1-0
FORFAR A	Nov26 3-1	Mar25 1-0	Aug27 4-1 Jan02 4-1	Oct19 1-2	Sep17 1-3 Apr01 2-1	Apr05 0-1	Apr29 3-3	Nov12 2-0 Mar22 2-2		Aug20 2-0	Dec17 3-1 Apr15 0-3	Aug13 1-0	Sep28 4-1 Mar04 1-1	Oct08 3-2 Apr25 3-1
MEADOWBANK T	Sep10 1-2 Dec17 0-3	Nov04 0-2	Nov26 0-0	Oct01 0-1 Feb04 1-1	Apr28 2-3	Mar24 2-4	Dec30 2-4 Apr08 1-2	Oct08 1-2	Oct29 1-0 Mar10 1-1		Sep17 1-1 Nov19 1-3	Mar04 0-0	Jan14 2-3	Oct19 2-2 Apr12 2-1
QUEEN'S PARK	Mar25 1-1	Oct15 0-0 Apr29 2-3	Nov12 0-2	Aug27 1-1 Jan02 0-1	Dec10 2-1	Oct29 1-1	Dec03 3-2 Feb08 0-0	Sep28 1-2 Mar04 1-1	Sep13 2-1	Apr01 1-1		Sep24 0-3 Mar21 0-0	Oct19 1-0 Apr11 1-0	Aug13 0-2 Apr08 2-0
RAITH R	Oct19 1-1 Apr12 2-0	Jan14 7-1	Mar25 3-1 Apr22 1-0	Dec10 1-1	Aug20 2-2 Mar11 2-2	Oct15 2-1 Dec24 0-1	Sep10 1-0	Mar29 1-1	Dec31 1-2 Apr08 2-0	Sep28 1-0 Feb25 4-0	Nov26 1-1		Nov05 3-0	Sep17 1-1
STENHOUSEMUIR	Sep17 2-4	Nov26 0-0 Apr18 1-1	Oct15 2-2 Dec24 1-0	Oct29 2-2 Mar11 0-2	Oct01 1-3 Feb04 0-4	Nov12 2-0	Oct08 4-1 Dec10 1-0	Aug13 1-1	Feb25 1-0	Sep14 2-2 Apr15 3-1	Mar18 0-2	Aug27 1-1 Jan02 1-2		Mar25 1-0
STRANRAER	Nov05 3-5	Sep28 0-1 Feb25 0-1	Feb04 1-1	Oct15 2-1 Dec24 2-1	Sep10 3-1	Sep24 1-1 Jan21 0-2	Aug20 3-2 Mar11 3-0	Sep14 0-2 Apr15 0-2	Dec10 4-1	Mar18 4-1	Dec31 1-1	Nov19 1-4 Apr01 1-0	Oct22 3-0 Apr22 1-2	

Scottish Football League Records
Season 1978-79

	ABERDEEN	CELTIC	DUNDEE U	HEARTS	HIBERNIAN	MORTON	MOTHERWELL	PARTICK T	RANGERS	ST MIRREN
ABERDEEN		Oct07 4-1 Mar03 0-1	Nov04 1-0 Mar17 0-2	Oct21 1-2 May02 5-0	Nov25 4-1 Apr07 0-0	Aug19 3-1 Dec30 1-2	Sep09 4-0 Mar26 8-0	Sep30 1-1 Feb28 2-1	Nov18 0-0 Apr25 2-1	Dec16 1-1 Apr28 1-2
CELTIC	Dec09 0-0 Apr21 1-1		Dec16 1-1 Apr28 2-1	Aug19 4-0 May14 1-0	Sep16 0-1 May02 3-1	Oct21 0-0 Mar28 3-0	Nov04 1-2 Mar17 2-1	Nov25 1-0 Apr07 2-0	Sep09 3-1 May21 4-2	Sep30 2-1 Apr25 2-1
DUNDEE U	Aug26 1-1 May05 2-2	Oct14 1-0 Apr11 2-1		Sep30 3-1 Apr25 2-1	Aug12 0-0 Dec23 2-1	Sep09 1-2 Mar10 4-1	Nov18 2-1 Mar31 2-1	Oct28 2-0 Mar14 2-1	Dec09 3-0 Apr21 1-2	Nov25 1-1 Apr07 2-0
HEARTS	Aug12 1-4 Dec23 0-0	Oct28 2-0 Apr18 0-3	Apr04 2-0 Apr14 0-3		Aug26 1-1 Mar28 1-2	Sep16 1-1 May07 0-1	Nov25 3-2 Apr07 3-0	Nov11 0-1 Apr11 0-2	Oct14 0-0 Feb24 3-2	Oct07 1-1 Feb10 1-2
HIBERNIAN	Sep23 2-1 Jan20 1-1	Nov18 2-2 Mar31 2-1	Oct21 1-1 Mar03 1-0	Nov04 1-2 Mar17 1-1		Sep30 1-1 Feb24 1-1	Dec09 2-2 Apr21 4-0	Dec16 0-0 Apr28 1-0	Aug19 0-0 May31 2-1	Sep09 1-0 Apr04 0-2
MORTON	Oct28 2-1 Apr04 0-1	Aug12 1-2 Dec23 1-0	Nov11 3-1 Mar24 3-1	Nov18 3-2 Mar31 2-2	Apr14 2-2 Apr18 3-0		Oct14 1-2 Mar14 6-0	Oct07 1-0 Feb17 2-2	Sep23 2-2 Jan20 0-2	Aug26 1-3 Apr11 1-0
MOTHERWELL	Nov11 1-1 Apr18 1-1	Aug26 1-5 Apr04 3-4	Sep16 0-1 Mar07 0-4	Sep23 0-1 Jan20 3-2	Oct07 2-3 Feb10 0-3	Dec16 1-1 Aug28 3-3		Aug12 0-1 Dec23 1-1	Apr14 2-0 May02 1-2	Oct28 1-2 Mar10 0-3
PARTICK T	Apr14 0-1 May11 1-2	Sep23 2-3 May07 1-2	Aug19 1-1 Mar28 1-2	Sep09 3-2 May05 2-0	Oct14 2-1 Apr25 6-1	Dec09 2-1 Apr21 2-1	Oct21 2-0 Mar03 0-0		Nov04 1-0 Mar17 0-2	Nov18 2-1 Mar31 3-1
RANGERS	Sep16 1-1 May07 2-0	Nov11 1-1 May05 1-0	Oct07 1-1 Feb10 1-0	Dec16 5-3 Apr28 4-0	Oct28 2-1 Mar14 1-0	Nov25 3-0 Apr07 1-1	Sep30 4-1 Apr10 3-0	Aug26 0-0 May23 1-0		Aug12 0-1 Dec23 1-0
ST MIRREN	Oct14 2-1 Feb24 2-2	Apr14 0-1 May11 0-2	Sep23 1-3 Jan20 2-1	Dec09 4-0 Apr21 2-1	Nov11 1-0 Mar24 2-3	Nov04 0-0 Mar17 3-1	Aug19 0-1 Feb17 1-0	Sep16 1-0 May02 1-1	Oct21 0-1 Mar27 1-2	

PREMIER DIVISION

	P	W	D	L	F	A	W	D	L	F	A	Pts
Celtic	36	12	4	2	32	13	9	2	7	29	24	48
Rangers	36	12	5	1	32	10	6	4	8	20	25	45
Dundee U	36	12	4	2	33	16	6	4	8	23	21	44
Aberdeen	36	9	4	5	38	16	4	10	4	21	20	40
Hibernian	36	7	9	2	23	16	5	4	9	21	32	37
St Mirren	36	8	3	7	23	20	7	3	8	22	21	36
Morton	36	9	4	5	34	23	3	8	7	18	30	36
Partick T	36	10	2	6	31	21	3	6	9	11	18	34
Hearts	36	5	5	8	19	25	3	2	13	20	46	23
Motherwell	36	2	5	11	20	38	3	2	13	13	48	17

LEAGUE TABLES

DIVISION 1

	P	W	D	L	F	A	W	D	L	F	A	Pts
Dundee	39	13	5	1	36	12	11	2	7	32	24	55
Kilmarnock	39	13	5	1	41	14	9	5	6	31	21	54
Clydebank	39	15	2	3	48	23	9	4	6	30	27	54
Ayr U	39	12	3	5	39	19	9	2	8	32	33	47
Hamilton A	39	13	4	2	39	17	4	5	11	23	43	43
Airdrie	39	9	4	7	44	33	7	4	8	28	28	40
Dumbarton	39	9	3	8	30	22	5	8	6	28	28	39
Stirling A	39	6	4	9	23	29	7	5	8	20	26	35
Clyde	39	8	3	8	30	29	5	5	10	24	36	34
Arbroath	39	8	6	6	33	26	3	5	11	17	35	33
Raith R	39	8	3	8	29	21	4	5	11	19	34	32
St Johnstone	39	6	8	6	32	28	4	3	12	25	38	31
Montrose	39	4	6	9	31	37	4	3	13	24	55	25
Queen of South	39	8	4	8	31	35	0	4	15	12	58	24

DIVISION 2

	P	W	D	L	F	A	W	D	L	F	A	Pts
Berwick R	39	11	6	3	45	22	11	4	4	37	22	54
Dunfermline A	39	13	6	1	41	19	6	8	5	25	21	52
Falkirk	39	13	4	3	39	16	6	8	5	27	21	50
East Fife	39	10	2	7	33	22	7	7	6	31	31	43
Cowdenbeath	39	10	5	4	37	22	6	5	9	26	36	42
Alloa	39	10	7	3	36	26	6	2	11	21	36	41
Albion R	39	9	6	4	28	17	6	4	10	29	39	40
Forfar A	39	9	7	4	35	25	4	5	10	20	27	38
Stranraer	39	11	1	7	32	27	7	1	12	20	39	38
Stenhousemuir	39	6	4	10	34	30	6	4	9	20	28	32
Brechin C	39	8	7	5	31	33	1	7	11	18	32	32
E. Stirling	39	10	4	5	42	31	2	4	14	19	56	32
Queen's Park	39	4	7	8	19	19	4	5	11	27	38	28
Meadowbank T	39	5	3	11	17	31	3	5	12	20	43	24

DIVISION 1

	AIRDRIE	ARBROATH	AYR U	CLYDE	CLYDEBANK	DUMBARTON	DUNDEE	HAMILTON A	KILMARNOCK	MONTROSE	QUEEN OF SOUTH	RAITH R	ST JOHNSTONE	STIRLING A
AIRDRIE		Oct14 1-1 Feb28 2-0	Sep06 2-4 Apr28 2-0	Dec09 2-2	Sep27 1-1 Apr07 1-3	Nov11 3-6	Dec23 0-2 Apr21 2-4	Aug26 4-1 Mar14 2-1	Oct20 4-1	Apr18 1-1 Apr05 8-2	Aug12 4-1	Sep16 3-0 Apr04 0-1	Nov25 0-1	Sep30 2-1
ARBROATH	Dec16 3-3		Mar24 4-1 Apr07 2-3	Oct21 0-2 Apr21 2-0	Apr28 1-1	Aug12 1-1 Mar03 1-1	Oct28 0-1	Nov11 3-0	Dec09 3-2 Feb10 0-1	Aug26 1-3 Feb21 4-0	Sep13 1-1	Sep30 0-5	Sep16 3-0 Apr04 3-1	Nov25 1-0 Jan20 0-0
AYR U	Mar10 0-0	Sep27 3-0		Nov25 2-0	Oct21 4-3	Sep16 2-5 Apr18 1-0	Aug12 0-1 Mar31 1-2	Sep13 1-2 Mar17 2-1	Aug26 0-0 Mar07 2-1	Dec16 5-0 Feb24 5-0	Oct28 1-1	Nov11 3-0	Sep30 1-0 Apr14 4-2	Dec09 0-1 Feb10 2-0
CLYDE	Oct07 2-1 Mar07 2-3	Dec23 1-0	Sep23 0-1 Feb28 0-5		Dec02 1-2 Apr14 0-1	Sep13 1-0	Nov18 2-1	Oct14 2-3	Sep26 1-1 Apr07 0-1	Oct28 2-4	Aug26 3-0 Feb21 3-0	Aug12 3-1 Mar31 1-1	Nov11 6-4	Mar10 0-0
CLYDEBANK	Mar24 4-1	Sep06 5-2 Mar10 2-2	Dec23 3-1 Apr21 0-1	Sep30 1-4		Aug26 1-1 Apr25 3-1	Nov25 2-1	Sep16 4-1 Feb17 3-1	Aug12 2-1 Mar31 1-2	Nov11 1-0	Oct14 2-0 Feb28 3-1	Oct28 2-1	Mar07 3-0 Apr18 1-0	Sep13 5-2
DUMBARTON	Sep09 1-1 May02 0-1	Mar31 0-1	Nov18 2-0	Mar17 3-0 Apr04 0-0	Nov04 1-2		Sep27 0-0 Apr07 3-2	Sep23 2-0 Apr16 3-0	Mar13 0-3 Apr28 1-3	Sep30 4-1	May05 4-1	Dec09 1-3 Mar28 3-1	Oct14 2-0	Aug19 0-1 May07 0-2
DUNDEE	Oct21 1-0	Aug19 2-0 May06 0-2	May10 2-2	Sep16 2-0 Apr18 2-0	Sep23 2-0 Feb21 2-1	Mar24 2-0		Dec02 1-1 Apr14 4-3	Nov11 0-0	Sep06 1-1 Apr28 1-0	Oct07 5-0 Apr04 4-0	May08 2-0	Nov04 1-1	Dec16 2-1
HAMILTON A	Nov04 2-0	Sep09 3-1 Mar07 2-0	Feb03 3-1	Dec16 3-3 Feb24 2-0	Nov18 1-0	Nov25 5-0	Sep30 1-2		Oct21 2-3 Apr21 1-0	Dec09 3-1	Sep27 3-2 Mar24 0-0	Sep06 1-1	Aug19 2-1 Dec30 2-1	Mar03 1-1 Mar31 2-0
KILMARNOCK	Aug19 2-0 Apr11 1-0	Oct07 3-1	Nov04 1-2	Mar24 2-1	Mar03 0-0	Sep06 0-0	Sep09 1-1 Apr25 2-1	Dec23 4-0		Sep23 2-2 Jan20 4-1	Dec02 0-0 Apr14 3-1	Oct14 3-0 Feb24 2-1	Feb03 3-2 Mar17 3-1	Nov18 5-0
MONTROSE	Sep13 2-2	Nov04 3-0	Oct14 4-6	Aug19 2-2 Apr11 4-0	Sep09 1-3 Mar28 1-2	Apr14 2-1 May09 0-2	Mar14 0-2	Oct07 1-1 Feb28 2-4	Nov28 0-4		Mar07 6-1	Dec23 0-0 Apr21 1-1	Mar03 1-3	Sep27 1-1 Mar24 0-2
QUEEN OF SOUTH	Mar03 1-3 Mar31 1-5	Feb24 1-1 Mar17 2-2	Aug19 1-0 Dec30 0-1	Nov04 3-0	Dec16 2-1	Oct21 0-2 Apr21 1-3	Dec09 3-1	Apr07 3-3	Sep30 2-1	Sep16 1-3 Nov18 2-1		Nov25 2-1	Sep06 1-1 Apr28 1-2	Sep09 1-2 May02 3-2
RAITH R	Nov18 2-0	Apr14 1-2 Apr18 1-0	Sep09 0-0 Mar14 2-0	Mar03 1-2	Aug19 4-2 May02 1-2	Oct07 0-0	Sep13 2-4 Apr11 1-2	Mar10 0-1 Apr28 2-0	Dec16 1-3	Oct21 3-1	Sep23 4-0 Jan20 3-0		Apr25 0-0	Nov04 1-2
ST JOHNSTONE	Sep23 0-2 Mar27 1-3	Nov18 1-1	May05 4-2	Sep09 1-1 Mar14 0-1	Oct07 2-3	Dec16 2-2 Mar20 2-2	Aug26 0-2 May02 3-2	Oct28 0-0	Sep13 0-0	Aug12 3-2 Mar31 4-0	Mar10 5-2	Sep27 1-1 Apr07 3-0		Oct21 0-0 Apr21 0-2
STIRLING A	Apr14 2-1 Apr25 1-2	Sep23 2-1	Oct07 1-2	Sep06 1-4 Apr28 3-2	Mar13 2-3 Mar17 0-0	Oct28 1-1	Oct14 1-0 Mar28 0-1	Aug12 0-0	Sep16 1-4 Apr04 0-0	Apr07 0-1	Nov11 4-1	Aug26 0-1 Mar07 3-0	Dec23 1-5	

DIVISION 2

	ALBION R	ALLOA	BERWICK R	BRECHIN C	COWDENBEATH	DUNFERMLINE A	EAST FIFE	E STIRLING	FALKIRK	FORFAR A	MEADOWBANK T	QUEEN'S PARK	STENHOUSEMUIR	STRANRAER
ALBION R		Sep23 1-2 May10 2-1	Apr25 0-2	Oct07 3-2 May03 2-2	Mar13 1-1	Mar10 1-1 Apr28 1-0	Mar31 2-0	May08 1-1	Aug19 1-1 May01 0-0	Sep13 3-0	Sep09 1-2 Apr03 2-0	Apr14 1-0 Apr18 4-0	Oct21 0-1	Nov04 2-1
ALLOA	Nov25 2-6		Sep13 2-1	Aug19 1-1 Apr19 1-0	Sep16 2-4 Nov18 4-0	Sep09 1-1 May05 2-0	Oct21 0-0 Apr21 4-3	Dec09 2-2	Mar10 3-3 Apr28 2-0	Feb24 2-0	Sep30 1-1	Sep27 1-0 Mar24 1-1	Nov04 2-1	Mar03 3-1 Mar31 0-1
BERWICK R	Sep16 2-0 Mar28 5-1	Feb03 0-1 Mar17 3-2		Nov25 2-0 Apr04 1-0	Sep27 4-1	Oct14 2-2 Feb24 0-0	Sep09 1-2	Sep30 5-2 Apr14 5-1	Mar31 1-1	Dec09 2-4 Feb10 1-0	Aug26 0-0	Mar10 1-1	Aug19 6-1 Apr10 3-2	Oct21 1-1
BRECHIN C	Dec09 1-1	Oct28 4-2	Sep23 1-2		Aug12 1-1 Mar31 2-1	Mar07 1-6 Apr16 0-0	Apr07 1-1	Sep16 1-1 Dec06 3-1	Sep30 1-4	Aug26 3-2 Apr23 1-0	Sep06 2-2 Apr28 2-1	Oct21 2-1 Apr21 1-1	Mar28 1-3 Apr30 2-1	Apr11 1-2
COWDENBEATH	Oct14 4-1 Feb24 3-1	Apr04 5-1	Apr07 1-3 Mar02 1-2	Mar03 0-0		Nov04 1-1	Sep23 1-0 Nov25 1-1	Mar05 1-2 May10 2-1	Apr21 1-1	Sep30 2-1	Aug19 2-1 Apr25 4-1	Dec09 2-2	Sep09 1-2	Sep06 2-0 Apr28 3-1
DUNFERMLINE A	Sep06 2-1	Nov11 2-2	May13 1-0	Sep13 1-1	Aug26 3-0 Apr18 2-0		Oct07 5-1 Mar28 1-1	Oct28 2-1	May16 1-1	Apr07 2-1 May02 2-2	Oct21 2-1 Feb28 1-0	Aug12 0-3 Mar03 2-2	Mar13 1-0 Apr14 2-1	Sep16 6-1 Mar18 3-0
EAST FIFE	Aug12 0-2 Mar03 1-2	Dec23 3-0	Nov11 2-4 Dec16 2-1	Sep27 0-0 Mar24 1-0	Jan20 0-1	Dec09 2-1		Sep06 5-0	Oct14 1-0	Oct28 1-2	Sep16 2-2 Nov18 2-3	Aug26 3-2 Apr10 3-0	Feb03 3-0	Sep30 2-0 Apr14 0-2
E STIRLING	Sep26 3-3 Apr07 0-1	Oct07 3-2 Feb10 3-1	Apr19 1-4	Feb28 3-2	Sep13 4-1	Aug19 1-1 Apr12 0-2	Mar10 0-1 Apr29 2-1		Nov04 1-1	Oct21 1-1 Apr21 3-1	Nov25 4-1	Sep09 4-2 Apr03 4-2	Mar31 1-3	Jan27 4-1
FALKIRK	Oct28 2-1	Sep06 1-0	Aug12 6-0 Mar03 1-1	Apr14 3-0 Apr25 2-0	Oct21 2-1 May08 0-3	Sep23 1-1 Nov25 4-1	Feb28 0-1 Apr18 2-5	Aug26 2-0 Mar28 1-1		Nov11 1-0	Oct07 6-0	Mar14 1-0	Sep16 1-0 Mar20 1-1	Mar24 2-0
FORFAR A	Apr16 1-1 May06 1-1	Oct14 2-1 Mar28 2-0	Oct07 2-2	Nov04 2-2	Dec02 4-2 Apr14 2-0	Sep26 1-2	Aug19 3-1 Mar06 1-1	Dec23 4-0	Sep09 1-0 Apr04 1-4		Mar31 2-3	Nov18 2-1	Sep06 1-1 Mar10 0-0	Sep23 1-3 Mar14 2-0
MEADOWBANK T	Nov11 2-0	Dec02 0-1 Apr14 1-1	Nov03 0-5 Mar07 0-1	Mar10 0-3	Oct28 0-2	Apr21 1-3	Mar20 1-3	Sep23 3-1 Jan20 3-1	Dec09 1-2 Feb10 1-1	Aug12 0-0 Mar03 1-0		Oct14 0-4	Sep27 2-0 Mar24 1-2	Sep13 0-1
QUEEN'S PARK	Sep30 2-0	Apr07 0-1	Sep06 0-1 Apr28 1-1	Dec23 1-1	Oct07 1-1 Apr30 1-2	Mar30 0-1	Nov04 1-1	Nov10 4-0	Sep13 0-3 Mar17 1-2	Sep16 1-1 Apr25 0-1	Feb24 1-1 Mar27 3-0		Nov25 0-0	Aug19 0-1 Dec16 2-1
STENHOUSEMUIR	Dec23 3-2 Apr21 2-3	Aug26 0-2 Mar06 0-1	Oct28 0-2	Oct14 4-2	Nov11 1-1 Feb28 0-0	Sep30 1-2	Sep13 1-2 Apr24 2-2	Aug12 0-2 Mar03 5-0	Nov18 1-2	Apr28 1-1	Apr07 2-0	Sep23 1-2 Jan20 5-1		Dec09 4-1 Apr03 1-2
STRANRAER	Aug26 3-1 Feb17 0-1	Aug12 4-0	Dec23 0-0 Apr21 1-5	Sep09 1-0 Nov11 4-2	Mar10 2-4	Apr24 1-0	Dec02 2-4	Oct14 1-0 Feb24 6-2	Sep27 1-0 Apr07 2-1	Nov25 0-3	Feb03 3-1 Mar17 1-0	Oct28 0-2	Oct07 0-1	

Scottish Football League Records
Season 1979-80

PREMIER

	ABERDEEN	CELTIC	DUNDEE	DUNDEE U	HIBERNIAN	KILMARNOCK	MORTON	PARTICK T	RANGERS	ST MIRREN
ABERDEEN		Sep22 1-2 Jan19 0-0	Mar19 3-0 Apr07 2-1	Nov03 0-3 Mar15 2-1	Aug18 3-0 Apr16 1-1	Oct13 3-1 Feb23 1-2	Nov10 1-2 Mar22 1-0	Oct20 1-1 Mar01 1-1	Sep15 3-1 Jan12 3-2	Dec15 2-0 Apr26 2-0
CELTIC	Apr05 1-2 Apr23 1-3		Oct13 3-0 Feb23 2-2	Sep08 2-2 Jan05 1-0	Nov17 3-0 Mar29 4-0	Aug25 5-0 Apr16 2-0	Aug11 3-2 Dec22 3-1	Dec15 5-1 Apr26 2-1	Oct27 1-0 Apr22 1-0	Sep29 3-1 Mar12 2-2
DUNDEE	Sep29 0-4 Feb02 1-3	Apr19 5-1 Apr30 0-2		Oct20 1-0 Mar01 1-1	Nov03 2-1 Mar15 3-0	Dec15 3-1 Apr26 0-2	Sep15 4-3 Jan12 1-0	Sep08 2-2 Jan05 1-1	Nov24 3-1 Apr05 1-4	Aug18 4-1 Apr02 1-3
DUNDEE U	Aug25 1-3 Apr29 1-1	Nov10 0-1 Apr08 3-0	Aug11 3-0 Dec22 2-0		Oct13 2-0 Feb23 1-0	Oct27 4-0 Mar08 0-0	Apr12 2-0 Apr23 2-0	Sep22 2-1 Mar12 0-0	Oct06 0-0 Mar19 0-0	Nov17 0-0 Mar29 0-0
HIBERNIAN	Oct27 1-1 May03 0-5	Sep15 1-3 Jan12 1-1	Aug25 5-2 Mar25 2-0	Apr02 0-2 Apr19 0-2		Nov10 1-1 Apr21 1-2	Oct06 1-1 Feb09 3-2	Dec01 2-1 May05 0-1	Aug11 1-3 Dec22 2-1	Sep22 0-2 Apr29 2-1
KILMARNOCK	Apr01 0-4 Apr19 1-3	Nov03 2-0 Mar15 1-1	Oct06 3-1 Feb09 1-1	Aug18 1-0 Dec29 0-0	Sep08 1-0 Jan05 3-1		Mar12 1-1 Apr05 0-2	Nov17 0-1 Mar29 0-1	Sep29 2-1 Apr23 1-0	Oct20 1-1 Mar01 1-1
MORTON	Sep08 3-2 Jan05 1-0	Oct20 1-0 Mar01 0-1	Nov17 2-0 Mar29 1-1	Sep29 4-1 May01 0-0	Dec15 2-0 Apr26 1-1	Sep22 3-1 Jan19 1-2		Aug18 2-1 Dec29 1-3	Dec08 0-1 Apr19 0-1	Nov03 0-0 Mar15 2-1
PARTICK T	Aug11 1-0 May07 1-1	Oct06 0-0 Feb09 1-1	Nov10 2-3 Apr13 3-0	Nov28 1-1 Apr05 2-2	Sep29 2-1 Apr23 1-0	Sep15 0-0 Jan12 1-1	Oct27 1-4 Apr02 0-1		Aug25 2-1 May03 4-3	Apr09 1-1 Apr19 1-2
RANGERS	Nov17 0-1 Mar29 2-2	Aug18 2-2 Dec29 1-1	Sep22 2-0 Mar12 1-0	Dec15 2-1 Apr26 2-1	Oct20 2-0 Mar01 1-0	Dec01 2-1 Apr30 1-0	Oct13 2-2 Feb23 3-1	Nov03 2-1 Mar15 0-0		Sep08 3-1 Jan05 1-2
ST MIRREN	Oct06 2-2 Feb09 1-1	Dec01 2-1 May03 0-0	Oct27 4-2 Mar08 2-1	Sep15 3-2 Jan12 2-1	Nov24 2-1 Apr05 2-0	Aug11 2-2 Apr12 3-1	Aug25 0-3 Jan01 2-2	Oct13 1-2 Feb23 3-0	Nov10 2-1 May07 4-1	

LEAGUE TABLES

PREMIER DIVISION

	P	W	D	L	F	A	W	D	L	F	A	Pts
Aberdeen	36	10	4	4	30	18	9	6	3	38	18	48
Celtic	36	13	3	2	44	17	5	8	5	17	21	47
St Mirren	36	11	5	2	37	23	4	7	7	19	26	42
Dundee U	36	9	7	2	23	6	3	6	9	20	24	37
Rangers	36	11	5	2	29	16	4	2	12	21	30	37
Morton	36	9	4	5	24	16	5	4	9	27	30	36
Partick T	36	6	8	4	24	22	5	6	7	19	25	36
Kilmarnock	36	7	6	5	19	19	4	5	9	17	33	33
Dundee	36	9	3	6	33	30	1	3	14	14	43	26
Hibernian	36	6	4	8	23	31	0	2	16	6	36	18

DIVISION 1

	P	W	D	L	F	A	W	D	L	F	A	Pts
Hearts	39	13	6	1	33	18	7	7	5	25	21	53
Airdrie	39	14	2	4	46	21	7	7	5	32	26	51
Ayr U	39	11	5	4	37	22	5	7	7	27	29	44
Dumbarton	39	10	4	5	34	22	9	2	9	25	29	44
Raith R	39	8	7	5	30	22	6	8	5	29	24	43
Motherwell	39	9	7	3	32	17	7	4	9	27	31	43
Hamilton A	39	11	5	3	39	20	4	5	11	21	39	40
Stirling A	39	7	6	7	23	19	6	7	6	17	21	39
Clydebank	39	9	6	5	32	21	5	2	12	26	36	36
Dunfermline A	39	7	7	5	23	24	4	6	10	16	33	35
St Johnstone	39	5	5	9	28	32	7	5	8	29	42	34
Berwick R	39	5	8	7	36	31	3	7	9	21	33	31
Arbroath	39	7	5	7	31	32	2	5	13	19	47	28
Clyde	39	3	6	10	22	34	3	7	10	21	35	25

DIVISION 2

	P	W	D	L	F	A	W	D	L	F	A	Pts
Falkirk	39	11	7	2	34	12	8	5	6	31	23	50
E. Stirling	39	10	3	6	28	20	11	4	5	27	20	49
Forfar A	39	9	6	5	35	27	10	2	7	28	24	46
Albion R	39	11	5	3	46	21	5	7	8	27	35	44
Queen's Park	39	8	5	6	32	21	8	4	8	27	26	41
Stenhousemuir	39	10	1	8	32	22	6	8	6	24	29	41
Cowdenbeath	39	9	7	4	33	24	5	5	9	21	28	40
Brechin C	39	9	4	6	35	23	6	6	8	26	36	40
Montrose	39	8	5	7	37	35	6	5	8	23	28	38
East Fife	39	9	6	5	26	21	3	3	13	19	36	33
Stranraer	39	7	4	8	26	25	5	4	11	25	40	32
Meadowbank T	39	7	2	11	17	29	5	6	8	25	41	32
Queen of South	39	6	6	8	29	29	5	3	11	22	40	31
Alloa	39	8	4	7	32	28	3	3	14	12	36	29

DIVISION 1

	AIRDRIE	ARBROATH	AYR U	BERWICK R	CLYDE	CLYDEBANK	DUMBARTON	DUNFERMLINE	HAMILTON A	HEARTS	MOTHERWELL	RAITH R	ST JOHNSTON	STIRLING A
AIRDRIE		Sep08 4-1 Jan05 5-2	Sep05 6-2 Apr26 2-1	Mar01 3-1 Mar29 2-1	Dec08 1-2	Mar15 1-0 Feb20 3-1	Sep15 1-0 Nov17 0-0	Sep29 5-1	Nov03 1-0	Apr05 0-1	Oct20 4-0 Apr19 3-1	Aug18 0-0 Dec29 0-3	Nov24 4-2	Dec15 1-2
ARBROATH	Nov10 1-0		Dec22 1-1	Dec01 1-1 Apr12 1-0	Oct13 3-2 Feb23 0-0	Sep19 3-2	Apr05 4-1	Sep15 1-1 Jan12 1-3	Sep05 1-2 Apr26 2-5	Aug11 1-2	Oct27 3-2	Oct06 3-1	Aug25 2-2 Jan01 1-2	Mar05 1-3 Mar15 1-2
AYR U	Mar08 1-2	Oct20 2-1 Apr19 5-0		Sep19 3-2 Mar25 1-0	Aug25 0-0 Mar12 2-1	Nov17 2-2	Aug11 1-2 Mar29 1-0	Sep11 3-0	Sep08 0-3 Jan05 4-1	Oct27 2-0	Dec15 0-0 Feb23 0-5	Dec01 3-0	Sep22 5-1 Apr05 2-2	Oct06 0-0
BERWICK R	Aug11 2-2	Sep29 7-2	Nov24 2-4		Dec22 1-1 Apr19 0-2	Oct13 2-3 Feb23 2-1	Feb02 0-2 Mar15 3-0	Oct27 0-1	Dec08 1-1	Aug25 1-3 Nov03 0-0	Nov10 2-2	Sep05 0-0 Apr26 3-3	Sep15 1-2 Jan12 5-0	Sep22 3-1 Apr05 1-1
CLYDE	Oct06 2-3 Feb09 1-3	Dec15 0-2	Nov03 3-3	Oct20 1-2		Aug18 1-0 Dec29 0-2	Sep05 0-2 Apr26 1-2	Nov10 1-1	Sep15 4-0 Jan12 2-2	Dec01 2-2 Apr13 2-1	Sep22 0-1 Apr16 0-2	Mar01 0-4	Mar15 1-1	Apr09 1-1
CLYDEBANK	Sep11 2-2	Jan19 5-1 Feb16 3-1	Sep15 1-0 Jan12 1-0	Dec15 0-0	Oct27 2-2		Aug25 2-1 Apr02 2-2	Mar19 3-1 Apr09 0-1	Oct20 4-0 Apr19 2-0	Nov10 1-1	Aug11 1-1 Mar01 1-2	Mar25 1-0 Apr05 0-3	Sep29 1-2	Apr26 0-1
DUMBARTON	Jan12 0-0	Sep22 1-0 Mar25 2-3	Mar01 0-3	Sep01 4-1	Mar08 3-1	Nov03 1-0		Nov24 2-1	Aug18 3-2 Dec29 4-0	Oct06 1-1 Feb09 1-1	Dec01 1-1 Apr12 1-0	Oct13 4-2	Feb16 0-1 Apr19 5-2	Sep08 1-2 Jan05 0-1
DUNFERMLINE A	Dec01 1-0 Apr12 3-3	Nov17 1-1	Mar05 2-2 Mar15 0-0	Aug18 1-2 Dec29 2-1	Sep08 1-1 Jan05 3-1	Oct06 1-3	Sep19 1-3 Mar12 0-2		Apr05 0-0	Mar25 0-3	Sep05 2-0	Nov03 1-0	Oct13 3-2 Feb23 1-0	Mar01 0-0
HAMILTON A	Aug25 4-3 Mar25 1-3	Mar08 1-0	Nov10 0-0	Oct06 1-2 Feb09 4-0	Nov28 3-1	Dec22 3-0	Oct27 1-0	Sep22 2-0 Apr15 4-0		Oct13 3-1	Sep11 3-2	Sep19 1-3 Jan19 1-1	Aug11 2-2 Mar29 1-1	Dec01 1-1 Apr12 3-0
HEARTS	Sep22 2-2 Apr30 1-0	Mar01 2-1 Mar29 1-0	Aug18 4-2 Apr01 0-1	Apr23 1-1	Sep29 4-1	Sep08 2-1 Jan05 3-3	Dec08 1-0	Oct20 2-1 Apr19 0-0	Dec15 0-0 Feb23 1-0		Nov24 2-1	Apr09 2-2	Sep05 2-1	Sep15 2-1 Nov17 1-0
MOTHERWELL	Dec22 2-1	Aug18 1-1 Oct29 0-0	Oct13 0-2	Sep08 1-1 Jan05 1-1	Apr05 3-0	Mar29 3-2	Sep29 3-0	Mar08 1-1 Apr26 1-1	Mar03 2-1 Mar15 4-0	Sep19 4-2 Jan19 0-0		Nov17 1-2	Dec08 3-0 Feb09 1-2	Nov03 1-0
RAITH R	Oct27 1-2	Dec08 1-1 Feb09 2-1	Sep29 2-2 Apr12 2-0	Mar19 2-1	Aug11 0-0 Mar29 1-1	Sep22 2-4	Dec15 0-1 Feb23 4-0	Sep25 0-0 Jan01 1-0	Feb16 2-1	Sep11 3-2 Mar15 0-0	Sep15 5-2 Jan12 0-1		Nov10 1-2	Oct20 1-1
ST JOHNSTONE	Sep19 1-1 Mar19 1-2	Nov03 3-0	Aug23 2-1	Nov17 3-3	Sep11 3-2 Apr02 1-2	Dec01 0-1 Apr12 3-1	Oct20 2-4	Dec15 1-3	Mar01 0-1	Apr16 0-1 Apr26 0-3	Oct06 1-3	Sep08 2-2 Mar08 2-2		Aug18 3-0 Mar12 0-0
STIRLING A	Oct13 0-0 Feb23 0-3	Sep11 1-1	Dec08 1-1 Feb09 0-2	Apr16 1-1	Sep19 2-0 Nov24 2-1	Sep05 2-0 Mar08 2-0	Nov10 2-3	Aug11 4-0 Mar29 1-0	Sep29 2-2	Jan12 0-1	Aug25 2-0 Mar19 0-1	Apr02 0-1 Apr19 0-0	Oct27 1-2	

DIVISION 2

	ALBION R	ALLOA	BRECHIN C	COWDENBEATH	EAST FIFE	E STIRLING	FALKIRK	FORFAR A	MEADOWBANK T	MONTROSE	QUEEN OF SOUTH	QUEEN'S PARK	STENHOUSEMUIR	STRANRAER
ALBION R		Sep11 2-0 Feb09 1-0	Feb16 4-0 Apr28 1-1	Sep08 2-1 Jan19 1-0	Mar08 5-1 Apr26 4-0	Mar04 1-4	Dec13 2-2	Nov03 5-0	Nov18 3-1	Dec29 1-1	Mar29 5-1	Aug18 3-0 Jan01 2-2	Sep29 1-2	Sep22 1-3 Apr05 2-2
ALLOA	Mar15 1-1		Aug11 8-3 Mar29 1-4	Oct06 1-0 Feb16 3-2	Sep22 1-0	Mar26 2-3	Sep08 3-2 Mar11 1-2	Dec01 0-3 Apr12 1-1	Sep19 4-0 Mar04 2-1	Aug25 0-1 Jan12 2-1	Dec29 0-1	Apr26 0-1	Oct27 1-1	Nov17 1-1
BRECHIN C	Oct06 2-0	Mar01 1-1		Nov17 1-3	Dec22 1-0	Mar08 2-0 Apr26 1-1	Apr23 1-1	Aug18 2-0 Mar26 0-1	Sep08 3-1 Jan19 1-1	Sep19 1-2 Mar12 2-3	Dec01 3-0 Apr12 4-1	Nov03 4-1	Oct20 2-3	Sep11 2-1 Apr02 2-3
COWDENBEATH	Nov10 2-2	Dec08 2-1	Sep15 1-0 Apr16 2-3		Oct27 2-2	Aug25 2-2 Feb20 0-1	Nov24 0-0	Sep22 1-0 Apr05 0-1	Sep05 1-2 Apr26 2-2	Aug11 4-2	Oct13 3-1 Feb23 2-2	Sep29 1-0	Mar04 3-1 Mar15 1-1	Mar25 2-0 Apr19 2-1
EAST FIFE	Sep05 1-0	Dec15 2-1 Apr05 1-0	Oct13 0-1 Feb23 2-1	Aug18 4-0 Jan01 2-1		Dec29 0-3	Jan12 1-0 Mar15 0-1	Mar01 2-2	Nov03 2-2	Dec01 1-1 Apr12 2-0	Oct06 1-2	Nov17 1-1	Sep19 1-1 Mar25 1-3	Sep08 1-0 Jan19 1-1
E STIRLING	Sep18 2-0 Jan05 1-1	Oct13 1-0 Feb23 1-2	Sep05 2-1	Nov03 0-1	Oct20 2-1 Aug19 1-0		Aug18 2-3 Jan01 2-1	Nov28 2-1	Apr01 4-1	Apr16 3-1	Sep08 0-1 Jan19 0-1	Mar01 0-0 Mar29 1-3	Feb16 1-1	Sep29 3-1
FALKIRK	Dec22 4-0 Feb23 1-0	Nov10 2-0	Sep22 3-2 Apr05 0-0	Sep19 3-0 Apr09 0-0	Sep11 0-0	Oct27 1-2		Oct06 1-2	Dec01 2-2	Mar08 0-0 Apr26 2-1	Nov17 3-1	Oct20 3-0 Apr19 2-1	Aug11 4-1 Mar29 0-0	Aug25 3-0 Jan26 0-0
FORFAR A	Aug25 6-2 Jan12 2-2	Sep29 0-2	Oct27 1-1	Apr21 2-1	Aug11 1-0 Mar29 0-4	Sep15 1-2 Jan26 1-1	Dec08 2-1 Feb16 2-0		Dec29 5-3 Apr19 0-0	Oct13 1-1 Feb23 1-2	Sep05 3-1 Mar08 0-0	Sep10 2-1	Nov10 2-3	Nov24 3-0
MEADOWBANK T	Sep15 1-2 Apr22 1-1	Nov24 2-1	Nov10 0-1	Mar08 0-2	Aug24 2-0 Jan30 3-1	Sep11 0-1 Mar15 0-1	Sep29 0-3 Apr12 0-5	Oct20 1-0		Oct27 2-1	Sep22 2-1	Feb16 0-2 Mar19 1-2	Dec22 0-0 Feb23 0-1	Aug11 2-1 Mar29 0-3
MONTROSE	Oct20 0-2 Apr19 1-4	Nov03 2-0	Nov24 2-2	Mar01 1-1 Mar29 1-1	Sep29 1-1	Sep22 2-0 Apr05 2-1	Sep05 1-3	Dec22 1-4	Aug18 3-0 Jan01 3-3		Feb09 1-3 Mar15 3-2	Sep08 2-1 Jan19 0-2	Sep15 0-2 Nov17 5-0	Dec08 6-3
QUEEN OF SOUTH	Aug11 2-1 Mar01 3-3	Oct20 0-1 Apr19 0-0	Sep29 1-1	Dec22 2-2	Dec08 2-4 Mar19 1-0	Nov10 1-2	Sep15 2-0 Mar25 0-2	Apr26 2-3	Apr05 0-2 Apr15 5-0	Sep11 1-2		Nov24 3-2 Mar04 0-0	Aug25 2-1 Mar12 1-1	Oct27 1-2
QUEEN'S PARK	Oct27 2-2	Sep05 7-0 Mar08 2-2	Aug25 1-3 Jan12 4-0	Nov28 1-1 Apr01 0-2	Sep15 1-2 Jan26 3-1	Aug11 2-0	Dec29 2-2	Feb09 1-0 Mar15 0-1	Oct06 0-1	Nov10 1-0	Sep18 2-1		Apr05 1-1	Oct13 0-2 Feb23 2-0
STENHOUSEMUIR	Dec01 1-3 Apr12 0-1	Aug18 3-1 Mar19 2-0	Apr08 2-0 Apr19 0-1	Sep11 4-1	Nov24 2-0	Oct06 0-1 Dec08 1-0	Mar01 1-1	Sep08 4-0 Jan19 1-5	Oct13 0-1	Jan26 2-1	Nov03 2-1	Sep22 0-1 Apr22 1-3		Mar08 6-1
STRANRAER	Apr16 2-0	Sep15 1-0 Apr09 4-0	Mar15 1-1	Oct20 0-2	Nov10 4-2	Dec01 1-2 Apr12 0-0	Nov03 1-2	Sep19 0-1 Feb02 0-3	Mar01 1-2	Oct06 1-2 Feb16 1-1	Aug18 5-1 Jan01 1-1	Dec22 0-4	Sep05 1-0 Apr26 2-1	

Scottish Football League Records
Season 1980-81

PREMIER

	ABERDEEN	AIRDRIE	CELTIC	DUNDEE U	HEARTS	KILMARNOCK	MORTON	PARTICK T	RANGERS	ST MIRREN
ABERDEEN		Nov01 4-1 Apr18 3-0	Sep27 2-2 Dec27 4-1	Aug16 1-1 Dec30 1-1	Mar07 4-1 Apr11 1-0	Oct11 2-0 May02 0-2	Sep06 6-0 Feb07 0-1	Nov15 2-1 Apr01 3-1	Dec13 2-0 Apr22 0-0	Oct18 3-2 Feb28 1-2
AIRDRIE	Aug23 0-4 Feb21 0-0		Nov15 1-4 Mar21 1-2	Sep13 0-0 Jan31 0-5	Oct25 3-0 Apr25 1-2	Sep27 1-0 Mar11 3-0	Oct11 1-0 May02 3-2	Nov29 0-0 Mar07 2-0	Aug09 1-1 Jan03 1-1	Dec06 1-2 Apr04 0-2
CELTIC	Nov08 0-2 Mar28 1-1	Sep20 1-1 Dec20 2-1		Oct04 2-0 Jan10 2-1	Dec13 3-2 Apr01 6-0	Oct25 4-1 Apr25 1-1	Aug09 2-1 Jan03 3-0	Sep06 4-1 Mar18 4-1	Aug23 1-2 Feb21 3-1	Nov22 1-2 Mar14 7-0
DUNDEE U	Oct25 1-3 Apr25 0-0	Dec13 1-0 Apr29 4-1	Nov29 0-3 Apr22 2-3		Sep27 1-1 Dec27 4-1	Aug09 2-2 Jan03 7-0	Aug23 1-1 Feb21 1-0	Oct11 0-0 May02 3-2	Sep06 2-4 Feb07 2-1	Nov15 2-0 Mar21 1-2
HEARTS	Oct04 0-1 Jan10 0-2	Aug16 0-2 Jan01 2-3	Sep13 0-2 Jan31 0-3	Nov08 0-3 Mar28 0-4		Dec06 2-0 Apr06 1-0	Sep20 0-1 Dec20 0-0	Oct18 0-1 Feb28 1-1	Nov22 0-0 Mar14 2-1	Nov01 1-1 Apr18 1-2
KILMARNOCK	Nov22 1-1 Mar14 1-0	Nov08 1-1 Mar28 0-1	Aug16 0-3 Jan01 1-2	Oct18 0-1 Feb28 0-1	Sep06 0-1 Mar24 2-0		Dec13 3-3 Apr15 0-0	Nov01 0-1 Apr18 0-1	Sep20 1-8 Dec20 1-1	Oct04 1-6 Jan10 2-0
MORTON	Dec06 1-0 Apr04 1-3	Nov22 3-1 Mar14 0-1	Oct18 2-3 Feb28 0-3	Nov01 0-2 Apr18 2-0	Nov15 2-2 Mar21 3-0	Sep13 2-0 Jan31 1-0		Sep27 1-2 Dec27 2-0	Oct04 2-2 Jan10 0-2	Aug16 1-4 Jan01 1-3
PARTICK T	Sep20 0-1 Dec20 1-1	Oct04 2-1 Jan10 1-0	Dec06 0-1 Apr05 0-1	Nov22 2-3 Mar14 0-2	Aug09 3-2 Jan03 1-0	Aug23 0-1 Feb21 1-1	Nov06 0-0 Mar28 3-1		Oct25 1-1 Apr25 1-1	Sep13 1-0 Jan31 0-0
RANGERS	Sep13 1-1 Jan31 1-0	Oct18 0-0 Feb28 2-0	Nov01 3-0 Apr18 0-1	Mar18 1-4 Apr04 2-1	Oct11 3-1 May02 4-0	Nov15 2-0 Mar21 2-0	Nov29 0-1 Apr01 4-0	Aug16 4-0 Jan01 1-1		Sep27 2-0 Apr15 1-0
ST MIRREN	Aug09 0-1 Jan03 1-1	Sep06 2-2 Mar04 2-1	Oct11 0-2 May02 3-1	Sep20 2-0 Dec20 3-3	Aug23 1-3 Feb21 2-1	Nov29 2-0 Mar07 1-1	Oct25 1-1 Apr25 2-0	Dec13 1-0 Apr11 3-2	Nov08 0-0 Mar28 2-1	

LEAGUE TABLES

PREMIER DIVISION

	P	W	D	L	F	A	W	D	L	F	A	Pts
Celtic	36	12	3	3	47	18	14	1	3	37	19	56
Aberdeen	36	11	4	3	39	16	8	7	3	22	10	49
Rangers	36	12	3	3	33	10	4	9	5	27	22	44
St Mirren	36	9	6	3	28	20	9	2	7	28	27	44
Dundee U	36	8	5	5	34	24	9	4	5	32	18	43
Partick T	36	6	6	6	17	17	4	4	10	15	31	30
Airdrie	36	6	5	7	19	25	4	4	10	17	30	29
Morton	36	7	2	9	24	28	3	6	9	12	30	28
Kilmarnock	36	3	5	10	14	31	2	4	12	9	34	19
Hearts	36	3	4	11	10	27	3	2	13	17	44	18

DIVISION 1

	P	W	D	L	F	A	W	D	L	F	A	Pts
Hibernian	39	14	4	2	38	9	10	5	4	29	15	57
Dundee	39	14	4	2	42	18	8	4	7	22	22	52
St Johnstone	39	12	3	5	31	21	8	8	3	33	24	51
Raith R	39	12	7	1	27	11	8	3	8	22	21	50
Motherwell	39	14	5	1	41	20	5	6	8	24	31	49
Ayr U	39	11	5	3	34	17	6	6	8	25	25	45
Hamilton A	39	9	5	6	39	27	6	2	11	22	30	37
Dumbarton	39	8	5	6	23	22	5	6	9	26	28	37
Falkirk	39	7	4	8	24	29	6	4	10	15	23	34
Clydebank	39	8	6	5	31	25	2	7	11	17	34	33
E. Stirling	39	4	10	6	20	24	2	7	10	21	32	29
Dunfermline A	39	6	3	10	17	27	4	4	12	24	31	27
Stirling A	39	4	6	9	13	21	2	5	13	5	27	23
Berwick R	39	5	6	8	18	27	0	6	14	13	55	22

DIVISION 2

	P	W	D	L	F	A	W	D	L	F	A	Pts
Queen's Park	39	9	9	2	30	19	7	9	3	32	24	50
Queen of South	39	7	8	4	31	29	9	6	5	35	24	46
Cowdenbeath	39	12	3	4	35	20	6	6	8	28	28	45
Brechin C	39	10	7	3	29	18	5	7	7	23	28	44
Forfar A	39	9	3	7	34	32	8	6	6	29	25	43
Alloa	39	10	4	6	29	25	5	8	6	32	29	42
Montrose	39	9	4	6	31	24	7	4	9	35	31	40
Clyde	39	10	6	4	45	31	4	6	9	23	32	40
Arbroath	39	3	9	8	20	29	10	3	6	38	25	38
Stenhousemuir	39	4	7	8	27	32	9	4	7	36	26	37
East Fife	39	6	9	4	21	21	4	6	10	23	32	35
Albion R	39	9	3	8	37	41	4	6	9	22	31	35
Meadowbank T	39	6	2	11	17	35	5	5	10	25	29	29
Stranraer	39	4	5	11	20	41	3	3	13	16	42	22

DIVISION 1

	AYR U	BERWICK R	CLYDEBANK	DUMBARTON	DUNDEE	DUNFERMLINE A	E STIRLING	FALKIRK	HAMILTON A	HIBERNIAN	MOTHERWELL	RAITH R	ST JOHNSTONE	STIRLING A
AYR U		Nov01 4-1	Nov15 1-0 Feb21 4-1	Dec13 0-0 Apr25 1-2	Dec27 1-0	Sep27 2-0 Mar07 2-1	Jan03 3-3	Nov29 3-1	Sep17 2-1	Sep13 1-3 Mar28 0-1	Aug09 5-0	Oct01 1-0	Oct11 0-0 Jan17 3-3	Aug23 0-0 Apr18 1-0
BERWICK R	Sep06 1-2 Mar14 1-1		Dec06 0-1	Nov08 2-2	Oct25 0-1	Aug16 1-1 Apr04 1-0	Nov22 1-2	Dec20 0-4 Apr18 1-2	Jan10 1-0	Jan01 0-2 Jan31 0-0	Sep20 3-2 Feb07 2-2	Oct18 1-4	Sep09 0-1	Oct04 1-0 Feb28 1-0
CLYDEBANK	Sep20 2-2	Oct11 2-1 Apr11 2-0		Aug23 1-4 May02 0-0	Sep06 3-0	Dec13 2-3	Aug09 3-2 Apr25 2-0	Oct25 2-1	Oct04 3-1 Feb28 1-2	Nov22 1-1	Sep09 2-2 Mar21 0-0	Apr22 3-0	Nov08 0-2 Mar24 1-3	Jan03 1-1
DUMBARTON	Oct18 0-1	Sep17 2-0 Feb21 1-1	Jan01 1-1		Nov29 1-2	Dec20 1-0 Apr18 2-1	Sep13 2-2 Jan31 1-0	Jan10 0-1	Nov01 2-1 Apr04 2-1	Oct01 2-0 Mar21 1-4	Sep27 1-2 Apr08 0-0	Nov15 2-2	Aug16 0-3	Dec06 2-0
DUNDEE	Aug16 0-0 Jan31 2-4	Sep13 2-2 Mar28 0-0	Nov01 2-1 Apr18 1-0	Oct04 3-1 Mar11 2-1		Mar18 2-0	Oct18 2-0	Sep20 4-0	Oct14 2-0	Sep09 1-2 Dec20 1-0	Nov08 2-1	Mar14 3-1 Apr01 2-1	Jan01 2-2 Apr04 4-1	Nov22 5-1
DUNFERMLINE A	Nov22 2-3	Apr22 1-1	Oct18 3-1 Apr01 2-1	Sep09 1-1	Aug09 1-0 Apr11 1-1		Nov01 1-0	Nov08 0-1 Mar04 0-1	Dec06 0-1	Oct04 0-2 Feb28 0-5	Mar28 1-3 Apr15 2-1	Aug23 0-2	Sep20 0-2	Sep13 2-0 Jan31 0-1
E STIRLING	Oct13 0-2 Apr04 1-3	Sep27 5-1 Apr07 0-0	Apr29 2-2	Oct25 2-1	Dec13 0-2 May02 0-1	Sep06 0-4 Mar21 0-0		Jan01 0-0 Feb21 1-1	Aug16 1-1	Nov08 1-1	Oct11 1-1	Mar24 0-1	Dec20 1-1 Apr18 2-2	Sep20 2-0 Apr01 1-0
FALKIRK	Oct04 3-1 Feb28 2-1	Sep03 6-0	Sep13 3-2 Jan31 0-0	Aug09 0-5 Apr11 1-3	Nov15 0-3 Apr25 1-2	Sep17 2-1	Aug23 1-1		Oct18 2-3 Mar14 2-1	Dec06 0-2	Mar18 0-1	Jan03 1-0	Nov22 0-3	Nov01 0-0 Mar21 0-0
HAMILTON A	Nov08 1-0 Mar04 0-0	Aug09 9-1 Apr25 4-1	Nov29 3-0	Sep06 1-1	Jan03 4-2 Mar21 1-3	Oct11 1-1 Feb14 1-4	Dec27 1-0 Mar28 2-2	Dec13 0-1		Sep20 1-1	Aug23 4-2 Apr18 1-2	Sep27 3-1 Mar07 0-2	Oct25 0-3	Sep09 2-0
HIBERNIAN	Oct25 1-0	Aug23 3-0	Sep27 4-1 Apr15 3-0	Jan03 1-0	Feb07 0-0	Nov29 1-0	Sep17 2-2 Apr11 2-0	Oct11 2-0 Jan17 1-0	Nov15 3-3 Feb21 4-0		Sep06 1-0	Aug09 0-1 Apr18 2-0	Dec13 4-0 Mar18 1-2	Dec27 3-0 Apr04 0-0
MOTHERWELL	Jan10 3-2 Apr11 1-0	Nov15 2-1	Dec20 3-0	Nov22 4-2	Sep17 3-2 Feb21 4-1	Oct01 2-0	Dec06 1-1 Mar14 2-1	Aug16 3-0 Apr04 1-0	Jan01 1-3	Nov01 2-0 Aug25 1-1		Sep13 1-1 Jan31 0-0	Oct04 2-2 Feb28 3-2	Oct18 2-1
RAITH R	Dec20 2-1 Mar21 1-1	Dec13 3-0 Feb14 1-1	Aug16 0-4 Apr04 1-1	Sep20 4-1 Feb07 1-0	Oct11 0-0	Jan01 1-0 Apr25 1-0	Oct04 2-1 Feb28 0-0	Sep09 2-1 Mar28 0-0	Nov22 1-0	Jan10 2-0	Oct25 2-0		Sep06 0-0	Nov08 3-0
ST JOHNSTONE	Dec06 1-0	Jan03 1-0 Mar21 6-2	Sep17 1-1	Dec27 2-0 Mar28 2-1	Aug23 1-0	Nov15 2-4 Feb21 4-1	Sep03 0-2	Sep27 0-0 Mar07 2-1	Sep13 1-0 Jan31 2-1	Oct18 1-2	Nov29 2-2	Nov01 0-3 Apr11 2-0		Aug09 0-1 Apr25 1-0
STIRLING A	Jan01 1-1	Nov29 1-0	Oct01 0-0 Mar28 0-0	Oct11 0-1 Mar14 0-0	Aug27 1-1 Mar24 0-1	Oct25 3-3	Nov15 4-2	Sep06 1-0	Mar11 0-2 Apr11 0-1	Aug16 0-2	Dec13 2-0 May02 0-3	Sep17 0-2 Feb21 0-1	Jan10 0-1	

DIVISION 2

	ALBION R	ALLOA	ARBROATH	BRECHIN C	CLYDE	COWDENBEATH	EAST FIFE	FORFAR A	MEADOWBANK T	MONTROSE	QUEEN OF SOUTH	QUEEN'S PARK	STENHOUSEMUIR	STRANRAER
ALBION R		Nov22 3-1	Oct04 1-6 Feb28 2-4	Sep20 2-3	Jan10 3-3	Sep13 2-0 Mar28 0-2	Nov08 0-0 Feb14 3-2	Sep24 2-4 Apr11 3-2	Aug24 3-1 Jan01 2-1	Nov01 2-1	Sep10 0-4 Mar14 1-0	Oct18 2-2	Apr18 0-2	Dec06 1-3 Mar17 5-0
ALLOA	Sep27 1-0 Mar11 0-1		Oct25 1-1	Oct11 5-0 Feb07 0-2	Sep06 2-0	Aug16 1-1	Dec20 2-1 Jan31 0-0	Sep09 1-0 Apr04 0-1	Jan10 2-1	Nov15 0-4 Feb21 1-0	Mar04 1-3 Apr18 1-5	Nov19 5-2	Jan01 3-2 Mar14 0-0	Sep17 3-1
ARBROATH	Dec13 2-2	Sep13 1-1 Mar28 0-3		Sep27 2-2 Mar07 0-0	Dec20 2-2	Mar04 0-1	Oct11 1-1	Aug23 2-3 Mar14 0-0	Nov01 0-1	Sep03 1-4	Dec27 1-2 Apr25 1-1	Sep17 1-4 Feb14 0-0	Apr11 0-1 May02 2-0	Nov15 3-1 Feb21 1-0
BRECHIN C	Nov15 2-2 Feb21 2-1	Dec06 1-1	Nov22 5-1		Dec27 3-1 Mar14 2-1	Nov01 0-2 Apr04 1-2	Oct04 0-1	Sep17 1-1 Feb14 0-0	Apr11 0-0 May02 2-1	Aug23 1-1 Jan01 3-1	Mar24 2-1 Apr14 1-0	Sep13 0-0	Sep03 2-1	Oct18 1-0
CLYDE	Oct01 1-1 Mar21 4-0	Nov01 0-3 Apr11 0-0	Oct18 0-2 Jan31 1-0	Aug16 3-0		Dec06 2-2	Aug09 3-1 Apr25 6-2	Sep27 2-1 Mar07 3-1	Nov15 2-1 Feb22 1-4	Sep13 4-3 Mar28 6-0	Apr01 1-4	Mar04 1-1	Sep15 2-2	May02 3-3
COWDENBEATH	Oct25 2-1	Mar21 5-2 Apr15 4-2	Aug09 2-1 Apr18 1-0	Sep06 2-1	Oct11 4-2 Mar18 2-0		Jan01 1-1	Apr01 1-2	Sep27 1-0 Apr29 1-0	Sep17 2-1	Jan31 1-1	May02 1-2	Nov15 0-1 Feb21 1-2	Sep03 1-1 Mar24 3-0
EAST FIFE	Sep17 1-1	Oct18 1-1	Dec06 2-1 Feb07 0-2	Nov29 0-2 Feb28 2-2	Mar24 0-1	Aug23 3-2 Mar14 1-0		Dec27 0-0	Sep03 2-1	Apr11 1-1 May02 0-0	Sep27 1-1	Nov15 0-2 Feb21 1-1	Nov01 1-1	Sep13 3-1 Mar11 2-1
FORFAR A	Aug09 1-1	May02 4-1	Apr08 2-1	Nov08 0-0	Nov22 3-2	Oct04 1-2 Mar11 1-0	Aug16 3-2 Mar21 1-2		Sep13 3-2 Mar28 3-1	Oct18 0-4	Sep20 1-2 Dec13 3-4	Sep03 1-1 Apr18 1-2	Dec06 2-1 Feb07 1-4	Nov01 3-0
MEADOWBANK T	Apr04 2-1	Aug09 0-3 Jan24 0-4	Aug20 1-4 Mar21 1-2	Sep09 2-0	Sep20 0-2	Nov22 1-4	Feb11 1-3 Apr18 1-0	Oct25 4-2		Oct04 0-2 Feb28 2-1	Nov08 0-2 Feb14 0-0	Dec06 1-1	Oct18 0-3 Jan31 1-0	Dec27 0-1
MONTROSE	Sep06 0-1 Apr25 1-1	Sep20 2-1	Jan10 1-2 Apr04 0-3	Apr18 3-2	Oct25 1-0	Nov08 3-2 Apr22 3-1	Sep09 1-0	Jan31 4-0 Mar24 0-0	Mar18 1-2		Oct11 1-1	Aug16 1-3	Sep27 1-3 Mar11 2-1	Aug09 0-0 Apr08 6-1
QUEEN OF SOUTH	May02 3-0	Sep02 1-1	Aug16 2-2	Aug09 3-2	Oct04 1-3 Feb28 0-0	Oct18 1-0 Apr08 2-2	Nov22 1-1 Mar07 2-1	Nov15 1-1	Sep17 1-1	Dec06 1-5 Feb07 4-1		Nov01 0-3 Jan24 1-0	Sep13 4-4 Mar28 0-2	Jan01 3-0
QUEEN'S PARK	Dec20 2-0 Jan31 3-1	Oct04 1-1 Feb28 2-1	Nov08 2-2	Oct25 1-1 Mar28 1-0	Aug23 0-1 Apr04 1-1	Sep09 1-1 Apr25 1-1	Sep20 2-1	Jan10 1-3	Oct11 1-1 Jan03 1-1	Mar14 1-1 Apr01 1-0	Sep06 5-1		Aug09 2-1	Nov22 1-0
STENHOUSEMUIR	Aug16 3-1 Feb24 0-3	Aug23 1-1	Sep09 1-2	Mar18 0-3 Apr25 1-1	Nov08 3-0 Feb14 3-3	Sep20 1-1	Sep06 2-0 Apr04 1-3	Oct11 0-1	Mar31 1-1	Nov22 1-2	Oct25 1-1	Feb10 2-2 Mar21 3-4		Oct04 1-2 Feb28 2-1
STRANRAER	Oct11 1-4	Nov08 1-3 Feb14 2-2	Sep20 0-2	Dec20 0-1 Jan31 1-1	Sep09 1-0 Apr18 1-1	Apr11 3-2	Mar28 1-1	Sep06 0-4 Apr25 0-3	Aug16 1-3 Mar14 1-2	Jan24 0-3	Aug23 1-0 Apr04 1-2	Sep27 2-1 Mar07 1-1	Nov29 2-5	

Scottish Football League Records
Season 1981-82

PREMIER

	ABERDEEN	AIRDRIE	CELTIC	DUNDEE	DUNDEE U	HIBERNIAN	MORTON	PARTICK T	RANGERS	ST MIRREN
ABERDEEN		Nov28 0-0 Apr24 2-0	Sep05 1-3 Jan30 1-3	Oct24 2-1 Feb27 0-0	Oct31 1-1 Mar20 2-1	Sep19 1-0 Mar10 3-1	Oct03 2-0 Feb06 0-0	Nov14 2-1 May03 3-1	Apr21 3-1 May15 4-0	Apr14 4-1 May08 5-1
AIRDRIE	Sep26 0-4 Feb20 0-3		Oct31 1-3 Apr14 1-5	Oct10 4-2 Mar13 0-2	Sep19 2-1 Feb09 2-0	Nov14 3-1 Apr03 0-2	Feb13 1-1 May08 1-1	Oct24 1-1 Feb27 3-1	Dec05 2-2 Apr17 0-1	Sep05 3-4 Apr21 0-2
CELTIC	Nov07 2-1 Mar27 0-1	Aug29 5-2 Mar20 2-0		Dec05 3-1 Apr17 4-2	Oct17 1-1 Apr21 3-1	Feb02 0-0 May01 6-0	Sep12 2-1 Mar03 1-0	Sep26 2-0 Feb20 2-2	Nov21 3-3 Apr10 2-1	May03 0-0 May15 3-0
DUNDEE	Mar17 0-3 May01 0-5	Dec12 3-1 May15 1-0	Oct03 1-3 Feb06 1-3		Nov14 1-3 Apr03 0-2	Oct31 0-0 Mar20 2-2	Nov28 4-1 Apr25 2-1	Sep05 4-2 Apr21 1-2	Oct11 2-3 Apr14 3-1	Sep19 3-0 Jan30 0-2
DUNDEE U	Aug29 4-1 May05 1-2	Nov21 4-0 Apr10 4-0	Mar31 0-2 May08 3-0	Sep12 5-2 Mar10 1-1		Dec05 1-0 Apr17 0-1	Nov07 3-0 Mar27 5-0	Oct10 0-0 Mar13 5-1	Nov11 2-0 Feb20 1-1	Oct24 0-2 Feb27 1-1
HIBERNIAN	Nov21 1-1 Apr10 0-3	Sep12 1-1 Jan16 1-0	Oct24 1-0 Feb27 1-0	Aug29 2-0 Jan02 2-1	Oct03 1-1 Feb06 0-1		Oct10 4-0 Mar13 2-2	Dec19 3-0 May08 1-1	Nov07 1-2 Mar27 0-0	Nov28 0-0 Apr24 2-1
MORTON	Dec05 2-1 Apr17 2-1	Oct17 3-0 Mar06 1-0	Nov14 1-1 Apr03 1-1	Sep26 2-0 Feb20 2-0	Sep05 1-0 Apr07 1-1	Apr14 2-1 May15 0-0		Sep19 1-0 Jan30 0-0	Mar17 0-0 May01 1-3	Oct31 0-2 Mar20 0-1
PARTICK T	Sep12 0-2 Feb03 0-0	Apr07 4-1 May01 0-0	Nov28 0-2 Apr24 0-3	Nov07 1-2 Mar27 0-2	Apr14 2-3 May15 1-2	Oct17 1-0 Mar06 1-2	Nov21 2-2 Apr10 4-0		Aug29 0-1 Feb17 2-0	Oct03 1-1 Feb06 0-0
RANGERS	Oct10 0-0 Mar13 1-3	Oct03 4-1 Mar31 1-0	Sep19 0-2 Jan09 1-0	Dec19 2-1 May08 4-0	Jan16 2-0 Apr24 1-1	Sep05 2-2 Jan30 1-1	Oct24 1-1 Feb27 3-0	Oct31 0-2 Mar20 4-1		Nov14 4-1 May05 3-0
ST MIRREN	Oct17 1-2 May12 0-2	Nov07 1-1 Mar27 3-0	Oct10 1-2 Mar13 2-5	Nov21 4-0 Apr10 0-1	Feb03 1-0 May01 2-2	Sep26 1-0 Feb20 2-2	Aug29 2-0 Jan03 3-1	Dec05 2-1 Apr17 2-0	Sep12 1-1 Mar10 2-3	

LEAGUE TABLES

PREMIER DIVISION

	P	W	D	L	F	A	W	D	L	F	A	Pts
Celtic	36	12	5	1	41	16	12	2	4	38	17	55
Aberdeen	36	12	4	2	36	15	11	3	4	35	14	53
Rangers	36	10	5	3	34	16	6	6	6	23	29	43
Dundee U	36	10	4	4	40	14	5	6	7	21	24	40
St Mirren	36	8	4	6	30	23	6	5	7	19	29	37
Hibernian	36	8	7	3	23	14	3	7	8	15	26	36
Morton	36	9	6	3	20	12	0	6	12	11	42	30
Dundee	36	7	2	9	28	34	4	2	12	18	38	26
Partick T	36	4	5	9	19	23	2	5	11	16	36	22
Airdrie	36	5	4	9	24	36	0	4	14	7	40	18

DIVISION 1

	P	W	D	L	F	A	W	D	L	F	A	Pts
Motherwell	39	12	7	0	41	17	14	2	4	51	19	61
Kilmarnock	39	6	12	2	25	11	11	5	3	35	18	51
Hearts	39	12	2	5	33	19	9	6	5	32	18	50
Clydebank	39	12	3	5	33	27	7	5	7	28	26	46
St Johnstone	39	12	3	4	44	29	5	5	10	25	31	42
Ayr U	39	12	6	1	39	20	3	6	11	17	30	42
Hamilton A	39	10	3	6	20	16	6	5	9	32	33	40
Queen's Park	39	11	5	4	32	17	2	5	12	9	24	36
Falkirk	39	8	8	4	26	19	3	6	10	23	33	36
Dunfermline A	39	3	9	7	24	31	8	5	7	22	25	36
Dumbarton	39	10	1	9	25	30	3	8	8	24	31	35
Raith R	39	5	2	13	13	32	6	5	8	18	27	29
E. Stirling	39	4	6	9	20	35	3	4	13	18	42	24
Queen of South	39	2	5	13	25	50	2	5	12	19	43	18

DIVISION 2

	P	W	D	L	F	A	W	D	L	F	A	Pts
Clyde	39	11	6	2	35	16	13	5	2	44	22	59
Alloa	39	9	6	4	33	25	10	6	4	33	17	50
Arbroath	39	12	5	2	34	16	8	5	7	28	34	50
Berwick R	39	14	4	2	46	15	6	4	9	20	23	48
Brechin C	39	9	5	5	28	19	9	5	6	33	24	46
Forfar A	39	11	6	3	35	12	4	9	6	24	23	45
East Fife	39	7	5	8	23	24	7	4	8	25	27	37
Cowdenbeath	39	8	6	6	34	26	3	7	9	17	31	35
Stirling A	39	9	5	6	25	18	3	6	10	14	26	35
Montrose	39	8	4	8	28	31	4	4	11	21	43	32
Albion R	39	8	3	8	28	28	5	2	13	24	46	31
Meadowbank T	39	8	6	6	34	29	2	4	13	15	33	30
Stenhousemuir	39	6	5	8	22	28	5	1	14	19	37	28
Stranraer	39	5	1	13	22	44	2	5	13	14	41	20

DIVISION 1

	AYR U	CLYDEBANK	DUMBARTON	DUNFERMLINE	E STIRLING	FALKIRK	HAMILTON A	HEARTS	KILMARNOCK	MOTHERWELL	QUEEN OF SOU	QUEEN'S PARK	RAITH R	ST JOHNSTONE
AYR U		Feb06 2-1	Sep30 3-2	Oct24 1-1	Oct17 5-1 Mar27 1-1	Nov14 4-1 Apr10 1-0	Sep05 2-0 Apr24 3-2	Sep23 0-0 Feb20 0-3	Mar17 1-1	Mar13 1-1 Apr14 4-3	Jan26 1-0 May08 5-2	Sep26 2-0	Dec05 2-0	Sep16 1-1
CLYDEBANK	Oct31 2-1 May15 2-0		Feb17 3-0	Sep16 4-1 May01 1-0	Jan30 2-1	Sep26 1-1 Feb27 0-2	Oct20 2-1	Mar27 2-1 Apr14 1-5	Sep08 0-0	Oct17 1-7	Dec05 2-1 Mar20 5-1	Nov14 2-1 Mar10 1-0	Feb03 0-1 Apr17 0-0	Sep05 2-3
DUMBARTON	Mar06 3-1 Apr07 3-1	Sep12 1-3 Mar13 0-2		Feb23 0-1	Aug29 0-3	Feb06 3-1 May08 1-0	Oct10 1-2	Nov28 3-1	Oct24 0-2 Apr24 0-2	Sep19 0-6	Nov07 1-0 Apr17 3-1	Apr14 1-0	Nov21 1-1 Apr03 0-2	Oct03 2-1 Feb20 2-0
DUNFERMLINE A	Feb03 0-0 Apr03 2-2	Nov21 3-6	Oct17 2-2 Mar20 0-0		Nov07 2-1 May15 1-1	Sep23 1-1	Feb10 1-3 Feb27 1-1	Aug29 1-1 Apr24 1-2	Dec05 1-2	Sep26 1-2	Sep12 1-1	Feb17 2-1	Feb06 2-3	Oct31 1-2 Apr17 1-0
E STIRLING	Feb10 2-1	Oct24 0-0 Apr10 0-1	Nov14 1-1 Feb27 2-2	Sep05 1-2		Sep08 2-2	Feb17 1-5 May08 2-1	Feb06 0-1	Sep29 2-1 May01 1-5	Dec05 0-6 Apr03 1-2	Sep23 3-1	Sep16 0-1	Mar03 0-1 Mar20 1-1	Oct10 1-1
FALKIRK	Aug29 1-2	Nov28 3-0	Oct31 1-1	Feb13 0-0 Mar13 1-0	Feb20 2-0 Apr07 0-3		Oct03 3-0	Sep12 0-0 Mar06 3-1	Feb17 2-2	Nov21 1-1 Apr17 1-3	Oct17 0-0	Jan30 0-0 May15 1-1	Nov07 1-2 Apr24 3-2	Sep19 1-0 Mar27 2-1
HAMILTON A	Nov07 1-0	Sep12 0-2 Feb20 3-1	Apr21 0-0 May15 1-0	Sep19 0-2	Sep12 1-1	Dec05 2-0 May01 1-0		Nov21 0-2 Apr10 0-2	Oct17 1-2	Feb13 1-0	Sep26 2-3	Oct31 2-1 Apr03 2-0	Aug29 1-0	Jan30 0-0 Mar13 2-0
HEARTS	Apr21 2-1	Sep19 1-0	Sep26 2-1 May01 2-5	Nov14 1-1	Oct31 0-1 Apr27 2-0	Feb09 3-0	Sep16 2-1		Sep05 0-1	Jan30 0-3 May15 0-1	Feb17 4-1	Dec05 1-1 Mar20 1-0	Oct07 2-1 Feb27 4-0	Oct17 3-1 Apr03 3-0
KILMARNOCK	Sep12 1-1 Feb27 1-1	Apr03 0-0 Apr21 2-0	Jan30 0-0	Oct03 0-1 Mar10 2-0	Nov28 2-0	Oct10 2-2 Mar20 4-1	Jan16 2-2 Apr17 0-0	Nov07 0-0 May08 0-0		Aug29 2-0	Nov21 0-0 May15 6-0	Sep19 0-0	Oct31 1-1	Dec12 0-2
MOTHERWELL	Oct10 1-1	Jan19 3-1 Apr24 0-0	Mar03 1-1 Apr10 1-0	Nov28 6-1 May08 2-2	Oct03 3-0	Sep16 3-2	Sep08 2-2 Mar20 3-2	Oct24 2-2	Nov14 2-0 Mar27 1-0		Feb06 2-1	Sep05 1-0 Feb27 3-0	Sep23 3-0	Feb17 2-2
QUEEN OF SOUTH	Sep19 1-2	Oct03 2-1	Sep05 0-4	Feb20 2-3 Apr14 0-3	Feb13 1-1 Mar06 4-0	Jan19 0-4 Apr03 1-1	Nov28 2-4 Mar27 0-3	Oct10 1-2 Mar13 1-5	Sep16 1-1	Oct31 0-2 May01 2-5		Sep08 1-1 Apr24 1-2	Jan30 2-3	Nov14 3-3
QUEEN'S PARK	Nov24 2-0 Apr17 0-0	Aug29 2-2	Sep23 3-0 Mar27 3-0	Oct10 0-1 Apr10 2-1	Nov21 2-1 Mar13 3-0	Oct24 2-2	Feb06 2-0	Oct03 1-0	Feb20 0-2 Mar30 2-3	Nov07 0-1	Feb02 1-1		Sep12 0-0 May08 2-0	Mar16 3-2 May01 2-1
RAITH R	Oct03 0-1 May01 1-0	Oct10 0-2	Sep16 1-3	Sep08 0-0 Mar27 0-1	Sep19 1-0	Sep05 0-3	Nov14 2-0 Mar06 1-2	Mar31 0-3	Mar13 0-3 Apr06 3-3	Feb20 0-2 Apr21 0-1	Oct24 2-1 Apr10 1-2	Feb09 1-0		Nov28 0-4 Mar15 0-1
ST JOHNSTONE	Nov21 2-0 Mar20 3-2	Nov07 1-3 May08 3-3	Dec05 5-2	Mar31 2-1	Mar24 3-2 Apr24 7-1	Mar10 2-0	Oct24 1-1	Feb23 2-1	Sep23 0-2 Apr10 1-3	Sep12 1-3 Mar06 3-2	Aug29 1-0 Feb27 3-3	Oct17 2-0	Sep26 2-0	

DIVISION 2

	ALBION R	ALLOA	ARBROATH	BERWICK R	BRECHIN C	CLYDE	COWDENBEATH	EAST FIFE	FORFAR A	MEADOWBANK T	MONTROSE	STENHOUSEMUIR	STIRLING A	STRANRAER
ALBION R		Oct31 1-5 Mar20 1-1	Sep22 2-0	Oct03 1-3	Jan23 1-2 Apr17 1-2	Feb10 0-1 May01 2-3	Aug29 2-0	Mar17 1-0	Oct17 3-3	Mar31 2-0	Nov07 0-2 Feb27 2-2	Nov21 1-4 May15 2-0	Nov28 1-0 Apr10 1-0	Sep12 4-0
ALLOA	Feb17 1-0		Oct03 2-1 Feb20 2-2	Oct10 1-0 Mar06 1-1	Oct24 1-3	Mar27 2-2 Apr21 0-3	Nov21 3-1 May08 2-2	Feb02 1-2	Aug29 1-2	Nov28 4-3 Apr10 2-0	Mar22 5-0	Sep12 1-0	Nov07 0-0	Sep23 3-2 May01 1-1
ARBROATH	Dec19 4-0 Apr24 2-0	Dec05 2-1		Oct24 2-1	Sep19 1-1	Oct17 0-1 Apr10 0-5	Sep12 1-1 Feb27 3-0	Feb13 3-1 May01 1-1	Jan02 1-1	Apr29 3-2 Mar27 0-0	Nov21 1-0 Mar13 2-0	Sep26 3-0	Jan23 1-0	Nov07 4-1
BERWICK R	Dec05 6-1 Mar13 4-1	Apr07 2-0	Feb06 3-0 Apr03 2-2		Oct17 3-1	Oct31 4-0	Sep26 1-2	Sep30 2-1 Mar27 3-0	Nov07 1-1 May08 2-1	Sep12 3-1 Feb27 2-2	Aug29 4-0	Feb23 1-0 Apr24 0-2	Nov21 1-0	Feb17 0-0 Apr17 2-0
BRECHIN C	Oct10 3-2	Feb06 0-4 Mar13 0-1	Feb17 2-2 May08 0-2	Feb03 2-0 May01 1-0		Oct20 2-2	Oct31 0-1	Oct03 2-1 Apr10 1-1	Nov21 0-0	Nov07 3-0	Sep12 3-0	Feb10 1-1 Mar27 0-1	Aug29 2-1	Nov28 3-0 Feb27 3-0
CLYDE	Oct24 1-2	Sep19 1-1	Mar17 1-1	Feb13 3-1 Mar20 1-2	Apr03 3-1 Apr14 1-0		Nov07 1-1 Apr17 2-0	Oct10 3-2	Sep12 1-1	Oct03 1-0	Nov28 3-0	Aug29 3-0 Mar13 1-0	Feb27 2-0 Mar30 3-3	Nov21 3-0 May08 1-1
COWDENBEATH	Nov14 2-0 Feb23 2-3	Sep16 1-2	Mar24 1-2	Nov28 2-1 Apr10 2-0	Feb13 0-0 May15 0-2	Sep05 0-4		Sep08 2-2 Mar06 1-2	Oct24 1-1 Mar13 3-1	Mar03 2-2	Oct03 6-0 Mar27 3-2	Sep23 3-1	Mar17 0-0 May01 2-0	Oct10 1-1
EAST FIFE	Sep19 3-0 May08 1-1	Oct17 1-2 Apr03 0-2	Oct31 0-1	Jan30 0-1	Dec05 2-2	Feb06 2-2 Apr25 1-1	Jan02 1-1		Sep26 0-4 Feb27 1-0	Nov21 2-0 Mar13 1-0	Feb10 0-1	Nov07 3-2 Apr17 1-0	Sep12 3-0 Mar20 1-2	Aug29 0-2
FORFAR A	Apr14 3-1 Apr28 3-0	Nov14 0-0 May15 0-1	Sep08 6-0 Apr21 1-1	Sep05 2-1	Oct27 0-1 Apr24 0-0	Feb20 0-0 Mar24 1-3	Feb06 4-0	Nov28 1-0		Oct10 1-1	Mar17 2-1 May01 0-0	Oct31 2-0	Oct20 3-1	Oct03 3-1 Mar20 3-0
MEADOWBANK T	Sep08 3-2 Mar06 0-2	Sep26 1-1	Nov14 1-2	Mar17 2-1	Sep05 1-0 Feb20 2-0	Dec05 2-3 May15 1-3	Oct17 1-1 Mar20 1-0	Sep16 1-1	Feb23 1-1 Apr17 2-5		Sep23 2-2	Feb06 6-1	Oct31 2-1 May08 0-1	Mar10 4-1 Apr03 1-1
MONTROSE	Sep05 4-2	Sep08 2-0 Apr17 0-3	Sep16 2-1	Nov14 0-2 Feb20 0-0	Jan02 2-2 Mar20 1-4	Sep26 0-3 Mar06 4-1	Dec05 2-2	Oct24 1-2 May15 1-2	Sep19 2-1	Dec19 1-0 Apr24 1-0		Jan23 2-1	Oct17 1-1 Apr03 1-2	Feb13 1-2
STENHOUSEMUIR	Sep15 2-2	Feb27 2-2 Mar30 0-1	Nov28 1-3 Mar20 0-2	Sep19 1-1	Sep08 0-4	Nov14 0-3	Apr03 3-0 Apr20 2-1	Sep05 2-0	Feb17 0-0 Apr10 0-1	Oct24 1-2 May01 3-1	Oct10 2-4 May08 2-1		Oct03 0-0	Jan30 1-0
STIRLING A	Sep26 1-0	Sep05 0-0 Apr24 3-2	Oct10 0-1 Apr17 3-2	Sep16 0-1 Mar15 0-0	Nov14 5-0 Mar06 0-2	Sep08 1-2	Sep19 0-0	Apr07 0-2	Mar10 0-0 Mar27 2-0	Feb17 1-0	Jan30 1-1	Dec05 2-3 Feb20 3-1		Oct24 1-0 Mar13 2-1
STRANRAER	Jan02 0-1 Mar27 1-4	Feb23 0-4	Sep05 4-0 May15 1-3	Sep08 2-4	Sep26 0-6	Sep16 0-2	Jan23 1-4 Apr24 1-0	Nov14 0-3 Feb20 1-2	Dec05 2-1	Sep19 0-1	Oct31 3-5 Apr10 2-0	Oct17 2-1 Mar06 0-1	Feb06 2-2	

Scottish Football League Records
Season 1982-83

PREMIER

	ABERDEEN	CELTIC	DUNDEE	DUNDEE U	HIBERNIAN	KILMARNOCK	MORTON	MOTHERWELL	RANGERS	ST MIRREN
ABERDEEN		Dec11 1-2 Apr23 1-0	Oct16 1-0 Feb26 3-1	Nov06 5-1 Mar19 1-2	Jan01 2-0 May14 5-0	Dec27 2-0 May04 5-0	Sep11 4-1 Jan08 2-0	Oct02 2-1 Feb08 5-1	Sep25 1-2 Jan22 2-0	Nov20 4-0 Apr02 0-1
CELTIC	Oct09 1-3 Feb12 1-3		Sep04 2-0 Jan03 2-2	Apr06 2-0 Apr20 2-3	Sep25 2-0 Jan22 4-1	Oct16 2-1 Feb26 4-0	Dec27 5-1 May07 2-0	Nov20 3-1 Apr02 3-0	Oct30 3-2 Mar23 0-0	Nov13 5-0 Mar26 1-1
DUNDEE	Dec18 0-2 Apr30 0-2	Nov06 2-3 Mar19 2-1		Jan01 0-2 May14 1-2	Oct09 2-1 Feb22 0-1	Nov27 5-2 Apr09 0-0	Sep18 2-0 Jan15 3-3	Sep11 3-1 Jan08 3-1	Mar02 1-0 May03 2-1	Oct23 1-1 Mar05 2-5
DUNDEE U	Sep04 2-0 Jan03 0-3	Oct02 2-2 Feb05 1-1	Oct30 1-0 Mar12 5-3		Nov20 3-0 Mar26 3-3	Dec11 7-0 Apr23 4-0	Oct16 6-0 Feb26 1-1	Dec27 5-0 May07 4-0	Nov13 4-2 Apr04 3-1	Sep25 3-0 Jan22 3-2
HIBERNIAN	Oct30 1-1 May02 0-0	Nov27 2-3 Apr09 0-3	Dec11 1-1 Apr23 0-0	Sep18 0-0 Jan15 0-0		Nov13 2-2 Apr02 8-1	Oct02 1-2 Feb05 2-0	Oct16 1-0 Feb26 1-1	Dec27 0-0 May07 1-2	Sep04 0-0 Jan03 1-1
KILMARNOCK	Oct23 0-2 Mar05 1-2	Dec18 0-4 Apr30 0-5	Sep25 0-0 Jan22 2-0	Oct09 1-1 Feb12 0-5	Sep11 1-1 Jan08 0-2		Nov06 3-1 Mar19 4-0	Jan01 0-2 May14 1-1	Nov20 0-0 Mar26 0-1	Dec04 2-2 Apr27 2-2
MORTON	Mar13 1-1 Mar26 1-2	Oct23 1-2 Mar05 0-3	Nov20 1-2 Apr07 1-0	Dec18 1-2 Apr30 0-4	Dec04 0-0 Apr16 0-1	Sep04 0-0 Jan03 3-0		Sep25 3-1 Jan22 0-1	Oct09 0-0 Feb12 0-5	Jan01 2-0 May14 0-2
MOTHERWELL	Dec04 0-2 Apr27 0-3	Sep18 0-7 Jan15 2-1	Nov13 1-0 Mar26 1-1	Oct23 0-2 Mar05 1-4	Dec18 0-1 Apr30 2-0	Oct30 4-1 Mar12 3-1	Nov27 3-1 Apr09 4-1		Sep04 2-2 Jan03 3-0	Oct09 2-0 Mar01 0-0
RANGERS	Nov27 0-1 Apr09 2-1	Jan01 1-2 May14 2-4	Oct02 1-1 Feb05 1-1	Sep11 0-0 Sep08 2-1	Oct23 3-2 Mar05 1-1	Sep18 5-0 Jan15 1-1	Dec11 1-1 Apr23 2-0	Nov06 4-0 Mar19 1-0		Dec18 1-0 Apr30 4-0
ST MIRREN	Jan15 1-1 Sep18 1-1	Sep11 1-2 Jan08 0-1	Dec27 0-0 May09 2-1	Nov27 0-2 Apr09 1-2	Nov06 3-0 Mar19 3-0	Oct02 3-2 Feb05 2-0	Oct30 1-1 Mar16 2-3	Dec11 3-0 Apr23 4-0	Oct16 2-2 Feb26 1-0	

LEAGUE TABLES

PREMIER DIVISION

	P	W	D	L	F	A	W	D	L	F	A	Pts
Dundee U	36	13	4	1	57	18	11	4	3	33	17	56
Aberdeen	36	14	0	4	46	12	11	5	2	30	12	55
Celtic	36	12	3	3	44	18	13	2	3	46	18	55
Rangers	36	9	6	3	32	16	4	6	8	20	25	38
St Mirren	36	8	5	5	30	18	3	7	8	17	33	34
Dundee	36	8	3	7	29	28	1	8	9	13	25	29
Hibernian	36	3	11	4	21	17	4	4	10	14	34	29
Motherwell	36	9	3	6	28	27	2	2	14	11	46	27
Morton	36	4	4	10	14	26	2	4	12	16	48	20
Kilmarnock	36	3	7	8	17	31	0	4	14	11	60	17

DIVISION 1

	P	W	D	L	F	A	W	D	L	F	A	Pts
St Johnstone	39	17	1	2	34	10	8	4	7	25	27	55
Hearts	39	13	4	3	46	20	9	6	4	33	18	54
Clydebank	39	8	5	6	32	27	12	5	3	40	22	50
Partick T	39	9	6	4	31	23	11	3	6	35	22	49
Airdrie	39	7	3	9	27	27	9	4	7	35	19	39
Alloa	39	8	7	5	31	21	6	4	9	21	31	39
Dumbarton	39	6	7	6	26	32	7	3	10	24	27	36
Falkirk	39	8	2	9	20	22	7	4	9	25	33	36
Raith R	39	8	3	8	32	29	5	5	10	32	34	34
Clyde	39	8	2	10	32	38	6	4	9	23	28	34
Hamilton A	39	7	6	7	27	32	4	6	9	27	34	34
Ayr U	39	9	4	7	29	26	3	4	12	16	35	32
Dunfermline A	39	5	9	6	19	30	2	8	9	20	39	31
Queen's Park	39	3	6	10	24	39	3	5	12	20	41	23

DIVISION 2

	P	W	D	L	F	A	W	D	L	F	A	Pts
Brechin C	39	13	5	2	46	17	8	8	3	31	21	55
Meadowbank T	39	13	2	4	37	20	10	6	4	27	25	54
Arbroath	39	14	4	2	45	23	7	3	9	33	28	49
Forfar A	39	8	9	2	31	16	10	3	7	27	22	48
Stirling A	39	12	5	2	35	17	6	5	9	22	24	46
East Fife	39	8	5	6	35	20	8	6	6	33	23	43
Queen of South	39	8	6	6	44	30	9	2	8	31	25	42
Cowdenbeath	39	10	4	5	35	25	3	8	9	19	28	38
Berwick R	39	6	7	6	25	30	7	3	10	22	30	36
Albion R	39	10	2	8	29	23	4	4	11	26	43	34
Stenhousemuir	39	4	8	8	22	33	3	7	9	21	33	29
Stranraer	39	6	4	10	21	32	4	3	12	25	47	27
E. Stirling	39	4	4	12	20	38	3	5	11	21	41	23
Montrose	39	5	2	12	18	33	3	4	13	19	53	22

DIVISION 1

	AIRDRIE	ALLOA	AYR U	CLYDE	CLYDEBANK	DUMBARTON	DUNFERMLINE A	FALKIRK	HAMILTON A	HEARTS	PARTICK T	QUEEN'S PARK	RAITH R	ST JOHNSTONE
AIRDRIE		Nov13 2-1 May14 0-1	Oct23 3-1	Oct16 3-4 Mar15 1-0	Nov27 2-2	Sep04 1-2	Oct02 1-1	Dec11 3-1 Feb26 0-2	Sep15 2-0	Jan03 0-1 Apr02 0-2	Sep18 1-3	Jan22 0-1	Dec27 1-2 Apr16 4-2	Jan15 2-0 Apr30 1-1
ALLOA	Sep08 1-2		Feb19 0-0 Apr16 3-0	Feb08 1-3	Sep11 2-0 Feb12 1-2	Oct30 2-0 Mar19 0-0	Nov06 2-2 Mar26 1-1	Jan01 0-2	Sep25 4-2	Jan15 0-0 Apr23 1-1	Oct16 2-1	Dec04 4-1 Mar05 3-1	Sep22 3-0	Nov20 0-2 May07 1-1
AYR U	Feb05 1-0 Mar19 1-1	Sep04 2-1		Jan03 2-0	Oct02 1-3 Mar05 1-0	Nov13 0-1 Apr02 1-2	Dec11 1-0 Apr09 2-3	Jan15 4-0	Sep18 1-1	Dec27 0-3	Sep15 2-1	Nov27 2-2 Apr30 4-0	Oct30 0-4 May07 3-2	Oct16 1-1 Feb26 0-1
CLYDE	Jan08 2-1	Oct23 2-0 Apr09 3-3	Nov06 3-1 May14 3-2		Sep18 3-5	Oct02 0-4 Mar05 1-0	Mar09 1-0	Sep04 0-1	Jan22 5-2	Dec11 2-3	Nov27 1-3 Feb26 0-2	Jan01 0-1 Mar19 2-1	Oct09 0-2 Apr30 3-3	Sep11 1-3 Apr16 0-1
CLYDEBANK	Sep22 0-4 Apr23 2-0	Dec27 2-2	Dec04 0-1	Nov20 2-2 Apr02 2-1		Sep15 5-1 Feb26 3-1	Oct16 1-1	Feb05 0-2	Jan03 2-1 Apr30 1-1	Nov13 0-3	Jan15 1-3 May14 1-2	Sep25 2-0	Sep04 1-1	Oct30 1-0 Mar12 6-1
DUMBARTON	Feb23 0-0 Mar26 1-1	Jan22 1-2	Sep29 1-0	Dec04 1-3	Jan01 0-4		Sep18 1-1 Mar12 1-3	Sep11 5-1	Oct09 1-5 Apr16 1-1	Nov27 1-1 May07 0-4	Oct23 1-1 Apr30 2-1	Nov06 1-1 Feb12 2-1	Jan08 2-1	Sep25 4-1
DUNFERMLINE A	Dec04 1-0 Apr05 0-4	Jan03 2-0	Sep05 1-0	Sep08 1-1 Apr23 0-0	Feb23 1-1 Mar19 1-1	Nov20 0-3		Oct30 0-0 May10 2-2	Dec27 1-1	Feb09 2-1	Nov13 0-4 Mar05 0-3	Oct09 1-1 Apr16 1-0	Sep14 1-2 Apr02 2-2	Sep22 2-4
FALKIRK	Sep25 1-3	Sep15 0-1 Apr30 2-1	Oct09 1-3 Mar12 2-0	Nov13 0-1 Mar23 1-2	Oct23 0-2 Apr09 0-2	Dec27 2-1 May14 1-2	Jan22 1-0		Nov27 1-0 Mar26 1-1	Sep18 1-1	Sep29 2-1	Jan08 2-0	Jan03 2-0	Dec04 0-1
HAMILTON A	Jan01 0-4 May05 0-3	Dec11 1-1 Apr02 2-0	Nov20 1-1 Apr23 1-0	Oct30 1-0 May07 4-1	Nov06 0-2	Jan15 0-3	Sep11 4-1 Feb26 4-0	Sep22 2-1		Oct16 1-3	Oct02 1-2 Apr09 0-0	Sep08 2-2	Feb05 2-2 Mar19 0-5	Dec18 1-1
HEARTS	Nov06 2-4	Oct09 3-0	Sep11 1-1 Feb12 5-1	Sep25 1-0 Mar26 3-1	Sep29 4-1 Apr16 2-2	Oct06 1-1	Oct23 4-1 Apr30 3-3	Nov20 3-1 Mar05 1-2	Jan08 2-1 Mar14 2-0		Jan22 0-1 Mar19 4-0	Dec04 2-0	Apr06 2-0	Jan01 1-0
PARTICK T	Nov20 1-0 May07 0-1	Jan08 1-1 Mar15 1-2	Jan01 2-2 Mar26 3-1	Oct05 2-1	Oct09 0-1	Feb05 3-2	Sep04 1-1	Apr06 1-1 Apr16 4-2	Dec04 1-1	Oct30 1-1		Sep11 2-3	Sep25 2-1 Mar22 1-0	Nov06 3-1 Apr02 2-1
QUEEN'S PARK	Oct30 1-1 Apr09 4-3	Oct02 1-2	Sep22 3-1	Sep14 0-0	Dec11 2-2 May07 1-3	Jan03 2-1	Jan15 2-2	Oct16 0-2 Apr02 1-1	Nov13 1-3 Mar15 1-4	Sep04 1-2 Feb26 0-3	Dec27 1-4 Apr23 0-1		Nov20 2-2	Feb05 1-2
RAITH R	Sep11 0-3	Nov27 0-1 Feb26 3-1	Jan22 0-1	Jan15 1-2	Dec18 0-3 Mar26 1-3	Oct16 3-0 Apr09 0-0	Jan01 6-0	Nov06 2-1 Apr23 0-3	Oct23 4-1	Oct02 1-0 Mar29 4-2	Dec11 2-2	Sep18 3-1 May14 2-2		Sep08 0-3
STJOHNSTONE	Oct09 1-0	Sep18 3-1	Jan08 2-0	Dec27 2-1	Jan22 0-1	Dec11 1-0 Apr23 1-0	Nov27 2-0 May14 1-0	Oct02 4-0 Mar19 1-0	Sep04 3-0 Feb12 0-2	Sep15 1-1 Apr09 2-1	Jan03 1-0	Oct23 4-1 Mar26 2-1	Nov13 2-1 Mar05 1-0	

DIVISION 2

	ALBION R	ARBROATH	BERWICK R	BRECHIN C	COWDENBEATH	EAST FIFE	E STIRLING	FORFAR A	MEADOWBANK T	MONTROSE	QUEEN OF SOUTH	STENHOUSEMUIR	STIRLING A	STRANRAER
ALBION R		Jan15 1-3 Apr23 0-2	Mar02 0-1 May14 2-1	Oct09 0-0	Sep25 0-2 Apr13 2-0	Sep11 1-0 Mar26 1-1	Dec04 3-1	Nov02 0-1 Mar19 1-0	Apr05 4-0 Apr16 1-3	Nov20 2-1	Sep22 3-1	Jan01 2-1	Sep08 3-0	Nov09 2-3 Mar05 1-2
ARBROATH	Sep04 3-1		Nov13 0-2 Mar19 3-1	Jan03 0-3 Apr16 1-1	Oct30 1-0	Dec18 3-1	Sep18 4-1 Apr09 4-0	Sep15 2-1 Feb23 3-3	Jan29 2-2	Oct16 3-1	Dec27 3-2	Nov27 0-0 May07 5-2	Oct02 1-0 Mar05 1-0	Feb05 3-0 Apr30 3-2
BERWICK R	Oct23 4-0	Sep08 2-1		Jan22 1-1 Mar12 1-1	Oct09 2-1 Apr30 1-1	Nov06 1-0	Feb12 0-3 Apr23 1-3	Nov27 1-2	Jan01 0-0	Sep25 1-1 Mar26 3-1	Dec04 0-4 Feb26 1-0	Jan15 2-4	Sep18 2-2 Apr09 0-3	Sep11 2-2
BRECHIN C	Feb23 3-0 Apr09 3-0	Nov06 3-1	Oct30 2-0		Sep22 1-1 Mar19 4-1	Sep08 0-0	Sep25 3-0	Oct16 1-1 Apr30 1-0	Nov20 1-1 May07 1-1	Jan01 4-0 Mar05 3-1	Mar09 2-3 Mar26 1-0	Dec04 5-2	Sep11 1-2 Feb19 3-1	Jan15 4-2
COWDENBEATH	Mar09 1-1	Jan22 2-1 Feb26 3-2	Feb05 2-0	Dec01 1-3		Jan01 2-4	Oct23 1-1 Mar12 3-1	Oct02 2-1	Jan15 3-1 May14 0-1	Sep11 2-3	Oct16 2-1 Apr09 2-3	Sep18 2-0 Mar26 1-1	Nov06 0-0	Sep29 2-1 Apr27 4-0
EAST FIFE	Dec27 4-3	Sep25 2-2 May14 4-0	Jan03 0-1 Apr02 3-0	Nov13 1-2 Apr23 1-2	Sep15 1-1 Mar05 0-2		Sep04 3-1	Mar09 0-2	Dec04 5-0	Sep22 0-1 Mar19 4-0	Nov20 0-0	Oct09 1-1	Feb12 1-0	Oct30 2-2 Feb23 3-0
E STIRLING	Oct02 1-1 Apr30 1-3	Nov20 1-3	Oct16 0-4	Mar15 0-3 Apr02 2-2	Mar01 2-0	Jan15 0-3 May07 1-1		Feb05 1-4 Mar05 0-1	Sep11 1-3 Mar19 1-2	Sep08 0-0 Feb19 3-1	Nov03 1-2 Apr16 0-1	Nov06 2-1	Jan01 2-1	Sep22 1-2
FORFAR A	Jan22 2-0	Jan01 1-1	Sep22 2-2 May07 1-1	Mar02 2-1	Dec04 0-0 Apr16 2-0	Oct23 4-1 Feb26 0-0	Oct09 5-1		Sep08 0-1 Apr02 0-3	Nov06 2-2	Sep25 1-0	Sep11 0-0 Mar12 2-2	Jan15 0-0 Mar26 2-0	Nov20 5-1
MEADOWBANK T	Oct16 4-3	Oct23 2-1 Mar26 0-3	Sep15 4-2 Feb19 5-0	Sep18 2-1	Sep14 2-0	Oct02 0-2 Apr30 0-3	Dec27 0-0	Nov13 1-0		Feb05 5-0 Apr09 2-0	Jan04 1-0 Mar05 1-2	Jan22 3-1 Apr23 1-1	Nov27 3-1	Apr13 1-0
MONTROSE	Sep18 3-3 Feb26 1-2	Feb16 2-1 Mar12 0-3	Dec18 1-0	Sep15 1-2	Dec27 0-4 May07 1-1	Nov27 0-2	Nov13 1-2	Jan03 1-2 May13 1-2	Oct09 0-1		Sep04 1-5	Oct23 1-0 Apr16 0-1	Jan22 0-1	Oct02 3-1 Apr02 1-0
QUEEN OF SOUTH	Nov27 5-0 May07 2-0	Sep11 2-1 Apr02 1-1	Oct02 1-2	Oct23 3-1	Feb16 0-0	Sep18 1-5 Dec11 1-2	Jan22 2-2	Mar29 1-1 Apr23 1-2	Nov06 1-1	Mar02 4-0 Apr30 6-0		Sep08 1-2 Feb19 2-2	Oct09 1-0 Mar19 3-5	Jan01 6-3
STENHOUSEMUIR	Sep14 1-0 Apr02 1-0	Sep22 1-6	Sep04 0-0 Mar05 0-1	Oct02 2-2 May14 0-0	Nov20 2-2	Feb09 3-2 Apr09 0-2	Jan03 2-2 Feb19 1-1	Dec27 0-1	Oct30 1-2	Feb23 3-1	Nov13 2-3		Mar09 0-0 Apr30 0-4	Oct16 2-3 Mar19 1-1
STIRLING A	Nov13 2-2 Mar12 1-2	Dec04 1-0	Nov20 3-1	Dec27 1-1	Jan03 2-2 Apr02 3-1	Oct16 1-0 Apr16 2-2	Sep15 2-0 May14 3-1	Sep04 2-0	Sep22 1-1 Feb26 2-0	Oct30 2-3 Apr23 1-0	Feb05 4-1	Sep25 1-0		Jan29 1-0
STRANRAER	Jan03 1-5	Oct09 0-1	Dec27 1-0 Apr16 0-3	Sep04 1-2 Feb26 1-3	Nov13 2-0	Jan22 2-2	Nov27 2-1 Mar26 1-0	Sep18 2-1 Apr09 1-2	Sep25 1-2 Mar12 0-2	Dec04 3-3	Sep15 0-3 May14 0-0	Feb12 2-0	Nov23 1-1 May10 0-1	

Scottish Football League Records
Season 1983-84

PREMIER

	ABERDEEN	CELTIC	DUNDEE	DUNDEE U	HEARTS	HIBERNIAN	MOTHERWELL	RANGERS	ST JOHNSTONE	ST MIRREN
ABERDEEN		Oct22 3-1 Feb04 1-0	Aug20 3-0 Dec31 5-2	Sep24 1-2 Apr18 5-1	Nov19 2-0 Apr02 1-1	Dec17 2-1 May05 2-2	Dec03 3-1 Apr07 2-1	Nov12 3-0 May09 0-0	Sep03 5-0 Mar30 1-0	Oct08 5-0 Mar03 2-0
CELTIC	Dec10 0-0 Mar31 1-0		Nov26 1-0 Apr24 3-0	Dec27 1-1 May12 1-1	Oct15 1-1 Feb25 4-1	Oct29 5-1 Apr28 3-2	Nov12 4-0 Apr10 4-2	Sep03 2-1 Apr02 3-0	Sep10 5-2 Feb11 5-2	Oct01 1-1 Feb14 2-0
DUNDEE	Oct29 1-3 Apr28 0-1	Sep24 2-6 Mar20 3-2		Sep03 1-4 Apr02 2-5	Sep17 1-2 Jan07 4-1	Dec10 0-3 Mar31 1-2	Nov19 2-0 Apr18 1-0	Oct15 3-2 Feb25 1-3	Dec27 0-1 May12 2-0	Dec03 2-2 Apr07 2-5
DUNDEE U	Nov26 0-2 May07 0-0	Oct08 2-1 Mar03 3-1	Nov05 0-1 Apr21 1-1		Oct22 1-0 Mar11 3-1	Sep10 5-0 Feb11 2-0	Aug20 4-0 Dec31 2-1	Oct01 0-2 May14 1-2	Nov12 7-0 Apr14 3-0	Apr30 2-0 May05 2-2
HEARTS	Oct01 0-2 May02 0-1	Dec17 1-3 May05 1-1	Nov13 1-3 May09 1-1	Dec10 0-0 Mar31 0-0		Sep03 3-2 Jan02 1-1	Oct08 0-0 Mar03 2-1	Sep10 3-1 Feb11 2-2	Oct29 2-0 Apr28 2-2	Nov26 2-2 Mar24 2-1
HIBERNIAN	Oct15 2-1 Feb25 0-2	Aug20 0-2 Dec31 0-1	Oct22 2-1 Feb29 3-1	Dec03 0-2 Apr07 1-0	Nov05 1-1 Apr21 0-0		Sep24 2-1 Mar10 1-2	Dec27 0-2 May12 0-0	Nov19 4-1 Mar18 1-2	Sep17 3-1 Jan07 1-1
MOTHERWELL	Sep10 1-1 Feb11 0-4	Sep17 0-3 Jan07 2-2	Oct01 1-3 Mar28 2-4	Oct29 2-2 Apr28 1-3	Dec26 1-1 May12 0-1	Nov26 1-2 Mar24 2-3		Dec10 0-3 Mar31 0-3	Oct15 0-1 Feb25 1-0	Nov05 0-0 Apr21 1-0
RANGERS	Sep17 0-2 Jan07 1-1	Nov05 1-2 Apr21 1-0	Dec17 2-1 May05 2-2	Nov19 0-0 May02 2-2	Dec03 3-0 Apr07 0-0	Oct08 1-0 Mar03 0-0	Oct22 1-2 Feb04 2-1		Sep24 6-3 Jan21 2-0	Aug20 1-1 Dec31 1-1
ST JOHNSTONE	Nov05 0-5 Apr21 0-2	Dec03 0-3 Apr07 0-0	Oct08 0-2 Mar03 1-0	Sep17 1-2 Jan07 1-2	Aug20 0-1 Dec31 1-2	Oct01 0-3 Feb18 1-0	Dec17 3-1 May05 3-1	Nov26 0-1 Mar06 1-4		Oct22 3-2 Mar31 4-2
ST MIRREN	Dec24 0-3 May12 3-2	Nov19 4-2 Apr18 2-4	Sep10 0-0 Feb11 4-0	Nov22 4-0 Feb25 2-2	Sep24 0-1 Mar17 1-1	Nov12 2-1 Mar21 3-1	Sep03 1-1 Jan03 2-1	Oct29 3-0 Apr28 1-1	Dec10 1-2 Feb04 1-1	

LEAGUE TABLES

PREMIER DIVISION

	P	W	D	L	F	A	W	D	L	F	A	Pts
Aberdeen	36	14	3	1	46	12	11	4	3	32	9	57
Celtic	36	13	5	0	46	15	8	3	7	34	26	50
Dundee U	36	11	3	4	38	14	7	8	3	29	25	47
Rangers	36	7	8	3	26	18	8	4	6	27	23	42
Hearts	36	5	9	4	23	23	5	7	6	15	24	36
St Mirren	36	8	6	4	34	23	1	8	9	21	36	32
Hibernian	36	7	4	7	21	21	5	3	10	24	34	31
Dundee	36	6	1	11	28	42	5	4	9	22	32	27
St Johnstone	36	6	1	11	19	33	4	2	12	17	48	23
Motherwell	36	2	5	11	15	36	2	2	14	16	39	15

DIVISION 1

	P	W	D	L	F	A	W	D	L	F	A	Pts
Morton	39	10	6	3	36	21	11	6	3	39	25	54
Dumbarton	39	13	4	3	37	19	7	7	5	29	25	51
Partick T	39	11	5	4	37	20	8	3	8	30	30	46
Clydebank	39	10	5	5	38	29	6	8	5	24	21	45
Brechin C	39	11	4	4	33	22	3	10	7	23	36	42
Kilmarnock	39	10	4	5	31	17	6	2	12	26	36	38
Falkirk	39	8	5	7	27	25	8	1	10	19	29	38
Clyde	39	6	8	5	28	23	6	5	9	25	27	37
Hamilton A	39	6	8	5	27	22	5	6	9	16	24	36
Airdrie	39	10	3	7	20	21	3	7	9	25	32	36
Meadowbank T	39	8	4	8	29	35	4	6	9	20	34	34
Ayr U	39	5	8	6	29	32	5	4	11	27	38	32
Raith R	39	6	6	8	33	30	4	5	10	20	32	31
Alloa	39	7	5	7	24	24	1	5	14	17	40	26

DIVISION 2

	P	W	D	L	F	A	W	D	L	F	A	Pts
Forfar A	39	16	4	0	45	13	11	5	3	28	18	63
East Fife	39	11	3	6	31	21	9	4	6	26	21	47
Berwick R	39	11	5	4	35	13	5	6	8	22	25	43
Stirling A	39	9	5	6	23	18	5	9	5	28	24	42
Arbroath	39	10	3	6	32	25	8	3	9	19	21	42
Queen of South	39	11	6	2	29	15	5	4	11	22	31	42
Stenhousemuir	39	10	5	4	30	25	4	6	10	17	32	39
Stranraer	39	9	7	3	25	16	4	5	11	22	31	38
Dunfermline A	39	7	7	5	25	16	6	3	11	19	29	36
Queen's Park	39	10	4	6	35	28	4	4	11	23	35	36
E. Stirling	39	4	4	11	23	37	6	7	7	28	29	31
Montrose	39	7	3	10	17	25	5	4	10	19	31	31
Cowdenbeath	39	5	5	10	21	29	5	4	10	23	29	29
Albion R	39	3	7	9	24	37	5	4	11	22	39	27

DIVISION 1

	AIRDRIE	ALLOA	AYR U	BRECHIN C	CLYDE	CLYDEBANK	DUMBARTON	FALKIRK	HAMILTON A	KILMARNOCK	MEADOWBANK T	MORTON	PARTICK T	RAITH R
AIRDRIE		Nov26 1-0	Nov19 2-0 Apr14 1-0	Sep09 1-0 Mar03 1-2	Dec10 0-4	Sep14 1-0 Mar31 3-3	Nov05 1-1 May05 1-4	Sep28 0-1	Jan03 1-0 Feb25 0-1	Oct15 1-0 Mar17 3-0	Dec27 1-2	Oct10 0-3	Feb22 0-0 Apr21 1-0	Jan07 1-0
ALLOA	Oct08 1-0 May12 0-0		Dec03 0-0	Sep28 4-1	Nov05 1-1 Mar10 0-0	Nov19 0-2	Feb21 1-0	Aug20 0-1 Feb11 3-1	Dec26 2-1 Mar24 3-1	Dec10 0-4	Sep03 0-1	Jan07 1-3	Sep14 3-4 Apr07 2-2	Oct15 1-2 Apr21 2-0
AYR U	Sep17 2-2	Oct01 4-2 Mar17 3-1		Dec10 1-1	Dec26 1-0 Feb25 2-1	Nov26 2-2	Sep03 1-2	Oct15 0-1 Apr28 1-2	Nov05 1-1 Apr21 1-1	Aug20 0-2	Jan21 2-2	Nov12 2-2 Mar31 1-2	Jan07 2-1 Mar14 1-5	Sep28 2-2
BRECHIN C	Dec31 3-1	Dec17 1-0 Feb25 1-1	Sep24 2-1 Mar10 4-1		Sep17 3-0 Apr10 3-2	Mar13 0-2 May12 2-2	Nov12 2-3 Apr21 0-3	Oct29 1-0	Mar06 1-0	Nov26 3-2	Oct22 0-0	Sep10 3-1 Apr07 1-2	Oct01 2-0	Aug20 1-1
CLYDE	Sep24 1-1 Apr07 1-1	Feb04 2-2	Sep10 1-1	Nov19 2-2		Dec31 2-2 Mar03 1-1	Feb29 0-0	Sep14 1-2 May05 1-0	Oct22 1-0 May12 0-1	Oct01 0-1 Apr21 2-1	Oct17 2-1	Oct29 2-3 Mar17 3-2	Aug20 1-2	Nov26 5-0
CLYDEBANK	Nov12 2-4	Sep17 2-7 Apr14 1-0	Oct08 4-1 Feb11 1-2	Nov05 1-0	Sep03 1-0		Jan02 0-2	Jan07 3-1 Mar24 1-2	Feb21 1-1	Sep28 4-0 Feb25 3-0	Dec03 3-0 Apr21 1-1	Oct15 3-3 Apr28 1-1	Dec10 1-0	Dec26 1-1 Mar10 4-3
DUMBARTON	Feb04 4-2	Oct29 1-1 Mar31 2-0	Dec31 2-1 May12 0-3	Sep14 1-2	Oct15 1-0 Apr28 2-2	Aug20 2-0 Apr07 2-1		Dec10 3-0 Mar03 2-0	Sep28 2-0	Jan07 4-3	Nov19 0-0 Mar17 3-0	Nov26 1-1	Sep10 0-1	Oct01 2-1 Feb25 3-1
FALKIRK	Dec17 2-0 Mar10 1-1	Feb29 1-1	Feb18 2-1	Feb21 0-1 Mar17 0-0	Nov12 0-2	Oct22 1-1	Sep24 4-1		Dec03 4-1	Dec26 1-3 Mar31 2-0	Oct08 2-1 Feb25 1-4	Sep17 0-2 Apr21 0-1	Nov05 2-2 May12 1-2	Sep03 2-1 Apr14 1-0
HAMILTON A	Aug20 1-1	Sep10 1-0	Feb04 0-0	Oct15 3-3 Apr14 3-2	Jan07 1-2	Oct29 1-0 Mar17 0-1	Dec17 4-1 Feb11 3-3	Oct01 1-2 Apr07 2-0		Sep17 0-1 Mar03 1-1	Sep24 1-1 May05 1-2	Dec31 1-1	Nov26 3-1	Nov12 0-0
KILMARNOCK	Jan14 4-1	Sep24 2-0 Apr28 2-0	Jan03 1-0 May05 3-0	Oct08 4-1 Feb11 1-1	Dec03 0-1	Dec17 0-1	Oct22 2-2 Mar10 0-0	Sep10 2-1	Nov19 2-1		Sep14 3-1 Apr07 1-1	Feb04 0-1	Dec31 1-2	Oct29 2-1 Mar24 1-2
MEADOWBANK T	Sep10 1-0 Apr28 0-4	Dec31 4-0 Mar03 2-1	Oct29 1-5 Mar24 2-2	Jan07 2-1 Mar31 2-2	Sep28 1-1 Apr14 3-1	Oct01 1-3	Sep17 0-2	Nov26 0-1	Dec10 2-0	Nov12 2-1		Aug20 1-4 Feb11 1-1	Oct15 2-1	Feb04 1-3 May12 1-2
MORTON	Dec03 3-2 Mar24 2-1	Oct22 1-0 May05 3-0	Sep14 2-3	Dec26 0-0	Feb21 2-1	Feb29 1-2	Oct08 2-2 Apr14 2-0	Nov19 3-1	Sep03 1-1 Mar20 0-0	Nov05 2-2 May12 3-2	Jan02 4-0		Sep28 1-2 Feb25 4-2	Dec10 0-0
PARTICK T	Oct29 2-1	Nov12 5-0	Oct22 4-3	Dec03 2-2 Apr28 1-1	Jan02 1-2 Feb11 1-2	Sep24 1-0 May05 1-1	Dec26 1-0 Mar24 0-0	Feb04 3-1	Oct08 0-0 Mar31 1-2	Sep03 2-0 Apr14 1-2	Feb18 4-1 Mar10 2-1	Dec17 3-1		Sep17 2-0
RAITH R	Oct22 0-0 Feb11 2-3	Feb17 1-1	Dec17 1-3 Apr07 5-0	Jan02 1-1 May05 6-0	Oct08 2-1 Mar31 2-2	Sep10 0-0	Dec03 1-3	Dec31 2-2	Sep14 1-2 Apr28 0-2	Feb29 2-1	Nov05 3-1	Sep24 1-3 Mar03 0-2	Nov19 1-2 Mar17 2-1	

DIVISION 2

	ALBION R	ARBROATH	BERWICK R	COWDENBEATH	DUNFERMLINE A	EAST FIFE	E STIRLING	FORFAR A	MONTROSE	QUEEN OF SOUTH	QUEEN'S PARK	STENHOUSEMUIR	STIRLING A	STRANRAER
ALBION R		Nov12 3-0	Feb14 4-4	Mar13 2-0	Sep17 1-1	Oct22 1-2	Sep24 2-3 May05 0-1	Oct29 2-2	Sep10 0-2 Mar24 0-4	Dec17 1-1 Feb25 1-4	Nov26 1-4 Apr07 0-0	Aug20 1-2 Apr21 1-1	Oct01 1-1 Mar10 1-4	Dec31 2-1
ARBROATH	Aug27 3-0 May12 0-1		Oct22 1-1	Sep03 3-2 Mar10 1-0	Feb21 3-0	Nov19 0-2 Apr28 0-1	Feb04 3-2	Jan02 0-1	Dec17 2-1 Feb25 1-1	Sep24 1-2 Apr21 6-3	Oct01 2-0 Mar31 0-5	Nov26 1-1	Mar20 2-1	Oct29 3-1
BERWICK R	Oct15 4-3 Apr14 0-0	Feb28 0-0 Mar17 2-0		Oct29 0-0	Nov12 1-1 May12 2-0	Dec17 1-0 Mar31 2-1	Dec31 1-2	Oct01 1-2 Mar10 0-1	Sep24 4-0	Feb04 2-0	Aug20 3-0	Sep10 3-0 Apr28 6-1	Nov26 1-1	Sep17 0-1 Feb18 2-0
COWDENBEATH	Nov05 0-1 Mar31 2-3	Dec31 0-1	Feb21 2-1 Apr07 0-1		Aug20 0-1 Mar03 1-2	Dec03 0-0 Mar17 1-5	Sep17 2-1	Mar06 0-1 May05 1-2	Nov12 5-2 Apr28 1-0	Oct08 0-0	Sep10 3-1	Dec26 1-1	Sep28 0-4 Feb18 0-0	Oct15 2-2
DUNFERMLINE A	Feb11 1-2 Apr28 5-0	Oct15 0-1 Apr07 2-0	Sep14 1-0	Mar20 0-0		Sep03 1-1 Apr21 0-1	Oct29 1-1 Mar10 1-2	Sep28 1-2 Apr09 3-1	Feb08 1-1	Nov19 1-0	Feb21 2-2	Oct01 2-0	Dec26 1-1	Nov26 1-1 Feb25 1-0
EAST FIFE	Jan14 1-0 Feb21 1-4	Sep17 0-1	Sep28 1-2	Oct01 2-1	Dec31 3-1		Nov12 2-1 Apr14 2-0	Nov26 2-3 Feb25 0-0	Aug20 1-0	Oct29 1-2 Mar10 0-0	Dec26 3-1 May05 3-0	Feb04 0-1 Apr07 3-1	Oct15 1-1 Mar24 4-2	Sep10 1-0
E STIRLING	Dec26 2-2	Nov05 0-3 Mar03 0-1	Sep03 0-2 Mar24 1-1	Nov19 3-1 May12 3-4	Feb15 0-2	Sep14 1-4		Feb11 3-1	Oct08 1-3	Dec03 1-0	Sep28 1-2	Oct15 1-3 Feb18 2-1	Aug20 0-1 Apr07 1-3	Mar14 1-1 Apr28 2-2
FORFAR A	Feb28 2-1 Mar17 1-0	Aug20 4-1 Feb18 1-1	Dec03 4-1	Oct22 1-0	Dec17 1-0	Oct08 3-1	Sep10 0-0 Apr21 4-3		Dec31 4-0 May12 2-0	Feb21 2-0 Apr28 3-0	Nov12 4-1 Mar03 0-0	Sep17 1-0	Nov05 1-1	Sep24 2-0 Apr07 5-3
MONTROSE	Nov19 3-1	Sep28 0-4	Dec10 0-1 May05 2-1	Sep14 1-2	Nov05 0-1 Mar31 2-0	Jan02 0-1 Mar03 1-1	Nov26 0-2 Mar17 0-1	Sep03 0-1		Feb11 1-0 Apr07 2-1	Oct15 1-2 Mar18 2-1	Feb15 0-0	Mar14 1-0 Apr21 0-0	Oct01 1-5
QUEEN OF SOUTH	Sep28 4-0	Dec24 2-1	Nov05 1-1 Mar03 2-1	Nov26 1-0 Apr14 0-2	Sep10 2-1 Feb18 1-0	Dec10 0-0	Oct01 2-1 Mar31 1-1	Oct15 1-1	Sep17 1-2		Dec31 2-1 Mar17 2-0	Nov12 2-0	Feb29 2-2	Aug20 3-1 Feb05 0-0
QUEEN'S PARK	Oct08 1-1	Dec03 2-1	Jan02 1-0 Apr21 1-1	Feb11 4-3 Mar27 0-4	Oct22 3-1 Apr17 1-2	Sep24 5-2	Dec17 5-4 Jan28 1-1	Sep14 0-1	Mar06 3-0	Sep03 0-2		Oct29 1-1 May12 3-1	Nov19 0-1 Apr28 3-1	Feb04 0-1 Mar10 1-0
STENHOUSEMUIR	Feb07 1-1	Oct08 0-0 Apr14 1-0	Feb11 3-2	Sep24 2-0 Feb25 0-1	Dec03 2-1 May05 2-1	Nov05 3-1	Mar06 1-1	Nov19 2-1 Mar31 0-4	Oct22 1-2 Mar10 0-0	Sep14 0-3 Mar24 2-2	Mar14 4-2		Sep03 4-3	Dec17 2-0
STIRLING A	Dec03 3-1	Sep10 2-1 May05 0-1	Oct08 0-2 Feb25 0-0	Dec17 4-1	Sep24 2-1 Mar17 1-2	Mar06 0-1	Feb21 0-0	Mar27 0-0 Apr14 1-1	Oct29 2-0	Oct22 2-0 May12 3-1	Sep17 1-0	Dec31 0-0 Mar03 0-3		Nov12 2-1 Mar31 0-2
STRANRAER	Sep03 3-1 Mar03 2-0	Feb15 0-1 Mar24 2-1	Nov19 1-0	Jan21 1-1 Apr21 1-1	Oct08 1-1	Feb11 1-0 May12 1-2	Oct22 1-1	Dec26 1-3	Dec03 2-1 Apr14 0-0	Jan02 2-1	Nov05 1-1	Aug27 2-0 Mar17 2-0	Sep14 1-1	

Scottish Football League Records
Season 1984-85

PREMIER

	ABERDEEN	CELTIC	DUMBARTON	DUNDEE	DUNDEE U	HEARTS	HIBERNIAN	MORTON	RANGERS	ST MIRREN
ABERDEEN		Dec08 4-2 Apr27 1-1	Nov24 1-0 Apr20 4-0	Aug11 3-2 Dec15 0-0	Dec22 0-1 Mar30 4-2	Sep29 4-0 Feb09 2-2	Sep01 4-1 Jan05 2-0	Nov10 3-1 Jan12 5-0	Sep15 0-0 Jan19 5-1	Oct20 4-0 Mar02 3-0
CELTIC	Oct06 2-1 Feb23 2-0		Nov10 2-0 May11 2-0	Dec01 5-1 May04 0-1	Aug18 1-1 Dec29 1-2	Sep15 1-0 Mar20 3-2	Oct13 3-0 Mar16 0-1	Sep01 5-0 Feb19 4-0	Dec22 1-1 May01 1-1	Nov24 7-1 Apr20 3-0
DUMBARTON	Sep22 0-2 Feb02 0-2	Sep08 1-1 Apr03 0-2		Aug25 2-1 Jan01 1-0	Dec08 2-2 Apr27 0-2	Nov03 0-1 Mar23 1-3	Nov17 2-2 Apr06 0-2	Oct13 3-1 Mar16 1-0	Aug18 1-2 Dec29 2-4	Sep29 0-1 Feb09 1-1
DUNDEE	Oct13 1-2 Mar16 0-4	Sep29 2-3 Feb09 2-0	Oct27 1-1 Apr13 1-0		Nov10 0-2 May11 1-0	Nov24 2-1 Apr20 3-0	Aug18 0-1 Dec29 2-0	Dec08 5-1 Apr27 0-0	Sep01 0-2 Jan05 2-2	Sep15 2-0 Feb20 1-0
DUNDEE U	Aug25 0-2 Jan02 2-1	Oct20 1-3 Mar02 0-0	Oct06 1-0 Feb23 4-0	Sep08 3-4 Apr03 4-0		Aug11 2-0 Dec15 5-2	Sep22 2-1 Feb02 2-0	Nov17 7-0 Apr06 5-0	Dec01 1-1 May04 2-1	Nov03 3-2 Mar23 3-1
HEARTS	Dec01 1-2 May04 0-3	Nov17 1-5 Apr06 0-2	Sep01 1-0 Jan05 5-1	Sep22 0-2 Feb03 3-3	Oct13 2-0 Mar16 0-1		Oct27 0-0 Apr02 2-2	Aug18 1-2 Dec29 1-0	Oct06 1-0 Feb23 2-0	Sep08 1-2 Jan12 0-1
HIBERNIAN	Nov06 0-3 Mar23 0-5	Aug11 0-0 Dec15 0-1	Sep15 2-3 Jan19 3-1	Oct20 2-0 Mar02 0-1	Nov24 0-0 Apr20 1-1	Aug25 1-2 Jan01 1-2		Sep29 3-1 Feb09 5-1	Nov10 2-2 May11 1-0	Dec08 2-3 Apr27 0-4
MORTON	Sep08 0-3 May11 1-2	Nov03 2-1 Mar23 2-7	Aug11 2-1 Dec15 2-4	Oct06 1-1 Feb23 0-1	Sep15 0-3 Mar13 0-3	Oct20 2-3 Mar02 0-1	Dec01 4-0 May04 1-2		Nov24 1-3 Apr20 0-3	Aug25 0-4 Jan01 0-2
RANGERS	Nov17 1-2 Apr06 1-2	Aug25 0-0 Jan01 1-2	Oct20 0-0 Mar02 3-1	Nov03 0-0 Mar23 1-3	Sep29 1-0 Feb09 0-0	Dec08 1-1 Apr27 3-1	Sep08 2-0 Jan12 1-2	Sep22 2-0 Feb02 2-0		Aug11 0-0 Dec15 2-0
ST MIRREN	Aug18 0-2 Dec29 2-2	Sep22 1-2 Feb02 0-2	Dec01 0-0 May04 1-0	Nov17 2-1 Apr06 4-2	Sep01 1-0 Jan05 1-0	Nov10 2-3 May11 5-2	Oct06 2-0 Feb23 2-1	Oct27 2-1 Apr02 2-3	Oct13 0-2 Mar16 2-1	

LEAGUE TABLES

PREMIER DIVISION

	P	W	D	L	F	A	W	D	L	F	A	Pts
Aberdeen	36	13	4	1	49	13	14	1	3	40	13	59
Celtic	36	12	3	3	43	12	10	5	3	34	18	52
Dundee U	36	13	2	3	47	18	7	5	6	20	15	47
Rangers	36	7	6	5	21	14	6	6	6	26	24	38
St Mirren	36	10	2	6	29	24	7	2	9	22	32	38
Dundee	36	9	3	6	25	19	6	4	8	23	31	37
Hearts	36	6	3	9	21	26	7	2	9	26	38	31
Hibernian	36	5	4	9	23	30	5	3	10	15	31	27
Dumbarton	36	4	4	10	17	29	2	3	13	12	35	19
Morton	36	3	1	14	18	44	2	1	15	11	56	12

DIVISION 1

	P	W	D	L	F	A	W	D	L	F	A	Pts
Motherwell	39	11	4	4	34	14	10	4	6	28	22	50
Clydebank	39	11	4	4	31	16	6	10	4	26	21	48
Falkirk	39	9	3	7	36	31	10	4	6	29	23	45
Hamilton A	39	8	5	7	23	24	8	6	5	25	25	43
Airdrie	39	11	1	7	43	33	6	7	7	27	26	42
Forfar A	39	9	7	4	27	18	5	6	8	27	31	41
Ayr U	39	9	6	5	31	25	6	3	10	26	27	39
Clyde	39	9	5	6	31	26	5	6	8	16	22	39
Brechin C	39	7	5	8	25	28	7	4	8	24	29	37
East Fife	39	6	6	8	26	25	6	6	7	29	31	36
Partick T	39	8	5	6	28	22	5	4	11	22	33	35
Kilmarnock	39	8	8	4	23	23	4	2	13	19	38	34
Meadowbank T	39	5	5	9	25	33	6	5	9	25	33	32
St Johnstone	39	4	4	11	23	33	6	1	13	28	45	25

DIVISION 2

	P	W	D	L	F	A	W	D	L	F	A	Pts
Montrose	39	11	5	3	29	21	11	4	5	28	19	53
Alloa	39	9	6	4	29	17	11	4	5	29	23	50
Dunfermline A	39	7	9	4	34	20	10	6	3	27	16	49
Cowdenbeath	39	10	5	4	36	17	8	6	6	32	22	47
Stenhousemuir	39	9	6	5	27	25	6	9	4	18	18	45
Stirling A	39	8	7	4	33	22	7	6	7	29	25	43
Raith R	39	9	1	9	30	25	9	5	6	39	32	42
Queen of South	39	6	7	7	27	25	4	7	8	15	31	34
Albion R	39	7	2	11	27	39	6	6	7	22	33	34
Queen's Park	39	7	5	7	24	19	5	4	11	24	36	33
Stranraer	39	7	2	11	30	33	6	4	9	22	34	32
E. Stirling	39	5	8	7	21	22	3	7	9	17	31	31
Berwick R	39	5	7	7	18	20	3	5	12	18	29	28
Arbroath	39	6	5	9	22	28	3	2	14	13	38	25

DIVISION 1

	AIRDRIE	AYR U	BRECHIN C	CLYDE	CLYDEBANK	EAST FIFE	FALKIRK	FORFAR A	HAMILTON A	KILMARNOCK	MEADOWBANK T	MOTHERWELL	PARTICK T	ST JOHNSTONE
AIRDRIE		Mar26 1-2	Dec22 2-2	Oct13 4-3 Apr20 1-2	Aug18 1-0	Nov05 2-3 May04 2-4	Sep22 1-0 Mar02 2-1	Mar13 4-2 Apr06 2-4	Sep08 1-2	Dec01 2-1	Dec29 5-0 Mar23 3-5	Oct06 2-0	Nov17 4-1	Sep01 2-1 Feb23 2-0
AYR U	Oct20 0-2 Apr13 5-1		Nov24 2-1 Feb23 0-1	Sep15 0-0	Dec08 4-4 Apr27 3-2	Dec15 2-1 Mar16 1-1	Oct27 2-0	Aug25 2-0	Aug11 1-1	Jan02 1-0 Mar30 0-0	Feb02 1-1 May11 1-3	Nov10 1-3 Mar02 1-2	Sep29 3-2	Mar06 1-0
BRECHIN C	Aug25 3-0 Apr27 0-0	Sep22 0-2		Dec29 1-0	Nov03 2-2	Sep08 2-2 Feb09 1-1	Oct06 2-3 May11 0-0	Aug18 0-2	Nov21 0-1 Mar16 2-0	Dec15 3-2 Mar02 2-1	Oct20 4-1 Apr20 1-2	Feb26 0-2	Jan19 0-4 Apr09 1-3	Dec01 1-0
CLYDE	Feb16 0-0	Nov17 2-1 Mar09 1-0	Aug11 1-3 Apr06 2-2		Sep08 2-0	Sep22 1-1	Dec01 1-2	Nov03 4-2 Apr13 2-1	Jan19 1-3	Aug25 4-1	Sep01 0-0 Apr27 0-1	Oct20 3-3 Mar23 1-0	Jan01 1-0 Feb09 1-0	Oct06 2-3 May11 2-3
CLYDEBANK	Jan01 1-0 Apr03 1-1	Oct06 2-1	Feb02 0-2 Apr13 5-1	Nov10 1-2 Mar02 2-0		Dec01 1-0	Dec22 1-3	Mar05 1-1	Sep01 0-0 Feb23 1-1	Sep15 5-0	Oct27 1-0	Nov24 2-1	Oct20 1-0 Mar23 1-2	Aug11 3-0 May04 2-1
EAST FIFE	Feb02 3-1	Sep01 1-1	Nov10 2-0	Nov24 1-1 Feb23 0-1	Sep29 4-4 May11 0-0		Aug11 2-4 Mar23 3-2	Dec08 0-0	Dec22 0-1	Oct20 0-1 Apr20 0-2	Sep15 1-1 Mar02 1-0	Oct27 1-2 Jan19 1-2	Jan12 3-1 Apr27 0-1	Jan01 3-0
FALKIRK	Nov24 4-2	Feb26 1-0 May04 0-1	Dec08 3-0	Sep29 2-0 Mar16 1-0	Aug25 0-2 Mar09 0-0	Dec29 1-2		Oct20 4-6	Nov03 6-4 Apr20 0-0	Mar13 3-2	Aug18 3-3	Sep15 0-3 Feb09 0-2	Dec15 5-1	Nov10 1-3 Apr03 2-0
FORFAR A	Oct27 0-0	Dec22 4-2 Feb09 0-5	Jan01 2-1 Mar19 1-0	Feb02 1-1	Oct13 0-0 Apr20 1-1	Oct06 1-0 Apr09 1-0	Jan05 0-0 Apr27 0-2		Dec01 1-1	Nov10 4-1	Nov24 2-1	Sep01 1-2 May11 0-0	Aug11 4-0	Sep15 4-0 Mar16 0-1
HAMILTON A	Nov10 1-1 Feb09 1-3	Dec29 3-1 Mar23 1-4	Sep15 0-1	Oct27 0-2 Mar30 1-0	Dec15 0-1	Aug25 2-4 Apr13 2-1	Feb02 0-0	Sep29 3-1 Mar02 0-1		Nov24 1-0	Jan12 0-0	Aug18 2-0 Apr27 1-1	Dec09 1-0 May11 1-1	Oct20 3-2
KILMARNOCK	Sep29 0-5 May11 1-4	Aug18 0-0	Sep01 1-1	Dec22 2-0 May04 2-0	Nov17 1-1 Feb26 0-0	Jan05 1-1	Oct13 3-1 Apr06 0-3	Sep08 2-1 Mar23 1-0	Sep22 1-2 Mar09 1-1		Dec08 2-1	Dec29 0-0	Nov03 0-0 Apr13 2-0	Jan19 3-2
MEADOWBANK T	Aug11 0-3	Nov07 3-0	Jan05 2-4	Sep01 0-0 Dec15 1-1	Jan19 1-3 Apr09 0-3	Nov17 0-3	Dec18 1-1 Apr13 0-1	Sep22 1-3 Feb23 0-0	Oct13 2-0 May04 2-4	Oct06 4-0 Mar16 2-1		Dec01 4-2	Sep08 1-1 Mar09 0-2	Dec22 1-1
MOTHERWELL	Dec08 1-1 Mar20 2-0	Sep08 1-1	Oct13 2-0 May04 2-1	Jan05 0-0	Sep22 0-1 Mar16 1-0	Apr06 5-0	Nov17 2-3	Dec15 2-0	Jan02 3-0	Aug11 2-0 Feb23 2-2	Sep29 3-1 Apr03 0-1		Aug25 2-1	Nov03 0-2 Apr24 4-0
PARTICK T	Sep15 0-1 Mar16 1-1	Dec01 2-0 Apr06 3-2	Oct27 1-2	Aug18 1-1	Feb20 0-1	Oct13 0-0	Sep01 3-0 Feb23 0-1	Dec29 1-1 May04 1-1	Oct06 1-0	Feb02 1-0	Nov10 2-0	Dec22 2-1 Apr20 0-1		Nov24 3-7 Mar02 6-2
ST JOHNSTONE	Dec15 2-1	Oct13 2-1 Apr20 0-2	Sep29 0-1 Mar23 1-1	Dec08 1-2	Feb16 1-1	Aug18 3-4 Mar09 3-1	Sep08 0-2	Nov17 1-1	Jan05 1-2 Apr06 1-2	Oct27 0-1 Apr27 2-4	Aug25 3-2 Feb26 0-2	Feb02 0-1	Sep22 2-2	

DIVISION 2

	ALBION R	ALLOA	ARBROATH	BERWICK R	COWDENBEATH	DUNFERMLINE A	E STIRLING	MONTROSE	QUEEN OF SOUTH	QUEEN'S PARK	RAITH R	STENHOUSEMUIR	STIRLING A	STRANRAER
ALBION R		Sep15 0-1 Apr13 4-1	Nov10 1-0 Feb16 3-0	Nov06 1-0 Mar16 3-2	Aug11 1-0 May11 1-2	Oct20 0-2 Apr16 1-1	Feb19 1-0	Feb02 1-4	Aug25 3-4	Mar05 3-3	Apr02 0-6 Apr27 2-4	Jan01 0-1	Dec01 0-4	Sep29 1-2 Mar09 1-2
ALLOA	Nov17 4-0		Nov03 3-0	Feb09 1-0 Apr23 0-0	Sep29 3-0 Mar16 1-1	Feb26 1-3 May04 0-0	Dec29 2-1 Apr20 1-3	Sep08 3-1	Sep22 1-1	Aug11 2-0 Mar09 2-1	Oct13 1-1	Aug25 0-0	Jan02 2-1	Dec01 1-2 Mar06 1-2
ARBROATH	Sep08 1-2	Jan26 0-0 May11 0-1		Dec15 0-5 Feb23 2-0	Oct27 1-1	Oct06 0-2 Mar09 1-3	Oct20 2-2 Apr27 3-0	Aug18 0-3	Jan12 3-0	Nov17 1-2	Dec29 2-1	Feb02 0-0 Apr20 1-1	Sep22 0-3 Mar16 0-1	Aug25 2-0 Apr10 3-1
BERWICK R	Apr10 0-1	Oct20 0-0	Oct29 2-1		Jan01 0-2 Apr20 0-4	Sep08 0-1	Dec01 0-0 Mar09 0-0	Sep22 0-1 Apr16 0-1	Feb02 0-0 Mar23 4-0	Aug25 4-1 Feb26 1-0	Aug11 2-1	Oct27 2-2	Nov17 1-1 Apr27 0-2	Dec29 2-2
COWDENBEATH	Jan12 0-0	Dec15 2-1	Feb26 3-2 Mar23 2-0	Aug18 1-0		Nov17 0-1	Feb02 5-1	Oct06 0-1	Oct20 4-1 Apr13 1-1	Sep08 2-3 Apr10 0-0	Aug25 5-1 Feb23 0-0	Mar09 0-1 Apr03 2-0	Nov03 3-3	Sep22 2-1 Apr27 4-0
DUNFERMLINE A	Feb09 1-1	Oct27 2-2	Dec01 1-2	Nov10 1-1 May11 2-1	Sep15 2-1 Mar02 1-2		Mar19 2-0	Dec22 1-1 Apr20 0-0	Sep29 1-1 Apr27 4-0	Oct13 4-0	Jan02 1-2 Apr23 2-3	Nov24 1-1 Mar23 0-0	Sep01 1-0 Feb16 2-2	Aug11 5-0
E STIRLING	Sep22 2-3 May04 0-0	Sep01 1-2	Feb09 2-0	Oct06 1-2	Oct13 0-0 Apr06 1-2	Nov03 2-0 Apr13 0-0		Nov17 0-1 Mar16 0-0	Sep08 0-0 Mar06 0-0	Dec26 3-2 Mar23 0-1	Dec15 1-3 Mar02 2-1	Aug11 1-1	Dec22 2-2	Feb25 3-2
MONTROSE	Oct13 1-0 Apr23 0-0	Nov10 2-1 Mar23 2-0	Jan01 2-1 Mar02 3-0	Nov24 1-1	Dec01 1-4 Feb16 2-1	Aug25 2-4	Sep15 4-2		Feb20 2-2	Apr27 1-4	Feb09 2-0	Sep29 1-0 May04 0-0	Aug11 1-0	Nov03 0-0 Apr13 2-1
QUEEN OF SOUTH	Dec22 3-2 Apr20 1-2	Nov24 1-2 Feb23 0-2	Aug11 1-1 May04 1-0	Oct13 3-0	Mar13 1-1	Dec15 0-0	Nov10 0-1	Sep01 3-1 Mar09 1-1		Oct06 2-2	Nov03 3-5 Mar16 3-0	Sep15 1-2 Mar30 1-1	Feb26 0-1 May11 2-1	Jan01 0-0
QUEEN'S PARK	Sep01 5-1 Feb23 1-1	Jan12 0-0	Sep15 0-1 Apr06 1-0	Dec22 1-0	Nov10 1-1	Feb02 4-1 Mar16 1-1	Aug18 4-1	Oct27 0-1 Jan19 2-1	Dec01 0-1 Mar02 0-2		Nov24 1-1 Apr20 1-2	Jan26 1-0	Sep29 1-2	Oct20 0-2
RAITH R	Oct27 3-0	Feb02 1-2 Apr09 2-0	Sep01 2-0 Apr13 2-1	Feb20 2-1 May04 3-0	Dec22 0-3	Aug18 1-3	Sep29 2-0	Oct20 0-1 May11 1-3	Mar26 3-0	Sep22 0-2		Dec01 3-0 Mar06 1-2	Sep08 1-1 Mar09 2-4	Nov17 1-2
STENHOUSEMUIR	Aug18 1-1 Mar02 2-1	Dec22 0-3 Apr27 2-4	Oct13 1-2	Mar20 2-1 Apr13 1-1	Sep01 0-4	Sep22 1-0	Feb16 1-1 Feb23 0-0	Dec15 1-2	Nov17 1-0	Nov03 3-2 May11 2-0	Oct06 1-1		Feb09 1-1 Apr10 3-0	Sep08 2-0 Mar16 2-1
STIRLING A	Oct06 2-3 Mar23 4-1	Aug18 0-1 Mar02 2-3	Nov24 1-1	Sep15 1-1	Mar06 1-1 May04 1-0	Dec29 2-2	Aug25 2-2 Apr03 1-0	Feb23 3-1 Mar12 3-1	Oct27 2-0	Dec15 3-0 Apr13 1-0	Nov10 1-1	Oct20 1-2		Feb02 2-2
STRANRAER	Mar26 2-3	Oct06 2-3	Dec22 7-1	Sep01 2-0 Mar02 1-2	Nov24 4-2	Feb23 0-1 Apr03 0-2	Oct27 1-1 May11 0-2	Jan26 0-3	Aug18 1-0 Apr06 1-2	Mar20 2-1 May04 0-0	Sep15 1-2 Mar23 1-4	Nov10 2-4	Oct13 2-0 Apr20 1-0	

Scottish Football League Records
Season 1985-86

PREMIER

	ABERDEEN	CELTIC	CLYDEBANK	DUNDEE	DUNDEE U	HEARTS	HIBERNIAN	MOTHERWELL	RANGERS	ST MIRREN
ABERDEEN		Nov02 4-1 Apr12 0-1	Oct05 3-1 Feb08 4-1	Nov09 4-1 Mar22 0-0	Oct19 3-2 Apr16 0-1	Sep07 3-0 Jan18 0-1	Aug10 3-0 Dec14 4-0	Aug24 1-1 Apr09 3-2	Feb19 1-0 Apr26 1-1	Sep21 1-1 Jan04 3-1
CELTIC	Sep14 2-1 Jan11 1-1		Nov16 2-0 Dec28 2-0	Apr02 2-1 Apr26 2-0	Oct26 0-3 Mar15 1-1	Oct12 0-1 Feb22 1-1	Nov23 1-1 Apr19 2-0	Aug17 2-1 Jan15 3-2	Aug31 1-1 Jan01 2-0	Oct05 2-0 Feb08 1-1
CLYDEBANK	Dec10 2-1 May03 0-6	Aug24 0-2 Mar29 0-5		Aug17 4-0 Dec23 0-0	Nov23 1-2 Apr19 1-1	Sep28 1-0 Feb01 1-1	Oct30 2-4 Mar15 1-3	Oct12 1-1 Apr05 1-1	Sep14 0-1 Apr12 2-1	Nov13 1-1 Mar22 0-2
DUNDEE	Aug31 1-3 Jan01 0-0	Sep28 0-2 Feb01 1-3	Oct19 2-0 Mar01 4-0		Nov16 0-3 Mar29 0-1	Dec07 1-1 May03 2-0	Sep14 1-0 Jan11 3-1	Oct26 3-1 Apr19 4-0	Nov23 3-2 Mar15 2-1	Aug10 2-1 Dec14 3-1
DUNDEE U	Aug17 1-1 Dec21 2-1	Dec23 1-0 Jan04 4-2	Sep07 2-1 Jan18 4-0	Aug24 2-0 Dec28 0-0		Nov02 1-1 Apr12 0-3	Oct05 2-2 Feb08 4-0	Nov09 3-0 Mar22 4-0	Oct12 1-1 Feb22 1-1	Apr08 5-0 Apr26 1-2
HEARTS	Oct30 1-0 Apr20 1-1	Aug10 1-1 Dec14 1-1	Nov30 4-1 Apr26 1-0	Oct05 1-1 Feb08 3-1	Sep14 2-0 Jan11 1-1		Aug31 2-1 Jan01 3-1	Nov23 3-0 Mar15 2-0	Nov16 3-0 Mar29 3-1	Oct19 3-0 Mar25 3-0
HIBERNIAN	Oct12 1-1 Feb22 0-1	Sep07 0-5 Jan18 2-2	Oct01 5-0 Jan04 2-3	Nov02 2-1 Apr12 1-0	Feb26 0-1 May03 1-2	Nov09 0-0 Mar22 1-2		Sep28 1-0 Feb01 4-0	Aug17 1-3 Dec21 1-1	Aug24 2-3 Mar12 3-0
MOTHERWELL	Nov16 1-1 Mar29 0-1	Oct19 1-2 Apr30 0-2	Aug10 0-0 Dec14 3-0	Sep07 1-3 Jan18 2-2	Aug31 0-1 Mar12 2-0	Sep21 2-1 Jan04 1-3	Mar18 2-0 Apr26 3-1		Oct05 0-3 Feb08 1-0	Nov02 3-1 Apr12 1-2
RANGERS	Sep28 0-3 Feb01 1-1	Nov09 3-0 Mar22 4-4	Nov02 0-0 Jan11 4-2	Sep21 0-1 Jan04 5-0	Aug10 1-0 Dec14 1-1	Aug24 3-1 Dec28 0-2	Oct19 1-2 Mar01 3-1	Dec07 1-0 May03 2-0		Sep07 3-0 Jan18 2-0
ST MIRREN	Nov23 1-0 Mar15 1-1	Apr05 1-2 May03 0-5	Aug31 0-2 Jan01 3-0	Oct12 1-0 Feb22 1-2	Sep28 1-0 Feb01 1-1	Aug17 6-2 Dec21 0-1	Nov16 1-3 Mar29 0-2	Sep14 4-1 Jan11 1-0	Oct26 2-1 Apr19 2-1	

LEAGUE TABLES

PREMIER DIVISION

	P	W	D	L	F	A	W	D	L	F	A	Pts
Celtic	36	10	6	2	27	15	10	4	4	40	23	50
Hearts	36	13	5	0	38	10	7	5	6	21	23	50
Dundee U	36	10	6	2	38	15	8	5	5	21	16	47
Aberdeen	36	11	4	3	38	15	5	8	5	24	16	44
Rangers	36	10	4	4	34	18	3	5	10	19	27	35
Dundee	36	11	2	5	32	20	3	5	10	13	31	35
St Mirren	36	9	2	7	26	24	4	3	11	16	39	31
Hibernian	36	6	4	8	27	25	5	2	11	22	38	28
Motherwell	36	7	3	8	23	23	0	3	15	10	43	20
Clydebank	36	4	6	8	18	32	2	2	14	11	45	20

DIVISION 1

	P	W	D	L	F	A	W	D	L	F	A	Pts
Hamilton A	39	14	3	2	43	17	10	5	5	34	27	56
Falkirk	39	6	8	6	26	24	11	3	5	31	15	45
Kilmarnock	39	12	4	4	37	17	6	4	9	25	32	44
Forfar A	39	11	4	4	28	18	6	6	8	23	25	44
East Fife	39	8	9	2	31	18	6	6	8	23	28	43
Dumbarton	39	8	6	5	32	23	8	5	7	27	29	43
Morton	39	10	3	7	32	27	4	8	7	25	36	39
Partick T	39	5	7	8	25	30	5	9	5	28	34	36
Airdrie	39	7	6	7	30	27	5	5	9	21	23	35
Brechin C	39	8	6	5	35	27	5	3	12	23	37	35
Clyde	39	7	7	5	28	28	2	10	8	21	31	35
Montrose	39	6	9	5	23	21	4	5	10	20	33	34
Ayr U	39	6	3	10	19	29	4	8	8	22	31	31
Alloa	39	2	8	10	27	39	4	6	9	22	35	26

DIVISION 2

	P	W	D	L	F	A	W	D	L	F	A	Pts
Dunfermline A	39	14	4	1	52	18	9	7	4	39	29	57
Queen of South	39	14	2	3	40	16	9	7	4	31	20	55
Meadowbank T	39	11	7	2	39	20	8	4	7	29	25	49
Queen's Park	39	14	3	3	37	15	5	5	9	24	24	46
Stirling A	39	10	6	4	31	17	8	2	9	26	26	44
St Johnstone	39	11	3	6	37	23	7	3	9	26	32	42
Stenhousemuir	39	11	4	4	34	26	5	4	11	21	37	40
Arbroath	39	9	5	5	29	26	6	4	10	27	24	39
Raith R	39	11	3	6	41	27	4	4	11	26	38	37
Cowdenbeath	39	9	4	7	32	26	5	5	9	20	27	37
E. Stirling	39	7	2	10	26	32	4	4	12	23	37	28
Berwick R	39	5	9	6	25	33	2	2	15	20	47	25
Albion R	39	4	5	10	19	34	4	3	13	19	52	24
Stranraer	39	5	1	13	21	38	4	4	12	20	45	23

DIVISION 1

	AIRDRIE	ALLOA	AYR U	BRECHIN C	CLYDE	DUMBARTON	EAST FIFE	FALKIRK	FORFAR A	HAMILTON A	KILMARNOCK	MONTROSE	MORTON	PARTICK T
AIRDRIE		Mar19 3-0 Apr05 2-2	Oct12 4-1 Apr19 2-1	Sep21 1-2 Mar08 4-2	Oct05 3-0	Aug10 0-2 Apr12 2-1	Nov30 1-2	Sep07 1-1	Nov16 0-0	Mar24 0-4 May03 1-2	Oct26 1-2 Mar22 1-0	Dec21 1-1	Feb01 1-2	Aug24 2-2 Feb22 0-0
ALLOA	Aug17 0-0		Sep07 1-1	Oct05 2-3	Oct19 1-1	Feb04 2-4 Apr15 1-3	Sep24 1-1 Apr26 1-2	Aug31 0-2 Mar08 0-2	Nov30 1-2 May03 2-2	Dec14 4-5	Jan11 1-4	Feb01 1-1 Apr08 1-3	Oct26 3-0 May05 2-0	Nov16 1-1 Mar22 2-2
AYR U	Dec14 0-4	Nov09 1-3 Apr12 1-1		Sep14 1-3	Jan11 1-0 Mar08 2-0	Sep28 0-1	Oct19 1-0	Aug17 0-3 Apr26 1-2	Dec28 0-0 Mar12 2-0	Jan18 1-1 Mar22 0-1	Aug31 3-0	Nov23 2-1	Dec07 0-3	Nov02 1-3 Apr05 2-3
BRECHIN C	Nov23 0-2	Mar25 1-1 Apr22 3-1	Nov19 4-1 Apr08 1-1		Apr15 1-2 Apr26 2-2	Oct26 3-1 Apr05 1-1	Aug10 4-0	Feb01 1-1	Aug31 1-0 Mar22 0-3	Mar12 1-3	Sep28 2-4	Sep07 3-1 Mar18 4-2	Oct12 1-1	Dec21 2-0
CLYDE	Dec07 3-2 Apr02 1-1	Apr19 1-1 Apr28 4-2	Aug10 0-0	Aug24 2-0		Oct12 0-0	Mar05 3-4 Mar22 0-0	Nov16 0-4 Feb08 0-2	Jan18 1-1	Nov02 1-0 Apr12 4-2	Nov23 1-3 Apr05 1-3	Sep28 2-0	Sep07 2-1	Mar12 2-2
DUMBARTON	Mar12 3-0	Aug24 4-0	Feb19 1-1 Mar05 2-0	Jan18 4-1	Dec14 1-1 Mar15 0-0		Oct05 2-1 Mar01 2-3	Sep21 2-0 Mar29 2-1	Nov02 1-1 Apr09 0-2	Sep07 2-2 Apr26 1-4	Oct19 1-0	Nov16 2-2	Jan01 1-2	Aug17 1-2
EAST FIFE	Sep28 1-1 Mar29 2-0	Nov23 1-0	Dec21 1-3 Mar15 0-0	Jan11 4-2 Apr12 1-0	Aug17 2-2	Dec07 1-0		Oct26 0-1	Sep07 1-1 Mar08 3-0	Nov16 1-1 Apr16 4-0	Feb01 2-2	Jan01 0-0 Apr19 2-0	Aug24 4-4	Oct12 1-1
FALKIRK	Nov09 0-1 Mar15 1-1	Jan01 3-1	Mar19 1-2	Nov02 0-1 Apr19 2-1	Sep14 0-0	Nov23 0-0	Jan18 1-0 May03 2-2		Oct12 5-3 Apr05 1-0	Aug10 0-0	Dec07 0-1 Mar25 1-1	Aug24 2-1	Dec21 1-1 Apr12 2-3	Sep28 2-3 Apr02 2-2
FORFAR A	Sep14 2-0 Apr15 1-1	Sep28 0-4	Aug24 1-0	Apr01 2-0	Oct26 2-1 Mar29 2-1	Feb01 4-0	Nov09 0-2	Dec14 2-1		Oct19 2-2 Apr22 2-0	Aug17 0-0 Apr12 1-0	Jan11 1-2 Mar15 1-2	Nov23 2-0	Dec07 1-1 Apr19 2-1
HAMILTON A	Aug31 3-1	Oct12 1-2 Apr02 1-1	Oct26 2-0	Aug17 0-0 Mar15 1-0	Feb01 3-0	Nov09 6-1	Sep14 2-1	Jan11 2-0 Apr09 0-3	Dec21 1-0		Dec28 4-1 Mar08 3-2	Dec07 4-2 Apr05 1-0	Sep28 5-0 Apr19 2-1	Nov23 2-2
KILMARNOCK	Jan18 0-2	Aug10 3-0 Mar15 2-0	Jan01 1-2 May03 3-2	Nov30 3-1 Mar29 1-2	Sep21 1-1	Dec21 1-4 Apr19 3-0	Nov02 2-2 Apr09 2-0	Oct05 1-0	Jan04 1-0	Aug24 1-0		Oct12 0-0 Mar01 3-0	Nov16 3-0 Feb08 1-1	Sep07 5-0
MONTROSE	Oct19 1-0 Apr26 2-1	Nov02 1-1	Sep25 2-2 Mar29 1-0	Nov09 1-1	Nov30 0-0 Mar25 1-1	Sep14 0-3 May03 0-0	Aug31 1-0	Mar11 1-2 Mar22 1-1	Aug10 1-2	Oct05 1-2	Dec14 4-1		Jan04 1-1 Mar08 1-1	Jan18 3-1 Apr12 0-1
MORTON	Nov02 1-4 Apr09 1-0	Jan18 2-0	Oct05 2-2 Mar01 0-1	Dec14 2-0 Feb22 3-2	Nov09 3-2 May03 3-2	Aug31 1-2 Mar25 1-0	Dec28 0-0 Apr05 2-2	Oct19 0-3	Sep23 2-3 Apr26 2-0	Nov30 0-1	Sep14 3-0	Aug17 1-2		Jan11 3-1
PARTICK T	Mar05 1-0	Sep14 1-2	Feb01 2-2	Oct19 2-1 May03 1-1	Aug31 1-3 Apr09 2-2	Mar08 1-2 Mar19 2-2	Dec14 1-0 Mar25 0-1	Nov30 1-2	Oct05 0-3	Sep21 1-2 Mar29 0-2	Nov09 1-1 Apr26 2-0	Oct26 2-0	Aug10 1-1 Mar15 3-3	

DIVISION 2

	ALBION R	ARBROATH	BERWICK R	COWDENBEATH	DUNFERMLINE A	E STIRLING	MEADOWBANK T	QUEEN OF SOUTH	QUEEN'S PARK	RAITH R	ST JOHNSTONE	STENHOUSEMUIR	STIRLING A	STRANRAER
ALBION R		Oct12 0-0	Jan11 0-0	Nov09 2-1	Mar31 0-3	Sep14 1-2 Apr29 2-1	Jan18 3-2 Apr26 0-2	Nov23 1-5 Mar25 2-2	Aug31 0-2 Mar29 1-1	Sep28 2-0	Dec14 2-4	Mar15 0-0 May06 0-1	Aug17 1-3 Apr08 0-2	Nov02 2-3
ARBROATH	Mar04 1-1 Apr05 2-0		Mar01 5-1	Sep14 0-5 Feb22 0-1	Aug10 3-3	Nov23 2-1	Aug17 3-0 Dec21 2-2	Feb01 2-2 Apr19 0-1	Oct26 1-0 Apr09 0-2	Dec14 2-2 Mar15 2-1	Aug31 1-0	Nov09 1-4	Oct19 1-0	Sep28 1-0
BERWICK R	Aug10 0-0 Mar08 1-2	Aug24 0-2 May03 0-4		Nov23 1-1	Dec21 4-4 Apr26 0-4	Sep28 1-1	Jan01 0-0	Dec14 0-1	Jan18 0-5	Oct12 4-3 Mar29 1-0	Feb01 3-1 Mar22 1-1	Sep14 1-1 Apr09 1-1	Oct26 1-0	Nov09 2-2 Mar04 4-0
COWDENBEATH	Sep07 3-0 Mar18 0-2	Nov16 1-0	Sep24 4-2 Apr22 1-0		Mar05 0-1 Mar15 0-2	Nov02 1-1 May03 1-1	Aug10 3-1 Apr05 1-0	Apr29 3-3	Oct05 2-2	Aug24 1-4	Mar11 1-3 Apr09 2-1	Oct19 2-0	Nov30 1-2 Apr26 0-1	Mar25 5-0
DUNFERMLINE A	Oct26 6-0 Apr12 4-0	Mar22 0-0 Apr22 2-0	Aug17 4-2	Aug31 3-2		Jan18 2-1 Apr19 4-0	Oct12 1-1	Nov09 2-1	Jan11 3-2 Mar08 0-0	Sep14 3-3	Nov23 4-0 Apr16 4-0	Sep28 3-2	Feb01 2-3	Dec14 1-0 Mar29 4-1
E STIRLING	Nov16 5-1	Sep21 1-2 Apr26 1-1	Mar18 0-2 Apr02 4-2	Feb01 2-1	Oct19 0-4		Oct05 1-3 Mar22 2-3	Aug17 0-0	Sep07 2-1	Oct26 0-2	Mar05 1-3	Aug31 0-2 Mar08 2-0	Dec28 0-2 Mar29 1-0	Jan11 3-1 Apr09 1-2
MEADOWBANK T	Oct19 1-1	Apr15 2-1	Aug31 0-3 Apr19 3-1	Dec28 1-1	Mar18 2-2 Apr08 4-0	Dec14 2-1		Oct26 0-0 Mar29 1-0	Feb01 2-1 Mar15 1-1	Nov09 6-0 Mar05 0-3	Sep28 4-1	Nov23 3-1 May03 1-0	Feb19 1-1 Mar08 4-1	Sep14 1-1
QUEEN OF SOUTH	Sep21 5-2	Nov02 2-0	Oct05 2-0 Mar15 2-1	Oct12 6-1 Mar08 3-0	Sep07 0-0 Apr05 3-1	Jan04 2-1 Apr12 3-1	Feb08 1-0		Feb05 0-1 Mar11 0-3	Jan18 2-0	Feb19 2-1	Aug10 2-0	Nov16 3-1	Aug31 1-1 Apr26 1-2
QUEEN'S PARK	Jan01 2-0	Feb08 1-2	Oct19 2-0 Apr12 5-0	Dec14 2-0 Apr19 0-1	Aug24 3-1	Nov09 1-0 Feb22 4-2	Nov02 2-1	Sep28 1-2		Nov23 0-0	Sep14 1-1 Mar01 2-0	Dec21 3-2 Apr04 1-1	Mar22 1-0 Apr01 2-0	Aug10 2-1 Dec28 2-1
RAITH R	Feb04 1-0 May03 5-2	Oct05 2-1	Feb18 3-1	Jan11 0-1 Mar22 2-1	Nov16 1-2 Feb15 3-3	Mar25 1-4 Apr05 2-0	Sep07 1-1	Oct19 0-1 Apr09 0-2	Sep24 3-1 Apr26 2-1		Aug10 0-2	Nov02 9-2	Aug31 1-1	Mar11 1-0 Apr22 4-1
ST JOHNSTONE	Oct05 7-1 Apr19 1-0	Jan04 1-0 Mar29 4-1	Nov02 3-2	Aug17 0-0	Sep24 1-2	Oct12 3-0 Mar15 1-1	Apr01 1-0 Apr12 1-3	Aug24 0-3 May03 1-1	Nov16 1-0	Dec28 4-1 Mar08 1-3		Mar25 1-3	Sep07 2-0 Mar18 0-2	Jan18 4-0
STENHOUSEMUIR	Aug24 4-2	Sep07 1-1 Mar18 2-1	Nov16 3-1	Jan18 1-0 Mar29 2-1	Mar12 1-1 Apr29 0-0	Apr22 4-3	Sep24 1-5	Mar22 1-2 Apr02 1-0	Aug17 4-0	Feb01 2-0 Apr12 1-0	Oct26 3-2 Apr26 0-0		Oct05 2-5	Oct12 1-2
STIRLING A	Dec21 2-0	Jan18 1-0 Apr12 1-0	Mar24 2-0 Apr05 2-2	Sep28 0-0	Nov02 0-1 May03 3-2	Aug10 0-1	Aug24 1-2	Sep14 2-2 Apr22 3-1	Oct12 0-0	Apr15 1-1 Apr19 3-1	Nov09 0-2	Dec14 1-0 Mar04 4-0		Nov23 3-0 Mar15 2-2
STRANRAER	Feb01 0-2 Mar22 2-3	Dec07 1-6 Mar08 1-5	Sep07 2-0	Oct26 1-2 Apr12 1-1	Oct05 1-3	Aug24 0-1	Nov16 0-1 Feb15 1-2	Jan01 0-2	May03 2-1	Aug17 3-2	Oct19 0-2 Apr05 1-2	Feb05 2-0 Apr19 0-1	Sep25 3-2	

Scottish Football League Records
Season 1986-87

PREMIER

PREMIER	ABERDEEN	CELTIC	CLYDEBANK	DUNDEE	DUNDEE U	FALKIRK	HAMILTON A	HEARTS	HIBERNIAN	MOTHERWELL	RANGERS	ST MIRREN
ABERDEEN		Nov26 1-1 Mar14 1-0	Nov19 5-0 Apr11 1-1	Aug30 2-0 Jan01 2-1	Oct11 2-0 Feb28 0-1	Dec03 1-0 May09 3-1	Aug16 2-0 Dec27 0-0	Sep13 0-1 Jan21 2-1	Aug13 4-0 Dec13 1-0	Oct04 2-2 Feb07 1-0	Nov22 1-0 May02 1-1	Nov08 0-0 Mar28 0-1
CELTIC	Aug23 1-1 Dec20 1-1		Oct29 6-0 Mar21 3-0	Aug09 1-0 Dec06 2-0	Nov15 1-0 Apr18 1-1	Nov22 4-2 May02 1-2	Sep06 4-1 Jan03 8-3	Oct08 2-0 Feb14 1-1	Sep20 5-1 Jan21 1-0	Oct18 3-1 Mar07 3-1	Nov01 1-1 Apr04 3-1	Oct14 2-0 Feb07 3-0
CLYDEBANK	Sep20 1-3 Jan27 0-5	Aug16 0-1 Dec27 1-1		Oct04 0-2 Feb07 1-1	Aug13 0-0 Dec13 1-2	Aug30 1-2 Jan01 2-1	Oct11 2-1 Feb28 2-3	Nov08 0-3 Mar28 1-1	Dec03 0-0 May09 1-2	Nov22 2-3 May02 0-0	Nov15 1-4 Apr18 0-3	Oct25 1-1 Mar24 2-1
DUNDEE	Nov01 0-2 Apr04 1-1	Oct11 0-3 Feb28 4-1	Nov29 3-3 Apr25 4-1		Sep06 0-2 Mar10 1-1	Oct25 3-0 Mar25 4-0	Dec03 3-3 May09 7-3	Sep27 0-0 Jan24 0-1	Aug16 3-0 Dec27 2-0	Nov15 1-1 Apr18 4-1	Sep20 1-0 Mar17 0-4	Aug13 2-1 Dec13 6-3
DUNDEE U	Aug09 2-1 Dec06 0-0	Sep13 2-2 Jan10 3-2	Oct18 2-0 Mar07 1-1	Nov08 0-3 Mar28 1-1		Oct04 2-0 Feb07 2-1	Nov19 3-0 Apr28 2-1	Aug23 1-0 Dec20 3-1	Nov22 1-0 May02 2-1	Oct08 4-0 Feb14 2-0	Oct29 0-0 Mar21 0-1	Aug30 3-0 Jan06 2-0
FALKIRK	Oct08 3-3 Feb21 0-3	Sep27 0-1 Jan24 1-2	Nov01 1-0 Apr04 0-0	Aug23 0-1 Apr21 0-0	Nov29 2-1 Apr25 1-2		Sep13 0-0 Feb25 0-2	Oct29 2-0 Mar21 0-0	Sep06 1-1 Jan03 1-3	Aug09 1-1 Dec06 1-0	Oct18 1-5 Mar07 1-2	Nov19 1-1 Apr14 0-0
HAMILTON A	Oct25 0-1 Mar21 0-2	Nov08 1-2 Mar28 2-3	Aug09 0-1 Dec06 0-0	Oct08 0-3 Feb14 1-1	Sep20 1-5 Apr14 0-0	Nov15 1-2 Apr18 0-1		Oct18 1-3 Mar07 0-1	Oct04 1-4 Feb07 0-1	Aug30 0-3 Jan01 4-2	Aug23 1-2 Dec20 0-2	Nov22 1-1 May02 1-0
HEARTS	Nov15 2-1 Apr18 1-1	Dec03 1-0 May09 1-0	Sep06 2-1 Jan03 3-0	Nov22 3-1 May02 1-3	Oct25 2-2 May11 1-1	Aug16 1-0 Dec27 4-0	Aug13 1-0 Dec13 7-0		Nov01 1-1 Apr04 2-1	Sep20 4-0 Feb25 1-1	Oct04 1-1 Feb07 2-5	Oct11 0-0 Feb28 1-0
HIBERNIAN	Oct18 1-1 Mar07 1-1	Nov19 0-1 Apr11 1-4	Oct08 3-2 Feb14 4-1	Oct29 0-3 Mar21 2-2	Sep27 1-1 Jan24 0-2	Nov08 1-0 Mar28 2-0	Nov29 1-3 Apr25 1-1	Sep30 1-3 Jan06 2-2		Sep23 0-0 Dec20 0-1	Aug09 2-1 Dec06 0-0	Sep13 0-1 Jan10 1-0
MOTHERWELL	Nov29 0-1 Apr25 0-2	Aug13 0-4 Dec13 1-1	Sep27 0-1 Jan24 3-2	Sep13 0-0 Jan27 2-0	Dec03 0-2 May09 1-0	Oct11 2-2 Feb28 1-0	Nov01 1-1 Apr04 3-0	Nov19 2-3 Apr15 0-1	Oct25 4-1 Mar24 2-1		Sep06 0-2 Jan06 0-1	Aug16 1-1 Dec27 1-2
RANGERS	Sep27 2-0 Jan24 0-0	Aug31 1-0 Jan01 2-0	Sep13 4-0 Jan10 5-0	Nov19 2-1 Apr14 2-0	Sep16 2-3 Dec27 2-0	Aug13 1-0 Dec13 4-0	Jan17 2-0 Mar14 2-0	Nov29 3-0 Apr25 3-0	Oct11 3-0 Feb28 1-1	Nov08 0-1 Mar28 1-0		Dec03 2-0 May09 1-0
ST MIRREN	Sep06 1-1 Feb25 1-0	Nov29 0-1 Apr25 1-3	Aug23 0-1 Dec20 3-1	Oct18 4-1 Mar07 0-1	Nov01 0-1 Apr04 2-1	Sep20 1-0 Jan27 1-0	Sep27 2-1 Jan24 0-1	Aug09 0-0 Dec06 0-0	Nov15 3-1 Apr18 1-1	Oct29 1-0 Mar21 1-1	Oct08 0-1 Feb14 1-3	

LEAGUE TABLES

PREMIER DIVISION

	P	W	D	L	F	A	W	D	L	F	A	Pts
Rangers	44	18	2	2	45	6	13	5	4	40	17	69
Celtic	44	16	5	1	57	17	11	4	7	33	24	63
Dundee U	44	15	5	2	38	15	9	7	6	28	21	60
Aberdeen	44	13	6	3	32	11	8	10	4	31	18	58
Hearts	44	13	7	2	42	19	8	7	7	22	24	56
Dundee	44	11	6	5	49	31	7	6	9	25	26	48
St Mirren	44	9	5	8	23	20	3	7	12	13	31	36
Motherwell	44	7	5	10	24	28	4	7	11	19	36	34
Hibernian	44	6	8	8	24	30	4	5	13	20	40	33
Falkirk	44	4	9	9	17	28	4	1	17	14	42	26
Clydebank	44	3	7	12	19	40	3	5	14	16	53	24
Hamilton A	44	2	4	16	15	40	4	5	13	24	53	21

DIVISION 1

	P	W	D	L	F	A	W	D	L	F	A	Pts
Morton	34	12	4	6	43	27	12	5	5	45	29	57
Dunfermline A	34	12	5	5	29	16	11	5	6	32	25	56
Dumbarton	34	12	6	4	37	25	11	1	10	30	27	53
East Fife	34	10	10	2	34	22	5	11	6	34	33	51
Airdrie	34	15	2	5	39	22	5	9	8	19	24	51
Kilmarnock	34	11	7	4	35	20	6	4	12	27	33	45
Forfar A	34	7	9	6	38	34	7	6	9	23	29	43
Partick T	34	7	7	8	27	25	5	8	9	22	29	39
Clyde	34	6	9	7	26	25	5	7	10	22	31	38
Queen of South	34	7	5	10	24	26	4	7	11	26	45	34
Brechin C	34	5	5	12	26	39	6	5	11	18	33	32
Montrose	34	7	5	10	24	30	2	6	14	13	44	29

DIVISION 2

	P	W	D	L	F	A	W	D	L	F	A	Pts
Meadowbank T	39	14	3	2	37	11	9	6	5	32	27	55
Raith R	39	8	10	1	34	19	8	10	2	39	25	52
Stirling A	39	11	5	3	27	13	9	7	4	28	20	52
Ayr U	39	13	3	4	38	24	9	5	5	32	25	52
St Johnstone	39	10	2	7	26	24	6	11	3	33	25	45
Alloa	39	9	3	8	26	27	8	4	7	22	23	41
Cowdenbeath	39	8	5	6	33	31	8	3	9	26	24	40
Albion R	39	6	5	9	28	29	9	4	6	20	22	39
Queen's Park	39	5	12	2	27	20	4	7	9	21	29	37
Stranraer	39	4	7	9	17	28	5	4	10	24	31	29
Arbroath	39	5	5	10	25	33	6	2	11	21	33	29
Stenhousemuir	39	5	6	9	21	28	5	3	11	16	30	29
E. Stirling	39	3	6	11	17	31	3	5	11	16	25	23
Berwick R	39	5	3	11	21	31	3	4	13	19	38	23

DIVISION 1

DIVISION 1	AIRDRIE	BRECHIN C	CLYDE	DUMBARTON	DUNFERMLINE A	EAST FIFE	FORFAR A	KILMARNOCK	MONTROSE	MORTON	PARTICK T	QUEEN OF SOUTH
AIRDRIE		Aug13 4-0 Dec13 3-1	Nov05 0-2 Apr11 3-2	Aug16 1-0 Dec27 1-0	Nov22 3-0 May02 2-1	Oct11 0-3 Mar14 0-0	Sep20 3-1 Feb24 0-0	Sep13 3-2 Apr18 4-3	Nov08 3-0 Mar28 4-1	Nov29 1-2 May09 1-0	Sep06 1-0 Jan03 1-0	Oct04 1-3 Feb28 0-1
BRECHIN C	Oct08 1-2 Mar07 0-2		Sep30 2-1 Feb14 0-1	Nov01 3-1 Apr04 1-2	Sep13 1-4 Feb24 0-2	Oct29 2-2 Apr11 3-2	Aug30 0-1 Jan01 1-1	Sep20 2-2 Feb17 1-0	Aug09 0-0 Dec06 2-3	Aug23 2-5 Dec20 1-3	Nov22 0-1 May02 1-1	Oct18 2-1 Mar21 1-2
CLYDE	Sep16 1-1 Feb21 1-0	Nov29 4-1 May09 2-1		Sep20 2-1 Jan24 1-2	Oct11 1-0 Mar14 0-1	Aug16 3-3 Dec27 0-1	Oct25 2-3 Apr18 1-2	Nov22 0-0 May02 0-1	Sep06 1-1 Feb25 0-0	Oct04 1-2 Feb28 0-0	Nov08 3-3 Mar28 1-1	Aug13 0-0 Dec13 2-1
DUMBARTON	Oct18 2-1 Mar21 2-2	Sep06 3-1 Mar31 1-1	Nov15 1-1 Apr25 2-1		Aug13 0-1 Dec13 1-2	Sep27 2-1 Feb07 1-1	Aug23 3-2 Dec20 0-1	Oct29 2-0 Apr11 3-2	Sep13 1-0 Feb21 2-1	Nov08 2-1 Mar28 2-3	Oct04 2-2 Feb28 1-0	Nov29 1-1 May09 3-0
DUNFERMLINE A	Sep27 0-0 Feb07 1-1	Oct25 4-0 Apr18 0-2	Aug23 2-0 Feb10 2-0	Oct08 0-1 Mar07 1-0		Aug30 2-4 Jan01 1-1	Aug09 1-0 Dec06 2-0	Nov01 1-0 Apr04 0-1	Sep30 1-0 Mar03 2-0	Oct18 1-1 Mar21 1-2	Sep16 2-0 Feb21 2-1	Nov15 2-2 Apr25 1-0
EAST FIFE	Aug23 1-1 Dec20 0-0	Sep16 1-0 Jan27 2-2	Oct18 1-1 Mar21 1-1	Nov22 0-0 May02 2-1	Nov08 2-1 Mar28 1-1		Sep30 1-2 Feb14 0-0	Aug09 1-4 Dec06 2-1	Oct08 2-2 Mar07 3-1	Sep06 1-0 Jan07 2-1	Sep20 2-0 Jan24 1-1	Oct25 3-2 Apr18 5-0
FORFAR A	Nov15 3-1 Apr25 1-0	Nov08 0-1 Mar28 0-0	Sep13 2-1 Mar31 1-2	Oct11 3-5 Mar17 0-2	Oct04 3-3 Feb28 3-1	Nov29 1-1 May09 1-4		Aug16 3-1 Dec27 1-1	Oct28 3-0 Apr11 4-1	Sep27 2-2 Feb07 3-3	Aug13 1-1 Dec13 1-2	Sep06 1-1 Jan03 1-1
KILMARNOCK	Oct25 2-0 Jan24 0-0	Nov15 0-1 Apr25 0-1	Sep27 0-0 Feb07 1-1	Sep16 2-1 Jan27 1-2	Sep06 1-2 Jan03 2-2	Oct04 1-1 Feb28 3-1	Oct18 3-0 Mar21 2-0		Aug23 3-0 Dec20 1-0	Aug13 2-2 Dec13 2-0	Nov29 3-2 May09 1-0	Nov08 3-2 Mar28 2-2
MONTROSE	Aug30 1-2 Jan01 0-1	Oct04 0-2 Feb28 1-1	Nov01 0-1 Apr04 2-1	Oct25 1-0 Apr18 2-0	Nov29 0-2 May09 1-0	Aug13 2-2 Dec13 2-1	Sep16 1-1 Feb10 0-1	Oct11 0-2 Mar14 1-1		Nov15 0-3 Apr25 1-4	Aug16 3-1 Dec27 0-0	Sep27 3-4 Feb07 3-0
MORTON	Sep30 2-1 Feb14 2-1	Oct11 2-3 Mar14 1-0	Aug09 3-0 Dec06 3-2	Aug30 0-3 Jan01 4-1	Aug16 0-1 Dec27 2-2	Nov01 1-1 Apr04 1-1	Nov22 0-0 May02 3-1	Oct08 2-0 Mar11 2-1	Sep20 0-2 Jan24 6-1		Oct25 1-2 Apr18 1-2	Sep16 5-2 Jan21 2-0
PARTICK T	Nov01 2-0 Apr04 2-2	Sep27 1-0 Feb07 0-0	Aug30 0-0 Mar17 0-2	Aug09 1-2 Dec06 0-2	Oct29 0-1 Apr11 0-2	Nov15 3-3 Apr25 2-0	Oct08 1-1 Mar07 2-1	Sep30 1-0 Mar03 1-2	Oct18 5-0 Mar21 0-0	Sep13 2-5 Feb10 0-1		Aug23 1-1 Jan27 3-0
QUEEN OF SOUTH	Aug09 0-0 Dec05 0-1	Aug16 2-0 Dec27 2-0	Oct08 1-1 Mar11 4-1	Sep30 1-3 Feb14 0-1	Sep20 1-1 Jan24 1-2	Sep13 2-0 Feb21 0-1	Nov01 2-1 Apr04 1-4	Aug30 2-1 Jan01 1-2	Nov22 1-0 May02 0-0	Oct29 0-2 Apr11 2-3	Oct11 1-1 Mar14 0-1	

DIVISION 2

DIVISION 2	ALBION R	ALLOA	ARBROATH	AYR U	BERWICK R	COWDENBEATH	E STIRLING	MEADOWBANK T	QUEEN'S PARK	RAITH R	ST JOHNSTONE	STENHOUSEMUIR	STIRLING A	STRANRAER
ALBION R		Aug30 1-2	Sep06 3-0 Mar07 0-1	Sep27 3-2 Mar21 0-1	Oct04 2-0 Apr04 2-1	Nov15 4-1 May09 0-1	Feb24 1-1	Mar10 1-1	Jan01 0-0	Nov01 2-4 Apr18 1-2	Nov22 0-2 Mar03 3-4	Aug16 1-4	Feb10 1-1	Oct18 1-1 Apr25 2-0
ALLOA	Nov29 1-3 Mar28 0-1		Nov15 2-3 Apr11 0-3	Aug23 1-0	Jan24 1-2	Aug16 2-1 Feb28 1-0	Nov01 1-0	Feb10 0-0 May09 0-1	Oct04 2-1	Oct18 2-2 Feb14 2-4	Sep20 3-3	Sep06 2-0 Mar21 0-1	Jan01 2-1 Apr25 2-1	Jan28 2-0
ARBROATH	Jan03 1-1	Aug09 2-4		Nov29 2-5 Feb14 2-0	Feb03 3-0 May02 1-1	Jan17 0-1	Oct04 0-0 Apr04 0-3	Sep27 1-2	Nov08 4-1	Dec20 2-1	Sep13 1-1 Jan31 1-4	Aug23 3-1 Feb28 1-1	Oct18 0-1 Mar21 0-1	Nov01 1-4 Apr18 0-1
AYR U	Jan24 3-1	Nov22 1-0 Feb21 2-0	Aug30 2-1		Sep06 4-2 Apr18 2-0	Dec13 1-3	Sep20 2-1	Oct25 2-0 Mar07 1-3	Aug09 1-0	Nov08 3-3 Apr25 0-0	Dec27 0-2 Mar14 1-1	Oct11 1-0 Apr04 3-1	Feb07 3-1 May09 2-3	Jan01 4-2
BERWICK R	Feb07 0-1	Sep27 1-2 Mar14 1-1	Oct11 2-0	Jan03 0-2		Oct25 1-3 Apr25 1-6	Aug23 2-2 Mar07 0-1	Sep13 1-1 Apr11 0-1	Dec27 2-1 Mar28 1-0	Feb10 1-0	Dec16 1-2	Nov15 2-3	Aug16 0-2 Feb14 2-3	Nov29 3-0
COWDENBEATH	Aug09 0-2	Nov08 1-0	Sep20 1-0 Mar28 1-3	Oct18 3-1 Apr11 1-3	Jan06 3-1		Nov29 1-1	Oct04 0-2	Jan31 2-2 May02 1-1	Sep13 1-2 Mar07 2-2	Feb03 4-3	Nov01 4-1 Feb21 3-1	Aug23 0-2	Jan24 2-1 Mar14 3-3
E STIRLING	Oct11 1-2 Apr11 1-0	Dec27 1-0 May02 0-1	Feb07 1-2	Jan28 1-2 Mar28 1-3	Nov22 0-1	Sep30 0-1 Mar10 0-2		Dec13 4-4	Oct25 2-0 May09 2-2	Sep27 0-5 Mar25 1-1	Aug16 1-1 Feb28 0-2	Jan01 0-1	Nov15 1-1	Sep06 0-0
MEADOWBANK T	Sep20 5-0 Feb28 3-0	Oct11 4-0	Jan24 2-1 Mar14 2-1	Dec20 2-2	Dec30 1-0	Feb07 1-0 Apr04 1-0	Oct18 1-0 Apr25 2-1		Sep06 0-0	Aug23 0-1	Nov15 1-1 Apr18 2-1	Nov29 5-0	Nov01 0-1	Aug16 1-0 Mar17 4-2
QUEEN'S PARK	Sep13 1-2 Feb21 0-0	Feb07 1-1 Apr18 1-1	Aug16 5-1 Apr25 2-0	Nov15 1-1 Feb28 0-0	Nov01 3-1	Oct11 2-2	Dec20 2-1	Jan06 2-2 Mar21 1-3		Nov29 2-2 Apr04 1-1	Jan24 0-0	Oct18 0-0	Sep20 0-0	Aug23 3-2
RAITH R	Dec27 2-0	Dec17 0-0	Oct25 3-0 Mar17 2-2	Aug16 5-0	Sep20 1-1 Mar21 3-2	Jan01 2-2	Jan24 2-0	Nov22 2-3 Mar28 1-1	Aug30 2-2		Oct11 2-2 Dec13 1-1	Feb07 1-0 Apr11 1-0	Sep06 0-0 Feb28 2-2	Nov15 2-1
ST JOHNSTONE	Aug23 1-2	Mar07 1-3 Mar17 2-1	Jan01 2-0	Nov01 2-2	Oct18 3-2 Feb24 2-0	Sep06 1-0 Mar21 1-0	Nov08 3-0	Aug09 1-5	Sep27 3-0 Apr11 0-2	May02 1-1		Dec20 1-0 Apr25 0-1	Nov29 2-1	Oct04 0-3 Mar28 0-1
STENHOUSEMUIR	Nov08 0-0 May02 2-3	Jan31 2-1	Nov22 0-1	Feb11 0-4	Aug09 0-0 May09 3-1	Dec27 0-1	Sep13 3-2 Apr18 1-0	Aug30 0-1 Feb14 3-1	Dec13 2-2 Mar14 0-2	Oct04 1-2	Oct25 1-1		Jan24 1-1 Mar28 1-2	Sep20 1-3 Mar07 0-0
STIRLING A	Oct25 0-2 Mar14 0-0	Sep13 1-2	Dec13 2-2	Oct04 0-1	Nov08 2-2	Nov22 4-1 Apr18 1-0	Aug09 3-0 Feb21 1-0	Dec27 2-0 May02 3-1	Mar07 1-0 Mar17 1-0	Feb03 1-1	Aug30 1-0 Apr04 1-1	Sep27 1-0		Feb24 2-0
STRANRAER	Dec13 1-0	Oct25 0-1 Apr04 1-2	Dec27 1-0	Sep13 0-0 May02 1-3	Aug30 2-1 Feb28 0-1	Sep27 1-1	Jan03 0-3 Mar21 0-0	Nov08 2-0	Nov22 2-3 Feb14 1-2	Aug09 1-1 May09 1-4	Mar11 1-1	Feb04 1-1	Oct11 1-1 Apr11 0-3	

Scottish Football League Records
Season 1987-88

PREMIER

	ABERDEEN	CELTIC	DUNDEE	DUNDEE U	DUNFERMLINE A	FALKIRK	HEARTS	HIBERNIAN	MORTON	MOTHERWELL	RANGERS	ST MIRREN
ABERDEEN		Oct31 0-1 Mar30 0-1	Oct10 0-0 Feb27 1-0	Aug29 1-1 Jan02 0-0	Oct03 3-0 Jan16 1-0	Dec09 3-1 Mar26 2-0	Nov14 0-0 Apr23 0-0	Nov24 1-1 May04 0-2	Aug12 3-1 Dec12 4-0	Nov21 1-0 May07 0-0	Aug15 2-0 Feb06 1-2	Sep12 2-0 Dec16 2-1
CELTIC	Sep19 2-2 Dec19 0-0		Nov14 5-0 Apr23 3-0	Oct24 1-2 Mar26 0-0	Nov21 4-0 May07 1-0	Oct28 3-2 Mar05 2-0	Aug12 1-0 Dec12 2-2	Oct03 1-1 Jan16 2-0	Oct10 3-1 Feb27 1-0	Aug15 4-1 Feb06 1-0	Aug29 1-0 Jan02 2-0	Nov25 1-0 Apr05 2-0
DUNDEE	Aug08 1-1 Dec05 1-2	Oct07 1-1 Feb13 1-2		Oct03 1-1 Jan16 0-2	Aug29 5-0 Jan01 2-0	Nov07 3-1 Apr16 4-2	Sep19 1-3 Dec19 0-0	Nov21 2-1 Apr30 0-0	Oct28 1-0 Mar05 1-0	Nov24 2-0 Apr06 1-2	Jan06 0-1 Mar26 2-3	Aug22 0-2 Mar01 2-1
DUNDEE U	Oct17 0-0 Mar19 0-2	Sep05 0-0 Dec26 1-2	Nov28 1-3 Apr02 1-0		Nov14 1-0 Apr23 2-2	Sep26 3-0 Jan09 0-0	Nov18 0-3 May07 0-0	Sep12 1-2 Dec16 1-2	Aug15 3-1 Feb06 2-0	Aug12 1-1 Dec12 3-1	Oct10 1-0 Feb27 1-1	Oct31 2-3 Mar26 5-1
DUNFERMLINE A	Nov28 0-3 Apr02 1-1	Aug22 2-1 Mar02 0-4	Oct17 0-1 Mar19 6-1	Oct06 0-0 Feb13 0-3		Nov17 0-0 Apr30 0-1	Sep26 0-1 Jan09 0-4	Aug08 3-3 Dec05 1-0	Sep19 4-1 Dec19 1-1	Sep05 0-1 Dec26 1-1	Oct28 0-4 Mar05 0-3	Nov07 2-0 Apr16 2-1
FALKIRK	Sep05 2-2 Dec26 0-2	Sep12 0-1 Dec22 0-2	Aug12 0-3 Dec12 0-6	Nov24 4-1 May04 1-2	Aug15 0-0 Feb06 1-0		Oct10 1-5 Feb27 2-0	Oct31 1-1 Mar12 1-0	Nov14 2-0 Apr23 4-1	Oct17 3-0 Mar19 0-0	Nov21 0-1 May07 0-5	Oct03 1-3 Jan16 3-0
HEARTS	Oct07 2-1 Feb13 2-2	Nov07 1-1 Apr16 2-1	Oct31 4-2 Mar30 2-0	Aug22 4-1 Feb03 1-1	Nov24 3-2 Apr13 2-1	Aug08 4-2 Dec05 1-0		Aug29 1-0 Jan02 0-0	Oct24 3-0 Mar26 2-0	Sep12 1-0 Dec16 1-1	Oct03 0-0 Jan16 1-1	Nov21 0-0 Apr30 0-1
HIBERNIAN	Sep26 0-2 Jan09 0-0	Nov28 0-1 Apr02 0-2	Aug15 0-4 Feb06 2-1	Oct28 0-1 Mar05 0-0	Oct10 4-0 Feb27 2-0	Sep19 1-0 Dec19 0-0	Oct17 2-1 Mar19 0-0		Nov18 0-0 May07 3-1	Nov14 1-0 Apr23 1-1	Aug12 1-0 Dec12 0-2	Sep05 1-1 Dec26 0-0
MORTON	Nov07 0-0 Apr16 0-2	Aug08 0-4 Dec05 0-4	Sep12 4-3 Dec16 1-7	Nov21 0-1 Apr30 0-4	Oct31 1-2 Mar23 0-3	Oct07 4-1 Feb16 0-0	Sep05 1-2 Dec26 0-0	Aug22 3-3 Jan23 1-1		Oct03 1-1 Jan16 0-2	Nov24 0-3 Apr09 3-2	Oct17 0-0 Mar19 0-2
MOTHERWELL	Aug22 0-1 Jan23 2-1	Nov17 0-2 Apr30 0-1	Sep26 0-2 Jan09 3-3	Nov07 2-1 Apr16 4-2	Oct24 3-2 Mar26 3-2	Aug29 1-2 Jan01 0-0	Oct27 0-3 Mar08 0-2	Oct06 1-0 Feb13 0-2	Nov28 1-0 Apr02 1-0		Sep19 0-1 Dec19 0-2	Aug08 2-1 Dec05 2-1
RANGERS	Nov17 0-1 Apr30 0-1	Oct17 2-2 Mar20 1-2	Sep05 2-1 Dec26 2-0	Aug08 1-1 Dec05 1-0	Sep12 4-0 Dec15 2-2	Aug22 4-0 Jan23 3-1	Nov28 3-2 Apr02 1-2	Nov07 1-0 Apr16 1-1	Sep26 7-0 Jan09 5-0	Oct31 1-0 Mar12 1-0		Oct06 3-1 Feb13 4-0
ST MIRREN	Oct28 1-3 Mar05 0-0	Sep26 0-1 Jan09 1-1	Nov17 1-2 May07 1-0	Sep19 2-0 Dec19 0-1	Aug11 1-1 Dec12 4-1	Nov28 2-2 Apr02 0-0	Aug15 1-1 Feb06 0-6	Oct24 2-2 Mar26 1-1	Aug29 2-1 Jan02 0-0	Oct10 1-0 Feb27 0-0	Nov14 2-2 Apr23 0-3	

DIVISION 1

	AIRDRIE	CLYDE	CLYDEBANK	DUMBARTON	EAST FIFE	FORFAR A	HAMILTON A	KILMARNOCK	MEADOWBANK T	PARTICK T	QUEEN OF SOUTH	RAITH R
AIRDRIE		Sep15 4-3 Dec19 0-2	Oct31 0-2 Mar19 1-0	Aug22 0-1 Feb06 1-1	Aug08 1-0 Nov28 2-1	Sep28 1-0 Feb13 3-0	Aug29 0-3 Jan02 1-4	Sep19 3-2 Jan09 3-3	Oct17 0-0 Mar05 0-1	Nov11 3-1 Apr30 1-0	Oct24 5-1 Apr09 1-1	Nov21 3-0 Apr16 1-2
CLYDE	Oct20 1-0 Apr22 4-2		Sep12 5-1 Dec12 0-1	Aug08 5-0 Nov28 3-4	Aug22 3-3 Feb24 0-4	Oct07 2-2 Apr30 0-1	Oct24 0-3 Apr02 0-4	Nov21 2-0 Apr16 0-0	Sep19 0-0 Jan26 2-2	Aug29 4-1 Jan01 1-2	Sep29 2-3 Mar01 2-1	Oct31 3-2 Mar19 1-2
CLYDEBANK	Sep05 2-3 Dec26 1-1	Oct17 2-0 Mar05 1-2		Nov07 3-1 Mar26 1-0	Sep29 2-1 Mar01 2-0	Oct24 1-0 Apr09 3-2	Oct06 0-2 Apr30 3-1	Sep15 2-0 Dec19 1-0	Nov21 2-1 Apr16 0-2	Aug22 0-2 Nov28 0-3	Aug08 1-1 Feb06 1-0	Sep19 1-2 Jan09 3-1
DUMBARTON	Oct10 0-0 Apr02 0-1	Oct03 1-1 Feb27 0-1	Aug29 1-1 Jan02 1-3		Nov14 1-1 Apr23 0-0	Sep12 1-1 Dec12 0-1	Oct31 2-1 Mar19 1-1	Aug15 1-3 Jan23 1-0	Aug11 2-3 Dec05 0-1	Oct20 4-2 Mar22 1-2	Sep26 2-2 Jan16 0-2	Oct27 1-3 May07 3-0
EAST FIFE	Oct03 1-3 Feb27 3-1	Oct10 0-2 Apr09 2-0	Oct28 1-2 May07 1-1	Sep19 1-2 Jan09 3-4		Oct20 2-3 Mar12 4-0	Nov21 0-1 Apr16 1-1	Aug12 2-1 Dec05 2-1	Aug15 3-3 Feb06 0-0	Oct31 2-1 Mar19 1-0	Sep12 0-3 Dec12 2-2	Aug29 2-1 Jan02 1-2
FORFAR A	Oct27 4-4 May07 3-0	Aug11 3-5 Dec05 4-2	Aug15 3-0 Jan27 2-2	Oct17 0-2 Mar05 4-0	Sep15 4-0 Dec19 1-1		Sep19 1-1 Jan09 0-0	Oct10 2-0 Apr02 1-1	Aug29 0-0 Jan01 1-2	Nov22 1-4 Apr16 1-0	Oct31 3-1 Mar19 1-1	Oct03 3-0 Feb27 2-2
HAMILTON A	Nov07 2-2 Mar26 1-1	Aug15 3-2 Feb06 2-0	Aug11 3-2 Dec05 4-0	Sep05 2-1 Dec26 2-0	Sep26 0-1 Jan16 1-0	Nov14 1-0 Apr23 0-1		Oct03 1-1 Feb27 1-0	Oct27 1-5 May07 1-1	Sep12 5-0 Dec12 1-0	Oct20 2-2 Mar12 1-2	Oct10 0-2 Apr09 2-1
KILMARNOCK	Nov14 1-0 Apr23 4-1	Sep26 2-0 Jan16 3-1	Oct20 1-3 Mar12 2-2	Oct24 1-0 Apr09 3-1	Oct06 2-0 Apr30 1-3	Aug22 2-2 Feb06 0-2	Aug08 0-2 Nov28 1-0		Oct31 2-4 Mar19 0-0	Sep29 1-1 Feb13 0-1	Aug29 0-2 Jan02 0-0	Sep12 3-4 Dec12 1-1
MEADOWBANK T	Sep12 1-2 Dec12 0-0	Nov14 0-2 Apr23 0-1	Sep26 0-0 Jan16 3-2	Oct07 0-0 Apr30 2-4	Oct24 2-3 Apr02 2-1	Nov07 3-0 Mar26 3-0	Sep29 1-1 Feb13 2-0	Sep05 2-1 Dec26 1-3		Aug08 3-2 Jan23 3-1	Aug22 1-0 Nov28 5-0	Oct20 4-3 Mar12 3-0
PARTICK T	Aug11 2-2 Dec05 2-0	Nov07 1-4 Mar26 1-0	Oct03 0-1 Feb27 3-0	Sep15 1-2 Dec19 1-3	Sep05 3-3 Dec26 4-2	Sep26 1-1 Jan16 0-1	Oct17 1-0 Mar05 0-0	Nov03 1-0 May07 0-1	Oct10 1-0 Apr09 2-1		Nov14 3-3 Apr23 0-3	Aug15 0-0 Feb06 5-0
QUEEN OF SOUTH	Aug15 2-2 Jan26 1-2	Oct28 3-1 May07 2-1	Oct10 2-0 Apr02 0-1	Nov21 2-0 Apr16 0-0	Oct17 2-1 Mar05 2-0	Sep05 1-1 Dec26 1-1	Sep15 0-3 Dec19 0-0	Nov07 1-4 Mar26 1-0	Oct03 0-2 Feb27 2-1	Sep19 0-0 Jan09 0-0		Aug12 0-3 Dec05 1-5
RAITH R	Sep26 3-2 Jan16 2-2	Sep05 1-3 Dec26 2-0	Nov14 1-0 Apr23 2-3	Sep29 4-1 Feb13 1-1	Nov07 7-1 Mar26 0-1	Aug08 1-4 Nov28 0-0	Aug22 1-2 Mar02 0-1	Oct17 0-2 Mar05 2-2	Sep15 2-0 Dec19 4-0	Oct24 4-3 Apr02 1-2	Oct07 3-1 Apr30 4-2	

LEAGUE TABLES

PREMIER DIVISION

	P	W	D	L	F	A	W	D	L	F	A	Pts
Celtic	44	16	5	1	42	11	15	5	2	37	12	72
Hearts	44	13	8	1	37	17	10	8	4	37	15	62
Rangers	44	14	4	4	49	17	12	4	6	36	17	60
Aberdeen	44	11	7	4	27	11	10	10	2	29	14	59
Dundee U	44	8	7	7	29	24	8	8	6	25	23	47
Hibernian	44	8	8	6	18	17	4	11	7	23	25	43
Dundee	44	9	5	8	31	25	8	2	12	39	39	41
Motherwell	44	10	2	10	25	31	3	8	11	12	25	36
St Mirren	44	5	11	6	22	28	5	4	13	19	36	35
Falkirk	44	8	4	10	26	35	2	7	13	15	40	31
Dunfermline A	44	6	6	10	23	35	2	4	16	18	49	26
Morton	44	3	7	12	19	47	0	3	19	8	53	16

DIVISION 1

	P	W	D	L	F	A	W	D	L	F	A	Pts
Hamilton A	44	12	5	5	36	24	10	7	5	31	15	56
Meadowbank T	44	12	4	6	41	26	8	8	6	29	25	52
Clydebank	44	13	2	7	32	25	8	5	9	27	36	49
Forfar A	44	9	9	4	44	28	7	7	8	23	30	48
Raith R	44	10	4	8	45	33	9	3	10	36	43	45
Airdrie	44	11	4	7	34	28	5	9	8	31	40	45
Queen of South	44	8	7	7	23	28	6	8	8	33	39	43
Partick T	44	9	6	7	32	27	7	3	12	28	37	41
Clyde	44	8	5	9	40	38	9	1	12	33	37	40
Kilmarnock	44	8	6	8	30	30	5	5	12	25	30	37
East Fife	44	8	5	9	34	34	5	5	12	27	42	36
Dumbarton	44	4	8	10	23	30	8	4	10	28	40	36

DIVISION 2

	P	W	D	L	F	A	W	D	L	F	A	Pts
Ayr U	39	15	2	2	52	14	12	5	3	43	17	61
St Johnstone	39	14	5	1	40	11	11	4	4	34	13	59
Queen's Park	39	10	6	4	30	20	11	3	5	34	24	51
Brechin C	39	12	3	5	33	20	8	5	6	23	20	48
Stirling A	39	12	4	4	34	23	6	6	7	26	28	46
E. Stirling	39	8	5	6	25	23	7	8	5	26	24	43
Alloa	39	10	4	6	30	19	6	4	9	20	27	40
Montrose	39	6	4	9	21	25	6	7	7	24	26	35
Arbroath	39	8	6	5	32	24	2	8	10	22	42	34
Stenhousemuir	39	5	6	8	19	25	7	3	10	30	33	33
Cowdenbeath	39	6	7	7	30	36	4	6	9	21	30	33
Albion R	39	6	5	8	21	33	4	6	10	24	42	31
Berwick R	39	3	4	13	18	38	3	0	16	14	39	16
Stranraer	39	2	6	11	22	42	2	2	16	12	42	16

DIVISION 2

	ALBION R	ALLOA	ARBROATH	AYR U	BERWICK R	BRECHIN C	COWDENBEATH	E STIRLING	MONTROSE	QUEEN'S PARK	ST JOHNSTONE	STENHOUSEMUIR	STIRLING A	STRANRAER
ALBION R		Sep26 1-0 Apr23 1-2	Dec26 1-1	Dec12 1-1	Jan30 0-2	Jan23 2-0 Mar12 1-5	Nov28 0-0	Aug15 1-1 Feb27 1-4	Nov14 0-1	Aug29 0-4 Apr09 1-2	Oct24 1-1	Oct31 3-2 Feb20 0-4	Sep12 2-1 Apr02 3-1	Oct10 2-1
ALLOA	Nov21 2-0		Sep19 3-1	Mar01 0-2 Apr16 1-3	Oct24 1-0 Apr02 2-0	Aug08 0-1 Feb13 3-0	Aug22 5-2	Sep12 1-2 May07 0-1	Dec12 1-0	Nov07 0-3 Feb27 1-0	Feb17 1-1 Apr30 1-1	Oct10 1-1	Aug29 4-0	Dec30 2-0 Mar22 1-1
ARBROATH	Sep05 3-0 Mar05 4-0	Nov28 1-1 Feb20 1-1		Jan16 2-4	Sep26 3-1	Oct24 1-2 Mar26 0-3	Feb09 2-1 Apr30 0-0	Oct03 1-1	Sep12 0-0 Apr09 1-1	Aug08 3-1 Mar12 1-2	Jan02 0-2	Dec12 3-0	Aug22 3-2	Nov07 3-2
AYR U	Sep15 3-0 Mar19 6-2	Oct17 2-1	Oct10 2-0 Apr02 3-0		Nov14 2-0	Nov28 1-2	Dec19 3-1 Mar05 5-0	Feb06 2-0 Apr23 0-0	Aug15 3-1	Sep26 4-1 Feb20 1-1	Oct31 0-3	Jan23 3-0	Dec26 4-0	Aug29 5-1 Apr09 3-1
BERWICK R	Oct17 0-3 Apr30 1-3	Feb23 1-2	Nov21 3-3 May07 4-0	Aug22 0-2 Feb13 0-1		Nov07 0-2 Feb27 0-0	Aug29 2-2	Jan19 1-1	Sep19 2-1	Dec26 0-1	Oct10 0-4 Apr09 0-2	Sep12 1-3 Mar19 1-3	Jan23 0-4	Aug08 0-1 Mar26 2-0
BRECHIN C	Oct03 2-1	Oct31 3-1	Feb16 1-1	Sep19 0-3 May07 2-1	Aug15 4-0		Dec26 1-0 Mar19 0-3	Jan16 2-3 Apr09 1-0	Aug29 2-0 Mar08 0-1	Sep12 1-1 Apr02 2-0	Nov14 2-1	Oct17 2-0	Dec12 1-2 Apr30 1-1	Nov21 2-0 Feb20 4-1
COWDENBEATH	Sep19 3-3 Mar26 1-0	Nov14 2-2 Apr09 0-1	Oct17 3-5	Sep12 1-6	Jan02 5-3 Apr23 3-0	Sep05 1-1		Oct31 0-0 Mar12 0-0	Jan16 1-1 May07 2-1	Oct03 2-4	Aug15 0-3 Feb20 1-0	Feb06 1-1	Nov21 2-4 Feb27 0-1	Dec12 2-0
E STIRLING	Nov07 2-2	Dec19 3-1	Jan23 1-1 Mar19 2-1	Oct24 0-2	Sep15 1-0 Mar01 2-1	Oct10 0-0	Aug08 0-1		Dec26 2-2 Apr30 3-2	Nov28 0-1	Sep26 0-2	Aug29 2-0 Mar26 1-2	Feb02 2-1 Apr16 1-3	Aug22 1-1 Mar05 2-0
MONTROSE	Aug22 1-2 Feb13 0-0	Sep15 2-0 Mar28 0-2	Dec29 1-1	Nov07 2-4 Mar12 1-1	Nov28 4-0 Apr16 1-0	Jan02 0-1	Oct10 2-1	Sep05 0-3		Oct24 0-2 Apr23 1-2	Feb23 0-1	Sep26 1-0 Feb27 1-1	Aug08 1-3	Jan23 3-1
QUEEN'S PARK	Jan02 1-1	Aug15 2-0	Oct31 1-1	Nov21 0-2	Sep05 3-2 Mar05 2-0	Dec19 2-0	Jan23 3-2 Apr16 1-1	Sep19 2-1 Feb13 1-2	Feb06 1-1		Sep15 0-1 Mar26 2-1	Nov14 0-2 May07 2-1	Oct10 1-1 Mar19 1-1	Oct17 3-0 Feb16 2-0
ST JOHNSTONE	Feb06 4-1 May07 2-0	Oct03 2-1	Aug29 3-1 Apr16 4-0	Aug08 0-0 Feb27 2-0	Jan16 2-1	Aug22 1-1 Apr23 2-0	Nov07 0-1	Nov21 3-1 Apr02 0-0	Oct17 1-1 Mar19 5-1	Dec12 2-0		Dec26 4-1	Sep19 1-1 Mar01 1-0	Sep12 1-0
STENHOUSEMUIR	Aug08 3-1	Jan16 0-1 Mar12 0-0	Sep15 1-1 Feb13 1-1	Oct03 0-6 Apr30 1-0	Dec19 1-2	Feb24 1-2 Apr16 2-1	Oct24 0-0 Apr02 2-0	Jan02 2-3	Nov21 0-2	Aug22 2-3	Sep05 0-0 Mar05 3-0		Aug15 0-0	Sep19 0-2
STIRLING A	Dec19 1-1	Jan02 2-0 Mar05 4-1	Nov14 3-0 Apr23 2-0	Sep05 1-1 Mar26 2-2	Oct03 1-0 Mar12 2-0	Sep15 2-1	Sep26 2-0	Oct17 3-0	Oct31 0-2 Feb20 0-2	Jan16 2-2	Nov28 0-6	Nov07 0-3 Apr04 3-2		Feb06 2-0 May07 2-0
STRANRAER	Jan16 1-2 Apr16 2-2	Sep05 0-3	Aug15 3-1 Feb27 0-3	Jan02 1-2	Oct31 0-2	Sep26 1-1	Sep15 2-2 Feb24 0-4	Nov14 3-3	Oct03 1-3 Apr02 1-1	Apr30 1-4	Dec19 1-2 Mar12 1-3	Nov28 2-3 Apr23 2-1	Oct24 0-0	

SCOTTISH FOOTBALL LEAGUE RECORDS
SEASON 1988-89

PREMIER

	ABERDEEN	CELTIC	DUNDEE	DUNDEE U	HAMILTON A	HEARTS	HIBERNIAN	MOTHERWELL	RANGERS	ST MIRREN
ABERDEEN		Nov02 2-2 Apr29 0-0	Nov16 1-0 Mar11 2-0	Nov12 1-1 Apr01 1-0	Dec03 1-1 Apr15 3-0	Sep24 1-0 Feb25 3-0	Sep03 0-0 Jan07 2-0	Nov19 2-1 May06 0-0	Oct08 2-1 Jan14 1-2	Aug20 1-1 Dec17 3-1
CELTIC	Sep17 1-3 Dec10 0-0		Oct29 2-3 Apr22 2-1	Oct12 1-0 Mar25 1-0	Sep03 2-1 Jan07 2-0	Aug13 1-0 Dec31 4-2	Nov19 1-0 May06 1-0	Sep28 3-1 Feb11 1-2	Nov12 3-1 Apr01 1-2	Oct08 7-1 Jan14 2-1
DUNDEE	Aug13 1-1 Dec31 2-0	Sep24 1-0 Feb25 0-3		Sep03 0-3 Jan07 0-1	Nov02 5-2 Apr29 1-0	Dec03 1-1 Apr15 2-1	Oct08 2-1 Jan14 1-2	Oct12 1-1 Mar25 2-1	Nov19 0-0 May06 1-2	Nov12 0-1 Apr01 2-1
DUNDEE U	Aug27 2-2 Jan03 1-1	Aug20 1-0 Dec17 2-0	Nov05 2-0 Apr08 2-1		Nov26 1-0 May13 0-1	Oct01 0-0 Jan21 0-0	Sep17 1-1 Dec10 4-1	Oct29 1-1 Apr22 1-1	Sep27 0-1 Feb11 1-1	Oct22 0-1 Mar11 1-4
HAMILTON A	Sep27 0-1 Feb14 0-2	Nov05 0-8 Apr08 2-0	Sep17 1-0 Dec10 1-0	Oct08 0-4 Jan14 0-5		Oct11 0-4 Mar25 0-2	Oct29 0-3 Apr22 0-3	Aug27 1-0 Jan03 0-2	Aug13 0-2 Dec31 0-1	Nov19 2-4 May06 2-1
HEARTS	Oct29 1-1 Apr22 1-0	Oct22 0-2 Mar11 0-1	Sep28 1-1 Feb11 3-1	Nov19 0-0 May06 0-0	Aug20 3-2 Dec17 2-0		Nov12 1-2 Apr01 2-1	Oct08 2-2 Jan14 0-0	Sep17 1-2 Dec10 2-0	Sep03 1-2 Jan07 2-0
HIBERNIAN	Nov05 1-2 Apr08 1-2	Oct01 3-1 Jan21 1-3	Nov26 1-1 May13 1-1	Nov02 1-1 Apr29 1-2	Sep24 1-0 Mar01 2-1	Aug27 0-0 Jan04 1-0		Aug13 1-0 Dec31 2-0	Oct12 0-1 Mar25 0-1	Dec03 2-0 Apr19 1-0
MOTHERWELL	Oct01 1-1 Jan21 0-2	Dec03 1-3 Apr12 2-2	Aug20 1-1 Dec17 1-0	Sep24 1-2 Mar14 1-2	Nov12 1-1 Apr01 1-0	Nov26 2-0 May13 1-1	Oct22 1-1 Mar11 0-0		Sep03 0-2 Jan07 2-1	Nov01 1-2 Apr29 4-0
RANGERS	Nov26 1-0 May13 0-3	Aug27 5-1 Jan03 4-1	Oct01 2-0 Jan21 3-1	Dec03 0-1 May02 2-0	Nov16 3-1 Mar11 3-0	Nov01 3-0 Apr29 4-0	Aug20 0-0 Dec17 1-0	Nov05 2-1 Apr08 1-0		Sep24 2-1 Feb25 3-1
ST MIRREN	Oct12 1-1 Mar25 1-3	Nov26 2-3 May13 0-1	Aug27 0-0 Jan03 1-1	Aug13 0-1 Dec31 0-1	Oct01 2-0 Jan21 1-0	Nov05 1-1 Apr08 1-1	Sep28 0-1 Feb21 3-1	Sep17 1-0 Dec10 2-1	Oct29 1-1 Apr22 0-2	

LEAGUE TABLES

PREMIER DIVISION

	P	W	D	L	F	A	W	D	L	F	A	Pts
Rangers	36	15	1	2	39	11	11	3	4	23	15	56
Aberdeen	36	10	7	1	26	10	8	7	3	25	15	50
Celtic	36	13	1	4	35	18	8	3	7	31	26	46
Dundee U	36	6	8	4	20	16	10	4	4	24	10	44
Hibernian	36	8	4	6	20	16	5	5	8	17	20	35
Hearts	36	7	6	5	22	17	2	7	9	13	25	31
St Mirren	36	5	6	7	17	19	6	1	11	22	36	29
Dundee	36	8	4	6	22	21	1	6	11	12	27	28
Motherwell	36	5	7	6	21	21	2	6	10	14	23	27
Hamilton A	36	5	0	13	9	42	1	2	15	10	34	14

DIVISION 1

	P	W	D	L	F	A	W	D	L	F	A	Pts
Dunfermline A	39	13	5	2	37	17	9	5	5	23	19	54
Falkirk	39	13	3	3	38	10	9	5	6	33	27	52
Clydebank	39	12	6	2	50	29	6	6	7	30	26	48
Airdrie	39	11	6	2	36	16	6	7	7	30	28	47
Morton	39	8	5	6	20	20	8	4	8	26	26	41
St Johnstone	39	11	4	4	30	16	3	8	9	21	26	40
Raith R	39	8	6	6	29	25	7	4	8	21	27	40
Partick T	39	7	6	6	26	24	6	5	9	31	34	37
Forfar A	39	6	9	5	24	24	4	7	8	28	32	36
Meadowbank T	39	8	4	7	26	26	5	6	9	19	24	36
Ayr U	39	8	6	6	39	37	5	3	11	17	35	35
Clyde	39	7	6	7	23	26	2	10	7	17	26	34
Kilmarnock	39	5	7	7	19	25	5	7	8	28	35	34
Queen of South	39	1	6	13	20	47	1	2	16	18	52	*10

DIVISION 2

	P	W	D	L	F	A	W	D	L	F	A	Pts
Albion R	39	14	5	1	39	19	7	3	9	26	29	50
Alloa	39	12	6	1	42	20	5	5	10	24	28	45
Brechin C	39	8	5	6	27	24	7	8	5	31	25	43
Stirling A	39	10	6	3	31	20	5	6	9	33	35	42
East Fife	39	9	8	3	31	21	5	5	9	25	34	41
Montrose	39	10	4	5	25	25	5	7	8	29	30	41
Queen's Park	39	8	7	4	26	20	2	11	7	24	29	38
Cowdenbeath	39	6	11	2	30	27	7	3	10	18	25	*38
E. Stirling	39	10	3	7	31	31	3	8	8	23	27	37
Arbroath	39	5	6	9	29	40	6	9	4	27	23	37
Stranraer	39	6	8	6	30	31	6	4	9	29	33	36
Dumbarton	39	10	2	8	28	27	2	8	9	17	28	34
Berwick R	39	5	7	7	18	26	5	6	9	32	33	33
Stenhousemuir	39	6	8	6	27	24	3	3	13	17	35	29

* 2 points deducted for breach of rules.

DIVISION 1

	AIRDRIE	AYR U	CLYDE	CLYDEBANK	DUNFERMLINE A	FALKIRK	FORFAR A	KILMARNOCK	MEADOWBANK T	MORTON	PARTICK T	QUEEN OF SOUTH	RAITH R	ST JOHNSTONE
AIRDRIE		Nov05 2-1	Oct15 1-1 Mar11 1-1	Dec17 1-1	Jan21 0-2	Jan14 2-0 Apr29 3-0	Dec10 0-3 Feb11 2-1	Sep10 5-1	Oct01 0-0	Aug20 1-1 Mar25 2-1	Sep24 5-1	Aug27 3-0 Apr01 3-0	Nov19 3-1	Dec31 1-0 Apr24 1-1
AYR U	Jan07 1-4 May06 3-1		Oct29 1-1	Aug13 3-2 Apr08 2-4	Oct15 2-2 Apr22 1-2	Sep10 3-4	Sep03 2-1	Jan03 4-1 Mar11 2-1	Dec03 2-2 Feb25 3-2	Dec17 3-1 May13 0-1	Nov19 1-3	Oct08 1-1	Feb04 1-1 Mar25 2-2	Sep24 2-1
CLYDE	Dec27 0-0	Dec10 4-2 Mar04 1-0		Sep10 0-5 Feb28 1-1	Oct01 1-1	Sep24 1-2	Aug20 1-1 Apr08 1-1	Nov19 0-2	Jan21 1-2	Jan17 0-1 Apr29 2-1	Aug27 1-0 Mar28 0-0	Nov05 3-1 Apr22 2-1	Dec31 0-1	Oct22 2-4 May13 2-0
CLYDEBANK	Oct22 3-3 May13 4-1	Jan18 5-1	Nov12 3-2		Sep17 2-1 Mar04 0-1	Aug20 2-2 Mar25 0-1	Oct01 2-2	Sep03 2-2 May06 3-2	Nov26 2-1	Jan03 1-1	Jan21 3-2 Apr22 4-2	Dec10 4-2 Feb14 3-0	Dec24 3-1	Nov05 2-0 Apr01 2-2
DUNFERMLINE A	Oct08 1-0 Apr08 1-1	Dec24 5-1	Feb04 3-0 May06 1-1	Nov19 2-2		Dec31 3-0	Nov05 2-1	Sep24 3-0 Mar25 0-0	Oct22 1-3 May13 1-1	Dec10 2-1 Apr15 1-0	Jan14 3-2	Sep10 4-2	Aug27 2-1 Mar11 0-1	Aug20 1-0 Feb11 1-0
FALKIRK	Aug13 0-0	Nov12 1-0 Mar28 2-0	Nov26 0-0 Apr15 3-1	Dec03 3-1	Sep03 2-1 Mar07 4-0		Oct22 1-2	Jan07 2-0	Jan03 3-0 Mar04 0-0	Sep17 0-1	Dec24 0-1	Feb07 2-0 May06 7-1	Oct29 3-1 Apr08 3-0	Oct08 2-1
FORFAR A	Oct29 1-1	Dec31 1-2 Apr01 0-0	Dec03 2-1	Feb04 2-4 Apr15 1-2	Jan07 2-1 Apr29 0-1	Dec17 0-0 May13 2-2		Oct08 2-2	Aug13 1-0 Mar25 2-1	Oct15 0-1 Feb25 0-0	Sep10 3-2	Nov19 2-2	Sep24 1-0	Aug27 1-1 Mar04 1-1
KILMARNOCK	Nov12 0-3 Mar04 1-1	Aug27 2-0	Sep17 1-2 Feb18 0-0	Dec31 1-0	Nov26 2-2	Oct05 0-2 Apr01 0-0	Jan21 2-1 Mar18 2-2		Dec24 1-0	Oct01 3-4	Aug20 0-1 Apr29 0-0	Jan14 2-1	Oct22 1-1 Apr15 1-2	Dec10 0-3
MEADOWBANK T	Feb04 3-2 Apr22 3-1	Aug20 1-2	Oct08 3-2 Mar18 2-0	Sep24 0-0 Mar11 1-1	Dec17 0-1	Aug27 2-1	Jan14 1-1	Oct15 0-2 Apr08 1-2		Jan07 2-1	Dec10 0-2	Dec31 1-2	Sep10 2-1 Feb11 1-3	Nov19 1-1 May06 2-1
MORTON	Dec03 0-2	Oct22 2-0	Aug13 0-2	Aug27 1-0 Apr04 1-0	Oct29 1-0	Nov19 1-5 Feb21 2-2	Dec24 1-1	Mar01 2-2 Apr22 3-0	Nov05 2-0 Apr01 0-2		Dec31 1-0 Mar04 1-1	Sep24 1-0	Oct08 0-1 May06 0-1	Sep10 1-1
PARTICK T	Nov26 0-2 Mar18 1-0	Sep17 2-2 Feb14 4-1	Jan03 0-0	Oct08 1-1	Aug13 1-2 Apr01 0-0	Oct15 1-3 Mar11 2-1	Nov12 1-2 May06 4-1	Dec03 0-1	Oct29 1-1 Apr15 2-1	Sep03 1-4		Dec17 2-1	Jan07 1-1	Feb08 2-0
QUEEN OF SOUTH	Jan03 2-4	Jan21 0-2 Apr15 1-2	Jan07 3-3	Oct29 0-3	Nov12 0-0 Mar21 0-2	Oct01 0-3	Sep17 2-1 Mar11 2-2	Aug13 2-2 May13 0-6	Sep03 0-1 Apr29 1-2	Nov26 2-3 Apr08 1-1	Oct22 1-4 Feb25 2-4		Dec03 0-1	Dec24 1-1
RAITH R	Sep17 1-2 Mar01 1-1	Oct01 0-0	Sep03 0-0 Apr01 2-0	Oct15 1-3 Apr29 3-0	Jan03 1-3	Dec10 1-3	Nov26 2-1 Apr22 2-3	Dec17 0-0	Nov12 1-0	Jan21 1-0	Nov05 5-3 Apr13 1-1	Aug20 2-1 Mar04 4-1		Jan14 1-1 Apr05 0-2
ST JOHNSTONE	Sep03 2-1	Nov26 2-0 Apr29 0-1	Dec17 0-0	Jan07 2-0	Dec03 0-1	Jan21 2-1 Apr22 0-1	Jan02 2-1	Oct29 2-0 Feb25 2-2	Sep17 0-0	Nov12 4-2 Mar11 0-1	Oct01 2-1 Apr08 1-1	Oct15 3-1 Mar25 3-1	Aug13 3-1	

DIVISION 2

	ALBION R	ALLOA	ARBROATH	BERWICK R	BRECHIN C	COWDENBEAT	DUMBARTON	EAST FIFE	E STIRLING	MONTROSE	QUEEN'S PARI	STENHOUSEM	STIRLING A	STRANRAER
ALBION R		Feb11 3-2	Oct15 3-1 May06 2-2	Oct08 3-1 May13 2-1	Sep10 1-1	Dec10 3-1 Apr08 2-1	Sep03 2-1 Apr22 2-0	Nov12 2-0 Mar04 1-2	Aug13 1-0	Oct29 2-1 Mar07 2-2	Sep24 1-1	Dec24 1-0	Jan31 1-0	Jan03 3-0 Mar18 2-2
ALLOA	Oct01 3-1 Apr29 2-0		Jan03 3-3 Mar01 3-0	Oct15 2-1	Nov19 2-2	Aug20 2-1 Mar25 2-1	Dec17 2-0	Nov26 2-1	Sep17 2-2	Jan31 1-0 Apr22 3-3	Dec31 0-0	Sep03 1-2 Mar04 4-0	Feb04 3-2 Apr08 4-0	Nov05 1-1
ARBROATH	Jan21 0-3	Aug27 2-2		Jan14 1-2 Feb25 0-3	Aug20 1-2	Dec31 0-1	Feb04 1-1 Apr29 1-3	Dec17 1-3 Mar18 1-3	Oct22 3-3 Apr22 2-2	Nov26 0-0	Nov05 2-2	Sep17 5-1 Apr08 2-1	Oct01 2-1 May13 0-4	Nov19 1-0 Mar11 4-3
BERWICK R	Feb04 2-1	Jan21 1-1 Mar22 1-0	Sep03 0-3		Dec31 4-4	Nov05 0-1 Apr15 0-0	Oct01 1-0	Oct22 1-2	Nov26 0-5 Mar04 2-0	Sep17 1-2 May06 1-1	Nov19 0-2 Apr01 1-1	Dec17 1-0	Jan07 0-0 Feb18 2-2	Aug20 0-1
BRECHIN C	Nov26 0-2 Apr01 2-1	Aug13 2-1 Mar07 1-2	Nov12 1-0 Mar15 3-4	Oct29 2-0 Apr22 0-2		Oct08 0-1	Sep17 1-1	Dec24 1-0 May06 1-0	Dec17 2-2	Jan03 1-1	Feb11 2-0	Feb01 3-1 Mar18 1-1	Sep03 2-3	Oct15 2-2
COWDENBEATH	Sep17 1-1	Nov12 1-1	Oct29 1-1 Apr01 1-1	Dec24 3-3	Feb08 3-3 Apr29 0-2		Oct22 2-0 Mar04 1-1	Jan03 1-1	Oct01 2-1	Aug13 2-6	Jan21 2-2 Mar18 3-1	Nov26 2-0 Feb18 2-1	Dec17 1-1	Sep03 1-0 Apr22 1-1
DUMBARTON	Apr04 1-0	Sep24 1-1 May13 0-2	Oct08 1-4	Mar07 2-2 Apr08 0-4	Dec13 0-2 Apr15 1-0	Jan31 3-0		Aug13 3-1 Feb18 4-0	Oct29 3-0	Dec24 3-2 Mar28 2-0	Aug27 0-3 Mar11 1-0	Nov12 0-2 May06 2-0	Oct15 1-2	Sep10 0-2
EAST FIFE	Aug20 1-2	Sep10 2-0 Mar11 1-0	Sep24 0-0	Jan28 2-2 Apr29 1-1	Nov05 1-0	Aug27 4-1 Feb25 1-0	Nov19 1-1		Jan14 2-2	Oct08 1-1 May13 1-4	Dec10 2-2	Oct15 2-1 Apr15 1-1	Dec31 2-0 Mar25 3-0	Feb11 1-2 Apr08 2-1
E STIRLING	Nov19 3-4 Mar11 0-1	Dec10 2-1 Apr15 2-0	Jan28 0-3	Sep10 3-2	Sep24 4-3 Feb18 1-1	Mar15 1-0 May13 0-2	Dec31 0-1 Mar25 1-0	Sep03 2-2 Apr01 4-2		Oct15 1-0	Aug20 2-1 Apr29 2-1	Jan03 0-3	Nov05 2-2	Oct08 1-2
MONTROSE	Dec31 1-0	Oct22 1-0	Sep10 0-1 Apr15 1-1	Dec10 2-1	Aug27 0-2 Mar25 1-0	Nov19 0-2 Mar11 2-1	Nov05 1-1	Feb04 2-2	Jan21 0-1 Apr08 2-1		Jan14 1-1	Oct01 3-1	Aug20 3-2 Apr29 0-6	Sep24 4-2 Feb22 1-0
QUEEN'S PARK	Dec17 0-0 Feb18 3-2	Oct29 0-2 May06 0-2	Dec24 2-0 Mar25 1-1	Aug13 2-0	Oct01 1-1 Apr08 1-2	Oct15 1-1	Jan03 2-1	Sep17 1-0 Apr22 1-2	Nov12 0-0	Sep03 2-0 Mar04 2-2		Feb04 1-1	Nov26 2-0	Feb07 4-3
STENHOUSEMUIR	Nov05 2-3 Mar25 1-2	Jan24 2-0	Dec10 0-0	Sep24 3-2 Mar11 0-0	Oct22 0-2	Sep10 0-0	Aug20 3-1	Jan21 1-1	Aug27 1-1 Mar06 1-0	Mar01 0-1 Apr01 2-3	Oct08 0-0 May13 1-1		Nov19 1-1 Apr22 4-2	Dec31 3-4 Apr29 2-0
STIRLING A	Oct22 4-2 Apr15 0-0	Oct08 3-1	Feb11 1-1	Aug27 2-1	Jan18 2-2 Mar11 0-0	Sep24 2-3 May06 0-1	Jan21 1-1 Apr01 3-1	Oct29 3-1	Dec24 1-0 Mar18 2-1	Nov12 2-0	Sep10 3-2 Feb27 0-0	Aug13 2-0		Dec14 0-3
STRANRAER	Aug27 3-1	Dec24 2-2 Apr01 1-4	Aug13 0-1	Nov12 2-2 Mar25 1-2	Jan21 0-1 May13 2-1	Jan25 2-0	Nov26 2-2 Feb25 1-1	Oct01 2-2	Feb04 1-2 May06 0-0	Dec17 1-0	Oct22 3-1 Apr15 3-3	Oct29 2-1	Sep17 1-1 Mar04 1-4	

Scottish Football League Records
Season 1989-90

PREMIER

	ABERDEEN	CELTIC	DUNDEE	DUNDEE U	DUNFERMLINE A	HEARTS	HIBERNIAN	MOTHERWELL	RANGERS	ST MIRREN
ABERDEEN		Sep30 1-1 Feb17 1-1	Aug26 1-0 Jan02 5-2	Dec09 2-0 Apr18 1-0	Sep16 2-1 Jan13 4-1	Oct14 1-3 Feb03 2-2	Aug12 1-0 Dec26 1-2	Oct28 1-0 Mar24 2-0	Nov22 1-0 Apr08 0-0	Nov25 5-0 Apr28 2-0
CELTIC	Dec02 1-0 May02 1-3		Dec16 4-1 Apr21 1-1	Nov18 0-1 Mar03 3-0	Aug19 1-0 Dec30 0-2	Oct21 2-1 Mar10 1-1	Oct04 3-1 Feb10 1-1	Sep23 1-1 Jan27 0-1	Aug26 1-1 Jan02 0-1	Nov22 1-1 Apr07 0-3
DUNDEE	Nov04 1-1 Mar31 1-1	Oct14 1-3 Feb03 0-0		Aug19 4-3 Dec30 1-1	Oct21 1-2 Mar10 1-0	Sep09 2-2 Jan06 0-1	Sep23 0-0 Jan27 2-0	Dec02 2-1 May05 1-2	Nov18 0-2 Mar03 2-2	Dec09 3-3 Apr14 1-2
DUNDEE U	Oct04 2-0 Feb10 1-1	Sep16 2-2 Jan13 2-0	Oct28 0-0 Mar24 1-2		Aug26 2-1 Jan03 1-0	Nov25 2-1 Apr28 1-1	Nov08 1-0 Apr07 1-0	Aug12 1-1 Dec23 1-1	Dec16 1-1 Apr21 0-1	Sep30 0-0 Feb17 2-0
DUNFERMLINE A	Oct18 0-3 Mar03 2-4	Oct28 2-0 Mar24 0-0	Aug12 2-1 Dec26 1-0	Nov04 1-1 Mar31 0-1		Dec09 0-2 Apr14 0-1	Dec02 0-0 May05 1-1	Sep09 1-1 Jan06 0-5	Sep23 1-1 Jan27 0-1	Oct14 5-1 Feb03 1-0
HEARTS	Dec20 1-1 Apr21 1-0	Aug12 1-3 Dec26 0-0	Nov11 6-3 Apr04 0-0	Sep23 1-1 Jan27 3-2	Oct04 1-2 Feb10 0-2		Aug26 1-0 Jan01 2-0	Nov18 3-0 Mar03 2-0	Dec02 1-2 May05 1-1	Oct28 4-0 Mar24 0-0
HIBERNIAN	Oct25 0-3 Mar10 3-2	Dec09 0-3 Apr17 1-0	Nov25 3-2 Apr28 1-1	Sep09 2-0 Jan06 0-0	Sep30 2-2 Feb17 2-1	Nov04 1-1 Mar31 1-2		Oct14 3-2 Feb03 1-2	Aug19 2-0 Dec30 0-0	Sep16 3-1 Jan13 0-1
MOTHERWELL	Aug19 0-0 Dec30 2-2	Nov25 0-0 Apr28 1-1	Sep30 3-0 Feb17 3-1	Oct21 3-2 Mar10 0-1	Nov08 1-1 Apr07 1-3	Sep16 1-3 Jan13 0-3	Jan09 0-2 Apr21 1-0		Oct03 1-0 Feb10 1-1	Aug26 3-1 Jan02 2-0
RANGERS	Sep09 1-0 Jan06 2-0	Nov04 1-0 Apr01 3-0	Sep16 2-2 Jan13 3-0	Oct14 2-1 Feb03 3-1	Nov25 3-0 Apr28 2-0	Sep30 1-0 Feb17 0-0	Oct28 3-0 Mar24 0-1	Dec09 3-0 Apr14 2-1		Aug12 0-1 Dec23 1-0
ST MIRREN	Sep23 0-2 Jan27 1-0	Sep09 1-0 Jan06 0-2	Oct04 3-2 Feb10 0-0	Dec13 1-0 May05 0-0	Jan10 2-0 Apr21 1-2	Aug19 1-2 Dec30 2-0	Nov18 0-0 Mar03 0-1	Nov04 2-2 Mar31 0-0	Oct25 0-2 Mar17 0-0	

LEAGUE TABLES

PREMIER DIVISION

	P	W	D	L	F	A	W	D	L	F	A	Pts
Rangers	36	14	2	2	32	7	6	9	3	16	12	51
Aberdeen	36	12	4	2	33	13	5	6	7	23	20	44
Hearts	36	8	6	4	28	17	8	6	4	26	18	44
Dundee U	36	8	8	2	21	12	3	5	10	15	27	35
Celtic	36	6	6	6	21	20	4	8	6	16	17	34
Motherwell	36	7	6	5	23	21	4	6	8	20	26	34
Hibernian	36	8	5	5	25	23	4	5	9	9	18	34
Dunfermline A	36	5	6	7	17	23	6	2	10	20	27	30
St Mirren	36	6	6	6	14	15	4	4	10	14	33	30
Dundee	36	4	8	6	23	26	1	6	11	18	39	24

DIVISION 1

	P	W	D	L	F	A	W	D	L	F	A	Pts
St Johnstone	39	13	3	4	40	16	12	5	2	41	23	58
Airdrie	39	12	6	2	45	23	11	2	6	32	22	54
Clydebank	39	10	4	5	39	29	7	6	7	35	35	44
Falkirk	39	11	5	3	38	17	3	10	7	21	29	43
Raith R	39	10	4	5	30	22	5	8	7	27	28	42
Hamilton A	39	9	5	5	33	27	5	8	7	19	26	41
Meadowbank T	39	7	6	7	22	25	6	7	6	19	21	39
Partick T	39	9	5	6	33	22	3	9	7	29	31	38
Clyde	39	5	9	5	18	20	5	6	9	21	26	35
Ayr U	39	6	8	5	24	23	5	5	10	17	39	35
Morton	39	4	10	6	21	20	5	6	8	17	26	34
Forfar A	39	5	7	7	29	33	3	8	9	22	32	*29
Albion R	39	4	8	8	31	38	4	3	12	19	40	27
Alloa	39	4	8	8	18	27	2	5	12	23	43	25

* 2 points deducted for breach of rules

DIVISION 2

	P	W	D	L	F	A	W	D	L	F	A	Pts
Brechin C	39	12	5	3	33	20	7	6	6	26	24	49
Kilmarnock	39	14	3	3	35	11	8	1	10	32	28	48
Stirling A	39	13	3	4	44	20	7	4	8	29	30	47
Stenhousemuir	39	10	2	7	30	29	8	6	6	30	24	44
Berwick R	39	13	4	3	36	19	5	1	13	30	38	41
Dumbarton	39	9	5	5	33	29	6	5	9	37	44	40
Cowdenbeath	39	7	6	6	35	30	6	7	7	23	24	39
Stranraer	39	8	4	8	32	31	7	4	8	25	28	38
East Fife	39	7	7	5	37	29	5	5	10	23	34	36
Queen's Park	39	10	5	5	26	23	3	5	11	14	28	36
Queen of South	39	8	8	3	40	34	3	6	11	18	35	36
Arbroath	39	9	5	5	26	18	3	5	12	21	43	34
Montrose	39	5	7	8	28	29	5	5	9	25	34	32
E. Stirling	39	8	3	8	20	25	0	7	13	14	41	26

DIVISION 1

	AIRDRIE	ALBION R	ALLOA	AYR U	CLYDE	CLYDEBANK	FALKIRK	FORFAR A	HAMILTON A	MEADOWBANK T	MORTON	PARTICK T	RAITH R	ST JOHNSTONE
AIRDRIE		Aug26 1-0	Sep30 2-1 Mar24 3-1	Dec09 1-1 Feb10 6-0	Dec26 1-0	Jan30 2-2 Apr03 3-4	Sep05 1-1	Oct28 4-1	Aug19 1-0 May05 3-1	Oct14 3-1 Apr14 1-1	Jan06 4-1	Nov25 1-1 Feb17 3-2	Nov11 3-2 Apr21 0-1	Sep16 2-2
ALBION R	Jan02 0-2 Mar03 1-2		Nov04 1-1	Aug12 3-1	Sep23 2-0	Sep02 3-4 May05 1-2	Dec02 2-1 Feb03 2-2	Oct07 0-2 Apr07 2-2	Jan09 0-0	Oct21 0-0 Mar31 1-2	Jan13 1-1	Dec30 5-4 Apr28 2-2	Nov18 2-2	Nov11 1-3 Mar10 2-5
ALLOA	Dec02 0-2	Sep05 4-1 Mar27 3-4		Sep23 1-1 May05 0-0	Nov11 1-1 Feb10 1-0	Oct28 1-4 Apr28 1-1	Aug26 1-1 Mar20 0-0	Dec23 0-2	Jan06 0-2 Mar31 1-1	Dec30 0-1	Nov18 1-1	Feb28 1-0	Oct07 2-0 Apr14 0-4	Aug12 0-1
AYR U	Oct07 1-3	Dec26 2-0 Apr14 0-2	Nov25 3-0		Jan06 1-0 Mar14 1-1	Sep16 3-2	Nov11 3-3 Mar24 1-1	Aug19 1-1 Feb28 1-1	Aug26 0-1	Jan13 0-0	Sep05 2-3	Sep30 0-0 Feb03 2-1	Dec16 1-0	Oct21 2-2 Apr28 0-2
CLYDE	Aug12 1-0 Feb03 0-1	Nov29 0-0 Apr04 2-1	Sep09 2-4	Sep02 2-2		Nov04 2-0	Oct28 2-0 Apr14 0-0	Sep16 0-0	Sep30 1-1 Mar27 0-1	Dec09 0-3 Apr28 1-1	Dec30 1-1	Jan02 3-3	Mar17 1-0 Mar21 0-0	Oct14 0-2
CLYDEBANK	Oct21 0-3	Jan06 1-3	Jan13 3-1	Nov18 4-1 Mar03 0-1	Sep05 2-1 Apr07 2-1		Dec23 3-3	Nov11 3-2 Feb10 3-2	Oct07 2-2	Sep23 1-1 Mar27 2-1	Aug26 3-1 Apr21 0-1	Aug12 1-2	Dec02 3-1 Mar24 2-2	Dec30 4-0
FALKIRK	Nov04 3-1 Apr07 3-1	Sep30 6-0	Jan02 1-0	Sep09 0-1	Jan13 3-0	Oct14 2-1 Feb21 0-1		Dec26 4-0 Apr21 2-2	Sep16 3-3	Sep02 1-1	Sep21 1-0 Mar31 2-0	Dec09 1-1 Mar17 2-0	Aug19 0-2	Nov25 3-3 Feb10 1-0
FORFAR A	Jan13 1-1 Mar10 2-3	Dec09 3-0	Oct14 3-3 Mar03 3-2	Dec30 1-0	Nov18 1-1 Mar31 2-2	Sep09 2-2	Aug12 1-2		Oct21 0-1 Apr28 2-0	Nov04 1-3	Dec02 0-1	Sep02 0-3 Apr14 2-0	Sep23 2-2 Feb03 2-2	Jan02 1-5
HAMILTON A	Apr07 3-2	Oct14 0-0 Apr21 1-2	Sep02 1-0	Jan02 4-0 Mar17 2-1	Dec02 0-1	Dec09 2-1 Feb03 1-3	Nov18 1-0 Mar03 2-2	Feb14 1-1		Aug12 2-0	Sep23 2-2 Apr14 2-0	Sep09 1-4	Oct28 3-2	Nov04 3-3 Mar24 2-3
MEADOWBANK T	Dec20 0-1	Jan27 3-2	Aug19 1-3 Apr07 1-1	Oct28 1-2 Apr21 1-0	Oct07 2-1	Nov25 1-1	Jan06 1-2 May05 1-0	Sep05 3-1 Mar17 0-3	Dec23 1-0 Feb10 1-1		Nov11 0-0 Mar03 1-0	Sep16 1-1 Mar24 1-1	Aug26 1-2	Sep30 1-3
MORTON	Sep02 0-1 Apr28 1-1	Oct28 0-0 Mar17 3-0	Sep16 3-2 Feb03 2-0	Nov04 1-1 Apr07 0-1	Aug19 0-1 May05 2-3	Jan03 2-2	Jan27 0-2	Sep30 1-1 Mar27 2-0	Nov25 0-0	Sep09 0-0		Oct14 2-2	Dec23 1-1	Dec09 0-0 Feb27 1-2
PARTICK T	Sep23 2-1	Aug19 4-0	Oct21 3-3 Apr21 1-0	Dec02 1-2	Aug26 2-2 Mar03 0-3	Dec26 1-1 Mar31 4-0	Oct07 1-0	Jan06 0-0	Nov11 3-1 Mar14 4-1	Nov18 2-0	Jan09 1-2 Feb10 0-1		Sep05 3-1 May05 1-1	Jan13 0-1 Apr07 0-2
RAITH R	Sep09 0-4	Sep16 2-1 Feb10 3-2	Dec09 1-1	Oct14 2-0 Mar31 5-2	Oct21 0-2	Sep30 1-0	Dec30 4-0 Apr28 1-1	Nov25 1-0	Jan13 1-3 Apr07 0-0	Jan02 1-2 Feb28 3-0	Aug12 2-0 Mar10 2-1	Nov04 1-1		Sep02 0-2
ST JOHNSTONE	Nov18 1-2 Mar31 3-1	Sep09 2-1	Dec26 3-0 Mar17 6-0	Jan27 4-0	Dec16 2-0 Apr21 1-1	Aug19 2-1 Apr17 1-3	Sep23 2-0	Aug26 3-1 May05 1-0	Sep05 3-0	Dec02 1-0 Feb03 1-2	Oct07 1-1	Oct28 2-1	Jan06 1-2 Mar03 0-0	

DIVISION 2

	ARBROATH	BERWICK R	BRECHIN C	COWDENBEATH	DUMBARTON	EAST FIFE	E STIRLING	KILMARNOCK	MONTROSE	QUEEN OF SOUT	QUEEN'S PARK	STENHOUSEMUI	STIRLING A	STRANRAER
ARBROATH		Oct28 1-0	Nov11 0-1 Feb27 0-2	Jan27 0-0 Apr21 0-1	Oct07 2-1	Jan31 3-0	Nov25 2-0	Aug19 1-1 Feb17 2-4	Sep16 2-2 Mar17 3-0	Jan13 1-0 Apr07 1-0	Sep30 2-2 Mar24 1-1	Aug26 2-1	Dec26 1-2	Dec20 2-0
BERWICK R	Feb03 3-1 May05 5-0		Oct21 1-1 Apr28 1-0	Aug12 2-0	Nov11 1-2 Mar31 3-2	Sep09 1-1 Mar10 2-0	Apr14 1-0	Nov25 3-2 Feb24 1-4	Sep30 2-0	Mar03 1-1	Jan06 2-0	Oct14 0-2 Feb10 1-0	Aug26 1-1	Jan16 3-1 Apr07 2-1
BRECHIN C	Sep02 2-2	Jan27 1-0		Dec02 1-0 Feb10 1-3	Aug19 4-0 Mar17 3-0	Nov25 2-1	Oct14 2-1 May05 0-0	Dec26 3-1	Jan01 1-1 Mar24 2-2	Sep16 3-1	Nov04 1-0 Mar03 1-0	Sep30 1-2	Jan13 3-1 Apr07 1-5	Oct28 1-0 Apr21 0-0
COWDENBEATH	Nov21 1-1	Dec26 2-1 Mar27 3-1	Nov07 1-1		Sep30 1-5	Aug26 0-1 Feb17 2-2	Feb03 4-0 Apr28 3-3	Jan13 2-1	Aug19 0-1 Apr07 2-4	Dec20 4-2 Mar07 2-1	Nov25 0-0	Jan06 0-1	Sep16 4-0 Mar13 1-1	Nov11 3-4
DUMBARTON	Dec02 0-0 Apr24 2-0	Sep02 1-5	Dec23 1-1	Nov18 2-2 Apr14 1-3		Apr21 3-1	Mar20 3-0 Apr17 2-1	Mar24 0-2 Apr03 1-3	Nov04 3-2	Aug12 2-1	Oct14 2-1	Oct21 1-0	Sep23 2-2 Apr28 1-2	Sep09 5-2 Apr10 1-1
EAST FIFE	Nov04 3-0 Mar03 2-3	Jan13 2-2	Sep23 3-1 Apr14 1-3	Jan02 0-0	Sep16 2-2 Mar14 3-1		Dec26 1-1 Mar17 1-1	Jan10 4-2	Oct28 4-1	Oct07 2-2 Mar24 1-2	Sep02 1-1 Feb10 3-2	Aug19 2-3	Jan27 1-0	Nov18 1-2
E STIRLING	Sep23 1-1 Feb10 1-0	Oct07 3-1 Dec02 2-1	Jan10 2-0	Oct28 1-1	Aug26 1-2	Aug12 0-2		Nov11 2-1	Oct21 0-2 Mar14 1-1	Nov18 1-0	Dec23 1-0	Sep09 0-3 Apr11 4-2	Jan06 0-2 Mar27 0-2	Apr04 0-3 Apr24 0-1
KILMARNOCK	Dec23 3-0	Sep23 2-0	Aug12 0-2 Mar31 2-2	Sep09 0-0 May05 2-1	Oct28 3-0	Oct14 1-0 Apr07 2-1	Sep02 2-0 Mar03 2-0		Dec02 1-1	Nov04 2-0 Apr21 4-1	Jan02 2-0 Mar10 3-0	Jan20 2-0	Nov18 1-2 Mar06 1-0	Jan27 0-1
MONTROSE	Jan20 4-2	Nov18 2-1 Feb28 0-2	Aug26 0-1	Dec23 2-0	Jan06 2-2 Mar27 1-2	Feb03 2-2 Mar31 0-2	Apr21 3-0	Oct07 0-1 Apr28 1-3		Sep23 0-0 May05 1-1	Sep09 4-1 Apr14 0-1	Nov11 0-2 Mar10 1-1	Dec20 3-3	Aug12 2-2
QUEEN OF SOUTH	Sep09 2-2	Aug19 4-2 Dec23 3-2	Feb07 3-1 Mar10 2-2	Oct14 2-4	Jan10 1-4 Feb10 1-1	Dec02 5-1	Sep30 2-2 Mar31 1-1	Mar13 2-1	Nov25 3-2		Oct21 3-1 Apr28 0-0	Feb03 1-1 Apr14 0-4	Nov11 3-1	Aug26 2-2
QUEEN'S PARK	Nov18 1-2	Sep16 3-1 Apr21 0-3	Jan17 0-3	Sep23 0-0 Mar17 0-2	Dec16 2-2 May05 1-0	Nov11 2-1	Aug19 3-2 Apr07 2-1	Aug26 1-0	Jan13 2-1	Jan27 0-0		Dec26 0-0 Feb27 1-1	Oct28 2-1 Mar31 3-1	Oct07 0-2 Feb20 3-0
STENHOUSEMUIR	Jan02 3-0 Mar31 1-0	Jan09 1-3	Nov18 2-0 Feb20 1-1	Nov04 3-1 Mar03 2-1	Jan27 4-3 Apr07 1-3	Dec23 2-2 Apr28 1-2	Jan13 2-0	Sep16 0-3 Mar17 2-1	Sep02 1-0	Oct28 1-3	Aug12 1-3		Oct07 2-1	Sep23 0-2
STIRLING A	Aug12 2-3 Apr14 3-2	Jan02 3-2 Apr04 4-0	Sep09 2-0	Feb07 1-1	Nov25 4-1	Oct21 3-1 May05 2-0	Nov04 4-0	Sep30 0-1	Oct14 2-0 Mar03 2-3	Sep02 5-0 Feb17 1-1	Feb03 1-0	Dec02 1-1 Apr21 1-3		Dec23 1-0 Mar24 2-1
STRANRAER	Oct14 2-1 Apr28 2-1	Nov04 1-3	Feb03 2-4	Sep02 3-1 Mar31 1-2	Jan13 4-4	Sep30 1-1 Feb28 0-2	Sep16 1-1	Oct21 1-0 Apr14 2-1	Dec26 1-2 Feb10 2-0	Jan02 0-2 Mar17 3-0	Dec02 0-1	Nov25 2-2 May05 4-1	Aug19 0-2	

Scottish Football League Records
Season 1990-91

PREMIER

	ABERDEEN	CELTIC	DUNDEE U	DUNFERMLINE A	HEARTS	HIBERNIAN	MOTHERWELL	RANGERS	ST JOHNSTONE	ST MIRREN
ABERDEEN		Nov03 3-0 Apr06 1-0	Sep15 1-1 Jan02 0-1	Dec01 3-2 Mar13 0-0	Oct20 3-0 Feb02 5-0	Aug25 2-0 Jan12 2-0	Dec15 1-1 Apr20 3-0	Oct06 0-0 Mar02 1-0	Nov17 0-0 May04 2-1	Sep22 2-1 Dec26 1-0
CELTIC	Sep01 0-3 Jan19 1-0		Oct20 0-0 Feb02 1-0	Dec15 1-2 Apr20 5-1	Sep22 3-0 Dec29 1-1	Sep08 2-0 Jan05 1-1	Nov06 2-1 Mar30 1-2	Nov25 1-2 Mar24 3-0	Oct06 0-0 Mar02 3-0	Nov17 4-1 May05 1-0
DUNDEE U	Nov24 2-3 Mar23 1-2	Dec08 3-1 Apr13 2-1		Oct10 3-0 Mar02 1-0	Nov17 1-1 May04 2-1	Oct13 1-0 Feb09 0-0	Sep01 1-0 Jan19 3-0	Sep22 2-1 Dec29 1-2	Oct27 1-2 Mar30 0-0	Sep08 1-0 Jan05 3-2
DUNFERMLINE A	Sep08 1-1 Jan05 1-4	Oct13 1-1 Mar06 0-1	Dec22 1-0 May11 1-0		Sep01 2-0 Feb23 3-1	Sep29 1-1 Mar16 1-1	Nov10 3-3 Apr27 2-5	Nov20 0-1 Mar30 0-1	Nov24 1-2 Mar23 3-2	Dec11 0-0 Apr13 2-2
HEARTS	Dec08 1-0 Apr13 1-4	Nov10 1-0 Apr27 0-1	Sep29 1-0 Feb16 2-1	Nov03 1-1 Apr06 4-1		Nov24 1-1 Mar23 3-1	Dec22 3-2 May11 2-1	Sep08 1-3 Jan05 0-1	Oct13 2-3 Mar06 2-1	Aug25 1-1 Jan12 2-0
HIBERNIAN	Oct27 1-1 Mar30 2-4	Dec01 0-3 Mar09 0-2	Dec15 0-0 Apr20 1-0	Nov17 1-1 May04 3-0	Sep15 0-3 Jan02 1-4		Oct20 1-0 Feb02 1-1	Sep01 0-0 Jan19 0-2	Sep22 1-0 Dec29 0-1	Oct06 1-0 Mar02 4-3
MOTHERWELL	Oct13 0-0 Mar05 0-2	Aug25 2-0 Jan30 1-1	Nov03 0-2 Apr16 1-0	Sep22 2-0 Feb27 1-0	Oct06 1-1 Mar02 1-3	Dec11 4-1 Apr13 1-0		Nov17 2-4 May04 3-0	Sep08 3-0 Jan05 2-2	Nov24 1-1 Mar23 3-1
RANGERS	Dec22 2-2 May11 2-0	Sep15 1-1 Jan02 2-0	Nov10 1-2 Apr24 1-0	Aug25 3-1 Jan12 2-0	Dec01 4-0 Mar09 2-1	Nov03 4-0 Apr06 0-0	Sep29 1-0 Feb16 2-0		Dec08 4-1 Apr13 3-0	Oct13 5-0 Feb09 1-0
STJOHNSTONE	Sep29 5-0 Feb13 0-1	Dec22 3-2 May11 2-3	Aug25 1-3 Feb19 0-1	Sep15 3-2 Jan02 0-1	Dec15 2-1 Apr20 0-2	Nov10 1-1 Apr27 0-0	Dec01 2-1 Mar09 1-4	Oct20 0-0 Feb26 1-1		Nov03 0-1 Apr09 2-1
ST MIRREN	Nov10 0-4 Apr27 0-1	Sep29 2-3 Mar12 0-2	Dec01 1-1 Mar09 0-1	Oct20 0-1 Feb19 2-2	Oct27 2-1 Mar30 0-0	Dec22 1-0 May11 1-0	Sep15 1-0 Jan02 2-2	Dec15 0-3 Apr20 0-1	Sep01 2-2 Jan19 0-1	

LEAGUE TABLES

PREMIER DIVISION

	P	W	D	L	F	A	W	D	L	F	A	Pts
Rangers	36	14	3	1	40	8	10	4	4	22	15	55
Aberdeen	36	12	5	1	30	7	10	4	4	32	20	53
Celtic	36	10	4	4	30	14	7	3	8	22	24	41
Dundee U	36	11	3	4	28	16	6	4	8	13	13	41
Hearts	36	10	3	5	28	22	4	4	10	20	33	35
Motherwell	36	9	5	4	28	18	3	4	11	23	32	33
St Johnstone	36	6	4	8	23	25	5	5	8	18	29	31
Dunfermline	36	5	7	6	23	26	3	4	11	15	35	27
Hibernian	36	6	5	7	17	25	0	8	10	7	26	25
St Mirren	36	4	5	9	14	25	1	4	13	14	34	19

DIVISION 1

	P	W	D	L	F	A	W	D	L	F	A	Pts
Falkirk	39	12	4	4	40	18	9	8	2	30	17	54
Airdrie	39	9	5	5	32	21	12	6	2	37	22	53
Dundee	39	12	3	4	33	15	10	5	5	26	18	52
Partick	39	7	6	6	25	24	9	7	4	31	29	45
Kilmarnock	39	10	6	3	32	21	5	7	8	26	27	43
Hamilton	39	8	6	6	25	20	8	4	7	25	21	42
Raith	39	7	5	8	22	26	7	4	8	32	38	37
Clydebank	39	6	6	8	40	39	7	4	8	25	31	36
Morton	39	6	7	6	25	22	5	6	9	23	33	35
Forfar	39	6	9	5	32	28	3	6	10	18	29	33
Meadowbank	39	4	7	8	25	33	6	6	8	31	35	33
Ayr	39	7	7	6	32	24	3	5	11	15	35	32
Clyde	39	6	4	10	24	32	3	5	11	17	29	27
Brechin	39	3	4	12	20	37	4	6	10	24	43	24

DIVISION 2

	P	W	D	L	F	A	W	D	L	F	A	Pts
Stirling A	39	12	3	4	39	11	8	11	1	23	13	54
Montrose	39	10	2	7	29	18	10	4	6	25	16	46
Cowdenbeath	39	9	4	7	31	26	9	5	5	33	24	45
Stenhousemuir	39	11	4	5	32	20	5	8	6	24	22	44
Queen's Park	39	11	6	2	27	12	6	2	12	21	30	42
Stranraer	39	8	3	8	30	30	10	1	9	31	30	40
Dumbarton	39	8	8	4	23	20	7	2	10	26	29	40
Berwick	39	9	6	4	27	18	6	4	10	24	39	40
Alloa	39	8	4	7	27	22	5	7	8	24	24	37
East Fife	39	7	7	6	30	31	7	2	10	27	34	37
Albion	39	8	5	6	31	30	3	8	9	17	33	35
Queen of South	39	7	6	7	31	29	2	6	11	15	33	30
E. Stirling	39	5	7	8	22	32	4	4	11	14	39	29
Arbroath	39	5	5	10	22	24	3	6	10	19	35	27

DIVISION 1

	AIRDRIE	AYR U	BRECHIN C	CLYDE	CLYDEBANK	DUNDEE	FALKIRK	FORFAR A	HAMILTON A	KILMARNOCK	MEADOWBANK T	MORTON	PARTICK T	RAITH R
AIRDRIE		Sep22 4-0	Sep08 3-0	Dec08 2-2 Apr20 1-1	Oct06 2-2	Nov24 0-1 Mar02 0-1	Oct27 1-3 Mar30 0-3	Jan19 1-1 Apr27 2-1	Jan02 2-1	Nov10 2-0 Mar16 2-0	Sep18 2-0	Aug25 4-0 Apr23 3-0	Mar12 0-0	Oct20 1-5
AYR U	Dec15 2-2 Apr13 0-1		Jan19 4-0	Oct20 4-1	Oct27 1-1 Apr06 0-1	Oct06 2-4	Nov24 1-1	Aug25 1-1	Nov20 2-2 Mar26 1-2	Jan02 1-2 May11 1-0	Sep08 1-1 Apr27 2-0	Dec29 1-0 Apr10 1-1	Sep18 0-1	Sep29 2-0 Mar02 5-3
BRECHIN C	Feb05 1-2 Feb16 1-1	Sep15 1-2 Mar23 2-2		Feb02 0-2 Mar30 2-0	Jan29 3-2	Oct27 1-3	Sep22 0-2	Oct13 2-1	Dec11 0-1 Mar02 2-2	Oct06 0-2	Jan05 1-3	Nov24 0-1 Apr20 1-3	Nov10 2-2 Apr27 1-2	Aug25 0-4
CLYDE	Sep29 1-4	Mar09 1-0 Apr02 2-2	Nov13 1-1		Aug25 0-1 Mar12 3-1	Mar23 4-2 Apr30 0-1	Oct06 1-3	Sep08 1-1 Apr06 0-1	Nov24 0-2	Feb26 1-1 Apr27 2-1	Dec15 1-0	Oct27 1-3 May11 0-1	Oct13 2-4 Apr13 2-1	Nov10 1-2
CLYDEBANK	Dec01 5-2 Mar09 1-3	Dec22 0-2	Nov03 3-4 Mar16 1-0	Nov17 2-1		Sep08 1-3 Mar30 1-1	Sep01 3-1 Feb27 2-2	Oct10 2-2	Oct20 3-1 Apr27 1-3	Sep18 1-3 Apr20 0-0	Sep29 2-2	Jan02 2-4	Jan19 2-3 May11 7-1	Dec15 1-1
DUNDEE	Oct09 0-1	Dec01 1-0 Mar05 4-0	Dec22 1-2 Mar09 0-1	Sep15 3-1	Feb05 1-0		Oct20 2-2	Dec18 4-1 Mar16 1-0	Feb02 3-2	Sep29 1-1	Nov03 1-2 Apr20 4-0	Nov20 1-0 Apr06 1-0	Aug25 1-1	Jan01 2-1 Apr27 2-0
FALKIRK	Dec22 1-1	Oct09 1-2 May08 4-1	Dec15 3-0 Apr06 2-1	Dec01 2-0 Mar02 1-0	Nov10 5-1	Jan05 1-0 Apr13 0-0		Sep29 1-0	Aug25 0-1 Mar16 3-0	Jan19 1-1	Oct13 2-2 May11 4-2	Sep18 2-1	Sep08 0-2	Nov03 7-1 Feb16 0-2
FORFAR A	Sep15 1-4	Nov17 3-1 Apr20 1-1	Mar05 0-0 May11 4-1	Feb23 1-3	Nov24 0-3 Mar23 2-2	Sep22 1-1	Dec12 1-2 Apr02 0-0		Dec29 0-0	Oct27 2-2 Mar12 1-1	Sep01 3-2 Mar30 2-0	Oct20 5-1 May04 2-2	Oct06 0-1	Feb02 3-1
HAMILTON A	Oct13 0-1 Mar23 1-1	Sep01 0-0	Sep29 2-1	Oct10 1-0 May04 3-1	Jan05 2-0	Sep18 1-0 May11 1-2	Nov17 0-2	Nov03 2-0 Mar20 0-1		Sep08 3-1	Mar09 1-1 Mar13 2-1	Nov10 1-1	Dec15 2-2 Apr06 0-1	Dec01 2-2 Apr20 1-2
KILMARNOCK	Sep01 3-4	Oct13 3-1	Dec01 2-1 Apr13 2-2	Nov03 2-1	Feb02 3-0	Dec08 2-1 May04 0-0	Sep15 1-1 Mar23 1-1	Dec22 1-0	Jan12 1-0 Mar30 1-0		Nov17 2-3	Sep22 3-1 Mar09 1-1	Jan05 2-3 Feb16 1-0	Oct09 1-1
MEADOWBANK T	Apr06 0-1 Apr03 2-4	Jan12 1-0	Oct20 6-1 May04 1-1	Sep22 0-2 Mar26 1-1	Dec08 0-3 Apr13 2-3	Dec29 0-1	Mar20 0-1	Nov10 2-2	Oct27 1-1	Aug25 1-0 Apr10 1-8		Oct31 1-1	Nov24 1-1	Sep15 1-1 Mar23 4-1
MORTON	Nov17 1-0	Nov03 2-1	Oct09 3-3	Mar05 0-0	Oct13 2-0 Apr02 2-2	Sep01 0-1	Feb02 0-0 Apr27 0-1	Mar26 1-1	Sep15 0-2 Apr13 0-4	Dec15 3-0	Dec01 0-3 Feb16 1-1		Sep29 4-0 Mar23 1-1	Mar30 4-0 Apr16 1-2
PARTICK T	Nov03 1-1 May04 0-2	Mar30 0-0 Apr23 2-0	Sep01 3-3	Apr16 2-0	Sep15 0-1	Nov17 1-3 Mar26 1-0	Mar05 2-0 Apr20 1-1	Dec01 3-2 Mar02 2-0	Sep22 0-1	Oct20 2-0	Nov06 1-1 Mar16 2-4	Dec08 2-2		Feb23 0-3
RAITH R	Jan05 1-1 May11 0-1	Dec08 3-0	Nov17 1-2 Feb19 1-0	Sep01 1-1 Mar16 1-0	Sep22 2-0 May04 1-2	Oct13 1-1	Dec29 1-4	Sep18 2-1 Apr13 1-2	Oct06 1-0	Nov24 1-1 Apr06 1-2	Mar06 1-3	Sep08 1-0	Oct27 0-0 Mar09 1-5	

DIVISION 2

	ALBION R	ALLOA	ARBROATH	BERWICK R	COWDENBEATH	DUMBARTON	EAST FIFE	E.STIRLING	MONTROSE	QUEEN OF SOUTH	QUEEN'S PARK	STENHOUSEMUIR	STIRLING A	STRANRAER
ALBION R		Nov17 3-1	Oct09 1-1 Mar09 1-3	Jan19 1-1 Apr27 4-2	Sep01 3-1	Sep15 3-2	Nov24 0-2 Feb23 3-1	Jan05 4-0	Oct27 0-3	Dec22 1-0 Apr06 2-2	Oct13 1-0	Sep18 1-4 Mar16 0-0	Mar23 2-2	Sep29 0-1 Apr13 1-4
ALLOA	Aug25 1-0 May04 1-2		Sep18 2-1 Apr06 2-2	Nov10 5-0 Apr20 1-1	Oct30 1-2	Oct20 0-1 Mar16 2-1	Mar12 3-6	Feb26 0-1	Dec01 1-0 Mar02 1-0	Sep08 4-1	Oct27 1-1	Jan22 1-0 Feb19 1-1	Sep29 0-1	Feb02 0-1
ARBROATH	Jan12 0-0	Jan29 1-1		Aug25 4-2 Feb23 0-1	Sep22 1-2	Nov10 2-1 Apr20 0-1	Feb09 1-1 May04 0-1	Oct06 3-0 Mar16 0-1	Jan02 0-1	Oct27 1-1	Dec22 3-0	Dec01 0-0 Mar30 0-2	Sep08 2-3 Mar02 0-1	Oct20 3-0 May11 1-5
BERWICK R	Oct06 3-0	Sep01 1-0	Nov17 1-1		Jan12 0-1 Mar09 1-1	Dec15 2-1	Oct20 1-0	Feb02 2-2 Mar30 2-0	Sep08 2-1 Apr13 0-1	Dec01 2-0 Feb26 3-3	Sep18 1-2 Mar16 2-1	Sep29 0-1	Dec08 1-1 May04 0-0	Nov03 3-2
COWDENBEATH	Nov10 2-0 Mar02 2-2	Mar06 1-1 May11 1-0	Feb02 0-1 Apr13 4-2	Oct10 0-1		Nov24 4-2 Feb27 1-3	Mar26 2-0	Sep18 2-1	Oct20 0-1	Sep29 2-1	Dec01 0-1 Apr06 2-1	Nov03 3-3 May04 1-1	Aug25 0-2	Dec15 2-3 Mar16 2-0
DUMBARTON	Dec01 2-2 Feb16 0-2	Jan26 0-0	Sep01 1-1	Oct27 1-1 Mar23 2-0	Sep08 1-3		Nov17 3-2 Mar02 2-1	Oct13 2-1	Dec22 1-1 Mar30 2-2	Jan12 0-2 May04 2-0	Sep29 1-0 May11 1-0	Feb02 0-0 Apr13 2-1	Oct06 0-0	Sep18 0-1
EAST FIFE	Sep08 2-2	Nov03 2-2 Apr27 1-3	Sep29 2-0	Feb19 4-1 May11 0-1	Oct13 1-1 Apr20 0-5	Aug25 2-1		Dec11 1-1	Jan12 1-3 Mar16 2-2	Sep18 2-0	Feb02 2-1	Oct06 2-1 Mar09 1-0	Dec01 1-1 Feb16 2-2	Nov10 1-2 Mar30 1-2
E.STIRLING	Oct20 0-3 May11 1-1	Oct09 0-0 Feb23 1-6	Jan19 1-1	Sep22 0-4	Jan29 1-3 Mar23 0-0	Jan22 2-1 Apr27 2-0	Oct27 3-1 Apr06 5-1		Sep29 0-1	Nov17 1-0 Apr20 1-1	Nov24 1-3 Mar09 1-1	Sep01 2-2	Mar05 0-1	Sep15 0-2
MONTROSE	Dec15 5-0 Apr20 3-0	Sep15 2-4	Oct13 3-0 Mar23 1-0	Nov24 1-2	Feb05 2-0 Feb16 1-0	Nov03 1-2	Oct09 0-2	Feb09 2-2 May04 2-0		Feb02 0-0	Sep01 1-0	Nov17 2-3	Oct23 0-1 Apr06 0-1	Jan19 1-0 Mar12 2-1
QUEEN OF SOUTH	Nov03 1-1	Nov24 1-3 Mar09 0-0	Dec15 1-0 Apr27 6-1	Sep15 2-0	Feb09 2-4 Mar30 2-2	Oct10 1-2	Mar06 3-0 Apr13 1-3	Aug25 1-2	Sep22 2-1 May11 0-3		Jan26 3-2	Oct20 3-2	Nov10 0-0 Mar16 0-0	Jan02 1-1 Feb23 1-2
QUEEN'S PARK	Jan02 1-1 Mar30 0-0	Dec18 1-0 Apr13 3-1	Nov03 2-1 Feb16 0-0	Feb05 2-1	Sep15 1-0	Feb09 1-1	Sep22 0-2 Mar23 2-0	Sep08 4-0	Nov10 0-0 Apr27 0-3	Oct06 3-1 Mar02 3-0		Jan12 1-0	Oct20 0-0	Aug25 3-1
STENHOUSEMUIR	Jan26 2-0	Oct13 1-0	Sep15 2-0	Mar05 2-1 Apr06 1-1	Dec22 1-4	Sep22 1-1	Feb27 2-0	Nov10 4-1 Mar02 0-0	Aug25 0-1 Feb23 0-1	Feb05 2-1 Mar23 0-1	Oct09 1-2 Apr20 4-1		Oct27 2-2 May11 2-1	Nov24 3-2 Apr27 2-0
STIRLING A	Sep22 2-0 Feb13 3-0	Feb09 2-0 Mar30 1-2	Nov24 3-1	Oct13 4-1	Nov17 5-1 Apr27 0-0	Jan19 2-0 Mar09 0-1	Sep15 1-2	Nov03 3-0 Aug13 4-0	Jan29 3-0	Sep01 0-0	Jan05 0-1 Feb23 2-0	Dec15 1-1		Oct09 3-1
STRANRAER	Feb09 2-1	Sep22 2-0 Mar23 0-0	Jan16 2-3	Dec22 1-2 Mar02 4-1	Oct27 1-3	Jan30 2-1 Apr10 1-4	Sep01 2-2	Dec01 1-2 Feb16 2-0	Oct06 1-0	Oct13 4-1	Nov17 2-1 May04 1-3	Sep08 1-2	Jan12 1-4 Apr20 0-0	

Scottish Football League Records Season 1991-92

PREMIER

	ABERDEEN	AIRDRIE	CELTIC	DUNDEE U	DUNFERMLII	FALKIRK	HEARTS	HIBERNIAN	MOTHERWEI	RANGERS	STJOHNSTOI	ST MIRREN
ABERDEEN		Oct12 3-1 Mar28 1-0	Aug24 1-0 Dec28 2-2	Nov02 0-1 Mar21 0-2	Aug17 3-0 Feb01 1-1	Nov30 1-1 Apr25 1-1	Nov20 0-2 Mar18 2-0	Sep21 1-1 Feb08 0-1	Oct30 3-1 Apr11 2-0	Dec04 2-3 May02 0-2	Sep07 1-2 Dec14 4-1	Oct05 4-1 Jan04 0-0
AIRDRIE	Aug10 1-2 Dec07 2-0		Nov23 0-3 Apr18 0-0	Oct26 1-3 Mar17 1-0	Nov12 3-1 Apr11 3-2	Nov02 0-0 Mar21 2-2	Aug13 2-3 Jan18 2-1	Sep07 0-1 Dec14 0-3	Aug24 0-1 Dec28 2-0	Oct05 0-4 Jan04 0-0	Sep28 1-2 Feb22 0-3	Oct19 4-1 Apr21 1-1
CELTIC	Nov09 2-1 Mar14 1-0	Sep21 3-1 Feb08 2-0		Oct12 4-1 Mar28 3-1	Nov30 1-0 Apr25 2-0	Aug17 4-1 Feb01 2-0	Oct05 3-1 Jan04 1-2	Dec04 0-0 May02 1-2	Nov20 2-2 Mar17 4-1	Aug31 0-2 Jan01 1-3	Oct30 4-0 Apr11 3-2	Sep07 0-0 Dec14 4-0
DUNDEE U	Aug31 0-0 Jan01 4-0	Oct08 0-0 Jan11 2-1	Aug10 3-4 Dec07 1-1		Sep07 3-0 Dec14 0-0	Nov16 2-1 Feb29 2-1	Nov23 0-1 Apr18 2-0	Nov09 1-1 Mar14 1-0	Sep28 2-2 Feb22 2-2	Oct29 3-2 Apr11 1-2	Oct19 1-2 Apr04 2-1	Aug13 4-1 Jan18 1-3
DUNFERMLINE A	Oct19 0-0 Apr04 0-0	Sep14 1-2 Jan15 0-0	Aug13 1-3 Jan18 0-1	Nov06 1-2 Mar07 0-1		Oct08 0-4 Jan11 1-0	Aug10 1-2 Dec07 0-2	Nov16 1-2 Feb29 0-0	Nov23 0-0 Apr18 3-1	Nov09 0-5 Mar14 1-3	Aug31 0-0 Jan01 0-3	Sep28 1-4 Feb22 0-0
FALKIRK	Aug14 0-1 Jan18 2-2	Aug31 3-2 Jan01 0-3	Oct19 4-3 Apr04 0-3	Oct05 0-4 Jan04 1-3	Nov20 0-1 Mar11 2-0		Sep28 1-2 Mar04 1-2	Nov12 3-2 Apr11 2-3	Aug10 1-1 Dec07 0-1	Sep07 0-2 Dec14 1-3	Nov23 2-3 Apr18 2-0	Nov09 3-0 Mar14 1-0
HEARTS	Oct09 1-0 Jan11 0-4	Nov30 1-0 Apr25 2-2	Nov16 3-1 Feb29 1-2	Sep21 1-1 Feb08 1-0	Oct12 1-0 Mar28 1-0	Dec04 1-1 May02 2-0		Aug31 0-0 Jan01 1-1	Sep07 2-0 Dec14 3-1	Aug17 1-0 Feb01 0-1	Nov09 2-1 Mar14 2-0	Oct30 0-0 Apr11 0-0
HIBERNIAN	Nov23 1-0 Apr18 1-1	Nov05 2-2 Apr07 0-2	Sep28 1-1 Feb22 0-2	Aug24 1-0 Dec28 3-2	Oct05 3-0 Jan04 5-0	Sep14 2-2 Dec21 0-1	Nov02 1-1 Mar21 1-2		Oct19 0-0 Apr04 0-0	Nov19 0-3 Mar10 1-3	Aug13 2-1 Jan18 0-1	Aug10 4-1 Dec07 0-0
MOTHERWELL	Sep14 0-1 Jan14 3-3	Nov09 1-2 Mar14 0-3	Oct08 0-2 Jan11 0-0	Dec03 1-1 May02 1-2	Sep21 3-0 Feb08 1-2	Oct12 4-2 Mar28 0-1	Oct26 0-1 Apr07 0-1	Aug17 1-1 Feb01 1-1		Nov30 0-2 Apr23 1-2	Nov16 1-1 Feb29 3-1	Aug31 1-0 Jan01 3-0
RANGERS	Sep28 0-2 Feb25 0-0	Nov16 4-0 Feb29 5-0	Nov02 1-1 Mar21 0-2	Sep14 1-1 Dec21 2-0	Aug24 4-0 Dec28 2-1	Oct26 1-1 Apr07 4-1	Oct19 2-0 Apr28 1-1	Oct08 4-2 Jan11 2-0	Aug13 2-0 Jan18 2-0		Aug10 6-0 Dec07 3-1	Nov23 0-1 Apr18 4-0
STJOHNSTONE	Oct26 1-3 Apr08 0-0	Dec04 1-0 May02 1-1	Sep14 1-0 Jan08 2-4	Aug17 1-1 Feb01 1-1	Nov02 3-2 Mar21 1-0	Sep21 2-3 Feb08 1-1	Aug24 0-1 Dec28 0-5	Nov30 0-1 Apr25 1-1	Oct05 0-1 Jan04 0-0	Oct12 2-3 Mar28 1-2		Nov20 1-0 Mar07 1-2
ST MIRREN	Nov16 0-1 Feb29 0-2	Aug17 1-2 Feb01 4-1	Oct26 0-5 Apr08 1-1	Nov30 1-1 Apr25 0-1	Dec04 0-0 May02 3-1	Aug24 0-0 Dec28 0-1	Sep14 2-3 Dec21 0-1	Oct12 0-1 Mar28 0-1	Nov02 1-2 Mar21 1-2	Sep21 1-2 Feb08 1-2	Oct09 1-1 Jan11 1-5	

DIVISION 1

	AYR U	CLYDEBANK	DUNDEE	FORFAR A	HAMILTON A	KILMARNOCK	MEADOWBANK	MONTROSE	MORTON	PARTICK T	RAITH R	STIRLING A
AYR U		Aug17 3-0 Feb01 3-1	Oct29 4-1 Apr11 0-0	Oct12 4-0 Mar28 1-0	Nov19 0-2 Mar07 2-0	Nov02 0-3 Mar21 0-2	Sep21 7-0 Feb08 0-0	Nov30 2-0 Apr25 0-0	Dec03 3-2 May02 1-0	Sep07 1-3 Dec14 0-2	Aug24 1-0 Dec28 1-1	Oct05 1-2 Jan04 1-2
CLYDEBANK	Oct19 3-2 Apr04 1-0		Aug10 1-2 Dec07 2-2	Oct29 3-3 Apr11 2-0	Nov23 1-1 Apr18 1-3	Sep07 1-1 Dec14 0-3	Oct05 1-1 Jan04 1-1	Aug24 4-1 Dec28 4-2	Nov02 3-1 Mar21 2-3	Nov19 0-0 Mar10 0-2	Aug13 0-2 Jan18 1-1	Sep28 0-1 Feb26 2-1
DUNDEE	Sep14 3-1 Jan07 1-1	Oct12 4-0 Mar28 3-0		Nov30 4-0 Apr25 3-1	Aug24 4-1 Dec28 1-2	Sep21 2-1 Feb08 1-1	Aug17 3-1 Feb01 2-1	Dec03 1-0 May02 1-2	Oct26 0-1 Apr07 2-2	Oct05 1-2 Jan04 1-0	Nov02 1-1 Mar21 3-2	Nov19 0-0 Mar07 5-0
FORFAR A	Aug10 2-3 Nov26 0-1	Sep14 2-1 Jan07 1-3	Aug13 2-4 Jan18 0-3		Oct26 0-0 Apr07 1-3	Oct05 0-1 Jan04 0-0	Nov19 0-0 Mar07 1-0	Nov02 2-2 Mar21 2-0	Aug24 1-4 Dec28 1-5	Sep28 0-3 Feb22 0-0	Oct19 0-1 Apr04 1-2	Nov23 1-1 Apr18 1-1
HAMILTON A	Oct09 3-1 Jan11 2-1	Sep21 0-0 Feb08 2-3	Nov09 1-3 Mar14 1-1	Sep07 4-0 Dec14 2-1		Nov30 2-2 Apr25 0-1	Dec04 3-1 May02 2-0	Oct12 2-0 Mar28 4-1	Aug17 1-1 Feb01 0-0	Aug31 1-1 Jan01 0-2	Nov16 4-1 Feb29 1-0	Oct30 3-1 Apr11 1-0
KILMARNOCK	Aug31 1-1 Jan01 1-1	Oct26 2-1 Apr07 1-0	Nov23 1-2 Apr18 2-0	Nov16 4-2 Feb29 2-0	Aug13 1-2 Jan18 0-2		Nov09 1-0 Mar14 2-1	Sep14 0-0 Jan07 5-1	Oct08 1-0 Jan11 0-1	Oct19 2-3 Apr04 1-3	Sep28 1-0 Feb26 1-0	Aug10 0-0 Dec07 2-0
MEADOWBANK T	Nov23 1-1 Apr18 0-1	Nov16 1-1 Feb29 2-0	Oct19 1-2 Apr04 0-0	Oct09 0-0 Jan11 2-0	Sep28 3-3 Feb22 1-2	Aug24 2-3 Dec28 1-0		Oct26 0-0 Apr08 0-1	Sep14 0-1 Feb12 1-2	Aug12 0-1 Jan18 0-0	Aug10 2-0 Dec07 0-1	Nov02 0-1 Mar21 0-0
MONTROSE	Aug13 1-3 Jan18 0-0	Nov09 1-3 Mar14 2-2	Sep28 1-2 Feb22 2-3	Aug31 2-1 Jan01 2-1	Aug10 2-2 Dec17 1-3	Oct29 2-2 Apr11 0-1	Sep07 2-2 Dec14 2-2		Nov16 1-1 Feb29 1-1	Nov23 0-2 Apr18 0-1	Oct08 0-3 Jan11 2-2	Oct19 4-1 Apr04 0-0
MORTON	Sep28 3-4 Mar17 2-0	Aug31 1-7 Jan14 5-0	Sep07 3-0 Dec14 0-0	Nov09 1-3 Mar14 1-1	Oct19 1-0 Apr04 1-1	Nov19 0-1 Mar24 0-0	Oct29 2-1 Apr11 3-1	Oct05 1-1 Jan04 2-2		Aug10 2-1 Dec07 0-1	Nov23 0-2 Apr18 0-1	Aug13 2-1 Jan18 2-0
PARTICK T	Oct26 3-0 Feb15 4-1	Oct08 0-3 Jan11 2-1	Nov16 2-6 Feb29 2-0	Dec03 1-1 May02 0-0	Nov02 1-1 Mar21 0-0	Aug17 1-0 Feb01 2-1	Nov30 0-2 Apr25 1-2	Sep21 1-0 Feb08 3-0	Oct12 3-4 Mar28 1-0		Sep14 5-0 Dec21 0-1	Aug24 1-0 Dec28 0-1
RAITH R	Nov09 0-0 Mar14 2-4	Nov30 4-0 Apr25 0-0	Aug31 0-1 Jan01 1-0	Aug17 2-0 Feb01 2-0	Oct05 1-3 Jan04 2-1	Dec03 1-1 May02 1-1	Oct12 1-1 Mar28 3-0	Nov19 2-1 Mar07 5-0	Sep21 1-1 Feb08 2-0	Oct29 1-0 Apr11 0-0		Sep07 1-0 Dec14 1-2
STIRLING A	Nov16 0-0 Feb29 1-2	Dec03 3-0 May02 2-0	Oct08 1-1 Jan11 1-1	Sep21 1-3 Feb08 4-1	Sep14 0-1 Jan08 3-0	Oct12 0-3 Mar28 1-0	Aug31 2-3 Jan01 0-0	Aug17 2-2 Feb01 4-1	Nov30 2-1 Apr25 4-3	Nov09 1-1 Mar14 1-1	Oct26 1-3 Apr07 1-2	

LEAGUE TABLES

PREMIER DIVISION

	P	W	D	L	F	A	W	D	L	F	A	Pts
Rangers	39	14	5	3	50	14	19	1	2	51	17	72
Hearts	39	12	7	3	26	15	15	2	5	34	22	63
Celtic	39	15	3	4	47	20	11	7	4	41	22	62
Dundee U	39	10	7	5	37	25	9	6	7	29	25	51
Hibernian	39	7	8	7	28	25	9	9	4	25	20	49
Aberdeen	39	9	6	7	32	23	8	8	6	23	19	48
Airdrie	39	7	5	10	25	33	6	5	11	25	37	36
St Johnstone	39	5	7	10	21	32	8	3	11	31	41	36
Falkirk	39	7	2	13	29	41	5	9	8	25	32	35
Motherwell	39	5	6	11	25	29	5	8	9	18	32	34
St Mirren	39	2	5	15	18	36	4	7	11	15	37	24
Dunfermline	39	2	7	13	11	35	2	3	17	11	45	18

DIVISION 1

	P	W	D	L	F	A	W	D	L	F	A	Pts
Dundee	39	13	5	4	46	20	10	7	5	34	28	58
Partick	39	11	4	7	33	24	12	7	3	29	12	57
Hamilton	39	12	6	4	39	21	10	7	5	33	27	57
Kilmarnock	39	12	4	6	31	20	9	8	5	28	17	54
Raith	39	11	7	4	33	16	10	4	8	26	26	53
Ayr	39	11	4	7	35	21	7	7	8	28	34	47
Morton	39	9	6	7	32	28	8	6	8	34	31	46
Stirling A	39	8	7	7	35	29	6	6	10	15	28	41
Clydebank	39	7	8	7	33	33	5	4	13	26	44	36
Meadowbank	39	4	8	10	17	20	3	8	11	20	39	30
Montrose	39	3	10	9	28	38	2	7	13	17	47	27
Forfar	39	3	7	12	18	38	2	5	15	18	47	22

DIVISION 2

	P	W	D	L	F	A	W	D	L	F	A	Pts
Dumbarton	39	9	8	3	29	20	11	4	4	36	17	52
Cowdenbeath	39	14	2	3	40	20	8	5	7	34	32	51
Alloa	39	13	4	3	34	15	7	6	6	24	23	50
East Fife	39	10	7	2	42	26	9	4	7	30	31	49
Clyde	39	11	4	4	38	15	7	3	10	23	28	43
E. Stirling	39	10	4	5	32	33	5	7	8	29	37	41
Arbroath	39	9	7	3	29	23	3	7	10	20	25	38
Brechin	39	7	7	6	27	24	6	5	8	27	31	38
Queen's Park	39	10	3	7	31	26	4	4	11	28	37	35
Stranraer	39	9	4	7	29	29	4	5	10	17	27	35
Queen of South	39	6	2	11	37	44	8	3	9	34	42	33
Berwick	39	4	6	10	20	32	6	5	8	30	33	31
Stenhousemuir	39	7	3	9	27	28	4	5	11	19	29	30
Albion	39	2	6	12	19	39	3	4	12	23	42	20

DIVISION 2

	ALBION R	ALLOA	ARBROATH	BERWICK R	BRECHIN C	CLYDE	COWDENBEATH	DUMBARTON	EAST FIFE	E.STIRLING	QUEEN OF SOUTH	QUEEN'S PARK	STENHOUSEMUIR	STRANRAER
ALBION R		Aug17 2-1 Mar10 1-3	Aug10 0-1	Jan11 1-2	Sep28 0-3 Apr18 1-2	Oct12 2-2 May02 0-2	Nov23 0-4 Apr04 1-2	Dec26 0-3 Feb15 1-1	Feb01 0-1	Sep17 1-1 Feb24 1-3	Aug24 1-1	Jan04 1-1 Mar21 3-4	Oct26 1-1	Sep14 2-1
ALLOA	Nov09 1-0		Jan18 0-0	Dec28 2-1	Nov05 1-0 Feb08 6-1	Nov16 4-2	Feb25 4-2 May02 0-0	Oct05 1-2	Nov30 0-0 Apr25 1-2	Oct19 0-1 Apr11 1-0	Nov23 3-1 Mar28 3-1	Jan25 1-0 Mar14 2-1	Mar03 1-0	Dec14 3-1 Feb29 0-0
ARBROATH	Nov02 2-1 Mar14 1-1	Sep28 2-2 Apr18 1-3		Nov16 1-1	Sep21 3-2	Nov30 0-0 Feb08 3-0	Aug31 2-1 Mar28 1-0	Dec28 1-0	Jan11 0-0	Sep07 3-3	Oct12 2-3 Apr11 0-3	Oct26 2-2 Feb22 2-1	Feb01 2-0	Aug17 1-0
BERWICK R	Oct05 3-1 Feb29 1-1	Sep17 0-1 Feb15 0-1	Aug24 0-0 Apr25 3-2		Sep07 1-1	Jan01 2-1	Jan18 1-3	Nov09 2-2 Mar28 1-5	Oct26 1-2 May02 1-4	Feb18 1-0	Dec21 1-1	Feb25 1-3	Aug10 0-1 Apr04 0-1	Oct19 0-0 Mar14 1-2
BRECHIN C	Jan18 1-2	Aug10 0-2	Jan01 1-1 Apr04 1-0	Nov23 2-2 Mar07 2-2		Sep17 1-0 Feb29 1-2	Oct05 0-1	Sep14 0-4	Aug24 4-4 Mar21 0-1	Jan07 0-0	Oct26 7-1 Feb15 1-1	Oct19 2-0 Apr25 1-0	Nov09 1-0 May02 0-0	Feb04 2-1
CLYDE	Feb04 6-2	Aug24 2-0 Apr04 0-1	Sep14 1-1	Sep10 2-0 Mar03 0-1	Dec28 0-0		Oct19 4-0	Nov23 0-1	Aug10 1-0 Feb15 4-0	Oct26 2-1	Dec07 2-3 Mar17 2-1	Oct05 3-1	Jan21 0-0 Apr18 4-0	Jan18 4-2 Mar21 1-1
COWDENBEATH	Sep07 1-0	Oct12 1-1	Feb18 3-1	Sep28 2-0 Mar21 4-1	Feb12 2-1 Apr11 2-1	Feb01 0-3 Mar14 3-1		Oct26 2-1	Sep21 3-3 Feb29 3-1	Nov09 3-2 Feb15 4-0	Aug10 0-1 Apr25 3-1	Nov30 0-2	Aug24 2-0	Dec28 2-0
DUMBARTON	Aug31 4-3	Jan11 2-2 Mar21 1-1	Sep17 2-1 May02 1-1	Aug17 1-1	Nov30 3-0 Feb25 1-3	Sep07 0-0 Apr11 2-1	Dec14 0-0 Apr18 2-1		Sep28 1-2	Jan14 1-1 Mar17 0-1	Feb01 3-1	Nov02 3-1	Oct12 1-0	Nov16 1-0 Feb08 0-0
EAST FIFE	Oct19 3-2 Mar28 3-1	Sep14 0-0	Oct05 2-2 Mar07 3-1	Dec14 3-1	Nov16 2-1	Nov02 1-2	Jan01 1-0	Jan18 2-2 Apr04 0-2		Feb04 2-2 Apr18 1-1	Sep17 4-1 Feb22 5-1	Aug17 2-0 Feb08 2-2	Nov23 4-4	Aug31 2-1
E.STIRLING	Dec28 2-1	Feb01 2-1	Nov23 1-1 Feb29 0-5	Sep14 4-1 Feb08 0-4	Aug31 3-3 Mar14 0-0	Dec14 2-1 Apr25 2-1	Aug17 2-3	Sep21 1-2	Oct12 4-2		Jan11 2-1	Nov16 2-1	Sep28 2-1 Mar28 0-3	Nov02 2-2 Apr04 1-0
QUEEN OF SOUTH	Nov16 2-4 Feb08 3-0	Sep07 1-3	Jan25 0-2	Aug31 0-3 Apr18 0-3	Dec14 4-2	Aug17 1-2	Nov02 3-3	Oct19 2-4 Mar14 1-2	Dec28 3-1	Oct05 5-1 Mar21 2-3		Jan18 2-2 Apr04 5-3	Sep14 2-1 Feb29 1-3	Sep21 0-2
QUEEN'S PARK	Sep23 1-1	Aug31 2-1	Dec14 1-0	Oct12 3-2 Apr11 4-1	Feb01 0-1	Jan11 0-1 Mar28 1-0	Sep14 2-3 Mar07 1-2	Aug10 0-3 Feb29 0-0	Nov09 1-0	Aug24 4-2 May02 1-1	Sep28 1-4		Dec28 2-1 Feb15 2-0	Nov23 0-1 Apr18 5-2
STENHOUSEMUIR	Dec14 1-1 Apr11 4-0	Sep21 4-0 Jan01 1-1	Oct19 2-1 Mar21 1-0	Nov02 0-2	Aug17 0-2	Aug31 1-2	Nov16 3-3 Feb08 2-4	Feb04 1-0 Apr25 0-1	Sep07 2-1 Mar14 1-2	Jan18 2-1	Nov30 1-3	Sep17 1-3		Oct05 0-1
STRANRAER	Nov30 1-2 Apr25 2-0	Oct26 1-0	Nov09 2-0 Feb15 1-0	Feb01 2-2	Oct12 1-3 Mar28 1-1	Sep28 2-0	Sep17 2-2 Feb22 1-0	Aug24 2-1	Jan08 0-2 Apr11 1-2	Aug10 3-5	Jan01 0-2 May02 1-3	Sep07 2-1	Jan11 3-2 Mar11 1-1	

Scottish Football League Records
Season 1992-93

PREMIER

	ABERDEEN	AIRDRIE	CELTIC	DUNDEE	DUNDEE U	FALKIRK	HEARTS	HIBERNIAN	MOTHERWELL	PARTICK T	RANGERS	ST JOHNSTONE
ABERDEEN		Sep02 0-0 Jan16 7-0	Aug05 1-1 Feb13 1-1	Aug22 2-1 Jan02 0-0	Oct03 0-1 Feb24 0-0	Oct17 3-1 Mar13 2-2	Nov28 6-2 Apr17 3-2	Aug01 3-0 Dec19 2-0	Nov11 2-0 Mar27 1-0	Sep19 2-0 Mar02 1-0	Feb02 0-1 May12 1-0	Dec05 3-0 May08 1-1
AIRDRIE	Oct31 1-2 Apr10 1-1		Aug29 1-1 Jan23 0-1	Aug08 0-0 Jan30 2-2	Sep12 1-2 Mar06 1-3	Aug22 2-0 Jan02 0-1	Sep26 1-0 Feb20 0-0	Nov21 2-0 Apr20 3-1	Dec12 0-2 May15 1-2	Oct10 2-2 Mar09 2-2	Dec01 1-1 May01 0-1	Nov14 0-2 Mar27 1-1
CELTIC	Dec02 2-2 May01 1-0	Oct24 2-0 Apr06 4-0		Dec12 1-0 May15 2-0	Aug15 2-0 Dec26 0-1	Nov21 3-2 Apr20 1-0	Oct07 1-1 Mar10 1-0	Sep12 2-3 Mar16 2-1	Aug08 1-1 Jan30 1-1	Sep26 1-2 Feb20 0-0	Nov07 0-1 Mar20 2-1	Sep02 3-1 Feb03 5-1
DUNDEE	Nov07 1-2 Mar20 1-2	Oct17 2-0 Mar13 1-1	Oct03 0-1 Feb23 0-1		Nov21 1-3 Apr20 0-4	Aug01 1-2 Dec19 2-1	Sep01 1-3 Feb03 1-0	Dec05 1-1 May08 3-1	Sep12 2-1 Mar06 1-1	Oct24 0-2 Apr03 0-1	Aug15 4-3 Dec26 1-3	Aug04 1-1 Feb13 1-0
DUNDEE U	Dec12 2-2 May15 1-4	Nov28 0-0 Apr17 3-0	Nov11 1-1 Mar27 2-3	Sep19 0-1 Feb27 1-0		Aug29 2-0 Jan23 2-1	Aug08 1-1 Jan30 0-1	Oct31 1-0 Apr13 0-3	Oct07 1-1 Mar09 0-0	Dec01 2-1 May01 3-1	Sep26 0-4 Feb20 0-0	Aug22 2-1 Jan02 1-2
FALKIRK	Aug08 0-1 Jan30 1-4	Nov07 5-1 Mar20 0-1	Sep19 4-5 Feb27 0-3	Oct10 2-2 Mar10 1-0	Oct24 1-1 Apr03 1-2		Dec02 2-1 May01 6-0	Aug15 2-1 Dec26 3-3	Sep26 1-0 Feb20 1-3	Sep05 0-1 Feb02 4-2	Dec12 1-2 May15 1-2	Nov28 2-2 Apr17 2-2
HEARTS	Sep12 1-0 May05 1-2	Dec05 1-3 May08 1-1	Aug01 0-1 Dec19 1-0	Oct31 1-0 Apr10 0-0	Oct17 1-0 Mar13 1-0	Aug05 3-0 Feb13 3-1		Nov07 1-0 Mar20 1-0	Aug29 1-0 Jan23 0-0	Aug15 2-1 Dec26 1-1	Nov21 1-1 Apr14 2-3	Oct03 1-1 Jan20 2-0
HIBERNIAN	Oct07 1-3 Mar09 1-2	Sep19 2-2 Feb27 3-1	Nov28 1-2 Apr17 3-1	Sep26 0-0 Feb20 1-3	Sep02 2-1 Jan16 2-1	Nov14 3-1 Mar27 1-1	Aug22 0-0 Jan02 0-0		Dec01 2-2 May01 1-0	Dec12 1-0 May15 0-1	Aug08 0-0 Jan30 3-4	Oct24 3-1 Apr06 2-2
MOTHERWELL	Aug15 2-1 Dec26 0-2	Oct03 2-0 Feb06 0-0	Oct17 1-3 Apr03 2-0	Nov28 1-3 Apr17 1-2	Aug01 0-1 Feb02 2-0	Dec05 3-1 May08 2-1	Oct24 1-3 Apr20 2-1	Aug04 1-2 Feb13 0-0		Nov07 0-2 Mar20 2-3	Sep02 1-4 Feb23 0-4	Sep19 3-3 Feb27 1-1
PARTICK T	Nov24 0-7 Apr20 1-3	Aug01 1-0 Dec19 1-1	Dec05 2-3 May08 0-1	Aug29 6-3 Jan27 2-0	Aug05 0-1 Feb13 0-4	Oct31 1-2 Apr10 0-1	Nov10 1-1 Mar27 1-1	Oct03 2-2 Feb16 0-3	Aug22 2-2 Jan02 0-1		Sep12 1-4 May04 3-0	Oct17 1-0 Mar13 1-1
RANGERS	Aug29 3-1 Mar30 2-0	Aug04 2-0 Feb13 2-2	Aug22 1-1 Jan02 1-0	Nov11 3-1 Mar27 3-0	Jan05 3-2 May08 1-0	Oct03 4-0 Feb09 5-0	Sep19 2-0 Feb27 2-1	Oct17 1-0 Mar13 3-0	Oct31 4-2 Apr10 1-0	Nov28 3-0 Apr17 3-1		Aug01 1-0 Dec19 2-0
STJOHNSTONE	Sep26 0-3 Feb20 0-2	Aug15 3-0 Dec26 1-0	Oct31 0-0 Apr10 1-1	Dec02 4-4 May01 1-1	Nov07 2-0 Mar20 1-4	Sep12 3-2 Mar16 1-0	Dec12 1-1 May15 3-1	Aug29 1-1 Jan23 2-0	Nov24 2-0 Apr24 0-0	Aug08 1-1 Jan30 0-0	Oct07 1-5 Mar10 1-1	

LEAGUE TABLES

PREMIER DIVISION

	P	W	D	L	F	A	W	D	L	F	A	Pts
Rangers	44	20	2	0	52	11	13	5	4	45	24	73
Aberdeen	44	13	7	2	41	13	14	3	5	46	23	64
Celtic	44	13	5	4	37	18	11	7	4	31	23	60
Dundee U	44	8	7	7	25	27	11	2	9	31	22	47
Hearts	44	12	6	4	26	15	3	8	11	20	36	44
St Johnstone	44	8	10	4	29	27	2	10	10	23	39	40
Hibernian	44	8	8	6	32	28	4	5	13	22	36	37
Partick T	44	5	6	11	26	41	7	6	9	24	30	36
Motherwell	44	7	4	11	27	37	4	9	9	19	25	35
Dundee	44	7	4	11	25	34	4	8	10	23	34	34
Falkirk	44	7	5	10	40	39	4	2	16	20	47	29
Airdrie	44	4	9	9	22	27	2	8	12	13	43	29

DIVISION 1

	P	W	D	L	F	A	W	D	L	F	A	Pts
Raith	44	17	5	0	54	14	8	10	4	31	27	65
Kilmarnock	44	13	6	3	43	14	8	6	8	24	26	54
Dunfermline	44	10	5	7	33	27	12	3	7	31	20	52
St Mirren	44	11	5	6	33	20	10	4	8	29	32	51
Hamilton	44	11	7	4	36	23	8	5	9	29	22	50
Morton	44	11	3	8	36	27	8	7	7	29	29	48
Ayr	44	9	9	4	27	19	5	9	8	22	25	46
Clydebank	44	10	8	4	42	22	6	5	11	29	44	45
Dumbarton	44	10	3	9	30	30	5	4	13	26	41	37
Stirling A	44	7	5	10	23	31	4	8	10	21	30	35
Meadowbank	44	6	6	10	23	32	5	4	13	28	48	32
Cowdenbeath	44	0	5	17	18	55	3	2	17	15	54	13

DIVISION 2

	P	W	D	L	F	A	W	D	L	F	A	Pts
Clyde	39	11	5	4	37	18	11	5	3	40	24	54
Brechin	39	13	3	3	37	13	10	4	6	25	19	53
Stranraer	39	8	9	2	33	21	11	6	3	36	23	53
Forfar	39	10	5	4	47	30	8	5	7	27	24	46
Alloa	39	8	4	7	25	28	8	8	4	38	26	44
Arbroath	39	8	6	6	34	26	10	2	7	25	24	44
Stenhousemuir	39	9	3	8	30	25	6	7	6	29	23	40
Berwick	39	8	5	6	30	25	8	2	10	26	39	39
East Fife	39	6	6	8	32	33	8	4	7	38	31	38
Queen of South	39	5	4	11	27	37	7	5	7	30	35	33
Queen's Park	39	6	6	7	29	32	2	6	12	22	41	28
Montrose	39	5	3	12	24	35	5	4	10	22	36	27
E. Stirling	39	4	4	12	24	39	4	5	10	26	46	25
Albion	39	4	5	10	22	36	2	5	13	14	40	22

DIVISION 1

	AYR U	CLYDEBANK	COWDENBEATH	DUMBARTON	DUNFERMLINE A	HAMILTON A	KILMARNOCK	MEADOWBANK T	MORTON	RAITH R	ST MIRREN	STIRLING A
AYR U		Oct17 2-1 Mar13 0-0	Sep12 0-1 Mar06 3-1	Nov21 5-3 Apr24 0-0	Aug01 1-1 Dec12 1-0	Oct31 0-0 Apr10 1-0	Aug22 2-0 Jan02 0-1	Aug04 1-2 Feb13 1-0	Sep05 0-2 Feb09 0-0	Nov07 1-1 Mar27 0-0	Dec05 2-0 May08 3-3	Oct03 2-1 Jan26 2-2
CLYDEBANK	Aug08 1-1 Jan30 1-1		Oct10 4-1 Mar09 5-0	Aug22 0-1 Jan02 3-1	Oct31 1-0 Apr10 1-1	Sep26 3-1 Feb20 0-1	Sep05 1-1 Feb16 2-0	Nov28 0-0 Apr17 3-1	Dec19 2-2 May01 2-2	Dec01 3-0 May15 4-1	Nov07 1-2 Mar27 0-3	Sep19 4-1 Feb27 1-1
COWDENBEATH	Dec08 2-2 Apr17 0-1	Aug01 3-3 Dec12 1-3		Sep05 0-1 Feb23 0-2	Aug05 2-5 Feb13 1-2	Nov07 0-3 Mar27 0-4	Dec05 2-3 May08 0-3	Aug22 1-5 Jan20 2-2	Oct31 1-3 Apr10 0-1	Sep19 0-3 Feb27 0-2	Oct03 1-2 Jan27 0-3	Oct17 1-1 Mar13 1-1
DUMBARTON	Sep19 0-3 Feb27 2-0	Nov14 3-1 Mar20 0-2	Oct24 1-0 Apr03 0-0		Dec05 0-1 May08 0-0	Nov28 2-2 Apr17 2-0	Aug04 1-3 Feb13 1-0	Oct03 3-2 Dec01 0-1	Aug15 0-1 Dec26 3-1	Aug29 1-2 Feb06 1-2	Oct17 4-2 Mar13 2-1	Aug01 4-3 Dec12 0-3
DUNFERMLINE A	Oct10 1-3 Mar10 1-1	Aug29 1-3 Feb02 2-0	Dec19 4-1 May01 0-2	Sep26 3-2 Feb20 2-2		Aug08 2-1 Jan30 2-1	Nov07 2-0 Mar27 2-2	Sep19 3-1 Feb27 3-2	Dec02 0-0 May15 1-2	Aug22 0-1 Jan02 0-0	Nov28 2-0 Apr17 1-2	Oct24 1-0 Apr03 0-1
HAMILTON A	Aug29 1-1 Mar02 1-3	Dec08 2-0 May08 2-1	Aug15 3-0 Dec26 4-0	Sep12 3-2 Mar06 1-1	Oct17 2-1 Mar13 0-2		Oct03 1-1 Jan27 1-2	Aug01 1-3 Jan06 2-0	Nov24 3-1 Apr24 2-1	Oct24 2-2 Apr03 2-2	Aug05 0-0 Feb13 0-0	Nov14 1-0 Mar20 2-0
KILMARNOCK	Nov14 3-0 Mar20 1-1	Oct24 3-3 Apr03 6-0	Sep26 3-0 Feb20 1-1	Dec19 1-0 May01 1-0	Aug15 0-1 Dec26 2-3	Dec01 1-0 May15 0-0		Aug29 1-0 Jan16 5-0	Oct10 3-0 Mar09 2-2	Aug08 1-1 Jan30 3-0	Sep19 1-2 Feb27 1-0	Nov28 1-0 Apr17 3-0
MEADOWBANK T	Dec19 1-0 May01 1-2	Sep12 1-0 Mar31 0-1	Nov14 2-0 Mar20 3-1	Jan27 3-3 May15 2-1	Nov21 3-2 Apr24 0-1	Oct10 0-4 Mar10 1-2	Oct31 1-1 Apr14 1-1		Aug08 0-3 Jan30 1-1	Sep26 0-2 Feb20 1-1	Sep05 0-2 Feb03 1-2	Aug15 0-1 Feb06 1-1
MORTON	Oct24 2-1 Apr03 1-0	Aug04 5-1 Feb13 2-0	Aug29 1-0 Feb02 3-2	Nov07 1-2 Mar27 2-1	Oct03 0-1 Feb06 0-1	Sep19 2-1 Feb27 1-2	Aug01 0-2 Dec29 2-0	Oct17 4-1 Mar13 2-0		Nov28 3-4 Apr17 1-1	Aug22 0-1 Jan02 1-1	Dec05 2-2 May08 1-3
RAITH R	Aug15 1-0 Dec26 1-1	Oct03 2-2 Jan26 4-2	Nov21 3-0 Apr24 4-1	Oct31 4-1 Apr10 2-0	Nov14 1-0 Mar20 2-0	Sep05 2-1 Feb02 1-1	Oct17 1-1 Mar13 2-0	Dec05 5-0 May08 3-2	Sep12 2-1 Mar06 2-0		Aug01 7-0 Dec12 3-1	Aug04 0-0 Feb13 2-0
ST MIRREN	Sep26 2-0 Feb20 1-0	Aug15 0-0 Dec26 3-2	Dec02 5-0 May15 1-2	Aug08 4-0 Jan30 2-1	Sep12 2-1 Mar06 0-1	Dec19 0-2 May01 2-1	Nov21 0-1 Apr24 2-1	Oct24 1-1 Apr03 1-2	Nov14 2-3 Mar20 2-0	Oct10 1-1 Mar10 1-1		Aug29 0-0 Jan16 1-0
STIRLING A	Dec01 0-0 May15 1-1	Nov21 0-1 Apr24 2-3	Aug08 2-1 Feb16 2-1	Oct10 1-2 Mar09 1-0	Sep05 0-5 Feb09 1-2	Aug22 0-2 Jan01 0-0	Sep12 0-1 Mar06 2-0	Nov07 4-1 Mar27 2-2	Sep26 1-1 Feb20 0-2	Dec29 0-3 May01 2-1	Oct31 0-1 Apr10 2-1	

DIVISION 2

	ALBION R	ALLOA	ARBROATH	BERWICK R	BRECHIN C	CLYDE	EAST FIFE	E.STIRLING	FORFAR A	MONTROSE	QUEEN OF SOUTH	QUEEN'S PARK	STENHOUSEMUIR	STRANRAER
ALBION R		Oct03 0-1	Feb13 0-1 May01 1-2	Sep05 1-1 Mar13 0-2	Nov07 1-4	Dec12 1-2	Oct31 0-5 Apr03 4-2	Jan30 2-2	Oct17 2-1	Sep12 2-2	Jan09 2-1 Mar27 1-3	Aug15 3-2	Feb16 0-0 Apr24 0-2	Nov21 1-1 Feb27 1-2
ALLOA	Dec26 4-0 Feb20 1-0		Sep12 0-2 Apr03 0-3	Aug08 2-0 Mar20 0-2	Sep26 3-2	Aug29 1-5 Apr24 1-1	Jan02 0-2	Nov21 1-0	Nov14 1-1	Jan26 3-0 Mar13 3-1	Feb06 2-2	Oct24 0-0	Aug22 2-1 May01 0-2	Oct10 1-4
ARBROATH	Oct10 2-0	Nov28 0-0		Jan05 0-1 Apr10 6-0	Aug08 0-0 Feb20 2-0	Nov14 1-1	Sep19 1-3 May08 3-0	Aug22 4-5 Mar16 0-0	Jan02 2-3 May15 0-0	Sep26 3-4	Oct24 0-0	Aug29 2-1	Feb10 3-2 Mar27 2-1	Jan20 2-1 Apr24 1-4
BERWICK R	Nov14 1-1	Dec12 2-2	Oct03 5-1		Feb06 0-2 Apr03 2-1	Jan16 0-3 Mar06 0-1	Jan30 3-0	Oct17 2-5 May01 0-0	Feb13 2-1	Nov07 3-0 Mar27 2-0	Nov28 1-4 Feb20 3-0	Sep19 1-0 Apr24 1-1	Jan02 1-1	Oct24 1-2
BRECHIN C	Aug29 2-0 May08 2-0	Jan30 4-2 Mar27 1-0	Dec12 2-0	Aug22 5-1		Oct24 2-1	Oct17 1-0	Oct03 2-1 Apr10 5-0	Feb02 1-2 Apr24 0-1	Aug15 3-1 Feb27 0-0	Nov14 3-0	Feb13 1-0	Nov21 2-2	Sep12 1-1 Mar13 0-1
CLYDE	Aug08 2-0 Apr17 4-0	Nov07 1-1	Sep05 2-0 Mar09 2-0	Oct31 2-0	Feb23 0-1 May15 1-2		Aug22 2-2	Jan02 5-1 Mar27 2-1	Sep19 0-0 May01 3-2	Oct10 1-2 Apr10 2-1	Feb16 2-1	Nov28 4-1 Feb20 2-3	Sep26 0-0	Feb06 0-0
EAST FIFE	Jan16 5-0	Aug15 2-0 Mar06 2-2	Nov21 1-3	Sep26 4-2 May15 1-2	Feb09 1-0 May01 1-2	Jan26 1-1 Feb27 2-3		Sep12 2-2	Aug29 0-3	Oct24 2-3 Apr24 0-0	Oct10 2-5	Nov14 2-1	Aug08 1-1 Apr10 2-1	Dec26 0-1 Mar27 1-1
E.STIRLING	Sep26 1-1 May15 0-1	Sep19 4-2 Feb27 0-2	Feb23 1-2	Feb10 2-0	Dec26 0-0	Aug15 1-2	Nov28 1-6 Mar20 1-3		Oct24 1-0 Mar13 0-2	Aug08 0-2 May08 0-0	Aug29 1-2 Apr24 1-2	Feb02 2-2 Apr03 4-1	Oct10 3-7	Nov14 1-2
FORFAR A	Feb06 3-2 Apr10 5-2	Sep05 1-1 May08 1-1	Aug15 1-1	Oct10 5-3 Apr17 0-2	Oct31 0-1	Nov21 2-4	Nov07 2-2 Feb20 1-2	Jan23 5-1		Jan19 4-3	Aug08 5-1	Jan26 2-0 Mar27 2-2	Sep12 3-1 Mar06 1-0	Sep26 4-1
MONTROSE	Nov28 2-1 Mar06 1-1	Oct31 1-4	Jan30 1-1 Apr17 2-0	Aug29 1-3	Jan02 0-2	Feb13 1-2	Jan23 1-3	Dec12 4-1	Oct03 0-0 Mar20 1-3		Sep19 5-1 Apr03 0-1	Oct17 0-2 May15 3-1	Sep05 0-1 Feb20 1-4	Aug22 0-2 May01 0-2
QUEEN OF SOUTH	Aug22 0-3	Oct17 1-2 May15 0-7	Feb02 0-1 Mar20 2-3	Sep12 1-0	Sep05 0-0 Mar06 1-2	Oct03 3-1 May08 2-3	Feb13 1-1 Apr17 2-0	Nov07 1-2	Dec12 1-1 Feb27 2-4	Nov21 0-1		Jan30 5-2	Oct31 0-1	Jan02 2-0 Apr10 3-3
QUEEN'S PARK	Jan02 1-0 Mar20 1-1	Feb09 0-3 Apr10 2-2	Nov07 0-1 Feb27 2-1	Nov21 4-0	Oct10 1-2 Apr17 1-0	Sep12 1-6	Sep05 1-3 Mar13 2-2	Oct31 4-2	Aug22 1-2	Feb06 3-1	Sep26 1-2 May01 1-1		Dec26 2-2	Aug08 1-1
STENHOUSEMUIR	Oct24 2-0	Feb02 0-1	Oct17 1-3	Aug15 1-3 Feb27 0-0	Sep19 2-4 Mar20 3-0	Jan30 0-2 Apr03 3-0	Dec12 3-1	Feb13 1-2 Apr17 2-0	Nov28 2-0	Nov14 2-0	Jan26 1-1 Mar13 2-1	Oct03 2-0 May08 0-0		Aug29 1-2 May15 2-5
STRANRAER	Sep19 1-1	Feb13 1-2 Apr17 3-3	Oct31 1-0	Jan23 1-3 May08 3-1	Nov28 0-0	Oct17 1-1 Mar20 1-1	Oct03 2-1	Sep05 4-1 Feb20 0-0	Jan30 2-0 Apr03 3-1	Jan09 3-1	Aug15 2-2	Dec12 1-1 Mar06 4-2	Nov07 0-0	

Scottish Football League Records
Season 1993-94

PREMIER

	ABERDEEN	CELTIC	DUNDEE	DUNDEE U	HEARTS	HIBERNIAN	KILMARNOCK	MOTHERWELL	PARTICK T	RAITH R	RANGERS	ST JOHNSTONE
ABERDEEN		Nov09 1-1 May14 1-1	Oct30 1-0 Apr30 1-1	Oct23 2-0 Mar26 1-0	Oct05 0-0 Mar05 0-1	Nov27 4-0 Mar29 2-3	Aug14 1-0 Dec18 3-1	Nov13 1-1 Apr16 0-0	Dec14 2-1 Apr23 2-0	Sep25 4-1 Feb12 4-0	Sep18 2-0 Jan22 0-0	Aug28 0-0 Jan08 1-1
CELTIC	Sep04 0-1 Jan19 2-2		Oct09 2-1 Apr06 1-1	Sep18 1-1 Jan22 0-0	Nov20 0-0 Apr09 2-2	Aug14 1-1 Dec18 1-0	Oct02 0-0 Mar01 1-0	Nov24 2-0 Mar26 0-1	Nov06 3-0 May07 1-1	Nov27 2-0 Mar30 2-1	Aug21 0-0 Jan01 2-4	Dec04 1-0 Apr27 1-1
DUNDEE	Aug21 1-1 Jan11 0-1	Dec11 1-1 Apr23 0-2		Dec07 1-2 Mar24 1-1	Oct02 2-0 Mar01 0-2	Nov06 3-2 May07 4-0	Oct23 1-0 Mar26 3-0	Aug14 1-2 Dec18 1-3	Oct05 2-2 Mar05 1-0	Sep18 0-1 Jan22 2-2	Sep04 1-1 Jan15 1-1	Nov20 0-1 Apr09 0-1
DUNDEE U	Aug07 1-1 Dec27 0-1	Nov30 1-0 Apr02 1-3	Sep11 1-0 Feb05 1-1		Aug28 0-0 Jan08 3-0	Nov13 2-2 Apr16 3-0	Dec04 0-0 Apr26 1-3	Sep25 0-0 Feb12 1-2	Oct16 2-2 Mar19 2-2	Nov09 2-2 May14 2-3	Oct09 1-3 Apr05 0-0	Oct30 2-0 Apr30 0-0
HEARTS	Dec04 1-1 Apr27 1-1	Sep25 1-0 Feb12 0-2	Nov13 1-2 Apr16 0-2	Nov06 1-1 Apr07 2-0		Aug21 1-0 Jan12 1-1	Sep18 0-1 Jan22 1-1	Dec15 2-3 Mar30 0-0	Sep04 2-1 Jan15 1-0	Aug14 1-0 Dec18 0-1	Nov03 2-2 Mar26 1-2	Oct09 1-1 Apr06 2-2
HIBERNIAN	Sep11 2-1 Feb05 3-1	Oct16 1-1 Mar19 0-0	Aug28 2-0 Jan08 2-0	Oct02 2-0 Feb26 0-1	Oct30 0-2 Apr30 0-0		Nov09 2-1 May14 0-0	Dec11 3-2 Apr23 0-2	Aug07 0-0 Dec27 5-1	Oct05 3-2 Mar05 3-0	Nov20 0-1 May03 1-0	Nov30 0-0 Apr02 0-0
KILMARNOCK	Oct16 1-1 Mar19 2-3	Nov13 2-2 Apr16 2-0	Aug07 1-0 Jan04 1-0	Oct05 1-1 Mar05 1-1	Nov30 0-0 Apr02 0-1	Sep04 1-1 Jan15 0-3		Aug21 0-1 Jan01 0-0	Sep25 3-1 Feb12 1-2	Dec11 1-0 Apr23 0-0	Nov06 0-2 May07 1-0	Sep11 0-0 Feb05 0-0
MOTHERWELL	Oct02 0-0 Mar08 1-1	Aug07 2-2 Jan11 2-1	Oct16 1-0 Mar19 3-1	Nov20 2-0 May03 1-2	Sep11 2-0 Feb05 1-1	Oct09 0-2 Mar12 0-0	Oct30 2-2 Apr30 1-0		Nov30 1-0 Apr02 2-2	Aug28 4-1 Jan25 3-1	Dec04 0-2 Apr26 2-1	Nov09 1-0 May14 0-1
PARTICK T	Oct09 3-2 Apr05 1-1	Aug28 0-1 Jan08 1-0	Dec04 3-2 Apr26 1-0	Aug14 1-2 Dec18 1-0	Oct23 0-0 May14 0-1	Nov02 0-0 Mar26 1-0	Nov20 0-1 Apr19 1-0	Sep18 1-0 Jan22 0-0		Oct30 1-1 Apr30 2-2	Nov27 1-1 Mar29 1-2	Oct02 4-1 Mar22 0-0
RAITH R	Dec07 1-1 May03 0-2	Sep11 1-4 Feb05 0-0	Nov30 2-1 Apr02 1-1	Sep04 1-1 Jan15 0-2	Oct16 1-0 Mar19 2-2	Dec04 1-2 Apr26 1-1	Oct09 2-2 Mar15 3-2	Nov06 0-3 May07 3-3	Aug21 2-2 Jan12 0-1		Oct02 1-1 Feb26 1-2	Aug07 1-1 Jan19 1-1
RANGERS	Nov30 2-0 Apr02 1-1	Oct30 1-2 Apr30 1-1	Nov10 3-1 May14 0-0	Dec11 0-3 Apr23 2-1	Aug07 2-1 Dec27 2-2	Sep25 2-1 Feb12 2-0	Aug28 1-2 Jan08 3-0	Oct06 1-2 Mar05 2-1	Sep11 1-1 Feb05 5-1	Nov13 2-2 Apr16 4-0		Oct16 2-0 Mar19 4-0
ST JOHNSTONE	Nov06 1-1 May07 0-1	Oct06 2-1 Mar05 0-1	Sep25 2-1 Feb12 1-1	Aug21 1-1 Jan25 1-1	Dec11 2-0 Apr23 0-0	Sep18 1-3 Jan22 2-2	Nov27 0-1 Mar30 0-1	Sep04 3-0 Feb08 2-1	Nov13 1-3 Apr16 1-0	Oct23 1-1 Mar26 2-0	Aug14 1-2 Dec18 0-4	

LEAGUE TABLES

PREMIER DIVISION

	P	W	D	L	F	A	W	D	L	F	A	Pts
Rangers	44	12	6	4	43	22	10	8	4	31	19	58
Aberdeen	44	11	9	2	33	12	6	12	4	25	24	55
Motherwell	44	11	7	4	31	20	9	7	6	27	23	54
Celtic	44	8	11	3	25	17	7	9	6	26	21	50
Hibernian	44	11	7	4	29	15	5	8	9	24	33	47
Dundee U	44	5	11	6	26	25	6	9	7	21	23	42
Hearts	44	6	9	7	22	24	5	11	6	15	19	42
Kilmarnock	44	6	10	6	18	19	6	6	10	18	26	40
Partick T	44	9	8	5	23	17	3	8	11	23	40	40
St Johnstone	44	7	7	8	24	26	3	13	6	11	21	40
Raith	44	3	12	7	25	35	3	7	12	21	45	31
Dundee	44	6	7	9	26	26	2	6	14	16	31	29

DIVISION 1

	P	W	D	L	F	A	W	D	L	F	A	Pts
Falkirk	44	16	4	2	47	16	10	10	2	34	16	66
Dunfermline	44	18	2	2	61	18	11	5	6	32	17	65
Airdrie	44	9	9	4	28	18	11	5	6	30	20	54
Hamilton	44	13	5	4	43	20	6	7	9	23	34	50
Clydebank	44	11	5	6	30	28	7	9	6	26	20	50
St Mirren	44	10	3	9	30	25	11	5	6	31	30	50
Ayr	44	6	8	8	20	28	8	6	8	22	24	42
Dumbarton	44	5	8	9	25	29	6	6	10	23	30	36
Stirling A	44	7	6	9	23	30	6	3	13	18	38	35
Clyde	44	6	7	9	18	20	4	5	13	17	38	32
Morton	44	3	11	8	22	29	3	6	13	22	46	29
Brechin	44	4	3	15	13	34	2	4	16	17	47	19

DIVISION 2

	P	W	D	L	F	A	W	D	L	F	A	Pts
Stranraer	39	15	2	3	38	18	8	8	3	25	17	56
Berwick	39	9	7	4	40	23	9	5	5	35	23	48
Stenhousemuir	39	10	6	3	35	15	9	3	8	27	29	47
Meadowbank	39	9	8	2	36	24	8	5	7	26	24	47
Queen of South	39	9	3	7	36	20	8	6	6	33	28	43
East Fife	39	9	5	5	33	23	6	6	8	25	29	41
Alloa	39	6	8	6	16	17	6	9	4	25	22	41
Forfar	39	6	6	8	27	32	8	5	6	31	26	39
E. Stirling	39	7	3	9	29	31	6	8	6	25	26	37
Montrose	39	6	5	8	24	25	8	3	9	32	36	36
Queen's Park	39	10	4	6	34	32	2	6	11	18	44	34
Arbroath	39	6	8	5	24	28	6	1	13	18	39	33
Albion	39	3	5	12	18	33	4	5	10	19	33	24
Cowdenbeath	39	1	4	15	19	39	5	4	10	21	33	20

Four Divisions created.

Falkirk promoted to Premier Division. The bottom 3 clubs in the Premier Division, 2nd to 7th in Division One and Stranraer promoted form Division Two formed the new Division One. The bottom 5 clubs in Division One and 2nd to 6th in Division Two formed the new Division Two. The bottom 8 clubs in Division Two plus new clubs Caledonian T and Ross Co formed the new Division Three.

DIVISION 1

	AIRDRIE	AYR U	BRECHIN C	CLYDE	CLYDEBANK	DUMBARTON	DUNFERMLINE A	FALKIRK	HAMILTON A	MORTON	ST MIRREN	STIRLING A
AIRDRIE		Oct02 1-1 Feb12 0-0	Aug14 1-0 Jan22 0-1	Sep14 2-1 Dec18 3-2	Nov30 2-1 Apr26 0-0	Nov20 0-1 Apr16 1-1	Nov06 1-1 May07 1-0	Oct23 1-1 Apr02 0-0	Aug21 4-0 Jan18 0-1	Sep04 2-0 Feb01 2-2	Oct09 1-1 Mar26 0-2	Sep18 3-2 Mar05 3-0
AYR U	Nov13 1-2 Apr09 2-3		Oct23 1-0 Apr02 0-0	Oct30 1-0 Apr30 1-1	Oct09 1-1 Mar26 0-0	Aug28 0-1 Jan08 1-1	Sep25 1-1 Mar12 0-4	Sep14 0-3 Dec18 0-3	Dec04 1-1 Apr23 1-0	Sep28 2-2 Mar01 2-1	Nov09 0-1 May14 0-1	Aug14 2-1 Jan22 3-1
BRECHIN C	Dec11 0-2 Mar29 0-2	Sep11 0-2 Feb05 1-4		Nov30 4-2 Apr26 0-1	Sep18 1-0 Mar05 0-1	Oct16 0-3 Mar19 0-0	Aug21 1-0 Jan04 0-1	Oct02 0-0 Feb12 0-2	Aug07 1-2 Jan11 0-0	Nov06 0-3 May07 1-2	Nov20 1-4 Apr16 0-1	Sep04 1-2 Jan15 2-0
CLYDE	Oct16 0-2 Mar19 0-1	Aug21 0-1 Jan11 0-0	Sep25 1-1 Mar12 1-0		Nov06 1-1 May07 1-1	Dec11 2-1 Mar29 1-2	Sep04 0-2 Feb19 0-1	Nov23 0-2 Apr16 1-1	Sep11 2-0 Feb05 0-2	Aug07 2-1 Feb22 0-0	Dec04 0-1 Mar23 3-0	Oct02 3-0 Feb12 0-0
CLYDEBANK	Sep25 1-2 Mar22 2-1	Aug07 1-0 Jan04 0-2	Dec04 3-2 Apr23 2-1	Aug28 2-1 Jan08 0-2		Oct30 2-1 Apr30 2-0	Dec11 0-3 Mar29 0-1	Nov09 1-1 May14 1-1	Oct16 2-2 Mar19 3-2	Sep11 3-0 Feb05 0-0	Oct02 1-1 Feb12 0-3	Nov20 2-1 Apr16 2-1
DUMBARTON	Sep28 0-1 Mar01 0-0	Nov06 1-1 May07 1-1	Sep14 1-0 Dec18 3-1	Aug14 3-0 Jan22 1-1	Aug21 2-4 Jan18 2-2		Nov13 1-5 Apr12 0-2	Sep18 0-1 Mar05 0-1	Sep04 0-0 Jan15 0-1	Nov27 2-0 Apr26 2-0	Oct23 3-3 Apr02 2-3	Oct09 1-2 Mar26 0-0
DUNFERMLINE A	Aug28 3-2 Jan25 0-0	Dec14 6-1 Apr26 1-0	Oct30 4-0 Apr30 2-1	Nov09 4-0 May14 5-0	Aug14 0-2 Jan22 2-0	Oct02 4-1 Feb12 3-2		Oct09 1-0 Mar26 1-1	Dec07 4-0 Apr16 2-1	Sep18 4-0 Mar05 3-0	Sep14 3-4 Dec18 4-2	Oct23 3-0 Apr02 2-1
FALKIRK	Sep11 2-1 Feb05 0-0	Oct16 2-0 Mar19 2-0	Nov13 2-0 Apr09 4-2	Sep29 0-1 Mar01 2-0	Sep04 0-4 Jan15 0-0	Dec04 1-1 Apr23 4-0	Aug07 3-2 Jan18 2-0		Nov06 3-3 May07 3-0	Jan11 5-1 Mar29 1-0	Sep25 2-0 Mar12 4-0	Aug21 2-0 Feb15 3-1
HAMILTON A	Oct30 3-2 Apr30 1-0	Sep18 2-1 Mar05 2-1	Oct09 5-0 Mar26 9-1	Oct23 2-0 Apr02 2-1	Sep15 2-3 Dec18 1-0	Nov10 2-0 May14 2-1	Sep29 0-2 Mar02 1-1	Aug28 1-1 Jan08 1-1		Nov13 4-1 Apr13 3-2	Aug14 0-0 Jan22 0-0	Feb02 0-1 Apr27 0-1
MORTON	Nov09 0-0 May14 1-3	Nov20 0-1 Apr16 0-1	Aug28 2-1 Jan08 1-1	Oct09 1-1 Mar26 2-0	Oct23 0-0 Apr02 1-1	Sep25 3-1 Mar12 0-0	Dec04 0-0 Apr23 2-2	Aug14 1-5 Jan22 1-1	Oct02 1-2 Feb12 2-2		Oct30 1-2 Apr30 1-2	Sep14 2-2 Dec18 0-1
ST MIRREN	Aug07 0-1 Jan11 3-0	Sep04 0-1 Jan25 3-1	Sep28 2-0 Feb26 1-1	Sep18 2-1 Mar05 0-0	Nov13 1-0 Apr09 2-0	Sep11 0-3 Feb05 0-3	Oct16 1-2 Mar19 0-2	Jan03 3-1 Apr26 0-3	Nov30 1-0 Mar29 0-2	Aug21 2-2 Jan18 5-1		Nov06 0-1 May07 4-0
STIRLING A	Dec04 0-4 Apr23 1-1	Dec11 0-0 Mar29 1-3	Nov09 2-1 May14 0-3	Nov13 1-1 Apr09 0-1	Sep28 0-3 Feb26 1-2	Aug07 2-0 Jan11 0-0	Sep11 2-0 Feb05 1-0	Oct30 3-4 Apr30 0-1	Sep25 3-1 Mar12 1-1	Oct16 1-1 Mar19 0-3	Aug28 1-0 Jan08 3-0	

DIVISION 2

	ALBION R	ALLOA	ARBROATH	BERWICK R	COWDENBEATH	EAST FIFE	E. STIRLING	FORFAR A	MEADOWBANK T	MONTROSE	QUEEN OF SOUTH	QUEEN'S PARK	STENHOUSEMUIR	STRANRAER
ALBION R		Aug07 0-2 Apr30 1-1	Oct09 0-1	Feb12 0-2	Nov13 0-1 Apr09 1-0	Jan29 1-1	Dec04 1-5 Feb19 3-1	Nov06 1-3 Apr23 1-3	Oct16 0-0 May14 0-2	Jan25 3-4 Mar05 0-1	Sep25 1-1	Aug21 2-0 Mar19 1-1	Sep11 1-2	Jan08 1-2
ALLOA	Dec18 1-1		Jan22 1-2	Oct23 1-0	Aug14 0-1 Apr16 1-0	Jan18 2-2 May14 1-1	Aug21 0-0 Mar05 0-1	Dec07 1-1 May07 1-3	Oct02 1-0	Sep25 0-1	Nov13 1-0 Mar15 1-0	Oct30 1-1 Apr12 0-0	Feb12 1-2	Sep11 1-0 Mar26 1-1
ARBROATH	Nov27 1-1 May07 1-0	Oct16 2-3 Mar12 0-0		Jan26 0-4	Oct02 2-2	Dec29 3-2	Feb02 1-1	Aug21 1-1	Nov20 3-2 Mar26 1-1	Nov06 2-0 Feb26 0-0	Aug07 2-5 Apr09 0-3	Sep11 2-0 Apr23 2-1	Sep18 1-2	Feb12 0-0
BERWICK R	Sep04 1-1 Apr16 3-0	Feb01 1-1 Mar19 1-1	Aug28 2-0 May14 5-0		Feb05 3-2	Aug07 0-1 Mar05 1-3	Nov06 2-2	Nov30 0-2 Apr09 2-2	Jan11 2-2	Oct16 3-3	Jan18 1-2	Oct09 6-0	Dec04 2-1 Apr30 3-0	Sep18 1-0 Feb23 1-0
COWDENBEATH	Sep18 0-1	Nov06 1-1	Dec04 0-1 Apr02 1-0	Sep11 1-2 Mar26 1-5		Aug21 1-2 Apr23 1-2	Oct09 1-3	Jan18 1-2	Aug07 1-2 Mar05 0-1	Mar22 0-1	Oct16 3-3 May14 0-2	Feb12 3-4 Apr30 1-1	Feb01 1-3 Mar16 1-1	Nov20 1-2
EAST FIFE	Oct23 1-1 Apr02 3-1	Aug28 4-1	Oct30 1-0 Apr30 1-2	Dec18 1-1	Jan11 2-0		Sep25 0-1 Mar26 1-0	Oct02 3-2 Feb26 1-1	Feb05 0-2	Nov27 5-2	Sep04 0-2 Apr16 0-1	Nov13 5-5 Mar12 1-0	Aug14 3-0	Jan25 1-1
E. STIRLING	Oct02 1-4	Jan11 0-1	Oct23 2-4 Mar19 2-0	Aug14 2-1 May07 1-3	Nov27 3-2 Mar12 4-0	Nov20 2-1		Sep18 1-2	Aug28 0-1 Mar15 1-0	Sep04 2-3	Feb05 0-0	Jan22 2-0	Dec18 0-2 Apr09 2-2	Oct30 2-2 Apr23 2-3
FORFAR A	Aug14 3-0	Oct09 0-3	Jan11 1-4 Mar05 3-2	Sep25 1-1	Oct30 3-2 Mar02 2-1	Dec04 1-0	Nov13 1-1 Apr16 0-2		Sep04 0-2 Apr02 0-0	Sep11 1-1 May14 0-2	Aug28 1-2 Mar19 4-4	Dec18 4-0	Jan22 1-1	Oct23 0-1 Apr30 1-3
MEADOWBANK T	Jan22 4-2	Dec04 1-1 Mar02 3-2	Sep25 3-0	Aug21 1-1 Apr23 1-2	Dec18 1-1	Sep11 1-0 Apr09 2-2	Jan15 1-1	Feb12 4-2		Nov13 5-3	Oct09 0-0 May07 2-1	Oct23 1-1	Oct30 3-1 Mar19 1-0	Aug14 1-3 Mar12 1-1
MONTROSE	Oct30 1-0	Nov20 1-2 Apr23 2-2	Aug14 0-0	Jan22 2-3 Mar12 3-1	Oct23 1-2 Mar19 1-1	Oct09 0-1 Feb19 3-0	Feb12 2-2 Apr02 0-2	Feb05 1-1	Sep18 0-3 Apr30 2-0		Dec04 2-1	Jan15 1-2	Aug21 2-0	Jan04 0-2
QUEEN OF SOUTH	Nov20 1-2 Mar12 1-2	Sep18 0-1	Dec18 6-0	Oct30 2-5 Apr02 0-0	Jan22 1-2	Feb12 0-0	Sep11 5-0 Apr30 1-1	Jan15 1-0	Nov30 5-1	Oct02 1-0 Mar26 1-0		Aug14 5-2 Feb19 3-0	Oct23 1-2 Apr23 2-1	Aug21 0-1
QUEEN'S PARK	Jan01 2-0	Dec27 2-1	Feb05 2-1	Nov27 0-0 Mar01 1-3	Sep04 1-3	Sep18 4-2	Oct16 1-1 May14 2-0	Aug07 0-3 Mar26 3-2	Jan29 3-2 Apr16 1-3	Aug28 2-1 May07 3-2	Nov06 3-1		Nov20 1-2 Mar05 2-4	Oct02 0-0 Apr02 1-1
STENHOUSEMUIR	Feb05 5-1 Mar26 0-0	Sep04 1-1 Apr02 1-0	Nov13 4-0 Feb19 2-0	Oct02 2-1	Aug28 1-1	Nov06 0-1 May07 1-1	Aug07 3-1	Oct16 2-0 Mar12 0-1	Jan25 1-1	Jan18 3-4 Apr16 2-0	Feb08 3-0	Sep25 2-0		Nov30 2-2
STRANRAER	Aug28 2-1 Feb26 2-1	Feb05 1-1	Sep04 2-1 Apr16 1-0	Nov13 3-0	Sep25 4-0 May07 2-0	Oct16 3-2 Mar19 2-1	Dec27 1-0	Feb02 2-0	Nov06 3-1	Aug07 2-4 Apr13 1-0	Jan01 1-2 Mar05 3-3	Dec04 2-0	Oct09 1-0 May14 0-1	

Richard Gough made 37 League appearances as Rangers clinched another championship title.

Alex McLeish was one of the major performers in Aberdeen's season in which they finished runners-up.

Mark Hateley (above) and Brian Laudrup (below) were just two of the many foreign imports Rangers acquired in the quest for European glory, culminating in the 1995 close season with the purchase of Paul Gascoigne from Lazio, of Italy.

PREMIER

	ABERDEEN	CELTIC	DUNDEE U	FALKIRK	HEARTS	HIBERNIAN	KILMARNOCK	MOTHERWELL	PARTICK T	RANGERS
ABERDEEN		Dec26 0-0 Apr15 2-0	Oct29 3-0 May06 2-1	Aug20 2-2 Jan07 0-0	Aug13 3-1 Dec31 3-1	Nov09 0-0 Mar18 0-0	Dec03 0-1 Apr01 0-1	Oct15 1-3 Feb25 0-2	Sep17 1-1 Jan14 3-1	Sep24 2-2 Feb12 2-0
CELTIC	Oct08 0-0 Mar05 2-0		Aug20 2-1 Jan07 1-1	Oct22 0-2 Dec31 2-0	Jan11 1-1 Apr19 0-1	Sep24 2-0 Feb11 2-2	Sep17 1-1 Jan14 2-1	Dec03 2-2 Apr01 1-1	Nov09 0-0 May02 1-3	Oct30 1-3 May07 3-0
DUNDEE U	Aug27 2-1 Jan01 0-0	Nov05 2-2 May13 0-1		Sep24 1-0 Feb21 1-0	Nov19 5-2 Mar21 1-1	Oct22 0-0 Apr29 0-1	Dec26 2-2 Apr15 1-2	Sep10 1-1 Jan21 6-1	Oct15 0-1 Feb25 2-0	Dec04 0-3 Apr01 0-2
FALKIRK	Nov05 2-1 May13 0-2	Aug13 1-1 Apr29 1-2	Nov26 1-3 Apr08 3-1		Oct01 2-1 Feb04 2-0	Oct15 0-0 Feb25 1-0	Nov08 3-3 Mar25 2-0	Dec26 0-1 Apr15 3-0	Aug27 2-1 Jan17 1-3	Sep17 0-2 Jan14 2-3
HEARTS	Oct22 2-0 Apr29 1-2	Oct15 1-0 Feb25 1-1	Sep17 2-1 Jan14 2-0	Dec03 1-1 Apr01 0-1		Aug27 0-1 Jan18 2-0	Sep24 3-0 Feb11 2-2	Nov05 1-2 May13 2-0	Dec26 3-0 Apr15 0-1	Nov09 1-1 Mar18 2-1
HIBERNIAN	Sep10 2-2 Jan21 4-2	Nov30 1-1 May10 1-1	Aug13 5-0 Dec31 4-0	Dec10 2-2 Apr19 0-2	Oct29 2-1 May06 3-1		Aug20 0-0 Jan07 2-1	Nov19 2-2 Mar22 2-0	Oct01 3-0 Feb04 1-2	Oct08 2-1 Mar04 1-1
KILMARNOCK	Oct01 2-1 Feb04 3-1	Nov19 0-0 Mar21 0-1	Oct08 0-2 Mar04 2-0	Sep10 1-1 Jan21 2-1	Nov26 3-1 Apr12 3-2	Nov05 0-0 May13 1-2		Aug27 0-1 Jan17 2-0	Oct22 2-0 Apr29 0-0	Dec10 1-2 Apr20 0-1
MOTHERWELL	Dec10 0-1 Apr18 2-1	Oct01 1-1 Feb04 1-0	Nov08 1-1 Mar18 2-1	Oct08 5-3 Mar07 2-2	Aug20 1-1 Jan08 1-2	Sep17 1-1 Jan13 0-0	Oct29 3-2 May06 2-0		Nov26 3-1 Apr08 1-2	Oct22 2-1 Dec31 1-3
PARTICK T	Nov19 2-1 Mar11 2-2	Sep10 1-2 Jan21 0-0	Mar07 2-0 Apr18 1-3	Oct29 1-2 May06 0-0	Oct08 0-1 Apr04 3-1	Dec03 2-2 Apr01 2-2	Aug13 2-0 Dec31 2-2	Sep24 2-2 Mar14 0-0		Aug20 0-2 Jan07 1-1
RANGERS	Nov25 1-0 Apr08 3-2	Aug27 0-2 Jan04 1-1	Oct01 2-0 Feb04 1-1	Nov19 1-1 Mar11 2-2	Sep11 3-0 Jan21 1-0	Dec26 2-0 Apr16 3-1	Oct15 2-0 Feb25 3-0	Aug13 2-1 Apr29 0-2	Nov05 3-0 May13 1-1	

DIVISION 1

	AIRDRIE	AYR U	CLYDEBANK	DUNDEE	DUNFERMLINE A	HAMILTON A	RAITH R	ST JOHNSTONE	ST MIRREN	STRANRAER
AIRDRIE		Sep10 0-0 Jan24 2-2	Sep24 2-0 Feb14 1-2	Nov19 2-1 Mar25 0-3	Aug13 0-0 Dec31 0-0	Oct29 1-0 May06 0-1	Oct08 0-0 Mar06 1-2	Aug20 0-0 Jan07 0-2	Jan10 2-0 Apr22 1-0	Dec03 8-1 Apr01 2-0
AYR U	Nov12 0-3 Mar18 0-2		Dec26 1-1 Apr15 1-0	Sep24 3-2 Feb11 1-0	Oct15 0-0 Feb25 1-2	Aug13 1-1 Dec31 1-2	Dec03 1-1 Apr01 0-1	Sep03 3-4 Jan14 1-3	Aug20 1-1 Jan07 2-0	Oct29 2-1 May06 3-0
CLYDEBANK	Nov26 0-1 Apr11 1-1	Oct08 3-0 Mar11 1-1		Sep10 5-2 Jan21 0-3	Aug20 0-1 Jan07 1-2	Jan10 0-0 Apr22 1-4	Nov19 0-3 Apr04 1-2	Oct01 0-0 Feb04 0-0	Oct29 1-1 May06 2-1	Aug13 2-0 Dec31 2-3
DUNDEE	Sep03 1-1 Jan14 0-1	Nov26 1-1 Apr08 1-1	Nov12 2-0 Mar18 3-2		Oct01 4-4 Feb04 2-3	Oct08 2-0 Mar04 2-0	Dec10 2-1 Apr22 0-2	Oct29 1-0 May06 2-1	Aug13 2-0 Dec31 4-0	Aug20 3-1 Jan07 2-0
DUNFERMLINE A	Oct22 2-2 Apr29 0-0	Dec10 6-0 Apr22 3-0	Nov05 4-1 May13 2-1	Dec03 0-1 Apr01 1-1		Sep10 4-0 Jan21 2-1	Aug27 1-0 Jan11 0-1	Oct08 3-0 Mar11 1-1	Nov19 1-0 Mar25 1-1	Sep24 1-0 Feb14 3-1
HAMILTON A	Aug27 2-6 Jan02 3-0	Oct22 2-0 Apr29 1-0	Oct15 0-0 Feb25 0-1	Dec26 0-1 Apr15 1-4	Nov12 3-1 Mar22 1-3		Nov05 0-3 May13 0-0	Nov26 3-1 Apr08 1-0	Oct01 2-2 Feb04 2-0	Sep03 1-0 Jan14 1-0
RAITH R	Dec26 3-2 Apr15 0-1	Oct01 3-0 Feb04 2-1	Sep03 1-1 Jan14 1-0	Oct15 1-1 Feb25 0-0	Oct29 2-5 May06 0-0	Aug20 1-1 Jan07 2-0		Aug13 1-1 Dec31 2-0	Dec06 1-1 Apr08 2-1	Nov12 4-2 Mar18 1-1
ST JOHNSTONE	Nov22 4-0 May13 2-1	Nov19 1-0 Mar25 1-1	Dec03 1-1 Apr01 1-0	Aug27 0-1 Jan11 2-2	Dec26 3-2 Apr15 1-1	Sep24 1-1 Feb18 3-0	Oct22 3-1 Apr29 1-2		Sep10 1-1 Jan21 5-1	Oct15 3-0 Feb25 3-0
ST MIRREN	Oct15 0-1 Feb25 0-1	Nov05 1-0 May13 2-1	Aug27 2-1 Jan02 0-0	Oct22 1-2 Apr29 1-0	Sep03 1-1 Jan14 2-2	Dec03 0-1 Apr01 3-2	Sep24 1-2 Feb11 1-2	Nov12 2-2 Mar21 0-0		Dec26 1-0 Apr15 2-0
STRANRAER	Oct01 0-1 Feb04 1-4	Aug27 2-1 Jan02 2-0	Oct22 0-1 Apr29 0-1	Nov23 0-2 May13 0-5	Nov26 0-0 Apr08 0-1	Nov19 2-0 Mar25 0-5	Sep10 0-0 Jan24 2-4	Dec10 2-2 Apr22 2-6	Oct08 1-1 Mar11 1-3	

Season 1994-95

DIVISION 2

	BERWICK R	BRECHIN C	CLYDE	DUMBARTON	EAST FIFE	MEADOWBANK T	MORTON	QUEEN OF SOUTH	STENHOUSEMUIR	STIRLING A
BERWICK R		Nov05 2-1 May13 2-0	Nov19 2-1 Mar25 1-1	Sep10 1-0 Feb04 1-2	Oct01 1-1 Feb25 0-0	Oct08 2-1 Mar04 1-0	Oct22 2-1 Apr29 3-4	Aug27 1-0 Jan10 3-1	Nov26 0-0 Apr08 0-0	Dec31 1-0 Apr22 0-0
BRECHIN C	Aug20 1-2 Jan21 1-0		Dec31 0-2 Apr22 0-0	Oct01 1-2 Feb25 0-0	Oct29 2-0 May06 1-1	Aug13 1-5 Jan14 3-1	Nov12 1-3 Mar18 1-1	Nov26 0-1 Apr08 0-2	Sep03 1-1 Feb14 0-2	Oct08 1-2 Mar04 2-1
CLYDE	Sep03 3-4 Feb11 1-3	Oct15 4-0 Mar11 1-0		Nov26 3-1 Apr08 1-0	Nov12 1-1 Mar18 1-1	Oct01 2-1 Feb25 4-1	Dec26 0-0 Apr15 1-3	Nov05 2-2 Jan21 3-4	Oct22 0-0 Apr29 3-2	Aug27 1-2 Jan17 2-0
DUMBARTON	Nov12 3-2 Mar21 1-0	Dec03 6-0 Apr01 4-1	Sep24 2-1 Feb18 2-2		Dec26 4-0 Apr15 2-0	Sep03 0-1 Feb11 4-0	Aug27 2-1 Jan24 2-1	Oct22 0-0 Apr29 2-2	Oct15 1-2 Mar14 5-1	Nov05 1-0 Jan21 2-2
EAST FIFE	Dec03 3-0 Apr01 0-1	Aug27 1-1 Jan02 4-0	Sep10 2-0 Feb04 1-3	Oct08 2-3 Mar04 0-2		Dec31 2-1 Apr22 1-1	Sep24 1-2 Feb28 1-1	Nov19 3-1 Mar25 3-1	Nov05 2-3 Jan21 0-2	Oct22 4-3 Apr29 1-2
MEADOWBANK T	Dec10 2-1 Apr15 0-3	Oct22 1-0 Apr29 2-1	Dec03 2-2 Apr01 0-1	Nov19 0-0 Mar25 1-0	Oct15 0-1 Mar11 1-3		Aug20 0-1 Jan21 1-0	Sep10 0-1 Feb04 1-2	Aug27 3-0 May05 1-0	Sep24 1-2 Mar08 0-3
MORTON	Aug13 1-1 Jan14 2-1	Sep10 2-0 Feb04 1-0	Oct08 0-1 Mar14 4-1	Oct29 1-0 May06 2-0	Nov26 3-0 Apr08 4-1	Nov05 4-0 May13 1-0		Dec31 1-1 Apr22 0-0	Oct01 3-2 Feb25 1-0	Nov22 1-1 Mar25 2-2
QUEEN OF SOUTH	Oct29 5-4 May06 2-0	Sep24 0-2 Feb18 0-1	Aug20 1-2 May13 1-0	Aug13 4-1 Jan14 0-0	Sep03 0-2 Feb14 3-3	Nov12 0-0 Mar18 2-3	Oct15 3-0 Mar11 1-0		Dec26 1-2 Apr15 1-2	Dec03 0-1 Apr01 1-3
STENHOUSEMUIR	Sep24 1-1 Mar07 2-2	Nov19 2-0 Mar25 3-0	Aug13 1-0 Jan14 2-2	Dec31 1-0 Apr22 0-0	Aug20 1-1 May13 2-1	Oct29 1-1 Jan10 2-1	Dec03 0-0 Apr01 1-1	Oct08 0-0 Mar21 2-2		Sep10 3-0 Feb04 0-2
STIRLING A	Oct15 3-2 Mar11 2-2	Dec24 2-0 Apr15 2-0	Oct29 0-1 May06 2-0	Aug20 1-1 May13 0-2	Aug13 0-1 Jan14 3-0	Nov26 2-3 Apr08 2-1	Sep03 2-0 Feb11 0-3	Oct01 3-0 Feb25 1-1	Nov12 0-2 Mar18 3-1	

DIVISION 3

	ALBION R	ALLOA	ARBROATH	CALEDONIAN T	COWDENBEATH	E. STIRLING	FORFAR A	MONTROSE	QUEEN'S PARK	ROSS Co
ALBION R		Aug13 0-4 Jan14 0-1	Oct08 1-2 Apr15 0-3	Sep03 0-1 Feb11 1-2	Sep24 2-4 Feb18 2-0	Nov12 0-2 Apr05 3-1	Dec03 0-1 Apr01 0-3	Aug20 2-4 Mar22 1-4	Oct29 3-2 May06 0-2	Dec31 0-1 Apr22 1-2
ALLOA	Oct22 1-0 Apr29 5-0		Sep10 3-1 Feb04 3-2	Sep24 1-1 Feb18 1-0	Dec03 1-0 Apr01 2-1	Aug27 1-3 Feb07 0-1	Nov05 0-1 Jan24 0-2	Oct08 1-1 Mar28 0-1	Dec31 2-3 Apr22 0-1	Nov19 1-1 Mar25 1-1
ARBROATH	Dec24 0-1 Mar04 2-0	Nov12 0-0 Mar18 2-1		Oct22 1-2 Apr29 2-0	Nov05 0-3 Jan21 0-3	Oct15 0-1 Mar11 5-2	Aug27 0-1 Jan28 1-1	Oct01 0-3 Feb25 4-1	Sep03 1-1 Feb15 3-1	Nov26 0-1 Apr08 0-1
CALEDONIAN T	Nov19 2-1 Apr11 0-2	Nov26 2-2 Apr08 0-1	Aug13 5-2 Jan14 1-1		Oct08 0-3 Mar04 3-1	Oct01 3-3 Feb25 3-3	Sep10 3-1 Feb04 1-1	Feb14 0-4 Apr22 0-3	Aug20 0-4 May13 1-1	Oct29 0-0 May06 3-0
COWDENBEATH	Nov26 2-2 Apr08 2-0	Oct01 1-3 Feb25 1-3	Aug20 6-2 May13 1-1	Dec26 1-1 Apr15 1-3		Sep03 1-1 Mar22 1-4	Oct15 1-0 Mar11 1-3	Oct29 1-1 May06 0-4	Nov12 2-0 Mar18 1-3	Aug13 0-2 Jan14 0-3
E. STIRLING	Sep10 4-0 Mar07 3-0	Oct29 1-2 May06 1-1	Dec31 1-0 Apr22 0-2	Dec03 2-0 Apr01 1-0	Nov19 0-2 Mar25 1-0		Sep24 3-1 Feb18 1-2	Oct22 1-2 Mar15 1-0	Oct08 3-2 Apr18 3-2	Aug20 2-2 Jan21 0-2
FORFAR A	Oct01 1-1 Feb25 4-0	Aug20 3-2 May13 2-0	Oct29 3-0 May06 4-1	Nov12 2-1 Mar18 4-1	Dec31 1-1 Apr22 2-2	Nov26 3-2 Apr08 1-0		Sep03 1-0 Apr04 1-3	Oct22 2-0 Jan14 3-0	Oct08 1-0 Mar04 4-2
MONTROSE	Nov05 4-1 May13 4-1	Dec24 1-2 Apr15 0-0	Dec03 3-1 Apr01 5-0	Oct15 3-1 Mar11 0-1	Aug27 2-0 Jan02 1-2	Aug13 2-0 Apr29 1-0	Nov19 2-0 Mar25 1-2		Sep24 1-1 Feb18 2-2	Sep10 0-2 Feb04 1-1
QUEEN'S PARK	Aug27 2-1 Jan02 0-0	Oct15 0-1 Mar11 2-1	Nov19 0-4 Mar25 2-3	Nov05 0-2 Jan21 4-1	Sep10 0-3 Feb04 1-0	Dec26 2-3 Apr15 1-0	Aug13 1-2 Apr29 0-2	Nov26 1-1 Apr11 1-0		Oct01 3-1 Feb25 1-2
ROSS Co	CO 3-0 Mar29 4-1	Oct15 3-3 Feb11 6-0	Sep03 1-4 Feb18 0-1	Sep24 1-3 Jan02 3-1	Aug27 4-0 Apr29 2-0	Oct22 1-4 May13 2-3	Nov05 2-1 Apr15 0-1	Jan11 0-1 Apr19 0-3	Nov12 2-0 Apr01 1-0	Dec03

LEAGUE TABLES

PREMIER DIVISION

	P	W	D	L	F	A	W	D	L	F	A	Pts
Rangers	36	11	5	2	31	14	9	4	5	29	21	69
Motherwell	36	8	6	4	29	23	6	6	6	21	27	54
Hibernian	36	9	7	2	37	19	3	10	5	12	18	53
Celtic	36	6	8	4	23	19	5	10	3	16	14	51
Falkirk	36	8	3	7	26	24	4	9	5	22	23	48
Hearts	36	9	4	5	26	14	3	3	12	18	37	43
Kilmarnock	36	8	4	6	22	16	3	6	9	18	32	43
Partick T	36	4	9	5	23	23	6	4	8	17	27	43
Aberdeen	36	7	7	4	24	16	3	4	11	19	30	*41
Dundee U	36	6	6	6	24	20	3	3	12	16	36	36

DIVISION 1

	P	W	D	L	F	A	W	D	L	F	A	Pts
Raith	36	8	8	2	27	18	11	4	3	27	14	69
Dunfermline	36	11	5	2	35	11	7	9	2	28	21	*68
Dundee	36	11	4	3	34	18	9	4	5	31	18	68
Airdrie	36	7	6	5	22	14	10	4	4	28	19	61
St Johnstone	36	10	6	2	36	15	4	8	6	23	24	56
Hamilton	36	9	3	6	23	22	5	4	9	19	26	49
St Mirren	36	7	5	6	20	18	1	7	10	14	32	36
Clydebank	36	4	6	8	20	25	4	5	9	13	22	35
Ayr	36	6	5	7	22	24	0	6	12	9	34	29
Stranraer	36	3	4	11	15	37	1	1	16	10	44	17

* Play-off between Aberdeen (Premier Division) and Dunfermline (Division One) 3-1, 3-1.

DIVISION 2

	P	W	D	L	F	A	W	D	L	F	A	Pts
Morton	36	12	5	1	33	11	6	5	7	22	22	64
Dumbarton	36	12	4	2	43	16	5	5	8	14	19	60
Stirling A	36	9	3	6	28	20	8	4	6	26	23	58
Stenhousemuir	36	7	10	1	24	14	7	4	7	22	25	56
Berwick	36	10	6	2	23	13	5	4	9	29	33	55
Clyde	36	8	5	5	33	25	6	5	7	20	23	52
Queen of South	36	6	3	9	25	26	5	8	5	21	25	44
East Fife	36	7	3	8	31	27	4	7	7	17	29	43
Meadowbank	36	7	2	9	16	21	4	3	11	16	33	*35
Brechin	36	4	5	9	15	21	2	1	15	7	39	24

*3 Points deducted

DIVISION 3

	P	W	D	L	F	A	W	D	L	F	A	Pts
Forfar	36	14	3	1	42	16	11	2	5	25	17	80
Montrose	36	9	4	5	33	17	11	3	4	36	15	67
Ross Co	36	9	1	8	35	26	9	5	4	24	18	60
E. Stirling	36	10	2	6	28	20	8	3	7	33	30	59
Alloa	36	7	4	7	23	20	8	5	5	27	25	54
Caledonian	36	5	7	6	27	33	7	2	9	21	28	45
Arbroath	36	6	3	9	21	23	7	2	9	30	39	44
Queen's Park	36	7	2	9	21	27	5	4	9	25	30	42
Cowdenbeath	36	4	5	9	23	36	7	2	9	25	24	40
Albion	36	3	0	15	16	39	2	3	13	11	43	18

Scottish Football League Records

Gordon Durie (above) and Ally McCoist (below) were Rangers top scorers. Durie's 17 goals included two penalties) while McCoist scored three goals from the spot in an overall tally of 16.

DIVISION PREMIER

	ABERDEEN	CELTIC	FALKIRK	HEARTS	HIBERNIAN	KILMARNOCK	MOTHERWELL	PARTICK	RAITH	RANGERS
ABERDEEN		Sep10 2-3 Jan14 1-2	Nov08 3-1 May04 2-1	Dec 16 1-2 Apr20 1-1	Nov04 1-2 Mar23 2-1	Dec 13 4-1 Mar02 3-0	Dec 09 1-0 Apr13 2-1	Oct21 3-0 Jan20 1-0	Sep30 3-0 Feb07 1-0	Oct07 0-1 Feb25 0-1
CELTIC	Oct28 2-0 Apr01 5-0		Dec 16 1-0 Apr20 4-0	Nov25 3-1 Mar02 4-0	Oct14 2-2 Feb03 2-1	Dec 02 4-2 Apr10 1-1	Sep16 1-1 Jan06 1-0	Oct07 2-1 Feb24 4-0	Nov08 0-0 May04 4-1	Sep30 0-2 Jan03 0-0
FALKIRK	Aug26 2-3 Jan16 1-1	Oct04 0-1 Feb10 0-0		Oct28 2-0 Mar30 0-2	Nov11 2-0 Apr27 1-1	Oct14 0-2 Feb03 4-2	Sep23 0-0 Jan23 0-1	Nov18 0-1 Mar16 1-2	Dec 02 2-1 Apr06 2-3	Sep16 0-2 Jan06 0-4
HEARTS	Oct04 1-2 Feb10 1-3	Sep23 0-4 Jan17 1-2	Sep09 4-1 Jan13 2-1		Nov19 2-1 Mar16 1-1	Nov11 2-1 Apr27 1-0	Aug26 1-1 Jan10 4-0	Nov04 3-0 Mar23 2-5	Oct14 4-2 Feb03 2-0	Dec 02 0-2 Apr10 2-0
HIBERNIAN	Sep16 1-1 Jan08 1-2	Dec 09 0-4 Apr14 1-2	Oct07 2-1 Feb24 2-1	Oct01 2-2 Jan01 2-1		Oct28 2-0 Mar30 1-1	Oct21 4-2 Jan20 0-0	Nov22 3-0 May04 1-0	Dec 16 1-2 Apr20 1-1	Nov25 1-4 Mar03 0-2
KILMARNOCK	Sep23 1-2 Jan23 1-1	Oct21 0-0 Jan20 0-0	Dec 09 4-0 Apr13 1-0	Oct07 3-1 Feb24 0-2	Sep09 0-3 Jan13 3-2		Nov18 1-1 Mar16 0-1	Dec 26 2-1 Apr20 2-1	Nov04 5-1 Mar23 2-0	Nov08 0-2 May04 0-3
MOTHERWELL	Oct14 2-1 Feb13 1-0	Nov04 0-2 Mar23 0-0	Nov25 1-1 Mar02 1-0	Nov07 0-0 May04 1-1	Dec 02 0-2 Apr06 3-0	Sep30 3-0 Jan16 0-1		Sep09 1-1 Jan13 0-2	Oct07 0-2 Feb24 1-0	Dec 19 0-0 Apr20 1-3
PARTICK	Dec 02 1-0 Apr16 1-1	Nov11 1-2 Apr27 2-4	Sep30 1-1 Jan09 0-3	Sep16 2-0 Jan06 0-1	Aug26 1-1 Jan16 0-0	Oct04 1-1 Feb10 0-1	Oct28 1-0 Mar30 0-2		Nov25 0-2 Mar02 0-3	Oct14 0-4 Feb03 1-2
RAITH	Nov18 1-0 Mar16 2-2	Aug26 0-1 Jan09 1-3	Oct21 0-1 Jan20 1-0	Dec 09 1-1 Apr13 1-3	Oct04 3-0 Feb10 1-0	Sep16 2-0 Jan06 1-1	Nov11 0-0 Apr27 2-0	Sep23 3-1 Jan23 0-2		Oct28 2-2 Mar30 2-4
RANGERS	Nov11 1-1 Apr28 3-1	Nov19 3-3 Mar17 1-1	Nov04 2-0 Mar23 3-2	Oct21 4-1 Jan20 0-3	Sep23 0-1 Dec 30 7-0	Aug26 1-0 Dec 26 3-0	Oct03 2-1 Feb10 3-2	Dec 09 1-0 Apr13 5-0	Sep09 4-0 Jan13 4-0	

DIVISION 1

	AIRDRIE	CLYDEBANK	DUMBARTON	DUNDEE	DUNDEE U	DUNFERMLINE	HAMILTON	MORTON	ST JOHNSTONE	ST MIRREN
AIRDRIE		Oct14 1-1 Feb13 1-1	Nov11 2-1 Mar30 5-1	Oct28 2-3 a27 0-0	Nov25 1-1 Mar02 1-1	Aug12 0-1 Feb10 1-2	S30 0-0 Mar06 3-0	S16 3-2 Jan23 0-2	Dec02 1-1 a06 1-3	S02 1-2 Jan16 1-3
CLYDEBANK	Jan09 1-1 a13 2-1		Sep30 2-1 Feb17 1-0	Sep02 1-1 Jan16 0-1	Sep16 1-2 Jan06 1-1	Nov11 0-4 Mar30 2-3	Oct28 2-0 a27 1-3	Oct07 1-0 Jan20 0-1	Nov25 2-0 Mar02 1-2	Aug12 1-1 Feb10 1-2
DUMBARTON	Sep09 1-2 Jan13 1-2	Nov18 1-2 Mar16 0-1		Sep23 1-5 Jan23 1-2	Oct07 1-0 Jan20 1-3	Sep02 0-4 Mar09 0-3	Aug12 1-0 Feb13 1-2	Oct28 0-2 a27 0-1	Nov04 1-3 Mar23 0-3	Dec09 0-0 a13 0-1
DUNDEE	Aug26 1-1 Feb24 2-0	Oct21 1-1 a20 3-0	Dec05 1-1 Mar02 3-0		Sep30 2-3 Jan09 0-2	Dec09 2-4 a13 1-1	Sep16 1-1 Jan06 2-1	Nov11 0-0 Mar30 1-1	Dec16 0-1 m04 0-0	Oct07 3-1 Jan20 1-2
DUNDEE U	Sep23 1-2 Dec30 2-2	Oct31 3-0 Mar23 6-0	Dec02 8-0 a06 6-1	Nov18 2-3 Mar16 2-0		Oct28 3-1 a27 0-1	Sep02 2-1 Dec26 1-1	Aug12 1-1 Feb27 4-0	Oct14 2-1 Feb03 1-3	Sep09 1-0 Jan13 2-1
DUNFERMLINE	Dec16 2-0 m04 2-1	Sep09 2-1 Jan13 4-3	Oct21 3-1 a20 4-1	Oct14 0-1 Mar06 1-1	Aug26 3-0 Feb24 2-2		Dec02 4-0 a06 1-3	Nov25 0-2 Mar02 4-1	Sep30 2-1 Feb28 3-2	Nov04 1-1 Mar23 2-2
HAMILTON	Nov18 1-2 Mar16 4-1	Aug27 0-2 Feb24 1-1	Dec16 3-0 m04 2-1	Nov04 1-2 Mar23 0-1	Oct21 0-1 a22 0-2	Oct07 1-3 Jan20 0-0		Dec09 2-3 a13 0-1	Sep09 0-3 Jan13 2-1	Sep23 2-2 Jan24 3-0
MORTON	Nov04 2-1 Mar23 3-0	Dec02 3-0 a06 0-0	Aug26 1-2 Feb24 2-0	Sep09 2-2 Jan13 1-0	Dec16 1-2 m04 2-2	Sep23 2-0 Mar19 1-1	Oct14 2-0 Mar09 4-1		Oct21 4-0 a20 1-0	Nov18 0-3 Mar16 1-2
ST JOHNSTONE	Oct07 1-0 Jan20 0-0	Sep23 2-2 Jan23 3-1	Sep16 4-1 Jan06 3-0	Aug12 0-2 Feb13 3-2	Dec09 0-0 a13 1-0	Nov18 1-0 Mar16 2-2	Nov11 2-0 Mar30 4-1	Sep02 0-2 Jan09 6-1		Oct28 0-0 a27 1-0
ST MIRREN	Oct21 1-2 a20 2-1	Dec16 2-1 m04 1-2	Oct14 3-2 Feb03 5-0	Dec02 1-2 a06 2-1	Nov11 1-1 Marar30 1-3	Sep16 0-2 Jan06 2-1	Nov25 0-3 Marar02 0-1	Sep30 1-4 Jan31 0-1	Aug26 0-0 Feb24 1-3	

SEASON 1995-96

DIVISION 2

	AYR	BERWICK	CLYDE	EAST FIFE	FORFAR	MONTROSE	QUEEN OF SOUTH	STENHOUSEMUIR	STIRLING A	STRANRAER
AYR		Sep02 1-4 Mar02 5-0	Aug12 1-1 Feb27 2-1	Oct28 0-1 Apr27 1-0	Sep09 1-3 Mar05 1-1	Nov25 2-0 Mar09 2-0	Dec02 2-0 Apr06 3-0	Oct14 1-2 Feb03 1-1	Nov04 1-2 Mar23 2-2	Sep30 0-0 Jan27 0-0
BERWICK	Jan16 2-2 m04 2-1		Nov11 0-0 Mar30 2-3	Oct07 0-1 Jan20 1-2	Sep23 1-0 Jan30 1-0	Dec16 2-2 Apr13 4-1	Nov21 0-0 Mar16 4-1	Sep16 3-1 Feb10 2-1	Aug26 3-0 Feb24 0-3	Oct21 4-0 Apr20 1-0
CLYDE	Oct21 1-2 Apr20 2-0	Sep09 3-1 Feb18 2-1		Dec16 0-1 Apr13 2-2	Aug26 1-2 Feb24 3-1	Nov04 3-0 Mar23 1-3	Mar05 2-1 m04 0-0	Sep23 0-1 Jan13 3-0	Nov18 1-2 Mar16 1-3	Oct07 1-1 Jan20 2-2
EAST FIFE	Aug26 1-0 Feb24 1-1	Dec02 1-0 Apr06 0-0	Oct14 0-0 Feb03 1-1		Oct21 1-1 Apr20 1-0	Sep09 3-0 Feb21 7-0	Sep23 2-1 Jan31 1-2	Nov18 0-2 Mar16 3-1	Jan17 0-3 m04 0-1	Nov04 3-3 Mar23 2-1
FORFAR	Nov11 2-1 Mar30 1-0	Nov25 1-4 Mar09 1-3	Oct28 1-0 Apr27 4-2	Aug12 0-2 Jan09 0-2		Sep30 0-0 Jan23 2-1	Sep16 2-1 Feb13 0-3	Sep02 1-0 Mar02 3-1	Oct07 0-6 Jan20 1-4	Dec16 0-0 Apr13 2-2
MONTROSE	Sep23 0-1 Jan13 0-1	Oct14 1-3 Feb03 1-2	Sep16 0-0 Mar12 2-3	Nov11 1-2 Mar30 0-1	Nov18 1-0 Mar16 3-1		Aug26 1-4 Feb24 0-6	Dec02 1-4 Apr06 1-3	Oct21 2-2 Apr20 0-3	Jan16 4-2 m04 0-1
QUEEN OF SOUTH	Oct07 0-0 Jan20 2-2	Sep30 1-4 Jan23 3-0	Sep02 0-3 Mar02 2-1	Nov25 0-2 Mar09 1-0	Nov04 1-1 Mar23 4-1	Oct28 4-2 Apr27 1-1		Aug12 2-2 Jan10 3-3	Dec16 1-5 Apr13 0-7	Sep09 0-3 Feb17 2-1
STENHOUSEMUIR	Dec16 1-1 Apr13 0-1	Oct31 4-1 Mar23 0-3	Nov25 0-1 Mar09 1-0	Sep30 0-1 Jan23 2-2	Jan16 3-1 m04 0-2	Oct07 3-1 Jan20 3-1	Oct21 2-1 Apr20 1-3		Sep09 1-1 Feb27 0-1	Aug26 3-0 Feb24 2-0
STIRLING A	Sep16 2-0 Feb14 2-0	Oct28 1-0 Apr27 4-3	Sep30 1-1 Jan24 3-0	Sep02 0-2 Mar02 2-2	Dec02 4-1 Apr06 1-0	Aug12 3-0 Dec23 2-0	Oct14 2-2 Feb03 4-1	Nov11 2-1 Mar30 0-1		Nov25 1-1 Mar09 2-0
STRANRAER	Nov18 2-0 Mar16 1-1	Aug12 0-0 Jan10 0-3	Dec02 0-0 Apr06 2-2	Sep16 2-0 Feb10 0-0	Oct14 1-1 Feb03 1-0	Sep02 4-1 Mar02 1-2	Nov11 0-0 Mar30 3-1	Oct28 2-1 Apr27 0-0	Sep23 0-0 Jan13 2-2	

DIVISION 3

	ALBION	ALLOA	ARBROATH	BRECHIN	CALEDONIAN	COWDENBEATH	E.STIRLING	LIVINGSTON	QUEEN'S PARK	ROSS
ALBION		Oct28 2-1 Apr27 1-0	Aug12 0-2 Mar02 1-1	Dec02 1-0 Apr06 0-0	Sep02 2-2 Feb28 0-2	Sep09 2-3 Feb17 2-0	Oct14 1-2 Mar20 2-2	Nov25 0-2 Mar09 0-1	Sep30 3-1 Mar16 0-2	Nov04 3-4 Mar23 0-3
ALLOA	Aug26 3-2 Feb24 3-1		Sep09 0-2 Feb17 0-3	Oct21 3-2 Apr20 0-3	Sep23 0-5 Jan13 0-2	Jan16 2-3 Apr30 2-1	Nov18 1-3 Mar16 2-2	Nov04 0-2 Mar23 1-1	Dec02 0-0 Apr06 0-1	Oct14 1-0 Feb03 0-4
ARBROATH	Jan06 2-0 Apr30 2-1	Nov11 1-1 Mar30 1-0		Nov18 1-1 Mar16 0-1	Sep16 2-1 Feb21 1-2	Dec02 2-1 Apr06 0-0	Sep23 2-2 Jan13 2-1	Aug26 1-3 Feb24 1-2	Oct17 1-1 Feb03 1-1	Oct21 1-2 Apr20 1-1
BRECHIN	Oct07 0-1 Jan20 1-0	Sep02 0-1 Jan23 3-0	Sep30 1-1 Jan31 0-1		Oct28 0-0 Apr27 0-1	Nov04 2-0 Mar23 2-0	Aug12 3-1 Dec09 4-1	Dec16 2-0 Apr13 0-1	Nov25 1-0 Mar09 4-0	Sep09 2-1 Feb17 0-0
CALEDONIAN	Oct21 6-1 Apr20 1-1	Nov25 1-1 Mar12 0-0	Nov04 5-1 Mar23 1-1	Aug26 1-2 Feb24 0-1		Oct14 3-2 Apr13 2-0	Dec02 1-1 Apr06 0-3	Aug12 0-3 Apr30 1-2	Sep09 3-1 Mar05 1-1	Sep30 1-1 Jan23 1-1
COWDENBEATH	Nov11 4-1 Mar30 1-1	Aug12 1-0 Mar02 3-0	Oct07 1-1 Jan20 1-2	Sep16 0-1 Feb14 0-0	Dec16 0-0 Feb03 2-1		Sep02 4-2 Jan09 1-4	Sep30 0-1 Feb28 0-3	Oct28 3-2 Apr27 2-3	Nov25 2-0 Mar09 1-1
E.STIRLING	Dec19 5-1 Apr13 1-1	Sep30 2-2 Jan31 1-0	Nov25 0-1 Mar09 1-0	Mar02 2-0 Apr30 3-0	Oct07 0-5 Jan20 1-5	Oct21 3-1 Apr20 1-1		Sep09 1-2 Feb17 0-3	Nov04 1-2 Mar23 1-2	Aug27 1-2 Feb24 2-4
LIVINGSTON	Sep23 2-1 Jan13 0-1	Sep16 2-0 Feb10 1-0	Oct28 0-1 Apr27 3-0	Oct14 0-0 Feb03 0-1	Jan17 0-2 Mar02 2-2	Nov18 0-1 Mar16 2-1	Nov11 1-1 Mar30 1-1		Sep20 2-0 Jan10 3-1	Dec02 0-0 Apr06 2-1
QUEEN'S PARK	Nov18 4-1 Jan01 5-1	Oct07 0-0 Jan20 0-0	Dec16 2-0 Apr13 0-0	Sep23 0-2 Jan13 0-0	Nov11 0-3 Mar30 1-2	Aug26 3-1 Feb24 2-1	Sep16 1-0 Feb10 2-2	Oct21 0-1 Apr20 0-0		Dec30 1-1 Mar02 0-0
ROSS	Sep16 5-1 May06 1-1	Dec16 2-2 Apr13 0-0	Sep02 4-2 Jan10 0-0	Nov11 0-0 Mar30 1-2	Nov18 2-0 Mar16 2-1	Sep23 2-2 Jan13 4-1	Oct28 1-1 Apr27 1-3	Oct07 1-1 Feb13 2-2	Aug12 2-0 Apr30 0-1	

LEAGUE TABLES

PREMIER DIVISION

	P	W	D	L	F	A	W	D	L	F	A	Pts
Rangers	36	13	3	2	47	16	14	3	1	38	9	87
Celtic	36	12	5	1	40	12	12	6	0	34	13	83
Aberdeen	36	11	1	6	31	17	5	6	7	21	28	55
Hearts	36	10	2	6	33	26	6	5	7	22	27	55
Hibernian	36	7	5	6	25	26	4	5	9	18	31	43
Raith	36	7	5	6	23	21	5	2	11	18	36	43
Kilmarnock	36	8	4	6	25	21	3	4	11	14	33	41
Motherwell	36	6	6	6	15	16	3	6	9	13	23	39
Partick T	36	3	5	10	12	28	5	1	12	17	34	*30
Falkirk	36	4	4	10	17	26	2	2	14	14	34	24

DIVISION 1

	P	W	D	L	F	A	W	D	L	F	A	Pts
Dunfermline	36	11	4	3	40	23	10	4	4	33	18	71
Dundee U	36	11	3	4	47	18	8	7	3	26	19	*67
Morton	36	10	4	4	32	16	10	3	5	25	23	67
St Johnstone	36	11	5	2	33	14	8	3	7	27	22	65
Dundee	36	5	8	5	24	20	10	4	4	29	20	57
St Mirren	36	6	2	10	23	30	7	6	5	23	21	47
Clydebank	36	6	4	8	20	24	4	6	8	19	34	40
Airdrie	36	4	7	7	24	25	5	4	9	19	29	38
Hamilton	36	5	3	10	22	26	5	3	10	18	31	36
Dumbarton	36	2	1	15	10	36	1	1	16	13	58	11

* Play-off between Partick T (Premier Division) and Dundee U (Division One) 1-1, 1-2.

DIVISION 2

	P	W	D	L	F	A	W	D	L	F	A	Pts
Stirling A	36	12	4	2	36	15	12	5	1	47	15	81
East Fife	36	8	6	4	27	17	11	4	3	23	12	67
Berwick	36	10	4	4	32	18	8	2	8	32	29	60
Stenhousemuir	36	8	3	7	26	21	6	4	8	25	28	49
Clyde	36	7	4	7	28	23	4	8	6	19	22	45
Ayr	36	7	6	5	26	18	4	6	8	14	22	45
Queen of South	36	6	6	6	27	38	5	4	9	27	29	43
Stranraer	36	6	10	2	21	14	2	8	8	17	29	42
Forfar	36	8	3	7	21	32	3	4	11	16	29	40
Montrose	36	3	2	13	18	39	2	3	13	15	47	20

DIVISION 3

	P	W	D	L	F	A	W	D	L	F	A	Pts
Livingston	36	8	5	5	21	14	13	4	1	30	10	72
Brechin	36	10	3	5	25	9	8	6	4	16	12	63
Caledonian	36	5	8	5	28	23	10	4	4	36	15	57
Ross	36	6	9	3	30	20	6	8	4	26	19	53
Arbroath	36	6	7	5	22	21	7	6	5	19	20	52
Queen's Park	36	6	8	4	21	15	6	4	8	19	28	48
E.stirling	36	6	3	9	26	32	5	8	5	32	30	44
Cowdenbeath	36	7	5	6	26	23	3	3	12	19	36	38
Alloa	36	5	3	10	18	37	1	8	9	8	21	29
Albion	36	5	4	9	20	28	2	4	12	17	46	29

Rangers' controversial England international Paul Gascoigne scored 14 goals in 28 League appearances.

Celtic's Dutch international Pierre Van Hooijdonk was their leading scorer with 26 goals which included four from the spot.

DIVISION PREMIER

	ABERDEEN	CELTIC	DUNDEE U	DUNFERMLINE	HEARTS	HIBERNIAN	KILMARNOCK	MOTHERWELL	RAITH	RANGERS
ABERDEEN		Aug10 2-2 Dec26 1-2	Nov16 3-3 Mar15 1-1	Oct12 3-0 Jan04 0-2	Aug25 4-0 Feb10 0-0	Sep21 0-2 Dec28 1-1	Sep14 3-0 Feb01 2-1	Dec14 0-0 Apr05 0-0	Oct26 1-0 May03 2-0	Dec01 0-3 Mar01 2-2
CELTIC	Nov02 1-0 Apr20 3-0		Dec21 1-0 May10 3-0	Sep21 5-1 Dec28 4-2	Nov30 2-2 Mar01 2-0	Sep07 5-0 Jan18 4-1	Jan08 6-0 May07 0-0	Oct12 1-0 Jan04 5-0	Aug17 4-1 Feb06 2-0	Nov14 0-1 Mar16 0-1
DUNDEE U	Sep28 1-0 Jan01 4-0	Sep14 1-2 Feb01 1-0		Nov30 1-1 Mar01 2-1	Oct26 1-0 May03 1-0	Aug17 0-1 Feb08 0-0	Oct12 0-0 Jan04 2-0	Aug10 1-1 Dec26 2-0	Nov23 1-2 Mar22 2-1	Dec10 1-0 May07 0-1
DUNFERMLINE	Dec07 2-3 Feb22 3-0	Jan29 0-2 Mar22 2-2	Oct19 1-1 Jan11 1-3		Sep10 2-1 Dec26 2-3	Dec11 2-1 Apr12 1-1	Oct26 2-1 May03 3-1	Sep14 1-1 Feb01 3-1	Sep28 3-1 Jan01 2-0	Aug17 2-5 Feb08 0-3
HEARTS	Dec11 1-2 Apr12 0-0	Oct20 2-2 Jan11 1-2	Sep07 1-0 Jan18 1-2	Nov02 2-0 Apr19 1-1		Nov16 0-0 Mar15 1-0	Aug17 3-2 Feb08 2-0	Sep21 1-1 Dec28 4-1	Dec07 0-0 Feb22 3-2	Dec21 1-4 May10 3-1
HIBERNIAN	Nov23 0-1 Mar22 3-1	Oct26 0-4 May04 1-3	Dec14 1-1 Apr05 2-0	Aug24 0-0 Mar08 1-0	Sep28 1-3 Jan01 0-4		Aug10 1-2 Dec26 0-1	Nov30 2-0 Mar01 1-1	Sep14 1-0 Feb01 1-1	Oct12 2-1 Jan04 1-2
KILMARNOCK	Dec21 3-0 May10 1-1	Aug24 1-3 Mar11 2-0	Dec07 0-2 Feb22 2-3	Sep07 2-2 Jan18 2-1	Dec14 2-0 Apr05 1-0	Nov01 4-2 Apr19 1-1		Nov16 2-4 Mar15 1-0	Oct19 2-1 Jan11 0-1	Sep21 1-4 Jan15 1-1
MOTHERWELL	Aug17 2-2 Feb08 2-2	Dec07 2-1 Feb22 0-1	Nov02 1-3 Apr19 1-1	Dec21 2-3 May10 2-2	Nov11 0-2 Mar22 0-1	Oct19 1-1 Jan11 2-1	Sep28 1-0 Jan21 2-0		Dec11 0-1 Apr12 5-0	Sep07 0-1 Jan18 1-3
RAITH	Sep07 1-4 Jan18 2-2	Jan14 1-2 Apr05 1-1	Sep21 3-2 Dec28 0-1	Nov16 1-2 Mar15 0-1	Oct12 1-1 Jan04 1-2	Dec21 0-3 May10 1-1	Nov30 1-0 Mar05 2-1	Aug24 0-3 Feb18 1-5		Nov02 2-2 Apr15 0-6
RANGERS	Oct19 2-2 Jan12 4-0	Sep28 2-0 Jan02 3-1	Aug24 1-0 Mar12 0-2	Dec14 3-1 Apr05 4-0	Sep14 3-0 Feb01 0-0	Dec07 4-3 Feb23 3-1	Dec17 4-2 Mar22 1-2	Oct26 5-0 May05 0-2	Aug10 1-0 Dec26 4-0	

DIVISION 1

	AIRDRIE	CLYDEBANK	DUNDEE	EAST FIFE	FALKIRK	G'NOCK MORTON	PARTICK	ST JOHNSTONE	ST MIRREN	STIRLING A
AIRDRIE		Dec11 3-1 Apr05 4-1	Nov09 0-0 Apr12 2-0	Aug24 0-0 Feb22 1-1	Nov16 0-1 Mar15 2-0	Sep14 1-2 Jan14 1-0	Sep21 4-4 Jan22 1-1	Dec18 0-1 May10 0-1	Oct15 2-2 Jan18 1-1	Oct19 3-1 Apr26 1-2
CLYDEBANK	Oct12 1-4 Feb01 1-1		Nov30 0-0 Mar22 0-0	Dec21 2-0 May10 0-4	Nov02 0-1 Apr19 1-2	Oct19 2-1 Apr26 0-1	Nov16 1-3 Mar15 4-1	Sep21 2-1 Feb04 1-1	Sep07 2-1 Feb15 0-1	Aug24 1-0 Feb22 1-2
DUNDEE	Sep07 0-1 Jan11 2-1	Oct05 2-1 Jan18 1-0		Sep21 2-0 Dec28 6-0	Dec07 2-0 Apr05 0-2	Aug24 2-1 Feb22 1-0	Oct19 0-2 Apr26 1-1	Nov16 0-1 Mar15 0-0	Nov02 0-1 Apr19 2-0	Dec14 1-1 May10 4-2
EAST FIFE	Oct26 0-4 May03 0-0	Sep03 1-1 Feb08 1-2	Dec17 1-7 Mar01 1-1		Oct05 3-1 Jan18 0-2	Dec11 0-3 Apr12 1-4	Jan07 1-3 Apr05 0-2	Sep14 1-4 Jan28 2-2	Aug17 0-4 Dec26 0-3	Sep28 2-2 Jan01 1-3
FALKIRK	Sep28 1-1 Feb25 0-3	Sep14 2-0 Jan04 1-1	Oct12 0-1 Feb01 1-1	Nov30 2-1 Mar22 3-1		Dec14 0-0 May10 3-0	Aug24 1-0 Feb22 2-1	Oct19 2-0 Apr26 1-4	Jan08 1-1 Mar11 1-1	Nov09 5-2 Apr07 2-2
G'NOCK MORTON	Nov02 1-1 Apr19 1-1	Aug17 3-0 Dec26 2-2	Oct26 0-0 May03 1-1	Sep07 0-0 Jan11 2-0	Aug31 1-0 Mar04 0-2		Oct05 1-0 Jan18 1-3	Dec07 0-2 Apr05 0-1	Sep28 1-3 Feb04 2-0	Nov23 3-2 Mar01 1-1
PARTICK	Nov23 0-0 Mar08 1-2	Sep28 1-0 Jan01 3-1	Aug17 0-0 Dec26 2-2	Oct12 6-0 Feb01 3-1	Oct26 3-0 May03 2-1	Nov30 0-0 Mar22 0-3		Nov19 0-4 Apr12 0-4	Aug31 1-1 Feb08 0-0	Sep14 1-1 Jan04 1-1
ST JOHNSTONE	Sep24 1-1 Feb08 2-2	Nov23 2-0 Mar01 1-0	Sep28 0-1 Jan01 7-2	Nov13 3-0 Apr19 3-2	Aug17 0-0 Dec26 3-1	Oct12 1-0 Feb01 1-0	Sep07 2-0 Jan13 0-0		Oct26 4-0 May03 1-0	Nov30 5-0 Mar22 1-1
ST MIRREN	Nov30 2-3 Mar22 1-2	Nov09 1-0 Apr12 1-0	Sep14 0-1 Jan28 3-2	Oct19 4-1 Apr26 1-0	Sep21 0-1 Jan14 1-0	Nov16 1-0 Mar15 3-1	Dec14 3-2 May10 2-0	Aug24 0-3 Feb22 2-1		Oct12 2-1 Feb01 1-3
STIRLING A	Aug17 0-1 Dec21 1-2	Oct26 2-0 May03 4-2	Aug31 1-1 Feb08 0-1	Nov16 2-1 Mar15 4-1	Sep07 1-0 Jan11 0-0	Sep21 1-3 Jan08 4-3	Nov02 1-2 Apr19 2-0	Oct15 1-3 Jan18 1-4	Dec10 1-1 Apr05 1-0	

SEASON 1996-97

DIVISION 2

	AYR	BERWICK	BRECHIN	CLYDE	DUMBARTON	HAMILTON	LIVINGSTON	QUEEN OF SOUTH	STENHOUSEMUIR	STRANRAER
AYR		Aug31 6-0 Mar01 2-0	Oct26 1-0 May03 2-0	Sep14 2-4 Feb08 3-1	Nov30 1-4 Mar22 1-1	Aug17 1-1 Jan28 1-0	Oct12 1-0 Feb01 1-0	Nov23 1-0 Mar08 2-2	Nov09 1-2 Apr12 2-1	Sep28 2-0 Jan21 2-0
BERWICK	Dec28 1-2 May10 0-2		Nov30 0-0 Mar22 1-0	Oct19 1-5 Apr26 0-2	Sep21 3-1 Jan11 0-3	Nov02 0-2 Apr19 0-5	Nov16 1-2 Mar15 1-1	Sep07 2-2 Feb15 1-1	Aug24 0-6 Feb22 1-0	Oct12 1-2 Feb01 2-0
BRECHIN	Aug24 1-1 Feb22 1-1	Oct05 3-2 Jan18 3-1		Nov16 1-2 Mar15 2-1	Dec28 2-1 May10 0-3	Sep21 0-2 Mar04 0-1	Nov09 0-0 Apr12 1-0	Dec14 3-3 Apr05 0-1	Oct19 0-0 Apr26 1-1	Sep14 0-2 Feb08 0-0
CLYDE	Nov02 2-3 Apr19 1-1	Aug17 2-1 Dec21 0-0	Sep28 1-0 Jan21 1-1		Sep07 0-1 Mar04 2-1	Oct26 1-1 May03 0-1	Nov30 2-0 Mar22 0-1	Aug31 0-2 Mar11 2-1	Oct12 0-4 Feb01 3-0	Dec10 1-0 Mar08 3-0
DUMBARTON	Oct05 1-3 Jan18 1-1	Nov23 1-0 Mar08 2-2	Aug31 1-1 Mar01 1-2	Nov09 2-2 Apr12 2-0		Dec14 1-3 Apr05 0-3	Sep14 2-4 Feb08 2-3	Oct26 1-2 May03 0-3	Sep28 1-1 Jan21 0-2	Aug17 1-1 Dec26 2-2
HAMILTON	Oct19 1-2 Apr26 1-1	Sep14 4-2 Feb08 4-1	Dec04 5-1 Mar08 4-0	Aug24 2-0 Feb22 4-0	Oct12 2-0 Feb01 4-0		Feb05 3-3 May10 0-0	Sep28 2-2 Jan22 4-1	Dec10 0-2 Mar22 1-1	Nov09 4-0 Apr12 2-1
LIVINGSTON	Dec14 1-0 Apr05 2-1	Sep28 2-1 Jan01 2-2	Sep07 2-1 Feb26 2-3	Oct05 0-0 Jan18 0-0	Nov02 5-0 Apr19 1-2	Aug31 1-0 Mar30 1-2		Aug17 3-1 Dec21 2-1	Dec07 2-1 Mar08 1-3	Oct26 2-0 May03 3-0
QUEEN OF SOUTH	Sep21 1-2 Feb05 1-3	Nov09 2-1 Apr12 2-0	Oct12 1-5 Feb01 2-1	Jan15 0-2 May10 0-1	Aug24 2-1 Feb22 4-0	Nov16 1-1 Mar15 1-0	Oct19 2-2 Apr26 1-2		Sep14 1-0 Feb08 2-3	Nov30 3-2 Mar22 1-1
STENHOUSEMUIR	Sep07 1-2 Feb15 1-2	Oct26 1-1 May03 1-1	Aug17 0-0 Dec21 3-1	Jan28 0-0 Apr05 1-1	Nov16 0-1 Mar15 1-4	Oct05 0-1 Jan18 3-1	Sep21 0-0 Jan11 1-3	Nov02 2-1 Apr19 0-3		Aug31 0-1 Mar04 4-0
STRANRAER	Nov16 0-1 Mar15 0-1	Dec14 1-1 Apr05 1-1	Dec07 0-1 Apr19 0-1	Sep21 0-0 Feb05 1-0	Oct19 2-0 Apr26 1-0	Sep07 0-3 Mar12 0-1	Aug24 1-2 Feb22 1-1	Oct05 2-1 Jan18 3-1	Jan25 2-2 May10 2-1	

DIVISION 3

	ALBION	ALLOA	ARBROATH	COWDENBEATH	E STIRLING	FORFAR	INVERNESS CAL	MONTROSE	QUEEN'S PARK	ROSS
ALBION		Sep21 1-1 Mar05 3-0	Nov02 1-0 Apr19 1-2	Aug31 2-0 Feb28 4-0	Oct27 4-3 May02 1-1	Aug17 2-0 Jan25 1-3	Sep07 0-0 Feb15 0-3	Oct05 1-2 Jan18 2-1	Nov16 1-1 Mar15 2-1	Dec21 0-2 Apr05 1-2
ALLOA	Dec03 2-0 Mar08 2-0		Aug24 1-1 Feb22 0-2	Sep14 1-1 Feb08 1-0	Sep28 1-0 Jan21 1-1	Oct12 3-4 Feb01 0-3	Mar11 0-2 May10 1-0	Oct19 3-1 Apr26 1-0	Nov30 2-1 Jan18 3-1	Nov09 1-3 Apr12 1-1
ARBROATH	Sep14 1-3 Feb18 1-2	Oct26 0-2 May03 1-2		Sep28 0-1 Jan01 1-0	Aug31 0-0 Mar04 1-2	Nov23 1-1 Mar08 3-3	Nov30 1-4 Mar22 0-0	Nov09 1-2 Apr12 1-1	Oct12 1-0 Feb01 0-0	Aug17 3-1 Dec26 2-1
COWDENBEATH	Feb04 1-1 May10 0-0	Nov02 2-0 Apr19 2-1	Nov16 2-2 Mar15 1-1		Oct12 1-0 Feb01 2-0	Dec10 1-3 Mar22 1-2	Oct19 3-4 Apr26 2-1	Aug24 1-0 Feb22 0-1	Sep07 1-1 Feb15 1-4	Sep21 0-1 Jan28 1-1
E STIRLING	Aug23 0-1 Feb21 1-4	Nov16 2-2 Mar15 0-3	Feb26 0-0 May10 3-0	Dec14 1-0 Apr05 2-2		Sep07 2-1 Feb15 0-3	Nov02 0-0 Apr19 0-3	Sep21 1-3 Feb04 4-2	Oct19 2-1 Apr26 1-0	Oct05 0-1 Jan18 2-3
FORFAR	Oct19 0-0 Apr26 3-1	Feb25 1-1 Apr05 1-0	Sep21 1-1 Feb04 1-1	Oct05 2-5 Jan18 3-0	Nov09 3-0 Apr12 1-0		Aug24 3-1 Oct26 2-0	Nov16 3-1 Mar15 5-3	Jan11 2-2 May10 4-0	Sep14 0-2 Feb08 0-1
INVERNESS CAL	Nov09 1-1 Apr12 4-1	Aug31 1-0 Mar01 3-1	Oct05 2-0 Jan18 4-1	Aug17 1-3 Dec21 2-1	Sep14 2-0 Feb08 3-2	Feb22 1-1 May03 0-4		Dec14 2-0 Apr05 3-2	Sep21 2-2 Jan22 1-0	Nov16 2-0 Mar15 3-0
MONTROSE	Nov30 2-1 Mar22 0-4	Aug17 1-2 Dec21 2-3	Sep07 0-0 Feb15 1-0	Oct26 0-2 May03 0-0	Nov26 1-0 Mar08 0-2	Sep28 4-1 Jan01 0-4	Oct12 2-2 Feb01 0-2		Nov02 3-2 Apr19 1-1	Aug31 2-1 Mar11 0-0
QUEEN'S PARK	Sep28 1-1 Jan28 0-0	Oct05 2-1 Mar22 0-4	Dec14 3-1 Apr05 3-1	Nov09 1-0 Apr12 2-1	Aug17 3-3 Dec21 3-0	Aug31 1-4 Mar01 4-0	Nov23 2-3 Mar08 1-2	Sep14 0-2 Feb08 0-1		Oct26 0-3 May03 1-2
ROSS	Oct12 3-2 Feb01 3-1	Sep07 1-2 Feb15 3-1	Oct19 2-0 Apr26 1-0	Nov23 1-0 Mar08 4-0	Nov30 1-1 Mar22 1-0	Nov02 1-1 Apr19 1-1	Sep28 1-3 Feb12 0-3	Dec07 4-4 May10 3-1	Aug24 1-2 Mar04 2-0	

LEAGUE TABLES

PREMIER DIVISION

	P	W	D	L	F	A	W	D	L	F	A	Pts
Rangers	36	13	2	3	44	16	12	3	3	41	17	80
Celtic	36	14	2	2	48	9	9	4	5	30	23	75
Dundee U	36	10	4	4	21	10	7	5	6	25	23	60
Hearts	36	8	6	4	27	20	6	4	8	19	23	52
Dunfermline	36	8	4	6	32	30	4	5	9	20	35	45
Aberdeen	36	6	8	4	25	19	4	6	8	20	35	44
Kilmarnock	36	8	4	6	28	26	3	2	13	13	35	39
Motherwell	36	5	5	8	24	25	4	6	8	20	30	38
Hibernian	36	6	4	8	18	25	3	7	8	20	30	*38
Raith	36	3	5	10	18	39	3	2	13	11	34	25

DIVISION 1

	P	W	D	L	F	A	W	D	L	F	A	Pts
St Johnstone	36	12	5	1	37	10	12	3	3	37	13	80
Airdrie	36	6	7	5	26	19	9	8	1	30	15	*60
Dundee	36	10	3	5	26	14	5	10	3	21	19	58
St Mirren	36	12	0	6	28	21	5	7	6	20	20	58
Falkirk	36	8	7	3	28	20	7	2	9	14	19	54
Partick T	6	6	8	4	24	21	6	4	8	25	27	48
Stirling A	36	8	3	7	27	25	4	7	7	27	36	46
Greenock M	36	6	7	5	20	19	6	2	10	22	22	45
Clydebank	36	6	4	8	19	24	1	3	14	12	35	28
East Fife	36	1	5	12	15	48	1	3	14	13	44	14

* Play-off between Hibernian (Premier Division) and Airdrie (Division One) 1-0, 4-2.

DIVISION 2

	P	W	D	L	F	A	W	D	L	F	A	Pts
Ayr	36	12	3	3	32	16	11	5	2	29	17	77
Hamilton	36	11	5	2	47	17	11	3	4	28	11	74
Livingston	36	11	3	4	32	18	7	7	4	24	20	64
Clyde	36	8	4	6	21	18	6	6	6	21	21	52
Queen of South	36	8	3	7	27	27	5	5	8	28	30	47
Stenhousemuir	36	4	6	8	19	23	7	5	6	30	20	44
Brechin	36	5	7	6	18	22	5	4	9	18	27	41
Stranraer	36	6	5	7	17	18	3	4	11	12	33	36
Dumbarton	36	2	7	9	21	35	7	1	10	23	31	35
Berwick	36	4	4	10	15	36	0	7	11	17	39	23

DIVISION 3

	P	W	D	L	F	A	W	D	L	F	A	Pts
Inverness Cal	36	13	3	2	37	19	10	4	4	33	18	76
Forfar	36	10	5	3	35	19	9	5	4	39	26	67
Ross	36	10	4	4	33	22	10	3	5	25	19	67
Alloa	36	9	4	5	24	21	7	3	8	26	26	55
Albion	36	8	4	6	27	22	5	6	7	23	25	49
Montrose	36	6	5	7	19	27	6	2	10	27	35	43
Cowdenbeath	36	6	6	6	22	23	4	3	11	16	28	39
Queen's Park	36	7	3	8	27	29	2	6	10	19	30	36
E Stirling	36	6	4	8	21	29	2	5	11	15	29	33
Arbroath	36	4	6	8	18	25	2	7	9	13	27	31

Scottish Football League Records

Henrik Larsson scored 16 goals to help Celtic to the championship in a thrilling climax as they prevented Rangers from recording their tenth successive Scottish League title.

Although Rangers finished in runners-up spot, Italian Marco Negri hit 32 goals for the Ibrox club.

DIVISION PREMIER

	ABERDEEN	CELTIC	DUNDEE U	DUNFERMLINE	HEARTS	HIBERNIAN	KILMARNOCK	MOTHERWELL	RANGERS	ST JOHNSTONE
ABERDEEN		Dec09 0-2 Mar21 0-1	Aug30 1-1 Jan03 1-0	Sep27 1-2 Jan28 2-0	Nov01 1-4 May02 2-2	Oct18 2-0 Feb07 3-0	Aug02 0-0 Feb29 0-0	Aug23 1-3 Dec27 3-0	Nov15 1-1 Apr19 1-0	Dec06 1-1 Apr04 0-1
CELTIC	Sep20 2-0 Feb02 3-1		Dec22 4-0 Mar15 1-1	Aug16 1-2 Feb25 5-1	Jan13 1-0 Mar28 0-0	Jan20 5-0 Apr25 0-0	Oct04 4-0 Feb21 4-0	Nov15 0-2 Apr18 4-1	Nov19 1-1 Jan02 2-0	Oct25 2-0 May09 2-0
DUNDEE U	Nov09 5-0 Apr11 0-0	Sep27 1-2 Jan27 1-2		Dec06 0-0 Apr07 2-2	Dec09 0-0 Mar21 0-1	Aug17 1-1 Feb24 1-1	Sep13 1-2 Jan10 1-1	Oct18 4-0 Feb07 1-0	Oct25 2-1 May09 1-2	Dec20 2-1 Apr25 0-2
DUNFERMLINE	Nov22 1-1 Mar14 3-3	Nov01 0-2 May03 1-1	Oct04 3-3 Feb21 2-2		Aug23 2-1 Dec27 1-3	Nov15 2-1 Apr18 1-1	Sep21 1-1 Jan31 3-2	Aug02 0-2 Mar07 2-1	Dec13 0-0 Mar28 2-3	Aug30 2-2 Jan03 0-1
HEARTS	Aug16 4-1 Feb25 3-1	Oct18 1-2 Feb08 1-1	Sep20 2-1 Jan31 2-0	Oct29 3-1 May09 2-0		Nov08 2-0 Jan01 2-2	Nov23 5-3 Mar14 1-1	Dec06 2-0 Apr08 1-1	Dec20 2-5 Apr25 0-3	Nov15 2-1 Apr18 1-1
HIBERNIAN	Dec13 2-2 Mar28 1-1	Aug03 2-1 Feb28 0-1	Nov01 1-3 May02 1-2	Sep13 5-2 Jan10 1-0	Aug30 0-1 Apr11 2-1		Aug23 4-0 Dec27 0-1	Nov29 1-1 Mar21 1-0	Oct04 3-4 Feb21 1-2	Sep27 1-1 Jan17 0-1
KILMARNOCK	Oct20 1-0 Apr25 2-1	Dec06 0-0 Apr08 1-2	Nov15 1-3 Apr18 1-0	Nov29 2-1 Mar21 3-0	Sep27 0-3 Jan17 2-2	Oct25 2-1 May09 1-1		Oct08 2-1 Jan03 4-1	Sep24 0-3 Feb24 1-1	Oct18 0-1 Feb07 1-0
MOTHERWELL	Oct25 1-2 May09 1-2	Sep13 2-3 Jan10 1-1	Dec13 1-0 Mar28 1-0	Dec20 2-0 Apr25 1-3	Oct04 1-4 Feb21 2-4	Sep20 1-1 Jan31 6-2	Nov08 0-1 Apr11 1-1		Nov22 1-1 Mar14 2-1	Aug16 0-1 Feb25 2-1
RANGERS	Sep13 3-3 Jan10 2-0	Nov08 1-0 Apr12 2-0	Aug23 5-1 Dec27 4-1	Oct18 7-0 Feb07 1-1	Aug04 3-1 Feb28 2-2	Dec07 1-0 Apr01 3-0	Nov01 4-1 May02 0-1	Sep27 2-2 Jan17 1-0		Nov29 3-2 Mar21 2-1
ST JOHNSTONE	Oct04 1-0 Feb21 0-1	Aug23 0-2 Dec27 1-0	Aug02 1-1 Feb28 1-1	Nov08 0-2 Apr11 0-0	Sep13 1-2 Jan12 2-3	Nov22 1-0 Mar14 1-1	Dec13 1-1 Mar28 1-0	Nov01 4-3 May02 3-2	Sep20 0-2 Jan31 2-0	

DIVISION 1

	AIRDRIE	AYR	DUNDEE	FALKIRK	GREENOCK	HAMILTON	PARTICK	RAITH	ST MIRREN	STIRLING A
AIRDRIE		Sep27 1-0 Feb10 2-0	Dec06 0-0 Apr04 1-2	Aug23 2-2 Mar03 0-1	Nov15 3-3 Apr18 1-1	Oct18 0-0 Feb07 3-2	Aug30 1-1 Jan06 2-1	Nov01 1-0 May02 1-0	Aug02 1-3 Dec27 2-1	Nov29 2-0 Mar21 1-0
AYR	Nov22 6-0 Mar14 0-2		Sep13 1-2 Jan10 2-5	Nov11 1-2 May02 1-3	Aug02 1-2 Dec27 2-1	Nov08 1-2 Apr11 2-1	Aug23 2-2 Feb28 2-2	Sep20 1-0 Jan31 0-0	Dec13 0-2 Mar23 2-2	Oct04 2-1 Feb21 1-0
DUNDEE	Oct04 1-0 Feb21 1-0	Nov15 4-0 Apr18 1-1		Aug02 3-0 Dec27 0-1	Nov22 0-1 Mar14 2-0	Sep20 0-2 Jan31 1-1	Nov01 0-0 May02 0-3	Aug30 2-2 Jan03 1-1	Aug23 1-0 Feb28 1-0	Dec13 0-0 Mar28 2-0
FALKIRK	Dec20 2-1 May09 0-1	Aug16 2-1 Feb25 4-0	Oct25 1-1 Apr25 1-0		Oct18 1-0 Feb07 1-1	Sep13 1-4 Jan10 3-1	Dec06 0-1 Mar24 1-1	Nov22 0-1 Mar14 0-1	Sep20 3-1 Jan31 2-2	Nov08 3-2 Apr11 1-0
GREENOCK	Sep13 1-1 Jan10 0-2	Oct25 1-1 Apr25 0-1	Sep27 0-2 Jan17 0-0	Dec13 0-2 Mar28 1-1		Aug16 0-2 Feb14 3-1	Nov29 3-2 Mar21 1-0	Oct04 1-3 Feb21 3-1	Nov08 3-0 Apr11 2-0	Dec20 1-3 May09 1-0
HAMILTON	Dec30 0-0 Mar28 0-2	Aug30 0-2 Feb17 1-1	Nov29 0-4 Mar21 1-2	Nov15 1-1 Apr18 1-2	Nov01 1-0 May02 0-3		Aug02 1-1 Dec27 0-1	Aug23 2-0 Mar17 1-4	Oct04 2-0 Feb23 1-1	Sep27 3-2 Mar03 2-2
PARTICK	Nov08 1-2 Apr11 2-0	Dec20 3-0 May09 1-3	Aug16 0-3 Feb25 1-2	Oct04 3-4 Feb21 0-0	Sep20 2-1 Jan31 3-3	Oct25 3-3 Apr25 0-0		Dec13 1-3 Mar28 1-2	Nov22 2-2 Mar14 1-2	Sep13 1-2 Jan10 1-3
RAITH	Aug16 1-1 Mar07 1-1	Nov29 0-1 Mar21 0-0	Nov08 0-1 Apr11 1-1	Sep27 2-0 Feb03 2-0	Dec06 0-0 Apr04 1-2	Dec20 3-1 May09 2-1	Oct18 2-0 Feb07 2-0		Sep13 2-1 Jan10 4-1	Oct25 2-0 Apr25 0-1
ST MIRREN	Oct25 0-2 Apr25 0-1	Oct18 1-1 Feb07 3-0	Dec20 0-2 May09 1-0	Nov29 2-0 Mar21 1-2	Aug30 2-1 Jan07 3-2	Dec06 2-1 Apr04 2-2	Sep27 1-0 Jan17 0-1	Nov15 2-3 Apr18 0-2		Aug16 2-2 Mar07 0-2
STIRLING A	Sep20 0-0 Jan31 2-2	Dec06 1-1 Apr04 2-0	Oct18 1-2 Feb07 1-3	Aug30 2-3 Jan03 0-6	Aug23 1-3 Feb28 2-2	Nov22 2-1 Mar14 0-1	Nov15 2-2 Apr18 0-1	Aug02 1-1 Dec27 3-2	Nov01 0-0 May02 0-1	

Season 1997-98

DIVISION 2

	BRECHIN	CLYDE	CLYDEBANK	EAST FIFE	FORFAR	INVERNESS	LIVINGSTON	QUEEN OF SOUTH	STENHOUSEMUIR	STRANRAER
BRECHIN		Nov29 2-1 Mar21 0-2	Jan10 0-1 May09 1-6	Oct18 0-0 Feb07 2-1	Oct25 2-0 Apr25 1-1	Aug16 2-2 Feb25 3-1	Sep13 0-2 Mar17 0-2	Sep27 0-3 Feb03 1-1	Dec20 1-1 Apr07 4-3	Nov08 2-2 Apr11 1-3
CLYDE	Sep20 1-1 Jan31 2-2		Oct25 0-1 Apr25 2-0	Nov08 3-0 Apr11 0-0	Aug16 1-2 Feb25 1-2	Nov22 4-3 Mar14 1-6	Oct04 1-0 Feb17 0-3	Dec16 0-0 Mar28 3-1	Sep13 2-0 Mar07 0-0	Jan13 0-1 May09 0-1
CLYDEBANK	Aug05 3-0 Feb21 2-1	Aug23 2-2 Dec27 2-1		Sep13 1-2 Mar17 0-3	Nov08 1-1 Apr11 0-1	Dec13 1-1 Mar28 1-0	Nov22 1-1 Mar14 0-2	Nov05 4-0 May02 1-1	Sep20 1-0 Jan31 1-0	Oct04 0-0 Feb14 0-1
EAST FIFE	Dec13 3-1 Mar28 4-1	Aug30 3-0 Feb28 1-1	Nov15 2-3 Apr18 0-2		Jan11 1-0 May09 0-1	Oct25 1-5 Apr25 0-1	Sep20 2-3 Jan31 2-0	Oct04 3-2 Feb15 1-5	Aug16 0-3 Feb25 2-1	Nov22 2-2 Mar14 0-3
FORFAR	Aug23 2-5 Dec27 5-0	Nov01 2-2 May02 0-1	Aug30 0-2 Feb28 0-0	Sep07 1-2 Feb21 1-0		Oct04 2-1 Mar10 1-2	Dec13 2-2 Mar28 2-1	Nov15 2-4 Apr18 2-4	Nov22 1-1 Mar14 0-1	Sep20 3-1 Jan31 2-1
INVERNESS	Nov01 0-0 May02 2-1	Sep27 1-2 Jan17 5-1	Oct18 0-0 Feb07 3-2	Aug23 0-1 Dec27 4-0	Dec20 2-2 Apr04 0-0		Aug06 1-1 Feb21 2-2	Nov29 2-1 Mar21 0-2	Nov08 4-1 Apr11 2-1	Sep13 2-2 Mar07 1-2
LIVINGSTON	Nov15 5-2 Apr18 1-0	Dec20 0-2 Apr07 4-0	Sep27 0-0 Feb10 0-3	Dec03 1-0 Mar21 2-2	Oct18 4-3 Feb07 4-0	Mar03 2-2 May09 1-2		Aug30 3-1 Mar25 1-1	Oct25 2-1 Apr25 1-1	Aug16 1-0 Feb25 0-1
QUEEN OF SOUTH	Nov22 0-0 Mar14 1-1	Oct18 4-3 Feb07 0-0	Aug16 2-2 Feb24 0-0	Dec20 2-1 Apr05 1-4	Sep13 0-1 Mar07 5-1	Sep20 2-1 Jan31 1-0	Nov08 1-0 Apr11 0-1		Jan20 0-1 May09 1-0	Oct25 2-1 Apr25 3-2
STENHOUSEMUIR	Oct04 3-2 Feb17 3-1	Nov15 0-0 Apr18 1-1	Nov29 2-3 Mar21 0-0	Nov01 0-0 May02 2-3	Sep27 1-4 Feb03 2-2	Aug30 3-2 Feb28 0-3	Aug23 1-1 Dec27 1-2	Aug05 2-1 Feb21 2-0		Dec13 3-0 Mar28 0-1
STRANRAER	Aug30 4-0 Mar04 0-2	Aug06 0-0 Feb21 3-0	Dec20 0-1 Apr04 2-1	Sep27 3-2 Jan17 2-3	Nov29 2-2 Mar21 4-0	Nov15 2-1 Apr18 3-1	Nov01 1-1 May02 2-0	Aug23 2-1 Dec27 3-4	Oct18 4-1 Feb07 1-2	

DIVISION 3

	ALBION	ALLOA	ARBROATH	BERWICK	COWDENBEATH	DUMBARTON	E STIRLING	MONTROSE	QUEEN'S PARK	ROSS
ALBION		Sep20 2-1 Jan31 3-3	Apr04 0-1 Apr29 0-2	Aug16 2-1 Apr13 5-0	Nov22 2-1 Mar14 0-1	Sep13 2-1 Mar07 2-2	Oct18 5-1 Feb07 3-2	Jan10 3-2 May09 4-2	Oct25 0-0 Apr25 1-2	Nov08 2-0 Apr11 1-3
ALLOA	Nov29 4-0 Mar21 3-1		Sep27 3-0 Feb03 3-1	Jan10 1-3 May09 1-0	Aug16 1-0 Feb24 2-0	Nov08 1-2 Apr11 3-0	Oct25 0-2 Apr25 5-2	Sep13 5-1 Mar07 3-2	Oct18 3-4 Feb07 2-0	Dec30 1-0 Apr04 1-1
ARBROATH	Oct04 3-0 Dec20 3-1	Nov22 2-3 Mar14 3-0		Nov08 4-1 Apr11 1-0	Dec13 3-2 Mar28 2-0	Sep20 2-1 Jan31 2-2	Aug16 2-0 Dec06 3-0	Oct25 1-2 Apr25 4-2	Jan10 2-2 May09 1-1	Sep13 2-2 Mar07 1-1
BERWICK	Nov01 1-1 May02 5-2	Aug05 0-2 Feb21 1-1	Aug30 1-3 Feb28 0-0		Oct04 2-1 Feb14 0-2	Aug23 5-3 Dec27 1-1	Sep27 2-3 Jan17 3-1	Dec13 1-2 Mar28 1-1	Nov15 2-1 Apr18 2-2	Nov29 0-0 Mar21 1-1
COWDENBEATH	Sep27 1-4 Feb10 2-0	Nov01 0-3 May02 1-3	Oct18 0-4 Feb07 3-1	Dec20 0-2 Apr07 1-0		Aug05 0-2 Feb21 2-0	Sep13 1-0 Mar09 0-1	Nov08 3-1 Apr11 0-0	Nov29 0-0 Mar21 1-2	Aug23 0-1 Dec27 0-2
DUMBARTON	Nov15 1-1 Apr18 2-0	Aug30 0-1 Feb28 0-3	Nov29 1-2 Mar21 1-2	Oct25 1-4 Apr25 0-2	Jan10 1-2 May09 2-3		Dec20 0-1 Apr04 1-0	Aug16 2-2 Feb25 2-3	Sep27 0-0 Jan17 0-0	Oct18 2-2 Feb07 0-1
E STIRLING	Dec13 1-0 Mar28 2-0	Aug23 2-1 Dec27 0-3	Nov01 1-2 May02 1-1	Nov22 4-0 Mar14 1-1	Nov15 4-0 Apr18 2-1	Oct04 3-1 Feb17 1-0		Sep20 4-1 Jan31 1-2	Aug30 1-0 Mar04 0-0	Aug05 1-3 Feb21 1-0
MONTROSE	Aug05 1-2 Feb21 1-3	Nov15 0-2 Apr18 0-3	Aug23 0-3 Dec27 1-0	Oct18 1-2 Feb07 2-2	Aug30 2-0 Feb28 3-1	Nov01 2-2 May02 2-1	Nov29 1-1 Mar21 1-1		Dec20 1-3 Apr04 4-3	Sep27 3-4 Mar10 0-2
QUEEN'S PARK	Aug23 5-1 Dec27 2-4	Dec13 3-0 Mar28 1-1	Sep09 3-2 Feb21 0-2	Sep13 0-0 Mar07 2-1	Sep20 1-0 Jan31 0-4	Nov22 2-3 Feb14 0-2	Nov08 0-1 Apr11 0-2	Oct04 1-1 Feb14 0-2		Nov01 0-3 May02 0-4
ROSS	Aug30 5-3 Mar17 6-2	Oct04 2-4 Mar24 0-2	Nov15 0-0 Apr18 1-0	Sep20 2-0 Jan31 0-0	Oct25 5-0 Apr25 1-0	Dec13 2-3 Mar28 0-0	Feb10 0-0 May09 5-2	Nov22 8-1 Mar14 2-1	Aug16 0-1 Oct11 2-1	

LEAGUE TABLES

PREMIER DIVISION

	P	W	D	L	F	A	W	D	L	F	A	Pts
Celtic	36	12	4	2	41	9	10	4	4	23	15	74
Rangers	36	13	4	1	46	16	8	5	5	30	22	72
Hearts	36	10	5	3	36	24	9	5	4	34	22	67
Kilmarnock	36	9	4	5	24	21	4	7	7	16	31	50
St Johnstone	36	7	5	6	20	21	6	4	8	18	21	48
Aberdeen	36	6	6	6	20	18	3	6	9	19	35	39
Dundee U	36	5	7	6	23	18	3	6	9	20	33	37
Dunfermline	36	4	9	5	26	30	4	4	10	17	38	37
Motherwell	36	6	4	8	26	28	3	3	12	20	36	34
Hibernian	36	6	4	8	26	24	0	8	10	12	35	30

DIVISION 1

	P	W	D	L	F	A	W	D	L	F	A	Pts
Dundee	36	8	6	4	20	12	12	4	2	32	12	70
Falkirk	36	9	4	5	26	19	10	4	4	30	22	65
Raith	36	9	5	4	25	12	8	4	6	26	21	60
Airdrie	36	9	6	3	24	17	7	6	5	18	18	60
Greenock	36	7	4	7	21	22	5	6	7	26	26	46
St Mirren	36	7	3	8	22	24	4	5	9	19	29	41
Ayr	36	6	4	8	27	29	4	6	8	13	27	40
Hamilton	36	4	6	8	17	28	5	5	8	26	28	38
Partick	36	3	5	10	26	35	5	7	6	19	20	36
Stirling A	36	3	7	8	20	31	5	3	10	20	25	34

DIVISION 2

	P	W	D	L	F	A	W	D	L	F	A	Pts
Stranraer	36	10	3	5	38	22	8	4	6	24	22	61
Clydebank	36	7	6	5	21	17	9	6	3	27	14	60
Livingston	36	9	5	4	32	21	7	6	5	24	19	59
Queen of South	36	9	5	4	25	19	6	4	8	32	32	54
Inverness	36	7	7	4	31	21	6	3	9	34	30	49
East Fife	36	7	2	9	27	34	7	4	7	24	25	48
Forfar	36	6	4	8	28	30	6	6	6	23	31	46
Clyde	36	6	5	7	21	23	4	7	7	19	30	42
Stenhousemuir	36	6	6	6	26	26	4	4	10	18	27	40
Brechin	36	5	6	7	22	32	2	5	11	20	41	32

DIVISION 3

	P	W	D	L	F	A	W	D	L	F	A	Pts
Alloa	36	13	1	4	42	19	11	3	4	36	20	76
Arbroath	36	11	5	2	41	20	9	3	6	26	19	68
Ross	36	10	4	4	41	20	9	6	3	30	16	67
E Stirling	36	11	3	4	30	16	6	3	9	20	32	57
Albion	36	9	3	6	35	25	4	2	12	25	48	44
Berwick	36	5	8	5	28	27	5	4	9	19	28	42
Queen's Park	36	5	3	10	20	33	5	8	5	22	22	41
Cowdenbeath	36	6	2	10	15	26	6	0	12	18	31	38
Montrose	36	5	4	9	25	35	5	4	9	28	45	38
Dumbarton	36	2	5	11	16	29	5	5	8	26	32	31

Scottish Football League Records

Andrei Kanchelskis was one of Rangers' star performers as they won back the Scottish League title from Celtic. He scored eight goals in 30 appearances (one as a sub).

Craig Burley missed the middle part of Celtic's season as the Parkhead club failed to hang on to the championship.

DIVISION PREMIER

	ABERDEEN	CELTIC	DUNDEE	DUNDEE U	DUNFERMLINE	HEARTS	KILMARNOCK	MOTHERWELL	RANGERS	ST JOHNSTONE
ABERDEEN		Aug16 3-2 Mar14 1-5	Oct17 2-2 May08 1-2	Nov28 0-3 Apr17 0-4	Nov07 2-1 Apr03 3-1	Dec12 2-0 May23 2-5	Sep27 0-1 Feb06 2-1	Sep12 1-1 Dec29 1-1	Sep23 1-1 Jan30 2-4	Nov21 0-1 May01 1-0
CELTIC	Oct24 2-0 May15 3-2		Nov07 6-1 Apr03 5-0	Aug22 2-1 Feb27 2-1	Aug01 5-0 Dec19 5-0	Sep26 1-1 Feb06 3-0	Sep12 1-1 Feb17 1-0	Nov28 2-0 Apr17 1-0	Nov21 5-1 May02 0-3	Sep23 0-1 Jan31 5-0
DUNDEE	Aug01 0-2 Dec19 1-2	Aug29 1-1 Dec27 0-3		Sep19 2-2 Jan02 1-3	Oct28 1-0 May15 3-1	Oct31 1-0 Mar20 2-0	Nov14 1-1 Apr24 2-1	Sep26 1-0 Feb06 1-0	Jan27 0-4 Apr18 1-1	Aug23 0-1 Feb27 0-1
DUNDEE U	Oct04 1-0 Feb20 3-0	Dec12 1-1 May23 1-2	Nov22 0-1 May01 0-2		Sep23 1-1 Jan30 1-1	Aug16 0-0 Apr06 1-3	Oct17 0-2 May08 0-0	Nov07 2-2 Apr03 0-3	Sep12 0-0 Dec30 1-2	Dec05 1-1 Apr20 0-1
DUNFERMLINE	Aug29 1-1 Dec26 1-2	Oct17 2-2 May08 1-2	Aug15 2-0 Mar13 2-0	Nov15 2-1 Apr24 2-2		Sep20 1-1 Jan02 0-0	Nov28 0-3 Apr17 0-6	Dec12 1-1 May23 1-2	Sep26 0-2 Feb07 0-3	Oct31 1-1 Mar20 1-0
HEARTS	Aug22 2-0 Feb27 0-2	Dec06 2-1 Apr14 2-4	Sep12 0-2 Dec30 1-2	Oct24 0-1 Apr15 4-1	Nov21 2-1 May03 2-0		Nov07 2-1 Apr03 2-2	Sep23 3-0 Jan30 0-2	Aug02 2-1 Dec19 2-3	Oct04 1-1 Feb20 0-2
KILMARNOCK	Feb05 4-0 Apr10 4-2	Oct31 2-0 Mar21 0-0	Sep23 2-1 Jan30 0-0	Aug01 2-0 Dec20 2-0	Oct03 0-0 Mar06 0-0	Aug30 3-0 Dec26 1-0		Nov21 0-0 May01 0-1	Aug22 1-3 Feb28 0-5	Oct24 2-2 May15 1-1
MOTHERWELL	Oct31 2-2 Mar20 1-1	Oct03 1-2 Feb21 1-7	Dec16 2-1 Apr10 1-2	Aug30 1-0 Dec26 2-0	Aug22 0-0 Feb27 1-1	Nov14 3-2 Apr24 0-4	Sep19 0-0 Jan01 1-2		Oct28 1-0 May15 1-5	Aug01 1-0 Dec19 1-2
RANGERS	Nov14 2-1 Apr25 3-1	Sep20 0-0 Jan03 2-2	Oct04 1-0 Feb20 6-1	Oct31 2-1 Mar20 0-1	Dec05 1-1 Apr14 1-0	Oct17 3-0 May09 0-0	Dec12 1-0 May23 1-1	Aug15 2-1 Mar13 2-1		Aug29 4-0 Dec26 1-0
ST JOHNSTONE	Sep19 2-0 Jan02 4-1	Nov14 2-1 Apr24 1-0	Dec12 1-1 May23 1-0	Sep26 1-3 Feb06 1-0	Sep12 1-1 Dec29 1-1	Dec09 1-1 Apr17 0-0	Aug15 0-0 Mar13 0-1	Oct17 5-0 May08 0-0	Nov08 0-7 Apr04 3-1	

DIVISION 1

	AIRDRIE	AYR	CLYDEBANK	FALKIRK	GREENOCK	HAMILTON	HIBERNIAN	RAITH	ST MIRREN	STRANRAER
AIRDRIE		Nov21 0-2 Apr03 0-2	Aug04 0-0 Feb05 2-0	Nov07 0-3 Apr10 1-2	Sep12 0-1 Jan19 0-2	Oct06 3-2 May01 1-0	Oct03 1-3 Jan30 1-4	Aug29 0-1 Dec26 2-2	Aug22 1-0 Feb23 0-3	Oct31 3-2 Mar13 2-0
AYR	Sep26 1-2 Jan16 0-1		Nov14 4-1 Apr18 0-0	Oct17 4-2 Apr24 1-2	Aug15 1-0 Feb06 1-0	Sep05 2-3 Dec19 5-0	Oct24 3-3 Feb27 1-3	Dec12 0-2 May08 1-0	Nov28 1-1 Mar20 2-2	Sep19 7-1 Jan02 4-0
CLYDEBANK	Oct17 0-1 Apr24 0-1	Sep12 0-1 Apr27 2-1		Aug15 0-1 Mar10 1-2	Oct27 2-1 Apr21 1-2	Nov07 0-0 Apr10 0-0	Sep05 2-2 Mar13 2-0	Nov28 1-1 Mar20 0-0	Sep26 1-0 Jan16 2-2	Dec12 2-1 May08 1-2
FALKIRK	Sep19 0-1 Jan02 1-1	Aug04 1-0 Dec05 3-0	Oct11 2-2 May01 0-2		Sep26 2-1 Jan16 1-2	Nov28 2-1 Mar20 6-1	Aug22 1-1 Feb20 1-2	Nov14 1-1 Apr17 1-0	Oct31 1-1 Mar13 1-0	Aug29 1-0 Dec26 3-2
GREENOCK	Nov14 0-0 Apr17 0-2	Oct11 1-2 May01 1-4	Aug29 2-2 Dec26 1-1	Nov21 0-3 Apr03 3-2		Aug22 1-2 Feb20 3-0	Aug04 0-1 Dec05 1-3	Oct31 2-0 Mar13 1-1	Sep19 0-1 Jan05 0-0	Oct03 3-0 Jan30 1-0
HAMILTON	Aug15 1-1 Feb06 0-2	Oct31 1-3 Mar24 0-2	Sep19 1-2 Jan12 0-1	Oct03 2-1 Jan30 0-2	Dec12 0-0 May08 0-2		Nov21 2-2 Apr03 0-2	Oct17 3-2 Apr24 1-2	Aug29 0-0 Dec26 0-0	Nov14 1-2 Apr17 1-0
HIBERNIAN	Nov28 1-0 Mar20 3-0	Aug29 4-2 Dec26 3-0	Oct31 2-1 Dec19 3-0	Dec12 2-1 May08 2-1	Oct17 2-1 Apr24 2-1	Sep26 0-0 Jan16 4-0		Sep19 3-1 Jan02 5-1	Nov24 4-1 Apr17 2-1	Aug15 1-2 Feb06 2-0
RAITH	Nov03 1-3 Feb27 0-1	Aug22 0-0 Feb20 2-4	Oct03 0-1 Jan30 2-1	Sep12 1-1 Jan09 2-1	Sep05 0-0 Dec19 1-3	Aug04 0-2 Dec08 1-1	Nov07 1-3 Apr10 1-3		Oct11 1-0 May01 1-1	Nov21 2-0 Apr03 3-2
ST MIRREN	Dec12 1-5 May08 3-0	Oct03 0-2 Jan30 1-0	Nov21 0-0 Apr03 1-1	Sep05 0-2 Dec19 0-3	Nov07 1-0 Apr10 1-5	Oct24 3-2 Feb27 1-0	Sep12 2-0 Jan09 1-2	Aug15 2-1 Feb06 3-1		Oct17 1-0 Apr24 5-1
STRANRAER	Sep05 1-2 Dec19 1-2	Nov07 0-1 Apr10 0-2	Aug22 0-2 Feb20 0-2	Oct28 1-2 Feb27 0-1	Nov28 2-3 Mar20 0-1	Sep12 2-1 Jan09 2-2	Oct10 0-1 May01 0-4	Sep26 2-2 Jan16 2-0	Aug05 0-1 Dec05 1-2	

SEASON 1998-99

DIVISION 2

	ALLOA	ARBROATH	CLYDE	EAST FIFE	FORFAR	INVERNESS	LIVINGSTON	PARTICK	QUEEN OF SOUTH	STIRLING A
ALLOA		Nov07 1-1 Apr10 1-2	Sep12 3-0 Feb16 1-0	Oct10 5-1 May01 3-1	Aug04 1-2 Dec19 3-1	Aug22 1-1 Feb20 1-4	Sep26 3-4 Jan16 1-3	Oct31 3-1 Mar06 0-1	Nov28 2-1 Mar20 3-5	Aug29 7-0 Dec29 2-2
ARBROATH	Sep19 0-2 Feb06 1-2		Oct03 0-0 Jan30 0-3	Aug04 0-2 Dec19 2-1	Aug29 2-1 Jan19 2-2	Oct31 0-1 Mar06 3-1	Nov14 2-2 Apr17 1-1	Nov21 1-0 Apr03 2-1	Oct10 2-1 May01 0-2	Aug22 0-3 Feb20 1-0
CLYDE	Nov14 2-1 Apr17 0-1	Nov28 3-0 Mar20 1-1		Aug22 0-0 Feb20 1-0	Oct31 3-1 Mar06 1-0	Sep26 4-1 Jan16 1-1	Sep19 1-1 Feb06 0-3	Aug29 1-2 Dec26 0-1	Aug04 2-0 Dec19 2-1	Oct10 2-1 May01 4-1
EAST FIFE	Aug15 2-2 Feb27 0-4	Oct17 0-3 Apr24 1-2	Dec12 0-0 May08 2-1		Nov14 1-0 Apr17 2-1	Aug29 1-5 Dec27 3-2	Oct31 2-3 Mar06 1-1	Sep19 1-3 Feb06 1-0	Sep27 2-0 Jan17 0-1	Nov28 2-3 Mar20 1-0
FORFAR	Oct17 1-2 Apr24 3-1	Oct26 1-3 Mar13 5-2	Sep05 2-2 Feb02 3-1	Sep12 1-2 Feb16 2-4		Nov28 2-2 Mar20 0-3	Dec12 1-2 May08 1-2	Aug15 0-1 Feb27 2-1	Nov07 1-0 Apr10 2-1	Sep26 1-2 Jan16 3-3
INVERNESS	Dec16 3-2 May08 1-1	Sep05 2-1 Jan09 2-0	Nov21 1-1 Apr03 3-0	Oct24 4-2 Mar13 4-0	Oct03 2-2 Jan30 2-0		Aug15 2-1 Feb27 3-1	Oct17 3-2 Apr24 3-2	Sep12 3-2 Feb13 1-0	Nov07 3-1 Apr10 2-2
LIVINGSTON	Nov21 2-1 Apr03 1-0	Sep12 2-1 Feb16 1-0	Nov07 2-0 Apr10 2-0	Sep05 3-1 Jan20 1-0	Aug22 1-1 Feb20 5-0	Oct10 2-1 May01 4-3		Oct03 1-0 Jan30 1-1	Oct24 2-0 Mar13 1-2	Aug04 1-1 Dec19 0-0
PARTICK	Sep05 1-0 Jan13 2-1	Sep26 2-0 Jan16 0-0	Oct24 0-2 Mar13 0-1	Nov07 0-1 Apr10 2-2	Oct11 2-0 May01 1-0	Aug04 0-1 Dec19 2-1	Nov28 1-3 Mar20 1-1		Aug22 2-2 Feb20 1-3	Sep12 1-0 Feb17 0-1
QUEEN OF SOUTH	Oct03 2-1 Jan30 0-0	Aug15 0-0 Feb27 3-0	Oct17 2-1 Apr24 2-1	Nov21 0-0 Apr03 2-0	Sep19 3-0 Feb06 0-3	Nov14 2-2 Apr17 1-1	Aug29 0-1 Dec27 2-2	Dec12 0-0 May08 2-2		Oct31 2-3 Mar06 3-0
STIRLING A	Oct24 4-2 Mar13 1-1	Dec12 0-1 May08 2-1	Aug15 1-2 Feb27 2-3	Oct03 3-2 Jan30 0-1	Nov21 3-1 Apr03 2-2	Sep19 0-1 Feb06 1-5	Oct17 1-3 Apr24 0-0	Nov14 2-0 Apr17 3-0	Sep05 1-0 Jan26 1-3	

DIVISION 3

	ALBION	BERWICK	BRECHIN	COWDENBEATH	DUMBARTON	E STIRLING	MONTROSE	QUEEN'S PARK	ROSS	STENHOUSEMUIR
ALBION		Oct17 1-1 Apr24 0-3	Sep19 1-4 Feb06 4-1	Sep26 0-1 Feb23 1-1	Dec12 0-2 May08 0-2	Nov14 3-1 Apr17 0-2	Oct31 4-1 Mar16 0-0	Aug29 2-1 Dec26 1-0	Aug15 0-8 Feb27 3-3	Nov28 1-3 Mar20 1-2
BERWICK	Aug22 2-1 Dec19 1-1		Nov28 3-0 Mar20 2-3	Nov14 3-1 Apr18 2-1	Oct24 3-1 Mar13 0-1	Sep19 1-2 Feb06 1-2	Oct11 1-1 May01 4-1	Aug04 0-3 Feb20 0-2	Sep05 0-2 Jan27 2-2	Sep26 1-2 Jan16 2-1
BRECHIN	Nov07 1-0 Apr10 3-1	Oct03 1-1 Jan30 0-3		Oct31 2-1 Mar06 1-1	Sep12 0-0 Feb13 3-3	Oct10 0-0 May01 1-0	Aug29 3-0 Feb16 2-3	Aug22 2-2 Dec19 1-0	Nov21 0-1 Apr03 0-1	Aug04 1-0 Feb20 0-2
COWDENBEATH	Nov21 2-3 Apr03 0-2	Sep12 1-1 Feb13 1-2	Sep05 0-1 Jan26 0-2		Nov07 0-2 Apr10 2-1	Aug22 2-1 Dec19 3-2	Aug04 4-1 Feb20 1-0	Oct03 0-3 Jan30 0-0	Oct28 1-2 Mar13 2-3	Oct09 0-2 May01 0-2
DUMBARTON	Aug04 2-0 Mar09 1-1	Aug29 0-0 Feb02 1-1	Nov14 1-2 Apr17 2-0	Sep19 5-0 Apr05 6-1		Oct31 2-2 Mar06 0-2	Nov25 0-2 Apr03 2-1	Oct10 1-0 May01 0-1	Oct03 1-2 Jan30 0-0	Aug22 0-2 Dec19 1-4
E STIRLING	Sep12 0-1 Feb13 4-1	Nov07 0-0 Apr10 3-3	Aug15 1-1 Feb27 4-1	Oct17 1-1 Apr24 0-0	Sep05 1-2 Jan26 1-2		Oct03 3-1 Jan30 2-1	Nov21 1-1 Jan16 1-1	Dec12 2-2 May08 1-2	Oct26 1-1 Mar13 1-1
MONTROSE	Sep05 1-2 Jan09 2-3	Aug15 1-1 Feb27 0-3	Oct27 1-2 Mar13 1-3	Dec12 1-1 May08 1-2	Sep26 1-1 Jan16 4-2	Nov28 2-0 Mar20 1-0		Sep19 1-0 Feb06 3-0	Oct17 3-6 Apr24 2-3	Nov14 0-0 Apr17 1-2
QUEEN'S PARK	Oct27 0-0 Mar13 0-0	Dec12 1-1 May08 1-1	Oct17 1-1 Apr24 0-2	Nov28 2-0 Mar20 2-1	Aug15 0-1 Feb27 1-1	Sep26 0-4 Apr03 2-1	Nov07 3-0 Apr10 1-2		Sep12 4-2 Feb13 0-3	Sep05 0-0 Jan26 4-1
ROSS	Oct10 1-2 May01 2-0	Oct31 3-1 Mar06 6-0	Sep26 0-1 Mar09 2-1	Aug29 2-0 D26 1-0	Nov28 2-0 Mar20 1-2	Aug04 1-0 Mar02 4-2	Aug22 3-1 Dec19 3-0	Nov14 5-1 Apr17 1-2		Sep19 0-1 Feb06 2-2
STENHOUSEMUIR	Oct03 4-1 Jan30 1-2	Nov21 1-2 Apr03 1-1	Dec15 0-1 May08 1-0	Aug15 1-2 Feb27 4-1	Oct17 0-3 Apr24 0-2	Aug29 1-0 Dec26 2-2	Sep12 4-0 Feb23 3-1	Oct31 2-1 Mar06 4-1	Nov07 2-4 Apr10 3-2	

LEAGUE TABLES

PREMIER DIVISION

	P	W	D	L	F	A	W	D	L	F	A	Pts
Rangers	36	12	5	1	32	11	11	3	4	46	20	77
Celtic	36	14	2	2	49	12	7	6	5	35	23	71
St Johnstone	36	8	7	3	24	18	7	5	6	15	20	57
Kilmarnock	36	8	7	3	24	15	6	7	5	23	14	56
Dundee	36	7	4	7	18	23	6	3	9	18	33	46
Hearts	36	8	2	8	27	26	3	7	8	17	24	42
Motherwell	36	6	5	7	20	31	4	6	8	15	23	41
Aberdeen	36	6	4	8	24	35	4	3	11	19	36	37
Dundee U	36	2	8	8	13	22	6	2	10	24	26	34
Dunfermline	36	4	7	7	18	29	0	9	9	10	30	28

DIVISION 1

	P	W	D	L	F	A	W	D	L	F	A	Pts
Hibernian	36	16	1	1	45	13	12	4	2	39	20	89
Falkirk	36	9	5	4	28	18	11	1	6	32	20	66
Ayr	36	8	4	6	38	23	11	1	6	28	19	62
Airdrie	36	6	2	10	17	29	12	3	3	25	14	59
St Mirren	36	10	2	6	26	25	4	8	6	16	18	52
Greenock	36	5	5	8	20	24	9	2	7	25	17	49
Clydebank	36	5	6	7	17	18	6	7	5	19	20	46
Raith	36	5	5	8	19	27	3	6	9	18	30	35
Hamilton	36	3	5	10	13	26	3	5	10	17	36	28
Stranraer	36	2	2	14	14	31	3	0	15	15	43	17

DIVISION 2

	P	W	D	L	F	A	W	D	L	F	A	Pts
Livingston	36	13	4	1	32	12	9	7	2	34	23	77
Inverness	36	14	4	0	44	20	7	5	6	36	28	72
Clyde	36	10	4	4	28	16	5	4	9	18	26	53
Queen of South	36	7	8	3	26	17	6	1	11	24	28	48
Alloa	36	8	3	7	41	30	5	4	9	24	26	46
Stirling A	36	7	3	8	27	28	5	5	8	23	35	44
Arbroath	36	7	4	7	19	25	5	4	9	18	27	44
Partick	36	7	4	7	18	19	5	3	10	18	26	43
East Fife	36	7	3	8	22	31	5	3	10	20	33	42
Forfar	36	6	3	9	31	34	2	4	12	17	36	31

DIVISION 3

	P	W	D	L	F	A	W	D	L	F	A	Pts
Ross	36	12	1	5	39	16	12	4	2	48	26	77
Stenhousemuir	36	9	2	7	34	26	10	5	3	28	16	64
Brechin	36	7	6	5	21	19	10	2	6	26	24	59
Dumbarton	36	6	5	7	25	21	10	4	4	28	19	57
Berwick	36	7	3	8	28	27	5	11	2	25	22	50
Queen's Park	36	6	7	5	22	21	5	4	9	19	25	44
Albion	36	5	4	9	22	36	7	4	7	21	27	44
E Stirling	36	4	10	4	27	22	5	3	10	23	26	40
Cowdenbeath	36	5	2	11	19	30	3	5	10	15	35	31
Montrose	36	5	4	9	26	31	3	2	13	16	43	30

Scottish Football League Records

Ranger's Rod Wallace and Celtic's Tom Boyd, both seem to have missed the ball in March 2000.

Celtic's Mark Viduka battles for the ball with Lorenzo Amoruso. Viduka was the Scottish Footballer of the Year, a rare bright spot in a worrying season for the Parkhead club.

DIVISION PREMIER

	ABERDEEN	CELTIC	DUNDEE	DUNDEE U	HEARTS	HIBERNIAN	KILMARNOCK	MOTHERWELL	RANGERS	ST JOHNSTONE
ABERDEEN		Aug01 0-5 Dec11 0-6	Aug14 0-2 Apr18 0-1	Sep18 1-2 Dec27 3-1	D08 3-1 Apr15 1-2	Oct02 2-2 Feb26 4-0	Oct23 2-2 May14 5-1	Jan26 1-1 Apr22 2-1	Oct30 1-5 Apr01 1-1	Aug29 0-3 Feb05 2-1
CELTIC	Oct16 7-0 May06 5-1		Mar01 6-2 Apr15 2-2	Dec18 4-1 May21 2-0	Aug29 4-0 Feb05 2-3	D04 4-0 Apr22 1-1	Oct30 5-1 Apr02 4-2	Oct27 0-1 Apr05 4-0	Dec27 1-1 Mar08 0-1	Aug07 3-0 Mar11 4-1
DUNDEE	Feb23 1-3 May21 0-2	Aug21 1-2 Feb12 0-3		Oct17 0-2 May06 3-0	Oct30T 1-0 Apr01 0-0	Aug08 3-4 May14 1-0	Jan26 0-0 Apr22 1-2	Nov20 0-1 Apr08 4-1	Oct02 2-3 Feb26 1-7	Sep19 1-2 Dec27 1-1
DUNDEE U	Nov06 3-1 Mar25 1-1	Aug15 2-1 May02 0-1	Jul31 2-1 Dec12 1-0		Sep25 0-2 Mar04 0-1	Sep11 3-1 Jan22 0-0	Aug29 0-0 Mar15 2-2	Oct23 0-2 May13 1-2	Feb02 0-4 Apr15 0-2	Nov27 1-0 Apr29 0-1
HEARTS	Aug22 3-0 Mar22 3-0	Nov20 1-2 Apr09 1-0	Sep11 4-0 Jan22 2-0	D05 3-0 Apr22 1-2		Dec19 0-3 May21 2-1	Oct27 2-2 Feb26 0-0	Nov06 1-1 Mar25 0-0	Aug07 0-4 Apr12 1-2	Oct16 1-1 May06 0-0
HIBERNIAN	Nov27 2-0 Apr29 1-0	Sep25 0-2 Mar05 2-1	Oct23 5-2 Mar21 1-2	Oct31 3-2 Apr01 1-0	Aug14 1-1 Mar18 3-1		Sep19 0-3 Dec27 2-2	Jul31 2-2 Dec11 2-2	Aug28 0-1 Feb06 2-2	Nov24 0-1 Apr15 3-3
KILMARNOCK	Aug07 2-0 Apr12 1-0	Sep12 0-1 Jan23 1-1	Sep25 0-2 Mar04 2-2	Nov20 1-1 Apr08 1-0	Nov27 2-2 Apr29 0-1	Nov06 0-2 Mar25 1-0		Aug21 0-1 Feb12 0-2	Oct16 1-1 May07 0-2	Dec18 1-2 May21 3-2
MOTHERWELL	Oct20 5-6 Mar04 1-0	Nov28 3-2 Apr29 1-1	Aug28 0-2 Feb05 0-3	Aug07 2-2 Apr19 1-3	Nov23 2-1 Mar01 0-2	Oct16 2-2 May06 2-0	Feb22 0-4 Apr16 2-0		Dec18 1-5 May21 2-0	Oct30 1-0 Apr01 2-1
RANGERS	Sep11 3-0 Jan22 5-0	Nov07 4-2 Mar26 4-0	Nov28 1-2 Apr30 3-0	Aug21 4-1 Apr04 3-0	Dec22 1-0 May13 1-0	Oct20 2-0 May03 5-2	Jul31 2-1 Dec11 1-0	Aug15 4-1 Mar18 6-2		Sep25 3-1 Mar04 0-0
ST JOHNSTONE	Nov21 1-1 May02 2-1	Oct24 1-2 May13 0-0	Nov06 0-1 Mar25 2-1	Oct27 0-1 Feb26 2-0	Jul31 1-4 Mar15 0-1	Aug21 1-1 Feb22 1-0	Aug15 2-0 Mar18 0-0	Sep11 1-1 Jan22 1-1	Feb15 1-1 Apr23 0-2	

DIVISION 1

	AIRDRIE	AYR	CLYDEBANK	DUNFERMLINE	FALKIRK	GREENOCK	INVERNESS	LIVINGSTON	RAITH	ST MIRREN
AIRDRIE		Oct30 2-1 Mar04 0-0	Oct23 1-0 Apr22 0-0	Aug14 2-2 Feb26 1-2	Sep18 0-0 Jan03 0-2	D07 1-0 Apr08 3-0	Oct02 1-1 Feb05 1-4	Dec14 2-3 May06 0-2	Aug28 1-4 Jan15 0-2	Nov12 0-2 Apr01 0-1
AYR	Sep11 2-0 Dec27 5-0		Nov06 0-0 Mar18 4-0	D04 0-3 Apr11 0-2	Dec11 1-1 May06 3-3	Oct02 3-0 Feb05 3-2	Aug28 1-0 Mar07 1-3	Aug14 1-2 Feb29 0-1	Nov14 0-1 Apr01 0-1	Oct23 0-3 Apr22 1-2
CLYDEBANK	Aug07 0-2 Dec18 1-1	Sep18 0-2 Jan03 0-2		Oct09 1-4 Feb05 1-3	Nov14 0-3 Apr02 0-1	Oct16 1-3 Apr29 0-3	Oct30 0-3 Mar04 0-1	D04 1-5 Apr08 1-2	Aug21 1-1 Mar07 2-1	Aug29 2- Mar25 0-0
DUNFERMLINE	Oct16 0-0 Apr29 1-0	Sep25 2-1 Jan22 2-0	Nov27 2-1 Aug15 6-0		Aug28 1-1 Jan15 2-2	Aug21 2-1 Feb12 1-1	Aug07 4-0 Dec18 1-0	Nov14 3-0 Apr01 4-1	Nov06 1-1 Mar18 0-2	Sep11 1-1 Feb19 1-1
FALKIRK	Nov06 2-0 Mar18 8-0	Aug21 2-1 Feb12 1-0	Sep04 3-2 Jan08 4-0	Nov20 1-3 Mar25 1-1		Aug07 2-4 Dec18 2-1	Oct16 0-2 Apr29 2-2	Sep11 0-2 Dec27 2-3	Nov27 2-1 Apr15 1-0	Sep25 3-1 Jan22 2-0
GREENOCK	Sep25 0-2 Jan22 4-0	Nov27 0-0 Apr15 1-2	Aug14 0-0 Feb26 1-0	Dec11 0-3 May06 2-0	Oct23 2-3 Apr22 0-2		Nov12 5-1 Apr01 0-2	Aug28 2-2 Mar14 1-0	Sep11 2-0 Dec27 1-0	Nov06 1-4 Mar18 0-2
INVERNESS	Nov27 2-0 Aug15 1-5	Nov30 1-1 Mar25 1-1	Sep11 1-0 Dec27 4-1	Oct23 1-1 Apr22 1-2	Aug14 2-3 Feb26 0-3	Sep04 1-1 Jan08 6-2		Nov06 2-0 Mar18 4-1	Sep25 0-2 Jan22 1-1	Dec11 1-1 May06 5-0
LIVINGSTON	Aug21 3-0 Apr04 3-2	Oct16 4-1 Apr29 3-1	Sep25 2-1 Jan22 3-0	Sep04 0-1 Jan08 1-0	Oct30 1-1 Mar04 0-1	Nov20 2-1 Mar25 1-0	Sep18 2-2 Jan03 1-1		Aug07 1-1 Mar11 0-0	Nov27 1-2 Apr15 1-2
RAITH	Nov20 1-1 Mar25 2-0	Sep04 5-1 Jan08 2-0	Jan18 1-0 May06 0-0	Sep18 2-2 Jan03 3-0	Oct02 2-1 Feb05 0-1	Oct30 3-1 Mar04 3-0	D04 4-2 Apr08 2-0	Oct23 3-1 Apr22 1-3		Aug14 0-6 Feb26 1-2
ST MIRREN	Sep04 5-0 Jan08 3-1	Aug07 1-1 Dec18 1-2	Nov20 2-1 Mar11 8-0	Oct30 3-1 Mar04 0-2	D04 2-1 Apr08 1-0	Sep18 3-2 Jan03 1-1	Aug21 3-2 Feb12 2-0	Oct02 1-1 Feb05 0-2	Oct16 3-2 Apr29 3-0	

Season 1999-2000

DIVISION 2

	ALLOA	ARBROATH	CLYDE	HAMILTON	PARTICK	QUEEN OF SOUTH	ROSS	STENHOUSEMUIR	STIRLING A	STRANRAER
ALLOA		Nov09 0-0 Apr01 2-1	Oct23 1-0 Apr22 2-1	Aug28 1-1 Apr04 2-0	Aug14 1-0 Feb26 1-1	Apr11 3-1 May06 6-1	Sep11 2-0 Mar14 1-2	Sep25 1-4 Mar07 3-1	Nov06 4-4 Mar18 1-0	Nov27 1-1 Apr15 4-0
ARBROATH	Sep04 2-2 Mar28 2-0		Aug14 2-1 Feb26 1-1	Nov27 1-1 Apr15 1-1	Dec27 0-0 May06 3-2	Oct23 5-2 Apr22 1-2	Nov20 0-1 Mar25 1-2	Nov06 0-3 Mar18 2-2	Sep11 2-1 Feb29 3-2	Sep25 1-2 Jan22 1-1
CLYDE	Aug07 0-1 Dec18 0-0	Oct16 0-0 Apr29 4-1		Sep25 2-1 Jan22 1'-0	Sep11 2-0 Feb29 1-0	Nov09 3-0 Apr01 3-1	Nov06 3-1 Mar18 0-0	Nov27 1-0 Apr15 7-0	Aug28 3-0 Feb12 4-1	Aug21 0-0 Mar28 1-1
HAMILTON	Nov16 1-2 Mar25 0-0	Oct02 2-2 Feb05 2-2	D04 2-3 Apr08 1-1		Nov06 0-0 Mar18 0-1	Aug14 0-3 Feb26 1-1	Oct09 1-0 Apr22 0-3	Sep05 1-1 Mar14 2-1	Dec27 0-2 May06 1-0	Sep11 2-1 Jan15 2-0
PARTICK	Oct16 2-2 Aug29 0-1	Aug21 1-3 Mar04 2-0	Oct30 0-0 Mar21 1-2	Sep18 0-1 Jan03 2-2		Aug28 2-0 Feb12 5-4	Sep25 0-2 Jan22 4-2	Aug07 0-1 Dec18 1-0	Nov27 1-0 Apr15 1-1	Nov14 2-0 Apr01 1-1
QUEEN OF SOUTH	Aug21 1-1 Mar04 2-1	Aug07 2-3 Dec18 1-0	Sep04 1-1 Mar14 3-0	Oct16 3-2 Apr29 1-1	Nov20 1-2 Mar25 1-1		Nov27 0-2 Apr15 0-3	Sep11 0-3 Jan15 3-1	Sep25 3-3 Jan22 2-3	Nov06 0-5 Mar18 0-0
ROSS	Oct30 1-0 Mar11 3-4	Aug28 2-0 Feb12 1-1	Sep18 2-0 Mar07 2-2	Aug07 2-1 Jan29 0-1	D04 2-1 Apr08 1-3	Oct02 1-1 Feb05 2-0		Aug21 0-0 Mar28 2-0	Nov12 1-3 Apr01 5-1	Oct16 1-1 Apr29 3-1
STENHOUSEMUIR	D04 1-3 Apr08 2-1	Sep18 1-3 Jan03 3-0	Oct02 1-3 Feb05 3-4	Nov10 0-0 Apr18 0-1	Oct23 0-1 Apr22 2-0	Oct30 2-1 Mar11 2-0	Mar21 0-2 May06 2-2		Aug14 2-1 Feb26 1-2	Aug28 1-1 Feb12 1-1
STIRLING A	Sep18 0-1 Jan03 1-1	Oct30 3-4 Mar11 1-1	Nov20 1-2 Mar25 3-6	Aug21 2-0 Mar04 1-4	Oct02 3-1 Feb05 0-2	Dec11 3-0 Apr08 2-2	Sep04 2-1 Feb19 3-1	Oct16 5-1 Apr29 1-0		Aug07 1-1 Dec18 2-5
STRANRAER	Oct02 0-0 Mar21 2-2	D04 2-2 Apr08 0-1	Dec27 2-2 May06 2-1	Oct30 0-2 Mar11 2-2	Sep04 1-1 Mar07 3-1	Sep18 1-0 Jan03 1-2	Aug14 0-0 Feb26 0-2	Nov20 2-0 Mar25 2-2	Oct23 2-1 Apr22 3-1	

DIVISION 3

	ALBION	BERWICK	BRECHIN	COWDENBEATH	DUMBARTON	EAST FIFE	E STIRLING	FORFAR	MONTROSE	QUEEN'S PARK
ALBION		Oct16 0-3 Apr29 0-0	Aug21 0-0 Mar04 0-2	Nov27 1-4 Apr15 0-3	Aug07 1-3 Dec18 3-0	Sep04 1-3 Feb19 3-1	Sep25 1-1 Jan22 0-1	Nov20 0-1 Mar25 0-1	Sep11 1-3 Mar07 0-2	Nov06 2-4 Mar18 0-3
BERWICK	Aug14 1-1 Feb26 2-1		Sep25 2-0 Jan22 3-1	Sep11 0-2 Jan15 0-0	Nov14 0-1 Apr01 0-0	Oct23 0-1 Apr22 0-1	Nov27 1-0 Apr15 3-0	Nov06 2-2 Mar18 2-0	Dec27 0-0 May06 2-1	Aug28 1-2 Feb12 1-1
BRECHIN	Dec11 8-1 May06 3-2	D07 0-3 Apr08 1-2		Nov14 2-0 Apr01 1-2	Aug28 0-2 Feb12 1-2	Oct02 1-3 Feb05 3-1	Sep11 1-2 Mar07 1-1	Oct23 0-2 Apr22 1-0	Nov06 1-0 Mar18 0-0	Aug14 1-2 Feb26 0-0
COWDENBEATH	Oct02 0-0 Feb05 5-0	Oct30 1-1 Mar11 1-3	Sep04 6-1 Feb19 1-1		D08 0-2 Apr08 1-2	Sep18 4-0 Jan03 1-0	Nov20 1-2 Mar25 0-0	Aug14 0-3 Feb26 4-1	Oct23 1-1 Apr22 2-1	Dec22 0-2 May06 2-3
DUMBARTON	Oct23 1-1 Apr22 0-0	Sep04 2-1 Mar14 0-2	Nov20 1-3 Mar25 2-1	Sep25 1-1 Jan22 2-0		Mar28 1-1 May06 2-1	Nov06 1-0 Mar18 3-0	Nov27 3-3 Apr15 0-0	Aug14 3-4 Feb26 3-2	Sep11 0-1 Jan29 1-1
EAST FIFE	Nov14 1-4 Apr01 2-1	Aug07 1-2 Mar21 3-1	Nov27 1-0 Apr15 1-1	Nov06 2-3 Mar18 1-1	Aug21 1-0 Mar04 2-1		Oct16 1-0 Apr29 3-1	Sep11 2-0 Jan15 1-1	Aug28 0-0 Feb15 2-0	Sep25 0-0 Jan22 0-0
E STIRLING	Feb29 4-3 Apr08 3-1	Oct02 0-3 Feb05 0-1	Oct30 0-0 Mar11 0-3	Aug28 0-1 Feb12 0-4	Sep18 1-3 Jan03 2-1	Aug14 0-2 Feb26 1-0		Jan29 0-2 May06 0-1	Nov14 2-0 Apr01 1-0	Oct23 1-1 Apr22 0-1
FORFAR	Aug28 2-0 Feb12 3-1	Sep18 1-1 Mar07 2-0	Aug07 0-0 Feb29 2-0	Oct16 3-1 Apr29 2-2	Oct02 5-0 Feb05 4-3	Oct30 3-2 Mar11 0-1	Aug21 1-1 Mar04 3-0		D07 1-2 Apr08 1-2	Nov14 2-2 Apr01 4-0
MONTROSE	Oct30 2-1 Mar11 1-2	Aug21 1-2 Mar04 2-3	Sep18 0-1 Jan03 1-0	Aug07 0-1 Dec18 1-3	Oct16 1-4 Apr29 2-1	Nov20 1-2 Mar25 1-1	Sep04 1-2 Feb19 0-0	Sep28 2-0 Jan22 1-5		Nov27 2-1 Apr15 0-2
QUEEN'S PARK	Sep18 2-0 Jan03 0-1	Nov20 1-4 Mar25 0-1	Oct16 5-3 Apr29 1-0	Aug21 1-0 Mar04 3-1	Oct30 3-2 Mar11 2-0	D04 0-1 Apr11 1-0	Aug07 2-1 Dec18 0-1	Sep04 1-1 Feb19 3-2	Oct02 2-1 Feb05 1-1	

LEAGUE TABLES

PREMIER DIVISION

	P	W	D	L	F	A	W	D	L	F	A	Pts
Rangers	36	16	1	1	52	12	12	5	1	44	14	90
Celtic	36	12	3	3	58	17	9	3	6	32	21	69
Hearts	36	7	6	5	25	18	8	3	7	22	22	54
Motherwell	36	8	3	7	27	34	6	7	5	22	29	52
St Johnstone	36	5	7	6	16	18	5	5	8	20	26	42
Hibernian	36	7	6	5	30	27	3	5	10	19	34	41
Dundee	36	4	3	11	20	33	8	2	8	25	31	41
Dundee U	36	6	4	8	16	22	5	2	11	18	35	39
Kilmarnock	36	5	5	8	16	22	3	8	7	22	30	37
Aberdeen	36	6	4	8	28	37	3	2	13	16	46	33

DIVISION 1

	P	W	D	L	F	A	W	D	L	F	A	Pts
St Mirren	36	12	3	3	42	19	11	4	3	33	20	76
Dunfermline	36	10	7	1	34	13	10	4	4	32	20	71
Falkirk	36	11	2	5	38	23	9	6	3	29	17	68
Livingston	36	9	5	4	29	17	10	2	6	31	28	64
Raith	36	11	3	4	35	21	6	5	7	20	19	59
Inverness	36	7	6	5	34	25	6	4	8	26	30	49
Ayr	36	6	3	9	25	24	4	5	9	17	28	38
Morton	36	7	3	8	22	23	3	3	12	23	38	36
Airdrie	36	4	5	9	15	26	3	3	12	14	43	29
Clydebank	36	1	3	14	11	40	0	4	14	6	42	10

DIVISION 2

	P	W	D	L	F	A	W	D	L	F	A	Pts
Clyde	36	12	5	1	35	7	6	6	6	30	30	65
Alloa	36	11	5	2	36	18	6	8	4	22	20	64
Ross	36	9	5	4	31	20	9	3	6	26	19	62
Arbroath	36	6	7	5	28	26	5	7	6	24	29	47
Partick	36	7	5	6	25	22	5	5	8	17	22	46
Stranraer	36	6	8	4	25	22	3	10	5	22	24	45
Stirling	36	7	4	7	34	33	4	3	11	26	39	40
Stenhousemuir	36	6	4	8	24	26	4	4	10	20	33	38
Queen of South	36	5	6	7	24	32	3	3	12	21	43	33
Hamilton	36	5	7	6	18	23	5	7	6	21	21	29*

*Hamilton deducted 15 points

DIVISION 3

	P	W	D	L	F	A	W	D	L	F	A	Pts
Queen's Park	36	11	2	5	28	20	9	7	2	26	17	69
Berwick	36	7	6	5	20	14	12	3	3	33	16	66
Forfar	36	10	5	3	39	18	7	5	6	25	22	61
East Fife	36	9	6	3	24	16	8	2	8	21	23	59
Cowdenbeath	36	6	5	7	30	23	9	4	5	29	20	54
Dumbarton	36	7	7	4	26	22	8	1	9	27	29	53
E Stirling	36	6	2	10	15	27	5	5	8	13	23	40
Brechin	36	6	3	9	25	25	4	5	9	17	26	38
Montrose	36	5	2	11	19	31	5	5	8	20	23	37
Albion	36	2	3	13	13	35	3	4	11	20	40	22

Scottish FA Cup Results 1873-2000

Season 1873-74

1st Round

Oct 18	Alexandra A	2	Callander	0
Oct 25	Clydesdale	6	Granville	0
	Dumbarton	*W*	Vale of Leven	*0*
	Eastern	4	Rovers	0
Oct 25	Queen's Park	7	Dumbreck	0
Oct 18	Renton	2	Kilmarnock	0
	T Lanark	*W*	Southern	*0*
	Western	0	Blythswood	1
	Alexandra A	0	Blythswood	2
Nov 8	Clydesdale	1	T Lanark	1
	Dumbarton	0	Renton	0
Nov 22	Queen's Park	1	Eastern	0

Replays

Nov 16	T Lanark	0	Clydesdale	0
Nov 29	Renton	1	Dumbarton	0
Dec 6	Clydesdale	2	T Lanark	0

played at Kinning Park

Semi-finals

Dec 20	Clydesdale	4	Blythswood	0
Dec 13	Queen's Park	2	Renton	0

Final

Mar 21	Clydesdale	0	Queen's Park	2

played at Hampden Park

Season 1874-75

1st Round

Oct 24	Clydesdale	0	Vale of Leven	0
Oct 17	Dumbarton	3	Arthurlie	0
Oct 24	Dumbreck	5	Alexandra A	1
Oct 17	Eastern	3	23rd Renfrew R	0
Oct 17	Helensburgh	3	3rd Edinburgh R	0
Oct 17	Kilmarnock	4	Vale of Leven R	0
Oct 24	Queen's Park	1	Western	0
	Rangers	2	Oxford	0
	Renton	*W*	Blythswood	*0*
	Rovers	*W*	Hamilton	*0*
Oct 17	T Lanark	0	Barrhead	0
	West End	3	Septar of Leven	0

Replays

	Clydesdale	*W*	Vale of Leven	*0*
Oct 24	T Lanark	1	Barrhead	0

2nd Round

	Clydesdale	2	Dumbreck	0
	Dumbarton	1	Rangers	0
Nov 21	Kilmarnock	0	Eastern	3
Nov 21	Queen's Park	7	West End	0
	Renton	2	Helensburgh	0
Nov 21	Standard	0	T Lanark	0

Replays

Nov 28	T Lanark	2	Standard	0

3rd Round

	Dumbarton	1	T Lanark	0
	Queen's Park	*W*	Rovers	*0*
Dec 26	Renton	1	Eastern	0

Semi-finals

Mar 20	Clydesdale	0	Queen's Park	0
Mar 27	Renton	1	Dumbarton	1

Replays

Mar 27	Queen's Park	2	Clydesdale	2
	Dumbarton	0	Renton	1
Apr 3	Clydesdale	0	Queen's Park	1

played at Kinning Park

Final

Apr 10	Queen's Park	3	Renton	0

played at Hampden Park

Season 1875-76

1st Round

Oct 9	Arthurlie	0	Levern	0
Oct 23	Caledonian	0	Western	0
Oct 16	Clydesdale	1	Eastern	0
	Drumpellier		Barrhead	
	Dumbarton	1	Lennox	0
	Dumbreck	*W*	Vale of Leven R	*0*
	Hamilton	1	Airdrie	0
Oct 9	Hearts		3rd Edinburgh	
	Helensburgh	1	Star of Leven	0
Oct 16	Kilbirnie	1	Ayr T	0
Oct 9	Kilmarnock	8	Ayr E	0
	Mauchline	*W*	Ardrossan	*0*
	Northern	4	Ramblers	0
Oct 16	Queen's Park	3	Alexandra A	0
	Rangers	7	1st Lanark R.v.	0
	Renton	1	Alclutha	0
	Renton T	*W*	Queen's Park J	*0*
	Rovers	*W*	Oxford	*0*
	Sandyford		23rd Renfrew Rv	
	St Andrew's	1	Telegraphists	0
Oct 16	Towerhill	2	Lancelot	0
	T Lanark	2	Havelock	0
	Vale of Leven	*W*	Vale of Leven R	*0*
	West End		Partick T	

Replays

Oct 16	Levern	4	Arthurlie	0
Oct 16	3rd Edinburgh R	0	Hearts	0
	Both Qualified			
Oct 23	Barrhead	0	Drumpellier	1
Oct 30	Western	3	Caledonian	0
	Partick T		West End	
	Both Qualified			
	23rd Renfrew Rv		Sandyford	
	Both Qualified			

2nd Round

Nov 13	3rd Edinburgh R	1	Edinburgh T	0
	Clydesdale	6	Kilmarnock	0
	Drumpellier	2	Hearts	0
	Dumbarton	2	Renton T	1
	Dumbreck	2	St Andrew's	0
	Helensburgh	1	23rd Renfrew Rv	0
Nov 6	Kilbirnie	0	Mauchline	0
Nov 13	Levern	3	Hamilton	0
	Partick T	2	Towerhill	0
Nov 6	Queen's Park	5	Northern	0
Nov 13	Rangers	1	T Lanark	2
	Rovers	6	West End	0
Nov 13	Vale of Leven	3	Renton	0
	Western	3	Sandyford	0

Replay

	Mauchline	*W*	Kilbirnie	*0*

3rd Round

Nov 27	Dumbarton	5	Drumpellier	1
Nov 27	Dumbreck	5	Partick T	0
Nov 27	Levern	0	T Lanark	3
Nov 27	Mauchline	0	Vale of Leven	6
	played at Victoria Park			
Nov 27	Queen's Park	2	Clydesdale	0
Nov 27	Rovers	4	3rd Edinburgh R	0
Nov 27	Western	2	Helensburgh	0

4th Round

Dec 18	Queen's Park	2	Dumbreck	0
Dec 18	T Lanark	5	Western	0
Dec 18	Vale of Leven	2	Rovers	0

Semi-finals

Jan 8	T Lanark	1	Dumbarton	1
Jan 8	Queen's Park	2	Vale of Leven	1

Replays

Jan 15	Dumbarton	1	T Lanark	1
	played at Alexandria			
	Dumbarton	0	T Lanark	3

Final

Mar 11	Queen's Park	1	T Lanark	1

played at Hamilton Cres

Replay

Mar 18	Queen's Park	2	T Lanark	0

played at Hamilton Cres

Season 1876-77

1st Round

Sep 30	1st Lanark R.v.	0	South Western	1
	23rd Rrv	2	Thornliebank	0
Sep 30	Arthurlie	3	Drumpellier	0
	Ayr T	1	Beith	0
Oct 7	Barrhead	4	Hamilton A	0
	Blythswood	2	Possilpark	1
	Busby	2	Renfrew	0
Sep 30	Caledonian	2	Standard	1
Oct 7	Clydesdale	6	Craig Park	0
	Crosshill	2	Hyde Park	1
Sep 30	Cumnock	1	Portland	2
Sep 30	Dumbarton	1	Renton	1
	Dumbreck	3	Dennistoun	1
	Dunfermline	*W*	Hearts	*0*
Sep 30	Eastern	1	Alexandria A	1
Sep 30	Edinburgh St A	1	Bonnybridge G	0
Sep 30	Edinburgh Swifts	2	Lenzie	1
Sep 30	Edinburgh T	5	Hanover	0
	Girvan	3	Dean	2
	Govan	*W*	Western	*0*
	Hamilton	2	Thornhill	0
Sep 23	Kilbirnie	5	Maybole Carrick	0
Sep 30	Lancefield	2	Parkgrove	0
	Lennox	3	Alclutha	0
Sep 30	Levern	0	Airdrie	1
	Mauchline	5	Winton	0
	Northern	12	Telegraphists	0
	Partick T	3	Havelock	1
	Queen of S'th	*W*	Ardrossan	*0*
Sep 30	Queen's Park	7	Sandyford	0
	Rangers	4	Queen's Park J	1
Sep 30	Renton T	0	Vale of Leven R	0
	St Andrew's	*W*	Ayr E	*0*
Sep 30	St Clements	1	3rd Edinburgh Rv	0
	Star of Leven	4	10th Dumbarton	0
	Stonelaw	3	Shotts	0
	Towerhill	2	Rovers	1
Sep 30	T Lanark	6	Ramblers	0
Sep 30	Vale of Leven	1	Helensburgh	0
	West End	2	4th Rrv	0

Replays

Oct 7	Alexandria A	1	Eastern	0
Oct 7	Renton	0	Dumbarton	2
Oct 7	Vale of Leven R	1	Renton T	1
	Both Qualified			

2nd Round

Oct 21	Barrhead	4	Airdrie	0
Oct 21	Clydesdale	0	T Lanark	0
	Dumbreck	2	South Western	0
Oct 21	Edinburgh Swifts	1	Edinburgh T	0
	Girvan	4	Dumfries	0
	Hamilton A	2	Dunfermline	1
Oct 21	Kilbirnie	0	Ayr T	1
	Lancefield	2	Crosshill	0
	Lennox	5	Renton T	1
	Mauchline	2	Kilmarnock	1
	Northern	4	Alexandria A	0
Oct 21	Partick T	5	Blythswood	1
Oct 21	Portland	2	Edinburgh St A	0
Oct 28	Queen's Park	7	Caledonian	0
Oct 21	Rangers	8	Towerhill	0
	St Clements	1	St Andrew's	1
	St Andrew's Scratched			
Oct 21	Star of Leven	0	Dumbarton	4
Oct 21	Stonelaw	0	Arthurlie	4

Oct 21	Vale of Leven	7	Vale of Leven R	0
	West End	1	Govan	0

Replay

Oct 28	T Lanark	4	Clydesdale	0

3rd Round

	Ayr T	1	Dumbreck	0
Nov 18	Edinburgh Swifts	1	West End	1
	West End Disqualified			
	Hamilton		Busby	
	Lancefield	3	Girvan	0
	Lennox	1	Dumbarton	0
Nov 11	Mauchline	7	Portland	0
	Northern	2	St Clements	1
Nov 18	Partick T	2	Barrhead	0
Nov 18	Queen's Park	7	Arthurlie	0
Nov 18	Vale of Leven	1	T Lanark	0

Replay

Nov 25	Busby	0	Hamilton	0
	Both Qualified			

4th Round

Dec 23	Ayr T	*W*	Partick T	*0*
	....Partick T Disqualified			
Dec 2	Lancefield	2	Hamilton	0
	Lennox	4	Edinburgh Swifts	0
Dec 2	Queen's Park	4	Northern	0
Dec 9	Rangers	3	Mauchline	0
Dec 2	Vale of Leven	4	Busby	0

5th Round

Dec 23	Lancefield	2	Ayr T	2
Dec 30	Queen's Park	1	Vale of Leven	2
	Rangers	3	Lennox	0

Replay

	Ayr T	1	Lancefield	0

Semi-finals

Jan 13	Ayr T	0	Vale of Leven	9
	played at Kinning Park			

Final

Mar 17	Rangers	1	Vale of Leven	1
	played at Hamilton Cres			

Replays

Apr 7	Rangers	1	Vale of Leven	1
	played at Hamilton Cres			
Apr 14	Rangers	2	Vale of Leven	3
	played at Hampden Park			

Season 1877-78

1st Round

Sep 29	10th Dumbarton	1	Star of Leven	0
	1st Lanark R.v.	1	Blythswood	0
	23rd Renfrew R	1	Levern	0
Sep 29	3rd Edinburgh R	0	Edinburgh Swifts	0
Sep 29	Alexandria	0	Milngavie	2
Sep 29	Alexandria A	2	Lancefield	0
	Arthurlie	3	Busby	0
	Ayr A	4	Vale of Calder	1
	Ayr T	*W*	St Andrew's	*0*
	Barrhead	7	Morton	0
	Beith	1	Catrine	0
	Blackfriars	*W*	Hyde Park	*0*
Sep 29	Clifton	2	Shaugraun	1
Sep 29	Clyde	0	T Lanark	1
Sep 29	Clydesdale	3	Dennistoun	0
	Derby	*W*	Dumbreck	*0*
Sep 29	Dumbarton	4	Waverly	0
	Glenkilloch	2	Wellington Park	0
	Govan	6	Albatross	0
Sep 29	Hanover	1	Edinburgh T	0
	Havelock	6	Craigpark	0
Sep 29	Hearts	0	Hibernian	0
Sep 22	Jordanhill	1	Queen's Park J	0
	Kelvinbank	3	Petershill	2
Sep 29	Kilbirnie	6	Dean	0
	Kilmarnock	5	Hurlford	1
	Kilmarnock C&FC	4	Maybole T	0
	Lennox	2	Helensburgh	0
	Lenzie	2	Ailsa	0
	Mauchline	6	Girvan	0
	Maybole C	3	Tarbolton	0
	Northern	3	Pollokshields A	0
Sep 22	Oxford	0	Sandyford	1
	Parkgrove	*W*	Winton	*0*
	Partick T	2	Union	0
Sep 29	Portland	1	Cumnock	0
Oct 6	Queen of S'th W	6	Stranraer	0
Sep 29	Queen's Park	1	Whiteinch	0
Sep 29	Ramblers	0	Stonefield	1
Oct 6	Rangers	13	Possilpark	0
	Renfrew	2	Pollokshaws	0
	Renton	*W*	Vale of Leven R	*0*
Oct 6	Renton T	2	Alclutha	0
	Rovers	0	John Elder	0
Oct 6	Shaftesbury	2	Roselyn	3
Sep 29	South Western	8	Our Boys	0
	St Clements	*W*	Dunfermline	*0*
	Strathclyde	5	West End	1
	Telegraphists	1	4th Rlv	0
	Thornliebank	1	Port Glasgow	0
	Vale of Leven	*W*	Kilmarnock T	*0*

Replays

Oct 6	Edinburgh Swifts	2	3rd Edinburgh R	1
Oct 6	Hibernian	2	Hearts	1
Oct 6	Rovers	2	John Elder	2
	Both Qualified			

2nd Round

	1st Lanark R	4	Telegraphists	0
Oct 20	Arthurlie 1	17	Renfrew R	0
	Ayr A	1	Kilmarnock	0
	Ayr T		Kilbirnie	
	Beith	1	Portland	0
Oct 27	Blackfriars	2	Rovers	2
	Caledonian	1	Rosslyn	0
Oct 20	Clydesdale	0	Queen's Park	2
	Glengowan	3	Stonelaw	1
	Govan	1	John Elder	0
	Grasshoppers	3	Clifton	0
Oct 20	Hanover	1	Hibernian	1
	Jordanhill	2	Lenzie	1
	Lennox	9	Milngavie	0
	Mauchline	1	Kilmarnock C&FC	0
	Maybole C	2	Queen of S'th W	0
	Parkgrove	2	Kelvinbank	1
Oct 20	Partick T	8	Strathclyde	1
Oct 27	Rangers	8	Alexandria A	0
	Renfrew	2	Glenkilloch	1
	Renton	3	10th Dumbarton	0
	Sandyford	2	Northern	1
Oct 20	South Western	2	Havelock	2
	St Clements	3	Dunmore	0
	Thornliebank	1	23rd Renfrew R	0
Oct 27	T Lanark	11	Derby	0
	Uddingston	3	Hamilton	0
Oct 27	Vale of Leven		Dumbarton	

Replays

Oct 27	Havelock	0	South Western	2
Oct 27	Hibernian	3	Hanover	0
Oct 27	Kilbirnie	3	Ayr T	1
Oct 27	Vale of Leven	4	Dumbarton	1
	Rovers	0	Blackfriars	0
	Both Qualified			

3rd Round

Nov 10	Arthurlie	0	Thornliebank	0
	Barrhead	2	Renfrew	1
	Barrhead Disqualified			
	Beith	3	Maybole C	0
Nov 10	Drumpellier	2	Glengowan	2
	Govan	5	Stonefield	2
Nov 10	Hibernian	2	Edinburgh Swifts	0
	Jordanhill	4	Grasshoppers	0
	Mauchline	3	Ayr A	1
	Parkgrove	3	Sandyford	2
	Partick T	3	Caledonian	0
	Rangers	13	Uddingston	0
Nov 17	Renton	2	Renton T	0
Nov 10	Rovers	1	Blackfriars	0
	South Western	4	1st Lanark Rv	0
Nov 10	T Lanark	1	Queen's Park	0
Nov 10	Vale of Leven	3	Lennox	0

Replay

Nov 17	Thornliebank	2	Arthurlie	0
	Glengowan		Drumpellier	
	Both Qualified			

4th Round

Dec 8	Barrhead	1	Partick T	0
	Barrhead Disqualified			
	Beith	*W*	St Clements	*0*
Dec 1	Kilbirnie	1	Mauchline	2
Dec 8	Parkgrove	3	Drumpellier	1
Dec 1	Rangers	0	Vale of Leven	0
Dec 8	Renton	4	Rovers	0
Dec 1	South Western	5	Glengowan	0
Dec 8	Thornliebank	1	Hibernian	2
Dec	A Draw			
Dec 1	T Lanark	7	Govan	0

Replays

Dec 8	Hibernian	2	Thornliebank	2
	Both Qualified			
Dec 15	Vale of Leven	5	Rangers	0

5th Round

Dec 29	Parkgrove	2	Partick T	1
Jan 5	Renfrew	0	Mauchline	2
Dec 29	Renton	2	Thornliebank	1
	South Western	3	Hibernian	1
	T Lanark	4	Beith	0
Dec 22	Vale of Leven	10	Jordanhill	0

6th Round

Jan 19	Renton	3	Mauchline	1
Jan 12	T Lanark	0	South Western	1
Jan 19	Vale of Leven	5	Parkgrove	0

Replay

Jan 19	South Western	1	T Lanark	2
	After Protest			

Semi-finals

Mar 9	Renton	1	T Lanark	1

Replay

Mar 16	T Lanark	1	Renton	0

Final

Mar 30	T Lanark	0	Vale of Leven	1
	played at Hampden Park			

Season 1878-79

1st Round

Sep 28	1st Lrv	0	Parkgrove	0
	3rd Edinburgh R	3	Brunswick	1
	Airdrie	7	Avondale	0
Sep 28	Alexandria	2	Renton T	2
	Alexandria A	3	Jordanhill	1
Oct 5	Annan	0	Queen of S'th W	3
Sep 28	Arbroath	3	Our Boys	0
	Arthurlie	4	Cartvale	1
	Ayr A	4	Cumnock	1
	Ayr T	2	Auchinleck	0
Sep 21	Barrhead	2	Wellington Park	0
	Beith	1	Hurlford	0
	Busby	3	Morton	1
Oct 5	Caledonian	0	South Western	2
	Catrine	*W*	Girvan	*0*
	Clyde	*W*	Blythswood	*0*
	Clydesdale	*W*	Dennistoun	*0*
	Cree R	*W*	Stranraer	*0*
Sep 28	Dumbarton	8	10th Dumbarton	1
	Edinburgh T	2	Hanover	1
	Falkirk	1	Campsie Glen	0
	Glengowan	4	Mount Vernon	3
	Govan	7	Ailsa	0
	Govanhill	*W*	Wellpark	*0*
	Hamilton A	3	Uddingston	1
Sep 28	Havelock	1	T Lanark	7
	Hearts	3	Swifts	1
	Helensburgh	4	Kilmarnock T	0
	Hibernian	5	Dunfermline	2
Sep 21	Jamestown	3	Lenzie	1
	John Elder	7	Blackfriars	0
	Kilbirnie	2	Kilmarnock	0
	Kilmarnock A		Lanemark	
Sep 28	Lenzie	3	Milngavie T	0
	Levern		23rd Rrv	
	Mauchline	*W*	Maybole C	*0*
	Maybole Ladywell	3	Tarbolton	0
	Oxford	0	Derby	0
	Partick T		Northern	
	Petershill	4	Albatross	2
	Portland	9	Dean	0
Sep 21	Possil Bluebell	8	19th Lrv	0
Sep 21	Queen's Park	8	Kelvinbank	0
Sep 28	Rangers	3	Shaftesbury	0
	Renfrew		17th Rrv	
	Renton	*W*	Star of Leven	*0*
	Rob Roy	1	Coupar Angus	0
Oct 5	Shotts	3	Drumpellier	0
	Stonefield	*W*	4th Rrv	*0*
	Stonelaw	4	East Kilbride	0
Oct 5	Strathblane	8	Grasshoppers	1
Sep 21	Thistle	2	Possilpark	0
	Thornliebank	3	Glenkilloch	0
Sep 28	Union	1	Rosslyn	0
Sep 28	Upp'r Clydesd'le	12	Newmains	0
	Vale of Leith	1	Clifton	0
Sep 21	Vale of Leven	6	Alclutha	0
Sep 28	Whitefield	10	Telegraphists	0
	Whiteinch	3	Pollokshields	3

Replays

Oct 5	Parkgrove	6	1st Lrv	2
Oct 5	Renton T	1	Alexandria	1
	Both Qualified			
Oct 5	17th Rrv	1	Renfrew	2
	Derby		Oxford	
	Both Qualified			
	Lanemark	0	Kilmarnock A	4
	Northern	0	Partick T	2
	Pollokshields	3	Whiteinch	3
	Both Qualified			
	23rd Rrv	0	Levern	1

2nd Round

	Alexandria A	3	Burnside	0
	Arbroath	*W*	St Clements	*0*
	Arthurlie	3	Busby	1
Oct 19	Barrhead	6	Port Glasgow	2
	Beith	3	Ayr T	1
	Catrine	3	Maybole Ladywell	1
	Derby	3	Whiteinch	1
Oct 26	Glengowan	2	Airdrie	0
	Both Disqualified			
Oct 12	Govan	2	Oxford	1
Oct 19	Hearts	1	Thistle	0
	Helensburgh	4	Alexandria	1

Oct 19 Hibernian 3 3rd Erv 0
Jamestown 7 Upper Clydesdale 0
John Elder 4 Stonefield 0
Oct 19 Kilbirnie 0 Kilmarnock A 2
Oct 19 Levern 1 Renfrew 2
Mauchline 5 Ayr A 1
Oct 19 Parkgrove 1 Union 0
Partick T 2 Possil Bluebell 1
Portland 4 Thornliebank 1
Queen of S'th W 3 Cree R 0
Oct 19 Queen's Park 6 Pollokshields A 0
Rangers 6 Whitefield 1
Oct 19 Renton 1 Dumbarton 6
Rob Roy 3 Vale of Teith 1
Oct 19 Shaugran 1 Lenzie 0
Oct 19 Shotts 1 Clarkston 1
Oct 19 South Western 5 Petershill 0
Stonelaw 2 Hamilton A 0
Oct 19 Strathblane 1 Falkirk 0
Thistle 4 Clyde 1
T Lanark 8 Wellpark 1
Oct 26 Vale of Leven 11 Renfrew T 0

Replays
Oct 26 South Western 8 Petershill 0
After Protest
Clarkston *W* Shotts *0*

3rd Round
Alexandria A 2 John Elder 0
Nov 9 Beith 7 Barrhead 1
Nov 9 Dumbarton 5 Strathblane 0
Nov 16 Edinburgh Univ 2 Hibernian 5
Govan 4 Derby 0
Nov 9 Hearts 2 Arbroath 1
Helensburgh 2 Shaugran 0
Kilmarnock A 5 Queen of S'th W 0
Mauchline 4 Arthurlie 1
Portland 3 Catrine 0
Queen's Park *W* Glasgow Univ *0*
Nov 9 Rangers 8 Parkgrove 2
Stonelaw 1 Clarkston 0
Thistle 2 Partick T 1
Thistle Disqualified
Nov 2 T Lanark 2 South Western 1
Nov 9 Vale of Leven 15 Jamestown 0

4th Round
Beith 9 Kilmarnock A 1
Nov 30 Helensburgh 2 Hearts 1
Hibernian 9 Rob Roy 0
Nov 30 Portland ... Dumbarton ...
Nov 30 Queen's Park 5 Mauchline 0
Nov 30 Rangers 3 Alexandria A 0
Nov 30 Renfrew 0 T Lanark 4
Stonelaw *W* Thistle *0*
Nov 30 Vale of Leven 11 Govan 1

Replays
Dec 7 Dumbarton 6 Portland 1

5th Round
Dumbarton 9 Stonelaw 1
Mar 8 Hibernian 1 Helensburgh 2
Mar 8 Queen's Park 5 T Lanark 0
Rangers 4 Partick T 0
Mar 8 Vale of Leven 6 Beith 1

6th Round
Mar 22 Queen's Park 0 Rangers 1
Mar 22 Vale of Leven 3 Dumbarton 1

Semi-finals
Mar 29 Helensburgh 0 Vale of Leven 3

Final
Apr 19 Rangers 1 Vale of Leven 1
played at Hampden Park

Rangers refused to replay
Cup awarded to Vale of Leven

SEASON 1879-80

1st Round
17th Renfrew Rv 4 Levern 1
19th Lanark Rv *W* Wellpark *0*
Ailsa *W* Burnside *0*
Airdrie 1 East Kilbride 0
Alexandria A 4 Albatross 0
Arbroath 5 Our Boys 1
Arthurlie 3 Busby 0
Atholl *W* Blythswood *0*
Sep 20 Ayr 0 Kilmarnock A 6
Sep 20 Barrhead 0 Renfrew 5
Sep 6 Beith ... Kilbirnie
Sep 20 Brunswick 5 Edinburgh Swifts 0
Cambuslang *W* Uddingston *0*
Sep 20 Campsie 3 King's Park 1
Sep 27 Campsie Glen 4 Milngavie T 1
Cartvale 5 Wellington Park 2
Sep 20 Clarkston 2 Stonelaw 1
Clyde *W* 1st Lanark Rv *0*
Sep 20 Cree R 0 Stranraer 2
Cumnock *W* Irvine *0*
Sep 6 Dumbarton 4 Vale of Leven 3
Sep 20 Dunfermline 2 Edinburgh T 0
Dunfermline 2 Thistle 0
Excelsior 2 Clydebank 1
Sep 20 Falkirk 4 Grasshoppers 2
Sep 20 Govan 2 Caledonian 1
Sep 20 Hamilton A 2 Glengowan 0
Harmonic *W* Stonefield *0*
Havelock *W* 4th Renfrew Rv *0*
Hearts *W* 3rd Erv *0*
Helensburgh 4 Alclutha 2
Sep 20 Hibernian 5 Hanover 1
Hurlsford 2 Catrine 0
Sep 20 Jamestown 2 Star of Leven 1
Later Disqualified
John Elder *W* Derby *0*
Johnstone A *W* Port Glasgow *0*
Jordanhill 2 Kelvinbank 1
Kennishead 2 Glenkilloch 1
Kilmarnock *W* Ayr A *0*
Ladywell 2 Auchinleck 0
Lennox *W* Renton T *0*
Mauchline 3 Dean 1
Maybole C *W* Girvan *0*
Netherlee ... Morton ...
Newmilns *W* Avondale *0*
Northern 3 Thistle 0
Parkgrove *W* Clydesdale *0*
Sep 27 Partick T 2 Petershill 0
Pollokshields A 4 Oxford 0
Portland *W* Lanemark *0*
Possil Bluebell *W* Telegraphists *0*
Possilpark ... City ...
Queen of S'th W *W* Annan *0*
Sep 20 Rangers 0 Queen's Park 4
Renfrew R *W* 23rd Renfrew Rv *0*
Sep 20 Renton 2 Kilmarnock T 2
Rob Roy 2 Coupar Angus 1
Rosslyn *W* Blackfriars *0*
Sep 27 Shotts 2 Drumpellier 1
South Western *W* Whiteinch *0*
Strathblane 1 Lenzie 0
Sep 20 Thornliebank 4 Yoker 0
T Lanark *W* Union *0*
Upper Clyd'dale *W* Mount Vernon *0*
Vale of Teith *W* Clifton *0*
Sep 27 Whitefield 7 Govanhill 0

Replays
Sep 27 Kilnbirnie 2 Beith 2
Both Qualified
Sep 27 Kilmarnock T 0 Renton 3
Sep 27 Queen's Park 5 Rangers 1
Oct 4 Campsie Glen 4 Milngavie 0
After Protest
Morton 7 Netherlee 4
Possilpark 3 City 1

2nd Round
Oct 18 Ailsa 3 Rosslyn 1
Oct 11 Alexandria A 5 Harmonic 0
Oct 11 Arthurlie 8 Morton 3
Oct 11 Barrhead R 2 Renfrew R 1
Cambuslang 4 Airdrie 1
Oct 11 Campsie 0 Campsie Glen 4
Clyde 2 Govan 1
Cumnock *W* Tarbolton *0*
Oct 11 Dumbarton 7 Helensburgh 0
Excelsior 2 Bellshill 1
Hamilton A 3 Upper Clydesdale 0
Hearts 2 Brunswick 1
Oct 11 Hibernian 4 Dunfermline 0
Oct 11 Johnstone A 6 Cartvale 0
Oct 25 Jordanhill 1 John Elder 2
Kennishead 5 Cartvale 0
Oct 18 Kilmarnock A 0 Kilbirnie 1
Oct 11 Kirkintilloch 0 Jamestown 1
Later Disqualified
Kirkintilloch A 5 Star of Leven 2
Ladywell 6 Stewarton 1
Mauchline 6 Kilmarnock 2
Oct 11 Maybole C 1 Hurlford 8
Oct 11 Northern 3 Whitefield 1
Partick T 3 Havelock 1
Plains Bluebell 2 Newmilns 0
Pollokshields A 5 Dennistown 1
Portland 2 Beith 1
Possilpark 4 High School 1
Queen of South 6 Stranraer 0
Oct 11 Queen's Park 14 19th Lrv 1
Renton ... Lennox ...
Rob Roy 3 Vale of Teith 0
Oct 11 Shotts 0 Clarkston 2
Oct 11 South Western 9 Atholl 0
Oct 11 Strathblane 1 Falkirk 0
Strathmore *W* St Clements *0*
Oct 11 Thornliebank 6 17th Rrv 1
Oct 11 T Lanark 0 Possil Bluebell 0

Replays
Lennox ... Renton ...
Both Qualified
T Lanark 1 Possil Bluebell 0

3rd Round
Arbroath 6 Strathmore 1
Nov 1 Arthurlie 1 Renfrew 2
Cambuslang 4 Clarkston 2
Clyde 6 Ailsa 1
Nov 1 Dumbarton 5 Renton 0
Nov 8 Hamilton A 7 Excelsior 1
Nov 15 Hibernian 2 Hearts 1
Hurlford 1 Cumnock 0
Nov 1 Jamestown 5 Lennox 1
Jamestown Disqualified
Nov 1 Johnstone A 3 Kennishead 1
Kilbirnie *W* Ladywell *0*
Kirkintilloch 6 Lennox 2
Lennox Reinstated
Nov 1 Mauchline 0 Portland 0
Nov 1 Parkgrove 6 Alexandria A 2
Plains Bluebell *W* Queen of S'th W *0*
Nov 1 Pollokshields A 2 Northern 1
Nov 1 Queen's Park 5 Partick T 1
Nov 8 Rob Roy 1 Edinburgh Univ 1
Nov 1 South Western 2 John Elder 1
Strathblane 2 Campsie Glen 1
Nov 1 Thornliebank 1 Barrhead R 0
Nov 8 T Lanark 1 Glasgow Univ 1

Replays
Nov 8 Portland 0 Mauchline 1
Nov 15 T Lanark 6 Glasgow Univ 0
Edinburgh Univ ... Rob Roy ...

4th Round
Cambuslang 3 Plains Bluebell 0
Nov 22 Dumbarton 11 Clyde 0
Nov 22 Hibernian 2 Parkgrove 2
Nov 29 Hurlford 1 Kilbirnie 1
Both Qualified
Nov 22 Johnstone A 2 Rob Roy 4
Mauchline 2 Hamilton A 0
Nov 22 Queen's Park 10 Strathblane 1
Nov 22 Renfrew 1 Pollokshields A 2
Nov 22 South Western 4 Arbroath 0
Nov 22 Thornliebank 12 Possilpark 0
Nov 29 T Lanark 5 Kirkintilloch A 1

Replays
Parkgrove 2 Hibernian 2
Both Qualified

5th Round
Dec 20 Dumbarton 6 Kilbirnie 2
Dec 20 Mauchline 0 Hibernian 2
Pollokshields A 4 Cambuslang 0
Dec 20 Queen's Park 15 Hurlford 1
Dec 20 South Western 1 Parkgrove 1
Dec 20 Thornliebank 12 Rob Roy 0

Replay
Dec 27 South Western 3 Parkgrove 2

6th Round
Jan 3 Dumbarton 6 Hibernian 2
Pollokshields A 6 South Western 1
Jan 3 Thornliebank 1 T Lanark 1

Replay
Jan 10 T Lanark 1 Thornliebank 2

Semi-finals
Jan 17 Queen's Park 1 Dumbarton 0
Jan 17 Thornliebank 2 Pollokshields A 1

Final
Feb 21 Queen's Park 3 Thornliebank 0
played at Cathkin Park

SEASON 1880-81

1st Round
17th Rrv 6 Wellington Park 1
5th KRV *W* Cree R *0*
Sep 18 Abercorn 7 Barrhead 1
Airdrie 2 Bellshill 0
Airdriehill *W* Airdrie Bluebell *0*
Sep 18 Alexandria A 4 Kelvinbank 1
Arbroath *W* Vale of Teith *0*
Sep 4 Arthurlie 2 Johnstone 0
Atholl *W* Whitefield *0*
After Protest
Sep 18 Auchinleck 1 Cumnock 7
Ayr 2 Catrine 0
Sep 11 Beith 4 Irvine 1
Sep 18 Caledonian 1 Clyde 2
Cambuslang *W* Upper Clydesdale *0*
Campsie 2 Grasshoppers 1
Sep 18 Cartside 6 Kennishead 2
Cartvale *W* Levern *0*
Central 2 Bridge of Allan 0
City *W* 19th Lanark Rv *0*
Sep 4 Clarkston 1 Plains Bluebell 0
Sep 18 Coupar Angus 4 Strathmore Dun 1
Cowlairs 4 Petershill 3
Sep 11 Dumbarton 7 Victoria 0
Sep 18 Dunfermline 5 Hanover 3
Dunkeld *W* St Clements *0*

Sep 11	Excelsior	3	Drumpellier	0
	Falkirk	*W*	Campsie A	*0*
	Hamilton A	*W*	Stonelaw	*0*
	Harmonic	*W*	Ailsa	*0*
Sep 11	Hearts	3	Brunswick	1
	Helensburgh	*W*	Lennox	*0*
	After Protest			
	Hurlford	*W*	Ayr T	*0*
Sep 11	Jamestown	6	Alclutha	0
	Jordanhill	1	Windsor	0
Sep 18	Kilbirnie	3	Lanemark	0
	Kilmarnock	*W*	Stewarton	*0*
	Kilmarnock A	*W*	Girvan	*0*
	King's Park	1	Strathblane	0
	Larkhall	5	Uddingston	0
	Lenzie	*W*	Thistle	*0*
	Mauchline	*W*	Dean	*0*
	Maybole	*W*	Rankinston	*0*
	After Protest			
	Morton	3	Glenkilloch	2
	Netherlee	*W*	Oakfield	*0*
Sep 11	Northern	3	T Lanark	1
Sep 11	Oxford	6	Maxwell	0
	Partick T	*W*	Dennistoun	*0*
Sep 18	Pilgrims	4	Lancefield	2
Sep 4	Pollok	5	Johnstone R	0
Sep 11	Pollokshields A	0	Partick T	4
	Portland	8	Coylton Coila	0
	Possilpark	*W*	High School	*0*
Sep 11	Queen's Park	7	John Elder	0
Sep 11	Rangers	4	Govan	1
Sep 4	Renfrew	1	Abercorn	5
	Renton	*W*	Kilmarnock T	*0*
	Rob Roy	2	Our Boys	1
	Shawlands	*W*	Clydesdale	*0*
Sep 11	Shotts	4	T Lanark	0
Sep 11	South Western	7	Ingram	0
Sep 4	St Mirren	3	Johnstone A	0
Sep 18	Star of Leven	3	Kirkintilloch A	2
Sep 11	Stranraer	3	Queen of S'th W	0
	Thistle	5	Tollcross	0
Sep 18	Thornliebank	3	Renfrew	0
	Yoker	*W*	Renfrew R	*0*

2nd Round

	5th KRV	4	Stranraer	3
Oct 2	Abercorn	4	Morton	2
Oct 2	Airdrie	3	Excelsior	2
Oct 2	Alexandria A	1	Atholl	0
Oct 2	Arthurlie	1	Cartvale	1
	Cambuslang	3	Hamilton A	1
Oct 2	Campsie C	5	Campsie	5
Oct 2	Clarkston	2	Airdriehill	1
Oct 2	Coupar Angus	1	Arbroath	2
Oct 9	Cowlairs	4	Oxford	3
Oct 2	Dumbarton	2	Jamestown	1
Oct 2	Falkirk	2	King's Park	1
	Glengowan	1	Thistle	1
Oct 2	Harmonic	1	Clyde	1
Oct 2	Helensburgh	5	Star of Leven	1
Oct 9	Hibernian	3	Dunfermline	1
	Hurlford	2	Cumnock	1
Oct 16	Kilbirnie	2	Kilmarnock A	1
Oct 9	Kilmarnock	6	Ayr	3
	Larkhall	1	Shotts	0
	Mauchline	6	Maybole	1
Oct 2	Netherlee	0	Yoker	2
	Partick T	1	Jordanhill	0
Oct 9	Pilgrims	7	City	0
Oct 2	Portland	0	Beith	1
Oct 2	Queen's Park	5	Possilpark	0
	Rangers	1	Northern	0
Oct 9	Renton	0	Vale of Leven	1
	Rob Roy	4	Dunkeld	0
	Shawlands A	*W*	Possil Bluebell	*0*
Oct 9	South Western	2	Partick T	0
Oct 2	St Mirren	3	17th Rrv	2
Oct 2	Thornliebank	0	Pollok	3

Replays

Oct 9	Cartvale	1	Arthurlie	2
Oct 9	Clyde	1	Harmonic	0
Oct 9	Campsie	1	Campsie C	3
	Thistle	6	Glengowan	1

3rd Round

Oct 23	Abercorn	1	St Mirren	4
Nov 6	Alexandria A	1	Cowlairs	2
	Arbroath	2	Rob Roy	1
Oct 23	Arthurlie	2	Pollok	0
Oct 23	Beith	17	5th KRV	2
Oct 30	Cartside	4	Yoker	3
	Central	6	Lenzie	1
Oct 23	Clyde	3	Shawlands A	0
	Dumbarton	7	Falkirk	1
Oct 23	Hearts	5	Hibernian	3
Oct 23	Helensburgh	1	Vale of Leven	4
Oct 30	Kilbirnie	0	Hurlford	2
Oct 23	Larkhall	0	Cambuslang	5
	Mauchline	*W*	Kilmarnock	*0*
	After Protest			
Oct 23	Queen's Park	8	Pilgrims	1
Oct 23	Rangers	3	Partick T	0
	Thistle	*W*	Airdrie	*0*

4th Round

Nov 13	Arthurlie	4	South Western	3
Nov 20	Cartside	1	Hurlford	3
Nov 13	Dumbarton	9	Glasgow Univ	0
Nov 13	Edinburgh Univ	0	Campsie C	1
Nov 13	Hearts	3	Cambuslang	0
	Mauchline	*W*	Clarkston	*0*
	After Protest			
Nov 13	Queen's Park	11	Beith	2
Nov 13	Rangers	11	Clyde	0
Nov 13	St Mirren	1	Cowlairs	0
	Vale of Leven	*W*	Arbroath	*0*

Replays

Nov 27	Arthurlie	1	South Western	1
	Tie to Arthurlie			

5th Round

Dec 11	Arthurlie	4	Hearts	0
	Hurlford	0	Rangers	3
Dec 11	Queen's Park	2	Mauchline	0
Dec 4	St Mirren	1	Dumbarton	5
Dec 4	Vale of Leven	7	Thistle	1

6th Round

Dec 25	Arthurlie	0	Vale of Leven	2
Dec 25	Rangers	1	Dumbarton	3
	Queen's Park	10	Campsie C	0

Semi-Final

Feb 5	Dumbarton	2	Vale of Leven	0
	played at Alexandria			

Final

Mar 26	Dumbarton	1	Queen's Park	2
	played at Kinning Park			
	Replay Ordered			

Replay

Apr 9	Dumbarton	1	Queen's Park	3
	played at Kinning Park			

SEASON 1881-82

1st Round

Sep 17	1st Lrv	0	Cowlairs	7
Sep 10	5th KRV		Moffat	
Sep 10	Abercorn	3	Arthurlie	3
	Airdrie	*W*	Tollcross	*0*
	Airdriehill	*W*	Bellshill	*0*
	Alexandria A	*W*	Possil Bluebell	*0*
	Auchinleck	*W*	Dean	*0*
Sep 10	Barrhead	0	Glenkilloch	2
Sep 10	Battlefield	1	Northern	3
	Beith	*W*	Coylton	*0*
Sep 10	Blairgowrie	0	Coupar Angus	4
Sep 17	Bridge of Allan	1	Thistle A	1
Sep 10	Cambuslang	5	Royal Albert	0
Sep 17	Cartvale	4	Renfrew	2
	Clarkston	*W*	T Lanark	*0*
	Clyde	*W*	Clydesdale	*0*
	Cumnock	1	Mauchline	1
Sep 10	Dumbarton	9	Alclutha	1
	Eastern A	*W*	Anfield	*0*
Sep 10	Falkirk	5	King's Park	0
	Grasshoppers	*W*	Campsie C	*0*
Sep 10	Hamilton A	1	Plains Bluebell	0
Sep 10	Hanover	1	Brunswick	2
	played at Tynecastle			
	Harmonic	*W*	Govan	*0*
	Hibernian	7	Addiewell	0
	Hurlford	*W*	Irvine	*0*
	Jamestown	*W*	Renton	*0*
	John Elder	*W*	Shawlands A	*0*
Sep 10	Johnstone	9	Greenock S	1
Sep 10	Kilbarchan	8	Ladyburn	1
	Kilbirnie	*W*	Catrine	*0*
	Kilmarnock	6	Largs A	0
Sep 10	Kilmarnock	2	Helensburgh	6
	Kilmarnock A	7	Ayr	1
	Kinning Park A	*W*	Kelvinbank	*0*
	Lenzie	*W*	Campsie A	*0*
Sep 10	Levern	4	Morton	2
Sep 10	Lugar Boswell	3	Lanemark	0
Sep 17	Maybole	7	Rankinston	0
Sep 10	Mousbank	1	Partick T	3
	Our Boys	2	Arbroath	1
Sep 17	Paisley A	6	Port Glasgow A	1
Sep 17	Partick T	5	Possilpark	1
	Pilgrims	*W*	Oxford	*0*
	Pollok	*W*	Cartside	*0*
Sep 10	Pollokshields A	1	Petershill	3
	Portland	10	Stewarton	0
Sep 17	Queen's Park	14	Caledonian	0
Sep 10	Rangers	2	T Lanark	1
	Rob Roy	*W*	Dunkeld	*0*
Sep 10	Shotts	5	Drumpellier	1
	South Western	*W*	Jordanhill	*0*
Sep 10	Southfield	0	Campsie	3
Sep 10	St Bernard's	1	Hearts	0
Sep 3	St Mirren	5	Johnstone R	1
	Star of Leven	*W*	Kirkintilloch	*0*
	Stranraer	*W*	Cree R	*0*
	Strathblane	7	Dunipace	0
	Strathmore	*W*	St Clements	*0*
	Thistle	*W*	Stonelaw	*0*
Sep 10	Thornliebank	5	Johnstone A	0
	Uddingston	*W*	Upper Clydesdale	*0*
	Vale of Leven	*W*	Lennox	*0*
	Vale of Teith	*W*	Aberfeldy	*0*
	Wellington Park	4	Netherlee	1
	West Benhar	4	Glengowan	2
Sep 17	West Calder	5	Kinleith	1
	Whitefield	*W*	Windsor	*0*
	Yoker	*W*	Kennishead	*0*

Replays

Sep 17	Arthurlie	4	Abercorn	0
Sep 17	Moffat	0	5th KRV	1
Sep 24	Thistle A		Bridge of Allan	
	Mauchline	5	Cumnock	1
Oct 1	Thistle A	8	Bridge of Allan	0

2nd Round

Oct 1	Airdrie	1	Airdriehill	1
Oct 1	Alexandria A	4	Whitefield	1
Oct 1	Arthurlie	3	Pollok	1
Oct 1	Beith	3	Hurlford	3
Oct 1	Cambuslang	6	Airdrie	2
Oct 15	Campsie	2	Lenzie	0
	Clyde	*W*	John Elder	*0*
Oct 8	Cowlairs	2	Queen's Park	2
	Glenkilloch	2	Yoker	0
Oct 8	Grasshoppers	0	Falkirk	5
	Helensburgh	*W*	Victoria	*0*
Oct 8	Hibernian	2	St Bernard's	1
Oct 8	Jamestown	5	Star of Leven	0
	Kilmarnock	7	Auchinleck	1
	Kilmarnock A	5	Maybole	0
Oct 1	Levern	3	Thornliebank	4
Oct 8	Lugar Boswell	3	Annbank	1
Oct 8	Mauchline		Portland	
Oct 1	Northern	9	Luton	1
Oct 15	Our Boys	5	Dundee H	3
Oct 8	Paisley A	3	St Mirren	1
	Partick FC	3	Kinning Park	0
Oct 1	Partick T	3	Pilgrims	1
	Queen of S'th	*W*	25th KRV	1
	Rangers	*W*	Harmonic	*0*
Oct 1	Rob Roy	3	Coupar Angus	1
Oct 8	Shotts	2	Hamilton A	1
	South Western	*W*	Eastern A	*0*
Oct 1	Thistle	10	Uddingston	0
	Thistle	3	Strathblane	2
Oct 1	Vale of Leven	0	Dumbarton	2
	Vale of Teith	6	Dunblane	2
Oct 8	Wellington Park	3	Kilbarchan	4
Oct 1	West Benhar	2	Clarkston	0
	West Calder	*W*	Dunfermline	*0*

Replays

Oct 8	Hurlford	4	Beith	4
	Both Qualified			
Oct 15	Partick T	7	Pilgrims	1
	After Protest			
Oct 15	Portland	1	Mauchline	5
Oct 15	Queen's Park	9	Cowlairs	0
	Airdrie	3	Airdriehill	2

3rd Round

Oct 29	Airdrie	4	Shotts	4
Oct 29	Arthurlie	7	Paisley A	1
	Cambuslang		West Benhar	
Oct 22	Dumbarton	5	Jamestown	0
Oct 29	Glenkilloch	0	Catvale	3
Oct 29	Kilbarchan	1	Johnstone	1
	Kilmarnock	2	Kilbirnie	0
Oct 22	Lugar Boswell	0	Beith	1
Oct 22	Mauchline	0	Hurlford	0
Oct 22	Northern	1	Clyde	2
Oct 22	Partick FC	1	South Western	2
Oct 22	Petershill	2	Partick T	2
Oct 22	Rangers	3	Alexandria A	1
	Stranraer	4	Queen of S'th W	1
Oct 29	Strathmore	1	Our Boys	4
Oct 22	Thistle	0	Falkirk	2
	Vale of Teith	6	Rob Roy	1
Oct 22	West Calder	4	Brunswick	1

Replays

Oct 29	Mauchline	2	Hurlford	0
Oct 29	Partick T	2	Petershill	0
Nov 5	Kilbarchan	2	Johnstone	2
Nov 5	Shotts	5	Airdrie	0
Nov 5	South Western	1	Partick T	0
Nov 5	West Benhar	3	Cambuslang	2
	After Protest			
Nov 5	Partick T	3	Petershill	2
	After Protest			
Nov 12	Johnstone	3	Kilbarchan	0

4th Round

	Cartvale	5	Glasgow Univ	4
Nov 12	Edinburgh Univ	2	Clyde	3
Nov 12	Falkirk	3	Campsie	1
Nov 12	Helensburgh	1	Arthurlie	1
	Kilmarnock	9	Our Boys	2
	Kilmarnock A	3	Mauchline	2
Nov 19	Queen's Park	3	Johnstone	2
Nov 12	Thistle	0	Partick T	1
Nov 12	Thornliebank	0	Rangers	2
Nov 19	West Benhar	4	Hibernian	4
	West Calder	*W*	Stranraer	*0*

Replays

Nov 19	Arthurlie	1	Helensburgh	0
Nov 26	Hibernian	8	West Benmar	0

5th Round

Dec 10	Arthurlie	4	Kilmarnock	1
Dec 3	Clyde	4	Cartvale	5
Dec 3	Hibernian	2	Dumbarton	6
Dec 3	Kilmarnock A	2	Beith	0
Dec 3	Queen's Park	10	Partick T	0
Dec 3	South Western	1	Rangers	2
Dec 3	Vale of Teith	0	Shotts	5
Dec 10	West Calder	4	Falkirk	2

Replays
Dec 24 Hibernian 2 Dumbarton 6
After Protest
Dec 24 Rangers 4 South Western 0
After Protest

6th Round
Jan 28 Dumbarton 2 Rangers 1
Jan 14 Kilmarnock A 5 Arthurlie 1
Jan 7 Queen's Park 15 Shotts 0
Dec 31 West Calder 3 Cartvale 5

Replay
Feb 4 Dumbarton 5 Rangers 1
After Protest

Semi-finals
Feb 18 Dumbarton 11 Cartvale 2
Feb 18 Kilmarnock A 2 Queen's Park 3

Final
Mar 18 Dumbarton 2 Queen's Park 2
played at Cathkin Park

Replay
Apr 1 Dumbarton 1 Queen's Park 4
played at Cathkin Park

Season 1882-83

1st Round
1st Dumfries Rv *W* Dumfries A *0*
Sep 16 1st Lrv 0 Northern 4
Sep 16 5th KRV 8 Thornhill 0
Sep 9 Abercorn 10 Ladyburn 1
Addiewell *W* Dunfermline *0*
Sep 9 Airdrie 5 Plains Bluebell 1
Sep 16 Airdriehill 0 Shotts 7
Sep 9 Airdrieonians 3 Royal Albert 3
Sep 9 Angus 1 Balgay 2
Annbank 7 Langs A 0
Arbroath 4 East End 3
Sep 9 Arthurlie 7 Bute R 0
Ayr 5 Stewarton 3
Sep 9 Battlefield 2 Partick T 4
Sep 9 Beith 4 Beith T 2
Clarkston Drumpellier
Sep 9 Clippens 2 Glenpatrick 4
Sep 9 Clyde 4 Luton 0
Sep 16 Coupar Angus 1 Dunblane 3
Sep 9 Cowlairs 4 Whitefield 1
Dumbarton *W* Kilmarnock T *0*
Dundee H 7 Perseverance 2
Sep 16 Dunipace 1 Falkirk 5
Sep 16 Hamilton A 0 Cambuslang 5
Sep 9 Hearts 1 St Bernard's 1
Hibernian 8 Brunswick 0
Sep 9 Jamestown 7 Vale of Leven 1
Sep 9 Johnstone 6 Paisley A 2
Sep 16 Johnstone A 0 Cartvale 4
Sep 9 Jordanhill 0 Rangers 4
Kilmarnock 2 Mauchline 0
Kilmarnock A 2 Cumnock 1
Sep 9 Lugar Boswell 4 Kilbirnie 1
Mavisbank 3 Granton 1
Maybole *W* Rankinstone *0*
Milngavie 2 E Stirling 1
Sep 16 Moffat 9 Dumfries R 0
Morton 2 Johnstone R 1
Our Boys 2 Dundee H 1
Sep 16 Partick T 5 Petershill 0
Sep 16 Pollok 3 Renfrew 2
Sep 9 Pollokshields A 6 Alexandria A 5
Port Glasgow A 3 Lochwinnoch 2
Sep 9 Portland 1 Hurlford 1
Sep 9 Possilpark 0 Pilgrims 6
Sep 9 Queen's Park 12 Thistle 1
Renton 3 Alclutha 1
Sep 9 South Western 0 T Lanark 3
Southfield *W* Aberfeldy *0*
Sep 9 St Mirren 8 Yoker 0
Strathblane 1 Lenzie 0
Sep 16 Thornliebank 7 Southern 1
Sep 16 Vale of Atholl 0 Vale of Teith 1
West Benhar 2 Belshill 1
West Calder *W* Kinleith *0*
West End 1 Strathmore 1
Winshaw 2 Holytown 0
Sep 9 Woodland 1 John Maxwell 1
Sep 16 Woodside 0 Kilbarchan 6

Replays
Sep 16 Hurlford 3 Portland 2
Sep 16 Royal Albert 3 Airdrieonians 3
Sep 16 John Maxwell 5 Woodford 3
Sep 16 St Bernard's 3 Hearts 4
Sep 23 Coupar Angus 1 Dumblane 6
After Protest
Sep 23 Drumpellier 2 Clarkston 5
Airdrieonians Royal Albert
Strathmore West End

2nd Round
Sep 30 5th KRV 5 Moffat 3
Sep 30 Abercorn 2 Pollok 2
Oct 7 Addiewell 0 Hearts 14
Airdrie 1 Wishaw 2
Cambuslang 3 Airdrieonians 1
Sep 30 Cartvale 2 Arthurlie 1
Sep 30 Cowlairs 13 Apsley 0
Sep 30 Dumbarton 8 King's Park 1
Dunblane 3 Arbroath 1
Dundee H 3 Aberdeen 1
Oct 7 Jamestown 12 Strathblane 1
Sep 30 John Maxwell 5 Port Glasgow A 3
Sep 30 Kilbarchan 0 Johnstone 7
Sep 30 Kilmarnock 2 Hurlford 6
Kilmarnock A 5 Annbank 4
Sep 30 Lugar Boswell 6 Beith 1
Maybole 6 Ayr 3
Sep 30 Morton 1 St Mirren 5
Sep 30 Northern 0 Pollokshields A 0
Our Boys 5 Balgay 3
Sep 30 Partick T 2 Pilgrims 1
Sep 30 Partick T 14 Mavisbank 2
Oct 7 Queen of S'th W 5 1st Dumfries Rv 3
Sep 30 Queen's Park 3 Rangers 2
Sep 30 Royal Albert 3 Clarkston 5
Sep 30 Southfield 1 Renton 14
Sep 30 Thornliebank 7 Glenpatrick 0
Sep 30 T Lanark 2 Clyde 0
Sep 30 Vale of Leven 16 Milngavie 0
Oct 7 West Banhar 10 Shotts 1
Oct 7 West Calder 2 Hibernian 3
Sep 30 West End 1 Vale of Teith 5

Replays
Oct 7 Cartvale 1 Arthurlie 3
After Protest
Oct 7 Pollok 2 Abercorn 2
Both Qualified
Oct 7 John Maxwell 2 Port Glasgow A 6
After Protest
Oct 7 T Lanark 3 Clyde 0
After Protest
Pollokshields A 4 Northern 0

3rd Round
Oct 28 Abercorn 8 Maybole 0
Oct 28 Arthurlie 0 Thornliebank 0
Oct 21 Cambuslang 3 Partick T 3
Oct 21 Dumbarton 8 Jamestown 1
Dunblane 5 Dundee H 0
Oct 21 Falkirk 1 Renton 1
Oct 28 Johnstone 2 Morton 1
Oct 21 Lugar Boswell 6 Pollok 0
Oct 21 Partick T 4 Cowlairs 0
Oct 21 Pollokshields A 3 West Benhar 0
Oct 28 Port Glasgow A 2 Kilmarnock A 5
Oct 28 Queen of S'th W 3 5th KRV 2
Oct 21 Queen's Park 13 Clarkston 0
Oct 21 T Lanark 3 Airdrie 0
Oct 21 Vale of Leven 8 Hearts 1
Oct 28 Vale of Teith 6 Our Boys 4

Replays
Oct 28 Partick T 3 Cambuslang 3
Both Qualified
Oct 28 Renton 4 Falkirk 1
Nov 4 Thornliebank 0 Arthurlie 0
Both Qualified

4th Round
Nov 18 Arthurlie 3 Queen of S'th W 1
Nov 11 Dunblane 1 T Lanark 7
Nov 11 Hibernian 2 Partick T 2
Nov 11 Johnstone 1 Pollokshields A 3
Nov 11 Kilmarnock A 5 Abercorn 2
Partick T *W* Glasgow Univ *0*
Nov 11 Queen's Park 5 Cambuslang 0
Nov 11 Renton 3 Lugar Boswell 5
Nov 11 Thornliebank 0 Dumbarton 3
Vale of Leven 2 Edinburgh Univ 0
Nov 11 Vale of Teith 2 Hurlford 3

Replays
Nov 18 Partick T 1 Hibernian 4

5th Round
Dec 2 Hibernian 3 Arthurlie 4
Abandoned Bad Light
Dec 2 Lugar Boswell 1 Vale of Leven 1
Dec 23 Queen's Park 7 Hurlford 2

Replays
Dec 23 Arthurlie 6 Hibernian 0
Dec 23 Vale of Leven 5 Lugar Boswell 1

6th Round
Dec 30 Arthurlie 1 Kilmarnock A 1
Feb 3 Dumbarton 3 Queen's Park 1
Feb 10 Partick T 0 Vale of Leven 4
Dec 23 T Lanark 1 Pollokshields A 1

Replay
Feb 3 Kilmarnock A 1 Arthurlie 2
Feb 3 Pollokshields A 5 T Lanark 2
Feb 10 Arthurlie 1 Kilmarnock A 1
After Protest
Feb 17 Arthurlie 0 Kilmarnock A 1
played at Cathkin Park

Semi-finals
Feb 24 Pollokshields A 0 Dumbarton 1
Feb 24 Vale of Leven 1 Kilmarnock A 1

Replays
Mar 17 Dumbarton 5 Pollokshields A 0
After Protest
Mar 17 Kilmarnock A 0 Vale of Leven 2

Final
Mar 31 Dumbarton 2 Vale of Leven 2
played at Hampden Park

Replay
Apr 7 Dumbarton 2 Vale of Leven 1
played at Hampden Park

Season 1883-84

1st Round
Sep 8 Abercorn 7 Levern 0
Sep 8 Airdrie 1 Tollcross 0
Sep 8 Alloa 0 Falkirk 5
Sep 8 Arbroath 2 Aberdeen 2
Sep 8 Arthurlie 3 Pollok 0
Sep 8 Balgay 2 Strathmore Arb 2
Sep 8 Battlefield 8 South Western 1
Sep 8 Benhar 2 Drumpellier 2
Bute R *W* Glenpatrick *0*
Sep 8 Cambuslang 8 Belshill 0
Sep 8 Cartvale 8 West End A 0
Clarkston *W* Plains Bluebell *0*
Sep 8 Clippens 3 Johnstone A 2
Sep 8 Dumbritton 1 Vale of Leven W 1
Sep 8 Dunblane 2 Vale of Teith 1
Sep 8 Dundee H 9 Angus 0
Sep 15 Dunfermline 1 St Bernard's 13
Sep 8 Dunipace 2 Campsie 1
East End R *W* Newton Stewart *0*
Sep 8 E Stirling 3 Tayavalla 0
Sep 8 Granton 3 Glencairn 1
Sep 8 Hamilton A 4 Airdrieonians 1
Sep 8 Hearts 8 Brunswick 0
Sep 8 Hibernian 5 West Calder 0
Hurlford *W* Beith T *0*
Jamestown *W* Kilmarnock T *0*
Sep 8 Johnstone 3 Thornliebank 4
Sep 8 Kilbarchan 3 Paisley A 4
Kilmarnock *W* Kilbirnie *0*
Kilmarnock A *W* Beith *0*
Sep 15 King's Park 11 Lenzie 0
Sep 8 Kinleith 1 Edina 2
Sep 8 Linwood 1 Woodland 4
Sep 8 Lugar Boswell 3 Ayr 1
Sep 8 Lyle A 2 Johnstone R 4
Sep 8 Mauchline 3 Annbank 1
Sep 8 Mavisbank 2 Dean Park 1
Sep 8 Maybole 0 Cumnock 4
Sep 8 Morton 1 Renfrew 0
Sep 8 Northern Greenoc 5 John Maxwell 3
Sep 8 Northern 0 Rangers 1
Sep 8 Our Boys 3 West End 2
Sep 8 Partick T 0 Queen's Park 8
Partick T *W* Pilgrims *0*
Sep 8 Pollokshields A 4 Thistle 1
Port Glasgow A *W* Lochwinnoch *0*
Sep 8 Possilpark 2 Orchard 4
Sep 8 Queen of S'th W 7 5th KRV 7
Sep 8 Renton 2 Dumbarton 1
Sep 8 Royal Albert 8 Shettleston 0
Sep 8 Southern 5 Netherlee 2
Sep 8 St Mirren 6 Caledonian 0
Sep 8 Stenhousemuir 3 Strathblane 2
Stewarton C *W* Portland *0*
Sep 8 Strathmore Dun 1 East End R 0
Sep 8 T Lanark 5 Clyde 2
Vale of Atholl *W* Aberfeldy *0*
Sep 8 Vale of Leven 12 Leverndale 0
Sep 8 Vale of Nith 2 Moffat 4
Whitefield *W* Luton *0*
Sep 8 Whitehill 3 Alexandria A 1
Sep 8 Yoker 0 Olympic 2

Replays
Strathmore Arb 1 Balgay 1
Both Qualified
Vale of Leven 0 Dumbritton 4
Sep 15 Arbroath 7 Aberdeen 0

Date	Team	Score	Team	Score
Sep 15	Benhar	12	Drumpellier	0
Sep 15	5th KRV	3	Queen of S'th W	1
Sep 22	Edina	4	Kinleith	0
	After Protest			
Sep 22	Tollcross	4	Airdrie	3
	After Protest			

2nd Round

Date	Team	Score	Team	Score
Sep 29	Abercorn	2	Paisley	0
	Arbroath	*W*	Perserverance	*0*
Sep 29	Balgay	1	Strathmore Dun	3
Sep 29	Battlefield	7	Whitefield	2
	Benhar	*W*	Vale of Avon	*0*
Sep 29	Cambuslang	7	Tollcross	0
Sep 29	Cartvale	6	Southern	2
Sep 29	Cowlairs	3	Granton	2
Sep 29	Drumlanrig R	2	East End R	3
Sep 29	Dunblane	4	Coupar Angus	1
	Dundee H	*W*	Vale of Atholl	*0*
Sep 29	E Stirling	2	Dunipace	2
Sep 29	Falkirk	9	Stenhousemuir	1
Sep 29	Hibernian	10	Edina	1
Sep 29	Jamestown	7	Dumbritton	1
Sep 29	Johnstone R	6	Northern	1
Sep 29	Kilmarnock	3	Hurlford	0
Sep 29	Kilmarnock A	9	Stewarton C	1
Sep 29	Mauchline	3	Lugar Boswell	1
Sep 29	Moffat	2	5th KRV	3
Sep 29	Newcastleton	1	Hearts	4
Sep 29	Olympic	5	Clippens	0
Sep 29	Our Boys	2	Strathmore Arb	0
Sep 29	Partick T	8	Orchard	1
Sep 29	Pollokshield A	6	Mavisbank	2
Sep 29	Port Glasgow A	1	Arthurlie	3
Sep 29	Rangers	14	Whitehill	2
Sep 29	Renton	6	King's Park	1
Sep 29	Royal Albert	8	Clarkston	1
Sep 29	Thornliebank	14	Bute R	0
Sep 29	T Lanark	2	Queen's Park	4
Sep 29	Woodland	0	St Mirren	7

Replays

Date	Team	Score	Team	Score
Oct 6	Dunipace	1	E Stirling	2

3rd Round

Date	Team	Score	Team	Score
Oct 20	Abercorn	7	Johnstone R	0
Oct 20	Arbroath	1	Dundee H	1
Oct 20	Arthurlie	3	St Mirren	1
Oct 20	Battlefield	4	Jamestown	2
Oct 20	Cambuslang	6	Hamilton A	0
Oct 20	Cartvale	4	Cumnock	1
Oct 20	Cowlairs	0	Queen's Park	5
Oct 20	East End R	1	5th KRV	6
Oct 20	Hearts	1	Hibernian	4
Oct 20	Morton	1	Kilmarnock A	2
Oct 20	Olympic	0	Mauchline	5
Oct 20	Partick T	6	E Stirling	0
Oct 20	Rangers	5	Falkirk	3
Oct 20	St Bernard's	7	Benhar	0
Oct 20	Strathmore Dun	2	Our Boys	2
Oct 20	Thornliebank		Kilmarnock	
Oct 20	Vale of Leven	4	Renton	1

Replays

Date	Team	Score	Team	Score
Oct 27	Dundee H	2	Arbroath	1
Oct 27	Our Boys	5	Strathmore Dun	1
Nov 3	Morton	0	Kilmarnock A	4
	After Protest			
Nov 3	Thornliebank	2	Kilmarnock	1
	After Protest			

4th Round

Date	Team	Score	Team	Score
Nov 10	5th KRV	1	Hibernian	8
	Battlefield	*W*	Edinburgh Univ	*0*
Nov 10	Cartvale	4	Abercorn	2
Nov 10	Dunblane	0	Rangers	6
Nov 10	Kilmarnock A	2	Cambuslang	3
Nov 10	Mauchline	4	Royal Albert	0
Nov 10	Partick T	0	Queen's Park	4
Nov 10	Pollokshields A	11	Our Boys	0
Nov 10	St Bernard's	2	Thornliebank	2
Nov 10	Vale of Leven	6	Dundee H	0

5th Round

Date	Team	Score	Team	Score
Dec 1	Arthurlie	0	Vale of Leven	0
Dec 1	Mauchline	2	Pollokshields A	3
Dec 1	St Bernard's	0	Rangers	3

Replays

Date	Team	Score	Team	Score
Dec 8	Vale of Leven	3	Arthurlie	1

6th Round

Date	Team	Score	Team	Score
Dec 22	Cambuslang	1	Rangers	5
Dec 22	Hibernian	6	Battlefield	1
Dec 22	Queen's Park	6	Cartvale	1
Dec 22	Vale of Leven	4	Pollokshields A	2

Semi-finals

Date	Team	Score	Team	Score
Feb 2	Hibernian	1	Queen's Park	5
Jan 19	Vale of Leven	3	Rangers	0

Final

Date	Team	Score	Team	Score
	Queen's Park		Vale of Leven	

Awarded To Queen's Park
Vale of Leven Did Not Appear

Season 1884-85

1st Round

Date	Team	Score	Team	Score
Sep 13	Airdrie	4	Shettleston	6
	Airdriehill	*W*	Vale of Avon	*0*
	Albion R	*W*	Dumbritton	*0*
Sep 13	Alloa	0	King's Park	4
Sep 13	Angus	1	Strathmore Dun	5
Sep 13	Arbroath	3	Dundee H	2
Sep 13	Arthurlie	2	Olympic	0
Sep 13	Battlefield	8	Kinning Park	0
Sep 13	Boness	0	Hibernian	2
Sep 13	Cartvale	12	Greenock Rangers	1
Sep 13	Clarkston	1	Hamilton A	4
Sep 13	Clippens	3	Greenock Rovers	1
Sep 13	Clyde	1	Cowlairs	2
Sep 13	Cumnock	3	Mauchline	2
Sep 13	Dalry	0	Annbank	4
Sep 13	Drumpellier	0	Airdrieonians	6
	Dumbarton	*W*	Leverndale	*0*
	Dumbarton A	*W*	Lenzie	*0*
Sep 13	Dunblane	8	Crieff J	0
Sep 13	Dunfermline	10	Newcastleton	2
Sep 13	East End	8	Coupar Angus	1
Sep 13	E Stirling	4	Campsie	2
	Falkirk	*W*	Strathblane	*0*
Sep 13	Glengowan	2	Albion R	1
Sep 13	Granton	1	Shawlands	0
Sep 13	Grasshoppers	4	Dunipace	0
Sep 13	Jamestown	1	Vale of Leven	1
Sep 13	Johnstone	9	Lyle A	1
Sep 20	Kilmarnock	6	Hurlford	1
	Kilmarnock A	14	Stewarton C	0
Sep 13	Lindertis	1	Aberdeen	4
Sep 13	Lugar Boswell	1	Ayr	4
Sep 13	Moffat	2	5th KRV	5
Sep 13	Morton	2	Abercorn	2
Sep 13	Northern	6	Glasgow Univ	4
Sep 13	Paisley A	2	Southern	3
Sep 13	Partick T	9	Eastern A	1
	Pollokshaw	*W*	Kilbarchan	*0*
Sep 13	Pollokshields	0	Queen's Park	4
Sep 13	Pollokshields A	6	Pilgrims	2
Sep 13	Port Glasgow A	6	1st KRV	1
Sep 13	Possilpark	7	Cyrus	0
Sep 13	Rangers	11	Whitehill	0
Sep 13	Renfrew	1	Johnstone R	0
Sep 13	Renton	2	Vale of Leven W	1
Sep 13	Royal Albert	1	Cambuslang	4
	Springburn H	*W*	Orchard	*0*
Sep 13	St Bernard's	6	Edina	0
Sep 13	St Mirren	4	Neilston	3
Sep 13	Stenhousemuir	1	Tayavalla	2
Sep 13	Strathmore Arb	1	Our Boys	4
Sep 13	Thornhill	0	Queen of S'th W	13
Sep 13	Thornliebank	6	Northern	0
Sep 13	T Lanark	3	Partick T	2
Sep 13	Vale of Teith	7	Breadalbane	0
Sep 13	Volunteer A	1	Vale of Nith	4
Sep 13	West Benhar	8	Chryston	1
Sep 13	West Calder	3	Norton Park	0
	West End	*W*	Perserverance	*0*
Sep 13	Westburn	6	Tollcross	2
Sep 13	Whitefield	3	Thistle	3
Sep 13	Wishaw S	2	Dykehead	1
Sep 13	Yoker	2	Rock	0

Replays

Date	Team	Score	Team	Score
Sep 20	Abercorn	3	Morton	4
	After Protest			
Sep 20	Thistle	3	Whitefield	1
Sep 20	Vale of Leven	4	Jamestown	1
Sep 27	Dykehead	2	Wishaw S	5
	After Protest			
Sep 27	Hurlford	3	Kilmarnock	1
	Hurlford Disqualified			
Sep 27	Neilston	1	St Mirren	4
	After Protest			
Sep 27	Abercorn	2	Morton	2
	Both Qualified			

2nd Round

Date	Team	Score	Team	Score
Oct 4	5th KRV	3	Queen of S'th W	4
Oct 4	Aberdeen	1	Arbroath	7
Oct 4	Airdrieonians	2	Cambuslang	2
Oct 4	Annbank	4	Kilmarnock	1
Oct 4	Arthurlie	1	Abercorn	0
Oct 4	Ayr	5	Cumnock	0
Oct 4	Clippens	1	Renfrew	7
Oct 4	Cowlairs	1	Pollokshields A	2
Oct 4	Dean Park	2	Springburn H	0
Oct 4	Dumbarton	2	Albion R	0
Oct 4	Dumbarton A	3	King's Park	1
Oct 4	Dunfermline	1	Hearts	11
	Hearts Disqualified			
Oct 4	E Stirling	2	Renton	10
Oct 4	Glengowan	4	Westburn	1
Oct 4	Granton	1	Northern	3
Oct 4	Grasshoppers	1	Falkirk	4
Oct 4	Hibernian	5	Vale of Teith	1
Oct 4	Maybole	1	Kilmarnock A	4
Oct 4	Our Boys	8	West End	1
Oct 4	Pollokshaws	2	Southern	2
Oct 4	Possilpark	0	Battlefield	3
Oct 4	St Mirren	3	Johnstone	0
Oct 4	Strathmore Dun	1	East End	1
Oct 4	Thistle	1	Queen's Park	4
Oct 4	Thornliebank	1	Port Glasgow A	0
Oct 4	T Lanark	2	Rangers	2
Oct 4	Vale of Leven	14	Central	0
Oct 4	West Benhar	9	Shettleston	1
Oct 4	West Calder	0	Dunblane	1
Oct 4	Wishaw S	8	Airdriehill	3
Oct 4	Yoker	17	Tayavalla	0

Replays

Date	Team	Score	Team	Score
Oct 11	Cambuslang	10	Airdrieonians	2
Oct 11	East End	2	Strathmore Dun	5
Oct 11	Rangers	0	T Lanark	0
	Both Qualified			
Oct 11	Southern	3	Pollokshaws	3
	Both Qualified			
Oct 18	Port Glasgow A	2	Thornliebank	2
	After Protest			
Oct 18	West Benhar	4	Shettleston	1
	After Protest			
Oct 25	Thornliebank	2	Port Glasgow A	1

3rd Round

Date	Team	Score	Team	Score
Oct 25	Arthurlie	3	Cartvale	0
Oct 25	Ayr	4	Kilmarnock A	2
Oct 25	Cambuslang	3	Hamilton A	0
Oct 25	Dean Park	2	Dumbarton	2
Oct 25	Dunblane	2	Arbroath	4
Oct 25	Hibernian	5	Glengowan	1
Oct 25	Morton	5	Southern	0
Oct 25	Our Boys	5	Strathmore Dun	1
Oct 25	Partick T	4	Falkirk	2
Oct 25	Pollokshields A	4	Dumbarton	1
Oct 25	Queen's Park	2	Battlefield	3
Oct 25	Renton	9	Northern	2
Oct 25	St Mirren	1	Renfrew	0
Nov 1	Thornliebank	4	Pollokshaws	0
Oct 25	T Lanark	0	Rangers	3
Oct 25	Vale of Leven	4	Yoker	1
Oct 25	Vale of Nith	0	Queen of S'th W	6
Oct 25	West Benhar	5	St Bernard's	1
Nov 1	Wishaw S	7	Dunfermline	1

Replays

Date	Team	Score	Team	Score
Nov 1	Dumbarton A	3	Deans Park	1
Nov 8	St Mirren	3	Renfrew	0
	After Protest			
Nov 13	St Mirren	6	Renfrew	3
	After Protest			

4th Round

Date	Team	Score	Team	Score
Nov 15	Annbank	5	Queen of S'th W	2
Nov 15	Arbroath	4	Rangers	3
Nov 15	Arthurlie	1	Vale of Leven	2
Nov 15	Cambuslang	2	Thornliebank	2
Nov 15	Dumbarton A	6	Partick T	3
Nov 15	Hibernian	5	Ayr	1
Nov 15	Our Boys	2	West Benhar	2
Nov 15	Pollokshields A	0	Battlefield	3
Nov 15	Renton	2	St Mirren	1
Nov 15	Wishaw S	1	Morton	2

Replays

Date	Team	Score	Team	Score
Nov 22	Thornliebank	0	Cambuslang	0
	Both Qualified			
Nov 22	West Banhar	8	Our Boys	3
Dec 20	Arbroath	1	Rangers	8
	After Protest			

5th Round

Date	Team	Score	Team	Score
Dec 6	Annbank	5	West Benhar	1
Dec 6	Cambuslang	4	Dumbarton A	1
Dec 6	Hibernian	4	Morton	0

6th Round

Date	Team	Score	Team	Score
Jan 10	Cambuslang	3	Battlefield	1
Dec 27	Hibernian	5	Annbank	0
Dec 27	Renton	5	Rangers	3
Dec 27	Thornliebank	3	Vale of Leven	4

Semi-finals

Date	Team	Score	Team	Score
Jan 24	Hibernian	2	Renton	3
Jan 31	Vale of Leven	0	Cambuslang	0

Replay

Date	Team	Score	Team	Score
Feb 7	Cambuslang	1	Vale of Leven	3

Final

Date	Team	Score	Team	Score
Feb 21	Renton	0	Vale of Leven	0
	played at Hampden Park			

Replay

Date	Team	Score	Team	Score
Feb 28	Renton	3	Vale of Leven	1
	played at Hampden Park			

Season 1885-86

1st Round

Date	Home		Away	
Sep 12	5th KRV	4	Vale of Nith	0
Sep 19	Abercorn	2	St Mirren	0
Sep 26	Airdrieonians	4	Royal Albert	2
Sep 12	Albion	4	Jamestown	4
Sep 12	Albion R	6	Drumpellier	2
Sep 12	Alpha	6	Cambuslang H	8
Sep 12	Arbroath	36	Bon Accord	0
	Arthurlie	*W*	Olympic	*0*
Sep 12	Ayr	7	Maybole	0
Sep 12	Ayr R	0	Dalry	8
	Battlefield	0	Cowlairs	2
Sep 12	Broxburn S	1	Boness	1
Sep 12	Cambridge	3	Southern A	1
Sep 12	Camelon	1	Falkirk	3
Sep 12	Cartvale	2	Morton	1
Sep 12	Clyde	1	Rangers	0
Sep 12	Clydevale	2	Tollcross	4
Sep 12	Coupar Angus	2	Our Boys	8
	Cowdenbeath	*W*	Aberfeldy	*0*
Sep 12	Crieff	0	Dunfermline A	7
Sep 19	Dumbarton	3	Vale of Leven W	1
	Dunblane	*W*	Dunfermline	*0*
Sep 12	Dunipace	4	Campsie C	2
Sep 12	East End	3	Strathmore Dun	3
Sep 12	E Stirling	6	Campsie	1
Sep 12	Forfar	3	Angus	1
	Glasgow Univ	*W*	Eastern	*0*
Sep 12	Granton	0	Partick T	11
Sep 12	Grasshoppers	2	Grahamston	2
Sep 12	Greenock S	1	Neilston	10
	Hamilton A	*W*	West Benhar	*0*
Sep 12	Harp	35	Aberdeen R	0
Sep 12	Hearts	5	St Bernard's	2
Sep 26	Helensburgh	2	Dumbarton A	3
Sep 12	Hibernian	9	Edina	0
Sep 12	Hurlford	5	Cumnock	1
Sep 12	Johnstone	1	Greenock R	1
Sep 12	Kilmarnock	7	Annbank	1
Sep 12	King's Park	3	Armadale	1
Sep 12	Kirkintilloch A	0	Renton	15
Sep 26	Lanemark	0	Monkcastle	2
Sep 12	Lenzie	1	Bonhill	1
Sep 12	Mauchline	2	Lugar Boswell	3
Sep 12	Northern	4	Linthouse	1
Sep 12	Norton P	6	Glencairn	2
Sep 12	Paisley H	2	Thornliebank	2
	Pollokshields A	*W*	Partick T	*0*
Sep 12	Port Glasgow A	4	1st Rrv	1
Sep 12	Queen's Park	16	St Peters	0
Sep 12	Renfrew	1	Greenock N	0
	Rock	*W*	Levendale	*0*
Sep 12	Shettleston	1	Cambuslang	7
	St Andrew's	*W*	10th Lrv	*0*
Sep 12	Strathmore Arb	7	Aberdeen	0
Sep 12	Thistle	11	Westbourne	1
	Thornliebank	*W*	Moffat	*0*
	Vale of Leven	*W*	Dunbritton	*0*
Sep 12	Vale of Teith	9	Oben	1
	West Calder	*W*	Newcastleton	*0*
Sep 12	West End	3	Broughty	3
Sep 12	Whitefield	3	Dennistoun A	1
Sep 12	Wishaw S	2	Rutherglen	0
Sep 12	Woodvale	3	Mearns A	2
Sep 12	Yoker	5	Union	1

Replays

Date	Home		Away	
Sep 19	Boness	5	Broxburn S	1
Sep 19	Bonhill	6	Lenzie	0
Sep 19	Broughty	3	West End	3
	Both Qualified			
Sep 19	Grahamston	2	Grasshoppers	4
Sep 19	Jamestown	0	Albion	1
Sep 19	Strathmore Dun	1	East End	4
Sep 19	Thornliebank	2	Paisley H	0
Sep 26	Hearts	1	St Bernard's	0
	After Protest			
Sep 26	Southern A	1	Cambridge	2
	After Protest			
Sep 26	Yoker	0	Union	1
	After Protest			
	Monkcastle	2	Lanemark	0
	After Protest			

2nd Round

Date	Home		Away	
Oct 3	5th KRV	3	Queen of S'th W	1
Oct 3	Airdrieonians	15	Cambuslang H	2
	Albion	*W*	Rock	*0*
Oct 3	Albion R	2	Wishaw S	2
Oct 3	Arbroath	9	Forfar A	1
Oct 3	Arthurlie	2	Woodvale	0
Oct 3	Boness	8	Norton Park	1
	Cambuslang	*W*	Hamilton A	*0*
Oct 3	Clyde	2	Thistle	3
Oct 3	Cowlairs	3	Pollokshields A	2
Oct 3	Dalry	6	Lugar Boswell	2
Oct 3	Dumbarton	7	Union	0
Oct 3	Dumbarton A	2	Renton	7
Oct 3	Dunblane	10	Dunfermline A	0
Oct 3	Dykehead	3	Tollcross	1
	Dykehead Disqualified			
Oct 3	East End	2	Broughty	2
Oct 3	Falkirk	0	Alloa	4
Oct 3	Glasgow Univ	1	T Lanark	8
Oct 3	Grasshoppers	1	E Stirling	6
Oct 3	Harp	4	Our Boys	1
Oct 3	Hibernian	2	Hearts	1
Oct 3	Johnstone	1	Thornliebank	2
Oct 3	Kilmarnock	3	Hurlford	4
Oct 3	King's Park	7	Dunipace	1
Oct 3	Monkcastle	2	Ayr	4
Oct 3	Northern	7	Whitefield	2
Oct 3	Port Glasgow A	1	Neilston	1
Oct 3	Queen's Park	1	Pilgrims	0
Oct 3	Renfrew	0	Abercorn	3
Oct 3	St Andrew's	6	Cambridge	0
Oct 3	Vale of Leven	10	Bonhill	0
	Vale of Teith	*W*	Cowdenbeath	*0*
Oct 3	West End	4	Strathmore Arb	5

Replays

Date	Home		Away	
Oct 10	Broughty	3	East End	8
	After Protest			
Oct 10	Neilston	0	Port Glasgow A	2
Oct 10	Wilshaw S	5	Albion R	0
Oct 17	Broughty	1	East End	2
	After Protest			
Oct 17	Kilmarnock	1	Hurlford	1
	After Protest			
Oct 17	Queen of S'th W	4	5th KRV	3
	After Protest			
Nov 7	Hurlford	2	Kilmarnock	2
Nov 14	Kilmarnock	1	Hurlford	5

3rd Round

Date	Home		Away	
Oct 24	Airdrieonians	8	Tollcross	2
Oct 24	Albion	0	Renton	1
Oct 24	Alloa	0	Partick T	12
Oct 24	Arbroath	7	East End	1
Nov 21	Arthurlie	5	Hurlford	0
Oct 24	Cartvale	1	Port Glasgow A	1
Oct 24	Cowlairs	2	Northern	1
Oct 24	Dalry	1	Ayr	6
Oct 24	Dumbarton	3	Thistle	0
Oct 24	E Stirling	0	Queen's Park	3
Oct 24	Harp	8	Vale of Teith	1
Oct 24	Hibernian	6	Boness	0
Oct 24	Strathmore Arb	3	Dunblane	1
Oct 24	Thornhill	0	Queen of S'th W	8
Oct 24	Thornliebank	1	Abercorn	5
Oct 31	T Lanark	11	St Andrew's	0
	Vale of Leven	*W*	King's Park	*0*
Oct 24	Wishaw S	3	West Calder	0

Replays

Date	Home		Away	
Oct 31	Port Glasgow A	4	Cartvale	2

4th Round

Date	Home		Away	
Nov 14	Abercorn	7	Strathmore Arb	2
Nov 14	Cambuslang	9	Wishaw S	0
Nov 14	Dumbarton	3	Partick T	0
Nov 14	Hibernian	5	Arbroath	3
Nov 28	Queen of S'th W	1	Arthurlie	3
Nov 14	Queen's Park	1	Airdrie	0
Nov 14	Renton	4	Cowlairs	0
Nov 14	T Lanark	3	Ayr	2
Nov 14	Vale of Leven	6	Harp	0

Replays

Date	Home		Away	
Nov 28	Ayr	3	T Lanark	3
	After Protest			
Dec 5	T Lanark	5	Ayr	1

5th Round

Date	Home		Away	
Dec 5	Abercorn	0	Cambuslang	1
Dec 5	Arthurlie	1	Queen's Park	2
Dec 5	Dumbarton	2	Hibernian	2
Dec 5	Renton	2	Vale of Leven	2
Dec 12	T Lanark	1	Port Glasgow A	1

Replays

Date	Home		Away	
Dec 12	Hibernian	4	Dumbarton	3
Dec 12	Renton	3	Vale of Leven	0
Dec 19	T Lanark	1	Port Glasgow A	1
Dec 26	T Lanark	4	Port Glasgow A	1

6th Round

Date	Home		Away	
Jan 16	Hibernian	3	Cambuslang	2

Semi-finals

Date	Home		Away	
Jan 23	Hibernian	0	Renton	2
Jan 16	T Lanark	0	Queen's Park	3

Final

Date	Home		Away	
Feb 13	Queen's Park	3	Renton	1
	played at Cathkin Park			

Season 1886-87

1st Round

Date	Home		Away	
	5th KRV	*W*	Thornhill	*0*
	Aberdeen	*W*	East End	*0*
Sep 11	Airdrie	5	Airdriehill	0
Sep 11	Albion	5	Rutherglen	1
Sep 11	Annbank	3	Kilbirnie	4
Sep 11	Arbroath	20	Orion	0
Sep 11	Armadale		Slamannan	
Sep 11	Ayr	2	Hurlford	3
Sep 11	Battlefield	0	Cowlairs	2
Sep 11	Bonhill	8	Kirkintilloch C	1
Sep 11	Broxburn S	1	Mossend S	2
Sep 11	Broxburn T	2	Bellstane	2
	Burntisland T	*W*	Dunfermline	*0*
Sep 11	Cambuslang	6	Motherwell	1
Sep 11	Campsie	10	Dunipace	1
Sep 11	Carrick	0	Westbourne	2
Sep 11	Clyde	5	St Peters	1
	Coupar Angus	*W*	Fair City A	*0*
Sep 11	Dalry	5	Ayr R	2
Sep 11	Dumbarton	5	Vale of Leven H	0
Sep 11	Dumbarton A	8	Duntocher	0
Sep 11	Dunblane	12	Crieff	0
	Dunbritton	*W*	Lenzie	*0*
Sep 11	Dundee W	2	Broughty	7
Sep 11	Dunfermline A	4	Alloa	8
Sep 11	Edina	1	Hearts	7
Sep 11	E Stirling	6	Camelon	3
Sep 11	Grahamston	0	Lawrieston	2
Sep 11	Grasshoppers	3	Vale of Bannock	3
Sep 11	Greenock R	3	1st Rrv	4
	Awarded To Greenock			
	Hamilton A	*W*	Wishaw S	*0*
Sep 11	Hibernian	6	Durhamstown R	1
Sep 11	Johnstone	6	Cartvale	2
Sep 11	Kelvinside A	1	Whitefield	2
	Kilmarnock	*W*	Cumnock	*0*
Sep 11	King's Park	1	Falkirk	3
Sep 11	Lindertis	3	Harp	4
Sep 11	Linthouse	4	Southern A	0
Sep 11	Lochwinnoch	0	Morton	6
	Lugar Boswell	*W*	Maybole	*0*
Sep 11	Monkcastle	1	Lanemark	3
	Newcastleton	*W*	Norton Park	*0*
Sep 11	Northern	1	T Lanark	4
	Oban	*W*	Our Boys	*0*
Sep 18	Our Boys	2	Forfar	5
Sep 11	Partick T	2	Queen's Park	3
Sep 11	Port Glasgow A	10	Johnstone H	1
	Queen of S'th W	*W*	Nithsdale W	*0*
Sep 11	Rangers	9	Govan A	1
Sep 11	Renfrew	3	Abercorn	3
	Renton	*W*	Kirkintilloch H	*0*
Sep 11	Rutherglen	2	Dumpellier	0
Sep 11	Shettleston	3	Carfin S	3
Sep 11	Slanannan	4	Avondale	3
Sep 11	St Andrew's	2	Pollokshields A	5
Sep 11	St Bernard's	3	Boness	2
Sep 11	St Johnstone	3	Erin R	3
Sep 18	St Mirren	5	Arthurlie	3
Sep 11	Strathmore Arb	3	Strathmore Dun	0
Sep 11	Thistle	13	Blairvaddick	0
Sep 11	Thornliebank	3	Neilston	2
Sep 11	Tollcross	0	Royal Albert	3
	R.Albert Disqualified			
Sep 11	Vale of Leven	9	Kirkintilloch A	0
Sep 11	Vale of Leven W	6	Jamestown	3
	Vale of Leven W Disqualified			
	Vale of Nith	*W*	Vale of Annan	*0*
Sep 11	West Calder	1	Armadale	3
	Woodvale	*W*	Pollokshaws A	*0*
Sep 11	Yoker	4	Union	2

Replays

Date	Home		Away	
Sep 18	Abercorn	9	Renfrew	0
Sep 18	Broxburn T	4	Bellstane	1
Sep 18	Carfin S	3	Shettleston	0
Sep 18	Erin R	7	St Johnstone	1
Sep 18	Vale of Bannock	2	Grasshoppers	0
Sep 25	St Andrew's	4	Pollokshields A	1
	After Protest			

2nd Round

Date	Home		Away	
Oct 2	Abercorn	8	Greenock R	2
Oct 2	Airdrie	3	Carfin S	2
	Airdrie Disqualified			
Oct 2	Albion	7	Dykehead	0
Oct 2	Bonhill	1	Jamestown	2
Oct 2	Broxburn T	1	Hearts	2
Oct 2	Caledonian R	4	Erin R	4
Oct 2	Cambuslang H	3	Hamilton A	1
Oct 2	Clyde	4	Cowlairs	3
Oct 2	Cowdenbeath	3	Burntisland	3
Oct 2	Dumbarton	4	Yoker	0
Oct 2	Dunblane	8	Oban	1
Oct 2	East End	5	Broughty	4
	E Stirling	*W*	Vale of Bannock	*0*
Oct 2	Falkirk	3	Laurieston	1
Oct 2	Forfar	2	Arbroath	5
Oct 2	Hurlford	3	Kilbirnie	2
Oct 2	Johnstone	4	Pollokshaws A	0
Oct 2	Kilmarnock	10	Lanemark	2
Oct 2	Lenzie	0	Vale of Leven	13
Oct 2	Linthouse	1	T Lanark	4
Oct 2	Lugar Boswell	3	Dalry	2
Oct 2	Moffat	3	5th KRV	5
Oct 2	Mossend S	1	Hibernian	1
Oct 2	Newcastleton	1	Armadale	5
Oct 2	Queen of S'th W	12	Vale of Nith	2
Oct 2	Queen's Park	7	Whitefield	0
Oct 2	Rangers	5	Westbourne	2
Oct 2	Renton	2	Dumbarton A	0
Oct 2	Rutherglen	1	Cambuslang	1
Oct 2	Slanannan	0	Campsie	3
Oct 2	St Mirren	2	Port Glasgow A	3
Oct 2	Strathmore Arb	3	Harp	3
Oct 2	Thistle	12	St Andrew's	0

Oct 2 Thornliebank 0 Morton 2

Replays
Oct 9 Cambuslang 6 Rutherglen 1
Oct 9 Erin R 6 Caledonian R 1
Oct 9 Harp 3 Strathmore Arb 3
Both Qualified
Oct 9 Hibernian 3 Mossend S 0
Oct 16 Cowdenbeath 3 Burntisland 1
Oct 16 Lugar Boswell 6 Dalry 1
After Protest

3rd Round
Oct 23 Abercorn 1 Port Glasgow A 5
Oct 23 Albion 4 Thistle 2
Oct 23 Cambuslang H 5 Jamestown 1
Oct 23 Cowdenbeath 6 Alloa 1
Dumbarton *W* Tollcross *0*
Oct 23 East End 3 Dunblane 3
East End Scratched
Oct 23 Erin R 3 Coupar Angus 2
Oct 23 E Stirling 1 Clyde 3
Oct 23 Falkirk 3 Queen's Park 8
Oct 23 Hibernian 5 Hearts 1
Oct 23 Johnstone 0 Hurlford 5
Oct 23 Kilmarnock 7 Lugar Boswell 2
Oct 23 Queen of S'th W 6 5th KRV 3
Oct 23 Rangers 0 Cambuslang 2
Oct 23 St Bernard's 5 Armadale 2
Oct 23 Strathmore Arb 1 Harp 8
Oct 23 T Lanark 3 Renton 1
Oct 23 Vale of Leven 7 Campsie 4

4th Round
Nov 13 Albion 1 Cambuslang 6
Nov 13 Cowdenbeath 0 Cambuslang H 3
Nov 6 Morton 11 Carfin S 0
Nov 13 Queen of S'th W 8 Arbroath 2
Nov 13 St Bernard's 5 Erin R 1

5th Round
Dec 4 Clyde 0 T Lanark 0
Dec 4 Harp 2 Dumbarton 2
Harp Scratched
Dec 4 Hibernian 7 Queen of S'th W 3
Dec 4 Hurlford 5 Morton 1
Dec 4 Kilmarnock 6 Dunblane 0
Dec 4 Port Glasgow A 6 St Bernard's 2
Dec 4 Queen's Park 1 Cambuslang 1
Nov 27 Vale of Leven 2 Cambuslang H 0

Replays
Dec 11 Cambuslang 4 Queen's Park 5
Dec 11 T Lanark 4 Clyde 2

6th Round
Dec 25 Hurlford 0 Dumbarton 0
Dec 25 Kilmarnock 0 Queen's Park 5
Dec 25 Port Glasgow A 1 Vale of Leven 3
Dec 25 T Lanark 1 Hibernian 2

Replays
Jan 8 Dumbarton 1 Hurlford 2
Jan 22 Dumbarton 3 Hurlford 1
After Protest

Semi-finals
Jan 22 Hibernian 3 Vale of Leven 1
Jan 29 Queen's Park 1 Dumbarton 2

Final
Feb 12 Dumbarton 1 Hibernian 2
played at Hampden Park

Season 1887-88

1st Round
Sep 3 1st Rrv 1 Renfrew 8
Sep 3 5th KRV 5 Thornhill 0
Sep 3 Abercorn 9 Johnstone H 0
Sep 3 Aberdeen 4 Our Boys 9
Sep 3 Airdrie 8 Dykehead 0
Sep 3 Albion 12 Airdriehill 0
Sep 3 Alloa 6 Cowdenbeath 2
Sep 3 Arbroath 18 Orion 0
Ayr *W* Monkcastle *0*
Sep 3 Boness 4 Leith A 1
Sep 3 Bonhill 1 Dumbarton A 6
Sep 3 Broughty 5 Montrose 7
Sep 3 Broxburn S 0 Mossend S 4
Mossend Disqualified
Sep 3 Burntisland 4 Dunfermline A 2
Burntisland Disqualified
Sep 3 Caledonian R 1 Crieff 7
Cambuslang *W* Hamilton A *0*
Sep 3 Cambuslang H 5 Hamilton 4
Sep 3 Carfin S 4 Shettleston 0
Both Qualified
Sep 3 Carrick 0 Thistle 10
Sep 3 Clyde 0 Queen's Park 7
Sep 3 Clydesdale 1 Rutherglen 4
Sep 3 Coupar Angus 9 Our Boys 2
Sep 3 Drumpellier 2 Motherwell 3
Sep 1 Dumbarton 10 Dunbritton 0
Sep 3 Dunblane 2 Fair City A 3
Sep 3 Dundee W 7 Lochee 0
Sep 3 Dunfermline A 3 Lassodie 2
Dunfermline Disqualified
Sep 3 Dykebar 5 Morton 2
Sep 3 Erin R Bath 5 Bellstane 0
Sep 3 Erin R Perth 3 St Johnstone 9
Sep 3 Falkirk 4 Kilsyth W 1
Sep 3 Grahamston 4 Redding A 3
Grahamston Disqualified
Sep 3 Grangemouth 2 E Stirling 5
Sep 3 Hearts 4 Norton Park 1
Sep 3 Hibernian 5 Broxburn T 0
Hurlford *W* Annbank *0*
Sep 3 Jamestown 3 Vale of Leven 2
Sep 3 Kelvinside A 6 St Andrew's 3
Sep 3 Kilbarchan 0 Arthurlie 4
Kilbirnie *W* Lanemark *0*
Sep 3 Kilmarnock 8 Ayr T 2
Sep 3 King's Park 1 Camelon 5
Sep 3 Kirkintilloch A 5 Kirkintilloch C 1
Sep 3 Lindertis 1 Harp 2
Harp Disqualified
Sep 3 Linthouse 3 Whitefield 3
Sep 3 Lochgilphead 1 Oban 9
Sep 3 Lochwinnoch 5 Pollokshaws 1
Sep 3 Lugar Boswell 9 Dalry 0
Sep 3 Maybole 3 Newmilns 2nd ARV 3
Sep 3 Moffat 7 Newcastleton 1
Neilston *W* Paisley A *0*
Sep 3 Northern 5 Govan A 1
Sep 3 Partick T 10 Westbourne 0
Plains *W* Tollcross *0*
Sep 3 Pollokshields A 4 United Abstainer 1
Aug 27 Port Glasgow A 11 Greenock R 0
Sep 3 Queen of S'th W 6 Vale of Nith 0
Sep 3 Rangers 4 Battlefield 1
Sep 3 Shanannan 5 Laurieston 4
Sep 3 St Bernard's 3 Armadale 2
Sep 3 Strathmore Arb 1 East End 13
Sep 3 Strathmore Dun 6 Forfar 3
Sep 3 Thornliebank 1 St Mirren 2
Sep 3 T Lanark 1 Cowlairs 2
Sep 3 Uddingston 2 Royal Albert 5
Sep 3 Union 0 Renton 6
Sep 3 Vale of Bannock 3 Campsie 4
Vale of Leven *W* Kirkintilloch H *0*
Sep 3 Vale of Leven W 7 Methlan Park 2
Sep 3 West Calder 9 Athenian 0

Replays
Sep 10 Motherwell 2 Drumpellier 0
After Protest
Sep 10 Newmilns 2nd ARV 4 Maybole 6
Sep 10 Whitefield 2 Linthouse 1
Sep 10 T Lanark 1 Cowlairs 4
After Protest
Sep 10 Vale of Leven 2 Jamestown 2
After Protest
Sep 25 Jamestown 3 Vale of Leven H 1

2nd Round
Sep 24 Abercorn 6 Neilston 0
Sep 24 Airdrie 3 Cambuslang H 0
Sep 24 Alloa 0 Dunfermline 1
Sep 24 Arbroath 3 Strathmore Dun 1
Sep 24 Arthurlie 3 St Mirren 3
Sep 24 Boness 5 West Calder 1
Sep 24 Cambuslang 2 Royal Albert 0
Sep 24 Carfin S 3 Motherwell 1
Coupar Angus *W* Crieff *0*
Sep 24 Cowlairs 9 Southern A 1
Sep 24 Dumbarton 1 Vale of Leven 5
Sep 24 Dundee W 10 Aberdeen R 0
Sep 24 Erin R Bath 0 Hibernian 6
Sep 24 Fair City A 3 St Johnstone 0
Sep 24 Falkirk 2 Campsie 2
Sep 24 Hurlford 9 Lugar Boswell 1
Jamestown 7 Kirkintilloch A 1
Sep 24 Kilbirnie 3 Mauchline 0
Sep 24 Lindertis 3 East End 2
Sep 24 Lochwinnoch 2 Dykebar 5
Sep 24 Maybole 0 Ayr 13
Sep 24 Moffat 4 Queen of S'th W 4
Sep 24 Nithsdale W 2 5th KRV 9
Sep 24 Northern 6 Shettleston 3
Sep 24 Our Boys 5 Montrose 3
Sep 24 Partick T 2 Rangers 1
Sep 24 Queen's Park 9 Kelvinside A 0
Sep 24 Redding A 0 Camelon 17
Sep 24 Renfrew 3 Port Glasgow A 3
Sep 24 Renton 4 Dumbarton A 2
Sep 24 Rutherglen 3 Albion R 6
Sep 24 Slanannan 1 E Stirling 6
Sep 24 St Bernard's 1 Broxburn S 1
Sep 24 Thistle 6 Glasgow Univ 0
Sep 24 Whitefield 2 Pollokshaws A 0

Replays
Oct 1 Campsie 2 Falkirk 2
Both Qualified
Oct 1 Port Glasgow A 5 Renfrew 3
Oct 1 Queen of S'th W 7 Moffat 4
Oct 1 St Bernard's 4 Broxburn S 1
Oct 1 St Mirren 4 Arthurlie 1

3rd Round
Oct 15 5th KRV 2 Queen of S'th W 6
Oct 15 Ayr 4 Port Glasgow A 0
Oct 15 Camelon 0 Renton 8
Oct 15 Cowlairs 9 Campsie 1
Oct 15 Dundee W 8 Coupar Angus 0
Oct 15 Dykebar 2 Kilmarnock 2
Oct 15 E Stirling 0 Cambuslang 0
Oct 15 Fair City A 0 Our Boys 5
Oct 15 Falkirk 2 Carfin S 2
Oct 15 Hearts 1 Hibernian 1
Oct 15 Hurlford 2 St Mirren 4
Oct 15 Kilbirnie 1 Abercorn 3
Oct 15 Lassodie 1 Boness 3
Oct 15 Northern 3 Albion R 4
Oct 15 Oban 1 Arbroath 5
Oct 15 Queen's Park 3 Jamestown 0
St Bernard's *W* Dunfermline *0*
Oct 15 Thistle 2 Whitefield 0
Oct 15 Vale of Leven 3 Airdrie 0
Oct 15 Vale of Leven W 9 Plains 0

Replays
Oct 22 Cambuslang 4 E Stirling 2
Oct 22 Carfin S 3 Falkirk 0
Oct 22 Hibernian 1 Hearts 3
Oct 22 Kilmarnock 9 Dykebar 1

4th Round
Nov 5 Ayr 3 Vale of Leven 2
Nov 5 Dundee W 4 Queen of S'th W 3
Nov 5 Hearts 1 St Mirren 1
Nov 5 Lindertis 1 Renton 13
Nov 5 Partick T 2 Kilmarnock 2
Nov 5 Vale of Leven W 2 Boness 0

Replays
Nov 12 Kilmarnock 1 Partick T 4
Nov 12 St Mirren 2 Hearts 2
Nov 19 Hearts 2 St Mirren 2
played at E Stirling
Nov 26 Hearts 2 St Mirren 4
played at Cathkin Park

5th Round
Nov 26 Abercorn 9 St Bernard's 0
Nov 26 Arbroath 5 Cowlairs 1
Nov 26 Cambuslang 10 Ayr 0
Nov 26 Dundee W 5 Carfin S 2
Nov 26 Our Boys 4 Albion R 2
Nov 26 Queen's Park 2 Partick T 0
Dec 3 St Mirren 2 Renton 3
Nov 26 Thistle 2 Vale of Leven W 9

6th Round
Dec 17 Abercorn 3 Arbroath 1
Dec 17 Cambuslang 6 Our Boys 0
Dec 17 Queen's Park 7 Vale of Leven W 1
Dec 17 Renton 5 Dundee W 1

Semi-finals
Jan 14 Abercorn 1 Cambuslang 1
Jan 14 Renton 3 Queen's Park 1

Replay
Jan 21 Cambuslang 10 Abercorn 1

Final
Feb 4 Cambuslang 1 Renton 6
played at Hampden Park

Season 1888-89

1st Round
Abercorn *W* Kilbarchan *0*
Sep 1 Aberdeen 3 Arbroath 4
Albion *W* Belshill *0*
Sep 1 Alva 6 Kilsyth W 2
Sep 1 Annbank 5 Britannia 1
Sep 1 Armadale 12 Champfleurie 0
Sep 1 Beith 2 Irving 3
Sep 1 Bellstane 2 Norton P 3
Sep 1 Bo'ness 0 Hearts 1
Sep 1 Broxburn S 3 West Calder 2
Sep 1 Cambuslang H 5 Coatbridge 0
Sep 1 Campsie 5 Camelon 1
Sep 1 Carfin S 6 Whifflet S 1
Sep 1 Celtic 5 Shettleston 1
Sep 1 Clydebank 3 Vale of Leven W 4
Sep 1 Clydesdale 1 Rutherglen 1
Sep 1 Coupar & Angus 6 Bridgend A 1
Sep 1 Cowdenbeath 3 Lassodie 1
Sep 1 Cowlairs 18 Temperance A 2
Sep 1 Crieff 10 Vale of Atholl 2
Sep 1 Dumbarton 13 Kirkintilloch C 1
Sep 1 Dumbarton A 15 Dumbarton U 0
Sep 1 Dunblane 6 St Johnstone 3

Sep 1 Dundee OB 5 Dundee East End 4
Dundee W W Aberdeen R 0
Dunfermline A W Dunfermline 0
Sep 1 Erin R Bathgate 6 Leith H 0
Sep 1 Erin R Perth 8 Blairgowrie OB 2
Sep 1 E Stirling 10 Stenhousemuir 1
Sep 1 Fair City A 5 Caledonian R 0
Sep 1 Falkirk 5 Dunipace 0
Sep 1 Forfar 14 Lindertis 1
Gairdoch W Redding A 0
Sep 1 Hamilton A 5 Airdrie 0
Sep 1 Hurlford 7 Ayr 0
Sep 1 Johnstone H 4 Woodvale 5
Sep 1 Kelvinside A 16 Govan A 0
Sep 1 Kilbirnie 3 Dalry 1
Sep 1 King's Park 4 Alloa 3
Sep 1 Kirkcaldy W 3 Townhill 0
Sep 1 Lanemark 7 Stevenston T 0
Sep 1 Linlithgow A 2 Adventurers 6
Sep 1 Linthouse 2 Clyde 4
Sep 1 Lochgilphead 15 Balaclava R 1
Sep 1 Lochwinnoch 0 Dykebar 5
Sep 1 Lugar Boswell 0 Kilmarnock 5
Maybole W Kilmarnock T 0
Sep 1 Methian P 5 Kirkintilloch A 0
Nov dale W Moffat 0
Sep 1 Montrose 8 Brechin C 1
Sep 1 Mossend S 2 Hibernian 1
Sep 1 Motherwell 3 Royal Albert 3
Sep 1 Neilston 3 St Mirren 4
Newmilns W Ayr T 0
Sep 1 Newton Stewart 13 Nithsdale W 0
Sep 8 Northern 2 Queen's Park 3
Oban W Campbeltown A 0
Sep 1 Pollokshaws 14 Carlton 0
Pollokshaws H W Greenock R 0
Sep 1 Port Glasgow A 3 Morton 7
Sep 1 Queen of South 9 5th KRV 4
Sep 1 Rangers 4 Partick T 2
Sep 8 Renfrew 0 Arthurlie 0
Sep 1 Renton 8 Bowling 0
Sep 1 Slamannan 5 Grangemouth 3
Sep 1 Southern A 1 Battlefield 9
Sep 1 St Bernard's 7 Leith A 0
Sep 1 Stewarton C 4 Rosebank 3
Sep 1 Strathmore Dun 3 Harp 4
Sep 1 Thistle 3 Maryhill 1
Sep 1 Thornhill 2 Vale of Nith 2
Thornliebank W Paisley 0
T Lanark W Whitefield 0
Sep 8 Union 2 Lochee 3
Sep 1 United Abstainer 2 Pollokshields A 1
Sep 1 Vale of Bannock 3 Laurieston 2
Sep 1 Vale of Leven 6 Jamestown 1
Sep 1 Wishaw 2 Cambuslang 4

Replays
Sep 8 Arthurlie 3 Renfrew 1
Sep 8 Royal Albert 1 Motherwell 2
Sep 8 Rutherglen 2 Clydesdale 2
Both Qualified
Sep 8 Thornhill 0 Vale of Nith 1
After Protest
Sep 15 West Calder 2 Broxburn S 1
After Protest
Vale of Nith W Thornhill 0

2nd Round
1st Rrv W Woodvale 0
Sep 22 Albion R 9 Rutherglen 1
Sep 22 Alva 0 Campsie 6
Sep 22 Arbroath 6 Montrose 2
Sep 22 Arthurlie 3 Pollokshaw 2
Sep 22 Battlefield 11 United Abstainer 0
Sep 22 Broughty 2 Harp 4
Sep 22 Broxburn 9 Adventurers 3
Sep 22 Cambuslang 4 Carfin S 2
Sep 22 Celtic 8 Cowlairs 0
Sep 22 Clyde 2 Rangers 2
Sep 22 Clydesdale 1 Uddingston 5
Sep 22 Coupar Angus 1 Erin R Perth 3
Sep 22 Cowdenbeath 2 Dunfermline A 4
Sep 22 Dumbarton A 4 Vale of Leven 2
Sep 22 Dundee OB 4 Lochee 2
Sep 22 Dykebar 1 St Mirren 6
Sep 22 E Stirling 11 Vale of Bannock 2
Sep 22 Fair City A 7 Crieff 1
Sep 22 Falkirk 8 Gairdoch 3
Sep 22 Forfar 6 Dundee W 5
Sep 22 Hearts 4 Erin R Bathgate 0
Sep 29 Hurlford 5 Annbank 4
Sep 22 Kelvinside A 0 T Lanark 8
Sep 22 Kilmarnock 1 Kilbirnie 3
Sep 22 Morton 1 Abercorn 4
Sep 22 Motherwell 5 Hamilton 1
Sep 22 Newmilns A 4 Maybole 4
Sep 22 Oban 4 Lochgilphead 2
Sep 22 Pollokshaws H 2 Thornliebank 5
Sep 22 Queen of S'th W 14 Newton Stewart 2
Sep 22 Queen's Park 6 Thistle 0
Sep 22 Slamannan 3 King's Park 3
Sep 29 St Bernard's 3 Norton P 1
Sep 22 Vale of Leven H 1 Methlan Park 3
Sep 22 Vale of Leven W 2 Renton 10
Sep 22 Vale of Nith 3 Mid-Annandale 1
Sep 22 West Calder 1 Mossend S 6

Replays
Sep 29 Clyde 3 Rangers 0
Sep 29 King's Park 13 Slamannan 1
Sep 29 Maybole 6 Newmilns 2
Oct 6 Hurlford 2 Annbank 2
After Protest
Oct 13 Annbank 2 Hurlford 3

3rd Round
Oct 13 1st Rrv 3 Kilbirnie 4
Oct 13 Arthurlie 0 St Mirren 7
Oct 13 Battlefield 1 Dumbarton A 3
Oct 13 Broxburn 2 Hearts 2
Oct 13 Celtic 4 Albion R 1
Oct 13 Clyde 4 Cambuslang H 0
Oct 13 Dunblane 4 Erin R Perth 4
Oct 13 Dundee OB 2 Harp 1
Oct 13 E Stirling 4 King's Park 0
Oct 13 Falkirk 2 Campsie 2
Oct 13 Forfar 1 Arbroath 2
Oct 20 Hurlford 4 Irvine 2
Oct 13 Kirkcaldy W 1 St Bernard's 2
Oct 13 Lanemark 4 Maybole 2
Oct 13 Mossend S 5 Armadale 2
Oct 13 Motherwell 2 Dumbarton 6
Oct 13 Queen of S'th W 11 Vale of Nith 1
Oct 13 Renton 4 Cambuslang 1
Oct 13 Thornliebank 0 Abercorn 8
Oct 13 T Lanark 2 Queen's Park 1
Oct 13 Uddingston 4 Glasgow U 0

Replays
Oct 20 Campsie 2 Falkirk 2
Both Qualified
Oct 20 Erin R Perth 0 Dunblane 6
Oct 20 Hearts 2 Broxburn 0
Oct 27 T Lanark 4 Queen's Park 2
After Protest

4th Round
Nov 3 Abercorn 11 Dundee OB 1
Nov 3 Campsie 3 Hearts 1
Nov 3 Dumbarton 9 Methlan P 0
Nov 3 Dumbarton A W Dunfermline A 0
Nov 3 Dunblane 4 E Stirling 4
Nov 3 Fair City A 1 Arbroath 3
Nov 3 Kilbirnie 1 St Mirren 6
Nov 3 Lanemark 0 Renton 8
Nov 3 Oban 0 Clyde 6
Nov 3 Queen of S'th W 10 Falkirk 2
Nov 3 St Bernard's 1 Celtic 4
Nov 3 T Lanark 7 Hurlford 1
Nov 3 Uddingston 1 Mossend S 4

Replays
Nov 10 E Stirling 4 Dunblane 0

5th Round
Nov 24 Arbroath 3 Renton 3
Nov 24 Celtic 0 Clyde 1
Dec 1 Dumbarton 3 Mossend S 1
Nov 24 St Mirren 3 Queen of S'th W 1
Nov 24 T Lanark 5 Abercorn 4

Replays
Dec 1 Renton 4 Arbroath 0
Dec 8 Celtic 9 Clyde 2
After Protest
Dec 8 T Lanark 2 Abercorn 2
After Protest
Dec 15 Abercorn 2 T Lanark 2
Dec 22 Abercorn 1 T Lanark 3
played at Ibrox

6th Round
Dec 15 Celtic 2 E Stirling 1
Dec 15 Dumbarton 2 St Mirren 2
Dec 15 Dumbarton A 1 Renton 2
Dec 29 T Lanark 6 Campsie 1

Replays
Dec 22 St Mirren 2 Dumbarton 2
Dec 29 Dumbarton 3 St Mirren 1
played at Ibrox

Semi-finals
Jan 12 Dumbarton 1 Celtic 4
Jan 12 T Lanark 2 Renton 0

Final
Feb 2 Celtic 0 T Lanark 3
played at Hampden Park

Replay
After Protest
Feb 9 Celtic 1 T Lanark 2
played at Hampden Park

SEASON 1889-90

1st Round
Aberdeen W Portland 0
Sep 7 Airdriehill 5 Motherwell 6
Sep 7 Alloa 5 Denny 1
Sep 7 Alva 3 King's Park 6
Sep 7 Arbroath 3 Dundee H 5
Sep 7 Armadale 2 Hibernian 3
Sep 7 Arthurlie 2 St Mirren 4
Sep 7 Ayr 16 Beith 0
Sep 7 Bathgate 3 Champfleurie 3
Sep 7 Bellstane 6 Norton Park 3
Sep 7 Bowling 1 Renton 8
Sep 7 Broughty 1 Dundee East End 6
Sep 7 Bute R 1 Kilbarchan 2
Sep 7 Carfin S 4 Albion R 0
Sep 7 Carrington 0 Maryhill 3
Sep 7 Celtic 0 Queen's Park 0
Abandoned
Sep 7 Clydebank 3 Vale of Leven 1
Clydebank Scratched
Sep 7 Clydesdale 1 Cambuslang 6
Sep 7 Cowdenbeath 8 Kirkcaldy W 0
Sep 7 Dalry 3 Kilbirnie 3
Sep 7 Dunblane 4 Caledonian R 1
Sep 7 Dundee OB 6 Strathmore 3
Sep 7 Dunipace 2 Laurieston 3
Sep 7 Duntocher H 5 Smithston H 0
Sep 7 Fair City A 8 Coupar Angus 0
Sep 7 Falkirk 11 Tillicoultry 1
Sep 7 Gairdoch 0 E Stirling 7
Sep 7 Glasgow H 1 Thistle 3
Greenock A W Renfrew 0
Sep 7 Hamilton A 0 Wishaw S 5
Sep 7 Irvine 2 Lugar Boswell 2
Sep 7 Jamestown 2 Methlan P 4
Kelvinside A W Southern A 0
Sep 7 Kilmarnock 2 Annbank 3
Sep 7 Kilsyth W 5 Stenhousemuir 1
Sep 7 Lassodie 3 Burntisland T 2
Sep 7 Leith A 6 Adventurers 2
Sep 7 Lindertis 0 Dundee W 5
Sep 7 Linthouse 7 Fairfield 2
Sep 7 Lochee 4 Brechin 1
Apr 31 Lochwinnoch 1 Abercorn 10
Sep 7 Mauchline 1 Newmilns 4
Sep 7 Maybole 6 Ayr A 6
Sep 7 Mid-Annandale 3 5th KRV 11
Sep 7 Moffat 8 Dumfries 0
Sep 7 Montrose 2 Forfar 4
Sep 7 Morton 8 Carlton 0
Sep 7 Mossend S 6 Bo'ness 0
Sep 7 Newton Stewart 3 Queen of South 4
Sep 7 Oban 5 Oban R 2
Sep 7 Old Kirkpatrick 1 Union 7
Sep 7 Orion 3 Victoria U 1
Sep 7 Perth OB 3 St Johnstone 5
Sep 7 Pollokshaw 3 Dykebar 1
Sep 7 Pollokshaw H 1 1st Rrv 7
Sep 7 Port Glasgow A 2 Neilston 1
Sep 7 Raith R 1 Dunfermline A 2
Sep 7 Rangers 6 United Abstainer 2
Sep 7 Royal Albert 12 Whifflet S 0
Sep 7 Rutherglen 2 Uddingston 8
Sep 7 Shettleston 1 Battlefield 7
Sep 7 Slamannan 0 Grangemouth 8
Sep 7 St Bernard's 0 Hearts 3
Sep 7 Stevenson T 4 Kilmarnock A 1
Sep 7 Stewarton C 0 Hurlford 5
Summerton A W Temperance A 0
Thornliebank W Johnstone H 0
Sep 7 T Lanark 3 Partick T 2
Vale of Atholl W Crieff 0
Sep 7 Vale of Bannock 3 Campsie 6
Sep 7 Vale of Leven 0 Dumbarton 0
Sep 7 Victoria 1 Cowlairs 21
Apr 31 West Calder 2 Broxburn 9
Sep 7 Whitefield 0 Northern 5

Replays
Champfleurie W Bathgate 0
Sep 14 Ayr 3 Maybole 1
Sep 14 Dumbarton 1 Vale of Leven 1
Both Qualified
Sep 14 Irvine 8 Lugar Boswell 0
Sep 14 Kilbirnie 5 Dalry 2
Sep 14 Queen's Park 2 Celtic 1

2nd Round
Sep 28 1st Rrv 2 Morton 10
Sep 28 Abercorn 10 Thornliebank 1
Sep 28 Aberdeen 2 Orion 1
Sep 28 Airdrie 5 Uddingston 2
Sep 28 Battlefield 0 Thistle 2
Sep 28 Bellstane 1 Hearts 4
Sep 28 Broxburn 2 Leith A 2
Sep 28 Camelon 4 Grangemouth 4
Sep 28 Campsie 3 Alloa 7
Sep 28 Carfin S 6 Motherwell 2
Sep 28 Clyde 1 Northern 2
Sep 28 Cowlairs 1 Linthouse 1
Sep 28 Dundee H 5 Dundee OB 6
Sep 28 Dundee W 0 Dundee East End 2
Dunfermline A W Dunfermline 0
Sep 28 Dumfries H 1 Queen of South 5
Sep 28 Duntocher H 3 Vale of Leven 4
Sep 28 Falkirk 5 King's Park 2
Sep 28 Hibernian 4 Mossend S 3
Sep 28 Kelvinside A 0 Rangers 13
Sep 28 Kilbirnie 5 Newmilns 0
Sep 28 Lanemark 2 Hurlford 1
Sep 28 Lassodie 3 Cowdenbeath 3
Sep 28 Laurieston 1 E Stirling 4
Sep 28 Lochee 1 Forfar A 7
Sep 28 Lugar Boswell 0 Ayr 2
Sep 28 Moffat 4 5th Rrv 1
Oban W Lochgilphead 0
Sep 28 Port Glasgow A 8 Greenock A 0
Sep 28 Renton 1 Dumbarton 2
Sep 28 Royal Albert 1 Cambuslang 1
Sep 28 St Johnstone 2 Fair City A 2
Sep 28 St Mirren 6 Kilbarchan 0
Sep 28 Stevenson T 3 Annbank 2
Sep 28 Summerton A 0 Queen's Park 11
Sep 28 T Lanark 9 Maryhill 3
Sep 28 Union 5 Kirkintilloch A 2
Sep 28 Vale of Atholl 4 Dunblane 9

Sep 28	Vale of Leven	4	Methlan Park	1

Replays

Oct 5	Cambuslang	4	Royal Albert	1
Oct 5	Fair City A	3	St Johnstone	2
Oct 5	Grangemouth	7	Camelon	2
Oct 5	Leith A	2	Broxburn	1
Oct 5	Linthouse	3	Cowlairs	2
	Cowdenbeath		Lassodie	

3rd Round

Oct 19	Abercorn	5	Stevenson T	2
Oct 19	Aberdeen	5	Forfar A	3
Oct 19	Alloa	3	Oban	0
Oct 19	Champfleurie	0	Hearts	5
Oct 19	Dumbarton	1	T Lanark	1
Oct 19	Dunblane	3	Fair City A	0
Oct 19	Dundee OB	2	Dundee East End	3
Oct 19	Dunfermline A	4	Hibernian	4
Oct 19	Edinburgh Univ	0	Leith A	9
Oct 19	Falkirk	1	E Stirling	6
Oct 19	Grangemouth	2	Kilsyth W	2
Oct 19	Lanemark	4	Ayr A	3
Oct 19	Moffat	0	Queen of S'th W	0
Oct 19	Morton	1	Ayr	4
Oct 19	Northern	2	Carfin S	1
Oct 19	Port Glasgow A	3	Kilbirnie	4
Oct 19	Queen's Park	8	Vale of Leven W	0
Oct 19	Rangers	0	Vale of Leven	0
Oct 19	St Mirren	5	Pollokshaw	1
Oct 19	Thistle	2	Airdrie	2
Oct 19	Union	1	Cambuslang	3
Oct 19	Wishaw T	8	Linthouse	5

Replays

Oct 26	Airdrie	3	Thistle	1
Oct 26	Hibernian	11	Dunfermline A	1
Oct 26	Kilsyth W	0	Grangemouth	1
Oct 26	Queen of S'th W	5	Moffat	5
	Both Qualified			
Oct 26	T Lanark	1	Dumbarton	0
Oct 26	Vale of Leven	3	Rangers	2
Nov 2	Cambuslang	6	Union	0
	After Protest			
Nov 2	Northern	3	Carfin S	4
	After Protest			

4th Round

Nov 9	Aberdeen	1	Queen's Park	13
Nov 9	Airdrie	2	Abercorn	3
Nov 9	Ayr	1	Leith A	1
Nov 9	Dunblane	4	Cowdenbeath	6
Nov 9	Dundee East End	3	Cambuslang	2
Nov 9	Grangemouth	1	Vale of Leven	7
Nov 9	Hearts	9	Alloa	1
Nov 9	Kilbirnie	5	E Stirling	2
Nov 9	Lanemark	2	St Mirren	8
Nov 9	Moffat	4	Carfin S	2
Nov 9	Queen of S'th W	3	Hibernian	7
Nov 9	T Lanark	2	Linthouse	0

Replays

Nov 16	Leith A	4	Ayr	1
Nov 23	Dundee East End	3	Cambuslang	2
	After Protest			

5th Round

Nov 30	Cowdenbeath	2	Abercorn	8
Nov 30	Moffat	2	Dundee East End	2
Nov 30	Queen's Park	1	St Mirren	0
Nov 30	Vale of Leven	3	Hearts	1

Replays

Dec 7	Dundee East End	5	Moffat	1

6th Round

Dec 21	Abercorn	6	Hibernian	2
Dec 21	Kilbirnie	1	T Lanark	4
Dec 21	Queen's Park	1	Leith A	0
Dec 21	Vale of Leven	4	Dundee East End	0

Semi-finals

Jan 27	Queen's Park	2	Abercorn	0
Jan 27	Vale of Leven	3	T Lanark	0

Final

Feb 15	Queen's Park	1	Vale of Leven	1
	played at Ibrox			

Replay

Feb 22	Queen's Park	2	Vale of Leven	1
	played at Ibrox			

Season 1890-91

1st Round

Sep 6	Abercorn	8	Irvine	0
Sep 6	Annan	2	Dumfries W	8
Sep 6	Arthurlie	2	St Mirren	5
	Ayr	*W*	Kilbarchan	*0*
Sep 6	Ayr Parkhouse	6	Kilbirnie	1
Sep 6	Bathgate	3	Dunfermline A	2
Sep 6	Battlefield	1	T Lanark	4
	Boness	*W*	Blair Adam	*0*
Sep 6	Brechin	3	Kirriemuir	4
Sep 6	Bridge of Allan	7	Southfield R	2
	Broxburn	*W*	West Calder	*0*
Sep 6	Burnbank S	11	United Abstainer	0
Sep 6	Burntisland T	4	Bonnyrigg R	2
Sep 6	Caledonian	2	Victoria U	1
Sep 6	Cambuslang	3	Glasgow W	1
Sep 6	Camelon	4	Alloa	3
Sep 6	Campsie	4	Laurieston	1
Sep 6	Campsie H	3	Clydebank A	6
	Carfin S	*W*	Cartha	*0*
	Carlton	*W*	Lugar Boswell	*0*
Sep 6	Carrington	1	Albion R	2
Sep 6	Cathcart	5	Pollokshaws H	3
Sep 6	Celtic	1	Rangers	0
Sep 6	Clackmannan	9	Milton	0
Sep 6	Clyde	7	Whitefield	2
Sep 6	Cowdenbeath	10	Linlithgow A	1
Sep 6	Cowlairs	1	Airdrie	3
	Crieff	*W*	Vale of Atholl	*0*
Sep 6	Dalry	5	Pollokshaws	2
Sep 6	Denny	1	Alloa	4
Sep 6	Douglas R	0	5th KRV	5
Sep 6	Dumbarton	8	Smithston H	2
Sep 6	Dumfries	9	Newton Stewart	0
	Dundee H	*W*	Lochee	*0*
Sep 6	Dundee W	3	Arbroath	3
Sep 6	E Stirling	8	Grangemouth	2
Sep 6	Fair City A	7	Dunblane	3
	Falkirk	*W*	Vale of Bannock	*0*
Sep 6	Forfar A	2	Dundee OB	7
Sep 6	Greenock Abst	0	Newmilns	13
Sep 6	Hamilton A	0	Linthouse	8
Sep 6	Hearts	7	Raith R	2
Sep 6	Inveraray	4	Lochgilphead	1
Sep 6	Inverness T	2	Inverness C	4
Sep 6	Kelvinside A	1	Glasgow H	1
Sep 6	Kilmarnock	4	Annbank	4
Sep 6	Kilsyth W	2	Renton	1
Sep 6	Kirkcaldy W	3	Hibernian	4
Sep 6	Kirkintilloch A	2	Clydebank	2
	Lanemark	*W*	Dykebar	*0*
Sep 6	Leith A	3	Armadale	2
	Maryhill	*W*	Southern A	*0*
Sep 6	Mauchline	1	Kilmarnock A	3
Sep 6	Maybole	3	Hurlford	4
Sep 6	Methlan Park	1	King's Park	0
Sep 6	Mid-Annandale	15	Rising T	0
Sep 6	Montrose	7	Broughty	1
Sep 6	Morton	7	Ayr A	2
	Mossend S	*W*	Lassodie	*0*
Sep 6	Motherwell S	3	Fairfield	7
Sep 6	Neilston	7	Bute R	3
Sep 6	Northern	5	Clydesdale	0
Sep 6	Oban	3	Oban R	0
Sep 6	Old Kilpatrick	1	Jamestown	6
Sep 6	Orion	1	Aberdeen	5
Sep 6	Penicuik A	5	Champfleurie	3
Sep 6	Port Glasgow A	0	Monkcastle	2
Sep 6	Royal Albert	5	Motherwell	4
	Rutherglen	*W*	St Brides	*0*
Sep 6	Saltcoats V	4	Lochwinnoch	3
Sep 6	Slamannan	6	Gairdoch	2
Sep 6	St Bernard's	7	Adventurers	0
	St Bernard's Disqualified			
Sep 6	St Johnstone	2	Coupar Angus	2
	Coupar A Disqualified			
Sep 6	Stevenston T	9	Stewarton C	2
	Stranraer	*W*	East End	*0*
	Summerton A	*W*	Whifflet S	*0*
Sep 6	Thistle	3	Queen's Park	5
Sep 6	Tillicoultry	1	Dalmuir T	5
Sep 6	Uddingston	6	Hamilton H	0
Sep 6	Union	12	Grasshoppers	1
	Vale of Leven	*W*	Stenhousemuir	*0*
	Vale of Leven W	*W*	Dunipace	*0*
Sep 6	Wishaw T	3	Partick T	2

Replays

Sep 13	Annbank	6	Kilmarnock	2
Sep 13	Arbroath	4	Dundee W	1
Sep 13	Clydebank	4	Kirkintilloch A	3
Sep 13	Glasgow H	5	Kelvinside A	1
	Northern	7	Clydesdale	1
	After Protest			

2nd Round

Sep 27	5th KRV	9	Mid-Annandale	1
Sep 27	Abercorn	12	Cathcart	0
Sep 27	Aberdeen	8	Caledonian	0
	Adventurers	*W*	Vale of Leven W	*0*
Sep 27	Airdrie	3	Annbank	1
Sep 27	Ayr Parkhouse	1	Summerton A	2
Sep 27	Bathgate	6	Union	2
Sep 27	Beith	2	Cambuslang	4
Oct 11	Boness	7	Bellstane	0
Sep 27	Bridge of Allan	1	Vale of Leven	5
Sep 27	Broxburn	5	Clackmannan	2
Sep 27	Burnbank S	2	Stevenston T	1
Sep 27	Camelon	2	Alva	1
Sep 27	Campsie	4	E Stirling	4
Sep 27	Celtic	2	Carfin S	2
Sep 27	Clyde	4	Hurlford	3
Sep 27	Clydebank A	3	Kilsyth W	5
Sep 27	Crieff	0	Fair City A	11
Sep 27	Dalmuir T	5	Cowdenbeath	7
Sep 27	Dumfries W	6	Dumfries	5
Sep 27	East End	4	St Johnstone	2
Sep 27	Fairfield	2	Royal Albert	5
	Glengowan	*W*	Carlton	*0*
Sep 27	Harp	1	Arbroath	5
	Hearts	*W*	Burntisland	*0*
Sep 27	Hibernian	1	Dumbarton	9
Sep 27	Inveraray	4	Oban	2
	Inverness C	*W*	Portland	*0*
Sep 27	Jamestown	2	Mossend S	5
Sep 27	Kirriemuir	0	Montrose	3
Sep 27	Leith A	7	Falkirk	2
Sep 27	Linthouse	7	Maryhill	2
Sep 27	Monkcastle	4	Dalry	3
Sep 27	Morton	3	Neilston	2
Sep 27	Newmilns	2	Uddingston	2
Sep 27	Penicuik A	3	Methlan P	4
Sep 27	Queen's Park	5	Northern	1
Sep 27	Rutherglen	1	Ayr	3
Sep 27	Saltcoats V	3	Lanemark	2
Sep 27	Slamannan	5	Clydebank	2
Sep 27	St Mirren	5	Albion R	1
Sep 27	T Lanark	8	Kilmarnock A	1
Sep 27	Wishaw T	4	Glasgow H	1

Replays

Oct 4	Campsie	1	E Stirling	3
Oct 4	Carfin S	1	Celtic	3
Oct 4	Uddingston	5	Newmilns	1
Oct 11	Burnbank S	3	Stevenston T	0
	After Protest			
Oct 11	Slamannan	3	Clydebank	5
	After Protest			

3rd Round

Oct 18	Airdrie	8	Glengowan	0
Oct 18	Bathgate	6	Broxburn	0
Oct 18	Bo'ness	1	Mossend S	1
Oct 18	Cambuslang	1	St Mirren	2
Oct 18	Clyde	3	Ayr	4
Oct 18	Dumbarton	6	Clydebank	0
	Dumfries W	*W*	Stranraer	*0*
Oct 18	E Stirling	3	Camelon	3
Oct 18	Edinburgh Univ	3	Cowdenbeath	2
Oct 18	Inverness C	6	Aberdeen	2
Oct 18	Kilsyth W	0	Vale of Leven	8
Oct 18	Leith A	12	Adventurers	0
Oct 18	Linthouse	3	Abercorn	4
Oct 18	Methlan Park	0	Hearts	3
Oct 18	Monkcastle	1	Burnbank S	7
Oct 18	Montrose	4	Fair City A	1
Oct 18	Morton	10	Inveraray	0
Oct 18	Dundee OB	4	Dundee East End	0
Oct 18	Queen's Park	6	Uddingston	0
Oct 18	Royal Albert	6	Saltcoats V	2
Oct 18	T Lanark	8	Summerton A	1
Oct 18	Wishaw T	2	Celtic	6

Replays

Oct 25	Camelon	6	E Stirling	10
Oct 25	Mossend S	9	Bo'ness	1

4th Round

Nov 8	5th KRV	6	Arbroath	2
Nov 8	Abercorn	8	Bathgate	0
Nov 8	Airdrie	1	St Mirren	2
Nov 8	Ayr	3	Hearts	4
Nov 8	Dumbarton	7	Mossend S	3
Nov 8	Dundee OB	1	Celtic	3
Nov 8	Edinburgh Univ	0	Queen's Park	7
Nov 8	E Stirling	2	Inverness C	0
Nov 8	Leith A	3	Vale of Leven	1
Nov 8	Montrose	0	T Lanark	3
Nov 8	Morton	6	Dumfries W	4
Nov 8	Royal Albert	1	Burnbank S	0

5th Round

Nov 29	Celtic	2	Royal Albert	2
Dec 6	Dumbarton	8	5th KRV	0
Nov 29	Hearts	5	Morton	1
Dec 6	St Mirren	2	Queen's Park	3

Replays

Dec 6	Royal Albert	0	Celtic	4
	Abandoned			
Dec 13	Celtic	2	Royal Albert	0
	played at Ibrox			

6th Round

Dec 20	Dumbarton	3	Celtic	0
Dec 20	Hearts	3	E Stirling	1
Dec 20	Leith A	2	Abercorn	3
Jan 10	Queen's Park	1	T Lanark	1

Replays

Jan 17	T Lanark	2	Queen's Park	2
Jan 24	Queen's Park	1	T Lanark	4

Semi-finals

Jan 17	Dumbarton	3	Abercorn	1
Jan 31	T Lanark	1	Hearts	4

Final

Feb 7	Dumbarton	0	Hearts	1
	played at Hampden Park			

Season 1891-92

1st Round

Sep 5	Adventurers	0	St Bernard's	5
Sep 5	Alva	1	Stenhousemuir	0
Sep 5	Annbank	5	Ayr Parkhouse	0
Sep 5	Armadale	3	Bathgate	3
Sep 5	Ayr	12	Pollokshaw	0
Sep 5	Beith	2	Arthurlie	2
	Arthurlie Awarded Tie			
Sep 5	Blairgowrie OB	0	Dunblane	5
Sep 5	Bonnyrigg R	1	Penicuik A	6
Sep 5	Bridge of Allan	7	Dumbarton U	2
Sep 5	Broughty	3	Montrose	3
Sep 5	Broxburn	2	Raith R	1
Sep 5	Burnbank S	5	Hamilton H	1
Sep 5	Burntisland T	4	Linlithgow A	6
Sep 5	Bute R	3	Monkcastle	4
Sep 5	Camelon	1	Dalmuir T	3
Sep 5	Campsie	7	Kilsyth W	3
Sep 5	Cathcart	1	Ayr A	3
Sep 5	Clacknacuddin	0	Inverness C	5
Sep 5	Clydebank	7	Grasshoppers	1
Sep 5	Clydesdale	2	Whitefield	2
Sep 5	Cronberry	2	Hurlford	4
Sep 5	Douglas R	0	Queen of South	14
Sep 12	Dundee	2	Dundee OB	0
Sep 5	Dunfermline A	4	Bo'ness	0
Sep 5	E Stirling	8	Jamestown	2
Sep 5	Forfar A	1	Dundee East End	3
Sep 5	Gairsloch	2	Grangemouth	4
Sep 5	Glasgow W	1	Partick T	2
Sep 5	Hamilton A	1	21st RS Fusilier	4
Sep 5	Inveraray	3	Oban	2
Sep 5	Johnstone	20	Greenock Abst	1
Sep 5	Kilbarchan	10	1st ARV	0
Sep 5	Kilbirnie	2	Morton	2
Sep 5	Kilsyth S	3	Dunipace	4
Sep 5	King's Park	5	Clydebank A	3
Sep 5	Kirkcaldy W	2	Polton Vale	3
Sep 5	Lassosie	0	Cowdenbeath	3
Sep 5	Laurieston	2	Denny	4
Sep 5	Linthouse	12	Carfin H	0
Sep 5	Lochee U	3	Johnstone W	4
Sep 5	Methlan Park	1	Slamannan R	3
Sep 5	Mid Annandale	5	Dumfries	4
Sep 5	Motherwell	1	Cowlairs	4
Sep 5	Muirhouse R	1	Mossend S	7
Sep 5	Neilston	3	Kilmarnock A	6
Sep 5	Newmilns	1	Dykebar	7
Sep 5	Old Kilpatrick	0	Kirkintilloch A	3
Sep 5	Port Glasgow A	6	Lanemark	3
Sep 5	Saltcoats V	6	Lochwinnoch	3
Sep 5	Smithston H	6	Alloa	3
Sep 5	Southern A	1	Royal Albert	6
Sep 5	St Johnstone	2	Fair City A	3
Sep 5	Stevenston T	5	Galston	2
Sep 5	Stewarton	3	Irving	3
Sep 5	Stonehaven	0	Bon Accord	8
Sep 5	Stranraer	2	5th KRV	3
Sep 5	Strathmore	3	Kirriemuir	7
Sep 5	Thistle	6	Shettleston S	1
Sep 5	Vale of Bannoch	5	Slamannan	3
Sep 5	Vale of Gala	3	Selkirk	4
Sep 5	Vale of Leven	1	Coupar Angus	6
Sep 5	Wishaw T	7	Albion R	3

Replays

Sep 12	Bathgate	3	Armadale	0
Sep 12	Brechin	3	Arbroath	9
Sep 12	Dalry	5	Catrine T	0
Sep 12	Montrose	5	Broughty	1
Sep 12	Morton	8	Kilbirnie	1
Sep 12	Orion	5	Victoria U	1
Sep 12	Whitefield	7	Clydesdale	0
	Irving		Stewarton	

2nd Round

Sep 26	Alva	3	Mossend S	9
Sep 26	Annbank	4	Rutherglen	0
Sep 26	Arbroath	7	Fair City A	1
Sep 26	Ayr	3	21st RS Fusilier	3
Oct 3	Ayr A	1	Kilbarchan	4
Sep 26	Bathgate	8	Slamannan R	1
Sep 26	Battlefield	9	Whitefield	0
Sep 26	Bon Accord	2	Aberdeen	5
Sep 26	Bridge of Allan	3	Clackmannan	0
Sep 26	Broxburn S	6	Campsie	4
Sep 26	Carrington	2	Burnbank S	8
Sep 26	Coupar Angus	4	Montrose	0
Sep 26	Dalry	9	Stewarton	0
Sep 26	Denny	2	Dunfermline A	1
Sep 26	Dundee H	5	Johnstone W	2
Sep 26	Duntocher H	4	Broxburn	2
Sep 26	Dykebar	1	Mauchline	4
Sep 26	E Stirling	3	King's Park	0
Sep 26	Grangemouth	0	Falkirk	2
Sep 26	Inveraray	4	Oban R	2
Sep 26	Johnstone	4	Thistle	7
Sep 26	Kirkintilloch A	4	Polton Vale	2
Sep 26	Kirriemuir	1	Dunblane	8
Sep 26	Morton	3	Airdrie	1
Sep 26	Newton Stewart	1	Mid-Annandale	1
Sep 26	Partick T	0	Hurlford	3
Sep 26	Penicuik A	2	Dalmuir T	3
Sep 26	Port Glasgow A	4	Glengowan	1
Sep 26	Queen of South	6	Moffat	1
Sep 26	Royal Albert	6	Cowlairs	6
Sep 26	Smithston H	11	Linlithgow A	1
Sep 26	St Bernard's	7	Dunipace	1
Sep 26	Stevenston T	3	Kilmarnock A	3
Sep 26	Vale of Atholl	1	Dundee East End	7
Sep 26	Vale of Bannoch	0	Clydebank	7
Sep 26	Wishaw T	5	Arthurlie	2

Replays

Oct 3	Broxburn S	3	Campsie	1
	After Protest			
Oct 3	Cowlairs	4	Royal Albert	4
	Both In Next Round			
Oct 3	E Stirling	7	King's Park	2
	After Protest			
Oct 3	Kilmarnock A	2	Stevenston T	2
	Both In Next Round			
Oct 3	Mid-Allondale	*W*	Newton Stewart	*O*
Oct 3	21st Rs Fusilier	1	Ayr	3

3rd Round

Oct 17	Aberdeen	3	Orion	1
Oct 17	Annbank	2	Hurlford	0
Oct 17	Ayr	6	Inveraray	1
Oct 17	Bathgate	5	Falkirk	5
Oct 17	Battlefield	4	Stevenston T	2
Oct 17	Bridge of Allan	4	Duntocher H	2
Oct 17	Burnbank S	5	Mauchline	0
Oct 17	Coupar Angus	2	Dunblane	3
Oct 17	Cowdenbeath	0	Clydebank	3
Oct 17	Cowlairs	5	Dalry	0
Oct 17	Denny	6	Edinburgh U	1
Oct 17	Dundee East End	1	Dundee H	1
Oct 17	Inverness T	2	Inverness C	1
Oct 17	Kilmarnock A	5	Port Glasgow A	4
Oct 17	Monkcastle	4	Morton	2
Oct 17	Mossend S	4	E Stirling	5
Oct 17	Queen of South	4	5th KRV	7
Oct 17	Saltcoats V	1	Linthouse	7
Oct 17	Smithston H	1	Broxburn S	2
Oct 17	St Bernard's	5	Kirkintilloch	1
Oct 17	Thistle	9	Kilbarchan	1
Oct 17	Wishaw T	3	Royal Albert	2

Replays

Oct 24	Dunblane	*W*	Coupar Angus	*O*
	After Protest			
Oct 24	Dundee H	0	Dundee East End	2
Oct 24	Falkirk	0	Bathgate	3

4th Round

Nov 7	Annbank		Wishaw T	
Nov 7	Arbroath	10	Denny	0
Nov 7	Bathgate	5	Clydebank	1
Nov 7	Cowlairs	9	5th KRV	3
Nov 7	Dalmuir T	1	Aberdeen	2
Nov 7	Dundee East End	3	Monkcastle	6
Nov 7	Inverness T	0	Battlefield	1
Nov 7	Thistle	5	Burnbank S	2

5th Round

Nov 28	Abercorn	2	Queen's Park	3
Nov 28	Annbank	2	Battlefield	1
Nov 28	Bathgate	6	Linthouse	0
Nov 28	Broxburn S	7	Northern	2
Dec 12	Cowlairs	3	Cambuslang	1
Nov 28	Dumbarton	4	Thistle	0
Nov 28	E Stirling	1	Kilmarnock	6
Nov 28	Hearts	3	Clyde	1
	Abandoned			
Nov 28	Kilmarnock A	7	Bridge of Allan	2
Nov 28	Leith A	5	Dunblane	0
Dec 5	Mid-Annandale	6	Aberdeen	2
Nov 28	Monkcastle	3	Arbroath	4
Nov 28	Rangers	5	St Bernard's	1
Nov 28	Renton	7	Ayr	4
Nov 28	St Mirren	2	Celtic	4
Nov 28	T Lanark	3	Vale of Leven	0

Replays

Dec 5	Hearts	8	Clyde	0
Dec 12	Cowlairs	3	Cambuslang	1
	After Protest			

6th Round

Dec 19	Annbank	2	Leith A	1
Dec 19	Arbroath	0	Renton	3
Dec 19	Broxburn S	4	Hearts	5
Dec 19	Celtic	3	Kilmarnock A	0
Dec 19	Cowlairs	11	Mid-Annandale	2
Dec 19	Queen's Park	6	Bathgate	0
Dec 19	Rangers	0	Kilmarnock	0
Dec 19	T Lanark	1	Dumbarton	3

Replays

Dec 26	Kilmarnock	1	Rangers	1
Jan 23	Kilmarnock	2	Rangers	3
	played at St Mirren			

7th Round

Jan 23	Celtic	4	Cowlairs	1
Jan 23	Dumbarton	2	Queen's Park	2
Jan 30	Rangers	2	Annbank	0
Jan 23	Renton	4	Hearts	4

Replays

Jan 30	Hearts	2	Renton	2
Jan 30	Queen's Park	4	Dumbarton	1
Feb 6	Hearts	2	Renton	3
	played at Hampden Park			

Semi-finals

Feb 6	Celtic	5	Rangers	3
Feb 13	Renton	1	Queen's Park	1

Replay

Feb 27	Queen's Park	3	Renton	0

Final

Mar 12	Celtic	1	Queen's Park	0
	played at Ibrox			

Replay Crowd Trouble

Apr 9	Celtic	5	Queen's Park	1
	played at Ibrox			

Season 1892-93

1st Round

Nov 26	5th KRV	5	Camelon	3
Nov 26	Abercorn	6	Renton	0
Nov 26	Aberdeen	4	St Mirren	6
Nov 26	Airdrie	3	T Lanark	6
Nov 26	Albion R	1	Kilmarnock	2
Nov 26	Celtic	3	Linthouse	1
Nov 26	Clyde	4	Dumbarton	1
Nov 26	Cowlairs	2	Queen's Park	5
Nov 26	Dunblane	0	Broxburn S	3
Nov 26	King's Park	6	Monkcastle	2
Nov 26	Motherwell	9	Campsie	2
Nov 26	Northern	1	Leith A	3
Nov 26	Rangers	7	Annbank	0
Nov 26	Royal Albert	6	Cambuslang	1
Nov 26	St Bernard's	5	Queen of S'th W	1
Nov 26	Stenhousemuir	1	Hearts	1

Replays

Dec 17	Dumbarton	6	Clyde	1
	After Protest			
Dec 17	Hearts	8	Stenhousemuir	0
Dec 17	Motherwell	6	Campsie	4
	After Protest			
Jan 21	Queen's Park	4	Cowlairs	1
	After Protest			

2nd Round

Dec 17	Abercorn	4	T Lanark	5
Dec 17	Broxburn S	3	King's Park	0
Dec 17	Celtic	7	5th KRV	0
Jan 28	Kilmarnock	0	Queen's Park	8
Dec 17	Leith A	0	St Mirren	2
Dec 24	Motherwell	2	Hearts	4
Jan 21	Rangers	1	Dumbarton	0
Dec 17	Royal Albert	1	St Bernard's	1

Replay

Dec 24	St Bernard's	5	Royal Albert	2

3rd Round

Jan 21	Broxburn S	4	St Mirren	3
Jan 21	Celtic	5	T Lanark	1
Feb 4	Hearts	1	Queen's Park	1
Jan 28	St Bernard's	3	Rangers	2

Replay

Feb 11	Queen's Park	5	Hearts	2

Semi-finals

Feb 4	Celtic	5	St Bernard's	0
Feb 18	Queen's Park	4	Broxburn S	2

Final

Feb 25	Celtic	1	Queen's Park	0
	played at Ibrox			

Replay Because of Pitch

Mar 11	Celtic	1	Queen's Park	2
	played at Ibrox			

Season 1893-94

1st Round

Nov 25	Abercorn	2	5th KRV	1
Nov 25	Albion R	6	Black Watch	0
Nov 25	Broxburn S	3	Arbroath	8
Nov 25	Cambuslang	3	E Stirling	2
Nov 25	Celtic	6	Hurlford	0
Nov 25	Clyde	5	King's Park	2
Nov 25	Grangemouth	1	Renton	7
Nov 25	Kilmarnock	1	St Bernard's	3

Nov 25	Leith A	11	Orion	2
Nov 25	Linthouse	1	Queen's Park	5
Nov 25	Port Glasgow A	7	Airdrie	5
Nov 25	Rangers	8	Cowlairs	0
Nov 25	St Mirren	1	Hearts	0
Nov 25	Thistle	1	Battlefield	3
Nov 25	T Lanark	9	Inverness	3
Nov 25	Vale of Leven	1	Dumbarton	2

2nd Round

Dec 16	Battlefield	3	Abercorn	3
Dec 16	Celtic	7	Albion R	0
Dec 16	Clyde	6	Cambuslang	0
Dec 16	Dumbarton	1	St Bernard's	3
Dec 16	Queen's Park	3	Arbroath	0
Dec 16	Rangers	2	Leith A	0
Dec 16	Renton	2	Port Glasgow A	2
Dec 16	T Lanark	3	St Mirren	2

Replays

Dec 23	Abercorn	3	Battlefield	0
Dec 23	Renton	1	Port Glasgow A	3

3rd Round

Jan 13	Abercorn	3	Queen's Park	3
Jan 13	Celtic	8	St Bernard's	1
Jan 13	Clyde	0	Rangers	5
Jan 13	T Lanark	2	Port Glasgow A	1

Replays

Jan 20	Queen's Park	3	Abercorn	3
Jan 27	Abercorn	0	Queen's Park	2
	played at Ibrox			

Semi-finals

Feb 3	Rangers	1	Queen's Park	1
Feb 3	T Lanark	3	Celtic	5

Replay

Feb 10	Queen's Park	1	Rangers	3

Final

Feb 17	Celtic	1	Rangers	3
	played at Hampden Park			

Season 1894-95

1st Round

Nov 24	Abercorn	1	Leith A	5
Nov 24	Annbank	5	T Lanark	4
Nov 24	Ayr Parkhouse	5	Polton Vale	3
Nov 24	Celtic	4	Queen's Park	1
Nov 24	Clyde	7	Stevenston T	2
Nov 24	Dumbarton	2	Galston	1
Nov 24	Dundee	5	Orion	1
	played at Aberdeen			
Nov 24	Hibernian	6	Forfar A	1
Nov 24	Kilmarnock	5	E Stirling	1
Nov 24	Lochee	2	King's Park	5
Nov 24	Motherwell	1	Mossend S	2
Nov 24	Raith R	6	5th KRV	3
Nov 24	Rangers	1	Hearts	2
Nov 24	Slamannan	2	Renton	3
Nov 24	St Bernard's	4	Airdrie	2
Nov 24	St Mirren	5	Battlefield	0

Replays

Dec 8	Abercorn	4	Leith	1
	After Protest			
Dec 8	Renton	4	Slamannan	0
	After Protest			
Dec 8	St Mirren	8	Battlefield	1
	After Protest			

2nd Round

Dec 15	Abercorn	1	Hearts	6
Dec 15	Ayr Parkhouse	3	Mossend S	1
Dec 15	Clyde	4	Annbank	2
Dec 15	Dundee	2	St Mirren	0
Dec 15	Hibernian	2	Celtic	0
Dec 15	King's Park	2	Dumbarton	1
Dec 15	Renton	6	5th KRV	0
Dec 15	St Bernard's	3	Kilmarnock	1

Replay

Dec 29	Celtic	2	Hibernian	0
	After Protest			

3rd Round

Jan 19	Ayr Parkhouse	2	Renton	3
Feb 2	Clyde	2	St Bernard's	6
Jan 19	Dundee	1	Celtic	0
Jan 12	Hearts	4	King's Park	2

Replay

Feb 23	Clyde	1	St Bernard's	2
	After Protest			

Semi-finals

Feb 16	Dundee	1	Renton	1
Mar 3	St Bernard's	0	Hearts	0

Replays

Feb 23	Dundee	3	Renton	3
	played at Hampden Park			
Mar 9	Dundee	0	Renton	3
	played at Celtic Park			
Mar 16	Hearts	0	St Bernard's	1
	played at Logie Green			

Final

Apr 20	Renton	1	St Bernard's	2
	played at Ibrox			

Season 1895-96

1st Round

Jan 18	Annbank	3	Kilmarnock	2
Jan 11	Arbroath	5	King's Park	0
Jan 18	Ayr	3	Abercorn	2
Jan 11	Blantyre	1	Hearts	12
Jan 18	Celtic	2	Queen's Park	4
Jan 18	Dumbarton	1	Rangers	1
Jan 11	E Stirling	2	Hibernian	3
Jan 11	Lochgelly U	2	Raith R	1
Jan 11	Morton	2	Dundee	3
Jan 11	Polton Vale	0	Clyde	3
Jan 18	Port Glasgow A	4	Arthurlie	2
Jan 11	Renton	1	Cowdenbeath	0
Jan 11	St Bernard's	8	Clackmannan	1
Jan 11	St Johnstone	4	Dundee W	3
Jan 11	St Mirren	7	Alloa	0
Jan 18	T Lanark	6	Leith A	0

Replay

Jan 25	Rangers	3	Dumbarton	1
Feb 1	Lochgelly U	2	Raith R	5
	After Protest			

2nd Round

Jan 25	Arbroath	3	St Johnstone	1
Feb 1	Ayr	1	Hearts	5
Feb 8	Hibernian	6	Raith R	1
Jan 25	Queen's Park	8	Port Glasgow A	1
Feb 1	Rangers	5	St Mirren	0
Jan 25	Renton	2	Clyde	1
Jan 25	St Bernard's	2	Annbank	0
Jan 25	T Lanark	4	Dundee	1

3rd Round

Feb 8	Arbroath	0	Hearts	4
Feb 8	Queen's Park	2	St Bernard's	3
Feb 15	Rangers	2	Hibernian	3
Feb 8	T Lanark	3	Renton	3

Replay

Feb 15	Renton	2	T Lanark	0

Semi-finals

Feb 22	Hearts	1	St Bernard's	0
Feb 22	Hibernian	2	Renton	1

Final

Mar 14	Hearts	3	Hibernian	1
	played at Logie Green			

Season 1896-97

1st Round

Jan 9	Abercorn	4	Hurlford	0
Jan 9	Arthurlie	4	Celtic	2
Jan 9	Blantyre	5	Bathgate	0
Jan 9	Dumbarton	2	Raith R	1
Jan 9	Duncrub Park	1	Hibernian	10
Jan 9	Dundee	7	Inverness T	1
Jan 9	Falkirk	2	Orion	0
Jan 9	Hearts	2	Clyde	0
Jan 9	Leith A	5	Dunblane	1
Jan 9	Lochgelly	1	King's Park	2
Jan 9	Morton	3	Johnstone	1
Jan 9	Motherwell	3	Kilmarnock	3
Jan 9	Partick T	2	Rangers	4
Jan 9	St Bernard's	2	Queen's Park	1
Jan 9	St Mirren	5	Renton	1
Jan 9	T Lanark	8	Newton Stewart	1

Replay

Jan 16	Kilmarnock	5	Motherwell	2

2nd Round

Jan 23	Abercorn	4	Blantyre	1
Feb 13	Arthurlie	1	Morton	5
Feb 6	Dumbarton	4	Leith A	4
Jan 30	Dundee	5	King's Park	0
Jan 23	Kilmarnock	3	Falkirk	1
Jan 23	Rangers	3	Hibernian	0
Jan 30	St Bernard's	5	St Mirren	0
Feb 6	T Lanark	5	Hearts	2

Replay

Feb 6	Kilmarnock	7	Falkirk	3
	After Protest			
Feb 13	Leith A	3	Dumbarton	3
Feb 20	Dumbarton	3	Leith A	2
	played at Motherwell			

3rd Round

Feb 27	Dumbarton	2	St Bernard's	0
Feb 13	Dundee	0	Rangers	4
Feb 13	Kilmarnock	3	T Lanark	1
Feb 20	Morton	2	Abercorn	2

Replay

Feb 27	Abercorn	2	Morton	3

Semi-finals

Mar 13	Dumbarton	4	Kilmarnock	3
Mar 13	Morton	2	Rangers	7

Final

Mar 20	Dumbarton	1	Rangers	5
	played at Hampden Park			

Season 1897-98

1st Round

Jan 8	Abercorn	1	Hibernian	1
Jan 8	Arthurlie	0	Celtic	7
Jan 8	Ayr Parkhouse	2	Kilmarnock A	1
Jan 8	Bo'ness	0	Queen's Park	6
Jan 8	Cartvale	4	Bathgate	2
Jan 15	Clyde	1	T Lanark	3
Jan 8	Dundee	2	Partick T	1
Jan 8	Dundee W	3	Orion	1
Jan 8	Hearts	8	Lochee U	0
Jan 8	Kilmarnock	5	6th GRV	1
Jan 8	Leith A	2	Port Glasgow A	0
Jan 8	Morton	7	Motherwell	1
Jan 8	Raith R	2	E Stirling	4
Jan 8	Rangers	8	Polton Vale	0
Jan 8	St Bernard's	1	Dumbarton	1
Jan 8	St Mirren	7	Dumfries	2

Replays

Jan 15	Dumbarton	1	St Bernard's	3
Jan 15	Hibernian	7	Abercorn	1

2nd Round

Jan 22	Dundee	2	St Mirren	0
Jan 22	Dundee W	3	Ayr Parkhouse	6
Jan 22	Hearts	4	Morton	1
Jan 22	Hibernian	3	E Stirling	1

Jan 22	Kilmarnock	9	Leith A	2
Jan 22	Rangers	12	Cartvale	0
Jan 22	St Bernard's	0	Queen's Park	5
Jan 22	T Lanark	3	Celtic	2

3rd Round

Feb 5	Ayr Parkhouse	2	Kilmarnock	7
Feb 5	Dundee	3	Hearts	0
Feb 5	Queen's Park	1	Rangers	3
Feb 5	T Lanark	2	Hibernian	0

Semi-finals

Feb 19	Kilmarnock	3	Dundee	2
Feb 19	Rangers	1	T Lanark	1

Replay

Feb 26	T Lanark	2	Rangers	2
Mar 12	Rangers	2	T Lanark	0
	played at Cathkin Park			

Final

Mar 26	Kilmarnock	0	Rangers	2
	played at Hampden Park			

Season 1898-99

1st Round

Jan 14	6th GRV	1	Celtic	8
Jan 14	Airdrie	3	Arbroath	3
Jan 14	Ayr Parkhouse	3	Dundee	1
Jan 14	Bo'ness	3	St Bernard's	3
Jan 14	Clyde	3	Wishaw T	0
Jan 14	E Stirling	4	Dumbarton	1
Jan 14	Forfar A	4	West Calder	5
Jan 14	Hibernian	2	Royal Albert	1
Jan 14	Morton	3	Annbank	1
Jan 14	Orion	0	Kilmarnock	2
Jan 14	Partick T	5	Irvine	0
Jan 14	Port Glasgow A	3	Renton	2
Jan 14	Queen's Park	4	Kilsyth W	0
Jan 14	Rangers	4	Hearts	1
Jan 14	St Mirren	7	Leith A	1
Jan 14	T Lanark	4	Arthurlie	1

Replays

Jan 21	Arbroath	3	Airdrie	2
Jan 21	St Bernard's	4	Bo'ness	2

2nd Round

Feb 11	Ayr Parkhouse	1	Rangers	4
Feb 4	Celtic	3	St Bernard's	0
Feb 4	Clyde	3	Arbroath	1
Feb 11	E Stirling	1	Kilmarnock	1
Feb 11	Partick T	2	Morton	2
Feb 4	Port Glasgow A	3	West Calder	1
Feb 11	Queen's Park	5	Hibernian	1
Feb 11	T Lanark	1	St Mirren	2

Replays

Feb 18	Kilmarnock	0	E Stirling	0
Feb 18	Morton	1	Partick T	2
Feb 25	E Stirling	2	Kilmarnock	4
	played at Cathkin Park			

3rd Round

Mar 11	Kilmarnock	1	St Mirren	2
Feb 25	Port Glasgow A	7	Partick T	3
Feb 25	Queen's Park	1	Celtic	2
Feb 18	Rangers	4	Clyde	0

Semi-finals

Mar 11	Celtic	4	Port Glasgow A	2
Apr 15	St Mirren	1	Rangers	2

Final

Apr 22	Celtic	2	Rangers	0
	played at Hampden Park			

Season 1899-1900

1st Round

Jan 13	Abercorn	5	Ayr Parkhouse	2
Jan 13	Airdrie	0	Clyde	1
Jan 13	Arbroath	0	St Bernard's	1
Jan 13	Celtic	7	Bo'ness	1
Jan 13	Dundee	8	Douglas W	0
Jan 13	Forfar A	3	Motherwell	4
Jan 13	Forres Mechanic	1	Orion	1
Jan 13	Galston	1	Partick T	2
Jan 13	Hearts	0	St Mirren	0
Jan 13	Hibernian	3	Hamilton A	2
Jan 13	Kilmarnock	2	E Stirling	0
Jan 13	Maybole	4	Wishaw T	2
Jan 13	Port Glasgow A	7	Falkirk	1
Jan 13	Queen's Park	3	Leith A	0
Jan 13	Rangers	4	Morton	2
Jan 13	T Lanark	5	Raith R	0

Replays

Jan 20	Orion	4	Forres Mechanic	1
Jan 20	St Mirren	0	Hearts	3

2nd Round

Jan 27	Celtic	5	Port Glasgow A	1
Jan 27	Dundee	3	Clyde	3
Jan 27	Hearts	1	Hibernian	1
Jan 27	Kilmarnock	10	Orion	0
Jan 27	Partick T	2	St Bernard's	1
Jan 27	Queen's Park	5	Abercorn	1
Jan 27	Rangers	12	Maybole	0
Jan 27	T Lanark	2	Motherwell	1

Replays

Feb 3	Hibernian	1	Hearts	2
Feb 17	Clyde	0	Dundee	3

3rd Round

Feb 17	Celtic	4	Kilmarnock	0
Feb 17	Partick T	1	Rangers	6
Feb 24	Queen's Park	1	Dundee	0
Feb 10	T Lanark	1	Hearts	2

Semi-finals

Mar 3	Queen's Park	2	Hearts	1
Feb 24	Rangers	2	Celtic	2

Replay

Mar 3	Celtic	4	Rangers	0

Final

Apr 14	Celtic	4	Queen's Park	3
	played at Ibrox			

Season 1900-01

1st Round

Jan 12	Ayr	2	Orion	2
Jan 12	Celtic	1	Rangers	0
Jan 5	Clyde	6	E Stirling	0
Jan 12	Dundee	3	Arthurlie	1
Dec 31	Dundee W	0	Abercorn	3
Jan 12	Forfar A	0	Leith A	4
Jan 12	Hearts	7	Mossend S	0
Jan 12	Hibernian	7	Dumbarton	0
Jan 12	Kilmarnock	3	Airdrie	2
Jan 12	Morton	10	Bo'ness	0
Jan 12	Port Glasgow A	9	Newton Stewart	1
Jan 12	Royal Albert	1	St Johnstone	1
Jan 12	St Bernard's	5	Partick T	0
Jan 12	St Mirren	10	Kilwinning	0
Jan 12	Stenhousemuir	1	Queen's Park	3
Jan 12	T Lanark	5	Douglas W	0

Replay

Jan 19	Orion	1	Ayr	3
Feb 9	St Johnstone	0	Royal Albert	2

2nd Round

Jan 26	Ayr	1	St Mirren	3
Feb 9	Celtic	6	Kilmarnock	0
Feb 9	Clyde	3	Dundee	5
Feb 9	Hearts	2	Queen's Park	1
Feb 9	Leith A	0	Port Glasgow A	3
Jan 26	Morton	1	St Bernard's	1
Feb 16	Royal Albert	1	Hibernian	1
Jan 26	T Lanark	1	Abercorn	1

Replays

Feb 9	Abercorn	0	T Lanark	1
Feb 9	Morton	3	St Bernard's	1
Feb 23	Hibernian	1	Royal Albert	0

3rd Round

Feb 16	Dundee	0	Celtic	1
Mar 2	Hibernian	2	Morton	0
Feb 16	Port Glasgow A	1	Hearts	5
Feb 16	St Mirren	0	T Lanark	0

Replay

Feb 23	T Lanark	1	St Mirren	1
Mar 2	St Mirren	3	T Lanark	3
	played at Hampden Park			
Mar 9	St Mirren	1	T Lanark	0
	played at Hampden Park			

Semi-finals

Mar 23	Celtic	1	St Mirren	0
Mar 9	Hearts	1	Hibernian	1

Replay

Mar 23	Hearts	2	Hibernian	1
	played at Easter Road			

Final

Apr 6	Celtic	3	Hearts	4
	played at Ibrox			

Season 1901-02

1st Round

Dec 28	Arbroath	3	Kilwinning	2
Jan 11	Arthurlie	1	Port Glasgow A	1
Jan 11	Ayr	0	Dundee	0
Jan 11	Celtic	3	Thornliebank	0
Jan 11	Cowdenbeath	0	Hearts	0
Jan 11	Forfar A	3	Abercorn	2
Jan 11	Hibernian	2	Clyde	0
Jan 11	Inverness C	6	Stranraer	1
Jan 11	Kilmarnock	4	Partick T	0
Jan 11	Lochgelly U	0	Falkirk	2
Jan 11	Queen's Park	7	Maxwelltown V	0
Jan 11	Rangers	6	Johnstone	1
Jan 11	St Bernard's	1	Motherwell	0
Jan 11	St Mirren	1	Airdrie	0
Jan 11	Stenhousemuir	6	Stanley	1
Jan 11	T Lanark	0	Morton	0

Replays

Jan 18	Dundee	2	Ayr	0
Jan 18	Hearts	3	Cowdenbeath	0
Jan 18	Morton	2	T Lanark	3
Jan 18	Port Glasgow A	3	Arthurlie	1

2nd Round

Jan 25	Arbroath	2	Celtic	3
Jan 25	Falkirk	2	St Bernard's	0
Jan 25	Forfar A	1	Queen's Park	4
Jan 25	Hearts	4	T Lanark	1
Jan 25	Kilmarnock	2	Dundee	0
Jan 25	Port Glasgow A	1	Hibernian	5
Jan 25	Rangers	5	Inverness C	1
Jan 25	St Mirren	6	Stenhousemuir	0

3rd Round

Feb 8	Falkirk	0	St Mirren	2
Feb 15	Hearts	1	Celtic	1
Feb 22	Queen's Park	1	Hibernian	7
Feb 22	Rangers	2	Kilmarnock	0

Replay

Feb 22	Celtic	2	Hearts	1

Semi-finals

Mar 22	St Mirren	2	Celtic	3
Mar 22	Rangers	0	Hibernian	2

Final

Apr 26	Celtic	0	Hibernian	1
	played at Celtic Park			

Season 1902-03

1st Round

Jan 24 Abercorn 2 Douglas W 2
Jan 17 Arbroath 1 Kilmarnock 3
Jan 10 Ayr U 2 Camelon 0
Jan 24 Celtic 0 St Mirren 0
Jan 10 Clyde 1 Hearts 2
Dundee *W* Barholm R *0*
Jan 24 Hamilton A 5 Airdrie 0
Jan 10 Hibernian 7 Morton 0
Jan 17 Leith A 4 Broxburn U 1
Jan 24 Nithsdale W 1 Orion 0
Jan 24 Queen's Park 1 Motherwell 2
Jan 10 Rangers 7 Auchterarder T 0
Jan 17 St Bernard's 1 Port Glasgow A 2
Jan 24 St Johnstone 1 T Lanark 10
Jan 2 Stenhousemuir 2 Inverness C 1
Jan 24 Vale of Leven 0 Partick T 4

Replays

Jan 31 Douglas W 3 Abercorn 1
Jan 31 St Mirren 1 Celtic 1
Feb 14 Celtic 4 St Mirren 0
played at Ibrox

2nd Round

Jan 24 Ayr U 2 Hearts 4
Feb 21 Celtic 2 Port Glasgow A 0
Jan 31 Dundee 7 Nithsdale W 1
Jan 31 Hamilton A 2 T Lanark 2
Jan 24 Hibernian 4 Leith A 1
Jan 31 Motherwell 0 Partick T 2
Jan 24 Rangers 4 Kilmarnock 0
Feb 14 Stenhousemuir 6 Douglas W 1

Replay

Feb 14 T Lanark 3 Hamilton A 1

3rd Round

Feb 28 Celtic 0 Rangers 3
Feb 7 Dundee 0 Hibernian 0
Feb 21 Hearts 2 T Lanark 1
Feb 21 Stenhousemuir 3 Partick T 0

Replay

Feb 14 Hibernian 0 Dundee 0
Feb 21 Dundee 1 Hibernian 0
played at Ibrox

Semi-finals

Feb 28 Dundee 0 Hearts 0
Mar 7 Stenhousemuir 1 Rangers 4

Replay

Mar 7 Hearts 1 Dundee 0

Final

Apr 11 Hearts 1 Rangers 1
played at Celtic Park

Replay

Apr 18 Hearts 0 Rangers 0
played at Celtic Park
Apr 25 Hearts 0 Rangers 2
played at Celtic Park

Season 1903-04

1st Round

Jan 23 Abercorn 2 Maxwelltown V 2
Jan 23 Albion R 2 Kilwinning 1
Jan 23 Alloa 2 Aberdeen 1
Jan 23 Ayr U 0 St Mirren 2
Celtic *W* Stanley *0*
Jan 23 Clyde 2 Arbroath 2
Jan 23 Dundee 3 Queen's Park 0
Jan 23 Hibernian 2 Airdrie 1
Jan 16 Morton 8 6th GRV 1
Jan 23 Motherwell 2 Partick T 1
Jan 23 Nithsdale 2 Kilmarnock 2
Jan 23 Port Glasgow A 1 Leith A 2
Jan 23 Rangers 3 Hearts 2
Jan 23 St Bernard's 1 West Calder S 1
Jan 23 St Johnstone 2 Hearts of Beath 0
T Lanark *W* Newton Stewart *0*

Replays

Jan 30 Arbroath 4 Clyde 0
Jan 30 Kilmarnock 1 Nithsdale W 1
Jan 30 Maxwelltown V 1 Abercorn 1
Jan 30 West Calder S 3 St Bernard's 3
Feb 6 Abercorn 2 Maxwelltown V 1
played at Ayr
Feb 6 Kilmarnock 2 Nithsdale W 1
played at Kilmarnock
Feb 6 St Bernard's 2 West Calder S 0
played at Bathgate

2nd Round

Feb 13 Dundee 4 Abercorn 0
Feb 6 Hibernian 1 Rangers 2
Feb 13 Kilmarnock 2 Albion R 2
Feb 6 Leith A 3 Motherwell 1
Feb 6 Morton 2 Arbroath 0
Feb 13 St Bernard's 0 Celtic 4
Feb 6 St Mirren 4 St Johnstone 0
Feb 6 T Lanark 3 Alloa 1

Replay

Feb 20 Albion R 0 Kilmarnock 1

3rd Round

Feb 20 Celtic 1 Dundee 1
Feb 20 Leith A 1 Morton 3
Feb 20 St Mirren 0 Rangers 1
Feb 27 T Lanark 3 Kilmarnock 0

Replays

Feb 27 Dundee 0 Celtic 0
Mar 5 Celtic 5 Dundee 0
played at Celtic Park

Semi-finals

Mar 19 Celtic 2 T Lanark 1
Mar 5 Rangers 3 Morton 0

Final

Apr 16 Celtic 3 Rangers 2
played at Hampden Park

Season 1904-05

1st Round

Jan 28 Aberdeen 2 Queen's Park 1
Jan 28 Airdrie 7 St Johnstone 0
Jan 28 Arthurlie 0 Motherwell 0
Jan 28 Bathgate 2 Arbroath 1
Jan 21 Cowdenbeath 2 6th GRV 0
Jan 28 Dumfries 1 Celtic 2
Jan 28 Dundee 1 Hearts 3
Jan 28 Hibernian 1 Partick T 1
Jan 28 Kilmarnock 2 Beith 2
Jan 21 Kirkcaldy U 3 Crieff 1
Jan 28 Lochgelly U 5 Inverness C 1
Jan 28 Morton 2 Renton 0
Jan 28 Port Glasgow A 3 Stranraer 0
Jan 28 Rangers 2 Ayr Parkhouse 1
Jan 28 St Mirren 1 Clyde 0
Jan 28 T Lanark 4 Leith A 1

Replays

Feb 4 Beith 3 Kilmarnock 1
Feb 4 Motherwell 1 Arthurlie 0
Feb 4 Partick T 4 Hibernian 2

2nd Round

Feb 18 Aberdeen 6 Bathgate 1
Feb 11 Airdrie 3 Port Glasgow A 0
Feb 11 Beith 4 Cowdenbeath 0
Feb 11 Celtic 3 Lochgelly U 0
Feb 11 Kirkcaldy U 0 Partick T 1
Feb 11 Morton 0 Rangers 6
Feb 11 Motherwell 0 T Lanark 1
Feb 11 St Mirren 2 Hearts 1

3rd Round

Feb 25 Celtic 3 Partick T 0
Feb 25 Rangers 5 Beith 1
Feb 25 St Mirren 0 Airdrie 0
Feb 25 T Lanark 4 Aberdeen 1

Replay

Mar 4 Airdrie 3 St Mirren 1

Semi-finals

Mar 25 Celtic 0 Rangers 2
Mar 25 T Lanark 2 Airdrie 1

Final

Apr 8 Rangers 0 T Lanark 0
played at Hampden Park

Replay

Apr 15 Rangers 1 T Lanark 3
played at Hampden Park

Season 1905-06

1st Round

Jan 27 Aberdeen 3 Dunfermline A 0
Jan 27 Airdrie 9 Maxwelltown V 0
Jan 27 Arbroath 1 Bo'ness U 4
Jan 27 Arthurlie 1 Rangers 7
Jan 27 Beith 2 Inverness T 0
Jan 27 Dundee 1 Celtic 2
Jan 27 Falkirk 1 Hibernian 2
Jan 27 Forfar A 0 Queen's Park 4
Jan 27 Hearts 4 Nithsdale W 1
Jan 27 Kilmarnock 2 Clyde 1
Jan 27 Leith A 1 Partick T 2
Jan 27 Morton 4 Lochgelly U 3
Jan 27 Motherwell 2 Hamilton A 3
Jan 27 Port Glasgow A 6 Dunblane 1
Jan 27 St Mirren 7 Black Watch 2
Jan 27 T Lanark 5 Galston 0

2nd Round

Feb 10 Aberdeen 2 Rangers 3
Feb 10 Beith 0 Hearts 3
Feb 10 Celtic 3 Bo'ness U 0
Feb 10 Hibernian 1 Partick T 1
Feb 10 Kilmarnock 2 Port Glasgow A 2
Feb 10 Queen's Park 1 Airdrie 2
Feb 10 St Mirren 3 Morton 1
Feb 10 T Lanark 2 Hamilton A 2

Replays

Feb 17 Hamilton A 1 T Lanark 3
Feb 17 Partick T 1 Hibernian 1
Feb 17 Port Glasgow A 0 Kilmarnock 0
Feb 24 Hibernian 2 Partick T 1
played at Ibrox
Feb 24 Kilmarnock 0 Port Glasgow A 0
played at Cathkin Park
Mar 3 Kilmarnock 0 Port Glasgow A 1
played at Celtic Park

3rd Round

Feb 24 Airdrie 0 St Mirren 0
Feb 24 Celtic 1 Hearts 2
Mar 10 Hibernian 2 T Lanark 3
Mar 10 Port Glasgow A 1 Rangers 0

Replay

Mar 3 St Mirren 2 Airdrie 0

Semi-finals

Mar 31 Port Glasgow A 0 Hearts 2
Mar 31 St Mirren 1 T Lanark 1

Replays

Apr 14 T Lanark 0 St Mirren 0
played at Ibrox
Apr 21 St Mirren 0 T Lanark 1
played at Ibrox

Final

Apr 28 Hearts 1 T Lanark 0
played at Ibrox

Season 1906-07

1st Round

Jan 26 Aberdeen 0 Johnstone 0
Jan 26 Arbroath 1 Queen's Park 1
Feb 2 Arthurlie 1 St Mirren 2
Jan 26 Ayr U 2 Cowdenbeath 0
Feb 2 Celtic 2 Clyde 1
Jan 26 Dumfries 2 P Glasgow A 2
Jan 26 Falkirk 1 Rangers 2
Feb 9 Galston 2 Motherwell 1
Jan 26 Hearts 0 Airdrie 0
Jan 23 Hibernian 5 Forfar 0
Feb 2 Kilmarnock 4 Clacknacuddin 0
Jan 26 Maxwelltown V 1 Morton 3
Feb 9 Partick T 2 Dundee 2
Jan 26 Raith R 5 Aberdeen Univ 1
Jan 26 Renton 0 St Bernard's 0
Jan 26 T Lanark 4 St Johnstone 1

Replays
Feb 2 Port Glasgow A 2 Dumfries 0
Feb 2 Queen's Park 4 Arbroath 0
Feb 2 St Bernard's 1 Renton 1
Feb 9 Airdrie 0 Hearts 2
Feb 9 Johnstone 2 Aberdeen 1
Feb 9 Renton 2 St Bernard's 0
played at Celtic Park
Feb 16 Dundee 5 Partick T 1

2nd Round
Feb 16 Galston 0 Rangers 4
Feb 16 Hibernian 1 Johnstone 1
Feb 16 Kilmarnock 0 Hearts 0
Feb 9 Morton 0 Celtic 0
Feb 9 Queen's Park 3 T Lanark 1
Feb 9 Raith R 4 Ayr U 0
Feb 23 Renton 1 Dundee 0
Feb 9 St Mirren 4 Port Glasgow A 0

Replays
Feb 16 Celtic 1 Morton 1
Feb 23 Celtic 2 Morton 1
played at Celtic Park
Feb 23 Hearts 2 Kilmarnock 1
Feb 23 Johnstone 0 Hibernian 5

3rd Round
Mar 9 Hearts 2 Raith 2
Mar 2 Hibernian 1 St Mirren 1
Mar 9 Queen's Park 4 Renton 1
Mar 9 Rangers 0 Celtic 3

Replays
Mar 9 St Mirren 1 Hibernian 1
Mar 23 Hibernian 2 St Mirren 0
played at Tynecastle
Mar 23 Raith 0 Hearts 1

Semi-finals
Mar 30 Celtic 0 Hibernian 0
Mar 30 Hearts 1 Queen's Park 0

Replays
Apr 6 Hibernian 0 Celtic 0
Apr 13 Celtic 3 Hibernian 0
played at Celtic Park

Final
Apr 20 Celtic 3 Hearts 0
played at Hampden Park

SEASON 1907-08

1st Round
Jan 25 Aberdeen 3 Albion R 0
Jan 25 Airdrie 0 Dundee 1
Jan 25 Celtic 4 Peebles R 0
Jan 25 Dumfries 0 Motherwell 4
Jan 25 Dunblane 8 Elgin C 3
Jan 25 Falkirk 2 Rangers 2
Jan 18 Galston 6 Uphall 0
Jan 25 Hearts 4 St Johnstone 1
Jan 25 Hibernian 5 Abercorn 0
Jan 25 Kilmarnock 2 Hamilton A 1
Jan 25 Morton 7 Vale of Atholl 0
Jan 25 Partick T 4 Bo'ness 0
Jan 25 Port Glasgow A 7 Ayr Parkhouse 2
Jan 25 Raith R 2 Inverness T 0
Jan 25 St Bernard's 1 Queen's Park 1
Jan 25 St Mirren 3 T Lanark 1

Replays
Feb 1 Queen's Park 1 St Bernard's 1
Feb 1 Rangers 4 Falkirk 1
Feb 5 Queen's Park 1 St Bernard's 0
played at Cathkin Park

2nd Round
Feb 8 Aberdeen 0 Dundee 0
Feb 8 Hearts 4 Port Glasgow A 0
Feb 8 Hibernian 3 Morton 0
Feb 8 Kilmarnock 3 Dunblane 0
Feb 8 Motherwell 2 St Mirren 2
Feb 8 Partick T 1 Raith R 1
Feb 8 Queen's Park 6 Galston 2
Feb 8 Rangers 1 Celtic 2

Replays
Feb 15 Dundee 2 Aberdeen 2
Feb 15 Raith R 2 Partick T 1
Feb 15 St Mirren 2 Motherwell 0
Feb 19 Aberdeen 3 Dundee 1
played at Hampden Park

3rd Round
Feb 22 Aberdeen 3 Queen's Park 1
Feb 22 Hibernian 0 Kilmarnock 1
Feb 22 Raith R 0 Celtic 3
Mar 21 St Mirren 3 Hearts 1

Semi-finals
Mar 21 Aberdeen 0 Celtic 1
Mar 28 Kilmarnock 0 St Mirren 0

Replay
Apr 11 St Mirren 2 Kilmarnock 0
played at

Final
Apr 18 Celtic 5 St Mirren 1
played at Hampden Park

SEASON 1908-09

1st Round
Jan 23 Alloa 2 St Mirren 2
Jan 23 Broxburn 1 Beith 1
Jan 23 Clyde 4 Dykehead 0
Jan 23 Dundee 9 Ayr Parkhouse 0
Jan 23 Falkirk 2 E Stirling 1
Jan 23 Hamilton A 0 Queen's Park 0
Jan 23 Hearts 2 Kilmarnock 1
Jan 23 Hibernian 2 Ayr 1
Jan 23 Leith A 2 Celtic 4
Jan 23 Morton 0 Aberdeen 4
Jan 23 Motherwell 6 Elgin C 1
Jan 23 Port Glasgow A 5 Dunblane 0
Jan 23 St Johnstone 0 Rangers 3
Jan 23 T Lanark 5 Brechin C 1
Jan 23 Vale of Leven 0 Airdrie 0
Jan 23 West Calder 0 Partick T 0

Replays
Partick T *W* West Calder *0*
Jan 30 Airdrie 1 Vale of Leven 0
Jan 30 Beith 0 Broxburn 0
Jan 30 Queen's Park 2 Hamilton A 0
Jan 30 St Mirren 5 Alloa 0
Feb 3 Beith 1 Broxburn 1
played at Ibrox
Feb 4 Beith 1 Broxburn 1
played at Ibrox
Feb 5 Beith 4 Broxburn 2
played at Love Street

2nd Round
Feb 6 Airdrie 2 Hearts 0
Feb 6 Celtic 4 Port Glasgow A 0
Feb 6 Clyde 1 Hibernian 0
Feb 6 Dundee 0 Rangers 0
Feb 6 Motherwell 1 Falkirk 3
Feb 6 Queen's Park 3 Partick T 0
Feb 6 St Mirren 3 Beith 0
Feb 6 T Lanark 4 Aberdeen 1

Replays
Feb 13 Rangers 1 Dundee 0

3rd Round
Feb 20 Celtic 3 Airdrie 1
Feb 20 Clyde 3 St Mirren 1
Feb 20 Rangers 1 Queen's Park 0
Feb 20 T Lanark 1 Falkirk 2

Semi-finals
Mar 20 Celtic 0 Clyde 0
Mar 20 Falkirk 0 Rangers 1

Replay
Mar 27 Celtic 2 Clyde 0

Final
Apr 10 Celtic 2 Rangers 2
played at Hampden Park

Replay
Apr 17 Celtic 1 Rangers 1
played at Hampden Park
Cup Withheld

SEASON 1909-10

1st Round
Feb 5 Aberdeen 3 Bo'ness 0
Jan 22 Ayr 3 Alloa 2
Jan 22 Bathgate 0 Hearts 4
Jan 22 Douglas W 0 Airdrie 6
Jan 22 Dumbarton 1 Celtic 2
Jan 22 Dundee 1 Beith 1
Jan 15 East Fife 4 Hurlford 0
Jan 22 Falkirk 3 Port Glasgow A 0
Jan 22 Hamilton A 0 Hibernian 0
Jan 22 Kilmarnock 0 T Lanark 0
Jan 22 Leith A 0 Clyde 1
Jan 22 Morton 4 Partick T 3
Jan 22 Motherwell 1 Forfar A 0
Jan 22 Queen's Park 0 Kircaldy U 0
Jan 22 Rangers 3 Inverness T 1
Jan 22 St Mirren 8 Elgin C 0

Replays
Jan 29 Dundee 1 Beith 0
Jan 29 Hibernian 2 Hamilton A 0
Feb 5 Queen's Park 6 Kircaldy U 1
Feb 5 T Lanark 2 Kilmarnock 0

2nd Round
Feb 12 Aberdeen 3 Airdrie 0
Feb 5 Ayr U 0 Hibernian 1
Feb 12 Celtic 3 T Lanark 1
Feb 5 Clyde 2 Rangers 0
Feb 5 Dundee 3 Falkirk 0
Feb 12 East Fife 2 Queen's Park 3
Feb 5 Motherwell 3 Morton 0
Feb 5 St Mirren 2 Hearts 2

Replays
Feb 12 Hearts 0 St Mirren 0
Feb 16 Hearts 4 St Mirren 0
played at Ibrox

3rd Round
Feb 19 Celtic 2 Aberdeen 1
Feb 19 Queen's Park 2 Clyde 2
Feb 26 Hearts 0 Hibernian 1
Feb 26 Motherwell 1 Dundee 3

Replays
Feb 26 Clyde 2 Queen's Park 2
Mar 2 Clyde 2 Queen's Park 1
played at Celtic Park

Semi-finals
Mar 12 Clyde 3 Celtic 1
Mar 12 Hibernian 0 Dundee 0

Replays
Mar 19 Dundee 0 Hibernian 0
Mar 23 Dundee 1 Hibernian 0
played at Celtic Park

Final
Apr 9 Clyde 2 Dundee 2
played at Ibrox

Replays
Apr 16 Clyde 0 Dundee 0
played at Ibrox
Apr 20 Clyde 1 Dundee 2
played at Ibrox

SEASON 1910-11

1st Round
Jan 28 Aberdeen 3 Brechin C 0
Jan 28 Airdrie 2 Bo'ness 0
Jan 28 Annbank 0 Motherwell 5
Jan 28 Celtic 2 St Mirren 0
Jan 28 Dundee 2 Hibernian 1
Jan 28 E Stirling 1 Morton 4
Jan 28 Forfar A 3 5th Ksob 0
Jan 28 Galston 8 Lochgelly 0
Jan 28 Hearts 1 Clyde 1
Jan 28 Inverness T 0 Johnstone 1
Jan 28 Leith A 2 Falkirk 2
Jan 28 Nithsdale W 3 Inverness C 1
Jan 28 Partick T 7 St Bernard's 2
Jan 28 Rangers 2 Kilmarnock 1
Jan 28 Stanley 1 Queen's Park 6
Jan 28 T Lanark 0 Hamilton A 1

Replays
Feb 4 Clyde 1 Hearts 0
Feb 4 Falkirk 4 Leith A 1

2nd Round
Feb 11 Aberdeen 1 Airdrie 0
Feb 11 Celtic 1 Galston 0
Feb 11 Clyde 4 Queen's Park 1
Feb 11 Forfar A 2 Falkirk 0
Feb 11 Hamilton A 1 Johnstone 1
Feb 11 Motherwell 0 Nithsdale W 0
Feb 11 Partick T 0 Dundee 3
Feb 11 Rangers 3 Morton 0

Replays
Feb 18 Motherwell 1 Nithsdale W 0
Feb 25 Johnstone 1 Hamilton A 3

3rd Round
Feb 25 Aberdeen 6 Forfar A 0
Feb 25 Celtic 1 Clyde 0
Feb 25 Dundee 2 Rangers 1
Mar 4 Hamilton A 2 Motherwell 1

Semi-finals
Mar 11 Celtic 1 Aberdeen 0
Mar 11 Hamilton A 3 Dundee 2

Final
Apr 8 Celtic 0 Hamilton A 0
played at Ibrox

Replay
Apr 15 Celtic 2 Hamilton A 0
played at Ibrox

Season 1911-12

1st Round
Feb 3 Armadale 2 Peterhead 1
Jan 27 Broxburn 6 Beith 0
Jan 27 Celtic 1 Dunfermline A 0
Jan 27 Clyde 2 Abercorn 0
Jan 20 E Stirling 3 Dumbarton 1
played at Falkirk
Jan 27 Falkirk 2 King's Park 2
Jan 27 Hearts 0 Hibernian 0
Jan 27 Kilmarnock 1 Hamilton A 0
Jan 27 Leith A 3 Ayr U 0
Jan 27 Morton 2 Clacknacuddin 0
Jan 27 Partick T 2 Dundee 2
Jan 27 Raith R 0 Airdrie 0
Jan 27 Rangers 3 Stenhousemuir 1
Jan 27 St Johnstone 0 Motherwell 2
Jan 27 St Mirren 3 Aberdeen 3
Jan 27 T Lanark 5 Renton 0

Replays
Feb 3 Dundee 3 Partick T 0
Feb 3 Airdrie 3 Raith R 1
Feb 3 Falkirk 6 King's Park 1
Feb 10 Aberdeen 4 St Mirren 0
Feb 10 Hibernian 1 Hearts 1
Feb 14 Hearts 3 Hibernian 1
played at Ibrox

2nd Round
Feb 17 Aberdeen 3 Armadale 0
Feb 10 Celtic 3 E Stirling 0
Feb 10 Clyde 3 Rangers 1
Abandoned - Rangers scratched
Feb 10 Falkirk 0 Morton 0
Feb 24 Hearts 1 Dundee 0
Feb 10 Leith A 0 Kilmarnock 2
Feb 10 Motherwell 5 Airdrie 1
Feb 10 T Lanark 6 Broxburn 1

Replay
Feb 17 Morton 3 Falkirk 1

3rd Round
Feb 24 Aberdeen 2 Celtic 2
Feb 24 Kilmarnock 1 Clyde 6
Mar 9 Morton 0 Hearts 1
Feb 24 T Lanark 3 Motherwell 1

Replay
Mar 9 Celtic 2 Aberdeen 0

Semi-finals
Mar 30 Celtic 3 Hearts 0
played at Ibrox
Mar 9 Clyde 3 T Lanark 1
played at Hampden Park

Final
Apr 6 Celtic 2 Clyde 0
played at Ibrox

Season 1912-13

1st Round
Jan 25 Hamilton A 0 St Bernard's 0
Jan 25 Kilmarnock 3 Nithsdale W 0

Replay
Feb 1 St Bernard's 0 Hamilton A 3

2nd Round
Feb 8 Aberdeen Univ 0 Peebles R 3
Feb 8 Ayr U 0 Airdrie 2
Feb 8 Celtic 4 Arbroath 0
Feb 8 Clyde 0 E Stirling 0
Feb 8 Dumbarton 2 Aberdeen 1
Feb 8 Dundee 5 Thornehill 0
Feb 8 Hamilton A 1 Rangers 1
Feb 8 Hearts 3 Dunfermline A 1
Feb 8 Kilmarnock 5 Abercorn 1
Feb 8 Morton 2 Falkirk 2
Feb 8 Motherwell 1 Hibernian 1
Feb 8 Partick T 4 Inverness C 1
Feb 8 Queen's Park 4 Dundee H 2
Feb 8 Raith R 5 Broxburn 0
Feb 8 St Johnstone 3 East Fife 0
Feb 8 St Mirren 0 T Lanark 0

Replays
Feb 15 E Stirling 1 Clyde 1
Feb 15 Falkirk 3 Morton 1
Feb 15 Hibernian 0 Motherwell 0
Feb 15 Rangers 2 Hamilton A 0
Feb 15 T Lanark 0 St Mirren 2
Feb 18 Clyde 1 E Stirling 0
played at Shawfields
Feb 19 Hibernian 2 Motherwell 1
played at Celtic Park

3rd Round
Feb 22 Celtic 3 Peebles R 0
Feb 22 Clyde 1 Queen's Park 0
Feb 22 Dumbarton 1 St Johnstone 0
Feb 22 Kilmarnock 0 Hearts 2
Feb 22 Partick T 0 Dundee 1
Feb 22 Raith R 2 Hibernian 2
Feb 22 Rangers 1 Falkirk 3
Feb 22 St Mirren 1 Airdrie 0

Replay
Mar 1 Hibernian 0 Raith R 1

4th Round
Mar 8 Celtic 0 Hearts 1
Mar 8 Dundee 0 Clyde 0
Mar 8 Falkirk 1 Dumbarton 0
Mar 8 Raith R 2 St Mirren 1

Replay
Mar 15 Clyde 1 Dundee 1
Mar 19 Clyde 2 Dundee 1
played at Hampden Park

Semi-finals
Mar 29 Clyde 1 Raith R 1
played at Tynecastle
Mar 29 Falkirk 1 Hearts 0
played at Ibrox

Replay
Apr 5 Clyde 0 Raith R 1
played at Tynecastle

Final
Apr 12 Falkirk 2 Raith R 0
played at Celtic Park

Season 1913-14

1st Round
Jan 24 Falkirk 1 Queen's Park 3
Jan 24 St Mirren 5 Inverness C 1

2nd Round
Feb 7 Aberdeen 4 Albion R 1
Feb 7 Airdrie 5 Dundee H 0
Feb 7 Broxburn U 5 Dumfries 1
Feb 7 Celtic 0 Clyde 0
Feb 7 E Stirling 1 Forfar A 1
Feb 7 Forres Mechanic 0 Peebles R 4
Feb 7 Kilmarnock 3 Hamilton A 1
Jan 31 Kirkcaldy U 0 Stevenston U 4
Feb 7 Leith A 1 Motherwell 1
Feb 7 Morton 1 Hibernian 1
Feb 7 Partick T 1 Nithsdale W 0
Feb 7 Queen's Park 1 Arthurlie 0
Feb 7 Raith R 2 Hearts 0
Feb 7 Rangers 5 Alloa 0
Feb 7 St Mirren 2 Dundee 1
Feb 7 T Lanark 2 Dumbarton 0

Replays
Feb 10 Clyde 0 Celtic 2
Feb 11 Hibernian 2 Morton 1
Feb 14 Forfar A 2 E Stirling 0
Feb 14 Motherwell 5 Leith A 2

3rd Round
Feb 21 Aberdeen 1 St Mirren 2
Feb 21 Airdrie 1 Queen's Park 1
Feb 21 Broxburn 0 Motherwell 2
Feb 21 Forfar A 0 Celtic 5
Feb 21 Hibernian 2 Rangers 1
Feb 21 Kilmarnock 1 Partick T 4
Feb 21 Stevenston U 3 Peebles R 2
Feb 21 T Lanark 4 Raith R 1

Replay
Feb 24 Queen's Park 2 Airdrie 1

4th Round
Mar 7 Motherwell 1 Celtic 3
Mar 7 Queen's Park 1 Hibernian 3
Mar 7 St Mirren 1 Partick T 0
Mar 7 T Lanark 0 Stevenston U 0

Replays
Mar 21 Stevenston U 1 T Lanark 1
Mar 24 Stevenston U 0 T Lanark 1
played at Cathkin Park

Semi-finals
Mar 28 Celtic 2 T Lanark 0
played at Ibrox
Mar 28 Hibernian 3 St Mirren 1
played at Tynecastle

Final
Apr 11 Celtic 0 Hibernian 0
played at Ibrox

Replay
Apr 16 Celtic 4 Hibernian 1
played at Ibrox

Season 1919-20

1st Round
Jan 24 Albion R 0 Dykehead 0
Jan 24 Armadale 1 Clyde 0
Jan 24 Cowdenbeath 0 Aberdeen 1
Jan 24 Dumbarton Harp 0 Alloa 0
Jan 24 Dundee 1 Airdrie 0
Jan 24 East Fife 4 Arthurlie 0
Jan 24 E Stirling 6 Thornhill 0
played at Falkirk
Jan 24 Galston 0 Hibernian 0
Jan 24 Hearts 5 Nithsdale W 1
Jan 24 Lochgelly U 2 Clacknacuddin 0
Jan 24 Morton 4 Forfar A 0
Jan 24 Partick T 3 Motherwell 1
Jan 24 Queen's Park 2 Hamilton A 0
Jan 24 Rangers 0 Dumbarton 0
Jan 24 Royal Albert 7 Forres Mechanic 0
Jan 24 Stevenston U 1 St Mirren 2
Jan 24 T Lanark 4 Inverness C 1

Replays

Jan 27	Rangers	1	Dumbarton	0
Jan 31	Alloa	1	Dumbarton H	0
Jan 31	Dykehead	1	Albion R	2
Jan 31	Hibernian	2	Galston	1

2nd Round

Feb 7	Aberdeen	2	Gala Fairydean	0
	Albion	*W*	Huntingtower	*0*
Feb 7	Alloa	0	Kilmarnock	2
Feb 7	Armadale	1	Hibernian	0
Feb 7	Ayr U	2	St Mirren	1
Feb 7	Broxburn U	1	Queen of South	0
Feb 7	Dundee	1	Celtic	3
Feb 7	E Stirling	0	Raith R	0
Feb 7	Hearts	2	Falkirk	0
Feb 7	Lochgelly U	2	Royal Albert	1
Feb 7	Partick T	5	East Fife	0
Feb 7	Queen's Park	3	Vale of Leithen	0
Feb 7	Rangers	5	Arbroath	0
Jan 24	St Bernard's	2	Bathgate	0
Feb 7	St Johnstone	1	Morton	1
Feb 7	T Lanark	2	Vale of Leven	1

Replays

Feb 11	Morton	5	St Johnstone	3
Feb 11	Raith R	1	E Stirling	1
Feb 18	E Stirling	0	Raith R	0
	played at Tynecastle			
Feb 19	E Stirling	0	Raith R	4
	played at Tynecastle			

3rd Round

Feb 21	Aberdeen	1	Hearts	0
Feb 21	Ayr U	1	Armadale	1
Feb 21	Celtic	2	Partick T	0
Feb 21	Kilmarnock	4	Queen of South	1
Feb 21	Lochgelly U	0	T Lanark	3
Feb 21	Raith R	2	Morton	2
Feb 21	Rangers	3	Broxburn U	0
Feb 21	St Bernard's	1	Albion R	1

Replays

Feb 25	Albion R	4	St Bernard's	1
Feb 25	Morton	3	Raith R	0
Feb 28	Armadale	1	Ayr U	0

4th Round

Mar 6	Albion R	2	Aberdeen	1
Mar 6	Armadale	1	Kilmarnock	2
Mar 6	Morton	3	T Lanark	0
Mar 6	Rangers	1	Celtic	0

Semi-finals

Mar 27	Albion R	1	Rangers	1
	played at Celtic Park			
Mar 27	Kilmarnock	3	Morton	2
	played at Hampden Park			

Replays

Mar 31	Albion R	0	Rangers	0
	played at Celtic Park			
Apr 7	Albion R	2	Rangers	0
	played at Celtic Park			

Final

Apr 17	Albion R	2	Kilmarnock	3
	played at Hampden Park			

Season 1920-21

1st Round

Jan 22	Alloa	0	Falkirk	0
Jan 22	Arbroath	2	Kilmarnock	4
Jan 22	Ayr U	1	Queen's Park	0
Jan 22	Boness	1	Galston	0
Jan 22	Clyde	1	Airdrie	1
Jan 22	Dundee	8	Inverness C	1
Jan 22	Hamilton A	3	Raith R	1
Jan 29	Johnstone	0	Stevenston U	2
Jan 22	Peterhead	0	Dykehead	3
Jan 22	Queen of South	8	Blairgowrie	0
Jan 22	St Mirren	2	Armadale	3
Jan 22	T Lanark	1	Hibernian	1

Replays

Jan 26	Airdrie	0	Clyde	1
Jan 26	Hibernian	1	T Lanark	1
Jan 29	Falkirk	1	Alloa	1
Feb 1	Hibernian	1	T Lanark	0
	played at Ibrox			
Feb 2	Falkirk	1	Alloa	1
	played at Firhill Park			
Feb 3	Alloa	1	Falkirk	0
	played at Firhill Park			

2nd Round

Feb 5	Albion R	3	Mid Annandale	1
Feb 5	Alloa	1	Clydebank	1
Feb 5	Ayr U	4	Dykehead	0
Feb 5	Boness	0	Armadale	0
Feb 5	Broxburn U	1	Hamilton A	2
Feb 5	Clyde	1	Hearts	1
Feb 5	Dumbarton	3	Elgin C	0
Feb 5	Dundee	1	Stenhousemuir	0
Feb 5	Hibernian	0	Partick T	0
Feb 5	Kilmarnock	1	Aberdeen	2
Feb 5	Motherwell	3	Renton	0
Feb 5	Queen of South	1	Nithsdale W	3
Feb 5	Rangers	2	Morton	0
Feb 5	Solway Star	1	E Stirling	5
Feb 5	Stevenston U	0	East Fife	0
Feb 5	Vale of Leven	0	Celtic	3

Replays

Feb 8	Partick T	0	Hibernian	0
Feb 9	Hearts	0	Clyde	0
Feb 12	Armadale	2	Boness	0
Feb 12	Clydebank	0	Alloa A	0
Feb 12	East Fife	2	Stevenston U	1
Feb 15	Hibernian	0	Partick T	1
	played at Celtic Park			
Feb 16	Alloa	1	Clydebank	0
	played at Ibrox			
Feb 16	Clyde	2	Hearts	3
	played at Shawfield			

3rd Round

Feb 19	Armadale	2	Albion R	2
Feb 19	Ayr U	1	Motherwell	1
Feb 19	Dumbarton	5	Nithsdale W	0
Feb 19	Dundee	0	Aberdeen	0
Feb 19	East Fife	1	Celtic	3
Feb 19	E Stirling	1	Partick T	2
Feb 19	Hamilton A	0	Hearts	1
Feb 19	Rangers	0	Alloa	0

Replays

Feb 23	Aberdeen	1	Dundee	1
Feb 23	Motherwell	1	Ayr U	1
Feb 26	Albion R	0	Armadale	0
Feb 26	Alloa	1	Rangers	4
	played at Ibrox			
Mar 1	Aberdeen	0	Dundee	2
	played at Ibrox			
Mar 2	Albion R	0	Armadale	0
	played at Hampden Park			
Mar 2	Ayr U	1	Motherwell	3
	played at Celtic Park			
Mar 3	Albion R	2	Armadale	0
	played at Hampden Park			

4th Round

Mar 5	Celtic	1	Hearts	2
Mar 5	Dumbarton	0	Rangers	3
Mar 5	Dundee	0	Albion R	2
Mar 5	Motherwell	2	Partick T	2

Replays

Mar 8	Partick T	0	Motherwell	0
Mar 15	Motherwell	1	Partick T	2
	played at Firhill Park			

Semi-finals

Mar 26	Albion R	1	Rangers	4
	played at Celtic Park			
Mar 26	Hearts	0	Partick T	0
	played at Ibrox			

Replays

Mar 30	Hearts	0	Partick T	0
	played at Ibrox			
Apr 5	Hearts	0	Partick T	2
	played at Ibrox			

Final

Apr 16	Partick T	1	Rangers	0
	played at Celtic Park			

Season 1921-22

1st Round

Jan 28	Aberdeen	1	Dumbarton	0
Jan 28	Airdrie	1	Dykehead	0
Jan 28	Albion R	6	Johnstone	0
Jan 28	Alloa	3	St Bernard's	1
Jan 28	Bathgate	3	Helensburgh	2
Jan 28	Blairgowrie Am	1	Queen of South	5
Jan 28	Bo'ness	6	Stranraer	0
Jan 28	Buckie T	1	Royal Albert	2
Jan 28	Celtic	4	Montrose	0
Feb 4	Clackmannan	3	Inver Citadel	5
Jan 28	Clacknacuddin	0	Rangers	5
Jan 28	Clydebank	1	Arbroath	1
Jan 28	Cowdenbeath	9	Vale of Atholl	1
Jan 28	Dundee H	0	Broxburn U	2
Jan 28	Dunfermline A	3	Stevenston U	1
Jan 28	East Fife	0	Motherwell	3
Jan 28	E Stirling	3	Douglas W	1
Jan 28	Forfar A	0	Falkirk	3
Jan 28	Hamilton A	9	Gala Fairydean	0
Jan 28	Hearts	2	Arthurlie	1
Jan 28	Hibernian	3	Armadale	0
Jan 28	Kilmarnock	5	Inverness Cal	1
Feb 4	King's Park	1	St Johnstone	1
	played at Falkirk			
Feb 1	Lochgelly U	1	Ayr U	5
Jan 28	Morton	4	Vale of Leithen	0
Jan 28	Partick T	7	Dumbarton H	0
Jan 28	Queen's Park	3	Nithsdale W	1
Jan 28	Raith R	2	Clyde	2
Jan 28	St Mirren	7	Solway Star	2
Jan 28	Stenhousemuir	0	Dundee	2
Jan 28	T Lanark	6	Leith A	0
Jan 28	Vale of Leven	1	Fraserburgh	0

Replays

Feb 1	Arbroath	0	Clydebank	1
Feb 1	Clyde	1	Raith R	0
Feb 8	St Johnstone	1	King's Park	1
Feb 15	King's Park	1	St Johnstone	0
	played at Dunfermline			

2nd Round

Feb 11	Aberdeen	1	Queen's Park	1
Feb 11	Albion R	1	Rangers	1
Feb 11	Ayr U	0	Partick T	1
Feb 11	Bathgate	1	Falkirk	0
Feb 11	Clyde	5	Bo'ness	1
Feb 11	Cowdenbeath	0	Airdrie	0
Feb 11	E Stirling	2	Dunfermline A	1
Feb 18	Hamilton A	4	King's Park	1
Feb 11	Hearts	2	Broxburn U	2
Feb 11	Inver Citadel	2	Queen of South	2
Feb 11	Kilmarnock	1	St Mirren	4
Feb 11	Morton	1	Clydebank	1
Feb 11	Motherwell	3	Hibernian	2
Feb 11	Royal Albert	0	Dundee	1
Feb 11	T Lanark	1	Celtic	1
Feb 11	Vale of Leven	0	Alloa	0

Replays

Feb 14	Alloa	1	Vale of Leven	0
Feb 14	Clydebank	1	Morton	3
Feb 14	Queen's Park	1	Aberdeen	2
Feb 15	Airdrie	4	Cowdenbeath	1
Feb 15	Broxburn U	2	Hearts	2
Feb 15	Rangers	4	Albion R	0
Feb 18	Queen of South	2	Inver Citadel	1
Feb 20	Broxburn U	1	Hearts	3
	played at Tynecastle			

3rd Round

Feb 25	Aberdeen	3	Dundee	0
Feb 25	Celtic	1	Hamilton A	3
Feb 25	Hearts	0	Rangers	4
Feb 25	Morton	4	Clyde	1
Feb 25	Motherwell	1	Alloa	0
Feb 25	Partick T	3	Bathgate	0
Feb 25	Queen of South	2	E Stirling	0
Feb 25	St Mirren	3	Airdrie	0

4th Round

Mar 11	Hamilton A	0	Aberdeen	0
Mar 11	Motherwell	1	Morton	2
Mar 11	Partick T	1	Queen of South	0
Mar 11	Rangers	1	St Mirren	1

Replays

Mar 14	St Mirren	0	Rangers	2
Mar 15	Aberdeen	2	Hamilton A	0

Semi-finals

Apr 1	Aberdeen	1	Morton	3
	played at Dens Park			
Mar 25	Partick T	0	Rangers	2
	played at Ibrox			

Final

Apr 15	Morton	1	Rangers	0
	played at Hampden Park			

Season 1922-23

1st Round

Jan 13	Aberdeen	1	Forfar A	0
Jan 13	Airdrie	2	Mid-Annandale	1
Jan 13	Alloa	0	Queen's Park	1
Jan 13	Arbroath A	0	Ayr U	3
Jan 13	Bo'ness	6	Clacknacuddin	0
Jan 13	Clyde	0	Rangers	4
Jan 13	Clydebank	0	Royal Albert	0
Jan 10	Cowdenbeath	10	St Andrew's Univ	1
Jan 13	Dumbarton	0	Dunfermline A	1
Jan 13	Dundee	6	Vale of Atholl	0
Jan 13	Dundee H	3	Beith	1
Jan 13	East Fife	7	Berwick R	1
Jan 13	E Stirling	1	Bathgate	1
Jan 13	Elgin C	0	St Mirren	3
Jan 13	Falkirk	10	Breadalbane	0
Jan 13	Galston	1	Stenhousemuir	0
Jan 13	Hamilton A	1	Albion R	0
Jan 13	Hearts	6	Thornhill	0
Jan 13	Hibernian	4	Clackmannan	0
Jan 13	Hurlford	2	Fraserburgh	1
Jan 13	Johnstone	2	Armadale	0
Jan 13	Kilmarnock	5	Broxburn U	0
Jan 13	Lochgelly U	2	Celtic	3
Jan 13	Moor Park	0	Peebles R	4
Jan 13	Nithsdale W	4	Arbroath	0
Jan 13	Partick T	1	T Lanark	1
Jan 13	Peterhead	3	Vale of Leithen	0
Jan 13	Queen of South	0	King's Park	1
Jan 13	Raith R	1	Morton	0
Jan 13	St Bernard's	8	Dalbeattie Star	1
Jan 13	St Johnstone	1	Motherwell	2
Jan 13	Vale of Leven	6	Inverness T	1

Replays

Jan 16	T Lanark	3	Partick T	2
Jan 17	Bathgate	3	E Stirling	2
Jan 17	Royal Albert	0	Clydebank	0
Jan 23	Clydebank	2	Royal Albert	0
	played at Firhill Park			

2nd Round

Jan 27	Airdrie	1	Aberdeen	1
Jan 27	Ayr U	2	Rangers	0
Jan 27	Bo'ness	3	Hearts	2
Jan 27	Celtic	4	Hurlford	0
Jan 27	Dundee	0	St Bernard's	0
Jan 27	Dunfermline A	1	Clydebank	0
Jan 27	Hamilton A	1	King's Park	0
Jan 27	Hibernian	0	Peebles R	0
Jan 27	Johnstone	0	Falkirk	1
Jan 27	Kilmarnock	1	East Fife	1
Jan 27	Motherwell	2	St Mirren	1
Jan 24	Nithsdale W	1	Dundee H	0
Jan 27	Peterhead	1	Galston	0
Jan 27	Queen's Park	1	Bathgate	1
Jan 27	Raith R	2	Cowdenbeath	0
Jan 27	Vale of Leven	2	T Lanark	2

Replays

Jan 30	Hibernian	3	Peebles R	0
Jan 30	T Lanark	2	Vale of Leven	1
Jan 31	Aberdeen	2	Airdrie	0
Jan 31	Bathgate	0	Queen's Park	2
Jan 31	East Fife	1	Kilmarnock	0
Jan 31	St Bernard's	2	Dundee	3

3rd Round

Feb 10	Aberdeen	13	Peterhead	0
Feb 10	Bo'ness	2	Nithsdale W	0
Feb 10	Celtic	2	East Fife	1
Feb 10	Dundee	0	Hamilton A	0
Feb 10	Dunfermline A	0	Raith R	3
Feb 10	Hibernian	2	Queen's Park	0
Feb 10	Motherwell	3	Falkirk	0
Feb 10	T Lanark	2	Ayr U	0

Replay

Feb 14	Hamilton A	0	Dundee	1

4th Round

Feb 24	Celtic	1	Raith R	0
Feb 24	Hibernian	2	Aberdeen	0
Feb 24	Motherwell	4	Bo'ness	2
Feb 24	T Lanark	1	Dundee	1

Replay

Feb 28	Dundee	0	T Lanark	0
Mar 6	Dundee	0	T Lanark	1
	played at Ibrox			

Semi-finals

Mar 10	Celtic	2	Motherwell	0
	played at Ibrox			
Mar 10	Hibernian	1	T Lanark	0
	played at Tynecastle			

Final

Mar 31	Celtic	1	Hibernian	0
	played at Hampden Park			

Season 1923-24

1st Round

Jan 26	Aberdeen	2	Dumbarton	1
Jan 26	Airdrie	2	Morton	1
Jan 26	Alloa	2	Buckie T	2
Jan 26	Ayr U	3	Albion R	1
Jan 26	Bathgate	1	Bo'ness	1
Jan 26	Clydebank	8	Blairgowrie	2
Jan 26	Coldstream	0	Armadale	1
Jan 26	Dundee	2	Dykehead	0
Jan 26	Dunfermline A	0	Arbroath	1
Jan 26	Falkirk	3	Brechin C	0
Jan 19	Galston	6	Gala Fairydean	2
Jan 26	Hibernian	1	Dundee U	0
Jan 26	Inverness Cal	0	Cowdenbeath	5
Jan 26	Inverness T	1	Forfar A	3
Jan 26	Johnstone	1	East Fife	3
Jan 26	Kilmarnock	2	Celtic	0
Jan 26	King's Park	0	Hamilton A	0
Jan 26	Mid-Annandale	3	Forres Mechanic	1
Jan 26	Motherwell	5	Breadalbane	0
Jan 26	Newton Stewart	1	E Stirling	8
Jan 12	Partick T	11	Dunkeld	0
Jan 26	Queen of South	8	Stranraer	0
Jan 26	Queen's Park	1	Dumbarton H	1
Jan 26	Raith R	3	Broxburn U	0
Jan 26	Rangers	4	Lochgelly U	1
Jan 26	St Bernard's	3	Fraserburgh	0
Jan 26	St Johnstone	3	Moor Park	0
Jan 26	St Mirren	3	Beith	2
Jan 26	Stenhousemuir	2	Clackmannan	1
Jan 26	Thornhill	0	Clyde	0
Jan 26	T Lanark	0	Hearts	0
Jan 26	Vale of Leven	0	Leith A	0

Replays

Jan 29	Clyde	4	Thornhill	0
Jan 29	Leith A	1	Vale of Leven	2
Jan 30	Alloa	3	Buckie T	0
	played at Aberdeen			
Jan 30	Bo'ness	1	Bathgate	0
Jan 30	Dumbarton H	1	Queen's Park	4
	played at Hampden Park			
Jan 30	Hamilton A	1	King's Park	0
Jan 30	Hearts	3	T Lanark	0

2nd Round

Feb 9	Airdrie	4	St Johnstone	0
Feb 9	Ayr U	1	Kilmarnock	0
Feb 9	Clyde	2	Vale of Leven	0
Feb 9	Clydebank	4	Arbroath	0
Feb 9	Cowdenbeath	0	Aberdeen	2
Feb 9	Dundee	0	Raith R	0
Feb 9	E Stirling	1	Mid-Annandale	0
Feb 9	Falkirk	2	East Fife	0
Feb 9	Forfar A	1	Motherwell	3
Feb 9	Hamilton A	2	Queen of South	1
Feb 9	Hearts	6	Galston	0
Feb 9	Hibernian	1	Alloa	1
Feb 9	Partick T	3	Bo'ness	0
Feb 9	Queen's Park	3	Armadale	1
Feb 9	St Bernard's	0	Stenhousemuir	0
Feb 9	St Mirren	0	Rangers	1

Replays

Feb 12	Alloa	0	Hibernian	5
Feb 13	Raith R	1	Dundee	0
Feb 13	Stenhousemuir	0	St Bernard's	0
Feb 20	St Bernard's	2	Stenhousemuir	0
	played at Tynecastle			

3rd Round

Feb 23	Aberdeen	2	E Stirling	0
Feb 23	Clydebank	2	Ayr U	3
Feb 23	Falkirk	0	Queen's Park	0
Feb 23	Hearts	3	Clyde	1
Feb 23	Motherwell	0	Airdrie	5
Feb 23	Partick T	1	Hamilton A	1
Feb 23	Raith R	0	St Bernard's	1
Feb 23	Rangers	1	Hibernian	2

Replays

Feb 27	Hamilton A	1	Partick T	2
Feb 27	Queen's Park	0	Falkirk	2

4th Round

Mar 8	Aberdeen	3	St Bernard's	0
Mar 8	Airdrie	1	Ayr U	1
Mar 8	Hearts	1	Falkirk	2
Mar 8	Hibernian	2	Partick T	2

Replays

Mar 12	Ayr U	0	Airdrie	0
Mar 12	Partick T	1	Hibernian	1
Mar 18	Hibernian	2	Partick T	1
	played at Celtic Park			
Mar 19	Airdrie	1	Ayr U	1
	played at Ibrox			
Mar 20	Airdrie	1	Ayr U	0
	played at Ibrox			

Semi-finals

Mar 22	Aberdeen	0	Hibernian	0
	played at Dens Park			
Mar 22	Airdrie	2	Falkirk	1
	played at Celtic Park			

Replays

Mar 26	Aberdeen	0	Hibernian	0
	played at Dens Park			
Apr 9	Aberdeen	0	Hibernian	1
	played at Dens Park			

Final

Apr 19	Airdrie	2	Hibernian	0
	played at Ibrox			

Season 1924-25

1st Round

Jan 24	Albion R	1	Clyde	1
Jan 24	Armadale	3	Civil Service	1
Jan 24	Arthurlie	3	Cowdenbeath	1
Jan 24	Ayr U	3	St Johnstone	1
Jan 24	Bathgate	0	Partick T	4
Jan 24	Bo'ness	1	Helensburgh	1
Jan 24	Broxburn U	3	Nithsdale W	2
Jan 24	Celtic	5	T Lanark	1
Jan 24	Clydebank	0	Queen's Park	1
Jan 24	Dundee	5	Johnstone	0
Jan 24	Dundee U	5	Aberdeen Univ	1
Jan 24	Dunfermline A	1	Arbroath	1
Jan 24	Dykehead	1	Forfar A	0
Jan 24	East Fife	1	Rangers	3
Jan 24	E Stirling	4	Clacknacuddin	0
Jan 24	Falkirk	1	Morton	1
Jan 24	Hamilton A	5	St Bernard's	2
Jan 24	Hearts	4	Leith A	1
Jan 24	Hibernian	0	Aberdeen	2
Jan 24	Kilmarnock	3	Arbroath A	0
Jan 24	King's Park	0	Airdrie	4
Jan 24	Lochgelly U	4	Bredalban	0
Jan 24	Montrose	6	Inver Citadel	2
Jan 24	Motherwell	6	Galston	3
Jan 24	Newton Stewart	0	Dumbarton	2
Jan 24	Queen of South	1	Alloa	1
Jan 24	Raith R	3	Clackmannan	0
Jan 24	Royal Albert	9	Stranraer	1
Jan 24	Solway Star	4	Stenhousemuir	2
Jan 24	St Cuthbert's	0	Peebles R	0
Jan 24	St Mirren	3	Peterhead	1
Jan 24	Vale of Leven	2	Inverness Cal	0

Replays

Jan 27	Alloa	2	Queen of South	0
Jan 28	Arbroath	1	Dunfermline A	0
Jan 28	Clyde	3	Albion R	1
Jan 28	Helensburgh	0	Bo'ness	0
Jan 28	Morton	0	Falkirk	3
Jan 28	Peebles R	5	St Cuthbert's	0
Feb 3	Bo'ness	2	Helensburgh	0
	played at Firhill Park			

2nd Round

Feb 7	Airdrie	4	Queen's Park	0
Feb 7	Arbroath	3	Clyde	0
Feb 7	Armadale	1	Aberdeen	1
Feb 7	Celtic	2	Alloa	1
Feb 7	Dundee	2	Lochgelly U	1
Feb 7	Dykehead	3	Peebles R	1
Feb 7	Falkirk	2	Dumbarton	0
Feb 7	Hamilton A	4	E Stirling	0
Feb 7	Kilmarnock	2	Hearts	1
Feb 7	Montrose	0	Rangers	2
Feb 7	Motherwell	2	Arthurlie	0
Feb 7	Partick T	5	Dundee U	1
Feb 7	Raith R	0	Bo'ness	0
Feb 7	Royal Albert	1	Broxburn U	3
Feb 7	St Mirren	1	Ayr U	0
Feb 7	Vale of Leven	2	Solway Star	2

Replays

Feb 11	Aberdeen	2	Armadale	0
Feb 11	Bo'ness	1	Raith R	3
Feb 12	Solway Star	3	Vale of Leven	3
Feb 16	Solway Star	2	Vale of Leven	1
	played at Cathkin Park			

3rd Round
Feb 21 Aberdeen 0 Motherwell 0
Feb 21 Broxburn U 2 Falkirk 1
Feb 21 Celtic 2 Solway Star 0
Feb 21 Dundee 3 Airdrie 1
Feb 21 Hamilton A 1 Raith R 0
Feb 21 Kilmarnock 5 Dykehead 0
Feb 21 Rangers 5 Arbroath 3
Feb 21 St Mirren 2 Partick T 0

Replay
Feb 25 Motherwell 1 Aberdeen 2

4th Round
Mar 7 Aberdeen 0 Hamilton A 2
Mar 7 Dundee 1 Broxburn U 0
Mar 7 Kilmarnock 1 Rangers 2
Mar 7 St Mirren 0 Celtic 0

Replays
Mar 10 Celtic 1 St Mirren 1
Mar 16 Celtic 1 St Mirren 0
played at Ibrox

Semi-finals
Mar 21 Celtic 5 Rangers 0
played at Hampden Park
Mar 21 Dundee 1 Hamilton A 1
played at Tynecastle

Replays
Mar 25 Dundee 2 Hamilton A 0
played at Easter Road

Final
Apr 11 Celtic 2 Dundee 1
played at Hampden Park

Season 1925-26

1st Round
Jan 23 Aberdeen 8 St Bernard's 1
Jan 23 Albion R 6 Nithsdale W 1
Jan 23 Arbroath 8 Berwick R 0
Jan 23 Arthurlie 5 Armadale 4
Jan 23 Bathgate 5 E Stirling 4
Jan 23 Bo'ness 2 East Fife 1
Jan 23 Brechin C 12 Thornhill 1
Jan 23 Clyde 3 Dunfermline A 0
Jan 23 Cowdenbeath 1 Hamilton A 2
Jan 23 Douglas W 1 Forfar A 4
Jan 23 Dumbarton 1 Buckie T 1
Jan 20 Dundee 2 Inverness Cal 0
Jan 23 Dundee U 1 Hearts 1
Jan 23 Dykehead 1 Morton 1
Jan 23 Falkirk 10 Breadalbane 0
Jan 23 Hibernian 1 Broxburn U 1
Jan 23 Kilmarnock 0 Celtic 5
Jan 23 King's Park 5 Peterhead 2
Jan 23 Leith A 2 Civil Service 0
Jan 23 Montrose 4 Clacknacuddin 0
Jan 23 Partick T 3 Motherwell 0
Jan 23 Peebles R 7 Keith 3
Jan 23 Queen of South 0 Airdrie 0
Jan 23 Queen's Park 4 Clydebank 2
Jan 23 Raith R 3 Ayr U 1
Jan 23 Rangers 3 Lochgelly U 0
Jan 23 Royal Albert 0 Alloa 1
Jan 23 Solway Star 2 Johnstone 2
Jan 23 St Johnstone 6 Nairn Co 1
Jan 23 St Mirren 4 Mid-Annandale 0
Jan 23 Stenhousemuir 1 Vale of Leven 1
Jan 23 T Lanark 7 Moor Park 0

Replays
Jan 26 Hibernian 1 Broxburn U 0
Jan 26 Johnstone 0 Solway Star 3
Jan 27 Airdrie 7 Queen of South 0
Jan 27 Buckie T 1 Dumbarton 2
Jan 27 Hearts 1 Dundee U 1
Jan 27 Morton 4 Dykehead 1
Jan 27 Vale of Leven 1 Stenhousemuir 2
Feb 1 Dundee U 6 Hearts 0
played at Tynecastle

2nd Round
Feb 6 Aberdeen 0 Dundee 0
Feb 6 Albion R 1 Peebles R 1
Feb 6 Alloa 2 Hearts 5
Feb 6 Arbroath 0 St Mirren 0
Feb 6 Arthurlie 2 Clyde 2
Feb 6 Bo'ness 1 Bathgate 1
Feb 6 Celtic 4 Hamilton A 0
Feb 6 Falkirk 5 Montrose 1
Feb 6 Forfar A 2 Dumbarton 2
Feb 6 Hibernian 2 Airdrie 3
Feb 6 Morton 3 Raith R 1
Feb 6 Partick T 4 King's Park 1
Feb 6 Rangers 1 Stenhousemuir 0
Feb 6 Solway Star 0 Brechin C 3
Feb 6 St Johnstone 7 Queen's Park 2
Feb 6 T Lanark 6 Leith A 1

Replays
Feb 9 Clyde 1 Arthurlie 0
Feb 9 St Mirren 3 Arbroath 0
Feb 10 Bathgate 3 Bo'ness 1
Feb 10 Dumbarton 4 Forfar A 1
Feb 10 Dundee 0 Aberdeen 3
Feb 10 Peebles R 0 Albion R 4

3rd Round
Feb 20 Aberdeen 2 St Johnstone 2
Feb 20 Bathgate 2 Airdrie 5
Feb 20 Dumbarton 3 Clyde 0
Feb 20 Falkirk 0 Rangers 2
Feb 20 Hearts 0 Celtic 4
Feb 20 Morton 1 Albion R 0
Feb 20 St Mirren 2 Partick T 1
Feb 20 T Lanark 4 Brechin C 0

Replay
Feb 24 St Johnstone 0 Aberdeen 0
Mar 1 Aberdeen 1 St Johnstone 0
played at Aberdeen

4th Round
Mar 6 Celtic 6 Dumbarton 1
Mar 6 Morton 0 Rangers 4
Mar 6 St Mirren 2 Airdrie 0
Mar 6 T Lanark 1 Aberdeen 1

Replays
Mar 10 Aberdeen 3 T Lanark 0

Semi-finals
Mar 20 Aberdeen 1 Celtic 2
played at Tynecastle
Mar 20 Rangers 0 St Mirren 1
played at Celtic Park

Final
Apr 10 Celtic 0 St Mirren 2
played at Hampden Park

Season 1926-27

1st Round
Jan 22 Aberdeen 4 Helensburgh 2
Jan 22 Alloa 3 Morton 0
Jan 22 Ayr U 2 Airdrie 2
Jan 22 Bathgate 2 Dunfermline A 2
Jan 22 Beith 7 Huntly 1
Jan 22 Bo'ness 3 Lochgelly U 0
Jan 22 Brechin C 8 Vale of Leithen 3
Jan 22 Broxburn U 2 Armadale 1
Jan 15 Buckie T 2 Fraserburgh 1
Jan 22 Clyde 3 Hearts 2
Jan 22 Clydebank 6 Douglas W 0
Jan 22 Cowdenbeath 3 Hibernian 0
Jan 22 Dundee 3 Motherwell 0
Jan 19 Dundee U 7 Arbroath A 0
Feb 5 Dykehead 3 Montrose 3
Jan 22 East Fife 8 Thornhill 1
Jan 22 E Stirling 0 Dumbarton 1
Jan 22 Elgin C 1 Albion R 0
Jan 22 Falkirk 1 St Johnstone 0
Jan 22 Forfar A 4 Raith R 2
Jan 22 Forres Mechanic 0 Mid-Annandale 2
Jan 22 Hamilton A 6 Stranraer 0
Jan 22 Kilmarnock 3 Peebles R 1
Jan 22 King's Park 1 T Lanark 0
Jan 22 Leith A 1 Rangers 4
Jan 25 Nithsdale W 0 Arthurlie 2
Jan 22 Partick T 3 Stenhousemuir 0
Jan 22 Queen of South 0 Celtic 0
Jan 22 Queen's Park 2 Inverness Cal 0
Jan 22 St Bernard's 3 Vale of Atholl 0
Jan 22 St Mirren 2 Arbroath 0
Jan 22 Vale of Leven 6 Johnstone 2

Replays
Jan 26 Airdrie 2 Ayr U 1
Jan 26 Celtic 4 Queen of South 1
Jan 26 Dunfermline A 5 Bathgate 2
Feb 7 Montrose 3 Dykehead 1

2nd Round
Feb 5 Alloa 1 Dumbarton 1
Feb 5 Bo'ness 2 Cowdenbeath 1
Feb 5 Brechin C 3 Celtic 6
Feb 12 Broxburn U 2 Montrose 2
Feb 5 Buckie T 2 Beith 0
Feb 5 Dundee U 4 Vale of Leven 1
Feb 5 Dunfermline A 2 Airdrie 1
Feb 5 East Fife 1 Aberdeen 1
Feb 5 Elgin C 2 Clyde 4
Feb 5 Falkirk 6 Queen's Park 3
Feb 5 Hamilton A 5 Clydebank 1
Feb 5 Kilmarnock 1 Dundee 1
Feb 5 King's Park 2 Partick T 4
Feb 5 Mid-Annandale 3 Forfar A 0
Feb 5 Rangers 6 St Mirren 0
Feb 5 St Bernard's 0 Arthurlie 3

Replays
Feb 9 Aberdeen 1 East Fife 2
Feb 9 Dumbarton 0 Alloa 4
Feb 9 Dundee 5 Kilmarnock 1
Feb 16 Montrose 1 Broxburn U 0

3rd Round
Feb 19 Alloa 0 Arthurlie 0
Feb 19 Buckie T 0 Bo'ness 3
Feb 19 Clyde 0 Partick T 1
Feb 19 Dundee 2 Celtic 4
Feb 23 Dundee U 2 Montrose 2
Feb 19 East Fife 2 Dunfermline A 0
Feb 19 Falkirk 3 Mid-Annandale 0
Feb 19 Rangers 4 Hamilton A 0

Replay
Feb 22 Arthurlie 3 Alloa 0
Feb 24 Montrose 1 Dundee U 3

4th Round
Mar 5 Arthurlie 0 East Fife 3
Mar 5 Bo'ness 2 Celtic 5
Mar 5 Falkirk 2 Rangers 2
Mar 5 Partick T 5 Dundee U 0

Replay
Mar 9 Rangers 0 Falkirk 1

Semi-finals
Mar 26 Celtic 1 Falkirk 0
played at Ibrox
Mar 26 East Fife 2 Partick T 1
played at Tynecastle

Final
Apr 16 Celtic 3 East Fife 1
played at Hampden Park

Season 1927-28

1st Round
Jan 21 Albion R 5 Glasgow Univ 1
Jan 21 Alloa 2 Fraserburgh 0
Jan 21 Arbroath 2 Nithsdale W 3
Jan 21 Armadale 3 Berwick R 1
Jan 21 Ayr U 2 Bo'ness 0
Jan 21 Beith 1 Airdrie 4
Jan 21 Brechin C 3 Lochgelly U 1
Jan 21 Celtic 3 Bathgate 1
Jan 21 Civil Service 0 King's Park 3
Jan 21 Clydebank 0 Dunfermline A 3
Jan 21 Cowdenbeath 12 Johnstone 0
Jan 25 Dumbarton 2 Hamilton A 3
Jan 21 East Fife 1 Dundee U 1
Jan 21 E Stirling 0 Rangers 6
Jan 21 Falkirk 3 St Bernard's 1
Jan 21 Forfar A 2 Queen of South 1
Jan 21 Forres Mechanic 2 Elgin C 1
Jan 21 Hearts 2 St Johnstone 2
Hibernian *W* Dykehead *0*
Jan 21 Huntly 0 Motherwell 3
Jan 21 Keith 5 Dalbeattie Star 2
Jan 21 Leith A 2 Kilmarnock 3
Jan 21 Montrose 0 Stenhousemuir 5
Jan 21 Morton 7 Mid-Annandale 3
Jan 21 Partick T 9 Inverness Cal 1
Jan 21 Queen's Park 2 Arthurlie 0
Jan 21 Raith R 4 Aberdeen 3
Jan 21 St Mirren 6 Clyde 1
Jan 21 Stranraer 2 Dundee 4
Jan 21 T Lanark 10 Clackmannan 0
Jan 21 Vale of Atholl 2 Newton Stewart 0
Jan 21 Vale of Leven 1 Leith Amat 2

Replays
Jan 25 Dundee U 2 East Fife 1
Jan 25 St Johnstone 0 Hearts 1

2nd Round

Feb 4 Airdrie 2 Hamilton A 1
Feb 4 Armadale 2 King's Park 4
Feb 4 Ayr U 2 Falkirk 4
Feb 4 Brechin C 1 Albion R 4
Feb 4 Dundee U 3 Dundee 3
Feb 4 Dunfermline A 3 Leith Amat 1
Feb 4 Forfar A 1 Kilmarnock 2
Feb 4 Hearts 7 Forres Mechanic 0
Feb 4 Keith 1 Celtic 6
Feb 4 Motherwell 2 Raith R 2
Feb 4 Partick T 4 Nithsdale W 0
Feb 4 Queen's Park 4 Morton 1
Feb 4 Rangers 4 Cowdenbeath 2
Feb 4 St Mirren 5 Vale of Atholl 1
Feb 4 Stenhousemuir 1 Alloa 2
Feb 4 T Lanark 0 Hibernian 2

Replays

Feb 8 Dundee 1 Dundee U 0
Feb 8 Raith R 1 Motherwell 2

3rd Round

Feb 18 Albion R 3 Airdrie 1
Feb 18 Celtic 2 Alloa 0
Feb 18 Dundee 1 Dunfermline A 2
Feb 18 Hearts 1 Motherwell 2
Feb 18 Hibernian 0 Falkirk 0
Feb 18 Kilmarnock 4 Queen's Park 4
Feb 18 Rangers 3 King's Park 1
Feb 18 St Mirren 0 Partick T 5

Replay

Feb 22 Falkirk 0 Hibernian 1
Feb 22 Queen's Park 1 Kilmarnock 0

4th Round

Mar 3 Albion R 0 Rangers 1
Mar 3 Dunfermline A 0 Hibernian 4
Mar 3 Motherwell 0 Celtic 2
Mar 3 Queen's Park 1 Partick T 0

Semi-finals

Mar 24 Celtic 2 Queen's Park 1
played at Ibrox
Mar 24 Hibernian 0 Rangers 3
played at Tynecastle

Final

Apr 14 Celtic 0 Rangers 4
played at Hampden Park

Season 1928-29

1st Round

Jan 19 Aberdeen 5 Solway Star 0
Jan 19 Albion R 7 Galston 1
Jan 19 Alloa 3 E Stirling 3
Jan 19 Arbroath 2 Inverness T 0
Jan 19 Armadale 9 Moor Park 2
Jan 19 Beith 2 Raith R 2
Jan 19 Berwick R 3 Ayr U 9
Jan 19 Bo'ness 7 Newton Stewart 1
Jan 26 Breadalbane 0 Brechin C 6
Jan 19 Buckie T 0 Queen's Park 3
Jan 19 Celtic 5 Arthurlie 1
Jan 12 Civil Service 1 Fraserburgh 1
Clackmannan *W* Dunkeld *0*
Jan 19 Clyde 4 Montrose 1
Jan 19 Dumbarton 6 Inver Citadel 1
Jan 19 Dundee 1 King's Park 1
Jan 19 Dundee U 3 Morton 1
Jan 19 Dunfermline A 1 Cowdenbeath 3
Jan 19 East Fife 1 Partick T 2
Jan 19 Hamilton A 2 Forfar A 1
Jan 19 Hearts 0 Airdrie 2
Jan 19 Hibernian 1 St Johnstone 2
Jan 19 Huntly 1 Stenhousemuir 3
Jan 19 Kilmarnock 8 Glasgow Univ 1
Jan 19 Motherwell 4 Leith A 1
Jan 19 Nithsdale W 0 St Mirren 4
Jan 19 Queen of South 2 Inverness Cal 2
Jan 19 Rangers 11 Edinburgh C 1
Jan 19 St Andrew's Univ 0 Bathgate 3
Jan 19 St Bernard's 1 Falkirk 2
Jan 12 Thornhill 0 Murrayfield A 4
Jan 19 T Lanark 6 Clydebank 2

Replays

Jan 19 Fraserburgh 4 Civil Service 3
Jan 23 E Stirling 2 Alloa 1
Jan 23 King's Park 1 Dundee 5
Jan 24 Inverness Cal 0 Queen of South 3
Jan 26 Raith R 4 Beith 1

2nd Round

Feb 2 Aberdeen 4 Queen's Park 0
Feb 2 Albion R 8 Clackmannan 1
Feb 2 Ayr U 5 Armadale 1
Feb 2 Bathgate 1 Raith R 1
Feb 2 Celtic 3 E Stirling 0
Feb 2 Clyde 1 Hamilton A 1
Feb 2 Cowdenbeath 0 Airdrie 0
Feb 2 Dundee 6 Brechin C 1
Feb 2 Fraserburgh 0 Dumbarton 3
Feb 2 Kilmarnock 3 Bo'ness 2
Feb 2 Murrayfield A 1 Arbroath 1
Feb 2 Queen of South 1 Falkirk 2
Feb 2 Rangers 5 Partick T 1
Feb 2 St Johnstone 2 Motherwell 3
Feb 2 Stenhousemuir 1 Dundee U 1
Feb 2 T Lanark 0 St Mirren 1

Replays

Feb 6 Airdrie 3 Cowdenbeath 2
Feb 6 Arbroath 5 Murrayfield A 2
Feb 6 Dundee U 2 Stenhousemuir 0
Feb 6 Hamilton A 1 Clyde 2
Feb 6 Raith R 5 Bathgate 2

3rd Round

Feb 16 Airdrie 1 Motherwell 1
Feb 16 Albion R 0 Kilmarnock 1
Feb 16 Ayr U 0 St Mirren 2
Feb 16 Celtic 4 Arbroath 1
Feb 16 Clyde 0 Rangers 2
Feb 16 Dundee 1 Dundee U 1
Feb 16 Falkirk 3 Aberdeen 5
Feb 16 Raith R 3 Dumbarton 2

Replays

Feb 20 Dundee U 1 Dundee 0
Feb 20 Motherwell 3 Airdrie 1

4th Round

Mar 6 Celtic 0 Motherwell 0
Mar 2 Raith R 2 Kilmarnock 3
Mar 2 Rangers 3 Dundee U 1
Mar 5 St Mirren 4 Aberdeen 3

Replay

Mar 13 Motherwell 1 Celtic 2

Semi-finals

Mar 23 Celtic 0 Kilmarnock 1
played at Ibrox
Mar 23 Rangers 3 St Mirren 2
played at Hampden Park

Final

Apr 6 Kilmarnock 2 Rangers 0
played at Hampden Park

Season 1929-30

1st Round

Jan 18 Airdrie 3 Dunfermline A 1
Jan 18 Albion R 4 Alloa 2
Jan 18 Arbroath 6 Galston 1
Jan 18 Ayr U 5 Mid-Annandale 0
Jan 18 Beith 4 Royal Albert 1
Jan 18 Bo'ness 0 St Johnstone 0
Jan 18 Buckie T 0 Falkirk 2
Jan 18 Clacknacuddin 2 Civil Service 0
Jan 18 Clyde 7 Keith 0
Jan 18 Dalbeattie Star 1 Partick T 6
Jan 18 Dumbarton 1 Cowdenbeath 4
Jan 18 Dundee 2 Morton 0
Jan 18 Falkirk A 0 Leith A 3
Jan 18 Forfar A 7 Brechin C 2
Jan 18 Hamilton A 6 Stenhousemuir 0
Jan 18 Hearts 1 Clydebank 0
Jan 18 Hibernian 2 Leith Amat 0
Jan 15 Inver Citadel 1 Armadale 0
Jan 18 Inverness Cal 0 Celtic 6
Jan 18 Kilmarnock 11 Paisley A 1
Jan 18 King's Park 6 Bathgate 2
Jan 18 Montrose 8 Solway Star 0
Jan 18 Motherwell 6 E Stirling 0
Jan 11 Murrayfield A 2 Burntisland 2
Jan 18 Nithsdale W 6 St Andrew's Univ 1
Jan 18 Peterhead 3 Vale of Leithen 3
Jan 18 Queen of South 2 East Fife 1
Jan 18 Queen's Park 0 Rangers 1
Jan 18 Raith R 3 Aberdeen 3
Jan 18 St Bernard's 5 T Lanark 3
Jan 18 St Cuthbert's W 1 St Mirren 5
Jan 18 Stranraer 0 Dundee U 2

Replays

Jan 18 Burntisland 0 Murrayfield A 3
Jan 22 Aberdeen 7 Raith R 0
Jan 22 St Johnstone 3 Bo'ness 1
Jan 25 Vale of Leithen 2 Peterhead 1

2nd Round

Feb 1 Aberdeen 5 Nithsdale W 1
Feb 1 Airdrie 8 Murrayfield A 3
Feb 1 Albion R 2 Beith 1
Feb 1 Ayr U 1 Hibernian 3
Feb 1 Celtic 5 Arbroath 0
Feb 1 Dundee 4 St Johnstone 1
Feb 1 Dundee U 0 Partick T 3
Feb 1 Falkirk 1 Queen of South 1
Feb 1 Forfar A 0 St Mirren 0
Feb 1 Hamilton A 4 Kilmarnock 2
Feb 1 Hearts 0 St Bernard's 0
Feb 1 Leith A 2 Clacknacuddin 0
Feb 1 Montrose 3 Inver Citadel 1
Feb 1 Motherwell 3 Clyde 0
Feb 1 Rangers 2 Cowdenbeath 2
Feb 1 Vale of Leithen 2 King's Park 7

Replays

Feb 4 St Mirren 3 Forfar A 0
Feb 5 Cowdenbeath 0 Rangers 3
Feb 5 St Bernard's 1 Hearts 5
Feb 6 Queen of South 3 Falkirk 4

3rd Round

Feb 15 Albion R 2 Montrose 2
Feb 15 Celtic 1 St Mirren 3
Feb 15 Dundee 0 Airdrie 0
Feb 15 Falkirk 0 Leith A 0
Feb 15 Hamilton A 4 King's Park 0
Feb 15 Hibernian 1 Hearts 3
Feb 15 Motherwell 2 Rangers 5
Feb 15 Partick T 3 Aberdeen 2

Replays

Feb 19 Airdrie 0 Dundee 0
Feb 19 Leith A 1 Falkirk 1
Feb 19 Montrose 3 Albion R 1
Feb 24 Airdrie 1 Dundee 2
played at Ibrox
Feb 24 Falkirk 1 Leith A 1
played at Tynecastle
Feb 25 Falkirk 1 Leith A 0
played at Tynecastle

4th Round

Mar 1 Dundee 2 Hearts 2
Mar 1 Partick T 3 Falkirk 1
Mar 1 Rangers 3 Montrose 0
Mar 1 St Mirren 3 Hamilton A 4

Replay

Mar 5 Hearts 4 Dundee 0

Semi-finals

Mar 22 Hamilton A 1 Partick T 3
played at Celtic Park
Mar 22 Hearts 1 Rangers 4
played at Hampden Park

Final

Apr 12 Partick T 0 Rangers 0
played at Hampden Park

Replay

Apr 16 Partick T 1 Rangers 2
played at Hampden Park

Season 1930-31

1st Round

Date	Team	Goals	Team	Goals
Jan 17	Aberdeen	6	Dumbarton	1
Jan 17	Albion R	6	Vale of Atholl	0
Jan 17	Alloa	2	Dalbeattie Star	0
Jan 17	Arbroath	7	Moor Park	1
Jan 17	Armadale	1	Rangers	7
Jan 17	Ayr U	11	Clackmannan	2
Jan 17	Bo'ness	3	Peterhead	0
Jan 17	Brechin C	1	Edinburgh C	3
Jan 17	Civil Service	2	Tarff R	0
Jan 17	Clyde	7	Leith A	0
Jan 17	Dundee	10	Fraserburgh	1
Jan 17	Dundee U	14	Nithsdale W	0
Jan 17	Dunfermline A	2	Airdrie	2
Jan 17	East Fife	1	Celtic	2
Jan 17	E Stirling	0	Hamilton A	2
Jan 17	Glasgow Univ	0	Inverness Cal	1
Jan 17	Hearts	9	Stenhousemuir	1
Jan 17	Hibernian	3	St Cuthbert's	1
Jan 17	Inver Citadel	0	Kilmarnock	7
Jan 17	King's Park	7	Falkirk A	0
Jan 17	Montrose	2	Mid-Annandale	0
Jan 17	Morton	1	Raith R	1
Jan 17	Motherwell	6	Bathgate	0
Jan 17	Murrayfield A	3	Beith	2
Jan 17	Partick T	16	Royal Albert	0
Jan 17	Peebles R	0	Falkirk	4
Jan 17	Queen of South	2	Cowdenbeath	3
Jan 17	Queen's Park	5	Elgin C	0
Jan 17	St Bernard's	6	Stranraer	2
Jan 17	St Johnstone	3	Forfar A	2
Jan 17	St Mirren	3	Clydebank	1
Jan 17	T Lanark	6	Buckie T	2

Replays

Date	Team	Goals	Team	Goals
Jan 21	Airdrie	6	Dunfermline A	1
Jan 21	Raith R	1	Morton	1
Jan 26	Morton	2	Raith R	0
	played at Firhill Park			

2nd Round

Date	Team	Goals	Team	Goals
Jan 31	Aberdeen	1	Partick T	1
Feb 7	Arbroath	2	Edinburgh C	0
Feb 4	Bo'ness	4	Alloa	2
Feb 3	Clyde	1	St Mirren	1
Feb 4	Cowdenbeath	1	St Johnstone	1
Feb 4	Dundee U	2	Celtic	3
Jan 31	Hamilton A	2	Hibernian	2
Jan 31	Inverness Cal	2	Falkirk	7
Jan 31	Kilmarnock	3	Hearts	2
Feb 4	King's Park	1	St Bernard's	1
Feb 7	Montrose	1	Civil Service	0
Jan 31	Motherwell	4	Albion R	1
Jan 31	Murrayfield A	0	Ayr U	1
Jan 31	Queen's Park	0	Morton	1
Jan 31	Rangers	1	Dundee	2
Jan 31	T Lanark	1	Airdrie	0

Replays

Date	Team	Goals	Team	Goals
Feb 4	Hibernian	5	Hamilton A	2
Feb 4	Partick T	0	Aberdeen	3
Feb 10	St Mirren	3	Clyde	1
Feb 11	St Bernard's	1	King's Park	0
Feb 11	St Johnstone	0	Cowdenbeath	4

3rd Round

Date	Team	Goals	Team	Goals
Feb 14	Bo'ness	1	Ayr U	0
Feb 14	Cowdenbeath	3	St Bernard's	0
Feb 14	Dundee	1	Aberdeen	1
Feb 14	Hibernian	0	Motherwell	3
Feb 14	Montrose	0	Kilmarnock	3
Feb 14	Morton	1	Celtic	4
Feb 14	St Mirren	2	Falkirk	0
Feb 14	T Lanark	4	Arbroath	2

Replay

Date	Team	Goals	Team	Goals
Feb 18	Aberdeen	2	Dundee	0

4th Round

Date	Team	Goals	Team	Goals
Feb 28	Bo'ness	1	Kilmarnock	1
Feb 28	Celtic	4	Aberdeen	0
Feb 28	Cowdenbeath	0	Motherwell	1
Feb 28	T Lanark	1	St Mirren	1

Replays

Date	Team	Goals	Team	Goals
Mar 3	St Mirren	3	T Lanark	0
Mar 4	Kilmarnock	5	Bo'ness	0

Semi-finals

Date	Team	Goals	Team	Goals
Mar 14	Celtic	3	Kilmarnock	0
	played at Hampden Park			
Mar 14	Motherwell	1	St Mirren	0
	played at Ibrox			

Final

Date	Team	Goals	Team	Goals
Apr 11	Celtic	2	Motherwell	2
	played at Hampden Park			

Replay

Date	Team	Goals	Team	Goals
Apr 15	Celtic	4	Motherwell	2
	played at Hampden Park			

Season 1931-32

1st Round

Date	Team	Goals	Team	Goals
Jan 16	Arbroath	2	Aberdeen	1
Jan 16	Armadale	3	Montrose	1
Jan 16	Ayr U	0	St Johnstone	3
Jan 16	Celtic	3	Falkirk	2
Jan 16	Clyde	4	T Lanark	0
Jan 16	Cowdenbeath	5	Alloa	1
Jan 16	Dalbeattie Star	2	Bo'ness	3
Jan 16	Dundee	4	Morton	1
Jan 16	Dunfermline A	5	E Stirling	2
Jan 13	Edinburgh C	3	Murrayfield A	0
	played at Tynecastle			
Jan 16	Forfar A	1	Airdrie	3
Jan 16	Hamilton A	2	Dumbarton	0
Jan 16	Hearts	13	Lochgelly U	3
Jan 16	Hibernian	2	Dundee U	3
Jan 16	Inver Citadel	0	Partick T	3
Jan 16	Kilmarnock	4	East Fife	1
Jan 16	King's Park	7	Thornhill	1
Jan 16	Leith A	1	Albion R	1
Jan 16	Motherwell	7	Stenhousemuir	2
Jan 16	Queen of South	11	Stranraer	1
Jan 16	Queen's Park	4	St Mirren	1
Jan 16	Raith R	8	Inverness T	1
Jan 16	Rangers	8	Brechin C	2
Jan 16	St Bernard's	4	Beith	3

Replays

Date	Team	Goals	Team	Goals
Jan 20	Albion R	4	Leith A	2
Jan 20	St Johnstone	2	Ayr U	0

2nd Round

Date	Team	Goals	Team	Goals
Jan 30	Airdrie	2	King's Park	2
Jan 30	Bo'ness	2	Partick T	2
Jan 30	Clyde	1	Arbroath	0
Jan 30	Dunfermline A	1	Dundee	0
Jan 30	Edinburgh C	2	St Bernard's	3
Jan 30	Hamilton A	5	Armadale	2
Jan 30	Hearts	4	Cowdenbeath	1
Jan 30	Kilmarnock	2	Albion R	0
Jan 30	Queen of South	2	Dundee U	2
Jan 30	Queen's Park	0	Motherwell	2
Jan 30	Raith R	0	Rangers	5
Jan 30	St Johnstone	2	Celtic	4

Replays

Date	Team	Goals	Team	Goals
Feb 3	Dundee U	1	Queen of South	1
Feb 3	King's Park	1	Airdrie	3
Feb 3	Partick T	5	Bo'ness	1
Feb 8	Dundee U	2	Queen of South	1
	played at Ibrox			

3rd Round

Date	Team	Goals	Team	Goals
Feb 13	Clyde	2	St Bernard's	0
Feb 13	Dundee U	1	Kilmarnock	1
Feb 13	Hearts	0	Rangers	1
Feb 13	Motherwell	2	Celtic	0

Replay

Date	Team	Goals	Team	Goals
Feb 17	Kilmarnock	3	Dundee U	0

4th Round

Date	Team	Goals	Team	Goals
Mar 5	Airdrie	4	Partick T	1
Mar 5	Clyde	0	Hamilton A	2
Mar 5	Dunfermline A	1	Kilmarnock	3
Mar 5	Rangers	2	Motherwell	0

Semi-finals

Date	Team	Goals	Team	Goals
Mar 26	Airdrie	2	Kilmarnock	3
	played at Firhill Park			
Mar 26	Hamilton A	2	Rangers	5
	played at Celtic Park			

Final

Date	Team	Goals	Team	Goals
Apr 16	Kilmarnock	1	Rangers	1
	played at Hampden Park			

Replay

Date	Team	Goals	Team	Goals
Apr 20	Kilmarnock	0	Rangers	3
	played at Hampden Park			

Season 1932-33

1st Round

Date	Team	Goals	Team	Goals
Jan 21	Aberdeen	1	Penicuik A	0
Jan 21	Airdrie	2	Alloa	1
Jan 21	Albion R	2	Inverness T	0
Jan 21	Armadale	0	Dundee U	2
Jan 21	Clyde	3	Fraserburgh	2
Jan 21	Cowdenbeath	1	Dundee	1
Jan 21	Dumbarton	3	Beith	1
Jan 21	Dunfermline A	1	Celtic	7
Jan 21	E Stirling	0	Montrose	2
Jan 18	Edinburgh C	1	Ayr U	3
	played at Tynecastle			
Jan 21	Hamilton A	0	Motherwell	2
Jan 21	Hearts	3	Solway Star	0
Jan 21	Hibernian	2	Forfar A	2
Jan 21	Kilmarnock	3	Lochgelly U	1
Jan 21	King's Park	0	St Mirren	0
Jan 21	Leith A	5	Brechin C	1
Jan 21	Queen of South	0	T Lanark	1
Jan 21	Queen's Park	4	Falkirk A	0
Jan 21	Raith R	1	Falkirk	2
Jan 23	Rangers	3	Arbroath	1
Jan 21	St Bernard's	2	Partick T	2
Jan 21	St Johnstone	2	East Fife	2
Jan 21	Stenhousemuir	1	Morton	0
Jan 21	Stranraer	1	Bo'ness	1

Replays

Date	Team	Goals	Team	Goals
Jan 24	St Mirren	5	King's Park	1
Jan 25	Dundee	3	Cowdenbeath	0
Jan 25	East Fife	1	St Johnstone	2
Jan 25	Partick T	3	St Bernard's	0
Jan 26	Forfar A	3	Hibernian	7
Jan 28	Bo'ness	3	Stranraer	0

2nd Round

Date	Team	Goals	Team	Goals
Feb 4	Aberdeen	1	Hibernian	1
Feb 4	Ayr U	1	Partick T	1
Feb 4	Celtic	2	Falkirk	0
Feb 4	Dumbarton	1	Albion R	2
Feb 1	Dundee	4	Bo'ness	0
Feb 4	Dundee U	3	St Johnstone	4
Feb 4	Hearts	6	Airdrie	1
Feb 4	Leith A	1	Clyde	1
Feb 4	Motherwell	7	Montrose	1
Feb 4	Rangers	1	Queen's Park	1
Feb 4	St Mirren	0	Kilmarnock	1
Feb 4	Stenhousemuir	2	T Lanark	0

Replays

Date	Team	Goals	Team	Goals
Feb 7	Clyde	5	Leith A	0
Feb 7	Partick T	2	Ayr U	0
Feb 8	Hibernian	1	Aberdeen	0
Feb 8	Queen's Park	1	Rangers	1
Feb 13	Queen's Park	1	Rangers	3
	played at Hampden Park			

3rd Round

Date	Team	Goals	Team	Goals
Feb 18	Celtic	2	Partick T	1
Feb 18	Hearts	2	St Johnstone	0
Feb 18	Kilmarnock	1	Rangers	0
Feb 18	Motherwell	5	Dundee	0

4th Round

Date	Team	Goals	Team	Goals
Mar 4	Albion R	1	Celtic	1
Mar 4	Clyde	3	Stenhousemuir	2
Mar 4	Hibernian	0	Hearts	0
Mar 4	Kilmarnock	3	Motherwell	3

Replays

Date	Team	Goals	Team	Goals
Mar 8	Celtic	3	Albion R	1
Mar 8	Hearts	2	Hibernian	0
Mar 8	Motherwell	8	Kilmarnock	3

Semi-finals

Date	Team	Goals	Team	Goals
Mar 18	Celtic	0	Hearts	0
	played at Hampden Park			
Mar 18	Clyde	0	Motherwell	2
	played at Ibrox			

Replay

Date	Team	Goals	Team	Goals
Mar 22	Celtic	2	Hearts	1
	played at Hampden Park			

Final

Date	Team	Goals	Team	Goals
Apr 15	Celtic	1	Motherwell	0
	played at Hampden Park			

Celtic in September 1932. They went on to win the SFA Cup that season, beating Motherwell in the Final. Back row (left to right): McGonagle, Geatens, Kennaway, Hughes, Cameron, Quiskley (trainer). Front row: McGrory, Cook, R.Thomson, McStay, Wilson, A.Thomson, Napier.

Season 1933-34

1st Round

Date	Home		Away	
Jan 20	Aberdeen	1	Raith R	0
Jan 20	Airdrie	1	Kilmarnock	1
Jan 20	Albion R	4	Vale Ocoba	1
Jan 20	Alloa	4	Dundee U	2
Jan 20	Arbroath	2	Dumbarton	1
Jan 20	Ayr U	2	Dunfermline A	0
Jan 20	Beith	1	Brechin C	2
Jan 20	Dalbeattie Star	0	Celtic	6
Jan 20	Falkirk	3	Leith Amat	0
Jan 20	Galston	8	Keith	2
Jan 20	Hearts	5	Montrose	1
Jan 20	Hibernian	5	Clyde	4
Jan 20	King's Park	0	Dundee	1
Jan 17	Leith A	0	Cowdenbeath	1
Jan 20	Motherwell	4	Gala Fairydean	0
Jan 20	Nithsdale W	0	E Stirling	2
Jan 20	Partick T	1	Morton	0
Jan 20	Penicuik A	2	St Mirren	2
Jan 20	Peterhead	0	Hamilton A	2
Jan 20	Queen of South	5	Edinburgh C	2
Jan 20	Queen's Park	1	Forfar A	0
Jan 20	Rangers	14	Blairgowrie	2
Jan 20	Ross Co	2	Burntisland	2
Jan 20	St Bernard's	3	Wick A	0
Jan 20	St Johnstone	3	East Fife	1
Jan 20	Stenhousemuir	1	T Lanark	1
Jan 20	Vale of Leithen	3	Rosyth Dockyard	0

Replays

Date	Home		Away	
Jan 23	St Mirren	4	Penicuik A	1
Jan 24	Kilmarnock	3	Airdrie	2
Jan 24	T Lanark	1	Stenhousemuir	0

2nd Round

Date	Home		Away	
Feb 3	Aberdeen	2	Dundee	0
Feb 3	Albion R	2	Kilmarnock	1
Feb 3	Ayr U	2	Celtic	3
Feb 3	Brechin C	0	St Mirren	4
Feb 3	Cowdenbeath	2	St Bernard's	1
Feb 3	East Stirling	1	Arbroath	1
Feb 3	Hamilton A	2	Falkirk	4
Feb 3	Hibernian	6	Alloa	0
Feb 3	Partick T	3	Motherwell	3
Feb 3	Queen's Park	1	Hearts	2
Feb 3	Ross Co	3	Galston	1
Feb 3	T Lanark	0	Rangers	3
Feb 3	Vale of Leithen	1	St Johnstone	3

Replays

Date	Home		Away	
Feb 7	Arbroath	0	E Stirling	3
Feb 7	Motherwell	2	Partick T	1

3rd Round

Date	Home		Away	
Feb 17	Albion R	6	Ross Co	1
Feb 17	Celtic	3	Falkirk	1
Feb 17	Hibernian	0	Aberdeen	1
Feb 17	Motherwell	5	E Stirling	0
Feb 17	Queen of South	3	Cowdenbeath	0
Feb 17	Rangers	0	Hearts	0

Replay

Date	Home		Away	
Feb 21	Hearts	1	Rangers	2

4th Round

Date	Home		Away	
Mar 3	Albion R	1	Motherwell	1
Mar 3	Rangers	1	Aberdeen	0
Mar 3	St Johnstone	2	Queen of South	0
Mar 3	St Mirren	2	Celtic	0

Replay

Date	Home		Away	
Mar 7	Motherwell	6	Albion R	0

Semi-finals

Date	Home		Away	
Mar 31	Motherwell played at Tynecastle	1	St Mirren	3
Mar 31	Rangers played at Hampden Park	1	St Johnstone	0

Final

Date	Home		Away	
Apr 21	Rangers played at Hampden Park	5	St Mirren	0

Season 1934-35

1st Round

Date	Home		Away	
Jan 26	Albion R	7	Paisley A	0
Jan 26	Ayr U	3	Queen of South	1
Jan 26	Berwick R	1	Rosyth Dockyard	3
Jan 26	Brechin C	3	Leith A	2
Jan 26	Buckie T	1	Beith	0
Jan 26	Celtic	4	Montrose	1
Jan 26	Dundee	1	Motherwell	2
Jan 26	Dunfermline A	1	Hamilton A	2
Jan 26	East Fife	1	Clyde	2
Jan 23	E Stirling	1	Raith R	2
Jan 26	Falkirk	2	Aberdeen	3
Jan 26	Forfar A	7	Chirnside U	1
Jan 26	Fraserburgh	2	Dundee U	6
Jan 26	Galston	0	Kilmarnock	1

Jan 26 Hearts 7 Solway Star 0
Jan 23 Hibernian 5 Vale of Atholl 0
Jan 26 Inver Citadel 1 Clacknacuddin 3
Jan 26 King's Park 3 Edinburgh 1
Jan 26 Morton 9 Bo'ness 0
Jan 26 Partick T 3 Stenhousemuir 0
Jan 26 Queen's Park 2 Alloa 1
Jan 26 Rangers 3 Cowdenbeath 1
Jan 26 St Bernard's 1 Airdrie 3
Jan 26 St Johnstone 1 Arbroath 0
Jan 26 St Mirren 3 Peebles R 1
Jan 26 T Lanark 6 Creetown 2
Jan 26 Vale Ocoba 1 Dumbarton 6

2nd Round

Feb 9 Aberdeen 4 Albion R 0
Feb 9 Airdrie 1 Rosyth Dockyard 0
Feb 9 Ayr U 1 King's Park 1
Feb 9 Brechin C 1 Raith R 1
Feb 9 Celtic 1 Partick T 1
Feb 9 Clyde 3 Hamilton A 3
Feb 9 Dundee U 6 Queen's Park 3
Feb 9 Hearts 2 Kilmarnock 0
Feb 9 Hibernian 7 Clacknacuddin 1
Feb 9 Motherwell 7 Morton 1
Feb 9 Rangers 2 T Lanark 0
Feb 9 St Johnstone 4 Dumbarton 0
Feb 9 St Mirren 3 Forfar A 0

Replays

Feb 13 Hamilton A 6 Clyde 3
Feb 13 Kings' Park 2 Ayr U 2
Feb 13 Partick T 1 Celtic 3
Feb 13 Raith R 2 Brechin C 4
Feb 18 Ayr U 4 King's Park 4
played at Firhill Park
Feb 19 Ayr U 1 King's Park 2
played at Hampden Park

3rd Round

Feb 23 Aberdeen 0 Hibernian 0
Feb 23 Airdrie 6 King's Park 2
Feb 23 Brechin C 2 Hamilton A 4
Feb 23 Buckie T 0 St Johnstone 1
Feb 23 Hearts 2 Dundee U 2
Feb 23 Rangers 1 St Mirren 0

Replays

Feb 27 Dundee U 2 Hearts 4
Feb 27 Hibernian 1 Aberdeen 1
Mar 4 Aberdeen 3 Hibernian 2
played at Easter Road

4th Round

Mar 9 Aberdeen 3 Celtic 1
Mar 9 Airdrie 2 Hearts 3
Mar 9 Hamilton A 3 St Johnstone 0
Mar 9 Motherwell 1 Rangers 4

Semi-finals

Mar 30 Aberdeen 1 Hamilton A 2
played at Celtic Park
Mar 30 Hearts 1 Rangers 1
played at Hampden Park

Replay

Apr 10 Hearts 0 Rangers 2
played at Hampden Park

Final

Apr 20 Hamilton A 1 Rangers 2
played at Hampden Park

SEASON 1935-36

1st Round

Jan 29 Aberdeen 4 Hamilton A 1
Jan 25 Albion R 7 Wigtown 1
Jan 29 Arbroath 1 Motherwell 3
Jan 25 Ayr U 2 St Mirren 3
Feb 1 Bo'ness 1 Airdrie 3
Jan 25 Burntisland 2 Dumbarton 2
Celtic *W* Berwick R *0*
Jan 25 Clyde 2 Forfar A 1
Jan 25 Dundee 6 Babcock & W 0
Jan 25 Dundee U 2 Alloa 2
Jan 29 Dunfermline A 6 Brechin C 2
Jan 29 E Stirling 2 Kilmarnock 5
Jan 25 Edinburgh C 2 Cowdenbeath 3
Feb 1 Elgin C 2 Chirnside U 2
Feb 1 Galston 5 Stranraer 3
Feb 1 King's Park 6 Wick A 1
Jan 25 Leith A 3 Buckie T 3
Jan 25 Montrose 0 Falkirk 2
Feb 1 Morton 11 Blairgowrie 1
Jan 25 Peebles R 3 Dalbeattie Star 3
Jan 25 Queen of South 2 Partick T 0
Jan 25 Raith R 2 St Johnstone 4
Jan 29 Rangers 3 East Fife 1
Feb 1 Ross Co 0 St Bernard's 5
Jan 29 Stenhousemuir 1 Queen's Park 0
Jan 29 T Lanark 2 Hearts 0
Feb 1 Vale Ocoba 1 Hibernian 3

Replays

Jan 29 Alloa 1 Dundee U 1
Jan 29 Buckie T 1 Leith A 2
Feb 1 Dalbeattie Star 1 Peebles R 0
Feb 1 Dumbarton 4 Burntisland 2
Feb 3 Alloa 1 Dundee U 2
played at Tynecastle
Feb 5 Chirnside U 3 Elgin C 4

2nd Round

Feb 8 Aberdeen 6 King's Park 0
Feb 8 Albion R 1 Rangers 3
Feb 8 Celtic 1 St Johnstone 2
Feb 8 Clyde 4 Hibernian 1
Feb 8 Cowdenbeath 5 Dundee U 3
Feb 8 Dalbeattie Star 0 St Mirren 1
Feb 8 Dundee 2 Airdrie 1
Feb 8 Dunfermline A 5 Galston 2
Feb 8 Elgin C 0 Queen of South 3
Feb 8 Falkirk 1 Kilmarnock 1
Feb 8 Morton 3 Stenhousemuir 0
Feb 8 Motherwell 3 St Bernard's 0
Feb 8 T Lanark 2 Leith A 0

Replay

Feb 12 Kilmarnock 1 Falkirk 3

3rd Round

Feb 22 Aberdeen 1 St Johnstone 1
Feb 22 Clyde 1 Dundee 1
Feb 22 Cowdenbeath 1 Motherwell 3
Feb 22 Morton 2 Queen of South 0
Feb 22 St Mirren 1 Rangers 2
Feb 22 T Lanark 8 Dumbarton 0

Replays

Feb 26 Dundee 0 Clyde 3
Feb 26 St Johnstone 0 Aberdeen 1

4th Round

Mar 7 Aberdeen 0 Rangers 1
Mar 7 Clyde 3 Motherwell 2
Mar 7 Falkirk 5 Dunfermline A 0
Mar 7 Morton 3 T Lanark 5

Semi-finals

Mar 28 Clyde 0 Rangers 3
played at Hampden Park
Mar 28 Falkirk 1 T Lanark 3
played at Tynecastle

Final

Apr 18 Rangers 1 T Lanark 0
played at Hampden Park

SEASON 1936-37

1st Round

Jan 30 Aberdeen 6 Inverness T 0
Jan 30 Airdrie 3 Dundee U 1
Feb 2 Alloa 2 Hibernian 5
Jan 30 Ayr U 0 Partick T 2
Jan 30 Babcock & W *0* Inverness Cal 1
Jan 30 Bo'ness 0 Cowdenbeath 6
Jan 30 Clyde 8 Vale Ocoba 0
Jan 30 Dalbeattie Star 1 Queen's Park 2
Jan 30 Dumbarton 3 Keith 1
Feb 3 Dundee 4 E Stirling 1
Feb 3 Dunfermline A 0 Arbroath 0
Feb 6 Edinburgh C 2 Duns 5
Jan 30 Falkirk 6 Peebles R 0
Feb 4 Forfar A 0 East Fife 3
Jan 30 Hearts 3 St Bernard's 1
Jan 30 Kilmarnock 1 Brechin C 2
Feb 6 King's Park 1 Elgin C 1
Jan 23 Larbert A 1 Solway Star 3
Feb 3 Leith A 4 Albion R 4
Jan 30 Montrose 1 T Lanark 1
Jan 27 Moor Park 1 Hamilton A 7
Jan 30 Motherwell 3 Galston 1
Jan 27 Murrayfield A 3 Morton 3

Play under way at Hampden Park in the 1937 Scottish Cup Final between Celtic and Aberdeen. The attendance of 146,433 is still a record for a club match in Europe.

Date	Home		Away	
Jan 30	Queen of South	1	Rangers	0
Feb 3	Raith R	0	St Johnstone	5
Jan 30	St Mirren	4	Beith	0
Jan 30	Stenhousemuir	1	Celtic	1

Replays

Date	Home		Away	
Jan 30	Morton	6	Murrayfield A	1
Feb 3	Celtic	2	Stenhousemuir	0
Feb 3	T Lanark	5	Montrose	0
Feb 10	Albion R	5	Leith A	3
Feb 10	Arbroath	1	Dunfermline A	0
Feb 10	Elgin C	3	King's Park	4

2nd Round

Date	Home		Away	
Feb 13	Aberdeen	4	T Lanark	2
Feb 13	Albion R	2	Celtic	5
Feb 13	Clyde	3	St Johnstone	1
Feb 13	Cowdenbeath	9	Solway Star	1
Feb 13	Dundee	2	Queen's Park	0
Feb 13	Duns	2	Dumbarton	1
Feb 13	Falkirk	0	Motherwell	3
Feb 13	Hamilton A	2	Hibernian	1
Feb 13	Hearts	15	King's Park	0
Feb 13	Inverness Cal	1	East Fife	6
Feb 13	Partick T	4	Arbroath	1
Feb 13	Queen of South	2	Airdrie	0
Feb 13	St Mirren	1	Brechin C	0

3rd Round

Date	Home		Away	
Feb 27	Clyde	0	Dundee	0
Mar 10	Duns	2	Motherwell	5
	played at Tynecastle			
Feb 27	East Fife	0	Celtic	3
Mar 3	Hamilton A	2	Hearts	1
Feb 27	Morton	1	Partick T	1
Feb 27	St Mirren	1	Cowdenbeath	0

Replays

Date	Home		Away	
Mar 3	Dundee	0	Clyde	1
Mar 3	Partick T	1	Morton	2

4th Round

Date	Home		Away	
Mar 17	Hamilton A	1	Aberdeen	2
Mar 13	Morton	4	Queen of South	1
Mar 17	Motherwell	4	Celtic	4
Mar 13	St Mirren	0	Clyde	3

Replay

Date	Home		Away	
Mar 24	Celtic	2	Motherwell	1

Semi-finals

Date	Home		Away	
Apr 3	Aberdeen	2	Morton	0
	played at Easter Road			
Apr 3	Celtic	2	Clyde	0
	played at Ibrox			

Final

Date	Home		Away	
Apr 24	Aberdeen	1	Celtic	2
	played at Hampden Park			

Season 1937-38

1st Round

Date	Home		Away	
Jan 22	Airdrie	1	East Fife	2
Jan 22	Albion R	4	Dundee	2
Jan 22	Alloa	1	Rangers	6
Jan 22	Ayr U	4	E Stirling	1
Jan 22	Bo'ness	0	Hamilton A	4
Jan 22	Chirnside U	2	Ross Co	3
Jan 22	Clyde	1	Motherwell	4
Jan 22	Cowdenbeath	4	Brechin C	1
Jan 22	Dundee U	3	Hearts	1
Jan 22	Dunfermline A	0	St Mirren	1
Jan 22	Elgin C	1	Aberdeen	6
Jan 22	Falkirk	6	Nithsdale W	0
Jan 22	Forfar A	7	Blairgowrie	4
Jan 22	Hibernian	2	Edinburgh C	3
Jan 22	Huntly	0	Nithsdale W	1
Jan 22	Kilmarnock	6	Dumbarton	0
Jan 22	Moor Park A	2	Larbert A	5
Jan 22	Morton	4	Peterhead	0
Jan 22	Penicuik A	1	King's Park	3
Jan 22	Queen of South	4	Leith A	2
Jan 22	Queen's Park	2	Galston	0
Jan 22	Raith R	1	Montrose	0
Jan 22	St Bernard's	1	Vale of Leithen	0
Jan 22	St Johnstone	1	Arbroath	1
Jan 22	Stenhousemuir	3	Babcock & W	1
Jan 22	Stranraer	2	Partick T	2
Jan 22	T Lanark	1	Celtic	2

Replays

Date	Home		Away	
Jan 26	Arbroath	1	St Johnstone	3
Jan 26	Partick T	8	Stranraer	0

2nd Round

Date	Home		Away	
Feb 12	Aberdeen	5	St Johnstone	1
Feb 12	Celtic	5	Nithsdale W	0
Feb 12	East Fife	5	Dundee U	0
Feb 12	Falkirk	3	St Mirren	2
Feb 12	Hamilton A	5	Forfar A	1
Feb 12	Larbert A	2	Morton	3
Feb 12	Partick T	1	Cowdenbeath	0
Feb 12	Queen's Park	1	Ayr U	1
Feb 12	Raith R	9	Edinburgh C	2
Feb 12	Rangers	3	Queen of South	1
Feb 12	Ross Co	2	Albion R	5
Feb 12	St Bernard's	1	King's Park	1
Feb 12	Stenhousemuir	1	Motherwell	1

Replays

Date	Home		Away	
Feb 16	Ayr U	2	Queen's Park	1
Feb 16	King's Park	3	St Bernard's	4
Feb 16	Motherwell	6	Stenhousemuir	1

3rd Round

Date	Home		Away	
Mar 5	Celtic	1	Kilmarnock	2
Mar 5	East Fife	1	Aberdeen	1
Mar 5	Falkirk	4	Albion R	0
Mar 5	Morton	1	Ayr U	1
Mar 5	Motherwell	2	Hamilton A	0
Mar 5	Partick T	1	Raith R	2

Replays

Date	Home		Away	
Mar 9	Aberdeen	1	East Fife	2
Mar 9	Ayr U	4	Morton	1

4th Round

Date	Home		Away	
Mar 19	East Fife	2	Raith R	2
Mar 19	Falkirk	1	Rangers	2
Mar 19	Kilmarnock	1	Ayr U	1
Mar 19	St Bernard's	3	Motherwell	1

Replay

Date	Home		Away	
Mar 23	Ayr U	0	Kilmarnock	5
Mar 23	Raith R	2	East Fife	3

Semi-finals

Date	Home		Away	
Apr 2	East Fife	1	St Bernard's	1
	played at Tynecastle			
Apr 2	Kilmarnock	4	Rangers	3
	played at Hampden Park			

Replays

Date	Home		Away	
Apr 6	East Fife	1	St Bernard's	1
	played at Tynecastle			
Apr 13	East Fife	2	St Bernard's	1
	played at Tynecastle			

Final

Date	Home		Away	
Apr 23	East Fife	1	Kilmarnock	1
	played at Hampden Park			

Replay

Date	Home		Away	
Apr 27	East Fife	4	Kilmarnock	2
	played at Hampden Park			

Season 1938-39

1st Round

Date	Home		Away	
Jan 21	Aberdeen	1	Albion R	0
Jan 21	Alloa	2	Ayr U	1
Jan 21	Blairgowrie	3	Dumbarton	2
Jan 21	Bo'ness	1	Hamilton A	4
Jan 21	Burntisland	3	Celtic	8
Jan 21	Clyde	2	St Johnstone	0
Jan 21	Cowdenbeath	3	Partick T	3
Jan 21	Dundee	2	St Bernard's	0
Jan 21	Dundee U	2	Stenhousemuir	0
Jan 21	Dunfermline A	5	Morton	2
Jan 21	Duns	4	Girvan	1
Jan 21	East Fife	1	Montrose	2
Jan 21	Edinburgh C	3	Stranraer	3
Jan 21	Falkirk	5	Brechin C	0
Jan 21	Falkirk A	2	Elgin C	4
Jan 21	Forfar A	0	Hibernian	3
Jan 21	Hearts	14	Penicuik A	2
Jan 21	Huntly	1	Motherwell	8
Jan 21	Kilmarnock	6	Berwick R	1
Jan 21	King's Park	5	Babcock & W	5
Jan 21	Leith A	0	Airdrie	2
Jan 21	Nithsdale W	5	Buckie T	5
Jan 21	Queen of South	5	Arbroath	4
Jan 21	Queen's Park	4	St Cuthbert's	1
Jan 21	Raith R	0	Rangers	1
Jan 21	St Mirren	7	E Stirling	0
Jan 21	T Lanark	8	Clacknacuddin	2

Replays

Date	Home		Away	
Jan 25	Babcock & W	3	King's Park	2
Jan 25	Partick T	1	Cowdenbeath	2
Jan 25	Stranraer	1	Edinburgh C	2
Jan 28	Buckie T	5	Nithsdale W	2

2nd Round

Date	Home		Away	
Feb 4	Aberdeen	5	Queen's Park	1
Feb 4	Blairgowrie	3	Buckie T	3
Feb 4	Dundee	0	Clyde	0
Feb 4	Dundee U	1	Motherwell	5
Feb 4	Dunfermline A	2	Duns	0
Feb 1	Edinburgh C	1	St Mirren	3
Feb 4	Falkirk	7	Airdrie	0
Feb 4	Hearts	14	Elgin C	1
Feb 4	Hibernian	3	Kilmarnock	1
Feb 4	Montrose	1	Celtic	7
Feb 4	Queen of South	5	Babcock & W	0
Feb 4	Rangers	2	Hamilton A	0
Feb 4	T Lanark	3	Cowdenbeath	0

Replays

Date	Home		Away	
Feb 8	Buckie T	4	Blairgowrie	1
Feb 8	Clyde	1	Dundee	0

3rd Round

Date	Home		Away	
Feb 18	Buckie T	0	T Lanark	6
Feb 18	Dunfermline A	1	Alloa	1
Feb 18	Falkirk	2	Aberdeen	3
Feb 18	Hearts	2	Celtic	2
Feb 18	Motherwell	4	St Mirren	2
Feb 18	Rangers	1	Clyde	4

Replays

Date	Home		Away	
Feb 22	Alloa	3	Dunfermline A	2
Feb 22	Celtic	2	Hearts	1

4th Round

Date	Home		Away	
Mar 4	Aberdeen	2	Queen of South	0
Mar 4	Clyde	1	T Lanark	0
Mar 4	Hibernian	3	Alloa	1
Mar 4	Motherwell	3	Celtic	1

Semi-finals

Date	Home		Away	
Mar 25	Aberdeen	1	Motherwell	1
	played at Ibrox			
Mar 25	Clyde	1	Hibernian	0
	played at Tynecastle			

Replay

Date	Home		Away	
Mar 29	Aberdeen	1	Motherwell	3
	played at Ibrox			

Final

Date	Home		Away	
Apr 22	Clyde	4	Motherwell	0
	played at Hampden Park			

Season 1946-47

1st Round

Date	Home		Away	
Jan 25	Aberdeen	2	Partick T	1
Jan 25	Albion R	3	Airdrie	0
Jan 25	Alloa	0	Hibernian	8
Jan 25	Arbroath	2	Stenhousemuir	2
Feb 1	Clacknacuddin	1	E Stirling	1
Jan 25	Dundee	2	Celtic	1
Jan 25	East Fife	6	Dunfermline A	2
Jan 25	Falkirk	2	Kilmarnock	0
Jan 25	Hamilton A	1	T Lanark	1
Jan 25	Hearts	3	St Johnstone	0
Jan 25	Morton	4	Edinburgh C	0
Jan 25	Motherwell	3	Forfar A	0
Jan 25	Peterhead	1	Ayr U	5
Jan 25	Queen of South	3	Raith R	4
Jan 25	Queen's Park	3	Dundee U	0
Jan 25	Rangers	2	Clyde	1
Jan 25	St Mirren	2	Dumbarton	3
Jan 25	Stranraer	0	Cowdenbeath	5

Replays

Date	Home		Away	
Feb 8	E Stirling	5	Clacknacuddin	1
Feb 8	Stenhousemuir	0	Arbroath	2
Feb 8	T Lanark	2	Hamilton A	1

2nd Round

Date	Home		Away	
Feb 8	Aberdeen	8	Ayr U	0
Feb 15	East Fife	5	E Stirling	1

3rd Round

Date	Home		Away	
Feb 22	Aberdeen	1	Morton	1
Feb 22	Arbroath	5	Raith R	4
Feb 22	Dumbarton	2	T Lanark	0
Feb 22	Dundee	3	Albion R	0
Feb 22	East Fife	3	Queen's Park	1
Feb 22	Falkirk	0	Motherwell	0
Mar 8	Hearts	2	Cowdenbeath	1

Feb 22 Rangers 0 Hibernian 0

Replays
Mar 8 Hibernian 2 Rangers 0
Mar 8 Morton 1 Aberdeen 2
Mar 8 Motherwell 1 Falkirk 0

4th Round
Mar 15 Arbroath 2 Hearts 1
Mar 29 Dundee 1 Aberdeen 2
Mar 15 East Fife 0 Motherwell 2
Mar 15 Hibernian 2 Dumbarton 0

Semi-finals
Apr 12 Aberdeen 2 Arbroath 0
played at Dens Park
Mar 29 Hibernian 2 Motherwell 1
played at Hampden Park

Final
Apr 19 Aberdeen 2 Hibernian 1
played at Hampden Park

Season 1947-48

1st Round
Jan 24 Albion R 0 Hibernian 2
Jan 24 Arbroath 9 Babcock & W 1
Jan 24 Ayr U 1 Morton 2
Jan 24 Berwick R 2 Cowdenbeath 4
Jan 17 Clacknacuddin 0 St Johnstone 2
Jan 24 Dundee 2 Hearts 4
Jan 24 East Fife 2 Kilmarnock 0
Jan 24 Inverness C 1 Falkirk 6
Jan 24 Motherwell 2 Hamilton A 2
Jan 24 Queen of South 1 Stenhousemuir 0
Jan 24 St Mirren 8 Shawfield 0
Jan 24 Stranraer 0 Rangers 1

Replays
Jan 31 Hamilton A 0 Motherwell 2

2nd Round
Feb 7 Airdrie 2 Hearts 1
Feb 7 Alloa 0 Queen of South 1
Feb 7 Celtic 3 Cowdenbeath 0
Feb 7 Clyde 2 Dunfermline A 1
Feb 7 East Fife 5 St Johnstone 1
Feb 7 Hibernian 4 Arbroath 0
Feb 7 Montrose 2 Duns 0
Feb 7 Morton 3 Falkirk 2
Feb 7 Motherwell 1 T Lanark 0
Feb 7 Nithsdale W 0 Aberdeen 5
Feb 7 Partick T 4 Dundee U 3
Feb 7 Peterhead 1 Dumbarton 2
Feb 7 Queen's Park 8 Deveronvale 2
Feb 7 Rangers 4 Leith A 0
Feb 7 St Mirren 2 E Stirling 0
Feb 7 Stirling A 2 Raith R 4

3rd Round
Feb 21 Airdrie 3 Raith R 0
Feb 21 Celtic 1 Motherwell 0
Feb 21 Dumbarton 0 East Fife 1
Feb 21 Hibernian 4 Aberdeen 2
Feb 21 Montrose 2 Queen of South 1
Feb 21 Morton 3 Queen's Park 0
Feb 21 Rangers 3 Partick T 0
Feb 21 St Mirren 2 Clyde 1

4th Round
Mar 6 Airdrie 0 Morton 3
Mar 6 Celtic 4 Montrose 0
Mar 6 Hibernian 3 St Mirren 1
Mar 6 Rangers 1 East Fife 0

Semi-finals
Mar 27 Celtic 0 Morton 1
played at Ibrox
Mar 27 Hibernian 0 Rangers 1
played at Hampden Park

Final
Apr 17 Morton 1 Rangers 1
played at Hampden Park

Replay
Apr 21 Morton 0 Rangers 1
played at Hampden Park

Season 1948-49

1st Round
Jan 22 Alloa 8 Montrose 3
Jan 22 Arbroath 3 Partick T 4
Jan 22 Ayr U 2 Queen's Park 1
Jan 22 Clyde 2 Fraserburgh 0
Jan 22 Cowdenbeath 6 Keith 2
Jan 22 Dumbarton 5 Kilmarnock 2
Jan 22 Dundee 5 St Johnstone 1
Jan 22 Dundee U 4 Celtic 3
Jan 22 East Fife 2 Falkirk 1
Jan 22 Forfar A 0 Hibernian 4
Jan 22 Hamilton A 1 Albion R 2
Jan 22 Hearts 4 Airdrie 1
Jan 22 Inverness Cal 2 Morton 2
Jan 22 Leith A 0 Raith R 1
Jan 22 Motherwell 3 Stranraer 0
Jan 22 Queen of South 2 E Stirling 0
Jan 22 Rangers 6 Elgin C 1
Jan 22 St Mirren 2 Stirling A 0
Jan 22 Stenhousemuir 2 Dunfermline A 0
Jan 22 T Lanark 2 Aberdeen 1

Replays
Jan 26 Morton 2 Inverness Cal 0

2nd Round
Feb 5 Ayr U 0 Morton 2
Feb 9 Clyde 3 Alloa 1
Feb 5 Cowdenbeath 1 East Fife 2
Feb 5 Dumbarton 1 Dundee U 1
Feb 5 Dundee 0 St Mirren 0
Feb 5 Hearts 3 T Lanark 1
Feb 5 Hibernian 1 Raith R 1
Feb 5 Motherwell 0 Rangers 3
Feb 5 Partick T 3 Queen of South 0
Feb 9 Stenhousemuir 5 Albion R 1

Replays
Feb 9 Dundee U 1 Dumbarton 3
Feb 9 Raith R 3 Hibernian 4
Feb 9 St Mirren 1 Dundee 2

3rd Round
Feb 19 Clyde 2 Morton 0
played at Ibrox
Feb 19 Hearts 3 Dumbarton 0

4th Round
Mar 5 Hearts 2 Dundee 4
Mar 5 Hibernian 0 East Fife 2
Mar 5 Rangers 4 Partick T 0
Mar 5 Stenhousemuir 0 Clyde 1

Semi-finals
Mar 26 Clyde 2 Dundee 2
played at Easter Road
Mar 26 East Fife 0 Rangers 3
played at Hampden Park

Replay
Apr 4 Clyde 2 Dundee 1
played at Hampden Park

Final
Apr 23 Clyde 1 Rangers 4
played at Hampden Park

Season 1949-50

1st Round
Jan 28 Alloa 0 Albion R 1
Jan 28 Brechin C 0 Celtic 3
Jan 28 Clacknacuddin 2 Stenhousemuir 3
Jan 28 Clyde 4 Newton Stewart 3
Feb 1 Cowdenbeath 1 Hamilton A 0
Jan 28 Dumbarton 1 Queen's Park 0
Jan 28 Dundee U 4 Ayr U 0
Jan 28 Dunfermline A 5 Forfar A 3
Jan 28 East Fife 4 Fraserburgh 0
Jan 28 Hearts 1 Dundee 1
Jan 28 Hibernian 0 Partick T 1
Jan 28 Inverness C 0 Queen of South 1
Jan 28 Kilmarnock 1 Stirling A 1
Jan 28 Motherwell 2 Rangers 4
Jan 28 Raith R 3 Airdrie 0
Jan 28 Ross Co 0 Morton 3
Jan 28 St Johnstone 7 Leith A 3
Jan 28 St Mirren 1 Aberdeen 2
Jan 28 Stranraer 1 Falkirk 3
Jan 28 T Lanark 2 Arbroath 1

Replays
Feb 1 Stirling A 3 Kilmarnock 1
Feb 6 Dundee 1 Hearts 2

2nd Round
Feb 11 Aberdeen 3 Hearts 1
Feb 15 Albion R 1 Dunfermline A 2
Feb 11 Falkirk 1 East Fife 3
Feb 14 Partick T 5 Dundee U 0
Feb 11 Queen of South 1 Morton 1
Feb 11 Raith R 3 Clyde 2
Feb 11 Rangers 8 Cowdenbeath 0
Feb 11 Stenhousemuir 2 St Johnstone 2
Feb 11 Stirling A 2 Dumbarton 2
Feb 15 T Lanark 1 Celtic 1

Replays
Feb 15 Dumbarton 1 Stirling A 1
Feb 15 Morton 0 Queen of South 3
Feb 15 St Johnstone 2 Stenhousemuir 4
Feb 20 Celtic 4 T Lanark 1
Feb 22 Dumbarton 2 Stirling A 6
played at Ibrox

3rd Round
Feb 25 Celtic 0 Aberdeen 1
Feb 25 Dunfermline A 1 Stenhousemuir 4

4th Round
Mar 11 Partick T 5 Stirling A 1
Mar 11 Queen of South 3 Aberdeen 3
Mar 11 Rangers 1 Raith R 1
Mar 11 Stenhousemuir 0 East Fife 3

Replay
Mar 15 Aberdeen 1 Queen of South 2
Mar 15 Raith R 1 Rangers 1
Mar 27 Raith R 0 Rangers 2
played at Ibrox

Semi-finals
Apr 1 East Fife 2 Partick T 1
played at Ibrox
Apr 1 Queen of South 1 Rangers 1
played at Hampden Park

Replay
Apr 5 Queen of South 0 Rangers 3
played at Hampden Park

Final
Apr 22 East Fife 0 Rangers 3
played at Hampden Park

Season 1950-51

1st Round

Date	Home		Away	
Jan 27	Aberdeen	6	Inverness Cal	1
Jan 27	Albion R	1	Stenhousemuir	1
Jan 27	Alloa	2	Hearts	3
Jan 27	Brechin C	3	Berwick R	2
Jan 27	Dumbarton	0	St Johnstone	2
Jan 27	Dundee	2	Dundee U	2
Jan 27	Dunfermline A	0	Clyde	3
Jan 27	Duns	3	Forres Mechanic	1
Jan 27	East Fife	2	Celtic	2
Jan 27	E Stirling	2	Kilmarnock	1
Jan 27	Falkirk	0	Airdrie	2
Jan 27	Hamilton A	2	Elgin C	2
Jan 27	Morton	2	Cowdenbeath	2
Jan 27	Partick T	1	Raith R	1
Jan 27	Peterhead	0	Motherwell	4
Jan 27	Queen's Park	3	Arbroath	1
Jan 27	Rangers	2	Queen of South	0
Jan 27	St Mirren	1	Hibernian	1
Jan 27	Stirling A	1	Ayr U	2
Jan 27	T Lanark	5	Forfar A	2

Replays

Date	Home		Away	
Jan 31	Celtic	4	East Fife	2
Jan 31	Cowdenbeath	1	Morton	2
Jan 31	Dundee U	0	Dundee	1
Jan 31	Elgin C	0	Hamilton A	3
Jan 31	Hibernian	5	St Mirren	0
Jan 31	Raith R	1	Partick T	0
Jan 31	Stenhousemuir	1	Albion R	2

2nd Round

Date	Home		Away	
Feb 10	Aberdeen	4	T Lanark	0
Feb 10	Albion R	0	Clyde	2
Feb 10	Celtic	4	Duns	0
Feb 10	E Stirling	1	Hearts	5
Feb 10	Morton	3	Airdrie	3
Feb 10	Motherwell	4	Hamilton A	1
Feb 10	Queen's Park	1	Ayr U	3
Feb 10	Raith R	5	Brechin C	2
Feb 10	Rangers	2	Hibernian	3
Feb 10	St Johnstone	1	Dundee	3

Replays

Date	Home		Away	
Feb 14	Airdrie	2	Morton	1

3rd Round

Date	Home		Away	
Feb 24	Airdrie	4	Clyde	0
Feb 24	Hearts	1	Celtic	2

4th Round

Date	Home		Away	
Mar 10	Airdrie	0	Hibernian	3
Mar 10	Ayr U	2	Motherwell	2
Mar 10	Celtic	3	Aberdeen	0
Mar 10	Dundee	1	Raith R	2

Replay

Date	Home		Away	
Mar 14	Motherwell	2	Ayr U	1

Semi-finals

Date	Home		Away	
Mar 31	Celtic	3	Raith R	2
	played at Hampden Park			
Mar 31	Hibernian	2	Motherwell	3
	played at Tynecastle			

Final

Date	Home		Away	
Apr 21	Celtic	1	Motherwell	0
	played at Hampden Park			

Season 1951-52

1st Round

Date	Home		Away	
Jan 26	Berwick R	7	Peebles R	0
Jan 26	Brechin C	0	Queen of South	6
Jan 30	Celtic	0	T Lanark	0
Jan 30	Deveronvale	1	Clyde	3
Jan 26	Dundee	4	Ayr U	0
Jan 26	Duns	1	Alloa	2
Jan 26	Eyemouth U	0	East Fife	4
Jan 26	Forfar A	2	Motherwell	4
Jan 26	Inverness Cal	3	Dundee U	3
Jan 26	Kilmarnock	2	Stenhousemuir	0
Jan 26	Montrose	1	Wigtown & Blad	2
Jan 26	Morton	2	E Stirling	0
Jan 26	Partick T	0	Hamilton A	1
Jan 26	Raith R	0	Hibernian	0

Replays

Date	Home		Away	
Jan 30	Dundee U	4	Inverness Cal	0
Jan 30	Hibernian	0	Raith R	0
Feb 4	Hibernian	1	Raith R	4
	played at Tynecastle			
Feb 4	T Lanark	2	Celtic	1

2nd Round

Date	Home		Away	
Feb 9	Aberdeen	2	Kilmarnock	1
Feb 9	Airdrie	2	East Fife	1
Feb 9	Albion R	1	Stranraer	1
Feb 9	Alloa	1	Berwick R	0
Feb 9	Clacknacuddin	1	Morton	2
Feb 9	Clyde	3	Dunfermline A	4
Feb 9	Cowdenbeath	1	Arbroath	4
Feb 9	Dumbarton	1	Queen's Park	0
Feb 9	Falkirk	3	Stirling A	3
Feb 9	Hamilton A	1	T Lanark	1
Feb 9	Hearts	1	Raith R	0
Feb 9	Leith A	1	Dundee U	4
Feb 9	Rangers	6	Elgin C	1
Feb 9	St Johnstone	2	Queen of South	2
Feb 9	St Mirren	2	Motherwell	3
Feb 9	Wigtown & Blad	1	Dundee	7

Replays

Date	Home		Away	
Feb 13	Queen of South	3	St Johnstone	1
Feb 13	Stirling A	1	Falkirk	2
Feb 13	Stranraer	3	Albion R	4
Feb 13	T Lanark	4	Hamilton A	0
Feb 14	Berwick R	4	Alloa	1

3rd Round

Date	Home		Away	
Feb 23	Airdrie	4	Morton	0
Feb 23	Albion R	1	T Lanark	3
Feb 23	Arbroath	0	Rangers	2
Feb 23	Dumbarton	1	Falkirk	3
Feb 23	Dundee	1	Berwick R	0
Feb 23	Dundee U	2	Aberdeen	2
Feb 23	Dunfermline A	1	Motherwell	1
Feb 23	Queen of South	1	Hearts	3

Replays

Date	Home		Away	
Feb 27	Aberdeen	3	Dundee U	2
Feb 27	Motherwell	4	Dunfermline A	0

4th Round

Date	Home		Away	
Mar 8	Airdrie	2	Hearts	2
Mar 8	Dundee	4	Aberdeen	0
Mar 8	Rangers	1	Motherwell	1
Mar 8	T Lanark	1	Falkirk	0

Replays

Date	Home		Away	
Mar 12	Hearts	6	Airdrie	4
Mar 12	Motherwell	2	Rangers	1

Semi-finals

Date	Home		Away	
Mar 29	Dundee	2	T Lanark	0
	played at Easter Road			
Mar 29	Hearts	1	Motherwell	1
	played at Hampden Park			

Replays

Date	Home		Away	
Apr 7	Hearts	1	Motherwell	1
	played at Hampden Park			
Apr 9	Hearts	1	Motherwell	3
	played at Hampden Park			

Final

Date	Home		Away	
Apr 19	Dundee	0	Motherwell	4
	played at Hampden Park			

Season 1952-53

1st Round

Date	Home		Away	
Jan 24	Berwick R	3	Dundee U	3
Jan 24	Dumbarton	1	Cowdenbeath	3
Jan 24	East Fife	7	Vale of Leithen	1
Jan 24	Elgin C	2	T Lanark	3
Jan 24	Eyemouth U	0	Celtic	4
Jan 24	Hibernian	8	Stenhousemuir	1
Jan 24	Leith A	1	Airdrie	8
Jan 24	Morton	3	Dunfermline A	1
Jan 24	Newton Stewart	2	Falkirk	2
Jan 24	Queen of South	2	Huntly	1
Jan 24	Raith R	5	Clacknacuddin	0
Jan 24	Rangers	4	Arbroath	0
Jan 24	St Mirren	1	Brechin C	1
Jan 24	Stranraer	0	Kilmarnock	4

Replays

Date	Home		Away	
Jan 28	Brechin C	0	St Mirren	1
Jan 28	Dundee U	2	Berwick R	3
Jan 28	Falkirk	4	Newton Stewart	0

2nd Round

Date	Home		Away	
Feb 7	Aberdeen	2	St Mirren	0
Feb 7	Airdrie	3	East Fife	0
Feb 7	Albion R	2	E Stirling	0
Feb 7	Alloa	0	Motherwell	2
Feb 7	Berwick R	2	Queen of South	3
Feb 7	Buckie T	1	Ayr U	5
Feb 7	Cowdenbeath	0	Morton	1
Feb 7	Dundee	0	Rangers	2
Feb 7	Forfar A	2	Falkirk	4
Feb 7	Hamilton A	2	Kilmarnock	2
Feb 7	Hibernian	4	Queen's Park	2
Feb 7	Partick T	0	Clyde	2
Feb 7	Raith R	0	Hearts	1
Feb 7	St Johnstone	1	Montrose	2
Feb 7	Stirling A	1	Celtic	1
Feb 7	Wigtown & Blad	1	T Lanark	3

Replays

Date	Home		Away	
Feb 11	Celtic	3	Stirling A	0
Feb 11	Kilmarnock	0	Hamilton A	2

3rd Round

Date	Home		Away	
Feb 21	Aberdeen	5	Motherwell	5
Feb 21	Airdrie	0	Hibernian	4
Feb 21	Clyde	8	Ayr U	3
Feb 21	Falkirk	2	Celtic	3
Feb 21	Hearts	3	Montrose	1
Feb 21	Morton	1	Rangers	4
Feb 21	Queen of South	2	Albion R	0
Feb 21	T Lanark	1	Hamilton A	0

Replay

Date	Home		Away	
Feb 25	Motherwell	1	Aberdeen	6

4th Round

Date	Home		Away	
Mar 14	Clyde	1	T Lanark	2
Mar 14	Hearts	2	Queen of South	1
Mar 14	Hibernian	1	Aberdeen	1
Mar 14	Rangers	2	Celtic	0

Replay

Date	Home		Away	
Mar 18	Aberdeen	2	Hibernian	0

Semi-finals

Date	Home		Away	
Apr 4	Aberdeen	1	T Lanark	0
	played at Ibrox			
Apr 4	Hearts	1	Rangers	2
	played at Hampden Park			

Replay

Date	Home		Away	
Apr 8	Aberdeen	2	T Lanark	1
	played at Ibrox			

Final

Date	Home		Away	
Apr 25	Aberdeen	1	Rangers	1
	played at Hampden Park			

Replay

Date	Home		Away	
Apr 29	Aberdeen	0	Rangers	1
	played at Hampden Park			

Season 1953-54

1st Round

Date	Home		Away	
Jan 30	Alloa	1	Clyde	3
Jan 30	Berwick R	7	E Stirling	0
Jan 30	East Fife	0	Queen of South	3
Jan 30	Fraserburgh	5	Leith A	4
Jan 30	Inverness T	3	Hamilton A	3
Jan 30	Montrose	0	Peebles R	1
Jan 30	Morton	3	Dundee U	2
Jan 30	Partick T	1	Airdrie	0
Jan 30	Rangers	2	Queen's Park	0
Jan 30	St Johnstone	1	Hibernian	2
Jan 30	St Mirren	1	Motherwell	2
Jan 30	Stirling A	2	Dumbarton	1
Jan 30	Stranraer	1	Dunfermline A	4
Jan 30	T Lanark	2	Stenhousemuir	2

Replays

Date	Home		Away	
Feb 3	Hamilton A	3	Inverness T	1
Feb 3	Stenhousemuir	0	T Lanark	0
Feb 8	Stenhousemuir	0	T Lanark	1
	played at Ibrox			

2nd Round

Date	Home		Away	
Feb 13	Albion R	1	Dundee	1
Feb 13	Berwick R	5	Ayr U	1
Feb 13	Brechin C	2	Hamilton A	3
Feb 13	Coldstream	1	Raith R	10
Feb 13	Duns	0	Aberdeen	8
Feb 17	Falkirk	1	Celtic	2
Feb 13	Fraserburgh	0	Hearts	3
Feb 13	Hibernian	7	Clyde	0
Feb 13	Morton	4	Cowdenbeath	0
Feb 13	Motherwell	5	Dunfermline A	2
Feb 13	Peebles R	1	Buckie T	1
Feb 13	Queen of South	3	Forfar A	0
Feb 13	Rangers	2	Kilmarnock	2
Feb 17	Stirling A	0	Arbroath	0
Feb 13	Tarff R	1	Partick T	9
Feb 13	T Lanark	7	Deveronvale	2

Replays

Date	Home		Away	
Feb 17	Dundee	4	Albion R	0
Feb 17	Kilmarnock	1	Rangers	3
Feb 20	Buckie T	7	Peebles R	2
Feb 22	Arbroath	1	Stirling A	3

3rd Round

Date	Home		Away	
Feb 27	Berwick R	3	Dundee	0
Feb 27	Hamilton A	2	Morton	0
Feb 27	Hibernian	1	Aberdeen	3
Feb 27	Motherwell	4	Raith R	1
Feb 27	Partick T	5	Buckie T	3
Feb 27	Queen of South	1	Hearts	2
Feb 27	Stirling A	3	Celtic	4
Feb 27	T Lanark	0	Rangers	0

Replays

Date	Home		Away	
Mar 3	Rangers	4	T Lanark	4
Mar 8	Rangers	3	T Lanark	2
	played at Ibrox			

4th Round

Date	Home		Away	
Mar 13	Aberdeen	3	Hearts	0
Mar 13	Hamilton A	1	Celtic	2
Mar 13	Partick T	1	Motherwell	1
Mar 13	Rangers	4	Berwick R	0

Replay

Date	Home		Away	
Mar 17	Motherwell	2	Partick T	1

Semi-finals

Date	Home		Away	
Apr 10	Aberdeen	6	Rangers	0
	played at Hampden Park			
Mar 27	Celtic	2	Motherwell	2
	played at Hampden Park			

Replay

Date	Home		Away	
Apr 5	Celtic	3	Motherwell	1
	played at Hampden Park			

Final

Date	Home		Away	
Apr 24	Aberdeen	1	Celtic	2
	played at Hampden Park			

Season 1954-55

1st Round

Date	Home		Away	
Sep 11	Aberdeen Univ	3	Girvan A	3
Sep 11	Babcock	3	Shawfield A	1
Sep 11	Burntisland	1	Forres Mechanic	7
Sep 11	Chirnside U	1	Peterhead	4
Sep 11	Civil Service S	2	Vale of Leithen	3
Sep 11	Deveronvale	0	Inverness T	4
Sep 11	Eyemouth	2	Buckie T	3
Sep 11	Fraserburgh	9	Edinburgh Univ	0
Sep 11	Gala Fairydean	5	Keith	3
Sep 11	Glasgow Univ	1	Huntly	5
Sep 11	Inverness C	7	Rothes	3
	Leith	*W*	Selkirk	*0*
Sep 11	Lossiemouth	6	Murrayfield A	0
Sep 11	Newton Stewart	3	Elgin C	5
Sep 11	Ross Co	2	Peebles R	2
Sep 11	St Cuthbert's	5	Vale of Atholl	1
Sep 11	Tarff R	1	Duns	1
Sep 11	Wick A	2	Coldstream	4

Replays

Date	Home		Away	
Sep 18	Duns	3	Tarff R	0
Sep 18	Girvan A	2	Aberdeen Univ	0
Sep 18	Peebles R	5	Ross Co	1

2nd Round

Date	Home		Away	
Sep 25	Brora R	2	Coldstream	0
Sep 25	Duns	1	Buckie T	1
Sep 25	Elgin C	1	Clacknacuddin	1
Sep 25	Forres Mechanic	5	Huntly	1
Sep 25	Inverness C	5	Wigtown	0
Sep 25	Inverness T	7	Selkirk	1
Sep 25	Lossiemouth	1	Gala Fairydean	0
Sep 25	Peebles R	4	Girvan A	3
Sep 25	Peterhead	7	Babcock	0
Sep 25	St Cuthbert's	4	Whithorn	2
Sep 25	Vale of Leithen	0	Fraserburgh	4

Replays

Date	Home		Away	
Sep 25	Clacknacuddin	7	Elgin C	1

3nd Round

Date	Home		Away	
Oct 9	Berwick R	3	Clacknacuddin	3
Oct 9	Brora R	3	Inverness C	3
Oct 9	Fraserburgh	4	E Stirling	2
Oct 9	Inverness T	2	Stranraer	1
Oct 9	Lossiemouth	3	Dumbarton	1
Oct 9	Peebles R	5	St Cuthbert's	2
Oct 9	Peterhead	0	Buckie T	4

Replays

Date	Home		Away	
Oct 16	Clacknacuddin	2	Berwick R	1
Oct 16	Forres Mechanic	5	Lossiemouth	3
Oct 16	Inverness C	8	Brora R	2

4th Round

Date	Home		Away	
Oct 23	Alloa	4	Fraserburgh	2
Oct 23	Arbroath	2	Brechin C	0
Oct 23	Buckie T	1	Queen's Park	1
Oct 23	Clacknacuddin	1	Inverness T	2
Oct 23	Cowdenbeath	2	Ayr U	2
Oct 23	Dundee U	1	Forfar A	3
Oct 23	Montrose	1	Inverness C	3
Oct 23	Peebles R	0	Forres Mechanic	2

Replays

Date	Home		Away	
Oct 30	Ayr U	3	Cowdenbeath	3
Oct 30	Queen's Park	1	Buckie T	2
Nov 10	Ayr U	3	Cowdenbeath	1
	played at Firhill Park			

5th Round

Date	Home		Away	
Feb 5	Airdrie	4	Forfar A	3
Feb 5	Alloa	2	Celtic	4
Feb 5	Arbroath	0	St Johnstone	4
Feb 5	Buckie T	2	Inverness T	0
Feb 5	Clyde	3	Albion R	0
Feb 5	Dunfermline A	4	Partick T	2
Feb 5	East Fife	1	Kilmarnock	2
Feb 5	Falkirk	4	Stenhousemuir	0
Feb 5	Forres Mechanic	3	Motherwell	4
Feb 5	Hamilton A	2	St Mirren	1
Feb 5	Hearts	5	Hibernian	0
Feb 5	Inverness C	1	Ayr U	1
Feb 5	Morton	1	Raith R	3
Feb 5	Rangers	0	Dundee	0
Feb 5	Stirling A	0	Aberdeen	6
Feb 5	T Lanark	2	Queen's Park	1

Replays

Date	Home		Away	
Feb 9	Ayr U	2	Inverness C	4
Feb 9	Dundee	0	Rangers	1

6th Round

Date	Home		Away	
Feb 19	Aberdeen	2	Rangers	1
Feb 19	Airdrie	7	Dunfermline A	0
Feb 19	Buckie T	0	Hearts	6
Feb 19	Clyde	3	Raith R	1
Feb 19	Inverness C	0	Falkirk	7
Feb 19	Kilmarnock	1	Celtic	1
Feb 19	St Johnstone	0	Hamilton A	1
Feb 19	T Lanark	1	Motherwell	3

Replays

Date	Home		Away	
Feb 23	Celtic	1	Kilmarnock	0

7th Round

Date	Home		Away	
Mar 5	Airdrie	4	Motherwell	1
Mar 5	Celtic	2	Hamilton A	1
Mar 5	Clyde	5	Falkirk	0
Mar 5	Hearts	1	Aberdeen	1

Replays

Date	Home		Away	
Mar 9	Aberdeen	2	Hearts	0

Semi-finals

Date	Home		Away	
Mar 26	Aberdeen	2	Clyde	2
	played at Easter Road			
Mar 26	Airdrie	2	Celtic	2
	played at Hampden Park			

Replay

Date	Home		Away	
Apr 4	Aberdeen	0	Clyde	1
	played at Easter Road			
Apr 4	Airdrie	0	Celtic	2
	played at Hampden Park			

Final

Date	Home		Away	
Apr 23	Celtic	1	Clyde	1
	played at Hampden Park			

Replay

Date	Home		Away	
Apr 27	Celtic	0	Clyde	1
	played at Hampden Park			

Season 1955-56

1st Round

Date	Home		Away	
Sep 10	Babcock	2	Clacknacuddin	5
Sep 10	Buckie T	2	Rothes	1
Sep 10	Chirnside U	1	Elgin C	9
Sep 10	Duns	3	Deveronvale	0
Sep 10	Edinburgh Univ	0	Inverness T	7
Sep 10	Eyemouth	5	Brora R	1
Sep 10	Forres Mechanic	3	Glasgow Univ	2
Sep 10	Fraserburgh	3	Aberdeen Univ	1
Sep 10	Gala Fairydean	2	Peterhead	1
Sep 10	Huntly	4	Civil Service S	2
Sep 10	Lossiemouth	7	Wick A	0
Sep 10	Murrayfield A	2	Shawfield A	2
Sep 10	Nairn Co	1	Inverness C	4
Sep 10	Newton Stewart	3	Peebles R	5
Sep 10	Ross Co	4	Coldstream	2
Sep 10	St Cuthbert's	3	Vale of Atholl	1
Sep 10	Selkirk	3	Burntisland	2
Sep 10	Tarff R	2	Girvan A	2
Sep 17	Whithorn	7	Vale of Leithen	0
Sep 10	Wigtown	0	Keith	7

Replays

Date	Home		Away	
Sep 17	Girvan A	0	Tarff R	1
Sep 17	Shawfield A	2	Murrayfield A	1

2nd Round

Date	Home		Away	
Sep 24	Clacknacuddin	3	St Cuthbert's	0
Sep 24	Gala Fairydean	6	Shawfield A	2
Sep 24	Huntly	2	Forres Mechanic	4
Sep 24	Inverness T	5	Buckie T	2
Sep 24	Keith	2	Elgin C	0
Sep 24	Lossiemouth	3	Duns	1
Oct 1	Peebles R	4	Eyemouth	3
Sep 24	Ross Co	3	Tarff R	2
Sep 24	Whithorn	2	Selkirk	3

3nd Round

Date	Home		Away	
Oct 8	Berwick R	3	Fraserburgh	0
Oct 8	Dumbarton	5	Inverness C	3
Oct 8	Forres Mechanic	2	Clacknacuddin	4
Oct 8	Gala Fairydean	4	Montrose	5
Oct 8	Inverness T	1	Peebles R	1
Oct 8	Keith	2	E Stirling	4
Oct 8	Lossiemouth	1	Selkirk	0
Oct 8	Ross Co	2	Stranraer	3

Replay

Date	Home		Away	
Oct 15	Peebles R	2	Inverness T	1

4th Round

Date	Home		Away	
Oct 22	Albion R	1	Alloa	1
Oct 22	Berwick R	5	Lossiemouth	1
Oct 22	Brechin C	1	Peebles	1
Oct 22	Cowdenbeath	6	Montrose	0
Oct 22	Dundee U	4	Dumbarton	1
Oct 22	E Stirling	0	Arbroath	2
Oct 22	Forfar A	5	Stranraer	2
Oct 22	Morton	5	Clacknacuddin	2

Replays

Date	Home		Away	
Oct 29	Alloa	4	Albion R	0
Oct 29	Peebles	4	Brechin C	4
Nov 2	Brechin C	0	Peebles	0
	played at Easter Road			
Nov 16	Brechin C	6	Peebles	2
	played at Tannadice			

5th Round

Feb 4	Airdrie	7	Hamilton A	1
Feb 4	Ayr U	5	Berwick R	2
Feb 4	Brechin C	1	Arbroath	1
Feb 8	Clyde	5	Dunfermline A	0
Feb 4	Dundee U	2	Dundee	2
Feb 8	East Fife	1	Stenhousemuir	3
Feb 4	Falkirk	0	Kilmarnock	3
Feb 4	Hearts	3	Forfar A	0
Feb 8	Hibernian	1	Raith R	1
Feb 4	Morton	0	Celtic	2
Feb 8	Motherwell	0	Queen's Park	2
Feb 4	Partick T	2	Alloa	0
Feb 4	Queen of South	3	Cowdenbeath	1
Feb 4	Rangers	2	Aberdeen	1
Feb 4	St Mirren	6	T Lanark	0
Feb 4	Stirling A	2	St Johnstone	1

Replays

Feb 8	Arbroath	2	Brechin C	3
Feb 8	Dundee	3	Dundee U	0
Feb 13	Raith R	3	Hibernian	1

6th Round

Feb 18	Airdrie	4	St Mirren	4
Feb 18	Ayr U	0	Celtic	3
Feb 18	Dundee	0	Rangers	1
Feb 18	Hearts	5	Stirling A	0
Feb 18	Kilmarnock	2	Queen of South	2
Feb 18	Partick T	3	Brechin C	1
Feb 18	Raith R	2	Queen's Park	2
Feb 18	Stenhousemuir	0	Clyde	1

Replays

Feb 21	St Mirren	1	Airdrie	3
Feb 22	Queen of South	2	Kilmarnock	0
Feb 22	Queen's Park	1	Raith R	2

7th Round

Mar 3	Celtic	2	Airdrie	1
Mar 3	Hearts	4	Rangers	0
Mar 3	Queen of South	2	Clyde	4
Mar 3	Raith R	2	Partick T	1

Semi-finals

Mar 24	Celtic	2	Clyde	1
	played at Hampden Park			
Mar 24	Hearts	0	Raith R	0
	played at Easter Road			

Replay

Mar 28	Hearts	3	Raith R	0
	played at Easter Road			

Final

Apr 21	Celtic	1	Hearts	3
	played at Hampden Park			

Season 1956-57

1st Round

Sep 8	Arbroath	10	Rothes	2
Sep 8	Babcock	6	Selkirk	3
Sep 8	Buckie T	4	Lossiemouth	0
Sep 8	Chirnside	1	Montrose	9
Sep 8	Civil Service S	0	Clacknacuddin	7
Sep 8	Coldstream	6	Whithorn	0
Sep 8	Edinburgh Univ	1	Duns	11
Sep 8	Elgin C	5	Shawfield A	1
Sep 8	Eyemouth	3	Burntisland	2
Sep 8	Forres Mechanic	6	Keith	1
Sep 8	Fraserburgh	5	Deveronvale	2
Sep 8	Peebles R	4	Murrayfield A	2
Sep 8	Peterhead	4	Huntly	2
Sep 8	Ross Co	6	Aberdeen Univ	3
Sep 8	Tarff R	1	Inverness C	7
Sep 8	Vale of Leithen	6	Glasgow Univ	1
Sep 8	Wick A	3	Girvan A	1
Sep 8	Wigtown	1	Brora R	4

2nd Round

Sep 22	Arbroath	6	Brora	1
Sep 22	Babcock	0	Inverness C	2
Sep 22	Elgin C	2	Clacknacuddin	2
Sep 22	Eyemouth	3	Duns	1
Sep 22	Fraserburgh	9	Gala Fairydean	0
Sep 22	Montrose	2	Buckie T	4
Sep 22	Peebles R	2	Albion R	2
Sep 22	Peterhead	2	Forres Mechanic	3
Sep 22	Ross Co	6	Coldstream	0
Sep 22	Vale of Leithen	7	Wick A	2

Replay

Sep 29	Albion R	6	Peebles R	0
Sep 29	Clacknacuddin	3	Elgin C	2

3rd Round

Oct 6	Buckie T	9	Newton S	2
Oct 6	Clacknacuddin	1	E Stirling	4
Oct 6	Eyemouth	0	Nairn Co	3
Oct 6	Forfar A	3	Arbroath	1
Oct 6	Fraserburgh	0	Forres Mechanic	2
Oct 6	Inverness T	0	Ross Co	2
Oct 6	St Cuthbert's	2	Inverness C	7
Oct 6	Vale of Leithen	0	Albion R	2

4th Round

Oct 20	Alloa	4	Forfar A	0
Oct 20	Buckie T	2	Hamilton A	3
Oct 20	Cowdenbeath	3	Inverness C	5
Oct 20	Dundee U	5	T Lanark	2
Oct 20	E Stirling	1	Morton	1
Oct 20	Forres Mechanic	3	Albion R	0
Oct 20	Nairn Co	5	Berwick R	5
Oct 20	Stranraer	3	Ross Co	0

Replays

Oct 27	Berwick R	3	Nairn Co	0
Oct 27	Morton	4	E Stirling	1

5th Round

Feb 2	Berwick R	1	Falkirk	2
Feb 2	Dundee	0	Clyde	0
Feb 2	Dunfermline A	3	Morton	0
Feb 2	East Fife	4	St Johnstone	0
Feb 2	Forres Mechanic	0	Celtic	5
Feb 2	Hamilton A	2	Alloa	2
Feb 2	Hearts	0	Rangers	4
Feb 2	Hibernian	3	Aberdeen	4
Feb 2	Inverness C	2	Raith R	3
Feb 2	Kilmarnock	1	Ayr U	0
Feb 2	Queen of South	2	Dumbarton	2
Feb 2	Queen's Park	3	Brechin C	0
Feb 2	St Mirren	1	Partick T	1
Feb 2	Stenhousemuir	1	Dundee U	1
Feb 2	Stirling A	1	Motherwell	2
Feb 2	Stranraer	1	Airdrie	2

After drawing the sixth-round tie 4-4 at Parkhead, Celtic went on to win the replay 2-0 with this headed goal from Mochan with Higgins getting the second. Celtic were themselves knocked out of the competition by finalists Kilmarnock.

Replays

Feb 6	Alloa	3	Hamilton A	5
Feb 6	Clyde	2	Dundee	1
Feb 6	Dumbarton	4	Queen of South	2
Feb 6	Dundee U	4	Stenhousemuir	0
Feb 6	Partick T	2	St Mirren	2
Feb 11	Partick T	1	St Mirren	5
	played at Hampden Park			

6th Round

Feb 16	Celtic	4	Rangers	4
Feb 16	East Fife	0	Kilmarnock	0
Feb 16	Falkirk	3	Aberdeen	1
Feb 16	Hamilton A	1	Airdrie	2
Feb 16	Motherwell	1	Dumbarton	3
Feb 16	Queen's Park	1	Clyde	1
Feb 16	Raith R	7	Dundee U	0
Feb 16	St Mirren	1	Dunfermline A	0

Replays

Feb 20	Clyde	2	Queen's Park	1
Feb 20	Kilmarnock	2	East Fife	0
Feb 20	Rangers	0	Celtic	2

7th Round

Mar 2	Celtic	2	St Mirren	1
Mar 2	Dumbarton	0	Raith R	4
Mar 2	Falkirk	2	Clyde	1
Mar 2	Kilmarnock	3	Airdrie	1

Semi-finals

Mar 23	Celtic	1	Kilmarnock	1
	played at Hampden Park			
Mar 23	Falkirk	2	Raith R	2
	played at Tynecastle			

Replay

Mar 27	Celtic	1	Kilmarnock	3
	played at Hampden Park			
Mar 27	Falkirk	2	Raith R	0
	played at Tynecastle			

Final

Apr 20	Falkirk	1	Kilmarnock	1
	played at Hampden Park			

Replay

Apr 24	Falkirk	2	Kilmarnock	1
	played at Hampden Park			

Season 1957-58

1st Round

Feb 1	Airdrie	3	Celtic	4
Feb 1	Albion R	3	Berwick R	1
Feb 1	Alloa	0	Dunfermline A	2
Feb 1	Ayr U	1	St Mirren	1
Feb 1	Brechin C	1	Montrose	1
Feb 1	Chirnside	0	T Lanark	4
Feb 1	Cowdenbeath	1	Rangers	3
Feb 1	Dumbarton	0	Clyde	5
Feb 1	East Fife	1	Hearts	2
Feb 1	E Stirling	3	Motherwell	7
Feb 1	Falkirk	2	Hamilton A	0
Feb 1	Raith R	4	Peebles R	0
Feb 1	Stranraer	6	Eyemouth U	2

Replays

Feb 5	Montrose	3	Brechin C	1
Feb 5	St Mirren	2	Ayr U	1

2nd Round

Feb 15	Celtic	7	Stirling A	2
Feb 15	Clyde	4	Arbroath	0
Feb 15	Dundee U	0	Hibernian	0
Feb 15	Falkirk	6	St Johnstone	3
Feb 15	Forfar A	1	Rangers	9
Feb 15	Hearts	4	Albion R	1
Feb 15	Inverness C	5	Stenhousemuir	2
Feb 15	Kilmarnock	7	Vale of Leithen	0
Feb 15	Montrose	2	Buckie T	2
Feb 15	Morton	0	Aberdeen	1
Feb 15	Motherwell	2	Partick T	2
Feb 15	Queen of South	7	Stranraer	0
Feb 15	Queen's Park	7	Fraserburgh	2
Feb 15	Raith R	0	Dundee	1
Feb 15	St Mirren	1	Dunfermline A	4
Feb 15	T Lanark	6	Lossiemouth	1

Replays

Feb 19	Buckie T	4	Montrose	1
Feb 19	Hibernian	2	Dundee U	0
Feb 19	Partick T	0	Motherwell	4

3rd Round

Mar 1	Buckie T	1	Falkirk	2
Mar 1	Celtic	0	Clyde	2
Mar 1	Dundee	1	Aberdeen	3
Mar 1	Dunfermline A	1	Rangers	2
Mar 1	Hearts	3	Hibernian	4
Mar 1	Inverness C	0	Motherwell	7
Mar 1	Kilmarnock	2	Queen of South	2
Mar 1	T Lanark	5	Queen's Park	3

Replay

Mar 5	Queen of South	3	Kilmarnock	0

4th Round

Mar 15	Clyde	2	Falkirk	1
Mar 15	Hibernian	3	T Lanark	2
Mar 15	Motherwell	2	Aberdeen	1
Mar 15	Queen of South	3	Rangers	4

Semi-finals

Apr 5	Clyde	3	Motherwell	2
	played at Celtic Park			
Apr 5	Hibernian	2	Rangers	2
	played at Hampden Park			

Replay

Apr 9	Hibernian	2	Rangers	1
	played at Hampden Park			

Final

Apr 26	Clyde	1	Hibernian	0
	played at Hampden Park			

Kilmarnock's goalkeeper is in a spot of bother in this Cup-tie against Queen of the South.

Season 1958-59

1st Round

Jan 31	Aberdeen	2	East Fife	1
Jan 31	Babcock & Wilcox	4	Forres Mechanic	0
Jan 31	Celtic	4	Albion R	0
Jan 31	Cowdenbeath	2	Dunfermline A	2
Jan 31	Dumbarton	4	Buckie T	0
Feb 9	E Stirling	1	Dundee U	1
Jan 31	Forfar A	1	Rangers	3
Jan 31	Fraserburgh	1	Dundee	0
Jan 31	Peebles R	2	Ross Co	0
Feb 4	Queen of South	1	Hearts	3
Jan 31	Raith R	1	Hibernian	1
Jan 31	Stenhousemuir	5	Eyemouth U	2
Jan 31	Stranraer	3	Berwick R	2

Replays

Feb 9	Dunfermline A	4	Cowdenbeath	1
Feb 9	Hibernian	2	Raith R	1
Feb 10	Dundee U	0	E Stirling	0
Feb 11	Dundee U	4	E Stirling	0
	played at Tynecastle			

2nd Round

Feb 14	Aberdeen	3	Arbroath	0
Feb 14	Airdrie	2	Motherwell	7
Feb 14	Ayr U	3	Stranraer	0
Feb 14	Babcock & Wilcox	0	Morton	5
Feb 14	Brechin C	3	Alloa	3
Feb 18	Celtic	1	Clyde	1
Feb 14	Coldstream	0	Hamilton A	4
Feb 14	Dumbarton	2	Kilmarnock	8
Feb 14	Dundee U	0	T Lanark	4
Feb 14	Fraserburgh	3	Stirling A	4
Feb 14	Hibernian	3	Falkirk	1
Feb 14	Montrose	0	Dunfermline A	1
Feb 14	Rangers	3	Hearts	2

The Duke of Gloucester greets Aberdeen's Jack Hather.

Date	Home		Away	
Feb 14	St Johnstone	3	Queen's Park	1
Feb 13	St Mirren	10	Peebles R	0
Feb 14	Stenhousemuir	1	Partick T	3

Replays

Date	Home		Away	
Feb 18	Alloa	3	Brechin C	1
Feb 23	Clyde	3	Celtic	4

3rd Round

Date	Home		Away	
Feb 28	Celtic	2	Rangers	1
Feb 28	Dunfermline A	2	Ayr U	1
Feb 28	Hamilton A	0	Kilmarnock	5
Feb 28	Hibernian	4	Partick T	1
Feb 28	St Johnstone	1	Aberdeen	2
Feb 28	St Mirren	3	Motherwell	2
Feb 28	Stirling A	3	Morton	1
Feb 28	T Lanark	3	Alloa	2

4th Round

Date	Home		Away	
Mar 14	Aberdeen	3	Kilmarnock	1
Mar 14	St Mirren	2	Dunfermline A	1
Mar 14	Stirling A	1	Celtic	3
Mar 14	T Lanark	2	Hibernian	1

Semi-finals

Date	Home		Away	
Apr 4	Aberdeen	1	T Lanark	1
	played at Ibrox			
Apr 4	Celtic	0	St Mirren	4
	played at Hampden Park			

Replay

Date	Home		Away	
Apr 8	Aberdeen	1	T Lanark	0
	played at Ibrox			

Final

Date	Home		Away	
Apr 25	Aberdeen	1	St Mirren	3
	played at Hampden Park			

Season 1959-60

1st Round

Date	Home		Away	
Jan 30	Aberdeen	0	Brechin C	0
Jan 30	Albion R	2	Tarff R	1
Jan 30	Berwick R	1	Rangers	3
Jan 30	Clyde	2	T Lanark	0
Jan 30	Dunfermline A	1	St Johnstone	1
Jan 30	East Fife	0	Partick T	2
Jan 30	Keith	3	Hamilton A	0
Jan 30	Kilmarnock	5	Stranraer	0
Jan 30	Morton	0	E Stirling	1
Jan 30	Queen of South	2	Dumbarton	1
Jan 30	Queen's Park	2	Raith R	0
Jan 30	St Mirren	15	Glasgow Univ	0
Jan 30	Stenhousemuir	2	Rothes	0

Replays

Date	Home		Away	
Feb 3	Brechin C	3	Aberdeen	6
Feb 3	St Johnstone	1	Dunfermline A	4

2nd Round

Date	Home		Away	
Feb 13	Aberdeen	0	Clyde	2
Feb 13	Alloa	1	Airdrie	5
Feb 13	Cowdenbeath	1	Falkirk	0
Feb 13	Dundee U	2	Partick T	2
Feb 13	Dunfermline A	2	Stenhousemuir	3
Feb 13	E Stirling	2	Inverness C	2
Feb 13	Elgin C	5	Forfar A	1
Feb 13	Eyemouth U	1	Albion R	0
Feb 22	Hearts	1	Kilmarnock	1
Feb 29	Hibernian	3	Dundee	0
Feb 13	Montrose	2	Queen's Park	2
Feb 13	Motherwell	6	Keith	0
Feb 22	Peebles R	1	Ayr U	6
Feb 13	Rangers	2	Arbroath	0
Feb 13	St Mirren	1	Celtic	1
Feb 13	Stirling A	3	Queen of South	3

Replays

Date	Home		Away	
Feb 17	Partick T	4	Dundee U	1
Feb 17	Queen of South	5	Stirling A	1
Feb 24	Celtic	4	St Mirren	4
Feb 24	Kilmarnock	2	Hearts	1
Feb 27	Inverness C	1	E Stirling	4
Feb 29	Celtic	5	St Mirren	2
	played at Celtic Park			
Feb 29	Queen's Park	1	Montrose	1
Mar 1	Montrose	1	Queen's Park	2
	played at Tynecastle			

3rd Round

Date	Home		Away	
Feb 27	Ayr U	4	Airdrie	2
Mar 5	Clyde	6	Queen's Park	0
Mar 5	E Stirling	0	Hibernian	3
Mar 5	Elgin C	1	Celtic	2
Feb 27	Eyemouth U	3	Cowdenbeath	0

Feb 27 Kilmarnock 2 Motherwell 0
Feb 27 Partick T 3 Queen of South 2
Feb 27 Stenhousemuir 0 Rangers 3

4th Round
Mar 12 Ayr U 0 Clyde 2
Mar 12 Celtic 2 Partick T 0
Mar 12 Eyemouth U 1 Kilmarnock 2
Mar 12 Rangers 3 Hibernian 2

Semi-finals
Apr 2 Celtic 1 Rangers 1
played at Hampden Park
Apr 2 Clyde 0 Kilmarnock 2
played at Ibrox

Replay
Apr 6 Celtic 1 Rangers 4
played at Hampden Park

Final
Apr 23 Kilmarnock 0 Rangers 2
played at Hampden Park

SEASON 1960-61

1st Round
Jan 28 Alloa 5 E Stirling 4
Jan 28 Berwick R 1 Dunfermline A 4
Jan 28 Clyde 0 Hibernian 2
Jan 28 Deveronvale 1 Stirling A 0
Jan 28 Elgin C 2 Airdrie 2
Jan 28 Falkirk 1 Celtic 3
Jan 28 Hearts 9 Tarff R 0
Jan 28 Keith 1 East Fife 2
Jan 28 Montrose 3 Albion R 1
Jan 28 Peebles 4 Gala Fairydean 2
Jan 28 Queen of South 1 St Johnstone 1
Jan 28 Queen's Park 2 Arbroath 3
Jan 28 T Lanark 2 Stenhousemuir 0

Replays
Feb 1 Airdrie 2 Elgin C 0
Feb 1 St Johnstone 1 Queen of South 2

2nd Round
Feb 11 Aberdeen 4 Deveronvale 2
Feb 11 Alloa 2 Dumbarton 0
Feb 11 Ayr U 0 Airdrie 0
Feb 11 Brechin C 5 Duns 3
Feb 11 Buckie T 0 Raith R 2
Feb 11 Celtic 6 Montrose 0
Feb 11 Cowdenbeath 1 Motherwell 4
Feb 11 Dundee 1 Rangers 5
Feb 11 Dundee U 0 St Mirren 1
Feb 11 East Fife 1 Partick T 3
Feb 11 Forfar A 2 Morton 0
Feb 11 Hibernian 15 Peebles 1
Feb 11 Kilmarnock 1 Hearts 2
Feb 11 Queen of South 0 Hamilton A 2
Feb 11 Stranraer 1 Dunfermline A 3
Feb 11 T Lanark 5 Arbroath 2

Replays
Feb 15 Airdrie 3 Ayr U 1

3rd Round
Feb 25 Aberdeen 3 Dunfermline A 6
Feb 25 Alloa 2 Forfar A 1
Feb 25 Brechin C 0 Airdrie 3
Feb 25 Hamilton A 0 Hibernian 4
Feb 25 Motherwell 2 Rangers 2
Feb 25 Partick T 1 Hearts 2
Feb 25 Raith R 1 Celtic 4
Feb 25 St Mirren 3 T Lanark 3

Replay
Feb 28 T Lanark 0 St Mirren 8
Mar 1 Rangers 2 Motherwell 5

4th Round
Mar 11 Celtic 1 Hibernian 1
Mar 11 Dunfermline A 4 Alloa 0
Mar 11 Hearts 0 St Mirren 1
Mar 11 Motherwell 0 Airdrie 1

Replay
Mar 15 Hibernian 0 Celtic 1

Semi-finals
Apr 1 Airdrie 0 Celtic 4
played at Hampden Park
Apr 1 Dunfermline A 0 St Mirren 0
played at Tynecastle

Replay
Apr 5 Dunfermline A 1 St Mirren 0
played at Tynecastle

Final
Apr 22 Celtic 0 Dunfermline A 0
played at Hampden Park

Replay
Apr 26 Celtic 0 Dunfermline A 2
played at Hampden Park

Dunfermline Athletic, winners of the Scottish Cup in 1961. Back row (left to right): Dickson, Sweeney, Fraser, Connachan, Smith, Miller, J.Stevenson (trainer). Front row: Peebles, Thomson, Mailer, Cunningham, Melrose.

SEASON 1961-62

1st Round
Dec 9 Aberdeen 5 Airdrie 2
Dec 9 Arbroath 2 Peterhead 1
Dec 9 Ayr U 3 Clyde 4
Dec 9 Berwick R 2 T Lanark 6
Dec 13 Celtic 5 Cowdenbeath 1
Dec 13 Dunfermline A 5 Forfar A 1
Dec 13 East Fife 3 Gala Fairydean 1
Dec 9 Eyemouth 1 Montrose 3
Dec 13 Falkirk 1 Rangers 2
Dec 9 Hamilton A 3 Elgin C 1
Dec 13 Motherwell 4 Dundee U 0
Dec 13 Partick T 2 Hibernian 2
Dec 9 Raith R 1 Queen's Park 1

Replays

Date	Team	Score	Team	Score
Dec 13	Queen's Park	1	Raith R	4
Jan 10	Hibernian	2	Partick T	3

2nd Round

Date	Team	Score	Team	Score
Jan 27	Alloa	1	Raith R	2
Jan 27	Brechin C	1	Kilmarnock	6
Jan 27	Clyde	2	Aberdeen	2
Jan 27	Dumbarton	2	Ross Co	3
Jan 27	Dundee	0	St Mirren	1
Jan 27	Dunfermline A	9	Wigtown	0
Jan 27	East Fife	1	Albion R	0
Jan 27	Hamilton A	0	T Lanark	2
Jan 27	Inverness C	3	E Stirling	0
Jan 27	Morton	1	Celtic	3
Jan 27	Motherwell	4	St Johnstone	0
Jan 27	Queen of South	0	Stenhousemuir	2
Jan 27	Rangers	6	Arbroath	0
Jan 27	Stirling A	3	Partick T	1
Jan 27	Stranraer	0	Montrose	0
Jan 27	Vale of Leithen	0	Hearts	5

Replays

Date	Team	Score	Team	Score
Jan 31	Aberdeen	10	Clyde	3
Jan 31	Montrose	0	Stranraer	1

3rd Round

Date	Team	Score	Team	Score
Feb 17	Aberdeen	2	Rangers	2
Feb 17	Dunfermline A	0	Stenhousemuir	0
Feb 17	Hearts	3	Celtic	4
Feb 17	Kilmarnock	7	Ross Co	0
Feb 17	Raith R	1	St Mirren	1
Feb 17	Stirling A	4	East Fife	1
Feb 17	Stranraer	1	Motherwell	3
Feb 17	T Lanark	6	Inverness C	1

Replay

Date	Team	Score	Team	Score
Feb 19	St Mirren	4	Raith R	0
Feb 21	Rangers	5	Aberdeen	1
Feb 26	Stenhousemuir	0	Dunfermline A	3

4th Round

Date	Team	Score	Team	Score
Mar 10	Celtic	4	T Lanark	4
Mar 10	Kilmarnock	2	Rangers	4
Mar 10	St Mirren	1	Dunfermline A	0
Mar 10	Stirling A	0	Motherwell	6

Replay

Date	Team	Score	Team	Score
Mar 14	T Lanark	0	Celtic	4
	played at Hampden Park			

Semi-finals

Date	Team	Score	Team	Score
Mar 31	Celtic	1	St Mirren	3
	played at Ibrox			
Mar 31	Motherwell	1	Rangers	3
	played at Hampden Park			

Final

Date	Team	Score	Team	Score
Apr 21	Rangers	2	St Mirren	0
	played at Hampden Park			

Season 1962-63

1st Round

Date	Team	Score	Team	Score
Mar 11	Airdrie	3	Stranraer	0
Jan 12	Arbroath	2	Dumbarton	0
Jan 26	Dundee U	3	Albion R	0
Jan 12	East Fife	5	Edinburgh Univ	0
Jan 26	E Stirling	2	Stirling A	0
Jan 28	Falkirk	0	Celtic	2
Jan 12	Forfar A	1	Hearts	3
Jan 19	Gala Fairydean	4	Keith	0
Jan 12	Inverness C	1	Dundee	5
Jan 12	Inverness T	0	Queen of South	2
Feb 4	Partick T	3	Morton	2
Jan 12	Raith R	2	Eyemouth	0
Mar 7	St Johnstone	1	Stenhousemuir	0

2nd Round

Date	Team	Score	Team	Score
Mar 13	Airdrie	0	Rangers	6
Feb 2	Ayr U	1	Dundee U	2
Jan 26	Berwick R	1	St Mirren	3
Jan 26	Brechin C	0	Hibernian	2
Mar 6	Celtic	3	Hearts	1
Mar 11	Cowdenbeath	2	Dunfermline A	3
Feb 4	Dundee	8	Montrose	0
Feb 4	East Fife	1	T Lanark	1
Mar 6	E Stirling	1	Motherwell	0
Jan 26	Gala Fairydean	1	Duns	1
Jan 26	Hamilton A	1	Nairn Co	1
Jan 26	Kilmarnock	0	Queen of South	0
Mar 4	Partick T	1	Arbroath	1
Jan 26	Queen's Park	5	Alloa	1
Jan 26	Raith R	3	Clyde	2
Mar 13	St Johnstone	1	Aberdeen	2

Replays

Date	Team	Score	Team	Score
Jan 30	Nairn Co	1	Hamilton A	2
Mar 6	T Lanark	2	East Fife	0
Mar 11	Duns	1	Gala Fairydean	2
Mar 11	Queen of South	1	Kilmarnock	0
Mar 13	Arbroath	2	Partick T	2
Mar 14	Arbroath	2	Partick T	3
	played at Gayfield			

3rd Round

Date	Team	Score	Team	Score
Mar 20	Aberdeen	4	Dunfermline A	0
Mar 13	Celtic	6	Gala Fairydean	0
Mar 18	Dundee	1	Hibernian	0
Mar 20	Queen of South	3	Hamilton A	0
Mar 11	Queen's Park	1	Dundee U	1
Mar 20	Rangers	7	E Stirling	2
Mar 19	St Mirren	1	Partick T	1
Mar 13	T Lanark	0	Raith R	1

Replay

Date	Team	Score	Team	Score
Mar 20	Dundee U	3	Queen's Park	1
Mar 22	Partick T	0	St Mirren	1

4th Round

Date	Team	Score	Team	Score
Mar 30	Dundee	1	Rangers	1
Mar 29	Dundee U	1	Queen of South	1
Mar 30	Raith R	2	Aberdeen	1
Mar 30	St Mirren	0	Celtic	1

Replay

Date	Team	Score	Team	Score
Apr 3	Rangers	3	Dundee	2
Apr 3	Queen of South	1	Dundee U	1
Apr 8	Dundee U	4	Queen of South	0
	played at Ibrox			

Semi-finals

Date	Team	Score	Team	Score
Apr 13	Celtic	5	Raith R	2
	played at Ibrox			
Apr 13	Dundee U	2	Rangers	5
	played at Hampden Park			

Final

Date	Team	Score	Team	Score
Mar 4	Celtic	1	Rangers	1
	played at Hampden Park			

Replay

Date	Team	Score	Team	Score
Mar 15	Celtic	0	Rangers	3
	played at Hampden Park			

In the 1962 Scottish Cup Final replay Ralph Brand puts Rangers ahead after only six minutes as he turns in a Henderson cross. Rangers went on to complete the double that season.

Ralph Brand drenches his Rangers teammates after their hat-trick of Scottish Cup Final wins in 1964. Shearer has the trophy.

Season 1963-64

1st Round

Date	Home		Away	
Jan 11	Aberdeen	5	Hibernian	2
Jan 11	Ayr U	3	Inverness T	2
Jan 11	Berwick R	5	St Cuthbert's W	2
Jan 11	Celtic	3	Eyemouth U	0
Jan 11	Dumbarton	4	Raith R	0
Jan 11	Dundee U	0	St Mirren	0
Jan 11	Forres Mechanic	3	Dundee	6
Jan 11	Kilmarnock	2	Gala Fairydean	1
Jan 11	Montrose	1	Alloa	1
Jan 11	Morton	0	Cowdenbeath	0
Jan 11	Stenhousemuir	1	Rangers	5
Jan 11	Stirling A	1	Brechin C	1
Jan 11	Stranraer	2	T Lanark	1

Replays

Date	Home		Away	
Jan 14	Alloa	3	Montrose	2
Jan 15	Brechin C	5	Stirling A	1
Jan 15	Cowdenbeath	1	Morton	4
Jan 15	St Mirren	1	Dundee U	2

2nd Round

Date	Home		Away	
Jan 25	Aberdeen	1	Queen's Park	1
Jan 25	Albion R	4	Arbroath	3
Jan 25	Alloa	1	Airdrie	3
Jan 25	Brechin C	2	Dundee	9
Jan 25	Buckie T	1	Ayr U	3
Jan 25	Clyde	2	Forfar A	2
Jan 25	Dunfermline A	7	Fraserburgh	0
Jan 25	East Fife	0	E Stirling	1
Jan 25	Falkirk	2	Berwick R	2
Jan 25	Hamilton A	1	Kilmarnock	3
Jan 25	Morton	1	Celtic	3
Jan 25	Motherwell	4	Dumbarton	1
Jan 25	Partick T	2	St Johnstone	0
Jan 25	Queen of South	0	Hearts	3
Jan 25	Rangers	9	Duns	0
Jan 25	St Mirren	2	Stranraer	0

Replays

Date	Home		Away	
Jan 29	Berwick R	1	Falkirk	5
Jan 29	Forfar A	3	Clyde	2
Jan 29	Queen's Park	1	Aberdeen	2

3rd Round

Date	Home		Away	
Feb 15	Aberdeen	1	Ayr U	2
Feb 15	Celtic	4	Airdrie	1
Feb 15	Dundee	6	Forfar A	1
Feb 15	E Stirling	1	Dunfermline A	6
Feb 15	Kilmarnock	2	Albion R	0
Feb 15	Motherwell	3	Hearts	3
Feb 15	Rangers	3	Partick T	0
Feb 15	St Mirren	0	Falkirk	1

Replay

Date	Home		Away	
Feb 19	Hearts	1	Motherwell	2

4th Round

Date	Home		Away	
Mar 7	Dundee	1	Motherwell	1
Mar 7	Dunfermline A	7	Ayr U	0
Mar 7	Falkirk	1	Kilmarnock	2
Mar 7	Rangers	2	Celtic	0

Replay

Date	Home		Away	
Mar 11	Motherwell	2	Dundee	4

Semi-finals

Date	Home		Away	
Mar 28	Dundee	4	Kilmarnock	0
	played at Ibrox			
Mar 28	Dunfermline A	0	Rangers	1
	played at Hampden Park			

Final

Date	Home		Away	
Apr 25	Dundee	1	Rangers	3
	played at Hampden Park			

Season 1964-65

1st Preliminary

Date	Home		Away	
Jan 9	Berwick R	2	Stenhousemuir	2
Jan 9	Brechin C	3	Albion R	4
Jan 9	Coldstream	2	Stranraer	4
Jan 9	Hamilton A	5	Clacknacuddin	3
Jan 9	Peebles	1	Stirling A	4

Replays

Date	Home		Away	
Jan 13	Stenhousemuir	1	Berwick R	0

2nd Preliminary

Date	Home		Away	
Jan 23	Cowdenbeath	2	Alloa	1
Jan 27	Edinburgh Univ	1	Forfar A	4
Jan 23	Hamilton A	3	Stranraer	0
Jan 23	Inverness C	2	Raith R	1
Jan 23	Keith	1	Ayr U	1
Jan 23	Queen's Park	0	Albion R	0
Feb 6	Stenhousemuir	4	Elgin C	1
Jan 23	Vale of Leithen	0	Stirling A	5

Replays

Date	Home		Away	
Jan 27	Ayr U	4	Keith	2
Feb 3	Albion R	1	Queen's Park	1
Feb 4	Albion R	0	Queen's Park	1
	played at Firhill Park			

1st Round

Date	Home		Away	
Feb 6	Aberdeen	0	East Fife	0
Feb 10	Airdrie	7	Montrose	3

Feb 6 Ayr U 1 Partick T 1
Feb 6 Clyde 0 Morton 4
Feb 6 Dumbarton 0 Queen's Park 0
Feb 6 Falkirk 0 Hearts 3
Feb 6 Forfar A 0 Dundee U 3
Feb 6 Hibernian 1 Clydebank 1
Feb 6 Inverness C 1 T Lanark 5
Feb 6 Kilmarnock 5 Cowdenbeath 0
Feb 13 Motherwell 3 Stenhousemuir 2
Feb 6 Queen of South 0 Dunfermline A 2
Feb 6 Rangers 3 Hamilton A 0
Feb 6 St Johnstone 1 Dundee 0
Feb 6 St Mirren 0 Celtic 3
Feb 6 Stirling A 2 Arbroath 1

Replays
Feb 10 Clydebank 0 Hibernian 2
Feb 10 East Fife 1 Aberdeen 0
Feb 10 Partick T 7 Ayr U 1
Feb 10 Queen's Park 2 Dumbarton 1

2nd Round
Feb 20 Dundee U 0 Rangers 2
Feb 20 East Fife 0 Kilmarnock 0
Feb 20 Hibernian 5 Partick T 1
Feb 20 Morton 3 Hearts 3
Feb 20 Motherwell 1 St Johnstone 0
Feb 20 Queen's Park 0 Celtic 1
Feb 20 Stirling A 1 Airdrie 1
Feb 20 T Lanark 1 Dunfermline A 1

Replays
Feb 24 Airdrie 0 Stirling A 2
Feb 24 Dunfermline A 2 T Lanark 2
Feb 24 Hearts 2 Morton 0
Feb 24 Kilmarnock 3 East Fife 0
Feb 26 Dunfermline A 4 T Lanark 2
played at Tynecastle

3rd Round
Mar 6 Celtic 3 Kilmarnock 2
Mar 6 Dunfermline A 2 Stirling A 0
Mar 6 Hibernian 2 Rangers 1
Mar 6 Motherwell 1 Hearts 0

Semi-finals
Mar 27 Celtic 2 Motherwell 2
played at Hampden Park
Mar 27 Dunfermline A 2 Hibernian 0
played at Tynecastle

Replays
Mar 31 Celtic 3 Motherwell 0
played at Hampden Park

Final
Apr 24 Celtic 3 Dunfermline A 2
played at Hampden Park

Season 1965-66

1st Preliminary
Jan 8 Berwick R 1 Stenhousemuir 0
Jan 8 Dumbarton 2 Peebles 2
Jan 8 Forfar A 1 Brechin C 1
Jan 8 Gala Fairydean 6 Selkirk 1
Jan 8 Raith R 1 Inverness C 0

Replays
Jan 12 Brechin C 1 Forfar A 3
Jan 12 Peebles 2 Dumbarton 3

2nd Preliminary
Jan 22 Arbroath 2 Cowdenbeath 2
Jan 22 Ayr U 1 Fraserburgh 0
Jan 22 Berwick R 0 Albion R 0
Jan 22 East Fife 1 Elgin C 0
Jan 22 Gala Fairydean 4 Montrose 5
Jan 22 Glasgow Univ 1 Dumbarton 2
Jan 22 Raith R 0 Alloa 1
Jan 22 Ross Co 4 Forfar A 3

Replays
Jan 26 Albion R 3 Berwick R 0
Jan 26 Cowdenbeath 1 Arbroath 1
Jan 31 Arbroath 2 Cowdenbeath 3
played at Tannadice

1st Round
Feb 10 Alloa 3 Ross Co 5
Feb 5 Ayr U 1 St Johnstone 1
Feb 5 Celtic 4 Stranraer 0
Feb 9 Cowdenbeath 1 St Mirren 0
Feb 9 Dumbarton 2 Montrose 1
Feb 9 Dundee 9 East Fife 1
Feb 7 Dundee U 0 Falkirk 0
Feb 5 Dunfermline A 3 Partick T 1
Feb 9 E Stirling 0 Motherwell 0
Feb 5 Hamilton A 1 Aberdeen 3
Feb 9 Hearts 2 Clyde 1
Feb 5 Hibernian 4 T Lanark 3
Feb 5 Morton 1 Kilmarnock 1
Feb 5 Queen of South 3 Albion R 0
Feb 5 Rangers 5 Airdrie 1
Feb 5 Stirling A 3 Queen's Park 1

Replays
Feb 9 Kilmarnock 3 Morton 0
Feb 14 Motherwell 4 E Stirling 1
Feb 14 St Johnstone 1 Ayr U 0
Feb 16 Falkirk 1 Dundee U 2

2nd Round
Feb 23 Aberdeen 5 Dundee U 0
Feb 28 Cowdenbeath 3 St Johnstone 3
Feb 23 Dumbarton 1 Queen of South 0
Feb 23 Dundee 0 Celtic 2
Feb 21 Hearts 2 Hibernian 1
Feb 21 Kilmarnock 5 Motherwell 0
Feb 28 Ross Co 0 Rangers 2
Feb 23 Stirling A 0 Dunfermline A 0

Replays
Feb 28 Dunfermline A 4 Stirling A 1
Mar 1 St Johnstone 3 Cowdenbeath 0

3rd Round
Mar 5 Dumbarton 0 Aberdeen 3
Mar 5 Dunfermline A 2 Kilmarnock 1
Mar 5 Hearts 3 Celtic 3
Mar 5 Rangers 1 St Johnstone 0

Replay
Mar 9 Celtic 3 Hearts 1

Semi-finals
Mar 26 Aberdeen 0 Rangers 0
played at Hampden Park
Mar 26 Celtic 2 Dunfermline A 0
played at Ibrox

Replays
Mar 29 Aberdeen 1 Rangers 2
played at Hampden Park

Final
Apr 23 Celtic 0 Rangers 0
played at Hampden Park

Replay
Apr 27 Celtic 0 Rangers 1
played at Hampden Park

Season 1966-67

1st Preliminary
Dec 17 Chirnside 1 Elgin C 7
Dec 17 Forfar A 1 E Stirling 0
Dec 17 Hawick 4 Gala Fairydean 1
Dec 17 Nairn Co 0 Stenhousemuir 3
Dec 17 Rothes 1 Clydebank 2
Dec 17 Vale of Leithen 1 Berwick R 8

2nd Preliminary
Jan 7 Albion R 0 Cowdenbeath 1
Jan 7 Alloa 2 Montrose 1
Jan 7 Berwick R 2 Forfar A 0
Jan 7 Brechin C 1 T Lanark 0
Jan 7 Dumbarton 2 Clydebank 0
Jan 14 Hawick 1 Elgin C 1
Jan 7 Inverness C 0 Stranraer 0
Jan 16 Queen's Park 3 Stenhousemuir 0

Replays
Jan 11 Stranraer 1 Inverness C 2
Jan 23 Elgin C 2 Hawick 0

1st Round
Jan 28 Aberdeen 5 Dundee 0
Jan 28 Berwick R 1 Rangers 0
Jan 28 Celtic 4 Arbroath 0
Feb 1 Elgin C 2 Ayr U 0
Jan 28 Falkirk 3 Alloa 1
Jan 28 Hearts 0 Dundee U 3
Jan 28 Hibernian 2 Brechin C 0
Jan 28 Inverness C 1 Hamilton A 3
Jan 28 Kilmarnock 2 Dunfermline A 2
Jan 28 Morton 0 Clyde 1
Jan 28 Motherwell 0 East Fife 1
Jan 28 Partick T 3 Dumbarton 0
Jan 28 Queen's Park 3 Raith R 2
Jan 28 St Johnstone 4 Queen of South 0
Jan 28 St Mirren 1 Cowdenbeath 1
Jan 28 Stirling A 1 Airdrie 2

Replays
Feb 1 Cowdenbeath 0 St Mirren 2
Feb 1 Dunfermline A 1 Kilmarnock 0

2nd Round
Feb 18 Aberdeen 5 St Johnstone 0
Feb 18 Celtic 7 Elgin C 0
Feb 18 Clyde 4 East Fife 1
Feb 18 Dundee U 1 Falkirk 0
Feb 18 Hibernian 1 Berwick R 0
Feb 18 Partick T 1 Dunfermline A 1
Feb 18 Queen's Park 1 Airdrie 1
Feb 18 St Mirren 0 Hamilton A 1

Replays
Feb 20 Airdrie 1 Queen's Park 2
Feb 22 Dunfermline A 5 Partick T 1

3rd Round
Mar 11 Celtic 5 Queen's Park 3
Mar 11 Clyde 0 Hamilton A 0
Mar 11 Dundee U 1 Dunfermline A 0
Mar 11 Hibernian 1 Aberdeen 1

Replays
Mar 22 Aberdeen 3 Hibernian 0
Mar 22 Hamilton A 1 Clyde 5

Semi-finals
Apr 1 Aberdeen 1 Dundee U 0
played at Dens Park
Apr 1 Celtic 0 Clyde 0
played at Hampden Park

Replays
Apr 5 Celtic 2 Clyde 0
played at Hampden Park

Final
Apr 29 Aberdeen 0 Celtic 2
played at Hampden Park

Season 1967-68

1st Preliminary
Dec 16 Dumbarton 0 Berwick R 0
Dec 16 Elgin C 3 Albion R 1
Dec 16 Fraserburgh 1 E Stirling 4
Dec 16 Hawick RA. 4 Vale of Leithen 0
Dec 16 Stranraer 2 Stenhousemuir 2

Replays
Dec 23 Berwick R 2 Dumbarton 1
Dec 23 Stenhousemuir 5 Stranraer 0

2nd Preliminary
Jan 6 Berwick R 2 Nairn Co 0
Jan 6 Brechin C 2 Montrose 1
Jan 17 Forfar A 3 Queen's Park 2
Jan 13 Keith 1 E Stirling 3
Jan 6 Queen of South 2 Clydebank 2
Jan 6 St Cuthbert's 2 Hawick RA. 6
Jan 6 Stenhousemuir 1 Alloa 3
Jan 6 Tarff R 2 Elgin C 3

Replays
Jan 17 Clydebank 2 Queen of South 2
Jan 18 Clydebank 0 Queen of South 1
played at Firhill Park

1st Round
Jan 27 Aberdeen 1 Raith R 1
Jan 27 Ayr U 0 Arbroath 2
Jan 27 Celtic 0 Dunfermline A 2
Jan 27 Clyde 2 Berwick R 0
Jan 27 Cowdenbeath 0 Dundee 1
Jan 27 Dundee U 3 St Mirren 1
Jan 27 East Fife 3 Alloa 0
Jan 27 E Stirling 3 Hibernian 5
Jan 27 Elgin C 3 Forfar A 1
Jan 27 Hearts 4 Brechin C 1
Jan 27 Morton 4 Falkirk 0
Jan 27 Motherwell 1 Airdrie 1
Jan 27 Partick T 0 Kilmarnock 0
Jan 27 Queen of South 1 Stirling A 1
Jan 27 Rangers 3 Hamilton A 1
Jan 27 St Johnstone 3 Hawick RA. 0

Replays
Jan 31 Airdrie 1 Motherwell 0
Jan 31 Kilmarnock 1 Partick T 2
Jan 31 Raith R 0 Aberdeen 1
Jan 31 Stirling A 1 Queen of South 3

2nd Round
Feb 17 Airdrie 1 Hibernian 0

Feb 17	Dundee	1	Rangers	1
Feb 17	Dundee U	5	Hearts	6
Feb 19	Dunfermline A	2	Aberdeen	1
Feb 17	East Fife	0	Morton	0
Feb 17	Elgin C	2	Arbroath	0
Feb 23	Partick T	3	Clyde	2
Feb 17	St Johnstone	5	Queen of South	2

Replays

Feb 21	Morton	5	East Fife	2
Mar 4	Rangers	4	Dundee	1

3rd Round

Mar 9	Dunfermline A	1	Partick T	0
Mar 9	Morton	2	Elgin C	1
Mar 9	Rangers	1	Hearts	1
Mar 9	St Johnstone	2	Airdrie	1

Replay

Mar 13	Hearts	1	Rangers	0

Semi-finals

Mar 30	Dunfermline A played at Tynecastle	1	St Johnstone	1
Mar 30	Hearts played at Hampden Park	1	Morton	1

Replays

Apr 2	Dunfermline A played at Tynecastle	2	St Johnstone	1
Apr 2	Hearts played at Hampden Park	2	Morton	1

Final

Apr 27	Dunfermline A played at Hampden Park	3	Hearts	1

A stretcher is called for as Dunfermline's Jim Fraser lies injured, while Celtic's Bertie Auld is booked for the foul. Dunfermline won this Scottish Cup-tie 2-0 and went on to collect the trophy by beating Hearts in the Final.

Season 1968-69

1st Preliminary

Dec 14	Alloa	6	Ross Co	1
Dec 14	Brechin C	1	Montrose	1
Dec 14	Cowdenbeath	1	Clydebank	0
Dec 14	Forfar A	1	Nairn Co	2
Dec 14	St Cuthbert's	1	Civil Service	0

Replay

Dec 18	Montrose	3	Brechin C	2

2nd Preliminary

Jan 4	Alloa	0	E Stirling	0
Jan 4	Dumbarton	3	Vale of Leithen	2
Jan 4	Glasgow Univ	5	St Cuthbert's	2
Jan 4	Hamilton A	0	Cowdenbeath	2
Jan 4	Montrose	6	Fraserburgh	1
Jan 4	Nairn Co	0	Berwick R	2
Jan 4	Stenhousemuir	1	Albion R	0
Jan 4	Stranraer	2	Elgin C	0

Replay

Jan 8	E Stirling	2	Alloa	1

1st Round

Jan 25	Aberdeen	3	Berwick R	0
Jan 25	Ayr U	1	Queen of South	0
Jan 25	Dumbarton	0	St Mirren	1
Jan 25	Dundee	1	Hearts	2
Jan 25	Dundee U	2	Queen's Park	1
Jan 25	E Stirling	2	Stirling A	0
Jan 25	Falkirk	1	Morton	2
Jan 25	Kilmarnock	6	Glasgow Univ	0
Jan 25	Montrose	1	Cowdenbeath	0
Jan 25	Motherwell	1	Clyde	1
Jan 25	Partick T	3	Celtic	3
Jan 25	Raith R	0	Dunfermline A	2
Jan 25	Rangers	1	Hibernian	0
Jan 25	St Johnstone	3	Arbroath	2
Jan 25	Stenhousemuir	0	Airdrie	3
Jan 25	Stranraer	3	East Fife	1

Replays

Jan 28	Clyde	2	Motherwell	1
Jan 29	Celtic	8	Partick T	1

2nd Round

Feb 25	Aberdeen	2	Dunfermline A	2
Feb 12	Airdrie	1	St Mirren	1
Feb 12	Clyde	0	Celtic	0
Feb 8	Dundee U	6	Ayr U	2
Feb 8	E Stirling	1	St Johnstone	1
Feb 8	Montrose	1	Kilmarnock	1
Feb 24	Rangers	2	Hearts	0
Feb 8	Stranraer	1	Morton	3

Replays

Feb 12	Kilmarnock	4	Montrose	1
Feb 24	Celtic	3	Clyde	0
Feb 24	St Johnstone	3	E Stirling	0
Feb 24	St Mirren	1	Airdrie	3
Feb 26	Dunfermline A	0	Aberdeen	2

3rd Round

Mar 1	Aberdeen	0	Kilmarnock	0
Mar 1	Celtic	3	St Johnstone	2
Mar 1	Dundee U	2	Morton	3
Mar 1	Rangers	1	Airdrie	0

Replay

Mar 5	Kilmarnock	0	Aberdeen	3

Semi-finals

Mar 22	Aberdeen played at Celtic Park	1	Rangers	6
Mar 22	Celtic played at Hampden Park	4	Morton	1

Final

Apr 26	Celtic played at Hampden Park	4	Rangers	0

Season 1969-70

1st Preliminary

Dec 6	Alloa	3	Peterhead	1
Dec 6	Berwick R	1	Brechin C	0
Dec 6	Forres Mechanic	0	Clydebank	2
Dec 6	Stenhousemuir	0	Gala Fairydean	1
Dec 6	Stranraer	3	E Stirling	1

2nd Preliminary

Dec 24	Albion R	1	Berwick R	0
Dec 24	Clydebank	1	Queen's Park	0
Dec 27	Gala Fairydean	1	Dumbarton	4
Dec 20	Inverness C	5	Ross Co	0
Dec 20	Montrose	2	Cowdenbeath	1
Dec 20	Stranraer	1	St Cuthbert's	1
Dec 27	Tarff R	1	Alloa	0
Dec 20	Vale of Leithen	1	Hamilton A	2

Replay

Dec 25	St Cuthbert's	0	Stranraer	5

1st Round

Jan 24	Aberdeen	4	Clyde	0
Jan 24	Airdrie	5	Hamilton A	0
Jan 24	Albion R	1	Dundee	2
Jan 24	Arbroath	1	Clydebank	2
Jan 24	Celtic	2	Dunfermline A	1
Jan 24	Dumbarton	1	Forfar A	2
Jan 24	Dundee U	1	Ayr U	0
Jan 24	East Fife	3	Raith R	0
Jan 24	Falkirk	3	Tarff R	0
Jan 24	Kilmarnock	3	Partick T	0
Jan 24	Montrose	1	Hearts	1
Jan 24	Morton	2	Queen of South	0
Jan 24	Motherwell	2	St Johnstone	1
Jan 24	Rangers	3	Hibernian	1
Jan 24	St Mirren	2	Stirling A	0
Jan 24	Stranraer	2	Inverness C	5

Replays

Jan 27	Hearts	1	Montrose	0

2nd Round

Feb 11	Aberdeen	2	Clydebank	1
Feb 7	Celtic	4	Dundee U	0
Feb 7	Dundee	3	Airdrie	0
Feb 7	East Fife	1	Morton	0
Feb 7	Falkirk	2	St Mirren	1
Feb 7	Forfar A	0	Rangers	7
Feb 7	Kilmarnock	2	Hearts	0
Feb 7	Motherwell	3	Inverness C	1

3rd Round

Feb 21	Celtic	3	Rangers	1
Feb 21	East Fife	0	Dundee	1
Feb 21	Falkirk	0	Aberdeen	1
Feb 21	Motherwell	0	Kilmarnock	1

Semi-finals

Mar 14	Aberdeen	1	Kilmarnock	0
	played at Muirton Park			
Mar 14	Celtic	2	Dundee	1
	played at Hampden Park			

Final

Apr 11	Aberdeen	3	Celtic	1
	played at Hampden Park			

SEASON 1970-71

Celtic, Scottish Cup winners in 1971.

Beaten 1970-71 Finalists of the Scottish Cup and winners of the League Cup, Glasgow Rangers' squad of 70-71: Back row (left to right): Conn, Stein, Donaldson, Neef, McCloy, Jackson, R.Watson, D.Stevenson, N.Stevenson, Fyfe, I.MacDonald. Middle row: J.Wallace (coach), T.Craig (physio), K.Watson, Mathieson, Renton, McKinnon, Miller, Jardine, Johnstone, Smith, McCallum, Craven (assistant trainer), S.Anderson (trainer). Front row: W.Waddell (manager), Henderson, Semple, A.MacDonald, Alexander, Greig, Parlane, Penman, Morrison, Johnston, W.Thornton (assistant manager).

1st Round

Dec 5	Brechin C	3	Nairn Co	1
Dec 5	E Stirling	0	Clydebank	2
Dec 5	Forfar A	2	Albion R	0
Dec 5	St Cuthbert's	1	Stranraer	3
Dec 5	Stenhousemuir	0	Elgin C	1

2nd Round

Dec 19	Brechin C	4	Glasgow Trans	1
Dec 19	Clacknacuddin	2	Glasgow Univ	1
Dec 19	Clydebank	2	Hamilton A	1
Dec 19	Elgin C	2	Berwick R	0
Dec 19	Forfar A	1	Gala Fairydean	0
Dec 19	Queen's Park	2	Montrose	1
Dec 19	Ross Co	1	East Fife	4
Dec 19	Stranraer	3	Dumbarton	2

3rd Round

Jan 25	Aberdeen	5	Elgin C	0
Jan 23	Airdrie	1	Alloa	1
Jan 23	Celtic	5	Queen of South	1
Jan 23	Clacknacuddin	0	Cowdenbeath	3
Jan 23	Clyde	2	Brechin C	0
Jan 23	Clydebank	0	Dundee U	0
Jan 23	Dundee	1	Partick T	0
Jan 23	Dunfermline A	3	Arbroath	1
Jan 23	East Fife	1	St Mirren	1
Jan 23	Hearts	3	Stranraer	0
Jan 23	Hibernian	8	Forfar A	1
Jan 23	Morton	2	Ayr U	0
Jan 23	Queen's Park	0	Kilmarnock	1
Jan 23	Rangers	3	Falkirk	0
Jan 23	St Johnstone	2	Raith R	2
Jan 23	Stirling A	3	Motherwell	1

Replays

Jan 26	Alloa	0	Airdrie	2
Jan 26	Raith R	4	St Johnstone	3
Jan 26	St Mirren	1	East Fife	1
Jan 27	Dundee U	5	Clydebank	1
Feb 1	St Mirren	3	East Fife	1

4th Round

Feb 13	Celtic	1	Dunfermline A	1
Feb 13	Cowdenbeath	0	Airdrie	4
Feb 13	Dundee	2	Stirling A	0
Feb 13	Dundee U	1	Aberdeen	1
Feb 13	Hearts	1	Hibernian	2
Feb 13	Morton	1	Kilmarnock	2
Feb 13	Raith R	1	Clyde	1
Feb 13	St Mirren	1	Rangers	3

Replays

Feb 17	Aberdeen	2	Dundee U	0
Feb 17	Clyde	0	Raith R	2
Feb 17	Dunfermline A	0	Celtic	1

5th Round

Mar 6	Celtic	7	Raith R	1
Mar 6	Hibernian	1	Dundee	0
Mar 6	Kilmarnock	2	Airdrie	3
Mar 6	Rangers	1	Aberdeen	0

Semi-finals

Apr 3	Airdrie	3	Celtic	3
	played at Hampden Park			
Mar 31	Hibernian	0	Rangers	0
	played at Hampden Park			

Replays

Apr 5	Hibernian	1	Rangers	2
	played at Hampden Park			
Apr 7	Airdrie	0	Celtic	2
	played at Hampden Park			

Final

May 8	Celtic	1	Rangers	1
	played at Hampden Park			

Replay

May 12	Celtic	2	Rangers	1
	played at Hampden Park			

SEASON 1971-72

1st Round

Dec 18	Burntisland	2	Coldstream	0
Dec 18	Elgin C	2	Stenhousemuir	0
Dec 18	Gala Fairydean	1	Queen of South	5
Dec 18	Queen's Park	2	E Stirling	1
Dec 18	St Cuthbert's	0	Brechin C	3

2nd Round

Jan 15	Albion R	3	Queen's Park	2
Jan 15	Burntisland	1	Elgin C	4
Jan 15	Forfar A	2	Stranraer	2
Jan 15	Huntly	0	Hamilton A	2
Jan 15	Inverness T	3	Inverness C	4
Jan 15	Queen of South	0	Berwick R	0
Jan 15	Raith R	2	Brechin C	1
Jan 15	Stirling A	1	Alloa	2

Replays

Jan 19	Berwick R	0	Queen of South	1
Jan 22	Stranraer	1	Forfar A	2

3rd Round

Feb 5	Arbroath	1	Airdrie	3
Feb 5	Celtic	5	Albion R	0
Feb 5	Clyde	0	Ayr U	1
Feb 5	Clydebank	1	East Fife	1
Feb 5	Dumbarton	3	Hamilton A	1
Feb 8	Dundee	3	Queen of South	0
Feb 5	Dundee U	0	Aberdeen	4
Feb 5	Elgin C	3	Inverness C	1
Feb 5	Falkirk	2	Rangers	2
Feb 5	Forfar A	0	St Mirren	1
Feb 5	Hearts	2	St Johnstone	0
Feb 5	Kilmarnock	5	Alloa	1
Feb 5	Morton	1	Cowdenbeath	0
Feb 5	Motherwell	2	Montrose	0

Feb 5	Partick T	0	Hibernian	2
Feb 5	Raith R	2	Dunfermline A	0

Replays

Feb 9	East Fife	0	Clydebank	1
Feb 9	Rangers	2	Falkirk	0

4th Round

Feb 26	Aberdeen	1	Morton	0
Feb 26	Ayr U	0	Motherwell	0
Feb 26	Celtic	4	Dundee	0
Feb 26	Dumbarton	0	Raith R	3
Feb 26	Elgin C	1	Kilmarnock	4
Feb 26	Hearts	4	Clydebank	0
Feb 26	Hibernian	2	Airdrie	0
Feb 26	St Mirren	1	Rangers	4

Replay

Mar 1	Motherwell	2	Ayr U	1

5th Round

Mar 18	Celtic	1	Hearts	1
Mar 18	Hibernian	2	Aberdeen	0
Mar 18	Motherwell	2	Rangers	2
Mar 18	Raith R	1	Kilmarnock	3

Replays

Mar 27	Hearts	0	Celtic	1
Mar 27	Rangers	4	Motherwell	2

Semi-finals

Apr 12	Celtic	3	Kilmarnock	1
	played at Hampden Park			
Apr 15	Hibernian	1	Rangers	1
	played at Hampden Park			

Replay

Apr 24	Hibernian	2	Rangers	0
	played at Hampden Park			

Final

May 6	Celtic	6	Hibernian	1
	played at Hampden Park			

SEASON 1972-73

1st Round

Dec 16	Babcock & Wilcox	0	Berwick R	2
Dec 16	Brechin C	0	Clydebank	0
Dec 16	E Stirling	1	Ross Co	0
Dec 16	Ferranti T	3	Duns	1
Dec 16	Montrose	2	Albion R	0

Replays

Dec 23	Clydebank	1	Brechin C	2

2nd Round

Jan 13	Alloa	0	Berwick R	2
Jan 13	Brechin C	0	E Stirling	0
Jan 13	Brora R	0	Hamilton A	4
Jan 13	Ferranti T	2	Elgin C	2
Jan 13	Inverness T	2	Queen's Park	1
Jan 25	Queen of South	2	Forfar A	0
Jan 13	Stenhousemuir	0	Raith R	0
Jan 13	Vale of Leithen	0	Montrose	3

Replays

Jan 17	Raith R	3	Stenhousemuir	0
Jan 20	Elgin C	2	Ferranti T	1
Jan 22	E Stirling	1	Brechin C	2

3rd Round

Feb 3	Ayr U	3	Inverness T	0
Feb 3	Berwick R	1	Falkirk	3
Feb 3	Brechin C	2	Aberdeen	4
Feb 3	Celtic	4	East Fife	1
Feb 3	Clyde	1	Montrose	1
Feb 3	Dumbarton	4	Cowdenbeath	1
Feb 3	Dunfermline A	0	Dundee	3
Feb 3	Elgin C	0	Hamilton A	1
Feb 3	Hearts	0	Airdrie	0
Feb 3	Hibernian	2	Morton	0
Feb 3	Kilmarnock	2	Queen of South	1
Feb 3	Motherwell	2	Raith R	1
Feb 3	Rangers	1	Dundee U	0
Feb 3	St Mirren	0	Partick T	1
Feb 3	Stirling A	3	Arbroath	3
Feb 3	Stranraer	1	St Johnstone	1

Replays

Feb 7	Airdrie	3	Hearts	1
Feb 7	Arbroath	0	Stirling A	1
Feb 7	Montrose	4	Clyde	2
Feb 7	St Johnstone	1	Stranraer	2

4th Round

Feb 28	Aberdeen	3	Falkirk	1
Feb 24	Ayr U	2	Stirling A	1
Feb 24	Dumbarton	2	Partick T	2
Feb 24	Kilmarnock	0	Airdrie	1
Feb 24	Montrose	2	Hamilton A	2
Feb 24	Motherwell	0	Celtic	4
Feb 24	Rangers	1	Hibernian	1
Feb 24	Stranraer	2	Dundee	9

Replays

Feb 28	Hamilton A	0	Montrose	1
Feb 28	Hibernian	1	Rangers	2
Feb 28	Partick T	3	Dumbarton	1

5th Round

Mar 17	Celtic	0	Aberdeen	0
Mar 17	Montrose	1	Dundee	4
Mar 17	Partick T	1	Ayr U	5
Mar 17	Rangers	2	Airdrie	0

Replays

Mar 21	Aberdeen	0	Celtic	1

Semi-finals

Apr 4	Ayr U	0	Rangers	2
	played at Hampden Park			
Apr 7	Celtic	0	Dundee	0
	played at Hampden Park			

Replay

Apr 11	Celtic	3	Dundee	0
	played at Hampden Park			

Final

May 5	Celtic	2	Rangers	3
	played at Hampden Park			

Rangers in 1973 with the Scottish FA Cup. Back row (left to right): D.Young, Struthers, Scott, Jackson, Hunter, McCloy, Kennedy, Forsyth, Burke, Donaldson, McNichol. Middle row: T.Craig (physiotherapist), McDonald, Hamilton, O'Hara, Conn, Smith, Johnstone, Miller, Thomson, Mathieson, Fyfe, McDougall, S.Anderson (trainer). Front row: J.Wallace (manager), Morris, McLean, MacDonald, Houston, Parlane, Greig, Jardine, Mason, Steel, Q.Young, Denny, W.Thornton (assistant manager).

Season 1973-74

1st Round

Date	Home		Away	
Dec 15	Berwick R	0	Albion R	0
Dec 24	E Stirling	0	Clydebank	0
Dec 15	Hamilton A	0	Alloa	0
Dec 15	Lossiemouth	3	Fraserburgh	3
Dec 17	Queen's Park	1	Edinburgh Univ	0

Replays

Date	Home		Away	
Dec 19	Albion R	2	Berwick R	0
Dec 19	Fraserburgh	6	Lossiemouth	0
Dec 19	Alloa	4	Hamilton A	1
Dec 25	Clydebank	1	E Stirling	0

2nd Round

Date	Home		Away	
Jan 5	Brechin C	5	Stenhousemuir	1
Jan 5	Clacknacuddin	1	Clydebank	1
Jan 5	Cowdenbeath	4	Fraserburgh	1
Jan 5	Ferranti T	1	Civil Service	0
Jan 5	Queen of South	1	Albion R	0
Jan 5	Queen's Park	6	Hawick RA	1
Jan 5	Ross Co	1	Forfar A	2
Jan 5	Stranraer	1	Alloa	0

Replay

Date	Home		Away	
Jan 12	Clydebank	3	Clacknacuddin	2

3rd Round

Date	Home		Away	
Jan 27	Aberdeen	0	Dundee	2
Jan 26	Arbroath	1	Dumbarton	0
Jan 27	Celtic	6	Clydebank	1
Jan 27	Cowdenbeath	0	Ayr U	5
Jan 26	Dundee U	4	Airdrie	1
Jan 27	Falkirk	2	Dunfermline A	2
Jan 27	Forfar A	1	St Johnstone	6
Jan 26	Hearts	3	Clyde	1
Jan 26	Hibernian	5	Kilmarnock	2
Jan 27	Montrose	1	Stirling A	1
Jan 27	Motherwell	2	Brechin C	0
Jan 27	Partick T	6	Ferranti T	1
Jan 27	Queen of South	1	East Fife	0
Jan 27	Raith R	2	Morton	2
Jan 26	Rangers	8	Queen's Park	0
Jan 26	Stranraer	1	St Mirren	1

Replays

Date	Home		Away	
Jan 29	Morton	0	Raith R	0
Jan 29	St Mirren	1	Stranraer	1
Jan 30	Dunfermline A	1	Falkirk	0
Jan 30	Stirling A	3	Montrose	1
Feb 3	Morton	1	Raith R	0
	played at Tynecastle			
Feb 4	St Mirren	2	Stranraer	3
	played at Somerset Park			

4th Round

Date	Home		Away	
Feb 16	Arbroath	1	Motherwell	3
Feb 17	Celtic	6	Stirling A	1
Feb 17	Dundee U	1	Morton	0
Feb 17	Dunfermline A	1	Queen of South	0
Feb 16	Hearts	1	Partick T	1
Feb 17	Rangers	0	Dundee	3
Feb 16	St Johnstone	1	Hibernian	3
Feb 16	Stranraer	1	Ayr U	7

Replay

Date	Home		Away	
Feb 19	Partick T	1	Hearts	4

5th Round

Date	Home		Away	
Mar 10	Celtic	2	Motherwell	2
Mar 10	Dunfermline A	1	Dundee U	1
Mar 9	Hearts	1	Ayr U	1
Mar 9	Hibernian	3	Dundee	3

Replays

Date	Home		Away	
Mar 12	Dundee U	4	Dunfermline A	0
Mar 13	Ayr U	1	Hearts	2
Mar 13	Motherwell	0	Celtic	1
Mar 18	Dundee	3	Hibernian	0

Semi-finals

Date	Home		Away	
Apr 3	Celtic	1	Dundee	0
	played at Hampden Park			
Apr 6	Dundee U	1	Hearts	1
	played at Hampden Park			

Replay

Date	Home		Away	
Apr 9	Dundee U	4	Hearts	2
	played at Hampden Park			

Final

Date	Home		Away	
May 4	Celtic	3	Dundee U	0
	played at Hampden Park			

Season 1974-75

1st Round

Date	Home		Away	
Dec 14	Clacknacuddin	8	Gala Fairydean	1
Dec 14	Montrose	5	Selkirk	1
Dec 14	Ross Co	2	Brechin C	0
Dec 14	St Cuthbert's	1	Albion R	4
Dec 14	Stenhousemuir	2	E Stirling	2

Replay

Date	Home		Away	
Dec 18	E Stirling	3	Stenhousemuir	1

2nd Round

Date	Home		Away	
Jan 4	Alloa	1	Albion R	1
Jan 4	Clacknacuddin	4	Stirling A	3
Jan 4	Cowdenbeath	0	Clydebank	2
Jan 4	E Stirling	2	St Mirren	1
Jan 4	Forfar A	2	Ross Co	3
Jan 4	Inverness C	2	Inverness T	0
Jan 4	Stranraer	2	Queen's Park	4
Jan 4	Vale of Leithen	0	Montrose	12

Replay

Date	Home		Away	
Jan 8	Albion R	2	Alloa	0

3rd Round

Date	Home		Away	
Jan 25	Aberdeen	1	Rangers	1
Jan 28	Airdrie	0	Morton	0
Jan 25	Arbroath	1	E Stirling	0
Jan 25	Ayr U	1	Queen's Park	2
Jan 25	Clyde	0	Dundee	1
Jan 28	Clydebank	2	Dunfermline A	1
Jan 29	Dumbarton	2	Clacknacuddin	1
Feb 4	Dundee U	1	Berwick R	1
Jan 29	Hearts	2	Kilmarnock	0
Jan 25	Hibernian	0	Celtic	2
Jan 25	Inverness C	0	Albion R	1
Jan 27	Montrose	0	Hamilton A	0
Jan 25	Motherwell	0	Partick T	0
Jan 25	Queen of South	2	Raith R	0
Jan 30	Ross Co	1	Falkirk	5
Jan 29	St Johnstone	1	East Fife	0

Replays

Date	Home		Away	
Feb 3	Hamilton A	3	Montrose	0
Feb 3	Morton	0	Airdrie	3
Feb 3	Partick T	0	Motherwell	1
Feb 5	Berwick R	0	Dundee U	1
Feb 10	Rangers	1	Aberdeen	2

4th Round

Date	Home		Away	
Feb 15	Airdrie	2	Falkirk	0
Feb 15	Arbroath	2	Albion R	0
Feb 15	Celtic	4	Clydebank	1
Feb 19	Dundee U	0	Aberdeen	1
Feb 15	Hamilton A	0	Dumbarton	1
Feb 15	Motherwell	4	Queen's Park	0
Feb 15	Queen of South	0	Hearts	2
Feb 15	St Johnstone	0	Dundee	1

5th Round

Date	Home		Away	
Mar 8	Aberdeen	0	Motherwell	1
Mar 8	Arbroath	2	Airdrie	2
Mar 8	Dumbarton	1	Celtic	2
Mar 8	Hearts	1	Dundee	1

Replays

Date	Home		Away	
Mar 12	Dundee	3	Hearts	2
Mar 12	Airdrie	3	Arbroath	0

Semi-finals

Date	Home		Away	
Apr 5	Airdrie	1	Motherwell	1
	played at Hampden Park			
Apr 2	Celtic	1	Dundee	0
	played at Hampden Park			

Replay

Date	Home		Away	
Apr 9	Airdrie	1	Motherwell	0
	played at Hampden Park			

Final

Date	Home		Away	
May 3	Airdrie	1	Celtic	3
	played at Hampden Park			

Season 1975-76

1st Round

Date	Home		Away	
Dec 13	Albion R	0	Hawick RA.	0
Dec 13	Brechin C	1	Berwick R	1
Dec 13	E Stirling	0	Alloa	5
Dec 13	Elgin C	0	Forres Mechanic	1
Dec 13	Peterhead	0	Raith R	2
Dec 13	Stranraer	1	Queen's Park	0

Replays

Date	Home		Away	
Dec 18	Hawick RA	0	Albion R	3
Dec 20	Berwick R	3	Brechin C	3
Dec 22	Berwick R	0	Brechin C	1

2nd Round

Date	Home		Away	
Jan 10	Albion R	1	Glasgow Univ	1
Jan 10	Cowdenbeath	2	Selkirk	0
Jan 10	Forfar A	2	Meadowbank T	1
Jan 10	Forres Mechanic	1	Alloa	2
Jan 10	Raith R	3	Clydebank	1
Jan 10	Stenhousemuir	2	Brechin C	2
Jan 10	Stirling A	4	Civil Service	0
Jan 10	Stranraer	2	Keith	3

Replays

Date	Home		Away	
Jan 14	Brechin C	0	Stenhousemuir	1
Jan 14	Glasgow Univ	0	Albion R	1

3rd Round

Date	Home		Away	
Jan 24	Albion R	1	Partick T	2
Jan 24	Alloa	0	Aberdeen	4
Jan 24	Ayr U	4	Airdrie	2
Jan 24	Cowdenbeath	3	St Mirren	0
Jan 24	Dumbarton	2	Keith	0
Jan 24	Dundee	1	Falkirk	2

After-match celebrations at Hampden as Rangers complete the treble of League and both Cups in 1975-76.

Date	Team	Score	Team	Score
Jan 24	Dundee U	4	Hamilton A	0
Jan 24	Hearts	2	Clyde	2
Jan 24	Hibernian	3	Dunfermline A	2
Jan 24	Motherwell	3	Celtic	2
Jan 24	Morton	1	Montrose	3
Jan 24	Queen of South	3	St Johnstone	2
Jan 24	Raith R	1	Arbroath	0
Jan 24	Rangers	3	East Fife	0
Jan 24	Stenhousemuir	1	Kilmarnock	1
Jan 24	Stirling A	2	Forfar A	1

Replays

Date	Team	Score	Team	Score
Jan 28	Clyde	0	Hearts	1
Jan 28	Kilmarnock	1	Stenhousemuir	0

4th Round

Date	Team	Score	Team	Score
Feb 14	Ayr U	2	Queen of South	2
Feb 14	Cowdenbeath	0	Motherwell	2
Feb 14	Hearts	3	Stirling A	0
Feb 14	Hibernian	1	Dundee U	1
Feb 14	Kilmarnock	3	Falkirk	1
Feb 14	Montrose	2	Raith R	1
Feb 14	Partick T	0	Dumbarton	0
Feb 14	Rangers	4	Aberdeen	1

Replays

Date	Team	Score	Team	Score
Feb 18	Queen of South	5	Ayr U	4
Feb 25	Dumbarton	1	Partick T	0
Feb 25	Dundee U	0	Hibernian	2

5th Round

Date	Team	Score	Team	Score
Mar 6	Dumbarton	2	Kilmarnock	1
Mar 6	Montrose	2	Hearts	2
Mar 6	Motherwell	2	Hibernian	2
Mar 6	Queen of South	0	Rangers	5

Replays

Date	Team	Score	Team	Score
Mar 9	Hearts	2	Montrose	2
Mar 10	Hibernian	1	Motherwell	1
Mar 15	Hibernian played at Ibrox	1	Motherwell	2
Mar 16	Hearts played at Muirton Park	2	Montrose	1

Semi-finals

Date	Team	Score	Team	Score
Apr 3	Dumbarton played at Hampden Park	0	Hearts	0
Mar 31	Motherwell played at Hampden Park	2	Rangers	3

Replay

Date	Team	Score	Team	Score
Apr 14	Dumbarton played at Hampden Park	0	Hearts	3

Final

Date	Team	Score	Team	Score
May 1	Hearts played at Hampden Park	1	Rangers	3

Season 1976-77

1st Round

Date	Team	Score	Team	Score
Dec 19	Clacknacuddin	1	Inverness T	2
Dec 22	Cowdenbeath	3	Clydebank	4
Dec 28	Elgin C	4	Vale of Leithen	0
Dec 27	Inverness C	3	Stenhousemuir	2
Dec 18	St Cuthbert's	0	Brechin C	1
Dec 18	Stranraer	1	Berwick R	0

2nd Round

Date	Team	Score	Team	Score
Jan 8	Albion R	2	Raith R	1
Jan 8	Brechin C	0	Inverness T	0
Jan 8	Clydebank	2	Selkirk	0
Jan 8	Forfar A	0	Elgin C	2
Jan 8	Girvan	0	Queen's Park	3
Jan 8	Inverness C	1	Alloa	1
Jan 8	Meadowbank T	1	E Stirling	2
Jan 8	Stranraer	0	Stirling A	0

Replays

Date	Team	Score	Team	Score
Jan 15	Inverness T	1	Brechin C	3
Jan 16	Alloa	3	Inverness C	1
Jan 24	Stirling A	2	Stranraer	1

3rd Round

Date	Team	Score	Team	Score
Jan 29	Airdrie	1	Celtic	1
Jan 29	Arbroath	1	Brechin C	0
Jan 29	Dunfermline A	0	Aberdeen	1
Jan 29	East Fife	2	Clyde	1
Jan 29	E Stirling	0	Albion R	3
Feb 2	Hamilton A	0	Clydebank	0
Jan 29	Hearts	1	Dumbarton	1
Feb 6	Hibernian	3	Partick T	0
Jan 29	Morton	0	Ayr U	1
Jan 29	Motherwell	3	Kilmarnock	0
Jan 29	Queen of South	3	Montrose	2
Jan 29	Queen's Park	0	Alloa	0
Jan 29	Rangers	3	Falkirk	1
Feb 7	St Johnstone	1	Dundee	1
Jan 29	St Mirren	4	Dundee U	1
Jan 29	Stirling A	1	Elgin C	1

Replays

Date	Team	Score	Team	Score
Feb 2	Celtic	5	Airdrie	0
Feb 2	Dumbarton	0	Hearts	1
Feb 2	Elgin C	3	Stirling A	2
Feb 6	Alloa	1	Queen's Park	0
Feb 7	Clydebank	3	Hamilton A	0
Feb 8	Dundee	4	St Johnstone	2

4th Round

Date	Team	Score	Team	Score
Feb 26	Arbroath	1	Hibernian	1
Feb 27	Celtic	1	Ayr U	1
Feb 26	Dundee	0	Aberdeen	0
Feb 26	East Fife	2	Albion R	1
Feb 26	Hearts	1	Clydebank	0
Feb 26	Motherwell	2	St Mirren	1
Feb 26	Queen of South	2	Alloa	1
Feb 26	Rangers	3	Elgin C	0

Replays

Date	Team	Score	Team	Score
Mar 2	Aberdeen	1	Dundee	2
Mar 2	Ayr U	1	Celtic	3
Mar 2	Hibernian	1	Arbroath	2

5th Round

Date	Team	Score	Team	Score
Mar 12	Arbroath	1	Dundee	3
Mar 13	Celtic	5	Queen of South	1
Mar 12	Hearts	0	East Fife	0
Mar 12	Rangers	2	Motherwell	0

Replay

Date	Team	Score	Team	Score
Mar 15	East Fife	2	Hearts	3

Semi-finals

Date	Team	Score	Team	Score
Apr 6	Celtic played at Hampden Park	2	Dundee	0
Mar 30	Hearts played at Hampden Park	0	Rangers	2

Final

Date	Team	Score	Team	Score
May 7	Celtic played at Hampden Park	1	Rangers	0

Season 1977-78

1st Round

Date	Team	Score	Team	Score
Dec 17	Brechin C	2	Falkirk	0
Dec 17	Burntisland	1	Berwick R	4
Dec 17	Civil Service	4	Selkirk	3
Dec 17	Dunfermline A	0	Clyde	0
Dec 17	Inverness C	5	Inverness T	0
Dec 17	Raith R	1	Stenhousemuir	0

Replays

Date	Team	Score	Team	Score
Dec 21	Clyde	0	Dunfermline A	3

2nd Round

Date	Team	Score	Team	Score
Jan 7	Albion R	1	Buckie T	0
Jan 7	Berwick R	6	Raith R	0
Jan 7	Brechin C	1	Dunfermline A	0
Jan 7	Inverness C	4	Civil Service	0
Jan 7	Meadowbank T	2	E Stirling	1
Jan 7	Peterhead	1	Cowdenbeath	1
Jan 7	Stranraer	0	Queen's Park	1
Jan 7	Vale of Leithen	4	Forfar A	1

Replays

Date	Team	Score	Team	Score
Jan 14	Cowdenbeath	5	Peterhead	0

3rd Round

Date	Team	Score	Team	Score
Feb 6	Aberdeen	2	Ayr U	0
Feb 6	Airdrie	2	Hearts	3
Feb 5	Albion R	0	Morton	1
Jan 29	Alloa	2	Dumbarton	2
Jan 28	Arbroath	0	Motherwell	4
Jan 28	Berwick R	2	Rangers	4
Feb 6	Celtic	7	Dundee	1
Jan 28	Hamilton A	1	Dundee U	4
Jan 28	Hibernian	4	East Fife	0
Jan 28	Meadowbank T	2	Inverness C	1
Feb 5	Partick T	1	Cowdenbeath	1
Jan 28	Queen of South	2	Montrose	2
Feb 7	St Johnstone	1	Brechin C	0
Feb 6	St Mirren	1	Kilmarnock	2
Feb 7	Stirling A	3	Clydebank	0
Feb 4	Vale of Leithen	0	Queen's Park	1

Replays

Date	Team	Score	Team	Score
Feb 6	Dumbarton	2	Alloa	1
Feb 6	Montrose	1	Queen of South	3
Feb 27	Cowdenbeath	0	Partick T	1

4th Round

Date	Team	Score	Team	Score
Feb 27	Aberdeen	3	St Johnstone	0
Feb 27	Celtic	1	Kilmarnock	1
Feb 18	Dumbarton	1	Hearts	1
Feb 27	Dundee U	3	Queen of South	0
Mar 4	Hibernian	0	Partick T	0
Feb 18	Morton	3	Meadowbank T	0
Feb 27	Motherwell	1	Queen's Park	3
Feb 18	Rangers	1	Stirling A	0

Replays

Date	Team	Score	Team	Score
Feb 27	Hearts	0	Dumbarton	1
Mar 6	Kilmarnock	1	Celtic	0
Mar 7	Partick T	2	Hibernian	1

5th Round

Date	Team	Score	Team	Score
Mar 11	Aberdeen	2	Morton	2
Mar 11	Dundee U	2	Queen's Park	0
Mar 11	Partick T	2	Dumbarton	1
Mar 11	Rangers	4	Kilmarnock	1

Replays

Date	Team	Score	Team	Score
Mar 15	Morton	1	Aberdeen	2

Semi-finals

Date	Team	Score	Team	Score
Apr 12	Aberdeen played at Hampden Park	4	Partick T	2
Apr 5	Dundee U played at Hampden Park	0	Rangers	2

Final

Date	Team	Score	Team	Score
May 6	Aberdeen played at Hampden Park	1	Rangers	2

McDonald's diving header nets Rangers their first goal in the 1977 Cup Final victory over Aberdeen.

Season 1978-79

1st Round

Date	Home		Away	
Dec 16	Dunfermline A	2	Albion R	2
Dec 16	Falkirk	2	Keith	0
Dec 16	Gala Fairydean	1	Cowdenbeath	3
Dec 16	Meadowbank T	1	Inverness C	1
Dec 16	Threave R	0	E Stirling	2
Dec 16	Vale of Leithen	1	Forfar A	4

Replays

Date	Home		Away	
Dec 19	Albion R	2	Dunfermline A	3
Dec 23	Inverness C	0	Meadowbank T	3

2nd Round

Date	Home		Away	
Jan 17	Cowdenbeath	0	Alloa	0
Jan 16	East Fife	2	Brechin C	1
Jan 21	E Stirling	2	Spartans	3
Jan 22	Forfar A	1	Berwick R	2
Feb 22	Inverness T	0	Falkirk	4
Jan 16	Meadowbank T	2	Stenhousemuir	1
Jan 17	Peterhead	2	Queen's Park	3
Jan 13	Stranraer	1	Dunfermline A	1

Replays

Date	Home		Away	
Jan 21	Alloa	2	Cowdenbeath	0
Jan 22	Dunfermline A	1	Stranraer	0

3rd Round

Date	Home		Away	
Jan 27	Arbroath	0	Airdrie	1
Feb 12	Ayr U	4	Queen of South	0
Jan 31	Clyde	1	Kilmarnock	5
Jan 31	Clydebank	3	Queen's Park	3
Feb 19	Dumbarton	1	Alloa	0
Feb 25	Dundee	1	Falkirk	0
Feb 26	Dundee U	0	St Mirren	2
Jan 28	Dunfermline A	1	Hibernian	1
Jan 27	East Fife	0	Berwick R	1
Jan 27	Hamilton A	0	Aberdeen	2
Jan 31	Meadowbank T	2	Spartans	1
Jan 31	Montrose	2	Celtic	4
Feb 19	Morton	1	St Johnstone	1
Jan 27	Raith R	0	Hearts	2
Feb 12	Rangers	3	Motherwell	1
Feb 19	Stirling A	0	Partick T	2

Replays

Date	Home		Away	
Feb 12	Hibernian	2	Dunfermline A	0
Feb 12	Queen's Park	0	Clydebank	1
Feb 26	St Johnstone	2	Morton	4

4th Round

Date	Home		Away	
Feb 21	Aberdeen	6	Ayr U	2
Feb 26	Celtic	3	Berwick R	0
Feb 24	Dumbarton	3	Clydebank	1
Mar 3	Dundee	4	St Mirren	1
Mar 3	Hearts	1	Morton	1
Feb 21	Meadowbank T	0	Hibernian	6
Feb 24	Partick T	3	Airdrie	0
Feb 21	Rangers	1	Kilmarnock	1

Replays

Date	Home		Away	
Feb 26	Kilmarnock	0	Rangers	1
Mar 5	Morton	0	Hearts	1

5th Round

Date	Home		Away	
Mar 10	Aberdeen	1	Celtic	1
Mar 10	Dumbarton	0	Partick T	1
Mar 10	Hibernian	2	Hearts	1
Mar 10	Rangers	6	Dundee	3

Replay

Date	Home		Away	
Mar 14	Celtic	1	Aberdeen	2

Semi-finals

Date	Home		Away	
Apr 11	Aberdeen played at Hampden Park	1	Hibernian	2
Apr 4	Partick T played at Hampden Park	0	Rangers	0

Replay

Date	Home		Away	
Apr 16	Partick T played at Hampden Park	0	Rangers	1

Final

Date	Home		Away	
May12	Hibernian played at Hampden Park	0	Rangers	0

Replay

Date	Home		Away	
May16	Hibernian played at Hampden Park	0	Rangers	0
May28	Hibernian played at Hampden Park	2	Rangers	3

Season 1979-80

1st Round

Date	Home		Away	
Dec 15	Annan A	1	Stranraer	3
Dec 15	Cowdenbeath	3	Albion R	1
Dec 15	E Stirling	1	Brechin C	1
Dec 15	Queen of South	1	Falkirk	1
Dec 15	Spartans	1	Forfar A	2
Dec 15	Stenhousemuir	4	Queen's Park	2

Replays

Date	Home		Away	
Dec 19	Brechin C	1	East Stirling	1
Dec 26	Brechin C played at Muirton Park	1	E Stirling	0
Dec 26	Falkirk	0	Queen of South	4

2nd Round

Date	Home		Away	
Jan 9	Alloa	1	East Fife	0
Jan 7	Brechin C	1	Montrose	1
Jan 5	Buckie T	0	Brora R	0
Jan 12	Coldstream	1	Queen of South	1
Jan 5	Cowdenbeath	3	Forfar A	2
Jan 5	Stenhousemuir	0	Peterhead	0
Jan 5	Stranraer	1	Meadowbank T	1
Jan 5	Threave R	2	Keith	3

Replays

Date	Home		Away	
Jan 12	Brora R	1	Buckie T	2
Jan 12	Meadowbank T	2	Stranraer	1
Jan 12	Peterhead	2	Stenhousemuir	0
Jan 14	Montrose	3	Brechin C	4
Jan 14	Queen of South	4	Coldstream	0

3rd Round

Date	Home		Away	
Jan 30	Airdrie	3	St Johnstone	1
Jan 30	Alloa	0	Hearts	1
Jan 26	Arbroath	1	Aberdeen	1
Jan 26	Berwick R	3	Peterhead	1
Jan 26	Celtic	2	Raith R	1
Jan 26	Clyde	2	Rangers	2
Jan 26	Clydebank	1	Stirling A	1
Jan 26	Dumbarton	1	Ayr U	2
Jan 30	Dundee U	5	Dundee	1
Jan 30	Dunfermline A	2	Buckie T	0
Jan 26	Hamilton A	2	Keith	3
Jan 30	Kilmarnock	0	Partick T	1
Jan 26	Meadowbank T	0	Hibernian	1
Jan 26	Morton	1	Cowdenbeath	0
Jan 26	Queen of South	2	Motherwell	0
Jan 26	St Mirren	3	Brechin C	1

Replays

Date	Home		Away	
Jan 30	Aberdeen	5	Arbroath	0
Jan 30	Rangers	2	Clyde	0
Jan 30	Stirling A	1	Clydebank	1
Feb 11	Clydebank played at Brockville	0	Stirling A	1

4th Round

Date	Home		Away	
Feb 16	Aberdeen	8	Airdrie	0
Feb 16	Celtic	1	St Mirren	1
Feb 16	Hearts	2	Stirling A	0
Feb 17	Hibernian	2	Ayr U	0
Feb 16	Keith	1	Berwick R	2
Feb 16	Morton	5	Dunfermline A	0
Feb 16	Queen of South	1	Partick T	3
Feb 16	Rangers	1	Dundee U	0

Replay

Date	Home		Away	
Feb 20	St Mirren	2	Celtic	3

5th Round

Date	Home		Away	
Mar 8	Berwick R	0	Hibernian	0
Mar 8	Celtic	2	Morton	0
Mar 8	Partick T	1	Aberdeen	2
Mar 8	Rangers	6	Hearts	1

Replay

Date	Home		Away	
Mar 12	Hibernian	1	Berwick R	0

Semi-finals

Date	Home		Away	
Apr 12	Aberdeen played at Celtic Park	0	Rangers	1
Apr 12	Celtic played at Hampden Park	5	Hibernian	0

Final

Date	Home		Away	
May10	Celtic played at Hampden Park	1	Rangers	0

Season 1980-81

1st Round

Date	Home		Away	
Dec 13	Alloa	1	Stenhousemuir	1
Dec 13	Brechin C	2	Keith	1
Dec 13	East Fife	2	Civil Service	1
Dec 13	Meadowbank T	2	Buckie T	2
Dec 13	Queen's Park	2	Montrose	2
Dec 13	Whitehill Welfare	1	Hawick RA	1

Replays

Date	Home		Away	
Dec 17	Hawick RA	4	Whitehill Welfare	1
Dec 17	Montrose	2	Queen's Park	0
Dec 17	Stenhousemuir	3	Alloa	2
Dec 20	Buckie T	3	Meadowbank T	2

2nd Round

Date	Home		Away	
Jan 12	Albion R	1	Arbroath	1
Jan 3	Forfar A	0	Brechin C	2
Jan 3	Hawick RA	2	Cowdenbeath	2
Jan 3	Inverness T	2	Montrose	0
Jan 10	Queen of South	1	East Fife	2
Jan 3	Rothes	1	Clyde	5
Jan 3	Stenhousemuir	0	Spartans	0
Jan 3	Stranraer	2	Buckie T	2

Replays

Date	Home		Away	
Jan 7	Spartans	1	Stenhousemuir	2
Jan 10	Buckie T	3	Stranraer	2

John MacDonald celebrates Cooper's opening goal against Dundee in the 1980-81 SFA Cup Final. Davie Cooper died suddenly in 1995 after a brain haemorrhage.

Jan 12 Cowdenbeath 3 Hawick RA 0
Jan 14 Arbroath 1 Albion R 0

3rd Round
Jan 24 Airdrie 0 Rangers 5
Jan 24 Arbroath 1 Cowdenbeath 1
Jan 24 Berwick R 0 Celtic 2
Jan 24 Brechin C 1 Dundee U 2
Jan 24 Buckie T 1 Stirling A 3
Jan 24 East Fife 0 Clydebank 0
Jan 24 E Stirling 4 Inverness T 1
Jan 24 Falkirk 1 Dundee 0
Jan 24 Hamilton A 0 St Johnstone 3
Jan 24 Hibernian 1 Dunfermline A 1
Jan 24 Kilmarnock 2 Ayr U 1
Jan 24 Morton 0 Hearts 0
Jan 24 Partick T 2 Clyde 2
Jan 24 Raith R 1 Aberdeen 2
Jan 24 St Mirren 0 Dumbarton 2
Jan 24 Stenhousemuir 1 Motherwell 1

Replays
Jan 28 Clyde 2 Partick T 4
Jan 28 Clydebank 5 East Fife 4
Jan 28 Cowdenbeath 4 Arbroath 0
Jan 28 Dunfermline A 1 Hibernian 2
Jan 28 Hearts 1 Morton 3
Jan 28 Motherwell 2 Stenhousemuir 1

4th Round
Feb 14 Celtic 3 Stirling A 0
Feb 14 Cowdenbeath 1 E Stirling 2
Feb 14 Dundee U 1 Partick T 0
Feb 14 Hibernian 1 Falkirk 0
Feb 14 Kilmarnock 0 Clydebank 0
Feb 14 Morton 1 Aberdeen 0
Feb 14 Motherwell 2 Dumbarton 1
Feb 14 St Johnstone 3 Rangers 3

Replays
Feb 18 Clydebank 1 Kilmarnock 1
Feb 18 Rangers 3 St Johnstone 1
Feb 23 Clydebank 1 Kilmarnock 0
played at Love Street

5th Round
Mar 8 Celtic 2 E Stirling 0
Mar 7 Dundee U 6 Motherwell 1
Mar 11 Morton 0 Clydebank 0
Mar 7 Rangers 3 Hibernian 1

Replay
Mar 16 Clydebank 0 Morton 6

Semi-finals
Apr 11 Celtic 0 Dundee U 0
played at Hampden Park
Apr 11 Morton 1 Rangers 2
played at Celtic Park

Replay
Apr 15 Celtic 2 Dundee U 3
played at Hampden Park

Final
May 9 Dundee U 0 Rangers 0
played at Hampden Park

Replay
May12 Dundee U 1 Rangers 4
played at Hampden Park

SEASON 1981-82

1st Round
Dec 12 Arbroath 0 Meadowbank T 2
Jan 21 Civil Service 3 Cowdenbeath 3
Dec 30 Fraserburgh 1 Clacknacuddin 1
Jan 21 Stenhousemuir 2 Berwick R 5
Jan 20 Stirling A 1 Clyde 2
Dec 23 Stranraer 1 East Fife 1

Replays
Jan 4 East Fife 4 Stranraer 1
Jan 25 Clacknacuddin 3 Fraserburgh 2
Jan 25 Cowdenbeath 6 Civil Service 1

2nd Round
Jan 30 Albion R 2 Clacknacuddin 1
Jan 23 Alloa 4 Hawick RA 1
Jan 23 Clyde 0 Berwick R 0
Jan 23 Coldstream 0 Meadowbank T 2
Jan 30 Cowdenbeath 1 Gala Fairydean 1
Jan 18 East Fife 2 Forfar 3
Jan 24 Inverness C 1 Brechin C 3
Jan 20 Montrose 0 Elgin C 0

Replays
Jan 25 Elgin C 0 Montrose 0
Jan 26 Berwick R 1 Clyde 3
Feb 3 Gala Fairydean 3 Cowdenbeath 2
Feb 1 Elgin C 1 Montrose 2
played at Keith

3rd Round
Jan 23 Airdrie 1 Queen's Park 2
Jan 30 Alloa 2 Ayr U 1
Jan 30 Brechin C 2 Dundee U 4
Jan 23 Celtic 4 Queen of South 0
Jan 30 Clyde 2 Meadowbank T 2
Jan 23 Clydebank 2 Dunfermline A 1
Jan 23 Dundee 1 Raith R 0
Jan 27 E Stirling 1 Hearts 4
Feb 6 Gala Fairydean 1 St Johnstone 2
Jan 23 Hamilton A 0 Forfar A 0
Jan 23 Hibernian 2 Falkirk 0
Feb 6 Kilmarnock 1 Montrose 0
Jan 23 Motherwell 0 Aberdeen 1
Jan 24 Partick T 1 Dumbarton 2
Feb 6 Rangers 6 Albion R 2
Jan 23 St Mirren 2 Morton 1

Replays
Jan 27 Forfar A 3 Hamilton A 2
Feb 3 Meadowbank T 4 Clyde 2

4th Round
Feb 13 Aberdeen 1 Celtic 0
Feb 13 Clydebank 0 St Mirren 2
Feb 14 Dundee 3 Meadowbank T 0
Feb 13 Dundee U 1 Hibernian 1
Feb 13 Hearts 0 Forfar A 1
Feb 13 Kilmarnock 3 St Johnstone 1
Feb 13 Queen's Park 2 Alloa 0
Feb 13 Rangers 4 Dumbarton 0

Replays
Feb 17 Hibernian 1 Dundee U 1
Feb 22 Dundee U 3 Hibernian 0
played at Easter Road

5th Round
Mar 6 Aberdeen 4 Kilmarnock 2
Mar 6 Queen's Park 1 Forfar A 2
Mar 6 Rangers 2 Dundee 0
Mar 6 St Mirren 1 Dundee U 0

Semi-finals
Apr 3 Aberdeen 1 St Mirren 1
played at Celtic Park
Apr 3 Forfar 0 Rangers 0
played at Hampden Park

Replays
Apr 7 Aberdeen 3 St Mirren 2
played at Dens Park
Apr 6 Forfar 1 Rangers 3
played at Hampden Park

Final
May22 Aberdeen 4 Rangers 1
played at Hampden Park

SEASON 1982-83

1st Round
Dec 11 Brechin C 2 Cowdenbeath 0
Dec 11 Meadowbank T 1 Elgin C 2
Dec 18 Peterhead 0 Forfar A 5
Dec 11 Selkirk 0 Brora R 2
Dec 18 Stirling A 1 E Stirling 0
Dec 18 Vale of Leithen 0 Stranraer 0

Replay
Dec 20 Stranraer 2 Vale of Leithen 0

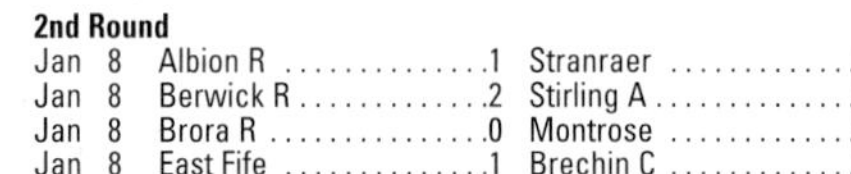

2nd Round
Jan 8 Albion R 1 Stranraer 0
Jan 8 Berwick R 2 Stirling A 0
Jan 8 Brora R 0 Montrose 0
Jan 8 East Fife 1 Brechin C 0

Aberdeen parade the Scottish Cup, along with the European Cup-winners' Cup, which they also won that year.

Jan 8	Elgin C	5	Gala Fairydean	2
Jan 8	Forfar A	3	Inverness C	0
Jan 8	Queen of South	3	Hawick RA	0
Jan 8	Stenhousemuir	1	Arbroath	0

Replays

Jan 15	Montrose	1	Brora R	1
Jan 17	Brora R	5	Montrose	2
	played at Inverness			

3rd Round

Jan 29	Alloa	1	Morton	2
Jan 29	Ayr U	1	Albion R	2
Jan 29	Clyde	0	Motherwell	0
Jan 29	Clydebank	0	Celtic	3
Jan 29	Dumbarton	0	Airdrie	1
Jan 29	Dundee	2	Brora R	1
Jan 29	Dunfermline A	5	Elgin C	0
Jan 29	East Fife	1	Raith R	0
Jan 29	Falkirk	0	Rangers	2
Jan 29	Forfar A	2	Berwick R	1
Jan 30	Hamilton A	0	St Johnstone	1
Jan 29	Hibernian	1	Aberdeen	4
Jan 29	Partick T	1	Kilmarnock	1
Jan 29	Queen of South	1	Hearts	1
Jan 29	Queen's Park	4	Stenhousemuir	1
Jan 29	St Mirren	1	Dundee U	0

Replays

Feb 2	Hearts	1	Queen of South	0
Feb 2	Kilmarnock	0	Partick T	0
Feb 2	Motherwell	3	Clyde	4
Feb 7	Partick T	2	Kilmarnock	2
	played at Firhill Park			
Feb 9	Kilmarnock	0	Partick T	1
	played at Rugby Park			

4th Round

Feb 19	Aberdeen	1	Dundee	0
Feb 19	Albion R	0	Airdrie	3
Feb 19	Celtic	3	Dunfermline A	0
Feb 20	Hearts	2	East Fife	1
Feb 19	Morton	0	St Mirren	2
Feb 19	Partick T	2	Clyde	2
Feb 19	Queen's Park	1	St Johnstone	0
Feb 19	Rangers	2	Forfar A	1

Replays

Feb 23	Clyde	1	Partick T	1
	Abandoned in Extra-time			
Feb 28	Clyde	0	Partick T	6

5th Round

Mar 12	Airdrie	0	St Mirren	5
Mar 12	Celtic	4	Hearts	1
Mar 12	Partick T	1	Aberdeen	2
Mar 12	Queen's Park	1	Rangers	2

Semi-finals

Apr 16	Aberdeen	1	Celtic	0
	played at Hampden Park			
Apr 16	Rangers	1	St Mirren	1
	played at Hampden Park			

Replay

Apr 19	Rangers	1	St Mirren	0
	played at Hampden Park			

Final

May21	Aberdeen	1	Rangers	0
	played at Hampden Park			

Season 1983-84

Pictured at the start of the 1983-84 season with the League Cup, won the previous year, Celtic went on to pick-up all three runners-up spots, losing to Aberdeen in the League and Scottish Cup, and to Rangers in the League Cup.

1st Round

Dec 10	Cowdenbeath	3	Vale of Leithen	0
Dec 10	Dalbeattie Star	1	Arbroath	5
Dec 10	E Stirling	1	Stenhousemuir	0
Dec 10	Elgin C	0	Queen's Park	2
Dec 10	Forfar A	4	Spartans	1
Dec 10	Inverness C	2	Albion R	1

2nd Round

Jan 7	Arbroath	0	Stirling	0
Jan 7	Cowdenbeath	2	Montrose	1
Jan 9	Dunfermline A	1	Forfar A	0
Jan 7	E Stirling	3	Fraserburgh	1
Jan 7	Gala Fairydean	0	Inverness C	2
Jan 7	Peterhead	1	East Fife	5
Jan 7	Stranraer	1	Queen's Park	2

Replays

Feb 6	Stirling A	0	Arbroath	0
Feb 8	Arbroath	1	Stirling A	2
	played at Arbroath			

3rd Round

Feb 13	Aberdeen	1	Kilmarnock	1
Feb 13	Airdrie	1	St Johnstone	0
Jan 28	Berwick R	0	Celtic	4
Feb 8	Clydebank	0	Brechin C	0
Feb 8	Cowdenbeath	0	Dundee	2
Feb 6	Dundee U	1	Ayr U	0
Feb 6	Falkirk	1	Clyde	2
Feb 2	Hamilton A	3	Alloa	1
Feb 6	Hearts	2	Partick T	0
Jan 28	Hibernian	0	East Fife	0
Feb 11	Inverness C	0	Stirling A	0
Jan 28	Meadowbank T	0	St Mirren	0
Feb 6	Morton	2	E Stirling	0
Feb 6	Motherwell	3	Queen's Park	0
Feb 6	Raith R	1	Dumbarton	4
Jan 28	Rangers	2	Dunfermline A	1

Replays

Jan 31	East Fife	2	Hibernian	0
Feb 6	St Mirren	2	Meadowbank T	2
Feb 13	Brechin C	0	Clydebank	3
Feb 15	Kilmarnock	1	Aberdeen	3
Feb 15	Meadowbank T	1	St Mirren	2
	played at Meadowbank			
Feb 15	Stirling A	1	Inverness C	2

4th Round

Feb 18	Clyde	0	Aberdeen	2
Feb 19	Dundee	2	Airdrie	1
Feb 18	Dundee U	2	Hearts	1
Feb 18	East Fife	0	Celtic	6
Feb 18	Inverness C	0	Rangers	6
Feb 18	Morton	2	Dumbarton	1
Feb 18	Motherwell	3	Clydebank	1
Feb 18	St Mirren	2	Hamilton A	1

5th Round

Mar 17	Aberdeen	0	Dundee U	0
Mar 10	Dundee	2	Rangers	2
Mar 17	Motherwell	0	Celtic	6
Mar 10	St Mirren	4	Morton	3

Replays

Mar 17	Rangers	2	Dundee	3
Mar 28	Dundee U	0	Aberdeen	1

Semi-finals

Apr 14	Aberdeen	2	Dundee	0
	played at Tynecastle			
Apr 14	Celtic	2	St Mirren	1
	played at Hampden Park			

Final

May19	Aberdeen	2	Celtic	1
	played at Hampden Park			

Season 1984-85

1st Round

Dec 8	Berwick R	3	Albion R	1
Dec 8	Dunfermline A	1	E Stirling	3
Dec 8	Queen of South	2	Arbroath	1
Dec 8	Stenhousemuir	2	Whitehill Welfare	1
Dec 8	Stirling A	20	Selkirk	0
Dec 8	Stranraer	2	Gala Fairydean	2

Replay

Dec 15	Gala Fairydean	0	Stranraer	1

2nd Round

Jan 5	Alloa	2	E Stirling	1
Jan 5	Berwick R	1	Inverness C	1
Jan 5	Cowdenbeath	2	Stirling A	1
Jan 5	Inverness T	1	Spartans	1
Jan 5	Keith	2	Brora R	0
Jan 5	Queen of South	3	Montrose	1
Jan 5	Queen's Park	0	Raith R	0
Jan 5	Stranraer	0	Stenhousemuir	0

Replays

Jan 12	Inverness C	3	Berwick R	3
Jan 21	Raith R	1	Queen's Park	0
Feb 2	Spartans	1	Inverness T	2
Feb 4	Stenhousemuir	0	Stranraer	2
Jan 21	Berwick R	0	Inverness C	3
	played at Bayview Park			

3rd Round

Jan 30	Aberdeen	5	Alloa	0
Feb 4	Airdrie	0	Falkirk	3
Jan 26	Ayr U	3	Keith	1
Jan 26	Brechin C	1	East Fife	1
Feb 4	Cowdenbeath	0	St Mirren	4
Feb 4	Dundee U	3	Hibernian	0
Feb 4	Forfar A	1	Clydebank	0
Jan 30	Hamilton A	1	Celtic	2
Jan 30	Hearts	6	Inverness C	0
Feb 9	Inverness T	3	Kilmarnock	0
Jan 30	Meadowbank T	4	Partick T	2
Jan 26	Morton	3	Rangers	3
Jan 30	Motherwell	4	Dumbarton	0
Jan 26	Raith R	2	Clyde	2
Feb 5	St Johnstone	1	Dundee	1
Feb 9	Stranraer	4	Queen of South	6

Replays

Jan 29	East Fife	0	Brechin C	4
Jan 30	Rangers	3	Morton	1
Feb 4	Clyde	1	Raith R	2
Feb 6	Dundee	2	St Johnstone	1

4th Round

Feb 16	Ayr U	0	St Mirren	1
Feb 16	Brechin C	1	Hearts	1
Feb 16	Celtic	6	Inverness T	0
Feb 16	Forfar A	2	Falkirk	1
Feb 20	Meadowbank T	0	Motherwell	2
Feb 16	Queen of South	0	Dundee U	3
Feb 16	Raith R	1	Aberdeen	2
Feb 16	Rangers	0	Dundee	1

Replay

Feb 20	Hearts	1	Brechin C	0

5th Round

Mar 9	Dundee	1	Celtic	1
Mar 9	Hearts	1	Aberdeen	1
Mar 9	Motherwell	4	Forfar A	1
Mar 9	St Mirren	1	Dundee U	4

Replays

Mar 13	Aberdeen	1	Hearts	0
Mar 13	Celtic	2	Dundee	1

Semi-finals

Apr 13	Aberdeen	0	Dundee U	0
	played at Tynecastle			
Apr 13	Celtic	1	Motherwell	1
	played at Hampden Park			

Replays

Apr 17	Aberdeen	1	Dundee U	2
	played at Tynecastle			
Apr 17	Celtic	3	Motherwell	0
	played at Hampden Park			

Final

May18	Celtic	2	Dundee U	1
	played at Hampden Park			

Danny McGrain passes the trophy back as Celtic embark on their lap of honour after beating Dundee United in the 1984 Final.

SEASON 1985-86

1st Round

Dec 7	Albion R	8	Gala Fairydean	1
Dec 7	Berwick R	0	Cowdenbeath	0
Dec 7	Dunfermline A	2	Raith R	0
Dec 7	Meadowbank T	3	East Stirling	2
Dec 7	Queen's Park	3	Buckie T	0
Dec 7	St Johnstone	1	Queen of South	0

Replay

Dec 11	Cowdenbeath	0	Berwick R	2

2nd Round

Jan 4	Fort William	0	Stirling A	0
Jan 11	Hawick RA	1	St Johnstone	2
Jan 11	Nairn Co	1	Meadowbank T	1
Jan 11	Peterhead	1	Arbroath	2
Jan 4	Queen's Park	2	Albion R	1
Jan 4	Stenhousemuir	0	Whitehill Welfare	0
Jan 4	Stranraer	1	Berwick R	2
Jan 4	Threave R	0	Dunfermline A	5

Replays

Jan 11	Stirling A	6	Fort William	0
Jan 11	Whitehill Welfare	2	Stenhousemuir	3
Jan 13	Meadowbank T	1	Nairn Co	2

3rd Round

Feb 5	Aberdeen	4	Montrose	1
Jan 25	Airdrie	0	Partick T	0
Jan 25	Arbroath	0	Clyde	0
Jan 25	Ayr U	1	Stenhousemuir	0
Jan 25	Berwick R	2	Alloa	3
Jan 25	Celtic	2	St Johnstone	0
Jan 25	Clydebank	0	Falkirk	0
Jan 25	Dundee U	4	Morton	0
Jan 25	East Fife	1	St Mirren	1
Feb 3	Hamilton A	2	Forfar A	1
Jan 25	Hearts	3	Rangers	2
Jan 26	Hibernian	2	Dunfermline A	0
Jan 25	Kilmarnock	1	Stirling A	0
Jan 25	Motherwell	1	Brechin C	1
Jan 25	Nairn Co	0	Dundee	7
Jan 25	Queen's Park	1	Dumbarton	0

Replays

Feb 3	Clyde	1	Arbroath	2
Feb 3	Falkirk	1	Clydebank	0
Feb 3	Partick T	1	Airdrie	2
Feb 4	St Mirren	3	East Fife	1
Feb 11	Brechin C	1	Motherwell	1
Feb 12	Brechin C	0	Motherwell	2
	played at Tannadice Park			

4th Round

Mar 5	Alloa	1	Motherwell	2
Feb 15	Arbroath	0	Aberdeen	1
Feb 15	Celtic	2	Queen's Park	1
Feb 19	Dundee	2	Airdrie	0
Feb 15	Dundee U	1	Kilmarnock	1
Mar 3	Hamilton A	1	Hearts	2
Feb 16	Hibernian	1	Ayr U	0
Mar 4	St Mirren	1	Falkirk	1

Replays

Feb 19	Kilmarnock	0	Dundee U	1
Mar 5	Falkirk	0	St Mirren	3

5th Round

Mar 8	Dundee	2	Aberdeen	2
Mar 9	Hearts	4	St Mirren	1
Mar 8	Hibernian	4	Celtic	3
Mar 8	Motherwell	0	Dundee U	1

Replay

Mar 12	Aberdeen	2	Dundee	1

Semi-finals

Apr 5	Aberdeen	3	Hibernian	0
	played at Dens Park			
Apr 5	Dundee U	0	Hearts	1
	played at Hampden Park			

Final

May10	Aberdeen	3	Hearts	0
	played at Hampden Park			

SEASON 1986-87

1st Round

Dec 6	Albion R	2	Arbroath	1
Dec 6	Ayr U	3	Annan A	1
Dec 13	Forres Mechanic	0	Berwick R	1
Dec 6	Inverness C	2	Alloa	2
Dec 6	Peterhead	1	E Stirling	0
Dec 6	Stirling A	3	Cowdenbeath	0

Replay

Dec 13	Alloa	0	Inverness C	1

2nd Round

Feb 4	Albion R	1	Whitehill Welfare	2
Jan 19	Inverness C	5	Spartans	0
Jan 26	Raith R	4	Vale of Leithen	0
Jan 10	Rothes	1	Peterhead	3
Jan 26	St Johnstone	4	Queen's Park	1
Jan 26	Stenhousemuir	0	Berwick R	0
Jan 21	Stirling A	0	Meadowbank T	1
Jan 10	Stranraer	1	Ayr U	1

Replay

Jan 21	Ayr U	2	Stranraer	0
Jan 28	Berwick R	2	Stenhousemuir	0

3rd Round

Feb 1	Aberdeen	2	Celtic	2
Jan 31	Berwick R	0	Morton	2
Jan 31	Brechin C	2	Dumbarton	2
Feb 3	Dundee	2	East Fife	2
Jan 31	Dundee U	1	Airdrie	1
Feb 3	Falkirk	0	Clydebank	0
Jan 31	Hearts	0	Kilmarnock	0
Jan 31	Hibernian	2	Dunfermline A	0
Feb 3	Meadowbank T	2	Ayr U	0
Jan 31	Montrose	1	Forfar A	2
Feb 3	Motherwell	3	Partick T	1
Jan 31	Peterhead	2	Clyde	0
Jan 31	Queen of South	0	Raith R	1
Jan 31	Rangers	0	Hamilton A	1
Feb 7	St Johnstone	4	Whitehill Welfare	0
Jan 31	St Mirren	3	Inverness C	0

Replays

Feb 4	Celtic	0	Aberdeen	0
Feb 4	Dumbarton	2	Brechin C	3
Feb 4	Kilmarnock	1	Hearts	1
Feb 9	Airdrie	1	Dundee U	2
Feb 9	Aberdeen	0	Celtic	1
	played at Dens Park			
Feb 9	Clydebank	3	Falkirk	1
Feb 9	East Fife	1	Dundee	4
Feb 9	Kilmarnock	1	Hearts	3

4th Round

Feb 21	Brechin C	0	Dundee U	1
Feb 21	Clydebank	1	Hibernian	0
Feb 21	Dundee	1	Meadowbank T	1
Feb 21	Hamilton A	1	Motherwell	2
Feb 21	Hearts	1	Celtic	0
Feb 21	Morton	2	St Mirren	3
Feb 21	Raith R	2	Peterhead	2
Feb 21	St Johnstone	1	Forfar A	2

Replays
Feb 25 Meadowbank T 1 Dundee 1
Feb 25 Peterhead 3 Raith R 3
Mar 2 Dundee 2 Meadowbank T 0
Mar 2 Peterhead 0 Raith R 3
played at Gayfield Park

5th Round
Mar 14 Clydebank 0 Dundee 4
Mar 14 Dundee U 2 Forfar A 2
Mar 14 Hearts 1 Motherwell 1
Mar 14 Raith R 0 St Mirren 2

Replays
Mar 17 Motherwell 0 Hearts 1
Mar 24 Forfar A 0 Dundee U 2

Semi-finals
Apr 11 Dundee 2 Dundee U 3
played at Tynecastle
Apr 11 Hearts 1 St Mirren 2
played at Hampden Park

Final
May16 Dundee 0 St Mirren 1
played at Hampden Park

Season 1987-88

1st Round
Dec 5 Albion R 1 St Johnstone 1
Dec 12 Inverness C 1 E Stirling 1
Dec 5 Montrose 0 Ayr U 2
Dec 5 Stirling A 1 Cowdenbeath 2
Dec 5 Threave R 0 Stranraer 6
Dec 5 Vale of Leithen 2 Brechin C 3

Replays
Dec 8 St Johnstone 2 Albion R 0
Dec 21 E Stirling 2 Inverness C 1

2nd Round
Jan 10 Alloa 0 Cowdenbeath 1
Jan 9 Berwick R 0 Brechin C 1
Jan 9 Buckie T 2 E Stirling 3
Jan 9 Fraserburgh 2 St Johnstone 5
Jan 9 Gala Fairydean 3 Civil Service 0
Jan 9 Queen's Park 2 Ayr U 3
Jan 9 Stenhousemuir 1 Arbroath 1
Jan 9 Stranraer 6 Keith 2

Replays
Jan 12 Arbroath 1 Stenhousemuir 1
Jan 18 Arbroath 1 Stenhousemuir 0
played at Muirton Park

3rd Round
Jan 30 Arbroath 0 Dundee U 7
Jan 30 Celtic 1 Stranraer 0
Jan 30 Clyde 0 Cowdenbeath 0
Jan 30 Dumbarton 0 Hibernian 0
Jan 30 Dundee 0 Brechin C 0
Jan 30 Dunfermline A 1 Ayr U 1
Jan 30 East Fife 1 Airdrie 2
Jan 30 Falkirk 1 Hearts 3
Feb 3 Forfar A 1 Partick T 1
Jan 30 Gala Fairydean 3 E Stirling 5
Jan 31 Hamilton A 2 Meadowbank T 0
Jan 30 Motherwell 0 Kilmarnock 0
Jan 30 Queen of South 1 Morton 2
Feb 8 Raith R 0 Rangers 0
Jan 30 St Johnstone 0 Aberdeen 1
Jan 30 St Mirren 0 Clydebank 3

Replays
Feb 2 Hibernian 3 Dumbarton 0
Feb 3 Ayr U 0 Dunfermline A 2
Feb 3 Brechin C 0 Dundee 3
Feb 3 Cowdenbeath 0 Clyde 1
Feb 3 Kilmarnock 1 Motherwell 3
Feb 10 Partick T 3 Forfar A 0
Feb 10 Rangers 4 Raith R 1

4th Round
Feb 20 Airdrie 0 Dundee U 2
Feb 21 Celtic 0 Hibernian 0
Feb 20 Clydebank 2 Partick T 2
Feb 20 Dundee 2 Motherwell 0
Feb 20 Dunfermline A 2 Rangers 0
Feb 20 E Stirling 2 Clyde 3
Feb 20 Hamilton A 0 Aberdeen 2
Feb 20 Hearts 2 Morton 0

Andy Walker of Celtic joyfully grabs the ball from the back of Hearts' net and Celtic are through to the Scottish Cup Final after being 1-0 down with only three minutes to play in this Hampden Park semi-final.

Replays
Feb 23 Partick T 4 Clydebank 1
Feb 23 Hibernian 0 Celtic 1

5th Round
Mar 12 Aberdeen 5 Clyde 0
Mar 12 Dundee 0 Dundee U 0
Mar 12 Hearts 3 Dunfermline A 0
Mar 12 Partick T 0 Celtic 3

Replays
Mar 15 Dundee U 2 Dundee 2
Mar 28 Dundee 0 Dundee U 3
played at Dens Park

Semi-finals
Apr 9 Aberdeen 0 Dundee U 0
played at Dens Park
Apr 9 Celtic 2 Hearts 1
played at Hampden Park

Replays
Apr 13 Aberdeen 1 Dundee U 1
played at Dens Park
Apr 20 Aberdeen 0 Dundee U 1
played at Dens Park

Final
May14 Celtic 2 Dundee U 1
played at Hampden Park

Season 1988-89

1st Round
Dec 3 Berwick R 1 Alloa 1
Dec 3 East Fife 4 Spartans 1
Dec 3 East Stirling 1 Gala Fairydean 0
Dec 3 Inverness T 0 Dumbarton 0
Dec 3 Montrose 2 Arbroath 0
Dec 3 Stranraer 2 Stirling A 2

Replays
Dec 7 Alloa 2 Berwick 1
Dec 10 Dumbarton 2 Inverness T 1
Dec 10 Stirling A 0 Stranraer 1

2nd Round
Jan 7 Annan A 1 Queen's Park 5
Jan 7 Caledonian T 1 Brechin C 1
Jan 7 Coldstream 1 Albion R 1
Jan 7 Cowdenbeath 1 Stenhousemuir 1
Jan 7 East Stirling 1 Montrose 2
Jan 7 Elgin C 2 Dumbarton 2
Jan 7 Forres Mechanic 1 Alloa 1
Jan 7 Stranraer 2 East Fife 1

Replays
Jan 14 Albion R 1 Coldstream 0
Jan 14 Alloa 2 Forres Mechanic 0
Jan 14 Brechin C 2 Caledonian T 1
Jan 14 Dumbarton 4 Elgin C 0
Jan 14 Stenhousemuir 3 Cowdenbeath 2

3rd Round
Jan 28 Alloa 3 Albion R 1
Jan 28 Celtic 2 Dumbarton 0
Jan 28 Clydebank 2 Montrose 1
Jan 28 Dundee 1 Dundee U 2
Jan 28 Dunfermline A 0 Aberdeen 0
Jan 28 Falkirk 1 Motherwell 1
Jan 28 Forfar A 1 Clyde 1
Jan 28 Hearts 4 Ayr U 1
Jan 28 Hibernian 1 Brechin C 0
Jan 29 Meadowbank T 2 Hamilton A 0
Jan 28 Morton 0 Airdrie 0
Jan 28 Partick T 0 St Mirren 0
Jan 28 Queen of South 2 Kilmarnock 2
Jan 28 Queen's Park 0 Stranraer 0
Jan 28 Raith R 1 Rangers 1
Jan 28 St Johnstone 2 Stenhousemuir 0

Replays
Jan 31 Clyde 0 Forfar A 1
Jan 31 St Mirren 1 Partick T 3
Feb 1 Aberdeen 3 Dunfermline A 1
Feb 1 Airdrie 0 Morton 1
Feb 1 Kilmarnock 0 Queen of South 1
Feb 1 Motherwell 2 Falkirk 1
Feb 1 Rangers 3 Raith R 0
Feb 1 Stranraer 1 Queen's Park 0

4th Round
Feb 18 Aberdeen 1 Dundee U 1
Feb 18 Celtic 4 Clydebank 1
Feb 18 Hearts 2 Partick T 0
Feb 18 Hibernian 2 Motherwell 1
Feb 18 Meadowbank T 0 Morton 1
Feb 18 Queen of South 0 Alloa 0
Feb 18 Rangers 8 Stranraer 0
Feb 18 St Johnstone 2 Forfar A 1

Replays
Feb 22 Alloa 4 Queen of South 2
Feb 22 Dundee U 1 Aberdeen 1
Feb 27 Dundee U 1 Aberdeen 0

5th Round
Mar 18 Celtic 2 Hearts 1
Mar 18 Hibernian 1 Alloa 0
Mar 22 Morton 2 St Johnstone 2
Mar 21 Rangers 2 Dundee U 2

Roy Aitken of Celtic holds the SFA Cup aloft after Celtic defeated Rangers in the all-Glasgow clash at Hampden Park in 1989.

Replays

Mar 27	Dundee U	0	Rangers	1
Mar 27	St Johnstone	3	Morton	2

Semi-finals

Apr 16	Celtic	3	Hibernian	1
	played at Hampden Park			
Apr 15	Rangers	0	St Johnstone	0
	played at Celtic Park			

Replay

Apr 18	Rangers	4	St Johnstone	0
	played at Celtic Park			

Final

May20	Celtic	1	Rangers	0
	played at Hampden Park			

Season 1989-90

1st Round

Dec 9	Berwick R	1	Stenhousemuir	1
Dec 9	Brechin C	3	Montrose	1
Dec 9	Elgin C	2	Arbroath	1
Dec 9	Queen of South	2	Cove R	1
Dec 9	Queen's Park	1	Dumbarton	2
Dec 9	Stirling A	4	Coldstream	0

Replay

Dec 12	Stenhousemuir	1	Berwick R	0

2nd Round

Dec 30	Dumbarton	0	Cowdenbeath	2
Dec 30	Elgin C	2	Brechin C	2
Dec 30	Gala Fairydean	2	Inverness C	2
Jan 7	Ross Co	1	East Fife	4
Dec 30	Stenhousemuir	0	Queen of South	1
Dec 30	Stirling A	3	Whitehill Welfare	0
	played at Firs Park			
Dec 30	Stranraer	1	Kilmarnock	1
Dec 30	Vale of Leithen	1	E Stirling	3

Replays

Jan 6	Brechin C	8	Elgin C	0
Jan 6	Inverness C	4	Gala Fairydean	1
Jan 6	Kilmarnock	0	Stranraer	0
	Penalties	3-4		

3rd Round

Jan 20	Airdrie	2	Inverness C	2
Jan 20	Albion R	0	Clydebank	2
Jan 20	Ayr U	0	St Mirren	0
Jan 20	Brechin C	0	Hibernian	2
Jan 20	Cowdenbeath	3	Stranraer	1
Jan 20	Dundee	0	Dundee U	0
Jan 20	Dunfermline A	0	Hamilton A	0
Jan 20	East Fife	3	Meadowbank T	1
Jan 29	E Stirling	0	Stirling A	1
Jan 20	Forfar A	1	Celtic	2
Jan 20	Hearts	2	Falkirk	0
Jan 20	Morton	2	Raith R	2
Jan 20	Motherwell	7	Clyde	0
Jan 20	Partick T	2	Aberdeen	6
Jan 20	Queen of South	0	Alloa	0
Jan 20	Rangers	3	St Johnstone	0

Replays

Jan 23	Dundee U	1	Dundee	0
Jan 24	Inverness C	1	Airdrie	1
	Penalties 5-4			
Jan 24	St Mirren	2	Ayr U	1
Jan 29	Alloa	2	Queen of South	3
Jan 29	Raith R	1	Morton	3
Jan 31	Hamilton A	0	Dunfermline A	1

4th Round

Feb 24	Aberdeen	2	Morton	1
Feb 25	Celtic	1	Rangers	0
Feb 27	Cowdenbeath	1	Dumbarton	2
Feb 26	Dundee U	2	Queen of South	1
Feb 24	Hearts	4	Motherwell	0
Feb 24	Hibernian	5	East Fife	1
Feb 28	St Mirren	1	Clydebank	1
Feb 28	Stirling A	6	Inverness C	2

Replay

Mar 12	Clydebank	3	St Mirren	2

5th Round

Mar 17	Aberdeen	4	Hearts	1
Mar 17	Clydebank	1	Stirling A	1
Mar 17	Dundee U	1	Hibernian	0
Mar 17	Dunfermline A	0	Celtic	0

Replays

Mar 21	Celtic	3	Dunfermline A	0
Mar 21	Clydebank	1	Stirling A	0
	played at Brockville Park			

Semi-finals

Apr 14	Aberdeen	4	Dundee U	0
	played at Tynecastle			
Apr 14	Celtic	2	Clydebank	0
	played at Hampden Park			

Final

May12	Aberdeen	0	Celtic	0
	Penalties 9-8			
	played at Hampden Park			

Season 1990-91

1st Round

Dec 8	E Stirling	1	Queen of South	3
Dec 8	Fraserburgh	3	Vale of Leithen	1
Dec 11	Montrose	0	Dumbarton	0
Dec 8	Ross Co	1	Alloa	1
Dec 15	Threave R	1	Spartans	2
Dec 15	Whitehill Welfare	0	East Fife	4

Replays

Dec 15	Alloa	1	Ross Co	3
Dec 17	Dumbarton	1	Montrose	4

2nd Round

Dec 29	Berwick R	1	Albion R	0
Dec 29	Fraserburgh	1	Cove R	4
Jan 5	Inverness T	1	East Fife	1
Dec 29	Montrose	0	Arbroath	2
Dec 29	Queen's Park	1	Stranraer	2
Jan 23	Ross Co	2	Queen of South	2
Jan 9	Spartans	0	Cowdenbeath	0
Dec 29	Stirling A	2	Stenhousemuir	0

Replays

Jan 7	East Fife	1	Inverness T	0
Jan 21	Cowdenbeath	2	Spartans	0
Jan 28	Queen of South	2	Ross Co	6

3rd Round

Jan 26	Aberdeen	0	Motherwell	1
Jan 26	Airdrie	2	Hearts	1
Jan 28	Clyde	0	Hibernian	2
Jan 26	Clydebank	0	Ayr U	1
Jan 26	Cove R	1	Cowdenbeath	2
Jan 26	Dundee	1	Brechin C	0
Jan 26	East Fife	1	Dundee U	1
Jan 26	Forfar A	0	Celtic	2
Jan 26	Kilmarnock	3	Arbroath	2
Jan 26	Partick T	0	Falkirk	0
Jan 26	Raith R	0	Hamilton A	1
Jan 29	Rangers	2	Dunfermline A	0
Feb 23	Ross Co	1	Meadowbank T	6
Jan 26	St Johnstone	0	Berwick R	0
Jan 26	Stirling A	0	Morton	1
Jan 26	Stranraer	1	St Mirren	5

Replays

Jan 29	Dundee U	2	East Fife	1
Jan 30	Berwick R	3	St Johnstone	4
Jan 30	Falkirk	4	Partick T	3

4th Round

Feb 23	Ayr U	0	Hamilton A	0
Feb 26	Celtic	3	St Mirren	0
Feb 23	Dundee	2	Kilmarnock	0
Feb 23	Dundee U	2	Airdrie	0
Mar 2	Morton	3	Meadowbank T	0
Feb 23	Motherwell	4	Falkirk	2
Feb 23	Rangers	5	Cowdenbeath	0
Feb 23	St Johnstone	2	Hibernian	1

Replays

Feb 27	Hamilton A	2	Ayr U	3

5th Round

Mar 17	Celtic	2	Rangers	0
Mar 13	Dundee U	3	Dundee	1
Mar 16	Motherwell	0	Morton	0
Mar 16	St Johnstone	5	Ayr U	2

Replay

Mar 19	Morton	1	Motherwell	1
	Penalties 4-5			

Semi-finals

Apr 3	Celtic	0	Motherwell	0
	played at Hampden Park			
Apr 6	Dundee U	2	St Johnstone	1
	played at East End Park			

Replay

Apr 9	Celtic	2	Motherwell	4
	played at Hampden Park			

Final

May18	Dundee U	3	Motherwell	4
	played at Hampden Park			

Season 1991-92

1st Round

Dec 7	Albion R	0	Arbroath	2
Dec 7	Alloa	7	Hawick	1
Dec 7	East Fife	6	Queen's Park	0
Dec 7	East Stirling	0	Dumbarton	2
Dec 14	Gala Fairydean	2	Ross Co	2
Dec 7	Vale of Leithen	1	Stranraer	2

Replay

Dec 16	Ross Co	3	Gala Fairydean	0

2nd Round

Jan 4	Alloa	0	Dumbarton	2
Jan 4	Berwick	7	Ross Co	4
Jan 4	Brechin	0	East Fife	0
Jan 14	Clyde	2	Arbroath	0

Mark Hateley celebrates after scoring in the 1992 Scottish Cup Final. Mikhailichenko shares his joy.

Date	Home		Away	
Jan 4	Huntly	4	Civil Service S	2
Jan 4	Peterhead	1	Cowdenbeath	1
Jan 4	Stenhousemuir	1	Caledonian T	4
Jan 4	Stranraer	4	Queen of South	1

Replays

Date	Home		Away	
Jan 11	Cowdenbeath	6	Peterhead	1
Jan 14	East Fife	3	Brechin	1

3rd Round

Date	Home		Away	
Jan 22	Aberdeen	0	Rangers	1
Jan 25	Airdrie	2	Stranraer	1
Jan 25	Ayr	1	Motherwell	1
Jan 25	Caledonian T	3	Clyde	1
Jan 25	Celtic	6	Montrose	0
Jan 25	Clydebank	3	Cowdenbeath	1
Jan 25	Dumbarton	0	Huntly	2
Feb 3	Dundee	1	Stirling A	1
Jan 26	Dundee U	6	Berwick	0
Jan 25	Forfar	0	Dunfermline A	0
Jan 25	Hamilton	0	Falkirk	1
Jan 25	Hibernian	2	Partick	0
Jan 25	Meadowbank	1	Kilmarnock	1
Jan 25	Morton	4	East Fife	2
Jan 25	Raith	0	St Johnstone	2
Jan 25	St Mirren	0	Hearts	0

Replays

Date	Home		Away	
Feb 4	Kilmarnock	1	Meadowbank	1
Feb 4	Motherwell	4	Ayr	1
Feb 5	Dunfermline A	3	Forfar	1
Feb 5	Hearts	3	St Mirren	0
Feb 5	Stirling A	0	Dundee	1

4th Round

Date	Home		Away	
Feb 15	Caledonian T	2	St Johnstone	2
Feb 11	Celtic	2	Dundee U	1
Feb 15	Clydebank	1	Hibernian	5
Feb 15	Dunfermline A	1	Hearts	2
Feb 15	Falkirk	0	Dundee	0
Feb 15	Huntly	1	Airdrie	3
Feb 15	Morton	2	Meadowbank	2
Feb 15	Rangers	2	Motherwell	1

Replays

Date	Home		Away	
Feb 24	Dundee	0	Falkirk	1
Feb 26	Meadowbank	2	Morton	3
Feb 26	St Johnstone	3	Caledonian T	0

5th Round

Date	Home		Away	
Mar 7	Celtic	3	Morton	0
Mar 8	Hearts	3	Falkirk	1
Mar 7	Hibernian	0	Airdrie	2
Mar 3	St Johnstone	0	Rangers	3

Semi-finals

Date	Home		Away	
Apr 4	Airdrie	0	Hearts	0
	played at Hampden Park			
Mar 31	Celtic	0	Rangers	1
	played at Hampden Park			

Replay

Date	Home		Away	
Apr 14	Airdrie	1	Hearts	1
	played at Hampden Park			
	Penalties 4-2			

Final

Date	Home		Away	
May 9	Airdrie	1	Rangers	2
	played at Hampden Park			

Season 1992-93

1st Round

Date	Home		Away	
Dec 8	Cove R	2	Peterhead	0
Dec 8	Forfar	5	Albion R	0
Dec 5	Huntly	4	Stranraer	2
Dec 5	Inverness T	3	Civil Service S	1
Dec 5	Queen of South	3	Spartans	0
Dec 5	Queen's Park	0	Clyde	1

2nd Round

Date	Home		Away	
Dec 19	Clyde	3	Brechin	1
Dec 19	Cove R	2	Montrose	0
Dec 19	East Fife	1	Alloa	1
Dec 19	Gala Fairydean	1	Arbroath	1
Jan 4	Huntly	2	Queen of South	1
Dec 26	Inverness T	0	Berwick	1
Dec 28	Stenhousemuir	2	Forfar	3
Dec 19	Vale of Leithen	2	East Stirling	2

Replays

Date	Home		Away	
Jan 28	Alloa	1	East Fife	1
	Penalties 5-6			
Jan 28	Arbroath	2	Gala Fairydean	0
Jan 28	East Stirling	3	Vale of Leithen	2

3rd Round

Date	Home		Away	
Jan 9	Aberdeen	4	Hamilton	1
Jan 9	Airdrie	0	Clydebank	0
Jan 9	Arbroath	3	Morton	0
Jan 9	Clyde	0	Celtic	0
Jan 9	Cove R	2	East Stirling	2
Jan 10	Dundee	2	Dumbarton	0
Jan 9	Dundee U	3	Meadowbank	1
Jan 9	Dunfermline A	1	Ayr	2
Jan 27	Falkirk	5	Berwick	2
Jan 9	Hearts	6	Huntly	0
Jan 9	Hibernian	5	St Mirren	2
Jan 9	Kilmarnock	5	Raith	0
Jan 9	Motherwell	0	Rangers	2
Jan 9	Partick	0	Cowdenbeath	1
Jan 9	St Johnstone	6	Forfar	0
Jan 9	Stirling A	1	East Fife	2

Replays

Date	Home		Away	
Jan 19	Clydebank	2	Airdrie	0
Jan 20	Celtic	1	Clyde	0
Jan 25	East Stirling	2	Cove R	1

4th Round

Date	Home		Away	
Feb 7	Aberdeen	2	Dundee U	0
Feb 6	Arbroath	0	East Fife	0
Feb 6	Ayr	0	Rangers	2
Feb 6	Cowdenbeath	0	Hibernian	0
Feb 6	East Stirling	1	Clydebank	2
Feb 6	Falkirk	2	Celtic	0
Feb 6	Hearts	2	Dundee	0
Feb 6	Kilmarnock	0	St Johnstone	0

Replays

Date	Home		Away	
Feb 10	Hibernian	1	Cowdenbeath	0
Feb 10	St Johnstone	1	Kilmarnock	0
Feb 16	East Fife	1	Arbroath	4

5th Round

Date	Home		Away	
Mar 6	Aberdeen	1	Clydebank	1
Mar 6	Arbroath	0	Rangers	3
Mar 6	Hearts	2	Falkirk	0
Mar 6	Hibernian	2	St Johnstone	0

Replay

Date	Home		Away	
Mar 16	Clydebank	3	Aberdeen	4

Semi-finals

Date	Home		Away	
Apr 3	Aberdeen	1	Hibernian	0
	played at Tynecastle			
Apr 3	Hearts	1	Rangers	2
	played at Hampden Park			

Final

Date	Home		Away	
May 29	Aberdeen	1	Rangers	2
	played at Hampden Park			

Season 1993-94

1st Round

Date	Home		Away	
Dec 11	Albion R	0	Huntly	0
Dec 11	Cowdenbeath	1	Queen's Park	1
Dec 11	East Fife	5	Rothes	0
Dec 11	Forfar	8	Queen of South	3
Dec 11	Ross Co	11	St Cuthbert's	0
Dec 11	Stranraer	3	Whitehill	3

Replays

Date	Home		Away	
Dec 14	Queen's Park	2	Cowdenbeath	3
Dec 18	Whitehill	0	Stranraer	4
Jan 15	Huntly	5	Albion R	3

2nd Round

Date	Home		Away	
Jan 15	Alloa	4	Gala	0
Jan 8	Berwick	1	East Fife	0
Jan 15	Cowdenbeath	1	Stenhousemuir	0
Jan 8	E.Stirling	4	Cove R	1
Jan 8	Forfar	0	Ross Co	4

Jan 8 Meadowbank 1 Montrose 2
Jan 15 Selkirk 0 Arbroath 3
Jan 22 Huntly 1 Stranraer 2

3rd Round
Jan 29 Airdrie 1 Dunfermline A 1
Feb 8 Alloa 2 Ross Co 0
Jan 29 Arbroath 2 Dundee U 3
Jan 29 Clydebank 1 Dundee 1
Feb 8 E.Stirling 1 Aberdeen 3
Jan 29 Hibernian 2 Clyde 1
Jan 29 Kilmarnock 2 Ayr 1
Jan 29 Morton 2 Cowdenbeath 2
Jan 29 Motherwell 1 Celtic 0
Jan 29 Partick 0 Hearts 1
Jan 29 Raith 2 Brechin 0
Jan 29 Rangers 4 Dumbarton 1
Jan 29 St Johnstone 2 Hamilton 0
Jan 29 St Mirren 2 Montrose 0
Jan 29 Stirling A 1 Berwick 0
Jan 29 Stranraer 2 Falkirk 1

Replays
Feb 8 Cowdenbeath 1 Morton 2
Feb 8 Dunfermline A 1 Airdrie 3
Feb 9 Dundee 2 Clydebank 1

4th Round
Feb 19 Aberdeen 1 Raith 0
Feb 19 Airdrie 1 Stranraer 0
Feb 20 Dundee 3 St Mirren 1
Feb 19 Dundee U 2 Motherwell 2
Feb 20 Hibernian 1 Heats 2
Feb 19 Morton 0 Kilmarnock 1
Feb 19 Rangers 6 Alloa 0
Feb 28 St Johnstone 3 Stirling A 3

Replays
Mar 1 Motherwell 0 Dundee U 1
Mar 1 Stirling A 0 St Johnstone 2

5th Round
Mar 12 Airdrie 0 Dundee U 0
Mar 12 Kilmarnock 1 Dundee 0
Mar 12 Rangers 2 Hearts 0
Mar 12 St Johnstone 1 Aberdeen 1

Replays
Mar 15 Aberdeen 2 St Johnstone 0
Mar 15 Dundee U 2 Airdrie 0

Semi-finals
Apr 9 Aberdeen 1 Dundee U 1
played at Hampden Park
Apr 10 Kilmarnock 0 Rangers 0
played at Hampden Park

Replays
Apr 12 Aberdeen 0 Dundee U 1
played at Hampden Park
Apr 13 Kilmarnock 1 Rangers 2
played at Hampden Park

Final
May21 Dundee U 1 Rangers 0
played at Hampden Park

Season 1994-95

1st Round
Dec 26 Albion R 2 Montrose 5
Dec 17 Caledonian T 1 Queen of South 2
Dec 17 Dumbarton 3 Stirling A 3
Dec 17 Stenhousemuir 3 E.Stirling 0

Replay
Dec 19 Stirling A 3 Dumbarton 0

2nd Round
Jan 7 Alloa 2 Ross Co 3
Jan 7 Brechin 2 Stirling A 3
Jan 7 Buckie 1 Berwick 3
Jan 7 Burntisland 6 St Cuthbert's 2
Jan 7 Cove R 2 Cowdenbeath 1
Jan 7 Forfar A 0 Meadowbank T 1
Jan 7 Gala Fairydean 2 East Fife 6
Jan 7 Keith 2 Huntly 2
Jan 7 Queen of South 0 Clyde 2
Jan 9 Queen's Park 2 Morton 2
Jan 7 Stenhousemuir 4 Arbroath 0
Jan 7 Whitehill Welfare 0 Montrose 0

Replays
Jan 14 Huntly 3 Keith 1
Jan 14 Montrose 5 Whitehill 2
Jan 17 Morton 2 Queen's Park 1

3rd Round
Jan 28 Aberdeen 1 Stranraer 0
Jan 28 Celtic 2 St Mirren 0
Feb 1 Clydebank 1 Hearts 1
Jan 28 Cove R 0 Dunfermline A 4
Jan 29 Dundee 2 Partick 1
Jan 28 Dundee U 0 Clyde 0
Feb 1 East Fife 1 Ross Co 0
Feb 6 Falkirk 0 Motherwell 2
Feb 6 Hamilton 1 Rangers 3
Jan 28 Huntly 7 Burntisland 0
Jan 28 Kilmarnock 0 Morton 0
Feb 6 Meadowbank 1 Berwick 1
Jan 28 Montrose 0 Hibernian 2
Jan 28 Raith 1 Ayr 0
Jan 31 St Johnstone 1 Stenhousemuir 1
Feb 1 Stirling A 1 Airdrie 2

Replays
Jan 31 Morton 1 Kilmarnock 2
Feb 7 Berwick R 3 Meadowbank 3
Penalties 6-7
Feb 7 Clyde 1 Dundee U 5
Feb 7 Hearts 2 Clydebank 1
Feb 7 Stenhousemuir 4 St Johnstone 0

4th Round
Feb 18 Airdrie 2 Dunfermline A 0
Feb 18 Celtic 3 Meadowbank 0
Feb 18 Dundee 1 Raith 2
Feb 20 Hearts 4 Rangers 2
Feb 18 Hibernian 2 Motherwell 0
Feb 18 Huntly 1 Dundee U 3
Feb 18 Kilmarnock 4 East Fife 0
Feb 18 Stenhousemuir 2 Aberdeen 0

5th Round
Mar 10 Celtic 1 Kilmarnock 0
Mar 12 Hearts 2 Dundee U 1
Mar 11 Raith 1 Airdrie 4
Mar 11 Stenhousemuir 0 Hibernian 4

Semi-finals
Apr 8 Airdrie 1 Hearts 0
Apr 7 Celtic 0 Hibernian 0

Replay
Apr 11 Celtic 3 Hibernian 1

Final
May27 Airdrie 0 Celtic 1
played at Hampden Park

Season 1995-96

1st Round
Dec 16 Albion 0 Deveronvale 2
Dec 16 Glasgow U 0 Spartans 1
Dec 12 Stenhousemuir 2 Arbroath 2
Dec 09 Stranraer 0 Livingston 3

Replay
Dec 18 Arbroath 0 Stenhousemuir 1

2nd Round
Jan 06 Ayr 0 Ross Co 2
Jan 06 Berwick 3 Annan 1
Jan 06 Caledonian 3 Livingston 2
Jan 06 Clyde 2 Brechin 2
Jan 06 Deveronvale 0 Keith 0
Jan 07 E Stirling 0 Stenhousemuir 1
Jan 06 Forfar 3 Lossiemouth 1
Jan 06 Montrose 2 Cowdenbeath 1
Jan 06 Queen Of South 2 Queen's Park 4
Jan 06 Spartans 0 East Fife 0
Jan 06 Stirling A 3 Alloa 1
Jan 06 Whitehill 2 Fraserburgh 2

Replays
Jan 13 Annan 1 Berwick 2
Jan 13 Fraserburgh 1 Whitehill 2
Jan 13 Keith 2 Deveronvale 0
Jan 14 East Fife 2 Spartans 1
Jan 15 Brechin 1 Clyde 3

3rd Round
Feb 14 Berwick 1 Dundee U 2
Jan 27 Caledonian 1 East Fife 1
Jan 31 Clyde 3 Dundee 1
Jan 30 Clydebank 0 Stirling A 1
Jan 30 Dumbarton 1 Airdrie 3
Feb 12 Dunfermline 3 St Mirren 0
Jan 30 Falkirk 0 Stenhousemuir 2
Jan 31 Hamilton 0 St Johnstone 1
Jan 31 Hearts 1 Partick 0
Jan 27 Hibernian 0 Kilmarnock 2
Jan 27 Keith 1 Rangers 10
Feb 13 Morton 1 Montrose 1
Jan 30 Motherwell 0 Aberdeen 2
Jan 27 Raith 3 Queen's Park 0
Jan 27 Ross 0 Forfar 3
Jan 28 Whitehill 0 Celtic 3

Replays
Feb 12 East Fife 1 Caledonian 1
Penalties 1-3
Feb 14 Montrose 3 Morton 2

4th Round
Feb 17 Airdrie 2 Forfar 2
Feb 17 Celtic 2 Raith 0
Feb 15 Clyde 1 Rangers 4
Feb 17 Dundee U 1 Dunfermline 0
Feb 17 Kilmarnock 1 Hearts 2
Feb 17 St Johnstone 3 Montrose 0
Feb 17 Stenhousemuir 0 Caledonian 1
Feb 17 Stirling A 0 Aberdeen 2

Replay
Feb 27 Forfar 0 Airdrie 0
Penalties 2-4

5th Round
Mar 09 Aberdeen 2 Airdrie 1
Mar 09 Caledonian 0 Rangers 3
Mar 10 Celtic 2 Dundee U 1
Mar 07 St Johnstone 1 Hearts 2

Semi-finals
Apr 06 Aberdeen 1 Hearts 2
played at Hampden Park
Apr 07 Celtic 1 Rangers 2
played at Hampden Park

Final
May 18 Hearts 1 Rangers 5
played at Hampden Park

Season 1996-97

1st Round
Dec 14 Albion 0 Forfar 0
Dec 07 Alloa 3 Hawick 1
Dec 07 Elgin 0 Whitehill 3
Dec 14 Huntly 1 Clyde 1

Replay
Dec 16 Clyde 3 Huntly 2
Dec 16 Forfar 4 Albion 0

2nd Round
Jan 07 Ayr 0 Clyde 2
Jan 04 Berwick 2 Peterhead 1
Jan 13 Brechin 2 Livingston 1
Jan 13 Cowdenbeath 1 Dumbarton 0
Jan 11 E Stirling 4 Brora 3
Jan 13 Forfar 0 Alloa 1
Jan 04 Queen's Park 2 Gala Fairydean 1
Jan 13 Ross 3 Montrose 0
Jan 11 Spartans 0 Arbroath 0
Jan 13 Stenhousemuir 1 Hamilton 2
Jan 13 Stranraer 1 Inverness 1
Jan 11 Whitehill 2 Queen Of South 3

Replays
Jan 13 Arbroath 3 Spartans 0
Jan 15 Inverness 0 Stranraer 0
Penalties 4-3

3rd Round
Jan 27 Airdrie 1 Raith 4
Jan 25 Arbroath 2 Morton 2
Feb 04 Brechin 3 Alloa 0
Jan 25 Clyde 3 St Mirren 1
Jan 26 Clydebank 0 Celtic 5
Jan 25 Dundee 3 Queen Of South 1
Jan 25 Dunfermline 4 Ross 0
Jan 25 Falkirk 1 Berwick 1
Jan 25 Hearts 5 Cowdenbeath 0
Jan 23 Hibernian 2 Aberdeen 2
Jan 25 Inverness 1 Hamilton 3
Jan 25 Kilmarnock 2 E Stirling 0
Jan 25 Partick 0 Motherwell 2
Jan 25 Queen's Park 1 East Fife 3
Jan 25 Rangers 2 St Johnstone 0
Jan 25 Stirling A 0 Dundee U 2

Replays
Jan 28 Aberdeen 0 Hibernian 0
Penalties 3-5
Jan 28 Morton 4 Arbroath 0
Feb 04 Berwick 1 Falkirk 2

4th Round
Feb 15 Brechin 1 Raith 2
Feb 15 Clyde 0 Kilmarnock 1
Feb 15 Falkirk 2 Dunfermline 1

Date	Home		Away	
Feb 16	Hearts	1	Dundee U	1
Feb 17	Hibernian	1	Celtic	1
Feb 15	Morton	2	Dundee	2
Feb 15	Motherwell	1	Hamilton	1
Feb 15	Rangers	3	East Fife	0

Replays

Date	Home		Away	
Feb 18	Dundee	0	Morton	1
Feb 25	Dundee U	1	Hearts	0
Feb 26	Celtic	2	Hibernian	0
Feb 26	Hamilton	0	Motherwell	2

5th Round

Date	Home		Away	
Mar 06	Celtic	2	Rangers	0
Mar 08	Dundee U	4	Motherwell	1
Mar 08	Falkirk	2	Raith	0
Mar 08	Morton	2	Kilmarnock	5

Semi-finals

Date	Home		Away	
Apr 12	Celtic	1	Falkirk	1
Apr 14	Dundee U	0	Kilmarnock	0
	played at Easter Road			

Replays

Date	Home		Away	
Apr 23	Celtic	0	Falkirk	1
	played at Ibrox			
Apr 22	Dundee U	0	Kilmarnock	1
	played at Easter Road			

Final

Date	Home		Away	
May 24	Falkirk	0	Kilmarnock	1
	played at Hampden Park			

Season 1997-98

1st Round

Date	Home		Away	
Dec 06	Cowdenbeath	0	Montrose	0
Dec 06	East Fife	2	Stranraer	3
Dec 13	Fraserburgh	1	Clyde	0
Dec 06	Inverness	3	Whitehill	1

Replay

Date	Home		Away	
Dec 09	Montrose	2	Cowdenbeath	1

2nd Round

Date	Home		Away	
Jan 03	Annan	3	Vale Of Leithen	1
Jan 06	Arbroath	1	Queen Of South	1
Jan 12	Clydebank	6	Montrose	0
Jan 10	E Stirling	1	Edinburgh	1
Jan 03	Forfar	1	Albion	2
Jan 03	Inverness	2	Queen's Park	0
Jan 07	Livingston	2	Berwick	1
Jan 03	Lossiemouth	0	Dumbarton	1
Jan 03	Peterhead	0	Alloa	2
Jan 03	Ross	3	Brechin	1
Jan 10	Stenhousemuir	4	Deveronvale	0
Jan 10	Stranraer	2	Fraserburgh	1

Replays

Date	Home		Away	
Jan 12	Edinburgh	0	E Stirling	0
	Penalties 4-3			
Jan 12	Queen Of South	4	Arbroath	0

3rd Round

Date	Home		Away	
Jan 24	Airdrie	2	Ross	2
Jan 24	Alloa	0	Ayr	3
Jan 24	Celtic	2	Morton	0
Jan 24	Dumbarton	1	Motherwell	1
Jan 25	Dundee	4	St Mirren	2
Jan 24	Dundee U	1	Aberdeen	0
Jan 24	Dunfermline	7	Edinburgh	2
Jan 24	Hamilton	1	Rangers	2
Jan 24	Hearts	2	Clydebank	0
Jan 24	Hibernian	1	Raith	2
Jan 24	Inverness	8	Annan	1
Jan 24	Livingston	3	Albion	3
Jan 24	Queen Of South	1	Stirling A	3
Jan 24	St Johnstone	1	Partick	0
Jan 24	Stenhousemuir	1	Falkirk	3
Jan 24	Stranraer	0	Kilmarnock	2

Replays

Date	Home		Away	
Jan 27	Motherwell	1	Dumbarton	0
Feb 02	Albion	0	Livingston	0
	Penalties 6-5			
Feb 03	Ross	1	Airdrie	0

4th Round

Date	Home		Away	
Feb 14	Ayr	2	Kilmarnock	0
Feb 14	Dundee U	1	Inverness	1
Feb 16	Dunfermline	1	Celtic	2
Feb 14	Hearts	3	Albion	0
Feb 14	Motherwell	2	Rangers	2
Feb 14	Raith	1	Falkirk	2
Feb 14	Ross	1	Dundee	1
Feb 14	St Johnstone	3	Stirling A	1

Replays

Date	Home		Away	
Feb 17	Dundee	3	Ross	0
Feb 17	Rangers	3	Motherwell	0
Feb 18	Inverness	2	Dundee U	3

5th Round

Date	Home		Away	
Mar 08	Dundee U	2	Celtic	3
Mar 07	Falkirk	3	St Johnstone	0
Mar 07	Hearts	4	Ayr	1
Mar 09	Rangers	0	Dundee	0

Replay

Date	Home		Away	
Mar 18	Dundee	1	Rangers	2

Semi-finals

Date	Home		Away	
Apr 05	Celtic	1	Rangers	2
	played at Celtic Park			
Apr 04	Falkirk	1	Hearts	3
	played at Ibrox			

Final

Date	Home		Away	
May 16	Hearts	2	Rangers	1
	played at Celtic Park			

Season 1998-99

1st Round

Date	Home		Away	
Dec 05	Arbroath	1	Partick	2
Dec 05	Dumbarton	1	Livingston	1
Dec 05	Queen's Park	2	Berwick	0
Dec 05	Stenhousemuir	1	Alloa	1

Replays

Date	Home		Away	
Dec 08	Livingston	3	Dumbarton	0
Dec 12	Alloa	0	Stenhousemuir	2

2nd Round

Date	Home		Away	
Jan 02	Civil Service	0	Albion	3
Jan 02	Dalbeattie	1	E Stirling	2
Jan 02	Forfar	2	East Fife	2
Jan 02	Huntly	3	Peterhead	0
Jan 02	Inverness	1	Livingston	2
Jan 02	Keith	0	Brechin	0
Jan 02	Montrose	0	Stirling A	0
Jan 02	Partick	5	Cowdenbeath	2
Jan 09	Queen Of South	1	Ross	3
Jan 18	Queen's Park	1	Clachnacuddin	1
Jan 02	Spartans	1	Clyde	1
Jan 02	Whitehill	1	Stenhousemuir	1

Replays

Date	Home		Away	
Jan 06	Clyde	5	Spartans	0
Jan 09	Brechin	3	Keith	1
Jan 09	East Fife	0	Forfar	1
Jan 09	Stenhousemuir	2	Whitehill	0
Jan 18	Stirling A	2	Montrose	1
Jan 23	Clachnacuddin	2	Queen's Park	3

3rd Round

Date	Home		Away	
Jan 23	Aberdeen	0	Livingston	1
Jan 23	Ayr	3	Kilmarnock	0
Jan 23	Brechin	1	Albion	1
Jan 23	Celtic	3	Airdrie	1
Feb 03	Clydebank	1	Ross	1
Jan 23	Falkirk	3	Huntly	0
Jan 23	Hibernian	1	Stirling A	1
Jan 23	Morton	2	Dundee	1
Jan 24	Motherwell	3	Hearts	1
Jan 23	Partick	1	Dunfermline	2
Feb 02	Queen's Park	0	Dundee U	0
Jan 23	Raith	0	Clyde	4
Jan 23	Rangers	2	Stenhousemuir	0
Jan 23	St Johnstone	1	Forfar	0
Jan 23	St Mirren	1	Hamilton	1
Jan 23	Stranraer	1	E Stirling	0

Replays

Date	Home		Away	
Feb 02	Albion	3	Brechin	1
Feb 02	Hamilton	1	St Mirren	0
Feb 02	Stirling A	2	Hibernian	1
Feb 09	Dundee U	1	Queen's Park	0
Feb 15	Ross	2	Clydebank	3

4th Round

Date	Home		Away	
Feb 13	Ayr	1	Albion	0
Feb 13	Celtic	4	Dunfermline	0
Mar 03	Clydebank	2	Dundee U	2
Feb 14	Hamilton	0	Rangers	6
Feb 13	Livingston	1	St Johnstone	3
Feb 14	Morton	6	Clyde	1
Feb 13	Motherwell	2	Stirling A	0
Feb 13	Stranraer	1	Falkirk	2

Replay

Date	Home		Away	
Mar 06	Dundee U	3	Clydebank	0

5th Round

Date	Home		Away	
Mar 13	Ayr	0	Dundee U	0
Mar 08	Morton	0	Celtic	3
Mar 06	Motherwell	0	St Johnstone	2
Mar 07	Rangers	2	Falkirk	1

Replay

Date	Home		Away	
Mar 16	Dundee U	2	Ayr	1

Semi-finals

Date	Home		Away	
Apr 10	Celtic	2	Dundee U	0
Apr 11	Rangers	4	St Johnstone	0

Final

Date	Home		Away	
May 29	Celtic	0	Rangers	1
	played at Hampden Park			

Season 1999-2000

1st Round

Date	Home		Away	
Dec 11	Hamilton	1	Clyde	2
Dec 11	Huntly	0	E Stirling	1
Dec 11	Ross	2	Forfar	2
Dec 27	Threave	1	Stenhousemuir	7

Replay

Date	Home		Away	
Jan 03	Forfar	0	Ross	0
	Penalties 4-2			

2nd Round

Date	Home		Away	
Jan 08	Albion	0	Dalbeattie	0
Jan 08	Arbroath	0	Fraserburgh	0
Jan 08	Brechin	2	Annan	2
Jan 08	Cowdenbeath	2	Clyde	3
Jan 08	Dumbarton	0	Stenhousemuir	2
Jan 08	Montrose	1	Queen of South	3
Jan 08	Partick	2	E Stirling	1
Jan 08	Peterhead	2	Forfar	1
Jan 08	Queen's Park	1	Berwick	2
Jan 08	Stirling A	2	East Fife	1
Jan 08	Stranraer	1	Clachnacuddin	0
Jan 08	Whitehill	2	Alloa	2

Replays

Date	Home		Away	
Jan 15	Annan	2	Brechin	3
Jan 15	Fraserburgh	1	Arbroath	3
Jan 19	Dalbeattie	1	Albion	5
Jan 29	Alloa	2	Whitehill	0

3rd Round

Date	Home		Away	
Jan 29	Albion	1	Partick	2
Feb 01	Arbroath	1	Motherwell	1
Feb 08	Celtic	1	Inverness	3
Jan 29	Clyde	3	Raith	1
Jan 29	Clydebank	1	Stirling A	0
Jan 29	Dundee	0	Ayr	0
Jan 30	Dundee U	4	Airdrie	1
Jan 29	Falkirk	3	Peterhead	1
Jan 29	Hearts	3	Stenhousemuir	2
Jan 29	Hibernian	4	Dunfermline	1
Feb 05	Kilmarnock	0	Alloa	0
Jan 30	Morton	1	Brechin	1
Jan 29	Queen of South	0	Livingston	7
Jan 30	St Johnstone	0	Rangers	2
Jan 29	St Mirren	1	Aberdeen	1
Jan 29	Stranraer	1	Berwick	2

Replays

Date	Home		Away	
Feb 08	Aberdeen	2	St Mirren	0
Feb 15	Ayr	1	Dundee	1
	Penalties 7-6			
Feb 08	Brechin	0	Morton	0
	Penalties 3-4			
Feb 09	Alloa	1	Kilmarnock	0
Feb 19	Motherwell	2	Arbroath	0

4th Round

Date	Home		Away	
Feb 19	Alloa	2	Dundee U	2
Feb 19	Berwick	0	Falkirk	0
Feb 19	Clyde	0	Hearts	2
Feb 19	Hibernian	1	Clydebank	1
Feb 20	Inverness	1	Aberdeen	1
Feb 19	Morton	0	Rangers	1
Feb 26	Motherwell	3	Ayr	4
Feb 19	Partick	2	Livingston	1

Replays

Date	Home		Away	
Feb 22	Dundee U	4	Alloa	0
Feb 29	Aberdeen	1	Inverness	0
Feb 29	Clydebank	0	Hibernian	3
Feb 29	Falkirk	3	Berwick	0

5th Round

Date	Home		Away	
Mar11	Ayr	2	Partick	0
Mar12	Dundee U	0	Aberdeen	1
Mar11	Hibernian	3	Falkirk	1
Mar12	Rangers	4	Hearts	1

Semi Finals

Date	Home		Away	
Apr 08	Ayr	0	Rangers	7
Apr 09	Hibernian	1	Aberdeen	2

Final

Date	Home		Away	
May 27	Aberdeen	0	Rangers	4

SCOTTISH LEAGUE CUP RESULTS 1946-2000

SEASON 1946-47

DIV 1 SECTION A

	Clyde	Hearts	Kilmarnock	Partick T
Clyde		Sep 21 1-2	Oct05 3-2	Oct19 3-1
Hearts	Oct12 2-1		Sep28 3-1	Oct26 1-1
Kilmarnock	Oct26 1-2	Oct19 2-0		Sep21 3-2
Partick T	Sep28 2-2	Oct05 4-4	Oct12 1-3	

DIV 1 SECTION B

	Morton	Queen's Park	Rangers	St Mirren
Morton		Sep21 2-1	Oct26 0-2	Oct19 6-1
Queen's Park	Oct12 0-6		Sep28 2-4	Oct05 2-2
Rangers	Oct05 3-0	Oct19 1-0		Sep21 4-0
St Mirren	Sep28 2-3	Oct26 2-0	Oct12 0-4	

DIV 1 SECTION C

	Celtic	Hamilton A	Hibernian	T Lanark
Celtic		Oct26 3-1	Oct12 1-1	Sep28 0-0
Hamilton A	Oct05 2-2		Sep28 3-6	Oct12 3-0
Hibernian	Sep21 4-2	Oct19 2-0		Oct05 1-2
T Lanark	Oct19 2-3	Sep21 3-5	Oct26 1-2	

DIV 1 SECTION D

	Aberdeen	Falkirk	Motherwell	Queen of South
Aberdeen		Sep21 4-3	Oct05 2-3	Oct19 1-0
Falkirk	Oct12 0-1		Sep28 1-1	Oct26 2-1
Motherwell	Oct26 3-0	Oct19 5-3		Sep21 0-1
Queen of South	Sep28 2-5	Oct05 0-2	Oct12 4-3	

DIV 2 SECTION A

	Alloa A	Dunfermline A	East Fife	St Johnstone
Alloa		Oct26 2-1	Oct19 0-2	Sep21 0-0
Dunfermline A	Oct05 3-1		Sep21 0-2	Oct19 3-2
East Fife	Sep28 6-0	Oct12 7-0		Oct26 3-0
St Johnstone	Oct12 1-0	Sep28 6-2	Oct05 0-2	

DIV 2 SECTION B

	Dundee	Raith R	Stenhousemuir
Dundee		Oct12 3-1	Sep28 4-0
Raith R	Sep21 0-2		Oct26 2-4
Stenhousemuir	Oct19 0-4	Oct05 1-2	

DIV 2 SECTION C

	Arbroath	Cowdenbeath	Dumbarton	Dundee U
Arbroath		Oct19 3-3	Sep21 4-1	Oct05 1-3
Cowdenbeath	Sep28 5-2		Oct26 2-3	Oct12 4-1
Dumbarton	Oct12 8-0	Oct05 0-4		Sep28 0-3
Dundee U	Oct26 3-2	Sep21 2-0	Oct19 2-1	

DIV 2 SECTION D

	Airdrie	Albion R	Ayr U
Airdrie		Sep28 6-1	Oct26 3-0
Albion R	Oct19 1-5		Sep21 5-4
Ayr U	Oct05 2-1	Oct12 4-3	

DIV 1 Section A	P	W	D	L	F	A	Pts
Hearts	6	3	2	1	12	10	8
Clyde	6	3	1	2	12	10	7
Kilmarnock	6	3	0	3	12	11	6
Partick T	6	0	3	3	11	16	3

DIV 1 Section B	P	W	D	L	F	A	Pts
Rangers	6	6	0	0	18	2	12
Morton	6	4	0	2	17	9	8
St Mirren	6	1	1	4	7	19	3
Queen's Park	6	0	1	5	5	17	1

DIV 1 Section C	P	W	D	L	F	A	Pts
Hibernian	6	4	1	1	16	9	9
Celtic	6	2	3	1	11	10	7
Hamilton A	6	2	1	3	14	16	5
T Lanark	6	1	1	4	8	14	3

DIV 1 Section D	P	W	D	L	F	A	Pts
Aberdeen	6	4	0	2	13	11	8
Motherwell	6	3	1	2	15	11	7
Falkirk	6	2	1	3	11	12	5
Queen of South	6	2	0	4	8	13	4

DIV 2 Section A	P	W	D	L	F	A	Pts
East Fife	6	6	0	0	22	0	12
St Johnstone	6	2	1	3	9	10	5
Dunfermline A	6	2	0	4	9	20	4
Alloa	6	1	1	4	3	13	3

DIV 2 Section B	P	W	D	L	F	A	Pts
Dundee	4	4	0	0	13	1	8
Raith R	4	1	0	3	5	10	2
Stenhousemuir	4	1	0	3	5	12	2

DIV 2 Section C	P	W	D	L	F	A	Pts
Dundee U	6	5	0	1	14	8	10
Cowdenbeath	6	3	1	2	18	11	7
Dumbarton	6	2	0	4	13	15	4
Arbroath	6	1	1	4	12	23	3

DIV 2 Section D	P	W	D	L	F	A	Pts
Airdrie	4	3	0	1	15	4	6
Ayr U	4	2	0	2	10	12	4
Albion R	4	1	0	3	10	19	2

Quarter-finals

Mar 1 Airdrie ....4 Hibernian 4
Mar 5 Hibernian ....1 Airdrie ....0 Agg 5-4
Mar 1 Dundee ....0 Aberdeen 1
Mar 5 Aberdeen ....3 Dundee ....2 Agg 4-2
Mar 1 Hearts ....0 East Fife 1
Mar 5 East Fife ....2 Hearts ....5 Agg 3-5
Mar 1 Rangers ....2 Dundee U 1
Mar 5 Dundee U ....1 Rangers ....1 Agg 2-3

Semi-finals

Mar 22 Aberdeen ....6 Hearts 2
played at Easter Road
Mar 22 Hibernian ....1 Rangers 3
played at Hampden Park

Final

Apr 5 Aberdeen ....0 Rangers 4
played at Hampden Park

SEASON 1947-48

DIV 1 SECTION A

	Aberdeen	Motherwell	Queen of South	ST Mirren
Aberdeen		Aug16 2-0	Sep13 9-0	Aug30 2-0
Motherwell	Sep06 2-0		Aug09 4-0	Aug23 3-1
Queen of South	Aug23 1-2	Aug30 0-1		Aug16 8-1
St Mirren	Aug09 0-1	Sep13 0-3	Sep06 7-1	

DIV 1 SECTION B

	Falkirk	Morton	Partick T	Queen's Park
Falkirk		Sep06 5-0	Aug09 5-6	Sep13 4-1
Morton	Aug16 1-2		Aug23 2-1	Aug30 3-1
Partick T	Aug30 3-3	Sep13 4-1		Aug16 3-1
Queen's Park	Aug23 0-4	Aug09 4-1	Sep06 4-3	

DIV 1 SECTION C

	Celtic	Dundee	Rangers	T Lanark
Celtic		Aug16 1-1	Aug30 2-0	Aug23 3-1
Dundee	Sep06 4-1		Sep13 1-1	Aug09 5-0
Rangers	Aug09 2-0	Aug23 3-0		Sep06 3-0
T Lanark	Sep13 3-2	Aug30 5-1	Aug16 1-3	

DIV 1 SECTION D

	Airdrie	Clyde	Hearts	Hibernian
Airdrie		Aug30 3-1	Aug16 3-2	Aug23 1-1
Clyde	Aug09 4-2		Sep13 5-2	Sep06 3-4
Hearts	Sep06 1-0	Aug23 1-0		Aug09 2-1
Hibernian	Sep13 5-0	Aug16 5-1	Aug30 1-2	

DIV 2 SECTION A

	Alloa A	Dunfermline A	Hamilton A	Raith R
Alloa		Sep13 1-1	Aug09 1-2	Sep06 1-2
Dunfermline A	Aug23 1-0		Sep06 1-3	Aug09 0-2
Hamilton A	Aug30 9-0	Aug16 3-2		Sep13 6-1
Raith R	Aug16 4-2	Aug30 6-1	Aug23 3-1	

DIV 2 SECTION B

	Albion R	Cowdenbeath	Dundee U	Leith A
Albion R		Sep06 4-1	Aug09 3-0	Sep13 1-1
Cowdenbeath	Aug16 2-3		Sep13 1-0	Aug30 0-1
Dundee U	Aug30 2-1	Aug23 0-2		Aug16 2-2
Leith A	Aug23 2-2	Aug09 2-1	Sep06 3-1	

DIV 2 SECTION C	Arbroath	Dumbarton	St Johnstone	Stenhousemuir
Arbroath		Aug16 1-3	Aug30 1-2	Sep13 5-1
Dumbarton	Sep06 4-2		Sep13 1-6	Aug09 5-5
St Johnstone	Aug09 5-1	Aug23 1-0		Sep06 0-1
Stenhousemuir	Aug23 2-0	Aug30 2-1	Aug16 3-2	

DIV 2 SECTION D	Ayr U	East Fife	Kilmarnock	Stirling A
Ayr U		Aug23 2-5	Aug09 2-2	Sep06 3-2
East Fife	Sep13 5-0		Sep06 1-3	Aug09 3-2
Kilmarnock	Aug30 1-2	Aug16 0-0		Sep13 3-2
Stirling A	Aug16 1-5	Aug30 2-5	Aug23 5-3	

DIV 1 Section A	P	W	D	L	F	A	Pts
Aberdeen	6	5	0	1	16	3	10
Motherwell	6	5	0	1	13	3	10
St Mirren	6	1	0	5	9	18	2
Queen of South	6	1	0	5	10	24	2

DIV 1 Section B	P	W	D	L	F	A	Pts
Falkirk	6	4	1	1	23	11	9
Partick T	6	3	1	2	20	16	7
Queen's Park	6	2	0	4	11	18	4
Morton	6	2	0	4	8	17	4

DIV 1 Section C	P	W	D	L	F	A	Pts
Rangers	6	4	1	1	12	4	9
Dundee	6	2	2	2	12	11	6
Celtic	6	2	1	3	9	11	5
T Lanark	6	2	0	4	10	17	4

DIV 1 Section D	P	W	D	L	F	A	Pts
Hearts	6	4	0	2	10	10	8
Hibernian	6	3	1	2	17	9	7
Airdrie	6	2	1	3	9	14	5
Clyde	6	2	0	4	14	17	4

DIV 2 Section A	P	W	D	L	F	A	Pts
Hamilton A	6	5	0	1	24	8	10
Raith R	6	5	0	1	18	11	10
Dunfermline A	6	1	1	4	6	15	3
Alloa	6	0	1	5	5	19	1

DIV 2 Section B	P	W	D	L	F	A	Pts
Leith A	6	3	3	0	11	7	9
Albion R	6	3	2	1	14	8	8
Cowdenbeath	6	2	0	4	7	10	4
Dundee U	6	1	1	4	5	12	3

DIV 2 Section C	P	W	D	L	F	A	Pts
Stenhousemuir	6	4	1	1	14	13	9
St Johnstone	6	4	0	2	16	7	8
Dumbarton	6	2	1	3	14	17	5
Arbroath	6	1	0	5	10	17	2

DIV 2 Section D	P	W	D	L	F	A	Pts
East Fife	6	4	1	1	19	9	9
Ayr U	6	3	1	2	14	16	7
Kilmarnock	6	2	2	2	12	12	6
Stirling A	6	1	0	5	14	22	2

Quarter-finals

Sep 27 Aberdeen . . . . .8 Leith A 2
Sep 27 Falkirk . . . . .3 Hamilton A 1
Sep 27 Hearts . . . . .3 East Fife 4
Sep 27 Rangers . . . . .2 Stenhousemuir . . .0

Semi-finals

Oct 11 Aberdeen . . . . .0 East Fife 1
played at Dens Park
Oct 11 Falkirk . . . . .1 Rangers 0
played at Hampden Park

Final

Oct 25 East Fife . . . . .0 Falkirk 0
played at Hampden Park

Replay

Nov 1 East Fife . . . . .4 Falkirk 1
played at Hampden Park

Season 1948-49

DIV 1 SECTION A	Celtic	Clyde	Hibernian	Rangers
Celtic		Oct09 3-6	Sep11 1-0	Sep25 3-1
Clyde	Sep18 0-2		Oct16 1-4	Oct02 1-3
Hibernian	Oct02 4-2	Sep25 4-0		Sep18 0-0
Rangers	Oct16 2-1	Sep11 1-1	Oct09 1-0	

DIV 1 SECTION B	Albion R	Dundee	Falkirk	Motherwell
Albion R		Oct02 2-3	Oct16 2-1	Sep18 0-1
Dundee	Sep11 2-1		Oct09 4-2	Oct16 0-1
Falkirk	Sep25 2-1	Sep18 2-3		Oct02 1-0
Motherwell	Oct09 8-3	Sep25 0-1	Sep11 1-0	

DIV 1 SECTION C	East Fife	Hearts	Partick T	Queen of South
East Fife		Sep18 4-0	Oct16 3-0	Oct02 3-1
Hearts	Oct09 6-1		Sep11 2-2	Oct16 4-0
Partick T	Sep25 2-5	Oct02 3-1		Sep18 9-0
Queen of South	Sep11 0-4	Sep25 2-3	Oct09 3-2	

DIV 1 SECTION D	Aberdeen	Morton	St Mirren	T Lanark
Aberdeen		Sep25 3-1	Sep11 3-1	Oct09 2-4
Morton	Oct16 3-1		Oct09 0-3	Sep11 2-1
St Mirren	Oct02 1-1	Sep18 1-1		Sep25 4-0
T Lanark	Sep18 1-1	Oct02 2-2	Oct16 4-2	

DIV 2 SECTION A	Cowdenbeath	Dunfermline A	Raith R	Stirling A
Cowdenbeath		Sep18 0-2	Oct02 0-6	Sep25 3-3
Dunfermline A	Oct09 3-2		Oct16 1-0	Sep11 1-1
Raith R	Sep11 3-3	Sep25 2-1		Oct09 6-2
Stirling A	Oct16 5-2	Oct02 4-3	Sep18 1-7	

DIV 2 SECTION B	Alloa	E Stirling	Kilmarnock	Queen's Park
Alloa		Sep18 1-0	Oct16 2-0	Oct02 1-0
E Stirling	Oct09 1-3		Sep11 2-1	Oct16 1-1
Kilmarnock	Sep25 4-3	Oct02 4-1		Sep18 3-3
Queen's Park	Sep11 4-1	Sep25 2-0	Oct09 2-2	

DIV 2 SECTION C	Dundee U	Hamilton A	St Johnstone	Stenhousemuir
Dundee U		Sep25 1-2	Oct02 4-2	Sep18 4-2
Hamilton A	Oct16 6-3		Sep18 2-2	Oct02 3-0
St Johnstone	Sep11 1-1	Oct09 0-0		Sep25 2-1
Stenhousemuir	Oct09 2-1	Sep11 1-1	Oct16 3-4	

DIV 2 SECTION D	Airdrie	Arbroath	Ayr U	Dumbarton
Airdrie		Oct09 3-2	Sep25 6-1	Sep11 8-1
Arbroath	Sep18 2-3		Oct02 1-1	Sep25 4-2
Ayr U	Oct16 1-4	Sep11 4-2		Oct09 2-1
Dumbarton	Oct02 0-5	Oct16 1-1	Sep18 1-2	

DIV 1 Section A	P	W	D	L	F	A	Pts
Rangers	6	3	2	1	8	6	8
Hibernian	6	3	1	2	12	5	7
Celtic	6	3	0	3	12	13	6
Clyde	6	1	1	4	9	17	3

DIV 1 Section B	P	W	D	L	F	A	Pts
Dundee	6	5	0	1	13	8	10
Motherwell	6	4	0	2	11	5	8
Falkirk	6	2	0	4	8	11	4
Albion R	6	1	0	5	9	17	2

DIV 1 Section C	P	W	D	L	F	A	Pts
East Fife	6	5	0	1	20	9	10
Hearts	6	3	1	2	16	12	7
Partick T	6	2	1	3	18	14	5
Queen of South	6	1	0	5	6	25	2

DIV 1 Section D	P	W	D	L	F	A	Pts
St Mirren	6	2	2	2	12	9	6
Aberdeen	6	2	2	2	11	11	6
T Lanark	6	2	2	2	12	13	6
Morton	6	2	2	2	9	11	6

DIV 2 Section A	P	W	D	L	F	A	Pts
Raith R	6	4	1	1	24	8	9
Dunfermline A	6	3	1	2	11	9	7
Stirling A	6	2	2	2	16	22	6
Cowdenbeath	6	0	2	4	10	22	2

DIV 2 Section B	P	W	D	L	F	A	Pts
Alloa	6	4	0	2	11	9	8
Queen's Park	6	2	3	1	12	8	7
Kilmarnock	6	2	2	2	14	13	6
E Stirling	6	1	1	4	5	12	3

DIV 2 Section C	P	W	D	L	F	A	Pts
Hamilton A	6	3	3	0	14	7	9
St Johnstone	6	2	3	1	11	11	7
Dundee U	6	2	1	3	14	15	5
Stenhousemuir	6	1	1	4	9	15	3

DIV 2 Section D	P	W	D	L	F	A	Pts
Airdrie	6	6	0	0	29	7	12
Ayr U	6	3	1	2	11	15	7
Arbroath	6	1	2	3	12	14	4
Dumbarton	6	0	1	5	6	22	1

Quarter-finals

Oct 30 Dundee . . . . .1 Alloa 1
Oct 30 Hamilton A . . . . .1 Airdrie 1
Oct 30 Raith R . . . . .5 East Fife 3
Oct 30 Rangers . . . . .1 St Mirren 0

Replays

Nov 3 Airdrie . . . . .1 Hamilton A 1
Nov 3 Alloa . . . . .1 Dundee 3
Nov 8 Airdrie . . . . .0 Hamilton A 1
played at Celtic Park

Semi-finals

Nov 20 Dundee . . . . .1 Rangers 4
played at Hampden Park
Nov 20 Hamilton A . . . . .0 Raith R 2
played at Celtic Park

Final

Mar 12 Raith R . . . . .0 Rangers 2
played at Hampden Park

Season 1949-50

DIV 1 SECTION A	Aberdeen	Celtic	Rangers	St Mirren
Aberdeen		Aug17 4-5	Sep03 1-1	Aug27 1-0
Celtic	Aug31 1-3		Aug13 3-2	Sep03 4-1
Rangers	Aug20 4-2	Aug27 2-0		Aug17 5-1
St Mirren	Aug13 3-1	Aug20 1-0	Aug30 1-1	

DIV 1 SECTION B	Falkirk	Hibernian	Queen of South	T Lanark
Falkirk		Aug27 2-1	Aug17 1-0	Aug20 1-2
Hibernian	Aug13 1-0		Sep03 5-3	Aug31 4-2
Queen of South	Aug31 0-0	Aug20 1-2		Aug13 2-4
T Lanark	Sep03 3-0	Aug17 0-2	Aug27 1-1	

DIV 1 SECTION C	Clyde	Dundee	Motherwell	Partick T
Clyde		Aug27 2-0	Aug20 2-2	Aug17 1-2
Dundee	Aug13 1-1		Aug31 0-1	Aug20 5-2
Motherwell	Sep03 1-1	Aug17 2-0		Aug27 1-1
Partick T	Aug31 3-1	Sep03 4-2	Aug13 2-0	

DIV 1 SECTION D	East Fife	Hearts	Raith R	Stirling A
East Fife		Sep03 4-3	Aug27 3-2	Aug17 3-1
Hearts	Aug20 1-1		Aug17 5-1	Aug27 4-5
Raith R	Aug13 0-3	Aug31 1-2		Aug20 6-2
Stirling A	Aug31 0-3	Aug13 1-5	Sep03 4-1	

DIV 2 SECTION A	Albion R	Forfar A	Hamilton A	Stenhousemuir
Albion R		Sep03 2-2	Aug17 1-0	Aug27 2-2
Forfar A	Aug20 3-2		Aug27 3-0	Aug17 2-2
Hamilton A	Aug31 1-1	Aug13 0-1		Aug20 0-0
Stenhousemuir	Aug13 0-1	Aug31 3-1	Sep03 3-0	

DIV 2 SECTION B	Airdrie	Arbroath	Dumbarton	Dundee U
Airdrie		Aug31 3-1	Aug20 2-2	Aug13 5-2
Arbroath	Aug17 1-2		Aug27 3-1	Aug20 2-4
Dumbarton	Sep03 0-4	Aug13 5-1		Aug31 3-1
Dundee U	Aug27 6-0	Sep03 4-1	Aug17 5-1	

DIV 2 SECTION C	Alloa	Ayr U	Cowdenbeath	Morton
Alloa		Aug17 2-2	Aug27 1-4	Aug20 0-4
Ayr U	Aug31 4-0		Aug20 2-2	Aug13 3-4
Cowdenbeath	Aug13 2-0	Sep03 2-0		Aug31 2-0
Morton	Sep03 7-1	Aug27 3-3	Aug17 1-0	

DIV 2 SECTION D	Dunfermline A	Kilmarnock	Queen's Park	St Johnstone
Dunfermline A		Aug20 5-1	Aug27 3-0	Aug17 1-2
Kilmarnock	Sep03 2-4		Aug17 2-0	Aug27 2-0
Queen's Park	Aug13 0-1	Aug31 3-1		Aug20 2-0
St Johnstone	Aug31 2-3	Aug13 3-2	Sep03 2-3	

DIV 1 Section A	P	W	D	L	F	A	Pts
Rangers	6	3	2	1	15	8	8
Celtic	6	3	0	3	13	13	6
Aberdeen	6	2	1	3	12	14	5
St Mirren	6	2	1	3	7	12	5

DIV 1 Section B	P	W	D	L	F	A	Pts
Hibernian	6	5	0	1	15	8	10
T Lanark	6	3	1	2	12	10	7
Falkirk	6	2	1	3	4	7	5
Queen of South	6	0	2	4	7	13	2

DIV 1 Section C	P	W	D	L	F	A	Pts
Partick T	6	4	1	1	14	10	9
Motherwell	6	2	3	1	7	6	7
Clyde	6	1	3	2	8	9	5
Dundee	6	1	1	4	8	12	3

DIV 1 Section D	P	W	D	L	F	A	Pts
East Fife	6	5	1	0	17	7	11
Hearts	6	3	1	2	20	13	7
Stirling A	6	2	0	4	13	22	4
Raith R	6	1	0	5	11	19	2

DIV 2 Section A	P	W	D	L	F	A	Pts
Forfar A	6	3	2	1	12	9	8
Stenhousemuir	6	2	3	1	10	6	7
Albion R	6	2	3	1	9	8	7
Hamilton A	6	0	2	4	1	9	2

DIV 2 Section B	P	W	D	L	F	A	Pts
Airdrie	6	4	1	1	16	12	9
Dundee U	6	4	0	2	22	12	8
Dumbarton	6	2	1	3	12	16	5
Arbroath	6	1	0	5	9	19	2

DIV 2 Section C	P	W	D	L	F	A	Pts
Cowdenbeath	6	4	1	1	12	4	9
Morton	6	4	1	1	19	9	9
Ayr U	6	1	3	2	14	13	5
Alloa	6	0	1	5	4	23	1

DIV 2 Section D	P	W	D	L	F	A	Pts
Dunfermline A	6	5	0	1	17	7	10
Queen's Park	6	3	0	3	8	9	6
St Johnstone	6	2	0	4	9	13	4
Kilmarnock	6	2	0	4	10	15	4

Quarter-finals

Sep 17 Airdrie . . . . .3 Dunfermline A 4
Sep 20 Dunfermline A . . . . .0 Airdrie . . . . .0 Agg 4-3
Sep 17 Forfar A . . . . .1 East Fife 3
Sep 21 East Fife . . . . .5 Forfar A . . . . .1 Agg 8-2
Sep 17 Partick T . . . . .4 Hibernian 2
Sep 21 Hibernian . . . . .4 Partick T . . . . . . .0 Agg 6-4
Sep 17 Rangers . . . . .2 Cowdenbeath 3
Sep 21 Cowdenbeath . . . . . .1 Rangers . . . . . . .3 Agg 4-5

Semi-finals

Oct 8 Dunfermline A . . . . .2 Hibernian 1
played at Tynecastle
Oct 8 East Fife . . . . .2 Rangers 1
played at Hampden Park

Final

Oct 29 Dunfermline A . . . . .0 East Fife 3
played at Hampden Park

Celtic in 1949-50, when they failed to qualify in their Section 'A' League Cup Group that included St Mirren, Aberdeen and Rangers. In the semi-final Rangers were to lose to East Fife, who collected the trophy that year. Rangers gained revenge later that season when they beat East Fife 3-0 in the SFA Cup. Rangers were also League champions for the second year running.

Season 1950-51

DIV 1 SECTION A	Celtic	East Fife	Raith R	T Lanark
Celtic		Aug12 2-0	Aug19 2-1	Aug30 3-1
East Fife	Aug26 1-1		Aug16 3-3	Aug19 2-5
Raith R	Sep02 2-2	Aug30 1-4		Aug12 3-2
T Lanark	Aug16 1-2	Sep02 3-3	Aug26 1-0	

DIV 1 SECTION B	Dundee	Falkirk	Hibernian	St Mirren
Dundee		Aug16 1-2	Aug26 0-2	Aug19 3-1
Falkirk	Aug30 1-2		Aug19 4-5	Aug12 1-1
Hibernian	Aug12 2-0	Sep02 4-0		Aug30 5-0
St Mirren	Sep02 3-1	Aug26 2-0	Aug15 0-6	

DIV 1 SECTION C	Airdrie	Hearts	Motherwell	Partick T
Airdrie		Sep02 1-3	Aug26 2-6	Aug16 2-3
Hearts	Aug19 3-2		Aug16 4-1	Aug26 2-0
Motherwell	Aug12 3-1	Aug30 3-2		Aug19 2-1
Partick T	Aug30 3-1	Aug12 1-1	Sep02 2-3	

DIV 1 SECTION D	Aberdeen	Clyde	Morton	Rangers
Aberdeen		Aug12 4-3	Sep02 6-1	Aug30 2-0
Clyde	Aug26 4-1		Aug16 3-3	Sep02 1-5
Morton	Aug19 0-2	Aug30 4-4		Aug12 1-2
Rangers	Aug16 1-2	Aug19 4-0	Aug26 6-1	

DIV 2 SECTION A	Ayr U	Dumbarton	Dunfermline A	Kilmarnock
Ayr U		Aug26 3-0	Aug19 1-0	Aug16 2-2
Dumbarton	Aug12 1-4		Aug30 1-1	Aug19 1-0
Dunfermline A	Sep02 2-5	Aug16 4-1		Aug26 5-4
Kilmarnock	Aug30 0-1	Sep02 0-0	Aug12 3-1	

DIV 2 SECTION B	Cowdenbeath	Dundee U	St Johnstone	Stenhousemuir
Cowdenbeath		Aug19 2-2	Aug12 0-2	Aug30 5-1
Dundee U	Sep02 4-1		Aug30 4-1	Aug12 2-1
St Johnstone	Aug26 2-2	Aug16 2-5		Aug19 6-2
Stenhousemuir	Aug16 2-2	Aug26 3-2	Sep02 1-2	

DIV 2 SECTION C	Hamilton A	Queen of South	Queen's Park	Stirling A
Hamilton A		Aug26 1-1	Aug16 2-1	Sep02 3-0
Queen of South	Aug12 3-2		Sep02 4-3	Aug30 2-2
Queen's Park	Aug30 3-1	Aug19 2-2		Aug12 1-0
Stirling A	Aug19 1-0	Aug16 1-3	Aug26 2-2	

DIV 2 SECTION D	Albion R	Alloa	Arbroath	Forfar A
Albion R		Aug19 1-3	Aug12 3-2	Aug30 1-2
Alloa	Sep02 2-2		Aug30 3-1	Aug12 6-0
Arbroath	Aug26 1-0	Aug16 1-1		Aug19 3-0
Forfar A	Aug16 0-2	Aug26 3-1	Sep02 4-1	

DIV 1 Section A	P	W	D	L	F	A	Pts
Celtic	6	4	2	0	12	6	10
T Lanark	6	2	1	3	13	13	5
East Fife	6	1	3	2	13	15	5
Raith R	6	1	2	3	10	14	4

DIV 1 Section B	P	W	D	L	F	A	Pts
Hibernian	6	6	0	0	24	4	12
St Mirren	6	2	1	3	7	16	5
Dundee	6	2	0	4	7	11	4
Falkirk	6	1	1	4	8	15	3

DIV 1 Section C	P	W	D	L	F	A	Pts
Motherwell	6	5	0	1	18	12	10
Hearts	6	4	1	1	15	8	9
Partick T	6	2	1	3	10	11	5
Airdrie	6	0	0	6	9	21	0

DIV 1 Section D	P	W	D	L	F	A	Pts
Aberdeen	6	5	0	1	17	9	10
Rangers	6	4	0	2	18	7	8
Clyde	6	1	2	3	15	21	4
Morton	6	0	2	4	10	23	2

DIV 2 Section A	P	W	D	L	F	A	Pts
Ayr U	6	5	1	0	16	5	11
Dunfermline A	6	2	1	3	13	15	5
Kilmarnock	6	1	2	3	9	10	4
Dumbarton	6	1	2	3	4	12	4

DIV 2 Section B	P	W	D	L	F	A	Pts
Dundee U	6	4	1	1	19	10	9
St Johnstone	6	3	1	2	15	14	7
Cowdenbeath	6	1	3	2	12	13	5
Stenhousemuir	6	1	1	4	10	19	3

DIV 2 Section C	P	W	D	L	F	A	Pts
Queen of South	6	3	3	0	15	11	9
Queen's Park	6	2	2	2	12	11	6
Hamilton A	6	2	1	3	9	9	5
Stirling A	6	1	2	3	6	11	4

DIV 2 Section D	P	W	D	L	F	A	Pts
Alloa	6	3	2	1	16	8	8
Forfar A	6	3	0	3	9	14	6
Albion R	6	2	1	3	9	10	5
Arbroath	6	2	1	3	9	11	5

Quarter-finals

Sep 16 Aberdeen ....4 Hibernian 1
Sep 20 Hibernian ....4 Aberdeen ....1 Agg 5-5
Sep 16 Ayr U ....3 Dundee U 0
Sep 20 Dundee U ....1 Ayr U ....2 Agg 1-5
Sep 16 Celtic ....1 Motherwell 4
Sep 20 Motherwell ....0 Celtic ....1 Agg 4-2
Sep 16 Queen of South ....1 Alloa 0
Sep 20 Alloa ....2 Queen of South ..2 Agg 2-3

Replays

Oct 2 Aberdeen ....1 Hibernian 1
played at Ibrox
Oct 3 Aberdeen ....1 Hibernian 5
played at Hampden Park

Semi-finals

Oct 7 Ayr U ....3 Motherwell 4
played at Ibrox
Oct 7 Hibernian ....3 Queen of South ..1
played at Tynecastle

Final

Oct 28 Hibernian ....0 Motherwell 3
played at Hampden Park

Season 1951-52

DIV 1 SECTION A	Airdrie	Celtic	Morton	T Lanark
Airdrie		Aug15 1-1	Aug25 1-3	Aug18 2-1
Celtic	Aug29 2-0		Aug18 2-0	Aug11 1-1
Morton	Aug11 2-1	Sep01 2-0		Aug29 5-2
T Lanark	Sep01 5-0	Aug25 0-1	Aug15 2-0	

DIV 1 SECTION B	Hibernian	Motherwell	Partick T	Stirling A
Hibernian		Aug15 0-4	Aug25 5-1	Aug18 4-2
Motherwell	Aug29 1-0		Sep01 3-2	Aug11 6-4
Partick T	Aug11 4-2	Aug18 0-0		Aug29 2-0
Stirling A	Sep01 1-1	Aug25 3-2	Aug15 0-1	

DIV 1 SECTION C	Dundee	Hearts	Raith R	St Mirren
Dundee		Aug15 2-1	Aug18 5-0	Aug25 0-1
Hearts	Aug29 5-2		Aug11 1-0	Sep01 3-1
Raith R	Sep01 1-3	Aug25 2-0		Aug15 3-2
St Mirren	Aug11 2-2	Aug18 5-5	Aug29 2-0	

DIV 1 SECTION D	Aberdeen	East Fife	Queen of South	Rangers
Aberdeen		Sep01 2-3	Aug11 5-4	Aug29 2-1
East Fife	Aug18 3-0		Aug29 1-0	Aug11 0-0
Queen of South	Aug25 2-0	Aug15 3-2		Aug18 0-3
Rangers	Aug15 2-1	Aug25 4-1	Sep01 5-2	

DIV 2 SECTION A	Cowdenbeath	Dundee U	Falkirk	Stenhousemuir
Cowdenbeath		Aug25 2-0	Aug15 0-5	Aug18 2-3
Dundee U	Aug11 1-1		Sep01 0-1	Aug29 4-2
Falkirk	Aug29 6-1	Aug18 3-0		Aug11 3-1
Stenhousemuir	Sep01 3-1	Aug15 1-1	Aug25 2-5	

DIV 2 SECTION B	Alloa	Dunfermline A	Hamilton A	Queen's Park
Alloa		Aug25 2-2	Sep01 1-2	Aug15 2-0
Dunfermline A	Aug11 4-1		Aug29 3-0	Sep01 2-1
Hamilton A	Aug18 0-1	Aug15 1-4		Aug25 2-3
Queen's Park	Aug29 2-1	Aug18 2-0	Aug11 1-2	

DIV 2 SECTION C

	Albion R	Arbroath	Clyde	St Johnstone
Albion R		Sep01 5-4	Aug29 0-2	Aug11 3-4
Arbroath	Aug18 0-1		Aug11 2-3	Aug29 2-2
Clyde	Aug15 4-0	Aug25 5-2		Sep01 0-1
St Johnstone	Aug25 0-1	Aug15 4-0	Aug18 3-2	

DIV 2 SECTION D

	Ayr U	Dumbarton	Forfar A	Kilmarnock
Ayr U		Aug15 5-0	Aug18 2-3	Aug25 1-2
Dumbarton	Aug29 1-3		Aug11 3-4	Aug18 1-0
Forfar A	Sep01 3-0	Aug25 1-1		Aug15 2-1
Kilmarnock	Aug11 3-0	Sep01 2-0	Aug29 1-0	

DIV 1 Section A	P	W	D	L	F	A	Pts
Celtic	6	3	2	1	7	4	8
Morton	6	4	0	2	12	8	8
T Lanark	6	2	1	3	11	9	5
Airdrie	6	1	1	4	5	14	3

DIV 1 Section B	P	W	D	L	F	A	Pts
Motherwell	6	4	1	1	16	9	9
Partick T	6	3	1	2	10	10	7
Hibernian	6	2	1	3	12	13	5
Stirling A	6	1	1	4	10	16	3

DIV 1 Section C	P	W	D	L	F	A	Pts
Dundee	6	3	1	2	14	10	7
Hearts	6	3	1	2	15	12	7
St Mirren	6	2	2	2	13	13	6
Raith R	6	2	0	4	6	13	4

DIV 1 Section D	P	W	D	L	F	A	Pts
Rangers	6	4	1	1	15	6	9
East Fife	6	3	1	2	10	9	7
Queen of South	6	2	0	4	11	16	4
Aberdeen	6	2	0	4	10	15	4

DIV 2 Section A	P	W	D	L	F	A	Pts
Falkirk	6	6	0	0	23	4	12
Stenhousemuir	6	2	1	3	12	16	5
Dundee U	6	1	2	3	6	10	4
Cowdenbeath	6	1	1	4	7	18	3

DIV 2 Section B	P	W	D	L	F	A	Pts
Dunfermline A	6	4	1	1	15	7	9
Queen's Park	6	3	0	3	9	9	6
Alloa	6	2	1	3	8	10	5
Hamilton A	6	2	0	4	7	13	4

DIV 2 Section C	P	W	D	L	F	A	Pts
St Johnstone	6	4	1	1	14	8	9
Clyde	6	4	0	2	16	8	8
Albion R	6	3	0	3	10	14	6
Arbroath	6	0	1	5	10	20	1

DIV 2 Section D	P	W	D	L	F	A	Pts
Forfar A	6	4	1	1	13	8	9
Kilmarnock	6	4	0	2	9	4	8
Ayr U	6	2	0	4	11	12	4
Dumbarton	6	1	1	4	6	15	3

Quarter-finals

Sep 15 Celtic . . . . .4 Forfar A 1
Sep 19 Forfar A . . . . .1 Celtic . . . . .1 Agg 2-5
Sep 15 Dunfermline A . . . . .1 Rangers 0
Sep 19 Rangers . . . . .3 Dunfermline A . . . . .1 Agg 3-2
Sep 15 Falkirk . . . . .0 Dundee 0
Sep 19 Dundee . . . . .2 Falkirk . . . . .1 Agg 2-1
Sep 15 St Johnstone . . . . . .0 Motherwell 4
Sep 19 Motherwell . . . . .3 St Johnstone . . . .0 Agg 7-0

Semi-finals

Oct 13 Celtic . . . . .0 Rangers 3
played at Hampden Park
Oct 13 Dundee . . . . .5 Motherwell 1
played at Ibrox

Final

Oct 27 Dundee . . . . .3 Rangers 2
played at Hampden Park

SEASON 1952-53

DIV 1 SECTION A

	Celtic	Hibernian	Partick T	St Mirren
Celtic		Aug16 2-0	Aug13 2-5	Aug23 3-1
Hibernian	Aug30 3-0		Aug23 3-1	Aug13 5-2
Partick T	Aug27 0-1	Aug09 1-5		Aug30 2-2
St Mirren	Aug09 0-1	Aug27 3-1	Aug16 5-1	

DIV 1 SECTION B

	East Fife	Falkirk	Queen of South	T Lanark
East Fife		Aug27 4-1	Aug09 2-0	Aug16 0-1
Falkirk	Aug13 3-3		Aug30 2-3	Aug23 2-1
Queen of South	Aug23 2-3	Aug16 2-2		Aug13 0-3
T Lanark	Aug30 2-0	Aug09 2-4	Aug27 3-1	

DIV 1 SECTION C

	Aberdeen	Hearts	Motherwell	Rangers
Aberdeen		Aug13 2-4	Aug23 0-1	Aug30 1-2
Hearts	Aug27 1-1		Aug16 0-1	Aug09 5-0
Motherwell	Aug09 5-2	Aug30 1-2		Aug27 3-3
Rangers	Aug16 3-1	Aug23 2-0	Aug13 2-0	

DIV 1 SECTION D

	Airdrie	Clyde	Dundee	Raith R
Airdrie		Aug23 4-0	Aug13 1-3	Aug16 0-1
Clyde	Aug09 1-1		Aug30 3-3	Aug27 6-1
Dundee	Aug27 3-2	Aug16 2-2		Aug09 2-1
Raith R	Aug30 1-1	Aug13 4-3	Aug23 1-2	

DIV 2 SECTION A

	Alloa	Arbroath	Dunfermline A	Kilmarnock
Alloa		Aug13 3-1	Aug16 2-2	Aug23 0-1
Arbroath	Aug27 1-1		Aug09 0-5	Aug16 2-0
Dunfermline A	Aug30 4-3	Aug23 3-1		Aug13 3-4
Kilmarnock	Aug09 3-1	Aug30 4-0	Aug27 3-2	

DIV 2 SECTION B

	Ayr U	Dumbarton	Dundee U	Stirling A
Ayr U		Aug13 11-1	Aug16 4-1	Aug23 1-2
Dumbarton	Aug27 1-1		Aug09 3-1	Aug30 2-1
Dundee U	Aug30 2-1	Aug23 1-0		Aug13 2-6
Stirling A	Aug09 2-0	Aug16 3-0	Aug27 6-1	

DIV 2 SECTION C

	Cowdenbeath	Forfar A	Hamilton A	Morton
Cowdenbeath		Aug09 2-0	Aug27 0-1	Aug16 2-3
Forfar A	Aug23 3-1		Aug30 1-1	Aug13 0-2
Hamilton A	Aug13 2-0	Aug16 2-2		Aug23 2-3
Morton	Aug30 2-2	Aug27 5-2	Aug09 4-1	

DIV 2 SECTION D

	Albion R	Queen's Park	St Johnstone	Stenhousemuir
Albion R		Aug09 2-0	Aug27 2-4	Aug30 4-4
Queen's Park	Aug23 2-0		Aug16 0-0	Aug13 1-2
St Johnstone	Aug13 6-3	Aug30 3-4		Aug23 1-0
Stenhousemuir	Aug16 1-0	Aug27 0-1	Aug09 1-5	

DIV 1 Section A	P	W	D	L	F	A	Pts
Hibernian	6	4	0	2	17	9	8
Celtic	6	4	0	2	9	9	8
St Mirren	6	2	1	3	13	13	5
Partick T	6	1	1	4	10	18	3

DIV 1 Section B	P	W	D	L	F	A	Pts
T Lanark	6	4	0	2	12	7	8
East Fife	6	3	1	2	12	9	7
Falkirk	6	2	2	2	14	15	6
Queen of South	6	1	1	4	8	15	3

DIV 1 Section C	P	W	D	L	F	A	Pts
Rangers	6	4	1	1	12	10	9
Hearts	6	3	1	2	12	7	7
Motherwell	6	3	1	2	11	9	7
Aberdeen	6	0	1	5	7	16	1

DIV 1 Section D	P	W	D	L	F	A	Pts
Dundee	6	4	2	0	15	10	10
Clyde	6	1	3	2	15	15	5
Raith R	6	2	1	3	9	14	5
Airdrie	6	1	2	3	9	9	4

DIV 2 Section A	P	W	D	L	F	A	Pts
Kilmarnock	6	5	0	1	15	8	10
Dunfermline A	6	3	1	2	19	13	7
Alloa	6	1	2	3	10	12	4
Arbroath	6	1	1	4	5	16	3

DIV 2 Section B	P	W	D	L	F	A	Pts
Stirling A	6	5	0	1	20	6	10
Ayr U	6	2	1	3	18	9	5
Dumbarton	6	2	1	3	7	18	5
Dundee U	6	2	0	4	8	20	4

DIV 2 Section C	P	W	D	L	F	A	Pts
Morton	6	5	1	0	19	9	11
Hamilton A	6	2	2	2	9	10	6
Forfar A	6	1	2	3	8	13	4
Cowdenbeath	6	1	1	4	7	11	3

DIV 2 Section D	P	W	D	L	F	A	Pts
St Johnstone	6	4	1	1	19	10	9
Queen's Park	6	3	1	2	8	7	7
Stenhousemuir	6	2	1	3	8	12	5
Albion R	6	1	1	4	11	17	3

Quarter-finals

Sep 13 Morton . . . . .0 Hibernian 6
Sep 17 Hibernian . . . . .6 Morton . . . . .3 Agg 12-3
Sep 13 Rangers . . . . .0 T Lanark 0
Sep 17 T Lanark . . . . .0 Rangers . . . . . . .2 Agg 0-2
Sep 13 St Johnstone . . . . . .1 Kilmarnock 3
Sep 17 Kilmarnock . . . . .4 St Johnstone . . . .1 Agg 7-2
Sep 13 Stirling A . . . . .3 Dundee 1
Sep 17 Dundee . . . . .5 Stirling A . . . . . . .0 Agg 6-3

Semi-finals

Oct 4 Dundee . . . . .2 Hibernian 1
played at Tynecastle
Oct 4 Kilmarnock . . . . .1 Rangers 0
played at Hampden Park

Final

Oct 25 Dundee . . . . .2 Kilmarnock 0
played at Hampden Park

Season 1953-54

DIV 1 SECTION A

	Falkirk	Hibernian	Queen of South	St Mirren
Falkirk		Aug26 1-2	Aug29 4-0	Aug08 1-1
Hibernian	Aug12 4-1		Aug22 2-1	Aug29 3-2
Queen of South	Aug15 1-4	Aug08 0-4		Aug26 1-0
St Mirren	Aug22 1-1	Aug15 2-2	Aug12 3-2	

DIV 1 SECTION B

	Aberdeen	Airdrie	Celtic	East Fife
Aberdeen		Aug12 2-0	Aug22 5-2	Aug29 3-4
Airdrie	Aug26 4-3		Aug15 2-1	Aug08 4-1
Celtic	Aug08 0-1	Aug29 2-0		Aug26 0-1
East Fife	Aug15 2-0	Aug22 5-1	Aug12 1-1	

DIV 1 SECTION C

	Hamilton A	Hearts	Raith R	Rangers
Hamilton A		Aug22 1-1	Aug12 1-2	Aug29 0-5
Hearts	Aug08 5-0		Aug15 2-0	Aug26 1-1
Raith R	Aug26 2-0	Aug29 3-1		Aug08 0-4
Rangers	Aug15 5-1	Aug12 4-1	Aug22 3-1	

DIV 1 SECTION D

	Clyde	Dundee	Partick T	Stirling A
Clyde		Aug12 2-4	Aug22 2-3	Aug15 4-1
Dundee	Aug26 4-2		Aug15 1-1	Aug08 6-1
Partick T	Aug08 4-1	Aug29 4-0		Aug26 3-0
Stirling A	Aug29 3-3	Aug22 0-2	Aug12 3-0	

DIV 2 SECTION A

	Alloa	Cowdenbeath	St Johnstone	T Lanark
Alloa		Aug26 3-1	Aug29 0-3	Aug08 0-10
Cowdenbeath	Aug12 2-1		Aug22 2-1	Aug15 4-2
St Johnstone	Aug15 2-0	Aug08 2-4		Aug26 4-1
T Lanark	Aug22 3-1	Aug29 7-0	Aug12 2-0	

DIV 2 SECTION B

	Albion R	Ayr U	Queen's Park	Stenhousemuir
Albion R		Aug12 1-4	Aug22 1-1	Aug29 2-2
Ayr U	Aug26 3-0		Aug29 3-1	Aug08 2-1
Queen's Park	Aug08 4-0	Aug15 0-0		Aug26 2-0
Stenhousemuir	Aug15 4-0	Aug22 4-2	Aug12 3-2	

DIV 2 SECTION C

	Dundee U	Kilmarnock	Morton	Motherwell
Dundee U		Aug29 0-3	Aug22 2-2	Aug12 0-5
Kilmarnock	Aug15 4-1		Aug12 1-0	Aug22 4-1
Morton	Aug08 5-3	Aug26 0-2		Aug29 2-3
Motherwell	Aug26 3-1	Aug08 3-0	Aug15 2-0	

DIV 2 SECTION D

	Arbroath	Dumbarton	Dunfermline A	Forfar A
Arbroath		Aug29 4-0	Aug22 3-1	Aug12 0-0
Dumbarton	Aug15 3-0		Aug12 1-3	Aug22 0-0
Dunfermline A	Aug08 2-1	Aug26 6-1		Aug29 3-0
Forfar A	Aug26 1-2	Aug08 2-1	Aug15 2-1	

DIV 1 Section A	P	W	D	L	F	A	Pts
Hibernian	6	5	1	0	17	7	11
Falkirk	6	2	2	2	12	9	6
St Mirren	6	1	3	2	9	10	5
Queen of South	6	1	0	5	5	17	2

DIV 1 Section B	P	W	D	L	F	A	Pts
East Fife	6	4	1	1	14	9	9
Aberdeen	6	3	0	3	14	12	6
Airdrie	6	3	0	3	11	14	6
Celtic	6	1	1	4	6	10	3

DIV 1 Section C	P	W	D	L	F	A	Pts
Rangers	6	5	1	0	22	4	11
Hearts	6	2	2	2	11	9	6
Raith R	6	3	0	3	8	11	6
Hamilton A	6	0	1	5	3	20	1

DIV 1 Section D	P	W	D	L	F	A	Pts
Partick T	6	4	1	1	15	7	9
Dundee	6	4	1	1	17	10	9
Clyde	6	1	1	4	14	19	3
Stirling A	6	1	1	4	8	18	3

DIV 2 Section A	P	W	D	L	F	A	Pts
T Lanark	6	4	0	2	25	9	8
Cowdenbeath	6	4	0	2	13	16	8
St Johnstone	6	3	0	3	12	9	6
Alloa	6	1	0	5	5	21	2

DIV 2 Section B	P	W	D	L	F	A	Pts
Ayr U	6	4	1	1	14	7	9
Stenhousemuir	6	3	1	2	14	10	7
Queen's Park	6	2	2	2	10	7	6
Albion R	6	0	2	4	4	18	2

DIV 2 Section C	P	W	D	L	F	A	Pts
Kilmarnock	6	5	0	1	14	5	10
Motherwell	6	5	0	1	17	7	10
Morton	6	1	1	4	9	13	3
Dundee U	6	0	1	5	7	22	1

DIV 2 Section D	P	W	D	L	F	A	Pts
Dunfermline A	6	4	0	2	16	8	8
Arbroath	6	3	1	2	10	7	7
Forfar A	6	2	2	2	5	7	6
Dumbarton	6	1	1	4	6	15	3

Quaretr-finals

Sep 12 East Fife . . . . .6 Dunfermline A . . .2
Sep 16 Dunfermline A . . . . .2 East Fife . . . . . . .3 Agg 4-9
Sep 12 Kilmarnock . . . . .4 Partick T 3
Sep 16 Partick T . . . . .4 Kilmarnock . . . . .0 Agg 7-4
Sep 12 Rangers . . . . .4 Ayr U 2
Sep 16 Ayr U . . . . .3 Rangers . . . . . . .2 Agg 5-6
Sep 12 T Lanark . . . . .0 Hibernian 4
Sep 16 Hibernian . . . . .4 T Lanark . . . . . . .0 Agg 8-0

Semi-finals

Oct 10 East Fife . . . . .3 Hibernian 2
played at Tynecastle
Oct 10 Partick T . . . . .2 Rangers 0
played at Hampden Park

Final

Oct 24 East Fife . . . . .3 Partick T 0
played at Hampden Park

Celtic were still awaiting success in the Scottish League Cup, having yet to even reach the Final. Here is the team that gained both the other domestic honours in 1953-54. Back row (left to right): Haughney, Meecham, Bonner, Evans, Stein, Peacock. Front row: Higgins, Fernie, Fallon, Tully, Mochan.

Season 1954-55

DIV 1 SECTION A	Kilmarnock	Motherwell	Raith R	St Mirren
Kilmarnock		Sep01 0-1	Aug14 3-2	Aug21 2-2
Motherwell	Aug18 4-0		Aug21 1-1	Aug28 3-1
Raith R	Aug28 0-1	Sep04 3-0		Aug18 2-2
St Mirren	Sep04 3-2	Aug14 4-4	Sep01 3-1	

DIV 1 SECTION B	Aberdeen	East Fife	Hibernian	Queen of South
Aberdeen		Sep04 5-1	Sep01 1-1	Aug14 4-0
East Fife	Aug21 0-3		Aug14 3-1	Sep01 3-0
Hibernian	Aug18 2-0	Aug28 1-2		Aug21 3-1
Queen of South	Aug28 3-0	Aug18 1-4	Sep04 3-5	

DIV 1 SECTION C	Clyde	Partick T	Rangers	Stirling A
Clyde		Aug28 2-0	Sep04 1-2	Aug18 0-1
Partick T	Aug14 3-2		Sep01 1-2	Sep04 9-1
Rangers	Aug21 1-3	Aug18 1-1		Aug28 2-0
Stirling A	Sep01 3-2	Aug21 0-2	Aug14 0-5	

DIV 1 SECTION D	Celtic	Dundee	Falkirk	Hearts
Celtic		Sep01 0-1	Aug14 3-0	Aug21 1-2
Dundee	Aug18 3-1		Aug21 3-1	Aug28 4-1
Falkirk	Aug28 2-2	Sep04 4-0		Aug18 2-6
Hearts	Sep04 3-2	Aug14 3-1	Sep01 4-1	

DIV 2 SECTION A	Forfar A	Hamilton A	St Johnstone	Stenhousemuir
Forfar A		Aug28 2-2	Sep04 3-3	Aug18 2-3
Hamilton A	Aug14 2-0		Sep01 0-0	Sep04 4-2
St Johnstone	Aug21 4-2	Aug18 2-0		Aug28 3-1
Stenhousemuir	Sep01 5-1	Aug21 4-3	Aug14 2-4	

DIV 2 SECTION B	Ayr U	Brechin C	Dundee U	Dunfermline A
Ayr U		Aug18 2-2	Aug28 3-1	Sep04 3-1
Brechin C	Sep01 2-4		Aug21 2-0	Aug14 1-1
Dundee U	Aug14 2-5	Sep04 0-1		Sep01 3-1
Dunfermline A	Aug21 4-0	Aug28 2-1	Aug18 3-1	

DIV 2 SECTION C	Airdrie	Cowdenbeath	Queen's Park	T Lanark
Airdrie		Aug18 2-1	Aug28 5-4	Aug21 2-0
Cowdenbeath	Sep01 1-2		Sep04 5-3	Aug14 1-0
Queen's Park	Aug14 2-4	Aug21 4-1		Sep01 1-2
T Lanark	Sep04 1-2	Aug28 4-0	Aug18 2-0	

DIV 2 SECTION D	Albion R	Alloa	Arbroath	Morton
Albion R		Sep01 2-2	Sep04 3-1	Aug14 1-0
Alloa	Aug18 0-0		Aug28 3-3	Sep04 1-0
Arbroath	Aug21 3-1	Aug14 2-3		Sep01 2-2
Morton	Aug28 3-0	Aug21 3-0	Aug18 5-2	

DIV 1 Section A	P	W	D	L	F	A	Pts
Motherwell	6	3	2	1	13	9	8
St Mirren	6	2	3	1	15	14	7
Kilmarnock	6	2	1	3	8	12	5
Raith R	6	1	2	3	9	10	4

DIV 1 Section B	P	W	D	L	F	A	Pts
East Fife	6	4	0	2	13	11	8
Aberdeen	6	3	1	2	13	7	7
Hibernian	6	3	1	2	13	10	7
Queen of South	6	1	0	5	8	19	2

DIV 1 Section C	P	W	D	L	F	A	Pts
Rangers	6	4	1	1	13	6	9
Partick T	6	3	1	2	16	8	7
Clyde	6	2	0	4	10	10	4
Stirling A	6	2	0	4	5	20	4

DIV 1 Section D	P	W	D	L	F	A	Pts
Hearts	6	5	0	1	19	11	10
Dundee	6	4	0	2	12	10	8
Celtic	6	1	1	4	9	11	3
Falkirk	6	1	1	4	10	18	3

DIV 2 Section A	P	W	D	L	F	A	Pts
St Johnstone	6	4	2	0	16	8	10
Hamilton A	6	2	2	2	11	10	6
Stenhousemuir	6	3	0	3	17	17	6
Forfar A	6	0	2	4	10	19	2

DIV 2 Section B	P	W	D	L	F	A	Pts
Ayr U	6	4	1	1	17	12	9
Dunfermline A	6	3	1	2	12	9	7
Brechin C	6	2	2	2	9	9	6
Dundee U	6	1	0	5	7	15	2

DIV 2 Section C	P	W	D	L	F	A	Pts
Airdrie	6	6	0	0	17	9	12
T Lanark	6	3	0	3	9	6	6
Cowdenbeath	6	2	0	4	9	15	4
Queen's Park	6	1	0	5	14	19	2

DIV 2 Section D	P	W	D	L	F	A	Pts
Morton	6	3	1	2	13	6	7
Alloa	6	2	3	1	9	10	7
Albion R	6	2	2	2	7	9	6
Arbroath	6	1	2	3	13	17	4

Quarter-finals

Sep 22 Ayr U ....2 Airdrie 1
Sep 25 Airdrie ....6 Ayr U ....1 Agg 7-3
Sep 22 Morton ....2 East Fife 2
Sep 25 East Fife ....2 Morton ....0 Agg 4-2
Sep 22 St Johnstone ......0 Hearts 5
Sep 25 Hearts ....2 St Johnstone ....0 Agg 7-0
Sep 22 Motherwell ....2 Rangers 1
Sep 25 Rangers ....1 Motherwell .....1 Agg 2-3

Semi-finals

Oct 9 Airdrie ....1 Hearts 4
played at Easter Road
Oct 9 East Fife ....1 Motherwell 2
played at Hampden Park

Final

Oct 23 Hearts ....4 Motherwell 2
played at Hampden Park

Season 1955-56

Section 1	Airdrie	Dundee	Kilmarnock	St Mirren
Airdrie		Aug13 4-0	Sep03 3-3	Aug31 2-4
Dundee	Aug27 2-2		Aug17 1-2	Aug20 2-0
Kilmarnock	Aug20 2-0	Aug31 0-0		Aug13 0-0
St Mirren	Aug17 3-2	Sep03 0-3	Aug27 3-0	

Section 2	East Fife	Hearts	Partick T	Raith R
East Fife		Aug20 1-0	Aug17 2-3	Aug27 0-2
Hearts	Sep03 4-0		Aug27 2-1	Aug17 5-0
Partick T	Aug31 2-1	Aug13 0-2		Aug20 4-0
Raith R	Aug13 2-4	Aug31 0-2	Sep03 0-1	

Section 3	Aberdeen	Clyde	Dunfermline A	Hibernian
Aberdeen		Aug20 3-2	Aug17 3-2	Aug27 2-1
Clyde	Sep03 1-2		Aug27 3-2	Aug17 2-2
Dunfermline A	Aug31 2-2	Aug13 4-2		Sep03 1-3
Hibernian	Aug13 0-1	Aug31 2-1	Aug20 3-1	

Section 4	Celtic	Falkirk	Queen of South	Rangers
Celtic		Aug20 5-1	Aug13 4-2	Aug31 0-4
Falkirk	Sep03 1-1		Aug31 4-0	Aug13 0-5
Queen of South	Aug17 0-2	Aug27 0-3		Aug20 1-2
Rangers	Aug27 1-4	Aug17 4-3	Sep03 6-0	

Section 5	Alloa	Arbroath	Cowdenbeath	Hamilton A
Alloa		Aug13 5-3	Aug31 5-3	Sep03 2-2
Arbroath	Aug27 1-2		Sep03 1-1	Aug17 1-2
Cowdenbeath	Aug17 5-3	Aug20 5-1		Aug27 1-2
Hamilton A	Aug20 1-1	Aug31 7-0	Aug13 6-1	

Section 6	Ayr U	Queen's Park	St Johnstone	Stirling A
Ayr U		Aug17 3-2	Aug27 3-2	Sep03 2-2
Queen's Park	Aug31 2-0		Aug20 1-2	Aug13 3-0
St Johnstone	Aug13 5-1	Sep03 3-0		Aug31 3-2
Stirling A	Aug20 3-1	Aug27 1-0	Aug17 0-1	

Section 7

	Albion R	Dundee U	Forfar A	Motherwell
Albion R		Aug27 3-3	Aug17 1-0	Aug20 0-2
Dundee U	Aug13 1-3		Sep03 3-2	Aug31 0-2
Forfar A	Aug31 2-1	Aug20 2-5		Aug13 1-6
Motherwell	Sep03 4-0	Aug17 7-1	Aug27 2-1	

Section 8

	Brechin C	Morton	Stenhousemuir	T Lanark
Brechin C		Sep03 4-0	Aug31 3-3	Aug13 2-1
Morton	Aug20 7-1		Aug13 3-1	Aug31 2-0
Stenhousemuir	Aug17 2-0	Aug27 2-4		Aug20 1-1
T Lanark	Aug27 1-4	Aug17 1-0	Sep03 3-0	

Section 9

	Berwick R	Dumbarton	E Stirling	Montrose	Stranraer
Berwick R				Sep03 1-2	Aug17 2-0
Dumbarton	Aug13 2-0		Sep03 6-1		
E Stirling	Aug27 3-2				Aug20 5-2
Montrose		Aug20 0-2	Aug17 2-5		
Stranraer		Aug27 3-3		Aug13 3-2	

DIV 1 Section 1	P	W	D	L	F	A	Pts
St Mirren	6	3	1	2	10	9	7
Kilmarnock	6	2	3	1	7	7	7
Dundee	6	2	2	2	8	8	6
Airdrie	6	1	2	3	13	14	4

DIV 1 Section 2	P	W	D	L	F	A	Pts
Hearts	6	5	0	1	15	2	10
Partick T	6	4	0	2	11	7	8
East Fife	6	2	0	4	8	13	4
Raith R	6	1	0	5	4	16	2

DIV 1 Section 3	P	W	D	L	F	A	Pts
Aberdeen	6	5	1	0	13	8	11
Hibernian	6	3	1	2	11	8	7
Dunfermline A	6	1	1	4	12	16	3
Clyde	6	1	1	4	11	15	3

DIV 1 Section 4	P	W	D	L	F	A	Pts
Rangers	6	5	0	1	22	8	10
Celtic	6	4	1	1	16	9	9
Falkirk	6	2	1	3	12	15	5
Queen of South	6	0	0	6	3	21	0

DIV 2 Section 5	P	W	D	L	F	A	Pts
Hamilton A	6	4	2	0	20	6	10
Alloa	6	3	2	1	18	15	8
Cowdenbeath	6	2	1	3	16	18	5
Arbroath	6	0	1	5	7	22	1

DIV 2 Section 6	P	W	D	L	F	A	Pts
St Johnstone	6	5	0	1	16	7	10
Stirling A	6	2	1	3	8	10	5
Ayr U	6	2	1	3	10	16	5
Queen's Park	6	2	0	4	8	9	4

DIV 2 Section 7	P	W	D	L	F	A	Pts
Motherwell	6	6	0	0	23	3	12
Dundee U	6	2	1	3	13	19	5
Albion R	6	2	1	3	8	12	5
Forfar A	6	1	0	5	8	18	2

DIV 2 Section 8	P	W	D	L	F	A	Pts
Morton	6	4	0	2	16	9	8
Brechin C	6	3	1	2	14	14	7
T Lanark	6	2	1	3	7	9	5
Stenhousemuir	6	1	2	3	9	14	4

DIV 2 SECTION 9	P	W	D	L	F	A	Pts
Dumbarton	4	3	1	0	13	4	7
E Stirling	4	3	0	1	14	12	6
Stranraer	4	1	1	2	8	12	3
Berwick R	4	1	0	3	5	7	2
Montrose	4	1	0	3	6	11	2

Play-offs

Sep 6 Dumbarton . . . . .2 Morton 1
Sep 8 Morton . . . . .0 Dumbarton . . . . .1 Agg 1-3

Quarter-finals

Sep 14 St Mirren . . . . .5 Dumbarton 1
Sep 17 Dumbarton . . . . .1 St Mirren . . . . . . .1 Agg 2-6
Sep 14 Aberdeen . . . . .5 Hearts 3
Sep 17 Hearts . . . . .2 Aberdeen . . . . . . .4 Agg 5-9
Sep 14 St Johnstone . . . . . .1 Motherwell 2
Sep 17 Motherwell . . . . .0 St Johnstone . . . .1 Agg 2-2
Sep 14 Hamilton A . . . . .1 Rangers 2
Sep 17 Rangers . . . . .8 Hamilton A . . . . .0 Agg 10-1

Replay

Sep 21 Motherwell . . . . .2 St Johnstone 0
played at Ibrox

Semi-finals

Oct 1 Aberdeen . . . . .2 Rangers 1
played at Hampden Park
Oct 1 Motherwell . . . . .3 St Mirren 3
played at Ibrox

Replay

Oct 8 Motherwell . . . . .0 St Mirren 2
played at Celtic Park

Final

Oct 22 Aberdeen . . . . .2 St Mirren 1
played at Hampden Park

The jubilant Aberdeen players tour the city in a 'make-do' open-top bus, with Paddy Buckley rising to the occasion after the Dons' 1956 League Cup success.

Season 1956-57

Section 1

	Airdrie	Dundee	Motherwell	Raith R
Airdrie		Sep01 1-7	Aug15 1-3	Aug25 3-1
Dundee	Aug18 3-1		Aug25 2-1	Aug15 1-0
Motherwell	Aug29 6-1	Aug11 0-1		Sep01 0-1
Raith R	Aug11 4-2	Aug29 2-2	Aug18 4-2	

Section 2

	Aberdeen	Celtic	East Fife	Rangers
Aberdeen		Aug11 1-2	Aug29 4-1	Aug18 2-6
Celtic	Aug25 3-2		Aug18 2-1	Aug15 2-1
East Fife	Aug15 2-1	Sep01 0-1		Aug25 1-4
Rangers	Sep01 4-1	Aug29 0-0	Aug11 3-0	

Section 3

	Dunfermline A	Kilmarnock	Queen of South	St Mirren
Dunfermline A		Aug25 5-1	Aug15 2-1	Sep01 2-0
Kilmarnock	Aug11 0-0		Aug18 2-3	Aug29 1-4
Queen of South	Aug29 1-1	Sep01 0-2		Aug11 0-0
St Mirren	Aug18 2-0	Aug15 2-2	Aug25 1-1	

Section 4

	Falkirk	Hearts	Hibernian	Partick T
Falkirk		Sep01 1-1	Aug29 4-0	Aug11 0-2
Hearts	Aug18 5-0		Aug11 6-1	Aug29 2-2
Hibernian	Aug15 0-1	Aug25 1-2		Sep01 2-2
Partick T	Aug25 2-0	Aug15 3-1	Aug18 4-1	

Section 5

	Alloa	Brechin C	Dumbarton	Hamilton A
Alloa		Aug29 1-3	Sep01 1-3	Aug11 3-1
Brechin C	Aug15 3-1		Aug25 3-4	Sep01 2-0
Dumbarton	Aug18 1-1	Aug11 1-8		Aug29 3-4
Hamilton A	Aug25 3-2	Aug18 1-1	Aug15 5-3	

Section 6

	Berwick R	Cowdenbeath	Morton	Stranraer
Berwick R		Aug15 0-3	Aug25 1-1	Sep01 2-0
Cowdenbeath	Aug29 3-1		Aug18 0-1	Aug11 1-1
Morton	Aug11 1-1	Sep01 0-1		Aug29 1-1
Stranraer	Aug18 5-2	Aug25 1-3	Aug15 1-4	

Section 7

	Clyde	Queen's Park	St Johnstone	Stirling A
Clyde		Aug29 2-2	Sep01 5-1	Aug11 2-1
Queen's Park	Aug15 0-1		Aug25 0-2	Sep01 2-0
St Johnstone	Aug18 1-6	Aug11 2-1		Aug29 1-0
Stirling A	Aug25 0-3	Aug18 0-2	Aug15 0-0	

Section 8

	Ayr U	Dundee U	Stenhousemuir	T Lanark
Ayr U		Aug25 1-1	Sep01 3-1	Aug15 3-3
Dundee U	Aug11 6-1		Aug29 3-4	Sep01 2-1
Stenhousemuir	Aug18 1-1	Aug15 3-2		Aug25 2-1
T Lanark	Aug28 1-5	Aug18 1-2	Aug11 8-2	

Section 9

	Albion R	Arbroath	E Stirling	Forfar A	Montrose
Albion R		Aug11 2-1	Aug18 9-2		
Arbroath				Aug18 3-0	Sep01 6-1
E Stirling		Aug25 0-3			Aug15 3-0
Forfar A	Aug15 4-2		Sep01 0-1		
Montrose	Aug25 3-5			Aug11 2-3	

Section 1	P	W	D	L	F	A	Pts
Dundee	6	5	1	0	16	5	11
Raith R	6	3	1	2	12	10	7
Motherwell	6	2	0	4	12	10	4
Airdrie	6	1	0	5	9	24	2

Section 2	P	W	D	L	F	A	Pts
Celtic	6	5	1	0	10	5	11
Rangers	6	4	1	1	18	6	9
Aberdeen	6	1	0	5	11	18	2
East Fife	6	1	0	5	5	15	2

Section 3	P	W	D	L	F	A	Pts
Dunfermline A	6	3	2	1	10	5	8
St Mirren	6	2	3	1	9	6	7
Queen of South	6	1	3	2	6	8	5
Kilmarnock	6	1	2	3	8	14	4

Section 4	P	W	D	L	F	A	Pts
Partick T	6	4	2	0	15	6	10
Hearts	6	3	2	1	17	8	8
Falkirk	6	2	1	3	6	10	5
Hibernian	6	0	1	5	5	19	1

Section 5	P	W	D	L	F	A	Pts
Brechin C	6	4	1	1	20	8	9
Hamilton A	6	3	1	2	14	14	7
Dumbarton	6	2	1	3	15	22	5
Alloa	6	1	1	4	9	14	3

Section 6	P	W	D	L	F	A	Pts
Cowdenbeath	6	4	1	1	11	4	9
Morton	6	2	3	1	8	5	7
Stranraer	6	1	2	3	9	13	4
Berwick R	6	1	2	3	7	13	4

Section 7	P	W	D	L	F	A	Pts
Clyde	6	5	1	0	19	5	11
St Johnstone	6	3	1	2	7	12	7
Queen's Park	6	2	1	3	7	7	5
Stirling A	6	0	1	5	1	10	1

Section 8	P	W	D	L	F	A	Pts
Dundee U	6	3	1	2	16	11	7
Ayr U	6	2	3	1	14	13	7
Stenhousemuir	6	3	1	2	13	18	7
T Lanark	6	1	1	4	15	16	3

Section 9	P	W	D	L	F	A	Pts
Arbroath	4	3	0	1	13	3	6
Albion R	4	3	0	1	18	10	6
Forfar A	4	2	0	2	7	8	4
E Stirling	4	2	0	2	6	12	4
Montrose	4	0	0	4	6	17	0

Play-offs

Sep 3 Arbroath ....2 Dundee U 0
Sep 5 Dundee U ....5 Arbroath ....0 Agg 5-2

Quarter-finals

Sep 12 Brechin C ....3 Clyde 2
Sep 15 Clyde ....3 Brechin C ......1 Agg 5-4
Sep 12 Dundee ....7 Dundee U 3
Sep 15 Dundee U ....2 Dundee ....1 Agg 5-8
Sep 12 Celtic ....6 Dunfermline A ...0
Sep 15 Dunfermline A .....3 Celtic ....0 Agg 3-6
Sep 12 Cowdenbeath ......1 Partick T 2
Sep 15 Partick T ....2 Cowdenbeath ....1 Agg 4-2

Semi-finals

Oct 6 Celtic ....2 Clyde 0
played at Hampden Park
Oct 6 Dundee ....0 Partick T 0
played at Ibrox

Replay

Oct 9 Dundee ....2 Partick T 3
played at Ibrox

Final

Oct 27 Celtic ....0 Partick T 0
played at Hampden Park

Replay

Oct 31 Celtic ....3 Partick T 0
played at Hampden Park

Celtic in 1957, showing off their League Cup trophy. Back row (left to right): Goldie, Fallon, Beattie, McPhail, Fernie, Evans. Front row: W.Johnstone (trainer), Tully, Collins, Peacock, Wilson, Mochan, J.McGrory (manager).

Season 1957-58

Section 1

	Aberdeen	Falkirk	Motherwell	Queen of S'h
Aberdeen		Aug28 2-1	Aug31 5-3	Aug10 5-1
Falkirk	Aug14 3-4		Aug24 1-3	Aug17 3-0
Motherwell	Aug17 2-3	Aug10 1-4		Aug28 2-1
Queen of South	Aug24 2-3	Aug31 1-1	Aug14 3-0	

Section 2

	Partick T	Raith R	Rangers	St Mirren
Partick T		Aug24 1-4	Aug14 0-1	Aug31 0-2
Raith R	Aug10 1-0		Aug31 4-3	Aug28 4-1
Rangers	Aug28 0-3	Aug17 4-3		Aug10 6-0
St Mirren	Aug17 1-0	Aug13 1-0	Aug24 0-4	

Section 3

	Airdrie	Celtic	East Fife	Hibernian
Airdrie		Aug24 1-2	Aug31 9-1	Aug14 4-1
Celtic	Aug10 3-2		Aug28 6-1	Aug31 2-0
East Fife	Aug17 1-3	Aug14 1-4		Aug24 2-2
Hibernian	Aug28 5-1	Aug17 3-1	Aug10 4-0	

Section 4

	Dundee	Hearts	Kilmarnock	Queen's Park
Dundee		Aug20 2-2	Aug14 0-3	Aug24 1-1
Hearts	Aug31 4-2		Aug24 1-1	Aug14 9-2
Kilmarnock	Aug28 1-1	Aug10 2-1		Aug17 3-1
Queen's Park	Aug10 2-5	Aug28 0-0	Aug31 2-2	

Section 5

	Clyde	Dumbarton	Dundee U	Stranraer
Clyde		Aug17 7-1	Aug24 8-1	Aug14 10-0
Dumbarton	Aug31 1-4		Aug14 2-4	Aug24 10-3
Dundee U	Aug10 1-4	Aug28 0-3		Aug31 3-0
Stranraer	Aug28 0-5	Aug10 3-1	Aug17 2-4	

Section 6

	Ayr U	Brechin C	Cowdenbeath	Dunfermline A
Ayr U		Aug24 4-2	Aug31 3-2	Aug14 4-1
Brechin C	Aug10 5-2		Aug28 7-1	Aug17 2-1
Cowdenbeath	Aug17 1-1	Aug14 1-1		Aug24 2-5
Dunfermline A	Aug28 3-0	Aug31 3-1	Aug10 1-1	

Section 7

	Morton	Stenhousemuir	Stirling A	T Lanark
Morton		Aug17 7-5	Aug10 0-1	Aug28 3-3
Stenhousemuir	Aug31 1-2		Aug28 4-0	Aug10 3-3
Stirling A	Aug24 1-3	Aug14 0-1		Aug31 0-1
T Lanark	Aug14 1-0	Aug24 3-0	Aug17 2-0	

Section 8

	Albion R	Arbroath	Hamilton A	St Johnstone
Albion R		Aug17 2-0	Aug28 1-1	Aug10 2-4
Arbroath	Aug31 4-1		Aug10 1-1	Aug28 3-1
Hamilton A	Aug14 3-2	Aug24 3-0		Aug31 4-1
St Johnstone	Aug24 6-2	Aug14 1-2	Aug17 0-3	

Section 9

	Alloa	Berwick R	E Stirling	Forfar A	Montrose
Alloa		Aug17 5-0	Aug14 3-3		
Berwick R				Aug10 3-5	Aug24 1-3
E Stirling		Aug31 5-1			Aug10 3-1
Forfar A	Aug24 2-3		Aug17 2-1		
Montrose	Aug31 3-1			Aug14 4-1	

Section 1	P	W	D	L	F	A	Pts
Aberdeen	6	6	0	0	22	12	12
Falkirk	6	2	1	3	13	11	5
Motherwell	6	2	0	4	11	17	4
Queen of South	6	1	1	4	8	14	3

Section 2	P	W	D	L	F	A	Pts
Rangers	6	4	0	2	18	10	8
Raith R	6	4	0	2	16	10	8
St Mirren	6	3	0	3	5	14	6
Partick T	6	1	0	5	4	9	2

Section 3	P	W	D	L	F	A	Pts
Celtic	6	5	0	1	18	8	10
Hibernian	6	3	1	2	15	10	7
Airdrie	6	3	0	3	20	13	6
East Fife	6	0	1	5	6	28	1

Section 4	P	W	D	L	F	A	Pts
Kilmarnock	6	3	3	0	12	6	9
Hearts	6	2	3	1	17	9	7
Dundee	6	1	3	2	11	13	5
Queen's Park	6	0	3	3	8	20	3

Section 5	P	W	D	L	F	A	Pts
Clyde	6	6	0	0	38	4	12
Dundee U	6	3	0	3	13	19	6
Dumbarton	6	2	0	4	18	21	4
Stranraer	6	1	0	5	8	33	2

Section 6	P	W	D	L	F	A	Pts
Brechin C	6	3	1	2	18	12	7
Dunfermline A	6	3	1	2	14	10	7
Ayr U	6	3	1	2	14	14	7
Cowdenbeath	6	0	3	3	8	18	3

Section 7	P	W	D	L	F	A	Pts
T Lanark	6	4	2	0	13	6	10
Morton	6	3	1	2	15	12	7
Stenhousemuir	6	2	1	3	14	15	5
Stirling A	6	1	0	5	2	11	2

Section 8	P	W	D	L	F	A	Pts
Hamilton A	6	4	2	0	15	5	10
Arbroath	6	3	1	2	10	9	7
St Johnstone	6	2	0	4	13	16	4
Albion R	6	1	1	4	10	18	3

Section 9	P	W	D	L	F	A	Pts
Montrose	4	3	0	1	11	6	6
E Stirling	4	2	1	1	12	7	5
Alloa	4	2	1	1	12	8	5
Forfar A	4	2	0	2	10	11	4
Berwick R	4	0	0	4	5	18	0

Play-offs

Sep 2 Montrose 1 Hamilton A 0
Sep 4 Hamilton A 3 Montrose 0 Agg 3-1

Quarter-finals

Sep 11 Celtic 6 T Lanark 1
Sep 14 T Lanark 0 Celtic 3 Agg 1-9
Sep 11 Kilmarnock 2 Rangers 1
Sep 14 Rangers 3 Kilmarnock 1 Agg 4-3
Sep 11 Aberdeen 1 Clyde 2
Sep 14 Clyde 4 Aberdeen 2 Agg 6-3
Sep 11 Hamilton A 2 Brechin C 4
Sep 14 Brechin C 1 Hamilton A 0 Agg 5-2

Semi-finals

Sep 28 Celtic 4 Clyde 2
played at Ibrox
Sep 28 Brechin C 0 Rangers 4
played at Hampden Park

Final

Oct 19 Celtic 7 Rangers 1
played at Hampden Park

Celtic retain the League Cup in emphatic style as Mochan beats Niven of Rangers for Celtic's second of seven goals.

Season 1958-59

Section 1

	Hearts	Raith R	Rangers	T Lanark
Hearts		Aug30 3-1	Aug23 2-1	Aug13 3-0
Raith R	Aug16 1-3		Aug13 3-1	Aug23 3-1
Rangers	Aug09 3-0	Aug27 6-0		Aug16 2-2
T Lanark	Aug27 4-5	Aug09 4-2	Aug30 0-3	

Section 2

	Airdrie	Celtic	Clyde	St Mirren
Airdrie		Aug27 1-2	Aug16 2-3	Aug09 3-4
Celtic	Aug13 3-3		Aug23 2-0	Aug16 3-0
Clyde	Aug30 3-1	Aug09 1-4		Aug27 6-1
St Mirren	Aug23 3-2	Aug30 6-3	Aug13 1-2	

Section 3

	Dundee	Motherwell	Partick T	Queen of South
Dundee		Aug27 2-3	Aug09 2-3	Aug30 2-0
Motherwell	Aug13 1-2		Aug16 2-5	Aug23 4-0
Partick T	Aug23 3-2	Aug30 1-1		Aug13 5-1
Queen of South	Aug16 1-0	Aug09 1-2	Aug27 3-0	

Section 4

	Aberdeen	Falkirk	Hibernian	Kilmarnock
Aberdeen		Aug16 5-1	Aug13 1-2	Aug23 0-2
Falkirk	Aug30 1-1		Aug23 0-4	Aug13 1-3
Hibernian	Aug27 4-2	Aug09 3-2		Aug16 0-3
Kilmarnock	Aug09 1-2	Aug27 1-2	Aug30 2-1	

Section 5

	Brechin C	Dunfermline A	East Fife	Stirling A
Brechin C		Aug30 1-2	Aug13 0-3	Aug23 2-5
Dunfermline A	Aug16 4-1		Aug23 5-2	Aug13 6-1
East Fife	Aug27 5-1	Aug09 1-3		Aug30 5-2
Stirling A	Aug09 3-2	Aug27 1-3	Aug16 1-0	

Section 6

	Cowdenbeath	Dundee U	Morton	St Johnstone
Cowdenbeath		Aug27 6-1	Aug09 2-1	Aug30 2-1
Dundee U	Aug13 1-3		Aug16 1-4	Aug23 5-3
Morton	Aug23 0-0	Aug30 6-1		Aug13 1-3
St Johnstone	Aug16 1-2	Aug09 1-2	Aug27 2-0	

Section 7

	Alloa	Arbroath	Dumbarton	Queen's Park
Alloa		Aug23 2-5	Aug13 1-3	Aug30 2-2
Arbroath	Aug09 3-1		Aug16 6-3	Aug27 4-0
Dumbarton	Aug27 3-1	Aug30 0-1		Aug09 3-3
Queen's Park	Aug16 5-2	Aug13 2-1	Aug23 0-3	

Section 8

	Ayr U	Forfar A	Hamilton A	Montrose
Ayr U		Aug16 4-0	Aug23 3-1	Aug13 7-1
Forfar A	Aug30 1-1		Aug13 1-0	Aug23 4-1
Hamilton A	Aug09 3-1	Aug27 2-0		Aug30 3-0
Montrose	Aug27 1-2	Aug09 2-2	Aug16 2-3	

Section 9

	Albion R	Berwick R	E Stirling	Stenhousemuir	Stranraer
Albion R			Aug23 4-1	Aug13 0-4	
Berwick R	Aug30 2-2		Aug13 3-2		
E Stirling				Aug09 0-5	Aug16 1-2
Stenhousemuir		Aug16 0-1			Aug27 3-4
Stranraer	Aug09 4-1	Aug23 2-1			

Section 1	P	W	D	L	F	A	Pts
Hearts	6	5	0	1	16	10	10
Rangers	6	3	1	2	16	7	7
Raith R	6	2	0	4	10	18	4
T Lanark	6	1	1	4	11	18	3

Section 2	P	W	D	L	F	A	Pts
Celtic	6	4	1	1	17	11	9
Clyde	6	4	0	2	15	11	8
St Mirren	6	3	0	3	15	19	6
Airdrie	6	0	1	5	12	18	1

Section 3	P	W	D	L	F	A	Pts
Partick T	6	4	1	1	17	11	9
Motherwell	6	3	1	2	13	11	7
Dundee	6	2	0	4	10	11	4
Queen of South	6	2	0	4	6	13	4

Section 4	P	W	D	L	F	A	Pts
Kilmarnock	6	4	0	2	12	6	8
Hibernian	6	4	0	2	14	10	8
Aberdeen	6	2	1	3	11	11	5
Falkirk	6	1	1	4	7	17	3

Section 5	P	W	D	L	F	A	Pts
Dunfermline A	6	6	0	0	23	7	12
East Fife	6	3	0	3	16	12	6
Stirling A	6	3	0	3	13	18	6
Brechin C	6	0	0	6	7	22	0

Section 6	P	W	D	L	F	A	Pts
Cowdenbeath	6	5	1	0	15	5	11
Morton	6	2	1	3	12	9	5
St Johnstone	6	2	0	4	11	12	4
Dundee U	6	2	0	4	11	23	4

Section 7	P	W	D	L	F	A	Pts
Arbroath	6	5	0	1	20	8	10
Dumbarton	6	3	1	2	15	12	7
Queen's Park	6	2	2	2	12	15	6
Alloa	6	0	1	5	9	21	1

Section 8	P	W	D	L	F	A	Pts
Ayr U	6	4	1	1	18	7	9
Hamilton A	6	4	0	2	12	7	8
Forfar A	6	2	2	2	8	10	6
Montrose	6	0	1	5	7	21	1

Section 9	P	W	D	L	F	A	Pts
Stranraer	4	4	0	0	12	6	8
Berwick R	4	2	1	1	7	6	5
Stenhousemuir	4	2	0	2	12	5	4
Albion R	4	1	1	2	7	11	3
E Stirling	4	0	0	4	4	14	0

Play-offs

Sep 1 Stranraer ....3 Arbroath 4
Sep 3 Arbroath ....1 Stranraer ....0 Agg 5-3

Quarter-finals

Sep 10 Ayr U ....1 Hearts 5
Sep 17 Hearts ....3 Ayr U ....1 Agg 8-2
Sep 10 Celtic ....2 Cowdenbeath 0
Sep 17 Cowdenbeath ......1 Celtic ....8 Agg 1-10
Sep 10 Kilmarnock ....4 Dunfermline A ...1
Sep 16 Dunfermline A .....3 Kilmarnock .....3 Agg 4-7
Sep 10 Partick T ....2 Arbroath 1
Sep 17 Arbroath ....1 Partick T ....1 Agg 2-3

Semi-finals

Oct 1 Celtic ....1 Partick T 2
played at Ibrox
Oct 1 Hearts ....3 Kilmarnock 0
played at Easter Road

Final

Oct 25 Hearts ....5 Partick T 1
played at Hampden Park

Season 1959-60

Section 1

	Airdrie	Celtic	Partick T	Raith R
Airdrie		Aug15 4-2	Aug22 4-0	Aug12 2-3
Celtic	Aug29 2-2		Aug12 1-2	Aug22 1-0
Partick T	Aug08 0-0	Aug26 0-2		Aug29 1-3
Raith R	Aug26 3-0	Aug08 2-1	Aug15 2-0	

Section 2

	Clyde	Dunfermline A	St Mirren	T Lanark
Clyde		Aug08 0-0	Aug15 4-2	Aug26 2-2
Dunfermline A	Aug22 1-4		Aug12 3-0	Aug29 2-3
St Mirren	Aug29 2-1	Aug26 1-2		Aug08 2-3
T Lanark	Aug12 2-0	Aug15 6-1	Aug22 3-1	

Section 3

	Aberdeen	Hearts	Kilmarnock	Stirling A
Aberdeen		Aug26 1-4	Aug29 2-4	Aug08 3-1
Hearts	Aug12 2-2		Aug22 2-0	Aug29 2-2
Kilmarnock	Aug15 2-3	Aug08 0-4		Aug26 5-0
Stirling A	Aug22 2-5	Aug15 1-2	Aug12 2-2	

Section 4

	Dundee	Hibernian	Motherwell	Rangers
Dundee		Aug12 4-3	Aug22 1-4	Aug29 2-3
Hibernian	Aug26 1-3		Aug15 1-3	Aug08 1-6
Motherwell	Aug08 4-2	Aug29 4-2		Aug26 2-1
Rangers	Aug15 2-0	Aug22 5-1	Aug12 1-2	

Section 5

	Ayr U	Berwick R	Falkirk	Hamilton A
Ayr U		Aug22 1-1	Aug12 2-1	Aug29 5-2
Berwick R	Aug08 2-3		Aug15 0-2	Aug26 2-2
Falkirk	Aug26 1-1	Aug29 3-0		Aug08 3-2
Hamilton A	Aug15 1-0	Aug12 3-3	Aug22 2-3	

Section 6

	Albion R	Arbroath	Dumbarton	Stenhousemuir
Albion R		Aug29 4-1	Aug26 1-0	Aug08 1-2
Arbroath	Aug15 0-3		Aug08 2-0	Aug26 1-0
Dumbarton	Aug12 3-3	Aug22 3-4		Aug29 1-2
Stenhousemuir	Aug22 3-0	Aug12 2-3	Aug15 0-2	

Section 7

	Brechin C	East Fife	Forfar A	Queen of South
Brechin C		Aug08 0-0	Aug26 6-1	Aug29 2-1
East Fife	Aug22 3-0		Aug29 4-1	Aug12 4-0
Forfar A	Aug12 2-2	Aug15 0-3		Aug22 4-4
Queen of South	Aug15 2-2	Aug26 0-2	Aug08 1-1	

Section 8

	Alloa	Cowdenbeath	Morton	St Johnstone
Alloa		Aug29 1-1	Aug08 4-2	Aug26 1-3
Cowdenbeath	Aug15 4-3		Aug26 3-1	Aug08 3-1
Morton	Aug22 0-1	Aug12 0-2		Aug15 2-4
St Johnstone	Aug12 6-3	Aug22 3-3	Aug29 3-1	

Section 9

	Dundee U	E Stirling	Montrose	Queen's Park	Stranraer
Dundee U		Aug08 2-0			Aug15 2-0
E Stirling			Aug15 5-1	Aug12 1-2	
Montrose	Aug12 1-1			Aug22 0-2	
Queen's Park	Aug29 0-4				Aug08 4-1
Stranraer		Aug22 2-1	Aug29 4-2		

Section 1 P	W	D	L	F	A	Pts
Raith R 6	5	0	1	13	5	10
Airdrie 6	2	2	2	12	10	6
Celtic 6	2	1	3	9	10	5
Partick T 6	1	1	4	3	12	3

Section 2 P	W	D	L	F	A	Pts
T Lanark 6	5	1	0	19	8	11
Clyde 6	2	2	2	11	9	6
Dunfermline A 6	2	1	3	9	14	5
St Mirren 6	1	0	5	8	16	2

Section 3 P	W	D	L	F	A	Pts
Hearts 6	4	2	0	16	6	10
Aberdeen 6	3	1	2	16	15	7
Kilmarnock 6	2	1	3	13	13	5
Stirling A 6	0	2	4	8	19	2

Section 4 P	W	D	L	F	A	Pts
Motherwell 6	6	0	0	19	8	12
Rangers 6	4	0	2	18	8	8
Dundee 6	2	0	4	12	17	4
Hibernian 6	0	0	6	9	25	0

Section 5 P	W	D	L	F	A	Pts
Falkirk 6	4	1	1	13	7	9
Ayr U 6	3	2	1	12	8	8
Hamilton A 6	1	2	3	12	16	4
Berwick R 6	0	3	3	8	14	3

Section 6 P	W	D	L	F	A	Pts
Arbroath 6	4	0	2	11	12	8
Albion R 6	3	1	2	12	9	7
Stenhousemuir . . .6	3	0	3	9	8	6
Dumbarton 6	1	1	4	9	12	3

Section 7 P	W	D	L	F	A	Pts
East Fife 6	5	1	0	16	1	11
Brechin C 6	2	3	1	12	9	7
Queen of South . . .6	0	3	3	8	15	3
Forfar A 6	0	3	3	9	20	3

Section 8 P	W	D	L	F	A	Pts
Cowdenbeath 6	4	2	0	16	9	10
St Johnstone 6	4	1	1	20	13	9
Alloa 6	2	1	3	13	16	5
Morton 6	0	0	6	6	17	0

Section 9 P	W	D	L	F	A	Pts
Dundee U 4	3	1	0	9	1	7
Queen's Park 4	3	0	1	8	6	6
Stranraer 4	2	0	2	7	9	4
E Stirling 4	1	0	3	7	7	2
Montrose 4	0	1	3	4	12	1

Play-offs

Aug 31 Falkirk . . . . .1 Dundee U 1
Sep 2 Dundee U . . . . .0 Falkirk . . . . .3 Agg 1-4

Quarter-finals

Sep 9 Cowdenbeath . . . . . .3 East Fife 1
Sep 16 East Fife . . . . .1 Cowdenbeath . . . .2 Agg 2-5
Sep 9 Motherwell . . . . .1 Hearts 1
Sep 16 Hearts . . . . .6 Motherwell . . . . .2 Agg 7-3
Sep 9 Raith R . . . . .2 Arbroath 2
Sep 16 Arbroath . . . . .2 Raith R . . . . .1 Agg 4-3
Sep 9 T Lanark . . . . .2 Falkirk 1
Sep 16 Falkirk . . . . .0 T Lanark . . . . . . .3 Agg 1-5

Semi-finals

Oct 7 Arbroath . . . . .0 T Lanark 3
played at Ibrox
Oct 7 Cowdenbeath . . . . . .3 Hearts 9
played at Easter Road

Final

Oct 24 Hearts . . . . .2 T Lanark 1
played at Hampden Park

Season 1960-61

Section 1

	Clyde	Hearts	Motherwell	St Mirren
Clyde		Aug17 2-0	Aug27 1-1	Aug20 4-0
Hearts	Aug31 6-2		Sep03 2-1	Aug13 1-1
Motherwell	Aug13 4-4	Aug20 2-3		Aug31 5-2
St Mirren	Sep03 0-0	Aug27 3-1	Aug17 0-4	

Section 2

	Celtic	Partick T	Rangers	T Lanark
Celtic		Aug31 1-2	Sep03 1-2	Aug13 2-0
Partick T	Aug17 1-1		Aug27 1-4	Sep03 0-4
Rangers	Aug20 2-3	Aug13 3-1		Aug31 3-2
T Lanark	Aug27 1-3	Aug20 3-1	Aug17 2-1	

Section 3

	Airdrie	Dunfermline A	Hibernian	Kilmarnock
Airdrie		Aug27 4-2	Sep03 3-1	Aug17 0-2
Dunfermline A	Aug13 5-2		Aug31 3-1	Sep03 2-0
Hibernian	Aug20 6-1	Aug17 3-0		Aug27 2-2
Kilmarnock	Aug31 2-0	Aug20 2-1	Aug13 4-2	

Section 4

	Aberdeen	Ayr U	Dundee	Raith R
Aberdeen		Aug13 4-3	Aug20 1-4	Aug31 3-0
Ayr U	Aug27 1-1		Aug17 1-2	Sep03 1-2
Dundee	Sep03 6-0	Aug31 3-0		Aug13 5-0
Raith R	Aug17 4-1	Aug20 1-1	Aug27 0-3	

Section 5

	Albion R	Montrose	Queen of South	Queen's Park
Albion R		Aug31 2-1	Aug13 0-3	Aug20 3-1
Montrose	Aug17 3-1		Sep03 1-2	Aug27 2-1
Queen of South	Aug27 5-2	Aug20 5-2		Aug17 2-0
Queen's Park	Sep03 0-1	Aug13 0-2	Aug31 0-1	

Section 6

	Arbroath	Falkirk	Hamilton A	St Johnstone
Arbroath		Aug27 2-2	Aug20 0-4	Aug17 0-0
Falkirk	Aug13 2-2		Aug31 2-1	Aug20 3-2
Hamilton A	Sep03 1-0	Aug17 4-1		Aug27 3-2
St Johnstone	Aug31 2-2	Sep03 7-1	Aug13 2-3	

Section 7

	Alloa	Berwick R	Dumbarton	Morton
Alloa		Sep03 2-1	Aug31 1-5	Aug13 1-2
Berwick R	Aug20 1-2		Aug13 2-2	Aug31 3-1
Dumbarton	Aug17 0-0	Aug27 3-0		Sep03 3-3
Morton	Aug27 3-2	Aug17 2-2	Aug20 1-3	

Section 8

	Brechin C	Dundee U	Stenhousemuir	Stirling A
Brechin C		Aug31 2-1	Aug13 1-3	Aug20 1-2
Dundee U	Aug17 2-1		Aug20 3-3	Aug27 0-3
Stenhousemuir	Aug27 2-1	Sep03 1-1		Aug17 2-0
Stirling A	Sep03 4-2	Aug13 1-2	Aug31 2-2	

Section 9

	Cowdenbeath	East Fife	E Stirling	Forfar A	Stranraer
Cowdenbeath			Aug20 3-0	Aug17 3-1	
East Fife	Aug13 2-5			Sep03 4-3	
E Stirling		Aug27 4-1			Aug17 1-3
Forfar A			Aug13 2-2		Aug27 5-1
Stranraer	Sep03 3-1	Aug20 2-2			

Section 1 P	W	D	L	F	A	Pts
Clyde 6	2	3	1	13	11	7
Hearts 6	3	1	2	13	11	7
Motherwell 6	2	2	2	17	12	6
St Mirren 6	1	2	3	6	15	4

Section 2 P	W	D	L	F	A	Pts
Rangers 6	4	0	2	15	10	8
Celtic 6	3	1	2	11	8	7
T Lanark 6	3	0	3	12	10	6
Partick T 6	1	1	4	6	16	3

Section 3 P	W	D	L	F	A	Pts
Kilmarnock 6	4	1	1	12	7	9
Dunfermline A 6	3	0	3	13	12	6
Hibernian 6	2	1	3	15	13	5
Airdrie 6	2	0	4	10	18	4

Section 4 P	W	D	L	F	A	Pts
Dundee 6	6	0	0	23	2	12
Aberdeen 6	2	1	3	10	18	5
Raith R 6	2	1	3	7	14	5
Ayr U 6	0	2	4	7	13	2

Section 5 P	W	D	L	F	A	Pts
Queen of South . . .6	6	0	0	18	5	12
Montrose 6	3	0	3	11	11	6
Albion R 6	3	0	3	9	13	6
Queen's Park 6	0	0	6	2	11	0

Section 6 P	W	D	L	F	A	Pts
Hamilton A 6	5	0	1	16	7	10
Falkirk 6	2	2	2	11	18	6
St Johnstone 6	1	2	3	15	12	4
Arbroath 6	0	4	2	6	11	4

Section 7	P	W	D	L	F	A	Pts
Dumbarton	6	3	3	0	16	7	9
Morton	6	2	2	2	12	14	6
Alloa	6	2	1	3	8	12	5
Berwick R	6	1	2	3	9	12	4

Section 8	P	W	D	L	F	A	Pts
Stenhousemuir	6	3	3	0	13	8	9
Stirling A	6	3	1	2	12	9	7
Dundee U	6	2	2	2	9	11	6
Brechin C	6	1	0	5	8	14	2

Section 9	P	W	D	L	F	A	Pts
Cowdenbeath	4	3	0	1	12	6	6
Stranraer	4	2	1	1	9	9	5
Forfar A	4	1	1	2	11	10	3
E Stirling	4	1	1	2	7	9	3
East Fife	4	1	1	2	9	14	3

Play-offs

Sep 5 Dumbarton . . . . .3 Cowdenbeath 0
Sep 7 Cowdenbeath . . . . . .2 Dumbarton . . . . .1 Agg 2-4
Sep 12 Clyde . . . . .2 Hearts 1

Quarter-finals

Sep 14 Clyde . . . . .1 Kilmarnock 2
Sep 21 Kilmarnock . . . . .3 Clyde . . . . .1 Agg 5-2
Sep 14 Hamilton A . . . . .4 Stenhousemuir 0
Sep 21 Stenhousemuir . . . . .5 Hamilton A . . . . .4 Agg 5-8
Sep 14 Queen of South . . . .2 Dumbarton 0
Sep 21 Dumbarton . . . . .2 Queen of South . . . .1 Agg 2-3
Sep 14 Rangers . . . . .1 Dundee 0
Sep 21 Dundee . . . . .3 Rangers . . . . . . .4 Agg 3-5

Semi-finals

Oct 12 Hamilton A . . . . .1 Kilmarnock 5
played at Ibrox
Oct 19 Queen of South . . . .0 Rangers 7
played at Celtic Park

Final

Oct 29 Kilmarnock . . . . .0 Rangers 2
played at Hampden Park

Brand of Rangers draws goalkeeper Brown out before scoring against Kilmarnock in the 1960-61 Scottish League Cup Final as the Killies went down 2-0 at Hampden.

Season 1961-62

Section 1	Celtic	Hibernian	Partick T	St Johnstone
Celtic		Sep02 2-1	Aug26 3-2	Aug16 0-1
Hibernian	Aug19 2-2		Aug16 2-1	Aug26 4-1
Partick T	Aug12 2-3	Aug30 2-1		Aug19 0-0
St Johnstone	Aug30 2-0	Aug12 1-1	Sep02 4-3	

Section 2	Aberdeen	Dundee U	Dunfermline A	Motherwell
Aberdeen		Sep02 2-2	Aug26 0-0	Aug16 3-4
Dundee U	Aug19 5-3		Aug16 0-0	Aug26 0-2
Dunfermline A	Aug12 1-2	Aug30 3-0		Sep02 2-0
Motherwell	Aug30 2-1	Aug12 5-3	Aug19 1-1	

Section 3	Airdrie	Dundee	Rangers	T Lanark
Airdrie		Aug26 0-5	Aug19 1-2	Aug16 2-2
Dundee	Aug12 2-0		Aug30 1-1	Sep02 2-2
Rangers	Sep02 4-1	Aug16 4-2		Aug26 5-0
T Lanark	Aug30 3-1	Aug19 3-2	Aug12 0-2	

Section 4	Hearts	Kilmarnock	Raith R	St Mirren
Hearts		Aug30 2-0	Aug12 1-0	Sep02 3-1
Kilmarnock	Aug16 1-2		Sep02 4-1	Aug26 6-1
Raith R	Aug26 3-1	Aug19 1-7		Aug16 0-3
St Mirren	Aug19 1-0	Aug12 1-0	Aug30 0-2	

Section 5	Alloa	Berwick R	Stirling A	Stranraer
Alloa		Sep02 4-4	Aug12 2-3	Aug30 2-0
Berwick R	Aug19 3-1		Aug30 0-2	Aug12 2-1
Stirling A	Aug26 3-1	Aug16 4-2		Aug19 4-1
Stranraer	Aug16 1-1	Aug26 1-2	Sep02 3-0	

Section 6	Clyde	Hamilton A	Montrose	Stenhousemuir
Clyde		Aug30 2-3	Aug19 3-2	Aug12 3-0
Hamilton A	Aug16 3-2		Aug26 2-0	Sep02 3-1
Montrose	Sep02 4-0	Aug12 2-2		Aug30 4-0
Stenhousemuir	Aug26 2-4	Aug19 1-3	Aug16 1-4	

Section 7	Arbroath	Brechin C	East Fife	Queen of South
Arbroath		Sep02 4-1	Aug16 1-4	Aug26 1-0
Brechin C	Aug19 1-2		Aug26 2-8	Aug16 0-4
East Fife	Aug30 6-0	Aug12 3-1		Sep02 1-0
Queen of South	Aug12 1-0	Aug30 5-1	Aug19 1-3	

Section 8	Ayr U	Cowdenbeath	Dumbarton	Falkirk
Ayr U		Aug30 3-1	Aug12 3-1	Aug19 1-1
Cowdenbeath	Aug16 2-3		Aug19 4-3	Aug26 1-1
Dumbarton	Aug26 1-2	Sep02 2-1		Aug16 0-1
Falkirk	Sep02 4-4	Aug12 2-2	Aug30 3-0	

Section 9	Albion R	E Stirling	Forfar A	Morton	Queen's Park
Albion R		Aug12 5-2		Sep02 3-1	
E Stirling			Aug26 1-0	Aug19 4-1	
Forfar A	Aug19 3-5				Aug12 1-3
Morton			Aug16 2-1		Aug26 1-3
Queen's Park	Aug16 1-3	Sep02 7-2			

Section 1	P	W	D	L	F	A	Pts
St Johnstone	6	3	2	1	9	8	8
Celtic	6	3	1	2	10	10	7
Hibernian	6	2	2	2	11	9	6
Partick T	6	1	1	4	10	13	3

Section 2	P	W	D	L	F	A	Pts
Motherwell	6	4	1	1	14	10	9
Dunfermline A	6	2	3	1	7	3	7
Aberdeen	6	1	2	3	11	14	4
Dundee U	6	1	2	3	10	15	4

Section 3	P	W	D	L	F	A	Pts
Rangers	6	5	1	0	18	5	11
Dundee	6	2	2	2	14	10	6
T Lanark	6	2	2	2	10	14	6
Airdrie	6	0	1	5	5	18	1

Section 4	P	W	D	L	F	A	Pts
Hearts	6	4	0	2	9	6	8
Kilmarnock	6	3	0	3	18	8	6
St Mirren	6	3	0	3	7	11	6
Raith R	6	2	0	4	7	16	4

Section 5	P	W	D	L	F	A	Pts
Stirling A	6	5	0	1	16	9	10
Berwick R	6	3	1	2	13	13	7
Alloa	6	1	2	3	11	14	4
Stranraer	6	1	1	4	7	11	3

Section 6	P	W	D	L	F	A	Pts
Hamilton A	6	5	1	0	16	8	11
Montrose	6	3	1	2	16	8	7
Clyde	6	3	0	3	14	14	6
Stenhousemuir	6	0	0	6	5	21	0

Section 7	P	W	D	L	F	A	Pts
East Fife	6	6	0	0	25	5	12
Queen of South	6	3	0	3	11	6	6
Arbroath	6	3	0	3	8	13	6
Brechin C	6	0	0	6	6	26	0

Section 8	P	W	D	L	F	A	Pts
Ayr U	6	4	2	0	16	10	10
Falkirk	6	2	4	0	12	8	8
Cowdenbeath	6	1	2	3	11	14	4
Dumbarton	6	1	0	5	7	14	2

Section 9	P	W	D	L	F	A	Pts
Albion R	4	4	0	0	16	7	8
Queen's Park	4	3	0	1	14	7	6
E Stirling	4	2	0	2	9	13	4
Morton	4	1	0	3	5	11	2
Forfar A	4	0	0	4	5	11	0

Play-offs

Sep 4 East Fife 4 Albion R 1
Sep 6 Albion R 1 East Fife 2 Agg 2-6

Quarter-finals

Sep 13 Ayr U 4 Stirling A 2
Sep 20 Stirling A 3 Ayr U 0 Agg 5-4
Sep 13 Hamilton A 1 Hearts 2
Sep 20 Hearts 2 Hamilton A 0 Agg 4-1
Sep 13 Motherwell 2 St Johnstone 3
Sep 20 St Johnstone 1 Motherwell 1 Agg 4-3
Sep 13 Rangers 3 East Fife 1
Sep 20 East Fife 1 Rangers 3 Agg 2-6

Semi-finals

Oct 11 Hearts 2 Stirling A 1
played at Easter Road
Oct 11 Rangers 3 St Johnstone 2
played at Celtic Park

Final

Oct 28 Hearts 1 Rangers 1
played at Hampden Park

Replay

Dec 18 Hearts 1 Rangers 3
played at Hampden Park

Season 1962-63

Section 1	Airdrie	Dunfermline A	Kilmarnock	Raith R
Airdrie		Aug18 2-4	Aug25 0-4	Aug15 1-1
Dunfermline A	Sep01 4-1		Aug15 3-3	Aug25 1-1
Kilmarnock	Aug11 4-0	Aug29 3-2		Sep01 3-1
Raith R	Aug29 3-1	Aug11 2-2	Aug18 2-3	

Section 2	Celtic	Dundee	Dundee U	Hearts
Celtic		Aug29 3-0	Aug18 4-0	Aug11 3-1
Dundee	Aug15 1-0		Aug25 2-1	Aug18 0-2
Dundee U	Sep01 0-0	Aug11 3-2		Aug29 2-0
Hearts	Aug25 3-2	Sep01 2-0	Aug15 3-1	

Section 3	Aberdeen	Falkirk	Motherwell	Partick T
Aberdeen		Aug18 3-0	Aug15 4-0	Aug25 0-3
Falkirk	Sep01 1-2		Aug25 0-1	Aug15 1-3
Motherwell	Aug29 4-1	Aug11 9-1		Sep01 0-1
Partick T	Aug11 1-2	Aug29 3-1	Aug18 1-1	

Section 4	Hibernian	Rangers	St Mirren	T Lanark
Hibernian		Aug11 1-4	Aug29 2-0	Aug18 3-2
Rangers	Aug25 0-0		Sep01 4-0	Aug15 5-2
St Mirren	Aug15 3-3	Aug18 2-1		Aug25 1-1
T Lanark	Sep01 1-4	Aug29 2-5	Aug11 1-2	

Section 5	Ayr U	Berwick R	E Stirling	Hamilton A
Ayr U		Aug15 2-2	Aug25 2-1	Sep01 3-2
Berwick R	Aug29 1-1		Sep01 2-0	Aug11 3-2
E Stirling	Aug11 4-1	Aug18 3-2		Aug29 0-1
Hamilton A	Aug18 4-4	Aug25 0-2	Aug15 4-4	

Section 6	Clyde	Cowdenbeath	St Johnstone	Stranraer
Clyde		Aug25 1-0	Aug15 5-1	Sep01 4-1
Cowdenbeath	Aug11 1-2		Aug18 0-7	Aug29 3-0
St Johnstone	Aug29 1-0	Sep01 4-1		Aug11 1-0
Stranraer	Aug18 3-5	Aug15 2-1	Aug25 1-4	

Section 7	East Fife	Montrose	Queen of South	Queen's Park
East Fife		Aug15 0-5	Aug25 1-0	Sep01 5-4
Montrose	Aug29 0-1		Sep01 0-0	Aug11 3-1
Queen of South	Aug11 3-1	Aug18 2-1		Aug29 4-4
Queen's Park	Aug18 3-0	Aug25 1-1	Aug15 0-4	

Section 8	Alloa	Arbroath	Morton	Stirling A
Alloa		Sep01 2-2	Aug15 2-3	Aug25 2-1
Arbroath	Aug18 3-0		Aug25 3-3	Aug15 3-2
Morton	Aug29 5-2	Aug11 2-2		Sep01 2-0
Stirling A	Aug11 1-1	Aug29 2-3	Aug18 1-4	

Section 9	Albion R	Brechin C	Dumbarton	Forfar A	Stenhousemuir
Albion R			Aug11 3-5		Sep01 1-2
Brechin C	Aug25 0-4		Aug18 3-5		
Dumbarton				Aug25 1-0	Aug15 1-1
Forfar A	Aug15 0-0	Sep01 1-1			
Stenhousemuir		Aug11 2-1		Aug18 2-3	

Section 1	P	W	D	L	F	A	Pts
Kilmarnock	6	5	1	0	20	8	11
Dunfermline A	6	2	3	1	16	12	7
Raith R	6	1	3	2	10	11	5
Airdrie	6	0	1	5	5	20	1

Section 2	P	W	D	L	F	A	Pts
Hearts	6	4	0	2	11	8	8
Celtic	6	3	1	2	12	5	7
Dundee U	6	2	1	3	7	11	5
Dundee	6	2	0	4	5	11	4

Section 3	P	W	D	L	F	A	Pts
Partick T	6	4	1	1	12	5	9
Aberdeen	6	4	0	2	12	9	8
Motherwell	6	3	1	2	15	8	7
Falkirk	6	0	0	6	4	21	0

Section 4	P	W	D	L	F	A	Pts
Rangers	6	4	1	1	19	7	9
Hibernian	6	3	2	1	13	10	8
St Mirren	6	2	2	2	8	12	6
T Lanark	6	0	1	5	9	20	1

Section 5	P	W	D	L	F	A	Pts
Berwick R	6	3	2	1	12	8	8
Ayr U	6	2	3	1	13	14	7
E Stirling	6	2	1	3	12	12	5
Hamilton A	6	1	2	3	13	16	4

Section 6	P	W	D	L	F	A	Pts
St Johnstone	6	5	0	1	18	7	10
Clyde	6	5	0	1	17	7	10
Stranraer	6	1	0	5	7	18	2
Cowdenbeath	6	1	0	5	6	16	2

Section 7	P	W	D	L	F	A	Pts
Queen of South	6	3	2	1	13	7	8
Montrose	6	2	2	2	10	5	6
East Fife	6	3	0	3	8	15	6
Queen's Park	6	1	2	3	13	17	4

Section 8	P	W	D	L	F	A	Pts
Morton	6	4	2	0	19	10	10
Arbroath	6	3	3	0	16	11	9
Alloa	6	1	2	3	9	15	4
Stirling A	6	0	1	5	7	15	1

Section 9	P	W	D	L	F	A	Pts
Dumbarton	4	3	1	0	12	7	7
Stenhousemuir	4	2	1	1	7	6	5
Forfar A	4	1	2	1	4	4	4
Albion R	4	1	1	2	8	7	3
Brechin C	4	0	1	3	5	12	1

Play-offs
Sep 3 Dumbarton . . . . .0 Berwick R 0
Sep 5 Berwick R . . . . .1 Dumbarton . . . . .2 Agg 1-2

Quarter-finals
Sep 12 Dumbarton . . . . .1 Rangers 3
Sep 19 Rangers . . . . .1 Dumbarton . . . . .1 Agg 4-2
Sep 12 Morton . . . . .0 Hearts 3
Sep 19 Hearts . . . . .3 Morton . . . . .1 Agg 6-1
Sep 12 Partick T . . . . .1 Kilmarnock 2
Sep 19 Kilmarnock . . . . .3 Partick T . . . . . . .1 Agg 5-2
Sep 12 Queen of South . . . . . .1 St Johnstone 0
Sep 19 St Johnstone . . . . . .4 Queen of South . . . .1 Agg 4-2

Semi-finals
Oct 10 Hearts . . . . .4 St Johnstone 0
played at Easter Road
Oct 10 Kilmarnock . . . . .3 Rangers 2
played at Hampden Park

Final
Oct 27 Hearts . . . . .1 Kilmarnock 0
played at Hampden Park

Season 1963-64

Section 1	Falkirk	Hearts	Motherwell	Partick T
Falkirk		Aug24 0-3	Aug17 0-6	Aug14 2-2
Hearts	Aug10 6-2		Aug28 0-0	Aug31 2-2
Motherwell	Aug31 4-0	Aug14 3-0		Aug24 2-0
Partick T	Aug28 3-2	Aug17 2-2	Aug10 0-2	

Section 2	Aberdeen	Dundee U	Hibernian	St Mirren
Aberdeen		Aug24 2-0	Aug31 0-2	Aug14 2-2
Dundee U	Aug10 1-1		Aug28 2-4	Aug31 3-2
Hibernian	Aug17 2-2	Aug14 3-2		Aug24 3-0
St Mirren	Aug28 0-3	Aug17 2-3	Aug10 1-1	

Section 3	Airdrie	Dundee	Dunfermline A	T Lanark
Airdrie		Aug28 4-1	Aug10 0-1	Aug17 2-3
Dundee	Aug14 2-1		Aug17 4-1	Aug24 3-2
Dunfermline A	Aug24 3-2	Aug31 3-4		Aug14 2-3
T Lanark	Aug31 2-1	Aug10 1-2	Aug28 0-3	

Section 4	Celtic	Kilmarnock	Queen of South	Rangers
Celtic		Aug28 2-0	Aug17 1-1	Aug10 0-3
Kilmarnock	Aug14 0-0		Aug24 2-0	Aug17 1-4
Queen of South	Aug31 2-3	Aug10 1-4		Aug28 2-5
Rangers	Aug24 3-0	Aug31 2-2	Aug14 5-2	

Section 5	Albion R	Alloa	Cowdenbeath	Stirling A
Albion R		Aug31 0-1	Aug24 2-0	Aug14 3-2
Alloa	Aug17 0-2		Aug14 1-2	Aug24 2-4
Cowdenbeath	Aug10 2-3	Aug28 1-0		Aug17 1-2
Stirling A	Aug28 2-0	Aug10 3-3	Aug31 3-2	

Section 6	Ayr U	Clyde	Morton	Stranraer
Ayr U		Aug28 2-4	Aug10 0-1	Aug31 1-2
Clyde	Aug14 3-4		Aug31 0-4	Aug24 4-1
Morton	Aug24 5-2	Aug17 3-1		Aug14 5-0
Stranraer	Aug17 2-1	Aug10 0-2	Aug28 1-2	

Section 7	E Stirling	Hamilton A	Queen's Park	St Johnstone
E Stirling		Aug31 1-0	Aug10 2-0	Aug28 2-1
Hamilton A	Aug17 2-3		Aug28 1-0	Aug10 2-3
Queen's Park	Aug24 0-1	Aug14 2-1		Aug17 0-3
St Johnstone	Aug14 3-1	Aug24 5-0	Aug31 1-0	

Section 8	Arbroath	Dumbarton	East Fife	Raith R
Arbroath		Aug10 1-1	Aug28 1-1	Aug31 2-0
Dumbarton	Aug24 1-2		Aug17 2-3	Aug14 3-0
East Fife	Aug14 3-0	Aug31 4-2		Aug24 3-0
Raith R	Aug17 3-4	Aug28 1-2	Aug10 1-1	

Section 9	Berwick R	Brechin C	Forfar A	Montrose	Stenhousemuir
Berwick R		Aug17 4-1	Aug24 3-1		
Brechin C				Aug24 2-2	Aug14 1-1
Forfar A		Aug31 3-3		Aug14 1-2	
Montrose	Aug10 3-0				Aug17 2-3
Stenhousemuir	Aug31 2-4		Aug10 2-2		

Section 1	P	W	D	L	F	A	Pts
Motherwell	6	5	1	0	17	0	11
Hearts	6	2	3	1	13	9	7
Partick T	6	1	3	2	9	12	5
Falkirk	6	0	1	5	6	24	1

Section 2	P	W	D	L	F	A	Pts
Hibernian	6	4	2	0	15	7	10
Aberdeen	6	2	3	1	10	7	7
Dundee U	6	2	1	3	11	14	5
St Mirren	6	0	2	4	7	15	2

Section 3	P	W	D	L	F	A	Pts
Dundee	6	5	0	1	16	12	10
Dunfermline A	6	3	0	3	13	13	6
T Lanark	6	3	0	3	11	13	6
Airdrie	6	1	0	5	10	12	2

Section 4	P	W	D	L	F	A	Pts
Rangers	6	5	1	0	22	7	11
Kilmarnock	6	2	2	2	9	9	6
Celtic	6	2	2	2	6	9	6
Queen of South	6	0	1	5	8	20	1

Section 5	P	W	D	L	F	A	Pts
Stirling A	6	4	1	1	16	11	9
Albion R	6	4	0	2	10	7	8
Cowdenbeath	6	2	0	4	8	11	4
Alloa	6	1	1	4	7	12	3

Section 6	P	W	D	L	F	A	Pts
Morton	6	6	0	0	20	4	12
Clyde	6	3	0	3	14	14	6
Stranraer	6	2	0	4	6	15	4
Ayr U	6	1	0	5	10	17	2

Section 7	P	W	D	L	F	A	Pts
St Johnstone	6	5	0	1	16	5	10
E Stirling	6	5	0	1	10	6	10
Hamilton A	6	1	0	5	6	14	2
Queen's Park	6	1	0	5	2	9	2

Section 8	P	W	D	L	F	A	Pts
East Fife	6	4	2	0	15	6	10
Arbroath	6	3	2	1	10	9	8
Dumbarton	6	2	1	3	11	11	5
Raith R	6	0	1	5	5	15	1

Section 9	P	W	D	L	F	A	Pts
Berwick R	4	3	0	1	11	7	6
Montrose	4	2	1	1	9	6	5
Stenhousemuir	4	1	2	1	8	9	4
Brechin C	4	0	3	1	7	10	3
Forfar A	4	0	2	2	7	10	2

Play-offs
Sep 2 St Johnstone . . . . . .2 Berwick R 2
Sep 4 Berwick R . . . . .4 St Johnstone . . . .2 Agg 6-4

Quarter-finals
Sep 11 Dundee . . . . .3 Hibernian 3
Sep 18 Hibernian . . . . .2 Dundee . . . . .0 Agg 5-3
Sep 11 East Fife . . . . .1 Rangers 1
Sep 18 Rangers . . . . .2 East Fife . . . . . . .0 Agg 3-1
Sep 11 Motherwell . . . . .0 Morton 0
Sep 18 Morton . . . . .2 Motherwell . . . . .0 Agg 2-0
Sep 11 Stirling A . . . . .2 Berwick R 2
Sep 18 Berwick R . . . . .4 Stirling A . . . . . . .3 Agg 6-5

Semi-finals
Oct 2 Berwick R . . . . .1 Rangers 3
played at Hampden Park
Oct 7 Hibernian . . . . .1 Morton 1
played at Ibrox

Replay
Oct 14 Hibernian . . . . .0 Morton 1
played at Ibrox

Final
Oct 26 Morton . . . . .0 Rangers 5
played at Hampden Park

Season 1964-65

Section 1

	Aberdeen	Rangers	St Johnstone	St Mirren
Aberdeen		Aug22 3-4	Aug12 2-1	Aug29 2-2
Rangers	Aug08 4-0		Aug29 3-1	Aug26 6-2
St Johnstone	Aug26 1-1	Aug15 1-9		Aug08 1-2
St Mirren	Aug15 3-3	Aug12 0-0	Aug22 2-0	

Section 2

	Airdrie	Dunfermline A	Hibernian	T Lanark
Airdrie		Aug08 1-4	Aug29 1-4	Aug26 1-2
Dunfermline A	Aug22 3-0		Aug12 2-0	Aug15 3-1
Hibernian	Aug15 5-0	Aug26 1-1		Aug08 3-0
T Lanark	Aug12 5-2	Aug29 0-1	Aug22 0-2	

Section 3

	Celtic	Hearts	Kilmarnock	Partick T
Celtic		Aug26 6-1	Aug15 4-1	Aug08 0-0
Hearts	Aug12 0-3		Aug22 0-1	Aug29 4-3
Kilmarnock	Aug29 2-0	Aug08 1-1		Aug26 4-0
Partick T	Aug22 1-5	Aug15 2-1	Aug12 0-0	

Section 4

	Dundee	Dundee U	Falkirk	Motherwell
Dundee		Aug08 2-3	Aug15 4-1	Aug26 6-0
Dundee U	Aug22 2-1		Aug12 3-0	Aug29 2-1
Falkirk	Aug29 1-3	Aug26 5-2		Aug08 1-1
Motherwell	Aug12 3-0	Aug15 0-1	Aug22 3-1	

Section 5

	East Fife	Montrose	Queen of South	Raith R
East Fife		Aug15 4-2	Aug12 5-0	Aug22 1-5
Montrose	Aug29 0-5		Aug22 1-6	Aug12 2-4
Queen of South	Aug26 1-1	Aug08 2-0		Aug15 1-1
Raith R	Aug08 1-4	Aug26 7-0	Aug29 2-3	

Section 6

	Clydebank	Hamilton A	Stenhousemuir	Stranraer
Clydebank		Aug15 2-4	Aug08 2-2	Aug26 3-3
Hamilton A	Aug29 0-0		Aug26 6-0	Aug08 2-2
Stenhousemuir	Aug22 1-2	Aug12 1-2		Aug15 3-3
Stranraer	Aug12 2-2	Aug22 2-1	Aug29 1-0	

Section 7

	Albion R	Arbroath	Clyde	Queen's Park
Albion R		Aug22 1-3	Aug15 0-5	Aug12 0-1
Arbroath	Aug08 1-3		Aug26 1-2	Aug29 2-2
Clyde	Aug29 5-1	Aug12 1-1		Aug22 4-1
Queen's Park	Aug26 0-2	Aug15 1-3	Aug08 0-0	

Section 8

	Ayr U	Berwick R	Dumbarton	Morton
Ayr U		Aug22 6-0	Aug15 2-1	Aug12 0-1
Berwick R	Aug08 3-1		Aug26 0-0	Aug15 0-5
Dumbarton	Aug29 2-1	Aug12 3-2		Aug22 1-1
Morton	Aug26 1-1	Aug29 5-2	Aug08 1-1	

Section 9

	Alloa	Brechin C	Cowdenbeath	Forfar A	Stirling A
Alloa			Aug12 0-0		Aug29 2-1
Brechin C	Aug15 3-5				Aug08 1-4
Cowdenbeath		Aug29 2-3		Aug08 1-2	
Forfar A	Aug22 3-0	Aug12 4-1			
Stirling A			Aug22 4-0	Aug15 1-2	

Section 1	P	W	D	L	F	A	Pts
Rangers	6	5	1	0	26	7	11
St Mirren	6	2	3	1	11	12	7
Aberdeen	6	1	3	2	11	15	5
St Johnstone	6	0	1	5	5	19	1

Section 2	P	W	D	L	F	A	Pts
Dunfermline A	6	5	1	0	14	3	11
Hibernian	6	4	1	1	15	4	9
T Lanark	6	2	0	4	8	12	4
Airdrie	6	0	0	6	5	23	0

Section 3	P	W	D	L	F	A	Pts
Celtic	6	4	1	1	18	5	9
Kilmarnock	6	3	2	1	9	5	8
Partick T	6	1	2	3	6	14	4
Hearts	6	1	1	4	7	16	3

Section 4	P	W	D	L	F	A	Pts
Dundee U	6	5	0	1	13	9	10
Dundee	6	3	0	3	16	10	6
Motherwell	6	2	1	3	8	11	5
Falkirk	6	1	1	4	9	16	3

Section 5	P	W	D	L	F	A	Pts
East Fife	6	4	1	1	20	9	9
Queen of South	6	3	2	1	13	10	8
Raith R	6	3	1	2	20	11	7
Montrose	6	0	0	6	5	28	0

Section 6	P	W	D	L	F	A	Pts
Hamilton A	6	3	2	1	15	7	8
Stranraer	6	2	4	0	13	11	8
Clydebank	6	1	4	1	11	12	6
Stenhousemuir	6	0	2	4	7	16	2

Section 7	P	W	D	L	F	A	Pts
Clyde	6	4	2	0	17	4	10
Arbroath	6	2	2	2	11	10	6
Albion R	6	2	0	4	7	15	4
Queen's Park	6	1	2	3	5	11	4

Section 8	P	W	D	L	F	A	Pts
Morton	6	3	3	0	14	5	9
Dumbarton	6	2	3	1	8	7	7
Ayr U	6	2	1	3	11	8	5
Berwick R	6	1	1	4	7	20	3

Section 9	P	W	D	L	F	A	Pts
Forfar A	4	4	0	0	11	3	8
Alloa	4	2	1	1	7	7	5
Stirling A	4	2	0	2	10	5	4
Brechin C	4	1	0	3	8	15	2
Cowdenbeath	4	0	1	3	3	9	1

Play-offs

Aug 31 Forfar A ....4 East Fife 3
Sep 2 East Fife ....4 Forfar A ....1 Agg 7-5

Quarter-finals

Sep 9 Clyde ....0 Morton 3
Sep 16 Morton ....0 Clyde ....2 Agg 3-2
Sep 9 Dundee U ....8 Hamilton A 0
Sep 16 Hamilton A ....1 Dundee U ......2 Agg 1-10
Sep 9 East Fife ....2 Celtic 0
Sep 16 Celtic ....6 East Fife ....0 Agg 6-2
Sep 14 Dunfermline A .....0 Rangers 3
Sep 16 Rangers ....2 Dunfermline A .....2 Agg 5-2

Semi-finals

Sep 29 Celtic ....2 Morton 0
played at Ibrox
Sep 30 Dundee U ....1 Rangers 2
played at Hampden Park

Final

Oct 24 Celtic ....1 Rangers 2
played at Hampden Park

Season 1965-66

Section 1

	Celtic	Dundee	Dundee U	Motherwell
Celtic		Aug21 0-2	Aug28 3-0	Aug18 1-0
Dundee	Sep04 1-3		Aug18 0-0	Aug28 1-2
Dundee U	Aug14 2-1	Sep01 1-3		Aug21 4-1
Motherwell	Sep01 2-3	Aug14 1-0	Sep04 3-2	

Section 2

	Aberdeen	Clyde	Hearts	Rangers
Aberdeen		Aug28 2-0	Aug18 1-1	Aug21 2-0
Clyde	Aug14 1-2		Sep04 1-2	Sep01 1-3
Hearts	Sep01 2-0	Aug21 1-2		Aug14 4-2
Rangers	Sep04 4-0	Aug18 3-0	Aug28 1-0	

Section 3

	Dunfermline A	Kilmarnock	Partick T	St Johnstone
Dunfermline A		Aug21 1-3	Aug28 6-2	Aug18 5-1
Kilmarnock	Sep04 0-1		Aug18 2-0	Aug28 3-0
Partick T	Aug14 0-0	Sep01 1-2		Aug21 0-1
St Johnstone	Sep01 3-1	Aug14 0-1	Sep04 2-0	

Section 4

	Falkirk	Hibernian	Morton	St Mirren
Falkirk		Aug14 3-1	Sep01 3-2	Aug21 0-1
Hibernian	Aug28 3-1		Sep04 3-0	Aug18 1-0
Morton	Aug18 1-1	Aug21 2-4		Aug28 0-1
St Mirren	Sep04 2-3	Sep01 0-3	Aug14 1-2	

Section 5

	Berwick R	Cowdenbeath	Hamilton A	T Lanark
Berwick R		Aug21 6-1	Sep01 1-1	Aug14 4-1
Cowdenbeath	Sep04 3-2		Aug14 1-1	Sep01 0-1
Hamilton A	Aug18 1-1	Aug28 0-1		Aug21 2-2
T Lanark	Aug28 3-2	Aug18 1-1	Sep04 5-1	

Section 6

	Arbroath	Queen's Park	Raith R	Stirling A
Arbroath		Aug28 3-0	Aug18 2-2	Aug21 1-3
Queen's Park	Aug14 2-2		Aug21 1-1	Sep01 2-1
Raith R	Sep01 4-2	Sep04 3-0		Aug14 3-1
Stirling A	Sep04 4-1	Aug18 0-2	Aug28 1-2	

Section 7

	Airdrie	Albion R	Queen of South	Stranraer
Airdrie		Aug18 6-1	Aug21 5-1	Aug28 3-0
Albion R	Sep01 8-2		Aug14 1-1	Sep04 2-1
Queen of South	Sep04 2-3	Aug28 2-0		Aug18 1-2
Stranraer	Aug14 1-3	Aug21 0-0	Sep01 1-1	

Section 8

	Alloa	Dumbarton	East Fife	E Stirling
Alloa		Aug21 2-1	Aug14 3-2	Sep01 2-1
Dumbarton	Sep04 4-1		Sep01 6-1	Aug14 2-1
East Fife	Aug28 1-2	Aug18 3-2		Aug21 4-1
E Stirling	Aug18 1-0	Aug28 1-0	Sep04 6-2	

Section 9

	Ayr U	Brechin C	Forfar A	Montrose	Stenhousemuir
Ayr U				Aug21 5-0	Aug14 5-2
Brechin C	Aug28 0-1		Aug21 1-0		
Forfar A	Sep04 1-3			Aug14 4-1	
Montrose		Aug18 2-0			Aug28 1-3
Stenhousemuir		Sep04 1-0	Aug18 2-1		

Section 1	P	W	D	L	F	A	Pts
Celtic	6	4	0	2	11	7	8
Motherwell	6	3	0	3	9	11	6
Dundee	6	2	1	3	7	7	5
Dundee U	6	2	1	3	9	11	5

Section 2	P	W	D	L	F	A	Pts
Rangers	6	4	0	2	13	7	8
Hearts	6	3	1	2	10	7	7
Aberdeen	6	3	1	2	7	8	7
Clyde	6	1	0	5	5	13	2

Section 3	P	W	D	L	F	A	Pts
Kilmarnock	6	5	0	1	11	3	10
Dunfermline A	6	3	1	2	14	9	7
St Johnstone	6	3	0	3	7	10	6
Partick T	6	0	1	5	3	13	1

Section 4	P	W	D	L	F	A	Pts
Hibernian	6	5	0	1	15	6	10
Falkirk	6	3	1	2	11	10	7
St Mirren	6	2	0	4	5	9	4
Morton	6	1	1	4	7	13	3

Section 5	P	W	D	L	F	A	Pts
T Lanark	6	3	2	1	13	10	8
Berwick R	6	2	2	2	16	10	6
Cowdenbeath	6	2	2	2	7	11	6
Hamilton A	6	0	4	2	6	11	4

Section 6	P	W	D	L	F	A	Pts
Raith R	6	4	2	0	15	7	10
Queen's Park	6	2	2	2	7	10	6
Stirling A	6	2	0	4	10	11	4
Arbroath	6	1	2	3	11	15	4

Section 7	P	W	D	L	F	A	Pts
Airdrie	6	5	0	1	22	13	10
Albion R	6	2	2	2	12	12	6
Queen of South	6	1	2	3	8	12	4
Stranraer	6	1	2	3	5	10	4

Section 8	P	W	D	L	F	A	Pts
Alloa	6	4	0	2	10	10	8
Dumbarton	6	3	0	3	15	9	6
E Stirling	6	3	0	3	11	10	6
East Fife	6	2	0	4	13	20	4

Section 9	P	W	D	L	F	A	Pts
Ayr U	4	4	0	0	14	3	8
Stenhousemuir	4	3	0	1	8	7	6
Forfar A	4	1	0	3	6	7	2
Montrose	4	1	0	3	4	12	2
Brechin C	4	1	0	3	1	4	2

Play-offs

Sep 6 T Lanark . . . . .1 Ayr U 2
Sep 8 Ayr U . . . . .1 T Lanark . . . . . . .0 Agg 3-1

Quarter-finals

Sep 15 Airdrie . . . . .1 Rangers 5
Sep 22 Rangers . . . . .4 Airdrie . . . . .0 Agg 9-1
Sep 15 Alloa . . . . .0 Hibernian 2
Sep 22 Hibernian . . . . .11 Alloa . . . . .2 Agg 13-2
Sep 15 Kilmarnock . . . . .2 Ayr U 0
Sep 22 Ayr U . . . . .2 Kilmarnock . . . . .2 Agg 2-4
Sep 15 Raith R . . . . .1 Celtic 8
Sep 22 Celtic . . . . .4 Raith R . . . . .0 Agg 12-1

Semi-finals

Oct 4 Celtic . . . . .2 Hibernian 2
played at Ibrox
Oct 6 Kilmarnock . . . . .4 Rangers 6
played at Hampden Park

Replay

Oct 18 Celtic . . . . .4 Hibernian 0
played at Ibrox

Final

Oct 23 Celtic . . . . .2 Rangers 1
played at Hampden Park

It's the first for Celtic as big John Hughes sends Rangers' goalkeeper Billy Ritchie the wrong way in the 1965-66 League Cup Final.

Season 1966-67

Section 1

	Aberdeen	Dundee	Dundee U	St Johnstone
Aberdeen		Aug31 2-0	Aug20 4-1	Aug13 3-0
Dundee	Aug17 3-4		Aug27 1-1	Aug20 2-0
Dundee U	Sep03 3-4	Aug13 2-0		Aug31 5-3
St Johnstone	Aug27 0-3	Sep03 2-2	Aug17 1-1	

Section 2

	Hibernian	Kilmarnock	Rangers	Stirling A
Hibernian		Aug17 2-1	Aug27 3-2	Sep03 3-0
Kilmarnock	Aug31 3-0		Sep03 0-1	Aug13 2-0
Rangers	Aug13 1-0	Aug20 0-0		Aug31 1-1
Stirling A	Aug20 2-4	Aug27 0-0	Aug17 0-8	

Section 3

	Dunfermline A	Falkirk	Motherwell	Partick T
Dunfermline A		Aug20 2-2	Aug13 2-1	Aug31 3-2
Falkirk	Sep03 1-2		Aug31 0-2	Aug13 0-0
Motherwell	Aug27 4-3	Aug17 2-2		Aug20 4-0
Partick T	Aug17 0-3	Aug27 1-0	Sep03 0-0	

Section 4

	Celtic	Clyde	Hearts	St Mirren
Celtic		Aug17 6-0	Aug27 3-0	Aug20 8-2
Clyde	Aug31 1-3		Sep03 1-3	Aug13 1-0
Hearts	Aug13 0-2	Aug20 4-3		Aug31 3-1
St Mirren	Sep03 0-1	Aug27 0-1	Aug17 0-0	

Section 5

	Ayr U	Berwick R	Cowdenbeath	Raith R
Ayr U		Aug27 2-0	Aug20 2-2	Aug17 0-0
Berwick R	Aug13 1-1		Aug31 1-1	Aug20 1-1
Cowdenbeath	Sep03 0-3	Aug17 0-0		Aug27 2-1
Raith R	Aug31 3-1	Sep03 2-0	Aug13 1-2	

Section 6

	Arbroath	East Fife	Morton	T Lanark
Arbroath		Aug31 2-1	Aug20 0-0	Aug13 2-0
East Fife	Aug17 0-0		Aug27 0-1	Aug20 2-2
Morton	Sep03 2-0	Aug13 2-1		Aug31 3-2
T Lanark	Aug27 1-1	Sep03 2-3	Aug17 0-1	

Section 7

	Airdrie	Dumbarton	Queen of South	Queen's Park
Airdrie		Aug13 3-0	Aug31 1-1	Sep03 3-2
Dumbarton	Aug27 1-2		Aug20 1-1	Aug17 1-2
Queen of South	Aug17 0-3	Sep03 4-2		Aug27 6-1
Queen's Park	Aug20 1-3	Aug31 0-3	Aug13 1-5	

Section 8

	Albion R	Alloa	Hamilton A	Montrose
Albion R		Aug27 1-0	Aug17 0-0	Aug20 0-0
Alloa	Aug13 4-0		Aug20 3-1	Aug31 1-0
Hamilton A	Aug31 3-0	Sep03 1-0		Aug13 1-3
Montrose	Sep03 2-2	Aug17 2-1	Aug27 2-0	

Section 9

	Brechin C	Clydebank	E Stirling	Forfar A	Stenhousemuir	Stranraer
Brechin C		Aug20 3-1			Aug13 4-0	
Clydebank			Aug13 3-0		Sep03 3-2	
E Stirling	Aug17 0-4				Aug27 1-1	Aug20 0-0
Forfar A	Aug27 1-1	Aug17 2-1	Sep03 5-1			
Stenhousemuir				Aug20 1-3		Aug17 1-1
Stranraer	Sep03 1-2	Aug27 1-0		Aug13 2-1		

Bobby Lennox slips the ball past Rangers' Ronnie McKinnon for the only goal of the game as the Parkhead boys retain the League Cup in 1966-67.

Section 1	P	W	D	L	F	A	Pts
Aberdeen	6	6	0	0	20	7	12
Dundee U	6	2	2	2	13	13	6
Dundee	6	1	2	3	8	11	4
St Johnstone	6	0	2	4	6	16	2

Section 2	P	W	D	L	F	A	Pts
Rangers	6	3	2	1	13	4	8
Hibernian	6	4	0	2	12	9	8
Kilmarnock	6	2	2	2	6	3	6
Stirling A	6	0	2	4	3	18	2

Section 3	P	W	D	L	F	A	Pts
Dunfermline A	6	4	1	1	15	10	9
Motherwell	6	3	2	1	13	7	8
Partick T	6	1	2	3	3	10	4
Falkirk	6	0	3	3	5	9	3

Section 4	P	W	D	L	F	A	Pts
Celtic	6	6	0	0	23	3	12
Hearts	6	3	1	2	10	10	7
Clyde	6	2	0	4	7	16	4
St Mirren	6	0	1	5	3	14	1

Section 5	P	W	D	L	F	A	Pts
Ayr U	6	2	3	1	9	6	7
Cowdenbeath	6	2	3	1	7	8	7
Raith R	6	2	2	2	8	6	6
Berwick R	6	0	4	2	3	7	4

Section 6	P	W	D	L	F	A	Pts
Morton	6	5	1	0	9	3	11
Arbroath	6	2	3	1	5	4	7
East Fife	6	1	2	3	7	9	4
T Lanark	6	0	2	4	7	12	2

Section 7	P	W	D	L	F	A	Pts
Airdrie	6	5	1	0	15	5	11
Queen of South	6	3	2	1	17	9	8
Dumbarton	6	1	1	4	8	12	3
Queen's Park	6	1	0	5	7	21	2

Section 8	P	W	D	L	F	A	Pts
Montrose	6	3	2	1	9	5	8
Alloa	6	3	0	3	9	5	6
Hamilton A	6	2	1	3	6	8	5
Albion R	6	1	3	2	3	9	5

Section 9	P	W	D	L	F	A	Pts
Brechin C	5	4	1	0	14	3	9
Forfar A	5	3	1	1	12	6	7
Stranraer	5	2	2	1	5	4	6
Clydebank	5	2	0	3	8	8	4
Stenhousemuir	5	0	2	3	5	12	2
E Stirling	5	0	2	3	2	13	2

Play-offs

Sep 5 Brechin C . . . . .1 Morton 2
Sep 7 Morton . . . . .5 Brechin C . . . . . .2 Agg 7-3

Quarter-finals

Sep 14 Ayr U . . . . .1 Rangers 1
Sep 21 Rangers . . . . .3 Ayr U . . . . .0 Agg 4-1
Sep 14 Celtic . . . . .6 Dunfermline A 3
Sep 21 Dunfermline A . . . . .1 Celtic . . . . .3 Agg 4-9
Sep 14 Montrose . . . . .3 Airdrie 3
Sep 21 Airdrie . . . . .5 Montrose . . . . . .1 Agg 8-4
Sep 14 Morton . . . . .3 Aberdeen 1
Sep 21 Aberdeen . . . . .3 Morton . . . . .0 Agg 4-3

Semi-finals

Oct 19 Aberdeen . . . . .2 Rangers 2
played at Hampden Park
Oct 17 Airdrie . . . . .0 Celtic 2
played at Hampden Park

Replay

Oct 24 Aberdeen . . . . .0 Rangers 2
played at Hampden Park

Final

Oct 29 Celtic . . . . .1 Rangers 0
played at Hampden Park

More action from the Final as Rangers' Alex Smith is foiled by Ronnie Simpson and Bobby Murdoch of Celtic, as they search for an equaliser.

Season 1967-68

Section 1	Airdrie	Dunfermline A	Kilmarnock	Partick T
Airdrie		Aug19 2-3	Aug16 1-2	Aug26 2-1
Dunfermline A	Sep02 2-1		Aug26 1-3	Aug16 1-1
Kilmarnock	Aug30 0-0	Aug12 2-2		Aug19 4-0
Partick T	Aug12 0-1	Aug30 3-2	Sep02 1-0	

Section 2	Aberdeen	Celtic	Dundee U	Rangers
Aberdeen		Sep02 1-5	Aug30 2-2	Aug12 1-1
Celtic	Aug19 3-1		Aug12 1-0	Aug30 3-1
Dundee U	Aug16 5-0	Aug26 0-1		Sep02 0-3
Rangers	Aug26 3-0	Aug16 1-1	Aug19 1-0	

Section 3	Clyde	Dundee	Hibernian	Motherwell
Clyde		Aug16 1-2	Sep02 0-2	Aug26 2-1
Dundee	Aug30 1-0		Aug12 0-0	Aug19 2-1
Hibernian	Aug19 3-1	Aug26 2-4		Aug16 1-0
Motherwell	Aug12 2-2	Sep02 2-5	Aug30 2-1	

Section 4	Falkirk	Hearts	St Johnstone	Stirling A
Falkirk		Aug19 0-2	Aug30 0-3	Aug12 0-2
Hearts	Sep02 3-1		Aug12 1-2	Aug30 4-1
St Johnstone	Aug16 0-0	Aug26 3-2		Aug19 2-1
Stirling A	Aug26 1-1	Aug16 0-1	Sep02 1-0	

Section 5	Ayr U	Berwick R	St Mirren	Stranraer
Ayr U		Sep02 2-1	Aug16 2-0	Aug26 1-0
Berwick R	Aug19 2-1		Aug26 1-3	Aug16 2-0
St Mirren	Aug30 1-2	Aug12 2-2		Sep02 2-1
Stranraer	Aug12 1-4	Aug30 1-0	Aug19 1-3	

Section 6	Cowdenbeath	Hamilton A	Montrose	Queen's Park
Cowdenbeath		Aug30 0-0	Aug19 3-0	Aug12 0-2
Hamilton A	Aug16 0-1		Aug26 3-1	Aug19 1-0
Montrose	Sep02 2-1	Aug12 2-3		Aug30 0-1
Queen's Park	Aug26 1-0	Sep02 1-1	Aug16 2-1	

Section 7	Dumbarton	Morton	Queen of South	Raith R
Dumbarton		Sep02 1-3	Aug16 1-2	Aug26 1-1
Morton	Aug19 6-0		Aug26 3-2	Aug16 3-1
Queen of South	Aug30 3-1	Aug12 0-4		Sep02 3-2
Raith R	Aug12 2-0	Aug30 2-3	Aug19 2-5	

Section 8	Albion R	Alloa	Arbroath	East Fife
Albion R		Sep02 4-3	Aug30 1-1	Aug12 2-4
Alloa	Aug19 1-4		Aug12 1-2	Aug30 0-2
Arbroath	Aug16 1-3	Aug26 1-1		Aug19 4-3
East Fife	Aug26 1-0	Aug16 3-1	Sep02 3-0	

Section 9	Brechin C	Clydebank	E Stirling	Forfar A	Stenhousemuir
Brechin C			Aug19 2-1	Aug26 2-1	
Clydebank	Aug12 2-0				Aug19 2-1
E Stirling		Aug16 0-1			Aug26 3-3
Forfar A		Sep02 1-2	Aug12 4-0		
Stenhousemuir	Sep02 2-4			Aug16 3-1	

Section 1	P	W	D	L	F	A	Pts
Kilmarnock	6	3	2	1	11	5	8
Dunfermline A	6	2	2	2	11	12	6
Airdrie	6	2	1	3	7	8	5
Partick T	6	2	1	3	6	10	5

Section 2	P	W	D	L	F	A	Pts
Celtic	6	5	1	0	14	4	11
Rangers	6	3	2	1	10	5	8
Dundee U	6	1	1	4	7	8	3
Aberdeen	6	0	2	4	5	19	2

Section 3	P	W	D	L	F	A	Pts
Dundee	6	5	1	0	14	6	11
Hibernian	6	3	1	2	9	7	7
Motherwell	6	1	1	4	8	13	3
Clyde	6	1	1	4	6	11	3

Section 4	P	W	D	L	F	A	Pts
St Johnstone	6	4	1	1	10	5	9
Hearts	6	4	0	2	13	7	8
Stirling A	6	2	1	3	6	8	5
Falkirk	6	0	2	4	2	11	2

Section 5	P	W	D	L	F	A	Pts
Ayr U	6	5	0	1	12	5	10
St Mirren	6	3	1	2	11	9	7
Berwick R	6	2	1	3	8	9	5
Stranraer	6	1	0	5	4	12	2

Section 6	P	W	D	L	F	A	Pts
Queen's Park	6	4	1	1	7	3	9
Hamilton A	6	3	2	1	8	5	8
Cowdenbeath	6	2	1	3	5	5	5
Montrose	6	1	0	5	6	13	2

Section 7	P	W	D	L	F	A	Pts
Morton	6	6	0	0	22	6	12
Queen of South	6	4	0	2	15	13	8
Raith R	6	1	1	4	10	15	3
Dumbarton	6	0	1	5	4	17	1

Section 8	P	W	D	L	F	A	Pts
East Fife	6	5	0	1	16	7	10
Albion R	6	3	1	2	14	11	7
Arbroath	6	2	2	2	9	12	6
Alloa	6	0	1	5	7	16	1

Section 9	P	W	D	L	F	A	Pts
Clydebank	4	4	0	0	7	2	8
Brechin C	4	3	0	1	8	6	6
Stenhousemuir	4	1	1	2	9	10	3
Forfar A	4	1	0	3	7	7	2
E Stirling	4	0	1	3	4	10	1

Play-offs

Sep 4 Ayr U ....1 Clydebank 1
Sep 6 Clydebank ....2 Ayr U ....4 Agg 3-5

Quarter-finals

Sep 13 Celtic ....6 Ayr U 2
Sep 27 Ayr U ....0 Celtic ....2 Agg 2-8
Sep 13 East Fife ....0 Dundee 1
Sep 20 Dundee ....4 East Fife ....0 Agg 5-0
Sep 13 Morton ....3 Kilmarnock 2
Sep 27 Kilmarnock ....1 Morton ....2 Agg 3-5
Sep 13 Queen's Park ......0 St Johnstone 5
Sep 27 St Johnstone ......3 Queen's Park ....1 Agg 8-1

Semi-finals

Oct 11 Celtic ....7 Morton 1
played at Hampden Park
Oct 11 Dundee ....3 St Johnstone 1
played at Tannadice

Final

Oct 28 Celtic ....5 Dundee 3
played at Hampden Park

Season 1968-69

Section 1	Falkirk	Hibernian	Raith R	St Johnstone
Falkirk		Aug31 0-2	Aug10 1-1	Aug28 2-2
Hibernian	Aug17 2-0		Aug28 3-0	Aug10 0-1
Raith R	Aug24 4-2	Aug14 0-1		Aug31 2-1
St Johnstone	Aug14 2-3	Aug24 2-2	Aug17 0-0	

Section 2	Airdrie	Dundee	Hearts	Kilmarnock
Airdrie		Aug31 0-3	Aug10 2-3	Aug28 2-0
Dundee	Aug17 1-1		Aug28 4-0	Aug10 4-0
Hearts	Aug24 0-2	Aug14 2-1		Aug31 0-0
Kilmarnock	Aug14 0-3	Aug24 2-2	Aug17 3-3	

Section 3	Aberdeen	Clyde	Dundee U	Dunfermline A
Aberdeen		Aug24 0-2	Aug17 4-1	Aug14 1-0
Clyde	Aug10 4-1		Aug28 0-4	Aug31 3-0
Dundee U	Aug31 1-0	Aug14 2-3		Aug24 2-1
Dunfermline A	Aug28 1-2	Aug17 2-1	Aug10 3-2	

Section 4	Celtic	Morton	Partick T	Rangers
Celtic		Aug14 4-1	Aug17 4-0	Aug24 1-0
Morton	Aug28 0-3		Aug10 1-3	Aug31 0-5
Partick T	Aug31 1-6	Aug24 2-0		Aug14 1-5
Rangers	Aug10 0-2	Aug17 2-0	Aug28 2-1	

Section 5	Arbroath	Ayr U	Cowdenbeath	Stirling A
Arbroath		Aug17 1-1	Aug28 2-0	Aug10 2-1
Ayr U	Aug31 3-1		Aug10 3-1	Aug28 1-0
Cowdenbeath	Aug14 1-1	Aug24 0-2		Aug31 3-6
Stirling A	Aug24 1-0	Aug14 2-4	Aug17 2-1	

Section 6	Berwick R	Clydebank	East Fife	Queen of South
Berwick R		Aug28 3-0	Aug31 1-4	Aug10 1-1
Clydebank	Aug14 2-4		Aug24 1-3	Aug31 1-1
East Fife	Aug17 1-0	Aug10 2-0		Aug28 1-1
Queen of South	Aug24 2-0	Aug17 1-2	Aug14 1-1	

Section 7

	Hamilton A	Montrose	Motherwell	St Mirren
Hamilton A		Aug31 2-0	Aug10 2-1	Aug28 2-1
Montrose	Aug17 0-2		Aug28 2-1	Aug10 1-2
Motherwell	Aug24 0-0	Aug14 1-2		Aug17 6-0
St Mirren	Aug14 3-0	Aug24 1-0	Aug31 2-0	

Section 8

	Albion R	Dumbarton	Forfar A	Queen's Park
Albion R		Aug24 5-0	Aug17 2-4	Aug14 3-2
Dumbarton	Aug10 0-4		Aug28 5-1	Aug17 4-3
Forfar A	Aug31 2-2	Aug14 1-0		Aug24 0-2
Queen's Park	Aug28 2-3	Aug31 1-0	Aug10 4-0	

Section 9

	Alloa	Brechin C	E Stirling	Stenhousemuir	Stranraer
Alloa				Aug10 0-1	Aug31 0-1
Brechin C	Aug14 2-3		Aug31 3-0		
E Stirling	Aug24 2-2			Aug17 3-0	
Stenhousemuir		Aug24 1-0			Aug14 1-3
Stranraer		Aug17 1-2	Aug10 2-1		

Section 1	P	W	D	L	F	A	Pts
Hibernian	6	4	1	1	10	3	9
Raith R	6	2	2	2	7	8	6
St Johnstone	6	1	3	2	8	9	5
Falkirk	6	1	2	3	8	13	4

Section 2	P	W	D	L	F	A	Pts
Dundee	6	3	2	1	15	5	8
Airdrie	6	3	1	2	10	7	7
Hearts	6	2	2	2	8	12	6
Kilmarnock	6	0	3	3	5	14	3

Section 3	P	W	D	L	F	A	Pts
Clyde	6	4	0	2	13	9	8
Dundee U	6	3	0	3	12	11	6
Aberdeen	6	3	0	3	8	9	6
Dunfermline A	6	2	0	4	7	11	4

Section 4	P	W	D	L	F	A	Pts
Celtic	6	6	0	0	20	2	12
Rangers	6	4	0	2	14	5	8
Partick T	6	2	0	4	8	18	4
Morton	6	0	0	6	2	19	0

Section 5	P	W	D	L	F	A	Pts
Ayr U	6	5	1	0	14	5	11
Stirling A	6	3	0	3	12	11	6
Arbroath	6	2	2	2	7	7	6
Cowdenbeath	6	0	1	5	6	16	1

Section 6	P	W	D	L	F	A	Pts
East Fife	6	4	2	0	12	4	10
Queen of South	6	1	4	1	7	6	6
Berwick R	6	2	1	3	9	10	5
Clydebank	6	1	1	4	6	14	3

Section 7	P	W	D	L	F	A	Pts
Hamilton A	6	4	1	1	8	5	9
St Mirren	6	4	0	2	9	9	8
Montrose	6	2	0	4	5	9	4
Motherwell	6	1	1	4	9	8	3

Section 8	P	W	D	L	F	A	Pts
Albion R	6	4	1	1	19	10	9
Queen's Park	6	3	0	3	14	10	6
Forfar A	6	2	1	3	8	15	5
Dumbarton	6	2	0	4	9	15	4

Section 9	P	W	D	L	F	A	Pts
Stranraer	4	3	0	1	7	4	6
Brechin C	4	2	0	2	7	5	4
Stenhousemuir	4	2	0	2	3	6	4
E Stirling	4	1	1	2	6	7	3
Alloa	4	1	1	2	5	6	3

Play-offs

Sep 2 Stranraer . . . . .3 Albion R 3
Sep 4 Albion R . . . . .0 Stranraer . . . . . . .2 Agg 3-5

Quarter-finals

Sep 11 Ayr U . . . . .0 Clyde 1
Sep 25 Clyde . . . . .2 Ayr U . . . . .0 Agg 3-0
Sep 11 Celtic . . . . .10 Hamilton A 0
Sep 25 Hamilton A . . . . .2 Celtic . . . . .4 Agg 2-14
Sep 11 East Fife . . . . .1 Hibernian 4
Sep 25 Hibernian . . . . .2 East Fife . . . . . . .1 Agg 6-2
Sep 11 Stranraer . . . . .0 Dundee 4
Sep 25 Dundee . . . . .6 Stranraer . . . . . . .0 Agg 10-0

Semi-finals

Oct 9 Celtic . . . . .1 Clyde 0
played at Hampden Park
Oct 9 Dundee . . . . .1 Hibernian 2
played at Tynecastle

Final

Apr 5 Celtic . . . . .6 Hibernian 2
played at Hampden Park

SEASON 1969-70

Section 1

	Airdrie	Celtic	Raith R	Rangers
Airdrie		Aug23 0-3	Aug13 3-1	Aug16 0-3
Celtic	Aug09 6-1		Aug16 5-0	Aug20 1-0
Raith R	Aug20 2-1	Aug27 2-5		Aug09 2-3
Rangers	Aug27 3-0	Aug13 2-1	Aug23 3-3	

Section 2

	Aberdeen	Clyde	Dunfermline A	Hibernian
Aberdeen		Aug20 3-0	Aug09 2-2	Aug16 2-2
Clyde	Aug13 0-0		Aug27 0-0	Aug23 3-1
Dunfermline A	Aug23 0-1	Aug16 0-0		Aug13 3-1
Hibernian	Aug27 0-0	Aug09 4-1	Aug20 2-0	

Section 3

	Dundee	Kilmarnock	Partick T	St Johnstone
Dundee		Aug16 0-0	Aug13 4-0	Aug23 1-2
Kilmarnock	Aug27 1-0		Aug23 6-0	Aug13 2-3
Partick T	Aug20 0-1	Aug09 0-2		Aug16 1-8
St Johnstone	Aug09 3-1	Aug20 2-1	Aug27 4-0	

Section 4

	Dundee U	Hearts	Morton	St Mirren
Dundee U		Aug09 2-3	Aug20 0-2	Aug27 2-1
Hearts	Aug23 1-0		Aug16 0-1	Aug13 0-0
Morton	Aug13 4-1	Aug27 0-2		Aug23 1-2
St Mirren	Aug16 0-1	Aug20 1-0	Aug09 1-1	

Section 5

	Albion R	East Fife	Montrose	Motherwell
Albion R		Aug19 2-1	Aug09 0-1	Aug27 2-4
East Fife	Aug13 1-1		Aug16 4-1	Aug23 0-0
Montrose	Aug23 1-1	Aug27 1-3		Aug13 1-4
Motherwell	Aug16 5-1	Aug09 2-0	Aug20 3-2	

Section 6

	Ayr U	E Stirling	Queen of South	Queen's Park
Ayr U		Aug20 0-0	Aug16 4-1	Aug09 2-0
E Stirling	Aug13 0-1		Aug23 0-0	Aug27 2-0
Queen of South	Aug27 2-1	Aug09 2-0		Aug20 2-1
Queen's Park	Aug23 0-1	Aug16 7-2	Aug13 1-4	

Section 7

	Clydebank	Cowdenbeath	Dumbarton	Stranraer
Clydebank		Aug16 3-1	Aug09 1-3	Aug20 3-2
Cowdenbeath	Aug27 2-1		Aug20 2-3	Aug09 2-2
Dumbarton	Aug23 1-0	Aug13 2-3		Aug27 2-0
Stranraer	Aug13 1-1	Aug23 3-3	Aug16 2-2	

Section 8

	Arbroath	Falkirk	Forfar A	Stirling A
Arbroath		Aug27 1-3	Aug20 1-0	Aug09 2-3
Falkirk	Aug16 1-2		Aug09 3-1	Aug20 4-3
Forfar A	Aug13 2-1	Aug23 1-1		Aug16 0-3
Stirling A	Aug23 4-1	Aug13 2-3	Aug27 1-2	

Section 9

	Alloa	Berwick R	Brechin C	Hamilton A	Stenhousemuir
Alloa			Aug20 2-0	Aug09 0-3	
Berwick R	Aug23 1-2			Aug16 2-0	
Brechin C		Aug09 1-0			Aug16 2-1
Hamilton A			Aug13 1-2		Aug23 2-0
Stenhousemuir	Aug12 3-3	Aug26 3-3			

Section 1	P	W	D	L	F	A	Pts
Celtic	6	5	0	1	21	5	10
Rangers	6	4	1	1	14	7	9
Raith R	6	1	1	4	10	20	3
Airdrie	6	1	0	5	5	18	2

Section 2	P	W	D	L	F	A	Pts
Aberdeen	6	2	4	0	8	4	8
Hibernian	6	2	2	2	10	9	6
Dunfermline A	6	1	3	2	5	6	5
Clyde	6	1	3	2	4	8	5

Section 3	P	W	D	L	F	A	Pts
St Johnstone	6	6	0	0	22	6	12
Kilmarnock	6	3	1	2	12	5	7
Dundee	6	2	1	3	7	6	5
Partick T	6	0	0	6	1	25	0

Section 4	P	W	D	L	F	A	Pts
Morton	6	3	1	2	9	6	7
Hearts	6	3	1	2	6	4	7
St Mirren	6	2	2	2	5	5	6
Dundee U	6	2	0	4	6	11	4

Section 5	P	W	D	L	F	A	Pts
Motherwell	6	5	1	0	18	6	11
East Fife	6	2	2	2	9	7	6
Albion R	6	1	2	3	7	13	4
Montrose	6	1	1	4	7	15	3

Section 6	P	W	D	L	F	A	Pts
Ayr U	6	4	1	1	9	3	9
Queen of South	6	4	1	1	11	7	9
E Stirling	6	1	2	3	4	10	4
Queen's Park	6	1	0	5	9	13	2

Section 7	P	W	D	L	F	A	Pts
Dumbarton	6	4	1	1	13	8	9
Cowdenbeath	6	2	2	2	13	14	6
Clydebank	6	2	1	3	9	10	5
Stranraer	6	0	4	2	10	13	4

Section 8	P	W	D	L	F	A	Pts
Falkirk	6	4	1	1	15	10	9
Stirling A	6	3	0	3	16	12	6
Forfar A	6	2	1	3	6	10	5
Arbroath	6	2	0	4	8	13	4

Section 9	P	W	D	L	F	A	Pts
Brechin C	4	3	0	1	5	4	6
Alloa	4	2	1	1	7	7	5
Hamilton A	4	2	0	2	6	4	4
Berwick R	4	1	1	2	6	6	3
Stenhousemuir . . .	4	0	2	2	7	10	2

Play-offs
Sep 1 Brechin C . . . . .1 Dumbarton 1
Sep 3 Dumbarton . . . . .5 Brechin C . . . . . .2 Agg 6-3

Quarter-finals
Sep 10 Aberdeen . . . . .0 Celtic 0
Sep 24 Celtic . . . . .2 Aberdeen . . . . . . .1 Agg 2-1
Sep 10 Dumbarton . . . . .1 Ayr U 4
Sep 24 Ayr U . . . . .1 Dumbarton . . . . .0 Agg 5-1
Sep 10 Morton . . . . .3 Motherwell 0
Sep 24 Motherwell . . . . .3 Morton . . . . .0 Agg 3-3
Sep 10 St Johnstone . . . . . .5 Falkirk 1
Sep 24 Falkirk . . . . .2 St Johnstone . . . .6 Agg 3-11

Replay
Sep 30 Morton . . . . .0 Motherwell 1
played at Ibrox

Semi-finals
Oct 8 Ayr U . . . . .3 Celtic 3
played at Hampden Park
Oct 1 Motherwell . . . . .0 St Johnstone 2
played at Hampden Park

Replay
Oct 13 Ayr U . . . . .1 Celtic 2
played at Hampden Park

Final
Oct 25 Celtic . . . . .1 St Johnstone 0
played at Hampden Park

Season 1970-71

Section 1	Celtic	Clyde	Dundee U	Hearts
Celtic		Aug12 5-3	Aug15 2-2	Aug22 4-2
Clyde	Aug19 0-2		Aug08 1-1	Aug26 1-5
Dundee U	Aug26 2-2	Aug22 1-1		Aug12 2-1
Hearts	Aug08 1-2	Aug15 1-2	Aug19 0-0	

Section 2	Dunfermline A	Morton	Motherwell	Rangers
Dunfermline A		Aug12 0-2	Aug26 1-1	Aug22 0-6
Morton	Aug19 3-2		Aug08 1-4	Aug26 0-2
Motherwell	Aug15 3-0	Aug22 0-2		Aug12 0-2
Rangers	Aug08 4-1	Aug15 0-0	Aug19 2-0	

Section 3	Ayr U	Dundee	Kilmarnock	St Mirren
Ayr U		Aug12 1-2	Aug22 0-0	Aug15 2-2
Dundee	Aug19 4-1		Aug15 2-0	Aug08 1-0
Kilmarnock	Aug08 1-0	Aug26 2-1		Aug19 2-0
St Mirren	Aug26 1-2	Aug22 0-2	Aug12 1-3	

Section 4	Aberdeen	Airdrie	Hibernian	St Johnstone
Aberdeen		Aug22 7-3	Aug15 1-1	Aug12 2-1
Airdrie	Aug08 1-1		Aug19 2-4	Aug26 1-0
Hibernian	Aug26 4-0	Aug12 3-2		Aug22 1-1
St Johnstone	Aug19 0-1	Aug15 0-1	Aug08 1-3	

Section 5	East Fife	Partick T	Queen of South	Stirling A
East Fife		Aug15 1-1	Aug22 2-1	Aug12 1-1
Partick T	Aug26 1-3		Aug12 4-1	Aug22 1-1
Queen of South	Aug08 1-1	Aug19 0-0		Aug26 1-1
Stirling A	Aug19 2-1	Aug08 2-3	Aug15 2-2	

Section 6	Alloa	Berwick R	Brechin C	Dumbarton
Alloa		Aug19 0-1	Aug26 2-0	Aug08 1-3
Berwick R	Aug12 1-1		Aug22 4-1	Aug15 0-2
Brechin C	Aug15 1-3	Aug08 2-3		Aug19 1-3
Dumbarton	Aug22 5-2	Aug26 3-2	Aug12 2-2	

Section 7	Cowdenbeath	E Stirling	Montrose	Raith R
Cowdenbeath		Aug08 1-1	Aug19 3-0	Aug15 3-1
E Stirling	Aug22 1-4		Aug15 1-2	Aug12 2-0
Montrose	Aug12 3-2	Aug26 2-1		Aug22 4-1
Raith R	Aug26 0-2	Aug19 2-1	Aug08 1-0	

Section 8	Albion R	Arbroath	Clydebank	Falkirk
Albion R		Aug15 2-1	Aug12 2-2	Aug22 0-3
Arbroath	Aug26 5-3		Aug22 4-0	Aug12 1-4
Clydebank	Aug19 5-1	Aug08 4-1		Aug15 0-3
Falkirk	Aug08 5-0	Aug19 2-1	Aug26 1-1	

Section 9	Forfar A	Hamilton A	Queen's Park	Stenhousemuir	Stranraer
Forfar A		Aug15 1-2		Aug08 2-1	
Hamilton A			Aug19 1-1		Aug08 2-3
Queen's Park	Aug12 1-1				Aug15 2-1
Stenhousemuir		Aug12 3-2	Aug22 1-4		
Stranraer	Aug22 1-0			Aug19 4-0	

Section 1	P	W	D	L	F	A	Pts
Celtic	6	4	2	0	17	10	10
Dundee U	6	1	5	0	8	7	7
Clyde	6	1	2	3	8	15	4
Hearts	6	1	1	4	10	11	3

Section 2	P	W	D	L	F	A	Pts
Rangers	6	5	1	0	16	1	11
Morton	6	3	1	2	8	8	7
Motherwell	6	2	1	3	8	8	5
Dunfermline A	6	0	1	5	4	19	1

Section 3	P	W	D	L	F	A	Pts
Dundee	6	5	0	1	12	4	10
Kilmarnock	6	4	1	1	8	4	9
Ayr U	6	1	2	3	6	10	4
St Mirren	6	0	1	5	4	12	1

Section 4	P	W	D	L	F	A	Pts
Hibernian	6	4	2	0	16	7	10
Aberdeen	6	3	2	1	12	10	8
Airdrie	6	2	1	3	10	15	5
St Johnstone	6	0	1	5	3	9	1

Section 5	P	W	D	L	F	A	Pts
Partick T	6	2	3	1	10	8	7
East Fife	6	2	3	1	9	7	7
Stirling A	6	1	4	1	9	9	6
Queen of South . . .	6	0	4	2	6	10	4

Section 6	P	W	D	L	F	A	Pts
Dumbarton	6	5	1	0	18	8	11
Berwick R	6	3	1	2	11	9	7
Alloa	6	2	1	3	9	11	5
Brechin C	6	0	1	5	7	17	1

Section 7	P	W	D	L	F	A	Pts
Cowdenbeath	6	4	1	1	15	6	9
Montrose	6	4	0	2	11	9	8
Raith R	6	2	0	4	5	12	4
E Stirling	6	1	1	4	7	11	3

Section 8	P	W	D	L	F	A	Pts
Falkirk	6	5	1	0	18	3	11
Clydebank	6	2	2	2	12	12	6
Arbroath	6	2	0	4	13	15	4
Albion R	6	1	1	4	8	21	3

Section 9	P	W	D	L	F	A	Pts
Stranraer	4	3	0	1	9	4	6
Queen's Park	4	2	2	0	8	4	6
Hamilton A	4	1	1	2	7	8	3
Forfar A	4	1	1	2	4	5	3
Stenhousemuir . . .	4	1	0	3	5	12	2

Play-offs
Aug 31 Partick T . . . . .2 Stranraer 1
Sep 2 Stranraer . . . . .2 Partick T . . . . . . .2 Agg 3-4

Quarter-finals
Sep 9 Dundee . . . . .2 Celtic 2
Sep 23 Celtic . . . . .5 Dundee . . . . .1 Agg 7-3
Sep 9 Falkirk . . . . .0 Cowdenbeath 1
Sep 23 Cowdenbeath . . . . . .0 Falkirk . . . . .0 Agg 1-0
Sep 9 Hibernian . . . . .1 Rangers 3
Sep 23 Rangers . . . . .3 Hibernian . . . . . .1 Agg 6-2
Sep 9 Partick T . . . . .3 Dumbarton 3
Sep 23 Dumbarton . . . . .3 Partick T . . . . . . .2 Agg 6-5

Semi-finals
Oct 7 Celtic . . . . .0 Dumbarton 0
played at Hampden Park
Oct 14 Cowdenbeath . . . . . .0 Rangers 2
played at Hampden Park

Replay
Oct 12 Celtic . . . . .4 Dumbarton 3
played at Hampden Park

Final
Oct 24 Celtic . . . . .0 Rangers 1
played at Hampden Park

Season 1971-72

Section 1

	Dundee U	Hibernian	Kilmarnock	Motherwell
Dundee U		Aug25 1-4	Aug14 1-0	Aug21 2-2
Hibernian	Aug18 2-0		Aug21 3-1	Aug28 2-1
Kilmarnock	Aug28 4-2	Sep01 0-0		Aug18 2-1
Motherwell	Sep01 1-3	Aug14 0-3	Aug25 2-0	

Section 2

	Aberdeen	Clyde	Dundee	Falkirk
Aberdeen		Aug25 5-0	Aug14 1-1	Aug21 1-0
Clyde	Aug18 0-2		Aug21 0-1	Aug28 0-1
Dundee	Aug28 3-1	Sep01 3-0		Aug18 2-2
Falkirk	Sep01 3-1	Aug14 5-2	Aug25 1-0	

Section 3

	Airdrie	Dunfermline A	Hearts	St Johnstone
Airdrie		Aug28 1-0	Aug18 1-3	Aug21 1-3
Dunfermline A	Aug14 2-1		Aug21 1-0	Aug25 0-2
Hearts	Aug25 1-2	Sep01 4-0		Aug14 4-1
St Johnstone	Sep01 0-1	Aug18 1-1	Aug28 1-0	

Section 4

	Ayr U	Celtic	Morton	Rangers
Ayr U		Aug21 0-3	Aug14 1-1	Aug25 0-4
Celtic	Aug30 4-1		Aug25 0-1	Aug14 2-0
Morton	Aug28 2-0	Aug18 0-1		Sep01 0-1
Rangers	Aug18 4-0	Aug28 0-3	Aug21 2-0	

Section 5

	Berwick R	Clydebank	Cowdenbeath	Queen's Park
Berwick R		Aug14 2-2	Aug25 0-1	Aug21 2-3
Clydebank	Aug28 5-0		Aug21 2-1	Aug18 3-2
Cowdenbeath	Aug18 2-2	Sep01 3-4		Aug28 1-1
Queen's Park	Sep01 0-1	Aug25 1-1	Aug14 1-0	

Section 6

	Dumbarton	Queen of South	Stenhousemuir	Stirling A
Dumbarton		Sep01 1-3	Aug25 1-2	Aug14 1-1
Queen of South	Aug21 1-0		Aug14 3-2	Aug25 1-2
Stenhousemuir	Aug18 2-3	Aug28 1-0		Aug21 1-3
Stirling A	Aug28 3-2	Aug18 2-1	Sep01 3-1	

Section 7

	Arbroath	East Fife	Partick T	Raith R
Arbroath		Aug21 2-2	Aug28 2-4	Aug18 4-0
East Fife	Sep01 0-2		Aug18 2-3	Aug28 1-1
Partick T	Aug14 4-0	Aug25 1-1		Sep01 5-0
Raith R	Aug25 1-1	Aug14 2-1	Aug21 1-1	

Section 8

	Albion R	Montrose	St Mirren	Stranraer
Albion R		Aug25 0-2	Sep01 2-1	Aug14 2-1
Montrose	Aug18 1-1		Aug28 0-1	Aug21 2-2
St Mirren	Aug21 1-0	Aug14 4-1		Aug25 3-0
Stranraer	Aug28 2-0	Sep01 2-4	Aug18 2-0	

Section 9

	Alloa	Brechin C	E Stirling	Forfar A	Hamilton A
Alloa		Aug21 1-1			Aug14 3-0
Brechin C			Aug25 1-4	Aug28 2-1	
E Stirling	Aug18 1-1				Aug28 2-6
Forfar A	Aug25 0-0		Aug14 2-2		
Hamilton A		Aug18 2-2		Aug21 1-4	

Section 1	P	W	D	L	F	A	Pts
Hibernian	6	5	1	0	14	3	11
Kilmarnock	6	2	1	3	7	9	5
Dundee U	6	2	1	3	9	13	5
Motherwell	6	1	1	4	7	12	3

Section 2	P	W	D	L	F	A	Pts
Falkirk	6	4	1	1	12	6	9
Dundee	6	3	2	1	10	5	8
Aberdeen	6	3	1	2	11	7	7
Clyde	6	0	0	6	2	17	0

Section 3	P	W	D	L	F	A	Pts
St Johnstone	6	3	1	2	8	7	7
Hearts	6	3	0	3	12	6	6
Airdrie	6	3	0	3	7	9	6
Dunfermline A	6	2	1	3	4	9	5

Section 4	P	W	D	L	F	A	Pts
Celtic	6	5	0	1	13	2	10
Rangers	6	4	0	2	11	5	8
Morton	6	2	1	3	4	5	5
Ayr U	6	0	1	5	2	18	1

Section 5	P	W	D	L	F	A	Pts
Clydebank	6	4	2	0	17	9	10
Queen's Park	6	2	2	2	8	8	6
Cowdenbeath	6	1	2	3	8	10	4
Berwick R	6	1	2	3	7	13	4

Section 6	P	W	D	L	F	A	Pts
Stirling A	6	5	1	0	14	7	11
Queen of South	6	3	0	3	9	8	6
Stenhousemuir	6	2	0	4	9	13	4
Dumbarton	6	1	1	4	8	12	3

Section 7	P	W	D	L	F	A	Pts
Partick T	6	4	2	0	18	6	10
Arbroath	6	2	2	2	11	11	6
Raith R	6	1	3	2	5	13	5
East Fife	6	0	3	3	7	11	3

Section 8	P	W	D	L	F	A	Pts
St Mirren	6	4	0	2	10	5	8
Montrose	6	2	2	2	10	10	6
Stranraer	6	2	1	3	9	11	5
Albion R	6	2	1	3	5	8	5

Section 9	P	W	D	L	F	A	Pts
Alloa	4	1	3	0	5	2	5
Forfar A	4	1	2	1	7	5	4
E Stirling	4	1	2	1	9	10	4
Brechin C	4	1	2	1	6	8	4
Hamilton A	4	1	1	2	9	11	3

Play-offs

Sep 6 Partick T ....4 Alloa 1
Sep 8 Alloa ....1 Partick T ....1 Agg 2-5

Quarter-finals

Sep 8 Clydebank ....0 Celtic 5
Sep 22 Celtic ....6 Clydebank ......2 Agg 11-2
Sep 8 Falkirk ....2 Hibernian 0
Sep 22 Hibernian ....1 Falkirk ....0 Agg 1-2
Sep 20 St Johnstone ......2 Partick T 0
Sep 22 Partick T ....5 St Johnstone ....1 Agg 5-3
Sep 8 St Mirren ....2 Stirling A 0
Sep 22 Stirling A ....0 St Mirren ....3 Agg 0-5

Semi-finals

Oct 6 Celtic ....3 St Mirren 0
played at Hampden Park
Oct 4 Falkirk ....0 Partick T 2
played at Hampden Park

Final

Oct 23 Celtic ....1 Partick T 4
played at Hampden Park

In 1971-72 Celtic, in the middle of a 14-year unbroken run of reaching the League Cup Final, were soundly beaten by unfancied Partick Thistle, who had just gained promotion to the First Division the previous season. Here, Lou Macari and Bobby Murdoch leave the field together with Partick's Alex Forsyth (right). Celtic successfully defended their League and SFA Cup trophies though.

Season 1972-73

Section 1	Cowdenbeath	Morton	Partick T	Stranraer
Cowdenbeath		Aug19 1-0	Aug12 1-5	Aug23 0-2
Morton	Aug30 7-2		Aug23 0-0	Aug12 1-5
Partick T	Aug26 2-2	Aug16 0-0		Aug30 2-0
Stranraer	Aug16 3-0	Aug26 1-3	Aug19 0-2	

Section 2	Aberdeen	Hibernian	Queen of South	Queen's Park
Aberdeen		Aug16 4-1	Aug26 2-1	Aug19 5-1
Hibernian	Aug23 2-1		Aug19 3-0	Aug12 4-2
Queen of South	Aug12 0-4	Aug30 1-3		Aug23 1-0
Queen's Park	Aug30 0-3	Aug26 0-1	Aug16 1-2	

Section 3	Ayr U	Clydebank	Rangers	St Mirren
Ayr U		Aug23 5-0	Aug30 1-2	Aug12 2-1
Clydebank	Aug16 1-0		Aug26 0-5	Aug30 3-3
Rangers	Aug19 2-1	Aug12 2-0		Aug23 1-4
St Mirren	Aug26 0-3	Aug19 4-2	Aug16 0-4	

Section 4	Dundee U	Dunfermline A	Kilmarnock	Stenhousemuir
Dundee U		Aug12 2-0	Aug23 2-1	Aug19 5-0
Dunfermline A	Aug26 0-1		Aug30 1-0	Aug16 2-2
Kilmarnock	Aug16 2-3	Aug19 2-1		Aug26 3-1
Stenhousemuir	Aug30 2-0	Aug23 5-2	Aug12 1-1	

Section 5	Falkirk	Montrose	Raith R	St Johnstone
Falkirk		Aug26 3-0	Aug19 1-0	Aug16 1-2
Montrose	Aug12 3-4		Aug23 2-1	Aug30 0-3
Raith R	Aug30 1-0	Aug16 1-2		Aug26 3-0
St Johnstone	Aug23 6-1	Aug19 4-1	Aug12 2-0	

Section 6	Airdrie	Berwick R	Dumbarton	Hearts
Airdrie		Aug12 0-0	Aug30 2-1	Aug23 2-1
Berwick R	Aug26 1-4		Aug16 1-0	Aug19 1-1
Dumbarton	Aug19 4-1	Aug23 2-2		Aug12 1-0
Hearts	Aug16 0-0	Aug30 3-0	Aug26 1-1	

Section 7	Clyde	Dundee	E Stirling	Motherwell
Clyde		Aug23 0-1	Aug19 3-1	Aug12 2-2
Dundee	Aug16 2-1		Aug26 3-0	Aug30 2-1
E Stirling	Aug30 0-2	Aug12 2-8		Aug23 1-5
Motherwell	Aug26 1-1	Aug19 1-3	Aug16 1-0	

Section 8	Arbroath	Celtic	East Fife	Stirling A
Arbroath		Aug19 0-5	Aug26 3-0	Aug16 1-2
Celtic	Aug28 3-3		Aug16 1-1	Aug26 3-0
East Fife	Aug12 2-1	Aug23 2-3		Aug19 0-0
Stirling A	Aug23 2-1	Aug12 0-3	Aug30 0-2	

Section 9	Albion R	Alloa	Brechin C	Forfar A	Hamilton A
Albion R			Aug19 3-0	Aug26 2-1	
Alloa	Aug16 4-3				Aug26 2-0
Brechin C		Aug23 1-2		Aug16 2-1	
Forfar A		Aug12 2-1			Aug19 1-0
Hamilton A	Aug22 4-3		Aug12 1-0		

Section 1	P	W	D	L	F	A	Pts
Partick T	6	3	3	0	11	3	9
Stranraer	6	3	0	3	11	8	6
Morton	6	2	2	2	11	9	6
Cowdenbeath	6	1	1	4	6	19	3

Section 2	P	W	D	L	F	A	Pts
Aberdeen	6	5	0	1	19	5	10
Hibernian	6	5	0	1	14	8	10
Queen of South	6	2	0	4	5	13	4
Queen's Park	6	0	0	6	4	16	0

Section 3	P	W	D	L	F	A	Pts
Rangers	6	5	0	1	16	6	10
Ayr U	6	3	0	3	12	6	6
St Mirren	6	2	1	3	12	15	5
Clydebank	6	1	1	4	6	19	3

Section 4	P	W	D	L	F	A	Pts
Dundee U	6	5	0	1	13	5	10
Stenhousemuir	6	2	2	2	11	13	6
Kilmarnock	6	2	1	3	9	9	5
Dunfermline A	6	1	1	4	6	12	3

Section 5	P	W	D	L	F	A	Pts
St Johnstone	6	5	0	1	17	6	10
Falkirk	6	3	0	3	10	12	6
Raith R	6	2	0	4	6	7	4
Montrose	6	2	0	4	8	16	4

Section 6	P	W	D	L	F	A	Pts
Airdrie	6	3	2	1	9	7	8
Dumbarton	6	2	2	2	9	7	6
Hearts	6	1	3	2	6	5	5
Berwick R	6	1	3	2	5	10	5

Section 7	P	W	D	L	F	A	Pts
Dundee	6	6	0	0	19	5	12
Motherwell	6	2	2	2	11	9	6
Clyde	6	2	2	2	9	7	6
E Stirling	6	0	0	6	4	22	0

Section 8	P	W	D	L	F	A	Pts
Celtic	6	4	2	0	18	6	10
East Fife	6	2	2	2	7	8	6
Stirling A	6	2	1	3	4	10	5
Arbroath	6	1	1	4	9	14	3

Section 9	P	W	D	L	F	A	Pts
Alloa	4	3	0	1	9	6	6
Albion R	4	2	0	2	11	9	4
Forfar A	4	2	0	2	5	5	4
Hamilton A	4	2	0	2	5	6	4
Brechin C	4	1	0	3	3	7	2

Play-offs

Sep 4 Alloa . . . . .0 Ayr U 0
Sep 6 Ayr U . . . . .0 Alloa . . . . .1 Agg 0-1
Sep 4 Motherwell . . . . .4 Albion R 1
Sep 6 Albion R . . . . .0 Motherwell . . . . .4 Agg 1-8

2nd Round

Sep 20 Aberdeen . . . . .8 Falkirk 0
Oct 4 Falkirk . . . . .3 Aberdeen . . . . . . .2 Agg 3-10
Sep 20 Dumbarton . . . . .3 Dundee 0
Oct 4 Dundee . . . . .4 Dumbarton . . . . .0 Agg 4-3
Sep 20 Dundee U . . . . .2 Hibernian 5
Oct 4 Hibernian . . . . .0 Dundee U . . . . . .0 Agg 5-2
Sep 20 East Fife . . . . .1 Partick T 0
Oct 4 Partick T . . . . .0 East Fife . . . . . . .0 Agg 0-1
Sep 20 Motherwell . . . . .0 Airdrie 1
Oct 4 Airdrie . . . . .1 Motherwell . . . . . . .1 Agg 2-1
Sep 20 St Johnstone . . . . . .2 Alloa 0
Oct 3 Alloa . . . . .0 St Johnstone . . . .1 Agg 0-3
Sep 20 Stenhousemuir . . . . .0 Rangers 5
Oct 4 Rangers . . . . .1 Stenhousemuir . .2 Agg 6-2
Sep 20 Stranraer . . . . .1 Celtic 2
Oct 4 Celtic . . . . .5 Stranraer . . . . . . .2 Agg 7-3

Quarter-finals

Oct 11 Aberdeen . . . . .3 East Fife 0
Nov 1 East Fife . . . . .1 Aberdeen . . . . . . .4 Agg 1-7
Oct 11 Airdrie . . . . .2 Hibernian 6
Nov 1 Hibernian . . . . .4 Airdrie . . . . .10 Agg 10-3
Oct 11 Dundee . . . . .1 Celtic 0
Nov 1 Celtic . . . . .3 Dundee . . . . .2 Agg 3-3
Oct 11 Rangers . . . . .1 St Johnstone 1
Nov 1 St Johnstone . . . . . .0 Rangers . . . . . . .2 Agg 1-3

Replay

Nov 20 Celtic . . . . .4 Dundee 1
played at Hampden Park

Semi-finals

Nov 27 Aberdeen . . . . .2 Celtic 3
played at Hampden Park
Nov 22 Hibernian . . . . .1 Rangers 0
played at Hampden Park

Final

Dec 9 Celtic . . . . .1 Hibernian 2
played at Hampden Park

Season 1973-74

Section 1	Arbroath	Celtic	Falkirk	Rangers
Arbroath		Aug29 1-3	Aug18 3-1	Aug15 1-2
Celtic	Aug11 2-1		Aug22 2-1	Aug25 1-3
Falkirk	Aug25 2-3	Aug15 0-2		Aug29 1-5
Rangers	Aug22 3-0	Aug18 1-2	Aug11 3-1	

Section 2	Ayr U	Dumbarton	Hibernian	Morton
Ayr U		Aug11 2-0	Aug22 0-2	Aug25 2-1
Dumbarton	Aug29 1-0		Aug25 4-1	Aug15 1-1
Hibernian	Aug15 1-0	Aug18 1-0		Aug29 2-1
Morton	Aug18 3-2	Aug22 1-0	Aug11 1-4	

Section 3	Dundee	Hearts	Partick T	St Johnstone
Dundee		Aug18 2-1	Aug22 4-0	Aug11 1-0
Hearts	Aug25 0-0		Aug11 2-0	Aug22 4-1
Partick T	Aug15 0-3	Aug29 0-0		Aug25 1-3
St Johnstone	Aug29 1-1	Aug15 2-1	Aug18 5-1	

Section 4	Aberdeen	Dundee U	East Fife	Motherwell
Aberdeen		Aug22 0-2	Aug18 1-1	Aug11 3-1
Dundee U	Aug15 0-0		Aug29 5-2	Aug25 0-3
East Fife	Aug25 0-2	Aug11 1-2		Aug22 3-0
Motherwell	Aug29 0-0	Aug18 4-0	Aug15 5-0	

Section 5	E Stirling	Hamilton A	Kilmarnock	Queen's Park
E Stirling		Aug18 2-0	Aug11 3-2	Aug22 1-3
Hamilton A	Aug25 0-0		Aug22 0-4	Aug11 2-2
Kilmarnock	Aug29 4-0	Aug15 0-0		Aug18 2-0
Queen's Park	Aug15 0-1	Aug29 1-3	Aug25 1-1	

Section 6	Cowdenbeath	Queen of South	Raith R	Stirling A
Cowdenbeath		Aug11 0-1	Aug27 1-0	Aug25 1-5
Queen of South	Aug29 5-1		Aug25 1-2	Aug15 2-1
Raith R	Aug15 5-1	Aug18 2-2		Aug29 1-0
Stirling A	Aug18 4-1	Aug22 2-0	Aug11 1-0	

Section 7	Airdrie	Alloa	Clyde	Montrose
Airdrie		Aug11 3-0	Aug22 1-1	Aug25 6-4
Alloa	Aug29 0-2		Aug25 0-2	Aug15 3-1
Clyde	Aug15 0-2	Aug18 1-0		Aug29 2-1
Montrose	Aug18 2-2	Aug22 3-0	Aug11 2-2	

Section 8	Berwick R	Dunfermline A	St Mirren	Stenhousemui
Berwick R		Aug22 1-2	Aug11 1-1	Aug25 3-1
Dunfermline A	Aug15 3-2		Aug18 5-1	Aug29 2-2
St Mirren	Aug29 2-1	Aug25 2-1		Aug15 2-0
Stenhousemuir	Aug18 0-1	Aug11 1-0	Aug22 1-2	

Section 9	Albion R	Brechin C	Clydebank	Forfar A	Stranraer
Albion R		Aug18 4-1	Aug15 3-1		
Brechin C			Aug25 2-2	Aug15 1-0	
Clydebank				Aug22 0-1	Aug18 3-0
Forfar A	Aug11 1-1				Aug25 2-1
Stranraer	Aug22 4-0	Aug11 2-1			

Section 1	P	W	D	L	F	A	Pts
Rangers	6	5	0	1	17	6	10
Celtic	6	5	0	1	12	7	10
Arbroath	6	2	0	4	9	13	4
Falkirk	6	0	0	6	6	18	0

Section 2	P	W	D	L	F	A	Pts
Hibernian	6	5	0	1	11	6	10
Dumbarton	6	2	1	3	6	6	5
Morton	6	2	1	3	8	11	5
Ayr U	6	2	0	4	6	8	4

Section 3	P	W	D	L	F	A	Pts
Dundee	6	4	2	0	11	2	10
St Johnstone	6	3	1	2	12	9	7
Hearts	6	2	2	2	8	5	6
Partick T	6	0	1	5	2	17	1

Section 4	P	W	D	L	F	A	Pts
Motherwell	6	3	1	2	13	6	7
Aberdeen	6	2	3	1	6	4	7
Dundee U	6	3	1	2	9	10	7
East Fife	6	1	1	4	7	15	3

Section 5	P	W	D	L	F	A	Pts
Kilmarnock	6	3	2	1	13	4	8
E Stirling	6	3	1	2	7	9	7
Hamilton A	6	1	3	2	5	9	5
Queen's Park	6	1	2	3	7	10	4

Section 6	P	W	D	L	F	A	Pts
Stirling A	6	4	0	2	13	5	8
Raith R	6	3	1	2	10	6	7
Queen of South	6	3	1	2	11	8	7
Cowdenbeath	6	1	0	5	5	20	2

Section 7	P	W	D	L	F	A	Pts
Airdrie	6	4	2	0	16	7	10
Clyde	6	3	2	1	8	6	8
Montrose	6	1	2	3	13	15	4
Alloa	6	1	0	5	3	12	2

Section 8	P	W	D	L	F	A	Pts
St Mirren	6	4	1	1	10	9	9
Dunfermline A	6	3	1	2	13	9	7
Berwick R	6	2	1	3	9	9	5
Stenhousemuir	6	1	1	4	5	10	3

Section 9	P	W	D	L	F	A	Pts
Albion R	4	2	1	1	8	7	5
Forfar A	4	2	1	1	4	3	5
Stranraer	4	2	0	2	7	6	4
Clydebank	4	1	1	2	6	6	3
Brechin C	4	1	1	2	5	8	3

Play-offs

Sep 3	Albion R	1	E Stirling	0	
Sep 5	E Stirling	0	Albion R	0	Agg 0-1
Sep 3	Clyde	4	Forfar A	0	
Sep 5	Forfar A	1	Clyde	3	Agg 1-7

2nd Round

Sep 12	Aberdeen	3	Stirling A	0	
Oct 10	Stirling A	0	Aberdeen	3	Agg 0-6
Sep 11	Albion R	3	Airdrie	0	
Oct 10	Airdrie	0	Albion R	1	Agg 0-4
Sep 12	Clyde	1	St Mirren	0	
Oct 10	St Mirren	4	Clyde	5	Agg 4-6
Sep 12	Dunfermline A	2	Dundee	3	
Oct 10	Dundee	2	Dunfermline A	2	Agg 5-4
Sep 12	Hibernian	3	Raith R	2	
Oct 10	Raith R	0	Hibernian	2	Agg 2-5
Sep 12	Motherwell	1	Celtic	2	
Oct 10	Celtic	0	Motherwell	1	Agg 2-2
Sep 12	Rangers	6	Dumbarton	0	
Oct 10	Dumbarton	1	Rangers	2	Agg 1-8
Sep 12	St Johnstone	1	Kilmarnock	0	
Oct 10	Kilmarnock	3	St Johnstone	1	Agg 3-2

Replay

Oct 29	Celtic	3	Motherwell	2

Quarter-finals

Oct 30	Albion R	2	Kilmarnock	0	
Nov 24	Kilmarnock	5	Albion R	2	Agg 5-4
Oct 31	Celtic	3	Aberdeen	2	
Nov 21	Aberdeen	0	Celtic	0	Agg 2-3
Oct 31	Dundee	1	Clyde	0	
Nov 21	Clyde	2	Dundee	2	Agg 2-3
Oct 31	Rangers	2	Hibernian	0	
Nov 21	Hibernian	0	Rangers	0	Agg 0-2

Semi-finals

Dec 5 Celtic ....3 Rangers 1
played at Hampden Park

Dec 3 Dundee ....1 Kilmarnock 0
played at Hampden Park

Final

Dec 15 Celtic ....0 Dundee 1
played at Hampden Park

Season 1974-75

Section 1	Arbroath	Clyde	Dumbarton	Partick T
Arbroath		Aug17 2-0	Aug14 3-3	Aug28 0-2
Clyde	Aug24 2-1		Aug28 1-1	Aug14 2-2
Dumbarton	Aug21 0-2	Aug10 2-3		Aug24 3-1
Partick T	Aug10 4-0	Aug21 3-1	Aug17 1-2	

Section 2	Dundee	Hibernian	Rangers	St Johnstone
Dundee		Aug14 2-1	Aug17 0-2	Aug28 6-1
Hibernian	Aug21 4-2		Aug10 3-1	Aug17 4-0
Rangers	Aug24 4-0	Aug28 0-1		Aug07 3-2
St Johnstone	Aug10 2-1	Aug24 1-3	Aug14 3-6	

Section 3	Aberdeen	Dunfermline A	Hearts	Morton
Aberdeen		Aug24 3-0	Aug10 0-1	Aug21 4-0
Dunfermline A	Aug17 1-1		Aug21 2-1	Aug10 1-1
Hearts	Aug28 2-1	Aug14 2-3		Aug24 2-0
Morton	Aug14 3-1	Aug28 1-1	Aug17 0-5	

Section 4	Ayr U	Celtic	Dundee U	Motherwel
Ayr U		Aug14 3-2	Aug28 2-2	Aug17 0-3
Celtic	Aug21 5-2		Aug17 1-0	Aug10 2-1
Dundee U	Aug10 3-1	Aug24 0-1		Aug21 1-0
Motherwell	Aug24 5-0	Aug28 2-2	Aug14 0-0	

Section 5	Berwick R	Hamilton A	Queen of South	Raith R
Berwick R		Aug28 0-2	Aug17 0-0	Aug14 2-0
Hamilton A	Aug10 4-0		Aug21 2-1	Aug17 1-0
Queen of South	Aug24 1-0	Aug14 0-2		Aug28 2-0
Raith R	Aug21 1-0	Aug24 2-1	Aug10 1-1	

Section 6	Kilmarnock	Montrose	Queen's Park	Stranrae
Kilmarnock		Aug10 2-0	Aug24 6-0	Aug21 2-0
Montrose	Aug28 1-1		Aug14 0-0	Aug24 2-0
Queen's Park	Aug17 0-2	Aug21 2-3		Aug10 0-0
Stranraer	Aug14 0-5	Aug17 2-4	Aug28 0-0	

Section 7

	Airdrie	Clydebank	St Mirren	Stirling A
Airdrie		Aug10 4-0	Aug17 0-1	Aug21 3-2
Clydebank	Aug28 1-2		Aug14 2-0	Aug17 3-1
St Mirren	Aug24 0-6	Aug21 1-0		Aug10 3-2
Stirling A	Aug14 2-1	Aug24 5-2	Aug28 0-4	

Section 8

	Alloa	Cowdenbeath	East Fife	Falkirk
Alloa		Aug21 1-0	Aug10 1-2	Aug17 0-1
Cowdenbeath	Aug14 0-0		Aug24 2-0	Aug28 1-3
East Fife	Aug28 5-1	Aug17 2-1		Aug14 1-4
Falkirk	Aug24 3-0	Aug10 4-0	Aug21 1-0	

Section 9

	Albion R	Brechin C	E Stirling	Forfar	Meadowbank T	Stenhousemuir
Albion R		Aug14 6-1				Aug24 5-1
Brechin C				Aug17 1-1		Aug10 2-2
E Stirling	Aug17 1-2	Aug24 3-2			Aug14 3-1	
Forfar A	Aug21 1-5		Aug10 3-3		Aug24 2-1	
Meadowbank T	Aug09 0-1	Aug28 1-4				
Stenhousemuir			Aug28 0-2	Aug14 3-0	Aug17 2-1	

Section 1	P	W	D	L	F	A	Pts
Partick T	6	3	1	2	13	8	7
Dumbarton	6	2	2	2	11	11	6
Clyde	6	2	2	2	9	11	6
Arbroath	6	2	1	3	8	11	5

Section 2	P	W	D	L	F	A	Pts
Hibernian	6	5	0	1	16	6	10
Rangers	6	4	0	2	16	9	8
Dundee	6	2	0	4	11	14	4
St Johnstone	6	1	0	5	9	23	2

Section 3	P	W	D	L	F	A	Pts
Hearts	6	4	0	2	13	6	8
Dunfermline A	6	2	3	1	8	9	7
Aberdeen	6	2	1	3	10	7	5
Morton	6	1	2	3	5	14	4

Section 4	P	W	D	L	F	A	Pts
Celtic	6	4	1	1	13	8	9
Motherwell	6	2	2	2	11	5	6
Dundee U	6	2	2	2	6	5	6
Ayr U	6	1	1	4	8	20	3

Section 5	P	W	D	L	F	A	Pts
Hamilton A	6	5	0	1	12	3	10
Queen of South	6	2	2	2	5	5	6
Raith R	6	2	1	3	4	7	5
Berwick R	6	1	1	4	2	8	3

Section 6	P	W	D	L	F	A	Pts
Kilmarnock	6	5	1	0	18	1	11
Montrose	6	3	2	1	10	7	8
Queen's Park	6	0	3	3	2	11	3
Stranraer	6	0	2	4	2	13	2

Section 7	P	W	D	L	F	A	Pts
Airdrie	6	4	0	2	16	6	8
St Mirren	6	4	0	2	9	10	8
Stirling A	6	2	0	4	12	16	4
Clydebank	6	2	0	4	8	13	4

Section 8	P	W	D	L	F	A	Pts
Falkirk	6	6	0	0	16	2	12
East Fife	6	3	0	3	10	10	6
Cowdenbeath	6	1	1	4	4	10	3
Alloa	6	1	1	4	3	11	3

Section 9	P	W	D	L	F	A	Pts
Albion R	5	5	0	0	19	4	10
E Stirling	5	3	1	1	12	8	7
Stenhousemuir	5	2	1	2	8	10	5
Brechin C	5	1	2	2	10	13	4
Forfar A	5	1	2	2	7	13	4
Meadowbank T	5	0	0	5	4	12	0

Play-offs

Sep 2 Albion R . . . . .1 Falkirk 2
Sep 4 Falkirk . . . . .6 Albion R . . . . . . .1 Agg 8-2

Quarter-finals

Sep 11 Celtic . . . . .2 Hamilton A 0
Sep 25 Hamilton A . . . . .2 Celtic . . . . .4 Agg 2-6
Sep 11 Hearts . . . . .0 Falkirk 0
Sep 25 Falkirk . . . . .1 Hearts . . . . .0 Agg 1-0
Sep 11 Kilmarnock . . . . .3 Hibernian 3
Sep 25 Hibernian . . . . .4 Kilmarnock . . . . . .1 Agg 7-4
Sep 11 Partick T . . . . .2 Airdrie 5
Sep 25 Airdrie . . . . .1 Partick T . . . . . . .1 Agg 6-3

Semi-finals

Oct 9 Airdrie . . . . .0 Celtic 1
played at Hampden Park
Oct 9 Falkirk . . . . .0 Hibernian 1
played at Tynecastle

Final

Oct 26 Celtic . . . . .6 Hibernian 3
played at Hampden Park

Celtic gain revenge for their 1972-73 League Cup Final defeat at the hands of Hibernian as goalkeeper McArthur is beaten by Celtic's Paul Wilson for their third goal in the 6-3 victory at Hampden Park, giving them the 'hat-trick' of domestic honours for that season.

Season 1975-76

The triumphant Rangers team in the dressing room after their 1-0 victory in the 1975-76 League Cup Final.

Section 1	Airdrie	Clyde	Motherwell	Rangers
Airdrie		Aug16 2-1	Aug13 2-1	Aug27 1-2
Clyde	Aug23 2-1		Aug27 1-2	Aug13 0-1
Motherwell	Aug20 2-0	Aug09 2-0		Aug23 2-2
Rangers	Aug09 6-1	Aug20 6-0	Aug16 1-1	

Section 2	Ayr U	Dundee	Dunfermline A	Hibernian
Ayr U		Aug16 1-1	Aug27 2-2	Aug13 2-1
Dundee	Aug23 2-4		Aug13 4-0	Aug27 1-2
Dunfermline A	Aug09 1-1	Aug20 1-1		Aug23 0-4
Hibernian	Aug20 2-1	Aug09 2-0	Aug16 3-0	

Section 3	Aberdeen	Celtic	Dumbarton	Hearts
Aberdeen		Aug27 0-2	Aug13 2-0	Aug16 1-2
Celtic	Aug09 1-0		Aug16 3-1	Aug20 3-1
Dumbarton	Aug20 0-1	Aug23 0-8		Aug09 2-1
Hearts	Aug23 1-0	Aug13 2-0	Aug27 6-2	

Section 4	Dundee U	Kilmarnock	Partick T	St Johnstone
Dundee U		Aug16 2-0	Aug20 1-2	Aug09 2-1
Kilmarnock	Aug23 1-0		Aug09 1-3	Aug20 1-0
Partick T	Aug13 3-1	Aug27 2-1		Aug23 3-0
St Johnstone	Aug27 1-2	Aug13 2-1	Aug16 2-4	

Section 5	Falkirk	Hamilton A	Queen of South	Stirling A
Falkirk		Aug09 0-1	Aug16 0-0	Aug20 2-1
Hamilton A	Aug27 2-2		Aug13 0-2	Aug16 0-0
Queen of South	Aug23 0-1	Aug20 0-3		Aug09 2-0
Stirling A	Aug13 3-0	Aug23 1-0	Aug27 2-3	

Section 6	East Fife	Montrose	Raith R	St Mirren
East Fife		Aug23 1-1	Aug13 2-2	Aug27 2-0
Montrose	Aug16 4-0		Aug27 2-1	Aug13 1-1
Raith R	Aug20 0-2	Aug09 2-1		Aug16 1-0
St Mirren	Aug09 2-1	Aug20 1-2	Aug23 1-1	

Section 7

	Arbroath	Berwick R	Clydebank	E Stirling
Arbroath		Aug23 2-0	Aug09 4-0	Aug20 3-1
Berwick R	Aug16 1-0		Aug20 0-1	Aug09 1-2
Clydebank	Aug27 1-0	Aug13 3-2		Aug16 1-1
E Stirling	Aug13 0-4	Aug27 2-2	Aug23 0-1	

Section 8

	Albion R	Morton	Stenhousemuir	Stranrae
Albion R		Aug09 0-1	Aug20 0-1	Aug23 2-1
Morton	Aug27 2-1		Aug16 4-1	Aug13 2-5
Stenhousemuir	Aug13 0-0	Aug23 2-1		Aug27 3-2
Stranraer	Aug16 3-2	Aug20 2-1	Aug09 0-0	

Section 9

	Alloa	Brechin C	Cowdenbeath	Forfar A	Meadowbank T	Queen's Park
Alloa			Aug09 1-3			Aug16 1-2
Brechin C	Aug23 2-1				Aug09 1-1	
Cowdenbeath		Aug13 5-2		Aug27 6-2	Aug16 0-2	
Forfar A	Aug13 2-1	Aug16 4-0				
Meadowbank T	Aug18 0-1			Aug23 4-1		Aug13 1-2
Queen's Park		Aug27 1-2	Aug23 0-1	Aug09 5-0		

Section 1	P	W	D	L	F	A	Pts
Rangers	6	4	2	0	18	5	10
Motherwell	6	3	2	1	10	6	8
Airdrie	6	2	0	4	7	14	4
Clyde	6	1	0	5	4	14	2

Section 2	P	W	D	L	F	A	Pts
Hibernian	6	5	0	1	14	4	10
Ayr U	6	2	3	1	11	9	7
Dundee	6	1	2	3	9	10	4
Dunfermline A	6	0	3	3	4	15	3

Section 3	P	W	D	L	F	A	Pts
Celtic	6	5	0	1	17	4	10
Hearts	6	4	0	2	13	8	8
Aberdeen	6	2	0	4	4	6	4
Dumbarton	6	1	0	5	5	21	2

Section 4	P	W	D	L	F	A	Pts
Partick T	6	6	0	0	17	6	12
Dundee U	6	3	0	3	8	8	6
Kilmarnock	6	2	0	4	5	9	4
St Johnstone	6	1	0	5	6	13	2

Section 5	P	W	D	L	F	A	Pts
Queen of South	6	3	1	2	7	6	7
Hamilton A	6	2	2	2	6	5	6
Falkirk	6	2	2	2	5	7	6
Stirling A	6	2	1	3	7	7	5

Section 6	P	W	D	L	F	A	Pts
Montrose	6	3	2	1	11	6	8
East Fife	6	2	2	2	8	9	6
Raith R	6	2	2	2	7	8	6
St Mirren	6	1	2	3	5	8	4

Section 7	P	W	D	L	F	A	Pts
Clydebank	6	4	1	1	7	7	9
Arbroath	6	4	0	2	13	3	8
E Stirling	6	1	2	3	6	12	4
Berwick R	6	1	1	4	6	10	3

Section 8	P	W	D	L	F	A	Pts
Stenhousemuir	6	3	2	1	7	7	8
Stranraer	6	3	1	2	13	10	7
Morton	6	3	0	3	11	11	6
Albion R	6	1	1	4	5	8	3

Section 9	P	W	D	L	F	A	Pts
Cowdenbeath	5	4	0	1	15	7	8
Queen's Park	5	3	0	2	10	5	6
Meadowbank T	5	2	1	2	8	5	5
Brechin C	5	2	1	2	7	12	5
Forfar A	5	2	0	3	9	16	4
Alloa	5	1	0	4	5	9	2

Play-offs

Sep 2 Cowdenbeath ......0 Clydebank 2
Sep 3 Clydebank ....2 Cowdenbeath ....0 Agg 4-0

Quarter-finals *Agg*

Sep 10 Hibernian ....1 Montrose 0
Sep 24 Montrose ....3 Hibernian ......1 Agg 3-2
Sep 10 Partick T ....4 Clydebank 0
Sep 24 Clydebank ....1 Partick T ....0 Agg 1-4
Sep 10 Rangers ....1 Queen of South ..0
Sep 24 Queen of South ....2 Rangers ....2 Agg 2-3
Sep 10 Stenhousemuir .....0 Celtic 2
Sep 24 Celtic ....1 Stenhousemuir ..0 Agg 3-0

Semi-finals

Oct 6 Celtic ....1 Partick T 0
played at Hampden Park
Oct 8 Montrose ....1 Rangers 5
played at Hampden Park

Final

Oct 25 Celtic ....0 Rangers 1
played at Hampden Park

Season 1976-77

Section 1

	Dundee	Hearts	Motherwell	Partick T
Dundee		Sep01 3-2	Aug18 2-1	Aug21 0-2
Hearts	Aug14 2-0		Aug21 2-1	Aug25 3-3
Motherwell	Aug25 3-3	Aug28 1-4		Aug14 1-1
Partick T	Aug28 0-1	Aug18 0-2	Sep01 2-0	

Section 2

	Aberdeen	Ayr U	Kilmarnock	St Mirren
Aberdeen		Aug21 1-0	Aug14 2-0	Aug25 4-0
Ayr U	Aug28 1-1		Aug25 3-1	Aug14 2-1
Kilmarnock	Sep01 2-1	Aug18 2-0		Aug21 1-1
St Mirren	Aug18 2-3	Sep01 2-2	Aug28 1-0	

Section 3

	Arbroath	Celtic	Dumbarton	Dundee U
Arbroath		Aug21 0-5	Sep01 0-3	Aug18 1-3
Celtic	Aug28 2-1		Aug18 3-0	Sep01 1-1
Dumbarton	Aug14 2-0	Aug25 3-3		Aug21 1-2
Dundee U	Aug25 2-0	Aug14 0-1	Aug28 1-1	

Section 4

	Hibernian	Montrose	Rangers	St Johnstone
Hibernian		Sep01 0-0	Aug18 1-1	Aug28 9-2
Montrose	Aug14 0-1		Aug28 0-3	Aug25 5-1
Rangers	Aug25 3-0	Aug21 4-0		Aug14 5-0
St Johnstone	Aug21 1-2	Aug18 0-0	Sep01 0-1	

Section 5

	Airdrie	Clyde	Queen's Park	Raith R
Airdrie		Aug28 1-0	Aug14 3-1	Aug25 7-1
Clyde	Aug21 2-3		Aug25 1-2	Aug14 1-1
Queen's Park	Sep01 2-1	Aug18 3-5		Aug28 0-4
Raith R	Aug18 1-4	Sep01 1-1	Aug21 0-1	

Section 6

	East Fife	Falkirk	Hamilton A	Stranraer
East Fife		Aug28 1-5	Aug25 1-1	Aug14 3-0
Falkirk	Aug21 1-2		Aug14 1-0	Aug25 5-1
Hamilton A	Aug18 5-0	Sep01 1-2		Aug21 6-1
Stranraer	Sep01 5-0	Aug18 5-0	Aug28 3-3	

Section 7

	Cowdenbeath	E Stirling	Morton	Stirling A
Cowdenbeath		Aug14 2-1	Aug28 0-0	Aug25 0-1
E Stirling	Sep01 4-0		Aug18 1-1	Aug28 0-6
Morton	Aug21 7-1	Aug25 1-1		Aug14 1-0
Stirling A	Aug18 0-0	Aug21 1-1	Sep01 3-2	

Section 8

	Alloa	Clydebank	Dunfermline A	Queen of South
Alloa		Aug14 1-0	Aug25 4-0	Aug28 1-0
Clydebank	Sep01 1-0		Aug28 2-0	Aug18 1-0
Dunfermline A	Aug18 3-0	Aug21 0-1		Sep01 0-0
Queen of South	Aug21 2-2	Aug25 1-4	Aug14 1-0	

Section 9

	Albion R	Berwick R	Brechin C	Forfar A	Meadowbank T	Stenhousemuir
Albion R				Aug18 1-0	Aug21 0-0	
Berwick R	Aug14 1-1			Aug21 1-1		
Brechin C	Aug28 0-2	Aug18 3-1				Aug21 2-0
Forfar A			Aug25 0-2		Aug28 2-3	Aug14 0-3
Meadowbank T		Aug25 1-1	Aug14 0-0			
Stenhousemuir	Aug25 1-3	Aug28 0-0			Aug18 1-1	

Section 1	P	W	D	L	F	A	Pts
Hearts	6	4	1	1	15	8	9
Dundee	6	3	1	2	9	10	7
Partick T	6	2	2	2	8	7	6
Motherwell	6	0	2	4	7	14	2

Section 2	P	W	D	L	F	A	Pts
Aberdeen	6	4	1	1	12	5	9
Ayr U	6	2	2	2	8	8	6
Kilmarnock	6	2	1	3	6	8	5
St Mirren	6	1	2	3	7	12	4

Section 3	P	W	D	L	F	A	Pts
Celtic	6	4	2	0	15	5	10
Dundee U	6	3	2	1	9	5	8
Dumbarton	6	2	2	2	10	9	6
Arbroath	6	0	0	6	2	17	0

Section 4	P	W	D	L	F	A	Pts
Rangers	6	5	1	0	17	1	11
Hibernian	6	3	2	1	13	7	8
Montrose	6	1	2	3	5	9	4
St Johnstone	6	0	1	5	4	22	1

Section 5	P	W	D	L	F	A	Pts
Airdrie	6	5	0	1	19	7	10
Queen's Park	6	3	0	3	9	14	6
Clyde	6	1	2	3	10	11	4
Raith R	6	1	2	3	8	14	4

Section 6	P	W	D	L	F	A	Pts
Falkirk	6	4	0	2	14	10	8
Hamilton A	6	2	2	2	16	8	6
Stranraer	6	2	1	3	15	17	5
East Fife	6	2	1	3	7	17	5

Section 7	P	W	D	L	F	A	Pts
Stirling A	6	3	2	1	11	4	8
Morton	6	2	3	1	12	6	7
E Stirling	6	1	3	2	8	11	5
Cowdenbeath	6	1	2	3	3	13	4

Section 8	P	W	D	L	F	A	Pts
Clydebank	6	5	0	1	9	2	10
Alloa	6	3	1	2	8	6	7
Queen of South	6	1	2	3	4	8	4
Dunfermline A	6	1	1	4	3	8	3

Section 9	P	W	D	L	F	A	Pts
Albion R	5	3	2	0	7	2	8
Brechin C	5	3	1	1	7	3	7
Meadowbank T	5	1	4	0	5	4	6
Stenhousemuir	5	1	2	2	5	6	4
Berwick R	5	0	4	1	4	6	4
Forfar A	5	0	1	4	3	10	1

Play-offs
Sep 6 Airdrie 3 Albion R 2
Sep 8 Albion R 3 Airdrie 1 Agg 5-4

Quarter-finals
Sep 22 Aberdeen 1 Stirling A 0
Oct 6 Stirling A 1 Aberdeen 0 Agg 1-1
Sep 22 Albion R 0 Celtic 1
Oct 6 Celtic 5 Albion R 0 Agg 6-0
Sep 22 Hearts 4 Falkirk 1
Oct 6 Falkirk 4 Hearts 3 Agg 5-7
Sep 22 Rangers 3 Clydebank 3
Oct 6 Clydebank 1 Rangers 1 Agg 4-4

Replays
Oct 18 Aberdeen 2 Stirling A 0
played at Dens Park
Oct 18 Rangers 0 Clydebank 0
Oct 19 Clydebank 1 Rangers 2
played at Firhill Park

Semi-finals
Oct 27 Aberdeen 5 Rangers 1
played at Hampden Park
Oct 25 Celtic 2 Hearts 1
played at Hampden Park

Final
Nov 6 Aberdeen 2 Celtic 1
played at Hampden Park

Season 1977-78

1st Round
Aug 17 Aberdeen 3 Airdrie 1
Aug 24 Airdrie 0 Aberdeen 2 Agg 1-5
Aug 17 Alloa 5 Stranraer 3
Aug 24 Stranraer 3 Alloa 0 Agg 6-5
Aug 17 Clydebank 5 East Fife 0
Aug 24 East Fife 0 Clydebank 1 Agg 0-6
Aug 17 Dundee U 5 Albion R 0
Aug 23 Albion R 1 Dundee U 5 Agg 1-10
Aug 17 Hibernian 1 Queen of South 2
Aug 24 Queen of South 0 Hibernian 0 Agg 2-1
Aug 17 Montrose 1 Dundee 3
Aug 24 Dundee 1 Montrose 0 Agg 4-1

2nd Round
Aug 31 Aberdeen 5 Cowdenbeath 0
Sep 3 Cowdenbeath 0 Aberdeen 5 Agg 0-10
Aug 30 Ayr U 1 Queen's Park 0
Sep 3 Queen's Park 1 Ayr U 0 Agg 1-1
Penalties 2-4
Aug 31 Celtic 0 Motherwell 0
Sep 3 Motherwell 2 Celtic 4 Agg 2-4
Aug 29 Clyde 0 Dunfermline A 0
Sep 3 Dunfermline A 2 Clyde 1 Agg 2-1
Aug 31 Clydebank 0 Stranraer 0
Sep 3 Stranraer 0 Clydebank 1 Agg 0-1
Aug 31 Dumbarton 4 Hamilton A 1
Sep 3 Hamilton A 6 Dumbarton 0 Agg 7-4
Aug 31 Dundee 4 Berwick R 0
Sep 3 Berwick R 1 Dundee 1 Agg 1-5
Aug 31 E Stirling 0 Stirling A 1
Sep 3 Stirling A 0 E Stirling 0 Agg 1-0
Aug 29 Hearts 1 Stenhousemuir 0
Sep 3 Stenhousemuir 0 Hearts 5 Agg 0-6
Aug 31 Kilmarnock 0 St Mirren 0
Sep 3 St Mirren 2 Kilmarnock 1 Agg 2-1
Aug 31 Meadowbank T 2 Forfar A 2
Sep 3 Forfar A 2 Meadowbank T 0 Agg 4-2
Aug 31 Morton 0 Falkirk 0
Sep 3 Falkirk 2 Morton 3 Agg 2-3
Aug 31 Partick T 0 Dundee U 0
Sep 3 Dundee U 1 Partick T 0 Agg 1-0
Aug 31 Queen of South 2 Brechin C 0
Sep 3 Brechin C 2 Queen of South 2 Agg 2-4
Aug 31 Raith R 0 Arbroath 1
Sep 3 Arbroath 3 Raith R 1 Agg 4-1
Aug 24 Rangers 3 St Johnstone 1
Sep 3 St Johnstone 0 Rangers 3 Agg 1-6

3rd Round
Oct 5 Arbroath 0 Dundee U 4
Oct 26 Dundee U 2 Arbroath 1 Agg 6-1
Oct 5 Ayr U 2 Forfar A 1
Oct 26 Forfar A 3 Ayr U 1 Agg 4-3
Oct 5 Dundee 0 Queen of South 0
Oct 26 Queen of South 6 Dundee 0 Agg 6-0
Oct 5 Dunfermline A 2 Clydebank 0
Oct 26 Clydebank 2 Dunfermline A 2 Agg 2-4
Oct 5 Hamilton A 0 St Mirren 2
Oct 26 St Mirren 1 Hamilton A 2 Agg 3-2
Oct 5 Hearts 3 Morton 0
Oct 26 Morton 2 Hearts 0 Agg 2-3
Oct 5 Rangers 6 Aberdeen 1
Oct 26 Aberdeen 3 Rangers 1 Agg 4-7
Oct 5 Stirling A 1 Celtic 2
Oct 26 Celtic 1 Stirling A 1 Agg 3-2

4th Round
Nov 9 Dundee U 3 Hearts 1
Nov 16 Hearts 2 Dundee U 0 Agg 3-3
Penalties 4-2
Nov 8 Queen of South 3 Forfar A 3
Nov 16 Forfar A 1 Queen of South 0 Agg 4-3
Nov 9 Rangers 3 Dunfermline A 1
Nov 16 Dunfermline A 1 Rangers 3 Agg 2-6
Nov 9 St Mirren 1 Celtic 3
Nov 16 Celtic 2 St Mirren 0 Agg 5-1

Semi-finals
Mar 1 Celtic 2 Hearts 0
played at Hampden Park
Feb 27 Forfar A 2 Rangers 5
played at Hampden Park

Final
Mar 18 Celtic 1 Rangers 2
played at Hampden Park

Season 1978-79

1st Round
Aug 16 Alloa 4 Stirling A 1
Aug 23 Stirling A 0 Alloa 1 Agg 1-5
Aug 16 Berwick R 2 St Johnstone 0
Aug 23 St Johnstone 0 Berwick R 0 Agg 0-2
Aug 16 Celtic 3 Dundee 1
Aug 23 Dundee 0 Celtic 3 Agg 1-6
Aug 16 Dumbarton 0 St Mirren 0
Aug 23 St Mirren 2 Dumbarton 0 Agg 2-0
Aug 16 Montrose 4 Queen of South 0
Aug 23 Queen of South 0 Montrose 1 Agg 0-5
Aug 16 Rangers 3 Albion R 0
Aug 23 Albion R 0 Rangers 1 Agg 0-4

2nd Round
Aug 30 Airdrie 3 Dunfermline A 0
Sep 2 Dunfermline A 0 Airdrie 5 Agg 0-8
Aug 30 Ayr U 1 Stranraer 0
Sep 2 Stranraer 1 Ayr U 3 Agg 1-4
Aug 30 Berwick R 1 St Mirren 3
Sep 2 St Mirren 5 Berwick R 1 Agg 8-2
Aug 30 Brechin C 0 Hibernian 3
Sep 2 Hibernian 3 Brechin C 1 Agg 6-1
Aug 30 Clyde 3 Motherwell 1
Sep 2 Motherwell 3 Clyde 0 Agg 4-3
Aug 30 Cowdenbeath 3 Hamilton A 2
Sep 2 Hamilton A 2 Cowdenbeath 0 Agg 4-3
Aug 30 Dundee U 2 Celtic 3
Sep 2 Celtic 1 Dundee U 0 Agg 4-2
Aug 30 East Fife 0 Arbroath 1
Sep 2 Arbroath 1 East Fife 0 Agg 2-0
Aug 30 Hearts 1 Morton 3
Sep 2 Morton 4 Hearts 1 Agg 7-2
Aug 30 Kilmarnock 2 Alloa 0
Sep 2 Alloa 1 Kilmarnock 1 Agg 1-3
Aug 30 Meadowbank T 0 Aberdeen 5
Sep 2 Aberdeen 4 Meadowbank T 0 Agg 9-0
Aug 28 Montrose 1 E Stirling 1
Sep 2 E Stirling 0 Montrose 2 Agg 1-3
Aug 30 Partick T 1 Falkirk 1
Sep 2 Falkirk 2 Partick T 2 Agg 3-3
Penalties
Aug 30 Raith R 4 Queen's Park 2
Sep 2 Queen's Park 4 Raith R 2 Agg 6-6
Penalties
Aug 30 Rangers 3 Forfar A 0
Sep 2 Forfar A 1 Rangers 4 Agg 1-7
Aug 30 Stenhousemuir 1 Clydebank 0
Sep 2 Clydebank 4 Stenhousemuir 1 Agg 4-2

3rd Round
Oct 4 Arbroath 1 Airdrie 1
Oct 10 Airdrie 1 Arbroath 2 Agg 2-3
Oct 4 Celtic 0 Motherwell 1
Oct 11 Motherwell 1 Celtic 4 Agg 2-4
Oct 4 Falkirk 0 Ayr U 2
Oct 11 Ayr U 1 Falkirk 1 Agg 3-1
Oct 4 Hamilton A 0 Aberdeen 1
Oct 11 Aberdeen 7 Hamilton A 1 Agg 8-1
Oct 4 Hibernian 1 Clydebank 0
Oct 11 Clydebank 1 Hibernian 1 Agg 1-2
Oct 4 Kilmarnock 2 Morton 0
Oct 11 Morton 5 Kilmarnock 2 Agg 5-4
Oct 4 Raith R 3 Montrose 0
Oct 11 Montrose 5 Raith R 1 Agg 5-4
Oct 4 Rangers 3 St Mirren 2
Oct 11 St Mirren 0 Rangers 0 Agg 2-3

4th Round
Nov 8 Ayr U 3 Aberdeen 3
Nov 15 Aberdeen 3 Ayr U 1 Agg 6-4
Nov 8 Montrose 1 Celtic 1
Nov 15 Celtic 3 Montrose 1 Agg 4-2
Nov 8 Morton 1 Hibernian 0
Nov 15 Hibernian 2 Morton 0 Agg 2-1
Nov 8 Rangers 1 Arbroath 0
Nov 15 Arbroath 1 Rangers 2 Agg 1-3

Semi-finals
Dec 13 Aberdeen 1 Hibernian 0
played at Dens Park
Dec 13 Celtic 2 Rangers 3
played at Hampden Park

Final
Mar 31 Aberdeen 1 Rangers 2
played at Hampden Park

Season 1979-80

1st Round
Aug 15 Aberdeen ....4 Arbroath 0
Aug 22 Arbroath ....2 Aberdeen ....1 Agg 2-5
Aug 15 Dumbarton ....1 St Johnstone 1
Aug 22 St Johnstone ......3 Dumbarton .....2 Agg 4-3
Aug 15 E Stirling ....1 Albion R 1
Aug 27 Albion R ....4 E Stirling ....1 Agg 5-2
Aug 15 Forfar A ....3 Berwick R 2
Aug 22 Berwick R ....2 Forfar A ....2 Agg 4-5
Aug 15 Kilmarnock ....2 Alloa 1
Aug 22 Alloa ....1 Kilmarnock .....1 Agg 2-3
Aug 15 Stranraer ....0 Dunfermline A ...0
Aug 22 Dunfermline A .....2 Stranraer ....4 Agg 2-4

2nd Round
Aug 29 Airdrie ....2 Dundee U 1
Sep 1 Dundee U ....2 Airdrie ....0 Agg 3-2
Sep 1 Ayr U ....2 Hearts 2
Sep 3 Hearts ....0 Ayr U ....1 Agg 2-3
Aug 29 Clyde ....1 Rangers 2
Sep 1 Rangers ....4 Clyde ....0 Agg 6-1
Aug 29 Clydebank ....0 Hamilton A 0
Sep 2 Hamilton A ....1 Clydebank ......0 Agg 1-0
Aug 29 Cowdenbeath ......1 Dundee 4
Sep 1 Dundee ....3 Cowdenbeath ....1 Agg 7-2
Aug 29 Falkirk ....1 Celtic 2
Sep 1 Celtic ....4 Falkirk ....1 Agg 6-2
Aug 29 Hibernian ....2 Montrose 1
Sep 1 Montrose ....1 Hibernian ......1 Agg 2-3
Aug 29 Kilmarnock ....2 Forfar A 0
Sep 1 Forfar A ....1 Kilmarnock .....1 Agg 1-3
Aug 29 Meadowbank T .....0 Aberdeen 5
Sep 1 Aberdeen ....2 Meadowbank T ..2 Agg 7-2
Aug 29 Motherwell ....1 Queen's Park 4
Sep 1 Queen's Park ......0 Motherwell .....2 Agg 4-3
Aug 29 Partick T ....2 Albion R 2
Sep 1 Albion R ....0 Partick T ....1 Agg 2-3
Aug 29 Queen of South ....0 Morton 1
Sep 1 Morton ....4 Queen of South ..0 Agg 5-0
Aug 29 Raith R ....1 East Fife 0
Sep 1 East Fife ....0 Raith R ....2 Agg 0-3
Aug 29 St Johnstone ......3 Stranraer 1
Sep 1 Stranraer ....3 St Johnstone ....3 Agg 4-6
Aug 28 Stenhousemuir .....1 St Mirren 4
Sep 1 St Mirren ....4 Stenhousemuir ..2 Agg 8-3
Aug 29 Stirling A ....3 Brechin C 1
Sep 1 Brechin C ....0 Stirling A ....1 Agg 1-4

3rd Round
Sep 26 Aberdeen ....3 Rangers 1
Oct 10 Rangers ....0 Aberdeen ....2 Agg 1-5
Sep 26 Dundee ....2 Ayr U 1
Oct 10 Ayr U ....0 Dundee ....1 Agg 1-3
Sep 26 Hamilton A ....1 St Mirren 3
Oct 10 St Mirren 0 Hamilton A .....2 Agg 3-3
Penalties 2-4
Sep 26 Hibernian ....1 Kilmarnock 2
Oct 10 Kilmarnock ....2 Hibernian ......1 Agg 4-2
Sep 26 Partick T ....0 Morton 1
Oct 10 Morton ....4 Partick T ....1 Agg 5-1
Sep 26 Queen's Park ......0 Dundee U 3
Oct 10 Dundee U ....2 Queen's Park ....1 Agg 5-1
Sep 26 Raith R ....1 St Johnstone 1
Oct 10 St Johnstone ......1 Raith R ....3 Agg 2-4
Sep 26 Stirling A ....1 Celtic 2
Oct 10 Celtic ....2 Stirling A ....0 Agg 4-1

4th Round
Oct 31 Aberdeen ....3 Celtic 2
Nov 24 Celtic ....0 Aberdeen ....1 Agg 2-4
Oct 31 Dundee U ....0 Raith R 0
Nov 14 Raith R ....0 Dundee U ......1 Agg 0-1
Oct 31 Hamilton A ....3 Dundee 1
Nov 14 Dundee ....1 Hamilton A .....0 Agg 2-3
Oct 31 Morton ....3 Kilmarnock 2
Nov 24 Kilmarnock ....3 Morton ....2 Agg 5-5
Penalties 4-5

Semi-finals
Dec 1 Aberdeen ....2 Morton 1
played at Hampden Park
Nov 24 Dundee U ....6 Hamilton A 2
played at East End Park

Final
Dec 8 Aberdeen ....0 Dundee U 0
played at Hampden Park

Replay
Dec 12 Aberdeen ....0 Dundee U 3
played at Dens Park

Season 1980-81

1st Round
Aug 13 Ayr U ....1 Morton 2
Aug 20 Morton ....0 Ayr U ....2 Agg 2-3
Aug 13 East Fife ....2 Dundee U 5
Aug 20 Dundee U ....4 East Fife ....0 Agg 9-2
Aug 13 Kilmarnock ....1 Airdrie 0
Aug 20 Airdrie ....0 Kilmarnock .....1 Agg 0-2
Aug 13 Queen's Park ......1 E Stirling 0
Aug 19 E Stirling ....0 Queen's Park ....4 Agg 0-5
Aug 13 Raith R ....3 Falkirk 2
Aug 20 Falkirk ....0 Raith R ....2 Agg 2-5
Aug 13 St Johnstone ......0 Clydebank 2
Aug 20 Clydebank ....0 St Johnstone ....0 Agg 2-0

2nd Round
Aug 27 Aberdeen ....8 Berwick R 1
Aug 30 Berwick R ....0 Aberdeen 4Agg 1-12
Aug 26 Albion R ....1 St Mirren 2
Aug 30 St Mirren ....5 Albion R ....0 Agg 7-1
Aug 27 Alloa ....0 Hibernian 2
Aug 30 Hibernian ....1 Alloa ....1 Agg 3-1
Aug 27 Brechin C ....0 Clyde 0
Aug 30 Clyde ....2 Brechin C ......1 Agg 2-1
Aug 27 Dumbarton ....0 Raith R 1
Aug 30 Raith R ....1 Dumbarton .....1 Agg 2-1
Aug 26 Dundee ....2 Arbroath 0
Aug 30 Arbroath ....0 Dundee ....3 Agg 0-5
Aug 27 Dundee U ....4 Cowdenbeath 0
Aug 30 Cowdenbeath ......1 Dundee U ......4 Agg 1-8
Aug 27 Forfar A ....0 Rangers 2
Aug 30 Rangers ....3 Forfar A ....1 Agg 5-1
Aug 27 Hamilton A ....5 Stranraer 1
Aug 30 Stranraer ....0 Hamilton A .....2 Agg 1-7
Aug 27 Hearts ....2 Montrose 1
Aug 30 Montrose ....1 Hearts ....3 Agg 2-5
Aug 27 Kilmarnock ....0 Dunfermline A ...0
Aug 30 Dunfermline A .....1 Kilmarnock .....2 Agg 1-2
Aug 27 Meadowbank T .....1 Clydebank 2
Aug 30 Clydebank ....2 Meadowbank T ..1 Agg 4-2
Aug 27 Partick T ....3 Queen's Park 1
Aug 30 Queen's Park ......1 Partick T ....1 Agg 2-4
Aug 27 Queen of South ....1 Ayr U 2
Aug 30 Ayr U ....1 Queen of South ..0 Agg 3-1
Aug 27 Stenhousemuir .....0 Motherwell 0
Aug 30 Motherwell ....6 Stenhousemuir ..1 Agg 6-1
Aug 27 Stirling A ....1 Celtic 0
Aug 30 Celtic ....6 Stirling A ....1 Agg 6-2

3rd Round
Sep 3 Clyde ....0 Hibernian 2
Sep 24 Hibernian ....2 Clyde ....1 Agg 4-1
Sep 3 Dundee ....0 Kilmarnock 0
Sep 24 Kilmarnock ....0 Dundee ....0 Agg 0-0
Penalties 3-5
Sep 22 Hamilton A ....1 Celtic 3
Sep 24 Celtic ....4 Hamilton A .....1 Agg 7-2
Sep 3 Hearts ....2 Ayr U 3
Sep 24 Ayr U ....4 Hearts ....0 Agg 7-2
Sep 3 Motherwell ....2 Dundee U 1
Sep 24 Dundee U ....4 Motherwell .....2 Agg 5-4
Sep 3 Partick T ....2 St Mirren 0
Sep 24 St Mirren ....0 Partick T ....0 Agg 0-2
Sep 3 Raith R ....0 Clydebank 1
Sep 24 Clydebank ....1 Raith R ....0 Agg 2-0
Sep 3 Rangers ....1 Aberdeen 0
Sep 24 Aberdeen ....3 Rangers ....1 Agg 3-2

4th Round
Oct 8 Ayr U ....2 Hibernian 2
Oct 22 Hibernian ....0 Ayr U ....2 Agg 2-4
Oct 8 Clydebank ....2 Dundee U 1
Oct 29 Dundee U ....4 Clydebank ......1 Agg 5-3
Oct 8 Dundee ....0 Aberdeen 0
Oct 29 Aberdeen ....0 Dundee ....1 Agg 0-1
Oct 8 Partick T ....0 Celtic 1
Oct 20 Celtic ....2 Partick T ....1 Agg 3-1

Semi-finals
Nov 5 Ayr U ....1 Dundee 1
Nov 19 Dundee ....3 Ayr U ....2 Agg 4-3
Nov 12 Dundee U ....1 Celtic 1
Nov 19 Celtic ....0 Dundee U ......3 Agg 1-4

Final
Dec 6 Dundee ....0 Dundee U 3
played at Dens Park

Season 1981-82

Section 1	Celtic	Hibernian	St Johnstone	St Mirren
Celtic		Aug15 4-1	Aug19 4-1	Aug08 1-3
Hibernian	Aug26 1-4		Aug08 1-2	Aug19 0-1
St Johnstone	Aug12 2-0	Aug22 1-2		Aug15 2-3
St Mirren	Aug22 1-5	Aug12 0-0	Aug26 2-0	

Section 2	Dundee	Morton	Raith R	Rangers
Dundee		Aug15 1-2	Aug08 1-2	Aug19 1-2
Morton	Aug26 3-2		Aug19 2-0	Aug08 1-1
Raith R	Aug22 1-1	Aug12 2-5		Aug26 1-3
Rangers	Aug12 4-1	Aug22 1-0	Aug15 8-1	

Section 3	Aberdeen	Airdrie	Hearts	Kilmarnock
Aberdeen		Aug15 3-0	Aug19 3-0	Aug08 3-0
Airdrie	Aug26 0-0		Aug08 0-1	Aug19 0-1
Hearts	Aug12 1-0	Aug22 2-3		Aug15 1-1
Kilmarnock	Aug22 0-3	Aug12 1-1	Aug26 2-0	

Section 4	Ayr U	Dundee U	Motherwell	Partick T
Ayr U		Aug08 3-4	Aug19 1-0	Aug15 1-0
Dundee U	Aug22 2-1		Aug26 1-1	Aug12 2-0
Motherwell	Aug12 2-3	Aug15 1-2		Aug22 0-1
Partick T	Aug26 1-5	Aug19 1-2	Aug08 2-0	

Section 5	Brechin C	Cowdenbeath	Dumbarton	Queen of South
Brechin C		Aug12 2-0	Aug15 2-1	Aug22 1-2
Cowdenbeath	Aug19 4-0		Aug08 2-0	Aug15 1-2
Dumbarton	Aug26 1-3	Aug22 3-0		Aug12 1-0
Queen of South	Aug08 1-3	Aug26 2-2	Aug19 3-2	

Section 6	Alloa	Falkirk	Forfar A	Stirling A
Alloa		Aug12 1-1	Aug22 0-2	Aug15 4-3
Falkirk	Aug19 3-0		Aug15 1-0	Aug08 4-1
Forfar A	Aug08 4-1	Aug26 3-2		Aug19 1-0
Stirling A	Aug26 2-2	Aug22 0-0	Aug12 0-1	

Section 7	Berwick R	Clyde	Clydebank	Queen's Park
Berwick R		Aug08 2-1	Aug19 3-1	Aug26 3-0
Clyde	Aug22 2-2		Aug15 3-0	Aug12 0-3
Clydebank	Aug12 2-2	Aug26 1-0		Aug22 4-1
Queen's Park	Aug15 2-0	Aug19 1-0	Aug08 1-0	

Section 8	Dunfermline A	E Stirling	Hamilton A	Montrose
Dunfermline A		Aug15 2-1	Aug22 2-3	Aug12 2-1
E Stirling	Aug26 0-1		Aug12 0-2	Aug22 1-2
Hamilton A	Aug08 2-0	Aug19 1-0		Aug26 4-2
Montrose	Aug19 0-1	Aug08 1-0	Aug15 1-2	

Section 9	Albion R	Arbroath	East Fife	Meadowbank T	Stenhousemuir	Stranraer
Albion R			Aug13 1-1		Aug15 5-2	
Arbroath	Aug22 4-0				Aug08 3-0	Aug15 4-0
East Fife		Aug19 1-1		Aug15 0-1		
Meadowbank T	Aug08 2-2	Aug12 1-3			Aug19 1-1	
Stenhousemuir			Aug22 2-3			Aug12 2-3
Stranraer	Aug19 2-0		Aug08 1-3	Aug22 1-2		

Section 1	P	W	D	L	F	A	Pts
St Mirren	6	4	1	1	10	8	9
Celtic	6	4	0	2	18	9	8
St Johnstone	6	2	0	4	8	12	4
Hibernian	6	1	1	4	5	12	3

Section 2	P	W	D	L	F	A	Pts
Rangers	6	5	1	0	19	5	11
Morton	6	4	1	1	13	7	9
Raith R	6	1	1	4	7	20	3
Dundee	6	0	1	5	7	14	1

Section 3	P	W	D	L	F	A	Pts
Aberdeen	6	4	1	1	12	1	9
Kilmarnock	6	2	2	2	5	8	6
Hearts	6	2	1	3	5	9	5
Airdrie	6	1	2	3	4	8	4

Section 4	P	W	D	L	F	A	Pts
Dundee U	6	5	1	0	13	7	11
Ayr U	6	4	0	2	14	9	8
Partick T	6	2	0	4	5	10	4
Motherwell	6	0	1	5	4	10	1

Section 5	P	W	D	L	F	A	Pts
Brechin C	6	4	0	2	11	9	8
Queen of South	6	3	1	2	10	10	7
Cowdenbeath	6	2	1	3	9	9	5
Dumbarton	6	2	0	4	8	10	4

Section 6	P	W	D	L	F	A	Pts
Forfar A	6	5	0	1	11	4	10
Falkirk	6	3	2	1	11	5	8
Alloa	6	1	2	3	8	15	4
Stirling A	6	0	2	4	6	12	2

Section 7	P	W	D	L	F	A	Pts
Berwick R	6	3	2	1	12	8	8
Queen's Park	6	4	0	2	8	7	8
Clydebank	6	2	1	3	8	10	5
Clyde	6	1	1	4	6	9	3

Section 8	P	W	D	L	F	A	Pts
Hamilton A	6	6	0	0	14	5	12
Dunfermline A	6	4	0	2	8	7	8
Montrose	6	2	0	4	7	10	4
E Stirling	6	0	0	6	2	9	0

Section 9	P	W	D	L	F	A	Pts
Arbroath	5	4	1	0	15	2	9
East Fife	5	2	2	1	8	6	6
Meadowbank T	5	2	2	1	7	7	6
Albion R	5	1	2	2	8	11	4
Stranraer	5	2	0	3	7	11	4
Stenhousemuir	5	0	1	4	7	15	1

Play-offs

Aug 31 Arbroath . . . . .1 Forfar A 2
Sep 2 Forfar A . . . . .2 Arbroath . . . . . . .2 Agg 4-3

Quarter-finals

Sep 2 Aberdeen . . . . .5 Berwick R 0
Sep 23 Berwick R . . . . .0 Aberdeen . . . . . . .3 Agg 0-8
Sep 2 Brechin C . . . . .0 Rangers 4
Sep 23 Rangers . . . . .1 Brechin C . . . . . .0 Agg 5-0
Sep 16 Forfar A . . . . .1 St Mirren 1
Sep 23 St Mirren . . . . .6 Forfar A . . . . .0 Agg 7-1
Sep 2 Hamilton A . . . . .0 Dundee U 4
Sep 23 Dundee U . . . . .5 Hamilton A . . . . .0 Agg 9-0

Semi-finals

Oct 7 Dundee U . . . . .0 Aberdeen 1
Oct 28 Aberdeen . . . . .0 Dundee U . . . . . .3 Agg 1-3
Oct 7 St Mirren . . . . .2 Rangers 2
Oct 28 Rangers . . . . .2 St Mirren . . . . . . .1 Agg 4-3

Final

Nov 28 Dundee U . . . . .1 Rangers 2
played at Hampden Park

Season 1982-83

Section 1	Alloa	Arbroath	Celtic	Dunfermline A
Alloa		Aug28 0-1	Aug18 0-5	Sep01 3-0
Arbroath	Aug14 1-2		Aug21 0-3	Aug25 1-0
Celtic	Aug25 4-1	Sep01 4-1		Aug14 6-0
Dunfermline A	Aug21 2-1	Aug18 0-0	Aug28 1-7	

Section 2	Aberdeen	Dumbarton	Dundee	Morton
Aberdeen		Aug21 3-0	Aug14 3-3	Aug25 3-0
Dumbarton	Sep08 1-2		Aug25 2-3	Aug14 1-3
Dundee	Aug28 1-5	Aug18 3-2		Sep01 3-3
Morton	Aug11 2-2	Aug28 4-1	Aug21 4-1	

Section 3	Airdrie	Clydebank	Hibernian	Rangers
Airdrie		Aug14 1-3	Sep01 3-1	Aug25 1-2
Clydebank	Aug28 1-2		Aug18 0-2	Aug21 1-4
Hibernian	Aug21 1-1	Aug25 1-1		Aug14 1-1
Rangers	Aug18 3-1	Sep01 3-2	Aug28 0-0	

Section 4	Dundee U	Falkirk	Raith R	St Johnstone
Dundee U		Aug25 4-0	Aug21 5-1	Aug14 3-0
Falkirk	Aug18 0-4		Aug28 2-0	Aug21 1-6
Raith R	Sep01 1-3	Aug14 0-0		Aug25 3-3
St Johnstone	Aug28 0-3	Sep01 1-0	Aug18 5-0	

Section 5	Clyde	Forfar A	Hearts	Motherwell
Clyde		Aug28 0-1	Aug21 1-7	Aug18 3-3
Forfar A	Aug14 2-0		Aug25 0-2	Sep01 0-1
Hearts	Sep01 3-0	Aug18 2-1		Aug28 1-0
Motherwell	Aug25 3-1	Aug21 1-1	Aug14 2-1	

Section 6	Ayr U	Queen of South	St Mirren	Stirling A
Ayr U		Aug21 0-2	Aug28 2-1	Aug18 0-0
Queen of South	Sep01 1-4		Aug18 0-1	Aug28 0-2
St Mirren	Aug14 3-1	Aug25 6-0		Sep01 0-0
Stirling A	Aug25 1-1	Aug14 2-0	Aug21 0-3	

Section 7	Brechin C	East Fife	E Stirling	Partick T
Brechin C		Aug28 4-0	Aug18 4-0	Sep01 1-1
East Fife	Aug14 0-0		Aug21 0-1	Aug25 0-3
E Stirling	Aug25 1-1	Sep01 0-0		Aug14 0-4
Partick T	Aug21 0-0	Aug18 0-0	Aug28 4-2	

Section 8	Berwick R	Hamilton A	Kilmarnock	Queen's Park
Berwick R		Aug21 0-1	Aug28 2-1	Aug18 1-0
Hamilton A	Sep01 0-1		Aug18 0-0	Aug28 1-2
Kilmarnock	Aug14 4-0	Aug25 1-0		Sep01 5-1
Queen's Park	Aug25 2-1	Aug14 1-1	Aug21 0-2	

Section 9	Albion R	Cowdenbeath	Meadowbank T	Montrose	Stenhousemuir	Stranraer
Albion R				Aug28 1-2	Aug21 0-0	Aug14 2-2
Cowdenbeath	Aug25 2-1			Aug14 0-1	Aug28 1-1	
Meadowbank T	Aug18 3-2	Aug21 0-1				
Montrose			Aug25 0-1			Aug21 1-0
Stenhousemuir			Aug14 1-1	Aug18 2-2		Aug25 0-4
Stranraer		Aug18 1-3	Aug28 0-2			

Section 1	P	W	D	L	F	A	Pts
Celtic	6	6	0	0	29	3	12
Arbroath	6	2	1	3	4	9	5
Alloa	6	2	0	4	7	13	4
Dunfermline A	6	1	1	4	3	18	3

Section 2	P	W	D	L	F	A	Pts
Aberdeen	6	4	2	0	18	7	10
Morton	6	3	2	1	16	11	8
Dundee	6	2	2	2	14	19	6
Dumbarton	6	0	0	6	7	18	0

Section 3	P	W	D	L	F	A	Pts
Rangers	6	4	2	0	13	6	10
Hibernian	6	1	4	1	6	6	6
Airdrie	6	2	1	3	9	11	5
Clydebank	6	1	1	4	8	13	3

Section 4	P	W	D	L	F	A	Pts
Dundee U	6	6	0	0	22	2	12
St Johnstone	6	3	1	2	15	10	7
Falkirk	6	1	1	4	3	15	3
Raith R	6	0	2	4	5	18	2

Section 5	P	W	D	L	F	A	Pts
Hearts	6	5	0	1	16	4	10
Motherwell	6	3	2	1	10	7	8
Forfar A	6	2	1	3	5	6	5
Clyde	6	0	1	5	5	19	1

Section 6	P	W	D	L	F	A	Pts
St Mirren	6	4	1	1	14	3	9
Stirling A	6	2	3	1	5	4	7
Ayr U	6	2	2	2	8	8	6
Queen of South	6	1	0	5	3	15	2

Section 7	P	W	D	L	F	A	Pts
Partick T	6	3	3	0	12	3	9
Brechin C	6	2	4	0	10	2	8
E Stirling	6	1	2	3	4	13	4
East Fife	6	0	3	3	0	8	3

Section 8	P	W	D	L	F	A	Pts
Kilmarnock	6	4	1	1	13	3	9
Berwick R	6	3	0	3	5	8	6
Queen's Park	6	2	1	3	6	11	5
Hamilton A	6	1	2	3	3	5	4

Section 9	P	W	D	L	F	A	Pts
Meadowbank T	5	3	1	1	7	4	7
Cowdenbeath	5	3	1	1	7	4	7
Montrose	5	3	1	1	6	4	7
Stenhousemuir	5	0	4	1	4	8	4
Stranraer	5	1	1	3	7	8	3
Albion R	5	0	2	3	6	9	2

Play-offs
Sep 1 Cowdenbeath . . . . . .3 Meadowbank T . .0
Sep 6 Kilmarnock . . . . .1 Cowdenbeath 0
Sep 8 Cowdenbeath . . . . . .1 Kilmarnock 0
Penalties 3-4

Quarter-finals
Sep 22 Aberdeen . . . . .1 Dundee U 3
Oct 6 Dundee U . . . . .1 Aberdeen . . . . . . .0 Agg 4-2
Sep 15 Celtic . . . . .4 Partick T 0
Sep 22 Partick T . . . . .0 Celtic . . . . .3 Agg 0-7
Sep 22 Kilmarnock . . . . .1 Rangers 6
Oct 6 Rangers . . . . .6 Kilmarnock . . . . .0 Agg 12-1
Sep 15 St Mirren . . . . .1 Hearts 1
Sep 22 Hearts . . . . .2 St Mirren . . . . . . .1 Agg 3-2

Semi-finals
Oct 27 Celtic . . . . .2 Dundee U 0
Nov 10 Dundee U . . . . .2 Celtic . . . . .1 Agg 2-3
Oct 27 Rangers . . . . .2 Hearts 0
Nov 10 Hearts . . . . .1 Rangers . . . . . . .2 Agg 1-4

Final
Dec 4 Celtic . . . . .2 Rangers 1
played at Hampden Park

Season 1983-84

1st Round
Aug 13 Albion R . . . . .0 Queen of South . .4
Aug 17 Queen of South . . . .2 Albion R . . . . . . .1 Agg 6-1
Aug 13 Arbroath . . . . .0 East Fife 1
Aug 17 East Fife . . . . .1 Arbroath . . . . . . .1 Agg 2-1
Aug 13 Berwick R . . . . .2 Stranraer 0
Aug 17 Stranraer . . . . .1 Berwick R . . . . . .1 Agg 1-3
Aug 13 Forfar A . . . . .1 Stenhousemuir . .0
Aug 17 Stenhousemuir . . . . .2 Forfar A . . . . .2 Agg 2-3
Aug 13 Montrose . . . . .1 E Stirling 0
Aug 17 E Stirling . . . . .1 Montrose . . . . . . .2 Agg 1-3
Aug 15 Stirling A . . . . .1 Cowdenbeath 1
Aug 17 Cowdenbeath . . . . . .2 Stirling A . . . . . . .0 Agg 3-1

2nd Round
Aug 24 Aberdeen . . . . .9 Raith R 0
Aug 27 Raith R . . . . .0 Aberdeen . . . . . . .3 Agg 0-12
Aug 24 Airdrie . . . . .2 Clyde 0
Aug 27 Clyde . . . . .1 Airdrie . . . . .0 Agg 1-2
Aug 24 Ayr U . . . . .1 Clydebank 2
Aug 27 Clydebank . . . . .1 Ayr U . . . . .0 Agg 3-1
Aug 24 Brechin C . . . . .0 Celtic 1
Aug 27 Celtic . . . . .0 Brechin C . . . . . .0 Agg 1-0
Aug 24 Cowdenbeath . . . . . .0 Hearts 0
Aug 27 Hearts . . . . .1 Cowdenbeath . . . .1 Agg 1-1
Penalties 4-2
Aug 24 Dundee U . . . . .6 Dunfermline A . . .1
Aug 27 Dunfermline A . . . . .0 Dundee U . . . . . .2 Agg 1-8
Aug 24 East Fife . . . . .1 St Johnstone 2
Aug 27 St Johnstone . . . . . .6 East Fife . . . . . . .3 Agg 8-4
Aug 24 Falkirk . . . . .2 Alloa 4
Aug 27 Alloa . . . . .2 Falkirk . . . . .2 Agg 6-4
Aug 24 Hamilton A . . . . .2 Morton 1
Aug 27 Morton . . . . .3 Hamilton A . . . . . .1 Agg 4-3
Aug 24 Hibernian . . . . .5 Dumbarton 0
Aug 27 Dumbarton . . . . .1 Hibernian . . . . . .2 Agg 1-7
Aug 23 Meadowbank T . . . . .2 Partick T 1
Aug 27 Partick T . . . . .1 Meadowbank T . .2 Agg 2-4
Aug 23 Montrose . . . . .1 Dundee 3
Aug 27 Dundee . . . . .4 Montrose . . . . . . .1 Agg 7-2
Aug 24 Motherwell . . . . .2 Berwick R 0
Aug 27 Berwick R . . . . .0 Motherwell . . . . .2 Agg 0-4
Aug 24 Queen's Park . . . . . .3 Kilmarnock 2
Aug 27 Kilmarnock . . . . .3 Queen's Park . . . .1 Agg 5-4
Aug 24 Rangers . . . . .4 Queen of South . .0
Aug 27 Queen of South . . . .1 Rangers . . . . . . .4 Agg 1-8
Aug 24 St Mirren . . . . .1 Forfar A 0
Aug 27 Forfar A . . . . .2 St Mirren . . . . . . .2 Agg 2-3

3rd Round

Section 1	Alloa	Dundee U	Morton	Motherwel
Alloa		Nov09 2-4	Nov30 1-0	Sep07 1-2
Dundee U	Aug30 5-0		Oct26 3-0	Oct05 4-2
Morton	Oct05 2-4	Sep07 1-1		Nov09 4-2
Motherwell	Oct26 2-2	Nov30 0-3	Aug31 3-0	

Section 2	Clydebank	Hearts	Rangers	St Mirren
Clydebank		Nov30 0-3	Nov09 0-3	Sep07 2-0
Hearts	Oct05 1-1		Sep07 0-3	Nov09 3-1
Rangers	Aug31 4-0	Oct26 2-0		Oct05 5-0
St Mirren	Oct26 3-3	Aug31 2-2	Nov30 0-1	

Section 3	Aberdeen	Dundee	Meadowbank T	St Johnstone
Aberdeen		Oct05 0-0	Aug31 4-0	Oct26 1-0
Dundee	Nov30 1-2		Oct25 1-1	Aug31 2-1
Meadowbank T	Nov09 1-3	Sep07 0-1		Nov30 0-0
St Johnstone	Sep07 0-1	Nov09 0-3	Oct04 1-2	

Section 4	Airdrie	Celtic	Hibernian	Kilmarnock
Airdrie		Aug31 1-6	Nov30 1-3	Oct26 1-2
Celtic	Nov09 0-0		Sep07 5-1	Oct05 1-1
Hibernian	Oct05 0-0	Oct26 0-0		Aug31 2-0
Kilmarnock	Sep07 3-0	Nov30 0-1	Nov09 3-1	

Section 1	P	W	D	L	F	A	Pts
Dundee U	6	5	1	0	20	5	11
Motherwell	6	2	1	3	11	14	5
Alloa	6	2	1	3	10	15	5
Morton	6	1	1	4	7	14	3

Section 2	P	W	D	L	F	A	Pts
Rangers	6	6	0	0	18	0	12
Hearts	6	2	2	2	9	9	6
Clydebank	6	1	2	3	6	14	4
St Mirren	6	0	2	4	6	16	2

Section 3	P	W	D	L	F	A	Pts
Aberdeen	6	5	1	0	11	2	11
Dundee	6	3	2	1	8	4	8
Meadowbank T	6	1	2	3	4	10	4
St Johnstone	6	0	1	5	2	9	1

Section 4	P	W	D	L	F	A	Pts
Celtic	6	3	3	0	13	3	9
Kilmarnock	6	3	1	2	9	6	7
Hibernian	6	2	2	2	7	9	6
Airdrie	6	0	2	4	3	14	2

Semi-finals
Feb 22 Aberdeen . . . . .0 Celtic 0
Mar 10 Celtic . . . . .1 Aberdeen . . . . . . .0 Agg 1-0
Feb 14 Dundee U . . . . .1 Rangers 1
Feb 22 Rangers . . . . .2 Dundee U . . . . . .0 Agg 3-1

Final
Mar 25 Celtic . . . . .2 Rangers 3
played at Hampden Park

Rangers pictured in 1984. Back row (left to right): Prytz, D.Ferguson, McFarlane, Kennedy, McPherson, McClelland, Paterson, McAdam, Mitchell, E.Ferguson, Munro, Fleck. Middle row: Stan Anderson (youth-team coach), Lindsay, Davies, Durrant, S.Fraser, Walker, McCloy, Bruce, Burns, McKinnon, Leeman, Connor, Bob Findlay (physiotherapist). Front row: Redford, Dawson, I.Ferguson, Williamson, Cooper, Alex Totton (first-team coach), Jock Wallace (manager), John Hagart (reserve coach), Clark, C.Fraser, McCoist, Russell, MacDonald.

Season 1984-85

1st Round

Date	Home		Away		
Aug 14	Albion R	2	Montrose	0	
Aug 15	Dunfermline A	4	Arbroath	0	
Aug 15	E Stirling	1	Berwick R	1	Penalties 4-3
Aug 15	Queen of South	2	Queen's Park	1	
Aug 15	Stirling A	2	Stenhousemuir	0	
Aug 15	Stranraer	0	Cowdenbeath	3	

2nd Round

Date	Home		Away		
Aug 22	Airdrie	3	Aberdeen	1	
Aug 22	Ayr U	1	Motherwell	0	
Aug 21	Cowdenbeath	3	Partick T	0	
Aug 22	Dundee	3	Hamilton A	0	
Aug 21	Dundee U	5	Forfar A	0	
Aug 22	Dunfermline A	2	Celtic	3	
Aug 22	Hearts	4	E Stirling	0	
Aug 22	Hibernian	1	East Fife	0	
Aug 22	Kilmarnock	1	Alloa	1	Penalties 3-2
Aug 21	Meadowbank T	2	Morton	1	
Aug 22	Queen of South	1	Dumbarton	2	
Aug 21	Raith R	2	Clydebank	0	
Aug 22	Rangers	1	Falkirk	0	
Aug 22	St Johnstone	2	Albion R	1	
Aug 22	St Mirren	1	Clyde	0	
Aug 22	Stirling A	1	Brechin C	4	

3rd Round

Date	Home		Away		
Aug 29	Airdrie	0	Celtic	4	
Aug 29	Brechin C	2	St Johnstone	4	
Aug 29	Cowdenbeath	2	St Mirren	0	
Aug 29	Dumbarton	0	Dundee U	4	
Aug 29	Dundee	1	Kilmarnock	1	Penalties 3-2
Aug 29	Hearts	1	Ayr U	0	
Aug 29	Hibernian	1	Meadowbank T	2	
Aug 29	Rangers	4	Raith R	0	

4th Round

Date	Home		Away		
Sep 5	Cowdenbeath	1	Rangers	3	
Sep 4	Dundee	0	Hearts	1	
Sep 5	Dundee U	2	Celtic	1	
Sep 5	Meadowbank T	2	St Johnstone	1	

Semi-finals

Date	Home		Away		
Sep 26	Hearts	1	Dundee U	2	
Oct 10	Dundee U	3	Hearts	1	Agg 5-2
Sep 26	Rangers	4	Meadowbank T	0	
Oct 9	Meadowbank T	1	Rangers	1	Agg 1-5; played at Tynecastle

Final

Date	Home		Away		
Oct 28	Dundee U	0	Rangers	1	played at Hampden Park

Season 1985-86

1st Round

Date	Home		Away		
Aug 14	Berwick R	1	Cowdenbeath	3	
Aug 19	Dunfermline A	4	Stenhousemuir	0	
Aug 14	E Stirling	1	Raith R	3	
Aug 14	Queen of South	3	Arbroath	0	
Aug 14	Queen's Park	1	Stirling A	2	
Aug 14	Stranraer	3	Albion R	0	

2nd Round

Date	Home		Away		
Aug 21	Aberdeen	5	Ayr U	0	
Aug 21	Alloa	0	Dundee U	2	
Aug 21	Brechin C	3	Falkirk	1	
Aug 21	Clydebank	7	Raith R	2	
Aug 20	Hamilton A	2	East Fife	0	
Aug 21	Hibernian	6	Cowdenbeath	0	
Aug 20	Meadowbank T	2	Forfar A	3	
Aug 20	Montrose	1	Hearts	3	
Aug 21	Morton	2	Dunfermline A	2	Penalties 4-3
Aug 21	Motherwell	1	Partick T	0	
Aug 21	Queen of South	1	Celtic	4	
Aug 21	Rangers	5	Clyde	0	
Aug 21	St Johnstone	1	Airdrie	0	
Aug 20	St Mirren	3	Kilmarnock	1	
Aug 21	Stranraer	2	Dundee	3	
Aug 21	Stirling A	1	Dumbarton	1	Penalties 4-2

3rd Round

Date	Home		Away		
Aug 28	Celtic	7	Brechin C	0	
Aug 28	Dundee U	2	Clydebank	0	
Aug 27	Forfar A	2	Rangers	2	Penalties 5-6
Aug 28	Hamilton A	2	Dundee	1	
Aug 27	Hearts	2	Stirling A	1	
Aug 28	Hibernian	6	Motherwell	1	
Aug 28	Morton	1	St Mirren	4	
Aug 28	St Johnstone	0	Aberdeen	2	

4th Round

Date	Home		Away		
Sep 4	Aberdeen	1	Hearts	0	
Sep 4	Dundee U	2	St Mirren	1	
Sep 4	Hamilton A	1	Rangers	2	
Sep 4	Hibernian	4	Celtic	4	Penalties 4-3

Semi-finals

Date	Home		Away		
Sep 25	Dundee U	0	Aberdeen	1	
Oct 9	Aberdeen	1	Dundee U	0	Agg 2-0
Sep 25	Hibernian	2	Rangers	0	
Oct 9	Rangers	1	Hibernian	0	Agg 1-2

Final

Date	Home		Away		
Oct 27	Aberdeen	3	Hibernian	0	played at Hampden Park

Aberdeen made two appearances at Hampden in 1985-86 and were victorious on both occasions, by the same scoreline of 3-0, beating their Edinburgh opponents Hearts in the SFA Cup and Hibernian in the League Cup. Here they are celebrating after their win against Hearts.

Season 1986-87

1st Round

Aug 12 Albion R . . . . .3 Berwick R 1
Aug 13 Arbroath . . . . .2 Raith R 1
Aug 13 Cowdenbeath . . . . . .0 St Johnstone 1
Aug 13 Meadowbank T . . . . .1 Stirling A 4
Aug 13 Stenhousemuir . . . . .1 Queen's Park 0
Aug 13 Stranraer . . . . .0 E Stirling 2

2nd Round

Aug 20 Aberdeen . . . . .4 Alloa 0
Aug 20 Albion R . . . . .2 Forfar A 2
Penalties 1-3
Aug 19 Brechin C . . . . .0 Hamilton A 1
Aug 20 Celtic . . . . .2 Airdrie 0
Aug 19 Clyde . . . . .2 Falkirk 1
Aug 20 Clydebank . . . . .3 St Johnstone 0
Aug 20 Dumbarton . . . . .1 Stirling A 0
Aug 20 Dunfermline A . . . . .0 St Mirren 2
Aug 19 Hearts . . . . .0 Montrose 2
Aug 20 Hibernian . . . . .1 E Stirling 0
Aug 20 Kilmarnock . . . . .1 Ayr U 2
Aug 20 Morton . . . . .2 Dundee 5
Aug 20 Motherwell . . . . .4 Arbroath 0
Aug 20 Partick T . . . . .0 East Fife 1
Aug 20 Queen of South . . . .0 Dundee U 1
Aug 20 Stenhousemuir . . . . .1 Rangers 4

3rd Round

Aug 27 Aberdeen . . . . .3 Clyde 1
Aug 27 Ayr U . . . . .0 Dundee U 3
Aug 27 Celtic . . . . .3 Dumbarton 0
Aug 27 Dundee . . . . .4 Montrose 0
Aug 27 East Fife . . . . .0 Rangers 0
Penalties 4-5
Aug 27 Forfar A . . . . .5 St Mirren 1
Aug 27 Hamilton A . . . . .0 Hibernian 1
Aug 27 Motherwell . . . . .2 Clydebank 0

4th Round

Sep 3 Aberdeen . . . . .1 Celtic 1
Penalties 2-4
Sep 3 Hibernian . . . . .0 Dundee U 2
Sep 3 Motherwell . . . . .2 Forfar A 1
Sep 3 Rangers . . . . .3 Dundee 1

Semi-finals

Sep 23 Celtic . . . . .2 Motherwell 2
Penalties 5-4
played at Hampden Park
Sep 24 Dundee U . . . . .1 Rangers 2
played at Hampden Park

Final

Oct 26 Celtic . . . . .1 Rangers 2
played at Hampden Park

As the tie went into a penalty competition, Aberdeen's Peter Nicholas blasts his spot-kick over the bar against Rangers in the 1987-88 Scottish League Cup Final.

Season 1987-88

1st Round

Aug 12 Arbroath . . . . .1 Ayr U 3
Aug 12 Berwick R . . . . .1 Stirling A 2
Aug 12 Cowdenbeath . . . . . .1 Queen's Park . . .3
Aug 12 St Johnstone . . . . . .4 Alloa 1
Aug 11 Stenhousemuir . . . . .1 E Stirling 3
Aug 12 Stranraer . . . . .0 Albion R 3

2nd Round

Aug 19 Aberdeen . . . . .5 Brechin C 1
Aug 19 Albion R . . . . .1 East Fife 1
Penalties 5-3
Aug 19 Ayr U . . . . .0 Dumbarton 1
Aug 19 Celtic . . . . .3 Forfar A 1
Aug 19 Dundee U . . . . .4 Partick T 1
Aug 18 E Stirling . . . . .1 Dunfermline A . . .3
Aug 19 Hearts . . . . .6 Kilmarnock 1
Aug 18 Hibernian . . . . .3 Montrose 2
Aug 18 Meadowbank T . . . . .1 Hamilton A 0
Aug 19 Morton . . . . .1 Clyde 5
Aug 19 Motherwell . . . . .3 Airdrie 1
Aug 18 Queen of South . . . .2 Falkirk 1
Aug 18 Queen's Park . . . . . .0 Dundee 3
Aug 19 Raith R . . . . .2 Clydebank 1
Aug 18 St Mirren . . . . .0 St Johnstone 1
Aug 19 Stirling A . . . . .1 Rangers 2

3rd Round

Aug 26 Aberdeen . . . . .3 St Johnstone 0
Aug 26 Dumbarton . . . . .1 Celtic 5
Aug 26 Dunfermline A . . . . .1 Rangers 4
Aug 25 Hearts . . . . .2 Clyde 0
Aug 25 Hibernian . . . . .3 Queen of South . .1
Aug 26 Meadowbank T . . . . .0 Dundee 3
Aug 26 Motherwell . . . . .4 Albion R 0
Aug 25 Raith R . . . . .1 Dundee U 2

4th Round

Sep 1 Aberdeen . . . . .1 Celtic 0
Sep 2 Dundee . . . . .2 Dundee U 1
Sep 1 Motherwell . . . . .1 Hibernian 0
Sep 2 Rangers . . . . .4 Hearts 1

Semi-finals

Sep 23 Aberdeen . . . . .2 Dundee 0
played at Tannadice
Sep 23 Motherwell . . . . .1 Rangers 3
played at Hampden Park

Final

Oct 25 Aberdeen . . . . .3 Rangers 3
Penalties 3-5
played at Hampden Park

Season 1988-89

1st Round
Aug 10 Alloa 2 Stirling A 4
Aug 10 Brechin C 3 Montrose 1
Aug 10 Cowdenbeath 0 Albion R 0
Penalties 3-4
Aug 11 E Stirling 0 Arbroath 1
Aug 10 Queen's Park 1 Stranraer 2
Aug 10 Stenhousemuir 3 Berwick R 0

2nd Round
Aug 17 Aberdeen 4 Arbroath 0
Aug 17 Airdrie 0 Motherwell 1
Aug 16 Albion R 2 Hamilton A 4
Aug 17 Brechin C 0 Morton 2
Aug 17 Celtic 4 Ayr U 1
Aug 17 Clyde 0 Rangers 3
Aug 17 Clydebank 2 Stenhousemuir 0
Aug 16 Dumbarton 1 St Mirren 3
Aug 17 Dundee 5 Queen of South 1
Aug 17 East Fife 1 Dunfermline A 1
Penalties 3-4
Aug 17 Falkirk 1 Raith R 1
Penalties 9-8
Aug 17 Hearts 5 St Johnstone 0
Aug 17 Hibernian 4 Stranraer 0
Aug 17 Kilmarnock 1 Forfar A 0
Aug 16 Meadowbank T 2 Stirling A 1
Aug 16 Partick T 0 Dundee U 2

3rd Round
Aug 24 Celtic 7 Hamilton A 2
Aug 24 Dundee 2 Falkirk 1
Aug 24 Dunfermline A 2 Motherwell 1
Aug 23 Hibernian 1 Kilmarnock 0
Aug 23 Meadowbank T 0 Hearts 2
Aug 23 Morton 1 Aberdeen 2
Aug 24 Rangers 6 Clydebank 0
Aug 24 St Mirren 1 Dundee U 3

4th Round
Aug 31 Dundee U 2 Celtic 0
Aug 31 Dunfermline A 1 Hearts 4
Aug 31 Hibernian 1 Aberdeen 2
Aug 31 Rangers 4 Dundee 1

Semi-finals
Sep 20 Aberdeen 2 Dundee U 0
played at Dens Park
Sep 21 Hearts 0 Rangers 3
played at Hampden Park

Final
Oct 23 Aberdeen 2 Rangers 3
played at Hampden Park

Season 1989-90

1st Round
Aug 9 Arbroath 1 E Stirling 0
Aug 9 Cowdenbeath 0 Montrose 4
Aug 8 Dumbarton 3 Stenhousemuir 0
Aug 9 East Fife 2 Queen's Park 2
Penalties 6-7
Aug 9 Stirling A 0 Berwick R 3
Aug 9 Stranraer 3 Brechin C 4

2nd Round
Aug 15 Airdrie 4 Forfar A 0
Aug 16 Albion R 0 Aberdeen 2
Aug 15 Ayr U 0 Hamilton A 1
Aug 15 Berwick R 0 St Mirren 2
Aug 16 Brechin C 0 Falkirk 3
Aug 16 Clydebank 3 Meadowbank T 1
Aug 15 Dumbarton 0 Celtic 3
Aug 15 Dundee 5 Clyde 1
Aug 16 Dundee U 1 Partick T 0
Aug 15 Dunfermline A 3 Raith R 0
Aug 16 Hearts 3 Montrose 0
Aug 15 Hibernian 2 Alloa 0
Aug 15 Kilmarnock 1 Motherwell 4
Aug 16 Queen of South 1 St Johnstone 0
Aug 15 Queen's Park 0 Morton 1
Aug 15 Rangers 4 Arbroath 0

3rd Round
Aug 23 Aberdeen 4 Airdrie 0
Aug 22 Celtic 2 Queen of South 0
Aug 23 Dunfermline A 1 Dundee 0
Aug 23 Falkirk 1 Hearts 4
Aug 23 Hamilton A 2 Dundee U 1
Aug 22 Hibernian 0 Clydebank 0
Penalties 5-3
Aug 23 Morton 1 Rangers 2
Aug 23 St Mirren 1 Motherwell 0

4th Round
Aug 30 Aberdeen 3 St Mirren 1
Aug 30 Hamilton A 0 Rangers 3
Aug 30 Hearts 2 Celtic 2
Penalties 1-3
Aug 29 Hibernian 1 Dunfermline A 3

Semi-finals
Sep 20 Aberdeen 1 Celtic 0
played at Hampden Park
Sep 19 Dunfermline A 0 Rangers 5
played at Hampden Park

Final
Oct 22 Aberdeen 2 Rangers 1
played at Hampden Park

Season 1990-91

1st Round
Aug 14 E Stirling 2 Dumbarton 2
Penalties 4-1
Aug 15 Montrose 1 Queen of South 2
Aug 14 Queen's Park 3 East Fife 3
Penalties 5-4
Aug 14 Stenhousemuir 0 Cowdenbeath 2
Aug 15 Stirling A 1 Arbroath 2
Aug 15 Stranraer 4 Berwick R 3

2nd Round
Aug 21 Airdrie 1 Stranraer 2
Aug 21 Alloa 0 Dundee U 3
Aug 21 Brechin C 0 Hamilton A 2
Aug 22 Celtic 4 Ayr U 0
Aug 22 Cowdenbeath 0 Hearts 2
Aug 21 Dunfermline A 4 Albion R 0
Aug 22 Falkirk 1 Partick T 1
Penalties 1-4
Aug 21 Forfar A 1 Raith R 2
Aug 21 Kilmarnock 3 Clydebank 2
Aug 22 Meadowbank T 0 Hibernian 1
Aug 21 Motherwell 4 Morton 3
Aug 21 Queen of South 2 Dundee 2
Penalties 4-1
Aug 21 Queen's Park 1 Aberdeen 2
Aug 21 Rangers 5 E Stirling 0
Aug 21 St Johnstone 0 Clyde 2
Aug 22 St Mirren 1 Arbroath 0

3rd Round
Aug 29 Aberdeen 4 Stranraer 0
Aug 28 Dunfermline A 1 Queen of South 2
Aug 29 Hamilton A 0 Celtic 1
Aug 28 Motherwell 2 Clyde 0
Aug 28 Partick T 1 Dundee U 3
Aug 29 Raith R 1 Hibernian 0
Aug 28 Rangers 1 Kilmarnock 0
Aug 29 St Mirren 0 Hearts 1

4th Round
Sep 5 Aberdeen 3 Hearts 0
Sep 5 Celtic 2 Queen of South 1
Sep 4 Dundee U 2 Motherwell 0
Sep 4 Rangers 6 Raith R 2

Semi-finals
Sep 26 Aberdeen 0 Rangers 1
played at Hampden Park
Sep 25 Celtic 2 Dundee U 0
played at Hampden Park

Final
Oct 28 Celtic 1 Rangers 2
played at Hampden Park

Season 1991-92

1st Round
Aug 13 Alloa 0 Stranraer 0
Penalties 8-7
Aug 14 Berwick R 0 Dumbarton 1
Aug 21 Cowdenbeath 1 Arbroath 0
Aug 13 East Fife 2 E Stirling 2
Penalties 2-4
Aug 13 Queen of South 0 Albion R 4
Aug 13 Queen's Park 4 Stenhousemuir 2

2nd Round
Aug 20 Brechin C 3 St Mirren 3
Penalties 4-5
Aug 21 Clyde 0 Aberdeen 4
Aug 26 Cowdenbeath 0 Kilmarnock 1
Aug 20 Dumbarton 1 Airdrie 2
Aug 21 Dundee 2 Ayr U 4
Aug 20 Dundee U 3 Montrose 2
Aug 20 Dunfermline A 4 Alloa 1
Aug 20 Falkirk 3 E Stirling 0
Aug 20 Hamilton A 2 Forfar A 0
Aug 20 Hearts 3 Clydebank 0
Aug 21 Meadowbank T 0 St Johnstone 2
Aug 21 Morton 2 Celtic 4
Aug 20 Partick 2 Albion R 0
Aug 20 Raith R 4 Motherwell 1
Aug 20 Rangers 6 Queen's Park 0
Aug 20 Stirling A 0 Hibernian 3

3rd Round
Aug 28 Aberdeen 0 Airdrie 1
Aug 27 Ayr U 2 St Johnstone 0
Aug 27 Celtic 3 Raith R 1
Aug 27 Dundee U 1 Falkirk 0
Aug 28 Dunfermline A 1 St Mirren 1
Penalties 3-2
Aug 28 Hamilton A 0 Hearts 2
Aug 28 Kilmarnock 2 Hibernian 3
Aug 28 Partick 0 Rangers 2

4th Round
Sep 3 Airdrie 0 Celtic 2
Penalties 4-2
Sep 3 Ayr U 0 Hibernian 2
Sep 3 Dunfermline A 3 Dundee U 1
Sep 4 Hearts 0 Rangers 1

Semi-finals
Sep 24 Airdrie 1 Dunfermline A 1
played at Tynecastle
Penalties 2-3
Sep 25 Hibernian 1 Rangers 0
played at Hampden Park

Final
Oct 27 Dunfermline A 0 Hibernian 2
played at Hampden Park

Season 1992-93

1st Round

Aug 4 Brechin C 2 Albion R 1
Aug 1 E Stirling 0 Alloa 1
Aug 4 Queen of South 3 Berwick R 0
Aug 4 Queen's Park 1 Clyde 3
Aug 1 Stenhousemuir 2 Arbroath 3
Aug 1 Stranraer 0 East Fife 0
Penalties 5-4

2nd Round

Aug 11 Airdrie 2 Stranraer 3
Aug 11 Alloa 1 St Johnstone 3
Aug 12 Arbroath 0 Aberdeen 4
Aug 11 Brechin C 4 Hamilton A 2
Aug 11 Dumbarton 0 Rangers 5
Aug 11 Dundee U 6 Queen of South 0
Aug 12 Falkirk 4 Forfar A 1
Aug 12 Hearts 1 Clydebank 0
Aug 12 Hibernian 4 Raith R 1
Aug 11 Meadowbank T 0 Dundee 3
Aug 12 Montrose 0 Dunfermline A 6
Aug 11 Morton 2 Kilmarnock 3
Aug 11 Motherwell 4 Clyde 2
Aug 11 Partick T 2 Ayr U 0
Aug 12 St Mirren 1 Cowdenbeath 0
Aug 12 Stirling A 0 Celtic 3

3rd Round

Aug 19 Aberdeen 1 Dunfermline A 0
Aug 19 Brechin C 1 Hearts 2
Aug 19 Celtic 1 Dundee 0
Aug 18 Dundee U 3 St Mirren 0
Aug 18 Kilmarnock 3 Hibernian 1
Aug 19 Motherwell 0 Falkirk 1
Aug 19 St Johnstone 2 Partick T 2
Penalties 4-3
Aug 19 Stranraer 0 Rangers 5

4th Round

Aug 25 Kilmarnock 1 St Johnstone 3
Aug 26 Dundee U 2 Rangers 3
Aug 26 Falkirk 1 Aberdeen 4
Aug 26 Hearts 1 Celtic 2

Semi-finals

Sep 23 Aberdeen 1 Celtic 0
played at Hampden Park
Sep 22 Rangers 3 St Johnstone 1
played at Hampden Park

Final

Oct 25 Aberdeen 1 Rangers 2
at Hampden Park

Season 1993-94

1st Round

Aug 3 Alloa 1 Berwick R 0
Aug 3 East Fife 1 Albion R 2
Aug 4 Montrose 0 E Stirling 1
Aug 4 Queen of South 1 Stranraer 2
Aug 3 Queen's Park 0 Arbroath 1
Aug 3 Stenhousemuir 3 Forfar A 1

2nd Round

Aug 10 Aberdeen 5 Clydebank 0
Aug 10 Airdrie 2 Cowdenbeath 1
Aug 11 Albion R 1 Partick T 11
Aug 10 Ayr U 0 Motherwell 6
Aug 10 Brechin C 0 St Mirren 1
Aug 11 Clyde 1 St Johnstone 2
Aug 11 Dunfermline A 2 E Stirling 0
Aug 10 Hamilton A 0 Dundee U 1
Aug 10 Hearts 2 Stranraer 0
Aug 10 Hibernian 2 Alloa 0
Aug 10 Kilmarnock 1 Morton 2
Aug 10 Meadowbank T 1 Dundee 1
Penalties
Aug 11 Raith R 1 Arbroath 2
Aug 11 Rangers 1 Dumbarton 0
Aug 10 Stenhousemuir 1 Falkirk 2
Aug 10 Stirling A 0 Celtic 2

3rd Round

Aug 24 Aberdeen 5 Motherwell 2
Aug 25 Arbroath 1 Celtic 9
Aug 24 Dunfermline A 0 Rangers 2
Aug 25 Hearts 0 Falkirk 1
Aug 24 Hibernian 2 Dundee 1
Aug 24 Morton 0 Partick T 1
Aug 25 St Johnstone 0 Airdrie 2
Aug 24 St Mirren 0 Dundee U 1

4th Round

Aug 31 Celtic 1 Airdrie 0
Aug 31 Dundee U 3 Falkirk 3
Penalties 4-2
Aug 31 Partick T 2 Hibernian 2
Penalties 2-3
Sep 1 Rangers 2 Aberdeen 1

Semi-finals

Sep 21 Dundee U 0 Hibernian 1
played at Hampden Park
Sep 22 Rangers 1 Celtic 2
played at Hampden Park

Final

Oct 24 Hibernian 1 Rangers 2
played at Hampden Park

Season 1994-95

1st Round

Aug 10 Arbroath 1 Alloa 1
Penalties 5-4
Aug 9 Berwick R 0 Montrose 0
Penalties 2-3
Aug 9 East Fife 1 Forfar A 0
Aug 9 E Stirling 0 Caledonian T 2
Aug 10 Queen of South 2 Albion R 0
Aug 10 Ross 3 Queen's Park 2
Aug 9 Stenhousemuir 0 Meadowbank T 4
Aug 10 Stranraer 2 Cowdenbeath 2
Penalties 4-2

2nd Round

Aug 17 Aberdeen 1 Stranraer 0
Aug 17 Arbroath 1 Rangers 6
Aug 16 Ayr U 0 Celtic 1
Aug 16 Dumbarton 0 Hearts 4
Aug 17 Dundee 3 Caledonian T 0
Aug 17 Dunfermline A 4 Meadowbank T 1
Aug 16 Falkirk 1 Montrose 1
Penalties 5-4
Aug 17 Hamilton A 5 Clyde 0
Aug 17 Kilmarnock 4 East Fife 1
Aug 16 Morton 1 Airdrie 1
Penalties 3-5
Aug 16 Motherwell 3 Clydebank 1
Aug 16 Partick T 5 Brechin C 0
Aug 17 Queen of South 0 Hibernian 3
Aug 17 Ross 0 Raith R 5
Aug 16 St Mirren 0 Dundee U 1
Aug 17 Stirling A 0 St Johnstone 2

3rd Round

Aug 31 Dundee 1 Celtic 2
Aug 31 Hamilton A 2 Dundee U 2
Penalties 3-5
Aug 30 Hibernian 2 Dunfermline A 0
Aug 31 Hearts 2 St Johnstone 4
Aug 31 Motherwell 1 Airdrie 2
Aug 30 Partick T 0 Aberdeen 5
Aug 31 Raith R 3 Kilmarnock 2
Aug 31 Rangers 1 Falkirk 2

4th Round

Sep 21 Celtic 1 Dundee U 0
Sep 21 Falkirk 1 Aberdeen 4
Sep 21 Hibernian 1 Airdrie 2
Sep 20 St Johnstone 1 Raith R 3

Semi-finals

Oct 25 Airdrie 1 Raith R 1
Penalties 4-5
played at Hampden Park
Oct 26 Celtic 1 Aberdeen 0
played at Hampden Park

Final

Nov 27 Celtic 2 Raith R 2
Penalties 5-6
played at Ibrox

Season 1995-96

1st Round

Aug 05 Albion 0 Cowdenbeath 1
Aug 05 Alloa 2 Forfar 1
Aug 05 Berwick 1 Caledonian T 1
Penalties 5-3
Aug 05 Brechin 2 East Fife 3
Aug 05 Clyde 1 E Stirling 2
Aug 05 Montrose 0 Livingston 2
Aug 05 Queen Of South 3 Queen's Park 1
Aug 05 Ross 0 Arbroath 2

2nd Round

Aug 19 Aberdeen 3 St Mirren 1
Aug 19 Ayr 0 Celtic 3
Aug 19 Berwick 0 Partick 7
Aug 19 Clydebank 1 Motherwell 1
Penalties 1-4
Aug 19 Cowdenbeath 0 Dundee U 4
Aug 19 Dunfermline 3 Stranraer 0
Aug 19 East Fife 2 Airdrie 3
Aug 19 E Stirling 0 Dundee 6
Aug 19 Hearts 3 Alloa 0
Aug 19 Hibernian 3 Stenhousemuir 1
Aug 19 Kilmarnock 1 Dumbarton 0
Aug 19 Queen Of South 0 Falkirk 2
Aug 19 Raith 2 Arbroath 1
Aug 19 Rangers 3 Morton 0
Aug 19 St Johnstone 1 Livingston 1
Penalties 2-4
Aug 19 Stirling A 2 Hamilton 0

3rd Round

Aug 29 Airdrie 2 Hibernian 0
Aug 31 Celtic 2 Raith 1
Aug 30 Dundee 3 Kilmarnock 1
Aug 29 Dundee U 1 Motherwell 2
Aug 30 Falkirk 1 Aberdeen 4
Aug 30 Hearts 2 Dunfermline 1
Aug 30 Livingston 1 Partick 2
Aug 30 Rangers 3 Stirling A 2

4th Round

Sep 20 Airdrie 1 Partick 1
Penalties 3-2
Sep 19 Celtic 0 Rangers 1
Sep 20 Dundee 4 Hearts 4
Penalties 5-4
Sep 20 Motherwell 1 Aberdeen 2

Semi-finals

Oct 24 Aberdeen 2 Rangers 1
played at Hampden Park
Oct 25 Airdrie 1 Dundee 2
played at Mcdiarmid Park

Final

Nov 26 Aberdeen 2 Dundee 0
played at Hampden Park

Season 1996-97

1st Round
Aug 04 Albion . . . . .4 Arbroath 0
Aug 04 Ayr . . . . .5 Livingston 2
Aug 04 Brechin . . . . .3 Montrose 0
Aug 04 Clyde . . . . .1 Inverness 0
Aug 04 Cowdenbeath . . . . . .1 Forfar 2
Aug 04 E Stirling . . . . .1 Alloa 3
Aug 04 Queen's Park . . . . . .3 Ross 1
Aug 04 Stranraer . . . . .2 Queen Of South . .0

2nd Round
Aug 13 Airdrie . . . . .3 Raith 2
Aug 13 Brechin . . . . .0 Hibernian 2
Aug 14 Clyde . . . . .1 Celtic 3
Aug 14 Clydebank . . . . .0 Rangers 3
Aug 13 Dundee . . . . .2 Dumbarton 1
Aug 13 East Fife . . . . .1 St Johnstone 5
Aug 13 Falkirk . . . . .2 Albion 3
Aug 14 Hearts . . . . .1 Stenhousemuir . .1
Penalties 5-4
Aug 13 Kilmarnock . . . . .0 Ayr 1
Aug 13 Morton . . . . .1 Hamilton 1
Penalties 4-3
Aug 13 Motherwell . . . . .0 Alloa 0
Penalties 2-4
Aug 13 Partick . . . . .3 Forfar 0
Aug 13 Queen's Park . . . . . .0 Aberdeen 2
Aug 13 St Mirren . . . . .4 Berwick 0
Aug 13 Stirling A . . . . .1 Dundee U 2
Aug 14 Stranraer . . . . .1 Dunfermline 2

3rd Round
Sep 03 Albion . . . . .0 Hibernian 2
Sep 04 Alloa . . . . .1 Celtic 5
Sep 03 Dundee U . . . . .2 Dundee 2
Penalties 2-4
Sep 04 Dunfermline . . . . . . .3 St Mirren 1
Sep 03 Morton . . . . .3 Aberdeen 7
Sep 03 Partick . . . . .1 Airdrie 0
Sep 04 Rangers . . . . .3 Ayr 1
Sep 03 St Johnstone . . . . . .1 Hearts 3

4th Round
Sep 17 Dundee . . . . .2 Aberdeen 1
Sep 17 Dunfermline . . . . . . .2 Partick 0
Sep 17 Hearts . . . . .1 Celtic 0
Sep 17 Rangers . . . . .4 Hibernian 0

Semi-finals
Oct 23 Dundee . . . . .1 Hearts 3
played at Easter Road
Oct 22 Dunfermline . . . . . . .1 Rangers 6
played at Celtic Park

Final
Nov 24 Hearts . . . . .3 Rangers 4
played at Hampden Park

Season 1997-98

1st Round
Aug 02 Arbroath . . . . .0 Queen Of South . .4
Aug 02 Berwick . . . . .2 Brechin 0
Aug 02 Cowdenbeath . . . . . .0 Alloa 2
Aug 02 Dumbarton . . . . .1 Queen's Park 1
Penalties 6-5
Aug 02 E Stirling . . . . .3 Stranraer 1
Aug 02 Forfar . . . . .1 Albion 0
Aug 02 Inverness . . . . .5 Stenhousemuir . .1
Aug 02 Ross . . . . .2 Montrose 1

2nd Round
Aug 09 Berwick . . . . .0 Celtic 7
Aug 09 Dumbarton . . . . .1 Aberdeen 5
Aug 09 Dundee . . . . .1 E Stirling 0
Aug 09 Dunfermline . . . . . . .5 Ayr 1
Aug 09 East Fife . . . . .0 Kilmarnock 2
Aug 07 Hamilton . . . . .0 Rangers 1
Aug 09 Hibernian . . . . .3 Alloa 1
Aug 09 Livingston . . . . .0 Hearts 2
Aug 09 Morton . . . . .4 Airdrie 1
Aug 09 Motherwell . . . . .2 Inverness 2
Penalties 4-1
Aug 09 Partick . . . . .2 Stirling A 3
Aug 09 Queen Of South . . . .2 Dundee U 4
Aug 09 Raith . . . . .5 Forfar 0
Aug 09 Ross . . . . .0 Falkirk 3
Aug 09 St Johnstone . . . . . .3 Clyde 0
Aug 09 St Mirren . . . . .2 Clydebank 0

3rd Round
Aug 19 Dundee . . . . .0 Aberdeen 3
Aug 20 Dundee U . . . . .2 Hibernian 1
Aug 20 Dunfermline . . . . . . .2 St Mirren 0
Aug 20 Motherwell . . . . .3 Morton 0
Aug 19 Raith . . . . .1 Hearts 2
Aug 19 Rangers . . . . .4 Falkirk 1
Aug 19 St Johnstone . . . . . .0 Celtic 1
Aug 20 Stirling A . . . . .6 Kilmarnock 2

4th Round
Sep 10 Celtic . . . . .1 Motherwell 0
Sep 09 Dunfermline . . . . . . .1 Hearts 0
Sep 09 Rangers . . . . .0 Dundee U 1
Sep 10 Stirling A . . . . .0 Aberdeen 2

Semi-finals
Oct 15 Aberdeen . . . . .1 Dundee U 3
played at Tynecastle
Oct 14 Celtic . . . . .1 Dunfermline 0

Final
Nov 30 Celtic . . . . .3 Dundee U 0
played at Hampden Park

Season 1998-99

1st Round
Aug 01 Arbroath . . . . .0 Clydebank 1
Aug 01 Brechin . . . . .2 Hamilton 2
Penalties 2-3
Aug 01 Clyde . . . . .1 Berwick 1
Penalties 3-4
Aug 01 Cowdenbeath . . . . . .0 Livingston 2
Aug 01 Dumbarton . . . . .0 Alloa 4
Aug 01 East Fife . . . . .3 Partick 2
Aug 01 Forfar . . . . .0 Stirling A 1
Aug 01 Queen Of South . . . .1 Inverness 4
Aug 01 Queen's Park . . . . . .1 Ayr 3
Aug 01 Ross . . . . .4 Montrose 1
Aug 01 Stenhousemuir . . . . .1 E Stirling 0
Aug 01 Stranraer . . . . .1 Albion 1
Penalties 4-3

2nd Round
Aug 08 Berwick . . . . .1 Falkirk 5
Aug 08 Dundee . . . . .0 Alloa 1
Aug 08 Dundee U . . . . .2 E Stirling 2
Penalties 3-0
Aug 08 East Fife . . . . .0 Motherwell 1
Aug 08 Hamilton . . . . .1 Hibernian 2
Aug 08 Inverness . . . . .0 Aberdeen 3
Aug 08 Livingston . . . . .1 Dunfermline 0
Aug 08 Morton . . . . .0 Ross 1
Aug 08 Raith . . . . .2 Clydebank 0
Aug 08 St Johnstone . . . . . .3 Stranraer 0
Aug 08 St Mirren . . . . .1 Ayr 3
Aug 08 Stenhousemuir . . . . .0 Airdrie 2

3rd Round
Aug 19 Airdrie . . . . .1 Celtic 0
Aug 18 Falkirk . . . . .0 St Johnstone 1
Aug 19 Hearts . . . . .4 Raith 2
Aug 19 Hibernian . . . . .1 Aberdeen 0
Aug 18 Kilmarnock . . . . .3 Livingston 1
Aug 18 Motherwell . . . . .0 Ayr 2
Aug 18 Rangers . . . . .4 Alloa 0
Aug 19 Ross . . . . .2 Dundee U 0

4th Round
Sep 08 Ayr . . . . .0 Rangers 2
Sep 09 Hearts . . . . .1 Ross 1
Penalties 3-0
Sep 08 Kilmarnock . . . . .0 Airdrie 1
Sep 08 St Johnstone . . . . . .4 Hibernian 0

Semi-finals
Oct 25 Airdrie . . . . .0 Rangers 5
Oct 27 Hearts . . . . .0 St Johnstone 3

Final
Nov 29 Rangers . . . . .2 St Johnstone 1
played at Celtic Park

Season 1999-2000

1st Round
Jul 31 Albion . . . . .0 Clyde 3
Jul 31 Brechin . . . . .0 Dumbarton 2
Jul 31 Clydebank . . . . .1 E Stirling 2
Jul 31 Cowdenbeath . . . . . .0 Livingston 2
Jul 31 East Fife . . . . .2 Stirling A 2
Penalties 8-7
Jul 31 Montrose . . . . .1 Hamilton 2
Jul 31 Partick . . . . .0 Alloa 2
Jul 31 Queen of South . . . . .1 Arbroath 0
Jul 31 Queen's Park . . . . . . .2 Berwick 1
Jul 31 Ross . . . . .2 Forfar 1
Jul 31 Stenhousemuir . . . . .1 Inverness 3
Jul 31 Stranraer . . . . .0 Raith 1

2nd Round
Aug 17 Aberdeen . . . . .1 Livingston 0
Aug 17 Ayr . . . . .2 Hamilton 1
Aug 17 Clyde . . . . .2 Hibernian 2
Aug 17 Dundee . . . . .4 Dumbarton 0
Aug 18 Dundee U . . . . .3 Ross 1
Aug 18 Dunfermline . . . . .4 Queen's Park 0
Aug 18 E Stirling . . . . .0 Falkirk 2
Aug 17 East Fife . . . . .2 Airdrie 2
Penalties 5-4
Aug 17 Inverness . . . . .2 St Mirren 0
Aug 17 Morton . . . . .1 Alloa 3
Aug 18 Queen of South . . . . .1 Hearts 3
Aug 18 Raith . . . . .2 Motherwell 2
Penalties 4-5

3rd Round
Oct 12 Aberdeen . . . . .1 Falkirk 1
Oct 12 Alloa . . . . .1 Dundee 3
Oct 13 Ayr . . . . .0 Celtic 4
Oct 12 East Fife . . . . .0 Hearts 2
Oct 12 Inverness . . . . .0 Motherwell 1
Oct 12 Kilmarnock . . . . .3 Hibernian 2
Oct 12 Rangers . . . . .1 Dunfermline 0
Oct 12 St johnstone . . . . . . .1 Dundee U 2

4th Round
Dec 01 Aberdeen . . . . .1 Rangers 0
Dec 01 Celtic . . . . .1 Dundee 0
Penalties 1-3
Dec 01 Dundee U . . . . .3 Motherwell 2
Feb 02 Kilmarnock . . . . .1 Hearts 0

Semi Finals
Feb 13 Aberdeen . . . . .1 Dundee U 0
Feb 16 Celtic . . . . .1 Kilmarnock 0

Final
Mar19 Aberdeen . . . . .0 Celtic 2